CHILDREN'S CORE COLLECTION

TWENTY-SECOND EDITION

CORE COLLECTION SERIES

**FORMERLY
STANDARD CATALOG SERIES**

MARIA HUGGER, GENERAL EDITOR

**CHILDREN'S CORE COLLECTION
MIDDLE AND JUNIOR HIGH CORE COLLECTION
SENIOR HIGH CORE COLLECTION
NONFICTION CORE COLLECTION
FICTION CORE COLLECTION
GRAPHIC NOVEL CORE COLLECTION**

CHILDREN'S CORE COLLECTION

TWENTY-SECOND EDITION

Volume 1

Nonfiction and E

EDITED BY

JULIE CORSARO

KENDAL SPIRES

AND

GABRIELA TOTH

H. W. Wilson

A Division of EBSCO Information Services

Ipswich, Massachusetts

2015

GREY HOUSE PUBLISHING

CONTENTS

CONTENTS

PREFACE

Children's Core Collection is a comprehensive list of fiction and nonfiction books recommended for children from preschool through grade six, together with professional aids for librarians and library media specialists. This list is available in full as an EBSCO*host* database and updated weekly. Printed versions are published approximately every two years and contain *Most Highly Recommended* and *Core Collection* books, the top recommended titles in the database. Additional metadata for these titles, plus all of the *Supplementary* and *Archival Materials* levels, appear only in the database available via EBSCO. Go to www.ebscohost.com/public/core-collections for more information or for a free trial.

What's New in this Edition?

For the first time, the *Children's Core Collection* is being published as two volumes in order to accommodate the growing number of titles. See "Organization" below for more detail. EBSCO invites feedback from Core Collections customers at corecollections@ebsco.com

This edition features library science titles specifically addressing children's librarianship in public and school libraries, collection development for the age group, or related issues. To find books on library services for adults and the general public, please refer to the *Nonfiction Core Collection*.

The *Children's Core Collection* at the time of the twenty-second edition contains over 15,000 titles at the *Most Highly Recommended* and *Core Collection* levels.

History

The first edition of the collection, originally called *Children's Catalog* and containing 3,000 books, was compiled by Marion E. Potter in 1909 and was based on 24 selected lists. The second edition, compiled by Corinne Bacon in 1917, contained 3,500 books and was based on 54 lists. It was also issued in two other editions of 2,000 and 1,000 titles respectively. In the third edition of 4,100 titles compiled by Minnie Earl Sears (for whom the *Sears List of Subject Headings* is named) in 1925, 35 additional lists were used, making a total of 89. The third edition was also issued in an abridged edition of 1,200 titles.

Scope

All books listed are published in the United States, or published in Canada or the United Kingdom and distributed in the United States.

The Core Collection excludes the following: non-English-language materials, with the exception of bilingual materials, dictionaries, and similar items; textbooks; and books about individual computer programs or versions of programs, and other topics that quickly become outdated.

Preparation

Books included in this edition were selected by experienced librarians representing public library systems and school libraries across the United States who also act as a committee of advisors on library policy and trends. The names of participating librarians and their affiliations are listed in the Acknowledgments.

Organization

Children's Core Collection is presented in two volumes for the first time. The Classified Collection is spread over both volumes and the index resides in volume two. As in previous editions, the *Children's Core Collection* contains a generous selection of graphic novels. Most fiction graphic novels are in 741.5 with nonfiction either in biography, 92, or under specific Dewey headings by subject. For the comprehensive list of recommended graphic novels, refer to the *Graphic Novels Core Collection* on EBSCO*host*.

Volume 1: Nonfiction and E Classified Collections. The first volume contains the nonfiction and E (picture books/easy readers) sections arranged according to Dewey Decimal Classification. Within classes, arrangement is by main entry, with complete bibliographical and cataloging information given for each book. The classified arrangement, along with the descriptive and critical annotations, provides a useful guide to book selection. Entries include such information as price and ISBN to facilitate acquisitions. Individual biographies are classed at 92 and precede the 920s (collective biography) in volume 1.

Volume 2: Fiction and SC Classified Collections and Index. The second volume contains fiction, SC (short story collections) and the index--a comprehensive key to the Classified List with entries for authors, titles, and subjects.

ACKNOWLEDGMENTS

H. W. Wilson and EBSCO Information Services express special gratitude to the following librarians who both advised the company in editorial matters and assisted in the selection and weeding of titles for this Core Collection:

Advisory Board

Heather Campbell Shock
West Virginia Library Commission
Charleston, West Virginia

Betty Carter
Library Consultant
Coppell, Texas

Julie Corsaro
Library Consultant
Williamsburg, VA

Gail de Vos
SLIS University of Alberta
Edmonton, Alberta, Canada

Crystal Faris
Kansas City Public Library
Kansas City, Missouri

Laura Harrington
North Andover High School
North Andover, Massachusetts

Pam Spencer Holley
Library Consultant
Hallwood, Virginia

Joquetta Johnson
Randallstown High School
Randallstown, Maryland

Angela Leeper
University of Richmond
Richmond, Virginia

John Peters
Children's Literature Specialist
Bronx, New York

Linda Ward-Callaghan
Joliet Public Library
Joliet, Illinois

The editors would like to thank EBSCO librarian Christi Showman Farrar whose help was instrumental in the creation of this collection.

DIRECTIONS FOR USE OF THE CORE COLLECTION

USES OF THE COLLECTION

CHILDREN'S CORE COLLECTION is designed to serve a number of purposes:

As an aid in purchasing. The Core Collection is designed to assist in the selection and ordering of titles. Annotations and grade level designations are provided for each title along with information concerning the publisher, ISBN, price, and availability. Since Part 1, Classified Collection, is arranged according to the Dewey Decimal Classification, the Core Collection may be used to identify parts of the library collection that should be updated or strengthened. In evaluating the suitability of a work each library will want to consider the special character of the school and community it serves.

As an aid in user service. Every title in this Core Collection is a recommended work of its kind and can be given with confidence to a user who expresses a need based on topic, genre, etc. Reference work and user service are further aided by information about grade level, sequels, and companion volumes; by the descriptive and critical annotations; and by the series and subject headings in the Index. In addition, the Index includes entries under names of illustrators and series.

As an aid in curriculum support. The classification, subject indexing, annotations, and grade level designations are helpful in identifying materials appropriate for classroom use.

As an aid in collection maintenance. Information about titles available on a subject facilitates decisions to rebind, replace, or discard items. If a book has been deleted from the Core Collection in this edition because it is no longer in print, that deletion is not intended as a sign that the book is no longer valuable or that it should necessarily be weeded from the collection.

As an aid in professional development. The Core Collection is useful in courses that deal with children's literature and book selection, especially in the creation of bibliographies and reading lists.

ORGANIZATION

The Core Collection consists of two parts: a Classified Collection, and an Author, Title, and Subject Index.

Part 1. Classified Collection

The Classified Collection is arranged with nonfiction books first, classified according to the Dewey Decimal Classification in numerical order from 000 to 999. Individual biographies are classed at 92 and precede the 920s (collective biography) in volume 1. Three sections follow nonfiction: Easy Books (E), consisting chiefly of picture books of interest to children from preschool to grade three; Fiction (Fic); and Story Collections (S C). The information supplied for each book includes bibliographic description, suggested subject headings, an annotation, and frequently, an evaluation from a quote source.

An Outline of Classification, which serves as a table of contents for the Classified Collection, is reproduced below. It should be noted that many topics can be classified in more than one discipline. If a particular title is not found where it might be expected, the Index should be consulted to determine if it is classified elsewhere.

Within classes, works are arranged alphabetically under main entry, usually the author. Works of individual biography are arranged alphabetically under the biography's subject.

Each listing consists of a full bibliographical description. Prices, which are always subject to change, have been obtained from the publisher, when available, and are as current as possible. Entries include recommended subject headings derived from the *Sears List of Subject Headings,* a suggested classification number from the *Abridged Dewey Decimal Classification and Relative Index,* a brief description of the contents, and, whenever possible, an evaluation from a quoted source. The following is an example of a typical entry and a description of its components:

> ★**Silverstein, Alvin**
> Wildfires; the science behind raging infernos; [by] Alvin and Virginia Silverstein and Laura Silverstein Nunn. Enslow Publishers 2010 48p il map (The science behind natural disasters) lib bdg $23.95
> Grades: 4 5 6 **634.9**
> 1. Wildfires
> ISBN 978-0-7660-2973-6 (lib bdg); 0-7660-2973-5 (lib bdg)
> LC 2004-13282
> "Examines the science behind wildfires, including what causes them, the different types of wildfires, their devastating effects, and how to stay safe during a wildfire" Publisher's note
> "Scientific explanations are accompanied by plentiful color diagrams that will help students to grasp causes and effect…. Photos…are effective, and are sometimes turning into helpful, lively diagrams by the addition of such features as wind-direction arrows." SLJ
> Includes glossary and bibliographical references

The star at the start of the entry indicates this is a "most highly recommended" title. The name of the author, Alvin Silverstein, is given in conformity with *Anglo-American Cataloguing Rules,* 2nd edition, 2002 revision. The title of the book is *Wildfires; the science behind raging infernos.* The book was published by Enslow Publishers in 2010.

The book has 48 pages and contains illustrations. It is published in the "The science behind natural disasters" series, in a library binding, and sells for $23.95. (Prices given were current when the Collection went to press.) The book is recommended for any of the following grade levels: 4 5 6.

At the end of the last line of type in the body entry is the figure 634.9 in bold face type. This is the classification number derived from the fifteenth edition of the *Abridged Dewey Decimal Classification.* The number 634.9 is the classification number for "Forestry".

The numbered term "1. Wildfires" is a recommended subject heading for this book based on *Sears List of Subject Headings.*

The ISBN (International Standard Book Number) is included to facilitate ordering. The Library of Congress control number is provided when available.

Following are three notes supplying additional information about the book. The first is a description of the book's content. The second is a critical note from *School Library Journal.* Such annotations are useful in evaluating books for selection and in determining which of several books on the same subject is best suited for the individual reader. The final note describes special features, in this case a glossary and a bibliography. Notes are also made to describe sequels and companion volumes, editions available, awards, and publication history.

Part 2. Author, Title, and Subject Index

The Index is a single alphabetical list of all the books entered in the Core Collection. Each book is entered under author; title (if distinctive); and subject. The classification number, displayed in boldface type, is the key to the location of the main entry for the book in the Classified Collection.

Appropriate added entries are made for joint authors and editors. "See" references are made from forms of names or subjects that are not used as headings. "See also" references are made to related or more specific headings.

The following are examples of Index entries for the book cited above:

Author	**Silverstein, Alvin** Wildfires	**634.9**
Title	**Wildfires;** the science behind raging infernos	**634.9**
Subject	**Wildfires** Silverstein, A. Wildfires	**634.9**
Publisher's series	**The science behind natural disasters** [series] Silverstein, A. Wildfires	**634.9**
Joint authors	**Silverstein, Virginia B.** (jt. auth) Silverstein, A. Wildfires	**634.9**

Standards Used

Anglo-American Cataloguing Rules, 2nd ed., 2002 revision, 2005 update. Chicago: American Library Association, 2005.

Dewey, Melvil. *Abridged Dewey Decimal Classification and Relative Index.* 15th ed. Edited by Joan S. Mitchell, et al. Dublin, Ohio: OCLC, 2012.

Bristow, Barbara and Christi Showman Farrar, eds. *Sears List of Subject Headings.* 21st ed. Ipswich, MA: H. W. Wilson, a division of EBSCO Information Services, 2014.

OUTLINE OF CLASSIFICATION

Reproduced below is the Second Summary of the Dewey Decimal Classification.* As Part 1 of this Core Collection is arranged according to this classification, the outline will serve as a table of contents for it. Please note, however, that the inclusion of this outline is not to be considered a substitute for consulting the Dewey Decimal Classification itself.

* Reproduced from Edition 15 of the Abridged Dewey Decimal Classification and Relative Index, published in 2012, by permission of OCLC Online Computer Library Center, Inc., owner of copyright.

OUTLINE OF CLASSIFICATION

Reproduced below is the Second Summary of the Dewey Decimal Classification.* As part of this Core Collection is arranged according to this classification, the outline will serve as a table of contents for it. Please note, however, that the inclusion of this outline is not to be considered a substitute for consulting the Dewey Decimal Classification itself.

000	Computer science, knowledge & systems	500	Science
010	Bibliographies	510	Mathematics
020	Library & information sciences	520	Astronomy
030	Encyclopedias & books of facts	530	Physics
040	[Unassigned]	540	Chemistry
050	Magazines, journals & serials	550	Earth sciences & geology
060	Associations, organizations & museums	560	Fossils & prehistoric life
070	News media, journalism & publishing	570	Life sciences; biology
080	Quotations	580	Plants (Botany)
090	Manuscripts & rare books	590	Animals (Zoology)
100	Philosophy	600	Technology
110	Metaphysics	610	Medicine & health
120	Epistemology	620	Engineering
130	Parapsychology & occultism	630	Agriculture
140	Philosophical schools of thought	640	Home & family management
150	Psychology	650	Management & public relations
160	Logic	660	Chemical engineering
170	Ethics	670	Manufacturing
180	Ancient, medieval & eastern philosophy	680	Manufacture for specific uses
190	Modern western philosophy	690	Building & construction
200	Religion	700	Arts
210	Philosophy & theory of religion	710	Landscaping & area planning
220	The Bible	720	Architecture
230	Christianity & Christian theology	730	Sculpture, ceramics & metalwork
240	Christian practice & observance	740	Drawing & decorative arts
250	Christian pastoral practice & religious orders	750	Painting
260	Christian organization, social work & worship	760	Graphic arts
270	History of Christianity	770	Photography & computer art
280	Christian denominations	780	Music
290	Other religions	790	Sports, games & entertainment
300	Social sciences, sociology & anthropology	800	Literature, rhetoric & criticism
310	Statistics	810	American literature in English
320	Political science	820	English & Old English literatures
330	Economics	830	German & related literatures
340	Law	840	French & related literatures
350	Public administration & military science	850	Italian, Romanian & related literatures
360	Social problems & social services	860	Spanish & Portuguese literatures
370	Education	870	Latin & Italic literatures
380	Commerce, communications & transportation	880	Classical & modern Greek literatures
390	Customs, etiquette & folklore	890	Other literatures
400	Language	900	History
410	Linguistics	910	Geography & travel
420	English & Old English languages	920	Biography & genealogy
430	German & related languages	930	History of ancient world (to ca. 499)
440	French & related languages	940	History of Europe
450	Italian, Romanian & related languages	950	History of Asia
460	Spanish & Portuguese languages	960	History of Africa
470	Latin & Italic languages	970	History of North America
480	Classical & modern Greek languages	980	History of South America
490	Other languages	990	History of other areas

CHILDREN'S CORE COLLECTION
TWENTY-SECOND EDITION
CLASSIFIED COLLECTION

000 COMPUTER SCIENCE, KNOWLEDGE & SYSTEMS

001.4 Research; statistical methods

Cefrey, Holly

★ **Researching** people, places, and events. Rosen Central 2010 48p il (Digital and information literacy) lib bdg $26.50

Grades: 5 6 7 8   **001.4**

1. Research 2. Report writing 3. Internet research

ISBN 978-1-4358-5317-1 lib bdg; 1-4358-5317-2 lib bdg

LC 2008-46785

Describes researching people, places, and events on the Internet, including using primary and secondary sources, evaluating source material, and avoiding plagiarism

"Colorful photos, diagrams, and sidebars and [a] lively [text creates an] appealing, user-friendly [presentation]. . . . Students and teachers will find [this title] useful in keeping up-to-date on and utilizing online resources and today's technology in a rapidly changing digital world." SLJ

Includes glossary and bibliographical references

Gaines, Ann

Ace your Internet research; [by] Ann Graham Gaines. Enslow Publishers 2009 48p il (Ace it! information literacy) lib bdg $23.93

Grades: 3 4 5   **001.4**

1. Internet research 2. Internet searching

ISBN 978-0-7660-3392-4 lib bdg; 0-7660-3392-9 lib bdg

LC 2008032351

"Readers will learn what the internet is, and how to do effective research while staying safe online" Publisher's note

Includes bibliographical references

Jakubiak, David J.

A **smart** kid's guide to doing Internet research. PowerKids Press 2009 24p il (Kids online) lib bdg $21.25; pa $8.25

Grades: 3 4 5 6   **001.4**

1. Internet research

ISBN 978-1-4042-8116-5 lib bdg; 1-4042-8116-9 lib bdg; 978-1-4358-3352-4 pa; 1-4358-3352-X pa

LC 2009002879

In this title "readers are shown how to read URL tags, use browsers, and develop search-term strings. Readers are told that Wikipedia is not reliable because anybody can add

to it. . . . [This is a] worthwhile [purchase] for . . . updating collections in this area." SLJ

Includes glossary

Randolph, Ryan P.

New research techniques; getting the most out of search engine tools. [by] Ryan Randolph. Rosen Central 2011 48p il (Digital and information literacy) lib bdg $27.95; pa $11.75

Grades: 5 6 7 8   **001.4**

1. Internet resources 2. Internet searching 3. Web search engines

ISBN 978-1-4488-1321-6 lib bdg; 1-4488-1321-2 lib bdg; 978-1-4488-2292-8 pa; 1-4488-2292-0 pa

LC 2010016912

Explains new research techniques and tools that are available for online searching. Among the topics covered are browser tools and search engine toolbars, browser add-ons, Web mashups, e-mail and text alerts, RSS feeds and readers, Boolean operators, and refining research results.

"Color illustrations, large fonts, clearly defined subheadings, and easy to read content encourage access to copious information. . . . Teachers and librarians should find this . . . to be a highly versatile teaching tool." Libr Media Connect

Includes glossary and bibliographical references

001.9 Controversial knowledge

Allen, Judy

Unexplained. Kingfisher 2006 144p il $19.95

Grades: 5 6 7 8   **001.9**

1. Parapsychology 2. Curiosities and wonders

ISBN 978-0-7534-5950-8; 0-7534-5950-7

This addresses such topics as ghosts, psychic phenomena, superstitions, mysterious natural phenomena, alleged monsters, disappearances, secrets and mysteries of ancient history, and possible extraterrestrials.

"A seamless combination of absorbing fact-filled text and stunning visuals in an investigation of mysteries that continue to baffle, tantalize, and spark endless debate." SLJ

Includes glossary

Arnosky, Jim

Monster hunt; exploring mysterious creatures with Jim Arnosky. Disney/Hyperion 2011 32p il $16.99

Grades: 2 3 4 5   **001.9**

1. Monsters

ISBN 978-1-4231-3028-4; 1-4231-3028-6

"Arnosky invites readers to join him on a cryptozoology adventure. . . . He compares legends to fact and asks if, for example, sharks could be the documented carcharodon from

13 millennia ago, or if the Loch Ness Monster might be a plesiosaur, thought extinct for 100 million years. The expansive format is appealing. A third of each full-page spread features accessible text, while two-thirds are given over to a painting of the subject. . . . This offers many opportunities for readers to speculate about these intriguing mysteries." Booklist

Erickson, Justin

Alien abductions. Bellwether Media 2011 24p il (Torque: The unexplained) lib bdg $15.95

Grades: 3 4 5 6　　　　　　　　　　　　**001.9**

   1. Extraterrestrial beings

   ISBN 978-1-60014-582-7; 1-60014-582-5

                  LC 2010034773

This book explores the history of alien abduction stories, some of the commonly reported themes, and whether or not the stories could be true.

"Designed for struggling readers, this . . . combines accessible writing, dynamic illustrations, and [a] high-interest [topic]. [A] snazzy [cover] and an abundance of glossy, full-color illustrations provide appeal. . . . The writing is succinct but informative." SLJ

Includes glossary and bibliographical references

Gee, Joshua

   ★ **Encyclopedia** horrifica; the terrifying truth! about vampires, ghosts, monsters, and more. Scholastic Inc. 2007 129p il $14.99

Grades: 4 5 6 7　　　　　　　　　　　　**001.9**

   1. Ghosts 2. Monsters 3. Vampires

   ISBN 978-0-439-92255-5; 0-439-92255-0

                  LC 2007061733

A visual reference contains true stories of such creatures as vampires, aliens, werewolves, and ghosts, accompanied by photographic evidence, eyewitness accounts, and original interviews.

"Each topic is replete with color illustrations and photos and is accompanied by a light, readable text that tries to separate fact from fiction." Voice Youth Advocates

Includes bibliographical references

Halls, Kelly Milner

   In search of Sasquatch; an exercise in zoological evidence. Houghton Mifflin Books for Children 2011 47p il map $16.99

Grades: 4 5 6　　　　　　　　　　　　**001.9**

   1. Animals 2. Sasquatch

   ISBN 978-0-547-25761-7; 0-547-25761-9

                  LC 2011005785

"This book does a fair job of presenting the evidence for Sasquatch through stories of people who have dedicated their lives to finding the cryptid. Evidence for its existence might leave many kids unconvinced, but they will likely be entertained anyway. Black-and-white and muted color illustrations and photos of people, lush forests, clues, and Sasquatch itself are scattered throughout." SLJ

   ★ **Tales** of the cryptids; mysterious creatures that may or may not exist. by Kelly Milner Halls, Rick Spears, Roxyanne Young; [illustrated by Rick Spears] Darby Creek 2006 72p il map $18.95

Grades: 4 5 6 7　　　　　　　　　　　　**001.9**

   1. Monsters

   ISBN 1-58196-049-2

This considers the existence of creatures such as Bigfoot, the Loch Ness Monster, Marozi of Kenya, the Orangpendek of Sumatra, and the Thylacine of Tasmania.

"The conversational text makes for fun reading, and a plethora of pictures . . . will prove enticing." SLJ

Helstrom, Kraig

   Crop circles. Bellwether Media 2011 24p il (Torque: The unexplained) lib bdg $15.95

Grades: 3 4 5 6　　　　　　　　　　　　**001.9**

   1. Crop circles

   ISBN 978-1-60014-583-4; 1-60014-583-3

                  LC 2010034776

This title explores the history of crop circles and looks into whether or not some could be of alien origin.

"Designed for struggling readers, this . . . combines accessible writing, dynamic illustrations, and [a] high-interest [topic]. [A] snazzy [cover] and an abundance of glossy, full-color illustrations provide appeal. . . . The writing is succinct but informative." SLJ

Includes glossary and bibliographical references

Karst, Ken

   Area 51; Ken Karst. Creative Education 2014 48 p. color illustrations, map (Enduring mysteries) (hardcover: alk. paper) $35.65

Grades: 5 6 7 8　　　　　　　　　　　　**001.9**

   1. Nevada 2. Air bases 3. Unidentified flying objects 4. Area 51 (Nev.)

   ISBN 1608183998; 9781608183999

                  LC 2013036073

This book, by Ken Karst, part of the "Enduring Mysteries" series, "takes an investigative approach to the curious phenomena and mysterious circumstances surrounding Area 51, from conspiracy theories to claims of extraterrestrial sightings to hard facts." (Publisher's note)

"With only the barest dashes of skepticism, these handsomely produced surveys present budding cryptozoologists and conspiracy theorists with rich arrays of historical anecdotes and encounters, supposed evidence, "scientific" explanations of varying plausibility, and tantalizing speculations...Karst goes beyond standard issue recaps—ensuring, for instance, that readers will come away from Atlantis knowing more than they did about Madame Blavatsky, as well as Mu and Lemuria, and also expanding his topics with references to, at best, tangentially relevant mysteries such as the fate of Amelia Earhart in Loch Ness Monster." SLJ

   Includes bibliographical references and index

   Other titles in the series are:

   Atlantis (2014)

   Bigfoot (2014)

   Loch Ness Monster (2014)

   Bermuda Triangle (2015)

Matthews, Rupert

   Strange animals. QEB Pub. 2011 30p il (Unexplained) lib bdg $28.50

Grades: 4 5 6 7　　　　　　　　　　　　**001.9**

   1. Monsters

   ISBN 978-1-59566-856-1; 1-59566-856-X

                  LC 2010017915

This discusses the possible existance of cryptids such as Bigfoot, the Loch Ness monster, the Bunyip, sea monsters, the Orang Pendek, and the Marozi.

"This well-written and thoughtfully designed [book] features [an] engrossing [topic]. . . . Though the pages are profusely illustrated with large, well-reproduced photographs and drawings, the layout is not cluttered. This [book] just might inspire kids to seek out more in-depth materials." SLJ

Includes glossary and bibliographical references

Michels, Troy
  Atlantis. Bellwether Media 2011 24p il (Torque: The unexplained) lib bdg $15.95
  Grades: 3 4 5 6   001.9
    1. Atlantis
    ISBN 978-1-60014-585-8; 1-60014-585-X

This book explores the story of Atlantis and the debate about the existence of this ancient civilization.

"Designed for struggling readers, this . . . combines accessible writing, dynamic illustrations, and [a] high-interest [topic]. [A] snazzy [cover] and an abundance of glossy, full-color illustrations provide appeal. . . . The writing is succinct but informative." SLJ

Includes glossary and bibliographical references

004.6   Interfacing and communications

Cornwall, Phyllis
  Online etiquette and safety. Cherry Lake Pub. 2010 32p il (Super smart information strategies) lib bdg $27.07
  Grades: 3 4 5 6   004.6
    1. Etiquette 2. Internet -- Social aspects 3. Internet -- Security measures
    ISBN 978-1-60279-956-1 lib bdg; 1-60279-956-3 lib bdg
                                                       LC 2010002023

This "teaches valuable lessons on why it's important to be responsible online citizens despite the misleading anonymity of the Web and offers tips on how to deal with cyberbullies and other online dangers." Booklist

Includes bibliographical references

Grayson, Robert
  Managing your digital footprint. Rosen Central 2011 48p il (Digital and information literacy) lib bdg $26.50; pa $11.75
  Grades: 5 6 7 8   004.6
    1. Internet 2. Etiquette 3. Right of privacy
    ISBN 978-1-4488-1319-3 lib bdg; 1-4488-1319-0 lib bdg; 978-1-4488-2290-4 pa; 1-4488-2290-4 pa
                                                       LC 2010025746

Though this "title is a broad overview of a sometimes-complex subject, the detail is significant. . . . Touches of blue enhance the clean design. . . . [This] discusses the permanence of impulsively posted material online, contrasting it with more retro forms of self-expression, such as keeping a paper diary." Booklist

Includes bibliographical references

005.8   Data security

Jakubiak, David J.
  A **smart** kid's guide to Internet privacy. PowerKids Press 2009 24p il (Kids online) lib bdg $21.25; pa $8.25
  Grades: 3 4 5 6   005.8
    1. Computer crimes 2. Right of privacy 3. Internet and children 4. Internet -- Security measures
    ISBN 978-1-4042-8118-9 lib bdg; 1-4042-8118-5 lib bdg; 978-1-4358-3356-2 pa; 1-4358-3356-2 pa
                                                       LC 2009005369

This title "is straightforward about not sharing information without parental permission and also gives support and suggestions in case something does happen. . . . [A] worthwhile [purchase] for teaching online safety and updating collections in this area." SLJ

Includes glossary and bibliographical references

006.7   Multimedia systems

Fontichiaro, Kristin
  Podcasting 101. Cherry Lake Pub. 2010 32p il (Super smart information strategies) lib bdg $27.07
  Grades: 3 4 5 6   006.7
    1. Podcasting
    ISBN 978-1-60279-953-0 lib bdg; 1-60279-953-9 lib bdg
                                                       LC 2010004533

"A knockout resource for media-fair projects, Podcasting 101 doles out page after page of useful information, from the equipment required to content ideas for those who might need a creative spark to tips for structuring and adding effects to a successful podcast." Booklist

Includes bibliographical references

Rowell, Rebecca
  YouTube; the company and its founders. ABDO Pub. Co. 2011 112p il (Technology pioneers) lib bdg $32.44
  Grades: 5 6 7 8   006.7
    1. Internet 2. YouTube, Inc.
    ISBN 978-1-61714-813-2 lib bdg; 1-61714-813-X lib bdg; 978-1-61758-971-3 e-book
                                                       LC 2010043379

This is an introduction to YouTube and its founders.

"Written in a clear, linear fashion, this series offers vivid, well-researched details about the development of technological advancements considered essential in today's society. . . . Readers who are interested in technology and inventions will be thoroughly engrossed." SLJ

Includes glossary and bibliographical references

Selfridge, Benjamin
  A **teen's** guide to creating Web pages and blogs; [by] Benjamin Selfridge, Peter Selfridge, and Jennifer Osburn. Prufrock Press 2009 148p il pa $16.95; OP
  Grades: 5 6 7 8 9 10   006.7
    1. Weblogs 2. Internet and teenagers 3. Web sites -- Design
    ISBN 978-1-59363-345-5; 1-59363-345-9
                                                       LC 2008-40044

First published 2004 by Zephyr Press with title: Kid's guide to creating Web pages for home and school

"This guide begins with basic step-by-step information about HTML, fonts, images, lists, and tables. . . . The book's last half introduces more advanced techniques, such as JavaScript, functions, loops, and applications like Flash and Instant Messenger. . . . Illustrated, with references and a glossary, this attractive paperback has lots of practical content." Voice Youth Advocates

Includes glossary and bibliographical references

Truesdell, Ann

Wonderful wikis; by Ann Truesdell. Cherry Lake Publishing 2013 32 p. (Information explorer) (library) $28.50; (paperback) $14.21

Grades: 4 5 6 7   **006.7**
    1. Wikis (Computer science)
    ISBN 1610804805; 9781610804806; 9781610806541
                        LC 2012001758

This juvenile nonfiction book, by Ann Truesdell, as part of the publisher's "Explorer Library" series, presents a profile and guidelines for school children to make use of wikis online for educational purposes. Topics addressed include definitions of what a wiki is, how to contribute to them properly, and what ways they are most useful.

Includes bibliographical references and index

Woog, Adam

YouTube. Norwood House Press 2008 48p il (A great idea) lib bdg $25.27

Grades: 3 4 5 6   **006.7**
    1. Internet 2. YouTube, Inc.
    ISBN 978-1-59953-198-4 lib bdg; 1-59953-198-4 lib bdg
                        LC 2008010724

This "offers a fresh topic and handles it extremely well. . . Woog's account is interesting and informative and written in simple yet uncondescending prose that's spot-on for the intended audience. . . . The attractive design features full-color photographs, while fast facts appear throughout the narrative in eye-catching sidebars." Booklist

Includes glossary and bibliographical references

011.6   General bibliographies and catalogs of works for young people and people with disabilities; for specific types of libraries

East, Kathy

★ **Across** cultures; a guide to multicultural literature for children. Libraries Unlimited 2007 342p il (Children's and young adult literature reference series) $55

Grades: Adult Professional   **011.6**
    1. Reference books 2. Multiculturalism -- Bibliography
    3. Children's literature -- Bibliography
    ISBN 978-1-59158-336-3; 1-59158-336-5
                        LC 2007013573

This is "user-friendly and extremely helpful both in terms of the choices and the descriptions." SLJ

This "introduces more than 400 . . . fiction and nonfiction multicultural resources for preschool through grade 6 . . . arranged in thematic groupings. . . . It presents both annotations and . . . advice on programming strategies. Connec-

tions are made to projects, graphic organizers, and activities." Publisher's note

Includes bibliographical references

Fichtelberg, Susan

★ **Primary** genreflecting; a guide to picture books and easy readers. [by] Susan Fichtelberg and Bridget Dealy Volz. Libraries Unlimited 2010 375p (Genreflecting advisory series) $48

Grades: Adult Professional   **011.6**
    1. Children's literature 2. Picture books for children 3. Children's literature -- Bibliography 4. Picture books for children -- Bibliography
    ISBN 1-56308-907-6; 978-1-56308-907-7
                        LC 2010036578

This "covers picture books and easy readers for children ages three to eight. . . . Fichtelberg and Volz . . . organize 2,500 annotated titles by theme. Most titles are positively reviewed and award-winning books published between 1999 and 2009. . . . Succinct descriptions of plot and style of illustration accompany bibliographic information, awards won, and grade level." Booklist

Includes bibliographical references

Freeman, Judy

★ **Books** kids will sit still for 3; a read-aloud guide. [by] Judy Freeman; Catherine Barr, series editor. Libraries Unlimited 2006 915p il (Children's and young adult literature reference series) $70; pa $55

Grades: Adult Professional   **011.6**
    1. Best books 2. Reference books 3. Children's literature -- Bibliography
    ISBN 1-59158-163-X; 1-59158-164-8 pa

First published 1984 by Alleyside with title: Books kids will sit still for

"This excellent resource will be a favorite with teachers who need assistance finding quality children's literature, and it will also aid librarians and media specialists." SLJ

Gillespie, John Thomas, 1928-

The **children's** and young adult literature handbook; a research and reference guide. Libraries Unlimited 2005 393p (Children's and young adult literature reference series) $55

Grades: Adult Professional   **011.6**
    1. Reference books 2. Children's literature -- Bibliography 3. Young adult literature -- Bibliography 4. Children's literature -- History and criticism 5. Young adult literature -- History and criticism
    ISBN 1-56308-949-1

"This reference should meet the needs of librarians, teachers, and scholars." Choice

This is "a selection guide and collection development aid for librarians, as well as a navigation tool for researchers. Describing and evaluating more than 1,000 publications, the book covers . . . general reference, bibliographies, and biographies to review sources, literary awards, professional organizations, and special library collections. Internet and other nonprint media are included, as are major English-language resources from Britain, Canada, Australia, and South Africa." Publisher's note

Matthew, Kathryn I.

Neal-Schuman guide to recommended children's books and media for use with every elementary subject; by Kathryn I. Matthew and Joy L. Lowe. 2nd ed; Neal-Schuman Publishers 2010 356p pa $75

Grades: Adult Professional   **011.6**

1. Best books 2. Books and reading 3. Audiovisual materials -- Catalogs 4. Children's literature -- Bibliography

ISBN 978-1-55570-688-3; 1-55570-688-6

LC 2010014082

First published 2002

"Listing more than 1,000 books, videos, software, CDs, and Web sites up through early 2010, this book offers elementary (and middle-school) librarians a wonderful collection-development and collaboration tool. Each chapter covers one elementary subject area. . . . The chapters are broken down into narrower topics; each section covers the book and media choices plus ideas for exploring many of the resources listed. Each chapter begins with relevant national standards and ends with teacher resources and references including books, professional organizations, and Web sites. The annotated listings are arranged by grade level from pre–K up through middle school and include full bibliographic information." Booklist

Includes bibliographical references

Meese, Ruth Lyn

Family matters; adoption and foster care in children's literature. Libraries Unlimited 2010 147p pa $35

Grades: Adult Professional   **011.6**

1. Adoption -- Bibliography 2. Foster home care -- Bibliography 3. Children's literature -- Bibliography

ISBN 978-1-59158-782-8 pa; 1-59158-782-4 pa

LC 2009040750

"Meese's goal is to help adults, particularly educators, select high-quality children's books about adoption and foster care and to raise awareness about the unique issues that adoptees often face. . . . Charts, Venn diagrams, and extensive annotations supplement the annotated list of books for children in kindergarten through grade eight. Meese explains her rationale for choosing these books so that readers have the tools to evaluate other selections." SLJ

Includes bibliographical references

Reid, Rob

Reid's read-alouds; selections for children and teens. American Library Association 2009 xiii, 121p pa $45

Grades: Adult Professional   **011.6**

1. Books and reading 2. Children's literature -- Bibliography 3. Young adult literature -- Bibliography

ISBN 978-0-8389-0980-5 pa; 0-8389-0980-9 pa

LC 2008045376

"Reid has collected 200 titles published between 2000 and 2008 that have both readability and general kid appeal. The titles are organized alphabetically by author, and the book includes subject and age-level indexes. Each selection has a cursory summary, grade-level range, and a suggestion for a 10-minute read-aloud, which either provides an introduction to the main characters or a glimpse into the story. . . . This last part is what makes the book so useful." SLJ

Includes bibliographical references

Reid's read-alouds 2; modern day classics from C.S. Lewis to Lemony Snicket. American Library Association 2011 160p

Grades: Adult Professional   **011.6**

1. Books and reading 2. Children's literature 3. Young adult literature 4. Children's literature -- Bibliography 5. Young adult literature -- Bibliography

ISBN 0-8389-1072-6; 978-0-8389-1072-6

LC 2010028985

"The very successful first edition of Reid's Read-Alouds (ALA, 2009) profiled children's and young adult books published between the years 2000 and 2008. This companion volume showcases 200 strong titles that were published from 1950 to 1999. Reid offers a variety of genres and age levels, and a good balance between male and female protagonists. . . . The focus is on books that are great to read to groups of young people. Each entry includes a brief plot summary, suggested grade level, and Reid's signature '10 Minute Selections,' which are engaging episodes from the books that can be read in one sitting. These alone make the book a valuable resource." SLJ

Includes bibliographical references

Safford, Barbara Ripp

Guide to reference materials for school library media centers; 6th ed; Libraries Unlimited 2010 236p $60

Grades: Adult Professional   **011.6**

1. Instructional materials centers 2. School libraries -- Catalogs 3. Reference books -- Bibliography

ISBN 978-1-59158-277-9; 1-59158-277-6

LC 2009-51190

First edition by Christine Gehrt Wynar published 1973 with title: Guide to reference books for school media centers

"This volume has been updated to include web-based reference offerings as well as listings of older sources, provided that their content is still valid. . . . This title profiles resources recommended for use by school librarians for collection management, readers' advisory, teaching, general reference materials, the social sciences and humanities, and science and technology. This volume is an excellent starting point for new school librarians, as well as for those who are building a library from scratch." SLJ

Includes bibliographical references

Schon, Isabel

Recommended books in Spanish for children and young adults, 2004-2008. Scarecrow Press 2009 414p $55

Grades: Adult Professional   **011.6**

1. Reference books 2. Spanish literature -- Bibliography 3. Children's literature -- Bibliography 4. Young adult literature -- Bibliography 5. Latin American literature -- Bibliography

ISBN 978-0-8108-6386-6; 0-8108-6386-3

LC 2008-33390

"Schon evaluates 1231 reference books, fiction, and nonfiction. . . . Entries are arranged alphabetically by author and include a grade level for each book. . . . Schon examines and recommends materials based on the quality of the Spanish language, literary appeal, and the versatility of the translators, paying special attention to the effective use of Peninsular Spanish or the Spanish from the Americas. This annotated bibliography will help selectors in public libraries and media centers to develop existing Spanish-language collections." SLJ

Spiegel, Carol

Book by book; an annotated guide to young people's literature with peacemaking and conflict resolution themes. Educators for Social Responsibility 2010 186p pa $35

Grades: Adult Professional   **011.6**

1. Peace -- Bibliography 2. Conflict management -- Bibliography 3. Children's literature -- Bibliography 4. Young adult literature -- Bibliography

ISBN 978-0-942349-93-1 pa; 0-942349-93-8 pa

"More than 900 books for preschool through high school have been organized by title into two sections, picture and chapter books; described; and assigned behavioral headings. Thematic clusters include making connections, emotional literacy, caring and effective communication, cultural competence and social responsibility, and conflict management and responsible decision making. . . . Useful especially in elementary and middle schools where character education is part of the curriculum without the explicit mandate." SLJ

011.62   Works for young people

Barr, Catherine

★ **Best** books for children; preschool through grade 6. Catherine Barr and John T. Gillespie. 9th ed. Libraries Unlimited/ABC-CLIO 2010 xv, 1901 p.p (hardcover: acid-free paper) $95

Grades: Adult Professional   **011.62**

1. Best books -- United States 2. Children's literature -- Bibliography 3. Children -- Books and reading -- United States

ISBN 1591585759; 9781591585756

LC 2009049873

First published 1978

Author Catherine Barr's book allows librarians to "build collections to make their young patrons--and their parents and teachers--happy." It is a "guide to the best recreational and educational reading for children in preschool through grade 6." The book "brings together information on nearly 25,000 of the best fiction and nonfiction for children in pre-school through grade 6." (Publisher's note)

Hearne, Betsy Gould

Choosing books for children; a commonsense guide. [by] Betsy Hearne with Deborah Stevenson. 3rd ed; University of Ill. Press 1999 229p il hardcover o.p. OP; pa $21

Grades: Adult Professional   **011.62**

1. Reference books 2. Books and reading 3. Children's literature -- Bibliography

ISBN 0-252-02516-4; 0-252-06928-5 pa

LC 99-6144

First published 1981 by Delacorte Press

"The focus is on books since 1950; the 14 chapter-opening illustrations mainly represent books of the last decade. Chapters divide books by age and genre; one chapter considers the value of controversial books while another affectionately revisits classics." Publ Wkly

Silvey, Anita

★ **Children's** book-a-day almanac; Anita Silvey. Roaring Brook Press 2012 388 p. $19.99

Grades: Adult Professional   **011.62**

1. Children's literature 2. Children -- Books and reading 3. Almanacs 4. Best books -- United States 5. Children's literature -- Bibliography 6. Children's literature -- Stories, plots, etc 7. Children -- Books and reading -- United States

ISBN 1596437081; 9781596437081

LC 2012013301

Author Anita Silvey presents a reference book of great children's books of the past and present. "Each page features an event of the day, a children's book that relates to that event, and a list of other events that took place on that day." The almanac includes 365 books for children of various ages, from picture books to counting books and read-along books. (Publisher's note)

Includes bibliographical references

016   Bibliographies and catalogs of works on specific subjects

Al-Hazza, Tami Craft

Books about the Middle East; selecting and using them with children and adolescents. [by] Tami Craft Al-Hazza and Katherine T. Bucher. Linworth Pub. 2008 168p pa $39.95

Grades: Adult Professional   **016**

1. Reference books 2. Middle East -- Bibliography 3. Children's literature -- Bibliography 4. Young adult literature -- Bibliography

ISBN 978-1-58683-285-8; 1-58683-285-9

LC 2007-40149

"This book examines the body of literature about the diverse groups of people who inhabit the Middle East, and it also explores a variety of ways in which this literature can be used. . . . It fills a huge gap and should not be overlooked. This powerhouse book will be tremendously helpful to media specialists, educators, and public librarians." Voice Youth Advocates

Includes bibliographical references

Child Study Children's Book Committee at Bank Street

The **best** children's books of the year; selected by the Children's Book Committee at Bank Street College of Education. Teacher's College Press

Grades: Adult Professional   **016**

1. Reference books 2. Children's literature -- Bibliography

First published 1998

"This is a comprehensive annotated book list for children, aged infant–14." Publisher's note

Crew, Hilary S.

Women engaged in war in literature for youth; a guide to resources for children and young adults. Scarecrow Press 2007 303p (Literature for youth) pa $51

Grades: Adult Professional   **016**

1. Reference books 2. War -- Bibliography 3. Women -- Bibliography 4. Children's literature -- Bibliography 5. Young adult literature -- Bibliography

ISBN 978-0-8108-4929-7; 0-8108-4929-1

LC 2006-101112

"Crew's guide to print and online sources documents women's roles in wars over the centuries and throughout the world, divided by time periods. . . . This is a great addition for libraries looking for a way to move Women's Studies beyond the month of March." SLJ

Includes bibliographical references

Garcha, Rajinder

The **world** of Islam in literature for youth; a selective annotated bibliography for K-12. [by] Rajinder Garcha, Patricia Yates Russell. Scarecrow Press 2006 xx, 221p (Literature for youth) pa $35

Grades: Adult Professional   **016**
1. Reference books 2. Islam -- Bibliography 3. Children's literature -- Bibliography 4. Young adult literature -- Bibliography

ISBN 978-0-8108-5488-8; 0-8108-5488-0

LC 2005-26645

"This highly useful bibliography fills a conspicuous gap in a much-needed cultural area." Voice Youth Advocates

Includes bibliographical references

Hall, Susan

★ **Using** picture storybooks to teach literary devices; recommended books for children and young adults. Libraries Unlimited 2007 282p (Using picture books to teach) pa $42

Grades: Adult Professional   **016**
1. Literature -- Study and teaching

ISBN 978-1-59158-493-3 pa; 1-59158-493-0 pa

"This fourth volume of the series, . . . gives teachers and librarians the . . . tool to teach literary devices in grades K–12. With this volume, the author has added: colloquialism; counterpoint; solecism; archetype; and others to the list of devices. The entries have been reorganized to include all the information under the book listing itself. Each entry includes an annotation, a listing of curricular tie-ins for the book and the art style used, and a listing and explanation of all the literary devices taught by that title." Publisher's note

Includes bibliographical references

Thomas, Rebecca L.

★ **Popular** series fiction for K-6 readers; a reading and selection guide. [by] Rebecca L. Thomas and Catherine Barr. 2nd ed; Libraries Unlimited 2008 1002p (Children's and young adult literature reference series) $65

Grades: Adult Professional   **016**
1. Reference books 2. Children's literature -- Bibliography

ISBN 978-1-59158-659-3; 1-59158-659-3

LC 2008-38124

First published 2004

"Using standard review sources and bibliographies as well as author, publisher, bookseller, and library Web sites, the authors have identified nearly 2,200 in-print series appropriate for K–6 readers. . . . Entries are arranged by the series title and contain author, most recent publisher, grade level, notation for availability of accelerated-reader resources, genre, a descriptive three to five-sentence annotation, and a list of individual titles in the series, arranged by publication date. Following the entries are author, title, and genre/subject indexes as well as appendixes that list books for boys, girls, and reluctant readers. . . . [This is] essential

as reference and selection tools in all school, public, and academic libraries." Booklist

Includes bibliographical references

Walter, Virginia A.

★ **War** & peace; a guide to literature and new media, grades 4-8. [by] Virginia A. Walter. Libraries Unlimited 2007 276p (Children's and young adult literature reference series) pa $40

Grades: Adult Professional   **016**
1. Reference books 2. War -- Bibliography 3. Peace -- Bibliography 4. Children's literature -- Bibliography 5. Young adult literature -- Bibliography

ISBN 1-59158-271-7 pa; 978-1-59158-271-7 pa

LC 2006030671

"Walter addresses the issue of war—and peace—by examining the information needs of children and how we as professionals can meet them. . . . The bulk of the book is the annotated listing of resources that is divided topically. . . . The well-annotated bibliography includes books, DVDs, Web sites, and CDs, as well as suggestions for using the materials. . . . This book should be a 'must purchase.'" SLJ

Includes bibliographical references

Wesson, Lindsey Patrick

Green reads; best environmental resources for youth, K-12. Libraries Unlimited 2009 219p (Children's and young adult literature reference series) $50

Grades: Adult Professional   **016**
1. Reference books 2. Children's literature -- Bibliography 3. Young adult literature -- Bibliography 4. Environmental protection -- Bibliography 5. Conservation of natural resources -- Bibliography

ISBN 978-1-59158-834-4; 1-59158-834-0

LC 2009-17353

"This well-organized bibliography offers 450 annotated resources that can be integrated into the classroom to introduce students to environmental concepts. The five chapters focus on global warming, pollution, the Earth's resources, recycling, and conservation. Subchapters follow a uniform organization, including fiction; DVDs and CDs; nonfiction; seminal works, which are labeled 'Recycled Favorites'; and a storytime lesson plan with a variety of activities including songs and tactile learning activities. . . . This reference will delight educators and professionals interested in making students aware of environmental issues and to help youngsters rediscover the outside and natural worlds around them." SLJ

Includes bibliographical references

016.098   Challenged books – United States -- Bibliography

★ **Books** under fire; a hit list of banned and challenged children's books. Pat Scales. ALA Editions, an imprint of the American Library Association 2015 xvi, 208 p.p (pbk.) $47

Grades: Adult Professional   **016.098**
1. Books -- Censorship 2. Children -- Books and reading -- United States 3. School libraries -- Censorship -- United States 4. Challenged books -- United States -- Bibliography 5. Prohibited books -- United States -- Bibliography 6. Children's literature -- Censorship

-- United States

ISBN 0838911099; 9780838911099

LC 2014023945

This book on banned and challenged books, by Pat R. Scales, "covers both children's and young adult books. The main section profiles 34 books (and series such as 'Harry Potter' and 'Captain Underpants') that have recently been challenged for library or curriculum suitability in the US. . . . Each entry includes a . . . synopsis, quotations from some reviews, details of known challenges, awards/accolades, and a 'Further Reading' section." (Choice: Current Reviews for Academic Libraries)

"Like death and taxes, book challenges are always with us, as noted intellectual-freedom advocate Scales implies in her splendid new book about censorship. . . . Books under Fire contains a veritable arsenal of information . . . a copiously annotated list of 34 often challenged children's books or series. Some of these are familiar (e.g., The Giver and the Captain Underpants series), and some may be surprising (e.g., the Wimpy Kid and Junie B. Jones series). Each featured title contains a gracefully written book summary, quotes from professional review sources, details of recorded challenges, lists of awards and accolades, official websites for the author and/or illustrator, suggestions for further reading, and references for listening and viewing. . . . this one is clearly indispensable and belongs in every library collection." Booklist

Includes bibliographical references and index

020   Library and information sciences

Fontichiaro, Kristin

Go straight to the source. Cherry Lake Pub. 2010 32p il (Super smart information strategies) lib bdg $27.07

Grades: 3 4 5 6   **020**

1. Research 2. Information resources 3. History -- Sources

ISBN 978-1-60279-640-9 lib bdg; 1-60279-640-8 lib bdg

LC 2009028057

"The appealing layout includes manageable paragraphs, a variety of engaging illustrations, and examples that clearly guide reader through each topic. . . . [This] provides an excellent introduction to primary sources and will create enthusiasm in readers for examining old photographs and ads." SLJ

Includes glossary and bibliographical references

Gaines, Ann

Master the library and media center; [by] Ann Graham Gaines. Enslow Publishers, Inc. 2009 48p il (Ace it! information literacy) lib bdg $23.93

Grades: 3 4 5   **020**

1. Research 2. Libraries 3. Information literacy 4. Information resources 5. Instructional materials centers

ISBN 978-0-7660-3393-1 lib bdg; 0-7660-3393-7 lib bdg

LC 2008024886

"Readers will learn about both the regular and electronic research materials available at the library" Publisher's note

Includes bibliographical references

Kenney, Karen Latchana

Librarians at work; by Karen L. Kenney; illustrated by Brian Caleb Dumm; content consultant, Judith Stepan-Norris. Magic Wagon 2010 32p il (Meet your community workers!) lib bdg $18.95

Grades: K 1 2 3   **020**

1. Librarians 2. Vocational guidance

ISBN 978-1-60270-649-1 lib bdg; 1-60270-649-2 lib bdg

LC 2009-2386

This book about librarians has "an uncluttered layout and consistent organization. . . . Chapter headings such as 'Problems on the Job,' and 'Technology at Work,' and 'Special Skills and Training' make it easy to pinpoint specific information." SLJ

Includes glossary

Pinborough, Jan

Miss Moore thought otherwise; the story of the lady who made libraries for children. by Jan Pinborough; illustrated by Debby Atwell. Houghton Mifflin Harcourt 2013 40 p. (reinforced) $16.99

Grades: 1 2 3 4 5   **020**

1. Librarians 2. Children's libraries 3. New York Public Library -- Biography 4. Children's libraries -- United States -- History 5. Children's librarians -- United States -- Biography

ISBN 054747105X; 9780547471051

LC 2012018092

This book is a biography of "children's advocate and librarian [Anne Carroll] Moore (1871-1961), celebrated for her pioneering work in making libraries and library services accessible to (and fun for) kids." Author Jan Pinborough "has selected highlights from Moore's life—her belief in letting children touch and borrow books, her ascent to the head of children's services for the New York Public Library—and streamlined them." (Publishers Weekly)

Includes bibliographical references

021   Relationships of libraries, archives, information centers

York, Sherry

Booktalking authentic multicultural literature; fiction and history for young readers. Linworth Pub. 2009 112p pa $39.95

Grades: Adult Professional   **021**

1. Book talks 2. Multicultural education 3. Youth -- Books and reading 4. Teenagers -- Books and reading 5. Multiculturalism -- Bibliography 6. Young adult literature -- Bibliography

ISBN 978-1-58683-300-8 pa; 1-58683-300-6 pa

LC 200843798

This title "highlights 101 contemporary books by a variety of U.S. authors. Arranged alphabetically by title, entries include the cultural background of author, illustrator, and translator; their Web sites when available; reading and interest levels; genre; related titles; and the single-paragraph booktalk itself. Over 20 ethnic groups are represented. . . . Librarians will find this book helpful in expanding their collections to reflect our global society." SLJ

021.2 Relationships with the community

Squires, Tasha

Library partnerships; making connections between school and public libraries. Information Today, Inc. 2009 203p pa $39.50

Grades: Adult Professional   **021.2**

1. Public libraries 2. School libraries 3. Library cooperation 4. Libraries and schools 5. Libraries and students

ISBN 978-1-57387-362-8; 1-57387-362-4

LC 2008-51647

"Squires's confident advice can get beleaguered librarians through . . . difficulties and into mutually productive partnerships." Voice Youth Advocates

Includes bibliographical references

021.7 Promotion of libraries, archives, information centers

Cole, Sonja

Booktalking around the world; great global reads for ages 9-14. Libraries Unlimited 2010 155p pa $35

Grades: Adult Professional   **021.7**

1. Book talks 2. Children's literature 3. Ethnology 4. Geography 5. World history 6. Children's literature -- Bibliography

ISBN 1-59884-613-2 pa; 978-1-59884-613-3 pa; 978-1-59884-614-0 ebook

LC 2010036580

"In this authoritative and highly readable text, [Cole] presents booktalks and reading lists of interest to children. The titles chosen are set in Africa, Asia, Europe, the Americas, Australia, New Zealand and the South Pacific Islands, and the Arctic and Antarctic. Each booktalk contains an enticing description of the book, bibliographic information, interest and reading levels, and awards. Those that have videos available are noted." SLJ

Includes bibliographical references

Keane, Nancy J.

★ The **tech**-savvy booktalker; a guide for 21st-century educators. [by] Nancy J. Keane and Terence W. Cavanaugh. Libraries Unlimited 2009 162p il pa $35

Grades: Adult Professional   **021.7**

1. Book talks 2. Information technology

ISBN 978-1-59158-637-1 pa; 1-59158-637-2 pa

LC 2008-38988

"Keane offers a way to enhance booktalks with technology and to invite students to explore new ways to talk about books using Web 2.0 tools. The volume is divided into 11 chapters from booktalking concepts to more advanced uses of technology including scanners, digital cameras, computer software, and audio recording. Also included are chapters on software programs such as PowerPoint and iMovie as well as Internet sites such as YouTube and Amazon. The sequence of chapters is designed to allow easy access to information for both novice and experienced computer users. . . . This excellent resource shows ways to use existing technology to augment booktalks and to expand the experience beyond the classroom." SLJ

Includes bibliographical references

Skaggs, Gayle

Look, it's books! marketing your library with displays and promotions. [by] Gayle Skaggs. McFarland & Co. 2008 188p il pa $45

Grades: Adult Professional   **021.7**

1. School libraries 2. Books and reading 3. Libraries -- Exhibitions

ISBN 978-0-7864-3132-8 pa; 0-7864-3132-6 pa

LC 2007049517

"A good basic resource for anyone needing ideas to promote reading to elementary students." Booklist

025.04 Information storage and retrieval systems

Porterfield, Jason

★ **Conducting** basic and advanced searches. Rosen Central 2010 48p il (Digital and information literacy) lib bdg $26.50

Grades: 5 6 7 8   **025.04**

1. Internet resources 2. Internet searching

ISBN 978-1-4358-5316-4 lib bdg; 1-4358-5316-4 lib bdg

LC 2008-46783

Describes how to conduct both basic and advanced searches on the Internet, from the basics of online search engines, boolean search terms, and evaluating the content of search results

"Colorful photos, diagrams, and sidebars and [a] lively [text creates an] appealing, user-friendly [presentation]. . . . Students and teachers will find [this title] useful in keeping up-to-date on and utilizing online resources and today's technology in a rapidly changing digital world." SLJ

Includes glossary and bibliographical references

Rabbat, Suzy

Find your way online. Cherry Lake Pub. 2010 32p il (Super smart information strategies) lib bdg $27.07

Grades: 3 4 5 6   **025.04**

1. Internet searching

ISBN 978-1-60279-639-3 lib bdg; 1-60279-639-4 lib bdg

LC 2009024549

"The appealing layout includes manageable paragraphs, a variety of engaging illustrations, and examples that clearly guide readers through each topic. . . . [This] begins with keywords, narrowing the search, and search engines. Then it shows students how to 'drill down' using subject directories and databases." SLJ

Scheeren, William O.

Technology for the school librarian; theory and practice. Libraries Unlimited 2010 223p il $50

Grades: Adult Professional   **025.04**

1. School libraries 2. Digital libraries 3. Information technology 4. Libraries -- Special collections

ISBN 978-1-59158-900-6; 1-59158-900-2

LC 2009-51922

"This title provides information on the practical aspects of technology in the school library as well as the theoretical framework to spark continued learning. Sharing actual case studies as well as practical tips on technology implentation and terminology, this title will be a valuable resource to any school librarian." Libr Media Connect

Includes bibliographical references

Truesdell, Ann

Find the right site. Cherry Lake Pub. 2010 32p il (Super smart information strategies) lib bdg $27.07

Grades: 3 4 5 6   **025.04**

1. Internet searching

ISBN 978-1-60279-638-6 lib bdg; 1-60279-638-6 lib bdg

LC 2009027083

"The appealing layout includes manageable paragraphs, a variety of engaging illustrations, and examples that clearly guide readers through each topic. . . . [This] is an excellent introduction to Web site evaluation and related pitfalls." SLJ

Includes glossary and bibliographical references

025.1 Administration

Farmer, Lesley S. Johnson

Neal-Schuman technology management handbook for school library media centers; by Lesley S. Johnson Farmer and Marc E. McPhee. Neal-Schuman Publishers 2010 289p il pa $59.95

Grades: Adult Professional   **025.1**

1. School libraries 2. Instructional materials centers

ISBN 978-1-55570-659-3; 1-55570-659-2

LC 2010-9301

"This informative, well-researched text is perfect for those in the early stages of integrating technology into their programs. The first chapter begins with an overview of the impact technology has had on society and defines technology and its role in the library, including past, present, and possible future changes, as well as managerial roles of the librarian. Other chapters examine planning for management, assessing, researching, developing a technology plan, acquiring all types of tech resources, and managing the physical space to accommodate equipment and networking." SLJ

Includes bibliographical references

The **frugal** librarian; thriving in tough economic times. edited by Carol Smallwood. American Library Association 2011 277p il

Grades: Adult Professional   **025.1**

1. Library finance 2. Libraries and community 3. Libraries -- United States

ISBN 0-8389-1075-0; 978-0-8389-1075-7

LC 2010034317

"The thirty-four chapters in Smallwood's collection address a myriad of issues faced by libraries and librarians when times get tough and money is tight. Written by practicing librarians from academic, public, and school libraries, the concise essays are easy to read, sometimes personal, and highly practical. . . . This issue is certainly timely, but in reality, sound management and creative budgeting never vanish from the library environment. The table of contents and descriptive title chapters, coupled with the index, allow for ease of use for the browser. This inexpensive volume from ALA will be particularly helpful to public and academic librarians." Voice Youth Advocates

Includes bibliographical references

Fullner, Sheryl Kindle

The **shoestring** library. Linworth Publishing 2010 139p il pa $30

Grades: Adult Professional   **025.1**

1. Library finance

ISBN 978-1-58683-520-0 pa; 1-58683-520-3 pa

LC 2010-718

"The book is divided into two sections. 'Library Management for Tough Times' has hints for taking advantage of free continuing-education opportunities, using volunteers, networking, and more. 'The Physical Plant' contains suggestions for sprucing up the library at little or no cost (for example: request mismatched or clearance paints from paint stores; then get students to do the painting)." (Booklist)

Independent school libraries; perspectives on excellence. Dorcas Hand, editor. Libraries Unlimited 2010 369p il (Libraries Unlimited professional guides in school librarianship) pa $45

Grades: Adult Professional   **025.1**

1. Private schools 2. School libraries

ISBN 978-1-59158-803-0 pa; 1-59158-803-0 pa; 978-1-59158-812-2 ebook

LC 2010-14567

"Twenty-one essays by prominent independent school librarians both address the current state of independent school librarianship in the United States and offer suggestions for the future. Pieces cover the library's role in the school, statistical comparisons, staffing, advocacy, assessment, technology, information commons, collaboration, college preparation, programming, traditions, collection development, minors' rights, budgeting, facilities, accreditation, and disaster planning. . . . Librarians from all schools will find a wealth of information here." Voice Youth Advocates

Includes bibliographical references

Johnson, Doug

★ The **indispensable** librarian; surviving and thriving in school libraries in the information age. Doug Johnson; illustrations by Brady Johnson. Linworth, an imprint of ABC-CLIO, LLC 2013 xix, 207 p.p illustrations (pbk.) $40

Grades: Adult Professional   **025.1**

1. Librarians 2. School libraries 3. School librarians -- United States 4. School libraries -- United States -- Administration

ISBN 161069239X; 9781610692397

LC 2012051394

This book, by Doug A. Johnson, "defines and clarifies the role of the school library media specialist in a technologically enhanced school, providing relevant examples and useful advice on a variety of topics; and underscores the importance of strong management skills, especially regarding collaborative planning and communications. The book is written especially for K-12 school librarians, both new and experienced, and is also suitable for pre-service librarians as a textbook." (Publisher's note)

"Johnson offers both theory and practical suggestions on ways to embed [librarians] and [their] jobs into the fabric of a school's culture and curriculum." Lib Med Con

Includes bibliographical references and index

MacDonell, Colleen

★ **Essential** documents for school libraries; 2nd ed.; Linworth 2010 xxiv, 156p il $50

Grades: Adult Professional   **025.1**
1. Libraries -- Administration
ISBN 978-1-58683-400-5

LC 2010-21241

First published 2004
"Each chapter begins with why the documents are needed, followed by practical advice for writing the documents, and examples of how the documents make an effective change in the library media program." Libr Media Connect [review of 2004 edition]
Includes bibliographical references

Martin, Barbara Stein
★ **Fundamentals** of school library media management; a how-to-do-it manual. [by] Barbara Stein Martin and Marco Zannier. Neal-Schuman Publishers 2009 172p il (How-to-do-it manuals for librarians) pa $59.95
Grades: Adult Professional   **025.1**
1. School libraries 2. Instructional materials centers
ISBN 978-1-55570-656-2; 1-55570-656-8

LC 2009-7930

This book "contains useful information to help school librarians manage a myriad of tasks and roles. . . . [The authors] have created a book that is helpful, accessible, and full of down-to-earth, concrete examples." Booklist
Includes bibliographical references

★ **School** library management; [edited by] Judi Repman and Gail Dickinson. 6th ed.; Linworth Pub. 2007 200p il pa $44.95
Grades: Adult Professional   **025.1**
1. School libraries 2. Libraries -- Administration
ISBN 978-1-58683-296-4; 1-58683-296-4

LC 2006-103468

First published 1987 with title: School library management notebook
"This collection of more than 35 articles written for Library Media Connection from 2003 to 2006 is a virtual treasure trove for library media specialists. . . . The book covers the very practical everyday issues such as scheduling and overdues, and also provides invaluable information on data gathering, facilities planning, professional development, the role of the library in the world of standardized testing, the technological future of libraries, and much more." SLJ
Includes bibliographical references

Tips and other bright ideas for elementary school libraries. Volume 4 Kate Vande Brake, editor. Linworth 2010 134p Volume 4 pa $35
Grades: Adult Professional   **025.1**
1. Elementary school libraries 2. Libraries -- Administration
ISBN 978-1-58683-416-6 pa; 1-58683-416-9 pa; 978-1-58683-417-3 ebook

LC 2010011049

This title includes "fun and informative management advice from fellow librarians. All of it has been taken from 2006-2009 Library Media Connection magazine. . . . [The introduction] reviews some of the many jobs and responsibilities in a librarian's day. Section one includes management hints to help maximize effectiveness, followed by sections on working with students, teaching skills, . . . working with teachers, technology, reading promotion, public relations, and working with helpers." SLJ

025.2   Acquisitions and collection developme

Baumbach, Donna
★ **Less** is more; a practical guide to weeding school library collections. American Library Association 2006 194p il pa $32
Grades: Adult Professional   **025.2**
1. Libraries -- Collection development
ISBN 978-0-8389-0919-5; 0-8389-0919-1

LC 2006-7490

"This outstanding, easy-to-use guide makes weeding realistic and achievable. . . . This is an indispensable resource for every school library." Booklist
Includes bibliographical references

Brenner, Robin E.
★ **Understanding** manga and anime. Libraries Unlimited 2007 335p il pa $40
Grades: Adult Professional   **025.2**
1. Anime 2. Manga -- Study and teaching 3. Libraries -- Collection development 4. Libraries -- Special collections -- Graphic novels
ISBN 978-1-59158-332-5; 1-59158-332-2

LC 2007-9773

The author "provides thorough explanations of manga and anime vocabulary, potential censorship issues because of cultural disparities, and typical Manga conventions. . . . No professional collection could possibly be complete without this all-inclusive and exceptional work." Voice Youth Advocates

Fagan, Bryan D:
Comic book collections for libraries; [by] Bryan D. Fagan and Jody Condit Fagan; foreword by Stan Sakai; cover art by Derek Steed. Libraries Unlimited 2011 162p pa $45; e-book $45
Grades: Adult Professional   **025.2**
1. Graphic novels -- Bibliography 2. Comic books; strips, etc. -- Bibliography 3. Libraries -- Special collections -- Graphic novels
ISBN 978-1-59884-511-2 pa; 1-59884-511-X pa; 978-1-59884-512-9 e-book

LC 2010052532

"Armed with this book, librarians should feel confident about knowledgeably creating and maintaining a successful comic-book collection." SLJ
Includes bibliographical references

Franklin, Patricia
School library collection development; just the basics. Claire Gatrell Stephens and Patricia Franklin. Libraries Unlimited 2012 x, 71 p.p ill. (Just the basics) (paperback) $35
Grades: Adult Professional   **025.2**
1. Libraries -- Collection development 2. Collection management (Libraries) -- United States 3. School libraries -- Collection development -- United States
ISBN 1598849433; 9781598849431

LC 2012016990

This book, by Claire Gatrell Stephens and Patricia Franklin, discusses collection development for school librarians. This volume offers a "manual that explains the fundamentals of purchasing, developing, and managing a collection. Containing information useful to anyone from a professional working under the guidance of a certified school librarian to a newcomer to the field to a certified media specialist, this book covers all of the basics through best practices." (Publisher's note)

Gallaway, Beth
★ **Game** on! gaming at the library. Neal-Schuman Publishers 2009 306p il pa $55
Grades: Adult Professional   025.2
1. Video games 2. Video games and children 3. Video games and teenagers 4. Multimedia library services 5. Electronic games -- Collections 6. Libraries -- Special collections
ISBN 1-55570-595-2; 978-1-55570-595-4
LC 2009-14110
"An essential guide for any librarian who plans on embracing the video-game phenomenon, or at the very least, understanding it. . . . [The chapters] are well organized and contain an abundance of practical information. The sections on selection, collection, and circulation of video games include relevant advice on policy, cataloging, marketing, storage, and displays. . . . The annotated list of video games for a core collection is wonderful for selection purposes." SLJ
Includes bibliographical references

Goldsmith, Francisca
The **readers'** advisory guide to graphic novels. American Library Association 2010 124p (ALA readers' advisory series) pa $45
Grades: Adult Professional   025.2
1. Graphic novels -- Bibliography 2. Libraries -- Special collections -- Graphic novels
ISBN 978-0-8389-1008-5; 0-8389-1008-4
LC 2009-25239
"After dispelling the two main myths that ghettoize graphic novels—they are just for adolescents and they are far less complex than texts without pictures—Goldsmith emphasizes that GNs are a format and not a genre. She suggests active and passive ways to offer readers' advisory (RA) from face-to-face encounters with patrons to book displays and book groups and offers guidance on helping established GN readers to find new titles they might enjoy. . . . All in all it is a valuable and quite readable resource that belongs in every library's professional collection." Voice Youth Advocates
Includes glossary and bibliographical references

Graphic novels beyond the basics; insights and issues for libraries. Martha Cornog and Timothy Perper, editors. Libraries Unlimited 2009 xxx, 281p il pa $45
Grades: Adult Professional   025.2
1. Graphic novels -- History and criticism 2. Comic books, strips, etc. -- History and criticism 3. Libraries -- Special collections -- Graphic novels
ISBN 978-1-59158-478-0; 1-59158-478-7
LC 2009-16189
Editors Cornog and Perper have collected essays by experts Robin Brenner, Francisca Goldsmith, Trina Robbins, Michael R. Lavin, Gilles Poitras, Lorena O'English, Michael Niederhausen, Erin Byrne, and Cornog herself, all about graphic novels in libraries. Topics covered range from the appeal of superheroes to manga, the appeal of comics to women and girls, anime, independent comics, dealing with challenges to the material, and more. Appendices provide resource information on African American-interest

graphic novels, Latino-Interest graphic novels, LGBT-interest graphic novels, religious-themed graphic novels, a bibliography of books about graphic novels in libraries, and online resources.

"Whether you are serious about the genre, interested in the history, or looking for ammunition, this book should be on your shelf. The wealth of knowledge and research that went into these essays is impressive, and reading this book will put you on the road to becoming an expert." Libr Media Connect
Includes bibliographical references

Herald, Nathan
Graphic novels for young readers; a genre guide for ages 4-14. Libraries Unlimited 2011 188p (Genreflecting advisory series) $40
Grades: Adult Professional   025.2
1. Graphic novels 2. Children's literature 3. Graphic novels -- Bibliography
ISBN 1-59884-395-8; 978-1-59884-395-8
LC 2010044947
"Librarians looking to beef up their graphic-novel collections will do well to get their hands on this valuable volume. The annotated entries are laid out in eight chapters organized by major genre, and from action and adventure to educational. Within chapters, the titles, 600 in all, are arranged alphabetically into popular subgenres such as superheroes, mythology, sports, and many more. . . . The intended audience for each title is clear, with bold icons providing an age range. Herald's writing style lends personality to what could easily be a dry overview. . . . A thorough, well-organized, one-stop shop for quality graphic novels." SLJ
Includes bibliographical references

Mayer, Brian
Libraries got game; aligned learning through modern board games. [by] Brian Mayer and Christopher Harris. American Library Association 2010 134p il pa $45
Grades: Adult Professional   025.2
1. Board games 2. Libraries -- Special collections
ISBN 978-0-8389-1009-2; 0-8389-1009-2
LC 2009-26839
"This is a valuable resource for K-12 librarians interested in building curriculum-aligned 'designer' game collections. The authors . . . explain how specific games enhance language-arts, social-studies, and math units, and build literacy skills. The two chapters devoted to promoting and justifying the inclusion of games in the library are well documented and a wonderful source to have to convince skeptical administrators. Suggestions for building a core collection, which highlights top recommended games for elementary school, middle school, and high school; a list of game publishers; a list of games discussed; and a glossary of terminology are included." SLJ
Includes bibliographical references

Scales, Pat R.
★ **Protecting** intellectual freedom in your school library; scenarios from the front lines. [by] Pat R. Scales for the Office for Intellectual Freedom. American Library Association 2009 148p (Intellectual freedom front lines) pa $55

Grades: Adult Professional **025.2**
1. School libraries 2. Intellectual freedom
ISBN 978-0-8389-3581-1; 0-8389-3581-8
LC 2008-39893

"Scales uses court opinions, federal and state laws, and ALA documents to offer solutions for responding to infringements. A broad range of potential scenarios—from challenges to materials in both the library and the classroom, the legality of film rating systems, using computerized reading programs as selection tools and labeling books by reading levels, policies for interlibrary loans and reserves to confidentiality of children's and teens' circulation records—are covered. . . . This resource should be in every school library's professional collection." Voice Youth Advocates

Includes bibliographical references

Serchay, David S.
★ The **librarian's** guide to graphic novels for children and tweens. Neal-Schuman Publishers 2008 272p pa $55
Grades: Adult Professional **025.2**
1. Graphic novels 2. Children -- Books and reading 3. Libraries -- Special collections -- Graphic novels
ISBN 978-1-55570-626-5 pa; 1-55570-626-5 pa
LC 2008-6487

This book provides a brief history of graphic novels, describes genres, discusses manga, gives librarians reasons to include graphic novels in library collections and in school curricula. It also discusses some of the major comic book publishers in the U.S., suggests how to purchase graphic novels, and how to process, catalog, and shelve them, and also how to use them in programming. Several lengthy appendices provide annotated lists of titles that are suitable for children and tween readers, online resources for purchasing, reviews, and news, and additional, comics-related books

"An insightful introduction to this format as well as an effective selection tool, this guide is highly recommended." Booklist

Includes bibliographical references

025.3 Bibliographic analysis and control

★ **Cataloging** correctly for kids; an introduction to the tools. edited by Sheila S. Intner, Joanna F. Fountain, and Jean Weihs. 5th ed.; Association for Library Collections and Technical Services, American Library Association 2011 224p pa $55
Grades: Adult Professional **025.3**
1. Cataloging 2. Reference books 3. Children's literature -- Cataloging
ISBN 978-0-8389-3589-7 pa; 0-8389-3589-3 pa
LC 2010012945

First published 1989 by the Cataloging for Children's Materials Committee

Among the topics discussed are: guidelines for standardized cataloging for children; how children search; using AACR2 and MARC 21; copy cataloging; using RDA; Sears List of Subject Headings; LC Children's headings; sources for Dewey numbers; cataloging nonbook materials; authority control; how the CIP program helps children; cataloging for kids in the academic library; cataloging for non-English-speaking children and preliterate children; au-

tomating the children's catalog; vendors of cataloging for children's materials.

Includes bibliographical references

025.4 Subject analysis and control

Donovan, Sandra, 1967-
Bob the Alien discovers the Dewey decimal system; by Sandy Donovan; illustrated by Martin Haake. Picture Window 2010 24p il (In the library) lib bdg $25.32
Grades: 2 3 4 **025.4**
1. Bibliographic instruction 2. Dewey Decimal Classification
ISBN 978-1-4048-5757-5 lib bdg; 1-4048-5757-5 lib bdg

Bob is from planet Plainold, where they have just discovered spiders. But planet Plainold doesn't have books, so Bob has traveled to Earth to find books about spiders. Join Allison Wonderland as she teaches Bob how to use the Dewey Decimal System to find books about spiders.

"What is wonderful about this . . . is that key terms and phrases are enlarged and placed in bold letters to stress their importance. . . . [This is a] vital resource for teaching library skills. All elementary librarians will appreciate the innovative way the author and illustrator combine their talents to create an exciting way to share specifics about libraries and books." Libr Media Connect

Bored Bella learns about fiction and nonfiction; by Sandy Donovan; illustrated by Leeza Hernandez. Picture Window 2010 24p il (In the library) lib bdg $25.32
Grades: 2 3 4 **025.4**
1. Library classification 2. Bibliographic instruction
ISBN 978-1-4048-5758-2 lib bdg; 1-4048-5758-3 lib bdg

Bored Bella thinks books are boring. When his class takes a trip to the library, Bella isn't thrilled. Join Ms. Paige Turner as she introduces fiction and nonfiction books to Bella and her class.

"What is wonderful about this . . . is that key terms and phrases are enlarged and placed in bold letters to stress their importance. . . . [This is a] vital resource for teaching library skills. All elementary librarians will appreciate the innovative way the author and illustrator combine their talents to create an exciting way to share specifics about libraries and books." Libr Media Connect

Includes glossary

025.5 Services for users

American Association of School Librarians
Standards for the 21st-century learner in action. American Association of School Librarians 2009 120p pa $39
Grades: Adult Professional **025.5**
1. Information literacy 2. Libraries -- Standards
ISBN 978-0-8389-8507-6 pa; 0-8389-8507-6 pa

"Standards in Action attempts to expand upon AASL's Standards for the 21st Century Learner by providing benchmarks and action examples. The original document was a nine-page brochure that outlined nine common beliefs, four learning standards, four strands, and indicators under each strand. It was an excellent starting point, but the addition of benchmarks at grades two, five, eight, ten, and twelve helps flesh out the original vision. . . . School libraries should own a copy of this professional, which has a role within any program." Voice Youth Advocates

Includes glossary and bibliographical references

Grassian, Esther S.
★ **Information** literacy instruction; theory and practice. [by] Esther S. Grassian and Joan R. Kaplowitz. 2nd ed; Neal-Schuman Publishers 2009 xxvii, 412p pa $75
Grades: Adult Professional **025.5**
1. Information literacy 2. Information literacy -- Study and teaching 3. Information retrieval -- Study and teaching 4. Bibliographic instruction -- College and university students
ISBN 978-155570-666-1; 1-55570-666-5
LC 2009-23647
First published 2001

This "is designed for anyone involved in the creation and management of information literacy programming. Sixteen well-written chapters, organized into five sections, provide both theory and practical applications, with the emphasis on the practical. . . . Several extras appear in the accompanying CD-ROM. . . . A timely, thorough, and endlessly useful must-have title for librarians, teaching librarians, and library schools." Booklist

Includes bibliographical references

Harper, Meghan
Reference sources and services for youth. Neal-Schuman Publishers 2011 307p $65
Grades: Adult Professional **025.5**
1. School libraries 2. Children's libraries 3. Young adults' libraries 4. Reference services (Libraries)
ISBN 978-1-55570-641-8; 1-55570-641-X
LC 2011004987

"The concept of school and public library collaboration is thoroughly explored in this excellent volume on providing reference services. The chapter on information literacy includes web links with information about standards, models, instruction and assessment, rubrics, web quests, graphic organizers, evaluation tools, and assessment. Additional chapters provide a discussion of online resources, government resources for youth, evaluation and marketing reference services, and managing them." SLJ

Includes bibliographical references

Intner, Carol F.
Homework help from the library; in person and online. American Library Association 2011 202p il pa $47
Grades: Adult Professional **025.5**
1. Homework 2. Library resources 3. Libraries and students
ISBN 978-0-8389-1046-7; 0-8389-1046-7
LC 2010042096

"Building on the concept that information services and education converge with homework help, the author sketches in the history of youth services and current learning theories. She offers practical suggestions for needs assessment and determining a guiding philosophy. Speaking to the public librarian, Intner outlines the points to consider in designing a homework help program and training staff. Possible workshop topics include an overview of student needs

and available resources, creating a comfortable and inviting space, considering the needs of different ages, understanding youth culture, and responding to various learning styles. . . . Youth librarians will want this comprehensive and practical guide within easy reach. " Voice Youth Advocates

Includes bibliographical references

Lanning, Scott
Essential reference services for today's school media specialists; [by] Scott Lanning and John Bryner. 2nd ed.; Libraries Unlimited 2010 141p il pa $45
Grades: Adult Professional **025.5**
1. School libraries 2. Reference services (Libraries)
ISBN 978-1-59158-883-2; 1-59158-883-9
LC 2009-39375

"The content focuses on core reference skills, electronic resources, and leadership. The first few chapters discuss information literacy, evaluation of resources, the role of print resources, and the reference interview. These are followed by chapters on the library catalog, electronic resources, and the Web as a reference tool. Finally, there are several chapters dealing with the teacher-librarians' instructional and leadership roles. The authors use a very accessible tone while providing the basics." Booklist

Includes bibliographical references

Peck, Penny
Readers' advisory for children and 'tweens. Libraries Unlimited 2010 190p pa $36
Grades: Adult Professional **025.5**
1. Children's libraries 2. Children's literature 3. Young adult literature 4. Children -- Books and reading 5. Children's literature -- Bibliography
ISBN 978-1-59884-387-3 pa; 1-59884-387-7 pa
LC 2010002589

"Written for novices, this useful guide will provide many valuable suggestions to library staff unfamiliar with the literature and how to go about recommending it to their young patrons and their caregivers. The first two chapters define readers' advisory and describe how to provide it successfully. The next few chapters are divided into age categories. . . . The concluding chapters are divided by type of literature. . . . All of the chapters include helpful booklists and websites, which are great collection development tools as well. There are some tips on promoting books. . . . This title is a valuable resource." SLJ

Includes bibliographical references

Wichman, Emily T.
Librarian's guide to passive programming; easy and affordable activities for all ages. Emily T. Wichman. Libraries Unlimited Inc. 2012 xvii, 152 p.p ill. (pbk.: acid-free paper) $40
Grades: Professional **025.5**
1. Librarians 2. Library finance 3. Library services
ISBN 159884895X; 9781598848953; 9781598848960
LC 2011045419

In her book, author Emily T. Wichman discusses library budget cuts, and how "librarians are seeking new ways to stretch their programming dollars and maximize staff resources. Passive programming allows libraries to inexpensively showcase their services while inviting visitors of all ages to enjoy the value that libraries bring to the community." (Publisher's note)

Includes bibliographical references and index.

027 General libraries, archives, information centers

Sawa, Maureen

The **library** book; the story of libraries from camels to computers. illustrated by Bill Slavin. Tundra Books 2006 72p il $18.95

Grades: 3 4 5 6   **027**

1. Libraries

ISBN 0-88776-698-6

"This information-packed picture book is an excellent tribute to libraries around the world, describing the development of libraries from ancient times to today. . . . The picture-book format, filled with earth-toned illustrations, adds appeal. . . . The book is also filled with interesting sidebars and highlighted sections of information." Voice Youth Advocates

Includes bibliographical references

Trumble, Kelly

The **Library** of Alexandria; illustrated by Robina MacIntyre Marshall. Clarion Bks. 2003 72p il maps $17

Grades: 5 6 7 8   **027**

1. Ancient civilization 2. Egypt -- Civilization 3. Alexandrian Library (Egypt)

ISBN 0-395-75832-7

LC 2003-150

An introduction to the largest and most famous library in the ancient world, discussing its construction in Alexandria, Egypt, its vast collections, rivalry with the Pergamum Library, famous scholars, and destruction by fire

This is a "well-organized and thorough resource." SLJ

Includes glossary and bibliographical references

027.4 Public libraries

King, M. G.

Librarian on the roof! a true story. illustrated by Stephen Gilpin. Albert Whitman 2010 un il $16.95

Grades: K 1 2 3   **027.4**

1. Libraries 2. Librarians

ISBN 978-0-8075-4512-6; 0-8075-4512-0

"King's writing is clear and often witty, and she does a credible job of capturing Laurell's determined and forthright personality, as well as the drama and excitement of this unusual approach to fund-raising. Gilpin's hand-drawn, vibrantly colored cartoon illustrations enliven the story." SLJ

027.6 Libraries for special groups and organizations

Alire, Camila

★ **Serving** Latino communities; a how-to-do-it manual for librarians. [by] Camila Alire, Jacqueline Ayala. 2nd ed; Neal-Schuman Publishers 2007 229p il (How-to-do-it manuals for librarians) pa $59.95

Grades: Adult Professional   **027.6**

1. Libraries and Hispanic Americans

ISBN 978-1-55570-606-7; 1-55570-606-1

LC 2007-7783

First published 1998

"The information covered helps library staff understand the needs of their library's Latino community; develop successful programs and services; obtain funding for projects and programs; prepare staff to work more effectively with Latinos; establish partnerships with relevant external agencies and organizations; improve collection development; and perform effective outreach and public relations. . . . There are few resources widely available on this topic and none as complete." Libr Media Connect

Includes bibliographical references

Diamant-Cohen, Betsy

Early literacy programming en Espanol; Mother Goose on the Loose programs for bilingual learners. Neal-Schuman Publishers 2010 xxii, 177p il pa $65

Grades: Adult Professional   **027.6**

1. Nursery rhymes 2. Bilingual education 3. Children's libraries

ISBN 978-1-55570-691-3; 1-55570-691-6

LC 2009049594

"Diamant-Cohen has developed this manual to encourage librarians to present Spanish-language MGOL programs. . . . The author proposes recruiting community partners fluent in Spanish who will be trained by the children's librarian and will copresent the sessions. Five parts cover the basics on how to run the program successfully. The manual is complemented with illustrations that can be replicated and used as flannel-board figures; bibliographies, worksheets, and a CD with instructions; nursery rhymes in English and Spanish; and graphics and templates of documents. This volume is infused with enthusiasm to serve the children of Spanish-speakers. It will not only help English-speaking librarians, but also the bilingual ones to present and enjoy MGOL." SLJ

Includes bibliographical references

Klipper, Barbara

Programming for children and teens with autism spectrum disorder; Barbara Klipper. ALA Editions 2014 168 p. illustrations (pbk) $45

Grades: Adult Professional   **027.6**

1. Autism 2. Autistic children 3. Libraries and people with disabilities 4. Children's libraries -- Activity programs 5. Youth with autism spectrum disorders -- Services for 6. Children with autism spectrum disorders -- Services for

ISBN 9780838912065; 0838912060

LC 2013044207

This book, by Barbara Klipper, is "[f]or librarians who offer or are thinking about offering programming to children and/or teens with autism spectrum disorders (ASD). . . . There are storytime models; programming for school-age children, teens, and families; and program plans for school libraries. Helpful side boxes include tips on ways to supplement or adapt existing programs and library spaces. . . . The appendixes include valuable resources such as vendors, websites, and publishers." (School Library Journal)

Includes bibliographical references and index

027.62 Libraries for specific age groups

Bauer, Caroline Feller

Leading kids to books through crafts. American Lib. Assn. 2000 145p (Mighty easy motivators) pa $30

Grades: Adult Professional 027.62

1. Handicraft 2. Reference books 3. Books and reading 4. Children's libraries 5. Children's literature -- Bibliography

ISBN 0-8389-0769-5

LC 99-41387

"Bauer gives basic, practical information on presenting programs that introduce preschool and primary-grade youngsters to stories and poems and demonstrates related crafts that are easy to prepare and execute." SLJ

Leading kids to books through magic; illustrated by Richard Laurent. American Lib. Assn. 1996 128p il (Mighty easy motivators) pa $35

Grades: Adult Professional 027.62

1. Magic tricks 2. Reference books 3. Books and reading 4. Children's libraries 5. Children's literature -- Bibliography

ISBN 978-0-8389-0684-2 pa; 0-8389-0684-2 pa

LC 95-53049

The author's "concise yet thorough directions accompanied by Richard Laurent's delightful line drawings make this book a useful tool for teachers and librarians looking for ways to promote children's enthusiasm for reading." J Youth Serv Libr

Includes bibliographical references

Leading kids to books through puppets; illustrated by Richard Laurent. American Lib. Assn. 1997 156p il (Mighty easy motivators) pa $35

Grades: Adult Professional 027.62

1. Reference books 2. Books and reading 3. Children's libraries 4. Puppets and puppet plays 5. Children's literature -- Bibliography

ISBN 978-0-8389-0706-1 pa; 0-8389-0706-7 pa

LC 97-1357

"Even the most reluctant performer will be encouraged by this practical, concise, easy-to-use book." SLJ

This "book suggests ways to promote books and reading to children through simple puppetry. . . . [It offers] a number of theme-based programs complete with stories to act out, poems, and lists of related books." Booklist

Includes bibliographical references

Benton, Gail

Ready-to-go storytimes; fingerplays, scripts, patterns, music, and more. [by] Gail Benton, Trisha Waichulaitis. Neal-Schuman 2003 239p il pa $65

Grades: Adult Professional 027.62

1. Storytelling 2. Children's libraries

ISBN 978-1-55570-449-0 pa; 1-55570-449-2 pa

LC 2002-5806

"This resource is excellent for beginning librarians and teachers and for any professionals who seek new ideas to freshen up their repertoires." Booklist

Includes bibliographical references

Bird, Elizabeth

Children's literature gems; choosing and using them in your library career. American Library Association 2009 125p pa $45

Grades: Adult Professional 027.62

1. Book selection 2. Children's libraries 3. Children -- Books and reading 4. Children's literature -- Bibliography

ISBN 978-0-8389-0995-9 pa; 0-8389-0995-7 pa

LC 2009003079

"Bird writes in a chatty tone reminiscent of her popular blog, A Fuse #8 Production, and her love of children's literature shines through on every page. This slim volume is not meant to be an in-depth textbook, but rather a brief overview of the field and an introduction to the stars of children's literature. . . . Highlighted boxes throughout feature questions and answers from seasoned professionals on how they handle various parts of their collections and aspects of their work. Readers who are new to the field may find this a comforting basic guide to managing their collections. " SLJ

Includes bibliographical references

Bromann, Jennifer

More storytime action! 2,000+ more ideas for making 500+ picture books interactive. Neal-Schuman Publishers 2009 326p pa $55

Grades: Adult Professional 027.62

1. Storytelling 2. Children's libraries 3. Picture books for children -- Bibliography

ISBN 978-1-55570-675-3 pa; 1-55570-675-4 pa

LC 2009031724

"Bromann presents more than 2,000 activities related to more than 500 picture books published since 2003. Beginning chapters cover 10 elements of interactive stories; storytelling, including how to select and prepare stories; and how to select books for interactive storytimes, identifying clues found in reviews. . . . The final chapter lists the more than 500 books alphabetically by author with bibliographic information, summary, and storytime activities. . . . For librarians looking to hold the attention of their youngest patrons or to spice up storytime, this title will be a welcome resource." Booklist

Includes bibliographical references

Cerny, Rosanne

★ **Outstanding** library service to children; putting the core competencies to work. [by] Rosanne Cerny, Penny Markey, and Amanda Williams. American Library Association 2006 94p pa $25

Grades: Adult Professional 027.62

1. Children's libraries

ISBN 978-0-8389-0922-5 pa; 0-8389-0922-1 pa

"This slim volume should be required reading for all future children's services librarians." Booklist

Includes bibliiographical references

Children's services; partnerships for success. edited by Betsy Diamant-Cohen. American Library Association 2010 126p il (ALA public library handbook series) pa $50

Grades: Adult Professional 027.62

1. Children's libraries 2. Libraries and schools 3.

Libraries and community
ISBN 978-0-8389-1044-3 pa; 0-8389-1044-0 pa
LC 2009045788

"Diamant-Cohen has created a valuable resource by providing practical examples of successful partnerships between libraries of various sizes and community organizations. Concrete scenarios include successful partnerships with law enforcement agencies, recreation departments, academic institutions, children's museums, cultural institutions, churches that attract mainly immigrant populations, businesses, and other agencies." SLJ

Includes bibliographical references

Cullum, Carolyn N.
★ The **storytime** sourcebook II; [a compendium of 3500+ new ideas and resources for storytellers] Neal-Schuman Publishers 2007 489p pa $75
Grades: Adult Professional   027.62
1. Storytelling 2. Children's libraries
ISBN 978-1-55570-589-3 pa; 1-55570-589-8 pa
LC 2006-35096

First published 1990 with title: The storytime sourcebook
"Each of the 146 themed programs, designed for children ages two to eight, appears on two facing pages that include appropriate calendar tie-ins, videos, books, music, movements, crafts, activities, and songs. . . . [The author] presents clear and simple directions for crafts and activities, quick and uncomplicated for librarians to prepare, and easy for children to follow. . . . This sourcebook is an essential purchase for libraries serving this audience." SLJ

Includes bibliographical references

De las Casas, Dianne
Tell along tales! playing with participation stories. illustrated by Soleil Lisette. Libraries Unlimited 2011 125p il pa $30
Grades: Adult Professional   027.62
1. Storytelling 2. Children's libraries
ISBN 978-1-59884-635-5; 1-59884-635-3
LC 2011000335

"In five chapters chock-full of storyteller tips and ideas, de las Casas explains various types of participation models from call-and-response to directed role-playing and covers how to direct questions to the group. She offers valuable clues for warming up an audience and for settling boisterous children back down. . . . The main body of the book contains the author's choices of suitable stories from around the world with suggested age levels and pointers for leaders. . . . Both novice and veteran storytellers will benefit from the myriad suggestions offered here." SLJ

Includes bibliographical references

Del Negro, Janice M.
Folktales aloud; practical advice for playful storytelling. Janice M. Del Negro. American Library Association 2014 212 p. (alk. paper) $47
Grades: Adult Professional   027.62
1. Fairy tales 2. Storytelling 3. Children's libraries -- Activity programs 4. Elementary school libraries -- Activity programs
ISBN 0838911358; 9780838911358
LC 2013028036

This book, by Janice M. Del Negro, "aims to show that storytelling is still vital in librarianship and throughout the greater community. . . . The text provides useful information for novice and seasoned storytellers alike while engaging the reader with its conversational tone. The chapters are broken down by audience age . . . and include information about audience needs and wants, stories, and resource information." (Booklist)

"Folktales are an integral part of children's literature and are the basis for many classic books librarians use daily in their work. These much loved tales are also the backbone of the art of storytelling...Del Negro leads novice tellers through the nuances of successful storytelling...Advice is offered in a very practical way on how to approach this group and suggestions are made as to how to grab and hold their interest with pacing, movement and suspense. If you have even a passing interest in the art of storytelling, this guide is not to be missed." SLJ

Includes bibliographical references and index

Diamant-Cohen, Betsy
Crash course in library services to preschool children. Libraries Unlimited 2010 137p pa $30
Grades: Adult Professional   027.62
1. Children's libraries
ISBN 978-1-59884-688-1 pa; 1-59884-688-4 pa
LC 2010024071

"This book presents 10 chapters to quickly immerse the librarian working with preschoolers into the field. An overview of children's services to preschoolers in public libraries is followed by chapters on programming, books, collections, reader's advisory and reference, and the children's room. . . . All librarians who deal with preschoolers, whether experienced public librarians or new school media specialist, will benefit from the ideas, concepts, and guidance provided here." SLJ

Includes bibliographical references

Ernst, Linda L.
Baby rhyming time; [by] Linda L. Ernst. Neal-Schuman Publishers 2008 235p il pa $59.95
Grades: Adult Professional   027.62
1. Children's libraries
ISBN 978-1-55570-540-4 pa; 1-55570-540-5 pa
LC 2007043246

"This useful resource provides background, logistics, and a wealth of practical ideas for programs. Ernst describes brain development and language acquisition clearly, with quotes and references for support. She does a good job of tying the science to infant/toddler growth and explaining the librarian's important role in sharing the information with caregivers. She discusses broader factors to consider when planning baby-time programs, including community, facilities, staffing, and potential partnerships." SLJ

Includes bibliographical references

Fasick, Adele M.
Managing children's services in the public library; [by] Adele M. Fasick and Leslie E. Holt. 3rd ed; Libraries Unlimited 2008 248p bibl il tab pa $45
Grades: Adult Professional   027.62
1. Public libraries 2. Children's libraries 3. Children -- Books and reading
ISBN 978-1-59158-412-4 pa; 1-59158-412-4 pa
LC 2007032759

First published 1991

"Excellent support for newbies and as a basis for professional development." Booklist

"Section I deals with planning services in the context of a community. Section II covers maintaining a productive work environment, recruiting and retaining staff, communicating with colleagues, annual reports, budgeting and fundraising, planning facilities, and keeping the department safe and secure. Section III focuses on collection development, electronic resources, intellectual freedom, and reaching out to the community through programs and special events, working with other youth service organizations, and marketing children's services. Section IV suggests ways in which children's librarians can participate in the larger professional community of librarians." Publisher's note

Includes bibliographical references

Fiore, Carole D.

Fiore's summer library reading program handbook. Neal-Schuman Publishers 2005 xxiii, 312p pa $65

Grades: Adult Professional   **027.62**

1. Books and reading 2. Children's libraries

ISBN 1-55570-513-8

                     LC 2004-31104

"This research-laden handbook . . . serves as a 'comprehensive program-planning and implementation tool' for public libraries seeking to revamp, revise, or develop a summer library reading program. . . . This is an invaluable resource, both for its concrete guidance and its abstract exploration of the meaning of summer library programs." Bull Cent Child Books

Includes bibliographical references

Ghoting, Saroj Nadkarni

STEP into storytime; using storytime effective practice to strengthen the development of newborns to five-year-olds. Saroj Nadkarni Ghoting and Kathy Fling Klatt. ALA Editions, an imprint of the American Library Association 2014 368 p. $59

Grades: Professional   **027.62**

1. Storytelling 2. Early childhood education 3. Children's libraries -- Activity programs 4. Storytelling -- United States 5. Libraries and preschool children -- United States 6. Children's libraries -- Activity programs -- United States

ISBN 0838912222; 9780838912225

                     LC 2014004162

This book, by Saroj Nadkarni Ghoting and Kathy Fling Klatt, focuses on "Story Time Effective Practice (STEP). . . . [It] is an approach that articulates the link between child development theory and storytimes. This important resource shows how presenters can use STEP to craft a storytime that is effective for mixed-age groups and adheres to best practices for emotional, social, physical, and cognitive support." (Publisher's note)

"It is a rare volume that could serve as both pleasure reading or as a textbook, but STEP into Storytime walks that fine line...The majority of children's librarians have studied childhood development and early literacy best practices; consider this book required reading to keep this knowledge fresh while reminding us of the importance—and delightful fun—of our work." Booklist

Includes bibliographical references and index

Kirker, Christine

Multicultural storytime magic; Kathy MacMillan and Christine Kirker. American Library Association 2012 241 p. $47

Grades: Professional   **027.62**

1. Storytelling 2. Multicultural education 3. Children's libraries -- Activity programs 4. Storytelling -- United States 5. Children's libraries -- Activity programs -- United States 6. Multicultural education -- Activity programs -- United States

ISBN 0838911420; 9780838911426

                     LC 2011043434

"Authors [Kathy] MacMillan and [Christine] Kirker offer a . . . paradigm for multicultural programs, one in which diversity is woven into any and every storytime, no matter what the topic. Arranged thematically around dozens of popular storytime themes, the authors . . . offer . . . book recommendations, fingerplays, and other activities that can be integrated into existing storytimes." (Publisher's note)

Includes bibliographical references and indexes

LibrarySparks: library lessons. Upstart Bks. 2011 200p $17.95

Grades: Adult Professional   **027.62**

1. Books and reading 2. Children's libraries 3. Bibliographic instruction

ISBN 1-60213-052-3; 978-1-60213-052-4

"Compiled from the first six volumes of the magazine LibrarySparks, this book contains 24 lessons by librarians and educators attuned to the interests, needs, and learning styles of youngsters from kindergarten through fifth grade. . . . Students are challenged to access information in a variety of formats. This fine collection will provide rich and rewarding lessons all year long." SLJ

MacDonald, Margaret Read

Look back and see; twenty lively tales for gentle tellers. illustrations by Roxane Murphy. Wilson, H.W. 1991 178p il $60

Grades: Adult Professional   **027.62**

1. Folklore 2. Storytelling

ISBN 978-0-8242-0810-3; 0-8242-0810-3

                     LC 91-2539

The author presents twenty non-violent folktales from around the world, with background notes and suggestions for storytelling uses

"Delightfully varied in mood, the tales range from silly and rowdy to contemplative and touching. . . . MacDonald's useful, informative, and entertaining notes follow each story. . . . The notes alone are worth the price of the book." J Youth Serv Libr

Includes bibliographical references

★ **When** the lights go out; twenty scary tales to tell. illustrations by Roxane Murphy. Wilson, H.W. 1988 176p il $70

Grades: Adult Professional   **027.62**

1. Folklore 2. Storytelling 3. Horror fiction

ISBN 0-8242-0770-X

                     LC 88-14197

"Divided into six sections—Not Too Scary, Scary in the Dark, Gross Stuff, Jump Tales, Tales to Act Out, and Tales to Draw or Stir Up—the selections will be especially useful around Halloween, although, as the author points out, the book can be used year round. Following each inclusion are helpful notes on telling the stories and a section that gives sources on origins and variants. Murphy's decorative drawings introduce chapters and are scattered throughout the text. Several concluding chapters list bibliographies and provide other helpful information." Booklist

Includes bibliographical references

MacMillan, Kathy

Storytime magic; 400 fingerplays, flannelboards, and other activities. [by] Kathy MacMillan and Christine Kirker. American Library Association 2009 139p il pa $45

Grades: Adult Professional   **027.62**

1. Storytelling 2. Children's libraries

ISBN 978-0-8389-0977-5 pa; 0-8389-0977-9 pa

LC 2008030266

"Both new and veteran storytellers will appreciate this book. Sixteen chapters are arranged by themes such as 'All About Me,' 'Animals,' and 'Holidays.' Whenever a flannelboard idea is listed, a thumbnail pen-and-ink sketch of the necessary pieces is included next to a Web icon. Readers can then proceed to an ALA Web page to view the actual-sized pattern. An appendix gives further instruction on how to use other props or costumes along with a story." SLJ

Includes bibliographical references

Marino, Jane

★ Babies in the library! Scarecrow Press 2003 149p hardcover o.p. pa $32

Grades: Adult Professional   **027.62**

1. Children's libraries

ISBN 0-8108-4576-8; 0-8108-6044-9 pa

LC 2002-12022

The author presents "arguments for holding library programs specifically geared toward babies. Organizing and presenting her ideas in a thoughtful and philosophical manner, she addresses many relevant topics: making babies feel comfortable in the library, creating programs for prewalkers and walkers, handling registration, and offering suggestions for planning and executing programs. She also includes various activities that introduce books, rhymes, puppets, and other tools that enhance language skills." SLJ

Includes bibliographical references

Nichols, Judy

Storytimes for two-year-olds; [by] Judy Nichols; illustrated by Lori D. Sears. 3rd ed; American Library Association 2007 252p bibl il pa $40

Grades: Adult Professional   **027.62**

1. Storytelling 2. Children's libraries

ISBN 0-8389-0925-6 pa; 978-0-8389-0925-6 pa

LC 2006023915

First published 1987

This outlines techniques for creating library programs for two-year-olds using books, rhymes, songs, fingerplays, puppets, and crafts on such themes as farms, animals, seasons, and bedtimes.

"The variety of programs, the diverse and excellent book selections, and the other program components . . . . make this book useful for librarians, nursery-school teachers, and homeschoolers." Booklist

Includes bibliographical references

Pavon, Ana-Elba

★ 25 Latino craft projects; [by] Ana-Elba Pavon, Diana Borrego. American Library Association 2003 80p il (Celebrating culture in your library) pa $35

Grades: Adult Professional   **027.62**

1. Handicraft 2. Children's libraries 3. Hispanic Americans -- Social life and customs

ISBN 978-0-8389-0833-4 pa; 0-8389-0833-0 pa

LC 2002-5750

Following a "chapter on planning, the projects are organized around important Latino holidays and are inspired by artesanias (Latino folk art). . . . For each celebration, there is a suggested program for preschoolers, after-schooler, and families; each program incorporates the craft with songs, poems, and books. Activities include making piñatas, paper flowers, sweet tamales, and salsa." SLJ

Includes glossary and bibliographical references

Peck, Penny

Crash course in storytime fundamentals. Libraries Unlimited 2009 154p (Crash course) pa $30

Grades: Adult Professional   **027.62**

1. Storytelling 2. Children's libraries

ISBN 978-1-59158-715-6 pa; 1-59158-715-8 pa

LC 2008031234

"Practical and concise, this well-organized and readable guide is for inexperienced staff members who are not necessarily children's librarians. . . . The 75 themed storytimes include different types of books and Web sites and sources for songs, musical instruments, fingerplays, games, puppets, and crafts. The author discusses best times and settings for programs; special issues, such as children's and parents' behavior; selection and training of volunteers; the 'registration' question, and more." SLJ

Includes bibliographical references

Reid, Rob

More family storytimes; twenty-four creative programs for all ages. American Library Association 2009 181p pa $45

Grades: Adult Professional   **027.62**

1. Storytelling 2. Children's libraries

ISBN 978-0-8389-0973-7

LC 2008015377

"This volume contains 24 programs, each lasting 30 minutes, that promote learning readiness and reading skills. . . . Clearly presented and easy to follow, this is an excellent resource for librarians who want to come up with winning story hours that have broad appeal." Booklist

Includes bibliographical references

Shake & shout; 16 noisy, lively story programs. Upstart Books 2008 110p il pa $17.95

Grades: Adult Professional   **027.62**

1. Dance 2. Songs 3. Storytelling 4. Children's libraries 5. Children -- Books and reading

ISBN 978-1-60213-006-7 pa; 1-60213-006-X pa

LC 2009535346

"This book centers on the idea of using one song as the jumping-off point for a thematic storytime. Each program features two to three picture books that support the theme, along with one or two movement activities. There's also a 'backup picture book' listed as well as more related songs. . . . The featured songs are listed within the programs, where recordings can be found, and are also printed at the end of the chapter with suggested guitar chords. The themes run the gamut from seasonal, to various animals and their environments, to pretend activities and emotions. This volume will spark creativity and imagination." SLJ

Includes bibliographical references

★ **What's** black and white and Reid all over? something hilarious happened at the library. Rob Reid. American Library Association 2012 xii, 175 p.p (softbound) $45
Grades: Professional   **027.62**
1. Storytelling 2. Humorous fiction 3. Children's libraries 4. Storytelling -- United States 5. Wit and humor, Juvenile -- Bibliography 6. Children's libraries -- Activity programs -- United States
ISBN 0838911471; 9780838911471

LC 2011043233

This book presents "10 humorous story programs -- five aimed at preschoolers and five for school-aged children. . . . Each one provides read-aloud suggestions and movement activities. There are also . . . storytelling tips that include everything from how to hold the book to what props to use. . . . Reid also includes an additional list of titles that can be substituted, jokes, call-and-response chants, short storybooks, songs, and musical activities." (School Library Journal)

"Those new to interactive book talking will appreciate his instructions for hamming up particular titles. Seasoned users will be grateful for the flexibility Reid provides to tailor programs to the tastes, time slots, and collection at hand." VOYA

Includes bibliographical references and index

Sierra, Judy
The **flannel** board storytelling book; 2nd ed rev & expanded; Wilson, H.W. 1997 241p il music $65
Grades: Adult Professional   **027.62**
1. Storytelling 2. Children's libraries
ISBN 978-0-8242-0932-2; 0-8242-0932-X

LC 97-15107

First published 1987

"Fifty stories, poems, and songs and over three hundred patterns are included for presenting stories to children in a flannel board medium, including classic children's stories, nursery rhymes, folk tales, and songs. . . . Sierra's experience telling stories with children is reflected throughout her book." J Youth Serv Libr

Sima, Judy
Raising voices; creating youth storytelling groups and troupes. [by] Judy Sima, Kevin Cordi. Libraries Unlimited 2003 xxviii, 241p pa $32.50
Grades: Adult Professional   **027.62**
1. Storytelling
ISBN 1-56308-919-X

LC 2003-47631

This offers a "blueprint for beginning and sustaining a successful group or troupe of storytellers from grades 4 to 12. . . . The book includes reproducible forms that will save a lot of work and lists of valuable resources. . . . Raising Voices is the complete, and essential, handbook for this special group of storytellers." SLJ

Includes bibliographical references

Sullivan, Michael
★ **Fundamentals** of children's services; by Michael Sullivan. American Library Association 2013 xx, 359 p.p (alk. paper) $52
Grades: Professional   **027.62**
1. Children's libraries 2. Libraries -- Collection development 3. Children's libraries -- United States
ISBN 0838911889; 9780838911884

LC 2013005037

This book, by Michael Sullivan, presents a reference on children's services at libraries. It covers "both innovative and standard practices in children's services. Fundamentals such as collection development and management, programming, homework support, and reference and reader's advisory are all thoroughly updated. [It] offers an expansive view of what it means to ensure that children are well-served in light of ongoing budgetary challenges." (Publisher's note)

Includes bibliographical references (pages 327-339) and index

Walter, Virginia A.
Twenty-first-century kids, twenty-first-century librarians. American Library Association 2010 104p pa $45
Grades: Adult Professional   **027.62**
1. Librarians 2. Children's libraries 3. Young adults' libraries
ISBN 978-0-8389-1007-8 pa; 0-8389-1007-6 pa

LC 2009016972

"This volume more than updates Walter's 2001 Children and Libraries; it revisits the nature of children, addressing social changes and encouraging a new generation of children's librarians. Chapter 1 provides a fine history about U.S. library services to children, primarily in public libraries. Subsequent chapters detail six enduring core values of children's library services and add two emerging themes: the need for information (and information literacy) and collaboration. Walter's main contribution lies in her description of five models of children relative to the library: as reader, as a child of the information age, as a community member, as global, and as an empowered person. Another chapter focuses on management principals. . . . Walter's core values are worth reading and implementing." Booklist

Includes bibliographical references

027.8   School libraries

Adams, Helen R.
★ **Ensuring** intellectual freedom and access to information in the school library media program. Libraries Unlimited 2008 xxi, 254p il map pa $40
Grades: Adult Professional   **027.8**
1. Censorship 2. School libraries 3. Freedom of information
ISBN 978-1-59158-539-8; 1-59158-539-2

LC 2008-16753

This is "an extremely helpful guide for dealing with intellectual-freedom and information-access issues. In chapters geared to school situations and covering topics including selection of resources, the First Amendment, privacy, challenges to resources, the Internet, and access for students with disabilities, Adams offers background on the topic and bulleted lists of strategies for dealing with the issue. . . . This is a book that every school librarian needs to keep handy and share with administrators, colleagues, and parents." Booklist

Includes bibliographical references

Bishop, Kay

The **collection** program in schools; concepts, practices, and information sources. 4th ed. Libraries Unlimited 2007 xx, 269p il (Library and information science text series) pa $50; $65

Grades: Adult Professional   **027.8**

1. School libraries 2. Libraries -- Collection development 3. School libraries -- Collection development 4. Children's literature -- Bibliography of bibliographies 5. Young adult literature -- Bibliography of bibliographies

ISBN 1-59158-360-8 pa; 1-59158-583-X; 978-1-59158-360-8 pa; 978-1-59158-583-1

LC 2007-9005

First published 1988 under the authorship of Phyllis J. Van Orden

"Media specialists who read this book will be renewed in their quest for excellence in their collections. . . . The book covers A-Z: Acquisitions, Evaluation, Ethical Issues, Inventory, Procedure Manual, Selection, Special Groups of Students, Weeding, etc. . . . This is a must purchase for every school library media center." Libr Media Connect

Includes bibliographical references

Buzzeo, Toni

Collaborating to meet standards: teacher/librarian partnerships for K-6; [by] Toni Buzzeo. 2nd ed.; Linworth Pub. 2007 246p pa $39.95

Grades: Adult Professional   **027.8**

1. School libraries

ISBN 1-58683-302-2 pa; 978-1-58683-302-2 pa

LC 2007015406

First published 2002

This "addresses the assessment-driven educational environment of the No Child Left Behind Act. In the first section, Buzzeo focuses on the benefits of an involved school librarian to the educational process and how best to achieve this collaboration. She includes a template for collaborative planning and instruction. Sample lessons for specific grades from librarians around the United States complete the book. Practical suggestions and examples from school librarians across the country appear in separate text boxes. . . . Buzzeo gives worthwhile advice." SLJ

Includes bibliographical references

The **collaboration** handbook. Linworth Pub. 2008 132p il pa $42.95

Grades: Adult Professional   **027.8**

1. School libraries

ISBN 978-1-58683-298-8 pa; 1-58683-298-0 pa

LC 2008-18119

"In this succinct guide, Buzzeo paints a picture of how media specialists can use instructional collaboration to transform a media program and increase student achievement. . . . Those new to the field will appreciate the step-by-step approach to increasing collaboration, while experienced media specialists will likely benefit most from the chapters on data-driven collaboration and assessment. The book concludes with a substantial amount of information on how to overcome common barriers to collaboration, the role of ad-

vocacy, and the importance of integrating new technologies into collaborative projects." SLJ

Includes bibliographical references

Erikson, Rolf

Designing a school library media center for the future; [by] Rolf Erikson and Carolyn Markuson. 2nd ed; American Library Association 2007 117p il pa $45

Grades: Adult Professional   **027.8**

1. School libraries -- Design and construction 2. Instructional materials centers -- Design and construction

ISBN 978-0-8389-0945-4; 0-8389-0945-0

LC 2006-37644

First published 2000

"The first chapter offers an overview of the various steps involved in any project. Succeeding chapters cover technology planning, space allocations, furniture and placement, lighting and acoustics, ADA requirements, specifications, and bids." Booklist

Includes bibliographical references

Grimes, Sharon

★ **Reading** is our business; how libraries can foster reading comprehension. American Library Association 2006 155p il pa $35

Grades: Adult Professional   **027.8**

1. School libraries 2. Books and reading 3. Reading comprehension

ISBN 0-8389-0912-4

LC 2005028263

Grimes "led a school-wide research study with classroom teachers to transform the reading program at Lansdowne Elementary School in Baltimore. The study resulted in dramatic and measurable gains in student reading achievement. This book can be used as a toolkit to duplicate those results. Grimes's work is informed by solid educational research in the field of reading comprehension. The text is lively and clearly written, accessible to teachers and librarians." SLJ

Includes bibliographical references

Harada, Violet H.

Assessing for learning; librarians and teachers as partners. [by] Violet H. Harada and Joan M. Yoshina. 2nd ed.; Libraries Unlimited 2010 242p il pa $45

Grades: Adult Professional   **027.8**

1. School libraries 2. Instructional materials centers

ISBN 978-1-59884-470-2; 1-59884-470-9

First published 2055 with title: Assessing learning

"Using assessment tools familiar to the classroom teacher, the authors show how to use them in the library setting. Starting with the challenges that face 21st century schools, the rationale for schools as learning organizations is laid out. The tools for assessment are the main points of this title and include checklists, rubrics, rating scales, conferences, logs, personal correspondence, exit passes, graphic organizers, and student portfolios. . . . The tools for better instruction and assessment of learning need to be used by all educators, and this title provides examples and models for all librarians." Libr Media Connect

Includes bibliographical references

Hughes-Hassell, Sandra

★ **School** reform and the school library media specialist; [by] Sandra Hughes-Hassell and Violet H. Harada. Libraries Unlimited 2007 xxiii, 204p il (Principles and practice series) pa $40

Grades: Adult Professional   **027.8**

1. School libraries

ISBN 978-1-59158-427-8; 1-59158-427-2

LC 2007-16437

"This volume covers critical issues impacting school libraries today and offers practical solutions to meet these challenges. Written by leaders in the field such as Pam Berger, Carol Gordon, Barbara Stripling, and Ross Todd, the articles expound on implications of No Child Left Behind legislation, 21st-century literacy requirements, population diversity, and professional growth. . . . This volume will empower current and future school librarians as they embrace its guidelines." SLJ

Morris, Betty J.

★ **Administering** the school library media center; 5th ed.; Libraries Unlimited 2010 580p il $75; pa $60

Grades: Adult Professional   **027.8**

1. School libraries 2. Instructional materials centers

ISBN 978-1-59158-685-2; 1-59158-685-2; 978-1-59158-689-0 pa; 1-59158-689-5 pa

LC 2010015939

First published 1973 under the authorship of John T. Gillespie and Diana L. Spirt with title: Creating a school media program

"This updated edition provides a comprehensive and current examination of the multiple and varied jobs media specialists do to manage today's school library media centers. . . . Sample job description statements, media center budgets, and budget justification tools are thorough and valuable references. Morris addresses the proactive and visible leadership role that today's media specialists must take on to remain viable and support student learning. . . . The title supports concepts on current standards. It is a forward thinking text for new or future library media specialists and a realistic, functional reference for practitioners." Libr Media Connect

Includes bibliographical references

Stephens, Claire Gatrell

Library 101; a handbook for the school library media specialist. [by] Claire Gatrell Stephens and Patricia Franklin. Libraries Unlimited 2007 233p il pa $35

Grades: Adult Professional   **027.8**

1. School libraries 2. Instructional materials centers 3. Libraries -- Handbooks, manuals, etc.

ISBN 978-1-59158-324-0; 1-59158-324-1

LC 2007-18420

"This handbook provides information for brand-new and inexperienced librarians preparing for a first job in a school library media center. Articles are divided into four subcategories covering day-to-day operations (library organization, circulation policies, media management, scheduling, staffing, and media center arrangement); collaboration with teachers; collection development and management; and equipment." Booklist

Includes bibliographical references

Sykes, Judith A.

Conducting action research to evaluate your school library; Judith Anne Sykes. Libraries Unlimited, an imprint of ABC-CLIO, LLC 2013 118 p. illustrations (hard copy) $40

Grades: Adult Professional   **027.8**

1. School libraries 2. Librarians -- Rating 3. Educational evaluation 4. School librarians 5. Teacher-librarians 6. Action research in education 7. School libraries -- Evaluation

ISBN 161069077X; 9781610690775

LC 2012051277

In this book, author Judith Anne Sykes "coalesces current expert opinions on the topic of action research in the school library environment and highlighting what other teacher librarians in the field have identified as the pros and cons of using the process. Readers are directed to focus on mitigating the 'cons' through the use of specific working pages and templates and by initially exploring 'five favorite' links." (Publisher's note)

"When budget issues hit, school librarianship can be in danger, and this text provides tools for professionals to evaluate their programs and make necessary changes to stay a vital part of their schools. . . This purchase would be worthwhile for any teacher-librarian interested in evaluating his or her program and taking advantage of Sykes' extensive research and expertise." Booklist

Includes bibliographical references and index

028.1   Reviews

Baxter, Kathleen A.

★ **From** cover to cover; evaluating and reviewing children's books. rev ed.; Collins 2010 229p $14.99

Grades: Adult Professional   **028.1**

1. Books -- Reviews 2. Children's literature -- History and criticism

ISBN 978-0-06-077757-9; 0-06-077757-5

First published 1997

The author addresses the distinctions between evaluation and review, and what makes a good children's book. She discusses categories of children's books including nonfiction; traditional literature (folktales, myths, legends, etc.); poetry, verse, rhymes, and songs; picture books; easy readers and transitional books; and fiction. She then describes the process of writing a review.

This is a "very complete resource that will continue to be the venerable reference tool and required reading for education and library-science students, youth librarians, teachers, and anyone else interested in kids, reading, and children's literature." SLJ

Naidoo, Jamie Campbell

★ **Rainbow** family collections; selecting and using children's books with lesbian, gay, bisexual, transgender, and queer content. Jamie Campbell Naidoo. Libraries Unlimited, an imprint of ABC-CLIO, LLC 2012 xvii, 260 p.p ill. (hardback) $50

Grades: Professional   **028.1**

1. Libraries and sexual minorities 2. Sexual minorities in literature 3. Libraries and sexual minorities -- United States 4. Libraries -- Special collections --

Sexual minorities 5. Children's libraries -- Collection development -- United States 6. Children's libraries -- Services to minorities -- United States 7. Children of sexual minority parents -- Books and reading -- United States
ISBN 1598849603; 9781598849608
LC 2012008362
This book by Jamie Campbell Naidoo "highlight[s] titles for children from infancy to age 11" featuring lesbian, gay, bisexual, transgender, and queer content. It "supplies a synopsis of the title's content, lists awards it has received, cites professional reviews, and provides suggestions for librarians considering acquisition. The book also provides a brief historical overview of LGBTQ children's literature along with the major book awards for this genre." (Publisher's note)
Includes bibliographical references and index

028.5 Reading and use of other information media by young people

Allyn, Pam
What to read when; the books and stories to read with your child, and all the best times to read them. Avery 2009 318p pa $16.95
Grades: Adult Professional 028.5
1. Children -- Books and reading
ISBN 978-1-58333-334-1
LC 2008-54501
The author "provides many ways to promote a love of reading to children and offers top-ten lists of reasons to read to kids that incorporate practical, easy-to-use tips to encourage literacy from a young age. . . . This is an indispensable guide to choosing age-appropriate books for children. Allyn provides a list of more than 300 titles on 50 themes including such issues as adoption, feelings about school, sharing, and coping with illness. This valuable resource for children's librarians, educators, and parents is highly recommended." Libr J

Baxter, Kathleen A.
Gotcha again for guys! more nonfiction books to get boys excited about reading. [by] Kathleen A. Baxter and Marcia Agness Kochel. Libraries Unlimited 2010 248p il pa $35
Grades: Adult Professional 028.5
1. Book talks 2. Boys -- Books and reading 3. Children's literature -- Bibliography
ISBN 978-1-59884-376-7 pa; 1-59884-376-1 pa; 978-1-59884-377-4 e-book
LC 2010036577
This "highlights books published mainly between 2007 and 2009. Twelve chapters cover themes such as sports, animals, gross/disgusting stuff, mysteries/disasters, and machines. Each one features anywhere from a few to two dozen ready-touse booktalks, most aimed at grades 3-8, along with extensive bibliographies (not annotated) of other titles that have received good reviews in Booklist, Horn Book Guide, and School Library Journal. New to this volume are enlightening interviews with male authors such as Kadir Nelson, Nic Bishop, and Seymour Simon, whose books are featured in the text. The introduction also lists ideas for promoting

books to boys in public libraries and school media centers." SLJ
Includes bibliographical references

Gotcha good! nonfiction books to get kids excited about reading. [by] Kathleen A. Baxter and Marcia Agness Kochel. Libraries Unlimited 2008 259p pa $35
Grades: Adult Professional 028.5
1. Books and reading 2. Children's literature -- Bibliography 3. Young adult literature -- Bibliography
ISBN 978-1-59158-654-8 pa; 1-59158-654-2 pa
LC 2008010350
"In addition to annotations for over 1000 nonfiction titles, [the authors] profile eight prolific authors and provide fun top-10 features for the various subjects covered. . . . The titles chosen are truly high quality, relevant, and up-to-date, with suggested ages provided, most ranging from grades three through eight. . . . A must-have for all librarians who want to get kids excited about nonfiction." SLJ
Includes bibliographical references

Bishop, Rudine Sims
Free within ourselves; the development of African American children's literature. Heinemann/Greenwood 2007 295p bibl il $65; pa $22
Grades: Adult Professional 028.5
1. African Americans in literature 2. Children -- Books and reading 3. Children's literature -- History and criticism 4. American literature -- African American authors -- History and criticism
ISBN 978-0-325-07135-0 Heinemann; 978-0-313-34093-2 pa Greenwood
LC 2007000612
"Bishop traces the evolution of fiction written for black children and by black authors and illustrators within the context of African-American social and literary history. . . . Her writing is precise and engaging, and it really comes alive when presenting primary-source material. . . . Librarians as well as teachers will be enriched by this work." SLJ
Includes bibliographical references

Brooks, Wanda M.
Embracing, evaluating, and examining African American children's and young adult literature; edited by Wanda M. Brooks, Jonda C. McNair; foreword by Rudine Sims Bishop. Scarecrow Press 2008 251p pa $45
Grades: Adult Professional 028.5
1. African Americans in literature 2. Children -- Books and reading 3. Children's literature -- History and criticism 4. Young adult literature -- History and criticism 5. American literature -- African American authors -- History and criticism
ISBN 978-0-8108-6027-8 pa; 0-8108-6027-9 pa
LC 2007025703
"Brooks and McNair have compiled 12 scholarly studies about the use of books by and about African-American children and young adults in classrooms across the United States. Selections include a detailed textual analysis of the work of Arna Bontemps and Langston Hughes; a sociolinguistic perspective on readers' response to books containing African-American Vernacular English; and a detailed study of the books used as classroom read-alouds by teachers in rural schools, which found that only three percent were about African Americans. While each study is complete in and of

itself, the text as a whole gives a broad picture of what is currently being done in this field, both in K-12 classrooms and college classes that emphasize children's literature." SLJ

Includes bibliographical references

Casement, Rose

Black history in the pages of children's literature. Scarecrow Press 2008 317p pa $55

Grades: Adult Professional   028.5

1. African Americans in literature 2. Children's literature -- Bibliography 3. Children's literature -- History and criticism

ISBN 978-0-8108-5843-5 pa; 0-8108-5843-6 pa
LC 2007018137

"Casement has organized her book along a time line from the initial presence of Africans in America before colonization to the present day. Each chapter begins with a brief description of important historical events that have often been left out of our history books. This is followed by an annotated bibliography that includes excerpts from each title and a description of the content. Books listed are primarily straight nonfiction but some fantasy, realistic fiction, biography, and poetry are included. The final two chapters address criteria for selecting children's literature for classroom use and introduce several talented African-American writers and illustrators. Putting this eminently accessible book into the hands of teachers should greatly increase the use of accurate books about African Americans and help to identify and pass on a more truthful historical picture than most of us were given in school." SLJ

Includes bibliographical references

Diamant-Cohen, Betsy

Booktalking bonanza; ten ready-to-use multimedia sessions for the busy librarian. American Library Association 2009 240p il pa $40

Grades: Adult Professional   028.5

1. Book talks 2. Books and reading 3. Children's literature

ISBN 978-0-8389-0965-2; 0-8389-0965-5
LC 2008-15371

"This volume is a collection of scripts for multimedia-enriched booktalks. After an introductory chapter that explains the reasoning for this approach, 10 scripts are outlined. Books, music, video, and Web sites are included for each one. The programs are geared toward elementary-aged children, although suggestions for adapting them for a middle or high school audience are included." SLJ

Includes bibliographical references

Embracing, evaluating, and examining African American children's and young adult literature; edited by Wanda M. Brooks, Jonda C. McNair; foreword by Rudine Sims Bishop. Scarecrow Press 2008 251p pa $45

Grades: Adult Professional   028.5

1. African Americans in literature 2. Children -- Books and reading 3. Children's literature -- History and criticism 4. Young adult literature -- History and criticism 5. American literature -- African American authors -- History and criticism

ISBN 978-0-8108-6027-8 pa; 0-8108-6027-9 pa
LC 2007025703

"Brooks and McNair have compiled 12 scholarly studies about the use of books by and about African-American

children and young adults in classrooms across the United States. Selections include a detailed textual analysis of the work of Arna Bontemps and Langston Hughes; a sociolinguistic perspective on readers' response to books containing African-American Vernacular English; and a detailed study of the books used as classroom read-alouds by teachers in rural schools, which found that only three percent were about African Americans. While each study is complete in and of itself, the text as a whole gives a broad picture of what is currently being done in this field, both in K-12 classrooms and college classes that emphasize children's literature." SLJ

Includes bibliographical references

Feinberg, Barbara

Welcome to Lizard Motel; children, stories, and the mystery of making things up: a memoir. Beacon Press 2004 256p $20

Grades: Adult Professional   028.5

1. Imagination 2. Children -- Books and reading

ISBN 0-8070-7144-7
LC 2004-710

"Feinberg, who's spent years working with children in a creativity workshop she designed, has the independence and experience to raise important questions. Her critique . . . should stir some much-needed controversy." Publ Wkly

Includes bibliographical references

Gilmore, Barry

★ **Speaking** volumes; how to get students discussing books, and much more. Heinemann 2006 128p pa $17.95

Grades: Adult Professional   028.5

1. Books and reading

ISBN 978-0-325-00915-5 pa; 0-325-00915-5 pa
LC 2005-28371

"Gilmore provides practical, hands-on methods to involve students in oral and written classroom conversations that encourage reflection and ultimately polished, coherent expression. . . . Both new and seasoned discussion leaders will want a copy for repeated reference." Voice Youth Advocates

Includes bibliographical references

Gilton, Donna L.

Multicultural and ethnic children's literature in the United States; [by] Donna L. Gilton. Scarecrow Press 2007 236p pa $45

Grades: Adult Professional   028.5

1. Multiculturalism 2. Minorities in literature 3. Children's literature -- History and criticism

ISBN 978-0-8108-5672-1 pa; 0-8108-5672-7 pa
LC 2007006391

"Gilton writes with authority, clarity, and conviction, presenting a strong rationale for the necessity for teachers to use multicultural literature whether or not their schools and/or classrooms have diverse populations. . . . The author offers a wealth of information. . . . She gives a history of multicultural literature in the U.S. . . . Gilton addresses current issues. . . . There is ample information on how to find the best books that appropriately represent a variety of cultures. Finally, Gilton looks closely at groups that are growing in the U.S." SLJ

Includes bibliographical references

Handbook of research on children's and young adult literature; edited by Shelby A. Wolf . . . [et al.] Routledge 2010 555p $295; pa $119.95

Grades: Adult Professional   **028.5**

1. Children's literature -- History and criticism 2. Young adult literature -- History and criticism

ISBN 978-0-415-96505-7; 0-415-96505-5; 978-0-415-96506-4 pa; 0-415-96506-3 pa; 978-0-203-84354-3 e-book

LC 2010-16339

"The book examines readers, texts, and cultural contexts of children's literature and across the three intersecting disciplines of Education, English, and Library and Information Science, in an effort to model a multidisciplinary approach to children's literature research. Thirty-seven scholarly articles, by figures such as Eliza Dresang, Rudine Sims Bishop, and Roderick McGillis . . . are counterpointed by responses that often provide more personal perspectives, including insights from noted authors such as Lois Lowry, M. T. Anderson, and Markus Zusak." Bull Cent Child Books

Herb, Steven

Connecting fathers, children, and reading; a how-to-do it manual for librarians. [by] Steven Herb, Sara Willoughby-Herb. Neal-Schuman 2001 196p (How-to-do-it manuals for librarians) pa $45

Grades: Adult Professional   **028.5**

1. Fathers 2. Books and reading

ISBN 1-55570-390-9

LC 2001-18315

This "book looks at both the importance and effect of father involvement in children's reading. . . . Case studies, anecdotes, and interesting sidebars abound in this well-organized, well-written source. . . . An extensive bibliography includes more than 450 children's books about fathers and fathering." SLJ

Hey! listen to this; stories to read aloud. edited by Jim Trelease. Viking 1992 414p hardcover o.p. pa $15

Grades: Adult Professional   **028.5**

1. Authors 2. Books and reading 3. Literature -- Collections

ISBN 0-14-014653-9 pa

LC 91-37668

"Divided into categories such as 'Animal Tales,' 'Children of Courage,' or 'Classic Tales,' the forty-eight selections cover a wide spectrum from folktales to fantasy, classics to contemporary stories. More than half are complete stories, while the remainder are one or two chapters from longer books. Trelease skillfully weaves his choices into a cohesive whole. Beyond merely categorizing them, he refers to other authors or stories in the discussions that precede and follow each story." J Youth Serv Libr

Includes bibliographical references

Keane, Nancy J.

101 great, ready-to-use book lists for children; Nancy J. Keane. Libraries Unlimited, an imprint of ABC-CLIO, LLC 2012 xiv, 246 p.p (paperback) $45

Grades: Adult Professional   **028.5**

1. Best books 2. Children -- Books and reading 3. School libraries -- Book lists 4. Children's libraries -- Book lists 5. Children's literature -- Bibliography 6.

Children -- Books and reading -- United States

ISBN 1610690834; 9781610690836

LC 2011051429

Includes bibliographical references and index

Kitain, Sandra

Shelf-esteem; [by] Sandra Kitain. Neal-Schuman Publishers 2008 183p pa $49.95

Grades: Adult Professional   **028.5**

1. Book talks 2. Reference books 3. Books and reading 4. Children's libraries 5. Children's literature -- Bibliography

ISBN 978-1-55570-568-8 pa; 1-55570-568-5 pa

LC 2007034737

"Kitain offers an array of books that 'help children relate to their personal lives and individual challenges.' Chapters are based on themes including but not limited to friendship, courage, emotions, moving, new siblings, physical challenges, and bullies. Tough subjects like alcoholism, illness and death, and homelessness are also included. . . . The quality and variety of texts are excellent. The remaining chapters of the book explore working with community partners. This text is highly recommended for all librarians, teachers, caregivers, and parents of younger readers." SLJ

Includes bibliographical references

Larson, Jeanette C.

Bringing mysteries alive for children and young adults; [by] Jeanette Larson. Linworth Pub. 2004 134p il pa $39.95

Grades: Adult Professional   **028.5**

1. Mystery fiction 2. Children -- Books and reading 3. Teenagers -- Books and reading

ISBN 1-58683-012-0

LC 2003-22064

"The book has excellent ideas for beginning as well as seasoned professionals." SLJ

Includes bibliographical references

Latrobe, Kathy Howard

The **children's** literature dictionary; definitions, resources, and teaching activities. [by] Kathy Latrobe, Carolyn S. Brodie, Maureen White. Neal-Schuman 2002 282p pa $59.95

Grades: Adult Professional   **028.5**

1. Reference books 2. Children's literature -- Dictionaries

ISBN 1-55570-424-7

LC 2001-44434

"The first section is an alphabetical dictionary of 325 terms found in reviews, lesson plans, and other resources. Definitions of terms contain meanings and examples from popular children's literature and activities related to the term. The activities descriptions provide a starting point for teaching or demonstrating the term. This reference book supports resources and materials that librarians or teachers should have in their collection." Book Rep

Lerer, Seth

★ **Children's** literature; a reader's history, from Aesop to Harry Potter. University of Chicago Press 2008 385p il

Grades: Adult Professional   **028.5**

1. Books and reading 2. Children's literature -- History

and criticism
ISBN 0-226-47300-7; 978-0-226-47300-0

LC 2007046708

The author sets out to "chart the makings of the Western literary imagination from Aesop's fables to Mother Goose, from Alice's Adventures in Wonderland to Peter Pan, from Where the Wild Things Are to Harry Potter. Lerer here explores the iconic books, ancient and contemporary alike, that have forged a lifelong love of literature in young readers during their formative years. Along the way, Lerer also looks at the changing environments of family life and human growth, schooling and scholarship, and publishing and politics in which children found themselves changed by the books they read." (Publisher's note) Index.

"This work presents a true critical history of [children's literature], from Aesop to the present. Scholarly, erudite, and all but exhaustive, it is also entertaining and accessible. . . . [Lerer] asks important questions about writers' intentions and readers' reactions, about why some texts endure and others do not, about the influence of science and religion on children's literature, and even about the impact of libraries and literary prizes upon the genre." Libr J

Includes bibliographical references

Marks, Diana F.

Children's book award handbook. Libraries Unlimited 2006 412p bibl il tab pa $40
Grades: Adult Professional   **028.5**
1. Children's literature -- Awards 2. Young adult literature -- Awards
ISBN 1-59158-304-7

The author "has compiled a valuable resource that will be much appreciated by teachers and school librarians. Her handbook provides details on the history and origins of 24 major children's book awards from the Jane Addams Book Award to the Charlotte Zolotow Award and includes lesson plans and student activity sheets for 21 of them." Libr J

McDaniel, Deanna

Gentle reads; great books to warm hearts and lift spirits, grades 5-9. [by] Deanna J. McDaniel. Libraries Unlimited 2008 318p (Children's and young adult literature reference series) $45
Grades: Adult Professional   **028.5**
1. Children's literature -- Bibliography 2. Young adult literature -- Bibliography
ISBN 978-1-59158-491-9

LC 2008018878

This includes "500 recommended titles. Here readers will find books with divorce, drug use, attempted suicides, and more but they all meet the criteria the author has set by being either inspiring, heartwarming, or in some way uplifting. . . . Arranged by genres, the entries include full bibliographic information, an annotation, and a description of why the book fits the 'gentle criteria.'" SLJ

Includes bibliographical references

Nespeca, Sue McCleaf

Picture books plus; 100 extension activities in art, drama, music, math, and science. [by] Sue McCleaf Nespeca, Joan B. Reeve. American Lib. Assn. 2003 133p il pa $38

Grades: Adult Professional   **028.5**
1. Books and reading 2. Picture books for children
ISBN 0-8389-0840-3

LC 2002-11822

"This book is intended for use by teachers, librarians, and others working with children in preschool through grade three and features extension activities for use with a variety of materials. . . . Each chapter includes titles with annotations, 20 activities, and a list of resource books that will introduce readers to further activities. . . . Librarians and teachers will find many useful ideas here." Booklist

Includes bibliographical references

Reid, Rob

★ **Cool** story programs for the school-age crowd. American Library Association 2004 181p il pa $32
Grades: Adult Professional   **028.5**
1. Books and reading 2. Children's literature
ISBN 0-8389-0887-X

LC 2004-9933

This offers plans for story programs which incorporate poetry, picture books, chapter book excerpts, and short stories

"Eighteen well-developed plans with wacky themes that kids will love will bring literature to life with a minimum of stress for public librarians, teachers, and school media specialists. . . . A useful book with surefire suggestions for winning programs." SLJ

Includes bibliographical references

Saccardi, Marianne

Books that teach kids to write; [by] Marianne C. Saccardi. Libraries Unlimited 2011 150p pa $30; e-book $30
Grades: Adult Professional   **028.5**
1. Creative writing 2. Books and reading 3. Literature -- Study and teaching
ISBN 978-1-59884-451-1 pa; 978-1-59884-452-8 e-book

LC 2011001866

"Divided into sections such as 'Making Stories Unique,' 'Creating Memorable Characters,' and 'Putting Passion and Voice into Nonfiction Writing,' this book gives countless recommendations for teaching various skills. Saccardi offers short, annotated summaries of mentor texts and describes how they can be used to model good writing techniques. . . . After reading this resource, educators will have a long wish list of materials to purchase." SLJ

Includes bibliographical references

Sullivan, Michael

★ **Connecting** boys with books 2; closing the reading gap. American Library Association 2009 119p il pa $40
Grades: Adult Professional   **028.5**
1. School libraries 2. Children's libraries 3. Young adults' libraries 4. Boys -- Books and reading
ISBN 978-0-8389-0979-9 pa; 0-8389-0979-5 pa

LC 2008-34925

"A must-read for all librarians and media specialists." SLJ

Includes bibliographical references (p. 105-110)

Raising boy readers; Michael Sullivan. Huron Street Press/ALA 2014 xiii, 193 p.p illustrations (pbk.) $19.95

Grades: Adult Professional **028.5**
1. Reading 2. Boys -- Education 3. Boys -- Books and reading 4. Reading -- Sex differences 5. Teenage boys -- Books and reading 6. Children's literature, American -- Bibliography 7. Young adult literature, American -- Bibliography
ISBN 1937589439; 9781937589431

LC 2013011537

This book, by Michael Sullivan, "conveys an understanding of the differences that are common among many boys and how these differences affect reading. It provides practical approaches to promote reading to boys, addressing physical differences, such as the different rates of early brain development between boys and girls; psychological issues, such as the outward focus of boys; and social issues, such as stress and confidence." (Publisher's note)

"So much more than just a compendium of annotated book lists (though they are here and well organized by genre and age level), Raising Boy Readers lays out the challenges of reaching reluctant readers, identifies common stumbling blocks, and systematically explores the how, when, why, what, and with whom of boys and their books." Booklist

Includes bibliographical references and index

Serving boys through readers' advisory. American Library Association 2010 152p (ALA readers' advisory series) pa $48
Grades: Adult Professional **028.5**
1. Children's literature 2. Reference services (Libraries) 3. Boys -- Books and reading 4. Boys
ISBN 978-0-8389-1022-1; 0-8389-1022-X

LC 2009-26841

"This volume was created to give a general direction when helping most boys select books. . . . Sullivan challenges us to throw out our preconceived notions about how to conduct such an interview. Methods of performing indirect readers' advisory with parents and teachers are included. The excellent booktalks for elementary, middle school, and high school boys alone make this a worthwhile purchase." SLJ

Includes bibliographical references

Temple, Charles A.
Children's books in children's hands; an introduction to their literature. [by] Charles Temple, Miriam Martinez, Junko Yokota; with contributions by Evelyn B. Freeman. 4th ed.; Pearson Allyn & Bacon 2010 572p pa $137.40
Grades: Adult Professional **028.5**
1. Books and reading 2. Children's literature -- History and criticism
ISBN 978-0-1370-7403-7 pa; 0-1370-7403-4 pa

LC 2010018237

First published 1998

The authors focus on creating an understanding of how literature works and how children respond to literature, they provide a wide range of good books to use with children, and they suggest ways to guide children into books and help them enjoy the experience.

Includes bibliographical references

Vardell, Sylvia M.
Children's literature in action; a librarian's guide. Libraries Unlimited 2008 323p (Library and information science text series) pa $50; $65

Grades: Adult Professional **028.5**
1. Children's literature 2. Children -- Books and reading 3. Children's literature -- History and criticism 4. Children's library services -- Activity projects
ISBN 1-59158-557-2 pa; 1-59158-657-7; 978-1-59158-557-2 pa; 978-1-59158-657-9

LC 2007038012

"This excellent introduction to children's literature and its various genres and forms offers many activities and practical applications. Each chapter includes 'Action' components that highlight literature, authors, specific book titles, or history. . . . It also includes evaluation criteria, writing reviews, collection development of various genres, awards, and other programs of merit as well as additional information in numerous bibliographies and lists of recommended reading and Web sites." SLJ

Includes bibliographical references

Yolen, Jane
Touch magic; fantasy, faerie & folklore in the literature of childhood. Expanded ed; August House 2000 128p pa $11.95
Grades: Adult Professional **028.5**
1. Folklore 2. Children's literature -- History and criticism
ISBN 0-87483-591-7

LC 00-27565

First published 1981 by Philomel Bks.

The author provides perspectives on reading, appreciating, and preserving fantasy and folklore for children. Among topics discussed are the morality of fairy tales, the definition of story, and the theme of time travel

Includes bibliographical references

Zbaracki, Matthew D.
Best books for boys; a resource for educators. foreward by Jon Scieszka. Libraries Unlimited 2008 189p il (Children's and young adult literature reference series)
Grades: Adult Professional **028.5**
1. Best books 2. Children's literature 3. Young adult literature 4. Reading interests 5. Boys -- Books and reading 6. Children's literature -- Book lists 7. Children's literature -- Bibliography 8. Young adult literature -- Bibliography
ISBN 1-59158-599-6; 978-1-59158-599-2

LC 2007-51065

"Good source notes guide readers to additional writings on the topic and speak to the author's significant research in his field. Nicely indexed by author, title, and subject, this [is an] easy-to-navigate resource." Voice Youth Advocates

Includes bibliographical references

Zvirin, Stephanie
Read with me; best books for preschoolers. Stephanie Zvirin. Huron Street Press 2012 171 p. (pbk.) $18.95
Grades: Adult Professional **028.5**
1. Reading readiness 2. Children -- Books and reading 3. Best books -- United States 4. Reading -- Parent participation 5. Libraries and preschool children
ISBN 193758903X; 9781937589035; 9781937589066; 9781937589073

LC 2012002405

This book, by Stephanie Zvirin, "offers more than 300 age-appropriate and subject-specific book selections from librarians for reading time with children. From board and picture books to hot new books, these recommendations reflect family, community, play, and the environment. Chapters include segments on reading together, friendship, places near and far, and making believe." (Publisher's note)

Includes bibliographical references and index

028.7   Use of books and other information media as sources of information

Callison, Daniel

★ The **blue** book on information age inquiry, instruction and literacy; [by] Daniel Callison and Leslie Preddy. Libraries Unlimited 2006 643p il pa $45
Grades: Adult Professional   **028.7**
1. Information literacy
ISBN 978-1-59158-325-7; 1-59158-325-X
LC 2006-23645

A revised edition of Key Words, Concepts and Methods for Information Age Instruction, published 2003 by LMS Associates

"Part 1 introduces the concepts of information inquiry, providing foundational documents and exploring search and use models, information literacy, standards, the instructional role of library media specialists, online inquiry learning, and resource management. Part 2 offers concrete examples of inquiry applied to the middle-school student research process and supplies reproducible pages for classroom use. Part 3 discusses and defines 51 key terms. Entries here are several pages in length and include citations and references. Indispensable for all school media specialists, this book will also appeal to other readers, who will be impressed by its well-organized design, thoroughness, and practicality." Booklist

Includes bibliographical references

030   General encyclopedic works

Anderson, Jennifer Joline

Wikipedia; the company and its founders. ABDO Pub. Co. 2011 112p il (Technology pioneers) lib bdg $34.22
Grades: 5 6 7 8   **030**
1. Electronic encyclopedias 2. Wikis (Computer science) 3. Wikimedia Foundation
ISBN 978-1-61714-812-5 lib bdg; 1-61714-812-1 lib bdg; 978-1-61758-970-6 e-book
LC 2010037886

This is an introduction to Wikipedia and its founders.

"Written in a clear, linear fashion, this series offers vivid, well-researched details about the development of technological advancements considered essential in today's society. . . . Readers who are interested in technology and inventions will be thoroughly engrossed." SLJ

Includes glossary and bibliographical references

031   General encyclopedic works in specific languages and language families

DK Publishing, Inc.

DK children's illustrated encyclopedia; 7th ed.; DK Pub. 2010 600p il map $34.99
Grades: 4 5 6 7   **031**
1. Encyclopedias and dictionaries
ISBN 978-0-7566-5759-8; 0-7566-5759-8
LC 2010279636

First published 1991 with title: Random House children's encyclopedia; a revised edition of Dorling Kindersley's children's illustrated encyclopedia 6th ed. published 2006

A highly illustrated one-volume encyclopedia containing entries ranging from Abolitionist movement to Zoos.

"This handsome revision features more than 3000 photographs, maps, time lines, and illustrations. . . . The attractive format encourages browsing." SLJ

Guinness world records 2015; by Guinness World Records. St. Martin's Press 2014 255 p. ill. (some col.) $28.95
Grades: 3 4 5 6 7 8 9 10 11 12   **031**
1. World records 2. World records -- Periodicals 3. Curiosities and wonders -- Periodicals
ISBN 1908843632; 9781908843630

This 2015 edition of the Guinness World Records book "presents thousands of new and updated records. . . . [It] showcases the very best of the most recent world records, with new subjects as diverse as castles, 3D printing, the search for alien life and the latest developments in AI and robotics. Plus, the Flashback features offer a look back at the archives to bring you the best of the classic and iconic records from the past 60 years." (Publisher's note)

The **Kingfisher** children's encyclopedia. Kingfisher 2012 480 p. (hardcover) $29.99
Grades: 3 4 5 6 7 8   **031**
1. Picture books for children 2. Encyclopedias and dictionaries
ISBN 075346814X; 9780753468142

The entries in this updated children's encyclopedia "range from one to four pages in length each, feature full-color illustrations and photos and subheadings in a large, easy-to-read font and sidebars and fact boxes of thought-provoking information." Topics include "continents and countries, technology, transportation, animal and plant life, religion, and space." (School Library Journal)

Knowledge Encyclopedia. Dk Pub 2013 360 p. $29.99
Grades: 4 5 6 7 8   **031**
1. Encyclopedias and dictionaries
ISBN 1465414177; 9781465414175

This book, by the Smithsonian Institution, is a "family reference using 3-D rendered images to explore the wonders of the world . . . . Divided into six chapters . . . a wide range of topics come to life. Illustrated with fascinating facts, maps, timelines, and graphics, the Knowledge Encyclopedia makes complex subjects easy to understand and is the perfect resource for kids, whether to help with homework or to pique their curiosity." (Publisher's note)

Turner, Tracey

World of the weird. Firefly Books 2009 144p il $14.95

Grades: 5 6 7 8   **031**
1. Curiosities and wonders
ISBN 978-1-55407-481-5; 1-55407-481-9
"A first-rate browsing item, from the bicycle-riding frog on the front cover to the recipe for chocolate-covered crickets at the end. . . . Turner presents barrages of snippets on extreme sports ('chessboxing'), uncommon maladies ('exploding head syndrome'), oddball festivals, bizarre beliefs ('Eating stolen bacon is a cure for constipation.' Do tell!), strange creatures real or otherwise, supernatural phenomena and . . . more. . . . Illustrated with photos that are often startling but never gory or gross, this compact page-turner will light up the imaginations of motivated young readers and jaded nonreaders alike." Kirkus

Wilkes, Angela
My world of discovery. Kingfisher 2007 192p il $14.95
Grades: 3 4 5 6   **031**
1. Reference books 2. Encyclopedias and dictionaries
ISBN 0-7534-5931-0
This "is an excellent resource for a young person developing an interest in a diverse number of science topics. Many colorful, clear illustrations accompany the text. . . . The text is easy to read and follow." Sci Books Films

The **World** Book Encyclopedia. World Book, Inc 22 v col ill, col maps
Grades: 4 5 6 7 8 9 10 11 12 Adult   **031**
1. Reference books 2. Encyclopedias and dictionaries
New editions published yearly; revised frequently
"A 22-volume, highly illustrated, A-Z general encyclopedia for all ages, featuring sections on how to use World Book, other research aids, pronunciation key, a student guide to better writing, speaking, and research skills, and comprehensive index." (Publisher's note)

031.02   Books of miscellaneous facts

Aronson, Marc
For boys only; the biggest, baddest book ever. [by] Marc Aronson [and] H.P. Newquist. Feiwel and Friends 2007 157p il map $14.95
Grades: 4 5 6 7   **031.02**
1. Boys 2. Curiosities and wonders
ISBN 978-0-312-37706-9; 0-312-37706-1
LC 2007-32847
"In a tone both light and humorous, Newquist and Aronson aim to please by assembling a tantalizing miscellany—codes, puzzles, best lists, brief history and science facts, instructions for making fake blood and playing Ultimate Frisbee. . . . This offers lots of good fun." Booklist

Buchanan, Andrea J.
The daring book for girls; [by] Andrea J. Buchanan, Miriam Peskowitz; illustrations by Alexis Seabrook. Collins 2007 279p il map $24.95
Grades: 4 5 6 7   **031.02**
1. Girls 2. Amusements 3. Recreation 4. Curiosities and wonders
ISBN 978-0-06-147257-2
LC 2007031986

"In the introduction, the authors invite girls to explore their world . . . and they deliver a resource that will help them to do just that. The pages that follow are filled with interesting activities to try and important facts they may not know, but are sure to keep them busy for hours. The authors cover everything from making a lemon-powered clock to the history of writing and cursive, from how to paddle a canoe to the Periodic Table of the Elements in clear, thoughtful language that readers of all ages are sure to embrace." SLJ

Farndon, John
Do not open; written by John Farndon. DK Publishing 2007 256p il $24.99
Grades: 4 5 6 7   **031.02**
1. Curiosities and wonders
ISBN 978-0-7566-3205-2; 0-7566-3205-6
LC 2007300131
This encyclopedic tome catalogues "the mysterious and unusual. . . . Flaps, foldout pages and varied styles of illustration—from photomontage to digital cartoons and more conventional line art—keep the book visually fresh and ably complement the subject matter. . . . Taking in everything from weird weather like St. Elmo's fire and raining frogs to possible locations of Atlantis, the book incites curiosity—and expansively rewards it." Publ Wkly

Iggulden, Conn
The dangerous book for boys; [by] Conn Iggulden, Hal Iggulden. Collins 2007 270p il map $24.95
Grades: 4 5 6 7   **031.02**
1. Boys 2. Amusements 3. Recreation 4. Curiosities and wonders
ISBN 0-06-124358-2; 978-0-06-124358-5
LC 2006-491918
"This eclectic collection addresses the undeniable boy-appeal of certain facts and activities. Dozens of short chapters, in fairly random order, cover a wide range of topics in conversational prose. Simple instructions for coin tricks and paper airplanes alternate with excerpts from history such as Famous Battles and facts about ancient wonders of the world and astronomy. . . . Tongue-in-cheek humor emerges throughout." SLJ

Kane, Joseph Nathan
★ Famous first facts; a record of first happenings, discoveries, and inventions in American history. [by] Joseph Nathan Kane, Steven Anzovin, & Janet Podell. 6th ed.; Wilson, H.W. 2006 1307p il $185
Grades: 5 6 7 8 9 10 11 12 Adult   **031.02**
1. Reference books 2. Encyclopedias and dictionaries 3. United States -- History -- Dictionaries
ISBN 978-0-8242-1065-6; 0-8242-1065-4
LC 2006-3096
First published 1933
Over 7500 entries cover first occurences in American history, organized into 16 chapters each divided into sections. Sections are alphabetically organized, and individual entries are organized chronologically within each section. Includes five indexes: subject index, index by years, index by days, index to personal names, and geographical index
"Besides serving as an essential ready-reference source, the book is also fun to read out loud to colleagues—when was bubble gum first manufactured in the U.S.? When was the spray can introduced?" Booklist

Masoff, Joy

Oh, yuck! the encyclopedia of everything nasty. illustrated by Terry Sirrell. Workman 2000 212p il pa $14.95

Grades: 4 5 6 7   **031.02**

1. Curiosities and wonders

ISBN 0-7611-0771-1

LC 99-43603

An alphabetical collection of articles about disgusting things, from acne, ants, and bacteria to worms, x-periments, and zits

"Amusing cartoons and well-chosen, black-and-white photographs with humorous captions support the text. . . . This delightful volume will be enjoyed by fans of grossness everywhere." SLJ

Includes bibliographical references

Murrie, Steve

While You Were Sleeping; Fun Facts That Happen at Night. by Steve Murrie and Matthew Murrie; illustrated by Tom Bloom. Turtleback Books 2012 224 p. col. ill. (paperback) $9.99; (prebind) $20.85

Grades: 2 3 4   **031.02**

1. Night 2. Sleep

ISBN 0545430283; 0606267468; 9780545430289; 9780606267465

This book "provides general observations about internal biological processes associated with sleep, nocturnal animals, nighttime jobs, and wee-hours activities--interleaved with mini-disquisitions on earthquakes, Mount Rushmore, bamboo, comets, space probes, the largest Lego tower every constructed, and an array of other subjects." (Booklist)

Ripley, Catherine

How? the most awesome question and answer book about nature, animals, people, places, and you! by Catherine Ripley; illustrated by Scot Ritchie. Owlkids Books 2012 192 p. col. ill. (hardcover) $19.95

Grades: 1 2 3   **031.02**

1. Shells 2. Hamsters 3. Questions and answers 4. Children's questions and answers

ISBN 1926973240; 9781926973241

LC 2012405052

Author Catherine Ripley uses humor to answer questions about how everyday subjects work for children. In "question-and-answer format, . . . [the questions] include how batter turns into cake and how birthday candles stay on fire, why hamsters run on wheels and why they stuff their cheeks with food, why you hear the sea in a seashell and why the ocean is salty." (Kirkus Reviews)

Shields, Amy

Little kids first big book of why. National Geographic 2011 127p (National geographic little kids) $14.95

Grades: K 1 2 3   **031.02**

1. Science 2. Curiosities and wonders

ISBN 978-1-4263-0793-5; 1-4263-0793-4

"Young readers will find clear answers to a variety of basic science, nature, technology, and human body questions in this random but potentially useful volume. . . . Crisp photographs illustrate the information, including brief explanations behind everything from curly hair to blue skies to purring cats to why planes fly." Horn Book Guide

★ The World almanac for kids. World Almanac il maps

Grades: 4 5 6 7   **031.02**

1. Almanacs 2. Reference books

Annual. First published 1995 for 1996

This volume contains information on animals, art, religion, sports, books, law, language, science and computers. Includes a section of full-color maps and flags. Illustrated throughout with pictures, diagrams, and charts

050   General serial publications

Botzakis, Stergios

Pretty in print; questioning magazines. by Stergios Botzakis. Fact Finders 2007 32p il (Media literacy) lib bdg $22.60; pa $7.95

Grades: 4 5 6 7   **050**

1. Periodicals 2. Publishers and publishing

ISBN 978-0-7368-6764-1 lib bdg; 0-7368-6764-3 lib bdg; 978-0-7368-7860-9 pa; 0-7368-7860-2 pa

LC 2006021443

This is "written in a breezy style and [has] plenty of popping colors and photos. . . . Useful and attractive." SLJ

"Describes what media is, how magazines are part of media, and encourages readers to question the medium's influential messages." Publisher's note

Includes bibliographical references

051   General serial publications in specific languages and language families

Hopkins, Lee Bennett

★ Days to celebrate; a full year of poetry, people, holidays, history, fascinating facts, and more. written and edited by Lee Bennett Hopkins; illustrated by Stephen Alcorn. Greenwillow Books 2005 112p il $17.99; lib bdg $18.89

Grades: 3 4 5   **051**

1. Almanacs 2. Holidays 3. Reference books 4. Poetry -- Collections

ISBN 0-06-000765-6; 0-06-000766-4 lib bdg

LC 2003-49288

"The writers represented include Robert Frost, Langston Hughes, Richard Wilbur, and Gwendolyn Brooks. Alcorn's large, vibrant, whimsical artwork perfectly enhances the prose and verse to make this book a delight to the eye and the ear." SLJ

069   Museology (Museum science)

Korrell, Emily B.

Awesome adventures at the Smithsonian; the official kids guide to the Smithsonian Institution. Emily B. Korrell. Smithsonian Books 2013 127 p. ill. (chiefly col.) (paperback) $14.95

Grades: 4 5 6   **069**

1. Museums -- Guidebooks 2. National Air and Space Museum 3. Washington (D.C.) -- Guidebooks 4. National Museum of Natural History (U.S.)

ISBN 1588343499; 9781588343499

LC 2012029119

This "guide offers children ages 8-12 years a way to navigate the Smithsonian. Engaging maps, photographs, and illustrations present the main museum halls along with puzzles, games, mad libs, and pages for journal entries, drawings, and superlatives that will help get kids ready for their big trip to the nation's capital and keep them focused and attentive as they navigate the world's largest museum complex that is the Smithsonian Institution." (Publisher's note)

Mark, Jan

The **museum** book; a guide to strange and wonderful collections. written by Jan Mark; illustrated by Richard Holland. Candlewick Press 2007 54p il $15

Grades: 3 4 5 6   **069**

1. Museums

ISBN 978-0-7636-3370-7; 0-7636-3370-4

LC 2006-49055

Explains what a museum is, and what fascinating things you might find there.

This "tome will launch readers on a leisurely and edifying journey of discovery. . . . Holland . . . jolts readers . . . with his mixed-media collages, which sparingly employ color and liberally combine to look like Victorian engravings, pencil sketches, Gorey-like figures, and photos of various locales." Publ Wkly

070.5   Publishing

Donovan, Sandra, 1967-

★ **Pingpong** Perry experiences how a book is made; by Sandy Donovan; illustrated by Martin Haake. Picture Window 2010 24p il (In the library) lib bdg $25.32

Grades: 1 2 3   **070.5**

1. Publishers and publishing

ISBN 978-1-4048-5759-9 lib bdg; 1-4048-5759-1 lib bdg

This volume "surprises and amuses with every page, while also neatly explaining the publishing process. . . . On the first page, Perry (digitally illustrated in an angular, retro-cool style) is clutching his own book: Perry's Practical Guide to the Pizza Picks of Popular Pingpong Players. Donovan then backtracks to relate Perry's meteoric transformation into publishing royalty. . . . The editing process, complete with a sample of a copyedited page, is admirably realistic, as is the portrayal of the savvy professional women Perry encounters at every turn." Booklist

Neuburger, Emily K.

Golden legacy; how Golden Books won children's hearts, changed publishing forever, and became an American icon along the way. Golden Books 2007 245p il $40

Grades: Adult Professional   **070.5**

1. Publishers and publishing 2. Golden Books Publishing Co. Inc. 3. Children's literature -- History and criticism

ISBN 978-0-375-82996-3; 0-375-82996-2

LC 2006-939312

Presents a history of Golden Books, discussing how it was founded in the midst of World War II providing quality books at inexpensive prices and used innovative writers and marketing techniques to establish itself as a highly successful publishing firm

This is a "lavishly illustrated, handsomely designed volume. . . . The author unearths some startling facts. . . . The highly readable narrative is documented with thorough and detailed footnotes. . . . This winning combination of nostalgia and clear-eyed, meticulously researched history breaks new ground." SLJ

★ **Minders** of make-believe; idealists, entrepreneurs, and the shaping of American children's literature. Houghton Mifflin Co. 2008 402p $28

Grades: Adult Professional   **070.5**

1. Publishers and publishing 2. Children -- Books and reading 3. Children's literature -- History and criticism

ISBN 978-0-395-67407-9; 0-395-67407-7

LC 2008-00589

"Marcus' approach and tone are always, and irresistibly, well informed, sensible, and intelligent. . . . It is hard to imagine any issue that he has overlooked, and the resulting book is, in word, indispensable." Booklist

Includes bibliographical references

Wickings, Ruth

Pop-up; everything you need to know to create your own pop-up book. paper engineering by Ruth Wickings; illustrated by Frances Castle. Candlewick Press 2010 un il $19.99

Grades: 3 4 5 6   **070.5**

1. Pop-up books

ISBN 978-0-7636-5056-8; 0-7636-5056-0

LC 2010-05488

"First outlining the basic building blocks of pop-up engineering (types of folds, mechanics like noisemakers and spirals), the book then uses the example of a pop-up robot to demonstrate how such components work together. The remaining sections offer four illustrated scenes, into which punch-put elements can be incorporated. . . . Completing the pop-ups will be tricky for younger readers (the difficulty level increases with each project) but the end result should be as gratifying as it is illuminating." Publ Wkly

081   General collections in specific languages and language families

Hudson, Wade

★ **Powerful** words; more than 200 years of extraordinary writing by African Americans. illustrated by Sean Qualls; foreword by Marian Wright Edelman. Scholastic Nonfiction 2004 178p il $19.95

Grades: 5 6 7 8   **081**

1. African Americans -- History 2. African Americans -- Biography 3. American literature -- African American authors

ISBN 0-439-40969-1

LC 2003-42792

A collection of speeches and writings by African Americans, with commentary about the time period in which each person lived, information about the speaker/writer, and public response to the words.

"Short enough to hold attention, the selections . . . are also long enough to show the writers' tone and style. Many sensitive full-page portraits are included. . . . This well-designed volume will be an excellent addition to many library collections." Booklist

Includes bibliographical references

098   Prohibited works, forgeries, hoaxes

Scales, Pat R.

Teaching banned books; 12 guides for young readers. American Library Association 2001 134p pa $28

Grades: Adult Professional   **098**

1. School libraries 2. Books -- Censorship 3. Children's literature -- Study and teaching

ISBN 0-8389-0807-1

LC 01-22340

"Scales knows her material inside out. She also knows how to inspire others to take up this cause and gives them an effective handbook to do just that." Booklist

Includes bibliographical references

100   PHILOSOPHY

100   Philosophy, parapsychology and occultism, psychology

Law, Stephen

Really, really big questions; about the weird, the wonderful, and everything else. illustrated by Nishant Choksi. Kingfisher 2009 62p il $16.99

Grades: 5 6 7 8   **100**

1. Philosophy

ISBN 978-0-7534-6309-3; 0-7534-6309-1

An introduction to philosophy which uses clear analogies to explore some of life's biggest moral and scientific questions, including the origins of the universe and the meaning of life

"Through a combination of vibrant colors; hip, retro illustrations; and interesting quotes, Law has produced a stimulating work for young minds that is sure to spark conversation and, of course, more questions." SLJ

133.1   Apparitions

Everett, J. H.

Haunted histories; creepy castles, dark dungeons, and powerful palaces. J. H. Everett and Marilyn Scott-Waters. 1st ed. Henry Holt and Company 2012 160 p. (hardcover) $14.99; (paperback) $5.99

Grades: 4 5 6   **133.1**

1. Castles 2. Torture 3. Historic sites 4. Ghosts 5. Haunted places

ISBN 0805089713; 9780805089714; 9781250027269

LC 2011033495

In this book, authors J.H. Everett and Marilyn Scott-Waters focus on "Virgil Dante, youngest Master Ghostorian in London," ghosts, and his raven, Thor, as they "tour history with the assistance of a cursed pocket watch and look in on castles, dungeons, palaces and graveyards. . . . The usual suspects get the eye: The Tower of London and the

Bastille figure prominently, but there are also lesser-known nests of nastiness like Himeji Castle in Japan and Castle Neuschwanstein in Bavaria." (Kirkus Reviews)

Gudgeon, Christopher

Ghost trackers; the unreal world of ghosts, ghost-hunting, and the paranormal. by Chris Gudgeon; foreword by Joe MacLeod. Tundra Books 2010 75p il pa $14.95

Grades: 4 5 6 7   **133.1**

1. Ghosts 2. Parapsychology

ISBN 978-0-88776-950-4; 0-88776-950-0

"Gudgeon thoroughly discusses all things ghostly. Chapters take on the history of sightings, scientists and paranormal research, haunted places around the world, and ghost tracking. . . . Side boxes offer other assorted information, and photographs and illustrations, some quite eerie, are sprinkled throughout. The writing is clear and the subject is presented in an evenhanded manner." SLJ

Hawes, Jason

Ghost hunt; chilling tales of the unknown. [by] Jason Hawes & Grant Wilson; with Cameron Dokey. Little Brown & Co. 2010 218p il $16.99

Grades: 4 5 6 7 8 9   **133.1**

1. Ghosts

ISBN 978-0-316-09959-2; 0-316-09959-7

"This collection of stories is based on case files from The [Atlantic] Paranormal Society, TAPS, founded by Hawes and Wilson. Each of the eight selections describes the sightings and paranormal activity from the perspective of the observer, then describes how members of TAPS researched, set up equipment, and discovered explanations for what happened. . . . The stories have enough elements of the unknown to make them spine-tingling, but they are more mystery than horror. . . . The easy-to-read format and subject matter will keep even the most reluctant of readers interested." SLJ

Followed by: Ghost hunt 2: more chilling tales of the unknown (2011)

Ghost hunt 2; more chilling tales of the unknown. by Jason Hawes and Grant Wilson; with Cameron Dokey. Little Brown & Co. 2011 297p il $16.99

Grades: 4 5 6 7 8   **133.1**

1. Ghosts

ISBN 978-0-316-09958-5; 0-316-09958-9

"From ghostly spirits roaming Alcatraz to glowing red eyes in the woods, The Atlantic Paranormal Society (aka the popular reality television series Ghost Hunters) is back with a compilation of even more chilling and terrifying tales. Selections include a restless spirit terrorizing a house-sitting victim through her dreams, ghosts reappearing in the O.K. Corral in Tombstone, AZ, and a saddened ghost revisiting a lighthouse where her family was eradicated long ago." SLJ

Matthews, Rupert

Ghosts and spirits. QEB Pub. 2011 32p il (Unexplained) lib bdg $28.50

Grades: 4 5 6 7   **133.1**

1. Ghosts 2. Apparitions

ISBN 978-1-59566-857-8; 1-59566-857-8

LC 2010014205

This discusses stories about ghosts and poltergeists.

"This well-written and thoughtfully designed [book] features [an] engrossing [topic]. . . . Though the pages are profusely illustrated with large, well-reproduced photographs and drawings, the layout is not cluttered. This [book] just might inspire kids to seek out more in-depth materials." SLJ

Includes glossary

Stefoff, Rebecca

Ghosts and spirits; [by] Rebecca Stefoff. Marshall Cavendish Benchmark 2007 94p il (Secrets of the supernatural) lib bdg $32.79

Grades: 5 6 7 8   **133.1**

1. Ghosts

ISBN 978-0-7614-2634-9 lib bdg; 0-7614-2634-5 lib bdg

LC 2006031652

This is a history of beliefs in ghosts and spirits throughout the world, including haunted houses, spiritualism, hauxes, and investigations into paranormal phenomena.

"Nearly every other page has an illustration. . . . The text is accessible." Libr Media Connect

Includes glossary and bibliographical references

Wetzel, Charles

Haunted U.S.A. written by Charles Wetzel; illustrated by Josh Cochran. Sterling 2008 86p il (Mysteries unwrapped) pa $5.95

Grades: 5 6 7 8   **133.1**

1. Ghosts

ISBN 978-1-4027-3735-0 pa; 1-4027-3735-1 pa

LC 2007045905

"Wetzel tells stories of haunted America from the White House to Hollywood. Although some of the places and people mentioned, such as the Amityville house and Rudolph Valentino, might be unfamiliar to younger readers, the selections are still good ghost stories. . . . [The book has] an ample number of clear black-and-white and full-color photographs and illustrations. . . . Perfect for libraries that need a boost or an update to their scary-story collections." SLJ

Includes bibliographical references

133.3 Divinatory arts

Doft, Tony

Nostradamus. Bellwether Media 2011 24p il (Torque: The unexplained) lib bdg $15.95

Grades: 3 4 5 6   **133.3**

1. Physicians 2. Prophecies 3. Astrologers 4. Futurologists

ISBN 978-1-60014-584-1; 1-60014-584-1

LC 2010034777

This considers the life and predictions of Nostradamus, who died in 1566.

"Designed for struggling readers, this . . . combines accessible writing, dynamic illustrations, and [a] high-interest [topic]. [A] snazzy [cover] and an abundance of glossy, full-color illustrations provide appeal. . . . The writing is succinct but informative." SLJ

Includes bibliographical references

Stefoff, Rebecca

Prophets and prophecy; [by] Rebecca Stefoff. Marshall Cavendish Benchmark 2007 79p il (Secrets of the supernatural) lib bdg $32.79

Grades: 5 6 7 8   **133.3**

1. Prophets 2. Prophecies

ISBN 978-0-7614-2638-7 lib bdg; 0-7614-2638-8 lib bdg

LC 2007008779

This is a history of prophecy and fortune-telling from ancient times to the present, discussing such topics as tarot cards, the Oracle of Delphi, astrology, fate, Nostradamus, Jean Dixon, omens, and the I Ching.

"Nearly every other page has an illustration. . . . The text is accessible." Libr Media Connect

Includes glossary and bibliographical references

133.4 Demonology and witchcraft

Hill, Douglas

Witches & magic-makers; written by Douglas Hill; photographed by Alex Wilson. Dorling Kindersley 2000 61p il (DK eyewitness books) $15.99; lib bdg $19.99

Grades: 4 5 6 7   **133.4**

1. Magic 2. Witchcraft

ISBN 0-7894-5878-0; 0-7894-6619-8 lib bdg

First published 1997 by Knopf

This book on "witchcraft, shamanism, and mysticism . . . introduces magical charms, talismans, and amulets from around the world. . . . This title gives a colorful overview of the topic." [review of 1997 edition]

Hirschmann, Kris

Demons. ReferencePoint Press 2011 80p il (Monsters and mythical creatures) $26.95

Grades: 5 6 7 8   **133.4**

1. Demonology

ISBN 978-1-60152-147-7; 1-60152-147-2

LC 2010029905

"Beginning with an introduction that explains the origins of the devilish creatures, the book discusses demon-like entities throughout cultures and religions. . . . The book's visuals, which include contemporary photos of ceremonies and artists' rendering of demons, can be quite startling. Excellent sidebars . . . cover topics such as the number of exorcists in the Catholic Church." Booklist

Includes bibliographical references

Jackson, Shirley

The witchcraft of Salem Village. Random House 1987 146p hardcover o.p. pa $5.99

Grades: 4 5 6 7   **133.4**

1. Witchcraft 2. Salem (Mass.) -- History

ISBN 0-394-89176-7 pa

LC 87-4543

A reissue of the title first published 1956

"A simple, chilling account of the witchcraft trials of 1692 and '93 when, because of testimony given by a group of little girls, twenty persons were executed as witches and others died in jail. There is good introductory background and though the story's subject is by nature horrifying the book does not play on the emotions. . . . It presents a difficult theme lucidly and without condescension." Horn Book

Kerns, Ann

Wizards and witches. Lerner Publications 2010 48p il (Fantasy chronicles) lib bdg $27.93

Grades: 4 5 6 7 **133.4**

1. Witches

ISBN 978-0-8225-9983-8 lib bdg; 0-8225-9983-X lib bdg

LC 2008050757

"The explanations and history behind . . . witches [and wizards] . . . will provide satisfaction for readers who want to know more about these familiar characters from myth, fantasy, and folk and fairy tales. Brief and concise." SLJ

Includes bibliographical references

Roach, Marilynne K.

In the days of the Salem witchcraft trials. Houghton Mifflin 1996 92p il map hardcover o.p. pa $5.95

Grades: 4 5 6 7 **133.4**

1. Witchcraft 2. Salem (Mass.) -- History

ISBN 0-395-69704-2; 0-618-39196-7 pa

LC 94-32383

"After discussing the Salem Witchcraft trials in one short chapter, this attractive volume explores the social history of the times to show the context that made such events possible. Topics include the law and punishment, magic, social status, clothing, food, household goods, occupations, recreation, common activities, government, and the political troubles leading to widespread tension and unrest. Readers will come away with a much fuller picture of who lived in Salem and how they lived. Small ink drawings decorate the pages." Booklist

Includes bibliographical references

133.5 Astrology

Young, Ed

Cat and Rat; the legend of the Chinese zodiac. Holt & Co. 1995 un il $15.95; pa $6.95

Grades: K 1 2 3 **133.5**

1. Zodiac 2. Cats -- Folklore 3. Rats -- Folklore 4. Folklore -- China

ISBN 0-8050-2977-X; 0-8050-6049-9 pa

LC 94-49147

"Young tells the story in lively, spare prose. . . . His charcoal and pastel drawings on dark blue and buff rice paper are elegant and full of action." SLJ

"Cat and Rat were best friends, according to this Chinese legend, until the Jade Emperor of Heaven held a race to determine which animals would be included in the zodiac. . . . In the author's note, Young comments on the Chinese New Year, the 12 traditional signs, and the birth years and personality traits for each one." Booklist

152.1 Sensory perception

Brocket, Jane

Spotty, stripy, swirly; what are patterns? [written and photographed by Jane Brocket] Millbrook Press 2012 31 p. (Jane brocket's clever concepts)

Grades: PreK K 1 2 **152.14**

1. Color 2. Pattern perception

ISBN 9780761346135

LC 2011022179

This illustrated children's book, a part of Jane Brocket's Clever Concepts Series, "examines patterns from almost every conceivable angle. There are patterns determined sometimes by shape, sometimes by color, sometimes by object. They run the gamut from simple to quite complex. There are man-made patterns such as brickwork or quilts, and patterns that occur in nature, such as geranium leaves." (School Libr J) "[Brocket's] up-close photos show a wide array of objects with their own distinctive patterns, from fabrics and architectural elements to food and plants. . . . [S]he delves into the reasons for patterns. They help us identify plants, stay organized, decorate and plan, but, most of all, they are pleasing to the eye." (Kirkus)

Includes bibliographical references

Cobb, Vicki

How to really fool yourself; illusions for all your senses. illustrated by Jessica Wolk-Stanley. Wiley 1999 120p il pa $12.95

Grades: 5 6 7 8 **152.1**

1. Perception 2. Optical illusions 3. Senses and sensation

ISBN 0-471-31592-3

LC 98-27723

A newly illustrated edition of the title first published 1981 by Lippincott

"The book begins with an explanation of perception and explores many different sensory aspects of it through experiments, definitions of important terms (italicized), background information and how illusions affect us in everyday life." SLJ

152.14 Visual perception

Banyai, Istvan

Zoom. Viking 1995 un il $16.99; pa $6.99

Grades: K 1 2 3 **152.14**

1. Stories without words

ISBN 0-670-85804-8; 0-14-055774-1 pa

LC 94-33181

A wordless picture book presents a series of scenes, each one from farther away, showing, for example, a girl playing with toys which is actually a picture on a magazine cover, which is part of a sign on a bus, and so on

"If the concept is not wholly new, the execution is superior. Readers are in for a perpetually surprising—and even philosophical—adventure." Publ Wkly

Pistoia, Sara

Patterns; by Sara Pistoia. Child's World 2007 24 p. (MathBooks) $25.64

Grades: PreK K 1 2 **152.14**

1. Pattern perception 2. Mathematics -- Study and teaching

ISBN 159296690X; 1623235332; 9781592966905; 9781623235338

LC 2005037838

This children's book on patterns, by Sara Pistoia, is part of the "Simply Math" series, which "offer[s] real-world introductions to basic math concepts suited for the youngest children." This book "focuses largely on animal markings but also includes demonstrations using calendars and colored candy." (Booklist)

"In the first book, children are introduced to the basic concepts of counting by ones, fives, and tens, and of place values. Groups of children use familiar objects such as rocks, buttons, and jelly beans to count...Each book concludes with a short list of key words (without definitions) facing an index that duplicates these words. Appropriate additions for the earliest readers in schools or public libraries." SLJ

Other titles in the series include:
Fractions
Graphs
Measurement
Money
Shapes

Simon, Seymour
★ Now you see it, now you don't; the amazing world of optical illusions. drawings by Constance Ftera. rev ed; Morrow Junior Bks. 1998 64p il $17.99
Grades: 4 5 6 7   **152.14**
1. Optical illusions
ISBN 0-688-16152-9
                                              LC 97-49855
First published 1976 by FourWinds Press with title: The optical illusion book
The author explains optical illusions involving lines and spaces, changeable figures, depth and distance, brightness and contrast, and color
"One of the clearest and most interesting discussions of optical illusions ever written for children." Booklist

Vry, Silke
Trick of the eye; art and illusion. Prestel 2010 89p il $14.95
Grades: 4 5 6   **152.14**
1. Art appreciation 2. Optical illusions
ISBN 978-3-7913-7026-2; 3-7913-7026-X
"From the Parthenon to the Mona Lisa to the Op-Art of the 1960s, images and text reveal the many ways our eyes play tricks on us. Perception of size and color is discussed using standard optical illusions, but this book includes much more. Anecdotes, such as the story of dueling Greek painters Zeuxis and Parrhasius, and unique reproductions, like portraits with altered facial features, lend excitement. The author has taken an interactive approach, filling the pages with questions, puzzles, and project ideas. . . . Text explains the images, which are large and clear. The broad range of styles represented and the fun of the interactive approach will no doubt appeal to young art lovers and curious kids alike." SLJ

Wick, Walter
★ Walter Wick's optical tricks; by Walter Wick. 10th anniversary edition; Cartwheel Books 2008 43p il $14.99
Grades: 4 5 6 7   **152.14**
1. Optical illusions
ISBN 978-0-439-85520-4; 0-439-85520-9
First published 1998
Presents a series of optical illusions and explains what is seen.

The author "has produced a stunning picture book of optical illusions. With crystal-clear photographs, he creates a series of scenes that fool the eye and the brain." Booklist [review of 1998 ed.]

152.4   Emotions

Aliki
★ Feelings. Greenwillow Bks. 1984 32p il $16; pa $5.95
Grades: K 1 2 3   **152.4**
1. Emotions
ISBN 0-688-03831-X; 0-688-06518-X pa
                                              LC 84-4098
"Small pen-and-ink cartoons with vivid coloring depict boys and girls interacting and experiencing the full range of feelings which evolve in everyday settings. This creative, unique book would be ideal for parent/child interaction or use by elementary teachers in language arts classes. Children will enjoy the comic book 'frame' format." Child Book Rev Serv

Freymann, Saxton
★ How are you peeling? foods with moods. [by] Saxton Freymann and Joost Elffers. Scholastic 1999 un il $16.95; pa $6.99
Grades: PreK K 1 2 3   **152.4**
1. Emotions
ISBN 0-439-10431-9; 0-439-59841-9 pa
                                              LC 99-18162
Brief text and photographs of carvings made from vegetables introduce the world of emotions by presenting leading questions such as "Are you feeling angry?"
"Kids will find the inherent silliness irresistible and be drawn in by the book's visual appeal: the colors are strong, the photography is excellent, and the expressions . . . are surprisingly masterful." Booklist

Graves, Sue
But what if? Sue Graves; illustrated by Desideria Guicciardini. Free Spirit Publishing 2013 25 p. $12.99
Grades: PreK K 1   **152.4**
1. Moving -- Fiction 2. Emotions 3. Worry in children
ISBN 1575424444; 9781575424446
                                              LC 2013012337
In this book, by Sue Graves, "Daisy's family is moving, and Daisy is very worried. What if she doesn't like her new home? What if her cat runs away? What if her new teacher isn't nice? A conversation with her grandpa helps Daisy learn that many worries don't come true--and if one does, someone will be there to help her solve the problem." (Publisher's note)
"Books in the Our Emotions and Behavior series offer young children and their caregivers help with hard-to-manage feelings and inappropriate actions...A fictional story portrays a child struggling with a particular emotion. Each story takes the main character through several misdeeds or scenarios, looking at the same theme in slightly different ways... In But What If?, Daisy worries about moving to a new house, neighborhood, and school. Bright but sometimes too intensely colored, the cartoon-style digital illustrations are generally easy to interpret. Advising adults on using

the book with children, the final two-page section suggests related activities. These purposeful books will be useful in many libraries." Booklist.

But why can't I? written by Sue Graves; illustrated by Desideria Guicciardini. Free Spirit Pub. 2011 25p il (Our emotions and behavior)

Grades: PreK K 1   152.4

1. Etiquette 2. Conduct of life

ISBN 1-57542-376-6; 978-1-57542-376-0

LC 2011001563

This book joins Noah and his babysitter, Jenny, who shows him how rules help keep people safe, healthy, and happy.

"Short sentences and [a] simple [plotline] create [an] excellent [lead-in] to talking about making good decisions what faced with new and difficult emotions. . . . The color cartoon illustrations help make the concepts easy to grasp. . . . Discussion questions are included in the back matter." SLJ

I hate everything! Sue Graves; illustrated by Desideria Guicciardini. Free Spirit Publishing 2013 28 p. (Our emotions and behavior) $12.99

Grades: K 1 2   152.4

1. Emotions in children 2. Picture books for children 3. Anger 4. Anger in children

ISBN 1575424436; 9781575424439

LC 2013012336

This book by Sue Graves is part of the Our Emotions and Behavior series, which offers "young children and their caregivers help with hard-to-manage feelings and inappropriate actions. . . . A fictional story portrays a child struggling with a particular emotion. Each story takes the main character through several misdeeds or scenarios, looking at the same theme in slightly different ways." Here, "Sam has difficulty controlling his anger . . . but Aunt Meg's suggestions give him some tools to try." (Booklist)

I'm not happy; written by Sue Graves; illustrated by Desideria Guicciardini. Free Spirit Pub. 2011 25p il (Our emotions and behavior)

Grades: PreK K 1   152.4

1. Kindness 2. Happiness

ISBN 1-57542-373-1; 978-1-57542-373-9

LC 2011001565

Ben helps cheer up his friends and shows how kids can turn sadness into smiles.

"Short sentences and [a] simple [plotline] create [an] excellent [lead-in] to talking about making good decisions when faced with new and difficult emotions. . . . The color cartoon illustrations help make the concepts easy to grasp. . . . Discussion questions are included in the back matter." SLJ

Not fair, won't share; written by Sue Graves; illustrated by Desideria Guicciardini. Free Spirit Pub. 2011 25p il (Our emotions and behavior)

Grades: PreK K 1   152.4

1. Conduct of life 2. Interpersonal relations

ISBN 1-57542-375-8; 978-1-57542-375-3

LC 2011001566

When Nora, Dan, and Henry have trouble sharing at school, they all end up feeling mad. With the help of their

teacher, the friends learn that when kids get frustrated, there are ways to calm down, share, and play fairly.

"Short sentences and [a] simple [plotline] create [an] excellent [lead-in] to talking about making good decisions when faced with new and difficult emotions. . . . The color cartoon illustrations help make the concepts easy to grasp. . . . Discussion questions are included in the back matter." SLJ

Take a deep breath; by Sue Graves; illustrated by Desideria Guicciardini. Free Spirit Publishing 2013 28 p. (Our emotions and behavior) $12.99

Grades: PreK K 1   152.4

1. Fear in children 2. Friendship -- fiction 3. Fear in children

ISBN 1575424460; 9781575424460

LC 2013012339

In this book by Sue Graves, "Lucy is afraid of dogs, Josh doesn't like to go in the pool, Dan doesn't want the nurse to touch his bruised knee, and Ben is afraid to go on stage in front of people. Follow along as these friends learn that when something scares them, they can take a deep breath and feel brave enough to get through their ordeals." (Publisher's note)

Who feels scared? written by Sue Graves; illustrated by Desideria Guicciardini. Free Spirit Pub. 2011 25p il (Our emotions and behavior) $12.99

Grades: PreK K 1   152.4

1. Fear

ISBN 978-1-57542-374-6; 1-57542-374-X

LC 2011001626

Everybody feels afraid sometimes—like Jack and his friends Ravi and Kevin when they have a sleepover. This book shows children that they can cope with their fears and be brave.

"Short sentences and [a] simple [plotline] create [an] excellent [lead-in] to talking about making good decisions when faced with new and difficult emotions. . . . The color cartoon illustrations help make the concepts easy to grasp. . . . Discussion questions are included in the back matter." SLJ

153.4 Thought, thinking, reasoning, intuition, value, judgment

Kelsey, Elin

Wild ideas; Elin Kelsey; illustrated by Soyeon Kim. Owlkids Books, Inc. 2015 32 p. color illustrations $18.95

Grades: K 1 2 3 4 5   153.4

1. Animal behavior 2. Problem solving

ISBN 1771470623; 9781771470629

LC 2014947497

This picture book by Elin Kelsey, illustrated by Soyeon Kim, "looks deep into the forests, skies and oceans to explore how animals solve problems. Whether it's weaving a safe place to rest and reflect, blowing a fine net of bubbles to trap fish, or leaping boldly into a new situation, the animals featured (including the orangutan, humpback whale and gibbon) can teach us a lot about creative problem solving tools and strategies." (Publisher's note)

"Finding solutions to sticky problems can be a mind-expanding adventure. The creative team behind You Are Stardust (2012) again blends science with a philosophical spark that demands thoughtful inquiry. Employing well-researched facts, Kelsey focuses on the rather remarkable adaptations and achievements of animals. . . . This is a work that will be read and examined again and again, with something new to be discovered at every turn. Profound and entirely wonderful." Kirkus

Watanabe, Ken

No problem! an easy guide to getting what you want. illustrated by Elwood H. Smith; adapted by Sarah L. Thomson. Viking 2010 70p il $16.99; pa $9.99

Grades: 4 5 6 **153.4**

1. Problem solving

ISBN 978-0-670-01203-9; 0-670-01203-3; 978-0-670-01254-1 pa; 0-670-01254-8 pa

Adaptation of: Problem solving 101, published 2009 for adults

"This little gem explains how to approach intimidating goals or jobs by breaking them down into simple tasks. Realistic scenarios such as finding money for a big purchase or choosing a high school are approached with data-driven evaluation tools. The author defines the steps involved along with terms such as hypotheses, logic trees, matrixes, and evaluation charts." SLJ

153.6 Communication

Jackson, Donna M.

★ Every body's talking; what we say without words. by Donna M. Jackson. Twenty-First Century Books 2014 64 p. illustrations (lib. bdg.: alk. paper) $30.60

Grades: 5 6 7 8 9 **153.6**

1. Body language 2. Nonverbal communication

ISBN 1467708585; 9781467708586

LC 2013019674

This book, by Donna M. Jackson, "explores the complexities of body language. Discover what is really being expressed when people stand, sit, or move in certain ways and learn how you can use your body and facial expressions to communicate more effectively in a variety of situations." (Publisher's note)

"Nonverbal clues including stance, facial expression, posture, eye contact, and others add meaning to our words, or sometimes contradict them. Using second-person narration to engage readers, suggestions for interpreting body language is followed by a chapter explaining how cultural differences affect interpretations. A final chapter encourages readers to practice physical positions to increase confidence. Plentiful full-color pictures illustrate concepts." Horn Book

Includes bibliographical references and index

153.7 Perceptual processes

Hillman, Ben

How big is it? a big book all about bigness. Scholastic 2007 47p il $14.99

Grades: 3 4 5 **153.7**

1. Size

ISBN 0-439-91808-1; 978-0-439-91808-4

LC 2006050609

"This oversize picture book . . . presents 22 giant creatures, objects, and plants, prehistoric and contemporary. On each double-page spread there is a panel of chatty information next to a huge, unframed color picture, which uses digitally blended images to show comparative size. . . . These clear, astonishing pictures [are] both a magnet to browsers as well as a device to demonstrate gradations of bigness." Booklist

Miller, Margaret

★ Big and little. Greenwillow Bks. 1998 un il $15.99

Grades: PreK **153.7**

1. Size

ISBN 0-688-14748-8

LC 97-17242

Photographs and easy text introduce the concepts of size and opposites

"This book uses cheerful, clear color photos of active toddlers to teach basic concepts." Booklist

155.45 Exceptional children; children by social and economic levels, by ethnic or national group

Fonseca, Christine

101 success secrets for gifted kids; the ultimate guide. Prufrock Press 2011 xi, 191p pa $14.95

Grades: 4 5 6 7 8 **155.45**

1. Gifted children

ISBN 978-1-59363-544-2; 1-59363-544-3

LC 2011004912

"Fonseca explains what it means to be labeled 'gifted,' how to cope in school, and how to interact with friends and family. Information is delivered in a friendly, conversational manner with firsthand advice from gifted kids and their parents. The myriad tips include how to deal with stress, how to complete homework assignments effectively, how to be respectful of others, how to accept oneself, and even how to deal with bullies. All are incredibly useful." SLJ

Includes bibliographical references

Gerstein, Mordicai

★ The wild boy; based on the true story of the Wild Boy of Aveyron. Foster Bks. 1998 39p il hardcover o.p. pa $6.95

Grades: K 1 2 3 **155.45**

1. Wild children

ISBN 0-374-38431-2; 0-374-48396-5 pa

LC 97-37246

Relates the story of a boy who grew up wild in the forests of France and was captured in 1800, studied and cared for and named Victor, but who never learned to speak

"Gerstein's prose finds power in its simplicity and emotional resonance in its declarative understatement. . . . The narrative strength and energy of the illustrations expand the inherent drama of Victor's situation. Together, Gerstein's text and pictures work to create an unforgettable story." Booklist

155.9   Environmental psychology

Brown, Laurene Krasny
When dinosaurs die; a guide to understanding death.
[by] Laurie Krasny Brown and Marc Brown. Little, Brown
1996 32p il hardcover o.p. pa $5.95
Grades: K 1 2 3   **155.9**
1. Death 2. Bereavement
ISBN 0-316-10917-7; 0-316-11955-5 pa
LC 95-14511
"The text explains the inevitability of death, various
reasons for death (including old age, sickness, accident, and
suicide), and the difference between death and sleep; it then
goes on to examine feelings about death and ways, both individual and cultural, of dealing with the loss of loved ones.
. . . The simple watercolor illustrations help to make some
scary situations more approachable. Quiet, respectful, and
unthreatening, this will probably become a primary-grades
standard on the subject." Bull Cent Child Books
Includes glossary

Krementz, Jill
How it feels when a parent dies. Knopf 1981 110p il
hardcover o.p. pa $16
Grades: 4 5 6 7   **155.9**
1. Death 2. Bereavement
ISBN 0-394-75854-4 pa
LC 80-8808
This book is "a hopeful tribute to the healing power
sustained by young survivors, who are competently interviewed and photographed in their widely varied reactions
and situations. The subjects range in age from 7 to 16 and
cope with a variety of deaths by suicide, accident, and illness. Adults helping children through a hard time will better understand their charges' problems through the honest
opinions expressed here, and young readers might feel less
alone." Booklist

Murphy, Patricia J.
Death; [by] Patricia J. Murphy. Heinemann Library
2008 32p il (Tough topics) lib bdg $25.36; pa $7.99
Grades: PreK K 1 2 3   **155.9**
1. Death 2. Bereavement
ISBN 978-1-4034-9778-9 lib bdg; 978-1-4034-9783-
3 pa
LC 2007007230
The author "discusses what death is, how it can happen,
how it affects people, funerals and memories, and different
ways of coping with such loss. . . . The two-page chapters
include full-color photos and two paragraphs of text that are
frank yet sensitive in their approach." SLJ
Includes glossary and bibliographical references

Raschka, Christopher
The purple balloon; [by] Chris Raschka. Schwartz &
Wade Books 2007 un il $16.99; lib bdg $19.99
Grades: PreK K 1 2   **155.9**
1. Death 2. Terminally ill
ISBN 978-0-375-84146-0; 0-375-84146-6; 978-0-375-
94259-4 lib bdg; 0-375-94259-9 lib bdg
LC 2006-23725
"Dying is the subject of this sensitive and somber book
intended for terminally ill children and their families and
friends. . . . The focus is first on how support from those

around us can help 'make dying not so hard' for an older
person. The same case is then made for a child who faces
death. . . . The illustrations are appropriately subdued, with
balloons as the characters, all of them given loving and supportive faces and postures. . . . The book ends with suggestions on how to help a friend who is terminally ill." Booklist

Simons, Rae
Survival skills; how to handle life's catastrophes. Mason Crest Publishers 2009 128p il (Survivors: ordinary
people, extraordinary circumstances) lib bdg $24.95
Grades: 5 6 7 8   **155.9**
1. Life skills 2. Survival skills
ISBN 978-1-4222-0456-6 lib bdg; 1-4222-0456-1
lib bdg
LC 2008-50320
"Begins with a brief and accessible discussion of the
psychology of stress and its role in adolescence, and offers
twelve pieces of advice for overcoming difficult experiences
and catastrophes. . . . [This book features] important, and
sometimes complex, information in an easy-to-read format,
offering high gloss photographs, marginal glossary notes,
concept definitions, a bibliography, and further reading
reccommendations." Voice Youth Advocates
Includes glossary and bibliographical references

158   Applied psychology

Andrews, Linda Wasmer
Meditation; [by] Linda Wasmer Andrews. F. Watts
2004 79p (Life balance) $19.50; pa $6.95
Grades: 5 6 7 8   **158**
1. Meditation
ISBN 0-531-12219-0; 0-531-16609-0 pa
LC 2003-7153
"Andrews emphasizes that meditation is not a flaky practice, or a particularly religious one, but one that's designed to
reduce stress and help individuals manage their lives. Four
chapters explain the why and how of meditating. . . . [This
offers] solid, easy-to-understand information" SLJ
Includes bibliographical references

Burstein, John
I said no! refusal skills. Crabtree Pub. Co. 2010 32p il
(Slim Goodbody's life skills 101) lib bdg $26.60; pa $8.95
Grades: 1 2 3 4 5   **158**
1. Peer pressure 2. Decision making 3. Risk-taking
(Psychology)
ISBN 978-0-7787-4789-5 lib bdg; 0-7787-4789-1 lib
bdg; 978-0-7787-4805-2 pa; 0-7787-4805-7 pa
LC 2009022850
In this book children are taught to understand when and
why they need to say "no," and how to refuse and still keep
their friends
This book offers "clear and simple advice for children
and [provides] adults with springboards for discussion and
role-playing. [It has] appealing color photographs of a variety of types of kids, . . . opening scenarios, concrete coping
suggestions, and solid reasoning." SLJ
Includes bibliographical references

Crist, James J.

What to do when you're sad & lonely; a guide for kids. [by] James J. Crist. Free Spirit Pub. 2006 124p il pa $9.95

Grades: 4 5 6 7   **158**

1. Solitude 2. Depression (Psychology)

ISBN 978-1-57542-189-6 pa; 1-57542-189-5 pa

LC 2005021794

"Advising his audience to read this book and work through negative feelings with an adult, Crist describes sad and lonely feelings, distinguishes them from more serious conditions such as depression, and then suggests 'Blues Busters' and ways to ask for help. . . . Crist's clear explanations and simple techniques . . . are relevant for both children and adults." Voice Youth Advocates

Includes bibliographical references

What to do when you're scared & worried; a guide for kids. [by] James Crist. Free Spirit Pub. 2004 128p il pa $9.95

Grades: 4 5 6 7   **158**

1. Fear 2. Worry

ISBN 1-57542-153-4

"Part one deals with normal anxiety, offering detailed steps for developing 10 coping mechanisms. Expert help is needed to deal with the more serious problems discussed in Part two (e.g., phobias, separation anxiety, obsessive-compulsive disorder). Throughout, the author provides information, case histories, and coping skills in a manner that is both reassuring and encouraging. . . . Illustrations lighten the tone of the subject matter." SLJ

Includes bibliographical references

Fox, Annie

Real friends vs. the other kind. Free Spirit Pub. 2009 90p il

Grades: 5 6 7 8   **158**

1. Friendship 2. Interpersonal relations

ISBN 1-57542-319-7 pa; 978-1-57542-319-7 pa

LC 2008031368

"Jack, Abby, Mateo, Jen, Chris, and Michelle are the middle school students of various ethnicities who take readers through this slim, interactive guide. Chapters cover such topics as friendship dilemmas, so-called friends, when friendships aren't working, crushes, and making new friends. Each chapter opens with a scene played out by the students in cartoon panels. Next, bits of text, along with a multitude of side boxes, address the topic at hand. . . . Lists of questions are offered, along with the answers. There's a lot packed into this colorful title that falls somewhere between self-help and peer advice." SLJ

McIntyre, Thomas

The **behavior** survival guide for kids; how to make good choices and stay out of trouble. [by] Thomas McIntyre. Free Spirit Pub. 2003 167p pa $14.95

Grades: 5 6 7 8   **158**

1. Conduct of life 2. Interpersonal relations

ISBN 1-57542-132-1

LC 2003-4565

"The author provides skills and activities to learn and practice so that new behaviors can replace those that have resulted in getting students into trouble. . . . Those motivated to make better choices for how they behave in school or

with friends and family will find much to help them." Voice Youth Advocates

Moss, Wendy

Being me; a kid's guide to boosting confidence and self-esteem. by Wendy L. Moss. Magination Press 2010 112p il $14.95; pa $9.95

Grades: 5 6 7 8   **158**

1. Self-esteem 2. Self-confidence

ISBN 978-1-4338-0883-8; 1-4338-0883-8; 978-1-4338-0884-5 pa; 1-4338-0884-6 pa

LC 2010014384

"Moss encourages her young audience to concentrate on two areas: focusing on inner self-esteem and building social confidence. Through procedure and practice . . . Moss reminds kids that real confidence doesn't come from being the smartest, prettiest, or the most popular one in the room but from the comfort one has with him- or herself. . . . Moss' offering gives great tips for the truly interested." Booklist

Rogers, Fred

Making friends; photographs by Jim Judkis. Putnam 1987 un il hardcover o.p. pa $6.99

Grades: PreK K 1   **158**

1. Friendship

ISBN 0-698-11409-4 pa

LC 86-12353

"From its opening lines ('When people like each other and like to do things together, they're friends. Can you think of someone who's your friend?'), Rogers's inimitable voice reaches out to his small readers with understanding and reassurance. He describes the pleasures of friendship as well as potential problem areas. . . . Judkis's large color photos capture the range of emotions Rogers writes about." Publ Wkly

Seuss

Oh, the places you'll go! Random House 1990 un il $17; lib bdg $20.99

Grades: PreK K 1 2   **158**

1. Stories in rhyme

ISBN 0-679-80527-3; 0-679-90527-8 lib bdg

LC 89-36892

Advice in rhyme for proceeding in life; weathering fear, loneliness, and confusion; and being in charge of your actions

"The combination of the lively text and wacky, offbeat pictures will delight both children and their parents." Child Book Rev Serv

158.2 Interpersonal relations

Brown, Laurene Krasny

How to be a friend; a guide to making friends and keeping them. [by] Laurie Krasny Brown and Marc Brown. Little, Brown 1998 31p il $15.99; pa $6.99

Grades: K 1 2 3   **158.2**

1. Friendship

ISBN 0-316-10913-4; 0-316-11153-8 pa

LC 97-10179

Dinosaur characters illustrate the value of friends, how to make friends, and how to be and not to be a good friend

"Dialogue balloons personalize, enrich, and add humor to the main text. . . . How to Be a Friend will be very useful to parents, teachers, and other caregivers of young children." Horn Book

170 Ethics (Moral philosophy)

MacGregor, Cynthia
Think for yourself; a kid's guide to solving life's dilemmas and other sticky problems. by Cynthia MacGregor; illustrator: Paula Becker. 2nd ed.; Lobster Press 2008 142p il pa $14.95
Grades: 3 4 5 6 **170**
1. Ethics 2. Conduct of life
ISBN 978-1-897073-90-2 pa; 1-897073-90-9 pa
First published 2003
This book "presents 53 real-life dilemmas that 21st century children might face. Topics range from cyberbullying, chat rooms, and online porn to situations with friends, family and adults. . . . Each dilemma is . . . followed by three questions. . . . The questions encourage readers to examine why the predicaments are dilemmas, to analyze possible solutions, and to arrive at acceptable decisions. . . . This indispensible book is recommended for school and public library collections." Libr Media Connect

Parker, Victoria
Making choices; [by] Vic Parker. Heinemann Library 2010 32p il (Exploring citizenship) $25.36; pa $7.99
Grades: 1 2 3 4 **170**
1. Decision making 2. Choice (Psychology)
ISBN 978-1-4329-3317-3; 1-4329-3317-5; 978-1-4329-3325-8 pa; 1-4329-3325-6 pa
LC 2008-55310
This describes the different choices and decisions people have to make every day and why it is important to think for yourself, what to do if you are bullied, and how to make the right choices for your health.
"The text presents a multitude of realistic situations to which young children will relate. There are 'Think About It' fact boxes and checklists that aid in understanding and that will spark discussion. All are filled with captioned, color photographs that relate to the text. The information is relevant and current. . . . Strongly consider this." Libr Media Connect
Includes glossary and bibliographical references

172 Applied ethics

Halperin, Wendy Anderson
Peace; Wendy Anderson Halperin. Atheneum Books for Young Readers 2013 40 p. $16.99
Grades: K 1 2 **172**
1. Picture books for children 2. Peace 3. Taoism
ISBN 0689825528; 9780689825521; 9781442467873
LC 2012030589
This picture book, by Wendy Anderson Halperin, offers a "compilation of . . . illustrations and wisely chosen words [which] reveals the heart of where peace truly must originate: within ourselves. . . . Intricate artwork, with tiny, precisely rendered details of life across the globe, complements

. . . text that includes quotations from famous peacemakers." (Publisher's note)

174 Occupational ethics

Hartman, Eve
Science ethics and controversies; [by] Eve Hartman and Wendy Meshbesher. Raintree 2009 48p il (Sci-hi: life science) $31.43; pa $8.99
Grades: 5 6 7 8 **174**
1. Science -- Ethical aspects
ISBN 978-1-4109-3330-0; 1-4109-3330-X; 978-1-4109-3338-6 pa; 1-4109-3338-5 pa
LC 2009003475
In this introduction to science ethics and controversies "clear language, embedded definitions, and interesting examples illustrate abstract concepts through both text and well-chosen photographs. . . . [It] discusses topics such as global warming and animal research, and their implications for decision-making by scientists, policy makers, and voters. Because so many issues are raised in this book, it will be especially useful as a research starter in both science and social-studies classes. . . . [The] book also includes suggested activities to test ideas as well as a thorough glossary and a Webliography." SLJ
Includes glossary and bibliographical references

175 Ethics of recreation, leisure, public performances, communication

Barraclough, Sue
Fair play. Heinemann Library 2010 32p il (Exploring citizenship) $25.36; pa $7.99
Grades: 1 2 3 4 **175**
1. Respect 2. Sportsmanship
ISBN 978-1-4329-3313-5; 1-4329-3313-2; 978-1-4329-3321-0 pa; 1-4329-3321-3 pa
LC 2008-55301
"The text presents a multitude of realistic situations to which young children will relate. There are 'Think About It' fact boxes and checklists that aid in understanding and that will spark discussion. All are filled with captioned, color photographs that relate to the text. The information is relevant and current. . . . Strongly consider this." Libr Media Connect
Includes glossary and bibliographical references

177 Ethics of social relations

Barraclough, Sue
Sharing. Heinemann Library 2010 32p il (Exploring citizenship) $25.36; pa $7.99
Grades: 1 2 3 4 **177**
1. Kindness 2. Etiquette
ISBN 978-1-4329-3312-8; 1-4329-3312-4; 978-1-4329-3320-3 pa; 1-4329-3320-5 pa
LC 2008-55300
"The text presents a multitude of realistic situations to which young children will relate. There are 'Think About It' fact boxes and checklists that aid in understanding and

that will spark discussion. All are filled with captioned, color photographs that relate to the text. The information is relevant and current. . . . Strongly consider this." Libr Media Connect

Includes glossary and bibliographical references

Graves, Sue

I didn't do it; Sue Graves; illustrated by Desideria Guicciardini. Free Spirit Publishing 2013 28 p. (Our emotions and behavior) $12.99

Grades: PreK K 1   **177**

    1. Emotions in children 2. Truthfulness and falsehood

    ISBN 1575424452; 9781575424453

                   LC 2013012340

This book by Sue Graves is part of the Our Emotions and Behavior series, which offers "young children and their caregivers help with hard-to-manage feelings and inappropriate actions. . . . A fictional story portrays a child struggling with a particular emotion. Each story takes the main character through several misdeeds or scenarios, looking at the same theme in slightly different ways." This entry looks at lying. (Booklist)

Parker, Victoria

Good relationships. Heinemann Library 2008 32p il (Exploring citizenship) $25.36; pa $7.99

Grades: 1 2 3 4   **177**

    1. Interpersonal relations

    ISBN 978-1-4329-3316-6; 1-4329-3316-7; 978-1-4329-3324-1 pa; 1-4329-3324-8 pa

                   LC 2008-55306

This describes how important it is to get along with the people around us and what can happen when people do not try to listen to or understand each other.

"The text presents a multitude of realistic situations to which young children will relate. There are 'Think About It' fact boxes and checklists that aid in understanding and that will spark discussion. All are filled with captioned, color photographs that relate to the text. The information is relevant and current. . . . Strongly consider this." Libr Media Connect

Includes glossary and bibliographical references

Pryor, Kimberley Jane

Cooperation; by Kimberley Jane Pryor. Marshall Cavendish Benchmark 2008 32p il (Values) lib bdg $19.95

Grades: 1 2 3   **177**

    1. Cooperation 2. Conduct of life

    ISBN 978-0-7614-3124-4 lib bdg; 0-7614-3124-1 lib bdg

                   LC 2008001617

In this book "cooperation is described as following instructions, sharing, and solving problems. [This] value is considered in a direct manner, which makes the [book] useful for the younger part of the age range, while the [title] will provide springboards for discussion among the older children. The brief [text is] accompanied by attractive, captioned color photographs." SLJ

Honesty; by Kimberley Jane Pryor. Marshall Cavendish Benchmark 2008 32p il (Values) lib bdg $19.95

Grades: 1 2 3   **177**

    1. Honesty 2. Conduct of life

    ISBN 978-0-7614-3125-1 lib bdg; 0-7614-3125-X lib bdg

                   LC 2008001673

This "well-executed [book provides a] simple [definition] of [honesty], examples of how it can be demonstrated, and a breakdown of the behavior into individual actions. . . . The brief [text is] accompanied by attractive, captioned color photographs." SLJ

Kindness; by Kimberley Jane Pryor. Marshall Cavendish Benchmark 2008 32p il (Values) lib bdg $19.95

Grades: 1 2 3   **177**

    1. Kindness 2. Conduct of life

    ISBN 978-0-7614-3126-8 lib bdg; 0-7614-3126-8 lib bdg

                   LC 2008001661

This "begins with a bulleted explanation of the word 'values.'. . . The rest of the text describes [kindness]. . . . The author then goes on to discuss examples of behaviors and emotions such as being kind to family and friends, feeling sympathy, and caring. The accompanying color photographs, showing children that appear to be unposed, are age-appropriate, culturally diverse, and complement the [narrative]." SLJ

Respect; by Kimberley Jane Pryor. Marshall Cavendish Benchmark 2008 32p il (Values) lib bdg $19.95

Grades: 1 2 3   **177**

    1. Respect 2. Conduct of life

    ISBN 978-0-7614-3128-2 lib bdg; 0-7614-3128-4 lib bdg

                   LC 2008001669

This "begins with a bulleted explanation of the word 'values.' . . . The rest of the text describes [respect]. . . . The author then goes on to discuss examples of behaviors and emotions such as being kind to family and friends, feeling sympathy, and caring. The accompanying color photographs, showing children that appear to be unposed, are age-appropriate, culturally diverse, and complement the [narrative]." SLJ

Tolerance; by Kimberley Jane Pryor. Marshall Cavendish Benchmark 2008 32p il (Values) lib bdg $19.95

Grades: 1 2 3   **177**

    1. Toleration 2. Conduct of life

    ISBN 978-0-7614-3129-9 lib bdg; 0-7614-3129-2 lib bdg

                   LC 2008001672

This "begins with a bulleted explanation of the word 'values.' . . . The rest of the text describes [tolerance]. . . . The author then goes on to discuss examples of behaviors and emotions such as being kind to family and friends, feeling sympathy, and caring. The accompanying color photographs, showing children that appear to be unposed, are age-appropriate, culturally diverse, and complement the [narrative]." SLJ

Verdick, Elizabeth

Words are not for hurting; illustrated by Marieka Heinlen. Free Spirit Pub. 2004 33p il pa $11.95; bd bk $7.95

Grades: K 1 2   **177**
1. Etiquette 2. Conversation 3. Interpersonal relations
ISBN 1-57542-156-9 pa; 1-57542-155-0 bd bk
LC 2003-21273
Encourages toddlers and preschoolers to express themselves using helpful, not hurtful, words. Includes a note for parents and caregivers

"The brightly colored drawings, which bring the minimal text to life, are especially effective at showing the range of emotions children experience when they hear unkind language. An excellent resource for sharing at home and at preschools." Booklist

179   Other ethical norms

Barraclough, Sue
Honesty. Heinemann Library 2010 32p il (Exploring citizenship) $25.36; pa $7.99
Grades: 1 2 3 4   **179**
1. Honesty 2. Citizenship
ISBN 978-1-4329-3311-1; 1-4329-3311-6; 978-1-4329-3319-7 pa; 1-4329-3319-1 pa
LC 2008-55297
"The text presents a multitude of realistic situations to which young children will relate. There are 'Think About It' fact boxes and checklists that aid in understanding and that will spark discussion. All are filled with captioned, color photographs that relate to the text. The information is relevant and current. . . . Strongly consider this." Libr Media Connect

Includes glossary and bibliographical references

Belanger, Jeff
What it's like; to climb Mount Everest, blast off into space, survive a tornado, and other extraordinary stories. Sterling Pub. Co. 2010 136p il pa $9.95
Grades: 5 6 7 8   **179**
1. Courage 2. Anecdotes 3. Adventure and adventurers
ISBN 978-1-4027-6711-1; 1-4027-6711-0
LC 2009040875
"This illustrated collection presents short, first-person accounts of high-octane adventures—and, in some cases, personal disasters—by the people who actually experienced them. . . . The stories are told in present-tense, straightforward language, filled in with many pertinent and fascinating details. . . . The exciting action and the entries' short length will draw reluctant readers, as will the many color photographs, which are imaginatively laid out. This attractive package will be an easy sell." Booklist

Burstein, John
Can we get along? dealing with differences. Crabtree Pub. Company 2010 32p il (Slim Goodbody's life skills 101) lib bdg $26.60; pa $8.95
Grades: 1 2 3 4 5   **179**
1. Toleration
ISBN 978-0-7787-4788-8 lib bdg; 0-7787-4788-3 lib bdg; 978-0-7787-4804-5 pa; 0-7787-4804-9 pa
LC 2009023634
This book helps students understand the need and importance for tolerance, and the steps they can take to increase peace in their lives and in the world.

These book offers "clear and simple advice for children and [provides] adults with springboards for discussion and roleplaying. All have appealing color photographs of a variety of types of kids, . . . opening scenarios, concrete coping suggestions, and solid reasoning." SLJ

Includes bibliographical references

Obama, Barack, 1961-
Of thee I sing; a letter to my daughters. illustrated by Loren Long. Alfred A. Knopf 2010 un il $17.99; lib bdg $20.99
Grades: 1 2 3 4   **179**
1. Conduct of life 2. Heroes and heroines 3. United States -- History
ISBN 0-375-83527-X; 0-375-93527-4 lib bdg; 978-0-375-83527-8; 978-0-375-93527-5 lib bdg
"In characteristically measured prose, the 44th President introduces 13 American icons and heroes as exemplars of personal virtues, from Georgia O'Keeffe (creativity) and Jackie Robinson (courage) to Helen Keller (strength) and Cesar Chavez (inspiration). . . . Long's superb technical gifts and gentle sense of humor shine in the pictures. . . . [This offers] thought-provoking choices and commentary. . . . This [is a] stately outing." SLJ

Parker, Victoria
Acting responsibly; [by] Vic Parker. Heinemann Library 2010 32p il (Exploring citizenship) $25.36; pa $7.99
Grades: 1 2 3 4   **179**
1. Responsibility
ISBN 978-1-4329-3315-9; 1-4329-3315-9; 978-1-4329-3323-4 pa; 1-4329-3323-X pa
LC 2008-55305
This describes how and why to behave in a responsible way

"The text presents a multitude of realistic situations to which young children will relate. There are 'Think About It' fact boxes and checklists that aid in understanding and that will spark discussion. All are filled with captioned, color photographs that relate to the text. The information is relevant and current. . . . Strongly consider this." Libr Media Connection

Includes glossary and bibliographical references

Pryor, Kimberley Jane
Courage; by Kimberley Jane Pryor. Marshall Cavendish Benchmark 2008 32p il (Values) lib bdg $19.95
Grades: 1 2 3   **179**
1. Courage 2. Conduct of life
ISBN 978-0-7614-3131-2 lib bdg; 0-7614-3131-4 lib bdg
LC 2008001662
This "well-executed [book provides a] simple [definition] of [courage], examples of how it can be demonstrated, and a breakdown of the behavior into individual actions. . . . The brief [text is] accompanied by attractive, captioned color photographs." SLJ

183 Sophistic, Socratic, related Greek philosophies

Jun Lim

Socrates; the public conscience of Golden Age Athens. by Jun Lim. 1st ed. Rosen Pub. 2006 112 p. col. ill., col. map (library) $34.60

Grades: 5 6 7 8 **183**

1. Philosophers

ISBN 1404205640; 9781404205642

LC 2005012259

This book by Jun Lim is part of the Library of Greek Philosophers series and looks at Socrates. "This series introduces students to the great philosophers and mathematicians who helped shape the intellectual world in modern times." Examples are given "of the kinds of knowledge these men taught to their students. The early years, travels, and education of each man are told, and the contributions to society are detailed in the context of the times." (Library Media Connection)

Includes bibliographical references (p. 107-108) and index.

200 RELIGION

200 Religion

Ajmera, Maya

Faith; [by] Maya Ajmera, Magda Nakassis, and Cynthia Pon. Charlesbridge 2009 un il lib bdg $16.95; pa $7.95

Grades: 1 2 3 **200**

1. Religion 2. Religions

ISBN 978-1-58089-177-6 lib bdg; 1-58089-177-2 lib bdg; 978-1-58089-178-3 pa; 1-58089-178-0 pa

LC 2008008282

This "explores through full-color photographs the many ways in which the world celebrates and practices religious belief, highlighting the common threads—praying and meditating, chants and songs, holy books, cleansing, holy places, holidays and festivals, important events, dress, food and drink, and helping others. Spare text accompanies the pictures of children and identifies the specific religion and practices. . . . The excellent photographs are clear and colorful and invite careful observation." SLJ

Osborne, Mary Pope

★ One world, many religions; the ways we worship. Knopf 1996 86p il map $19.95

Grades: 4 5 6 7 **200**

1. Islam 2. Taoism 3. Judaism 4. Buddhism 5. Hinduism 6. Religions 7. Christianity 8. Confucianism

ISBN 0-679-83930-5

LC 96-836

"The presentation is notable for its respect to each group, succinctness, and clarity. . . . The artful, full-page, color and black-and-white photographs tell much of the story." SLJ

Includes glossary and bibliographical references

What do you believe? religion and faith in the world today. DK Pub. 2011 96p il map $16.99

Grades: 4 5 6 7 **200**

1. Religions 2. Philosophy

ISBN 978-0-7566-7228-7; 0-7566-7228-7

"This extensive guidebook covers the beliefs and history of the world's major religions. Focusing in particular on Buddhism, Christianity, Hinduism, Islam, Judaism, and Sikhism, the book also explores atheism and agnosticism, indigenous belief systems, East Asian religions, philosophy, and morality. . . . The graphically bold format—which mixes photographs, cartoons, and sidebars—will keep kids' attention, whether they are seeking truth, knowledge, or more to ponder." Publ Wkly

201 Specific aspects of religion

Hamilton, Virginia

★ In the beginning; creation stories from around the world; told by Virginia Hamilton; illustrated by Barry Moser. Harcourt Brace Jovanovich 1988 161p il hardcover o.p. pa $20

Grades: 5 6 7 8 **201**

1. Creation 2. Mythology

ISBN 0-15-238740-4; 0-15-238742-0 pa

LC 88-6211

A Newbery Medal honor book, 1989

"Hamilton has gathered 25 creation myths from various cultures and retold them in language true to the original. Images from the tales are captured in Moser's 42 full-page illustrations, tantalizing oil paintings that are rich with somber colors and striking compositions. Included in the collection are the familiar stories (biblical creation stories, Greek and Roman myths), and some that are not so familiar (tales from the Australian aborigines, various African and native American tribes, as well as from countries like Russia, China, and Iceland). At the end of each tale, Hamilton provides a brief commentary on the story's origin and originators." Booklist

Includes bibliographical references

Reinhart, Matthew

Gods & heroes; [by] Matthew Reinhart and Robert Sabuda. Candlewick Press 2010 un il (Encyclopedia mythologica) $29.99

Grades: K 1 2 3 **201**

1. Mythology 2. Gods and goddesses 3. Pop-up books

ISBN 978-0-7636-3171-0; 0-7636-3171-X

LC 2009-15140

This is "a global tour of gods and other deities. Multiple stories unfold on each page within layered tableaus in miniature booklets, like treasures to be unveiled. . . . A fun and engaging assemblage that seamlessly marries its form and content." Publ Wkly

204 Religious experience, life, practice

Pelham, Sophie

Food and faith; [by] Susan Reuben and Sophie Pelham. Frances Lincoln Children's Books 2011 45 p. ill. $18.99

Grades: 3 4 5   **204**

1. Food 2. Religions 3. Religious holidays

ISBN 1845079868; 9781845079864

Author Susan Reuben presents a cookbook for "people of various ethnic backgrounds [and religious celebrations] . . . [The book discusses] the Jewish Shabbat, as well as Chanukah, Rosh Hashanah, Yom Kippur, Purim and Passover, [in addition to] the Muslim Eid ul Fitr . . . and Christingle . . . Recipes for one representative dish per religion are included, [such as] Hinduism and Sikhism." (Kirkus)

220   Bible

Brown, Alan

The **Bible** and Christianity; by Alan Brown. Smart Apple Media 2003 30p il (Sacred texts) $27.10

Grades: 5 6 7 8   **220**

1. Christianity 2. Bible (as subject)

ISBN 1-58340-243-8

LC 2003-41645

Explains how the Old and New Testaments came to be part of the Bible used by Christians and discusses some of the important messages found in the holy scriptures.

"Colorful strips of symbolic patterns adorn the pages and accent the informative text boxes. . . . The clear captioned . . . illustrations (photos and historical art) provide additional background." Horn Book Guide

Includes glossary

220.5   Modern versions and translations

The **Bible**: Authorized King James Version; with an introduction and notes by Robert Carroll and Stephen Prickett. Oxford University Press 2008 lxxiv, 1039, 248, 445p il map (Oxford world's classics) pa $18.95

Grades: 5 6 7 8 9 10 11 12 Adult   **220.5**

ISBN 978-0-19-953594-1

LC 2008-273825

This Oxford World's Classics version first published 1997

The authorized or King James Version originally published 1611.

Includes bibliographical references

The **Holy** Bible; containing the Old and New Testaments with the Apocryphal/Deuterocanonical books: New Revised Standard Version. Oxford University Press 1989 xxi, 996, 298, 284p map $29.99

Grades: 5 6 7 8 9 10 11 12 Adult   **220.5**

ISBN 0-19-528330-9; 978-0-19-528330-3

LC 90-222105

"Intended for public reading, congregational worship, private study, instruction, and meditation, it attempts to be as literal as possible while following standard American English usage, avoids colloquialism, and prefers simple, direct terms and phrases." Sheehy. Guide to Ref Books. 10th edition. suppl

220.8   Nonreligious subjects treated in Bible

Animals of the Bible; a picture book by Dorothy P. Lathrop; with text selected by Helen Dean Fish from the King James Bible. Harper & Row 1987 65p il $17.95; lib bdg $18.89

Grades: 1 2 3 4   **220.8**

1. Animals 2. Bible -- Natural history

ISBN 0-397-31536-8; 0-397-30047-6 lib bdg

A reissue of the title first published 1937 by Lippincott

Awarded the Caldecott Medal, 1938

"Dorothy Lathrop's love and understanding of animals, the sensitiveness and joy with which she draws them, make her the ideal artist for such a volume. It is more than a beautiful picture book, for she has studied the fauna and flora of Bible lands until each animal and bird, each flower and tree, is true to natural history." NY Times Book Rev

220.9   Geography, history, chronology, persons of Bible lands in Bible times

Barnes, Trevor

The **Kingfisher** children's illustrated Bible; illustrated by Vanessa Card . . . [et al.] 2011 256p il map $14.99

Grades: 3 4 5 6   **220.9**

1. Bible stories

ISBN 978-0-7534-6490-8; 0-7534-6490-X

"In the straightforward style of a practiced storyteller, Barnes recreates the ancient world of the Israelites peopled by patriarchs, prophets, kings, the Messiah, and his disciples. Beginning with Creation and concluding the first portion of the book with a selection of psalms and proverbs, he pays homage to key Old Testament figures. . . . The second section focuses on the New Testament stories of Jesus' life and teachings and the spread of Christianity. . . . The one to two-page stories flow together seamlessly from Genesis to Revelation. Each entry includes a citation to the corresponding scripture passages and is complemented by illustrations replete with historically correct cultural details. A supplementary reference section featuring commentary, maps, and captioned photographs puts the sacred stories in historical and geographical context." SLJ

Brown, Laaren

The **Children's** illustrated Jewish Bible; retold by Laaren Brown & Lenny Hort; illustrated by Eric Thomas. rev ed; DK Pub. 2007 192p il map $19.99

Grades: 1 2 3 4 5 6   **220.9**

1. Bible stories

ISBN 978-0-7566-2665-5

"This is indeed a Jewish Bible, written by Jewish authors, and successful in its inclusion of many popular stories retold in a lively, child-friendly style. Realistic and colorful pencil-drawn illustrations add to the telling, and as a treat for curious minds, the small photographs on the sidebars are really interesting." SLJ

Delval, Marie-Helene

The **Bible** for young children; [illustrated by] Götting. Eerdmans Books for Young Readers 2010 88p il $16.50

Grades: K 1 2 3   **220.9**
　　1. Bible stories
　　ISBN 978-0-8028-5383-7; 0-8028-5383-8
　　　　　　　　　　　　　　　　LC 2010005164
　　Original French edition 2002
　　"This introduction to the Christian Bible uses simple format that is accessible both to younger children and new readers. Forty Bible stories are retold with just a few sentences for each story or incident. . . . The text is set in large type on the left-hand pages against an attractive corresponding illustration on the right-hand pages. The paintings used for the illustrations use a variety of perspectives and a palette of deep shades that suggests an ancient setting. The clear and simple format provides an accessible introduction to major stories and characters in the Bible." Kirkus
　　Includes bibliographical references

DePaola, Tomie, 1934-
　　★ **Tomie** dePaola's book of Bible stories. Putnam 1989 127p il $24.99; pa $12.99
Grades: 2 3 4 5   **220.9**
　　1. Bible stories
　　ISBN 0-399-21690-1; 0-698-11923-1 pa
　　　　　　　　　　　　　　　　LC 88-26468
　　"A collection of 17 stories from the Old Testament, 15 from the New Testament, and 4 psalms. The text is from the New International Version. . . . De Paola uses the text as written with some abridgement to make the stories an appropriate length. Done in his typical style, the illustrations feature stylized people and objects. . . . There are several illustrations for each story, many of which are full page, and most make dramatic use of color. The large format enhances the impact of the pictures." SLJ

Lottridge, Celia Barker
　　Stories from Adam and Eve to Ezekiel; retold from the Bible. by Celia Barker Lottridge; illustrated by Gary Clement. Douglas & McIntyre/Groundwood 2004 192p il $24.95
Grades: 4 5 6 7   **220.9**
　　1. Bible stories
　　ISBN 0-88899-490-7
　　"Lottridge uses her storyteller's ear to bring ancient stories from the Hebrew Bible to a young audience, tailoring them to make them more age appropriate. . . . The numerous, well-drawn ink-and-watercolor illustrations are reminiscent of Warwick Hutton's work. Some pictures . . . are quite spectacular." Booklist

Osborne, Mary Pope
　　The **Random** House book of Bible stories; by Mary Pope Osborne and Natalie Pope Boyce; illustrated by Michael Welply. Random House 2009 165p il $24.99; lib bdg $27.99
Grades: 2 3 4 5   **220.9**
　　1. Bible stories
　　ISBN 978-0-375-82281-0; 0-375-82281-X; 978-0-375-92281-7 lib bdg; 0-375-92281-4 lib bdg
　　　　　　　　　　　　　　　　LC 2007047308
　　"The retellers do a credible job of adapting more than 50 Old and New Testament selections in sequential order. Each story is related in language that evokes biblical storytelling, giving the collection the feel of a real Bible with the accessibility of a shared read-aloud. . . . Welply's realistic

illustrations . . . will help readers contextualize the place and time." SLJ

Pirotta, Saviour
　　Children's stories from the Bible; stories retold. color art by Anne Yvonne Gilbert; monochrome art by Ian Andrew. Templar Books 2009 292p il map $19.99
Grades: 4 5 6   **220.9**
　　1. Bible stories
　　ISBN 978-0-7636-4551-9; 0-7636-4551-6
　　　　　　　　　　　　　　　　LC 2008944069
　　Recounts over seventy stories from the Bible, including "The Walls of Jericho," "The Prodigal Son," "Jesus and the Children," and "Rahab and the Spies"
　　Pirotta "adds, for example, kid-friendly details about the weather on the day Mary and Joseph travel to Bethlehem, and he resolves each story with a tidy ending. Softly textured illustrations enhance the mood of the tales." Horn Book Guide

Watts, Murray
　　The **Bible** for children from Good Books; retold by Murray Watts; illustrated by Helen Cann. Good Bks. (Pa.) 2002 352p il map $23.99
Grades: 3 4 5 6   **220.9**
　　1. Bible stories
　　ISBN 1-56148-362-1
　　　　　　　　　　　　　　　　LC 2002-20243
　　A collection of approximately two hundred and fifty illustrated stories from the Old and New Testaments, retold for children
　　"Watts' retellings from the Old and New Testaments are vivid and evocative. . . . The handsome pictures and decorated borders employ a rich palette of colors and patterns, giving the book a contemporary look." Booklist

220.95　History

Ehrlich, Amy, 1942-
　　With a mighty hand; the story of the Torah. Amy Ehrlich, Daniel Nevins. Candlewick Press 2013 224 p. $29.99
Grades: 2 3 4 5 6 7 8   **220.95**
　　1. Bible 2. Bible stories 3. Picture books for children
　　ISBN 0763643955; 9780763643959
　　　　　　　　　　　　　　　　LC 2012947723
　　This book is an interpretation of the Torah for children. Amy Ehrlich has "changed the traditional phrasing" of the Bible's first five books. She "describes Moses' basket as "a little ark of papyrus," reminding readers of how much danger the baby was in, floating in the middle of the Nile. . . . Not every word of the Bible has been included, the text having been pared down to a series of interconnected stories." (Kirkus Reviews)

221.9　Geography, history, chronology, persons of Old Testament lands in Old Testament times

Hanft, Joshua E.
　　Miracles of the Bible; by Josh Hanft; illustrated by Seymour Chwast. Blue Apple Books 2007 un il $16.95

Grades: K 1 2   **221.9**
   1. Miracles 2. Bible stories
   ISBN 978-1-59354-617-5; 1-59354-617-3

                        LC 2007007093

   This retells "such familiar Bible stories as 'Daniel in the Lion's Den' and 'Jonah and the Fish' and 'Noah's Ark.' He also includes such dramatic episodes as the parting of the Red Sea and the conquests of Samson and David. . . . It's Chwast's full-page-and-more compositions, rendered in creamy, pastel-toned ink-and-watercolor that stand out—literally. A number of these illustrations, in Chwast's signature comics-influenced style, appear on foldout pages that boldly expand the scene, vertically or horizontally. Children will likely flock to this hands-on reading experience." Publ Wkly

Sasso, Sandy Eisenberg
   But God remembered; stories of women from creation to the promised land. illustrated by Bethanne Andersen. Jewish Lights Pub. 1995 31p il $16.95
Grades: 3 4 5   **221.9**
   1. Bible stories 2. Women in the Bible
   ISBN 1-879045-43-5

                        LC 95-3591

   "Although part of the pleasure of the book lies in its strong feminist voice, Sasso also tells good stories; and these will have even more value for the discussions they can generate. Andersen's evocative paintings are beautiful additions to this carefully designed book." Booklist

Ward, Elaine M.
   Old Testament women; [by] Elaine Ward. Enchanted Lion 2004 32p il (Art revelations) $18.95
Grades: 5 6 7 8   **221.9**
   1. Bible stories 2. Women in the Bible
   ISBN 1-59270-011-X

   These Old Testament stories about women include "explanatory paragraphs, sidebars, and captions by the author. Art masterpieces . . . illustrate each story. . . . The captions provide background on the artist and the significance of each painting or mosaic. . . . The 18 women . . . include Rachel, Leah, Ruth, and Bathsheba. . . . Bosch, Botticelli, and Poussin are among the painters whose work appears here. . . . Visually stunning." SLJ

222   Historical books of Old Testament

Feiler, Bruce S.
   ★ **Walking** the Bible; an illustrated journey for kids through the greatest stories ever told. by Bruce Feiler; illustrated by Sasha Meret. HarperCollinsPublishers 2004 108p il map $16.99; lib bdg $17.89
Grades: 5 6 7 8   **222**
   1. Bible (as subject) 2. Middle East
   ISBN 0-06-051117-6; 0-06-051118-4 lib bdg

                        LC 2003-15861

   The author describes his journey through places mentioned in the Old Testament
   "In this version of his adult book with the same title (Morrow, 2001), Feiler largely succeeds in slimming rather than dumbing down his account of his trip across the 10,000-mile setting of the earliest Bible stories. The author's unpre-

tentious . . . tone and astute pacing help make the volume accessible, and his sincerity is palpable." SLJ

Fischer, Chuck
   ★ **In** the beginning: the art of Genesis; a pop-up book. by Chuck Fischer. Little, Brown 2008 un il $35
Grades: 5 6 7 8   **222**
   1. Bible stories 2. Religious art 3. Pop-up books 4. Bible -- O.T. -- Genesis
   ISBN 978-0-316-11842-2; 0-316-11842-7

                        LC 2007045411

   Fischer "presents an impressive, three-dimensional view of the Book of Genesis. . . . Fischer and his collaborators offer a Garden of Eden scene executed in an artistic style that recalls ancient tile work; a huge Noah's Ark landed atop a mountain; and a Tower of Babel impressively high. . . . The text, more commentary than story, is hidden in inset mini-books and is accompanied by reproductions of biblical masterpieces. . . . This book becomes more amazing as the pages are turned." Booklist

Hodges, Margaret
   ★ **Moses**; illustrated by Barry Moser. Harcourt, Inc. 2006 un il $16
Grades: 3 4 5   **222**
   1. Prophets 2. Bible stories 3. Biblical characters
   ISBN 978-0-15-200946-5; 0-15-200946-9

   Retells the story of Moses, from his birth and trip in a boat of bulrushes to his bringing of the Ten Commandments down from Mount Sinai.
   "The venerable story of Moses gets a brisk yet compelling treatment by Hodges. . . . The book is beautiful to page through, with cream-colored pages and the bordered watercolors in Moser's signature style." Booklist

Jules, Jacqueline
   Abraham's search for God; by Jacqueline Jules; illustrated by Natascia Ugliano. Kar-Ben Pub. 2007 un il lib bdg $17.95
Grades: K 1 2 3   **222**
   1. God 2. Prophets 3. Biblical characters
   ISBN 978-1-58013-243-5 lib bdg; 1-58013-243-X lib bdg

                        LC 2006027429

   "Jules retells a midrash (a legend based on biblical text) in which the youthful Abraham discovers the concept of monotheism. Rejecting worship of unresponsive idols, Abraham spends time outdoors where he senses an unseen hand directing the movements of the moon, sun, storm, and rainbow. He concludes that 'God is everywhere. God is in everything. God is something we know with our hearts.' . . . The energetic pastel illustrations are cheerful and warm. . . . This simply told tale is an excellent introduction to the concept of monotheism, and would be a great discussion starter for talking about God." SLJ
   Includes bibliographical references

   Benjamin and the silver goblet; illustrated by Natascia Ugliano. Kar-Ben Pub. 2009 un il $17.95; pa $8.95
Grades: K 1 2 3   **222**
   1. Bible stories
   ISBN 978-0-8225-8757-6; 0-8225-8757-2; 978-0-8225-8758-3 pa; 0-8225-8758-0 pa

                        LC 2007048344

"When Jacob's sons arrive home from their travels in Egypt, they tell their father that one brother is being held as a hostage by the governor, who demands that they return with the youngest brother, Benjamin. The child, aching to see the world, is only too happy to oblige, though Jacob fears that he will lose this son the way he lost his eldest, Joseph, years before. . . . Well paced and well told, this familiar story makes itself fresh with a folkloric feel and a satisfying ending. Ugliano's heavily textured, colorful pastel illustrations ably support and extend the text." Kirkus

Miriam in the desert; illustrated by Natascia Ugliano. Kar-Ben Pub. 2010 un il lib bdg $17.95; pa $8.95
Grades: K 1 2 3   **222**
  1. Bible stories 2. Biblical characters
  ISBN 978-0-7613-4494-0 lib bdg; 0-7613-4494-2 lib bdg; 978-0-7613-4496-4 pa; 0-7613-4496-9 pa
                              LC 2009001874
"Miriam, Moses's sister, is featured in [this book] . . . , offering encouragement and guidance to the Israelites as they continue their seemingly endless thirst- and hunger-filled journey through the desert following their escape from Egypt. . . . Deeply colored pastel-and-acrylic double-page paintings effectively portray a legendary biblical setting in a guileless and unsophisticated style. . . . They effectively match the original and simple dialogue-driven text." Kirkus

Sarah laughs; by Jacqueline Jules; illustrated by Natascia Ugliano. Kar-Ben Pub. 2008 32p il $17.95; pa $8.95
Grades: K 1 2 3   **222**
  1. Prophets 2. Bible stories 3. Biblical characters
  ISBN 978-0-8225-7216-9; 0-8225-7216-8; 978-0-8225-9934-0 pa; 0-8225-9934-1 pa
                              LC 2006039738
"Through poetic language and sweeping illustrations, this picture book tells the story of the biblical patriarch and matriarch Abraham and Sarah from Sarah's point of view. . . . Sarah is portrayed as graceful, loving, and faithful. However, her sadness about remaining childless through the years has made her lose her bright laughter. With the birth of Isaac, when she is gray-haired and wrinkled, she finally laughs again. . . . This lovely retelling deserves a place on the shelves of any library that collects religious materials." SLJ
  Includes bibliographical references

Kimmel, Eric A.
  ★ The **story** of Esther; retold by Eric A. Kimmel; illustrated by Jill Weber. Holiday House 2010 un il $16.95
Grades: K 1 2   **222**
  1. Purim 2. Queens 3. Bible stories 4. Biblical characters
  ISBN 978-0-8234-2223-4; 0-8234-2223-2
                              LC 2008048490
"Kimmel and Weber turn their considerable talents to the Book of Esther and its corresponding Jewish holiday. . . . As always, Kimmel is an effortless storyteller, his learnedness leavened with an expert sense of pacing for young audiences—even the book's longer passages feel like they're exactly the right length. In vibrant mixed-media paintings, Weber proves once again that she's an excellent match for this unflashy master." Publ Wkly

Koralek, Jenny
  The **coat** of many colors; illustrated by Pauline Baynes. Eerdmans Books for Young Readers 2004 un il $16
Grades: K 1 2 3   **222**
  1. Bible stories 2. Biblical characters
  ISBN 0-8028-5277-7
                              LC 2004-6575
This "retelling of the story from the Book of Genesis highlights the key events in the life of Joseph . . . , and explores timeless themes of sibling rivalry and the power of forgiveness. . . . Baynes enhances the straightforward text with atmospheric illustrations rendered in muted desert shades. . . . This appealing rendition of a well-known tale is perfect for reading aloud." SLJ

  The **story** of Queen Esther; written by Jenny Koralek; illustrated by Grizelda Holderness. Eerdmans Books for Young Readers 2008 un il $17.50
Grades: K 1 2 3   **222**
  1. Queens 2. Bible stories 3. Biblical characters
  ISBN 978-0-8028-5348-6; 0-8028-5348-X
                              LC 2008017713
This is a "retelling of the biblical story of the Jewish queen of ancient Persia who saved her people from the plotting of the king's evil vizier, Haman. . . . The Jewish holiday of Purim, which commemorates the story of Queen Esther, is mentioned on the final spread. . . . The illustrations are the highlight of the book. Stylized, dreamy pastel spreads sing with deep color. . . . The dignified pictures support the solemn tone of the text." SLJ

Manushkin, Fran
  Miriam's cup; a Passover story. illustrated by Bob Dacey. Scholastic 1998 un il hardcover o.p. pa $6.99
Grades: K 1 2 3   **222**
  1. Passover 2. Bible stories 3. Biblical characters
  ISBN 0-590-67720-9; 0-439-81111-2 pa
                              LC 96-2480
A Jewish mother preparing for Passover tells her young children, the story of Miriam, the Biblical woman who prophesied the birth of Moses
  "The text and the lush double-spread watercolors, which are painted to reflect a child's perspective, are framed on a papyrus background. Each illustration bursts with movement, immersing readers and pre-readers alike in the sequence and drama of the story." Booklist
  Includes bibliographical references

Ray, Jane
  Adam and Eve and the Garden of Eden; written and illustrated by Jane Ray. Eerdmans Books for Young Readers 2005 un il $17
Grades: K 1 2 3   **222**
  1. Bible stories 2. Biblical characters
  ISBN 0-8028-5278-5
                              LC 2004-6804
"Adam and Eve live harmoniously with the animals that have been named by the first man, until Eve is tempted by the serpent. In rich prose, the author describes the garden in lyrical detail. The descriptive passages are complemented by exquisite illustrations that lend a mystical aura to the narrative." SLJ

Sasso, Sandy Eisenberg

★ **Cain** & Abel; finding the fruits of peace. illustrated by Joani Keller Rothenberg. Jewish Lights Pub. 2001 32p il $16.95

Grades: K 1 2 3   **222**

1. Bible stories 2. Biblical characters

ISBN 1-58023-123-3

LC 2001-2206

Retells the story of two brothers who, after years of sharing everything, become angry enough to lose control and bring violence into the world

"In this simple yet effective book, Sasso leads children to think not only about how the brothers' personal relationship failed but also about the story's connection to today's violence. The eye-catching, folk-art-style illustrations, with thick swathes of color and inventive background designs, make as strong a statement as the text." Booklist

Spier, Peter

★ **Noah's** ark; illustrated by Peter Spier. Doubleday 1977 un il $16.95; pa $7.99

Grades: K 1 2   **222**

1. Noah's ark 2. Bible stories

ISBN 0-385-09473-6; 0-440-49693-8 pa

LC 76-43630

Awarded the Caldecott Medal, 1978

"A seventeenth-century Dutch poem, 'The Flood' by Jacobus Revius, opens the otherwise almost wordless book. Skillfully translated by the artist and set in a readable, appropriately archaic type, the artlessly reverent verses add an unexpected dimension to the full-color pictures. Peter Spier's characteristic panoramas are marvels of minute detail, activity, vitality, and humor." Horn Book

Stewig, John W.

The **animals** watched; by John Warren Stewig; illustrated by Rosanne Litzinger. Holiday House 2007 un il $16.95

Grades: K 1 2   **222**

1. Alphabet 2. Noah's ark

ISBN 978-0-8234-1906-7; 0-8234-1906-1

LC 2006004784

"A simple account of the story of Noah's ark. The language is easy enough for young children to understand, but remains true to the basics of the Genesis text.... In alphabetical order from aardvarks to jaguars to zebras, animals tell a part of the tale.... The appealing illustrations are done in pencil, watercolor, gouache, and colored pencil." SLJ

Wolf, Gita

The **Enduring** Ark; by Gita Wolf; illustrated by Joydeb Chitrakar. Pgw 2013 34 p. ill. (hardcover) $21.95

Grades: 1 2 3 4   **222**

1. Toy and movable books 2. Noah's Ark

ISBN 9380340184; 9789380340180

This children's book, by Gita Wolf, illustrated by Joydeb Chitrakar, offers an "Indian version of the Biblical tale [of the Flood and Noah's Ark, which] ... leads the reader from a deluge of water to a rainbow of hope. A book that can be leafed through in the traditional way or unfolded out as an accordion." (Publisher's note)

223   Poetic books of Old Testament

Delval, Marie-Helene

Psalms for young children; by Marie-Helene Delval; illustrated by Arno. Eerdmans Books for Young Readers 2008 un il $16

Grades: K 1 2 3   **223**

1. Bible. Old Testament 2. Bible -- O.T. -- Psalms

ISBN 978-0-8028-5322-6; 0-8028-5322-6

LC 2006031831

"Each psalm expresses feelings familiar to children: fear and uncertainty, comfort and contentment, amazement and gratitude. The sacred songs, paraphrased in simple, child-friendly language, celebrate the beautiful world, which is protected by God's all-encompassing love, and provide a sense of reassurance.... Organized in numerical order, the selections are printed in a large, readable font.... The magical paintings feature exotic settings, bold outlines, and rich hues. They are filled with images of children and the natural world." SLJ

Dillon, Leo

★ **To** every thing there is a season; verses from Ecclesiastes. illustrations by Leo and Diane Dillon. Blue Sky Press (NY) 1998 un il $16.95

Grades: 4 5 6 7 8   **223**

ISBN 0-590-47887-7

LC 97-35124

"The words of Ecclesiastes I:4 and III:1-8, adapted from the King James Version of the Bible, are ... {illustrated here in} 16 full- and double-page paintings.... Kindergarten and up." (SLJ)

"The Dillons compellingly convey the relevance of the Ecclesiastes verse throughout history, via a stunning array of artwork that embraces motifs from cultures the world over." Publ Wkly

Lindbergh, Reeve

On morning wings; adapted from Psalm 139 by Reeve Lindbergh; illustrated by Holly Meade. Candlewick Press 2002 un il $15.99

Grades: K 1 2 3   **223**

1. God 2. Bible -- O.T. -- Psalms

ISBN 0-7636-1106-9

LC 2001-58169

"On morning wings" was previously published in the anthology In every tiny grain of sand: a child's book of prayers and praise, collected by Reeve Lindbergh, published by Candlewick Press, 2000

Retells, in simple words, a psalm of God's knowledge of and love for each of us

"Meade's visual story line shows four children spending an idyllic summer day together outdoors. The striking use of light, reflected in water or filtered by campfire, conveys the natural reverence of the text with seeming spontaneity." Publ Wkly

Moser, Barry

Psalm 23; illustrated by Barry Moser. Zonderkidz 2008 un il $14.99

Grades: K 1 2   **223**

1. Bible. Old Testament 2. Bible -- O.T. -- Psalms

ISBN 978-0-310-71085-1; 0-310-71085-5

LC 2006027616

"In a two-page introduction, Moser invites readers to see the venerable poem through a new prism: that of a boy tending goats and sheep on a Caribbean island such as Antigua, where the author-illustrator has spent much time. While watching the island animals, Moser says he has often recited the psalm, which he writes here in simple words. . . . Moser strives to accentuate mood and nature, and the paintings in this book . . . highlight the feeling that as God watches over us, we watch over those in our charge." Booklist

226   Gospels and Acts

Warren, Rick

The **Lord's** prayer; [illustrated by] Richard Jesse Watson; commentary by Rick Warren. Zonderkidz 2011 un il (Master illustrator series) $16.99
Grades: PreK K 1 2   **226**
  1. Prayer
  ISBN 978-0-310-71086-8; 0-310-71086-3
                                          LC 2009037508

"With vibrant illustrations featuring children of all ages and nationalities, Watson illuminates the message of love and worship contained within the lines of the King James Version of The Lord's Prayer. Each spread focuses on a single line, which is printed in elegant font and incorporated into the painting. Images of animals and the sun recur throughout the book. Some of the pictures are painted in rich colors while others appear to be shadowy, gray pencil sketches. . . . Warren explains the meaning behind the words Jesus taught his disciples with line-by-line commentary, teaching young readers the value of prayer. The artist also offers a reflection on what this prayer means to him. This lovely picture book is a fine choice to help parents introduce the practice of prayer into their children's daily lives." SLJ

230   Christianity

Nardo, Don

Christianity. Compass Point Books 2010 48p il map (World religions) lib bdg $27.99
Grades: 5 6 7 8   **230**
  1. Christianity
  ISBN 978-0-7565-4237-5 lib bdg; 0-7565-4237-5 lib bdg
                                          LC 2009-15811

"The colorful, attractive layout includes high-quality reproductions of photographs, maps, and paintings. Students who are new to religious studies, as well as those doing reports, will find that this . . . meets their needs." SLJ

Includes glossary and bibliographical references

Self, David

  ★ **Christianity**; [by] David Self. World Almanac Library 2005 48p il map (Religions of the world) lib bdg $30
Grades: 5 6 7 8   **230**
  1. Christianity
  ISBN 0-8368-5866-2
                                          LC 2005041712

This is a summary of the Christian religion including history, beliefs, worship, festivals, practice, and current disagreements.

"Wonderfully colorful in images, language, and fact. . . . [This is] enumerated with full-color photographs on every page, charts, maps, and tables." SLJ

Includes bibliographical references

231   Christian doctrinal theology

Delval, Marie-Helene

Images of God for young children; illustrated by Barbara Nascimbeni. Eerdmans Books for Young Readers 2011 88p il $16.50
Grades: K 1 2 3   **231**
  1. God
  ISBN 978-0-8028-5391-2; 0-8028-5391-9

This "sets out to explain the concept of God to children in creative, often metaphorical ways. . . . The explanatory text is written in a thoughtful, calm voice with a comforting view of God as kind, loving and all-encompassing. This modern point of view is complemented by Nascimbeni's bright, imaginative illustrations on the right-hand pages, using children and images from nature painted in a cheery surrealistically childlike style." Kirkus

Fitch, Florence Mary

  A **book** about God; illustrated by Henri Sorensen. Lothrop, Lee & Shepard Bks. 1998 24p il hardcover o.p. lib bdg $15.93
Grades: K 1 2 3   **231**
  1. God
  ISBN 0-688-16128-6; 0-688-16129-4 lib bdg
                                          LC 97-48682

A newly illustrated edition of the title first published 1953

The "text explains how people can understand God's nature by observing the world he created. Fitch describes the ways that characteristics of the sun, air, trees, mountains, and oceans reflect the character of God. Proponents of many faiths will embrace this book's message." Horn Book Guide

231.7   Relation to the world

DePaola, Tomie, 1934-

  ★ **Let** the whole earth sing praise. G. P. Putnam's Sons 2011 un il $15.99
Grades: PreK K 1   **231.7**
  1. Creation
  ISBN 978-0-399-25478-9; 0-399-25478-1
                                          LC 2010011565

"In this small-format book, dePaola masterfully pairs simple words and resonant images. Rendered in acrylics and inspired by the folk art of the Otomi people from Puebla, Mexico, the pictures offer primitive depictions of natural phenomena. . . . Based on two pieces of Old Testament scripture—the Canticle of the Three Young Men from the Book of Daniel and Psalm 148—dePaola's narrative bids specific creatures and forces of nature to give praise, before issuing a cumulative call-out: 'Let everything in heaven and on earth bless and praise God.' The very largeness of the loose, hand-lettered text, which appears in all caps, amplifies the message, while the joy that emanates from the cheerful spreads confirms its value." Publ Wkly

232.9   Family and life of Jesus

Castillo, Lauren

★ **Christmas** is here; words from the King James Bible; illustrated by Lauren Castillo. Simon & Schuster 2010 un il $12.99
Grades: PreK K 1 2   **232.9**
1. Christmas
ISBN 978-1-4424-0822-7; 1-4424-0822-7

"This touching interpretation of the Christmas story wordlessly follows a modern-day family as they journey through a snowy town in the evening to view a live Nativity scene. . . . The setting shifts in time and place to Bethlehem of long ago, accompanied by the traditional words from the King James Bible, before returning to the contemporary setting. Gorgeous watercolor illustrations in a subdued palette of twilight grays set off the falling snowflakes in the modern scenes, while the biblical scenes are brilliantly lit by starlight. Castillo's smudgy style infuses all with wonder." Kirkus

Crossley-Holland, Kevin

★ **How** many miles to Bethlehem? illustrated by Peter Malone. Arthur A. Levine Books 2004 un il $16.95
Grades: K 1 2 3   **232.9**
1. Jesus Christ 2. Jesus Christ -- Nativity
ISBN 0-439-67642-8

LC 2003-28079

This is a telling of the Nativity story, told from the perspectives of Mary, the innkeeper, the ox, the donkey, the shepherds, the Wise Men, King Herod, the child, the lamb, and the angels.

"The language is both colloquial and lyrical. . . . Malone's illustrations are reminiscent of early Renaissance and medieval Eastern art in their wealth of detail and color. . . . The paintings evoke both sumptuous glory and a serene stillness." SLJ

Demi

★ **Jesus**; written and illustrated by Demi. Margaret K. McElderry Books 2005 un il $19.95
Grades: 3 4 5 6   **232.9**
1. Jesus Christ
ISBN 0-689-86905-3

LC 2004-12854

This life of Jesus is based "on Isaiah and the four Gospels from the King James version of the Bible. . . . Grades three to six." (Bull Cent Child Books)

"Brilliantly colored artwork and text based on the King James version of the Bible tell the story of the life of Jesus, beginning with the prophesies and the annunciation and ending with his ascension into Heaven. Demi's paintings are full of bright, intricate patterns, and bold touches of gold produce a feeling of awe and splendor." SLJ

Johnson, Pamela

The **story** of Christmas; from the King James Bible. illustrations by Pamela Dalton. Handprint Books 2011 un il $17.99

Grades: 1 2 3   **232.9**
1. Jesus Christ 2. Jesus Christ -- Nativity
ISBN 978-1-4521-0470-6; 1-4521-0470-0

LC 2011025407

"Delicate paper-cut illustrations provide a lovely, solemn backdrop to the King James Bible's account of the Nativity story. . . . As shepherds, wise men, and angels gather to honor the birth of Jesus, Dalton sets her tableaus against black backgrounds, which both focus attention on the story's major players and make logical sense given the nocturnal setting of much of the story's events. The iconic nature of Dalton's scenes is ideally suited to the traditional Biblical translation used." Publ Wkly

Lottridge, Celia Barker

Stories from the life of Jesus; retold from the Bible by Celia Barker Lottridge; illustrated by Linda Wolfsgruber. Douglas & McIntyre 2004 140p il $24.95
Grades: 4 5 6 7   **232.9**
1. Bible stories 2. Jesus Christ
ISBN 0-88899-497-4

A retelling of selected events from the life of Christ based on biblical accounts

This is an "exceptional collection. . . . Each story is retold in three or four pages of clear, concise prose that is meant to be read aloud. . . . Each selection is enhanced by dramatic and atmospheric, mixed-media illustrations that are executed in warm earth tones." SLJ

Menotti, Gian Carlo

Amahl and the night visitors; illustrated by Michèle Lemieux. Morrow 1986 64p il $21
Grades: 2 3 4   **232.9**
1. Magi -- Fiction 2. Jesus Christ 3. Jesus Christ -- Fiction
ISBN 0-688-05426-9

LC 84-27196

Relates how a crippled young shepherd comes to accompany the three Kings on their way to pay hommage to the newborn Jesus

"Some of the pictures, which are dominated by reddish brown, have rich tension and composition, as in the one of Amahl's mother contemplating theft, or in the portrait of Melchior describing the Christ child. . . . There is a great deal to look at, and the story, popular since the opera's 1951 debut, has sentimental appeal, humor, and some commanding moments." Bull Cent Child Books

Paterson, Katherine

★ The **light** of the world; the life of Jesus for children. [by] Katherine Paterson; [illustrated by] Francois Roca. Arthur A. Levine Books 2008 un il $17.99
Grades: K 1 2 3   **232.9**
1. Jesus Christ
ISBN 978-0-545-01172-3; 0-545-01172-8

LC 2007-06811

"The incisive text . . . deftly moves through the story of Jesus' life and death, and also highlights several of the best-known parables. . . . Roca presents . . . close-ups of the various people surrounding Jesus and . . . handsome landscapes that give import to events." Booklist

Skevington, Andrea

The **story** of Jesus; illustrated by Angelo Ruta. Lion Children's 2009 127p il $16.95

Grades: 2 3 4 5   **232.9**

   1. Bible stories 2. Jesus Christ

   ISBN 978-0-7459-4982-6; 0-7459-4982-7

            LC 2008278094

"Skevington's collection of key New Testament stories chronicles the life of Jesus beginning with his birth in a humble stable in Bethlehem and concluding with the feast of Pentecost when the Holy Spirit descends upon the disciples. Retelling stories from all four gospels, the author fictionalizes the scripture passages, adding dialogue and cultural details to enliven the characters and the setting. . . . Explanatory margin notes supplement the stories, and the neatly drawn illustrations portray Jesus and his followers in a palette of soft pastels." SLJ

Slegers, Liesbet

The **child** in the manger. Clavis Pub. 2010 un il $15.95

Grades: PreK K 1   **232.9**

   1. Jesus Christ 2. Jesus Christ -- Nativity

   ISBN 978-1-60537-084-2; 1-60537-084-3

"This is a short version of the Nativity story, told in simple language that very young children can understand. . . . The cheerful, colorful paintings, rendered in primary colors with bold outlines, feature childlike animals and smiley-faced Biblical people. This is a fine choice for sharing with toddlers and preschoolers one-on-one, as well as in a religious preschool storytime." SLJ

Spirin, Gennady

★ **Jesus**; his life in verses from the King James Holy Bible. art by Gennady Spirin. Marshall Cavendish Children 2010 un il $21

Grades: 5 6 7 8   **232.9**

   1. Jesus Christ

   ISBN 978-0-7614-5630-8; 0-7614-5630-9

            LC 2009005956

"In an unusual project, a tempera painting by Spirin has been digitally dissected to create individual images for this picture book that portrays 13 events from the life of Jesus. . . . Details from the larger work illustrate key moments—including the Annunciation, Jesus' baptism, and the raising of Lazarus, among others—beside passages from the King James Bible (Jesus' words are printed in red). The result is an elegant, large-format volume that offers a reverent and arresting visual interpretation of biblical events." Publ Wkly

Wildsmith, Brian

Jesus. Eerdmans Bks. for Young Readers 2000 un il $20

Grades: K 1 2 3   **232.9**

   1. Jesus Christ

   ISBN 0-8028-5212-2

            LC 00-55126

"Wildsmith's pictures are framed in windowlike arches, set against backgrounds of pure colors. As with his other works, gold embellishments add majesty." Booklist

This "picture book gives an overview of Jesus' life beginning with the angel Gabriel's visit to Mary and ending with Jesus' ascension into Heaven." Horn Book Guide

Williams, Sophy

The **first** Christmas; a changing picture book. Templar Books 2010 un il $12.99

Grades: PreK K 1 2   **232.9**

   1. Jesus Christ 2. Jesus Christ -- Nativity

   ISBN 978-0-7636-5013-1; 0-7636-5013-7

            LC 2010004644

"This lovely presentation of the Nativity story includes four 'changing-pictures,' which are created by overlaying two images divided into vertical slats. In this case, the images change when a flap is opened. Williams's pastel illustrations are both luminous and child-centric, conveying a sense of mystery, awe, and gentle humor." SLJ

232.91   Mary, mother of Jesus

Bernier-Grand, Carmen T.

Our Lady of Guadalupe; retold by Carmen T. Bernier-Grand; illustrated by Tonya Engel. 1st ed. Marshall Cavendish Children 2012 31 p. ill. (hardcover) $17.99

Grades: 1 2 3   **232.91**

   1. Aztecs -- Folklore 2. Religious biography 3. Guadalupe, Our Lady of

   ISBN 9780761461357; 9780761461371

            LC 2011016398

Author Carmen Bernier-Grand "describes the Aztec Juan Diego's three encounters with the Virgin Mary on Tepeyac Hill, near Tlatelolco (now Mexico City). Mary requests that Juan Diego tell the local bishop to build her a shrine on the hill . . . [and he] carries a sign from the Virgin to the bishop: roses in December. . . . The author concludes the tale with details on the significance of the shrine, the origins of the name 'Our Lady of Guadalupe' and other relevant historical facts and dates." (Kirkus Reivews)

Córdova, Amy, 1953-

Talking Eagle and the Lady of Roses; the story of Juan Diego and Our Lady of Guadalupe. illustrated by Amy Cordova; written by Amy Cordova, with Eugene Gollogly. SteinerBooks 2010 un il

Grades: K 1 2   **232.91**

   1. Christian saints

   ISBN 0-88010-719-7; 978-0-88010-719-8

            LC 2010032329

This "story tells of the appearance of Our Lady of Guadalupe to an indigenous healer, Talking Eagle, who had converted to Catholicism, becoming Juan Diego. . . . Rendered in dazzling jewel tones, Córdova's drawings possess a quiet radiance." Publ Wkly

Demi

Mary; written and illustrated by Demi. Margaret K. McElderry Books 2006 un il $19.95

Grades: 3 4 5 6   **232.91**

   1. Saints

   ISBN 0-689-87692-0; 978-0-689-87692-9

            LC 2005005844

"Demi begins her story before Mary is born, when her parents, Anna and Joachim, learn that their prayers have been heard, and that they will have a child whom they will dedicate to the service of the Lord. . . . The words simply serve as a backdrop for the glorious artwork. . . . Along with her familiar beautiful borders and diminutive characters, she incorporates many Jewish and Christian symbols that tie the religions together." SLJ

242 Devotional literature

Billingsley, Mary

The **life** of Jesus; an illustrated rosary. written and illustrated by Mary Billingsley; foreword by Benedict J. Groeschel. Eerdmans Books for Young Readers 2010 56p il $19.99

Grades: 3 4 5 6   **242**

1. Prayer 2. Jesus Christ

ISBN 978-0-8028-5362-2; 0-8028-5362-5

"Billingsley has divided this book according to the four 'Mysteries' that are emblematic of Christ's life—'Joyful,' 'Luminous,' 'Sorrowful,' and 'Glorious,' and then into subsections about each of its five parts. The book is remarkable in the accessibility it offers to readers of all ages. The introductory page provides visual instruction—a painting of a rosary with labels and arrows indicating which beads are meant for each prayer—followed by the prayers themselves. . . . Billingsley's unusual technique is what stands out; she has created 'shrines' of everyday objects, flowers, puppets, children's toys arranged in a vignette, and then reproduced them in gouache. The overall effect is child-friendly but also intensely emotionally evocative." SLJ

Brooks, Jeremy

Let there be peace; prayers from around the world. illustrated by Jude Daly. Frances Lincoln 2009 un il $16.95

Grades: PreK K 1 2 3   **242**

1. Peace 2. Prayers

ISBN 978-1-8450-7530-9; 1-8450-7530-7

"This picture-book collection of prayers sends universal messages of peace and global unity. Brooks . . . . has pulled from diverse religious traditions. . . . Almost all of the selections are simple, immediate, and rhythmic. . . . Daly's delicately rendered, brightly hued paintings greatly increase the impact of the words. . . . Children of many backgrounds will be stirred by these prayers." Booklist

My first prayers. Albert Whitman 2009 un il $16.95

Grades: K 1 2   **242**

1. Prayers

ISBN 978-1-84507-535-4; 1-84507-535-8

"Brooks has collected prayers from a variety of nations including Poland, South Africa, the United States, and France, as well as several from his native England. The book features prayers of thanks, requests for guidance, blessings, and bedtime prayers. . . . Young readers will appreciate Brooks's gentle message of acceptance and inclusiveness." SLJ

A **world** of prayers; illustrated by Elena Gomez. Eerdmans Books for Young Readers 2006 un il $16

Grades: 1 2 3 4   **242**

1. Prayers

ISBN 0-8028-5285-8

LC 2004017482

"A collection of 26 prayers assembled under the headings, Prayers for the Morning, Mealtime Graces, Prayers

for Nighttime, and Blessings. A brief introduction and comments at the beginning of each chapter reflect on the place of prayer in our lives. Written in simple, easy-to-read language, the entreaties are recited by children in a variety of lands. . . . Dreamlike, decorative paintings that reflect the various cultures greatly enhance the selections and emphasize the books message of inclusiveness." SLJ

A **child's** book of prayers; collected and illustrated by Juli Kangas. Dial Books for Young Readers 2007 un il $12.99

Grades: PreK K   **242**

1. Prayers

ISBN 978-0-8037-3054-0; 0-8037-3054-3

LC 2006017595

"Simple meditations, both familiar and less well known, are presented along with warmhearted illustrations for the purpose of exposing children to the spiritual benefits of prayer. The well-chosen selections begin at the start of the day and follow different youngsters and their families through school, meals, and other typical pursuits, offering prayers of blessing, thanksgiving, or praise suited to each endeavor. The pencil, watercolor, and oil-wash artwork skillfully depicts the charismatic characters, who hale from a variety of ethnic backgrounds and live in both city and rural settings." SLJ

Field, Rachel

Prayer for a child; pictures by Elizabeth Orton Jones. Diamond anniversary ed; Simon & Schuster Books for Young Readers 2004 un il $10.95

Grades: K 1 2   **242**

1. Prayers

ISBN 0-689-87356-5

LC 2004-5259

A reissue of the title first published 1944 by Macmillan

Awarded the Caldecott Medal, 1945

"The complete prayer, written in rhymed couplets, appears on the first page; then a few lines per page accompany serene illustrations of a girl in tender moments—stargazing out a window or smiling up at her parents. . . . This lovely book lends itself to nightly repetition (a reference to Jesus tags it for a Christian audience)." Publ Wkly

Goble, Paul

Song of creation; written and illustrated by Paul Goble. Eerdmans Books for Young Readers 2004 un il $16

Grades: K 1 2 3   **242**

1. Prayers 2. Creation

ISBN 0-8028-5271-8

LC 2004-6576

"In striking graphic compositions, Goble creates magical, yet concrete, scenes of birds, beasts, fish, and more, conveying a personal and a universal reverence for and connection to nature. A beautiful, praiseworthy volume that does, indeed, sing." Booklist

Jordan, Deloris

Baby blessings; a prayer for the day you are born. illustrated by James E. Ransome. Simon & Schuster Books for Young Readers 2010 un il $16.99

Grades: PreK K 242
1. Prayers
ISBN 1-4169-5362-0; 978-1-4169-5362-3
LC 2008017131
Jordan "offers a colloquial prayer to greet the newborn child, offers advice, and gives reassurance of family love and support as well as God's blessings. . . . Ransome's handsome . . . oil paintings follow an African American child growing from infancy to the start of kindergarten under the watchful eyes of his loving parents. . . . Tenderly portraying a child growing up within a warmhearted family, this appealing picture book clearly expresses the faith, love, and hopes that surround him." Booklist

Piper, Sophie
I can say a prayer; illustrated by Emily Bolam. IPG/Lion 2011 un il $12.99
Grades: PreK 242
1. Prayers
ISBN 978-0-7459-6233-7; 0-7459-6233-5
"This collection of 12 rhyming prayers for the young child is accompanied by simple pen, ink, and watercolor illustrations that are right up preschoolers' alleys. Some of the prayers are original and some are familiar, such as the Lord's Prayer. A few are accompanied by verses from the Bible that serve to introduce that particular prayer. The prayers include familiar preschool concepts like counting, sharing, and making music. The bright, smiley illustrations, meanwhile, depict children going about their everyday activities. . . . This book does its job and does it well." Booklist

Prayers for a better world; [illustrated by] Mique Moriuchi. Lion Children's 2010 63p il $9.99
Grades: 1 2 3 242
1. Prayers 2. Religious poetry
ISBN 978-0-7459-6929-9; 0-7459-6929-1
"This brightly colored little book offers 38 short prayers in verse that reflect on the earth, its animals and plants, and living in harmony with other people and with nature. Most are original . . . while a few of the entries are attributed to other poets. The verses are lyrical and thought-provoking but still accessible to a young audience. . . . Moriuchi's naive artwork illustrates children and the natural world in joyful, colorful, and occasionally playful collages of painted papers." Booklist

Rivett, Rachel
I imagine; a child's book of prayers. illustrated by Mique Moriushi. Lion/Trafalgar 2011 il $12.99
Grades: PreK K 1 242
1. Prayers
ISBN 978-0-7459-6208-5; 0-7459-6208-4
"An unusual, whimsical collection of 12 short prayers offers an imaginative approach with a patterned text and creative responses from the children narrating the prayers. Each prayer follows a similar pattern, describing a particular circumstance or challenge familiar to young children ('if life is stormy'), followed by the child narrator's imagined action ('I imagine I'm a tree, tossed and tumbled in the wind'). In alternating spreads, there is also a comforting response from God ('you show me how my roots are getting stronger'). . . . Moriuchi's pleasing collage illustrations of chubby-cheeked children incorporate textured papers, fabrics and snippets of print along with painted elements. . . . The light, soothing at-mosphere created by the well-matched prayers and illustrations is deceptively simple, effectively conveying powerful images and a strong sense of comfort." Kirkus

Rock, Lois
A **child's** first book of prayers; illustrated by Alison Jay. IPG/Lion 2012 il $12.99
Grades: K 1 2 3 4 242
1. Prayers
ISBN 978-0-7459-4474-6; 0-7459-4474-4
First published 2002 in the United Kingdom
"With its portable size, thick binding, comforting illustrations, and more than 150 prayers, this book is an appealing package. . . . The book's strength is that has something for everyone. The table of contents provides a quick guide, offering chapters like 'This Fragile World' and 'Prayers for Sad Times.' . . . The often attributed prayers, some of which rhyme, run the gamut from aspirational to celebratory to comforting and are uniformly short. . . . Jay's omnipresent soft watercolors add a further peacefulness." Booklist

263   Days, times, places of religious observance

Fisher, Aileen Lucia
The **story** of Easter; by Aileen Fisher; illustrated by Stefano Vitale. HarperCollins Pubs. 1997 un il hardcover o.p. pa $5.95
Grades: 3 4 5 263
1. Easter 2. Jesus Christ 3. Jesus Christ -- Resurrection
ISBN 0-06-027296-1; 0-06-443490-7 pa
LC 96-17395
A newly illustrated edition of Easter published 1968 by Crowell
"This book begins with the story of Jesus' crucifixion and resurrection, but focuses on the origins of various Easter and vernal equinox traditions, with an emphasis on the history of egg decorating. . . . The folk-art illustrations are defined by strong black outlines, simple shapes, and natural colors." Horn Book Guide

264   Public worship

Alexander, Cecil Frances
★ All things bright and beautiful; based on the hymn by Cecil F. Alexander. Atheneum Books for Young Readers 2010 un il $16.99
Grades: PreK K 1 2 3 264
1. Hymns 2. Religious poetry
ISBN 978-1-4169-8939-4; 1-4169-8939-0
LC 2009032628
Bryan "interprets Cecil F. Alexander's 19th century hymn with cut-paper art defined by swirling geometrical shapes in neon hues, contributing to a pervasively jubilant atmosphere. Every spread is a riot of colors, movement, and natural splendors." Publ Wkly

Granfield, Linda
Out of slavery; the journey to Amazing Grace. illustrated by Janet Wilson. Tundra Books 2009 un il map $15.95

Grades: 4 5 6 7　　　　　　　　　　**264**
1. Hymns 2. Clergy 3. Slave trade 4. Amazing grace
(Hymn)
ISBN 978-0-88776-915-3; 0-88776-915-2
　　　　　　　　　　　　　　　LC 2009502001
First published 1997 with title: Amazing Grace
This story of the hymn Amazing Grace "and its writer
is beautifully written, evocative, and heart-wrenching. With
an emphasis on John Newton and his years as a slave trader,
Granfield shares how the events in his life led him to become
an abolitionist, a pastor, and a writer of hymns. . . . Quotations from Newton's own writings are peppered throughout.
Full-color, full-page illustrations add grandeur and appeal to
the story. Rich in texture and color, the artwork is somber in
tone and content." SLJ

266　Missions

Perritano, John
　Spanish missions. Children's Press 2010 48p il map
(True book) lib bdg $35; pa $6.95
Grades: 3 4 5　　　　　　　　　　**266**
1. Franciscans 2. Native Americans 3. Missions 4.
Southwestern States 5. Spaniards -- United States
ISBN 978-0-531-20575-4 lib bdg; 0-531-20575-4 lib
bdg; 978-0-531-21238-7 pa; 0-531-21238-6 pa
　　　　　　　　　　　　　　　LC 2009017742
This "takes a look at the Christianity-fueled Spanish side
of New World colonization. Beginning with a pithy account
that delves into the conquer-and-cash-in strategy of Spanish exploration, it then nicely outlines what missions are . . .
. who built them . . . and why they were built. . . . With an
evenhanded tone, Perritano also touches on important Spanish priests, . . . native revolts, and various missions in what is
now Mexico and the southwestern U.S. . . . The colorful, amply illustrated design make for an accessible read." Booklist
　Includes glossary and bibliographical references

270　History, geographic treatment, biography of Christianity; Church history; Christian denominations and sects

Demi
　The legend of Saint Nicholas. Margaret K. McElderry
Bks. 2003 un il $19.95
Grades: 3 4 5 6　　　　　　　　　　**270**
1. Saints 2. Bishops 3. Santa Claus 4. Christian saints
ISBN 0-689-84681-9
　　　　　　　　　　　　　　　LC 2002-8426
Recounts pivotal events in the history and life of Saint
Nicholas, including how he came to be associated with
Christmas and Santa Claus
　"The gilded paintings are full of absorbing . . . details. . .
. The greatest strength of this book is its straightforward, af-
fectionate depiction of a person who, by his deep love for the
young and the needy, embodies the spirit of Christmas." SLJ

270.1　Historical periods

Sabuda, Robert
　Saint Valentine; retold and illustrated by Robert Sabuda. Atheneum Pubs. 1992 un il $16.95; pa $5.99
Grades: 1 2 3　　　　　　　　　　**270.1**
1. Saints 2. Christian saints
ISBN 0-689-31762-X; 0-689-82429-7 pa
　　　　　　　　　　　　　　　LC 91-25012
Recounts an incident in the life of St. Valentine, a physician who lived some 200 years after Christ, in which he
treated a small child for blindness
　"The fluid, straightforward retelling of the legend is accompanied by evocative, mosaiclike illustrations created
from colored cut paper. Varying sizes of illustrations, careful
page placement, and effective use of white space create the
impression of the large-scale period mosaics. A fine melding
of text and art." SLJ

271　Religious congregations and orders in church history

Kennedy, Robert Francis
　Saint Francis of Assisi; a life of joy. written by Robert F. Kennedy, Jr.; illustrated by Dennis Nolan. Hyperion
Books for Children 2004 31p il $18.99
Grades: 2 3 4　　　　　　　　　　**271**
1. Saints 2. Christian saints 3. Writers on religion
ISBN 0-7868-1875-1
　　　　　　　　　　　　　　　LC 2003-60420
　"The book paints Francis in glowing terms . . . . weaving
together the major threads of his life: his early kindness to
beggars in his family's fabric shop; his call to and ultimate
rejection of a military career; his estrangement from his
wealthy father; and his ministry to lepers, the impoverished,
and animals. . . . Nolan's oil paintings render realistic figures
in carefully staged scenes." SLJ

Norris, Kathleen
　★ The holy twins: Benedict and Scholastica; written
by Kathleen Norris; illustrated by Tomie De Paola. Putnam
2001 un il $16.99
Grades: 3 4 5　　　　　　　　　　**271**
1. Monks 2. Saints 3. Christian saints 4. Writers on
religion
ISBN 0-399-23424-1
　　　　　　　　　　　　　　　LC 00-40294
　"This fictionalized biography of Saints Benedict and
Scholastica, twins who lived in sixth-century Italy, is told in
a lively, authoritative manner. . . . dePaola's elegant, stylized
artwork seems particularly well suited to the eternal quality
of religious subjects. The framed spreads are painted in soft,
warm acrylics on tea-stained watercolor paper, which gives
the semblance of an old manuscript." SLJ

Visconti, Guido
　Clare and Francis; text by Guido Visconti, inspired by
the biographies and written works of the two saints of Assisi
collected in the Franciscan Sources. Eerdmans Books for
Young Readers 2004 un il $20
Grades: 4 5 6 7　　　　　　　　　　**271**
　1. Nuns 2. Saints 3. Christian saints 4. Writers on

religion
ISBN 0-8028-5269-6

LC 2003-13441

Reviews the lives and works of two members of Assisi society, Francis and Clare, who renounced their wealth and founded religious orders dedicated to relying on God and living in peace, poverty, and humility.

"The familiar story of Francis (and to a lesser extent, Clare) is beautifully treated in this book, with luminous iconic artwork and a text that is both down-to-earth and stroking the stars." Booklist

282 Roman Catholic Church

Hawker, Frances

Christianity in Mexico; written by Frances Hawker and Noemi Paz; photography by Bruce Campbell. Crabtree Pub. Co. 2010 32p il (Families and their faiths) lib bdg $26.60; pa $8.95
Grades: 3 4 5   **282**
1. Catholics 2. Mexico
ISBN 978-0-7787-5007-9 lib bdg; 0-7787-5007-8 lib bdg; 978-0-7787-5024-6 pa; 0-7787-5024-8 pa

LC 2009-14157

This "book introduces a child who practices [Christianity]. . . . Provides a solid introduction without overwhelming readers with complex regional variations in practices and beliefs. . . . Words and phrases that are unique to the faith appear in bold font and are defined at greater length in the glossary." SLJ

Includes glossary

282.092 Cardinals (Clergy)

Schmidt, Gary D.

Martin de Porres; the rose in the desert. written by Gary D. Schmidt; illustrated by David Diaz. Clarion Books 2012 32 p. col. ill. (reinforced) $16.99
Grades: 1 2 3   **282.092**
1. Picture books for children 2. Christian saints -- Biography 3. Christian saints -- Peru -- Biography
ISBN 0547612184; 9780547612188

LC 2011025721

Pura Belpré Illustrator Award (2013)

This children's picture book offers a biography of the Catholic saint Martin de Porres. The "illegitimate son of a former slave and a Spanish conquistador in 1579 in Lima, Peru," he "was the first black saint of the Americas." Author Gary Schmidt focuses on the saint's "extreme humility . . . emphasizing his humble servitude and great empathy." (School Library Journal)

289.3 Latter-Day Saints (Mormons)

Bial, Raymond

Nauvoo; Mormon city on the Mississippi River. [by] Raymond Bial. Houghton Mifflin Co. 2006 44p il map $17
Grades: 5 6 7 8   **289.3**
1. Mormons 2. Church of Jesus Christ of Latter-day

Saints 3. Illinois -- History
ISBN 978-0-618-39685-6; 0-618-39685-3

LC 2005027528

"Bial introduces readers to a city that was established by the Church of Jesus Christ of Latter Day Saints in 1839. . . . This effectively written account provides a sympathetic but balanced introduction to Mormon beliefs. . . . Excellent color photographs grace almost every page." SLJ

George, Charles

What makes me a Mormon? by Charles George. KidHaven Press 2004 48p il map (What makes me a--?) $27
Grades: 3 4 5   **289.3**
1. Mormons 2. Church of Jesus Christ of Latter-day Saints
ISBN 978-0-7377-3083-8; 0-7377-3083-8

LC 2004-13636

This describes Morman origins, beliefs, practices, and holidays

"Presenting information about religion objectively for younger audiences poses a difficult challenge, but [this title does] an excellent job of it." Booklist

Includes bibliographical references

289.6 Society of Friends (Quakers)

Woog, Adam

What makes me a Quaker? by Adam Woog. KidHaven Press 2004 48p il (What makes me a--?) $27
Grades: 3 4 5   **289.6**
1. Society of Friends
ISBN 978-0-7377-3082-1; 0-7377-3082-X

LC 2004-13096

This explains Quakerism's origins, beliefs, practices, and future

"Presenting information about religion objectively for younger readers poses a difficult challenge, but [this title does] an excellent job of it." Booklist

Includes glossary and bibliographical references

292 Classical religion (Greek and Roman religion)

Aliki

★ The **gods** and goddesses of Olympus; written and illustrated by Aliki. HarperCollins Pubs. 1994 48p il $16; pa $6.95
Grades: 2 3 4 5   **292**
1. Classical mythology
ISBN 0-06-023530-6; 0-06-446189-0 pa

LC 93-17834

"This large-format book provides a quick, brightly illustrated introduction to the ancient Greek gods and goddesses." Booklist

"After the Uranus-Gaea, Cronus-Rhea background is sketched, the occupants of the 12 golden thrones are each described, along with Hades (underground), Hestia (hearthbound) and Eros (hovering). The author outlines the deities' characters and attributes, sometimes including a brief incident from their lives." SLJ

Bryant, Megan E.

Oh my gods! a look-it-up guide to the gods of mythology. Franklin Watts 2009 128p il map (Mythlopedia) lib bdg $39; pa $13.95

Grades: 4 5 6 7   292

1. Gods and goddesses 2. Classical mythology
ISBN 978-1-60631-026-7 lib bdg; 1-60631-026-7 lib bdg; 978-1-60631-058-8 pa; 1-60631-058-5 pa
LC 2009-17169

Presents a guide to Greek mythology, providing profiles of gods and goddesses along with information on monsters, heroes, and the underworld.

"The book is organized around entries on major gods and titans, each with vital stats and a Top 10 Things to Know about Me, followed by a few highlights from their lore and sidebars that delve into their cultural relevance. Illustrations abound, from embellished stock images to original cartoons, and the pastel-heavy color scheme may entice readers otherwise resistant to the grays and ivories that tend to dominate classicism." Booklist

Includes glossary and bibliographical references

She's all that! a look-it-up guide to the goddesses of mythology. Franklin Watts 2009 128p il map (Mythlopedia) lib bdg $39; pa $13.95

Grades: 4 5 6 7   292

1. Gods and goddesses 2. Classical mythology
ISBN 978-1-60631-027-4 lib bdg; 1-60631-027-5 lib bdg; 978-1-60631-059-5 pa; 1-60631-059-3 pa
LC 2009-17168

Presents a guide to Greek mythology, providing profiles of goddesses and the myths surrounding them.

This "spices things up with sassy artwork, a pastel color scheme, and an OMG sensibility. . . . Aside from the heaps of information coming from all angles on just about every page, . . . [this] book also contains a decent family tree, a rudimentary star chart, and lists of further reading. . . . For kids unconvinced that anything so old and gray could have any bearing on their lives, . . . [this provides] a feisty . . . guide to the many cultural references lingering from antiquity." Booklist

Includes glossary and bibliographical references

Clayton, Sally Pomme

Greek myths; stories of sun, stone, and sea. Sally Pomme Clayton; illustrated by Jan Ray. Frances Lincoln Children's Books 2012 77 p. $19.99

Grades: 2 3 4   292

1. Greek mythology
ISBN 1847802273; 9781847802279

This children's book by Sally Pomme Clayton presents a "collection of Greek myths with special emphasis on adventure and heroic quests. The ten stories include: Creation of the Gods, Pandora's Box, Atalanta, Perseus, Pegasus and Bellerophon, King Midas and the Gift of Gold, King Midas and the Donkey's Ears, How Arachne Became a Spider." (Publisher's note)

★ Persephone; a journey from winter to spring. by Sally Pomme Clayton; illustrated by Virginia Lee. Eerdmans Books for Young Readers 2009 un il $18

Grades: 2 3 4   292

1. Persephone (Greek deity)
ISBN 0-8028-5349-8; 978-0-8028-5349-3
LC 2008018391

"Approaching the Greek myth of Persephone with the respect that a good storyteller holds for a great story, Clayton retells the tale with drama and grace. The mixed-media artwork creates a series of scenes defined by sweeping lines, broad views, and restrained use of color." Booklist

Curlee, Lynn

Mythological creatures; a classical bestiary: tales of strange beings, fabulous creatures, fearsome beasts, & hideous monsters from ancient Greek mythology. Atheneum Books for Young Readers 2008 35p il $17.99

Grades: 3 4 5   292

1. Mythical animals 2. Classical mythology
ISBN 978-1-4169-1453-2; 1-4169-1453-6
LC 2006-16980

"A preponderance of these sixteen fabulous beasts are half human (or, like Pan, minor deities). Most are monstrous in behavior as well as body; only the purely animal Pegasus and Phoenix possess some sort of nobility. Confining each within a broad, sober border, Curlee depicts all as classically statuesque. . . . Staightforward and clean, the accompanying text outlines without dramatization what these mythical beings were and their role in Greek lore. . . . The book is an eye-catching introduction to the world of ancient myth." Horn Book

Karas, G. Brian

★ Young Zeus. Scholastic Press 2010 un il $17.99

Grades: 2 3 4 5   292

1. Classical mythology 2. Zeus (Greek deity)
ISBN 978-0-439-72806-5; 0-439-72806-1
LC 2009-10148

Karas "opens this spirited embellishment of Zeus's little-documented boyhood with an author's note explaining that he drew form early accounts of the Greek gods and 'true to the nature of myths, imagined the rest.' . . . But Kara's imagination serves him well in making Zeus a relatable character. . . . Droll dialogue and asides mitigate the tale's dark undertones [and] . . . energetic, airy gouache and pencil cartoons playfully skew scale and also keep the tone light." Publ Wkly

Kimmel, Eric A.

★ The McElderry book of Greek myths; [by] Eric A. Kimmel; illustrated by Pep Montserrat. M.K. McElderry Books 2008 96p il $21.99

Grades: K 1 2 3   292

1. Classical mythology
ISBN 1-4169-1534-6; 978-1-4169-1534-8
LC 2005031010

In this collection of retellings of Greek myths "Kimmel uses spare, direct language and lots of exciting action. . . . Montserrat's stylish computer-generated artwork picks up on ancient Greek design motifs and creates memorable characters from the mythical archetypes." Booklist

Lupton, Hugh

The adventures of Odysseus; [by] Hugh Lupton and Daniel Morden; [illustrated by] Christina Balit. Barefoot Books 2006 un il $19.99

Grades: 3 4 5 6   **292**
1. Classical mythology 2. Odysseus (Greek mythology)
ISBN 1-84148-800-3

LC 2005032532

This "book retells Homer's epic of Odysseus' perilous journey home in a immediate, fast-paced narrative. . . . The text is beautifully framed with crisp, brightly colored, mosaic-style illustrations of the heroes and monsters, rendered in watercolor, gouache, and gold ink." Booklist

Mayer, Marianna
★ **Pegasus**; as told by Marianna Mayer; illustrated by K. Y. Craft. Morrow Junior Bks. 1998 un il $17.99
Grades: 4 5 6   **292**
1. Classical mythology 2. Pegasus (Greek mythology)
ISBN 0-688-13382-7; 0-688-13383-5 lib bdg

LC 96-32442

Retells how Bellerophon, son of the King of Corinth, secures the help of the winged horse Pegasus in order to fight the monstrous Chimera

"Dark, painterly illustrations set in gold frames heighten the mysticism in this lyrical interpretation of the Greek myth." Horn Book Guide

McCaughrean, Geraldine
★ **Hercules**; retold by Geraldine McCaughrean. Cricket Books 2005 142p il (Heroes) $16.95
Grades: 5 6 7 8   **292**
1. Classical mythology 2. Hercules (Legendary character)
ISBN 978-0-8126-2737-4; 0-8126-2737-7

LC 2005004524

First published 2003 by Oxford University Press

This is a retelling of the twelve labors of Hercules including his battles with the Cretan Bull, the many-headed Hydra, the Nemean Lion, and the three-headed guardian of hell, Cerberus.

"This volume does a creditable job of making Hercules a dimensional character whose struggles against fate and the vindictiveness of the gods arouse readers' sympathy. . . McCaughrean enlivens the familiar story with arresting imagery." SLJ

★ **Odysseus**; retold by Geraldine McCaughrean. Cricket Books 2004 148p il (Heroes) $16.95
Grades: 5 6 7 8   **292**
1. Classical mythology 2. Odysseus (Greek mythology)
ISBN 978-0-8126-2721-3; 0-8126-2721-0

LC 2004-10734

"With mounting suspense, wild action, and simple, rhythmic prose, this dramatic retelling of Homer's classic makes a gripping read-aloud as well as an exciting introduction to the story." Booklist

★ **Perseus**; retold by Geraldine McCaughrean. Cricket Books 2005 118p il (Heroes) $16.95
Grades: 5 6 7 8   **292**
1. Classical mythology 2. Perseus (Greek mythology)
ISBN 978-0-8126-2735-0; 0-8126-2735-0

This "makes a thrilling read-aloud. . . . McCaughrean blends the colloquial and contemporary into the heroic quest." Booklist

This follows the story of "Perseus as he lives the fate the oracles have declared, an impossible quest to kill the hideous, snake-haired Medusa to save his mother from marriage to an evil king." Publisher's note

Osborne, Mary Pope
Favorite Greek myths; retold by Mary Pope Osborne; illustrated by Troy Howell. Scholastic 1989 81p il lib bdg $18.95
Grades: 3 4 5 6   **292**
1. Classical mythology
ISBN 0-590-41338-4

LC 87-32332

Retells twelve tales from Greek mythology, including the stories of King Midas, Echo and Narcissus, the Golden Apples, and Cupid and Psyche

"Osborne's retellings are both lively and descriptive, while Howell's full-color, often iridescent illustrations set the scene and mood at the start of each tale." Publ Wkly

Includes glossary and bibliographical references

Otfinoski, Steven
All in the family; a look-it-up guide to the in-laws, outlaws, and offspring of mythology. F. Watts 2009 128p il (Mythlopedia) lib bdg $39; pa $13.95
Grades: 4 5 6 7   **292**
1. Classical mythology
ISBN 978-1-60631-025-0 lib bdg; 1-60631-025-9 lib bdg; 978-1-60631-057-1 pa; 1-60631-057-7 pa

LC 2009-20999

"Jam-packed with trivia, brief profiles, god and goddess relationships, stories, 'Top 10 Things to Know About Me' facts, and entertaining illustrations, this title explores 20 heroes and mortals of classic Greek mythology. The selections include the well-known Achilles, Heracles, Odysseus, and Pandora and the more obscure Meleager, Orion, Atalanta, and Bellerophon; each one is given lively treatment. . . . The lighthearted style and humorous collage and cartoon illustrations may draw even the most reluctant of readers. " SLJ

Includes glossary and bibliographical references

Rylant, Cynthia
The beautiful stories of life; six Greek myths, retold. illustrated by Carson Ellis. Harcourt 2009 71p il $16
Grades: 5 6 7 8   **292**
1. Classical mythology
ISBN 978-0-15-206184-5; 0-15-206184-3

LC 2007-34808

"Rylant retells the stories of Pandora, Persephone, Orpheus, Pygmalion, Narcissus, and Psyche in this trim, handsome book. Written in a modern style with an old-fashioned feel, the selections sit well with other titles in the genre. . . . Accompanied by full-page black-and-white illustrations and sprinkled with decorations, the whole package is nicely done." SLJ

Steer, Dugald
The mythology handbook; a course in ancient Greek myths. by Hestia Evans; edited by Dugald A. Steer and Clint Twist. Candlewick Press 2009 71p il map $12.99
Grades: 4 5 6 7   **292**
1. Classical mythology
ISBN 978-0-7636-4291-4

"This follow-up to Mythology (Candlewick, 2007) again uses the voice of a fictional 19th-century scholar. Here, Lady Hestia Evans offers a guide to elements of Greek myth for her two children, providing information in 'lessons' ... with exercises based on each topic. Some of the activities encourage students to do further research ... while others suggest that they draw new monsters, write hymns with the Muses' help, or design a new pentathlon for the Olympics. Mazes and a word search (using Greek letters) are also included.... The activities are engaging, and the illustrations of creatures and maps of the ancient world will add to the knowledge of even more experienced myth fans." SLJ

Townsend, Michael
Michael Townsend's amazing Greek myths of wonder and blunders. Dial Books for Young Readers 2010 160p il $14.99
Grades: 4 5 6 7   292
1. Greek mythology -- Graphic novels 2. Graphic novels 3. Mythology, Greek
ISBN 978-0-8037-3308-4; 0-8037-3308-9
"Ten familiar myths—the stories of Pandora, Arachne, Midas, Perseus, and others—are embellished with humor, the gory parts glossed over, and served up in blazing color for fans of either comic books or Percy Jackson, or both. ... Conversational, up-to-date language and broad jokes help to make the stories accessible and coordinate well with the simple, cartoon illustration style." SLJ

Turnbull, Ann
★ Greek myths; retold by Ann Turnbull; illustrated by Sarah Young. Candlewick Press 2011 165p il
Grades: 5 6 7 8 9 10   292
1. Classical mythology 2. Mythology, Greek
ISBN 0-7636-5111-7; 978-0-7636-5111-4
                                          LC 2010-39178
Turnbull divides sixteen Greek myths "under three headings: Earth, the Heavens, and the Underworld; Monsters and Heroes; Gods and Mortals. . . . Grades five to ten." (Bull Cent Child Books)
"Sixteen Greek myths . . . are retold here with stylistic grace well matched to beautiful visual presentation. . . . Turnbull narrates with . . . vibrancy. . . . Sarah Young's mixed-media artwork—regal, yet sensuous compositions in richly textured earthtones touch[ed] with gold—is sufficiently representational to assist younger readers with context clues, and sufficiently elegant and sophisticated to satisfy seasoned readers." Bull Cent Child Books

292.1 Specific elements

Craft, Marie
★ Cupid and Psyche; as told by M. Charlotte Craft; illustrated by K. Y. Craft. Morrow Junior Bks. 1996 un il $16
Grades: 4 5 6 7   292.1
1. Classical mythology 2. Eros (Greek deity) 3. Psyche (Greek deity)
ISBN 0-688-13163-8
                                          LC 95-14895
"In this Greek myth, Cupid falls in love with Psyche and treats her royally but does not reveal himself. When Psyche tries to discover his identity, Cupid leaves her, but she wins him back by accomplishing three difficult tasks. Recalling an earlier artistic era, the occasionally ornate romantic

paintings—some of them quite dramatic—feature detailed landscapes and beautiful figures in flowing drapery." Horn Book Guide

293 Germanic religion

Fisher, Leonard Everett
Gods and goddesses of the ancient Norse. Holiday House 2001 un il $16.95
Grades: 3 4 5 6   293
1. Norse mythology
ISBN 0-8234-1569-4
                                          LC 00-32040
In this guide each "double-page spread is devoted to one or two of the major gods or goddesses, accompanied by a succinct description that includes significant characteristics and responsibilities. A pronunciation guide and family tree are appended." Horn Book Guide
Includes bibliographical references

Lunge-Larsen, Lise
The adventures of Thor the Thunder God; retold by Lise Lunge-Larsen; illustrated by Jim Madsen. Houghton Mifflin 2007 76p il $19.95
Grades: 3 4 5 6   293
1. Norse mythology
ISBN 0-618-47301-7; 978-0-618-47301-4
                                          LC 2004015765
"Madsen's . . . majestic digitally rendered illustrations bring the tales to life, echoing their humor. . . . These retellings offer an accessible and engaging doorway into the world of Norse mythology." Publ Wkly

294 Religions of Indic origin

Ollhoff, Jim
Indian mythology. ABDO Pub. 2012 32 p. il map (The world of mythology) lib bdg $27.07
Grades: 5 6 7 8   294
1. Hinduism 2. Indic mythology 3. India -- Religion
ISBN 978-1-61714-722-7; 1-61714-722-2
                                          LC 2010041628
'This book offers information about Indian mythology, answering questions such as "Who is Devi? What is Ganesha? Why are myths so important in our lives? Myths are a rich source of history. People use them to make sense of our world. Even before myths were written down, people told and retold the stories of the gods and goddesses of their homeland. Readers of Indian Mythology will learn the history of myths, as well as their deeper meaning." (Publisher's note) The book "introduces Brahma, Vishnu, Shiva, Kali, and other Hindu gods and goddesses while also discussing how the deities often took on different forms called avatars." (Booklist)
"Ollhoff writes in a clear and engaging fashion, presenting complex issues in a way that will be easy for youngsters to grasp. . . . The photographs and reproductions of art tie directly to the [text]." SLJ

294.3 Buddhism

Chodzin, Sherab

The **wisdom** of the crows and other Buddhist tales; retold by Sherab Chödzin & Alexandra Kohn; illustrated by Marie Cameron. Tricycle Press 1998 80p il pa $16.95

Grades: 4 5 6 7 **294.3**

1. Buddhism

ISBN 1-883672-68-6

LC 97-30441

First published 1997 in the United Kingdom with title: The Barefoot book of Buddhist tales

A collection of thirteen retold Buddhist tales from all over Asia, illustrating various aspects of Buddhist thought

"Folktale lovers will find much to like here. Marie Cameron's clear, fresh watercolors, incorporating Asian artistic motifs and bordered with waves and origami, are handsomely rendered." Booklist

Includes bibliographical references

Demi

★ **Buddha**. Holt & Co. 1996 un il $21.95

Grades: 4 5 6 **294.3**

1. Philosophers 2. Buddhist leaders

ISBN 0-8050-4203-2

LC 95-16906

Demi "uses clear, uncomplicated storytelling to present complex philosophical concepts. . . . The gilded illustrations (based, according to the jacket, on 'Indian, Chinese, Japanese, Burmese, and Indonesian paintings, sculptures, and sutra illustrations') are delicate, yet the colors and composition are bold, with central figures and action cascading beyond the careful borders." Bull Cent Child Books

Buddha stories. Holt & Co. 1997 un il $21.95

Grades: 3 4 5 6 **294.3**

1. Jataka stories

ISBN 0-8050-4886-3

LC 96-31253

This "is a picture-book collection of eleven Jataka tales retold in a formal yet straightforward style. . . . An author's note gives the source of the tales as well as the historical basis for the design concept behind the elegantly sophisticated artwork. Both text and illustrations are done in gold ink on deep indigo paper, resulting in a striking visual impact." Bull Cent Child Books

Ganeri, Anita

★ **Buddhism**; [by] Anita Ganeri. World Almanac Library 2006 48p il map (Religions of the world) lib bdg $30.60

Grades: 5 6 7 8 **294.3**

1. Buddhism

ISBN 0-8368-5865-4

LC 2005041708

The author "presents a survey of Buddhist history, beliefs, sacred texts, festivals, and lifecycle events. . . . There is discussion of the art and folk literature associated with the religious tradition. Colorful photographs, illustrations, and art reproductions appear throughout." SLJ

Includes bibliographical references

George, Charles

What makes me a Buddhist? by Charles George. KidHaven Press 2004 48p il (What makes me a--?) $23.70

Grades: 3 4 5 **294.3**

1. Buddhism

ISBN 0-7377-2269-X

LC 2003-24344

This describes the beliefs, origins, practices, holidays and future of Buddhism.

"An attractive, colorful design is the background for a map and numerous color photographs and diagrams. But best of all is the straightforward organization and the clarity of the text." Booklist

Includes bibliographical references

Hawker, Frances

Buddhism in Thailand; written by Frances Hawker and Sunantha Phusomsai; photography by Bruce Campbell. Crabtree Pub. Co. 2009 32p il map (Families and their faiths) lib bdg $26.60; pa $8.95

Grades: 3 4 5 **294.3**

1. Buddhism 2. Thailand

ISBN 978-0-7787-5006-2 lib bdg; 0-7787-5006-X lib bdg; 978-0-7787-5023-9 pa; 0-7787-5023-X pa

LC 2009-14156

This "book introduces a child who practices [Buddhism]. . . . Provides a solid introduction without overwhelming readers with complex regional variations in practices and beliefs. . . . Words and phrases that are unique to the faith appear in bold font and are defined at greater length in the glossary." SLJ

Includes glossary

Nardo, Don

Buddhism. Compass Point Books 2009 48p il map (World religions) lib bdg $27.99

Grades: 5 6 7 8 **294.3**

1. Buddhism

ISBN 978-0-7565-4236-8 lib bdg; 0-7565-4236-7 lib bdg

LC 2009-11453

"The colorful, attractive layout includes high-quality reproductions of photographs, maps, and paintings. Students who are new to religious studies, as well as those doing reports, will find that this . . . meets their needs." SLJ

Includes glossary and bibliographical references

294.5 Hinduism

Ganeri, Anita

The **Ramayana** and Hinduism. Smart Apple Media 2003 30p il (Sacred texts) $27.10

Grades: 5 6 7 8 9 **294.5**

1. Hinduism

ISBN 1-58340-242-X

LC 2003-42352

Explains the history and practices of the religion of Hinduism, especially as revealed through its sacred book, the Ramayana

George, Charles

What makes me a Hindu? by Charles George. Kid-Haven Press 2004 48p il map (What makes me a--?) $27
Grades: 3 4 5   **294.5**
1. Hinduism
ISBN 978-0-7377-2267-3; 0-7377-2267-3
LC 2003-24346
This describes Hindu origins, beliefs, practices, and holidays
"Presenting information about religion objectively for younger audiences poses a difficult challenge, but [this title does] an excellent job of it." Booklist
Includes bibliographical references

Hawker, Frances

Hinduism in Bali; written by Frances Hawker and Putu Resi; photography by Bruce Campbell. Crabtree Pub. Company 2009 32p il (Families and their faiths) lib bdg $26.60; pa $8.95
Grades: 3 4 5   **294.5**
1. Hinduism 2. Indonesia 3. Bali Island (Indonesia)
ISBN 978-0-7787-5008-6 lib bdg; 0-7787-5008-6 lib bdg; 978-0-7787-5008-6 pa; 0-7787-5008-6 pa
LC 2009-14297
This "book introduces a child who practices [Hinduism]. . . . Provides a solid introduction without overwhelming readers with complex regional variations in practices and beliefs. . . . Words and phrases that are unique to the faith appear in bold font and are defined at greater length in the glossary," SLJ
Includes glossary

Heiligman, Deborah

★ Celebrate Diwali; [by] Deborah Heiligman; consultant, Dr. Vasudha Narayanan. National Geographic 2006 32p il map (Holidays around the world) $15.95; lib bdg $23.90
Grades: K 1 2 3   **294.5**
1. Divali
ISBN 0-7922-5922-X; 0-7922-5923-8 lib bdg
LC 2006003426
This "focuses on the Hindu celebration in India but mentions observance by the Sikh and Jain faiths and also show customs in four other countries. . . . Each spread features up to three high-quality color photographs." SLJ

Jani, Mahendra

What you will see inside a Hindu temple; [by] Mahendra Jani and Vandana Jani; with photographs by Neirah Bhargava and Vijay Dave. Skylight Paths 2005 32p il (What you will see inside) $17.99
Grades: 3 4 5 6   **294.5**
1. Hinduism
ISBN 978-1-59473-116-7; 1-59473-116-0
"This introduces the beliefs and practices of the Hindu religion. The book opens with a traditional Sanskrit word of greeting . . . setting the respectful, inviting tone of the text, which leads readers into a temple. The book explains what can be seen there and discusses Hindu beliefs, worship practices, scriptures, celebrations, blessing ceremonies, and family shrines in homes. A typical double-page spread includes one large color photograph and a few small ones illustrating several paragraphs of clear, concise text." Booklist

Plum-Ucci, Carol

Celebrate Diwali; [by] Carol Plum-Ucci. Enslow Publishers 2008 128p il map (Celebrate holidays) $31.93
Grades: 5 6 7 8   **294.5**
1. Divali
ISBN 978-0-7660-2778-7; 0-7660-2778-3
LC 2006028106
This describes the history, cultural significance, customs, symbols and celebrations around the world of the Hindu holiday of Diwali.
"Captioned photographs, maps, drawings, and sidebars combine with accessible text to present a thorough discussion of [Diwali]. . . . This . . . is a useful resource." Horn Book Guide
Includes glossary and bibliographical references

Rasamandala Das

★ Hinduism. World Almanac Library 2006 48p il map (Religions of the world) $30.60
Grades: 5 6 7 8   **294.5**
1. Hinduism
ISBN 0-8368-5867-0
Hinduism is "explored in an accessible introductory manner, including information on [its] history, teachings, religious practices, culture and lifestyle, and the [faith's role] in today's global society. Vibrant full-color photographs are appropriately placed within the [text]. Ideal for . . . school reports or for general interest." SLJ
Includes bibliographical references

294.6 Sikhism

Hawker, Frances

Sikhism in India; written by Frances Hawker and Mohini Kaur Bhatia; photography by Bruce Campbell. Crabtree Pub. Company 2009 32p il (Families and their faiths) lib bdg $26.60; pa $8.95
Grades: 3 4 5   **294.6**
1. Sikhs 2. Sikhism 3. India
ISBN 978-0-7787-5011-6 lib bdg; 0-7787-5011-6 lib bdg; 978-0-7787-5028-4 pa; 0-7787-5028-0 pa
LC 2009-14160
This "book introduces a child who practices [Sikhism]. . . . Provides a solid introduction without overwhelming readers with complex regional variations in practices and beliefs. . . . Words and phrases that are unique to the faith appear in bold font and are defined at greater length in the glossary." SLJ
Includes glossary

296 Judaism

Hawker, Frances

Judaism in Israel; written by Frances Hawker and Daniel Taub; photography by Bruce Campbell. Crabtree Pub. 2010 32p il (Families and their faiths) lib bdg $26.60; pa $8.95

Grades: 3 4 5 **296**

   1. Judaism 2. Israel

   ISBN 978-0-7787-5010-9 lib bdg; 0-7787-5010-8 lib bdg; 978-0-7787-5027-7 pa; 0-7787-5027-2 pa

                       LC 2009-14159

This "book introduces a child who practices [Judaism]... Provides a solid introduction without overwhelming readers with complex regional variations in practices and beliefs.... Words and phrases that are unique to the faith appear in bold font and are defined at greater length in the glossary." SLJ

Includes glossary

Keene, Michael

   ★ **Judaism**; [by] Michael Keene. World Almanac Library 2006 48p il map (Religions of the world) lib bdg $30.60

Grades: 5 6 7 8 **296**

   1. Judaism

   ISBN 0-8368-5869-7

                       LC 2005041734

This "volume presents fundamental beliefs and faith foundations, current status and practices of [Judaism] around the globe, and a time line of historically significant events.... The [book is] enumerated with full-color photographs on every page, charts, maps, and tables.... [This title] will enhance the education of diverse populations." SLJ

Includes bibliographical references

Rosinsky, Natalie M.

   Judaism. Compass Point Books 2009 48p il map (World religions) lib bdg $27.99

Grades: 5 6 7 8 **296**

   1. Judaism

   ISBN 978-0-7565-4240-5 lib bdg; 0-7565-4240-5 lib bdg

                       LC 2009-15813

"The colorful, attractive layout includes high-quality reproductions of photographs, maps, and paintings. Students who are new to religious studies, as well as those doing reports, will find that this... meets their needs." SLJ

Includes glossary and bibliographical references

296.1 Sources

Chaikin, Miriam

   Angels sweep the desert floor; Bible legends about Moses in the wilderness. illustrated by Alexander Koshkin. Clarion Bks. 2002 102p il $19

Grades: 4 5 6 7 **296.1**

   1. Prophets 2. Bible stories 3. Jewish legends 4. Angels -- Fiction 5. Biblical characters

   ISBN 0-395-97825-4

                       LC 2001-47501

A collection of eighteen stories based on the Bible which tell how angels respond to God's commands to ease the way for Moses and the Israelites as they cross the wilderness after being freed from slavery in Egypt

"The full-page watercolor, tempera, and gouache illustrations have a fanciful formality that complements the narrative. Capable of exciting the creative, as well as the spiritual imagination, these wonderful stories make great read-alouds." SLJ

Includes bibliographical references

Heiman, Diane

   It's a-- it's a-- it's a mitzvah! Diane Heiman and Liz Suneby; Illustrations by Laurel Molk. Jewish Lights Publishing 2012 32 p. $18.99

Grades: PreK K 1 2 **296.1**

   1. Judaism 2. Kindness 3. Judaism -- Customs and practices 4. Commandments (Judaism)

   ISBN 1580235093; 9781580235099

                       LC 2012003703

This book by Liz Suneby and Diane Heiman, illustrated by Laurel Molk, is an "introduction to the joys of doing mitzvoth. Join Mitzvah Meerkat and friends as they introduce children to the everyday kindnesses that mark the beginning of ... a lifetime commitment to 'tikkun olam' (repairing the world).... Children engage with Jewish wisdom as they share in welcoming new friends, forgiving mistakes, respecting elders, sharing food with the hungry, and much, much more." (Publisher's note)

Pinsker, Marlee

   In the days of sand and stars; illustrated by Francois Thisdale. Tundra Books 2006 87p il $22.95

Grades: 5 6 7 8 **296.1**

   1. Bible stories 2. Jewish legends 3. Women in the Bible

   ISBN 978-0-88776-724-1; 0-88776-724-9

This is a collection of stories from the Midrash about women including Eve, Naamah, Sarai, Sarah, Rebecca, Leah, Rachel, Dina, and Yocheved.

"Pinsker works like a musician, playing with words instead of notes, but the result is just as lilting and lyrical. The stories are matched by unusual illustrations. Thisdale blends traditional artwork with digital technology. Pieces of photographs mix with ancient elements, giving the pictures a fresh, compelling look." Booklist

296.4 Traditions, rites, public services

Balsley, Tilda

   Maccabee! the story of Hanukkah. illustrated by David Harrington. Kar-Ben Pub. 2010 un il lib bdg $17.95; pa $7.95

Grades: K 1 2 3 **296.4**

   1. Hanukkah 2. Stories in rhyme

   ISBN 978-0-7613-4507-7 lib bdg; 0-7613-4507-8 lib bdg; 978-0-7613-4508-4 pa; 0-7613-4508-6 pa

                       LC 2009001877

Judah and his small army of Maccabees fight to free Jerusalem from the cruel King Antiochus in this rhyming version of the Hanukkah story.

"Balsley's rhythmic narration includes basic characterization and dialogue for the key players to make the story come alive. Bold opaque paintings of brave, bearded men with flowing hair... provide a cinematic view of this legend of heroism and determination." Kirkus

Bernhard, Durga Yael

Around the world in one Shabbat; Jewish people celebrate the Sabbath together. [by] Durga Yael Bernhard. Jewish Lights Pub. 2011 32p il $18.99

Grades: K 1 2 3   **296.4**

1. Jews 2. Sabbath

ISBN 978-1-58023-433-7; 1-58023-433-X

LC 2010041803

"Bernhard uses a global, child-centric approach to explore traditions and rituals that accompany the Sabbath. Each spread tells the story of a different child; in Buenos Aires, Alicia awakens from a nap and helps her sister braid challah, while in Istanbul Leyla joins her brother and parents around the table. . . . As Bernhard moves from France and Canada to Ethiopia and Thailand, warm, genial paintings add to an overall sense of serenity and community. The lyricism of the vignettes belies just how much information Bernhard packs into the book—it's an excellent resource." Publ Wkly

Chaikin, Miriam

★ **Menorahs,** mezuzas, and other Jewish symbols; illustrated by Erika Weihs. Clarion Bks. 1990 102p il $17; pa $5.95

Grades: 5 6 7 8   **296.4**

1. Jewish art and symbolism 2. Judaism -- Customs and practices

ISBN 0-89919-856-2; 0-618-37835-9 pa

LC 89-77719

Explains the history and significance of many Jewish symbols, such as the Shield of David, the menorah, and the mezuza, and discusses holiday symbols and rituals

"Embellished with bibliographical references as well as Weihs' simple yet elegant and wonderfully dramatic scratchboard illustrations, this smoothly woven patchwork of history and culture is a fine introduction that will attract browsers and be useful for children investigating the subject of symbolism in school." Booklist

Cooper, Ilene

★ **Jewish** holidays all year round; a family treasury. written by Ilene Cooper; illustrations by Elivia Savadier; captions by Josh Feinberg; in association with the Jewish Museum, New York. Abrams 2002 80p il $19.95

Grades: 4 5 6 7   **296.4**

1. Handicraft 2. Jewish cooking 3. Jewish holidays

ISBN 0-8109-0550-7

LC 2001-56741

As the author "explores the history and significance of the holidays and festivals of the Jewish year, she . . . links these to traditions and rituals. . . . Instructions for holiday activities (crafts, recipes, etc.) are also included. . . . Savadier's vignettes, mostly of busy, happy people, underscore the liveliness of Jewish faith." Publ Wkly

Includes bibliographical references

Had gadya; a Passover song. paintings by Seymour Chwast; afterword by Michael Strassfeld. Roaring Brook Press 2005 un il $16.95; pa $7.95

Grades: K 1 2 3   **296.4**

1. Songs 2. Passover

ISBN 1-59643-033-8; 1-59643-298-5 pa

LC 2003-17831

"The bright, acrylic folk-art paintings express the rhythm of the chant. . . . The book, complete with musical notation and Hebrew and English words, is bound to add to the pleasure of the seder." Booklist

This is an illustrated version of "a folk song often sung at the end of the Passover Seder. [It] tells a cumulative story that begins with a man's purchase of a goat. In the tradition of chain folk stories, the cat eats the goat, the dog chases the cat, the stick beats the dog, and so on. . . . The Angel of Death appears, but then God comes and destroys the Angel of Death." Bull Cent Child Books

Hanft, Josh

The **miracles** of Passover; [by] Josh Hanft; illustrated by Seymour Chwast. Blue Apple Books 2007 un il $15.95

Grades: PreK K 1 2   **296.4**

1. Passover

ISBN 978-1-59354-600-7; 1-59354-600-9

LC 2006031585

"The story of Moses, Pharaoh, the 10 plagues, and the crossing of the Red Sea is explained in child-friendly language with additional information included about the traditions of the Seder. What distinguishes this book from others of its kind is the overall excellence of the colorful artwork." SLJ

Heiligman, Deborah

★ **Celebrate** Hanukkah; [by] Deborah Heiligman; consultant, Shira Stern. National Geographic 2006 32p il (Holidays around the world) $15.95; lib bdg $23.90

Grades: K 1 2 3   **296.4**

1. Hanukkah

ISBN 0-7922-5924-6; 0-7922-5925-4 lib bdg

LC 2005032427

This "introduces children to the Jewish Festival of Lights. Heiligman recounts the holiday's history and origins and describes how it is celebrated today. . . . The main text is succinct and appropriate for reading aloud. . . . Decorating the pages are sumerous crisp, full-color photos." Booklist

Includes glossary and bibliographical references

★ **Celebrate** Passover; [by] Deborah Heiligman. National Geographic 2007 32p il (Holidays around the world) $15.95; lib bdg $23.90

Grades: K 1 2 3   **296.4**

1. Passover

ISBN 978-1-4263-0018-9; 978-1-4263-00196 lib bdg

LC 2006020676

This "begins with a short recitation of the Passover story and then moves directly into how the holiday is celebrated. . . . A concluding essay by a rabbi offers thoughts on the meaning of the holiday. The clean format evokes the spring holiday, but the book's visual emphasis is also on Jewish communities in Africa, Asia, the Middle East, and elsewhere." Booklist

Includes bibliographical references

★ **Celebrate** Rosh Hashanah and Yom Kippur; [by] Deborah Heiligman; consultant, Shira Stern. National Geographic 2007 31p il (Holidays around the world) $15.95; lib bdg $23.90

Grades: K 1 2 3   **296.4**
1. Yom Kippur 2. Rosh ha-Shanah
ISBN 978-1-4263-0076-9; 978-1-4263-0077-6 lib bdg
LC 2006100317

"Lush color photographs show the diversity of the celebrants and bring an immediacy to these observances. Clear, simple [text provides] history and background information, descriptions of customs, and basic analyses of each celebration's deeper meaning. . . . Exemplary back matter includes quick facts and extra information to provide context. There is even a map showing where all of the fascinating photos were taken." SLJ

Includes glossary and bibliographical references

Heller, Esther Susan
   Menorah under the sea; photographs by David Ginsburg. Kar-Ben Pub. 2009 29p il lib bdg $17.95
Grades: K 1 2 3   **296.4**
1. Hanukkah 2. Marine biology 3. Antarctica
ISBN 978-0-8225-7386-9 lib bdg; 0-8225-7386-5
lib bdg
LC 2007043175

Describes how, while studying sea urchins in Antarctica, marine biologist David Ginsburg celebrated Hanukkah by creating his own menorah on the sea floor

"The vibrant color photography and surprising thematic juxtaposition—readers will learn as much about urchins as about the holiday—makes this a memorable selection, even for readers who don't celebrate Hanukkah." Publ Wkly

Hoffman, Lawrence A.
   What you will see inside a synagogue; [by] Lawrence Hoffman and Ron Wolfson; with photographs by Bill Aron. SkyLight Paths 2004 31p il (What you will see inside--) $17.99
Grades: 3 4 5 6   **296.4**
1. Judaism
ISBN 1-59473-012-1
LC 2004-11178

"This book provides a warm and thorough welcome to the center of Jewish life. . . . Numerous clear color photos and pronunciation guides for Hebrew words are included. . . . An excellent overview." SLJ

Kimmel, Eric A.
   The **Chanukkah** guest; illustrated by Giora Carmi. Holiday House 1990 un il $15.95; pa $6.95
Grades: K 1 2 3   **296.4**
1. Jews -- Fiction 2. Bears -- Fiction 3. Hanukkah
-- Fiction
ISBN 0-8234-0788-8; 0-8234-0978-3 pa
LC 89-20073

On the first night of Chanukkah, Old Bear wanders into Bubba Brayna's house and receives a delicious helping of potato latkes when she mistakes him for the rabbi

"In this comical story, Kimmel captures the kindness of an old woman and the innocence of a hungry bear in an unusual visit. Carmi's airy pastel illustrations shade the tale with a golden glow appropriate for the Festival of Lights." Publ Wkly

   ★ **Wonders** and miracles; a Passover companion. illustrated with art spanning three thousand years; written and

compiled by Eric A. Kimmel. Scholastic Press 2004 136p il $18.95
Grades: 4 5 6 7   **296.4**
1. Passover
ISBN 0-439-07175-5
LC 2002-4732

Presents the steps performed in a traditional Passover Seder, plus stories, songs, poetry, and pictures that celebrate the historical significance of this holiday to Jews all over the world.

"The marvelous selection of art—paintings, photographs, artifacts, and illustrations from historical Haggadahs—illuminates each step in the service. . . . Both the presentation of information and the overall design attest to the careful and loving attention given to every detail. This inviting, handsome, and informative compendium should find a place of honor in every library." SLJ

Includes bibliographical references

Lehman-Wilzig, Tami
   Hanukkah around the world; by Tami Lehman-Wilzig; illustrated by Vicki Wehrman. Kar-Ben Pub. 2009 48p il map $16.95
Grades: 2 3 4 5   **296.4**
1. Hanukkah
ISBN 978-0-8225-8761-3; 0-8225-8761-0
LC 2008031196

"This tour of Hanukkah includes information on its historical significance and the ways in which it is celebrated in places like New York City, Turin, Sydney and Warsaw. After an introductory section about the history, terminology and customs associated with the holiday, the book features a story of a child living in each city." Publ Wkly

Melmed, Laura Krauss
   Eight winter nights; a family Hanukkah book. illustrated by Elisabeth Schlossberg. Chronicle Books 2010 un il $16.99
Grades: PreK K 1   **296.4**
1. Hanukkah
ISBN 978-0-8118-5552-5; 0-8118-5552-X
LC 2009019574

Short verses describe symbols, foods, and family fun associated with the festival of Hanukkah. Includes facts about the history and traditions.

"The verse and illustrations work well together. . . . Created with pencil and pastels, the illustrations use plenty of curved lines and deep, warm colors to depict the celebrations in this lively, amiable household." Booklist

Metter, Bert
   Bar mitzvah, bat mitzvah; the ceremony, the party, and how the day came to be. by Bert Metter; illustrated by Joan Reilly. Clarion Books 2007 un il $16; pa $5.95
Grades: 4 5 6 7   **296.4**
1. Bar mitzvah 2. Bat mitzvah
ISBN 978-0-618-76772-4; 0-618-76772-X; 978-0-
618-76773-1 pa; 0-618-76773-8 pa
LC 2006032942

The author "describes a typical ceremony and explains how this custom began for boys during the Middle Ages and how it was adapted for girls beginning in 1922. He also discusses the recent custom of adult bar and bat mitzvahs and celebratory parties. The writing is clear and concise; ink illustrations . . . help break up the text." Booklist

Includes bibliographical references

Podwal, Mark H.

Built by angels; the story of the old-new synagogue. by Mark Podwal. Harcourt Children's Books 2009 un il $16

Grades: 1 2 3 4   **296.4**

1. Synagogues 2. Jews -- Czech Republic

ISBN 978-0-15-206678-9; 0-15-206678-0

LC 2007052091

"Legend, history and spiritual significance intertwine in Podwal's illustrated free-verse poem paying homage to Prague's Altneuschul, or Old-New Synagogue, which is the oldest in Europe, dating back to 1270, and is treasured for its early Gothic architecture. . . . Childlike yet abstract drawings in acrylic, gouache and colored pencil-dominated by a combination of reds . . . delineate the building's history as a haven for worship throughout the centuries. . . . A beautiful, Impressionistic introduction to a portion of Judaic lore and a European architectural marvel." Kirkus

★ A **sweet** year; a taste of the Jewish holidays. [by] Mark Podwal. Doubleday Bks. for Young Readers 2003 un il hardcover o.p. lib bdg $14.99

Grades: K 1 2 3   **296.4**

1. Food 2. Jewish holidays

ISBN 0-385-74637-7; 0-385-90869-5 lib bdg

LC 2002-155442

Pictures and easy-to-read text introduce Jewish holidays, focusing on the foods associated with each

This offers "beautifully crafted poetic text and symbolic paintings in gouache and acrylics." SLJ

Includes bibliographical references

Schecter, Ellen

★ The **family** Haggadah; illustrated by Neil Waldman. Viking 1999 66p il music pa $13.99

Grades: 4 5 6 7   **296.4**

1. Passover

ISBN 0-670-88341-7

LC 98-28597

"Although really intended for parents to use with their children at a family Passover seder, this attractive book may also be useful to children wanting to plan their own model celebration." Booklist

The **story** of Hanukkah; illustrated by Jill Weber. Holiday House 2011 un il $14.95

Grades: PreK K 1 2   **296.4**

1. Hanukkah 2. Hanukkah stories 3. Children's literature -- Works -- Preschool through grade two

ISBN 978-0-8234-2295-1; 0-8234-2295-X

This retells the Hanukkah story of the Maccabees and the miracle that took place in the Temple in Jerusalem. Includes a recipe for latkes and directions for playing dreidel.

"The events commemorated in the holiday of Hanukkah are retold simply for young ears. . . . Weber's full-spread color illustrations, with an emphasis on traditional holiday blue, convey the epic scope of the story." Publ Wkly

Walker, Robert

Bar and bat mitzvahs; Robert Walker. Crabtree Pub. Co. 2012 32 p. (reinforced library binding: alk. paper) $26.60

Grades: 1 2 3   **296.4**

1. Bar mitzvah 2. Bat mitzvah 3. Rites and ceremonies

ISBN 0778740862; 0778740919; 1427178453; 1427179603; 9780778740865; 9780778740919; 9781427178459; 9781427179609

LC 2012004070

This book looks at bar and bat mitzvahs. Chapters explore themes including the "history of the ceremony," "the Sabbath," "important religious texts," "the Hebrew language," and how "girls get their own day." The post-ceremony reception and party is also considered. (WorldCat)

Includes bibliographical references and index

Woog, Adam

What makes me a Jew? Kidhaven Press 2004 48p il (What makes me a-- ?) $23.70

Grades: 3 4 5   **296.4**

1. Judaism

ISBN 0-7377-2266-5

LC 2003-20951

This describes Jewish origins, beliefs, practices, foods, and holidays.

"Presenting information about religion objectively for younger audiences poses a difficult challenge, but [this title does] and excellent job of it." Booklist

Includes bibliographical references

Ziefert, Harriet

★ **Hanukkah** haiku; [by] Harriet Ziefert; paintings by Karla Gudeon. Blue Apple Books 2008 un il $16.95

Grades: PreK K 1   **296.4**

1. Haiku 2. Hanukkah

ISBN 978-1-934706-33-6; 1-934706-33-7

LC 2008005877

"Combining festive illustrations and a playful format, this title uses haiku to celebrate the eight nights of Hanukkah. . . . Each turn of the stepped pages brings fresh excitement as another lit candle and verse are revealed. Illustrations have a lovely folkloric quality in which Chagall-like figures, surrounded by richly colored flowers and stars, float across a fibrous tan background." SLJ

Passover; celebrating now, remembering then. paintings by Karla Gudeon. Blue Apple Books 2010 un il $17.99

Grades: PreK K 1 2 3   **296.4**

1. Passover

ISBN 978-1-60905-020-7; 1-60905-020-7

"Ziefert provides a simplified adaptation of Exodus, a description of holiday preparations, and a concise Haggadah, or service for this ritual meal. Throughout, Ziefert contrasts current practice . . . with ancient origins. . . . On every page, Gudeon's Chagall-like paintings exhibit a folkloric style. . . . This title is one that families with young children will appreciate and want to own." Booklist

297 Islam, Babism, Bahai Faith

Barnard, Bryn

★ The **genius** of Islam; how Muslims made the modern world. Alfred A. Knopf 2011 37p il map $17.99; lib bdg $20.99

Grades: 4 5 6 7   **297**

1. Islamic civilization 2. Islam -- History

ISBN 978-0-375-84072-2; 0-375-84072-9; 978-0-375-94072-9 lib bdg; 0-375-94072-3 lib bdg

LC 2010-12777

This is a "concise and eloquent exploration of the far-reaching influence of Islam over the centuries. Each spread is devoted to a different subject (writing, Arabic numerals, architecture, astronomy, agriculture), while captioned spot art homes in on specific inventions and innovations (the zither, the astrolabe, advanced medical knowledge)." Publ Wkly

Includes bibliographical references

Cooper, Alison

Facts about Islam. Rosen Central 2010 45p il map (World religions) lib bdg $26.50

Grades: 3 4 5 6   **297**

1. Islam

ISBN 978-1-61532-322-7 lib bdg; 1-61532-322-8 lib bdg

LC 2009052445

"This book describes who Muslims are, the beginning of Islam, beliefs and leaders, the Qur'an, Sunna, family life, worship, the Islamic calendar, Hajj, festivals, and how the religion spread. . . . Colorful photographs, maps, and illustrations appear on every chapter spread, and the language is easy to understand, making this a useful resource for children." SLJ

Includes glossary and bibliographical references

Demi

★ **Muhammad**; written and illustrated by Demi. Margaret K. McElderry Bks. 2003 un il $19.95

Grades: 4 5 6 7   **297**

1. Islam 2. Prophets 3. Islamic leaders 4. Writers on religion

ISBN 0-689-85264-9

LC 2002-2985

"With dramatic scenes extending past the borders of the intricately patterned frames, the art will be a continual source of interest for young people. . . . [An] excellent retelling of the Prophet's life that combines beauty and scholarship." Booklist

Includes bibliographical references

Hawker, Frances

Islam in Turkey; written by Frances Hawker and Leyla Alicavusoglu; photography by Bruce Campbell. Crabtree Pub. Company 2010 32p il (Families and their faiths) lib bdg $26.60; pa $8.95

Grades: 3 4 5   **297**

1. Islam 2. Turkey

ISBN 978-0-7787-5009-3 lib bdg; 0-7787-5009-4 lib bdg; 978-0-7787-5026-0 pa; 0-7787-5026-4 pa

LC 2009-14158

This "book introduces a child who practices [Islam]. . . . Provides a solid introduction without overwhelming readers with complex regional variations in practices and beliefs. . . .

Words and phrases that are unique to the faith appear in bold font and are defined at greater length in the glossary." SLJ

Includes glossary

Raatma, Lucia

Islam. Compass Point Books 2010 48p il map (World religions) lib bdg $27.99

Grades: 5 6 7 8   **297**

1. Islam

ISBN 978-0-7565-4239-9 lib bdg; 0-7565-4239-1 lib bdg

LC 2009-15812

"The colorful, attractive layout includes high-quality reproductions of photographs, maps, and paintings. Students who are new to religious studies, as well as those doing reports, will find that this . . . meets their needs." SLJ

Includes glossary and bibliographical references

297.09 History, geographic treatment, biography

Whiting, Jim

The **role** of religion in the early Islamic world; Jim Whiting. Crabtree Pub. Company 2012 48 p. (Life in the early islamic world) (reinforced library binding: alk. paper) $30.60

Grades: 4 5 6   **297.09**

1. Islam -- History 2. Picture books for children 3. Islamic Empire -- History

ISBN 0778721698; 9780778721697; 9780778721765; 9781427195623; 9781427198419

LC 2012000075

This book looks at the role of religion in the early Islamic world. "Information is presented in concise chapters. . . . The main texts are supplemented with blue boxes of information, subsections, and many . . . reproductions, maps, and paintings. Each book contains time lines and short biographies of important historical figures." (School Library Journal)

297.3 Islamic worship

Brown, Tricia

Salaam; a Muslim American boy's story. Henry Holt 2006 un il $17.95

Grades: K 1 2 3   **297.3**

1. Islam 2. Muslims

ISBN 978-0-8050-6538-1; 0-8050-6538-5

LC 2005013147

"A gentle and informative look at a Muslim-American boy and the way he practices his faith. The book does a good job of explaining each of the Five Pillars of Islam. . . . Good-quality black-and-white photos enhance the presentation and effectively show the warmth of Imran's family life." SLJ

Includes glossary

Bullard, Lisa

Rashad's Ramadan and Eid al-Fitr; by Lisa Bullard; illustrated by Holli Conger. Millbrook Press 2012 24 p. col. ill. (lib. bdg.: alk. paper) $23.93; (ebook) $35.93; (paperback) $6.95

Grades: 1 2 3   **297.3**
1. Muslims 2. Islamic holidays 3. Picture books for
children 4. Ramadan 5. Eid al-Fitre
ISBN 0761350799; 9780761350798; 9780761388425;
9780761385837

     LC 2011024545

Author Lisa Bullard's book focuses on Muslim holidays and celebrations. "For Muslims, Ramadan is a time
for fasting, prayer, and thinking of others. Rashad tries to
be good all month. When it's time for Eid al-Fitr, he feasts
and plays! Find out how people celebrate this special time of
year. Learn the history behind the days people celebrate in
the Holidays and Special Days series, part of the Cloverleaf
Books collection." (Publisher's note)

Dickmann, Nancy
    Ramadan and Id-ul-Fitr. Heinemann Library 2010
24p il (Holidays and festivals) $21.50; pa $5.99
Grades: PreK K 1   **297.3**
1. Islam 2. Ramadan 3. Id al-Adha
ISBN 978-1-4329-4049-2; 1-4329-4049-X; 978-1-
4329-4068-3 pa; 1-4329-4068-6 pa

     LC 2009054305

This is a "clear introduction to Islam's holy month. .
. Large photos dominate the top two-thirds of each page,
while a single line of large-print text delivers information. .
. Even lesser known to Americans is the celebration of Id-ul-
Fitr at the end of Ramadan, and it is here where the book's
photographs are particularly effective." Booklist

Includes bibliographical references

Douglass, Susan L.
    ★ **Ramadan**; illustrations by Jeni Reeves. Carolrhoda
Books 2004 48p il (On my own holidays) lib bdg $23.93;
pa $4.95
Grades: 1 2 3   **297.3**
1. Islam 2. Ramadan 3. Id al-Adha
ISBN 0-87614-932-8 lib bdg; 1-57505-584-8 pa

     LC 2002-6781

An introduction to Islamic observances during the month
of Ramadan and the subsequent festival of Eid-al-Fitr

"Reeves's abundant, framed illustrations in pastel colors
provide detailed windows on the observance. . . . An easy-to-
read, well-organized introduction." SLJ

Heiligman, Deborah
    ★ **Celebrate** Ramadan & Eid al-Fitr; [by] Deborah
Heiligman; consultant, Neguin Yavari. National Geographic
2006 31p il map (Holidays around the world) $15.95; lib
bdg $23.90
Grades: K 1 2 3   **297.3**
1. Islam 2. Ramadan 3. Id al-Adha
ISBN 0-7922-5926-2; 0-7922-5927-0 lib bdg

     LC 2006008889

"Heiligman offers a simple, accessible introduction to
the traditions of this solemn month and its concluding festival. Numerous clear, expressive photos feature captions that
describe the experiences of children from varying countries
and cultures and how they observe Ramadan." Publ Wkly

Includes glossary and bibliographical references

Hoyt-Goldsmith, Diane
    ★ **Celebrating** Ramadan; Ramadan al-mu'azzam.
photographs by Lawrence Migdale. Holiday House 2001
32p il map $16.95
Grades: 3 4 5   **297.3**
1. Islam 2. Ramadan
ISBN 0-8234-1581-3

     LC 2001-16643

"This picture book for older readers follows devout muslim Ibraheem, a fourth-grader living in New Jersey, through
the holy month of Ramadan. . . . This is a sensitive introduction to Ramadan; the quality of the photographs and the
eloquent text make the book the one of the best introductions
in recent memory." Booklist

Jeffrey, Laura S.
    Celebrate Ramadan; [by] Laura S. Jeffrey. Enslow
Publishers 2007 112p il (Celebrate holidays) lib bdg
$31.93
Grades: 5 6 7 8   **297.3**
1. Islam 2. Ramadan 3. Id al-Adha
ISBN 978-0-7660-2774-9 lib bdg; 0-7660-2774-0
lib bdg

     LC 2006028107

"This book opens by introducing a contemporary Muslim, Bushra, who celebrated Ramadan as a girl growing up
in England [and] later immigrated to the United States. . .
. An informative chapter surveys the history, beliefs, and
practices of Islam. . . . The remainder of the book offers a
detailed discussion of Ramadan, prayer, and spiritual awareness, and of l'Id al Fitr. . . . Punctuated by sidebars and illustrated with color photos, this clearly written book offers a
good overview of how the holidays of Islam are celebrated."
Booklist

Includes glossary and bibliographical references

Khan, Aisha Karen
    What you will see inside a mosque; photographs by
Aaron Pepis. Skylight Paths Pub. 2003 31p il (What you
will see inside--) $16.95; pa $8.99
Grades: 3 4 5 6   **297.3**
1. Islam 2. Mosques
ISBN 1-893361-60-8; 1-594732-57-4 pa

     LC 2002-153436

Describes what happens inside a mosque and introduces
the Muslim faith

This is an "excellent introduction. . . . Full-page photographs are supplemented by smaller photos with informative
captions." SLJ

MacMillan, Dianne M.
    Ramadan and Id al-Fitr; [by] Dianne M. MacMillan.
rev and updated ed.; Enslow Elementary 2008 48p il map
(Best holiday books) $23.93
Grades: 2 3 4   **297.3**
1. Islam 2. Ramadan 3. Id al-Adha
ISBN 978-0-7660-3045-9; 0-7660-3045-8

     LC 2007002425

First published 1994

This describes the history of the Muslim holidays of
Ramadan and Id al-Fitr and how they are celebrated in the
United States

"The well-written [text] aptly [describes] the traditions
and customs and capture the flavor of the [holidays]. The

open, spacious format makes the [book] accessible, and the full-color and black-and-white photos lend interest." SLJ

Includes glossary and bibliographical references

Murray, Julie

Ramadan. ABDO Pub. Company 2011 24p il (Holidays) $25.26

Grades: 2 3 4   **297.3**

1. Ramadan

ISBN 978-1-61783-041-9; 1-61783-041-0

LC 2011002287

"This short, concise introduction is simple enough for the target audience, and it is accurate. Each two-page chapter introduces an aspect of Ramadan that is rooted in religious practices that are common to all Muslims: Sunnis and Shi'ites, Salafis and Sufis, liberals and conservatives. Each spread has a large, full-color picture. The publisher's website provides further reading with links to additional, credible Internet resources. This title succeeds where others have been undermined by cultural bias. An excellent addition." SLJ

Petrini, Catherine M.

★ **What** makes me a Muslim? [by] Catherine M. Petrini. KidHaven Press 2005 48p il map (What makes me a-- ?) $27

Grades: 3 4 5   **297.3**

1. Islam

ISBN 978-0-7377-2265-9; 0-7377-2265-7

LC 2004014526

"This overview explains what Islam is, where it came from, and how it has spread over time. Petrini provides a look at the background, beliefs, practices, holidays, and challenges of the religion today. . . . The full-color photographs and religious paintings throughout the book are as informative as they are appealing." SLJ

Includes bibliographical references

Whitman, Sylvia

Under the Ramadan moon; [by] Sylvia Whitman; illustrated by Sue Williams. A. Whitman & Co. 2008 un il $15.99

Grades: PreK K 1 2   **297.3**

1. Ramadan 2. Moon

ISBN 978-0-8075-8304-3; 0-8075-8304-9

LC 2008001307

"This delightful picture book describes the month-long Muslim observance of Ramadan by a modern family. . . . The images of the waxing, full, and waning moon progress along with the spare, lyrical text. Practices such as fasting, speaking kind words, giving to the poor, decorating with bright lights, and praying all take place, 'under the moon, under the Ramadan moon.' Williams uses soft, luminous pastels in richly textured, detailed spreads." SLJ

299 Religions not provided for elsewhere

Fisher, Leonard Everett

★ The **gods** and goddesses of ancient China. Holiday House 2003 un il $16.95

Grades: 3 4 5 6   **299**

1. Gods and goddesses 2. China -- Religion

ISBN 0-8234-1694-1

LC 2002-68802

"Beginning with an introduction that mentions Qin Shi Huangdi, China's First Supreme Emperor, Fisher offers very brief historical and cultural background to China's deities. . . . Profiles of 17 gods and goddesses follow, each one presented on a double-page spread that includes a roughly brushed portrait opposite a few paragraphs summarizing the figure's corresponding legend. . . . Fisher combines concise, accessible language, colorful art, and exciting stories about figures that aren't often covered in books for youth." Booklist

Includes bibliographical references

299.31 Ancient Egyptian Religion

Kramer, Ann

Egyptian myth; a treasury of legends, art, and history. M. E. Sharpe 2008 96p il map (The world of mythology) $35.95

Grades: 5 6 7 8   **299.31**

1. Egyptian art 2. Egyptian mythology 3. Egypt -- History

ISBN 978-0-7656-8105-8; 0-7656-8105-6

LC 2007005876

This "handsomely designed [book is] illustrated with works of art from the culture. [It] is a well-organized presentation that includes information and tales about the gods and the pharoahs as well as magical stories and legends, providing an excellent introduction to this fascinating culture." SLJ

Includes glossary and bibliographical references

Napoli, Donna Jo

★ **Treasury** of Egyptian Mythology; Classic Stories of Gods, Goddesses, Monsters & Mortals. by Donna Jo Napoli and illustrated by Christina Balit. National Geographic Children's books 2013 192 p. $24.95

Grades: 3 4 5 6   **299.31**

1. Egyptian mythology 2. Gods and goddesses

ISBN 1426313802; 9781426313806

Author Donna Jo Napoli presents a "tableau of Egyptian myths, including those of pharaohs, queens, the boisterous Sun God Ra, and legendary creatures like the Sphinx. The stories are embellished with sidebars that provide historical, cultural, and geographic context and a mapping feature that adds to the fun and fascination. Resource notes and ample back matter direct readers to discover more about ancient Egypt." (Publisher's note)

Williams, Marcia

Ancient Egypt; tales of gods and pharaohs. Candlewick Press 2011 un il $16.99

Grades: 4 5 6   **299.31**

1. Egyptian mythology 2. Egypt -- Religion

ISBN 978-0-7636-5308-8; 0-7636-5308-X

LC 2010040745

"The highpoints of Egyptian mythology—creation, the divinity of Ra, the death of Osiris, and the vengeance of his son Horus—as well as the stories of four great pharaohs—are presented in this lighthearted picture book/graphic novel. . . . This book makes them all seem like fun. Williams utilizes a beautiful, sun-soaked palette of gold, turquoise, lapis, jade, and carnelian lifted right off a sarcophagus. . . . Expressive postures, smiling faces, and playful interactions among them keep readers scouring the pages for every little joke. . . . Each figure in this book . . . fairly leaps off the page in order to grab readers' attention." SLJ

299.5   Religions of East and Southeast Asian origin

Demi
★ The **legend** of Lao Tzu and the Tao te ching. Margaret K. McElderry Books 2007 un il $21.99
Grades: 4 5 6 7   **299.5**
1. Taoism 2. Philosophers
ISBN 1-4169-1206-1; 978-1-4169-1206-4
LC 2005029695
"This is the legend of Lao Tzu . . . who may or may not have founded Taoism, one of the greatest religions of the world. Demi's elegant picture-book introduction to the legendary Chinese philosopher . . . combines nuggets of his purported life with 20 verses from the Tao Te Ching. . . . The narrative and graceful paintings are contained in a gold circular frame on each parchment shaded page." SLJ

Levin, Judith
Japanese mythology; [by] Judith Levin. The Rosen Pub. Group 2008 64p il map (Mythology around the world) $29.95
Grades: 5 6 7 8   **299.5**
1. Shinto 2. Buddhism 3. Japanese mythology 4. Japan -- Civilization
ISBN 978-1-4042-0736-3; 1-4042-0736-8
LC 2005035279
This "presents not only an introduction to Shinto and Buddhist beliefs, but also Japanese history and mythology in general. . . . The most remarkable part of [this book] . . . is the respect [it shows] for the mythological customs, treating them throughout with the same care that writers of books on major religions might offer. The illustrations show both ancient and modern incarnations of the deities and heroes." SLJ

Includes glossary and bibliographical references

299.7   Religions of North American native origin

Swamp, Jake
Giving thanks; a Native American good morning message. by Chief Jake Swamp; illustrated by Erwin Printup, Jr. Lee & Low Bks. 1995 un il $16.95; pa $6.95
Grades: K 1 2 3   **299.7**
1. Human ecology 2. Mohawk Indians 3. Native Americans
ISBN 1-880000-15-6; 1-880000-54-7 pa
LC 94-5955
"Its simple, timeless language bears witness to the Native American reverence for the natural world and sense of unity with all living things. . . . The gifts of the earth . . . are richly depicted in paintings of wildlife and bountiful harvests." Publ Wkly

300   SOCIAL SCIENCES, SOCIOLOGY & ANTHROPOLOGY

302.23   Media (Means of communication)

Milich, Zoran
City signs. Kids Can Press 2002 un il $15.95; pa $6.95
Grades: PreK K 1 2   **302.23**
1. Signs and signboards
ISBN 1-55337-003-1; 1-55337-748-6 pa
"Milich took to the streets with his camera, looking for printed words found in various outdoor environments. The 30 photographs here demonstrate that even children who can't yet read a book understand many of the words they see around them. The quality of the pictures is very good. They are nicely composed, clear, and often colorful." Booklist

302.3   Social interaction within groups

Burstein, John
Why are you picking on me? dealing with bullies. Crabtree Pub. Company 2009 32p il (Slim Goodbody's life skills 101) lib bdg $26.60; pa $8.95
Grades: 1 2 3 4 5   **302.3**
1. Bullies
ISBN 978-0-7787-4792-5 lib bdg; 0-7787-4792-1 lib bdg; 978-0-7787-4808-3 pa; 0-7787-4808-1 pa
LC 2009022427
This book about dealing with bullies offers "clear and simple advice for children and [provides] adults with springboards for discussion and roleplaying. All have appealing color photographs of a variety of types of kids, . . . opening scenarios, concrete coping suggestions, and solid reasoning." SLJ

Includes bibliographical references

Ellis, Deborah
★ **We** want you to know; kids talk about bullying. Coteau Books 2010 120p il $19.95; pa $15.95
Grades: 5 6 7 8 9 10   **302.3**
1. Bullies
ISBN 978-1-55050-417-0; 1-55050-417-7; 978-1-55050-463-7 pa; 1-55050-463-0
"As part of her work with an anti-bullying campaign in her local Canadian community, Ellis interviewed young people between the ages of 9 and 19 about their experiences. In honest, straightforward prose, she shares their stories, many as targets and some as perpetrators or bystanders. . . . Each story is written from the first-person point of view, some with real names and photos, providing an intimacy and immediacy that are critical with these kinds of issues. Readers will find at least one or two stories they can relate to, and educators should be able to use many of the narratives to jumpstart conversation." SLJ

Includes bibliographical references

Fox, Debbie

★ **Good**-bye bully machine; written by Debbie Fox and Allan L. Beane; illustrated by Debbie Fox. Free Spirit Pub. 2009 39p il pa $8.95; $12.99

Grades: K 1 2 3 4 5   **302.3**
1. Bullies
ISBN 978-1-57542-321-0 pa; 1-57542-321-9 pa; 978-1-57542-326-5; 1-57542-326-X

LC 2008-41025

Kids learn what bullying is, why it hurts, and what they can do to end it with this fresh, compelling book including contemporary collage art, lively layout, and straightforward text.

"The authors provide tips for dealing with negative behaviors and encourage readers to take a stand against bullying and unplug the bully machine. Fox's enticing, edgy, collage artwork will draw readers in. . . . This offering will be a great discussion springboard for teachers and counselors." SLJ

Jakubiak, David J.

A **smart** kid's guide to online bullying. PowerKids Press 2009 24p il (Kids online) lib bdg $21.25; pa $8.95
Grades: 3 4 5 6   **302.3**
1. Bullies 2. Safety education 3. Internet -- Security measures
ISBN 978-1-4042-8114-1 lib bdg; 978-1-4358-3348-7 pa

LC 2009000695

This describes how to identify bullies online, how to deal with them, and how to avoid becoming a bully.

"This . . . is easy to read, has vibrant photos on each page, and offers Tips. Additional links can be found at the publisher's portal, which is regularly updated." Libr Media Connect

Includes glossary

Kevorkian, Meline

★ **101** facts about bullying; what everyone should know. [by] Meline Kevorkian and Robin D'Antona. Rowman & Littlefield Pub. 2008 148p $32.95
Grades: Adult Professional   **302.3**
1. Bullies
ISBN 978-1-57886-849-0; 1-57886-849-1

"A user-friendly, accessible, and well-organized resource. . . . The format will lend itself well to group discussions and give teachers and others who work with young people a solid basis upon which to explore the issues surrounding this prevalent problem." SLJ

Lutz, Lisa

How to negotiate everything; David Spellman with Lisa Lutz; illustrated by Jaime Temairik. Simon & Schuster Books for Young Readers 2012 32 p. (hardcover) $16.99
Grades: K 1 2 3   **302.3**
1. Wit and humor 2. Negotiation
ISBN 144245119X; 9781442451193

LC 2011038386

This humorous juvenile picture book, by Lisa Lutz, illustrated by Jaime Temairik, "teaches you how to get everything you want. . . . Through several simple steps, you will learn the best way to ask for what you want, how to ask for more of what you want, and the importance of not overreaching. With helpful illustrations and a complete glos-

sary, there is no end to what these skills can get you." (Publisher's note)

Shapiro, Ouisie

Bullying and me; schoolyard stories. illustrated by Steven Vote. Albert Whitman & Company 2010 un il $16.99
Grades: 4 5 6 7   **302.3**
1. Bullies
ISBN 978-0-8075-0921-0; 0-8075-0921-3

LC 2010000754

"Thirteen individuals, including some adults, who have been bullied at school share their painful experiences. . . . Vote's full-color portraits sensitively depict the faces at the receiving end of abuse. . . . An educational psychologist specifically addresses each individual's dilemma, but the book's strength lies in the honestly conveyed through the personal stories." Publ Wkly

302.302   Computer applications

Schwartz, Heather E.

Safe social networking; by Heather E. Schwartz. Capstone Press 2013 32 p. col. ill. (Fact finders. Tech safety smarts) (library) $26.65
Grades: 4 5 6 7   **302.302**
1. Online social networks 2. Internet -- Security measures 3. Social networking
ISBN 1429699434; 9781429699433; 9781620658024

LC 2012026027

This children's resource book, by Heather E. Schwartz, is part of the publisher's "Fact Finders" series, providing guidance for young children to safely use and navigate online social media. "If a strange person asks to be your online friend, do you know what to do? . . . This book is here to help! Learn tech-savvy ways to keep your social networking sites safe sites without taking away all the fun!" (Publisher's note)

Includes bibliographical references (p. 31) and index.

303.3   Coordination and control

Barraclough, Sue

Leadership. Heinemann Library 2009 32p il (Exploring Citizenship) $25.36; pa $7.99
Grades: 1 2 3 4   **303.3**
1. Leadership
ISBN 978-1-4329-3314-2; 1-4329-3314-0; 978-1-4329-3322-7 pa; 1-4329-3322-1 pa

LC 2008-55302

"The text presents a multitude of realistic situations to which young children will relate. There are 'Think About It' fact boxes and checklists that aid in understanding and that will spark discussion. All are filled with captioned, color photographs that relate to the text. The information is relevant and current. . . . Strongly consider this." Libr Media Connect

Includes glossary and bibliographical references

303.4 Social change

Solway, Andrew

Communication; the impact of science and technology. Gareth Stevens Pub. 2010 64p il (Pros and cons) lib bdg $35

Grades: 5 6 7 8   **303.4**
1. Communication 2. Telecommunication 3. Information technology
ISBN 978-1-4339-1986-2 lib bdg; 1-4339-1986-9 lib bdg

LC 2009-12435

An "active layout that features color photographs, maps, graphs or charts on every spread, this . . . [book] has much to offer. . . . It conveniently outlines the range of views . . . helping students to learn how to view both sides of [the] issue[s]." SLJ

Includes glossary and bibliographical references

303.48 Causes of change

Scandiffio, Laura

People who said no; courage against oppression. Laura Scandiffio. Annick Press 2012 168 p. $24.95

Grades: 5 6 7   **303.48**
1. Demonstrations 2. Protest movements 3. Civil disobedience 4. Resistance to government
ISBN 1554513839; 9781554513833

This book, by Laura Scandiffio, profiles activists who broke the law to protest injustices. "Sometimes it's okay to ignore the rules or break the law. . . . This . . . book features people who did just that: Sophie and Hans Scholl . . . and Andrei Sakharov. . . . Also included are Helen Suzman, . . . Aung San Suu Kyi, . . . and the people of Egypt, who recently brought down the repressive government of Hosni Mubarak." (Publisher's note)

Slade, Suzanne

Friends for freedom; the Story of Susan B. Anthony & Frederick Douglass. Suzanne Slade; illustrated by Nicole Tadgell. Charlesbridge 2014 40 p. color illustrations (reinforced) $16.95

Grades: 1 2 3 4   **303.48**
1. Suffragists 2. Social problems 3. Abolitionists -- Biography 4. Social reformers -- United States -- Biography
ISBN 1580895689; 9781607346517; 9781607347491; 9781580895682

LC 2013022795

In this children's book, by Suzanne Slade, "no one thought Susan B. Anthony and Frederick Douglass would ever become friends. The former slave and the outspoken woman came from two different worlds. But they shared deep-seated beliefs in equality and the need to fight for it. Despite naysayers, hecklers, and even arsonists, Susan and Frederick became fast friends and worked together to change America." (Publisher's note)

"Tadgell's carefully drafted and evocative watercolors capture both the past and present obstacles Anthony and Douglass faced, from Douglass's youth as a slave to rotten eggs hurled at the two when they appeared in public together and combative differences of opinion, as when the Fifteenth Amendment proposed to give voting rights to black men but not to women." Pub Wkly

303.6 Conflict and conflict resolution

Ellis, Deborah

Off to war; voices of soldiers' children. Groundwood Books/House of Anansi Press 2008 175p il $15.95; pa $9.95

Grades: 5 6 7 8   **303.6**
1. Children and war 2. Iraq War, 2003-2011 3. Afghanistan War, 2001-
ISBN 978-0-88899-894-1; 0-88899-894-5; 978-0-88899-895-8 pa; 0-88899-895-3 pa

The wars in Iraq and Afghanistan have impacted the children of soldiers—men and women who have been called away from their families to fight in a faraway war. In their own words, some of these children describe how their experience has marked and shaped their lives

"Accessible and utterly readable. . . . The book is an excellent resource for opening discussions about the current events." SLJ

Includes glossary and bibliographical references

Gilley, Jeremy

★ **Peace** one day; illustrated by Karen Blessen. Putnam 2005 48p il $16.99 **303.6**
1. Peace
ISBN 0-399-24330-5

LC 2004-20475

The author "tells how he persuaded world leaders to establish World Peace Day. . . . His personal account of filming the consequences of war in several countries . . . draws attention to the issue, as do his accounts of meeting with world leaders. . . . Most powerful are the double-page collage illustrations . . . which blend some of Gilley's film images of kids caught up in war and portraits of world peace leaders with colored pencil drawings, posters, and even news headlines. [This offers] passionate prose and stirring images." Booklist

Walker, Niki

Why do we fight? conflict, war, and peace. Niki Walker. Owlkids Books 2013 80 p. $16.95

Grades: 5 6 7 8   **303.6**
1. War 2. Culture conflict 3. Conflict management
ISBN 1926973860; 9781926973869

LC 2013930981

In this book, Niki Walker explains "different types of conflict and then contemplat[es] ways conflict can escalate." (Kirkus Reviews) "Using real-world examples, such as the 1979 peace deal between Egypt and Israel or the history of Afghanistan over multiple centuries, Walker offers . . . explanations of power and resource inequities, cultural divisions, the global role of the United Nations, bias, prejudice, and more." (Publishers Weekly)

304.2 Human ecology

McCarthy, Pat

Friends of the earth; a history of American environmentalism. Pat McCarthy. 1st ed. Chicago Review Press 2012 132 p. ill. (paperback) $16.95

Grades: 3 4 5   **304.2**

1. Environmentalists 2. Environmental movement -- United States 3. Environmentalism -- United States -- History 4. Environmental protection -- United States -- History

ISBN 1569767181; 9781569767184

LC 2012039334

This book provides "10 profiles of American naturalists and environmentalists" that "offer a broad overview of the movement's past highlights." Also included are "photos, sidebars, resource lists, and a quick closing survey of current environmental issues." Figures mentioned include John Muir, Henry David Thoreau, and Rachel Carson. (Booklist)

Urrutia, María Cristina

Who will save my planet? Maria Cristina Urrutia. Tundra Books of Northern New York 2012 32 p. (hardcover) $10.95

Grades: 3 4 5   **304.2**

1. Human influence on nature

ISBN 177049281X; 9781770492813

LC 2011923291

This book by Maria Cristina Urrutia "uses striking photos to show the impact of humans on the environment. . . . On every spread we are shown a treasure that nature has given us beside a picture of how we've abused that treasure. We see a beautiful forest glade beside a devastated patch of burned-out wood, a gorgeous green parrot beside a dull-feathered caged bird, a sparkling waterfall beside a garbage-clogged river." (Publisher's note)

304.6 Population

Barber, Nicola

Coping with population growth; Nicola Barber. Raintree 2011 48 p. col. ill.

Grades: 4 5 6 7   **304.6**

1. Population 2. Population -- Environmental aspects

ISBN 9781410942968; 9781410943033

LC 2010052702

"Barber examines the pressures exerted on the environment and global resources due to population growth... Color photographs add interest, and helpful diagrams effectively convey statistical concepts." Horn Book

Includes bibliographical references (p. 46-47) and index

Smith, David J.

If the World Were a Village; 2 A Book About the World's People. by David J. Smith and illustrated by Shelagh Armstrong. Kids Can Press 2011 32 p. $18.95

Grades: 3 4 5   **304.6**

1. Population 2. Citizenship

ISBN 1554535956; 9781554535958

This book, by David J. Smith and illustrated by Shelagh Armstrong, promotes "world-mindedness by imagining the world's population, all 6.8 billion of us, as a village of just 100 people. Now, 'If the World Were a Village' has been newly revised with updated statistics, several new activities and completely new material on food security, energy and health. By exploring the lives of the 100 villagers, children will discover that life in other nations is often very different from their own." (Publisher's note)

304.8 Movement of people

Kenney, Karen Latchana

Ellis Island; illustrated by Judith A. Hunt. Magic Wagon 2011 32p il (Our nation's pride) lib bdg $28.50

Grades: 2 3 4   **304.8**

1. Ellis Island Immigration Station 2. United States -- Immigration and emigration

ISBN 978-1-61641-150-3; 1-61641-150-3

LC 2010013995

"The author describes how the existing island was built up and expanded to accomodate the station to process immigrants coming into the United States and the various buildings that were constructed. . . . The full-color artwork not only explains the text but also gives almost photographic rendering of the [topic]." SLJ

Lawlor, Veronica

★ I was dreaming to come to America; memories from the Ellis Island Oral History Project. selected and illustrated by Veronica Lawlor; foreword by Rudolph W. Giuliani. Viking 1995 38p il hardcover o.p. pa $6.99

Grades: 4 5 6 7   **304.8**

1. Ellis Island Immigration Station 2. United States -- Immigration and emigration

ISBN 0-670-86164-2; 0-14-055622-2 pa

LC 95-1281

"Begun in 1975, the Ellis Island Oral History Project is . . . {a} collection of interviews with individuals who immigrated to the U.S. through Ellis Island. Short selections—each 1 or 2 paragraphs long—from 15 of those interviews are reprinted here. The subjects were for the most part children when they arrived in the period 1900-1925. . . . Grades four to six." (SLJ)

"There is a flavor of Chagall in the peasant figures dancing above the ship or hopping ashore near the turreted towers of the huge building on Ellis Island. The elegant rendering offers a timeless view of this significant journey that is at once personal and universal." Horn Book

Ollhoff, Jim

Exploring immigration. ABDO Pub. Co. 2011 32p il (Your family tree) $18.95

Grades: 4 5 6 7   **304.8**

1. Genealogy 2. Immigrants 3. United States -- Immigration and emigration

ISBN 978-1-61613-463-1; 1-61613-463-1

LC 2009050807

This book about immigration is "great . . . for kids interested in genealogy. [It does] a wonderful job of presenting the fundamentals of genealogical research in a clear and exciting manner. . . . Understanding and properly using primary documents is stressed throughout. . . . [An] attractive, spacious [layout]; full-color, sharp images; clearly labeled

diagrams; and scattered maps add information and appeal."
SLJ

Includes glossary

305.23   Young people

Freedman, Russell

★ **Children** of the Great Depression. Clarion Books
2005 118p il lib bdg $20
Grades: 4 5 6 7   **305.23**
1. Great Depression, 1929-1939 2. Children -- United
States 3. United States -- Social conditions
ISBN 0-618-44630-3
LC 2005-06506

"This stirring photo-essay combines . . . . unforgettable
personal details with a clear historical overview of the period and black-and-white photos by Dorothea Lange, Walker
Evans, and many others." Booklist

Kerley, Barbara

★ **One** world, one day. National Geographic 2009 un
il map $17.95; lib bdg $26.90
Grades: PreK K 1 2   **305.23**
1. Children -- Pictorial works
ISBN 978-1-4263-0460-6; 1-4263-0460-9; 978-1-
4263-0461-3 lib bdg; 1-4263-0461-7 lib bdg
LC 2008-29315

"An arresting, eye-opening compilation." Publ Wkly

Kindersley, Anabel

★ **Children** just like me; by Barnabas & Anabel
Kindersley. Dorling Kindersley 1995 79p il maps $19.95
Grades: 3 4 5 6   **305.23**
1. Children -- Pictorial works
ISBN 0-7894-0201-7
LC 95-10199

"A delightful, attractive look at children from around the
world. . . . This book is factual, respectful, and insightful.
It provides just the right balance of information and visual
interest for the intended audience." SLJ

Pinkney, Sandra L.

★ **Shades** of black; a celebration of our children.
photographs by Myles C. Pinkney. Scholastic 2000 un il
$14.95; bd bk $6.99
Grades: PreK K 1   **305.23**
1. African Americans
ISBN 0-439-14892-8; 0-439-80251-2 bd bk
LC 99-86593

Photographs and text celebrate the beauty and diversity
of African American children

"Wonderful, clear, full-color photographs of youngsters
illustrate a poetic, vivid text that describes a range of skin
and eye colors and hair textures." SLJ

Smith, David J.

This child, every child; a book about the world's children. written by David J. Smith; illustrated by Shelagh Armstrong. Kids Can Press 2011 36p il (CitizenKid) $18.95
Grades: 4 5 6 7   **305.23**
1. Children
ISBN 978-1-55453-466-1; 1-55453-466-6

This title "takes a global look at the lives of contemporary children. Balancing statistics with fictional profiles of
kids, Smith's concise narrative focuses on such topics as
families, homes, health, work, war, and play. Each spread
contains accessible summaries of articles from 1989's United Nations Convention on the Rights of the Child, underscoring the disparity between many children's lives and that
document's vision and goals. . . . Rendered in acrylics with
digital textures, Armstrong's gauzy paintings sometimes
span multiple cultures in a single illustration . . . reinforcing
the universal nature of children's needs." Publ Wkly

UNICEF

A **Life** like mine. DK Pub. 2002 127p il maps hard-
cover o.p. pa $12.99
Grades: 3 4 5 6   **305.23**
1. Children
ISBN 0-7894-8859-0; 0-7566-1803-7 pa
LC 2002-11197

Looks at what life is like for children of different countries and how each child can fulfill his or her hopes and
ambitions no matter how little or much their human rights
are infringed

"This book gives the reader a remarkable look at the
lives of children around the world. . . . The text is varied
within each page and is written in language easy for a child
to understand. The photographs are dispersed throughout all pages and enhance the meaning of the text." Libr
Media Connect

Wilson, Janet

One peace; true stories of young activists. written and
illustrated by Janet Wilson. Orca Book Publishers 2008
43p il $19.95
Grades: 4 5 6 7   **305.23**
1. Peace 2. Children and war
ISBN 978-1-55143-892-4; 1-55143-892-5

"The stories of young people who have been refugees
from war, injured by land mines, or learned about the consequences of violence through other means are interspersed
with children's poems, quotes, artwork, and photographs.
The brief, powerful accounts document how these children
ages 8 to 15 worked for or became symbols of peace." SLJ

305.4   Women

Carosella, Melissa

Founding mothers; women who shaped America.
Teacher Created Materials 2011 il (Primary source read-
ers: focus on women in U.S. history)
Grades: 3 4 5 6   **305.4**
1. Women -- United States -- History
ISBN 143331505X; 978-1-43331505-3

"This introduction to influential women in early American history begins with the colonial period and closes with
the Civil War. . . . The clear text is enhanced with archival
illustrations and sidebars that highlight notable items about
the women discussed in the narrative. A glossary, an index,
and two suggested extension activities conclude this informative book." Booklist

Coster, Patience

A **new** deal for women; the expanding roles of women, 1938-1960. Chelsea House 2011 il (A cultural history of women in America) $35

Grades: 5 6 7 8 **305.4**

1. Feminism 2. Women -- Social conditions 3. Women -- United States -- History 4. United States -- Social conditions

ISBN 978-1-6041-3934-1; 1-6041-3934-X

LC 2010045959

An "eye-catching [layout] with good use of color, photographs, and informative sidebars, many of which use primary-source quotations, are the highlights of [this] appealing [volume]. . . . After a succinct overview of contemporary events, the chapters describe women's lives at home, at work, in education, in politics, in the arts, and their role in the general culture. . . . New opportunities for women were a part of the New Deal and World War II and together changed American culture—these topics are explored [this] volume covering the years 1938-1960." SLJ

Includes glossary and bibliographical references

Gelletly, LeeAnne

A **woman's** place in early America; LeeAnne Gelletly. Mason Crest Publishers 2013 64 p. (Finding a voice: women's fight for equality in U.S. society) (hc) $22.95

Grades: 4 5 6 7 8 **305.4**

1. Women -- United States -- History 2. United States -- Social conditions 3. United States -- Politics and government 4. United States -- Social life and customs 5. Women -- United States -- Social conditions

ISBN 1422223558; 9781422223550; 9781422223659

LC 2011043480

Author LeeAnne Gelletly's book focuses on women in Early America. "In early America, married women had no rights under law. They belonged to their husbands. Their voices were not heard in public. But with the War of Independence, women found a voice as patriots. They supported the rebellion with boycotts. During wartime, women spied on the enemy. They served as messengers. They tended the wounded. Some even served as soldiers. Women performed daring feats of bravery. And they proved they were capable of doing much more than 18-century society allowed them." (Publisher's note)

Includes bibliographical references and index

Gorman, Jacqueline Laks

The **modern** feminist movement; sisters under the skin, 1961-1979. Chelsea House 2011 il (A cultural history of women in America) $35

Grades: 5 6 7 8 **305.4**

1. Feminism 2. Women -- Social conditions 3. Women -- United States -- History

ISBN 978-1-6041-3935-8; 1-6041-3935-8

LC 2010045990

An "eye-catching [layout] with good use of color, photographs, and informative sidebars, many of which use primary-source quotations, are the highlights of [this] appealing [volume]. . . . After a succinct overview of contemporary events, the chapters describe women's lives at home, at work, in education, in politics, in the arts, and their role in the general culture. . . . [This book] delves into the years of protest and quest for equal rights." SLJ

Includes glossary and bibliographical references

Heinemann, Sue

★ The **New** York Public Library amazing women in American history; a book of answers for kids. Wiley 1998 192p (New York Public Library answer books for kids series) pa $12.95

Grades: 5 6 7 8 **305.4**

1. Women -- United States -- History

ISBN 0-471-19216-3

LC 97-18465

Consists of short answers to questions about the roles and achievements of women in America from prehistory to the end of the twentieth century

"The text is succinct, easy to read, and informative. . . . Pertinent black-and-white photos appear throughout." SLJ

Includes glossary and bibliographical references

Stearman, Kaye

Women of today; contemporary issues and conflicts, 1980-present. [by] Kaye Stearman and Patience Coster. Chelsea House 2011 il (A cultural history of women in America) $35

Grades: 5 6 7 8 **305.4**

1. Feminism 2. Women -- United States 3. Women -- Social conditions

ISBN 978-1-6041-3936-5; 1-6041-3936-6

LC 2010046014

An "eye-catching [layout] with good use of color, photographs, and informative sidebars, many of which use primary-source quotations, are the highlights of [this] appealing [volume]. . . . After a succinct overview of contemporary events, the chapters describe women's lives at home, at work, in education, in politics, in the arts, and their role in the general culture. . . . [This book] highlights women's achievements, including U.S. Supreme Court justices, Speaker of the U.S. House of Representatives, and presidential candidates." SLJ

Includes glossary and bibliographical references

305.5 People by social and economic levels

Adler, David A.

A **picture** book of Harriet Tubman; illustrated by Samuel Byrd. Holiday House 1992 un il $17.95; pa $6.95

Grades: 1 2 3 **305.5**

1. Abolitionists 2. Underground railroad 3. African American women -- Biography

ISBN 0-8234-0926-0; 0-8234-1065-X pa

LC 91-19628

Biography of the black woman who escaped from slavery to become famous as a conductor on the Underground Railroad

This book features "brief, easy-to-read text. . . . Byrd's appealing, colorful illustrations convey the quiet dignity of a brave heroine." Booklist

A **picture** book of Sojourner Truth; illustrated by Gershom Griffith. Holiday House 1994 un il $17.95; pa $6.95

Grades: 1 2 3 **305.5**

1. Feminism 2. Abolitionists 3. Memoirists 4. African

American women -- Biography
ISBN 0-8234-1072-2; 0-8234-1262-8 pa

LC 93-7478

An introduction to the life of the woman born into slavery who became a well-known abolitionist and crusader for the rights of African Americans in the United States

The author "portrays his subject in a realistic manner, discussing slavery and other issues in an easy-to-read style. The quotes, while undocumented, are simple enough for the target audience and help to place events in context. Excellent-quality watercolor illustrations capture the action and provide effective representations and details of the time period." SLJ

Horn, Geoffrey M.

Sojourner Truth; speaking up for freedom. by Geoffrey Michael Horn. Crabtree Pub. Co. 2010 64 p. ill. (some col.) (pbk.: alk. paper) $10.95

Grades: 4 5 6 7 8   305.5
1. Abolitionists -- United States -- Biography 2. African American women -- Biography 3. African American abolitionists -- Biography 4. Social reformers -- United States -- Biography
ISBN 0778748405; 9780778748243; 9780778748403

LC 2009022428

This children's picture book by Geoffrey M. Horn in the Voices for Freedom: Abolitionist Views series looks at abolitionist Sojourner Truth. It "relates and details Truth's life and times, from her often-brutal treatment as a slave, named Isabella at birth, to her freedom, religious influences, and self-determination . . . and path to outspoken, sometimes provocative, and influential traveling speaker on a mission to raise awareness of and support for abolitionism." (Booklist)

"Combining accessible, lively prose and abundant visuals, this title . . . offers an engaging, informative introduction to the early advocate for the rights of African Americans and women." Booklist

Schroeder, Alan

Minty: a story of young Harriet Tubman; pictures by Jerry Pinkney. Dial Bks. for Young Readers 1996 un il hardcover o.p. pa $6.99

Grades: 1 2 3 4   305.5
1. Abolitionists 2. Slavery -- Fiction
ISBN 0-8037-1888-8; 0-14-056196-X pa

LC 95-23499

Coretta Scott King Award for illustration

Pinkney's "paintings, done in pencil, colored-pencils, and watercolor, use light and shadow to great effect. . . . This is a dramatic story that will hold listeners' interest and may lead them to biographical material." SLJ

305.8 Ethnic and national groups

Bolden, Tonya

Tell all the children our story; memories and mementos of being young and Black in America. Abrams 2001 128p il $24.95

Grades: 5 6 7 8   305.8
1. African American children 2. United States -- Race

relations
ISBN 0-8109-4496-0

LC 2001-1353

"This compilation of the African American experience, from colonial times through the twentieth century, reads and looks like a family scrapbook. . . . Photographs, excerpts from diaries and memoirs, and reproductions of artwork by black artists such as Charles Alston beautifully bring the story of each generation to life. Bolden vibrantly delivers her historical message through a contemporary perspective." Booklist

Includes bibliographical references

Cha, Dia

★ **Dia's** story cloth; written by Dia Cha; stitched by Chue and Nhia Thao Cha. Lee & Low Bks. 1996 un il $15.95; pa $6.95

Grades: 3 4 5   305.8
1. Hmong (Asian people)
ISBN 1-880000-34-2; 1-880000-63-6 pa

LC 95-41465

The story cloth made for her by her aunt and uncle chronicles the life of the author and her family in their native Laos and their eventual emigration to the United States

"An interesting and unusual title that resists neat categorization. . . . Part autobiography, part history, part description of a changing culture adapting life and art to new circumstances, the book serves as a brief introduction to the Hmong people." SLJ

Includes bibliographical references

Lester, Julius

★ **Let's** talk about race; illustrated by Karen Barbour. HarperCollinsPublishers 2005 un il $15.99; lib bdg $16.89

Grades: K 1 2 3   305.8
1. Racism 2. Prejudices
ISBN 0-06-028596-6; 0-06-028598-2 lib bdg

LC 2002-10979

This "picture book introduces race as just one of many chapters in a person's story. . . . Throughout the narrative, [the author] asks questions that young readers can answer, creating a dialogue about who they are and encouraging them to tell their own tales. He also discusses 'stories' that are not always true, pointing out that we create prejudice by perceiving ourselves as better than others. . . . The pairing of text and dazzling artwork is flawless." SLJ

Masoff, Joy

★ The **African** American story; the events that shaped our nation--and the people that changed our lives. Five Ponds 2007 95p il map $26.50

Grades: 4 5 6 7   305.8
1. African Americans -- History
ISBN 978-0-9727156-9-0

This "covers the history of the African people in America from the 1400s to the present. Historical photographs, archival documents, maps, and a fact-filled time line provide a visually stimulating introduction to the subject. . . . Masoff provides a tremendous amount of material in an exciting, appealing title that is useful for browsing, introductory lessons, quick reference, and beginning research." SLJ

Includes bibliographical references

Myers, Walter Dean, 1937-2014

★ **Now** is your time! the African-American struggle for freedom. HarperCollins Pubs. 1991 292p il hardcover o.p. pa $14.99

Grades: 6 7 8 9 **305.8**

    1. African Americans -- History

    ISBN 0-06-446120-3 pa

                              LC 91-314

Coretta Scott King Award for text

A history of the African-American struggle for freedom and equality, beginning with the capture of Africans in 1619, continuing through the American Revolution, the Civil War, and into contemporary times

"Myers's unique episodic approach makes this history a compelling exploration of the African-American experience. . . . This fascinating book will engender pride in heritage for young African Americans and provide insight into American history for all of us." Horn Book

Includes bibliographical references

Nelson, Kadir

★ **Heart** and soul; words and paintings by Kadir Nelson. Balzer + Bray 2011 108p. col. ill. $19.99; lib bdg $20.89

Grades: 3 4 5 6 **305.8**

    1. African Americans -- History

    ISBN 978-0-06-173074-0; 0-06-173074-2; 978-0-06-173076-4 lib bdg; 0-06-173076-9 lib bdg

                    LC 2010046236

Coretta Scott King Award (Authors) (2012)

"Nelson knits together the nation's proudest moments with its most shameful, taking on the whole of African-American history, from Revolutionary-era slavery up to the election of Barack Obama. He handles this vast subject with easy grace. . . . In jaw-dropping portraits, Nelson paints heroes like Frederick Douglass and Joe Louis, conferring equal dignity on the slaves, workers, soldiers, and students. . . . A tremendous achievement." Publ Wkly

Include bibliographical references (p. 104) and index.

Petrillo, Valerie

★ **A kid's** guide to Latino history; more than 70 activities. Chicago Review Press 2009 214p il pa $14.95

Grades: 4 5 6 7 **305.8**

    1. Hispanic Americans -- History

    ISBN 978-1-55652-771-5 pa; 1-55652-771-3 pa

                  LC 2008040433

"This big, lively overview examines the history of Latinos in the U.S. . . . The chatty, informative text, presented in readable, spacious layouts, will draw kids with lots of fun, illustrated instructions for related activities. . . . The accessible facts and the individual portraits of notable authors, athletes, entertainers, and politicians portray Latinos' rich contribution to U.S. heritage, and kids will want to talk about the well-presented issues." Booklist

Includes bibliographical references

Rappaport, Doreen

★ **Free** at last! stories and songs of Emancipation. illustrated by Shane W. Evans. Candlewick Press 2004 63p il $19.99; pa $7.99

Grades: 3 4 5 6 **305.8**

    1. African Americans -- History 2. African Americans

-- Civil rights 3. Southern States -- Race relations

    ISBN 0-7636-1440-8; 0-7636-3147-7 pa

                  LC 2003-43853

"Stories, poems, and songs about events from the Emancipation Proclamation of 1863 through the Brown v. Board of Education decision of 1954 are perfectly matched with vibrant oil paintings. The result is a glorious tribute to the lives of African-American heroes and heroines." SLJ

Reynolds, Jan

Only the mountains do not move; a Maasai story of culture and conservation. Lee & Low Books 2011 40p il $18.95; pa $9.95

Grades: 2 3 4 **305.8**

    1. Agriculture 2. Kenya -- Social life and customs

    ISBN 978-1-60060-333-4; 1-60060-333-5; 978-1-60060-844-5 pa; 1-60060-844-2 pa

                  LC 2010050879

"With many clear color photos and an appended glossary with pronunciation, this is an excellent addition to classroom units on Africa today." Booklist

"A photographic essay about the Maasai people in Kenya, traditionally nomadic herders, exploring the contemporary challenges they face—focusing on environmental changes such as the overgrazing of land and the threat of wildlife extinction—and how the Maasai are adapting their agricultural practices and lifestyle while preserving their culture." Publisher's note

Slade, Suzanne

Climbing Lincoln's steps; the African American journey. illustrated by Colin Bootman. Albert Whitman 2010 un il $16.99

Grades: 2 3 4 5 **305.8**

    1. United States -- Race relations 2. African Americans -- Civil rights 3. Lincoln Memorial (Washington, D.C.)

    ISBN 978-0-8075-1204-3; 0-8075-1204-4

                  LC 2010004962

"This attractive, accessible title uses the Lincoln Memorial as a vehicle to outline the history of the Civil Rights Movement from the Emancipation Proclamation to Dr. King's 'I Have a Dream' speech to the 2008 presidential election. Other pivotal moments include world-renowned singer Marian Anderson's 1939 performance at the memorial when she was barred from singing at Constitution Hall. . . . Bootman's realistic watercolor spreads are striking." SLJ

Stefoff, Rebecca, 1951-

A **different** mirror for young people; a history of multicultural America. by Ronald Takaki; adapted by Rebecca Stefoff. Seven Stories Press 2012 vi, 377 p.p ill. (paperback: alk. paper) $18.95; (hardcover: alk. paper) $40.00; (ebook) $18.95

Grades: 7 8 9 10 **305.8**

    1. Letters 2. Multiculturalism 3. United States -- History 4. United States -- Race relations 5. United States -- Ethnic relations 6. Minorities -- United States -- History 7. Cultural pluralism -- United States -- History

    ISBN 1609804163; 9781609804169; 9781609804848; 9781609804176

                  LC 2012017004

Through studies of "American ethnic history . . . multiculturalism studies . . . and diversity" author Ronald Takaki "brings ethnic history alive through the words of people, including teenagers, who recorded their experiences in letters, diaries, and poems." The book "offers a rich and rewarding 'people's view' perspective on the American story." (Publisher's note)

Includes bibliographical references and index.

305.896   Africans and people of African descent

King, Martin Luther, Jr., 1929-1968

★ **I** have a dream; foreword by Coretta Scott King; paintings by fifteen Coretta Scott King Award and Honor Book artists, Ashley Bryan . . . [et al.] Scholastic 1997 40p il $16.95

Grades: K 1 2 3   **305.896**

1. Illustration of books 2. United States -- Race relations 3. African Americans -- Civil rights

ISBN 0-590-20516-1

LC 95-45189

"Martin Luther King, Jr.'s classic speech is creatively illustrated by 15 Coretta Scott King Award-winning artists. Signed statements from the artists explain the emotions they were trying to capture and why and how they used certain colors and tones. . . . From cover to cover this is a beautiful book." SLJ

306.3   Economic institutions

Kimmel, Allison Crotzer

A **primary** source history of slavery in the United States; by Allison Crotzer Kimmel. Capstone Press 2015 32p illustrations, map (pbk) $7.95; (lib bdg) $26.65

Grades: 3 4 5 6   **306.3**

1. Slavery -- United States 2. African Americans -- History

ISBN 9781491418437; 9781491418390

"Uses primary sources to tell the story of slavery in the United States." (Publisher's note)

"Well designed and informative, these books are ideal for those new to primary source documents. The fonts--large, plain, and bold--are offset by plain backgrounds. An apt and clearly captioned photograph appears on each page." SLJ

Includes bibliographical references and index

Lester, Julius

★ **From** slave ship to freedom road; paintings by Rod Brown. Dial Bks. 1998 40p il hardcover o.p. pa $6.99

Grades: 5 6 7 8   **306.3**

1. Slavery -- United States

ISBN 0-8037-1893-4; 0-14-056669-4 pa

LC 96-44422

"Lester's impassioned questions grow from his visceral response to Brown's narrative paintings. . . . The combination of history, art, and commentary demands interaction." Booklist

306.76   Sexual orientation, transgenderism, intersexuality

Seba, Jaime

Gallup guides for youth facing persistent prejudice; The LGBT community. by Jaime Seba. Mason Crest Publishers 2013 64 p. col. ill., photographs (library) $22.95

Grades: 5 6 7 8   **306.76**

1. LGBT people -- Civil rights 2. Homophobia 3. Gay youth -- United States 4. Homophobia -- United States 5. Sexual minorities -- Civil rights -- United States

ISBN 1422224678; 9781422224670

LC 2012017108

This book by Jaime Seba on the LGBT community "discusses the history of prejudice toward this group, the laws that protect people against discrimination-and what you can do to fight the prejudice you find in the world." (Publisher's note) As part of the "Gallup Guides for Youth Facing Persistent Prejudice" series, it "emphasiz[es] recent violence and other problems, such as bullying and depression, which are, unfortunately, still routine for many LGBT youth." (Booklist)

Includes bibliographical references (p. 62) and index.

306.8   Marriage and family

Ajmera, Maya

Our grandparents; a global album. [by] Maya Ajmera, Sheila Kinkade, Cynthia Pon; with a foreword by Archbishop Desmond Tutu. Charlesbridge 2010 un il $16.95

Grades: PreK K 1 2   **306.8**

1. Grandparents

ISBN 978-1-57091-458-4; 1-57091-458-3

LC 2009005494

"Clear, colorful photographs show the two generations engaged in a variety of activities and invite careful observation. The pictures are clearly labeled with the name of the families' countries and highlight common threads, e.g., 'listening,' in Tibet, India, Mexico, and USA. Spare text defines the actions represented. The book concludes with 'Five Things to Do with Your Grandparents.'" SLJ

Crist, James J.

Siblings; you're stuck with each other so stick together. by James J. Crist & Elizabeth Verdick; illustrated by Steve Mark. Free Spirit Pub. 2010 118p il (Laugh & learn) pa $8.95

Grades: 3 4 5 6   **306.8**

1. Siblings

ISBN 978-1-57542-336-4 pa; 1-57542-336-7 pa

"Starting with the wry subtitle and the colorful cover cartoon of two fuming kids standing back to back, this lively title uses accessible humor to approach sibling-related topics, such as birth order, privacy, jealousy, bullying, and bonding. The authors discuss each subject in a child-centered, casual, and humorous tone. . . . The book's open design and interactive features, such as quick checklists and quizzes, help make this a great choice for kids and grownups to talk and laugh about together." Booklist

Includes bibliographical references

Guillain, Charlotte

A **new** brother or sister. Heinemann Library 2011 24p
il (Growing up) lib bdg $22; pa $6.49

Grades: PreK K 1 2   **306.8**

1. Infants 2. Siblings

ISBN 978-1-4329-4803-0 lib bdg; 1-4329-4803-2 lib
bdg; 978-1-4329-4813-9 pa; 1-4329-4813-X pa

LC 2010024197

Brief text and photographs explain what happens when
a new baby joins your family, the special care babies need,
and how you can help take care of your new brother or sister.

Includes bibliographical references

Hoffman, Mary

★ The **great** big book of families; pictures by Ros
Asquith. Dial Books for Young Readers 2011 un il $16.99

Grades: PreK K 1 2   **306.8**

1. Family 2. Single-parent families

ISBN 978-0-8037-3516-3; 0-8037-3516-2

LC 2010-12141

"In matter-of-fact prose and genial pen-and-ink drawings, Hoffman and Asquith reassure readers [that] . . . there's
no one right way to be a family. What sets their survey of
familyhood apart . . . is the collaborators' expansive take on
demographics. They cover not only a wide range of parental
and domestic arrangements, but also schooling, homes, con-
sumerism, employment—or lack of it—and psychographics.
. . . Asquith's spreads have a lively, encyclopedic feel, with
whimsical themed borders." Publ Wkly

Konrad, Marla Stewart

Grand. Tundra Books 2010 un il (World vision early
readers) $12.95

Grades: PreK K   **306.8**

1. Grandparents

ISBN 978-0-88776-997-9; 0-88776-997-7

This features color photographs of children around the
world engaged in activities with their grandparents.

This book's "simple, sharp aesthetic will capture the
imagination of a good number of children." Booklist

Mom and me. Tundra Books 2009 un il (World vision
early readers) $12.95

Grades: PreK K   **306.8**

1. Mother-child relationship

ISBN 978-0-88776-866-8; 0-88776-866-0

"A spare easy-to-read text combined with high-quality,
full-color photographs highlights youngsters and mothers
throughout the world involved in universal activities such as
bathing, feeding, and providing comfort and support. Each
spread demonstrates strong emotions and provides evidence
of the woman's love and pride in her child. The vivid photos
present a variety of settings, including many different cultures, and draw viewers into the pages." SLJ

Sheldon, Annette

★ **Big** sister now; a story about me and our new baby.
written by Annette Sheldon; illustrated by Karen Maizel.
Magination Press 2006 32p il $14.95; pa $8.95

Grades: PreK   **306.8**

1. Infants 2. Siblings

ISBN 1-59147-243-1; 1-59147-244-X pa

LC 2005005839

"Among the flood of titles about older siblings and new
babies, this book, published under the auspices of the American Psychological Association, stands out for its appealing
illustrations and direct story, which wraps a clear, comforting message. . . . An appended section offers parents solid
ideas for helping a child adjust to a new baby." Booklist

306.846   Interracial marriages, partnerships, unions

Alko, Selina

★ The **case** for loving; fighting for interracial marriage.
by Selina Alko; illustrated by Sean Qualls and Selina Alko.
Arthur A. Levine Books, an imprint of Scholastic Inc. 2015
40 p. illustrations (chiefly color) (jacketed hardcover: alk.
paper) $18.99

Grades: K 1 2 3 4   **306.846**

1. Family 2. Interracial marriage -- Law and legislation
3. Interracial marriage

ISBN 0545478537; 9780545478533

LC 2014005329

This children's book by Selina Alko is "story of one
brave family: Mildred Loving, Richard Perry Loving, and
their three children. It is the story of how Mildred and Richard fell in love, and got married in Washington, D.C. But
when they moved back to their hometown in Virginia, they
were arrested (in dramatic fashion) for violating that state's
laws against interracial marriage." (Publisher's note)

"Many children's books tackle landmark events in U.S.
history, but this one is an especially needed addition. The
story of Richard and Mildred Loving, the interracial couple
whose fight for the right to be married led to the Supreme
Court's ruling that ended anti-miscegenation laws, is relayed
here as a love story that does not sugarcoat the virulent racism of the time...An author's note grounds the Lovings' story in the present as Alko recognizes that her own interracial
marriage is part of the trajectory of change, which continues
today in the LGBTQ community's fight for equality. Inspirational, never heavy-handed, and appropriate for just about
everyone. " Booklist

Includes bibliographical references

306.85   Family

Rotner, Shelley

Families; by Shelley Rotner and Sheila M. Kelly; photographs by Shelley Rotner. Holiday House 2015 32 p.
color illustrations (hardcover) $17.95

Grades: PreK K 1 2   **306.85**

1. Family 2. Families

ISBN 0823430537; 9780823430536

LC 2013032957

This book, by Shelley Rotner and Sheila M. Kelly, is "a
picture book for very young children about the many faces
of contemporary families. . . . This inclusive look at many
varieties of families will help young readers see beyond
their own immediate experiences and begin to understand
others." (Publisher's note)

"Rotner and Kelly describe all kinds of familial units:
those with only one parent or one child, those in which the
parents and children resemble one another, those with mem-

bers of different races, those with same and opposite sex parents, and those with adopted children. Winsome, clear photographs are accompanied by brief, large-font text. This celebration of differences is further enhanced by the inclusion of women in head scarves, a dad in a wheelchair, and multigenerational groupings." SLJ

306.874 Parent-child relationship

Joosse, Barbara M.
★ **Mama,** do you love me? illustrated by Barbara Lavallee. Chronicle Bks. 1991 un il $15.99; bd bk $6.99
Grades: PreK K   **306.874**
1. Inuit -- Fiction 2. Mother-daughter relationship -- Fiction
ISBN 978-0-87701-759-2; 0-87701-759-X; 978-0-8118-2131-5 bd bk; 0-8118-2131-5 bd bk
LC 90-1863
"A young girl asks how much her mother loves her, even when she is naughty, and receives warm, reassuring answers. The twist on this familiar theme is that the two are Inuits, and the text and pictures draw on their unique culture. . . . Two pages of back matter define and explain the functions of various terms in Inuit life past and present. Charming, vibrant watercolor illustrations expand the simple rhythmic text, adding to the characters' personalities and to the cultural information." SLJ

Thomas, Pat
This is my family; a first look at same-sex parents. by Pat Thomas. 1st ed. Barron's Educational Series, Inc. 2012 29 p. ill. (A first look at) (paperback) $7.99
Grades: K 1 2   **306.874**
1. Same-sex marriage 2. Families 3. Gay parents 4. Children of gay parents 5. Gay fathers -- Family relationships 6. Lesbian mothers -- Family relationships
ISBN 1438001878; 9781438001876
LC 2012940639
This book by Pat Thomas is part of the "A First Look At" series, which "encourages kids of preschool through early school age to understand and overcome problems that might trouble them in social and family relationships." It "takes a child's point of view in its discussion of same-sex marriage. Its message is intended both for children of gay or lesbian parents, as well as for the kids and parents of the children's friends and playmates." (Publisher's note)
Includes bibliographical references (p. 29).

306.875 Sibling relationships

Cole, Joanna
★ The **new** baby at your house; photographs by Margaret Miller. rev ed; Morrow Junior Bks. 1998 un il hardcover o.p. pa $6.99
Grades: K 1 2 3   **306.875**
1. Infants 2. Siblings
ISBN 0-688-13897-7; 0-688-13898-5 lib bdg; 0-688-16698-9 pa
LC 97-29267
A revised and newly illustrated edition of the title first published 1985

Describes the activities and changes involved in having a new baby in the house and the feelings experienced by the older brothers and sisters
"Miller captures many intimate and touching moments with her pictures. . . . There is a good balance of families from varied ethnic backgrounds. . . . This book opens with a clear and precise note to parents that gives honest, practical advice." SLJ
Includes bibliographical references

306.89 Separation and divorce

Brown, Laurene Krasny
★ **Dinosaurs** divorce; a guide for changing families. [by] Laurene Krasny Brown and Marc Brown. Atlantic Monthly Press 1986 31p il $15.95; pa $7.95
Grades: K 1 2 3   **306.89**
1. Divorce
ISBN 0-316-11248-8; 0-316-10996-7 pa
LC 86-1079
Text and illustrations of dinosaur characters introduce aspects of divorce such as its causes and effects, living with a single parent, spending holidays in two separate households, and adjusting to a stepparent
"The picture-book, almost comic-book, format, the touches of humor, and the distancing effect of the dinosaurs as surrogate humans may make the book accessible to young or extremely anxious children. A thoughtful, useful book." Horn Book

Cook, Julia
The "D" word; [illustrated by Phillip W. Rodgers] National Center for Youth Issues 2011 32 p. $9.95
Grades: K 1 2 3 4   **306.89**
ISBN 1931636761; 9781931636766
Otis used to have the "perfect" family. That all changed when his parents told him that they were getting a D... D... D... The "D" Word - he can't even say it! At first Otis blames himself. With the help of his Gram, Otis discovers the reasons why people get divorced.

Holyoke, Nancy
A **smart** girl's guide to her parents' divorce; how to land on your feet when your world turns upside down. illustrated by Scott Nash. American Girl Pub. 2009 120p il pa $9.95
Grades: 3 4 5   **306.89**
1. Divorce 2. Children of divorced parents
ISBN 978-1-59369-488-3 pa; 1-59369-488-1 pa
"Short chapters illustrated with bright cartoon drawings cover many important concerns and offer explanations of the divorce process. Topics range from how to deal with negative emotions, family changes, and new living arrangements, to tougher issues such as violence and financial troubles. The text has a compassionate tone, and sprinkled throughout are answers to questions that readers might have as well as snippets of advice from girls who have found what works for them." SLJ

306.9 Institutions pertaining to death

Thornhill, Jan

I found a dead bird; the kids' guide to the cycle of life & death. Maple Tree Press 2006 64p il $21.95; pa $9.95
Grades: 4 5 6   **306.9**
1. Death 2. Bereavement
ISBN 1-897066-70-8; 1-897066-71-6 pa

Explores the cycle of life and death, and how the process is necessary in nature, while also commenting on how death effects people personally, and the skills they use to cope with such a trauma when it occurs.

"This straightforward, no holds barred approach to the subject will captivate children. Chock-full of color photographs, the well-designed book contains boxes with tidbits of information on a wide variety of topics, such as death of a species, human destruction, plant decomposition, trapped in time, and learning from death." SLJ

307 Communities

Ajmera, Maya

Be my neighbor; [by] Maya Ajmera & John D. Ivanko. Shakti for Children, Charlesbridge 2004 un il $15.95; pa $6.95
Grades: K 1 2   **307**
1. Community life
ISBN 1-57091-504-0; 1-57091-685-3 pa
                              LC 2003-21230
A simple introduction to the characteristics of a neighborhood

"This beautifully crafted book explores the concept of community, using well-chosen words from the late Mr. Rogers as a starting point. . . . Illustrated with bright, beautiful full-color photos of children around the world, the gorgeous spreads are organized by themes." SLJ

Hopkinson, Deborah

Shutting out the sky; life in the tenements of New York, 1880-1924. Orchard Bks. 2003 134p il $17.95
Grades: 5 6 7 8 9 10   **307**
1. Poor 2. Immigrants -- United States 3. Lower East Side (New York, N.Y.)
ISBN 0-439-37590-8
                              LC 2002-44781
Photographs and text document the experiences of five individuals who came to live in the Lower East Side of New York City as children or young adults from Belarus, Italy, Lithuania, and Romania at the turn of the twentieth century.

"The text is supported by numerous tinted archival photos of living and working conditions. Although this book will appeal to students looking for material for projects, the writing lends immediacy and vivid images make it simply a fascinating read." SLJ

Includes bibliographical references

307.76 Urban communities

Reilly, Kathleen M.

Cities; Discover How They Work. by Kathleen M. Reilly, illustrated by Tom Casteel. Pgw 2014 128 p. $16.95

Grades: 4 5 6   **307.76**
1. Urban ecology 2. Cities and towns 3. City planning 4. Civil engineering
ISBN 1619302136; 1619302179; 9781619302136; 9781619302174

This book, by Kathleen M. Reilly and illustrated by Tom Casteel, "will give kids a view into the inner functioning of . . . urban areas. They'll learn about all the parts that come together to make cities work and how they've grown and changed since the very first riverside settlements. . . . Sidebars, unique illustrations, . . . and fun . . . facts combine with age-appropriate hands-on activities to make learning about complex urban environments fun and reinforce learning." (Publisher's note)

"According to the 2010 Census, 80% of Americans live in urban areas." But do they know what it takes to make a city run? From this well-organized and engaging text, readers will learn how cities developed and grew...The simple black-and-white illustrations are helpful, but young readers accustomed to photos might pass on it when leafing through the book. Even so, this is a worthy title for any library collection." SLJ

320 Political science (Politics and government)

Giesecke, Ernestine

National government; 2nd ed; Heinemann Library 2010 32p il map (Kids' guide to government) $29.29; pa $7.99
Grades: 3 4 5   **320**
1. United States -- Politics and government
ISBN 978-1-4329-2708-0; 1-4329-2708-6; 978-1-4329-2713-4 pa; 1-4329-2713-2 pa
First published 2000

Introduces the purpose and function of national government, the significance of the Constitution, the three branches of government, how the government raises money, and how a bill becomes a law

"This . . . would be a great asset. . . . Students will learn about a different, but related government every two pages. The font is large and easy to read. The photos, diagrams, charts, maps, and illustrations supplement the text well." Libr Media Connect

Includes glossary

320.3 Comparative government

Giesecke, Ernestine

Governments around the world; 2nd ed; Heinemann Library 2010 32p il map (Kids' guide to government) $29.29; pa $7.99
Grades: 3 4 5   **320.3**
1. Comparative government
ISBN 978-1-4329-2705-9; 1-4329-2705-1; 978-1-4329-2710-3 pa; 1-4329-2710-8 pa
First published 2000

Introduces the concept of government, exploring various types of systems, including democracy, communism, and socialism, and presenting international organizations such as the UN and NATO

"This . . . would be a great asset. . . . Students will learn about a different, but related government every two pages. The font is large and easy to read. The photos, diagrams, charts, maps, and illustrations supplement the text well." Libr Media Connect

Includes glossary and bibliographical references

Who's in charge? how governments make the world go round. foreword by Andrew Marr; [editors, Alexander Cox, Deborah Lock, Fleur Star; US editor, Margaret Parrish] DK 2010 96p il $16.99

Grades: 3 4 5 6   **320.3**

1. Political science

ISBN 978-0-7566-6278-3; 0-7566-6278-8

LC 2010280417

Introduces politicians and how laws are made, what happens in government and how the reader can get involved.

"The book explains ideas like democracy, monarchy, communism, and capitalism in a way that is accessible to children. Information is presented with DK's signature bright, colorful graphics. . . . This book is a timely and useful addition." Libr Media Connect

Includes glossary

320.4   Structure and functions of government

Wyatt, Valerie

How to build your own country; written by Valerie Wyatt; illustrated by Fred Rix. Kids Can Press 2009 40p il (CitizenKid) $17.95

Grades: 3 4 5   **320.4**

1. Citizenship 2. Political science

ISBN 978-1-55453-310-7; 1-55453-310-4

"This unique, odd, and informative book offers a guide for readers to create their own personal countries. Everything from finding unclaimed land and coming up with a name . . . to holding elections and serving one's citizens is covered. Despite the silliness, useful information is given, teaching readers about the value of diplomacy and how actual governments function." Horn Book Guide

Includes glossary

320.8   Local government

Giesecke, Ernestine

Local government; 2nd ed; Heinemann Library 2009 32p il map (Kids' guide to government) $29.29; pa $7.99

Grades: 3 4 5   **320.8**

1. Local government 2. United States -- Politics and government

ISBN 978-1-4329-2706-6; 1-4329-2706-X; 978-1-4329-2711-0 pa; 1-4329-2711-6 pa

First published 2000

Introduces the purpose and function of local governments, explores the three branches of government at the city and county level, and presents the relationships between city and suburban governments and between various governments and schools

"This . . . would be a great asset. . . . Students will learn about a different, but related government every two pages. The font is large and easy to read. The photos, diagrams,

charts, maps, and illustrations supplement the text well." Libr Media Connect

Includes glossary

322.4   Political action groups

Schwartz, Heather E.

Political activism; how you can make a difference. by Heather E. Schwartz. Capstone Press 2009 32p il (Take action) lib bdg $19.99

Grades: 3 4 5 6   **322.4**

1. Lobbying 2. Social action 3. Political activists

ISBN 978-1-4296-2799-3 lib bdg; 1-4296-2799-9 lib bdg

LC 2008026939

"Whether the issue is animal rights, global warming, or student representation in government, this lively hands-on title . . . combines personal profiles of activist teens with the politics of what they are fighting for, and includes realistic advice about how to do research, set goals, ask questions, and take one step at a time to reach those in power. The open, attractive design will draw readers with color photos of young activists." Booklist

Includes bibliographical references

323   Civil and political rights

Marzollo, Jean

★ **Happy** birthday, Martin Luther King; illustrated by J. Brian Pinkney. Scholastic 1993 un il pa $6.99; $15.95

Grades: K 1 2 3   **323**

1. Clergy 2. Nonfiction writers 3. Civil rights activists 4. Nobel laureates for peace 5. African Americans -- Biography 6. African Americans -- Civil rights 7. Biography, Individual

ISBN 0-439-78224-4 pa; 0-590-44065-9

LC 91-42137

This biography of the Baptist minister discusses "his education, his life as a pastor, and his involvement in the civil rights movement. . . . Ages four to eight." (Booklist)

"This very easy biography of Martin Luther King is distinguished by its succinct explanations of King's achievements. . . . The narrative of King's life is smooth and accessible. Pinkney's scratchboard paintings are fluidly drawn, warm, and dignified." Bull Cent Child Books

National Geographic Society (U.S.)

★ **Every** human has rights; a photographic declaration for kids. based on the United Nations Universal Declaration of Human Rights; with poetry from the ePals community; foreword by Mary Robinson. National Geographic 2009 30p il $26.90

Grades: 4 5 6 7 8   **323**

1. Human rights

ISBN 978-1-4263-0511-5; 1-4263-0511-7

"On the sixtieth anniversary of the Universal Declaration of Human Rights, this full-color photo-essay combines prize-winning poems by young people with beautiful photographs from all over the world. . . . The stirring pictures will stimulate classroom discussion about the declaration, which is quoted in full at the back." Booklist

Thomas, William David

What are citizens' basic rights? [by] William David Thomas. Gareth Stevens Pub. 2008 32p il (My American government) lib bdg $23.93; pa $8.95

Grades: 3 4 5 **323**

1. Civil rights

ISBN 978-0-8368-8861-4 lib bdg; 0-8368-8861-8 lib bdg; 978-0-8368-8866-9 pa; 0-8368-8866-9 pa

LC 2007032425

This describes the basic legal rights of United States citizens

This book has "an accessible format and clear writing. . . . Black-and-white and full-color vintage and more recent photographs appear throughout." SLJ

Includes glossary and bibliographical references

323.1 Civil and political rights of nondominant groups

Aretha, David

Sit-ins and freedom rides. Morgan Reynolds Pub. 2009 128p il lib bdg $28.95

Grades: 5 6 7 8 **323.1**

1. African Americans -- Civil rights 2. Southern States -- Race relations

ISBN 978-1-59935-098-1 lib bdg; 1-59935-098-X lib bdg

LC 2008039600

"Aretha opens with an introduction to the four college students who orchestrated the famous sit-in at Woolworth's in Greensboro, NC, in 1960. He follows that with chapters that describe slavery, Reconstruction, and Jim Crow in terms of how they set the stage for the resistance efforts. . . . [The book] offers insight into to workings of the protests at the grassroots level. Individual anecdotes interspersed thoughout the detailed narrative provide personal and effective accounts that go beyond mere facts. Black-and-white and some color photographs appear on almost every page." SLJ

Includes bibliographical references

Bass, Hester

Seeds of freedom; the peaceful integration of Huntsville, Alabama. Hester Bass, illustrated by E.B. Lewis. Candlewick Press 2014 32 p. color illustrations $16.99

Grades: K 1 2 3 **323.1**

1. Blacks -- Segregation 2. Alabama -- Race relations 3. African Americans -- Civil rights

ISBN 0763669199; 9780763669195

LC 2013955948

This children's book by Hester Bass tells "a little-known story of the civil rights movement, in which black and white citizens in [Huntsville,] Alabama city worked together nonviolently to end segregation. Bass and illustrator E. B. Lewis show children how racial discrimination, bullying, and unfairness can be faced successfully with perseverance and ingenuity." (Publisher's note)

"This picture book opens by telling of life in Huntsville, Alabama, in 1962, during the Jim Crow era. While the city takes pride in its world-renowned space center, a black family cannot eat in a whites-only restaurant... Capturing the period with finesse, Lewis' expressive watercolor paintings record the events and settings in beautifully composed scenes.

His portrayal of people is particularly fine, conveying the personalities, attitudes, and emotions of individuals as well as the essential dignity of the nonviolent protesters. A valuable introduction to the civil rights period." Booklist

Bausum, Ann

Freedom Riders; John Lewis and Jim Zwerg on the front lines of the civil rights movement. by Ann Bausum; forewords by Freedom Riders Congressman John Lewis and Jim Zwerg. National Geographic 2006 79p il por $18.95; lib bdg $28.90

Grades: 5 6 7 8 **323.1**

1. Members of Congress 2. Civil rights activists 3. African Americans -- Civil rights 4. Southern States -- Race relations

ISBN 0-7922-4173-8; 0-7922-4174-6 lib bdg

LC 2005012947

"Bausum's narrative style, fresh, engrossing, and at times heart-stopping, brings the story of the turbulent and often violent dismantling of segregated travel alive in vivid detail. The language, presentation of material, and pacing will draw readers in and keep them captivated." SLJ

Includes bibliographical references

Brimner, Larry Dane, 1949-

★ Birmingham Sunday. Calkins Creek 2010 48p il

Grades: 5 6 7 8 **323.1**

1. Bombings 2. Hate crimes 3. Racism 4. African Americans -- Civil rights 5. Birmingham (Ala.) -- Race relations 6. Sixteenth Street Baptist Church (Birmingham, Ala.) 7. Hate crimes -- Birmingham (Ala.)

ISBN 1590786130; 9781590786130

LC 2009035716

This book describes the bombing of the Sixteenth Street Church in 1963 by Ku Klux Klan members, which killed four girls, and discusses how the event contributed to the civil rights movement. "Grades five to eight." (Bull Cent Child Books)

"This moving photo-essay covers much more than just an account of the Birmingham, Alabama, Baptist Church bombing that killed four young girls in 1963. The detailed text, illustrated with black-and-white photos on every spacious double-page spread, sets the shocking assassination of the children within a general overview of both the racist segregation of the times and the struggle against it." Booklist

Freedman, Russell

★ Freedom walkers; the story of the Montgomery bus boycott. Holiday House 2006 114p il $18.95

Grades: 4 5 6 7 **323.1**

1. Clergy 2. Historians 3. College teachers 4. Nonfiction writers 5. Civil rights activists 6. Nobel laureates for peace 7. African Americans -- Civil rights 8. Montgomery (Ala.) -- Race relations

ISBN 978-0-8234-2031-5; 0-8234-2031-0

LC 2006-41148

This account of the Montgomery bus boycott of 1955 focuses on Jo Ann Robinson, Claudette Colvin, Rosa Parks, Martin Luther King, and other participants.

This offers "expertly paced text, balanced but impassioned. . . . The narrative arc is compelling; well-cap-

tioned black-and-white photographs enhance the impact."
Horn Book

Includes bibliographical references

Holland, Leslie J.

Dr. Martin Luther King Jr.'s I have a dream speech in
translation; what it really means. Capstone Press 2009 32p
il (Fact finders. Kids' translations) lib bdg $23.99; pa
$7.95

Grades: 3 4 5　　　　　　　　　　　　　　**323.1**

1. Clergy 2. American speeches 3. Nonfiction writers
4. Civil rights activists 5. Nobel laureates for peace 6.
African Americans -- Civil rights

ISBN 978-1-4296-2793-1 lib bdg; 1-4296-2793-X lib
bdg; 978-1-4296-3449-6 pa; 1-4296-3449-9 pa

LC 2008-32867

"Presents Dr. Martin Luther King Jr.'s speech and explains its meaning using everyday language. Describes the
events that led to the speech and its significance through history." Publisher's note

Includes glossary and bibliographical references

Kittinger, Jo S.

Rosa's bus; illustrated by Steven Walker. Boyds Mills
Press 2010 un il $17.95

Grades: 1 2 3 4　　　　　　　　　　　　　**323.1**

1. Buses 2. Civil rights activists 3. African Americans
-- Civil rights 4. Montgomery (Ala.) -- Race relations

ISBN 978-1-59078-722-9; 1-59078-722-6

LC 2010005091

"In an inventive approach, this handsome picture book
frames the biography of Rosa Parks with the story of the
bus on which she famously refused to give up her seat to a
white passenger. . . . The free-verse narrative and dramatic
oil paintings tell the larger story of discrimination in daily
life." Booklist

Includes bibliographical references

McWhorter, Diane

★ **A dream** of freedom; the Civil Rights Movement
from 1954 to 1968. foreword by Reverend Fred Shuttles-
worth. Scholastic Nonfiction 2004 160p il $19.95

Grades: 5 6 7 8　　　　　　　　　　　　　**323.1**

1. United States -- Race relations 2. African Americans
-- Civil rights

ISBN 0-439-57678-4

The author discusses "the national civil rights movement
from Brown v. the Board of Education to the assassination
of Martin Luther King Jr. . . . This account is both factual
and personal. She discusses her feelings as a white child in
the South, and she focuses in on the many ways in which
both white and black children were involved in the movement. . . . The breadth and depth of McWhorter's book is
exemplary." Booklist

Pinkney, Andrea Davis

Martin and Mahalia; his words, her song. by Andrea
Davis Pinkney; illustrated by Brian Pinkney. 1st ed. Little,
Brown and Co. 2013 40 p. ill. (reinforced) $17.99

Grades: 1 2 3 4　　　　　　　　　　　　**323.092**

1. Picture books for children 2. African Americans
-- Civil rights -- History -- 20th century -- literature 3.
Civil rights movements -- United States -- History --

20th century

ISBN 0316070130; 9780316070133

LC 2012005499

This children's picture book weaves together "the stories
of two giants of the American civil rights movement," Martin Luther King, Jr. and Mahalia Jackson. "At first the stories
are distinct, with alternating, dedicated spreads tracing the
individuals' paths as gospel preacher and singer until they
meet and combine forces at the Montgomery bus boycott
in 1955 and forge a collaboration that takes them through
Martin's most famous speech, at the Lincoln Memorial."
(Booklist)

★ **Sit-in**; how four friends stood up by sitting down.
[by] Andrea Davis Pinkney and Brian Pinkney. Little,
Brown and Company 2010 un il $16.99

Grades: K 1 2 3　　　　　　　　　　　　**323.1**

1. African Americans -- Civil rights 2. Southern States
-- Race relations 3. Civil rights movements

ISBN 0-316-07016-5; 978-0-316-07016-4

LC 2009-19470

Flora Stieglitz Straus Award for Nonficton 2011

"This picture book is a celebration of the 50th anniversary of the . . . Woolworth's lunch counter sit-in, when four
college students staged a peaceful protest." (Publisher's
note) "Grades three to five." (Bull Cent Child Books)

"This compelling picture book is based on the historic
sit-in 50 years ago by four college students who tried to integrate a Woolworth's lunch counter in Greensboro, North
Carolina. Food-related wordplay adds layers to free verse. .
. . At the core of the exciting narrative are scenes that show
the difficulty of facing hatred. . . . Even young children will
grasp the powerful, elemental, and historic story." Booklist

Rappaport, Doreen

★ **Nobody** gonna turn me 'round; stories and songs of
the civil rights movement. illustrated by Shane W. Evans.
Candlewick Press 2006 63p il $19.99

Grades: 3 4 5 6　　　　　　　　　　　　**323.1**

1. United States -- Race relations 2. African Americans
-- Civil rights

ISBN 0-7636-1927-2; 978-0-7636-1927-5

LC 2005-53184

"Rappaport draws on songs, poems, memories, letters,
court testimony, and first-person accounts to provide a moving portrayal of the experiences of African Americans from
the 1955 Montgomery Bus Boycott to the Voting Rights Act
in July 1965. . . . Evans's earth-toned oil paintings enhance
the stories with images that are by turns poignant, sad, hurtful, resigned, determined, hopeful, and triumphant." SLJ

Includes bibliographical references

Shelton, Paula Young

★ **Child** of the civil rights movement; illustrated by
Raul Colón. Schwartz & Wade Books 2010 un il $17.99;
lib bdg $20.99

Grades: K 1 2 3　　　　　　　　　　　　**323.1**

1. Clergy 2. Mayors 3. Members of Congress 4. Civil
rights activists 5. United Nations officials 6. Selma
(Ala.) -- Race relations 7. African Americans -- Civil
rights

ISBN 978-0-375-84314-3; 0-375-84314-0; 978-0-375-
95414-6 lib bdg; 0-375-95414-7 lib bdg

LC 2008045855

The daughter of Andrew Young recalls her memories of her father and other African American Civil Rights activists, including Martin Luther King Jr., Dorothy Cotton and Ralph Abernathy, and the march from Selma to Montgomery Alabama.

"Colón's . . . soft-focus art features his customarily rich textural backdrop of speckles, scratches, and waves. Both contributors evoke the drama and emotion of the times . . . and a triumphal sense of community and family." Publ Wkly

Includes bibliographical references

Watkins, Angela Farris

My Uncle Martin's words of love for America; Martin Luther King Jr.'s niece tells how he made a difference. by Angela Farris Watkins, PhD; Illustrated by Eric Velasquez. Abrams Books for Young Readers 2011 40p il

Grades: 2 3 4   **323.1**

1. Clergy 2. Nonfiction writers 3. Civil rights activists 4. Nobel laureates for peace 5. African Americans -- Civil rights

ISBN 1-4197-0022-7; 978-1-4197-0022-4

LC 2011003888

"Explaining Jim Crow laws and the Civil Rights movement to a very young audience is not easy, but Watkins and Velasquez rise to the challenge with grace and warmth. Using a childlike voice, Martin Luther King Jr.'s niece simply and clearly emphasizes themes of love, nonviolence, freedom and equality. The repetitive text instills the message 'people listened, and things changed' and focuses on the positive. While the prejudice and violence of segregation is broached, . . . the intensity and extent of that violence is omitted. . . . Though picture books about Dr. King by his family members and others abound, this stands out for its graceful, age-appropriate treatment of the Movement." Kirkus

Includes bibliographical references

Weatherford, Carole Boston

★ The beatitudes; from slavery to civil rights. written by Carole Boston Weatherford; illustrated by Tim Ladwig. Eerdmans Books for Young Readers 2010 un il $16.99

Grades: 1 2 3 4   **323.1**

1. African Americans -- History 2. African Americans -- Civil rights

ISBN 978-0-8028-5352-3; 0-8028-5352-8

"Using the Beatitudes of blessings found in the Sermon on the Mount as an underpinning, Weatherford . . . highlights the faith that bolstered the African American struggle for freedom and civil rights. . . . The words serve as a refrain to puncuate Ladwig's elegant watercolors and lend a dreamlike quality to the stirring depictions." Booklist

323.11   Ethnic and national groups

Rubin, Susan Goldman

Freedom Summer; the 1964 Struggle for Civil Rights in Mississippi. by Susan Rubin. Holiday House 2014 120 p. illustrations (hardcover) $18.95

Grades: 5 6 7 8 9 10   **323.11**

1. African Americans -- Civil rights 2. Mississippi Freedom Project 3. African Americans -- Suffrage 4. Civil rights workers -- Mississippi 5. Civil rights

movements -- Mississippi

ISBN 0823429202; 9780823429202

LC 2013020208

"Rubin has created a narrative retelling of the events and occurrences from the summer of 1964. Chock-full of primary sources, such as photographs, memos sent to applicants regarding the growing tensions in Mississippi, and pencil drawings depicting various settings from Neshoba County, Mississippi, Freedom Summer is organized in a time-line fashion, from June 1964 until late August 1964." (VOYA)

"This work gives a real sense of the time and place, the issues and the opposing sides, and the impact on the nation. Including myriad period photos and drawings, facsimiles of reports and records, meticulous source notes, an extensive bibliography, picture credits, and an extensive index, this title is the epitome of excellent historical reporting, with the human element never forgotten." SLJ

Includes bibliographical references and index

323.3   Civil and political rights of other social groups

Serres, Alain

I have the right to be a child; author, Alain Serres; illustrator, Aurélia Fronty; translator, Helen Mixter. Groundwood Books 2012 48 p.

Grades: 3 4 5 6 7   **323.3**

1. Treaties 2. Human rights 3. Children -- Civil rights

ISBN 1554981492; 9781554981496

In this children's book, "a young narrator describes what it means to be a child with rights -- from the right to food, water and shelter, to the right to go to school, to the right to be free from violence, to the right to breathe clean air, and much more. The book emphasizes that these rights belong to every child on the planet. . . . A brief afterword explains that the rights outlined in the book come from the Convention on the Rights of the Child." (Publisher's note)

323.6   Citizenship and related topics

Raatma, Lucia

Citizenship; by Lucia Raatma. Children's Press 2012 64 p. ill. (chiefly col.), col. map (Cornerstones of freedom) (library) $30; (paperback) $8.95

Grades: 4 5 6   **323.6**

1. Citizenship -- United States

ISBN 0329917374; 0531230643; 0531281647; 9780329917371; 9780531230640; 9780531281642

LC 2011031340

This book on citizenship by Lucia Raatma "covers everything from basic facts about naturalization to debates over hot issues such as gun control." It is part of the "Cornerstones of Freedom" series for students in grades 4 to 6. Included are "a two-page map of 'What Happened Where?'; a two-page epilogue; glossary-style identifications of significant people; a page of primary sources; a bibliography of books; a glossary; and an index plus author bio." (Booklist)

Includes bibliographical references (p. 61) and index.

Raum, Elizabeth

The **Pledge** of Allegiance in translation; what it really means. by Elizabeth Raum. Capstone Press 2009 32p il map (Fact finders. Kids' translations) lib bdg $23.93; pa $7.95

Grades: 3 4 5   323.6

1. Pledge of Allegiance

ISBN 978-1-4296-1931-8 lib bdg; 1-4296-1931-7 lib bdg; 978-1-4296-2846-4 pa; 1-4296-2846-4 pa

LC 2007-51304

Provides "a nearly line-by-line translation that makes . . . the written word accessible and meaningful." SLJ

Includes glossary and bibliographical references

324.6   Election systems and procedures; suffrage

Fritz, Jean

You want women to vote, Lizzie Stanton? illustrated by DyAnne DiSalvo-Ryan. Putnam 1995 88p il $16.99; pa $5.99

Grades: 2 3 4   324.6

1. Feminism 2. Suffragists 3. Women -- Suffrage

ISBN 0-399-22786-5; 0-698-11764-6 pa

LC 94-30018

This is a biography of the 19th century feminist and advocate of women's suffrage

"With remarkable clarity, sensitivity, and momentum, Fritz has captured—but never imprisoned [Stanton's] spirit in an accessible, fascinating portrait." Horn Book

Includes bibliographical references

Hollihan, Kerrie Logan

Rightfully ours; how women won the vote: 21 activities. Kerrie Logan Hollihan. 1st ed. Chicago Review Press 2012 xiii, 130 p.p ill. (some col.) (paperback) $16.95

Grades: 4 5 6 7 8   324.6

1. Women -- Suffrage 2. Women -- United States -- History 3. Suffragists -- United States -- History 4. Women's rights -- United States -- History 5. Women -- Suffrage -- United States -- History 6. Women's rights -- Study and teaching -- Activity programs -- United States 7. Women -- Suffrage -- Study and teaching -- Activity programs -- United States

ISBN 1883052890; 9781883052898

LC 2012006044

This book is an "account of the struggle for women's suffrage. The first three chapters focus on notable activists Lucy Stone, Elizabeth Cady Stanton, and Susan B. Anthony. [Kerrie Logan] Hollihan recounts how this battle was inexorably tied to the antislavery movement and the role played by women of color in both movements, including Harriett Tubman, Sojourner Truth, and Ida Wells-Barnett." (School Library Journal)

Includes bibliographical references (p. 121-124) and index

Van Rynbach, Iris

The **taxing** case of the cows; a true story about suffrage. by Iris Van Rynbach and Pegi Deitz Shea; illustrated by Emily Arnold McCully. Clarion Books 2010 32p il $16.99

Grades: 1 2 3   324.6

1. Cattle 2. Taxation 3. Suffragists 4. Women -- Suffrage

ISBN 978-0-547-23631-5; 0-547-23631-X

"This title introduces the little-known story of two elderly sisters, Abby and Julia Smith, who fought against the taxation levied upon them as nonvoting citizens in nineteenth-century Connecticut. . . . The sisters' beloved cows became pawns in the arguments, used as collateral and bargaining chips by both sides. . . . McCully's watercolor illustrations of the historical scenes enhance this account of a pivotal event in women's long struggle for equality." Booklist

Wallner, Alexandra

Susan B. Anthony; by Alexandra Wallner. Holiday House 2011 32 p. col. ill. (hardcover) $16.95

Grades: K 1 2 3   324.6

1. Women -- Suffrage 2. Picture books for children 3. Women's rights -- United States 4. Feminists -- United States -- Biography 5. Suffragists -- United States -- Biography

ISBN 0823419533; 9780823419531

LC 2009017815

This "picture-book biography focuses on America's foremost champion for women's rights," Susan B. Anthony. It covers her life, "from her strict upbringing in Massachusetts to her death after 58 years of working for reform, and her passionate role in the women's-suffrage movement." (School Library Journal)

Includes bibliographical references

324.7   Conduct of election campaigns

Donovan, Sandy

Getting elected; a Look at running for office. Robin Nelson and Sandy Donovan. Lerner Publications 2012 40 p. (Searchlight books. How government does works) (lib. bdg.: alk. paper) $27.93

Grades: 3 4 5   324.7

1. Politics 2. Elections -- United States 3. Campaign management -- United States 4. Political campaigns -- United States

ISBN 0761365192; 9780761365198

LC 2010041859

Author Robin Nelson's book focuses on information regarding elections, government, and politics in the United States. "What does it mean to be elected to political office? It means you get to decide how to make a town, a state, or even the whole country a better place to live. But how does someone get elected? And what are the challenges of running for office?" (Publisher's note)

Includes bibliographical references (p. 39) and index

324.9   History and geographic treatment of elections

Christelow, Eileen

★ **Vote!** Clarion 2003 47p il $16

Grades: K 1 2 3 **324.9**
1. Politics 2. Elections
ISBN 0-618-24754-8
LC 2002-152288

Using a campaign for mayor as an example, shows the steps involved in an election, from the candidate's speeches and rallies, to the voting booth where every vote counts, to the announcement of the winner

"It's hard to imagine a more accessible introduction to voting. The words are straightforward, the art whimsical and creative, and two darling dogs provide color commentary on the action." Booklist

Includes glossary

325 International migration and colonization

Bial, Raymond
Ellis Island; coming to the land of liberty. Houghton Mifflin Books for Children 2009 56p il $18
Grades: 4 5 6 7 **325**
1. Ellis Island Immigration Station 2. United States -- Immigration and emigration
ISBN 978-0-618-99943-9; 0-618-99943-4
LC 2008-36794

"Bial examines the history of the famed immigration station. . . . He looks at the socio-historical roots of the mass exodus to America and provides a detailed look at the immigrant experience from ship to shore, with Ellis Island in between. Primary-source quotes and period photos pair eloquently with the modern narrative voice and color photographs of the museum exhibits. . . . The generously sized period photos and Bial's museum shots tell a vivid and poignant tale." SLJ

Includes bibliographical references

Freedman, Russell
★ **Immigrant** kids. Dutton 1980 72p il hardcover o.p. pa $8.99
Grades: 4 5 6 7 **325**
1. City and town life 2. Children of immigrants 3. United States -- Immigration and emigration
ISBN 0-14-037594-5 pa
LC 79-20060

The author has "assembled an interesting collection of old photographs for a book that gives a broad view of the experiences of immigrant children in an urban environment. The text is divided into such areas as the journey to America, schools, play, work (much of it illegal), and home life. Photographs are carefully placed in relation to textual references, and the text itself is enlivened by quotations from the reminiscences of several people about their first days in the United States as child immigrants. Large, clear print and an index add to the book's usefulness." Horn Book

Levine, Ellen
★ **. . . if** your name was changed at Ellis Island; illustrated by Wayne Parmenter. Scholastic 1993 80p il hardcover o.p. pa $6.99
Grades: 3 4 5 **325**
1. Immigrants -- United States 2. Ellis Island (N.J. and N.Y.) 3. Ellis Island Immigration Station 4. United

States -- Immigration and emigration
ISBN 0-590-43829-8 pa
LC 92-27940

Describes, in question and answer format, the great migration of immigrants to New York's Ellis Island, from the 1880s to 1914. Features quotes from children and adults who passed through the station

The author "writes in a clear, direct style that's packed with information and lively case histories. . . . There are many illustrations, sometimes full-page, sometimes small, in acrylic earth colors . . . they are an attractive part of a clear and accessible design." Booklist

Maestro, Betsy
★ **Coming** to America: the story of immigration; illustrated by Susannah Ryan. Scholastic 1996 un il $15.95
Grades: K 1 2 3 **325**
1. Immigrants -- United States 2. Ellis Island Immigration Station 3. United States -- Immigration and emigration
ISBN 0-590-44151-5
LC 94-31110

"In an introductory look at immigration, all inhabitants of the United States are considered immigrants or descendants of immigrants, whether they crossed the land bridge from Asia, came across the oceans voluntarily, or were brought as slaves. The clear, simple text and bright, animated illustrations convey excitement and adventure as well as hardship and loss." Horn Book Guide

Solway, Andrew
Graphing immigration. Raintree 2010 32p il (Real world data) $28.21; pa $7.99
Grades: 4 5 6 7 **325**
1. Statistics 2. Graphic methods 3. Immigrants -- United States 4. United States -- Immigration and emigration
ISBN 978-1-4329-2617-5; 1-4329-2617-9; 978-1-4329-2626-7 pa; 1-4329-2626-8 pa
LC 2009001185

"A line graph in [this] title shows the estimated number of illegal immigrants in the U.S. from 1980 to 2005. Arguments about costs and benefits of all kinds of immigrants include a pie chart that shows where immigrants in the U.S. come from and pairs thoughts on why people migrate with a discussion of costs and benefits. . . . The clear design, with lots of full-color photos and sidebars, will encourage browsers as much as the up-to-date examples and the clear directions for remaining 'chart smart.'" Booklist

Includes glossary and bibliographical references

Staton, Hilarie
Ellis Island. Chelsea Clubhouse 2009 48p il (Symbols of American freedom) $30
Grades: 3 4 5 **325**
1. Immigrants -- United States 2. Ellis Island (N.J. and N.Y.) 3. New York (N.Y.) 4. Ellis Island Immigration Station 5. United States -- Immigration and emigration
ISBN 978-1-60413-519-0; 1-60413-519-0
LC 2009-12067

This book about Ellis Island Immigration Station "provides nearly as much information as a guided tour by a park ranger. [It begins] with the story of how the place came to be, and where it fits into U.S. history. Information boxes offer additional background and some surprising facts, such as the stages an immigrant would pass through at Ellis Island. . . . The final chapter shows the landmark today and includes maps and photographs of the visitors' center and some of the things individuals might see or do while visiting the site. Much information is packed into [this] slim [book]. Excellent . . . for state reports or to complement U.S. history units." SLJ

Includes glossary

326   Slavery and emancipation

Bial, Raymond

The **Underground** Railroad. Houghton Mifflin 1995 48p il map hardcover o.p. pa $6.95
Grades: 4 5 6 7   **326**
1. Underground railroad 2. Slavery -- United States
ISBN 0-395-69937-1; 0-395-97915-3 pa
LC 94-19614

"Although the text covers ground often trodden by other works on this popular subject, Bial's shots of places and things which now appear tidy and innocent conjure spirits of desperate freedom-seekers as handily as do more detailed narratives." Bull Cent Child Books

Includes bibliographical references

Hamilton, Virginia

★ **Many** thousand gone; African Americans from slavery to freedom. illustrated by Leo and Diane Dillon. Knopf 1993 151p il hardcover o.p. pa $12.95
Grades: 5 6 7 8   **326**
1. Underground railroad 2. Slavery -- United States
ISBN 0-394-92873-3; 0-679-87936-6 pa
LC 89-19988

In this book the author tells "the story of slavery through a series of dramatic biographical vignettes. . . . Her book includes such famous historical figures as Frederick Douglass, Sojourner Truth and Harriet Tubman. She also presents some more obscure individuals. . . . All of these profiles drive home the sickening realities of slavery in a personal way. . . . These are powerful stories eloquently told." N Y Times Book Rev

Includes bibliographical references

Haskins, James

Get on board: the story of the Underground Railroad. Scholastic 1993 152p il map hardcover o.p. pa $4.50
Grades: 5 6 7 8   **326**
1. Slaves 2. Abolitionists 3. Underground railroad 4. Slavery -- United States
ISBN 0-590-45419-6; 0-590-45418-8 pa
LC 92-13247

"Weaving together poignant personal stories and carefully researched historical data, Haskins has produced a stirring account of the founding and the workings of the Underground Railroad." Publ Wkly

Includes bibliographical references

Heinrichs, Ann

★ The **Underground** Railroad. Compass Point Bks. 2001 48p il map (We the people) lib bdg $21.26

Grades: 2 3 4   **326**
1. Underground railroad 2. Slavery -- United States
ISBN 0-7565-0102-4
LC 00-11020

This book briefly describes the Underground Railroad, slavery, and important abolitionists in the U.S.

"Short chapters, succinct text, large print, and well-chosen illustrations make this book a good starting point for young readers embarking on a study of the topic." SLJ

Includes glossary and bibliographical references

Lester, Julius

★ **To** be a slave; paintings by Tom Feelings. 30th anniversary ed; Dial Bks. 1998 160p il hardcover o.p. pa $6.99
Grades: 6 7 8 9   **326**
1. Slavery -- United States
ISBN 0-8037-2347-4; 0-14-131001-4 pa
LC 98-5213

A reissue of the title first published 1968

"Through the words of the slave, interwoven with strongly sympathetic commentary, the reader learns what it is to be another man's property; how the slave feels about himself; and how he feels about others. Every aspect of slavery, regardless of how grim, has been painfully and unrelentingly described." Read Ladders for Hum Relat. 6th edition

Includes bibliographical references

327   International relations

Deedy, Carmen Agra

14 cows for America; [by] Carmen Agra Deedy in collaboration with Wilson Kimeli Naiyomah; illustrated by Thomas Gonzalez. Peachtree 2009 un il $17.95
Grades: K 1 2 3   **327**
1. Masai (African people) 2. September 11 terrorist attacks, 2001 3. Kenya
ISBN 978-1-56145-490-7; 1-56145-490-7

"A native of Kenya, Naiyomah was in New York City on September 11, 2001. In his and Deedy's . . . lyrical account, he returns to his homeland and tells the members of his Maasai tribe the story that had 'burned a hole in his heart.' . . . Featuring luminous images . . . Gonzalez's pastel, colored pencil and airbrush paintings appear almost three-dimensional in their realism. A moving tale of compassion and generosity." Publ Wkly

327.1   Foreign policy and specific topics in international relations

Kerley, Barbara

A **little** peace; by Barbara Kerley; with a note by Richard H. Solomon. National Geographic 2007 un il $16.95; lib bdg $25.90
Grades: 1 2 3 4   **327.1**
1. Peace
ISBN 978-1-4263-0086-8; 1-4263-0086-7; 978-1-4263-0087-5 lib bdg; 1-4263-0087-5 lib bdg
LC 2006026367

Juxtaposes photographs from around the world with a simple message about our responsibilities for making and keeping peace on the planet.

This is a "simple, beautiful photo-essay. . . . The colorful pictures are supported by limited, yet powerful text, illustrating how each person can work to achieve peace." SLJ

Includes bibliographical references

327.12   Espionage and subversion

Earnest, Peter

The **real** spy's guide to becoming a spy; by Peter Earnest and Suzanne Harper, in association with the Spy Museum. Abrams Books for Young Readers 2009 144p il $16.95

Grades: 4 5 6 7   327.12

1. Spies 2. Espionage 3. Intelligence service

ISBN 978-0-8109-8329-8; 0-8109-8329-X

LC 2009-00518

"This guide, written by the executive director of the International Spy Museum, gives readers a glimpse at how spies work. Along with descriptions of the different types of intelligence officers and agencies and the tasks they perform, the text includes brief stories of spies in action." Horn Book Guide

Gilbert, Adrian

Secret agents. Firefly 2009 32p il (Spy files) pa $6.95

Grades: 3 4 5 6   327.12

1. Spies 2. Secret service

ISBN 978-1-55407-574-4; 1-55407-574-2

First published 2008 in the United Kingdom

Discusses American, British, and Russian spies and secret agents, and the history of espionage. Includes profiles of famous spies and double agents.

The text's "short paragraphs and great pictures are combined in a collage style that will draw readers quickly through the information. Useful for reports and browsing." SLJ

Includes glossary

Spy school. Firefly 2009 32p il (Spy files) pa $6.95

Grades: 3 4 5 6   327.12

1. Spies 2. Espionage

ISBN 978-1-55407-575-1 pa; 1-55407-575-0 pa

"Gilbert reveals how spies are recruited and trained, discussing methods of disguise, surveillance, interrogation, evasion, and escape. . . . The [text's] short paragraphs and great pictures are combined in a collage style that will draw readers quickly through the information. Useful for reports and browsing." SLJ

Includes glossary

Janeczko, Paul B.

The **dark** game; true spy stories. Candlewick Press 2010 248p il $16.99

Grades: 5 6 7 8   327.12

1. Espionage

ISBN 978-0-7636-2915-1; 0-7636-2915-4

"From Benedict Arnold and Mata Hari to the lesser-known Elizabeth Van Lew and Juan Pujol, Janeczko delves

into [spies'] stories with delicious detail, drawing readers into a world of intrigue and danger. Did you ever wonder why invisible ink works? How a code breaker deciphers a message? Or whether dentistry could affect a secret agent's success? The answers to these questions and more can be found here. Each chapter covers a historical era and chronicles the maturation of spying, while primary-source photographs are interspersed throughout, lending an authentic feel to each section." SLJ

Mitchell, Susan K.

Spies and lies; famous and infamous spies. Enslow Publishers 2011 48p il (The secret world of spies) lib bdg $23.93

Grades: 4 5 6   327.12

1. Spies 2. Espionage

ISBN 978-0-7660-3713-7

LC 2010044126

"Archival photographs, sidebars, and multiple fact-filled features (sidebars, text boxes, etc.) combine with accessible texts to present a thorough (albeit busy) introduction to the history and current enterprise of spies and spying." Horn Book

Includes glosssary and bibliographical references

Spies, double agents, and traitors. Enslow Publishers 2011 48p il (The secret world of spies) lib bdg $23.93

Grades: 4 5 6   327.12

1. Spies 2. Espionage

ISBN 978-0-7660-3711-3

LC 2010006178

Discusses double agents and traitors throughout history, such as Benedict Arnold, Dusan Popov, Kim Philby, and Robert Hanssen, and includes information on becoming a spy catcher (counterintelligence agent).

Includes glossary bibliographical references

Spy gizmos and gadgets. Enslow Publishers 2011 48p il (The secret world of spies) lib bdg $23.93

Grades: 4 5 6   327.12

1. Espionage 2. Electronic surveillance

ISBN 978-0-7660-3710-6

LC 2010006177

Discusses different gadgets used by spies, such as invisible ink, hidden cameras, small guns made to look like ordinary objects, and bugs, and includes career information.

Includes glossary and bibliographical references

★ **Spyology**; the complete book of spycraft. Candlewick Press 2008 un il $22.99

Grades: 3 4 5 6   327.12

1. Spies 2. Espionage

ISBN 978-0-7636-4048-4; 0-7636-4048-4

This "poses as a collection of items assembled in 1958 and stored in national archives, now declassified under the 'fifty-year rule.' Agent K, a British spy, is tracking down the evil international Operation Codex, using his mission to ground a training manual for spies. Readers can match wits with Agent K as they pick up clues." Publ Wkly

328   The legislative process

Hamilton, John

How a bill becomes a law; [by] John Hamilton. ABDO Pub. Co. 2004 32p il (Government in action!) lib bdg $15.95

Grades: 3 4 5   **328**

1. Law 2. Legislation

ISBN 1-59197-646-4

LC 2003-69305

This describes the steps in passing a federal law in the United States

This "book has an interesting assortment of vintage and recent color photos, all well captioned, and is logically arranged." SLJ

328.73   Legislative process – United States

Bow, James

What is the legislative branch? by James Bow. Crabtree Publishing Company 2013 32 p. (Your guide to government) (reinforced library binding) $26.60

Grades: 4 5 6 7   **328.73**

1. Legislative bodies 2. United States. Congress 3. United States -- Politics and government

ISBN 0778708799; 9780778708797; 9780778709053

LC 2013001277

This book, by James Bow "provide[s] solid introductory material about the U.S. government. [The] book discusses the purpose of [the legislative] branch; the different positions, . . . the work done; and the strengths and the challenges of each branch and how they interact." (School Library Journal)

330   Economics

Hlinka, Michael

Follow Your Money; Who Gets It, Who Spends It, Where Does It Go? by Kevin Sylvester and Michael Hlinka; illustrated by Kevin Sylvester. Annick Press 2013 56 p. col. ill. (paperback) $14.95; (hardcover) $24.95

Grades: 5 6 7 8   **330**

1. Economics 2. Money

ISBN 1554514800; 1554514819; 9781554514809; 9781554514816

This book by Kevin Sylvester and Michael Hlinka answers the questions "what happens to your money after you hand it to the cashier? Who actually pockets it or puts it into the bank? Was the price you paid fair? Why do things cost what they do? Kids will also discover the trail their money takes through advertising, banks [and] charitable giving. [It is an] introduction to the . . .people and companies that we influence and are influenced by when we pay for a product or service." (Publisher's note)

330.9   Economic situation and conditions

Heinrichs, Ann

★ The **great** recession. Children's Press 2011 il (Cornerstones of freedom) lib bdg $30; pa $8.95

Grades: 4 5 6 7   **330.9**

1. Recessions 2. Financial crises 3. Economic policy -- United States

ISBN 978-0-531-25035-8 lib bdg; 0-531-25035-0 lib bdg; 978-0-531-26560-4 pa; 0-531-26560-9 pa

LC 2011010824

This "offers simplified but not simplistic explanations of the current great recession's course and immediate causes. The . . . design has . . . visually stimulating pages that combine big color photos, boxed side essays, and blocks of large text with bright-red headers and highlights. In simple language and a judicious, matter-of-fact tone, Heinrichs describes the origins and growth of the housing bubble and the trade in mortgage-backed securities that magnified the effects of its eventual collapse; summarizes the federal government's palliative measures; surveys the effects of hard times on general patterns of living and spending; and notes the creation of a 'Generation R,' for whom high unemployment and financial insecurity are likely to become ways of life." Booklist

Includes bibliographical references

Mooney, Carla

The **Industrial** Revolution; investigate how science and technology changed the world with 25 projects. illustrated by Jen Vaughn. Nomad Press 2011 120p il (Build it yourself) $21.95; pa $15.95

Grades: 4 5 6 7   **330.9**

1. Industrial revolution

ISBN 978-1-936313-81-5; 1-936313-81-2; 978-1-936313-80-8; 1-936313-80-4 pa

This "gives on overview of the era known as the Industrial Revolution as well as the consequences, good and bad, of each new development upon the average citizen. Topics covered include the transformation of textiles from homespun to manufactured, the birth of labor unions, advances in transportation and communication, the inventions of Thomas Edison, and brief profiles of 'Captains of Industry,' such as Carnegie, Vanderbilt, and Rockefeller. Each chapter ends with enticing projects related to the topic. . . . The crisp, clear format, featuring ample black-and-white sketches and diagrams and pleasingly arranged type in a large font, is in sync with the straightforward text." Booklist

331.1   Labor force and market

Lynette, Rachel

What to do when your parent is out of work. PowerKids Press 2010 24p il (Let's work it out) lib bdg $21.25; pa $8.25

Grades: 2 3 4   **331.1**

1. Unemployed

ISBN 978-1-4358-9338-2 lib bdg; 1-4358-9338-7 lib bdg; 978-1-4358-9764-9 pa; 1-4358-9764-1 pa

LC 2009-23067

A guide to unemployment, what it is, what it may mean for your family, and how you can help.

"Full-page color photographs appear opposite the [narrative], depicting multicultural children, parents, grandparents, social workers, and others, whose demeanors match the hopeful tone of the [title]. This . . . will help promote empathy and understanding for the plight of others and is a key purchase." SLJ

Includes glossary

331.3 Labor force by personal attributes

Bartoletti, Susan Campbell

★ Growing up in coal country. Houghton Mifflin 1996 127p il $17; pa $7.95

Grades: 5 6 7 8   **331.3**

1. Child labor 2. Coal mines and mining 3. Immigrants 4. Coal miners 5. Coal mines and mining 6. Pennsylvania -- History 7. Children -- Employment -- United States

ISBN 0-395-77847-6; 0-395-97914-5 pa

LC 96-3142

This is an "account of working and living conditions in Pennsylvania coal towns. The first half of the volume . . . {describes} various duties in the mines, from jobs performed by the youngest boys to the tasks of adult miners, while the second half describes the company village, common customs and recreational activities, and the accidents and diseases that frequently beset the workers. Preceding each chapter and within the text {are} quotes from personal interviews with miners, as well as taped interviews and transcripts." (Horn Book) Bibliography. "Grade five and up." (Booklist)

"With compelling black-and-white photographs of children at work in the coal mines of northeastern Pennsylvania about 100 years ago, this handsome, spacious photo-essay will draw browsers as well as students doing research on labor and immigrant history." Booklist

Includes bibliographical references

Freedman, Russell

★ Kids at work; Lewis Hine and the crusade against child labor. with photographs by Lewis Hine. Clarion Bks. 1994 104p il $20; pa $9.95

Grades: 5 6 7 8   **331.3**

1. Child labor 2. Photographers

ISBN 0-395-58703-4; 0-395-79726-8 pa

LC 93-5989

Freedman "does an outstanding job of integrating historical photographs with meticulously researched and highly readable prose." Publ Wkly

Includes bibliographical references

331.4 Women workers

Colman, Penny

★ Rosie the riveter; women working on the home front in World War II. Crown 1995 120p il hardcover o.p. pa $10.99

Grades: 5 6 7 8   **331.4**

1. Women -- Employment 2. World War, 1939-1945 -- United States

ISBN 0-517-59790-X; 0-517-88567-0 pa

LC 94-3614

"A thoughtfully prepared look at women's history and wartime society, this dynamic book is characterized by extensive research." Horn Book

Includes bibliographical references

Warren, Sarah

Dolores Huerta; a hero to migrant workers. by Sarah E. Warren; illustrated by Robert Casilla. Marshall Cavendish Children 2012 32 p. (hardcover) $17.99

Grades: 3 4 5   **331.4**

1. Labor unions 2. Migrant labor 3. Women political activists 4. Mexican American women -- Biography 5. Women labor leaders -- United States -- Biography 6. Mexican American women labor union members -- Biography 7. Migrant agricultural laborers -- Labor unions -- United States -- History 8. Mexican American migrant agricultural laborers -- Labor unions -- Organizing -- History

ISBN 0761461078; 9780761461074; 9780761461081

LC 2011016403

This picture-book, by Sarah E. Warren, "chronicles the campaigns of the Latina activist who advocated for the rights of agricultural laborers in 1960s and '70s California. . . . Each double-page spread begins with 'Dolores is a . . . ' and adds a noun that embodies an aspect of her advocacy. . . . An appended timeline offers expanded details of Huerta's personal life and her collaboration with Cesar and Richard Chavez." (Bulletin of the Center for Children's Books)

"While the book alone will work with younger children, the backmatter makes this title an exceptional resource for both Hispanic Heritage and Woman's History months. A welcome title for children and educators alike." Kirkus

331.7 Labor by industry and occupation

Coulter, Laurie

★ Cowboys and coffin makers; one hundred 19th-century jobs you might have feared or fancied. by Laurie Coulter; art by Martha Newbigging. Annick Press 2007 96p il $25.95; pa $16.95

Grades: 3 4 5 6   **331.7**

1. Occupations 2. World history -- 19th century

ISBN 978-1-55451-068-9; 1-55451-068-6; 978-1-55451-067-2 pa; 1-55451-067-8 pa

"Short job descriptions, usually one or two per page, are written in an entertaining style and grouped according to headings. . . . The author considers a variety of economic and social classes, from robber barons to forced laborers and slaves, and acknowledges how locations affect available occupations. . . . Bright watercolor, cartoon-style illustrations accompany each job description." SLJ

Hopkinson, Deborah

★ Up before daybreak; cotton and people in America. Scholastic Nonfiction 2005 120p il $18.99

Grades: 5 6 7 8   **331.7**

1. Cotton 2. Working class 3. Textile industry -- History

ISBN 0-439-63901-8

LC 2005-8128

"From the industrial revolution to the 1950s demise of the Lowell cotton mills, Hopkinson discusses the history and sociology of king cotton, frequently emphasizing the children who labored under slave masters, endured dead-end mill jobs, or helped sharecropping parents claw out a living. . . . Stories of real people . . . sharply focus the dramatic history, as do arresting archival photos of stern youngsters manipulating hoes, cotton sags, or bobbins." Booklist

Hord, Colleen
My safe community. Rourke 2011 il (Little world social studies)
Grades: K 1 2 3   331.7
1. Occupations
ISBN 1-61741-795-5; 1-61741-997-4 pa; 978-1-61741-795-5 lib bdg; 978-1-61741-997-3 pa
This "introduces various community workers such as the mayor, police, or sanitation workers. . . . The [book has] minimal text but still [manages] to impart basic information and even raise questions. The full-page color photographs that face the text pages are crisp." Booklist

Miller, Margaret
★ Guess who? Greenwillow Bks. 1994 un il $16.99
Grades: PreK   331.7
1. Occupations
ISBN 0-688-12783-5
LC 93-26704
A child is asked who delivers the mail, gives haircuts, flies an airplane, and performs other important tasks. Each question has several different answers from which to choose
"Gender and ethnic representation are deftly handled. The author's sharp, clear full-color photographs are well composed, and her use of cropped photos and white space alternating with bled photos is an effective tool for involving youngsters." SLJ

Tsiang, Sarah
Warriors and wailers; one hundred ancient Chinese jobs you might have relished or reviled. Annick Press 2012 96 p.
Grades: 4 5 6   331.7
1. China -- History 2. Occupations -- History 3. Professions -- History
ISBN 155451391X; 9781554513918
This book, by Sarah Tsiang, is part of the "Jobs in History" series. "China was one of the most advanced societies in the ancient world. Whether in medicine, the arts, or education, the Chinese far outpaced the Europeans. Although most people were peasants, society included a myriad of other jobs. . . . Other jobs included wailer, . . . noodle maker, . . . or Shaolin warrior monk." (Publisher's note)

331.702   Choice of vocation

Zephaniah, Benjamin, 1958-
When I Grow Up; poems by Benjamin Zephaniah; photographs by Prodeepta Das. Pgw 2012 32 p. $17.99
Grades: 1 2 3 4 5   331.702
1. Occupations 2. Vocational guidance
ISBN 1847800599; 9781847800596
This book by Benjamin Zephaniah "takes an alternative look at 12 occupations and the people who fill them. Its aim is to open up children's imaginations to the possibil-

ity that there are many more roles open to them than they may think. It . . . depict[s] . . .broad-ranging examples of unusual people doing unusual jobs, such as Sikh lollipop man, a female clown and a black British Space Scientist." (Publisher's note)

331.8   Labor unions, labor-management bargaining and disputes

Brill, Marlene Targ
Annie Shapiro and the clothing workers' strike; illustrated by Jamel Akib. Millbrook Press 2010 48p il (History speaks: picture books plus reader's theater) lib bdg $27.93; pa $9.95
Grades: 2 3 4   331.8
1. Strikes 2. Labor unions 3. Readers' theater 4. Clothing industry 5. Labor leaders
ISBN 978-1-58013-672-3 lib bdg; 1-58013-672-9 lib bdg; 978-0-7613-6132-9 pa; 0-7613-6132-4 pa
LC 2009051812
"This partly fictionalized picture-book story is followed by an eight-page script for reader's theater. In 1910, Hannah 'Annie' Shapiro, a teenage Russian immigrant, led a walkout in Chicago to protest pay cuts and poor conditions in the clothing factory where she worked. . . . Dramatic double-page spreads in deep shades of red and brown focus on Annie as they show the confrontations. . . . After the story, an author's note fills in more historical facts, and a reader's theater section features roles for Annie, two narrators, and two additional readers and includes practical notes about costumes, props, and performance." Booklist
Includes bibliographical references

331.892   Strikes

Bartoletti, Susan Campbell
★ Kids on strike! Houghton Mifflin 1999 208p il $20; pa $8.95
Grades: 5 6 7 8   331.892
1. Strikes 2. Child labor 3. Centenarians 4. Labor leaders
ISBN 0-395-88892-1; 0-618-36923-6 pa
LC 98-50575
Describes the conditions and treatment that drove workers, including many children, to various strikes, from the mill workers strikes in 1828 and 1836 and the coal strikes at the turn of the century to the work of Mother Jones on behalf of child workers
"This well-researched and well-illustrated account creates a vivid portrait of the working conditions of many American children in the 19th and early 20th centuries." SLJ
Includes bibliographical references

Markel, Michelle
★ Brave girl; Clara and the Shirtwaist Makers' Strike of 1909. written by Michelle Markel; pictures by Melissa Sweet. Balzer + Bray 2013 32 p. (hardcover bdg.) $17.99
Grades: K 1 2 3 4   331.892
1. Picture books for children 2. Strikes -- United States -- History 3. Shirtwaist Makers' Strike, New York, N.Y., 1909 4. Women clothing workers -- New York (State)

-- New York 5. Women in the labor movement -- New York (State) -- New York 6. Strikes and lockouts -- Clothing trade -- New York (State) -- New York
ISBN 0061804428; 9780061804427

LC 2012025439

Amelia Bloomer Project (2014)

Orbis Pictus Awards Honor Book (2014)

This children's picture book offers a biography of Clara Lemlich, early 20th-century union organizer. "She not only worked to support her family in a factory that made women's clothing, but read and studied at night. When the male workers talked about a strike to protest their fearsome working conditions," Clara "called for a general strike. She was arrested 17 times and beaten, but the strike won the right to unionize for workers in many factories." (Kirkus Reviews)

332.02 Miscellany and personal finance

Brennan, Linda Crotta

Managing money; by Linda Crotta Brennan and illustrated by Rowan Barnes-Murphy. Childs World 2012 24 p. (library reinforced: alk. paper) $27.07

Grades: 2 3 4 5   332.02

1. Economics 2. Personal finance

ISBN 1614732418; 9781614732419

LC 2012932818

This book, by Linda Crotta Brennan and illustrated by Rowan Barnes-Murphy, "introduces money management, including how to create a budget and the importance of spending, saving, and donating. [It also] features a glossary and lists resources to explore the subject further." (Publisher's note)

332.024 Personal finance

Bochner, Rose

The **new** totally awesome money book for kids (and their parents) [by] Arthur Bochner & Rose Bochner; foreword by Adriane G. Berg. 3rd ed., rev & updated.; Newmarket Press 2007 189p il pa $9.95

Grades: 4 5 6 7   332.024

1. Personal finance

ISBN 978-1-55704-738-0

LC 2006038930

First published 1993 with title: The totally awesome money book for kids (and their parents)

An introduction to money for kids including the basics of saving, investing, working, and taxes.

"Using an easy and comfortable style that young people will find unthreatening, the book presents a wealth of information. . . . The cute illustrations are also fun." Voice of Youth Advocates

Includes bibliographical references

Chatzky, Jean

Not your parents' money book; making, saving, and spending your own money. [by Jean Sherman Chatzky]; illustrated by Erwin Haya. Simon & Schuster Books for Young Readers 2010 162p il pa $12.99

Grades: 5 6 7 8   332.024

1. Money 2. Personal finance

ISBN 978-1-4169-9472-5 pa; 1-4169-9472-6 pa

LC 2010008840

"Written in a light, somewhat jocular tone and sprinkled with amusing but eye-opening and conversation-starting quotes from 12, 13, and 14-year-olds, this book is sure to hold readers' attention. The content includes how you get money, via allowances and jobs, and notes the difference between cash-only and paychecks. Tracking typical teen expenditures, both long-term and short, is juxtaposed against keeping money in checking, savings, and money-market accounts. . . . Chatzky's presentation is engaging. . . . Cartoons appear on almost every page, adding humor and some additional material." SLJ

Includes bibliographical references

Hall, Alvin

★ **Show** me the money; [by] Alvin Hall. DK 2008 96p il $15.99

Grades: 4 5 6   332.024

1. Money 2. Personal finance

ISBN 978-0-7566-3762-0; 0-7566-3762-7

"Four main sections cover the history of money, expenses/income, the basics of economics, and the world of work and business. Brief profiles of eight wealthy entrepreneurs and their paths to prosperity and eight significant economists and their theories are included. The lively writing features real-life examples that will be meaningful to students and is presented in a balanced, nonjudgmental style that encourages them to decide for themselves among the various ideas concerning economic policies. . . . Color photos and graphics excel at conveying the concepts presented and represent diversity well." SLJ

Includes glossary

Hall, Margaret

Your allowance; [2nd ed]; Heinemann Library 2008 32p il (Earning, saving, spending) $25.36; pa $7.99

Grades: 3 4 5   332.024

1. Personal finance

ISBN 978-1-4034-9817-5; 1-4034-9817-2; 978-1-4034-9822-9 pa; 1-4034-9822-9 pa

LC 2007015113

First published 2000

Offers young people information on how to manage the money they have, providing advice on spending, saving, and donating money to help others

Includes bibliographical references

Hord, Colleen

Need it or want it? Rourke 2011 il (Little world social studies) $22.79; pa $7.95

Grades: K 1 2 3   332.024

1. Personal finance

ISBN 978-1-61741-793-1; 1-61741-793-9; 978-1-61741-995-9 pa; 1-61741-995-8 pa

This book "brings up the provocative question of whether you desire something because it will be useful or just because it will be fun. Examples of both are given, and a page reminds readers they can give back to their communities by donating needed goods. The [book has] minimal text but still [manages] to impart basic information and even raise questions. The full-page color photographs that face the text pages are crisp." Booklist

Larson, Jennifer S.

Do I need it? or do I want it? making budget choices. Lerner 2010 32p il (Exploring economics) lib bdg $25.26; pa $7.95

Grades: K 1 2   **332.024**

1. Personal finance

ISBN 978-0-7613-3914-4 lib bdg; 0-7613-3914-0 lib bdg; 978-0-7613-5664-6 pa; 0-7613-5664-9 pa

An introduction to budgeting that explains how to make a budget and stick to it, how to decide if something is a need or a want, why it is important to have a budget, and how to save and spend money wisely.

"Clear, age-appropriate language explains new concepts well. . . . The [book's] layout is interesting and fresh, and each page features a large, well-chosen photograph with a boxed caption." SLJ

What can you do with money? earning, spending, and saving. Lerner Pub. 2010 32p il (Exploring economics) lib bdg $25.26; pa $7.95

Grades: K 1 2   **332.024**

1. Personal finance

ISBN 978-0-7613-3910-6 lib bdg; 0-7613-3910-8 lib bdg; 978-0-7613-5666-0 pa; 0-7613-5666-5 pa

Provides an introduction to earning, spending, and saving and discusses goods, services, and how people choose what to buy.

"Clear, age-appropriate language explains new concepts well. . . . The [book's] layout is interesting and fresh, and each page features a large, well-chosen photograph with a boxed caption." SLJ

Lynette, Rachel

What to do when your family has to cut costs. PowerKids Press 2010 24p il (Let's work it out) lib bdg $21.25; pa $8.25

Grades: 2 3 4   **332.024**

1. Personal finance

ISBN 978-1-4358-9340-5 lib bdg; 1-4358-9340-9 lib bdg; 978-1-4358-9768-7 pa; 1-4358-9768-4 pa

LC 2009-23737

Learn about prioritizing needs over wants and ways to be cost-conscious and frugal.

"Full-page color photographs appear opposite the [narrative], depicting multicultural children, parents, grandparents, social workers, and others, whose demeanors match the hopeful tone of the [title]. This . . . will help promote empathy and understanding for the plight of others and is a key purchase." SLJ

Includes glossary

What to do when your family is in debt. PowerKids Press 2010 24p il (Let's work it out) lib bdg $21.25; pa $8.25

Grades: 2 3 4   **332.024**

1. Debt 2. Consumer credit

ISBN 978-1-4358-9341-2 lib bdg; 1-4358-9341-7 lib bdg; 978-1-4358-9770-0 pa; 1-4358-9770-6 pa

A guide to debt, what it is, what it may mean for your family, and how you can help.

"Full-page color photographs appear opposite the [narrative], depicting multicultural children, parents, grandparents, social workers, and others, whose demeanors match the hopeful tone of the [title]. This . . . will help promote empathy and understanding for the plight of others and is a key purchase." SLJ

Includes glossary

Mitten, Ellen K.

Goods or services? Ellen K. Mitten. Rourke 2011 24 p. col. ill. (library) $22.79; $15.95; (paperback) $7.95

Grades: K 1 2 3   **332.024**

1. Personal finance

ISBN 9781617417917; 9781612367095; 9781617419935

LC 2011924836

In this book "the concept of different ways to use money is introduced, with pages showing how you can buy something, like an apple, or have a service provided to you, like getting a haircut. Readers are told families must make choices about how to spend their money. . . . The [book has] minimal text but still [manages] to impart basic information and even raise questions. The full-page color photographs that face the text pages are crisp." Booklist

Includes bibliographical references and index.

Morrison, Jessica

Saving. Weigl Publishers 2009 32p il (Everyday economics) lib bdg $26; pa $9.95

Grades: 5 6 7   **332.024**

1. Saving and investment

ISBN 978-1-60596-647-2 lib bdg; 1-60596-647-9 lib bdg; 978-1-60596-648-9 pa; 1-60596-648-7 pa

LC 2009018567

This "informative [book introduces savings in] U.S. economic theory and practices using everyday language and real-life examples. [It] includes history, a brief annotated chronology, sidebar and intext explanations of terminology, and helpful diagrams. . . . With brief paragraphs; large, captioned photographs; ample margins; and well-organized graphics, the [book's] design makes economics accessible without sacrificing content. . . . [This is] easy to navigate and full of solid information and interesting facts." SLJ

Includes glossary

Roderick, Stacey

Centsibility; the Planet Girl guide to money. [by] Stacey Roderick and Ellen Warwick; illustrated by Monika Melnychuk. Kids Can Press 2008 80p il (Planet girl) $12.95

Grades: 5 6 7 8   **332.024**

1. Personal finance

ISBN 978-1-55453-208-7

"This book presents handy methods for managing money. . . . Chapters are broken down into subsections . . . which are peppered with quizzes and craft projects to keep readers engaged. . . . The book's sound advice is both practical and approachable." Horn Book Guide

Schwartz, David M.

If you made a million; pictures by Steven Kellogg. Lothrop, Lee & Shepard Bks. 1989 un il hardcover o.p. pa $6.99

Grades: PreK K 1 2 3   **332.024**
1. Personal finance
ISBN 0-688-07017-5; 0-688-13634-6 pa
     LC 88-12819
"The concepts of banks and banking . . . are all explained with absurd and humorous examples involving Ferris wheels, ogres, and rhinoceroses. . . . The best advice of all is 'Enjoying your work is more important than money.' Steven Kellogg's splendidly funny illustrations contain a troupe of two cats, one dog, numerous kids, a unicorn, and the wonderful magician Marvelosissimo." Horn Book

Wiseman, Blaine
     Budgeting. Weigl Publishers 2009 32p il (Everyday economics) lib bdg $26; pa $9.95
Grades: 5 6 7   **332.024**
1. Budget
ISBN 978-1-60596-643-4 lib bdg; 1-60596-643-6 lib bdg; 978-1-60596-644-1 pa; 1-60596-644-4 pa
     LC 2009018439
This "informative [book introduces budgeting in] U.S. economic theory and practices using everyday language and real-life examples. [It] includes history, a brief annotated chronology, sidebar and intext explanations of terminology, and helpful diagrams. . . . With brief paragraphs; large, captioned photographs; ample margins; and well-organized graphics, the [book's] design makes economics accessible without sacrificing content. . . . [This is] easy to navigate and full of solid information and interesting facts." SLJ
     Includes glossary

332.1   Banks

Brennan, Linda Crotta
     Banking; by Linda Crotta Brennan; illustrated by Rowan Barnes-Murphy. Childs World 2012 24 p. (library reinforced: alk. paper) $27.07
Grades: 2 3 4 5   **332.1**
1. Banks and banking 2. Picture books for children
ISBN 1614732396; 9781614732396
     LC 2012932816
Author Linda Crotta Brennan's book focuses on teaching concepts related to financial literacy and economics. It "introduces banking and explains services such as savings accounts and loans, banking insurance, and being a dependable borrower." The book also "features a glossary . . . and lists resources to explore the subject further." (Publisher's note)
     Includes bibliographical references (p. 24) and index

332.4   Money

Adler, David A.
     ★ **Money** madness; by David A. Adler; illustrated by Edward Miller. Holiday House 2009 un il $16.95
Grades: PreK K 1 2   **332.4**
1. Money
ISBN 978-0-8234-1474-1; 0-8234-1474-4
     LC 2008004223
"This brightly illustrated picture book introduces the concept of money, first by looking at its development as an alternative to bartering and then by explaining the many forms of money, from primitive rocks, feathers, and metal lumps to the familiar coins and paper bills to alternatives such as checks, credit cards, and digital forms of payment. Adler does a particularly good job explaining the inconvenience of bartering through child-friendly examples. . . . Using flat colors and stylized designs, Miller's upbeat digital artwork helps to clarify points made in the text, while adding occasional bits of visual humor. Photos of coins and bills are incorporated where appropriate." Booklist

Blobaum, Cindy
     Explore money! With 25 Great Projects. by Cindy Blobaum; illustrated by Bryan Stone. Nomad Press 2014 90 p. color illustrations $19.95
Grades: 3 4 5 6   **332.4**
1. Money
ISBN 1619302853; 9781619302853
In this book, by Cindy Blobaum, "young readers explore the cultural aspect of money as well as its physical properties, discovering how these properties have affected business and global relationships throughout history. Kids experiment with various substances to clean coins, scientifically test coin components, design their own currency, and plan how to allocate their own money." (Publisher's note)

Brennan, Linda Crotta
     Payment methods; by Linda Crotta Brennan and illustrated by Rowan Barnes-Murphy. Childs World 2012 24 p. (library reinforced: alk. paper) $27.07
Grades: 2 3 4 5   **332.4**
1. Economics 2. Personal finance
ISBN 1614732426; 9781614732426
     LC 2012932820
This book, by Linda Crotta Brennan and illustrated by Rowan Barnes-Murphy, "introduces payment methods including cash, checks, and credit. [It also] features a glossary and lists resources to explore the subject further." (Publisher's note)

Cleary, Brian P., 1959-
     A dollar, a penny, how much and how many? by Brian P. Cleary; illustrated by Brian Gable. Millbrook Press 2012 31 p. col. ill. (Math is Categorical) (reinforced) $16.95
Grades: K 1 2   **332.4**
1. Money 2. Mathematics 3. Coins
ISBN 0822578824; 9780822578826
     LC 2011045864
This nonfiction children's book was written by Brian P. Cleary. "In rhyming text young readers are introduced to the world of currency and coins, and more subtly, to the economic concepts of value and compensation. In this new series called 'Math is CATegorical,' the popular cats from the 'Words are CATegorical' series show how to combine bills and coins of various denominations in order to pay for goods and services." (Children's Literature)

Cribb, Joe
     ★ **Money**; written by Joe Cribb. rev ed; DK Pub. 2005 72p il (DK eyewitness books) lib bdg $15.99
Grades: 4 5 6 7   **332.4**
1. Money
ISBN 0-7566-1389-2
First published 1990 by Knopf

Examines, in text and photographs, the symbolic and material meaning of money, from shekels, shells, and beads to gold, silver, checks, and credit cards. Also discusses how coins and banknotes are made, the value of money during wartime, and how to collect coins

Forest, Christopher

The **dollar** bill in translation; what it really means. Capstone Press 2009 32p il (Fact finders. Kids' translations) lib bdg $23.99; pa $7.95

Grades: 3 4 5   **332.4**

1. Money 2. Dollar 3. Paper money 4. Signs and symbols

ISBN 978-1-4296-2794-8 lib bdg; 1-4296-2794-8 lib bdg; 978-1-4296-3448-9 pa; 1-4296-3448-0 pa

LC 2008-28981

"Presents the dollar bill and explains its meaning and symbolism using everyday language. Describes the events that led to the creation of currency and its significance through history." Publisher's note

Includes glossary and bibliographical references

Jenkins, Martin

The **history** of money; from bartering to banking. Martin Jenkins, illustrated by Satoshi Kitamura. First U.S. Edition Candlewick Press 2014 64 p. color illustrations $16.99

Grades: 4 5 6 7 8   **332.4**

1. Money -- History

ISBN 0763667633; 9780763667634

LC 2013952840

"Martin Jenkins and Satoshi Kitamura take readers on a . . . . tour of the history of money. What can take the form of a stone with a hole in the middle, a string of shells, a piece of paper, or a plastic card? The answer is money, of course. But when did we start using it? And why? What does money have to do with writing? And how do taxes and interest work?" (Publisher's note)

"This cleverly designed picture book uses just the right balance of information and explanation to guide students through both the global history of currency and the application of market pressures on exchange methods." Booklist

Includes bibliographical references and index

Larson, Jennifer S.

What is money, anyway? why dollars and coins have value. Lerner Pub. 2010 32p il (Exploring economics) lib bdg $25.26

Grades: K 1 2   **332.4**

1. Money

ISBN 978-0-7613-3915-1 lib bdg; 0-7613-3915-9 lib bdg

An introduction to money that discusses what it is made of, the values of coins and bills, how it is used, and other related topics.

"Clear, age-appropriate language explains new concepts well. . . . The [book's] layout is interesting and fresh, and each page features a large, well-chosen photograph with a boxed caption." SLJ

Leedy, Loreen

★ **Follow** the money! written and illustrated by Loreen Leedy. Holiday House 2002 un il $16.95; pa $6.95

Grades: K 1 2 3   **332.4**

1. Coins 2. Money

ISBN 0-8234-1587-2; 0-8234-1794-8 pa

LC 2001-39418

A quarter describes all the ways it is used from the time it is minted until it is taken back to a bank

"Leedy includes a good deal of information, while keeping the book light, energetic, and entertaining." Booklist

Includes glossary

Orr, Tamra

Coins and other currency; a kid's guide to coin collecting. by Tamra Orr. Mitchell Lane Publishers 2009 48p il map (Money matters: a kid's guide to money) lib bdg $29.95

Grades: 4 5 6   **332.4**

1. Coins 2. Money

ISBN 978-1-58415-640-6 lib bdg; 1-58415-640-6 lib bdg

LC 2008-2262

"Photos feature multigenerational and diverse subjects and illustrate related locations and historical figures, while graphs and sidebars enhance the [text]. Well-documented and informative." SLJ

Includes glossary and bibliographical references

332.6   Investment

Minden, Cecilia

Investing; making your money work for you. Cherry Lake Pub. 2008 32p il (Real world math: personal finance) lib bdg $25.26

Grades: 3 4 5 6   **332.6**

1. Investments 2. Personal finance

ISBN 978-1-60279-003-2 lib bdg; 1-60279-003-5 lib bdg

LC 2007005917

This "examines the importance of short-term and long-term savings and explains the pros and cons of savings accounts, certificates of deposit, government bonds, and stocks. Engaging full-color photographs on every page feature diverse children and families, and plenty of white space." SLJ

Includes bibliographical references

Morrison, Jessica

Investing. Weigl Publishers 2009 32p il (Everyday economics) lib bdg $26; pa $9.95

Grades: 5 6 7   **332.6**

1. Investments

ISBN 978-1-60596-649-6 lib bdg; 1-60596-649-5 lib bdg; 978-1-60596-650-2 pa; 1-60596-650-9 pa

LC 2009018568

This explains the advantages of investing money, how to read a stock report, interest, and the types of investments provided by different companies.

This "informative [book introduces] U.S. economic theory and practices using everyday language and real-life examples. . . . [This is] easy to navigate and full of solid information and interesting facts." SLJ

Includes glossary

332.7 Credit

Hall, Margaret

Credit cards and checks; [by] Margaret Hall. 2nd ed.; Heinemann Library 2008 32p il (Earning, saving, spending) lib bdg $28.21; pa $7.99

Grades: 1 2 3   332.7

1. Debit cards 2. Credit cards 3. Personal finance

ISBN 978-1-4034-9816-8 lib bdg; 978-1-4034-9821-2 pa

LC 2007015150

First published 2000

This offers an overview of spending money without using cash, including details on credit, checkbooks, debt and interest.

"Illustrated with sharp, clear photographs, each spread presents a different concept in a logical procession. The author uses simple sentences, highlighting important words." SLJ

Includes glossary and bibliographical references

Tomljanovic, Tatiana

Borrowing. Weigl Pubs. 2009 32p il (Everyday economics) lib bdg $26; pa $9.95

Grades: 5 6 7   332.7

1. Credit

ISBN 978-1-60596-645-8 lib bdg; 1-60596-645-2 lib bdg; 978-1-60596-646-5 pa; 1-60596-646-0 pa

LC 2009018444

This "informative [book introduces borrowing in] U.S. economic theory and practices using everyday language and real-life examples. [It] includes history, a brief annotated chronology, sidebar and intext explanations of terminology, and helpful diagrams. . . . With brief paragraphs; large, captioned photographs; ample margins; and well-organized graphics, the [book's] design makes economics accessible without sacrificing content. . . . [This is] easy to navigate and full of solid information and interesting facts." SLJ

Includes glossary

333.7 Natural resources and energy

Gazlay, Suzy

Managing green spaces; careers in wilderness and wildlife management. Crabtree 2010 64p il (Green-collar careers) lib bdg $30.60; pa $10.95

Grades: 4 5 6 7   333.7

1. Wildlife 2. Wilderness areas 3. Vocational guidance

ISBN 978-0-7787-4855-7 lib bdg; 0-7787-4855-3 lib bdg; 978-0-7787-4866-3 pa; 0-7787-4866-9 pa

LC 2009-28145

"Passions often lead to professions, as this upbeat title . . . shows. . . . There is inevitable overlap among the categories: government-run parks and forestry, outdoor adventure, science, and wildlife sanctuaries. The browsable format, combining many crisp color photos with blocks of narrative texts and sidebars featuring specific ecoprofessionals, will easily lead students through the survey of nature-focused careers." Booklist

Yasuda, Anita

Explore Natural Resources! with 25 great projects. Anita Yasuda, illustrated by Jennifer Keller. Pgw 2014 96 p. illustrations pbk $13.95

Grades: 2 3 4   333.7

1. Science projects 2. Natural resources

ISBN 1619302233; 9781619302235

LC 2014497629

"The 25 projects inspire young readers ages 6-9 to have fun while learning why natural resources are important to all living things and how every child can take care of the earth's resources through reducing, reusing, and recycling. Kids will read about national parks and early environmentalists, Earth celebrations, and the science behind renewable and nonrenewable resources." (Publisher's note)

"Words to know, listed in the sidebar of each chapter, are boldface in the text, underscored in the illustrations, and defined in a glossary. Activities follow each chapter and include art projects, experiments, building plans, and challenges." Booklist

Includes bibliographical references and index

333.72 Conservation and protection

Black, Jess

A year in the life of Bindi; Australia's Favorite Wildlife Warrior. Random House Australia 2012 95 p.

Grades: 4 5 6   333.72

1. Wildlife

ISBN 1864718382; 9781864718386

This book gives "the inside scoop on how Bindi Irwin, daughter of Steve Irwin the Crocodile Hunter, spends her time. Appearing on 'Oprah' in Sydney one day, helping out at the Australia Zoo Wildlife Hospital the next, spending weeks croc tagging in the Cape York Peninsula--she's an Australian girl with a life like no other." (Publisher's note)

Bullard, Lisa

Earth Day every day; illustrated by Xiao Xin. Millbrook Press 2011 24p col. ill. (Planet protectors) lib bdg $23.93

Grades: K 1 2 3   333.72

1. Earth Day 2. Environmental protection

ISBN 978-0-7613-6109-1; 0-7613-6109-X

LC 2010053466

On Earth Day Trina plants trees with her class. She forms an Earth Day club with her friends and explains what can you do to make every day Earth Day.

"The bright colors used in the illustrations . . . will attract young readers to the environmental science content. . . . [The] facts are written in child-friendly language and the information should be attainable by young children. . . . [This book] will raise the environmental awareness of young children." Sci Books Films

Dell, Pamela

Protecting the planet; environmental activism. Compass Point Books 2010 64p il (Green generation) lib bdg $31.99; pa $6.95

Grades: 5 6 7 8 9   333.72

1. Environmental movement 2. Environmental

protection
ISBN 978-0-7565-4248-1 lib bdg; 0-7565-4248-0 lib bdg; 978-0-7565-4295-5 pa; 0-7565-4295-2 pa

LC 2009-8782

"The cover design, layout, and graphics feel hip and of the moment. The clear writing is easy to understand and includes many concrete examples of environmentally friendly practices. . . . [A] good choice[s] for both leisure reading and reports." SLJ

"Opening with the famous 1972 "blue marble" photograph of the earth and a rather persuasive quote reminding readers that earth is the only home we have, this title focuses on the effects of climate change and the government initiatives in place to protect our planet." Booklist

Includes glossary and bibliographical references

Farquhar, Jackie
Try this at home; planet-friendly projects for kids. Jackie Farquhar, D.I.Y. editor. Owlkids 2009 93p il pa $10.95

Grades: 5 6 7 8 **333.72**
1. Environmental protection
ISBN 978-2-89579-192-8 pa; 2-89579-192-9 pa

"Many of these projects are unique or innovative, featuring ideas like growing your own pizza ingredients and making a foosball game out of recycled corks, clothespins, and plastic fruit baskets. One of the best projects provides tips on making sure a bike is road ready, offering advice on checking the cables, gears, and oiling the chain. The book also includes sections designed to increase environmental awareness, including information on carbon footprint and 'eco all-stars.' Interactive elements, like a game board, should appeal to children. Illustrations are hip collages of full-color photographs and cartoons." SLJ

Includes bibliographical references

Fuoco, Gina Dal
Earth. Compass Point Books 2009 40p il (Mission: science) lib bdg $26.60

Grades: 4 5 6 **333.72**
1. Earth
ISBN 978-0-7565-4070-8 lib bdg; 0-7565-4070-4 lib bdg

LC 2008-37575

Discusses the basic parts systems (atmosphere, hydrosphere, and geosphere) of Earth and how important it is to protect Earth's resources

Includes glossary

Hewitt, Sally
Your local environment. Crabtree Pub. Co. 2009 32p il (Green team) lib bdg $26.60; pa $8.95

Grades: 3 4 5 6 **333.72**
1. Environmental protection
ISBN 978-0-7787-4100-8 lib bdg; 0-7787-4100-1 lib bdg; 978-0-7787-4107-7 pa; 0-7787-4107-9 pa

LC 2008023292

This offers suggestions for improving local environments, such as keeping schools and playgrounds clean and tidy, planning and creating gardens, attracting wildlife, controlling litter, planting trees, and maintaining parks

"The color graphics and layouts are highly appealing and will definitely be attractive to young readers. . . . This . . . is

an excellent resource for school libraries, science teachers, and community sponsors." Libr Media Connect

Hirsch, Rebecca E.
Protecting our natural resources; by Rebecca Hirsch. Cherry Lake Pub. 2010 32p il (Save the planet) lib bdg $27.07

Grades: 3 4 5 6 **333.72**
1. Conservation of natural resources
ISBN 978-1-60279-661-4 lib bdg; 1-60279-661-0 lib bdg

LC 2009-38097

Explains what natural resources are, how they are being exploited, and what should be done to protect them

"At the beginning of . . . [the] book, readers are given a mission and advised to be alert to the facts provided so that they can successfully answer the questions at the end. . . . Children are made to feel part of the process; suggestions for how they can become involved abound." SLJ

Includes glossary and bibliographical references

Kelsey, Elin
★ **Not** your typical book about the environment; illustrated by Clayton Hammer. Owlkids 2010 64p il $22.95; pa $10.95

Grades: 4 5 6 7 **333.72**
1. Environmental protection 2. Ecology 3. Sustainable living
ISBN 978-1-897349-79-3; 1-897349-79-3; 978-1-897349-84-7 pa; 1-897349-84-X pa

Written to allay children's fears about the environment, this book shows how smart technologies, innovative ideas, and a growing commitment to alternative lifestyles are exploding around the world, creating a future that will be brighter than we sometimes might think. Includes profiles of unexpected personalities.

"Imaginative, comic-booklike illustrations add to a lively layout that will keep readers moving from one paragraph to the next, and funny wordplay prevents the facts from becoming overwhelming or dry. . . . This hilarious, information-packed work is an excellent addition." SLJ

Kriesberg, Daniel A.
Think green, take action; books and activities for kids. illustrated by Kathleen A. Price. Libraries Unlimited 2010 136p il pa $30; e-book $30

Grades: Adult Professional **333.72**
1. Environmental sciences -- Study and teaching
ISBN 978-1-59884-378-1 pa; 1-59884-378-8 pa; 978-1-59884-379-8 e-book

LC 2010014409

"A resource for teaching environmental understanding and activism through stewardship, this book outlines teaching strategies for ages 6-10, provides resources for understanding environmental concerns for ages 10-13, and promotes action and growth for ages 13+. Chapters focus on local ecology, endangered species, resource depletion, and pollution. Extensive annotated bibliographies of both recent and older fiction and nonfiction selections . . . supplement the activities." SLJ

Includes bibliographical references

McKay, Kim

True green kids; 100 things you can do to save the planet. [by] Kim McKay and Jenny Bonnin. National Geographic 2008 143p il $15.95

Grades: 4 5 6 7   **333.72**

1. Environmental protection

ISBN 978-1-4263-0442-2; 1-4263-0442-0

Presents an overview of global warming and describes 100 simple ways to be more environmentally friendly in the bedroom, in the house, at school, and on vacation.

"Accompanied by attractive, up-to-date pictures in a lively design, the one hundred suggestions are direct . . . and generally practical." Horn Book Guide

Includes glossary

Parr, Todd

The **Earth** book. Little, Brown Books for Young Readers 2010 un il $15.99

Grades: PreK K 1   **333.72**

1. Environmental protection

ISBN 978-0-316-04265-9; 0-316-04265-X

LC 2008047562

"With illustrations that look as though they might have been done by enthusiastic children themselves, Parr's book offers first-person advice about ways to take care of the earth. . . . The strong appeal comes from the simple artwork done in Parr's signature style, which features pure colors, objects and people outlined in thick black ink, and kids whose round faces are comprised of two dots for eyes and upturned lines for mouths. Young children will get a kick out of the vivid art." Booklist

Raatma, Lucia

Green living; no action too small. Compass Point Books 2009 64p il (Green generation) lib bdg $31.99; pa $6.95

Grades: 5 6 7 8 9   **333.72**

1. Environmental movement 2. Environmental protection

ISBN 978-0-7565-4245-0 lib bdg; 0-7565-4245-6 lib bdg; 978-0-7565-4293-1 pa; 0-7565-4293-6 pa

LC 2009-8779

Shows children how can they make a difference. From fighting global warming to protecting wildlife, this book contains the information young environmentalists need to change the world

"The cover design, layout, and graphics feel hip and of the moment. The clear writing is easy to understand and includes many concrete examples of environmentally friendly practices. . . . [A] good [choice] for both leisure reading and reports." SLJ

Includes glossary and bibliographical references

★ **Recycle** this book; 100 top children's book authors tell you how to go green. edited by Dan Gutman. Yearling 2009 267p pa $5.99

Grades: 5 6 7 8   **333.72**

1. Authors 2. Recycling 3. Environmental protection

ISBN 978-0-385-73721-0 pa; 0-385-73721-1 pa

LC 2008-10800

"This lively collection of brief essays (and a poem) by 100 outstanding children's and young adult authors teaches through example. Each selection highlights a small step (or steps) taken by the writer toward a greener Earth. . . . The essays also provide insight into the lives and thoughts of many familiar and beloved authors such as Laurie Halse Anderson, Ralph Fletcher, Gary Schmidt, Lois Lowry, Susan Patron, and Rick Riordan. Several pages of Web sites offer a starting point for action and information. Highly useful for classroom and family discussions and science-project ideas." SLJ

Reilly, Kathleen M.

Planet Earth; 25 environmental projects you can build yourself. Nomad Press 2008 122p il (Projects you can build yourself) $21.95; pa $14.95

Grades: 4 5 6 7   **333.72**

1. Science projects 2. Environmental sciences

ISBN 978-1-934670-05-7; 1-934670-05-7; 978-1-934670-04-0 pa; 1-934670-04-9 pa

"Both comprehensive and approachable, this title . . . . combines explanations of science concepts and environmental issues with hands-on projects. . . . Elementary- and middle-school students will find the succinct overview of the facts very useful, and they'll welcome the clearly presented projects." Booklist

Ride, Sally

Mission: save the planet; things you can do to help fight global warming. [by] Sally Ride and Tam O'Shaughnessy; illustrated by Andrew Arnold. Roaring Brook Press 2009 61p il (Sally Ride science) pa $7.99

Grades: 5 6 7 8   **333.72**

1. Environmental protection

ISBN 978-159643-379-3 pa; 1-59643-379-5 pa

LC 2009-29254

"The first chapter in this slim volume discusses our energy use, dependence on fossil fuels, and the environmental impact of these practices. The remaining chapters are packed with facts and suggestions on reducing our carbon footprint. . . . The authors' background in science education is evident, as the writing style is clear, precise, and kid-friendly. Black-and-white cartoon illustrations provide excellent visuals for many of the recommendations." SLJ

Rohmer, Harriet

★ **Heroes** of the environment; true stories of people who are helping to protect our planet. illustrated by Julie McLaughlin. Chronicle Books 2009 109p il map $16.99

Grades: 4 5 6   **333.72**

1. Environmentalists

ISBN 978-0-8118-6779-5; 0-8118-6779-X

LC 2009004366

"Engaging graphics and clear writing combine to provide a compelling reading experience." Sci Books Films

"This title spotlights 12 contemporary conservationists who are working to fight pollution in cities, oceans, and wetlands, from Alaska to Mexico City. Many of the featured activists are young people." Booklist

Smalley, Carol Parenzan

Green changes you can make around your home. Mitchell Lane Publishers 2010 47p il (Tell your parents) lib bdg $21.50

Grades: 4 5 6 7   **333.72**

1. Environmental movement 2. Environmental

protection
ISBN 978-1-58415-764-9 lib bdg; 1-58415-764-X
lib bdg

LC 2009-4527

This book that explains how to be environmentally friendly "offers numerous facts and statistics, all of which are cited. . . . Chapters cover present-day issues and . . . are interspersed with full-color photographs and short 'Did You Know' trivia boxes. . . . Back matter includes detailed resource lists and 'Try This!' experiments." SLJ

Includes glossary and bibliographical references

Walsh, Melanie

  ★ **10** things I can do to help my world. Candlewick Press 2008 un il $15.99

Grades: PreK K 1   **333.72**

  1. Waste minimization

  ISBN 978-0-7636-4144-3; 0-7636-4144-8

LC 2007051888

"A thoroughly successful presentation on how even small changes in lifestyle can make a big difference. On each spread, a large and colorful acrylic painting is accompanied by a sturdy die-cut flap and eco-friendly tips. Each suggestion opens with 'I,' followed by a verb, such as 'remember,' 'try,' and 'always.' The sentence is completed under the flap, along with a reason why the tip is conservation friendly. The recommendations are those that children can easily relate to, such as turning off the water while brushing your teeth, . . . using both sides of the paper, recycling, etc. Visually appealing and effective in its presentation, this title will serve as an introduction to environmental studies." SLJ

Wilson, Janet

  ★ **Our** earth; how kids are saving the planet. written and illustrated by Janet Wilson. Second Story Press 2010 un il $18.95

Grades: 2 3 4 5   **333.72**

  1. Environmentalists

  ISBN 978-1-897187-84-5; 1-897187-84-X

"Packed with inspiring, true-life stories on every spread, this collective biography introduces contemporary kids around the world who have made remarkable efforts to help protect the earth. . . . The spreads combine both paintings and photos of the young activists with brief, lively descriptions of their environmental work, including web links when available so that readers can learn more." Booklist

333.78   Recreational and wilderness areas

Carson, Mary Kay

  The **park** scientists; Mary Kay Carson; with photographs by Tom Uhlman. Houghton Mifflin Harcourt 2014 80 p. (Scientists in the field) $18.99

Grades: 4 5 6 7 8 9   **333.78**

  1. Science 2. National parks and reserves -- United States 3. Park rangers -- United States 4. Interpretation of cultural and natural resources -- United States

  ISBN 0547792689; 9780547792682

LC 2013039895

Written by Mary Kay Carson and illustrated by Tom Uhlman, this children's book describes how "America's National Parks are protected places and have become living

museums for as many as 270 million visitors per year! In addition, researchers are able to perform long term studies of a wide number of subjects from salamanders the size of thumbnails to gigantic geothermal geysers. These parks are natural laboratories for scientists." (Publisher's note)

"The National Park System is often known as the nation's own backyard due to the possibilities it provides for leisure, recreation, and scientific study. This entry into the long-running Scientists in the Field series celebrates this by focusing on three specific parks: Yellowstone, Saguaro, and the Great Smoky Mountains... With a conservationist bent, Carson describes just how accessible these real-life "natural laboratories and living museums" are and how each individual can act with the same spirit of inquiry as the scientist-explorers detailed here." Booklist

Part of the non fiction "Scientists in the Field" series.

McHugh, Erin

  National Parks; A Kid's Guide to America's Parks, Monuments and Landmarks. Erin McHugh; Art by Neal Aspinall, Doug Leen, and Brian Maebius. Black Dog & Leventhal Publishers 2012 128 p. col. ill., col. map (hbk.) $19.95; (hbk.) $19.95

Grades: 4 5 6   **333.78**

  1. National parks and reserves -- United States

  ISBN 157912884X; 9781579128845

This book, "arranged alphabetically by state . . . tours more than 75 U.S. parks, monuments, and landmarks, from the rocky shores of Maine's Acadia National Park to the ancient redwood groves of Northern California. Also included is a removable, fold-out collector map to house" the commemorative quarters from the America the Beautiful series. (Publisher's note)

333.79   Energy

Bailey, Gerry

  Out of energy. Gareth Stevens 2011 48p il (Planet SOS) lib bdg $31.95; pa $14.05

Grades: 4 5 6   **333.79**

  1. Energy resources 2. Renewable energy resources

  ISBN 978-1-4339-4978-4 lib bdg; 1-4339-4978-4 lib bdg; 978-1-4339-4979-1 pa; 1-4339-4979-2 pa

LC 2010032889

This book "has separate chapters on fossil fuels, renewable energy, nuclear energy, and more. The many large, colorful photos will engage readers and assist them in understanding the important concepts introduced." SLJ

Includes glossary

Brezina, Corona

  Jobs in sustainable energy. Rosen Pub. 2010 80p il (Green careers) lib bdg $30

Grades: 5 6 7 8   **333.79**

  1. Vocational guidance 2. Renewable energy resources

  ISBN 978-1-4358-3569-6 lib bdg; 1-4358-3569-7 lib bdg

LC 2009021855

This "well-conceived [introduction focuses] on various jobs in [sustainable energy], the education and experience required, and expected earnings. The [book is] well organized, making it easy to gain an overview of the major aspects of the work. . . . [This book] will make [a] good [addition] to career collections. Photographs from the field and website and contact information for professional organizations add value." SLJ

Includes glossary and bibliographical references

Bullard, Lisa

Go easy on energy; illustrated by Wes Thomas. Millbrook Press 2011 24p il (Planet protectors)
Grades: K 1 2 3   **333.79**
   1. Energy conservation
   ISBN 0-7613-6107-3; 978-0-7613-6107-7
                    LC 2010053302

A boy named Tyler shows how we can use energy wisely.

"The bright colors used in the illustrations . . . will attract young readers to the environmental science content. . . . [The] facts are written in child-friendly language and the information should be attainable by young children. . . . [This book] will raise the environmental awareness of young children." Sci Book Films

Includes bibliographical references

Caduto, Michael J.

★ **Catch** the wind, harness the sun; 22 super-charged science projects for kids. Storey Pub. 2011 223p il $26.95; pa $16.95
Grades: 5 6 7 8   **333.79**
   1. Energy conservation 2. Renewable energy resources
   3. Science -- Experiments
   ISBN 978-1-60342-971-9; 1-60342-971-9; 978-1-
   60342-794-4 pa; 1-60342-794-5 pa; 1603427945 pa;
   1603429719; 9781603427944 pa; 9781603429719
                    LC 2010051169

"The eco-themed activities that Caduto lays out here are only the beginning, as he embeds them in short but clear explanations of relevant scientific facts, profiles of young eco-activitists, provocative follow-up questions, photos and cartoon spot art aplenty, folktales, and other enhancements." Booklist

Farrell, Courtney

Using alternative energies. Cherry Lake Pub. 2010 32p il (Save the planet) lib bdg $27.07
Grades: 3 4 5 6   **333.79**
   1. Renewable energy resources
   ISBN 978-1-60279-663-8 lib bdg; 1-60279-663-7
   lib bdg

Examines the climate change and the problems caused by the use of traditional fossil fuels, and looks at alternatives such wind, solar, and hydroelectric energy

"At the beginning of . . . [the] book, readers are given a mission and advised to be alert to the facts provided so that they can successfully answer the questions at the end. . . . Children are made to feel part of the process; suggestions for how they can become involved abound." SLJ

Includes glossary and bibliographical references

Gaarder-Juntti, Oona

What in the world is green energy? ABDO Pub. Company 2010 24p il (Going green) lib bdg $24.21

Grades: 1 2 3 4   **333.79**
   1. Renewable energy resources
   ISBN 978-1-61613-191-3 lib bdg; 1-61613-191-8
   lib bdg
                    LC 2010004320

"The lively layout design, featuring colorful headings, short paragraphs, and attractive photographs, has a scrapbook-like quality. . . . [The title explains] how all our choices require energy and resources, and encourage readers to make changes in their lifestyles. . . . [This] . . . will inspire and empower readers to make a difference." SLJ

Includes glossary and bibliographical references

Guillain, Charlotte

Saving energy; [by] Charlotte Guillain. Heinemann Library 2008 24p il (Help the environment) $21.70; pa $5.99
Grades: PreK K 1 2   **333.79**
   1. Energy conservation
   ISBN 978-1-4329-0887-4; 1-4329-0887-1; 978-1-
   4329-0893-5 pa; 1-4329-0893-6 pa
                    LC 2007-41172

This describes ways to save energy.

"A great jumping-off point for a broader discussion of environmentalism. . . . The bright, vibrant photographs will grab readers' attention as they reinforce the simple sentences." Libr Media Connect

Includes glossary

Hewitt, Sally

Using energy. Crabtree Pub. Co. 2009 32p il (Green team) $26.60; pa $8.95
Grades: 3 4 5 6   **333.79**
   1. Energy resources 2. Energy conservation
   ISBN 978-0-7787-4096-4; 0-7787-4096-X; 978-0-
   7787-4103-9 pa; 0-7787-4103-6 pa
                    LC 2008023288

"The color graphics and layouts are highly appealing and will definitely be attractive to young readers. . . . This . . . is an excellent resource for school libraries, science teachers, and community sponsors." Libr Media Connect

Leedy, Loreen

The **shocking** truth about energy; written and illustrated by Loreen Leedy. Holiday House 2010 32p il $17.95
Grades: 1 2 3   **333.79**
   1. Energy resources
   ISBN 978-0-8234-2220-3; 0-8234-2220-8

An imaginary bolt of pure energy named Erg introduces the nature of energy, offers tips on how to use energy sensibly, and shows different ways energy can be harnessed.

"Leedy's experience selecting facts that are most relevant and engaging for young readers is evident, and the information is eminently digestible. The design moves from energetic to near-frenetic. Her brightly colored mixed-media illustrations are filled with animated appliances, bursts of information, and decorated fonts." Booklist

Mulder, Michelle, 1976-

Brilliant! earth-friendly energy for a healthier planet. Michelle Mulder. Orca Book Publishers 2013 48 p. (Orca footprints) (pbk.) $19.95
Grades: 4 5 6   **333.79**
   1. Energy resources 2. Energy development 3.

Sustainable development
ISBN 1459802217; 9781459802216; 9781459802223; 9781459805200

LC 2013935381

This book on sustainable energy "begins with a very basic explanation of how energy is created and transmitted, beginning with the moment a light switch is flicked. Our current dependence on fossil fuels is discussed, and the disadvantages of their use are laid out as the impetus for exploring alternative sources of energy. Environmental problems are treated as exciting opportunities for ingenuity, rather than a scary future menace." (Booklist)

Ollhoff, Jim

Geothermal, biomass, and hydrogen. ABDO Pub. 2010 32p il (Future energy) lib bdg $18.95
Grades: 3 4 5 6　　　　　　　　　　　　　**333.79**
1. Renewable energy resources
ISBN 978-1-60453-937-0 lib bdg; 1-60453-937-2 lib bdg

Discusses the advantages and disadvantages of alternative energy sources and the promise of harnessing other renewable energy sources, such as hydrogen fuel cells, geothermal power, and biomass.

"Liberally filled with bright photographs, the text provides examples with accurate data and narrative. . . . Inquiring readers will find this . . . valuable." Libr Media Connect
Includes glossary

Nuclear energy. ABDO Pub. 2010 32p il (Future energy) lib bdg $18.95
Grades: 3 4 5 6　　　　　　　　　　　　　**333.79**
1. Nuclear energy 2. Nuclear engineering 3. Nuclear power plants
ISBN 978-1-60453-936-3; 1-60453-936-4

Discusses fusion energy and the possible future of nuclear power.

"Liberally filled with bright photographs, the text provides examples with accurate data and narrative. . . . Inquiring readers will find this . . . valuable." Libr Media Connect
Includes glossary

Solar power. ABDO Pub. 2010 32p il (Future energy) lib bdg $18.95
Grades: 3 4 5 6　　　　　　　　　　　　　**333.79**
1. Solar energy
ISBN 978-1-60453-938-7; 1-60453-938-0

Discusses the history and the possible future of solar power.

"Liberally filled with bright photographs, the text provides examples with accurate data and narrative. . . . Inquiring readers will find this . . . valuable." Libr Media Connect
Includes glossary

World in crisis. ABDO Pub. 2010 32p il (Future energy) lib bdg $18.95
Grades: 3 4 5 6　　　　　　　　　　　　　**333.79**
1. Energy policy 2. Energy resources
ISBN 978-1-60453-940-0; 1-60453-940-2

Discusses what can be done and the possible future of energy.

"Liberally filled with bright photographs, the text provides examples with accurate data and narrative. . . . Inquiring readers will find this . . . valuable." Libr Media Connect
Includes glossary

Rau, Dana Meachen

Alternative energy beyond fossil fuels. Compass Point Books 2010 64p il (Green generation) lib bdg $31.99; pa $6.95
Grades: 5 6 7 8 9　　　　　　　　　　　　**333.79**
1. Energy resources 2. Renewable energy resources
ISBN 978-0-7565-4247-4 lib bdg; 0-7565-4247-2 lib bdg; 978-0-7565-4289-4 pa; 0-7565-4289-8 pa

LC 2009-08778

"This great little book introduces the topics of fossil fuel usage, the limited nature of fossil fuels, and alternative energy options. It is particularly praiseworthy for its refreshingly objective, but still enthusiastic, presentations on solar, wind, geothermal, hydro, and biomass energy. . . . Interesting, well-written, and appropriately illustrated, the book is entertaining enough for general reading, but factual enough for use as a science text." Sci Books Films
Includes glossary and bibliographical references

Slade, Suzanne

What can we do about the energy crisis? PowerKids Press 2010 24p il (Protecting our planet) lib bdg $21.25; pa $8
Grades: 2 3 4　　　　　　　　　　　　　　**333.79**
1. Energy resources 2. Energy development
ISBN 978-1-4042-8081-6 lib bdg; 1-4042-8081-2 lib bdg; 978-1-4358-2481-2 pa; 1-4358-2481-4 pa

LC 2008-51935

This book provides "straightforward information . . . complemented by full-page, color photographs. . . . Links for further information . . . are housed at the publisher's Web site (which allows feedback so that readers can suggest more sites)." SLJ
Includes glossary

Solway, Andrew

Renewable energy sources. Raintree 2010 48p il (Sci-hi: Earth and space science) lib bdg $31.43; pa $8.99
Grades: 4 5 6 7　　　　　　　　　　　　　**333.79**
1. Renewable energy resources
ISBN 978-1-4109-3351-5 lib bdg; 1-4109-3351-2 lib bdg; 978-1-4109-3361-4 pa; 1-4109-3361-X pa

LC 2009-3535

"Multiple colorful sidebars and large and small diagrams and photographs will help students to grasp the fundamentals being discussed, and the easy but interesting science experiments will act as further reinforcements." SLJ
Includes glossary and bibliographical references

Vogel, Julia

Power up! Learn about energy; illustrated by Jane Yamada. The Child's World 2010 24p il (Science definitions) lib bdg $22.79
Grades: PreK K 1 2　　　　　　　　　　　　**333.79**
1. Energy resources
ISBN 978-1-60253-512-1; 1-60253-512-4

LC 2010010980

This book about energy is "attractive and succinct. . . . Large, eye-catching photos cover the recto of each spread.

. . Varying, jewel-toned accents are used in headings, highlighted glossary terms, and in a sidebar on each spread." SLJ

Includes glossary

Weakland, Mark

Onion juice, poop, and other surprising sources of alternative energy. Capstone Press 2010 32p il (Fact finders. Nasty (but useful!) science) lib bdg $25.99

Grades: 3 4 5   333.79

1. Biomass energy 2. Renewable energy resources

ISBN 978-1-4296-4536-2; 1-4296-4536-9

This informative guide also explains "relevant chemical processes, medical rationales, and ecological functions in reasonably specific detail. . . . A list of relevant web resources is maintained on the publisher's page." SLJ

Includes glossary and bibliographical references

333.8   Subsurface resources

Bang, Molly

★ Buried sunlight; how fossil fuels have changed the Earth. by Molly Bang and Penny Chisholm. The Blue Sky Press, an imprint of Scholastic Inc. 2014 48 p. $18.99

Grades: 2 3 4 5 6   333.8

1. Sunshine 2. Fossil fuels

ISBN 0545577853; 9780545577854

LC 2014000215

This children's book, by Molly Bang and Penny Chisholm, tells the "story of fossil fuels. What are fossil fuels, and how did they come to exist? This . . . book explains how coal, oil, and gas are really 'buried sunlight,' trapped beneath the surface of our planet for millions and millions of years. Now, in a very short time, we are digging them up and burning them, changing the carbon balance of our planet's air and water. What does this mean, and what should we do about it?" (Publisher's note)

"Bang and Chisholm explain the production and consumption of fossil fuels, along with the consequences of all that energy use: climate change. The sun serves as narrator describing the relationship between photosynthesis (plants) and respiration (animals) and energy; a slight imbalance produces fossil fuels. Bang's illustrations brilliantly represent the chemistry: bright yellow dots of energy against a deep-blue background hover over their producers." Horn Book

Hartman, Eve

Fossil fuels; [by] Eve Hartman and Wendy Meshbesher. Raintree 2010 48p il map (Sci-hi: Earth and space science) lib bdg $31.43; pa $8.99

Grades: 4 5 6 7   333.8

1. Coal 2. Oils and fats

ISBN 978-1-4109-3350-8 lib bdg; 1-4109-3350-4 lib bdg; 978-1-4109-3360-7 pa; 1-4109-3360-1 pa

LC 2009-3548

"Multiple colorful sidebars and large and small diagrams and photographs will help students to grasp the fundamentals being discussed, and the easy but interesting science experiments will act as further reinforcements." SLJ

Includes glossary and bibliographical references

Ollhoff, Jim

Fossil fuels. ABDO Pub. 2010 32p il (Future energy) lib bdg $18.95

Grades: 3 4 5 6   333.8

1. Fuel 2. Energy resources

ISBN 978-1-60453-935-6; 1-60453-935-6

LC 2009-29857

Discusses how coal is mined and burned and the possible future of fossil fuels.

"Liberally filled with bright photographs, the text provides examples with accurate data and narrative. . . . Inquiring readers will find this . . . valuable." Libr Media Connect

Includes glossary

White, Nancy

Using Earth's underground heat. Bearport Pub. 2009 32p il (Going green) lib bdg $25.27

Grades: 4 5 6 7   333.8

1. Geothermal resources

ISBN 978-1-59716-963-9 lib bdg; 1-59716-963-3 lib bdg

LC 2009-15119

"Color photographs (most full page) and a few diagrams accompany the informative text[s]. . . . Overall, the [book] . . . is user-friendly and covers topics that are not easily found elsewhere." SLJ

Includes glossary and bibliographical references

333.9   Other natural resources

Dobson, Clive

Wind power; 20 projects to make with paper. Firefly Books 2010 96p il $24.95; pa $12.95

Grades: 5 6 7 8   333.9

1. Wind power 2. Paper crafts

ISBN 978-1-55407-659-8; 1-55407-659-5; 978-1-55407-749-6 pa; 1-55407-749-4 pa

"In this informative craft book, a celebration of wind and of innovative efforts to harness its energy, Dobson describes the geometric and aerodynamic principles behind windmills, sails, and wind turbines, then implements these concepts via 20 paper projects, ranging from a two-blade pinwheel to a dramatic 'Squirrel Cage' turbine. . . . Readers should gain a more palpable understanding of the subject matter by building and watching the graceful compositions function." Publ Wkly

Drummond, Allan

★ Energy island; how one community harnessed the wind and changed their world. Farrar, Straus and Giroux 2011 un il $16.99

Grades: K 1 2 3   333.9

1. Wind power 2. Renewable energy resources 3. Denmark

ISBN 978-0-374-32184-0; 0-374-32184-1

This is an "account of how the residents of a Danish island made large and small changes to switch to renewable energy sources. . . . Now people from around the world come to Samsø to learn about ways to harness renewable energy and reduce carbon emissions. Informative sidebars supply information on global warming, renewable and nonrenewable energy, and conservation. What is most remarkable about this island . . . is how ordinary people achieved an extraordinary 140 percent reduction in carbon emissions in just 10 years. The illustrations further personalize the story with energy of their own as they bring Samsø and its residents to life." SLJ

Includes bibliographical references

Ollhoff, Jim

Wind and water. ABDO Pub. 2010 32p il (Future energy) lib bdg $18.95

Grades: 3 4 5 6　　　　　　　　　　　　　**333.9**

1. Wind power 2. Water power

ISBN 978-1-60453-939-4; 1-60453-939-9

Discusses the possible future of energy from wind and water.

"Liberally filled with bright photographs, the text provides examples with accurate data and narrative. . . . Inquiring readers will find this . . . valuable." Libr Media Connect

Includes glossary

333.91　　Water and lands adjoining bodies of water

Bullard, Lisa

Watch over our water; illustrated by Xiao Xin. Millbrook Press 2011 il (Planet protectors) lib bdg $23.93

Grades: K 1 2 3　　　　　　　　　　　　　**333.91**

1. Water 2. Water pollution

ISBN 978-0-7613-6106-0; 0-7613-6106-5

LC 2010053299

A girl named Trina shows how to care for Earth's water.

"The bright colors used in the illustrations . . . will attract young readers to the environmental science content. . . . [The] facts are written in child-friendly language and the information should be attainable by young children. . . . [This book] will raise the environmental awareness of young children." Sci Books Films

Mulder, Michelle, 1976-

★ **Every** last drop; bringing clean water home. Michelle Mulder. Orca Book Pub 2014 48 p. illustrations (some color) (Orca footprints) (hardcover) $19.95

Grades: 4 5 6 7　　　　　　　　　　　　　**333.91**

1. Water conservation 2. Water resources development 3. Water quality management

ISBN 9781459802247; 9781459807129; 1459802233; 9781459802230

LC 2013951377

This book, by Michelle Mulder, "looks at why the world's water resources are at risk and how communities around the world are finding innovative ways to quench their thirst and water their crops. Maybe you're not ready to drink fog, as they do in Chile, or use water made from treated sewage, but you can get a low-flush toilet, plant a tree, protect a wetland or just take shorter showers." (Publisher's note)

"Divided into four chapters, this book explores the history of water use by humans; the natural cycle of water on earth; how people access, clean, and desalinate water; and ways in which we can conserve and preserve our water resources. Plenty of well-captioned photos, including some from the author's own travels, illustrate and personalize the accessible text." Horn Book

333.95　　Biological resources

Arnosky, Jim

★ **Crinkleroot's** guide to giving back to nature; by Jim Arnosky. G.P. Putnam's Sons 2012 48 p. $17.99

Grades: K 1 2　　　　　　　　　　　　　**333.95**

1. Hermits 2. Nature 3. Nature conservation

ISBN 0399255206; 9780399255205

LC 2011028758

This children's nature book, by Jim Arnosky, shows "[f]orest-dweller Crinkleroot . . . lead[ing] 21st-century readers outdoors, urging them to appreciate and give back to nature. Arnosky's bearded guide [was] inspired by 19th-century naturalist John Burroughs. . . . In this . . . title, the author focuses on things children can do on their own for their environment." (Kirkus)

Guerive, Gaelle

Extraordinary endangered animals; by Sandrine Silhol & Ga["e]lle Guérive; illustrated by Marie Doucedame. Abrams 2011 il $24.95

Grades: 5 6 7 8　　　　　　　　　　　　　**333.95**

1. Endangered species

ISBN 978-1-4197-0034-7; 1-4197-0034-0

"Detailed, large-scale photographs and intricate drawings depict 35 endangered species from around the globe, including the California condor, the sea otter, the golden lion tamarin, and the sawfish. Silhol and Guérive describe the habitat, behavior, and endangered status of each animal, while sidebars place each in human context, implicating our role in their endangerment. . . . Honest but not downbeat, this informative collection encourages readers to take action before these species disappear." Publ Wkly

Guillain, Charlotte

Caring for nature; [by] Charlotte Guillain. Heinemann Library 2008 24p il (Help the environment) $21.70; pa $5.99

Grades: PreK K 1 2　　　　　　　　　　　**333.95**

1. Nature conservation

ISBN 978-1-4329-0889-8; 1-4329-0889-8; 978-1-4329-0895-9 pa; 1-4329-0895-2 pa

LC 2007-41174

This book is "a great jumping–off point for a broader discussion of environmentalism. . . . The bright, vibrant photographs will grab readers' attention as they reinforce the simple sentences." Libr Media Connect

Includes glossary

Laidlaw, Rob

★ **Saving** lives & changing hearts; animal sanctuaries and rescue centres. Fitzhenry & Whiteside 2012 62 p. $19.95

Grades: 4 5 6 7 8　　　　　　　　　　　**333.95**

1. Wildlife refuges 2. Wildlife rehabilitation

ISBN 1554552125; 9781554552122

This book "profiles a variety of sanctuaries throughout the world and the people who work to safeguard the wildlife. . . . The author offers the . . . stories behind the founding of many of these sanctuaries and presents . . . conclusions to the many . . . stories of rescued animals. A section showing the difference between true sanctuaries and those neither meeting the needs of animals in their care nor preparing them for rehabilitation into the wild is" included. (School Library Journal)

Reptiles and amphibians; edited by Tim Harris. Brown Bear Books 2012 64 p. (Facts at your fingertips: endangered animals) (library binding) $35.65

Grades: 5 6 7 8   **333.95**

1. Reptiles 2. Amphibians 3. Endangered species 4. Rare reptiles 5. Rare amphibians

ISBN 1936333368; 9781936333363

LC 2010053968

This book "profiles a global sampling of reptiles and amphibians in various degrees of endangerment . . . . Twenty-one species are described in . . . detail that includes information on their classification, distribution, physical characteristics, habitat, diet, and reproduction." The book is part of "the 'Facts at Your Fingertips: Endangered Animals' series, which profiles various groups of endangered species from all parts of the planet." (National Science Teachers Association)

Includes bibliographical references and index

Salmansohn, Pete, 1947-

Saving birds; heroes around the world. [by] Pete Salmansohn and Stephen W. Kress. Tilbury House 2003 39p il $16.95; pa $7.95

Grades: 5 6 7 8   **333.95**

1. Endangered species 2. Wildlife conservation 3. Birds -- Protection

ISBN 0-88448-237-5; 0-88448-276-6 pa

LC 2002-6710

Profiles adults and children working in six habitats around the world to save wild birds, some of which are on the brink of extinction.

"As a teaching aid, this volume is an exceptional supplement. The six articles relating the heroic rescue of the endangered birds are accurate and enhanced by appropriate color photographs." Sci Books Films

Sheehan, Sean

Endangered species; by Sean Sheehan. Gareth Stevens Pub. 2009 48p il map (What if we do nothing?) lib bdg $31

Grades: 5 6 7 8   **333.95**

1. Endangered species

ISBN 978-1-4339-0086-0 lib bdg; 1-4339-0086-6 lib bdg

LC 2008029167

"Using intelligent, focused text; an open design; vivid photos; and excellent maps, [this] book demands attention." Booklist

"Some scientists predict that, if we do nothing, half of all species alive today will be extinct by 2100. This book looks at the many animals and plants that have become endangered through hunting, poaching, pollution, habitat loss, and climate change. It also discusses the steps conservationists are taking to protect threatened species." Publisher's note

Includes bibliographical references

342   **Branches of law; laws, regulations, cases;**

law of specific jurisdictions, areas, socioeconomic regions

Cheney, Lynne V.

We the people; the story of our Constitution. by Lynne Cheney; illustrated by Greg Harlin. Simon & Schuster Books for Young Readers 2008 30p il pbk. $7.99

Grades: 3 4 5   **342**

1. United States -- Constitution 2. Constitutional history -- United States 3. United States -- Politics and government -- 1783-1809 4. United States -- Politics and government -- 1775-1783, Revolution

ISBN 9781442444225

LC 2008-8871

In May 1787 delegates from across the country-including George Washington, James Madison, and Benjamin Franklin-gathered in Philadelphia and, meeting over the course of a sweltering summer, created a new framework for governing: the Constitution of the United States

This book is written "in clear, cogent prose. . . . The vocabulary is rich, and the author incorporates fascinating details. . . . [It is illustrated with] Harlin's impressive artwork, described as being done in 'various water media.' The sweep of these realistic paintings across the pages highlights the drama of each situation, and the artist makes remarkable use of perspective." SLJ

Includes bibliographical references

Fritz, Jean

★ **Shh!** we're writing the Constitution; illustrated by Tomie dePaola. Putnam 1987 64p il $15.99; pa $5.99

Grades: 2 3 4   **342**

1. Constitutional history -- United States

ISBN 0-399-21403-8; 0-698-11624-0 pa

LC 86-22528

"Jean Fritz gives a vivid, vibrant picture of the 1787 Constitutional Convention. The wonderful, full-color illustrations are a perfect match for the captivating text." Child Book Rev Serv

Krull, Kathleen

A **kid's** guide to America's Bill of Rights; curfews, censorship, and the 100-pound giant. illustrated by Anna DiVito. Avon Bks. 1999 226p il $15.99

Grades: 4 5 6 7   **342**

1. Civil rights 2. United States -- Constitution -- 1st-10th amendments

ISBN 0-380-97497-5

LC 99-17324

"After describing how the first 10 amendments came to be added to the Constitution, the book considers each one from a historical point of view, examining Supreme Court cases and famous challenges, and explaining in what ways each amendment applies to children and teenagers. Anna DiVito's cartoonlike drawings add a visually appealing touch." Booklist

Includes bibliographical references

Leavitt, Amie Jane

The **Bill** of Rights in translation; what it really means. by Amie Jane Leavitt. Capstone Press 2009 32p il (Fact finders. Kids' translations) lib bdg $23.93; pa $7.95

Grades: 3 4 5   **342**

1. Civil rights 2. United States -- Constitution -- 1st-

10th amendments
ISBN 978-1-4296-1928-8 lib bdg; 1-4296-1928-7 lib bdg; 978-1-4296-2843-3 pa; 1-4296-2843-X pa
LC 2007-51307

Provides "a nearly line-by-line translation that makes . . . the written word accessible and meaningful." SLJ

Includes glossary and bibliographical references

Maestro, Betsy

A **more** perfect union; the story of our Constitution. illustrated by Giulio Maestro. Lothrop, Lee & Shepard Bks. 1987 48p il hardcover o.p. pa $7.99
Grades: 2 3 4　　　　　　　　　　　　　　　**342**
1. Constitutional history -- United States
ISBN 0-688-10192-5 pa
LC 87-4083

"A simple, straightforward account using an oversize format with full-color illustration throughout. There is an excellent, fact-filled addenda that also includes the Preamble, chronologies and summaries of the Articles of the Constitution, the Bill of Rights, the Amendments and the Connecticut Compromise. This fine book places important events in historical context." Publ Wkly

Mortensen, Lori

★ **Writing** the U.S. Constitution; illustrated by Siri Weber Feeney. Picture Window Books 2010 32p il (Our American story) lib bdg $23.99
Grades: 2 3 4　　　　　　　　　　　　　　　**342**
1. Constitutional history 2. United States -- Constitution -- History 3. United States -- Politics and government -- 1783-1809
ISBN 978-1-4048-5540-3 lib bdg; 1-4048-5540-8 lib bdg
LC 2009-6895

Discusses the history of the writing of the United States Constitution

This title is "illustrated with well-executed, full-page, color illustrations, maps, and photos. . . . [It has] accurate, clearly written information that students can use for either leisure reading or reports." SLJ

Includes glossary and bibliographical references

Thomas, William David

What is a constitution? [by] William David Thomas. Gareth Stevens Pub. 2008 32p il (My American government) lib bdg $23.93; pa $8.95
Grades: 3 4 5　　　　　　　　　　　　　　　**342**
1. Democracy 2. Constitutions 3. United States -- Constitution
ISBN 978-0-8368-8863-8 lib bdg; 0-8368-8863-4 lib bdg; 978-0-8368-8868-3 pa; 0-8368-8868-5 pa
LC 2007027281

This describes the United States constitution as well as the constitutions of state governments.

This book has "an accessible format and clear writing. . . Black-and-white and full-color vintage and more recent photographs appear throughout." SLJ

Includes glossary and bibliographical references

342.73　Constitutional law -- United States

Baxter, Roberta

The **Bill** of Rights; by Roberta Baxter. Heinemann Library 2012 48 p. (hbk) $32
Grades: 4 5 6 7　　　　　　　　　　　　　**342.73**
1. Legislation 2. United States -- Politics and government 3. Constitutional history -- United States 4. Civil rights -- United States -- History 5. United States. Constitution. 1st-10th Amendments
ISBN 1432967517; 9781432967512; 9781432967604
LC 2011037780

In this book, Roberta Baxter, readers can "learn about the Bill of Rights, one of the most significant documents in U.S. history. [They can] find out about those who were involved in its creation and why studying this primary source is [considered] so important." (Publisher's note)

Includes bibliographical references (p. 47) and index

Sonneborn, Liz

The **Articles** of Confederation; by Liz Sonneborn. Heinemann Library 2013 48 p. (Documenting U.S. history) (hb) $32
Grades: 4 5 6 7　　　　　　　　　　　　　**342.73**
1. United States -- Politics and government -- 1775-1783, Revolution 2. Constitutional history -- United States 3. United States. Articles of Confederation 4. United States -- Politics and government -- 1775-1783
ISBN 1432967495; 9781432967499; 9781432967581
LC 2011037709

In this book, written by Liz Sonneborn, readers can "learn about the Articles of Confederation, one of the most significant documents in U.S. history. [They can] find out about those who were involved in its creation and why studying this primary source is [considering] so important." (Publisher's note)

Includes bibliographical references and index

The **United** States Constitution; by Liz Sonneborn. Heinemann-Raintree 2012 48 p. (hb) $32
Grades: 4 5 6 7　　　　　　　　　　　　　**342.73**
1. United States. Constitution 2. Constitutional law -- United States 3. Constitutional history -- United States
ISBN 1432967525; 9781432967529; 9781432967611
LC 2011037781

In this book, by Liz Sonneborn, readers can "learn about the United States Constitution, one of the most significant documents in U.S. history. [They can also] find out about those who were involved in its creation and why studying this primary source is [considered] so important." (Publisher's note)

Includes bibliographical references and index

344　Labor, social service, education, cultural law

Chmara, Theresa

★ **Privacy** and confidentiality issues; a guide for libraries and their lawyers. American Library Association 2009 98p pa $40
Grades: Adult Professional　　　　　　　　**344**
1. Library services 2. Right of privacy 3. Libraries

-- Law and legislation
ISBN 978-0-8389-0970-6; 0-8389-0970-1

LC 2008-34902

"This slim title is a must read. Chmara, a First Amendment attorney and litigation expert, clarifies privacy and confidentiality issues such as requests or subpoenas for patron-use records (both book and Internet), hostile-work-environment issues, state and federal privacy and confidentiality statutes, and minors' First Amendment rights and rights to privacy." Booklist

Includes bibliographical references

345 Criminal law

Coleman, Wim
   Racism on trial; From the Medgar Evers murder case to 'Ghosts of Mississippi' [by] Wim Coleman and Pat Perrin. Enslow Publishers 2009 112p il lib bdg $31.93
Grades: 5 6 7 8   **345**
   1. Lynching 2. Trials (Homicide) 3. Murderers
4. White supremacists 5. Civil rights activists 6. Mississippi -- Race relations
   ISBN 978-0-7660-3059-6; 0-7660-3059-8

LC 2008-21483

"Examines the Byron De La Beckwith murder trials, including the mistrials and his eventual conviction, key figures in the case, and the inspiration for the movie Ghosts of Mississippi." Publisher's note

346 Private law

Butler, Rebecca P.
   Copyright for teachers & librarians in the 21st century. Neal-Schuman Publishers 2011 274p il pa $70
Grades: Adult Professional   **346**
   1. Copyright 2. Fair use (Copyright)
   ISBN 978-1-55570-738-5

LC 2011012600

First published 2004 with title: Copyright for teachers and librarians

"Library educator Rebecca Butler explains fair use, public domain, documentation and licenses, permissions, violations and penalties, policies and ethics codes, citations, creation and ownership, how to register copyrights, and gives tips for staying out of trouble." Publisher's note

Includes bibliographical references

Popek, Emily
   Copyright and digital ethics. Rosen Central 2011 48p il (Digital and information literacy) lib bdg $26.50; pa $11.75
Grades: 5 6 7 8   **346**
   1. Ethics 2. Internet 3. Copyright
   ISBN 978-1-4488-1323-0 lib bdg; 1-4488-1323-9; 978-1-4488-2294-2 pa; 1-4488-2294-7 pa

LC 2010027018

Though this "title is a broad overview of a sometimes-complex subject, the detail is significant. . . . Touches of blue enhance the clean design. . . . [This] explains concepts like

fair use and tries to persuade readers of the damage done by digital piracy and plagiarism." Booklist

Includes bibliographical references

346.04 Property

Crews, Kenneth D.
   Copyright law for librarians and educators; creative strategies and practical solutions. with contributions from Dwayne K. Buttler . . . [et al.] 2nd ed; American Library Association 2012 xii, 192 p.p ill. (alk. paper) $57
Grades: Adult Professional   **346.04**
   1. Copyright 2. Sound recordings 3. Fair use (Copyright) 4. Copyright -- United States 5. Fair use (Copyright) -- United States 6. Teachers -- United States -- Handbooks, manuals, etc 7. Librarians -- United States -- Handbooks, manuals, etc
   ISBN 0838910920; 9780838910924

LC 2011027604

First published 2000 with title: Copyright essentials for librarians and educators

Author Kenneth D. Crews' book "allows readers to get up to speed on current interpretations of the Digital Millennium Copyright Act from a librarian-educator viewpoint." It also "draws on cutting-edge case law in 18 discrete areas of copyright, including specialized and controversial music and sound recording issues. [This guide offers] information professionals . . . the tools they need to take control of their rights and responsibilities as copyright owners and users." (Publisher's note)

The author "addresses 18 areas of copyright in 5 parts. He begins with the scope of protectable works as well as works without copyright protection. Next, he discusses the rights of ownership, including duration and exceptions. He then explains fair use and its related guidelines. Part 4 focuses on the TEACH Act, Section 108, and responsibilities and liabilities. Lastly, Crews examines special issues such as the Digital Millennium Copyright Act." Booklist

Includes bibliographical references and index.

Russell, Carrie
   Complete copyright for K-12 librarians and educators; Carrie Russell. American Library Association 2012 xi, 173 p.p ill. (chiefly col.) (alk. paper) $50
Grades: Professional   **346.04**
   1. Copyright 2. Fair use (Copyright) 3. Segregation -- Law and legislation 4. Copyright -- United States 5. Fair use (Copyright) -- United States 6. Librarians -- Legal status, laws, etc. -- United States 7. School libraries -- Law and legislation -- United States
   ISBN 0838910831; 9780838910832

LC 2012016674

This book by Carrie Russell "is designed as a resource for educators, offering guidance for providing material to students while carefully observing copyright law. The book offers detailed advice on distinctive issues of intellectual property in the school setting; explores scenarios often encountered by educators . . . and precisely defines 'fair use,' by showing readers exactly what's possible within the law." (Education Digest)

Includes bibliographical references and index

347   Procedure and courts

Adler, David A.

A **picture** book of Thurgood Marshall; illustrated by Robert Casilla. Holiday House 1997 un il $16.95; pa $6.95

Grades: 1 2 3   347

1. Judges 2. Lawyers 3. Solicitors general 4. Civil rights activists 5. Supreme Court justices 6. African Americans -- Biography 7. United States -- Supreme Court

ISBN 0-8234-1308-X; 0-823-41506-6 pa

LC 96-37248

Follows the life of the first African American to serve as a judge on the United States Supreme Court

"Adler presents the high points of Marshall's life with enough detail to humanize the man. . . . Sensitive line-and-watercolor illustrations on every page add warmth to the story as they define people and settings." Booklist

347.73   Civil procedure and courts of the United States

Rodger, Ellen

What is the judicial branch? by Ellen Rodger. Crabtree Publishing Company 2013 32 p. (Your guide to government) (reinforced library binding) $26.60

Grades: 4 5 6 7   347.73

1. Law -- United States 2. Courts -- United States 3. Procedure (Law) -- United States

ISBN 0778708802; 9780778708803; 9780778709060

LC 2013001275

This book, by Ellen Rodger "provide[s] solid introductory material about the U.S. government. [The] book discusses the purpose of [the judicial] branch; the different positions, . . . the work done; and the strengths and the challenges of each branch and how they interact." (School Library Journal)

351   Public administration

Bow, James

What is the executive branch? by James Bow. Crabtree Publishing Company 2013 32 p. (Your guide to government) (reinforced library binding) $26.60

Grades: 4 5 6 7   351

1. Presidents -- United States 2. Executive power -- United States 3. Executive departments -- United States

ISBN 0778709027; 9780778709022; 9780778709077

LC 2013001276

This book, by James Bow "provide[s] solid introductory material about the U.S. government. [The] book discusses the purpose of [the executive] branch; the different positions, ... the work done; and the strengths and the challenges of each branch and how they interact." (School Library Journal)

352.13   Administration of subordinate jurisdictions

Giesecke, Ernestine

State government; Rev. and updated; Heinemann Library 2010 32p il map (Kids' guide to government) $29.29; pa $7.99

Grades: 3 4 5   352.13

1. State governments 2. United States -- Politics and government

ISBN 978-1-4329-2707-3; 1-4329-2707-8; 978-1-4329-2712-7 pa; 1-4329-2712-4 pa

First published 2000

Introduces the purpose and function of state government, the function of the three branches, how states raise money, how state government operates. and how a bill becomes a state law.

"This . . . would be a great asset. . . . Students will learn about a different, but related government every two pages. The font is large and easy to read. The photos, diagrams, charts, maps, and illustrations supplement the text well." Libr Media Connect

Includes glossary

352.23   Chief executives

Obama, Barack

Our enduring spirit; President Barack Obama's first words to America. with illustrations by Greg Ruth. Harper 2009 un il $17.99; lib bdg $18.89

Grades: 2 3 4 5 6   352.23

1. United States -- Politics and government 2. Presidents -- United States -- Inaugural addresses

ISBN 978-0-06-183455-4; 0-06-183455-6; 978-0-06-183456-1 lib bdg; 0-06-183456-4 lib bdg

LC 2009014361

"The selected excerpts from Obama's speech (also printed in its entirety at the end of the book) only obliquely note the nation's current crises, but make ample use of Obama's numerous historical references. . . . Dramatic washes of color are juxtaposed with Ruth's inky paintings of the president and of Americans past and present, as strong brushstrokes define their subjects while creating a tangible sense of movement. With the book's emphasis on common values and backgrounds, readers are likely to come away with a sense of pride, hope and belonging, while recognizing that freedom doesn't come without work." Publ Wkly

355   Military science

Chapman, Caroline

Battles & weapons: exploring history through art; [by] Caroline Chapman. Two-Can 2007 64p il (Picture that!) $19.95

Grades: 5 6 7 8   355

1. War in art 2. Military history 3. Military art and science

ISBN 978-1-58728-588-2

LC 2006033229

"High quality reproductions of paintings, murals, sculptures, and artifacts show military customs and equipment over the centuries. . . . The lively, informative text creates a 'you are there' sense that will engage even reluctant readers." SLJ

Includes bibliographical references

Murrell, Deborah Jane

Greek warrior; by Deborah Murrell. QEB Pub. 2010 32p il map (QEB warriors) lib bdg $28.50

Grades: 4 5 6 7   **355**

1. Greece -- Military history 2. Military art and science -- History

ISBN 978-1-59566-759-5 lib bdg; 1-59566-759-8 lib bdg

LC 2009-3542

"Bold, comprehensible type and full-color and black-and-white illustrations; reproductions; and photographs will make this offering a hit with its target audience, including reluctant readers." SLJ

Includes glossary

Park, Louise

The **Japanese** samurai; [by] Louise Park and Timothy Love. Marshall Cavendish Benchmark 2010 32p il map (Ancient and medieval people) lib bdg $28.50

Grades: 4 5 6   **355**

1. Samurai 2. Japan -- History -- 0-1868 3. Military art and science -- History

ISBN 978-0-7614-4448-0 lib bdg; 0-7614-4448-3 lib bdg

LC 2009-3573

This title has "a simple and elegant design with the proper balance of quality writing and quantity of information. . . . Handy time lines, well-chosen photos of ruins and artifacts, quality illustrations, inset 'Quick Facts', and 'What You Should Know About' features will grab reluctant readers and captivate even those with short attention spans." SLJ

Includes glossary

The **Pharaohs'** armies; by Louise Park and Timothy Love. Marshall Cavendish Benchmark 2009 32p il map (Ancient and medieval people) lib bdg $28.50

Grades: 4 5 6   **355**

1. Egypt -- Civilization 2. Military art and science -- History

ISBN 978-0-7614-4451-0 lib bdg; 0-7614-4451-3 lib bdg

This title has "a simple and elegant design with the proper balance of quality writing and quantity of information. . . . Handy time lines, well-chosen photos of ruins and artifacts, quality illustrations, inset 'Quick Facts', and 'What You Should Know About' features will grab reluctant readers and captivate even those with short attention spans." SLJ

Includes glossary

Solway, Andrew

Graphing war and conflict. Raintree 2010 32p il (Real world data) $28.21; pa $7.99

Grades: 4 5 6 7   **355**

1. Graphic methods 2. Military history

ISBN 978-1-4329-2620-5; 1-4329-2620-9; 978-1-4329-2629-8 pa; 1-4329-2629-2 pa

LC 2009001188

This "uses graphs and charts to talk about global conflicts between 1990 and 2005, from guerilla warfare and civ-

il war to nuclear attacks, with a special section on terrorism, including 9/11 and suicide bombers. . . . The clear design, with lots of full-color photos and sidebars, will encourage browsers as much as the up-to-date examples and the clear directions for remaining 'chart smart.'" Booklist

Includes glossary and bibliographical references

Souter, Janet

War in Afghanistan and Iraq; the daily life of the men and women serving in Afghanistan and Iraq. [by] Janet Souter and Gerry Souter. Carlton Books 2011 47p il map $16.95

Grades: 2 3 4   **355**

1. Afghan War, 2001- 2. Iraq War, 2003-2011

ISBN 978-1-84732-895-3; 1-84732-895-4

"An overview of these wartorn countries' physical and religious make-ups leads to the review of current political instability in the region. The discussion of combat techniques illustrates America's military power, though a nod to numerous international organizations (from NATO to ISAF) conveys the global scope. Double-page spreads address the perceived catalysts for conflict and the United States' accompanying responses (including Osama Bin Laden's recent death). . . . Despite its slimness, a remarkably effective and timely treatment." Kirkus

Inlcudes glossary

355.02 War and warfare

Benoit, Peter

The **nuclear** age; by Peter Benoit. Children's Press 2012 64 p. ill. (chiefly col.), col. map (Cornerstones of freedom) (library) $30.00; (paperback) $8.95

Grades: 4 5 6   **355.02**

1. Nuclear energy -- History 2. Nuclear weapons -- History 3. Nuclear energy -- History

ISBN 0531230627; 0531281620; 9780531230626; 9780531281628

LC 2011031341

This book by Peter Benoit, part of the "Cornerstones of Freedom" series, "offers comprehensive coverage of all concepts related to the nuclear age beginning in the late 1800s through current times. . . . Four chapters highlight issues that emerge--birth of the new age, cold war, atom's legacy and human dilemma." Topics include "the atomic bomb, [Adolf] Hitler versus allies, international competitions, precautions, peaceful pursuits and cleaner sources of energy." (Children's Literature)

Includes bibliographical references (p. 61) and index.

355.1 Military life and customs

Biden, Jill, 1951-

Don't forget, God bless our troops; Jill Biden; illustrated by Raúl Colón. Simon & Schuster Books for Young Readers 2012 40 p. (hbk.) $16.99

Grades: K 1 2   **355.1**

1. Children and war 2. Afghan War, 2001- 3. Father-daughter relationship 4. Children of military personnel -- United States 5. Families of military personnel -- United States 6. Soldiers -- Family relationships --

United States
ISBN 144245735X; 1442457376; 9781442457355;
9781442457379

LC 2012008493

In the book by author Jill Biden, "when her father leaves for a year of being at war, Natalie knows that she will miss him. Natalie is proud of her father but there is nothing to stop her from wishing he was home. Some things do help her feel better. Natalie works with her Nana to send her dad and the other service men and women cookies and treats they have made. Natalie, her mom, and brother can see and talk to Dad over the computer, and the kindness of friends at school and at church help her feel supported and loved. But there is nothing like the day when her Dad comes home at last." (Publisher's note)

Includes bibliographical references.

355.4   Military operations

Durman, Laura
Siege; by Laura Durman. Arcturus Pub. 2012 32 p. col. ill. (Knights and castles) (library) $28.50
Grades: 4 5 6   355.4
1. Middle Ages 2. Military art and science 3. Sieges
4. Castles 5. Siege warfare
ISBN 1848585624; 9781848585621

LC 2011051446

This book by Laura Durman is part of the Knights and Castles series and looks at sieges. In "two-page spreads filled with photos, staged reenactments, diagrams, and line drawings, Durman . . . outlines how both sides prepared and fared in a siege. Chapters on castle defense, defense tactics, and personal protection" are included as is an "in-depth look at the precision and force at work with such siege machines as the trebuchet, mangonel, battering ram, and belfry." (Children's Literature)

Includes bibliographical references (p. 31) and index.

Grayson, Robert
Military. Marshall Cavendish Benchmark 2010 62p il (Working animals) lib bdg $28.50
Grades: 4 5 6 7   355.4
1. Animals -- War use
ISBN 978-1-60870-164-3 lib bdg; 1-60870-164-6 lib bdg
"Describes animals, including elephants, dogs, horses, mules, sea lions, dolphins, rats, and homing pigeons, which provide valuable service to the military." Publisher's note
Includes glossary and bibliographical references

Patent, Dorothy Hinshaw
Dogs on duty; soldiers' best friends on the battlefield and beyond. by Dorothy Hinshaw Patent. Walker & Co. 2012 48 p. (hardcover) $16.99
Grades: 3 4 5 6   355.4
1. Working dogs 2. Dogs -- War use
ISBN 0802728456; 9780802728456

LC 2012004457

Author Dorothy Hinshaw Patent reports that "nine thousand dogs served in World War II, . . . four thousand dogs served in Vietnam, and hundreds died in combat. . . . [She] sketches the history of dogs in war from ancient times to World Wars I and II and on to modern wars--Vietnam, Iraq and Afghanistan. It's dogs' 'super senses' of sight, sound and smell, and their capacity to bond with soldiers that make them so useful in military theaters. They uncovered hidden tunnels in Vietnam, find dangerous land mines in Afghan villages, and locate weapons, explosives and drugs at home and abroad." (Kirkus Reviews)

"The straightforward text and color photographs celebrate the bonds between dogs and handlers that are so crucial in modern warfare. A sure hit with dog lovers everywhere." Kirkus

355.8   Military equipment and supplies (Materiel)

Byam, Michele
Arms & armor; written by Michéle Byam. rev ed; DK Pub. 2004 72p il (DK eyewitness books) $15.99
Grades: 4 5 6 7   355.8
1. Armor 2. Weapons
ISBN 0-7566-0654-3

LC 2004-558979

First published 1988 by Knopf

A photo essay examining the design, construction, and uses of hand weapons and armor from a Stone Age axe to the revolvers and rifles of the Wild West

358.4   Air forces and warfare

Schwartz, Heather E.
Women of the U.S. Air Force; aiming high. Capstone Press 2011 32p (Women in the U.S. Armed Forces) lib bdg $26.65
Grades: 4 5 6 7   358.4
1. Women air pilots 2. Women in the armed forces 3. United States -- Air Force
ISBN 978-1-4296-5449-4; 1-4296-5449-X

LC 2010040749

Describes the past, present, and future of women in the U.S. Air Force.

The book has "a snappy design and eye-catching photographs, and the [text is] written with struggling readers in mind. The content is engaging, the material is worthy, and the [package is] attractive." SLJ

Includes glossary and bibliographical references

359   Sea forces and warfare

Llanas, Sheila Griffin
Women of the U.S. Navy; making waves. Capstone Press 2011 32p il (Women in the U. S. Armed Forces) lib bdg $26.65
Grades: 4 5 6 7   359
1. Sailors 2. United States -- Navy 3. Women in the armed forces
ISBN 978-1-4296-5448-7; 1-4296-5448-1

LC 2010040801

This book explains "how women's roles in the U.S. [Navy] have evolved over the years. [The] volume starts with an account of one specific servicewoman and then delves into her branch's history. [The book has] a snappy design and eye-catching photographs, and the [text is] written with struggling readers in mind. The content is engaging, the material is worthy, and the [package is] attractive." SLJ

Includes glossary and bibliographical references

361.2 Social action

Olien, Rebecca

Kids care! 75 ways to make a difference for people, animals & the environment. [by] Rebecca Olien; illustrations by Michael Kline. Williamson Books 2007 128p il (Williamson kids can! book) $16.99; pa $12.99

Grades: 3 4 5 6   **361.2**

1. Social action 2. Interpersonal relations
ISBN 978-0-8249-6793-2; 0-8249-6793-3; 978-0-8249-6792-5 pa; 0-8249-6792-5 pa

LC 2006036186

"This book is filled with ideas that children can implement in order to make a positive impact on the world around them. It is divided into five sections: people, pets, wildlife, environment, and kids joining together. . . . Throughout, material is neatly organized and the book has plenty of factual insets; color cartoon illustrations appear on every spread. . . . This is an excellent resource." SLJ

Includes bibliographical references

361.3 Social work

O'Neal, Claire

Volunteering in your school. Mitchell Lane Publishers 2011 47p (How to help: a guide to giving back) lib bdg $29.95

Grades: 4 5 6   **361.3**

1. Volunteer work
ISBN 978-1-58415-920-9; 1-58415-920-0

LC 2010011982

This suggests ways in which young people can volunteer to do such tasks as participating in a clean-up day, setting up a recycling center, or planting a garden to enhance and contribute to the school community.

This "well-organized [book] will encourage children to contribute to the world around them. [The] title is filled with examples of volunteer opportunities that can be accomplished with some adult involvement and supervision to guide, steer, and maintain focus so that youngsters will have varied and successful experiences." SLJ

Includes bibliographical references

Ways to help in your community. Mitchell Lane 2010 47p il (How to help: a guide to giving back) lib bdg $29.95

Grades: 4 5 6   **361.3**

1. Community life 2. Volunteer work
ISBN 978-1-58415-921-6 lib bdg; 1-58415-921-9 lib bdg

This "well-organized [book] will encourage children to contribute to the world around them. [The] title is filled with examples of volunteer opportunities that can be accomplished with some adult involvement and supervision to guide, steer, and maintain focus so that youngsters will have varied and successful experiences. . . . [The book] offers spe-

cific examples and steps for making a neighborhood safer, organizing yard sales, spending time with an elderly person, helping at a soup kitchen, or offering to do storyhours at a library." SLJ

Includes bibliographical references

361.7 Private action

Reusser, Kayleen

Celebrities giving back. Mitchell Lane Publishers 2011 47p (How to help: a guide to giving back) lib bdg $29.95

Grades: 4 5 6   **361.7**

1. Charities 2. Celebrities 3. Philanthropists
ISBN 978-1-58415-922-3 lib bdg; 1-58415-922-7 lib bdg

LC 2010014904

"Reusser writes about 17 people, including Bono and his interest in eliminating world hunger and poverty, President Carter's dreams of building homes for the homeless, and charitable works by Rihanna, Shakira, Tony Hawk, and others." SLJ

Includes bibliographical references

Shoveller, Herb

Ryan and Jimmy; and the well in Africa that brought them together. Kids Can Press 2006 55p il $16.95; pa $9.95

Grades: 3 4 5 6   **361.7**

1. Wells 2. Children 3. Social action 4. International cooperation 5. Uganda 6. Humanitarians
ISBN 978-1-55337-967-6; 1-55337-967-5; 978-1-55453-271-1 pa; 1-55453-271-X pa

This is an account of the a Canadian boy named Ryan Hreljac, whose efforts helped provide clean drinking water to a village in Uganda, and who befriended and ultimately rescued a boy named Akana Jimmy from Ugandan rebels

"Clearly written and illustrated with full-color family photographs set against colorful backgrounds, this story is both personal and representative of the many people living in developing countries, the individuals working against all odds to help them, and the power of young people to make a difference." SLJ

362.1 People with illnesses and disabilities

Barber, Nicola

Going to the hospital. PowerKids Press 2009 24p il (The big day!) lib bdg $21.25; pa $8.25

Grades: PreK K 1   **362.1**

1. Hospitals 2. Medical care
ISBN 978-1-4358-2840-7 lib bdg; 1-4358-2840-2 lib bdg; 978-1-4358-2896-4 pa; 1-4358-2896-8 pa

LC 2008025812

"Children in kindergarten will enjoy [this book] as a read-aloud] . . . while those at the end of first grade will be able to read [it] independently. The writing is straightforward and reassuring, and the content provides a realistic view of what youngsters might experience in [a hospital]. . . .

[The book] discusses sickness, admission and surroundings, fasting for surgery, and blood tests." SLJ

Includes bibliographical references

Fleischman, John

★ **Phineas** Gage: a gruesome but true story about brain science. Houghton Mifflin 2002 86p il $16; pa $8.95

Grades: 5 6 7 8 9　　　　　　　　　　　　**362.1**

1. Railroad workers 2. Brain -- Wounds and injuries

ISBN 0-618-05252-6; 0-618-49478-2 pa

LC 2001-39253

"The author deftly introduces readers to a diverse range of relevant scientific history as well as more specific beliefs that influenced the medical establishment's understanding of Gage, then goes on to examine subsequent neurological discoveries that have changed and enhanced our understanding of Gage's fate. The book's present-tense narrative is inviting and intimate, and the text is crisp and lucid." Bull Cent Child Books

Includes glossary and bibliographical references

Parker, Victoria

Going to the hospital; [by] Vic Parker. Heinemann Library 2011 24p il (Growing up) lib bdg $22; pa $6.49

Grades: PreK K 1 2　　　　　　　　　　　　**362.1**

1. Hospitals 2. Medical care

ISBN 978-1-4329-4797-2 lib bdg; 1-4329-4797-4 lib bdg; 978-1-4329-4807-8 pa; 1-4329-4807-5 pa

LC 2010024191

This describes the experience of being a patient in a hospital.

Includes bibliographical references

362.18　Emergency services

Shepherd, Jodie

A **day** with paramedics; by Jodie Shepherd. Children's Press 2013 32 p. (pbk.) $5.95

Grades: K 1 2　　　　　　　　　　　　　　**362.18**

1. Emergency medical technicians 2. Emergency medical services

ISBN 0531289540; 9780531289549; 9780531292549

LC 2012013358

This book describes the job of paramedics. "In four short chapters dominated by photos of stretchers, oxygen masks, and neck braces . . . and a couple lines of text, [Jodie] Shepherd . . . list[s] where you find paramedics (football games, fairs) and establish[es] their professionalism: "They work quickly and calmly.' After stating that paramedics sometimes restart hearts or lungs, we go inside the ambulance . . . before wrapping up with some odder means of rescue (skis and helicopters)." (Booklist)

362.29　Substance abuse

Gottfried, Ted

Marijuana; by Ted Gottfried with Lisa Harkrader. Marshall Cavendish Benchmark 2010 32p il (Drug facts) $19.95

Grades: 4 5 6 7　　　　　　　　　　　　**362.29**

1. Marijuana

ISBN 978-0-7614-4351-3; 0-7614-4351-7

LC 2008-52761

"Provides clear explanations about effects, followed by diagrams of the body to clarify the specific organs/body systems that suffer the most damage. . . . An excellent starting point." SLJ

Includes glossary

LeVert, Suzanne

Ecstasy; by Suzanne LeVert with Jeff Hendricks. Marshall Cavendish Benchmark 2010 32p il (Drug facts) $19.95

Grades: 4 5 6 7　　　　　　　　　　　　**362.29**

1. Drug abuse 2. Designer drugs 3. Ecstasy (Drug)

ISBN 978-0-7614-4349-0; 0-7614-4349-5

LC 2008-52753

"Provides clear explanations about effects, followed by diagrams of the body to clarify the specific organs/body systems that suffer the most damage. . . . An excellent starting point." SLJ

Includes glossary

Steroids; by Suzanne LeVert with Jim Whiting. Marshall Cavendish Benchmark 2010 32p il (Drug facts) $19.95

Grades: 4 5 6 7　　　　　　　　　　　　**362.29**

1. Steroids 2. Sports -- Corrupt practices

ISBN 978-0-7614-4352-0; 0-7614-4352-5

LC 2008-52752

"Provides clear explanations about effects, followed by diagrams of the body to clarify the specific organs/body systems that suffer the most damage. . . . An excellent starting point." SLJ

Includes glossary

Menhard, Francha Roffe

The **facts** about inhalants; by Francha Roffe Menhard with Laura Purdie Salas. Marshall Cavendish Benchmark 2010 32p il (Drug facts) $19.95

Grades: 4 5 6 7　　　　　　　　　　　　**362.29**

1. Inhalant abuse

ISBN 978-0-7614-4350-6; 0-7614-4350-9

LC 2008-52739

"Provides clear explanations about effects, followed by diagrams of the body to clarify the specific organs/body systems that suffer the most damage. . . . An excellent starting point." SLJ

Includes glossary

Schaefer, Adam

Steroids; [by] A.R. Schaefer. Cherry Lake Pub. 2009 32p il (Health at risk) lib bdg $27.07

Grades: 4 5 6 7　　　　　　　　　　　　**362.29**

1. Steroids 2. Athletes -- Drug use

ISBN 978-1-60279-287-6 lib bdg; 1-60279-287-9 lib bdg

LC 2008017502

This describes how steroids affect the body and what sports groups are doing to halt their use.

"Great for reports or reluctant readers." Booklist

Includes bibliographical references

362.292   Alcohol

Bjornlund, Lydia D.

Alcohol; [by] Lydia Bjornlund. Cherry Lake Pub. 2009 32p il (Health at risk) lib bdg $27.07

Grades: 4 5 6 7   **362.292**

1. Alcohol 2. Alcoholism

ISBN 978-1-60279-280-7 lib bdg; 1-60279-280-1 lib bdg

LC 2008017495

This describes the effects of alcohol, the dangers of driving drunk, how to get help, and how to make good choices.

"Great for reports or reluctant readers." Booklist

Includes bibliographical references

Gottfried, Ted

Alcohol; by Ted Gottfried with Katherine Follett. Marshall Cavendish Benchmark 2010 32p il (Drug facts) $19.95

Grades: 4 5 6 7   **362.292**

1. Alcoholism 2. Drinking of alcoholic beverages 3. Alcohol -- Physiological effect

ISBN 978-0-7614-4348-3; 0-7614-4348-7

LC 2008-52751

"Provides clear explanations about effects, followed by diagrams of the body to clarify the specific organs/body systems that suffer the most damage. . . . An excellent starting point." SLJ

Includes glossary

362.4   People with physical disabilities

Bozzo, Linda

Guide dog heroes. Enslow Publishers 2010 48p il (Amazing working dogs with American Humane) lib bdg $23.93

Grades: 2 3 4   **362.4**

1. Guide dogs

ISBN 978-0-7660-3198-2; 0-7660-3198-5

This describes the work of guide dogs, the breeds that are best suited to the job, the training required, the tasks the dogs perform, and what happens to them after they retire.

"Full-color photos, some full page, appear throughout. [This book is] clearly written in a personable style, with plenty of anecdotal and factual information, which makes [it] suitable for report writing and enjoyable for general reading." SLJ

Includes glossary and bibliographical references

Service dog heroes. Enslow Publishers 2010 48p il (Amazing working dogs with American Humane) lib bdg $23.93

Grades: 2 3 4   **362.4**

1. Working dogs 2. Animals and people with disabilities

ISBN 978-0-7660-3199-9; 0-7660-3199-3

This describes the work of service dogs who help people with disabilities, the breeds that are best suited to the work, the training required, the tasks the dogs perform, and what happens to them after they retire.

"Full-color photos, some full page, appear throughout. [This book is] clearly written in a personable style, with plenty of anecdotal and factual information, which makes [it] suitable for report writing and enjoyable for general reading." SLJ

Includes glossary and bibliographical references

Goldish, Meish

Prison puppies. Bearport Pub. 2011 32p il (Dog heroes) lib bdg $25.27

Grades: 3 4 5   **362.4**

1. Prisoners 2. Animals and people with disabilities

ISBN 978-1-61772-151-9; 1-61772-151-4

LC 2010037154

In this book, "readers learn about the 'Puppies Behind Bars' program, where inmates train dogs for careers as service animals. While the future work duties of the dogs are evident, the real story here is how they give the inmates an opportunity to contribute to society in a positive way. . . . [This book is] engaging not just because the content is so compelling, but also because the [author has] highlighted specific dogs currently working in [this field]. The use of real names and full-color photographs on every page, many contributed by the individuals who work with these dogs, makes reading [this book] a personal experience. . . . [An] excellent [introduction] to [this] new [development] in service-dog training." SLJ

Includes glossary and bibliographical references

Hoffman, Mary Ann

Helping dogs. Gareth Stevens Pub. 2011 24p il (Working dogs) lib bdg $22.60; pa $8.15

Grades: 2 3 4   **362.4**

1. Animals and people with disabilities

ISBN 978-1-4339-4651-6 lib bdg; 1-4339-4651-3 lib bdg; 978-1-4339-4652-3 pa; 1-4339-4652-1 pa

LC 2010035242

This describes helping "dogs and the training they receive. The short chapters, complemented by numerous color photographs, provide examples of particular breeds that do [this] job and show how their characteristics are suited for the tasks. The charts provided are especially helpful, covering commands and more specific tasks. There is enough information to make the [text] feel fresh. . . . A solid choice for readers looking for more than cute pictures." SLJ

Hopkinson, Deborah

Annie and Helen; by Deborah Hopkinson; illustrated by Raul Colón. Schwartz & Wade Books 2012 48 p. $17.99

Grades: 2 3 4 5   **362.4**

1. Reading 2. Female friendship 3. Deafblind women -- United States -- Biography

ISBN 0375857060; 9780375857065; 9780375957062

LC 2010031443

Author Deborah Hopkinson presents a picture-book biography on Helen Keller. "Focusing on the relationship between Helen and her teacher, Annie Sullivan, the book is interspersed with excerpts of Annie's letters home, written as she struggled with her angry, wild pupil. But slowly, with devotion and determination, Annie teaches Helen finger spelling and braille, letters, and sentences. As Helen comes to understand language and starts to communicate, she connects for the first time with her family and the world around her." (Publisher's note)

Includes bibliographical references.

Lambert, Joseph

The **Center** for Cartoon Studies presents Annie Sullivan and the trials of Helen Keller; by Joseph Lambert; with an introduction by TK. Disney Hyperion Books 2012 96 p.

Grades: 5 6 7　　　　　　　　　　　　　　**362.4**

1. Women authors -- Biography 2. Female friendship -- Graphic novels 3. People with disabilities -- Graphic novels 4. Graphic novels 5. Women -- United States -- History 6. Women -- United States -- Biography 7. Female friendship -- United States -- History

ISBN 9781423113362

LC 2011036324

This nonfiction graphic novel about Annie Sullivan and Helen Keller "focuses on the trials both Annie and Helen struggle with in their lives," particularly the incident when Helen was accused of plagiarism in her story 'The Frost King' and interrogated at the Perkins Institution. "Helen's perspective is . . . communicated in dialogue-free black panels in which she is represented as only a gray silhouette" by author/illustrator Joseph Lambert. (Kirkus) Bibliography.

Martin, Claudia

Helpers. Marshall Cavendish Benchmark 2010 64p il (Working animals) lib bdg $28.50

Grades: 4 5 6 7　　　　　　　　　　　　　　**362.4**

1. Animals and people with disabilities

ISBN 978-1-60870-163-6 lib bdg; 1-60870-163-8 lib bdg

"Attractively designed and packed with information. . . . The composition of each page is attractively set up with well-selected and reproduced stock and historical photos." SLJ

Montalvan, Luis Carlos

Tuesday tucks me in; the loyal bond between a soldier and his service dog. Luis Carlos Montalvan, Bret Witter; [photographs by] Dan Dion. Roaring Brook Press 2014 40 p. (hardback) $16.99

Grades: K 1 2 3 4　　　　　　　　　　　　　**362.4**

1. Service dogs 2. Human-animal relationship 3. Human-animal relationships 4. Service dogs -- United States

ISBN 1596438916; 9781596438910

LC 2013032042

Written by Luis Carlos Montalván and Bret Witter, with photography by Dan Dion, "'Tuesday Tucks Me In' is a day in the life of this service dog extraordinaire and tail-wagging ambassador for all things positive and uplifting in the world. The book takes us through a typical day of adventures, starting with Tuesday waking Luis in the morning and greeting him with dog breath in the face, and then ending with Tuesday cuddling up to Luis on their bed." (Publisher's note)

"Montalván, the best-selling author of the adult memoir Until Tuesday: A Wounded Warrior and the Golden Retriever Who Saved Him (2011), is a 17-year army veteran and advocate for veterans with disabilities. Yet this is not his story but that of his golden retriever service dog, Tuesday... Tuesday typifies the unbreakable bond between humans and canines and in a kid-friendly way, manages to dispel some of the stigma of post-traumatic stress disorder and invisible war wounds." Booklist

Patent, Dorothy Hinshaw

★ The **right** dog for the job; Ira's path from service dog to guide dog. photographs by William Muñoz. Walker & Co. 2004 un il $16.95

Grades: 2 3 4　　　　　　　　　　　　　　**362.4**

1. Guide dogs 2. Animals and people with disabilities 3. Animals -- Training

ISBN 0-8027-8914-5

LC 2003-65785

This "photo-essay follows a puppy from his training to become a service dog to becoming a guide dog. . . . The author . . . manages to slip in an extraordinary amount of information about the raising and training of guide dogs. . . . Myriad full-color photographs that will capture kids' interest accompany the text." SLJ

Rappaport, Doreen, 1939-

★ **Helen's** big world; the life of Helen Keller. written by Doreen Rappaport; illustrated by Matt Tavares. Disney/Hyperion Books 2012 48 p. $17.99

Grades: K 1 2 3 4　　　　　　　　　　　　**362.4**

1. Disabilities 2. Picture books for children 3. Deafblind women -- United States -- Biography 4. Deafblind people -- United States -- Biography

ISBN 078680890X; 9780786808908

LC 2011053516

In this children's picture-book biography of Helen Keller, author Doreen Rappaport and illustrator Matt Tavares begin "when Keller was a healthy baby . . . and end . . . with her death at 87, when she had long been a national icon and social activist." Her teacher Annie Sullivan is featured throughout the book, which "conveys . . . both the catastrophic nature of Helen's disabilities and the steely will that raged to be unleashed." (Publishers Weekly)

Includes bibliographical references.

362.5　Poor people

Lynette, Rachel

What to do when your family loses its home. PowerKids Press 2010 24p il (Let's work it out) lib bdg $21.25; pa $8.25

Grades: 2 3 4　　　　　　　　　　　　　　**362.5**

1. Homeless persons

ISBN 978-1-4358-9339-9 lib bdg; 1-4358-9339-5 lib bdg; 978-1-4358-9766-3 pa; 1-4358-9766-8 pa

"Full-page color photographs appear opposite the [narrative], depicting multicultural children, parents, grandparents, social workers, and others, whose demeanors match the hopeful tone of the [title]. This . . . will help promote empathy and understanding for the plight of others and is a key purchase." SLJ

Includes glossary

Mason, Paul, 1967-

Poverty; [by] Paul Mason. Heinemann Library 2006 48p il map (Planet under pressure) lib bdg $31.43

Grades: 4 5 6 7　　　　　　　　　　　　　　**362.5**

1. Poverty

ISBN 1-4034-7743-4

LC 2005017166

"Mason presents common factors for poverty worldwide, such as lack of money and education, as well as natural disasters. He also addresses the effects of outsourcing jobs from wealthier countries to poorer ones and how poverty affects environment. The book should make the global situation clearer. [This has] numerous quality color visuals, and sidebars. Up-to-date and informative." SLJ

Includes bibliographical references

362.7 Young people

Krementz, Jill

How it feels to be adopted. Knopf 1982 107p il hardcover o.p. pa $15

Grades: 4 5 6 7   **362.7**
1. Adoption
ISBN 0-394-75853-6 pa
LC 82-48011

This "is an important contribution to literature on adoption and the question of searching for biological parents." SLJ

Includes bibliographical references

Lynette, Rachel

What to do when your family is on welfare. PowerKids Press 2010 24p il (Let's work it out) lib bdg $21.25; pa $8.25

Grades: 2 3 4   **362.7**
1. Public welfare
ISBN 978-1-4358-9337-5 lib bdg; 1-4358-9337-9 lib bdg; 978-1-4358-9762-5 pa; 1-4358-9762-5 pa
LC 2009-19863

"Full-page color photographs appear opposite the [narrative], depicting multicultural children, parents, grandparents, social workers, and others, whose demeanors match the hopeful tone of the [title]. This . . . will help promote empathy and understanding for the plight of others and is a key purchase." SLJ

Includes glossary

Parr, Todd

We belong together; a book about adoption and families. Little, Brown 2007 32p il $15.99

Grades: PreK K   **362.7**
1. Family 2. Adoption
ISBN 0-316-01668-3

"Parr illustrates the rewards of family ties in this heartfelt, supportive book geared toward adopted children and their parents. In each double-page spread, Parr completes the phrase 'We belong together because . . .' with poignant explanations that touch upon basic, tangible needs . . . as well as emotional ones. . . . Cheerful, friendly artwork, with thickly outlined forms and characters and a bold rainbow palette, inclusively depicts an array of children and families—including one with a single parent and one with two dads." Booklist

Rotner, Shelley

I'm adopted! by Shelley Rotner and Sheila M. Kelly; photographs by Shelley Rotner. Holiday House 2011 un il $16.95

Grades: PreK K 1   **362.7**
1. Adoption
ISBN 978-0-8234-2294-4; 0-8234-2294-1
LC 2010029561

"This introduction to adoption for very young children stands out in its clear, accessible approach to [the] topic. . . . Engaging, full-color photos portray kids and parents of varying ethnicities and families of varying compositions. The process of adoption is explained in simple language that children understand. . . . Both domestic and international adoption are addressed, making this suitable for all kinds of adoptive families. The photo album-like design . . . adds to the appeal." Kirkus

Saul, Laya

Ways to help disadvantaged youth. Mitchell Lane Publishers 2011 47p (How to help: a guide to giving back) lib bdg $29.95

Grades: 4 5 6   **362.7**
1. Poor 2. Social action
ISBN 978-1-58415-918-6; 1-58415-918-9
LC 2010006536

This "well-organized [book] will encourage children to contribute to the world around them. [This] title is filled with examples of volunteer opportunities that can be accomplished with some adult involvement and supervision to guide, steer, and maintain focus so that youngsters will have varied and successful experiences. . . . [The book] suggests tutoring, having a toy or food drive, etc." SLJ

Includes bibliographical references

Stewart, Sheila

A house between homes; kids in the foster care system. by Sheila Stewart and Camden Flath. Mason Crest Publishers 2010 48p il (Kids have troubles too) lib bdg $19.95; pa $7.95

Grades: 3 4 5 6   **362.7**
1. Foster home care
ISBN 978-1-4222-1692-7 lib bdg; 1-4222-1692-6 lib bdg; 978-1-4222-1905-8 pa; 1-4222-1905-4 pa
LC 2010012756

"The prose is respectable in its dialogue, character development, and pacing... This series will be well placed in a school media center, as well as in any institution that serves high-risk children." SLJ

Includes bibliographical references

362.73 Institutional and related services

Warren, Andrea

★ We rode the orphan trains. Houghton Mifflin 2001 132p il $18; pa $8.95

Grades: 4 5 6 7   **362.73**
1. Orphans
ISBN 0-618-11712-1; 0-618-11712-1 pa
LC 00-47279

"This is powerful nonfiction for classroom and personal reading and for discussion." Booklist

Includes bibliographical references

362.82   Families

Stewart, Sheila

When Daddy hit Mommy; by Sheila Stewart and Rae Simons. Mason Crest Publishers 2011 48p il (Kids have troubles too) lib bdg $19.95; pa $7.95

Grades: 3 4 5   **362.82**

1. Child abuse 2. Domestic violence

ISBN 978-1-4222-1696-5 lib bdg; 1-4222-1696-9 lib bdg; 978-1-4222-1909-6 pa; 1-4222-1909-7 pa

LC 2010029346

"These slender volumes open with fictional vignettes followed by honest discussions of the facts in order to inform and reassure kids in tough situations, as well as help children not undergoing these troubles empathize with those who are. The prose is respectable in its dialogue, character development, and pacing; the nonfiction sections are conversational in tone but include enough facts for research. Unfamiliar words are defined in sidebars. This series will be well placed in a school media center, as well as in any institution that serves high-risk children." SLJ

Includes bibliographical references

363.1   Public safety programs

Aronson, Marc

★ **Trapped**; how the world rescued 33 miners from 2,000 feet below the Chilean desert. Atheneum 2011 144p il

Grades: 4 5 6 7   **363.1**

1. Rescue work 2. Gold mines and mining 3. Copper mines and mining 4. Mine accidents -- Chile

ISBN 1-4169-1397-1; 978-1-4169-1397-9

LC 2011000777

This title is about thirty-three miners trapped in a copper-gold mine in San Jose, Chile and how experts from around the world, from drillers, to astronauts, to submarine specialists, came together to make their remarkable rescue possible.

This is "a riveting, in-depth recounting of the events that held the world rapt. . . . Twelve short chapters with photos and diagrams keep the story well-paced." Publ Wkly

Includes bibliographical references

Benoit, Peter

The **Hindenburg** disaster. Children's Press 2011 48p il map (True book) lib bdg $28

Grades: 3 4 5   **363.1**

1. Airships 2. Aircraft accidents 3. Hindenburg (Airship)

ISBN 978-0-531-20626-3 lib bdg; 0-531-20626-2 lib bdg; 978-0-531-29025-5 pa; 0-531-29025-5 pa

LC 2010045931

This describes how the Hindenburg blimp crashed and burned in New Jersey on May 6, 1937.

"Benoit provides unbiased information that is on target for the intended audience. . . . The photographs and reproductions enhance the [text]. . . . [This book is] well-conceived." SLJ

Includes bibliographical references

Nuclear meltdowns. Children's Press 2011 48p il (True book: disasters) lib bdg $28; pa $6.99

Grades: 3 4 5   **363.1**

1. Chernobyl Nuclear Accident, Chernobyl, Ukraine, 1986 2. Nuclear power plants -- Security measures 3. Three Mile Island Nuclear Power Plant (Pa.)

ISBN 978-0-531-25422-6 lib bdg; 0-531-25422-4; 978-0-531-26627-4 pa; 0-531-26627-3 pa

LC 2011007142

This describes nuclear power plant accidents at Three Mile Island, Chernobyl, and in Japan.

This is "thoughtfully designed. . . . The information . . . is right on target: concise, accurate, and thorough. . . . The photographs . . . are especially effective at putting a human face on large-scale devastation." Booklist

Includes glossary and bibliographical references

363.11   Occupational and industrial hazards

Scott, Elaine

★ **Buried** alive! how 33 miners survived 69 days deep under the Chilean desert. Elaine Scott. Houghton Mifflin Harcourt 2012 80 p. col. ill., col. maps (hardcover) $17.99; (ebook) $17.99

Grades: 4 5 6 7 8   **363.11**

1. Miners 2. Disasters 3. Industrial accidents 4. San José Mine Accident, Chile, 2010 5. Mine rescue work -- Chile -- Copiapó Region 6. San José Mine Accident, Chile, 2010 7. Gold mines and mining -- Accidents -- Chile -- Copiapó Region 8. Copper mines and mining -- Accidents -- Chile -- Copiapó Region

ISBN 0547707789; 9780547707785; 9780547691787

LC 2011025945

Author Elaine Scott chronicles the events that took place "[o]n August 5, 2010, [when] a copper mine in Chile collapsed, trapping 33 miners nearly half a mile underground . . . [The author] describes the choices the miners' strong leader advised that prolonged their survival long enough to be rescued and the creative solutions that effected that rescue. They drilled through over 2,000 feet of especially hard rock, delivered supplies to the trapped men through a tiny bore hole and then invented a way to carry the men, one at a time, to the surface in a very small capsule." (Kirkus)

Includes bibliographical references (p. 78) and index.

363.12   Transportation hazards

Verstraete, Larry

Surviving the Hindenburg; by Larry Verstraete; illustrated by David Geister. Sleeping Bear Press 2012 32 p. col. ill.

Grades: 2 3 4   **363.12**

1. Airships 2. Aeronautics 3. Aircraft accidents 4. Hindenburg (Airship) 5. Cabin boys -- Germany -- Biography 6. Airships -- Germany -- History -- 20th century 7. Survival -- New Jersey -- History -- 20th century 8. Aircraft accident victims -- New Jersey -- Biography 9. Aircraft accidents -- New Jersey -- History -- 20th century

ISBN 1585367877; 9781585367870

LC 2011027879

This historical story, by Larry Verstraete and David Geister, relates the story of the German airship "Hindenburg." "On May 6, 1937, the . . . airship . . . exploded. . . . 62 survived, including Werner Franz, the ship's 14-year-old cabin boy. . . . Verstrate recounts young Werner's story. . . . Through Werner's memories young readers will explore the inner workings of the giant airship . . . and hold their breath during Werner's terrifying escape from the fiery devastation." (Publisher's note)

363.2 Police services

Arroyo, Sheri L.
How crime fighters use math; math curriculum consultant: Rhea A. Stewart. Chelsea Clubhouse 2010 32p il (Math in the real world) lib bdg $28
Grades: 4 5 6 **363.2**
1. Mathematics 2. Vocational guidance 3. Criminal investigation
ISBN 978-1-60413-602-9 lib bdg; 1-60413-602-2 lib bdg
LC 2009-23330
"The layout for [this] slim [title] is bright and colorful with a photograph and a 'You Do the Math' problem to solve and large, easy-to-read text on every spread. An answer key is included in the back matter, along with a page detailing the career choices and the educational requirements. [It] touches on crime-scene grids, the importance of shoe prints in tracking a criminal, cracking secret codes, and more. . . . [This title] would be useful to supplement lessons on mathematics. [It] will also appeal to students wanting to learn more about math as it relates to specific careers." SLJ
Includes glossary and bibliographical references

Bozzo, Linda
Police dog heroes. Enslow Publishers 2010 48p il (Amazing working dogs with American Humane) lib bdg $23.93
Grades: 2 3 4 **363.2**
1. Working dogs 2. Animals in police work
ISBN 978-0-7660-3197-5; 0-7660-3197-7
LC 2008048017
"Full-color photos, some full page, appear throughout. [This book is] clearly written in a personable style, with plenty of anecdotal and factual information, which makes [it] suitable for report writing and enjoyable for general reading." SLJ
Includes glossary and bibliographical references

Graham, Ian
Forensic technology. Smart Apple Media 2011 il (New technology) lib bdg $34.25
Grades: 4 5 6 7 **363.2**
1. Forensic sciences 2. Criminal investigation
ISBN 978-1-599-20532-8; 1-599-20532-7
LC 2010044238
Describes the technology used by forensic scientists to gather and analyze evidence from crime scenes.
This "offers a fine overview for reports, and its attractive design may also entice middle-grade readers to learn more." Booklist

Hoffman, Mary Ann
Police dogs. Gareth Stevens Pub. 2011 24p il (Working dogs) lib bdg $22.60; pa $8.15
Grades: 2 3 4 **363.2**
1. Dogs
ISBN 978-1-4339-4659-2 lib bdg; 1-4339-4659-9 lib bdg; 978-1-4339-4660-8 pa; 1-4339-4660-2 pa
LC 2010035244
This describes police "dogs and the training they receive. The short chapters, complemented by numerous color photographs, provide examples of particular breeds that do [this] job and show how their characteristics are suited for the tasks. The charts provided are especially helpful, covering commands and more specific tasks. There is enough information to make the [text] feel fresh. . . . A solid choice for readers looking for more than cute pictures." SLJ

Jackson, Donna M.
★ The wildlife detectives; how forensic scientists fight crimes against nature. by Donna M. Jackson; photographs by Wendy Shattil and Bob Rozinski. Houghton Mifflin 2000 47p il $16
Grades: 4 5 6 7 **363.2**
1. Game protection 2. Forensic sciences 3. U.S. Fish and Wildlife Service -- Forensics Laboratory
ISBN 0-395-86976-5
LC 99-34857
Describes how the wildlife detectives at the National Fish and Wildlife Forensics Laboratory in Ashland, Oregon, analyze clues to catch and convict people responsible for crimes against animals
This book features "a smoothly written text that unfolds almost like a mystery novel. . . . Engaging full-color photographs help clarify the text and will appeal to browsers. A list of follow-up suggestions and a glossary of terms are appended. A book that will be welcomed by mystery fans and anyone who cares about animals." Booklist

Kenney, Karen Latchana
Police officers at work; by Karen L. Kenney; illustrated by Brian Caleb Dumm; content consultant: Judith Stepan-Norris. Magic Wagon 2009 32p il (Meet your community workers!) lib bdg $18.95
Grades: K 1 2 3 **363.2**
1. Police 2. Vocational guidance
ISBN 978-1-60270-652-1 lib bdg; 1-60270-652-2 lib bdg
LC 2009-2391
This book about police officers has "an uncluttered layout and consistent organization. . . . Chapter headings such as 'Problems on the Job,' and 'Technology at Work,' and 'Special Skills and Training' make it easy to pinpoint specific information." SLJ
Includes glossary

Mezzanotte, Jim
Police. Marshall Cavendish Benchmark 2010 64p il (Working animals) lib bdg $28.50
Grades: 4 5 6 7 **363.2**
1. Animals in police work
ISBN 978-1-60870-166-7 lib bdg; 1-60870-166-2 lib bdg
LC 2010007006

Describes animals, such as dogs and horses, which work with police in such areas as search-and-rescue, tracking criminals, and sniffing out explosives

"Attractively designed and packed with information. . . . The composition of each page is attractively set up with well-selected and reproduced stock and historical photos." SLJ

Perritano, John

Science beats crime. Marshall Cavendish Benchmark 2010 48p il (Cool science) lib bdg $28.50

Grades: 5 6 7 8   **363.2**

1. Forensic sciences 2. Criminal investigation

ISBN 978-1-60870-078-3 lib bdg; 1-60870-078-X lib bdg

LC 2009053774

"Perritano briefly traces the history of forensic science, . . . discusses different subspecialities, such as toxicology and forensic anthropology, and then gets into the good stuff—fingerprinting, DNA profiling, ballistics, splatter patterns, even a gross-out spread of how studying maggots can determine time of death. Interspersed throughout are real-life case studies. . . . This solid, amply illustrated, and easy-reading introduction to forensic science ends with a look at the future of the field." Booklist

Includes glossary and bibliographical references

Spilsbury, Richard

Counterfeit! stopping fakes and forgeries. Enslow Publishers 2009 48p il (Solve that crime!) lib bdg $23.93

Grades: 5 6 7 8   **363.2**

1. Fraud 2. Forgery

ISBN 978-0-7660-3378-8 lib bdg; 0-7660-3378-3 lib bdg

LC 2008-33310

This "title boasts in-depth information, sidebars detailing events of true crime, and activities that will increase understanding. . . . Photographs are colorful, well-captioned, and related to the text." SLJ

Includes glossary and bibliographical references

Townsend, John

Famous forensic cases. Amicus 2011 il (Amazing crime scene science) $19.95

Grades: 4 5 6 7   **363.2**

1. Forensic sciences 2. Criminal investigation

ISBN 978-1-60753-169-2; 1-60753-169-0

In this book "readers will find a straight presentation of fascinating information. Loosely organized by era, the book opens with a history of fingerprinting . . . which focuses on the 1920s and 1930s. Other topics include hair science in the 1950s, voiceprints in the 1970s, and recent advancements in DNA forensics. Scatter throughout are case studies. . . . This entry features an eye-catching layout, plenty of sidebars, and well-chosen photos. . . . Kids will go for this one." Booklist

363.25   Detection of crime (Criminal investigation)

MacLeod, Elizabeth

Bones Never Lie; How Forensics Helps Solve History's Mysteries. Elizabeth MacLeod. Firefly Books Ltd 2013 iv, 156 p.p (hardcover) $24.95

Grades: 4 5 6 7 8   **363.25**

1. Forensic sciences -- Encyclopedias

ISBN 1554514835; 9781554514830

This children's book, by Elizabeth MacLeod, explores how through "forensics--the scientific way of examining physical evidence--we now know what killed Napoleon and whether Anastasia survived the massacre of the Russian royal family. Seven intriguing stories about historical royal figures whose demise was suspicious, and hard scientific facts about crime-solving techniques make each event seem like an episode of CSI rather than a history lesson." (Publisher's note)

"In real life, forensics can be slow and tedious, but MacLeod invests these high-profile deaths with considerable vim and drama. A good selection of staged and archival photographs and artwork accompany the stories. A fully fleshed and crisply told story of forensics at its romantic best." Kirkus

363.28   Services of special kinds of security and law enforcement agencies

Butts, Ed

Bodyguards! from gladiators to the secret service. Annick Press 2012 121 p. $24.95

Grades: 3 4 5   **363.28**

1. Bodyguards 2. Gladiators 3. Guard animals 4. Secret service

ISBN 1554514371; 9781554514373

This book "includes all the information you need to become a bodyguard" as well as facts about the bodyguards of the Egyptian pharaoh and animals with hearing that makes them good alert systems. "Aside from ancient Egyptian priests and animals, other types of bodyguards mentioned include, among others, the Vatican's Swiss Guard, Abraham Lincoln's tippling police guard and Elvis' Memphis Mafia." (Kirkus)

363.3   Other aspects of public safety

Nolan, Janet

★ The firehouse light; illustrations by Marie Lafrance. Tricycle Press 2010 un il lib bdg $18.95; $15.99

Grades: K 1 2 3   **363.3**

1. Electric lamps 2. Fire departments

ISBN 978-1-58246-346-9 lib bdg; 1-58246-346-8 lib bdg; 978-1-58246-298-1; 1-58246-298-4

LC 2009-7964

The true story of a lightbulb in a firehouse located in Livermore, California, that has stayed lit for more than one hundred years.

"The narrative successfully knits firefighting and history into a fast dash through the twentieth century. . . . Flat, folk-style acrylic illustrations feature fluid, sinewy human figures amid a variety of vintage fire trucks." Booklist

363.34 Disasters

Bailey, Gerry

Fragile planet. Gareth Stevens Pub. 2011 48p il map (Planet SOS) lib bdg $31.95; pa $14.05

Grades: 4 5 6   **363.34**

1. Natural disasters

ISBN 978-1-4339-4974-6 lib bdg; 1-4339-4974-1 lib bdg; 978-1-4339-4975-3 pa; 1-4339-4975-X pa

LC 2010032886

This "well-designed [book]. . . . discusses natural events and disasters, such as avalanches, earthquakes, floods, hurricanes, lightning, volcanoes, and windstorms. . . . The many large, colorful photos will engage readers and assist them in understanding the important concepts introduced." SLJ

Includes glossary

Fradin, Judith Bloom

★ **Droughts**; [by] Judy & Dennis Fradin. National Geographic 2008 48p il map (Witness to disaster) $16.95; lib bdg $20.90

Grades: 4 5 6 7   **363.34**

1. Droughts

ISBN 978-1-4263-0339-5; 1-4263-0339-4; 978-1-4263-0340-1 lib bdg; 1-4263-0340-8 lib bdg

LC 2008020424

"This book examines the lessons from the Dust Bowl droughts for farmers, including the importance of topsoil. The history of droughts around the world compares impacts on a wide variety of societies. The final chapter looks at the latest tools and technologies developed to help us survive future droughts." Publisher's note

Includes glossary and bibliographical references

Hurricane Katrina; [by] Judith Bloom Fradin, Dennis Brindell Fradin. Marshall Cavendish Benchmark 2009 47p il map (Turning points in U.S. history) lib bdg $21.95

Grades: 3 4 5   **363.34**

1. Hurricane Katrina, 2005

ISBN 978-0-7614-4261-5 lib bdg; 0-7614-4261-8 lib bdg

LC 2008038268

This book provides "accurate, nonsensationalized information in [a] well-organized, clearly written, and politically neutral [text]. The photos are crisp, and, due to the subject matter, heartrending." SLJ

Includes glossary and bibliographical references

Garbe, Suzanne

The **Worst** wildfires of all time; by Suzanne Garbe. Capstone Press 2013 32 p. ill. (chiefly col.), col. maps (library) $27.32

Grades: 4 5 6 7   **363.34**

1. Wildfires 2. Natural disasters

ISBN 1429684186; 9781429684187

LC 2011053150

This book by Suzanne Garbe is part of the Epic Disasters series and looks at the worst wildfires of all time. "These uncontrolled fires can strike in the blink of an eye and spread just as quickly. Put out the flames and read about the worst wildfires in history." The series allows readers to "witness the destructive power of hurricanes, earthquakes, and more." (Publisher's note)

Includes bibliographical references and index.

Karwoski, Gail

Tsunami; the true story of an April Fools' Day disaster. [by] Gail Langer Karwoski; illustrated by John MacDonald. Darby Creek Pub. 2006 64p il $17.95

Grades: 4 5 6 7   **363.34**

1. Tsunamis 2. Hawaii -- History

ISBN 1581960441

The author "opens with a description of the tsunami waves that struck the northern coast of the Hawaiian Islands in 1946, destroying a school and sweeping many children and adults out to sea. The book goes on to provide broader information about tsunamis, from scientific understanding of how they occur to ongoing efforts at early warning systems. . . . Clearly written and informative." Booklist

Langley, Andrew

Hurricanes, tsunamis, and other natural disasters; [by] Andrew Langley. Kingfisher 2006 63p il map (Kingfisher knowledge) $12.95

Grades: 5 6 7 8   **363.34**

1. Natural disasters

ISBN 978-0-7534-5975-1; 0-7534-5975-2

LC 2005027200

This briefly describes such natural disasters as hurricanes, tsunamis, avalanches, brush fires, earthquakes, floods, tornadoes, drought and famine, pandemics, with many color illustrations and maps

"This book presents a high-interest topic in an attractively designed format that features colorful, eye-catching graphics and a solidly written text." Booklist

Includes glossary and bibliographical references

Markle, Sandra

★ **Rescues!** Millbrook Press 2006 88p il map lib bdg $25.26

Grades: 4 5 6 7   **363.34**

1. Rescue work 2. Survival after airplane accidents, shipwrecks, etc.

ISBN 978-0-8225-3413-6 lib bdg; 0-8225-3413-4 lib bdg

LC 2005-09707

"From the collapse of a Pennsylvania coal mine in 2002 to the tsunami that struck 11 countries in 2004 to Hurricane Katrina in 2005, the 11 disasters Markle describes are straight from news headlines. In this full-color photo-essay, she uses individual experiences of rescue and survival to bring each drama close." Booklist

Includes bibliographical references

Meyer, Susan

Adapting to flooding and rising sea levels; Susan Meyer. 1st ed. Rosen Central 2012 64 p. col. ill., col. maps (Science to the rescue: Adapting to climate change) (library) $31.95

Grades: 4 5 6   **363.34**

1. Sea level 2. Climate change 3. Global warming 4. Floods 5. Climatic changes 6. Sea level -- Climatic

factors

ISBN 1448868475; 9781448868476

LC 2011045624

This book is part of the Science to the Rescue: Adapting to Climate Change series. It "focuses on the devastation to coastal regions worldwide caused by storms and global warming and how those issues are being addressed in various countries. A succinct explanation of the reasons for global warming and the rising sea level is followed by a section on the methods of adaptation . . . and a rundown of the current research being conducted." (Booklist)

Includes bibliographical references and index

Miller, Mara

Hurricane Katrina strikes the Gulf Coast; disaster & survival. [by] Mara Miller. Enslow Publishers 2006 48p il map (Deadly disasters) $23.93

Grades: 4 5 6 7   363.34

1. Hurricanes 2. Rescue work 3. Hurricane Katrina, 2005

ISBN 0-7660-2803-8

LC 2005030989

"Miller begins with an account of the development of Hurricane Katrina as it struck Florida and then threatened the Gulf Coast. She discusses the subsequent flooding of New Orleans, the damage it caused, rescue and recovery attempts, and planning for the aftermath of future hurricanes. The author includes a clear scientific description of hurricanes, defining key terms. Color photos and graphics help explain concepts such as the structure of a hurricane, Katrina's path, and the conditions endured by the victims." SLJ

Includes glossary and bibliographical references

Reilly, Kathleen M.

Natural disasters; investigate Earth's most destructive forces. by Kathleen M. Reilly; illustrated by Tom Casteel. Nomad Press 2012 121 p. (paperback) $15.95

Grades: 4 5 6 7   363.34

1. Weather 2. Natural disasters

ISBN 1619301466; 9781619301467

In this book, "spiraling winds, surging waters, eruptions, blazing forests, and chilling snows are discussed." Topics include "the MMS Scale and the Enhanced Fujita Scale." In addition to an "explanation of each type of phenomenon, safety tips, historical incidences, pen-and-ink line drawings, and correlative projects using simple materials are included." (School Library Journal)

Rusch, Elizabeth

★ **Eruption!** volcanoes and the science of saving lives. text by Elizabeth Rusch; illustrated by Tom Uhlman. Houghton Mifflin Harcourt 2013 76 p. col. ill. (hardcover) $18.99

Grades: 5 6 7 8   363.34

1. Disaster response and recovery 2. Volcanoes 3. Natural disasters 4. Volcanic eruptions

ISBN 0547503504; 9780547503509

LC 2012034055

This book by Elizabeth Rusch contains "photographs and sidebars [which] reveals the perilous . . . life-saving work of an international volcano crisis team (VDAP) and the sleeping giants they study, from Colombia to the Philippines, from Chile to Indonesia. [It presents an] stunning account of volcanologists Andy Lockhart, John Pallister,

and their group of scientists who risk their lives, investigating deadly volcanoes that remain constant threats to people around the world." (Publisher's note)

Includes bibliographical references (pages 74-75) and index.

Saul, Laya

Ways to help after a natural disaster; by Laya Saul. Mitchell Lane Publishers 2011 47 p. col. ill. (library) $29.95

Grades: 4 5 6   363.34

1. Volunteer work 2. Disaster relief

ISBN 1584159170; 9781584159179

LC 2010006538

"This focuses on various activities in which children can participate to help families be prepared in the event of a natural disaster or in its aftermath, when citizens experience the devastating results. The brief sections on teaching preparedness include advice for putting together supply kits and a sample list for collecting emergency numbers. The bulk of the information is sound, practical, commonsense recommendations. . . . Included are simple measures, such as offering emotional support, as well as those that are more complicated, such as organizing drives for collecting blood or food and clothing. The design is inviting, with text appealingly laid out and offset by blocks of color." Booklist

Includes bibliographical references and index.

Somervill, Barbara A.

Graphing natural disasters. Heinemann Library 2010 32p il (Real world data) $28.21; pa $7.99

Grades: 5 6 7 8   363.34

1. Graphic methods 2. Natural disasters

ISBN 978-1-4329-2622-9; 1-4329-2622-5; 978-1-4329-2631-1 pa; 1-4329-2631-4 pa

LC 2009001290

This describes natural disasters such as tornadoes and volcanic eruptions using graphs and charts.

The book is "colorful, easy to read, and well designed." SLJ

Includes glossary and bibliographical references

363.37   Fire hazards

Cooper, Michael L., 1950-

Fighting fire! ten of the deadliest fires in American history and how we fought them. Michael L. Cooper. Henry Holt and Co. 2014 224 p. illustrations, maps (hardback) $19.99

Grades: 5 6 7 8   363.37

1. Fires 2. Fire fighting 3. Fire extinction -- United States -- History

ISBN 0805097147; 9780805097146

LC 2013043580

This book, by Michael L. Cooper, "brings to life ten of the deadliest infernos . . . [the United States] has ever endured: the great fires of Boston, New York, Chicago, Baltimore, and San Francisco, the disasters of the Triangle Shirtwaist Factory, the General Slocum, and the Cocoanut Grove nightclub, the wildfire of Witch Creek in San Diego County, and the catastrophe of 9/11." (Publisher's note)

"Throughout history, fires have wreaked destruction but have also sparked innovation and reform. The Great Chicago Fire (1871) destroyed a third of the city but brought about a new architecture style; the Triangle Shirtwaist Factory Fire (1911) killed 146 people but led to the passage of laws protecting workers. Entries are lively, with dramatic illustrations to match." Horn Book

Includes bibliographical references and index

363.6 Public utilities and related services

Brown, Cynthia Light
Discover National Monuments, National Parks; natural wonders. illustrated by Blair Shedd. Nomad Press 2009 106p il (Discover your world) pa $19.95
Grades: 5 6 7 8   363.6
  1. National parks and reserves
  ISBN 978-1-9346702-8-6 pa; 1-9346702-8-6 pa
"With an inviting, browsable design and a chatty style, this large-sized volume . . . covers 15 national monuments and parks in the U.S. that celebrate and protect natural phenomena . . . . The science will excite readers, with detailed explanations of tectonic plates, radiometric dating, and dendrochronology." Booklist

Burgan, Michael
Not a drop to drink; water for a thirsty world. Peter H. Gleick, consultant. National Geographic 2008 64p il map (National Geographic investigates) $17.95
Grades: 4 5 6 7   363.6
  1. Water 2. Water supply
  ISBN 978-1-4263-0360-9; 1-4263-0360-2
Explores the important connections between human activity and the water cycle and shows how researchers are working to understand such issues as how climate change affects water supplies and how the oceans can help solve the water crisis.

Hollyer, Beatrice
  ★ Our world of water; children and water around the world. foreword by Zadie Smith. Henry Holt and Co. 2009 47p il map $16.99
Grades: 3 4 5   363.6
  1. Water 2. Water supply
  ISBN 978-0-8050-8941-7; 0-8050-8941-1
                                                    LC 2008040596
"Seven and eight-year-olds share what water means to them by revealing their everyday uses of it. An opening spread introduces the children and their countries—Peru, Ethiopia, Mauritania, Tajikistan, Bangladesh, and the United States—on an outline world map. Locations vary from mountaintop to seaside and from scarcity to abundance. . . . There is no order to the countries and the text is matter-of-fact, leaving readers to draw their own conclusions about the subjects' varying circumstances. Several full-color, captioned photos appear on each spread. . . . Questions will inevitably arise from this revealing look at the status of water in the world." SLJ

  Includes bibliographical references

Kerley, Barbara
  A cool drink of water. National Geographic Soc. 2002 un il map $16.95; pa $7.95
Grades: K 1 2 3   363.6
  1. Water 2. Water supply
  ISBN 0-7922-6723-0; 0-7922-5489-9 pa
                                                    LC 2001-2479
Depicts people around the world collecting, chilling, and drinking water
"Children will be entranced by the beautiful images of a basic substance that connects us all. Excellent for cross-cultural discussions." Booklist

363.7 Environmental problems

Aitken, Stephen
Earth's fever; written and illustrated by Stephen Aitken. Magic Wagon 2011 il (Climate change) $28.50
Grades: K 1 2 3   363.7
  1. Greenhouse effect 2. Climate -- Environmental aspects
  ISBN 1-61641-670-X; 978-1-61641-670-6
                                                    LC 2011001872
This "strikes a perfect balance for young readers. Aitken presents scientific facts straightforwardly and offers practical, age-appropriate suggestions for environmentally friendly activities. . . . The earnest cartoon illustrations . . . are generally helpful." Booklist

Albee, Sarah
  ★ Poop happened! a history of the world from the bottom up. illustrated by Robert Leighton. Walker 2010 170p il lib bdg $20.89; pa $15.99
Grades: 4 5 6 7   363.7
  1. Feces 2. Toilets 3. Sanitation 4. Refuse and refuse disposal
  ISBN 978-0-8027-9825-1 lib bdg; 0-8027-9825-X lib bdg; 978-0-8027-2077-1 pa; 0-8027-2077-3 pa
"Albee deposits a heaping history of human sanitation— or rather lack thereof— and its effects. . . . She pumps out a steady stream of comments on the miasmic effects of urbanization, waste disposal, and the roles of (not) bathing in ancient Greece, Rome, medieval Europe, . . . and the 'Reeking Renaissance.' She then digs into the gradual adoption of better practices in the nineteenth century. . . . The cartoon illustrations feature sludgy green highlights." Booklist

Barnham, Kay
  ★ Recycle; [by] Kay Barnham. Crabtree Pub. 2008 32p il (Environment action!) lib bdg $22.60; pa $7.95
Grades: K 1 2 3   363.7
  1. Recycling
  ISBN 978-0-7787-3659-2 lib bdg; 0-7787-3659-8 lib bdg; 978-0-7787-3669-1 pa; 0-7787-3669-5 pa
                                                    LC 2007030000
This book "exposes young children to concepts that can truly make a difference. . . . [The book has] plenty of colorful, relevant, and interesting glossy color photographs." Sci Books Films
  Includes glossary

Barraclough, Sue

Reusing things; by Sue Barraclough. Sea to Sea Publications 2008 30p il (Making a difference) lib bdg $27.10

Grades: 1 2 3   **363.7**

1. Recycling 2. Environmental protection

ISBN 978-1-59771-109-8 lib bdg; 1-59771-109-8 lib bdg

LC 2006051277

This suggests ways in which people can reduce waste by reusing paper or junk, repairing or repainting old items, borrowing or giving away things, and buying or using second-hand things.

This features "clear, concise information that is simple to read and understand, alternating between giving simple facts and dispersing helpful hints and suggestions. The full-color photographs are crisp and attractive." SLJ

Benoit, Peter

The **BP** oil spill. Children's Press 2011 48p il map (True book) lib bdg $28; pa $6.95

Grades: 3 4 5   **363.7**

1. Gulf of Mexico oil spill, 2010 2. BP (Firm).

ISBN 978-0-531-20630-0 lib bdg; 0-531-20630-0 lib bdg; 978-0-531-28999-0 pa; 0-531-28999-0 pa

LC 2010045927

Photographs, maps, time lines, and text describe the events surrounding the 2010 British Petroleum oil spill in the Gulf of Mexico.

"Benoit provides unbiased information that is on target for the intended audience. . . . The photos are realistic and well chosen to show that current events can be examined as critically as historical events." SLJ

Includes bibliographical references

Bridges, Andrew

Clean air. Roaring Brook Press 2009 40p il (Sally Ride science) pa $7.99

Grades: 5 6 7 8   **363.7**

1. Air pollution 2. Greenhouse effect

ISBN 978-1-59643-576-6 pa; 1-59643-576-3 pa

This is a "well-written, engaging book. . . . The [book's] best feature is the conversational tone that simply and clearly conveys important, and sometimes complicated, scientific concepts. Illustrations and layout are well done, and include colorful photographs and charts. Excellent." SLJ

Bullard, Lisa

Power up to fight pollution; illustrated by Wes Thomas. Lerner 2011 24p il (Planet protectors) lib bdg $23.93

Grades: K 1 2 3   **363.7**

1. Pollution 2. Environmental protection

ISBN 978-0-7613-6108-4; 0-7613-6108-1

LC 2010048862

A boy named Tyler shows what makes Earth's land, air, and water dirty and ways to clean up our world.

"The bright colors used in the illustrations . . . will attract young readers to the environmental science content. . . . [The] facts are written in child-friendly language and the information should be attainable by young children. . . . [This book] will raise the environmental awareness of young children." Sci Books Films

Includes bibliographical references

Cherry, Lynne

★ **How** we know what we know about our changing climate; scientists and kids explore global warming. by Lynne Cherry and Gary Braasch; with a foreword by David Sobel. Dawn Publications 2008 66p il $18.95; pa $11.95

Grades: 4 5 6 7   **363.7**

1. Greenhouse effect 2. Climate -- Environmental aspects

ISBN 978-1-58469-103-7; 0-1-58469-103-4; 978-1-58469-130-3 pa; 1-58469-130-1 pa

LC 2007-37255

"The can-do emphasis helps to make the topic less depressing, and the intriguing color photographs are thoughtful and upbeat." Booklist

"This volume describes where scientists look to find evidence of climate change—from changes in bird migration patterns and fruit blossom dates, to obtaining tree rings and mud cores—and especially how students and other citizen-scientists are assisting to monitor climate change, as well as what can be done to mitigate global warming." Publisher's note

Cole, Joanna

The **magic** school bus and the climate challenge; illustrated by Bruce Degen. Scholastic 2010 37p il $16.99

Grades: 2 3 4   **363.7**

1. Environmental protection 2. Greenhouse effect 3. Climate -- Environmental aspects

ISBN 978-0-590-10826-3; 0-590-10826-3

"Ms. Frizzle and her class challenge readers to go green. After traveling in their bus-plane and showing in storyboard style example after example of the Earth's changing climate, Ms. Frizzle, reluctant traveler Arnold, new South Korean classmate Joon, and the gang ride sun rays to the Earth, and then get back on the bus as those rays (and riders) get caught by heat-trapping gases." SLJ

David, Laurie

★ The **down**-to-earth guide to global warming; [by] Laurie David and Cambria Gordon. Orchard Books 2007 112p il map pa $15.99

Grades: 4 5 6 7   **363.7**

1. Greenhouse effect 2. Climate -- Environmental aspects

ISBN 978-0-439-02494-5 pa; 0-439-02494-3 pa

LC 2006-35705

The authors "put forth the basics on global warming, climate change, and how readers can green up the environment. They temper the book's often troubling subject matter with kid-friendly humor, some celebrity shout-outs, and explanations of the scientific underpinnings. An amply illustrated layout, featuring attention-grabbing sidebars, dramatic photos, and diagrams, will sustain reader interest." Booklist

Includes bibliographical references

Davies, Nicola

Gaia warriors; urgent; the fight is on! with an afterword by James Lovelock. Candlewick Press 2011 192p il $14.99

Grades: 5 6 7 8   **363.7**

1. Gaia hypothesis 2. Environmental protection 3. Greenhouse effect 4. Climate -- Environmental aspects

6. Gaia hypothesis 7. Climatic changes
ISBN 978-0-7636-4808-4; 0-7636-4808-6
LC 2010-40126

This "offers a dynamic overview of global warming's causes and concerns. Davies . . . devotes half the book to exciting profiles of individuals . . . who are working to slow climate change. . . . They include scientists, rock musicians, food distributors, architects, and youth organizers, and their broad variety reinforces the sense that every creative individual effort matters. Highly browsable layouts combine color photos and quotes printed in varied, eye-catching fonts. . . . [This has a] humorous, conversational tone." Booklist

Includes glossary

Delano, Marfe Ferguson
★ **Earth** in the hot seat; bulletins from a warming world. National Geographic 2009 63p il (Preserve our planet) $19.95; lib bdg $28.90
Grades: 5 6 7 8   363.7
1. Greenhouse effect 2. Climate -- Environmental aspects
ISBN 978-1-4263-0434-7; 1-4263-0434-X; 978-1-4263-0435-4 lib bdg; 1-4263-0435-8 lib bdg
LC 2008029317

"This book lays out . . . the evidence for global warming and the part that human activity plays in it. Five chapters lay out the signs and evidences of a warming world. . . . Subsequent chapters of the book are devoted to what humankind can expect in a warming world and steps that must be taken to avert catastrophe for humans and the planet. . . . The illustrative photos are fully up to National Geographic high standards. This [is a] fine book, reasonably priced and carefully researched." Voice Youth Advocates

Includes bibliographical references

Farrell, Courtney
Keeping water clean. Cherry Lake Pub. 2010 32p il (Save the planet) lib bdg $27.04
Grades: 3 4 5 6   363.7
1. Water pollution
ISBN 978-1-60279-659-1 lib bdg; 1-60279-659-9 lib bdg

Teaches young readers the importance of unpolluted water, and describes how to keep water clean by using gray water processes, conserving drinking water, and reducing overall pollution

"At the beginning of . . . [the] book, readers are given a mission and advised to be alert to the facts provided so that they can successfully answer the questions at the end. . . . Children are made to feel part of the process; suggestions for how they can become involved abound." SLJ

Includes glossary and bibliographical references

Geiger, Beth
Clean water. Roaring Brook Press 2009 40p il (Sally Ride science) pa $7.99
Grades: 5 6 7 8   363.7
1. Water supply 2. Water pollution
ISBN 978-1-59643-577-3 pa; 1-59643-577-1 pa
This is a "well-written, engaging book. . . . The [book']s best feature is the conversational tone that simply and clearly conveys important, and sometimes complicated, scientific concepts. Illustrations and layout are well done, and include colorful photographs and charts. Excellent." SLJ

Gore, Al
★ An **inconvenient** truth; the crisis of global warming. adapted for young readers by Jane O'Connor. rev ed.; Viking 2007 191p il map $23; pa $16
Grades: 5 6 7 8   363.7
1. Greenhouse effect 2. Climate -- Environmental aspects
ISBN 978-0-670-06271-3; 978-0-670-06272-0 pa
Adapted from the title for adults published 2006 by Rodale Press

This explains what global warming is, what causes it, and explains how to take action to stop this crisis.

This is illustrated with "easy-to-grasp graphics and revealing before-and-after photos. . . . O'Connor rephrases Gore's arguments in briefer, simpler language without compromising their flow." SLJ

Guiberson, Brenda Z.
★ **Earth** feeling the heat; illustrated by Chad Wallace. Henry Holt and Company 2010 un il map $16.99
Grades: K 1 2 3   363.7
1. Animals 2. Greenhouse effect 3. Climate -- Environmental aspects
ISBN 978-0-8050-7719-3; 0-8050-7719-7
LC 2009012219

"This handsome picture book shows the threat of global warming, one creature at a time. . . . On each double-page spread, the detailed oil paintings pair with rhythmic text. . . . An accompanying world map shows the habitat of each creature and emphasizes the sense of global connections among living beings, while a final page features detailed suggestions for kids to practice conservation in their daily lives." Booklist

Hanel, Rachael
Climate fever; stopping global warming. Compass Point Books 2010 64p il (Green generation) lib bdg $31.99; pa $6.95
Grades: 5 6 7 8 9   363.7
1. Greenhouse effect 2. Climate -- Environmental aspects
ISBN 978-0-7565-4246-7 lib bdg; 0-7565-4246-4 lib bdg; 978-0-7565-4291-7 pa; 0-7565-4291-X pa
LC 2009-11448

"The cover design, layout, and graphics feel hip and of the moment. The clear writing is easy to understand and includes many concrete examples of environmentally friendly practices. . . . [A] good choice[s] for both leisure reading and reports." SLJ

Includes glossary and bibliographical references

Hunter, Nick
How carbon footprints work; Nick Hunter. Gareth Stevens Publishing 2014 32 p. (Ecoworks) (library binding) $26.60
Grades: 3 4 5   363.7
1. Sustainability 2. Energy conservation 3. Environmental protection 4. Sustainable living
ISBN 1433995522; 1433995530; 9781433995521; 9781433995538
LC 2012277824

This book, by Nick Hunter, explains "what exactly is a carbon footprint. . . . Content . . . takes on climate change, vehicle emissions, and wasting electricity. Practical solutions to reducing readers' carbon footprints compliment social studies and science information that augment what they encounter in the classroom." (Publisher's note)

"Carbon footprint is a term few people knew a decade ago, and now it is used constantly. But what exactly does it mean? This title from the EcoWorks series gives kids a good understanding of the term, but more importantly it shows how each individual's carbon footprint affects the environment...Illustrated with stock color photos, the text is occasionally broken up by "Eco Facts" and other sidebars. A thought-provoking overview, and the good back matter will lead kids to more." Booklist

Includes bibliographical references (page 31) and index
Other titles include:
How a solar-powered home works
How community gardens work
How electric and hybrid cars work
How recycling works
How renewable energy works
Carbon footprints

Jakab, Cheryl

Waste management. Marshall Cavendish Benchmark 2010 32p il map (Environment in focus) lib bdg $28.50
Grades: 4 5 6   363.7
1. Refuse and refuse disposal
ISBN 978-1-60870-093-6; 1-60870-093-3

"The layout gives each topic the look of a file folder, with the first spread going to a case-study problem and the second going to a 'Toward a Sustainable Future' case-study solution. . . . Photos bring home the heartbreaking litter, human-waste treatment plants, etc." Booklist

Includes glossary

Jakubiak, David J.

What can we do about acid rain? PowerKids Press 2011 24p il (Protecting our planet) lib bdg $21.25; pa $8.25
Grades: 2 3 4   363.7
1. Acid rain
ISBN 9781448849840 lib bdg; 9781448851164 pa
LC 2010053329

This explains how acid rain forms, how it affects the environment, and what can be done about it.

"Every spread has a full-page, thoughtfully captioned color photograph. . . . School and public libraries will want [this title] to round out collections or as [an update] to replace older books." SLJ

Includes glossary and bibliographical references

What can we do about nuclear waste? PowerKids Press 2011 24p il (Protecting our planet) lib bdg $21.25; pa $8.25
Grades: 2 3 4   363.7
1. Nuclear engineering 2. Radioactive waste disposal
ISBN 978-1-4488-4983-3 lib bdg; 978-1-4488-5114-0 pa
LC 2010052216

This describes nuclear waste, how nuclear energy is used, how nuclear waste is stored, and how it affects the environment.

Includes glossary

What can we do about oil spills and ocean pollution? PowerKids Press 2011 24p il (Protecting our planet) lib bdg $21.25; pa $8.25
Grades: 2 3 4   363.7
1. Oil spills 2. Marine pollution
ISBN 978-1-4488-4982-6 lib bdg; 978-1-4488-5112-6 pa
LC 2010047319

This explains the importance of oceans, how they can be polluted, and the damage caused by oil spills.

Includes glossary

What can we do about ozone loss? PowerKids Press 2011 24p il (Protecting our planet) lib bdg $21.25; pa $8.25
Grades: 2 3 4   363.7
1. Pollution 2. Ozone layer 3. Greenhouse effect
ISBN 978-1-4488-4985-7 lib bdg; 978-1-4488-5118-8 pa
LC 2011000156

This explains the depletion of the ozone layer and its affect on the environment.

Includes glossary

Landau, Elaine

★ Oil spill! disaster in the Gulf of Mexico. Millbrook Press 2011 32p il lib bdg $25.26
Grades: 3 4 5   363.7
1. Oil spills 2. Gulf of Mexico oil spill, 2010
ISBN 978-0-7613-7485-5; 0-7613-7485-X
LC 2010029390

"Landau documents the mind-boggling scope of the 2010 oil spill in the Gulf of Mexico, and the urgent progression of measures taken to contain the calamity. . . . Throughout, Landau applies the clearsighted, nonalarmist tone of a veteran science writer but still manages to infuse the narrative with nearly the same urgency as an edge-of-your-seat disaster flick. Diagrams and photos present a revealing look at the fascinating science and technology behind deep-sea drilling and complex, one-step-forward/two steps back cleanup efforts." Booklist

Includes glossary and bibliographical references

Martin, Laura C.

Recycled crafts box; [by] Laura C. Martin. Storey Publishing 2004 88p il $19.95; pa $10.95
Grades: 3 4 5 6   363.7
1. Recycling 2. Handicraft
ISBN 1-58017-523-6; 1-58017-522-8 pa
LC 2003-16703

Discusses recycling and provides information and instructions for making art projects from a variety of recycled materials

"Illustrated with cheerful cartoon drawings and color photos of the finished projects, and bolstered by many resource lists, this is a surprisingly attractive, substantive offering." Booklist

Metz, Lorijo

What can we do about global warming? Rosen Pub. Group 2010 24p il (Protecting our planet) lib bdg $21.25; pa $8
Grades: 2 3 4   363.7
1. Environmental protection 2. Greenhouse effect 3.

Climate -- Environmental aspects
ISBN 978-1-4042-8079-3 lib bdg; 1-4042-8079-0 lib bdg; 978-1-4358-2479-9 pa; 1-4358-2479-2 pa
LC 2008-50766

This book provides "straightforward information . . . complemented by full-page, color photographs. . . . Links for further information . . . are housed at the publisher's Web site (which allows feedback so that readers can suggest more sites)." SLJ

Includes glossary

What can we do about trash and recycling? PowerKids Press 2010 24p il (Protecting our planet) lib bdg $21.25; pa $8

Grades: 2 3 4   **363.7**

1. Recycling
ISBN 978-1-4042-8082-3 lib bdg; 1-4042-8082-0 lib bdg; 978-1-4358-2483-6 pa; 1-4358-2483-0 pa
LC 2008-53812

This book provides "straightforward information . . . complemented by full-page, color photographs. . . . Links for further information . . . are housed at the publisher's Web site (which allows feedback so that readers can suggest more sites)." SLJ

Includes glossary

Minden, Cecilia
  Reduce, reuse, and recycle. Cherry Lake Pub. 2010 32p il (Save the planet) lib bdg $27.07

Grades: 3 4 5 6   **363.7**

1. Recycling 2. Waste minimization 3. Conservation of natural resources
ISBN 978-1-60279-662-1 lib bdg; 1-60279-662-9 lib bdg

Presents tips for how to reduce the amount of garbage thrown away, from buying items that have less packaging at the store to precycling and making art from trash

"At the beginning of . . . [the] book, readers are given a mission and advised to be alert to the facts provided so that they can successfully answer the questions at the end. . . . Children are made to feel part of the process; suggestions for how they can become involved abound." SLJ

Includes glossary and bibliographical references

Morgan, Sally
  Pollution. Cherrytree Books 2011 30p il (Helping our planet) lib bdg $28.50

Grades: 1 2 3   **363.7**

1. Pollution
ISBN 978-1-84234-607-5; 1-84234-607-5
LC 2010000036

This book "discusses activities that are harming the planet and how individuals can prevent or minimize their effects. . . . The [book features] large, full-color photos with one or two paragraphs of large-print text per page. 'Find Out More' boxes scattered throughout give additional facts with related websites and 'You Choose' boxes ask students questions regarding important choices they can make. . . . [This] well-designed [book] will be useful for reports and general interest." SLJ

Includes glossary

Waste and recycling. Cherrytree Books 2010 30p il (Helping our planet) lib bdg $28.50

Grades: 1 2 3   **363.7**

1. Recycling 2. Refuse and refuse disposal
ISBN 978-1-84234-608-2
LC 2010000037

This book "suggests how discarded items can be reduced, reused, and recycled. The [book features] large, full-color photos with one or two paragraphs of large-print text per page. 'Find Out More' boxes scattered throughout give additional facts with related websites and 'You Choose' boxes ask students questions regarding important choices they can make. . . . [This] well-designed [book] will be useful for reports and general interest." SLJ

Includes glossary

Morris, Neil
  ★ **Global** warming. World Almanac Library 2007 48p il (What if we do nothing?) lib bdg $22.95; pa $11.95

Grades: 5 6 7 8   **363.7**

1. Greenhouse effect 2. Climate -- Environmental aspects
ISBN 978-0-8368-7755-7 lib bdg; 0-8368-7755-1 lib bdg; 978-0-8368-155-4 pa; 0-8368-8155-9 pa
LC 2006-30444

This "boasts an attractive format, with large pages that allow room for pictures, excellent charts and graphs, as well as a thoughtful, clear discussion of the topic." Booklist

Includes bibliographical references

Nardo, Don
  Climate crisis; the science of global warming. by Don Nardo. Compass Point Books 2009 47p il map (Headline science) lib bdg $27.93; pa $7.95

Grades: 5 6 7   **363.7**

1. Greenhouse effect 2. Climate -- Environmental aspects
ISBN 978-0-7565-3571-1 lib bdg; 0-7565-3571-9 lib bdg; 978-0-7565-3948-1 pa; 0-7565-3948-X pa
LC 2008-7259

"Color photos and graphics provide visual information; a timeline is helpful to find fast facts, and the Facthound Web site provides students with additional information." Libr Media Connect

Includes glossary and bibliographical references

Oil spill; disaster. Scholastic Press 2010 31p il pa $5.99

Grades: 4 5 6 7 8   **363.7**

1. Oil spills 2. Gulf of Mexico oil spill, 2010
ISBN 978-0-545-31776-4; 0-545-31776-2

Explores the immediate and future consequences of the Gulf of Mexico oil spill in April 2010, when the offshore oil rig Deepwater Horizon exploded, causing major environmental and economical damage along the Gulf coast of the United States.

"While text and color photographs convey the extent of the devastation to the Gulf, the book also highlights some innovative attempts to clean up oil spills and profiles two middle school students, who researched cleaning up oil in their own neighborhood." Publ Wkly

Parker, Steve, 1952-
  Population. QEB Pub. 2010 32p il (QEB changes in . . .) lib bdg $28.50

Grades: 3 4 5 6   363.7
1. Human ecology 2. Human influence on nature
ISBN 978-1-59566-774-8 lib bdg; 1-59566-774-1
lib bdg

LC 2008-56070

"The information is presented in brief paragraphs and sidebars. Suggestions for kids to help improve the planet are sprinkled throughout. . . . Students will enjoy this appealing layout and the information can spark further research on the topic[s]. . . . Either digitally or on paper, students could make fantastic presentations using a similar design." Libr Media Connect

Includes glossary

Paul, Miranda
One plastic bag; Isatou Ceesay and the recycling women of the Gambia. by Miranda Paul; illustrated by Elizabeth Zunon. Millbrook Press 2015 32 p. color illustrations, color map
Grades: K 1 2 3 4   363.7
1. Plastics 2. Recycling 3. Wolof (African people) 4. Pollution -- Africa, West 5. Plastic bags -- Africa, West 6. Plastic bag craft -- Africa, West 7. Recycling (Waste, etc.) -- Africa, West
ISBN 1467716081; 9781467716086

LC 2014009382

In this children's book by Miranda Paul, "distressed by the problem of plastic-bag disposal, a Gambian woman organizes her neighbors to turn trash into treasure. When Isatou Ceesay first discovered plastic bags in the Gambia in West Africa, in the 1980s, they seemed wonderfully useful and sturdy. But in her village, they soon became a nuisance. . . . Her solution was to collect and clean used bags, cut them into strips and crochet the strips into useful plastic purses." (Kirkus Reviews)

"One woman's efforts to rid her Gambian village of trash sparks a recycling movement in this uplifting tale inspired by true events... Incorporating real plastic bags into her mixed-media collages, Zunon, who grew up in West Africa, juxtaposes the brown, dusty landscape against splashes of color and vibrant printed dresses and head coverings worn by the village women. A glossary and list of suggested reading are included." PW

Potts, Aiden
The **smash!** smash! truck; recycling as you've never heard it before. by Professor Potts. David Fickling Books 2009 un il $16.99; lib bdg $19.99
Grades: PreK K 1 2   363.7
1. Recycling
ISBN 978-0-385-75143-8; 0-385-75143-5; 978-0-385-75144-5 lib bdg; 0-385-75144-3 lib bdg

Rapp, Valerie
Protecting Earth's air quality; by Valerie Rapp. Lerner Publications 2009 72p il map (Saving our living Earth) lib bdg $30.60
Grades: 5 6 7 8   363.7
1. Air pollution
ISBN 978-0-8225-7558-0 lib bdg; 0-8225-7558-2 lib bdg

LC 2008-907

"Provides a thorough, interesting discussion of multiple aspects of [protecting Earth's air quality], including histori-cal origins, the current situation, and potential solutions. . . . Photos from around the world accompany discussions. . . . [This is a] solid choice to replace outdated books." SLJ
Includes glossary and bibliographical references

Rockwell, Anne F.
★ **Why** are the ice caps melting? the dangers of global warming. by Anne Rockwell; illustrated by Paul Meisel. HarperCollins 2006 33p il (Let's-read-and-find-out science) $15.99; pa $4.99
Grades: K 1 2 3   363.7
1. Greenhouse effect 2. Climate -- Environmental aspects
ISBN 0-06-054669-7; 0-06-054671-9 pa

LC 2005-17972

Tells about the greenhouse effect, recycling, and what you can do to help fight global warming
"The information is detailed, but not overwhelming. . . . Colorful illustrations provide details that support the [text]." SLJ

Royston, Angela
Global warming. Heinemann 2008 32p il (Protect our planet) lib bdg $25.36; pa $7.99
Grades: 1 2 3   363.7
1. Greenhouse effect 2. Climate -- Environmental aspects
ISBN 978-1-4329-0924-6 lib bdg; 1-4329-0924-X lib bdg; 978-1-4329-0930-7 pa; 1-4329-0930-4 pa
This is a "very basic introduction to some of the causes and effects of global warming. . . . [The author] discusses extreme weather, changing climates, melting ice caps, alternative sources of energy . . . and low-carbon living. Young readers will come away not frightened, but understanding why they should be concerned." Booklist
Includes glossary and bibliographical references

Silverstein, Alvin
Smog, oil spills, sewage, and more; the yucky pollution book. by Alvin Silverstein, Virginia Silverstein, and Laura Silverstein Nunn; illustrated by Gerald Kelley. Enslow Publishers 2010 48p il (Yucky science) lib bdg $23.93
Grades: 3 4 5 6   363.7
1. Pollution 2. Environmental protection
ISBN 978-0-7660-3313-9 lib bdg; 0-7660-3313-9 lib bdg

LC 2009021274

"With conversational prose and zany, retro-gross illustrations, . . . [this volume provides] a painless intro to . . . pollution. Filthy air, polluted water, . . . nonbiodegradable landfills, asbestos, greenhouse gases, and the scourge of 'cow farts' are all here. . . . Kelley's art . . . is a perfect fit for the material, and 'Yikes!' sidebars keep things gregariously gross." Booklist

Simon, Seymour
★ **Global** warming. Collins 2010 31p il $17.99; lib bdg $18.89
Grades: 3 4 5   363.7
1. Greenhouse effect 2. Climate -- Environmental aspects
ISBN 978-0-06-114250-5; 0-06-114250-6; 978-0-06-114251-2 lib bdg; 0-06-114251-4 lib bdg

LC 2009001265

This takes "on the timely matter of climate change. Informative and noncondescending, this boils down large, complex issues into understandable concepts, even as it covers the range of current understanding on how we are impacting the planet. . . . Thoughtfully chosen full-page photos complement and reflect the text." Booklist

Includes glossary, bibliographical references and index

Wells, Robert E.

Polar bear, why is your world melting? Albert Whitman & Co. 2008 un il $16.99; pa $6.99

Grades: 1 2 3 4 **363.7**

1. Ice 2. Arctic regions 3. Greenhouse effect
ISBN 978-0-8075-6598-8; 0-8075-6598-9; 978-0-8075-6599-5 pa; 0-8075-6599-7 pa

LC 2008-01308

"Two children sail in a red research vessel through the pages of this clear and simple explanation of global warming. Colorful, cartoon drawings show the youngsters rescuing a mother polar bear and her two cubs by hauling them onto their boat. Then, beginning with an explanation of the sun's effect on the Earth's atmosphere, they pursue the reasons that the Arctic ice is melting. Without oversimplifying, Wells makes the large concepts of the Greenhouse Effect and the sources of CO2 understandable for young children. . . . An excellent introduction to the topic." SLJ

363.738 Pollutants

Arnold, Caroline

A **warmer** world; from polar bears to butterflies, how global warming is changing lives. Caroline Arnold; illustrated by Jamie Hogan. Charlesbridge 2012 31 p.

Grades: 3 4 5 **363.738**

1. Ecology 2. Wildlife 3. Climate change 4. Global warming 5. Adaptation (Biology) 6. Climatic changes
ISBN 9781580892667

LC 2011000811

The focus of this book is how "[a] warmer world is the new reality for many animals and plants . . . and how they are reacting to climbing temperatures. . . . [Caroline] Arnold looks at the . . . impact of melting ice on polar bears and at the broadening range of Edith's checkerspot butterflies. . . . The speed of this change is leaving many species unable to adapt, and as many as a million species are feared to face extinction. A few might actually benefit from a wider habitable range, but often at a cost to other species. Combining general information on rising seas, melting ice caps, and warmer water with specific emphasis on individual animals such as loggerhead turtles, marmots, penguins, and walruses, this book offers students the opportunity to examine a natural world in flux." (School Libr J)

364 Criminology

Somervill, Barbara A.

Graphing crime. Raintree 2010 32p il (Real world data) $28.21; pa $7.99

Grades: 4 5 6 7 **364**

1. Crime 2. Statistics 3. Graphic methods
ISBN 978-1-4329-2623-6; 1-4329-2623-3; 978-1-4329-2632-8 pa; 1-4329-2632-2 pa

LC 2009001292

This "discusses juvenile offenders, drug money, terrorism, and more, and teaches readers how to evaluate statistics in the various charts, such as the difference between crimes committed and crimes reported, or between total numbers and rate per population. . . . The clear design, with lots of full-color photos and sidebars, will encourage browsers as much as the up-to-date examples and the clear directions for remaining 'chart smart.'" Booklist

Includes glossary and bibliographical references

364.15 Offenses against the person

Schroeder, Andreas

Robbers! true stories of the world's most notorious thieves. by Andreas Schroeder, illustrated by Remy Simard. Annick Press 2012 166 p. $21.95

Grades: 4 5 6 **364.15**

1. Picture books for children 2. Crime 3. Thieves
ISBN 155451441X; 9781554514410

This juvenile book, by Andreas Schroeder, illustrated by Remy Simard, offers true stories of historical thieves. In it accounts are given for "eight cunning master thieves, including master-of-disguise Willie Sutton, who robbed banks in costume, . . . D. B. Cooper, who hijacked a plane, demanded $200,000, and parachuted to safety, . . . [and] London's Great Train Robbers, who held up a moving train to pull off one of the largest ever hauls of banknotes." (Publisher's note)

364.16 Offenses against property

Guillain, Charlotte

Great art thefts; by Charlotte Guillain. Capstone Raintree 2013 48 p. col. ill. (Treasure hunters) (library) $29.33; (paperback) $8.99

Grades: 5 6 7 8 **364.16**

1. Theft -- History 2. Art thefts
ISBN 1410949583; 9781410949516; 9781410949585

LC 2012012759

This book by Charlotte Guillain, part of the Treasure Hunters series, looks at art thefts. "After . . . introductions that lay foundations so children will understand why thieves might want to steal art or treasure hunters take such risks, each volume contains chapters that follow the discovery and/or quests for objects such as 'Roman Riches' or locations such as the legendary city of Troy." (School Library Journal)

Includes bibliographical references and index.

368.3 Old-age insurance and insurance against death, illness, injury

Lynette, Rachel

What to do when your family can't afford healthcare. PowerKids Press 2010 24p il (Let's work it out) $21.25; pa $8.25

Grades: 2 3 4   368.3
1. Medicaid 2. Health insurance
ISBN 978-1-4358-9342-9; 1-4358-9342-5; 978-1-
4358-9772-4 pa; 1-4358-9772-2 pa
This book explains what healthcare and insurance are
and why they are so crucial. It also explains the many different low-cost insurance options that are available so that
every family can get the care they need.

"Full-page color photographs appear opposite the [nar-
rative], depicting multicultural children, parents, grandparents, social workers, and others, whose demeanors match
the hopeful tone of the [title]. This . . . will help promote
empathy and understanding for the plight of others and is a
key purchase." SLJ

Includes glossary

369.463   Girl Scouts and Girl Guides

Corey, Shana
Here come the Girl Scouts! by Shana Corey; illustrated
by Hadley Hooper. Scholastic Press 2012 40 p.
Grades: 2 3 4   369.463
1. Girl Scouts -- History 2. Women -- United States
-- Biography 3. Girl Scouts of the United States of
America -- History
ISBN 0545342783; 9780545342780
                                   LC 2011008690
This book, a "celebration of the life of [Juliette] Low,
founder of the Girl Scouts, reveals a gutsy, active girl growing up in Savannah, Ga., at a time when "proper young ladies were supposed to be dainty and delicate." Low craved
"adventure and excitement," and, as an adult, she traveled
extensively and decided that she "wanted to be useful, to
make a difference in the world." . . . [S]he launched the Girl
Scouts and, at an inaugural meeting, told the girls what to
expect: "They'd hike and camp and swim! They'd do good
deeds. They'd learn to tie knots and survive in the wilderness and even save lives!" [Shana Corey] . . . conveys Low's
gumption and optimism, and . . . quotations from the first
Girl Scout handbook impart . . . tenets for living and scouting." (Publishers Weekly)

Includes bibliographical references

Wadsworth, Ginger
★ First Girl Scout; Ginger Wadsworth. Clarion Books
2012 xiii, 210p ill. $17.99
Grades: 7 8 9 10 11 12   369.463
1. Biography 2. Girl Scouts 3. Philanthropists 4.
Scout leaders 5. Girl Scouts of the United States of
America
ISBN 978-0-547-24394-8; 0-547-24394-4
                                   LC 2011009642
This book offers a biography of the founder of the Girl
Scouts organization. "Juliette (Daisy) Gordon Low [who]
was a . . . woman with ideas that were ahead of her time. She
witnessed important eras in U.S. history, from the Civil War
and Reconstruction to westward expansion to post–World
War I. And she made history by founding the first national
organization to bring girls from all backgrounds into the out-
of-doors. Daisy created controversy by encouraging them to
prepare not only for traditional homemaking but also for
roles as professional women—in the arts, sciences, and

business—and for active citizenship outside the home. Her
group also welcomed girls with disabilities at a time when
they were usually excluded." (Publisher's note)

"This well-documented biography introduces readers to
the founder of the Girl Scouts. . . . Low's personality really
comes to life through the details in the narrative. Wadsworth
shows readers that this remarkable woman was a skilled
leader and hostess in spite of having suffered severe hearing
loss that made conversation difficult. . . . The attractive book
design features chapter headings that look like Girl Scout
badges, and most spreads include period photos or reproductions of primary-source documents. Exemplary nonfiction."
SLJ

Includes bibliographical references (p. 201-204)
and index.

370.1   Philosophy and theory, education for
specific objectives, educational psychology

Barker, Dan
Maybe right, maybe wrong; a guide for young thinkers.
by Dan Barker; illustrated by Brian Strassburg. Prometheus
Bks. 1992 76p il pa $17.98
Grades: 4 5 6   370.1
1. Human rights 2. Conduct of life 3. Moral education
ISBN 978-0-87975-731-1 pa; 0-87975-731-0 pa
                                   LC 92-416
Discusses learning right from wrong, stressing such as-
pects as the difference between rules and principles and the
importance of an individual's rights

370.71   Education

Growing schools; librarians as professional developers.
Debbie Abilock, Kristin Fontichiaro, and Violet H. Ha-
rada, editors. Libraries Unlimited 2012 390 p. (pbk.)
$45
Grades: Professional   370.71
1. Teachers -- Training 2. Educational technology 3.
School libraries -- Information technology 4. Libraries
and teachers -- United States -- Case studies 5. Teachers
-- Training of -- United States -- Case studies 6.
Educational technology -- Study and teaching -- Case
studies 7. Information technology -- Study and teaching
-- Case studies 8. Technological literacy -- Study
and teaching -- Case studies 9. Teachers -- In-service
training -- United States -- Case studies 10. School
librarian participation in curriculum planning -- Case
studies 11. Academic libraries -- Relations with faculty
and curriculum -- Case studies
ISBN 1610690419; 9781610690416
                                   LC 2012016191
In this book, "editors [Debbie] Abilock, [Kristin] Fontichiaro, and [Violet H.] Harada examine ways school librarians can act as professional developers within their peda-
gogical communities. Thirty-two articles in sixteen thematic
chapters offer real-world examples of how teacher librarians
have leveraged their skills and expertise to provide learning
experiences for other teachers, community members, and
students." (Voice of Youth Advocates)

"This book promotes the role of the school librarian as a leader in school, district, and online professional development in 16 essays written by school librarians, school district personnel, and professors...A rich smorgasbord of ideas, this book would be invaluable for an individual librarian looking to become a professional development leader, and for district librarians to use in planning and implementing meaningful district-wide professional development." (Library Media Connection)

Includes bibliographical references and index

McKeown, Rosalyn

Into the classroom; a practical guide for starting student teaching. Rosalyn McKeown. University of Tennessee Press 2011 xv, 165 p.p (pbk.) $14.95

Grades: Adult Professional   **370.71**

1. Teaching 2. Student teaching -- United States
ISBN 1572338164; 9781572338166

LC 2011011282

This book offers suggestions to those "just starting out in a secondary school classroom. . . . After exploring the pitfalls of inexperience and providing . . . guidance on maintaining order in the classroom, [Rosalyn] McKeown focuses on teaching skills. She advises readers on writing objectives and lesson plans, creating interesting ways to start and end class, introducing variety into the classroom, lecturing, asking meaningful questions, and using visual aids." (Amazon. com)

Includes bibliographical references and index.

370.9   History, geographic treatment, biography

Aillaud, Cindy Lou

★ Recess at 20 below. Alaska Northwest Books 2005 un il hardcover o.p. pa $8.95

Grades: K 1 2 3   **370.9**

1. Schools -- Alaska
ISBN 0-88240-604-3; 0-88240-609-4 pa

"Aillaud, who wrote the text and took the photos here, teaches elementary physical education in Delta Junction, Alaska, a town at the end of the Alaska Highway, above the Arctic Circle. By focusing on one school activity—outdoor recess . . . she demonstrates how cold things get and how kids deal with it and still have plenty of fun. . . . Twenty-five color photographs capture marvelous details." Booklist

Ruurs, Margriet

My school in the rain forest; how children attend school around the world. Boyds Mills Press 2009 31p il map $17.95

Grades: 1 2 3 4 5   **370.9**

1. Schools 2. Students
ISBN 978-1-59078-601-7; 1-59078-601-7

LC 2009000366

"The book introduces 13 schools, including home schools in Australia and the U.S., a floating school on a Cambodian lake, a village school in Guatemala, a monastery school in Myanmar, and one operated by a global charity. Each double-page spread includes several paragraphs of text, four color photos, and fact box with information about the country, a drawing of its flag, and a map. . . . The book

as a whole gives a good sense of the vastly different educational experiences of children around the world." Booklist

370.92   Education biography

Asim, Jabari

★ Fifty cents and a dream; by Jabari Asim; illustrated by Bryan Collier. Little, Brown and Co. 2012 48 p. $16.99

Grades: 2 3 4   **370.92**

1. Biography 2. United States -- History 3. Education -- United States -- History 4. African Americans -- Biography 5. Educators -- United States -- Biography
ISBN 0316086576; 9780316086578

LC 2012007265

Author Jabari Asim tells the story of Booker T. Washington. "Born into slavery, young Booker T. Washington could only dream of learning to read and write. After emancipation, Booker began a five-hundred-mile journey, mostly on foot, to Hampton Institute, taking his first of many steps towards a college degree. When he arrived, he had just fifty cents in his pocket and a dream about to come true." (Publisher's note)

McKissack, Pat, 1944-

Mary McLeod Bethune; woman of courage. Patricia and Frederick McKissack. Enslow Publishers 2013 24 p. (Famous African Americans) (library) $21.26

Grades: 1 2 3   **370.92**

1. African American women 2. African Americans -- Education 3. Teachers -- United States -- Biography 4. African American women educators -- Biography 5. African American women social reformers -- Biography
ISBN 0766041034; 9780766041035

LC 2012007620

This book, part of the Famous African Americans series, looks at Mary McLeod Bethune. She was "her parents' fifteenth child but the first born free. Determined to read the family Bible, she went to school, then college, and then, with just $1.50 in her pocket, opened the first school for black girls in Daytona Beach, Florida." (Booklist)

371   Schools and their activities; special education

Guillain, Charlotte

My first day at a new school. Heinemann Library 2011 24p il (Growing up) lib bdg $22; pa $6.49

Grades: PreK K 1 2   **371**

1. Schools
ISBN 978-1-4329-4796-5 lib bdg; 1-4329-4796-6 lib bdg; 978-1-4329-4806-1 pa; 1-4329-4806-7 pa

LC 2010024189

This book examines a "common, often scary [event] in children's lives and [guides] readers through [it] step-by-step. The [author discusses] the who, what, and why of [the] experience. . . . By confronting . . . fears head-on, children will feel 'in the know' and be prepared to experience [this first]. The text—two sentences per page in a large font and placed on white space—is accompanied by large color photos of children, families, and adults of a variety of ethnic backgrounds. [The] volume includes boldface vocabulary words, a picture glossary, and dos and don'ts." SLJ

Includes glossary and bibliographical references

Hughes, Susan

Off to class; incredible and unusual schools around the world. Owlkids Books 2011 64p il map $22.95; pa $12.95

Grades: 2 3 4 5   **371**

1. Schools 2. Students

ISBN 978-1-926818-85-6; 1-926818-85-7; 978-1-926818-86-3 pa; 1-926818-86-5 pa

"This book examines innovative schools around the world, the educators who brought them about, and the students who attend them. The book has three chapters. 'Working with the Environment' features boat schools, rainforest schools, and tent schools; 'No School? No Way!,' focuses on educational opportunities for disenfranchised populations; and 'One Size Doesn't Fit All' is about unconventional programs in nontraditional settings. Each spread is devoted to one school, with five to seven paragraphs of text, vivid full-color photographs, and a map indicating its general area of the world. The strong emphasis on humanitarianism will move, excite, and inspire those reading about Hurricane Katrina survivors planting gardens, homeless children in India hearing stories on a train platform, and Maasai girls going to school instead of being sold into marriage." SLJ

Mara, Wil

The **schoolmaster**. Marshall Cavendish Benchmark 2010 48p il (Colonial people) lib bdg $29.93

Grades: 3 4 5 6   **371**

1. Teachers 2. Schools -- United States -- History 3. United States -- History -- 1600-1775, Colonial period

ISBN 978-0-7614-4801-3; 0-7614-4801-2

This describes the life of a colonial schoolmaster and his importance to the community, as well as everyday life, responsibilities, and social practices during that time.

"The type font, just slightly larger than usual, makes the text very visually appealing. . . . [The] book is liberally illustrated with artwork dating from the colonial period . . . [and] information boxes offer supplemental material." Libr Media Connect

Includes glossary and bibliographical references

371.1 Schools and their activities

Harada, Violet H.

Inquiry learning through librarian-teacher partnerships; [by] Violet H. Harada and Joan M. Yoshina. Linworth Pub. 2004 172p il pa $39.95

Grades: Adult Professional   **371.1**

1. Teaching teams 2. School libraries

ISBN 1-58683-134-8

LC 2004-662

"The authors describe what happens in an inquiry-based classroom and library media center and show teachers/librarians how to develop a curriculum that incorporates essential questions and important habits of mind, all aligned with content standards. . . . The volume contains everything

a teacher-librarian team would need to create, teach, research, and assess major interdisciplinary units." SLJ

Includes bibliographical references

Houston, Gloria

My great-aunt Arizona; illustrated by Susan Condie Lamb. HarperCollins Pubs. 1992 un il $15.99; pa $6.99

Grades: K 1 2 3   **371.1**

1. Teachers 2. Appalachian region

ISBN 0-06-022606-4; 0-06-022607-2 lib bdg; 0-06-443374-9 pa

LC 90-44112

"The pleasant, conversational rhythm of the prose, the unobtrusive use of repetition, and the ability to sum up the unique quality of a life in a few telling phrases give the writing its substance. . . . Sunny and lively, the watercolor paintings have a naive quality that suits the story well." Booklist

Kenney, Karen Latchana

Teachers at work; by Karen L. Kenney; illustrated by Brian Caleb Dumm; content consultant, Judith Stepan-Norris. Magic Wagon 2009 32p il (Meet your community workers!) lib bdg $18.95

Grades: K 1 2 3   **371.1**

1. Teachers 2. Vocational guidance

ISBN 978-1-60270-653-8 lib bdg; 1-60270-653-0 lib bdg

LC 2009-2395

This book about teachers has "an uncluttered layout and consistent organization. . . . Chapter headings such as 'Problems on the Job,' and 'Technology at Work,' and 'Special Skills and Training' make it easy to pinpoint specific information." SLJ

Includes glossary

371.3 Methods of instruction and study

Fox, Janet S.

Get organized without losing it; by Janet S. Fox; edited by Pamela Espeland. Free Spirit Pub. 2006 105p il (Laugh & learn) pa $8.95

Grades: 5 6 7 8   **371.3**

1. Life skills 2. Study skills 3. Time management

ISBN 978-1-57542-193-3 pa; 1-57542-193-3 pa

LC 2005032809

"In this handbook for students, Fox uses humor to provide practical, easy-to-follow ideas for organizing desks, backpacks, and lockers; managing time for homework and after school activities; planning long-term projects; and taking better notes. . . . Fox writes in a conversational style. . . . Humorous illustrations complement the text." Voice Youth Advocates

Includes bibliographical references

Green, Julie

Write it down. Cherry Lake Pub. 2010 32p il (Super smart information strategies) lib bdg $27.07

Grades: 3 4 5 6   **371.3**

1. Note-taking

ISBN 978-1-60279-645-4 lib bdg; 1-60279-645-9 lib bdg

LC 2009024741

"The appealing layout includes manageable paragraphs, a variety of engaging illustrations, and examples that clearly guide readers through each topic. . . . Effective note taking and highlighting are the focus of [this book], but the book also suggests using sticky notes and creating diagrams and charts." SLJ

Includes glossary and bibliographical references

Kraus, Jeanne
   Annie's plan; taking charge of schoolwork and homework. written by Jeanne Kraus; illustrated by Charles Beyl. Magination Press 2007 47p il $14.95; pa $8.95
Grades: 2 3 4 5   **371.3**
   1. Homework 2. Study skills 3. Attention deficit disorder
   ISBN 978-1-59147-481-4; 1-59147-481-7; 978-1-59147-482-1 pa; 1-59147-482-5 pa
                                          LC 2006009948
"Annie is smart but she just can't stay focused on anything so she is always behind in class. With the help of her parents and teacher, she learns how to organize her work and is given other tips for completing her assignments. The book offers 10 easy-to-follow steps that begin with a clean, organized desk at school and a quiet, organized work space at home, and end with a signed reward contract. . . . Comical color illustrations and a conversational tone explain that a youngster with ADHD is neither dumb nor an incurable behavioral problem. . . . An extensive note for adults is included. This is an excellent resource for school libraries, professional collections, and parenting collections, and a great shared read for parent and child." SLJ

November, Alan C.
   Empowering students with technology; 2nd ed.; Corwin Press 2010 115p il pa $25.95
Grades: Adult Professional   **371.3**
   1. Internet in education 2. Computer-assisted instruction
   ISBN 978-1-4129-7425-7; 1-4129-7425-9
                                          LC 2009-43649
First published 2001 by Skylight Professional Development
"Discusses the relationship of technology to today's learning environment and the potential for technology to encourage students to learn collaboratively. This . . . edition emphasizes current topics such as information literacy, global connectivity, and the educational applications of utilities such as digital cameras and cell phones. The book's usefulness is as a reasource for teachers and librarians to consult in creating, planning, and assisting with school projects in all subjects." Libr Media Connect

   Includes bibliographical references

Richardson, Will
   Blogs, wikis, podcasts, and other powerful Web tools for classrooms; 3rd ed.; Corwin 2010 171p il pa $31.95
Grades: Adult Professional   **371.3**
   1. Weblogs 2. Podcasting 3. Internet in education 4. Online social networks 5. Wikis (Computer science) 6. Teaching -- Aids and devices
   ISBN 978-1-4129-7747-0; 1-4129-7747-9
                                          LC 2009-51376
First published 2006
"The book is well-written and comprehensive. The author's engaging writing style will instill confidence in read-

ers that they will be able to easily integrate the same technologies with the same results in their classrooms. Readers will not want to stop reading this eye-opening and inspirational book. It is jam-packed with proven ideas, and individuals, especially educators, will want to try out these technologies." Libr Media Connect

   Includes bibliographical references

Teehan, Kay
   Wikis; the educator's power tool. Linworth 2010 78p il pa $30
Grades: Adult Professional   **371.3**
   1. Internet in education 2. Electronic encyclopedias 3. Wikis (Computer science) 4. Computer-assisted instruction
   ISBN 978-1-58683-530-9 pa; 1-58683-530-0 pa; 978-1-58683-531-6 e-book; 1-58683-531-9 e-book
                                          LC 2010020285
"This book breaks down three types of wikis: library wikis, which are usually content and link-to-content focused; reciprocal wikis, which are collaborative in nature; and student-produced wikis that are developed to share projects and research. . . . There is also a wiki to complement the guidelines in the book. This is a simple to use quick-start guide and a great resource for school technology teachers and librarians." Libr Media Connect

   Includes bibliographical references

371.5   School discipline and related activities

Beaudoin, Marie-Nathalie
   Responding to the culture of bullying and disrespect; new perspectives on collaboration, compassion, and responsibility. [by] Marie-Nathalie Beaudoin, Maureen Taylor. rev 2nd ed.; Corwin Press 2009 281p il $76.95; pa $36.95
Grades: Adult Professional   **371.5**
   1. Bullies 2. School discipline
   ISBN 978-1-4129-6853-9; 1-4129-6853-4; 978-1-4129-6854-6 pa; 1-4129-6854-2 pa
                                          LC 2008-55933
First published 2004 with title: Breaking the culture of bullying and disrespect
"This profound resource explores the behaviors that cultivate a culture of bullying and disrespect. . . . Concrete solutions to issues are offered, and the authors make sure to load this title with practical suggestions for affecting change. They delve into ways to work directly with young people to better address their concerns. . . . This purchase is essential for any educator, counselor, or parent. It should be a staple of the school library reference collection because the information provided should be used daily. It will be a title that can be referenced for years to come and will help with adults struggling to overcome bullying." Voice Youth Advocates

   Includes glossary and bibliographical references

Bott, C. J.
   More bullies in more books. Scarecrow Press 2009 197p il pa $35
Grades: Adult Professional   **371.5**
   1. Bullies 2. Reference books 3. Children's literature --

Bibliography 4. Young adult literature -- Bibliography
ISBN 978-0-8108-6654-6 pa; 0-8108-6654-4 pa

LC 2009-923

This "offers more than 350 annotated titles published since 2000 to create awareness of the many types of harassment and bullying. . . . Although the text is written for educators and librarians for use in classroom settings, the information is equally helpful for parents, caregivers, and public librarians." SLJ

Includes bibliographical references

★ **Bully**; an action plan for teachers and parents to combat the bullying crisis. edited by Lee Hirsch and Cynthia Lowen; with Dina Santorelli. Perseus Books Group 2012 viii, 295 p.p ill. $15.99
Grades: Adult Professional   371.5
1. Bullies 2. Bullying 3. Bullying -- Prevention 4. Cyberbullying -- Prevention 5. Bullying in schools -- Prevention
ISBN 1602861846; 1602861854; 9781602861848; 9781602861855

LC 2012289039

"This companion book to the documentary film Bully was edited by filmmaker [Lee]Hirsch and writer/producer [Cynthia] Lowen, with contributing chapters by a number of celebrities, authors, experts, government officials, and educators. Part homage to the film, part resource, the book interweaves the stories of children who have been bullied with practical information and advice for parents and other readers." (Publishers Weekly)

Includes bibliographical references (p. 281-289) and index

Myers, Jill J.
Responding to cyber bullying; an action tool for school leaders. [by] Jill J. Myers, Donna S. McCaw, Leaunda S. Hemphill. Corwin Press 2011 195p pa $33.95
Grades: Adult Professional   371.5
1. Bullies 2. Cyberbullying 3. School violence
ISBN 978-1-4129-9484-2; 1-4129-9484-5

LC 2010040679

"The book's introduction addresses the nature of 'digital generation' students. The problem of cyberbullying is introduced in light of the generational reality. The book covers decisions made to resolve real-life situations, practical principles about censorship, and the capacity and limitations of school authority. Included is a matrix that serves as a decision-making tool for administration. This resource is a healthy blend of the theoretical and practical." Libr Media Connect

Includes bibliographical references

371.6   Physical plant; materials management

Gaarder-Juntti, Oona
What in the world is a green school? ABDO Pub. Company 2011 24p il (Going green) lib bdg $24.21
Grades: 1 2 3 4   371.6
1. School buildings 2. Environmental protection
ISBN 978-1-61613-190-6 lib bdg; 1-61613-190-X lib bdg

LC 2010004324

"The lively layout design, featuring colorful headings, short paragraphs, and attractive photographs, has a scrapbook-like quality. . . . [The title explains] how all our choices require energy and resources, and encourage readers to make changes in their lifestyles. . . . [This] . . . will inspire and empower readers to make a difference." SLJ

Includes glossary and bibliographical references

371.7   Student welfare

Curtis, Andrea
What's for lunch? How schoolchildren eat around the world. Andrea Curtis; Yvonne Duivenvoorden. Red Deer Press 2012 40 p. $12.95
Grades: 3 4 5   371.7
1. School children -- Food
ISBN 0889954828; 9780889954823

This book by Andrea Curtis and Yvonne Duivenvoorden "reveals the variety and inequality to be found in the food consumed by young people in typical school lunches from thirteen countries around the world, including Japan, Kenya, Russia, United States, Canada, Mexico, Brazil and Afghanistan. In some countries, the meals are nutritious and well-balanced. In others they barely satisfy basic nutrition standards." (Publisher's note)

371.82   Specific groups of students; schools for specific groups of students

Finkelstein, Norman H.
Schools of hope; the Rosenwald Schools of the American South. Norman H. Finkelstein. Calkins Creek 2014 80 p. illustrations $16.95
Grades: 5 6 7 8   371.82
1. African Americans -- History 2. African Americans -- Education
ISBN 1590788419; 9781590788417

LC 2013951346

"When Booker T. Washington, the famed African American educator, asked Julius Rosenwald, the wealthy president of Sears, Roebuck and Company and noted philanthropist, to help him build well-designed and fully equipped schools for black children, the face of education in the South changed for the better. . . . In this inspiring story, noted nonfiction writer Norman H. Finkelstein spotlights one man's legacy and the power of community action." (Publisher's note)

"This straightforward narrative is substantially supported with many photographs of the period, especially of the schools and the students. Source notes, a bibliography (which could have used a few more titles for the target readership), a list of websites, an index and picture credits add to its authenticity. Clean layout and design augment a quality introduction to an important chapter in the history of American education." -Kirkus

Marx, Trish
Kindergarten day USA and China; a flip-me-over book. by Trish Marx and Ellen B. Senisi. Charlesbridge 2010 un il $16.95; pa $7.95
Grades: PreK K 1   371.82
1. Kindergarten 2. Schools -- China 3. Schools --

United States

ISBN 978-1-58089-219-3; 1-58089-219-1; 978-1-58089-220-9 pa; 1-58089-220-5 pa

"Half of this book narrates a day at a kindergarten in Schenectady, NY; when flipped, it details a day with Chinese children in Beijing. Although there are some differences between the two classes, the book focuses on illustrating their similarities. . . . Large, bright photographs and a limited number of words per page make this a good choice for storytime." SLJ

UNICEF

A **school** like mine; a unique celebration of schools around the world. DK 2007 79p il map $19.99

Grades: 3 4 5 6   **371.82**

1. Schools 2. Children

ISBN 978-0-7566-2913-7; 0-7566-2913-6

LC 2007298451

Introduces children from around the world and discusses where they live, how they play, and what their schools are like

Winter, Jeanette

★ **Nasreen's** secret school; a true story from Afghanistan. Beach Lane Books 2009 un il $16.99

Grades: 2 3 4   **371.82**

1. Girls -- Education 2. Schools -- Afghanistan 3. Afghanistan -- Social conditions

ISBN 978-1-4169-9437-4; 1-4169-9437-8

LC 2009-08285

"This story begins with an author's note that succinctly explains the drastic changes that occurred when the Taliban came to power in Afghanistan in 1996. The focus is primarily on the regime's impact on women, who were no longer allowed to attend school or leave home without a male chaperone, and had to cover their heads and bodies with a burqa. After Nasreen's parents disappeared, the child neither spoke nor smiled. Her grandmother, the story's narrator, took her to a secret school, where she slowly discovered a world of art, literature, and history obscured by the harsh prohibitions of the Taliban. . . . Winter manages to achieve that delicate balance that is respectful of the seriousness of the experience, yet presents it in a way that is appropriate for young children. Winter's acrylic paintings make effective use of color. . . . This is an important book that makes events in a faraway place immediate and real." SLJ

371.829   Ethnic groups - education

Jordan-Fenton, Christy

When I was eight; Christy Jordan-Fenton, Margaret Pokiak-Fenton, illustrated by Gabrielle Grimard. Annick Press 2013 32 p. (reinforced) $21.95

Grades: 1 2 3 4   **371.829**

1. Girls -- Education 2. Inuit -- Biography

ISBN 1554514916; 9781554514915

In this children's book, by Christy Jordan-Fenton, Margaret Pokiak-Fenton, "Olemaun is eight and knows a lot of things. But she does not know how to read. She must travel to the outsiders' school to learn. . . . The nuns at the school take her Inuit name and call her Margaret. . . . Margaret's tenacious character draws the attention of a black-cloaked nun

who tries to break her spirit at every turn. But she is more determined than ever to read." (Publisher's note)

371.9   Special education

Lauren, Jill

That's like me! stories about amazing people with learning differences. foreword by Jerry Pinkney. Star Bright Books 2009 un il $17.95; pa $7.95

Grades: 3 4 5   **371.9**

1. Learning disabilities

ISBN 978-1-59572-207-2; 1-59572-207-6; 978-1-59572-208-9 pa; 1-59572-208-4 pa

LC 2009028647

"This colorful book spotlights people of different ages, backgrounds, and interests who have coped with learning disabilities and succeeded in their chosen fields. . . . Each entry includes several photos showing the person at different ages. A good resource for encouraging children with learning disabilities." Booklist

Includes bibliographical references

Stanley, Jerry

★ **Children** of the Dust Bowl; the true story of the school at Weedpatch Camp. Crown 1992 85p il map hardcover o.p. pa $9.95

Grades: 5 6 7 8   **371.9**

1. Migrant labor 2. Great Depression, 1929-1939 3. Education -- Social aspects

ISBN 0-517-88094-6; 0-517-58782-3 pa

LC 92-393

Describes the plight of the migrant workers who traveled from the Dust Bowl to California during the Depression and were forced to live in a federal labor camp and discusses the school that was built for their children

"Stanley's text is a compelling document. . . . The story is inspiring and disturbing, and Stanley has recorded the details with passion and dignity." Booklist

Includes bibliographical references

371.91   Students with physical disabilities

Hauser, Peter C.

★ **How** deaf children learn; what parents and teachers need to know. Marc Marschark Peter C. Hauser. Oxford University Press 2012 156 p. $26.50

Grades: Adult Professional   **371.91**

1. Teaching 2. Deaf children 3. Elementary education 4. Deaf -- Education 5. Deaf -- Means of communication

ISBN 0195389751; 9780195389753

LC 2011012553

This book is "about teaching deaf children. Written primarily for parents and teachers of deaf or hard-of-hearing children, this work covers general information about their education, gives insights into their cognitive development, and provides steps to their school success. The authors also discuss issues such as the value of cochlear implants and the debate over signing vs. speaking." (Library Journal)

Includes bibliographical references.

372 Specific levels of education

Barber, Nicola

First day of school. PowerKids Press 2009 24p il (The big day!) lib bdg $21.25; pa $8.25

Grades: PreK K 1   **372**

1. Schools

ISBN 978-1-4358-2839-1 lib bdg; 1-4358-2839-9 lib bdg; 978-1-4358-2895-7 pa; 1-4358-2895-X pa

LC 2008025816

"Children in kindergarten will enjoy [this book] as [a read-aloud] . . . while those at the end of first grade will be able to read [it] independently. The writing is straightforward and reassuring, and the content provides a realistic view of what youngsters might experience in [school]. . . .The author discusses the activities of a typical day as well as feelings of sadness or loneliness that may occur." SLJ

Includes bibliographical references

Brooks-Young, Susan

Teaching with the tools kids really use; learning with Web and mobile technologies. Corwin 2010 137p pa $26.95

Grades: Adult Professional   **372**

1. Web 2.0 2. Teachers -- Training

ISBN 978-1-4129-7275-8 pa; 1-4129-7275-2 pa

LC 2009-43856

"In this book, we see how technology can be used, but we also see the reponsibility of the educator to make sure it is done appropriately, so 21st-century skills are addressed. The author addresses technologies and applications, and also discusses their ethical uses and how to think ahead to make adjustments for the future. . . . This book will be incredibly useful for those who are unsure about Web 2.0 tools, want to explore their possibilities, and would like to educate themselves further about usage in their own schools." Libr Media Connect

Includes bibliographical references

Carlow, Regina

Exploring the connection between children's literature and music. Libraries Unlimited 2008 124p il pa $30

Grades: Adult Professional   **372**

1. Music -- Study and teaching 2. Children's literature -- Bibliography

ISBN 978-1-59158-439-1 pa; 1-59158-439-6 pa

LC 2007-40134

"Carlow sees music as part of developmental human activity and issues a plea to introduce it as direct participation. . . . This collection of methods and lessons encourages adults to broaden the possibilities of interacting with music, thereby using it to introduce young children to language, literature, and culture. Text is divided into chapters on singing and other ways to be musical. . . . The succeeding chapters are devoted to specific grade levels. . . . Each chapter includes an explanation of methods appropriate for the age group, followed by numerous lesson ideas for classrooms. The organization of this book makes it a solid addition to enhance curriculum materials." SLJ

Includes bibliographical references

Gates, Pamela

Cultural Journeys; Multicultural Literature for Elementary and Middle School Students. Rowman & Littlefield Pub Inc 2010 258 p. (paperback) $29.95

Grades: Adult Professional   **372**

1. Best books 2. Multicultural literature

ISBN 144220687X; 9781442206878

This book looks at multicultural literature for elementary and middle school students. The first chapter asks "the question of 'why.' Why use multicultural literature? . . . The 'why' is further developed as the chapter continues with a definition of multicultural literature." The seventh chapter looks at "works that challenge stereotypes and go beyond the common one-dimensional diversity theme." (Alberta Journal of Educational Research)

Libresco, Andrea S.

Every book is a social studies book; how to meet standards with picture books, K-6. [by] Andrea S. Libresco, Jeannette Balantic, and Jonie C. Kipling. Libraries Unlimited 2011 269p il pa $30

Grades: Adult Professional   **372**

1. Social sciences -- Study and teaching

ISBN 978-1-59884-520-4; 1-59884-520-9

LC 2010053649

"Based on observations and instructional surveys, the authors theorize that consistent social studies instruction no longer occurs due to the time requirements of reading and math instruction. They recommend teaching reading and social studies concurrently by using trade picture books. Each of the national standards' thematic strands is featured along with essential questions to frame classroom discussion. Three representative titles are featured for each theme, followed by social studies concepts and supporting discussion questions. Thoughtful hands-on, student-centered activities are provided for each title as well as reproducibles, study sheets, and graphic organizers." Libr Media Connect

Includes bibliographical references

Lukenbill, W. Bernard

Health information in a changing world; practical approaches for teachers, schools, and school librarians. [by] W. Bernard Lukenbill and Barbara Froling Immroth. Libraries Unlimited 2010 244p il $45

Grades: Adult Professional   **372**

1. Health education 2. Youth -- Health and hygiene 3. Health -- Information services

ISBN 978-1-59884-398-9; 1-59884-398-2

LC 2010-7505

"This is quite an impressive book and a real treasure for any professional involved with health education, whether for the classroom, public health, or personal counseling." Voice Youth Advocates

Includes bibliographical references

MacDonell, Colleen

Thematic inquiry through fiction and nonfiction, PreK to grade 6. Linworth Pub. 2009 121p il pa $44.95

Grades: Adult Professional   **372**

1. Active learning 2. Education -- Curricula

ISBN 978-1-58683-350-3 pa; 1-58683-350-2 pa

LC 2008-33365

"This is an excellent guide for classroom teachers and school media specialists interested in adding inquiry-based collaborative lessons to their repertoire." Libr Media Connect

This describes "how outstanding fiction and nonfiction titles can be integrated into thematic inquiry in preschool and elementary classrooms. Each thematic inquiry unit has four sections: Read it! describes a sample dialogic reading of one of the fiction or nonfiction books; Integrate it! gives concrete examples of how specialized subjects and technology can be integrated with the fiction or nonfiction selections; Do it! describes hands-on activities that are integral to the use of fiction and nonfiction for inquiry; and Assess it! enumerates across-the-curriculum standards met in the thematic inquiry." Publisher's note

Includes bibliographical references

Mackey, Bonnie
   A **librarian's** guide to cultivating an elementary school garden; [by] Bonnie Mackey and Jennifer Mackey Stewart. Linworth Pub. 2009 124p il pa $39.95
Grades: Adult Professional   372
   1. Gardening 2. School libraries -- Activity projects
   ISBN 978-1-58683-328-2 pa; 1-58683-328-6 pa
                                        LC 2008-34963
"Its unusual topic makes this book a standout." Libr Media Connect
Includes bibliographical references

372.21 Preschool education

Howe, James
   ★ **When** you go to kindergarten; text by James Howe; photographs by Betsy Imershein. rev & updated ed; Morrow Junior Bks. 1994 un il hardcover o.p. pa $6.99
Grades: PreK K   372.21
   1. Kindergarten
   ISBN 0-688-12912-9; 0-688-14387-3 pa
                                        LC 93-48152
First published 1986 by Knopf
"The author tells youngsters what school might look like and how they might get there, and describes some of the possible activities. . . . Multicultural children are welcomed and taught by both male and female teachers. Smiling, busy kids engaged in many activities portray school as an exciting, interesting, and happy place." SLJ

372.4 Reading

Grover, Sharon
   Listening to learn; audiobooks supporting literacy. by Sharon Grover and Lizette D. Hannegan. American Library Association 2011 xi, 188 p.p (alk. paper) $45
Grades: Adult Professional   372.4
   1. Literacy 2. Audiobooks 3. Educational technology 4. Reading -- United States 5. Children -- Books and reading 6. Libraries -- Special collections -- Audiobooks 7. Literacy -- Study and teaching -- United States 8. School librarian participation in curriculum planning
   ISBN 0838911072; 9780838911075
                                        LC 2011041814

Authors Sharon Grover and Lizette D. Hannegan "make the case that audiobooks not only present excellent opportunities to engage the attention of young people but also advance literacy. 'Listening to Learn' connects audiobooks with K-12 curricula and demonstrates how the format can support national learning standards and literacy skills." (Publisher's note)

"This informative resource establishes the literacy benefits of audiobooks as an alternate reading delivery method... Discussions of audiobook formats and recommended sources for building an audiobook collection are also included. The authors provide a collaborative resource that would benefit a classroom, library, or home setting." (Library Media Connection)

Includes bibliographical references (p. 175-178) and index

Hutchins, Darcy J.
   Family reading night; [by] Darcy J. Hutchins, Marsha D. Greenfeld, Joyce L. Epstein. Eye on Education 2008 126p il pa $29.95
Grades: Adult Professional   372.4
   1. Reading 2. Family literacy programs
   ISBN 978-1-59667-063-1 pa; 1-59667-063-0 pa
                                        LC 2007034492
"This guide presents clear examples of how to plan and implement thematic, monthly programs to help engage families with elementary-age children in literacy activities that they can do together. . . . This title would be an excellent tool for any school librarian, educator, or administrator working to devise a successful and strategically planned school-wide family reading program." SLJ

Moreillon, Judi
   Collaborative strategies for teaching reading comprehension; maximizing your impact. [by] Judi Moreillon. American Library Association 2007 170p il $38
Grades: Adult Professional   372.4
   1. Reading comprehension
   ISBN 978-0-8389-0929-4; 0-8389-0929-9
                                        LC 2006036132

This "begins by emphasizing the importance of collaboration between classroom teachers and teacher-librarians. . . . The bulk of the book focuses on seven reading comprehension strategies and how to teach them. . . . Overall this book is a cut above other 'how-to' books with its plethora of suggestions and resources for teachers and librarians." Voice Youth Advocates

Includes glossary and bibliographical references

372.47 Reading comprehension strategies

Bradbury, Judy
   The **read**-aloud scaffold; best books to enhance content area curriculum, grades pre-K-3. by Judy Bradbury. Libraries Unlimited 2011 xi, 180 p.p (pbk.: acid-free paper) $40
Grades: Adult Professional   372.47
   1. Books and reading 2. Curriculum planning 3. Children's literature 4. Content area reading -- United States 5. Reading (Elementary) -- United States 6.

Language arts (Elementary) -- United States
ISBN 1598846841; 9781598846843

LC 2011023169

This book, by Judy Bradbury, "offers teachers and librarians over 700 content area connections through carefully selected, recently published children's trade books. These selections include fiction and non-fiction titles that represent outstanding read-aloud choices that will augment the instructional curriculum, covering subjects ranging from history to holidays to special events, and from biographies and memoirs to poetry and character education." (Publisher's note)

Includes bibliographical references and indexes

372.5   The arts

Press, Judy

★ **Around**-the-world art & activities; visiting the 7 continents through craft fun. illustrations by Betsy Day. Williamson 2001 128p il (Williamson Little Hands book) pa $12.95

Grades: K 1 2   **372.5**

1. Handicraft
ISBN 1-88559-345-7

LC 00-60030

"North American totem poles, Hawaiian leis, Aboriginal bark painting, Japanese dolls in kimonos, Korean drums, egg-carton camels, Masai beaded necklaces, nesting Russian dolls, and South American gaucho belts are among the projects. While the ideas will not be new to veteran crafters, they are basic and solid for the intended audience." SLJ

372.6   Language arts (Communication skills)

Bauer, Caroline Feller

★ **Caroline** Feller Bauer's new handbook for storytellers; with stories, poems, magic, and more. illustrations by Lynn Gates Bredeson. American Library Association 1993 550p il hardcover o.p. pa $45

Grades: Adult Professional   **372.6**

1. Storytelling
ISBN 0-8389-0664-8 pa

LC 93-14959

First published 1977 with title: Handbook for storytellers

Bauer's introduction "incorporates a broad variety of media and props into the storytelling process. . . . Beginners and veterans alike can benefit from this practical approach to program planning and promotion, story selection and preparation, and activities extending various themes or occasions." Bull Cent Child Books

Includes bibliographical references

Briggs, Diane

Preschool favorites; 35 storytimes kids love. [by] Diane Briggs; illustrated by Thomas Briggs. American Library Association 2007 227p bibl il pa $40

Grades: Adult Professional   **372.6**

1. Storytelling
ISBN 0-8389-0938-8 pa; 978-0-8389-0938-6 pa

LC 2006103159

"This book presents suggestions and resources for a variety of themes, from 'Animal Oddballs' to 'A Woggle of Witches.' Each session includes a variety of books and activities per topic. . . . Several fingerplays and folk rhymes per theme come with clear instructions for accompanying motions. . . . A useful discography provides sources for musical selections. Each theme also incorporates a flannel board poem, story, or song, with simple reproducible patterns and instructions on how to present them. . . . The thematic groupings and quantity of ideas should be useful to beginners and some experienced presenters looking to freshen up their programs." SLJ

Includes bibliographical references

Toddler storytimes II; [by] Diane Briggs; illustrations by Thomas Briggs. Scarecrow Press 2008 165p il pa $45

Grades: Adult Professional   **372.6**

1. Storytelling
ISBN 978-0-8108-6057-5 pa; 0-8108-6057-0 pa

LC 2008006243

"With 25 theme-based chapters, this is a handy resource. Each theme includes book recommendations, often 10 or more, with a nice mixture of classic and newer titles, and a suggestion to choose two or three per session. Words and instructions for fingerplays, rhymes, and songs are provided, while a discography provides melody sources for all songs. Each theme includes a flannel-board activity, complete with reproducible patterns and brief directions on how to present the story or song on the board." SLJ

Includes discography and bibliographical references

Cavanaugh, Terence W.

Bookmapping; lit trips and beyond. [by] Terence W. Cavanaugh, Jerome Burg. International Society for Technology in Education 2011 228p il pa $34.95

Grades: Adult Professional   **372.6**

1. Audiovisual education 2. Literature -- Study and teaching 3. Maps -- Study and teaching -- Activities and projects

ISBN 978-1-56484-283-1; 1-56484-283-5

LC 2010051664

This book "provides ideas on how teachers can use elements from different disciplines in their own classrooms. . . . Other information includes using Google Earth, sources for images, Bing maps, information on creating your own bookmaps, instruction for bookmaps done individually and in cooperation with another teacher's class or classes, how to set up mapping in the classroom, and exploring existing bookmaps available on the Web. . . . This book should be in the professional collection of every middle and high school library, preferably in every classroom." Voice Youth Advocates

Includes bibliographical references

Chatton, Barbara

Using poetry across the curriculum; learning to love language. 2nd ed; Libraries Unlimited 2010 241p pa $40

Grades: Adult Professional   **372.6**

1. Poetry -- Study and teaching
ISBN 978-1-59158-697-5; 1-59158-697-6

LC 2009-36711

First published 1993

"With the emphasis in most schools on improving literacy, fluency, and reading and writing test scores, this book is extremely valuable. Sections are divided into various curricula areas. Each section begins with the national standards for that discipline, then a few paragraphs explain how the poetry in the extensive listing can be used. . . . Because all teachers must incorporate writing into their teaching, having relevant poetry for their curriculum and ideas on how to use it, will make this book popular." Libr Media Connect

Includes bibliographical references

Greene, Ellin

Storytelling: art & technique; [by] Ellin Greene and Janice Del Negro. 4th ed.; Libraries Unlimited 2010 xxvii, 455p il $55

Grades: Adult Professional   **372.6**

1. Storytelling

ISBN 978-1-59158-600-5; 1-59158-600-3

First published 1977 by Bowker under the authorship of Augusta Baker and Ellin Greene

"The fourth edition of this storytelling standby includes a wealth of updated and new materials." Bull Cent Child Books

Includes bibliographical references

Heitman, Jane

★ **Once** upon a time; fairy tales in the library and language arts, [by] Jane Heitman. Linworth Pub. 2007 132p pa $36.95

Grades: Adult Professional   **372.6**

1. Reading 2. Fairy tales 3. Language arts

ISBN 1-58683-231-X pa; 978-1-58683-231-X pa

LC 2007006890

"Heitman presents a well-organized and comprehensive look at how fairy tales can be infused into the curriculum. . . . The book includes ways in which various lessons can be adapted for special and English-language learners, as well as numerous templates for writing, speaking, and listening activities. . . . This excellent resource deserves a place in most professional collections." SLJ

Includes bibliographical references

Hostmeyer, Phyllis

Storytelling and QAR strategies; [by] Phyllis Hostmeyer and Marilyn Adele Kinsella. Libraries Unlimited 2010 123p pa $30

Grades: Adult Professional   **372.6**

1. Storytelling

ISBN 978-1-59884-494-8 pa; 1-59884-494-6 pa; 978-1-59884-495-5 e-book

LC 2010036576

"The authors, both storytellers with backgrounds in education and library work, present 18 stories based on six aspects of character development. These selections, which include folktales, fables, and myths, are just right for youngsters in third through eighth grades. Each one is followed by telling tips, a story path, and questions using the QAR (Question-Answer Relationships) model." SLJ

Includes bibliographical references

MacDonald, Margaret Read

Shake-it-up tales! stories to sing, dance, drum, and act out. August House 2000 174p il music $24.95; pa $14.95

Grades: Adult Professional   **372.6**

1. Folklore 2. Storytelling

ISBN 0-87483-590-9; 0-87483-570-4 pa

LC 00-36228

This is a collection of "participation tales from different cultures. Each of the 20 stories is easy to learn and MacDonald provides wonderful ideas on how to inspire elementary-aged children to join in and become part of the storytelling tradition." SLJ

Includes bibliographical references

Miller, Donalyn

★ The **book** whisperer; awakening the inner reader in every child. [by] Donalyn Miller; foreword by Jeff Anderson. Jossey-Bass 2009 227p

Grades: Adult Professional   **372.6**

1. Books and reading

ISBN 0-4703-7227-3; 978-0-4703-7227-2

LC 2008055666

Donalyn Miller's approach to reading promotion "is simple yet provocative: affirm the reader in every student, allow students to choose their own books, carve out extra reading time, model authentic reading behaviors, discard time-worn reading assignments such as book reports and comprehension worksheets, and develop a classroom library filled with high-interest books. . . . Miller provides many tips for teachers and parents and includes a useful list of ultimate reading suggestions picked by her students. This outstanding contribution to the literature is highly recommended." Libr J

Includes bibliographical references

Roth, Rita

The **story** road to literacy; [by] Rita Roth. Teacher Ideas Press 2006 176p il pa $30

Grades: Adult Professional   **372.6**

1. Language arts 2. Children of immigrants 3. English language -- Study and teaching

ISBN 1-59158-323-3

LC 2005030835

"Roth advances the idea that using traditional literature with students who are learning English will help them acquire critical communication skills while tying unfamiliar new places to familiar elements of their own heritages. The author provides practical, ready-to-use lesson plans, story samples, and suggested activities." SLJ

Includes bibliographical references

Sawyer, Ruth

The **way** of the storyteller. Viking 1962 360p il hardcover o.p. pa $16

Grades: Adult Professional   **372.6**

1. Storytelling 2. Literature -- Collections

ISBN 0-14-004436-1 pa

First published 1942

"This is not primarily a book on how to tell stories; it is rather the whole philosophy of story telling as a creative art. From her own rich experience the author writes inspiringly of the background, experience, creative imagination, technique and selection essential to this art. A part of the book is devoted to a few well-loved stories with suggestions and comments." Booklist

Includes bibliographical references

Spaulding, Amy E.

The **art** of storytelling; telling truths through telling stories. Scarecrow Press, Inc. 2011 210p $49.95

Grades: Adult Professional   **372.6**

1. Storytelling

ISBN 978-0-8108-7776-4; 0-8108-7776-7; 978-0-8108-7777-1 ebook

LC 2010039697

"Spaulding's passion for storytelling is evident as she shares the skills she has learned over the years. . . . She offers practical advice on selecting and learning stories, matching the story to the audience, and avoiding common performance pitfalls. . . . The presentation is conversational, filled with personal insights, interesting quotes, and thorough documentation." SLJ

Includes bibliographical references

372.61   Grammar

An **ambush** of tigers; a wild gathering of collective nouns. By Betsy R. Rosenthal; Illustrated by Jago. Millbrook Press 2015 32 p. (lib. bdg.: alk. paper) $19.99

Grades: K 1 2 3 4   **372.61**

1. Animals 2. English language 3. English language -- Rhymes 4. English language -- Grammar 5. English language -- Collective nouns

ISBN 146771464X; 9781467714648

LC 2014009383

This children's book, by Betsy R. Rosenthal and illustrated by Jago, "introduces collective nouns for animals through wordplay. Clever rhymes and humorous illustrations bring these collective nouns to life in funny ways, making it easy to remember which terms and animals go together." (Publisher's note)

"While several picture books have tackled collective nouns, Rosenthal and Jago's collaboration stands out for the sheer inventiveness they bring to the subject. Rosenthal frames her rhymes as rhetorical questions that often make surprising (and wonderful) interspecies connections . . . Witty delights abound as a shiver of sharks bundles up in winter knitwear and a bouquet of pheasants peers glumly out of a tall vase." Pub Wkly

372.62   Written and spoken expression

Ellis, Sarah

From reader to writer; teaching writing through classic children's books. Douglas & McIntyre 2000 176p hardcover o.p. pa $14.95

Grades: Adult Professional   **372.62**

1. Poets 2. Artists 3. Authors 4. Novelists 5. Dramatists 6. Librarians 7. Theologians 8. Illustrators 9. Mathematicians 10. Editors 11. Essayists 12. Linguists 13. Satirists 14. Biographers 15. Philologists 16. Travel writers 17. Fantasy writers 18. Literary critics 19. Children's authors 20. Nonfiction writers 21. Writers on science 22. Short story writers 23. Young adult authors 24. Science fiction writers 25. Rhetoric -- Study and teaching 26. Children's literature -- Study and teaching

ISBN 0-88899-372-2; 0-88899-440-0 pa

The author discusses the work of seventeen British, Canadian and American authors of children's literature. "With each classic book, there's a 'sneak preview' (i.e., booktalk), a suggested read-aloud, exercises to help students and adult writers find their own stories, and a short annotated bibliography of related children's books." Booklist

372.63   Spelling and handwriting

Cunha, Stephen F.

How to ace the National Geographic Bee; official study guide. by Stephen F. Cunha. 4th ed. National Geographic 2012 127 p. ill., maps (library) $18.90; (paperback) $9.95

Grades: 4 5 6 7 8   **372.63**

1. Maps 2. Geography 3. Examinations -- Study guides 4. Contests 5. Geography -- Competitions 6. School contests -- United States 7. Geography -- Competitions -- United States

ISBN 1426309856; 1426309864; 9781426309854; 9781426309861

LC 2012419185

This book "is a study guide to prepare the reader for test questions in geographic trivia. . . . The book then separates into six distinct chapters. It begins with defining geography and giving the reader an overall understanding of how the bee is conducted. Chapter 3 . . . defines the various types of maps and how they should be interpreted and also explains map features and landforms." (Voice of Youth Advocates)

Includes bibliographical references (p. 109-117).

372.64   Literature appreciation

MacDonald, Margaret Read

★ The **storyteller's** start-up book; finding, learning, performing, and using folktales including twelve tellable tales. August House 1993 215p $26.95; pa $14.95

Grades: Adult Professional   **372.64**

1. Folklore 2. Storytelling

ISBN 0-87483-304-3; 0-87483-305-1 pa

LC 93-1580

The author's advice on storytelling "covers the practical ground, from selection, learning (in one hour!), performance, and setting to classroom applications. . . . A dozen texts of proven success follow, with performance tips and source notes. Equally valuable are the selected and annotated bibliographies appended to every chapter." Libr J

Includes bibliographical references

Pellowski, Anne

★ The **storytelling** handbook; a young people's collection of unusual tales and helpful hints on how to tell them. illustrated by Martha Stoberock. Simon & Schuster Bks. for Young Readers 1995 129p il hardcover o.p. pa $7.99

Grades: Adult Professional   **372.64**

1. Storytelling

ISBN 0-689-80311-7; 978-1-4169-7598-4 pa; 1-4169-7598-5 pa

LC 95-2991

This work "addresses the young person who wants to tell stories in a public setting. It is similar in format to many adult books on storytelling how-tos, with sections on getting started and selecting and preparing stories, as well as a selection of sample tales. Pellowski's notes are extensive and will be very useful to novices looking for ways to research stories." Booklist

Includes bibliographical references

372.66 Drama (Theater)

Bany-Winters, Lisa

On stage; theater games and activities for kids. Lisa Bany-Winters. Chicago Review Press 2012 227 p. il (pbk.) $16.95

Grades: 3 4 5 **372.66**

1. Educational games 2. Drama in education 3. Play 4. Children's plays, American

ISBN 1613740735; 9781613740736

LC 2012012741

This book, by Lisa Bany-Winters, is a theater teaching resource for young actors, offering "more than 125 theater games that spark creativity, boost confidence, and encourage collaboration. They'll learn all about how to make a stage performance great with improvisational games, . . . they'll make puppets, discover makeup secrets, and design and build a set." (Publisher's note)

Includes bibliographical references

Champlin, Connie

★ **Storytelling** with puppets; 2nd ed; American Library Association 1998 249p il pa $35

Grades: Adult Professional **372.66**

1. Storytelling 2. Puppets and puppet plays

ISBN 0-8389-0709-1

LC 97-24810

First published 1985 under the authorship of Connie Champlin and Nancy Renfro

This book covers "such topics as puppet types and styles, developing a puppet collection, participatory storytelling, and presentation formats. . . . A very useful choice for professional shelves in both school and public libraries." Booklist

Includes bibliographical references

372.7 Mathematics

Long, Ethan

★ The **Wing** Wing brothers math spectacular! Ethan Long. Holiday House 2012 32 p. (hardcover) $15.95

Grades: PreK K 1 2 **372.7**

1. Vaudeville -- Fiction 2. Mathematics 3. Numeration -- Study and teaching (Primary) 4. Numbers, Natural -- Study and teaching (Primary)

ISBN 0823423204; 9780823423200

LC 2011018256

The protagonists of this children's picture book, "Wilber, Wendell, Willy, Walter, and Woody really know how to put on a show. Five hilarious ducks juggle pies . . . spin plates . . . and show off their magic box. . . . Their slapstick routine is also a math lesson. They introduce the concepts greater than, less than, and equal to as well as addition and subtraction." (Publisher's note)

"[Long's] humorous illustrations—black pencil outlines with digital color that are reminiscent of Mo Willems' pigeon—will keep kids riveted with the birds' fantastically expressive faces. This is how learning math should be—painless, comical and, yes, spectacular." Kirkus

Long, Lynette

Measurement mania; games and activities that make math easy and fun. Wiley 2001 122p il (Magical math) pa $12.95

Grades: 3 4 5 6 **372.7**

1. Measurement

ISBN 0-471-36980-2

LC 00-43383

In this introduction to measurement "the activities range from using hands and feet to measure distance to making a sundial. . . . [This book provides] valuable activities and games to help children learn about the concepts." SLJ

"Brimming with fun and educational games and activities, the Magical Math series provides everything you need to know to become a master of mathematics! In each of these books, Lynette Long uses her own unique style to help you truly understand mathematical concepts as you play with everyday objects such as playing cards, dice, coins, and paper and pencil." Publisher's Note

VanCleave, Janice Pratt

Janice VanCleave's play and find out about math; easy activities for young children. Wiley 1998 122p il $29.95; pa $12.95

Grades: K 1 2 **372.7**

1. Mathematics

ISBN 0-471-12937-2; 0-471-12938-0 pa

LC 96-53002

"Fifty simple activities that involve basic arithmetic such as using one's fingers to do simple addition and subtraction. . . . Most procedures are between four and eight steps and are clearly written and accompanied by pencil drawings." SLJ

372.89 History and geography

Panchyk, Richard

New York City history for kids; from New Amsterdam to the Big Apple, with 21 activities. Richard Panchyk. Chicago Review Press 2012 134 p. $16.95

Grades: 4 5 6 **372.89**

1. Picture books for children 2. Historic buildings -- New York (N.Y.) 3. New York (N.Y.) -- History 4. New York (N.Y.) -- History -- Study and teaching (Primary) -- Activity programs

ISBN 1883052939; 9781883052935

LC 2012029893

"In this . . . 400-year history [of New York City, by Richard Panchyk,] kids will read about Peter Stuyvesant and the enterprising Dutch colonists, follow the . . . patriots as they rebel against the British during the American Revolution, . . . journey through the notorious Five Points slum with its tenements and street vendors, and soar to new heights with the Empire State Building and New York City's other . . . skyscrapers." (Publisher's note)

Includes bibliographical references and index

373.1 Organization and activities in secondary education

Glasser, Debbie

New kid, new scene; a guide to moving and switching schools. by Debbie Glasser and Emily Schenck. Magination Press 2012 112p il $14.95; pa 9.95

Grades: 5 6 7 8 **373.1**

1. Moving 2. Students

ISBN 978-1-4338-1039-8; 1-4338-1039-5; 978-1-4338-1038-1 pa; 1-4338-1038-7 pa

LC 2011013608

"Students making the transition to new schools, new communities, or new homes will always experience a bit of anxiety, and this self-help book offers practical advice on how to make those changes smoother. The ideas and suggestions are sound and practical. . . . The eye-catching layout will keep students flipping through the pages." SLJ

375 Curricula

Bishop, Kay

Connecting libraries with classrooms; the curricular roles of the media specialist. 2nd. ed.; Linworth 2011 122p pa $45

Grades: Adult Professional **375**

1. Librarians 2. School libraries 3. Instructional materials centers

ISBN 978-1-59884-599-0; 1-59884-599-3

LC 2010051623

This book provides an . . . exploration of the topics that are currently relevant in K-12 curricula, including the school librarian's role in dealing with these issues, collaborating with teachers, and connecting to classrooms.

"Kay Bishop's book covers a wide range of topics and issues within the school library field. . . . Collaborative planning between classroom teacher, principal, students, and the community is also addressed. This material will be a welcome addition to the Library Media Specialist's arsenal of resources to stay current and involved." Libr Media Connect

Includes bibliographical references

379 Public policy issues in education

Morrison, Toni

Remember; the journey to school integration. Houghton Mifflin Co. 2004 78p il $18

Grades: 3 4 5 **379**

1. School integration 2. Discrimination in education 3. African Americans -- Education 4. United States -- Race relations

ISBN 978-0-618-39740-2; 0-618-39740-X

LC 2003-22884

Historical real photo/portraits combined with simple factual statement from the point of view of African American children tells the history of the school integration in this country

"The provocative, candid images and conversational text should spark questions and discussion, a respect for past sacrifices, and inspiration for facing future challenges." SLJ

Walker, Paul Robert

★ Remember Little Rock; the time, the people, the stories. by Paul Robert Walker. National Geographic 2008 61p il map $17.95; lib bdg $27.90

Grades: 5 6 7 8 9 **379**

1. School integration 2. Segregation in education 3. Arkansas -- Race relations 4. African Americans -- Education 5. Central High School (Little Rock, Ark.)

ISBN 978-1-4263-0402-6; 1-4263-0402-1; 978-1-4263-0403-3 lib bdg; 1-4263-0403-X lib bdg

LC 2008-24959

"The story of the battle to integrate Central High School in 1957 Little Rock, Arkansas, is presented through photographs and firsthand accounts from those who were there. . . . The multitude of eyewitness accounts, the poignant photographs, and the contextual background make this text a must-have addition to any classroom or library." Voice Youth Advocates

Includes bibliographical references

379.2 Specific policy issues in public education

Tonatiuh, Duncan

★ Separate is never equal; Sylvia Mendez & her family's fight for desegregation. by Duncan Tonatiuh. Abrams Books for Young Readers 2014 40 p. illustrations (hardback) $18.95

Grades: 2 3 4 5 **379.2**

1. School integration 2. Latinos (U.S.) -- History -- 20th century 3. Hispanic Americans -- Education 4. Hispanic Americans -- Civil rights 5. School integration -- United States 6. Civil rights movements -- United States

ISBN 1419710540; 9781419710544

LC 2013032089

Robert F. Sibert Honor Book (2015)

Pura Belpré (Illustrator) Honor Book (2015)

This children's book by Duncan Tonatiuh describes how "Sylvia Mendez and her parents helped end school segregation in California. An American citizen of Mexican and Puerto Rican heritage who spoke and wrote perfect English, Mendez was denied enrollment to a 'Whites only' school. Her parents took action by organizing the Hispanic community and filing a lawsuit in federal district court. Their success eventually brought an end to the era of segregated education in California." (Publisher's note)

"Tonatiuh's multimedia artwork showcases period detail, such as the children's clothing and the differences between the school facilities, in his unique folk art style. An endnote essay recapping the events, photos of Sylvia and her schools, and a glossary and resource list for further research complete this thorough exploration of an event that is rarely taught." Booklist

Includes bibliographical references and index

381 Commerce (Trade)

Freese, Susan M.

Craigslist; the company and its founder. ABDO Pub. Co. 2011 112p il (Technology pioneers) lib bdg $34.22

Grades: 5 6 7 8 **381**
1. Advertising 2. Businessmen 3. Internet marketing 4. Online social networks 5. Webmasters 6. Craigslist Inc. 7. Software engineers
ISBN 978-1-61714-806-4 lib bdg; 1-61714-806-7 lib bdg; 978-1-61758-964-5 e-book
LC 2010042448
This is an introduction to Craigslist and its founder, Craig Newmark.
"Written in a clear, linear fashion, this series offers vivid, well-researched details about the development of technological advancements considered essential in today's society. . . . Readers who are interested in technology and inventions will be thoroughly engrossed." SLJ
Includes glossary and bibliographical references

Krull, Kathleen
Supermarket; illustrated by Melanie Hope Greenberg. Holiday House 2001 un il $16.95
Grades: K 1 2 3 **381**
1. Supermarkets
ISBN 0-8234-1546-5
LC 99-88042
Explains modern supermarkets and how they work, discussing how they organize, display, and keep track of the items they sell
"Written in a clear and lively style. . . . Best of all, however, are the vibrant double-page gouache cartoon-style pictures using flat, decorative forms." SLJ

Lanz, Helen
Shopping choices; Helen Lanz. Sea-to-Sea Publications 2012 30 p. col. ill. (Go green) (library) $28.50
Grades: 3 4 5 **381**
1. Commerce -- Environmental aspects 2. Consumers -- Environmental aspects 3. Shopping 4. Sustainable living 5. Shopping -- Environmental aspects
ISBN 159771304X; 9781597713047
LC 2011005509
This entry in the Go Green series "reminds readers that all goods come from a finite supply of natural resources." It looks at "where products come from and how commerce contributes to global warming and impacts forests, while also suggesting solutions like frequenting thrift stores, purchasing products made from recycled materials, and identifying items approved by the Forest Stewardship Council." (Booklist)

Larson, Jennifer S.
Who's buying? Who's selling? understanding consumers and producers. Lerner Pub. 2010 32p il (Exploring economics) lib bdg $25.26; pa $7.95
Grades: K 1 2 **381**
1. Commerce
ISBN 978-0-7613-3912-0 lib bdg; 0-7613-3912-4 lib bdg; 978-0-7613-5665-3 pa; 0-7613-5665-3 pa
Photographs and simple text introduce young readers to how people buy and sell goods.
"Clear, age-appropriate language explains new concepts well. . . . The [book's] layout is interesting and fresh, and each page features a large, well-chosen photograph with a boxed caption." SLJ

Lassieur, Allison
Trade and commerce in the early Islamic world; Allison Lassieur. Crabtree Pub. Company 2012 48 p. (Life in the early Islamic world) (reinforced library binding: alk. paper) $30.60
Grades: 4 5 6 **381**
1. Commerce 2. Islam -- History 3. Islamic Empire -- Commerce 4. Islamic Empire -- Economic conditions
ISBN 0778721728; 9780778721727; 9780778721796; 9781427195654; 9781427198426
LC 2012000078
This book is part of a series where "each book covers a particular aspect of life in the early Islamic world. . . . The main texts are supplemented with blue boxes of information, subsections, and many . . . reproductions, maps, and paintings. Each book contains time lines and short biographies of important historical figures." (School Library Journal)

McClure, Nikki
★ **To** market, to market. Abrams Books for Young Readers 2011 un il $17.95
Grades: K 1 2 3 **381**
1. Food 2. Markets 3. Farm produce
ISBN 0-8109-9738-X; 978-0-8109-9738-7
LC 2010032946
"As a mother and son meander through the Olympia, WA, market, a full-page illustration shows them at a farmer's table while the facing page names the food sold there and briefly introduces the person who grows it. On the next page the farmer is illustrated at work and several paragraphs of elegant prose describe each process, ending with a simple 'thank you.' In this way, youngsters learn about apple-tree grafting and pruning, growing kale, beekeeping, smoking fish, baking, making batik napkins, and the art of cheesemaking. . . . McClure's mysterious and beautiful images are cut from black paper with an X-Acto knife; the lacelike result is scanned and colored. McClure's art and life intersect in this stirring tribute to the connections among nature, people, and the food that nourishes them." SLJ

383 Communications and transportation

Brown, Craig McFarland
★ **Mule** train mail. Charlesbridge Pub. 2009 un il lib bdg $16.95; pa $7.95
Grades: 1 2 3 **383**
1. Grand Canyon (Ariz.) 2. Postal service -- West (U.S.)
ISBN 978-1-58089-187-5 lib bdg; 1-58089-187-X lib bdg; 978-1-58089-188-2 pa; 1-58089-188-8 pa
LC 2008007252
"Brown relates the daily trip made by Anthony the Postman from the top of the Grand Canyon to the village of Supai far below on the canyon floor. . . . An author's note gives additional details that children will appreciate. . . . He also describes the expedition he made with Anthony Paya, lead muleteer, to appreciate firsthand the journey and the rigors of the landscape. Brown's wonderful pastel and colored pencil illustrations are a testament to the time he spent on the trail. . . . A fascinating and informative addition." SLJ

Kay, Verla

Whatever happened to the Pony Express? illustrated by Kimberley Bulcken Root & Barry Root. G. P. Putnam's Sons 2010 un il $16.99

Grades: K 1 2 3   **383**

1. Pony express 2. Postal service 3. West (U.S.) -- History

ISBN 978-0-399-24483-4; 0-399-24483-2

"Through a series of letters between a brother and sister, Kay examines changes in mail delivery during the time period 1851-1870. . . . The rhymed text flows well. . . . While the brief phrases provide the larger historical context, the illustrations, rendered in pencil, ink, gouache, and watercolor, are crucial in developing the personal drama of the siblings and their families. . . . Libraries will want to accept delivery of this attractive and informative package." SLJ

Kenney, Karen Latchana

Mail carriers at work; by Karen L. Kenney; illustrated by Brian Caleb Dumm; content consultant: Judith Stepan-Norris. Magic Wagon 2009 32p il (Meet your community!) lib bdg $18.95

Grades: K 1 2 3   **383**

1. Letter carriers 2. Vocational guidance

ISBN 978-1-60270-650-7 lib bdg; 1-60270-650-6 lib bdg

LC 2009-2398

This book about mail carriers has "an uncluttered layout and consistent organization. . . . Chapter headings such as 'Problems on the Job,' and 'Technology at Work,' and 'Special Skills and Training' make it easy to pinpoint specific information." SLJ

Includes glossary

Spradlin, Michael P.

Off like the wind! the first ride of the pony express. illustrated by Layne Johnson. Walker Books for Young Readers 2010 un il map $17.99; lib bdg $18.89

Grades: 3 4 5   **383**

1. Pony express 2. Postal service 3. West (U.S.) -- History

ISBN 978-0-8027-9652-3; 0-8027-9652-4; 978-0-8027-9653-0 lib bdg; 0-8027-9653-2 lib bdg

LC 2009-10827

"Basing his book, as much as possible, on scanty historical records . . . Spradlin re-creates the Pony Express' first rides east from Sacramento and west from St. Joseph, Missouri—naming riders and horses when he can, and providing a composite of various Express riders' adventures. Johnson heightens the drama with evocative full-bleed oils." Booklist

Includes bibliographical references

Thompson, Gare

Riding with the mail; the story of the Pony Express. by Gare Thompson. National Geographic 2007 40p il map (National Geographic history chapters) lib bdg $17.90

Grades: 2 3 4   **383**

1. Pony express 2. West (U.S.) -- History

ISBN 978-1-4263-0192-6 lib bdg; 1-4263-0192-8 lib bdg

LC 2007007897

"After an introduction sets the historical scene, this engaging volume provides a comprehensive introduction to the rise and fall of America's first postal service, the Pony Ex-

press. . . . Archival photographs, . . . maps, and . . . sidebars extend the text." Horn Book Guide

384.55   Television

Hirschmann, Kris

HDTV; high definition television. Norwood House Press 2010 48p il (A great idea) lib bdg $25.27

Grades: 3 4 5 6   **384.55**

1. High definition television

ISBN 978-1-59953-379-7 lib bdg; 1-59953-379-0 lib bdg

LC 2010008699

This "book is peppered with clear, current photographs, useful websites, and [a] complete [index]. Students do not need prior knowledge to appreciate [this] worthy [title]." SLJ

Includes glossary and bibliographical references

385   Railroad transportation

Curlee, Lynn

★ **Trains**. Atheneum Books for Young Readers 2009 40p il $19.99

Grades: 4 5 6   **385**

1. Railroads -- History

ISBN 978-1-4169-4848-3; 1-4169-4848-1

LC 2007-40425

"Curlee illuminates . . . trains . . . with stunning, clean-lined illustrations and informative narration. He opens with a romantic reminiscence about the mighty engines that rumbled through his North Carolina hometown. . . . Launching into a chronological account of the evolution of the 'iron horse,' subsequent pages highlight major developments in (mostly American) railroad history, from the first steam engines to run on rails to the high-speed trains of Europe and Asia. Flatly styled and employing limited color palettes, several of Curlee's acrylic paintings will impress and awe readers." Publ Wkly

Floca, Brian

★ **Locomotive**; written and illustrated by Brian Floca. Atheneum Books for Young Readers 2013 64 p. ill. (hardcover) $17.99

Grades: K 1 2 3 4 5   **385**

1. Picture books for children 2. Locomotives 3. Railroads -- United States -- History -- 19th century 4. Locomotives -- United States -- History -- 19th century

ISBN 1416994157; 9781416994152; 9781442485228

LC 2012042295

Robert F. Sibert Honor Book (2014)

Caldecott Medal (2014)

Orbis Pictus Award Honor Book (2014)

In this children's picture book, Brian Richard Floca "invites readers to join a family—mother, daughter and son—on one of the first passenger trips from Omaha to Sacramento after the meeting of the Union Pacific and the Central Pacific in May 1869. . . . Floca visually documents the trip, vignettes illustrating the train's equipment as well as such . . . details as toilet and sleeping conditions." (Kirkus Reviews)

Halpern, Monica

★ **Railroad** fever; building the Transcontinental Railroad, 1830-1870. [by] Monica Halpern. National Geographic 2004 40p il map (Crossroads America) $21.90; pa $12.95

Grades: 4 5 6   385

1. Frontier and pioneer life 2. Railroads -- History 3. Central Pacific Railroad 4. Union Pacific Railroad Company

ISBN 0-7922-6767-2; 0-7922-6767-2 pa

LC 2003-17858

Presents a history of the building of the transcontinental railroad and its effects on American life

"This is a first-choice purchase for its visually appealing presentation and its succinct yet thorough treatment of the topic." SLJ

Includes glossary

McMahon, Peter

Ultimate trains. Kids Can Press 2010 40p il (Machines of the future) $16.95

Grades: 4 5 6 7   385

1. Railroads 2. Science -- Experiments

ISBN 978-1-55453-366-4; 1-55453-366-X

"In simple engaging text and illustrations, McMahon and Mora present a brief history of [railroads]. Integral to the book are five experiments children can create. . . . Each experiment ties in well with a particular type of train, features clear instructions, and offers safety precautions." Booklist

Includes glossary

Murphy, Jim

Across America on an emigrant train. Clarion Bks. 1993 150p il hardcover o.p. pa $10.95

Grades: 5 6 7 8   385

1. Poets 2. Authors 3. Novelists 4. Authors, Scottish 5. Essayists 6. Travel writers 7. Short story writers 8. Railroads -- History 9. United States -- Description and travel

ISBN 0-395-63390-7; 0-395-76483-1 pa

LC 92-38650

"Murphy presents a forthright and thoroughly engrossing history of the transcontinental railway, with entries from Robert Louis Stevenson's 1879 journal as he rode cross country. It's also an inviting introduction to Stevenson, with a romance in the bargain." SLJ

Includes bibliographical references

Perritano, John

The **transcontinental** railroad. Children's Press 2010 48p il map (True book) lib bdg $26; pa $6.95

Grades: 3 4 5   385

1. Railroads -- History 2. Central Pacific Railroad 3. West (U.S.) -- Exploration 4. Union Pacific Railroad Company

ISBN 978-0-531-20585-3 lib bdg; 978-0-531-21248-6 pa

LC 2009014185

This introduction to the history of the transcontinental railroads provides "elementary readers with clear explanations, maps, illustrations, time lines, and engaging reproductions of primary resources. [This] volume contains eye-catching quick facts; illustrations and photographs are representational of regional Native Americans, pioneers, and explorers. This is ideal material for reports on the Westward expansion." SLJ

Includes bibliographical references

Simon, Seymour

★ **Seymour** Simon's book of trains. HarperCollins Pubs. 2002 un il $16.99; lib bdg $17.89; pa $6.99

Grades: K 1 2 3   385

1. Railroads

ISBN 0-06-028475-7; 0-06-028476-5 lib bdg; 0-06-446223-4 pa

LC 2001-24020

"Each double-page spread in this picture book sets a dramatic close-up photo of a moving train opposite a few sentences about the train's source of power (steam, diesel, electric) and how it works. The full-color, close-up pictures by a number of photographers will grab even young preschoolers. . . . The astonishing facts will interest older train buffs." Booklist

Steele, Phillip W.

Legendary journeys: trains. Kingfisher 2010 30p $19.99

Grades: 3 4 5   385

1. Railroads -- History

ISBN 978-0-7534-6465-6; 0-7534-6465-9

"The squat, wide format of this book is already well-suited to its subject matter, and it becomes even more so when its trick is revealed: five pages pull out, almost tripling the scenes' width and unveiling additional railroad cars. Steele provides an informative chronology of locomotive history from the advent of steam power to the rise of luxury trains." Publ Wkly

Zimmermann, Karl R.

★ **All** aboard! passenger trains around the world. [by] Karl Zimmermann; photography by the author. Boyds Mills Press 2006 48p il $19.95

Grades: 5 6 7 8   385

1. Railroads

ISBN 1-59078-325-5

LC 2005-24990

Zimmermann "has traveled by train across six continents, and his beautiful, big color photos appear on every double-page spread of this enthusiastic account, which blends history, geography, business, and engineering with his personal focus." Booklist

★ **Steam** locomotives; whistling, chugging, smoking iron horses of the past. Boyds Mills Press 2004 48p il $19.95

Grades: 4 5 6 7   385

1. Locomotives 2. Steam engines

ISBN 1-59078-165-1

"In this photo-essay, Zimmermann shares his excitement for steam locomotives with young readers, tracing the development of the early engines and their impact on the history of the U.S. He includes a clear explanation . . . of how a steam engine works. The photographs, some archival and some from the present day, are excellent. . . . The engaging text clearly imparts the author's enthusiasm and love for the subject." SLJ

Includes glossary

386 Inland waterway and ferry transportation

Harness, Cheryl

★ The **amazing** impossible Erie Canal. Macmillan Bks. for Young Readers 1995 un il map hardcover o.p. pa $5.99

Grades: 3 4 5 **386**

1. Erie Canal (N.Y.)

ISBN 0-02-742641-6; 0-689-82584-6 pa

LC 94-11114

"Harness has done a wonderful job of making the history and construction of the Erie Canal come alive. . . . The narrative is matched with illustrations that cover each page." SLJ

Includes bibliographical references

Kendall, Martha E.

The **Erie** Canal; by Martha E. Kendall. National Geographic 2008 128p il $18.95; lib bdg $28.90

Grades: 4 5 6 **386**

1. Erie Canal (N.Y.)

ISBN 978-1-4263-0022-6; 978-1-4263-0023-3 lib bdg

LC 2007029386

"This handsomely packaged introduction to our country's first great public works project pairs plenty of period prints and photos to a fluidly written account of the canal's origins, construction, uses and the folklore surrounding it." Booklist

387.1 Ports

House, Katherine L.

Lighthouses for kids; history, science, and lore with 21 activities. [by] Katherine L. House. Chicago Review Press 2008 118p il pa $14.95

Grades: 4 5 6 7 8 **387.1**

1. Lighthouses

ISBN 978-1-55652-720-3 pa; 1-55652-720-9 pa

LC 2007-27093

"This book is noteworthy for the way in which the activities are related to the information in the text. . . . Readers learn about the challenges of building . . . [lighthouses], inventions to make them more reliable, and how lighthouses function as historical relics today." SLJ

Includes glossary and bibliographical references

387.2 Ships

Barton, Byron

★ **Boats**. Crowell 1986 un il lib bdg $16.89; bd bk $6.99

Grades: K 1 **387.2**

1. Ships 2. Boats and boating

ISBN 0-690-04536-0 lib bdg; 0-694-01165-7 bd bk

LC 85-47900

Depicts a variety of boats and a cruise ship docking and unloading passengers

"Thick black outlines contain vivid colors . . . clean lines, bright hues, and undemanding text." Booklist

Floca, Brian

★ **Lightship**. Atheneum Books for Young Readers 2007 un il $16.99

Grades: K 1 2 **387.2**

1. Lightships

ISBN 978-1-4169-2436-4; 1-4169-2436-1

LC 2005-28028

"Lightships—floating lighthouses—were retired in 1983, but they live on in Floca's handsome picture book, which uses simple words and repeated phrases to emphasize the vessels' purpose and uniqueness as well as their day-to-day operation. . . . Some pictures include elements of humor, while other scenes are notable for their quiet beauty." Booklist

Lavery, Brian

Legendary journeys: ships; illustrated Sebastian Quigley. Kingfisher 2011 il $19.99

Grades: 3 4 5 **387.2**

1. Ships

ISBN 978-0-7534-6681-0; 0-7534-6681-3

"Compelling details and interactive effects appear throughout this guide to ships. . . . Recreations of Greek triremes, Viking longships, and the Titanic, among others, are enhanced by slide-out pages that double (or more) the spreads' width, providing a sense of the boats' scale. Flaps reveal cross-sections of ships' interiors, while depictions of naval, cargo, and other commercial vessels emphasize our continued reliance on ships. A thorough and well-constructed guide for boat fanatics." Publ Wkly

Zimmermann, Karl R.

★ **Ocean** liners; crossing and cruising the seven seas. photographs by the author. Boyds Mills Press 2008 48p il $17.95

Grades: 5 6 7 8 **387.2**

1. Ocean liners 2. Ocean travel

ISBN 978-1-59078-552-2; 1-59078-552-5

LC 2007049323

This is "a comprehensive overview of ships from sail to steam to diesel, from the important modes of transportation to the modern resorts at sea. The information is organized in chapters about the history and development of the ships, the star ships of the Atlantic crossings and the conversion to modern cruising. . . . All is accompanied by photographs taken over the years by the author and supplemented by historic drawings, photos and documents. . . . A fascinating voyage." Kirkus

Includes glossary

387.7 Air transportation

Barton, Byron

★ **Airplanes**. Crowell 1986 un il lib bdg $15.89

Grades: PreK K 1 **387.7**

1. Airplanes

ISBN 0-690-04532-8

LC 85-47899

Brief text and illustrations present a variety of airplanes and what they do, "as well as some of the usual scenes surrounding each (e.g., workers checking a passenger plane). Brightly colored illustrations outlined in heavy black convey a bold and simple first impression, yet they portray a good number of accurate details that preschoolers find so fascinating." SLJ

★ **Airport**. Crowell 1982 un il lib bdg $18.89; pa $6.99

Grades: PreK K 1   **387.7**

  1. Airports 2. Airplanes

  ISBN 0-690-04169-1 lib bdg; 0-06-443145-2 pa

                                       LC 79-7816

"In a brightly illustrated book, the author/artist captures the hustle and bustle of passenger traffic from arrival at the terminal to take off." Kobrin Letter

"Byron Barton introduces young readers to the fun of the airport in this bold and colorful book. From the excitement of arrival to the wonder of taking off, Airport captures all the magic of an airport with joyous and powerful images and simple text. Perfect for fans of Richard Scarry and Tom Lichtenheld!" Publisher's Note

Parker, Steve

  By air. Marshall Cavendish Benchmark 2011 il (Future transport)

Grades: 4 5 6   **387.7**

  1. Aeronautics 2. Forecasting

  ISBN 1608707776; 9781608707775

                                   LC 2011000998

"Beginning with a speculative illustration featuring people of the future traveling through the air in carlike personal jets, this title . . . offers a fascinating look at prototypes for all sorts of aircraft, from small planes to passenger airliners to lighter-than-air vehicles. . . . The various possibilities for future aircraft are covered in double-page spreads that are well laid out and easy to digest. Illustrated with plenty of striking, digitally enhanced color pictures, this will probably be of equal interest to those doing reports and browsers." Booklist

Includes bibliographical references

  My first trip on an airplane. Heinemann Library 2011 24p il (Growing up) lib bdg $22; pa $6.49

Grades: PreK K 1 2   **387.7**

  1. Airports 2. Airplanes 3. Aeronautics

  ISBN 978-1-4329-4801-6 lib bdg; 1-4329-4801-6 lib bdg; 978-1-4329-4811-5 pa; 1-4329-4811-3 pa

                                   LC 2010024195

This book examines a "common, often scary [event] in children's lives and [guides] readers through [it] step-by-step. The [author discusses] the who, what, and why of [the] experience . . . [including] what happens before and during a flight. . . . By confronting . . . fears head-on, children will feel 'in the know' and be prepared to experience [this first]. The text—two sentences per page in a large font and placed on white space—is accompanied by large color photos of children, families, and adults of a variety of ethnic backgrounds. [The] volume includes boldface vocabulary words, a picture glossary, and dos and don'ts." SLJ

Includes glossary and bibliographical references

388 Transportation

Flatt, Lizann

  Let's go! the story of getting from there to here. [by] Lizann Flatt; illustrated by Scot Ritchie. Maple Tree 2007 un il $16.95

Grades: K 1 2   **388**

  1. Transportation

  ISBN 978-1-897349-02-1; 1-897349-02-5

"A breezy picture book introduction to modes of North American transportation from foot power to space vehicle. The book is rich in descriptive language and follows a logical time line. . . . Vivid, double-page spreads of artwork, rendered in rainbow colors, provide added details." SLJ

Gaarder-Juntti, Oona

  What in the world is green transportation? ABDO Pub. Company 2011 24p il (Going green) lib bdg $24.21

Grades: 1 2 3 4   **388**

  1. Transportation -- Environmental aspects

  ISBN 978-1-61613-193-7 lib bdg; 1-61613-193-4 lib bdg

                                   LC 2010004310

"The lively layout design, featuring colorful headings, short paragraphs, and attractive photographs, has a scrapbook-like quality. . . . [The title explains] how all our choices require energy and resources, and encourage readers to make changes in their lifestyles. . . . [This] . . . will inspire and empower readers to make a difference." SLJ

Includes glossary and bibliographical references

Konrad, Marla Stewart

  Getting there. Tundra Books 2009 un il (World vision early readers) $12.95

Grades: PreK K   **388**

  1. Transportation

  ISBN 978-0-88776-867-5; 0-88776-867-9

"This book depicts an ordinary aspect of every child's life—getting from one place to another. . . . What makes it extraordinary are the images that depict the journey: a child in Africa sitting on his mother's shoulders, for example, or a little girl riding a yak to her destination. Each spread includes an easy, large-font sentence or phrase, but it is the stunning color photographs that tell the richer story. Sure to spark questions, observations, and awe." SLJ

Mulder, Michelle, 1976-

  Pedal it! how bicycles are changing the world. Michelle Mulder. Orca Book Publishers 2013 48 p. (Footprints) (hardcover) $19.95

Grades: 3 4 5 6 7 8   **388**

  1. Cycling 2. Bicycles

  ISBN 1459802195; 9781459802193

                                   LC 2012953464

This book, by Michelle Mulder, "celebrates the humble bicycle--from the very first boneshakers to the sleek racing bikes of today, from handlebars to spokes to gear sprockets--and shows you why and how bikes can make the world a better place. Not only can bikes be used to power computers and generators, they can also reduce pollution, promote wellness and get a package across a crowded city--fast!" (Publisher's note)

Wooldridge, Connie Nordhielm

Just fine the way they are; from dirt roads to rail roads to interstates. illustrated by Richard Walz. Calkins Creek 2011 un il $17.95

Grades: 2 3 4 5   388

1. Roads 2. Transportation

ISBN 978-1-59078-710-6; 1-59078-710-2

"Wooldridge's picture book traces the development of the National Road in the United States. . . . Wooldridge interjects the public's positive and negative opinions regarding the road's development and describes how the inventions of the steam engine and automobile influenced changes in the highway, which ultimately became Route 40 and crossed the country. As the story winds down, Wooldridge raises the problem of air pollution. Her folksy, conversational writing style incorporates flavorful language. . . . Muscular horses, changing modes of transportation, and caricatured people populate the bright artwork." SLJ

Includes bibliographical references

388.4   Local transportation

Miller, Heather

★ Subway ride; illustrated by Sue Rama. Charlesbridge 2009 un il lib bdg $15.95

Grades: PreK K 1   388.4

1. Subways

ISBN 978-1-58089-111-0 lib bdg; 1-58089-111-X lib bdg

LC 2008-7249

"Take a ride on subway trains all around the world. Beginning in Cairo, a multicultural group of children rides the trains in ten cities, zigzagging from stop to stop around the globe. . . . Vivid colors and blurred lines evoke a bustling cheer. Cleverly composed to suggest both depth and action, the pictures tell most of the story. . . . The offbeat idea is deftly handled and should trigger further study." Kirkus

389   Metrology and standardization

Adler, David A.

Time zones; illustrated by Edward Miller. Holiday House 2010 31p il map $16.95

Grades: 3 4 5   389

1. Time

ISBN 978-0-8234-2201-2; 0-8234-2201-1

LC 2009007733

"Adler offers a simple but thorough explanation of time zones and why people experience different parts of the day simultaneously depending on their location around the globe. Illustrations of an astronaut and his robot dog provide a perspective from high above Earth, which helps readers visualize the way sunlight reaches different parts of the planet as it rotates. . . . Numerous maps and diagrams help visualize these abstract boundaries, including the international date line in the Pacific. . . . Adler explains the impact of daylight savings time and includes a simple experiment for readers to see for themselves how noon and midnight occur simultaneously on opposite sides of the globe." SLJ

Bernhard, Durga

While you are sleeping; a lift-the-flap book of time around the world. Charlesbridge 2011 un il map $14.95

Grades: PreK K 1 2 3   389

1. Time 2. Time -- Systems and standards 3. Children's literature -- Works -- Preschool

ISBN 978-1-57091-473-7; 1-57091-473-7

LC 2010007589

"A clever design allows readers to travel the world, one page turn at a time. . . . The illustrations show an Alaskan child curled up in bed with a parent at 10 p.m., facing a map of Africa, Nigeria highlighted, with an inset gatefold. A flip reveals a young Nigerian girl at 9 a.m. Turning the page reveals that same Nigerian girl opposite a Japanese child . . . and so on until the circular tale returns to Alaska. Teachers will appreciate Bernhard's incorporation of 12- and 24-hour digital clocks, as well as the analog clock hiding under each gatefold. The final page is a map of the world delineated by time zone and includes thumbnails from each highlighted country. A small text block explains the reason for the time zones and tells how they work. Gorgeous illustrations combine beautiful colors with a glimpse of life in other countries." Kirkus

Murphy, Stuart J.

Mighty Maddie; comparing weights. illustrated by Bernice Lum. HarperCollins Publishers 2004 31p il (MathStart) hardcover o.p. pa $4.99

Grades: K 1 2   389

1. Cleanliness 2. Weights and measures

ISBN 0-06-053159-2; 0-06-053161-4 pa

LC 2003-17610

As Maddie cleans up her room, she learns how to compare the weights of various objects

"Childlike line drawings with bright colors give readers a sense of action. This appealing book has uses beyond the math concept, and offers messages about family life, self-image, and responsibility." SLJ

391   Customs

Bliss, John

Preening, painting, and piercing; body art. Raintree 2010 32p il (Culture in action) lib bdg $29

Grades: 5 6 7 8   391

1. Body art 2. Cosmetics 3. Tattooing 4. Theatrical makeup

ISBN 978-1-4109-3924-1; 1-4109-3924-1

LC 2009051182

"This book covers different looks achieved through makeup, body painting, tattoos, and piercing. Photographs, advertisements, paintings, and artifacts show a variety of cultures and time periods and help readers see the huge changes in the fashion of physical appearance. . . . The author does a good job of explaining that some cultures have negative stereotypes of tattooed people being criminals and some piercing can be dangerous to people with allergies. Fun activities are included. . . . This book . . . is well written and has few biases." SLJ

Includes glossary and bibliographical references

DeCarufel, Laura

Learn to speak fashion; a guide to creating, showcasing, and promoting your style. DeCarufel, Laura. Owlkids Books, Inc. 2012 96 p. (hardcover) $22.95

Grades: 4 5 6 391

1. Fashion 2. Fashion -- Handbooks, manuals, etc. 3. Clothing and dress

ISBN 1926973372; 9781926973371

LC 2011941966

Author Laura deCarufel "takes preteen readers with her on the 'clothes + art = fashion' formula. She starts with finding one's own style and continues with learning to see: using visual curiosity to examine design, pattern, color and so on to find what inspires. Window shopping, building a wardrobe, preparing a sketchbook and learning to sew are all part of the plan. She gives advice about runway shows, models, fashion shoots, stylists and so on." (Kirkus)

Jaber, Pamela

When royals wore ruffles; a funny & fashionable alphabet! written by Chesley McLaren and Pamela Jaber; illustrated by Chesley McLaren. Schwartz & Wade Books 2009 un il $16.99; lib bdg $19.99

Grades: K 1 2 3 391

1. Alphabet 2. Fashion -- History 3. Clothing and dress -- History

ISBN 978-0-375-85166-7; 0-375-85166-6; 978-0-375-95166-4 lib bdg; 0-375-95166-0 lib bdg

LC 2008017374

McLaren and "Jaber cover the fashion waterfront, enlightening readers on both history . . . and the less tangible aspects of glamour. . . . The commentary is smart and accessible. . . . Witty as the writing may be, the illustrations are irresistible. Like the best fashion, the lines and colors feel effortlessly right." Publ Wkly

Krull, Kathleen

★ **Big** wig; a little history of hair. illustrated by Peter Malone. Arthur A. Levine Books 2011 un il $18.99

Grades: 3 4 5 6 391

1. Hair 2. Fashion

ISBN 978-0-439-67640-3; 0-439-67640-1

LC 2010031005

"Krull delivers a fascinating and quite funny 'history' of humankind's relationship with hair, from furry prehistory to the advent of punk style. . . . Equally wonderful are Malone's gouache illustrations, rife with humor." Publ Wkly

Includes bibliographical references

Morris, Ann

Hats, hats, hats; photographs by Ken Heyman. Lothrop, Lee & Shepard Bks. 1989 un il $16; pa $4.95

Grades: PreK K 1 391

1. Hats

ISBN 0-688-06338-1; 0-688-12274-4 pa

LC 88-26676

This book introduces a variety of hats worn around the world

"The vivid color photographs, one or two per page, show people engaged in lively activities while . . . wearing their hats. Each picture offers a strong ethnic identity or a thought-provoking human interaction, with captions of only a few words in large print. An unusual index . . . gives background information about the pictures, citing the countries of origin and a few facts about each . . . kind of hat." SLJ

Shoes, shoes, shoes. Lothrop, Lee & Shepard Bks. 1995 32p il hardcover o.p. pa $4.95

Grades: PreK K 1 391

1. Shoes

ISBN 0-688-13666-4; 0-688-16166-9 pa

LC 94-46649

"Morris gives a world-tour of shoes . . . in [a] picture book illustrated by various photographers. In rhyming text, she talks about shoes for all kinds of activities. . . . [The] book includes a map and a photograph key of the places visited." Bull Cent Child Books

Platt, Richard

They wore what?! the weird history of fashion and beauty. [by] Richard Platt. Two-Can 2007 48p il $16.95; pa $9.95

Grades: 4 5 6 391

1. Personal appearance 2. Fashion -- History

ISBN 978-1-58728-582-0; 1-58728-582-7; 978-1-58728-584-4 pa; 1-58728-584-3 pa

LC 2006039159

Published in the United Kingdom with title: Would you believe in 1500, platform shoes were outlawed?

"Busy, colorful pages recount the historical, social, and political sides of clothing, hair, hats, and shoes, from legal and moral issues such as wearing fur to dangerous practices like cinched waists and bound feet. . . . Ever-fluctuating ideas of beauty and body image are also explored." Horn Book Guide

Includes glossary and bibliographical references

Rowland-Warne, L.

Costume; written by L. Rowland-Warne; [special photography, Liz McAulay] Dorling Kindersley 2000 63p il (DK eyewitness books) $15.99; lib bdg $19.99

Grades: 4 5 6 7 391

1. Costume 2. Clothing and dress 3. Fashion -- History

ISBN 0-7894-5586-2; 0-7894-6584-1 lib bdg

First published 1992 by Knopf

Photographs and text document the history and meaning of clothing, from loincloths to modern children's clothes

Swain, Ruth Freeman

Underwear; what we wear under there. by Ruth Freeman Swain; illustrated by John O'Brien. Holiday House 2008 32p il $16.95

Grades: 2 3 4 5 391

1. Underwear 2. Fashion -- History

ISBN 978-0-8234-1920-3; 0-8234-1920-7

LC 2008-4041

"Swain packs a lot of detail into the text as she quickly and chronologically progresses through a discussion of different types of underwear throughout the ages and how it has accommodated people's lifestyles. Children will find a multitude of interesting historical tidbits. . . . The winsome, imaginative illustrations vary in size and are rendered in watercolor over ink." SLJ

391.4   Kinds of garments; accessories; buttons

Kyi, Tanya Lloyd

   50 underwear questions; a bare-all history. by Tanya Kyi and illustrated by Ross Kinnaird. Annick Press 2011 116 p. $21.95

Grades: 4 5 6 7   **391.4**

   1. Underwear 2. Clothing and dress -- History

   ISBN 1554513537; 9781554513536

This book, by Tanya Kyi and illustrated by Ross Kinnaird, examines the history of underwear. "The format, as the title indicates, is question-and-answer. Beginning with 'ancient undies,' the questions cover everything from what's worn under certain kinds of dress to how the modern bra came into being, and reasons for wearing underclothes in the first place." (Booklist)

392   Customs of life cycle and domestic life

Laroche, Giles

   ★ If you lived here; houses of the world. Houghton Mifflin Harcourt 2011 un il $16.99

Grades: K 1 2 3   **392**

   1. Houses

   ISBN 978-0-547-23892-0; 0-547-23892-4

                       LC 2010044361

   "Laroche applies his signature bas-relief cut-paper collage technique to sixteen different dwellings that illustrate the range of places that people call home. . . . Each . . . is introduced with a paragraph that begins with the phrase 'If you lived here,' enticing the reader to imagine how it might be. . . . For young readers, these profiles not only provide glimpses into the lives of people who might live very differently from us but also expand and broaden their worldview." Horn Book

Lauber, Patricia

   ★ What you never knew about beds, bedrooms, and pajamas; illustrated by John Manders. Simon & Schuster Books for Young Readers 2007 un il (Around-the-house history) $16.95

Grades: 2 3 4   **392**

   1. Sleeping customs

   ISBN 0-689-85211-8

                       LC 2004-20654

   "Focusing on sleeping customs through the ages, Lauber begins with the Stone Age and moves up to the 1700s, but includes some more contemporary facts as well. . . . Manders's engaging artwork varies between full-page and spot illustrations. The humorous asides from characters in the comic-style pictures will entertain youngsters." SLJ

   Includes bibliographical references

393   Death customs

Carney, Elizabeth

   Mummies. National Geographic 2009 31p il (National Geographic readers) lib bdg $11.90; pa $3.99

Grades: 1 2 3   **393**

   1. Mummies

   ISBN 978-1-4263-0529-0 lib bdg; 1-4263-0529-X lib bdg; 978-1-4263-0528-3 pa; 1-4263-0528-1 pa

                       LC 2009-3630

   "In challenging but readable text for early independent readers, Carney highlights mummies discovered all over the world. Details such as a 2,300-year-old vegetable soup in one mummy's stomach and another's still-soft hair and skin raise the bar on an already high-interest topic. Photographs don't shy away from showing human remains." Horn Book Guide

Deem, James M.

   ★ Bodies from the ice; melting glaciers and the recovery of the past. Houghton Mifflin 2008 58p il map $17

Grades: 5 6 7 8 9 10   **393**

   1. Mummies 2. Glaciers

   ISBN 978-0-618-80045-2; 0-618-80045-X

                       LC 2008-01868

   A Sibert Medal honor book, 2009

   This describes the discovery of human remains preserved in glaciers in the Alps, the Andes, The Himalayas, and other places around the world and what can be learned from them

   "Full-color photographs, reproductions, and maps are clearly captioned; grand images of glaciated mountain peaks span entire pages, and detailed pictures of recovered objects . . . are presented. . . . [This] is a fantastic resource. Deem superbly weaves diverse geographical settings, time periods, and climate issues into a readable work that reveals the increasing interdisciplinary dimensions of the sciences." SLJ

   Includes bibliographical references

Halls, Kelly Milner

   Mysteries of the mummy kids. Darby Creek Pub. 2007 72p il map $18.95

Grades: 4 5 6 7   **393**

   1. Mummies

   ISBN 978-1-58196-059-4; 1-58196-059-X

   "Halls presents an eerily fascinating exploration of mummified children and teens found in South and North America, Europe, and Asia. . . . The writing style is plain yet absorbing, presenting scientific and historical information in simple terms." Voice Youth Advocates

   Includes bibliographical references

Knapp, Ron

   Mummy secrets uncovered. Enslow Publishers 2011 48p il (Bizarre science) lib bdg $23.93

Grades: 5 6 7 8   **393**

   1. Mummies

   ISBN 978-0-7660-3670-3; 0-7660-3670-7

                       LC 2010000976

   First published 1996 with title: Mummies

   This describes mummies such as the Iceman found in the Italian Alps in 1991, King Tut of Egypt, the people of Pompeii killed by the eruption of Mount Vesuvius, Tollund Man found in Denmark in 1950, and the Ice Maiden found in the Siberian Steppes

   "Aimed at reluctant readers, [this title is] sure to disgust and delight in equal measure. . . . [The title] will pique interest and get kids lining up at the reference desk looking for

more. The text is complemented by illustrations and magnified photos of things that you would hope never to see." SLJ
Includes glossary and bibliographical references

Markle, Sandra
★ **Outside** and inside mummies. Walker & Co. 2005 40p il $17.95; lib bdg $18.85
Grades: 4 5 6 7   **393**
1. Mummies
ISBN 0-8027-8966-8; 0-8027-8967-6 lib bdg
LC 2004-66128
"Markle explores a global smorgasbord of mummy varieties, both those created by human procedures and those caused by nature. Crisp (if gruesome) color photos accompany the readable, informative text, which discusses not only the mummification process, but also the cutting-edge technologies used by forensic anthropologists and others to study the mummies themselves." SLJ
Includes glossary

Rau, Dana Meachen
Mummies. Marshall Cavendish Benchmark 2010 24p il (Surprising science) lib bdg $22.79
Grades: 2 3 4   **393**
1. Mummies
ISBN 978-0-7614-4869-3; 0-7614-4869-1
LC 2009053761
"Colorfully illustrated with photographs on each page, this . . . will be well received by elementary students and educators." Libr Media Connect
Includes glossary and bibliographical references

Robson, David
The **mummy**. ReferencePoint Press 2011 il (Monsters and mythical creatures) $27.95
Grades: 6 7 8 9   **393**
1. Mummies
ISBN 978-1-60152-182-8; 1-60152-182-0
LC 2011022437
This is "an ideal starting point for young researchers interested in the weird, mysterious, and paranormal. Using fleet, descriptive prose to communicate the impressively researched (and sourced) information, [this] medium-length [work manages] to rope in just about everything, from folklore to history to pop culture. . . . TheMummy begins with the seminal 1932 Boris Karloff film before backtracking into the worldwide 'mummy lust' that began with the 1922 discovery of King Tut's tomb and and the subsequent curses and legends. . . . The illustrations are fine and varied, the sidebars always illuminating, and the back matter robust." Booklist
Includes bibliographical references

Sloan, Christopher
Mummies. National Geographic 2010 48p il (National Geographic Kids) $17.95; lib bdg $26.90
Grades: 4 5 6 7   **393**
1. Mummies
ISBN 978-1-4263-0695-2; 1-4263-0695-4; 978-1-4263-0696-9 lib bdg; 1-4263-0696-2 lib bdg
LC 2010-08498
"A gratifyingly grisly album of choice photos accompanies Sloan's lucid, informative text as he describes not only the mummification processes but also individual mummies

produced whether by intent or by chance. From the dried Beauty of Krorän in China to the bundled Lady of Cao in a Peruvian pyramid or the familiar Boy King Tut in Egypt, a global variety is offered to fascinated readers. . . . [This is a] well-written, heavily illustrated glimpse into the world of after-death preservation, either by accident or design." SLJ
Includes glossary and bibliographical references

394   General customs

Gibbons, Gail
★ **Knights** in shining armor. Little, Brown 1995 un il hardcover o.p. pa $7.99
Grades: K 1 2 3   **394**
1. Medieval civilization 2. Knights and knighthood
ISBN 0-316-30948-6 lib bdg; 0-316-30038-1 pa
LC 94-35525
The author "covers tournaments, chivalry, and what happened when a bad knight was caught. Legendary knights such as Sir Gawain and the knights of the Round Table are briefly described, as is St. George and the dragon, and Gibbons also discusses present-day knights. The watercolor-and-ink pictures are some of Gibbons' liveliest and most attractive." Booklist

394.1   Eating, drinking; using drugs

Ancona, George
Come and eat. Charlesbridge 2011 il $16.95; pa $7.95
Grades: K 1 2   **394.1**
1. Eating customs
ISBN 158089366X; 1580893678; 9781580893664; 9781580893671
LC 2010033632
"This introduces food customs around the world for younger children. As focused on culture as on food, the brief, chatty text discusses the varied ways foods are eaten. . . . The clean design features full-color photos." Booklist

Augustin, Byron
The **food** of Mexico. Marshall Cavendish Benchmark 2011 il (Flavors of the world) $21.95
Grades: 4 5 6 7   **394.1**
1. Mexican cooking 2. Festivals -- Mexico 3. Mexico -- Social life and customs
ISBN 978-1-6087-0237-4
LC 2010013830
Includes bibliographical references

Ichord, Loretta Frances
★ **Double** cheeseburgers, quiche, and vegetarian burritos; American cooking from the 1920s through today. by Loretta Frances Ichord; illustrated by Jan Davey Ellis. Millbrook Press 2007 63p il (Cooking through time) lib bdg $25.26
Grades: 3 4 5 6   **394.1**
1. Cooking 2. Eating customs
ISBN 978-0-8225-5969-6 lib bdg; 0-8225-5969-2 lib bdg
LC 2005-24535

"Each chapter, illustrated with lighthearted drawings, presents a quick, cogent overview of an American eating trend—from the first processed foods through TV dinners, fast food, the mainstreaming of organic foods, and more—ending with the influential fad diets of the 1990s. The examples are clear and lively, and relevant recipes close each chapter." Booklist

Includes bibliographical references

Kras, Sara Louise

The **food** of Italy. Marshall Cavendish Benchmark 2011 il (Flavors of the world) $21.95

Grades: 4 5 6 7   **394.1**

1. Italian cooking 2. Festivals -- Italy 3. Italy -- Social life and customs

ISBN 978-1-6087-0236-7

LC 2010021542

This explores the culture, traditions, and festivals of Italy through its food.

Includes bibliographical references

Kummer, Patricia K.

The **food** of Thailand. Marshall Cavendish Benchmark 2011 il (Flavors of the world) $21.95

Grades: 4 5 6 7   **394.1**

1. Thai cooking 2. Festivals -- Thailand 3. Thailand -- Social life and customs

ISBN 978-1-6087-0238-1

LC 2010023508

This explores the culture, traditions, and festivals of Thailand through its food.

Includes bibliographical references

Lauber, Patricia

★ **What** you never knew about fingers, forks, & chopsticks; illustrated by John Manders. Simon & Schuster Bks. for Young Readers 1999 un il (Around-the-house history) $16

Grades: 2 3 4   **394.1**

1. Tableware 2. Eating customs 3. Table etiquette

ISBN 0-689-80479-2

LC 97-17041

Describes changes in eating customs throughout the centuries and the origins of table manners

"A delicious blend of humor and fascinating facts. . . . The lively, linear drawings incorporate amusing asides in dialogue balloons that will entertain readers as the text enlightens them about the subject." SLJ

Includes bibliographical references

Orr, Tamra

The **food** of Greece; [by] Tamra B. Orr. Marshall Cavendish Benchmark 2011 il (Flavors of the world) $21.95

Grades: 4 5 6 7   **394.1**

1. Greek cooking 2. Festivals -- Greece 3. Greece -- Social life and customs

ISBN 978-1-6087-0235-0; 978-1-6087-0688-4 e-book

LC 2010035820

This explores the culture, traditions, and festivals of Greece through its food.

Includes bibliographical references

Orr, Tamra B.

The **food** of China; [by] Tamra B. Orr. Marshall Cavendish Benchmark 2011 il (Flavors of the world)

Grades: 4 5 6 7   **394.1**

1. Chinese cooking 2. Festivals -- China 3. China -- Social life and customs

ISBN 1-608-70234-0; 978-1-608-70234-3; 978-1-608-70687-7 e-book

LC 2010039293

This explores the culture, traditions, and festivals of China through its food.

"Numerous high-quality, close-up color photos of outdoor vegetable markets, food in various stages of preparation, and families gathering around the table will keep readers engaged (and hungry) throughout the accessible and enlightening food tour." Booklist

Includes bibliographical references

Silverstein, Alvin

Chocolate ants, maggot cheese, and more; the yucky food book. by Alvin and Virginia Silverstein and Laura Silverstein Nunn; illustrated by Gerald Kelley. Enslow Publishers 2010 48p il (Yucky science) lib bdg $23.93

Grades: 4 5 6 7   **394.1**

1. Eating customs

ISBN 978-0-7660-3315-3 lib bdg; 0-7660-3315-5 lib bdg

LC 2009012283

"Written in an engaging and conversational style and full of revolting descriptions and entertaining cartoon illustrations . . . [this is] sure to turn even the strongest stomach. An introduction . . . puts 'yucky' in perspective, reminding kids that our world is diverse and that everyone has a different definition of repulsive." SLJ

Includes glossary and bibliographical references

394.12   Eating and Drinking

Mogren, Molly

Andrew Zimmern's field guide to exceptionally weird, wild, & wonderful foods; an intrepid eater's digest. by Andrew Zimmern. 1st ed. Feiwel & Friends 2012 197 p. ill. (paperback) $14.99; (hardcover) $19.99

Grades: 5 6 7   **394.12**

1. Food 2. Cooking

ISBN 0312606613; 125001929X; 9780312606619; 9781250019295

LC 2012289475

This book is a "guide to world cuisine." The authors Andrew Zimmern and Molly Mogren "focus on 40 unusual foodstuffs including cockroaches, guinea pigs, headcheese, lutefisk, turducken, and Twinkies. Recipes, interviews, and a great many facts . . . lead to . . . digressions, including suggestions on how to survive a zombie outbreak . . . and a time line of popular dances, following a discussion of eating 'dancing' (live) shrimp." (Publishers Weekly)

394.2   Special occasions

Ancona, George

Powwow; photographs and text by George Ancona. Harcourt Brace Jovanovich 1993 un il hardcover o.p. pa $10

Grades: 3 4 5 6   **394.2**

1. Crow Fair (Crow Agency, Mont.) 2. Native Americans -- Rites and ceremonies

ISBN 0-15-263268-9; 0-15-263269-7 pa

LC 92-15912

A photo essay on the pan-Indian celebration called a powwow, this particular one being held on the Crow Reservation in Montana

The book is "illustrated with well-placed, full-color photos that clearly reflect the text. . . . An exquisite kaleidoscope of Native American music, customs, and crafts." SLJ

Johnston, Tony

Day of the Dead; illustrated by Jeanette Winter. Harcourt Brace & Co. 1997 un il hardcover o.p. pa $6

Grades: PreK K 1 2   **394.2**

1. Mexico -- Fiction 2. All Souls' Day -- Fiction

ISBN 0-15-222863-2; 0-15-202446-8 pa

LC 96-2276

Describes a Mexican family preparing for and celebrating the Day of the Dead

"Spanish phrases are a natural part of the storytelling as the children ask questions about the cooking and preparations. . . . Winter's brilliantly colored, acrylic illustratons in folk-art style express the magic realism that is part of the ceremony under the stars." Booklist

394.26   Holidays

Chocolate, Debbi

My first Kwanzaa book; illustrated by Cal Massey. Scholastic 1992 un il hardcover o.p. pa $5.99

Grades: K 1 2   **394.26**

1. Kwanzaa 2. African Americans -- Social life and customs

ISBN 0-590-45762-4; 0-439-12926-5 pa

LC 92-1200

Introduces Kwanzaa, the holiday in which Afro-Americans celebrate their cultural heritage

"The book effectively conveys the spirit of the holiday through the text and the acrylic paint and colored-pencil illustrations, all outlined in a thin line of earthy brown." SLJ

Includes glossary

Craats, Rennay

Columbus Day; American celebrations. AV2 by Weigl Pubs. 2011 24p il (American celebrations) lib bdg $27.13; pa $11.95

Grades: 3 4 5   **394.26**

1. Explorers 2. Columbus Day 3. America -- Exploration

ISBN 978-1-60596-775-2 lib bdg; 1-60596-6775-0 lib bdg; 978-1-60596-933-6 pa; 1-60596-933-8 pa; 978-1-60596-940-4 e-book

LC 2009050986

First published 2004

This book about Columbus Day "is well positioned to plug holes in school units on holidays, with [a] punchy, informative [entry] on the past and present [history] of [the holiday]. The colorful [layout features] an ever-shifting mix of period and modern photographs, while sidebars keep things from settling too comfortably into the organizing structure, which is: . . . introduction, history, key personalities, celebrations, symbols, and activities." Booklist

Demi

Happy, happy Chinese New Year! Crown Pubs. 2003 un il $8.95

Grades: K 1 2 3   **394.26**

1. Chinese New Year 2. China -- Social life and customs

ISBN 0-375-82642-4

LC 2003-43469

First published in different form 1997 with title: Happy New Year! Kung-Hsi Fa-ts'ai!

Examines the customs, traditions, food, and lore associated with the celebration of Chinese New Year

Farmer, Jacqueline

O Christmas tree; its history and holiday traditions. illustrated by Joanne Friar. Charlesbridge 2010 un il lib bdg $16.95; pa $7.95

Grades: 1 2 3 4   **394.26**

1. Christmas trees

ISBN 978-1-58089-238-4 lib bdg; 1-58089-238-8 lib bdg; 978-1-58089-239-1 pa; 1-58089-239-6 pa

LC 2009027788

"This slender but informative book traces the roots and history of the Christmas tree through pagan and Christian practices over thousands of years. . . . Then the focus shifts to Christmas tree agriculture in North America: the varieties of trees grown, the stages of growing them, and the challenges of tree farming. . . . The clearly written text shows respect for its audience by introducing some stories . . . as legends rather than history. . . . Colorful gouache paintings brighten the presentation and provide visual information that complements the text." Booklist

Includes bibliographical references

Foran, Jill

Martin Luther King, Jr. Day; American celebrations. AV2 by Weigl Pubs. 2011 24p il (American celebrations) lib bdg $27.13; pa $11.95

Grades: 3 4 5   **394.26**

1. Clergy 2. Martin Luther King Day 3. Nonfiction writers 4. Civil rights activists 5. Nobel laureates for peace

ISBN 978-1-60596-772-1 lib bdg; 1-60596-772-6 lib bdg; 978-1-60596-779-0 pa; 1-60596-779-3 pa; 978-1-60596-937-4 e-book

LC 2009050988

First published 2004

This book about Martin Luther King Day "is well positioned to plug holes in school units on holidays, with [a] punchy, informative [entry] on the past and present histories of [the holiday]. The colorful [layout features] an ever-shifting mix of period and modern photographs, while sidebars keep things from settling too comfortably into the organizing structure: . . . introduction, history, key personalities, celebrations, symbols, and activities." Booklist

Gibbons, Gail

Easter. Holiday House 1989 un il lib bdg $16.95; pa $6.95

Grades: K 1 2 3 **394.26**

1. Easter

ISBN 0-8234-0737-3 lib bdg; 0-8234-0866-3 pa

LC 88-23292

Examines the background, significance, symbols, and traditions of Easter

Gibbons "simplifies complex beliefs and traditions in a straightforward way, though transitions are occasionally abrupt. Pleasing watercolors outlined in black ink illustrate the text." Booklist

Groundhog day! shadow or no shadow? by Gail Gibbons. Holiday House 2007 32p il $16.95

Grades: K 1 2 3 **394.26**

1. Marmots 2. Groundhog Day

ISBN 978-0-8234-2003-2; 0-8234-2003-5

LC 2006003456

"A look at some fascinating facts about this red-letter day, presented in Gibbons's signature style. Readers will learn about the traditions that led to the big celebration now held each year on February 2nd in Punxsutawney, PA. The author includes tidbits about the groundhog's diet, habitat, burrows, newborns/kits and looks at past cultures that depended on hibernating animals to help them determine the arrival of spring." SLJ

Halloween is-- Holiday House 2002 un il $16.95; pa $6.95

Grades: K 1 2 3 **394.26**

1. Halloween

ISBN 0-8234-1758-1; 0-8234-1797-2 pa

LC 2001-59429

Describes the origins and history of Halloween traditions and festivities from ancient times to the present day

"The new version of Gibbons' Halloween (1984) features a larger format, new illustrations, and a revised and slightly longer text as well as the new title. . . . Libraries with multiple copies of the earlier book will still find this version useful when the holiday rush is on, and given a choice, children will reach for this bigger, brighter, new edition." Booklist

St. Patrick's Day. Holiday House 1994 un il lib bdg $16.95; pa $6.95

Grades: K 1 2 3 **394.26**

1. Saint Patrick's Day

ISBN 0-8234-1119-2 lib bdg; 0-8234-1173-7 pa

LC 93-29570

"A basic introduction to the holiday—how it began, the life and works of St. Patrick, and the various ways in which the day is celebrated. The text is clear and concise, and the pages are full of information. Gibbons's simple, clean, full-page watercolor-and-ink illustrations flow logically from one to the next." SLJ

Hamilton, Lynn

Presidents' Day; American celebrations. AV2 by Weigl Pubs. 2011 24p il (American celebrations) lib bdg $27.13; pa $11.95

Grades: 3 4 5 **394.26**

1. Presidents' Day 2. Presidents -- United States

ISBN 978-1-60596-773-8 lib bdg; 1-60596-773-4 lib bdg; 978-1-60596-931-2 pa; 1-60596-931-1 pa; 978-1-60596-938-1 e-book

LC 2009050991

First published 2004

This book about Presidents' Day "is well positioned to plug holes in school units on holidays, with [a] punchy, informative [entry] on the past and present histories of [the holiday]. The colorful [layout features] an ever-shifting mix of period and modern photographs, while sidebars keep things from settling too comfortably into the organizing structure: . . . introduction, history, key personalities, celebrations, symbols, and activities. . . . With its fascinating account of the frequently renamed and repositioned holiday, Presidents' Day is a series standout and expands the idea of 'symbols' to include not just Mount Rushmore but also U.S. currency." Booklist

Heiligman, Deborah

★ Celebrate Christmas; [by] Deborah Heiligman; consultant, Reverend Father Nathan J.A. Humphrey. National Geographic 2007 31p il (Holidays around the world) $15.95; lib bdg $23.90

Grades: K 1 2 3 **394.26**

1. Christmas

ISBN 978-1-4263-0122-3; 978-1-4263-0123-0 lib bdg

LC 2007012659

"Brief text accompanies captivating and colorful photographs that demonstrate customs around the world. The use of bonfires and candles, Nativity plays, Advent wreaths, Three Kings Day, and Yule logs are among the topics touched upon. . . . A solid addition." SLJ

Includes glossary and bibliographical references

★ Celebrate Halloween; [by] Deborah Heiligman; consultant, Jack Santino. National Geographic Society 2007 31p il (Holidays around the world) $15.95; lib bdg $23.90

Grades: K 1 2 3 **394.26**

1. Halloween

ISBN 978-1-4263-0120-9; 978-1-4263-0121-6 lib bdg

LC 2007003121

In this introduction to Halloween "children will recognize familiar customs, such as carving pumpkins, dressing up, and hanging decorations, explained in simple, yet satisfying, text. The holiday is made accessible and inviting. . . . Lovely, well-captioned color photographs feature children around the world joyfully taking part in festivities." SLJ

Includes glossary and bibliographical references

★ Celebrate Independence Day; [by] Deborah Heiligman; consultant, Matthew Dennis. National Geographic 2007 31p il map (Holidays around the world) $15.95; lib bdg $23.90

Grades: K 1 2 3 **394.26**

1. Fourth of July

ISBN 978-1-4263-0074-5; 978-1-4263-0075-2 lib bdg

LC 2006100316

"Heiligman captures the festiveness of Independence Day, also reminding readers of its origin and relevence. . . . Her writing is clear and easy to read. . . . Plentiful photographs depict varied community celebrations." Horn Book Guide

Includes glossary and bibliographical references

★ **Celebrate** Thanksgiving; [by] Deborah Heiligman; consultant, Elizabeth Pleck. National Geographic 2006 32p il map (Holidays around the world) $15.95; lib bdg $23.90

Grades: K 1 2 3 **394.26**

1. Thanksgiving Day

ISBN 0-7922-5928-9; 0-7922-5929-7 lib bdg

LC 2006008685

This briefly describes the history of Thanksgiving Day and how it is celebrated.

Includes glossary and bibliographical references

Hoyt-Goldsmith, Diane

★ **Cinco** de Mayo; celebrating the traditions of Mexico. by Diane Hoyt-Goldsmith; photographs by Lawrence Migdale. Holiday House 2007 30p il $16.95

Grades: 3 4 5 **394.26**

1. Cinco de Mayo 2. Mexico -- Social life and customs

ISBN 978-0-8234-2107-7; 0-8234-2107-4

LC 2006101433

"This colorful photo-essay introduces Rosie, whose family celebrates their Mexican American traditions in California. After discussing Benito Juárez, the history of Cinco de Mayo, and three major waves of immigration from Mexico, Hoyt-Goldsmith presents elements of Rosie's heritage such as food, language, and mariachi music. . . . The clearly written text and the many fine, color photos provide readers with information as well as glimpses of the life in Rosie's community." Booklist

Includes glossary

★ **Three** Kings Day; a celebration at Christmastime. photographs by Lawrence Migdale. Holiday House 2004 30p il map $16.95

Grades: 3 4 5 **394.26**

1. Epiphany 2. Puerto Ricans -- United States

ISBN 0-8234-1839-1

LC 2003-67625

This "photo-essay introduces Three Kings Day, or Dia de los Tres Reyes, and shows the celebration as experienced by a 10-year-old girl in New York's Puerto Rican community. . . . The clearly written text conveys a good deal of information in a lively, accessible manner. The many photographs capture the joyful spirit of the holiday." Booklist

Includes glossary

Jango-Cohen, Judith

Chinese New Year; illustrations by Jason Chin. Carolrhoda Books 2005 48p il (On my own holidays) lib bdg $23.93; pa $5.95

Grades: 1 2 3 **394.26**

1. Chinese New Year

ISBN 1-57505-653-4 lib bdg; 1-57505-763-8 pa

LC 2004-4472

This "book describes the celebration of Chinese New Year. . . . Among the topics discussed are the Chinese zodiac, traditional symbols of the new year, family feasts and traditions for the holiday, and community activities, such as parades. . . . Clearly written, informative, and child-centered without talking down to children, this provides a good introduction to the holiday." Booklist

Jeffrey, Laura S.

Celebrate Martin Luther King, Jr., Day; [by] Laura S. Jeffrey. Enslow 2006 104p il (Celebrate holidays) lib bdg $31.93

Grades: 5 6 7 8 **394.26**

1. Clergy 2. Martin Luther King Day 3. Nonfiction writers 4. Civil rights activists 5. Nobel laureates for peace 6. African Americans -- Civil rights

ISBN 0-7660-2492-X

LC 2005028110

This offers a brief introduction to the life of Martin Luther King and the Civil Rights movement in the United States and how Martin Luther King Day became a holiday and is celebrated.

Includes glossary and bibliographical references

Celebrate Tet; [by] Laura S. Jeffrey. Enslow Publishers 2008 104p il map (Celebrate holidays) lib bdg $31.93

Grades: 5 6 7 8 **394.26**

1. Vietnamese New Year

ISBN 978-0-7660-2775-6 lib bdg; 0-7660-2775-9 lib bdg

LC 2006031922

"Captioned photographs, maps, drawings, and sidebars combine with an accessible text to present a thorough discussion of the Vietnamese New Year celebration. Jeffrey discusses the holiday's legendary origins and ancient traditions along with people's modern-day observances." Horn Book Guide

Includes glossary and bibliographical references

Jones, Lynda

Kids around the world celebrate! the best feasts and festivals from many lands. Wiley 1999 124p il pa $12.95

Grades: 4 5 6 **394.26**

1. Holidays 2. Festivals

ISBN 0-471-34527-X

LC 99-14639

Introduces a variety of festivals celebrated around the world. Includes recipes and hands-on activities to give a taste of what it is like to be part of a feast or ceremony in another country

Lankford, Mary D.

★ **Christmas** around the world; illustrated by Karen Dugan. Morrow Junior Bks. 1995 47p il map hardcover o.p. pa $5.95

Grades: 3 4 5 **394.26**

1. Christmas

ISBN 0-688-12166-7; 0-688-12167-5 lib bdg; 0-688-16323-8 pa

LC 93-38566

This book "looks at the rich diversity of Christmas traditions found in 12 distinctly different cultures. A small amount of pertinent background information serves as an introduction to each entry, but the majority of the text discusses the special ways each culture celebrates the holiday. The book's attractive layout effectively uses repetition of color and theme, with each double-page spread of text and art surrounded by a decorative border. . . . The book features a small selection of craft activities. . . . A helpful pronunciation guide, and an interesting selection of Christmas superstitions." Booklist

Includes bibliographical references

Lewis, Anne Margaret

What am I? Halloween; illustrated by Tom Mills. Albert Whitman 2011 un il $9.99

Grades: PreK   **394.26**

1. Halloween

ISBN 978-0-8075-8959-5; 0-8075-8959-4

LC 2010049643

"When looking for a simple yet entertaining introduction to Halloween for the very youngest readers, search no further. . . . A friendly witch, pumpkin to carve, funny bat, silly scarecrow, hooting owl, happy monster, black cat, dancing skeleton, busy spider and trick-or-treater are all included in this easy interactive guessing game. . . . This nonthreatening approach will surely satisfy those who wish to avoid the scary or creepy Halloween offerings that abound. A solid introduction for toddlers." Kirkus

MacMillan, Dianne M.

Diwali--Hindu festival of lights; [by] Dianne M. MacMillan. rev and updated ed.; Enslow Elementary 2008 48p il (Best holiday books) lib bdg $23.93

Grades: 2 3 4   **394.26**

1. Divali 2. Hindu holidays

ISBN 978-0-7660-3060-2 lib bdg; 0-7660-3060-1 lib bdg

LC 2007002420

First published 1997

This describes the history of the Hindu festival of Diwali and how it is celebrated in the United States

Includes glossary and bibliographical references

Mattern, Joanne

Celebrate Christmas; [by] Joanne Mattern. Enslow Publishers 2007 112p il (Celebrate holidays) lib bdg $31.93

Grades: 5 6 7 8   **394.26**

1. Christmas

ISBN 978-0-7660-2776-3 lib bdg; 0-7660-2776-7 lib bdg

LC 2006025258

The author "devotes several pages to the origins of Christmas, first as a pagan holiday, then as a celebration of Jesus' birth, and its evolution into the holiday as it is observed today. Symbols of Christmas, important people, and traditions from around the world are explored, and there is a fair amount of discussion about the commercialization of the holiday. . . . Full-color photos and reproductions appear throughout. There is plenty here for reports." SLJ

Includes glossary and bibliographical references

Celebrate Cinco de Mayo; [by] Joanne Mattern. Enslow Pub. 2006 104p il map (Celebrate holidays) lib bdg $31.93

Grades: 5 6 7 8   **394.26**

1. Cinco de Mayo 2. Mexico -- History 3. Mexico -- Social life and customs

ISBN 0-7660-2579-9

LC 2005028107

This describes the history of Cinco de Mayo and how it is celebrated.

Includes glossary and bibliographical references

Nelson, Vaunda Micheaux

★ Juneteenth; by Vaunda Micheaux Nelson and Drew Nelson; illustrations by Mark Schroder. Millbrook Press 2006 48p il (On my own holidays) lib bdg $23.93

Grades: 2 3 4   **394.26**

1. Juneteenth 2. African Americans -- Social life and customs

ISBN 978-1-57505-876-4 lib bdg; 1-57505-876-6 lib bdg

LC 2005-15334

This is an introduction to the holiday "which celebrates the belated arrival of emancipation news to Texas slaves on June 19, 1865. . . . [This] offers a solid introduction to the holiday for independent readers or for presenting to small groups." Booklist

Otto, Carolyn

★ Celebrate Chinese New Year; [by] Carolyn Otto; consultant, Haiwang Yuan. National Geographic 2008 32p il (Holidays around the world) $15.95; lib bdg $23.90

Grades: K 1 2 3   **394.26**

1. Chinese New Year 2. China -- Social life and customs

ISBN 978-1-4263-0381-4; 1-4263-0381-5; 978-1-4263-0382-1 lib bdg; 1-4263-0382-3 lib bdg

LC 2008024678

"Vivid, colorful photographs of fireworks, lion dancers, and food fill the pages of this introduction to Chinese New Year. The concise but informative narrative notes when the event occurs, cites a few of the countries where it is observed, and explains the reasons behind the customs and symbols, especially those traditions involving children. The well-captioned pictures capture the intense excitement and raucous exuberance of the festivities." Booklist

Includes glossary and bibliographical references

★ Celebrate Cinco de Mayo; [by] Carolyn Otto; consultant, Jose M. Alamillo. National Geographic 2008 32p il map (Holidays around the world) $15.95; lib bdg $23.90

Grades: K 1 2 3   **394.26**

1. Cinco de Mayo 2. Mexico -- Social life and customs

ISBN 978-1-4263-0215-2; 1-4263-0215-0; 978-1-4263-0216-9 lib bdg; 1-4263-0216-9 lib bdg

This "combines a clear, read-aloud-friendly text with big, beautiful color photos. After introducing Cinco de Mayo's 1862 origins, Otto shows and tells how the celebration has become an annual, joyous festival of Mexican culture, both north and south of the border. . . . Excellent back matter includes bibliography, recipes, a glossary and an informative afterword." Booklist

★ Celebrate Kwanzaa; [by] Carolyn Otto; consultant, Keith A. Mayes. National Geographic 2007 32p il (Holidays around the world) $15.95; lib bdg $23.90

Grades: K 1 2 3   **394.26**

1. Kwanzaa 2. African Americans -- Social life and customs

ISBN 978-1-4263-0319-7; 978-1-4263-0320-3 lib bdg

LC 2007041221

This describes the history of the African American holiday of Kwanzaa and how it is celebrated and includes a craft activity and a recipe.

Includes glossary and bibliographical references

★ **Celebrate** Valentine's Day; [by] Carolyn Otto; consultant, Jack Santino. National Geographic 2008 32p il map (Holidays around the world) $15.95; lib bdg $23.90

Grades: K 1 2 3 **394.26**

1. Valentine's Day

ISBN 978-1-4263-0213-8; 1-4263-0213-4; 978-1-4263-0214-5 lib bdg; 1-4263-0214-2 lib bdg

LC 2007033764

This describes how Valentine's Day is celebrated and includes a game and a recipe

Includes glossary and bibliographical references

Peppas, Lynn

Cultural traditions in Mexico; Lynn Peppas. Crabtree Publishing Company 2012 32 p. (Cultural traditions in my world) (reinforced library binding: alk. paper) $26.60

Grades: 3 4 5 **394.26**

1. Holidays 2. Festivals -- Mexico 3. Holidays -- Mexico 4. Festivals -- Mexico 5. Mexico -- Social life and customs

ISBN 0778775879; 9780778775874; 9780778775942; 9781427178664; 9781427179814

LC 2012003079

Author Lynn Peppas's "book describes how the blending of native and Spanish traditions, beliefs, and rituals has resulted in many of the lively and colorful festivals celebrated today. . . . Mexico's culture is a unique mixture of ancient traditions passed down by the native Maya and Aztec peoples, and the religion and culture of Mexico's Spanish conquerors. . . . Young readers will also learn how the Mexican people celebrate family occasions with fiestas." (Publisher's note)

Pfeffer, Wendy

The **longest** day; celebrating the summer solstice. illustrated by Linda Bleck. Dutton Children's Books 2010 un il $17.99

Grades: K 1 2 3 **394.26**

1. Summer 2. Summer solstice

ISBN 978-0-525-42237-2; 0-525-42237-4

"Science, myth and custom merge into a celebratory introduction to the Summer Solstice. . . . Bleck's sprightly, colorful illustrations offer a visual celebration as they faithfully track the text. A comfortable, multidimensional investigation of the Summer Solstice that transcends time and place." Kirkus

A **new** beginning; celebrating the spring equinox. illustrated by Linda Bleck. Dutton Children's Books 2008 un il $17.99

Grades: K 1 2 3 **394.26**

1. Spring 2. Vernal equinox

ISBN 978-0-525-47874-4; 0-525-47874-4

LC 2007-18123

This "covers the spring equinox and how people mark its passage in the northern hemisphere. . . . [It includes] five multicultural activities. The free-verse text is clear and simple, and the colorful illustrations blanket every page with celebrants clad in traditional, festive clothing." Booklist

Includes bibliographical references

The **shortest** day; celebrating the winter solstice. illustrated by Jesse Reisch. Dutton Children's Books 2003 un il $16.99

Grades: K 1 2 3 **394.26**

1. Winter solstice

ISBN 0-525-46968-0

LC 2003-40811

Describes how and why daylight grows shorter as winter approaches, the effect of shorter days on animals and people, and how the winter solstice has been celebrated throughout history. Includes activities

This uses "clear, concise language. . . . Pfeffer uses an easy, comfortable tone for conveying the basic information. . . . Reisch's realistic craypas illustrations provide serviceable interpretations of the author's ideas." SLJ

Rissman, Rebecca

Martin Luther King, Jr. Day. Heinemann Library 2011 24p il (Holidays and festivals) $21.50; pa $5.99

Grades: PreK K **394.26**

1. Clergy 2. Martin Luther King Day 3. Nonfiction writers 4. Civil rights activists 5. Nobel laureates for peace 6. African Americans -- Civil rights

ISBN 978-1-4329-4055-3; 1-4329-4055-4; 978-1-4329-4074-4 pa; 1-4329-4074-0 pa

LC 2009052855

This introduction to Martin Luther King Day offers "large pictures on the top three-fourths of the page and a simple line or two of text below. . . . Pictures of segregation—in particular, a 'For Colored Only' water fountain—still retain their power to shock and will compel children to ask questions. Rissman uses five very short chapters to take the youngest readers through some simple facts about slavery . . . before touching on King's life. . . . This is . . . a fine introduction." Booklist

Includes bibliographical references

Simonds, Nina

★ **Moonbeams,** dumplings & dragon boats; a treasury of Chinese holiday tales, activities & recipes. [by] Nina Simonds, Leslie Swartz, & the Children's Museum of Boston; illustrated by Meilo So. Harcourt 2002 74p il $20

Grades: 4 5 6 7 **394.26**

1. Handicraft 2. Chinese cooking 3. Chinese New Year 4. Folklore -- China 5. Festivals -- China

ISBN 0-15-201983-9

LC 2001-4280

Presents background information, related tales, and activities for celebrating five Chinese festivals—Chinese New Year, the Lantern Festival, Qing Ming, the Dragon Boat Festival, and the Moon Festival

"The ample white space surrounding the text is filled with small, whimsical watercolor illustrations. . . . [This] is a useful, visually appealing addition to any holiday collection." SLJ

Includes bibliographical references

Tait, Leia

Cinco de Mayo. AV2 by Weigl Pubs. 2011 24p il (American celebrations) lib bdg $27.13; pa $8.95

Grades: 3 4 5 **394.26**

1. Cinco de Mayo 2. Mexico -- Social life and customs

3. Mexican Americans -- Social life and customs
ISBN 978-1-6059-6776-9 lib bdg; 1-60596-776-9 lib
bdg; 978-1-60596-934-3 pa; 1-60496-934-6 pa
LC 2009050985

This book about Cinco de Mayo "is well positioned to
plug holes in school units on holidays, with [a] punchy, informative [entry] on the past and present [history] of [the
holiday]. The colorful [layout features] an ever-shifting mix
of period and modern photographs, while sidebars keep
things from settling too comfortably into the organizing
structure: . . . introduction, history, key personalities, celebrations, symbols, and activities. . . . Cinco de Mayo does an
admirable job explaining this all-too-infrequently-explained
holiday." Booklist

Tokunbo, Dimitrea
The **sound** of Kwanzaa; illustrated by Lisa Cohen.
Scholastic Press 2009 un il $16.99
Grades: PreK K 1 2   **394.26**
1. Kwanzaa 2. African Americans -- Social life and
customs
ISBN 978-0-545-01865-4; 0-545-01865-X
LC 2007025916

"This picture book provides readers with an introduction
to Kwanzaa's seven principles. . . . Rhythmic text includes
the definitions, pronunciations, and significances of the principles. Uncluttered, vibrantly colored illustrations extend the
meanings of each of the seven candles of Kwanzaa." Horn
Book Guide
Includes bibliographical references

Waters, Kate
Lion dancer: Ernie Wan's Chinese New Year; by Kate
Waters and Madeline Slovenz-Low; photographs by Martha
Cooper. Scholastic 1990 un il hardcover o.p. pa $4.99
Grades: K 1 2 3   **394.26**
1. Chinese New Year 2. Chinese Americans -- Social
life and customs
ISBN 0-590-43047-5 pa
LC 89-6423

Describes six-year-old Ernie Wan's preparations, at
home and in school, for the Chinese New Year celebrations
and his first public performance of the lion dance

"While some of the pictures look posed, the marvelously
colorful photographs successfully capture Ernie's pride and
anticipation as he is dressed in his gorgeous costume and
the excitement and swirling movement of the subsequent
parade. Illustrations of a Chinese lunar calendar and a Chinese horoscope are extra dividends in a useful and appealing
book." Horn Book

394.264 Thanksgiving

Grace, Catherine O'Neill
★ **1621**; a new look at Thanksgiving. [by] Catherine
O'Neill Grace and Margaret M. Bruchac with Plimoth Plan-
tation; photographs by Sisse Brimberg and Cotton Coulson.
National Geographic Soc. 2001 47p il map $17.95; pa
$7.95
Grades: 3 4 5   **394.264**
1. Thanksgiving Day 2. Wampanoag Indians 3.
Pilgrims (New England colonists) 4. Plimoth Plantation,

Inc. (Plymouth, Mass.)
ISBN 0-7922-7027-4; 0-7922-6139-1 pa
LC 2001-124

This is a "pictorial presentation of the reenactment of
the first Thanksgiving, held at Plimoth Plantation museum
in October, 2000. Countering the prevailing, traditional story
of the first Thanksgiving . . . this lushly illustrated photo-
essay presents a more measured, balanced, and historically
accurate version of the three-day harvest celebration in
1621." SLJ
Includes bibliographical references

395 Etiquette (Manners)

Aliki
★ **Manners**. Greenwillow Bks. 1990 un il $16; lib
bdg $15.93; pa $5.95
Grades: K 1 2 3   **395**
1. Etiquette
ISBN 0-688-09198-9; 0-688-09199-7 lib bdg; 0-688-
04579-0 pa
LC 89-34622

The author discusses etiquette and good manners
"Aliki makes manners accessible to children through
colorful cartoon-style illustrations. . . . Her lively primer
sparkles with examples of the proper and the poor." Booklist

Joslin, Sesyle
★ **What** do you do, dear? pictures by Maurice Sendak.
Harper & Row 1985 un il hardcover o.p. pa $6.95
Grades: PreK K 1 2   **395**
1. Etiquette
ISBN 0-06-443113-4 pa
LC 84-43139

First published 1961 by Addison-Wesley
A "wonderful spoof on manners in a hilarious picture-
book made for laughing aloud." Child Study Assoc of Am

★ **What** do you say, dear? pictures by Maurice Sen-
dak. Harper & Row 1986 un il lib bdg $15.89; pa $5.95
Grades: PreK K 1 2   **395**
1. Etiquette
ISBN 0-06-023074-6 lib bdg; 0-06-443112-6 pa
LC 84-43140

First published 1958 by Addison-Wesley
A Caldecott Medal honor book, 1959
"A rollicking introduction to manners for the very young.
A series of delightfully absurd situations—being introduced
to a baby elephant, bumping into a crocodile, being rescued
from a dragon—are posed and appropriately answered. The
illustrations are among Sendak's best—and funniest." Bull
Cent Child Books

★ **Manners** mash-up: a goofy guide to good behavior;
story and pictures. featuring Tedd Arnold [et al.] Dial
Books for Young Readers 2010 un il $16.99
Grades: 2 3 4 5   **395**
1. Etiquette 2. Etiquette for children and teenagers 3.
Children's literature -- Works -- Grades two through six
ISBN 0-8037-3480-8; 978-0-8037-3480-7
LC 2010-11882

This "picture-book look at manners showcases the . . . [work] of fourteen illustrators, each of whom get a spread to explore a particular area of behavior. . . . Grades two to four." (Bull Cent Child Books)

"This follow-up to Why Did the Chicken Cross the Road? (2006) and Knock Knock (2007) rounds up 14 of the usual suspects—the most gifted illustrators working today—and gives them one spread to explain the hows and whys of etiquette. . . . The results are top-notch." Publ Wkly

Post, Peggy

Emily Post's table manners for kids. Collins 2009 96p $15.99

Grades: 4 5 6 7   **395**

1. Etiquette

ISBN 978-0-06-111709-1; 0-06-111709-9

LC 2008010655

"This deceptively slim guide teems with advice about everything from meal courses to table settings, from the art of conversation to dining out. The tone is measured and mildly proscriptive, offset by Bjorkman's amusing cartoons. . . . A strength: the excellent troubleshooting for specific concerns, such as eating fondue and using chopsticks." Kirkus

Emily Post's The guide to good manners for kids; by Peggy Post & Cindy Post Senning. HarperCollins 2004 144p il $15.99; lib bdg $16.89

Grades: 4 5 6 7   **395**

1. Etiquette

ISBN 0-06-057196-9; 0-06-057197-7 lib bdg

LC 2003-26426

This offers advice on etiquette at home, at school, and other places, including letter writing and on-line communication, table manners, phone answering, and behavior at social gatherings, and public places.

"The writing is clear, friendly, and sometimes clever. . . . The advice is consistently practical and simple." SLJ

Emily's everyday manners; [by] Peggy Post and Cindy Post Senning; illustrated by Steve Bjorkman. HarperCollins 2006 un il $16.99; lib bdg $17.89

Grades: PreK K 1 2   **395**

1. Etiquette

ISBN 0-06-076174-1; 0-06-076177-6 lib bdg

"Cheerful illustrations set the upbeat (and updated) tone for this introduction to manners. A succinct running text introduces young Emily and her neighbor Ethan and comments on how and why they use manners as well as how etiquette can differ according to the time and place." Booklist

Other titles in this series are:

Emily's magic words (2007)

Emily's Christmas gifts (2008)

Emily's sharing and caring book (2008)

Emily's out and about book (2009)

Emily's new friend (2010)

Emily's magic words; please, thank you, and more. by Peggy Post and Cindy Post Senning; illustrated by Leo Landry. Collins 2007 un il $15.99; lib bdg $16.89

Grades: PreK K   **395**

1. Etiquette

ISBN 978-0-06-111680-3; 0-06-111680-7; 978-0-06-111681-0 lib bdg; 0-06-111681-5 lib bdg

LC 2006019582

Emily explains how just a few little words please, thank you, hello, goodbye, and excuse me can work magic!

This is a "chipper, earnest etiquette primer. . . . Landry's . . . crisp, winsome ink and watercolor spot illustrations keep the mood light. . . . Parents will welcome the useful, encouraging advice supplied in an endnote." Publ Wkly

Includes bibliographical references

Senning, Cindy Post

Emily's new friend; by Cindy Post Senning and Peggy Post; illustrated by Steve Björkman. Collins 2010 un il $16.99

Grades: PreK K   **395**

1. Etiquette 2. Friendship

ISBN 978-0-06-111706-0; 0-06-111706-4

LC 2009011767

Emily and a new neighbor become friends by treating one another with generosity, kindness, and good manners. Includes a note for parents on the importance of teaching principles of etiquette at home.

"Björkman's brightly colored watercolor-and-ink illustrations add a welcome touch of levity to the . . . text; readers will especially enjoy the antics of the two dogs. Small vignettes allow the artwork to match the many activities of the characters." Kirkus

Emily's out and about book; by Cindy Post Senning and Peggy Post; illustrated by Leo Landry. Collins 2009 un il $16.99

Grades: PreK K   **395**

1. Etiquette

ISBN 978-0-06-111700-8; 0-06-111700-5

LC 2008029286

"Emily and her mother visit the library and the doctor's office, eat tacos from an outdoor stand, and greet a neighbor. Along the way, Emily remembers her manners, and that helps make the day a good one for everyone. The genial story and pictures will please children who like to see their everyday activities mirrored in their books. . . . This closes with a note to parents, here encouraging them to teach preschoolers not just how to behave but why they should do so." Booklist

Emily's sharing and caring book; by Cindy Post Senning and Peggy Post; illustrated by Leo Landry. HarperCollins Children's Books 2008 un il $16.99; lib bdg $17.89

Grades: PreK K   **395**

1. Etiquette 2. Interpersonal relations

ISBN 978-0-06-111697-1; 0-06-111697-1; 978-0-06-111698-8; 0-06-111698-X

LC 2006102927

"This appealing and practical picture book . . . encourages young children to share with others and to show other people that they care about them. . . . The section on sharing defines the term broadly to include sharing time or even a good mood with someone, as well as sharing toys or food. The section on caring shows young Emily and her friend thinking about others and doing things to make them feel good. The book's potentially weighty message is buoyed by the simplicity and lightness of its delivery in both the text and the inviting line-and-watercolor artwork." Booklist

Verdick, Elizabeth

Don't behave like you live in a cave. Free Spirit Pub. 2010 120p il (Laugh & learn) pa $8.95

Grades: 4 5 6   **395**

1. Etiquette 2. Child psychology

ISBN 978-1-57542-353-1 pa; 1-57542-353-7 pa

LC 2010010441

Explains how children can make smarter, more positive choices about how they behave at home and at school and, as a result, stay out of trouble, feel good about themselves, and get along better with family, friends, and teachers.

"Not only are the antics of a cartoon Cave Boy and Cave Girl used to represent bad behavior throughout the book, but they are also part of the infusion of humor that makes the tone light, accessible, and soapbox free. Verdick keeps the dialogue conversational." SLJ

395.2   Etiquette for stages in life cycle

Hoyt-Goldsmith, Diane

★ **Celebrating** a Quinceanera; a Latina's 15th birthday celebration. photographs by Lawrence Migdale. Holiday House 2002 30p il $16.95

Grades: 3 4 5   **395.2**

1. Quinceañera (Social custom) 2. Mexican Americans -- Social life and customs

ISBN 0-8234-1693-3

LC 2001-59424

Describes the customs and traditions connected with the celebration of a Mexican-American girl's fifteenth birthday, marking her coming of age

This offers "eye-catching, full-color photos. . . . The clearly written, engaging text conveys both the social and religious significance of the event." SLJ

398   Folklore

Beeler, Selby B.

Throw your tooth on the roof; tooth traditions from around the world. illustrated by G. Brian Karas. Houghton Mifflin 1998 un il $16; pa $6.95

Grades: K 1 2 3   **398**

1. Teeth -- Folklore

ISBN 0-395-89108-6; 0-618-15238-5 pa

LC 97-46042

Consists of brief statements relating what children from around the world do with a tooth that has fallen out. Includes facts about teeth

"This book will be an eye-opener for young Americans who may have assumed that the Tooth Fairy holds a worldwide visa." Publ Wkly

Berk, Ariel

Secret history of mermaids and creatures of the deep; or the Liber Aquaticum. written and collected by Ari Berk, magister and scribe; illuminated by Wayne Anderson, Gary Chalk, Matt Dangler, Virginia Lee. Candlewick Press 2009 un il $16.99

Grades: 4 5 6   **398**

1. Mermaids and mermen

ISBN 978-0-7636-4515-1; 0-7636-4515-X

"This volume details merfolk from tales and mythologies around the world. A wide variety of creatures, their customs, and habitats are touched on. The often ornately scripted text is accompanied by intricate illustrations and numerous foldouts." Horn Book Guide

Kallen, Stuart A.

The **sphinx**; part of the Monsters and mythical creatures series. by Stuart A. Kallen. ReferencePoint Press 2012 80 p. ill. (chiefly col.) (Monsters and mythical creatures series) (hardback) $27.95

Grades: 4 5 6 7 8   **398**

1. Sphinxes (Mythology)

ISBN 1601522223; 9781601522221

LC 2011026636

This book, part of the "Monsters and Mythical Creatures" series, looks at the "history . . . [and] associated mythology" of the Sphinx. (School Library Journal). It "reveals the significant symbolic role this creature has played in human civilization from ancient Egypt through classical Greece and the Renaissance into the twenty-first century. . . . The ancient mythical creature has been an inspiration for artists, writers, architects, scholars, and theologians for millennia." (Publisher's note)

"Children will get a well-rounded look at the featured subjects and how they have evolved into the creatures that still fascinate many today." SLJ

Includes bibliographical references and index

Kelly, Sophia

What a beast! a look-it-up guide to the monsters and mutants of mythology. Scholastic 2010 128p il map (Mythlopedia) lib bdg $39; pa $13.95

Grades: 4 5 6 7   **398**

1. Monsters 2. Classical mythology

ISBN 978-1-60631-028-1 lib bdg; 1-60631-028-3 lib bdg; 978-1-60631-060-1 pa; 1-60631-060-7 pa

LC 2009-20998

Describes some of the creatures and monsters in Greek mythology.

This "spices things up with sassy artwork, a pastel color scheme, and an OMG sensibility. . . . [This title is] loaded with information on the inspired methods with which various nasty creatures could put an end to bothersome heroes. Aside from the heaps of information coming from all angles on just about every page, . . . [the] book also contains a decent family tree, a rudimentary star chart, and lists of further reading. . . . For kids unconvinced that anything so old and gray could have any bearing on their lives, . . . [this book provides] a feisty . . . guide to the many cultural references lingering from antiquity." Booklist

Includes glossary and bibliographical references

Knudsen, Shannon

Fairies and elves. Lerner 2010 48p il (Fantasy chronicles) lib bdg $27.93

Grades: 4 5 6 7   **398**

1. Fairies

ISBN 978-0-8225-9979-1 lib bdg; 0-8225-9979-1 lib bdg

LC 2008050207

"The explanations and history behind . . . fairies [and elves] . . . will provide satisfaction for readers who want to know more about these familiar characters from myth, fantasy, and folk and fairy tales. Brief and concise." SLJ

Includes bibliographical references

Fantastical creatures and magical beasts. Lerner Publications 2010 48p il (Fantasy chronicles) lib bdg $27.93
Grades: 4 5 6 7   **398**
  1. Mythical animals
  ISBN 978-0-8225-9987-6 lib bdg; 0-8225-9987-2
lib bdg

LC 2009004794

This describes mythical beasts such as dragons, unicorns, Hydra, Medusa, the labyrinth, and basilisks

"The explanations and history behind well-known fantastical creatures . . . will provide satisfaction for readers who want to know more about these familiar characters from myth, fantasy, and folk and fairy tales. Brief and concise." SLJ

Includes bibliographical references

Losure, Mary
  The **Fairy** Ring, or, Elsie and Frances Fool the World; Mary Losure. Candlewick Press 2012 184 p. ill.
Grades: 5 6 7 8   **398**
  1. Deception 2. Fairies 3. Fairies -- England
  ISBN 9780763656706; 0763656704

LC 2011046081

This book offers explores an event that occurred "[t]owards the end of World War I, [when] two girls in Yorkshire took photographs that purported to capture the fairies they regularly saw, and these pictures . . . became a national sensation when . . . Sir Arthur Conan Doyle . . . championed them as authentic. . . . [The] book . . . conveys the widening of the ripples from the event and . . . the impulses behind the creation of the photographs." (Bulletin of the Center for Children's Books)

Ogburn, Jacqueline K.
  A **dignity** of dragons; collective nouns for magical beasts. by Jacqueline K. Ogburn, Nicoletta Ceccoli; illustrated by Nicoletta Ceccoli. Houghton Mifflin Books for Children 2010 un il $16
Grades: 2 3 4   **398**
  1. Mythical animals
  ISBN 978-0-618-86254-2; 0-618-86254-4

"Gorgeous mixed-media illustrations complement dozens of inventive collective nouns. . . . These creative descriptions comprise the only text in the book. A four-page glossary defines each fantastic creature and identifies the culture(s) of its origin. Ceccoli has created a stylized and luminous fantasyland energetically inhabited by Ogburn's enchanting bestiary. Fans of mythology and fantasy as well as budding lexophiles will savor this sophisticated picture book." SLJ

Reinhart, Matthew
  ★ **Dragons** & Monsters; [by] Matthew Reinhart and Robert Sabuda. Candlewick Press 2011 un il (Encyclopedia mythologica)
Grades: K 1 2 3   **398**
  1. Dragons 2. Monsters 3. Pop-up books
  ISBN 0-7636-3173-6; 978-0-7636-3173-4

LC 2010015485

"The pop-up book veterans continue to push the envelope in this addition to the Encyclopedia Mythologica se-

ries, with infamous figures like Medusa . . . joining more general creatures such as dragons, sea monsters, and vampires. Minibooks and sidebars profile less recognizable monsters—the golem, sharklike 'taniwha,' and 'wendigo,' known to Algonquian tribes. . . . Once again, Reinhart and Sabuda have created an offering distinguished by clever details; superb execution, and a sense of wonder."

"The pop-up book veterans continue to push the envelope in this addition to the Encyclopedia Mythologica series, with infamous figures like Medusa . . . joining more general creatures such as dragons, sea monsters, and vampires. Minibooks and sidebars profile less recognizable monsters—the golem, sharklike 'taniwha,' and 'wendigo,' known to Algonquian tribes. . . . Once again, Reinhart and Sabuda have created an offering distinguished by clever details; superb execution, and a sense of wonder." Publ Wkly

  ★ **Fairies** and magical creatures; [by] Matthew Reinhart and Robert Sabuda. Candlewick Press 2008 un il (Encyclopedia mythologica) $27.99
Grades: K 1 2 3   **398**
  1. Fairies 2. Mythical animals 3. Pop-up books
  ISBN 978-0-7636-3172-7; 0-7636-3172-8

This pop-up book depicts and describes such magical creatures as Shakespeare's fairy queen Titania, hobgoblins, trolls, a humanoid magical tree, brownies, Pegasus, satyrs, Serbian enchanted birds, and merfolk.

"A dramatic pop-up towers over each spread, surrounded by flaps and corner gatefolds that open up more surprises. . . . The paper engineering consistently enhances the text. . . . The emphasis on global legends as well as a palette heavy on blues, purples and reds widen the audience way past the girly-girl set." Publ Wkly

Scieszka, Jon
  ★ The **Stinky** Cheese Man and other fairly stupid tales; [by Jon Scieszka & Lane Smith] Viking 1992 un il $17.99
Grades: 2 3 4 5   **398**
  1. Fairy tales 2. Short stories
  ISBN 0-670-84487-X

LC 91-48194

A Caldecott Medal honor book, 1993

"The picture-book set will probably recognize the stories enough to know that what's going on isn't what's 'supposed' to happen. But The Stinky Cheese Man isn't a book for little ones. It will take older children (that's teens along with 10s) to follow the disordered story lines and appreciate the narrative's dry wit, wordplay, and wacky, sophomoric jokes. . . . Smith's New Wave art is an intricate part of the whole, extending as well as reinforcing the narrative; the pictures are every bit as comically insolent and deliberately clever as the words." Booklist

  ★ The **true** story of the 3 little pigs; pictures by Lane Smith. Viking Kestrel 1989 un il $16.99; pa $7.99
Grades: K 1 2 3 4   **398**
  1. Pigs -- Fiction 2. Wolves -- Fiction
  ISBN 0-670-82759-2; 0-14-054451-8 pa

LC 89-8953

The wolf gives his own outlandish version of what really happened when he tangled with the three little pigs

"The 'excited and funky' illustrations match the hilarious revisionist text to a standard story." N Y Times Book Rev

Sierra, Judy

The **gruesome** guide to world monsters; illustrated by Henrik Drescher. Candlewick Press 2005 63p il $18.99

Grades: 5 6 7 8　　　**398**

1. Folklore 2. Monsters

ISBN 0-7636-1727-X

LC 2004-57470

This presents "brief introductions to dozens of ugly customers from world folklore. . . . [The author] offers wonderfully provocative warnings against creatures as diverse as the giant skunk Aniwye, the bloodsucking bat Mansusopsop, and Bloody Mary, an evil specter who lives on the other side of mirrors." SLJ

Thong, Roseanne

Wish; wishing traditions around the world. illustrated by Elisa Kleven. Chronicle Books 2008 un il $16.99

Grades: K 1 2 3　　　**398**

1. Wishes

ISBN 978-0-8118-5716-1

LC 2007038299

"'The many ways to make a wish wherever home may be' come in for lighthearted yet respectful exploration in this attractive square-format book. Thong . . . entices readers with consistently well-rhymed verses . . . following up each with a brief description of a national custom. . . . Rendered in Kleven's . . . kaleidoscopic style, many of the full-bleed spreads nearly shimmer. . . . Endnotes include more information along with an invitation to find 15 lucky symbols hidden in the pictures." Publ Wkly

398.2　Folk literature

Aardema, Verna

★ **Borreguita** and the coyote; a tale from Ayutla, Mexico. retold by Verna Aardema; illustrated by Petra Mathers. Knopf 1991 un il hardcover o.p. pa $6.99

Grades: K 1 2 3　　　**398.2**

1. Coyote (Legendary character) 2. Sheep -- Folklore 3. Folklore -- Mexico

ISBN 0-679-88936-1 pa

LC 90-33302

A little lamb uses her clever wiles to keep a coyote from eating her up

This folk tale "is energetically told and comfortably packed with many recognizable motifs. Mathers enlarges upon the humorous elements of the story in her boldly colored paintings. . . . Aardema and Mathers are felicitously paired in a tale of trickery rewarded that begs to be read aloud." Horn Book

Includes glossary

★ **Bringing** the rain to Kapiti Plain; a Nandi tale. retold by Verna Aardema; pictures by Beatriz Vidal. Dial Bks. for Young Readers 1981 un il $16.99; pa $5.99

Grades: K 1 2 3　　　**398.2**

1. Stories in rhyme 2. Folklore -- Africa 3. Droughts -- Folklore

ISBN 0-8037-0809-2; 0-8037-0904-8 pa

LC 80-25886

"Effective both in the rhythm of its metered storytelling and in the brilliance of its stylized paintings, the panoramic picture book quickly engages both eye and ear." Horn Book

Who's in Rabbit's house? a Masai tale. retold by Verna Aardema; pictures by Leo and Diane Dillon. Dial Bks. for Young Readers 1977 un il hardcover o.p. pa $6.99

Grades: K 1 2 3　　　**398.2**

1. Animals -- Folklore 2. Folklore -- East Africa 3. Masai (African people) -- Folklore

ISBN 0-14-054724-X pa

LC 77-71514

This "tale relates the attempts of Rabbit to regain possession of her house after it is taken over by an intruder. Rabbit's friends offer suggestions on how to solve the problem, but the solution comes from 'an unexpected source.' The story, adapted from the Masai tale 'The Long One,' uses repetition of key phrases to produce a rhythmic read-aloud text. The Dillons skillfully present their artistry in a vivid, colorful and impressive manner which contributes to the story and sets the tone." Child Book Rev Serv

★ **Why** mosquitoes buzz in people's ears; a West African tale retold. pictures by Leo and Diane Dillon. Dial Bks. for Young Readers 1975 un il $16.99; pa $6.99

Grades: K 1 2 3　　　**398.2**

1. Animals -- Folklore 2. Mosquitoes -- Folklore 3. Folklore -- West Africa

ISBN 0-8037-6089-2; 0-14-054905-6 pa

Awarded the Caldecott Medal, 1976

"Stunning full-color illustrations—watercolor sprayed with air gun, overlayed with pastel, cut out and repasted—give an eye-catching abstract effect and tell the story with humor and power." SLJ

Alley, Zoe B.

★ **There's** a princess in the palace; pictures by R.W. Alley. Roaring Brook Press 2010 34p il $19.99

Grades: 1 2 3 4　　　**398.2**

1. Graphic novels 2. Humorous graphic novels 3. Folklore -- Graphic novels 4. Princesses -- Graphic novels

ISBN 978-1-59643-471-4; 1-59643-471-6

"Within a graphic-novel format, the tales of Cinderella, Sleeping Beauty, Snow White, the Frog Prince and the Princess and the Pea develop familial and hilarious interconnections while retaining the stories' traditional structures. . . . Smartly hysterical." Kirkus

★ **There's** a wolf at the door; pictures by R. W. Alley. Roaring Brook Press 2008 40p il $19.95

Grades: K 1 2 3　　　**398.2**

1. Graphic novels 2. Humorous graphic novels 3. Wolves -- Folklore -- Graphic novels

ISBN 978-1-59643-275-8; 1-59643-275-6

LC 2007-44025

As his plans are spoiled over and over again, the wolf keeps trying to find his dinner, in this retelling of five well-known stories and fables.

This is a "hilarious romp. . . . Illustrated with softly colored pen-and-ink drawings, these five stories meld seamlessly together. The text is full of puns, alliteration, and occasional rhymes." SLJ

Andrews, Jan

Rude stories; illustrations by Francis Blake. Tundra Books 2010 87p il $19.95

Grades: 3 4 5   **398.2**

1. Folklore

ISBN 978-0-88776-921-4; 0-88776-921-7

"Andrews has added her own special touches to a collection of humorous, traditional tales from cultures around the world. The rudeness in the stories takes different forms: in an original tale, two sisters compete in a belching contest. In a Swahili tale, a girl known for her kindness finally speaks her mind to her family, and in another from Japan, a man receives a magical fan from a goblin. Its special power? Waving it will increase or decrease the size of someone's bottom. . . . A selection of witty, original poems is interspersed among the stories, . . . The selections have the flavor of the oral tradition. Blake's colorful spot art and occasional full-page illustrations are a perfect match for the irreverent humor." SLJ

Includes bibliographical references

★ **When** apples grew noses and white horses flew; tales of Ti-Jean. illustrations by Dusan Petricic. Groundwood Books/House of Anansi Press 2011 67p il $16.95

Grades: 2 3 4 5   **398.2**

1. Folklore -- Canada

ISBN 978-0-88899-952-8; 0-88899-952-6

This is a retelling of three stories featuring "Quebec's traditional folktale hero, Ti-Jean. He's an endearing character who is both wise and foolish, and though he does find himself in hard situations (often of his own making), in the end, he somehow manages to do what needs to be done. In 'Ti-Jean and the Princess of Tomboso,' he outwits a greedy princess; in 'Ti-Jean the Marble Player,' he gets the best of a pint-sized scoundrel; and in 'How Ti-Jean Became a Fiddler,' he turns the tables on a too-clever-for-her-own-good seigneur's daughter, and finds true love in the process." (Publisher's note) "Ages seven to ten." (Quill Quire)

"Ti-Jean, the cheerful, hapless, ultimately triumphant stripling of French-Canadian folklore . . . makes a winning appearance in three tales of European origin lightly transposed to a New World setting. . . . These zesty, well-paced texts virtually read themselves. . . . Sly Petricic drawings underpin the fun throughout." Horn Book

The **August** House book of scary stories; spooky tales for telling out loud. edited by Liz Parkhurst. August House 2009 144p $15.95

Grades: 4 5 6 7 8   **398.2**

1. Folklore 2. Storytelling 3. Short stories 4. Horror fiction

ISBN 978-0-87483-915-9; 0-87483-915-7

LC 2009008711

An anthology of spooky stories drawn from folklore, local history, and the storytellers' imaginations, and divided into the categories "Just Desserts and Lessons Learned," "Ghostly Guardians," "Dark Humor," "Urban Legends and Jump Tales," and "Fearless Females."

"Each of these 20 chilling tales is meant to be told out loud and includes author notes about how to maximize the spooky effect. Middle schoolers will relish reading and sharing these tales, hoping to creep each other out." SLJ

Aylesworth, Jim

Goldilocks and the three bears; retold by Jim Aylesworth; illustrated by Barbara McClintock. Scholastic Press 2003 un il $15.95

Grades: K 1 2 3   **398.2**

1. Folklore 2. Bears -- Folklore

ISBN 0-439-39545-3

LC 2002-15964

A little girl walking in the woods finds the house of the three bears and helps herself to their belongings

"Aylesworth's text is faithful to the traditional elements of the original, juicing up the plot with folksy, conversational asides. . . . The artist's watercolor, sepia ink, and gouache illustrations are pastel and dainty yet full of life and action." SLJ

★ The **mitten**; retold by Jim Aylesworth; illustrated by Barbara McClintock. Scholastic Press 2009 un il $16.99

Grades: PreK K 1 2   **398.2**

1. Winter -- Folklore 2. Animals -- Folklore 3. Folklore -- Ukraine

ISBN 978-0-439-92544-0; 0-439-92544-4

LC 2006-37115

A retelling of the traditional tale of how a boy's lost mitten becomes a refuge from the cold for an increasing number of animals.

"Aylesworth's polished story together with McClintock's energetic pictures prove that The Mitten can hold one more. Aylesworth's text shows its storytelling roots with its perfect pacing, precisely chosen details, and most of all its particapatory repetition." Horn Book

Badoe, Adwoa

The **pot** of wisdom: Ananse stories; pictures by Baba Wagué Diakité. Douglas & McIntyre 2001 63p il hardcover o.p. pa $12.95

Grades: 3 4 5 6   **398.2**

1. Anansi (Legendary character) 2. Folklore -- West Africa

ISBN 0-88899-429-X; 0-88899-869-4 pa

"Badoe remembers hearing these trickster stories in her youth in Ghana, and she retells them with the freshness and verve of the spoken word. . . . Each tale is illustrated with a brilliantly colored polychrome tile by Diakite, the Mali-born illustrator. The tiles employ strong black linear motifs and sun-and-earth colors: gold, orange, brown, blue, lemon." Booklist

Barrager, Brigette

The **twelve** dancing princesses; written and illustrated by Brigette Barrager. Chronicle Books 2011 un il $16.99

Grades: K 1 2 3   **398.2**

1. Fairy tales 2. Folklore -- Germany

ISBN 978-0-8118-7696-4; 0-8118-7696-9

LC 2010011580

A retelling of the Grimm brothers' tale of twelve princesses who dance secretly all night long and how their secret is eventually discovered.

"With art resembling that of animated film and several graceful dance scenes, this story could easily be set to a sound track. The plot is true to that told by the Grimms, and nice bits of dialogue and observations by Pip thread easily through the narrative, bringing the characters to life." SLJ

Barton, Byron

★ The **little** red hen. HarperCollins Pubs. 1993 un il $15.95; lib bdg $15.89; pa $24.99; bd bk $7.99

Grades: K 1 2   **398.2**

1. Folklore 2. Chickens -- Folklore

ISBN 0-06-021675-1; 0-06-021676-X lib bdg; 0-06-443379-X pa; 0-694-00999-7 bd bk

LC 91-4051

The little red hen finds none of her lazy friends willing to help her plant, harvest, or grind wheat into flour, but all are eager to eat the bread she makes from it. "Preschool." (SLJ)

"Barton here skillfully pares down a well-known tale for the youngest readers and listeners. Vibrant hues abound in his full-page, collage-like illustrations." Publ Wkly

★ The **three** bears. HarperCollins Pubs. 1991 un il $15.95; lib bdg $15.89; bd bk $7.99

Grades: K 1   **398.2**

1. Folklore 2. Bears -- Folklore

ISBN 0-06-020423-0; 0-06-020424-9 lib bdg; 0-694-00998-9 bd bk

LC 90-43151

While the three bears are away from home, Goldilocks ventures inside their house, tastes their porridge, tries their chairs, and finally falls asleep in Baby Bear's bed. "Ages two to four." (Bull Cent Child Books)

"Here's the familiar tale of the three bears and their blond gal pal drawn for the very youngest. Byron uses large simple shapes, bright colors, and a spare text to tell his story. . . . The size of the art makes this a good choice for mother-toddler story hours." Booklist

Bateman, Teresa

The **Frog** with the Big Mouth; retold by Teresa Bateman; illustrated by Will Terry. Albert Whitman & Co. 2008 un il $16.99

Grades: K 1 2   **398.2**

1. Frogs -- Folklore 2. Folklore -- South America 3. Rain forest animals -- Folklore

ISBN 978-0-8075-2621-7; 0-8075-2621-5

LC 2007052157

An Argentine wide-mouthed frog sets out through the rain forest to brag about his fly-eating abilities and encounters a toco toucan, a coati, a capybara, and a jaguar. Includes a note about the animals.

"Terry's shiny, verdant rain forest capably offsets myriad greens with shadows of lavender, an electric-blue beetle, and wine-red berries. The spreads swirl with movement and beckon forward via fluid lines. . . . This is an inventive version of a long-favored tale." SLJ

Baynes, Pauline

Questionable creatures; a bestiary. [by] Pauline Baynes. Eerdmans Books for Young Readers 2006 47p il $18

Grades: 4 5 6 7   **398.2**

1. Bestiaries 2. Mythical animals

ISBN 978-0-8028-5284-7; 0-8028-5284-X

LC 2005033658

"Baynes introduces readers to the creatures and myths found in medieval bestiaries and explains how the books were made and how they were viewed by the general public. The rest of the volume details the commonly held beliefs that both peasants and scholars embraced about specific animals. . . . Baynes's detailed gouache and colored-pencil illustrations . . . are done in the style of medieval illuminations. . . . The artist shows great respect for the early bestiary creators while also giving the stories relevance for modern readers." SLJ

Includes bibliographical references

Berner, Rotraut Susanne

Definitely not for little ones; some very Grimm fairy-tale comics. translated by Shelley Tanaka. House of Anansi Press 2009 un il $18.95

Grades: 4 5 6   **398.2**

1. Authors 2. Folklore 3. Fairy tales 4. Folklorists 5. Philologists 6. Short story writers

ISBN 978-0-88899-957-3; 0-88899-957-7

"In a comic book format, Berner retells the Brothers Grimm tales of the Frog Prince, Mother Holle, Tom Thumb, Rapunzel, Jorinda & Jorindel, Lucky Hans, Hans the Hedgehog, and Little Red Cap, using a humorous, breezy and somewhat ironic tone. . . . Older elementary-school readers who like sneaky humor, slightly violent demises of villains, and humorous takes on familiar tales will enjoy these comics. . . . Tanaka's translation lets the narration and dialogue flow seamlessly." Booklist

Blackstone, Stella

Storytime; first tales for sharing. told by Stella Blackstone; illustrated by Anne Wilson. Barefoot Books 2005 94p il $19.99; pa $12.99

Grades: K 1   **398.2**

1. Folklore 2. Animals -- Folklore

ISBN 1-84148-345-1; 1-84686-165-9 pa

LC 2004029542

"Seven familiar nursery tales are accompanied by bright, stylized, folk-art illustrations, done in paper collage and acrylic. Selections include The Cock, the Mouse and the Little Red Hen, The Gingerbread Man, The Ugly Duckling, Goldilocks, The Timid Hare (a Henny Penny story from India), The Three Little Pigs, and Stone Soup. The retellings are straightforward; most are faithful to the most commonly known versions and retain the familiar refrains. . . . The collection as a whole is delightful; the art is fresh, vibrant, and full of child appeal." SLJ

Includes bibliographical references

Blackwood, Gary L.

Legends or lies? Marshall Cavendish Benchmark 2006 72p il (Unsolved history) lib bdg $34.21

Grades: 4 5 6 7   **398.2**

1. Legends

ISBN 978-0-7614-1891-7 lib bdg; 0-7614-1891-1 lib bdg

Describes several legends that have intrigued people for centuries: the lost civilization of Atlantis, the Amazons, King Arthur, St Brendon, Pope Joan, and El Dorado

This collection "of tidbits about lingering mysteries of the past . . . [offers] more substance than most. . . . [It offers] a full-page illustration opening each chapter; reproductions, many in color; and a generously spaced format." SLJ

Includes glossary and bibliographical references

Blia Xiong

Nine-in-one, Grr! Grr! a folktale from the Hmong people of Laos. told by Blia Xiong; adapted by Cathy Spagnoli;

illustrated by Nancy Hom. Children's Bk. Press 1989 30p
il hardcover o.p. pa $7.95
Grades: K 1 2 **398.2**
  1. Folklore -- Laos 2. Tigers -- Folklore 3. Hmong
(Asian people) -- Folklore
ISBN 0-89239-048-4; 0-89239-110-3 pa
LC 89-9891
When the great god Shao promises Tiger nine cubs each
year, Bird comes up with a clever trick to prevent the land
from being overrun by tigers
  "Simply and eloquently told, this pourquoi tale from
a minority Laotian culture is boldly illustrated in a style
adapted from the multi-imaged embroidered story cloths of
the Hmong people. Its rhythmic text and appealing, brightly
colored pictures make it a good choice for preschool story
hours." Booklist

Brett, Jan
  Beauty and the beast; retold and illustrated by Jan
Brett. Clarion Bks. 1989 un il lib bdg $16; pa $6.95
Grades: 1 2 3 **398.2**
  1. Fairy tales 2. Folklore -- France
ISBN 0-89919-497-4 lib bdg; 0-395-55702-X pa
LC 88-16965
This is a retelling of the French fairy tale. Through her
great capacity to love, a kind and beautiful maid releases
a handsome prince from the spell which has given him the
appearance of a wild beast and turned his servants into animals. "Ages four to eight." (Booklist)
  "A Beauty of distinguished appearance, a delightful set
of animal servants, and a suitably hideous Beast are presented in Jan Brett's distinctive, decorative style. Small details,
such as tapestries mirroring the action of the tale, add to the
effect of the simply written story." Horn Book Guide

  Gingerbread baby. Putnam 1999 un il $16.99
Grades: K 1 2 3 **398.2**
  1. Folklore
ISBN 0-399-23444-6
LC 98-52310
  A young boy and his mother bake a gingerbread baby
that escapes from their oven and leads a crowd on a chase
  "Although the story remains true to the original tale,
Brett has added her own touches and a surprise ending. . .
. The illustrations are pure Brett and feature warm colors
against a snow-white landscape." SLJ

  Goldilocks and the three bears; retold and illustrated by
Jan Brett. Putnam 1992 48 p. col il $17.99
Grades: PreK K 1 2 **398.2**
  1. Folklore 2. Bears -- Folklore
ISBN 039922033X; 9780399220333
LC 87565
This children's story, retold and illustrated by Jan Brett,
presents the classic "story of the curious little girl named
Goldilocks, who made herself quite at home in the house of
the three bears. Jan Brett's lavish illustrations for this classic
tale, full of details and surprises, gives this edition a special
flair." (Publisher's note)
  "Brett's beautifully executed retelling of this classic story is distinguished by the use of luxuriant color and a wealth
of visual detail...with such a display before them, readers
will hardly blame Goldilocks for her lack of restraint."
Publishers Weekly

  The **mitten**; a Ukrainian folktale. adapted and illustrated by Jan Brett. anniversary ed.; Penguin Young Readers Group 2009 un il $17.99
Grades: K 1 2 **398.2**
  1. Animals -- Folklore 2. Folklore -- Ukraine
ISBN 978-0-399-25296-9; 0-399-25296-7
First published 1989 by Putnam
After Nicki accidentally drops his mitten in the forest it
becomes an object of curiosity for a mole, a rabbit, a badger,
a tiny brown mouse, and a big brown bear, as they all crawl
into it
  "Readers will enjoy the charm and humor in the portrayal of the animals as they make room for each newcomer
in the mitten and sprawl in the snow after the big sneeze."
Horn Book

  The **three** snow bears; [by] Jan Brett. G. P. Putnam's
Sons 2007 un il $16.99
Grades: K 1 2 3 **398.2**
  1. Inuit -- Folklore 2. Polar bear -- Folklore
ISBN 978-0-399-24792-7
LC 2007007373
Retells the story of Goldilocks, set in an Inuit village and
featuring a family of polar bears.
  "Filled with the gorgeously detailed watercolor and
gouache illustrations that distinguish her work, this Arctic
version of the classic tale is pure Brett. . . . The plot remains
true to the progression of the traditional tale and the narrative moves swiftly." SLJ

  Who's that knocking on Christmas Eve. Putnam 2002
un il $16.99
Grades: K 1 2 **398.2**
  1. Folklore -- Norway 2. Christmas -- Fiction
ISBN 0-399-23873-5
LC 2001-48253
  A boy from Finnmark and his ice bear help scare away
some hungry trolls so that Kyri and her father can enjoy their
Christmas Eve meal
  This is a "vivid, well-paced retelling of an old Norwegian folktale. . . . Gorgeous endpapers depicting night-sky
constellations studded with trolls, bears, and other mythical
symbols complement the exquisitely detailed winter-won-
derland artistry within." Booklist

Brown, Marcia
  Once a mouse; a fable cut in wood. Atheneum Pubs.
1961 un il $16; pa $5.99
Grades: K 1 2 3 **398.2**
  1. Fables 2. Folklore -- India
ISBN 0-684-12662-1; 0-689-71343-6 pa
Awarded the Caldecott Medal, 1962
  "The illustrations are remarkably beautiful. The emo-
tional elements of the story . . . are conveyed with just as
much intensity as the purely visual ones." New Yorker

  Stone soup; an old tale. told and pictured by Marcia
Brown. Scribner 1947 un il $16.95; pa $6.99
Grades: K 1 2 3 **398.2**
  1. Folklore -- France
ISBN 0-684-92296-7; 0-689-71103-4 pa
A Caldecott Medal honor book, 1948

"When the people in a French village heard that three soldiers were coming, they hid all their food for they knew what soldiers are. However, when the soldiers began to make soup with water and stones the pot gradually filled with all the vegetables which had been hidden away. The simple language and quiet humour of this folktale are amplified and enriched by gay and witty drawings of clever lighthearted soldiers, and the gullible 'light-witted' peasants." Cont Libr Rev

Bruchac, James

★ The **girl** who helped thunder and other Native American folktales; retold by James Bruchac and Joseph Bruchac; illustrated by Stefano Vitale. Sterling Pub. Co. 2008 96p il (Folktales of the world) $14.95

Grades: 3 4 5 6   **398.2**

1. Native Americans -- Folklore

ISBN 978-1-4027-3263-8; 1-4027-3263-5

LC 2007-16876

"The Bruchacs retell Native North American folktales in a clear yet bold voice. The anthology is arranged geographically, a logical organization that reveals the diversity of Native peoples. . . . Descriptions of each region introduce the original inhabitants of those places, as the authors provide succinct yet enriching historical and cultural context for the stories that follow. . . . Vitale's stylized oil-on-wood illustrations vividly reveal the colorful spirit of the tales, as bright blues and reds complement the earth tones found throughout." SLJ

Bruchac, Joseph

Between earth & sky; legends of Native American sacred places. written by Joseph Bruchac; illustrated by Thomas Locker. Harcourt Brace & Co. 1996 un il map hardcover o.p. pa $7

Grades: 3 4 5   **398.2**

1. Native Americans -- Folklore

ISBN 0-15-200042-9; 0-15-202062-4 pa

LC 95-10862

"Each tale is a model of economy, gracefully distilling its message, while Locker's landscapes capture the mysticism inherent in each setting." Horn Book Guide

★ The **first** strawberries; a Cherokee story. retold by Joseph Bruchac; pictures by Anna Vojtech. Dial Bks. for Young Readers 1993 un il hardcover o.p. pa $6.99

Grades: K 1 2 3   **398.2**

1. Strawberries -- Folklore 2. Cherokee Indians -- Folklore

ISBN 0-8037-1331-2; 0-14-05409-8 pa

LC 91-31058

A quarrel between the first man and the first woman is reconciled when the Sun causes strawberries to grow out of the earth

"This retelling . . . is simply and clearly written, and as sweet as the berries the woman stops to taste. The attractive watercolors and colored-pencil illustrations show an idealized pastoral world." SLJ

How Chipmunk got his stripes; a tale of bragging and teasing. as told by Joseph Bruchac & James Bruchac; pictures by Jose Aruego & Ariane Dewey. Dial Bks. for Young Readers 2001 un il hardcover o.p. pa $6.99

Grades: K 1 2 3   **398.2**

1. Bears -- Folklore 2. Chipmunks -- Folklore 3. Squirrels -- Folklore 4. Native Americans -- Folklore

ISBN 0-8037-2404-7; 0-14-250021-6 pa

LC 99-16793

"This pourquoi story is succinctly written in simple, concrete language, and repeated chants give listeners an opportunity to participate actively in the narrative's unfolding. . . . The pictures are large enough to be seen and enjoyed by a group." Bull Cent Child Books

Thirteen moons on a turtle's back; a Native American year of moons. by Joseph Bruchac and Jonathan London; illustrated by Thomas Locker. Philomel Bks. 1992 un il $16.95; pa $5.99

Grades: K 1 2 3 4   **398.2**

1. Seasons -- Poetry 2. Native Americans -- Poetry 3. Native Americans -- Folklore 4. Poetry -- By individual authors

ISBN 0-399-22141-7; 0-698-11584-8 pa

LC 91-3961

"Locker . . . has created a dramatic oil painting for each short tale. His artwork portrays seasonal changes in the land as well as the specific seasonal activities of humans and animals. The large format with minimal text will appeal to younger children, while the alternative calendar, based on changes in nature, will interest middle readers. An unusual, easy-to-use resource for librarians, teachers, and others wishing to incorporate multicultural activites throughout the year." Booklist

Turtle's race with Beaver; a traditional Seneca story. as told by Joseph Bruchac & James Bruchac; pictures by Jose Aruego & Ariane Dewey. Dial Bks. for Young Readers 2003 un il $15.99; pa $5.99

Grades: K 1 2 3   **398.2**

1. Beavers -- Folklore 2. Turtles -- Folklore 3. Seneca Indians -- Folklore

ISBN 0-8037-2852-2; 0-14-240466-7 pa

LC 2002-4001

When Beaver challenges Turtle to a swimming race for ownership of the pond, Turtle outsmarts Beaver, and Beaver learns to share

"Done in pen and ink, gouache, and pastel, the cheerful artwork is a wonderful match for this well-told tale." SLJ

Bryan, Ashley

★ **Ashley** Bryan's African tales, uh-huh. Atheneum Bks. for Young Readers 1998 198p $22

Grades: 4 5 6   **398.2**

1. Folklore -- Africa

ISBN 0-689-82076-3

LC 97-77743

This volume combines three previously published titles: The ox of the wonderful horns and other African folktales (1971), Beat the story-drum, pum-pum (1980), Lion and the ostrich chicks and other African folktales (1986)

This collection of African folktales is "told with Bryan's distinctive rhythmic word patterns and filled with humor, life lessons, and the antics of trickster Ananse. . . . Quality reproductions of the original woodcuts enrich this handsome volume." Horn Book Guide

★ **Beautiful** blackbird. Atheneum Bks. for Young Readers 2003 un il $16.95
Grades: K 1 2 3 **398.2**
1. Birds -- Folklore 2. Folklore -- Zambia 3. Folklore -- Africa
ISBN 0-689-84731-9
LC 2002-5290
In a story of the Ila people, the colorful birds of Africa ask Blackbird, whom they think is the most beautiful of birds, to decorate them with some of his blackening brew. "Ages five to nine." (Bull Cent Child Books)
"Bryan employs boldly colored, cut-paper artwork to dramatize the action. The overlapping collage images fill the pages with energy. . . . Ready-made for participative story-telling." Booklist

Buehner, Caralyn
Goldilocks and the three bears; [by] Caralyn Buehner; pictures by Mark Buehner. Dial Books for Young Readers 2007 un il $16.99
Grades: PreK K 1 2 **398.2**
1. Folklore 2. Bears -- Folklore
ISBN 0-8037-2939-1
LC 2005036401
In this variation on the classic folktale, a rhyming, rope-skipping, little girl rudely helps herself to the belongings of a genteel family of bears.
"This warm and pleasing retelling of the classic include a rope-jumping Goldilocks in red cowboy boots who bursts with personality. . . . The luminous oil-over-acrylic illustrations enhance the story with delightful details." SLJ

Bunting, Eve
Finn McCool and the great fish; written by Eve Bunting; illustrated by Zachary Pullen. Sleeping Bear Press 2010 un il $16.95
Grades: K 1 2 3 **398.2**
1. Fishes -- Folklore 2. Giants -- Folklore 3. Folklore -- Ireland
ISBN 1-58536-366-9; 978-1-58536-366-7
LC 2009036936
Irish giant Finn McCool is told that in order to become wise he much catch and eat the salmon that possesses knowledge, but Finn finds that he cannot bring himself to kill the miraculous fish
"Bunting makes this unfamiliar story accessible to readers. The art beautifully illustrates the green Irish countryside and makes Finn a real gentle giant." SLJ

Burningham, John
Tug-of-war; John Burningham. Candlewick Press 2013 32 p. $16.99
Grades: K 1 2 3 **398.2**
1. Tricksters -- Folklore 2. Picture books for children
ISBN 0763665754; 9780763665753
LC 2012947722
This children's picture book offers an illustrated retelling of a West African folktale. Hare is teased by Hippopotamus and Elephant, so "Hare is keen to defeat his tormenters using his superior wits. Hare finds Elephant in the forest, challenges him to a tug-of-war, and gives him an end of rope. Hare meets Hippopotamus at the river and gives him the other end. Sight unseen, both creatures believe Hare is pull-ing against them, and fail to realize their error until Hare" has disappeared. (Publishers Weekly)

Burns, Batt
★ The **king** with horse's ears and other Irish folktales; [by] Batt Burns; illustrated by Igor Oleynikov. Sterling Pub. Co. 2009 96p il (Folktales of the world) $14.95
Grades: 4 5 6 7 **398.2**
1. Fairy tales 2. Folklore -- Ireland
ISBN 978-1-4027-3772-5; 1-4027-3772-6
LC 2007035258
"These 13 Irish tales retold by storyteller Burns follow fairies and warriors, heroes and clever thieves. . . . The stories are cleanly retold in contemporary, accessible language, and each is introduced with a short paragraph providing cultural or other information. . . . Oleynikov's paintings have a rough texture that suits the energy of the retellings and adds to the lively tone. This is a hearty collection, handsomely produced with Celtic-knot borders and gouache full-page and spot illustrations." Booklist
Includes glossary

Caduto, Michael J.
Keepers of the night; Native American stories and nocturnal activities for children. [by] Michael J. Caduto and Joseph Bruchac; story illustrations by David Kanietakeron Fadden; chapter illustrations by Jo Levasseur and Carol Wood; foreword by Merlin D. Tuttle. Fulcrum 1994 146p il pa $15.95
Grades: Adult Professional **398.2**
1. Nature study 2. Night -- Folklore 3. Native Americans -- Folklore
ISBN 1-55591-177-3
LC 94-2602
"The well-written chapters include discussions with illuminating scientific information." Sci Books Films
"Caduto and Bruchac use stories from various American Indian tribes as the basis for activities and lessons about the nighttime world. Written as a guide for teachers, outdoor education leaders, and other adults working with children in a nature setting, the guide gives detailed instructions for preparing, conducting, and evaluating a variety of activities that focus on the nocturnal habits of animals, on astronomy and nighttime weather, and on campfire activities, such as storytelling, dances, and games." Booklist
Includes glossary and bibliographical references

Campoy, F. Isabel
★ **Tales** our abuelitas told; a Hispanic folktale collection. [by] F. Isabel Campoy and Alma Flor Ada; illustrated by Felipe Dávalos . . . [et al.] Simon & Schuster 2006 118p il $19.95
Grades: 3 4 5 6 **398.2**
1. Folklore -- Latin America 2. Hispanic Americans -- Folklore
ISBN 0-689-82583-5
Presents the authors', retellings of twelve traditional tales accompanied by information on origins and different versions
"All of the selections are peppered with energetic dialogue and witty detail. Children will relish their humor, especially if read aloud." SLJ

Cardenas, Teresa

Oloyou; pictures by Margarita Sada; translated by Elisa Amado. Groundwood Books 2008 un il $18.95

Grades: 2 3 4 5   **398.2**

1. Cats -- Folklore 2. Folklore -- Cuba 3. Bilingual books -- English-Spanish 4. Yoruba (African people) -- Folklore

ISBN 978-0-88899-795-1; 0-88899-795-7

"In this striking bilingual retelling of a Yoruba myth, Oloyou the Cat is the very first creature created by the God-child while he is still too young to know what he is doing. More importantly, Oloyou becomes God's first friend. They are happy until Oloyou falls into Nothing, which is an oceanic kingdom presided over by Okun Aró. . . . The clarity of the writing makes this book suitable for reading aloud, while the complexity of the story will hold the interest of older readers. The oil-on-canvas illustrations are rich and bold with a mythic scope that incorporates the story's African-Caribbean roots." SLJ

Casey, Dawn

The **Barefoot** book of Earth tales; retold by Dawn Casey; illustrated by Anne Wilson. Barefoot Books 2009 95p il $19.99

Grades: 2 3 4 5 6   **398.2**

1. Folklore 2. Ecology -- Folklore

ISBN 978-1-84686-224-3; 1-84686-224-8

"This enchanting collection of folk tales and creation myths from different cultures encourages readers to live a more harmonious life with nature. . . . Well chosen and crafted with broad appeal, the tales are woven with subtle morals and wisdom. Each story is introduced by a brief overview about the featured locale and culture . . . and followed by a related, easy-to-replicate activity or craft. Full-page and spot illustrations and colorful decorative borders reflect the spirit and origins of each offering. Done with collaged papers with acrylic and printed backgrounds." SLJ

The **great** race; the story of the Chinese zodiac. written by Dawn Casey; illustrated by Anne Wilson. Barefoot Books 2006 un il $16.99

Grades: 1 2 3 4   **398.2**

1. Zodiac 2. Folklore -- China 3. Animals -- Folklore

ISBN 1-905236-77-8

LC 2005032544

Relates how the Jade Emperor chose twelve animals to represent the years in his calendar. Also discusses the Chinese calendar, zodiac, the qualities associated with each animal, and what animal rules the year in which the reader was born

"In this retelling of the ancient legend, Casey maintains the pace well. . . . The book is a visual treat, with illustrations in simple collage designs on acrylic and painted backgrounds placed in such a way as to keep the eye engaged and moving." SLJ

Cech, John

Jack and the beanstalk; retold by John Cech; illustrated by Robert Mackenzie. Sterling Pub. Co. 2008 un il $14.95

Grades: 1 2 3   **398.2**

1. Fairy tales 2. Giants -- Folklore 3. Folklore -- Great Britain

ISBN 978-1-4027-3064-1; 1-4027-3064-0

LC 2007001783

A boy climbs to the top of a giant beanstalk where he uses his quick wits to outsmart an ogre and make his and his mother's fortune. Includes historical notes on versions of this tale, other heroic stories, and alternate "ascension" tales.

Cech "knits fresh strands into the . . . story. This smoothly paced version, which begins with some hilarious wordplay, runs close to traditional tellings until the end, when the giant's wife joins Jack in his hasty escape. . . . MacKenzie ably ramps up the drama in the pencil-and-paint scenes." Booklist

Puss in boots; retold by John Cech; illustrated by Bernhard Oberdieck. Sterling Pub. 2010 un il (Classic fairy tale collection) $14.95

Grades: K 1 2 3   **398.2**

1. Fairy tales 2. Folklore -- France

ISBN 978-1-4027-4436-5; 1-4027-4436-6

LC 2008052496

A clever cat helps his poor master win fame, fortune, and the hand of a beautiful princess. Includes historical notes on versions of this tale and other fairy tales

This "offers an enjoyable retelling of the timeless story. . . . The narrative is descriptive, lively, and droll, and the colorful watercolor-and-ink illustrations, filled with period details, are intricately rendered." Booklist

Rapunzel; retold by John Cech; illustrated by Fiona Sansom. Sterling 2010 un il (Classic fairy tale collection) $14.95

Grades: K 1 2 3   **398.2**

1. Folklore 2. Fairy tales

ISBN 978-1-4027-6911-5; 1-4027-6911-3

A retelling of a folktale in which a beautiful girl with long golden hair is kept imprisoned in a lonely tower by a witch. Includes a note on the origins of the story.

"Cech employs clear, descriptive language that is fresh and appealing to modern readers, at times seeming to speak directly to his audience. Varying in size from inserts to double-page spreads, with the text often placed in frames, Sansom's lovely medieval paintings complement and enhance the text, depicting the action while concentrating on emotional content. . . . A spendid candidate for a crowd-pleasing read-aloud." Kirkus

Chase, Richard

Grandfather tales; American-English folk tales. selected and edited by Richard Chase; illustrated by Berkeley Williams, Jr. Houghton Mifflin 1948 239p il pa $7.95

Grades: 4 5 6 7   **398.2**

1. Folklore -- Southern States

ISBN 0-395-06692-1; 0-618-34690-2 pa

Folklore gathered in Alabama, "North Carolina, Virginia and Kentucky. Written down only after many tellings, these [twenty-four] humorous tales are told in the vernacular of the region with added touches of local color provided by the storytellers as they meet together to keep Old-Christmas Eve. . . . Of special interest to storytellers." Booklist

The **Jack** tales; told by R.M. Ward and his kindred in the Beech Mountain section of western North Carolina and by other descendants of Council Harmon (1803-1896) elsewhere in the southern mountains; with three tales from Wise County, Virginia; set down from these sources and edited by Richard Chase; with an appendix compiled by Herbert

Halpert; and illustrated by Berkeley Williams, Jr. Houghton Mifflin 2003 216p il pa $7.95

Grades: 5 6 7 8 Adult Professional **398.2**

1. Folklore -- Southern States

ISBN 978-0-618-34692-9 pa; 0-618-34692-9 pa

LC 2003276676

First published 1943

A collection of folk tales from the southern Appalachians that center on a single character, the irrepressible Jack

"Humor, freshness, colorful American background, and the use of one character as a central figure in the cycle mark these 18 folk tales, told here in the dialect of the mountain country of North Carolina. A scholarly appendix by Herbert Halpert, giving sources and parallels, increases the book's value as a contribution to American folklore. Black-and-white illustrations in the spirit of the text." Booklist

Includes bibliographical references

Chichester-Clark, Emma

★ **Goldilocks** and the three bears. Candlewick Press 2010 un il $14.99

Grades: PreK K 1 **398.2**

1. Folklore 2. Bears -- Folklore

ISBN 978-0-7636-4680-6; 0-7636-4680-6

LC 2009-14601

A retelling of the adventures of a nosy, naughty, and sassy little girl who finds the house of the three bears and helps herself to their belongings.

"This large-format edition of the traditional story offers plenty of scope for Clark's colorful illustrations. While the plot remains the same, the telling is a little more elaborate here than in most versions, with a couple of new refrains and added dialogue. . . . The controlled profusion of patterns gives the pencil-and-acrylic illustrations a busy but cheerful look. . . . Recommended for the freshness and energy of its artwork." Booklist

Cinderella; [illustrated by K.Y. Craft] SeaStar Books 2000 32 p. col. ill. $16.99

Grades: K 1 2 3 **398.2**

1. Fairy tales -- Fiction 2. Cinderella (Legendary character) -- Fiction 3. Folklore 4. Fairy tales

ISBN 1587170043; 9781587170041

LC 00024540

This retold fairy tale of Cinderella is illustrated by K.Y. Craft. "Inspired by the opulent styles of 17th- and 18th-century France, the paintings are confections of luxurious clothing, densely vegetated woods and regally appointed ballrooms. . . . The story, adapted from Arthur Rackham's and Andrew Lang's versions, contains pleasing touches as well as a moral." (Publishers Weekly)

"In this fresh retelling, Cinderella is tending to a wounded bird in the woods when she accidentally meets the prince for the first time. The bird later transforms into her fairy godmother and makes it possible for her to attend the ball, where she captures the prince's heart. Ornate illustrations, echoed by elaborate marginalia that swirl around the text, place the tale in seventeenth-century France." Horn Book

Clayton, Sally Pomme

Amazons! women warriors of the world. illustrated by Sophie Herxheimer. Frances Lincoln 2009 93p il $19.95

Grades: 3 4 5 6 **398.2**

1. Folklore 2. Women -- Folklore

ISBN 978-1-84507-660-3; 1-84507-660-5

"This handsome collection of folktales showcases seven empowering females, each with her own unique strengths and abilities. . . . Filled with lively language and fast-paced action, the tales introduce a pleasing range of characters and moods. . . . The illustrations employ swirling lines and vibrant color washes to reflect the setting and tone of each tale. The stories are separated by two-page interludes that provide brief facts or activities." SLJ

Includes glossary

Tales told in tents; stories from central Asia. written by Sally Pomme Clayton; illustrated by Sophie Herxheimer. Frances Lincoln 2005 64p il map $16.95; pa $8.95

Grades: 2 3 4 **398.2**

1. Folklore -- Asia

ISBN 978-1-84507-066-3; 1-84507-066-6; 978-1-84507-278-0 pa; 1-84507-278-2 pa

"In 12 traditional stories from the nomadic cultures of Central Asia, folklorist Clayton retells myth and folklore she heard in Kazakhstan, Afghanistan, and elsewhere. The lively tales include epic creation myths, rhyming riddles, trickster tales, songs, and stories of magic carpets and music. The large picture book is illustrated with richly colored line-and-watercolor paintings that evoke Central Asian traditional culture. . . . A rich resource, even for older readers, this anthology has stories that travel across the world." Booklist

Includes glossary

Climo, Shirley

The **Egyptian** Cinderella; illustrated by Ruth Heller. Crowell 1989 un il $15.95; pa $5.95

Grades: K 1 2 3 **398.2**

1. Fairy tales 2. Folklore -- Egypt

ISBN 0-690-04822-X; 0-06-443279-3 pa

LC 88-37547

This picture book tells the legend of Rhodopis, a Greek slave who married the sixth-century B.C. pharaoh Amasis. This "is accomplished through the intercession of the great falcon, symbol of the god Horus. When the majestic bird deposits one of Rhodopis' rosy-gold slippers, a gift from her master, in the lap of the Pharaoh, he determines this to be a signal from the gods to marry the maiden whose foot it fits. . . . Kindergarten to grade three." (SLJ)

"The beauty of the language is set off to perfection by Heller's arresting full-color illustrations." SLJ

Coburn, Jewell Reinhart

Domitila; a Cinderella tale from the Mexican tradition. adapted by Jewell Reinhart Coburn; illustrated by Connie McLennan. Shen's Bks. 2000 un il $16.95

Grades: 2 3 4 **398.2**

1. Folklore -- Mexico

ISBN 1-88500-813-9

LC 99-56173

By following her mother's admonition to perform every task with care and love, a poor young Mexican girl wins the devotion of the governor's son

"The full-page oil-on-cavas illustrations are bright, sumptuous, and visually enticing. The text is bordered by proverbs rendered in both Spanish and English. Well-written and strongly illustrated." SLJ

Cohen, Caron Lee

The **mud** pony; a traditional Skidi Pawnee tale. retold
by Caron Lee Cohen; illustrated by Shonto Begay. Scholastic 1988 un il hardcover o.p. pa $4.99

Grades: K 1 2 3   **398.2**

1. Horses -- Folklore 2. Pawnee Indians -- Folklore
ISBN 0-590-41526-3 pa

LC 87-23451

A poor boy becomes a powerful leader when Mother
Earth turns his mud pony into a real one, but after the pony
turns back to mud, he must find his own strength

"The text is powerful because it is spare and unadorned.
It is extended well by the softly toned, full-color, impressionistic pictures." Helbig. This land is our land

Cousins, Lucy

★ **Yummy**; eight favorite fairy tales. Candlewick Press
2009 121p il $18.99

Grades: PreK K 1   **398.2**

1. Folklore 2. Fairy tales
ISBN 978-0-7636-4474-1; 0-7636-4474-9

"Beloved classics are successfully served by these bold,
striking renditions. . . . Large, arresting gouache spreads in
Cousins's signature style utilize saturated colors and thick,
dark outlines against solid backgrounds. Expressive characters enhance the stories' shifting moods. Large type accentuates the dynamic texts, building each spare entry to its
powerful climax." SLJ

Crews, Nina

Jack and the beanstalk. Henry Holt 2011 32p il
$16.99

Grades: K 1 2   **398.2**

1. Fairy tales 2. Giants -- Folklore 3. Folklore -- Great
Britain 4. Folklore
ISBN 978-0-8050-8765-9; 0-8050-8765-6

LC 2010026951

Photo-collage illustrations and updated text provide a
new look at the traditional tale of a boy who plants magic
beans, climbs the beanstalk, and is captured by a giant and
his wife.

"The images are quite keen, photographs and the occasional line drawing manipulated and layered to shape the
story. . . . Crews' fans will be delighted; others will be drawn
in by the nifty mix of folktale and photo-collage." Kirkus

Cummings, Pat

★ **Ananse** and the lizard; a West African tale. retold
and illustrated by Pat Cummings. Holt & Co. 2002 un il
$16.95

Grades: K 1 2 3   **398.2**

1. Anansi (Legendary character) 2. Folklore -- Ghana
ISBN 0-8050-6476-1

LC 2001-1679

Ananse the spider thinks he will marry the daughter of
the village chief, but instead he is outsmarted by Lizard

"Cummings' lively prose and humor are a perfect match
for the story. The boxed text is accompanied by gorgeous
watercolor, gouache, and pencil illustrations, rich in color
and lively pattern." Booklist

Curry, Jane Louise

Hold up the sky: and other Native American tales from
Texas and the Southern Plains; illustrated by James Watts.
Margaret K. McElderry Bks. 2003 159p il $17.95

Grades: 4 5 6 7   **398.2**

1. Folklore -- Southern States 2. Native Americans --
Folklore
ISBN 0-689-85287-8

LC 2002-16519

Retells twenty-six tales from Native Americans whose
traditional lands were in Texas and the Southern Plains, and
provides a brief introduction to the history of each tribe

"Curry has carefully researched and sensitively retold
tales from fourteen Native American nations. Attractive pencil drawings enhance the stories." Horn Book Guide

Includes bibliographical references

D'Aulaire, Ingri

The **terrible** troll-bird; [by] Ingri and Edgar Parin
d'Aulaire. New York Review Books 2007 41p il $15.95

Grades: K 1 2 3   **398.2**

1. Trolls 2. Fairy tales 3. Folklore -- Norway
ISBN 978-1-59017-252-0; 1-59017-252-3

LC 2007-13020

First published 1976 by Doubleday

When four children defeat the terrible troll-bird who
has terrified their Norwegian valley for years, everyone celebrates in a merry feast.

"The d'Aulaires illustrate this rousing Scandinavian
folktale in exuberant pictures using both sketchy black-and-
white lines and mottled color." Horn Book Guide

Dabcovich, Lydia

The **polar** bear son; an Inuit tale. retold and illustrated
by Lydia Dabcovich. Clarion Bks. 1997 37p il hardcover
o.p. pa $5.95

Grades: K 1 2 3   **398.2**

1. Inuit -- Folklore 2. Polar bear -- Folklore
ISBN 0-395-72766-9; 0-395-97567-0 pa

LC 96-4780

An old woman adopts and raises a polar bear cub which
grows up and provides for her even after she has had to send
it away to save it from the jealous men of the village

"Illustrated in muted pastel colors, the pictures capture
this stark, yet beautiful, winter world." SLJ

Dayrell, Elphinstone

★ **Why** the Sun and the Moon live in the sky; an African folktale. illustrated by Blair Lent. Houghton Mifflin
1968 26p il $16; pa $6.95

Grades: K 1 2 3   **398.2**

1. Sun -- Folklore 2. Moon -- Folklore 3. Folklore
-- Nigeria
ISBN 0-395-29609-9; 0-395-53963-3 pa

First told by the author in his book: Folk stories from
Southern Nigeria, West Africa, published 1910 in England

A Caldecott Medal honor book, 1969

"The beautifully detailed and stylized art work is based
on African sources; the artist uses cool colors for the water,
a pale blue-grey for the moon, and shades of gold and white
for the sun." Sutherland. The Best in Child Books

De las Casas, Dianne

The **gigantic** sweet potato; illustrated by Marita Gentry. Pelican Pub. Co. 2010 un il $16.99
Grades: K 1 2 3   **398.2**
   1. Folklore -- Russia
ISBN 978-1-58980-755-6; 1-58980-755-3
                  LC 2010009434

Ma Farmer craves sweet potato pie but needs help to harvest a homegrown sweet potato—in this version of the Russian folktale, The Giant Turnip. Includes recipe and directions to make sweet potato pie.

"Colorful watercolors accompany the rhythmic text and add a touch of foreshadowing. . . . Children will happily join in the repetitive, cumulative text and enjoy the satisfying end. . . . This tasty selection is a solid interpretation of the classic tale, with appealing pictures and a strong female character." Kirkus

De Regniers, Beatrice Schenk

Little sister and the month brothers; retold by Beatrice Schenk de Regniers; pictures by Margot Tomes. Marshall Cavendish Children 2009 un il $17.99
Grades: K 1 2 3   **398.2**
   1. Fairy tales 2. Slavs -- Folklore
ISBN 978-0-7614-5546-2; 0-7614-5546-9

A reissue of the title first published 1976 by Seabury Press

A retelling of the Slavic fairy tale in which the Month Brothers' magic helps Little Sister fulfill seemingly impossible tasks which prove the undoing of her greedy stepmother and stepsister.

"Tomes's intimate, unpretentious illustrations extend the text brilliantly. A timeless treasure." Horn Book Guide

Deedy, Carmen Agra

★ **Martina** the beautiful cockroach; a Cuban folktale. retold by Carmen Agra Deedy; illustrated by Michael Austin. Peachtree 2007 un il $16.95
Grades: 2 3 4 5   **398.2**
   1. Folklore -- Cuba 2. Cockroaches -- Folklore
ISBN 978-1-56145-399-3
                  LC 2007003108

In this humorous retelling of a Cuban folktale, a cockroach interviews her suitors in order to decide whom to marry

"Deedy's masterful retelling . . . has a rollicking voice imbued with sly tongue-in-cheek humor. The acrylic illustrations, in a hyperrealistic style . . . are rendered in a vivid tropical palette." Booklist

Demi

★ The **hungry** coat; a tale from Turkey. Margaret K. McElderry Books 2004 un il $19.95
Grades: K 1 2 3   **398.2**
   1. Folklore -- Turkey
ISBN 0-689-84680-0
                  LC 2002-155129

After being forced to change to a fancy new coat to attend a party, Nasrettin Hoca tries to feed his dinner to the coat, reasoning that it was the coat that was the invited guest.

"Demi's retelling of this tale is compelling and includes many details that help bring both time and place into focus. Her paint-and-ink illustrations are resplendent with her trademark gold leaf and intricate borders." SLJ

King Midas; the golden touch. Margaret K. McElderry Bks. 2002 un il $19.95
Grades: 2 3 4   **398.2**
   1. Midas (Legendary character)
ISBN 0-689-83297-4
                  LC 99-89389

A king finds himself bitterly regretting the consequences of his wish that everything he touches would turn to gold

Demi's "unsourced but briskly amusing retelling begins with the contest when Midas's preference for Pan's shrill discord so angers the great musician Apollo that he gives the king donkey's ears. . . . The gilded special effects take center stage; still, Demi's glowing colors, decorative figures, and delicate drafting are also worthy of note. . . . This handsome book breathes new life into one of the oldest of cautionary tales." Horn Book

DePaola, Tomie, 1934-

★ **Adelita**; a Mexican Cinderella story. written and illustrated by Tomie de Paola. Putnam 2002 un il hardcover o.p. pa $6.99
Grades: K 1 2 3   **398.2**
   1. Fairy tales 2. Folklore -- Mexico
ISBN 0-399-23866-2; 0-14-240187-0 pa
                  LC 2001-57873

After the death of her mother and father, Adelita is badly mistreated by her stepmother and stepsisters until she finds her own true love at a grand fiesta

"The prose is straightforward and crisp. . . . Making perfect use of clear, warm hues, the full-color acrylic illustrations are a feast for the eye." SLJ

The **clown** of God; an old story. told and illustrated by Tomie de Paola. Harcourt Brace Jovanovich 1978 un il $16; pa $7
Grades: K 1 2 3   **398.2**
   1. Legends 2. Miracles -- Folklore 3. Christmas --
   Folklore
ISBN 0-15-219175-5; 0-15-618192-4 pa
                  LC 78-3845

An orphan whose juggling skill led him to a career as a traveling entertainer has grown old and clumsy and returns as a hungry beggar to his birthplace. On Christmas Eve in the monastery church a miracle occurs as he summons his last strength to make his only possible offering

"Mr. de Paola has written the tale with love, tenderness, and joy. He has executed authentic Renaissance illustrations that are magnificent in design and beauty." Child Book Rev Serv

Jamie O'Rourke and the big potato; an Irish folktale. retold and illustrated by Tomie dePaola. Putnam 1992 un il hardcover o.p. pa $5.99; bd bk $5.99
Grades: K 1 2 3   **398.2**
   1. Folklore -- Ireland
ISBN 0-399-22257-X; 0-698-11603-8 pa; 0-448-
45090-9 bd bk
                  LC 91-10626

The laziest man in all of Ireland catches a leprechaun, who offers a potato seed instead of a pot of gold for his freedom

"Illustrated in dePaola's signature style, this has an inviting look. Buoyant watercolors are framed by thin orange borders, but the potato simply can't be contained and bulges beyond the boundaries, graphic proof of its enormous size, an engaging read-aloud choice for Saint Patrick's Day." Booklist

★ The **legend** of the Indian paintbrush; retold and illustrated by Tomie dePaola. Putnam 1988 un il $16.99; pa $7.99
Grades: K 1 2 3   398.2
1. Native Americans -- Folklore
ISBN 0-399-21534-4; 0-698-11360-8 pa
LC 87-20160
"The native American motifs are rendered simply and authentically; the night sky and glorious sunset spreads are truly beautiful with line, color, and form perfectly balanced to capture the text." Horn Book

Tomie dePaola's Favorite nursery tales. Putnam 1986 127p il $24.99
Grades: K 1 2 3   398.2
1. Fables 2. Folklore
ISBN 0-399-21319-8
LC 85-28302
"DePaola's droll, witty, and very funny illustrations capture the essence of each story from a child's point of view. . . . The beautiful layout of these pages, in which the print and pictures are perfectly at ease with one another, invites confident new readers as well as adults for reading aloud." SLJ

DiPrimio, Pete
The **sphinx**. Mitchell Lane Publishers 2010 48p il map (Monsters in myth) lib bdg $29.95
Grades: 4 5 6 7   398.2
1. Sphinxes (Mythology)
ISBN 978-1-58415-931-5; 1-58415-931-6
LC 2010006560
This describes the mythic Sphinx that has appeared in both Egyptian and Greek myth.
This book is "thorough and respectful of a number of ancient and modern sources and [bends] over backward to navigate often contradictory, interlinked legends. . . . A number of paintings and photos break up the otherwise text-heavy pages, and copious chapter notes and reading suggestions conclude. This is by no means entry-level stuff, but for kids handy with the basics and ready to delve deeper, [this book] will be of great use." Booklist
Includes glossary and bibliographical references

Doherty, Berlie
Fairy tales; told by Berlie Doherty; illustrated by Jane Ray. Candlewick Press 2000 223p il $19.99
Grades: 4 5 6   398.2
1. Folklore 2. Fairy tales
ISBN 0-7636-0997-8
LC 99-89380
A collection of well-known fairy tales, such as Cinderella, Rapunzel, Aladdin and the enchanted lamp, and The fire-bird
These are "superb retellings on the earliest available sources in fresh versions sure to captivate readers anew. Ray's gold paint and folk art motifs prevail, but she also peppers the spreads with striking silhouette-collage compositions in a sumptuously designed volume." Publ Wkly

Downard, Barry
The **race** of the century; retold, written, and illustrated by Barry Downard. Simon & Schuster Books for Young Readers 2008 un il $15.99
Grades: 2 3 4   398.2
1. Fables 2. Rabbits -- Folklore 3. Turtles -- Folklore
ISBN 978-1-4169-2509-5; 1-4169-2509-0
LC 2006028791
Fed up with his incessant taunting, Tom Tortoise challenges Flash Harry Hare to the race of the century, which turns into a worldwide media event complete with television and newspaper coverage, photographers, and many other distractions.
"Digitally created photocollages of an animal cast, [the illustrations are] packed with silly exaggeration and humorous visual personification. . . . The sheer ludicrousness of this scenario will elicit snickering even in kids allergic to fables." Bull Cent Child Books

Eastman, Mary Huse
Index to fairy tales; including folklore, legends, and myths in collections. Scarecrow Press 1985 4v
Grades: Adult Professional   398.2
1. Fairy tales 2. Reference books 3. Legends -- Indexes
4. Folklore -- Indexes 5. Mythology -- Indexes
Volumes covering 1949-1972 and 1973-1977 first published by Faxon 1973 and 1979 respectively
"Although this is an essential reference book for the children's department, it is also a valuable source for the location of much folklore and fairy-tale material and should be available in adult book collections as well." Ref Sources for Small & Medium-sized Libr. 6th edition

Ehlert, Lois
★ **Cuckoo.** Cucu; a Mexican folktale. translated into Spanish by Gloria de Aragón Andújar. Harcourt Brace & Co. 1997 un il $16; pa $7
Grades: K 1 2 3   398.2
1. Mayas -- Folklore 2. Folklore -- Mexico 3. Bilingual books -- English-Spanish
ISBN 0-15-200274-X; 0-15-202428-X pa
LC 95-39560
A traditional Mayan tale which reveals how the cuckoo lost her beautiful feathers
"This tale, charmingly told in both English and Spanish, is boldly illustrated with large, brightly colored, cut-paper pictures. Inspired by folk art and crafts, the images evoke the tin work and cutout fiesta banners of Mexico." SLJ

Mole's hill; a woodland tale. Harcourt Brace & Co. 1994 un il $17; pa $7
Grades: PreK K 1 2   398.2
1. Moles (Animals) -- Fiction
ISBN 0-15-255116-6; 0-15-201890-5 pa
LC 93-31151
When Fox tells Mole she must move out of her tunnel to make way for a new path, Mole finds an ingenious way to save her home
"Ehlert's language is compact and telling. . . . The art . . . is dark-hued, appropriately nocturnal without losing spirit or contrast, and the beads stippled across the cutout cloth shapes lend interesting texture to the planes of color. . . . The story (which Ehlert says she based on a fragment of a Seneca

tale, with source completely cited in the book) has charm and vigor." Bull Cent Child Books

Ehrlich, Amy

A **treasury** of princess stories; retold by Amy Ehrlich; illustrated by Gary Blythe; [paper engineering by Keith Finch] Candlewick Press 2009 un il lib bdg $19.99
Grades: 1 2 3   **398.2**
1. Folklore 2. Fairy tales 3. Pop-up books 4. Princesses -- Fiction
ISBN 978-0-7636-4478-9 lib bdg; 0-7636-4478-1 lib bdg

"Six fairy tales previously retold by Ehlrich are here compiled, repackaged, and reillustrated with pop-ups. Each begins with a sort of title page/frontispiece designed to resemble a miniature book; when the cover is opened, a beautifully rendered pop-up illustration is revealed. The stories themselves are recounted faithfully and rhythmically. Each features at least two lush illustrations as well as spot decorations." Horn Book Guide

Elya, Susan Middleton, 1955-

★ **Rubia** and the three osos; illustrated by Melissa Sweet. Disney/Hyperion Books 2010 un il $15.99
Grades: PreK K 1 2   **398.2**
1. Folklore 2. Stories in rhyme 3. Bears -- Folklore 4. Spanish language -- Vocabulary
ISBN 978-1-4231-1252-5; 1-4231-1252-0
LC 2009028131

Retells the story of Goldilocks and the three bears in rhyming text interspersed with Spanish words, which are defined in a glossary.

"Pencil, watercolor and collage illustrations are packed with Southwest detail and rendered in fiesta colors, adding a Latin flair, while the overtly comic depiction of the three osos and Rubia in her red cowgirl boots contributes to the lighthearted humor." Kirkus

Emberley, Ed

★ **Chicken** Little. Roaring Brook Press 2009 un il $16.95
Grades: PreK K 1 2   **398.2**
1. Folklore 2. Animals -- Folklore
ISBN 978-1-59643-464-6; 1-59643-464-3
LC 2008-49329

A retelling of the classic story of Chicken Little, who has an acorn fall on his head and runs in a panic to his friends Henny Penny, Lucky Ducky, and Loosey Goosey, to tell them the sky is falling.

"The punchy text is perfectly complemented by high-impact illustrations in collage-like planes of electric hues. The bold splashes of countless colors, contrasted against sharp fields of white, briliantly jump out from the square pages. This is certain to become a favorite version of this story, and young readers will gleefully welcome an ending that offers no pedantic lesson." Bull Cent Child Books

★ The **red** hen; by Rebecca Emberley and Ed Emberley. Roaring Brook Press 2010 1 v. (unpaged)
Grades: PreK K 1 2   **398.2**
1. Folklore
ISBN 1596434929; 9781596434929
LC 2010284450

"When Red Hen finds a recipe for 'simply splendid cake,' she repeatedly asks the cat, the rat, and the frog for help gathering the ingredients. . . . The cat and the rat provide the familiar 'not I' but the frog croaks out a humorous 'bribbit.' . . . Set against white backgrounds, the zany characters, each with uniquely distinct eyes, pop off the pages. . . . The short, simple text allows for instant audience participation and offers a satisfying lesson on cooperation and fairness." SLJ

Endredy, James

The **journey** of Tunuri and the Blue Deer; a Huichol Indian story. illustrated by Maria Hernández de la Cruz and Casimiro de la Cruz López. Bear Cub Books 2003 32p il $15.95
Grades: 1 2 3   **398.2**
1. Native Americans -- Folklore -- Mexico
ISBN 1-59143-016-X
LC 2003-52298

Retells a traditional Huichol folktale in which the young Tunuri learns his place in the natural world when he meets the magical Blue Deer, and follows him on an enlightening journey.

"The colorful artwork is made from yarn that is applied to a piece of wood, an elaborate process that is a long-practiced art of the Huichol. The illustrations enhance the feel and authenticity of the story. Elaborate notes explain the sacred symbols, who the Huichol are, and how the art was created. A strong addition to folktale collections." SLJ

English folktales; edited by Dan Keding and Amy Douglas. Libraries Unlimited 2005 231p il map (World folklore series) $35
Grades: Adult Professional   **398.2**
1. Folklore -- Great Britain
ISBN 1-59158-260-1
LC 2005016075

"This collection of more than 50 English folktales contains a variety of stories arranged by common themes: The Fool in All His Glory, Wily Wagers and Tall Tales, Dragons and Devils, etc. The work of 22 storytellers is represented and their tellings are lively and inflected with the rhythms and speech of the regions from which their stories emanate. It is a delightful compendium for storytellers." SLJ

Ernst, Lisa Campbell

Little Red Riding Hood: a newfangled prairie tale. Simon & Schuster Bks. for Young Readers 1995 un il $16; pa $5.99
Grades: K 1 2 3   **398.2**
1. Folklore 2. Wolves -- Folklore
ISBN 0-689-80145-9; 0-689-82191-3 pa
LC 94-45723

In this "contemporary rendering of the old tale, Little Red Riding Hood wears a hooded sweatshirt and rides her bicycle, while Grandma is a robust farmer who turns the tables on the wolf. Ernst's inventive plot, enjoyable characters, and characteristic cartoon-style drawings demonstrate her mastery of the picture-book form." Horn Book Guide

Fleischman, Paul

★ **Glass** slipper, gold sandal; a worldwide Cinderella. illustrated by Julie Paschkis. Henry Holt 2007 un il $16.95

Grades: K 1 2 3 4   **398.2**
1. Folklore 2. Fairy tales
ISBN 978-0-8050-7953-1; 0-8050-7953-X
LC 2006-30615

"This inspired retelling blends many versions of Cinderella into a single, extraordinary tale. . . . As . . . Fleischman's . . . strong storytelling voice incorporates sometimes small details from different traditions, text and illustrations nimbly morph from one Cinderella story to the next, creating this brand-new version. Paschkis . . . makes use of folk art and textile patterns throughout the world in the clever background paintings behind each of her vibrant panel illustrations." Publ Wkly

Forest, Heather

The **contest** between the Sun and the Wind; an Aesop's fable. retold by Heather Forest; illustrated by Susan Gaber. August House Little Folk 2008 un il $16.95
Grades: K 1 2 3   **398.2**
1. Fables 2. Authors 3. Folklore 4. Storytellers
ISBN 978-0-87483-832-9; 0-87483-832-0
LC 2007018813

The sun and the wind test their strength by seeing which of them can cause a man to remove his coat, demonstrating the value of using gentle persuasion rather than force as a means of achieving a goal.

"Forest recasts this fable from Aesop in simple, crystalline language and occasional rhyme. . . . Gaber's wild and vivid images reflect, augment, and illuminate the story." Booklist

★ The **little** red hen; an old fable. retold by Heather Forest; illustrated by Susan Gaber. August House Little Folk 2006 un il $16.95
Grades: K 1 2 3   **398.2**
1. Folklore 2. Animals -- Folklore 3. Chickens -- Folklore
ISBN 0-87483-795-2
LC 2006040727

A rhymed retelling of the traditional tale about the industrious little red hen and her lazy friends

"Gaber's bold acrylic artwork and varied use of space . . . and the infectious, familiar refrain . . . make this an appealing storytime and readers' theater selection." SLJ

French, Vivian

Henny Penny; [by] Vivian French; illustrated by Sophie Windham. Bloomsbury Children's Books 2006 un il $16.95
Grades: PreK K 1 2   **398.2**
1. Folklore 2. Animals -- Folklore
ISBN 1-58234-706-9
LC 2005053688

Henny Penny and her barnyard friends are on their way to tell the king that the sky is falling when they meet a hungry fox, but Henny Penny's quick thinking saves the day

"A charmingly fleshed-out version of the traditional story. . . . Brightly colored and skillfully drawn illustrations balance perfectly with the delightful text and draw readers into their depths." SLJ

Galdone, Joanna

★ The **tailypo**; a ghost story. told by Joanna Galdone; illustrated by Paul Galdone. Clarion Bks. 1984 un il hardcover o.p. pa $7.95
Grades: K 1 2 3   **398.2**
1. Folklore -- United States
ISBN 0-395-30084-3 pa
LC 77-23289
First published by Seabury Press

"An old man lives in the Tennessee backwoods with his three hunting dogs. . . . The old man sees an odd animal squeezing through a crack in his cabin and grabs it. All he gets is its tail but he makes a snack of that and gets into bed with a satisfied appetite. But the dismembered [creature] wants its tail back." Publ Wkly

Galdone, Paul

The **elves** and the shoemaker; retold and illustrated by Paul Galdone. Clarion Bks. 1984 un il hardcover o.p. pa $6.95
Grades: PreK K 1 2   **398.2**
1. Fairy tales 2. Folklore -- Germany
ISBN 0-89919-422-2 pa
LC 83-14979

A pair of elves help a poor shoemaker become successful, and the shoemaker and his wife reward them with elegant outfits

"The pictures in flashing hues emphasize the secret helpers' impishness; they seem to be performing the service more for a lark than in the name of sweet charity." Publ Wkly

★ The **gingerbread** boy. Clarion Bks. 1975 un il $16; pa $6.95
Grades: PreK K 1 2   **398.2**
1. Folklore 2. Fairy tales
ISBN 0-395-28799-5; 0-89919-163-0 pa
First published by Seabury Press

"A lively version of the tale of the gingerbread boy who sprang into action as soon as he was baked and gleefully eluded all would-be captors until he was finally outwitted by a fox. The artist's gingerbread boy is a strong-legged, cocky individual, who sets out on a merry race through the countryside. The action of the tale is well-paced; large, humorous illustrations with stone fences, a covered bridge, and hearty rural folk suggest a New England background, while the triumphant fox is the epitome of all slyness." Horn Book

★ **Henny** Penny; retold and illustrated by Paul Galdone. Clarion Bks. 1968 un il $16; pa $6.95
Grades: PreK K 1 2   **398.2**
1. Folklore 2. Animals -- Folklore
ISBN 0-395-28800-2; 0-89919-225-4 pa
First published by Seabury Press

A folktale also popularly known as Chicken Little. "The simple retelling has a different ending which makes the fox seem somewhat less villainous—when Henny Penny and her credulous friends follow Foxy Loxy into the cave they are never seen again and the king is never told that the sky is falling, but Foxy Loxy, his wife, and seven little foxes (appealingly portrayed in a picture as a family group) still remember the fine feast they had that day." Booklist

★ The **little** red hen; a folk tale classic. Houghton Mifflin Harcourt 2011 un il $8.99

Grades: K 1 2 3 **398.2**
1. Folklore 2. Animals -- Folklore 3. Chickens -- Folklore
ISBN 978-0-547-37018-7; 0-547-37018-0

A reissue of the edition first published 1973 by Seabury Press

The little red hen finds none of her lazy friends willing to help her plant, harvest, or grind wheat into flour, but all are eager to eat the cake she makes from it.

Galdone's retelling is "straightforward and his unassuming loose-lined pictures provide just enough embellishment." Horn Book Guide

★ The **monkey** and the crocodile; a Jataka tale from India. Clarion Bks. 1969 un il hardcover o.p. pa $6.95
Grades: PreK K 1 2 **398.2**
1. Fables 2. Jataka stories 3. Folklore -- India 4. Monkeys -- Folklore 5. Crocodiles -- Folklore
ISBN 0-89919-524-5 pa

First published by Seabury Press

Illustrated by Galdone, this is a retelling of one of the Jataka fables about Buddha in his animal incarnations. "The crocodile wants a meal of monkey, but the intended prey is far wilier than his antagonist." SLJ

★ **Puss** in boots. Clarion Bks. 1976 un il hardcover o.p. pa $7.95
Grades: K 1 2 **398.2**
1. Fairy tales 2. Cats -- Folklore 3. Folklore -- France
ISBN 0-89919-192-4 pa

First published by Seabury Press

"Galdone follows Perrault's story line faithfully, as Puss works mischief to obtain a fortune for his master. The writing, fluid and readable, makes even this familiar tale sound fresh—no mean feat. Galdone's large, humorous caricatures—easily seen for story hour—have great gusto, and Puss is the embodiment of cleverness and knavery." SLJ

★ The **teeny**-tiny woman; a ghost story. Clarion Bks. 1984 un il $16; pa $5.95
Grades: PreK K 1 2 **398.2**
1. Ghost stories 2. Folklore -- Great Britain
ISBN 0-89919-270-X; 0-89919-463-X pa
LC 84-4311

Retold and illustrated by Galdone, this is an English folk tale about a "teeny-tiny woman who lives in a teeny-tiny house in a teeny-tiny village goes for a teeny-tiny walk, etc. Opening the gates to a churchyard, she finds a bone that will add flavor to the soup she plans for supper. Back home, she goes to bed but is alarmed by a voice . . . demanding, 'Give me back my bone!'" Publ Wkly

★ The **three** bears. Clarion Bks. 1972 un il $15; pa $6.95
Grades: PreK K 1 2 **398.2**
1. Folklore 2. Bears -- Folklore
ISBN 0-395-28811-8; 0-89919-401-X pa

First published by Seabury Press

In Galdone's illustrations for his retelling of the tale of Goldilocks, "his three bears are beautifully groomed, civilized creatures, living a life of rustic contentment in an astonishingly verdant forest, while his Goldilocks is a horrid,

be-ringletted, overdressed child who rampages wantonly through the bears' tidy home." Times Lit Suppl

★ The **three** Billy Goats Gruff. Clarion Bks. 1973 un il $16; pa $6.95
Grades: PreK K 1 2 **398.2**
1. Goats -- Folklore 2. Folklore -- Norway
ISBN 0-395-28812-6; 0-89919-035-9 pa

First published by Seabury Press

In this retelling of the old Norwegian folk tale, "the goats flummox the wicked troll and send him over the rickety bridge to a watery grave." Publ Wkly

★ The **three** little pigs; a folk tale classic. Houghton Mifflin Harcourt 2011 un il $8.99
Grades: K 1 2 3 **398.2**
1. Pigs -- Folklore 2. Wolves -- Folklore
ISBN 978-0-547-37020-0; 0-547-37020-2
LC 2011281137

A reissue of the edition published 1970 by Clarion Books

Retells the fatal episodes in the lives of two foolish pigs and how the third pig managed to avoid the same pigfalls.

Galdone's retelling is "straightforward and his unassuming loose-lined pictures provide just enough embellishment." Horn Book Guide

Gavin, Jamila
Tales from India; illustrated by Amanda Hall. Candlewick Press 2011 il
Grades: 5 6 7 8 **398.2**
1. Hindu mythology 2. Folklore -- India
ISBN 0-7636-5564-3; 978-0-7636-5564-8
LC 2010047651

"Gavin, . . . presents 10 classic Hindu stories, accompanied by Hall's lush and elegant gouache illustrations. . . . Readers should be drawn toward the valor, action, and dramatic transformations in these powerful tales." Publ Wkly

Gerson, Mary-Joan
Why the sky is far away; a Nigerian folktale. retold by Mary-Joan Gerson; pictures by Carla Golembe. Little, Brown 1992 un il hardcover o.p. pa $5.95
Grades: K 1 2 3 **398.2**
1. Folklore -- Nigeria
ISBN 0-316-30874-9 pa
LC 91-24949

A revised and newly illustrated edition of the title first published 1974 by Harcourt

The sky was once so close to the Earth that people cut parts of it to eat, but their waste and greed caused the sky to move far away

"Golembe's simple, theatrical illustrations combine monotype prints and collages in brilliant colors. . . . With its playfulness and drama, this is a fine book for story hour, especially in an ecology program." Booklist

Ginsburg, Mirra
Clay boy; adapted from a Russian folk tale by Mirra Ginsburg; pictures by Jos. A. Smith. Greenwillow Bks. 1997 un il $16
Grades: K 1 2 3 **398.2**
1. Folklore -- Russia
ISBN 0-688-14409-8; 0-688-14410-1 lib bdg
LC 96-33820

Wanting a son, an old man and woman make a clay boy who comes to life and begins eating everything in sight until he meets a clever goat

"The tale is adapted from a Russian folktale, and the storytelling voice is very simple and immediate. . . . In their play with scale, the illustrations express a wonderful combination of the monstrous and the cozy." Booklist

Goble, Paul

Buffalo woman; story and illustrations by Paul Goble. Bradbury Press 1984 un il hardcover o.p. pa $5.99
Grades: 2 3 4 **398.2**
  1. Bison -- Folklore 2. Native Americans -- Folklore
  ISBN 0-02-737720-2; 0-689-71109-3 pa
LC 83-15704

A young hunter marries a female buffalo in the form of a beautiful maiden, but when his people reject her he must pass several tests before being allowed to join the buffalo nation

"Each page sparkles with the lupins and yuccas of the Southwest and teems with native birds, butterflies, and small animals, the richness of detail never detracting from the overall design of the handsome illustrations. The author-artist successfully combines a compelling version of an old legend with his own imaginative and striking visual interpretation." Horn Book
  Includes bibliographical references

The **girl** who loved wild horses; story and illustrations by Paul Goble. Bradbury Press 1978 un il $14.95; pa $5.99
Grades: K 1 2 3 **398.2**
  1. Horses -- Folklore 2. Native Americans -- Folklore
  ISBN 0-02-736570-0; 0-689-71696-6 pa
LC 77-20500
  Awarded the Caldecott Medal, 1979

"Elaborate double-page spreads burst with life, revealing details of flowers and insects, animals and birds. . . . The story is told in simple language, and the author has included verses of a Navaho and Sioux song about horses. Both storytelling and art express the harmony with and the love of nature which characterize Native American culture." Horn Book

The **legend** of the White Buffalo Woman. National Geographic Soc. 1998 un il hardcover o.p. pa $7.95
Grades: 3 4 5 **398.2**
  1. Native Americans -- Folklore
  ISBN 0-7922-7074-6; 0-7922-6552-1 pa
LC 97-24086

A Lakota Indian legend in which the White Buffalo Woman presents her people with the Sacred Calf Pipe which gives them the means to pray to the Great Spirit

"In his fluid retelling of the legend of the first peace pipe, Goble . . . handles sweeping Lakota history succinctly and assuredly, largely due to his compelling artwork." Publ Wkly
  Includes bibliographical references

The **woman** who lived with wolves, & other stories from the tipi; told and illustrated by Paul Goble; foreword by Vivian Arviso Deloria. World Wisdom, Inc. 2011 un $14.95

Grades: 3 4 5 6 **398.2**
  1. Native Americans -- Folklore
  ISBN 978-1-935493-20-4; 1-935493-20-5
LC 2010029180

"Goble has collected and retold 27 stories, poems, and song lyrics from a variety of Native American tribes. . . . Depictions of how animals and man worked in harmony with one another permeate the stories and convey Goble's message that humans must live with tolerance and understanding of the natural world in order for both to survive. This collection is unique in its simplicity. The tales are accessible to young listeners as they beg to be read aloud. Most are only a page long. The accompanying illustrations are vintage Goble, finely detailed and painstakingly painted in rich tones of morning sky blues, orange-hued sunsets, and myriad chestnut, black, and amber horses." SLJ
  Includes bibliographical references

Goldman, Judy

Whiskers, tails, and wings; animal folktales from Mexico. Judy Goldman; illustrated by Fabricio Vanden Broeck. Charlesbridge 2012 58 p. (reinforced for library use) $16.95
Grades: 2 3 4 5 **398.2**
  1. Native Americans -- Folklore -- Mexico 2. Native American mythology 3. Tales -- Mexico 4. Animals -- Mexico -- Folklore 5. Indians of Mexico -- Folklore
  ISBN 1580893724; 9781580893725
LC 2012024636

This book is a "selection of Mexican folktales from five indigenous groups includes trickster tales, origin stories, and brief narratives about the triumphs of unconventional heroes. In a story from the Triqui people, the God of Creation creates the irritating flea in order to prevent Man and Woman from lying about lazily; a story from the Huichol tribe tells how the opossum lost its tail hair." Glossaries are provided. (Publishers Weekly)
  Includes bibliographical references and index

Green, Roger Lancelyn

King Arthur and his Knights of the Round Table; retold out of the old romances. with illustrations by Aubrey Beardsley. Knopf 1993 355p il $14.95
Grades: 5 6 7 8 **398.2**
  1. Arthurian romances 2. Kings
  ISBN 0-679-42311-7
LC 92-55073

A newly illustrated edition of the title first published 1953 in the United Kingdom
  Relates the exploits of King Arthur and his knights from the birth of Arthur to the destruction of Camelot

Gregorowski, Christopher

Fly, eagle, fly! an African tale. retold by Christopher Gregorowski; pictures by Niki Daly. Margaret K. McElderry Bks. 2000 un il hardcover o.p. pa $12.99
Grades: K 1 2 3 **398.2**
  1. Eagles -- Folklore 2. Folklore -- Africa
  ISBN 0-689-82398-3; 1-4169-7599-3 pa
LC 98-45302

Original two-color illustrated edition published 1982 in South Africa

A farmer finds an eagle and raises it to behave like a chicken, until a friend helps the eagle learn to find its rightful place in the sky

This "is a powerful celebration of the human spirit and its need for independence. It is beautifully complemented by watercolors, rich in the vibrant tones of earth and sky." Booklist

Grifalconi, Ann

The **village** of round and square houses. Little, Brown 1986 un il lib bdg $16.95

Grades: K 1 2 3   **398.2**

1. Folklore -- Africa

ISBN 0-316-32862-6

LC 85-24150

A Caldecott Medal honor book, 1987

A grandmother explains to her listeners why in their village on the side of a volcano the men live in square houses and the women in round ones

The author "illustrates her own tale, told to her by a young girl who grew up in Tos. The resting purple volcano, suddenly erupting into orange; the eerie orange sun; the villagers covered with ash; the fiery colored skies; the dense, lush jungles—all are captured beautifully by Grifalconi's art." Publ Wkly

Grimm, Jacob, 1785-1863

★ **Fairy** tales of the Brothers Grimm; edited by Noel Daniel; translated by Matthew R. Price. Taschen 2011 il $39.99

Grades: 4 5 6   **398.2**

1. Fairy tales 2. Folklore -- Germany

ISBN 978-3-8365-2672-2; 3-8365-2672-7

"This gorgeous treasury pairs new translations of 27 of the Grimm brothers' fairy tales with vintage illustrations dating from the 1820s to the 1950s. Brief introductions offer insight into the symbolism, themes, and contemporary relevance of each tale. Though Price and Daniel's translations feel modern . . . they honor the darkness that characterizes 'Little Red Riding Hood,' 'Snow White,' and other tales. The images show striking range. . . . The elegant presentation should entice readers to discover the cornucopia within." Publ Wkly

Grimm's fairy tales; illustrated by Arthur Rackam. Seastar Books 2001 160p il $19.95

Grades: 4 5 6   **398.2**

1. Fairy tales 2. Folklore -- Germany

ISBN 978-158717-092-8; 1-58717-092-2

A collection of twenty-two favorite fairy tales from the Brothers Grimm, including "Rapunzel," "The Bremen Town Musicians," "The Valiant Tailor", "The Frog Prince," "Ashenputtel," and "The Elves and the Shoemanker."

"This handsome facsimile of the 1909 edition is illustrated with twenty-one color plates and twenty-eight black-and-white drawings with an afterword by Peter Glassman." Horn Book Guide

Little Red Riding Hood; [by] the Brothers Grimm; illustrated by Bernadette Watts. North-South 2009 un il $16.95

Grades: K 1 2 3   **398.2**

1. Fairy tales 2. Wolves -- Folklore 3. Folklore --

Germany

ISBN 978-0-7358-2256-6; 0-7358-2256-5

A reissue of the edition first published 1968

A sweet little girl meets a hungry wolf in the forest while on her way to visit her grandmother.

"The well-known story is told simply and without embellishment, including some violent elements (e.g., the wolf's belly is slit open and filled with stones). The expansive illustrations use Old World folk-art elements to envelope readers in the forest landscapes." Horn Book Guide

Snow White; [by] the Brothers Grimm; illustrated by Charles Santore. Sterling 2010 un il $16.95

Grades: 1 2 3   **398.2**

1. Fairy tales 2. Folklore -- Germany

ISBN 978-1-4027-7157-6; 1-4027-7157-6

A reissue of the edition published 1996 by Random House

Retells the tale of the beautiful princess whose lips were red as blood, skin was white as snow, and hair was black as ebony.

"Lovely, broad paintings provide a rich sense of place and characters in this faithful rendering of the well-known tale. Snow White is a pretty child, the envious queen is haughty and wonderfully wizened in her disguises, and the dwarfs are distinctive individuals." SLJ

The **story** of Little Red Riding Hood; [by] The Brothers Grimm; illustrated by Christopher Bing. Handprint Books 2010 un il $18.99

Grades: K 1 2 3   **398.2**

1. Folklore 2. Fairy tales 3. Wolves -- Folklore

ISBN 978-0-8118-6986-7; 0-8118-6986-5

LC 2009019577

"This newly illustrated fairy tale includes three versions of an old favorite. The first and primary telling is Grimm's story. The grandmother and Little Red Riding Hood are consumed by the wolf, but freed by the hunter. . . . A second, lesser-known tale shows a resourceful girl who outfoxes the wolf, and all ends happily. In Perrault's shorter, darker version, which appears on the back endpaper with its original art, the old woman and girl are eaten and not saved. . . . The new, yet traditionally styled illustrations for the first two tales are well matched to the old stories. . . . [Bing] successfully takes the story back to its traditions." SLJ

Tales from the Brothers Grimm; selected & illustrated by Lisbeth Zwerger. Minedition 2013 96 p. (hbk.) $29.99

Grades: 4 5 6 7 8   **398.2**

1. Fairy tales 2. Fairy tales -- Germany

ISBN 9789888240531; 9888240536

In this book, Lisbeth Zwerger selects and illustrates stories "from the well-known collection of fairy tales by the Brothers Grimm. Old favorites such as 'Hansel and Gretel' and 'The Bremen Town Musicians' are included as are some lesser-known stories such as 'The Seven Ravens' and 'Hans My Hedgehog.'" (Publisher's note)

"High production values give this mix of new and recycled translations and illustrations a suitably sumptuous air...Like Zwerger's figures, which are nearly all small on the page and tend to look off into the distance, Bell's translations are more often lyrical than intimate or earthy: "Once upon a time, when wishes could still come true, there was a king whose daughters were all beautiful, but the youngest was so lovely that the sun itself, although it had seen so much, marveled at her beauty whenever it shone on her face.'...A belated companion to Zwerger's Hans Christian Andersen's Fairy Tales (1992, 2006), similarly elegant of design and equally fine for reading alone or aloud." (Kirkus)

The **twelve** dancing princesses; [originally] written by the Brothers Grimm; [adapted and] illustrated by Rachel Isadora. G.P. Putnam's Sons 2007 un il $16.99
Grades: K 1 2 3   **398.2**
1. Folklore 2. Fairy tales 3. Folklore -- Germany
ISBN 0-399-24744-0; 978-0-399-24744-6
                                          LC 2007-08160
This is a retelling of the story of twelve princesses who dance secretly all night long and how their secret is eventually discovered. "Age four and up." (N Y Times Book Rev)
"Working in collages of painted, textured paper, Isadora evokes an archetypal African kingdom through sumptuous, kente cloth textiles and Serengenti-like landscapes that pop vibrantly agains primarily white backgrounds." Booklist

Haley, Gail E.
★ A **story,** a story; an African tale retold and illustrated by Gail E. Haley. Atheneum Pubs. 1970 un il $18; pa $7.99
Grades: K 1 2 3   **398.2**
1. Anansi (Legendary character) 2. Folklore -- Africa
ISBN 0-689-20511-2; 0-689-71201-4 pa
Awarded the Caldecott Medal, 1971
"The story explains the origin of that favorite African folk material, the spider tale. Here Ananse, the old spider man, wanting to buy the Sky God's stories, completes by his cleverness three seemingly impossible tasks set as the price for the golden box of stories which he takes back to earth." Sutherland. The Best in Child Books

Hamilton, Martha
The **ghost** catcher; a Bengali folktale. [by] Martha Hamilton & Mitch Weiss; illustrated by Kristen Balouch. August House Little Folk 2008 un il $16.95
Grades: PreK K 1 2   **398.2**
1. Folklore -- India 2. Ghosts -- Folklore
ISBN 978-0-87483-835-0; 0-87483-835-5
                                          LC 2007-14308
A retelling of a traditional Bengali tale in which a kind and generous Indian barber, pressed by his father then his wife to earn more money, cleverly persuades a ghost to bring him riches.
"Hamilton and Weiss relate the tale with economy and wit. . . . The illustrations' lyrical lines, colorful forms, and linen-textured backdrop create a distinctive look." Booklist

Hamilton, Virginia, 1934-2002
★ The **people** could fly: American Black folktales; told by Virginia Hamilton; illustrated by Leo and Diane Dillon. 2009 178p il $24.99; pa $13
Grades: 5 6 7 8   **398.2**
1. African Americans -- Folklore
ISBN 978-0-394-86925-4; 0-394-86925-7; 978-0-679-84336-8 pa; 0-679-84336-1 pa
A reissue of the title first published 1985
Coretta Scott King honor book for illustration, 1986
The author "has been successful in her efforts to write these tales in the Black English of the slave storytellers. Her

scholarship is unobtrusive and intelligible. She has provided a glossary and notes concerning the origins of the tales and the different versions in other cultures. Handsomely illustrated." NY Times Book Rev
In this retelling of a folktale, a group of slaves, unable to bear their sadness and starvation any longer, calls upon the African magic that allows them to fly away. "Age four and up." (N Y Times Book Rev)
"Familiar as it is, we have never seen the story like this. Not with all these evocative images, vivid, bright and moving, leading us on a journey through territory we thought we knew." NY Times Book Rev
Includes bibliographical references

Han, Suzanne Crowder
The **rabbit's** tail; a story from Korea. illustrated by Richard Wehrman. Holt & Co. 1999 un il $16.95
Grades: K 1 2 3   **398.2**
1. Folklore -- Korea 2. Tigers -- Folklore 3. Rabbits -- Folklore
ISBN 0-8050-4580-5
                                          LC 98-16627
Tiger is afraid of being eaten by a fearsome dried persimmon, but when Rabbit tries to convince him he is wrong, Rabbit loses his long tail
"The tale is vividly retold. . . . An amusing entertainment about misperceptions." SLJ

Harris, John
My monster notebook; [by] John Harris & Mark Todd. J. Paul Getty Museum 2011 un il $16.95
Grades: 4 5 6   **398.2**
1. Folklore 2. Monsters
ISBN 978-1-60606-050-6; 1-60606-050-3
                                          LC 2010025302
"At its core, the volume is a descriptive list of mythological monsters, from the immortal half-woman, half-serpent Echidna to Python, the dangerous snake sent to kill baby Apollo. The notebook-style layout includes doodles, photographs, and scrap papers, making the book appear to be a relic unearthed from the ruins of a modern school locker." Horn Book Guide

Strong stuff; Herakles and his labors. fierce words by John Harris; powerful art by Gary Baseman. J. Paul Getty Museum 2005 un il map $16.95
Grades: 4 5 6 7   **398.2**
1. Classical mythology 2. Hercules (Legendary character)
ISBN 0-89236-784-9
                                          LC 2004-7904
This is a "simplified version of the 12 labors of Hercules (Herakles as the Greeks called him). . . . Each labor is allotted a spread with bright and bold illustrations featuring Herakles locked in mortal combat with the monster of the moment, accompanied by a chatty, humorous commentary." SLJ

Hartman, Bob
The **Lion** storyteller book of animal tales; animal tales old and new especially for reading aloud. illustrated by Krisztina Kállai Nagy. Lion 2011 128p il $19.99

Grades: K 1 2 3   398.2
1. Fables 2. Folklore 3. Animals -- Fiction
ISBN 978-0-74596-131-6; 0-74596-131-2

"Hartman vibrantly retells and updates 36 animal fables hailing from ancient Greece, Africa, Japan, India, and other world cultures. The selections include trickster, morality, and animal-origin tales . . . along with a few original stories. Nagy's bright and friendly illustrations mimic Hartman's descriptive but accessible tone. A thoughtful collection that might inspire some readers to create animal stories of their own." Publ Wkly

Mr. Aesop's story shop; illustrated by Jago Silver. Lion/Trafalgar 2011 48p il $14.99
Grades: K 1 2 3   398.2
1. Fables 2. Authors 3. Storytellers
ISBN 0-7459-6915-1; 978-0-7459-6915-2

"This title re-frames 10 familiar fables . . . to add new context and setting to the stories. Each entry is narrated in first person, as if Aesop himself were speaking. . . . The introduction informs young readers about what is known, and what is not, about Aesop and defines what makes a story a fable. . . . The painterly illustrations look as if they are done on textured paper and incorporate Greek architectural details. . . . A worthwhile addition to collections." Booklist

Hausman, Gerald
Horses of myth; [by] Gerald and Loretta Hausman; pictures by Robert Florczak. Dutton Children's Books 2004 100p il $12
Grades: 4 5 6 7   398.2
1. Folklore 2. Horses -- Folklore
ISBN 0-525-46964-8
LC 2002-40809

"These five tales each feature a different type of horse, remarkable for both its individuality and the qualities representative of its breed. . . . Florczak's illustrations adapt characteristics appropriate to the locations and time periods of each selection's origins. . . . This is an attractive volume, useful to teachers and librarians for read-alouds and of interest to horse-loving youngsters." SLJ

Hayes, Joe
The **coyote** under the table; = El coyote debajo de la mesa: folktales told in Spanish and English. illustrations by Antonio Castro L. Cinco Puntos Press 2011 il $19.95; pa $12.95
Grades: 3 4 5 6   398.2
1. Folklore -- New Mexico 2. Bilingual books -- English-Spanish
ISBN 978-1-935955-21-4; 1-935955-21-7; 978-1-935955-06-1 pa; 1-935955-06-3 pa
LC 2011011430

"Eight tales of tricksters and magical transformations are given a Southwestern setting by a veteran storyteller and paired to Spanish versions on facing pages. . . . Each tale opens with a realistically detailed black-and-white scene to set the comic or dramatic mood. . . . These wise and witty tales continue to repay fresh encounters." Kirkus

Dance, Nana, dance; Cuban folktales in English and Spanish. retold by Joe Hayes; illustrated by Mauricio Trenard Sayago. Cinco Puntos Press 2008 128p il $20.95

Grades: 5 6 7 8 9   398.2
1. Folklore -- Cuba 2. Bilingual books -- English-Spanish
ISBN 978-1-933693-17-0; 1-933693-17-7
LC 2007-38295

A collection of stories from Cuban folklore, representing the cultures of Spain, Africa, and the Caribbean.

"Each tale is accompanied by a full-page illustration that is colorful and contributes to the text. This book is a great addition to folktale and Spanish language collections. Students will enjoy these stories that could easily be incorporated into the curriculum." Libr Media Connect

Little Gold Star; a Cinderella cuento/Estrellita de oro. retold in Spanish & English by Joe Hayes; illustrated by Gloria Osuna Perez & Lucia Angela Perez. Cinco Puntos Press 2000 30p il $15.95
Grades: K 1 2 3   398.2
1. Fairy tales 2. Hispanic Americans -- Folklore 3. Bilingual books -- English-Spanish
ISBN 0-938317-49-0
LC 99-57104

In this variation of the Cinderella story, coming from the Hispanic tradition in New Mexico, Arciá and her wicked stepsisters have different encounters with a magical hawk and are left physically changed in ways that will affect their meeting with the prince

"The English text, which is made full-bodied by its many details, appears with a Spanish translation. The impressive acrylic illustrations, done in a sturdy folk-art style, are thick with color and bright with humor." Booklist

Hennessy, B. G.
The **boy** who cried wolf; retold by B.G. Hennessy; illustrated by Boris Kulikov. Simon & Schuster Books for Young Readers 2006 un il $15.95
Grades: K 1 2   398.2
1. Folklore 2. Sheep -- Folklore 3. Wolves -- Folklore
ISBN 0-689-87433-2
LC 2004-21672

A boy tending sheep on a lonely mountainside thinks it a fine joke to cry "wolf" and watch the people come running—and then one day a wolf is really there, but no one answers his call

"The story begs to be read aloud, and the large, colorful, and amusing watercolor-and-gouache paintings are perfect for group viewing. . . . A clever take on an old favorite." SLJ

Henrichs, Wendy
I am Tama, lucky cat; a Japanese legend. illustrated by Yoshiko Jaeggi. Peachtree 2011 un il $16.95
Grades: K 1 2 3   398.2
1. Cats -- Folklore 2. Folklore -- Japan
ISBN 978-1-56145-589-8; 1-56145-589-X
LC 2010052072

A retelling of the traditional Japanese tale describing the origins of the beckoning cat and how it came to be a symbol of good luck.

"Evocative watercolor illustrations capture ancient Japan in this picture book retelling of the lucky-cat legend. . . . The story's tone is formal but not stilted. . . . The artist studied in Osaka and her traditional training comes through, blending formal composition with light comic touches. . . .

With its compelling story and stunning art, this is a worthy addition." SLJ

Hickox, Rebecca

The **golden** sandal; a Middle Eastern Cinderella story. illustrated by Will Hillenbrand. Holiday House 1998 un il $16.95; pa $6.95

Grades: K 1 2 3   **398.2**

1. Fairy tales 2. Folklore -- Iraq

ISBN 0-8234-1331-4; 0-8234-1513-9 pa

LC 97-5071

An Iraqi version of the Cinderella story in which a kind and beautiful girl who is mistreated by her stepmother and stepsister finds a husband with the help of a magic fish

"The story is charmingly told and illustrated with paintings on vellum, giving the pictures a soft, luxurious quality." N Y Times Book Rev

Hirsh, Marilyn

The **rabbi** and the twenty-nine witches. Marshall Cavendish Children 2009 un il $17.99

Grades: K 1 2 3   **398.2**

1. Rain -- Fiction 2. Jews -- Folklore 3. Moon -- Folklore 4. Witches -- Folklore

ISBN 978-0-7614-5586-8; 0-7614-5586-8

LC 2008022985

A reissue of the title first published 1976 by Holiday House

A wise old rabbi finally rids the village of the witches that terrorize it every night that the moon is full.

Hoberman, Mary Ann

Very short fables to read together; adapted by Mary Ann Hoberman; illustrated by Michael Emberley. Little Brown & Company 2010 32p il (You read to me, I'll read to you) $16.99

Grades: K 1 2 3   **398.2**

1. Fables 2. Poetry -- By individual authors

ISBN 978-0-316-04117-1; 0-316-04117-3

"The team behind the collaborative reading series turns their attention to Aesop's fables. Two readers can recite alternating passages differentiated by color, with the closing morals to be read in unison. Emberley's pencil and watercolor spot illustrations bring fresh energy to the classic tales as well as a softening tone. . . . The jaunty rhymes and theatrical element of adopting a persona should spark enthusiasm from reluctant readers." Publ Wkly

Hodges, Margaret

★ **Dick** Whittington and his cat; retold by Margaret Hodges; illustrated by Melisande Potter. Holiday House 2006 un il $16.95

Grades: K 1 2 3   **398.2**

1. Mayors 2. Cats -- Folklore 3. Folklore -- Great Britain

ISBN 0-8234-1987-8

LC 2005-46222

Retells the legend of the poor boy in medieval England who trades his beloved cat for a fortune in gold and jewels and eventually becomes Lord Mayor of London.

"In this spare retelling of the British legend, the narrative keeps buoyant with droll dialogue. The humorous illustrations, created with colorful inks and gouache, enhance the

story with expressive faces and movement that delight the eye." SLJ

★ **Saint** George and the dragon; a golden legend. adapted by Margaret Hodges from Edmund Spenser's Faerie Queene; illustrated by Trina Schart Hyman. Little, Brown 1984 32p il $16.95; pa $6.95

Grades: 2 3 4 5   **398.2**

1. Saints 2. Martyrs 3. Soldiers 4. Dragons -- Folklore 5. Knights and knighthood -- Folklore

ISBN 0-316-36789-3; 0-316-36795-8 pa

LC 83-19980

Awarded the Caldecott Medal, 1985

Retells the segment from Spenser's The Faerie Queene, in which George, the Red Cross Knight, slays the dreadful dragon that has been terrorizing the countryside for years and brings peace and joy to the land

"Hyman's illustrations are uniquely suited to this outrageously romantic and appealing legend. . . . The paintings are richly colored, lush, detailed and dramatic. . . . This is a beautifully crafted book, a fine combination of author and illustrator." SLJ

Hogrogian, Nonny

The **contest**; adapted and illustrated by Nonny Hogrogian. Greenwillow Bks. 1976 un il lib bdg $15.89

Grades: K 1 2 3   **398.2**

1. Folklore -- Armenia

ISBN 0-688-84042-6

A Caldecott Medal honor book, 1977

"The symmetrical elements of the tale, which create arabesques of humor, are well-served by the full-color, full-page illustrations and by the pencil drawings scattered through the text. Some of the colored illustrations are bordered by oriental rug patterns, and all of the paintings and drawings are strong in their depiction of Armenian physiognomy." Horn Book

★ **One** fine day. Macmillan 1971 un il $16; pa $5.99

Grades: K 1 2 3   **398.2**

1. Foxes -- Folklore 2. Folklore -- Armenia

ISBN 0-02-744000-1; 0-02-043620-3 pa

Awarded the Caldecott Medal, 1972

When a fox drinks the milk in an old woman's jug, she chops off his tail and refuses to sew it back on unless he gives her milk back. The author-illustrator's cumulative tale, based on an Armenian folktale, tells of the many transactions the fox must go through before his tail is restored

"A charming picture book that is just right for reading aloud to small children, the scale of the pictures also appropriate for group use." Sutherland. The Best in Child Books

Huck, Charlotte S.

Princess Furball; retold by Charlotte Huck; illustrated by Anita Lobel. Greenwillow Bks. 1989 un il hardcover o.p. pa $6.99

Grades: 1 2 3   **398.2**

1. Fairy tales

ISBN 0-688-13107-7 pa

LC 88-18780

This book is about a "princess who rebels against her tyrannical father and makes the most of her gifts to survive in another kingdom and win the hand of the king. This narrative focuses on the ingenuity of a girl who plots her own destiny." N Y Times Book Rev

Huling, Jan

Ol' Bloo's boogie-woogie band and blues ensemble; illustrated by Henri Sorensen. Peachtree 2010 un il $16.95

Grades: 2 3 4   **398.2**

1. Animals -- Folklore 2. Folklore -- Germany 3. Musicians -- Folklore

ISBN 978-1-56145-436-5; 1-56145-436-2

Set in Louisiana, four aging animals who are no longer of any use to their masters find a new home after outwitting a gang of robbers.

"The story of the Bremen Town Musicians works just as well in the American South as it does in the Black Forest. . . . In contrast to the antic narration, Sørensen . . . contributes thoughtful, painterly landscapes of the tin-roofed buildings and dry scrub of the South, and realistic portraits of the animals. . . . Small black silhouettes adjacent to the main paintings add another layer of visual interest. Read-aloud audiences will giggle at the dialect, nonstop action, and atmospheric descriptions of Huling's . . . retelling." Publ Wkly

Hyman, Trina Schart

★ **Little** Red Riding Hood; by the Brothers Grimm retold and illustrated by Trina Schart Hyman. Holiday House 1983 un il lib bdg $16.95; pa $6.95

Grades: K 1 2   **398.2**

1. Wolves -- Folklore 2. Folklore -- Germany

ISBN 0-8234-0470-6 lib bdg; 0-8234-0653-9 pa

LC 82-7700

On her way to deliver a basket of food to her sick grandmother, Elisabeth encounters a sly wolf. "Grades two to four." (Bull Cent Child Books)

This retelling "basically follows the Grimm story, although the text has been fleshed out with some extraneous details (for instance, the little girl is called Elisabeth). . . . The illustrations seem to be a labor of love; richly colored paintings of the forest teem with exquisitely detailed plant and animal life, and the interior scenes, awash with atmospheric light, are beautifully composed and executed." Horn Book

Isadora, Rachel

The **fisherman** and his wife; written by the Brothers Grimm; retold and illustrated by Rachel Isadora. G. P. Putnam's Sons 2008 un il $16.99

Grades: K 1 2 3   **398.2**

1. Folklore 2. Fairy tales

ISBN 978-0-399-24771-2; 0-399-24771-8

LC 2007-18385

The fisherman's greedy wife is never satisfied with the wishes granted her by an enchanted fish.

"Isadora uses collages of paint-striated paper in tropical colors, plus occasional scraps of fabric, to give this familiar tale a generic African setting. . . . Compared to other retellings, dialogue here is minimal, suiting the story to listeners and beginning readers. . . . It's a handsome book, and a tale that sits comfortably in its new setting." Horn Book

Hansel and Gretel; written by the Brothers Grimm; retold and illustrated by Rachel Isadora. G.P. Putnam's Sons 2009 un il $16.99

Grades: PreK K 1 2   **398.2**

1. Folklore 2. Fairy tales

ISBN 978-0-399-25028-6; 0-399-25028-X

LC 2008018580

When they are left in the woods by their parents, two children find their way home despite an encounter with a wicked witch.

"Isadora's abbreviated retelling of the popular Grimm Brothers tale closely follows the original in both plot and detail while making the story more accessible to a younger audience. . . . She again sets her tale in Africa, piecing colorfully patterned and hand-painted papers together to create bold, busy eye-catching scenes with a strong ethnic feel." SLJ

Rapunzel; written by the Brothers Grimm; retold and illustrated by Rachel Isadora. G. P. Putnam's Sons 2008 un il $16.99

Grades: K 1 2 3   **398.2**

1. Fairy tales 2. Folklore -- Germany

ISBN 978-0-399-24772-9; 0-399-24772-6

LC 2007047104

Recasts in an African setting the familiar fairy tale in which a beautiful girl with extraordinarily long hair is imprisoned in a lonely tower by a witch.

"The story remains true to the original. . . . Colorful, vibrant oil paints and collages brighten up the story. The artwork has rich brushstrokes and is heavily patterned, and details abound." SLJ

Jacobs, Joseph

English fairy tales; with illustrations by John Batten. Knopf 1993 428p il $13.95

Grades: 4 5 6   **398.2**

1. Fairy tales 2. Folklore -- Great Britain

ISBN 0-679-42809-7

LC 93-13878

A reissue in one volume of the author's English fairy tales (1891) and More English fairy tales (1894)

A collection of more than eighty traditional stories that recount the adventures of giants, witches, princes, princesses, and animals

James, Alison

The **star** child; translated & adapted from German by J. Alison James; illustrated by Bernadette Watts. North-South 2010 un il $16.95

Grades: PreK K 1   **398.2**

1. Fairy tales 2. Folklore -- Germany

ISBN 978-0-7358-2330-3; 0-7358-2330-8

"Poor in worldly goods but possessing 'a loving and courageous heart,' orphaned Mathilde spends a day giving away her meager possessions and reaps a splendid return. The original tale is often known as 'The Shower of Gold,' but apart from the title change and naming the girl, this sunny version faithfully recounts the story and its lesson. Watts's simply drawn and warmly colored figures encounter one another in appealing rural scenes." SLJ

James, Elizabeth

The **woman** who married a bear; retold by Elizabeth James; illustrated by Atanas. Simply Read Books 2008 un il $16.95

Grades: 2 3 4   **398.2**

1. Bears -- Folklore 2. Native Americans -- Folklore
ISBN 978-1-894965-49-1; 1-894965-49-3

"In this retelling of a West Coast First Nations' myth, a young woman tells her friends that bears are ugly, filthy, dumb animals. The Chief of the Bear People wants to punish her, but his nephew asks for her as his wife. From Mouse Woman she learns that bears can transform into humans and then into bears again. . . . Atanas's exquisite watercolor illustrations capture the natural beauty of the Pacific Coast and the distinctive culture of the First Nations people. . . . This is a welcome addition to units on Native American cultures." SLJ

Jeffers, Susan

Hansel and Gretel; by Susan Jeffers. Rev. ed.; Dutton Children's Books 2011 il $17.99

Grades: 2 3 4   **398.2**

1. Fairy tales 2. Folklore -- Germany
ISBN 978-0-525-42221-1

LC 2011005246

A revised version of the edition published 1980 by Dial Press

When they are left in the woods by their parents, two children find their way home despite an encounter with a wicked witch.

"Those familiar with Jeffers's 1980 version (Dial) will notice that this edition includes a few changes in the illustrations and a simplified text. . . . The artwork, done once again in pen, ink, and dyes, is for the most part from the earlier edition. . . . The pictures are slightly more muted overall, but are still presented in Jeffers's very recognizable style." SLJ

Johnson, Paul Brett

★ **Fearless** Jack; adapted and illustrated by Paul Brett Johnson. Margaret K. McElderry Bks. 2001 un il hardcover o.p. pa $10.99

Grades: K 1 2 3   **398.2**

1. Folklore -- Appalachian Mountains
ISBN 0-689-83296-6; 1-416-96833-4 pa

LC 99-89184

In this Appalachian folktale, Jack wins fame and fortune after killing ten yellow jackets with one whack

"In an Appalachian twang, complete with distinct vocabulary and speech patterns, Johnson's colorful, comical, sturdy pictures are just as energetic as the story which is told." Booklist

★ **Jack** outwits the giants; adapted and illustrated by Paul Brett Johnson. Margaret K. McElderry Bks. 2002 un il hardcover o.p. pa $11.99

Grades: K 1 2 3   **398.2**

1. Giants -- Folklore 2. Folklore -- Appalachian Mountains
ISBN 0-689-83902-2; 1-4169-7861-5 pa

LC 2001-30811

Companion volume to Fearless Jack

In this Appalachian folktale, Jack outwits two giants who want fresh meat for breakfast

"Johnson interweaves several familiar motifs from many traditions while bringing an authentic mountain twang to his telling. Johnson's lively acrylics leave no doubt that these events are as comical as they are suspenseful; the equally lively dialogue makes this an especially good read-aloud." Horn Book Guide

Kajikawa, Kimiko

★ **Tsunami!** illustrated by Ed Young. Philomel Books 2009 un il $16.99

Grades: K 1 2 3   **398.2**

1. Folklore -- Japan 2. Tsunamis -- Folklore
ISBN 978-0-399-25006-4; 0-399-25006-9

LC 2008-25747

A wealthy man in a Japanese village, who everyone calls Ojiisan, which means grandfather, sets fire to his rice fields to warn the innocent people of an approaching tsunami.

"Kajikawa imbues the story with a sense of nobility. . . . Young's rough, impressionistic collages of handpainted papers, fabric, and organic material are dark and stirring." Booklist

Karlin, Barbara

James Marshall's Cinderella; illustrated by James Marshall; retold by Barbara Karlin. Dial Bks. for Young Readers 2001 un il hardcover o.p. pa $6.99

Grades: K 1 2   **398.2**

1. Folklore 2. Fairy tales
ISBN 0-8037-2730-5; 0-14-230048-9 pa

LC 2001-23097

This is a reissue of Barbara Karlin's Cinderella, published 1989 by Little, Brown

"Those seeking a condensed version of the classic fairy tale will find just what they want in Karlin's brief retelling; . . . James Marshall's witty, warts-and-all illustrations add the sparkle that brings out the best in Karlin's straightforward retelling." Horn Book

Keats, Ezra Jack

John Henry; an American legend. story and pictures by Ezra Jack Keats. Pantheon Bks. 1965 un il hardcover o.p. pa $5.99

Grades: K 1 2 3   **398.2**

1. John Henry (Legendary character) 2. Folklore -- United States 3. African Americans -- Folklore
ISBN 0-394-89052-3 pa

LC 86-27453

This is a picture book retelling of the legend of the Black American folk hero who drove spikes for the railroads

"The dynamic power with which John Henry wields his hammer is matched by the strong illustrations: brilliant oranges and reds contrast with grays and blacks that are often silhouettes; unusual backgrounds produce startling effects. A good picture-story to show to a group." Horn Book

Kellogg, Steven

Chicken Little; retold & illustrated by Steven Kellogg. Morrow 1985 un il hardcover o.p. pa $5.95

Grades: K 1 2 3   **398.2**

1. Folklore 2. Animals -- Folklore
ISBN 0-688-07045-0 pa

LC 84-25519

In this adaptation of Joseph Jacobs' fable, Chicken Little and his feathered friends, alarmed that the sky seems to be falling, are easy prey to hungry Foxy Loxy when he poses as a police officer in hopes of tricking them into his truck. "Grades one to three." (SLJ)

"Kellogg has enlivened the text [by] giving it some modern touches (Turkey Lurkey carries golf clubs, Foxy Loxy is caught when a 'hippoliceman' tumbles out of a patrol helicopter to land him). Children have always enjoyed the repetition and cumulation of the story, as well as the silliness of the fowls who believe the sky is falling; here there's added fun." Bull Cent Child Books

★ **Paul** Bunyan; a tall tale. retold and illustrated by Steven Kellogg. Morrow 1984 un il lib bdg $16.89; pa $5.95

Grades: K 1 2 3   **398.2**
  1. Tall tales 2. Bunyan, Paul (Legendary character)
  ISBN 0-688-03850-6 lib bdg; 0-688-05800-0 pa
                             LC 83-26684
"Kellogg uses oversize pages for busy, detail-crowded illustrations that have vitality and humor, echoing the exaggeration and ebullience of the story." Bull Cent Child Books

Pecos Bill; a tall tale. retold and illustrated by Steven Kellogg. Morrow 1986 un il $17; pa $5.95

Grades: K 1 2 3   **398.2**
  1. Tall tales 2. Pecos Bill (Legendary character)
  ISBN 0-688-05871-X; 0-688-09924-6 pa
                             LC 86-784
Incidents from the life of Pecos Bill, from his childhood among the coyotes to his unusual wedding day

"Although there's a lot going on in these pictures, they're not cluttered; both the gradations of color and the page design smooth the lines of continuous action and tumult of humorous detail. Kellogg's portrayal of Pecos Bill as a perpetual boy will appeal to children. The retelling is a smooth adaptation for introducing young listeners to longer versions or to accompany storytelling sessions centered around tall-tale heroes." Bull Cent Child Books

★ **Sally** Ann Thunder Ann Whirlwind Crockett; a tall tale. retold and illustrated by Steven Kellogg. Morrow Junior Bks. 1995 un il hardcover o.p. $17

Grades: K 1 2 3   **398.2**
  1. Tall tales
  ISBN 0-688-14042-4; 0-688-14043-2 lib bdg; 0-688-17113-3 pa
                             LC 94-43782
Sally Ann is "Davy's wife and a match for any bear, alligator, or macho man in the West. As retold (and scrupulously sourced) by Kellogg, Sally Ann's early life outracing and outswimming her nine big brothers and beating all comers at the state fair . . . is but a prelude to her flight to the frontier and subsequent rescue of and marriage to Davy Crockett. . . . Kellogg's characteristically energetic paintings meet their match in this story's kinetic hyperbole; the fact that his Sally Ann and Davy look like rambunctious big kids will only add to their story-hour appeal." Bull Cent Child Books

Kim, So-Un
  Korean children's favorite stories; retold by Kim So-un; illustrated by Jeong Kyoung-Sim. Tuttle 2004 95p il $16.95

Grades: 3 4 5 6   **398.2**
  1. Folklore -- Korea
  ISBN 0-8048-3591-8
A newly illustrated edition of The story bag, published 1955

This collection of 13 Korean folktales "includes elements shared by many cultures, such as a flood story, and others with a unique sensibility. A variety of animals appear, including tigers, both good and bad, and snakes, depicted as dragons. The delicate watercolor illustrations make the stories accessible to children." SLJ

Kimmel, Eric A.
  Anansi and the moss-covered rock; retold by Eric A. Kimmel; illustrated by Janet Stevens. Holiday House 1988 un il lib bdg $17.95

Grades: 1 2 3 4   **398.2**
  1. Anansi (Legendary character) 2. Animals -- Folklore
  3. Spiders -- Folklore 4. Folklore -- West Africa
  ISBN 0-8234-0689-X
                             LC 87-31766
Anansi the Spider uses a strange moss-covered rock in the forest to trick all the other animals, until Little Bush Deer decides he needs to learn a lesson

"The text is rhythmic, nicely building suspense to the inevitable conclusion. Stevens' complementary, colorful illustrations add detail, humor, and movement to the text." SLJ

Anansi's party time; by Eric A. Kimmel; illustrated by Janet Stevens. Holiday House 2008 un il $16.95; pa $6.95

Grades: K 1 2 3   **398.2**
  1. Anansi (Legendary character) 2. Spiders -- Folklore
  3. Turtles -- Folklore 4. Folklore -- West Africa
  ISBN 978-0-8234-1922-7; 0-8234-1922-3; 978-0-8234-2241-8 pa; 0-8234-2241-0 pa
                           LC 2007002206
When Anansi the spider invites Turtle to a party just to play a trick on him, Turtle gets revenge at a party of his own

"Children will delight in hearing this tale of the spider's comeuppance. . . . Almost every page, illustrated in acrylic ink and colored pencils, has some comical element." SLJ

Even higher! Holiday House 2009 un il $16.95

Grades: K 1 2 3   **398.2**
  1. Jews -- Folklore 2. Rosh ha-Shanah -- Fiction
  ISBN 978-0-8234-2020-9; 0-8234-2020-5
                           LC 2008019710
A skeptical visitor to the village of Nemirov finds out where its rabbi really goes just before the Jewish New Year, when the villagers claim he goes to heaven to speak to God.

"Kimmel's wise, reassuring voice embellishes the story with wonderful details. . . . while keeping the narrative taut. . . . Weber's colorful, openhearted drawings immerse readers in a lost world where piety defined life and the quest for truth was the biggest adventure of all." Publ Wkly

The fisherman and the turtle; adapted by Eric A. Kimmel; illustrated by Martha Aviles. Marshall Cavendish Children 2008 un il $16.99

Grades: K 1 2   **398.2**
  1. Folklore 2. Fairy tales 3. Aztecs -- Folklore 4. Turtles -- Folklore
  ISBN 978-0-7614-5387-1; 0-7614-5387-3
A retelling of the Grimm tale about the fisherman's greedy wife, set in the land of the Aztecs

"The vivid colors of the acrylic-and-watercolor illustrations and pages bordered with motifs from Aztec art give the tale an authentic flavor." Booklist

The **flying** canoe; a Christmas story. retold by Eric A. Kimmel; illustrated by Daniel San Souci and Justin San Souci. Holiday House 2011 un il $16.95
Grades: K 1 2 3   398.2
1. Folklore -- Canada 2. Christmas -- Folklore 3. French Canadians -- Folklore
ISBN 0823417301; 9780823417308; 978-0-8234-1730-8; 0-8234-1730-1
LC 2011001919

On Christmas Eve, six French-Canadian trappers meet a mysterious stranger who gives them the gift of a trip to their homes in Montreal, if only they agree not to speak until they cross their own thresholds.

"This French-Canadian folktale is brought to luminous life by the San Soucis. The atmospheric artwork, done in traditional and digital media, conveys the mystery and wonder of the snowy journey. Kimmel's storytelling is rich and straightforward." SLJ

★ **Gershon's** monster; a story for the Jewish New Year. retold by Eric A. Kimmel; illustrated by Jon J. Muth. Scholastic Press 2000 un il $16.95
Grades: K 1 2 3   398.2
1. Jews -- Folklore 2. Rosh ha-Shanah -- Fiction
ISBN 0-439-10839-X
LC 99-46986

When his sins threaten the lives of his beloved twin children, a Jewish man finally repents of his wicked ways

"This presentation of a Hasidic legend has everything a reader could want: a suspenseful story, an insightful lesson and brilliantly conceived, airy pictures that accelerate the delivery of both." Publ Wkly

★ **Hershel** and the Hanukkah goblins; written by Eric A. Kimmel; illustrated by Trina Schart Hyman. Holiday House 1989 un il $16.95; pa $6.95
Grades: K 1 2 3   398.2
1. Jews -- Fiction 2. Fairies -- Fiction 3. Hanukkah -- Fiction
ISBN 0-8234-0769-1; 0-8234-1131-1 pa
LC 89-1954

A Caldecott Medal honor book, 1990

This "will fit companionably with haunted castle variants. Hyman is at her best with windswept landscapes, dark interiors, close portraiture, and imaginatively wicked creatures. Both art and history are charged with energy." Bull Cent Child Books

Medio Pollito; a Spanish tale. adapted by Eric A. Kimmel; illustrated by Valeria DoCampo. Marshall Cavendish 2010 un il $17.99
Grades: PreK K 1 2   398.2
1. Folklore -- Spain 2. Chickens -- Folklore
ISBN 978-0-7614-5705-3; 0-7614-5705-4

In this version of the Spanish folktale, Medio Pollito, the half-chick, ventures from his safe barnyard home all the way to Madrid, aided by the friends that he helped along the way.

"Richly colored, cheerful paintings show the endearing, plucky half chick with one leg and one wing, hopping along the road." Booklist

The **runaway** tortilla; illustrated by Randy Cecil. Winslow Press (Delray Beach) 2000 un il $16.95
Grades: K 1 2 3   398.2
1. Folklore 2. Fairy tales 3. Hispanic Americans -- Folklore
ISBN 1-89081-718-X
LC 00-20487

In this Southwestern version of the Gingerbread Man, a tortilla runs away from Tia Lupe and Tio Jose in Texas

"The primitive oil paintings feature a palette of sunset colors, a rotund Tia and Tio, and a lipsticked, scowling tortilla. . . . Kimmel's saucy story joins a swarm of similar, albeit popular, retellings of traditional tales with a Southwestern setting." SLJ

The **spider's** gift; a Ukrainian Christmas story. retold by Eric A. Kimmel; illustrated by Katya Krenina. Holiday House 2010 un il $16.95
Grades: K 1 2 3   398.2
1. Folklore -- Ukraine 2. Spiders -- Folklore 3. Christmas -- Folklore
ISBN 978-0-8234-1743-8; 0-8234-1743-3
LC 2004054162

Katrusya's family cannot afford Christmas, but they cut a small pine tree in the forest, decorate it with buttons, and, when baby spiders hatch in its branches, they especially enjoy the silvery webs that appear.

"Painterly illustrations work well with a charmingly retold text to introduce American children to this unusual yet appealing holiday fable." Booklist

Kimmelman, Leslie
★ The **Little** Red Hen and the Passover matzah; illustrated by Paul Meisel. Holiday House 2010 un il $16.95
Grades: PreK K 1 2   398.2
1. Folklore 2. Jews -- Folklore 3. Animals -- Folklore 4. Chickens -- Folklore 5. Passover -- Folklore
ISBN 978-0-8234-1952-4; 0-8234-1952-5
LC 2008-48488

No one will help the Little Red Hen make the Passover matzah, but they all want to help her eat it. Includes information about Passover, a recipe for matzah, and a glossary of Yiddish words used in the story.

"Such a clever idea! . . . By the time Kimmelman, . . . a terrifically conversational storyteller, and Meisel, . . . a slyly astute cartoonist, . . . are done, readers of all faiths will know a lot more than some emotionally evocative Yiddish words." Publ Wkly

Knutson, Barbara
Love and roast chicken; a trickster tale from the Andes. Lerner Pub. Group 2004 un il map lib bdg $16.95
Grades: K 1 2 3   398.2
1. Folklore -- Peru 2. Foxes -- Folklore 3. Guinea pigs -- Folklore 4. Native Americans -- South America -- Folklore
ISBN 1-57505-657-7
LC 2003-18045

In this folktale from the Andes, a clever guinea pig repeatedly outsmarts the fox that wants to eat him for dinner

"Knutson's boldly outlined, vibrant woodcut-and-water-color artwork captures the mischievous nature of the guinea pig.... A thoroughly enjoyable tale that deserves a place in most libraries." SLJ

Kopisch, August

The **helpful** elves; illustrated by Beatrice Braun-Fock. Floris 2011 il $17.95

Grades: PreK K 1 2   **398.2**

1. Fairies -- Fiction 2. Folklore -- Germany

ISBN 978-0-86315-815-5; 0-86315-815-3

"According to legend, the city of Cologne once had tiny helpers who would sneak into homes at night and complete the daily chores while the townsfolk slept. . . . Until one day the tailor's wife grew curious to see these mysterious helpers. . . . Based on a well-known poem by Kopisch (1799-1853) and illustrated in muted tones by Braun-Fock (1898-1973), the charm of this tale lies in the tiny elf tabs found at the top of each page. Together in a row, 10 elves are perched expectantly—each made distinct with a different smile or a long white beard-forming a miniature audience to watch readers.... An enchanting ... piece of German lore brought to a new audience." Kirkus

Krasno, Rena

Cloud weavers; ancient Chinese legends. [by] Rena Krasno and Yeng-Fong Chiang; illustrations from the collection of Yeng-Fong Chiang. Pacific View Press 2003 96p il $22.95

Grades: 5 6 7 8   **398.2**

1. Folklore -- China

ISBN 1-881896-26-9

LC 2002-35911

Presents legends and tales from China, including ancient folktales, stories that reflect Chinese traditions and virtues, historical tales, and selections from literature

This collection "provides a showcase for some remarkable pieces of Chinese calendar art and advertising posters from the 1920s and 1930s. . . . Prefaces provide cultural insight for some stories, and the brisk retellings weave important background unobtrusively into the narrative." Booklist

Krensky, Stephen

Anansi and the box of stories; a West African folktale. adapted by Stephen Krensky; illustrations by Jeni Reeves. Millbrook Press 2007 48p il (On my own folklore) lib bdg $25.26

Grades: 1 2 3 4   **398.2**

1. Anansi (Legendary character) 2. Folklore -- West Africa

ISBN 978-0-8225-6741-7

LC 2006037783

Long ago in Africa, the sky god Nyame keeps all of the stories to himself, but when Anansi the spider asks their price, Nyame agrees to trade his stories if Anansi can perform four seemingly impossible tasks

"Krensky's retelling is simple and fast-moving, ably supported by Reeve's illustrations." SLJ

John Henry; adapted by Stephen Krensky; illustrations by Mark Oldroyd. Millbrook Press 2007 48p il (On my own folklore) lib bdg $25.26

Grades: 1 2 3 4   **398.2**

1. John Henry (Legendary character) 2. Folklore --

United States 3. African Americans -- Folklore

ISBN 978-1-57505-887-0 lib bdg; 1-57505-887-1 lib bdg

LC 2005010187

Retells the life of the legendary African American hero who raced against a steam drill to cut through a mountain.

This is "written in a comfortably folksy tone. . . . While the narrative has its moments of understated humor, it also involves readers. . . . Full of light and movement, Oldroyd's impressionistic pictures effectively illustrate the story." Booklist

Paul Bunyan; adapted by Stephen Krensky; illustrated by Craig Orback. Millbrook Press 2007 42p il (On my own folklore) lib bdg $25.26

Grades: 1 2 3 4   **398.2**

1. Tall tales 2. Bunyan, Paul (Legendary character) 3. Folklore -- United States

ISBN 978-1-57505-888-7 lib bdg; 1-57505-888-X lib bdg

LC 2005033157

Relates some of the exploits of Paul Bunyan, a lumberjack said to be taller than the trees whose pet was a blue ox named Babe.

"With simple vocabulary and some dialogue, Krensky gives children a feeling for the characters as well as the flavor of the time and the story's setting." SLJ

Includes bibliographical references

Pecos Bill; adapted by Stephen Krensky; illustrations by Paul Tong. Millbrook Press 2007 44p il (On my own folklore) lib bdg $25.26

Grades: 1 2 3 4   **398.2**

1. Tall tales 2. Pecos Bill (Legendary character) 3. Folklore -- United States

ISBN 978-1-57505-889-4 lib bdg; 1-57505-889-8 lib bdg

LC 2005033174

Relates some of the exploits of Pecos Bill, the extraordinary cowboy who was raised by coyotes, rode a mountain lion, and used a rattle snake as a rope.

"With simple vocabulary and some dialogue, Krensky gives children a feeling for the characters as well as the flavor of the time and the story's setting." SLJ

Kurtz, Jane

Fire on the mountain; illustrated by E. B. Lewis. Simon & Schuster Bks. for Young Readers 1994 un il hardcover o.p. pa $5.99

Grades: 1 2 3 4   **398.2**

1. Folklore -- Ethiopia

ISBN 0-689-81896-3 pa

LC 93-11477

A clever young shepherd boy uses his wits to gain a fortune for himself and his sister from a haughty rich man

"Lewis uses color to achieve intriguing contrast and articulates characters' faces with expression and power. Kurtz, who heard the story as a child in Ethiopia, retells it in a strong narrative voice: her language is simple and spare yet evocative." Booklist

L'Homme, Erik

Tales of a lost kingdom; a journey into Northwest Pakistan. written by Erik L'Homme; illustrated by Francois

Place; translated by Claudia Zoe Bedrick. Enchanted Lion Books 2007 47p il $17.95

Grades: 3 4 5 6   **398.2**

1. Folklore -- Pakistan

ISBN 978-1-59270-072-1; 1-59270-072-1

A collection of three authentic folktales from the ancient kingdom of Chitral at the border between Pakistan and Afghanistan. Includes a travelogue with photographs, illustrations, and a map.

"Sardonic, bittersweet, and often tragic, these three tales reflect the hardscrabble life of this country. . . . The retellings are flavored with detail and language suitable to the oral tradition. . . . Place's elegantly simple, naive watercolor and pen-and-ink illustrations add to the attractive, hand-crafted design." SLJ

Lagercrantz, Rose

My Heart Is Laughing; by Rose Lagercrantz; illustrated by Eva Eriksson. Lerner Pub Group 2014 120 p. $16.95

Grades: 1 2 3   **398.2**

1. Moving -- Fiction 2. Bullies -- Fiction 3. Friendship -- Fiction 4. Schools -- fiction 5. Bullying -- fiction

ISBN 1877579521; 9781877579523

LC 2011012226

In this children's book, by Rose Lagercrantz and illustrated by Eva Eriksson, "Dani's been trying her best to stay happy ever since her best friend Ella moved away. But some girls are cruel to her . . . It would all be okay if only Ella would move back." (Publisher's note)

"This new adaptation of the Yiddish folk song presented in Simms Taback's Joseph Had a Little Overcoat (Viking, 1999) and Phoebe Gilman's Something from Nothing (Scholastic, 1992) is a fresh rhythmic retelling with charming cartoon-style illustrations that deserves a place even in collections that own the other two. Aylesworth's story, told in the voice of the main character's granddaughter, recounts highlights of her grandfather's life . . . McClintock's pen-and-ink detailed watercolor illustrations highlight four generations of family history. . . . The paintings highlight McClintock's special skill for aging grandpa. Her eye for detail is apparent in ever-changing clothing styles; in a sole coming loose from young grandpa's shoe; and the evolution of his sewing machines from treadle to modern motorized. This is a tale worth reading again and again." SLJ

Laird, Elizabeth

★ **Pea** boy; and other stories from Iran. illustrated by Shirin Adl. Frances Lincoln Children's Books 2010 61p il $22.95

Grades: 3 4 5   **398.2**

1. Folklore -- Iran

ISBN 978-1-84507-912-3; 1-84507-912-4

Retells folktales and fables from Iran, including the story of a mouse and a cockroach who fell in love, a foolish weaver's apprentice, and a boy with the head of a chickpea.

"Adl, who grew up in Iran, creates collages with quirky characters, a naive folk quality and a modern artistic sensibility. . . . A wonderful blend of traditional stories and original art that reflects the customs of this country." Kirkus

Lang, Andrew

The **Arabian** nights entertainments; selected and edited by Andrew Lang; with numerous illustrations by H. J. Ford. Dover Publs. 1969 424p il pa $9.95

Grades: 5 6 7 8   **398.2**

1. Fairy tales 2. Arabs -- Folklore

ISBN 0-486-22289-6

First published 1898 in the United Kingdom

"A collection of popular tales assembled over many centuries, and well known in Europe from the 18th cent. It contains the stories of 'Aladdin, Alibaba, and Sindbad the sailor.' . . . The framing story in which the tales are set concerns Scheherazade, who is determined to delay her royal husband's plan of killing her—he has taken to murdering his wives because the first was unfaithful to him—by telling him a story every evening. She leaves each evening's tale incomplete until the next day, so that he has to spare her life in order to hear its conclusion. He is so entertained that he finally abandons his murderous plan." Oxford Companion to Child Lit

The **Blue** fairy book; edited by Andrew Lang; with numerous illustrations by H. J. Ford and G. P. Jacomb Hood. Dover Publs. 1965 390p il pa $10.95

Grades: 4 5 6   **398.2**

1. Folklore 2. Fairy tales

ISBN 0-486-21437-0

Also available in paperback $10.95 each: The Green fairy book; The Grey fairy book; The Lilac fairy book; The Olive fairy book; The Orange fairy book; The Pink fairy book; The Red fairy book; The Yellow fairy book

A reprint of the title first published 1889 by Longmans

A collection of thirty-seven fairy tales from various countries, consisting largely of old favorites from such sources as Perrault, the Brothers Grimm, Madame D'Aulnoy, Asbjörnsen and Möe, the Arabian Nights and Swift's Gulliver's travels

Lee, H. Chuku

Beauty and the beast; a retelling. by H. Chuku Lee; illustrations by Pat Cummings. Harper 2014 32 p. color illustrations (hardcover bdg.) $17.99

Grades: K 1 2 3   **398.2**

1. Fairy tales 2. Love stories 3. Folklore -- France

ISBN 0688148190; 9780688148195

LC 2013021852

This book, by H. Chuku Lee and illustrated by Pat Cummings, is a retelling of the Beauty and the Beast fairy tale. The book creates a "fairy-tale world flavored by the art, architecture, and culture of West Africa. . . . When her father is taken prisoner by a fearsome Beast, Beauty begs the captor to take her instead. . . . Though he will give her whatever her heart desires . . . she is forbidden to leave. Over time, however, Beauty sees the gentler side of the Beast, and an unexpected bond forms." (Publisher's note)

"Beautifully executed full- and double-page folk-style illustrations combine the vivid hues of watercolor, the softness of pastel, and the texture of gouache. Bold African patterns; elegance in design of clothing, jewelry and coiffures; and the unique architectural style of the Beast's enchanted palace, with influences from the ancient Dogon buildings of Mali, add to the book's distinctiveness." SLJ

Lesser, Rika

★ **Hansel** and Gretel; illustrated by Paul O. Zelinsky; retold by Rika Lesser. Dutton Children's Bks. 1999 un il $16.99; pa $6.99

Grades: K 1 2 3   **398.2**
1. Fairy tales 2. Folklore -- Germany
ISBN 0-525-46152-3; 0-698-11407-8 pa
LC 99-10198
A reissue of the edition first published 1984 by Dodd,
Mead
A Caldecott Medal honor book, 1985
A retelling of the well-known tale in which two children
are left in the woods but find their way home despite an en-
counter with a wicked witch
"Direct and unembellished, Lesser's retelling resembles
that of the earliest German edition of Grimm, published in
1812. . . . A visual feast, the illustrations frequently recall
Flemish and French genre painting of the seventeenth centu-
ry, while the idyllic woodland scenes reflect a later Romantic
mood." Horn Book Guide

Lester, Julius
★ **John** Henry; pictures by Jerry Pinkney. Dial Bks.
for Young Readers 1994 un il $17.99; pa $6.99
Grades: K 1 2 3   **398.2**
1. John Henry (Legendary character) 2. Folklore --
United States 3. African Americans -- Folklore
ISBN 0-8037-1606-0; 0-14-056622-8 pa
LC 93-34583
A Caldecott Medal honor book, 1995
"The original legend of John Henry and how he beat the
steam drill with his sledgehammer has been enhanced and
enriched, in Lester's retelling, with wonderful contemporary details and poetic similes that add humor, beauty, and
strength. Pinkney's evocative illustrations—especially the
landscapes, splotchy and impressionistic, yet very solid and
vigorous—are little short of magnificent." Horn Book Guide

The **tales** of Uncle Remus; the adventures of Brer Rabbit. as told by Julius Lester; illustrated by Jerry Pinkney.
Dial Bks. 1987 151p il $19.99; pa $8.99
Grades: 4 5 6 7   **398.2**
1. Animals -- Folklore 2. African Americans -- Folklore
ISBN 0-8037-0271-X; 0-14-130347-6 pa
LC 85-20449
This adaptation of 48 Brer Rabbit stories "is the work
of a writer familiar with the methodology of folkloristic and
historical research but also with the techniques of flavoring
fiction. . . . Pinkney's illustrations—black-and-white drawings with occasional double-page spreads in full color—are
well drafted, fresh, and funny." Bull Cent Child Books

★ **Uncle** Remus, the complete tales; with a new in-
troduction. as told by Julius Lester; illustrated by Jerry
Pinkney. 1999 xxi, 686p il lib bdg $35
Grades: 4 5 6 7   **398.2**
1. Animals -- Folklore 2. African Americans -- Folklore
ISBN 0-8037-2451-9
LC 99-17121
Reprint in one volume of works originally published
separately, 1987-1994
Lester retells stories of the trickster rabbit from African
American folklore collected by Joel Chandler Harris
"This is a landmark collection. . . . Lester's retellings
are sharp and flavorful and grounded in the here and now."
[review of book 1] Booklist

Livo, Norma J.
Tales to tickle your funny bone; humorous tales from
around the world. [by] Norma J. Livo; foreward by Pat
Mendoza. Libraries Unlimited 2007 xxvii, 206p il pa $30
Grades: Adult Professional   **398.2**
1. Folklore 2. Wit and humor
ISBN 978-1-59158-504-6
LC 2007003331
"Tall tales, noodlehead stories, urban legends, riddles,
and songs fill this delightful collection of humorous tales.
The selections are in shortened but lively formats for easy
reading or telling. Introductory notes discuss folklore and
the healing power of humor. The more than 70 stories are
arranged by genre and labeled with the country of origin. .
. . The bibliography includes books and Internet sources as
well as VHS and DVD materials. An excellent resource for
teachers, librarians, and students." SLJ
Includes bibliographical references

Louie, Ai-Ling
★ **Yeh**-Shen; a Cinderella story from China. retold
by Ai-Ling Louie; illustrated by Ed Young. Philomel Bks.
1982 un il $16.99; pa $6.99
Grades: 2 3 4   **398.2**
1. Fairy tales 2. Folklore -- China
ISBN 0-399-20900-X; 0-698-11388-8 pa
LC 80-11745
This version of the Cinderella story, in which a young
girl overcomes the wickedness of her stepsister and stepmother to become the bride of a prince, is based on ancient
Chinese manuscripts written 1000 years before the earliest
European version
"The reteller has cast the tale in well-cadenced prose,
fleshing out the spare account with elegance and grace. In
a manner reminiscent of Chinese scrolls and of decorated
folding screens, the text is chiefly set within vertical panels, while the luminescent illustrations—less narrative than
emotional—often increase their impact by overspreading
the narrow framework or appearing on pages of their own."
Horn Book

Lowery, Linda
The **tale** of La Llorona; a Mexican folktale. adapted by
Linda Lowery and Richard Keep; illustrations by Janice Lee
Porter. Millbrook Press 2008 48p il (On my own folklore)
lib bdg $25.26
Grades: 1 2 3 4   **398.2**
1. Ghost stories 2. Folklore -- Mexico
ISBN 978-0-8225-6378-5 lib bdg; 0-8225-6378-9
lib bdg
LC 2006005478
Expands on a popular Mexican folktale about a ghost
that haunts riverbanks at night, crying as she searches for
her lost children
"The illustrations are done in soft earth tones in a style
reminiscent of Mexican folk art. . . . Given the limitations
of the easy-reader format and the necessity of not terrifying young audiences too much, this is a creditable retelling."
SLJ
Includes bibliographical references

Luna, James
The **runaway** piggy; illustrated by Laura Lacamara.
Pinata Books 2010 un il

Grades: PreK K 1 2   **398.2**
1. Folklore 2. Bilingual books -- English-Spanish
ISBN 1-55885-586-6; 978-1-55885-586-1

LC 2009053971

A Mexican piggy cookie escapes from the bakery before
it can be eaten and eludes an ever-growing line of people
pursuing it. Includes recipe for piggy cookies.

"The story of The Gingerbread Man gets a lively Mexican makeover in this bilingual tale." Publ Wkly

Lunge-Larsen, Lise

The **troll** with no heart in his body and other tales of
trolls from Norway; retold by Lise Lunge-Larsen; woodcuts
by Betsy Bowen. Houghton Mifflin 1999 92p il hardcover
o.p. pa $7.95
Grades: 3 4 5 6   **398.2**
1. Folklore -- Norway
ISBN 0-395-91371-3; 0-618-35403-4 pa

LC 98-43244

"Lunge-Larsen presents nine Norwegian tales about the
greed and foolishness of trolls in a casual style that makes
these stories ripe for reading aloud and storytelling. Her liveliness of language and easy turn of phrase give these retellings a comforting tone despite the sometimes scary events.
Bowen's colored-ink woodblock prints, inspired by traditional Norwegian woodcarving and design, suit the monumental nature of the subject." Bull Cent Child Books

Includes bibliographical references

MacDonald, Margaret Read

Bat's big game; retold by Margaret Read MacDonald;
illustrated by Eugenia Nobati. Albert Whitman & Co. 2008
un il $16.95
Grades: K 1 2 3   **398.2**
1. Fables 2. Bats -- Folklore 3. Soccer -- Folkore 4.
Animals -- Folklore
ISBN 978-0-8075-0587-8; 0-8075-0587-0

"In this retelling of a traditional fable, Bat cannot decide
whether he wants to be on the Animals' or the Birds' soccer
team. At first he chooses the Animals, but when they start to
fall behind, he switches to the Birds. When they start to lose,
he tries to switch back. . . . The text is compact and has an
innate rhythm characteristic of a veteran storyteller. Nobati's
full-page, digitally created color illustrations are highly stylized. . . . The pictures are full of action and recreate the mood
of a heated soccer game." SLJ

★ The **boy** from the dragon palace; a folktale from
Japan. retold by Margaret Read MacDonald; illustrated by
Sachiko Yoshikawa. Albert Whitman 2011 un il
Grades: K 1 2 3   **398.2**
1. Folklore -- Japan
ISBN 0-8075-7513-5; 978-0-8075-7513-0

LC 2010045965

A magical boy grants a poor flower-seller's every wish
until the greedy and ungrateful man grows tired of the boy's
unpleasant behavior and sends him away.

"The digitally enhanced, watercolor collage art is typically Japanese in setting, clothing and the wide-eyed . . .
boy's black topknot. The text is nicely repetitive and includes satisfyingly disgusting nose-blowing effects that
children will love." Kirkus

Conejito; a folktale from Panama. illustrated by Geraldo Valério. August House 2006 un il $16.95
Grades: K 1 2 3   **398.2**
1. Folklore -- Panama 2. Rabbits -- Folklore
ISBN 0-87483-779-0

LC 2005-52567

In this folktale from Panama, a little rabbit and his Tia
Monica outwit a fox, a tiger, and a lion, all of whom want to
eat him for lunch.

"Rhyming refrains invite the participation of young listeners. . . . Valerio's splashy tropical colors and elongated,
rubbery characters . . . capture the tale's bouncing energy."
Booklist

Five-minute tales; more stories to read and tell when
time is short. [by] Margaret Read MacDonald. August
House Publishers 2007 159p $24.94; pa $14.95
Grades: Adult Professional   **398.2**
1. Folklore 2. Storytelling
ISBN 978-0-87483-781-0; 0-87483-781-2; 978-0-
87483-782-7 pa; 0-87483-782-0 pa

LC 2007014511

"Quick tales in storytellers' pockets are like money in
the bank. They fill in when programs are delayed, and when
class periods are cut short or interrupted so that lengthier
stories are no longer suitable. . . . This collection fits the bill
with participation, animal, origin, riddle, romance, strange,
trickster, and moral tales from around the world and for all
ages. . . . Her practical guidance enables newer as well as
veteran tellers to proceed confidently with these engaging
stories." SLJ

Includes bibliographical references

Go to sleep, Gecko! a Balinese folktale. retold by Margaret Read MacDonald; illustrated by Geraldo Valério. August House Little Folk 2006 un il $16.95
Grades: K 1 2   **398.2**
1. Geckos -- Folklore 2. Folklore -- Indonesia
ISBN 978-0-87483-780-3; 0-87483-780-4

LC 2006-40748

Retells the folktale of the gecko who complains to the
village chief that the fireflies keep him awake at night but
then learns that in nature all things are connected

"MacDonald's lyrical language and use of repetition
help bring this folktale to life. There is just the right touch
of humor in both the text and the art. The pacing is perfectly
matched to the richly colored acrylic illustrations." SLJ

The **great** smelly, slobbery, small-tooth dog; a folktale
from Great Britain. retold by Margaret Read MacDonald; illustrated by Julie Paschkis. August House Little Folk 2007
un il $16.95
Grades: PreK K 1 2   **398.2**
1. Dogs -- Folklore 2. Folklore -- Great Britain
ISBN 978-0-87483-808-4

LC 2007005504

In this British variant of a traditional tale, a great smelly,
slobbery, small-tooth dog rescues a rich man from bandits
and demands that the man bring his beautiful daughter to
live in his castle.

"The text is perfectly paced for interactive read-alouds
. . . but the active, richly colored gouache paintings, which

include beautiful details, . . . will work best with small groups." Booklist

How many donkeys? an Arabic counting tale. retold by Margaret Read MacDonald and Nadia Jameel Taibah; illustrations by Carol Liddiment. Albert Whitman 2009 un il $16.99

Grades: K 1 2   **398.2**

1. Counting 2. Arabs -- Folklore
ISBN 978-0-8075-3424-3; 0-8075-3424-2

LC 2008056047

When Jouha counts the ten donkeys carrying his dates to market, he repeatedly forgets to count the one he is riding on, causing him great consternation. Includes numbers written out in Arabic and in English transliteration, as well as the numerals one through ten, and a note on the origins and other versions of the story

"Bright, painterly illustrations depict the sunny desert setting; jewel-toned robes, turban, and blankets enliven the sandy palette. . . . . A winning, witty, and surprisingly effective combination." Booklist

Little Rooster's diamond button; retold by Margaret Read MacDonald; illustrated by Will Terry. Albert Whitman 2007 un il $16.95

Grades: K 1 2 3   **398.2**

1. Folklore -- Hungary 2. Roosters -- Fiction
ISBN 0807546445; 9780807546444

LC 2006-23979

In this Hungarian folktale, a rooster with a magic stomach retrieves the diamond button which was stolen from him by a greedy king

"This fine paean to cleverness and persistence is given extra zest by Terry's acrylic illustrations, which are as colorful as sparkling gems." Booklist

Surf war! a folktale from the Marshall Islands. illustrated by Geraldo Valerio. August House LittleFolk 2009 un il $16.95

Grades: K 1 2   **398.2**

1. Ecology -- Folklore 2. Folklore -- Marshall Islands
ISBN 978-0-87483-889-3; 0-87483-889-4

LC 2008042589

A bragging contest between Whale and Sandpiper turns into a battle over the beach and sea, until both parties realize that the beach and the sea, as well as sea creatures and shorebirds, are interdependent

"The illustrations dominate the pages, with the birds and their backgrounds painted with bright shades of yellow, pink, and orange, while the sea and its creatures are deeper blues, grays, and purples. This charming story provides a moral about getting along with others and caring for the environment." SLJ

Three-minute tales; stories from around the world to tell or read when time is short. August House 2004 160p $24.95; pa $17.95 **398.2**

1. Folklore 2. Storytelling
ISBN 0-87483-728-6; 0-87483-729-4 pa

LC 2004-46257

"Easy to tell, easy to teach to children and adults, and easy to remember, the 80 very short tales in this global collection are for sharing in the classroom, library, and home

and around the campfire. . . . The informal, highly practical suggestions for beginners make storytelling sound easy." Booklist

Includes bibliographical references

Too many fairies; a Celtic Tale. retold by Margaret Read MacDonald; illustrated by Susan Mitchell. Marshall Cavendish Children 2010 un il $17.99

Grades: K 1 2 3   **398.2**

1. Fairies -- Folklore 2. Folklore -- Scotland
ISBN 978-0-7614-5604-9; 0-7614-5604-X

LC 2009007128

An old woman complains about all the housework she has to do, but when some fairies come to help her she finds that they are more trouble than they are worth

"This Scottish folktale is subtle but effective in its message of humility. The illustrations are folksy and warm with amusing detail. . . . A fun read-aloud." SLJ

Tunjur! Tunjur! Tunjur! a Palestinian folktale. retold by Margaret Read MacDonald; collected by Ibrahim Muhawi and Sharif Kanaana; illustrated by Alik Arzoumanian. Marshall Cavendish Children 2006 un il $16.95

Grades: K 1 2   **398.2**

1. Theft -- Fiction 2. Palestinian Arabs -- Folklore
ISBN 978-0-7614-5225-6; 0-7614-5225-7

LC 2005009719

"In this lively Palestinian tale, a woman wishes for a child to love, 'even if it is nothing more than a cooking pot.' Voila! Her wish comes true, and red Little Pot appears. . . . Reluctantly, the mother lets her pot outdoors, and its adventures include meetings with a merchant and even the royal family. Little Pot manages to roll away from each encounter with valuable stolen goods tucked inside her lid, but after her petty thefts are discovered, she receives a stinky comeuppance that is sure to please read-aloud crowds. Folklorist MacDonald's briskly paced text brims with repetitive phrases that evoke the sounds and rhythm of Little Pot's tumbling, rolling movement, and Arzoumanian's richly hued, stylized acrylics, bordered with Islamic motifs, add subtle cultural detail." Booklist

Mahy, Margaret

★ The **seven** Chinese brothers; illustrated by Jean and Mou-Sien Tseng. Scholastic 1990 un hardcover o.p. pa $5.99

Grades: 1 2 3   **398.2**

1. Fairy tales 2. Folklore -- China
ISBN 0-590-42057-7 pa

LC 88-33668

A story about "seven brothers, each of whom was blessed with an extraordinary power. Together, they use their amazing talents to avoid death at the hands of Emperor Ch'in Shih Huang, while trying to help the exhausted conscripted laborers working on the Great Wall." Child Book Rev Serv

Malam, John

Fairies. QEB Pub. 2010 32p il (QEB mythologies) lib bdg $28.50

Grades: 4 5 6 7   **398.2**

1. Fairies
ISBN 978-1-59566-979-7; 1-59566-979-5

LC 2008-56083

"A wealth of sidebars and captions . . . . adds depth to the compelling [narrative]. Supported by vibrant color illustrations, . . . [this] fascinating and well-written [tale] will integrate well with social-science curriculums." SLJ

Includes glossary

Giants. QEB Pub. 2010 32p il (QEB mythologies) lib bdg $28.50

Grades: 4 5 6 7　　　　　　　　　　　　**398.2**

1. Giants -- Folklore

ISBN 978-1-59566-980-3; 1-59566-980-9

LC 2009000389

"A wealth of sidebars . . . adds depth to the compelling [narrative]. Supported by vibrant color illustrations, . . . [this] fascinating and well-written [tale] will integrate well with social-science curriculums." SLJ

Includes glossary

Monsters. QEB Pub. 2010 32p il map (QEB mythologies) $28.50

Grades: 4 5 6 7　　　　　　　　　　　　**398.2**

1. Monsters

ISBN 978-1-59566-981-0; 1-59566-981-7

LC 2008056090

This "is filled with some of the weirdest creatures ever conceived. . . . Take the Hambaba (Iraqi myth), the hideous giant with a face of coiled intestines. Or the Flying Head (Iroquois folktale). . . . The layout, designed as if printed upon an ancient map or scroll, is great, and Follenn's artwork is a rousing example of graphic novel-style menace." Booklist

Mandell, Muriel

A **donkey** reads; adapted from a Turkish folktale by Muriel Mandell from a Turkish folktale; art by André Letria. Star Bright Books 2011 un il $16.95; pa $6.95

Grades: K 1 2 3　　　　　　　　　　　　**398.2**

1. Donkeys -- Fiction 2. Folklore -- Turkey 3. Books and reading -- Fiction

ISBN 978-1-59572-255-3; 1-59572-255-6; 978-1-59572-256-0 pa; 1-59572-256-4 pa

LC 2010002989

In a small village in Anatolia, even the poorest villager is expected to pay tribute to a tyrranical Mongol ruler, but the wiseman, Nasreddin Hoca, finds a way to make an aged donkey seem most valuable.

"The story's clever trickery and triumph-over-wickedness elements are satisfying. The vivid illustrations have a playful reverence. . . . The last page provides some historical context for Nasreddin." Horn Book Guide

Manna, Anthony L.

The **orphan**; a Cinderella story from Greece. [by] Anthony L. Manna and Soula Mitakidou; illustrated by Giselle Potter. Schwartz & Wade 2011 un il $16.99; lib bdg $19.99

Grades: K 1 2 3　　　　　　　　　　　　**398.2**

1. Fairy tales 2. Folklore -- Greece

ISBN 978-0-375-86691-3; 0-375-86691-4; 978-0-375-96691-0 lib bdg; 0-375-96691-9 lib bdg

LC 2010044480

In this variation on the Cinderella story set in Greece, a girl mistreated by her stepmother and stepsisters manages to captivate the prince, with help from Mother Nature and her children.

"The doll-like faces and stiff limbs of Potter's naïve-style watercolor figures suit the fairy-tale setting, and the pictures of tiny tailors and jewelers fawning before the pudgy stepsisters give the otherwise earnest story mordant humor. This Cinderella somehow seems more resourceful than her French counterpart, and her happy ending more dearly earned." Publ Wkly

Marshall, James

★ **Goldilocks** and the three bears; retold and illustrated by James Marshall. Dial Bks. for Young Readers 1988 un il $15.99; pa $5.99

Grades: PreK K 1 2　　　　　　　　　　**398.2**

1. Folklore 2. Bears -- Folklore

ISBN 0-8037-0542-5; 0-14-056366-0 pa

LC 87-32983

A Caldecott Medal honor book, 1989

Three bears return home from a walk to find a little girl asleep in baby bear's bed. "Preschool to grade two." (SLJ)

"Marshall's Goldilocks, the naughty little girl who disrupts a placid bear household, is no adorable blond moppet led more by curiosity than by mischievous intent. Instead, she is a sturdy, brazen, mini-hussy who stomps over the doorsill with a determined set to her mouth and a confident bounce in her step. . . . The big cartoonlike pictures depict a cozy modern setting for the respectable, suburban bears with snug rooms cluttered with books, bulbous upholstered furniture and a messy little bear's room. . . . The story contains a genuine enjoyment of Goldilock's adventures as they are reflected in Marshall's usual slapdash and rollicking illustrations." Horn Book

Hansel and Gretel; retold and illustrated by James Marshall. Dial Bks. for Young Readers 1990 un il hardcover o.p. pa $5.99

Grades: PreK K 1 2　　　　　　　　　　**398.2**

1. Fairy tales 2. Folklore -- Germany

ISBN 0-14-050836-8 pa

LC 89-26011

A poor woodcutter's children, lost in the forest, come upon a house made of cookies, cakes, and candy, occupied by a wicked witch who likes to have children for dinner

"Marshall's trademark wit and slyness mark every page of this effervescent interpretation. Never has there been a more horribly magnificent witch than his—an overstuffed, cackling harridan resplendent in scarlet costume, lipstick and rouge, her hair bedecked with incongruously delicate bows." Publ Wkly

★ **Red** Riding Hood; retold and illustrated by James Marshall. Dial Bks. for Young Readers 1987 un il $15.99; pa $5.99

Grades: PreK K 1 2　　　　　　　　　　**398.2**

1. Wolves -- Folklore 2. Folklore -- Germany

ISBN 0-8037-0344-9; 0-14-054693-6 pa

LC 86-16722

A little girl meets a hungry wolf in the forest on her way to visit her grandmother. "Preschool to grade three." (SLJ)

A "retelling of the familiar tale . . . maintaining the integrity of the Grimm Brothers' version, with both Grandma and Red Riding Hood eaten and later rescued by a hunter." SLJ

★ The **three** little pigs; retold and illustrated by James Marshall. Dial Bks. for Young Readers 1989 un il hardcover o.p. pa $6.99

Grades: PreK K 1 2 **398.2**

1. Pigs -- Folklore 2. Wolves -- Folklore 3. Folklore -- Great Britain

ISBN 0-8037-0591-3; 0-14-055742-3 pa

LC 88-33411

"In his spiffed-up version of the story, the three porkers follow the traditional course of straw, sticks, and bricks with the traditional results, but the players and accoutrements have a bit more zip than those in other versions. . . . The large, exuberant, cartoonlike illustrations provide much additional entertainment, jouncing readers along delightfully from one amusing scene to the next." Horn Book

Martin, Rafe

★ The **world** before this one; a novel told in legend. with paper sculpture by Calvin Nicholls. Levine Bks. 2002 195p il hardcover o.p. pa $5.99

Grades: 4 5 6 7 **398.2**

1. Seneca Indians -- Folklore

ISBN 0-590-37976-3; 978-0-590-37980-9 pa; 0-590-37980-1 pa

LC 2001-23403

"Written in the style of a novel, this collection of 14 Seneca tales is presented through the retelling of one central story into which all of the others are artfully woven. . . . Martin offers sources for the tales along with an introductory note by Seneca Elder Peter Jemison. Each chapter includes a painstakingly detailed white paper sculpture of a character (often an animal) from one of the stories." SLJ

Mayer, Marianna

Baba Yaga and Vasilisa the brave; as told by Marianna Mayer; illustrated by K. Y. Craft. Morrow Junior Bks. 1994 un il $16.95

Grades: 3 4 5 **398.2**

1. Fairy tales 2. Folklore -- Russia

ISBN 0-688-08500-8

LC 90-38514

This is a retelling of a Russian fairy tale. "After the death of her father, Vasilisa is mistreated by her stepmother and stepsisters; her only comfort is the magical doll made by her mother before she died. Sent to Baba Yaga's house to fetch a light, the girl . . . is given a series of impossible tasks to perform. With the help of her doll, she pleases the demanding hag, who sends her home with the precious light. After it destroys her stepmother and stepsisters, Vasilisa goes to live with an elderly woman and learns to spin and weave. She creates an exquisite piece of cloth that catches the attention of the tsar, . . . {who} asks for her hand in marriage." (SLJ) "Ages four to eight." (Booklist)

"Mayer's graceful prose conveys both the wonder and power of the tale. Complementing the text are Craft's illustrations done in a mixture of watercolor, gouache, and oils. The palette of red and gold set against a dark background resembles Russian folk-art paintings on black-lacquered wood." SLJ

The **twelve** dancing princesses; as told by Marianna Mayer; illustrated by K.Y. Craft. Morrow Junior Bks. 1988 [40] p. col. ill. $17.99

Grades: K 1 2 3 **398.2**

1. Dance -- Fiction 2. Shoes -- Fiction 3. Princesses -- Fiction 4. Fairy tales -- Fiction 5. Fairy tales

ISBN 0688020267; 0688080510; 9780688080518

LC 83001034

This children's book, by Marianna Mayer, illustrated by K.Y. Craft, tells the "enchanting story of the twelve beautiful princesses and the handsome young lad who solves the mystery of their tattered shoes." (Publisher's note)

"Craft's richly hued illustrations create a magical setting for Mayer's polished version of this romantic fairy tale... With skillful use of lighting, texture and detail and a fine sense of mood, Craft captures both the regal opulence of the King's court and the shimmery, ethereal beauty of the subterranean world of the all-night dancing, resulting in a lavish feast for the eyes and the imagination. All ages."

McCaughrean, Geraldine

★ The **epic** of Gilgamesh; retold by Geraldine McCaughrean; illustrated by David Parkins. Eerdmans Bks. for Young Readers 2003 95p il $18

Grades: 5 6 7 8 **398.2**

1. Gilgamesh 2. Folklore -- Iraq

ISBN 0-8028-5262-9

LC 2003-1086

A retelling, based on seventh-century B.C. Assyrian clay tablets, of the wanderings and adventures of the god king, Gilgamesh, who ruled in ancient Mesopotamia (now Iraq) in about 2700 B.C., and of his faithful companion, Enkidu

This is "clearly a telling for our time, but one that honors its source. Parkins captures the epic's primitive power and universal emotions in rough, broadly rendered portraits." Horn Book

McDermott, Gerald

★ **Anansi** the spider; a tale from the Ashanti. adapted and illustrated by Gerald McDermott. Holt & Co. 1972 un il $16.95; pa $6.95

Grades: K 1 2 3 **398.2**

1. Anansi (Legendary character) 2. Folklore -- Ghana 3. Ashanti (African people) -- Folklore

ISBN 0-8050-0310-X; 0-8050-0311-8 pa

A Caldecott Medal honor book, 1973

The adaptation of this traditional tale of Ghana is based on an animated film by McDermott. It tells of Anansi, a spider, who is saved from terrible fates by his six sons and is unable to decide which of them to reward. The solution to his predicament is also an explanation for how the moon was put into the sky

This offers "brief poetic text, complemented by geometric African folk-style illustrations in pure, bold colors." SLJ

★ **Arrow** to the sun; a Pueblo Indian tale. adapted and illustrated by Gerald McDermott. Viking 1974 un il $16.99; pa $6.99

Grades: K 1 2 3 **398.2**

1. Pueblo Indians -- Folklore

ISBN 0-670-13369-8; 0-14-050211-4 pa

Awarded the Caldecott Medal, 1975

This myth tells how Boy searches for his immortal father, the Lord of the Sun, in order to substantiate his paternal heritage. Shot as an arrow to the sun, Boy passes through the four chambers of ceremony to prove himself. Accepted by his father, he returns to earth to bring the Lord of the Sun's spirit to the world of men

"The simple, brief text—which suggests similar stories in religion and folklore—is amply illustrated in full-page and doublespread pictures.... The strong colors and the bold angular forms powerfully accompany the text." Horn Book

★ **Coyote**: a trickster tale from the American Southwest; told and illustrated by Gerald McDermott. Harcourt Brace & Co. 1994 un il $15; pa $6
Grades: K 1 2 3　　　　　　　　　　　　**398.2**
　　1. Coyote (Legendary character) 2. Native Americans -- Folklore
　　ISBN 0-15-220724-4; 0-15-201958-8 pa
　　　　　　　　　　　　　　　　　LC 92-32979

"Coyote persuades the crows to help him fly, but he becomes so obnoxious and boastful that they abandon him in midair, so he falls back to earth. Told with playful illustrations against the glowing orange of a desert sky, the humorous Zuni tale explains how Coyote, who once had blue fur, got his dust-colored coat and black-tippped tail." Horn Book Guide

Jabuti the tortoise; a trickster tale from the Amazon. told and illustrated by Gerald McDermott. Harcourt 2001 un il hardcover o.p. pa $7
Grades: K 1 2 3　　　　　　　　　　　　**398.2**
　　1. Turtles -- Folklore 2. Native Americans -- Folklore 3. Amazon River valley -- Folklore
　　ISBN 0-15-200496-3; 0-15-205374-3 pa
　　　　　　　　　　　　　　　　　LC 00-11977

All the birds enjoy the song-like flute music of Jabuti, the tortoise, except Vulture who, jealous because he cannot sing, tricks Jabuti into riding his back toward a festival planned by the King of Heaven

"The story succeeds by embracing what McDermott refers to as a universal trickster theme.... Utilizing a radiant palette to evoke the brilliance and vitality of the region, McDermott's spreads feature his familiar geometrically drawn characters that seem to vibrate against the lush-green stylized foliage set upon hot-pink backgrounds." SLJ

★ **Monkey**; a trickster tale from India. Harcourt Children's Books 2011 un il $16.99
Grades: K 1 2 3　　　　　　　　　　　　**398.2**
　　1. Folklore -- India 2. Monkeys -- Folklore 3. Crocodiles -- Folklore
　　ISBN 978-0-15-216596-3; 0-15-216596-7
　　　　　　　　　　　　　　　　　LC 2009007977

Crocodile wants to feast on Monkey's heart and Monkey must outsmart him if he is to enjoy eating mangoes all day.

"Playfully told with succinct text and illustrations, this tale will appeal to a wide audience. It is both simple and sophisticated with subtle and not-so-subtle levels of irony. The cut/torn paper illustrations are inseparable from the text." SLJ

Pig-Boy; a trickster tale from Hawai'i. Harcourt Children's Books 2009 un il $16
Grades: PreK K 1 2 3　　　　　　　　　　**398.2**
　　1. Pigs -- Folklore 2. Folklore -- Hawaii
　　ISBN 978-0-15-216590-1; 0-15-216590-8
　　　　　　　　　　　　　　　　　LC 2006-35426

The mischievous, shape-shifting Pig-Boy gets in trouble with both the King and Pele, the goddess of fire, but always manages to slip away as his grandmother has told him to do.

"The boldly colored art is dynamic and reflects both the humor of the sprightly text and the author/illustrator's background as an animator in its visual pacing. The tale itself has just enough folkloric elements to convey action, character and setting without bogging down in detail.... Good rascally fun." Kirkus

Raven; a trickster tale from the Pacific Northwest. told and illustrated by Gerald McDermott. Harcourt Brace Jovanovich 1993 un il $16; pa $7
Grades: K 1 2 3　　　　　　　　　　　　**398.2**
　　1. Native Americans -- Folklore
　　ISBN 0-15-265661-8; 0-15-202449-2 pa
　　　　　　　　　　　　　　　　　LC 91-14563
A Caldecott Medal honor book, 1994
Raven, a Pacific Coast Indian trickster, sets out to find the sun

"Raven, whether he appears as a bird or child, is always marked with a distinctive design of clear-cut red, green, and blue on black, sharply contrasting with the softer hues and forms of the backgrounds and the other characters. In this way, Raven is always recognizable, even when he shifts his shape to human form. . . . Read this picture book aloud for the full effect of its simple, rhythmic text and striking artwork." Booklist

McGill, Alice
　　Way up and over everything; illustrated by Jude Daly. Houghton Mifflin 2008 un il $16
Grades: 2 3 4 5　　　　　　　　　　　　**398.2**
　　1. Slavery -- Folklore 2. Folklore -- United States 3. African Americans -- Folklore
　　ISBN 978-0-618-38796-0; 0-618-38796-X
　　　　　　　　　　　　　　　　　LC 2003-19384

In this retelling of a folktale, five Africans escape the horrors of slavery by flying away

"Daly's delicate and elongated figures, small in scale against the vast watercolor landscapes of the Georgia countryside, present a bird's eye view of the story and suggest the enormity of such an escape." Booklist

McGovern, Ann
　　Too much noise; illustrated by Simms Taback. Houghton Mifflin 1967 44p il $16; pa $6.95
Grades: K 1 2 3　　　　　　　　　　　　**398.2**
　　1. Folklore
　　ISBN 0-395-18110-0; 0-395-62985-3 pa

"The too crowded house of a familiar old tale becomes a too noisy house in this entertaining picture-book story. Bothered by the noises in his house, an old man follows the advice of the village wise man by first acquiring and then getting rid of a cow, donkey, sheep, hen, dog, and cat. Only then can he appreciate how quiet his house is. The simplicity and straightforwardness of the folktale are evident in both the telling of the cumulative story and in the amusing colored illustrations." Booklist

Menchu, Rigoberta
　　The **honey** jar; [by] Rigoberta Menchu with Dante Liano; pictures by Domi; translated by David Unger. Groundwood Books/House of Anansi Press 2006 64p il $18.95

Grades: 4 5 6 **398.2**
1. Mayas -- Folklore
ISBN 978-0-88899-670-1; 0-88899-670-5
This is a collection of 12 Mayan folktales that the author "heard as a child. The stories range from creation stories and pourquoi tales about animals to selections that reflect a distinctive worldview, a broad awareness of nature, and a sense of humor. Using vivid colors, the naturalistic, folk-art oil paintings . . . illustrate the stories in a manner that reflects the simple spirit and directness of the tellings. An expressive collection that lends insight into the Mayan culture in which Menchu grew up." Booklist
Includes glossary

The **secret** legacy; [by] Rigoberta Menchu with Dante Liano; pictures by Domi; translated by David Unger. Groundwood Books/House of Anansi Press 2008 64p il $19.95
Grades: 4 5 6 7 8 **398.2**
1. Mayas -- Folklore 2. Folklore -- Guatemala
ISBN 978-0-88899-896-5; 0-88899-896-1
"On her first day watching over her Mayan grandfather's cornfields, young Ixkem is invited by the b'e'n, spirits in the form of small humans, to visit them underground. They feed her generously and she tells them stories that explain Mayan customs and include bits of folklore. . . . The Mexican artist Domi has provided bright paintings in a naturalistic, folk-art style. The lyrical translation preserves the storyteller's voice." SLJ

Mhlophe, Gcina
African tales; a Barefoot collection. written by Gcina Mhlophe; illustrated by Rachel Griffin. Barefoot Books 2009 95p il map
Grades: 5 6 7 8 **398.2**
1. Folklore -- Africa
ISBN 1-84686-118-7; 978-1-84686-118-5
LC 2008028042
"Each of these eight tales is preceded by information and interesting facts about the country from which it originated. A basic map of Africa helps orient readers to the location of the various countries represented. Extensive source notes are appended. . . . There are many choices that could be read aloud or told using a call-and-response format. The book design . . . is a feast for the eyes. Griffin employs a collage technique using colored beads, sewn fabric, and textured papers, and incorporates them into shapes and faces of animals and humans. . . . This compilation contains a wealth of information and will enhance folklore collections." SLJ
Includes bibliographical references

Miller, Bobbi
Davy Crockett gets hitched; retold by Bobbi Miller; illustrated by Megan Lloyd. Holiday House 2009 un il $16.95
Grades: K 1 2 3 **398.2**
1. Tall tales 2. Folklore -- United States
ISBN 978-0-8234-1837-4; 0-8234-1837-5
LC 2006050063
An accidental encounter with a thorn bush on his way to the spring dance has Davy Crockett kicking up his heels and out-dancing even the audacious Miss Sally Ann Thunder Ann Whirlwind.

"Lloyd's energetic artwork propels the narrative with effective use of light and line. . . . The text sings with rich vocabulary, making this tall tale a great choice for reading aloud." Booklist

One fine trade; retold by Bobbi Miller; illustrated by Will Hillenbrand. Holiday House 2009 un il $16.95
Grades: K 1 2 3 **398.2**
1. Weddings -- Folklore 2. Folklore -- United States 3. Peddlers and peddling -- Folklore
ISBN 978-0-8234-1836-7; 0-8234-1836-7
LC 2007-25493
Georgy Piney Woods, the best peddler who ever lived, makes several trades so his daughter can buy a wedding dress.
"This is an "entertaining romp. . . . The ink and pencil scenes were scanned and digitally manipulated, with colored pencil and gouache additions to the final work. This creates a convincing depth. . . . The outlandish events and droll caricatures are supported by lively language that is full of rhythm and fun to read aloud." SLJ

Milligan, Bryce
Brigid's cloak; an ancient Irish story. written by Bryce Milligan; illustrated by Helen Cann. Eerdmans Bks. for Young Readers 2002 un il $16; pa $8
Grades: K 1 2 3 **398.2**
1. Nuns 2. Saints 3. Folklore -- Ireland
ISBN 0-8028-5224-6; 0-8028-5297-1 pa
LC 2001-40174
Relates a legend about the Irish slave girl who became Saint Brigid, beginning with a celestial song, a mysterious gift, and a prophecy on the night of her birth
"Borders of Celtic designs frame Cann's mixed-media pictures and add both authenticity and wonder to the tale." Booklist

Mitchell, Stephen
Iron Hans; a Grimm's fairy tale. retold by Stephen Mitchell; illustrated by Matt Tavares. Candlewick Press 2007 un il $16.99
Grades: K 1 2 3 **398.2**
1. Fairy tales 2. Folklore -- Germany
ISBN 978-0-7636-2160-5; 0-7636-2160-9
LC 2006047520
With the help of Iron Hans, the wild man of the forest, a young prince makes his own way in the world and wins the hand of a princess
"Clamoring knights, galloping steeds and scenes of palace splendor crowd the pages, which rise in a vertical format as if to stress Iron Hans's nine-foot stature. . . . Complex and muscular, this is a good bet for readers who demand lots of action." Publ Wkly

Mitton, Tony
The **storyteller's** secrets; illustrated by Peter Bailey. David Fickling Books 2010 118p il $15.99
Grades: 4 5 6 **398.2**
1. Folklore 2. Storytelling -- Fiction
ISBN 978-0-385-75190-2; 0-385-75190-7
"In a handsome volume profusely illustrated with a mix of silhouettes and vigorous line drawings, Mitton presents verse renditions of European tales and legends. . . . Written in ballad-style quatrains with unforced, natural sounding rhymes and cadences, the stories offer enthralling, easy-to-

follow plots with clear themes. . . . Mitton links all of his selections with prose encounters between two marveling children and a mysterious old Storyteller. . . . This gathering will cast the same sort of profound spell on readers and listeners." Booklist

Moerbeek, Kees

Aesop's fables: a pop-up book of classic tales; paper engineering by Kees Moerbeek; illustrated by Chris Beatrice & Bruce Whatley. Little Simon 2011 il $27.99
Grades: K 1 2 3 4   **398.2**
1. Fables 2. Folklore 3. Pop-up books
ISBN 978-1-4169-7146-7; 1-4169-7146-7

"This book makes good use of the format to showcase 10 traditional tales. Five of the fables are presented on handsomely illustrated spreads, each including a dramatic 3D sculpture that takes center stage and two smaller foldouts embellished with movable parts that contain the bulk of the text. . . . Each centerpiece pop-up does an excellent job of grabbing readers' attention and drawing them into the story. . . . Throughout, rich earthy hues, lush forest landscapes, and vivid detail make the illustrations appealing. The straightforward text aptly conveys the gist of each tale, and a brief section offers background about Aesop." SLJ

Montes, Marisa

★ Juan Bobo goes to work; a Puerto Rican folktale. retold by Marisa Montes; illustrated by Joe Cepeda. HarperCollins Pubs. 2000 un il $15.95; lib bdg $15.89
Grades: K 1 2 3   **398.2**
1. Folklore -- Puerto Rico
ISBN 0-688-16233-9; 0-688-16234-7 lib bdg
LC 99-28799

Although he tries to do exactly as his mother tells him, foolish Juan Bobo keeps getting things all wrong

"The funny, well-paced retelling smoothly incorporates Spanish words and phrases. . . . Using bold, bright Caribbean colors, Cepeda's oil paintings amplify Juan's silliness and charm. Brush strokes add texture, and background details establish the Puerto Rican setting." Booklist
Includes glossary

Montileaux, Donald F.

Tatanka and the Lakota people; a creation story. illustrated by Donald F. Montileaux. South Dakota State Historical Society Press 2006 un il $16.95
Grades: 1 2 3 4   **398.2**
1. Creation -- Folklore 2. Teton Indians -- Folklore
ISBN 0-9749195-8-6
LC 2006016009

The transformaton of the Buffalo Nation into the Ordinary People and their salvation by Tatanka comes from this traditional creation story of the Lakota, or Sioux, Indians.

"Montileaux, an Oglala Lakota artist, illustrates the text with paintings rendered in a two-dimensional format that reflects traditional buffalo-hide paintings. The colorful, stylized images match the formal tone of the story. The English telling is clear and concise, with the corresponding Lakota text appearing alongside." SLJ

Morales, Yuyi

★ Just a minute; a trickster tale and counting book. Chronicle Books 2003 un il $15.95

Grades: K 1 2 3   **398.2**
1. Counting 2. Folklore -- Mexico 3. Bilingual books -- English-Spanish
ISBN 0-8118-3758-0
LC 2002-151386

In this version of a traditional tale, Senor Calavera arrives at Grandma Beetle's door, ready to take her to the next life, but after helping her count, in English and Spanish, as she makes her birthday preparations, he changes his mind

"Like the text, the rich, lively artwork draws strongly upon Mexican culture. . . . The splendid paintings and spirited storytelling—along with useful math and multicultural elements—augur a long, full life for this original folktale." Booklist

Morpurgo, Michael

★ Beowulf; illustrated by Michael Foreman. Candlewick Press 2006 92p il $17.99
Grades: 5 6 7 8   **398.2**
1. Beowulf 2. Folklore -- Europe 3. Monsters -- Folklore
ISBN 978-0-7636-3206-9; 0-7636-3206-6

"Morpurgo retells the classic story of the courageous young warrior . . . who used his brute strength to save the neighboring Danes, then his own kinsmen, by slaying two horrible monsters, a sea serpent, and a massive dragon. . . . Many attractive full-page watercolor and pastel paintings illustrate important action-filled scenes. . . . This is a fine retelling." SLJ

Hansel and Gretel; retold by Michael Morpurgo; illustrated by Emma Chichester Clark. Candlewick Press 2008 un il $18.99
Grades: 2 3 4   **398.2**
1. Fairy tales 2. Folklore -- Germany
ISBN 978-0-7636-4012-5; 0-7636-4012-3
LC 2007052335

When they are left in the woods by their parents, Hansel and Gretel find their way home despite an encounter with a wicked witch

"Leaving the basic framework of the Grimm Brothers' tale intact, Morpurgo has altered details of the plot, creating a story in which strong familial bonds allow the innocent brother and sister to overcome evil. . . . Folk-art-style paintings, in watercolor with colored-pencil outlines and facial features, range in size from small decorations and vertical strips of various widths to full-page scenes." SLJ

★ The McElderry book of Aesop's fables; illustrations by Emma Chichester Clark. Margaret K. McElderry Books 2005 94p il $19.95
Grades: K 1 2   **398.2**
1. Fables 2. Authors 3. Storytellers
ISBN 1-4169-0290-2
LC 2004-58160

First published 2004 in the United Kingdom with title: The Orchard book of Aesop's fables

Retellings of twenty-one classic Aesop fables, including "The Hare and the Tortoise" and "Belling the Cat," in updated language.

"This large, spacious hardcover is perfectly designed for reading aloud. The text appears in big, clear type on thick paper, and Clark's gorgeous watercolors show the characters. . . . Morpurgo's adaptations of 21 short tales stay true to the tradition of humanlike animal characters and lessons that eschew heavy philosophizing in favor of warnings about ordinary folk and their foolishness." Booklist

The **Pied** Piper of Hamelin; [retold by] Michael Morpurgo; illustrated by Emma Chichester Clark. Candlewick Press 2011 il $16.99
Grades: K 1 2   **398.2**
1. Folklore -- Germany 2. Pied Piper of Hamelin
ISBN 978-0-7636-4824-4; 0-7636-4824-8
LC 2010050683
The Pied Piper pipes a village free of rats, and when the villagers refuse to pay him for the service, he pipes away their children as well.
"Chichester Clark's pencil-and-acrylic illustrations are bright and beautifully composed; the teeming rats radiate menace without being actively scary. An evocative and effective retelling of an old classic." Kirkus

★ **Sir** Gawain and the Green Knight; as told by Michael Morpurgo; illustrated by Michael Foreman. Candlewick Press 2004 114p il $18.99
Grades: 5 6 7 8   **398.2**
1. Arthurian romances 2. Gawain (Legendary character)
ISBN 0-7636-2519-1
LC 2003-65527
The quest of Sir Gawain for the Green Knight teaches him a lesson in pride, humility, and honor
"Morpurgo's sprightly writing brings out all the humor as well as the horror of the original tale, and Foreman's profuse, evocative watercolor-and-pastel illustrations highlight the drama in each scene." SLJ

Mosel, Arlene
The **funny** little woman; retold by Arlene Mosel; pictures by Blair Lent. Dutton 1972 un il hardcover o.p. pa $5.99
Grades: K 1 2   **398.2**
1. Folklore -- Japan
ISBN 0-14-054753-3 pa
Awarded the Caldecott Medal, 1973
While chasing a dumpling, a little lady is captured by wicked creatures from whom she escapes with the means of becoming the richest woman in Japan
"The tale unfolds in a simple tellable style. . . . Using elements of traditional Japanese art, the illustrator has made marvelously imaginative pictures. . . . All the inherent drama and humor of the story are manifest in the illustrations." Horn Book

Tikki Tikki Tembo; retold by Arlene Mosel; illustrated by Blair Lent. Holt & Co. 1968 un il $16.95; pa $6.95
Grades: K 1 2   **398.2**
1. Folklore -- China 2. Personal names -- Folklore
ISBN 0-8050-0662-1; 0-312-36748-1 pa
A "Chinese folk tale about a first son with a very long name. When Tikki Tikki Tembo-No Sa Rembo-Chari Bari Ruchi-Pip Peri Pembo fell into the well, it took his little brother so long to say his name and get help that Tikki almost drowned." Hodges. Books for Elem Sch Libr

Mueller, Doris L.
The **best** nest; by Doris L. Mueller; illustrated by Sherry Neidigh. Sylvan Dell 2008 un il $16.95; pa $8.95

Grades: 2 3 4   **398.2**
1. Birds -- Nests 2. Birds -- Folklore 3. Folklore -- Great Britain
ISBN 978-1-934359-09-9; 1-934359-09-2; 978-1-934359-25-9 pa; 1-934359-25-4 pa
LC 2007-935084
In this retelling of an old English folktale featuring birds native to the U.S., Magpie explains to the other birds how to build a nest. Some birds are impatient and fly off without listening to all the instructions, however. That is why, to this day, birds' nests come in different shapes and sizes
"The author provides support for additional activities, information about each bird, 'bird math' (problems based upon the number of broods and eggs for each species), bird care, and a 'match the nest' activity. Illustrations show each bird in mixed media with watercolor and pen and ink details." SLJ

Muller, Gerda
Goldilocks and the three bears. Floris 2011 il $17.95
Grades: PreK K 1 2   **398.2**
1. Bears -- Folklore
ISBN 978-0-86315-795-0
"This delicately illustrated version of this tale, first published in France, removes some of the familiar oppositions (too hard, too soft, just right) found in earlier versions and gives the heroine a contemporary backstory (she lives in a traveling circus caravan). The charm of the book lies primarily in Muller's detailed illustrations, which are set against tan backgrounds and include an inviting fairy tale woods dotted with wildflowers and a rustic abode for the bears. . . . The story's size motif is emphasized both textually and in the art, with big, medium, and small objects appearing throughout." Publ Wkly

Muth, Jon J.
★ **Stone** soup; retold and illustrated by Jon J. Muth. Scholastic Press 2003 un il $16.95
Grades: K 1 2 3   **398.2**
1. Folklore 2. China -- Fiction
ISBN 0-439-33909-X
LC 2002-3776
"Muth's muted blue-and-gray watercolors are ideally suited to portraying the inhospitable village. . . . His respect for Chinese people and their culture makes this serving of fusion cuisine delicious and satisfying." Horn Book

Myers, Christopher
Lies and other tall tales; collected by Zora Neale Hurston; adapted and illustrated by Christopher Myers. HarperCollins Pub. 2005 un il $15.99; lib bdg $16.89 **398.2**
1. Authors 2. Novelists 3. Dramatists 4. Tall tales 5. Memoirists 6. Folklorists 7. Short story writers 8. African Americans -- Folklore
ISBN 0-06-000655-2; 0-06-000656-0 lib bdg
LC 2004-22252
"Myers has adapted and illustrated some of the wild, very short, wicked stories collected by . . . Zora Neale Hurston. . . . True to the spirit of the tall-tale oral tradition, Myers' quiltlike pictures in paper and fabric collage are minimalist and exaggerated, magical and mundane. . . . Perfect for sharing with many age groups." Booklist

Myers, Tim

The **furry**-legged teapot; retold by Tim Myers; illustrated by Robert McGuire. Marshall Cavendish Children 2007 un il $16.99

Grades: 1 2 3 4   **398.2**

    1. Folklore -- Japan

    ISBN 978-0-7614-5295-9

                    LC 2005016935

In ancient Japan, a young tanuki, a raccoon dog that can change shapes, becomes stuck in the form of a teapot

"McGuire's acrylic spreads place the farmer's hut and monk's quarters in a lush Japanese countryside with mountains in the background. . . . Myers provides source notes for his entertaining version of the tanuki-turned-teapot story." SLJ

Naidoo, Beverley

    ★ **Aesop's** fables; [illustrated by] Piet Grobler. Frances Lincoln Children's Books 2011 48p il $18.95

Grades: 2 3 4 5   **398.2**

    1. Fables 2. Authors 3. Storytellers 4. Africa -- Fiction

    ISBN 978-1-84780-007-7; 1-84780-007-6

"Wearing a deliberate African patina, this refreshing collection of 16 Aesop fables takes place in the South African veld, giving these timeless moral tales a visual and verbal facelift. . . . In typical Aesop fashion, animals serve as lead characters, but Naidoo adds to the African texture by populating the tales with distinctive African animals. . . . The single-action narrative of each fable preserves the impersonal moral tone of the originals. . . . Primitive, whimsical watercolor-and-pencil illustrations preserve the African theme." Kirkus

Namm, Diane

    Greek myths; retold from the classic originals by Diane Namm; illustrated by Eric Freeberg. Sterling 2011 152p il (Classic starts) $5.95

Grades: 2 3 4 5   **398.2**

    1. Greek mythology

    ISBN 978-1-4027-7312-9; 1-4027-7312-9

                    LC 2010039803

From Icarus's legendary flight to Orpheus's trip to the underworld, this introduces young readers to classic Greek myths.

"Namm retells 15 familiar myths in the simple, straightforward style that makes this series so accessible for emerging readers. . . . Motivations and feelings are described directly, allowing children to easily grasp the deeper meaning of the stories. The book ends with discussion questions and a note for parents and educators. . . . It will likely become a fixture in most libraries." SLJ

Nanji, Shenaaz

    Indian tales; written by Shenaaz Nanji; illustrated by Christopher Corr. Barefoot Books 2007 92p il $19.99

Grades: 3 4 5 6   **398.2**

    1. Folklore -- India

    ISBN 978-1-846860-83-6

                    LC 2006100357

"This anthology presents eight fluid retellings of folktales from different Indian states. . . . An introduction offers a brief overview of the country's history. . . . Each folktale is preceded by a note with facts about the state from which it originated, including explanations of festivals or terms that appear in the text. Illustrations and page borders support the texts perfectly as the folk-style paintings reflect colors of rural life." SLJ

Napoli, Donna Jo, 1948-

    ★ **Treasury** of Greek mythology; classic stories of gods, goddesses, heroes & monsters. National Geographic Society 2011 191p il map $24.95; lib bdg $33.90

Grades: 5 6 7 8   **398.2**

    1. Greek mythology

    ISBN 978-1-4263-0844-4; 1-4263-0844-2; 978-1-4263-0845-1 lib bdg; 1-4263-0845-0 lib bdg

                    LC 2011024327

"Napoli presents 25 tales introducing the major players of the Greek pantheon along with an assortment of celebrated heroes and mortals. . . . At once eloquent and elemental, these lyrically written portraits deftly detail each character's origins, realm of power, and legendary story lines. Filled with sensual imagery, the language is poetic, yet balanced by amusing asides and wry observations that add a contemporary, almost conversational accessibility. . . . Stunning stylized paintings featuring luminous colors, rich patterns, and star-infused motifs add depth and drama to the text. . . . Interesting sidebars appear throughout, providing historical, scientific, and cultural information." SLJ

Nesbit, E.

    Jack and the beanstalk; [by] E. Nesbit; illustrated by Matt Tavares. Candlewick Press 2006 un il $16.99

Grades: 2 3 4   **398.2**

    1. Fairy tales 2. Giants -- Folklore 3. Folklore -- Great Britain

    ISBN 0-7636-2124-2

                    LC 2005050190

After climbing to the top of a huge beanstalk, a boy uses his quick wits to outsmart a giant and gain a fortune for himself and his mother

"First published in Nesbit's The Old Nursery Stories (1908), this lively retelling adds character and wit to the timeless fairy tale, and Tavares' large pencil-and-watercolor illustrations, in shades of dusky brown and green, are a fitting accompaniment to the young boy's scary encounter with the giant." Booklist

Nishizuka, Koko

    The **beckoning** cat; based on a Japanese folktale. illustrated by Rosanne Litzinger. Holiday House 2009 un il $16.95

Grades: K 1 2 3   **398.2**

    1. Cats -- Folklore 2. Folklore -- Japan

    ISBN 978-0-8234-2051-3; 0-8234-2051-5

                    LC 2008007266

A retelling of the traditional Japanese tale describing the origins of the beckoning cat and how it came to be a symbol of good luck.

Litzinger's "full-bleed pictures—a highly tactile mix of watercolor, colored pencil, ink and gouache—combine comfortably rounded, stylized forms and a gently shaded palette to evoke a contemplative mood." Publ Wkly

O'Malley, Kevin

    The **great** race. Walker Books for Young Readers 2011 un il $16.99

Grades: K 1 2   **398.2**
1. Fables 2. Folklore 3. Rabbits -- Folklore 4. Turtles -- Folklore
ISBN 978-0-8027-2158-7; 0-8027-2158-3
                                    LC 2010031075
Retells the traditional tale of the tortoise and the hare as a match between the very vain Lever Lapin and Nate Turtle, who is tired of all of the publicity Lever's speed generates.

"Working in watercolor and ink, O'Malley makes fine use of the wide trim, alternating sprawling crowd shots with extreme close-ups that really distill the mano a mano dislike brewing between the opponents. A simple tale, enjoyably told." Booklist

Oberman, Sheldon
Solomon and the ant; and other Jewish folktales. retold by Sheldon Oberman; introduction and commentary by Peninnah Schram. Boyds Mills Press 2006 165p $19.95
Grades: 5 6 7 8   **398.2**
1. Jews -- Folklore
ISBN 1-59078-307-7
                                    LC 2005020115
"This collection of 43 traditional Jewish stories is authoritative as well as immensely entertaining. . . . The stories, from both Ashkenazi and Sephardic traditions, are arranged more or less chronologically—from biblical days through the talmudic period to more contemporary times. There are legends, medieval fables, trickster tales, and more. . . . The stories, wonderful for storytelling and sharing, are accessible even to listeners younger than the target audience, and the notes and commentary will provide older children with context and history." Booklist
Includes bibliographical references

Ollhoff, Jim
Japanese mythology. ABDO Pub. 2011 32p il lib bdg $27.07
Grades: 5 6 7 8   **398.2**
1. Japanese mythology
ISBN 978-1-61714-723-4
                                    LC 2010042019
'This book offers information about Japanese mythology, answering questions such as "Who is Hachiman? What is the Seven Gods of Fortune? Why are myths so important in our lives? Myths are a rich source of history. People use them to make sense of our world. Even before myths were written down, people told and retold the stories of the gods and goddesses of their homeland. Readers of Japanese Mythology will learn the history of myths, as well as their deeper meaning." (Publisher's note) "A Shinto creation story forms the backbone of [this book], which also introduces the sun goddess Amaterasu; the fabled first emperor of Japan, Jimmu; and the impish Oni." (Booklist)

"Ollhoff writes in a clear and engaging fashion, presenting complex issues in a way that will be easy for youngsters to grasp. . . . The photographs and reproductions of art tie directly to the [text]." SLJ

Olson, Arielle North
Ask the bones: scary stories from around the world; selected and retold by Arielle North Olson and Howard Schwartz; illustrated by David Linn. Viking 1999 145p il hardcover o.p. pa $5.99

Grades: 4 5 6 7   **398.2**
1. Folklore
ISBN 0-670-87581-3; 0-14-230140-X pa
                                    LC 98-19108
A collection of scary folktales from countries around the world including China, Russia, Spain, and the United States

"David Linn's bone-chilling black-and-white illustrations . . . will stay with the reader long after the book is closed. Excellent for reading aloud, this collection will satisfy even jaded genre fans." Booklist
Includes bibliographical references

More bones; scary stories from around the world. selected and retold by Arielle North Olson and Howard Schwartz; illustrated by E.M. Gist. Viking 2008 162p il $15.99
Grades: 4 5 6 7   **398.2**
1. Folklore
ISBN 978-0-670-06339-0; 0-670-06339-8
"This tour of the world's shadowy corners is full of dark wizards, unkind witches, and other untrustworthy creatures. . . . The 22 tales, as retold by Olson and Schwartz, give a vivid glimpse into unfamiliar, unnerving territory. . . . The atmospheric illustrations, while not intricately detailed, are somewhat startling in their imagery." Booklist

Onyefulu, Ifeoma
The **girl** who married a ghost; and other tales from Nigeria. illustrated by Julia Cairns. Frances Lincoln Children's 2010 109p il $15.95
Grades: 2 3 4 5   **398.2**
1. Folklore -- Nigeria
ISBN 978-1-84780-176-0; 1-84780-176-5
A collection of nine Nigerian tales from a world where spirits rule and animals talk.

"Onyefulu retells these tales in an informal, chatty style that captures the drama. . . . The stated morals are heavy. . . . But the stories and occasional, appealing pencil drawings move beyond the lessons, with surprising twists and turns and animal characters that steal, lie, and get their comeuppances." Booklist

Orgel, Doris
Doctor All-Knowing; a folk tale from the Brothers Grimm. retold by Doris Orgel; illustrated by Alexandra Boiger. Atheneum Books for Young Readers 2008 un il $16.99
Grades: PreK K 1 2   **398.2**
1. Folklore -- Germany
ISBN 978-1-4169-1246-0; 1-4169-1246-0
Desperate to provide enough food for himself and his daughter, a poor man sets himself up as Doctor All-Knowing and is soon called upon by a rich man to find a thief.

"Consistent in style, yet varied in size, composition, and perspective, the watercolor paintings use comic exaggeration to good effect. Vivid in both the telling and art." Booklist

Orr, Tamra
The **monsters** of Hercules. Mitchell Lane Publishers 2011 48p il map (Monsters in myth) lib bdg $29.95

Grades: 4 5 6 7 **398.2**
1. Monsters 2. Hercules (Legendary character)
ISBN 978-1-58415-927-8; 1-58415-927-8
LC 2010028764

This book about the monsters of Hercules is "thorough and respectful of a number of ancient and modern sources and [bends] over backward to navigate often contradictory, interlinked legends. . . . A number of paintings and photos break up the otherwise text-heavy pages, and copious chapter notes and reading suggestions conclude. This is by no means entry-level stuff, but for kids handy with the basics and ready to delve deeper, [this book] will be of great use." Booklist

Includes glossary and bibliographical references

The **sirens**. Mitchell Lane Publishers 2011 48p il map (Monsters in myth) lib bdg $29.95
Grades: 4 5 6 7 **398.2**
1. Sirens (Mythology)
ISBN 978-1-58415-930-8; 1-58415-930-8
LC 2010026965

This book examines the various stories that surround the myths of the Sirens.

This book is "thorough and respectful of a number of ancient and modern sources and [bends] over backward to navigate often contradictory, interlinked legends. . . . A number of paintings and photos break up the otherwise text-heavy pages, and copious chapter notes and reading suggestions conclude. This is by no means entry-level stuff, but for kids handy with the basics and ready to delve deeper, [this book] will be of great use." Booklist

Includes glossary and bibliographical references

Osborne, Mary Pope
★ **American** tall tales; wood engravings by Michael McCurdy. Knopf 1991 115p il map $22
Grades: 3 4 5 6 **398.2**
1. Tall tales 2. Folklore -- United States
ISBN 0-679-80089-1
LC 89-37235

A collection of tall tales about such American folk heroes as Sally Ann Thunder Ann Whirlwind, Pecos Bill, John Henry, and Paul Bunyan

"As tantalizing as Osborne's storytelling are McCurdy's . . . elaborate, full-color wood engravings, which in their robust stylization dramatically render the grandeur of these engrossing yarns." Publ Wkly

Includes bibliographical references

★ The **brave** little seamstress; written by Mary Pope Osborne; illustrated by Giselle Potter. Atheneum Bks. for Young Readers 2002 un il hardcover o.p. $16
Grades: K 1 2 3 **398.2**
1. Folklore 2. Fairy tales
ISBN 0-689-84486-7; 1-4169-1620-2 pa
LC 2001-33018

A seamstress who kills seven flies with one blow outwits the king and, with the help of a kind knight, becomes a wise and kind queen

"The whimsically perky, generous text is perfectly matched to the illustrations, in Potter's signature ink-gouache-gesso-water-colors, which affix just the right amount of sauciness to the cheeky heroine." Booklist

★ **Kate** and the beanstalk; written by Mary Pope Osborne; illustrated by Giselle Potter. Atheneum Bks. for Young Readers 2000 un il pa $7.99
Grades: K 1 2 3 **398.2**
1. Fairy tales 2. Giants -- Folklore 3. Folklore -- Great Britain
ISBN 0-689-82550-1; 1-4169-0818-8 pa
LC 99-27029

In this version of the classic tale, a girl climbs to the top of a giant beanstalk, where she uses her quick wits to outsmart a giant and make her and her mother's fortune

"The text is straightforward but punctuated by some delicious dialogue. . . . Using a variety of mediums—pencil, ink, gouache, and watercolor—the illustrations are executed in Potter's signature folk-art style. They are immediate, innovative, and just the right size for story hours." Booklist

Osborne, Will
★ **Sleeping** Bobby; [by] Will Osborne and Mary Pope Osborne; illustrated by Giselle Potter. Atheneum Books for Young Readers 2005 un il $16.95
Grades: K 1 2 3 **398.2**
1. Fairy tales 2. Folklore -- Germany
ISBN 0-689-87668-8
LC 2004-06346

A retelling of the Grimm tale featuring a handsome prince who is put into a deep sleep by a curse until he is awakened by the kiss of a brave princess.

This "is written in a breezy, readable style, and most details of the original story have been included. . . . Potter's folk-style characters are dressed in Elizabethan garb with details such as puffed sleeves, high lace collars, and ruffs." SLJ

Palatini, Margie
★ **Lousy** rotten stinkin' grapes; illustrated by Barry Moser. Simon & Schuster Books for Young Readers 2009 un il $15.99
Grades: PreK K 1 2 **398.2**
1. Fables 2. Authors 3. Folklore 4. Storytellers 5. Foxes -- Folklore
ISBN 978-0-689-80246-1; 0-689-80246-3
LC 2007015727

Retells the fable of a frustrated fox that, after many tries to reach a high bunch of grapes, decides they must be sour anyway.

"Moser's wonderful watercolor illustrations of the doubting animals executing Fox's convoluted plans are rich in humor. . . . Matched by a text that rolls off the tongue and is full of action and repetitive phrases, the book is a delight." SLJ

Paterson, Katherine
Parzival; the quest of the Grail Knight. retold by Katherine Paterson. Lodestar Bks. 1998 127p hardcover o.p. pa $5.99
Grades: 5 6 7 8 **398.2**
1. Arthurian romances
ISBN 0-525-67579-5; 0-14-130573-8 pa
LC 97-23891

A retelling of the Arthurian legend in which Parzival, unaware of his noble birth, comes of age through his quest for the Holy Grail

"Nearly 800 years old, the story has freshness, humor, grace, and depth. . . . Paterson clarifies much of the Christian doctrine that is the basis of the story, but she is never dull or pedantic." SLJ

Paye, Won-Ldy

★ **Head,** body, legs; a story from Liberia. retold by Won-Ldy Paye & Margaret H. Lippert; illustrated by Julie Paschkis. Holt & Co. 2002 un il $16.95; pa $7.95
Grades: K 1 2 3   **398.2**
   1. Folklore -- Liberia
   ISBN 0-8050-6570-9; 0-8050-7890-8 pa
                                              LC 00-44856
In this tale from the Dan people of Liberia, Head, Arms, Body, and Legs learn that they do better when they work together

"This simple fable about working together is told in a straightforward text; humor is inherent in the situation. Enticing illustrations in ripe fruit colors enhance the strange, silly tale." Horn Book Guide

★ **Mrs.** Chicken and the hungry crocodile; [by] Won-Ldy Paye & Margaret H. Lippert; illustrated by Julie Paschkis. Holt & Co. 2003 un il $16.95
Grades: K 1 2 3   **398.2**
   1. Folklore -- Liberia 2. Chickens -- Folklore 3. Crocodiles -- Folklore
   ISBN 0-8050-7047-8
                                             LC 2002-1755
When a crocodile captures Mrs. Chicken and takes her to an island to fatten her up, clever Mrs. Chicken claims that she can prove they are sisters and that, therefore, the crocodile shouldn't eat her

"Told in straightforward language this trickster tale is smart and funny. . . . The stylized gouache artwork is strong and streamlined. . . . The flat paintings recall folk art, and Crocodile's checkerboard skin reflects the patterns found in her home." SLJ

Perrault, Charles

Cinderella; or, The little glass slipper. a free translation from the French of Charles Perrault; with pictures by Marcia Brown. Scribner 1954 un il $16; pa $5.99
Grades: K 1 2 3   **398.2**
   1. Fairy tales 2. Folklore -- France
   ISBN 0-684-12676-1; 0-689-81474-7 pa
   Awarded the Caldecott Medal, 1955
This is the classic story of the poor, good-natured girl who works for her selfish step-sisters until a fairy godmother transforms her into a beautiful 'princess' for just one night

"With soft, delicate colors and lines that subtly suggest, Miss Brown creates a thoroughly fairyland atmosphere, at the same time recreating the sophistication of the French Court with its golden coach, canopied bed, dazzling chandeliers, liveried footmen, curled and pompadoured ladies, and peruked (bewigged) courtiers." Libr J

Pinkney, Jerry

★ The **little** red hen. Dial Books for Young Readers 2006 un il $16.99
Grades: K 1 2 3   **398.2**
   1. Folklore 2. Animals -- Folklore 3. Chickens --

Folklore
ISBN 0-8037-2935-9
                                             LC 2005-13301
A newly illustrated edition of the classic fable of the hen who is forced to do all the work of baking bread and of the animals who learn a bitter lesson from it.

This is "a lush, light-filled rendition of a folktale staple. . . . The animal's names appear in color-coded font (red for the hen, brown for the dog, etc.), making it extra-easy even for pre-readers to chime in, and the glorious, generous paintings are a real gift." SLJ

★ **Little** Red Riding Hood; [written and illustrated by] Jerry Pinkney. Little, Brown 2007 un il $16.99
Grades: PreK K   **398.2**
   1. Fairy tales 2. Wolves -- Folklore 3. Folklore -- Germany
   ISBN 978-0-316-01355-0; 0-316-01355-2
                                           LC 2006025291
This is an adaptation of the fairy tale by the Brothers Grimm. "Preschool, primary." (Horn Book)

This is a "delightful, old-fashioned version of a familiar tale. . . . With lively detail . . . and lots of pattern and colors, Pinkney's watercolors show the predator in nightcap and glasses under Grandmother's patchwork quilt." Booklist

Pirotta, Saviour

Firebird; paintings by Catherine Hyde. Candlewick Press 2010 40p il $18.99
Grades: 2 3 4 5   **398.2**
   1. Fairy tales 2. Folklore -- Russia
   ISBN 978-0-7636-5076-6; 0-7636-5076-5
                                           LC 2010006608
With the aid of Gray Wolf, young Prince Ivan fulfills a series of tasks set for him by his father and two other kings, winning the legendary firebird, a magical horse, and the hand of Princess Helen by his efforts.

"Large and lavish, this handsome presentation builds nicely on European folktale elements. . . . Hyde's acrylic paintings are soft in focus and deep with luminous portrayals of the featured animals and dusky views of the nighttime and woodland journeys. The book's expansive layout nicely varies the use of white space and painting size. . . . A welcome choice for storytelling and reading aloud." SLJ

The **McElderry** book of Grimms' fairy tales; retold by Saviour Pirotta; illustrated by Emma Clark. Margaret K. McElderry Books 2006 126p il $19.95
Grades: 2 3 4   **398.2**
   1. Authors 2. Fairy tales 3. Folklorists 4. Philologists 5. Folklore -- Germany 6. Short story writers
   ISBN 1-4169-1798-5
First published 2002 in the United Kingdom with title: The sleeping princess and other fairy tales from Grimm

"An appealing collection of 10 fairy tales. . . . Pirotta writes like a storyteller, with great imagery and description, and the lively stories read aloud beautifully. . . . Clark's dark, twisty branches in the forest enhance the mood of this story. The large typeface, generous use of white space, and overall design make this book one children can read themselves, and the artist's expressive illustrations contribute to the appeal." SLJ

Polacco, Patricia

★ **Luba** and the wren. Philomel Bks. 1999 un il hardcover o.p. pa $6.99

Grades: K 1 2 3 **398.2**

1. Fairy tales 2. Birds -- Folklore 3. Folklore -- Russia
ISBN 0-399-23168-4; 0-698-11922-3 pa

LC 98-16353

In this variation on the story of "The Fisherman and His Wife," a young Ukrainian girl must repeatedly return to the wren she has rescued to relay her parents' increasingly greedy demands

"Polacco's signature illustrations are lush and vibrant. The regal colors of royal blue and crimson play against deep green, dappled brown, and ocher of the natural world." SLJ

Princess stories; a classic illustrated edition. compiled by Cooper Edens. Chronicle Books 2004 133p il $19.95

Grades: 2 3 4 **398.2**

1. Folklore 2. Fairy tales
ISBN 0-8118-4032-8

LC 2003-20890

"This edition of classic princess stories showcases artists from the Golden Age of Illustration, roughly the 1880s to the 1920s. . . . Arthur Rackham, Walter Crane, Jesse Wilcox Smith, Charles Robinson, Kay Nielsen, and Edmund Dulac are among the American and European artists represented. The edition is rich in language, tone, and picture and despite the disparate nature of each artist's style, it somehow comes together as a classic whole." SLJ

Pringle, Laurence P.

Imagine a dragon; [by] Laurence Pringle; illustrated by Eujin Kim Neilan. Boyds Mills Press 2008 un il $16.95

Grades: 3 4 5 **398.2**

1. Dragons
ISBN 978-1-56397-328-4; 1-56397-328-6

LC 2007017575

This is a history of dragons in various world cultures

"The book is interesting with lots of materials without being overwhelming. It provides a good introduction to dragon myths in world literature. The pictures, done in acrylic, are strong and powerful." Libr Media Connect

Puttapipat, Niroot

The **musicians** of Bremen; a brothers Grimm tale. retold and illustrated by Niroot Puttapipat. Candlewick Press 2005 un il $15.99

Grades: K 1 2 3 **398.2**

1. Animals -- Folklore 2. Folklore -- Germany
ISBN 0-7636-2758-5

LC 2005-46907

While on their way to Bremen, four aging animals who are no longer of any use to their masters find a new home after outwitting a gang of robbers

"Puttapipat makes music the strong focus of this lively version of the old Grimm folktale. . . . The dramatic ink-and-watercolor illustrations show the characters as real barnyard animals." Booklist

Ramsden, Ashley

Seven fathers; retold by Ashley Ramsden; illustrated by Ed Young. Roaring Brook Press 2011 32p il $16.99

Grades: 2 3 4 5 **398.2**

1. Fairy tales 2. Folklore -- Norway 3. Fathers --

Folklore 4. Old age -- Folklore
ISBN 978-1-59643-544-5; 1-59643-544-5

LC 2010009674

A lone traveler, tired, hungry, and cold, finds a house and asks for a room for the night, but the old man to whom he speaks refers him to his father, and that man to his father, until he is finally rewarded for his efforts by the eldest.

"Striking collage art accompanies a fluid retelling of a lesser-known Norwegian folktale. . . . Young's minimalist yet highly expressive illustrations use a strong black line to artfully convey the wintry setting and the stranger's encounters with the fathers." SLJ

Ray, Jane

Snow White. Candlewick Press 2009 un il $19.99

Grades: 3 4 5 **398.2**

1. Fairy tales 2. Pop-up books 3. Folklore -- Germany
ISBN 978-0-7636-4473-4; 0-7636-4473-0

LC 2009007774

Retells, in six dioramas with accompanying text, the tale of the beautiful princess whose lips were red as blood, skin was white as snow, and hair was black as ebony.

"Unusual paper engineering makes this a particularly memorable version of the familiar tale. . . . Birds, squirrels, and other wildlife join viewers in looking through a die-cut screen of trees (or in interior scenes an archway) at gracefully posed, richly clad figures. The jewel-like colors, as well as Ray's almond-eyed Snow White and dusky-skinned Prince, give the tale an otherworldly air." SLJ

Robbins, Ruth

Baboushka and the three kings; illustrated by Nicolas Sidjakov; adapted from a Russian folk tale. Houghton Mifflin 1960 un il $16; pa $6.95

Grades: 1 2 3 4 **398.2**

1. Folklore -- Russia 2. Christmas -- Folklore
ISBN 0-395-27673-X; 0-395-42647-2 pa

First published by Parnassus Press

Awarded The Caldecott Medal, 1961

A retelling of the Christmas legend about the old woman who declined to accompany the three kings on their search for the Christ Child and has ever since then searched for the Child on her own. Each year as she renews her search she leaves gifts at the homes she visits, acting, in this respect, as a Russian equivalent to Santa Claus

"Mystery and dignity are in the retelling. . . . At the end of the book is the story in verse set to original music." Horn Book

Rodgers, Greg

Chukfi Rabbit's big, bad bellyache; a trickster tale. told by Greg Rodgers; illustrated by Leslie Stall Widener. Cinco Puntos Press 2014 40 p. color illustrations (hardback) $16.95

Grades: K 1 2 3 **398.2**

1. Food -- Fiction 2. Choctaw Indians -- Folklore 3. Rabbit (Legendary character) -- Legends
ISBN 1935955268; 9781935955269; 9781935955276

LC 2013010568

"Deep in Choctaw Country, Chukfi Rabbit is always figuring out some way to avoid work at all costs. When Bear, Turtle, Fox, and Beaver agree on an everybody-work-together day to build Ms. Possum a new house, Chukfi Rabbit says he's too busy to help. Until he hears there will be a feast to eat after the work is done." (Publisher's note)

"Choctaw illustrator Widener dresses her animal characters in a mélange of traditional and contemporary attire; Chula Fox and Luksi Turtle sport black, brimmed hats and tasseled belts, while Kinta Beaver wears a denim work shirt and a baseball cap. Both text and illustrations positively exude good humor." Kirkus

Rohmer, Harriet

Uncle Nacho's hat; adapted by Harriet Rohmer; illustrations by Veg Reisberg; Spanish version, Rosalma Zubizarreta. Children's Bk. Press 1989 31p il hardcover o.p. pa $7.95

Grades: K 1 2 3   **398.2**
   1. Folklore -- Nicaragua 2. Bilingual books -- English-Spanish
   ISBN 0-89239-112-X pa
                                          LC 88-37090

"Adaptation of a Nicaraguan folktale. . . . When his niece, Ambrosia, gives Uncle Nacho a new hat, he tries unsuccessfully several times to get rid of the old, holey one. Seeing him dejected because his hat keeps coming back, Ambrosia suggests he put his mind on the new one instead. Flattened primitive paintings in brilliant, clear tropical colors and motifs enhance the fun of this comedy of errors." Helbig. This land is our land

Rumford, James

★ Beowulf; a hero's tale retold. Houghton Mifflin Company 2007 un il $17

Grades: 4 5 6 7   **398.2**
   1. Beowulf 2. Folklore -- Europe 3. Monsters -- Folklore
   ISBN 0-618-75637-X; 978-0-618-75637-7

A simplified and illustrated retelling of the exploits of the Anglo-Saxon warrior, Beowulf, and how he came to defeat the monster Grendel, Grendel's mother, and a dragon that threatened the kingdom.

"Superb on all counts—from the elegant bookmaking to the vigorous, evocative prose . . . to the pen-and-ink and watercolor illustrations that strikingly recall the work of Edmund Dulac." Horn Book

Sabuda, Robert

Beauty & the beast; a pop-up book of the classic fairy tale. Little Simon 2010 un il $29.99

Grades: 1 2 3 4   **398.2**
   1. Folklore 2. Fairy tales 3. Pop-up books
   ISBN 978-1-4169-6079-9; 1-4169-6079-1

"Paper-craft-pro Sabuda extends the familiar fairy tale into a moody 3-D romance that captures, in particular, the mystery and opulence of the Beast's castle. . . . Shrewdly designed mini books package the lengthy, smoothly phrased text." Booklist

Sage, Alison

★ Rapunzel; [illustrations by] Sarah Gibb; based on the original story by the Brothers Grimm. Albert Whitman 2011 un il $16.99

Grades: 1 2 3 4   **398.2**
   1. Folklore 2. Fairy tales
   ISBN 978-0-8075-6804-0; 0-8075-6804-X

Beautiful Rapunzel is locked away in a tall, tall tower, visited only by the little creatures of the forest and the witch who has imprisoned her. Until one day a handsome prince, passing by on his horse, is transfixed by the magical sound of Rapunzel singing to her animals friends and knows he must reach her.

"Reminiscent of elaborate embroidery or tapestries, the pictures create and sustain the tale's magical atmosphere. . . . Children and adults alike will be spellbound, poring over the pages again and again, delighting each time in new details and discoveries." Kirkus

Sakade, Florence

Japanese children's favorite stories; compiled by Florence Sakade; illustrated by Yoshisuke Kurosaki. 3rd ed; Tuttle 2003 109p il $16.95

Grades: 2 3 4   **398.2**
   1. Folklore -- Japan
   ISBN 0-8048-3449-0
   First published 1953
   A collection of Japanese folktales.

"This enduring collection presents 20 stories to enchant and enlighten young readers. . . . Minor text revisions have little effect on the stories. . . . The text remains simple, clear, and accessible to beginning readers and storytellers alike. The 'sparkling new color illustrations' are simply Kurosaki's original stylized scenes, repainted in bright dabs of watercolor." SLJ

San Souci, Robert

As luck would have it; from the Brothers Grimm. [by] Robert D. San Souci; illustrated by Daniel San Souci. August House/Little Folk 2008 un il $16.95

Grades: K 1 2 3 4   **398.2**
   1. Folklore -- Germany
   ISBN 978-0-87483-833-6; 0-87483-833-9
                                          LC 2008000965

"Lively, comical illustrations enhance the abundant droll humor in this noodle-head tale that plays off the Grimm Brothers' 'Clever Elsie.' . . . The expressive, lucent watercolors highlighted with Prismacolor pencils portray the foolish escapades adeptly, and the anthropomorphized animal characters evocatively represent human characteristics and foibles." SLJ

★ Cendrillon; a Caribbean Cinderella. [by] Robert D. San Souci; illustrated by Brian Pinkney. Simon & Schuster Bks. for Young Readers 1998 un il hardcover o.p. pa $8.99

Grades: K 1 2 3   **398.2**
   1. Fairy tales 2. Folklore -- Martinique
   ISBN 0-689-80668-X; 0-689-84888-9 pa
                                          LC 96-53142

A Creole variant of the familiar Cinderella tale set in Martinique and narrated by the godmother who helps Cendrillon find true love

"The narrative is full of French Creole words and phrases. . . . A fruit`a pain   (breadfruit) is transformed into the coach; six agoutis (a kind of rodent) become the horses. . . . Pinkney's art perfectly conveys the lush beauty and atmosphere of the island setting." SLJ

★ Cut from the same cloth; American women of myth, legend, and tall tale. collected and told by Robert D. San

Souci; illustrated by Brian Pinkney; introduction by Jane Yolen. Philomel Bks. 1993 140p il hardcover o.p. pa $6.99

Grades: 4 5 6 7   **398.2**

1. Tall tales 2. Women -- Folklore 3. Folklore -- United States

ISBN 0-399-21987-0; 0-698-11811-1 pa

LC 92-5233

A collection of fifteen stories about legendary American women from Anglo-American, African American, and Native American folklore

"San Souci's language is vigorous and action verbs abound; Pinkney's black-and-white block prints match the strength of the telling. The inclusion of notes on the sources and a general bibliography make this an academic resource as well as a good collection of rolicking stories." Child Book Rev Serv

Little Gold Star; a Spanish American Cinderella tale. retold by Robert D. San Souci; illustrated by Sergio Martinez. HarperCollins Pubs. 2000 un il $15.95; lib bdg $15.89

Grades: 2 3 4   **398.2**

1. Fairy tales 2. Folklore -- Southern States 3. Hispanic Americans -- Folklore

ISBN 0-688-14780-1; 0-688-14781-X lib bdg

LC 99-50290

A Spanish American retelling of the familiar story of a kind girl who is mistreated by her jealous stepmother and stepsisters. In this version, the Virgin Mary replaces the traditional fairy godmother

"Martinez' watercolors depict homes with Spanish architectural influences in an arid, southwest desert landscape; his characters have lively, expressive faces and evocative body language. . . . This is effective fairy-tale magic transported to new terrain." Bull Cent Child Books

★ **Robin** Hood and the golden arrow; retold by Robert D. San Souci; illustrations by E.B. Lewis. Orchard Books 2010 un il $17.99

Grades: K 1 2 3   **398.2**

1. Robin Hood (Legendary character) 2. Folklore -- Great Britain

ISBN 978-0-439-62538-8; 0-439-62538-6

LC 2009015624

Retells, in easy text, of the Sheriff of Nottingham's plot to hold an archery contest in order to capture the outlaw Robin Hood, but Robin and his band of merry men arrive in disguise with a plan of their own.

"Lewis draws young readers in with the splendid cover image of Robin. . . . The watercolor pictures, reminiscent of both Pyle and N. C. Wyeth, are full of mottled greens and dappled light, with powerful figures running, shooting arrows or standing nobly. It is a feast to look upon." Kirkus

Short & shivery; thirty chilling tales. retold by Robert D. San Souci; illustrated by Katherine Coville. Doubleday 1987 175p il hardcover o.p. pa $5.50

Grades: 4 5 6 7   **398.2**

1. Folklore 2. Ghost stories

ISBN 0-440-41804-6 pa

LC 86-29067

"A collection of spooky stories, competently adapted and retold (sometimes quite freely) from world folklore, including Japan, Africa, and Latin America, as well as Europe and the U.S. . . . The stories drawn from collections of regional American folklore are not only the freshest, but often the scariest. Sources are fully documented. . . . There are some delicious shivers here, with plenty of fodder for an active imagination, as well as excitement." SLJ

★ **Sister** tricksters; rollicking tales of clever females. retold by Robert D. San Souci; illustrated by Daniel San Souci. August House Pubs. 2006 69p il $19.95

Grades: 3 4 5 6   **398.2**

1. Animals -- Folklore 2. Folklore -- Southern States

ISBN 978-0-87483-791-9; 0-87483-791-X

LC 2006-40793

"These eight stories, featuring characters like Molly Cottontail, Miz Grasshopper, and Miz Goose, are energetically retold from Anne Virginia Culbertsons long out-of-print At the Big House (Bobbs-Merrill, 1904). . . . Delicious dialect and expressions convey a rural Southern flavor, yet the text is never hard to read or understand. . . . Stunning, richly colored, detailed, and playful paintings showing animals dressed in lavish finery introduce each lively tale." SLJ

Sootface; an Ojibwa Cinderella story. retold by Robert D. San Souci; illustrated by Daniel San Souci. Doubleday Bks. for Young Readers 1994 un il hardcover o.p. pa $6.99

Grades: 1 2 3 4   **398.2**

1. Ojibwa Indians -- Folklore

ISBN 0-440-41363-X pa

LC 93-10553

In this Ojibwa version of the Cinderella story, "Sootface is a young woman who does all the cooking, mending, and fire tending for her father and her two mean and lazy older sisters. When the mysterious invisible warrior announces through his sister that he will take for his bride a woman with a kind and honest heart, only Sootface proves worthy." (Booklist) "Kindergarten to grade four." (SLJ)

"The San Souci version reads aloud well, and the watercolor artwork illustrates the story with quiet grace." Booklist

★ **Sukey** and the mermaid; [by] Robert D. San Souci; illustrated by Brian Pinkney. Four Winds Press 1992 un il hardcover o.p. pa $5.95

Grades: 1 2 3 4   **398.2**

1. Mermaids and mermen 2. African Americans -- Folklore

ISBN 0-02-778141-0; 0-689-80718-X pa

LC 90-24559

Unhappy with her life at home, Sukey receives kindness and wealth from Mama Jo the mermaid

San Souci "outdoes himself here with pungent, lyrical prose that reverberates with the cadences of the South Carolina islands. . . . The supple lines of Pinkney's fluid scratchboard technique capture the grace and spirit of this magical tale and serve as the perfect foil to its darker undertones." Publ Wkly

★ The **talking** eggs; a folktale from the American South. retold by Robert D. San Souci; pictures by Jerry Pinkney. Dial Bks. for Young Readers 1989 un il $16

Grades: K 1 2 3   **398.2**
1. Folklore -- Southern States
ISBN 0-8037-0619-7

LC 88-33469

A Caldecott Medal honor book, 1990

A Southern folktale in which kind Blanche, following the instructions of an old witch, gains riches, while her greedy sister makes fun of the old woman and is duly rewarded

"Adapted from a Creole folk tale originally included in a collection of Louisiana stories by folklorist Alcee Fortier, this tale captures the flavor of the nineteenth-century South in its language and story line. . . . Jerry Pinkney's watercolors are chiefly responsible for the excellence of the book; his characters convey their moods with vivid facial expressions." Horn Book

Sanfield, Steve

The **adventures** of High John the Conqueror; [illustrated by John Ward] August House 1995 113p il hardcover o.p. pa $11.95
Grades: 4 5 6 7   **398.2**
1. Folklore -- United States 2. African Americans -- Folklore
ISBN 0-87483-433-3; 0-87483-774-X pa

LC 95-35825

A reissue of the title first published 1988 by Orchard Books

A collection of folk tales about High John the Conqueror, the traditional trickster hero of blacks during and immediately after the time of slavery

"Simply told in language comprehensible to very young readers, these tales are short, funny, and entertaining. . . . Fourteen full-page black-and-white pencil drawings illustrate some of the more dramatic moments in the stories." SLJ

Includes bibliographical references

Schlitz, Laura Amy

★ The **Bearskinner**; a tale of the Brothers Grimm. retold by Laura Amy Schlitz; illustrated by Max Grafe. Candlewick Press 2007 un il $16.99
Grades: 3 4 5 6   **398.2**
1. Fairy tales 2. Folklore -- Germany
ISBN 978-0-7636-2730-0; 0-7636-2730-5

LC 2007-22787

A retelling of the Grimm fairy tale in which a despondent soldier makes a pact to do the devil's bidding for seven years in return for as much money and property as he could ever want

"Schlitz narrates with clarity, grace, and sensitivity. . . . Except for the devil's coat of darkest green, Grafe's atmospheric full-page illustrations are almost monochromatic. . . . A provocative edition that should set older children thinking about the meaning of endurance and heroism." Horn Book

Schram, Peninnah

The **magic** pomegranate; by Peninnah Schram; illustrated by Melanie Hall. Millbrook Press 2008 48p il (On my own folklore) lib bdg $25.26; pa $6.95
Grades: 1 2 3 4   **398.2**
1. Fairy tales 2. Jews -- Folklore 3. Pomegranates

-- Folklore
ISBN 978-0-8225-6742-4 lib bdg; 0-8225-6742-3 lib bdg; 978-0-8225-6746-2 pa; 0-8225-6746-6 pa

LC 2006036722

Three handsome and clever brothers compete to find the world's most unusual gift. Includes a note on doing good deeds, or mitzvah, and discusses the symbolism of the pomegranate in Judaism

The "tale is paired with an illustration style that nicely reflects the culture." Horn Book Guide

Includes bibliographical references

Schwartz, Alvin, 1927-1992

★ **Ghosts!** ghostly tales from folklore. retold by Alvin Schwartz; illustrated by Victoria Chess. HarperCollins Pubs. 1991 63p il (I can read book) lib bdg $15.89; pa $3.95
Grades: K 1 2   **398.2**
1. Folklore 2. Ghost stories
ISBN 0-06-021797-9 lib bdg; 0-06-444170-9 pa

LC 90-21746

Presents seven, easy-to-read ghost stories based on traditional folk tales and legends from various countries

"All of the pen-and-watercolor illustrations are tidy and cheery and creepy. . . . Retold in a style that is simple but not choppy . . . and accompanied by a page of brief notes, all the tales will lend themselves to elaboration and innovation." Bull Cent Child Books

I saw you in the bathtub, and other folk rhymes; collected by Alvin Schwartz; pictures by Syd Hoff. Harper & Row 1989 64p il (I can read book) hardcover o.p. pa $3.99
Grades: K 1 2   **398.2**
1. Folklore
ISBN 0-06-444151-2 pa

LC 88-16111

Presents an illustrated collection of traditional folk rhymes, some composed by children

"Kids may be surprised to see their recess yells on the printed page but will relish the confirmation of significance. Hoff's full-color cartoons interpret the rhymes literally, an approach that leads to some pretty surreal results." Bull Cent Child Books

★ **In** a dark, dark room, and other scary stories; retold by Alvin Schwartz; illustrated by Dirk Zimmer. Harper & Row 1984 63p il (I can read book) $15.95; pa $3.95
Grades: K 1 2   **398.2**
1. Folklore 2. Ghost stories 3. Horror fiction
ISBN 0-06-025271-5; 0-06-444090-7 pa

LC 83-47699

This is a collection of "seven traditional tales from around the world retold in simple yet effective language. . . . The chill here springs from suspense, an eerie setting or a ghostly surprise, rather than from blood and gore. Though pared down somewhat from longer versions, the stories retain their genuine creepiness. . . . The colorfully dark illustrations are sinister without being gruesome and add a comic touch." SLJ

★ **More** scary stories to tell in the dark; collected from folklore and retold by Alvin Schwartz; illustrated by Brett Helquist. Reillustrated Harper Trophy ed Harper 2010 111 p. ill. (hardcover) $15.99

Grades: 4 5 6 7　　　　　　　　　　　**398.2**
1. Ghost stories 2. Horror fiction 3. Folklore -- United
States
ISBN 9780060835217; 0060835214
　　　　　　　　　　　　　LC 2010922248
Originally published in 1984 by Lippincott, with illustra-
tions by Stephen Gammell.

This volume contains stories of ghosts, murders, graveyards and other horrors.

"Helquist's new illustrations for Schwartz's classic [col-
lection] of ghost stories inhabit an altogether more benign
universe than the nightmarish Stephen Gammell originals.
[This edition is] handsome and accessible, ceding the stories
themselves pride of place." Horn Book Guide

Includes bibliographical references (pages 105-111).

★ **Scary** stories 3; more tales to chill your bones. collected from folklore and retold by Alvin Schwartz; drawings
by Stephen Gammell. HarperCollins Pubs. 1991 115p il
music $15.99; lib bdg $16.89; pa $5.99
Grades: 4 5 6 7　　　　　　　　　　　**398.2**
1. Ghost stories 2. Horror fiction 3. Folklore -- United
States
ISBN 0-06-021794-4; 0-06-021795-2 lib bdg; 0-06-
440418-8 pa
　　　　　　　　　　　　　LC 90-47474
Traditional and modern-day stories of ghosts, haunts, superstitions, monsters, and horrible scary things

"The book is well paced and continually captivates,
surprises, and entices audiences into reading just one more
page. Gammell's gauzy, cobwebby, black-and-white pen-
and-ink drawings help to sustain the overall creepy mood."
SLJ

Includes bibliographical references

★ **There** is a carrot in my ear, and other noodle tales;
retold by Alvin Schwartz; pictures by Karen Ann Weinhaus.
Harper & Row 1982 64p il (I can read book) hardcover
o.p. pa $3.95
Grades: K 1 2　　　　　　　　　　　**398.2**
1. Folklore 2. Wit and humor
ISBN 0-06-025234-0; 0-06-444103-2 pa
　　　　　　　　　　　　　LC 80-8442
This "is a collection of six stories from sources . . . as
diverse as American 'Little Moron' stories, ancient Greek
tales and vaudeville pieces. Explaining in his foreword that a
'noodle is a silly person,' reteller Alvin Schwartz goes on to
introduce the noodly Brown family and reveal their various
foibles. . . . Most of the stories don't appear in other beginning noodle collections and will provide laughs for readers
who catch the puns and absurdities the stories hinge on. The
drawings by Karen Ann Weinhaus . . . show funny, pointy-
proboscised folk blissfully unaware of their own goofiness."
SLJ

Schwartz, Howard

A **coat** for the moon and other Jewish tales; selected
and retold by Howard Schwartz and Barbara Rush; illustrated by Michael Iofin. Jewish Publ. Soc. 1999 81p il
hardcover o.p. pa $13
Grades: 4 5 6 7　　　　　　　　　　　**398.2**
1. Jews -- Folklore
ISBN 0-8276-0596-X; 0-8276-0736-9 pa
　　　　　　　　　　　　　LC 98-52704

A collection of Jewish folktales from around the world,
including "The Lamp on the Mountain," "The Witch Baru-
sha," "The Sabbath Walking Stick," and "The Fisherman
and the Silver Fish"

"These tales incorporate everything from the magical to
the bizarre, all the while imparting specific Jewish values
that have transcended time and cultural dispersion. . . . Each
retelling opens with a delightfully detailed pen-and-ink illustration encircled by a key sentence or phrase from the text
that gives a hint of what's to come." SLJ

Scott, Nathan Kumar

The **sacred** banana leaf; an Indonesian trickster tale,
by Nathan Kumar Scott; illustrated by Radhashyam Raut.
Tara 2008 un il $16.95
Grades: 2 3 4　　　　　　　　　　　**398.2**
1. Animals -- Folklore 2. Folklore -- Indonesia
ISBN 978-81-86211-28-1; 81-86211-28-4
"Scott's retelling has verve and humor, and the illustrations, rendered in patachitra (a traditional style of temple
painting originating in eastern India) are both accessible and
graceful. Saturated colors gleam from sand-toned pages, and
the patterned skins of the clearly delineated animals add texture." Booklist

Seeger, Pete

★ **Abiyoyo**; based on a South African lullaby and folk
story. text by Pete Seeger; illustrations by Michael Hays.
Simon & Schuster Bks. for Young Readers 2001 un il
$19.95; pa $6.99
Grades: K 1 2 3　　　　　　　　　　　**398.2**
1. Giants -- Folklore 2. Folklore -- South Africa
ISBN 0-689-84693-2; 0-689-71810-1 pa
A reissue of the title first published 1986 by Macmillan
Banished from the town for making mischief, a little boy
and his father are welcomed back when they make the giant
Abiyoyo disappear

"Told in the familiar Seeger style, with brief musical phrases of the one-word song incorporated in the text
and printed complete at the end, and with illustrations full
of light and color, this rendering of a South African tale is
a pleasure. The giant is imposing but not too scary for the
youngest listener leaning over the book while a parent tells
the story." N Y Times Book Rev

Shannon, George

★ **More** stories to solve; fifteen folktales from around
the world. told by George Shannon; illustrated by Peter Sis.
Greenwillow Bks. 1991 64p il hardcover o.p. pa $4.99
Grades: 3 4 5 6　　　　　　　　　　　**398.2**
1. Riddles 2. Folklore
ISBN 0-688-09161-X; 0-380-73261-0 pa
"Shannon combines the folktale and the riddle in a brief
collection that brings together 15 international stories."
Booklist

Includes bibliographical references

Rabbit's gift; a fable from China. told by George
Shannon; illustrated by Laura Dronzek. Harcourt 2007 un
il $16
Grades: PreK K 1　　　　　　　　　　　**398.2**
1. Fables 2. Folklore -- China 3. Animals -- Folklore

4. Rabbits -- Folklore
ISBN 978-0-15-206073-2; 0-15-206073-1
LC 2006-04789
Woodland animals, each thinking of his neighbor, share
a turnip left on their doorstep.

"The uncluttered illustrations, many framed in purple to
compliment the purple of the turnip, perfectly capture the
action of the story. The expressive faces of the animals are
charming." Booklist

★ **Stories** to solve; folktales from around the world.
illustrated by Peter Sis. Greenwillow Bks. 1985 55p il
hardcover o.p. pa $4.99
Grades: 3 4 5 6   **398.2**
1. Riddles 2. Folklore
ISBN 0-688-04303-8; 0-380-73260-2 pa
LC 84-18656
"Each of these 14 delightful folktales is a short puzzle to
be solced through clevernes, common sense or careful observations of details in the text. . . . Sis' pointillistic pen-and-
ink drawings illustrate each puzzle, and sometimes clarify
the solutions." SLJ

Sharpe, Leah Marinsky
★ The **goat**-faced girl; a classic Italian folktale. retold
by Leah Marinsky Sharpe; illustrated by Jane Marinsky. David R. Godine 2009 un il $16.95
Grades: K 1 2 3   **398.2**
1. Fairy tales 2. Folklore -- Italy
ISBN 978-1-56792-393-3; 1-56792-393-3
LC 2009-22383
When Isabella, a beautiful but lazy young woman,
agrees to marry an equally lazy prince, the sorceress who
raised her gives her the head of a goat in hopes that she will
learn to do things for herself.

"Rich storytelling and intricately imagined artwork
make this debut a standout. . . . Marinsky's paintings, in the
chalky, sun-bleached colors of the Italian renaissance, contain many small pleasures." Publ Wkly

Shelby, Anne
The **adventures** of Molly Whuppie and other Appa-
lachian folktales; [by] Anne Shelby; illustrations by Paula
McArdle. The University of North Carolina Press 2007
88p il $14.95
Grades: 4 5 6 7   **398.2**
1. Folklore -- Appalachian Mountains
ISBN 978-0-8078-3163-2
LC 2007013789
A collection of Appalachian folktales featuring Molly
Whuppie and her adventures.

"Shelby has captured the language of Appalachia. .
. . Her adaptations are true to the traditional folktales. . .
. Young readers and listeners will make these stories their
own and enjoy retelling them." SLJ

Includes bibliographical references

Shepard, Aaron
★ **One**-Eye! Two-Eyes! Three-Eyes! a very Grimm
fairy tale. pictures by Gary Clement. Atheneum Books for
Young Readers 2007 un il $16.95

Grades: K 1 2 3   **398.2**
1. Folklore 2. Fairy tales
ISBN 978-0-689-86740-8; 0-689-86740-9
LC 2005-00459
A retelling of the Grimm's fairy tale about a little girl
who has two eyes and is horribly teased by her sisters who
have one and three eyes respectively.

"The alterations to the story are consistent with the lighthearted watercolor-and-pencil illustrations. . . . Children will
enjoy the humor in this reincarnation, and it will make excellent fodder for reader's theater, with a script available on the
author's Web site." SLJ

★ The **princess** mouse; a tale of Finland. told by
Aaron Shepard; illustrated by Leonid Gore. Atheneum Bks.
for Young Readers 2003 un il hardcover o.p. pa $13.99
Grades: K 1 2 3   **398.2**
1. Fairy tales 2. Mice -- Folklore 3. Folklore -- Finland
ISBN 0-689-82912-4; 1-4169-8969-2 pa
LC 2001-55273
A retelling of a Finnish folk tale about a young man who
plans to marry his mouse sweetheart

"Shepard's charmingly droll version of a Finnish folktale
combines classic elements with unexpected, witty details. .
. . The jewel-toned art has beautiful luminescence; the elongated, somewhat blocky look of the characters reinforces the
fantasy; and the mice are downright irresistible." Booklist

The **sea** king's daughter; a Russian legend. retold by
Aaron Shepard; illustrated by Gennady Spirin. Atheneum
Bks. for Young Readers 1997 28p il pa $11.99
Grades: 3 4 5 6   **398.2**
1. Folklore -- Russia 2. Musicians -- Folklore
ISBN 0-689-80759-7; 0-689-84259-7 pa
LC 96-3391
A talented musician from Novgorod plays so well that
the Sea King wants him to marry one of his daughters

"The telling is descriptive yet very accessible, with the
art, in Spirin's majestic signature style, evoking both the
mythical feel of the legend and the folk-music roots from
which the story sprang." Booklist

Sherman, Pat
The **sun's** daughter; a story based on an Iroquois legend. illustrated by R. Gregory Christie. Clarion Bks. 2005
31p il $16
Grades: 2 3 4   **398.2**
1. Iroquois Indians -- Folklore
ISBN 0-618-32430-5
LC 2004-17820
"Inspired by Iroquois tales of the Corn Maiden and her
sisters, this original story tells how Maize, Red Bean, and
Pumpkin walked the earth spreading a bounty of food in
their wake. . . . The story is charmingly told with eloquent
phrasing and vocabulary. The artwork, done in a folk-art
style, is energetic and exuberant, and the brush strokes are
used to dramatic effect across the spreads." SLJ

Shulevitz, Uri
★ The **treasure**. Farrar, Straus & Giroux 1978 un il
hardcover o.p. pa $6.95
Grades: K 1 2 3   **398.2**
1. Folklore
ISBN 0-374-37740-5; 0-374-47955-0 pa

A Caldecott Medal honor book, 1980

"Although the story is known in many cultures the retelling suggests the Hassidic tradition. . . . The eastern European influence is extended in the illustrations." Horn Book

Sierra, Judy

Can you guess my name? traditional tales around the world. selected and retold by Judy Sierra; illustrated by Stefano Vitale. Clarion Bks. 2002 110p il $20
Grades: 3 4 5 6   **398.2**
1. Folklore
ISBN 0-618-13328-3

LC 2002-3509

A collection of fifteen folktales from all over the world, including stories that resemble "The Three Pigs," "The Bremen Town Musicians," "Rumpelstiltskin," "The Frog Prince," and "Hansel and Gretel"

"All of the selections have dramatic dialogue and repetitive phrases and refrains, and are easy to learn. . . . Vitale's engaging folk illustrations are painted on wood. . . . This collection provides a fascinating experience with comparative literature, one that can open doors to other cultures. A must purchase for most collections." SLJ

Includes bibliographical references

The **gift** of the Crocodile; a Cinderella story. illustrated by Reynold Ruffins. Simon & Schuster Bks. for Young Readers 2000 un il $17
Grades: K 1 2 3   **398.2**
1. Fairy tales 2. Folklore -- Indonesia
ISBN 0-689-82188-3

LC 98-40592

In this Indonesian version of the Cinderella story, a girl named Damura escapes her cruel stepmother and stepsister and marries a handsome prince with the help of Grandmother Crocodile

"Sierra's unadorned retelling is straightforward. . . . Ruffins's brightly colored, patterned paintings, with their angular figures and wavy landscapes, express and evoke the story's island setting." Horn Book

★ **Nursery** tales around the world; selected and retold by Judy Sierra; illustrated by Stefano Vitale. Clarion Bks. 1996 114p il $20
Grades: K 1 2 3 4 5   **398.2**
1. Folklore
ISBN 0-395-67894-3

LC 93-2068

Presents eighteen simple stories from international folklore, grouped around six themes, such as "Runaway Cookies," "Slowpokes and Speedsters," and "Chain Tales." Includes background information and storytelling hints

"This richly illustrated compendium of folktales does double duty as a nursery story book for lap-sharing and as a sourcebook for parents and professionals. . . . Most entries feature strong rhythms and repetition that invite audience participation and develop memory. . . . Top this engaging text with Vitale's lavish oil-on-wood ethnic borders, motif vignettes, and full-page illustrations, and you have a handsome work to be valued by readers and treasured by listeners." Bull Cent Child Books

Includes bibliographical references

Singer, Isaac Bashevis

Zlateh the goat, and other stories; pictures by Maurice Sendak; translated from the Yiddish by the author and Elizabeth Shub. Harper & Row 1966 90p il $15.95; pa $6.95
Grades: 4 5 6 7   **398.2**
1. Jews -- Folklore
ISBN 0-06-028477-3; 0-06-440147-2 pa

A Newbery Award honor book, 1967

"Seven tales drawn from middle-European Jewish village life, with illustrations which extend the humor and subtlety of the situations." Hodges. Books for Elem Sch Libr

Singh, Rina

Nearly nonsense; Hoja tales from Turkey. illustrated by Farida Zaman. Tundra Books 2011 48p il $17.95
Grades: 2 3 4 5   **398.2**
1. Folklore -- Turkey
ISBN 978-0-88776-974-0; 0-88776-974-8

"Turkey has a particularly vibrant oral tradition, and the stories of Nasrudin Hoja—a foolish/wise man—are legion and deservedly popular. . . . When he and his son take their donkey to market, they are ridiculed whether they ride, walk, or carry the animal on their backs, proving that you can't please everyone. When Hoja wears fancy clothing, he is treated more deferentially than when he wears patched clothing, so he 'feeds' his coat to show the error of his host's behavior. Lesser-known stories are also included. . . . These retellings are unembellished, but their humor and intention are clear." SLJ

Smith, Chris

★ **One** city, two brothers; written by Chris Smith, illustrated by Aurélia Fronty. Barefoot Books 2007 un il $16.99
Grades: 2 3 4   **398.2**
1. Brothers -- Folklore 2. Jerusalem -- Folklore 3. Folklore -- Middle East
ISBN 978-1-846860-42-3

To settle an inheritance dispute between two brothers, King Solomon tells a tale of how Jerusalem came to be founded.

"Based on a folktale told by both Jews and Arabs, this picture book beautifully captures the spirit of brotherhood. . . . The accomplished folk-style artwork, in shades of verdant green, heavenly blue, and harvest orange . . . adds an air of peace and hope." Booklist

Snyder, Dianne

The **boy** of the three-year nap; illustrated by Allen Say. Houghton Mifflin 1988 32p il $16.95; pa $6.95
Grades: 1 2 3   **398.2**
1. Folklore -- Japan
ISBN 0-395-44090-4; 0-395-66957-X pa

LC 87-30674

A Caldecott Medal honor book, 1989

"Japan's contribution to the trickster folktale, in which a lazy son cons a rich man, only to be outsmarted by his own, even trickier mother. Lilting prose and shimmering illustrations combine in perfect harmony." SLJ

Souhami, Jessica

King Pom and the fox; [by] Jessica Souhami. Frances Lincoln 2007 un il $16.95

Grades: K 1 2 3   **398.2**
1. Folklore
ISBN 978-1-84507-478-4; 1-84507-478-5

"In this Chinese version of 'Puss in Boots,' a young man is called King Pom because he owns a grand pomegranate tree. When a fox is caught stealing its fruit, he strikes a bargain. The fox arranges for King Pom to be rescued from the river and presented to the Emperor as a rich man, unfortunately attacked by robbers. . . . Souhami's bright, uncluttered collages are made of Ingres papers adorned with watercolor, ink, and pencil and lightly positioned on creamy backgrounds. . . . The spareness of the text matches the simplicity of the artwork." SLJ

The **little,** little house. Frances Lincoln 2006 32p il $15.95
Grades: K 1 2   **398.2**
1. Jews -- Folklore
ISBN 1-84507-108-5

"A delightful retelling. . . . The vibrant colors and strong contrast of the cut-paper shapes against neutral backgrounds provide great visual energy. The simple yet dramatic text makes it especially well suited to reading aloud." SLJ

"Souhami's adaptation of this eastern European Jewish folktale features a poor man named Joseph, his wife, and three children, who live together in a cramped little house. Joseph seeks advice from wise Aunty Bella, who recommends that he bring his six chickens, his rooster, his cow, and his goat inside. The results are predictably disastrous. . . . Finally, Aunty Bella gives permission to turn the animals outside again, and, suddenly, the house seems just the right size for Joseph's family." Booklist

Sausages. Frances Lincoln Children's Books 2006 un il hardcover o.p. pa $8.95
Grades: PreK K 1 2   **398.2**
1. Folklore
ISBN 978-1-84507-397-8; 1-84507-397-5; 978-1-84507-601-6 pa; 1-84507-601-X pa

"In this vibrant retelling of the Grimms' The Three Wishes, brilliantly designed paper collages capture every trace of humor in this cautionary tale. . . . A woodcutter rescues an elf from a rosebush and is granted three wishes. . . . The woodcutter asks for sausages. His wife responds with an angry reply that leaves the sausages stuck on his nose, and, of course, the last wish must be used to remove them. The story begs to be read aloud or told—the language is rich with sound effects." SLJ

Spirin, Gennady
Goldilocks and the three bears; retold and illustrated by Gennady Spirin. Marshall Cavendish Children 2009 un il $17.99
Grades: PreK K 1 2   **398.2**
1. Folklore 2. Bears -- Folklore
ISBN 978-0-7614-5596-7; 0-7614-5596-5

LC 2008026984

A simplified retelling of the adventures of a little girl walking in the woods who finds the house of the three bears and helps herself to their belongings. Includes a note on the history of the tale

"Spirin's version of this classic pairs a simple, straightforward retelling with lush Renaissance costumes and elegant page designs. The bears, rendered in watercolor and colored pencil, are solid, realistic creatures, revealing sharp teeth and claws. . . . The setting is created with richly realized essentials: solid porridge bowls, carved chairs, ornate beds, a massive stucco and wood-trimmed dwelling. . . . This . . . will be embraced for its visual clarity and sumptuous style." SLJ

★ **Little** Red Riding Hood; adapted from the Brothers Grimm by Gennady Spirin. Marshall Cavendish 2010 un il $17.99
Grades: 2 3 4   **398.2**
1. Fairy tales 2. Wolves -- Folklore 3. Folklore -- Germany
ISBN 0761457046; 978-0-7614-5704-6

A retelling of Little Red Riding Hood's encounter with a wicked wolf while visiting her grandmother.

"This classic Grimm tale has had many interpretations over the years, but Spirin's splendid version is inspired by the lavish Dutch paintings of the 17th century. The jacket, with windmills and Renaissance cathedral spires in the background, sets the scene. . . . Grandmother, who is garbed in lace and flounces, and the hunters with their long rifles and Cavalier hats fit well into the setting. . . . Spirin places his characters up front on the page against plentiful white space, giving intensity to the unfolding drama. A simply retold and richly illustrated addition." SLJ

★ **The tale** of the Firebird; translated by Tatiana Popova. Philomel Bks. 2002 32p il $16.99
Grades: 2 3 4   **398.2**
1. Fairy tales 2. Birds -- Folklore 3. Folklore -- Russia
ISBN 0-399-23584-1

LC 2001-36660

When Prince Ivan sets out to find the Firebird for his father the tsar, he must complete a series of tasks before obtaining the Firebird and winning the hand of a beautiful princess. "Ages six to ten." (Bull Cent Child Books)

"The storytelling is dramatic and controlled, the language rising and falling in a cadence that encourages reading aloud. . . . Detailed and dramatic, with a golden palette that echoes crown jewels, the illustrations have an adventurous fairy-tale sweep." Bull Cent Child Books

Steptoe, John
★ **Mufaro's** beautiful daughters; an African tale. Lothrop, Lee & Shepard Bks. 1987 un il $15.95; lib bdg $15.89
Grades: K 1 2 3   **398.2**
1. Folklore -- Africa
ISBN 0-688-04045-4; 0-688-04046-2 lib bdg

LC 84-7158

A Caldecott Medal honor book, 1988; Coretta Scott King Award for illustration, 1988; Boston Globe-Horn Book Award, picture book 1987

Mufaro's two beautiful daughters, one bad-tempered, one kind and sweet, go before the king, who is choosing a wife

"The pace of the text matches the rhythm of the illustrations—both move in dramatic unity to the climax. By changing perspective the artist not only captures the lush, rich background but also the personalities of the characters with revealing studies of their faces." Horn Book

★ The **story** of Jumping Mouse; a native American legend. retold and illustrated by John Steptoe. Lothrop, Lee & Shepard Bks. 1984 un il $15.95; pa $5.95

Grades: 1 2 3   **398.2**

1. Mice -- Folklore 2. Native Americans -- Folklore

ISBN 0-688-01902-1; 0-688-08740-X pa

LC 82-14848

A Caldecott Medal honor book, 1985

"By keeping hope alive within himself, a mouse is successful in his quest for the far-off land. Steptoe's retelling of an unattributed tribal legend is exquisite in its use of language and in its expansive drawings which employ dazzling subtleties of light and shadow." SLJ

Steven, Kenneth C.

Stories for a fragile planet; [written by] Kenneth Steven; [illustrated by] Jane Ray. Trafalgar Square 2011 48p il $16.99

Grades: 3 4 5 6   **398.2**

1. Folklore

ISBN 978-0-7459-6157-6; 0-7459-6157-6

"This appealing collection consists of 10 brief stories each with a nature theme. Settings include Ancient Greece, ... Africa, ... Greenland, ... Russia, Asia, South America, and Ireland. ... Although there are no source notes, each smoothly written story is preceded by a brief statement about its origins. The book is beautifully designed, with most of the stories illustrated with crisp, jewel-toned paintings in a primitive style." Booklist

Stevens, Janet

Coyote steals the blanket; an Ute tale. retold and illustrated by Janet Stevens. Holiday House 1993 un il lib bdg $17.95; pa $6.95

Grades: K 1 2 3   **398.2**

1. Coyote (Legendary character) 2. Ute Indians -- Folklore

ISBN 0-8234-0996-1 lib bdg; 0-8234-1129-X pa

LC 92-54415

"When Coyote swipes a blanket, thus angering the spirit of the desert, he is pursued by a rock on a rampage. This traditional trickster tale features a scraggly, scruffy yet lovable character, a narrative that will roll right off storytellers' tongues, and hilarious pictures of boastful animals trying to halt the furious boulder." SLJ

★ **Tops** and bottoms; adapted and illustrated by Janet Stevens. Harcourt Brace & Co. 1995 un il $16

Grades: K 1 2 3   **398.2**

1. Bears -- Folklore 2. Rabbits -- Folklore 3. African Americans -- Folklore

ISBN 0-15-292851-0

LC 93-19154

A Caldecott Medal honor book, 1996

"Bear agrees to enter into a farming partnership with Hare, but first Hare makes Bear choose which half he will receive at harvest time: tops or bottoms. Because Bear picks tops, Hare sows all root vegetables. For the second crop, Bear chooses bottoms; this time Hare grows lettuce, broccoli, and celery. Finally, the frustrated Bear demands tops and bottoms from the final season's crop. But Hare is still the winner: he grows corn [and] keeps the ears 'in the middle' for his family. ... Steven's bold, well-composed watercolor,

pencil, and gesso illustrations cover every inch of each vertically oriented double-page spread. ... The story contains enough sly humor and reassuring predictability to captivate listeners." Horn Book

Sturges, Philemon

★ The **Little** Red Hen (makes a pizza) retold by Philemon Sturges; illustrated by Amy Walrod. Dutton Children's Bks. 1999 un il $15.99

Grades: K 1 2 3   **398.2**

1. Folklore 2. Chickens -- Folklore

ISBN 0-525-45953-7

LC 99-20066

In this version of the traditional tale, the duck, the dog, and the cat refuse to help the Little Red Hen make a pizza but do get to participate when the time comes to eat it and then they wash the dishes

"There's a keen sense of the absurd here, and the hilarious cut-paper illustrations are right in tune with the zany plot." SLJ

Taback, Simms

★ **Joseph** had a little overcoat. Viking 1999 un il music $15.99

Grades: K 1 2 3   **398.2**

1. Jews -- Fiction 2. Toy and movable books 3. Folklore -- Europe, Eastern 4. Clothing and dress -- Fiction 5. Toy and movable books -- Specimens

ISBN 0-670-87855-3

LC 98-47721

A newly illustrated edition of the title first published 1977 by Random House

Awarded the Caldecott Medal, 2000

This is an "adaptation of a Yiddish folk song (a newly illustrated version of a book Taback first did in 1977). ... {It} tells the story of resourceful Joseph, a farmer/tailor of Yehupetz, Poland, who recycles his worn overcoat into ever-smaller elements (jacket, vest, scarf, tie, handkerchief, and button)." (Horn Book) "Ages four to seven." (Booklist)

"Taback's inventive use of die-cut pages shows off his signature artwork. ... This diverting, sequential story unravels as swiftly as the threads of Joseph's well-loved, patch-covered plaid coat." Publ Wkly

Talbott, Hudson

King Arthur and the Round Table; written and illustrated by Hudson Talbott. Books of Wonder 1995 un il $18.99

Grades: 3 4 5   **398.2**

1. Arthurian romances 2. Kings

ISBN 0-688-11340-0

LC 94-43766

"The rich watercolor tableaux ... paint war as bloody and painful, not all glorious. The love scenes glow golden. The Round Table, huge and decorated with the signs of the zodiac, exhibits its power more than the words do. Overall, this is a rousing addition to the current pickings of Arthurian stories." SLJ

Tarnowska, Wafa'

★ **Arabian** nights; written by Wafa' Tarnowska; illustrated by Carole Hénaff. Barefoot Books 2010 125p il $24.99

Grades: 5 6 7 8 **398.2**
1. Fairy tales 2. Arabs -- Folklore
ISBN 978-1-84686-122-2; 1-84686-122-5

LC 2008028159

"With bright, lush, stylized acrylic illustrations, this collection of eight stories from A Thousand and One Nights is designed for reading aloud. . . . Throughout, the spacious paintings capture the sense of the supernatural in daily life, including magical images of people taking flight above city, trees, and desert." Booklist

Taylor, C. J.
Spirits, fairies, and merpeople; Native stories of other worlds. Tundra Books 2009 39p il $19.95
Grades: 3 4 5 6 **398.2**
1. Native Americans -- Folklore
ISBN 978-0-88776-872-9; 0-88776-872-5

"The seven brief legends in this collection hail from a range of Native cultures. Mohawk artist/storyteller Taylor includes one from her own heritage, along with one each from the Mi'kmaq, Dakota, Coos, Ojibwa, Ute, and Cree. . . . Taylor's retellings are crisp and lend themselves well to reading aloud. Each story is accompanied by a lushly hued, surrealistic painting. The powerful images featuring fearsome creatures and tiny human figures balance the taut economy of the text." SLJ

Tchana, Katrin Hyman
Changing Woman and her sisters; stories of goddesses from around the world. retold by Katrin Hyman Tchana; illustrated by Trina Schart Hyman. Holiday House 2006 80p il $18.95
Grades: 5 6 7 8 **398.2**
1. Folklore 2. Gods and goddesses
ISBN 978-0-8234-1999-9; 0-8234-1999-1

LC 2005-52504

An illustrated collection of traditional tales which feature goddesses from different cultures, including Navajo, Mayan, and Fon. Notes explain each goddess's place in her culture, the reason for the book, and how the illustrations were developed

"This large, handsome volume assembles well-chosen, well-told stories. . . . Hyman . . . contributed distinctive portrayals of the goddesses using a technique that melded photographs and found materials into full-page ink and acrylic paintings." Booklist

Includes bibliographical references

Tracy, Kathleen
Cerberus. Mitchell Lane Publishers 2011 48p il map (Monsters in myth) lib bdg $29.95
Grades: 4 5 6 7 **398.2**
1. Classical mythology
ISBN 978-1-58415-924-7; 1-58415-924-3

LC 2010026968

This describes myths of Cerberus, Hades three-headed watchdog who guarded the gates of the Greek Underworld.

This book is "thorough and respectful of a number of ancient and modern sources and [bends] over backward to navigate often contradictory, interlinked legends. . . . A number of paintings and photos break up the otherwise text-heavy pages, and copious chapter notes and reading suggestions conclude. This is by no means entry-level stuff, but for kids

handy with the basics and ready to delve deeper, [this book] will be of great use." Booklist

Includes glossary and bibliographical references

★ **Trickster:** Native American tales; a graphic collection. edited by Matt Dembicki. Fulcrum 2010 231p il pa $22.95
Grades: 5 6 7 8 **398.2**
1. Graphic novels 2. Folklore -- Graphic novels 3. Native Americans -- Folklore
ISBN 978-1-55591-724-1 pa; 1-55591-724-0 pa

LC 2009-49668

"More than 40 storytellers and cartoonists have contributed to this original and provocative compendium of traditional folklore presented in authentic, colorful, and engaging sequential art. The stories are drawn from a variety of Native peoples across North America, and so the trickster character appears variously as Rabbit, a raccoon, Coyote, and in other guises; landscapes, clothing and rhythms of speech and action also vary in keeping with distinct traditions. Realistic, impressionistic, painterly, and cartoon styles of art are employed to echo and announce the tone of each tale and telling style, making this a rich visual treasure as well as cultural trove." SLJ

Vallverdu, Josep
Aladdin and the magic lamp; from The thousand and one nights. adaptation by Josep Vallverdu; illustrated by Pep Montserrat. Chronicle Books 2006 un il $14.95; pa $6.95
Grades: K 1 2 **398.2**
1. Fairy tales 2. Arabs -- Folklore 3. Bilingual books -- English-Spanish
ISBN 0-8118-5061-7; 0-8118-5062-5 pa

Aladdin outwits an evil magician who first tries to trick him into handing over an old lamp with a genie inside and later steals Aladdin's wife and possessions.

"Told in a simple but richly descriptive style, the story is both entertaining and lends itself very well to reading out loud. . . . This is a handsomely executed English-Spanish version that will make a great addition to a child's library of favorite bedtime readings." Booklist

Wada, Stephanie
Momotaro and the island of ogres; a Japanese folktale. as told by Stephanie Wada; paintings by Kano Naganobu. George Braziller 2005 47p il $19.95
Grades: 3 4 5 6 **398.2**
1. Folklore -- Japan
ISBN 0-8076-1552-8

Found floating on the river inside a peach by an old couple, Momotaro grows up and fights the terrible demons who have terrorized the village for years.

"Nineteenth-century silk handscrolls, painted by master Naganobu and housed in the New York Public Library's Spencer Collection, illustrate this handsome retelling of a much-loved Japanese folktale." Booklist

Waldman, Debby
Clever Rachel; story by Debby Waldman; illustrations by Cindy Revell. Orca Book Publishers 2009 un il $19.95
Grades: K 1 2 3 **398.2**
1. Jews -- Folklore 2. Riddles -- Fiction
ISBN 978-1-55469-081-7; 1-55469-081-1

Retells a traditional Jewish folktale about a clever girl named Rachel who clashes with a boy named Jacob when he challenges her with his riddles, until a woman with an urgent problem shows them that they are at their best when they work together.

"The lighthearted text includes occasional Yiddish words. Energetic illustrations convey Rachel and Jacob's competitive spirits." Horn Book Guide

A **sack** full of feathers; story by Debby Waldman; illustrations by Cindy Revell. Orca Book Publishers 2006 un il $19.95

Grades: K 1 2 3   **398.2**
1. Jews -- Folklore 2. Gossip -- Folklore
ISBN 1-55143-332-X

"Yankel loves to tell stories and repeat the gossip that he hears in his father's store in the shtetl. . . . Unfortunately, Yankel only hears the bits and pieces that make trouble, not how things turn out. So the rabbi decides to teach the boy a lesson by making him see that stories spread and that they can be hurtful. The fun in this retelling of a Jewish folktale is not in the lesson, but in the setting, the people, and the stories they tell. The bright acrylic folk art shows the characters gossiping, quarreling . . . and, finally, getting together." Booklist

Wang Ping
The **dragon** emperor; a Chinese folktale. retold by Wang Ping; illustrations by Tang Ge. Millbrook Press 2008 48p il (On my own folklore) lib bdg $25.26

Grades: 1 2 3 4   **398.2**
1. Folklore -- China 2. Dragons -- Folklore
ISBN 978-0-8225-6740-0 lib bdg; 0-8225-6740-7 lib bdg

LC 2006036718
A jealous warrior challenges the leadership of the dragon emperor. End note discusses the dragon in Chinese folklore and culture.

The "tale is paired with an illustration style that nicely reflects the culture." Horn Book Guide

Wargin, Kathy-Jo
The **frog** prince; by the Brothers Grimm; as retold by Kathy-jo Wargin; illustrated by Anne Yvonne Gilbert. Mitten Press 2007 un il $18.95

Grades: K 1 2 3   **398.2**
1. Fairy tales 2. Folklore -- Germany
ISBN 978-1-58726-279-1; 1-58726-279-7

LC 2006020283
As payment for retrieving the princess's ball, the frog exacts a promise which the princess is reluctant to fulfill

"Intricate, gloriously lush illustrations highlight this retelling of the familiar tale. Wargin has preserved much of the tone of the original text while editing the length to make it more palatable for younger audiences." Booklist

Waters, Fiona
Aesop's fables; retold by Fiona Waters; illustrated by Fulvio Testa. Trafalgar Square 2011 il $24.99

Grades: 1 2 3 4   **398.2**
1. Fables
ISBN 978-1-84939-049-1; 1-84939-049-5

"Waters deftly adds a contemporary tone in description and dialogue to her smooth rendering of 60 familiar and less-well-known tales. The terse moral of each fable, concluding each one in customary style, is usually set in traditional terms. . . . Testa's pen and watercolor drawings are fun, portraying all animals with the large eyes currently popular in cartoon art. . . . With its many comic touches, this anthology presents once again the humor, folly, ingenuity, and wisdom that make Aesop so durable." SLJ

Willey, Margaret
★ The **3** bears and Goldilocks; illustrated by Heather M. Solomon. Atheneum Books for Young Readers 2008 un il $16.99

Grades: PreK K 1 2 3   **398.2**
1. Folklore 2. Bears -- Folklore
ISBN 978-1-4169-2494-4; 1-4169-2494-9

LC 2007-13857
Goldilocks, ignoring her father's warning not to rush in where she does not belong, enters a cabin in the woods, cleans it to meet her standards, plucks from the porridge items unappealing to her before eating a bowlful, and falls asleep on the bed that suits her best.

"There is a rustic feel to the illustrations, rendered in watercolor, collage, colored pencil, acrylic, and oil paint. . . . This satisfying read-aloud offers a new twist on an old favorite." SLJ

Clever Beatrice; an Upper Peninsula conte. illustrated by Heather McWhorter. Atheneum Bks. for Young Readers 2001 un il $16

Grades: K 1 2 3   **398.2**
1. Giants -- Folklore 2. Folklore -- United States
ISBN 0-689-83254-0

LC 00-42019
A small, but clever young girl outwits a rich giant and wins all his gold

"Set in Michigan's Upper Peninsula, this is a winning tale of brain vs. brawn. . . . Willey's telling is simple but spirited, and her dialogue, with its slight French-Canadian cadence, is pitch perfect. Heather Solomon's illustrations are remarkable: watercolors augmented with collage, they have unusual texture and depth." Horn Book

Other titles about Clever Beatrice by this author are:
Clever Beatrice and the best little pony (2004)
A Clever Beatrice Christmas (2006)

Wisniewski, David
Rain player; story and pictures by David Wisniewski. Clarion Bks. 1991 un il pa $7.95; $17

Grades: 1 2 3 4   **398.2**
1. Games -- Fiction 2. Mayas -- Fiction
ISBN 0-395-72083-4 pa; 0-395-55112-9

LC 90-44101
To bring rain to his thirsty village, Pik challenges the rain god to a game of pok-a-tok

"This original tale combines research on Mayan history and legend with a suspenseful sports story. . . . Intricate and dramatic cut-paper illustrations powerfully re-create the foliage, landscape, architecture, and clothing of the Mayan classical period. . . . An author's note provides fascinating background information on Mayan civilization and gives in-depth explanations of some of the words and phrases used in the text." Horn Book

Wolf, Gita

Gobble You Up! Pgw 2013 40 p. $34.95

Grades: PreK K   **398.2**

1. Jackals 2. Folk literature 3. Animals -- Fiction

ISBN 8192317145; 9788192317144

Author Gita Wolf's book "is an adaptation of an oral trickster tale from Rajasthan, north India. It is illustrated with finger painting by . . . Sunita, a young woman artist who hails from the Meena tribe. In this handmade, silkscreen printed children's book, Sunita adapts a traditional Meena art form called Mandna, which is traditionally painted by women on the walls and floors of their village homes." (Publisher's note)

Wormell, Christopher

Mice, morals, & monkey business; lively lessons from Aesop's Fables. Running Press 2005 un il $18.95

Grades: K 1 2 3   **398.2**

1. Fables 2. Authors 3. Storytellers

ISBN 0-7624-2404-4

"Wormell uses linocut prints to illuminate 21 of Aesop's famous life lessons. . . . The bold, black lines of the expertly rendered images and colorful accents primarily in earth tones create instantly recognizable figures. The subtle use of light and shadow adds clarity, expression, and often drama without extraneous detail." SLJ

Yolen, Jane

Sister Bear; a Norse tale. adapted by Jane Yolen; illustrated by Linda Graves. Marshall Cavendish Children 2011 un il

Grades: K 1 2 3   **398.2**

1. Bears -- Folklore 2. Folklore -- Norway

ISBN 0-7614-5958-8; 978-0-7614-5958-3

LC 2010024235

Halva is traveling with her trained bear to visit the King of Denmark when they stop for the night at a cottage where, they learn, a pack of trolls is about to make its annual Christmas Eve visit, causing trouble and making a big mess. Includes author's note about the story's origins.

"There isn't a dull moment in Yolen's rousing retelling of this Norwegian folktale. . . . Grave's . . . characters have the attraction of costumed toys, and nearly every spread features a loving look at a traditional Scandinavian garment and its inticate needlework. . . . Yolen knows a good story when she sees one." Publ Wkly

Young, Ed

★ **Lon** Po Po; a Red-Riding Hood story from China. translated and illustrated by Ed Young. Philomel Bks. 1989 un il $16.99; pa $6.99

Grades: 1 2 3   **398.2**

1. Folklore -- China 2. Wolves -- Folklore

ISBN 0-399-21619-7; 0-698-11382-9 pa

LC 88-15222

Awarded the Caldecott Medal, 1990

This folktale "involves three little sisters who outsmart the wolf (lon or long in Cantonese) who has gained entry to their home under the false pretense of being their maternal grandmother (Po Po). The clever animal blows out the candle before the children can see him, and is actually in bed with them when they start asking the traditional 'Why Grandma!' questions. The eldest realizes the truth and tricks the wolf into letting them go outside to pick gingko nuts,

and then lures him to his doom." (SLJ) "Ages six to nine." (Booklist)

"The text possesses that matter-of-fact veracity that characterizes the best fairy tales. The watercolor and pastel pictures are remarkable: mystically beautiful in their depiction of the Chinese countryside, menacing in the exchanges with the wolf, and positively chilling in the scenes inside the house." SLJ

★ The **sons** of the Dragon King; a Chinese legend. Atheneum Bks. for Young Readers 2004 un il $16.95

Grades: 3 4 5   **398.2**

1. Folklore -- China

ISBN 0-689-85184-7

LC 2002-154321

The nine immortal sons of the Dragon King set out to make something of themselves, and each, with help from a watchful father, finds a role that suits his individual strengths.

"The text is engrossing and includes an informative author's note. The illustrations, rendered in brush, ink, and cut paper, use softly smudged lines for the part of the story focused on the legend, and sharper, cleaner lines augmented by a minimal but dramatically effective use of color for the present-day segments. This elegant addition to folklore shelves should be a first purchase for most libraries." SLJ

Zelinsky, Paul O.

Rumpelstiltskin; from the German of the Brothers Grimm. retold & illustrated by Paul O. Zelinsky. Dutton 1986 un il lib bdg $16.99; pa $6.99

Grades: K 1 2 3   **398.2**

1. Fairy tales 2. Folklore -- Germany

ISBN 0-525-44265-0 lib bdg; 0-14-055864-0 pa

LC 86-4482

A Caldecott Medal honor book, 1987

A strange little man helps the miller's daughter spin straw into gold for the king on the condition that she will give him her first-born child. This adaptation is based mainly on the 1819 edition of the Grimm brothers' Kinder-und Hausmärchen. "Kindergarten to grade four." (SLJ)

"Zelinsky's painterly style and rich colors provide an evocative backdrop to this story. The medieval setting and costumes and the spools of gold thread which shine on the page like real gold are suggestive of an illuminated manuscript. . . . Zelinsky's smooth retelling and glowing pictures cast the story in a new and beautiful light." SLJ

Zemach, Margot

The **three** little pigs; an old story. Farrar, Straus & Giroux 1989 un il hardcover o.p. pa $5.95

Grades: K 1 2   **398.2**

1. Pigs -- Folklore 2. Wolves -- Folklore 3. Folklore -- Great Britain

ISBN 0-374-37527-5; 0-374-47717-5 pa

LC 87-73488

This is an adaptation of the traditional folktale about a hungry wolf who "attempts to wile his way to three pork chop dinners." (Horn Book) "Preschool to grade two." (SLJ)

Zemach "has brought a familiar, often-told tale to life with marvelous ink-and-watercolor illustrations. Her wolf, wearing a dapper green hat and radiating slyness with every inch of his furry self, cuts a spendidly sinister figure as he attempts to wile his way to three pork chop dinners. With simple, lively sentences Zemach has related the complete story, including the apple-picking and country fair episodes." Horn Book

Ziefert, Harriet

Little Red Riding Hood; retold by Harriet Ziefert; illustrated by Emily Bolam. Viking 2000 un il (Viking easy-to-read) hardcover o.p. pa $3.99

Grades: K 1 2   **398.2**
1. Fairy tales 2. Wolves -- Folklore 3. Folklore -- Germany
ISBN 0-670-88389-1; 0-14-056529-9 pa
LC 99-23210

A little girl meets a hungry wolf in the forest while on her way to visit her gandmother

This adaptation of the Grimm's fairy tale "tells the story in a brisk, straightforward style . . . [with] simple, colorful illustrations. . . . The vocabulary is appropriate for beginning readers. The lively illustrations and familiarity of the story should provide a successful reading experience." SLJ

398.209 History, geographic treatment, biography

Aardema, Verna

★ Anansi does the impossible! an Ashanti tale. retold by Verna Aardema; illustrated by Lisa Desimini. Atheneum Bks. for Young Readers 1997 un il $16; pa $5.99

Grades: K 1 2 3   **398.209**
1. Anansi (Legendary character) 2. Folklore -- West Africa
ISBN 0-689-81092-X; 0-689-83933-2 pa
LC 96-20033

"Vivid, stylized collage illustrations convey the frightening force and power of the Sky God yet also reveal Anansi's own pluck and boldness. Perfect for reading or telling aloud." Booklist

Includes glossary and bibliographical references

Beneduce, Ann

Jack and the beanstalk; retold by Ann Keay Beneduce; illustrated by Gennady Spirin. Philomel Bks. 1999 32p il $16.99

Grades: 2 3 4   **398.209**
1. Fairy tales 2. Folklore -- Great Britain
ISBN 0-399-23118-8
LC 98-5722

A boy climbs to the top of a giant beanstalk, where he uses his quick wits to outsmart an ogre and make his and his mother's fortune

"Beneduce bases her version of Jack and the Beanstalk on a Victorian version, complete with a fairy guardian. . . . Spirin contributes some glorious borders for the text as well as many impressively detailed paintings, notable for their dark muted colors and mysterious, foggy look." Booklist

Bodkin, Odds

The crane wife; retold by Odds Bodkin; illustrated by Gennady Spirin. Gulliver Bks. 1998 un il hardcover o.p. pa $7

Grades: 3 4 5   **398.209**
1. Folklore -- Japan
ISBN 0-15-201407-1; 0-15-216350-6 pa
LC 96-35488

A retelling of the traditional Japanese tale about a poor sail maker who gains a beautiful but mysterious wife skilled at weaving magical sails

"Capturing the tale's mystery and tragedy, Spirin's watercolor-and-gouache paintings take their inspiration from Japanese art. Delicate shades of tawny gray and burnished gold predominate in the illustrations." Booklist

Casanova, Mary

The hunter; a Chinese folktale. retold by Mary Casanova; illustrations by Ed Young. Atheneum Bks. for Young Readers 2000 un il $16.95

Grades: K 1 2 3   **398.209**
1. Folklore -- China
ISBN 0-689-82906-X
LC 99-32166

After learning to understand the language of animals, Hai Li Bu the hunter sacrifices himself to save his village

Casanova "tells the tale in a dignified yet moving way that is complemented by the stark artwork. Arid-looking, dun-colored paper is the background for Young's masterful brush strokes." Booklist

Craft, Charlotte

★ King Midas and the golden touch; as told by Charlotte Craft; illustrated by K.Y. Craft. Morrow 1999 32p il $16; pa $6.99

Grades: 2 3 4   **398.209**
1. Midas (Legendary character)
ISBN 0-688-13165-4; 0-06-054063-X pa
LC 98-24035

A king finds himself bitterly regretting the consequences of his wish that everything he touches would turn to gold

"This sophisticated retelling, set in the Middle Ages, places King Midas in a sumptuous palace. . . . The elaborate oil-over-watercolor illustrations show the wondrous, tragic effects of the golden touch." Horn Book Guide

Defelice, Cynthia

Nelly May has her say; Cynthia DeFelice; pictures by Henry Cole. Margaret Ferguson Books 2013 32 p. col. ill. $16.99

Grades: K 1 2 3   **398.209**
1. Picture books for children 2. Folklore -- England
ISBN 0374398992; 9780374398996
LC 2011018484

In this children's picture book, Nelly May Nimble leaves her childhood home and 12 siblings to work for Lord Ignasius Pinkwinkle. Lord Pinkwinkle "agrees with one condition; the master of the house has special names for things, and Nelly must use those names when she speaks to him. . . . But when Lord Pinkwinkle's 'fur-faced fluffenbarker's wigger-wagger' catches fire, Nelly has to wake him and announce the fire before the house burns down. Can she remember all those silly names?" (School Library Journal)

Delacre, Lulu

Golden tales; myths, legends, and folktales from Latin America. [retold by] Lulu Delacre. Scholastic 1996 73p hardcover o.p. pa $5.99

Grades: 5 6 7 8 **398.209**
1. Folklore -- Latin America 2. Native Americans --
Folklore
ISBN 0-439-24398-X pa

LC 94-36724

This includes 12 "stories from four native cultures
(Taino, Zapotec, Muisca, and Quechua), including pourquoi
tales, legends of the conquistadores, and folktales from before and after the age of Columbus. . . . [The author's] . . .
retellings are done in a clear and confident voice and are accompanied by her robust, colorful oil paintings. . . . This impressively presented and referenced collection will inspire
readers and tellers alike." Booklist
Includes bibliographical references

Demi
★ The **empty** pot. Holt & Co., 1990 un il $16.95;
pa $6.95
Grades: K 1 2 3 **398.209**
1. Folklore -- China
ISBN 0-8050-1217-6; 0-8050-4900-2 pa

LC 89-39062

"This simple story with its clear moral is illustrated with
beautiful paintings. . . . A beautifully crafted book that will
be enjoyed as much for the richness of its illustrations as for
the simplicity of its story." SLJ

Doyle, Malachy
Tales from old Ireland; retold by Malachy Doyle; illustrated by Niamh Sharkey. Barefoot Bks. (NY) 2000 95p
il $19.99; pa $16.99
Grades: 3 4 5 6 **398.209**
1. Folklore -- Ireland
ISBN 978-1-902283-97-5; 1-902283-97-X; 978-1-
905236-32-9 pa; 1-905236-32-8 pa
A collection of seven Irish folk tales
Doyle's "retellings are simple and economical, yet contain all the lilting rhythm and musical quality for which Irish
tales are famous. Sharkey's illustrations, prepared in oil and
gesso on canvas, are a perfect match." SLJ
Includes bibliographical references

Fang, Linda
The **Ch'i**-lin purse; a collection of ancient Chinese stories. retold by Linda Fang; pictures by Jeanne M. Lee. Farrar, Straus & Giroux 1994 127p il hardcover o.p. pa $5.95
Grades: 5 6 7 8 **398.209**
1. Folklore -- China
ISBN 0-374-31241-9; 0-374-41189-1 pa

LC 94-9909

A collection of "Chinese stories derived from the history of the Warring States Period (770-221 B.C.E.) and
from operatic versions of popular tales. Retellings are vivid,
lively, and read aloud well. Many have a moral, and all are
entertaining. . . . The black-and-white illustrations—one per
selection—are graceful, depicting widely different epochs
with amazing accuracy." SLJ
Includes glossary and bibliographical references

Garland, Sherry
Children of the dragon; selected tales from Vietnam.
with illustrations by Trina Schart Hyman. Harcourt 2001
58p il $18

Grades: 3 4 5 6 **398.209**
1. Folklore -- Vietnam
ISBN 0-15-224200-7

LC 00-8300

An illustrated collection of Vietnamese folktales with
explanatory notes following each story
"This handsome volume gathers six well-told traditional tales not readily available elsewhere. . . . [The book is]
greatly enhanced by Hyman's strong color work, romantic
sensibility, and dramatic characterizations." SLJ

Gavin, Jamila
School for princes; stories from the Panchatantra. re-
told by Jamila Gavin; illustrated by Bee Willey. Reprint
Frances Lincoln Children's Books 2012 64 p. ill. (hard-
cover) $19.99
Grades: 4 5 6 **398.209**
1. Indic mythology 2. Indian literature (English) 3.
Indic literature -- Collections 4. Conduct of life --
Literary collections
ISBN 1845079906; 9781845079901
This children's book presents "a series of newly created
stories in combination with five traditional tales to reveal the
Panchatantra's themes. . . . Three arrogant princes change
their tune in six short months as a sage uses stories to teach
them the art of ruling. These fables have been introduced
to people of all classes for generations to spread ideas of
wisdom, kindness, friendship and unity, and self-control."
(Kirkus Reviews)

Heo, Yumi
The **green** frogs; a Korean folktale. retold by Yumi
Heo. Houghton Mifflin 1996 un il $16; pa $6.95
Grades: K 1 2 3 **398.209**
1. Folklore -- Korea 2. Frogs -- Folklore
ISBN 0-395-68378-5; 0-618-43228-8 pa

LC 95-19129

"Using delicate tones, flat perspectives, and somewhat
abstract figures set against busy backgrounds, [Heo] creates a quaint, comic effect. . . . This is a quirkier pourquoi
tale than most, but it's too mischievous to be morbid."
Horn Book

Jiang, Ji-li
★ The **magical** Monkey King; mischief in heaven.
classic Chinese tales retold by Ji-Li Jiang; illustrated by Hui
Hui Su-Kennedy. HarperCollins Pubs. 2002 122p il hard-
cover o.p. pa $4.95
Grades: 3 4 5 **398.209**
1. Folklore -- China 2. Monkeys -- Folklore
ISBN 0-06-029544-9 lib bdg; 0-06-442149-X pa

LC 2001-39672

The mischievous Monkey King attempts to achieve im-
mortality the easy way, gains god-like powers, and wreaks
havoc in heaven
The author "provides a lively telling, and the stories
move briskly. Accompanying black-and-white pictures have
the look of woodcuts." Booklist

MacDonald, Margaret Read
★ **Fat** cat; a Danish folktale. retold by Margaret Read
MacDonald; illustrated by Julie Paschkis. August House
2001 un il $15.95; pa $7.95

Grades: K 1 2 3   **398.209**

1. Cats -- Folklore 2. Mice -- Folklore 3. Folklore -- Denmark

ISBN 0-87483-616-6; 0-87483-765-0 pa

LC 00-68939

A greedy cat grows enormous as he eats everything in sight, including his friends and neighbors who call him fat

"The book's huge, bright illustrations are glorious. . . . The large, funny illustrations will carry well for a bigger crowd and, combined with refrain that invites chanting along, make this a surefire hit for reading aloud." Booklist

★ **Mabela** the clever; retold by Margaret Read MacDonald; illustrated by Tim Coffey. Whitman, A. 2001 un il music hardcover o.p. pa $6.95

Grades: K 1 2 3   **398.209**

1. Cats -- Folklore 2. Mice -- Folklore 3. Folklore -- Africa

ISBN 0-8075-4902-9; 0-8075-4903-7 pa

LC 00-8307

An African folktale about a mouse who pays close attention to her surroundings and avoids being tricked by the cat

"MacDonald's retelling of this Limba tale is engineered for storytime success. . . . Coffey's thatch-strewn paintings, rendered in acrylic on watercolor paper textured with gesso, feature lots of visibly clueless, wide-eyed mice, and his cat oozes predatory shrewdness to the very end." SLJ

O'Connor, George

Hades. First Second 2012 76p col. ill. (Olympians)

Grades: 4 5 6   **398.209**

1. Graphic novels 2. Greek mythology 3. Mother-daughter relationship -- Fiction 4. Hades (Greek deity) -- Comic books, strips, etc.

ISBN 9781596434349

LC 2011017563

In this book, a "tempestuous mother-daughter relationship makes up the centerpiece of [author and illustrator George] O'Connor's . . . Olympian portrait. Snatched down to the Underworld in the wake of a screaming fight with her mother Demeter, . . . raging adolescent Kore (meaning, generically 'The Maiden') initially gives her quiet, gloomy captor Hades a hard time too. After grabbing the opportunity to give herself a thorough makeover and changing her name to Persephone ('Bringer of Destruction'), though, she takes charge of her life--so surely that, when offered the opportunity to return to her remorseful mom, she lies about having eaten those pomegranate seeds so she can spend half of each year as Queen of the Dead." (Kirkus)

Includes bibliographical references.

Ollhoff, Jim

Middle Eastern Mythology; by Jim Ollhoff. ABDO Publishing Company 2011 32p il (The world of mythology) lib bdg $27.07

Grades: 5 6 7 8   **398.209**

1. Children -- Books and reading 2. Mythology -- Middle East

ISBN 1617147257; 9781617147258; 1-61714-725-7; 978-1-61714-725-8

LC 2010042977

This describes the history of myths of the Middle East, their meaning, and their gods and goddesses including

Mithra, Mot, the Mesopotamian goddess Ishtar, and the Canaanite thunder god, Baal.

"Ollhoff writes in a clear and engaging fashion, presenting complex issues in a way that will be easy for youngsters to grasp. . . . The photographs and reproductions of art tie directly to the [text]." SLJ

Tolman, Marije

The island; Ronald Tolman; Marije Tolman. Lemniscaat USA 2012 32 p. $17.95

Grades: PreK K   **398.209**

1. Picture books for children 2. Islands fiction 3. Polar bears

ISBN 1935954199; 9781935954194

In this "wordless picture book" by Marije Tolman and Ronald Tolman "you swim along with a bear on a journey through a unique archipelago. . . . With every island lies a whole new world to discover, until the bear finds the ultimate island. Has he finally come across his home, or is he merely passing through?" (Publisher's note)

Wisniewski, David

★ **Sundiata**; lion king of Mali. story and pictures by David Wisniewski. Clarion Bks. 1992 un il hardcover o.p. pa $5.95

Grades: 1 2 3 4   **398.209**

1. Kings 2. Mali -- History

ISBN 0-395-61302-7; 0-395-76481-5 pa

LC 91-27951

The story of Sundiata, who overcame physical handicaps, social disgrace, and strong opposition to rule Mali in the thirteenth century

"Passed down through oral tradition, this historical account has the drama and depth of a folktale. The illustrations—elaborate collages inspired by the artifacts and culture of the Malinke—create a series of dramatic images. The intricacy of the paper-cuts and the richness of the colors and patterns give the artwork visual as well as narrative strength." Booklist

398.21   Tales and lore on a specific topic

Cruz, Alejandro

The woman who outshone the sun; the legend of Lucia Zenteno. from a poem by Alejandro Cruz Martinez; pictures by Fernando Olivera; story by Rosalma Zubizarreta, Harriet Rohmer, David Schecter. Children's Bk. Press 1991 30p hardcover o.p. pa $7.95

Grades: K 1 2 3   **398.21**

1. Zapotec Indians -- Folklore 2. Bilingual books -- English-Spanish

ISBN 0-89239-101-4; 0-89239-126-X pa

LC 91-16646

Retells the Zapotec legend of Lucia Zenteno, a beautiful woman with magical powers who is exiled from a mountain village and takes its water away in punishment

This "Hispanic folktale is skillfully told, and is solid and colorfully steeped with imagery of the earth and sky. Both the Spanish and English read gracefully, and the poetic use of language suits the story well for telling. The illustrations have a sense of volume that is reminiscent of Orozco." SLJ

Egielski, Richard

★ The **gingerbread** boy. HarperCollins Pubs. 1997 un il $15.95; pa $5.95

Grades: K 1 2 3   **398.21**

  1. Folklore 2. New York (N.Y.) -- Fiction

  ISBN 0-06-026030-0; 0-06-443708-6 pa

          LC 95-50026

"Egielski's retelling is straightforward and retains the traditional refrain: 'Run run run as fast as you can'—it sounds just right, making a satisfying modern variation. The illustrations . . . adroitly evoke the city setting while giving a solid three-dimensionality and unique individuality to the Gingerbread Boy and his pursuers." SLJ

Hong, Lily Toy

★ **Two** of everything; a Chinese folktale. retold and illustrated by Lily Toy Hong. Whitman, A. 1993 un il $15.95

Grades: K 1 2 3   **398.21**

  1. Folklore -- China

  ISBN 0-8075-8157-7

          LC 92-29880

A poor old Chinese farmer finds a magic brass pot that doubles or duplicates whatever is placed inside it, but his efforts to make himself wealthy lead to unexpected complications

The author "here paints with muted colors, defining rounded forms with broad outlines. Retold with verve and gentle humor, this Chinese folktale could become a read-aloud favorite." Booklist

Kellogg, Steven

Jack and the beanstalk; retold and illustrated by Steven Kellogg. Morrow Junior Bks. 1991 un il $16; lib bdg $16.89; pa $6.95

Grades: K 1 2 3   **398.21**

  1. Fairy tales 2. Giants -- Folklore 3. Folklore -- Great Britain

  ISBN 0-688-10250-6; 0-688-10251-4 lib bdg; 0-688-15281-3 pa

          LC 90-45990

Jack climbs to the top of a giant beanstalk, where he uses his quick wits to outsmart an ogre and make his and his mother's fortune. "Kindergarten to grade three." (SLJ)

"Seldom has the ogre at the top of the beanstalk been depicted with such gusto! The warty, fanged, pug-nosed lout dressed in animal skins and a necklace of teeth is a wonder to behold. Steven Kellogg's humorous detail provides witty embellishment for savoring. His story line is quite faithful to the Joseph Jacobs version of the story, the sturdy text offering a strong framework for the energetic illustrations." Horn Book

Kimmel, Eric A.

The **gingerbread** man; retold by Eric A. Kimmel; illustrated by Megan Lloyd. Holiday House 1993 un il $16.95; pa $6.95

Grades: K 1 2   **398.21**

  1. Folklore

  ISBN 0-8234-0824-8; 0-8234-1137-0 pa

          LC 90-33202

A freshly baked gingerbread man escapes when he is taken out of the oven and eludes a number of animals until he meets a clever fox. "Preschool." (SLJ)

"This version softens the ending with a final page of fresh, recently baked gingerbread men. This is a story that calls for energetic art, and Lloyd provides just that in warm-toned watercolors that feature the gingerbread man zipping across the pages. A compact text and suitably large pictures make this just right for groups." Booklist

Mollel, Tololwa M.

The **orphan** boy; a Maasai story. illustrated by Paul Morin. Clarion Bks. 1990 un il hardcover o.p. pa $6.95

Grades: K 1 2 3   **398.21**

  1. Folklore -- Africa 2. Masai (African people) -- Folklore

  ISBN 0-89919-985-2; 0-395-72079-6 pa

          LC 90-2358

"Infused with an aura of mystery, Mollel's compelling story is told skillfully and dramatically. Morin's richly textured paintings, evoking in bold colors an Africa of both parched desert and lush vegetation, are worthy companions." Publ Wkly

Salley, Coleen

Epossumondas; written by Coleen Salley; illustrated by Janet Stevens. Harcourt 2002 un il $16

Grades: K 1 2 3   **398.21**

  1. Opossums -- Folklore 2. Folklore -- Southern States

  ISBN 0-15-216748-X

          LC 2001-4906

A retelling of a classic tale in which a well-intentioned young possum continually takes his mother's instructions much too literally. "Ages four to seven." (Bull Cent Child Books)

"All of the elements of a good story are here. . . . Salley's text rolls off the page (and off the tongue) easily, and is accompanied by delightful watercolor and colored-pencil art." SLJ

Other titles about Epossumondas are:

Epossumondas saves the day (2006)

Epossumondas plays possum (2009)

Why Epossumondas has no hair on his tail (2004)

San Souci, Robert

The **faithful** friend; [by] Robert D. San Souci; illustrated by Brian Pinkney. Simon & Schuster Bks. for Young Readers 1995 un il $16; pa $5.99

Grades: 2 3 4   **398.21**

  1. Folklore -- Martinique

  ISBN 0-02-786131-7; 0-689-82458-0 pa

          LC 93-40672

A Caldecott Medal honor book, 1996

"Pinkney's scratchboard and oil artwork switches from bright daytime hues for most of the book to purples and grays for scenes with the zombies and snakes, which are very effective. . . . This excellent title contains all the elements of a well-researched folktale, and convincingly conveys the richness of the West Indian culture." SLJ

Includes bibliographical references

Wisniewski, David

★ **Golem**; story and pictures by David Wisniewski. Clarion Bks. 1996 un il $15.95; pa $6.95

Grades: 3 4 5   **398.21**
1. Jews -- Folklore 2. Monsters -- Folklore
ISBN 0-395-72618-2; 0-618-89424-1 pa

LC 95-21777

Awarded the Caldecott Medal, 1997

"The fiery, crisply layered paper illustrations, portraying with equal drama and precision the ornamental architecture of Prague and the unearthly career of the Golem, match the specificity and splendor of the storytelling." Publ Wkly

398.22   Tales and lore of persons without paranormal powers

Hodges, Margaret

The **kitchen** knight; a tale of King Arthur. retold by Margaret Hodges and illustrated by Trina Schart Hyman. Holiday House 1990 un il $16.95
Grades: 3 4 5 6   **398.22**
1. Arthurian romances 2. Gareth (Legendary character)
ISBN 0-8234-0787-X

LC 89-11215

A retelling of the Arthurian legend of how Sir Gareth becomes a knight and rescues the lady imprisoned by the fearsome Red Knight of the Red Plain

"Hyman's richly romantic illustrations are lush watercolors, framed and broken with framed insets for closeups and framed text inside the panoramic picture. The format is horizontal, capturing the sweep of the story. While not a tale of King Arthur, it's a wonderful taste of Arthurian legend, hopefully whetting young appetites for more." SLJ

Kellogg, Steven

Mike Fink; a tall tale. retold and illustrated by Steven Kellogg. Morrow Junior Bks. 1992 un il hardcover o.p. pa $6.95
Grades: K 1 2 3   **398.22**
1. Tall tales 2. Pioneers
ISBN 0-688-07003-5; 0-688-13577-3 pa

LC 91-46014

Relates the extraordinary deeds of the frontiersman who became King of the Keelboatmen on the Mississippi River

"Steven Kellogg's ebullient retelling of Mike's tall-tale feats—illustrated with large, glowing scenes suffused with blue and yellow and with smaller vignettes emphasizing comic detail—follows Mike's prodigious childhood exploits, his teenage wrestling practice with Rocky Mountain grizzlies, and his years as King of the Keelboatmen, and closes with a final showdown with enormous steamboats taking over the river trade." Horn Book

Yolen, Jane

Not one damsel in distress; world folktales for strong girls. collected and told by Jane Yolen; with illustrations by Susan Guevara. Silver Whistle Bks. 2000 116p il $17
Grades: 4 5 6 7   **398.22**
1. Fairy tales 2. Women -- Folklore
ISBN 0-15-202047-0

LC 99-18509

A collection of thirteen traditional tales from various parts of the world, each of whose main character is a fearless, strong, heroic, and resourceful woman

"This is a spirited collection with a lively pace. . . . The stories sing and soar in Yolen's supple language, and each is contained enough for a read-aloud." Booklist

Includes bibliographical references

Zelinsky, Paul O.

★ **Rapunzel**; retold and illustrated by Paul O. Zelinsky. Dutton Children's Bks. 1997 un il $16.99
Grades: 3 4 5   **398.22**
1. Folklore 2. Fairy tales
ISBN 0-525-45607-4

LC 96-50260

Awarded the Caldecott Medal, 1998

A retelling of the folktale in which a beautiful girl with long golden hair is kept imprisoned in a lonely tower by a sorceress

"An elegant and sophisticated retelling that draws on early French and Italian versions of the tale. Masterful oil paintings capture the Renaissance setting and flesh out the tragic figures." SLJ

398.24   Tales and lore of plants and animals

Brett, Jan

Town mouse, country mouse. Putnam 1994 un il $16.99; pa $6.99
Grades: K 1 2 3   **398.24**
1. Fables 2. Authors 3. Storytellers 4. Mice -- Folklore
ISBN 0-399-22622-2; 0-698-11986-X pa

LC 93-41227

"A mouse couple living in a town are enchanted by the simple life of the country, and, while on a picnic, meet a pair of local mice who long for the luxury and convenience of the city. Homes are swapped, but they find that reality is different from their expectations. Both couples end up fleeing from unfamiliar predators—a cat in town and an owl in the country—all the way home. The owl and cat collide, and . . . negotiate a territorial swap of their own. . . . Kindergarten to grade three." (SLJ)

"In Brett's version, the town mice are as charming and naive as their country cousins. . . . Brett's narrative alternates the parallel mishaps of the two sets of mice with lively, smooth writing and a deft touch of humor. . . . The illustrations are rich with meticulous detail." SLJ

DePaola, Tomie, 1934-

The **legend** of the poinsettia; retold and illustrated by Tomie de Paola. Putnam 1994 un il $16.99; pa $6.99
Grades: K 1 2 3   **398.24**
1. Folklore -- Mexico 2. Flowers -- Folklore 3. Christmas -- Folklore
ISBN 0-399-21692-8; 0-698-11567-8 pa

LC 92-20459

When Lucida is unable to finish her gift for the Baby Jesus in time for the Christmas procession, a miracle enables her to offer the beautiful flower we now call the poinsettia

"dePaola establishes a sense of place in his use of glowing colors and architectural details as he retells another legend of miraculous transcendence." Horn Book

Hirschmann, Kris

The **werewolf**; by Kris Hirschmann. ReferencePoint Press 2012 80 p. (hardback) $27.95

Grades: 4 5 6 7 8 **398.24**

1. Werewolves

ISBN 160152238X; 9781601522382

LC 2011036347

This book on werewolves "examines these legendary creatures . . . describing their bodies, their behavior, and their monstrous transformations. It also goes snout to snout with some of history's most infamous real-life werewolves and discusses the many books and films these encounters have inspired." (Publisher's note)

"Children will get a well-rounded look at the featured subjects and how they have evolved into the creatures that still fascinate many today." SLJ

Includes bibliographical references and index

Johnston, Tony

The **tale** of Rabbit and Coyote; illustrated by Tomie de Paola. Putnam 1994 un il hardcover o.p. pa $5.99

Grades: K 1 2 3 **398.24**

1. Coyote (Legendary character) 2. Rabbit (Legendary character) 3. Zapotec Indians -- Folklore

ISBN 0-399-22258-8; 0-698-11630-5 pa

LC 92-43652

Rabbit outwits Coyote in this Zapotec tale which explains why coyotes howl at the moon

"DePaola's vivid, spicy palette of gold, red, and turquoise tones and his use of folk-art borders evoke the desert setting and complement the broad humor of Johnston's text. A glossary of the Spanish phrases that pepper the illustrations is appended." Booklist

Kellogg, Steven

★ The **three** little pigs; retold and illustrated by Steven Kellogg. Morrow Junior Bks. 1997 un il hardcover o.p. pa $6.99

Grades: K 1 2 3 **398.24**

1. Folklore 2. Pigs -- Folklore 3. Wolves -- Folklore

ISBN 0-688-08731-0; 0-688-08732-9 lib bdg; 0-06-443779-5 pa

LC 96-34434

In this retelling of a well-known tale, Serafina Sow starts her own waffle-selling business in order to enable her three offspring to prepare for the future, which includes an encounter with a surly wolf

"Much of the broad humor is carried in the lively, colorful illustrations, though there's wordplay aplenty in the text and pictures too." Booklist

Kimmel, Eric A.

Anansi and the magic stick; illustrated by Janet Stevens. Holiday House 2001 un il $16.95; pa $6.95

Grades: K 1 2 3 **398.24**

1. Anansi (Legendary character) 2. Folklore -- Africa

ISBN 0-8234-1443-4; 0-8234-1763-8 pa

LC 00-39608

Anansi the Spider steals Hyena's magic stick so he won't have to do the chores, but when the stick's magic won't stop, he gets more than he bargained for

"Kimmel tells it with cheerful energy, and Stevens' chaotic mixed-media illustrations, with lots of bright pink and

green, show Anansi's friends and neighbors . . . caught up in the mess." Booklist

Anansi and the talking melon; retold by Eric A. Kimmel; illustrated by Janet Stevens. Holiday House 1994 un il $16.95; pa $6.95

Grades: K 1 2 3 **398.24**

1. Anansi (Legendary character) 2. Folklore -- Africa

ISBN 0-8234-1104-4; 0-8234-1167-2 pa

LC 93-4239

In this African folktale, the trickster hero "Anansi the spider outwits all the great galumphing gullible animals, including Elephant, Hippo, Warthog, and even the stupid king. Hiding inside a melon, the wily spider tricks the animals, one by one, into believing that the melon can talk, and what he says is usually an insult. . . . Ages four to eight." (Booklist)

"The snappy narration is well suited for individual reading or group sharing. The colorful line-and-wash illustrations are filled with movement and playful energy." SLJ

★ **Anansi** goes fishing; retold by Eric A. Kimmel; illustrated by Janet Stevens. Holiday House 1992 un il $16.95; pa $6.95

Grades: K 1 2 3 **398.24**

1. Anansi (Legendary character) 2. Folklore -- Africa

ISBN 0-8234-0918-X; 0-8234-1022-6 pa

LC 91-17813

This is an African etiological tale explaining the origin of spider webs and playing on the motif of the trickster tricked. Anansi the spider "decides to trick turtle into catching a fish for him. But Turtle has his own plans: 'One of us can work while the other gets tired.' Anansi doesn't want to get tired, so he weaves a net, sets it in the river, and catches and cooks the fish. When the fish is ready, Turtle tells Anansi: 'One of us should eat while the other gets full.' Of course, Anansi wants to get full, so Turtle eats the whole fish. . . . {Anansi} never understands Turtle's deception; however, he does share his newly acquired weaving skills with his friends, and today spiders everywhere weave webs. . . . Ages five to eight." (Booklist)

"Children able to comprehend the wordplay will be delighted when the lazy but lovable trickster figure is outwitted by the clever turtle, and Stevens' colorful, comical illustrations are perfect for this contemporary rendition of the tale." Booklist

Mayor, Adrienne

The **Griffin** and the Dinosaur; How Adrienne Mayor Discovered a Fascinating Link Between Myth and Science. Natl Geographic Soc Childrens books 2014 48 p. col. ill. $18.99

Grades: 5 6 7 8 **398.24**

1. Griffins 2. Dinosaurs

ISBN 1426311087; 9781426311086

"Could Griffins have been real? When [author] Adrienne Mayor carefully read the ancient Greek and Roman descriptions, this mythic hybrid of a lion and an eagle sounded like something people had actually seen." Co-written by Mayor and Marc Aronson, with illustrations by Chris Muller, "Here is the story of one insightful, curious, and determined woman who solved the mystery of the Griffin, and invented a new science. Now she and others travel the world matching myths and fossils." (Publisher's note)

"With the suspense of a detective story, the narrative details Mayor's research process as she consults with experts, conducts fieldwork, and seeks out ancient documents, artifacts, and stories." - PM reviews

McDermott, Gerald

★ **Zomo** the Rabbit; a trickster tale from West Africa. told and illustrated by Gerald McDermott. Harcourt Brace Jovanovich 1992 un il $14.95; pa $6

Grades: K 1 2 3   **398.24**

1. Folklore -- Africa 2. Rabbits -- Folklore

ISBN 0-15-299967-1; 0-15-201010-6 pa

LC 91-14558

"Like the spare text, the shapes here are boldly controlled—ideal for sharing with a group of very young children. Because of their rich patterns and sharp color contrasts, the images in the gouache paintings, although simple, never become simplistic." Bull Cent Child Books

Paterson, Katherine

The **tale** of the mandarin ducks; illustrated by Leo & Diane Dillon. Lodestar Bks. 1989 un il hardcover o.p. pa $6.99

Grades: 1 2 3   **398.24**

1. Ducks -- Folklore 2. Folklore -- Japan

ISBN 0-525-67283-4; 0-14-055739-3 pa

LC 88-30484

"A Japanese fairy tale, in picture-book format, about a Mandarin duck caught and caged at the whim of a wealthy Japanese lord. Separated from his mate, the bird languishes in captivity until a compassionate servant girl sets him free. The lord sentences the girl and her beloved to death, but they in turn are freed and rewarded with happiness." Booklist

Perrault, Charles

Puss in boots; illustrated by Fred Marcellino; translated by Malcolm Arthur. Farrar, Straus & Giroux 1990 un il $16; pa $8.95

Grades: K 1 2 3   **398.24**

1. Fairy tales 2. Cats -- Folklore 3. Folklore -- France

ISBN 0-374-36160-6; 0-374-46034-5 pa

LC 90-82136

A Caldecott Medal honor book, 1991

This is a new illustrated version of the French fairy tale in which a clever cat wins for his master a castle and the hand of a princess. "Ages five to nine." (Booklist)

"Opulently designed and handsomely illustrated, this picture book provides a fitting showcase for Perrault's artful tale of deceit and resourcefulness. Unsullied by type, the striking front of the book features a close-up portrait of the cat's face. Befitting a fairy tale, the artwork inside is suffused with a golden light that proclaims the story to be from a sunnier, more dreamlike world." Booklist

Taylor, Harriet Peck

Coyote places the stars; retold and illustrated by Harriet Peck Taylor. Bradbury Press 1993 un il hardcover o.p. pa $5.99

Grades: K 1 2 3   **398.24**

1. Coyote (Legendary character) 2. Stars -- Folklore 3. Chinook Indians -- Folklore

ISBN 0-689-81535-2 pa

LC 92-46431

"Taylor's batik-and-dye paintings are a good match for the casual, playful rhythm of her retelling." Booklist

Trivizas, Eugene

The **three** little wolves and the big bad pig; illustrated by Helen Oxenbury. Margaret K. McElderry Bks. 1993 un il $18.99; pa $7.99

Grades: PreK K 1 2   **398.24**

1. Pigs -- Fiction 2. Wolves -- Fiction

ISBN 0-689-50569-8; 0-689-81528-X pa

LC 92-24829

"Trivizas laces the text with funny, clever touches. . . . Oxenbury's watercolors capture the story's broad humor and add a wealth of supplementary details, with exquisite renderings of the wolves' comic temerity and the pig's bellicose stances." Publ Wkly

Young, Ed

Seven blind mice. Philomel Bks. 1992 un il $17.99; pa $7.99

Grades: K 1 2 3   **398.24**

1. Fables 2. Mice -- Folklore 3. Folklore -- India 4. Elephants -- Folklore 5. Folklore -- India

ISBN 0-399-22261-8; 0-698-11895-2 pa

LC 90-35396

A Caldecott Medal honor book, 1993

In this retelling of the "Indian folktale of the blind men and the elephant, seven blind mice approach an elephant, {and} ask what it is. . . . On Monday, Red Mouse feels the elephant's leg and proclaims 'It's a pillar.' On Tuesday, Green Mouse jumps onto the elephant's trunk and decides, 'It's a snake.' On Wednesday, Yellow Mouse checks out the tusk and says, 'It's a spear.' But on the seventh day, White Mouse scampers all over the creature and puts all the clues together. The author offers this moral, 'Knowing in part may make a fine tale, but wisdom comes from seeing the whole.' . . . Ages three to eight." (Booklist)

"In Young's version of the familiar Indian folktale of the blind men and the elephant, seven blind mice approach an elephant, ask what it is, explore various parts of the beast, and arrive at different conclusions. . . . Many preschool and primary grade teachers will find that the book reinforces their students' learning of colors, days of the week, and ordinal numbers, while heeding the story's admonition not to lose sight of the whole in their enthusiasm for identifying the parts. Graphically, this picture book is stunning, with the cut-paper figures of the eight characters dramatically silhouetted against black backgrounds. . . . At once profound and simple, intelligent and playful." Booklist

398.25   Ghost stories

Schwartz, Alvin, 1927-1992

★ **Scary** stories to tell in the dark; collected from folklore by Alvin Schwartz; edited by Rachel Abrams; illustrated by Brett Helquist. Newly illustrated ed. Harper 2010 113 p. ill. (paperback) $5.99; (hardcover) $16.99

Grades: 4 5 6 7   **398.25**

1. Ghost stories 2. Horror fiction 3. Folklore -- United States

ISBN 9780060835200; 0060835192; 0060835206; 9780060835194

Stories of ghosts and witches, "jump" stories, scary songs, and modern-day scary stories.

"Helquist's new illustrations for Schwartz's classic [collection] of ghost stories inhabit an altogether more benign universe than the nightmarish Stephen Gammell originals. [This edition is] handsome and accessible, ceding the stories themselves pride of place." Horn Book Guide

398.8   Rhymes and rhyming games

Ada, Alma Flor

Ten little puppies; adapted from a traditional nursery rhyme in Spanish. [by] Alma Flor Ada; F. Isabel Campoy; English version by Rosalma Zubizarreta; illustrated by Ulises Wensell. Rayo 2011 un il $16.99; lib bdg $17.89
Grades: PreK   398.8
   1. Counting 2. Nursery rhymes 3. Dogs -- Poetry 4. Bilingual books -- English-Spanish
   ISBN 978-0-06-147043-1; 0-06-147043-0; 978-0-06-147044-8 lib bdg; 0-06-147044-9 lib bdg
                                          LC 2010015930
Ten little puppies are lost, one by one, for different reasons, until only one little puppy remains.

This is "one of the most popular counting rhymes in Spanish folklore. . . . Vibrant colored-pencil and watercolor illustrations are done in deep hues of green, pastels, and earth tones to create realistic images that capture the spontaneous, playful, and affectionate nature of the pups. The text can be sung or spoken in Spanish or English. The English translation skillfully utilizes rhyme to maintain the story's authenticity while accurately reflecting the original poem." SLJ

Baker, Keith

   ★ **Big** fat hen; illustrated by Keith Baker. Harcourt Brace & Co. 1994 un il $15; pa $6; bd bk $6.95
Grades: PreK K 1 2   398.8
   1. Counting 2. Nursery rhymes 3. Chickens -- Folklore
   ISBN 0-15-200294-4; 0-15-201951-0 pa; 0-15-201331-8 bd bk
                                          LC 93-19160
"The text is the old rhyme, 'One, two, buckle my shoe,' and the double-page spreads show the hen and her chicks (first appearing as eggs) enacting the words. . . . Children who want to skip the counting altogether can just enjoy the singsong text and the pictures executed in acrylic paints. The big fat hen is very large and quite beautiful, with iridescent green feathers accented with purple and red; her friends are just as lovely, all colors, some with delicate patterns in their feathers." Booklist

Bodden, Valerie

Nursery rhymes. Creative Education 2010 32p il (Poetry basics) $28.50
Grades: 5 6 7 8   398.8
   1. Nursery rhymes
   ISBN 978-1-58341-778-2; 1-58341-778-8
                                          LC 2008009157
This book describes nursery rhymes' "history, characteristics, and variations. Many examples are provided as well as ideas for how children can write their own pieces. The information is accessible, and the writing is sufficiently lively

to engage readers. The well-designed pages feature a variety of art reproductions from different literary eras and some photographs." Horn Book Guide
Includes glossary and bibliographical references

Brown, Marc

Marc Brown's playtime rhymes; a treasury for families to learn and play together. by Marc Brown. Little, Brown and Co. 2013 48 p. (hc) $18
Grades: PreK K Professional   398.8
   1. Nursery rhymes 2. Finger play 3. Children's poetry
   ISBN 0316207357; 9780316207355
                                          LC 2012048542
This book presents "a treasury of twenty favorite finger rhymes compiled and illustrated by . . . artist Marc Brown. These are rhymes to say and sing aloud, each with pictorial instructions for the correlating finger movements. 'Playtime Rhymes' [is designed to] get little hands wiggling, jiggling, pointing, pounding, bending, stretching, and dancing as children animate the rhymes, pore over the vibrant pictures, and share the fun with family and friends." (Publisher's note)
   Playtime rhymes

Chapman, Jane

Sing a song of sixpence; a pocketful of nursery rhymes and tales. [by] Jane Chapman. Candlewick Press 2004 61p il $15.99
Grades: K 1   398.8
   1. Nursery rhymes
   ISBN 0-7636-2545-0
                                          LC 2003-69565
An illustrated collection of twenty-five traditional nursery rhymes and stories, including "Jack and Jill," "Wee Willie Winkie," "Little Miss Muffet," "Three Blind Mice," "Goldilocks and the Three Bears," and "The Little Red Hen"

"With clear, bright acrylic pictures, Chapman brings an action-packed collection to preschoolers. . . . The type is large and clear, and lots of boisterous pictures decorate the big, spacious pages." Booklist

Cleary, Brian P., 1959-

Six sheep sip thick shakes; and other tricky tongue twisters. illustrations by Steve Mack. Millbrook Press 2011 31p il
Grades: 1 2 3   398.8
   1. Tongue twisters
   ISBN 1580135854 lib bdg; 9781580135856 lib bdg
                                          LC 2010014421
This is an illustrated collection of tongue twisters. "Grades two to four." (Bull Cent Child Books)

"This high-energy collection of pleasantly rhythmic tongue twisters features a screwball cast of cartoon animals rendered in digital collages. . . . An appended guide provides tips for creating effective tongue twisters-something readers are likely to try out once they master the satisfying sounds of these silly, slippery, serpentine selections." Publ Wkly

Cole, Joanna

Anna Banana: 101 jump-rope rhymes; compiled by Joanna Cole; illustrated by Alan Tiegreen. Morrow Junior Bks. 1989 64p il hardcover o.p. pa $7.95

Grades: 3 4 5　　　　　　　　　　　**398.8**
1. Games 2. Jump rope rhymes
ISBN 0-688-08809-0 pa

　　　　　　　　　　　　　　　LC 88-29108

An illustrated collection of jump rope rhymes arranged according to the type of jumping they are meant to accompany

"Heavily inked drawings provide cartoon-style humor; sources for jump-rope rhymes and an index of first lines are appended." Booklist

Collins, Heather

Out came the sun; a day in nursery rhymes. Kids Can Press 2007 91p il $19.95
Grades: PreK K　　　　　　　　　**398.8**
1. Nursery rhymes
ISBN 978-1-55337-881-5; 1-55337-881-4

"Collins arranges 45 mostly familiar nursery rhymes in a sun-up to sun-down romp starring a multi-species stuffed animal family. . . . Collins's watercolors display just enough verve and domestic humor to keep her subjects from turning twee. . . . The manageable size and good-natured fun make this volume stand out." Publ Wkly

Crews, Nina

★ The **neighborhood** Mother Goose; [illustrated by] Nina Crews. Greenwillow Books 2004 63p il $15.99; lib bdg $16.89
Grades: PreK K 1 2 3　　　　　　　**398.8**
1. Nursery rhymes
ISBN 0-06-051573-2; 0-06-051574-0 lib bdg
　　　　　　　　　　　　　　　LC 2003-41763

"Nina Crews' urban photographs and photo montages . . . {illustrate} over forty . . . verses and chants from Mother Goose. . . . Ages two to seven." (Bull Cent Child Books)

"Nina Crews' clear, beautiful color photographs and computer manipulations bring children closeup to people like them. . . . She uses computer tools to combine photos of joyful kids in her Brooklyn neighborhood with all kinds of scenarios, realistic and wild." Booklist

Delacre, Lulu Arrorro

★ **Arrorro** mi nino; Latino lullabies and gentle games. selected and illustrated by Lulu Delacre; musical arrangements by Cecilia Esqivel and Diana Sáez. Lee & Low Books 2004 un il $16.95
　Grades: K 1 2 3　　　　　　　　**398.8**
　1. Lullabies 2. Finger play 3. Nursery rhymes 4. Lullabies, Spanish -- Texts 5. Nursery rhymes, Spanish American 6. Bilingual books -- English-Spanish 7. Spanish language materials -- Bilingual 8. Children's songs -- Latin America -- Texts
　ISBN 1-58430-159-7
　　　　　　　　　　　　　　　LC 2003-9234

An illustrated collection of nursery rhymes, finger play games, and lullabies from the major Latino groups living in the United States today

"The bright, beautiful oil-wash illustrations . . . reflect the diversity of the Latino experience. . . . The bilingual text appears first in Spanish, with the English translation beneath or by its side. . . . Musical notation and comments about the melodies are at the back." Booklist

DePaola, Tomie, 1934-

Tomie dePaola's Mother Goose. Putnam 1985 127p il $24.99
Grades: PreK K　　　　　　　　　**398.8**
1. Nursery rhymes
ISBN 0-399-21258-2

　　　　　　　　　　　　　　　LC 84-26314

This "is a large, ample, unfussy edition of every child's first staple of literature. . . . The neat, flat illustrations are darkly outlined and colored generally in the illustrator's favorite palette of clear pinks, blues, and violets and surrounded with a lot of white space. Each verse is pictured in a simple and unmistakable interpretation. . . . A perfectly basic and lovely Mother Goose, lavish yet simple, and a splendid beginning for the youngest listener." Horn Book

Emberley, Barbara

Drummer Hoff; adapted by Barbara Emberley; illustrated by Ed Emberley. Simon & Schuster 1987 un il $16; pa $5.95
Grades: PreK K 1 2　　　　　　　**398.8**
1. Nursery rhymes
ISBN 0-671-66248-1; 0-671-66249-X pa
　　　　　　　　　　　　　　　LC 87-35755

First published 1967 by Prentice-Hall
Awarded the Caldecott Medal, 1968

"A cumulative folk rhyme is adapted in spirited style and illustrated with arresting black woodcuts accented with brilliant color. The characters who participate in the building and firing of a cannon—'Sergeant Crowder brought the powder, Corporal Farrell brought the barrel,' etc.—are hilariously rugged characters, while 'Drummer Hoff who fired it off stands by, deadpan, waiting to touch off the marvelously satisfying explosion.'" Hodges. Books for Elem Sch Libr

Fitzgerald, Joanne, 1956-

Yum! yum!! delicious nursery rhymes. [compiled and illustrated by] Joanne Fitzgerald. Fitzhenry & Whiteside 2007 un il $18.95
Grades: PreK　　　　　　　　　　**398.8**
1. Nursery rhymes 2. Food -- Poetry
ISBN 978-1-55041-888-0; 1-55041-888-2

This Mother Goose collection pairs illustrated nursery rhymes with the story of a little pig on his way to market. In addition to This Little Piggy, the rhymes include: "Little Tommy Tucker, Jack Sprat, Hey Diddle Diddle, Peter Piper, Pease Porridge Hot, I Eat My Peas with Honey, If All the World were Apple Pie, I Had a Little Nut Tree, Polly Put the Kettle On, Higgledy, Piggledy, Little Jack Horner, [and] Little Miss Muffet ." (Publisher's note) "Ages two to six." (Quill Quire)

"A farmer's market is the setting for this charming story, set around 13 well-known nursery rhymes that deal with food. The characters are animals dressed in human clothes. Listeners will have fun hunting for the piggy who appears in every scene. . . . The small pictures, all in light pastels, are beautifully detailed. . . . Subtle humor abounds." SLJ

Galdone, Paul

The **cat** goes fiddle-i-fee; adapted and illustrated by Paul Galdone. Clarion Bks. 1985 un il hardcover o.p. pa $6.95

Grades: K 1 **398.8**
1. Nursery rhymes 2. Animals -- Poetry
ISBN 0-89919-705-1 pa

LC 85-2686

An old English rhyme names all the animals a farm boy
feeds on his daily rounds

"Galdone's line-and-watercolor illustrations have all the
verve and accessible good humor associated with his work,
and the varied and irresistible rhythm of the verses carries
the nonsense along at a good pace, enhancing its appeal to
the very young. Whether told or sung, this is a diverting selection for preschool story times." Booklist

Three little kittens. Clarion Bks. 1986 un il $15;
pa $5.95
Grades: PreK K 1 2 **398.8**
1. Nursery rhymes 2. Cats -- Poetry
ISBN 0-89919-426-5; 0-89919-796-5 pa

LC 86-2655

Three little kittens lose, find, soil, and wash their mittens
"Galdone's characteristically exuberant pen-and-wash
drawings fill these pages with feline faces, first rueful then
joyful, then repentant, and finally excited about the prospects of catching 'a rat close by.' This is one of those sustained nursery rhymes that initiates youngest listeners into
the concentration required for stories, and there's enough
dramatic movement and color contrast in the art to hold toddlers' attention." Bull Cent Child Books

Griego, Margot C.
Tortillitas para mama and other nursery rhymes; Span-
ish and English. selected and translated by Margot C.
Griego . . . [et al.]; illustrated by Barbara Cooney. Holt &
Co. 1981 un il hardcover o.p. pa $5.95
Grades: PreK K 1 2 **398.8**
1. Nursery rhymes 2. Folklore -- Latin America 3.
Bilingual books -- English-Spanish
ISBN 0-8050-0317-7

LC 81-4823

A bilingual collection of 13 popular Latin American
nursery rhymes

The purpose of this book "is to preserve a unique aspect of Hispanic culture which deserves to be passed down
to all children. . . . The illustrations are strikingly beautiful,
capturing the rich color and texture of some parts of South
America. . . . [But their] homogenized view of Latin Americans can easily lead to the perpetuation of some familiar stereotypes." Interracial Books Child Bull

Gustafson, Scott
Favorite nursery rhymes from Mother Goose; illustrated by Scott Gustafson. Greenwich Workshop Press 2007
96p il $19.95
Grades: PreK K 1 **398.8**
1. Nursery rhymes
ISBN 978-0-86713-097-3; 0-86713-097-0

This book contains forty-five nursery rhymes. "Age two
and up." (N Y Times Book Rev)

"These 45 rhymes include the very well known (Itsy
Bitsy Spider) and the somewhat familiar (Hickety, Pickety,
My Black Hen). . . . [The illustrations include] an anthropomorphic baking bear, a pelican sea captain, and Peter Piper
as a pug on two legs." Publisher's note

Hillenbrand, Will
★ **Mother** Goose picture puzzles. Marshall Cavendish
Children's Books 2011 40p il $17.99
Grades: K 1 2 3 **398.8**
1. Puzzles 2. Nursery rhymes 3. Children's poetry
4. Rebuses
ISBN 978-0-7614-5808-1; 0-7614-5808-5

LC 2010-23111

This is a "collection of nursery rhymes—jazzed up by a
rebus format. . . . Playful tweaks in visually depicting both
verse and action make this outing special. Each uncluttered,
mixed-media spread features a rhyme . . . which appears in
large font with pictures in place of some of the words. . . .
Gently humorous touches abound. . . . This volume works as
a nifty guessing game for early readers . . . and the beloved
rhymes and detail-rich artwork should earn the project an
enthusiastic audience." Publ Wkly

Hoberman, Mary Ann
Miss Mary Mack; a hand-clapping rhyme. adapted by
Mary Ann Hoberman; illustrated by Nadine Bernard Westcott. Little, Brown 1998 un il music hardcover o.p. pa
$6.99; bd bk $6.99
Grades: PreK K 1 **398.8**
1. Nursery rhymes
ISBN 0-316-93118-7; 0-316-07614-7 pa; 0-316-
36642-0 bd bk

LC 96-34829

"In this expanded version of the popular hand-clapping
rhyme, the elephant (who's 'jumped so high' . . ./ He reached
the sky/) . . . lands in the middle of a picnic where Mary
Mack promises him her silver buttons if he doesn't go back
to the zoo. Westcott's loose and humorous illustrations add
to the necessarily limited text. A melody line and instructions for hand-clapping are included on the front endpapers." Horn Book Guide

If you love a nursery rhyme; illustrated by Susanna Lock-
heart. Barrons Educational Series 2009 un il $18.99
Grades: PreK K **398.8**
1. Nursery rhymes
ISBN 978-0-7641-6186-5; 0-7641-6186-5

"This large-format volume features just a dozen nursery
rhymes but illustrates them with grace, style, and imaginative details. Some of the rhymes are featured on single
pages, but five appear on double-page spreads accompanied
with gatefold pages that, when opened out, move the vertical
panels in the picture's central, cur-out oval to reveal a new
scene. . . . Well designed and illustrated for active toddlers as
well as older preschoolers." Booklist

Kubler, Annie
Hop a little, jump a little! illustrated by Annie Kubler.
Child's Play 2010 un il bd bk $4.99
Grades: PreK **398.8**
1. Nursery rhymes 2. Board books for children
ISBN 978-1-84643-341-2; 1-84643-341-X

"These board books are appealing introductions to nursery rhymes. Most pages or spreads have just one line of text,
allowing the soft, lively watercolors to take center stage."
SLJ

Pat-a-cake; illustrated by Annie Kubler. Child's Play
2010 un il bd bk $4.99

Grades: PreK   **398.8**
1. Nursery rhymes 2. Board books for children
ISBN 978-1-84643-338-2; 1-84643-338-X
"The rhymes stay true to the originals. One of the best aspects of the illustrations is that many different babies and toddlers are represented, including children with disabilities." SLJ

Lipchenko, Oleg
Humpty Dumpty and friends; nursery rhymes for the young at heart. selected and illustrated by Oleg Lipchenko. Tundra Books 2010 un $17.95
Grades: PreK K   **398.8**
1. Nursery rhymes
ISBN 978-1-77049-205-9; 1-77049-205-4
"Mother Goose rhymes are smartly paired and dreamily illustrated in this beguiling collection from Lipchenko. Each page features two poems, which often have shared elements or themes. . . . Classics are far outnumbered by rarer rhymes of equal charm. . . . The highly detailed and surreal nature of Lipchenko's illustrations will keep readers poring over the pages." Publ Wkly

Long, Sylvia
Sylvia Long's Mother Goose. Chronicle Bks. 1999 109p il $22.95
Grades: PreK   **398.8**
1. Nursery rhymes
ISBN 0-8118-2088-2
LC 98-52311
"Human beings are replaced by animals, reptiles, and insects, all elegantly dressed, in this exuberant nursery-rhyme collection, which includes 82 familiar and less familiar verses." SLJ

Morris, Jackie
★ The **cat** and the fiddle; a treasury of nursery rhymes. Francis Lincoln 2011 il $19.95
Grades: PreK K   **398.8**
1. Nursery rhymes
ISBN 978-1-84507-987-1; 1-84507-987-6
"Animals figure prominently in this collection of 40 nursery rhymes, distinguished by Morris's dreamlike watercolor illustrations. For 'Lavender's Blue' and 'Lilies Are White' a king and queen ride a polar bear, all three crowned with botanicals mentioned in the verse. Later, a woman in vibrant robes knits yarn carried 'three bags full' by her enormous, shaggy black sheep. Morris places nomadic, magisterial figures against pastoral backdrops, peppered with castles and cottages, creating moments of strange, bewitching beauty." Publ Wkly

Moses, Will
Will Moses Mother Goose. Philomel Bks. 2003 61p il $17.99
Grades: PreK K   **398.8**
1. Nursery rhymes
ISBN 0-399-23744-5
LC 2003-731
Folk art paintings accompany this compilation of over sixty of the best-loved Mother Goose rhymes
"In a marvelous match of style and content Moses's . . . sprightly folk-art oil paintings make this a 'must have' Mother Goose volume. The book's tempo is set from the first

page, which intersperses thumbnail vignettes with individual rhymes. . . . A turn of the page then blends the vignettes into a full-bleed panorama of busy village life." Publ Wkly

Opie, Iona Archibald
★ **Here** comes Mother Goose; edited by Iona Opie; illustrated by Rosemary Wells. Candlewick Press 1999 107p il $21.99
Grades: PreK K 1 2   **398.8**
1. Nursery rhymes
ISBN 0-7636-0683-9
LC 99-14256
This selection presents some sixty traditional nursery rhymes, including Old Mother Hubbard, I'm a Little Teapot, and One, Two, Buckle My Shoe, accompanied by illustrations of various animals. "Age two and up." (Commonweal)
"Wells's watercolor-and-ink pictures of somersaulting guinea pigs, mischievous rabbits, and fluffy ducklings capture the sheer joy and exuberance of the rhymes. . . . Make room on the shelves for this must-have title." SLJ

I saw Esau; the schoolchild's pocket book. edited by Iona and Peter Opie; illustrated by Maurice Sendak. Candlewick Press 1992 160p il $19.99; pa $9.99
Grades: Adult Professional   **398.8**
1. Folklore -- Great Britain 2. English poetry -- Collections
ISBN 1-56402-046-0; 0-7636-1199-9 pa
LC 91-71845
A revised and newly illustrated edition of the title first published 1947 in the United Kingdom
A collection of rhymes and riddles traditionally passed on orally from child to child
"From lamentation, pun, and insult to rebuttal, tongue-twister, and comic complaint, these schoolyard folk rhymes are vulgar, absurd, fierce, and utterly compelling. . . . [The book features] Sendak's wicked, joyful illustrations. Blending the factual and the surreal, the pictures (most in color, some in sepia or in black and white) extend the rhymes with characters and scenarios that are gross and tender. Sendak knows kids' ferocity and their fear." Booklist

Mother Goose's little treasures; [edited by] Iona Opie; illustrated by Rosemary Wells. Candlewick Press 2007 52p il $17.99
Grades: PreK K   **398.8**
1. Nursery rhymes
ISBN 978-0-7636-3655-5; 0-7636-3655-X
LC 2007-24959
This is a collection of nursery rhymes featuring such characters as the wee melodie man and Handy Spandy, Mrs. Whirly and little bonny Button-cap. "Age three and up." (N Y Times Book Rev)
"This gem . . . shines with the charm of old-time rhymes and with Wells' beloved animal and child characters, set down in her signature style." Booklist

★ **My** very first Mother Goose; edited by Iona Opie; illustrated by Rosemary Wells. Candlewick Press 1996 107p il $21.99

Grades: PreK K 1 2 **398.8**
1. Nursery rhymes
ISBN 1-56402-620-5

LC 96-4904

For this nursery rhyme collection, the British folklorist Iona Opie "has chosen 68 rhymes . . . and arranged them in the loose framework of a day's activities, from morning till night. The book opens with Jack and Jill's disastrous trip to fetch a pail of water and concludes with a prayer for a safe journey." (N Y Times Book Rev) Index of first lines. "Preschool to kindergarten." (SLJ)

"The 60 plus rhymes in this collection are mostly the old-time favorites, but include some more recent ones such as 'Shoo Fly' and 'Down by the Station.' Wells illustrates the selections with her usual winsome, quirky, anthropomorphic mice, rabbits, cats, pigs, bears, etc., and even includes some people. The lavish ink-and-watercolors are filled with action and delightful details." SLJ

Over the hills and far away; a treasury of nursery rhymes from around the world. [edited by] Elizabeth Hammill. Candlewick Press 2015 160 p. color illustrations $21.99
Grades: PreK K 1 2 3 **398.8**
1. Nursery rhymes
ISBN 0763677299; 9780763677299

LC 2014934992

This children's anthology, edited by Elizabeth Hammill, presents a "treasury of 150 classic nursery rhymes. . . . [It contains] rhymes from the English-speaking world as well as verse that entered English from Chinese, Latino, African, and other cultures. With illustrations from seventy-seven artists, many celebrated throughout the world, and some just emerging, this volume is . . . an adventure in language, image, and imagination." (Publisher's note)

"Hammill's skills as collector are especially sharp in juxtaposing cultural variants of rhymes--for example, a spread with the English Little Miss Muffet includes the Jamaican Lickle Muss Julie, the American Little Miss Tuckett and the Australian Little Miss Muffet, who gets frightened away by a pugnacious wombat rather than a spider." Kirkus
Includes bibliographical references and index

The **Oxford** dictionary of nursery rhymes; edited by Iona and Peter Opie. 2nd ed; Oxford Univ. Press 1997 xxix, 559p il $55
Grades: Adult Professional **398.8**
1. Reference books 2. Nursery rhymes -- Dictionaries
ISBN 0-19-860088-7

LC 98-140995

First published 1951
"The novice as well as the professional will find it an enjoyable read, as well as a learning experience." Am Ref Books Annu, 1999

Oxenbury, Helen
★ The **Helen** Oxenbury nursery collection. Alfred A. Knopf 2004 91p il $19.95; lib bdg $21.99
Grades: K 1 2 3 **398.8**
1. Nursery rhymes 2. Poetry -- Collections
ISBN 0-375-82992-X; 0-375-92992-4 lib bdg

LC 2004-58446

"The stories all feature Oxenbury's trademark winsome pencil-and-watercolor pictures. They include such favorites

as 'Little Red Riding Hood,' 'Henny-Penny,' and 'The Three Little Pigs,' and are retold with drama and humor." SLJ

Pinkney, J. Brian, 1961-
Three little kittens. Dial Books for Young Readers 2010 un il
Grades: PreK K **398.8**
1. Nursery rhymes
ISBN 0803735332; 9780803735330

LC 2009051660

Presents the classic tale of three youngsters who are careless with their mittens, but who turn out to be good little kittens after all.

"Pinkney offers another masterful visual interpretation of a classic narrative. . . . Rendered in graphite, color pencil, and watercolor, Pinkney's sparkling-eyed young cats . . . are almost impossibly . . . cuddly and precious, exuding boundless energy and capricious emotions." Publ Wkly

★ **Pocketful** of posies; a treasury of nursery rhymes. [illustrated by] Salley Mavor. Houghton Mifflin Harcourt 2010 62p il $21.99
Grades: PreK K **398.8**
1. Nursery rhymes
ISBN 978-0-618-73740-6; 0-618-73740-5

LC 2009049700

An illustrated collection of sixty-four traditional nursery rhymes.

"Rarely have classic childhood verses been depicted with so much care and detail—and fabric. Loosely organizing the rhymes over the course of the day , . . Mavor creates a miniature world using wood felt, various stitching techniques, and found materials like acorn caps and seashells. . . . Mavor's intricate and colorful embroidered work of art makes even the best-known childhood poems feel special and new again." Publ Wkly

Polacco, Patricia
Babushka's Mother Goose. Philomel Bks. 1995 64p il hardcover o.p. pa $7.99
Grades: PreK **398.8**
1. Nursery rhymes
ISBN 0-399-22747-4; 0-698-11860-X pa

LC 94-32332

"Polacco credits her story-telling Babushka as the reshaper of many of the 24 rhymes and stories in this collection, borrowed from such sources as Aesop, Moldavian folktales, and Mother Goose. . . . Preschool to grade one." (SLJ)

"The collection includes original rhymes written by Polacco as well as Ukrainian folktales and retellings from Mother Goose and Aesop that Polacco heard as a child from her own Babushka. The distinctive and humorous folk-art illustrations and delightful verses and stories make this book a joy to share with children." Horn Book Guide

Ranson, Claire
Sally go round the stars; favourite rhymes for an Irish childhood. compiled by Sarah Webb & Claire Ranson; illustrated by Steve McCarthy. O'Brien 2011 64 p.
Grades: PreK K 1 2 3 **398.8**
1. Nursery rhymes
ISBN 1847172113; 9781847172112

LC 2012418512

This book by Sarah Webb and Claire Ranson, illustrated by Steve McCarthy, is a "collection of favourite nursery rhymes known and loved throughout Ireland. It includes favourite international, British and Irish rhymes as well as special Irish favourites." The book "Includes Sally Go Round the Moon; Diddly, Diddle, Dumpling; Two Little Dicky Birds; Are Ye Right There, Michael?; Half a Pound of Tuppeny Rice; Adam and Eve and Pinch Me; and many, many more!" (Publisher's note)

Reinhart, Matthew

A pop-up book of nursery rhymes. Little Simon 2009 un il (Classic collectible pop-up) $26.99

Grades: PreK K　　　　　　　　　　　**398.8**

1. Nursery rhymes 2. Pop-up books

ISBN 978-1-4169-1825-7; 1-4169-1825-6

Matthew Reinhart adapts Mother Goose's nursery rhymes, as the characters spring to life as intricate pop-up surprises.

"Ingenious details abound—the thoughtfulness put into every movement is evident." Pub Wkly

Ross, Tony

Three little kittens and other favorite nursery rhymes; selected and illustrated by Tony Ross. Henry Holt and Co. 2009 90p il $16.95

Grades: PreK　　　　　　　　　　　**398.8**

1. Nursery rhymes

ISBN 978-0-8050-8885-4; 0-8050-8885-7

LC 2008-925587

This is a "collection of nearly fifty classic nursery verses. . . . Illustrator Ross has sensibly taken a broad and pragmatic interpretation of the genre, so classic anonymous verse rubs shoulders with Lewis Carroll and lullabies. The presentation is invitingly simple. . . . Ross' visual style remains his usual rumply, comfortable , personable line and watercolor, his figures imbued with a gentle sense of comedy and individuality, and the illustrative vignettes are spirited and deft, sometimes approaching the masterful." Bull Cent Child Books

Schertle, Alice

★ Pio peep! traditional Spanish nursery rhymes. selected by Alma Flor Ada & F. Isabel Campoy; English adaptations by Alice Schertle; illustrated by Vivi Escrivá. HarperCollins Pubs. 2003 64p il $14.99; lib bdg $16.89

Grades: K 1 2 3　　　　　　　　　　**398.8**

1. Nursery rhymes 2. Bilingual books -- English-Spanish

ISBN 0-688-16019-0; 0-688-16020-4 lib bdg

LC 2001-51641

A collection of more than two dozen nursery rhymes in Spanish, from Spain and Latin America, with English translations

"Deeply rhythmic verses, compelling rhyme schemes, and words that 'play trippingly on the tongue' characterize every verse. Schertle's excellent English adaptations are not literal translations but poetic re-creations. They retain the rhythm, meter, and general meaning of the originals. . . . Escrivá's watercolor and colored-pencil illustrations use brilliant hues and detail to reconstruct a young child's world." SLJ

Seibold, J. Otto

Other goose; re-nurseried, and re-rhymed, re-mothered, and re-goosed . . . Chronicle Books 2010 69p il $19.99

Grades: 2 3 4 5　　　　　　　　　　**398.8**

1. Nursery rhymes

ISBN 978-0-8118-6882-2; 0-8118-6882-6

"In the spirit of Mother Goose rhymes, many of which started as parodies, the funny rhymes and wild, vibrantly colored pictures in this picture-book collection bring the nonsense up to date with technological and cultural references kids will recognize and silliness that is universal. . . . Most if the farce and the wordplay are for sharing and reading aloud with older grade-schoolers, who will best appreciate the satire and puns as well as the busy, full-page computer graphics." Booklist

Taback, Simms

★ This is the house that Jack built. Putnam 2002 un il $15.99; pa $6.99

Grades: K 1 2 3　　　　　　　　　　**398.8**

1. Nursery rhymes

ISBN 0-399-23488-8; 0-14-240200-1 pa

LC 00-28057

The cumulative nursery rhyme about the chain of events that started when Jack built a house

"Taback's version of the age-old cumulative rhyme is an explosion of color, energy, zaniness, and pore-over-able detail." Horn Book

★ This little piggy; lap songs, finger plays, clapping rhymes, and pantomime rhymes. edited by Jane Yolen; illustrated by Will Hillenbrand; musical arrangements by Adam Stemple. Candlewick Press 2006 80p il $19.99

Grades: PreK K 1 2　　　　　　　　　**398.8**

1. Songs 2. Finger play 3. Nursery rhymes

ISBN 0-7636-1348-7

An "anthology of approximately 60 lap rhymes, songs, clapping rhymes, and finger and foot rhymes, all presented with explanations and simple instructions for parents to play with their babies and toddlers. . . . Hillenbrand has framed the rhymes with lovely mixed-media pictures in an array of sherbet pastel colors with happy piggy families acting out the rhymes. . . . A delightful accompanying CD includes 13 songs from the text, beautifully done with vivacious accompaniment. The result is a perfect book for one-on-one sharing." SLJ

Tildes, Phyllis Limbacher

Will you be mine? a nursery rhyme romance. compiled and illustrated by Phyllis Limbacher Tildes. Charlesbridge 2011 un il lib bdg $17.95; pa $7.95

Grades: PreK K 1　　　　　　　　　　**398.8**

1. Nursery rhymes

ISBN 978-1-58089-244-5 lib bdg; 1-58089-244-2; 978-1-58089-245-2 pa; 1-58089-245-0 pa

LC 2010007590

"Tildes has compiled and illustrated 18 traditional nursery rhymes that trace an 18th-century courtship to honeymoon of a farmer tabby cat and his long-lashed poodle love. The pastoral scenes of preparation for the nuptials include mice tailors, a piggy florist, and a hedgehog minister. Gouache paintings in pastel colors accompany favorites like 'Hickory, Dickory, Dock' and less-familiar poems such as 'Pretty John Watts.' . . . this picture book offers nursery rhymes in a fresh way." SLJ

Trapani, Iza

Rufus and friends: rhyme time; traditional poems extended and illustrated by Iza Trapani. Charlesbridge 2008 33p il $16.95; pa $7.95

Grades: PreK K   **398.8**

1. Nursery rhymes

ISBN 978-1-58089-206-3; 978-1-58089-207-0 pa

LC 2007026200

In this collection of tongue-twisting nursery rhymes, the reader is asked to find hidden objects in the illustrations.

"The lively artwork was created using watercolor, ink, and colored pencils. Each actor/pooch is a different breed; they all have priceless facial expressions and vary with the situations. Children will ask for repeated readings as they search for the pictures again and again." SLJ

Rufus and friends: school days; extended and illustrated by Iza Trapani. Charlesbridge 2010 35p il lib bdg $16.96; pa $7.95

Grades: PreK K   **398.8**

1. Nursery rhymes

ISBN 978-1-58089-248-3; 1-58089-248-5; 978-1-58089-249-0 pa; 1-58089-249-3 pa

LC 2009-4307

A collection of traditional rhymes illustrated and adapted to a school setting, with hidden objects for the reader to find in the illustrations.

"Many of the source poems will be unfamiliar, but Trapani's inventive and precise verse allows each rhyme to stand on its own. Similarly, her illustrations, in watercolor, ink and colored pencil, are bright and distinct. . . . A winner." Kirkus

Wright, Blanche Fisher

The **real** Mother Goose; illustrated by Blanch Fisher Wright. Scholastic 1994 128p il $9.95

Grades: PreK K 1 2   **398.8**

1. Nursery rhymes

ISBN 0-590-22517-0

First published 1916 by Rand McNally

A comprehensive collection of over three-hundred traditional nursery rhymes

398.9 Proverbs

The **Night** has ears; African proverbs. selected and illustrated by Ashley Bryan. Atheneum Bks. for Young Readers 1999 un il $16

Grades: K 1 2 3   **398.9**

1. Proverbs 2. Folklore -- Africa

ISBN 0-689-82427-0

LC 98-48772

A collection of twenty-six proverbs, some serious and some humorous, from a variety of African tribes

"Illustrated in Bryan's distinctive multishape, multicolor style, the tempera-and-gouache art resembles stained glass. . . . A worthy supplement to cultural studies, this will also

inspire students to write and illustrate their own proverbs." Booklist

400 LANGUAGE

401 Philosophy and theory

Lunge-Larsen, Lise

★ **Gifts** from the gods; written by Lise Lunge-Larsen; illustrated by Gareth Hinds. Houghton Mifflin Harcourt/Childrens 2011 90p. $18.99

Grades: 4 5 6 7   **401**

1. Vocabulary 2. Classical mythology

ISBN 978-0-547-15229-5; 0-547-15229-9

LC 2010031635

In this book "[Lise] Lunge-Larsen and [Gareth] Hinds explain what words like echo, grace, hypnotize, and janitor have in common, tracing the origins of common words and expressions to Greek and Roman myths. Readers may know that 'arachnid' derives from the story of Arachne and that modern-day 'sirens' have mythical antecedents, but this collection . . . [also explains] the roots of 'nemesis' (the goddess of justice) or 'tantalize,' after doomed Tantalus. Lunge-Larsen provides additional context, including dictionary definitions, and quotes from children's literature. Hinds incorporates graphic novel–style elements into his . . . illustrations, including dialogue balloons and filmic perspectives." (Publishers Weekly)

411 Writing systems of standard forms of languages

Agee, Jon

★ **Z** goes home. Hyperion Bks. for Children 2003 un il $16.95

Grades: PreK K 1 2   **411**

1. Alphabet

ISBN 0-7868-1987-1

LC 2002-114205

"The letter Z abandons its allotted spot in the City Zoo sign and heads off in Agee's innovative alphabet book. Children can track the red Z's journey past an Alien, over a Bridge, into some Cake, and over Hurdles until the red-letter moment when it finally finds its way to its similarly colored friends. . . . Each letter is exemplified by a noun . . . but to make matters more interesting, the object is also shaped like the letter. . . . Bold shapes and lines create a clean, comical look." Booklist

Bayer, Jane

A **my** name is Alice; pictures by Steven Kellogg. Dial Bks. for Young Readers 1984 un il $16.99; pa $6.99

Grades: PreK K 1 2   **411**

1. Alphabet 2. Stories in rhyme

ISBN 0-8037-0123-3; 0-14-054668-5 pa

LC 84-7059

"It is a superlative blend of visual and textual nonsense because the visual surprises keep the repetitive pattern in the text from becoming tedious. The verbal parts gradually expand in their ludicrousness, in their cataloging of zany characters and occupations." Wilson Libr Bull

Donoughue, Carol
The **story** of writing; [by] Carol Donoughue. Firefly Books 2007 48p il map $19.95
Grades: 4 5 6 7   **411**
   1. Writing -- History 2. Alphabet -- History
ISBN 978-1-55407-306-1; 1-55407-306-5
This is an "introduction to the history of the Roman alphabet. . . . Beginning sections about early civilizations' alphabets, starting with Sumerian cuniforms, include a you-are-there narrative. . . . Later spreads cover European illuminated manuscripts and the development of printing technology. A final section [covers] Chinese characters. . . . Numerous carefully chosen color photos of artifacts . . . greatly enhance the book's appeal." Booklist
   Includes bibliographical references

Ehlert, Lois
   ★ **Eating** the alphabet; fruits and vegetables from A to Z. Harcourt Brace Jovanovich 1989 un il $17; pa $7; bd bk $6.95
Grades: PreK K 1   **411**
   1. Fruit 2. Alphabet 3. Vegetables
ISBN 0-15-224435-2; 0-15-224436-0 pa; 0-15-201036-X bd bk
                                        LC 88-10906
An alphabetical tour of the world of fruits and vegetables, from apricot and artichoke to yam and zucchini
   "The objects depicted, shown against a white ground, are easily identifiable for the most part, and represent the more common sounds of the letter shown. . . . Both upper- and lower-case letters are printed in large, black type. A nice added touch is the glossary which includes the pronunciation and interesting facts about the origin of each fruit and vegetable, how it grows, and its uses. An exuberant, eye-catching alphabet book." SLJ

Fleming, Denise
   ★ **Alphabet** under construction. Holt & Co. 2002 un il $16.95
Grades: PreK K 1 2   **411**
   1. Alphabet 2. Mice -- Fiction
ISBN 0-8050-6848-1
                                        LC 2001-5210
   Companion volume to Lunch
   A mouse works his way through the alphabet as he folds the "F," measures the "M," and rolls the "R"
   "Fleming has poured colored cotton fiber through hand-cut stencils to make her illustrations, which are thus bold in outline and shape and vivid with an almost incandescent coloring. Although this has the simplicity of many alphabet books, it also has momentum . . . and ingenuity in its execution." Booklist

Floca, Brian
   The **racecar** alphabet. Atheneum Bks. for Young Readers 2003 un il $15.95
Grades: PreK K 1 2   **411**
   1. Alphabet 2. Automobile racing -- Fiction
ISBN 0-689-85091-3
                                        LC 2002-2198
   Automobile races highlight the letters of the alphabet

"The alphabetical text often uses alliterative phrases. . . . Although a single race appears to proceed throughout the book, the cars, drivers, tracks, and spectators change considerably from the book's opening in 1901 . . . to the conclusion in 2001. . . . Large in scale, the ink-and-watercolor artwork is bold enough to share with a story hour or classroom group, yet young racing fans will find the details absorbing. Floca's introductory note on the history of racing may interest them as well." Booklist

Jeffrey, Laura S.
   All about Braille; reading by touch. Enslow Publishers 2004 48p il (Transportation & communication series) lib bdg $23.93
Grades: 2 3 4   **411**
   1. Blind -- Books and reading
ISBN 0-7660-2184-X
                                        LC 2003-17617
   This offers a brief history of braille, describes the braille alphabet and how it is used for communication for the blind.

Johnson, Stephen
   ★ **Alphabet** city; [by] Stephen T. Johnson. Viking 1995 un il $16.99; pa $6.99
Grades: PreK K 1   **411**
   1. Alphabet
ISBN 0-670-85631-2; 0-14-055904-3 pa
                                        LC 95-12335
   A Caldecott Medal honor book, 1995
   "Only after careful scrutiny will viewers realize that these arresting images aren't photographs but compositions of pastels, watercolors, gouache and charcoal. A visual tour de force, Johnson's ingenious alphabet book transcends the genre by demanding close inspection of not just letters, but the world." Publ Wkly

Lobel, Anita
   Alison's zinnia. Greenwillow Bks. 1990 un il hardcover o.p. pa $6.99
Grades: PreK K 1 2   **411**
   1. Alphabet 2. Flowers -- Fiction
ISBN 0-688-08865-1; 0-688-14737-2 pa
                                        LC 89-23700
   Alison acquired an amaryllis for Beryl who bought a begonia for Crystal—and so on through the alphabet, as full-page illustrations are presented of each flower. "Preschool to grade two." (SLJ)
   "More than two dozen little girls, a full alphabet of them, pick flowers for their friends: 'Alison acquired an Amaryllis for Beryl' and 'Nancy noticed a Narcissus for Olga' and so on till 'Zena zeroed in on a Zinnia for Alison.' Underneath each large handsome floral illustration is a smaller picture of the named child and her flower. Charming." N Y Times Book Rev

Macdonald, Suse
   Alphabatics. Bradbury Press 1986 un il $19.95; pa $7.99
Grades: PreK K 1 2   **411**
   1. Alphabet
ISBN 0-02-761520-0; 0-689-71625-7 pa
                                        LC 85-31429
   A Caldecott Medal honor book, 1987

In this book the letters of the alphabet are transformed and incorporated into twenty-six illustrations, so that the hole in "b" becomes a balloon and "y" turns into the head of a yak. "Ages two to five." (Christ Sci Monit)

MacDonald "maneuvers each letter to create a visual image as well as an object that begins with that letter." Child Book Rev Serv

Pelletier, David

The **graphic** alphabet. Orchard Bks. 1996 un il $17.95

Grades: PreK K 1 2   **411**

1. Alphabet

ISBN 0-531-36001-6

LC 96-4001

A Caldecott Medal honor book, 1997

For this "alphabet book, {Pelletier} decided that 'the illustration of the letterform had to retain the natural shape of the letter as well as represent the meaning of the word.'" (Publisher's note) "Ages four to eight." (N Y Times Book Rev)

In this alphabet book "a stylized letter Y, pink against a black background, is turned on its side and looks like a mouth open in a yawn. . . . The letter Q is repeated in squares, becoming a handsome quilt, and a three-dimensional golden H hovers over a darkened sky. Even for those who know their letters very well, some of the pictures demand a second look before the artist's view is clear. But that's the point; things can be more than or different from what they seem. An engaging book that will certainly have art-class relevance." Booklist

Robb, Don

★ **Ox,** house, stick; the history of our alphabet. illustrated by Anne Smith. Charlesbridge 2007 48p il $16.95; pa $7.95

Grades: 4 5 6 7   **411**

1. Writing -- History 2. Alphabet -- History

ISBN 978-1-57091-609-0; 978-1-57091-610-6 pa

LC 2005-06015

"Robb traces the history of each letter from its origin to its modern appearance in the Roman alphabet. He explains the birth of writing in pictogram form and the eventual transition to written symbols that stand for sounds. . . . Smith's whimsical paintings are a fitting companion to Robb's light-hearted text." SLJ

Van Allsburg, Chris

The **Z** was zapped; a play in twenty-six acts. performed by the Caslon Players; written and directed by Chris Van Allsburg. Houghton Mifflin 1987 un il $18.95

Grades: K 1 2 3   **411**

1. Alphabet

ISBN 0-395-44612-0

LC 87-14988

One by one the letters of the alphabet appear on stage, where each suffers a mishap, from "A was in an avalanche" to "Z was zapped." "Ages five to eight years." (Bull Cent Child Books)

"Children can try to guess what action has occured, thereby increasing their vocabulary and the fun, or they can turn the page and read the text, or better yet—do both. This clever romp resembles old vaudeville theater, with one curious act following the next." SLJ

Werner, Sharon

Alphabeasties and other amazing types; by Sharon Werner and Sarah Forss. Blue Apple Books 2009 un il $19.99

Grades: K 1 2 3   **411**

1. Animals 2. Alphabet

ISBN 978-1-934706-78-7; 1-934706-78-7

LC 2009-12599

"An alphabet of animals is presented, each one cleverly composed of its initial letter in a typeface that often suits the characteristics of that creature—a spiky alligator, shaggy sheep, etc. Foldout pages allow for the impressive height of the giraffe or the length of the alligator to be revealed. . . . Young readers will enjoy the animals while older children will have a greater appreciation for the book's artistry." SLJ

413   Dictionaries of standard forms of languages

Evans, Lezlie

Can you greet the whole wide world? 12 common phrases in 12 different languages. by Lezlie Evans; illustrated by Denis Roche. Houghton Mifflin 2006 un il $16

Grades: K 1 2 3   **413**

1. Vocabulary 2. Polyglot materials

ISBN 0-618-56327-X

LC 2005020612

Introduces young readers to common phrases such as "good morning," "thank you," and "please" in German, Hebrew, Spanish, Arabic, Russian, Hindi, Chinese, Zulu, Japanese, Italian, French, and Portuguese.

"This book is a great way to introduce the many similarities and interests of children around the world. . . . Flat, cartoon-style illustrations done in bright colors reinforce action and concepts." SLJ

Includes bibliographical references

Ogburn, Jacqueline K.

Little treasures; endearments from around the world. Houghton Mifflin 2012 il $16.99

Grades: PreK K 1 2   **413**

1. Love 2. Polyglot materials

ISBN 978-0-547-42862-8; 0-547-42862-6

"Ogburn and Raschka give families a whole new vocabulary with which to express their love, exploring terms of endearment used around the globe. Impish, doe-eyed figures rendered in broad, calligraphic brushstrokes wear with pride terms like 'ducky,' used in England, and 'kullan-muru,' which means 'nugget of gold' in Finland. Raschka forgoes painting his characters with black, brown, or white skin, instead using gleeful pinks, blues, teals, and greens. The phrases appear both in English and in their original languages . . . with phonetic pronunciations provided. . . . The message about familial love being a universal human trait is clearly and joyfully articulated; it's hard to imagine a sweeter concept." Publ Wkly

Padmanabhan, Manjula

I am different; can you find me? Charlesbridge Publishing 2011 un il $16.95; pa $7.95

Grades: K 1 2 3   **413**

1. Vocabulary 2. Picture puzzles 3. Polyglot materials

4. Language and culture
ISBN 978-1-57091-639-7; 1-57091-639-X; 978-1-57091-640-3 pa; 1-57091-640-3 pa

LC 2010007579

First published in India

"An informational picture book presenting diverse languages to child readers, this offering . . . is a tour de force. Each page opening includes a brightly colored picture puzzle image with one item differing from the others, accompanied by the question 'Can you find me?' written in one of 16 languages from page to page and supported by phonetic pronunciation guides. Supplemental text provides information about each language, including words potentially familiar to English speakers . . . or words and phrases for readers to learn. . . . The resulting whole broadens readers' awareness of how languages evolve and adopt words from one another. . . . A substantive, engaging title." Kirkus

Park, Linda Sue
Mung-mung! a foldout book of animal sounds. illustrated by Diane Bigda. Charlesbridge 2004 un il $9.95
Grades: K 1 2   **413**
1. Vocabulary 2. Polyglot materials
ISBN 1-57091-486-9

LC 2003-3765

"A multilingual guessing game for the youngest children. Each spread begins with the question, 'What kind of animal says.' and features a variety of sounds in playful handwritten typefaces. Opening a flap reveals the answer. Several languages from Europe, Asia, and the Middle East are included, as well as the sound in English to tip off youngsters. Bigda's cotton-candy-colored gouache artwork displays a lightness of line and a jazzy, freeform feel that blends well with the simple fare." SLJ

Yum! Yuck! a foldout book of people sounds from around the world. [by] Linda Sue Park, Julia Durango; illustrated by Sue Rama. Charlesbridge 2005 un il $9.95
Grades: K 1 2   **413**
1. Vocabulary 2. Polyglot materials
ISBN 1-57091-659-4

LC 2004-18955

Presenting sounds that people make to utter or cry out abruptly in various languages to express such emotion as distaste, excitement, and surprise

"This original offering is a delightful addition to the canon of multicultural picture books and a fun read-aloud guessing game." SLJ

Stojic, Manya
Hello world! greetings in 42 languages around the globe! Scholastic 2002 38p il $14.95
Grades: K 1 2   **413**
1. Vocabulary 2. Polyglot materials
ISBN 0-439-36202-4

LC 2001-43615

Children from around the world say "hello" in forty-two languages, from Amharic to Zulu

"Greetings appear with a bold nearly full-page acrylic painting of a child. . . . This deceivingly simple book encourages interest in and awareness of other languages." SLJ

Weinstein, Ellen
Everywhere the cow says Moo! [by] Ellen Weinstein; illustrated by Kenneth Andersson. Boyds Mills Press 2008 un il $14.95
Grades: PreK K   **413**
1. Vocabulary 2. Polyglot materials
ISBN 978-1-59078-458-7; 1-59078-458-8

LC 2007-17566

"Via simple text and illustrations, children are told what a dog, frog, duck, rooster, and cow say in English, Spanish, French, and Japanese. . . . Each phrase has its own page featuring the animal and an iconic item (the Eiffel Tower, a bullfighter, etc.). . . . The spare and colorful cartoonlike pictures mix the look of folk art and digital precision. Bold primary colors and heavy black lines abound. A glossary includes proper and phonetic spellings." SLJ

Includes glossary

419   Sign languages

Ault, Kelly
★ Let's sign! every baby's guide to communicating with grownups. written by Kelly Ault; illustrated by Leo Landry. Houghton Mifflin Co. 2005 77p il $17
Grades: PreK K 1   **419**
1. Sign language
ISBN 0-618-50774-4

"After a brief and informative introduction that details the benefits of using sign language with babies, Ault presents three simple stories: Mealtime, Playtime, and Bedtime. . . . Landry's pencil-and-watercolor illustrations are child-friendly, and his depictions of the signs are both appealing and informative. . . . The signs are well chosen to reflect a child's world." SLJ

Gordon, Jean M.
★ The Gallaudet children's dictionary of American Sign Language; Jean Gordon, editorial consultant; color illustrations by Debbie Tilley; sign illustrations by Peggy Swartzel Lott, Daniel Renner, and Rob Hills. Gallaudet University Press 2014 384 p. illustrations (some color) (hardcover: alk. paper) $39.95
Grades: K 1 2 3 4   **419**
1. Deaf children 2. Sign language -- Dictionaries 3. American Sign Language -- Dictionaries 4. Deaf children -- United States -- Education
ISBN 1563686317; 9781563686313

LC 2014004275

This book, Jean M. Gordon, "is a bilingual dictionary that serves a twofold purpose-to increase and improve deaf children's English vocabulary skills and to teach American Sign Language to hearing children. . . . This dictionary will help deaf children make the connections between the signs they already know and the written English words that express the same concept. . . . Hearing children will learn a new language and a new way to communicate." (Publisher's note)

"This long-anticipated and colorfully designed reference work is the first comprehensive American Sign Language dictionary for children published to date. It boasts more than 1,000 signs and includes a searchable DVD, which features young native signers demonstrating each sign and 150 of the practice sentences... The comprehensive introduction relays important information about ASL, including regional differences, and explains the arrows used to depict the motions of the signs. Highly recommended." SLJ

Children's dictionary of American Sign Language

Heller, Lora

★ **Sign** language for kids; a fun & easy guide to American sign language. [by] Lora Heller. Sterling 2004 95p il $14.95

Grades: 3 4 5 6   **419**

1. Sign language

ISBN 1-4027-0672-3

LC 2003-19011

Color photos illustrate sign language for numbers, letters, colors, feelings, animals, and clothes

"Clear color photos and simple text combine to form an excellent introduction to American Sign Language (ASL)." SLJ

Lowenstein, Felicia

All about sign language; talking with your hands. Enslow Publishers 2004 48p il (Transportation & communication series) lib bdg $23.93

Grades: 2 3 4   **419**

1. Sign language

ISBN 0-7660-2028-2

LC 2003-26608

This discusses "how sign language came about, the jobs where it is useful to know sign language, and people who are important to sign language. Also {includes} the manual alphabet." Publisher's note

Includes glossary and bibliographical references

Warner, Penny

Signing fun; American sign language vocabulary, phrases, games & activities. illustrated by Paula Gray. Gallaudet Univ. Press 2006 225p il pa $19.95

Grades: 4 5 6 7 8   **419**

1. Sign language

ISBN 1-56368-292-3

"This book is a great resource for readers who want to learn more signs, or for teachers and librarians looking for fun ways to share them with kids." SLJ

420 Specific languages

Dubosarsky, Ursula

The **word** snoop; illustrated by Tohby Riddle. Dial Books 2009 246p il $16.99

Grades: 5 6 7 8   **420**

1. English language -- History

ISBN 978-0-8037-3406-7; 0-8037-3406-9

LC 2009-8306

First published 2008 in Australia with title: The word spy

A tour of the English language from the beginning of the alphabet in 4000 BC to modern text messaging and emoticons

"Short chapters, clear explanations, and humorous examples bring the subject to life, while word puzzles and coded messages at the end of each section invite reader participation. The attractive design adds to the appeal." Booklist

422 Etymology of standard English

Baker, Rosalie F.

In a word; 750 words and their fascinating stories and origins. by Rosalie Baker; illustrated by Tom Lopes. Cobblestone Pub. 2003 221p il $17.95

Grades: 5 6 7 8   **422**

1. English language -- Etymology

ISBN 0-8126-2710-5

LC 2003-25582

"The entries in this book discuss the meanings and derivations of 750 words and phrases. . . . While exploring word origins, Baker also touches on interesting facets of European history and Greek mythology. The jaunty illustrations are reproduced in black and shades of gray. . . . This informative book fosters an appreciation for the richness of the English language." Booklist

423 Dictionaries of standard English

★ The **American** Heritage children's dictionary; by the editors of the American Heritage dictionaries. Houghton Mifflin Harcourt 2010 885 p. $19.95

Grades: 3 4 5 6   **423**

1. Vocabulary 2. Encyclopedias and dictionaries 3. English language -- Dictionaries 4. English language -- Dictionaries, Juvenile

ISBN 0547212550; 0547659555; 9780547212555; 9780547659558

LC 2009012324

This book is a dictionary for children. It "covers all the vocabulary young readers need today. More than 2,000 new words and senses" are included. It's an "illustrated reference book including an A-Z vocabulary listing, a thesaurus, and special sections on synonyms, word histories, vocabulary builders, and phonics." (Publisher's note)

★ The **American** Heritage first dictionary; rev ed; Houghton Mifflin 2009 405p il $17.95

Grades: PreK K 1 2   **423**

1. Reference books 2. English language -- Dictionaries

ISBN 978-0-547-21597-6; 0-547-21597-5

First published 2007

This dictionary includes more than 2,000 entry words, and 850 full-color photographs and drawings

"This clear, easy-to-use reference opens with a five-page introduction to dictionary use and contains more than 2000 common words and 850 color photographs and drawings. Entries feature full-sentence definitions and sample usage. Occasional sidebars offer opposites, rhyming, or related words... Users, especially second-language learners, will appreciate the dictionary's clarity and simplicity...appealing choice for home libraries." SLJ

Bollard, John K.

Scholastic children's thesaurus; illustrated by Mike Reed. [new and updated ed]; Scholastic Reference 2006 240p il $16.99

Grades: 4 5 6 7   **423**

1. Reference books 2. English language -- Synonyms

and antonyms
ISBN 0-43979-831-0

LC 2005050010

First published 1998

An illustrated thesaurus for young readers defines more than five hundred headwords and 2,500 synonyms, providing example sentences for each synonym and including an extensive cross-referencing index.

DK Merriam-Webster children's dictionary; rev ed; Dorling Kindersley 2005 911p il map $19.99

Grades: 3 4 5 6   **423**

1. Reference books 2. English language -- Dictionaries
ISBN 0-7566-1143-1

First published 2000

Presents definitions for over 32,000 entries and includes some 3,000 illustrations interspersed throughout the text

Ferris, Jeri Chase

Noah Webster and his words; by Jeri Chase Ferris; illustrated by Vincent X. Kirsch. Houghton Mifflin Harcourt 2012 32 p. col. ill. (reinforced) $16.99

Grades: 2 3 4   **423**

1. English language -- Spelling 2. Educators -- United States -- Biography 3. Lexicographers -- United States -- Biography
ISBN 0547390556; 9780547390550

LC 2011013018

In this picture-book biography, author Jeri Chase Ferris tells the story of Noah Webster, who "entered Yale University and became a teacher [at age 15]. When the Revolutionary War was over, he wanted to write . . . an American spelling book that would systematize American spelling. . . . He followed his speller with a grammar text, and eventually, at age 70, published his American Dictionary of the English Language." (Kirkus Reviews)

Foster, John

Barron's junior rhyming Dictionary; illustrated by Melanie Williamson and Rupert Van Wyk. Barron's 2006 160p il pa $12.99

Grades: 3 4 5   **423**

1. Poetics 2. Reference books 3. English language -- Rhyme
ISBN 0-7641-3424-8

First published 2005 in the United Kingdom with title: Oxford junior rhyming dictionary

"Young poets will have fun perusing this book in search of the perfect rhyme. . . . Short rhymes scattered throughout are likely to encourage and inspire readers to try their hand at creating their own poems. [Illustrated with] fanciful cartoons. . . . Tips for writing limericks, nonsense nursery rhymes, and various other rhymes are included in this useful resource." SLJ

Hellweg, Paul

★ The **American** Heritage Children's Thesaurus; by Paul Hellweg with the editors of the American Heritage dictionaries. Houghton Mifflin Harcourt 2012 280 p. il $18.95

Grades: 3 4 5 6   **423**

1. Vocabulary 2. English language -- Synonyms and

antonyms
ISBN 0395849772; 0547659547; 9780547659541

LC 9712396

This book is a thesaurus for children. The "entries appear in dark purple type and are followed by the part of speech in smaller italic black type. A solid diamond then indicates in bold type the best choices of synonyms. Next, an open diamond gives other synonyms that don't fit the example sentence as well as the first group or are related words. Lastly, a sentence is given as a usage example. If a word can be more than one part of speech, each part is treated separately." (School Library Journal)

"Each entry word is printed in dark purple, followed by part of speech. Best choices are listed first, followed by other choices. . . . Homographs are entered separately and are numbered. . . . Recommended for breadth, attractiveness, and usefulness." Booklist

Hillerich, Robert L.

★ The **American** Heritage picture dictionary; illustrations by Maggie Swanson. Houghton Mifflin Harcourt 2012 138 p. col il $15.95

Grades: K 1 2   **423**

1. Picture dictionaries 2. Picture books for children 3. Encyclopedias and dictionaries 4. Picture dictionaries, English
ISBN 0547659571; 9780547659572

LC 8615279

This book was "created especially for preschoolers and children in the first years of school." This "dictionary lists 900 words, arranged alphabetically and illustrated with lively full-color drawings. The A-to-Z list is complemented by nine thematic illustrations at the back of the book that feature related vocabulary grouped in settings such as a classroom, a supermarket, and an apartment." (Publisher's note)

The **Kingfisher** children's illustrated dictionary & thesaurus; 2nd ed.; Kingfisher 2011 320p il $16.99

Grades: 2 3 4 5   **423**

1. Reference books 2. English language -- Dictionaries
ISBN 978-0-7534-6469-4; 0-7534-6469-1

First published 2003

"One of the challenges when designing books for children is to present information in a way that is appealing to them. The second edition of The Kingfisher Children's Illustrated Dictionary and Thesaurus meets this challenge. The design of the book makes it intuitive for students to use. . . . The illustrations and information on these pages will spark the imagination of the reader. . . . This book would be a good resource for elementary-school-age students and is recommended for both elementary-school and public libraries." Booklist

Kingfisher first thesaurus. Kingfisher 2004 144 p. $10.99

Grades: 1 2 3 4   **423**

1. Vocabulary 2. English language -- Synonyms and antonyms
ISBN 075345808X; 0753465868; 9780753465868

LC 2004274244

This book is a thesaurus for young children. An "introduction gives a basic review of specific word choices and synonyms. It includes directions for using the thesaurus and clearly describes the organization by key words and cross references. A discussion of antonyms and homonyms follows with the promise of games on special topic pages." (Children's Literature)

★ **Macmillan** dictionary for children; general editor, Christopher G. Morris. [rev and updated ed.]; Simon & Schuster Books for Young Readers 2007 832p il map $19.99
Grades: 2 3 4 5 **423**
1. Reference books 2. English language -- Dictionaries
ISBN 978-1-4169-3959-7; 1-4169-3959-8
LC 2007297593
First published 1975

"With 35,000 entries and more than 3,000 full-color illustrations, this attractive dictionary is a browser's delight. An introductory section explains how to find a word and includes a helpful spelling guide. . . . Eye-catching feature panels provide detailed information about words of particular interest to children. . . . An accessible and enticing addition." SLJ

The **McGraw-Hill** children's dictionary; by the Wordsmyth Collaboratory. McGraw-Hill Children's Pub. 2003 various paging il (Wordsmyth reference series) $24.95
Grades: 4 5 6 7 **423**
1. Reference books 2. English language -- Dictionaries
ISBN 1-57768-298-X
LC 2002-18796

A dictionary with word histories, synonyms, illustrations, and spelling, grammar, and usage features

"The more than 30,000 entries are easy to read, with definitions arranged in three columns. 'Word History,' 'Homophone Note,' and 'Synonyms' boxes give extra information about some words. . . . This attractive dictionary is a fine work." Booklist

The **McGraw-Hill** children's thesaurus; by the Wordsmyth Collaboratory. McGraw-Hill Children's Pub. 2003 294p (Wordsmyth reference series) $19.95
Grades: 4 5 6 7 **423**
1. Reference books 2. English language -- Synonyms and antonyms
ISBN 1-57768-296-3
LC 2002-18797

Presents an alphabetical list of more than 3000 entries, with explanations of the different meanings of each headword and its synonyms

This is "a valuable addition to the upper elementary classroom, library, or any place where children write or do homework." Am Ref Books Annu, 2003

McIllwain, John
DK Children's illustrated dictionary. Dorling Kindersley 2009 256p il $19.99
Grades: K 1 2 3 **423**
1. Reference books 2. English language -- Dictionaries
ISBN 978-0-7566-5196-1; 0-7566-5196-4

First published 1994 with title: The Dorling Kindersley children's illustrated dictionary

This dictionary offers concise definitions with numerous illustrations, and information about abbreviations, spelling, word building, facts and figures, and countries of the world

Merriam-Webster's elementary dictionary; New and expanded ed.; Merriam-Webster 2009 24a, 824p il map $17.95
Grades: 3 4 5 6 **423**
1. English language -- Dictionaries
ISBN 978-0-87779-675-6; 0-87779-675-0
LC 2008041753
First published 1986 with title: Webster's elementary dictionary

More than 36,000 entries with expanded definitions, usage examples, and nearly 1,300 quotes from classic and contemporary children's literature.
Includes bibliographical references

Merriam-Webster's first dictionary; with illustrations by Ruth Heller. Merriam-Webster 2012 [12a], 436 p.p (alk. paper) $16.95
Grades: K 1 2 3 **423**
1. Vocabulary 2. Encyclopedias and dictionaries 3. English language -- Dictionaries, Juvenile
ISBN 0877792747; 9780877792741
LC 2011017950

This book is "a beginner's dictionary written for children in grades K-2, ages 5-7. Formerly Merriam-Webster's Primary Dictionary, [it] introduces young readers to almost 3,000 words using 1,000 entries—many new and revised for 2012—with hundreds of captivating illustrations by Ruth Heller." (Publisher's note)

★ **Merriam-Webster's** intermediate dictionary. Merriam-Webster 2011 18a, 1005 p.p $18.95
Grades: 5 6 7 8 **423**
1. Vocabulary 2. Encyclopedias and dictionaries 3. English language -- Dictionaries 4. English language -- Dictionaries, Juvenile
ISBN 0877796793; 9780877796794
LC 2011534122

This dictionary is "written especially for the needs of students grades 6-8, ages 11-14" and has "nearly 70,000 entries including new words and definitions from the fields of science, technology, entertainment, and health" as well as "more than 22,000 usage examples." The book also "provides definitions, pronunciation, etymology, part of speech designation, and other appropriate information." (Publisher's note)

★ **Scholastic** children's dictionary. Scholastic Inc 2010 800p il $19.99
Grades: 3 4 5 6 **423**
1. Reference books 2. English language -- Dictionaries
ISBN 978-0-545-21858-0; 0-545-21858-6
LC 2010001521
First published 1996

Offers a dictionary that includes pronunciations, definitions, parts of speech, sample sentences, etymologies, synonyms, and cross-references

"The most noticeable changes in the new edition of this perennial favorite are stylistic; the design is more restrained and less cutesy than that of the 2007 edition, with smaller print. The volume appears to be targeted at children who are more visually savvy than previous generations...oxes feature more word histories and sample sentences than in previous editions, and a directory of U.S. presidents, complete with pictures and facts, joins the thesaurus, grammar, punctuation, idiom, acronym, and flag information in the supplementary material." SLJ

Scholastic first dictionary; updated ed; Scholastic Reference 2006 256p il $16.99

Grades: 1 2 3   **423**

1. Reference books 2. English language -- Dictionaries

ISBN 0-439-79834-5

LC 2005049911

First published 1998

This offers definitions for approximately 1,500 words, illustrated with approximately 600 full-color photographs, and includes alternate forms for nouns, verbs, and adjectives, illustrative example sentences, and a phonetic pronunciation guide for each word

★ **Scholastic** dictionary of idioms; new & updated; Scholastic 2006 298p il pa $19.85

Grades: 4 5 6 7   **423**

1. Reference books 2. English language -- Idioms

ISBN 978-0-439-77083-5 pa; 0-439-77083-1 pa

First published 1996

This "introduction to American slang and phrase origins identifies and defines more than six hundred commonly used idioms, complementing the entries with . . . sample sentences and . . . illustrations." Publisher's note

Scholastic first picture dictionary; rev ed; Scholastic Reference 2009 92p il $15.99

Grades: PreK K 1   **423**

1. Reference books 2. Picture dictionaries 3. English language -- Dictionaries

ISBN 978-0-545-13769-0; 0-545-13769-1

First published 2005

This visual dictionary "features more than 700 clearly labeled images of inanimate objects, food items and living things. A section called 'The Living Room' contains common items including a remote control, telephone and DVD player. . . . The artwork (and assorted reader-directed questions) will engage the curious." Publ Wkly

Seuss, Dr., 1904-1991

The **Cat** in the Hat beginner book dictionary; by the Cat himself and P. D. Eastman. Beginner Bks. 1964 133p il $21

Grades: K 1 2 3   **423**

1. Reference books 2. Picture dictionaries 3. English language -- Dictionaries

ISBN 0-394-81009-0; 978-0-394-91009-3

"This alphabetically arranged dictionary, illustrated with rollicking funny drawings, explains word meanings with sentences and pictures. It intends to help pre-schoolers 'recognize, remember, and really enjoy a basic vocabulary of 1,350 words.' Despite its age, this book will still appeal to young children." Peterson. Ref Books for Child. 4th edition

Terban, Marvin

Mad as a wet hen! and other funny idioms; illustrated by Giulio Maestro. Clarion Bks. 1987 64p il hardcover o.p. pa $7.95

Grades: 3 4 5   **423**

1. English language -- Idioms 2. English language --

Terms and phrases

ISBN 0-89919-479-6 pa

LC 86-17575

Illustrates and explains over 100 common English idioms, in categories including animals, body parts, and colors

"Maestro's two-color cartoonlike illustrations are amusing and informative themselves, providing visual clues that support the textual explanations. . . . Although some of the expressions included are dated, the alphabetical index enables teachers and librarians to pick and choose. This book might be particularly beneficial in schools having a large ESL program, especially for older, more advanced students." SLJ

Webster's New World children's dictionary; editor in chief, Michael Agnes. 2nd ed., rev.; Wiley Pub. 2006 928p il map $17.95

Grades: 3 4 5 6   **423**

1. Reference books 2. English language -- Dictionaries

ISBN 978-0-471-78688-7; 0-471-78688-8

LC 2005053750

First published 1991

This dictionary includes more than 33,000 entries, more than 800 notes and tips on synonyms, homonyms, prefixes, spelling, and word histories, over 750 photographs and illustrations, a thesaurus, an album of U.S. presidents, tables of weights and measures, an atlas of the world, and an album of U.S. states

"This dictionary is almost three reference books in one. . . . [It] is enjoyable to read and makes learning easy." Libr Media Connect

425   Grammar of standard English

Cleary, Brian P., 1959-

But and for, yet and nor; what is a conjunction? illustrated by Brian Gable. Millbrook Press 2010 31p il (Words are categorical) lib bdg $15.95

Grades: 2 3 4   **425**

1. English language -- Grammar

ISBN 978-0-8225-9153-5 lib bdg; 0-8225-9153-7 lib bdg

LC 2009015861

"This colorful book offers information about conjunctions and examples of how they work, all in easy-to-read rhymes. . . . The cartoon-style artwork depicts brightly colored, catlike creatures in human dress dramatizing a variety of situations. The high-energy illustrations rev up the comic intensity of the lightly humorous verse and promise to engage children in the subject." Booklist

Pre- and re-, mis- and dis; what is a prefix? by Brian P. Cleary; Illustrated by Martin Goneau. Millbrook Press 2013 31 p. (lib. bdg.: alk. paper) $16.95

Grades: 2 3 4   **425**

1. Word skills 2. English language -- Grammar 3. Language arts (Primary) 4. English language -- Suffixes and prefixes

ISBN 0761390316; 9780761390312

LC 2013001050

This book, by Brian P. Cleary and illustrated by Martin Goneau, is part of the Words are CATegorical series. It "presents the concept of prefixes for young readers. For easy identification, key prefixes appear in color and comical cats reinforce each idea. [It] turns traditional grammar lessons on end!." (Publisher's note)

Heller, Ruth

Fantastic! wow! and unreal! a book about interjections and conjunctions. written and illustrated by Ruth Heller. Grosset & Dunlap 1998 un il hardcover o.p. pa $7.99

Grades: K 1 2   **425**

1. English language -- Grammar

ISBN 0-448-41862-2; 0-698-11875-8 pa

LC 98-36361

Rhyming text and illustrations introduce and explain various interjections and conjunctions, including "awesome," "alas," and "yet."

Lawlor, Laurie

Muddy as a duck puddle and other American similes; illustrated by Ethan Long. Holiday House 2010 un il $16.95

Grades: 1 2 3   **425**

1. Simile

ISBN 978-0-8234-2229-6; 0-8234-2229-1

LC 2009-29944

"Sly and irreverent, the folk sayings collected here, one for each letter of the alphabet, stretch back over history and reflect Americans' restlessness. . . . For each letter, big, clear, brightly colored cartoons show the literal meaning in the imagery expressed in such phrases as 'crooked as a barrel of snakes,' as well as the words' sly double meanings. . . . Kids will relish the boisterous insults and ornery frontier references in both the words and the pictures." Booklist

427 Historical and geographic variations, modern nongeographic variations of English

O'Reilly, Gillian

Slangalicious; where we got that crazy lingo. text by Gillian O'Reilly; illustrations by Krista Johnson. Annick Press 2004 84p il $24.95; pa $12.95

Grades: 4 5 6 7   **427**

1. English language -- Slang 2. English language -- Etymology

ISBN 1-55037-765-5; 1-55037-764-7 pa

"This volume explores the origins and meanings of slang words by tracing the efforts of a fictional student doing an assignment. . . . After a general introduction to slang, succeeding chapters explore the colorful terminology used in the food industry, in different types of work, and in the world of sports. Also discussed are words used for money, musical terms, criminal jargon, and slang used during wartime and in different countries. . . . This is a clever way for younger students to learn about the topic. . . . Colorful, amusing illustrations appear throughout." SLJ

Includes bibliographical references

428 Standard English usage (Prescriptive linguistics)

Agee, Jon

Jon Agee's palindromania! Farrar, Straus & Giroux 2002 un il hardcover o.p. pa $6.96

Grades: 3 4 5 6   **428**

1. Palindromes

ISBN 0-374-35730-7; 0-374-40025-3 pa

LC 2002-101771

This "book on word play is a creative, comedic gem." Booklist

In this collection "the pages are filled with whimsical black-and-white drawings of absurd or nonsensical situations. Some of the approximately 170 palindromes are monologues, some are comic-strip stories, and others are simply descriptive situations. From 'How Palindromes Are Formed in the Atmosphere' to 'AIBOHPHOBIA: Unusual Fear of Palindromes.'" SLJ

Bacon, Pamela S.

100 + literacy lifesavers; a survival guide for librarians and teachers K-12. [by] Pamela S. Bacon and Tammy K. Bacon. Libraries Unlimited 2009 363p il pa $40

Grades: Adult Professional   **428**

1. Reading 2. Teaching teams

ISBN 978-1-59158-669-2 pa; 1-59158-669-0 pa

LC 2008-45514

"This wonderful professional resource's focus is mainly school librarians and teachers, but it could be used by public librarians to generate ideas for educational programs. . . . This book is an insightful tool that provides the skills and plans for successful collaboration and evaluation of literacy efforts between teachers and librarians." Voice Youth Advocates

Includes glossary and bibliographical references

Bruno, Elsa Knight

A **punctuation** celebration! illustrated by Jenny Whitehead. Henry Holt and Co. 2009 un il $17.95

Grades: 1 2 3 4   **428**

1. Punctuation

ISBN 978-0-8050-7973-9; 0-8050-7973-4

LC 2008018337

"Young readers will receive a better-than-average introduction to punctuation marks and their uses in this cheerfully illustrated collection of poems. Each selection presents an individual punctuation mark through rhyming verse. . . . Bruno's writing is clear and lively throughout. . . . Bright collages of children of various ethnicities engaged in diverse activities complement the text." SLJ

Budzik, Mary

Punctuation: the write stuff! [created by Basher; written by Mary Budzik] Kingfisher 2010 64p il (Basher basics) pa $7.99

Grades: 4 5 6 7   **428**

1. Punctuation

ISBN 978-0-7534-6420-5 pa; 0-7534-6420-9 pa

"This slim volume uses catchy graphic design and an informal narrative to spark interest in the subject. In a presentation reminiscent of manga and Saturday-morning cartoons, each punctuation mark is introduced as a unique character who conveys his job through chatty dialogue. . . . The book explains the various uses of each mark and some basics of sentence structure." SLJ

Includes glossary

Cleary, Brian P., 1959-
Cool! whoa! ah! and oh! what is an interjection? illustrated by Brian Gable. Millbrook Press 2010 32p il (Words are CATegorical) lib bdg $16.98
Grades: 2 3 4 **428**
1. English language -- Grammar
ISBN 978-1-58013-594-8 lib bdg; 1-58013-594-3 lib bdg

LC 2010026263

The "defines an interjection as a 'word or phrase spoken suddenly and used to show emotion,' then demonstrates its uses in a rhyming, rhythmic text. Throughout, the level of Cleary's inventive verbal humor is greatly magnified by Gable's madcap drawings of dressed animals dramatizing the sentences with cartoon-style exaggeration." Booklist

★ **Hairy,** scary, ordinary; what is an adjective? illustrated by Jenya Prosmitsky. Carolrhoda Bks. 2000 32p il (Words are categorical) hardcover o.p. $12.95
Grades: 2 3 4 **428**
1. English language -- Grammar
ISBN 1-57505-401-9; 1-57505-419-1 pa

LC 98-32132

"Descriptive words of many kinds are presented in bouncy, rhyming text. . . . The adjectives are colorfully highlighted and readers will see their function demonstrated in a wide variety of contexts. Little round cats and quirky humans, both with fat noses and wide eyes, humorously illustrate the meanings." SLJ

★ **How** much can a bare bear bear? what are homonyms and homophones? by Brian P. Cleary; illustrated by Brian Gable. Millbrook Press 2005 un il (Words are categorical) lib bdg $15.95
Grades: 2 3 4 **428**
1. English language -- Homonyms
ISBN 1-57505-824-3

LC 2004031106

"Through rhyming wordplay, Cleary explains two parts of speech that are often difficult to understand. . . . Gable took ample advantage of the pairings to create zany cartoons that provide visual clues for readers. The grouping of each set of homophones and homonyms by color is also a helpful tool." SLJ

Lazily, crazily, just a bit nasally; more about adverbs. by Brian P. Cleary; illustrations by Brian Gable. Millbrook Press 2008 31p il (Words are categorical) lib bdg $15.95
Grades: 2 3 4 **428**
1. English language -- Grammar
ISBN 978-0-8225-7848-2 lib bdg; 0-8225-7848-4 lib bdg

LC 2006033800

"A professorial feline opens this offbeat lecture with a definition of adverbs and a color-coded guide to the types found throughout the book. Readers are then drawn into another of Cleary's signature rhyming narratives, which tumbles across each page verbally and visually. . . . Knob-nosed felines done in a rainbow of colors mime numerous

examples of actions that can be performed with adverbial panache." SLJ

The **punctuation** station; illustrations by Joanne Lew-Vriethoff. Millbrook Press 2010 37p il lib bdg $16.95
Grades: K 1 2 3 **428**
1. Punctuation
ISBN 978-0-8225-7852-9 lib bdg; 0-8225-7852-2 lib bdg

LC 2009015860

"Perky rhymes, animal characters, and a chaotic train-station setting provide an entertaining introduction to seven oft-used punctuation marks: periods, commas, apostrophes, quotation marks, question marks, hyphens, and exclamation points. . . . . The young audience will enjoy learning the concepts as they pore over the details in the cheerful, wittily detailed cartoon art." Booklist

Quirky, jerky, extra-perky; more about adjectives. by Brian P. Cleary; illustrations by Brian Gable. Millbrook Press 2007 30p il (Words are categorical) lib bdg $15.95
Grades: 2 3 4 **428**
1. English language -- Grammar
ISBN 978-0-8225-6709-7 lib bdg; 0-8225-6709-1 lib bdg

LC 2006010756

"Cleary offers more examples of the descriptive words in this upbeat, energetically illustrated book. Beginning with a straightforward definition of the word adjective, Cleary takes off with a series of imaginative examples presented in rhythmic, rhyming verses. . . . Colorful, comical, cartoon-style illustrations help create the madcap quality that distinguishes the series." Booklist

Stop and go, yes and no; what is an antonym? by Brian P. Cleary; illustrations by Brian Gable. Millbrook Press 2006 un il (Words are categorical) lib bdg $15.95
Grades: 2 3 4 **428**
1. Opposites 2. English language -- Synonyms and antonyms
ISBN 978-1-57505-860-3 lib bdg; 1-57505-860-X lib bdg

LC 2005013991

"Cleary describes and illustrates antonyms from the obvious stop and go, yes and no, front and back, fast and slow, to the more obscure: excite and soothe, hefty and diminutive. He elaborates on reasons for celebrating opposites and also describes how to create them through the use of powerful prefixes such as un, dis, im, and non. . . . The bouncy lettering style enhances the whimsical rhymes and makes for yet another strong addition to collections of books about the English language." SLJ

Stroll and walk, babble and talk; more about synonyms. by Brian P. Cleary; illustrated by Brian Gable. Millbrook Press 2008 31p il (Words are categorical) lib bdg $15.95
Grades: 2 3 4 **428**
1. English language -- Synonyms and antonyms
ISBN 978-0-8225-7850-5 lib bdg; 0-8225-7850-6 lib bdg

LC 2007040360

This book "shows the fun of words with light nonsense rhymes and color cartoons of animal characters that brag and boast, lie and deceive.... With all the slapstick fun, the pages show and tell about shades of meaning and the importance of choosing just the right word." Booklist

Edwards, Wallace

The **cat's** pajamas. Kids Can Press 2010 un il $18.95

Grades: 3 4 5   **428**

1. English language -- Idioms

ISBN 978-1-55453-308-4; 1-55453-308-2

"Edwards begins this picture book with a definition of 'idiom,' and English teachers will thrill to find a book that deals with this elusive idea.... Edwards's illustrations show the literal meaning, which is effective in its own way.... A list of the real meanings is provided at the end of the book. The illustrations are handsome and detailed, which adds to the ridiculous nature of the literal interpretations. This is a useful book to introduce this figure of speech." SLJ

Fuhrken, Charles

What every middle school teacher needs to know about reading tests (from someone who has written them) Charles Fuhrken. Stenhouse Publishers 2012 vii, 237 p.p ill. (pbk.: alk. paper) $24

Grades: Professional   **428**

1. Achievement tests 2. Examinations -- Study guides 3. Educational tests and measurements 4. Reading (Middle school) -- Ability testing

ISBN 1571108858; 1571109455; 9781571108852; 9781571109453

LC 2011037287

This book's author, "Charles Furhrken, has spent years working with several major testing companies and contributing to the reading assessments of various testing programs." He "offers . . . strategies to help students perform well on test day." Particular focus is given to "information about reading tests, including . . . preparation materials, samples of the most frequently assessed reading standards, and . . . core-reading activities." (Publisher's note)

Includes bibliographical references and index.

Heinrichs, Ann

Adjectives; illustrated by Dan McGeehan and David Moore. The Child's World 2011 24p il (Language rules!) lib bdg $27.07

Grades: 2 3 4   **428**

1. English language -- Grammar

ISBN 978-1-60253-425-4; 1-60253-425-X

LC 2010011445

This explains the ways adjectives work in reading, writing, and speaking.

This "tackles the usually humdrum mechanics of grammar using fun examples, silly sentences, and cute little monster artwork.... Through humor and clear and concise examples the sometimes mysterious world of grammar becomes so much easier to understand. Illustrations complement the text well, with silly characters in bright and lively colors speaking sentences using the parts of speech." Libr Media Connect

Includes glossary and bibliographical references

Adverbs; illustrated by Dan McGeehan and David Moore. The Child's World 2011 24p il (Language rules!) lib bdg $27.07

Grades: 2 3 4   **428**

1. English language -- Grammar

ISBN 978-1-60253-426-1; 1-60253-426-8

LC 2010011456

This explains the ways adverbs work in reading, writing, and speaking.

This "tackles the usually humdrum mechanics of grammar using fun examples, silly sentences, and cute little monster artwork.... Through humor and clear and concise examples the sometimes mysterious world of grammar becomes so much easier to understand. Illustrations complement the text well, with silly characters in bright and lively colors speaking sentences using the parts of speech." Libr Media Connect

Includes glossary and bibliographical references

Interjections; written by Ann Heinrichs; illustrated by Dan McGeehan and David Moore. Child's World 2010 24p il (Language rules!) lib bdg $27.07

Grades: 2 3 4   **428**

1. English language -- Grammar

ISBN 978-1-60253-428-5 lib bdg; 1-60253-428-4 lib bdg

LC 2010011458

This explains the ways interjections work in reading, writing, and speaking.

The book is "well organized and attractive, and [injects] humor into what might overwise be [a] fairly dry [subject]. . . . The brightly colored cartoon illustrations are amusing and clearly demonstrate . . . [the] part of speech . . . being explored. A purple-and-green monster levitates off his chair after spotting a mouse beneath it in Interjections —'Eek!.'" SLJ

Includes bibliographical references

Nouns; illustrated by Dan McGeehan and David Moore. Child's World 2011 24p il (Language rules!) lib bdg $27.07

Grades: 2 3 4   **428**

1. English language -- Grammar

ISBN 978-1-60253-429-2; 1-60253-429-2

LC 2010011459

This explains the ways nouns work in reading, writing, and speaking.

This "tackles the usually humdrum mechanics of grammar using fun examples, silly sentences, and cute little monster artwork.... Through humor and clear and concise examples the sometimes mysterious world of grammar becomes so much easier to understand. Illustrations complement the text well, with silly characters in bright and lively colors speaking sentences using the parts of speech." Libr Media Connect

Includes glossary and bibliographical references

Prefixes and suffixes; written by Ann Heinrichs; illustrated by Dan McGeehan and David Moore. Child's World 2010 24p il (Language rules!) lib bdg $27.07

Grades: 2 3 4   **428**

1. English language -- Grammar

ISBN 978-1-60253-430-8 lib bdg; 1-60253-430-6 lib bdg

LC 2010012343

This explains the ways prefixes and suffixes work in reading, writing, and speaking.

The book is "well organized and attractive, and [injects] humor into what might otherwise be [a] fairly dry [subject]. . . . The brightly colored cartoon illustrations are amusing and clearly demonstrate [prefixes and suffixes]." SLJ

Includes bibliographical references

Prepositions; written by Ann Heinrichs; illustrated by Dan McGeehan and David Moore. Child's World 2010 24p il (Language rules!) lib bdg $27.07
Grades: 2 3 4   **428**
1. English language -- Grammar
ISBN 978-1-60253-431-5 lib bdg; 1-60253-431-4
lib bdg

LC 2010011460

This explains the ways prepositions work in reading, writing, and speaking.

The book is "well organized and attractive, and [injects] humor into what might otherwise be [a] fairly dry subject. . . . The brightly colored cartoon illustrations are amusing and clearly demonstrate [prepositions]." SLJ

Includes bibliographical references

Pronouns; illustrated by Dan McGeehan and David Moore. The Child's World 2011 24p il (Language rules!) lib bdg $27.07
Grades: 2 3 4   **428**
1. English language -- Grammar
ISBN 978-1-60253-432-2; 1-60253-432-2

LC 2010011461

This explains the ways pronouns work in reading, writing, and speaking.

This "tackles the usually humdrum mechanics of grammar using fun examples, silly sentences, and cute little monster artwork. . . . Through humor and clear and concise examples the sometimes mysterious world of grammar becomes so much easier to understand. Illustrations complement the text well, with silly characters in bright and lively colors speaking sentences using the parts of speech." Libr Media Connect

Includes glossary and bibliographical references

Punctuation; illustrated by Dan McGeehan and David Moore. The Child's World 2011 24p il (Language rules!) lib bdg $27.07
Grades: 2 3 4   **428**
1. English language -- Grammar
ISBN 978-1-60253-433-9; 1-60253-433-0

LC 2010012344

This explains the proper use of punctuation and why it's important.

This "tackles the usually humdrum mechanics of grammar using fun examples, silly sentences, and cute little monster artwork. . . . Through humor and clear and concise examples the sometimes mysterious world of grammar becomes so much easier to understand. Illustrations complement the text well, with silly characters in bright and lively colors speaking sentences using the parts of speech." Libr Media Connect

Includes glossary and bibliographical references

Similes and metaphors; written by Ann Heinrichs; illustrated by Dan McGeehan and David Moore. Child's World 2010 24p il (Language rules!) lib bdg $27.07
Grades: 2 3 4   **428**
1. Simile 2. Metaphor
ISBN 978-1-60253-434-6 lib bdg; 1-60253-434-9
lib bdg

LC 2010012346

This explains the ways similes and metaphors work in reading, writing, and speaking.

The book is "well organized and attractive, and [injects] humor into what might otherwise be [a] fairly dry subject. . . . The brightly colored cartoon illustrations are amusing and clearly demonstrate [similes and metaphors]." SLJ

Includes bibliographical references

Synonyms and antonyms; illustrated by Dan McGeehan and David Moore. The Child's World 2011 24p il (Language rules!) lib bdg $27.07
Grades: 2 3 4   **428**
1. English language -- Synonyms and antonyms
ISBN 978-1-60253-435-3; 1-60253-435-7

LC 2010012347

This explains the ways synonyms and antonyms work in reading, writing, and speaking.

This "tackles the usually humdrum mechanics of grammar using fun examples, silly sentences, and cute little monster artwork. . . . Through humor and clear and concise examples the sometimes mysterious world of grammar becomes so much easier to understand. Illustrations complement the text well, with silly characters in bright and lively colors speaking sentences using the parts of speech." Libr Media Connect

Includes glossary and bibliographical references

Verbs; illustrated by Dan McGeehan and David Moore. The Child's World 2011 24p il (Language rules!) lib bdg $27.07
Grades: 2 3 4   **428**
1. English language -- Grammar
ISBN 978-1-60253-436-0; 1-60253-436-5

LC 2010011462

This explains the ways verbs work in reading, writing, and speaking.

This "tackles the usually humdrum mechanics of grammar using fun examples, silly sentences, and cute little monster artwork. . . . Through humor and clear and concise examples the sometimes mysterious world of grammar becomes so much easier to understand. Illustrations complement the text well, with silly characters in bright and lively colors speaking sentences using the parts of speech." Libr Media Connect

Includes glossary and bibliographical references

Heller, Ruth
Behind the mask; a book about prepositions. written and illustrated by Ruth Heller. Grosset & Dunlap 1995 un il hardcover o.p. pa $7.99
Grades: K 1 2   **428**
1. English language -- Grammar
ISBN 0-448-41123-7; 0-698-11698-4 pa

LC 95-9535

Explores through rhyming text the subject of prepositions and how they're used

"Large, colorful drawings illustrate the words imaginatively." Booklist

A **cache** of jewels and other collective nouns; written and illustrated by Ruth Heller. Grosset & Dunlap 1987 un il hardcover o.p. pa $7.99
Grades: K 1 2   428
1. English language -- Grammar
ISBN 0-448-19211-X; 0-698-11354-3 pa
LC 87-80254

"In light verse and brightly colored pictures, Heller provides an introduction to a specialized part of speech, the collective noun. She lists and depicts more than 25, including such familiar terms as 'batch of bread' and 'bunch of bananas,' as well as more unusual phrases. . . . The concept will stimulate the curiosity and imaginations of children with an ear for language. The illustrations, containing large, bold objects in simple yet striking compositions, ensure a visually inspiring exploration as well." Publ Wkly

Kites sail high: a book about verbs; written and illustrated by Ruth Heller. Grosset & Dunlap 1988 un il hardcover o.p. pa $7.99
Grades: K 1 2   428
1. English language -- Grammar
ISBN 0-448-10480-6; 0-698-11389-6 pa
LC 87-82718

This "book explicates and celebrates verbs of all kinds, in ebullient verses which themselves sail and soar. . . . The verses are accompanied by bold, gaily colored graphics that are especially striking for their skillful use of pattern and design." Publ Wkly

Many luscious lollipops: a book about adjectives; written and illustrated by Ruth Heller. Grosset & Dunlap 1989 un il hardcover o.p. pa $7.99
Grades: K 1 2   428
1. English language -- Grammar
ISBN 0-448-03151-5; 0-698-11641-0 pa
LC 88-83045

"The text begins: 'An adjective's terrific/when you want to be specific/It easily identifies/by number, color or by size/ TWELVE LARGE, BLUE, GORGEOUS butterflies.' And there they are, blue and yellow, filling a double-page spread. . . . There is great diversity and technical brilliance in the art work, and the text has rhyme, rhythm, humor, and a very clear presentation of the concepts of different kinds of adjectives and what they do." Bull Cent Child Books

Merry-go-round; a book about nouns. written and illustrated by Ruth Heller. Grosset & Dunlap 1990 un il hardcover o.p. pa $7.99
Grades: K 1 2   428
1. English language -- Grammar
ISBN 0-448-40085-5; 0-698-11642-9 pa
LC 90-80645

Rhyming text and illustrations present explanations of various types of nouns and rules for their usage

"While the text will be helpful to children struggling with noun usage, the large, bountiful illustrations will appeal to everyone." Horn Book Guide

Mine, all mine; a book about pronouns. written and illustrated by Ruth Heller. Grosset & Dunlap 1997 un il hardcover o.p. pa $7.99
Grades: K 1 2   428
1. English language -- Grammar
ISBN 0-448-41606-9; 0-698-11797-2 pa
LC 97-10051

Introduces various types of pronouns, explains how and when to use them, and provides whimsical glimpses of what our language would be without them

"Heller has taken a part of speech and made its function perfectly and entertainingly clear. . . . The stylishly drawn, brilliantly colored, double-paged illustrations grab readers and don't let go. The exceptionally fluent, rhythmic text is printed in an unobtrusive font with pronouns highlighted in bright blue." SLJ

Up, up and away; a book about adverbs. written and illustrated by Ruth Heller. Grosset & Dunlap 1991 un il hardcover o.p. pa $7.99
Grades: K 1 2   428
1. English language -- Grammar
ISBN 0-448-40249-1; 0-698-11663-1 pa
LC 91-70668

"Here the author explains concisely how adverbs answer precisely the questions of How? How often? When? and Where? The adverbs, in capital letters, stand out boldly and cannot be missed. . . . In the large, appealing illustrations, her penguins stand proudly, her pandas eat daintily, and her cat stares piercingly. . . . The cheerful volume . . . offers a clever introduction to kinds of words." Booklist

Hellweg, Paul
★ The **American** Heritage student thesaurus; Paul Hellweg, Joyce LeBaron, Susannah LeBaron. Houghton Mifflin Harcourt 2012 vi, 378 p.p $18.95
Grades: 5 6 7 8 9 10   428
1. Vocabulary 2. English language -- Synonyms and antonyms
ISBN 0547659164; 9780547659169
LC 2012462955

This newly updated student thesaurus "includes advice to teen writers about choosing the best word for their purpose, how synonyms are presented in the text, and the use of other words like antonyms. . . . Pages are large, with the entry word in a blue sans-serif type, while the synonyms appear in a smaller black boldface type. An even smaller type is used for each explanatory sentence, followed by antonyms (marked with a blue arrow) where appropriate." (Children's Literature)

Hoban, Tana
★ **Exactly** the opposite. Greenwillow Bks. 1990 un il $17.99; pa $6.99
Grades: PreK K   428
1. English language -- Synonyms and antonyms
ISBN 0-688-08861-9; 0-688-15473-5 pa
LC 89-27227

"Using a variety of people, animals, and objects found in outdoor settings of both the city and the country, [the author] introduces and expands on the concept of opposites in this wordless photographic book. The photographs are clear, bright, and enticing. Pairs of opposites are presented on facing pages." SLJ

Jenkins, Emily

Small, medium, large; a book about relative sizes. illustrated by Tomek Bogacki. Star Bright Books 2011 un il $19.95

Grades: PreK K 1 **428**

1. Size 2. Vocabulary

ISBN 978-1-59572-278-2; 1-59572-278-5

LC 2010050853

"Four colorful mouselike beings of varied sizes represent the concepts of small, medium, large, and extra large in bold, posterlike spreads rendered in black line and swathes of thick, textured paints. Similar characters, larger and smaller, join the original four to expand the notion of size at both ends of the scale (e.g., 'huge,' 'enormous,' 'colossal'; and 'tiny,' 'minuscule,' and 'itty-bitty' and demonstrate how many smaller sizes can stack up to equal one 'colossal' size in a splendid, culminating vertical gatefold. . . . The generous trim size, large font, simple ideas, and eye-popping shapes and colors add up to a cheerful concept book ideal for sharing with a group of young children or as a lapsit." SLJ

L is for lollygag; quirky words for a clever tongue. Chronicle Books 2008 125p $12.99

Grades: 4 5 6 7 **428**

1. Vocabulary

ISBN 978-0-8118-6021-5; 0-8118-6021-3

LC 2007021061

"Budding and accomplished wordsmiths will delight in this specialized dictionary showcasing oft-overlooked gems of the English language. . . . Each definition is related with humor, sometimes including word origination and listing equally interesting synonyms. . . . Black-and-white engravings juxtaposed with cartoons in Picassoesque profile give an old-fashioned yet offbeat air to this unusual compendium." SLJ

Includes bibliographical references

Leedy, Loreen

There's a frog in my throat; 440 animal sayings a little bird told me. written by Loreen Leedy & Pat Street; illustrated by Loreen Leedy. Holiday House 2003 48p il $16.95

Grades: 2 3 4 5 **428**

1. Animals -- Folklore 2. English language -- Terms and phrases

ISBN 0-8234-1774-3

LC 2002-68920

"The sayings are loosely grouped by types of animals—domestic, barnyard, winged, etc.—and each adage is accompanied by a short definition. For example, 'It's raining cats and dogs. It's raining hard.' . . . Children will pore over the pages. The collaboration of text and art makes the volume lively and humorous." SLJ

Moses, Will

Raining cats and dogs; [by] Will Moses. Philomel Books 2008 un il $17.99

Grades: 1 2 3 4 5 **428**

1. English language -- Idioms

ISBN 978-0-399-24233-5; 0-399-24233-3

LC 2008-10339

"In this highly appropriate pairing of folk art and sayings, Moses explains many common idioms. A colorful definition . . . a sample sentence, and one of Moses's old-fashioned Americana-style oil paintings accompany each phrase. The lesson is kept lighthearted through examples that play upon the literal meanings of each phrase, often to comedic effect." SLJ

National Geographic Society (U.S.)

Word book; learning the words in your world. National Geographic 2011 64p il (National Geographic little kids) $15.95; lib bdg $23.99

Grades: PreK **428**

1. Vocabulary

ISBN 978-1-4263-0789-8; 1-4263-0789-6; 978-1-4263-0790-4 lib bdg; 1-4263-0790-X lib bdg

LC 2010049462

Presents hundreds of words with images representing each word, grouped together by such themes as shapes, food, games, pets, music, and seasons.

"Small, clearly labeled photos set against single-colored squares enhance the easy-to-follow design." Horn Book Guide

O'Conner, Patricia T.

Woe is I Jr; the junior grammarphobes' guide to better English in plain English. [by] Patricia O'Conner; drawings by Tom Stiglich. G.P. Putnam's Sons 2007 152p il $16.99

Grades: 4 5 6 7 8 **428**

1. English language -- Usage 2. English language -- Grammar

ISBN 978-0-399-24331-8

LC 2006020575

An adaptation of Woe is I, published 2003 for adults by Riverhead Books

The author "covers pronouns, plurals, possessives, verb usage, subject-verb agreement, capitalization, and punctuation with jargon-free explanations and entertaining examples. . . . She knows her subject, can convey her message with wit and ease, and does it all in a compact, easy-to-read format." SLJ

Reid, Alastair

Ounce, dice, trice; drawings by Ben Shahn. New York Review Books 2009 57p il $15.95

Grades: K 1 2 3 **428**

1. Vocabulary 2. Wit and humor

ISBN 978-1-59017-320-6; 1-59017-320-1

LC 2008050325

A reissue of the title first published 1958 by Atlantic-Little

"'Words have a sound and shape, in addition to their meanings. Sometimes the sound is the meaning.' This 'odd collection of words and names' includes 'light words' (lissom, sibilant), 'heavy words' (befuddled), and other fascinating categories. The author's poetic lists have been turned into picture-and-word amusement through collaboration with an illustrator whose Lear-like sketches have originality, joy, and absurdity." Horn Book Guide

Roy, Jennifer Rozines

You can write using good grammar; [by] Jennifer Rozines Roy. Enslow 2004 64p il (You can write) lib bdg $22.60

Grades: 4 5 6 **428**
1. English language -- Grammar
ISBN 0-7660-2084-3

LC 2002-156035

This "discusses parts of speech, punctuation, and proof-reading. A list of 'Common Grammar Goofs' is appended. . . . Students will find [this book] useful." Horn Book Guide
Includes glossary and bibliographical references

Terban, Marvin
★ **Scholastic** dictionary of spelling; rev ed; Scholastic Reference 2006 272p il pa $9.99
Grades: 4 5 6 **428**
1. Spellers 2. Reference books
ISBN 978-0-439-76421-6; 0-439-76421-1
First published 1998

This spelling dictionary gives instructions for looking up a word the reader does not know how to spell, offers more than 150 memory tricks to correct commonly misspelled words, explains general spelling rules and their exceptions, and includes sections such as "The Four Longest Words in the English Language" and "The Spelling Words That Made Kids Champions." To aid pronunciation, each word is divided into syllables with the accented syllable in boldface.

Scholastic guide to grammar; [by] Marvin Terban as Professor Grammar. Scholastic Inc. 2011 255p il pa $9.99
Grades: 4 5 6 7 **428**
1. English language -- Grammar
ISBN 978-0-545-35669-5; 0-545-35669-5

This guide to English language grammar covers the parts of speech, sentences and paragraphs, spelling, capitalization, punctuation, communicating ideas through vocabulary, homonyms, homophones, homographs, figures of speech, alliteration, hyperbole, similes, personification, and idioms, and includes a thesaurus.

Truss, Lynne
Eats, shoots & leaves; why, commas really do make a difference! illustrated by Bonnie Timmons. G.P. Putnam's Sons 2006 un il $15.99
Grades: 2 3 4 **428**
1. Punctuation
ISBN 0-399-24491-3

LC 2005-28559

This version of Truss's work on punctuation is intended for children. It includes only the section on comma usage. "Primary." (Horn Book)

"Truss's picture-book version of her adult bestseller tackles the topic of commas and what can go wrong when they are misused. . . . Versions of two identically worded sentences are presented side by side, demonstrating the difference in meaning achieved when a comma is added or subtracted. Timmons's humorous watercolor cartoons bring the point home." SLJ

The **girl's** like spaghetti; why, you can't manage without apostrophes! illustrated by Bonnie Timmons. G. P. Putnam's Sons 2007 un il $16.99
Grades: 2 3 4 **428**
1. Punctuation
ISBN 978-0-399-24706-4; 0-399-24706-8

LC 2006-34456

This is a guide to the use of the apostrophe. "Age six and up." (N Y Times Book Rev)

"This book presents readers with two identical sentences whose meaning changes with the simple placement of the apostrophe. The plural versus the possessive is depicted through lively cartoons illustrating the sentences. Truss . . . manages to keep her lessons funny and full of kid appeal." SLJ

Twenty-odd ducks; why, every punctuation mark counts! [by] Lynne Truss; illustrated by Bonnie Timmons. G.P. Putman's Sons 2008 un il $16.99
Grades: 2 3 4 **428**
1. Punctuation
ISBN 978-0-399-25058-3; 0-399-25058-1

LC 2007045386

This "emphasizes the importance of punctuation in general. Truss . . . makes the case that careless application can dramatically change one's meaning. To prove her point, she provides contrasting examples of the same sentence, punctuated in different ways. Timmons's charming watercolors make the change in meaning clearer." SLJ

428.1   Vocabulary – English language -- usage

Cleary, Brian P., 1959-
Breezier, cheesier, newest, and bluest; what are comparatives and superlatives? by Brian P. Cleary; illustrations by Brian Gable. Millbrook Press 2013 31 p. col. ill. (Words are CATegorical) (reinforced) $16.95
Grades: 2 3 4 **428.1**
1. Picture books for children 2. English language -- Grammar 3. Comparison (Grammar) 4. Grammar, comparative and general -- Adjective
ISBN 0761353623; 9780761353621

LC 2012019105

This book is part of the Words Are CATegorical series and "presents a quick grammar lesson through a fast-paced, rhyming text and . . . cartoon-style illustrations. The introductory page defines (in prose) the terms 'comparatives' and 'superlatives.' An appended page tells (in prose) how to form comparative and superlative adjectives. And in between come the rhyming verses, briefly explaining these parts of speech and providing . . . many examples." (Booklist)

Escoffier, Michael
Take away the A; by Michaël Escoffier; illustrated by Kris Di Giacomo. Enchanted Lion Books 2014 56 p. color illustrations (alk. paper) $17.95
Grades: 2 3 4 5 **428.1**
1. Alphabet 2. Vocabulary 3. Wit and humor 4. Plays on words 5. Grammar, Comparative and general -- Word formation
ISBN 1592701566; 9781592701568

LC 2014014890

This juvenile book, by Michaël Escoffier and illustrated by Kris Di Giacomo "is a . . . romp through the alphabet. The idea behind the book is that within every language there are words that change and become a different word through the simple subtraction of a single letter. In other words, without the 'A,' the Beast is Best. Or, without the 'M,' a chomp becomes a chop." (Publisher's note)

"Amid the flood of alphabet books, now and then one rises to the surface. This one is a prize catch. In a distinctive, refreshing approach, the text takes a word and subtracts one letter, turning it into a different word. "Without the A / the BEAST is the BEST." The stylized illustration on the double-page spread gives form to the concept by depicting a photographer (a buzzard) focusing on the winners of a competition . . . Altogether, the fascinating illustrations, crafty composition and tall format give the book real flair. Without a doubt, these inventive images are imaginative and engaging—chock full of inspiration for kids to try their own wordplay and a boon to teachers." Kirkus

Könnecke, Ole

The **big** book of words and pictures; Ole Könnecke; translated by Monika Smith. Gecko Press 2012 22 p. $14.95
Grades: K 1   **428.1**
1. Children's literature 2. Picture books for children 3. Vocabulary
ISBN 187757905X; 9781877579059

This children's picture book, written and illustrated by Ole Konnecke, "is a large format board book of early concept words and pictures. . . ." multiple vocabulary words and their contextual concepts are demonstrated by illustrated scenarios with animals and people, each with their own simple story to tell. (Publisher's note)

430   German and related languages

Hettinga, Donald R.

The **Brothers** Grimm; two lives, one legacy. Clarion Bks. 2001 180p il $22
Grades: 5 6 7 8   **430**
1. Authors 2. Folklorists 3. Philologists 4. Folklore -- Germany 5. Short story writers
ISBN 0-618-05599-1
LC 00-65598

A biography of the brothers famous for collecting German folk tales

"No book for young readers presents the Grimms' intertwined lives against the larger background of early 19th-century Europe in such fascinating detail as this absorbing new biography. . . . Students will find it an excellent resource for term papers, yet it is written so clearly that it makes for enjoyable pleasure reading." SLJ

Includes bibliographical references

433   Dictionaries of standard German

Kudela, Katy R.

My first book of German words. Capstone Press 2010 32p il (A+ books: bilingual picture dictionaries) lib bdg $25.99
Grades: K 1 2 3   **433**
1. German language 2. Picture dictionaries
ISBN 978-1-4296-3296-6; 1-4296-3296-8
LC 2009005516

Simple text paired with themed photos invite the reader to learn German vocabulary and phrases.

"Ideal for children encountering multicultural friends at school and at play. . . . [This] makes simple language exchanges fun and easy. . . . The pictures are full-bleed and have the brilliant, bright look of a catalogue. . . . [This] makes for good kindergarten ready reference." Booklist

Includes bibliographical references

439   Other Germanic languages

Sussman, Joni Kibort

My first Yiddish word book; edited by Joni Kibort Sussman; pictures by Pepi Marzel. Kar-Ben Pub. 2008 32p il $17.95
Grades: K 1 2   **439**
1. Reference books 2. Yiddish language 3. Picture dictionaries
ISBN 978-0-8225-8755-2
LC 2007028347

"With this [Yiddish] picture dictionary, select vocabulary is accessible to young readers. Basic words for parts of the body, members of the family, clothing, the house, school, playground, city, grocery store, bedtime, the zoo, colors, etc., are included. All are written in block letters with English transliteration and translation. Each spread includes a large, detailed illustration with the individual items clearly identified along the bottom. The pictures are cheerful and contemporary." SLJ

443   Dictionaries of standard French

Corbeil, Jean-Claude

★ My first French English visual dictionary; [by] Jean-Claude Corbeil; Ariane Archambault. Firefly Books 2006 80p il $14.95
Grades: 3 4 5 6   **443**
1. Reference books 2. Picture dictionaries 3. French language -- Dictionaries
ISBN 978-1-55407-193-7; 1-55407-193-3

"There are 36 themes-among them 'Clothing,' 'Colors and Shapes,' 'Dinosaurs,' 'Space,' and 'Sports' selected to appeal to primary-age children. Each theme has a double-page spread of small to medium-sized individual illustrations of items allied to the theme. The other 1,300 illustrations are large and in full color and are accompanied by the English word in boldface letters with the word in the other language underneath. The typeface is large and uncluttered and easy to see. . . . Separate English and French indexes complete the book." Booklist

Kudela, Katy R.

My first book of French words; translator, Translations. com. Capstone Press 2009 32p il (A+ books: bilingual picture dictionaries) lib bdg $23.99
Grades: K 1 2 3   **443**
1. Picture dictionaries 2. French language -- Dictionaries
ISBN 978-1-4296-3295-9 lib bdg; 1-4296-3295-X lib bdg
LC 2009005510

"This simple bilingual picture dictionary is illustrated with attractive, colorful photos. Each themed spread introduces 10 words, first in English and then in French, followed by the approximate French pronunciation. . . . The 130 words cover family, body parts, clothes, toys, bedroom, bathroom, kitchen, food, farm, garden, colors, classroom, city, numbers, and useful phrases. . . . Overall, this book is appealing, useful, and easy to comprehend." SLJ

Includes bibliographical references

463 Dictionaries of standard Spanish

Corbeil, Jean-Claude

★ My first Spanish English visual dictionary; [by] Jean-Claude Corbeil; Ariane Archambault. Firefly Books 2006 80p il $14.95

Grades: 3 4 5 6   **463**

1. Reference books 2. Picture dictionaries 3. Spanish language -- Dictionaries

ISBN 978-1-55407-194-4; 1-55407-194-1

A Spanish/English visual dictionary for children: 1,600 terms annotate 1,300 realistic illustrations organized in 36 themes that children experience in their lives. Two indexes, by language, and Spanish terms include gender.

Kudela, Katy R.

My first book of Spanish words. Capstone Press 2009 32p il (A+ books: bilingual picture dictionaries) lib bdg $23.99

Grades: K 1 2 3   **463**

1. Picture dictionaries 2. Spanish language -- Dictionaries

ISBN 978-1-4296-3298-0 lib bdg; 1-4296-3298-4 lib bdg

LC 2009005518

This picture dictionary introduces common Spanish words with color photos.

Includes bibliographical references

492.4 Hebrew

Groner, Judyth Saypol

My first Hebrew word book; [by Judye Groner and Madeline Wikler]; pictures by Pepi Marzel. Kar-Ben Pub. 2005 32p il lib bdg $17.95

Grades: K 1 2   **492.4**

1. Hebrew language 2. Reference books 3. Picture dictionaries

ISBN 1-58013-126-3

LC 2004-13504

"Basic Hebrew words . . . are included. All are written in block letters with English transliteration and translation. Each spread includes a large, detailed illustration with the individual items clearly identified along the bottom. The color cartoon art is cheerful and contemporary. At the back of the book, a word list is organized alphabetically in English and includes the Hebrew words and corresponding page numbers. All in all, this is a wonderful resource." SLJ

493 Non-Semitic Afro-Asiatic languages

Giblin, James

★ The **riddle** of the Rosetta Stone; key to ancient Egypt. [by] James Cross Giblin. Crowell 1990 85p il hardcover o.p. pa $7.99

Grades: 5 6 7 8   **493**

1. Hieroglyphics 2. Rosetta stone 3. Egyptian language

ISBN 0-06-446137-8 pa

LC 89-29289

Describes how the discovery and deciphering of the Rosetta Stone unlocked the secret of Egyptian hieroglyphics

"Suspense keeps the reader glued to this fine piece of nonfiction as the mystery of hieroglyphs is slowly unraveled. . . . The author has done a masterful job of distilling information, citing the highlights, and fitting it all together in an interesting and enlightening look at a puzzling subject." Horn Book

Includes bibliographical references

495.1 Chinese

Kudela, Katy R.

My first book of Mandarin Chinese words. Capstone Press 2010 32p il (A+ books: bilingual picture dictionaries) lib bdg $25.99

Grades: K 1 2 3   **495.1**

1. Chinese language 2. Picture dictionaries

ISBN 978-1-4296-3297-3; 1-4296-3297-6

LC 2009005517

Simple text paired with themed photos invite the reader to learn Mandarin Chinese vocabulary and phrases.

"Ideal for children encountering multicultural friends at school and at play. . . . [This] makes simple language exchanges fun and easy. . . . The pictures are full-bleed and have the brilliant, bright look of a catalogue. . . . [This] makes for good kindergarten ready reference." Booklist

Includes bibliographical references

Lee, Huy Voun

1, 2, 3 go! Holt & Co. 2000 un il $17.95

Grades: K 1 2 3   **495.1**

1. Counting 2. Chinese language

ISBN 0-8050-6205-X

LC 99-48326

An introduction to Chinese writing describing the construction, meaning, and pronunciation of simple characters used for a variety of words and the numbers one through ten

"Lee effectively displays boldly contrasted cut-paper shapes on stark white backgrounds. . . . With masterful simplicity, Lee leads readers to a preliminary appreciation of Chinese culture." Booklist

At the beach; written and illustrated by Huy Voun Lee. Holt & Co. 1994 un il hardcover o.p. pa $7.95

Grades: K 1 2 3   **495.1**

1. Chinese language

ISBN 0-8050-2768-8; 0-8050-5822-2 pa

LC 93-25462

A mother amuses her young son at the beach by drawing in the sand Chinese characters, many of which resemble the objects they stand for

"The intricate, visually captivating cut-paper collages have borders with sea motifs. Useful for beginning language study and interesting due to its artistic innovation, the book includes a pronunciation guide." Horn Book Guide

Other titles in this series are:

In the leaves (2005)

In the park (1998)

In the snow (1995)

495.6   Japanese

Kudela, Katy R.

My first book of Japanese words. Capstone Press 2010 32p il (A+ books: bilingual picture dictionaries) lib bdg $25.99

Grades: K 1 2 3   **495.6**

1. Japanese language 2. Picture dictionaries

ISBN 978-1-4296-3916-3; 1-4296-3916-4

LC 2009028665

Simple text paired with themed photos invite the reader to learn Japanese vocabulary and phrases.

"Ideal for children encountering multicultural friends at school and at play. . . . [This] makes simple language exchanges fun and easy. . . . The pictures are full-bleed and have the brilliant, bright look of a catalogue. . . . [This] makes for good kindergarten ready reference." Booklist

Includes bibliographical references

500   SCIENCE

500   Natural sciences and mathematics

★ The **big** idea science book; incredible concepts that show how science works in the real world. editor, Matilda Gollon; consultant, Lisa Burke. DK Pub. 2010 304p il $29.99

Grades: 4 5 6 7   **500**

1. Science

ISBN 978-0-7566-6287-5; 0-7566-6287-7

LC 2010-281143

"Aimed at grabbing readers' general interest in science, this lively overview is split into sections on life, earth, and physical science; within each category, specific subjects are plainly labeled for easy reference. . . . Full-color photographs, drawings, and diagrams further inform, and readers can visit an interactive Web site for more exploration. For breadth of material and clarity, it's hard to beat." Publ Wkly

Bryson, Bill

A **really** short history of nearly everything. Delacorte Press 2009 169p il $19.99

Grades: 4 5 6 7   **500**

1. Science

ISBN 978-0-385-73810-1; 0-385-73810-2

A newly illustrated, abridged and adapted edition of A short history of nearly everything, published 2003 by Broadway Books for adults; this edition first published in the United Kingdom 2008

Bryson "whirls through mind-numbing notions such as the creation of the universe and the life span of an atom with

good cheer and accessible, even exciting, writing. The two-page speads meander their way through the various recesses of science with a combination of explanatory prose, historical anecdotes, wry asides, and illustrations that range from helpful to comical." Booklist

Cleary, Brian P., 1959-

Mrs. Riley Bought Five Itchy Aardvarks and other painless tricks for memorizing science facts; illustrated by J. P. Sandy. Millbrook Press 2008 48p il (Adventures in memory) lib bdg $23.93

Grades: 3 4 5 6   **500**

1. Memory 2. Science 3. Scientific recreations

ISBN 978-0-8225-7819-2 lib bdg; 0-8225-7819-0 lib bdg

LC 2007-52125

"This short (48 pages), well-written, often cleverly phrased, entertaining, humorous, engaging, colorfully illustrated book should be in every school and public library. . . . [It includes] a short, informative chapter on the scientific method." Sci Books Films

Cobb, Vicki

What's the big idea? amazing science questions for the curious kid. Skyhorse 2010 197p il $19.95

Grades: 3 4 5 6   **500**

1. Science 2. Questions and answers

ISBN 978-1-61608-013-6; 1-61608-013-2

LC 2009-46866

"The four main topics—energy, motion, matter, and life—are presented as 'big ideas' and explained through a series of two to four-page chapters that open with a kid-friendly question designed to provide insight into some of the great scientific breakthroughs. . . . Each question is introduced with an illustrated page of four students reacting (in speech bubbles) with humor and sarcasm to the question. . . . Spots of black-line cartoon-style artwork filled with color break up most pages and keep the large-point sans-serif text from overwhelming the spreads. This will be a quality addition to any collection." SLJ

Dotlich, Rebecca Kai

What is science? illustrated by Sachiko Yoshikawa. H. Holt 2006 un il $16.95

Grades: K 1 2   **500**

1. Science

ISBN 978-0-8050-7394-2; 0-8050-7394-9

LC 2005-20050

"Dotlich begins and ends with the line, What is science?/ So many things. In between, she enumerates some of the areas of study—astronomy, geology, paleontology, oceanography, botany, meteorology, and zoology. Each page has just a few words, in large print, superimposed on a background of boldly colored acrylic, pastel, and collage art. The rhyming text flows nicely. . . . With its large illustrations, simple text, and important concepts, this title will be enjoyed by newly independent readers, or will ignite excitement in a group. A unique look at the topic." SLJ

Goldsmith, Mike

Everything you need to know about science. Kingfisher 2009 160p il $18.99

Grades: 1 2 3 4 5 **500**
1. Science
ISBN 978-0-7534-6302-4; 0-7534-6302-4

"This broad, accessible encyclopedia will appeal to browsers because of the 500-plus highly realistic computer-generated illustrations, large fonts, and short paragraphs. . . . Science enthusiasts will enjoy browsing this smorgasbord of information." SLJ

Hillman, Ben

How weird is it; a freaky book all about strangeness. Scholastic 2009 47p il $15.99
Grades: 5 6 7 8 **500**
1. Science
ISBN 978-0-439-91868-8; 0-439-91868-5

LC 2008-09787

Strange but facinating facts about everyday things that turn out to be extraordinary.

"Humor adds interest to the random but readable text. Large, vivid computer-manipulated photographs illustrate the information." Horn Book Guide

Isabella, Jude

Hoaxed! fakes & mistakes in the world of science. by the editors of YES mag; illustrated by Howie Woo. Kids Can Press 2009 48p il lib bdg $16.95; pa $8.95
Grades: 5 6 7 8 **500**
1. Fraud 2. Science
ISBN 978-1-55453-206-3 lib bdg; 1-55453-206-X lib bdg; 978-1-55453-207-0 pa; 1-55453-207-8 pa

This title examines hoaxes, fakes and mistakes from the world of science, including crop circles, Bigfoot and the Loch Ness monster, and UFOs reported at Roswell, New Mexico. Index. "Ages nine to twelve." (Quill Quire)

"Piltdown man, Richard Meinertzhagen the light-fingered bird collector, 'Stone Age' Tasaday in the Philippines, crop circles in England, cold fusion energy and UFOs in Roswell, N.M., are the fakes and mistakes described in this lively introduction to fraud in science. The breezy text opens with a clear description of the scientific process of hypothesis, experiment, publication in professional magazines and replication of results before proceeding to the many colorful fakes exposed." Kirkus

Includes index.

Murphy, Glenn

Why is snot green; and other extremely important questions (and answers) Roaring Brook Press 2009 236p il pa $9.95
Grades: 4 5 6 7 **500**
1. Science 2. Technology
ISBN 978-1-59643-500-1 pa; 1-59643-500-3 pa

"Conservation, evolution, technology, animal life, space travel, physics, and much more are discussed in this lively science book. . . . [This offers] chatty questions and answers . . . with text that is compelling, never intimidating, and sometimes deliberately outrageous. . . . Children will have fun browsing the spacious pages and sharing what they read with adults." Booklist

O'Meara, Stephen James

Are you afraid yet? the science behind scary stuff; written by Stephen James O'Meara; illustrated by Jeremy Kaposy. Kids Can Press 2009 78p il $17.95; pa $9.95

Grades: 5 6 7 8 **500**
1. Science 2. Supernatural
ISBN 978-1-55453-294-0; 1-55453-294-9; 978-1-55453-295-7 pa; 1-55453-295-7 pa

"This book cleverly weaves together the supernatural and the scientific in an entertaining read that answers questions about ghosts, UFOs, vampires, werewolves, and how long a decapitated head can remain conscious. Examples depicting such things in classical fiction and popular movies are seamlessly interjected between the factual explanations. Each page is filled with detailed black-and-white illustrations, emphasizing the sometimes-humorous, yet often-macabre descriptions." SLJ

Richardson, Gillian

Kaboom! explosions of all kinds. Annick Press 2009 83p il $22.95; pa $12.95
Grades: 4 5 6 7 **500**
1. Science 2. Explosions
ISBN 978-1-55451-204-1; 1-55451-204-2; 978-1-55451-203-4 pa; 1-55451-203-4 pa

"With comic-style sound-effect headings and fact boxes galore, Kaboom! highlights the supercharged of the natural and manmade worlds, from astronomy, geology, biology, herbology, and entomology to chemistry, mechanics, pyrotechnics, and art. Text is broken into asymmetrical panels for bite-size explanations. Some explosions are captured in sequence and detail with historical and high-speed photography and illustrations in comic-style panel frames. . . . Kaboom! is an engrossing attention-getter, effectively tapping the sensationalism of all types of blasts." SLJ

Schwartz, David M.

Q is for quark; a science alphabet book. written by David M. Schwartz; illustrated by Kim Doner. Tricycle Press 2001 64p il $15.95
Grades: 4 5 6 7 **500**
1. Science 2. Alphabet
ISBN 1-58246-021-3

LC 00-10659

Explains the meaning of scientific terms which begin with the different letters of the alphabet such as atom, black hole, and clone

"The text is filled with readable and clear explanations for some very complex concepts. . . . [Readers] will enjoy browsing through this funny and informative book." SLJ

Watts, Claire

The most explosive science book in the universe; by the Brainwaves; illustrated by Lisa Swerling and Ralph Lazar; written by Claire Watts. DK Pub. 2009 60p il $19.99
Grades: 3 4 5 6 **500**
1. Science
ISBN 978-0-7566-5152-7; 0-7566-5152-2

The Brainwaves are pint-sized pals that explore the world of science including the building blocks of matter, chemistry, light, electricity and the future of science

"A sprawling, unique overview of the various scientific fields. Although students will have to hunt through the dense layout to find facts, they will likely encounter what they are searching for. . . . Appealing enough to inspire pleasure reading, the book will also serve those looking for scientific facts." SLJ

502   Miscellany

Murphy, Glenn

    How loud can you burp? more extremely important questions (and answers!) Roaring Book Press 2009 284p il pa $10.99

Grades: 4 5 6 7   **502**

    1. Science 2. Questions and answers

    ISBN 978-1-59643-506-3 pa; 1-59643-506-2 pa

    "'Why does pollen give you hay fever?' 'Why don't big metal ships just sink?' These are but a couple of the questions that Murphy received on the Web site he set up to solicit inquiries from kids. Written in an informal, question-and-answer format, he delivers serious scientific information in an easygoing, humorous manner, with several pages dedicated to each topic. . . . A few line drawings break up the text and sidebars highlight interesting facts or are, at times, simply funny. . . . This is an entertaining, accessible approach to science that's sure to appeal to science buffs and general browsers alike." SLJ

502.8   Auxiliary techniques and procedures; apparatus, equipment, materials

Kramer, Stephen

    Hidden worlds; looking through a scientist's microscope; photographs by Dennis Kunkel. Houghton Mifflin 2001 57p il (Scientists in the field) $16; pa $5.95

Grades: 4 5 6 7   **502.8**

    1. Microscopes 2. Microscopists

    ISBN 0-618-05546-0; 0-618-35405-0 pa

                     LC 00-58083

    This book takes a "look at the work of a microscopist. Kunkel works with microscopes to explore science. . . . This book contains many of his photos, most taken with electron microscopes. . . . Several opening pages, along with the front and back endpapers, are visually dazzling. The heart of the book, though, is what readers learn about how Kunkel produces these images, and to what uses scientists put them. . . . This title offers a wealth of scientific information along with an insightful look at the world of an individual scientist." SLJ

    Includes bibliographical references

Levine, Shar

    ★ The ultimate guide to your microscope; [by] Shar Levine & Leslie Johnstone. Sterling Pub. 2008 143p il pa $9.95

Grades: 5 6 7 8 9   **502.8**

    1. Microscopes

    ISBN 978-1-4027-4329-0 pa; 1-4027-4329-7 pa

                 LC 2006-100967

    "Through this fun and inviting book, readers can begin to explore the world using a microscope. Students are encouraged to learn the basics in the two first chapters and then undertake the 41 hands-on activities in the next eight chapters. Activities are presented in manageable one or two-page uniformly formatted modules." SLJ

503   Dictionaries, encyclopedias, concordances

    ★ DK first science encyclopedia; [senior editors, Currie Love, Caroline Stamps and Ben Morgan] DK Publishing 2008 127p il map $16.99

Grades: K 1 2 3 4   **503**

    1. Science -- Encyclopedias

    ISBN 978-0-7566-4296-9; 0-7566-4296-5

                 LC 2009277384

    Provides a basic reference guide to life, materials, physical, earth, and space science

    "On flipping to any page, readers' first impressions will be the vibrancy and beauty of the photography, but further examination reveals a wealth of interesting facts and information about the topics presented, along with real-world context for their importance." Sci Books Films

Everything you need to know; an encyclopedia for inquiring young minds. Kingfisher 2007 320p il map $24.95

Grades: PreK K 1 2 3 4   **503**

    1. Reference books 2. Science -- Encyclopedias 3. Technology -- Encyclopedias

    ISBN 978-0-7534-6089-4; 0-7534-6089-0

    "The encyclopedia is arranged thematically into 10 sections ('Our Earth,' 'Plants,' 'Animals,' 'Dinosaurs,' 'People and Places,' 'People Through Time,' 'My Body,' 'Science,' 'Space,' and 'Machines') with between 11 and 17 topics grouped under each. Most topics are treated in two-page spreads. . . . There is plenty of worthwhile information to answer questions and spark curiosity. . . . The volume is visually appealing, with full-color illustrations." Booklist

Jakab, Cheryl

    ★ The encyclopedia of junior science; [by] Cheryl Jakab, David Keystone. Chelsea Clubhouse 2009 10v il map set $230

Grades: 4 5 6 7   **503**

    1. Reference books 2. Science -- Encyclopedias

    ISBN 978-1-60413-554-1 set; 1-60413-554-9 set

                 LC 2008-38113

    "This set introduces students to basic science concepts. Approximately 270 entries are arranged alphabetically. . . . The writing is basic, and much of the information is presented in the form of charts and bulleted lists. . . . This set would be useful for school and public libraries seeking a science encyclopedia." Booklist

The **Kingfisher** science encyclopedia; general editor, Charles Taylor. 3rd ed. Kingfisher 2011 vii, 488 p.p ill. (some col.) (hardcover) $34.99

Grades: 5 6 7 8   **503**

    1. Science -- Encyclopedias

    ISBN 0753466880; 9780753466889

                 LC 2011047026

    This book is a science encyclopedia edited by Charles Taylor. The book is arranged thematically and "most topics are presented on . . . two-page spreads, with relevant charts, timelines, and other illustrations surrounding the text. In the bottom right corner of the spread is a 'See Also Pages' box that directs readers to related topics with their page numbers." (Voice of Youth Advocates)

    Topical chapters present "basic surveys of physics, geology, chemistry, biology, anatomy, the environment, and space. . . . Articles are generally, though not rigidly, confined to a spread each, and all have see-also references. . . . The illustrations are a plus; they are crisply reproduced, finely detailed, and labeled, enhancing the text rather than competing with it." SLJ

507 Education, research, related topics

Glass, Susan
Analyze this! understanding the scientific method. [by] Susan Glass. Heinemann Library 2007 48p il (How to be a scientist) lib bdg $21; pa $8.99
Grades: 3 4 5 6 **507**
1. Science -- Methodology
ISBN 978-1-4034-8358-4 lib bdg; 978-1-4034-8362-1 pa
LC 2006010638
Includes bibliographical references

Prove it! the scientific method in action. [by] Susan Glass. Heinemann Library 2007 48p il (How to be a scientist) hardcover o.p. lib bdg $21
Grades: 3 4 5 6 **507**
1. Science -- Experiments 2. Science -- Methodology
ISBN 978-1-4034-8359-1 lib bdg; 978-1-4034-8363-8 pa
LC 2006010639
"Introduces the scientific method, explains the role of the experiment, shows the steps involved in setting up an experiment, and looks at careers which use the scientific method." Publisher's Note
Includes bibliographical references

Kramer, Stephen
How to think like a scientist; answering questions by the scientific method. [by] Stephen P. Kramer; illustrated by Felicia Bond. Crowell 1987 44p il $16.89
Grades: 3 4 5 **507**
1. Science -- Methodology
ISBN 978-0-690-04565-9; 0-690-04565-4
LC 85-43604
"This is a pleasant book with an open format; an amusing halftone cartoon on almost every page illustrates the child oriented experiments and supports the light tone of the book." SLJ
An "exploration of the ways questions are asked and how scientists try to make sure that the questions are answered correctly. Relying on concrete story examples, Kramer shows how observed information can result in different or incorrect conclusions. Examples are also used to explain the principles of the scientific method." Booklist

Science detectives; how scientists solved six real-life mysteries. by the editors of Yes Mag; illustrated by Rose Cowles. Kids Can Press 2006 48p il $15.95; pa $8.95
Grades: 4 5 6 **507**
1. Science -- Methodology
ISBN 978-1-55337-994-2; 1-55337-994-2; 978-1-55337-995-9; 1-55337-995-0 pa
This describes how scientists solved mysteries such as the spread of typhoid in 1906, the death of vultures in India in 1999, and the crash of a Swissair flight in 1998. Includes related projects.

507.21 Research methods

★ **Mesmerized**; How Ben Franklin Solved a Mystery That Baffled All of France. Mara Rockliff, illustrated by Iacopo Bruno. Candlewick Press 2015 48 p. col ill, col map hbk $17.99
Grades: 2 3 4 **507.21**
1. Hypnotism 2. Science -- Methodology
ISBN 0763663514; 9780763663513
LC 2014939337
Includes bibliographical references
In this book, Mara Rockliff "tells the story of how Benjamin Franklin debunked Dr. [Anton Franz] Mesmer's magical cure-all. . . . With a heavy emphasis on his use of the scientific method, Rockliff shows how Franklin's experiment-blindfolding subjects so that they don't know they're being mesmerized--led to the discovery of the placebo effect, a vital component of medical testing to this day." (Booklist)
"The tale is nicely pitched to emphasize the importance of a hypothesis, testing and verification, and several inset text boxes are used to explain these scientific tools. Rockliff points out that Franklin's blind-test technique is in use today for medical treatments, and both the placebo effect and hypnosis are studied today." Kirkus

507.8 Use of apparatus and equipment in study and teaching

Becker, Helaine
★ **Science** on the loose; amazing activities and science facts you'll never believe. illustrated by Claudia Dávila. Maple Tree Press 2008 64p il $22.95; pa $10.95
Grades: 3 4 5 6 **507.8**
1. Science -- Experiments
ISBN 978-1-897349-18-2; 1-897349-18-1; 978-1-897349-19-9 pa; 1-897349-19-X pa
LC 2007939081
This "is thought provoking, imaginative, and engaging, with a wonderful blend of intelligent writing, intriguing ideas and easy-to-perform experiments. There is also plenty of humor." Sci Books Films

Bell-Rehwoldt, Sheri
Science experiments that surprise and delight; fun projects for curious kids. Capstone Press 2011 32p il (Edge books: kitchen science) lib bdg $26.65; pa $7.95
Grades: 3 4 5 6 **507.8**
1. Science -- Experiments
ISBN 978-1-4296-5428-9 lib bdg; 1-4296-5428-7 lib bdg; 978-1-4296-6253-6 pa; 1-4296-6253-0 pa
LC 2010025205
Provides step-by-step instructions for science projects using household materials and explains the science behind the experiments.
"Attractive, colorful, and full of photos, [this title] will appeal to a wide range of kids. . . . Anyone looking for a straightforward, fun, and easy science experiment will want [this title] close by." SLJ
Includes bibliographical references

Burke, Lisa

Backyard; fun experiments for budding scientists. DK Pub. 2010 23p il (I'm a scientist) $12.99

Grades: K 1 2 3   **507.8**

1. Nature 2. Science -- Experiments

ISBN 978-0-7566-6306-3; 0-7566-6306-7

LC 2010459418

"Each spread offers a science experiment with foldout flaps that demonstrate the science behind the project which introduces natural phenomena and the outside world in backyards and gardens." Publisher's note

Kitchen. DK Pub. 2010 23p il (I'm a scientist) $12.99

Grades: K 1 2 3   **507.8**

1. Science -- Experiments

ISBN 978-0-7566-6307-0; 0-7566-6307-5

"Each spread contains a kid-friendly science experiment for very young readers which they can perform right in their own kitchen, with foldout flaps that demonstrate the science behind the project." Publisher's note

Burns, Kylie

What's going on? collecting and recording your data. Crabtree 2010 32p il (Step into science) lib bdg $26.60; pa $8.95

Grades: 4 5 6   **507.8**

1. Science -- Methodology

ISBN 978-0-7787-5155-7 lib bdg; 0-7787-5155-4 lib bdg; 978-0-7787-5170-0 pa; 0-7787-5170-8 pa

This "shows the reader how to collect and record data in a journal, as well as how to organize the data by using graphs, charts, and diagrams. . . . The colorful photographs and illustrations enhance the text. A time line showing scientific discoveries and inventions, a glossary, a list of books and websites for further information, and an index are presented at the back of the book. This . . . would be a wonderful addition to a school classroom." Sci Books Films

Includes glossary and bibliographical references

Challen, Paul C.

What just happened? reading results and making inferences. [by] Paul Challen. Crabtree 2010 32p il (Step into science) lib bdg $26.60; pa $8.95

Grades: 4 5 6   **507.8**

1. Science -- Methodology

ISBN 978-0-7787-5156-4 lib bdg; 0-7787-5156-2 lib bdg; 978-0-7787-5171-7 pa; 0-7787-5171-6 pa

This "shows the reader how to make sense of the data that have been collected and recorded during the experiment. . . . The examples of charts and graphs, along with colorful photographs and illustrations, enhance the text. A time line showing scientific discoveries and inventions, a glossary, a list of books, and websites for further information, and an index are presented at the back of the book. This . . . would be a wonderful addition to a school classroom." Sci Books Films

Includes glossary and bibliographical references

What's going to happen? making your hypothesis. [by] Paul Challen. Crabtree 2010 32p il (Step into science) lib bdg $26.60; pa $8.95

Grades: 4 5 6   **507.8**

1. Science -- Methodology

ISBN 978-0-7787-5157-1 lib bdg; 0-7787-5157-0 lib bdg; 978-0-7787-5172-4 pa; 0-7787-5172-4 pa

Learn how scientists make educated guesses called hypotheses to test their theories. . . . Readers will learn how to construct a measurable and focused hypothesis to test in an experiment.

"A time line showing important hypotheses, a glossary, a list of books and websites for further information, and an index are provided at the back of the book. This . . . would be a wonderful addition to a school classroom." Sci Books Films

Includes glossary and bibliographical references

Cobb, Vicki

Science experiments you can eat; illustrated by David Cain. rev & updated; HarperCollins Pubs. 1994 214p il hardcover o.p. pa $5.95

Grades: 5 6 7 8   **507.8**

1. Cooking 2. Science -- Experiments

ISBN 0-06-023551-9; 0-06-446002-9 pa

LC 93-13679

First published 1972

Experiments with food demonstrate various scientific principles and produce an eatable result. Includes rock candy, grape jelly, cupcakes, and popcorn

Includes glossary

See for yourself; more than 100 amazing experiments for science fairs and school projects. illustrated by Dave Klug. 2nd ed; Skyhorse Pub. 2010 192p il pa $14.95

Grades: 4 5 6 7   **507.8**

1. Science -- Experiments

ISBN 978-1-61608-083-9; 1-61608-083-3

LC 2010020800

First published 2001 by Scholastic

This is an "accessible and often intriguing collection of activities and experiments. . . . The experiments are grouped by their source of inspiration: humans, the supermarket, the toy store, drugstore, and hardware and stationery stores. . . . Cartoon-style illustrations are . . . in full color." SLJ

We dare you! hundreds of science bets, challenges, and experiments you can do at home. [by] Vicki Cobb and Kathy Darling. Skyhorse Pub. 2007 321p il hardcover o.p. pa $14.94

Grades: 4 5 6 7   **507.8**

1. Science -- Experiments

ISBN 978-1-60239-225-0; 1-60239-225-0; 978-1-60239-775-0 pa; 1-60239-775-9 pa

LC 2007-51236

"Divided into chapters with titles such as 'The Human Wonder,' 'Fluid Feats,' 'Energy Entrapments,' and 'Mathematical Duplicity,' this volume has more than 200 experiments with clear how-to instructions. All of the projects are doable and the science behind them is explained in a kid-accessible manner. . . . Black-and-white line drawings add humor and clarify instructions. This is a great resource for teachers, parents, and budding scientists—and for any youngster who can't resist a challenge." SLJ

Includes bibliographical references

Connolly, Sean

The **book** of potentially catastrophic science; 50 experiments for daring young scientists. Workman Pub. 2010 305p il

Grades: 5 6 7 8   **507.8**

1. Science -- Experiments 2. Science -- Experiments

ISBN 0-7611-5687-9; 978-0-7611-5687-1

LC 2010-07044

This book presents thirty-four experiments. "Each chapter starts with a brief outline of the scientific advances of the time, followed by a clarification of the science and then one or more hands-on experiments to illustrate the object or concept presented. . . . Grades five to eight." (Sci Books Films)

"This volume approaches science historically, spotlighting certain periods, processes, individuals, discoveries, and inventions. Each of the 34 chapters includes a discussion and one or two related activities, such as making a Stone Age tool, creating an earthquake in Jell-O, building a parachute for an egg drop, and extracting a banana's DNA. Safety concerns are addressed for each project, and adult help will be necessary to complete some of the experiments successfully. . . . Connolly's writing is engaging, and the historical approach works well, offering kids a quick introduction to science history and the opportunity to explore certain ideas along the way." Booklist

Gabrielson, Curt

Stomp rockets, catapults, and kaleidoscopes; 30+ amazing science projects you can build for less than $1. Chicago Review Press 2008 159p il $16.95

Grades: 3 4 5 6   **507.8**

1. Science projects 2. Science -- Experiments

ISBN 978-1-55652-737-1; 1-55652-737-3

LC 2007-37917

"Projects include building a working model of the human hand's muscles, bones, and tendons using drinking straws, tape, and string; using a pair of two-liter bottles and a length of rubber tubing to learn how a toilet flushes; and discovering how musical instruments make sounds by fashioning a harmonica, saxophone, drum, flute, or oboe. All devices are designed to use recycled or nearly free materials and common tools." Publisher's note

Goodstein, Madeline

Ace your sports science project; great science fair ideas. [by] Madeline Goodstein, Robert Gardner, and Barbara Gardner Conklin. Enslow Publishers 2009 128p il (Ace your physics science project) lib bdg $31.93

Grades: 5 6 7 8   **507.8**

1. Sports 2. Physics 3. Science projects 4. Science -- Experiments

ISBN 978-0-7660-3229-3 lib bdg; 0-7660-3229-9 lib bdg

LC 2008-4689

"Presents several science experiments and project ideas dealing with the physics of sports." Publisher's note

"These three series offer a wealth of information and differ only in the topics they include. All begin with an introduction that discusses science-fair projects and the scientific method and lists safety tips. The texts consist of five chapters of themed experiments–for example, some of those in Animal Science Project are "Clever Lab and Field Studies" and "Studying Human Behavior.". . Each experiment includes a materials list, steps to follow, questions to con-

sider, and diagrams that clarify the directions. When something potentially dangerous is involved, an adult is listed as the first material in the list and a reminder is included in the experiment. Worthwhile purchases." SLJ

Includes bibliographical references

Goal! science projects with soccer. Enslow Publishers 2009 104p il (Score! Sports science projects) lib bdg $31.93

Grades: 5 6 7 8   **507.8**

1. Motion 2. Soccer 3. Force and energy 4. Science projects 5. Science -- Experiments

ISBN 978-0-7660-3106-7 lib bdg; 0-7660-3106-3 lib bdg

LC 2008-2999

"Introductions include information about the history of the sport, safety steps to follow, and the scientific method. . . . Detailed diagrams help clarify many of the directions." SLJ

Includes glossary and bibliographical references

Hammond, Richard

Super science lab. DK Pub. 2009 96p il pa $8.99

Grades: 3 4 5   **507.8**

1. Science -- Experiments

ISBN 978-0-7566-5341-5 pa; 0-7566-5341-X pa

"With more than 30 scientific experiments, ranging from more traditional science-fair projects . . . , this fun book has plenty of ideas to sample. Also offered are magnified images. . . . In between experiments, Hammond explores the science behind the subjects. . . . The active approach to science and scrapbook-style design, with plenty of photos, notes and asides, should win over curious kids." Publ Wkly

Hopwood, James

Cool distance assistants; fun science projects to propel things. [by] James Hopwood. ABDO Pub. 2008 32p il (Cool science) lib bdg $25.65

Grades: 4 5 6   **507.8**

1. Science projects 2. Science -- Experiments

ISBN 978-1-59928-906-9 lib bdg; 1-59928-906-7 lib bdg

LC 2007015625

This offers science projects about propulsion, including "Awesome Air & Water Rockets"

The experiments "will attract boys and girls. [The] book begins with [an] upbeat introduction and three chapters about the scientific method, keeping a journal, and safety. . . . Background on the science concepts involved is presented along with a complete list of supplies. . . . The numbered instructions are easy to follow and are accompanied by small, closeup photos." SLJ

Cool dry ice devices; fun science projects with dry ice. [by] James Hopwood. ABDO Pub. 2008 32p il (Cool science) lib bdg $25.65

Grades: 4 5 6   **507.8**

1. Science projects 2. Science -- Experiments

ISBN 978-1-59928-907-6 lib bdg; 1-59928-907-5 lib bdg

LC 2007010257

This offers science projects using dry ice, including "Fast Frozen Confections"

The experiments "will attract boys and girls. [The] book begins with [an] upbeat introduction and three chapters about the scientific method, keeping a journal, and safety. . . . Background on the science concepts involved is presented along with a complete list of supplies. . . . The numbered instructions are easy to follow and are accompanied by small, closeup photos." SLJ

Hyde, Natalie

What's the plan? designing your experiment. Crabtree 2010 32p il (Step into science) lib bdg $26.60; pa $8.95
Grades: 4 5 6   **507.8**
1. Science -- Methodology
ISBN 978-0-7787-5154-0 lib bdg; 0-7787-5154-6 lib bdg; 978-0-7787-5169-4 pa; 0-7787-5169-4 pa
            LC 2009-44172

This "shows readers how to gather materials and create a step-by-step procedure to test their hypotheses. . . . Colorful photographs and illustrations enhance the text. A time line showing scientific discoveries and inventions, a glossary, a list of books and websites for further information, and an index are presented at the back of the book. This . . . would be a wonderful addition to a school classroom." Sci Books Films

Includes glossary and bibliographical references

Johnson, Robin R.

What do we know now? drawing conclusions and answering the question. Crabtree 2010 32p il (Step into science) lib bdg $26.60; pa $8.95
Grades: 4 5 6   **507.8**
1. Science -- Methodology
ISBN 978-0-7787-5153-3 lib bdg; 0-7787-5153-8 lib bdg; 978-0-7787-5168-7 pa; 0-7787-5168-6 pa
            LC 2009-44171

This book illustrates fun and interesting ways in which to report your results, from a science fair demonstration to a written report.

"This title . . . would be a wonderful addition to a school classroom." Sci Books Films

Includes glossary and bibliographical references

Leavitt, Loralee

Candy experiments; Loralee Leavitt. Andrews McMeel Pub., LLC 2012 146 p. $14.99
Grades: 4 5 6   **507.8**
1. Candy 2. Science -- Experiments
ISBN 1449418368; 9781449418366
            LC 2011944678

This book presents science activities for children involving candy. "Grouped by physical properties that include 'Color,' 'Secret Ingredients,' and 'Sticky' or processes like 'Blow It Up,' 'Squash It,' and 'Dissolve This,' the activities begin with an introductory question and tend to flow incrementally. Each one includes the time required, a list of ingredients . . . step-by-step directions, and a discussion, including a cursory scientific explanation." (School Library Journal)

Lew, Kristi

Science experiments that fly and move; fun projects for curious kids. Capstone Press 2011 32p il (Edge books: kitchen science) lib bdg $26.65; pa $7.95

Grades: 3 4 5 6   **507.8**
1. Science -- Experiments
ISBN 978-1-4296-5426-5; 1-4296-5426-0; 978-1-4296-6252-9 pa; 1-4296-6252-2 pa
            LC 2010025206

Provides step-by-step instructions for science projects using household materials and explains the science behind the experiments.

"Attractive, colorful, and full of photos, [this title] will appeal to a wide range of kids. . . . Anyone looking for a straightforward, fun, and easy science experiment will want [this title] close by." SLJ

Includes glossary and bibliographical references

Margles, Samantha

Mythbusters science fair book. Scholastic 2011 128p il pa $9.99
Grades: 4 5 6 7   **507.8**
1. Science projects 2. Science -- Experiments
ISBN 978-0-545-23745-1; 0-545-23745-9

This offers "50 original ideas for science fair projects or long, boredom-riddled summer days. Much like the popular television program on which it's based, the book stays true to the scientific method. . . . Divided into chapters on chemical reactions, temperature, energy and force, and more, the two- to three-page experiments on busily designed pages feature easy step-by-step procedures." Booklist

Murphy, Pat

Exploratopia; by Pat Murphy, Ellen Macaulay, and the staff of the Exploratorium; illustrated by Jason Gorski. Little, Brown and Co. 2006 373p il $29.99
Grades: 3 4 5 6   **507.8**
1. Science -- Experiments
ISBN 978-0-316-61281-4; 0-316-61281-2
            LC 2006-40942

"Practiced young experimenters ready to strike out on their own will find enticing science demonstrations on nearly every page of this inviting collection. Each of the 21 sections contains a half dozen or more entries that feature easily gathered ingredients, clear directions, and color photos or diagrams that are not only informative but often arresting as well." SLJ

Includes bibliographical references

Science activities for all students; edited by Aviva Ebner. Facts on File 2009 2v il loose-leaf $370
Grades: Adult Professional   **507.8**
1. Science projects 2. Science -- Experiments
ISBN 978-0-8160-7396-2 loose-leaf; 0-8160-7396-1 loose-leaf
            LC 2008043827

Replaces Science Projects for All Students and More Science Projects for All Students, published 1998 and 2002 respectively

These "binders enable students in grades 4 through 9 with developmental or physical challenges to join their classmates in . . . hands-on [science] activities. There are 60 experiments in each binder—designed to be as inclusive as possible—in the areas of basic skills, Earth science, weather, space science, life science, and physical science. Each binder is also enhanced by approximately 250 black-and-white line illustrations." Publisher's note

Includes glossary and bibliographical references

Shores, Lori

How to build flipsticks. Capstone Press 2011 24p il (Hands-on science fun) lib bdg $23.99; pa $6.95
Grades: PreK K 1   **507.8**
1. Science -- Experiments
ISBN 978-1-4296-5292-6 lib bdg; 1-4296-5292-6 lib bdg; 978-1-4296-6213-0 pa; 1-4296-6213-1 pa
Simple text and full-color photos instruct readers on how to make two drawings act like a cartoon and explain the science behind the activity.
"Bright, glossy photos and irresistible ideas make these science lessons effortless fun." Booklist

How to make a bouncing egg. Capstone Press 2011 24p il (Hands-on science fun) lib bdg $23.99; pa $6.95
Grades: PreK K 1   **507.8**
1. Science -- Experiments
ISBN 978-1-4296-5291-9 lib bdg; 1-4296-5291-8 lib bdg; 978-1-4296-6214-7 pa; 1-4296-6214-X pa
Simple text and full-color photos instruct readers on how to make a bouncing egg.
"Bright, glossy photos and irresistible ideas make these science lessons effortless fun." Booklist

How to make a liquid rainbow. Capstone Press 2011 24p il (Hands-on science fun) lib bdg $23.99; pa $6.95
Grades: PreK K 1   **507.8**
1. Science -- Experiments
ISBN 978-1-4296-6216-1 lib bdg; 1-4296-6216-6 lib bdg; 978-1-4296-6216-1 pa; 1-4296-6216-6 pa
Simple text and full-color photos instruct readers on how to make a rainbow in a jar.
"Bright, glossy photos and irresistible ideas make these science lessons effortless fun." Booklist

How to make a mystery smell balloon. Capstone Press 2011 24p il (Hands-on science fun) lib bdg $23.99; pa $6.95
Grades: PreK K 1   **507.8**
1. Science -- Experiments
ISBN 978-1-4296-4494-5 lib bdg; 1-4296-4494-X lib bdg; 978-1-4296-5579-8 pa; 1-4296-5579-8 pa
LC 2010009483
Simple text and full-color photos instruct readers how to make a mystery smell balloon and explain the science behind the activity.
"Bright, glossy photos and irresistible ideas make these science lessons effortless fun." Booklist
Includes bibliographical references

Spangler, Steve

Naked eggs and flying potatoes; unforgettable experiments that make science fun. Greenleaf Book Group Press 2010 155p il (Steve Spangler science) pa $14.95
Grades: 3 4 5 6   **507.8**
1. Scientific recreations 2. Science -- Experiments
ISBN 978-1-60832-0608 pa; 1-60832-060-X pa
"Spangler uses cheap, everyday materials to invent entertaining, highly kid-appealing activities. . . . Heavily illustrated with color photos and described in funny, casual prose, the experiments will easily engage a young audience, and each is followed by a succinct explanation of the science concepts at play." Booklist

Tocci, Salvatore

More simple science fair projects, grades 3-5; illustrated by Bob Wiacek. Chelsea House Pub. 2006 48p il (Scientific American winning science fair projects) $27
Grades: 3 4 5   **507.8**
1. Science projects 2. Science -- Experiments
ISBN 0-7910-9055-8
LC 2005-57097
This "begins by describing how to exhibit information on a trifold display with the following information: background, the experimental question, materials, procedures, results, and explanations. The author then describes 18 experiments following that format. The language is clear and easy to follow. Simple drawings add a great deal to the explanations." Sci Books Films

VanCleave, Janice Pratt

★ Janice VanCleave's 201 awesome, magical, bizarre & incredible experiments. Wiley 1994 118p $12.95
Grades: 4 5 6 7   **507.8**
1. Science -- Experiments
ISBN 0-471-31011-5
LC 93-29807
The experiments in this book "are organized by field: astronomy, biology, chemistry, earth science, and physics; the purpose, materials needed, procedure, results, and an explanation are included for each demonstration. The author writes in a clear, easy-to-understand style. . . . The book will be especially useful to teachers looking for ideas that can be adapted as hands-on activities." SLJ
Includes glossary

★ Janice VanCleave's 202 oozing, bubbling, dripping & bouncing experiments. Wiley 1996 120p pa $12.95
Grades: 4 5 6 7   **507.8**
1. Science -- Experiments
ISBN 0-471-14025-2
LC 95-46398
Provides instructions for over 200 short experiments in astronomy, biology, chemistry, earth science, and physics
"Some activities consist merely of observation, such as 'To study parts of a feather.' Some are more complex, but all are clearly and concisely explained. Many are repeats from prior VanCleave books, but 40 are supposedly new." SLJ
Includes glossary

★ Janice VanCleave's 203 icy, freezing, frosty, cool & wild experiments. Wiley 1999 122p pa $12.95
Grades: 4 5 6 7   **507.8**
1. Science -- Experiments
ISBN 0-471-25223-9
LC 98-49721
This includes "experiments in astronomy, biology, chemistry, earth science, and physics. . . . Each activity includes a purpose, a list of materials, a step-by-step procedure, results, and an explanation. Experiments address such topics as the Moon's 'changing' size, how environment affects body temperature, and why ice pops are softer than ice. An excellent resource." SLJ

Janice VanCleave's big book of play and find out science projects. Wiley 2007 213p il pa $19.95

Grades: K 1 2 3   507.8
1. Science projects 2. Science -- Experiments
ISBN 978-0-7879-8928-6 pa; 0-7879-8928-2 pa
LC 2006-52572

This "is a compilation of 56 hands-on activities based on authentic questions asked by children. The four-part book contains activities in each of the following content areas: 'Physical Science,' 'Nature,' 'Bugs,' and 'Human Body.' . . . Adults and children will likely find it a useful tool." Sci Books Films

Includes glossary and bibliographical references

Janice VanCleave's engineering for every kid; easy activities that make learning science fun. Jossey-Bass 2007 205p il (Science for every kid series) pa $14.95
Grades: 4 5 6 7   507.8
1. Engineering 2. Science projects 3. Science -- Experiments
ISBN 978-0-471-47182-0 pa; 0-471-47182-8 pa
LC 2006-10540

Explains some of the basic physical principles of engineering, accompanied by activities that illustrate those principles

★ **Janice** VanCleave's guide to the best science fair projects; [by] Janice VanCleave. Wiley 1997 156p il pa $14.95
Grades: 4 5 6 7   507.8
1. Science projects 2. Science -- Experiments
ISBN 0-471-14802-4
LC 96-27512

"In the first section, VanCleave discusses scientific methodology: how to organize a project from selecting a topic through the investigatory process, the importance of keeping records, writing a final report, and the value of a nicely crafted presentation. . . . The next section—the largest by far—presents a number of double-page projects in a variety of fields. . . . A clear and informative addition." SLJ

Includes glossary and bibliographical references

Janice VanCleave's science around the year. Wiley 2000 122p il pa $12.95
Grades: 4 5 6 7   507.8
1. Science -- Experiments
ISBN 0-471-33096-5
LC 99-53778

Presents experiments and activities in such fields as astronomy, biology, chemistry, earth science, and physics that are in some way related to one of the four seasons

Wheeler-Toppen, Jodi
Science experiments that explode and implode; fun projects for curious kids. Capstone Press 2011 32p il (Edge books: kitchen science) lib bdg $26.65; pa $7.95
Grades: 3 4 5 6   507.8
1. Explosions 2. Science -- Experiments
ISBN 978-1-4296-5427-2; 1-4296-5427-9; 978-1-4296-6250-5 pa; 1-4296-6250-6 pa
LC 2010027687

Provides step-by-step instructions for science projects using household materials and explains the science behind the experiments.

"Attractive, colorful, and full of photos, [this title] will appeal to a wide range of kids. . . . Anyone looking for a straightforward, fun, and easy science experiment will want [this title] close by." SLJ

Includes glossary and bibliographical references

Science experiments that fizz and bubble; fun projects for curious kids. Capstone Press 2011 32p il (Edge books: kitchen science) lib bdg $26.65; pa $7.95
Grades: 3 4 5 6   507.8
1. Gases 2. Bubbles 3. Science -- Experiments
ISBN 978-1-4296-5425-8 lib bdg; 1-4296-5425-2 lib bdg; 978-1-4296-6251-2 pa; 1-4296-6251-4 pa
LC 2010027684

Provides step-by-step instructions for science projects using household materials and explains the science behind the experiments.

"Attractive, colorful, and full of photos, [this title] will appeal to a wide range of kids. . . . Anyone looking for a straightforward, fun, and easy science experiment will want [this title] close by." SLJ

Includes glossary and bibliographical references

Williams, Jennifer
★ **Oobleck,** slime, & dancing spaghetti; twenty terrific at-home science experiments inspired by favorite children's books. by Jennifer Williams. Bright Sky Press 2009 192 p. ill. (paperback) $14.95
Grades: 4 5 6   507.8
1. Children's literature 2. Science -- Experiments
ISBN 1933979348; 9781933979342
LC 2009000876

This book "provides a series of science experiments designed to explore concepts and ideas that spring from various stories. At the beginning of each chapter, a children's book is . . . summarized. The author then explains a related science concept, suggests discussion questions that connect the experiment to the story, and offers ideas for taking the project further. . . . The experiments cover concepts including polymers, chemical reactions, and non-Newtonian fluids." (School Library Journal)

"Using children's literature as a springboard, this title provides a series of science experiments designed to explore concepts and ideas that spring from various stories. At the beginning of each chapter, a children's book is nicely summarized. The author then explains a related science concept, suggests discussion questions that connect the experiment to the story, and offers ideas for taking the project further. This is serious science. . . . The experiments do a really wonderful job of emphasizing the importance of observation and data collection. The writing is relatively clear. . . . This book is great choice for home use and science units." SLJ

Includes bibliographical references.

Young, Karen Romano
Experiments to do on your family; 20 projects and experiments about sisters, brothers, parents, pets, and the rest of the gang. illustrations by David Goldin. National Geographic 2010 80p il (Science fair winners) $24.90; pa $12.95
Grades: 3 4 5 6   507.8
1. Psychology 2. Science -- Experiments
ISBN 978-1-4263-0692-1; 1-4263-0692-X; 978-1-4263-0691-4 pa; 1-4263-0691-1 pa

This volume provides "outlines for science fair projects in the behavioral . . . sciences. The procedures include just enough structure to help novice experimenters get started. . . . Well-placed questions encourage creativity and further thinking. [The] volume includes humorous cartoon spot illustrations and a section on preparing presentations." Horn Book Guide

Junkyard science; 20 projects and experiments about junk, garbage, waste, things we don't need anymore, and ways to recycle or reuse it--or lose it. illustrations by David Goldin. National Geographic 2010 80p il (Science fair winners) $24.90; pa $12.95

Grades: 3 4 5 6 **507.8**

1. Recycling 2. Environmental sciences 3. Science -- Experiments

ISBN 978-1-4263-0690-7; 1-4263-0690-3; 978-1-4263-0689-1 pa; 1-4263-0689-X pa

This volume provides "outlines for science fair projects in the . . . environmental . . . sciences. The procedures include just enough structure to help novice experimenters get started. . . . Well-placed questions encourage creativity and further thinking. [The] volume includes humorous cartoon spot illustrations and a section on preparing presentations." Horn Book Guide

508 Natural history

Baker, Stuart

In the Antarctic. Marshall Cavendish Benchmark 2009 32p il map (Climate change) lib bdg $19.95

Grades: 5 6 7 8 **508**

1. Antarctica 2. Greenhouse effect

ISBN 978-0-7614-4438-1 lib bdg; 0-7614-4438-6 lib bdg

LC 2009-5766

The book about climate change in the Antarctic "is perfectly organized for students. . . . Unique layout features serve as signposts and will help focus readers' attention. . . . [The book] features an outstanding chart of possible effects of global warming on the area in question, listing 'Possible Event', 'Predicted Result', and 'Impact' in short, bulleted statements." SLJ

Includes glossary

In the tropics. Marshall Cavendish Benchmark 2010 32p il map (Climate change) lib bdg $19.95

Grades: 5 6 7 8 **508**

1. Tropics 2. Greenhouse effect

ISBN 978-0-7614-4440-4 lib bdg; 0-7614-4440-8 lib bdg

LC 2009-5768

The book about climate change in the Tropics "is perfectly organized for students. . . . Unique layout features serve as signposts and will help focus readers' attention. . . . [The book] features an outstanding chart of possible effects of global warming on the area in question, listing 'Possible Event', 'Predicted Result', and 'Impact' in short, bulleted statements." SLJ

Includes glossary

Banes, Graham L.

★ The **Kingfisher** encyclopedia of life; minutes, months, millennia--how long is a life on Earth? Kingfisher 2012 160 p. $19.99

Grades: 3 4 5 6 **508**

1. Biology 2. Longevity

ISBN 0753468913; 9780753468913

This book "focuses on 230 species . . . , categorizing them according to lifespan. The chapters start with 'Here today . . . ,' which includes bacteria that survive for less than an hour, and close with 'Time Is on My Side,' which mentions champions of longevity such as the Great Barrier Reef. . . . Spreads focusing on a life span or on species are interspersed with features highlighting biodiversity, habitats, genetics, and other influences on Earth's lifeforms." (School Library Journal)

Bardhan-Quallen, Sudipta

Nature science experiments; what's hopping in a dust bunny? illustrated by Edward Miller. Sterling 2010 64p il (Mad science) $12.95

Grades: 4 5 6 **508**

1. Nature study 2. Science -- Experiments

ISBN 978-1-4027-2412-1; 1-4027-2412-8

"The first chapter of this attractive book, 'The Stuff of Life,' jumps right in by outlining the materials needed and the step-by-step process to follow to collect and isolate DNA by rinsing one's mouth out with salt water. . . . Youngsters can turn to the table of contents or detailed index to choose experiments based on interest and availability of resources. . . . The chapters on bacteria and protists include color photomicrographs of the organisms, and amusing cartoon illustrations appear throughout. This exploration of the natural world will spark readers' interest in experimenting and questioning results." SLJ

Burnie, David

The **Kingfisher** nature encyclopedia; rev ed.; Kingfisher 2010 320p il $27.99

Grades: 4 5 6 7 **508**

1. Nature 2. Natural history 3. Reference books

ISBN 978-0-7534-6503-5; 0-7534-6503-5

First published 2004 with title: The Kingfisher illustrated nature encyclopedia

"Organized into three sections—the first on our planet's origin and the evolution of life, the second surveying the five biotic kingdoms, the third taking closer looks at 14 biomes . . .—each spread offers a topical discussion that ranges in scope from 'Seasons and Weather' or 'How Fungi Feed' to 'Protozoans' and 'Tropical Forests.' Color photos on every page add visual interest while playing supporting roles to information presented in captions and columns of lucid, not heavily technical narrative text. . . . This is a first-rate overview of its topic." SLJ

Chin, Jason

★ **Island**; a story of the Galapagos. Jason Chin. 1st ed. Roaring Brook Press 2012 40 p. (alk. paper) $16.99

Grades: 3 4 5 6 **508**

1. Birds 2. Droughts 3. Reptiles 4. Natural history -- Galapagos Islands 5. Galapagos Islands 6. Natural history -- Galapagos Islands

ISBN 1596437162; 9781596437166

LC 2011033797

The author, Jason Chin, explains "how species of reptiles and birds on the Galapagos have evolved. He begins with the birth of the islands themselves, a process in which volcanic eruptions punch successive holes in the Earth's surface as tectonic plates move over them, [and] the adaptations of the islands' animals. . . . [Chin also provides information on the] droughts [that] become more common [due to the] climate and geology." (Publishers Weekly)

Includes bibliographical references and index.

Cole, Henry

I took a walk. Greenwillow Bks. 1998 un il $16.99
Grades: PreK K 1 2 **508**
1. Nature -- Fiction 2. Animals -- Fiction
ISBN 0-688-15115-9

LC 97-6692

A visit to woods, pasture, and pond brings encounters with various birds, insects, and other creatures of nature. Flaps fold out to reveal the animals hidden on each two-page spread

"Executed in acrylic paint, the realistic nature scenes invite close and careful inspection." Horn Book Guide

Gates, Phil

Nature got there first; 2nd ed.; Kingfisher 2010 64p il $16.99
Grades: 3 4 5 6 **508**
1. Nature 2. Inventions 3. Technology
ISBN 978-0-7534-6410-6; 0-7534-6410-1

First published 1995

"This browsable title presents fascinating facts about inventions inspired by nature, showing the similarities between the workings of I beams and the make-up of dinosaur vertebrae; the mechanics of sailboats and the physiognomy of jellyfish; and the movements of giant squids and jet engine design. . . . The well-chosen images are both inviting and clearly illustrate the points made in the text and captions. . . . This is an informative, appealing look at the connections between natural and human design." Booklist

Includes glossary

Granström, Brita

Nature adventures; [by] Mick Manning & Brita Granstr["o]m. Frances Lincoln Children's Books 48p il $18.95
Grades: 2 3 4 5 **508**
1. Nature study
ISBN 978-1-84780-088-6; 1-84780-088-2

"Highly illustrated, information-packed pages entice readers to explore nature wherever they might find themselves and to take an active look at the world around them. Chapters include 'In the Town,' 'Fresh Water,' 'Woodland,' 'Field and Hedgerow,' 'Wild Country,' 'The Seashore,' and 'Through the Seasons.' Beautifully drawn artwork in pencil and watercolor provides field-guide references for budding explorers." SLJ

Includes glossary

Kalman, Bobbie

What are opposites in nature? Crabtree Pub. Co. 2010 24p il (Looking at nature) lib bdg $21.27; pa $6.95

Grades: K 1 2 **508**
1. Nature 2. Opposites
ISBN 978-0-7787-3326-3 lib bdg; 0-7787-3326-2 lib bdg; 978-0-7787-3346-1 pa; 0-7787-3346-7 pa

LC 2010016399

This book explores opposites found in nature.

"Bright, colorful photographs were selected with young readers in mind, and the type is large—perfect for reading together. . . Throughout the book are questions that challenge the reader to identify the opposites shown on the pages. . . . Parents and teachers will find . . . [this book] a great addition to a child's library." Sci Books & Films

The **Kid's** Guide to Exploring Nature; Brooklyn Botanic Garden Educators; illustrated by Laszlo; Veres. Sterling Pub Co Inc 2014 120 p. color illustrations $16.95
Grades: 3 4 5 6 **508**
1. Nature 2. Nature conservation
ISBN 1889538884; 9781889538884

AAAS/Subaru SB & F Prize in Excellence in Science Books Finalists, Hands-on Science (2014)

This children's book, by the educators of the Brooklyn Botanic Garden and illustrated by László Veres, part of the "BBG Guides for a Greener Planet" series, "will inspire kids to look closely at the world around them! . . . It teaches children how to observe environments as a naturalist does and leads them on 24 adventures that reveal the complex ecosystems of plants and animals in the woods, at the beach, and in a city park." (Publisher's note)

"This addition to the BBG Guides for a Green Planet series walks readers through the basics of becoming a naturalist. Divided by season, the chapters introduce a variety of ecosystems, such as the beach, woods, city, and meadow. Nature-themed activities appear alongside guides to the flora and fauna of the regions, scavenger hunts, naturalist careers, and introductions to concepts like symbiotic relationships, all of which encourage readers to observe the intricacies of the natural world. Despite the project's New York City origins, readers from just about any geographical location will be able to find information for identifying local wildlife." PW

Lynch, Wayne

The **Everglades**; text and photographs by Wayne Lynch. NorthWord Books for Young Readers 2007 64p il (Our wild world: ecosystems) $16.95; pa $8.95
Grades: 4 5 6 7 **508**
1. Everglades (Fla.) 2. Natural history -- Florida
ISBN 978-1-55971-970-4; 1-55971-970-2; 978-1-55971-971-1 pa; 1-55971-971-0 pa

LC 2006-101497

This "provides an up-close look at the fascinating flora and fauna of the world-famous Everglades. . . . Lynch . . . smoothly pairs engaging prose with numerous color photographs that capture the beauty of the region in both sweeping panorama and close-up detail." Booklist

Morrison, Gordon

★ Nature in the neighborhood; [by] Gordon Morrison. Houghton Mifflin Company 2004 32p il $16
Grades: 3 4 5 6 **508**
1. Seasons 2. Natural history
ISBN 0-618-35215-5

LC 2004-2354

"Morrison offers another quiet, layered view of a natural world that is familiar to many children. . . . His precise, pencil-and-watercolor artwork encourages viewers to look closely at common neighborhood scenes." Booklist

Potter, Jean

Nature in a nutshell for kids; over 100 activities you can do in ten minutes or less. Wiley 1995 136p il pa $12.95

Grades: 2 3 4   508

1. Nature study

ISBN 0-471-04444-X

LC 94-28953

"Each of the 102 experiments is easy, uses safe and mostly readily available household supplies, and is fun at the same time. Divided into seasonal sections, the activities have catchy titles, state hypotheses, list materials, lay out procedures, and finish with clear explanations. Among the noteworthy investigations are: how duck feathers react to water, how mountains are formed, what keeps a seal from freezing in icy weather, whether ants prefer sugar or aspertame, and more." SLJ

Includes glossary and bibliographical references

Rau, Dana Meachen

Day and night. Marshall Cavendish Benchmark 2010 31p il (Bookworms. Nature's cycles) lib bdg $22.79

Grades: PreK K 1   508

1. Day 2. Night

ISBN 978-0-7614-4094-9 lib bdg; 0-7614-4094-1 lib bdg

LC 2008-42512

"Well composed, simple sentences tie directly to colorful, carefully chosen photos [and] . . . accurate information flows naturally. . . . A great resource for sharing one-on-one with the youngest readers." Libr Media Connect

Includes glossary

Schwartz, David M.

★ What in the wild? mysteries of nature concealed and revealed: ear-tickling poems. by David M. Schwartz andYael Schy; eye-tricking photos by Dwight Kuhn. Tricycle Press 2010 un il $16.99; lib bdg $19.99

Grades: K 1 2 3 4   508

1. Animals 2. Nature study 3. Nature poetry

ISBN 978-1-58246-310-0; 1-58246-310-7; 978-1-58246-359-9 lib bdg; 1-58246-359-9 lib bdg

"A nifty combo of poetry (often of the concrete variety), super color photos, scientific information, and a guessing game (complete with whole-page flaps for lifting). . . . Fun as a read-alone or for one-on-one sharing, this tidy package from a talented trio will delight children (and teachers of whole curriculum, too)." SLJ

Includes bibliographical references

Wood, A. J.

Charles Darwin and the Beagle adventure; countries visited during the voyage round the world of HMS Beagle under the command of Captain Fitzroy, Royal Navy, including extracts from the works of Charles Darwin. written by A.J. Wood & Clint Twist. Candlewick Press 2009 un il map $19.99

Grades: 4 5 6 7 8   508

1. Evolution 2. Naturalists 3. Travel writers 4. Writers

on science 5. Beagle Expedition (1831-1836)

ISBN 978-0-7636-4538-0; 0-7636-4538-9

LC 2009-921214

"This beautifully illustrated large-format book immediately appeals to both the eye and the mind. Imitating a 19th-century scrapbook to a certain extent, including various pull-outs . . . the book draws the young reader in. . . . Included are copious quotes from Darwin's journals and other writings, as well as reproductions . . . of numerous 19th-century engravings, drawings, and watercolors, some from the Beagle voyage itself. . . . Integrated into the 19th-century material are modern illustrations and well-written narratives relating background information, the story of the Beagle's voyage . . . and notes on Darwin's life and work. . . . This volume provides an excellent introduction to Darwin and his accomplishments." Sci Books Films

508.2   Seasons

Anderson, Maxine

Explore spring! 25 great ways to learn about spring. [by Maxine Anderson; illustrated by Alexis Frederick-Frost] Nomad Press 2007 92p il pa $12.95

Grades: 2 3 4 5   508.2

1. Spring 2. Science -- Experiments

ISBN 978-0-9785037-4-1

Explains what spring is and why it occurs. Includes projects, activities, and experiments.

"Bold, black-and-white cartoons and occasional jokes add levity to the science. . . . The information is sound, with engaging activities to test and illuminate spring events." SLJ

Includes glossary and bibliographical references

Explore winter! 25 great ways to learn about winter. [by Maxine Anderson; illustrated by Alexis Frederick-Frost] Nomad Press 2007 92p il pa $12.95

Grades: 2 3 4 5   508.2

1. Winter 2. Science -- Experiments

ISBN 978-0-9785037-5-8

Explains what winter is and why it occurs. Includes projects, activities, and experiments.

"Pages of basic information are interspersed with 'Wow' facts, black-and-white cartoon illustrations, and jokes. . . . Curious readers will gain a new level of understanding about winter after reading, laughing at, and experimenting with this book." SLJ

Includes glossary and bibliographical references

Anderson, Sheila

Are you ready for fall? by Sheila M. Anderson. Lerner Publications 2010 32p il (Lightning bolt books. Seasons) lib bdg $25.26; pa $7.95

Grades: PreK K 1 2   508.2

1. Autumn

ISBN 978-0-7613-4586-2 lib bdg; 0-7613-4586-8 lib bdg; 978-0-7613-5672-1 pa; 0-7613-5672-X pa

LC 2009-16408

"The book explores, in simplest terms, things that we see and experience in the fall. . . . Vivid photographs accompany the text, with explanatory balloons to highlight certain points. . . . This would be an excellent book to read, chapter by chapter, to younger preschoolers and to be read by older

readers and used for research up to third grade. It lends itself
well to science and social studies lessons, as well as other
activities." Sci Books Films

Includes glossary

Are you ready for spring? by Sheila M. Anderson. Lerner Publications 2010 32p il (Lightning bolt books. Seasons) lib bdg $25.26; pa $7.95

Grades: PreK K 1 2   **508.2**

1. Spring

ISBN 978-0-7613-4584-8 lib bdg; 0-7613-4584-1 lib
bdg; 978-0-7613-5670-7 pa; 0-7613-5670-3 pa

LC 2009-16409

This "explores those attributes we most often associate with spring. The book has a lot of 'kid appeal' with its
pictures and descriptions of mud puddles, rain, and flying
kites. Changes in nature are subtly woven in with everyday
experiences to provide a full overview of the season. The
descriptions and explanations are scientifically accurate, and
a diversity of ethncity and climates is shown in the colorful
pictures." Sci Books Films

Includes glossary

Branley, Franklyn Mansfield

★ **Sunshine** makes the seasons; illustrated by Michael
Rex. newly illustrated ed; HarperCollins Pubs. 2005 31p il
(Let's-read-and-find-out science) hardcover o.p. pa $4.99

Grades: K 1 2 3   **508.2**

1. Seasons

ISBN 0-06-059203-6; 0-06-059205-2 pa

LC 2003-25457

First published 1974; this is a newly illustrated edition of
the text revised for the 1985 edition

Describes how sunshine and the tilt of the earth's axis are
responsible for the changing seasons

Includes bibliographical references

Crausaz, Anne

Seasons. Kane/Miller 2011 un il $15.99

Grades: K 1 2   **508.2**

1. Seasons

ISBN 1-61067-006-X; 978-1-61067-006-7

"Spring is when everything looks green, blooming trees
smell fragrant, 'blackbirds are singing about their favorite
season,' a ladybug on your hand 'might tickle,' and cherries
are sweet. . . . Preschool." (Horn Book)

"With an emphasis on taste, smell, and outdoor activity,
Crausaz guides readers through the seasons of the year in
this understated and evocative French import. Crisp, delicate
digital artwork set against mostly plain backgrounds keeps
the focus on the freckled, rosy-cheeked girl." Publ Wkly

Esbaum, Jill

Everything spring. National Geographic 2010 15p il
(Picture the seasons) pa $5.95

Grades: PreK K 1   **508.2**

1. Spring

ISBN 978-1-4263-0607-5; 1-4263-0607-5

"These pages burst with vibrant photographs of baby animals and closeups of buds and growth. Esbaum uses poetic
prose to connect children with the joy of the season." SLJ

Hawk, Fran

Count down to Fall; illustrated by Sherry Neidigh.
Sylvan Dell 2009 un il $16.95

Grades: PreK K 1 2 3   **508.2**

1. Trees 2. Autumn 3. Counting 4. Forest animals

ISBN 978-1-934359-94-5; 1-934359-94-7

"Bold, full-spread illustrations with inset details feature
a variety of trees and woodland animals in this informational
picture book. As the facts about trees count down, the images represent the numbers 10 to 1, while corner insets show
the tree, spring and fall leaves, a seed, and occasionally the
flower of the specific tree pictured, such as birch, dogwood,
oak, and maple. Children will be drawn to examine the expressive images of animals and find additional ones along
the detailed border featuring closeups of the tree's bark."
SLJ

McKneally, Ranida

Our seasons; [by] Grace Lin and Ranida McKneally;
illustrated by Grace Lin. Charlesbridge 2006 un il $15.95

Grades: K 1 2 3   **508.2**

1. Seasons

ISBN 978-1-57091-360-0; 1-57091-360-9

LC 2005-06016

"Following a brief explanation of the science behind the
seasons, Lin takes readers from autumn to summer, pairing haiku verses on one page with explanations of seasonal
changes on the other. . . . The gouache illustrations have
plenty of child appeal and effectively tie together the poetry
and the facts." SLJ

Rau, Dana Meachen

Seasons. Marshall Cavendish Benchmark 2009 31p il
(Bookworms. Nature's cycles) lib bdg $22.79

Grades: PreK K 1   **508.2**

1. Seasons

ISBN 978-0-7614-4098-7 lib bdg; 0-7614-4098-4
lib bdg

LC 2008-42507

"Well composed, simple sentences tie directly to colorful, carefully chosen photos [and] . . . accurate information
flows naturally. . . . A great resource for sharing one-on-one
with the youngest readers." Libr Media Connect

Includes glossary

Rustad, Martha E. H.

Fall weather; cooler temperatures. illustrated by
Amanda Enright. Millbrook Press 2011 24p il (Fall's
here!) lib bdg $23.93

Grades: K 1 2 3   **508.2**

1. Autumn

ISBN 978-0-7613-5063-7; 0-7613-5063-2

LC 2010048309

This book about Fall weather is "outstanding for . . .
its clear description of seasons and the word 'equinox.' . . .
Colorful illustrations fill the spreads with active, cartoonlike
boys and girls surrounded by the green, brown, and orange
hues of autumn." SLJ

Schuette, Sarah L.

Let's look at fall; by Sarah L. Schuette. Capstone Press
2007 24p il (Investigate the seasons) $19.93

Grades: K 1 2   **508.2**
1. Autumn 2. Animal behavior
ISBN 978-0-7368-6705-4; 0-7368-6705-8
         LC 2006020449
"The format consists of about three descriptive sentences per page in a large font, a vivid color photograph opposite, and colorful chapter titles in a larger typeface.... [This book is] excellent ... for unit study and wonderful for sharing or browsing." SLJ
Includes bibliographical references

Let's look at spring; by Sarah L. Schuette. Capstone Press 2007 24p il (Investigate the seasons) $19.93
Grades: K 1 2   **508.2**
1. Spring 2. Animal behavior
ISBN 978-0-7368-6707-8; 0-7368-6707-4
         LC 2006020451
"The format consists of about three descriptive sentences per page in a large font, a vivid color photograph opposite, and colorful chapter titles in a larger typeface.... [This book is] excellent ... for unit study and wonderful for sharing or browsing." SLJ
Includes bibliographical references

Let's look at summer; by Sarah L. Schuette. Capstone Press 2007 24p il (Investigate the seasons) $19.93
Grades: K 1 2   **508.2**
1. Summer 2. Animal behavior
ISBN 978-0-7368-6708-5; 0-7368-6708-2
         LC 2006020452
"The format consists of about three descriptive sentences per page in a large font, a vivid color photograph opposite, and colorful chapter titles in a larger typeface.... [This book is] excellent ... for unit study and wonderful for sharing or browsing." SLJ
Includes bibliographical references

Let's look at winter; by Sarah L. Schuette. Capstone Press 2007 24p il (Investigate the seasons) $19.93
Grades: K 1 2   **508.2**
1. Winter 2. Animal behavior
ISBN 978-0-7368-6706-1; 0-7368-6706-6
         LC 2006020508
"The format consists of about three descriptive sentences per page in a large font, a vivid color photograph opposite, and colorful chapter titles in a larger typeface.... [This book is] excellent ... for unit study and wonderful for sharing or browsing." SLJ
Includes bibliographical references

Smith, Sian
  Fall. Heinemann Library 2009 24p il (Seasons) lib bdg $20.71; pa $5.99
Grades: K 1   **508.2**
1. Autumn
ISBN 1-4329-2732-9 pa; 978-1-4329-2727-1 lib bdg; 1-4329-2727-2 lib bdg; 978-1-4329-2732-5 pa
         LC 2008049155
This describes the clothing, weather, and human and animal activities of the Autumn.
"What distinguishes [this book] from others on the same [subject is] the vibrant, eye-catching photographs. The sentences are simple and repetitive.... Reading teachers will want to use this ... for instructional purposes while early

readers will feel successful mastering the text. Students will delight in the color photographs of animals and children enjoying the activities." SLJ

  Spring. Heinemann Library 2009 24p il (Seasons) lib bdg $20.71; pa $5.99
Grades: K 1   **508.2**
1. Spring
ISBN 978-1-4329-2728-8 lib bdg; 1-4329-2728-0 lib bdg; 978-1-4329-2733-2 pa; 1-4329-2733-7 pa
         LC 2008049156
This describes the clothing, weather, and human and animal activities of spring
"What distinguishes [this book] from others on the same [subject is] the vibrant, eye-catching photographs. The sentences are simple and repetitive.... Reading teachers will want to use this ... for instructional purposes while early readers will feel successful mastering the text. Students will delight in the color photographs of animals and children enjoying the activities." SLJ

  Summer. Heinemann Library 2009 24p il (Seasons) lib bdg $20.71; pa $5.99
Grades: K 1   **508.2**
1. Summer
ISBN 978-1-4329-2729-5 lib bdg; 1-4329-2729-9 lib bdg; 978-1-4329-2734-9 pa; 1-4329-2734-5 pa
         LC 2008049157
This describes the clothing, weather, and human and animal activities of summer
"What distinguishes [this book] from others on the same [subject is] the vibrant, eye-catching photographs. The sentences are simple and repetitive.... Reading teachers will want to use this ... for instructional purposes while early readers will feel successful mastering the text. Students will delight in the color photographs of animals and children enjoying the activities." SLJ

  Winter. Heinemann Library 2009 24p il (Seasons) lib bdg $20.71; pa $5.99
Grades: K 1   **508.2**
1. Winter
ISBN 978-1-4329-2730-1 lib bdg; 1-4329-2730-2 lib bdg; 978-1-4329-2735-6 pa; 1-4329-2735-3 pa
         LC 2008049162
This describes the clothing, weather, and human and animal activities of winter
"What distinguishes [this book] from others on the same [subject is] the vibrant, eye-catching photographs. The sentences are simple and repetitive.... Reading teachers will want to use this ... for instructional purposes while early readers will feel successful mastering the text. Students will delight in the color photographs of animals and children enjoying the activities." SLJ

509   Science - History, geographic treatment, biography

Beshore, George W.
  ★ **Science** in ancient China; [by] George Beshore. Watts 1998 63p il map (Science of the past) hardcover o.p. pa $8.95

Grades: 4 5 6 7　　　　　**509**

1. Science and civilization 2. Science -- China -- History

ISBN 0-531-11334-5 lib bdg; 0-531-15914-0 pa

LC 97-3519

First published 1988 in the First book series

Surveys the achievements of the ancient Chinese in science, medicine, astronomy, and cosmology, and describes such innovations as rockets, wells, the compass, water wheels, and movable type

Includes glossary and bibliographical references

Cole, Joanna

★ The **magic** school bus and the science fair expedition; illustrated by Bruce Degen. Scholastic Press 2006 45p il $15.99

Grades: 2 3 4　　　　　**509**

1. Scientists 2. Science -- History

ISBN 0-590-10824-7

Ms. Frizzle takes her class on a tour through the history of science so they can get ideas for their science fair

"This has all the hallmarks of the winning series: humorous cartoon speech bubbles; instructive, funny, appealing illustrations; and clear language that explains basic concepts without condescension." Booklist

Eamer, Claire

Before the World Was Ready; Stories of Daring Genius in Science. by Claire Eamer. Firefly Books Ltd 2013 125 p. (paperback) $14.95; $24.95

Grades: 5 6 7 8　　　　　**509**

1. Inventions 2. Scientists

ISBN 1554515351; 9781554515356; 9781554515363

This book looks at eight scientists and inventors. "Alfred Wegener struggled to convince geologists that the ground beneath our feet is moving. . . . Nikola Tesla's futuristic ideas about electricity were dismissed. Charles Darwin delayed publishing his controversial theory of evolution for decades." Also included are Charles Babbage, Ada Lovelace, Rachel Carson, and George Cayley. (Publisher's note)

Harris, Jacqueline L.

★ **Science** in ancient Rome. Watts 1998 64p il map (Science of the past) hardcover o.p. pa $8.95

Grades: 4 5 6 7　　　　　**509**

1. Science and civilization 2. Science -- Rome -- History

ISBN 0-531-20354-9; 0-531-15916-7 pa

LC 97-1901

First published 1988 in the First book series

Describes how the Romans put to use and expanded the scientific achievements of earlier civilizations

This "includes clear, easy-to-read text; simple yet effective topic headings; excellent-quality, full-color photographs and reproductions; and Internet sites." SLJ

Includes glossary and bibliographical references

Jackson, Donna M.

★ **Extreme** scientists; exploring nature's mysteries from perilous places. Houghton Mifflin Harcourt 2009 63p il (Scientists in the field) $18

Grades: 5 6 7 8　　　　　**509**

1. Botanists 2. Explorers 3. Scientists 4. Spelunkers 5. Meteorologists 6. Microbiologists 7. College teachers

ISBN 978-0-618-77706-8; 0-618-77706-7

LC 2008-36796

This volume "profiles three scientists working far out in the field. Hurricane hunter Paul Flaherty, . . . Hazel Barton, a microbiologist specializing in single-cell organisms living in extreme conditions, . . . [and] ecologist and college professor Steve Sillett, who . . . climbs into the canopies to study redwoods. While the clearly written text includes vivid passages about the dangers these scientists face, it goes on to discuss what drives them to pursue their subjects and what they have discovered along the way. . . . The many excellent color photos portray these adventures as scientists intently focused on their work." Booklist

Includes glossary and bibliographical references

Woods, Geraldine

★ **Science** in ancient Egypt. Watts 1998 64p il (Science of the past) hardcover o.p. pa $8.95

Grades: 4 5 6 7　　　　　**509**

1. Science and civilization 2. Science -- Egypt -- History

ISBN 0-531-20341-7; 0-531-15915-9 pa

LC 97-649

First published 1988 in the First book series

Discusses the achievements of the ancient Egyptians in science, mathematics, astronomy, medicine, agriculture, and technology

"Well-researched and easy-to-understand. . . . Woods offers a fascinating look at the ancient Egyptians' accomplishments." SLJ

Includes glossary and bibliographical references

509.2　Scientists

Davidson, Tish

African American scientists and inventors; by Tish Davidson. Mason Crest Publishers 2013 64 p. ill. (some col.) (Major Black contributions from Emancipation to civil rights) (library) $22.95

Grades: 4 5 6　　　　　**509.2**

1. African American inventors -- Biography 4. African American scientists -- Biography

ISBN 1422223752; 9781422223758

LC 2011051942

This book by Tish Davidson profiles African American scientists and inventors. "Some of them were elementary school dropouts. Others became medical doctors or college professors. Some were famous, while some toiled in obscurity. . . . Lewis Latimer devised a manufacturing process that made electric lights affordable for ordinary people. Charles Drew did pioneering work in blood storage, helping save countless lives. Garrett Woods figured out how to send messages from moving trains." (Publisher's note)

Includes bibliographical references (pages 60-61) and index.

Di Domenico, Kelly

Women scientists who changed the world; by Kelly Di Domenico. Rosen Pub. 2012 106 p. col. ill. (library) $34.60

Grades: 5 6 7 8 **509.2**
1. Women scientists -- Biography 2. Women in science -- Biography
ISBN 1448859999; 9781448859993
LC 2011032120
In this collective biography by Kelly Di Domenico, "readers meet eleven women scientists, whose research and discoveries are outstanding in their fields. . . . Readers are introduced to each scientist's life and work, including the obstacles each woman had to overcome to achieve success. Profiles include biologist Rachel Carson, orangutan researcher Birute Galdikas, and Nobel Prize-winning biochemist Ada Yonath." (Publisher's note)
Includes bibliographical references (p. 101) and index.

Krull, Kathleen
Lives of the scientists; experiments, explosions (and what the neighbors thought) Kathleen Krull, Illustrated by Kathryn Hewitt. Houghton Mifflin Harcourt 2013 96 p. $20.99
Grades: 4 5 6 7 **509.2**
1. Science -- History 2. Scientists -- Biography
ISBN 0152059091; 9780152059095
LC 2012953333
The author Kathleen Krull's book focuses on the history of science. "This latest in the Lives of . . . series is summed up by the subtitle's 'What the Neighbors Thought.' The authors delve into intriguing, obscure, and peculiar facts about 20 famous scientists from all fields of study, regions of the globe, and eras of history." Topics include James D. Watson, Francis Crick, Marie Curie, Edwin Hubble, Barbara McClintock, and Grace Murray Hopper." (Booklist)

Miles, Liz
Louis Pasteur; by Liz Miles. Raintree 2009 48 p. ill. (chiefly col.) (Great scientists) (library) $32.00
Grades: 4 5 6 **509.2**
1. Science -- History -- 19th century 2. Scientists -- France -- Biography 3. Microbiologists -- France -- Biography
ISBN 141093229X; 9781410932297
LC 2007050125
This book by Liz Miles is part of the Leveled Biographies series and looks at Louis Pasteur. "What is Pasteurization? How has Pasteur's work helped treat many diseases? The 'Leveled Biographies' series offers leveled, high-interest nonfiction in a range of text genres. Each title tells the story of one memorable life, using pictures, maps, sidebars, and engaging text to make each person's story come alive." (Publisher's note)
Includes bibliographical references (p. 46) and index.

509.56 Science – Islamic Empire -- History

Romanek, Trudee
Science, medicine, and math in the early Islamic world; Trudee Romanek. Crabtree Pub. Company 2012 48 p. (reinforced library binding: alk. paper) $30.60
Grades: 4 5 6 7 **509.56**
1. Science -- History 2. Medicine -- History 3. Mathematics -- History 4. Islamic civilization 5.

Science -- Islamic Empire -- History
ISBN 0778721701; 9780778721703; 9780778721772; 9781427195630; 9781427198402
LC 2012000077
This children's educational book, by Trudee Romanek, describes "the scientific contributions of the early Islamic empires to science, medicine, and mathematics. . . . This . . . book explores their public hospitals, libraries, and universities; their achievements in mathematics and astronomy, and the pursuit of alchemy; Arabic numbers; optics; music and musical instruments; poetry; and education." (Publisher's note)

510 Mathematics

Bodach, Vijaya
Bar graphs; by Vijaya Khisty Bodach. Capstone Press 2008 32p il (Making graphs) lib bdg $23.93; pa $7.95
Grades: K 1 2 **510**
1. Graphic methods
ISBN 978-1-4296-0040-8 lib bdg; 1-4296-0040-3 lib bdg; 978-1-4296-2870-9 pa; 1-4296-2870-7 pa
LC 2007004670
This "book illustrates how to sort items and represent quantity using horizontal and vertical bars on a graph. Toy animals, fruit, pet type, and hair color are used as examples. . . . [The] title encourages readers to create their own graphs. Large, colorful photographs depict the concepts and feature ethnically diverse children. The photos and graphs complement the controlled-vocabulary [text]." SLJ
Includes glossary and bibliographical references

Pictographs; by Vijaya Khisty Bodach. Capstone Press 2008 32p il (Making graphs) lib bdg $23.93; pa $7.95
Grades: K 1 2 **510**
1. Graphic methods
ISBN 978-1-4296-0041-5 lib bdg; 1-4296-0041-1 lib bdg; 978-1-4296-2871-6 pa; 1-4296-2871-5 pa
LC 2007006948
This "introduces the idea of organizing data to 'show how many' with picture representations. Comparisons are made on a variety of topics: spotted and solid-color bunnies, how students get to school (walking, bus, and bikes), beverage preferences, and the kinds of flowers in an arrangement. . . . [The] title encourages readers to create their own graphs. Large, colorful photographs depict the concepts and feature ethnically diverse children. The photos and graphs complement the controlled-vocabulary [text]." SLJ
Includes glossary and bibliographical references

Pie graphs; by Vijaya Khisty Bodach. Capstone Press 2007 32p il (Making graphs) lib bdg $23.93; pa $7.95
Grades: K 1 2 **510**
1. Graphic methods
ISBN 978-1-4296-0042-2 lib bdg; 1-4296-0042-X lib bdg; 978-1-4296-2872-3 pa; 1-4296-2872-3 pa
LC 2007011075
"It's hard to find books that effectively explain math concerts for young children; this crystal clear entry in the Making Graphs series does just that. The book sensibly opens with an episode involving slices of strawberry pie, then points out that 'pie graphs are not just for pies.' The

examples, eight in all, stay close to children's immediate concerns. . . . A big strength of this title are the pictures, primarily professional photographs of children in scenes set up to closely match the text." Booklist

Includes bibliographical references

Tally charts; by Vijaya Khisty Bodach. Capstone Press 2008 32p il (Making graphs) lib bdg $23.93; pa $7.95
Grades: K 1 2 **510**
1. Counting 2. Graphic methods
ISBN 978-1-4296-0043-9 lib bdg; 1-4296-0043-8 lib bdg; 978-1-4296-2873-0 pa; 1-4296-2873-1 pa
LC 2007010814

This "is devoted to keeping count with tally marks recorded in groups of five. This concept is illustrated with pickup sticks and then translated to pen and paper. Sports preferences, the probability of heads or tails on coin flips, and score keeping are shown. [The] title encourages readers to create their own graphs. Large, colorful photographs depict the concepts and feature ethnically diverse children. The photos and graphs complement the controlled-vocabulary [text.]" SLJ

Includes glossary and bibliographical references

Connolly, Sean
The **book** of perfectly perilous math; 24 death-defying challenges for young mathematicians. by Sean Connolly. Workman Pub. 2012 xiii, 240 p.p ill. (alk. paper) $12.95
Grades: 4 5 6 **510**
1. Mathematical recreations 2. Word problems (Mathematics) 3. Mathematics -- Study and teaching 4. Mathematics -- Problems, exercises, etc 5. Problem solving -- Problems, exercises, etc
ISBN 0761163743; 9780761163749
LC 2012003443

This children's book by Sean Connolly "blends middle school math with fantasy. . . . These word problems are perilous, do-or-die scenarios of blood-sucking vampires . . . or [of] a rowboat of 5 shipwrecked sailors with a single barrel of freshwater. . . . They test readers on fractions, algebra, geometry, probability, expressions and equations, and more." (Publisher's note)

D'Amico, Joan
The **math** chef; over 60 math activities and recipes for kids. [by] Joan D'Amico, Karen Eich Drummond; illustrations by Tina Cash-Walsh. Wiley 1997 180p il pa $12.95
Grades: 4 5 6 **510**
1. Cooking 2. Mathematics
ISBN 0-471-13813-4
LC 96-22143

Relates math and cookery by presenting math concepts and reinforcing them with recipes. Provides practice in converting from English to metric system, multiplying quantities, measuring area, estimating, and more

"The instructional value of this book is excellent. . . . The illustrations and content are accurate and very well depicted." Sci Books Films

Includes glossary

Flatt, Lizann
Sorting through spring; Lizann Flatt, Ashley Barron. Owlkids Books Inc. 2013 32 p. (Math in nature) $14.95

Grades: 1 2 3 **510**
1. Nature 2. Mathematics
ISBN 1926973593; 9781926973593
LC 2012945652

"The aim of this . . . picture book is to introduce mathematical concepts such as patterning, data management, and probability by using occurrences in nature as examples. It examines events in springtime, such as rain, bird nests, budding flowers, and baby rabbits, and asks mathematical questions about them. . . . This is the second in the 'Math in Nature' series." (Children's Literature)

Green, Dan
Math; a book you can count on! created by Basher; written by Dan Green. Kingfisher 2010 64p il $12.99; pa $7.99
Grades: 4 5 6 7 **510**
1. Mathematics
ISBN 978-0-7534-6620-9; 0-7534-6620-1; 978-0-7534-6419-9 pa; 0-7534-6419-5 pa

This "introduces basic mathematical terms such as zero, line, pi, quadrilaterals, ratio, bar graph, and x (representing unknown quantities). Each one, personified in the accompanying digital illustration, speaks for itself. . . . Reminiscent of Japanese cartoons, the colorful, iconic illustrations of the characters are appealing enough to disarm many mathphobic students, while those who love the subject will be in their element. . . . Appealing to a broad range of readers, this little book introduces plenty of ideas to build on while presenting familiar concepts in a fresh way." Booklist

Lee, Cora
The **great** number rumble; [a story of math in surprising places] [by] Cora Lee & Gillian O'Reilly; illustrations by Virginia Gray. Annick Press 2007 104p il $24.95; pa $14.95
Grades: 4 5 6 **510**
1. Mathematics
ISBN 978-1-55451-032-0; 1-55451-032-5; 978-1-55451-031-3 pa; 1-55451-031-7 pa

"When the schools in Jeremy's town ban math, there are loud cheers from the kids. . . . But Jeremy's best friend Sam, a self-proclaimed mathnik, sets out to prove that math is not only important, but fun. In the chapters that follow, Sam reveals math's presence in everyday places, including sports (types of triangles determine how a bike functions), art (artist M.C. Escher combined math patterns with imagination), even in nature (ants instinctively calculate dead reckoning—a navigation tool also used by astronauts). . . . In the end, Jeremy, his teachers, and even the Director of Education have to admit that school minus math equals all sorts of trouble." (Publisher's note) Index. "Ages nine to eleven." (Quill Quire)

"Interspersed with the story line are one-page biographies of Pythagoras, Archimedes, Hypatia of Alexandria, Sophie Germain, Charles Ludwig Dodgson, Srinivasa Ramanujan, and Andrew Wiles. Sidebars with Jeremy's thoughts on chaos theory, cash prizes for new prime numbers, laws of probability, and palindrome numbers add to the information. Full-color cartoons, diagrams, and photos appear throughout." SLJ

McKellar, Danica

Math doesn't suck; how to survive middle school math without losing your mind or breaking a nail. [by] Danica McKellar. Hudson Street Press 2007 297p il $23.95

Grades: 5 6 7 8   **510**

1. Mathematics

ISBN 978-1-59463-039-2; 1-59463-039-9

LC 2007017091

This "covers some of the most basic ideas of middle-grade math, including concepts relating to fractions, decimals, and ratios, making each comprehensible, interesting, and fun. Using real-world constructions, such as tangled necklaces, boyfriends, and pizza, concepts are thoroughly explained." Voice Youth Advocates

Merriam, Eve

12 ways to get to 11; written by Eve Merriam; illustrated by Bernie Karlin. Simon & Schuster Bks. for Young Readers 1993 un il hardcover o.p. pa $6.99

Grades: K 1 2 3   **510**

1. Counting 2. Mathematics

ISBN 0-689-80892-5 pa

LC 91-25810

Uses ordinary experiences to present twelve combinations of numbers that add up to eleven. Example: At the circus, six peanut shells and five pieces of popcorn

"Some of the double-page spreads are simpler to solve than others, which allows children to progress as they learn more about counting. The huge, vibrant cut-paper and colored-pencil pictures make the book fun, lively, and painlessly educational." Horn Book Guide

Schwartz, David M.

★ G is for googol; a math alphabet book. written by David M. Schwartz; illustrated by Marissa Moss. Tricycle Press 1998 57p il $15.95

Grades: 4 5 6 7   **510**

1. Alphabet 2. Mathematics

ISBN 1-883672-58-9

LC 98-15162

Explains the meaning of mathematical terms which begin with the different letters of the alphabet from abacus, binary, and cubit to zillion

"The text is lively and clear and will appeal to even those who think math is as dull as the kitchen floor. . . . The cartoon illustrations are colorful, amusing, and informative." SLJ

Includes glossary

Tang, Greg

Math-terpieces; the art of problem-solving. illustrated by Greg Paprocki. Scholastic Press 2003 31p il $16.95

Grades: 2 3 4   **510**

1. Counting 2. Set theory 3. Art appreciation

ISBN 0-439-44388-1

LC 2002-5361

A series of rhymes about artists and their works introduces counting and grouping numbers, as well as such artistic styles as cubism, pointillism, and surrealism

"Clearly written solutions to these exercises are given at the end of the book along with art definitions and brief explanations. This math-concept book is far more appealing than most." SLJ

510.92   Mathematics biography

Heiligman, Deborah

★ The boy who loved math; the improbable life of Paul Erdos. Deborah Heiligman; illustrated by LeUyen Pham. Roaring Brook Press 2013 48 p. (hardcover) $17.99

Grades: 1 2 3 4   **510.92**

1. Mathematics 2. Mathematicians -- Hungary -- Biography

ISBN 1596433078; 9781596433076

LC 2012029744

Orbis Pictus Awards Honor Book (2014)

This book is a biography of mathematician Paul Erdös. He was a child prodigy who had to be homeschooled due to his inability to sit still and follow rules. "High school was a better fit, and he made friends with students who shared his love of math. His skills became famous, but Erdös didn't know how to do laundry, cook, or even butter his own bread. He 'didn't fit into the world in a regular way.' So, he created a life that fit him instead." (School Library Journal)

"Heiligman's joyful, warm account invites young listeners and readers to imagine a much-loved boy completely charmed by numbers... The polished, disarming text offers Pham free rein for lively illustration that captures Erdos' childlike spirit." Kirkus

511   General principles of mathematics

Murphy, Stuart J.

The sundae scoop; illustrated by Cynthia Jabar. HarperCollins Pubs. 2003 33p il (Mathstart) hardcover o.p. pa $4.99

Grades: 1 2 3   **511**

1. Mathematics

ISBN 0-06-028924-4; 0-06-028925-2 lib bdg; 0-06-446250-1 pa

LC 2001-24322

This "presents the concept of combinations in a story about a group of children who host an ice-cream booth at their school picnic. With two flavors of ice cream, two sauces, and two choices of toppings, the children are surprised that eight different sundaes are available. . . . Murphy easily folds the math concepts into a lively story that will capture young readers, and Jabar reinforces the lesson with colorful , whimsical drawings of delectable ice-cream scoops." Booklist

Nagda, Ann Whitehead

★ Tiger math; learning to graph from a baby tiger. by Ann Whitehead Nagda and Cindy Bickel. Holt & Co. 2000 un il $17.95; pa $7.95

Grades: 2 3 4   **511**

1. Tigers 2. Graphic methods

ISBN 0-8050-6248-3; 0-8050-7161-X pa

LC 99-46686

Describes the growth of an orphan Siberian tiger cub, by means of words and graphs

"Easy-to-understand picture, pie or circle, bar, or line graphs, all with explanations, appear on the left; facing pages of text and clear full-color photographs are on the right." SLJ

511.3   Mathematical logic (Symbolic logic)

Berry, Minta

What comes in sets? Minta Berry. Crabtree Pub. Co. 2012 24 p. lib bdg $22.60

Grades: K 1 2   **511.3**
    1. Set theory
    ISBN 0778752682 pa; 0778752798 lib bdg;
    9780778752684 pa; 9780778752790 lib bdg;
    9781427196507 e-books; 9781427198099 e-books
                                            LC 2011040391

This children's book by Minta Berry "introduces young readers to the concept of equal sets. Readers will learn to identify familiar things that come in pairs, sets of threes, fours, fives, and more." (Publisher's note) "The basic idea of sets is introduced through familiar objects: clothing, toys, kitchen items, and body parts. The activities encourage children to search through their homes for sets and make comparisons." (School Library Journal)

Murphy, Stuart J.

Dave's down-to-earth rock shop; illustrated by Cat Bowman Smith. HarperCollins Pubs. 2000 33p il (MathStart) hardcover o.p. pa $4.95

Grades: K 1 2 3   **511.3**
    1. Set theory 2. Rocks -- Collectors and collecting
    ISBN 0-06-028018-2; 0-06-028019-0 lib bdg; 0-06-446729-5 pa
                                              LC 98-32128

As they consider sorting their rock collection by color, size, type, and hardness, Josh and Amy learn that the same objects can be organized in many different ways

"Murphy's forte is explaining complex topics in a down-to-earth manner, and that's just what he's done here. Along the way, he also includes a good deal of information about rocks, minerals, and the scientific method. Smith's full-color illustrations capture the excitement of rock hunting and include many geological and equipment details." Booklist

Seaweed soup; by Stuart Murphy; illustrated by Frank Remkiewicz. HarperCollins Pubs. 2001 31p il (MathStart) hardcover o.p. pa $4.95

Grades: K 1 2 3   **511.3**
    1. Set theory
    ISBN 0-06-028032-8; 0-06-028033-6 lib bdg; 0-06-028036-8 pa
                                              LC 99-87634

As he asks more and more friends to join him for lunch, Turtle must make up sets of dishes to accommodate them

"A graph will help children review what they've learned, and two pages of ideas for extending the book are appended. Remkiewicz's appealing illustrations encourage children to match sets and count items in each set." Booklst

512   Algebra

Adler, David A., 1947-

Mystery math; a first book of algebra. by David A. Adler; illustrated by Edward Miller. Holiday House 2011 1 v.

Grades: 2 3 4   **512**
    1. Algebra
    ISBN 0823422895; 9780823422890
                                            LC 2010024188

Adler tackles the "topic of algebra, starting with the basics and working up from there. . . . Easy-to-understand mathematical notations guide readers through the solution to each problem, which are originally posed as word problems involving two children, Mandy and Billy, and Igor, the caretaker of a haunted house. The Halloween theme echoes the idea of algebra as the solving of mathematical mysteries, and Miller's digital artwork ups the ante with a palette strong on blacks, dark blues and lime greens." Kirkus

Anno, Masaichiro

Anno's mysterious multiplying jar; [by] Masaichiro and Mitsumasa Anno; illustrated by Mitsumasa Anno. Philomel Bks. 1983 un il $19.99; pa $7.99

Grades: 2 3 4 5   **512**
    1. Factorials 2. Mathematics
    ISBN 0-399-20951-4; 0-698-11753-0 pa
                                              LC 82-22413

Simple text and pictures introduce the mathematical concept of factorials

This book "begins with a painting of a handsome blue and white lidded jar, moves into fantasy with pictures of the water in the jar becoming a sea on which an old sailing ship is moving, transfers to an island on the sea, and goes on to describe the rooms in the houses in the kingdoms on the mountains in the countries on the island. Each time the number grows: one island, two countries, three mountains, etc. How many jars, then, were in the boxes that were in the cupboards in the rooms? . . . The explanation is in itself clear, and is expanded by other examples of factorials." Bull Cent Child Books

512.9   Foundations of algebra

Murphy, Stuart J.

Safari Park; illustrated by Steve Björkman. HarperCollins Pubs. 2002 31p il (Mathstart) hardcover o.p. pa $4.99

Grades: 2 3 4   **512.9**
    1. Equations
    ISBN 0-06-028914-7; 0-06-028915-5 lib bdg; 0-06-446245-5 pa
                                              LC 00-63201

"At the new amusement park, Grandpa gives his grandkids twenty tickets each. With a little help, the kids add up the cost in tickets for rides and figure out the 'unknowns,' the number of tickets left over for snacks and games. Cartoony watercolors keep up the carnival atmosphere, while a plot about Paul's lost tickets and the Terrible Tarantula ride adds a hint of suspense. Related activities are appended." Horn Book Guide

513   Arithmetic

Adler, David A.

Fractions, decimals, and percents; illustrated by Edward Miller. Holiday House 2010 un il $16.95

Grades: 2 3 4 **513**

   1. Fractions 2. Percentage 3. Decimal fractions

   ISBN 978-0-8234-2199-2; 0-8234-2199-6

                     LC 2008048464

"This brightly illustrated book . . . quickly presents several math concepts related to fractions, decimals, and percents. Using a county fair as a backdrop, Adler discusses how to change a number in one form to its equivalent in another; and how the value of a digit depends upon its placement in relation to a decimal point. Miller's digital artwork illustrates the ideas clearly." Booklist

   Fun with Roman numerals; by David A. Adler; illustrated by Edward Miller. Holiday House 2008 un il lib bdg $16.95

Grades: 2 3 4 **513**

   1. Roman numerals

   ISBN 978-0-8234-2060-5 lib bdg; 0-8234-2060-4 lib bdg

                     LC 2007-43531

"This book provides basic information on the symbols, arrangements, and mathematical processes involving Roman numerals. Details are shared in a clear and logical manner with appropriate graphics to illustrate the concepts." Sci Books Films

Anno, Mitsumasa

   Anno's magic seeds; written and illustrated by Mitsumasa Anno. Philomel Bks. 1995 un il hardcover o.p. pa $6.99

Grades: K 1 2 3 **513**

   1. Mathematics

   ISBN 0-399-22538-2; 0-698-11618-6 pa

                     LC 92-39309

The reader is asked to perform a series of mathematical operations integrated into the story of a lazy man who plants magic seeds and reaps an increasingly abundant harvest

"Anno has succeeded in combining both the moral issue of conservation of resources and arithmetical games in a charming story for young readers. A tour de force from a most original author-illustrator." Horn Book

Bang, Molly

   ★ **Ten,** nine, eight. Greenwillow Bks. 1983 un il $16.99; lib bdg $17.89; pa $6.99; bd bk $6.99

Grades: PreK K 1 **513**

   1. Counting 2. Bedtime -- Fiction

   ISBN 0-688-00906-9; 0-688-00907-7 lib bdg; 0-688-10480-0 pa; 0-688-14901-4 bd bk

                     LC 81-20106

A Caldecott Medal honor book, 1984

"In countdown style, the text of this counting book begins with '10 small toes all washed and warm,' and ends with '1 big girl all ready for bed.' The captions rhyme . . . and the pictures—warm, bright paintings—show a black father and child snuggling in a chair, the child yawning, and the child hugging her toy bear after some loving good night kisses." Bull Cent Child Books

Campbell, Sarah C.

   ★ **Growing** patterns; Fibonacci numbers in nature. photographs by Sarah C. Campbell and Richard P. Campbell. Boyds Mills Press 2010 32p il $17.95

Grades: 2 3 4 5 **513**

   1. Numbers 2. Nature study

   ISBN 978-1-59078-752-6; 1-59078-752-8

                     LC 2009-24075

The authors "turn their attention to the Fibonacci sequence of numbers, employing photographs from nature, basic addition, and reader-directed text to explain it. . . . Besides being eye-catching, the photographs ought to prove invaluable for visual learners. . . . Kids should be left with a clear understanding of the pattern and curious about its remarkable prevalence in nature." Publ Wkly

   Includes glossary

Caron, Lucille

   Fraction and decimal smarts! [by] Lucille Caron, Philip M. St. Jacques. Enslow Publishers 2011 64p il lib bdg $27.93

Grades: 5 6 7 8 **513**

   1. Fractions 2. Decimal fractions

   ISBN 978-0-7660-3936-0

                     LC 2011008382

"This clearly written series provides definitions and examples of many concepts... examples are realistic and appropriate for the target age group." SLJ

   Percent and ratio smarts! [by] Lucille Caron, Philip M. St. Jacques. Enslow Publishers 2011 64p il lib bdg $27.93

Grades: 5 6 7 8 **513**

   1. Fractions 2. Ratios (Statistics)

   ISBN 978-0-7660-3940-7

                     LC 2011008164

"This clearly written series provides definitions and examples of many concepts... examples are realistic and appropriate for the target age group." SLJ

Cleary, Brian P., 1959-

   The **action** of subtraction; by Brian P. Cleary; illustrated by Brian Gable. Millbrook Press 2006 30p il lib bdg $15.95

Grades: 2 3 4 **513**

   1. Subtraction

   ISBN 978-0-7613-9461-7 lib bdg; 0-7613-9461-3 lib bdg

                     LC 2005025881

"Subtraction is explained in rhyming text and simple, silly cartoons with excellent examples that range from angry bulldogs, hornets, and bowling pins to pieces of birthday cake, sports time-outs, and stuffed animals. . . . The illustrations are colorful and attractive." SLJ

   A **fraction's** goal; parts of a whole. illustrated by Brian Gable. Millbrook Press 2011 31p il (Math is categorical) lib bdg $16.95

Grades: 2 3 4 5 **513**

   1. Fractions

   ISBN 978-0-8225-7881-9; 0-8225-7881-6

                     LC 2010051518

This "title presents fractions as a way to express parts of an entity (pizza) or group (jugglers). The rhyming lines of text bounce along in a genial way. . . . Brightened with eye-catching color combinations, Gable's cartoon-style illustrations express the simple mathematical ideas clearly, while his wacky critters add a good deal of humor." Booklist

Clements, Andrew

A **million** dots; illustrated by Mike Reed. Simon & Schuster Books for Young Readers 2006 un il $16.95

Grades: K 1 2 3   **513**

1. Million (The number)

ISBN 0-689-85824-8

LC 2004-05349

"With one million dots printed on its pages, this large-format picture book shows how big a million really is. Along the way, the text and illustrations offer plenty to look at and think about besides the rows and rows of tiny dots. On each page, Clements selects one number and connects it to a numerical fact." Booklist

Dodds, Dayle Ann

Full house; an invitation to fractions. [by] Dayle Ann Dodds; illustrated by Abby Carter. Candlewick Press 2007 un il $16.99

Grades: 1 2 3   **513**

1. Fractions 2. Stories in rhyme

ISBN 978-0-7636-2468-2; 0-7636-2468-3

LC 2006051847

Miss Bloom uses fractions as the six-room Strawberry Inn fills with guests and she divides her pie into sixths

"Fresh, whimsical watercolor illustrations fairly float off the pages in this title. Rhyming text invites readers to enjoy every moment at the Strawberry Inn." SLJ

Fisher, Valorie

How high can a dinosaur count? and other math mysteries. [by] Valorie Fisher. Schwartz & Wade Books 2006 un il $16.95

Grades: 1 2 3   **513**

1. Counting 2. Arithmetic

ISBN 0-375-83608-X

LC 2005010851

"The text for each of the 15 problems is presented on the left, using a large, clean font on a spectrum of soft pastel backgrounds. The problems are clearly explained, but lots of alliteration and some unexpected vocabulary make for interesting reading. The illustration on the right features Fisher's unique photographic technique. Richly textured patterns and hand-drawn objects are cut out and arranged, then photographed in such a way as to create whimsical tableaux with a three-dimensional feel. The characters are charming." SLJ

Fleming, Denise

★ **Count!** Holt & Co. 1992 un il $17.95; pa $7.95

Grades: PreK K 1 2   **513**

1. Animals 2. Counting

ISBN 0-8050-1595-7; 0-8050-4252-0 pa

LC 91-25686

The antics of lively and colorful animals present the numbers one to ten, twenty, thirty, forty, and fifty

"A fresh, upbeat concept book. Lizards, giraffes, toucans, butterflies are available for counting—if only they'll hold still long enough! Fuchsias and oranges, teals and purples, roll over the pages blending into each other in Fleming's beautiful couched paper with hand cut-stencil illustrations. Her explosions of color and motion are captivating and energizing." SLJ

Franco, Betsy

★ **Zero** is the leaves on the tree; illustrations by Shino Arihara. Tricycle Press 2009 un il $15.99

Grades: PreK K 1 2   **513**

1. Zero (The number)

ISBN 978-1-58246-249-3; 1-58246-249-6

LC 2008042185

Using "evocative examples from children's everyday experiences throughout the seasons, Franco explores the concept of zero. The gouache illustrations are done in soft, muted tones and have a naive charm that will have substantial child appeal." SLJ

Giganti, Paul

How many snails? a counting book. by Paul Giganti, Jr.; pictures by Donald Crews. Greenwillow Bks. 1988 un il $16.99; pa $6.99

Grades: PreK K 1 2   **513**

1. Counting

ISBN 0-688-06369-1; 0-688-13639-7 pa

LC 87-26281

"Instead of inviting children to count static objects, Mr. Giganti poses a series of simple, direct questions designed to encourage youngsters to determine the often subtle differences between those objects. Donald Crews . . . concentrates here on decorating each page with objects that supply the necessary links to the text. Some of the pages—depicting a collection of motley dogs at the park or beautiful toy boats and trucks, cars and airplanes at a toy store—are a joy to look at." N Y Times Book Rev

Lewis, J. Patrick

Arithme-tickle; an even number of odd riddle-rhymes. illustrated by Frank Remkiewicz. Harcourt 2002 32p il $16

Grades: 2 3 4   **513**

1. Arithmetic 2. Mathematical recreations

ISBN 0-15-216418-9

LC 2001-3228

"Wordplay, riddles, and math problems test readers' skill at addition, subtraction, multiplication, division, telling time, logic, and even general knowledge in this colorfully illustrated collection. Clearly meant to make math more approachable and enjoyable, this compilation includes enough genuinely complex puzzles to keep hardcore young math buffs entertained." Booklist

Long, Lynette

Marvelous multiplication; games and activities that make math easy and fun. Wiley 2000 122p il (Magical math) pa $12.95

Grades: 3 4 5 6   **513**

1. Multiplication

ISBN 0-471-36982-9

LC 00-20473

Presents a series of activities, arranged in order of difficulty, that teach the operation of multiplication

"The cheerful ink drawings help make the [book] more inviting." Booklist

Markel, Michelle

Tyrannosaurus math; illustrations by Doug Cushman. Tricycle Press 2009 un il $15.99

Grades: 1 2 3 **513**
1. Dinosaurs 2. Arithmetic 3. Mathematics
ISBN 978-1-58246-282-0; 1-58246-282-8
LC 2008042389
"From the moment he bursts out of his shell, T-Math thinks mathematically, making number sentences to express how many digits he has and the number of kids in his family. He counts footprints by twos and uses fives and tens to group and count a herd of triceratops. He checks his subtraction with addition, draws pictures to solve word problems, creates pictographs and thinks in pie graphs. And it is his estimation skills that save his sister, who gets stranded on the wrong side of a canyon after an earthquake. . . . Cushman's brightly colored acrylic illustrations nicely show readers the math involved without diminishing in any way the personalities of the dinosaurs. The ultimate melding of a topic kids love with knowledge they need." Kirkus

Mattern, Joanne
Even or odd? Rourke Pub. 2010 24p il (Little world math concepts) lib bdg $22.79; pa $7.95
Grades: PreK K **513**
1. Number concept
ISBN 978-1-61590-292-7 lib bdg; 1-61590-292-9 lib bdg; 978-1-61590-531-7 pa; 1-61590-531-6 pa
LC 2010009893
"Aimed at both preliterate preschoolers and emerging readers, the minimal text and images present questions and answers that introduce even and odd numbers. Magnified color photos show organized groups of everyday items . . . providing numerous opportunities for young children to practice counting by twos and identify the orphans when the groups represent odd numbers. . . . This book is a focused, one-stop resource for helping young children grasp the single, essential math concept it presents." Booklist
Includes bibliographical references

Murphy, Stuart J.
★ **Divide** and ride; illustrated by George Ulrich. HarperCollins Pubs. 1997 32p il (MathStart) hardcover o.p. pa $4.95
Grades: 1 2 3 **513**
1. Division
ISBN 0-06-026776-3; 0-06-026777-1 lib bdg; 0-06-446710-4 pa
LC 95-26134
"Eleven friends climb aboard the Dare-Devil roller coaster and three other rides, but before each ride can begin, all of the seats must be filled. Readers follow the children as they solve each problem by dividing and then filling the empty seats with new friends. Watercolor, pen, and ink illustrations and follow-up activities accompany the story." Horn Book Guide

★ **Double** the ducks; illustrated by Valeria Petrone. HarperCollins Pubs. 2003 31p il (MathStart) hardcover o.p. lib bdg $16.89; pa $4.99
Grades: K 1 **513**
1. Multiplication
ISBN 0-06-028922-8; 0-06-028923-6 lib bdg; 0-06-446249-8 pa
LC 2001-24321
"A young cowboy cares for his five little ducks, and he scurries around to bring them three sacks of food and four bundles of hay with his two hands. When each duck brings a friend, the boy has double the ducks, so he needs to double the hay and double the food. . . . In a double-page spread at the back of the book, Murphy suggests lots of activities and games for parents to use in the kitchen and at play to make preschoolers' first steps into addition and multiplication more fun." Booklist

Earth Day-hooray! illustrated by Renee Andriani. HarperCollins Pubs. 2004 32p il (MathStart) $15.99; pa $4.99
Grades: 1 2 3 **513**
1. Recycling 2. Place value (Mathematics)
ISBN 0-06-000127-5; 0-06-000129-1 pa
LC 2002-155234
A drive to recycle cans on Earth Day teaches the children of the Maple Street School Save-the-Planet Club about place value
"Andriani's cheerful illustrations fairly teem with information about recycling and add humor and human interest to the story." SLJ
Includes bibliographical references

★ **Elevator** magic; illustrated by G. Brian Karas. HarperCollins Pubs. 1997 32p il (MathStart) hardcover o.p. pa $4.95
Grades: K 1 2 **513**
1. Subtraction
ISBN 0-06-026775-5; 0-06-446709-0 pa
LC 96-5672
"A boy meets his mother on the 10th floor of a high rise. On the way down, Mom needs to do some errands. The first stop, two floors down, is to cash a check at the Farm Bank and Trust, which is (lo and behold!) filled with horses, barns, and hay fields. Farther down is the Hard Rock Candy Store, which is not only full of candy but also the sounds and lights of a heavy metal band. Karas's zany illustrations support the main concept being taught, while picking up on the humor in the word play." SLJ

The **Grizzly** Gazette; illustrated by Steve Björkman. HarperCollins Pubs. 2003 31p il (MathStart) $15.99; lib bdg $16.89; pa $4.99
Grades: 1 2 3 **513**
1. Percentage
ISBN 0-06-000027-9; 0-06-000025-2 lib bdg; 0-06-000026-0 pa
LC 2001-24633
At Camp Grizzly the camp newspaper takes a poll each day to see who has the greatest percentage of the vote so far in the election to chose a mascot. Includes activities for learning about percentages

Henry the fourth; illustrated by Scott Nash. HarperCollins Pubs. 1999 33p il (MathStart) $15.95; lib bdg $15.89; pa $4.95
Grades: K 1 **513**
1. Numbers
ISBN 0-06-027610-X; 0-06-027611-8 lib bdg; 0-06-446719-8 pa
LC 98-4960
A simple story about four dogs at a dog show introduces the ordinal numbers: first, second, third, and fourth

"The numerical concepts are sequential and simple enough for young children to follow. The watercolor cartoons fill the pages with action." SLJ

★ **Jack** the builder; illustrated by Michael Rex. HarperCollins Pubs. 2006 33p il (MathStart) hardcover o.p. pa $4.99

Grades: K 1   513

1. Counting

ISBN 0-06-055774-5; 0-06-055775-3 pa

"Jack stacks 2 blocks taken from a big pile. Turn the page, and a wild, colorful double-page spread shows what his simple stack becomes with the addition of a little imagination—a robot. A third block makes a hot-dog stand . . . and 2 more build 'a ferryboat out on the sea.' Eight blocks become a lookout tower, and, using 17, Jack creates a rocket ship. . . . Murphy begins and ends with simple hands-on activities for adults to help bring the math into kids' everyday life. Rex's bright illustrations will encourage even young preschoolers to point at shapes and colors as they count and add on." Booklist

Jump, kangaroo, jump! illustrated by Kevin O'Malley. HarperCollins Pubs. 1999 un il (MathStart) hardcover o.p. pa $4.95

Grades: 1 2 3   513

1. Division 2. Fractions

ISBN 0-06-027614-2; 0-06-446721-X pa

LC 97-45814

Kangaroo and his Australian animal friends divide themselves up into different groups for the various field day events at camp

"The simple story line presents a real-world application of fractions and division, neatly reinforced by O'Malley's expressive illustrations. Related activities are suggested." Horn Book Guide

Less than zero; illustrated by Frank Remkiewicz. HarperCollins Pubs. 2003 33p il (MathStart) $15.99; pa $4.99

Grades: K 1 2 3   513

1. Arithmetic 2. Zero (The number)

ISBN 0-06-000124-0; 0-06-000126-7 pa

LC 2002-20732

While trying to save enough money to buy a new ice scooter, Perry the Penguin learns about managing his money and about negative numbers

Includes bibliographical references

Mall mania; illustrated by Renée Andriani. HarperCollins 2006 33p il (MathStart) $15.99; pa $4.99

Grades: K 1 2   513

1. Addition 2. Counting

ISBN 0-06-055776-1; 0-06-055776-X pa

"The 100th person to enter Parkside Mall will get lots of promotional gifts, and four kids from Wilson Elementary School's chess club are on hand to count up the shoppers and add the numbers together. . . . The counters use a variety of addition strategies and activities, as always, Murphy adds greatly to the math lesson by making it seem a part of daily life. Suggestions for follow-up activities, both complex and easy . . . are appended." Booklist

Includes bibliographical references

More or less; illustrated by David T. Wenzel. HarperCollinsPublishers 2005 33p il (MathStart) $15.99; pa $4.99

Grades: K 1 2 3   513

1. Arithmetic

ISBN 0-06-053165-7; 0-06-053167-3 pa

LC 2003-27847

"In this story, Eddie works the 'guess the age' booth at the fair. . . . The way Eddie progresses . . . leads children into the world of logical, educated guesses. . . . Youngsters who need to understand the math concept in more depth will find several activities at the conclusion of the book. . . . Sprightly watercolor artwork makes math look like fun. " Booklist

Sluggers' car wash; illustrated by Barney Saltzberg. HarperCollins Pubs. 2002 33p il (MathStart) hardcover o.p. lib bdg $17.89; pa $4.99

Grades: 1 2 3   513

1. Addition

ISBN 0-06-028920-1; 0-06-028921-X lib bdg; 0-06-446248-X pa

LC 00-54062

When the 21st Street Sluggers, a baseball team, have a car wash to raise money, they learn to keep careful track of their dollars and cents

"Colorful illustrations both enhance the story line and elucidate the math lesson with clear tabulations for the money counting and change." SLJ

Nagda, Ann Whitehead

Cheetah math; learning about division from baby cheetahs. by Ann Whitehead Nagda in collaboration with the San Diego Zoo. Henry Holt 2007 29p il $16.95

Grades: 2 3 4   513

1. Cheetahs 2. Division

ISBN 978-0-8050-7645-5; 0-8050-7645-X

LC 2006030069

"Each spread includes division problems that revolve around the big cats on the left and facts about the birth and development of two baby cheetahs, Majani and Kubali, on the right. The color photography is outstanding. . . . This is a wonderful cross-curricular book and an appealing way to introduce math." SLJ

Panda math; learning about subtraction from Hua Mei and Mei Sheng. Holt & Co. 2005 29p il lib bdg $17.95

Grades: 2 3 4   513

1. Giant panda 2. Subtraction

ISBN 0-8050-7644-1

"This wonderful title featuring panda cubs born in the San Diego Zoo does double duty as a math book. The right side of each spread offers a captioned color photograph and text describing the growth and development of Hua Mei and Mei Sheng. The green left-hand pages provide additional details about pandas in general and these two specifically: their eating and sleeping habits, weight, and life expectancy and incorporates this information into a subtraction word problem." SLJ

Polar bear math; learning about fractions from Klondike and Snow. by Ann Whitehead Nagda and Cindy Bickel. H. Holt and Co. 2004 29p il $16.95

Grades: 2 3 4   **513**

1. Fractions 2. Polar bear
ISBN 0-8050-7301-9

LC 2003-20996

"Following the lives of two cubs that were born at the Denver Zoo and abandoned by their mother, this book provides information about polar bears and fractions. Right-hand pages tell the story of Snow and Klondike, with excellent, full-color photos showing how zoo personnel raised them from newborns until their first birthday. . . . The explanations, which combine text with pictographs, are clear and well formulated." SLJ

Rubin, Alan

How many fish? Yellow Umbrella Bks. 2003 17p il (Yellow umbrella books for early readers) $14.60
Grades: PreK K 1 2   **513**

1. Fishes 2. Counting
ISBN 0-7368-2013-2

LC 2003-924

Introduces counting by showing different numbers of fish and other creatures swimming in the sea

"Not only can beginning readers feel successful at mastering the short, repetitive sentences, but they can also excel at counting the human feet and fish under the water. Colorful illustrations enhance the text." SLJ

Schwartz, David M.

★ **How** much is a million? pictures by Steven Kellogg. Lothrop, Lee & Shepard Bks. 1985 un il $16.99; lib bdg $17.89; pa $6.99
Grades: PreK K 1 2 3   **513**

1. Billion (The number) 2. Million (The number) 3. Trillion (The number) 4. Counting 5. Number concept
ISBN 0-688-04049-7; 0-688-04050-0 lib bdg; 0-688-09933-5 pa

LC 84-5736

Text and pictures seek to provide conceptualization of a million, a billion, and a trillion. "Grades one to four." (SLJ)

"Marvelosissimo the Mathematical Magician leads the reader through Steven Kellogg's scenes of fantasy to express the concepts of a million, a billion and a trillion. The text is all printed in capital letters to point out the expanding scenes portrayed in the fabulous illustrations. The idea is to make possible to children the awesome concept of large numbers. It is a delightful fantasy as a picture book, but it is even more compelling as a first reader." Okla State Dept of Educ

Slade, Suzanne

What's new at the zoo? an animal adding adventure. illustrated by Joan Waites. Sylvan Dell 2009 un il $16.95
Grades: PreK K 1 2   **513**

1. Zoos 2. Animals 3. Addition
ISBN 978-1-934359-93-8; 1-934359-93-9

"On a visit to the zoo, a young boy counts the animal babies and parents in each enclosure, the accompanying rhyme encouraging readers to do the math along with him. . . Slade slyly sneaks in some great vocabulary, working the animal baby names into each verse. . . . Backmatter teaches two methods for adding all the numbers, a section about fact families and a matching game wherein readers can test their memories of baby names against some paragraphs of information about each animal's development. The solid math

and informative backmatter make this a worthwhile addition to libraries and math programs." Kirkus

Tang, Greg

★ **The** best of times; math strategies that multiply. illustrated by Harry Briggs. Scholastic Press 2002 un il $16.95
Grades: 2 3 4   **513**

1. Multiplication
ISBN 0-439-21044-5

LC 2002-23043

Simple rhymes offer hints on how to multiply any number by zero through ten without memorizing the multiplication tables

"Encouraging rhymes and colorful, jaunty illustrations bolster the multiplication lesson." Booklist

★ **Math** fables; lessons that count. illustrated by Heather Cahoon. Scholastic Press 2004 un il $16.95
Grades: K 1 2   **513**

1. Science 2. Counting
ISBN 0-439-45399-2

LC 2002-5360

A series of rhymes about animals introduces counting and grouping numbers, as well as examples of such behaviors as cooperation, friendship, and appreciation.

"The text and perky, computer-generated cartoons show youngsters that there are many different ways of putting numbers together. . . . The enriching vocabulary is an added bonus. A fine addition to math shelves." SLJ

513.2   Arithmetic operations

Adler, David A.

Fraction fun; illustrated by Nancy Tobin. Holiday House 1996 un il $16.95; pa $6.95
Grades: 2 3 4   **513.2**

1. Fractions
ISBN 0-8234-1259-8; 0-8234-1341-1 pa

LC 96-10773

"Adler presents the concept of fractions with the tried-and-true example of dividing a pie (pizza pie, in this case), then directs readers to draw lines across paper plates and color the eight resultant wedges in various color combinations. . . . Adler doesn't shy away from correct terminology—numerators and denominators—in this primary-grade introduction. Next he launches into some hands-on experimentation. . . . Tobin supplies a jazzy, eye-popping color scheme and diagrams of exceptional clarity to illuminate the straightforward text." Bull Cent Child Books

Browne, Anthony

One gorilla; a counting book. Anthony Browne. Candlewick Press 2013 32 p. $16.99
Grades: PreK K 1   **513.2**

1. Counting 2. Picture books for children 3. Primates
ISBN 0763663522; 9780763663520

LC 2012942388

This children's book by Anthony Browne provides children with an "array of creatures for kids to count." The book offers a "presentation of primates from gorillas to gibbons, macaques to mandrills, ring-tailed lemurs to spider monkeys

... [and] extends the basic number concept into a look at similarities and differences -- portraying an extended family we can count ourselves part of." (Publisher's note)

Hoban, Tana

★ **Let's** count. Greenwillow Bks. 1999 un il $17.99
Grades: PreK K   **513.2**
1. Counting
ISBN 0-688-16008-5

LC 98-44739

Photographs and dots introduce the numbers one to one hundred

"Hoban brings us another dazzling picture book. . . . Her photos range from the simple—1 hen, 8 Dalmatian puppies—to the more sophisticated—6 twirling rings on the arms of a circus performer; 12 rolls of toilet paper unpacked and stored on a pantry shelf." Booklist

Leedy, Loreen

2 x 2; a set of spooky multiplication stories. written and illustrated by Loreen Leedy. Holiday House 1995 32p il $17.95; pa $6.95
Grades: K 1 2 3   **513.2**
1. Multiplication
ISBN 0-8234-1190-7; 0-8234-1272-5 pa

LC 94-46711

This is an "introduction to basic multiplication, with witches, cats, and monsters demonstrating the consequences of multiplying numbers from 0 to 5. The illustrations are done in muted, autumnal tones of black, blue, orange, and mustard, and arranged in a comic-strip format. . . . The concepts are clear and understandable. . . . Leedy's book presents an entertaining alternative to rote memorization." SLJ

★ **Fraction** action; written and illustrated by Loreen Leedy. Holiday House 1994 31p il $17.95; pa $6.95
Grades: K 1 2 3   **513.2**
1. Fractions
ISBN 0-8234-1109-5; 0-8234-1244-X pa

LC 93-22800

Miss Prime and her animal students explore fractions by finding many examples in the world around them

"Thickly pigmented paintings loaded with sporty animal figures add to the humorous presentation, which should make fractions not only more understandable, but also more fun for young children." Bull Cent Child Books

★ **Mission**: addition; written and illustrated by Loreen Leedy. Holiday House 1997 un il $17.95; pa $6.95
Grades: K 1 2 3   **513.2**
1. Addition
ISBN 0-8234-1307-1; 0-8234-1412-4 pa

LC 96-37149

Miss Prime and her animal students explore addition by finding many examples in the world around them

"Flat chalk-box colors predominate in the illustrations, which will please kids with their liveliness, their informality, and their cartoonlike speech balloons. . . . An attractive picture book to support the math curriculum." Booklist

★ **Subtraction** action. Holiday House 2000 32p il $17.95; pa $6.95

Grades: K 1 2 3   **513.2**
1. Subtraction
ISBN 0-8234-1454-X; 0-8234-1244-X pa

LC 99-49803

Introduces subtraction through the activities of animal students at a school fair. Includes problems for the reader to solve

This is "an action-packed volume that is perfectly suited to its audience. The softly hued cartoon animals and dialogue balloons are skillfully combined on pages divided into framed sequences." SLJ

Long, Lynette

Fabulous fractions; games and activities that make math easy and fun. Wiley 2001 122p il (Magical math) pa $12.95
Grades: 3 4 5 6   **513.2**
1. Fractions
ISBN 0-471-36981-0

LC 00-43386

This introduction to fractions includes activities using such materials as sandwiches, paper plates, cards, and dominoes

This book includes "lists of the required materials, clear and complete procedures, and a black-and-white illustration." SLJ

Marzollo, Jean

Help me learn subtraction; by Jean Marzollo; photographs by Chad Phillips. 1st American ed. Holiday House 2012 32 p. col. ill. (hardcover) $15.95; (paperback) $6.99
Grades: K 1 2   **513.2**
1. Visual literacy 2. Word problems (Mathematics) 3. Mathematics -- Study and teaching 4. Subtraction 5. Counting-out rhymes
ISBN 0823424014; 9780823424016; 9780823428229

LC 2011046540

Author Jean Marzollo's book "in the photograph-based Help Me Learn series . . . uses puppets, figurines, and other playful items to demonstrate [subtraction] math equations, which are presented both numerically and in words. . . . [The book utilizes] finger puppets, pipe cleaner dogs, and other objects" to help children visualize the problems. (Publishers Weekly)

Menotti, Andrea

How many jelly beans? Andrea Menotti; illustrator, Yancey Labat. Chronicle Books 2012 28 p. ill. (hardcover) $18.99
Grades: 2 3 4   **513.2**
1. Candy 2. Numbers 3. Calendars 4. Counting 5. Jellybeans 6. Mathematics
ISBN 1452102066; 9781452102061

LC 2011030673

Author Andrea Menotti "takes on big numbers . . . [in this oversized book] using jelly beans as counters. When Emma and Aiden are asked how many jelly beans they want, they carry on a boasting match, resulting in escalating amounts of candy. . . . Five hundred beans cover a coffee table, and 1,000 beans are divided out over the days of a year on calendar pages." (Publishers Weekly)

Murphy, Stuart J.

Just enough carrots; illustrated by Frank Remkiewicz. HarperCollins Pubs. 1997 31p il (MathStart) $14.95; lib bdg $15.89; pa $4.95

Grades: K 1 **513.2**

1. Counting

ISBN 0-06-026778-X; 0-06-026779-8 lib bdg; 0-06-446711-2 pa

LC 96-19495

While a bunny and his mother shop in a grocery store for lunch guests, the reader may count and compare the amounts of carrots, peanuts, and worms in the grocery carts of other shoppers

"Bright, colorful illustrations, a surprise ending, and two pages of activities for adults and children extend and enhance the book's appeal." SLJ

Perritano, John

Mummies in the library; divide the pages. by John Perritano and David Hughes. Norwood House Press 2012 32 p. (iMath readers) (library edition: alk. paper) $22.60

Grades: 2 3 4 **513.2**

1. Mummies 2. Division 3. Reading

ISBN 1599535580; 9781599535586; 9781603575270

LC 2012023839

Authors John Perritano and David T. Hughes presents a "fictional story line involving a young boy's visit to the library for a book on mummies (thus the title) to introduce the concept of division. Division problems are woven into the story (for example, how many days will it take the narrator to read his 160-page book?), followed by information about Egyptian mummies and a few more division problems. The information about mummies connects a range of topics to curriculum segments." (Publisher's note)

Includes bibliographical references and index

Pistoia, Sara

Fractions; by Sara Pistoia. Child's World 2007 24 p. (MathBooks) $25.64

Grades: PreK K 1 2 **513.2**

1. Fractions 2. Mathematics -- Study and teaching 3. Fractions

ISBN 1592966861; 1623235294; 9781623235291

LC 2005037833

This children's book on fractions, by Sara Pistoia, is part of the "Simply Math" series, which "offer[s] real-world introductions to basic math concepts suited for the youngest children." This book "uses foods, such as pie, pizza, a candy bar, fruit, a sandwich, and cookies, as well as everyday objects like traffic lights, to show how a whole can be divided into even parts. (They encourage sharing, too.)" (Booklist)

"In the first book, children are introduced to the basic concepts of counting by ones, fives, and tens, and of place values. Groups of children use familiar objects such as rocks, buttons, and jelly beans to count...Each book concludes with a short list of key words (without definitions) facing an index that duplicates these words. Appropriate additions for the earliest readers in schools or public libraries." SLJ

Other titles in the series include:

Graphs

Measurement

Patterns

Shapes

Money

Rose, Deborah Lee

★ **One** nighttime sea; an ocean counting rhyme. pictures by Steve Jenkins. Scholastic 2003 un il $16.95

Grades: PreK K 1 2 **513.2**

1. Night 2. Counting 3. Marine animals

ISBN 0-439-33906-5

LC 2002-8127

A counting book featuring nocturnal sea creatures, from one blue whale calf to ten turtle hatchlings, and back down to one seal pup. Includes facts about each of the twenty featured animals

"In a lapping, sealike rhythm, this enchanting counting book lulls its audience into the world beneath the waves. . . . Vivid cut-paper collages beautifully interplay with the rhymes." SLJ

Schmandt-Besserat, Denise

The **history** of counting; illustrated by Michael Hays. Morrow Junior Bks. 1999 45p il $17; lib bdg $16.93

Grades: 4 5 6 7 **513.2**

1. Counting 2. Mathematics

ISBN 0-688-14118-8; 0-688-14119-6 lib bdg

LC 96-35316

"Beginning with a look at primitive expressions of numbers, the text goes on to explain abstract counting and the methods used by the Sumerians, the Phoenicians, the Greeks, the Romans, and finally the Arabs, who brought Hindu numerals from India to Europe about 1,000 years ago. . . . Imaginatively conceived and well composed, Hays' acrylic paintings feature warm, harmonious colors and delicate plays of light and shadow against textured-linen backings. Cogently written and beautifully made." Booklist

Includes glossary

Weill, Cynthia

Count me in; a parade of numbers in English and Spanish. by Cynthia Weill; figurines by the Aguilar Sisters: Guillermina, Josefina, Irene and Concepción. Cinco Puntos Press 2012 32 p. (hardback: alk. paper) $14.95

Grades: PreK **513.2**

1. Counting 2. Mexican art 3. Picture books for children 4. Parades 5. Numerals

ISBN 193595539X; 9781935955399

LC 2012004538

This children's picture book helps children "practice [their] numbers in English and Spanish when [they] count the beautiful dancers, playful musicians, and happy children of Oaxaca as the Guelaguetza parade goes by! Pronounced Gal-a-get-zah, the lively celebration—full of traditional dancing and music—takes place every July deep in the heart of southern Mexico." (Publisher's note)

Winter, Jeanette

Josefina. Harcourt Brace & Co. 1996 un il $16

Grades: PreK K 1 2 **513.2**

1. Counting 2. Mexico -- Fiction 3. Women artists -- Fiction

ISBN 0-15-201091-2

LC 95-34110

"In a sunny patio in Mexico, there is one rising sun in a sky where two angels keep watch over three houses. . . . Throughout her life—from her childhood through the deaths of her parents, her marriage to José, and the birth of their nine children, Josefina works the soft clay into figures to create this world. . . . Inspired by the painted clay figures decorating Josefina Aguilar's patio in Ocotlán, Mexico, Winter has crafted a picture-book vision of the folk artist's life that cleverly turns into a bilingual counting story. . . . Paired with a simple prose narrative, the artwork creates an effect that is both elegant and soothing." Booklist

513.211　Addition

Pistoia, Sara

Counting; by Sara Pistoia. Child's World 2007 24 p. (MathBooks.) $25.64

Grades: PreK K 1 2　　　　　　　　　　**513.211**

1. Counting

ISBN 1592966853; 1623235286; 9781623235284

LC 2005037832

This educational illustrated children's book, by Sara Pistoia, as part of the publisher's "MathBooks" series, presents the concept of counting with illustrations and photographs of everyday objects such as buttons, rocks, and peanuts. The text then expands onward to teach children how to count in groups.

"—In the first book, children are introduced to the basic concepts of counting by ones, fives, and tens, and of place values. Groups of children use familiar objects such as rocks, buttons, and jelly beans to count...Each book concludes with a short list of key words (without definitions) facing an index that duplicates these words. Appropriate additions for the earliest readers in schools or public libraries." SLJ

513.5　Numeration systems

Geisert, Arthur

Roman numerals I to MM; Numerabilia romana uno ad duo mila: liber de difficillimo computando numerum. Houghton Mifflin 1996 xxxii $16

Grades: K 1 2 3　　　　　　　　　　**513.5**

1. Counting 2. Roman numerals

ISBN 0-395-74519-5

LC 95-36247

"Geisert's detailed etchings reward extended perusal, and children will revel in the sheer abundance of pigs. A great lesson in Roman numerals." Publ Wkly

Giganti, Paul

★ Each orange had 8 slices; a counting book. by Paul Giganti, Jr.; pictures by Donald Crews. Greenwillow Bks. 1992 un il $16.99; lib bdg $17.89; pa $6.99

Grades: PreK K 1 2　　　　　　　　　　**513.5**

1. Counting 2. Mathematics

ISBN 0-688-10428-2; 0-688-10429-0 lib bdg; 0-688-13985-X pa

LC 90-24167

"This bright, well-designed book challenges young children to think analytically about what's on its pages. . . . Since the objects are organized into sets and subsets, this could be used to introduce the concept of multiplication as well as counting and addition." Booklist

Schwartz, David M.

On beyond a million; an amazing math journey. illustrated by Paul Meisel. Doubleday Bks. for Young Readers 1999 un il hardcover o.p. pa $6.99

Grades: 2 3 4　　　　　　　　　　**513.5**

1. Counting

ISBN 0-385-32217-8; 0-440-41177-7 pa

LC 98-52990

"The design is busy, with sidebars and balloon comments. Each double-page spread is clearly meant to be talked about, and the discussions aren't overwhelming. . . . Awesome and yet accessible." Booklist

515　Analysis

Cleary, Brian P.

A-B-A-B-A--a book of pattern play; illustrated by Brian Gable. Millbrook Press 2010 31p il (Math is categorical) lib bdg $16.95

Grades: 2 3 4 5　　　　　　　　　　**515**

1. Patterns (Mathematics)

ISBN 978-0-8225-7880-2 lib bdg; 0-8225-7880-8 lib bdg

LC 2009-49386

"Through rhyming text and colorful illustrations, readers are given examples of simple visual and numerical patterns—from circle-square-circle-square to 1-3-5-7. . . . The buoyant narrative calls for reading aloud and the images are large enough for a modest group setting." SLJ

Murphy, Stuart J.

Beep beep, vroom vroom! illustrated by Chris Demarest. HarperCollins Pubs. 2000 33p il (MathStart) hardcover o.p. pa $4.95

Grades: K 1　　　　　　　　　　**515**

1. Patterns (Mathematics)

ISBN 0-06-028016-6; 0-06-028017-4 lib bdg; 0-06-446728-7 pa

LC 98-51907

"Molly loves playing with cars, but her brother, Kevin, tells her she's too young. He lines up his 12 cars—four red, four green, four yellow—in special order on the shelf and tells her not to touch them while he's gone. . . . At the back are practical suggestions for adults and kids to find patterns on the pages and make their own patterns with pebbles, buttons, coins, and kitchen utensils. Demarest's clear, simple pastel pictures express the fun of playing with cars as the vrooming action reveals the patterns in everyday things." Booklist

Includes bibliographical references

516　Geometry

Adler, David A.

Perimeter, area, and volume; a monster book of dimensions. by David A. Adler; illustrated by Edward Miller. 1st ed. Holiday House 2012 32 p. col. ill. (hardcover) $16.95

Grades: 3 4 5　　　　　　　　　　**516**

1. Mathematics 2. Measurement 3. Dimensions 4.

Weights and measures
ISBN 0823422909; 9780823422906

LC 2010048653

This educational children's book by David A. Adler, illustrated by Edward Miller, provides lessons in measurement-taking within the context of a film set crewed by monsters. The book is "aligned with the Common Core State Standards for third-grade, fourth-grade, and fifth-grade mathematics in measurement and data. . . . Grab your jumbo popcorn and 3-D glasses, because you're invited to the premiere of a 3-D movie! The star-studded cast of monsters will help you calculate the perimeter of the set, the area of the movie screen, and the volume of your popcorn box." (Publisher's note)

★ **Shape** up! illustrated by Nancy Tobin. Holiday House 1998 un il $16.95; pa $6.95
Grades: 2 3 4   **516**
    1. Shape 2. Geometry
    ISBN 0-8234-1346-2; 0-8234-1638-0 pa

LC 97-22236

Uses cheese slices, pretzel sticks, a slice of bread, graph paper, a pencil, and more to introduce various polygons, flat shapes with varying numbers of straight sides

"Tobin's colorful diagrams and lanky, baseball-capped tour guide make each definition and direction crystal clear, making this a useful and appealing title for extending classroom lessons or encouraging beginners to charge beyond circle-square-triangle." Bull Cent Child Books

Brocket, Jane
    Circles, stars, and squares; looking for shapes. by Jane Brocket; photographs by Jane Brocket. Millbrook Press 2013 30 p. col. ill. (library) $26.60
Grades: K 1 2   **516**
    1. Shape 2. Plane geometry 3. Shapes 4. Geometry, Plane
    ISBN 0761346112; 9780761346111

LC 2011050199

This children's picture book by Jane Brocket "teaches readers about two- and three-dimensional shapes. . . . The first of two loose sections looks at 'flat' shapes--circles, ovals, squares, rectangles, triangles, diamonds, and a brief mention of pentagons, hexagons and octagons--the second at 'solid' shapes--spheres, cylinders, cubes, cones, rings and eggs." (Kirkus Reviews)

Caron, Lucille
    Geometry smarts! [by] Lucille Caron, Philip M. St. Jacques. Enslow Publishers 2011 64p il lib bdg $27.93
Grades: 5 6 7 8   **516**
    1. Geometry
    ISBN 978-0-7660-3935-3

LC 2011008384

Ehlert, Lois
    ★ **Color** farm. Lippincott 1990 un il $17.99; lib bdg $18.89
Grades: PreK K 1   **516**
    1. Color 2. Shape
    ISBN 0-397-32440-5; 0-397-32441-3 lib bdg

LC 89-13561

"A delightful die-cut exploration of how shapes and colors can be layered and overlapped to create the faces of farm animals. Includes geometric pictures of a rooster, a chicken, a goose, a duck, a cat, a dog, a sheep, a pig, and a cow." Sci Child

Henkes, Kevin
    ★ **Circle** dogs; illustrated by Dan Yaccarino. Greenwillow Bks. 1998 un il $18.99; pa $6.99
Grades: PreK K 1 2   **516**
    1. Dogs -- Fiction 2. Shape -- Fiction
    ISBN 0-688-15446-8; 0-06-443757-4 pa

LC 97-33037

Circle dogs live in a square house with a square yard and spend a busy day eating circle snacks, digging circle holes, and sleeping

"The text is simple, almost primer-like, with lots of onomatopoetic words. . . . The lively gouache paintings in large flat areas of color have a retro look." SLJ

Hoban, Tana
    Is it larger? Is it smaller? Greenwillow Bks. 1985 un il hardcover o.p. pa $6.99
Grades: PreK K   **516**
    1. Size
    ISBN 0-688-15287-2 pa

LC 84-13719

"In each full-color photograph of the wordless picture book Hoban juxtaposes similar objects of differing size. In the simplest pictures only one kind of object is shown, such as three bright plastic sand cups in graduated sizes or three maple leaves. More complex compositions group several related items: measuring cups, bowls, and utensils; fish, shells, and pebbles in an aquarium. Still others contrast dissimilar objects that have common features. . . . In the photographs, Hoban demonstrates once again her mastery of the elements of composition, such as color, texture, and balance." Horn Book

Shapes, shapes, shapes. Greenwillow Bks. 1986 un il $16.99; lib bdg $17.89; pa $6.99
Grades: PreK K   **516**
    1. Shape
    ISBN 0-688-05832-9; 0-688-05833-7 lib bdg; 0-688-14740-2 pa

LC 85-17569

Photographs of familiar objects such as chair, barrettes, and manhole cover present a study of rounded and angular shapes

"Tana Hoban has created an excellent concept book that will encourage children to look for specific shapes in everyday urban scenes. . . . The photographs not only serve to teach shapes and colors but are works of art themselves." Appraisal

    ★ **So** many circles, so many squares. Greenwillow Bks. 1998 un il $16
Grades: PreK K   **516**
    1. Shape
    ISBN 0-688-15165-5

LC 97-10110

The geometric concepts of circles and squares are shown in photographs of wheels, signs, pots, and other familiar objects

"Teachers and young children will find plenty to talk about as they look at the colorful, well-composed, and clearly defined images." Booklist

Leedy, Loreen

Seeing symmetry; written and illustrated by Loreen Leedy. Holiday House 2012 32 p. ill. (chiefly col.) (hardcover) $17.95

Grades: PreK K 1 2   **516**

  1. Symmetry 2. Ratio and proportaion

  ISBN 0823423603; 9780823423606

LC 2011024038

This book presents an "introduction" to the concept of symmetry, "us[ing] a host of natural and manmade objects, as well as purely geometric designs, to illustrate horizontal, vertical, and rotational symmetry." The author asks "readers to consider whether all animals are symmetrical, to examine words for different types of symmetry in their lettering, to identify rotational symmetry in a display of buildings and furniture." (Bulletin of the Center for Children's Books)

Loughrey, Anita

Circles. QEB Pub. 2010 23p il (Shapes around me) lib bdg $24.25

Grades: PreK K 1 2   **516**

  1. Shape

  ISBN 978-1-59566-918-6; 1-59566-918-3

LC 2010005380

This "has a good grasp of how children best learn new math concepts. [The] book begins with a bright illustration of the shape and asks children to trace it with a finger. Subsequent pages present the shape in a variety of colorful sizes, places where it can be found, and activities. Well-thought-out, age appropriate, and attractive." Horn Book Guide

Rectangles. QEB Pub. 2010 23p il (Shapes around me) lib bdg $24.25

Grades: PreK K 1 2   **516**

  1. Shape

  ISBN 978-1-59566-915-5; 1-59566-915-9

LC 2010005381

This "has a good grasp of how children best learn new math concepts. [The] book begins with a bright illustration of the shape and asks children to trace it with a finger. Subsequent pages present the shape in a variety of colorful sizes, places where it can be found, and activities. Well-thought-out, age appropriate, and attractive." Horn Book Guide

Squares. QEB Pub. 2010 23p il (Shapes around me) lib bdg $24.25

Grades: PreK K 1 2   **516**

  1. Shape 2. Square

  ISBN 978-1-59566-917-9; 1-59566-917-5

LC 2010005382

This "has a good grasp of how children best learn new math concepts. [The] book begins with a bright illustration of the shape and asks children to trace it with a finger. Subsequent pages present the shape in a variety of colorful sizes, places where it can be found, and activities. Well-thought-out, age appropriate, and attractive." Horn Book Guide

Triangles. QEB Pub. 2010 23p il (Shapes around me) lib bdg $24.25

Grades: PreK K 1 2   **516**

  1. Shape

  ISBN 978-1-59566-916-2; 1-59566-916-7

LC 2010005383

This "has a good grasp of how children best learn new math concepts. [The] book begins with a bright illustration of the shape and asks children to trace it with a finger. Subsequent pages present the shape in a variety of colorful sizes, places where it can be found, and activities. Well-thought-out, age appropriate, and attractive." Horn Book Guide

Murphy, Stuart J.

★ **Bigger**, Better, BEST! illustrated by Marsha Winborn. HarperCollins Pubs. 2002 33p il (MathStart) hardcover o.p. pa $4.99

Grades: K 1 2 3   **516**

  1. Size 2. Measurement

  ISBN 0-06-028918-X; 0-06-028919-8 lib bdg; 0-06-446247-1 pa

LC 00-54034

"Jeff and Jenny are always fighting about who has something bigger or better, while Jill just ignores them. When the family moves to a bigger house with a separate room for each child, the two start arguing about whose room and windows are bigger. Mom then has them measure the windows with sheets of paper and the floor with newspaper. . . . [The story] carefully incorporates math without being overwhelming. The colorful and humorous illustrations add to the story." SLJ

★ **Captain** Invincible and the space shapes; illustrated by Rémy Simard. HarperCollins Pubs. 2001 33p il (MathStart) hardcover o.p. pa $4.95

Grades: K 1 2 3   **516**

  1. Shape 2. Geometry

  ISBN 0-06-028022-0; 0-06-028023-9 lib bdg; 0-06-446731-7 pa

LC 00-39609

While piloting his spaceship through the skies, Captain Invincible encounters three-dimensional shapes, including cubes, cylinders, and pyramids

"An excellent tool for introducing a unit on three-dimensional shapes. . . . The bold cartoon art in deep, bright colors draws readers into this fun and exciting story. . . . The concluding reinforcement strategies and activities are very good." SLJ

★ **Hamster** champs; by Stuart J. Murphy; illustrated by Pedro Martin. HarperCollins 2005 31p il (MathStart) $15.99; pa $4.99

Grades: 1 2 3   **516**

  1. Angles 2. Cats -- Fiction 3. Hamsters -- Fiction

  ISBN 0-06-055772-9; 0-06-055773-7 pa

LC 2004-22471

"The humorous cartoonlike characters are fun, and plenty of good-natured banter between the hamsters and the cat helps make the concept clear." Booklist

This "book offers a lesson on angles. Three rodents that are racing-car enthusiasts create a series of ramps in an attempt to get the feisty house cat with attitude to stop bothering them." SLJ

★ **Let's** fly a kite; illustrated by Brian Floca. HarperCollins Pubs. 2000 33p il (MathStart) hardcover o.p. pa $4.95

Grades: K 1 2 3   **516**

1. Kites 2. Symmetry

ISBN 0-06-028034-4; 0-06-028035-2 lib bdg; 0-06-446737-6 pa

LC 99-26550

Two squabbling siblings learn about symmetry when their babysitter helps them build and fly a kite

"Floca's watercolor-and-inkline cartoons enhance the story and ably depict the method used to divide everyday objects into two equal parts." SLJ

★ **Polly's** pen pal; illustrated by Remy Simard. HarperCollins 2005 30p il (MathStart) $15.99; pa $4.99

Grades: K 1 2 3   **516**

1. Measurement 2. Metric system

ISBN 0-06-053168-1; 0-06-053170-3 pa

LC 2003-27526

"Polly has an e-mail pen pal in Montreal. As Ally uses metrics to discuss height, weight, and distances, Polly learns what they mean. No comparisons to English measurements are made but the metric measurements are likened to common objects that kids will recognize. This title features colorful ... computer-generated cartoons." SLJ

Olson, Nathan

Cones; by Nathan Olson. Capstone Press 2008 32p il (3-D shapes) lib bdg $23.93

Grades: K 1 2   **516**

1. Cones 2. Shape 3. Geometry

ISBN 978-1-4296-0048-4 lib bdg; 1-4296-0048-9 lib bdg

LC 2006037424

This gives examples of cones such as megaphones, tops, and castle towers, and describes a simple activity.

Includes glossary and bibliographical references

Cubes; by Nathan Olson. Capstone Press 2008 32p il (3-D shapes) lib bdg $23.93

Grades: K 1 2   **516**

1. Cubes 2. Shape 3. Geometry

ISBN 978-1-4296-0049-1 lib bdg; 1-4296-0049-7 lib bdg

LC 2006037423

This gives examples of cubes, such as blocks, dice, sugar cubes, and ice cubes, and describes a simple activity.

Includes glossary and bibliographical references

Cylinders; by Nathan Olson. Capstone Press 2008 32p il (3-D shapes) lib bdg $23.93

Grades: K 1 2   **516**

1. Shape 2. Geometry 3. Cylinders

ISBN 978-1-4296-0050-7 lib bdg; 1-4296-0050-0 lib bdg

LC 2006037421

"Large color photographs show real-world examples of . . . cylinders (canned goods, birthday candles). Short descriptions flank each photo. . . . A hands-on activity will appeal to kids." Horn Book Guide

Includes glossary and bibliographical references

Pyramids; by Nathan Olson. Capstone Press 2008 32p il (3-D shapes) lib bdg $23.93

Grades: K 1 2   **516**

1. Shape 2. Geometry 3. Pyramids

ISBN 978-1-4296-0051-4 lib bdg; 1-4296-0051-9 lib bdg

LC 2006037420

"Large color photographs show real-world examples of pyramids (Hindu temple, toy tepee). . . . Short descriptions flank each photo. . . . A hands-on activity will appeal to kids." Horn Book Guide

Includes glossary and bibliographical references

Spheres; by Nathan Olson. Capstone Press 2008 32p il (3-D shapes) lib bdg $23.93

Grades: K 1 2   **516**

1. Shape 2. Geometry 3. Spheres

ISBN 978-1-4296-0052-1 lib bdg; 1-4296-0052-7 lib bdg

LC 2006037247

This offers examples of spheres such as bubbles, snowballs, oranges, and soccer balls, and describes a simple activity.

Includes glossary and bibliographical references

Rissman, Rebecca

Shapes in art. Heinemann Library 2009 24p il (Spot the shape) $14.50; pa $5.99

Grades: PreK K 1   **516**

1. Art 2. Shape

ISBN 978-1-4329-2169-9; 1-4329-2169-X; 978-1-4329-2175-0 pa; 1-4329-2175-4 pa

LC 2008043206

This describes the shapes that can be found in works of art.

This offers "vibrant photography and clarion text." Booklist

Shapes in buildings. Heinemann Library 2009 24p il (Spot the shape) $14.50; pa $5.99

Grades: PreK K 1   **516**

1. Shape 2. Buildings

ISBN 978-1-4329-2172-9; 1-4329-2172-X; 978-1-4329-2178-1 pa; 1-4329-2178-9 pa

LC 2008043210

This describes the shapes that can be found in buildings.

This offers "vibrant photography and clarion text." Booklist

Shapes in music. Heinemann Library 2009 24p il (Spot the shape) $14.50; pa $5.99

Grades: PreK K 1   **516**

1. Shape 2. Musical instruments

ISBN 978-1-4329-2171-2; 1-4329-2171-1; 978-1-4329-2177-4 pa; 1-4329-2177-0 pa

LC 2008043209

This describes the shapes that can be found in musical instruments.

This offers "vibrant photography and clarion text." Booklist

★ **Shapes** in sports. Heinemann Library 2009 24p il (Spot the shape) $14.50; pa $5.99

Grades: PreK K 1   **516**
1. Shape 2. Sports
ISBN 978-1-4329-2170-5; 1-4329-2176-2; 978-1-
4329-2176-7 pa; 1-4329-2176-2 pa
LC 2008043208
This describes the shapes that can be found in sports.

This "is a near-perfect union of concept and execution.
Using . . . vibrant photography and clarion text . . . . Rissman lays out a simple premise ('Shapes are all around us.')
before introducing seven shapes to come: rectangle, square,
semicircle, diamond, and so forth. . . . What is most impressive . . . are the stunning aerial photographs that turn baseball diamonds and tennis courts into dazzling intersections
of geometric patterns. This is the kind of book that will wake
readers up to the complexity of everyday items." Booklist

Shapes in the garden. Heinemann Library 2009 24p il
(Spot the shape) $14.50; pa $5.99
Grades: PreK K 1   **516**
1. Shape 2. Gardens
ISBN 978-1-4329-2168-2; 1-4329-2168-1; 978-1-
4329-2174-3 pa; 1-4329-2174-6 pa
LC 2008043205
This describes the shapes that can be found in gardens.
This offers "vibrant photography and clarion text."
Booklist

Somervill, Barbara A.
Distance, area, and volume. Heinemann Library 2010
32p il map (Measure it!) lib bdg $29; pa $7.99
Grades: 3 4 5   **516**
1. Measurement 2. Volume (Cubic content)
ISBN 978-1-4329-3763-8 lib bdg; 1-4329-3763-4 lib
bdg; 978-1-4329-3769-0 pa; 1-4329-3769-3 pa
LC 2009-35191
"Size of text and font is suitable for this age group with
uncluttered pages designed so that text is set off with the illustrations, graphs, or drawings placed vertically. Key words
appear in bold." Libr Media Connect
Includes glossary and bibliographical references

VanCleave, Janice Pratt
Janice VanCleave's geometry for every kid; easy activities that make learning geometry fun. Wiley 1994 221p
il hardcover o.p. pa $12.95
Grades: 4 5 6 7   **516**
1. Geometry
ISBN 0-471-31142-1; 0-471-31141-3 pa
LC 93-43049
This "introductory text covers many topics in geometry, from lines, optical illusions, and art-related activities
to applications with protractors and the construction of basic solids. Terms are presented in a simplified fashion and
are easily understood. Graphics are clear. The hands-on activities encourage learning, creativity, and excitement." Sci
Books Films
Includes glossary

Waxman, Laura Hamilton
Prisms; by Laura Hamilton Waxman; illustrated by
Kathryn Mitter. Magic Wagon 2012 24 p. $27.07
Grades: 1 2 3   **516**
1. Shape 2. Prisms 3. Solid geometry 4. Shapes 5.

Geometry, Solid
ISBN 1616418753; 9781616418755
LC 2012007117
This young children's book, by Laura Hamilton Waxman, illustrated by Kathryn Mitter, is part of the "Everyday
3-D Shapes" series, exploring various shapes seen in objects
of daily life. In this entry, "rhyming text and creative illustrations draw attention to prisms that are found in the world
around us." (Publisher's note)

516.15   Geometric configurations

Adler, David A., 1947-
★ **Triangles;** by David A. Adler; illustrated by Edward
Miller. Holiday House 2014 32 p. (hardcover) $17.95
Grades: 2 3 4   **516.15**
1. Triangle
ISBN 0823423786; 9780823423781
LC 2012037371
This children's book, written by David A. Adler and il-
lustrated by Edward Miller, "tackle[s] questions about dif-
ferent kinds of triangles with . . . text and . . . illustrations
starring two friendly kids and one savvy robot." (Publisher's
note) "Beginning with the definition of a triangle and a
breakdown of its parts--sides, angles, vertices--[David A.]
Adler quickly launches into a discussion of angles, even
teaching kids how they are named, measured and classified."
(Kirkus Reviews)

"A straightforward and easy introduction to triangles and
angles. There is a lot of repeated information, which will
work well with students with different learning styles, and
the bold, exciting illustrations will hold kids' attention...A
recommended purchase for any math collection, this title
serves as a great update on the subject." SLJ

Campbell, Sarah C.
★ **Mysterious** patterns; finding fractals in nature.
Sarah C. Campbell. First edition Boyds Mills Press 2014
32 p. $16.95
Grades: 2 3 4 5   **516.15**
1. Fractals 2. Mathematical models 3. Nature 4.
Shapes 5. Pattern perception 6. Mathematics in nature
ISBN 1620916274; 9781620916278
LC 2013951286
This book, by Sarah C. Campbell, is an "introduction to
fractals through examples that can be seen in parks, rivers,
and our very own backyards. Readers will . . . learn that
broccoli florets are fractals - just like mountain ranges, river
systems, and trees--and will share in the wonder of math as it
is reflected in the world around us." (Publisher's note)

"Here's a clear, fluid, concise introduction to fractals,
identified in 1975 by scientist Benoit Mandelbrot, who
noticed that the shapes of trees, broccoli, and ferns share a
common pattern: each has "smaller parts that look like the
whole shape." Well-designed pages feature crisp, up-close
photographs, which pair perfectly with the accessible text.
Includes an activity and an afterword by a Mandelbrot col-
league." Horn Book

Pistoia, Sara
Measurement; by Sara Pistoia. Child's World 2007 24
p. (MathBooks) $25.64

Grades: PreK K 1 2 **516.15**
1. Measurement 2. Mathematics -- Study and teaching
ISBN 1592966888; 1623235316; 9781623235314
LC 2005037835

This children's book on measurement, by Sara Pistoia, is part of the "Simply Math" series, which "offer[s] real-world introductions to basic math concepts suited for the youngest children." This book "shows how to use common household objects such as a ruler, tape measure, measuring cup, scale, and measuring spoons to explore different types and units of measurement." (Booklist)

"In the first book, children are introduced to the basic concepts of counting by ones, fives, and tens, and of place values. Groups of children use familiar objects such as rocks, buttons, and jelly beans to count...Each book concludes with a short list of key words (without definitions) facing an index that duplicates these words. Appropriate additions for the earliest readers in schools or public libraries." SLJ

Other titles in the series include:
Fractions
Graphs
Patterns
Shapes
Money

Shapes; by Sara Pistoia. Child's World 2007 24 p. (MathBooks) $25.64
Grades: PreK K 1 2 **516.15**
1. Shape 2. Mathematics -- Study and teaching 3. Geometry
ISBN 1592966918; 1623235340; 9781623235345
LC 2005037839

This educational illustrated children's book, by Sara Pistoia, as part of the publisher's "MathBooks" series, presents the concept of shapes with illustrations and photographs of everyday objects and in nature, such as watermelon wedges, soccer balls, and square birthday gift boxes. The text then expands onward to teach children various related skills and activities relating mathematics to the shapes.

"In the first book, children are introduced to the basic concepts of counting by ones, fives, and tens, and of place values. Groups of children use familiar objects such as rocks, buttons, and jelly beans to count...Each book concludes with a short list of key words (without definitions) facing an index that duplicates these words. Appropriate additions for the earliest readers in schools or public libraries." SLJ

Other titles in the series include:
Fractions
Graphs
Measurement
Money
Patterns

Wild About Shapes; by Jeremie Fischer. Flying Eye Books 2015 70 p. chiefly color illustrations $16.99
Grades: PreK K 1 2 **516.15**
1. Color 2. Shape 3. Animals
ISBN 1909263389; 9781909263383

This children's book, written and illustrated by Jérémie Fischer, "is playfully designed so that animals hide and reveal themselves within pages of overlapping color and alternating pages of printed acetate. From crocodiles and giraffes to snails and mice, each page offers a fresh surprise!" (Publisher's note)

"Acetate inserts—printed with abstract shapes in pink, teal, and yellow—transform Fischer's equally abstract screen prints into animals in a process that's graceful in its execution and delightful in its simplicity. . . . Clever and rewarding, this ranks with Hervé Tullet's Press Here and Rufus Butler Seder's Scanimation series as a book whose deceptively simple interactivity creates a reading experience that's nothing short of magic." Pub Wkly

516.2 Euclidean geometry

Green, Dan
Algebra & geometry; anything but square. illustrated by Simon Basher. Kingfisher 2011 il (Basher science) $14.99; pa $8.99
Grades: 4 5 6 **516.2**
1. Algebra 2. Geometry
ISBN 978-0-7534-6627-8; 978-0-7534-6597-4 pa

518.2 Specific numerical methods

Pistoia, Sara
Graphs; by Sara Pistoia. Child's World 2007 24 p. (MathBooks) $25.64
Grades: PreK K 1 2 **518.2**
1. Graphic methods 2. Mathematics -- Study and teaching
ISBN 159296687X; 1623235308; 9781623235307
LC 2005037834

This educational illustrated children's book, by Sara Pistoia, as part of the publisher's "MathBooks" series, presents the concept of graphs and other visual representations of mathematical data with illustrations and photographs of everyday objects such as fruit and cookies. The text then expands onward to teach children related applications of graphs in their lives.

"In the first book, children are introduced to the basic concepts of counting by ones, fives, and tens, and of place values. Groups of children use familiar objects such as rocks, buttons, and jelly beans to count...Each book concludes with a short list of key words (without definitions) facing an index that duplicates these words. Appropriate additions for the earliest readers in schools or public libraries." SLJ

Other titles in the series include:
Fractions
Measurement
Patterns
Shapes
Money

519.2 Probabilities

Aboff, Marcie
Pigs, cows, and probability. Capstone Press 2011 24p il (First facts. Data mania) lib bdg $23.99
Grades: 3 4 5 6 **519.2**
1. Mathematics 2. Probabilities
ISBN 978-1-4296-4529-4; 1-4296-4529-6
LC 2010000551

"Information is presented in a few pages in a clear, concise manner. The definitions provided for words will help readers learn the [subject]. This is an excellent introduction to elementary statistics and statistical analysis." Libr Media Connect

Includes glossary and bibliographical references

Goldstone, Bruce

★ **That's** a possibility! a book about what might happen. Bruce Goldstone. 1st ed. Henry Holt & Co 2013 32 p. ill. (hardcover) $16.99

Grades: 1 2 3 4　　　　　　　　　　　　**519.2**

1. Picture books for children 2. Probabilities

ISBN 0805089985; 9780805089981

LC 2012036691

This children's picture book looks at probability. "Starting with basic concepts of possibility, certainty, and impossibility ('Will an elephant hatch from this egg? That's impossible!'), [Bruce Goldstone] stages highly specific situations in photographic and digital illustrations. 'Will this butterfly land on one of the purple flowers?' he asks. 'That's probable. Can you see why?' (Spiky purple thistles dwarf and outnumber two yellow flowers, helping readers make the connection.)" (Publishers Weekly)

Leedy, Loreen

It's probably Penny; written and illustrated by Loreen Leedy. Henry Holt 2007 un il $16.95

Grades: 1 2 3　　　　　　　　　　　　　**519.2**

1. Probabilities

ISBN 978-0-8050-7389-8; 0-8050-7389-2

LC 2006-02872

"Lisa's teacher assigns the class to study probability by writing down predictions, determining results, and recording them. He demonstrates by using (and eating) jellybeans. Choosing Penny as her focal point, Lisa begins to calculate her results. . . . Leedy clearly and cleverly depicts the possibilities and choices in panels and segmented pages that feature Penny in funny poses." Booklist

Murphy, Stuart J.

★ **Probably** pistachio; illustrated by Marsha Winborn. HarperCollins Pubs. 2001 30p il (MathStart) hardcover o.p. pa $4.95

Grades: K 1 2 3　　　　　　　　　　　　**519.2**

1. Probabilities

ISBN 0-06-028028-X; 0-06-028029-8 lib bdg; 0-06-446734-1 pa

LC 99-27695

Readers are introduced to the concept of probability in a story about a boy who has a day in which nothing goes right

"Winborn's watercolors playfully depict Jack's misery as things go from bad to worse. . . . A closing section has follow-up activities to extend and enrich the lesson, as well as a short list of books with related themes." Booklist

519.5　Statistical mathematics

Goldstone, Bruce

★ **Great** estimations. H. Holt 2006 32p il $16.95

Grades: 1 2 3 4　　　　　　　　　　　　**519.5**

1. Approximate computation

ISBN 978-0-8050-7446-8; 0-8050-7446-5

LC 2005-19776

"Laying out a mixed assemblage of toys, pipe cleaners, marbles, peanuts, and other small items, Goldstone helps viewers train themselves to estimate the size of groups of about 10 things on sight, then goes on to present similar, often fetchingly arranged, materials by hundreds and (!) thousands. He also describes 'clump counting' and 'box and count' methods. . . . This book lends itself equally well to skill building and to casual reading." Booklist

★ **Greater** estimations. Henry Holt and Company 2008 31p il $16.95

Grades: 1 2 3 4　　　　　　　　　　　　**519.5**

1. Approximate computation

ISBN 0-8050-8315-4; 978-0-8050-8315-6

LC 2007-40894

"Goldstone builds on the topics introduced in Great Estimations (Holt, 2006) and also discusses how to estimate length, weight, area, and volume. He does an exceptional job of breaking down the process of so that even early elementary students can comprehend it. The author also effectively introduces different methods of estimation. . . . The vivid, eye-catching photographs are the highlight of the book. . . . This lively book would be an excellent addition." SLJ

Murphy, Stuart J.

Betcha! illustrated by S.D. Schindler. HarperCollins Pubs. 1997 33p il (MathStart) hardcover o.p. pa $4.95

Grades: 1 2 3　　　　　　　　　　　　　**519.5**

1. Arithmetic 2. Approximate computation

ISBN 0-06-026768-2; 0-06-026769-0 lib bdg; 0-06-446707-4 pa

LC 96-15486

"On their way to a store sponsoring a contest that involves guessing the number of jellybeans in a jar, two friends encounter situations that involve numerical determinations. . . One boy counts one by one to obtain the answers, whereas the other one uses simple techniques to come up with near estimations. The easy-to-read picture-book format with only one or two sentences per page will appeal to reluctant readers. . . . The uncomplicated drawings show how the boy's brain is processing data and the skills he employs to arrive at an educated guess." SLJ

★ **Coyotes** all around; illustrated by Steve Björkman. HarperCollins Pubs. 2003 31p il (MathStart) $15.99; pa $4.99

Grades: 1 2 3　　　　　　　　　　　　　**519.5**

1. Coyotes 2. Counting 3. Roadrunners 4. Approximate computation

ISBN 0-06-051529-5; 0-06-051531-7 pa

LC 2002-151776

A pack of coyotes tries to determine how many roadrunners and other creatures are in their vicinity, and while some count different groups and add their totals together, Clever Coyote rounds off and estimates

"Humorous watercolor cartoons depict the action and clarify the concept. . . . Factoids about coyotes and other desert creatures appear throughout, so readers learn not only math, but also get their fair share of science sprinkled into the mix." SLJ

520 Astronomy and allied sciences

Carson, Mary Kay

★ **Beyond** the solar system; exploring galaxies, black holes, alien planets, and more: a history with 21 activities. by Mary Kay Carson. Chicago Review Press 2013 vii, 127 p.p col. ill. (paperback) $18.95

Grades: 5 6 7 8   520

1. Creative activities 2. Astronomy -- History
ISBN 1613745443; 9781613745441

LC 2012046330

In this book, "Mary Kay Carson traces the evolution of humankind's astronomical knowledge, from the realization that we are not at the center of the universe to recent telescopic proof of planets orbiting stars outside our solar system. . . . This book contains 21 hands-on projects to further explore the subjects discussed" as well as "minibiographies of famous astronomers, a time line of major scientific discoveries . . .[and] a glossary of technical terms." (Publisher's note)

Includes bibliographical references (p. 121) and index.

Gardner, Robert

Ace your space science project; great science fair ideas. [by] Robert Gardner and Madeline Goodstein. Enslow Publishers 2009 128p il (Ace your science project) lib bdg $31.93

Grades: 5 6 7 8   520

1. Space sciences 2. Science projects 3. Science -- Experiments
ISBN 978-0-7660-3230-9 lib bdg; 0-7660-3230-2 lib bdg

LC 2008-04688

"Informative, practical, and not without dry wit, this is a good bet for replacing older books of science projects related to astronomny." Booklist

"Presents several science experiments and project ideas about space." Publisher's note

Includes bibliographical references

Goldsmith, Mike

The **Kingfisher** space encyclopedia; Dr. Mike Goldsmith. Kingfisher 2012 159 p. (hardcover) $18.99

Grades: 4 5 6   520

1. Astronomy -- Encyclopedias
ISBN 0753468050; 9780753468050

In this book, "[Mike] Goldsmith skims the history of astronomy and space exploration, tours the solar system and the universe beyond, then closes with glances at dark matter and other undiscovered territory." A "spread on Global Positioning Systems" is included along with "digital images" as illustrations. (Kirkus)

Green, Dan

Astronomy; out of this world! illustrated by Simon Basher. Kingfisher 2009 128p il pa $8.95

Grades: 5 6 7 8   520

1. Astronomy
ISBN 978-0-7534-6290-4 pa; 0-7534-6290-7 pa

"Basher has created a portrait gallery of personified planets, comets, space probes, galaxies, several kinds of stars, and an array of other celestial bodies in a hyper-cute, pastel cartoon style. . . . Along with short bulleted lists of additional information, each figure offers a fact-based self-description. . . . Green's astro-narrative is both accurate and spiced with seldom-mentioned details." SLJ

Includes glossary

Jankowski, Connie

Space exploration. Compass Point Books 2009 40p il (Mission: science) lib bdg $26.60

Grades: 4 5 6   520

1. Astronomy 2. Outer space -- Exploration
ISBN 978-0-7565-3958-0 lib bdg; 0-7565-3958-7 lib bdg

LC 2008-7722

Discusses outer space exploration and examines future possibilities such as a permanent space station, colonies in space, and journeys outside the solar system

Includes glossary

Lasky, Kathryn

★ The **librarian** who measured the earth; illustrated by Kevin Hawkes. Little, Brown 1994 48p il $16.95

Grades: 2 3 4 5   520

1. Astronomers 2. Geographers 3. Writers on science
ISBN 0-316-51526-4

LC 92-42656

Describes the life and work of Eratosthenes, the Greek geographer and astronomer who accurately measured the circumference of the Earth

"Illustrating the text with warmth and humor, Hawkes' acrylic paintings capture the period details of the setting and clarify the geometric concepts used in the measurement. The often dramatic compositions vary from page to page, while the sunlit reds, oranges, and yellows glow brightly against the cooler blues and greens. . . . Entertaining as well as instructional." Booklist

Includes bibliographical references

Pinkney, Andrea Davis

★ **Dear** Benjamin Banneker; illustrated by Brian Pinkney. Harcourt Brace & Co. 1994 un il hardcover o.p. pa $7

Grades: 2 3 4   520

1. Astronomers 2. Mathematicians 3. Nonfiction writers 4. Clock and watch makers 5. African Americans -- Biography
ISBN 0-15-200417-3; 0-15-201892-1 pa

LC 93-31162

This offers "lucid text and striking illustrations, rendered on scratchboard and colored with oil paint." Publ Wkly

"The Pinkneys chronicle Banneker's work on his almanac and, most particularly, his letter to Thomas Jefferson, then secretary of state, protesting the country's—and Jefferson's—involvement in slavery." Bull Cent Child Books

Sis, Peter, 1949-

★ **Starry** messenger; a book depicting the life of a famous scientist, mathematician, astronomer, philosopher, physicist, Galileo Galilei. created and illustrated by Peter Sis. Farrar, Straus & Giroux 1996 un il $18; pa $7.99

Grades: 2 3 4 5   520

1. Astronomers 2. Writers on science 3. Biography, Individual
ISBN 0-374-37191-1; 0-374-47027-8 pa

LC 95-44986

A Caldecott Medal honor book, 1997

This book traces "the astronomer's life from his birth, . . . to his childhood, . . . and finally to his years as a celebrated scientist whose experiments culminated in his construction of the first complete astronomical telescope. . . . Age six and up." (N Y Times Book Rev)

"Large, beautiful drawings reflect the ideas, events, books, maps, world view, and symbolism of the times. These intricate ink drawings, idiosyncratic in concept and beautifully tinted with delicate watercolor washes, are complemented by smaller drawings and prints that illustrate a side-text of significant dates, time lines, quotations, comments, and explanations. . . . Those drawn to the book will find that it works on many levels, offering not just facts but intuitive visions of another world." Booklist

Space: a visual encyclopedia. DK Pub. 2010 254p il $24.99

Grades: 5 6 7 8 **520**
1. Astronomy 2. Astronautics 3. Space sciences
ISBN 978-0-7566-6277-6; 0-7566-6277-X

"Any reader wishing to gain a fair introductory understanding of astronomy in one concise book will find much satisfaction in this work. An abundance of fascinating information is contained within these pages, and the format is such that excellent and attractive related photographs and diagrams directly accompany the text. . . . The book is very well organized and very well written." Sci Books & Films

VanCleave, Janice Pratt, 1942-
Step-by-step science experiments in astronomy; by Janice VanCleave. Rosen Pub. 2013 80 p. col. ill. (Janice Vancleave's first-place science fair projects) (library) $33.25; (paperback) $14.15

Grades: 5 6 7 8 **520**
1. Science -- Experiments 2. Science projects 3. Astronomy -- Experiments
ISBN 1448869781; 9781448869787; 9781448884612
LC 2012000715

This book by Janice VanCleave presents 22 science experiments in astronomy for children. "Van Cleave states the basic goal of the experiments, followed by a list of necessary materials. . . . Step-by-step instructions are . . . accompanied by diagrams where needed. The results section states exactly what is expected to happen and the 'Why?' section explains in accessible terms why those specific results were achieved." (School Library Journal)

Includes bibliographical references (p. 77-78) and index

520.92 Astronomers

Christensen, Bonnie
I, Galileo; Bonnie Christensen. Alfred A. Knopf 2012 40 p.

Grades: 3 4 5 **520.92**
1. Inventors -- Biography 2. Physicists -- Biography 3. Astronomers -- Biography 4. Picture books for children 5. Galilei, Galileo, 1564-1642
ISBN 0375867538; 9780307974402; 9780375867538; 9780375967535
LC 2011025100

"In this . . . picture book, blind, elderly Galileo sits . . . tells the story of his life. After speaking of his childhood and education, he recalls his scientific work, including developing an improved telescope that enabled him . . . to conclude that Copernicus' 'sun-centered theory' was correct. The church reacted . . . by placing him under house arrest and banning his books. The narrative . . . touches on many of Galileo's accomplishments." (Booklist)

522 Techniques, procedures, apparatus, equipment, materials

Cole, Michael D.
Eye on the universe; the incredible hubble space telescope. Michael D. Cole. Enslow Publishers 2013 48 p. $23.93

Grades: 4 5 6 7 8 **522**
1. Hubble Space Telescope 2. Outer space -- Exploration 3. Picture books for children 4. Astronomy -- Research 5. Astronautics in astronomy 6. Hubble Space Telescope
ISBN 0766040771; 9780766040779
LC 2011047074

This book looks at the Hubble Space Telescope. "Orbiting high above Earth, the Hubble Telescope captures . . . wonders of space. . . . Photographs are relayed back to Earth, allowing scientists and astronomers to study parts of space that were once completely unknown. Michael D. Cole explores the . . . journey of launching this telescope into space and how it has unlocked many of the . . . mysteries in the universe." (Publisher's note)

Includes bibliographical references and index

Jefferis, David
Star spotters; telescopes and observatories. Crabtree Pub. 2009 32p il (Exploring our solar system) lib bdg $26.60; pa $8.95

Grades: 3 4 5 **522**
1. Astronomy 2. Telescopes 3. Outer space -- Exploration
ISBN 978-0-7787-3725-4 lib bdg; 0-7787-3725-X lib bdg; 978-0-7787-3742-1 pa; 0-7787-3742-X pa
LC 2008-49242

"Focuses on important observatories—earthbound and orbiting—along with types of telescopes—and concludes with brief observations about binoculars and cameras. . . . [This book is] designed with easily digestible blocks of question-and-answer text sharing page space with large, sharply reproduced space photos and graphic art." SLJ

Includes glossary

Scott, Elaine
★ Space, stars, and the beginning of time; what the Hubble telescope saw. Clarion Books 2011 66p il $17.99

Grades: 5 6 7 8 **522**
1. Astronomy 2. Hubble Space Telescope 3. Outer space -- Exploration
ISBN 0-547-24189-5; 978-0-547-24189-0
LC 2010-08040

This book examines data collected from the Hubble Space Telescope. Index. "Grades four to eight." (Bull Cent Child Books)

This examines "some of the data that has been collected over the two decades of the Hubble Telescope's operation.

Opening chapters discuss the satellite's instrumentation and its 2009 repairs, and then the real fun begins with sections on calculating the age of the universe and its speed of expansion; the nature of dark matter, dark energy, and black holes; star formation; and planet formation, particularly outside our solar system. . . . Gasp-worthy photographs should fire up the most sluggish imaginations." Bull Cent Child Books

523   Specific celestial bodies and phenomena

Gardner, Robert

Far-out science projects about Earth's sun and moon; illustrations by Tom Labaff. Enslow Publishers 2007 48p il (Rockin' earth science experiments) lib bdg $23.93

Grades: 3 4 5   **523**

1. Science projects 2. Sun 3. Moon 4. Science -- Experiments

ISBN 978-0-7660-2736-7 lib bdg; 0-7660-2736-8 lib bdg

LC 2006-13789

A collection of science experiments such as getting direction and time from the sun, finding locations of sunrise and sunset, measuring heat from the sun, and observing the phases of the moon

This is "just right for students with limited experience looking for projects that are fairly interesting and manageable." SLJ

Includes glossary and bibliographical references

523.1   The universe, galaxies, quasars

Asimov, Isaac

The Milky Way and other galaxies; by Isaac Asimov; with revisions and updating by Richard Hantula. Gareth Stevens Pub. 2005 32p (Isaac Asimov's 21st century library of the universe) lib bdg $24.67

Grades: 4 5 6   **523.1**

1. Galaxies 2. Milky Way

ISBN 0-8368-3968-4

LC 2004-58313

This "examines various galactic types, structures, and superstructures, as observed by a wide array of specialized telescopes. . . . The pictures . . . are striking. . . . [An] excellent collection [enhancer]." SLJ

Includes bibliographical references

Fox, Karen C.

Older than the stars; [by] Karen C. Fox; illustrated by Nancy Davis. Charlesbridge 2010 un il lib bdg $15.95

Grades: 2 3 4 5   **523.1**

1. Atoms 2. Cosmology 3. Big bang theory

ISBN 978-1-57091-787-5 lib bdg; 1-57091-787-6 lib bdg

LC 2009-04304

"Fox and Davis tackle the challenge of creating an engaging read-aloud about the Big Bang theory with energy and style. Employing the structure of a familiar nursery rhyme, the text takes readers through the steps of the universe's expansion. . . . A text box on each spread offers a clear, concise explanation of what happened in that particular stage of the universe. . . . Perfect for the classroom, this

is an intriguing introduction to a difficult-to-understand concept." SLJ

Gibbons, Gail

Galaxies, galaxies! Holiday House 2006 32p il $16.95

Grades: K 1 2 3   **523.1**

1. Galaxies

ISBN 978-0-8234-2002-5; 0-8234-2002-7

LC 2006-02504

"Between an opening description of the Milky Way and a closing claim that galaxy formation is still going on, the author depicts ancient astronomers at work, describes several kinds of telescopes, and profiles five distinctive galactic forms, from irregular to lenticular. Pairing brief, matter-of-fact generalizations leavened with digestible doses of specific information to painted scenes that link diverse groups of human observers to galaxies seen in blobby, broadly brushed portraits, this introduction to some of the universe's largest structures will put stars in the eyes of the most Earthbound young readers." SLJ

Goldsmith, Mike

Universe; journey into deep space. Mike Goldsmith; illustrated by Mark A. Garlick. Kingfisher 2012 48 p. (hardcover) $17.99

Grades: 4 5 6 7   **523.1**

1. Universe 2. Astronomy 3. Outer space

ISBN 075346876X; 9780753468760

This book, by Mike Goldsmith, illustrated by Mark A. Garlick, profiles "some of the Universe's most intriguing places, and along the way . . . [describes] the amazing history of the Cosmos. A series of . . . spreads give . . . snapshots of distant galactic locations as the reader journeys . . . from red cold Mars (3 light minutes away) to a massive Supernova (10,000 light years away) and beyond." (Publisher's note)

Jefferis, David

Galaxies; immense star islands. Crabtree Pub. 2009 32p il (Exploring our solar system) lib bdg $26.60; pa $8.95

Grades: 3 4 5   **523.1**

1. Galaxies 2. Milky Way

ISBN 978-0-7787-3723-0 lib bdg; 0-7787-3723-3 lib bdg; 978-0-7787-3740-7 pa; 0-7787-3740-3 pa

LC 2008-46248

This "begins with a summary look at galactic types and origins, then goes on to describe cores, halos, and other structures with special reference to the Milky Way. It closes with a smattering of advice for young sky watchers and a spread of general facts about galaxies. . . . Designed with easily digestible blocks of question-and-answer text sharing page space with large, sharply reproduced space photos and graphic art." SLJ

Includes glossary

Simon, Seymour

★ Galaxies. Morrow Junior Bks. 1988 un il hardcover o.p. pa $6.95

Grades: 3 4 5 6   **523.1**

1. Galaxies

ISBN 0-688-08002-2; 0-688-10992-6 pa

LC 87-23967

"This fine introduction to an awe-inspiring subject will surely stimulate interest in stargazing, further reading, and investigation." Horn Book

523.2   Planetary systems

Aguilar, David A.

13 planets; the latest view of the solar system. National Geographic 2011 60p il $16.95; lib bdg $25.99

Grades: 5 6 7 8   **523.2**

1. Planets 2. Solar system

ISBN 9781426307706; 1426307705; 9781426307713 lib bdg; 1426307713 lib bdg

LC 2010032510

Updated and revised edition of: 11 planets: A new view of the Solar System (2008)

Profiles each of the planets in Earth's solar system, including Pluto, Ceres, Eris, Haumea, MakeMake, the sun, the Oort cloud, comets, and more.

"Aguilar offers an amended volume reflecting the findings of the International Astronomical Union, which currently classifies eight objects in the solar system as planets and, with the addition of Haumea and Makemake, five as dwarf planets. . . . Aguilar has not only added sections on Haumea and Makemake, he has also used this opportunity to rewrite portions of the text and captions throughout the book and, in some cases, to substitute new illustrations or improve old ones for the new volume. The result is a more readable, more accurate, and more handsome edition of the previous work." Booklist

Includes bibliographical references and index.

Bredeson, Carmen

What is the solar system? Enslow Elementary 2008 32p il (I like space!) lib bdg $22.60

Grades: K 1 2 3   **523.2**

1. Planets 2. Solar system

ISBN 978-0-7660-2944-6 lib bdg; 0-7660-2944-1 lib bdg

LC 2007-02745

This book "is beautifully illustrated, with photographs from NASA and other sources, and is well organized." Sci Books Films

This answers such questions as "Is Pluto a planet? Do all planets have moons? What are asteroids and comets?" Publisher's note

Includes glossary and bibliographical references

Carson, Mary Kay

Exploring the solar system; a history with 22 activities. by Mary Kay Carson. Chicago Review Press 2008 vii, 168 p.p ill. (paperback) $17.95

Grades: 4 5 6 7   **523.2**

1. Astronomy 2. Solar system

ISBN 1556527152; 9781556527159

This book by Mary Kay Carson is a "mix of facts, history, and hands-on activities [about the solar system]. Beginning with a two-page table of contents with chapters arranged as planets in our solar system and an introductory time line, the author takes readers on a historical journey of what was known and/or discovered in each of eight time periods." (School Library Journal)

Goldsmith, Mike

Solar system. Kingfisher 2010 56p il (Discover science) $9.99

Grades: 1 2 3   **523.2**

1. Solar system

ISBN 978-0-7534-6447-2; 0-7534-6447-0

First published in the series Kingfisher young knowledge in 2006

"With glossy color pages, abundant visuals, and descriptive prose, this . . . title provides an accessible introduction to earth's solar system. Printed in large font, the text is well suited to newly independent readers' abilities . . . and occasionally uses familiar comparisons to aid comprehension. . . . The visual-laden pages feature a wide range of images, from stock photos to detailed renderings of planetary surfaces." Booklist

Includes glossary and bibliographical references

Greathouse, Lisa E.

Solar system. Compass Point Books 2009 40p il (Mission: science) lib bdg $26.60

Grades: 4 5 6   **523.2**

1. Solar system

ISBN 978-0-7565-4071-5 lib bdg; 0-7565-4071-2 lib bdg

LC 2008-35728

Introduces the solar system and the specific characteristics of its planets

Includes glossary

Kops, Deborah

Exploring exoplanets. Lerner Publications 2011 40p il (What's amazing about space?) lib bdg $27.93

Grades: 4 5 6   **523.2**

1. Extrasolar planets

ISBN 978-0-7613-5444-4; 0-7613-5444-1

LC 2010046109

This explains how scientists have discovered other planets in the universe similar to those in our solar system.

Includes glossary and bibliographical references

Kudlinski, Kathleen V.

Boy were we wrong about the solar system! illustrated by John Rocco. Dutton Children's Books 2008 un il $15.99

Grades: K 1 2 3   **523.2**

1. Solar system

ISBN 978-0-525-46979-7; 0-525-46979-6

LC 2007-50557

This is a "debunking of such erstwhile astronomical theories as solar revolution around the Earth, concentric glass spheres dividing planetary orbits, Martian canals, and, of course, the overly elevated status of Pluto. . . . [This is illustrated with] jewel-hued, cartoonishly exaggerated paintings. . . . The concept of adults getting it dead wrong is realiably engaging." Bull Cent Child Books

Portman, Michael

Are there other Earths? Michael Portman. Gareth Stevens Publishing 2013 32 p. (Space mysteries) (library binding) $25.25

Grades: 3 4 5 **523.2**
1. Extrasolar planets 2. Solar system
ISBN 1433982579; 9781433982576; 9781433982583
LC 2012019207

Author Michael Portman presents information "about the other planets that scientists have discovered through accessible text, fun fact boxes, and amazing photographs. They will be introduced to amazing scientific tools including the Kepler telescope, which has assisted in locating many planets outside of our solar system. The question of other planets sustaining life, as it is on earth, has been plaguing scientists and . . . readers will speculate whether there are habitable planets and if people could move to them or not." (Publisher's note)

Simon, Seymour
★ **Our** solar system; [by] Seymour Simon. updated ed.; Collins 2007 62p il $19.99; lib bdg $20.89
Grades: 3 4 5 6 **523.2**
1. Solar system
ISBN 978-0-06-114008-2; 0-06-114008-2; 978-0-06-114009-9 lib bdg; 0-06-114009-0 lib bdg
LC 2007279969
First published 1992
Describes the origins, characteristics, and future of the sun, planets, moons, asteroids, meteoroids, and comets
This "is a fine, comprehensive work on the solar system. . . . [The book includes] excellent photographs. Beautifully designed and a pleasure to use." Horn Book Guide

Tourville, Amanda Doering
Exploring the solar system. Rourke Pub. 2010 48p il (Let's explore science) $32.79; pa $9.95
Grades: 4 5 6 7 **523.2**
1. Solar system
ISBN 978-1-61590-323-8; 1-61590-323-2; 1-61590-562-6 pa; 9781615905621 pa
LC 2010009910
This "moves from basic definitions . . . to more technical information, such as the formula for calculating the speed of light. Also included is up-to-date coverage of Pluto's demotion from planet to plutoid, as well as a section on dwarf planets. . . . In [this] title, well-chosen boxed examples, abundant color photos, diagrams, and an appended glossary add interest and support the engaging [text]." Booklist
Includes glossary and bibliographical references

Trammel, Howard K.
★ **The** solar system. Children's Press 2009 48p il (True book) lib bdg $26; pa $6.95
Grades: 3 4 5 **523.2**
1. Solar system
ISBN 978-0-531-16898-1 lib bdg; 0-531-16898-0 lib bdg; 978-0-531-22805-0 pa; 0-531-22805-3 pa
LC 2008049376
"The Solar System begins with a lineup of the usual suspects (yes, Pluto is off the hook). The way the chapters move from inner to outer planets is no surprise, but the called-out details are cunningly illustrated and plenty fascinating. . . . Short but solid back matter closes out [this] impressive [offering]." Booklist

Wittenstein, Vicki Oransky
Planet hunter; Goeff Marcy and the search for other earths. Boyds Mills Press 2010 48p il $17.95
Grades: 5 6 7 8 **523.2**
1. Extrasolar planets 2. Life on other planets 3. Astrophysicists 4. College teachers
ISBN 978-1-59078-592-8; 1-59078-592-4
"The profound thrill of searching for (and finding!) planets orbiting stars other than our own is deftly captured in this profile of Geoff Marcy, one of the great hunt's most successful practitioners. Matched to big, sharp color photos of scientists (mostly) at work and compelling speculative views of exotic suns and landscapes, Wittenstein's matter-of-fact narrative first introduces readers to Marcy and his team on the night shift . . . at the W. M. Keck Observatory atop Hawaii's Mauna Kea. . . . This handsomely packaged introduction is just the ticket for turning earthbound (for now) children into budding skywatchers." SLJ
Includes glossary and bibliographical references

523.3 Specific parts of solar system

Carson, Mary Kay
Far-out guide to the moon. Enslow Publishers 2010 48p il (Far-out guide to the solar system) lib bdg $23.93; pa $7.95
Grades: 3 4 5 **523.3**
1. Moon 2. Solar system
ISBN 978-0-7660-3189-0 lib bdg; 0-7660-3189-6 lib bdg; 978-1-59845-184-9 pa; 1-59845-184-7 pa
LC 2009006487
"Presents information about the moon, including fast facts, history, and technology used to study it." Publisher's note
Includes glossary and bibliographical references

Gibbons, Gail
The **moon** book. Holiday House 1997 un il $16.95; pa $6.95
Grades: K 1 2 3 **523.3**
1. Moon
ISBN 0-8234-1297-0; 0-8234-1364-0 pa
LC 96-36826
Identifies the moon as our only natural satellite, describes its movement and phases, and discusses how we have observed and explored it over the years
"Gibbons presents a great deal of information in a deceptively simple format by combining inviting illustrations with clear writing." Horn Book Guide

Landau, Elaine
The **moon**; [by] Elaine Landau. Children's Press 2007 48p il (True book) lib bdg $26
Grades: 2 3 4 **523.3**
1. Moon
ISBN 0-531-12562-9 lib bdg; 978-0-531-12562-5 lib bdg
LC 2007004183
This describes the phases of the moon, its composition and geography, and moon exploration.

This "matches a clearly reasoned, matter-of-fact text to plenty of small but sharply reproduced photos." SLJ

Includes glossary and bibliographical references

Simon, Seymour

★ The **moon**; rev ed.; Simon & Schuster Bks. for Young Readers 2003 un il $17.95

Grades: 4 5 6 7   **523.3**

1. Moon 2. Moon -- Exploration

ISBN 0-689-83563-9

LC 2001-31303

First published 1984 by Four Winds Press

A basic introduction to Earth's closest neighbor, its composition, and man's missions to it

"The digitally remastered color photographs in this update are incredible. . . . The text has undergone minimal change. . . . The facts remain true and relevant, and the writing reflects the graphics: beautiful. This is a must-have for astronomy sections." SLJ

Tomecek, Steve

★ **Moon**; illustrated by Liisa Chauncy Guida. National Geographic 2005 31p il (Jump into science) $16.95; lib bdg $25.90

Grades: K 1 2   **523.3**

1. Moon

ISBN 0-7922-5123-7; 0-7922-8304-X lib bdg

LC 2004-8761

This book presents facts about the moon. "Kindergarten to grade two." (Sci Books Films)

"A cartoon cat and bug explain scientific history and concepts regarding the Earth's moon: its ever-changing appearance, composition, comparisons to Earth and the sun, Galileo's observations and discoveries in 1609, astronauts, orbits, and other topics." SLJ

523.4 Planets, asteroids, trans-Neptunian objects of solar system

Bjorklund, Ruth

Venus. Marshall Cavendish Benchmark 2009 64p il (Space!) lib bdg o.p.; ebook $33

Grades: 4 5 6 7   **523.4**

1. Venus (Planet)

ISBN 978-0-7614-4251-6; 9780761445616

LC 2009014665

"Describes Venus, including its history, its composition, and its role in the solar system." Publisher's note

Includes glossary and bibliographical references

Capaccio, George

Jupiter. Marshall Cavendish Benchmark 2009 64p il (Space!) lib bdg $22.95

Grades: 4 5 6 7   **523.4**

1. Jupiter (Planet)

ISBN 978-0-7614-4244-8 lib bdg; 0-7614-4244-8 lib bdg; 9780761445555

LC 2008037276

"Describes Jupiter, including its history, its composition, and its role in the solar system." Publisher's note

Includes glossary and bibliographical references

Mars. Marshall Cavendish Benchmark 2010 64p il (Space!) lib bdg $22.95

Grades: 4 5 6 7   **523.4**

1. Mars (Planet)

ISBN 978-0-7614-4247-9 lib bdg; 0-7614-4247-2 lib bdg; 9780761445579

LC 2008037280

Describes Mars, including its history, its composition, and its role in the solar system

Includes glossary and bibliographical references

Carson, Mary Kay

Far-out guide to asteroids and comets. Enslow Publishers 2010 48p il (Far-out guide to the solar system) lib bdg $23.93; pa $7.95

Grades: 3 4 5   **523.4**

1. Comets 2. Asteroids 3. Solar system

ISBN 978-0-7660-3188-3 lib bdg; 0-7660-3188-8 lib bdg; 978-1-59845-191-7 pa; 1-59845-191-X pa

LC 2009006484

"Lively writing with specific facts systematically presented and plenty of dramatic space art and photography add up to a winning formula. . . . Carson offers a thrillingly alarmist view . . . of the (relatively) small rocks and comets that hurtle through local space to, on occasion, collide spectacularly with Earth or other planets." SLJ

Includes glossary and bibliographical references

Far-out guide to Jupiter. Enslow Publishers 2010 48p il (Far-out guide to the solar system) lib bdg $23.93; pa $7.95

Grades: 3 4 5   **523.4**

1. Jupiter (Planet) 2. Solar system

ISBN 978-0-7660-3184-5 lib bdg; 0-7660-3184-5 lib bdg; 978-1-59845-186-3 pa; 1-59845-186-3 pa

LC 2008050036

"Presents information about Jupiter, including fast facts, history, and technology used to study the planet." Publisher's note

Includes glossary and bibliographical references

Far-out guide to Mars. Enslow Publishers 2010 48p il (Far-out guide to the solar system) lib bdg $23.93; pa $7.95

Grades: 3 4 5   **523.4**

1. Mars (Planet) 2. Solar system

ISBN 978-0-7660-3183-8 lib bdg; 0-7660-3183-7 lib bdg; 978-1-59845-185-6 pa; 1-59845-185-5 pa

LC 2009006485

"Presents information about Mars, including fast facts, history, and technology used to study the planet." Publisher's note

Includes glossary and bibliographical references

Far-out guide to Mercury. Enslow Publishers 2010 48p il (Far-out guide to the solar system) lib bdg $23.93; pa $7.95

Grades: 3 4 5   **523.4**

1. Mercury (Planet) 2. Solar system

ISBN 978-0-7660-3180-7 lib bdg; 0-7660-3180-2 lib bdg; 978-1-59845-181-8 pa; 1-59845-181-2 pa

LC 2009006486

"Presents information about Mercury, including fast facts, history, and technology used to study the planet." Publisher's note

Far-out guide to Neptune. Enslow Publishers 2010 48p il (Far-out guide to the solar system) lib bdg $23.93; pa $7.95
Grades: 3 4 5   **523.4**
1. Neptune (Planet) 2. Solar system
ISBN 978-0-7660-3186-9 lib bdg; 0-7660-3186-1 lib bdg; 978-1-59845-189-4 pa; 1-59845-189-8 pa
LC 2008050037
"Presents information about Neptune, including fast facts, history, and technology used to study the planet." Publisher's note
Includes glossary and bibliographical references

Far-out guide to Saturn. Enslow Publishers 2010 48p il (Far-out guide to the solar system) lib bdg $23.93; pa $7.95
Grades: 3 4 5   **523.4**
1. Saturn (Planet) 2. Solar system
ISBN 978-0-7660-3178-4 lib bdg; 0-7660-3178-0 lib bdg; 978-1-59845-187-0 pa; 1-59845-187-1 pa
LC 2008050038
"Presents information about Saturn, including fast facts, history, and technology used to study the planet" Publisher's note
Includes glossary and bibliographical references

Far-out guide to the icy dwarf planets. Enslow Publishers 2010 48p il (Far-out guide to the solar system) lib bdg $23.93; pa $7.95
Grades: 3 4 5   **523.4**
1. Planets
ISBN 978-0-7660-3187-6 lib bdg; 0-7660-3187-X lib bdg; 978-1-59845-190-0 pa; 1-59845-190-1 pa
LC 2009037810
"Lively writing with specific facts systematically presented and plenty of dramatic space art and photography add up to a winning formula." SLJ
Includes glossary and bibliographical references

Far-out guide to Uranus. Enslow Publishers 2010 48p il (Far-out guide to the solar system) lib bdg $23.93; pa $7.95
Grades: 3 4 5   **523.4**
1. Uranus (Planet) 2. Solar system
ISBN 978-0-7660-3185-2 lib bdg; 0-7660-3185-3 lib bdg; 978-1-59845-188-7 pa; 1-59845-188-X pa
LC 2008050040
"Presents information about Uranus, including fast facts, history, and technology used to study the planet." Publisher's note
Includes glossary and bibliographical references

Far-out guide to Venus. Enslow Publishers 2010 48p il (Far-out guide to the solar system) lib bdg $23.93; pa $7.95

Grades: 3 4 5   **523.4**
1. Venus (Planet) 2. Solar system
ISBN 978-0-7660-3181-4 lib bdg; 0-7660-3181-0 lib bdg; 978-1-59845-182-5 pa; 1-59845-182-0 pa
LC 2008050041
"Presents information about Venus, including fast facts, history, and technology used to study the planet" Publisher's note
Includes glossary and bibliographical references

Colligan, L. H.
Mercury. Marshall Cavendish Benchmark 2009 64p il (Space!) lib bdg $22.95
Grades: 4 5 6 7   **523.4**
1. Mercury (Planet)
ISBN 0-7614-4239-1 lib bdg; 9780761442394 lib bdg; 9780761445517
LC 2008037278
"Describes Mercury, including its history, its composition, and its role in the solar system." Publisher's note
Includes glossary and bibliographical references

Hicks, Terry Allan
Saturn. Marshall Cavendish Benchmark 2010 64p il (Space!) lib bdg $22.95
Grades: 4 5 6 7   **523.4**
1. Saturn (Planet)
ISBN 978-0-7614-4249-3 lib bdg; 0-7614-4249-9 lib bdg; 9780761445593
LC 2008037453
"Describes Saturn, including its history, its composition, and its role in the solar system." Publisher's note
Includes glossary and bibliographical references

Landau, Elaine
Beyond Pluto; [by] Elaine Landau. Children's Press 2007 48p il (True book) lib bdg $26
Grades: 2 3 4   **523.4**
1. Planets
ISBN 0-531-12565-3 lib bdg; 978-0-531-12565-6 lib bdg
LC 2007012280
This "looks past Pluto into the Kuiper Belt, the Oort Cloud, and the search for extrasolar planets. . . . [This] matches a clearly reasoned, matter-of-fact text to plenty of small but sharply reproduced color photos." SLJ
Includes glossary and bibliographical references

Jupiter; [by] Elaine Landau. Children's Press 2007 48p il (True book) lib bdg $26; pa $6.95
Grades: 2 3 4   **523.4**
1. Jupiter (Planet)
ISBN 978-0-531-12559-5 lib bdg; 0-531-12559-9 lib bdg; 978-0-531-14789-4 pa; 0-531-14789-4 pa
LC 2007003869
First published 1991
This describes the atmosphere and geographic features of Jupiter and the missions which have explored the planet
This "matches a clearly reasoned, matter-of-fact text to plenty of small but sharply reproduced color photos." SLJ
Includes glossary and bibliographical references

Mars; [by] Elaine Landau. Children's Press 2007 48p il (True book) lib bdg $26; pa $6.95

Grades: 2 3 4　　　　　　　　　　**523.4**
1. Mars (Planet)
ISBN 978-0-531-12560-1 lib bdg; 0-531-12560-2 lib
bdg; 978-0-531-14790-0 pa; 0-531-14790-8 pa
LC 2007-12260
This book contains information about Mars's orbit, its
size, its moons, its climate, its relative position in the solar
system, and the space missions that have explored its surface.
Glossary. Index. "Grades three to six." (Sci Books Films)
This "matches a clearly reasoned, matter-of-fact text to
plenty of small but sharply reproduced color photos." SLJ
Includes glossary and bibliographical references

Neptune; [by] Elaine Landau. Children's Press 2007
48p il (True book) lib bdg $26; pa $6.95
Grades: 2 3 4　　　　　　　　　　**523.4**
1. Neptune (Planet)
ISBN 978-0-531-12563-2 lib bdg; 0-531-12563-7 lib
bdg; 978-0-531-14793-1 pa; 0-531-14793-2 pa
LC 2007008257
This describes Neptune's place in the solar system, its
atmosphere and composition
This "matches a clearly reasoned, matter-of-fact text to
plenty of small but sharply reproduced color photos." SLJ
Includes glossary and bibliographical references

Pluto; from planet to dwarf. [by] Elaine Landau. Children's Press 2007 48p il (True book) lib bdg $26; pa
$6.95
Grades: 2 3 4　　　　　　　　　　**523.4**
1. Pluto (Dwarf planet) 2. Pluto (Planet)
ISBN 978-0-531-12566-3 lib bdg; 0-531-12566-1 lib
bdg; 978-0-531-14794-8 pa; 0-531-14794-0 pa
LC 2007012279
This describes Pluto's place in the solar system, its
change in status from planet to dwarf, its moons, and missions to Pluto
This "matches a clearly reasoned, matter-of-fact text to
plenty of small but sharply reproduced color photos." SLJ
Includes glossary and bibliographical references

Saturn; [by] Elaine Landau. Children's Press 2007
48p il (True book) lib bdg $26; pa $6.95
Grades: 2 3 4　　　　　　　　　　**523.4**
1. Saturn (Planet)
ISBN 978-0-531-12567-0 lib bdg; 0-531-12567-X lib
bdg; 978-0-531-14795-5 pa; 0-531-14795-9 pa
LC 2007004181
This describes Saturn's place in the solar system, its
composition, its moons and rings and missions to Saturn
This "matches a clearly reasoned, matter-of-fact text to
plenty of small but sharply reproduced color photos." SLJ
Includes glossary and bibliographical references

Uranus; [by] Elaine Landau. Children's Press 2007
48p il (True book) lib bdg $26; pa $6.95
Grades: 2 3 4　　　　　　　　　　**523.4**
1. Uranus (Planet)
ISBN 978-0-531-12569-4 lib bdg; 0-531-12569-6 lib
bdg; 978-0-531-14797-9 pa; 0-531-14797-5 pa
LC 2007012258
This describes Uranus's place in the solar system, its atmosphere, moons, and rings, and exploration

This "matches a clearly reasoned, matter-of-fact text to
plenty of small but sharply reproduced color photos." SLJ
Includes glossary and bibliographical references

Venus; [by] Elaine Landau. Children's Press 2007 48p
il (True book) lib bdg $26; pa $6.95
Grades: 2 3 4　　　　　　　　　　**523.4**
1. Venus (Planet)
ISBN 978-0-531-12564-9 lib bdg; 0-531-12564-5 lib
bdg; 978-0-531-14798-6 pa; 0-531-14798-3 pa
LC 2007004449
This describes Venus's place in the solar system, its at-
mosphere and composition, and missions to Venus
This "matches a clearly reasoned, matter-of-fact text to
plenty of small but sharply reproduced color photos." SLJ
Includes glossary and bibliographical references

Leedy, Loreen
Messages from Mars; by Loreen Leedy and Andrew
Schuerger; illustrated by Loreen Leedy. Holiday House
2006 40p il $16.95
Grades: K 1 2 3　　　　　　　　　　**523.4**
1. Space flight to Mars 2. Mars (Planet)
ISBN 978-0-8234-1954-8; 0-8234-1954-1
LC 2005-50267
"In 2106 six children, their team leader, and a 'hover-
bot' (floating robot) take a voyage to Mars. . . . Along the
way, they send messages back home, informally relaying
information about space travel and conditions on the red
planet. Cartoonlike images of the fictional characters and
their spacecraft are digitally combined with photos of Mars.
. . . Clever, and a good starting point for those intrigued by
Mars." Booklist
Includes glossary

Miller, Ron
Seven wonders of the gas giants and their moons.
Twenty-First Century Books 2011 80p il (Seven wonders)
lib bdg $33.26
Grades: 5 6 7 8　　　　　　　　　　**523.4**
1. Planets
ISBN 978-0-7613-5449-9 lib bdg; 0-7613-5449-2 lib
bdg; 9780761372813
LC 2010-15558
This book describes seven phenomena about the outer
planets of the solar system and their moons, including the
great red spot of Jupiter and the underground sea of Europa.
Index. "Grades five to eight." (Sci Books Films)
This "celebrates the most unique features of Jupiter,
Saturn, Uranus and Neptune, including companion moons
and Saturn's mysterious rings. . . . [This] volume makes basic concepts clear in lively, energetic language that, along
with the mesmerizing color photos and artists' renderings of
space, will easily captivate a young audience, while up-to-
date examples, including discoveries made in the last five
years, will only increase the sense of immediacy and excitement." Booklist
Includes glossary and bibliographical references

Seven wonders of the rocky planets and their moons.
Twenty-First Century Books 2011 80p il (Seven wonders)
lib bdg $33.26

Grades: 4 5 6   **523.4**
  1. Planets
  ISBN 978-0-7613-5448-2 lib bdg; 0-7613-5448-4 lib bdg; 9780761372837

LC 2010-15553

This book shows "views of features on Mercury, Venus, Earth (and its moon), and Mars. [Glossary. Index.] Grades five to eight." (Sci Books Films)

This "compares the fascinating diversity of Earth's land masses with those on Mars, Venus and Mercury. . . . [This] volume makes basic concepts clear in lively, energetic language that, along with the mesmerizing color photos and artists' renderings of space, will easily captivate a young audience, while up-to-date examples, including discoveries made in the last five years, will only increase the sense of immediacy and excitement." Booklist

Includes glossary and bibliographical references

Poynter, Margaret
  Doomsday rocks from space. Enslow Publishers 2011 48p il (Bizarre science) lib bdg $23.93
Grades: 5 6 7 8   **523.4**
  1. Comets 2. Asteroids 3. Meteorites
  ISBN 978-0-7660-3673-4; 0-7660-3673-1

LC 2009053601

First published 1996 with title: Killer asteroids

"Aimed at reluctant readers, [this title is] sure to disgust and delight in equal measure. . . . [The title] will pique interest and get kids lining up at the reference desk looking for more. The text is complemented by illustrations and magnified photos of things that you would hope never to see." SLJ

Includes glossary and bibliographical references

Scott, Elaine
  ★ **When** is a planet not a planet? the story of Pluto. Clarion Books 2007 43p il $17
Grades: 3 4 5 6   **523.4**
  1. Planets
  ISBN 978-0-618-89832-9; 0-618-89832-8

"Scott takes the 2006 downgrading of Pluto from planet to dwarf planet as a teachable moment for discussing questions such as how the number of planets has changed through the centuries, what can be called a planet, and how scientists come to conclusions—and occasionally change their minds. . . . Beautifully designed, the book includes many well-captioned, color illustrations, from period portraits to NASA images to artist's conceptions." Booklist

Sherman, Josepha
  Asteroids, meteors, and comets. Marshall Cavendish Benchmark 2009 64p il (Space!) lib bdg $22.95
Grades: 4 5 6 7   **523.4**
  1. Comets 2. Meteors 3. Asteroids
  ISBN 978-0-7614-4252-3 lib bdg; 0-7614-4252-9 lib bdg

LC 2008037281

This stands out for its "clear, accurate [presentation] of basic facts punctuated by lively turns of phrase and, sometimes, details not commonly found in the plethora of similar tours of the solar system and beyond." SLJ

Includes glossary and bibliographical references

Neptune. Marshall Cavendish Benchmark 2009 63p il (Space!) lib bdg $22.95

Grades: 4 5 6 7   **523.4**
  1. Neptune (Planet)
  ISBN 978-0-7614-4246-2 lib bdg; 0-7614-4246-4 lib bdg; 9780761445562

LC 2008037279

"Describes Neptune, including its history, its composition, and its role in the solar system." Publisher's note

Includes glossary and bibliographical references

Uranus. Marshall Cavendish Benchmark 2010 63p il (Space!) lib bdg $22.95
Grades: 4 5 6 7   **523.4**
  1. Astronomers 2. Uranus (Planet)
  ISBN 978-0-7614-4248-6 lib bdg; 0-7614-4248-0 lib bdg; 9780761445586

LC 2008037274

"Describes Uranus, including its history, its composition, and its role in the solar system." Publisher's note

Includes glossary and bibliographical references

Sparrow, Giles
  Destination Uranus, Neptune, and Pluto. PowerKids Press 2010 32p il (Destination solar system) lib bdg $23.95; pa $10
Grades: 3 4 5 6   **523.4**
  1. Uranus (Planet) 2. Neptune (Planet) 3. Pluto (Dwarf planet) 4. Pluto (Planet)
  ISBN 978-1-4358-3446-0 lib bdg; 978-1-4358-3463-7 pa

LC 2009-2985

Examines the outer planets, and discusses their moons, interiors, atmospheres, locations, and exploration.

Includes glossary

Winrich, Ralph
  Pluto; a dwarf planet. by Ralph Winrich; revised and updated by Thomas K. Adamson. rev and updated; Capstone Press 2007 24p il (First facts: the solar system) lib bdg $21.26
Grades: K 1 2 3   **523.4**
  1. Pluto (Dwarf planet) 2. Pluto (Planet)
  ISBN 978-1-4296-0727-8 lib bdg; 1-4296-0727-0 lib bdg

LC 2006037427

First published 2005

This describes the dwarf planet Pluto, as well as other dwarf planets Ceres and Eris

"Information present in the simply phrased [narrative] is supplemented by boxes of facts . . . and sharply reproduced photos or other art." SLJ

Includes glossary and bibliographical references

523.43   Mars

Rusch, Elizabeth
  ★ The **mighty** Mars rovers; the incredible adventures of Spirit and Opportunity. by Elizabeth Rusch. Houghton Mifflin Books for Children 2012 79 p. ill. (chiefly col.) (hardcover) $18.99; (hardcover) $18.99
Grades: 4 5 6   **523.43**
  1. Mars probes 2. Mars (Planet) -- Exploration 3. Astronautics 4. Mars probes 5. Mars (Planet) --

Exploration 6. Roving vehicles (Astronautics)
ISBN 054747881X; 9780547478814

LC 2011012159

In this book, "[Elizabeth] Rusch covers not only the scientific aspects of Mars exploration but also the personalities of the people who made it happen, and profiles the rovers themselves, Spirit and Opportunity." She looks at "the behind-the-scenes efforts of launching a scientific mission." Also included are "[f]ull-color photographs," a glossary, and a list of further resources. (School Library Journal)

Includes bibliographical references (p. 76), discography (p. 78), filmograophy (p. 78), and index.

523.45   Jupiter

Mist, Rosalind

Jupiter and Saturn; by Rosalind Mist. QEB Pub. 2012 24 p. col. ill. (Up in space) (hardcover) $25.65
Grades: K 1 2   523.45
1. Saturn (Planet) 2. Jupiter (Planet)
ISBN 1609923219; 9781609923211

LC 2012007023

This book by Rosalind Mist, part of the Up in Space series, looks at Jupiter and Saturn. "Each planet is discussed individually, while a separate page on the solar system shows the relative size of the planets." Photographs from the Hubble Space Telescope and other space missions are included. (Booklist)

523.46   Saturn

Miller, Ron

Saturn; Ron Miller. Twenty-First Century Books 2003 80p ill. (library) $27.93
Grades: 5 6 7 8   523.46
1. Saturn (Planet)
ISBN 9780761323600; 0761323600

Chronicles the discovery and exploration of the planet Saturn and discusses its rings and moons, its place in the solar system, and more.

"Concepts are explained clearly, and helpful diagrams and carefully chosen illustrations assist understanding." SLJ

Includes bibliographical references

523.49   Trans-Neptunian objects

Devorkin, David

Pluto's secret; an icy world's tale of discovery. by Margaret Weitekamp with David DeVorkin; illustrated by Diane Kidd. Abrams Books for Young Readers 2013 40 p. (reinforced) $16.95
Grades: 2 3 4   523.49
1. Picture books for children 2. Pluto (Dwarf planet)
ISBN 1419704230; 9781419704239

LC 2012033546

This children's picture book looks at Pluto. "The ninth planet from its discovery in 1930 to its demotion in 2006, Pluto has been revealing more of its 'secrets' as technology improved, and is now considered a 'dwarf planet' in the Kuiper belt. . . . The book provides a factual history of our far-

away 'dwarf,' and on its companion icy worlds, and on the discovery of Kuiper-like bands around other stars." (School Library Journal)

Includes bibliographical references.

523.5   Meteors, solar wind, zodiacal light

Hartland, Jessie

★ How the meteorite got to the museum; by Jessie Hartland. Blue Apple Books 2013 40 p. (hardcover) $17.99
Grades: 1 2 3 4   523.5
1. Meteorites 2. Museums and schools 3. American Museum of Natural History 4. Meteorites -- New York (State) -- Peekskill
ISBN 1609052528; 9781609052522

LC 2013007801

This children's picture book looks at "the travels of the Peekskill meteorite to the American Museum of Natural History." Here, "a science teacher chronicles for her students the travels of a meteoroid from outer space to the atmosphere over the United States, across several states, into a parked car in Peekskill, N.Y., and on to the museum." (Kirkus Reviews)

523.6   Comets

Simon, Seymour

★ Comets, meteors, and asteroids. Morrow Junior Bks. 1994 un il hardcover o.p. pa $6.95
Grades: 3 4 5 6   523.6
1. Comets 2. Meteors 3. Asteroids
ISBN 0-688-15843-9 pa

LC 93-51251

"Simon presents basic information about comets, meteors, and asteroids in an attractive oversize book. . . . Blocks of text appear in fairly large type, usually facing a full-page illustration. . . . Simon writes in plain language, without talking down to his audience. The intriguing photographs include shots of comets and meteor showers in the sky, a meteorite in Antarctica, and an enormous impact crater in Arizona." Booklist

523.7   Sun

Branley, Franklyn Mansfield

★ The sun, our nearest star; by Franklyn M. Branley; illustrated by Edward Miller. HarperCollins Pubs. 2002 25p il (Let's-read-and-find-out science) hardcover o.p. pa $4.95
Grades: K 1 2   523.7
1. Sun
ISBN 0-06-028534-6; 0-06-028535-4 lib bdg; 0-06-445202-6 pa

LC 2001-24951

A revised and newly illustrated edition of the title first published 1961

Describes the sun and how it provides the light and energy which allow plant and animal life to exist on the earth

"This edition marks the third incarnation of an old stand-by. . . . The gently edited text reads better than the old one. The new design features a larger format, bolder typography, and eye-catching artwork." Booklist

Capaccio, George
The **sun**. Marshall Cavendish Benchmark 2009 64p il (Space!) lib bdg $22.95
Grades: 4 5 6 7   **523.7**
1. Sun
ISBN 978-0-7614-4242-4 lib bdg; 0-7614-4242-1 lib bdg
LC 2008037275

"Describes the Sun, including its history, its composition, and its role in the solar system." Publisher's note
Includes glossary and bibliographical references

Carson, Mary Kay
Far-out guide to the sun. Enslow Publishers 2010 48p il (Far-out guide to the solar system) lib bdg $23.93; pa $7.95
Grades: 3 4 5   **523.7**
1. Sun 2. Solar system
ISBN 978-0-7660-3179-1 lib bdg; 0-7660-3179-9 lib bdg; 978-1-59845-180-1 pa; 1-59845-180-4 pa
LC 2008050039

"Presents information about the sun, including fast facts, history, and technology used to study it." Publisher's note
Includes glossary and bibliographical references

Gibbons, Gail
Sun up, sun down; written and illustrated by Gail Gibbons. Harcourt Brace Jovanovich 1983 un il hardcover o.p. pa $7
Grades: K 1 2 3   **523.7**
1. Sun
ISBN 0-15-282781-1; 0-15-282782-X pa
LC 82-23420

This book provides a "look at the sun's effect on the daily life of a little girl, told in first person. From the sun's first beam through her window in the morning to the dark night, the little girl focuses on the sun. She sees patterns (from the sun's beams through the window) on her floor; shades her eyes from looking at the sun and eats cereal made of wheat ('My dad tells me the sun made the wheat grow'). . . . Grades one to three." (SLJ)

The author explains "the sun and its effect on the earth. Narrated by a little girl who notices the sun shining when she wakes up one morning, this . . . [book covers] what the sun does, what makes shadows, how the sun helps form rain clouds, and how it keeps the planet warm." Booklist

Landau, Elaine
The **sun**; [by] Elaine Landau. Children's Press 2007 48p il (True book) lib bdg $26; pa $6.95
Grades: 2 3 4   **523.7**
1. Sun
ISBN 978-0-531-12568-7 lib bdg; 0-531-12568-8 lib bdg; 978-0-531-14796-2 pa; 0-531-14796-7 pa
LC 2007012259

This describes the sun as a star, the sun's place in the solar system, its relationship to Earth, and how astronomers study the sun

This "matches a clearly reasoned, matter-of-fact text to plenty of small but sharply reproduced color photos." SLJ
Includes glossary and bibliographical references

Wells, Robert E.
★ **Why** do elephants need the sun? Albert Whitman & Co. 2010 un il $16.99
Grades: 2 3 4   **523.7**
1. Sun 2. Water 3. Photosynthesis
ISBN 0-8075-9081-9; 978-0-8075-9081-2

This "book, on the sun, provides an approachable introduction to the subject while laying the groundwork for understanding topics (gravity, nuclear fusion) that students will tackle in later years. Beginning with the sun itself, the presentation quickly comes down to earth in a child-friendly way, with an elephant who needs our closest star. . . . The discussion of gravity starts with the elephant, then shifts to the solar system and the sun's core. Wells also shows how people have used the sun. . . . The book's naive ink-and-watercolor illustrations are often playful in approach. Simple diagrams are often used to clarify more abstract concepts. . . . This title offers an appealing introduction to the sun, as well as a solid stepping-stone toward scientific literacy." Booklist

523.8 Stars

Abramson, Andra Serlin
Inside stars; by Andra Serlin Abramson and Mordecai-Mark Mac Low. Sterling Children's Books 2011 48p il (Inside . . .) $16.95; pa $9.95
Grades: 5 6 7 8   **523.8**
1. Stars
ISBN 978-1-4027-7709-7; 1-4027-7709-4; 978-1-4027-8162-9 pa; 1-4027-8162-8 pa
LC 2011283564

Presents an illustrated overview of stars, including information on how they affect the Earth, how scientists study them, how they are classified, how they form and die, and specific information about our star, the Sun.

"On full but not crowded-looking pages, the captions, vocabulary words and digestible blocks of text are set into and around an engagingly diverse mix of cutaway views, digital paintings and eye-widening deep-space photographs. . . . There's plenty here to stimulate both random browsers and confirmed young sky watchers." Kirkus
Includes bibliographical references

Aguilar, David A.
Super stars; the biggest, hottest, brightest, and most explosive stars in the Milky Way. National Geographic 2010 48p il $16.95; lib bdg $27.90
Grades: 4 5 6 7   **523.8**
1. Stars
ISBN 978-1-4263-0601-3; 1-4263-0601-6; 978-1-4263-0602-0 lib bdg; 1-4263-0602-4 lib bdg
LC 2009-37124

"Pairing dramatic space art with souped-up prose, Aguilar introduces more than a dozen types of stars and stellar phenomena. . . . Aside from the occasional alien or interstellar spacecraft set against glowing star fields, the information in both pictures and texts sticks to the facts, accurately reflecting current knowledge without ever coming close to turning into a dry recitation of data. . . . [This is an] un-usually exuberant ticket to ride for young sky watchers and armchair space travelers." SLJ

Includes glossary and bibliographical references

Asimov, Isaac

The **life** and death of stars; by Isaac Asimov. rev and updated ed; Gareth Stevens Pub. 2005 32p il lib bdg $24.67

Grades: 4 5 6   **523.8**

1. Stars

ISBN 0-8368-3967-6

LC 2004-57842

This "begins with the birth of stars in dust cloud nurser-ies; goes on to profile the different types of stars; describes supernovas, neutron stars, and other late-stage develop-ments; then closes with an account of our Sun's probable fate. . . . [This is an] excellent collection [enhancer]." SLJ

Includes bibliographical references

Branley, Franklyn Mansfield

The **Big** Dipper; by Franklyn M. Branley; illustrated by Molly Coxe. rev ed; HarperCollins Pubs. 1991 32p il (Let's-read-and-find-out science book) hardcover o.p. pa $4.95

Grades: K 1   **523.8**

1. Ursa Major

ISBN 0-06-445100-3 pa

LC 90-31199

A revised and newly illustrated edition of the title first published 1962

Explains basic facts about the Big Dipper, including which stars make up the constellation, how its position changes in the sky, and how it points to the North Star

Croswell, Ken

★ The **lives** of stars. Boyds Mills Press 2009 72p il $19.95

Grades: 5 6 7 8   **523.8**

1. Stars 2. Astronomy

ISBN 978-1-59078-582-9; 1-59078-582-7

LC 2008033913

"Extensive, detailed information about stars is coupled with amazing colorful photographs, many from the Hubble Space Telescope, in this stunning book. Packed with facts about the stars and their life cycle, the text often relates them to situations or objects familiar to readers." SLJ

Includes glossary

DeCristofano, Carolyn Cinami

★ A **black** hole is not a hole; Carolyn Cinami DeCris-tofano; Illustrated by Michael Carroll. Charlesbridge 2012 v, 74 p.p col ill. (reinforced for library use) $18.95

Grades: 4 5 6 7   **523.8**

1. Stars 2. Universe 3. Black holes (Astronomy)

ISBN 9781570917837; 9781570917844

LC 2010022764

In this non-fiction children's book, Carolyn Cinami De-Cristofano discusses black holes. "Covering the life cycles of stars; the formation of black holes and weird optical and physical effects associated with them; more recent revela-tions of super-sized black holes at the centers of galaxies; and the general effects of mass on space, light, and matter,

she presents a . . . picture of the strange structure and strang-er physics of black holes." (Booklist)

Jackson, Ellen B.

★ The **mysterious** universe; supernovae, dark energy, and black holes. text by Ellen Jackson; photographs and il-lustrations by Nic Bishop. Houghton Mifflin 2008 60p il (Scientists in the field) $18

Grades: 5 6 7 8 9   **523.8**

1. Supernovas 2. Black holes (Astronomy)

ISBN 978-0-618-56325-8; 0-618-56325-3

LC 2007-41165

"Splitting its attention evenly between the scientist and his field, this handsomely designed volume displays the joys of being fascinated by one's work in a way that will encour-age students to seek similar professional satisfaction for themselves." Booklist

Includes glossary and bibliographical references

Jefferis, David

The **stars**; glowing spheres in the sky. Crabtree Pub. 2009 32p il (Exploring our solar system) lib bdg $26.60; pa $8.95

Grades: 3 4 5   **523.8**

1. Stars

ISBN 978-0-7787-3726-1 lib bdg; 0-7787-3726-8 lib bdg; 978-0-7787-3743-8 pa; 0-7787-3743-8 pa

LC 2008-46250

"Provides an interesting, well-illustrated introduction." Sci Books Films

Inlcudes glossary

Kim, F. S.

★ **Constellations**. Children's Press 2009 48p il (True book) lib bdg $26; pa $6.95

Grades: 3 4 5   **523.8**

1. Constellations

ISBN 978-0-531-16895-0 lib bdg; 0-531-16895-6 lib bdg; 978-0-531-22802-9 pa; 0-531-22802-9 pa

LC 2008050629

Though this title "dabbles in the science of planetary or-bits and early stargazing gear, . . . it mostly focuses on the rich myths surrounding the constellations, in one illustration transforming the night sky into a draped tapestry of monsters and gods. . . . Short but solid back matter closes out [this] impressive [offering]." Booklist

Mack, Gail

The **stars**. Marshall Cavendish Benchmark 2009 64p il (Space!) lib bdg $32.79

Grades: 4 5 6 7   **523.8**

1. Stars 2. Galaxies

ISBN 978-0-7614-4250-9 lib bdg; 0-7614-4250-2 lib bdg

LC 2009014655

This stands out for its "clear, accurate [presentation] of basic facts punctuated by lively turns of phrase and, some-times, details not commonly found in the plethora of similar tours of the solar system and beyond." SLJ

Includes glossary and bibliographical references

Miller, Ron

Seven wonders beyond the solar system. Twenty-First Century Books 2011 80p il (Seven wonders) lib bdg $33.26

Grades: 5 6 7 8   **523.8**

1. Extrasolar planets 2. Solar system

ISBN 978-0-7613-5454-3; 0-7613-5454-9

LC 2010028446

This "discusses how stars and galaxies form and how scientists search for 'the most Earthlike planet,' as well as the noteworthy nebulae, pulsars, and superclusters. . . . [This] volume makes basic concepts clear in lively, energetic language that, along with the mesmerizing color photos and artists' renderings of space, will easily captivate a young audience, while up-to-date examples, including discoveries made in the last five years, will only increase the sense of immediacy and excitement." Booklist

Includes glossary and bibliographical references

Mitton, Jacqueline

★ **Once** upon a starry night; a book of constellations. [illustrated by] Christina Balit. National Geographic 2004 un il $16.95

Grades: K 1 2 3   **523.8**

1. Constellations 2. Classical mythology

ISBN 0-7922-6332-4

LC 2003-10993

Companion volume to Zoo in the sky (1998)

First published 2003 in the United Kingdom

Presents facts about stars, nebulas, galaxies, and constellations and recounts the Greek myths that provided widely-known names for ten constellations, from Andromeda to Pegasus.

"Although the stories are quite short, Mitton's vivid word choices make the text as dynamic as Balit's striking pictures. Partly abstract and partly representational, the artwork features bold figures of mythological characters with silver-foil stars highlighting the points of light that make up the constellations." Booklist

Rau, Dana Meachen

Black holes; by Dana Meachen Rau. Compass Point Books 2005 32p il (Our solar system) $22.60

Grades: 3 4 5   **523.8**

1. Black holes (Astronomy)

ISBN 0-7565-0849-5

LC 2004-15567

"Rightly noting . . . that black holes by their very nature can neither be seen nor directly measured, [the author] discusses what we can infer and theorize from indirect observations, then closes with a revealing 2004 discovery. . . . [This earns] high marks for visual appeal, and for clear, specific presentation of material." SLJ

Includes glossary and bibliographical references

Rey, H. A.

★ **Find** the constellations; 2nd ed.; Houghton Mifflin Harcourt 2008 72p il $20; pa $9.99

Grades: 3 4 5 6   **523.8**

1. Stars 2. Constellations

ISBN 978-0-547-13140-5; 0-547-13140-2; 978-0-547-13178-8 pa; 0-547-13178-X pa

First published 1954

"This much-needed update of Rey's classic work . . . features a cleaner typeface but retains the layout and most of the graphics of the previous edition. . . . The primary update . . . involves the change in Pluto's status; a great touch is the inclusion of definitions for 'planet' and 'dwarf planet.' . . . Statistical data . . . are updated; the planet finder now covers the years 2007 through 2016; and there is a new list of books for further reading. With its enduring appeal, current information, and exceptional sky charts . . . this revision should be an essential purchase for all libraries." SLJ

Rockwell, Anne F.

Our stars; written and illustrated by Anne Rockwell. Silver Whistle Bks. 1999 un il hardcover o.p. pa $6.99

Grades: K 1 2   **523.8**

1. Stars 2. Planets 3. Outer space

ISBN 0-15-201868-9; 0-15-216360-0 pa

LC 97-49518

A simple introduction to the stars, planets, and outer space

"This book clearly explains many science facts without 'talking down' to youngsters. The storybook-style illustrations, . . . invite children to look at the night sky and think about the information presented in the text." Sci Books Films

Than, Ker

★ **Stars**. Children's Press 2009 48p il (True book) lib bdg $26; pa $6.95

Grades: 3 4 5   **523.8**

1. Stars

ISBN 978-0-531-16899-8 lib bdg; 0-531-16899-9 lib bdg; 978-0-531-22806-7 pa; 0-531-22806-1 pa

LC 2008051630

This introduction to stars "is simply gorgeous. The ghostly veils of the Cat's Eye Nebula, the ominous gas pillars of the Eagle Nebula, the coral-reef depths of the Crab Nebula—the only complaint will be that the photos aren't bigger. The diagrams (including the cradle-to-grave 'A Star's Life') are remarkably educational. Short but solid back matter closes out [this] impressive [offering]." Booklist

Waxman, Laura Hamilton

Exploring black holes. Lerner Publications Company 2011 40p il (What's amazing about space?) lib bdg $27.93

Grades: 4 5 6   **523.8**

1. Black holes (Astronomy)

ISBN 978-0-7613-5442-0; 0-7613-5442-5

LC 2010035378

This book about black holes in space is "written in simple language, [and] illustrated nicely. . . . The information presented is factually correct. . . . Every page includes a well-chosen illustration or photograph." Sci Books Films

525   Earth (Astronomical geography)

Bailey, Jacqui

Sun up, sun down; the story of day and night. written by Jacqui Bailey; illustrated by Matthew Lilly. Picture Window Books 2004 31p il (Science works) lib bdg $23.93

Grades: 2 3 4   **525**
1. Day 2. Night 3. Sun 4. Moon 5. Earth
ISBN 1-4048-0567-2

LC 2003-20119

Follows the sun from dawn to dusk to explain how light rays travel, how shadows are formed, how the moon lights up the night sky, and more

This "excellent science [book explains its subject] lucidly and sometimes amusingly.... Children will be illuminated and engaged." SLJ

Includes bibliographical references

Carson, Mary Kay

Far-out guide to Earth. Enslow Publishers 2010 48p il (Far-out guide to the solar system) lib bdg $23.93; pa $7.95

Grades: 3 4 5   **525**
1. Earth 2. Solar system
ISBN 978-0-7660-3182-1 lib bdg; 0-7660-3182-9 lib bdg; 978-1-59845-183-2 pa; 1-59845-183-9 pa

LC 2008049781

"Lively writing with specific facts systematically presented and plenty of dramatic space art and photography add up to a winning formula." SLJ

Includes glossary and bibliographical references

Gibbons, Gail

The **reasons** for seasons. Holiday House 1995 un il $16.95; pa $6.95

Grades: K 1 2 3   **525**
1. Seasons 2. Earth
ISBN 0-8234-1174-5; 0-590-90735-2 pa

LC 94-32904

"Gibbons uses simple words and clear, colorful pictures to explain the seasons, the solstices, and the equinoxes. Besides discussing the earth's tilt and orbit, she also comments on what people and animals do in each season of the year." Booklist

The **seasons** of Arnold's apple tree. Harcourt Brace Jovanovich 1984 un il $17; pa $7

Grades: PreK K 1 2   **525**
1. Trees -- Fiction 2. Seasons -- Fiction
ISBN 0-15-271246-1; 0-15-271245-3 pa

LC 84-4484

Arnold enjoys his apple tree through the changing year: its springtime blossoms, the swing and tree-house it supports, its summer shade, its autumn harvest; in the winter, the tree's branches hold strings of popcorn and berries for the birds

"Two major concepts emerge here, the first being the passage of the seasons, the second the valuable resource Arnold has in his apple tree.... Gibbons' crisp pictures ensure that the multifaceted lesson is explicit, bright and cheery." Booklist

Hicks, Terry Allan

Earth and the moon. Marshall Cavendish Benchmark 2009 64p il (Space!) lib bdg $22.95

Grades: 4 5 6 7   **525**
1. Moon 2. Earth
ISBN 978-0-7614-4254-7 lib bdg; 0-7614-4254-5 lib bdg

LC 2009014663

"Describes Earth and its Moon, including their history, their composition, and their roles in the solar system." Publisher's note

Includes glossary and bibliographical references

Karas, G. Brian

★ On Earth; written and illustrated by G. Brian Karas. Putnam 2005 un il $16.99

Grades: K 1 2   **525**
1. Earth
ISBN 0-399-24025-X

LC 2004-18204

This book describes the Earth's cycles of rotation and revolution, plus how they affect our lives through the days and seasons. "Ages five to eight." (Bull Cent Child Books)

"Karas covers the earth's rotation and revolution, space and time, hemispheres, and gravity. The spare text alternates between technical descriptions and personal experiences. Artistic renderings of the earth and its cycles introduce diagrams and offer concrete images showing what happens as day turns to night, seasons change, and the earth rotates on its axis." Horn Book Guide

Landau, Elaine

Earth; [by] Elaine Landau. Children's Press 2007 48p il (True book) lib bdg $26; pa $6.95

Grades: 2 3 4   **525**
1. Earth
ISBN 978-0-531-12558-8 lib bdg; 0-531-12558-0 lib bdg; 978-0-531-14788-7 pa; 0-531-14788-6 pa

LC 2007012278

Describes the planet Earth, exploring its composition, the conditions which support life, theories about how it formed, and its relationship with the moon

This "matches a clearly reasoned, matter-of-fact text to plenty of small but sharply reproduced color photos." SLJ

Includes glossary and bibliographical references

Martin, Bill

I love our Earth; [by] Bill Martin, Jr., and Michael Sampson; photographs by Dan Lipow. Charlesbridge 2006 un il $14.95

Grades: PreK K 1 2   **525**
1. Earth
ISBN 978-1-58089-106-6; 1-58089-106-3

LC 2005-06008

This is a celebration of the Earth in text and in photographs. "Kindergarten to grade six." (Sci Books Films)

"Martin's simple poem celebrates the colors of varied landscapes and the glories of the seasons. Each line of text appears on half a page, under a photo of a child. The rest of each spread is devoted to a panoramic vista. The boys and girls, of varying ages, come from many racial and ethnic groups from around the globe." SLJ

Includes glossary and bibliographical references

Miller, Ron

Earth and the moon. 21st Cent. Bks. (Brookfield) 2003 96p il (Worlds beyond) lib bdg $25.90

Grades: 5 6 7 8   **525**
1. Moon 2. Earth
ISBN 0-7613-2358-9

LC 2001-8479

This book chronicles the origin, evolution, and exploration of the Earth and the Moon, and discusses their composition, their place in the solar system, along with other topics. Glossary. Index. "Grades five to eight." (Sci Books Films)

This is illustrated "with a mix of NASA photos and wide-angle, computer-generated art. . . . Students with a serious interest in the physical history of the Earth and its moon will be engrossed by his account of our planet's first few billion years, the Moon's probable origin, and the rise of life." SLJ

Includes glossary and bibliographical references

Ride, Sally

Mission: planet Earth; our world and its climate--and how humans are changing them. [by] Sally Ride & Tam O'Shaughnessy. Roaring Brook Press 2009 80p il map (Sally Ride science) $19.95

Grades: 5 6 7 8   **525**

1. Earth 2. Climate -- Environmental aspects

ISBN 978-1-59643-310-6; 1-59643-310-8

         LC 2009-29253

"This environmental-science primer introduces a range of important concepts necessary to understand climate change and global warming. Topics include the carbon cycle, water cycle, long-range carbon emissions data, biological evidence of climate change, and much more. The authors have an extensive background in science education, and their text exhibits an excellent balance of concept thoroughness with ease of comprehension. Attractive photographs and colorful graphics, including many charts and diagrams, are incorporated throughout." SLJ

Ross, Michael Elsohn

Earth cycles; illustrated by Gustav Moore. Millbrook Press 2001 un il (Cycles) hardcover o.p. pa $7.95

Grades: K 1 2 3   **525**

1. Earth

ISBN 0-7613-1815-1; 0-7613-1977-8 pa

         LC 00-41860

"Ross discusses Earth's daily cycle of light and dark, the thirteen lunar cycles, and Earth's yearly trip around the sun. The simple text provides very basic information about periodicity and uses familiar examples to introduce new concepts. . . . Pleasing watercolors expand the text." Horn Book Guide

Simon, Seymour

★ **Earth**: our planet in space; rev ed; Simon & Schuster Bks. for Young Readers 2003 un il $17.95

Grades: 4 5 6 7   **525**

1. Earth

ISBN 0-689-83562-0

         LC 2001-31304

First published 1984 by Four Winds Press

This describes the relationship between the Earth, the sun, and the moon and explains the seasons, day and night, the atmosphere, and changes in the planet's surface. Illustrated with photographs taken from space

Wells, Robert E.

What's so special about planet Earth? Albert Whitman & Co. 2009 un il $16.99

Grades: K 1 2 3   **525**

1. Earth

ISBN 978-0-8075-8815-4; 0-8075-8815-6

         LC 2008056045

"Wells elaborates on the idea that our planet is 'a pretty good place for people to live' by, first, giving each of the other seven planets a quick flyby, then explaining how Earth's water and atmosphere create conditions suitable for life. His lively cartoon illustrations feature a pair of overall-clad young explorers (and a spaniel) boarding a jalopy-like spaceship for their spin around the solar system, then landing back on their home planet to demonstrate recycling, energy conservation, and other environmentally friendly activities." Booklist

525.022   Earth (Planet) – Photographs from space

Nardo, Don

The **Blue** marble; how a photograph revealed Earth's fragile beauty. by Don Nardo. Compass Point Books 2014 64 p. (Compass point books. Captured history) (library binding) $33.99

Grades: 5 6 7 8 9   **525.022**

1. Earth 2. Photographs 3. Apollo project 4. Apollo 17 (Spacecraft) 5. Photographs -- History 6. Earth (Planet) -- Photographs from space

ISBN 0756547326; 9780756547325; 9780756547882

         LC 2013031184

This middle grades book by Don Nardo describes how "The astronauts headed to the moon in December 1972 thought they knew what to expect. . . . But what they didn't expect came as a huge bonus. The astronauts of Apollo 17 would produce an amazing photograph of planet Earth--a lonely globe floating in inky black space. Their stunning Blue Marble image was destined to become one of the most reproduced and recognizable photos in history." (Publisher's note)

"—This outstanding follow-up to Capstone's "Captured History" series continues the same format, focusing on a single, emblematic photograph that defines an era or event... This set will show students how a single image can "capture" history and influence the perceptions and actions of those who see it. The books will certainly draw a large readership and are must-buys for all middle-level and secondary collections." SLJ

Includes bibliographical references (page 63) and index
Other titles in the series include:
Assassination and its Aftermath (2014)
Summitting Everest (2014)
Breaker Boys (2012)
Civil War Witness (2014)
Hitler in Paris (2014)
Little Rock Girl 1957 (2012)
Man on the Moon (2011)
Migrant Mother (2011)
Raising the Flag (2011)
Tank Man (2014)

526   Mathematical geography

Boothroyd, Jennifer

Map my home; by Jennifer Boothroyd. Lerner Publications Company 2014 24 p. (First step nonfiction - map it out) (lib. bdg.: alk. paper) $22.60

Grades: PreK K 1 2 **526**

1. Maps 2. Cartography

ISBN 1467711101; 9781467711104

LC 2012042554

In this children's book, by by Jennifer Boothroyd, "see how a boy makes a map of his home showing fire escape routes. Simple text takes early readers step by step through the types of features a fire safety map needs to have." (Publisher's note)

"These easy-to-read titles are for youngsters just learning about maps. Color photographs intermingle with hand-drawn diagrams to help readers understand the vocabulary... Good examples of beginning narrative nonfiction that includes well-explained hands-on activities." SLJ

Other titles in the series include:

Map my Continent (2014)

Map my Country (2014)

Map my Room (2014)

Map my State (2014)

May my Neighborhood (2014)

Map my neighborhood; by Jennifer Boothroyd. Lerner Publications Co. 2014 24 p. $6.95

Grades: PreK K 1 2 **526**

1. Maps

ISBN 146771111X; 146771531X; 9781467711111; 9781467715317

LC 2012037533

In this children's book, by Jennifer Boothroyd, "a child narrator shown in a photograph sets up a situation, such as a grandma coming to visit, and creates a map to fit that situation. The maps, drawn with colored markers in a childlike style, follow the same steps in each volume: planning the map and then drawing it. 'Map My Neighborhood' features a girl helping her visiting grandma by drawing a map to various local spots." (Booklist)

Other titles in the series include:

Map my Continent (2014)

Map my Country (2014)

Map my Room (2014)

Map my State (2014)

May my Home (2014)

Borden, Louise

Sea clocks; the story of longitude. illustrated by Erik Blegvad. Margaret K. McElderry Bks. 2003 un il $18.95

Grades: 3 4 5 6 **526**

1. Longitude 2. Navigation 3. Clocks and watches 4. Mechanical engineers 5. Clock and watch makers

ISBN 0-689-84216-3

LC 00-45599

This "picture book introduces John Harrison, the 18th-century English carpenter turned clockmaker who spent more than 40 years perfecting a device that solved the centuries-old problem of determining longitude. . . . The writing has a measured pace that helps readers to keep the details straight and the scientific concepts are clearly explained and smoothly incorporated into the text. Blegvad's precise illustrations create a strong sense of time and place." SLJ

Galat, Joan Marie

The **discovery** of longitude; by Joan Marie Galat; illustrated by Wes Lowe. Pelican Pub. Co. 2012 32 p. (hardcover: alk. paper) $16.99

Grades: 3 4 5 **526**

1. Inventors 2. Longitude 3. Clocks and watches 4. Measuring instruments 5. Picture books for children 6. Chronometers -- History 7. Longitude -- Measurement -- History 8. Clock and watch makers -- Great Britain -- Biography

ISBN 1455616370; 9781455616374; 9781455616381

LC 2011052911

This children's book tells "the story of inventing a watch to compute longitude aboard the great sailing ships." Joan Galat explains that 300 years ago, the British government sought a way to measure longitude that was better than the current two clock system. "Enter John Harrison, carpenter and clockmaker, who toiled for over 40 years to make just such a clock." (Kirkus)

Lasky, Kathryn

★ The **man** who made time travel; pictures by Kevin Hawkes. Farrar, Straus & Giroux 2003 un il $17

Grades: 3 4 5 **526**

1. Longitude 2. Navigation 3. Clocks and watches 4. Mechanical engineers 5. Clock and watch makers

ISBN 0-374-34788-3

LC 2001-33266

Describes the need for sailors to be able to determine their position at sea and the efforts of John Harrison, an eighteenth century man who spent his life refining instruments to enable them to do this

"With Hawkes's luminous full-color paintings on every page, its clear science, and its compelling social commentary, this title is not to be missed." SLJ

Includes bibliographical references

526.9 Surveying

Petersen, Christine

The **surveyor**. Marshall Cavendish Benchmark 2010 48p il (Colonial people) lib bdg $29.93

Grades: 3 4 5 6 **526.9**

1. Surveying 2. United States -- History -- 1600-1775, Colonial period

ISBN 978-0-7614-4805-1; 0-7614-4805-5

This describes the life of a colonial surveyor and his importance to the community, as well as everyday life, responsibilities, and social practices during that time.

"The type font, just slightly larger than usual, makes the text very visually appealing. . . . [The] book is liberally illustrated with artwork dating from the colonial period . . . [and] information boxes offer supplemental material." Libr Media Connect

Includes glossary and bibliographical references

529 Chronology

Adamson, Thomas K.

How do you measure time? by Thomas K. and Heather Adamson. Capstone Press 2011 32p il (Measure it!) lib bdg $25.99

Grades: PreK K 1 2 **529**
1. Time 2. Calendars 3. Measurement
ISBN 978-1-4296-4459-4; 1-4296-4459-1

LC 2010002787

Simple text and color photographs describe the units and tools used to measure time.

"The large picture-book format and inviting color photographs make [this] clearly written [title a] welcome [addition]. . . . The [author uses] common objects, giving readers recognizable points of reference. . . . Solid." SLJ

Includes glossary and bibliographical references

Formichelli, Linda
Timekeeping; Explore the History and Science of Telling Time With 15 Projects. by Linda Formichelli, W. Eric Martin; illustrated by Sam Carbaugh. Independent Pub Group 2012 128 p. (hardcover) $21.95
Grades: 4 5 6 7 8 **529**
1. Time 2. Science -- Experiments
ISBN 1619301369; 9781619301368

This juvenile activity book, by Linda Formichelli, W. Eric Martin, with illustrations by Sam Carbaugh, is part of the "Build It Yourself" series. It teaches "the cultural history of time" through providing several activities and projects such as "making a shadow clock, tracking time like an ancient Egyptian, using a protractor to create a sundial, measuring time with water, and making a candle clock." (Publisher's note)

Gleick, Beth
Time is when; [by] Beth Gleick; illustrated by Marthe Jocelyn. Tundra Books 2008 un il $15.95
Grades: PreK K 1 **529**
1. Time
ISBN 978-0-88776-870-5; 0-88776-870-9

A newly illustrated edition of the title first published 1960 by Rand McNally

"Gleick successfully answers the age-old question, 'What is time?.'. . . Breaking down time into all of its components, the author explains each one, using events that children face daily. . . . The story then builds upon each part of time as it is woven back together to make up the four seasons, explaining that a year is the time between one birthday and the next—a concept readers are sure to grasp. Jocelyn's illustrations give this account a fresh look with multicultural characters and digital clocks while still keeping an old-fashioned, nostalgic feel in the paper and fabric collages, which have bright colors and fun, busy patterns. The simple, lyrical text has a timeless quality that works well as a read-aloud and is still easy enough for beginning readers to work out on their own." SLJ

Hutchins, H. J.
A **second** is a hiccup; a child's book of time. by Hazel Hutchins; illustrated by Kady MacDonald Denton. Arthur A. Levine Books 2007 un il $16.99
Grades: PreK K 1 2 **529**
1. Time
ISBN 0-439-83106-7

LC 2006007561

"The abstract concept of time is explained in child-friendly terms. . . . Denton's charming watercolor-and-ink vignettes, showing three friends interacting with one another and with their families, celebrate their joys and accomplish-ments with warmth and affection. The lyrical, rhyming text answers deceptively simple childhood questions with great flair." SLJ

Jenkins, Steve
★ **Just** a second. Houghton Mifflin Books for Children 2011 un il $16.99
Grades: PreK K 1 2 **529**
1. Time 2. Nature
ISBN 978-0-618-70896-3; 0-618-70896-0

LC 2011002104

This non-fiction picture book explores time and how we think about it in a different way—as a series of events in the natural world (some of them directly observable, others not) that take place in a given unit of time.

"Jenkins brings fresh perspective to the passage of time in a thought-provoking picture book that features his typically elegant cut-paper collages. . . . Back matter offers information about life spans, population growth, and Earth's history. This subtly philosophical examination of time, scale, and the mechanics of life is all but certain to leave readers reconsidering the world and their place in it." Publ Wkly

Koscielniak, Bruce
★ **About** time; a first look at time and clocks. by Bruce Koscielniak. Houghton Mifflin 2004 un il map $16
Grades: 3 4 5 **529**
1. Time 2. Calendars 3. Clocks and watches
ISBN 0-618-39668-3

LC 2003-17469

Describes the concept of time and how it has been measured throughout history, using water clocks, sundials, calendars, and atomic vibrations.

"Koscielniak gives an instructive yet entertaining march through the ages. . . . Attractive watercolor illustrations in green and tan tones enhance the text." SLJ

Maestro, Betsy
The **story** of clocks and calendars; marking a millennium. illustrated by Giulio Maestro. Lothrop, Lee & Shepard Bks. 1999 48p il hardcover o.p. pa $9.99
Grades: 3 4 5 6 **529**
1. Time 2. Calendars 3. Clocks and watches
ISBN 0-688-14548-5; 0-688-14549-3 lib bdg; 0-06-058945-0 pa

LC 98-21305

"This overview of timekeeping begins with prehistoric 'calendar sticks' and stone structures, and continues through today's ultra-precise atomic clocks. The text takes a broad multicultural approach, showing how science, history, and societal differences have influenced the calendar; the color illustrations are executed in styles that match the eras and cultures discussed in the volume." Horn Book Guide

Murphy, Stuart J.
★ **It's** about time! illustrated by John Speirs. HarperCollins Publishers 2005 33p il (MathStart) $15.99; pa $4.99
Grades: K 1 2 **529**
1. Day 2. Time 3. Night
ISBN 0-06-055768-0; 0-06-055769-9 pa

LC 2003-27524

"Each page shows an analog clock and a digital clock displaying the time, from seven o'clock one morning through the day and night to seven the next morning. The illustrations show the child's activities and, in the night, his dreams. . . . Soft pencil drawings deliniate the rounded forms of children engaged in their daily activities. The rich colors of the washes glow against the white backgrounds." Booklist

Rodeo time; by Stuart J. Murphy; illustrated by David T. Wenzel. HarperCollins 2006 33p il (MathStart) $15.99; pa $4.99
Grades: 2 3 4   **529**
  1. Time 2. Rodeos
  ISBN 0-06-055779-6; 0-06-055778-8 pa
                                                         LC 2005002665
"Katie and Cameron visit a rodeo with their uncle, Cactus Joe. . . . Joe gives Katie and Cameron some chores and activities, and Katie makes out a schedule to keep track of them all. Then, Katie and Cameron have to keep watch so that they don't miss any of the rodeo events. . . . The short length, light tone, and bright illustrations will help put across the concept." Booklist
Includes bibliographical references

Nagda, Ann Whitehead
  Chimp math; learning about time from a baby chimpanzee. by Ann Whitehead Nagda and Cindy Bickel. Holt & Co. 2002 29p il $16.95
Grades: 2 3 4   **529**
  1. Time 2. Chimpanzees
  ISBN 0-8050-6674-8
                                                            LC 00-57529
"The details of the chimp's young life will fascinate readers. . . . The time lines, in particular, illuminate the narrative and can lead to classroom projects." SLJ
The authors "integrate the elementary-level mathematical skills of telling and representing time with the story of [a] . . . chimp, Jiggs. . . . Jiggs's growth and feeding are shown through representations of time: timelines, graphs of variables over time, calendars, and daily charts." Horn Book

Older, Jules
  Telling time; how to tell time on digital and analog clocks! written by Jules Older; illustrated by Megan Halsey. Charlesbridge Pub. 2000 un il $16.95; pa $6.95
Grades: K 1 2 3   **529**
  1. Time 2. Clocks and watches
  ISBN 0-88106-396-7; 0-88106-397-5 pa
                                                          LC 99-18764
Humorous text explains the concept of time, from seconds to hours on both analog and digital clocks, from years to millennia on the calendar
"The cartoon illustrations, showing children and many, many types of clocks are colorful, plentiful, and inviting. . . . This jovial look at time and time telling is as handy as they come." SLJ

Raum, Elizabeth
  The **story** behind time. Heinemann Library 2009 32p il (True stories) lib bdg $28.21
Grades: 3 4 5   **529**
  1. Time 2. Calendars 3. Clocks and watches
  ISBN 978-1-4329-2343-3 lib bdg; 1-4329-2343-9 lib bdg
                                                         LC 2008037393

This offers information about time, including a history of time measurement
Includes bibliographical references

Skurzynski, Gloria
  On time; from seasons to split seconds. National Geographic Soc. 2000 41p il $17.95
Grades: 4 5 6 7   **529**
  1. Time
  ISBN 0-7922-7503-9
                                                          LC 99-33927
Examines the ways humans have measured time throughout history and discusses the various units that are used to keep track of it
"This attractive offering is brimming with information. . . . The conversational tone helps readers get through the more difficult concepts. . . . The book is heavily illustrated with full-color drawings, photographs, and diagrams." SLJ

529.2 Intervals of time

Perrin, Clotilde
  At the same moment, around the world; by Clotilde Perrin. Chronicle Books 2014 36 p. chiefly color illustrations (alk. paper) $17.99
Grades: K 1 2 3   **529.2**
  1. Time 2. Space and time 3. Time -- Systems and standards
  ISBN 1452122083; 9781452122083
                                                        LC 2013028005
In this children's book, by Clotilde Perrin, "discover Benedict drinking hot chocolate in Paris, France; Mitko chasing the school bus in Sofia, Bulgaria; and Khanh having a little nap in Hanoi, Vietnam! . . . Perrin takes readers eastward from the Greenwich meridian, from day to night, with each page portraying one of (the original) 24 time zones." (Publisher's note)
"Published first in French in 2011, Perrin's elegant construction looks at children and young people around the globe eastward from the Greenwich meridian. At 6 a.m. in Dakar, Senegal, Keita is helping his father with his catch of fish. . . . The moment unfolds with Yasmine in Baghdad, Lilu in the Himalyas, Chen in Shanghai, Allen and Kiana in Honolulu, and so on. . . . The pictures, in pencil and digital color, fill the tall oblong shape of the book dramatically. . . . A brief but excellent description of time zones and timekeeping closes the volume. . . . A very fine working of story, information, art and culture. (Picture book. 5-9)." Kirkus

530 Physics

Adams, Tom
  Feel the force! full of pop-up physics fun! illustrated by Thomas Flintham. Candlewick 2011 20p il (Super science)
Grades: 2 3 4   **530**
  1. Physics 2. Pop-up books
  ISBN 0-7636-5566-X; 978-0-7636-5566-2
"This high-energy pop-up takes a hands-on approach to physics. The text explains such concepts as force, gravity, friction, sound waves, light, and magnetism. . . . Cartoons,

pop-ups, mini-books, flaps, tabs, and sidebars further elaborate on the various topics, and numerous experiments encourage further exploration and scrutiny."

"This high-energy pop-up takes a hands-on approach to physics. The text explains such concepts as force, gravity, friction, sound waves, light, and magnetism. . . . Cartoons, pop-ups, mini-books, flaps, tabs, and sidebars further elaborate on the various topics, and numerous experiments encourage further exploration and scrutiny." Publ Wkly

Baxter, Roberta

The **particle** model of matter. Raintree 2009 48p il (Sci-hi: physical science) lib bdg $31.43; pa $8.99

Grades: 4 5 6 7   **530**

1. Atoms 2. Matter

ISBN 978-1-4109-3244-0 lib bdg; 978-1-4109-3259-4 pa

LC 2008030582

This takes a look at atoms, the building blocks of matter. It describes the different kinds of atoms, the particles that make up an atom, and the different states that matter can take

Includes bibliographical references

Bonnet, Robert L.

Home run! science projects with baseball and softball. [by] Robert L. Bonnet and Dan Keen. Enslow Publishers 2009 104p il (Score! Sports science projects) lib bdg $31.93

Grades: 5 6 7 8   **530**

1. Motion 2. Baseball 3. Force and energy 4. Science projects 5. Science -- Experiments

ISBN 978-0-7660-3365-8 lib bdg; 0-7660-3365-1 lib bdg

LC 2008-3005

"In addition to colorful, digital drawings illustrating the projects, a few photos and period prints also brighten the pages. . . . [This] will appeal to those looking for fresh science-project ideas." Booklist

Includes glossary and bibliographical references

Gaff, Jackie

Looking at solids, liquids, and gases; how does matter change? [by] Jackie Gaff. Enslow Publishers 2008 32p il (Looking at science: how things change) lib bdg $22.60

Grades: 1 2 3   **530**

1. Matter

ISBN 978-0-7660-3092-3 lib bdg; 0-7660-3092-X lib bdg

LC 2007-24514

"Fills a huge void in elementary science collections. . . . Text is arranged in succinct 'chunks,' giving important facts without overwhelming readers. . . . [This] is an essential addition." Libr Media Connect

Includes glossary and bibliographical references

Gardner, Robert

Ace your physical science project; great science fair ideas. [by] Robert Gardner, Madeline Goodstein, and Thomas R. Rybolt. Enslow Publishers 2009 128p il (Ace your physics science project) lib bdg $31.93

Grades: 5 6 7 8   **530**

1. Physics 2. Science projects 3. Science -- Experiments

ISBN 978-0-7660-3225-5 lib bdg; 0-7660-3225-6 lib bdg

LC 2008-29637

"Dozens of . . . science activities are presented with background information, step-by-step instructions, and suggestions for extending to the science fair level. . . . Color illustrations and important safety information are included." Horn Book Guide

Includes bibliographical references

Slam dunk! science projects with basketball; [by] Robert Gardner and Dennis Shortelle. Enslow Publishers 2009 104p il (Score! sports science projects) lib bdg $31.93

Grades: 5 6 7 8   **530**

1. Physics 2. Basketball 3. Science projects 4. Science -- Experiments

ISBN 978-0-7660-3366-5 lib bdg; 0-7660-3366-X lib bdg

LC 2008-24879

"Introductions include information about the history of the sport, safety steps to follow, and the scientific method. . . . Detailed diagrams help clarify many of the directions." SLJ

Includes glossary and bibliographical references

Goodstein, Madeline

Wheels! science projects with bicycles, skateboards, and skates. Enslow Publishers 2009 104p il (Score! sports science projects) lib bdg $31.93

Grades: 5 6 7 8 9 10   **530**

1. Wheels 2. Physics 3. Science projects 4. Science -- Experiments

ISBN 978-0-7660-3107-4 lib bdg; 0-7660-3107-1 lib bdg

LC 2008-24880

"Introductions include information about the history of the sport, safety steps to follow, and the scientific method. . . . Detailed diagrams help clarify many of the directions." SLJ

"Presents several science experiments and science project ideas using physics and bicycles, skateboards, and roller skates." Publisher's note

Includes glossary and bibliographical references

Green, Dan

Physics; why matter matters! [by] Dan Green; Simon Basher, illustrator. Kingfisher 2008 128p il pa $8.95

Grades: 5 6 7 8   **530**

1. Physics

ISBN 978-0-7534-6214-0 pa; 0-7534-6214-1 pa

LC 2007-31805

This "introduces the elements of physics as anthropomorphic, cartoon-style characters. . . . Each of the groupings begins with an introduction and each concept is given its own spread that shows the cartoon figure and describes its 'personality.' The information is presented in a chatty and conversational tone. . . . Along with the narrative, which is written in the first person from the concept's point of view, other key facts are presented. This book would be handy as a supplement to a physics curriculum." SLJ

Includes glossary

Hartman, Eve

Light and sound; [by] Eve Hartman and Wendy Mesh-besher. Raintree 2008 48p il (Sci-hi: physical science) lib bdg $22; pa $8.99

Grades: 5 6 7 8   **530**

1. Light 2. Sound

ISBN 978-1-4109-3378-2 lib bdg; 1-4109-3378-4 lib bdg; 978-1-4109-3383-6 pa; 1-4109-3383-0 pa

LC 2009-3506

A "compelling read for both browsers and science buffs. . . . Information is clearly presented and flows smoothly. . . . A treasure trove of information." SLJ

Includes glossary and bibliographical references

Lee, Cora

The great motion mission; a surprising story of physics in everyday life. illustrated by Steve Rolston. Annick Press 2009 114p il $24.95; pa $14.95

Grades: 4 5 6   **530**

1. Physics

ISBN 978-1-55451-185-3; 1-55451-185-2; 978-1-55451-184-6 pa; 1-55451-184-4 pa

"This book is a combination of narrative and concepts about physics. . . . Jeremy and his friends are distraught when the local summer fair is canceled in order to host a physics conference. While Jeremy helps his uncle campaign to save the fair, his new neighbor, Aubrey, sets out to prove that physics isn't only necessary, but also fun. The text is chatty and accessible to students. Topics include 'Physics and Sight,' 'Physics and Sound,' and 'Physics in Motion.' Each chapter profiles a featured physicist, from Albert Einstein to Richard Feynman. . . . Cartoon illustrations help to explain concepts such as the water cycle and wave patterns. Photographs are scattered throughout, and boxed areas highlight specific topics. This title would be especially useful for students wanting a good introduction to physics." SLJ

Includes glossary and bibliographical references

Mason, Adrienne

Change it! solids, liquids, gases and you. written by Adrienne Mason; illustrated by Claudia Davila. Kids Can Press 2006 32p il (Primary physical science) $12.95; pa $5.95

Grades: K 1 2   **530**

1. Matter 2. Science -- Experiments

ISBN 978-1-55337-837-2; 1-55337-837-7; 978-1-55337-838-9 pa; 1-55337-838-5 pa

This describes the three states of matter and includes experiments

This uses "colorful eye-catching graphics." Sci Books Films

Includes glossary

Motion, magnets and more; the big book of primary physical science. written by Adrienne Mason; illustrated by Claudia Dávila. Kids Can Press 2011 127p il $18.95

Grades: PreK K 1 2   **530**

1. Physical sciences

ISBN 978-1-55453-707-5; 1-55453-707-X

This book "is divided into four chapters that start readers off with the easy and familiar and work up to some larger science concepts, introducing and defining proper vocabulary along the way. . . . Short sentences, simple vocabulary and only a few paragraphs per page make this accessible

for even the youngest of science explorers, while the 19 activities scattered throughout will deepen their understanding and hold their focus. . . . Dávila's charming digital illustrations depict rosy, round-faced multiethnic children in a variety of settings exploring the world around them." Kirkus

Mercer, Bobby

Junk drawer physics; 50 awesome experiments that don't cost a thing. Bobby Mercer. First edition Chicago Review Press, Inc. 2014 208 p. (trade paper) $14.95

Grades: 5 6 7 8   **530**

1. Physics 2. Science -- Experiments 3. Physics -- Experiments

ISBN 1613749201; 9781613749203

LC 2013046726

In this book, Bobby Mercer "provides readers with more than 50 . . . hands-on experiments. . . . Turn a plastic cup into a pinhole camera using waxed paper, a rubber band, and a thumbtack. Build a swinging wave machine using a series of washers suspended on strings from a yardstick. . . . Each project has a materials list, detailed step-by-step instructions with illustrations, and a brief explanation of the scientific principle being demonstrated." (Publisher's note)

"This book is filled with practical and easy experiments that demonstrate many different principles of physics. Though it joins a crowded market of similar at-home science books, this title offers experiments that are fresh and different." SLJ

Silverstein, Alvin

Matter; by Alvin Silverstein, Virginia Silverstein, Laura Silverstein Nunn. Twenty-First Century Books 2009 112p il (Science concepts) lib bdg $31.93

Grades: 5 6 7 8   **530**

1. Matter

ISBN 978-0-8225-7515-3 lib bdg; 0-8225-7515-9 lib bdg

LC 2007049493

This is a "simple and straightforward [discussion] of the [subject]. The layout . . . is attractive and inviting, with full-color photographs and/or diagrams on almost every spread. In addition, the authors make good use of fact boxes. . . . [This] discusses the states of matter, the elements, chemical reactions, and more. [This title] will interest browsers and provide ample information for reports." SLJ

Includes glossary and bibliographical references

Sullivan, Navin

Weight. Marshall Cavendish Benchmark 2007 48p il (Measure up!) lib bdg $20.90

Grades: 4 5 6 7   **530**

1. Gravity 2. Weights and measures

ISBN 978-0-7614-2324-9 lib bdg; 0-7614-2324-9 lib bdg

"Examples using familiar objects and excellent full-color graphics help to bring concepts to life." SLJ

This "explains how molecules react to heat, how different types of thermometers measure heat energy, and shows the immense impact temperature has on every part of our lives." Publisher's note

Includes glossary and bibliographical references

Taylor-Butler, Christine

Think like a scientist in the gym. Cherry Lake 2011 32p il (Science explorer junior) $27.07

Grades: 3 4 5   **530**

1. Sports 2. Physics 3. Science -- Experiments

ISBN 978-1-61080-163-8; 1-61080-163-6

"This is a kid-friendly approach to physics in particular and the scientific method in general, arranging much of the information around places and ideas kids can relate to: the gym, the track, and sports. . . . Five short chapters highlight how scientists and kids can find out how things work through experiments. . . . Photos of kids playing sports and simple but bright cartoon illustrations make this a lively read." Booklist

Weir, Jane

Matter. Compass Point Books 2009 40p il (Mission: science) lib bdg $26.60

Grades: 4 5 6   **530**

1. Matter

ISBN 978-0-7565-4069-2 lib bdg; 0-7565-4069-0 lib bdg

LC 2008-37624

An introduction to the scientific concept of matter, including elements, atoms, and molecules

Includes glossary

530.1   Theories and mathematical physics

Rand, Casey

Time. Heinemann Library 2011 32p il map (Measure it!) lib bdg $29; pa $7.99

Grades: 3 4 5   **530.1**

1. Space and time

ISBN 978-1-4329-3766-9 lib bdg; 1-4329-3766-9 lib bdg; 978-1-4329-3772-0 pa; 1-4329-3772-3 pa

LC 2009-35210

"This book teaches the concept of time (including seasons, daylight savings, time zones)." Publisher's note

Includes glossary and bibliographical references

530.11   Relativity theory

Whiting, Jim

Space and time; Jim Whiting; photographs by Getty Images; folio illustration, Alex Ryan. 1st ed. Creative Education 2013 48 p. col. ill., col. maps (library) $35.65

Grades: 4 5 6 7   **530.11**

1. Physics 2. Space and time 3. Relativity (Physics)

ISBN 1608181928; 9781608181926

LC 2011040146

This book, by Jim Whiting, explores the concepts of space and time as part of the "Mysteries of the Universe" series. It appeals "to report writers and serious astronomy students. Each book carefully examines the history behind attempts to unravel explanations for the subjects, going back to Anaxagoras's work on energy in 450 B.C. all the way up to the contemporary findings of Stephen Hawking." (School Library Journal)

Includes bibliographical references (p. 46-47) and index.

530.4   States of matter

Boothroyd, Jennifer

What is a gas? by Jennifer Boothroyd. Lerner Publications Co. 2007 23p il (First step nonfiction: states of matter) lib bdg $21.27

Grades: K 1 2   **530.4**

1. Gases

ISBN 978-0-8225-6837-7 lib bdg; 0-8225-6837-3 lib bdg

LC 2006006303

"This small book introduces a single state of matter: a gas. Each page in the main section offers one or more colorful photographs and a brief line or two of large-print text. After a brief introduction to matter, the discussion moves on to the characteristics of gases and a few examples." Booklist

What is a liquid? by Jennifer Boothroyd. Lerner Publications Co. 2007 23p il (First step nonfiction: states of matter) lib bdg $21.27; pa $5.95

Grades: K 1 2   **530.4**

1. Liquids

ISBN 978-0-8225-6838-4 lib bdg; 0-8225-6838-1 lib bdg; 978-0-8225-6817-9 pa; 0-8225-6817-9 pa

LC 2006006304

This explains liquids "along with basic vocabulary. The layout is bright with many color photographs featuring children of different ethnicities. The text is spare; each spread includes, on average, three sentences." SLJ

What is a solid? by Jennifer Boothroyd. Lerner Publications Co. 2007 23p il (First step nonfiction: states of matter) lib bdg $21.27; pa $5.95

Grades: K 1 2   **530.4**

1. Solids

ISBN 978-0-8225-6836-0 lib bdg; 0-8225-6836-5 lib bdg; 978-0-8225-6816-2 pa; 0-8225-6816-0 pa

LC 2006006307

This explains solids "along with basic vocabulary. The layout is bright with many color photographs featuring children of different ethnicities. The text is spare; each spread includes, on average, three sentences." SLJ

Bradley, Kimberly Brubaker

Pop! a book about bubbles. photographs by Margaret Miller. HarperCollins Pubs. 2001 33p il (Let's-read-and-find-out science) hardcover o.p. pa $4.95

Grades: K 1   **530.4**

1. Bubbles

ISBN 0-06-028700-4; 0-06-028701-2 lib bdg; 0-06-445208-5 pa

LC 99-57794

Simple text explains how soap bubbles are made, why they are always round, and why they pop

"A simple, accurate text that is also fun to read. . . . Delightful color photographs of charming children making bubbles and of bubbles floating freely reinforce and extend the text. . . . This is science learning at its best." SLJ

Claybourne, Anna

The nature of matter; [by] Anna Claybourne. Gareth Stevens Pub. 2007 48p il (Gareth Stevens vital science: physical science) lib bdg $26.60; pa $11.95

Grades: 4 5 6 7   **530.4**
1. Matter
ISBN 978-0-8368-8088-5 lib bdg; 978-0-8368-8097-7 pa

LC 2006033732

This describes uses for matter and what happens when it changes from one form to another, the basic physical laws and properties of matter, and the various ways in which we control how matter behaves.

This is "straightforward and clear. . . . The layout is bright and colorful, with photographs and illustrations on almost every page." SLJ

Includes glossary and bibliographical references

Gardner, Robert
Melting, freezing, and boiling science projects with matter; [by] Robert Gardner. Enslow Elementary 2006 48p il (Fantastic physical science experiments) lib bdg $23.93
Grades: 4 5 6   **530.4**
1. Matter 2. Temperature 3. Science -- Experiments
ISBN 0-7660-2589-6

LC 2005033753

This offers experiments on the nature of solids, liquids, and gases and temperature.

"The ink-and-wash pictures illustrate the scientific principles as well as the equipment used in various activities. . . . Gardner's explanations are clear and his discussions lead readers to think about causes as well as what is happening to matter . . . as it changes form." Booklist

Includes glossary and bibliographical references

Hurd, Will
Changing states; solids, liquids, and gases. Heinemann Library 2009 48p il (Do it yourself) lib bdg $31.43; pa $8.99
Grades: 3 4 5 6   **530.4**
1. Gas 2. Matter 3. Solids 4. Liquids
ISBN 978-1-4329-2312-9 lib bdg; 1-4329-2312-9 lib bdg; 978-1-4329-2319-8 pa; 1-4329-2319-6 pa

LC 2008034939

The describes the fluctuating states of matter and includes experiments

This "would make an ideal supplement to science classes. A modular layout and dynamic photos keep things moving, while the experiments . . . feature lists of readily available materials, steps required to pull off the magic, and warnings as the when adult supervision is required." Booklist

Includes bibliographical references

Lawrence, Ellen
Water; by Ellen Lawrence. Bearport Publishing 2013 24 p. (Science Slam: Fundamental experiments) (library binding) $23.93
Grades: 1 2 3   **530.4**
1. Water 2. Science -- Experiments 3. Change of state (Physics)
ISBN 1617727369; 9781617727368

LC 2012046342

In this book by Ellen Lawrence, readers "will get the opportunity to conduct experiments that show how water can be a liquid, a gas, or a solid. Kids will also investigate questions such as 'What floats in water?' and 'What dissolves in water?' Using everyday items that kids can easily find around the house, students will turn into scientists as they carry out step-by-step experiments to answer interesting questions." (Publisher's note)

Includes bibliographical references (page 24) and index

Mason, Adrienne
Touch it! materials, matter and you. written by Adrienne Mason; illustrated by Claudia Dávila. Kids Can Press 2005 32p il (Primary physical science) $12.95; pa $5.95
Grades: K 1 2   **530.4**
1. Matter 2. Materials
ISBN 1-55337-760-5; 1-55337-761-3 pa

"Large-scale digital illustrations show children, animals, and adults commenting on and exploring the properties of matter. Some sections discuss ideas such as mass, buoyancy, or magnetism, while others suggest informal activities, for example describing different foods. Five double-page spreads present very simple science projects, beginning with a question-and-answer section followed by a short list of materials, a few steps to follow, and a brief concluding paragraph. . . . This colorful beginning science series is suitable for primary-grade students in groups and even younger children one-on-one." Booklist

Includes glossary

Oxlade, Chris
★ **Changing** materials; [by] Chris Oxlade. Crabtree Publishing Company 2008 32p il (Working with materials) lib bdg $26.60; pa $7.95
Grades: 2 3 4   **530.4**
1. Matter 2. Chemical reactions 3. Strength of materials
ISBN 978-0-7787-3638-7 lib bdg; 0-7787-3638-5 lib bdg; 978-0-7787-3648-6 pa; 0-7787-3648-2 pa

LC 2007027419

This describes how materials change by such processes as bending, breaking, melting, boiling, evaporating, dissolving, and burning

This "title has numerous captioned color photographs. . . . The [book offers] three simple, easy, and safe reproducible experiments. . . . Students will appreciate the pleasing design, easy-to-read font, and direct, clear writing style." Libr Media Connect

Includes glossary and bibliographical references

Cooling. Heinemann Library 2009 32p il (Changing materials) lib bdg $25.36; pa $7.99
Grades: K 1 2   **530.4**
1. Cold
ISBN 978-1-4329-3273-2 lib bdg; 1-4329-3273-X lib bdg; 978-1-4329-3278-7 pa; 1-4329-3278-0 pa
Introduces the concept of freezing points.

"A few simple activities provide opportunities to experiment. The color photographs are engaging." SLJ

Includes glossary and bibliographical references

Heating. Heinemann Library 2009 32p il (Changing materials) lib bdg $25.36; pa $7.99
Grades: K 1 2   **530.4**
1. Heat
ISBN 978-1-4329-3272-5 lib bdg; 1-4329-3272-1 lib bdg; 978-1-4329-3277-0 pa; 1-4329-3277-2 pa
Introduces the concept of boiling points.

"A few simple activities provide opportunities to experiment. The color photographs are engaging." SLJ

Includes glossary and bibliographical references

Shores, Lori

How to make bubbles. Capstone Press 2011 24p il (Hands-on science fun) lib bdg $23.99; pa $6.95

Grades: PreK K 1   530.4

1. Bubbles 2. Science -- Experiments

ISBN 978-1-4296-5293-3 lib bdg; 1-4296-5293-4 lib bdg; 978-1-4296-6215-4 pa; 1-4296-6215-8 pa

Simple text and full-color photos instruct readers on how to make bubbles.

"Bright, glossy photos and irresistible ideas make these science lessons effortless fun." Booklist

Spilsbury, Richard

What are solids, liquids, and gases? exploring science with hands-on activities. [by] Richard and Louise Spilsbury. Enslow Elementary 2008 32p il (In touch with basic science) lib bdg $22.60

Grades: 3 4 5   530.4

1. Matter 2. Science -- Experiments

ISBN 978-0-7660-3094-7 lib bdg; 0-7660-3094-6 lib bdg

LC 2007024516

This book "covers the three phases of matter described in its title. . . . Properties of each are explored. . . . The activities are all doable with simple household items, and they definitely reinforce the concepts being explored. This volume would a plus for budding scientists." Sci Books Films

Includes glossary and bibliographical references

Weakland, Mark

Bubbles float, bubbles pop. Capstone Press 2011 32p il (Science starts) lib bdg $25.99; pa $7.95

Grades: 1 2 3   530.4

1. Bubbles

ISBN 978-1-4296-5250-6 lib bdg; 1-4296-5250-0 lib bdg; 978-1-4296-6141-6 pa; 1-4296-6141-0 pa

LC 2010038874

Simple text and photographs explain the basic science behind bubbles.

"The text is simple and easily understood. . . . The large, up-close photographs are informative, . . . funny, . . . and intriguing." Booklist

Includes bibliographical references

Zoehfeld, Kathleen Weidner

What is the world made of? all about solids, liquids, and gases. illustrated by Paul Meisel. HarperCollins Pubs. 1998 32p il (Let's-read-and-find-out science) hardcover o.p. pa $4.95

Grades: K 1 2 3   530.4

1. Matter

ISBN 0-06-027143-4; 0-06-027144-2 lib bdg; 0-06-445163-1 pa

LC 97-30658

In simple text, presents the three states of matter, solid, liquid, and gas, and describes their attributes

"The explanations are clear with a simple, informal text for the new reader, and the lively line-and-water-color pictures bring in humor and common-sense." Booklist

530.8 Measurement

Adamson, Thomas K.

How do you measure length and distance? by Thomas K. and Heather Adamson. Capstone Press 2011 32p il (Measure it!) lib bdg $25.99

Grades: PreK K 1 2   530.8

1. Measurement

ISBN 978-1-4296-4456-3; 1-4296-4456-7

LC 2010002811

Simple text and color photographs describe the units and tools used to measure length and distance.

"The large picture-book format and inviting color photographs make [this] clearly written [title a] welcome [addition]. . . . The [author uses] common objects, giving readers recognizable points of reference. . . . Solid." SLJ

Includes glossary and bibliographical references

How do you measure liquids? by Thomas K. and Heather Adamson. Capstone Press 2011 32p il (Measure it!) lib bdg $25.99

Grades: PreK K 1 2   530.8

1. Liquids 2. Measurement

ISBN 978-1-4296-4457-0; 1-4296-4457-5

LC 2010002812

Simple text and color photographs describe the units and tools used to measure liquids.

"The large picture-book format and inviting color photographs make [this] clearly written [title a] welcome [addition]. . . . The [author uses] common objects, giving readers recognizable points of reference. . . . Solid." SLJ

Includes glossary and bibliographical references

How do you measure weight? by Thomas K. and Heather Adamson. Capstone Press 2011 32p il (Measure it!) lib bdg $25.99

Grades: PreK K 1 2   530.8

1. Weights and measures

ISBN 978-1-4296-4458-7; 1-4296-4458-3

LC 2010002784

Simple text and color photographs describe the units and tools used to measure weight.

"The large picture-book format and inviting color photographs make [this] clearly written [title a] welcome [addition]. . . . The [author uses] common objects, giving readers recognizable points of reference. . . . Solid." SLJ

Includes glossary and bibliographical references

Adler, David A.

★ How tall, how short, how faraway; illustrated by Nancy Tobin. Holiday House 1999 un il $16.95; pa $6.95

Grades: K 1 2 3   530.8

1. Measurement

ISBN 0-8234-1375-6; 0-8234-1632-1 pa

LC 98-18802

Introduces several measuring systems such as the Egyptian system, the inch-pound system, and the metric system

"In this wonderful hands-on concept book, easy technological measuring tools are superbly introduced and explained. . . . The informative text and colorful illustrations clearly explain the difference between customary and metric systems." Sci Child

Ball, Johnny

Why pi; how math applies to everyday life. DK Pub. 2009 93p il map $16.99

Grades: 4 5 6 7 **530.8**

1. Pi 2. Mathematics 3. Measurement

ISBN 978-0-7566-5164-0; 0-7566-5164-6

"Author Johnny Ball focuses on how people have used numbers to measure things through the ages, from the ways the ancient Egyptians measured the pyramids to how modern scientists measure time and space." Publisher's note

Cleary, Brian P., 1969-

How long or how wide? a measuring guide. illustrated by Brian Gable. Millbrook Press 2007 30p il (Math is categorical) lib bdg $15.95

Grades: K 1 2 **530.8**

1. Measurement

ISBN 978-0-8225-6694-6 lib bdg; 0-8225-6694-X lib bdg

LC 2006-10754

A rhyming text filled with humorous examples explains how to use and compare metric and U.S. customary units of length and introduces such tools of measurement as rulers and yardsticks.

"The book is very kid friendly, whimsical, vivid, and lively." Sci Books Films

On the scale; a weighty tale. by Brian P. Cleary; illustrated by Brian Gable. Millbrook Press 2008 31p il (Math is categorical) lib bdg $15.95

Grades: 2 3 4 5 **530.8**

1. Weights and measures

ISBN 978-0-8225-7851-2 lib bdg; 0-8225-7851-4 lib bdg

LC 2007033670

"In bubbly verse, Cleary presents a basic introduction to weights and measures. . . . Cheery, child-friendly examples are used for both English and metric measurements, progressing from smaller to larger weights in this approachable explanation of the topic. . . . Gable's watercolor cartoons depict rainbow-hued cats engaged in all manner of activities. This humorous title should prove useful in both classroom and family discussions." SLJ

Gardner, Robert

Ace your math and measuring science project; great science fair ideas. Enslow Publishers 2009 128p il (Ace your physics science project) lib bdg $31.93

Grades: 5 6 7 8 **530.8**

1. Measurement 2. Science projects 3. Weights and measures 4. Science -- Experiments

ISBN 978-0-7660-3224-8 lib bdg; 0-7660-3224-8 lib bdg

LC 2008-23926

"Dozens of . . . science activities are presented with background information, step-by-step instructions, and suggestions for extending to the science fair level. . . . Color illustrations and important safety information are included." Horn Book Guide

Includes bibliographical references

Super-sized science projects with volume; how much space does it take up? Enslow Pubs. 2003 48p il (Sensational science experiments) lib bdg $18.95

Grades: 3 4 5 6 **530.8**

1. Measurement 2. Science projects 3. Volume (Cubic content) 4. Science -- Experiments

ISBN 0-7660-2014-2

LC 2002-153850

This "explores topics ranging from determining the volume of a quart and a liter to the amount of air in a container of sand. Gardner's clear, informal explanations are echoed in LaBaff's colorful illustrations." Booklist

Includes bibliographical references and index

Murphy, Stuart J.

★ Room for Ripley; illustrated by Sylvie Wickstrom. HarperCollins Pubs. 1999 33p il (MathStart) hardcover o.p. pa $4.95

Grades: 1 2 3 **530.8**

1. Aquariums 2. Measurement

ISBN 0-06-027621-5 lib bdg; 0-06-446724-4 pa

LC 98-26109

Uses a story about a young boy who is getting a fish bowl ready for his new pet to introduce various units of liquid measure

"The writing is breezy and reads like a story about a boy who wants a pet, but the text constantly reinforces the mathematical concepts (how many cups in a pint, a quart, etc.). The illustrations are painted in muted primary colors against a lot of white space. . . . A fun, painless math lesson." SLJ

Parker, Victoria

How big is big? comparing plants. [by] Vic Parker. Heinemann Library 2011 32p il (Measuring and comparing) lib bdg $26; pa $7.99

Grades: 2 3 4 **530.8**

1. Plants 2. Weights and measures

ISBN 978-1-4329-3959-5 lib bdg; 1-4329-3959-9 lib bdg; 978-1-4329-3967-0 pa; 1-4329-3967-X pa

LC 2010000932

This "contains vivid photographs, charts, and diagrams with captions, explanations, and examples. Questions are posed throughout . . . to entice young learners to 'stop and think' or continue reading for more information. . . . [This] would make an excellent addition to any classroom library." Libr Media Connect

Includes glossary and bibliographical references

How full is full? comparing bodies of water. [by] Vic Parker. Heinemann Library 2011 32p il map (Measuring and comparing) lib bdg $26; pa $7.99

Grades: 2 3 4 **530.8**

1. Volume (Cubic content)

ISBN 978-1-4329-3957-1 lib bdg; 1-4329-3957-2 lib bdg; 978-1-4329-3965-6 pa; 1-4329-3965-3 pa

LC 2010000927

This "contains vivid photographs, charts, and diagrams with captions, explanations, and examples. Questions are posed throughout . . . to entice young learners to 'stop and think' or continue reading for more information. . . . [This] would make an excellent addition to any classroom library." Libr Media Connect

Includes glossary and bibliographical references

How heavy is heavy? comparing vehicles. [by] Vic Parker. Heinemann Library 2011 32p il (Measuring and comparing) lib bdg $26; pa $7.99

Grades: 2 3 4 **530.8**
1. Vehicles 2. Weights and measures
ISBN 978-1-4329-3954-0 lib bdg; 1-4329-3954-8 lib bdg; 978-1-4329-3962-5 pa; 1-4329-3962-9 pa
LC 2010000923
This "contains vivid photographs, charts, and diagrams with captions, explanations, and examples. Questions are posed throughout . . . to entice young learners to 'stop and think' or continue reading for more information. . . . [This] would make an excellent addition to any classroom library." Libr Media Connect

Includes glossary and bibliographical references

How long is long? comparing animals. [by] Vic Parker. Heinemann Library 2011 32p il (Measuring and comparing) lib bdg $26; pa $7.99
Grades: 2 3 4 **530.8**
1. Size 2. Measurement
ISBN 978-1-4329-3958-8 lib bdg; 1-4329-3958-0 lib bdg; 978-1-4329-3966-3 pa; 1-4329-3966-1 pa
LC 2010000930
This "contains vivid photographs, charts, and diagrams with captions, explanations, and examples. Questions are posed throughout . . . to entice young learners to 'stop and think' or continue reading for more information. . . . [This] would make an excellent addition to any classroom library." Libr Media Connect

Includes glossary and bibliographical references

Robbins, Ken
★ **For** good measure; the ways we say how much, how far, how heavy, how big, how old. Roaring Brook Press 2010 un il $17.99
Grades: 3 4 5 6 **530.8**
1. Measurement
ISBN 978-1-59643-344-1; 1-59643-344-2
"By tossing in tidbits of history, word origins and meanings, Robbins takes the everyday subject of measurement and makes it accessible, interesting and memorable. Beginning with the units for lengths and distances, readers will not only learn about feet and inches, but also hands . . . and cubits. . . . From distances, the author moves on to area—measured in acres, hectares and sections—and then on to weigh—pound, ounce, ton, stone, dram and carat. . . . Liquid measures, dry capacity and time round out the volume. The photographs are a good complement, clearly illustrating the concepts without distracting from the text." Kirkus

Includes glossary and bibliographical references

Schwartz, David M.
★ **Millions** to measure; pictures by Steven Kellogg. HarperCollins Pubs. 2003 un il $16.99; lib bdg $17.89
Grades: 2 3 4 **530.8**
1. Measurement 2. Metric system 3. Weights and measures
ISBN 0-688-12916-1; 0-06-623784-X lib bdg
LC 2001-39683
Marvelosissimo the Magician explains the development of standard units of measure, and shows the simplicity of calculating length, height, weight, and volume using the metric system
"Schwartz not only manages to impart a good deal of basic information . . . but also entertains the reader. He receives ample support from illustrator Kellogg, who contributes enough merry madness to make learning fun. Bright with shining colors, the large, detailed pictures brim with action and humor as well as history and math." Booklist

Somervill, Barbara A.
Mass and weight. Heinemann Library 2011 32p il (Measure it!) lib bdg $29; pa $7.99
Grades: 3 4 5 **530.8**
1. Measurement 2. Weights and measures
ISBN 978-1-4329-3765-2 lib bdg; 1-4329-3765-0 lib bdg; 978-1-4329-3771-3 pa; 1-4329-3771-5 pa
LC 2009-35208
"Size of text and font is suitable for this age group with uncluttered pages designed so that text is set off with the illustrations, graphs, or drawings placed vertically. Key words appear in bold." Libr Media Connect

Includes glossary and bibliographical references

Vogel, Julia
Measuring volume; by Julia Vogel; illustrated by Luanne Marten. The Child's World 2013 24 p. col. ill. (library) $27.07
Grades: 2 3 4 **530.8**
1. Picture books for children 2. Volume (Cubic content) 3. Volume (Cubic content) -- Measurement
ISBN 1614732833; 9781614732839
LC 2012933675
In this book, part of the Simple Measurement series, Julia Vogel "addresses the topic of measuring volume with a number of . . . examples. Pouring milk? Taking medicine? Filling the backyard pool? Well, then you're participating in figuring out volume." It includes a "What Equals What?" page with equivalency charts. (Booklist)

Includes bibliographical references (p. 24) and index.

531 Classical mechanics

Bradley, Kimberly Brubaker
Energy makes things happen; illustrated by Paul Meisel. HarperCollins Pubs. 2003 33p il (Let's-read-and-find-out science) hardcover o.p. lib bdg $16.89; pa $4.99
Grades: K 1 2 3 **531**
1. Force and energy
ISBN 0-06-028908-2; 0-06-028909-0 lib bdg; 0-06-445213-1 pa
LC 2001-39520
This book shows how energy comes originally from the sun and can be transferred from one thing to another
"This worthy title uses familiar examples and a clear focus to introduce basic scientific concepts. . . . Meisel's color illustrations of cheerful multiethnic children match the level and tone of the text perfectly, make it more comprehensible, and add to the book's appeal." SLJ

Forces make things move; illustrated by Paul Meisel. HarperCollins 2005 33p il (Let's-read-and-find-out science) $15.99; lib bdg $16.89; pa $4.99
Grades: K 1 2 3 **531**
1. Gravity 2. Force and energy
ISBN 0-06-028906-6; 0-06-028907-4 lib bdg; 0-06-445214-X pa
LC 2002-14763

Simple language and humorous illustrations show how forces make things move, prevent them from starting to move, and stop them from moving

"Colorful line-and-watercolor-wash illustrations brighten the pages. . . . A practical starting place for understanding forces." Booklist

Claybourne, Anna

Forms of energy. Raintree 2008 48p il (Sci-hi: physical science) lib bdg $22; pa $8.99

Grades: 5 6 7 8   531
1. Force and energy
ISBN 978-1-4109-3377-5 lib bdg; 1-4109-3377-6 lib bdg; 978-1-4109-3382-9 pa; 1-4109-3382-2 pa
LC 2009-3504

A "compelling read for both browsers and science buffs. . . . Information is clearly presented and flows smoothly. . . . A treasure trove of information." SLJ

Includes glossary and bibliographical references

Gut-wrenching gravity and other fatal forces; Anna Claybourne. Crabtree Publishing Company 2013 32 p. (Disgusting & dreadful science) (pbk.; alk. paper) $9.95

Grades: 4 5 6   531
1. Gravity 2. Physics 3. Force and energy
ISBN 0778709574; 9780778709503; 9780778709572
LC 2012043529

This book by Anna Claybourne is part of the Disgusting & Dreadful Science series and focuses on gravity and other physical forces. It shares facts including that "a mouse can survive a 328-foot fall, black holes have superstrong gravity that causes 'spaghettification,' and" more. Illustrations are included. (Booklist)

Includes bibliographical references and index

Pushes and pulls. QEB Pub. 2008 24p il (Why it works) $24.25

Grades: 2 3 4 5   531
1. Force and energy 2. Power (Mechanics)
ISBN 978-1-59566-558-4; 1-59566-558-7
LC 2008-11713

This is "colorfully illustrated and should help young students relate better to the concepts being presented. A glossary of key words and a page of suggestions for parents and teachers to extend the learning experience round out the text." Sci Books & Films

Includes glossary and bibliographical references

Cobb, Vicki, 1938-

I fall down; illustrated by Julia Gorton. HarperCollins Publishers 2004 un il (Science play) $17.99; lib bdg $18.89

Grades: K 1 2   531
1. Gravity 2. Science -- Experiments 3. Gravity
ISBN 0-688-17842-1; 0-688-17843-X lib bdg
LC 2003-1822

Simple experiments introduce the basic concept of gravity and its relationship to weight

"The digital illustrations offer clearly defined images with a distinctive, retro look. Their eye-catching pizzazz will help hold the attention of the audience. . . . Attuned to the learning style of young children, Cobb's questions and suggestions offer kids the experience of the scientific process." Booklist

Conrad, David

Gravity all around. Capstone Press 2011 24p il (Pebble plus: physical science) lib bdg $23.99

Grades: PreK K 1 2   531
1. Gravity
ISBN 978-1-4296-6606-0; 1-4296-6606-4
LC 2010034310

This describes the science of gravity.

This book "addresses its topic in a direct and simple manner. . . . [The] title includes a hands-on experiment with both textual and visual directions." SLJ

Includes glossary and bibliographical references

Gardner, Robert

Ace your forces and motion science project; great science fair ideas. [by] Robert Gardner and Madeline Goodstein. Enslow Publishers 2009 128p il (Ace your physics science project) lib bdg $31.93

Grades: 5 6 7 8   531
1. Force and energy 2. Science projects 3. Science -- Experiments
ISBN 978-0-7660-3222-4 lib bdg; 0-7660-3222-1 lib bdg
LC 2008-49778

"Presents several science experiments and project ideas about forces and motion." Publisher's note

Includes bibliographical references

Gray, Susan Heinrichs

Experiments with motion; [by] Susan H. Gray. Children's Press 2011 48p il (True books: experiments) lib bdg $28; pa $6.95

Grades: 4 5 6   531
1. Motion 2. Science -- Experiments
ISBN 978-0-531-26346-4 lib bdg; 0-531-26346-0 lib bdg; 978-0-531-26646-5 pa; 0-531-26646-X pa
LC 2011011971

"In just four short chapters with glossy pages and plentiful color photographs, the author breaks down some fairly complicated concepts and takes readers through laws governing motion and scientific investigation. . . . Multiethnic upper elementary children demonstrate experiments using readily available everyday materials, while the text gives clear explanations." Booklist

Includes glossary and bibliographical references

Hillman, Ben

How fast is it? a zippy book all about speed. Scholastic 2008 47p il $14.99

Grades: 3 4 5   531
1. Speed
ISBN 978-0-439-91867-1; 0-439-91867-7
LC 2007039983

"Twenty-two full-color, full-page spreads convey the quickness (or lack) of the most ordinary things in a unique and amazing way. Examples: * How fast is a bullet-bike? * Which one is faster? A coyote or a roadrunner? * Can a sneeze be faster than a tennis serve? * How fast is the population growing? * What is the fastest-growing plant?" Publisher's note

Hopwood, James

Cool gravity activities; fun science projects about balance. [by] James Hopwood. ABDO Pub. 2008 32p il (Cool science) lib bdg $16.95

Grades: 4 5 6   **531**

1. Gravity 2. Science projects 3. Science -- Experiments

ISBN 978-1-59928-908-3 lib bdg; 1-59928-908-3 lib bdg

LC 2007010204

This offers science projects about gravity, including "The Old Cane Trick"

The projects "will attract boys and girls. [The] book begins with [an] upbeat introduction and three chapters about the scientific method, keeping a journal, and safety. . . . Background on the science concepts involved is presented along with a complete list of supplies. . . . The numbered instructions are easy to follow and are accompanied by small, closeup photos." SLJ

Lawrence, Ellen

Motion; by Ellen Lawrence. Bearport Publishing 2013 22 p. (Science Slam: Fundamental experiments) (library binding) $23.93

Grades: K 1 2 3   **531**

1. Motion

ISBN 1617727393; 9781617727399

LC 2012049188

This book by Ellen Lawrence presents information on motion, including friction, force, and gravity, through the use of toy cars and milk cartons. It "contains seven experiments about motion with detailed, age -- appropriate instructions, background information, facts about motion, and a glossary of science words relating to motion. The book is written for students in kindergarten to grade three." (NSTA Recommends)

Includes bibliographical references and index

Macdonald, Wendy

Galileo's leaning tower experiment; a science adventure. illustrated by Paolo Rui. Charlesbridge 2009 32p il $16.95; pa $7.95

Grades: 3 4 5   **531**

1. Gravity 2. Physics 3. Astronomers 4. Writers on science

ISBN 978-1-57091-869-8; 1-57091-869-4; 978-1-57091-870-4 pa; 1-57091-870-8 pa

LC 2008010652

"In this fictionalized account of Galileo's legendary experiments on the speed of falling objects, the young professor meets a poor farm boy, Massimo, who drops bread and cheese to his uncle passing under a bridge in a boat. Stunned that the bread and cheese hit the boat at the same time, contradicting Aristotle's teachings, Galileo begins experimenting with other pairs of falling objects. . . . The story excels at teaching the concept involved and is admirably enhanced by Rui's attractive, colorful, and informative acrylics." SLJ

Mason, Adrienne

Move it! motion, forces and you. written by Adrienne Mason; illustrated by Claudia Dávila. Kids Can Press 2005 32p il (Primary physical science) $12.95; pa $5.95

Grades: K 1 2   **531**

1. Motion 2. Force and energy

ISBN 1-55337-758-3; 1-55337-759-1 pa

This explores the physics of why and how things move with simple activities such as pushing, pulling or lifting objects.

Includes glossary

O'Leary, Denyse

What are Newton's laws of motion? Crabtree Pub. Co. 2011 64p il (Shaping modern science) lib bdg $30.60; pa $10.95

Grades: 5 6 7 8   **531**

1. Motion 2. Physicists 3. Mathematicians 4. Writers on science

ISBN 978-0-7787-7200-2 lib bdg; 0-7787-7200-4 lib bdg; 978-0-7787-7207-1 pa; 0-7787-7207-1 pa

LC 2010-52629

This book examines how Sir Isaac Newton developed three basic laws that govern the way in which objects move. It explains how Newton expanded on the work of other scientists, including Galileo and Copernicus, to make his discovery. The book also explains how Newton's laws have influenced modern science and technology in areas such as sports and transportation.

This title is "not only written and organized well, but [it is] also gorgeous in design. Full-color photographs and illustrations are set over colorful backgrounds that add depth but not distraction. [The title] includes thought-provoking quotes from famous authors and scientists and some eyebrow-raising 'Quick Facts' throughout." SLJ

Includes glossary and bibliographical references

Phelan, Glen

Invisible force; the quest to define the laws of motion. [by] Glen Phelan. National Geographic 2006 59p il (Science quest) $17.95; lib bdg $25.90

Grades: 5 6 7 8   **531**

1. Motion 2. Gravity

ISBN 0-7922-5539-9; 0-7922-5540-2 lib bdg

LC 2005027350

This "traces the historical and scientific path to man's understanding of motion and gravity." Publisher's note

Includes glossary and bibliographical references

Riley, Peter D.

Forces; [by] Peter Riley. Sea-to-Sea Publications 2011 32p il (The real scientist investigates) lib bdg $28.50

Grades: 3 4 5   **531**

1. Force and energy 2. Science -- Methodology 3. Children's literature -- Works -- Grades two through six

ISBN 978-1-59771-280-4 lib bdg; 1-59771-280-9 lib bdg

LC 2010-05371

In this book about forces "solid scientific material is presented in accessible language and a visually engaging, boldly colored layout. Budding scientists are encouraged to hone their skills by recording observations, making predictions, and analyzing results. Hands-on activities are included on almost every spread. . . . The many color photos feature diverse children demonstrating the activities." SLJ

Includes glossary and bibliographical references

Royston, Angela

Looking at forces and motion; how do things move? [by] Angela Royston. Enslow Publishers 2008 32p il (Looking at science: how things change) lib bdg $22.60

Grades: 1 2 3   **531**
1. Motion 2. Force and energy
ISBN 978-0-7660-3089-3 lib bdg; 0-7660-3089-X
lib bdg

LC 2007-24508

"Fills a huge void in elementary science collections. . . .
Text is arranged in succinct 'chunks,' giving important facts
without overwhelming readers. . . . [This] is an essential addition." Libr Media Connect

Includes glossary and bibliographical references

Silverstein, Alvin

Forces and motion; [by Alvin & Virginia Silverstein &
Laura Silverstein Nunn] Twenty-First Century Books 2008
112p il (Science concepts) lib bdg $31.93

Grades: 5 6 7 8   **531**
1. Motion 2. Force and energy
ISBN 978-0-8225-7514-6 lib bdg; 0-8225-7514-0
lib bdg

LC 2007-48826

"The breadth of material the authors cover in this volume is impressive. They discuss energy (kenetic and potential), forces (friction, gravity, electricity, and magnetism),
simple machines (lever, wheel, pulley, ramp, and wedge),
motion in fluids, and Newton's laws of motion. . . . [This
offers] simple writing, many colorful pictures, and lots of
examples." Sci Books Films

Includes glossary and bibliographical references

Somervill, Barbara A.

Speed and acceleration. Heinemann Library 2011 32p
il (Measure it!) lib bdg $29; pa $7.99

Grades: 3 4 5   **531**
1. Speed 2. Measurement
ISBN 978-1-4329-3764-5 lib bdg; 1-4329-3764-2 lib
bdg; 978-1-4329-3770-6 pa; 1-4329-3770-7 pa

LC 2009-35204

"Size of text and font is suitable for this age group with
uncluttered pages designed so that text is set off with the illustrations, graphs, or drawings placed vertically. Key words
appear in bold." Libr Media Connect

Includes glossary and bibliographical references

Spilsbury, Richard

What are forces and motion? exploring science with
hands-on activities. [by] Richard and Louise Spilsbury. Enslow Publishers 2008 32p il (In touch with basic science)
lib bdg $22.60

Grades: 3 4 5   **531**
1. Motion 2. Force and energy 3. Science --
Experiments
ISBN 978-0-7660-3095-4 lib bdg; 0-7660-3095-4
lib bdg

LC 2007024517

This book "introduces children to forces through a simple introduction to Newton's three laws, simple machines,
the relationship of energy and motion through potential and
kinetic energy, buoyant forces, and structural forces. . . . This
volume is an excellent resource for any child who is interested in science." Sci Books Films

Includes glossary and bibliographical references

VanCleave, Janice Pratt, 1942-

Step-by-step science experiments in energy; by Janice
VanCleave. Rosen Pub. 2013 80 p. col. ill. (Janice Van-
Cleeve's first-place science fair projects) (library) $33.25;
(paperback) $14.15

Grades: 5 6 7 8   **531**
1. Energy 2. Science -- Experiments 3. Science
projects 4. Force and energy -- Experiments
ISBN 144886979X; 9781448869794; 9781448884711

LC 2012006835

This book by Janice VanCleave is part of the First-Place
Science Fair Projects series. The books have an introduction to the subject—here, energy, followed by 22 simple .
. . experiments. Van Cleave states the basic goal of the experiments, followed by a list of necessary materials, most of
which can be found around the house or easily acquired with
minimal cost. Step-by-step instructions are clearly detailed
and accompanied by diagrams where needed." (School
Library Journal)

Includes bibliographical references and index.

Waters, Jennifer

All kinds of motion. Capstone Press 2011 24p il (Pebble plus: physical science) lib bdg $23.99

Grades: PreK K 1 2   **531**
1. Motion 2. Kinematics
ISBN 978-1-4296-6607-7; 1-4296-6607-2

LC 2010034309

This decribes the science of motion.

This book "addresses its topic in a direct and simple
manner. . . . [The] title includes a hands-on experiment with
both textual and visual directions." SLJ

Includes glossary and bibliographical references

531.14   Mass and gravity

Chin, Jason

★ **Gravity**; Jason Chin. Roaring Brook Press 2014 32
p. (hardcover) $16.99

Grades: PreK K 1 2   **531.14**
1. Gravity
ISBN 1596437170; 9781596437173

LC 2013001634

This children's book, by Jason Chin, focus on gravity.
The book will answer children's questions such as: "What
keeps objects from floating out of your hand? What if your
feet drifted away from the ground? What stops everything
from floating into space?" It is aimed at children from age 5
to 8. (Publisher's note)

"This book's images of space and objects floating or
falling therein are hypnotically arresting. However, the science here is oversimplified to the point of inaccuracy. Objects do not "have gravity"; they have mass. To say "without
gravity, everything would float away" misses the essential
point--without gravity there would be no anything to float
anywhere. Appended "More About Gravity" provides fuller
explanations. Bib." (Horn Book)

532 Fluid mechanics

Adler, David A., 1947-

Things that float and things that don't; by David A. Adler; illustrated by Anna Raff. Holiday House 2013 32 p. (hardcover) $16.95

Grades: PreK K 1 2 **532**

1. Density 2. Science -- Experiments 3. Hydrostatics 4. Floating bodies 5. Buoyant ascent (Hydrodynamics)

ISBN 0823428621; 9780823428625

LC 2012045827

This book by David A. Adler is an "introduction to density." The "examples provide extension activities that can be done at home or in the classroom. . . . Readers meet a boy, a girl, and their dog as they embark on an adventure to discover what will float and what won't. For example, a spread . . . shows the dog looking over a kitchen sink full of water as a piece of aluminum foil floats as a loose ball and sinks as a tight one." (School Library Journal)

Cobb, Vicki

I get wet; illustrated by Julia Gorton. HarperCollins Pubs. 2002 un il $15.99; lib bdg $17.89

Grades: K 1 2 **532**

1. Water 2. Science -- Experiments

ISBN 0-688-17838-3; 0-688-17839-1 lib bdg

LC 00-49882

"The simple yet well-conceived activities engage children in more than just observations—the questions and explanations are constructed to help young kids draw conclusions from their observations. Remarkably, all this is accomplished in a child-friendly, straightforward text. The illustrations are bright and energetic." Horn Book

Parker, Steve, 1952-

The **science** of water; projects with experiments with water and power. [by] Steve Parker. Heinemann Library 2005 32p il (Tabletop scientist) lib bdg $29.29; pa $7.85

Grades: 4 5 6 7 **532**

1. Water 2. Science -- Experiments

ISBN 1-4034-7282-3 lib bdg; 1-4034-7289-0 pa

LC 2005007027

This "has experiments on the water cycle, water density, water as a solvent, surface tension, capillary action, buoyancy, water power, and water propulsion. . . . The colorful illustrations, organization, and ease of use of [this title makes it an] excellent [addition]." SLJ

Includes glossary

534 Specific forms of energy

Gardner, Robert

Jazzy science projects with sound and music; [by] Robert Gardner. Enslow Publishers 2006 48p il (Fantastic physical science experiments) lib bdg $23.93

Grades: 4 5 6 **534**

1. Sound 2. Science -- Experiments

ISBN 0-7660-2588-8

LC 2005018729

This offers science experiments illustrating such concepts as pitch, vibration, how sound travels and how it is perceived

Includes glossary and bibliographical references

Guillain, Charlotte

Different sounds. Heinemann Library 2009 24p il (Sounds all around us) lib bdg $20.71; pa $5.99

Grades: PreK K 1 **534**

1. Sound 2. Sound waves

ISBN 978-1-4329-3202-2 lib bdg; 1-4329-3202-0 lib bdg; 978-1-4329-3208-4 pa; 1-4329-3208-X pa

LC 2008-51740

This book "introduces the basics of sound through vibrant photographs, large text, and simple sentences. . . . [A] great introduction[s] and worthy addition[s]." SLJ

Includes glossary and bibliographical references

Making sounds. Heinemann Library 2008 24p il (Sounds all around us) lib bdg $20.71; pa $5.99

Grades: PreK K 1 **534**

1. Sound

ISBN 978-1-4329-3200-8 lib bdg; 1-4329-3200-4 lib bdg; 978-1-4329-3206-0 pa; 1-4329-3206-3 pa

LC 2008-51682

This book "introduces the basics of sound through vibrant photographs, large text, and simple sentences. . . . [A] great introduction[s] and worthy addition[s]." SLJ

Includes glossary and bibliographical references

What is sound? Heinemann Library 2009 24p il (Sounds all around us) lib bdg $20.71; pa $5.99

Grades: PreK K 1 **534**

1. Sounds 2. Sound waves

ISBN 978-1-4329-3199-5 lib bdg; 1-4329-3199-7 lib bdg; 978-1-4329-3205-3 pa; 1-4329-3205-5 pa

LC 2008-51681

This describes vibrations, sound waves, and echoes.

This book "introduces the basics of sound through vibrant photographs, large text, and simple sentences. . . . [A] great introduction[s] and worthy addition[s]." SLJ

Inlcudes glossary

Oxlade, Chris

Experiments with sound; explaining sound. Heinemann Library 2009 48p il (Do it yourself) $22; pa $8.99

Grades: 3 4 5 6 **534**

1. Sound 2. Science -- Experiments

ISBN 978-1-4329-2311-2; 978-1-4329-2318-1 pa

LC 2008034938

This explains the science of sound and includes such experiments as making a pan flute from straws and a homemade record player

This "would make an ideal supplement to science classes. A modular layout and dynamic photos keep things moving, while the experiments . . . feature lists of readily available materials, the steps required to pull off the magic, and warnings when adult supervision is required." Booklist

Includes bibliographical references

Riley, Peter D.

Sound; [by] Peter Riley. Sea-to-Sea Publications 2011 32p il (The real scientist investigates) lib bdg $28.50

Grades: 3 4 5 **534**

1. Sound

ISBN 978-1-59771-283-5; 1-59771-283-3

LC 2010005374

In this book about sound "solid scientific material is presented in accessible language and a visually engaging, boldly colored layout. Budding scientists are encouraged to hone their skills by recording observations, making predictions, and analyzing results. Hands-on activities are included on almost every spread. . . . The many color photos feature diverse children demonstrating the activities." SLJ

Includes glossary and bibliographical references

535   Light and related radiation

Branley, Franklyn Mansfield

★ **Day** light, night light; where light comes from. by Franklyn M. Branley; illustrated by Stacey Schuett. newly il ed; HarperCollins Pubs. 1998 32p col il (Let's-read-and-find-out science) hardcover o.p. pa $4.95

Grades: K 1 2 3 **535**

1. Light

ISBN 0-06-027294-5; 0-06-027295-3 lib bdg; 0-06-445171-2 pa

LC 96-33316

First published 1975 with title: Light and darkness

Discusses the properties of light, particularly its source in heat

"This is a beautifully illustrated children's book about a basic concept in science. The pictures add to the clearly written text." Sci Books Films

Bulla, Clyde Robert

What makes a shadow? illustrated by June Otani. rev ed; HarperCollins Pubs. 1994 32p il (Let's-read-and-find-out science) lib bdg $15.89

Grades: K 1 **535**

1. Shades and shadows

ISBN 0-06-022916-0

LC 92-36350

A revised and newly illustrated edition of the title first published 1962 by Crowell

"Using short sentences and developmentally appropriate language, the author explains how shadows are formed, gives numerous examples of shadows, and describes how to make shadow pictures on the wall. Each page is illustrated with bright, colorful drawings, and the gender and cultural representation is excellent." Sci Books Films

Burnie, David

Light; written by David Burnie. DK Pub. 1999 64p il (DK eyewitness books) $15.99

Grades: 5 6 7 8 **535**

1. Light

ISBN 978-0-7894-4885-9; 0-7894-4885-8

A guide to the origins, principles, and historical study of light.

Caes, Charles J.

★ **Discovering** the speed of light; by Charles J. Caes. 1st ed. Rosen Pub. 2012 112 p. ill. (chiefly col.) (Scientist's guide to physics) (library) $34.60

Grades: 5 6 7 8 **535**

1. Light -- Speed   2. Light -- Study and teaching -- History 3. Light -- Speed -- Measurement

ISBN 1448846994; 9781448846993

LC 2010048426

This book by Charles J. Caes is part of the "Scientist's Guide to Physics" series. It "uncovers the earliest study of the speed of light, around 550 BCE in classical Greece. From classical Greece to Galileo and later Albert Einstein, this title also details the history of the discovery of light speed measurement and theories." (VOYA)

Includes bibliographical references (p. 107-108) and index.

Claybourne, Anna

Light and dark. QEB Pub. 2008 24p il (Why it works) $24.25

Grades: 2 3 4 5 **535**

1. Light 2. Shades and shadows

ISBN 978-1-59566-556-0; 1-59566-556-0

LC 2008-11709

This is "colorfully illustrated and should help young students relate better to the concepts being presented. A glossary of key words and a page of suggestions for parents and teachers to extend the learning experience round out the text." Sci Books & Films

Includes glossary and bibliographical references

Cobb, Vicki

I see myself; illustrated by Julia Gorton. HarperCollins Pubs. 2002 un il (Science play) $15.99; lib bdg $17.89

Grades: K 1 2 **535**

1. Light 2. Optics

ISBN 0-688-17836-7; 0-688-17837-5 lib bdg

LC 00-57220

"The simple yet well-conceived activities engage children in more than just observations—the questions and explanations are constructed to help young kids draw conclusions from their observations. Remarkably, all this is accomplished in a child-friendly, straightforward text. The illustrations are bright and energetic." Horn Book

Farndon, John

Light and optics. Benchmark Bks. 2000 32p il (Science experiments) lib bdg $16.95

Grades: 3 4 5 6 **535**

1. Light 2. Optics 3. Science -- Experiments

ISBN 0-7614-1090-2

LC 99-89898

A collection of experiments that explore the nature of light and how it is measured and perceived. Activities include making a shadow theater, a periscope, a microscope, a telescope, and a pinhole camera

Includes glossary

Gardner, Robert

Dazzling science projects with light and color. Enslow Elementary 2006 48p il (Fantasic physical science experiments) lib bdg $23.93

Grades: 4 5 6 **535**

1. Color 2. Light 3. Science -- Experiments

ISBN 0-7660-2587-X

LC 2005-09498

This "title is devoted to light and seeing, mixing colors, and more. Each of 10 chapters includes an experiment, followed by an explanation of why it works, and offers ideas for devising projects to present at a science fair. . . . Large colorful, cartoonlike drawings complement the [text]. . . . [This offers] solid information." SLJ

Includes glossary and bibliographical references

Lauw, Darlene
   Light; [by Darlene Lauw & Lim Cheng Puay; series illustrator, Roy Chan Yoon Loy] Crabtree 2002 31p il (Science alive!) $25.27; pa $7.95
Grades: 3 4 5 6   **535**
   1. Light 2. Optics 3. Science -- Experiments
   ISBN 0-7787-0560-9; 0-7787-0606-0 pa
                    LC 2001-42423

Presents activities that demonstrate how light works in our everyday lives. History boxes feature the scientists who made significant discoveries in the field of light

This book explains its subject matter "in a colorful and easy to understand format. . . . All experiments use easily obtainable parts and in some cases actual household items." Sci Books Films

Includes glossary

Meiani, Antonella
   Light. Lerner Publs. 2003 40p il (Experimenting with science) lib bdg $23.93
Grades: 4 5 6 7   **535**
   1. Light 2. Science -- Experiments
   ISBN 0-8225-0084-1
                    LC 2001-38947

Experiments with light explain shadows and colors, and demonstrate such concepts as reflection and refraction

This offers "straightforward, well-designed experiments. . . . Numerous clear diagrams, some photos, and occasional historical sidebars extend this material, which is notable for its substance." Horn Book Guide

Includes glossary and bibliographical references

Riley, Peter D.
   Light; [by] Peter Riley. Sea-to-Sea Publications 2011 32p il (The real scientist investigates ...) lib bdg $28.50
Grades: 3 4 5   **535**
   1. Light 2. Science -- Experiments
   ISBN 9781597712811; 1597712817
                    LC 2010005372

"The design of, and concepts presented . . . are exciting and appropriate for third-and-fourth grade students. Each page is filled with colorful descriptions that are appropriate for exploring light. The scientific method is outlined for each exploration, and simple techniques are offered for how to conduct exciting experiments. . . . The safety aspects of doing science experiments are covered in clear details. Any science class or children's library would be an appropriate place for this beautifully designed book." Sci Books & Films

Includes bibliographical references

Spilsbury, Louise
   What is light? exploring science with hands-on activities. [by] Richard and Louise Spilsbury. Enslow Publishers 2008 32p il (In touch with basic science) lib bdg $22.60

Grades: 3 4 5   **535**
   1. Light 2. Optics 3. Science -- Experiments
   ISBN 978-0-7660-3097-8 lib bdg; 0-7660-3097-0 lib bdg
                    LC 2007024550

This book "introduces the reader to concepts such as reflection, refraction, taking pictures, using lenses, and light waves—specifically as manifested in rainbows and spectrometers. . . . What makes this volume so useful is that children are learning while they are doing the experiments. The graphics are excellent." Sci Books Films

Includes glossary and bibliographical references

535.6   Color

Barton, Chris
   ★ The **Day**-Glo brothers; the true story of Bob and Joe Switzer's bright ideas and brand-new colors. illustrated by Tony Persiani. Charlesbridge 2009 un il $18.95
Grades: K 1 2 3   **535.6**
   1. Color 2. Paint 3. Inventors 4. Fluorescence 5. Chemical industry executives
   ISBN 1-57091-673-X; 978-1-57091-673-1
                    LC 2008-26959
   ALA ALSC Siebert Medal Honor Book (2010)

This is the story of Joe and Bob Switzer who experimented with ultraviolet lights and flurorescent paints and invented a new king of color called Day-Glo. "Ages seven to ten." (N Y Times Book Rev)

"Still in their teens in 1933, brothers Bob and Joe Switzer began experimenting with fluorescent colors and trying to create paints that would glow in the dark. . . . After years of experimentation, they succeeded in creating paints that glowed in daylight as well as ultraviolet light. . . . In stylized, digital artwork with a retro feel, Persiani illustrates early scenes of the Switzers' life in black, white, and shades of gray, then gradually introduces colors. . . . Organizing his material well and writing with a sure sense of what will interest children, Barton creates a picture book that celebrates ingenuity and invention." Booklist

Brocket, Jane
   Ruby, violet, lime; looking for color. [text and photographs by Jane Brocket] Millbrook Press 2012 30p il (Jane Brocket's clever concepts) lib bdg $25.26
Grades: PreK K   **535.6**
   1. Color
   ISBN 978-0-7613-4612-8; 0-7613-4612-0
                    LC 2010051757

Presents brightly colored photograph illustrations that demonstrate the three primary colors and three secondary colors, as well as brown, pink, black, white, gray, silver, and gold.

"Isolating each featured color in snapshots (often close-ups) of everyday objects, the spreads are completely filled with a grid of three to five photos that prove to readers that colors can be found anywhere and everywhere. . . . Worthy of even the most overflowing of colorful collections, this is sure to be the beginning of many a color adventure, both in school and out." Kirkus

Color; illustrations and photos by Ella Doran, David Goodman & Zoe Miller. Abrams 2006 un il $19.95

Grades: K 1 2 3   **535.6**

1. Color

ISBN 978-1-85437-697-8; 1-85437-697-7

"This riotous and bold concept book presents the basic ideas about color with simple text and clear, inviting images. . . . Arty photo collages [introduce] each of the three primary colors. . . . [The book introduces] the idea of color mixing, followed by spreads for each of the secondary colors. . . . Black and white provide an introduction to the concepts of shading and tinting. The language of color, including word associations (e.g., blue: cool, calm, sad), and different shades printed in their appropriate hues are included as are some craft activities and a few trompe l'oeils." SLJ

Hoban, Tana

★ **Colors** everywhere. Greenwillow Bks. 1995 un il $18.99; lib bdg $17.89

Grades: PreK K   **535.6**

1. Color

ISBN 0-688-12762-2; 0-688-12763-0 lib bdg

LC 93-24847

"Very young children will enjoy naming the pictured objects, while older readers will be drawn into exploring the colors' varying tones. A book children will come back to over and over." Horn Book

★ **Of** colors and things. Greenwillow Bks. 1989 un il hardcover o.p. pa $7.99

Grades: PreK K   **535.6**

1. Color

ISBN 0-688-04585-5 pa

LC 88-11101

Photographs of toys, food, and other common objects are grouped on each page according to color

"Hoban hits on a simple device to heighten a child's awareness, but what lifts this above the average concept book is the quality of its design and illustration." Booklist

Houblon, Marie

A **world** of colors; seeing colors in a new way. National Geographic 2009 43p il $16.95; lib bdg $25.90

Grades: K 1 2 3   **535.6**

1. Color

ISBN 978-1-4263-0556-6; 1-4263-0556-7; 978-1-4263-0559-7 lib bdg; 1-4263-0559-1 lib bdg

Original French edition, 2004

"This sophisticated book shows the uses of color and encourages children to find examples in their own environments. Most hues are allotted two spreads. The first one features a solid, saturated page with the color's name in a contrasting shade, facing a closeup photograph framed in black. The second includes two or three additional photos with engaging commentary or questions. . . . The images are unexpected and captivating." SLJ

Lawrence, Ellen

Color; by Ellen Lawrence; consultants: Suzy Gazlay, MA, Recipient, Presidential Award for Excellence in Science Teaching, Kimberly Brenneman, PhD, National Institute for Early Education Research, Rutgers University, New Brunswick, New Jersey. Bearport Publishing 2013 24 p.

col. ill. (Science Slam: Fundamental experiments) (library) $23.93

Grades: K 1 2 3   **535.6**

1. Color

ISBN 1617727385; 9781617727382

LC 2012050812

In this book by Ellen Lawrence "students will have the opportunity to conduct experiments that help them investigate what color is, as well as why things in our world are different colors. Using everyday items that kids can easily find around their homes, young students will turn into scientists as they carry out step-by-step experiments to answer intriguing questions." (Publisher's note)

Includes bibliographical references (page 24) and index

536 Heat

Auch, Alison

All about temperature. Capstone Press 2011 24p il (Pebble plus: physical science) lib bdg $23.99

Grades: PreK K 1 2   **536**

1. Temperature

ISBN 978-1-4296-6608-4; 1-4296-6608-0

LC 2010034308

This explains the science of temperature.

This book "addresses its topic in a direct and simple manner. . . . [The] title includes a hands-on experiment with both textual and visual directions." SLJ

Includes glossary and bibliographical references

Gardner, Robert

Easy genius science projects with temperature and heat; great experiments and ideas. by Robert Gardner and Eric Kemer. Enslow Publishers 2009 128p il (Easy genius science projects) lib bdg $31.93

Grades: 5 6 7 8   **536**

1. Heat 2. Temperature 3. Science projects 4. Science -- Experiments

ISBN 978-0-7660-2939-2 lib bdg; 0-7660-2939-5 lib bdg

LC 2008-4675

"Presents several science experiments and science project ideas dealing with temperature and heat." Publisher's note

Includes glossary and bibliographical references

Sizzling science projects with heat and energy; [by] Robert Gardner. Enslow Elementary 2006 48p il (Fantastic physical science experiments) $23.93

Grades: 4 5 6   **536**

1. Heat 2. Force and energy 3. Science -- Experiments

ISBN 0-7660-2586-1

LC 2005033755

This offers science experiments concerning heat and temperature, kinetic energy, elastic potential energy, light and electric energy, insulation, and ice.

Includes glossary and bibliographical references

Rand, Casey

Temperature. Heinemann Library 2011 32p il (Measure it!) lib bdg $29; pa $7.99

Grades: 3 4 5 **536**
1. Measurement 2. Temperature
ISBN 978-1-4329-3767-6 lib bdg; 1-4329-3767-7 lib
bdg; 978-1-4329-3773-7 pa; 1-4329-3773-1 pa
LC 2009-35275
"Size of text and font is suitable for this age group with
uncluttered pages designed so that text is set off with the illustrations, graphs, or drawings placed vertically. Key words
appear in bold." Libr Media Connect
Includes glossary and bibliographical references

Sullivan, Navin
Temperature; [by] Navin Sullivan. Marshall Caven-
dish Benchmark 2007 48p il (Measure up!) lib bdg $20.90
Grades: 4 5 6 7 **536**
1. Heat 2. Temperature 3. Thermometers
ISBN 978-0-7614-2322-5 lib bdg; 0-7614-2322-2
lib bdg
LC 2006011981
This is "engaging and informative. . . . The excellent
blend of photographs, charts, and diagrams complements
the [text]." SLJ
Includes glossary and bibliographical references

537 Electricity and electronics

Berger, Melvin
Switch on, switch off; illustrated by Carolyn Croll.
Crowell 1989 32p il (Let's-read-and-find-out science
book) hardcover o.p. pa $4.95
Grades: K 1 2 3 **537**
1. Electricity
ISBN 0-690-04786-X lib bdg; 0-06-445097-X pa
LC 88-17638
"This book presents rudimentary exploration of electricity and how electrical current flows to the light switch in
a child's room. Follow the current from the generator to a
power plant to the switch on the wall. Includes instructions
for a simple generator. A good, first look at a topic that mys-
tifies young scientists." Sci Child

Claybourne, Anna
Electricity. QEB Pub. 2008 24p il (Why it works)
$24.25
Grades: 2 3 4 5 **537**
1. Electricity
ISBN 978-1-59566-559-1; 1-59566-559-5
LC 2008-11708
This is "colorfully illustrated and should help young
students relate better to the concepts being presented. A
glossary of key words and a page of suggestions for parents
and teachers to extend the learning experience round out the
text." Sci Books & Films
Includes glossary and bibliographical references

Farndon, John
Electricity. Benchmark Bks. 2001 32p il (Science
experiments) lib bdg $16.95
Grades: 3 4 5 6 **537**
1. Electricity 2. Science -- Experiments
ISBN 0-7614-1086-4
LC 00-39752

A collection of activities that explore electricity "discussing charges, circuits, conductors, and insulators. Activities include creating a Xerox effect and making an electro-
scope." SLJ
Includes glossary

Gardner, Robert
Easy genius science projects with electricity and mag-
netism; great experiments and ideas. Enslow Publishers
2009 128p il (Easy genius science projects) lib bdg $31.93
Grades: 5 6 7 8 **537**
1. Magnetism 2. Electricity 3. Science projects 4.
Science -- Experiments
ISBN 978-0-7660-2923-1 lib bdg; 0-7660-2923-9
lib bdg
LC 2007-38470
"Science projects and experiments about electricity and
magnetism." Publisher's note
Includes glossary and bibliographical references

Energizing science projects with electricity and magnetism; [by] Robert Gardner. Enslow Elementary 2006 48p
il (Fantastic physical science experiments) lib bdg $23.93
Grades: 4 5 6 **537**
1. Magnetism 2. Electricity 3. Science -- Experiments
ISBN 0-7660-2584-5
LC 2005018730
This offers science experiments concerning electric
charges, magnetism and compasses, batteries, electric bulbs,
and wires, and electromagnets
Includes glossary and bibliographical references

Riley, Peter D.
Electricity; [by] Peter Riley. Sea-to-Sea Publications
2011 32p il (The real scientist investigates) lib bdg $28.50
Grades: 3 4 5 **537**
1. Electricity
ISBN 978-1-59771-279-8; 1-59771-279-5
LC 2010005370
In this book about electricity "solid scientific material
is presented in accessible language and a visually engaging,
boldly colored layout. Budding scientists are encouraged to
hone their skills by recording observations, making predictions, and analyzing results. Hands-on activities are included
on almost every spread. . . . The many color photos feature
diverse children demonstrating the activities." SLJ
Includes glossary and bibliographical references

Van Vleet, Carmella
Explore Electricity! With 25 Great Projects. Nomad
Press 2013 96 p. $13.95
Grades: 2 3 4 **537**
1. Magnetism 2. Electricity
ISBN 1619301806; 9781619301801
This activity book, by Carmella Van Vleet, "explains the
workings of batteries, simple circuits, conductors and insulators, motors and generators, electricity and magnetism,
and the steps being taken toward more Earth-friendly electricity. The 25 simple projects . . . will reinforce the lessons
through fun and experience, and young readers will advance
their understanding of electricity further with the fun bits
of trivia, sidebars, and jokes found throughout the book."
(Publisher's note)

VanCleave, Janice Pratt

Janice VanCleave's electricity; mind-boggling experiments you can turn into science fair projects. [by] Janice VanCleave. Wiley 1994 89p il $10.95

Grades: 4 5 6 7 **537**

1. Electricity 2. Science projects 3. Science -- Experiments

ISBN 0-471-31010-7

LC 93-40913

"The experiments move from the simple, which do not require the use of batteries, to those that require small batteries, sizes AA, AAA, C, or D. An appendix shows how to make strips of aluminum foil that can be used to form the electrical circuits that are part of some of the experiments. By encouraging students to move beyond the basic problems (with adult supervision), the author encourages them to be creative in designing science fair projects." Booklist

Includes glossary

Woodford, Chris

Experiments with electricity and magnetism. Gareth Stevens Pub. 2010 32p il (Cool science) lib bdg $28; pa $10.50

Grades: 4 5 6 7 **537**

1. Magnetism 2. Electricity 3. Science -- Experiments

ISBN 9781433934445 lib bdg; 1433934442 lib bdg; 9781433934452 pa; 1433934450 pa

LC 2009037141

"The book [is] written in an easy-to-understand, straightforward style with helpful real-life photographs... Students who need simple experiments or those who need more advanced projects will find [it] helpful." Library Media Connection

Includes bibliographical references

538 Magnetism

Branley, Franklyn Mansfield

What makes a magnet? by Franklyn M. Branley; illustrated by True Kelley. HarperCollins Pubs. 1996 31p il (Let's-read-and-find-out science) hardcover o.p. pa $4.95

Grades: K 1 2 3 **538**

1. Magnets

ISBN 0-06-026441-1; 0-06-445148-8 pa

LC 95-32181

Describes how magnets work and includes instructions for making a magnet and a compass

"Kelley's happy line drawings incorporate a humorous mouse to add safety warnings and goofy side comments. The clear diagrams and lucid explanations are both informative and engaging." Horn Book

539.7 Atomic and nuclear physics

Campbell, Margaret Christine

★ Discovering atoms; Margaret Christine Campbell, Natalie Goldstein. 1st ed. Rosen Pub. 2012 112 p. ill. (The scientist's guide to physics) (library) $34.60

Grades: 5 6 7 8 9 **539.7**

1. Atoms 2. Atomic theory -- History 3. Atomic

structure 4. Matter -- Constitution

ISBN 1448847001; 9781448847006

LC 2010048416

This book by Margaret Christine Campbell is part of the "Scientist's Guide to Physics" series. It "presents the . . . story of the atom's discovery, which is full of bizarre theories, false starts, dead ends, and . . . intellectual insight." (Publisher's note) "Campbell includes a . . . chronological foundation upon which the discovery of elements and the creation of the periodic table build up to the discovery of the atom, atomic rays, particles, models . . . and subatomic particles." (VOYA)

Includes bibliographical references and index.

Cregan, Elizabeth R.

The atom. Compass Point Books 2009 40p il (Mission: science) lib bdg $26.60

Grades: 4 5 6 **539.7**

1. Atoms 2. Atomic theory 3. Nuclear energy

ISBN 978-0-7565-3953-5 lib bdg; 0-7565-3953-6 lib bdg

LC 2008007724

"Cregan discusses the structure of the atom, key scientists, cathode rays and electrons, radioactivity, and atom smashers. . . . The [book has an] open [layout] and large, easy-to-read type. . . . Large eye-catching and colorful photographs and illustrations appear on every page. The [book] includes a simple activity." SLJ

Includes glossary and bibliographical references

Jerome, Kate Boehm

Atomic universe; the quest to discover radioactivity. by Kate Boehm Jerome. National Geographic 2006 59p il (Science quest) $17.95; lib bdg $25.90

Grades: 5 6 7 8 **539.7**

1. Radioactivity 2. Nuclear physics

ISBN 0-7922-5543-7; 0-7922-5544-5 lib bdg

LC 2006001316

The text offers "key concepts in a pleasing and readable format that would appeal to reluctant readers." SLJ

Includes glossary and bibliographical references

Lepora, Nathan

Atoms and molecules. Marshall Cavendish Benchmark 2010 48p il (Invisible worlds) lib bdg $28.50

Grades: 4 5 6 7 **539.7**

1. Atoms 2. Molecules 3. Nanotechnology

ISBN 978-0-7614-4192-2 lib bdg; 0-7614-4192-1 lib bdg

LC 2008037237

This describes the details and characteristics of atoms and molecules that are too small for the unaided eye to see.

The narrative is "clear, well written, broken down into manageable pieces, and peppered with eye-opening facts. The numerous photographs are so phenomenal that they will inspire kids to read the text . . . so that they can wrap their minds around what they see." SLJ

Includes glossary and bibliographical references

McLean, Adam

What is atomic theory? Crabtree Pub. Co. 2011 64p il (Shaping modern science) lib bdg $30.60; pa $10.95

Grades: 5 6 7 8 **539.7**

1. Atoms 2. Chemists 3. Physicists 4. Atomic theory

5. Nuclear energy 6. Writers on science
ISBN 978-0-7787-7197-5 lib bdg; 0-7787-7197-0 lib bdg; 978-0-7787-7204-0 pa; 0-7787-7204-7 pa

This title is "not only written and organized well, but [it is] also gorgeous in design. Full-color photographs and illustrations are set over colorful backgrounds that add depth but not distraction. [The title] includes thought-provoking quotes from famous authors and scientists and some eyebrow-raising 'Quick Facts' throughout." SLJ

Includes glossary and bibliographical references

540 Chemistry and allied sciences

Van Gorp, Lynn
Elements. Compass Point Books 2009 40p il (Mission: science) lib bdg $26.60
Grades: 4 5 6 **540**
1. Chemical elements
ISBN 978-0-7565-3951-1 lib bdg; 0-7565-3951-X lib bdg
LC 2008007284

"Van Gorp provides an overview of matter and the elements and how the latter combine to form compounds; ionic and covalent bonds; the periodic table of the elements; reactions; and mixtures and solutions. The [book has an] open [layout] and large, easy-to-read type. . . . Large eye-catching and colorful photographs and illustrations appear on every page. . . . The [book] includes a simple activity." SLJ

Includes glossary and bibliographical references

540.7 Education, research, related topics

Gardner, Robert
Ace your chemistry science project; great science fair ideas. [by] Robert Gardner, Salvatore Tocci, and Kenneth G. Rainis. Enslow Publishers 2009 112p il (Ace your science project) lib bdg $31.93
Grades: 5 6 7 8 **540.7**
1. Chemistry 2. Science projects 3. Science -- Experiments
ISBN 978-0-7660-3227-9 lib bdg; 0-7660-3227-2 lib bdg
LC 2008-30800

"Presents several science projects and science project ideas about chemistry." Publisher's note
Includes bibliographical references

Ace your science project using chemistry magic and toys; great science fair ideas. Enslow Publishers 2009 128p il (Ace your science project) lib bdg $31.93
Grades: 5 6 7 8 **540.7**
1. Toys 2. Chemistry 3. Science projects 4. Science -- Experiments
ISBN 978-0-7660-3226-2 lib bdg; 0-7660-3226-4 lib bdg
LC 2008-4685

"Dozens of . . . science activities are presented with background information, step-by-step instructions, and suggestions for extending to the science fair level. . . . Color

illustrations and important safety information are included." Horn Book Guide
Includes bibliographical references

Easy genius science projects with chemistry; great experiments and ideas. Enslow Publishers 2009 112p il (Easy genius science projects) lib bdg $31.93
Grades: 5 6 7 8 **540.7**
1. Chemistry 2. Science projects 3. Science -- Experiments
ISBN 978-0-7660-2925-5 lib bdg; 0-7660-2925-5 lib bdg
LC 2007-38469

This book offers science projects and experiments about chemistry divided into the following chapters: atoms, molecules, elements, and compounds; chemical reactions; oxygen and oxidation; separating and testing substances

"Illustrations are bright and useful in explaining the techniques presented. . . . An excellent resource." Sci Books Films
Includes glossary and bibliographical references

541 Chemistry

Ballard, Carol
Mixtures and solutions. Raintree 2010 48p il (Sci-hi: physical science) lib bdg $22; pa $8.99
Grades: 5 6 7 8 **541**
1. Chemistry 2. Molecules
ISBN 978-1-4109-3376-8 lib bdg; 1-4109-3376-8 lib bdg; 978-1-4109-3381-2 pa; 1-4109-3381-4 pa
LC 2009-13452

A "compelling read for both browsers and science buffs. . . . Information is clearly presented and flows smoothly. . . . A treasure trove of information." SLJ
Includes glossary and bibliographical references

Baxter, Roberta
Chemical reaction. Kidhaven Press 2005 48p il (Kidhaven science library) $27
Grades: 4 5 6 7 **541**
1. Chemistry
ISBN 0-7377-2072-7

"Baxter defines her subject and describes many different types of reactions, including acid-base reactions, oxidation, and photosynthesis. The explanations are clear and succinct. The final chapter presents some potential uses for chemical reactions, citing the development of molecular computers." SLJ
Includes glossary and bibliographical references

Coelho, Alexa
Why Is Milk White? & 200 Other Curious Chemistry Questions. Alexa Coelho and Simon Quellen Field. Independent Pub Group 2013 288 p. ill. (paperback) $14.95
Grades: 4 5 6 7 8 **541**
1. Chemistry -- Miscellanea
ISBN 1613744528; 9781613744529
LC 2012040205

This juvenile chemistry book, by Alexa Coelho and Simon Quellen Field, is a "question-and-answer primer [that] provides straightforward, easy-to-understand explanations for inquisitive young scientists' questions. . . . From lifting latent fingerprints from a 'crime scene' using super glue (for smooth surfaces) or iodine (for paper) to hollowing out the zinc interior of a penny using muriatic acid . . . , this handy guide is [a] . . . resource for the budding chemist." (Publisher's note)

Green, Dan

Chemistry; getting a big reaction. created by Basher; written by Dan Green. Kingfisher 2010 128p il $14.99; pa $8.99

Grades: 4 5 6 7   541

1. Chemistry

ISBN 978-0-7534-6615-5; 0-7534-6615-5; 978-0-7534-6413-7 pa; 0-7534-6413-6 pa

This "begins with a short overview of [chemistry] and information on Antoine Lavoisier's 18th-century scientific findings. Concepts are grouped by associations: 'Basic States' (solid, liquid, etc.), 'Nuts and Bolts' (atom, ion, etc.), 'Nasty Boys' (acid, base, etc.), and more. The individual concepts are each introduced over a spread that features a computer-generated cartoon of a character representing the idea and a brief introduction to its characteristics and personality. . . . The information is presented in a chatty, first-person voice." SLJ

Kyi, Tanya Lloyd

50 burning questions; a sizzling history of fire. illustrated by Ross Kinnaird. Annick Press 2010 104p il (50 questions series) $21.95; pa $12.95

Grades: 3 4 5 6   541

1. Fire

ISBN 978-1-55451-221-8; 1-55451-221-2; 978-1-55451-220-1 pa; 1-55451-220-4 pa

The author answers "questions in engagingly written vignettes that reveal how important fire has been and continues to be in nearly every aspect of human life. . . . Interspersed throughout the text are simple fire-related activities readers can perform utilizing a few common household items. . . . Kinnaird's colorful cartoon illustrations complement the text's humorous tone. . . . Accessibly written and appealingly designed." Kirkus

Includes bibliographical references

Newmark, Ann

Chemistry; written by Ann Newmark. rev ed; DK Pub. 2005 72p il (DK eyewitness books) $15.99

Grades: 4 5 6 7   541

1. Chemistry

ISBN 0-7566-1385-X

First published 1993

Explores the world of chemical reactions and shows the role that chemistry plays in our world.

Oxlade, Chris

Mixing and separating. Heinemann Library 2009 32p il (Changing materials) lib bdg $25.36; pa $7.99

Grades: K 1 2   541

1. Materials

ISBN 978-1-4329-3274-9 lib bdg; 1-4329-3274-8 lib bdg; 978-1-4329-3279-4 pa; 1-4329-3279-9 pa

LC 2008-55124

"Discusses the ideas of mixtures, materials that combine to form a new marterial, and materials that cannot be combined. A few simple activities provide opportunities to experiment. The color photographs are engaging." SLJ

Includes glossary and bibliographical references

546   Inorganic chemistry

Angliss, Sarah

Gold; [by] Sarah Angliss. Benchmark Bks. 2000 32p il (The elements) lib bdg $28.50

Grades: 5 6 7 8   546

1. Gold

ISBN 978-0-7614-0887-1; 0-7614-0887-8

LC 98-46800

Explores the history of the precious metal gold and explains its chemistry, how it reacts, its uses, and its importance in our lives.

Includes glossary

Beatty, Richard

Phosphorus; by Richard Beatty. Benchmark Books 2001 32p il (The elements) lib bdg $28.50

Grades: 5 6 7 8   546

1. Phosphorus

ISBN 978-0-7614-0946-5; 0-7614-0946-7

LC 99-88821

Explores the history of the nonmetallic element phosphorus and explains its chemistry, its reactions with other substances, its uses, and its importance in our lives

Offers "clear, basic information, without oversimplification, in an appealing format." SLJ

Includes glossary

Sulfur; [by] Richard Beatty. Benchmark Books 2000 32p il (The elements) lib bdg $28.50

Grades: 5 6 7 8   546

1. Sulphur

ISBN 978-0-7614-0948-9; 0-7614-0948-3

LC 99-86992

Explores the history of the element sulfur and explains its chemistry, its reactions with other substances, its uses, and its importance in our lives

Offers "clear, basic information, without oversimplification, in an appealing format." SLJ

Includes glossary

Dingle, Adrian

The periodic table; elements with style! [created by Simon Basher; written by Adrian Dingle] Kingfisher 2007 128p il pa $8.95

Grades: 4 5 6 7   546

1. Chemical elements

ISBN 978-0-7534-6085-6 pa; 0-7534-6085-8 pa

LC 2006022515

"After a brief introduction to Mendeleev's famous table and a spread on the chart-topping loner, hydrogen, Dingle presents the elements by group. . . . Data on featured elements includes symbol, atomic number and weight, color, standard state, classification, density, boiling and melting points, . . . a diagram of the position in the periodic table, a full-page original anime-styled icon, . . . and descriptive paragraphs that rise from informative all the way to entertaining." Bull Cent Child Books

Gray, Leon

Iodine; [by] Leon Gray. Benchmark Books 2005 32p
il (The elements) lib bdg $28.50

Grades: 5 6 7 8 **546**

1. Iodine

ISBN 978-0-7614-1812-2; 0-7614-1812-1

LC 2004-47644

"After discussing the structure of the iodine atom and its
place on the periodic table, Gray considers its special characteristics, the history of its discovery, and its production
and uses, particularly in the medical field. . . . The color illustrations include well-designed, clearly labeled diagrams
and many excellent photographs. A solid choice for science
collections." Booklist

Includes glossary

Zinc; [by] Leon Gray. Marshall Cavendish Benchmark
2006 32p il (The elements) lib bdg $28.50

Grades: 5 6 7 8 **546**

1. Zinc

ISBN 978-0-7614-1922-8; 0-7614-1922-5

LC 2005-42163

Discusses zinc and where it can be found, how it was
discovered, its special characteristics, and their importance.

"Numerous captioned photos and sidebars augment the
accurate and well-organized text." Horn Book Guide

Includes glossary

Higgins, Nadia

Splash! Learn about water; illustrated by Jane Yamada.
Child's World 2010 24p il (Science definitions) lib bdg
$22.79

Grades: PreK K 1 2 **546**

1. Water

ISBN 978-1-60253-514-5 lib bdg; 1-60253-514-0
lib bdg

LC 2010010982

This book about water is "attractive and succinct. . . .
Large, eye-catching photos cover the recto of each spread. .
. . Varying, jewel-toned accents are used in headings, high-
lighted glossary terms, and in a sidebar on each spread." SLJ

Includes glossary

Just add water; science projects you can sink, squirt, splash
& sail. Children's Press 2008 32p il (Experiment with
science) lib bdg $25; pa $7.95

Grades: 5 6 7 8 **546**

1. Water 2. Science -- Experiments

ISBN 978-0-531-18545-2 lib bdg; 0-531-18545-1 lib
bdg; 978-0-531-18762-3 pa; 0-531-18762-4 pa

LC 2007-21682

"The book consists of nine hands-on activities that target physical science concepts inherent in water (e.g. density,
buoyancy, and hardness.) . . . Students . . . will likely find
the age-appropriate activities engaging and purposeful. . . .
The colorful photos augment the narrative and the science is
sound." Sci Books Films

Includes glossary and bibliographical references

Lepora, Nathan

Molybdenum; [by] Nathan Lepora. Marshall Cavendish Benchmark 2007 32p il (The elements) lib bdg
$28.50

Grades: 5 6 7 8 **546**

1. Molybdenum

ISBN 978-0-7614-2201-3; 0-7614-2201-3

LC 2005-57096

Introduces the element of molybdenum, discussing its
physical and chemical properties, where it is found, and
what processes or objects it is used in.

"Provides a comprehensive, yet easy-to-read overview
in large, bold print. Explanations are concise and clear without being oversimplified, and the arrangement is attractive."
SLJ

Includes glossary

O'Daly, Anne

Sodium; [by] Anne O'Daly. Benchmark Books 2001
32p il (The elements) lib bdg $28.50

Grades: 5 6 7 8 **546**

1. Sodium

ISBN 978-0-7614-1271-7; 0-7614-1271-9

LC 2001-25253

Discusses the characteristics, sources, and uses
of sodium.

Includes glossary

Oxlade, Chris

★ Mixing and separating; [by] Chris Oxlade. Crabtree Pub. 2008 32p il (Working with materials) lib bdg
$26.60; pa $7.95

Grades: 2 3 4 **546**

1. Matter 2. Materials

ISBN 978-0-7787-3640-0 lib bdg; 0-7787-3640-7 lib
bdg; 978-0-7787-3650-9 pa; 0-7787-3650-4 pa

LC 2007027421

This defines and gives examples of mixtures and describes how materials are mixed or separated by such processes as sieving, dissolving, straining, using magnets, settling and skimming, filtering, and evaporating.

This "title has numerous captioned color photographs.
. . . The [book offers] three simple, easy, safe reproducible experiments. . . . Students will appreciate the pleasing
design, easy-to-read font, and direct, clear writing." Libr
Media Connect

Includes glossary and bibliographical references

Sparrow, Giles

Iron; [by] Giles Sparrow. Benchmark Bks. 1999 32p
il (The elements) lib bdg $28.50

Grades: 5 6 7 8 **546**

1. Iron

ISBN 978-0-7614-0880-2; 0-7614-0880-0

LC 97-48524

Discusses the origin, discovery, special characteristics,
and uses of iron.

Includes glossary

Uttley, Colin

Magnesium; [by] Colin Uttley. Benchmark Bks. 2000
32p il (The elements) lib bdg $28.50

Grades: 5 6 7 8 **546**

1. Magnesium

ISBN 978-0-7614-0889-5; 0-7614-0889-4

LC 98-53200

Explores the history of the bright-colored metal magnesium and explains its chemistry, how it reacts, its uses, and its importance in our lives.

Includes glossary

Watt, Susan

Mercury; [by] Susan Watt. Benchmark Books 2005 32p il (The elements) lib bdg $28.50

Grades: 5 6 7 8 9 10 11 12   **546**

1. Mercury

ISBN 978-0-7614-1814-6; 0-7614-1814-8

LC 2004-47633

This book is part "of the 28-title The Elements series. Mercury tells the history of mercury, where it is found in nature, its place in mythology, how it is mined and refined, how it forms compounds, its uses, and its position in the periodic table." Sci Books Films

Includes glossary

West, Krista

Bromine; [by] Krista West. Marshall Cavendish Benchmark 2008 32p il (The elements) lib bdg $28.50

Grades: 5 6 7 8   **546**

1. Bromine

ISBN 978-0-7614-2685-1; 0-7614-2685-X

LC 2006-51812

Introduces the element of bromine and its compoinds, discussing its physical and chemical properties, where it is found, and how it is used.

"Provides a comprehensive, yet easy-to-read overview. . . . The explanations are succinct and clear, without being oversimplified, and the layout is attractive. Diagrams and photographs complement the text on every page." SLJ

Includes glossary

Yasdua, Anita

Explore water! 25 Great Projects, Activities, Experiments. Nomad Press 2011 92 p.

Grades: 2 3 4   **546**

1. Water 2. Aqueducts 3. Water pollution 4. Water conservation 5. Water resources development

ISBN 1936313421; 9781936313426

This book for children looks at the "world of water," offering a "guide that features hands-on activities, . . . illustrations, and . . . projects about this . . . natural resource. A deluge of . . . facts and . . . information about the history and science of water teach children about topics such as the water cycle, pollution and conservation, water folklore and festivals, and the latest in water technology. With projects ranging from a rain harvester made out of plastic containers to an edible aqueduct, this . . . guide brings the world of water straight into kids' hands." (Amazon.com)

549 Mineralogy

Spilsbury, Richard

Crystals; [by] Richard and Louise Spilsbury. Heinemann Library 2011 32p il (Let's rock) $29; pa $7.99

Grades: 4 5 6   **549**

1. Crystals

ISBN 978-1-4329-4684-5; 1-4329-4684-6; 978-1-4329-4692-0 pa; 1-4329-4692-7 pa

LC 2010022241

"Enhanced by plenty of photos, digital paintings, and diagrams, [this examination] of [crystals treats its topic] in unusual detail. [It] describes distinguishing characteristics, creation, history, . . . and human uses in [a] central [narrative] with additional notes, suggestions for activities during walks outside, and occasional thumbnail biographies of scientists in side boxes. [The] volume ends with a simple activity." SLJ

Includes bibliographical references

Minerals; [by] Richard and Louise Spilsbury. Heinemann Library 2011 32p il (Let's rock) $29; pa $7.99

Grades: 4 5 6   **549**

1. Minerals

ISBN 978-1-4329-4683-8; 1-4329-4683-8; 978-1-4329-4691-3 pa; 1-4329-4691-9 pa

LC 2010022235

"Enhanced by plenty of photos, digital paintings, and diagrams, [this examination] of [minerals treats its topic] in unusual detail. [It] describes distinguishing characteristics, creation, history, . . . and human uses in [a] central [narrative] with additional notes, suggestions for activities during walks outside, and occasional thumbnail biographies of scientists in side boxes. [The] volume ends with a simple activity." SLJ

Includes bibliographical references

550 Earth sciences

Bow, James

Earth's secrets. Marshall Cavendish Benchmark 2010 48p il (Invisible worlds) lib bdg $28.50

Grades: 4 5 6 7   **550**

1. Earth sciences

ISBN 978-0-7614-4196-0 lib bdg; 0-7614-4196-4 lib bdg

The narrative is "clear, well written, broken down into manageable pieces, and peppered with eye-opening facts. The numerous photographs are so phenomenal that they will inspire kids to read the text . . . so that they can wrap their minds around what they see." SLJ

Includes glossary and bibliographical references

Dorion, Christiane

How the world works; a hands-on guide to our amazing planet. written by Christiane Dorion; illustrated by Beverley Young. Templar Books 2010 un il $17.99

Grades: 3 4 5   **550**

1. Earth sciences 2. Pop-up books

ISBN 978-0-7636-4801-5; 0-7636-4801-9

"This pop-up survey devotes pages or spreads to Earth's history and structure, the origins of life, plate tectonics, the water cycle, weather, ocean currents, the carbon cycle, greenhouse effect, plants, and food chains. In snippets of text tucked into every available nook, Dorion provides commentary ranging from basic information on seasons and other cycles to abbreviated catalogs of cloud types and kinds of boundaries between tectonic plates." SLJ

Gaff, Jackie

Looking at earth; how does it change? [by] Jackie Gaff. Enslow Publishers 2008 32p il (Looking at science: how things change) lib bdg $22.60

Grades: 1 2 3 **550**

1. Earth

ISBN 978-0-7660-3088-6 lib bdg; 0-7660-3088-1 lib bdg

LC 2007-24507

"Fills a huge void in elementary science collections. . . . Text is arranged in succinct 'chunks,' giving important facts without overwhelming readers. . . . [This] is an essential addition." Libr Media Connect

Includes glossary and bibliographical references

Gibbons, Gail

Planet earth/inside out. Morrow Junior Bks. 1995 un il maps hardcover o.p. pa $4.95

Grades: K 1 2 3 **550**

1. Geology 2. Earth

ISBN 0-688-09681-6 lib bdg; 0-688-15849-8 pa

LC 94-41926

Gibbons' "explanations of the earth's interior are enlivened by comparisons . . . and her plentiful pictures, with their sharp outlines and broad blocks of color, will help clarify the concepts for the youngest learners." Booklist

Gilpin, Daniel

Planet Earth; what planet are you on? created by Basher; written by Dan Gilpin. Kingfisher 2010 128p il $14.99; pa $8.99

Grades: 5 6 7 8 **550**

1. Earth sciences

ISBN 978-0-7534-6616-2; 0-7534-6616-3; 978-0-7534-6412-0 pa; 0-7534-6412-8 pa

LC 2010015976

Presents concepts in earth sciences using lively descriptions and cartoon illustrations personifying each concept.

"The authors blend a surprising wealth of facts into the chatty, humorous text, which is filled with analogies kids can relate to. . . . The highly approachable language, animated cast of characters, awe-inspiring facts, and conservation messages make this an appealing starting point for students seeking basic earth-science information." Booklist

Simon, Seymour

Seymour Simon's extreme earth records; by Seymour Simon. San Francisco 2012 57 p. (hbk.: alk. paper) $17.99

Grades: 2 3 4 **550**

1. Earth 2. Earth sciences 3. Natural disasters

ISBN 1452107858; 9781452107851

LC 2011045937

This book, by Seymour Simon, "explor[es] the most extreme parts of our amazing planet--trekking though the driest desert, climbing the snowiest mountaintops, and diving to the deepest regions of the ocean floor. Seymour Simon . . . investigates Earth's biggest, smallest, deepest, and coldest environments, animals, plants, and most severe weather." (Publisher's note)

Includes bibliographical references (p. 57) and index

Solway, Andrew

Understanding cycles and systems. Raintree 2008 48p il map (Sci-hi: Earth and space science) lib bdg $31.43; pa $8.99

Grades: 4 5 6 7 **550**

1. Earth sciences 2. Earth

ISBN 978-1-4109-3348-5 lib bdg; 1-4109-3348-2 lib bdg; 978-1-4109-3358-4 pa; 1-4109-3358-X pa

LC 2009-3531

"Multiple colorful sidebars and large and small diagrams and photographs will help students to grasp the fundamentals being discussed, and the easy but interesting science experiments will act as further reinforcements." SLJ

Includes glossary and bibliographical references

Strother, Ruth

B is for blue planet; an earth science alphabet. written by Ruth Strother and illustrated by Bob Marstall. Sleeping Bear Press 2011 40 p.

Grades: 1 2 **550**

1. Earth 2. Geology 3. Earth sciences 4. Picture books for children 5. English language -- Alphabet

ISBN 9781585364541

LC 2010030635

In this picture book, "[t]he . . . poetic text and . . . illustrations provide an . . . entree into . . . Earth science topics . . . while sidebars provide . . . . information on each topic." (Science & Children) "Planet Earth has been home to mankind for hundreds of thousands of years and while scientists have learned a lot about it, they're still unraveling many of its mysteries. "B is for Blue Planet: An Earth Science Alphabet" explains what we do know about our planet and what more we have to learn. [It e]xamine[s] Earth's diverse ecosystems (deserts), . . . geological wonders (karst caves), . . . weather phenomena (hurricanes), and much more." (Publisher's note)

VanCleave, Janice Pratt, 1942-

Janice VanCleave's earth science for every kid; 101 easy experiments that really work. Wiley 1991 231p il hardcover o.p. pa $12.95

Grades: 4 5 6 7 **550**

1. Earth sciences 2. Science -- Experiments

ISBN 0-471-53010-7 pa

LC 90-42724

Instructions for experiments, each introducing a different earth science concept

"An entertaining, educational, and nonthreatening aid to understanding earth science. The easy experiments are carefully organized." SLJ

Woodward, John

Planet Earth; written by John Woodward; consultant Kim Bryan. DK Pub. 2009 123p il (One million things) $18.99

Grades: 5 6 7 8 **550**

1. Earth

ISBN 978-0-7566-5235-7; 0-7566-5235-9

This book features "photographic spreads that . . . showcase the rocks, minerals, streams, oceans, layers, clouds, ancient sediments, and brand-new islands that make up our planet." Publisher's note

550.78   Earth sciences – experiments

VanCleave, Janice Pratt, 1942-

Step-by-step science experiments in earth science; by Janice VanCleave. Rosen Pub. 2013 80 p. col. ill. (library) $33.25; (paperback) $14.15

Grades: 5 6 7 8   **550.78**

1. Earth sciences 2. Science -- Experiments 3. Earth sciences -- Experiments

ISBN 1448869838; 9781448869831; 9781448884674

LC 2012007944

This book by Janice VanCleave is part of the First-Place Science Fair Projects series. The books have an introduction to the subject—here, earth science, followed by 22 simple . . . experiments. Van Cleave states the basic goal of the experiments, followed by a list of necessary materials, most of which can be found around the house or easily acquired with minimal cost. Step-by-step instructions are clearly detailed and accompanied by diagrams where needed." (School Library Journal)

Includes bibliographical references (p. 78) and index.

551   Geology, hydrology, meteorology

Blobaum, Cindy

Geology rocks! 50 hands-on activities to explore the earth. illustrations by Michael Kline. Williamson 1999 96p il pa $10.95

Grades: 4 5 6   **551**

1. Geology 2. Science -- Experiments

ISBN 1-885593-29-5

LC 98-53299

Presents fifty hands-on activities to introduce the science of geology and explain the formation and history of the earth

"The text is witty but conveys much factual material. The experiments can be done easily with household items and include safety precautions. . . . The book is illustrated with red-and-purple tinted cartoons and photographs." SLJ

Includes bibliographical references

Gray, Susan H.

Geology the study of rocks; Susan H. Gray. Children's Press 2012 48 p. (pbk.) $6.95

Grades: 2 3 4 5   **551**

1. Rocks 2. Geology 3. Drilling and boring (Earth and rocks)

ISBN 0531282708; 9780531246764; 9780531282700

LC 2011031091

Author Susan Heinrichs Gray presents a book on geography, the history of the earth, and the study of rocks.

"Much like the other subsets, these volumes in the A True Book: Earth Science series are models of introducing a broad range of topics while still being concise—and graphically pleasing to boot... bright, appealing package perfect for writing reports or for following individual interests." Booklist

Includes bibliographical references and index.

Kelly, Erica

★ Evolving planet; [by] Erica Kelly & Richard Kissel. Harry N. Abrams 2008 136p il map $19.95

Grades: 5 6 7 8   **551**

1. Evolution 2. Earth 3. Field Museum of Natural History

ISBN 978-0-8109-9486-7; 0-8109-9486-0

LC 2007-36342

"Based on a exhibit at Chicago's Field Museum, this big spacious volume packs in a wealth of information about evolution over four billion years. . . . There are detailed, beautiful photographs and glorious paintings on every double-page spread and the chatty text is accessible for grade-schoolers." Booklist

Includes glossary and bibliographical references

551.1   Gross structure and properties of the earth

Saunders, Craig

What is the theory of plate tectonics? Crabtree Pub. Co. 2011 64p il (Shaping modern science) lib bdg $30.60; pa $10.95

Grades: 5 6 7 8   **551.1**

1. Plate tectonics 2. Geophysicists 3. Meteorologists 4. College teachers

ISBN 978-0-7787-7202-6 lib bdg; 0-7787-7202-0 lib bdg; 978-0-7787-7209-5 pa; 0-7787-7209-8 pa

LC 2010-52622

This title is "not only written and organized well, but [it is] also gorgeous in design. Full-color photographs and illustrations are set over colorful backgrounds that add depth but not distraction. [The title] includes thought-provoking quotes from famous authors and scientists and some eyebrow-raising 'Quick Facts' throughout." SLJ

Includes glossary and bibliographical references

Snedden, Robert

Earth's shifting surface. Raintree 2010 48p il (Sci-hi: Earth and space science) lib bdg $31.43; pa $8.99

Grades: 4 5 6 7   **551.1**

1. Plate tectonics 2. Earth -- Surface

ISBN 978-1-4109-3349-2 lib bdg; 1-4109-3349-0 lib bdg; 978-1-4109-3359-1 pa; 1-4109-3359-8 pa

LC 2009-3532

"Multiple colorful sidebars and large and small diagrams and photographs will help students to grasp the fundamentals being discussed, and the easy but interesting science experiments will act as further reinforcements." SLJ

Includes glossary and bibliographical references

551.2   Volcanoes, earthquakes, thermal waters and gases

Benoit, Peter

The Krakatau eruption. Children's Press 2011 48p il (True book) lib bdg $28; pa $6.99

Grades: 3 4 5   **551.2**

1. Volcanoes 2. Indonesia

ISBN 978-0-531-20628-7 lib bdg; 978-0-531-29027-9 pa

LC 2010045930

This describes the 1883 volcanic eruption on the island of Krakatau.

"Benoit provides unbiased information that is on target for the intended audience. . . . The photographs and reproductions enhance the [text]. . . . [This book is] well-conceived." SLJ

Includes bibliographical references

Branley, Franklyn Mansfield

Earthquakes; by Franklyn M. Branley; illustrated by Megan Lloyd. newly il ed.; HarperCollinsPublishers 2005 33p il (Let's-read-and-find-out science) hardcover o.p. pa $4.99

Grades: K 1 2 3   551.2

1. Earthquakes

ISBN 0-06-028008-5; 0-06-028009-3 lib bdg; 0-06-445188-7 pa

LC 2003-25458

A newly illustrated edition of the title first published 1990

"The most effective pictures are those that show the unseen and unseeable, such as cross-sections of mountains, volcanoes, and faults in the earth's moving crust." Booklist

Volcanoes; by Franklyn M. Branley; illustrated by Megan Lloyd. newly illustrated ed.; Collins 2008 30p il map (Let's-read-and-find-out science) $16.99; pa $5.99

Grades: 2 3 4   551.2

1. Volcanoes

ISBN 978-0-06-028011-6; 0-06-028011-5; 978-0-06-445189-5 pa; 0-06-445189-5 pa

LC 2006000465

A newly illustrated edition of the title first published 1985

Discusses volcanoes, what causes an eruption, and the warning signs

"The new illustrations excel at depicting ideas presented in the text and include scenes of destruction. . . . This work remains a sound, basic introduction to the topic." SLJ

Burleigh, Robert

Volcanoes; journey to the crater's edge. photographs by Philippe Bourseiller; adapted by Robert Burleigh; text by Helene Montardre; drawings by David Giraudon. H.N. Abrams 2003 75p il map $14.95

Grades: 4 5 6 7   551.2

1. Volcanoes

ISBN 0-8109-4590-8

LC 2003-971

Over thirty photographs and accompanying text reveal the facts about the world's volcanoes

"Photographer Bourseiller takes young readers to the crater's edge with truly spectacular full-color photographs. . . . The book does an excellent job of documenting the effect of volcanoes on the lives of those who live close to them, and small watercolor paintings further enliven the sense of human history." Booklist

Dwyer, Helen

Earthquakes! Marshall Cavendish Benchmark 2010 32p il map (Eyewitness disaster) lib bdg $28.50

Grades: 4 5 6   551.2

1. Earthquakes

ISBN 978-1-60870-001-1; 1-60870-001-1

Provides information about earthquakes through eyewitness accounts from survivors and rescue workers.

"Bold subheadings and color captions break information into readable chunks for the younger learner. Important vocabulary is in bold print. . . . An excellent addition to your science collection." Libr Media Connect

Includes glossary and bibliographical references

Fradin, Judith Bloom

★ **Earthquakes**; witness to disaster. by Judy and Dennis Fradin. National Geographic 2008 48p map (Witness to disaster) $16.95; lib bdg $26.90

Grades: 4 5 6 7   551.2

1. Earthquakes

ISBN 978-1-4263-0211-4; 1-4263-0211-8; 978-1-4263-0212-1 lib bdg; 1-4263-0212-6 lib bdg

LC 2007044164

"The combination of good writing and excellent graphics paired with archival and personal perspectives makes this book a valuable addition." SLJ

"The first chapter documents the 1964 Alaskan quake that shook Prince William Sound with a 9.2 magnitude force, and set off a tsunami that ultimately caused most of the deaths attributed to this frightening act of nature. The following chapters explore the deadly history of earthquakes and the seismic and geological science of this phenomenon." Publisher's note

Includes glossary and bibliographical references

Volcano! the Icelandic eruption of 2010 and other hot, smoky, fierce, and fiery mountains. [by] Judy & Dennis Fradin. National Geographic 2010 48p il map (National Geographic kids) pa $6.95

Grades: 4 5 6 7   551.2

1. Volcanoes

ISBN 978-1-4263-0815-4 pa; 1-4263-0815-9 pa

"The format includes text, quotes, and facts in sidebars, as well as photographs on each page, with a colorful layout. The photographs and maps that are shown are of good quality." Sci Books & Films

Includes glossary and bibliographical references

★ **Volcanoes**; by Judy and Dennis Fradin. National Geographic 2007 48p il map (Witness to disaster) $16.95; lib bdg $26.90

Grades: 4 5 6 7   551.2

1. Volcanoes

ISBN 978-0-7922-5376-1; 0-7922-5376-0; 978-0-7922-5377-8 lib bdg; 0-7922-5377-9 lib bdg

LC 2006-102817

This "introduces readers to these violent eruptions, using eyewitness accounts to explain the history and science involved. They begin with a report of the 1943 birth of a volcano in Paricutín, Mexico. . . . Subsequent chapters describe other celebrated volcanoes, explain their causes and types, note the benefits of these eruptions, and clarify how they are currently predicted. . . . Numerous clear, well-chosen photographs and diagrams help to convey the great power of volcanic activity and the consequences to humans. . . . This will be useful for report writers, and a fascinating pick for browsers." Booklist

Includes bibliographical references

Hague, Bradley

Alien deep; Revealing the Mysterious Living World at the Bottom of the Ocean. by Bradley Hague. National Geographic 2012 48 p. col. ill. (hardcover: alk. paper) $17.95

Grades: 5 6 7 8 **551.2**
1. Oceanography -- Research 2. Hydrothermal vent ecology 3. Natural history -- Galapagos Islands 4. Hydrothermal vents 5. Hydrothermal vent animals
ISBN 1426310676; 9781426310676; 9781426310683
LC 2012012939

This book by Bradley Hague "depicts adventurous and thrilling elements in oceanographic fieldwork in conjunction with a National Geographic television show." (Publisher's note) "The book takes readers along on the 2011 exploration of vents in the Galapagos Reef area of the Pacific Ocean. . . . Future scientists will be hooked by the excitement of finding newly developing vents and the disappointment of finding older vents that once disappeared under layers of magma." (Booklist)

Includes bibliographical references and index.

Jennings, Terry
Earthquakes and tsunamis. Smart Apple Media 2010 32p il map (Amazing planet earth) lib bdg $28.50
Grades: 4 5 6 **551.2**
1. Tsunamis 2. Earthquakes
ISBN 978-1-59920-372-0 lib bdg; 1-59920-372-3 lib bdg
LC 2008-55496

This book shows readers how the shifting plates far below the earth's surface can result in violent earthquakes and tsunamis

"Chapters are labeled as 'Case Study' or 'Science Report,' making the presentation lively. The concise explanations include just the right number of examples and clear diagrams, and have perfect color photo accompaniments." SLJ

Includes glossary

Violent volcanoes. Smart Apple Media 2010 32p il map (Amazing planet earth) lib bdg $28.50
Grades: 4 5 6 **551.2**
1. Volcanoes
ISBN 978-1-59920-374-4 lib bdg; 1-59920-374-X lib bdg
LC 2008-55499

This explains how powerful forces beneath the Earth's crust cause volcanoes to erupt

"Chapters are labeled as 'Case Study' or 'Science Report,' making the presentation lively. The concise explanations include just the right number of examples and clear diagrams, and have perfect color photo accompaniments." SLJ

Includes glossary

Levy, Matthys
Earthquakes, volcanoes, and tsunamis; projects and principles for beginning geologists. [by] Matthys Levy and Mario Salvadori. Chicago Review Press 2009 136p il pa $14.95
Grades: 5 6 7 8 **551.2**
1. Tsunamis 2. Volcanoes 3. Earthquakes
ISBN 978-1-55652-801-9 pa; 1-55652-801-9 pa
LC 2008040143

This "is an excellent introduction for young minds to the subject of earthquakes, volcanoes, and related phenomena. . . . The book is filled with projects to help young people understand the occurrence and consequences of earthquakes, volcanoes, and tsunamis." Sci Books Films

Nault, Jennifer
Volcanoes. AV2 by Weigl Pubs. 2010 24p il map (Earth science) $27.13; pa $11.95
Grades: 3 4 5 **551.2**
1. Volcanoes
ISBN 978-1-60596-970-1; 1-60596-970-2; 978-1-60596-971-8 pa; 1-60596-971-0 pa

This book about volcanoes "intelligently mixes history, science, geography, careers, and even myths. . . . The book [is] . . . an ideal starting point for student researchers with its breakdown of different types of volcanoes, a large map of the planet's active volcanoes, an impressive time line of notable eruptions, and details of life as a volcanologist." Booklist

Person, Stephen
Devastated by a volcano! Bearport Pub. 2010 32p il map (Disaster survivors) lib bdg $25.27
Grades: 4 5 6 7 **551.2**
1. Volcanoes
ISBN 978-1-936087-50-1 lib bdg; 1-936087-50-2 lib bdg

"Captivating photos and illustrations and sidebars present interesting facts or brief anecdotes. . . . [This] should be purchased for all school and public libraries as . . . [it gives] a new perspective on the topic." Libr Media Connect

Includes glossary and bibliographical references

Reingold, Adam
Leveled by an earthquake! Bearport Pub. 2010 32p il map (Disaster survivors) lib bdg $25.27
Grades: 4 5 6 7 **551.2**
1. Earthquakes
ISBN 978-1-936087-53-2 lib bdg; 1-936087-53-7 lib bdg
LC 2009-36961

"Introduces earthquakes, describing what causes them to occur and how they are measured, along with stories of survivors who were the victims of famous earthquakes of the past." Publisher's note

Includes glossary and bibliographical references

Silverstein, Alvin
Earthquakes; the science behind seismic shocks and tsunamis. [by] Alvin Silverstein, Virginia Silverstein, and Laura Silverstein Nunn. Enslow Publishers 2010 48p il map (The science behind natural disasters) lib bdg $23.93
Grades: 4 5 6 **551.2**
1. Tsunamis 2. Earthquakes
ISBN 978-0-7660-2975-0 lib bdg; 0-7660-2975-1 lib bdg
LC 2008-38589

"Scientific explanations are accompanied by plentiful color diagrams that will help students to grasp causes and effects. . . . Photos . . . are effective, and are sometimes turned into helpful, lively diagrams by the addition of such features as wind-direction arrows." SLJ

Includes glossary and bibliographical references

Volcanoes; the science behind fiery eruptions. [by] Alvin Silverstein, Virginia Silverstein, and Laura Silverstein Nunn. Enslow Publishers 2010 48p il map (The science behind natural disasters) lib bdg $23.93

Grades: 4 5 6 **551.2**
1. Volcanoes
ISBN 978-0-7660-2972-9 lib bdg; 0-7660-2972-7
lib bdg
LC 2008-42866

"Scientific explanations are accompanied by plentiful color diagrams that will help students to grasp causes and effects. . . . Photos . . . are effective, and are sometimes turned into helpful, lively diagrams by the addition of such features as wind-direction arrows." SLJ

Includes glossary and bibliographical references

Simon, Seymour
★ **Earthquakes**; rev ed.; Collins 2006 30p il map pa $6.99
Grades: 3 4 5 6 **551.2**
1. Earthquakes
ISBN 978-0-06-087715-6 pa; 0-06-087715-4 pa
LC 2006279219
First published 1991 by Morrow Junior Books
Examines the phenomenon of earthquakes, describing how and where they occur, how they can be predicted, and how much damage they can inflict

Spilsbury, Louise
Shattering earthquakes; [by] Louise and Richard Spilsbury. rev and updated.; Heinemann Library 2010 32p il map (Awesome forces of nature) lib bdg $29; pa $7.99
Grades: 3 4 5 6 **551.2**
1. Earthquakes
ISBN 978-1-4329-3784-3 lib bdg; 1-4329-3784-7 lib bdg; 978-1-4329-3791-1 pa; 1-4329-3791-X pa
LC 2009037565
First published 2004
This book about earthquakes discusses "causes, characteristics, and relevant science, including progress in predicting the events. Case studies illustrate the human response. Numerous color photographs and sidebars are interwoven into the well-organized and absorbing [narrative]." SLJ

Includes glossary and bibliographical references

Violent volcanoes; [by] Louise and Richard Spilsbury. rev and updated; Heinemann Library 2010 32p il map (Awesome forces of nature) lib bdg $29; pa $7.99
Grades: 3 4 5 6 **551.2**
1. Volcanoes
ISBN 978-1-4329-3783-6 lib bdg; 1-4329-3783-9 lib bdg; 978-1-4329-3790-4 pa; 1-4329-3790-1 pa
LC 2009-37564
First published 2004
This book about volcanoes "is sure to catch the eyes of students and educators. . . . The interesting and accurate facts are presented in an easily understood vocabulary. . . . Incredible eye-catching photographs, diagrams, or maps are tastefully positioned on every page." Libr Media Connect

Includes glossary and bibliographical references

Stewart, Melissa
Inside Earthquakes. Sterling Publishing Co., Inc. 2011 48p il map (Inside . . .) $16.95; pa $9.95
Grades: 5 6 7 8 **551.2**
1. Earthquakes
ISBN 978-1-4027-5877-5; 978-1-4027-8163-6 pa
LC 2010046452

This book about earthquakes "explores its topic in an engaging way, and the many illustrations work well with adjacent text and captions. . . . The [book's] varied page layouts and attractive and the quality of photos, computer-generated images, original illustrations, and charts is . . . excellent. . . . [The book] looks at the geology of the earth's crust as well as the effects of quakes on people and cities, landforms and coastlines." Booklist

Includes bibliographical references

Inside Volcanoes. Sterling Publishing Co. 2011 48p il map (Inside) $16.95; pa $9.95
Grades: 5 6 7 8 **551.2**
1. Volcanoes
ISBN 978-1-4027-5876-8; 1-4027-5876-6; 978-1-4027-8164-3 pa; 1-4027-8164-4 pa
LC 2010046451
Examines the nature of volcanoes, how they are formed, what they look like, and how they are measured, in a text with ten foldout pages.

"With pages that fold out or flip up, well-reproduced photographs of volcanoes at rest and in action, diagrams, maps, charts, timelines and short explanations, there is much to look at and to learn. . . . Appropriately for a book that is clearly designed to stimulate interest, there are solid suggestions for both books and websites for further exploration. A good starting-place for volcano explorations." Kirkus

Stille, Darlene R.
Great shakes; the science of earthquakes. Compass Point Books 2009 43p il map (Headline science) lib bdg $27.93; pa $7.95
Grades: 5 6 7 8 **551.2**
1. Earthquakes
ISBN 978-0-7565-3947-4 lib bdg; 0-7565-3947-1 lib bdg; 978-0-7565-3368-7 pa; 0-7565-3368-6 pa
LC 2008-05739
This "is an accessible, technically accurate introduction to [earthquakes]. . . . In addition to the ludic writing, this slim volume offers . . . readers comprehensive coverage of the fundamentals of earthquakes, including the effects, plate tectonics, fault systems, seismic waves, forecasting, and safer building designs. . . . The many charts and graphs enrich the volume and clarify technical issues." Sci Books Films

Includes glossary and bibliographical references

Tagliaferro, Linda
How does a volcano become an island? Raintree 2010 32p il (How does it happen?) lib bdg $27.50; pa $7.99
Grades: 3 4 5 **551.2**
1. Islands 2. Volcanoes
ISBN 978-1-4109-3447-5 lib bdg; 1-4109-3447-0 lib bdg; 978-1-4109-3455-0 pa; 1-4109-3455-1 pa
LC 2008-52652
"Information is clearly presented using a large font, diagrams, and photographs formatted to resemble Polaroid pictures. . . . A first-rate job answering some important scientific questions." SLJ

Includes glossary and bibliographical references

Woods, Michael
Volcanoes; by Michael Woods and Mary B. Woods. Lerner Publications Co. 2007 64p il map (Disasters up close) lib bdg $27.93

Grades: 4 5 6   **551.2**
1. Volcanoes
ISBN 978-0-8225-4715-0 lib bdg; 0-8225-4715-5 lib bdg

LC 2005-17132

"Each page of the colorful, eye-catching book has several paragraphs of text, sidebars, and small photos, with a large photo or graphic on the facing page." Sci Books Films

Includes bibliographical references

551.21   Volcanoes

Rusch, Elizabeth

Volcano rising; Elizabeth Rusch; illustrated by Susan Swan. Charlesbridge 2013 32 p. (reinforced for library use) $17.95

Grades: 2 3 4   **551.21**
1. Picture books for children 2. Volcanoes
ISBN 1580894089; 9781580894081; 9781580894098; 9781607346166

LC 2012000793

This children's picture book by Elizabeth Rousch explores volcanoes. "Blowing their tops off, growing taller and wider, and forming new mountains and islands, volcanoes can be both destructive and creative. . . . A dual-level narrative provides both a simple explanation of how volcanoes work and longer paragraphs that go into greater depth." Examples of eight volcanoes from around the world are discussed. (Kirkus Reviews)

551.3   Surface and exogenous processes and their agents

Harrison, David Lee

Glaciers; nature's icy caps. [by] David L. Harrison; illustrated by Cheryl Nathan. Boyds Mills Press 2006 un il (Earthworks) $15.95

Grades: K 1 2 3   **551.3**
1. Glaciers
ISBN 1-59078-372-7

LC 2005-24988

The author "provides a straightforward introduction to glaciers. Opening with the sinking of the Titanic, he explains how they form, move, and drop icebergs into the sea, going on to discuss where glaciers can be found and how their range shifts as Earth cycles in and out of ice ages. . . . The text reads like clear, informational prose. Nathan's digital illustrations vary in quality, but the best double-page spreads . . . are exceptionally fine." Booklist

Sepehri, Sandy

Glaciers; [by] Sandy Sepehri. Rourke Pub. 2008 32p il (Landforms) lib bdg $28.50; pa $7.95

Grades: 1 2 3 4   **551.3**
1. Glaciers
ISBN 978-1-60044-544-6 lib bdg; 1-60044-544-6 lib bdg; 978-1-60044-705-1 pa; 1-60044-705-8 pa

LC 2007012143

"The illustrations and photographs are plentiful and colorful. . . . The [volume is] well written and successfully [conveys] the basics of the topic." Sci Books Films

Includes glossary and bibliographical references

Silverman, Buffy

Exploring dangers in space; asteroids, space junk, and more. Lerner Publications 2011 40p il (What's amazing about space?) $27.93

Grades: 4 5 6   **551.3**
1. Comets 2. Meteors 3. Asteroids 4. Space debris
ISBN 978-0-7613-5446-8

LC 2010046078

This discusses meteoroids, space junk, comets and asteroids that fall to Earth, how scientists watch out for large collisions, and what they might do if Earth is in danger.

This book is "written in simple language, [and] illustrated nicely. . . . The information presented is factually correct. . . . Every page includes a well-chosen illustration or photograph." Sci Books Films

Includes bibliographical references

Simon, Seymour

★ **Icebergs** and glaciers. Morrow 1987 un il hardcover o.p. pa $6.99

Grades: 3 4 5 6   **551.3**
1. Glaciers 2. Icebergs
ISBN 0-688-16705-5 pa

LC 86-18142

The author "chronicles the development of glaciers and icebergs with a wonderfully clear, almost Spartan text that receives all of the support necessary from the magnificent color photographs which accompany it. . . . This book would be an excellent addition to any elementary school library or any personal juvenile collection." Appraisal

551.4   Geomorphology and hydrosphere

Henzel, Cynthia Kennedy

Great Barrier Reef. ABDO Pub. Co. 2011 32p il (Troubled treasures: world heritage sites) $25.65

Grades: 3 4 5   **551.4**
1. Coral reefs and islands 2. Great Barrier Reef (Australia)
ISBN 978-1-61613-564-5; 1-61613-564-6

LC 2010021310

This "book describes in general terms [the Great Barrier Reef's] . . . creation, distinctive features, and history, as well as threats to its continued existence and both current and past restoration intitiatives. Revealing color photos taken from different heights and angles are supplemented by maps and by graphic reconstructions. . . . Henzel's distinctive approach gives this [book] unusual value for both assignment and general reading." SLJ

Includes glossary

Hughes, Catherine D.

First big book of the ocean; by Catherine D. Hughes. National Geographic Children's Books 2013 128 p. $14.95

Grades: K 1 2 3   **551.4**
1. Marine animals 2. Marine biology
ISBN 9781426313684; 1426313683

This book, by Catherine D. Hughes, presents an "animal reference that includes the sea's high-interest animals, such as dolphins, sharks, sea otters, and penguins, and introduces kids to some of its lesser-known creatures. More than 100 . . . animal photos illustrate the profiles, with facts about the creatures' sizes, diets, homes, and more." (Publisher's note)

Jennings, Terry

Massive mountains. Smart Apple Media 2010 32p il map (Amazing planet earth) lib bdg $28.50

Grades: 4 5 6 **551.4**

1. Mountains

ISBN 978-1-59920-370-6 lib bdg; 1-59920-370-7 lib bdg

LC 2008-55497

This book explains how mountains form and change over time

"Chapters are labeled as 'Case Study' or 'Science Report,' making the presentation lively. The concise explanations include just the right number of examples and clear diagrams, and have perfect color photo accompaniments." SLJ

Includes glossary

Sheehan, Thomas F.

Islands; [by] Thomas F. Sheehan. Rourke Pub. 2008 32p il map (Landforms) lib bdg $28.50; pa $7.95

Grades: 1 2 3 4 **551.4**

1. Islands

ISBN 978-1-60044-545-3 lib bdg; 1-60044-545-4 lib bdg; 978-1-60044-706-8 pa; 1-60044-706-6 pa

LC 2007012183

"The illustrations and photographs are plentiful and colorful. . . . The [volume is] well written and successfully [conveys] the basics of the topic." Sci Books Films

Includes glossary and bibliographical references

Mountains; [by] Thomas Sheehan. Rourke Pub. 2008 32p il map (Landforms) lib bdg $28.50; pa $7.95

Grades: 1 2 3 4 **551.4**

1. Mountains

ISBN 978-1-60044-547-7 lib bdg; 1-60044-547-0 lib bdg; 978-1-60044-708-2 pa; 1-60044-708-2 pa

LC 2007012290

"The illustrations and photographs are plentiful and colorful. . . . The [volume is] well written and successfully [conveys] the basics of the topic." Sci Books Films

Includes glossary and bibliographical references

Simon, Seymour

★ **Mountains**. Morrow Junior Bks. 1994 un il hardcover o.p. pa $6.99

Grades: 4 5 6 7 **551.4**

1. Mountains

ISBN 0-688-15477-8 pa

LC 93-11398

Introduces various mountain ranges, how they are formed and shaped, and how they affect vegetation and animals, including humans

"The striking color photographs work well with the clear text to illustrate key points and highlight the diversity among the Earth's mountain ranges." Horn Book Guide

Wilson, Hannah

Seashore; illustrated by Simon Mendez. Kingfisher 2010 18p il (Flip the flaps) $9.99

Grades: PreK K 1 **551.4**

1. Seashore

ISBN 978-0-7534-6445-8; 0-7534-6445-4

This "features beautiful spreads by Mendez, who paints his coastal scenes with a soft realism so accurate they are occasionally indistinguishable from photographs. Wilson, meanwhile, introduces readers to the plants and wildlife present at shorelines everywhere—not just the classic sandy beach but also salt marsh, arctic region, and mangrove swamp. Each top flap presents three questions . . . which are answered underneath. . . . Perfect for light, educational browsing." Booklist

Zoehfeld, Kathleen Weidner

How mountains are made; illustrated by James Graham Hale. HarperCollins Pubs. 1995 29p il maps (Let's-read-and-find-out science) hardcover o.p. pa $4.95

Grades: K 1 2 3 **551.4**

1. Geology 2. Mountains

ISBN 0-06-024510-7; 0-06-445128-3 pa

LC 93-45436

"The text and illustrations work together well in this sequential, well-organized book. Much credit goes to Hale's engaging watercolor illustrations done in cheery colors; they are simply drawn but add effective examples and diagrams." SLJ

551.46 Oceanography and submarine geology

Adamson, Thomas K.

Tsunamis; with Walter C. Dudley, consultant. Capstone Press 2005 24p il $22.26

Grades: 2 3 4 **551.46**

1. Tsunamis

ISBN 0-7368-5248-4

LC 2005-01640

"Adamson explains how tsunamis are caused and how they move through the ocean and grow in height as they approach the shore. He describes the damage they cause, the kinds of warning systems used to detect them, and the impact of the 2004 Indian Ocean disaster. The writing is concise but clear, and the layout features a full-page illustration facing each page of easy-to-read text. Excellent photos of the 2004 tsunami are featured, and the diagrams of the earth's plates and earthquakes are simple but informative." SLJ

Includes bibliographical references

Aronin, Miriam

Slammed by a tsunami! Bearport Pub. 2010 32p il map (Disaster survivors) lib bdg $25.27

Grades: 4 5 6 7 **551.46**

1. Tsunamis

ISBN 978-1-936087-48-8 lib bdg; 1-936087-48-0 lib bdg

LC 2009-34574

"Introduces tsunamis, discussing how they form and when they tend to occur, and describing the devastating effects of the 2004 tsunami in Sumatra and of some of the other well-known tsunamis of the past." Publisher's note

Includes glossary and bibliographical references

Basher, Simon

Oceans; [making waves!] designed and created by Simon Basher; text written by Dan Green. Kingfisher 2012 128 p. ill. (paperback) $8.99; (hardcover) $14.99

Grades: 5 6 7 8   **551.46**

1. Oceanography 2. Marine ecology 3. Aquatic animals

ISBN 0753468220; 9780753468227; 9780753468210

"Following a brief introduction to oceans, the text employs an easy-to-navigate field guide like format, where facts and figures about ocean habitats, processes, and animals that live in various areas (e.g., shore, reef, deep water) face illustrations in manga style" Horn Book

"A rewarding wade, particularly for readers who think oceanography is a dry study." Booklist

Bodden, Valerie

To the ocean deep; by Valerie Bodden. Creative Education 2011 48 p. col. ill. (Great expeditions) (library) $34.25

Grades: 5 6 7 8   **551.46**

1. Ocean 2. Underwater exploration 3. Explorers -- Biography 4. Trieste (Bathyscaphe) -- History 5. Bathyscaphe -- History -- 20th century

ISBN 1608180670; 9781608180677

LC 2010033416

This book by Valerie Bodden is part of the Great Expeditions series and looks at oceanic exploration expeditions. "Bodden includes brief biographies of major people involved in each expedition, interspersed with the text. There are also numerous photographs or reproductions of paintings and woodcuts from the time of the expeditions." (Library Media Connection)

Includes bibliographical references (p. 46-47) and index.

Burns, Loree Griffin

★ Tracking trash; flotsam, jetsam, and the science of ocean motion. Houghton Mifflin 2007 56p il map (Scientists in the field) $18

Grades: 5 6 7 8   **551.46**

1. Pollution 2. Ocean currents 3. Oceanographers 4. Marine debris

ISBN 0-618-58131-6; 978-0-618-58131-3

LC 2006-11534

This book describes "Curt Ebbesmeyer's ongoing work. . . . The oceanographer has been tracing the surface currents of the seas via the movement of plastic rubbish that has escaped from broken cargo containers. [Index.] Grades five to nine." (Bull Cent Child Books)

"The book profiles two oceanographers who devised experiments using computer-modeling programs of ocean surface current movement to predict the landfall of . . . drifting objects. . . . Spacious layout, exceptionally fine color photos, and handsome maps give this book an inviting look. . . . A unique and often fascinating book." Booklist

Includes glossary and bibliographical references

Dwyer, Helen

Tsunamis! Marshall Cavendish Benchmark 2010 32p il map (Eyewitness disaster) lib bdg $28.50

Grades: 4 5 6   **551.46**

1. Tsunamis

ISBN 978-1-60870-005-9; 1-60870-005-4

LC 2010001801

Provides information about tsunamis through eyewitness accounts from survivors and rescue workers.

"Bold subheadings and color captions break information into readable chunks for the younger learner. Important vocabulary is in bold print. . . . An excellent addition to your science collection." Libr Media Connect

Includes glossary and bibliographical references

Earle, Sylvia A., 1935-

Dive! my adventures in the deep frontier. National Geographic Soc. 1999 64p il map $18.95

Grades: 4 5 6   **551.46**

1. Underwater exploration 2. Submarine diving

ISBN 0-7922-7144-0

LC 98-11480

The author relates some of her adventures studying and exploring the world's oceans, including tracking whales, living in an underwater laboratory, and helping to design a deep water submarine

"In this extraordinary photo-essay, an eminent marine biologist and ocean explorer combines personal adventure and scientific fact with glorious color action pictures." Booklist

Includes glossary

Fradin, Judith Bloom

★ Tsunamis; witness to disaster. [by] Judy & Dennis Fradin. National Geographic 2008 48p il map (Witness to disaster) $16.95; lib bdg $20.90

Grades: 4 5 6 7   **551.46**

1. Tsunamis

ISBN 978-0-7922-5380-8; 0-7922-5380-9; 978-0-7922-5381-5 lib bdg; 0-7922-5381-7 lib bdg

LC 2008010536

This "explores the science, history, and personal experience of tsunamis and shows kids what scientists are doing to develop early warning systems so we can survive such disasters in the future." Publisher's note

Includes glossary and bibliographical references

Gray, Susan H.

Oceanography the study of oceans; Susan H. Gray. Children's Press 2012 48 p.

Grades: 2 3 4 5   **551.46**

1. Oceanography

ISBN 0531246795; 0531282732; 9780531246795; 9780531282731

LC 2011031074

This book by Susan Heinrichs Gray is an introduction to oceanography for young readers. "Earth's oceans are almost like a foreign world, filled with millions of strange, fascinating animals and plants. Oceanographers dive into the watery depths to learn more about the incredible ocean ecosystems that make up the majority of our planet. Readers will discover how the ocean changes as it goes deeper, how deep sea animals survive in harsh environments, and more." (Google Books)

Includes bibliographical references (p. 44-45) and index

Green, Jen

The **world's** oceans. Smart Apple Media 2010 32p il map (Amazing planet earth) lib bdg $28.50

Grades: 4 5 6   **551.46**

1. Ocean

ISBN 978-1-59920-373-7 lib bdg; 1-59920-373-1 lib bdg

LC 2008-55500

This covers how ocean waves shape the seashore, the makeup of the ocean bed, underwater hazards, storm surges, and the effects of global warming. Interspersed with these are six "Case Study" chapters, which take an in-depth look at various oceanic events throughout history such as the creation of Iceland or the deadly tsunami that hit Indonesia in December, 2004

"Chapters are labeled as 'Case Study' or 'Science Report,' making the presentation lively. The concise explanations include just the right number of examples and clear diagrams, and have perfect color photo accompaniments." SLJ

Includes glossary

Hamilton, John

Tsunamis; [by] John Hamilton. ABDO Pub. Co. 2006 32p il map lib bdg $27.07

Grades: 2 3 4   **551.46**

1. Tsunamis

ISBN 1-59679-333-3

LC 2005040427

"Hamilton describes the 2004 Indian Ocean disaster and explains the causes and nature of tsunamis. . . . The brief but readable text adequately presents the phenomenon and the specific events. Excellent, informative color photos include several that are not common to many of the other recent books on the topic." SLJ

Includes bibliographical references

Mallory, Kenneth

Adventure beneath the sea; living in an underwater science station. [photographs by Brian Skerry] Boyds Mills Press 2010 48p il map $18.95

Grades: 4 5 6 7   **551.46**

1. Underwater exploration

ISBN 978-1-59078-607-9; 1-59078-607-6

The author "invites readers to squeeze into Aquarius, a venerable science-station habitat resting on the sea floor at a depth of 60 feet in the Florida Keys. The readable text explains the complexities of training for a weeklong stay, the aims of the scientists on the team, and what it is like to spend 24/7 in squashed companionship in a 43' × 9' cylinder as part of a crew of seven. . . . Sidebars contain interesting information. . . . Full-color photos abound." SLJ

Includes glossary and bibliographical references

★ **Diving** to a deep-sea volcano. Houghton Mifflin Company 2006 60p il map (Scientists in the field) $17

Grades: 5 6 7 8   **551.46**

1. Ocean bottom 2. Marine biology 3. Underwater exploration

ISBN 978-0-618-33205-2; 0-618-33205-7

LC 2005-25449

This describes the exploration by marine biologist Rich Lutz and his crew of deep sea hydrothermal vents and the creatures that survive there.

"The profile of an enthusiastic scientist injects excitement into even unassuming facts." Booklist

Includes glossary and bibliographical references

Marsico, Katie

★ **Puget** Sound; by Katie Marsico. Cherry Lake Pub. 2013 32 p. (It's cool to learn about America's waterways) (lib. bdg.) $28.50

Grades: 3 4 5   **551.46**

1. Puget Sound region (Wash.) 2. Puget Sound (Wash.)

ISBN 162431015X; 9781624310157; 9781624310393; 9781624310638

LC 2012034741

This book by Katie Marsico is part of a series that "provide[s] a wealth of information regarding each waterway's history, geographical characteristics, wildlife, and influence on the development of nearby towns and cities. Conservation is emphasized in all the titles. The importance of each waterway commercially and recreationally is also discussed." (Publisher's note) "In 'Puget Sound,' they graph local wildlife." (Booklist)

Includes bibliographical references and index

MacQuitty, Miranda

Eyewitness ocean; written by Miranda MacQuitty; photographed by Frank Greenaway. DK Publishing 2008 72 p. illustrations (chiefly color) $9.99

Grades: 4 5 6 7   **551.46**

1. Ocean 2. Marine animals 3. Marine biology 4. Marine ecology 5. Ocean

ISBN 1465420541; 1465420967; 9780756637767; 9781465420541

LC 2008276032

In this book, by Miranda MacQuitty, "dive in and discover the watery world covering most of our earth and the amazing wildlife in its depths. . . . Through images, maps and informative text learn about life on the shore to the darkest depths of the ocean floor, including predators and prey, gas and oil exploration, products of the ocean, brave explorers and what the human race can do to help preserve one of the earth's most valuable resources." (Publisher's note)

"The DK Eyewitness series exemplifies what the publisher does best: taking a broad topic and slicing it into two-page chapters that, while they contain no narrative thread, make for excellent museum-type browsing... The photos are stunning and wonderfully arranged. Each book rounds out the guided tour with an FAQ of sorts, profiles, and plenty of places for interested readers to keep looking. Just the thing to whet appetites before trucking down to the local real-life museum." Booklist

Ocean

Part of the DK Eyewitness series.

Nivola, Claire A.

★ **Life** in the ocean; Claire A. Nivola. Frances Foster Books, Farrar Straus Giroux 2012 1 v. (unpaged) col. ill.

Grades: K 1 2 3 4   **551.46**

1. Biography 2. Explorers 3. Oceanography 4. Marine biologists -- United States 5. Women marine biologists -- United States 6. Women explorers -- United States -- Biography

ISBN 9780374380687

LC 2011016645

This picture book presents a "biography of oceanographer Sylvia Earle, a pioneer and entrepreneur in her field who also set an example for women of the mid–20th century." It covers life on her "childhood farm," her "relocat[ion] to the Gulf Coast, and her interest [in]ocean exploration. . . . The . . . narrative highlights Earle's career and also provides a few . . . closeups from specific dives." (Publishers Weekly)

Includes bibliographical references and index

Rizzo, Johnna

Oceans; dolphins, sharks, penguins, and more!: meet 60 cool sea creatures and explore their amazing watery world. introduction by Sylvia A. Earle. National Geographic 2010 64p il $14.95; lib bdg $24.90

Grades: 4 5 6   551.46
1. Ocean 2. Marine animals
ISBN 978-1-4263-0686-0; 1-4263-0686-5; 978-1-4263-0724-9 lib bdg; 1-4263-0724-1 lib bdg

"A colorful olio of marine animals in eye-catching photos accompanies a cheerful conversational text. . . . Information boxes pop up all over the place as well, but it is the bright photos that steal the show. . . . This splashy volume is a nice introduction to a salty water-world." SLJ

Includes glossary

Schuh, Mari C.

Tsunamis. Capstone Press 2010 24p il (Earth in action) lib bdg $21.32

Grades: K 1 2   551.46
1. Tsunamis
ISBN 978-1-4296-3438-0 lib bdg; 1-4296-3438-3 lib bdg

LC 2009-2175

This book "boasts a full-page color photograph. . . . [It shows] the aftermath of a disaster . . . but there are also some diagrams showing physical mechanisms and maps highlighting commonly affected places. The left side of each spread provides a few sentences of large-print text, with short, clear explanations." SLJ

Includes glossary and bibliographical references

Simon, Seymour

Seymour Simon's extreme oceans; Seymour Simon. Chronicle Books 2013 60 p. col. ill. (reinforced) $17.99

Grades: 4 5 6   551.46
1. Ocean
ISBN 1452108331; 9781452108339

LC 2012012590

In this work of children's nonfiction, author "[Seymour] Simon examines the things that are 'most,' pertaining to oceans: the tallest sea mounts, the largest waves, the highest tides in the world, the most dangerous and largest animals, the coldest and warmest waters, the biggest storms and tsunamis, and the longest journeys, as well as a closing chapter predicting scenarios if sea levels continue to rise." (School Library Journal)

Spilsbury, Louise

Sweeping tsunamis; [by] Louise and Richard Spilsbury. rev ed.; Heinemann Library 2010 32p il map (Awesome forces of nature) lib bdg $29; pa $7.99

Grades: 3 4 5 6   551.46
1. Tsunamis
ISBN 978-1-4329-3785-0 lib bdg; 1-4329-3785-5 lib bdg; 978-1-4329-3792-8 pa; 1-4329-3792-8 pa

LC 2009037567

First published 2004

This book about tsunamis "causes, characteristics, and relevant science, including progress in predicting the events. Case studies illustrate the human response. Numerous color photographs and sidebars are interwoven into the well-organized and absorbing [narrative]." SLJ

Includes glossary and bibliographical references

Stille, Darlene R.

Oceans. Children's Press 1999 47p il maps (True book) $22; pa $6.95

Grades: 2 3 4   551.46
1. Ocean
ISBN 0-516-21510-8; 0-516-26768-X pa

LC 98-53857

An introduction to the ocean describing its physical characteristics, the plants and animals that live in or near it, and its importance to life on Earth

Includes bibliographical references

Tagliaferro, Linda

How does an earthquake become a tsunami? Raintree 2008 32p il map (How does it happen?) lib bdg $27.50; pa $7.99

Grades: 3 4 5   551.46
1. Waves 2. Tsunamis 3. Earthquakes 4. Plate tectonics
ISBN 978-1-4109-3446-8 lib bdg; 1-4109-3446-2 lib bdg; 978-1-4109-3454-3 pa; 1-4109-3454-3 pa

LC 2008-52643

"Information is clearly presented using a large font, diagrams, and photographs formatted to resemble Polaroid pictures. . . . A first-rate job answering some important scientific questions." SLJ

Includes glossary and bibliographical references

VanCleave, Janice Pratt, 1942-

Janice VanCleave's oceans for every kid; easy activities that make learning science fun. Wiley 1996 245p il map (Science for every kid series) hardcover o.p. pa $12.95

Grades: 4 5 6 7   551.46
1. Oceanography
ISBN 0-471-12453-2 pa

LC 95-9201

Includes information on techniques and technologies of oceanography, the topology of the ocean floor, movement of the sea, properties of sea water, and life in the sea

"An engaging overview of marine sciences. Each chapter explores a topic in two to four pages, then poses questions accompanied by lucid explanations." SLJ

Includes glossary

Woodward, John

The deep, deep ocean. Brown Bear Books 2009 32p il map (Oceans alive!) lib bdg $28.50

Grades: 2 3 4 5   551.46
1. Oceanography
ISBN 978-1-933834-63-4 lib bdg; 1-933834-63-3 lib bdg

This describes "deep parts of the ocean. Colored drawings, photos, and themed factual sidebars all enhance the story, navigated by a variety of submarines. . . . Differences in temperatures from the surface to the midnight zone are elegantly explained." Sci Books Films

Includes glossary and bibliographical references

On the seabed. Brown Bear Books 2009 32p il map (Oceans alive!) lib bdg $28.50

Grades: 2 3 4 5 **551.46**

1. Oceanography

ISBN 978-1-933834-64-1 lib bdg; 1-933834-64-1 lib bdg

Describes plants, animals, and different habitats that are found on the ocean's floor, and offers information on kelp forests, sunken treasure, and hydrothermal vents.

"From deep hot areas to cold places, strange, but wonderful, events and organisms are discussed. . . . Through the various photos and the text, the reader should develop an appreciation for the diversity found on the sea floor." Sci Books Films

Includes glossary and bibliographical references

Under the waves. Brown Bear Books 2009 32p il map (Oceans alive!) lib bdg $28.50

Grades: 2 3 4 5 **551.46**

1. Oceanography 2. Marine animals

ISBN 978-1-933834-62-7 lib bdg; 1-933834-62-5 lib bdg

Explores and describes both different oceans and different parts of the ocean.

"Explanations on notebook-style illustrations offer asides, a delightful extra along with appropriate maps and impressive photos. . . . Accurate details are given for such wonders as the Portuguese man-of-war, red tides, manta rays, and lion-fish." Sci Books Films

Includes glossary and bibliographical references

551.48 Hydrology

Dorros, Arthur

Follow the water from brook to ocean; written and illustrated by Arthur Dorros. HarperCollins Pubs. 1991 32p il (Let's-read-and-find-out science book) $13.95; lib bdg $13.89

Grades: K 1 2 3 **551.48**

1. Water

ISBN 0-06-021598-4; 0-06-021599-2 lib bdg

LC 90-1438

Explains how water flows from brooks, to streams, to rivers, over waterfalls, through canyons and dams, to eventually reach the ocean

"An excellent presentation of introductory material about water. . . . The illustrations are simple, almost childlike, in soft colors." SLJ

Dwyer, Helen

Floods! Marshall Cavendish Benchmark 2010 32p il map (Eyewitness Disaster) lib bdg $28.50

Grades: 4 5 6 **551.48**

1. Floods

ISBN 978-1-60870-002-8; 1-60870-002-X

Provides information about floods through eyewitness accounts from survivors and rescue workers.

"Bold subheadings and color captions break information into readable chunks for the younger learner. Important vocabulary is in bold print. . . . An excellent addition to your science collection." Libr Media Connect

Includes glossary and bibliographical references

Gallant, Roy A.

Water. Benchmark Bks. 2001 48p il (Kaleidoscope) lib bdg $15.95

Grades: 3 4 5 **551.48**

1. Water

ISBN 0-7614-1040-6

LC 99-49627

Explains why water, although common, has characteristics which make it an unusual substance

"The large-print [text is] easy to read, and the explanations are clear and concise. Outstanding full-page, full-color photographs appear throughout." SLJ

Includes glossary and bibliographical references

Green, Jen

Mighty rivers. Smart Apple Media 2010 32p il map (Amazing planet earth) lib bdg $28.50

Grades: 4 5 6 **551.48**

1. Rivers

ISBN 978-1-59920-371-3 lib bdg; 1-59920-371-5 lib bdg

LC 2008-55498

Starting with a quick introduction to the water cycle, this book shows readers how rivers are formed, and how they, in turn, form waterfalls, carve out canyons, create fertile deltas, cause flooding, and have a great impact on the daily lives of people all over the world

"Chapters are labeled as 'Case Study' or 'Science Report,' making the presentation lively. The concise explanations include just the right number of examples and clear diagrams, and have perfect color photo accompaniments." SLJ

Includes glossary

Lyon, George Ella

★ **All** the water in the world. Atheneum Books for Young Readers 2011 un il $15.99

Grades: K 1 2 3 **551.48**

1. Water 2. Hydrologic cycle

ISBN 978-1-4169-7130-6; 1-4169-7130-0

LC 2010-29530

"Lyrical text compactly describes the hydrological cycle and global contrast between plenty and dearth of the key life-giving substance. . . . The text . . . [is] lucid yet imaginative, turning scientific and geographical explanation into sonorous sound play. . . . Visuals are strong and supple: the text is creatively laid out with pattern-poem precision, and the digital art effortlessly balances crisp collage-style composite . . . and splashy, fluid splatters of pigment, providing impeccable rhythm and flow." Bull Cent Child Books

Paul, Miranda

Water is water; a book about the water cycle. Miranda Paul; illustrated by Jason Chin. Roaring Brook Press 2015 40 p. (hardback) $17.99

Grades: PreK K 1 2 **551.48**

1. Water 2. Cycles 3. Hydrologic cycle

ISBN 159643984X; 9781596439849

LC 2014031493

This picture book, by Miranda Paul and illustrated by Jason Chin, "highlights various forms water takes as it follows a brother and sister through the year. It includes autumn fog and rain, frozen ponds and falling snow, steam from cups of cocoa, and snowmelt turning dirt to mud." (School Library Journal)

Rauzon, Mark J.

Water, water everywhere; [by] Mark J. Rauzon and Cynthia Overbeck Bix. Sierra Club Bks. for Children 1994 32p il $14.95; pa $6.95

Grades: K 1 2 3 **551.48**

1. Water

ISBN 0-87156-598-6; 0-87156-383-5 pa

LC 92-34521

Describes the forms water takes, how it has shaped Earth, and its importance to life

"Water's vital role in the life of our planet is vividly portrayed in a crisp, economical text that cultivates respect for the environment. . . . Striking, often full-page, color photographs will engage the imagination of young readers." Horn Book Guide

Spilsbury, Louise

Raging floods; [by] Louise and Richard Spilsbury. Heinemann Library 2010 32p il (Awesome forces of nature) lib bdg $29; pa $7.99

Grades: 3 4 5 6 **551.48**

1. Floods

ISBN 978-1-4329-3782-9 lib bdg; 1-4329-3782-0 lib bdg; 978-1-4329-3789-8 pa; 1-4329-3789-8 pa

LC 2009-37562

First published 2004

This book about floods "is sure to catch the eyes of students and educators. . . . The interesting and accurate facts are presented in an easily understood vocabulary. . . . Incredible eye-catching photographs, diagrams, or maps are tastefully positioned on every page." Libr Media Connect

Includes glossary and bibliographical references

Waldman, Neil

The **snowflake**; a water cycle story. [by] Neil Waldman. Millbrook Press 2003 un il $14.95

Grades: K 1 2 3 **551.48**

1. Snow 2. Water

ISBN 0-7613-2347-3

LC 2003-4806

Follows the journey of a water droplet through the various stages of the water cycle, from precipitation to evaporation and condensation

"The clear text is undeniably lyrical. . . . The real stunners here, though, are the dazzling, cool-toned paintings that convey the wonders of nature with delicate precision." SLJ

Wells, Robert E.

Did a dinosaur drink this water? A. Whitman 2006 un il $15.95; pa $6.95

Grades: K 1 2 3 **551.48**

1. Water

ISBN 978-0-8075-8839-0; 978-0-8075-8840-6 pa

LC 2006-01039

This describes "the water cycle, explaining that the earth's water has been constantly recycled not just since dinosaur days but for billions of years. The simple text asks good questions and offers clearly worded answers, enhanced by lively, colorful ink-and-watercolor illustrations." Booklist

551.5 Meteorology

Branley, Franklyn Mansfield

Air is all around you; by Franklyn M. Branley; illustrated by John O'Brien. newly illustrated ed.; HarperCollinsPublishers 2006 36p il (Let's-read-and-find-out science) hardcover o.p. pa $4.99

Grades: K 1 2 **551.5**

1. Air

ISBN 0-06-059413-6; 0-06-059414-4 lib bdg; 0-06-059415-2 pa

LC 2004005043

A revised and newly illustrated edition of the title first published 1962

This "title introduces the concept of air, its presence in our world, and its importance to the environment. The text describes several interesting facts, clearly explaining ideas and incorporating experiments that are easy to reproduce at home or in the classroom. The appealing artwork supports the narrative. . . . Produced in pen and warm, earthy watercolors, the pictures are filled with amusing details." SLJ

Carson, Mary Kay

Weather projects for young scientists; experiments and science fair ideas. Chicago Review Press 2007 134p il $14.95

Grades: 4 5 6 7 **551.5**

1. Weather 2. Science -- Experiments

ISBN 978-1-55652-629-9; 1-55652-629-6

LC 2006-16430

This "presents difficult concepts in a very concrete, basic manner." Sci Books Films

This covers "fundamentals about the water cycle and seasons as well as more sophisticated topics, such as pressure systems, greenhouse gases, and forecasting. The information alternates with more than 40 activities." Booklist

Cosgrove, Brian

Weather; written by Brian Cosgrove. rev ed; DK Publishing 2007 72p il map (DK eyewitness books) $15.99; lib bdg $19.99

Grades: 4 5 6 7 **551.5**

1. Climate 2. Weather 3. Atmosphere

ISBN 978-0-7566-3006-5; 0-7566-3006-1; 978-0-7566-0737-1 lib bdg; 0-7566-0737-X lib bdg

LC 2007-281112

First published 1991 by Knopf

"Discover the world's weather—from heat waves and droughts to blizzards and floods"—Cover. Includes discussion of why the climate may change in the future.

"Accompanying the book are a poster, additional images on CD-ROM, and a useful glossary. Altogether, this book and its supplements are well crafted to motivate young learners about the importance of weather, to deepen their conceptual understanding of it, and to pique their interest in participating in its study." Sci Books Films

Includes glossary

DeLallo, Laura

Hammered by a heat wave! consultants, Daphne Thompson, Keith C. Heidorn. Bearport Pub. 2010 32p il map (Disaster survivors) lib bdg $25.27

Grades: 4 5 6 7   551.5

1. Meteorology

ISBN 978-1-936087-51-8 lib bdg; 1-936087-51-0 lib bdg

"Captivating photos and illustrations and sidebars present interesting facts or brief anecdotes. . . . [This] should be purchased for all school and public libraries as . . . [it gives] a new perspective on the topic." Libr Media Connect

Includes glossary and bibliographical references

Gardner, Robert

Ace your weather science project; great science fair ideas. [by] Robert Gardner and Salvatore Tocci. Enslow Publishers 2009 104p il (Ace your physics science project) lib bdg $31.93

Grades: 5 6 7 8   551.5

1. Weather 2. Science projects 3. Science -- Experiments

ISBN 978-0-7660-3223-1 lib bdg; 0-7660-3223-X lib bdg

LC 2008-49779

"Presents several science experiments and project ideas about weather." Publisher's note

Includes bibliographical references

Easy genius science projects with weather; great experiments and ideas. Enslow Publishers 2009 128p il (Easy genius science projects) lib bdg $31.93

Grades: 5 6 7 8   551.5

1. Weather 2. Science projects 3. Science -- Experiments

ISBN 978-0-7660-2924-8 lib bdg; 0-7660-2924-7 lib bdg

LC 2008-23972

"Science experiments and science project ideas about weather." Publisher's note

Includes glossary and bibliographical references

Stellar science projects about Earth's sky; [by] Robert Gardner; illustrations by Tom Labaff. Enslow Elementary 2007 48p il (Rockin' earth science experiments) lib bdg $23.93

Grades: 3 4 5   551.5

1. Sky 2. Science projects 3. Science -- Experiments

ISBN 978-0-7660-2732-9 lib bdg; 0-7660-2732-5 lib bdg

LC 2006-13790

This offers experiments on topics such as the weight of air, air pressure, why the sky is blue, why sunsets are red, clouds, stars, and balloons in sky and water

This is "just right for students with limited experience looking for projects that are fairly interesting and manageable." SLJ

Includes glossary and bibliographical references

Wild science projects about Earth's weather; illustrations by Tom LaBaff. Enslow 2007 48p il (Rockin' earth science experiments) lib bdg $23.93

Grades: 3 4 5   551.5

1. Weather 2. Science projects 3. Science -- Experiments

ISBN 978-0-7660-2734-3 lib bdg; 0-7660-2734-1 lib bdg

LC 2006-05897

This presents experiments on such topics as air temperature and pressure, wind direction, rainfall, and clouds.

"Each experiment is enhanced by a topical fact box and includes a supply list and step-by-step explanation." SLJ

Includes glossary and bibliographical references

VanCleave, Janice Pratt,1942-

Janice VanCleave's weather; mind-boggling experiments you can turn into science fair projects. [by] Janice VanCleave. Wiley 1995 89p il (Spectacular science projects series) pa $10.95

Grades: 4 5 6 7   551.5

1. Weather 2. Science projects 3. Science -- Experiments

ISBN 0-471-03231-X

LC 94-25646

"Using everyday household items, the reading audience can demonstrate to itself such phenomena as differences in climate at different points on the Earth, lightning, wind direction and intensity, clouds, rain, fronts, etc. Through excellent directions and adequate illustrations, the reader can do 20 simple experiments at little or no cost that demonstrate many aspects of the weather." Sci Books Films

Includes glossary

Whitt, Kelly Kizer

Solar system forecast; by Kelly Kizer Whitt; illustrated by Laurie Allen Klein. Sylvan Dell Publishing 2012 1 v. (unpaged) col. ill. (hardcover) $17.95; (paperback) $9.95; (English ebook) $9.95

Grades: 1 2 3   551.5

1. Weather forecasting 2. Pluto (Dwarf planet) 3. Planets -- Exploration 4. Solar system 5. Planetary meteorology

ISBN 9781607185239; 9781607185321; 9781607185413

LC 2012007599

Author Kelly Kizer Whitt's book is narrated by "a friendly, green-skinned TV weatheralien . . . [who] begins with the Sun . . . and moves on to each planet in turn. There are additional reports for the moon Titan . . . and the dwarf planet Pluto. . . . [The story features] space-suited commuters, melted or frozen science gear and views of prominent storms, from a hurricane on Earth to Jupiter's Great Red Spot. . . . Charts, tables, diagrams, quizzes and other . . . material" provide information on "meteorological data." (Kirkus Reviews)

551.51 Composition, regions, dynamics of atmosphere

Bauer, Marion Dane

Wind; illustrated by John Wallace. Aladdin 2004 32p il (Ready-to-read) hardcover o.p. pa $3.99

Grades: K 1 2   **551.51**

1. Winds

ISBN 0-689-85442-0; 0-689-85443-9 pa

LC 2002-9656

Illustrations and simple text explain what wind is, how it is used by plants, birds, and people, and how wind can become a storm

Cobb, Vicki

I face the wind; illustrated by Julia Gorton. HarperCollins Pubs. 2003 un il (Science play) $16.99

Grades: K 1 2   **551.51**

1. Winds 2. Science -- Experiments

ISBN 0-688-17840-5; 0-688-17841-3 lib bdg

LC 2001-26480

Introduces the characteristics and actions of the wind through simple hands-on activities

"All demonstrations . . . are conducted with readily available materials. . . . Streamlined and jargon-fee though the text may be, it gets the basics across in kid-friendly terms. . . . Gorton's strong, angular graphics feature a red-headed little gal with wide-set eyes and a powerful curiosity who alternately serves as wind-tousled subject of forces real but unseen and as demonstrator for each experiment." Bull Cent Child Books

Gallant, Roy A.

Atmosphere; sea of air. Benchmark Bks. 2002 79p il (Earthworks) lib bdg $19.95

Grades: 5 6 7 8   **551.51**

1. Atmosphere 2. Meteorology

ISBN 0-7614-1366-9

LC 2001-43301

Describes the atmosphere which makes life on earth possible, explores its effects on weather and climate, and examines what causes air pollution and what can be done it

"Gallant's prose is nearly conversational in its easy delivery, but his facts are always thorough and his ideas clearly explained. . . . Crisp graphs, maps, and excellent color photos illustrate [this] fine [volume]." Booklist

Includes glossary and bibliographical references

Kaner, Etta

Who likes the wind? written by Etta Kaner; illustrated by Marie Lafrance. Kids Can Press 2006 un il (Exploring the elements) $14.95

Grades: PreK K 1 2   **551.51**

1. Winds

ISBN 1-55337-839-3

"On each double-page spread, a child expresses why he or she likes the wind ('because it pushes my boat'). The child then wonders how the event happens ('I wonder why the wind blows') and lifts a flap for a scientific explanation. The narrative sections are illustrated in child-friendly acrylics, with the explantions set off in white. Clear diagrams supplement the scientific details." Horn Book Guide

Sayre, April Pulley

★ Stars beneath your bed; the surprising story of dust. pictures by Ann Jonas. Greenwillow Books 2005 un il $15.99; lib bdg $16.89

Grades: K 1 2 3   **551.51**

1. Dust

ISBN 0-06-057188-8; 0-06-057189-6 lib bdg

LC 2004-2108

"Dust gets a poetic treatment in a picture book that tells all about dust's what and where, and sometimes its why. Using free verse, Sayre explains how dust is made everywhere. . . . The watercolors in the well-composed two-page spreads sometimes soar . . . but there are also smaller images . . . that are equally effective." Booklist

551.55 Atmospheric disturbances and formations

Aronin, Miriam

Mangled by a hurricane! consultant, James L. Franklin. Bearport Pub. 2010 32p il map (Disaster survivors) lib bdg $25.27

Grades: 4 5 6 7   **551.55**

1. Hurricanes 2. Hurricane Katrina, 2005

ISBN 978-1-936087-49-5 lib bdg; 1-936087-49-9 lib bdg

"Captivating photos and illustrations and sidebars present interesting facts or brief anecdotes. . . . [This] should be purchased for all school and public libraries as . . . [it gives] a new perspective on the topic." Libr Media Connect

Includes glossary and bibliographical references

Bailer, Darice

Why does it thunder and lightning? Marshall Cavendish Benchmark 2011 32p il (Tell me why, tell me how) lib bdg $29.93

Grades: 2 3 4 5   **551.55**

1. Lightning 2. Thunderstorms

ISBN 978-0-7614-4825-9; 0-7614-4825-X

This offers information about thunder and lightning.

This title has "clear explanations of natural phenomena, beautiful full-color illustrations, and an uncluttered design. [The] book approaches its topic in a methodical, logical fashion, using examples from a child's world." SLJ

Branley, Franklyn Mansfield

Flash, crash, rumble, and roll; by Franklyn M. Branley; illustrated by True Kelley. newly il ed; HarperCollins Pubs. 1999 32p il (Let's-read-and-find-out science) hardcover o.p. pa $4.95

Grades: K 1 2 3   **551.55**

1. Lightning 2. Thunderstorms

ISBN 0-06-027858-7; 0-06-027859-5 lib bdg; 0-06-445179-8 pa

LC 97-43599

A revised and newly illustrated edition of the title first published 1964 by Crowell

Explains how and why a thunderstorm occurs and gives safety steps to follow when lightning is flashing

This offers "clear and informative explanations . . . [and] colorful cartoonlike pictures." Horn Book Guide

Carson, Mary Kay

★ **Inside** hurricanes. Sterling 2010 48p il map (Inside) $16.95; pa $9.95

Grades: 5 6 7 8   **551.55**

1. Hurricanes

ISBN 978-1-4027-5880-5; 1-4027-5880-4; 978-1-4027-7780-6 pa; 1-4027-7780-9 pa

"This trip into the eye of the storm is enveloping in more ways than one. . . . The pages fold up, or down, or left, or right, with every turn guided by an icon familiar to anyone who lives in a storm zone: a circular blue 'Hurricane Evacuation Route' road sign. This constant motion can't help but engage. . . . The design and layout is well above par, featuring excellent cutaways of storm systems, meteorological maps, thrilling photography, and a spectacular foldout Saffir-Simpson Hurricane Scale. The text is packed with info, data, and case studies broken into digestible chunks, and boxes and sidebars . . . make this . . . very appealing." Booklist

Demarest, Chris L.

Hurricane hunters! riders on the storm. [by] Chris L. Demarest. Margaret K. McElderry Books 2006 un il $17.95

Grades: K 1 2 3   **551.55**

1. Hurricanes 2. Weather forecasting

ISBN 978-0-689-86168-0; 0-689-86168-0

LC 2005011292

This "picture book explains the work of the large converted cargo planes that fly into hurricanes to collect weather data. . . . The pastels are particularly effective at capturing the look and feel of the powerful winds and swirling water caused by a hurricane at its height." SLJ

Includes bibliographical references

Fleisher, Paul

Lightning, hurricanes, and blizzards; the science of storms. Lerner Publications 2011 48p il (Weatherwise) lib bdg $29.27

Grades: 4 5 6 7   **551.55**

1. Blizzards 2. Lightning 3. Hurricanes

ISBN 978-0-8225-7536-8; 0-8225-7536-1

LC 2009044918

This describes how storms form, where they strike, and what makes them so powerful.

"Chapters are well-organized and contain clear explanations. The crisp layout contains plenty of captioned photos and diagrams, as well as sidebars that feature interesting facts and suggestions for observations readers can record in their backyards." Horn Book Guide

Includes glossary and bibliographical references

Fradin, Dennis Brindell

Tornado! the story behind these twisting, turning, spinning, and spiraling storms. by Judith Bloom Fradin & Dennis Brindell Fradin. National Geographic 2011 63p il map (National Geographic kids) $16.95; lib bdg $26.90

Grades: 4 5 6 7   **551.55**

1. Tornadoes

ISBN 978-1-4263-0779-9; 1-4263-0779-9; 978-1-4263-0780-5 lib bdg; 1-4263-0780-2 lib bdg

LC 2010042813

"Two of the four chapters describe deadly twisters in the U.S., while the others discuss the science and predictability of tornadoes. Throughout, there are first-person accounts. . . . Excellent color photos make this book a magnet for browsers, while the informative text and diagrams bring meaning to the images and provide content that students will find helpful for reports." Booklist

Includes glossary and bibliographical references

Fradin, Judith Bloom

★ **Hurricanes**; by Judy and Dennis Fradin. National Geographic 2007 48p il (Witness to disaster) $16.95; lib bdg $26.90

Grades: 4 5 6 7   **551.55**

1. Hurricanes

ISBN 978-1-4262-0111-0; 1-4262-0111-7; 978-1-4262-0112-7 lib bdg; 1-4262-0112-5 lib bdg

LC 2006-103003

This describes Hurricane Katrina, the science of hurricanes, some hurricanes of the past, and the prediction of hurricanes.

This offers "dramatic first-person quotes and an array of impressive photographs." Horn Book Guide

Includes glossary and bibliographical references

Gibbons, Gail

Hurricanes! Holiday House 2009 32p il $17.95

Grades: K 1 2   **551.55**

1. Hurricanes

ISBN 978-0-8234-2233-3; 0-8234-2233-X

LC 2009-8761

"Gibbons uses a picture-book format to detail [hurricanes'] destructive power without the information ever becoming too frightening. . . . Gentle watercolors are Gibbons' main weapons here, and the painted panoramas . . . are engagingly tumultuous. . . . Famous hurricanes, from Andrew to Katrina, are among the multitude of . . . topics broached in this intriguing introduction." Booklist

Tornadoes! Holiday House 2009 32p il $16.95

Grades: K 1 2 3   **551.55**

1. Tornadoes

ISBN 978-0-8234-2216-6; 0-8234-2216-X

LC 2008035828

"Gibbons uses her trademark watercolor cartoon images and simple text to introduce readers to scientific information. . . . Gibbons's style is appealing and accessible." SLJ

Godkin, Celia

Hurricane! Fitzhenry & Whiteside 2008 un il $19.95

Grades: 2 3 4   **551.55**

1. Hurricanes

ISBN 978-1-55455-080-7; 1-55455-080-7

"An attractive, simple introduction to the effects of a hurricane on humans and on wildlife. . . . Godkin's gentle illustrations—paintings in water-soluble oil on canvas and drawings in ink and watercolor on paper—add luminous grace to this simple look at the effects of violent tropical storms. Handsome and useful." SLJ

Goin, Miriam Busch

Storms. National Geographic 2009 32p il (National Geographic kids) lib bdg $11.90; pa $3.99

Grades: K 1 2 **551.55**
1. Storms
ISBN 978-1-4263-0395-1 lib bdg; 978-1-4263-0394-4 pa
LC 2008-51883

"Blizzards, monsoons, hurricanes: the excitement of wild, stormy weather will draw beginning readers to this dramatic title with color photos and an interactive text." Booklist

Harris, Caroline
Wild weather. Kingfisher 2005 53p il map (Kingfisher voyages) $14.95
Grades: 4 5 6 7 **551.55**
1. Storms 2. Weather
ISBN 0-7534-5931-0; 978-0-7534-5911-9

This describes weather phenomena such as monsoons, tsunamis, blizzards, tornadoes, cyclones, mirages, and El Niño.

This "book has bright and exciting pictures. . . . The organization . . . is great, and the text is easy to read." Sci Books Films

Includes glossary

Markovics, Joyce L.
Blitzed by a blizzard! by Joyce Markovics; consultant, Daphne Thompson. Bearport Pub. 2010 32p il map (Disaster survivors) lib bdg $25.27
Grades: 4 5 6 7 **551.55**
1. Blizzards
ISBN 978-1-936087-54-9 lib bdg; 1-936087-54-5 lib bdg
LC 2009-36960

"Captivating photos and illustrations and sidebars present interesting facts or brief anecdotes. . . . [This] should be purchased for all school and public libraries as . . . [it gives] a new perspective on the topic." Libr Media Connect

Includes glossary and bibliographical references

Royston, Angela
Hurricanes! Marshall Cavendish Benchmark 2010 32p il map (Eyewitness disaster) lib bdg $28.50
Grades: 4 5 6 **551.55**
1. Hurricanes
ISBN 978-1-60870-003-5; 1-60870-003-8
LC 2010001800

Provides information about hurricanes through eyewitness accounts from survivors and rescue workers.

"Bold subheadings and color captions break information into readable chunks for the younger learner. Important vocabulary is in bold print. . . . An excellent addition to your science collection." Libr Media Connect

Includes glossary and bibliographical references

Storms! Marshall Cavendish Benchmark 2010 32p il map (Eyewitness disaster) lib bdg $28.50
Grades: 4 5 6 **551.55**
1. Storms
ISBN 978-1-60870-004-2; 1-60870-004-6
LC 2009041697

Provides information about storms through eyewitness accounts from survivors and rescue workers.

"Bold subheadings and color captions break information into readable chunks for the younger learner. Important vo-

cabulary is in bold print. . . . An excellent addition to your science collection." Libr Media Connect

Includes glossary and bibliographical references

Rudolph, Jessica
Erased by a tornado! Bearport Pub. 2010 32p il map (Disaster survivors) lib bdg $25.27
Grades: 4 5 6 7 **551.55**
1. Tornadoes
ISBN 978-1-936087-52-5 lib bdg; 1-936087-52-9 lib bdg
LC 2009-34363

"Captivating photos and illustrations and sidebars present interesting facts or brief anecdotes. . . . [This] should be purchased for all school and public libraries as . . . [it gives] a new perspective on the topic." Libr Media Connect

Includes glossary and bibliographical references

Schuh, Mari C.
Tornadoes. Pebble Plus 2010 24p il map (Earth in action) lib bdg $21.32
Grades: K 1 2 **551.55**
1. Tornadoes
ISBN 978-1-4296-3434-2 lib bdg; 1-4296-3434-0 lib bdg
LC 2009-2174

This book "boasts a full-page color photograph. . . . [It shows] the aftermath of a disaster . . . but there are also some diagrams showing physical mechanisms and maps highlighting commonly affected places. The left side of each spread provides a few sentences of large-print text, with short, clear explanations." SLJ

Includes glossary and bibliographical references

Shores, Lori
How to build a tornado in a bottle. Capstone Press 2011 24p il (Hands-on science fun) lib bdg $17.99; pa $6.95
Grades: PreK K 1 **551.55**
1. Tornadoes 2. Science -- Experiments
ISBN 978-1-4296-4493-8 lib bdg; 1-4296-4493-1 lib bdg; 978-1-4296-5577-4 pa; 1-4296-5577-1 pa
LC 2010013585

Simple text and full-color photos instruct readers how to build a tornado in a bottle and explain the science behind the activity.

"Bright, glossy photos and irresistible ideas make these science lessons effortless fun." Booklist

Includes bibliographical references

Silverstein, Alvin
Hurricanes; the science behind killer storms. [by] Alvin Silverstein, Virginia Silverstein, and Laura Silverstein Nunn. Enslow Publishers 2009 48p il map (The science behind natural disasters) lib bdg $23.93
Grades: 4 5 6 **551.55**
1. Hurricanes
ISBN 978-0-7660-2971-2 lib bdg; 0-7660-2971-9 lib bdg
LC 2008-26264

"Examines the science behind hurricanes, including how and where tropical storms form, the various types of tropical storms, how scientists track hurricanes, and provides hurricane safety tips." Publisher's note

Includes glossary and bibliographical references

Tornadoes; the science behind terrible twisters. [by] Alvin Silverstein, Virginia Silverstein, and Laura Silverstein Nunn. Enslow Publishers 2009 48p il map (The science behind natural disasters) lib bdg $23.93

Grades: 4 5 6   **551.55**

1. Tornadoes

ISBN 978-0-7660-2976-7 lib bdg; 0-7660-2976-X lib bdg

LC 2008-29635

"Scientific explanations are accompanied by plentiful color diagrams that will help students to grasp causes and effects. . . . Photos . . . are effective, and are sometimes turned into helpful, lively diagrams by the addition of such features as wind-direction arrows." SLJ

Includes glossary and bibliographical references

Simon, Seymour

★ **Hurricanes**; updated ed; Collins 2007 31p il map $16.99; pa $6.99

Grades: 3 4 5 6   **551.55**

1. Hurricanes

ISBN 978-0-06-117072-0; 0-06-117072-0; 978-0-06-117071-3 pa; 0-06-117071-2 pa

LC 2007-280766

First published 2003

Discusses where and how hurricanes are formed, the destruction caused by legendary storms, and the precautions to take when a hurricane strikes

This is written "in a simple and precise manner. . . . The photos include computer-enhanced radar images and shots of storm damage from recent (Katrina in 2005) and historical (Glaveston in 1900) times." Sci Books Films

Includes bibliographical references

Storms. Morrow Junior Bks. 1989 un il hardcover o.p. pa $5.95

Grades: 4 5 6 7   **551.55**

1. Storms

ISBN 0-688-11708-2 pa

LC 88-22045

This book describes the atmospheric conditions which create thunderstorms, hailstorms, lightning, tornadoes, and hurricanes and how violent weather affects the environment and people

"The half- to full-page glossy color photographs are sure to attract young readers as will the subject. Storms is an excellent way to introduce the science of meteorology to children." Sci Books Films

★ **Tornadoes**. Morrow Junior Bks. 1999 un il map hardcover o.p. pa $6.99

Grades: 4 5 6 7   **551.55**

1. Tornadoes

ISBN 0-688-14646-5; 0-06-443791-4 pa

LC 98-27953

Describes the location, nature, development, measurement, and destructive effects of tornadoes, as well as how to stay out of danger from them

"Incredible full-color photographs and diagrams, clearly portraying the different formations and devastating power of the windstorms, complement the text perfectly." Booklist

Spilsbury, Louise

Howling hurricanes; [by] Louise and Richard Spilsbury. rev ed.; Heinemann Library 2010 32p il map (Awesome forces of nature) lib bdg $29; pa $7.99

Grades: 3 4 5 6   **551.55**

1. Hurricanes

ISBN 978-1-4329-3781-2 lib bdg; 1-4329-3781-2 lib bdg; 978-1-4329-3788-1 pa; 1-4329-3788-X pa

LC 2009037483

First published 2004

This book about hurricanes discusses "causes, characteristics, and relevant science, including progress in predicting the events. Case studies illustrate the human response. Numerous color photographs and sidebars are interwoven into the well-organized and absorbing [narrative]." SLJ

Includes glossary and bibliographical references

Terrifying tornadoes; [by] Louise and Richard Spilsbury. Heinemann Library 2010 32p il map (Awesome forces of nature) lib bdg $29; pa $7.99

Grades: 3 4 5 6   **551.55**

1. Tornadoes

ISBN 978-1-4329-3786-7 lib bdg; 1-4329-3786-3 lib bdg; 978-1-4329-3793-5 pa; 1-4329-3793-6 pa

LC 2009-37459

First published 2004

This book about tornadoes "is sure to catch the eyes of students and educators. . . . The interesting and accurate facts are presented in an easily understood vocabulary. . . . Incredible eye-catching photographs, diagrams, or maps are tastefully positioned on every page." Libr Media Connect

Includes glossary and bibliographical references

Stewart, Mark

Blizzards and winter storms. Gareth Stevens Pub. 2009 48p il map (The ultimate 10. Natural disasters) lib bdg $31

Grades: 5 6 7 8   **551.55**

1. Storms 2. Blizzards

ISBN 978-0-8368-9150-8 lib bdg; 0-8368-9150-3 lib bdg

LC 2008-28230

Blizzards and winter storms "are described, while color photos illustrate the resulting damage, conveying a significant part of the information through their captions. . . . An especially useful book." SLJ

Includes glossary and bibliographical references

551.56 Atmospheric electricity and optics

Kramer, Stephen

Lightning; photographs by Warren Faidley. Carolrhoda Bks. 1992 48p il (Nature in action) hardcover o.p. pa $7.95

Grades: 4 5 6   **551.56**

1. Lightning

ISBN 0-87614-659-0; 0-87614-617-5 pa

LC 91-21793

"Diagrams supplement the well-written narrative in describing scientific concepts. Exceptionally fine, full-color photographs—each a work of art—perfectly illustrate the text, powerfully and spectacularly showing the majesty and might of this phenomenon." SLJ

Includes glossary

Person, Stephen

Struck by lightning! Bearport Pub. 2010 32p il map (Disaster survivors) lib bdg $25.27

Grades: 4 5 6 7   **551.56**

1. Lightning

ISBN 978-1-936087-47-1 lib bdg; 1-936087-47-2 lib bdg

"Captivating photos and illustrations and sidebars present interesting facts or brief anecdotes. . . . [This] should be purchased for all school and public libraries as . . . [it gives] a new perspective on the topic." Libr Media Connect

Includes glossary and bibliographical references

Simon, Seymour

Lightning. Morrow Junior Bks. 1997 un il hardcover o.p. pa $6.99

Grades: 4 5 6 7   **551.56**

1. Lightning

ISBN 0-688-14638-4; 0-06-088435-5 pa

LC 96-16962

Photographs and text explore the natural phenomenon of lightning

"The subject is exciting, the information is amazing, and the full-color photographs are riveting. . . . Simon's explanations are concise but thorough." Booklist

Stewart, Melissa

★ **Inside** lightning; illustrations by Cynthia Shaw. Sterling 2011 48p il (Inside . . .) $16.95

Grades: 5 6 7 8   **551.56**

1. Lightning

ISBN 978-1-4027-5878-2; 1-4027-5878-2

This book about lightning "explores its topic in an engaging way, and the many illustrations work well with adjacent text and captions. . . . The [book's] varied page layouts and attractive and the quality of photos, computer-generated images, original illustrations, and charts is . . . excellent. . . . Featuring a step-by-step, illustrated explanation of lightning formation as well as comments from people who have had close encounters with the phenomenon, Inside Lightning provides a vivid and unusually informative introduction to the subject." Booklist

Includes bibliographical references

551.57 Hydrometeorology

Branley, Franklyn Mansfield

Down comes the rain; by Franklyn M. Branley; illustrated by James Graham Hale. HarperCollins Pubs. 1997 31p il (Let's-read-and-find-out science) hardcover o.p. pa $4.95

Grades: K 1 2 3   **551.57**

1. Rain 2. Clouds

ISBN 0-06-025338-X; 0-06-445166-6 pa

LC 96-3519

A revised and newly illustrated edition of Rain & hail published 1983 by Crowell

The author explains "how water is recycled, how clouds are formed, and why rain and hail occur. A few easy science activities are included. . . . The pen-and-ink with watercolor wash paintings clearly interpret the concepts presented on each page." SLJ

Snow is falling; by Franklyn M. Branley; illustrated by Holly Keller. HarperCollins Pubs. 2000 33p il (Let's-read-and-find-out science) hardcover o.p. pa $4.95

Grades: K 1   **551.57**

1. Snow

ISBN 0-06-027990-7; 0-06-027991-5 lib bdg; 0-06-445186-0 pa

LC 98-23106

A revised and newly illustrated edition of the title first published 1963 by Crowell

Describes snow's physical qualities and how quantities of it can be fun as well as dangerous

"Keller's new illustrations are a good match for the spare, informative text. A few easy activities explore snow's different properties, and a list of websites is appended." Horn Book Guide

Cassino, Mark

★ The **story** of snow; the science of winter's wonder. by Mark Cassino, with Jon Nelson; illustrations by Nora Aoyagi. Chronicle Books 2009 33p il $16.99

Grades: 2 3 4 5   **551.57**

1. Snow

ISBN 978-0-8118-6866-2; 0-8118-6866-4

LC 2009-04368

"Aoyagi's clean ink-and-watercolor diagrams and backgrounds allow the spectacular photographs to take center stage and provide supplemental information. Sure to get young scientists outside in the cold, particularly as it helpfully includes crystal-catching instructions." Kirkus

DePaola, Tomie, 1934-

The **cloud** book; words and pictures by Tomie de Paola. Holiday House 1975 30p il lib bdg $16.95; pa $6.95

Grades: K 1 2 3   **551.57**

1. Clouds

ISBN 0-8234-0259-2 lib bdg; 0-8234-0531-1 pa

The author instructs "young readers about the ten most common types of clouds, how they were named, and what they mean in terms of changing weather. Actually a very good text to use for early science instruction. Includes a scattering of traditional myths that have clouds as a basis." Adventuring with Books

Ehlert, Lois

★ **Snowballs**. Harcourt Brace & Co. 1995 un il $17; pa $7; bd bk $6.95

Grades: PreK K 1   **551.57**

1. Snow -- Fiction

ISBN 0-15-200074-7; 0-15-202095-0 pa; 0-15-216275-5 bd bk

LC 94-47183

"Using 'good stuff' like seeds, nuts, corn kernels, and colorful yarn kids create a wonderful snow family. Placed on vertical page spreads, the snow characters extend the full length of the book, a perspective that enhances the drama of their inevitable demise when the sun comes out. Large, well-designed illustrations effectively blend open space, colorful paper cutouts, and real objects." Horn Book Guide

Gibbons, Gail

It's snowing! Holiday House 2011 32p il $17.95

Grades: K 1 2 3   551.57

1. Snow

ISBN 978-0-8234-2237-1

LC 2010029570

Introduces snow, discussing how snowflakes are formed, what causes it to snow, where snow occurs around the world, different types of snowstorms, and what to do during a heavy winter storm.

"This is a crystal-clear introduction that illustrates how snow can be dangerous, but plenty of fun, too." Booklist

Kaner, Etta

Who likes the rain? written by Etta kaner; illustrated by Marie Lafrance. Kids Can Press 2007 un il (Exploring the elements) $14.95

Grades: PreK K 1 2   551.57

1. Rain

ISBN 978-1-55337-841-9; 1-55337-841-5

On each double-page spead, a child expresses why he or she likes the rain ("because I can jump in puddles"). The child then wonders how the event happens ("I wonder where puddles come from") and lifts a flap for a scientific explanation

"An attractive, straight-forward presentation of concepts related to rain." Booklist

Who likes the snow? written by Etta Kaner; illustrated by Marie Lafrance. Kids Can Press 2006 un il (Exploring the elements) $14.95

Grades: PreK K 1 2   551.57

1. Snow

ISBN 978-1-55337-842-6; 1-55337-842-3

"This slim book is packed with fascinating information about snow. Each spread is divided into three parts: a statement, a query, and, with the turn of a flap, a simply stated scientific explanation.... Lafrance's naive acrylic paintings have a flat appearance, as if they were carved of wood, and clearly depict the topics being discussed." SLJ

Libbrecht, Kenneth G.

The secret life of a snowflake; an up-close look at the art & science of snowflakes. [by] Kenneth Libbrecht. Voyageur Press 2010 48p il $17

Grades: 3 4 5 6   551.57

1. Snow

ISBN 978-0-7603-3676-2; 0-7603-3676-8

LC 2009-07892

"Extraordinary photographs of individual snowflakes are the true highlight of this informational book. With crisp detail and lit up with colored light, the crystals are mesmerizing in their clarity and brilliance. Libbrecht uses a first-person narration to describe the microphotography process that he uses to create the images and then goes on to outline the life cycle of a snowflake.... A solid addition to any science collection, this book will draw in young enthusiasts, and the beautiful photographs will engage casual browsers." SLJ

Marsico, Katie

Snowy weather days; [by] Katie Marsico. Children's Press 2007 24p il (Scholastic news nonfiction readers) lib bdg $19

Grades: K 1 2 3   551.57

1. Snow

ISBN 978-0-531-16773-1 lib bdg; 0-531-16773-9 lib bdg

LC 2006013306

Simple facts about snow.

"Young readers will take pleasure in learning simple facts while discovering new words along the way.... These full-color pictures show the featured conditions, as well as a variety of outdoor scenes of children and adults enjoying nature." SLJ

Includes glossary and bibliographical references

Martin, Jacqueline Briggs

★ Snowflake Bentley; illustrated by Mary Azarian. Houghton Mifflin 1998 un il $16; pa $7.99

Grades: K 1 2 3   551.57

1. Snow 2. Farmers 3. Scientists 4. Photographers 5. Meteorologists

ISBN 0-395-86162-4; 0-547-24829-6 pa

LC 97-12458

Awarded the Caldecott Medal, 1999

A biography of a self-taught scientist who photographed thousands of individual snowflakes in order to study their unique formations

"Azarian's woodblock illustrations, hand tinted with watercolors, blend perfectly with the text and recall the rural Vermont of Bentley's time.... The story of this man's life is written with graceful simplicity." SLJ

Rockwell, Anne F.

Clouds; by Anne Rockwell; illustrated by Frané Lessac. Collins 2008 33p il (Let's-read-and-find-out-science) $16.99; pa $5.99

Grades: 1 2 3   551.57

1. Clouds

ISBN 978-0-06-029101-3; 0-06-029101-X; 978-0-06-445220-5 pa; 0-06-445220-4 pa

"Rockwell introduces 11 different types of clouds according to their positions in the atmosphere.... The author describes each type of cloud formation, explains where it is found in the sky, and tells what kind of weather is associated with it. Attractive folk-art-style paintings show the clouds and children playing or working outside. The information is solid." SLJ

Schuh, Mari C.

Avalanches. Pebble Plus 2010 24p il (Earth in action) lib bdg $21.32

Grades: K 1 2   551.57

1. Avalanches

ISBN 978-1-4296-3437-3 lib bdg; 1-4296-3437-5 lib bdg

LC 2009-2163

Describes avalanches, how they occur, and the damage they cause

This book "boasts a full-page color photograph.... [It shows] the aftermath of a disaster ... but there are also some diagrams showing physical mechanisms and maps highlighting commonly affected places. The left side of each spread provides a few sentences of large-print text, with short, clear explanations." SLJ

Includes glossary and bibliographical references

551.6 Climatology and weather

Aitken, Stephen

Ecosystems at risk; Stephen Aitken. Marshall Cavendish Benchmark 2013 63 p. (Climate crisis) (print) $31.36
Grades: 4 5 6 7   **551.6**
1. Ecology 2. Climate change 3. Biodiversity conservation 4. Climatic changes 5. Climatic changes -- Environmental aspects
ISBN 1608704637; 9781608704637; 9781608706341
LC 2011025243

In this book, by Stephen Aitken, "readers are introduced to topics relating to climatology, thermal expansion, and biodiversity. . . . The case studies . . . provide a global perspective on the ecological concepts being presented. In addition, teachers may find the book helpful in meeting several Common Core literacy standards. . . .The book concludes with . . . ways that individuals can take action to prevent species extinctions, followed by a glossary of conservation-related terms." (Science & Children)

"These sobering overviews present current observable results of climate change and offer scientific predictions about its future effects on the Earth's ecosystems and inhabitants...Suggested websites from educational and action-oriented organizations offer more options. These books should be considered to update collections on this important topic." SLJ

Includes bibliographical references and index
Other titles include:
Animal Life
People
Ocean Life
Plants and Insects

Bailey, Gerry

Changing climate. Gareth Stevens Pub. 2011 48p il map (Planet SOS) lib bdg $31.95; pa $14.05
Grades: 4 5 6   **551.6**
1. Climate -- Environmental aspects
ISBN 978-1-4339-4962-3 lib bdg; 1-4339-4962-8 lib bdg; 978-1-4339-4963-0 pa; 1-4339-4963-6 pa
LC 2010032885

This "well-designed [book presents changing climate] . . . and how [it affects] human beings. With information about water supplies and melting ice and their impact on ecosystems, the discussion . . . of global water levels is especially enlightening. . . . The many large, colorful photos will engage readers and assist them in understanding the important concepts introduced." SLJ

Includes glossary

Baker, Stuart

In temperate zones. Marshall Cavendish Benchmark 2009 32p il map (Climate change) lib bdg $19.95

Grades: 5 6 7 8   **551.6**
1. Forest ecology 2. Greenhouse effect
ISBN 978-0-7614-4441-1 lib bdg; 0-7614-4441-6 lib bdg
LC 2009-5769

The book about climate change in the temperate zones "is perfectly organized for students. . . . Unique layout features serve as signposts and will help focus readers' attention. . . . [The book] features an outstanding chart of possible effects of global warming on the area in question, listing 'Possible Event', 'Predicted Result', and 'Impact' in short, bulleted statements." SLJ

Includes glossary

Evans, Bill

It's raining fish and spiders; by Bill Evans. Forge 2012 xiv, 223 p.p col. ill. (paperback) $18.99
Grades: 5 6 7 8   **551.6**
1. Extreme weather 2. Weather forecasting
ISBN 0765321327; 9780765321329
LC 2011278417

This book offers "information, lists, and accounts of personal experiences involving extreme weather by meteorologist and TV personality [Bill] Evans. Included are sections on tornadoes, hurricanes, and blizzards, with a good amount of information on each and . . . photos and diagrams sprinkled throughout." (Booklist)

Includes bibliographical references (p.221-222)

Gibbons, Gail

Weather words and what they mean. Holiday House 1990 un il $16.95; pa $6.95
Grades: K 1 2 3   **551.6**
1. Weather
ISBN 0-8234-0805-1; 0-8234-0952-X pa
LC 89-39515

The author discusses the meaning of meteorological terms such as temperature, air pressure, thunderstorm and moisture

"Gibbons' easily identifiable artistic style works well with her explanations of sometimes misunderstood weather-related terms. Drawings are appealing, attractively arranged, and closely matched to the textual information. . . . An attractive introduction for weather units in the primary grades." SLJ

Hartman, Eve

Climate change; [by] Eve Hartman and Wendy Meshbesher. Raintree 2010 48p il map (Sci-hi: Earth and space science) lib bdg $31.43; pa $8.99
Grades: 4 5 6 7   **551.6**
1. Greenhouse effect 2. Climate -- Environmental aspects
ISBN 978-1-4109-3352-2 lib bdg; 1-4109-3352-0 lib bdg; 978-1-4109-3362-1 pa; 1-4109-3362-8 pa
LC 2009-3538

Examine the causes of climate change, and how scientists gather data about global warming. Learn about the different ways people and nations are combating climate change, and how people and animals adapt to a new climate.

"Multiple colorful sidebars and large and small diagrams and photographs will help students to grasp the fundamentals being discussed, and the easy but interesting science experiments will act as further reinforcements." SLJ

Includes glossary and bibliographical references

Parker, Steve, 1952-

Climate. QEB Pub. 2010 32p il (QEB changes in . . .) lib bdg $28.50

Grades: 3 4 5 6   **551.6**

1. Climate

ISBN 978-1-59566-776-2 lib bdg; 1-59566-776-8 lib bdg

LC 2008-56068

"The information is presented in brief paragraphs and sidebars. Suggestions for kids to help improve the planet are sprinkled throughout. . . . Students will enjoy this appealing layout and the information can spark further research on the topic[s]. . . . Either digitally or on paper, students could make fantastic presentations using a similar design." Libr Media Connect

Includes glossary

Royston, Angela

Looking at weather and seasons; how do they change? [by] Angela Royston. Enslow Publishers 2008 32p il (Looking at science: how things change) lib bdg $22.60

Grades: 1 2 3   **551.6**

1. Seasons 2. Weather

ISBN 978-0-7660-3093-0 lib bdg; 0-7660-3093-8 lib bdg

LC 2007-24515

"Fills a huge void in elementary science collections. . . . Text is arranged in succinct 'chunks,' giving important facts without overwhelming readers. . . . [This] is an essential addition." Libr Media Connect

Includes glossary and bibliographical references

Rupp, Rebecca

Weather; with journal illustrations by Melissa Sweet and experiment illustrations by Dug Nap. Storey Kids 2003 136p il map hardcover o.p. pa $14.95

Grades: 4 5 6 7   **551.6**

1. Weather

ISBN 1-58017-469-8; 1-58017-420-5 pa

LC 2002-152310

This includes facts about weather with instructions for 22 science projects

"A lively, upbeat presentation. Chock-full of solid information, this compendium includes lots of slightly offbeat, appealing observations. . . . Numerous, attention-grabbing visuals illustrate experiments." SLJ

Includes glossary

Simpson, Kathleen

★ **Extreme** weather; science tackles global warming and climate change. by Kathleen Simpson; Jonathan D.W. Kahl, consultant. National Geographic 2008 64p il map (National Geographic investigates) $17.95; lib bdg $27.90

Grades: 4 5 6 7   **551.6**

1. Greenhouse effect 2. Climate -- Environmental aspects

ISBN 978-1-4263-0359-3; 1-4263-0359-9; 978-1-4263-0281-7 lib bdg; 1-4263-0281-9 lib bdg

This "is a well-written and engaging book. . . . Excellent descriptions of how and why these various weather patterns

occur are presented. The book includes dramatic photographs and clear diagrams." Sci Books Films

Includes glossary and bibliographical references

551.609   History, geographic treatment, biography

Christie, Peter

50 climate questions; a blizzard of blistering facts. Peter Christie; illustrated by Ross Kinnaird. Annick Press 2012 117 p. ill. (50 Questions) (paperback) $14.95; (hardcover) $22.95; (ebook) $10.99

Grades: 4 5 6 7   **551.609**

1. Climate 2. Climate change 3. Climate -- History

ISBN 155451374X; 9781554513741; 9781554513758; 9781554515165

This book by Peter Christie presents a "survey of the effects of climate through history and prehistory." (Kirkus Reviews) "Topics include global warming's effect on the Arctic . . . and how a cooling climate 2.5 million years ago forced early humans to diversify their diets. Christie also provides insight into weather events throughout history -- for example, how weather change contributed to civil unrest that spawned the French Revolution." (Publishers Weekly)

551.63   Weather forecasting and forecasts, reporting and reports

Breen, Mark

★ The **kids'** book of weather forecasting; build a weather station, read the sky & make predictions. with meteorologist Mark Breen and Kathleen Friestad; illustrations by Michael Kline. Williamson 2000 140p il maps music pa $12.95

Grades: 4 5 6 7   **551.63**

1. Weather forecasting 2. Science -- Experiments

ISBN 1-88559-339-2

LC 99-89954

A hands-on introduction to the science of meteorology, explaining how to make equipment to measure rainfall, wind direction, and humidity, record measurements and observations in a weather log, make weather predictions, and perform other related activities

"A useful, accessible book illustrated with black-and-white diagrams and cartoons." SLJ

Includes bibliographical references

Fleisher, Paul

Doppler radar, satellites, and computer models; the science of weather forecasting. Lerner Publications 2010 48p il map (Weatherwise) lib bdg $29.27

Grades: 4 5 6   **551.63**

1. Weather forecasting

ISBN 978-0-8225-7535-1; 0-8225-7535-3

LC 2009-44919

This describes how scientists predict the weather, the tools and instruments that help them make forecasts, and how far in advance can they make good predictions.

"Chapters are well-organized and contain clear explanations. The crisp layout contains plenty of captioned photos and diagrams, as well as sidebars that feature interesting facts and suggestions for observations readers can record in their backyards." Horn Book Guide

Includes glossary and bibliographical references

Gibbons, Gail

Weather forecasting. Four Winds Press 1987 un il hardcover o.p. pa $5.99
Grades: K 1 2 3   **551.63**
1. Weather forecasting
ISBN 0-689-71683-4 pa
LC 86-7602

"Any child can learn the basic concepts from the text at the bottom of each page, while the precocious can garner an impressive weather vocabulary by absorbing the terms labeled and defined within the artwork. Brightly illustrated with the artist's usual bold, flat colors, this book will serve as an appealing introduction to weather forecasting for young children." Booklist

552 Petrology

Aston, Dianna Hutts

A **rock** is lively; Dianna Hutts Aston, Sylvia Long. Chronicle Books 2012 40 p. (alk. paper) $16.99
Grades: 3 4 5 6   **552**
1. Rocks 2. Minerals
ISBN 1452106452; 9781452106458
LC 2011048375

This book by Dianna Hutts Aston explores "seemingly sedentary world of rocks and minerals, showing them to be anything but (when you know your geology). Boiling underground, freezing in space, colorful or drab, enormous or minuscule, health food (grits for gizzards), tools for prehistoric man and modern chimps, canvas for paleolithic art or construction material for the Taj Mahal -- rocks get around." (School Library Journal)

Davis, Barbara J.

Minerals, rocks, and soil. Raintree 2010 48p il map (Sci-hi: Earth and space science) lib bdg $31.43; pa $8.99
Grades: 4 5 6 7   **552**
1. Rocks 2. Minerals 3. Petrology
ISBN 978-1-4109-3347-8 lib bdg; 1-4109-3347-4 lib bdg; 978-1-4109-3357-7 pa; 1-4109-3357-1 pa
LC 2009-13459

"Multiple colorful sidebars and large and small diagrams and photographs will help students to grasp the fundamentals being discussed, and the easy but interesting science experiments will act as further reinforcements." SLJ

Includes glossary and bibliographical references

Faulkner, Rebecca

Igneous rock; [by] Rebecca Faulkner. Raintree 2007 48p il (Geology rocks!) lib bdg $31.43; pa $8.99
Grades: 4 5 6   **552**
1. Rocks
ISBN 978-1-4109-2747-7 lib bdg; 1-4109-2747-4 lib bdg; 978-1-4109-2755-2 pa; 1-4109-2755-5 pa
LC 2006037174

This "describes all three categories of rocks and what distinguishes them from each other, minerals, identification of igneous rocks, and their formation through volcanic activ-

ity. . . . [The book] includes quality color photographs and diagrams that do an exemplary job of expanding on the topics covered." SLJ

Includes glossary and bibliographical references

Metamorphic rock. Raintree 2007 48p il (Geology rocks!) lib bdg $31.43; pa $8.99
Grades: 4 5 6   **552**
1. Rocks
ISBN 978-1-4109-2749-1 lib bdg; 1-4109-2749-0 lib bdg; 978-1-4109-2757-6 pa; 1-4109-2757-1 pa
LC 2006037063

"This title covers the following: Squeeze and heat; Crust, mantle, and core; The world's rocks; Marvelous Metamorphism; Metamorphic rock types; Hard beauty; Metamorphic landforms." Publisher's note

Includes glossary and bibliographical references

Sedimentary rock; [by] Rebecca Faulkner. Raintree 2007 48p il (Geology rocks!) lib bdg $31.43; pa $8.99
Grades: 4 5 6   **552**
1. Rocks
ISBN 978-1-4109-2748-4 lib bdg; 1-4109-2748-2 lib bdg; 978-1-4109-2756-9 pa; 1-4109-2756-3 pa
LC 2006037173

This "covers the Earth's structure, how these rocks are formed, fossils, and the various types. [The] book includes quality color photographs and diagrams that do an exemplary job of expanding on the topics covered." SLJ

Includes glossary and bibliographical references

Gans, Roma

Let's go rock collecting; illustrated by Holly Keller. newly il ed; HarperCollins Pubs. 1997 31p il (Let's-read-and-find-out science) hardcover o.p. pa $5.99
Grades: K 1 2   **552**
1. Rocks -- Collectors and collecting
ISBN 0-06-027282-1; 0-06-027283-X lib bdg; 0-06-027283-X pa
LC 95-44999

A revised and newly illustrated edition of Rock collecting, published 1984 by Crowell

Describes the formation and characteristics of igneous, metamorphic, and sedimentary rocks and how to recognize and collect them

"The excellent diagrams, full-color photographs of specimens, and minor textual changes clarify the concepts (for example, Mohs' scale of hardness) and extend the presentation. . . . The pair of youngsters featured in Keller's brightly colored illustrations . . . convey the joys of being a rock hound." SLJ

Green, Dan

Rocks and minerals; a gem of a read! by Dan Green and Simon Basher; illustrated by Simon Basher. Kingfisher 2009 128p il pa $8.99
Grades: 5 6 7 8   **552**
1. Rocks 2. Minerals
ISBN 978-0-7534-6314-7 pa; 0-7534-6314-8 pa

This "presents a portrait gallery of 56 rocks and minerals (plus four kinds of fossils) composed of smiling, round-headed, usually peanut-shaped cartoon figures wearing or bearing distinctive identifiers. . . . The entries make light-hearted but unexpectedly meaty reading." Booklist

Rocks and minerals; facts at your fingertips. DK Pub. 2012
156 p. col. ill., map (Pocket genius) (hardcover) $7.99
Grades: 5 6 7 8 **552**
1. Rocks 2. Minerals
ISBN 0756692857; 9780756692858
LC 2011277725
This book, part of the "Pocket Genius" encyclopedia series, "profiles nearly 200 types of rocks and minerals from
volcanic rocks and granite to sparkling diamonds and explosive sulfur, and tells what they are made of, how they are
formed and what they are used for." It "offers a . . . catalog-
style presentation, which clearly lays out individual subcategories." (Publisher's note)

Salas, Laura Purdie
A **rock** can be . . . by Laura Purdie Salas; illustrated by
Violeta Dabija. Millbrook Press 2015 32 p. color illustra-
tions (lib. bdg) $17.99
Grades: PreK K 1 2 3 **552**
1. Rocks 2. Stories in rhyme
ISBN 1467721107; 9781467721103
LC 2014009377
"Laura Purdie Salas's lyrical rhyming text and Violeta
Dabija's . . . illustrations show how rocks decorate and
strengthen the world around them. Rocks may seem like boring, static objects--until you discover that a rock can spark a
fire, glow in the dark, and provide shelters of all shapes and
sizes." (Publisher's note)
"The ideas expressed in this picture book's pithy text
are varied and wide-ranging. Each two-word phrase appears
on its own page, accompanied by a luminous illustration. .
. . The sometimes cryptic phrases create a natural guessing
game, and an appended section offers a paragraph of text
explaining each one." Booklist

Smithsonian Institution
Extreme rocks & minerals! Q & A. Collins 2007 47p
il $17.99; pa $6.99
Grades: 4 5 6 **552**
1. Rocks 2. Minerals
ISBN 978-0-06-089982-0; 0-06-089982-4; 978-0-06-
089981-3 pa; 0-06-089981-6 pa
LC 2007001760
This describes types of rocks and minerals, how they are
formed, and how people use them.
"It's hard to beat this title for a clear, accurate, and ap-
pealing survey. Illustrations are key to this subject, and the
range of crisp photos is excellent." SLJ
Includes bibliographical references

Symes, R. F.
Rocks & minerals; written by R.F. Symes and the staff
of the Natural History Museum, London; special photography by Colin Keates and Andreas Einsiedel. Revised ed.
DK Pub. 2008 72 p. ill. (some col.) (hardcover: boxed;
package) $29.99; (hardcover) $16.99
Grades: 5 6 7 8 **552**
1. Gems 2. Rocks 3. Geology
ISBN 9780756631321 out of print; 0756637775;
9780756637774
LC 2009499083
This book is a guide to "rocks, fossils, minerals, precious
metals, crystals, jewels and gemstones." Readers "see rocks
that have come from outer space, stalactites as old as dino-

saurs, the strange and beautiful shapes of natural crystals and
priceless nuggets of gold, silver and platinum. Learn what
the Earth is made of and how its rocks were formed, how
early humans made the first flint tools and how diamonds
and precious stones are cut, polished, and made into jewelry." (Publisher's note)

Tomecek, Steve
Everything rocks and minerals. National Geographic
2011 64p il (National Geographic kids) lib bdg $25.90;
pa $12.95
Grades: 3 4 5 6 **552**
1. Rocks 2. Minerals
ISBN 978-1-4263-0801-7 lib bdg; 1-4263-0801-9 lib
bdg; 978-1-4263-0768-3 pa; 1-4263-0768-3 pa
LC 2010038112
A book about rocks and minerals.
"Exploding with astounding full-color photographs and
written in an appealing conversational tone, [this book is]
for every kid. . . . The [text] will keep kids interested and
turning pages to discover more and more facts. . . . [This]
compelling, browseable, and completely engrossing [title]
will delight readers." SLJ
Includes glossary and bibliographical references

Rocks & minerals; illustrated by Kyle Poling. National
Geographic 2010 32p il (Jump into science) $16.95; lib
bdg $25.90
Grades: 1 2 3 **552**
1. Rocks 2. Minerals
ISBN 978-1-4263-0538-2; 1-4263-0538-9; 978-1-
4263-0539-9 lib bdg; 1-4263-0539-7 lib bdg
LC 2010-07145
"Playful and interactive, this picture-book title . . . makes
geology accessible with colorful diagrams, photos, and computer graphics. The spreads discuss how the three main types
of rock are formed, as well as facts about fossils and the
more than 2,500 different minerals on the planet. The visuals
will capture kids." Booklist

VanCleave, Janice Pratt, 1942-
Janice VanCleave's rocks and minerals; mind-boggling
experiments you can turn into science fair projects. Wiley
1996 90p il (Spectacular science projects series) pa $10.95
Grades: 4 5 6 7 **552**
1. Rocks 2. Minerals 3. Science projects 4. Science
-- Experiments
ISBN 0-471-10269-5
LC 95-10324
"VanCleave presents stunningly clear, direct, and infor-
mative projects. They are generally simple enough for self-
directed students to do on their own, but a teacher's guid-
ance would be helpful." SLJ
Includes glossary

553.2 Carbonaceous materials

Green, Robert
Coal. Cherry Lake Pub. 2010 32p il (21st century
skills library. Power up!) lib bdg $27.07

Grades: 4 5 6   **553.2**
1. Coal
ISBN 978-1-60279-508-2 lib bdg; 1-60279-508-8
lib bdg
                                          LC 2008-44184

This "provides a basic introduction to [coal]. . . . The writing is clear and succinct, and the information is accurate, timely and unbiased. The plentiful photographs are outstanding and reinforce the text. . . . Certain to appeal to young readers and their teachers." Libr Media Connect

Includes glossary and bibliographical references

Tagliaferro, Linda

How does a plant become oil? Raintree 2010 32p il (How does it happen?) lib bdg $27.50; pa $7.99
Grades: 3 4 5   **553.2**
1. Gasoline 2. Petroleum
ISBN 978-1-4109-3443-7 lib bdg; 1-4109-3443-8 lib bdg; 978-1-4109-3451-2 pa; 1-4109-3451-9 pa
                                          LC 2008-52290

"Information is clearly presented using a large font, diagrams, and photographs formatted to resemble Polaroid pictures. . . . A first-rate job answering some important scientific questions." SLJ

Includes glossary and bibliographical references

553.4   Metals and semimetals

Raum, Elizabeth

The story behind gold. Heinemann Library 2009 32p il map (True stories) lib bdg $28.21
Grades: 3 4 5   **553.4**
1. Gold 2. Gold mines and mining
ISBN 978-1-4329-2340-2 lib bdg; 1-4329-2340-4 lib bdg
                                          LC 2008037525

This offers history, ephemera, and basic facts about gold, gold mining, and the uses of gold

Includes bibliographical references

553.6   Other economic materials

Kurlansky, Mark

★ The story of salt; [illustrated by] S. D. Schindler. G.P. Putnam's Sons 2006 48p il map $16.99
Grades: 3 4 5 6   **553.6**
1. Salt
ISBN 0-399-23998-7
                                          LC 2005-032629

An adaptation of the author's title for adults: Salt: a world history (2002)

"The informal narrative and the exquisitely detailed, sometimes playful ink-and-watercolor illustrations dramatize the sweeping world history of salt's essential role in human life—from prehistoric times and the early voyages of discovery through the breakthrough of refrigeration and the latest drilling technology." Booklist

Includes bibliographical references

Moore, Heidi

The story behind salt. Heinemann Library 2009 32p il map (True stories) lib bdg $28.21
Grades: 3 4 5   **553.6**
1. Salt
ISBN 978-1-4329-2348-8 lib bdg; 1-4329-2348-X lib bdg
                                          LC 2008037390

This describes the properties of salt and how it is used, including its history and miscellaneous facts, answering such questions as: Why is the sea salty? Why is it so easy to float in the Dead Sea? Why do people put salt on icy roads?

Includes bibliographical references

553.7   Water

Lauw, Darlene

Water; {by Darlene Lauw and Lim Cheng Puay} Crabtree 2003 31p il (Science alive!) lib bdg $21.28; pa $7.95
Grades: 3 4 5 6   **553.7**
1. Water 2. Science -- Experiments
ISBN 0-7787-0567-6 lib bdg; 0-7787-0613-3 pa
                                          LC 2002-11640

Uses simple experiments to demonstrate the properties of water

"The directions are kid friendly, and the graphics that support them are very helpful. . . . The science content is within the range of understanding of an upper elementary school student." Sci Books Films

Includes glossary

Strauss, Rochelle

★ One well; the story of water on Earth. written by Rochelle Strauss; illustrated by Rosemary Woods. Kids Can Press 2007 32p il $17.95
Grades: 4 5 6   **553.7**
1. Water
ISBN 978-1-55337-954-6; 1-55337-954-3

"Looking at all the water on Earth . . . as 'One Well' into which all life dips to survive, Strauss presents a timely discussion of the use and abuse of a not-so-limitless resource. Liberally sprinkled with interesting facts, . . . [the book has a] readable text. . . . Woods's delicate paintings keep perfect step and provide a gentle framework for the plentiful statistical snippets." SLJ

Wick, Walter

★ A drop of water; a book of science and wonder. written and photographed by Walter Wick. Scholastic 1997 40p il $16.95
Grades: 4 5 6   **553.7**
1. Water
ISBN 0-590-22197-3
                                          LC 95-30068

"This title is an elegant synthesis of science and art. . . . The close-up photographs are breathtakingly distinct; and the clarity provided by the combination of concept, text, and photography of this quality is noteworthy." Bull Cent Child Books

553.8 Gems

Moore, Heidi
The **story** behind diamonds. Heinemann Library 2009
32p il (True stories) lib bdg $28.21
Grades: 3 4 5 **553.8**
1. Diamonds
ISBN 978-1-4329-2345-7 lib bdg; 1-4329-2345-5
lib bdg
LC 2008043374
This describes the history, ephemera, basic facts, and uses of diamonds
Includes bibliographical references

560 Paleontology

Aliki
Fossils tell of long ago; rev ed; Crowell 1990 32p il
(Let's-read-and-find-out science book) hardcover o.p. pa
$4.95
Grades: K 1 2 3 **560**
1. Fossils
ISBN 0-06-445093-7 pa
LC 89-17247
First published 1972
"Information about how fossils are formed and discovered is presented in simple text and an appealing variety of colorful illustrations. Includes directions for creating a fossil." Sci Child

Barner, Bob
Dinosaurs roar, butterflies soar! Chronicle Books 2009
un il $16.99
Grades: K 1 2 3 **560**
1. Fossils 2. Dinosaurs 3. Butterflies
ISBN 978-0-8118-5663-8; 0-8118-5663-1
LC 2008016783
"This gently informative book describes the role butterflies played in helping dinosaurs and their environment flourish. The main text offers a simpler narrative than the supplementary and more detailed one in small type that appears below or next to it. . . . A few of the predominant theories about the dinosaurs' extinction and explanations of the continuing survival of butterflies are put forth. . . . Barner's illustrations are, as always, fantastically bright, eye-catching cut-paper collages. A useful, engaging, and illuminating book." SLJ

Bonner, Hannah
★ **When** fish got feet, sharks got teeth, and bugs began to swarm; a cartoon prehistory of life long before dinosaurs. written and illustrated by Hannah Bonner. National Geographic 2007 45p il $16.95; lib bdg $25.90
Grades: 2 3 4 5 **560**
1. Prehistoric animals
ISBN 978-1-4263-0078-3; 1-4263-0078-6; 978-1-4263-0079-0 lib bdg; 1-4263-0079-4 lib bdg
LC 2006-20768
"Bonner explores life on Earth during the Silurian and Devonian periods. . . . Bonner's clear, engaging writing conveys plenty of information without overwhelming readers,

and her illustrations offer fascinating visual representations of unusual creatures and landscapes." SLJ

Bradley, Timothy J.
★ **Paleo** bugs; survival of the creepiest. written and illustrated by Timothy J. Bradley. Chronicle Books 2008 44p il $15.99
Grades: 4 5 6 7 **560**
1. Fossils 2. Insects 3. Prehistoric animals
ISBN 978-0-8118-6022-2; 0-8118-6022-1
LC 2007-18174
This offers an "eye-widening gallery of extinct arthropods, from the mayfly-like heptagenia to a seven-foot-long arthropleura. . . . Bradley decks out each of his painted figures in bright hues, poses them in natural settings . . . and sets them aside a human hand or body in silhouette to suggest scale. . . . Readers will . . . pore over the pictures and come away knowing more about both these extinct animals and their modern descendants." Booklist
Includes glossary and bibliographical references

Brown, Charlotte Lewis
Beyond the dinosaurs; monsters of the air and sea. by Charlotte Lewis Brown; pictures by Phil Wilson. HarperCollinsPublishers 2007 30p il (I can read!) $15.99; lib bdg $16.89
Grades: K 1 2 3 **560**
1. Fossils 2. Prehistoric animals
ISBN 978-0-06-053056-3; 0-06-053056-1; 978-0-06-053057-0 lib bdg; 0-06-053057-X lib bdg
LC 2007014462
"This introduction to creatures 'just as strange and wonderful as any dinosaur' pairs a straightforward text with action-packed, life-like illustrations. . . . [It has] a spread devoted to each of 11 prehistoric animals, including the Elasmosaurus, Hainosaurus , and Archaeopteryx. Helpful pronunciation guides are included. Readers of this book will get a closeup feel for life millions of years ago." SLJ

Brown, Don
★ **Rare** treasure: Mary Anning and her remarkable discoveries. Houghton Mifflin 1999 un il hardcover o.p. pa $5.95
Grades: K 1 2 3 **560**
1. Fossils 2. Paleontologists
ISBN 0-395-92286-0; 0-618-31081-9 pa
LC 98-32372
Describes the life of the English girl whose discovery of an Ichthyosaurus fossil led to a lasting interest in other prehistoric animals
"Brown dwells on Mary's self-determination, focusing on her adventurous spirit . . . and lifelong quest for knowledge in her chosen field of study. . . . The understated watercolors suit the mood. Their subdued palette (ocean blues, sand browns) and simple compositions are undistracting." Bull Cent Child Books

Burton, Virginia Lee
Life story; updated ed.; Houghton Mifflin 2009 67p
il $22; pa $7.99
Grades: 3 4 5 **560**
1. Fossils 2. Evolution 3. Natural history
ISBN 978-0-547-19508-7; 0-547-19508-7; 978-0-547-20359-1 pa; 0-547-20359-4 pa

First published 1962

"Burton's 1962 exploration of the history of life on Earth, framed as a five-act play, returns in a newly updated edition that takes current scientific information into account (Pluto, for instance, is not among the planets shown orbiting the sun). Beginning with the birth of the Sun and continuing through the Earth's creation, the emergence and evolution of animal life, up to the changing seasons of the present, it's a lyrical and informative journey." Publ Wkly

Camper, Cathy

★ **Bugs** before time; prehistoric insects and their relatives. illustrated by Steve Kirk. Simon & Schuster Bks. for Young Readers 2002 un il $16.95

Grades: 4 5 6 7 **560**

1. Fossils 2. Insects

ISBN 0-689-82092-5

LC 98-22872

Describes the physical characteristics, habits, and natural environment of various prehistoric insects some of which, including cockroaches, centipedes, and dragonflies, have survived into the present day

"A handsome introduction to prehistoric insects and other arthropods. . . . [Includes] up-to-date, conversational text and informative captions and date boxes. . . . Kirk's eye-catching, realistic watercolors portray a fascinating array of creatures." SLJ

Includes glossary and bibliographical references

Faulkner, Rebecca

Fossils; [by] Rebecca Faulkner. Raintree 2007 48p il map (Geology rocks!) lib bdg $31.43; pa $8.99

Grades: 4 5 6 **560**

1. Fossils

ISBN 978-1-4109-2752-1 lib bdg; 1-4109-2752-0 lib bdg; 978-1-4109-2760-6 pa; 1-4109-2760-1 pa

LC 2006037065

This "discusses plate tectonics, common fossils and where they are found, dinosaurs, fossil fuels, and the contributions of the study of these relics to paleontology. . . . [The] book includes quality color photographs and diagrams that do an exemplary job of expanding on the topics covered." SLJ

Includes glossary and bibliographical references

Forbes, Scott

How to be a dinosaur hunter; your globe-trotting, time-travelling guide. Lonely Planet 2013 159 p. ill., maps. $17.99

Grades: 3 4 5 6 **560**

1. Fossils 2. Dinosaurs

ISBN 1743219083; 9781743219089

". . . Assuming that readers are embarking on a journey through both time and space to learn about and find dinosaurs, this guide supplies tips for budding paleontologists on everything from what to pack to how to outrun an enormous meat eater. Children are invited to explore three periods of time . . . Triassic, Jurassic, and Cretaceous. Scientific data is made easily accessible, including new discoveries. . . . The full-color, cartoon illustrations offer numerous sidebars with supplemental facts and asides filled with puns, jokes, and other humorous elements that will appeal to children. Though the volume is best suited for casual browsing, a

thorough index makes it a useful tool for research projects as well. Recommended for most collections." SLJ.

Goldish, Meish

The **fossil** feud; Marsh and Cope's bone wars. by Meish Goldish. Bearport Pub. 2007 32p il map (Fossil hunters) lib bdg $23.96

Grades: 3 4 5 6 **560**

1. Fossils 2. Zoologists 3. Paleontologists

ISBN 978-1-59716-256-2 lib bdg; 1-59716-256-6 lib bdg

LC 2006011319

This "tells of the Bone Wars, a clash between two American paleontologists. In 1868, at the Haddonfield, New Jersey, marl pit, Othniel Marsh and Edward Cope established a cooperative relationship, but it deteriorated rapidly. Over the next two decades, each man established dinosaur digs in Wyoming and Colorado, spied on the other's work, and engaged in bribery, theft, and sabotage, even dynamiting fossil sites. Finally, their newspaper attacks on each other's expertise, honor, and sanity alienated the scientific community and led to the end of the Bone Wars. Goldish writes in a clear, straightforward manner, letting the story's inherent drama speak for itself. . . . The presentation is enhanced by attractive page design, which includes a paragraph or two on each page and a photo of an artifact, individuals, sites, or fossils." Booklist

Includes bibliographical references

Gray, Susan H.

Paleontology the study of prehistoric life; Susan H. Gray. Children's Press 2012 48 p.

Grades: 2 3 4 5 **560**

1. Paleontology

ISBN 0329917145; 0531246809; 0531282740; 9780329917142; 9780531246801; 9780531282748

LC 2011030965

This book by Susan H. Gray provides an introduction to paleontology for young readers. It "presents general information about paleontologists . . . [and] what they learn about prehistoric animals and vegetation by studying them." (Open Library)

Includes bibliographical references (p. 44) and index

Holmes, Thom

★ **Dinosaur** scientist; careers digging up the past. Enslow Publishers 2009 128p il (Wild science careers) lib bdg $31.93

Grades: 5 6 7 8 **560**

1. Fossils 2. Vocational guidance

ISBN 978-0-7660-3053-4 lib bdg; 0-7660-3053-9 lib bdg

LC 2008-19634

"A great read for middle school students, the book provides vocational guidance while introducing the reader to a challenging, but very exciting, career as a paleontologist." Sci Books Films

Includes glossary and bibliographical references

Jenkins, Steve

★ **Prehistoric** actual size. Houghton Mifflin Co. 2005 un il $16

Grades: K 1 2 3 **560**
1. Prehistoric animals 2. Dinosaurs
ISBN 0-618-53578-0

LC 2004-25124

Jenkins "provides portraits of animals that flourished long, long ago. . . . [Each animal] receives a caption including common name or scientific name (pronunciation provided), general era of its flourishing, and its overall body size. . . . Grades three to seven." (Bull Cent Child Books)

Illustrated with cut-paper artwork, "the animals pictured here include the minuscule protozoa; . . . the eight-foot-tall 'terror bird'; and the Giganotosaurus. . . . The most arresting spreads are those in which the animal is too large to picture in its entirety. . . . Information about and an illustration of the entire creature (not to scale) completes this colorful volume." Booklist

Leedy, Loreen
My teacher is a dinosaur; and other prehistoric poems, jokes, riddles, and amazing facts. written and illustrated by Loreen Leedy. Marshall Cavendish Childrens 2010 47p il $17.99
Grades: 3 4 5 6 **560**
1. Geology 2. Earth sciences 3. Prehistoric animals
ISBN 978-0-7614-5708-4; 0-7614-5708-9

LC 2009052901

This "introduces readers to the history of the Earth and its plants and animals. Children will have no problem following the succession of life through the pages. . . . Each spread presents one topic with a poem conveying the primary information; surrounding that poem are goofy riddles, factlets and question-limericks that expand on it. The pages are unapologetically jam-packed with information, but they never overwhelm." Kirkus

Spilsbury, Richard
Fossils; [by] Richard and Louise Spilsbury. Heinemann Library 2011 32p il (Let's rock) $29; pa $7.99
Grades: 4 5 6 **560**
1. Fossils
ISBN 978-1-4329-4682-1; 1-4329-4682-X; 978-1-4329-4690-6 pa; 1-4329-4690-0 pa

LC 2010022233

"Enhanced by plenty of photos, digital paintings, and diagrams, [this examination] of [fossils treats its topic] in unusual detail. [It] describes distinguishing characteristics, creation, history, . . . and human uses in [a] central [narrative] with additional notes, suggestions for activities during walks outside, and occasional thumbnail biographies of scientists in side boxes. [The] volume ends with a simple activity." SLJ

Includes bibliographical references

Stewart, Melissa
How does a bone become a fossil? Raintree 2010 32p il (How does it happen?) lib bdg $27.50; pa $7.99
Grades: 3 4 5 **560**
1. Fossils
ISBN 978-1-4109-3445-1 lib bdg; 1-4109-3445-4 lib bdg; 978-1-4109-3453-6 pa; 1-4109-3453-5 pa

LC 2008-52596

"Information is clearly presented using a large font, diagrams, and photographs formatted to resemble Polaroid pic-

tures. . . . A first-rate job answering some important scientific questions." SLJ

Includes glossary and bibliographical references

Taylor, Paul D.
Fossil; written by Paul D. Taylor. rev ed; DK Pub. 2004 72p il map (DK eyewitness books) $15.99; lib bdg $19.99
Grades: 4 5 6 7 **560**
1. Fossils
ISBN 0-7566-0682-9; 0-7566-0681-0 lib bdg
First published 1990 by Knopf

This book describes different types of fossils, from algae to birds and mammals

560.9 History, geographic treatment, biography

Fern, Tracey
★ Barnum's bones; how Barnum Brown discovered the most famous dinosaur in the world. Tracey Fern; pictures by Boris Kulikov. Farrar Straus Giroux 2012 40 p. $17.99
Grades: 2 3 4 5 **560.9**
1. Fossils 2. Picture books for children 3. Paleontologists -- United States -- Biography
ISBN 9780374305161

LC 2010048846

This book tells the story of "Barnum Brown," who "had a nose for fossils, trudging along behind his father as he plowed his Kansas fields, picking up ancient clams and corals. And that nose, according to [Tracey] Fern, . . . led to a lifetime of work for the American Museum of Natural History in New York. . . . A brief glimpse at Brown's early years leads to his expeditions to Patagonia and the American West, and the discovery . . . [of the] Tyrannosaurus rex." (School Library Journal)

Includes bibliographical references.

560.973 Paleontology – United States -- History

Johnson, Rebecca L.
Battle of the dinosaur bones; Othniel Charles Marsh vs. Edward Drinker Cope. by Rebecca L. Johnson. Twenty-First Century Books 2013 64 p. ill., plates, charts (Scientific rivalries and scandals) (library) $33.27
Grades: 5 6 7 8 **560.973**
1. Paleontologists -- United States -- Biography 3. Paleontology -- United States -- History -- 19th century
ISBN 0761354883; 9780761354888

LC 2011045648

"This entry in the Scientific Rivalries and Scandals series focuses on the bitter antagonism between two pioneering nineteenth-century paleontologists. Marsh and Cope. Their contentious rivalry to discover the largest and most unusual dinosaur fossils of the American West became know as the Bone Wars and was at the forefront of American science for decades. The moral of the story is clear, revealing how rivalry can be positive and detrimental." (Booklist)

Includes bibliographical references (p. 58 - 60) and index.

567.9   Reptiles

Abramson, Andra Serlin

Inside dinosaurs; by Andra Serlin Abramson, Jason Brougham, and Carl Mehling; illustrated by Jason Brougham. Sterling Innovation 2010 48p il (Inside) $16.95; pa $9.95

Grades: 5 6 7 8   **567.9**

1. Birds 2. Fossils 3. Dinosaurs

ISBN 978-1-4027-7074-6; 1-4027-7074-X; 978-1-4027-7778-3 pa; 1-4027-7778-7 pa

LC 2010010122

"This pleasantly specific overview covers not only the dinosaurs' distinctive physical characteristics (the authors include modern birds in the group), but the work of paleontologists in both field and lab, the types and typical life cycles of what are carefully dubbed 'non-avian' dinos within each 'clade,' the mass extinction of 65,000,000 years ago . . . and how new discoveries have refined theories about wings and feathers. . . . The art mixes small color photos with soft-edged paint-and-pencil reconstructions of bones, individual live portraits and prehistoric herds in natural settings. . . . [This is an] above average series entry." Kirkus

Includes glossary and bibliographical references

Bacchin, Matteo

Giant vs. giant; Argentinosaurus and Giganotosaurus. drawings and story, Matteo Bacchin; essays, Marco Signore; translated from the Italian by Marguerite Shore. Abbeville Kids 2010 61p il (Dinosaurs) $15.95

Grades: 4 5 6 7   **567.9**

1. Fossils 2. Dinosaurs

ISBN 978-0-7892-1013-5; 0-7892-1013-4

LC 2010-21120

This "book is split into two sections: the first contains parts . . . of a serial graphic novel about dinosaur survival, complete with dramatic narrative and grisly, to-the-death battles. The second half is a higher-level traditional nonfiction text with color photographs and diagrams, focusing on the science behind the comics. The unique format is generally engaging and effective." Horn Book Guide

T. rex and the great extinction; drawings and story, Matteo Bacchin; essays, Marco Signore; translated from the Italian by Marguerite Shore. Abbeville Kids 2010 il (Dinosaurs) $15.95

Grades: 4 5 6 7   **567.9**

1. Fossils 2. Dinosaurs

ISBN 9780789210142; 0789210142

LC 2010021123

This "book is split into two sections: the first contains parts . . . of a serial graphic novel about dinosaur survival, complete with dramatic narrative and grisly, to-the-death battles. The second half is a higher-level traditional nonfiction text with color photographs and diagrams, focusing on the science behind the comics. The unique format is generally engaging and effective." Horn Book Guide

Bailey, Jacqui

Monster bones; the story of a dinosaur fossil. written by Jacqui Bailey; illustrated by Matthew Lilly. Picture Window Books 2004 31p il (Science works) lib bdg $23.93

Grades: 2 3 4   **567.9**

1. Fossils 2. Dinosaurs

ISBN 1-4048-0565-6

LC 2003-20117

Describes how the bones of a dinosaur became fossilized, were discovered by a paleontologist, and were ultimately displayed in a museum.

This "excellent science [book explains its subject] lucidly and sometimes amusingly. . . . Children will be illuminated and engaged." SLJ

Barton, Byron

★ Bones, bones, dinosaur bones. Crowell 1990 un il $16.99

Grades: PreK K   **567.9**

1. Fossils -- Fiction 2. Dinosaurs -- Fiction

ISBN 0-690-04825-4

LC 89-71306

"From the field search for dinosaur bones to reconstructed skeletons for museum display, paleontology as process is revealed in simple text, bold print, and flat illustrations with heavy, black outlines. Includes labeled illustrations of eight dinosaurs." Sci Child

Basher, Simon

Dinosaurs; the bare bones. written by Dan Green; illustrations by Simon Basher. Kingfisher 2012 64 p. (paperback) $7.99; (hardcover) $12.99; (prebind) $16.99

Grades: 2 3 4   **567.9**

1. Dinosaurs 2. Picture books for children

ISBN 0753468247; 9780753468241; 9780753468234; 9781451766288

This children's picture book by Dan Green presents a "one-stop guide to the world of dinosaurs. . . . Join the primeval party and meet terrifying Tyrannosaurus rex, huge Giganotosaurus and tiny Compsognathus. Also includes lots of information from the Triassic, Jurassic, and Cretaceous Periods, including dinosaur dinners, habitats, and fossil discoveries." (Publisher's note)

Benton, Mike

The Kingfisher dinosaur encyclopedia. Kingfisher 2010 159p il $19.99

Grades: 3 4 5 6   **567.9**

1. Fossils 2. Dinosaurs

ISBN 978-0-7534-6440-3; 0-7534-6440-3

"This thorough, fact-filled dinosaur encyclopedia contains full-color digital images of dinosaurs, in order of their appearance through geological time. . . . Profiles offer descriptions of various species' anatomy and speculations on issues like mobility, diet, and predation. Easy-to-read time lines and charts discuss the origins of and extinctions of species, while abundant photographs of skeletans, dig sites, and paleontogists at work integrate relevance and texture." Publ Wkly

Berkowitz, Jacob

★ Jurassic poop; what dinosaurs (and others) left behind. written by Jacob Berkowitz; illustrated by Steve Mack. Kids Can Press 2006 40p il $14.95; pa $7.95

Grades: 4 5 6 7   **567.9**

1. Feces 2. Fossils 3. Dinosaurs

ISBN 978-1-55337-860-0; 1-55337-860-1; 978-1-55337-867-9 pa; 1-55337-867-9 pa

This describes fossilized feces, or coprolites, and what we can learn from them

"Berkowitz' style is goofy and lighthearted, but there's plenty of real information. . . . The browsable format combines cartoony digital art, photographs . . . and design elements such as a spiky borders and background shading." Bull Cent Child Books

Includes glossary

Bishop, Nic

★ **Digging** for bird-dinosaurs; an expedition to Madagascar. Houghton Mifflin 2000 48p il $16; pa $4.95
Grades: 4 5 6 7   **567.9**
1. Birds 2. Fossils 3. Dinosaurs 4. Madagascar
ISBN 0-395-96056-8; 0-618-1982-X pa
                                                            LC 99-36145

The story of Cathy Forster's experiences as a member of a team of paleontologists who went on an expedition to the island of Madagascar in 1998 to search for fossil birds

"Throughout the engaging, personal story, Bishop presents a great deal of information in highly readable, age-appropriate language, well matched by exceptional full-color images of scientists at work and the Malagasy landscape and people." Booklist

Includes bibliographical references

Bonner, Hannah

When dinos dawned, mammals got munched, and Pterosaurs took flight; a cartoon pre-history of life in the Triassic. Hannah Bonner. National Geographic Children's Books 2012 44 p. col. ill., col. maps (hardback) $25.90
Grades: 3 4 5 6 7   **567.9**
1. Dinosaurs 2. Triassic Period 3. Graphic novels 4. Paleontology -- Triassic -- Comic books, strips, etc.
ISBN 9781426308628; 9781426308635
                                                          LC 2011029212

In this book Hannah Bonner "chronicles developments in the Triassic Period, during which life got a fresh lease on the planet in the wake of the massive Permian extinction. She tracks an explosion of biological diversity as the oceans were repopulated, lush forests grew and the dominant kinds of land animals went from clumsy-looking therapsids to sleek archosaurian dinosaurs and proto-crocodiles. Early mammals are already waiting in the wings." (Kirkus Reviews)

Includes bibliographical references and index

Brewster, Hugh

Dinosaurs in your backyard; illustrated by Alan Barnard. Abrams Books for Young Readers 2009 32p il $15.95
Grades: 3 4 5   **567.9**
1. Dinosaurs
ISBN 978-0-8109-7099-1; 0-8109-7099-6
                                                          LC 2008030406

First published 2008 in Canada with title: Breakout dinosaurs

"This informative book . . . transports readers back to a time when North America was defined by substantially different coastlines and divided by a broad inland seaway. Introducing some of the dinosaurs living there . . . the book uses double-page spreads that typically describe one animal in a paragraph of descriptive or dramatic text as well as a section of fast facts relating its size, weight, era, diet, and

range. Large, painterly illustrations set the tone, supported by smaller maps and photos of fossils. The occasional dramatic tooth-and-claw scene is more than balanced by the weight of accessible, interesting information." Booklist

Includes bibliographical references

Brown, Charlotte Lewis

The **day** the dinosaurs died; written by Charlotte Lewis Brown; illustrated by Phil Wilson. HarperCollins Publishers 2006 48p il (I can read book) $15.99; lib bdg $16.89
Grades: K 1 2 3   **567.9**
1. Dinosaurs
ISBN 978-0-06-000528-3; 0-06-000528-9; 978-0-06-000529-0 lib bdg; 0-06-000529-7 lib bdg
                                                           LC 2005-15135

"Beginning with a pronunciation guide for the names of various dinosaurs, this book describes what probably happened to those reptiles 65 million years ago, when a comet or an asteroid most likely slammed into the Earth in the area of the Yucatán Peninsula . . . Second graders will be able to read this book independently, and with its expressive, fairly naturalistic illustrations, younger children will find that it answers the question of how the dinosaurs became extinct." SLJ

Dixon, Dougal

Plant-eating dinosaurs; by Dougal Dixon. North American ed. New Forest Press 2010 48 p. col. ill., col. maps (library) $28.50
Grades: 4 5 6 7   **567.9**
1. Fossils 2. Dinosaurs 3. Herbivores
ISBN 1848983336; 9781848983335
                                                          LC 2010925201

This volume "contains detailed information about dinosaurs and other prehistoric life, covering species development in chronological order. Careful links to the fossil finds that helped scientists with their explanations are found throughout. Additional text boxes cover topics from structure-function to footprints, and interpretive color illustrations and photographs further enhance the [text]." Horn Book Guide

Includes bibliographical references (p. 44-45) and index.

Prehistoric oceans. New Forest Press 2010 48p il map (Dinosaur files) lib bdg $28.50
Grades: 4 5 6 7   **567.9**
1. Fossils 2. Dinosaurs 3. Marine animals
ISBN 978-1-8489-8332-8; 1-8489-8332-8

This volume "contains detailed information about dinosaurs and other prehistoric life, covering species development in chronological order. Careful links to the fossil finds that helped scientists with their explanations are found throughout. Additional text boxes cover topics from structure-function to footprints, and interpretive color illustrations and photographs further enhance the [text]." Horn Book Guide

Includes glossary

Prehistoric skies. New Forest Press 2010 48p il map (Dinosaur files) lib bdg $28.50
Grades: 4 5 6 7   **567.9**
1. Fossils 2. Dinosaurs 3. Prehistoric animals
ISBN 978-1-8489-8331-1; 1-8489-8331-X

Discusses the physical characteristics, behavior, diet, and fossil evidence of prehistoric animals that lived in the sky.

This volume "contains detailed information about dinosaurs and other prehistoric life, covering species development in chronological order. Careful links to the fossil finds that helped scientists with their explanations are found throughout. Additional text boxes cover topics from structure-function to footprints, and interpretive color illustrations and photographs further enhance the [text]." Horn Book Guide

Includes glossary

DK first dinosaur encyclopedia. DK Pub. 2007 127p il $15.99

Grades: 2 3 4 5　　　　　　　　　　**567.9**

1. Reference books 2. Dinosaurs -- Encyclopedias

ISBN 978-0-7566-2539-9

LC 2006016039

"Solid introductory information and strong visual appeal make this a fine choice for dinosaur fans. Crystal-clear photographs of models and artifacts fill every spread. . . . The text is clear, with enough intriguing facts to fascinate without overwhelming." SLJ

Farlow, James Orville

★ **Bringing** dinosaur bones to life; how do we know what dinosaurs were really like? [by] James O. Farlow; with illustrations by James E. Whitcraft. Watts 2001 63p il lib bdg $25

Grades: 5 6 7 8　　　　　　　　　　**567.9**

1. Fossils 2. Dinosaurs

ISBN 0-531-11403-1

LC 00-38150

"Clearly written and well organized, this book will interest children intrigued by the process of scientific thinking as well as its results." Booklist

This "describes how paleontologists draw conclusions from the dinosaur fossils they study. Separate chapters examine physical appearance, diet, fighting, and reproduction." SLJ

Includes glossary and bibliographical references

Forss, Sarah

Alphasaurs and other prehistoric types; by Sharon Werner and Sarah Forss. Blue Apple Books 2012 56 p. (hardback) $22.99

Grades: 1 2 3 4　　　　　　　　　　**567.9**

1. Alphabet 2. Picture books for children 3. Animals 4. Dinosaurs 5. Alphabet books

ISBN 1609051939; 9781609051938

LC 2012023718

Author Sharon Werner presents a picture book for children. "Like the creatures so artfully rendered in the best-selling Alphabeasties, the dinosaurs in this stylish book are ingeniously engineered out of letters. A different typeface comprises each animal. Factual information about each dinosaur appears in multiple entries and fonts, making for an eye-catching and witty way to look at the ABC-DINO's." (Publisher's note)

French, Vivian

T. Rex; illustrated by Alison Bartlett. Candlewick Press 2004 29p il $15.99; pa $6.99; pa with audio CD $8.99

Grades: K 1 2 3　　　　　　　　　　**567.9**

1. Dinosaurs

ISBN 978-0-7636-2184-1; 0-7636-2184-6; 978-0-7636-3177-2 pa; 0-7636-3177-9 pa; 978-0-7636-3999-0 pa with audio CD; 0-7636-3999-0 pa with audio CD

LC 2003-69563

In a "dialogue with his grandfather, a boy discovers the thrill of the intellectual hunt while touring a T. Rex exhibition. . . . Bartlett . . . working in saturated acrylics and bold shapes, travels back to the era when T. Rex was indeed king. . . . The author eloquently makes the case that a willingness to seek answers, rather than merely receive them, has its own rewards." Publ Wkly

Funston, Sylvia

Dino-why? the dinosaur question and answer book. updated and rev.; Maple Tree Press 2008 64p il $22.95; pa $10.95

Grades: 4 5 6 7　　　　　　　　　　**567.9**

1. Dinosaurs

ISBN 978-1-897349-24-3; 1-897349-24-6; 978-1-897349-25-0 pa; 1-897349-25-4 pa

LC 2007-939082

First published 1992 by Joy Street Books with title: The dinosaur question and answer book

"This book is an excellent and highly readable introduction to dinosaurs. . . . The questions are well conceived, and the answers . . . are scientifically sound and up to date. . . . The illustrations, a few of them cartoon-like, are nicely drawn and useful." Sci Books Films

Gibbons, Gail

Dinosaurs! by Gail Gibbons. Holiday House 2008 32p il $16.95

Grades: K 1 2 3　　　　　　　　　　**567.9**

1. Dinosaurs

ISBN 978-0-8234-2143-5; 0-8234-2143-0

LC 2007034425

Simple text and illustrations introduce young readers to dinosaurs

"The combination of clear writing and lively artwork makes this an accessible choice for young dinosaur enthusiasts." Booklist

Greenwood, Marie

Amazing giant dinosaurs; [written by Marie Greenwood; illustrated by Peter Minister] DK 2012 15 p. $19.99

Grades: 2 3 4　　　　　　　　　　**567.9**

1. Dinosaurs 2. Paleontology 3. Picture books for children 4. Toy and movable books 5. Toy and movable books -- Specimens

ISBN 075669308X; 9780756693084

LC 2011279215

This book features "large foldout flaps" that create pop-up illustrations of dinosaurs. "Each dinosaur appears in a . . . graphic along with a bulletin board collection of facts about its diet, habitat, behavior, and other characteristics. . . . Profiles of 'Dinosaur hunters' provide insight into the paleontology profession." (Publishers Weekly)

Guiberson, Brenda Z., 1946-

★ The **greatest** dinosaur ever; by Brenda Guiberson and illustrated by Gennady Spirin. Henry Holt and Company 2013 32 p. (hardcover) $17.99

Grades: PreK K 1 2 3   **567.9**

1. Dinosaurs 2. Dinosaurs -- Pictorial works

ISBN 0805096256; 9780805096255

LC 2013001725

This book, by Brenda Z. Guiberson and illustrated by Gennady Spirin, features "facts and . . . illustrations [designed to] inspire young readers to choose their own favorite dinosaurs! Which dinosaur was the greatest? Was it the tallest, the biggest, the strongest, the smartest, the weirdest, the fastest, or the smallest? Or was it the oldest bird, the best parent, the one with the best night vision, the best armor, or the longest tail spikes?" (Publisher's note)

"Here a dozen dinosaurs compete for the title of "greatest dinosaur that ever lived" by giving their credentials, from the Sauroposeidon as the tallest and biggest herbivore to the Microraptor as the smallest of all. The compact, information-light text is dwarfed by Spirin's lavish, detailed paintings--a double-spread for each candidate. The package includes pronunciation keys and concludes with a fact page." (Horn Book)

Includes bibliographical references

Hartland, Jessie

★ How the dinosaur got to the museum. Blue Apple Books 2011 un il $17.99

Grades: 1 2 3 4   **567.9**

1. Fossils 2. Museums 3. Dinosaurs 4. National Museum of Natural History (U.S.)

ISBN 978-1-60905-090-0; 1-60905-090-8

LC 2011018921

"This cumulative narrative follows the journey of a set of dinosaur bones belonging to a Diplodocus longus that lived 145 million years ago to its present home in the display halls of the Smithsonian National Museum of Natural History in Washington, DC. . . . It . . . describes the work of many hands involved, . . . starting with the dinosaur hunter who discovered the bones and the paleontologist who went to Utah to identify them and culminating with the museum director who opened the exhibit. . . . [The author's] verbs are interestingly varied, as are the many things these people do. The text is printed on double-page illustrations, painted in a childlike manner but detailed enough to show all the people and activities." Kirkus

Henry, Michel

Raptor; the life of a young deinonychus. illustrations by Rich Penney. Abrams Books for Young Readers 2007 un il map $15.95

Grades: 2 3 4   **567.9**

1. Dinosaurs

ISBN 978-0-8109-5775-6; 0-8109-5775-2

LC 2004-12588

This "is a beautifully illustrated book that brings a dinosaur and his environment to life. Based on informed speculation . . . this book follows the life experiences of several raptors that are part of a pack that lived in the western part of North America 100 million years ago." Sci Books Films

Includes glossary and bibliographical references

Hughes, Catherine D.

First big book of dinosaurs. National Geographic 2011 127p (National Geographic little kids) $14.95; lib bdg $21.90

Grades: PreK K 1 2   **567.9**

1. Dinosaurs

ISBN 978-1-4263-0846-8; 1-4263-0846-9; 978-1-4263-0847-5 lib ed; 1-4263-0847-7 lib bdg

LC 2011015051

"A bright, eye-catching format, naturalistic illustrations, and concise prose introduce readers to 52 dinosaur species, organized by size—small, big, giant, or gigantic. Distinguishing characteristics of each dinosaur . . . appear in a large font like a headline on each spread; informative sidebars, charts that compare each dino's size to a human, phonetic pronunciations, and lively interactive prompts . . . make this an especially engaging primer." Publ Wkly

Judge, Lita

★ **Born** to be giants; how baby dinosaurs grew to rule the world. Flash Point 2010 un il $17.99

Grades: 2 3 4   **567.9**

1. Dinosaurs

ISBN 978-1-59643-443-1; 1-59643-443-0

"Expanding on the idea that the hugest dinosaurs hatched from (relatively speaking) small eggs, Judge depicts cute hatchlings with outsized heads and feet wobbling about as their gargantuan parents look on indulgently. Along with a full measure of visual appeal, she also delivers a terse but clear explanation of how scientists gain insight into dino parenting from both fossil evidence." Booklist

Includes glossary and bibliographical references

How big were dinosaurs? Lita Judge. Roaring Brook Press 2013 40 p. (hardback) $17.99

Grades: 1 2 3 4   **567.9**

1. Picture books for children 2. Dinosaurs -- Size

ISBN 1596437197; 9781596437197

LC 2013001327

This children's picture book by Lita Judge looks at dinosaur size. "Moving from smallest to largest, [Judge's] illustrations juxtapose 12 dinos with modern-day objects and animals for comparison. A close-up of a fierce microraptor is followed by a scene showing the same microraptor cowering in the presence of a crowing rooster," for example. (Publishers Weekly)

Kelsey, Elin

Canadian dinosaurs; Elin Kelsey. Reprint Maple Tree Press 2009 96 p. ill. (prebind) $28.95

Grades: 4 5 6   **567.9**

1. Fossils 2. Dinosaurs

ISBN 1442060409; 9781442060401

This book offers a "history of fossil hunting north of the border, including bio-material on dino-hunters past and present, followed by a compendium of carnivores and herbivores. . . . Illustrations, mainly in color, appear on every page. . . . The whole is rounded out with a list of dino locations, a time line, and a listing of institutions where these splendid fossils may be examined at leisure." (School Library Journal)

Kerley, Barbara

★ The **dinosaurs** of Waterhouse Hawkins; an illuminating history of Mr. Waterhouse Hawkins, artist and lecturer. with drawings by Brian Selznick, many of which are based on the original sketches of Mr. Hawkins. Scholastic 2001 un il

Grades: 3 4 5 **567.9**

1. Artists 2. Dinosaurs 3. Sculptors 4. Modelmakers -- Great Britain

ISBN 0-439-11494-2

LC 00058376

A Caldecott Medal honor book, 2002

This is the true story of Victorian artist Benjamin Waterhouse Hawkins, who built life-sized models of dinosaurs in the hope of educating the world about these ancient animals and what they were like. "Ages five to eight." (Bull Cent Child Books)

"Kerley suffuses her text with a sense of wonder and amazement, a tone well-matched by Selznick's lush, dramatic illustrations." Publ Wkly

Kudlinski, Kathleen V., 1950-

★ **Boy,** were we wrong about dinosaurs! illustrated by S. D. Schindler. Dutton Children's Books 2005 un il $15.99

Grades: K 1 2 3 **567.9**

1. Dinosaurs

ISBN 0-525-46978-8

LC 2003-53140

This book examines what is known about dinosaur bones, behavior, and other characteristics and how different the facts often are from what scientists, from ancient China to the recent past, believed to be true. "Ages six to ten." (Bull Cent Child Books)

"Intelligently designed and imaginatively conceived, the artwork makes the text more understandable and the whole book more beautiful. . . . Best of all, the closing paragraph acknowledges that the search is not over yet." Booklist

Includes bibliographical references

Lessem, Don

The **fastest** dinosaurs; by Don Lessem; illustrations by John Bindon. Lerner Publications 2005 32p il (Meet the dinosaurs) lib bdg $23.93; pa $6.95

Grades: 2 3 4 **567.9**

1. Dinosaurs

ISBN 0-8225-1422-2 lib bdg; 0-8225-2620-4 pa

LC 2004-7055

This "looks at how paleontologists determine living speed when only the fossil record remains, and cites some prime examples of dinosprinters, such a Gallimimus and Troodon. The realistic, soft illustrations . . . are lively enough to please budding paleontologists. Simple, eye-catching, and informative." SLJ

Feathered dinosaurs; by Don Lessem; illustrations by John Bindon. Lerner Publications 2005 32p il (Meet the dinosaurs) lib bdg $23.93; pa $6.95

Grades: 2 3 4 **567.9**

1. Birds 2. Dinosaurs

ISBN 0-8225-1423-0 lib bdg; 0-8225-2621-2 pa

LC 2004-19651

This covers the "links between dinosaurs and birds. . . . Lessem writes in simple language and short sentences appropriate for children transitioning out of early readers. But the brief text . . . . will also read well to younger dino fans. . . . Bindon's detailed illustrations imagine the creatures in

dramatic settings that will bring the drama of the ancient age alive." Booklist

Flying giants of dinosaur time. Lerner Publications Co. 2005 32p il map (Meet the dinosaurs) lib bdg $23.93; pa $6.95

Grades: 2 3 4 **567.9**

1. Pterosaurs 2. Pterodactyls

ISBN 0-8225-1424-9 lib bdg; 0-8225-2622-0 pa

LC 2004-17918

This "covers the pterosaurs and pterodactyls, extrapolating some behaviors using modern birds as models, and speculates on beak shapes and sizes in the food-gathering process. . . . The realistic, soft illustrations . . . are lively enough to please budding paleontologists. Simple, eye-catching, and informative." SLJ

Sea giants of dinosaur time. Lerner Publications Co. 2005 32p il map (Meet the dinosaurs) lib bdg $23.93; pa $6.95

Grades: 2 3 4 **567.9**

1. Dinosaurs

ISBN 0-8225-1425-7 lib bdg; 0-8225-2623-9 pa

LC 2004-17916

"A quick glimpse at eight of the larger prehistoric marine reptiles, ranging in eras from 220 million to 65 million years ago. The simple text presents a time line for these creatures, a global map of fossil finds, and some details of their physiology and distribution. The colorful double-page illustrations on blue backgrounds are accompanied by a paragraph or two of particulars." SLJ

The **smartest** dinosaurs; by Don Lessem; illustrations by John Bindon. Lerner Publications 2005 32p il (Meet the dinosaurs) lib bdg $23.93; pa $6.95

Grades: 2 3 4 **567.9**

1. Dinosaurs

ISBN 0-8225-1373-0 lib bdg; 0-8225-2618-2 pa

LC 2004-11152

"After a discussion of brain/body-size ratios, Lessem goes on to describe the importance of fossil finds in determining intelligence possibilities, leading to brief descriptions of seven dinosaurs that scientists feel may have been brighter than their contemporaries. . . . This is a clear look at a facet of dinosaur makeup not often touched on in other works." SLJ

The **ultimate** dinopedia; the most complete dinosaur reference ever. illustrated by Franco Tempesta; with a foreword by Rodolfo Coria. National Geographic 2010 272p il map $24.95; lib bdg $34.90

Grades: 3 4 5 6 **567.9**

1. Dinosaurs

ISBN 978-1-4263-0164-3; 1-4263-0164-2; 978-1-4263-0165-0 lib bdg; 1-4263-0165-0 lib bdg

LC 2010-07146

In the opening chapter, Lessem "presents broad basics on [dinosaur] behavior and habitats as well as a look at major discoveries in paleontology. However, it's the later chapters, which devote two pages each to specific dinosaurs, that will hook hard-core dino lovers. . . . Tempesta's full-page illustrations appear on every spread and jump off the page, and the dynamic layout . . . is immensely appealing. . . .

Lessem's comprehensive overview will satisfy the interested browser as much as the ardent dinosaur enthusiast." Booklist

Includes bibliographical references

Long, John A.

★ **Dinosaurs**; [by] John Long. Simon & Schuster Books for Young Readers 2007 64p il (Insiders) lib bdg $16.99

Grades: 4 5 6 7   567.9

1. Dinosaurs

ISBN 978-1-4169-3857-6 lib bdg; 1-4169-3857-5 lib bdg

LC 2007-61735

"Richly hued, crisp computer-generated art and 3D model imagery serve as a stunning and sophisticated graphic counterpoint to the educational text." Publ Wkly

"The first section includes paleontological periods, extinction theories, and a . . . pictorial time line tracing the first bird archaeopteryx to the earliest feathered dinosaurs. The second section contains profiles of a diverse selection of species." Booklist

Includes glossary

Macken, JoAnn Early

The **dinosaur** museum. Amicus 2010 24p il (My community) lib bdg $14.95

Grades: K 1 2   567.9

1. Fossils 2. Museums 3. Dinosaurs

ISBN 978-1-6075-3023-7 lib bdg; 1-6075-3023-6 lib bdg

LC 2010010554

The design offers "clear font, colorful layout, and glossy photos. . . . What's most delightful about the museum images are the juxtapositions of the fantastic (a giant dinosaur skeleton) paired with the mundane (a guy on a step-ladder using a vacuum to clean the bones. . . . A solid effort." Booklist

MacLeod, Elizabeth

Monster fliers; from the time of the dinosaurs. written by Elizabeth MacLeod; illustrated by John Bindon. Kids Can Press 2010 31p il $16.95

Grades: K 1 2 3   567.9

1. Birds 2. Dinosaurs 3. Pterosaurs

ISBN 978-1-55453-199-8; 1-55453-199-3

"This attractive picture book [is] sure to appeal to dinophiles eager to learn more about dinosaurs' flying cousins. Nineteen pterosaurs, a few early birds, and a dromaeosaur (a dinosaur that both walked and flew) are briefly described and illustrated in their presumed native habitats. . . . The realistic illustrations [are] painted with remarkable detail." Booklist

Markle, Sandra

★ **Outside** and inside dinosaurs. Atheneum Bks. for Young Readers 2000 40p il hardcover o.p. pa $7.99

Grades: 2 3 4   567.9

1. Fossils 2. Dinosaurs

ISBN 0-689-82300-2; 0-689-85778-0 pa

LC 99-45808

Describes the inner and outer workings of dinosaurs, discussing what has been learned about their anatomy, diet, and behavior from fossils

"Excellent, large color photos march hand in hand with Markle's readable, informative text." SLJ

Includes glossary

McGowan, Chris

Dinosaur discovery; everything you need to be a paleontologist. illustrated by Erica Lyn Schmidt. Simon & Schuster Books for Young Readers 2011 48p il $17.99

Grades: 4 5 6 7   567.9

1. Fossils 2. Dinosaurs

ISBN 978-1-4169-4764-6; 1-4169-4764-7; 1416947647; 9781416947646

LC 2009044604

"In-depth facts about 13 dinosaurs are interspersed with activities that teach readers about anatomy and how paleontologists understand body structure. . . . The 27 activities and experiments illustrate the concepts presented and focus on the featured dinosaurs. By following the well-written directions as well as the picture steps, budding paleontologists will explore how a tail affects balance, discover binocular vision and learn how the two parts of a bone make them both stiff and elastic. . . . Schmidt's acrylic illustrations give life to the dinosaurs, and her scientific renderings of bones could have come straight out of an anatomy textbook. . . . A thinking, active alternative for readers who fall between adult nonfiction and all the rhyming dino fare meant for the younger set." Kirkus

Munro, Roxie

Inside-outside dinosaurs. Marshall Cavendish Children 2009 un il $17.99

Grades: PreK K   567.9

1. Dinosaurs

ISBN 978-0-7614-5624-7; 0-7614-5624-4

LC 2008055322

"This large-format book offers paired double-page spreads showing each featured dinosaur twice. In the first spread, a black-and-gray skeleton in a dramatic pose stands out clearly against a white background. . . . The second spread portrays the living dinosaur within its habitat. Typically these pictures, india-ink drawings washed with colors, depict action in the background or foreground. . . . An appended section offers a bit of information about each species and identifies all the dinosaurs in the action scenes. . . . Eye-catching illustrations and minimal text make this a good choice for young dino fans." Booklist

Includes bibliographical references

Myers, Tim

If you give a T-rex a bone; illustrated by Anisa Claire Hovemann. Dawn Publications 2007 un il (A sharing nature with children book) $16.95; pa $8.95

Grades: PreK K 1 2   567.9

1. Dinosaurs

ISBN 978-1-58469-097-9; 1-58469-097-6; 978-1-58469-098-6 pa; 1-58469-098-4 pa

LC 2007-08332

"The book is illustrated throughout with bright, and quite beautiful, watercolors. . . . This is a fine first introduction to prehistoric reptiles for the very young." Sci Books Films

"Dinosaurs and other ancient reptiles appear in their ancient habitats as if witnessed by a modern day child. Includes information about the animals and resources for additional learning." Publisher's note

Includes bibliographical references

Parker, Steve

Age of the Dinosaur; by Steve Parker. Trafalgar Square 2014 48 p. $7.99

Grades: 1 2 3   **567.9**

1. Dinosaurs 2. Paleontology

ISBN 0565093290; 9780565093297

This book, by Steve Parker, "explains what the world looked like when dinosaurs existed and how it changed; which . . . creatures, plants, and animals lived then; who survived to live another day; and how scientists know all this. Each colorful double-page spread explores a different dinosaur subject, from a particular period of time or group of animals to dinosaur diets and the study of fossils." (Publisher's note)

"Learn about dinosaur diets, fossils, and— - hooray! - — poop in this introduction to dinosaurs and the time in which they lived. This UK import provides an overview of the Mesozoic era by giving snapshots of the climate, landscape, and dinosaurs common to each of the era's periods: the Triassic, Jurassic, and Cretaceous. Information is distilled and simply explained, ensuring that readers will not be overwhelmed by a page's content." (Booklist)

Peterson, Sheryl

Pterodactyl. Creative Education 2010 48p il (Age of dinosaurs) lib bdg $34.25

Grades: 5 6 7 8   **567.9**

1. Dinosaurs

ISBN 978-1-58341-975-5 lib bdg; 1-58341-975-6 lib bdg

     LC 2009025175

"Peterson nicely balances the known with conjecture. . . . The inviting design, on glossy pages, elegantly detours from the main text into details tantalizing . . .; informative . . . and incredible. . . . The illustrations, from sharp diagrams to dramatic paintings to B-movie-worthy recreation scenes, add some nice flair to this solid entry." Booklist

Podesto, Martine

Dinosaurs; by Martine Podesto. Gareth Stevens 2009 102p il (My science notebook) lib bdg $31

Grades: 4 5 6   **567.9**

1. Dinosaurs

ISBN 978-0-8368-9213-0 lib bdg; 0-8368-9213-5 lib bdg

     LC 2008-12427

"Designed to resemble a notebook with illustrated paper clips, pasting, and tape appearing on most pages, this [book] . . . offers comprehensive information. . . . supplemented by colorful drawings, diagrams, and photographs." SLJ

Includes glossary and bibliographical references

Prap, Lila

Dinosaurs?! North South Books 2010 un il $16.95

Grades: K 1 2 3   **567.9**

1. Birds 2. Dinosaurs 3. Evolution

ISBN 978-0-7358-2284-9; 0-7358-2284-0

"In this humorous look at evolution, Prap makes the case that all modern-day birds, including chickens, are descended from dinosaurs. The book's illustrations are fun and well-

laid-out, and the witty text is chock-full of information. A group of chickens makes snarky comments about their disparate relatives . . . and side notes provide interesting details about the 'terrible lizards.' Dino lovers will clamor for this title." SLJ

Ray, Deborah Kogan

★ Dinosaur mountain; digging into the Jurassic Age. Frances Foster Books 2010 un il map $16.99

Grades: 3 4 5 6   **567.9**

1. Fossils 2. Dinosaurs 3. Paleontologists 4. Dinosaur National Monument (Colo. and Utah)

ISBN 978-0-374-31789-8; 0-374-31789-5

     LC 2008027877

This describes how, beginning in 1908, Earl Douglass set out to discover "a mountain in Utah that would reveal some of the grandest dinosaur skeletons anyone had ever seen. . . . Ray's expressive art . . . excels in capturing the grandeur and wonder of key moments. . . . Excited journal entries from Douglass enliven the informative text, and small sketch book-style drawings of fossils and tools add a scholarly touch." Booklist

Includes glossary and bibliographical references

Sloan, Christopher

Bizarre dinosaurs; some very strange creatures and why we think they got that way. [by] Christopher Sloan; with a foreword by James Clark and Cathy Forster. National Geographic 2008 31p il $16.95; lib bdg $25.90

Grades: 4 5 6 7   **567.9**

1. Dinosaurs

ISBN 978-1-4263-0330-2; 1-4263-0330-0; 978-1-4263-0331-9 lib bdg; 1-4263-0331-9 lib bdg

This "book should engage children of all ages who are fascinated by dinosaurs. . . . The illustrations are of uniformly high quality. . . . Each species gets two pages of text, including a full-page illustration; an inset with basic facts such as range, diet, and geological period in which it lived; a silhouette comparing their size with that of humans; and a paragraph of text." Sci Books Films

★ How dinosaurs took flight; the fossils, the science, what we think we know, and the mysteries yet unsolved. foreword by Dr. Xu Xing. National Geographic 2005 64p il $17.95

Grades: 5 6 7 8   **567.9**

1. Birds 2. Fossils 3. Dinosaurs

ISBN 0-7922-7298-6

This explains the evolutionary relationships between dinosaurs and birds, based on fossils and the latest research.

Includes glossary and bibliographical references

Supercroc and the origin of crocodiles; introduction by Paul Sereno. National Geographic Soc. 2002 55p il map $18.95

Grades: 5 6 7 8   **567.9**

1. Crocodiles 2. Fossil reptiles

ISBN 0-7922-6691-9

     LC 2001-3976

Discusses prehistoric crocodiles, including the discovery of SuperCroc in the Sahara Desert, and the lifestyles, habitats, and conservation of modern crocodiles

"Fans of paleontology or of crocodiles will find a great deal of information clearly explained. The illustrations are up to the high National Geographic standard." Booklist

Includes glossary

Snow, Alan

How Dinosaurs Really Work! written and illustrated by Alan Snow. Atheneum Books 2013 32 p. $17.99

Grades: K 1 2 3   **567.9**

1. Dinosaurs

ISBN 144248294X; 9781442482944

This book, written and illustrated by Alan Snow, examines dinosaurs and attempts to answer questions such as "what color were the dinosaurs? Where did they all go? And just how sharp were their teeth?" (Publisher's note)

Tanaka, Shelley

New dinos; The latest finds! The coolest dinosaur discoveries! written by Shelley Tanaka; illustrated by Alan Barnard. Atheneum Bks. for Young Readers 2003 48p il maps hardcover o.p. pa $9.95

Grades: 3 4 5 6   **567.9**

1. Fossils 2. Dinosaurs

ISBN 0-689-85183-9; 1-897330-55-3 pa

LC 2002-9809

Describes some of the newly discovered dinosaurs and what paleontologists have learned about these prehistoric creatures in recent years

"Vivid, dramatic illustrations are a sure draw to an already hot topic. . . . Tanaka's lively, brief text provides enough data to satisfy many readers, including true aficionados." SLJ

Includes glossary and bibliographical references

Thimmesh, Catherine

★ Scaly spotted feathered frilled; how do we know what dinosaurs really looked like? by Catherine Thimmesh. Houghton Mifflin Books for Children, Houghton Mifflin Harcourt 2013 64 p. $17.99

Grades: 4 5 6 7   **567.9**

1. Dinosaurs 2. Paleontology 3. Paleoart

ISBN 0547991347; 9780547991344

LC 2012048466

Author Catherine Thimmesh "explores the border between science and speculation in this [book about] how paleontologists . . . reconstruct prehistoric creatures from fossil evidence. . . . [She] explains how surviving evidence—including fossilized bone fragments, plant matter, bits of skin and, recently, feathers, prehistoric 'trackways' (preserved pathways of dino footprints) and similar physical features in modern animals—is assembled and interpreted by scientists." (Kirkus Reviews)

Includes bibliographical references (page 55) and index

Williams, Judith

The discovery and mystery of a dinosaur named Jane. Enslow Publishers 2007 48p il map

Grades: 3 4 5 6   **567.9**

1. Fossils 2. Dinosaurs 3. Tyrannosaurus rex

ISBN 0766027090 pa; 0766027309 lib bdg; 9780766027091 pa; 9780766027305 lib bdg

LC 2006010475

This book deals with how paleontologists and researchers discovered, excavated and put on display a Tyranno-

saurus skeleton found in Montana's Hell Creek formation. Glossary. Index. "Grades three to eight." (Sci Books Films)

This describes "the 2001 discovery of a fossilized dinosaur skeleton in Montana's Hell Creek Formation. . . . Williams carefully reports the entire event, from discovery through excavation and preparation to exhibition at the Burpee Museum of Natural History in Rockford, IL. Small color photos and artwork, simple diagrams, and a map help readers to visualize the complex process." SLJ

Includes bibliographical references

Woodward, John

Dinosaurs eye to eye; zoom in on the world's most incredible dinosaurs. digital sculptor Peter Minister. Dorling Kindersley 2010 96p il map $19.99

Grades: 3 4 5 6   **567.9**

1. Fossils 2. Dinosaurs

ISBN 978-0-7566-5760-4; 0-7566-5760-1

"This oversize reference book features striking digital images of dinosaurs, along with abundant information about them and the Triassic, Jurassic, and Cretaceous periods in which they thrived. . . . Action scenes . . . offer visual excitement, while diagrams, sidebars with dino-stats, and photographs of fossils emphasize the educational." Publ Wkly

Zoehfeld, Kathleen Weidner

Dinosaur parents, dinosaur young; uncovering the mystery of dinosaur families. with full-color paintings by Paul Carrick and line drawings by Bruce Shillinglaw. Clarion Bks. 2001 58p il map $17

Grades: 4 5 6 7   **567.9**

1. Fossils 2. Dinosaurs

ISBN 0-395-91338-1

LC 00-43101

"High-quality, color photographs of fossils of eggs and embryos and of paleontologists at work as well as line drawings and full-color paintings add to this inviting, thought-provoking book." SLJ

Includes glossary and bibliographical references

Dinosaur tracks; by Kathleen Weidner Zoehfeld; illustrated by Lucia Washburn. HarperCollinsPublishers 2007 33p il (Let's-read-and-find-out science) $15.99; lib bdg $16.89; pa $5.99

Grades: K 1 2 3   **567.9**

1. Fossils 2. Dinosaurs

ISBN 0-06-029024-2; 978-0-06-02904-5; 0-06-029025-0 lib bdg; 978-0-06-029025-2 lib bdg; 0-06-445217-4 pa; 978-0-06-445217-5 pa

LC 2004-06242

Describes how footprints made by the dinosaurs have been preserved and what these impressions tell scientists about the animals which made them.

"The clear text is illustrated with informal, colorful spreads of kids at play on the beach where millions of years earlier dinosaurs may have 'splooshed through gloppy mud . . . [leaving] footprints behind them.'" Booklist

Where did dinosaurs come from? illustrated by Lucia Washburn. HarperCollinsPublishers 2010 40p il (Let's-read-and-find-out science book) **567.9**

1. Fossils 2. Dinosaurs

ISBN 978-0-06-029022-1; 978-0-06-445216-8 pa

LC 2009020543

Presents information about the evolution of the dinosuars, from the earliest four-limbed tetrapos of the Paleozoic age, to the meat-eating eoraptors of early Triassic, to the fully-developed dinosaurs of the Jurassic and Cretaceous periods.

"Zoehfeld is remarkably precise with language, no easy feat when writing on this topic for beginning readers, providing outstanding explanations of key evolution concepts in the finest tradition of the series. The color illustrations include anatomical details, a helpful phylognetic timeline, and imagined portrayals of dinosaurs active in verdant habitats." Horn Book

Includes glossary

567.91   Specific dinosaurs and other archosaurs

Sloan, Christopher

Tracking Tyrannosaurs; meet T. rex's fascinating family, from tiny terrors to feathered giants. by Christopher Sloan. National Geographic 2013 48 p. (trade hard cover) $18.95

Grades: 5 6 7 8   **567.91**
1. Tyrannosaurus rex
ISBN 1426313748; 9781426313745; 9781426313752
                   LC 2013004988

This book, by Christopher Sloan, "highlights a newly discovered T. rex relative in China with a coat of downy feathers! This one-ton predator is the largest known animal to ever have walked the Earth. [Readers] meet 19 kinds of tyrannosaurs--including seven new species discovered in the last two years--that came before T. rex." (Publisher's note)

567.912   Specific dinosaurs

Dixon, Dougal

Meat-eating dinosaurs; by Dougal Dixon. North American ed. New Forest Press 2010 47 p. col. ill., col. maps (Dinosaur files) (library) $28.50

Grades: 4 5 6 7   **567.912**
1. Fossils 2. Dinosaurs 3. Carnivorous animals
ISBN 9781848983342; 1848983344
                   LC 2010925204

This volume "contains detailed information about dinosaurs and other prehistoric life, covering species development in chronological order. Careful links to the fossil finds that helped scientists with their explanations are found throughout. Additional text boxes cover topics from structure-function to footprints, and interpretive color illustrations and photographs further enhance the [text]." Horn Book Guide

Includes bibliographical references (p. 44-45) and index.

568   Fossil birds

Zoehfeld, Kathleen Weidner

Did dinosaurs have feathers? illustrated by Lucia Washburn. HarperCollins Publishers 2004 33p il (Let's-read-and-find-out science) $15.99; lib bdg $16.89; pa $4.99

Grades: K 1 2 3   **568**
1. Birds 2. Fossils 3. Dinosaurs 4. Archaeopteryx
ISBN 0-06-029026-9; 0-06-029027-7 lib bdg; 0-06-029027-7 pa
                   LC 2002-10585

Discusses the discovery and analysis of Archaeopteryx, a feathered dinosaur which may have been an ancestor of modern birds

"Using short sentences and simple words, Zoehfeld clearly explains what we know about dinosaurs with feathers. . . . Iridescent shades of blue and orange give the theropods and their settings an appealing glow." Horn Book Guide

569   Fossil mammals

Aliki

Wild and woolly mammoths; written and illustrated by Aliki. rev ed; HarperCollins Pubs. 1996 32p il hardcover o.p. pa $6.95

Grades: K 1 2 3   **569**
1. Mammoths
ISBN 0-06-446179-3 pa
                   LC 94-48217

A revised and newly illustrated edition of the title first published 1977

An easy-to-read account of the woolly mammoth, a giant land mammal which has been extinct for over 11,000 years

"With concise text and informative art, Aliki illuminates the timeless appeal of these long-gone animals—and drops a gentle warning about the possible fate of tusked decendants." Publ Wkly

Arnold, Caroline

★ **When** mammoths walked the earth; illustrated by Laurie Caple. Clarion Bks. 2002 40p il $16

Grades: 3 4 5 6   **569**
1. Mammoths
ISBN 0-618-09633-7
                   LC 2001-47192

Describes the physical characteristics, known habits, and fossil sites of mammoths, prehistoric animals closely related to the elephant

"The information is brief but thorough, with realistic watercolor illustrations depicting the giant animals and their surroundings." Booklist

Bardoe, Cheryl

Mammoths and mastodons; titans of the Ice Age. Abrams Books for Young Readers 2010 43p il map

Grades: 4 5 6 7   **569**
1. Fossils 2. Mammoths 3. Mastodon 4. Mastodons
ISBN 0-8109-8413-X lib bdg; 978-0-8109-8413-4 lib bdg
                   LC 2009-22006

The author presents a "case study in how paleontologists examine both ancient and modern clues for insights into the diets, physical development and behavior of extinct animals. Cousins to modern elephants, mammoths and mastodons once roamed large portions of the Earth, but for reasons that are not completely understood . . . vanished relatively suddenly. Focusing particularly on . . . remnants like the 55 fossilized skeletons found near one sinkhole in South Dakota and 'Lyuba,' the well preserved 'prehistoric popsicle' discovered in 2007 in Siberia, the author presents both facts and educated guesses--while leaving it clear that there is much still to be learned." (Kirkus)

"This well-designed book opens with two boys finding a strange animal dead on the arctic tundra. Their father hikes four days to a village where the news can be spread; then scientists take away the frozen baby mammoth, the first example found intact, and study it intensively. The book intersperses accounts of the scientists' research and deductions with general information about mammoths and mastodons as well as imagined scenes taking place when they walked the earth. . . . A handsome introduction." Booklist

Includes glossary and bibliographical references

Brown, Charlotte Lewis

  After the dinosaurs; mammoths and fossil mammals. written by Charlotte Lewis Brown, pictures by Phil Wilson. HarperCollinsPublishers 2006 un il (I can read!) $15.99; lib bdg $16.89

  Grades: K 1 2 3   569

    1. Fossil mammals

    ISBN 978-0-06-053053-2; 0-06-053053-7; 978-0-06-053054-9 lib bdg; 0-06-053054-5 lib bdg

    LC 2005028662

  "This title examines a variety of ancient mammals. It opens with a brief introduction, followed by a spread devoted to each animal. . . . The pronunciation guide is a welcome feature. The finely detailed watercolor illustrations emphasize the unusual features of each species." SLJ

Lister, Adrian

  The **Ice** Age tracker's guide; illustrated by Martin Ursell. Frances Lincoln Children's Books 2010 31p il map $17.95

  Grades: 4 5 6 7   569

    1. Ice Age 2. Fossil mammals

    ISBN 978-1-84507-718-1; 1-84507-718-0

  "'Hunters' of Ice Age fauna will find the tawny pages in this 'guide' a trove of pointers for identifying a round dozen of predators and prey. What does a giant ground sloth's poop look like? Just how big is a dwarf elephant? . . . Size, shape, food, fur (if any), locations, and other tidbits are scattered about the watercolor and ink illustrations, and are reinforced by two pages of solid paragraphs of text on each creature. Lister . . . writes with authority in this lighthearted, informational work." SLJ

Manning, Mick

  Woolly mammoth; [by] Mick Manning [and] Brita Granström. Frances Lincoln 2009 un il $16.95

  Grades: K 1 2 3   569

    1. Mammoths

    ISBN 978-1-84507-860-7; 1-84507-860-8

  "Manning and Granström pair rhyming couplets, in this case describing the life of a mammoth, alongside columns of information. Simple pencil drawings fill sidebars with specific details about these huge beasts, including their habitat and natural enemies, their physical characteristics and behavior. . . . Bright watercolor-over-pencil paintings dominate the pages, which feature simple stanzas that deliver the mammoth's side of the story." SLJ

Markle, Sandra

  ★ **Outside** and inside woolly mammoths. Walker & Co. 2007 40p il $17.95; lib bdg $18.85

  Grades: 4 5 6   569

    1. Mammoths

    ISBN 978-0-8027-9589-2; 0-8027-9589-7; 978-0-8027-9590-8 lib bdg; 0-8027-9590-0 lib bdg

    LC 2006027621

  "Markle explains what scientists have discovered from the preserved remains of mammoths: their food, and the structure of their hair, their soft tissues, and even their DNA. Asking readers leading questions and systematically noting similarities to and differences from modern elephants, she speculates about why mammoths became extinct. . . . Except for the cover picture, the illustrations are all big, sharp color photos and digital tomography images rather than artistic re-creations. A closing multimedia resource list that is accurately pitched to the level of her intended audience makes this as valuable for student use as for pleasure reading." Booklist

Parker, Steve, 1952-

  Ice age giants. QEB Pub. 2011 32p il (Wild age) lib bdg $28.50

  Grades: 2 3 4   569

    1. Fossils 2. Ice Age 3. Fossil mammals

    ISBN 978-1-59566-911-7; 1-59566-911-6

    LC 2010001152

  This describes prehistoric mammals of the ice age, including giant sloths, mammoths, giant deer, giant cats, Neanderthals and modern humans.

  "Vivid writing . . . lifts [this] otherwise ordinary [survey] a bit above average. . . . The art combines photos of fossils, distribution maps, illustrations of prehistoric monsters . . . and, on each spread, a human silhouette to indicate scale." SLJ

  Includes glossary

Sloan, Christopher

  Baby mammoth mummy; frozen in time: a prehistoric animal's journey into the 21st century. National Geographic 2011 il map $17.95; lib bdg 26.90

  Grades: 4 5 6 7   569

    1. Fossils 2. Mammoths

    ISBN 978-1-4263-0865-9; 1-4263-0865-5; 978-1-4263-0866-6 lib bdg; 1-4263-0866-3 lib bdg

    LC 2010044003

  "From CAT scans to the use of surgical cameras, the mummy of a baby mammoth found dislodged from Siberian ice undergoes veritable CSI treatment in the Netherlands, Japan, the U.S., and in her Russian homeland as scientists scramble to discover her historic age (42,000 years), her chronological age (32 days), her diet (mother's milk), and the cause of her demise (suffocation in mud). Sloan's clear, readable text follows this journey in nicely defined stages, with explanations along the way for possibly unfamiliar processes. Plentiful photos, a pair of maps, some diagrams, and colorful artwork accompany the information." SLJ

  Includes glossary and bibliographical references

Turner, Alan

  ★ **National** Geographic prehistoric mammals; illustrated by Mauricio Antón. National Geographic 2004 192p il map $29.95; lib bdg $49.90

Grades: 5 6 7 8   **569**
1. Fossil mammals
ISBN 0-7922-7134-3; 0-7922-6997-7 lib bdg
LC 2004-1189
This describes the Age of Mammals and profiles over 100 prehistoric mammals, including time lines, fact boxes, distribution maps, photos of fossils, and illustrations

"Dramatic full-color pictures . . . and captions enhance the brief, informative text." SLJ

Wheeler, Lisa
Mammoths on the move. Harcourt, Inc. 2006 un il $16
Grades: K 1 2   **569**
1. Mammoths
ISBN 0-15-204700-X
LC 2004-19112
"The text describes a group of female mammoths and their young traveling south for the winter, reaching their destination only to turn around and begin their long trek back. Wheeler uses wordplay skillfully, her verse shows originality. . . . The beautifully composed scratchboard illustrations offer strong line work, subtle use of color, and a fine sense of what migrating mammoths may have looked like." Booklist

569.9 Humans and related genera

Aronson, Marc
★ The **skull** in the rock; how a scientist, a boy, and Google Earth opened a new window on human origins. by Marc Aronson and Lee Berger. National Geographic 2012 64 p. (hardcover: alk. paper) $18.95
Grades: 5 6 7 8 9 10   **569.9**
1. Human origins 2. Fossil hominids 3. Excavations (Archeology) 4. Paleoanthropology 5. Human beings -- Origin 6. Fossil hominids -- South Africa -- Witwatersrand Region 7. Human evolution -- South Africa -- Witwatersrand Region 8. Excavations (Archaeology) -- South Africa -- Witwatersrand Region
ISBN 1426310102; 9781426310102; 9781426310539
LC 2012012943
This book by Marc Aronson and Lee R. Berger tells the story of how "in 2008 [Berger]--with the help of his curious 9-year-old son--discovered two remarkably well preserved, two-million-year-old fossils . . . known as 'Australopithecus sediba'; a previously unknown species of ape-like creatures that may have been a direct ancestor of modern humans." (Publisher's note)

Includes bibliographical references and index.

570 Biology

Green, Dan
Extreme biology; from superbugs to clones... get to the edge of science. written and illustrated by Simon Basher. Kingfisher 2013 64 p. col. ill. (hardcover) $12.99
Grades: 4 5 6 7   **570**
1. Biology
ISBN 0753470519; 9780753470510
This book written and illustrated by Simon Basher is designed to help readers "learn about the amazing research

that is revolutionizing biology, from advances in medicine to genetic engineering. [Readers will] meet the world's toughest bacterium and a biologically immortal flatworm whilst learning about epigenetics, superbugs, nanomedicine and cloning. 'Extreme Biology' is a compelling guide to developments at the very forefront of science." (Publisher's note)

Kalman, Bobbie
What is symmetry in nature? Crabtree Pub. Co. 2010 24p il (Looking at nature) lib bdg $21.27; pa $6.95
Grades: K 1 2   **570**
1. Nature 2. Symmetry
ISBN 978-0-7787-3327-0 lib bdg; 0-7787-3327-0 lib bdg; 978-0-7787-3347-8 pa; 0-7787-3347-5 pa
LC 2010016400
Reveals examples of symmertry found in nature.

"Bright, colorful photographs were selected with young readers in mind, and the type is large—perfect for reading together. . . Throughout the book are questions that challenge the reader to identify the opposites shown on the pages. . . . Parents and teachers will find . . . [this book] a great addition to a child's library." Sci Books & Films

Includes glossary

McManus, Lori
Cell systems. Heinemann Library 2011 48p il (Investigating cells) lib bdg $32
Grades: 5 6 7 8   **570**
1. Cells 2. Life (Biology)
ISBN 978-1-4329-3879-6; 1-4329-3879-7
LC 2009049974
This book looks at cell systems, including the cell, tissues, organ, and organ system hierarchy.

"The abundant graphic matter—photographs, diagrams, charts and graphs—work together with the text to create visually appealing pages. . . . [This] would be very useful in any kind of formal investigation of the topic and yet attractive enough to encourage browsing. . . . [This] . . . is exceptionally well done." Libr Media Connect

Includes glossary and bibliographical references

VanCleave, Janice Pratt, 1942-
Janice VanCleave's play and find out about nature; easy experiments for young children. Wiley 1997 122p il $29.95; pa $12.95
Grades: K 1 2   **570**
1. Nature 2. Biology 3. Science -- Experiments
ISBN 0-471-12939-9; 0-471-12940-2 pa
LC 96-2865
Provides instructions for fifty nature experiments and activities involving both plants and animals

"VanCleave's explanations are straightforward and concise. The book has a clear and uncluttered look." SLJ
Includes glossary

Step-by-step science experiments in biology; by Janice VanCleave. Rosen 2013 80 p. col. ill. (Janice Vancleave's first-place science fair projects) (library) $33.25; (paperback) $14.15
Grades: 5 6 7 8   **570**
1. Biology 2. Science -- Experiments 3. Biology -- Experiments
ISBN 144886982X; 9781448869824; 9781448884636
LC 2012007943

This book by Janice VanCleave presents 22 science experiments in biology for children. "Van Cleave states the basic goal of the experiments, followed by a list of necessary materials. . . . Step-by-step instructions are . . . accompanied by diagrams where needed. The results section states exactly what is expected to happen and the 'Why?' section explains in accessible terms why those specific results were achieved." (School Library Journal)

Includes bibliographical references and index.

Winston, Robert

Life as we know it; Robert Winston. 1st American ed. DK Publishing 2012 96 p. col. ill. (hardcover) $16.99

Grades: 4 5 6   **570**

1. Ecology 2. Zoology 3. Food chains (Ecology) 4. Life (Biology)

ISBN 0756691699; 9780756691691

LC 2011277462

Author Robert Winston "begins with Earth's formation billions of years ago and continues to the present day, exploring cells, the animal kingdom, ecosystems, food chains, and creatures that tolerate extreme conditions (including bacteria that thrive in volcanic pools and coffinfish that live under high pressure on the sea floor). The book's . . . design incorporates numerous photographs, sidebars, . . . digital art, and light humor, usually in the form of speech-bubble captions for the animals." (Publishers Weekly)

570.78   Biology - student experiments

Latham, Donna

★ **Backyard** Biology; Investigate Habitats Outside Your Door With 25 Projects. by Donna Latham; illustrated by Beth Hetland. Nomad Press 2013 128 p. ill. (Build it yourself) (paperback) $15.95

Grades: 4 5 6 7   **570.78**

1. Biology 2. Front yards and backyards

ISBN 1619301512; 9781619301511

This book, part of the Built It Yourself series, "incorporates 25 projects for kids to try as they explore the 'ecosystems that are outside your door.' The book's eight chapters cover biology (and microbiology), cells, and the life cycles of both plants and animals, among other topics; definitions of key terms appear throughout, as do [illustrator Beth] Hetland's cartoons and diagrams." (Publishers Weekly)

571   Internal biological processes and structures

Green, Jen

Inside animals. Marshall Cavendish Benchmark 2010 48p il (Invisible worlds) $28.50

Grades: 4 5 6 7   **571**

1. Cells 2. Anatomy 3. Physiology 4. Microorganisms

ISBN 978-0-7614-4195-3; 0-7614-4195-6

LC 2008037241

This describes the animal details that are too small for the unaided eye to see, and how these microscopic systems work to keep the animal alive and healthy.

The narrative is "clear, well written, broken down into manageable pieces, and peppered with eye-opening facts. The numerous photographs are so phenomenal that they will

inspire kids to read the text . . . so that they can wrap their minds around what they see." SLJ

Includes glossary and bibliographical references

571.1   Animals

Singer, Marilyn

A **strange** place to call home; the world's most dangerous habitats & the animals that call them home. Marilyn Singer & Ed Young. Chronicle Books 2012 44 p. ill.

Grades: 3 4 5   **571.1**

1. Habitat (Ecology) 2. Exotic animals 3. Animals -- Habitations

ISBN 1452101205; 9781452101200

LC 2011046379

This book, describes how "[u]nder the desert's cracked and barren skin, spadefoot toads are waiting for rain. In the endless black of the deepest caves, blind fish find their way. Even in the frozen hearts of glaciers, ice worms by the billion flourish. In this . . . look at fourteen animals who defy the odds by thriving in Earth's most dangerous places, . . . poet Marilyn Singer and . . . artist Ed Young show that of all the miracles of life, it is life's persistence that astounds the most." (Publisher's note)

571.4   Biophysics

Chisholm, Sallie W., 1947-

★ **Ocean** sunlight; how tiny plants feed the seas. by Molly Bang and Penny Chisholm; illustrated by Molly Bang. Blue Sky Press 2012 48 p. (hardcover: alk. paper) $18.99

Grades: K 1 2 3 4   **571.4**

1. Oceanography 2. Marine biology 3. Photosynthesis 4. Sunshine 5. Photobiology 6. Plants -- Effect of light on 7. Marine life -- Effect of light on

ISBN 0545273226; 9780545273220

LC 2011024823

AAAS/Subaru SB&F Prize for Excellence in Science Books: Children's Science Picture Book (2013)

In this book, the authors "turn their attention to the ocean and its vast population of phytoplankton. . . . The . . . text follows the food chain from the tiniest of green plants (powered into life by the sun) to the biggest predators dependent on plankton-gobblers for food. The authors explain photosynthesis and the ocean layer exchange wrought by sunlight-driven currents, and even touch on the life below, where the strongest sunbeam cannot reach." (School Library Journal)

Winner, Cherie

Cryobiology. Lerner Publications Co. 2006 48p il (Cool science) lib bdg $26.60

Grades: 4 5 6   **571.4**

1. Cryobiology

ISBN 978-0-8225-2907-1 lib bdg; 0-8225-2907-6 lib bdg

LC 2005006158

This book "discusses how different life forms survive low temperatures, e.g., hibernating animals. . . . [The book provides] clear explanations of the science and [covers] possible benefits to humans. A variety of photos and information boxes provide an eye-catching . . . . layout." Horn Book Guide

Includes glossary and bibliographical references

571.6 Cell biology

Cohen, Marina

What is cell theory? Crabtree Pub. Co. 2011 64p il (Shaping modern science) lib bdg $30.60; pa $10.95

Grades: 5 6 7 8   571.6

1. Cells

ISBN 978-0-7787-7199-9 lib bdg; 0-7787-7199-9 lib bdg; 978-0-7787-7206-4 pa; 0-7787-7206-3 pa

LC 2010052633

This title is "not only written and organized well, but [it is] also gorgeous in design. Full-color photographs and illustrations are set over colorful backgrounds that add depth but not distraction. [The title] includes thought-provoking quotes from famous authors and scientists and some eyebrow-raising 'Quick Facts' throughout." SLJ

Includes glossary and bibliographical references

Johnson, Rebecca L.

Mighty animal cells; [by] Rebecca L. Johnson; illustrations by Jack Desrocher; diagrams by Jennifer E. Fairman. Millbrook Press 2007 48p il (Microquests) lib bdg $29.27

Grades: 4 5 6   571.6

1. Cells

ISBN 978-0-8225-7137-7 lib bdg; 0-8225-7137-4 lib bdg

LC 2006-36394

In this introduction to animal cells, "Johnson builds one scientific concept at a time using authentic terminology and connecting new information to familiar things. . . . Full-color microscope images, drawings, and cartoons appear in a clean, uncluttered format, combining solid science with humor." Horn Book Guide

Includes glossary and bibliographical references

Lee, Kimberly Fekany

Cells. Compass Point Books 2009 40p il (Mission: science) lib bdg $26.60

Grades: 4 5 6   571.6

1. Cells

ISBN 978-0-7565-3954-2 lib bdg; 0-7565-3954-4 lib bdg

LC 2008007719

"Lee describes the difference between plant and animal cells, and their contents; diffusion; and cell storage, movement, and reproduction. . . . Large eye-catching and colorful photographs and illustrations appear on every page. . . . The [book] includes a simple activity." SLJ

Includes glossary and bibliographical references

571.8 Reproduction, development, growth

Mitchell, Susan K.

Animal body-part regenerators; growing new heads, tails, and legs. by Susan K. Mitchell. Enslow Publishers 2009 48p il (Amazing animal defenses) lib bdg $23.93

Grades: 4 5 6   571.8

1. Regeneration (Biology)

ISBN 978-0-7660-3295-8 lib bdg; 0-7660-3295-7 lib bdg

LC 2008-11453

"The closeup photos are frequent and well chosen, and accompanied by clear, simply phrased [text], which [is] more detailed than average and [takes] up most or all of the space on each page." SLJ

Includes glossary and bibliographical references

Royston, Angela

Looking at life cycles; how do plants and animals change? [by] Angela Royston. Enslow Publishers 2008 32p il (Looking at science: how things change) lib bdg $22.60

Grades: 1 2 3   571.8

1. Life cycles (Biology)

ISBN 978-0-7660-3091-6 lib bdg; 0-7660-3091-1 lib bdg

LC 2007-24513

"Fills a huge void in elementary science collections. . . . Text is arranged in succinct 'chunks,' giving important facts without overwhelming readers. . . . [This] is an essential addition." Libr Media Connect

"An explanation of life cycles of different types of plants and animals, as well as people." Publisher's note

Includes glossary and bibliographical references

Silverstein, Virginia B.

★ Growth and development; by Alvin Silverstein, Virginia Silverstein, and Laura Silverstein Nunn. Twenty-First Century Books 2008 112p il (Science concepts) lib bdg $31.93

Grades: 4 5 6 7   571.8

1. Growth 2. Biology

ISBN 978-0-8225-6057-9 lib bdg; 0-8225-6057-7 lib bdg

LC 2006030299

This "considers the growth process, animals with and without skeletons, human and plant growth, and future trends as a result of medical technology. Clear organization, engaging anecdotes, and generally good photos and diagrams are strengths of the [volume]." Horn Book Guide

Includes glossary and bibliographical references

Wade, Mary Dodson

Plants grow! Enslow Elementary 2009 24p il (I like plants!) lib bdg $21.26; pa $6.95

Grades: K 1 2   571.8

1. Growth 2. Plants

ISBN 978-0-7660-3152-4 lib bdg; 0-7660-3152-7 lib bdg; 978-0-7660-3612-3 pa; 0-7660-3612-X pa

LC 2007039453

"The life cycle and parts of a plant are discussed in a clear, concise manner. Beautifully detailed professional photographs of plants, animals, and people complement the subject matter. [The] book includes a simple activity." SLJ

Includes glossary and bibliographical references

571.9   Diseases

Stewart, Melissa

Germ wars! the secrets of keeping healthy. illustrated by Janet Hamlin. Marshall Cavendish Benchmark 2010 48p il (The gross and goofy body) $29.95

Grades: 2 3 4   **571.9**

1. Bacteria 2. Immune system

ISBN 978-0-7614-4165-6; 0-7614-4165-4

LC 2008033562

This offers information on the role the immune system plays in the body science of humans and animals.

572   Biochemistry

Bang, Molly

★ **Living** sunlight; how plants bring the Earth to life. by Molly Bang & Penny Chisholm; illustrated by Molly Bang. Blue Sky Press 2009 un il $16.99

Grades: PreK K 1 2 3   **572**

1. Photosynthesis 2. Sun

ISBN 978-0-545-04422-6; 0-545-04422-7

LC 2008-14238

This book "talks to young children about photosynthesis . . . in a way that tells what is actually happening on a molecular level. It also tells children why this process matters and leads them into a broad understanding of their personal connection with plant life and energy from the sun. . . . The amiable, well-informed narrator is the sun. Alight with unusual intensity, the artwork fills the pages with vibrant images. . . . Each double-page spread illustrates its lines of text with intelligence and originality." Booklist

Includes bibliographical references

Lunis, Natalie

Glow-in-the-dark animals. Bearport Pub. 2011 24p il (Animals with super powers) lib bdg $22.61

Grades: 3 4 5   **572**

1. Bioluminescence

ISBN 978-1-61772-119-9; 1-61772-119-0

LC 2010038281

This describes animals which glow in the dark including fireflies, glowworms, fireworms, deep-sea jellyfish, anglerfish, cucujos, and dinoflagellates.

"Large color photos of animals in natural settings and clear, cogent presentations of information combine to boost this [book] well above the average for both assignments and casual browsing." SLJ

Includes glossary and bibliographical references

Sitarski, Anita

★ **Cold** light; creatures, discoveries, and inventions that glow. Boyds Mills Press 2007 48p il $16.95

Grades: 5 6 7 8   **572**

1. Light 2. Bioluminescence

ISBN 1-59078-468-5; 978-1-59078-468-6

"A clearly written, chatty text not only discusses the expected bioluminescent critters (think fireflies), but delves into the realms of chemiluminescence, photoluminescence, and LEDs (light-emitting diodes) as well. . . . The text lays out the historical hows and whys of cold light, its success in the natural world, and its application in medicine and do-mestic/industrial illumination. Clear color photos and information boxes abound." SLJ

572.8   Biochemical genetics

Johnson, Rebecca L.

Amazing DNA; [by] Rebecca L. Johnson; illustrations by Jack Desrocher; diagrams by Jennifer E. Fairman. Millbrook Press 2008 48p il (Microquests) lib bdg $29.27

Grades: 4 5 6   **572.8**

1. DNA 2. Genetics

ISBN 978-0-8225-7139-1 lib bdg; 0-8225-7139-0 lib bdg

LC 2006-102324

This describes DNA structure, cell replication and genetic transmission.

"Johnson builds one scientific concept at a time using authentic terminology and connecting new information to familiar things. . . . Full-color microscope images, drawings, and cartoons appear in a clean, uncluttered format, combining solid science with humor." Horn Book Guide

Includes glossary and bibliographical references

Rand, Casey

DNA and heredity. Heinemann Library 2011 48p il (Investigating cells) lib bdg $32

Grades: 5 6 7 8   **572.8**

1. DNA 2. Cells 3. Heredity

ISBN 978-1-4329-3880-2; 1-4329-3880-0

LC 2009049978

Learn about cells, DNA and scientists who made an impact in cell research.

"The abundant graphic matter—photographs, diagrams, charts and graphs—work together with the text to create visually appealing pages. . . . [This] would be very useful in any kind of formal investigation of the topic and yet attractive enough to encourage browsing. . . . [This] . . . is exceptionally well done." Libr Media Connect

Includes glossary and bibliographical references

573.3   Digestive system

Collard, Sneed B.

Beaks! illustrated by Robin Brickman. Charlesbridge Pub. 2002 un il hardcover o.p. pa $6.95

Grades: K 1 2 3   **573.3**

1. Birds

ISBN 1-57091-387-0; 1-57091-388-9 pa

LC 2001-4362

Simple text describes various bird beaks and how birds use them to eat, hunt, and gather food. Includes a quiz

"The intricate characteristics of a variety of birds' beaks are presented skillfully through words and vividly painted, cut-and-sculpted-paper illustrations. . . . The clear text is easy to follow." SLJ

Includes bibliographical references

Deem, James M.

★ **Bodies** from the bog. Houghton Mifflin 1998 42p il hardcover o.p. pa $5.95

Grades: 4 5 6 7　　　　　　　　　　**573.3**

1. Mummies 2. Archeology 3. Prehistoric peoples
ISBN 0-395-85784-8; 0-618-35402-6 pa

LC 97-12010

Describes the discovery of bog bodies in northern Europe and the evidence which their remains reveal about themselves and the civilizations in which they lived

"The text is engaging and accessible, and the starkly dramatic photos are given dignity by the spacious and understated page design." Horn Book Guide

Includes bibliographical references

573.8　Nervous and sensory systems

Jenkins, Steve

★ **What** do you do with a tail like this? [by] Steve Jenkins & Robin Page. Houghton Mifflin 2003 un il $15
Grades: K 1 2 3　　　　　　　　　　**573.8**

1. Senses and sensation
ISBN 0-618-25628-8

LC 2002-11673

A Caldecott Medal honor book, 2004

"Jenkins' handsome paper-cut collages are both lovely and anatomically informative. . . . This is a striking, thoughtfully created book with intriguing facts made more memorable through dynamic art." Booklist

573.88　Eyes

Jenkins, Steve

★ **Eye** to eye; how animals see the world. Steve Jenkins. Houghton Mifflin Books for Children, Houghton Mifflin Harcourt 2014 32 p. $17.99
Grades: K 1 2 3 4 5　　　　　　　　**573.88**

1. Vision in animals
ISBN 0547959079; 9780547959078

LC 2013024004

In this picture book, author Steve Jenkins "explains how for most animals, eyes are the most important source of information about the world in a biological sense. The simplest eyes—clusters of light-sensitive cells—appeared more than one billion years ago, and provided a big survival advantage to the first creatures that had them. Since then, animals have evolved an amazing variety of eyes, along with often surprising ways to use them." (Publisher's note)

"...Toward the end of the book, Jenkins devotes a page to describing the "evolution of the eye," enabling readers to easily follow the changes. Jenkins's outstanding torn- and cut-paper illustrations offer a fascinating look at these important organs, which range in size from the tiniest holes (starfish) to basketballs (colossal squid)...Animal facts, a bibliography, and a glossary round out this slim volume that will captivate readers of all ages." SLJ

Includes bibliographical references

574.5　Rain forest ecology

Cobb, Vicki, 1938-

This place is wet; by Vicki Cobb; illustrated by Barbara Lavallee. Walker 1989 32 p. col. ill. (Imagine living here) (hardcover) $12.95; (library) $13.85; (paperback) $8.99
Grades: 1 2 3　　　　　　　　　　**574.5**

1. Brazil -- Description and travel 2. Rain forests 3. Amazon River valley 4. Rain forest ecology -- Amazon River Region 5. Amazon River Region -- Description and travel
ISBN 9780802768803; 0802734006; 0802768814; 9780802734006

LC 89032445

This book by Vicki Cobb is part of the "Imagine Living Here geography series" which "introduc[es] the land, climate, plants, animals,and people of various places. . . . This volume transports readers to the Amazon rain forest around Manaus, Brazil. The book, in addition to the aforementioned subjects, discusses rain forest destruction, mining, pollution, and global warming." (Booklist)

575　Specific parts of and physiological systems in plants

Farndon, John

Leaves. Blackbirch Press 2006 24p il (World of plants) lib bdg $24.90
Grades: 2 3 4 5　　　　　　　　　　**575**

1. Leaves
ISBN 978-1-4103-0422-3 lib bdg; 1-4103-0422-1 lib bdg

LC 2005047048

This book examines leaf shapes, the process of photosynthesis, the turning of leaves in the fall season, and unusual leaves that can trap insects

This uses "clear language and short sentences. . . . Helpful diagrams and sharp, colorful photographs supplement the [text]. . . . [This book offers] solid information in an attractive format." SLJ

Includes bibliographical references

Hicks, Terry Allan

Why do leaves change color? Marshall Cavendish Benchmark 2011 32p il (Tell me why, tell me how) lib bdg $29.93
Grades: 2 3 4 5　　　　　　　　　　**575**

1. Leaves
ISBN 978-0-7614-4827-3; 0-7614-4827-6

This offers information about why leaves change color.

This title has "clear explanations of natural phenomena, beautiful full-color illustrations, and an uncluttered design. [The] book approaches its topic in a methodical, logical fashion, using examples from a child's world." SLJ

Includes glossary

575.9　Animal-like physiological processes

Lawrence, Ellen

Meat-eating plants; toothless wonders. by Ellen Lawrence. Bearport Pub. 2013 24 p. (library binding) $23.93

Grades: 1 2 3 **575.9**
1. Carnivorous plants
ISBN 1617725897; 9781617725890

LC 2012014335

This juvenile reference book, by Ellen Lawrence, "explores the world of carnivorous plants that obtain nutrients by 'eating' animals. From plants that act like sticky flypaper to trap their prey, to other plants that lure their victims into deep pitchers of liquid from which the animals will never escape, children will learn about a variety of plants that employ interesting techniques to capture food." (Publisher's note)

Includes bibliographical references and index

576.5 Genetics

Duke, Shirley Smith
You can't wear these genes. Rourke Pub. LLC 2010 48p il (Let's explore science) $32.79
Grades: 4 5 6 7 **576.5**
1. Genetics
ISBN 978-1-61590-324-5; 1-61590-324-0

LC 2010009911

This "offers a clear introduction to the complexities of genetics while inviting students to think about how their own DNA shaped who they are. In [this] title, well chosen boxed examples, abundant color photos, diagrams, and an appended glossary add interest and support the engaging [text]." Booklist

Includes glossary and bibliographical references

Simpson, Kathleen
★ Genetics; from DNA to designer dogs. Sarah Tishkoff, consultant. National Geographic 2008 64p il map (National Geographic investigates) $27.90
Grades: 4 5 6 7 **576.5**
1. Genetics
ISBN 978-1-4263-0361-6; 1-4263-0361-0; 978-1-4263-0327-2 lib bdg; 1-4263-0327-0 lib bdg

This discusses topics in genetics such as the identification of an Egyptian mummy by DNA testing, the genetics of pea plants studied by Gregor Mendel, cloning, the Human Genome Project, and stem cell research.

"The content is fairly exciting and should grab the attention of its target audience. . . . The photographs throughout are of high quality. . . . An engaging look at a complex topic." Booklist

576.8 Evolution

Berkowitz, Jacob
Out of this world; the amazing search for an alien earth. Kids Can Press 2009 48p il $16.95; pa $8.95
Grades: 4 5 6 7 **576.8**
1. Life on other planets 2. Outer space -- Exploration
ISBN 978-1-55453-197-4; 1-55453-197-7; 978-1-55453-198-1 pa; 1-55453-198-5 pa

The author "has written a miniencyclopedic, profusely illustrated, picture book that describes, in much detail, what we all know about the universe in which we live and about the conditions that must be present on any planet in our solar

system, or on an exoplanet . . . for life as we know it to exist." Sci Books Films

Bortz, Alfred B.
Astrobiology. Lerner Publications 2008 48p il map (Cool science) lib bdg $26.60
Grades: 4 5 6 **576.8**
1. Space biology 2. Life on other planets
ISBN 978-0-8225-6771-4 lib bdg; 0-8225-6771-7 lib bdg

LC 2006033268

This describes "the search for life in the universe. Astrobiologists compare life on Earth to signs of life on other planets. They test meteorites for evidence of alien bacteria. They collect soil and atmospheric samples from other planets. They study photographs taken on space missions. And they listen for signals from alien civilizations on enormous radio dishes." Publisher's note

Includes bibliographical references

Brake, Mark
Alien Hunter's Handbook; How to Look for Extra-terrestrial Life. by Mark Brake; illustrated by Colin Jack and Geriant Ford. Kingfisher 2012 111 p. (paperback) $10.99
Grades: 4 5 6 7 **576.8**
1. Extraterrestrial beings
ISBN 0753468859; 9780753468852

This book on extra-terrestrial life by Mark Brake "opens with an overview of the defining characteristics of life and some of Earth's remarkable creatures, such as the microscopic tardigrade, which can exist in the vacuum of space. Topics like the development of solar systems, the speed of evolution, and the formation of language also get attention, laying factual groundwork for suppositions about what alien life could look like." (Publishers Weekly)

Branley, Franklyn Mansfield
Is there life in outer space? illustrated by Edward Miller. HarperCollins Pubs. 1999 31p il (Let's-read-and-find-out science) hardcover o.p. pa $4.95
Grades: K 1 2 3 **576.8**
1. Life on other planets 2. Outer space -- Exploration
ISBN 0-06-028146-4; 0-06-028145-6 lib bdg; 0-06-445192-5 pa

LC 99-10904

A newly illustrated edition of the title first published 1984 by Crowell

Discusses some of the ideas and misconceptions about life in outer space and speculates on the existence of such life in light of recent space explorations

"Children curious about the possibility of life on distant planets will find much to think about in this speculative yet scientifically accurate text. The new illustrations, which incorporate photographs of planets, are bright and colorful." Horn Book Guide

Gamlin, Linda
Evolution; written by Linda Gamlin. rev ed.; DK Pub. 2009 72p il (DK eyewitness books) $16.99
Grades: 4 5 6 7 **576.8**
1. Evolution
ISBN 978-0-7566-5028-5; 0-7566-5028-3
First published 1993

Text about and photography of experiments, animals, plants, bones, and fossils reveal the ideas and discoveries that have changed our understanding of the natural world and how life began. Includes a CD and wall chart.

Hartman, Eve

Changing life on Earth; [by] Eve Hartman and Wendy Meshbesher. Raintree 2009 48p il (Sci-hi: life science) lib bdg $31.43; pa $8.99

Grades: 5 6 7 8   **576.8**

1. Evolution

ISBN 978-1-4109-3324-9 lib bdg; 1-4109-3324-5 lib bdg; 978-1-4109-3332-4 pa; 1-4109-3332-6 pa

     LC 2009003459

In this introduction to evolution "clear language, embedded definitions, and interesting examples illustrate abstract concepts through both text and well-chosen photographs. . . . [The book] provides a clear and useful explanation of the theory of evolution, with multiple sources of evidence and a discussion of how it helps scientists to predict the implications of changes to the environment. . . . [The] book also includes suggested activities to test ideas as well as a thorough glossary and a Webliography." SLJ

Includes glossary and bibliographical references

Mehling, Randi

Great extinctions of the past; by Randi Mehling. Chelsea House 2007 72p il (Scientific American) lib bdg $30

Grades: 5 6 7 8   **576.8**

1. Dinosaurs 2. Mass extinctions 3. Prehistoric animals 4. Mass extinction of species

ISBN 978-0-7910-9049-7 lib bdg; 0-7910-9049-3 lib bdg

     LC 2006014851

Examines extinctions of prehistoric species including the dinosaurs, looks at the five largest extinctions ever, and explores the idea of a future mass extinction.

"The ideas in this book are . . . clearly explained. . . . [The book has] captioned color photos thoughout." SLJ

Includes glossary and bibliographical references

Newland, Sonya

Extinction! by Jim Pipe. Crabtree Publishing Company 2013 48 p. col. ill. (Crabtree chrome) (library) $30.60; (paperback) $9.95

Grades: 4 5 6   **576.8**

1. Extinct animals 2. Mass extinctions 3. Extinction (Biology)

ISBN 0778779254; 9780778779254; 9780778779346

     LC 2012032046

This book by Sonya Newland "explores both the history of extinction--dating back to the mass extinction of the Ordovician period 450 million years ago and the extinction of the dinosaurs 65 million years ago--as well as the possibility of the extinction of species in existence today. . . . In addition . . . Newland considers possible scenarios that might end life on Earth: an asteroid colliding with our planet . . . or an exploding nuclear bomb that blocks out the sun." (School Library Journal)

Includes bibliographical references and index

Pringle, Laurence P.

★ **Billions** of years, amazing changes; the story of evolution. Boyds Mills Press 2011 102p il $17.95

Grades: 4 5 6 7   **576.8**

1. Evolution

ISBN 978-1-59078-723-6; 1-59078-723-4

"Pringle provides an accessible introduction to complex concepts such as natural selection and genetics, paired with Jenkins's characteristically elegant collages. . . . Compelling photographs of fossils and living creatures, as well as Jenkins's paper collages, augment the substantial text. The presentation should help children gain a confident grasp on the fundamentals of evolution." Publ Wkly

Skurzynski, Gloria

★ **Are** we alone? scientists search for life in space. National Geographic Society 2004 92p il $18.95

Grades: 5 6 7 8   **576.8**

1. Life on other planets

ISBN 0-7922-6567-X

     LC 2003-17732

The author begins with a "history of how the idea of flying saucers and extraterrestrials became part of the American consciousness. Later chapters trace specific quests . . . for signs of life beyond earth. . . . The text remains readable even while explaining intricate scientific concepts and complex . . . ideas. The vibrant full-color photos enhance the work impressively." Booklist

Includes glossary and bibliographical references

Solway, Andrew

Why is there life on Earth? Raintree 2012 48p il (Earth, space, and beyond) $32; pa $8.99

Grades: 5 6 7 8   **576.8**

1. Life on other planets 2. Earth 3. Life -- Origin

ISBN 978-1-4109-4160-2; 978-1-4109-4166-4 pa

     LC 2010040160

"Delivering compact but broad summations about...life on Earth, [this] survey [is] well suited for review or reinforcement reading." SLJ

Includes glossary and bibliographical references

Turner, Pamela S.

★ **Life** on earth--and beyond; an astrobiologist's quest. Charlesbridge 2008 109p il map lib bdg $19.95; pa $11.95

Grades: 5 6 7 8   **576.8**

1. Space biology 2. Life on other planets 3. Astrophysicists

ISBN 978-1-58089-133-2 lib bdg; 1-58089-133-0 lib bdg; 978-1-58089-134-9 pa; 1-58089-134-9 pa

     LC 2007-01475

"Astrobiologists look outward from the Earth seeking evidence of life elsewhere in the universe. But, as this fascinating book shows, they also travel to places on Earth where extreme conditions may be similar to those on distant worlds. Turner follows astrobiologist Chris McKay as he looks for life in apparently hostile environments. . . . Illustrated with many excellent color photos and other images." Booklist

Includes bibliographical references

Walker, Robert

What is the theory of evolution? Crabtree Pub. Co. 2011 64p il (Shaping modern science) lib bdg $30.60; pa $10.95

Grades: 5 6 7 8   **576.8**
1. Evolution 2. Naturalists 3. Travel writers 4. Writers on science
ISBN 978-0-7787-7198-2 lib bdg; 0-7787-7198-9 lib bdg; 978-0-7787-7205-7 pa; 0-7787-7205-5 pa
LC 2010052628

This title is "not only written and organized well, but [it is] also gorgeous in design. Full-color photographs and illustrations are set over colorful backgrounds that add depth but not distraction. [The title] includes thought-provoking quotes from famous authors and scientists and some eyebrow-raising 'Quick Facts' throughout." SLJ

Includes glossary and bibliographical references

Weaver, Anne H.
The **voyage** of the beetle; a journey around the world with Charles Darwin and the search for the solution to the mystery of mysteries, as narrated by Rosie, an articulate beetle. [by] Anne H. Weaver; illustrated by George Lawrence. University of New Mexico Press 2007 80p il map $16.95
Grades: 4 5 6   **576.8**
1. Evolution 2. Naturalists 3. Travel writers 4. Writers on science 5. Beagle Expedition (1831-1836)
ISBN 978-0-8263-4304-8; 0-8263-4304-X
LC 2007008924

This book "is playful, creative, and beautifully conceived and executed, in terms of both the writing and the wonderful illustrations. . . . Through the eyes and narration of Darwin's fictional beetle friend Rosie, the reader is taken on the outer journey of Darwin's voyage (1831-1836) on the H.M.S. Beagle and the inner intellectual journey of Darwin's formulation of the theory of natural selection and the origin of the species." Sci Books Films

Includes bibliographical references

Winston, Robert M. L.
★ **Evolution** revolution; [by] Robert Wilson. DK Pub. 2009 96p il $16.99
Grades: 5 6 7 8   **576.8**
1. Evolution
ISBN 978-0-7566-45243-; 0-7566-4524-7

"The first two thirds of the book are devoted to the history of thought and research on evolution, from stories of Creation, through Darwin, to genetics. The last third looks at 'Evolution in Action.' Information on the fetuses of related species rubs shoulders with variations within species and a time line of the Earth. Visually, the book snaps with colored backgrounds, cool graphics, topflight photos, and clever word balloons coming from vintage black-and-white reproductions." SLJ

577 Ecology

Ecology; the delicate balance of life on earth. edited by Sherman Hollar. Rosen Educational Services, LLC 2012 87 p. col. ill. (library) $31.70
Grades: 5 6 7 8   **577**
1. Ecology 2. Environmentalism
ISBN 1615305076; 9781615305070
LC 2010052490

This book on ecology, edited by Sherman Hollar, "explores the formation of ecological communities and exam-ines the biological diversity that forms the backbone of life on the planet. . . . By parsing the natural world into various ecosystems and biomes" it looks at "interaction among species and between organisms and their natural habitats". (Publisher's note)

Includes bibliographical references (p. 84) and index.

Gardner, Robert
Ace your ecology and environmental science project; great science fair ideas. [by] Robert Gardner, Phyllis J. Perry, and Salvatore Tocci. Enslow Publishers 2009 128p il (Ace your science project) lib bdg $31.93
Grades: 5 6 7 8   **577**
1. Ecology 2. Science projects 3. Environmental sciences 4. Science -- Experiments
ISBN 978-0-7660-3216-3 lib bdg; 0-7660-3216-7 lib bdg
LC 2008-4683

"Dozens of . . . science activities are presented with background information, step-by-step instructions, and suggestions for extending to the science fair level. . . . Color illustrations and important safety information are included." Horn Book Guide

Includes bibliographical references

Godkin, Celia
Wolf island. Fitzhenry & Whiteside 2007 un il $17.95; pa $9.95
Grades: K 1 2 3   **577**
1. Ecology 2. Food chains (Ecology)
ISBN 1-55455-007-6; 1-55455-008-4 pa

A newly formatted edition of the title first published 1989 in Canada; first U.S. edition 1993 by Scientific American Books for Young Readers

When a family of wolves is removed from the food chain on a small island, the impact on the island's ecology is felt by the other animals living there.

"The food chain, especially its harsher aspects, can be difficult to explain to young children, but this gentle narrative conveys the realism without mawkish sentimentality. . . With a large format, arresting cover, and beautiful soft-edged illustrations, this presentation offers an effective balance between a documentary and a nature story." Booklist

Gray, Susan H.
Ecology the study of ecosystems; Susan H. Gray. Children's Press 2012 48 p. (pbk.) $6.95
Grades: 2 3 4 5   **577**
1. Environment 2. Biodiversity 3. Environmental sciences 4. Ecology
ISBN 0531282694; 9780531246757; 9780531282694
LC 2011030963

Author Susan Heinrichs Gray presents a children's book on ecology and ecosystems. She provides a history of ecology and discusses how ecosystems impact human beings. Gray also looks at the research being done by ecologists on the environment today and compares different ecosystems to one another, focusing on the importance of the rain forest to our environment.

Includes bibliographical references and index.

Housel, Debra J.
Ecosystems. Compass Point Books 2009 40p il map (Mission: science) lib bdg $26.60

Grades: 4 5 6 **577**
1. Ecology
ISBN 978-0-7565-4068-5 lib bdg; 0-7565-4068-2
lib bdg

LC 2008-35730

An introduction to the ways in which plants and animals interact with each other
Includes glossary

Larsen, Laurel
One night in the Everglades; Laurel Larsen; illustrated by Joyce Mihran Turley. Moonlight Pub./Taylor Trade Pub. 2012 30 p. (cloth: alk. paper) $15.95
Grades: 4 5 6 **577**
1. Nature study 2. Wetland ecology 3. Natural history -- Florida 4. Everglades (Fla.) 5. Ecologists -- Florida -- Everglades 6. Long-Term Ecological Research Program 7. Nature study -- Florida -- Everglades 8. Natural history -- Florida -- Everglades 9. Wetland ecology -- Florida -- Everglades 10. Everglades (Fla.) -- Environmental conditions
ISBN 0981770045; 9780981770048; 9780981770062
LC 2012007375

This children's book, by Laurel Larsen, illustrated by Joyce Mihran Turley, "follow[s] two scientists as they spend a night in the Everglades collecting water samples, photographing wildlife, and sloshing through marshes in an attempt to understand this mysterious ecosystem. Part of a long-term effort to return the Everglades to a natural state after a century of development, the scientists try to figure out what the 'river of grass' was like prior to human settlement." (Publisher's note)

Latham, Donna
Amazing biome projects you can build yourself; illustrated by Farah Rizvi. Nomad Press 2009 122p il map (Build it yourself) pa $15.95
Grades: 4 5 6 7 **577**
1. Ecology 2. Handicraft 3. Earth sciences 4. Science -- Experiments
ISBN 978-1-934670-40-8; 1-934670-40-5

"Although the text addresses young 'eco explorers' directly, this book will likely be used as much by teachers, parents, and organization leaders in planning group activities. Offering an overview of eight terrestrial biomes as well as the ocean, Latham crams a lot of information about climate, plants, animals, soil, and other characteristics onto every page. . . . Instructions for hands-on activities related to different biomes include craft projects such as pictographs and a cornhusk doll. Students can learn how to make a glacier, an erupting volcano, and a tornado in a bottle." SLJ
Includes glossary and bibliographical references

Ecology. Raintree 2009 48p il (Sci-hi: life science) lib bdg $31.43; pa $8.99
Grades: 5 6 7 8 **577**
1. Ecology
ISBN 978-1-4109-3328-7 lib bdg; 1-4109-3328-8 lib bdg; 978-1-4109-3336-2 pa; 1-4109-3336-9 pa
LC 2009003465

In this introduction to ecology "clear language, embedded definitions, and interesting examples illustrate abstract concepts through both text and well-chosen photographs.

. . [It] includes suggested activities to test ideas as well as a thorough glossary and a Webliography." SLJ
Includes glossary and bibliographical references

Lauber, Patricia
Who eats what? food chains and food webs. illustrated by Holly Keller. HarperCollins Pubs. 1995 32p il (Let's-read-and-find-out science) hardcover o.p. pa $4.95
Grades: K 1 2 3 **577**
1. Food chains (Ecology)
ISBN 0-06-022981-0; 0-06-022982-9 lib bdg; 0-06-445130-5 pa
LC 93-10609

"Clear, simple ink-and-watercolor drawings illustrate the clear, simple text. Informative and intriguing, this basic science book leads children to think about the complex and interdependent web of life on Earth." Booklist

The author "demonstrates the interconnectedness of nature by showing how creatures form chains through the foods they eat. . . . Lauber gives several examples, from short chains (apple to child) to the web of connections between sea creatures. She uses sea otters to show how the disappearance of one link in the chain can disrupt the flow of food both up and down." Bull Cent Child Books

Sayre, April Pulley
Trout are made of trees; [by] April Pulley Sayre; illustrated by Kate Endle. Charlesbridge 2008 un il lib bdg $15.95; pa $6.95
Grades: K 1 2 3 **577**
1. Food chains (Ecology)
ISBN 978-1-58089-137-0 lib bdg; 1-58089-137-3 lib bdg; 978-1-58089-138-7 pa; 1-58089-138-1 pa
LC 2007-02268

"A boy and girl, one white, one black, are exploring the stream and its inhabitants with their parents. In clear sentences, young readers follow autumn leaves as they fall from a tree into the water, are softened by algae and eaten by other creatures, which are then consumed by the trout. A more detailed explanation is included at the end of the book. Attractive collage illustrations in natural colors fill the spreads and help to explain the text. This unique introduction to how changes in nature create the food web illustrates how the whole world is interconnected." SLJ
Includes bibliographical references

Stille, Darlene R.
Nature interrupted; the science of environmental chain reactions. Compass Point Books 2009 48p il map (Headline science) lib bdg $27.93
Grades: 5 6 7 8 **577**
1. Ecology 2. Food chains (Ecology) 3. Environmental degradation
ISBN 978-0-7565-3949-8 lib bdg; 0-7565-3949-8 lib bdg
LC 2008007282

This "reviews the importance of subtle links in the environmental chain and the far-reaching consequences of its disruption. The possible harm to the food chain caused by the use of antibacterial soap is one case study. The flow of energy from one organism to the next in the food web and the unexpected results when this relationship is disrupted are shown in examinations of monarch butterflies, zebra mussels, and algal blooms. The color illustrations and charts . . .

are clear and helpful, and the text, although information rich, is not overly difficult." SLJ

Includes glossary and bibliographical references

Suzuki, David T.

★ **You** are the Earth; know your world so you can make it better. [by] David Suzuki and Kathy Vanderlinden; art by Wallace Edwards; diagrams by Talent Pun. rev ed; Greystone Books 2010 159p il $16.95

Grades: 4 5 6 7   577

1. Ecology 2. Human ecology

ISBN 978-1-55365-476-6; 1-55365-476-5

First published 1999 with title: You are the Earth: from dinosaur breath to pizza from dirt

"After devoting a chapter to each of life's necessities—air, water, soil (earth), energy (fire), love, and a spiritual connection with the universe—the authors close with a look at three social and environmental initiatives by young people; a set of review questions (with answers); and 10 consciousness-raising activities, from science projects to storytelling. Sourced, briefly told versions of folktales from several traditions are interspersed throughout, and the plentiful illustrations include color diagrams, comics, and crisply reproduced photos. . . . [The authors'] eloquent plea to see ourselves and the Earth as interdependent will inspire readers to sit up, look around, and take a little less for granted." SLJ

Includes glossary

VanCleave, Janice Pratt, 1942

Janice Vancleave's ecology for every kid; easy activities that make learning science fun. Wiley 1996 219p il maps (Science for every kid series) hardcover o.p. pa $10.95

Grades: 4 5 6 7   577

1. Ecology 2. Habitat (Ecology) 3. Science -- Experiments

ISBN 0-471-10100-1; 0-471-10086-2 pa

LC 95-6112

This book of science activities covers "25 topics, ranging from plant and animal food chains to the effect of plastics on the environment. Subjects are introduced in a 'What You Need to Know' section that gives explanation of the scientific principles, plus plenty of everyday examples. A brief preparatory exercise follows, usually in the form of an imaginative game. . . . Simple black-line drawings are crisp, uncluttered, and well placed. . . . Solid information and a generous portion of fun are combined to elevate this selection above the standard collection of experiments." SLJ

Includes glossary

Woodford, Chris

Arctic tundra and polar deserts; Revised ed. Raintree 2011 64p il map $34

Grades: 5 6 7 8 9   577

1. Tundra ecology 2. Polar regions

ISBN 978-1-4329-4172-7; 1-4329-4172-0

LC 2010012428

"...Provides detailed information suitable for middle school research projects, and browsing potential is high due to the colorful, graphic nature." Library Media Connection

577.078   Ecology - Experiments

VanCleave, Janice Pratt, 1942-

Step-by-step science experiments in ecology; by Janice VanCleave. Rosen Pub. 2013 80 p. col. ill. (Janice VanCleave's first-place science fair projects) (library) $33.25; (paperback) $14.15

Grades: 5 6 7 8   577.078

1. Ecology 2. Science -- Experiments 3. Ecology -- Experiments

ISBN 1448869803; 9781448869800; 9781448884698

This book by Janice VanCleave is part of the First-Place Science Fair Projects series. The books have an introduction to the subject—here, ecology, followed by 22 simple . . . experiments. Van Cleave states the basic goal of the experiments, followed by a list of necessary materials, most of which can be found around the house or easily acquired with minimal cost. Step-by-step instructions are clearly detailed and accompanied by diagrams where needed." (School Library Journal)

Includes bibliographical references (p. 76-78) and index.

577.09   Ecology - History, geographic treatment, biography

Pelletier, Mia

Avati; discovering Arctic ecology. Inhabit Media 2013 32 p. $14.95

Grades: 3 4 5   577.09

1. Arctic regions 2. Tundra ecology

ISBN 1927095131; 9781927095133

This book on arctic ecology by Mia Pelletier describes "a complex ecosystem that contains many thriving habitats, each supported by dozens of ecological relationships between plants and animals. From the many animals that live and hunt at the floe edge to the hundreds of insects that abound on the summer tundra, this book gives a . . . bird's-eye view of the . . . ways that animals, plants, and insects coexist in the Arctic ecosystem." (Publisher's note)

577.16   Food chains

Schwartz, David M.

Rotten pumpkin; A Rotten Tale in 15 Voices. David Schwarz; photographs by Dwight Kuhn. Creston Books 2013 32 p. $16.99

Grades: 1 2 3 4 5   577.16

1. Compost 2. Pumpkin

ISBN 1939547032; 9781939547033

In this book, by David Schwarz, with photographs by Dwight Kuhn, "Compost won't mean the same thing after readers have seen the . . . transformation of Jack from grinning pumpkin to mold-mottled wreckage. . . . The story of decomposition is . . . told so that science comes to life (and death)." The book "features a teacher guide in the back of the book, and additional material." (Publisher's note)

"What's scarier than a grinning jack-o'-lantern? How about what happens to it after Halloween? Kuhn's upbeat prose poems are written from the perspectives of 15 scavengers, insects, and molds that aid in a gourd's decomposition, which Kuhn captures in gruesomely vivid photographs.

As the pumpkin transforms from a crisp orange specimen to a blackened, sunken puddle of mush, the speakers include a mouse, "black rot" mold, and a fly ("You're gonna love hearing how I eat. I vomit on the pumpkin flesh. My vomit dissolves pumpkin nutrients so I can lap them up"). The inventive concept combines a Halloween theme with science that readers can easily replicate— - if they have the stomach for it." (Publishers Weekly)

577.2   Specific factors affecting ecology

Godkin, Celia

    Fire! Fitzhenry & Whiteside 2006 un il $17.95

Grades: 2 3 4   **577.2**

    1. Forest fires 2. Forest ecology

    ISBN 1-55041-889-0

"Focusing on events in one location, this handsome volume presents the cycle of forest fires in words and pictures. . . . Clear, concise writing and vivid artwork make this a fine presentation on the subject." Booklist

Peluso, Beth A.

    The **charcoal** forest; how fire helps animals and plants. written and illustrated by Beth A. Peluso. Mountain Press Pub. Co. 2007 56p il pa $12

Grades: 3 4 5 6   **577.2**

    1. Forest fires 2. Forest plants 3. Forest animals 4. Forest ecology 5. Rocky Mountains

    ISBN 978-0-87842-532-7 pa; 0-87842-532-2 pa

                         LC 2007003358

This "explores the new habitat created by [a forest] fire. Focusing on the Northern Rocky Mountains of the United States and Canada, the book describes twenty species of animals and plants that contribute to the reclamation and renewal of the charcoal forest." Publisher's note

Simon, Seymour

    Wildfires. Morrow Junior Bks. 1996 un il hardcover o.p. pa $6.99

Grades: 4 5 6 7   **577.2**

    1. Forest fires 2. Forest ecology

    ISBN 0-688-17530-9 pa

                         LC 95-12653

"Exploring the place of fire in nature, Simon explains that . . . forest fires have important functions in the ecosystem. With a brilliantly clear and colorful photograph facing each page of text, the book describes the causes and the progression of the wildfires that burned areas of Yellowstone National Park in 1988, explains how the fires were beneficial in many ways. . . . Lucid writing and excellent book design." Booklist

577.3   Ecology of specific environments

Brenner, Barbara

    One small place in a tree; illustrated by Tom Leonard. HarperCollins Publishers 2004 un il $15.99; lib bdg $16.89

Grades: 2 3 4   **577.3**

    1. Forest ecology

    ISBN 0-688-17180-X; 0-688-17181-8 lib bdg

                         LC 2002-1181

A child visitor observes as one tiny scratch in a tree develops into a home for a variety of woodland animals over many years, even after the tree has fallen.

"Brenner makes the science enjoyable and understandable, and Leonard's highly detailed, realistic illustrations provide great visual aid." Booklist

Collard, Sneed B.

    Forest in the clouds; by Sneed Collard III; illustrated by Michael Rothman. Charlesbridge Pub. 2000 un il map $16.95; pa $7.95

Grades: 2 3 4   **577.3**

    1. Cloud forests 2. Forest ecology 3. Natural history -- Costa Rica

    ISBN 0-88106-985-X; 0-88106-986-8 pa

                         LC 98-6150

Describes some of the exotic plants and animals that live in the cloud forest of Costa Rica, and discusses some environmental threats faced by this region

"Rothman's detailed acrylic paintings, dominated by rich greens and browns, cover the better part of each spread. . . . Although valuable for reports, Collard's book will interest browsers as well." SLJ

Fleisher, Paul

    Forest food webs. Lerner Publications Co. 2008 48p il (Early bird food webs) lib bdg $26.60

Grades: 2 3 4 5   **577.3**

    1. Forest ecology 2. Food chains (Ecology)

    ISBN 978-0-8225-6729-5

                       LC 2007-01373

"This colorful volume introduces the forest, with an emphasis on food webs. Clearly written chapters focus on topics such as plants, herbivores, carnivores, decomposers, and people's enjoyment, use, and destruction of forests in the U.S." Booklist

    Includes glossary and bibliographical references

Fusco Castaldo, Nancy

    Rainforests; an activity guide for ages 6-9. {by} Nancy F. Castaldo. Chicago Review Press 2003 133p il $14.95

Grades: 2 3 4 5   **577.3**

    1. Rain forest ecology

    ISBN 1-55652-476-5

                       LC 2002-152661

Provides facts and activities that explore tropical and temperate ancient forests, discusses how individuals can help preserve them, and describes well-known and unfamiliar creatures of the rain forest

"The activities are varied and interesting, ranging from science projects to crafts to recipes. . . . The book would serve as a valuable resource." SLJ

    Includes bibliographical references

Gibbons, Gail

    Nature's green umbrella; tropical rain forests. Morrow Junior Bks. 1994 un il maps hardcover o.p. pa $5.95

Grades: K 1 2 3   **577.3**

1. Rain forest ecology
ISBN 0-688-12353-8; 0-688-12354-6 lib bdg; 0-688-15411-5 pa

LC 93-17569

Describes the climatic conditions of the rain forest as well as the different layers of plants and animals that comprise the ecosystem

The language is "simple, yet poetic and evocative. . . . Colorful maps pinpoint the locations of these global resources. Green vines entwine around the borders of each page and enclose the text and bright illustrations." Sci Books Films

Jackson, Kay

Rain forests; by Kay Jackson. KidHaven Press 2007 48p il (Our environment) lib bdg $23.70

Grades: 5 6 7 8   **577.3**

1. Rain forests 2. Rain forest ecology
ISBN 978-0-7377-3624-3

LC 2007006892

"Jackson defines rain forests. . . . She explains why rain forests are important, . . . the causes of rain forest destruction, and current efforts to save diverse ecosystems. The writing is clear and succinct. . . . Full-color, captioned photographs and drawings appear on nearly every page." Booklist

Includes bibliographical references

Johnson, Rebecca L.

A **walk** in the boreal forest; with illustrations by Phyllis V. Saroff. Carolrhoda Bks. 2001 48p il map (Biomes of North America) lib bdg $23.93

Grades: 3 4 5 6   **577.3**

1. Forest ecology
ISBN 1-57505-156-7

LC 00-8240

Describes the climate, seasons, plants, animals, and soil of the boreal forest, a biome or land zone, which stretches across the northern parts of North America, Europe, and Asia

"A fine overview of the plant and animal life of the boreal forest. . . . Excellent full-color photographs." SLJ

Includes glossary and bibliographical references

A **walk** in the deciduous forest; with illustrations by Phyllis V. Saroff. Carolrhoda Bks. 2001 48p il map (Biomes of North America) lib bdg $23.93

Grades: 3 4 5 6   **577.3**

1. Forest ecology
ISBN 1-57505-155-9

LC 00-8243

Takes readers on a walk through a forest of trees that lose their leaves in the fall, showing examples of how the animals and plants depend on each other and their environment to survive

"The simple design and clearly written, informative text will appeal to readers who enjoy nature." Horn Book Guide

Includes glossary and bibliographical references

Lasky, Kathryn

The **most** beautiful roof in the world; exploring the rainforest canopy. photographs by Christopher G. Knight. Harcourt Brace & Co. 1997 un il hardcover o.p. pa $9

Grades: 4 5 6 7   **577.3**

1. Botanists 2. Rain forest ecology
ISBN 0-15-200893-4; 0-15-200897-7 pa

LC 95-48193

Describes the work of Meg Lowman in the rainforest canopy, an area unexplored until the last ten years and home to previously unknown species of plants and animals

"Fresh in out-look and intriguing in details, this memorable book features colorful photographs that reflect the you-are-there quality of the text." Booklist

Includes glossary

Levy, Janey

Discovering rain forests; [by] Janey Levy. PowerKids Press 2007 32p il map (World habitats) lib bdg $23.95

Grades: 3 4 5   **577.3**

1. Rain forests 2. Rain forest ecology
ISBN 978-1-4042-3782-7 lib bdg; 1-4042-3782-8 lib bdg

LC 2006036867

This book about rain forest ecology "includes 10 chapters with information on climate, location, plants, animals, people, conservation, and page of relevant facts and figures. Clear, colorful photographs show the landscape and the varied plants and wildlife." SLJ

Includes glossary

Lundgren, Julie K.

Forest fare; studying food webs in the forest. [by] Julie K. Lundgren. Rourke Pub. 2009 32p il map (Studying food webs) lib bdg $28.50

Grades: 3 4 5   **577.3**

1. Forest ecology 2. Food chains (Ecology)
ISBN 978-1-60472-316-8 lib bdg; 1-60472-316-5 lib bdg

LC 2008-24858

This book has "stunning photos, fascinating facts, and intriguing examples. . . . Herbivores, omnivores, and carnivores specific to . . . [the forest] ecosystem are presented. . . . 'Chew on this' insets add further interest and information. . . . [This] will appeal to readers." SLJ

Includes glossary and bibliographical references

Pfeffer, Wendy

A **log's** life; illustrations by Robin Brickman. Simon & Schuster Bks. for Young Readers 1997 un il $16

Grades: K 1 2 3   **577.3**

1. Oak 2. Forest ecology
ISBN 0-689-80636-1

LC 95-30020

This is an "introduction to the life, death, and decay of an oak tree. The simple, informative text presents the complex cast of characters residing in or on the living tree as well as the decomposing log. . . . The verbal descriptions of this rich ecosystem are enhanced by striking illustrations of three-dimensional paper sculptures, often so realistic as to seem to be preserved natural specimens." SLJ

Pyers, Greg

The **biodiversity** of rain forests. Marshall Cavendish 2010 32p il (Biodiversity) lib bdg $28.50

Grades: 4 5 6   577.3
1. Rain forest ecology
ISBN 978-1-60870-073-8 lib bdg; 1-60870-073-9
lib bdg
"Page format is attractive, filled with easy-to-understand
fact boxes, charts, graphs, maps and diagrams, and interesting captioned color photographs, all well-balanced within
the main text." Libr Media Connect
Includes glossary

The **biodiversity** of woodlands. Marshall Cavendish
2010 32p il (Biodiversity) lib bdg $28.50
Grades: 4 5 6   577.3
1. Forest ecology
ISBN 978-1-60870-074-5 lib bdg; 1-60870-074-7
lib bdg
"Page format is attractive, filled with easy-to-understand
fact boxes, charts, graphs, maps and diagrams, and interesting captioned color photographs, all well-balanced within
the main text." Libr Media Connect
Includes glossary

Simon, Seymour
Tropical rainforests. Collins 2010 30p il $16.99; lib
bdg $17.89
Grades: 3 4 5 6   577.3
1. Rain forests 2. Rain forest ecology
ISBN 978-0-06-114253-6; 0-06-114253-0; 978-0-06-
114254-3 lib bdg; 0-06-114254-9 lib bdg
"Simon's short overview has a familiar format: large
pages of oversize text facing sharp color photos of trees, animals, and plants provide an inviting overview of the biome
that is populated by the largest variety of plant and animal
species on the planet, with many of them yet to be discovered. . . . Simon's careful descriptions hold a great deal of
appeal for young people." SLJ
Includes glossary

Slade, Suzanne
What if there were no gray wolves? a book about the
temperate forest ecosystem. illustrated by Carol Schwartz.
Picture Window Books 2011 24p il map (Food chain reactions) lib bdg $25.99; pa $8.95
Grades: 2 3 4   577.3
1. Wolves 2. Forest ecology
ISBN 978-1-4048-6020-9 lib bdg; 1-4048-6020-7 lib
bdg; 978-1-4048-6395-8 pa; 1-4048-6395-8 pa
LC 2010009877
Discusses the temperate forest ecosystem and the role of
the gray wolf in helping to maintain it, describing the wolf's
place on the food chain and what would happen to the temperate forest if the gray wolf were to become extinct.
"Radiant illustrations are paired with simple, perceptive sentences to underscore the impact of the loss of [gray
wolves]. . . . In a very effective convention extinct plants and
animals are placed in silhouettes within many illustrations—
the black void left by the loss of each species increases with
each page. This . . . will engage readers on many levels." SLJ
Includes glossary and bibliographical references

Tagliaferro, Linda
Explore the tropical rain forest; by Linda Tagliaferro.
Capstone Press 2007 32p il map (Explore the biomes)
$16.95; pa $6.95

Grades: PreK K 1 2   577.3
1. Rain forest ecology
ISBN 978-0-7368-6407-7; 0-7368-6407-5; 978-0-
7368-9630-6 pa; 0-7368-9630-9 pa
LC 2006004107
This is an introduction to the tropical rain forest habitat
and some of its plants and animals.
This book "uses vivid, sense-appealing language. . . .
An attractive . . . format displays the captions to colorful
photographs." Sci Books Films
Includes bibliographical references

Vogt, Richard Carl
★ **Rain** forests. Simon & Schuster Books for Young
Readers 2009 64p il (Insiders) $16.99
Grades: 4 5 6 7   577.3
1. Rain forests
ISBN 978-1-4169-3866-8; 1-4169-3866-4
LC 2008061111
"The layers of a rain forest are drawn with exacting detail in every imaginable shade of green, while circular inserts
zoom in on flora with accompanying stats. Running down
the length of the spread are markers delineating the cutoff
points for each layer—emergent, canopy, and so on. The rest
of the book is similarly fine, bringing animals, reptiles, and
insects into the mix. . . . Some photographs join the mostly
hand-illustrated affair. . . . What will grab browsers are the
3D cover and vivid drawings on thick, oversize pages, but
what will keep them reading is a cumulative sense of the
rain forest as a verdant universe nearly festering with life."
Booklist

577.34   Rain forest ecology

Duke, Kate
In the rainforest; written and illustrated by Kate Duke.
HarperCollins Publishers 2014 40 p. color illustrations
(hardcover) $17.99
Grades: K 1 2 3   577.34
1. Rain forests 2. Rain forests -- Pictorial works
ISBN 0060282592; 9780060282592; 9780064451970
LC 2013047947
"The rainforest is home to millions of plant and ani-
mal species. Some animals live high up in the trees, some
crawl across the forest floor, and some tunnel underground,
but they all depend on one another and the rain to survive."
(Publisher's note)
"This informative volume from the dependable Let's-
Read-and-Find-Out science series offers an uncommonly
readable introduction to rain forests. Instructions for making
a terrarium are appended." Booklist

Welsbacher, Anne
Protecting Earth's rain forests; by Anne Welsbacher.
Lerner Publications 2009 72p il map (Saving our living
Earth) lib bdg $30.60
Grades: 5 6 7 8   577.34
1. Rain forests 2. Environmental protection
ISBN 978-0-8225-7562-7 lib bdg; 0-8225-7562-0
lib bdg
LC 2007-38859

"Provides a thorough, interesting discussion of multiple aspects of [rain forest protection], including historical origins, the current situation, and potential solutions. . . . Photos from around the world accompany discussions. . . . Solid choice to replace outdated books." SLJ

Includes glossary and bibliographical references

577.4   Grassland ecology

Bateman, Donna M.

Out on the prairie; Donna M. Bateman; illustrated by Susan Swan. Charlesbridge 2012 32 p. (reinforced for library use) $15.95

Grades: PreK K 1 2   **577.4**

1. Counting 2. Prairie animals 3. Picture books for children 4. Badlands National Park (S.D.) 5. Prairie animals -- South Dakota -- Badlands National Park 6. Prairie ecology -- South Dakota -- Badlands National Park

ISBN 1580893775; 9781580893770; 9781580893787

LC 2011025782

For this counting book, "[Donna M.] Bateman Bateman has chosen representative features and creatures" of the mixed-grass prairie of Badlands National Park in South Dakota "to introduce a remarkable ecosystem. Counting from one to 10, she goes on to include pronghorns, meadowlarks, prairie dogs, grasshoppers, grouse, owls, rattlesnakes, coyotes and toads in a series of verses that also span the day from dawn to night." (Kirkus)

Collard, Sneed B.

The **prairie** builders; reconstructing America's lost grasslands. written and photographed by Sneed B. Collard III. Houghton Mifflin Co. 2005 66p il (Scientists in the field) $17; pa $8.95

Grades: 4 5 6 7   **577.4**

1. Prairies 2. Nature conservation

ISBN 978-0-618-39687-0; 0-618-39687-X; 978-0-547-01441-8 pa; 0-547-01441-4 pa

LC 2004-13201

This describes an effort to restore part of the native tall-grass prairie in the the 8,000-acre Neal Smith National Wildlife Refuge in Iowa

"The engaging text is accompanied by large, inviting color photographs. . . . An essential purchase for libraries in prairie regions and a worthwhile choice for others." SLJ

Includes bibliographical references

Jackson, Kay

Explore the grasslands; by Kay Jackson. Capstone Press 2007 32p il map (Explore the biomes) $16.95; pa $6.95

Grades: PreK K 1 2   **577.4**

1. Grassland ecology

ISBN 978-0-7368-6405-3; 0-7368-6405-9; 978-0-7368-9628-3 pa; 0-7368-9628-7 pa

LC 2006005641

This is a introduction to grassland ecology and some of its plants and animals

This book "uses vivid, sense-appealing language. . . . An attractive . . . format displays the captions to colorful photographs." Sci Books Films

Includes bibliographical references

Johnson, Rebecca L.

A **walk** in the prairie; with illustrations by Phyllis V. Saroff. Carolrhoda Bks. 2001 48p il map (Biomes of North America) lib bdg $23.93

Grades: 3 4 5 6   **577.4**

1. Prairie ecology

ISBN 1-57505-153-2

LC 00-8252

Describes the climate, soil, seasons, plants, and animals of the North American prairie and the ways in which the plants and animals depend on each other and their environment to survive

Includes glossary and bibliographical references

Levy, Janey

Discovering the tropical savanna; [by] Janey Levy. PowerKids Press 2008 32p il map (World habitats) lib bdg $23.95

Grades: 3 4 5   **577.4**

1. Grassland ecology

ISBN 978-1-4042-3783-4 lib bdg; 1-4042-3783-6 lib bdg

LC 2006103368

This book about the ecology of the tropical savanna "includes 10 chapters with information on climate, location, plants, animals, people, conservation, and page of relevant facts and figures. The [text is] concise and accessible. Clear, colorful photographs show the landscape and the varied plants and wildlife." SLJ

Includes glossary

Pattison, Darcy

Prairie storms; by Darcy Pattison; illustrated by Kathleen Rietz. Sylvan Dell Pub. 2011 un il map $16.95; pa $8.95

Grades: K 1 2 3   **577.4**

1. Storms 2. Prairie animals 3. Prairie ecology

ISBN 978-1-60718-129-3; 1-60718-129-0; 978-1-60718-139-2 pa; 1-60718-139-8 pa; 978-1-60718-149-1 e-book; 1-60718-149-5 english e-book; 978-1-60718-159-0 spanish e-book; 1-60718-159-2 spanish e-book

LC 2011016339

This describes the prairie ecosystem through its ever-changing weather. Each month features a storm typical of that season and a prairie animal who must shelter, hide, escape, or endure those storms.

"Beautiful two-page framed spreads do a good job of showing an animal or bird of the plains and the weather conditions that might be currently affecting. The book gives a unique look at the differing plains habitats." Sci Books Films

Sill, Cathryn P.

Grasslands; written by Cathryn Sill; illustrated by John Sill. Peachtree Publishers 2011 un il (About habitats) $16.95

Grades: K 1 2 3 4   **577.4**
1. Grasslands 2. Grassland ecology
ISBN 978-1-56145-559-1; 1-56145-559-8
LC 2010026690

"With simple, informative sentences paired with beautifully detailed watercolor paintings, this title . . . will introduce young grade-schoolers to grassland ecology across the world: the climate, plants that grow there, and the wildlife that have adapted to survive in the large open spaces. . . . Great for classroom sharing." Booklist

Slade, Suzanne
What if there were no bees? a book about the grassland ecosystem. illustrated by Carol Schwartz. Picture Window Books 2010 24p il map (Food chain reactions) lib bdg $25.99; pa $8.95
Grades: 2 3 4   **577.4**
1. Bees 2. Grassland ecology 3. Fertilization of plants
ISBN 978-1-4048-6019-3 lib bdg; 1-4048-6019-3 lib bdg; 978-1-4048-6394-1 pa; 1-4048-6394-X pa
LC 2010006035

"Radiant illustrations are paired with simple, perceptive sentences to underscore the impact of the loss of [bees]. . . . In a very effective convention extinct plants and animals are placed in silhouettes within many illustrations—the black void left by the loss of each species increases with each page. This . . . will engage readers on many levels." SLJ
Includes glossary and bibliographical references

Stille, Darlene R.
Grasslands. Children's Press 1999 47p il (True book) lib bdg $22; pa $6.95
Grades: 2 3 4   **577.4**
1. Grassland ecology
ISBN 0-516-21509-4 lib bdg; 0-516-26762-0 pa
LC 98-49728

Examines the different types of grasslands and the plant and animal life they support
Includes glossary and bibliographical references

577.5 Ecology of miscellaneous environments

Banting, Erinn
Caves; Erinn Banting. AV2 by Weigl 2012 32 p. col. ill., col. map (Ecosystems) (hardcover) $28.55; (paperback) $13.95
Grades: 4 5 6   **577.5**
1. Caves 2. Cave ecology
ISBN 1616906391; 1616906456; 9781616906399; 9781616906450
LC 2010050985

This book by Erinn Banting is part of the "Biomes" series. "Caves are unique ecosystems that are found on all seven continents. This book explores the plants and animals that have adapted to life in this unique environment." (Publisher's note) "Explanations of climate and physical characteristics are accompanied by appropriate diagrams and illustrations." (School Library Journal)

Callery, Sean
Polar lands. Kingfisher 2011 il (Life cycles) $12.99

Grades: 2 3 4   **577.5**
1. Food chains (Ecology) 2. Antarctica 3. Arctic regions
ISBN 978-0-7534-6691-9; 0-7534-6691-0

"This focuses on 11 Arctic and Antarctic animals, exploring their life cycles and the ways in which they are interconnected by a food chain. The first food chain Callery presents is hermit crab, Arctic tern, Arctic fox, polar bear. Each spread is devoted to a single animal. . . . Beautiful closeup photographs show the animals in their natural habitats eating, playing and interacting with one another. . . . A great beginning look at the lifecycles of some fascinating animals and a solid tool for learning about food chains." Kirkus

Johansson, Philip
The **dry** desert; a web of life. Enslow Publishers 2004 48p il (World of biomes) lib bdg $18.95
Grades: 3 4 5   **577.5**
1. Desert ecology
ISBN 0-7660-2200-5
LC 2003-20443

This describes the plants, animals, and ecology of deserts of the world
Includes glossary and bibliographical references

The **frozen** tundra; a web of life. Enslow Pubs. 2004 48p il map (World of biomes) lib bdg $18.95
Grades: 3 4 5   **577.5**
1. Tundra ecology
ISBN 0-7660-2176-9
LC 2003-2271

This describes the ecology of the arctic tundra
This book is "extremely well written, and [it contains] ample information presented in a way that is easy to understand." Sci Books Films
Includes glossary and bibliographical references

Johnson, Rebecca L.
A **walk** in the tundra; with illustrations by Phyllis V. Saroff. Carolrhoda Bks. 2001 48p il map (Biomes of North America) lib bdg $23.93; pa $8.95
Grades: 3 4 5 6   **577.5**
1. Tundra ecology
ISBN 1-57505-157-5 lib bdg; 1-57505-526-0 pa
LC 00-8245

Takes readers on a walk in the tundra, showing examples of how the animals and plants of the tundra are connected and dependent on each other and the tundra's soil and climate
"A visually pleasing title with plenty of clear, colorful photographs of the biome's flora and fauna throughout the year." SLJ
Includes glossary and bibliographical references

Levy, Janey
Discovering mountains; [by] Janey Levy. PowerKids Press 2008 32p il map (World habitats) lib bdg $23.95
Grades: 3 4 5   **577.5**
1. Mountains 2. Mountain ecology
ISBN 978-1-4042-3785-8 lib bdg; 1-4042-3785-2 lib bdg
LC 2006103369

This book about mountain ecology "includes 10 chapters with information about climate, location, plants, animals, people, conservation, and a page of relevant facts and figures. The [text is] concise and accessible. Clear, colorful photographs show the landscape and the varied plants and wildlife." Booklist

Includes glossary

Discovering the Arctic tundra; [by] Janey Levy. PowerKids Press 2008 32p il map (World habitats) lib bdg $23.95

Grades: 3 4 5   **577.5**

1. Tundra ecology 2. Arctic regions

ISBN 978-1-4042-3787-2 lib bdg; 1-4042-3787-9 lib bdg

LC 2006103405

This book about the ecology of the Arctic tundra "includes 10 chapters with information on climate, location, plants, animals, people, conservation, and a page of relevant facts and figures. The [text is] concise and accessible. Clear, colorful photographs show the landscape and the varied plants and wildlife." Booklist

Includes glossary

Lynch, Wayne

Sonoran Desert; text and photographs by Wayne Lynch; assisted by Aubrey Lang. NorthWord Books 2009 64p il (Our wild world ecosystems) $16.95

Grades: 5 6 7 8   **577.5**

1. Desert ecology 2. Sonoran Desert 3. Natural history -- Sonoran Desert

ISBN 978-1-58979-389-7; 1-58979-389-7

LC 2008036635

"An in-depth look at a vibrant ecosystem. Spilling over the Mexican border into Arizona and New Mexico, the Sonoran Desert is especially rich in varied plants, animals, insects, and other critters that call it home. Lynch shares his expertise and experiences in a clearly written, conversational text, lavishly illustrated with his own crisp color photos." SLJ

Marsico, Katie

A **home** on the tundra; by Katie Marsico. Children's Press 2007 24p il (Scholastic news nonfiction readers) $20

Grades: 1 2 3   **577.5**

1. Tundra ecology

ISBN 0-516-25345-X; 978-0-516-25345-9

LC 2006002306

An introduction to tundra ecology

"Simple, easy-to-read. . . . Everything students need for reports is beautifully depicted with scenic full-color photographs of the land, the plants, and the animals that live there." SLJ

Includes bibliographical references

Moss, Miriam

This is the mountain; illustrated by Adrienne Kennaway. Frances Lincoln 2011 un il $17.95

Grades: K 1 2 3   **577.5**

1. Mountain ecology 2. Natural history -- Africa 3. Mount Kilimanjaro (Tanzania)

ISBN 978-1-84507-984-0; 1-84507-984-1

"Illustrated with attractive accessible watercolors, this picture book introduces Mount Kilimanjaro, from the people and animals living on the plains around it to the mountainside and the glaciers at its peak. . . . The book has real value

for children. Not only does it show life on and around Mount Kilimanjaro, it shows how the landforms and ecosystems change as one moves up the mountain." Booklist

Pyers, Greg

The **biodiversity** of coasts. Marshall Cavendish 2010 32p il map (Biodiversity) lib bdg $28.50

Grades: 4 5 6   **577.5**

1. Coasts 2. Seashore ecology

ISBN 978-1-60870-069-1 lib bdg; 1-60870-069-0 lib bdg

"Page format is attractive, filled with easy-to-understand fact boxes, charts, graphs, maps and diagrams, and interesting captioned color photographs, all well-balanced within the main text." Libr Media Connect

Includes glossary

The **biodiversity** of deserts. Marshall Cavendish 2010 32p il (Biodiversity) lib bdg $28.50

Grades: 4 5 6   **577.5**

1. Desert ecology

ISBN 978-1-60870-071-4 lib bdg; 1-60870-071-2 lib bdg

"Page format is attractive, filled with easy-to-understand fact boxes, charts, graphs, maps and diagrams, and interesting captioned color photographs, all well-balanced within the main text." Libr Media Connect

Includes glossary

The **biodiversity** of polar regions. Marshall Cavendish 2010 32p il (Biodiversity) lib bdg $28.50

Grades: 4 5 6   **577.5**

1. Polar regions

ISBN 978-1-60870-072-1 lib bdg; 1-60870-072-0 lib bdg

"Page format is attractive, filled with easy-to-understand fact boxes, charts, graphs, maps and diagrams, and interesting captioned color photographs, all well-balanced within the main text." Libr Media Connect

Includes glossary

Slade, Suzanne

What if there were no lemmings? a book about the tundra ecosystem. illustrated by Carol Schwartz. Picture Window Books 2011 24p il map (Food chain reactions) lib bdg $25.99; pa $8.95

Grades: 2 3 4   **577.5**

1. Lemmings 2. Tundra ecology 3. Animals -- Arctic regions

ISBN 978-1-4048-6021-6 lib bdg; 1-4048-6021-5 lib bdg; 978-1-4048-6396-5 pa; 1-4048-6396-6 pa

LC 2010009878

Discusses the tundra ecosystem and the role of lemmings as a keystone species in helping to maintain it, describing the lemmings' place on the food chain and what would happen to the tundra if they were to become extinct.

"Radiant illustrations are paired with simple, perceptive sentences to underscore the impact of the loss of [lemmings]. . . . In a very effective convention extinct plants and animals are placed in silhouettes within many illustrations— the black void left by the loss of each species increases with each page. This . . . will engage readers on many levels." SLJ

Includes glossary and bibliographical references

Tagliaferro, Linda

Explore the tundra; by Linda Tagliaferro. Capstone Press 2007 32p il map (Explore the biomes) $16.95; pa $6.95

Grades: PreK K 1 2   **577.5**

1. Tundra ecology

ISBN 978-0-7368-6408-4; 0-7368-6408-3; 978-0-7368-9631-3 pa; 0-7368-9631-7 pa

LC 2006004108

This is an introduction to the tundra and some of its plants and animals.

This book "uses vivid, sense-appealing language. . . . An attractive . . . format displays the captions to colorful photographs." Sci Books Films

Includes bibliographical references

Wojahn, Rebecca Hogue

An **Australian** outback food chain; a who-eats-what adventure. [by] Rebecca Hogue Wojahn, Donald Wojahn. Lerner Publications 2009 64p il map (Follow that food chain) lib bdg $30.60

Grades: 3 4 5 6   **577.5**

1. Food chains (Ecology) 2. Animals -- Australia 3. Natural history -- Australia

ISBN 978-0-8225-7499-6 lib bdg; 0-8225-7499-3 lib bdg

LC 2008021117

"Numerous photos of plants and animals in their habitats appear on these pages, accompanied by an explanation of the basic elements of a food chain and definitions of terms such as predators, consumers, producers, and decomposers. What sets [this book] apart . . . is [its] 'choose your own adventure' style. . . . The authors instruct [readers] to choose one of the region's carnivores and explore its food chain. . . . [including the] dingo, saltwater crocodile, wedge-tailed eagle, [and] Gould's monitor. . . . Choices result in returning to some pages more than once and sometimes discovering a 'dead end,' a critically endangered or extinct animal. . . . The interconnections created by the choices effectively illustrate the complexity of food webs while providing information about the plants and animals that form the components. Lively, engaging writing helps sustain interest." SLJ

Includes glossary and bibliographical references

A **tundra** food chain; a who-eats-what adventure in the Arctic. [by] Rebecca Hogue Wojahn, Donald Wojahn. Lerner Publications 2009 64p il map (Follow that food chain) lib bdg $30.60

Grades: 3 4 5 6   **577.5**

1. Tundra ecology 2. Food chains (Ecology) 3. Animals -- Arctic regions

ISBN 978-0-8225-7500-9 lib bdg; 0-8225-7500-0 lib bdg

LC 2008027092

"Numerous photos of plants and animals in their habitats appear on these pages, accompanied by an explanation of the basic elements of a food chain and definitions of terms such as predators, consumers, producers, and decomposers. What sets [this book] apart . . . . is [its] 'choose your own adventure' style. . . . The authors instruct [readers] to choose one of the region's carnivores and explore its food chain. Six animals (grizzly bear, snowy owl, Arctic wolf, polar bear, wolverine, and peregrine falcon) are presented. . . . Choices result in returning to some pages more than once and sometimes

discovering a 'dead end,' a critically endangered or extinct animal. . . . The interconnections created by the choices effectively illustrate the complexity of food webs while providing information about the plants and animals that form the components. Lively, engaging writing helps sustain interest." SLJ

Includes glossary and bibliographical references

577.54   Desert ecology

Johnson, Rebecca L.

A **walk** in the desert; with illustrations by Phyllis V. Saroff. Carolrhoda Bks. 2001 48p il map (Biomes of North America) lib bdg $23.93; pa $8.95

Grades: 3 4 5 6   **577.54**

1. Desert ecology

ISBN 1-57505-152-4 lib bdg; 1-57505-529-5 pa

LC 00-8251

Describes the climate, soil, plants, and animals of North American deserts and the ways in which the plants and animals depend on each other and their environment to survive

"The many full-color, close-up photographs and black-and-white drawings are sure to engage readers' interest." SLJ

Includes glossary and bibliographical references

577.6   Aquatic ecology

Hooks, Gwendolyn

Freshwater feeders; studying food webs in freshwater. Rourke Pub. 2009 32p il map (Studying food webs) lib bdg $28.50

Grades: 3 4 5   **577.6**

1. Freshwater ecology 2. Food chains (Ecology)

ISBN 978-1-60472-317-5 lib bdg; 1-60472-317-3 lib bdg

LC 2008-24857

This book has "stunning photos, fascinating facts, and intriguing examples. . . . Herbivores, omnivores, and carnivores specific to . . . [the freshwater] ecosystem are presented. . . . 'Chew on this' insets add further interest and information. . . . [This] will appeal to readers." SLJ

Includes glossary

Johansson, Philip

Lakes and rivers; a freshwater web of life. [by] Philip Johansson. Enslow Elementary 2007 48p il (Wonderful water biomes) lib bdg $23.93

Grades: 3 4 5   **577.6**

1. Lakes 2. Rivers 3. Freshwater ecology

ISBN 978-0-7660-2812-8 lib bdg; 0-7660-2812-7 lib bdg

LC 2006100470

This describes the plants, animals, and ecology of lakes and rivers.

Includes glossary and bibliographical references

Marshes and swamps; a wetland web of life. [by] Philip Johansson. Enslow Elementary 2007 48p il (Wonderful water biomes) lib bdg $23.93

Grades: 3 4 5   **577.6**
1. Wetlands 2. Marsh ecology
ISBN 978-0-7660-2814-2 lib bdg; 0-7660-2814-3
lib bdg
LC 2006039769
This describes the plants, animals, and ecology of
marshes and swamps.
This has "good-quality color photos. . . . Well written
and engaging." SLJ
Includes glossary and bibliographical references

Lynette, Rachel
River food chains. Heinemann Library 2011 48p il
map (Protecting food chains) lib bdg $32; pa $8.99
Grades: 4 5 6 7   **577.6**
1. River ecology 2. Food chains (Ecology)
ISBN 978-1-4329-3861-1 lib bdg; 1-4329-3861-4 lib
bdg; 978-1-4329-3868-0 pa; 1-4329-3868-1 pa
LC 2009049552
This book explores the species found in river food chains
and webs, and discusses why these food chains and webs
need to be protected.
"Featuring colorful, glossy images and accessible prose,
this . . . offers a good introduction to the web of life in rivers. . . . Conservation issues are highlighted throughout,
with specific suggestions for youth to get involved. . . . An
informative, thought-provoking resource that conveys the
fragile, interconnected web that holds ecosystems together."
Booklist
Includes glossary and bibliographical references

Marx, Trish
★ Everglades forever; restoring America's great wetland. photographs by Cindy Karp. Lee & Low Books 2004
40p il map $17.95; pa $8.95
Grades: 3 4 5 6   **577.6**
1. Wetlands 2. Everglades (Fla.)
ISBN 978-1-58430-164-6; 1-58430-164-3; 978-1-
60060-339-6 pa; 1-60060-339-4 pa
LC 2004-2934
The author offers an "introduction to the natural history and environment of the Everglades by documenting the
studies of a fifth-grade class. . . . Complementing the excellent, informative text are high-quality color photographs and
maps." Booklist

Root, Phyllis
Big belching bog; illustrations by Betsy Bowen. University of Minnesota Press 2010 un il $15.95
Grades: 2 3 4   **577.6**
1. Marshes 2. Minnesota
ISBN 978-0-8166-3359-3; 0-8166-3359-2
LC 2010018733
"Couching the adaptations of plants, insects, and animals
that live in the Big Bog in Minnesota as secrets of survival,
this oversize picture book becomes a real page-turner. . . .
The stunning full-color woodblocks, many full spread, are
beautiful enough to frame. The deep purples, browns, and
teals are highlighted with stark white circles." SLJ

Sill, Cathryn P.
Wetlands; written by Cathryn Sill; illustrated by John
Sill. Peachtree 2008 un il (About habitats) $16.95

Grades: K 1 2 3 4   **577.6**
1. Wetlands
ISBN 978-1-56145-432-7; 1-56145-432-X
LC 2007031280
This introduction to wetland ecology "features full-page
watercolor paintings that strikingly illustrate the factual
information conveyed by a sentence or two on the facing
pages. . . . The artwork is stunning, filled with realistic details and a beautiful balance of colors. The format would
work well as a read-aloud choice. . . . Independent readers
or browsers could enjoy perusing the book themselves." SLJ

Toupin, Laurie
Freshwater habitats; life in freshwater ecosystems. F.
Watts 2005 63p il map (Biomes and habitats) lib bdg
$25.50; pa $8.95
Grades: 4 5 6 7   **577.6**
1. Freshwater ecology
ISBN 0-531-12305-7 lib bdg; 0-531-16675-9 pa
LC 2003-16572
A look at the plants, animals, locations, and various habi-
tats that make up the freshwater ecosystems of the world

Trumbore, Cindy
★ The mangrove tree; planting trees to feed families.
Lee & Low Books 2011 40p il $19.95
Grades: 2 3 4   **577.6**
1. Mangrove ecology 2. Eritrea
ISBN 978-1-60060-459-1; 1-60060-459-5
LC 2010034501
"Roth's artwork is a treat, cut-paper and fabric collages
of intense, shimmering color on a ground of paper that is
electric with thick veins of fiber (photos join glossary in
backmatter). . . . Hitting home hard is the project's simple
practicality: no high-tech, no great infusions of capital or
energy—in a word, motivating, in the best possible way."
Kirkus

Wechsler, Doug
Frog heaven; ecology of a vernal pool. [by] Doug
Wechsler; photographs by the author. Boyds Mills Press
2006 48p il $17.95
Grades: 3 4 5 6   **577.6**
1. Frogs 2. Vernal pool ecology 3. Natural history
-- Delaware
ISBN 978-1-59078-253-8; 1-59078-253-4
LC 2005037562
"Wechsler offers a close-up view of a vernal pool in
Delaware as it cycles through the year. . . . Wechsler's clear,
color photos provide an excellent visual counterpoint to the
text. This well-focused book will open readers' eyes." Book-
list
Includes glossary and bibliographical references

577.63 Lake and pond ecology

Ridley, Kimberly
The secret pool; by Kimberly Ridley; illustrated by
Rebekah Raye. Tilbury House 2013 32 p. (hardcover: alk.
paper) $16.95
Grades: K 1 2 3   **577.63**
1. Forest ecology 2. Vernal pool ecology 3. Pond

animals 4. Vernal pools
ISBN 0884483398; 9780884483397

LC 2013006032

This book, by Kimberly Ridley and illustrated by Rebekah Raye, "introduces young readers to the wonders right underfoot as the voice of a vernal pool shares its secrets through the seasons, and sidebars provide fun facts on its inhabitants and the crucial role these small, often overlooked wetlands play in maintaining a healthy environment." (Publisher's note)

577.68　　Wetland ecology

Gibbons, Gail

Marshes & swamps. Holiday House 1998 un il $16.95; pa $6.95

Grades: K 1 2 3　　　**577.68**

1. Ecology 2. Wetlands
ISBN 0-8234-1347-0; 0-8234-1515-5 pa

LC 97-17995

Defines marshes and swamps, discusses how conditions in them may change, and examines the life found in and around them

"Gibbons balances a succinct, informative text with well-labeled watercolors." Horn Book Guide

577.690　　Saltwater wetland and seashore ecology

Yezerski, Thomas

Meadowlands; a wetlands survival story. Thomas F. Yezerski. Farrar, Straus, Giroux 2011 40 p. il

Grades: 2 3　　　**577.690**

1. Wetland ecology 2. Meadowlands (N.J.) 3. New Jersey -- History 4. Natural history -- New Jersey 5. Hackensack Meadowlands (N.J.) 6. Wetland ecology -- New Jersey -- Hackensack Meadowlands 7. Nature conservation -- New Jersey -- Hackensack Meadowlands 8. Wetland conservation -- New Jersey -- Hackensack Meadowlands

ISBN 0374349134; 9780374349134

LC 2010005503

This is an "ecological history of the Meadowlands of New Jersey, an estuary trapped in a dense industrial, commercial, and residential area. . . . Primary." (Horn Book)

This picture book explores the Meadowlands region of New Jersey, "a vast wetlands west of New York City [that] . . . was diked and drained by early European settlers and later developed and trashed. In the last 40 years, with dumping stopped and restoration begun, some wildlife has returned. . . . [Thomas F.] Yezerski surveys human uses as well as the disappearance and reappearance of other forms of life. . . . [The illustrations depict] industrial products and means of transport, . . . the varied contents of a trash mountain and . . . modern residential and commercial development. These are followed by pages showing marsh plants, worms and insects, some of the many varieties of fish that visit the waters, animals that live on the banks and birds that live there or stop by during migration." (Kirkus)

"Yezerski adroitly captures the tensions and hope in the sometimes adversarial, sometimes beneficial relationship between humans and the environment in this marvelous eco-logical history of the Meadowlands of New Jersey, an estuary trapped in a dense industrial, commercial, and residential area. . . . Despite humans' best efforts, the relationship is still fragile, and here captured beautifully in the expansive watercolor illustrations. . . . Each main double-page-spread illustration is bordered by tiny images with a wealth of additional taxonomical information (and sly humor) about the diverse flora and fauna (and mobsters and sports enthusiasts) of northern New Jersey." Horn Book

Includes bibliographical references

577.7　　Marine ecology

Becker, Helaine

The big green book of the big blue sea; written by Helaine Becker; illustrated by Willow Dawson. Kids Can Press 2012 80 p. $15.95

Grades: 3 4 5　　　**577.7**

1. Science -- Experiments 2. Marine biology 3. Marine ecology 4. Environmental protection
ISBN 1554537460; 9781554537464

This book, by Helaine Becker, "shows how the ocean works and why this immense ecosystem needs our protection. Experiments using everyday materials help explain scientific concepts. . . . A focus on pollution and other ecological hazards raises awareness. Young scientists will gain a hands-on understanding of how 'booms' clean oil spills and how a garbage patch roughly twice the size of Texas came to exist in the middle of the Pacific Ocean." (Publisher's note)

Callery, Sean

Ocean. Kingfisher 2011 32p il (Life cycles)

Grades: 2 3 4　　　**577.7**

1. Marine animals 2. Marine ecology 3. Food chains (Ecology)
ISBN 0-7534-6577-9; 978-0-7534-6577-6

After a brief introduction to the ocean ecosystem "examples of three actual food chains within that ecosystem are presented. . . . Well-designed double-page spreads . . . provide brief information about each creature and its place in the chain. Vivid photos and vibrantly colored pages are eye-catching. Useful food web charts summarizing content are appended." Horn Book Guide

Chin, Jason

Coral reefs. Roaring Brook Press 2011 un il $16.99

Grades: K 1 2 3　　　**577.7**

1. Coral reefs and islands
ISBN 978-1-5964-3563-6; 1-5964-3563-1

LC 2010045189

"Chin, who pioneered this hybrid form of straightforward nonfiction text and fanciful pictures with Redwoods (2009), offers another a statement about the power of reading for an imaginative child with this appealing introduction to a complex world. He opens and closes his narrative with accurate and clearly labeled pencil sketches of a large variety of reef-dwellers. Inside, realistic watercolor images, some in panels, some in full-bleed pages and even double-page spreads, complement the text." Kirkus

Cousteau, Philippe, 1980-

Make a splash! a kid's guide to protecting our oceans, lakes, rivers & wetlands. by Cathryn Berger Kaye; with Philippe Cousteau and EarthEcho International. Free Spirit Pub. Inc. 2013 125 p. ill. (chiefly col.) (paperback) $13.99

Grades: 3 4 5 6 **577.7**

1. Environmentalists 2. Water conservation 3. Marine ecology 4. Environmentalism 5. Marine pollution -- Prevention

ISBN 1575424177; 9781575424170

LC 2012032120

This book for elementary-age readers has "colorful photos and digital drawings [that] illustrate many aspects of water on Earth, while the text provides information and tells stories of children in elementary schools around the world who have translated their own environmental concerns into action." (Booklist)

Crenson, Victoria

★ **Horseshoe** crabs and shorebirds; the story of a food web. illustrated by Annie Cannon. Marshall Cavendish 2003 un il lib bdg $16.95

Grades: 2 3 4 **577.7**

1. Crabs 2. Food chains (Ecology) 3. Delaware Bay (Del. and N.J.)

ISBN 0-7614-5115-3

LC 2002-156473

Presents a portrait of the Delaware Bay in the spring when a wide variety of animals, including minnows, mice, turtles, raccoons, and especially migrating shorebirds, come to feed on the billions of eggs laid by horseshoe crabs

"Crenson's text is highly descriptive and reads like an adventure story, conveying the action and excitement of nature. Cannon's watercolors fill the pages with atmosphere and motion." SLJ

Gibbons, Gail

Coral reefs. Holiday House 2007 32p il $16.95

Grades: K 1 2 3 **577.7**

1. Coral reefs and islands

ISBN 978-0-8234-2080-3; 0-8234-2080-9

LC 2006-37959

"Gibbons introduces a complex ecosystem with accessible words and inviting watercolor-washed pictures. . . . [The author explains] coral types and anatomy, how reefs form, and the symbiotic . . . relationship among reef creatures." Booklist

Hooks, Gwendolyn

Makers and takers; studying food webs in the ocean. [by] Gwendolyn Hooks. Rourke Pub. 2009 32p il map (Studying food webs) lib bdg $28.50

Grades: 3 4 5 **577.7**

1. Marine ecology 2. Food chains (Ecology)

ISBN 978-1-60472-319-9 lib bdg; 1-60472-319-X lib bdg

LC 2008-24860

This book has "stunning photos, fascinating facts, and intriguing examples. . . . Herbivores, omnivores, and carnivores specific to . . . [The ocean] ecosystem are presented. . . 'Chew on this' insets add further interest and information. . . . [This] will appeal to readers." SLJ

Includes glossary and bibliographical references

Jackson, Kay

Explore the ocean; by Kay Jackson. Capstone Press 2007 32p il (Explore the biomes) $16.95; pa $6.95

Grades: PreK K 1 2 **577.7**

1. Marine ecology

ISBN 978-0-7368-6406-0; 0-7368-6406-7; 978-0-7368-9629-0 pa; 0-7368-9629-5 pa

LC 2006004110

This an introduction to the ocean habitat and some of its plants and animals.

This book "uses vivid, sense-appealing language. . . . An attractive . . . format displays the captions to colorful photographs." Sci Books Films

Includes bibliographical references

Parker, Steve, 1952-

Seashore; written by Steve Parker. rev ed; DK Pub. 2004 72p il (DK eyewitness books) $15.99

Grades: 4 5 6 7 **577.7**

1. Seashore 2. Marine plants 3. Marine animals

ISBN 0-7566-0721-3; 0-7566-0720-5 lib bdg

First published 1989 by Knopf

Brief text and photos introduce the animal inhabitants of the seashore, including fish, crustaceans, snails, and shorebirds

Pfeffer, Wendy

★ **Life** in a coral reef; illustrated by Steve Jenkins. Collins 2009 32p il (Let's-read-and-find-out science) $16; pa $5.99

Grades: K 1 2 3 **577.7**

1. Coral reefs and islands

ISBN 978-0-06-029553-0; 0-06-029553-8; 978-0-06-445222-9 pa; 0-06-445222-0 pa

LC 2008000498

"Jenkins' striking paper-collage illustrations nicely complement Pfeffer's clear and engaging text in this successful explanation of what lies beneath the surface of the ocean in and around a coral reef." Booklist

Pyers, Greg

The **biodiversity** of coral reefs. Marshall Cavendish 2010 32p il map (Biodiversity) lib bdg $28.50

Grades: 4 5 6 7 **577.7**

1. Coral reefs and islands

ISBN 978-1-60870-070-7 lib bdg; 1-60870-070-4 lib bdg

"Discusses the variety of living things in a coral reef's ecosystem." Publisher's note

Includes glossary

Slade, Suzanne

What if there were no sea otters? a book about the ocean ecosystem. illustrated by Carol Schwartz. Picture Window Books 2011 24p il map (Food chain reactions) lib bdg $25.99; pa $8.95

Grades: 2 3 4 **577.7**

1. Otters 2. Marine ecology

ISBN 978-1-4048-6018-6 lib bdg; 1-4048-6018-5 lib bdg; 978-1-4048-6397-2 pa; 1-4048-6397-4 pa

LC 2010009879

Discusses the ocean ecosystem and the role of the sea otter as a keystone species in helping to maintain it, describing the otter's place on the food chain and what would happen if the sea otter were to become extinct.

"Radiant illustrations are paired with simple, perceptive sentences to underscore the impact of the loss of [sea otters]. . . . In a very effective convention extinct plants and animals are placed in silhouettes within many illustrations—the black void left by the loss of each species increases with each page. This . . . will engage readers on many levels." SLJ

Includes glossary and bibliographical references

Taylor-Butler, Christine

A **home** in the coral reef; by Christine Taylor-Butler. Childrens Press 2007 24p il (Scholastic news nonfiction readers) $20

Grades: 1 2 3   **577.7**

1. Coral reefs and islands
ISBN 0-516-25344-1; 978-0-516-25344-2
       LC 2006002305

An introduction to coral reef ecology

"Simple, easy-to-read. . . . Everything students need for reports is beautifully depicted with scenic full-color photographs of the land, the plants, and the animals that live there." SLJ

Includes bibliographical references

578   Natural history of organisms and related subjects

Kelsey, Elin

Strange new species; astonishing discoveries of life on earth. Maple Tree Press 2005 96p il $24.95; pa $16.95

Grades: 5 6 7 8   **578**

1. Biology 2. Scientists 3. Natural history
ISBN 1-897066-31-7; 1-897066-32-5 pa

"This large-format book showcases new species . . . and the scientists who have discovered them. . . . The discussion ends with information on cloning, genetically modified food, and the future of life. . . . With many excellent photos, this introductory book on new species will be an intriguing addition to classroom units on classification or biology." Booklist

Strauss, Rochelle

Tree of life; the incredible biodiversity of life on Earth. Kids Can Press 2004 40p il $16.95

Grades: 5 6 7 8   **578**

1. Biological diversity 2. Biology -- Classification
ISBN 1-55337-669-2

The "text first introduces the concept of a family tree for all living things, then goes on to name the five kingdoms of scientific classification. . . . The author describes the life-forms included in each species, with specific examples shown in the softly colorful illustrations accompanied by informative captions. . . . Striking, lucid, and deceptively simple." SLJ

578.4   Adaptation

Rustad, Martha E. H.

Animals in fall; preparing for winter. illustrated by Amanda Enright. Millbrook Press 2011 24p il (Fall's here!) lib bdg $23.93

Grades: K 1 2 3   **578.4**

1. Autumn 2. Winter 3. Animal behavior
ISBN 978-0-7613-5066-8; 0-7613-5066-7
       LC 2010053468

This "relates the animals preparation for winter through pictures and text. . . . At the end of the book an activity that children can do to understand how extra fat can keep you warm is featured. . . . Children will enjoy the colorful, expressive illustrations." Sci Books Films

Includes glossary and bibliographical references

Silverstein, Alvin

★ **Adaptation**; by Alvin Silverstein, Virginia Silverstein, and Laura Silverstein Nunn. Twenty-First Century Books 2008 112p il (Science concepts) lib bdg $31.93

Grades: 4 5 6 7   **578.4**

1. Adaptation (Biology)
ISBN 978-0-8225-3434-1 lib bdg; 0-8225-3434-7 lib bdg
       LC 2007-02862

This "provides an accessible introduction to how living beings adapt to survive in diverse habitats. . . . The narrative gains clarity from abundant examples, colorful photos and diagrams, and fascinating sidebars." Booklist

Includes bibliographical references

578.6   Miscellaneous nontaxonomic kinds of organisms

Batten, Mary

Aliens from Earth; when animals and plants invade other ecosystems. written by Mary Batten; illustrated by Beverly Doyle. Peachtree Pubs. 2003 un il $15.95

Grades: 3 4 5 6   **578.6**

1. Nonindigenous pests 2. Biological invasions
ISBN 1-56145-236-X
       LC 2002-13170

Explores how and why plants and animals enter ecosystems to which they are not native, as well as the consequences of these invasions for other animals, plants, and humans

"From the book title and first line of text . . . to the information-packed, full-page color illustrations, this overview of ecological missteps is nonstop intriguing." Booklist

Drake, Jane

Alien invaders; species that threaten our world. [by] Jane Drake & Ann Love; illustrated by Mark Thurman. Tundra Books 2008 56p il map $19.95

Grades: 3 4 5 6   **578.6**

1. Nonindigenous pests 2. Biological invasions
ISBN 0-88776-798-2; 978-0-88776-798-2

The authors examine invasive species and their effects on ecosystems. Index. "Ages nine to twelve." (Quill Quire)

"This book discusses non-native flora and fauna that endanger native species. The authors present historical cases (Irish potato blight, toad invasion in Australia), the most notorious invasive species, and threatened communities. Each double-page spread features a detailed gouache illustration, a conversational overview of problems, and some species-specific facts." Horn Book Guide

Jackson, Cari

Alien invasion; invasive species become major menaces. Gareth Stevens Pub. 2010 48p il (Current science) lib bdg $31

Grades: 4 5 6   **578.6**

1. Nonindigenous pests 2. Biological invasions

ISBN 978-1-4339-2057-8 lib bdg; 1-4339-2057-3 lib bdg

LC 2009002279

This "lively, well-organized [text profiles] dozens of organisms that threaten our health and well-being. Jackson succinctly describes the characteristics of more than three dozen invasive species of plants and animals. . . . One or more illustrations accompany the text on every page—a mix of sharp, color photographs and some color drawings, maps, life cycle diagrams, etc." SLJ

Includes glossary and bibliographical references

Johnson, Rebecca L.

★ **Zombie** makers; true stories of nature's undead. Rebecca L. Johnson. Millbrook Press 2013 48 p.

Grades: 4 5 6   **578.6**

1. Zombies 2. Invertebrates 3. Parasites 4. Host-parasite relationships

ISBN 0761386335; 9780761386339

LC 2011046181

In this book, by Rebecca L. Johnson, real biological examples of "zombies" in nature are profiled. "[D]ead people do not come back to live and start walking around, looking for trouble. But there are things that can take over the bodies and brains of innocent creatures, turning them into senseless slaves. Meet nature's zombie makers--including a fly-enslaving fungus, a suicide worm, and a cockroach-taming wasp--and their victims." (Publisher's note)

Includes bibliographical references (p. 46-47) and index

Metz, Lorijo

What can we do about invasive species? PowerKids Press 2010 24p il (Protecting our planet) lib bdg $21.25; pa $8

Grades: 2 3 4   **578.6**

1. Nonindigenous pests 2. Biological invasions

ISBN 978-1-4042-8084-7 lib bdg; 1-4042-8084-7 lib bdg; 978-1-4358-2487-4 pa; 1-4358-2487-3 pa

LC 2008-55828

This book provides "straightforward information . . . complemented by full-page, color photographs. . . . Links for further information . . . are housed at the publisher's Web site (which allows feedback so that readers can suggest more sites)." SLJ

Includes glossary

Owen, Ruth

Gross body invaders. Bearport Pub. 2011 24p il (Up close and gross) lib bdg $22.61

Grades: 3 4 5   **578.6**

1. Parasites

ISBN 978-1-61772-127-4; 1-61772-127-1

LC 2010044416

This describes small creatures which can invade the body, including head lice, eyelash mites, mosquitoes, ticks, fleas, hookworms, tapeworms, and horseflies.

"Never have the wonders of electron microscopy been more thrillingly displayed. . . . These knife-sharp, all-too-explicit photos are riveting. The [text doesn't] trail far behind in appeal either." SLJ

Includes glossary and bibliographical references

Icky house invaders. Bearport Pub. 2011 24p il (Up close and gross) lib bdg $22.61

Grades: 3 4 5   **578.6**

1. Microbiology 2. Household pests

ISBN 978-1-61772-124-3; 1-61772-124-7

LC 2010041241

This describes insects and other small creatures which can inhabit a home, including houseflies, fleas, dust mites, bedbugs, moths, cockroaches, woodworms, and silverfish.

"Never have the wonders of electron microscopy been more thrillingly displayed. . . . These knife-sharp, all-too-explicit photos are riveting. The [text doesn't] trail far behind in appeal either." SLJ

Includes glossary and bibliographical references

578.68 Rare and endangered species

Pobst, Sandy

★ **Animals** on the edge; science races to save species threatened with extinction. by Sandra Pobst; Todd K. Fuller, consultant. National Geographic 2008 64p il (National Geographic investigates) $17.95; lib bdg $27.90

Grades: 4 5 6 7   **578.68**

1. Endangered species 2. Wildlife conservation

ISBN 978-1-4263-0358-6; 1-4263-0358-0; 978-1-4263-0265-7 lib bdg; 1-4263-0265-7 lib bdg

This "eye-catching [title features] full-color photographs. . . . The approach is to understand the challenges to protecting endangered animals, including global warming, destruction of habitat, tagging and tracking, poaching, captive breeding, and cloning." Voice Youth Advocates

Includes glossary and bibliographical references

578.7 Organisms characteristic of specific kinds of environments

Arnosky, Jim

★ **Beachcombing**; exploring the seashore. Dutton Children's Bks. 2004 un il $15.99

Grades: K 1 2 3   **578.7**

1. Seashore

ISBN 0-525-47104-9

Illustrations and text describe some of the many things that can be found on a walk along a beach, including coconuts, shark teeth, jellyfish, crabs and different kinds of shells.

"Young beachcombers will discover old and new ideas about collecting or just identifying their finds, and the book will appeal to those children who are looking for relaxing fun." SLJ

Cerullo, Mary M.

Life under ice; photography by Bill Curtsinger. Tilbury House 2003 37p il map $16.95

Grades: 3 4 5 **578.7**

1. Marine plants 2. Marine animals 3. Natural history -- Antarctica

ISBN 0-88448-246-4

LC 2002-154451

Follows marine photographer Bill Curtsinger as he dives under the ice at Antarctica to learn about the plants and animals that thrive in this extreme habitat

"Illustrated with stunning color undersea photographs, this offers a fascinating look at the many creatures living near and beneath the waters of Antarctica. . . . The text is clear and well written, but it is the wonderful photography that distinguishes the book." Booklist

Includes glossary and bibliographical references

Conlan, Kathy

Under the ice. Kids Can Press 2002 55p il $16.95; pa $8.95

Grades: 4 5 6 7 **578.7**

1. Marine biology 2. Marine pollution 3. Polar regions

ISBN 1-55337-001-5; 1-55337-060-0 pa

"The first-person text creates a feeling of immediacy. . . . Well-captioned, color photos appear throughout the book. . . . Conlan . . . offers readers an engaging account of her adventurous career in scientific field research." Booklist

Ernst, Lisa Campbell

How things work in the yard. Blue Apple Books 2011 un il $14.99

Grades: K 1 2 3 **578.7**

1. Urban ecology

ISBN 978-1-60905-009-2; 1-60905-009-6

LC 2010046821

"Graph paper style backgrounds emphasize the schematic approach to nature that Campbell-Ernst uses to explain how different items and creatures—such as birds, butterflies, rocks, and dirt—that can be found in a typical backyard 'work.' There's a playful aesthetic in evidence, from the bright palette and friendly cut-paper artwork to the innate humor in some of the questions themselves. . . . The various parts of the animals, plants, and objects are labeled, and brief facts about each subject dot the spreads. . . . It's an elegantly designed primer to the natural world." Publ Wkly

Guiberson, Brenda Z.

★ **Life** in the boreal forest; paintings by Gennady Spirin. Henry Holt and Co. 2009 un il $16.99

Grades: 2 3 4 5 **578.7**

1. Forest ecology

ISBN 978-0-8050-7718-6; 0-8050-7718-9

LC 2008-18329

"Gorgeously intricate illustrations perfectly complement equally evocative text in this introduction to the great northern, or boreal, forest, which sprawls across the entire northern hemisphere. . . . Any child interested in animals or the outdoors will be fascinated by the array portrayed here in a series of vignettes, each of which intersperses factual information information with lively action scenes." Booklist

Kirby, Richard R.

Ocean drifters; a secret world beneath the waves. Firefly Books 2011 192p il $29.95

Grades: 5 6 7 8 9 10 11 12 Adult **578.7**

1. Marine plankton

ISBN 978-1-55407-982-7; 1-55407-982-9

LC 2011284690

"Kirby (Marine Inst. Research Fellow, Plymouth Univ., UK), who has published widely in scientific journals, combines in this book his area of expertise-plankton-with magnificent color photography of each species. He details the importance of the ocean's plankton layer to the health of the globe and its effects on sea and human life in the photos' descriptions...Recommended for readers interested in the smaller denizens of the natural world, the ocean, or microphotography." (Library Journal)

Includes bibliographical references

O'Neill, Michael Patrick

Ocean magic. Batfish 2008 45p il $19.95

Grades: 1 2 3 4 **578.7**

1. Ocean 2. Marine animals

ISBN 978-0-9728653-5-7; 0-9728653-5-7

LC 2007-904079

"O'Neill introduces readers to coral reefs, kelp forests, and the ocean bottom. Especially stunning are the photos of the Hairy Frogfish, an incredibly camouflaged member of the Anglerfish family that prowls off the coast of Florida. Nevertheless, the colorful creatures of the coral reef are the stars of this book. The author's strong support of conservation comes through loud and clear in his narrative, and photographs amplify this message by showing the amazing life-forms that could be lost." SLJ

Owen, Ruth

Creepy backyard invaders. Bearport Pub. 2011 24p il (Up close and gross) lib bdg $22.61

Grades: 3 4 5 **578.7**

1. Insects 2. Agricultural pests

ISBN 978-1-61772-125-0; 1-61772-125-5

LC 2010041212

This describes organisms which can inhabit a backyard, including earwigs, honeybees, aphids, ants, lacewings, jumping spiders, woodlice, and stinging nettles.

"Never have the wonders of electron microscopy been more thrillingly displayed. . . . These knife-sharp, all-too-explicit photos are riveting. The [text doesn't] trail far behind in appeal either." SLJ

Includes glossary and bibliographical references

Person, Stephen

The **coral** reef; a giant city under the sea. consultant, Rod Salm. Bearport Pub. 2009 32p il map (Spectacular animal towns) lib bdg $25.27

Grades: 2 3 4 **578.7**

1. Coral reefs and islands

ISBN 978-1-59716-869-4 lib bdg; 1-59716-869-6 lib bdg

LC 2009-12952

"Through excellent photographs, high-interest texts, sidebars, maps, and other material, children learn about both the animals and their habitats. The . . . book also provides brief profiles of animals with similar habitats. . . . [This book is] much better than average 'report' titles." SLJ

Includes glossary and bibliographical references

Santoro, Lucio

Wild oceans; [by] Lucio and Meera Santoro. Little Simon 2010 un il $27.99

Grades: 2 3 4 5   578.7

1. Marine biology 2. Pop-up books

ISBN 978-1-4169-8467-2; 1-4169-8467-4

"Using the ocean as their milieu, the Santoros . . . provide solid information along with amazing visuals. Beginning with a 3-D re-creation of a tide pool, the book then moves to the open sea, where a whale rises out of the pages. An explanation of light zones underwater is illustrated by an anglerfish that lives 3,000 feet below the water's surface. Views of a coral reef and life in the frozen sea complete the treatment. Fact-filled fun." Booklist

Serafini, Frank

Looking closely across the desert. Kids Can Press 2008 un il (Looking closely) $16.95

Grades: K 1 2 3   578.7

1. Deserts

ISBN 978-1-55453-211-7; 1-55453-211-6

"An extreme closeup color photo of a section of a plant, animal, or other natural object set in a circle on a black background challenges readers to guess its identity. Turning the page reveals a large photo of the item in its natural setting, accompanied by two paragraphs of descriptive and informative text." SLJ

Looking closely along the shore; [by] Frank Serafini. Kids Can Press 2008 un il (Looking closely) $16.95

Grades: K 1 2 3   578.7

1. Seashore

ISBN 978-1-55453-141-7; 1-55453-141-1

This title about plants and animals of the seashore "will pique the interest of children and encourage them to seek out more information. . . . [It is] set up like a guessing game, allowing for interaction. . . . Each entry opens with a white page with large black type that asks viewers to 'Look very closely. What do you see?' The facing page is black with what seems like a hole to peep through to the next spread. . . . Readers are given a couple of possibilities to start them guessing on what image might be depicted, and, when the page is turned, an enlarged closeup is in full view, along with a few interesting facts about the plant or animal." SLJ

Looking closely around the pond. Kids Can Press 2010 un il (Looking closely) $16.95

Grades: K 1 2 3   578.7

1. Ponds

ISBN 978-1-55337-395-7; 1-55337-395-2

"Close-ups of a portion of a pond animal, insect, or plant on a spread invite children to guess the featured subject. . . . The animal, insect, or plant is then described in a couple of jaunty paragraphs on a page facing a full-color photograph." SLJ

Looking closely in the rain forest. Kids Can Press 2010 un il (Looking closely) $16.95

Grades: K 1 2 3   578.7

1. Rain forests

ISBN 978-1-55337-543-2; 1-55337-543-2

This "spotlights life in the tropical rain forest, including a squirrel monkey, a banana plant, a moth orchid, and a scarlet macaw. The crisp, beautiful photos and the interactive text will draw kids into both the interactive fun and scientific facts." Booklist

Looking closely inside the garden. Kids Can Press 2008 un il (Looking closely) $16.95

Grades: K 1 2 3   578.7

1. Gardens

ISBN 978-1-55453-210-0; 1-55453-210-8

"An extreme closeup color photo of a section of a plant, animal, or other natural object set in a circle on a black background challenges readers to guess its identity. Turning the page reveals a large photo of the item in its natural setting, accompanied by two paragraphs of descriptive and informative text." SLJ

Looking closely through the forest. Kids Can Press 2008 un il (Looking closely) $16.95

Grades: K 1 2 3   578.7

1. Forest plants 2. Forest animals

ISBN 978-1-55453-212-4; 1-55453-212-4

This book about forest plants and animals "will pique the interest of children and encourage them to seek out more information. . . . [It is] set up like a guessing game, allowing for interaction. . . . Each entry opens with a white page with large black type that asks viewers to 'Look very closely. What do you see?' The facing page is black with what seems like a hole to peep through to the next spread. . . . Readers are given a couple of possibilities to start them guessing on what image might be depicted, and, when the page is turned, an enlarged closeup is in full view, along with a few interesting facts about the plant or animal." SLJ

Somervill, Barbara A.

Marine biologist. Cherry Lake Pub. 2009 32p il (Cool science careers) lib bdg $27.07

Grades: 3 4 5 6   578.7

1. Marine biology 2. Vocational guidance

ISBN 978-1-60279-504-4 lib bdg; 1-60279-504-5 lib bdg

LC 2008045234

This describes the career of marine biologist, including ways to become involved in the profession, the interests and skills required, and activities for learning more

This is "highly readable. . . . Colorful photographs illustrate [the] book." SLJ

Includes glossary and bibliographical references

Thomas, William David

Marine biologist. Gareth Stevens Pub. 2010 32p il (Cool careers: cutting edge) lib bdg $26; pa $8.95

Grades: 4 5 6   578.7

1. Marine biology 2. Vocational guidance

ISBN 978-1-4339-1957-2 lib bdg; 1-4339-1957-5 lib bdg; 978-1-4339-2156-8 pa; 1-4339-2156-1 pa

LC 2009000239

Describes the work of a marine biologist.

This title offers "clear, solid information in a large font. . . . [This] short [book is] packed with relevant, current material." SLJ

Includes glossary and bibliographical references

Wallace, Marianne D.
America's forests; guide to plants and animals. Fulcrum Pub. 2009 47p il (America's ecosystems) pa $11.95
Grades: 5 6 7 8   578.7
1. Forest plants 2. Forest animals 3. Forest ecology 4. Forests and forestry
ISBN 978-1-55591-595-7 pa; 1-55591-595-7 pa
LC 2008041005
This "is a guide to plants and animals within the context of forest communities. Marianne Wallace . . . expertly crafts this introduction to forests. . . . The book contains abundant illustrations." Sci Books Films
Includes glossary

Wechsler, Doug
Marvels in the muck; life in the salt marshes. Boyds Mills Press 2008 48p il $17.95
Grades: 4 5 6 7   578.7
1. Salt marshes 2. Marsh ecology
ISBN 978-1-59078-588-1
LC 2007052583
"A season-by-season look at the ecology of an oft-overlooked habitat. Wechsler's lucid text introduces the insects, birds, reptiles, crustaceans, and other critters that claim this salty expanse as home. . . . Clear color photos present species mentioned in the text." SLJ
Includes glossary and bibliographical references

Winner, Cherie
Life on the edge. Lerner Publications Co. 2006 48p il (Cool science) lib bdg $26.60
Grades: 4 5 6   578.7
1. Adaptation (Biology)
ISBN 978-0-8225-2499-1 lib bdg; 0-8225-2499-6 lib bdg
LC 2005011071
This book "introduces creatures in extreme conditions such as thermal pools, Antarctica, and the deep sea. [The book provides] clear explanations of the science and [covers] possible benefits to humans. A variety of photos and information boxes provide an eye-catching . . . layout." Horn Book Guide

Includes glossary and bibliographical references

578.757   Soil biology

Lawrence, Ellen
Dirt; by Ellen Lawrence; consultants, Suzy Gazlay, MA, recipient of the Presidential Award for Excellence in Science Teaching and Kimberly Brenneman, PhD, National Institute for Early Education Research, Rutgers University, New Brunswick, New Jersey. Bearport Pub. Co. 2013 24 p. col. ill. (library) $23.93
Grades: K 1 2 3   578.757
1. Soils 2. Soil biology
ISBN 1617727377; 9781617727375
LC 2012046349

This book on dirt by Ellen Lawrence "includes in the materials list a notebook for children to keep records of predictions, observations, and conclusions. There are seven experiments with detailed, age -- appropriate instructions complete with pictures to support the experiments. There are also graphics that provide students with additional instructions. The author answers the questions in an appendix." (NSTA Recommends)

Includes bibliographical references and index.

579   Natural history of microorganisms, fungi, algae

Arato, Rona
Protists; algae, amoebas, plankton, and other protists. Crabtree Pub. Co. 2010 48p il (A class of their own) lib bdg $29.27; pa $9.95
Grades: 5 6 7 8   579
1. Algae 2. Protists 3. Protozoa
ISBN 978-0-7787-5377-3 lib bdg; 0-7787-5377-8 lib bdg; 978-0-7787-5391-9 pa; 0-7787-5391-3 pa
LC 2009-51386
Looks at the protist kingdom, providing information and examples of species from the major phyla, as well as information about the role of protists in the food chain and in various diseases.
"Lively section headings . . . and notes on uncommon achievements, . . . lighten the substantial load of biological terminology. Illustrated with a plethora of closeup color photos and microphotos, and closing with annotated lists of recommended Web sites, . . . [this captures] the remarkable diversity of life." SLJ
Includes glossary and bibliographical references

Brown, Jordan
Micro mania; a really close-up look at bacteria, bedbugs & the zillions of other gross little creatures that live in, on & all around you! [by] Jordan D. Brown. Imagine! 2010 80p il $19.95
Grades: 4 5 6   579
1. Microorganisms
ISBN 978-0-9823064-2-0; 0-9823064-2-3
"This engrossing book goes into squirm-inducing detail about the bacteria, microbes, and other assorted mini-organisms that dwell in our bodies and our homes. Each spread is well laid out with plenty of white space, large text, and colorful photos of these little critters . . . and the havoc they wreak. The writing is vivid without being breathless." SLJ

Davies, Nicola, 1958-
★ Tiny creatures; the world of microbes. Nicola Davies, illustrated by Emily Sutton. Candlewick Press 2014 40 p. $15.99
Grades: PreK K 1 2 3   579
1. Microorganisms 2. Science
ISBN 0763673153; 9780763673154
LC 2013953401
Written by Nicola Davies and illustrated by Emily Sutton, this children's book describes how "All around the world--in the sea, in the soil, in the air, and in your body--there are living things so tiny that millions could fit on an ant's antenna. They're busy doing all sorts of things, from

giving you a cold and making yogurt to eroding mountains and helping to make the air we breathe." (Publisher's note)

"A pleasant, picture book-style look at a rather icky topic: microbes, the teeny tiny critters that live on us and in us and everywhere around us, with an impact that belies their minute size...This really is an enjoyable beginner's look at these miniscule organisms and the effect they can have on everything from our bodies to the soil to the clouds in the sky." SLJ

Weakland, Mark
Gut bugs, dust mites, and other microorganisms you can't live without. Capstone Press 2010 32p il (Fact finders. Nasty (but useful!) science) lib bdg $25.99
Grades: 3 4 5   579
1. Bacteria 2. Microorganisms
ISBN 978-1-4296-4538-6 lib bdg; 1-4296-4538-5 lib bdg
This informative guide also explains "relevant chemical processes, medical rationales, and ecological functions in reasonably specific detail. . . . A list of relevant web resources is maintained on the publisher's page." SLJ
Includes glossary and bibliographical references

Wearing, Judy
Fungi; mushrooms, toadstools, molds, yeasts, and other fungi. Crabtree 2010 48p il (A class of their own) lib bdg $29.27; pa $9.95
Grades: 5 6 7 8   579
1. Fungi
ISBN 978-0-7787-5375-9 lib bdg; 0-7787-5375-1 lib bdg; 978-0-7787-5389-6 pa; 0-7787-5389-1 pa
Features an examination of the four major groups of fungi: yeasts, toadstools, chytrids, and bread molds.
"Lively section headings . . . and notes on uncommon achievements, . . . lighten the substantial load of biological terminology. Illustrated with a plethora of closeup color photos and microphotos, and closing with annotated lists of recommended Web sites, . . . [thi scaptures] the remarkable diversity of life." SLJ
Includes glossary and bibliographical references

Zabludoff, Marc
The protoctist kingdom. Benchmark Books 2006 95p il (Family trees) lib bdg $29.92
Grades: 5 6 7 8   579
1. Protoctista
ISBN 0-7614-1818-0
LC 2004-21821
This examines the physical traits, adaptations, diets, habitats, and life cycles of such life forms as bacteria, amoebas, slime nets, molds, algae, coccoliths, forams, and diatoms.
"Fact-filled, yet surprisingly readable. . . . [This] title contains a wide variety of excellent-quality, full-color photographs; interesting sidebars; and diagrams." SLJ

Zamosky, Lisa
Simple organisms. Compass Point Books 2009 40p il (Mission: science) lib bdg $26.60
Grades: 4 5 6   579
1. Microorganisms
ISBN 978-0-7565-3955-9 lib bdg; 0-7565-3955-2 lib bdg
LC 2008-7723

An introduction to microscopic organisms, including germs
Includes glossary and bibliographical references

579.3 Prokaryotes (Bacteria)

Barker, David M.
Archaea; salt-lovers, methane-makers, thermophiles, and other archaeans. by David Barker. Crabtree Pub. 2010 48p il (A class of their own) lib bdg $29.27; pa $9.95
Grades: 5 6 7 8   579.3
1. Bacteria
ISBN 978-0-7787-5373-5 lib bdg; 0-7787-5373-5 lib bdg; 978-0-7787-5387-2 pa; 0-7787-5387-5 pa
LC 2009-51393
Looks at the archaea domain, providing information and examples of species from the three major phyla, as well as information about why so little is known about this diverse domain.
"Lively section headings . . . and notes on uncommon achievements, . . . lighten the substantial load of biological terminology. Illustrated with a plethora of closeup color photos and microphotos, and closing with annotated lists of recommended Web sites, . . . [this captures] the remarkable diversity of life." SLJ
Includes glossary and bibliographical references

Wearing, Judy
Bacteria; staph, strep, clostridium, and other bacteria. Crabtree 2010 48p il (A class of their own) lib bdg $29.27; pa $9.95
Grades: 5 6 7 8   579.3
1. Bacteria
ISBN 978-0-7787-5374-2 lib bdg; 0-7787-5374-3 lib bdg; 978-0-7787-5388-9 pa; 0-7787-5388-3 pa
Examines bacteria that are found in virtually every environment-including those that are characterized by extreme heat, cold, and depth-and, of course, bacteria that are found inside our bodies.
"Lively section headings . . . and notes on uncommon achievements, . . . lighten the substantial load of biological terminology. Illustrated with a plethora of closeup color photos and microphotos, and closing with annotated lists of recommended Web sites, . . . [this captures] the remarkable diversity of life." SLJ
Includes glossary and bibliographical references

579.6 Mushrooms

Royston, Angela
Life cycle of a mushroom; rev and updated ed.; Heinemann Library 2009 32p il (Life cycle of a) $25.36; pa $7.99
Grades: 2 3 4   579.6
1. Mushrooms
ISBN 978-1-4329-2530-7; 1-4329-2530-X; 978-1-4329-2547-5 pa; 1-4329-2547-4 pa
LC 2009517694
Introduces the life cycle of a mushroom, from formation of spores through underground growth of the mycelia to formation of mature mushrooms

This offers "easily accessible information in [an] attractive [package]." SLJ

Includes glossary and bibliographical references

579.8 Algae

Cerullo, Mary M.

★ Sea soup: phytoplankton; photography by Bill Curtsinger. Tilbury House 1999 39p il $16.95

Grades: 5 6 7 8   **579.8**

1. Phytoplankton

ISBN 0-88448-208-1

LC 99-39210

Discusses the microscopic organisms known as phytoplankton and the important functions they serve in replenishing earth's atmosphere, in the marine food chain, and more

"Outstanding full-color photomicroscopy dominates this slim volume on the microscopic plants at the bottom of the ocean food chain. The clearly presented information is not available in another single volume for this audience." SLJ

Includes glossary and bibliographical references

580 Natural history of plants and animals

Goodman, Emily

Plant secrets; illustrated by Phyllis Limbacher Tildes. Charlesbridge 2009 un il $16.95; pa $7.95

Grades: PreK K 1 2   **580**

1. Plants

ISBN 978-1-58089-204-9; 1-58089-204-3; 978-1-58089-205-6 pa; 1-58089-205-1 pa

LC 2008-07256

"Children will look at plants with new eyes after reading this fresh introduction. The plant cycle is introduced, beginning and ending with seeds. . . . The text will draw readers into the wonder of the topic. Bold color-coded headings introduce each of the four stages. Realistic spot illustrations, beginning with the endpapers, present the variety described in the text." SLJ

Gould, Margee

Giant plants. The Rosen Pub. Group 2011 24p il (The strangest plants on Earth) lib bdg $21.25

Grades: 3 4 5   **580**

1. Size 2. Plants

ISBN 978-1-4488-4990-1; 1-4488-4990-X

LC 2010052217

This "colorful [introduction has] bright, full-color photographs that are detailed enough to enable identification in the field. . . . [The book] includes not only the tallest and most massive plants, but also those with giant odors. One of the illustrations for the corpse flower shows kids at a greenhouse holding their noses as they observe the huge flower that smells like rotting meat. . . . Useful for reports and fun to browse, read, and learn." SLJ

Includes glossary

Levine, Shar

Plants; flowering plants, ferns, mosses, and other plants. by Shar Levine and Leslie Johnstone. Crabtree Pub. 2010 48p il (A class of their own) lib bdg $29.27; pa $9.95

Grades: 5 6 7 8   **580**

1. Plants

ISBN 978-0-7787-5376-6 lib bdg; 0-7787-5376-X lib bdg; 978-0-7787-5390-2 pa; 0-7787-5390-5 pa

LC 2009-51342

Describes the main groups of plants, including mosses, ferns, conifers, and flowering plants.

"Lively section headings . . . and notes on uncommon achievements, . . . lighten the substantial load of biological terminology. Illustrated with a plethora of closeup color photos and microphotos, and closing with annotated lists of recommended Web sites, . . . [this captures] the remarkable diversity of life." SLJ

Includes glossary and bibliographical references

Taylor, Barbara

Inside plants. Marshall Cavendish Benchmark 2010 48p il (Invisible worlds) lib bdg $28.50

Grades: 4 5 6 7   **580**

1. Plants

ISBN 978-0-7614-4189-2 lib bdg; 0-7614-4189-1 lib bdg

LC 2008037247

This describes the plant details that are too small for the unaided eye to see, and how these microscopic systems work to keep the plant alive and healthy.

The narrative is "clear, well written, broken down into manageable pieces, and peppered with eye-opening facts. The numerous photographs are so phenomenal that they will inspire kids to read the text . . . so that they can wrap their minds around what they see." SLJ

Includes glossary and bibliographical references

Wade, Mary Dodson

Trees, weeds, and vegetables--so many kinds of plants! Enslow Elementary 2009 24p il (I like plants!) lib bdg $21.26; pa $6.95

Grades: K 1 2   **580**

1. Plants

ISBN 978-0-7660-3156-2 lib bdg; 0-7660-3156-X lib bdg; 978-0-7660-3616-1 pa; 0-7660-3616-2 pa

LC 2007039460

This does "an excellent job of introducing basic concepts about seeds and plants. Large text on colored pages explains terms and covers a lot of ground in the simplest manner imaginable. The full-color illustrations amplify the narrative." SLJ

Includes glossary and bibliographical references

580.7 Plants - Education, research, related topics

Benbow, Ann

Lively plant science projects; [by] Ann Benbow and Colin Mably; illustrations by Tom Labaff. Enslow Publishers 2009 48p il (Real life science experiments) lib bdg $23.93

Grades: 3 4 5   **580.7**

1. Botany 2. Plants 3. Science projects

ISBN 978-0-7660-3146-3 lib bdg; 0-7660-3146-2 lib bdg

LC 2008-01745

"Color drawings, photographs, a glossary, and suggestions for further research enliven . . . [this] title . . . [and provide] solid curricular support." Booklist

"Presents several easy-to-do science experiments using plants." Publisher's note

Includes glossary and bibliographical references

Sprouting seed science projects; [by] Ann Benbow and Colin Mably; illustrations by Tom Labaff. Enslow Publishers 2009 48p il (Real life science experiments) lib bdg $23.93

Grades: 3 4 5   **580.7**
1. Seeds 2. Germination 3. Science projects
ISBN 978-0-7660-3147-0 lib bdg; 0-7660-3147-0 lib bdg

LC 2008-1731

"Color drawings, photographs, a glossary, and suggestions for further research enliven . . . [this] title . . . [and provide] solid curricular support." Booklist

"Presents several easy-to-do science experiments using seeds." Publisher's note

Includes glossary and bibliographical references

Gardner, Robert
  Ace your plant science project; great science fair ideas. [by] Robert Gardner and Phyllis J. Perry. Enslow Publishers 2009 104p il (Ace your biology science project) lib bdg $31.93

Grades: 5 6 7 8   **580.7**
1. Plants 2. Science projects 3. Science -- Experiments
ISBN 978-0-7660-3221-7 lib bdg; 0-7660-3221-3 lib bdg

LC 2008-4687

"Presents several science experiments and project ideas using plants." Publisher's note

Includes bibliographical references

581 Specific topics in natural history of plants

Wade, Mary Dodson
  Plants live everywhere! Enslow Elementary 2009 24p il (I like plants!) lib bdg $21.26; pa $6.95

Grades: K 1 2   **581**
1. Plants
ISBN 978-0-7660-3155-5 lib bdg; 0-7660-3155-1 lib bdg; 978-0-7660-3615-4 pa; 0-7660-3615-4 pa

LC 2007039457

This book does "an excellent job of introducing basic concepts about seeds and plants. Large text on colored pages explains terms and covers a lot of ground in the simplest manner imaginable. The full-color illustrations amplify the narrative." SLJ

Includes glossary and bibliographical references

581.4 Adaptation

Aston, Dianna Hutts
  ★ A **seed** is sleepy; by Dianna Hutts Aston; illustrated by Sylvia Long. Chronicle Books 2007 un il $16.95

Grades: K 1 2 3   **581.4**
1. Seeds
ISBN 978-0-8118-5520-4; 0-8118-5520-1

LC 2006-13302

"The topic is seeds, and . . . Long's masterful watercolors dominate each spread, which includes text on two levels. Short poetic phrases in large print, airmed at younger children, give seeds accessible, anthropomorphic qualities. . . . Paragraphs in smaller print, which tackle science concepts and expand on the phrases, are geared to older readers." Booklist

Farndon, John
  Seeds. Blackbirch Press 2006 24p il (World of plants) lib bdg $27.44

Grades: 2 3 4 5   **581.4**
1. Seeds
ISBN 978-1-4103-0419-3 lib bdg; 1-4103-0419-1 lib bdg

LC 2005047047

This book examines germination, the ways seeds are spread, types and sizes of seeds, and the role of seeds in the diets of both humans and animals

This uses "clear language and short sentences. . . . Helpful diagrams and sharp, colorful photographs supplement the [text]. . . . [This book offers] solid information in an attractive format." SLJ

Includes bibliographical references

  Stems. Blackbirch Press 2006 24p il (World of plants) lib bdg $27.44

Grades: 2 3 4 5   **581.4**
1. Stems (Plants)
ISBN 978-1-4103-0420-9 lib bdg; 1-4103-0420-5 lib bdg

LC 2005047049

This book examines how stems grow, the sizes of various types of stems, underground stems, and the ways people and animals use stems for food and shelter

This uses "clear language and short sentences. . . . Helpful diagrams and sharp, colorful photographs supplement the [text]. . . . [This book offers] solid information in an attractive format." SLJ

Includes bibliographical references

Galbraith, Kathryn O.
  Planting the wild garden; written by Kathryn O. Galbraith; illustrated by Wendy Anderson Halperin. Peachtree 2011 32 p. il

Grades: K 1   **581.4**
1. Seeds 2. Wild plants 3. Picture books for children 4. Plants
ISBN 1561455636; 9781561455638

LC 2010026898

This picture book answers the question "how do wild plants grow and spread? In . . . prose punctuated with sound effects ("Per-chik-o-ree! Per-chiko-ree!" cries a goldfinch) . . . [Kathryn O.] Galbraith . . . explains that seeds from wild plants float in the wind, snap off plants, fall in the rain, and get carried--intentionally or unintentionally--by animals to new places where they sprout and thrive. "A family of raccoons feasts on blackberries. . . . When they amble home again, bits of berries and seeds go with them. Next spring, new prickly canes will pop up everywhere." [Wendy Anderson] Halperin's . . . spreads are divided into contiguous panels tinted in the lightest of watercolors, with delicate pencil shading that conveys the force of wind and rain alike." (Publishers Weekly)

"Seeds grow in wild meadows because they are carried by wind and water, birds and animals, plants and people. This title celebrates the power of these tiny wonders—so delicate, so hardy—with simple, poetic words. . . . The soft, pencil-and-watercolor images alternate expansive landscapes with small, framed details that show tiny, dramatic stories. . . . A natural choice for curriculum connections." Booklist

Gould, Margee

Prickly plants. PowerKids Press 2011 24p il (The strangest plants on Earth) lib bdg $21.25

Grades: 3 4 5   **581.4**

1. Cactus 2. Plants

ISBN 978-1-4488-4991-8; 1-4488-4991-8

LC 2010053141

This describes prickly plants including cacti, stinging nettles, the silk floss tree and the honey locust tree.

This "colorful [introduction has] bright, full-color photographs that are detailed enough to enable identification in the field. . . . Useful for reports and fun to browse, read, and learn." SLJ

Includes glossary

Heneghan, Judith

Once there was a seed; written by Judith Anderson; illustrated by Mike Gordon. Barron's 2010 32p il (Nature's miracles) pa $5.99

Grades: K 1 2   **581.4**

1. Seeds 2. Plants

ISBN 978-0-7641-4493-6 pa; 0-7641-4493-6 pa

First published 2009 in the United Kingdom

Introduces the life cycle of plants, describing how a plant is grown from a seed, sprouts roots and leaves, and eventually forms a mature plant or flower which contains new seeds.

"This proves that science for even the very youngest readers can retain the same nonfiction qualities as that for older students and still be captivating as well as educational." Libr Media Connect

Includes bibliographical references

Kim, Sue

How does a seed grow? a book with fold-out pages. photos by Tilde. Little Simon 2010 un il bd bk $7.99

Grades: PreK   **581.4**

1. Seeds 2. Board books for children 3. Plants -- Growth

ISBN 978-1-4169-9435-0; 1-4169-9435-1

"From seed to sprout to finished fruit, plants spring to life in this inventive picture book that folds out into four scenes on every spread. In a question-and-answer format, the smooth, rhyming text introduces botany basics. . . . Right-hand pages fold out to show the emerging plant in bright color photos, finally reaching an oversize scene of a child enjoying the mature fruit. . . . Both entertaining and informative." Booklist

Macken, JoAnn Early

Flip, float, fly; seeds on the move. by JoAnn Early Macken; illustrated by Pam Paparone. Holiday House 2008 un il $16.95

Grades: K 1 2 3   **581.4**

1. Seeds

ISBN 978-0-8234-2043-8; 0-8234-2043-4

LC 2006-37278

This book introduces "methods of seed distribution. Each is introduced on a double-page spread, in which a few lines of poetic text provide information succinctly. . . . Pleasing in their colors, compositions, and decorative elements, the pictures clearly show points made in the text. . . . Satisfying and well designed for both classroom sharing and individual reading." Booklist

Includes glossary and bibliographical references

Richards, Jean

A fruit is a suitcase for seeds; illustrated by Anca Hariton. Millbrook Press 2002 un il lib bdg $21.90

Grades: K 1 2   **581.4**

1. Fruit 2. Seeds

ISBN 0-7613-1622-1

LC 2001-32959

Provides an illustrated description of seed dispersal by which plants, most specifically fruits, travel from one place to another

"Richard's carefully worded information provides an excellent introduction to seeds, their purpose, and growth that should be easy for young children to grasp. . . . Hariton's use of bright watercolors adds sensual appeal to her illustrations." SLJ

Robbins, Ken

★ **Seeds**; text and pictures by Ken Robbins. Atheneum Books for Young Readers 2005 un il $15.95

Grades: K 1 2 3   **581.4**

1. Seeds

ISBN 0-689-85041-7

This "book focuses on seed basics: differences in shapes and sizes, and links between structure and function. . . . Seeds are show alongside the whole plants and fruits they come from. . . . The superb photographs lend themselves to scientific scrutiny: the details are sharp and clear." Horn Book

Rustad, Martha E. H.

Fall leaves; colorful and crunchy. illustrated by Amanda Enright. Millbrook Press 2011 24p il (Fall's here!) lib bdg $23.93

Grades: K 1 2 3   **581.4**

1. Autumn 2. Leaves

ISBN 978-0-7613-5062-0; 0-7613-5062-4

LC 2010053301

In this book "a young girl spies leaves changing color in the fall. She explores how different weather and amounts of sunlight allow the leaves to grow, get food and water, change color, and then fall as the seasons change. . . . In the back of the book, instructions are given for making a leaf print. . . . Children will enjoy the colorful, expressive illustrations." Sci Books Films

Includes glossary and bibliographical references

Wade, Mary Dodson

Seeds sprout! Enslow Elementary 2009 24p il (I like plants!) lib bdg $21.26; pa $6.95

Grades: K 1 2   **581.4**

1. Seeds 2. Plants

ISBN 978-0-7660-3154-8 lib bdg; 0-7660-3154-3 lib bdg; 978-0-7660-3614-7 pa; 0-7660-3614-6 pa

LC 2007039461

This book does "an excellent job of introducing basic concepts about seeds and plants. Large text on colored pages explains terms and covers a lot of ground in the simplest manner imaginable. The full-color illustrations amplify the narrative." SLJ

Includes glossary and bibliographical references

581.6   Miscellaneous nontaxonomic kinds of plants

Farrell, Courtney

Plants out of place. Rourke Pub. 2010 48p il (Let's explore science) $32.79

Grades: 4 5 6 7   **581.6**

1. Plants 2. Biological invasions 3. Food chains (Ecology)

ISBN 978-1-61590-322-1; 1-61590-322-4

LC 2010009909

This "takes a lively look at invasive plants . . . and shows both the destruction that non-native plants cause and what can be done about it. . . . In [this] title, well-chosen boxed examples, abundant color photos, diagrams, and an appended glossary add interest and support the engaging [text]." Booklist

Includes glossary and bibliographical references

Gould, Margee

Poisonous plants. PowerKids Press 2011 24p il (The strangest plants on Earth) lib bdg $21.25

Grades: 3 4 5   **581.6**

1. Poisonous plants

ISBN 978-1-4488-4989-5; 1-4488-4989-6

LC 2010050512

This "colorful [introduction has] bright, full-color photographs that are detailed enough to enable identification in the field, especially of such common poisonous plants as poison ivy, oak, and sumac. . . . Useful for reports and fun to browse, read, and learn." SLJ

Includes glossary

Rockwell, Lizzy

Plants feed me; by Lizzy Rockwell. Holiday House 2014 32 p. col. ill. (hardcover) $16.95

Grades: PreK K 1   **581.6**

1. Plants

ISBN 0823425266; 9780823425266

LC 2012007674

This children's book, by Lizzy Rockwell, features "illustrations [that] show plants and the parts we harvest for food—leaves from lettuce and chard plants; roots and tubers from carrot and potato plants; fruits from apple trees, tomato plants, blueberry bushes, and pumpkin vines; seeds from wheat grass and walnut trees; and all kinds of beans from pods of many shapes." (Booklist)

"It's easy to forget where everyday food comes from, but this gentle, colorful picture book explains, simply and accurately, how food gets from the garden and farm onto dining-room tables." Booklist

Souza, D. M.

Plant invaders; [by] D. M. Souza. F. Watts 2003 63p il (Watts library) lib bdg $25.50; pa $8.95

Grades: 3 4 5   **581.6**

1. Plant ecology 2. Nonindigenous pests 3. Biological invasions

ISBN 0-531-12211-5 lib bdg; 0-531-16247-8 pa

LC 2002-8887

Discusses non-native plants, such as the kudzu vine and the tree-of-heaven, which were imported from other countries and now pose a significant threat to the ecosystems of North America

"Large, brightly colored close-up photos ranging from beautiful to bizarre are nicely placed to support the well-written [narrative.]" SLJ

Wade, Mary Dodson

People need plants! Enslow Elementary 2009 24p il (I like plants!) lib bdg $21.26; pa $6.95

Grades: K 1 2   **581.6**

1. Plants

ISBN 978-0-7660-3153-1 lib bdg; 0-7660-3153-5 lib bdg; 978-0-7660-3613-0 pa; 0-7660-3613-8 pa

LC 2007039458

"Beautifully detailed professional photographs of plants, animals, and people complement the subject matter. [The] book includes a simple activity." SLJ

Includes glossary and bibliographical references

582   Plants noted for specific vegetative characteristics and flowers

Schaefer, Lola M.

★ Pick, pull, snap! where once a flower bloomed. illustrated by Lindsay Barrett George. Greenwillow Bks. 2003 un il $15.99

Grades: K 1 2 3   **582**

1. Fruit 2. Seeds 3. Plants 4. Flowers

ISBN 0-688-17834-0

LC 2002-66818

Describes how raspberries, peanuts, corn, and other foods are produced as various plants flower, create seeds, and finally bear fruit

"On each spread, rhythmic, poetic text describes a plant's flower or husk and shows a cross section that reveals the seeds inside. A few lines of text explain a plant's growth, and then the page folds out to reveal the mature plant. . . . George's inviting, realistic color art brings youngsters up close to plants that produce familiar foods." Booklist

Includes glossary

582.13   Plants noted for their flowers

Souza, D. M.

Freaky flowers. Watts 2002 63p il (Watts library) lib bdg $24.50; pa $8.95

Grades: 5 6 7 8　　　　　　　　　　　**582.13**
1. Flowers
ISBN 0-531-11981-5 lib bdg; 0-531-16221-4 pa
LC 2001-17573

"The book begins with a short course in botany that stresses vocabulary and processes. Subsequent chapters discuss different ways plants attract pollinators through colors, odors, and habitats. The last chapter acts as a warning that many plants are endangered because their pollinators are threatened, emphasizing the balance of nature. The outstanding full-color photos feature some of the most spectacular flowers found anywhere. Small sidebars offer interesting bits of trivia about similar plants. The text is packed with biological information and pertinent vocabulary." SLJ

Includes bibliographical references

Wade, Mary Dodson
Flowers bloom! Enslow Elementary 2009 24p il (I like plants!) lib bdg $21.26; pa $6.95
Grades: K 1 2　　　　　　　　　　　**582.13**
1. Flowers
ISBN 978-0-7660-3157-9 lib bdg; 0-7660-3157-8 lib bdg; 978-0-7660-3617-8 pa; 0-7660-3617-0 pa
LC 2007039462

"Beautifully detailed professional photographs of plants, animals, and people complement the subject matter. [The] book includes a simple activity." SLJ

Includes glossary and bibliographical references

582.16　Trees

Bulla, Clyde Robert
A **tree** is a plant; illustrated by Stacey Schuett. HarperCollins Pubs. 2001 31p il (Let's-read-and-find-out science) hardcover o.p. pa $4.95
Grades: K 1 2　　　　　　　　　　　**582.16**
1. Trees 2. Apples
ISBN 0-06-028171-5; 0-06-028172-3 lib bdg; 0-06-445196-8 pa
LC 00-40797

A newly illustrated edition of the title first published 1960 by Crowell

The text "follows an apple plant from seed to sprout to tree, including the development of blossoms, leaves, and fruit. The functions of roots, trunk, branches, and leaves are also discussed, as well as the seasonal changes in the tree. Schuett's colorful paintings clearly illustrate topics explained in the text, while their pleasing colors, rounded forms, and small, playful animals will help keep children involved in the topic." Booklist

Ehlert, Lois
★ **Red** leaf, yellow leaf. Harcourt Brace Jovanovich 1991 un il $16
Grades: K 1 2 3　　　　　　　　　　**582.16**
1. Trees
ISBN 0-15-266197-2
LC 90-21195

"In a quiet, first-person narrative, a young child details the life cycle of a sugar maple tree. . . . The story is quite brief, and the choice of a very large typeface makes the main portion of the book accessible to beginning readers. The

concluding section offers more detailed and concrete botanical information and provides hints on selecting and planting one's own tree. . . . Ehlert has combined many media to create the book's dazzling illustrations." Horn Book

Galat, Joan Marie
Branching out; How Trees Are Part of Our World. Joan Marie Galat. Owlkids Books, Inc. 2014 64 p. color illustrations (hardcover) $18.95
Grades: 4 5 6 7　　　　　　　　　　**582.16**
1. Trees
ISBN 1771470496; 9781771470490; 9781771470827
LC 2014932714

This book, by Joan Marie Galat, " takes an in-depth look at [trees], introducing the basics of tree biology and profiling 11 different trees from around the world, including familiar ones such as the Red Maple and lesser-known trees like the Tall-Stilted Mangrove. Showcasing the inextricable ways in which trees are part of our society, culture, and economy, this illustrated volume also outlines how animals need trees and how, sometimes, they even help trees survive through symbiosis." (Publisher's note)

"This short, lively introduction to the subject focuses on 11 trees from all over the world...This title is truly worldwide in its coverage; only one tree, the Red Maple, is a native of North America. Appended glossary and index are extensive and complete. A solid overview." SLJ

Gerber, Carole
Winter trees; illustrated by Leslie Evans. Charlesbridge 2008 un il $15.95
Grades: PreK K 1 2　　　　　　　　　**582.16**
1. Trees 2. Winter
ISBN 978-1-58089-168-4; 1-58089-168-3
LC 2007-26197

"Alone in the snowy woods with his dog, a boy discovers the wonder of winter trees. . . . On every double-page spread, four lines of simple verse and bright linoleum block prints decorated with watercolor and collage capture the stark outlines and the details of what he sees, hears, and touches. . . . The blend of play, science, poetry, and art is beautiful; and notes at the back provide more facts about each tree." Booklist

Gibbons, Gail
Tell me, tree; all about trees for kids. Little, Brown 2002 un il $15.95
Grades: K 1 2 3　　　　　　　　　　**582.16**
1. Trees
ISBN 0-316-30903-6
LC 00-64967

"The bright, watercolor illustrations show cheerful children and adults observing, planting, using, and enjoying many kinds of trees. In this simple, informative book, Gibbons provides a basic guide that is sure to please parents and teachers as well as children." Booklist

Howse, Jennifer
Trees. Weigl Publishers 2010 24p il (World of wonder: watch them grow) lib bdg $25.70; pa $9.95

Grades: 1 2   582.16
1. Trees
ISBN 978-1-60596-916-9 lib bdg; 1-60596-916-8 lib bdg; 978-1-60596-917-6 pa; 1-60596-917-6 pa
LC 2009-52098
Learn about the parts of a tree, how it matures from a tiny sprout, and how to learn its age.

The text "is simple without being simplistic; it is thoughtful and comprehensive without being overwhelming. The real appeal for teachers, students, and independent young readers, however, will be the photographs that fill the facing pages. Bold, bright, and colorful, the photographs bring you marvelously close to the subject. . . . On many different levels, this is a very appealing [book]." Libr Media Connect

Includes glossary

Lauber, Patricia
Be a friend to trees; illustrated by Holly Keller. HarperCollins Pubs. 1994 32p il (Let's-read-and-find-out science) hardcover o.p. pa $4.95
Grades: K 1 2 3   582.16
1. Trees
ISBN 0-06-021529-1 lib bdg; 0-06-445120-8 pa
LC 92-24082
"This conveys a lot of information in a simple text with clear line-and-watercolor illustrations." Booklist

In this book "photosynthesis is explained, as well as the beauty and usefulness of trees. Easy conservation suggestions are also offered." Horn Book Guide

Maestro, Betsy
Why do leaves change color? illustrated by Loretta Krupinski. HarperCollins Pubs. 1994 32p il (Let's-read-and-find-out science) hardcover o.p. pa $4.95
Grades: K 1 2 3   582.16
1. Autumn 2. Leaves
ISBN 0-06-022874-1 lib bdg; 0-06-445126-7 pa
LC 93-9611
Explains how leaves change their colors in autumn and then separate from the tree as the tree prepares for winter

"This is an informative concept book. . . . Krupinski's bright gouache-and-colored pencil illustrations show a boy and a girl playing in a country landscape that changes with weather and light. There are also detailed pictures of leaves in different sizes, shapes, and colors. Maestro includes simple instructions for making a leaf rubbing and for pressing leaves, as well as suggestions for places to visit where the fall foliage is special." Booklist

Pallotta, Jerry
Who will plant a tree? written by Jerry Pallotta; illustrated by Tom Leonard. Sleeping Bear Press 2010 un il $15.95
Grades: PreK K 1 2   582.16
1. Seeds 2. Trees
ISBN 978-1-58536-502-9; 1-58536-502-5
LC 2009037411
"Each spread features an animal in a different habitat that, by simply going about its everyday activities, unknowingly plants a tree. . . . The range of habitats and animals shown is impressive, from monkeys throwing figs in the jungle to Amazon River fish excreting seeds from their fruit dinners. . . . With simple, rhythmic language and engaging illustrations, this book encourages readers to see how the ac-

tions of each creature impact the Earth. An excellent accompaniment to science lessons." SLJ

Preus, Margi
Celebritrees; historic & famous trees of the world. illustrated by Rebecca Gibbon. Henry Holt & Co. 2011 un il $16.99
Grades: 2 3 4   582.16
1. Trees
ISBN 978-0-8050-7829-9; 0-8050-7829-0
"Preus introduces 14 trees famous in history or legend. Some are renowned for their age, height, girth, or other physical characteristics. For example, Methuselah, a bristlecone pine in California, is more than 4000 years old, while the Tule Tree in Mexico measures 177 feet around. Others are associated with historic events. . . . Each featured specimen receives a spread with several paragraphs of text plus Gibbon's charming colored pencil and watercolor illustrations. Readers who want to learn more about one or more of the tree varieties can find additional information at the book's end." SLJ

Includes bibliographical references

Rene, Ellen
Investigating why leaves change their color. Rosen/PowerKids 2008 24p il (Science detectives) lib bdg $15.95
Grades: 3 4 5   582.16
1. Trees 2. Leaves
ISBN 978-1-4042-4485-6 lib bdg; 1-4042-4485-9 lib bdg
"With a chatty text, oversize font, and beautiful, full-page color photos, the open design of this . . . book . . . will invite young readers to look at the astonishing science happening around them. The page headings are appealing . . . leading into text that details the process of photosynthesis and chlorophyll's role in trapping sunlight; the botany is quite technical and will encourage kids to talk about it in the classroom and at home. . . . [This is a] fine account of one of nature's most vibrant transformations, leading kids to an elementary understanding of how the sun and sky affect each and every leaf." Booklist

583 Dicotyledons

Aaseng, Nathan
Weird meat-eating plants. Enslow Publishers 2011 48p il (Bizarre science) lib bdg $23.93
Grades: 5 6 7 8   583
1. Carnivorous plants
ISBN 978-0-7660-3672-7; 0-7660-3672-3
LC 2010016602
First published 1996 with title: Meat-eating plants

This describes meat-eating plants such as butterworts, sundews, byblis, pitcher plants, cobra lilies, venus flytraps, and bladderworts.

"Aimed at reluctant readers, [this title is] sure to disgust and delight in equal measure. . . . [The title] will pique interest and get kids lining up at the reference desk looking for more. The text is complemented by illustrations and magnified photos of things that you would hope never to see." SLJ

Includes glossary and bibliographical references

Bash, Barbara

Desert giant; the world of the saguaro cactus. Sierra Club Bks. 1989 un il hardcover o.p. pa $6.95

Grades: 3 4 5   **583**

1. Cactus 2. Desert ecology

ISBN 1-57805-085-5 pa

LC 88-4706

"Animals find food and shelter in the towering plant of the Sonoran desert, and the local Tohono O'odom Indians have multiple uses for it. The cactus's 200-year life cycle is depicted as part of the ecosystem with colorful illustrations and clear text." Sci Child

Dickmann, Nancy

A **bean's** life. Heinemann Library 2010 24p il (Watch it grow) lib bdg $21.50; pa $5.99

Grades: PreK K 1   **583**

1. Beans

ISBN 978-1-4329-4142-0 lib bdg; 1-4329-4142-9 lib bdg; 978-1-4329-4151-2 pa; 1-4329-4151-8 pa

LC 2009-49158

"Practically unique among early introductions to life cycles because death is mentioned . . . this . . . follows [a bean] . . . from . . . seed to maturity with a set of close-up color photographs, one per page, paired to large-type, one or two-sentence captions. . . . Offers nourishing fare for young naturalists." SLJ

Includes glossary

An **oak** tree's life. Heinemann Library 2010 24p il (Watch it grow) lib bdg $21.50; pa $5.99

Grades: PreK K 1   **583**

1. Oak

ISBN 978-1-4329-4143-7 lib bdg; 1-4329-4143-7 lib bdg; 978-1-4329-4152-9 pa; 1-4329-4152-6 pa

LC 2009-49159

"Practically unique among early introductions to life cycles because death is mentioned . . . this . . . follows [an oak tree] . . . from . . . seed to maturity with a set of close-up color photographs, one per page, paired to large-type, one or two-sentence captions. . . . Offers nourishing fare for young naturalists." SLJ

Includes glossary and bibliographical references

A **sunflower's** life. Heinemann Library 2010 24p il (Watch it grow) lib bdg $21.50; pa $5.99

Grades: PreK K 1   **583**

1. Sunflowers

ISBN 978-1-4329-4144-4 lib bdg; 1-4329-4144-5 lib bdg; 978-1-4329-4153-6 pa; 1-4329-4153-4 pa

LC 2009-49161

"Practically unique among early introductions to life cycles because death is mentioned . . . this . . . follows [a sun-flower] . . . from . . . seed to maturity with a set of close-up color photographs, one per page, paired to large-type, one or two-sentence captions. . . . Offers nourishing fare for young naturalists." SLJ

Includes glossary and bibliographical references

Gould, Margee

Meat-eating plants. PowerKids Press 2011 24p il (The strangest plants on Earth) lib bdg $21.25

Grades: 3 4 5   **583**

1. Carnivorous plants

ISBN 978-1-4488-4988-8; 1-4488-4988-8

LC 2010047870

This describes meat-eating plants including the venus flytrap, the bladderwort, the pitcher plant, and the sundew.

This "colorful [introduction has] bright, full-color photographs that are detailed enough to enable identification in the field. . . . Useful for reports and fun to browse, read, and learn." SLJ

Includes glossary

Guiberson, Brenda Z.

Cactus hotel; illustrated by Megan Lloyd. Holt & Co. 1991 un il $16.95; pa $6.95

Grades: K 1 2 3   **583**

1. Cactus 2. Desert ecology

ISBN 0-8050-1333-4; 0-8050-2960-5 pa

LC 90-41748

Describes the life cycle of the giant saguaro cactus, with an emphasis on its role as a home for other desert dwellers

"Guiberson's simple, understandable text gives an enjoyable lesson in desert ecology. Crisply attractive illustrations in color pencil and watercolor show the beauty of the desert landscape and its variety of wildlife." Booklist

Hall, Zoe

The **apple** pie tree; illustrated by Shari Halpern. Blue Sky Press (NY) 1996 un il $15.95

Grades: K 1   **583**

1. Apples

ISBN 0-590-62382-6

LC 95-31134

"From bud to fruit, two children follow the cycle of an apple tree as it is nurtured through the seasons. . . . The story ends with a nice, warm apple pie being taken from the oven. The large pictures and text are suitable for young children. The colorful, clear-cut illustrations use a paint and paper collage technique. An end note shows how bees pollinate the tree's flowers and offers a recipe for apple pie." SLJ

Johnson, Jinny

Dandelion; illustrations by Graham Rosewarne. Smart Apple Media 2010 32p il (How does it grow?) lib bdg $28.50

Grades: 1 2 3   **583**

1. Dandelions

ISBN 978-1-59920-351-5 lib bdg; 1-59920-351-0 lib bdg

LC 2009-5693

Explains the life cycle of a dandelion

"Each stage is described on a spread that features clearly written, oversized text and a caption opposite a full-page, realistic watercolor, or, occasionally, a photograph. . . . A worthwhile purchase." SLJ

Includes glossary

Oak tree; illustrations by Graham Rosewarne. Smart Apple Media 2010 32p il (How does it grow?) lib bdg $28.50

Grades: 1 2 3   **583**

1. Oak

ISBN 978-1-59920-356-0 lib bdg; 1-59920-356-1 lib bdg

LC 2009-3399

Presents a basic overview of how an acorn grows into an oak tree and explains each stage in its development

"Each stage is described on a spread that features clearly written, oversized text and a caption opposite a full-page, realistic watercolor, or, occasionally, a photograph. . . . A worthwhile purchase." SLJ

Includes glossary and bibliographical references

Pfeffer, Wendy

From seed to pumpkin; illustrated by James Graham Hale. HarperCollins 2004 33p il (Let's-read-and-find-out science) hardcover o.p. lib bdg $16.89; pa $4.99

Grades: K 1   **583**

1. Pumpkin

ISBN 0-06-028038-7; 0-06-028039-5 lib bdg; 0-06-445190-9 pa

LC 00-54039

This explains the stages in the development of a seed into a pumpkin

Written "in simple, clear language. . . . A couple of easy recipes and experiments are appended. Appealing watercolor-and-pencil illustrations show children involved in planting and tending the pumpkins, and help make the process and the passage of time understandable to this audience." SLJ

Posada, Mia

Dandelions; stars in the grass. Carolrhoda Bks. 2000 un il lib bdg $15.95

Grades: 2 3 4   **583**

1. Dandelions

ISBN 1-57505-383-7

LC 98-53000

Rhyming text presents the dandelion, not as a weed, but as a flower of great beauty. Includes information about the flower, a recipe, and science activities

"This cheerful book is a nice combination of rhyme and information. . . . Bright and pleasing acrylic illustrations extend the text. . . . Posada includes just enough botanical detail for beginning dandelion pickers." SLJ

Includes bibliographical references

Root, Phyllis

Plant a pocket of prairie; Phyllis Root; illustrations by Betsy Bowen. University of Minnesota Press 2014 40 p. chiefly color illustrations (hc: alk. paper) $14.95

Grades: 1 2 3 4   **583.73**

1. Gardening 2. Prairie ecology 3. Prairie plants

ISBN 0816679800; 9780816679805

LC 2013040345

AAAS/Subaru SB & F Prize in Excellence in Science Books Finalists, Hands-on Science (2014)

In this book, "free verse poems invite readers to plant flowers and reconstruct pockets of lost prairie in backyards and on balconies to entice insects and birds to return, such as butterfly weed to attract monarch butterflies or rough blazing star for great spangled fritillaries. A map shows the once extensive prairie in Minnesota and the less than one percent now remaining, while the plant list will inspire the planting

of at least some of the 14 recommended flowers and grasses." (School Library Journal)

"There isn't much prairie left in the U.S., thanks to human farming and development. Readers are encouraged to reverse this trend by planting native plants in their own backyards and watching what animals are attracted by each plant species. Mixed-media illustrations are placed on white backgrounds, their chunky outlines a modern twist on botanical illustration. The conservation and restoration message is universal." Horn Book

Royston, Angela

Life cycle of an oak tree; rev and updated ed.; Heinemann Library 2009 32p il (Life cycle of a) $25.36; pa $7.99

Grades: 2 3 4   **583**

1. Oak

ISBN 978-1-4329-2531-4; 1-4329-2531-8; 978-1-4329-2548-2 pa; 1-4329-2548-2 pa

LC 2009517688

First published 2000

Introduces the life cycle of an oak tree, from the sprouting of an acorn through its more than 100 years of growth

This offers "easily accessible information in [an] attractive [package]." SLJ

Includes glossary and bibliographical references

585 Gymnosperms

Chin, Jason

★ **Redwoods**. Roaring Brook Press 2009 un il $16.95

Grades: PreK K 1 2   **585**

1. Redwood

ISBN 978-1-59643-430-1; 1-59643-430-9

"The framing story opens with a boy finding a copy of Redwoods on a subway station bench (he's even on the cover). He delves in, and facts about the ancient trees spring to life around him. . . . Emerging from the station to find himself in the middle of a redwood forest, his adventures mirror what he's learning. . . . The straightforward narrative is given enormous energy by the inventive format and realistic watercolor illustrations. . . . Chin adeptly captures the singular and spectacular nature of redwoods in this smartly layered book." Publ Wkly

586 Seedless plants

Pascoe, Elaine

Plants without seeds; photography by Dwight Kuhn. PowerKids Press 2003 32p il (Kid's guide to the classification of living things) $20.65

Grades: 2 3 4 5   **586**

1. Ferns 2. Mosses

ISBN 0-8239-6315-2

LC 2001-7794

An introduction to the life cycles and characteristics of bryophytes, or plants without seeds, such as mosses and ferns

This "slim, well-organized . . . {introduction is} a must for schools in which plant studies are a part of the curricu-

lum. . . . Useful for reports, with browsing appeal as well."
SLJ

Includes glossary and bibliographical references

590 Animals

125 true stories of amazing animals; [inspiring tales of animal friendship & four-legged heroes, plus crazy animal antics] National Geographic Publishers Group UK [distributor] 2012 112 p. (pbk.) $12.95

Grades: 4 5 6   **590**
   1. Animals 2. Rescue work 3. Animal behavior 4.
Animals -- Anecdotes
   ISBN 142630918X; 9781426309182
                           LC 2012471745
This book is a "collection of favorite animal antics from 'National Geographic Kids' 'Amazing Animals' column [and] has a little of everything: dramatic rescues, incredible adventures, mistaken identities, strange bedfellows, odd couples, and much more." Among those featured are a "hippo that opens doors with his lips, a bison that rides in cars, an owl that goes on bike rides, and a group of elephants that play in an orchestra." (School Library Journal)

Ablow, Gail
   A **horse** in the house, and other strange but true animal stories; illustrated by Kathy Osborn. Candlewick Press 2007 un il $17.99

Grades: 2 3 4 5   **590**
   1. Animals
   ISBN 978-0-7636-2838-3; 0-7636-2838-7
                           LC 2006051855
"Some of these 16 short tales would be very hard to believe, had Ablow, a journalist, not provided specific source notes for each at the end. It wouldn't be too hard to buy the moose that does laps in a Spokane swimming pool . . . —but a man successfully giving mouth-to-mouth to a distressed ornamental fish? . . . Osborn's stylized paintings capture the humor in each report. . . . Even skeptical young readers will come back for more." Booklist

Includes bibliographical references

Animals alive; the fight for survival in the wild. DK Pub. 2011 80p il map $15.99

Grades: 3 4 5 6   **590**
   1. Animals
   ISBN 978-0-7566-7213-3; 0-7566-7213-9
Explains biodiversity, discusses the role animals play in ecosystems, describes the threats affecting the lives of animals, and profiles various animals, including jaguars, black rhinoceros, and bluefin tuna.

This is an "excellently crafted book. . . . The layout invites readers in through the use of different fonts and bolded words, small paragraphs, circular quotes, and fact blurbs. Each spread has stunning photos of the animals and simple illustrations. A good choice for reports, and a great read for anyone interested in endangered species." SLJ

Arnosky, Jim
   ★ **Wild** tracks! a guide to nature's footprints. [by] Jim Arnosky. Sterling Pub. Co. 2008 32p il $14.95

Grades: 1 2 3   **590**
   1. Animal tracks
   ISBN 978-1-4027-3985-9; 1-4027-3985-0
                           LC 2007033972
"Tracks are separated into categories (bear, deer, cat, and so on), each presented in a two-page spread. On the left, a full-color painting displays an animal, and its tracks, in its natural habitat. On the right, information about the tracks, and how to read them, appears as pencil-sketch reproductions from Arnosky's own notebook. . . . Arnosky supplements the track identification information with fascinating related material in notebook-style entries. . . . The uniformly lovely illustrations and the compelling concept make this a book that young naturalists will enjoy year-round." Booklist

Baby animal pop! with 5 incredible, life-size foldouts. National Geographic 2011 il (National Geographic little kids) $14.95

Grades: PreK K 1 2   **590**
   1. Animal babies
   ISBN 978-1-4263-0765-2; 1-4263-0765-9
"This well-written book has exquisite life-size photos. Between the appealing pictures, an educational text for older children details the environment, anatomy, food, and homes of bunnies, ducklings, piglets, lambs, and ponies. The diagrams and photos give youngsters insight into the first year of the animals' lives." SLJ

Bayrock, Fiona
   Bubble homes and fish farts; illustrated by Carolyn Conahan. Charlesbridge 2009 45p il $16.95; pa $7.95

Grades: 2 3 4   **590**
   1. Animals 2. Bubbles
   ISBN 978-1-57091-669-4; 1-57091-669-1; 978-1-57091-670-0 pa; 1-57091-670-5 pa
                           LC 2008-06151
"Fast Repetitive Tick (FaRT) is the term scientists use to describe the flatulencelike noise that herring make as they communicate their locations to one another other. That might be the most amusing description of the uses of bubbles in the natural world, but this entire book is enjoyable and engaging. . . . The illustrations are pale and less-detailed versions of scientifically accurate drawings overlaid with entertaining comments. . . . Creative, accessible, and fact-filled." SLJ

Berger, Gilda
   101 animal records. Scholastic Inc. 2013 112 p. ill. (paperback) $8.99; (prebind) $19.65

Grades: 2 3 4 5   **590**
   1. Picture books for children 2. Animals
   ISBN 0545427967; 0606315055; 9780545427968; 9780606315050
In this book, "readers will find a list of 101 animal superlatives. . . . There are such accolades as 'Loudest Insect' (the cicada) and 'Strongest Tongue' (the anteater) and 'Most Useful Insect' (the honeybee). The authors [Melvin Berger and Gilda Berger] skip an introduction, diving straight in with #1, then present a new superlative on each page accompanied by a paragraph of explanatory text." (Booklist)

Berkes, Marianne Collins
   Animalogy; animal analogies. by Marianne Berkes; illustrated by Cathy Morrison. Sylvan Dell 2011 un il

$16.95; pa $8.95; English ebook $9.95; Spanish ebook $9.95

Grades: PreK K 1 2 3 4   **590**
1. Animals 2. Analogy
ISBN 978-1-60718-127-9; 1-60718-127-4; 978-1-60718-137-8 pa; 1-60718-137-1 pa; 978-1-60718-147-7 English ebook; 978-1-60718-157-6 Spanish ebook

LC 2011006510

"Use this rhyming book about animals with students to explain the concept of analogies. 'Robin is to wing, as goldfish is to fin. Beaver is to build, as spider is to spin.' Body parts, size, sounds, actions, and animal classification are all included in the examples. Detailed and realistic illustrations give moose, bears, and frogs a ready-to-jump-off-the-page appearance. . . . This book makes learning about analogies, new vocabulary, and animals easy to understand and fun." SLJ

BishopRoby, Joshua
Animal kingdom. Compass Point Books 2009 40p il (Mission: science) lib bdg $26.60

Grades: 4 5 6   **590**
1. Animals -- Classification
ISBN 978-0-7565-4057-9 lib bdg; 0-7565-4057-7 lib bdg

LC 2008-37574

An introduction to the animal kingdom, which is made up of a variety of animals that are organized into categories based on physical attributes or ancestors

Includes glossary

Broom, Jenny
Animalium; Jenny Broom, illustrated by Katie Scott. Candlewick Press 2014 112 p. color illustrations (reinforced) $35

Grades: 3 4 5 6 7   **590**
1. Animals 2. Museums
ISBN 9780763675080; 0763675083

LC 2013952848

"Open 365 days a year and unrestricted by the constraints of physical space, each title in this series is organized into galleries that display more than 200 full-color specimens accompanied by lively, informative text. Offering hours of learning, this first title within the series--[Jenny Broom's book] Animalium--presents the animal kingdom in glorious detail with illustrations from Katie Scott." (Publisher's note)

"Each basic group includes several spreads offering examples from subgroups within the class as well as a spread with a connected habitat: coastal waters, coral reefs, rain forest, deserts, woodlands and tundra. No information sources are given, but there are good suggestions for general websites for further learning." Kirkus

Cusick, Dawn
Get the scoop on animal poop; from lions to tapeworms, 251 cool facts about scat, frass, dung & more. Dawn Cusick. Imagine Pub. 2012 80 p.

Grades: 3 4 5   **590**
1. Feces 2. Wildlife 3. Excretion 4. Digestive system 5. Animal droppings
ISBN 9781936140428

LC 2011025982

This book is a "guide to coprology, the study of feces. . . . Every page is packed with colorful photographs, and the text is an accumulation of snippets, a few sentences about each of the hundreds of topics." (Kirkus) "Topics covered include digestive systems of various animals, parasites, animals that eat feces, and bathroom habits. Back matter includes a guide to identify types of animal feces, a "poo interview" with a veterinarian, activity ideas, a glossary and reading list . . ., a subject index, and an index by organism." (School Libr J)

Davies, Nicola, 1958-
Everything you need to know about animals. Kingfisher 2010 160p il $16.99

Grades: 1 2 3   **590**
1. Animals
ISBN 978-0-7534-6433-5; 0-7534-6433-0

Presents a brief overview of animal life, including types of animals and the ways their bodies are different, their means of locomotion, their food and how they find it, their senses, and how they reproduce themselves.

"As a beginner's encyclopedia of animals, this book is outstanding. The text is divided into five color-coded sections which range from the variety of animals in the world to how animals get around and get their food. . . . The text is full of colorful illustrations and the language is very readable. This is the type of book that the reader will come to again and again." Libr Media Connect

★ **Extreme** animals; the toughest creatures on Earth. illustrated by Neal Layton. Candlewick Press 2006 61p il $12.99; pa $7.99

Grades: 3 4 5 6   **590**
1. Animals 2. Adaptation (Biology)
ISBN 978-0-7636-3067-6; 0-7636-3067-5; 978-0-7636-4127-6 pa; 0-7636-4127-8 pa

LC 2005-43544

"There is life everywhere on Earth . . . and much of that life thrives in conditions that humans could not endure for five minutes or less. This funny and appealing little book describes who these amazing life-forms are and how they manage to survive. Simple and inviting cartoon drawings enliven the text and convey the types of extremes in an easy-to-understand manner." SLJ

Includes glossary

Who's like me? by Nicola Davies and illustrated by Marc Boutavant. Candlewick Press 2012 24 p. (alk. paper) $9.99

Grades: PreK K   **590**
1. Animals -- Classification 2. Anatomy
ISBN 0763658022; 9780763658021

LC 2011047180

This book, by Nicola Davies and illustrated by Marc Boutavant, examines how "some animals have fins to swim with, some have feathers and a beak, some have skin that is scaly, or smooth and wet. But whatever features a creature has, someone else has them, too. Can [readers] guess who? Big flaps and a matching spread at the end [are designed to] make animal classification fun." (Publisher's note)

Faulkner, Mark
★ **A zeal** of zebras; an alphabet of collective nouns. by Woop Studios. Chronicle Books 2011 un il

Grades: PreK K   **590**
1. Animals 2. Alphabet
ISBN 1452104921; 9781452104928
    LC 2011008011
"From the graphic designers of the Harry Potter franchise, this ABC book of collective nouns couples informative text with digitally created tableaus reminiscent of vintage posters that wryly play on the terms. . . . The thoughtful and provocative portraits will leave readers teasing out their subtleties." Publ Wkly

Gannij, Joan
    Hidden hippo; written by Joan Gannij; illustrated by Clare Beaton. Barefoot Books 2008 un il $15.99
Grades: PreK K 1 2   **590**
1. Animals 2. Hippopotamus
ISBN 978-1-84686-170-3; 1-84686-170-5
    LC 2007042677
"On safari, an unseen narrator hopes 'to see/A hippo or two,/Perhaps even three?' Clever rhyming verse details the spectacular sights along the way, such as lions, chimpanzees, and sleepy leopards. . . . This expansive tour of the African Plains is brought to life through Beaton's signature fabric appliqué collages. . . . The vibrant colors capture the hot, arid habitat. . . . Young adventurers and conservationists alike will pore over this visually stunning story." SLJ

Gibbs, Edward
    ★ **I** spy with my little eye. Candlewick Press 2011 un il $14.95
Grades: PreK K 1   **590**
1. Animals -- Color
ISBN 978-0-7636-5284-5; 0-7636-5284-9
    LC 2010039167
"A classic childhood guessing game gets an elegant treatment from newcomer Gibbs in this introduction to colors and animals. . . . Defined by joyful scribbled outlines, the exuberant, friendly animal portraits dazzle." Publ Wkly

Hearst, Michael
    Unusual creatures; a mostly accurate account of some of the Earth's strangest animals. by Michael Hearst; illustrations by Jelmer Noordeman. Chronicle Books 2012 109 p. (alk. paper) $16.99
Grades: 3 4 5   **590**
1. Animals -- Miscellanea
ISBN 1452104670; 9781452104676
    LC 2011048646
In "this guide to 'unusual creatures' . . . [Michael] Hearst introduces species like the echidna, flying snake, and narwhal, describing their physical characteristics, habitats, and behaviors, with tidbits, quizzes, and even poems. . . . Each animal appears in a matte illustration that combines naturalistic features with subtle hints of personality." (Publishers Weekly)

Hestermann, Josh
    Zoology for kids; understanding and working with animals: with 21 activities. Josh and Bethanie Hestermann. Chicago Review Press, Incorporated 2015 144 p. color illustrations $18.95
    Grades: 5 6 7 8 9   **590**
1. Zoology 2. Vocational guidance 3. Zoology -- Vocational guidance 4. Zoology -- Study and teaching

-- Activity programs
ISBN 1613749619; 9781613749616
    LC 2014042745
This book, by Josh and Bethanie Hestermann, "invites the next generation of zoologists to discover the animal kingdom through clear, entertaining information and anecdotes, lush color photos, hands-on activities, and peer-reviewed research. Young minds are introduced to zoology as a science by discussing animals' forms, functions, and behaviors as well as the history behind zoos and aquariums." (Publisher's note)
    "Studded with fun activities and attractive animal photos, this comprehensive resource will excite those not already smitten with the animal world to enthusiastically join in the delightful exploration of what it means to study and care for animals in today's world...Charming photos, hand-drawn graphics, highlighted words, and a correlative glossary enhance the clear-cut writing style." SLJ
    Includes bibliographical references and index

Hughes, Catherine D.
    Little kids first big book of animals. National Geographic 2010 128p il map $14.95
Grades: K 1 2 3   **590**
1. Animals
ISBN 9781426307041; 1426307047; 9781426307218 lib bdg; 1426307217 lib bdg
"This book, well organized by type of habitat . . . introduces animals from all over the world. The easy-to-follow text consists of somewhat random facts about the creatures; the real stars of the show are the many vivid nature photographs." Horn Book Guide

Hynes, Margaret
    Picture This! Animals; Amazing Information-right Before Your Eyes. by Margaret Hynes. Kingfisher 2014 64 p. color illustrations $12.99
Grades: 3 4 5 6   **590**
1. Animals
ISBN 0753468875; 9780753468876
This book, by Margaret Hynes, is a "reference book all about the animal world. Designed for . . . middle schoolers, fascinating facts and important information alike about all types of animals is presented both visually and in text form. . . . Topics covered include animal characteristics, defense, habitats, migration patterns, food webs, adaptation, birth and growth, and conservation." (Publisher's note)
    "This eclectic but organized book presents comparative data about animals, such as depth distribution of deep-sea life and flying abilities of bird species, through minimal text and busy, colorful infographics (tables, graphs, maps, callout labels, etc.). The volume requires careful study instead of light browsing, but occasional humor heightens the appeal. Though generally correct, there are few inaccuracies." Horn Book

Jenkins, Steve
    ★ The **Animal** Book; A Collection of the Fastest, Fiercest, Toughest, Cleverest, Shyest--and Most Surprising--animals on Earth. by Steve Jenkins. Houghton Mifflin Harcourt 2013 208 p. col. ill. (hardcover) $21.99
Grades: K 1 2 3 4 5   **590**
1. Picture books for children 2. Animals
ISBN 054755799X; 9780547557991

Boston Globe-Horn Book Honor: Nonfiction (2014)
This children's picture book by Steve Jenkins provides an "introduction to the vast animal kingdom. After a chapter of definition, information is presented in sections on animal families, senses, predators, defenses, extremes and the story of life. More facts appear in the final chapter, which serves both as index (with page numbers and thumbnails) and quick reference." (Kirkus Reviews)

★ **Biggest,** strongest, fastest. Ticknor & Fields Bks. for Young Readers 1995 un il $16; pa $5.95
Grades: K 1 2   590
1. Animals -- Miscellanea
ISBN 0-395-69701-8; 0-395-86136-5 pa
LC 94-21804
Jenkins uses "cut-paper collages to explore extremes—including longest lived, smallest, and slowest—in the animal world. These 'record holders' include the largest kind of spider, the bird-spider; the strongest for its size, the ant; and the biggest animal that has ever lived, the blue whale... . The book closes with a chart that includes brief facts about the animals' diet, range, and size." (Horn Book) "Ages four to nine." (Booklist)
"A helpful chart at the end contains further information about each creature, such as diet and habitat. An all-round superlative effort." SLJ

Johnson, Jinny
★ **Animal** tracks & signs. National Geographic Society 2008 192p il $24.95; lib bdg $32.90
Grades: 5 6 7 8   590
1. Animals 2. Animal tracks 3. Tracking and trailing
ISBN 978-1-4263-0253-4; 1-4263-0253-3; 978-1-4263-0254-1 lib bdg; 1-4263-0254-1 lib bdg
"This attractive book describes the tracks (paw prints, bird claw prints, slimy trails) and signs (molted skin, food remains, scat, tree markings) that animals leave in their wake... . A typical two-page layout includes a photo and short paragraph about the animal category, three or four colored boxes containing a photo or drawing of a specific animal (serval, bobcat), and a description of its size, geographic range, habitat, food, tracks and signs, and comments. ... The beautiful photos vary from action ... to informational. ... The language is simple and readable." Voice Youth Advocates
Includes glossary and bibliographical references

Komiya, Teruyuki
Life-size zoo; from tiny rodents to gigantic elephants, an actual-size animal encyclopedia. editorial supervisor of Japanese edition, Teruyuki Komiya; photographer, Toyofumi Fukuda; Japanese translation by Makiko Oku; English language adaptation by Kristin Earhart. Seven Footer Kids 2009 43p il $17.95
Grades: PreK K 1 2   590
1. Size 2. Zoos 3. Animals
ISBN 978-1-934734-20-9; 1-934734-20-9
"The claim to fame for this oversize collection of animal portraits is that each animal is shown at 'actual size.' The striking photographs, taken at Japanese zoos, provide a rare opportunity to see animal faces up close. ... Animal facts are provided in side panels that feature stick figures who engage readers. ... The stellar photographs, playful format

and informative content create a highly appealing package." Publ Wkly

More life-size zoo; lion, hippopotamus, polar bear and more: an all-new actual-size animal encyclopedia. photographer, Toshimitsu Matsuhashi; Japanese translation by Junko Miyakoshi; English language adaptation by Kristin Earhart. Seven Footer Press 2010 47p il $18.95
Grades: PreK K 1 2   590
1. Size 2. Zoos 3. Animals
ISBN 978-1-934734-19-3; 1-934734-19-5
This volume highlights "a second batch of zoo animals . . . in crisp, full-color photos. Some like . . . a large fruit bat, can be shown in entirety, but many others, like a fully maned African lion . . . require foldout pages for even a partial view. The eye-catching photos are the main thrust, while extra data flows along the edges of the page. . . . This is a great introduction to animals." SLJ

Levine, Shar
Animals; mammals, birds, reptiles, amphibians, fish, and other animals. by Shar Levine and Leslie Johnstone. Crabtree Pub. 2010 48p il (A class of their own) lib bdg $29.27; pa $9.95
Grades: 5 6 7 8   590
1. Animals -- Classification
ISBN 978-0-7787-5372-8 lib bdg; 0-7787-5372-7 lib bdg; 978-0-7787-5386-5 pa; 0-7787-5386-7 pa
Looks at the animal kingdom, providing information and examples of species from the major phyla and classes, as well as case histories of newly discovered endangered species.
"Lively section headings . . . and notes on uncommon achievements, . . . lighten the substantial load of biological terminology. Illustrated with a plethora of closeup color photos and microphotos, and closing with annotated lists of recommended Web sites, . . . [this captures] the remarkable diversity of life." SLJ
Includes glossary and bibliographical references

Lewin, Ted
★ **Look!** by Ted Lewin. Holiday House 2013 32 p. col. ill.
Grades: PreK K 1   590
1. Animals -- Africa 2. Animal ecology -- Africa
ISBN 9780823426072
LC 2011049607
" A satisfying challenge and a fun animal adventure made thrilling by Lewin's characteristically spectacular use of light." Kirkus

What am I? where am I? written and illustrated by Ted Lewin. Holiday House 2013 32 p. (I like to read) (hardcover) $14.95
Grades: PreK K 1   590
1. Biomes 2. Animals 3. Habitat (Ecology)
ISBN 0823428567; 9780823428564
LC 2012039289
This book, by Ted Lewin, uses drawings to "illustrate a guessing game that fosters an appreciation of both art and science, while introducing animals in the five major biomes: Grassland, desert, forest, tundra, and water. Inspired by his many travels, classically inspired compositions communicate the regal magnificence of five stunning animals: lion, camel, tiger, reindeer, and sea otter." (Publisher's note)

McGuinness, Lisa

The **dictionary** of ordinary extraordinary animals; by Lisa McGuinness and Leslie Jonath; illustrated by Lisa Congdon. Running Press 2011 un il $18.95

Grades: K 1 2 3   **590**

1. Animals -- Encyclopedias

ISBN 978-0-7624-4063-4; 0-7624-4063-5

LC 2010935841

"An alphabetically organized discussion of 150 animals, this informative guidebook combines casual descriptions of the animals with grainy illustrations reminiscent of vintage flashcards. . . . Congdon's paintings are characterized by naturalistic details and touches of surprising whimsy . . . communicating a palpable sense of wonder." Publ Wkly

McKay, Sindy

Animals under our feet; illustrated by Judith Hunt. Treasure Bay 2007 40p il (We both read) $7.99; pa $3.99

Grades: K 1 2   **590**

1. Burrowing animals

ISBN 978-1-60115-003-5; 1-60115-003-2; 978-1-60115-004-2 pa; 1-60115-004-0 pa

LC 2006-932224

This "is a marvelous series for beginning readers. . . . The parent reads the left-hand page, which has complex text and new or complex words in boldface print. The child's side has supporting, but less complex, text. . . . The illustrations are well done, and the boldface type used to introduce new words to the young reader is invaluable." Sci Books Films

Montgomery, Heather L.

★ **Wild** discoveries; wacky new animals. by Heather L. Montgomery. Scholastic, Inc. 2013 62 p. (pbk.) $6.99

Grades: 3 4 5 6 7   **590**

1. Discoveries in science 2. Animals

ISBN 0545477670; 9780545477673

LC 2012285070

This book by Heather Montgomery features "newly discovered species from around the world--such as the Shocking Pink Dragon and the Green Bomber. These . . . species are organized by region with . . . facts about each one's . . . abilities and traits. The book . . . has a special section featuring new species discovered by kids." (Publisher's note)

Myers, Jack

The **puzzle** of the platypus; and other explorations of science in action. [by] Jack Myers; illustrated by John Rice. Boyds Mills Press 2008 64p il map (Scientists probe 11 animal mysteries) $17.95

Grades: 3 4 5 6   **590**

1. Animals

ISBN 978-1-59078-556-0; 1-59078-556-8

LC 2007023741

"This collection of 11 articles originally appeared in Highlights magazine during the 1990s and early 2000s. Each article tells how a scientist was able to unravel a mystery about some kind of animal. Myers's stories about dolphins, polar bears, elephants, and other animals contain many interesting scientific facts and are written in accessible and engaging prose. . . . Most of the pages have attractive watercolor illustrations." SLJ

Pittau, Francisco

★ **Out** of sight; [by] Pittau & Gervais. Chronicle Books 2010 16p il $19.99

Grades: PreK K 1   **590**

1. Animals

ISBN 9780811877121; 0811877124

LC 2010016150

"In this sophisticated guess-the-animal book, oversize pages feature large flaps offering visual clues about the animals concealed underneath. . . . The unexpected details about each animal . . . should fascinate even adults, but the core appeal is in the abstract elements that challenge readers' way of seeing." Publ Wkly

Selsam, Millicent Ellis

Big tracks, little tracks; following animal prints. illustrated by Marlene Hill Donnelly. rev ed; HarperCollins Pubs. 1999 31p il (Let's-read-and-find-out science) hardcover o.p. pa $4.95

Grades: K 1 2 3   **590**

1. Animal tracks 2. Tracking and trailing

ISBN 0-06-028209-6; 0-06-445194-1 pa

LC 98-18315

First published with this title 1995; originally published with title How to be a nature detective

This book "teaches young readers how to track animals by finding footprints and other clues. . . . Included is a new Find Out More page with lots of hands-on activites." Publisher's note

Seuling, Barbara

Cows sweat through their noses; and other freaky facts about animal habits, characteristics, and homes. by Barbara Seuling; illustrated by Matthew Skeens. Picture Window Books 2008 40p il (Freaky facts) lib bdg $16.95

Grades: 2 3 4 5   **590**

1. Animals

ISBN 978-1-4048-3749-2 lib bdg; 1-4048-3749-3 lib bdg

LC 2007004028

"This delightful little book contains a potpourri of facts about many members of the animal kingdom, large and small, from insects to elephants. . . . The information presented . . . is . . . fascinating." Sci Books Films

Includes glossary and bibliographical references

Silverman, Buffy

Can an old dog learn new tricks? and other questions about animals. illustrations by Colin W. Thompson. Lerner 2010 40p il (Is it a fact?) lib bdg $26.60

Grades: 4 5 6   **590**

1. Questions and answers 2. Animals -- Miscellanea

ISBN 978-0-8225-9083-5; 0-8225-9083-2

LC 2009-20587

Includes glossary and bibliographical references

Silverstein, Alvin

Dung beetles, slugs, leeches, and more; the yucky animal book. by Alvin and Virginia Silverstein, and Laura Silverstein Nunn; illustrated by Gerald Kelley. Enslow Publishers 2010 48p il (Yucky science) lib bdg $23.93

Grades: 4 5 6 7   **590**

1. Insects 2. Invertebrates 3. Animal behavior

ISBN 978-0-7660-3317-7 lib bdg; 0-7660-3317-1 lib bdg

LC 2009012281

"Written in an engaging and conversational style and full of revolting descriptions and entertaining cartoon illustrations . . . [this is] sure to turn even the strongest stomach. An introduction . . . puts 'yucky' in perspective, reminding kids that our world is diverse and that everyone has a different definition of repulsive." SLJ

Includes glossary and bibliographical references

Siwanowicz, Igor

Animals up close; zoom in on the world's most incredible creatures. DK Pub. 2009 96p il $19.99

Grades: 4 5 6   **590**

1. Animals

ISBN 978-0-7566-4513-7; 0-7566-4513-1

"An eye-catching cover will attract readers to this amazing look at some of the world's insects, fish, mammals, reptiles, amphibians, and birds. The focus is on animals small enough to fit in a child's hand. Siwanowicz showcases each creature with a spread containing a full-color, high-quality, close-up photo surrounded by multiple factual asides. . . . The book is packed with interesting material that captures the author's fascination for small creatures." SLJ

Includes glossary

Swanson, Diane

Animal aha! thrilling discoveries in wildlife science. Annick Press 2009 48p il $19.95; pa $9.95

Grades: 4 5 6   **590**

1. Animals

ISBN 978-1-55451-165-5; 1-55451-165-8; 978-1-55451-164-8 pa; 1-55451-164-X pa

"An olio of 'AHA!' moments in natural science. Who knew that a Burmese python's heart enlarges to aid in digestion? Or that a parrot might comprehend human language and be able to use it creatively? Such are the tidbits in this browsable book. 'Fun Facts' and 'Fast Facts' boxes abound, and a color photo pops up on almost every page. With a lively text, this interesting pastiche will be enjoyed by kids pawing through the classroom library seeking an engaging nonfiction read." SLJ

Thomas, Keltie

Animals that changed the world. Annick Press 2010 112p il map $21.95; pa $12.95

Grades: 4 5 6   **590**

1. Animals

ISBN 978-1-55451-243-0; 1-55451-243-3; 978-1-55451-242-3 pa; 1-55451-242-5 pa

"Thomas takes a breezy, conversational look at more than 20 species—from microbes to codfish—that have impacted the Earth in extreme ways. . . . Animals profiled include the cat, dog, beaver, pigeon, and horse. . . . The busy format features narrow columns of text layered on color backgrounds alongside visually stimulating photographs, an occasional drawing, and 'Fact Track' and 'Speak of the Beast' sections, which explain the etymology of animal idioms." SLJ

Twist, Clint

A **little** book of slime; Clint Twist. Firefly Books 2012 80 p. $9.95

Grades: 3 4 5 6 7   **590**

1. Algae 2. Mucus 3. Molds (Fungi)

ISBN 1770850066; 9781770850064

Contents: What is slime? -- Slimy stuff in water -- Pond slime -- Slime tube -- Red tide -- Lungfish -- Horrible hagfish -- Jellyfish -- Sea cucumber -- Sea slug -- Sea hare -- Frogspawn -- Slimy stuff on land -- Poison arrow frog -- Foam-nest frog -- California newt -- Water-holding frog -- Cane toad -- Velvet worm -- Slime light -- Snail -- Banana slug -- Slime mold beetle -- Froghopper -- Starfish stinkhorn -- Other slimy stuff -- Saliva -- Phlegm -- Sundew plant -- Slime flux -- Decomposing vegetables -- Jelly fungus -- Lattice stinkhorn -- Creeping slime -- Living snot mold.

This book "provides a[n] . . . introduction to slime in the natural world. From pond slime and red tide to phlegm and living snot mold, the author surveys the slick, sticky substance produced by living organisms for protection, digestion, defense and more. In some cases the organism itself is the slime. This disparate material has been organized into three sections: 'Slimy Stuff in Water,' 'Slimy Stuff on Land' and 'Other Slimy Stuff.' . . . A . . . glossary defines terms bolded in the text. There's an index but no sources or suggestions for further research for those who want more". (Kirkus Reviews)

590.7   Education, research, related topics

Benbow, Ann

Awesome animal science projects; [by] Ann Benbow and Colin Mably; illustrations by Tom Labaff. Enslow Publishers 2010 48p il (Real life science experiments) lib bdg $23.93

Grades: 3 4 5   **590.7**

1. Animal behavior 2. Science projects

ISBN 978-0-7660-3148-7 lib bdg; 0-7660-3148-9 lib bdg

LC 2008-23932

"Color drawings, photographs, a glossary, and suggestions for further research enliven . . . [this] title . . . [and provide] solid curricular support." Booklist

"Presents several easy-to-do science experiments about animals and animal behavior." Publisher's note

Includes glossary and bibliographical references

Gardner, Robert

Ace your animal science project; great science fair ideas. [by] Robert Gardner . . . [et al.] Enslow Publishers 2009 128p il (Ace your biology science project) lib bdg $31.93

Grades: 5 6 7 8   **590.7**

1. Animal behavior 2. Science projects 3. Science -- Experiments

ISBN 978-0-7660-3220-0 lib bdg; 0-7660-3220-5 lib bdg

LC 2008-4234

"Dozens of . . . science activities are presented with background information, step-by-step instructions, and suggestions for extending to the science fair level. . . . Color

illustrations and important safety information are included."
Horn Book Guide

Includes bibliographical references

590.72   Research

Burns, Loree Griffin

Citizen scientists; be a part of scientific discovery from
your own backyard. Loree Griffin Burns; photographs by
Ellen Harasimowicz. H. Holt 2012 80 p. col. ill., col. maps
Grades: 3 4 5 6 7 8   590.72

1. Suburbs 2. Animals -- Classification 3. Research
-- Citizen participation 4. Wildlife -- Geographical
distribution 5. Suburban animals -- Research -- Citizen
participation 6. Suburban animals -- Monitoring --
Citizen participation

ISBN 0805090622; 9780805090628; 9780805095173
                                          LC 2011021673

AAAS/Subaru SB&F Prize for Excellence in Science
Books: Hands On Science Book (2013)

In this children's book, Loree Griffin Burns "brings . .
. attention to four . . . scientific projects that enlist regular
people in data collection. . . . The projects include . . . the
Monarch Watch butterfly tagging project, . . . the Audubon
Christmas Bird Count," and a "project documenting ladybug
species . . . . For each project, Burns gives detailed accounts
of the procedures employed by citizen scientists." (Horn
Book Magazine)

Includes bibliographical references and index

590.73   Collections and exhibits of living mammals

Krull, Kathleen

★ What's new? the zoo! a zippy history of zoos. by
Kathleen Krull; illustrated by Marcellus Hall. Arthur A.
Levine Books, an imprint of Scholastic, Inc. 2014 40 p.
(alk. paper) $17.99
Grades: K 1 2 3 4   590.73

1. Human-animal relationship 2. Zoos -- History
ISBN 0545135710; 9780545135719; 9780545135726
                                          LC 2013021189

This illustrated children's book, by Kathleen Krull, illustrated by Marcellus Hall, presents a history of zoos and
provides several entertaining trivia facts surrounding them.
The book brings "jazzy style and a globe-trotting eye to our
millennia-long history of keeping animals -- and the ways
animals have changed us in turn." (Publisher's note)

" whirlwind, episodic tour of zoos around the world
through the ages. Krull takes readers back 4000 years to zoos
in Sumeria and ancient China, India, Greece, and Ethiopia,
as well as to the menageries of Kublai Khan, Charlemagne,
Pope Leo, and Aztec emperor Moctezuma II straight through
to modern times...This thoroughly researched title cites
sources that include books and websites, making it ideal for
browsing purposes or for school reports." SLJ

Includes bibliographical references

What is new? the zoo!

Zippy history of zoos

590.92   Animal biography

Roop, Connie

Tales of Famous Animals; Peter Roop and Connie
Roop. Scholastic 2012 112 p. (reinforced) $17.99
Grades: 4 5 6 7 8   590.92

1. Pets 2. Animals
ISBN 0545430291; 9780545430296

This children's book, by Peter and Connie Roop, illustrated by Zachary Pullen, offers an "illustrated introduction
to some of the most fascinating and admirable animals we've
ever known! Everyone knows about President Obama's first
dog Bo, but would you believe President Adams had a pet alligator . . . ? . . . Readers will also learn about heroic animals
like Balto the sled dog and unique animals like Koko the
gorilla." (Publisher's note)

591   Specific topics in natural history of animals

George, Lindsay Barrett

In the woods: who's been here? Greenwillow Bks.
1995 un il hardcover o.p. pa $7.99
Grades: PreK K 1 2   591

1. Forest animals
ISBN 0-688-12318-X; 0-688-16163-4 pa
                                          LC 93-16244

A boy and girl in the autumn woods find an empty nest,
a cocoon, gnawed bark, and other signs of unseen animals
and their activities

"Children will be drawn to George's vivid gouache
paintings, especially those depicting the animals in their
natural surroundings. . . . For most childen this will be an excellent introduction to classroom nature units and the perfect
prelude to a walk in the woods." Booklist

Other titles in this series are:

Around the pond: who's been here? (1996)

Around the world: who's been here? (1999)

In the garden: who's been here? (2006)

In the snow: who's been here? (1995)

Thurlby, Paul

Paul Thurlby's wildlife; Paul Thurlby. Candlewick
Press 2013 32 p. $17.99
Grades: PreK K 1   591

1. Picture books for children 2. Animals
ISBN 0763665630; 9780763665630
                                          LC 2012943660

This children's picture book looks at wildlife. "A menagerie of animals is introduced," with "snippets of information
[that] provide unique facts about 24 individual species; for
example, 'monkeys split bananas from the bottom up—it's
easier that way!' Blocky digital cartoon characters saturated
in rich colors against faded backgrounds vibrantly exemplify each unique trait." (School Library Journal)

591.03 Dictionaries, encyclopedias, concordances

Spelman, Lucy
Animal encyclopedia; 2,500 animals with photos, maps, and more! National Geographic 2012 303 p. col. ill., col. maps (hardcover) $24.95; (library) $33.90
Grades: 5 6 7 **591.03**
1. Animals -- Encyclopedias 2. Animals
ISBN 1426310226; 9781426310225; 9781426310232
LC 2012023783

This encyclopedia about animals "is separated into vertebrate and invertebrate animals and then further subdivided by phylum. Each species gets its own page with dynamic color photos of creatures in their natural habitat, while . . . information on variations within the species celebrates the diversity of animals across the globe." (Booklist)

Includes bibliographical references (p. 295) and index.

591.3 Genetics, evolution, age characteristics

Bleiman, Andrew
ZooBorns; zoo babies from around the world. [written by] Andrew Bleiman and [photographed by] Chris Eastland. Beach Lane Books 2010 un il $12.99
Grades: PreK K 1 **591.3**
1. Animal babies
ISBN 978-1-4424-1272-9; 1-4424-1272-0
LC 2010009590

"If a picture is worth 1,000 words, then these stunning photographs starring precious animal tykes may be priceless. The range of real-life infants featured is extraordinary in its breadth, covering such unusual zoo or aquarium residents as the crowned sifaka and the tawny frogmouth. The captivating, clear photographs pose every cub, kit and so on at its most adorable." Kirkus

Carle, Eric
★ Does a kangaroo have a mother, too? HarperCollins Pubs. 2000 un il $16.99; lib bdg $18.89; pa $6.99; bd bk $7.99
Grades: PreK K 1 **591.3**
1. Animals
ISBN 0-06-028768-3; 0-06-028767-5 lib bdg; 0-06-443642-X pa; 0-694-01456-7 bd bk
LC 99-36147

"The repetitious text is perfect for the toddler set. 'Does a lion have a mother, too? Yes! A lion has a mother. Just like me and you.' The text is repeated on every spread as the author showcases a dozen different animal mothers and their babies. . . . The vibrant artwork is classic Carle and should delight its audience." SLJ

Jenkins, Steve
My first day; written by Steve Jenkins and Robin Page; illustrated by Steve Jenkins. Houghton Mifflin 2013 32 p. $16.99
Grades: PreK K 1 **591.3**
1. Picture books for children 2. Animal babies 3. Animal behavior 4. Animals -- Infancy
ISBN 054773851X; 9780547738512
LC 2011048210

Authors Steve Jenkins and Robin Page present a picture book on animals. "The first day of life is different for every animal. Human newborns don't do much at all, but some animals hit the ground running." Their book reveals "how twenty two different species, from the emperor penguin to the Siberian tiger, adapt to that traumatic first few hours of life, with or without parental help." (Publisher's note)

Judge, Lita
★ Born in the wild; Lita Judge. Roaring Brook Press 2014 48 p. (hardcover) $18.99
Grades: PreK K 1 2 3 **591.3**
1. Mammals 2. Animal babies 3. Mammals -- Infancy 4. Animals -- Infancy 5. Familial behavior in animals
ISBN 1596439254; 9781596439252
LC 2013044934

This children's book by Lita Judge describes how "Every baby mammal, from a tiny harvest mouse 'pinky' to a fierce lion cub, needs food, shelter, love, and a family. Filled with illustrations of some of the most adorable babies in the kingdom, this awww-inspiring book looks at the traits that all baby mammals share and proves that, even though they're born in the wild, they're not so very different from us, after all!" (Publisher's note)

"This charming picture book presents more than 20 baby animals and their parents...This title will surely be popular in the library as a beginning research tool, but some may find it quite appropriate as bedtime reading, too." SLJ

Kajikawa, Kimiko
Close to you; how animals bond. [by] Kimiko Kajikawa. Henry Holt 2008 un il $16.95
Grades: PreK K 1 **591.3**
1. Animal babies
ISBN 978-0-8050-8123-7; 0-8050-8123-2
LC 2007002959

"This tender title about the bonding between baby and adult animals gets some punch from additional facts appended at the end. The body of the book has a brief rhyming text, notable for its precise and engaging verbs. . . . Large, heart-warming stock photos of animal families clearly illustrate each verse. . . . The information seems carefully selected to be understandable and interesting to young children." SLJ

Kalman, Bobbie
Baby mammals; by Bobbie Kalman. Crabtree Publishing Company 2013 24 p. col. ill. (library) $22.60; (paperback) $6.95
Grades: 1 2 3 4 **591.3**
1. Mammals 2. Animals -- Infancy
ISBN 0778710084; 9780778710080; 9780778710134
LC 2012043723

In this book by Bobbie Kalman "close-up images of baby animals highlight the basic facts about different kinds of mammals, such as hoofed mammals, elephants, rodents, rabbits, marsupials, and primates. Children will learn about the bodies of mammals, the kinds of foods they eat, and how they are raised by their mothers after they are born. The books also show how mammals survive in different habitats." (Publisher's note)

Includes bibliographical references and index.

Patkau, Karen

Creatures yesterday and today; [by] Karen Patkau. Tundra Books 2008 un il $18.95

Grades: K 1 2 3   **591.3**

1. Animals 2. Fossils 3. Evolution 4. Prehistoric animals

ISBN 978-0-88776-833-0; 0-88776-833-4

"On the first page of this oversize book a huge diplodocus speaks. . . . Turn the page, and his descendant, a little skylark high in a tree, speaks. . . . Then there are the mollusks. . . . With large computer-created graphics in dramatic colors and a few lines of text, each double-page spread makes a similar connection for reptiles, fish, arachnids, birds, amphibians, mammals, crustaceans, and insects. . . . The amazing science will engage dinosaur fans with the wonder of evolution and the evidence of fossils." Booklist

Includes glossary

Rose, Deborah Lee

Ocean babies; illustrations by Hiroe Nakata. National Geographic 2005 un il $16.95; lib bdg $25.90

Grades: K 1 2   **591.3**

1. Animal babies 2. Marine animals

ISBN 0-7922-6669-2; 0-7922-8312-0 lib bdg

LC 2003-14075

Describes baby animals that live in the ocean, pointing out their many differences as well as the most important similarity.

"Nakata's cheerful watercolor paintings clearly illustrate the book's ideas while creating a beautiful undersea setting, bright with colors, teeming with varied creatures, and studded with intriguing details. Many books present information in this format, but few manage to stay as focused on the topic and sensitive to the intended audience as this one." Booklist

591.4   Physical adaptation

Aston, Dianna Hutts

★ An egg is quiet; illustrated by Sylvia Long. Chronicle Books 2006 un il $16.95

Grades: K 1 2 3   **591.4**

1. Eggs 2. Animals 3. Embryology

ISBN 0-8118-4428-5; 978-0-8118-4428-4

LC 2005-12090

This book introduces some 60 types of eggs and various egg facts. "Kindergarten to grade four." (Sci Books Films)

"An exceptionally handsome book on eggs, from the delicate ova of the green lacewing to the rosy roe of the Atlantic salmon to the mammoth bulk of an ostrich egg. Aston's simple, readable text celebrates their marvelous diversity, commenting on size, shape, coloration, and where they might be found." SLJ

Baines, Rebecca

What's in that egg? a book about life cycles. by Becky Baines. National Geographic 2009 27p il $16.95; lib bdg $25.90

Grades: PreK K 1   **591.4**

1. Eggs 2. Animals

ISBN 978-1-4263-0408-8; 1-4263-0408-0; 978-1-4263-0409-5 lib bdg; 1-4263-0409-9 lib bdg

LC 2008-47895

This describes the eggs of various animals, including turtles, frogs, fish, butterflies, and swans

This title engages "children through humor, clear language, interesting facts, and abundant photos. . . . [An] excellent [introduction] for young science students." SLJ

Burnie, David

How animals work. Dorling Kindersley 2010 132p il $24.99

Grades: 5 6 7 8   **591.4**

1. Animals 2. Animal behavior

ISBN 978-0-7566-5897-7; 0-7566-5897-7

Describes the anatomy of many animal species and explains how their bodies work to help them survive. Covers such animals as birds, butterflies, elephants, crocodiles, and wolves, and includes color photos, illustrations, and diagrams.

"This beautifully photographed encyclopedia of animals is divided into categories that include movement, diet, senses, and animal families. . . . Diagrams showing internal organs and intimate closeups of eyes, skin, fur, and wings, should engage budding biologists." Publ Wkly

Cusick, Dawn

Animal eggs; an amazing clutch of mysteries & marvels! [by] Dawn Cusick & Joanne O'Sullivan. Charlesbridge 2011 48p il $14.95

Grades: K 1 2 3   **591.4**

1. Eggs 2. Animals -- Infancy

ISBN 978-0-9797455-3-9; 0-9797455-3-5

"Cusick and O'Sullivan compare the egg-laying and -hatching habits of a broad spectrum of animals. . . . Each tidily composed double-page spread offers color photographs of three or four examples of the topic under discussion, with brief descriptive paragraphs that will do double duty as quick captions for casual browsers. Although the emphasis is on protective adaptations and strategies that maximize chances for survival, the predator's point of view is not neglected. . . . [This is an] inviting offering." Bull Cent Child Books

Davies, Nicola, 1958-

Just the right size; why big animals are big and little animals are little. illustrated by Neal Layton. Candlewick Press 2009 61p il $14.99

Grades: 3 4 5 6   **591.4**

1. Size 2. Animals

ISBN 978-0-7636-3924-2; 0-7636-3924-9

This "book uses the 'Big Thing, Little Thing' rule (which explains how the length, surface area and cross section of an object or creature are relative to its volume and weight) . . . to explore how size affects living things. Davies's often humorous text and Layton's energetic illustrations demonstrate why humans don't have superpowers . . . and later spreads discuss the advantages and limitations of being very small or very big. . . . The spot-on comic delivery and readily comprehensible explanations make this a prime pick for readers curious about physical science in the natural world." Publ Wkly

Eamer, Claire

Lizards in the sky; animals where you least expect them. Annick 2010 97p il $21.95; pa $12.95

Grades: 3 4 5   **591.4**
1. Animals -- Habitations
ISBN 978-1-55451-265-2; 1-55451-265-4; 978-1-55451-264-5 pa; 1-55451-264-6 pa

"Eamer looks at animals living unexpected lives in unanticipated habitats. Birds and spiders underwater, snakes far out in the open ocean, fish on land, burrowing owls, and shrimp in the desert are just a few of the creatures introduced. The physiological adaptations they have made to survive are described. . . . Text boxes with factual tidbits add to the narrative. The drawings and photographs on every page are in full color. . . . Overall, an enjoyable and fascinating title." SLJ

Fielding, Beth
Animal eyes. EarlyLight Books 2011 36p il $14.95
Grades: 1 2 3 4   **591.4**
1. Eye 2. Animals
ISBN 0979745551; 9780979745553; 978-0-9797455-5-3; 0-9797455-5-1

This book explores the morphology and behavior of animal eyes. Included are mammals, insects, birds, reptiles, amphibians, and mollusks. Glossary. Index. "Grades one to four." (Sci Books Films)

"Children who pick up this appealing book will instantly have their curiosity piqued. Each spread features a different animal and includes a full-color photo of it, close-ups of its eyes, and a few photographs of text. 'Test It Out' experiments using easily accessible materials such as colored pencils add a participatory element to the book. . . . An attractive, informative title." SLJ

★ Animal tails. EarlyLight Books 2011 36p il
Grades: 1 2 3   **591.4**
1. Tails 2. Animals
ISBN 0-9797455-8-6; 978-0-9797455-8-4

"Fielding describes how tails work for elephants, kangaroos, primates, cats, squirrels, chameleons, lizards, snakes, birds, whales, stingrays, and caterpillars. More than 13 styles of tails, such as scaly, stinging, and spraying, are paired with various functions performed by these animals. . . . The full-color photography is quite bright, clear, and eye-catching. . . . A visually appeal and interesting introduction." SLJ

Halfmann, Janet
Eggs 1 2 3; Who will the babies be? Janet Halfmann; illustrated by Betsy Thompson. 1st ed. Blue Apple Books 2012 32 p. col. ill. (hardcover) $17.99
Grades: K 1 2   **591.4**
1. Counting 2. Eggs -- Fiction 3. Picture books for children
ISBN 1609051912; 9781609051914
LC 2011038907

Author Janet Halfmann presents a picture book for children that focuses on counting skills. In the book, "words curve above and below large numbers, mimicking the subject matter: eggs and the hatchlings inside, which include newborn platypus, robins, turtles, and more . . . Gatefolds open to the right or upward, revealing the answers." (Publishers Weekly)

Hodgkins, Fran
Amazing eggs; with illustrations by Wendy Smith. Treasure Bay 2011 41p il (We both read)

Grades: K 1 2   **591.4**
1. Eggs
ISBN 1-60115-251-5; 1-60115-252-3 pa; 978-1-60115-251-0; 978-1-60115-252-7 pa

"A colorful and scientific explanation of eggs and the development of insects, reptiles, birds, and fish. The well-written, easy-to-understand text and the inviting format will encourage emerging readers to pick up the book on their own. Intended as a shared reading experience for adult and child, the dual differentiated text appears on each page, accompanied by clear, informative, full-color photos. An attractive addition that covers an important science-curriculum subject." SLJ

Hulbert, Laura
Who has these feet? illustrated by Erik Brooks. Henry Holt 2011 un il $16.99
Grades: PreK K 1 2   **591.4**
1. Foot 2. Animals
ISBN 978-0-8050-8907-3; 0-8050-8907-1
LC 2010033429

"This guess-the-animal book asks readers to identify species by looking at their feet. Hulbert describes how each animal's treads are acclimated to its particular environment: a tree frog's toes are sticky; a squirrel uses the claws on its toes to scamper along trees; and a sea turtle has flippers for swimming. A gatefold features all of the animals together. . . . Brooks's naturalistic yet affable animals will likely inspire readers to take a closer look at their own feet." Publ Wkly

Jenkins, Steve
★ Actual size. Houghton Mifflin 2004 un il $16
Grades: K 1 2 3   **591.4**
1. Size 2. Animals
ISBN 0-618-37594-5
LC 2003-17462

In "torn-and-cut paper collages, Jenkins depicts 18 animals and insects—or a part of their body—in actual size. . . . The end matter offers full pictures of the creatures and more details about their habitats and habits. Mixing deceptive simplicity with absolute clarity, this beautiful book is an enticing way to introduce children to the glorious diversity of our natural world, or to illustrate to budding scientists the importance of comparison, measurement, observation, and record keeping. A thoroughly engaging read-aloud and a must-have for any collection." SLJ

Big & little. Houghton Mifflin 1996 un il $16
Grades: K 1 2   **591.4**
1. Size 2. Animals
ISBN 0-395-72664-6
LC 95-41162

Jenkins "points out the differences in size between animals who are similar in other ways. The artwork combines cuttings of colored, textured papers to form animals that stand out strikingly against white backgrounds. . . . One line of text comments on the two animals' sizes, habits, or habitats. The final pages include a presentation of the comparative sizes of all the animals, [and] a paragraph of additional information about each species." Booklist

Includes bibliographical references

Johnson, Jinny

Animal Planet atlas of animals; by Jinny Johnson. Millbrook Press 2013 128 p. (lib. bdg.: alk. paper) $35.93
Grades: 1 2 3 4 5   **591.4**
   1. Atlases 2. Animals 3. Zoogeography
   ISBN 1467713279; 9781467713276
                                    LC 2013001746
   This children's book is an atlas of animals. "Grouped by continent and then by habitat type, the selected animals share space on full but not congested spreads with maps, labels and . . . notes on size, diet, memorable physical features or behavior. Though generally trimmed or cut out, the photos all seem to have been taken in natural settings, and they show each creature at revealing angles or in action poses." (Kirkus Reviews)

Kaner, Etta

Have you ever seen a hippo with sunscreen? written by Etta Kaner; illustrated by Jeff Szuc. Kids Can Press 2010 il $14.95
Grades: K 1 2 3   **591.4**
   1. Animals
   ISBN 978-1-55453-337-4; 1-55453-337-6
   "People may wear sunscreen, sunglasses, and snowshoes, but the seven featured animals have their own physical adaptations to their environments. Large type, very brief question-and-answer text . . . and humorous illustrations make the volume accessible and entertaining for young readers." Horn Book Guide

Lunis, Natalie

Electric animals. Bearport Pub. 2011 24p il (Animals with super powers) lib bdg $22.61
Grades: 3 4 5   **591.4**
   1. Platypus 2. Electric fishes
   ISBN 978-1-61772-121-2; 1-61772-121-2
                                    LC 2010034521
   This describes electric animals including eels, rays, platypuses, and great white sharks.
   "Large color photos of animals in natural settings and clear, cogent presentations of information combine to boost this [book] well above the average for both assignments and casual browsing." SLJ
   Includes glossary and bibliographical references

Messner, Kate

★ **Over** and under the snow. Chronicle Books 2011 un il $16.99
Grades: PreK K 1 2   **591.4**
   1. Winter 2. Animals -- Habitations
   ISBN 978-0-8118-6784-9; 0-8118-6784-6
                                    LC 2009028984
   "The lyrical descriptions of the text and the gray/brown/ ice-blue palette of the illustrations leave readers with a retro feel that harkens back to earlier days of children's books and bygone times when life seemed simpler. Utterly charming, and informative, to boot; readers brought up on a diet of rhymes, bright colors and adorable fluffy animals will find its simple beauty a balm." Kirkus

Miller, Debbie S.

Arctic lights, arctic nights; illustrations by Jon Van Zyle. Walker & Co. 2003 un il map $16.95; pa $7.95

Grades: 2 3 4   **591.4**
   1. Animals -- Arctic regions 2. Natural history -- Alaska
   ISBN 0-8027-8856-4; 0-8027-9636-2 pa
                                    LC 2002-191047
   Describes the unique light phenomena of the Alaskan Arctic and the way animals adapt to the temperature and daylight changes each month of the year
   The "brief text includes not only lyrical messages about light and its partner, darkness, but also references to the reaction of wildlife to the waxing and waning. . . . Wrapped about this unfamiliar (to many of us) swirl of seasons of light are Van Zyle's superb and quietly beautiful acrylic paintings, which capture both light and dark in perfect harmony with the text." SLJ
   Includes glossary

Miller, Sara Swan

★ **All** kinds of ears. Marshall Cavendish Benchmark 2007 48p il (All kinds of . . .) lib bdg $29.93
Grades: 3 4 5 6   **591.4**
   1. Ear 2. Animals
   ISBN 978-0-7614-2518-2 lib bdg; 0-7614-2518-7 lib bdg
   This describes the various forms and functions of animal ears
   Includes glossary and bibliographical references

★ **All** kinds of eyes. Marshall Cavendish Benchmark 2007 48p il (All kinds of . . .) lib bdg $29.93
Grades: 3 4 5 6   **591.4**
   1. Eye 2. Animals
   ISBN 978-0-7614-2519-9 lib bdg; 0-7614-2519-5 lib bdg
   This describes the various forms and functions of eyes in animals
   "The excellent content and rare photographs will appeal to children, whether for research or leisure reading." SLJ
   Includes glossary and bibliographical references

★ **All** kinds of feet. Marshall Cavendish Benchmark 2007 48p il (All kinds of . . .) lib bdg $29.93
Grades: 3 4 5 6   **591.4**
   1. Foot 2. Animals
   ISBN 978-0-7614-2520-5 lib bdg; 0-7614-2520-9 lib bdg
   This describes the various forms and functions of animal feet
   "The excellent content and rare photographs will appeal to children, whether for research of leisure reading." SLJ
   Includes glossary and bibliographical references

★ **All** kinds of mouths. Marshall Cavendish Benchmark 2007 48p il (All kinds of . . .) lib bdg $29.93
Grades: 3 4 5 6   **591.4**
   1. Mouth 2. Animals
   ISBN 978-0-7614-2521-2 lib bdg; 0-7614-2521-7 lib bdg
   This describes the various forms and functions of animal mouths
   "The excellent content and rare photographs will appeal to children, whether for research or leisure reading." SLJ
   Includes glossary and bibliographical references

★ **All** kinds of noses. Marshall Cavendish Benchmark 2007 48p il (All kinds of . . .) lib bdg $29.93
Grades: 3 4 5 6   591.4
1. Nose 2. Animals
ISBN 978-0-7614-2522-9 lib bdg; 0-7614-2522-5 lib bdg
This describes the various forms and functions of animal noses
"The excellent content and rare photographs will appeal to children, whether for research or leisure reading." SLJ
Includes glossary and bibliographical references

★ **All** kinds of skin. Marshall Cavendish Benchmark 2007 48p il (All kinds of . . .) lib bdg $29.93
Grades: 3 4 5 6   591.4
1. Skin 2. Animals
ISBN 978-0-7614-2713-1 lib bdg; 0-7614-2713-9 lib bdg
This describes the shapes and functions of animal exteriors found in nature, including skin, feathers, fur, and scales
Includes glossary and bibliographical references

Parker, Victoria
How small is small? comparing body parts. [by] Vic Parker. Heinemann Library 2011 32p il (Measuring and comparing) lib bdg $26; pa $7.99
Grades: 2 3 4   591.4
1. Size 2. Weights and measures
ISBN 978-1-4329-3960-1 lib bdg; 1-4329-3960-2 lib bdg; 978-1-4329-3968-7 pa; 1-4329-3968-8 pa
LC 2010000938
"Measure length and width and see how different parts of the body compare." Publisher's note
Includes glossary and bibliographical references

Patkau, Karen
Creatures great and small. Tundra Books 2006 un il $17.95
Grades: K 1 2 3   591.4
1. Size 2. Animals
ISBN 978-0-88776-754-8; 0-88776-754-0
"Each spread in this informational picture book shows a large animal filling a page-and-a-half scene and a small one from a similar classification on the right edge. . . . Sharp lines, bold colors, and careful composition of the computer-generated art successfully convey the rich variety of creatures and environments, accentuating similarities and differences. . . . Labeled illustrations at the back of the book introduce concepts of scale in a clear and inviting way." SLJ
Includes glossary

Posada, Mia
Guess what is growing inside this egg. Millbrook Press 2007 un il lib bdg $15.95
Grades: K 1 2 3   591.4
1. Eggs 2. Animals
ISBN 978-0-8225-6192-7 lib bdg; 0-8225-6192-1 lib bdg
LC 2006-16250
"This attractive picture book presents six animals that hatch from eggs: penguins, alligators, ducklings, sea turtles, spiders, and octopuses. . . . The first spread is a guessing game, telling a little about the animal in two rhymed couplets, showing a closeup of an egg in its natural setting, and

asking 'Can you guess what is growing inside this egg?' The next spread reveals the answer to the riddle and offers information about the featured animal's physical attributes and behaviors. Distinctive collage-and-watercolor artwork offers eye-catching views of the animals within their habitats." Booklist

Schaefer, Lola M.
★ **Just** one bite; 11 animals and their bites at life size! by Lola Schaefer; illustrated by Geoff Waring. Chronicle Books 2010 un il $17.99
Grades: K 1 2 3   591.4
1. Animals -- Food
ISBN 978-0-8118-6473-2; 0-8118-6473-1
"In this bold, oversized picture book, readers will see— at actual size—how much tasty giant squid a sperm whale can eat in one gulp . . . and how much dirt a worm can eat at once. . . . Nine other animals and their eating habits are illustrated. . . . The terrific, artfully composed brush, crayon and computer-aided artwork is lavish, the perspectives dramatically up-close. The text is lively, minimal and perfect for reading aloud." Kirkus

Schwartz, David M.
Where else in the wild? more camouflaged creatures concealed and revealed. by David M. Schwartz and Yael Schy; eye-tricking photographs by Dwight Kuhn. Tricycle Press 2009 un il $16.99
Grades: 2 3 4   591.4
1. Animals 2. Camouflage (Biology) 3. Poetry -- By individual authors
ISBN 978-1-58246-283-7; 1-58246-283-6
Presents poems and brief facts about eleven animals that rely on the ability to camouflage within nature to survive in the wilderness
"Poetry and photography work well together in this beautifully illustrated book. . . . Notable for its finesse and variety, the poetry includes rhymed verse, as well as haiku and concrete poems. A playful, informative introduction to camouflage in nature." Booklist

Where in the wild? camouflaged creatures concealed-and-revealed. ear-tickling poems by David M. Schwartz and Yael Schy; eye-tricking photos by Dwight Kuhn. Tricycle Press 2007 un il $15.95
Grades: 2 3 4   591.4
1. Animals 2. Camouflage (Biology) 3. Poetry -- By individual authors
ISBN 978-1-58246-207-3; 1-58246-207-0
LC 2006-101406
"The well-crafted, short poems . . . offer clues to the hidden animals' identities. Beautifully photographed and designed with great attention to detail, this book will intrigue and challenge children." Booklist

Singer, Marilyn
Eggs; illustrated by Emma Stevenson. Holiday House 2008 un il $16.95
Grades: 1 2 3 4   591.4
1. Eggs 2. Animals
ISBN 978-0-8234-1727-8; 0-8234-1727-1
Explains the varieties, functions, and characteristics of the eggs of a multitude of creatures, including insects, birds, and reptiles

"Smoothly written, the text creates an even, almost conversational flow from page to page. . . . Stevenson contributes large and small gouache paintings in a precise yet fluid style that suits the subject well." Booklist

Includes glossary

Stewart, Melissa

Give me a hand; the secrets of hands, feet, arms, and legs. illustrated by Janet Hamlin. Marshall Cavendish Benchmark 2010 48p il (The gross and goofy body) lib bdg $20.95

Grades: 2 3 4   **591.4**

1. Foot 2. Hand 3. Human body

ISBN 978-0-7614-4158-8 lib bdg; 0-7614-4158-1 lib bdg

LC 2008033618

This offers information on the role hands, feet, arms, and legs play in the body science of humans and animals

This "offers detailed science facts in a fashion approachable enough to make a welcome supplement to school textbooks. . . . The layout is fresh, clean, and colorful, sidebars keep things conversational, and the back matter is solid." Booklist

Includes glossary and bibliographical references

Zoehfeld, Kathleen Weidner

What lives in a shell? illustrated by Helen K. Davie. HarperCollins Pubs. 1994 32p il (Let's-read-and-find-out science) hardcover o.p. pa $5.99

Grades: K 1   **591.4**

1. Shells 2. Animal defenses

ISBN 0-06-445124-0 pa

LC 93-12428

Describes such animals as snails, turtles, and crabs, which live in shells and use these coverings as protection

This book uses "interesting and accurate illustrations and just the right words. . . . The science here is good, and the explanations should cause young readers to want to learn more." Sci Books Films

591.47 Protective and locomotor adaptations, color

Collard, Sneed B.

Teeth; illustrated by Phyllis Saroff. Charlesbridge 2008 32p il lib bdg $16.95; pa $7.95

Grades: 1 2 3   **591.47**

1. Teeth 2. Animals

ISBN 978-1-58089-120-2 lib bdg; 1-58089-120-9 lib bdg; 978-1-58089-121-9 pa; 1-58089-121-7 pa

LC 2007-02266

This describes types of animal teeth, how they are used, how they grow, and the differences between teeth and horns or antlers

"Packed with exciting information, this large-size picture book combines chatty prose . . . and clear, full-color illustrations to tell amazing facts." Booklist

Wings; illustrated by Robin Brickman. Charlesbridge 2008 31p il lib bdg $16.95; pa $7.95

Grades: 1 2 3   **591.47**

1. Wings 2. Flight 3. Animals

ISBN 978-1-57091-611-3 lib bdg; 1-57091-611-X lib bdg; 978-1-57091-612-0 pa; 1-57091-612-8 pa

LC 2007-02265

This "looks at wing design and the shapes of birds, insects, and mammals, as well as at prehistoric flyers and birds that no longer fly. Human fascination with flying rounds out the discussion. Brickman's paper collages of winged animals are . . . impressive in texture and color." SLJ

Includes glossary and bibliographical references

Fielding, Beth

Animal colors; a rainbow of colors from animals around the world. EarlyLight Books 2009 32p il $14.95

Grades: K 1 2 3 4 5   **591.47**

1. Color 2. Animals

ISBN 978-0-9797455-4-6; 0-9797455-4-3

"A gorgeous, in-depth look at animal colors as they occur in nature. Highly graphic and visually appealing, the book is organized first by singular colors, followed by common combinations. . . . For the youngest readers, this book can be enjoyed as simply an excellent introduction to color and to identifying the animals. For older readers, this book holds appeal as it also provides factual information, such as habitat, behavior, and diet, in bite-size doses beneath each picture. The photography is sharp and clear. . . . Simply stunning." SLJ

Halpern, Monica

Underground towns, treetops, and other animal hiding places; by Monica Halpern. National Geographic 2007 40p (National Geographic science chapters) lib bdg $17.90

Grades: 3 4 5 6   **591.47**

1. Animal defenses 2. Animals -- Habitations

ISBN 978-1-4263-0183-4 lib bdg; 1-4263-0183-9 lib bdg

LC 2007007894

This is an introduction to hidden animal habitats, such as underground burrows, underwater, or treetops

This "book provides a clear, engaging introduction to the topic. . . . The [book's] clear design features many well-captioned photographs . . . charts, and diagrams." Horn Book Guide

Helman, Andrea

Hide and seek; nature's best vanishing acts. photographs by Gavriel Jecan. Walker Pub. Co. 2008 un il $16.95; lib bdg $17.85

Grades: 2 3 4   **591.47**

1. Animal defenses 2. Camouflage (Biology)

ISBN 978-0-8027-9690-5; 0-8027-9690-7; 978-0-8027-9691-2 lib bdg; 0-8027-9691-5 lib bdg

LC 2007024242

"Animals' camouflage is equally effective at hiding prey from predators and predators from prey. This large-format book offers plenty of excellent photographs of animals in each category, arranged by type of habitat. . . . Throughout the book, the words seem to elaborate on the pictures." Booklist

Jenkins, Steve

★ Living color. Houghton Mifflin 2007 un il $17

Grades: 3 4 5 6 **591.47**
1. Animals -- Color 2. Color
ISBN 0-618-70897-9; 978-0-618-70897-0

LC 2007-12751

"Each of seven colors gets a spread or two featuring animals in that color. . . . Grades three to five." (Bull Cent Child Books)

This "offers a pageant of the most stunning, vividly hued creatures on the planet. . . . This book opens by explaining that bright coloration goes beyond mere decoration. . . . Arranged by color, subsequent spreads feature a rainbow of animals rendered in Jenkins' celebrated cut-paper style. Each picture is accompanied by a paragraph of nicely distilled information." Booklist

★ **What** do you do when something wants to eat you? Houghton Mifflin 1997 un il $16
Grades: K 1 2 3 **591.47**
1. Animal defenses
ISBN 0-395-82514-8

LC 96-44993

Describes how various animals, including an octopus, a bombadier beetle, a puff adder, and a gliding frog, escape danger

"Jenkins achieves remarkable anatomical detail in his boldly textured cut-paper collages; simple backgrounds keep attention tightly focused on the animals and their survival strategies." Bull Cent Child Books

Johnson, Rebecca L.
★ **When** lunch fights back; wickedly clever animal defenses. by Rebecca L. Johnson. Millbrook Press 2015 48 p. (lib. bdg.: alk. paper) $29.27
Grades: 4 5 6 7 **591.47**
1. Animal defenses
ISBN 1467721093; 9781467721097

LC 2013046646

This book, by Rebecca L. Johnson, explains that "in nature, good defenses can mean the difference between surviving a predator's attack and becoming its lunch. Some animals rely on sharp teeth and claws or camouflage. But that's only the beginning. Meet creatures with some of the strangest defenses known to science." (Publisher's note)

"Along with the ever popular hagfish (aka "snot eel") and the horned lizard—which can indeed squirt blood from one or both eyes—Johnson... profiles 10 animals with particularly noxious defense mechanisms... This is an outstanding way for readers to meet scientists at work in both field and lab, as well as to learn that, for instance, fulmar chicks can project vomit up to 6 feet and, creepily, that a school of the Amazonian two-spot astyanax will attack and eject one of its own to distract an approaching predator.Thrilling reading for budding biologists." Kirkus

Includes bibliographical references and index

Lunis, Natalie
See-through animals. Bearport Pub. 2011 24p il (Animals with super powers) lib bdg $22.61
Grades: 3 4 5 **591.47**
1. Camouflage (Biology)
ISBN 9781617721205; 1617721204

LC 2010045408

This describes see-through animals including the clearwing butterfly, the glass frog, transparent anemone shrimp, jellyfish, the transparent sea butterfly, glass squid, transparent octopus and zebrafish and frog.

"Large color photos of animals in natural settings and clear, cogent presentations of information combine to boost this [book] well above the average for both assignments and casual browsing." SLJ

Includes bibliographical references and index.

Mitchell, Susan K.
Animal chemical combat; poisons, smells, and slime. [by] Susan K. Mitchell. Enslow Publishers 2009 48p il (Amazing animal defenses) lib bdg $23.93
Grades: 4 5 6 **591.47**
1. Animal defenses
ISBN 978-0-7660-3294-1 lib bdg; 0-7660-3294-9 lib bdg

LC 2008-11075

"The closeup photos are frequent and well chosen, and accompanied by clear, simply phrased [text], which [is] more detailed than average and [takes] up most or all of the space on each page." SLJ

Includes glossary and bibliographical references

Animal mimics; look-alikes and copycats. [by] Susan K. Mitchell. Enslow Publishers 2009 48p il (Amazing animal defenses) lib bdg $23.93
Grades: 4 5 6 **591.47**
1. Animal defenses
ISBN 978-0-7660-3293-4 lib bdg; 0-7660-3293-0 lib bdg

LC 2008-11449

"The closeup photos are frequent and well chosen, and accompanied by clear, simply phrased [text], which [is] more detailed than average and [takes] up most or all of the space on each page." SLJ

Includes glossary and bibliographical references

Animals with awesome armor; shells, scales, and exoskeletons. [by] Susan K. Mitchell. Enslow Publishers 2009 48p il (Amazing animal defenses) lib bdg $23.93
Grades: 4 5 6 **591.47**
1. Animal defenses
ISBN 978-0-7660-3296-5 lib bdg; 0-7660-3296-5 lib bdg

LC 2008-11456

"The closeup photos are frequent and well chosen, and accompanied by clear, simply phrased [text], which [is] more detailed than average and [takes] up most or all of the space on each page." SLJ

Includes glossary and bibliographical references

Animals with crafty camouflage; hiding in plain sight. [by] Susan K. Mitchell. Enslow Publishers 2009 48p il (Amazing animal defenses) lib bdg $23.93
Grades: 4 5 6 **591.47**
1. Animal defenses 2. Camouflage (Biology)
ISBN 978-0-7660-3291-0 lib bdg; 0-7660-3291-4 lib bdg

LC 2008-11073

"The closeup photos are frequent and well chosen, and accompanied by clear, simply phrased [text], which [is]

more detailed than average and [takes] up most or all of the space on each page." SLJ

Includes glossary and bibliographical references

Animals with wicked weapons; stingers, barbs, and quills. [by] Susan K. Mitchell. Enslow Publishers 2009 48p il (Amazing animal defenses) lib bdg $23.93

Grades: 4 5 6   **591.47**

1. Animal defenses

ISBN 978-0-7660-3292-7 lib bdg; 0-7660-3292-2 lib bdg

           LC 2008-11075

"The closeup photos are frequent and well chosen, and accompanied by clear, simply phrased [text], which [is] more detailed than average and [takes] up most or all of the space on each page." SLJ

Includes glossary and bibliographical references

Morlock, Lisa

Track that scat! written by Lisa Morlock; illustrated by Carrie Anne Bradshaw. Sleeping Bear Press 2012 32 p. col. ill $15.95

Grades: K 1 2   **591.47**

1. Feces 2. Animal tracks 3. Animal behavior 4. Animal droppings

ISBN 158536536X; 9781585365364

           LC 2011028148

In this book, "for young Finn and her hound, . . . exploring the outdoors becomes . . . a vehicle to introduce readers to identifying commonly known animals through their tracks and, particularly, droppings. From the onset, the pair encounters -- and sometimes steps in -- a progression of animal excrement, . . . includ[ing] goose, raccoon, and bird poop." (Booklist)

"The large spreads are inviting, and the dog, a basset hound, is cute, cute, cute, and the gross factor is likely to draw kids in." SLJ

Pryor, Kimberley Jane

Amazing armor. Marshall Cavendish Benchmark 2009 32p il (Animal attack and defense) $19.95

Grades: 2 3 4   **591.47**

1. Animal defenses

ISBN 978-0-7614-4424-4; 0-7614-4424-6

           LC 2009-4996

"Students will enjoy the large vivid photographs that allow for a closeup look at the animal, along with the excellent descriptions of the different survival methods. . . . Pryor does a good job of bringing the information down to a level that an elementary student would understand without losing any of the important details. . . . [This] would be a great addition to any nonfiction collection." Libr Media Connect

Includes glossary

Clever camouflage. Marshall Cavendish Benchmark 2009 32p il (Animal attack and defense) $19.95

Grades: 2 3 4   **591.47**

1. Animal defenses 2. Camouflage (Biology)

ISBN 978-0-7614-4420-6; 0-7614-4420-3

           LC 2009-4997

"Students will enjoy the large vivid photographs that allow for a closeup look at the animal, along with the excellent descriptions of the different survival methods. . . . Pryor does a good job of bringing the information down to a level that

an elementary student would understand without losing any of the important details. . . . [This] would be a great addition to any nonfiction collection." Libr Media Connect

Includes glossary

Mimicry and relationships. Marshall Cavendish Benchmark 2009 32p il (Animal attack and defense) $19.95

Grades: 2 3 4   **591.47**

1. Animal defenses

ISBN 978-0-7614-4421-3; 0-7614-4421-1

           LC 2009-4995

"Students will enjoy the large vivid photographs that allow for a closeup look at the animal, along with the excellent descriptions of the different survival methods. . . . Pryor does a good job of bringing the information down to a level that an elementary student would understand without losing any of the important details. . . . [This] would be a great addition to any nonfiction collection." Libr Media Connect

Includes glossary

Tricky behavior. Marshall Cavendish Benchmark 2009 32p il (Animal attack and defense) $19.95

Grades: 2 3 4   **591.47**

1. Animal defenses

ISBN 978-0-7614-4425-1; 0-7614-4425-4

           LC 2009-4993

"Students will enjoy the large vivid photographs that allow for a closeup look at the animal, along with the excellent descriptions of the different survival methods. . . . Pryor does a good job of bringing the information down to a level that an elementary student would understand without losing any of the important details. . . . [This] would be a great addition to any nonfiction collection." Libr Media Connect

Inlcudes glossary

Warning colors. Marshall Cavendish Benchmark 2009 32p il (Animal attack and defense) $19.95

Grades: 2 3 4   **591.47**

1. Animal defenses

ISBN 978-0-7614-4419-0; 0-7614-4419-X

           LC 2009-4992

"Students will enjoy the large vivid photographs that allow for a closeup look at the animal, along with the excellent descriptions of the different survival methods. . . . Pryor does a good job of bringing the information down to a level that an elementary student would understand without losing any of the important details. . . . [This] would be a great addition to any nonfiction collection." Libr Media Connect

Includes glossary

Racanelli, Marie

Animals with armor. PowerKids Press 2010 24p il (Crazy nature) lib bdg $21.25; pa $8.25

Grades: 2 3 4 5   **591.47**

1. Animal defenses

ISBN 978-1-4358-9386-3 lib bdg; 1-4358-9386-7 lib bdg; 978-1-4358-9864-6 pa; 1-4358-9864-8 pa

           LC 2009036527

This describes the different animals that have adapted defensive coverings, from turtles and snakes to armadillos, snails, and bugs

This book "combines attention-grabbing information with a well-organized format. . . . [The book has] spectacular color photography and eye-popping facts." SLJ

Camouflaged creatures. PowerKids 2010 24p il (Crazy nature) lib bdg $21.25; pa $8.25
Grades: 2 3 4 5   **591.47**
1. Animals 2. Camouflage (Biology)
ISBN 978-1-4358-9383-2 lib bdg; 1-4358-9383-2 lib bdg; 978-1-4358-9858-5 pa; 1-4358-9858-3 pa
This explains how color, texture, and body shape allow animals to blend in seamlessly with their surroundings, with examples of camouflage in lizards, moths, beetles and other creatures
This book "combines attention-grabbing information with a well-organized format. . . . [The book has] spectacular color photography and eye-popping facts. . . . Excellent for reports." SLJ

Stewart, Melissa
The **skin** you're in; the secrets of skin. illustrated by Janet Hamlin. Marshall Cavendish Benchmark 2010 48p il (The gross and goofy body) lib bdg $29.93
Grades: 2 3 4   **591.47**
1. Skin
ISBN 978-0-7614-4169-4; 0-7614-4169-7
LC 2008033620
This provides information on the role skin plays in the body science of humans and animals.
This "offers detailed science facts in a fashion approachable enough to make it a welcome supplement to school textbooks. . . . The layout is fresh, clean, and colorful, sidebars keep things conversational, and the back matter is solid." Booklist
Includes glossary and bibliographical references

World's fastest animals; Melissa Stewart. Sterling Children's 2014 32 p. $9.95
Grades: 1 2 3   **591.47**
1. Speed 2. Animals 3. Animal locomotion
ISBN 1454906332; 9781402777936; 9781454906339
LC 2013028735
Written by Melissa Stewart, this children's book in the American Museum of Natural History Easy Readers series asks "Which creature moves so rapidly it can even run on water? Which bird's heart beats 1,200 times a minute?" It invites readers to "Come learn about the world's fastest animals, from speedy cheetahs and swiftly swinging tree gibbons to colorful chameleons whose tongues grab an insect quicker than you can blink an eye." (Publisher's note)
"With nonfiction early readers often in short supply compared to their fictional counterparts, these titles in the American Museum of Natural History Easy Readers series fill a gap in early literacy...Books in the series offer many surprises in the form of unfamiliar animals that take the idea of the "most" of something in new and unexpected directions, and conclude with a profile of a herpetologist from the American Museum of Natural History." Booklist
Other titles in the series include:
Penguins Are Cool! (2012)
Deadly and Dangerous (2013)
Extreme Survivors (2014)
Snakes up Close! (2012)
Strangest Animals (2013)

Stockdale, Susan
Stripes of all types; written and illustrated by Susan Stockdale. Peachtree Publishers 2013 32 p. $15.95
Grades: PreK K 1   **591.47**
1. Stripes 2. Animals -- Color 3. Camouflage (Biology)
ISBN 1561456950; 9781561456956
LC 2012025541
In this children's picture book "[Susan] Stockdale pairs . . .acrylic illustrations with . . . verse to depict 19 striped animals. . . . The accompanying images show purple-striped jellyfish, an eastern garter snake, ring-tailed lemurs, and an American bittern. Elsewhere . . . a poison frog in shocking orange, yellow, and red stripes is 'propped on a log.' Closer to home, two children cuddle with striped cats." (Publishers Weekly)

Yaw, Valerie
Color-changing animals. Bearport Pub. 2011 24p il (Animals with super powers) lib bdg $22.61
Grades: 3 4 5   **591.47**
1. Animal defenses 2. Animal communication 3. Camouflage (Biology)
ISBN 978-1-61772-122-9; 1-61772-122-0
LC 2010038283
This describes color-changing animals including gray tree frogs, snowshoe hares, cuttlefish, the mimic octopus, the golden tortoise beetle, chameleons, seahorses, and golden crab spiders.
"Large color photos of animals in natural settings and clear, cogent presentations of information combine to boost this [book] well above the average for both assignments and casual browsing." SLJ
Includes glossary and bibliographical references

591.5 Behavior

Barner, Bob
Animal baths. Chronicle Books 2011 un il $15.99
Grades: PreK K 1   **591.5**
1. Baths 2. Animal behavior
ISBN 978-1-4521-0056-2; 1-4521-0056-X
LC 2011008001
"Eleven colorful two-page spreads (illustrated in cut paper, ribbon and pastel) show a variety of animals bathing, with accompanying two-line verses. . . . Finally, there's a little boy in a tub rub-a-dubbing and covered in bubbles. Then, a fitting encore: A longer poem against a background of bubbles and a child's bathtime accessories goes through the child's whole bath routine with shoutouts to some of the animals. . . . Barner's text is crisp and age-appropriate, but his well-composed, clever pictures really carry the story. . . . Well-conceived in its simplicity from beginning to end; even pre-readers can follow along." Kirkus

Batten, Mary
Please don't wake the animals; a book about sleep. written by Mary Batten; illustrated by Higgins Bond. Peachtree 2008 un il $16.95
Grades: PreK K 1 2 3   **591.5**
1. Sleep 2. Animal behavior
ISBN 978-1-56145-393-1; 1-56145-393-5
LC 2007-31904

"This big bright picture book is an exciting way to talk about the biology that connects humans with many kinds of animals. 'All animals sleep,' and in all kinds of places. Predators can sleep quite safely. . . . Their prey, however, must stay alert, hardly daring to sleep at all. . . . There's also information about animals that hibernate." Booklist

Fielding, Beth

Animal baths; wild & wonderful ways animals get clean! illustrations by Susan Greenelsh. EarlyLight Books 2009 47p il $14.95

Grades: 3 4 5   591.5

1. Baths 2. Cleanliness 3. Animal behavior

ISBN 978-0-9797455-2-2; 0-9797455-2-7

"Written in a conversational tone, this book is divided into three parts based on how animals clean themselves. . . . Each section begins with a brief description of how and why they engage in specific activities, followed by a spread about which ones utilize this method. A full-page, softly colored drawing of the animals 'bathing' faces each page of text. This fascinating book provides some unusual details about the unique behavior of the featured creatures." SLJ

Hile, Lori

Animal survival. Raintree 2011 56p il (Extreme survival) lib bdg $33.50

Grades: 4 5 6 7   591.5

1. Pets 2. Animals 3. Animal behavior 4. Natural disasters

ISBN 978-1-4109-3973-9; 1-4109-3973-1

LC 2010028842

This book is "fun and informative. [This] well-organized title starts with an overview [of animal survival], offers some specific examples, and includes additional facts or tips and resources. . . . [It features] dramatic archival and full-color photos on nearly every page. . . . The first chapter introduces resilient creatures that beat the odds and then follows with their journeys, animal heroes, and their work while surviving natural disasters. . . . [This is a book] that youngsters will enjoy and talk about." SLJ

Includes glossary and bibliographical references

Jenkins, Steve

★ **How** many ways can you catch a fly? [by] Steve Jenkins & Robin Page. Houghton Mifflin Company 2008 un il $16

Grades: PreK K 1 2 3   591.5

1. Animal behavior 2. Food chains (Ecology)

ISBN 978-0-618-96634-9; 0-618-96634-X

LC 2008-01864

"This picture book is about the food chain. . . . The facts about how particular animals escape danger and evade predators to stay alive are just as exciting as the facts about hunting. With clear, gorgeous, freestanding images in cut- and torn-paper collage, each double-page spread shows detailed species close up, as well as the connections between animals." Booklist

Includes bibliographical references

★ **Time** to eat; written and illustrated by Steve Jenkins and Robin Page. Houghton Mifflin 2011 un il $12.99

Grades: PreK K 1 2 3   591.5

1. Animals -- Food

ISBN 978-0-547-25032-8; 0-547-25032-0

LC 2010025127

"This small, square picture book presents an exciting introduction to what animals eat and how they collect, store, and digest their food. . . . The beautiful cut- and torn-paper collage illustrations are . . . expertly colored, detailed, and expressive . . . and the layout, featuring plenty of white space, nicely spotlights each animal in action." Booklist

Time to sleep; written and illustrated by Steve Jenkins and Robin Page. Houghton Mifflin 2011 un il $12.99

Grades: K 1 2 3   591.5

1. Sleep 2. Animal behavior

ISBN 978-0-547-25040-3; 0-547-25040-1

LC 2010025128

"Jenkins and Page introduce an array of creatures, showcasing how they . . . sleep. [The title concludes] with an appendix detailing further information about the featured animals. The illustrations are rendered in torn- and cut-paper collage, with each animal against a white background. . . . [The book] introduces animals from the familiar red fox to the lesser-known basilisk. Fascinating behaviors are detailed with explanations. . . . Readers will be captivated." SLJ

Knapp, Ron

Bloodsucking creatures. Enslow Publishers 2011 48p il (Bizarre science) lib bdg $23.93

Grades: 5 6 7 8   591.5

1. Bloodsucking animals

ISBN 978-0-7660-3671-0; 0-7660-3671-5

LC 2010009761

First published 1996 with title: Bloodsuckers

This describes bloodsucking animals such as mosquitoes, vampire bats, and fleas.

"Aimed at reluctant readers, [this title is] sure to disgust and delight in equal measure. . . . [The title] will pique interest and get kids lining up at the reference desk looking for more. The text is complemented by illustrations and magnified photos of things that you would hope never to see." SLJ

Includes glossary and bibliographical references

Lunde, Darrin

★ **After** the kill; [by] Darrin Lunde; illustrated by Catherine Stock. Charlesbridge 2011 un il lib bdg $16.95; pa $7.95

Grades: 2 3 4 5   591.5

1. Food chains (Ecology) 2. Animals -- Food 3. Animals -- Africa 4. Predatory animals

ISBN 978-1-57091-743-1 lib bdg; 1-57091-743-4 lib bdg; 978-1-57091-744-8 pa; 1-57091-744-2 pa

LC 2010007524

This is a "blunt portrayal of animal life in the Seregeti. A lioness stalks and faltering zebra, kills it, and eats it with her family; meanwhile, white-backed vultures arrive. . . . Then come hyenas, jackals, two other types of vultures, and ultimately meat-eating beetles, until all that remains of the zebra is bones. . . . Given the inherent grisliness of the topic, the text is notably reined in and matter-of-fact, and the pictures, expansive horizontal spreads, are almost impressionistic, focusing more on the ferocity of the predators than on the details of their prey." Horn Book

Newman, Aline Alexander

Animal superstars; and more true stories of amazing animal talents. by Aline Alexander Newman. National Geographic Society 2013 111 p. col. ill. (National geographic kids. Chapters) (paperback) $5.99; (library) $14.90

Grades: 2 3 4 5   **591.5**

1. Animals 2. Animal intelligence
ISBN 1426310919; 1426310927; 9781426310911; 9781426310928

LC 2012277240

This book by Aline Alexander Newman "will feature animals who can perform amazing acts like riding motocross, foretelling the weather, and playing a guitar. These stories [may] empower them to devour the more text-heavy 'grown up' style of the book, while still keeping the story easily digestible for a hesitant reader." (Publisher's note)

Includes bibliographical references (p. 111) and index.

Page, Robin

Animals upside down; A Pull, Pop, Lift & Learn Book! Steve Jenkins and Robin Page. Houghton Mifflin Harcourt 2013 24 p. $24.99

Grades: K 1 2 3   **591.5**

1. Picture books for children 2. Animal behavior
ISBN 054734127X; 9780547341279

This children's picture book looks at animals that spend time upside down. The "three-toed sloth is topsy-turvy most of the time. The upside-down jellyfish rests on its back to feed. Skunks do stink-warning headstands and mallards upend in this colorful, interactive exploration of the hows and whys of upside-down animal behavior." (Publisher's note)

Pipe, Jim

Swarms; written by Jim Pipe; created and designed by David Salariya. Franklin Watts 2009 32p il (Scary creatures) lib bdg $26; pa $8.95

Grades: 3 4 5   **591.5**

1. Animal behavior
ISBN 978-0-531-21674-3 lib bdg; 0-531-21674-8 lib bdg; 978-0-531-21045-1 pa; 0-531-21045-6 pa

LC 2009010800

This describes the behavior of large groups of similar animals such as insects, birds, or fish, all moving in the same direction

This title has "two-page chapters of accessible, large-type text and bright color photos and illustrations. . . . The series distinguishes itself with 'X-Ray Vision.' When readers hold the page with this prompt up to the light, an image emerges. The X-rays mostly show the skeletal structures of the animals. Text boxes throughout add to the visual appeal. . . . [This is an] excellent [resource] for school assignments and browsing." SLJ

Includes glossary

Racanelli, Marie

Animal mimics. PowerKids Press 2010 24p il (Crazy nature) lib bdg $21.25; pa $8.25

Grades: 2 3 4 5   **591.5**

1. Animal behavior
ISBN 978-1-4358-9382-5 lib bdg; 1-4358-9382-4 lib bdg; 978-1-4358-9856-1 pa; 1-4358-9856-7 pa

Mimicry is an animal adaptation used both by prey and predators to disguise them in their habitats. The different kinds of mimicry are explored, along with specific examples of each type

This book "combines attention-grabbing information with a well-organized format. . . . [The book has] spectacular color photography and eye-popping facts. . . . Excellent for reports." SLJ

Underground animals. PowerKids 2010 24p il (Crazy nature) lib bdg $21.25; pa $8.25

Grades: 2 3 4 5   **591.5**

1. Animals
ISBN 978-1-4358-9384-9 lib bdg; 1-4358-9384-0 lib bdg; 978-1-4358-9860-8 pa; 1-4358-9860-5 pa

This describes animals that live underground from burrowers to cave-dwellers, such as earthworms, moles, ants, badgers, desert tortoises

This book "combines attention-grabbing information with a well-organized format. . . . [The book has] spectacular color photography and eye-popping facts. . . . Excellent for reports." SLJ

Ruurs, Margriet

Amazing animals; the remarkable things creatures do. illustrated by W. Allan Hancock. Tundra Books 2011 32p il $17.95

Grades: 2 3 4 5   **591.5**

1. Animal behavior
ISBN 978-0-88776-973-3; 0-88776-973-X

Detailed illustrations and short descriptions present facts about animals from around the world, including their home-building, diet, and hunting.

"Though only a few lines are devoted to each animal, the detailed paintings and surprising details should captivate readers." Publ Wkly

Stewart, Melissa

Beneath the sun; by Melissa Stewart; illustrated by Constance Bergum. Peachtree Publishers 2014 32 p. illustrations $16.95

Grades: PreK K 1 2 3   **591.5**

1. Heat 2. Sun 3. Animal behavior 4. Animals -- Adaptation
ISBN 1561457337; 9781561457335

LC 2013026214

This children's book, written by Melissa Stewart and illustrated by Constance Bergum, asks "how do wild animals react to . . . heat? Journey from your neighborhood to a field where an earthworm loops its long body into a ball underground, to a desert where a jackrabbit loses heat through its oversized ears, to a wetland where a siren salamander burrows into the mud to stay cool, and to a seashore where a sea star hides in the shade of a seaweed mat." (Publisher's note)

"The framing of illustrations within the double-page spreads gives readers a sense of spatiality within the environment depicted. A well-designed, well-written book that offers readers a greater awareness of and sense of relationship to the other inhabitants in their environments." Kirkus

Thimmesh, Catherine

True Stories of Extraordinary Friendship; written by Catherine Thimmesh. Houghton Mifflin 2011 un il $16.99

Grades: K 1 2 3   **591.5**
1. Animal behavior
ISBN 0547390106; 9780547390109; 978-0-547-
39010-9; 0-547-39010-6
LC 2010025122
This book offers a photo exploration of unlikely
animal friendships.
"The photos radiate trust and warmth, and the text is
soothing and reassuring." SLJ

Zelch, Patti R.
★ **Ready,** set . . . wait! what animals do before a hurricane. illustrated by Connie McLennan. Sylvan Dell 2010
un il $16.95; pa $8.95
Grades: 1 2 3 4   **591.5**
1. Hurricanes 2. Animal behavior
ISBN 978-1-60718-072-2; 1-60718-072-3; 978-1-
60718-083-8 pa; 1-60718-083-9 pa
"Superbly illustrated, . . . the book presents scientifically
verified information on the behaviors that many animals .
. . display in the days just prior to hurricanes. Prereaders
will enjoy both hearing the stories and looking at the illustrations, while early readers will be able to advance through the
text on their own." Sci Books Films

591.56   Behavior relating to life cycle

Bancroft, Henrietta
Animals in winter; by Henrietta Bancroft and Rich-
ard G. Van Gelder; illustrated by Helen K. Davie. rev ed;
HarperCollins Pubs. 1997 32p il (Let's-read-and-find-out
science) hardcover o.p. pa $4.95
Grades: K 1   **591.56**
1. Winter 2. Animal behavior
ISBN 0-06-027158-2; 0-06-445165-8 pa
LC 95-36246
First published 1963
Describes the many different ways animals cope with
winter, including migration, hibernation, and food storage
"The words are immediate . . . and the clear, active il-
lustrations will draw new readers to a popular subject."
Booklist

Berkes, Marianne Collins
Going home; the mystery of animal migration. illustrated by Jennifer DiRubbio. Dawn 2010 un il map
$16.95; pa $8.95
Grades: 2 3 4   **591.56**
1. Animals -- Migration
ISBN 978-1-58469-126-6; 1-58469-126-3; 978-1-
58469-127-3 pa; 1-58469-127-1 pa
LC 2009-38568
"The illustrations enhance the text with softly colored
two-page spreads. This book is perfect for a read-aloud
to introduce the topic of migration. The rhyming verse
flows smoothly, enhanced by the informational text." Libr
Media Connect
Includes bibliographical references

Carney, Elizabeth
Great migrations; whales, wildebeests, butterflies, elephants, and other amazing animals on the move. National

Geographic 2010 45p il map (National Geographic kids)
$17.95; lib bdg $27
Grades: 3 4 5   **591.56**
1. Animals -- Migration
ISBN 9781426307003; 1426307004; 9781426307010
lib bdg; 1426307012 lib bdg
LC 2010008501
"This colorful book offers excellent photos of eight
migrating animals: Mali elephants, red crabs, monarch butterflies, golden jellyfish, zebras, army ants, wildebeests, and
sperm whales. . . . The writing style is often lively, tha maps
are excellent, and the photos are exceptionally clear and vibrant." Booklist

Collard, Sneed B.
Animal dads; [by] Sneed B. Collard III; illustrated by
Steve Jenkins. Houghton Mifflin 1997 un il $15.95; pa
$5.95
Grades: K 1 2 3   **591.56**
1. Animal behavior
ISBN 0-395-83621-2; 0-618-03299-1 pa
LC 96-22171
"Each father and his offspring are presented on a single
or double-page spread, illustrated with striking, cut-paper
collage figures. The large, lifelike creatures are set against
backgrounds that are true to each animal's natural habitat."
SLJ

Dowson, Nick
North, the Amazing Story of Arctic Migration; the
story of Arctic migration. illustrated by Patrick Benson.
Candlewick Press 2011 56p il $16.99
Grades: 1 2 3   **591.56**
1. Arctic regions 2. Animals -- Migration
ISBN 978-0-7636-5271-5; 0-7636-5271-7
LC 2010048131
"In the dark Arctic winters, few species can survive, but
in short, lush summers, millions of animals return to reproduce. This combination of lyrical prose and striking illustrations conveys the mystery and magic of the far North and the
cycle of darkness and rebirth that includes some astonishing
migratory journeys. . . . Simple but effective, this is a beautiful introduction to a remarkable region that should encourage any child's sense of wonder." Kirkus

Fraser, Mary Ann
How animal babies stay safe. HarperCollins Pubs.
2002 33p il (Let's-read-and-find-out science) hardcover
o.p. pa $4.95
Grades: K 1   **591.56**
1. Animal babies
ISBN 0-06-028803-5; 0-06-445211-5 pa
LC 00-57267
The author "describes how animal babies are cared for
by their parents, including alligator babies who are carried
about in their mother's mouth and young elephants who are
placed in the middle of the herd for protection. Watercolor
illustrations in muted colors help expand the simple text."
Horn Book Guide

Jenkins, Steve
★ **Sisters** & brothers; sibling relationships in the ani-
mal world. [by] Steve Jenkins & Robin Page. Houghton
Mifflin 2008 un il $16

Grades: 2 3 4   **591.56**
  1. Siblings 2. Animal behavior
  ISBN 978-0-618-37596-7; 0-618-37596-1
                  LC 2007-34305
  "This riveting picture book . . . is packed with amazing facts. . . . [The subjects are] depicted in crisp, gorgeous, cut-and-torn paper collages set against lots of white space. . . . The sibling focus is a way to include a wealth of fascinating facts." Booklist

  Time for a bath; written and illustrated by Steve Jenkins and Robin Page. Houghton Mifflin 2011 un il $12.99
Grades: K 1 2 3   **591.56**
  1. Baths 2. Animal behavior
  ISBN 978-0-547-25037-3; 0-547-25037-1
                  LC 2010025126
  "Jenkins and Page introduce an array of creatures, showcasing how they bathe. . . . [The title concludes] with an appendix detailing further information about the featured animals. The illustrations are rendered in torn- and cut-paper collage, with each animal . . . set against a white background. . . . Readers are informed that animals bathe for different reasons: to clean themselves, to cool off, to warm up, to dissuade parasites. . . . Readers will be captivated." SLJ

Marsh, Laura
  Amazing animal journeys. National Geographic 2010 48p il (Great migrations) $11.90; pa $3.99
Grades: 1 2 3   **591.56**
  1. Crabs 2. Zebras 3. Walruses 4. Animals -- Migration
  ISBN 978-1-4263-0742-3; 1-4263-0742-X; 978-1-4263-0741-6 pa; 1-4263-0741-1 pa
                  LC 2010017958
  This describes the migration patterns of zebras, red crabs, and walruses.
  "Dynamic full-color photographs, informative writing, and consistent organization work well together in [this volume]. . . . Along with the many photographs, the fascinating details are supported by boxes of related information, helpful definitions of new terms, and a sprinkling of entertaining jokes/riddles." SLJ
  Includes glossary

Roemer, Heidi B.
  Whose nest is this? by Heidi Bee Roemer; illustrated by Connie McLennan. NorthWord Books for Young Readers 2009 un il $16.95
Grades: PreK K 1 2   **591.56**
  1. Birds -- Nests 2. Animals -- Habitations
  ISBN 978-1-58979-386-6; 1-58979-386-2
                  LC 2007021870
  "This picture book describes the nests of various birds, insects, mammals, fish, and reptiles. Whether it's an elf owl's cavity in a giant Saguaro, a Caribbean flamingo's mound of mud in shallow water, or a sea turtle's sandy pit, these shelters are described in brief rhymed texts. . . . The creatures are brought to life in the engaging rhymes and vivid art." SLJ

Stockdale, Susan
  Carry me! animal babies on the move. written and illustrated by Susan Stockdale. Peachtree Publishers 2005 un il $15.95

Grades: PreK K 1   **591.56**
  1. Animal behavior
  ISBN 1-56145-328-5
                  LC 2004-16585
  "The facts of zoology are both exciting and cuddly in this science picture book with clear, bright acrylic illustrations that show how various animals carry their babies. The settings give the big picture—from the African savannah and Antarctica to South America. Then children can look closely and find animal babies tucked into pouches, clinging to bellies, propped on shoulders, perched on feet, gripped between teeth." Booklist
  Includes bibliographical references

591.59   Animals - Communication

Baines, Rebecca
  What did one elephant say to the other; a book about communication. by Becky Baines. National Geographic Society 2008 26p il (Zig zag) $14.95; lib bdg $19.90
Grades: PreK K 1   **591.59**
  1. Animal communication
  ISBN 978-1-4263-0307-4; 1-4263-0307-6; 978-1-4263-0308-1 lib bdg; 1-4263-0308-4 lib bdg
                  LC 2008-07218
  "Curiosity will be piqued by the vibrant color photographs, accommodating illustrations, large font size, and helpful captions. Special features include drawings superimposed over photographs, and a zigzag path at the end of . . . [the] book prompting readers to further explore the topic in new and fun ways." SLJ

Davies, Nicola, 1958-
  Talk talk squawk; How and Why Animals Communicate. illustrated by Neal Layton. Walker & Company 2011 64 p.
Grades: 3 4 5   **591.59**
  1. Animal communication
  ISBN 0763650889 (Candlewick); 1406321184 (Walker & Co.); 9780763650889 (Candlewick); 9781406321180 (Walker & Co.)
                  LC 2010040794
  "Davies and Layton turn to animal communication, describing how animals send and receive messages by sound, sight, smell and touch, for a variety of purposes. . . . Cartoonlike illustrations, almost doodles, done in ink and colored digitally, add humor to every page, even in the backmatter. They often include speech balloons demonstrating the animals' messages. . . . Something to crow about." Kirkus

591.6   Miscellaneous nontaxonomic kinds of animals

Claybourne, Anna
  100 deadliest things on the planet. Scholastic 2012 112 p. $7.99
Grades: 4 5 6   **591.6**
  1. Tsunamis 2. Volcanoes 3. Animal attacks 4. Animal behavior 5. Natural disasters
  ISBN 0545434378; 9780545434379

This book by Anna Claybourne looks at Earth's deadliest animals and natural disasters. "There are animals that can use an arsenal of deadly weapons--teeth, claws, stinging spines, powerful pincers, or scary suckers--to fight, hunt, or defend themselves. There are natural disasters--from towering tsunamis to massive volcanic eruptions--that can destroy whole cities in the blink of an eye." The book "includes side panels, a 'deadly factor' rating, and photos throughout." (Publisher's note)

Davies, Nicola, 1958-
What's eating you? parasites--the inside story. [by] Nicola Davies; illustrated by Neal Layton. Candlewick Press 2007 60p il $12.99
Grades: 3 4 5 6   591.6
1. Parasites
ISBN 978-0-7636-3460-5; 0-7636-3460-3
LC 2007-25634
"Davies uses a conversational approach to introduce readers to those weird critters that consider their host to be 'just a pantry.' . . . The subject is inherently fascinating for kids and those who settle into read will find a good deal of information about some of the more familiar parasites. . . . The artwork adds a welcome comic veneer." Booklist

Graham, Ian
Microscopic scary creatures; written by Ian Graham; created and designed by David Salariya. Franklin Watts 2009 32p il (Scary creatures) lib bdg $26; pa $8.95
Grades: 3 4 5   591.6
1. Protozoa 2. Parasites 3. Microorganisms
ISBN 978-0-531-21673-6 lib bdg; 0-531-21673-X lib bdg; 978-0-531-21044-4 pa; 0-531-21044-8 pa
LC 2009-11224
This defines microscopic creatures and describes their habitats and life cycles, and their relationships to humans.
This title has "two-page chapters of accessible, large-type text and bright color photos and illustrations. . . . The series distinguishes itself with 'X-Ray Vision.' When readers hold the page with this prompt up to the light, an image emerges. The X-rays mostly show the skeletal structures of the animals. Text boxes throughout add to the visual appeal. . . . [This title is an] excellent [resource] for school assignments and browsing." SLJ
Includes glossary

Jenkins, Steve
★ Never smile at a monkey; and 17 other important things to remember. Houghton Mifflin Books for Children 2009 un il $16
Grades: 1 2 3 4   591.6
1. Dangerous animals
ISBN 978-0-618-96620-2; 0-618-96620-X
LC 2009-32964
"A visually stunning book illustrated with cut paper and torn collages. . . . This superlative illustrator has given children yet another work that educates and amazes." SLJ
"Eighteen alliterative rules showcase the dangerous defense mechanisms of animals found in the wild." Kirkus

Pryor, Kimberley Jane
Venom, poison, and electricity. Marshall Cavendish Benchmark 2009 32p il (Animal attack and defense) $19.95

Grades: 2 3 4   591.6
1. Animal defenses 2. Poisonous animals
ISBN 978-0-7614-4422-0; 0-7614-4422-X
LC 2009-4994
"Students will enjoy the large vivid photographs that allow for a close-up look at the animal, along with the excellent descriptions of the different survival methods. . . . Pryor does a good job of bringing the information down to a level that an elementary student would understand without losing any of the important details. . . . [This] would be a great addition to any nonfiction collection." Libr Media Connect
Inlcudes glossary

Racanelli, Marie
Albino animals. PowerKids Press 2010 24p il (Crazy nature) lib bdg $21.25; pa $8.25
Grades: 2 3 4 5   591.6
1. Albinos and albinism 2. Animals -- Color
ISBN 978-1-4358-9381-8 lib bdg; 1-4358-9381-6 lib bdg; 978-1-4358-9854-7 pa; 1-4358-9854-0 pa
This explains why different types of animals are born without skin pigmentation and about the challenges they must face in their natural environments
This book "combines attention-grabbing information with a well-organized format. . . . [The book has] spectacular color photography and eye-popping facts. . . . Excellent for reports." SLJ

Stewart, Melissa
Deadliest animals. National Geographic 2011 48p il (National Geographic readers) lib bdg $11.90; pa $3.99
Grades: K 1 2 3   591.6
1. Dangerous animals
ISBN 978-1-4263-0758-4 lib bdg; 1-4263-0758-6 lib ed; 978-1-4263-0757-7 pa; 1-4263-0757-8 pa
LC 2011284182
This describes 12 dangerous species including sharks, snakes, jellyfish, bears, tigers and mosquitoes.
"Vivid nature photos show the deadly creatures in action. Silly jokes . . . and . . . sidebars maintain readers' attention." Horn Book Guide

Tourville, Amanda Doering
Animal invaders. Rourke Pub. 2010 48p il (Let's explore science) $32.79
Grades: 4 5 6 7   591.6
1. Animals 2. Biological invasions
ISBN 978-1-61590-319-1; 1-61590-319-4
LC 2010009906
This describes non-native animal species.
Includes bibliographical references

591.68   Rare and endangered animals

Allgor, Marie
Endangered desert animals; by Marie Allgor; edited by Jennifer Way. PowerKids Press 2013 24 p. col. ill. (Save Earth's animals!) (library) $22.60; (paperback) $8.25
Grades: 1 2 3   591.68
1. Desert animals 2. Desert ecology 3. Endangered

species 4. Wildlife conservation
ISBN 9781448874231; 9781448874965

LC 2011051875

This book on endangered desert animals by Marie Allgor is part of the "Save the Earth's Animals!" series. "Before launching into the individual creatures, the title explores the region's climate and the various habitats: shrubs, cacti, and so on. The five featured animals are the slender-horned gazelle, the Egyptian vulture. Nelson's antelope squirrel, the Bactrian camel, and the desert tortoise." (Booklist)

Includes bibliographical references (p. 24) and index

Barry, Frances

Let's save the animals; a flip-the-flap book. Candlewick Press 2010 un il $12.99

Grades: PreK K   **591.68**

1. Endangered species 2. Wildlife conservation
ISBN 978-0-7636-4501-4; 0-7636-4501-X

LC 2009-22117

"Barry's engaging entry brings young children into the conversation [about wildlife conservation] without sacrificing an ounce of kid appeal. Sporting a rounded cover, sturdy pages, and inventive die-cut flaps, this primer presents 10 endangered species in their natural habitats. . . . Barry's superb, colorful paper-collage illustrations feature close-ups of friendly looking animals." Booklist

Hirsch, Rebecca E.

Helping endangered animals; by Rebecca Hirsch. Cherry Lake Pub. 2010 32p il (Save the planet) lib bdg $27.07

Grades: 3 4 5 6   **591.68**

1. Endangered species
ISBN 978-1-60279-658-4 lib bdg; 1-60279-658-0 lib bdg

LC 2009-38094

Examines endangered species, how human activities have contributed to shrinking numbers, and what is being done to protect animals for the future

"At the beginning of . . . [the] book, readers are given a mission and advised to be alert to the facts provided so that they can successfully answer the questions at the end. . . . Children are made to feel part of the process; suggestions for how they can become involved abound." SLJ

Includes glossary and bibliographical references

Jenkins, Martin

★ **Can** we save the tiger? Candlewick Press 2011 50p il $16.99

Grades: 1 2 3   **591.68**

1. Tigers 2. Extinct animals 3. Wildlife conservation 4. Extinction (Biology)
ISBN 0763649090; 9780763649098; 978-0-7636-4909-8; 0-7636-4909-0

LC 2010008899

"Magnificent artwork and a careful balance of good and bad news are the strengths of this examination of endangered species. . . . Conversational text . . . explains difficult nuances of politics and sociology with verve. White's animals—meticulously drafted and shaded with the subtlest of earth tones—could almost walk off the page. The book's large trim size allows the inclusion of many sketches of creatures in a variety of positions, while intelligent design and

typography decisions make each page worth lingering over. An excellent resource." Publ Wkly

Jenkins, Steve

★ **Almost** gone; the world's rarest animals. HarperCollins Pubs. 2006 33p il (Let's-read-and-find-out science) $16.99; pa $5.99

Grades: K 1 2 3   **591.68**

1. Rare animals 2. Endangered species
ISBN 0-06-053598-9; 0-06-053600-4 pa

LC 2004-30199

"This engaging title is informative as well as visually stunning." SLJ

The author "shows 21 endangered species, accompanying each image with a few sentences about the animal's habitat, a particular characteristic, and, sometimes, the reason for its endangered status." Booklist

591.7 Animal ecology, animals characteristic of specific environments

Arnosky, Jim

Watching desert wildlife. National Geographic Soc. 1998 un il hardcover o.p. pa $7.95

Grades: 3 4 5 6   **591.7**

1. Desert animals
ISBN 0-7922-7304-4; 0-7922-6737-0 pa

LC 98-13189

Illustrations and text describe some of the animals the author encountered in the deserts of the American Southwest

"An informative and well-illustrated addition to science units on desert wildlife." Booklist

Barnhill, Kelly Regan

Monsters of the deep; deep sea adaptation. by Kelly Regan Barnhill. Capstone Press 2008 32p il (Fact finders. Extreme life) lib bdg $22.60

Grades: 2 3 4   **591.7**

1. Ocean bottom 2. Marine animals
ISBN 978-1-4296-1264-7 lib bdg; 1-4296-1264-9 lib bdg

LC 2007-20897

This reveals "the world of deep-sea creatures. A conversational text explains how the animals have adapted to the incredible depth and darkness of the ocean's 'midnight zone.' Readers will be fascinated—or terrified—by the unusual-looking fish." Horn Book Guide

Includes glossary and bibliographical references

Bateman, Donna M.

Deep in the swamp; [by] Donna M. Bateman; illustrated by Brian Lies. Charlesbridge 2007 un il lib bdg $15.95; pa $6.95

Grades: K 1 2 3   **591.7**

1. Counting 2. Swamp animals
ISBN 978-1-57091-596-3 lib bdg; 978-1-57091-597-0 pa

LC 2006009026

"This stunning book spotlights the flora and fauna of Florida's Okefenokee Swamp. . . . The text is a version of the familiar poem 'Over in the Meadow,' with impeccable meter. . . . Lie's meticulous and glowing acrylic illustrations feature myriad shades of green, yellow, and blue." SLJ

Bredeson, Carmen

Baby animals of lakes and ponds. Enslow Elementary 2011 24p il (Nature's baby animals) lib bdg $21.26
Grades: 1 2 3   591.7
1. Lakes 2. Ponds 3. Animal babies
ISBN 978-0-7660-3563-8; 0-7660-3563-8
LC 2009037899

"The large, close-up photos . . . are irresistibly cute. The text . . . stayed focused and gives just the right amount of interesting information." Booklist

Includes glossary and bibliographical references

Baby animals of the frozen tundra. Enslow Publishers 2009 24p il map (Nature's baby animals) lib bdg $21.26
Grades: 1 2 3   591.7
1. Animal babies 2. Animals -- Arctic regions
ISBN 978-0-7660-3002-2 lib bdg; 0-7660-3002-4
lib bdg
LC 2007039472

"Up-close photos and information about baby animals of the tundra biome" Publisher's note

Includes glossary and bibliographical references

Baby animals of the grasslands. Enslow Publishers 2008 23p il map (Nature's baby animals) lib bdg $21.26
Grades: 1 2 3   591.7
1. Grasslands 2. Animal babies
ISBN 978-0-7660-3006-0 lib bdg; 0-7660-3006-7
lib bdg
LC 2007-29284

"Well chosen, exceedingly enderaring photos highlight this [book]. . . . Accessible to new readers." SLJ

Includes glossary and bibliographical references

Baby animals of the mountains. Enslow Elementary 2011 24p il (Nature's baby animals) lib bdg $21.26
Grades: 1 2 3   591.7
1. Animal babies 2. Mountain animals
ISBN 978-0-7660-3562-1; 0-7660-3562-X
LC 2009037898

"The large, closeup photos . . . are irresistibly cute. The text . . . stayed focused and gives just the right amount of interesting information." Booklist

Includes glossary and bibliographical references

Baby animals of the ocean. Enslow Publishers 2009 24p il (Nature's baby animals) lib bdg $21.26
Grades: 1 2 3   591.7
1. Animal babies 2. Marine animals
ISBN 978-0-7660-3003-9 lib bdg; 0-7660-3003-2
lib bdg
LC 2007039469

"Up-close photos and information about baby animals of the ocean biome" Publisher's note

Includes glossary and bibliographical references

Baby animals of the seashore. Enslow Elementary 2011 24p il (Nature's baby animals) lib bdg $21.26

Grades: 1 2 3   591.7
1. Seashore 2. Animal babies 3. Marine animals
ISBN 978-0-7660-3565-2; 0-7660-3565-4
LC 2009037901

"The large, closeup photos . . . are irresistibly cute. The text . . . stayed focused and gives just the right amount of interesting information." Booklist

Includes glossary and bibliographical references

Baby animals of the wetlands. Enslow Elementary 2011 24p il (Nature's baby animals) lib bdg $21.26
Grades: 1 2 3   591.7
1. Wetlands 2. Animal babies
ISBN 978-0-7660-3564-5 lib bdg; 0-7660-3564-6
lib bdg
LC 2009037900

"The large, closeup photos . . . are irresistibly cute. The text . . . stayed focused and gives just the right amount of interesting information." Booklist

Includes glossary and bibliographical references

Carlson-Voiles, Polly

Someone walks by; the wonders of winter wildlife. story and illustrations by Polly Carlson-Voiles. Raven Productions 2008 un il $18.95; pa $12.95
Grades: K 1 2 3   591.7
1. Winter 2. Forest animals
ISBN 978-0-9801045-5-4; 0-9801045-5-6; 978-0-9801045-6-1 pa; 0-9801045-6-4 pa
LC 2008036871

"Set in the northern woodland in winter, this picture book shows how a variety of animals adapt to the frigid, snowy environment. . . . Poetic metaphors, internal rhymes, and repeated sounds give a lyrical tone to the prose. A typical double-page spread introduces several animals . . . in a few lines of text and two collage illustrations that combine cut papers into effective compositions enhanced with ink drawings and watercolors for details and patterns." Booklist

Himmelman, John

Who's at the seashore? written and illustrated by John Himmelman. NorthWord Books 2009 un il $15.95
Grades: K 1   591.7
1. Animal behavior 2. Seashore ecology
ISBN 978-1-58979-387-3; 1-58979-387-0
LC 2008038264

"This quiet little book introduces some seaside creatures via a simple rhyming text and realistic illustrations. A ruddy turnstone uncovers a sand hopper, a watchful gull hits on the hopper, while a moon snail creates a sand collar to hold her eggs, and so on in a soft litany of beach denizens and their activities. Himmelman's larger-than-life watercolors spread across the facing pages, revealing not only the action described in the text, but also the participants in the next sequence." SLJ

Hodge, Deborah

Desert animals; written by Deborah Hodge; illustrated by Pat Stephens. Kids Can Press 2008 24p il (Who lives here?) $14.95; pa $5.95
Grades: K 1 2 3   591.7
1. Desert animals
ISBN 978-1-55453-047-2; 1-55453-047-4; 978-1-55453-048-9 pa; 1-55453-048-2 pa

This introduces animals that are built for living in the extremes of deserts, including Elf owls, sand cats, and scorpions.

Forest animals; written by Deborah Hodge; illustrated by Pat Stephens. Kids Can Press 2009 24p il (Who lives here?) $14.95; pa $5.95
Grades: K 1 2 3   **591.7**
  1. Forest animals
  ISBN 978-1-55453-070-0; 1-55453-070-9; 978-1-55453-071-7 pa; 1-55453-071-7 pa
"This mini-guide to creatures of the northern forest features one animal per spread. A brief introduction . . . includes facts about the animal's home, diet, young, unique features and abilities, and/or survival techniques. The text provides enough detail to engage readers without overwhelming them. Uncluttered design and finely crafted realistic illustrations are strengths." Horn Book Guide

Polar animals; written by Deborah Hodge; illustrated by Pat Stephens. Kids Can Press 2008 24p il (Who lives here?) $14.95; pa $5.95
Grades: K 1 2 3   **591.7**
  1. Animals -- Arctic regions
  ISBN 978-1-55453-043-4; 1-55453-043-1; 978-1-55453-044-1 pa; 1-55453-044-X pa
This book describes "the animal inhabitants of [the arctic region]. . . . Each double-page spread highlights a specific animal [and] . . . muted illustrations . . . effectively supplement and help explain the text." Horn Book Guide

Rain forest animals; written by Deborah Hodge; illustrated by Pat Stephens. Kids Can Press 2008 24p il (Who lives here?) $14.95; pa $5.95
Grades: K 1 2 3   **591.7**
  1. Rain forest animals
  ISBN 978-1-55453-041-0; 1-55453-041-5; 978-1-55453-042-7 pa; 1-55453-042-3 pa
This book describes "the animal inhabitants of [the rain forest]. . . . Each double-page spread highlights a specific animal [and] . . . muted illustrations . . . effectively supplement and help explain the text." Horn Book Guide

Savanna animals; written by Deborah Hodge; illustrated by Pat Stephens. Kids Can Press 2009 24p il (Who lives here?) $14.95; pa $5.95
Grades: K 1 2 3   **591.7**
  1. Grassland ecology 2. Animals -- Africa
  ISBN 978-1-55453-072-4; 1-55453-072-5; 978-1-55453-073-1 pa; 1-55453-073-3 pa
"This well-illustrated book introduces . . . readers to . . . animals that live in the African savanna. . . . Basic information about the elephant, wildebeest (aka, the gnu), giraffe, meerkat, zebra, black mamba (a snake), lion, and ostrich is presented to two-page spreads. . . . The highlight of the book is the excellent illustrations that complement the brief text." Sci Books Films

Wetland animals; written by Deborah Hodge; illustrated by Pat Stephens. Kids Can Press 2008 24p il (Who lives here?) $14.95; pa $5.95

Grades: K 1 2 3   **591.7**
  1. Wetlands 2. Freshwater animals
  ISBN 978-1-55453-045-8; 1-55453-045-8; 978-1-55453-046-5 pa; 1-55453-046-6 pa
Introduces the animals that are built for living in or on the water of swamps, ponds, bogs, and marshes, including hippos, moose, capybaras, and bullfrogs.

Jenkins, Steve
  ★ **Down,** down, down; a journey to the bottom of the sea. Houghton Mifflin Harcourt 2009 un il $17
Grades: 2 3 4 5   **591.7**
  1. Ocean bottom 2. Marine animals
  ISBN 978-0-618-96636-3; 0-618-96636-6
                               LC 2008-36082
"Starting at the surface of the Pacific Ocean, Jenkins introduces some of the animals that inhabit descending layers of water all the way down to the Marianas Trench. At nearly 36,000 feet, this zone has been visited only once, by human passengers of a research vessel. Depicted in Jenkins's signature handsome collages, the denizens of each level swim against ever-darkening backgrounds ranging from sunny blue to deepest black. . . . The repeated message that humans have much to explore and learn in the deeper ocean is intriguing and inviting. " SLJ

  ★ **How** to clean a hippopotamus; a look at unusual animal partnerships. [by] Steve Jenkins & Robin Page. Houghton Mifflin Books for Children 2010 un il lib bdg $16
Grades: K 1 2 3   **591.7**
  1. Symbiosis
  ISBN 978-0-547-24515-7 lib bdg; 0-547-24515-7 lib bdg
                                 LC 2009-45452
This picture book "explores unexpected animal partnerships. . . . The spreads have an exciting, comics-inspired feel. Each page combines panels of multiple images, rendered in Jenkins' superbly crafted paper-collage style, with brief lines of concise, clear text and attention-grabbing headlines. . . . These fascinating stories from the natural world will easily interest young people." Booklist

  ★ **I** see a kookaburra! discovering animal habitats around the world. [by] Steve Jenkins & Robin Page. Houghton Mifflin Co. 2005 un il map $16
Grades: K 1 2 3   **591.7**
  1. Animals 2. Habitat (Ecology)
  ISBN 0-618-50764-7
                                 LC 2004-13188
A pictorial introduction to desert, tide pool, jungle, savana, forest, and pond habitats, with examples of the animals that live in each
"Filled with vibrant colors and palpable textures, the illustrations are breathtaking and give a real sense of the vitality, diversity, and beauty of nature. A first-rate foray into ecology that will encourage readers to explore the world around them." SLJ
Includes bibliographical references

Johnson, Rebecca L.
  ★ **Journey** into the deep; discovering new ocean creatures. with a foreword by Sylvia A. Earle. Millbrook Press 2010 64p il lib bdg $31.93

Grades: 4 5 6 7 **591.7**

1. Ocean bottom 2. Marine animals 3. Scientific expeditions

ISBN 978-0-7613-4148-2 lib bdg; 0-7613-4148-X lib bdg

LC 2009049603

"This strikingly illustrated book takes its readers on a series of research voyages exploring the ocean from its shallow edges to unfathomable depths during the recently completed ten-year International Census of Marine Life. Clearly organized text and pictures combine to introduce newly discovered marine creatures of all kinds. . . . The excitement and challenge of discovery in tangible. Scientific photographs printed on blue-to-black background . . . illustrate animals mentioned in a nicely legible text. . . . Rich, revealing and rewarding." Kirkus

Includes glossary and bibliographical references

Landstrom, Lee Ann

Nature's yucky! 2: the desert southwest; by Lee Landstrom and Karen I. Shragg; illustrated by Rachel Rogge. Mountain Press Pub. Co. 2007 48p il pa $12

Grades: K 1 2 3 **591.7**

1. Desert animals 2. Natural history -- Southwestern States

ISBN 978-0-87842-529-7 pa; 0-87842-529-2 pa

LC 2006032479

This explains "the significance of adaptations of animals of the southwestern desert. . . . The illustrations are detailed and well done. . . . Each of the animals is well described." Sci Books Films

Lynette, Rachel

Who lives in a colorful coral reef? PowerKids Press 2011 24p il map (Exploring habitats) lib bdg $21.25; pa $8.25

Grades: 2 3 **591.7**

1. Animals 2. Coral reefs and islands

ISBN 978-1-4488-0677-5 lib bdg; 1-4488-0677-1 lib bdg; 978-1-4488-1281-3 pa; 1-4488-1281-X pa

LC 2009-54350

Presents the various types of animals that live in a coral reef, including sea anemones, sea stars, cleaner shrimp, clown fish, and sponges.

"Sharp color photographs provide visual interest. Text is arranged in photo caption boxes or is well divided into frames spaced between the photographs in a visually pleasing array. Loads of information is packed into fairly short sentences, containing vocabulary that can be easily read by second or third graders." Libr Media Connect

Includes glossary

Who lives in a deep, dark cave? PowerKids Press, 2011 24p il map (Exploring habitats) lib bdg $21.25; pa $8.25

Grades: 2 3 **591.7**

1. Caves 2. Animals 3. Cave dwellers

ISBN 978-1-4488-0676-8 lib bdg; 1-4488-0676-3 lib bdg; 978-1-4488-1277-6 pa; 1-4488-1277-1 pa

Introduces several types of animals that live in caves.

"Sharp color photographs provide visual interest. Text is arranged in photo caption boxes or is well divided into frames spaced between the photographs in a visually pleasing array. Loads of information is packed into fairly short sentences, containing vocabulary that can be easily read by second or third graders." Libr Media Connect

Includes glossary

Who lives in a wet, wild rain forest? PowerKids Press 2011 24p il map (Exploring habitats) lib bdg $21.25; pa $8.25

Grades: 2 3 **591.7**

1. Rain forest animals 2. Rain forest ecology

ISBN 978-1-4488-0678-2 lib bdg; 1-4488-0678-X lib bdg; 978-1-4488-1283-7 pa; 1-4488-1283-6 pa

LC 2010000423

Introduces some of the animals of rain forests and how they live.

"Sharp color photographs provide visual interest. Text is arranged in photo caption boxes or is well divided into frames spaced between the photographs in a visually pleasing array. Loads of information is packed into fairly short sentences, containing vocabulary that can be easily read by second or third graders." Libr Media Connect

Includes glossary

Who lives on a towering mountain? PowerKids Press 2010 24p il map (Exploring habitats) lib bdg $21.25; pa $8.25

Grades: 2 3 **591.7**

1. Mountain animals

ISBN 978-1-4488-0680-5 lib bdg; 1-4488-0680-1 lib bdg; 978-1-4488-1287-5 pa; 1-4488-1287-9 pa

LC 2010003466

Presents the various types of animals that live in the mountains, including snow leopards, bighorn sheep, elk, marmots, and mountain lions

"Sharp color photographs provide visual interest. Text is arranged in photo caption boxes or is well divided into frames spaced between the photographs in a visually pleasing array. Loads of information is packed into fairly short sentences, containing vocabulary that can be easily read by second or third graders." Libr Media Connect

Includes glossary

Who lives on the icy, cold tundra. PowerKids Press 2011 24p il map (Exploring habitats) lib bdg $21.25; pa $8.25

Grades: 2 3 **591.7**

1. Animals 2. Tundra ecology

ISBN 978-1-4488-0675-1 lib bdg; 1-4488-0675-5 lib bdg; 978-1-4488-1279-0 pa; 1-4488-1279-8 pa

LC 2009-54351

Presents the various types of animals that live on the tundra, including polar bears, the arctic fox, the giant petrel, the emperor penguin, and musk oxen.

"Sharp color photographs provide visual interest. Text is arranged in photo caption boxes or is well divided into frames spaced between the photographs in a visually pleasing array. Loads of information is packed into fairly short sentences, containing vocabulary that can be easily read by second or third graders." Libr Media Connect

Includes glossary

McLimans, David

Gone fishing; ocean life by the numbers. [by] David McLimans. Walker 2008 un il $16.99; lib bdg $17.89

Grades: 3 4 5 **591.7**
1. Marine animals 2. Endangered species
ISBN 978-0-8027-9770-4; 0-8027-9770-9; 978-0-8027-9564-9 lib bdg; 0-8027-9564-1 lib bdg
LC 2008014475

"Using animal-shaped numbers from 1 to 10 and back again, McLimans introduces various marine creatures and their survival status. An African penguin, sea lamprey, tiger tail sea horse, and blue-ringed octopus are among the featured species. . . . The black silhouetted numbers are sinuous and compelling in this unique and imaginative description of the dangers facing ocean life today." SLJ

Includes bibliographical references

Miller, Debbie S.
Survival at 120 above; by Debbie S. Miller; illustrations by Job Van Zyle. Walker & Co. 2012 40 p. col. ill. (hardback) $17.99; (reinforced) $18.89
Grades: 3 4 5 **591.7**
1. Animals 2. Climate 3. Desert animals 4. Adaptation (Biology) 5. Desert animals -- Australia -- Simpson Desert 6. Desert ecology -- Australia -- Simpson Desert 7. Heat adaptation -- Australia -- Simpson Desert
ISBN 0802798136; 9780802798138; 9780802798145
LC 2011021943

Author Deborah S. Miller "records a day in the life of . . . Australia's Simpson Desert . . . as birds, mammals, reptiles, amphibians, insects and plants revel in the glory of water and relative coolness of the world's longest parallel sand dunes. . . . The book introduces young readers to many animals children have likely never seen nor heard of and helps them understand the . . . ways in which animals and other life-forms have adapted to this extreme climate. . . . [P]ronunciation guides are incorporated within the text." (Kirkus Reviews)

Includes bibliographical references

Survival at 40 below; illustrations by Jon Van Zyle. Walker & Co. 2010 un il $17.99; lib bdg $18.89
Grades: 2 3 4 **591.7**
1. Animals -- Arctic regions 2. Natural history -- Alaska
ISBN 978-0-8027-9815-2; 0-8027-9815-2; 978-0-8027-9816-9 lib bdg; 0-8027-9816-0 lib bdg
LC 2009013328

"Miller describes the terrain of Alaska's Gates of the Arctic National Park and explains how the seasonal changes affect a diverse array of animals . . . that live in the area year-round. . . . The text moves smoothly and quickly, offering interesting glimpses of varied hibernation patterns and the physical characteristics enabling some animals to survive winter's deep chill aboveground. . . . Van Zyle's acrylic paintings span the spreads, offering good impressionistic views of varied landscapes and fauna." SLJ

Miller, Sara Swan
Secret lives of burrowing beasts. Marshall Cavendish Benchmark 2010 48p il (Secret lives) lib bdg $29.93
Grades: 3 4 5 6 **591.7**
1. Burrowing animals
ISBN 978-0-7614-4221-9 lib bdg; 0-7614-4221-9 lib bdg

"The bright, sharp color photos . . . enhance, but take second fiddle to Miller's lively, well-knit [narrative]. . . .

[This] volume closes with a generous selection of print and web resources." SLJ

"Describes the life cycles and habits of burrowing mammals, amphibians, reptiles, and birds." Publisher's note
Includes glossary

Secret lives of cave creatures. Marshall Cavendish Benchmark 2010 48p il (Secret lives) lib bdg $29.93
Grades: 3 4 5 6 **591.7**
1. Animals 2. Cave dwellers
ISBN 978-0-7614-4224-0 lib bdg; 0-7614-4224-3 lib bdg

"The bright, sharp color photos . . . enhance, but take second fiddle to Miller's lively, well-knit [narrative]. . . . [This] volume closes with a generous selection of print and web resources." SLJ
Includes glossary

Secret lives of deep-sea creatures. Marshall Cavendish Benchmark 2010 48p il (Secret lives) lib bdg $29.93
Grades: 3 4 5 6 **591.7**
1. Marine animals
ISBN 978-0-7614-4226-4 lib bdg; 0-7614-4226-X lib bdg
LC 2010000376

"The bright, sharp color photos . . . enhance, but take second fiddle to Miller's lively, well-knit [narrative]. . . . [This] volume closes with a generous selection of print and web resources." SLJ
Includes glossary

Secret lives of soil creatures. Marshall Cavendish Benchmark 2010 48p il (Secret lives) lib bdg $29.93
Grades: 3 4 5 6 **591.7**
1. Animals 2. Soil ecology
ISBN 978-0-7614-4229-5 lib bdg; 0-7614-4229-4 lib bdg

"The bright, sharp color photos . . . enhance, but take second fiddle to Miller's lively, well-knit [narrative]. . . . [This] volume closes with a generous selection of print and web resources." SLJ
Includes glossary

Mitton, Tony
Ocean odyssey; [illustrated by] Ant Parker. Kingfisher 2010 un il (Amazing animals) $9.99
Grades: K 1 2 3 **591.7**
1. Marine animals
ISBN 978-0-7534-3006-4; 0-7534-3006-1

"Three animal friends in human garb . . . explore the undersea world to introduce young readers to various animals in [that habitat]. The bouncy rhymed [text] and colorful cartoonlike illustrations, along with being entertaining, offer some surprisingly substantive facts about the creatures." Horn Book Guide

Rainforest romp; [by] Tony Mitton and [illustrated by] Ant Parker. Kingfisher 2009 un il (Amazing animals) $9.99 **591.7**
1. Rain forest animals
ISBN 978-0-7534-6298-0; 0-7534-6298-2

"In bouncy rhymes, Mitton describes animals that live in the rainforest. . . . Parker's vibrant cartoon illustrations show three animal friends, dressed in safari gear, exploring in the rainforest, along with the smiling creatures they encounter." Horn Book Guide

Parker, Steve, 1952-
Animal habitats. QEB Pub. 2010 32p il (QEB changes in . . .) lib bdg $28.50
Grades: 3 4 5 6   **591.7**
1. Habitat (Ecology)
ISBN 978-1-59566-773-1 lib bdg; 1-59566-773-3 lib bdg
    LC 2008-56067
"Outstanding photography and informative summaries uniquely combine to make this text a must have for any elementary school library. . . . Short, succinct paragraphs and marginalia combine to appeal to readers of all ages and literary abilities. The author guides the juvenile reader through a series of environmental concerns such as the preservation of rare and endangered species, sustainability, overpopulation, biodiversity hot spots, conservation techniques, and introduced and invasive species." Sci Books Films
Includes glossary

Stewart, Melissa
Under the snow; written by Melissa Stewart; illustrated by Constance R. Bergum. Peachtree 2009 un il $16.95
Grades: K 1 2 3   **591.7**
1. Snow 2. Winter 3. Animal behavior
ISBN 978-1-56145-493-8; 1-56145-493-1
This describes how animals live under the snow in fields, forests, ponds, and wetlands
This is a "lyrical portrait. . . . Bergum's watercolor illustrations painted in panels suggest the passage of time and include close-up insets of wildlife in various habitats. . . . Many of the facts will wow children . . . and pique interest to read more." Booklist

When rain falls; written by Melissa Stewart; illustrated by Constance R. Bergum. Peachtree 2008 un il $16.95
Grades: PreK K 1 2   **591.7**
1. Rain 2. Animal behavior
ISBN 978-1-56145-438-9; 1-56145-438-9
    LC 2007-31395
"After two children hurry inside to escape the rain, they gaze outdoors and wait for the end of the storm. Stewart elaborates on how various animals react to rain in different habitats: a forest, a field, a wetland, and a desert. The examples are clearly presented and interesting. . . . Bergum's well-rendered watercolors will facilitate group sharing." SLJ

Swinburne, Stephen R.
Ocean soup; tide pool poems. illustrated by Mary Peterson. Charlesbridge 2010 un il lib bdg $16.95
Grades: 1 2 3   **591.7**
1. Marine animals 2. Tide pool ecology 3. Animals -- Poetry
ISBN 978-1-58089-200-1 lib bdg; 1-58089-200-0 lib bdg
    LC 2008026960
"This brightly illustrated, large-format book offers a collection of poems in the voices of tide-pool animals. . . . Each species is presented through first-person verse and a paragraph of information. . . . Clean, curving pencil lines with

digitally added colors portray the animals in child-friendly, cartoon-style pictures." Booklist
Includes glossary and bibliographical references

Turner, Pamela S.
Prowling the seas; exploring the hidden world of ocean predators. Walker & Co. 2009 39p il map $17.99; lib bdg $18.89
Grades: 4 5 6   **591.7**
1. Ocean 2. Marine animals 3. Predatory animals
ISBN 978-0-8027-9748-3; 0-8027-9748-2; 978-0-8027-9749-0 lib bdg; 0-8027-9749-0 lib bdg
"In each chapter, a clearly delineated map makes it easy to follow the animals' routes, and many clear color photos show the animals and the scientists who study them. . . . A clearly written presentation of an unusual topic." Booklist

Webb, Sophie
Far from shore; a naturalist explores the deep ocean. written and illustrated by Sophie Webb. Houghton Mifflin Books for Children 2011 80p il $17.99
Grades: 4 5 6 7   **591.7**
1. Dolphins 2. Water birds 3. Marine animals
ISBN 978-0-618-59729-1; 0-618-59729-8
    LC 2010025121
Webb "returns with another richly detailed journal of her travels as a naturalist, combining scientific information, field guide-like illustrations, and a thorough account of the day-to-day experiments of a field scientist. The setting is a four-month-long research cruise on a National Ocean and Atmospheric Administration ship to study the impact of fishing on two dolphin populations that reside in the Eastern Tropical Pacific." Horn Book
Includes glossary

591.734   Rain forest animals

Lawler, Janet
Rain Forest Colors; Janet Lawler; photographs by Tim Laman. Natl Geographic Soc Childrens books 2014 32 p. color illustrations, color map $16.99
Grades: PreK K 1 2 3   **591.734**
1. Color 2. Animals -- Color 3. Rain forest animals
ISBN 1426317336; 9781426317330
Janet Lawler presents "a color concept book [for children]. It features their favorite animals that illustrate 10 basic colors. Lyrical text is sprinkled with 'Did You Know?' animal facts. The photography is by National Geographic field biologist and wildlife photojournalist Tim Laman." (Publisher's note)
"Stunning animal photos introduce children to 10 basic colors in this latest from National Geographic Kids. From the brilliant blue Ulysses butterfly and yellow orb weaver spider to the scarlet ibis and purple honeycreeper, the colors of these animals are never in doubt, and the photos get readers so close that the scales on the iguana are visible, as are the hairs and bumps on the fiddler crab...Readers will not only practice their colors, they'll get an inkling of what a colorful and wonderful world we live in." Kirkus
Part of the National Geographic Kids series of informational picture books.

591.75   Urban animals

Downer, Ann
Wild animal neighbors; sharing our urban world. Ann Downer. Twenty-First Century Books 2014 64 p. (library binding: alkaline paper) $33.27

Grades: 5 6 7 8   591.75
1. Wildlife 2. Urban ecology 3. Suburban life 4. Urban animals 5. City and town life 6. Human-animal relationships 7. Nature -- Effect of human beings on
ISBN 0761390219; 9780761390213

LC 2012043817

This book, by Ann Downer, explains that "as the human population tops seven billion, animals are running out of space. Their natural habitats are surrounded and sometimes even replaced by highways, shopping centers, office parks, and subdivisions. The result? A wildlife invasion of our urban neighborhoods. What kinds of animals are making cities their new home? How can they survive in our ecosystem of concrete, steel, and glass? And what does their presence there mean for their future and ours?" (Publisher's note)

"Although this book's editorial stance advocates for wild animals in city habitats, it's candid about problems such animals cause humans--from messy raccoons that may carry rabies to potentially dangerous mountain lions in Los Angeles. Accurate information unhampered by a rigid template and supported by good documentation is presented in readable, balanced prose; compelling photographs illustrate the text." (Horn Book)

Includes bibliographical references (page 62) and index

591.754   Desert animals

Pattison, Darcy
Desert baths; by Darcy Pattison; illustrated by Kathleen Rietz. Sylvan Dell Pub. 2012 32 p. (hardcover) $17.95

Grades: K 1 2 3 4   591.754
1. Baths -- Fiction 2. Animal behavior -- Juvenile fiction 3. Desert animals 4. Baths5. Desert animals -- Habitat
ISBN 1607185253; 9781607185253; 9781607185345; 9781607185437; 9781607185529

LC 2012004377

In author Darcy Pattison's book, "all animals bathe to keep their bodies clean and healthy. Humans might use soap and water, but what do animals, especially those living in dry climates, do to keep clean?" This book explores "the desert to find out how snakes, spiders, and birds bathe. This . . . book teaches children about hygiene and how some exciting desert creatures manage to stay clean without the help of soap and water." (Publisher's note)

591.77   Marine animals

Amazing giant sea creatures; swim with the whales, dolphins, and sharks. written by Marie Greenwood; illustrated by Peter Minister. DK Publishing 2014 15 p. color illustrations $19.99

Grades: PreK K 1 2   591.77
1. Marine animals 2. Toy and movable books 3. Lift-the-flap books
ISBN 1465419012; 9781465419019

LC 2014395931

NSTA Outstanding Science Trade Books for Students K-12 (2015)

This preschool reference book "provides an introduction to the biggest creatures found in the ocean, including the lion's mane jellyfish, the great white shark, the sperm whale, and the giant squid." (Publisher's note)

Arnosky, Jim
Shimmer & splash; the sparkling world of sea life. Jim Arnosky. Sterling Children's Books 2013 41 p. col. ill. (hardcover) $14.95

Grades: 2 3 4 5   591.77
1. Picture books for children 2. Marine biology 3. Marine animals
ISBN 1402786239; 9781402786235

LC 2012012863

In this book, author and illustrator Jim Arnosky explores life in the sea. With foldout pages and many life-size illustrations, this overview" touches "on sea life from coral reefs to sailfish, from sea jellies to fiddler crabs, all depicted in a . . . blues and greens with splashes of yellow." The text features "personal experiences as Arnosky wades, kayaks, boats, and fishes in the 'sparkling' world of water." (School Library Journal)

Includes bibliographical references (p. 41).

Hoyt, Erich
★ Weird sea creatures; Erich Hoyt. Firefly Books 2013 63 p. (pbk.) $9.95; (bound) $19.95

Grades: 5 6 7 8 9 10   591.77
1. Marine biology 2. Abyssal zone 3. Deep-sea animals -- Pictorial works
ISBN 9781770851917; 1770851917; 1770851976; 9781770851979

LC 2012554415

This book celebrates "odd and recently discovered [undersea] species. Through 50 . . . photos, readers are introduced to a yeti crab; a spined pigmy shark; Dumbo, the octopod; and many other deep-sea dwellers." The introduction "presents the physical characteristics of the abyssal ocean—its cold darkness, its cruel pressure—and of the difficulties in finding, collecting, and photographing the creatures that call it home." (School Library Journal)

"Eerie, riveting eye candy for budding biologists and casual browsers alike." Kirkus

Johnson, Jinny
Coral reef life; Jinny Johnson. Smart Apple Media 2012 32 p. col. ill., col. map (Watery worlds) (library) $28.50

Grades: 4 5 6   591.77
1. Coral reef ecology 2. Coral reef animals
ISBN 1599205025; 9781599205021

LC 2011012947

This book by Jinny Johnson is part of the "Watery Worlds" series. "In this book, we find out how coral reefs are formed and learn why they are so important. We look at the amazing variety of fish around the reefs and discover why the reefs themselves are in danger." (Publishers note) It "contains a map and a 'facts' page." (Library Media Connection)

Woodward, John

Ocean; an amazing window on our world. written by John Woodward; illustrations by Gary Hanna. DK Pub. 2012 59 p. col. ill. (Look closer) (hardcover) $10.99
Grades: 4 5 6 **591.77**

1. Picture books for children 2. Ocean 3. Marine biology 4. Marine animals

ISBN 0756692377; 9780756692377

LC 2011277622

This book is part of DK Publishing's Look Closer series and allows readers to "explore different perspectives of . . . underwater scenes as they zoom in, zoom out, and go sideways, forward, and backward. . . . Specially commissioned computer-generated imagery" is included. (Publisher's note)

592 Specific taxonomic groups of animals

Cerullo, Mary M.

Sea soup: zooplankton; [by] Mary M. Cerullo; photography by Bill Curtsinger. Tilbury House 2001 39p il $16.95
Grades: 5 6 7 8 **592**

1. Zooplankton

ISBN 0-88448-219-7

LC 00-46721

This book "opens a pellucid window into the drifting world of mostly minute animals that, along with phytoplankton, form an aqueous 'soup' that nourishes a wide variety of sea creatures. . . . Curtsinger's often extraordinary color photos allow readers to envision the often microscopically small creatures delineated in the text. . . . This is a fascinating look at a watery zoo of creatures whose ecological importance is far beyond the measure of their size." SLJ

Includes glossary and bibliographical references

Dixon, Norma

Lowdown on earthworms. Fitzhenry & Whiteside 2005 32p il $16.95
Grades: 3 4 5 **592**

1. Worms

ISBN 1-55041-114-8

"This project-oriented study combines basic facts about worm anatomy and behavior with general instructions for building, maintaining, and performing simple experiments with both a 'plastic-bottle wormery'; and a more ambitious compost bin. A mix of color photos and simple paintings offer cutaways views of worms and their burrows, representations of several types of earthworms, and pictures of finished projects." Booklist

Includes bibliographical references

Parker, Steve, 1952-

Sponges, jellyfish & other simple animals; by Steve Parker. Compass Point Books 2006 p. cm. (Animal kingdom classification)
Grades: 5 6 7 8 **592**

1. Sponges 2. Jellyfishes 3. Invertebrates

ISBN 0-7565-1614-5 (hard cover)

LC 2005029183

"Smoothly written, well-organized... With succinct text and colorful formats, [this] will appeal to students and browsers alike." SLJ

Includes bibliographical references

Pfeffer, Wendy

Wiggling worms at work; illustrated by Steve Jenkins. HarperCollins Publishers 2004 33p il (Let's-read-and-find-out science) $15.99; lib bdg $16.89; pa $4.99
Grades: K 1 2 3 **592**

1. Worms

ISBN 0-06-028448-X; 0-06-028449-8 lib bdg; 0-06-445199-2 pa

"This book is filled with clear explanations. . . . The concluding activities . . . are important because Jenkins's cut-paper illustrations, while lovely, include only a few anatomical details." Horn Book Guide

Trueit, Trudi Strain

Worms. Marshall Cavendish Benchmark 2009 23p il (Benchmark rebus. Creepy critters) lib bdg $22.79
Grades: PreK K 1 **592**

1. Worms

ISBN 978-0-7614-3966-0 lib bdg; 0-7614-3966-8 lib bdg

LC 2008-15997

"Brilliant closeup photos will help beginning readers make meaning and appeal to students who like these creatures. . . . Glossary, print and media resources for further learning, and an about the author section conclude . . . [the] book. Reading specialists will want to be advised about [this book] . . . as will teachers. . . . This . . . is an excellent resource for beginning research projects." Publisher's note

Includes glossary and bibliographical references

593 Miscellaneous marine and seashore invertebrates

Gilpin, Daniel

Starfish, urchins & other echinoderms; by Daniel Gilpin. Compass Point Books 2006 48 p. (Animal kingdom classification)
Grades: 4 5 6 **593**

1. Starfishes 2. Sea urchins 3. Echinodermata

ISBN 0-7565-1611-0 (hard cover)

LC 2005029184

Introduces the physical characteristics, habitat, and types of echinoderms, including starfish, sea urchins, and sea cucumbers.

Includes bibliographical references

593.4 Sponges

Coldiron, Deborah

Sea sponges; by Deborah Coldiron. ABDO Pub. 2008 32p il (Underwater world) lib bdg $24.21
Grades: 2 3 4 **593.4**

1. Sponges

ISBN 978-1-59928-812-3 lib bdg; 1-59928-812-5 lib bdg

LC 2007-17851

"Present[s] basic information about [sea sponges]. . . . Vibrant captioned photos enhance the accessible text." Horn Book Guide

Includes glossary

593.5   Coelenterates

Gray, Susan Heinrichs

Australian spotted jellyfish; [by] Susan H. Gray. Cherry Lake Pub. 2010 32p il map (Animal invaders) $27.07

Grades: 5 6 7 8   **593.5**

1. Jellyfishes 2. Biological invasions

ISBN 978-1-60279-628-7; 1-60279-628-9

LC 2009024168

This offers "an introduction to the problems caused by [the Australian spotted jellyfish], a discussion of its physical characteristics and habits, a history of how it arrived in its new habitat, and an analysis of challenges encountered by those trying to limit its spread. . . . [This] stinging jelly [was] brought by cargo ships to the Gulf of Mexico and some Atlantic coastal waters." Booklist

Includes glossary and bibliographical references

Metz, Lorijo

Discovering jellyfish. PowerKids Press 2011 24p il (Along the shore) lib bdg $21.25

Grades: 3 4 5   **593.5**

1. Jellyfishes

ISBN 978-1-4488-4997-0; 1-4488-4997-7

LC 2011000159

This book about jellyfish "briefly describes the major physical and behavioral characteristics common to all [jellyfish] and one or two distinctive characteristics of about a half dozen species. . . . One or two sharp color photographs of representative species, most of which are close-ups, accompany the text on every page. . . . [This is] well organized and smoothly written in an engaging style." SLJ

Includes glossary

Spilsbury, Louise

Jellyfish. Heinemann Library 2010 24p il (A day in the life. sea animals) lib bdg $22; pa $6.49

Grades: 1 2   **593.5**

1. Jellyfishes

ISBN 978-1-4329-4000-3 lib bdg; 1-4329-4000-7 lib bdg; 978-1-4329-4007-2 pa; 1-4329-4007-4 pa

LC 2010000624

Introduces jellyfish, describing their physical characteristics, feeding habits, senses, and defense mechanisms.

This pairs "well-chosen color photos . . . with one or two sentences of simple commentary for each. . . . [Though this title] includes references to several varieties of the chosen creature, one species in particular is highlighted. . . . [Good choice] for pleasure or purpose reading." SLJ

Includes glossary and bibliographical references

593.6   Anthozoa

Collard, Sneed B.

★ **One** night in the Coral Sea; [by] Sneed B. Collard III; illustrated by Robin Brickmann. Charlesbridge 2005 32p il $15.95; pa $6.95

Grades: 3 4 5   **593.6**

1. Corals 2. Coral reefs and islands

ISBN 1-57091-389-7; 1-57091-390-0 pa

LC 2004-3307

"On a single spring night . . . the coral in the Great Barrier Reef releases millions of eggs into the ocean. . . . Collard explains the unique spawning event and provides some background about coral and the sea creatures that share the reef. . . . Whether or not children understand the specifics of fertilization, they will be captivated by Brickman's realistic, astonishingly detailed colored-paper collages of the brilliant underwater world." Booklist

Includes glossary and bibliographical references

593.9   Echinoderms and hemichordates

Halfmann, Janet

Star of the sea; a day in the life of a starfish. illustrated by Joan Paley. H. Holt 2011 un il $16.99

Grades: K 1 2 3   **593.9**

1. Starfishes

ISBN 978-0-8050-9073-4; 0-8050-9073-8

LC 2010024952

"Simple, elegant text allows readers to follow a female ochre sea star as she comes ashore during high tide, finds and eats mussels, and is herself seized by a gull, escaping with only one ray lost. Accurate information is nicely embedded in the lyrical narration, while rich-hued watercolor collages . . . give both large-scale and close-up views." Horn Book Guide

Includes bibliographical references

Meister, Cari

Sea stars; by Cari Meister. Bullfrog Books 2012 24 p. (hardcover) $25.65

Grades: K 1 2 3   **593.9**

1. Starfishes

ISBN 1620310120; 9781620310120

LC 2012008430

This book, by author Cari Meister, presents a "photo-illustrated nonfiction story for young readers [that] describes the body parts of sea stars and how they are adapted to find food in the ocean. Picture glossaries introduce new vocabulary and simple quizzes and activities [to] help solidify comprehension." (Publisher's note)

Includes bibliographical references (p. 24) and index

Metz, Lorijo

Discovering starfish. PowerKids Press 2011 24p il (Along the shore) lib bdg $21.25

Grades: 3 4 5   **593.9**

1. Starfishes

ISBN 978-1-4488-4996-3; 1-4488-4996-9

LC 2011000152

This book about starfish "briefly describes the major physical and behavioral characteristics common to all [starfish] and one or two distinctive characteristics of about a half dozen species. . . . One or two sharp color photographs of representative species, most of which are closeups, accompany the text on every page. . . . [This is] well organized and smoothly written in an engaging style." SLJ

594 Mollusks and molluscoids

Bodden, Valerie

  Slugs; Valerie Bodden. Creative Education 2013 24 p. col. ill. (library) $25.65

Grades: 1 2 3 4   **594**

  1. Picture books for children 2. Slugs (Mollusks)

  ISBN 1608182339; 9781608182336

                       LC 2011050283

This book is part of the Creepy Creatures series by Valerie Bodden. The series uses "clear white backgrounds to showcase . . . magnified photos, while the simple, educational text is . . . arranged around the page." This entry looks at slugs, discussing "the slimy textures and spotted patterns of this mollusk, which are hermaphroditic and can produce from 20 to 100 eggs each." (Booklist)

Includes bibliographical references and index

Campbell, Sarah C.

  ★ Wolfsnail; a backyard predator. photographs by Sarah C. Campbell and Richard P. Campbell. Boyds Mills Press 2008 32p il $16.95

Grades: PreK K 1 2   **594**

  1. Snails

  ISBN 978-1-59078-554-6; 1-59078-554-1

                       LC 2007-30838

A Geisel Award honor book, 2009

"The tiny wolfsnail eats garden snails and slugs. This dramatic photo-essay . . . shows the predator stalking its prey, . . . eating it, and leaving the empty shell behind. The back matter includes a small photo of the tiny wolfsnail at its true size and lots of fascinating facts about where snails live, how they mate, and more." Booklist

Cerullo, Mary M.

  Giant squid; searching for a sea monster. by Mary M. Cerullo with Clyde F.E. Roper. Capstone Press 2012 48 p. ill. (chiefly col.) (Smithsonian) (library) $26.86; (paperback) $8.95

Grades: 4 5 6   **594**

  1. Giant squids

  ISBN 1429680237; 9781429675413; 9781429680233

                       LC 2011029181

This book "recounts some of the legends and historical clues that led to the giant squid's identification in the 19th century before focusing on Dr. Clyde Roper, a renowned specialist on cephalopods. . . . The text describes how Roper gathered facts by autopsying the carcasses of giant squids and sperm whales (its chief predator), examining other squid species, etc.; it also outlines several expeditions he led in search of a live specimen." (School Library Journal)

Coldiron, Deborah

  Octopuses. ABDO Pub. 2008 32p il (Underwater world) lib bdg $24.21

Grades: 2 3 4   **594**

  1. Octopuses

  ISBN 978-1-59928-815-4 lib bdg; 1-59928-815-X lib bdg

                       LC 2007-14852

This presents "basic information about [the octopus]. . . . Vibrant captioned photos enhance the accessible text." Horn Book Guide

Includes glossary

Gilpin, Daniel

  ★ Snails, shellfish & other mollusks; by Daniel Gilpin. Compass Point Books 2006 48 p. (Animal kingdom classification)

Grades: 4 5 6   **594**

  1. Snails 2. Mollusks 3. Shellfish 4. Snails

  ISBN 0-7565-1613-7 (hard cover)

                       LC 2005029182

"...Smoothly written, well-organized...With succinct texts and colorful formats, [this] will appeal to students and browsers alike." SLJ

Includes bibliographical references

Gray, Susan Heinrichs

  Giant African snail. Cherry Lake Pub. 2009 32p il map (Animal invaders) lib bdg $27.07

Grades: 3 4 5   **594**

  1. Snails 2. Biological invasions

  ISBN 978-1-60279-241-8 lib bdg; 1-60279-241-0 lib bdg

                       LC 2008000803

Looks at the qualities of giant African snails and examines how they became an invasive species in many of the world's tropical and subtropical regions, how they cause problems in their new environments, and the ways that people have attempted to deal with them

"Clear color photographs, most of which are closeups, accompany the [text] on about every other page. . . . [This title provides] report writers with in-depth and up-to-date information on these invaders and the serious problems they cause." SLJ

Includes glossary and bibliographical references

Markle, Sandra

  ★ Octopuses. Lerner Pubs. 2007 39p il (Animal prey) lib bdg $25.26

Grades: 3 4 5   **594**

  1. Octopuses

  ISBN 978-0-8225-6063-0 lib bdg; 0-8225-6063-1 lib bdg

                       LC 2005-36350

"This title about octopuses, both predator and prey, features eye-popping color photographs of the animals on nearly every spread. Markel's lively prose brings readers right into the underwater world with sensory descriptions and details kids can relate to." Booklist

Includes bibliographical references

Metz, Lorijo

  Discovering clams. PowerKids Press 2011 24p il (Along the shore) lib bdg $21.25

Grades: 3 4 5 **594**
1. Clams
ISBN 978-1-4488-4994-9; 1-4488-4994-2
LC 2011000158

This book about clams "briefly describes the major physical and behavioral characteristics common to all [clams] and one or two distinctive characteristics of about a half dozen species. . . . One or two sharp color photographs of representative species, most of which are closeups, accompany the text on every page. . . . [This is] well organized and smoothly written in an engaging style." SLJ

Miller, Sara Swan
Secret lives of seashell dwellers. Marshall Cavendish Benchmark 2010 48p il (Secret lives) lib bdg $29.93
Grades: 3 4 5 6 **594**
1. Mollusks
ISBN 978-0-7614-4228-8 lib bdg; 0-7614-4228-6 lib bdg
LC 2010000377

"The bright, sharp color photos . . . enhance, but take second fiddle to Miller's lively, well-knit [narrative]. . . . [This] volume closes with a generous selection of print and web resources." SLJ
Includes glossary

Newquist, H. P.
Here there be monsters; the legendary kraken and the giant squid. Houghton Mifflin Harcourt 2010 73p il map $18
Grades: 4 5 6 7 **594**
1. Squids
ISBN 978-0-547-07678-2; 0-547-07678-9

"This intriguing book offers a chronological account of giant squids, beginning with sailors' tales about krakens and leading up to the groundbreaking discoveries of the past few decades. . . . The many illustrations, in color when available, include photos, engravings, and maps. . . . An attractive, informative book on an underrepresented topic." Booklist

Owens, L. L.
The **life** cycle of a snail. Child's World 2011 il (Life cycles) $27.07
Grades: K 1 2 3 **594**
1. Snails
ISBN 978-1-60973-191-5; 1-60973-191-3

"The life cycle of a snail is divided as follows: egg, hatchling, and adult. With big, clear full-page photos . . . as well as straightforward text, readers can follow along on the slimy journey from egg to snail. . . . This title features beautiful photos and text simple enough for very young gastropod lovers." Booklist

Rand, Casey
Glass squid and other spectacular squid. Raintree 2011 32p il (Creatures of the deep) lib bdg $29; pa $7.99
Grades: 3 4 5 6 **594**
1. Squids
ISBN 978-1-4109-4194-7 lib bdg; 978-1-4109-4201-2 pa
LC 2010038186

"This informative and colorful series will engage younger children to learn more about the sea and its creatures." Library Media Connection
Includes glossary and bibliographical references

Redmond, Shirley-Raye
Tentacles! tales of the giant squid. illustrated by Bryn Barnard. Random House 2003 44p il (Step into reading) $11.99; pa $3.99
Grades: 1 2 3 **594**
1. Squids
ISBN 0-375-91307-6; 0-375-81307-1 pa
LC 2002-10238

Describes some of the exaggerated stories that have been told about giant squids and also what scientists have learned about their real physical characteristics and behavior

"An excellent choice to introduce early elementary students to nonfiction titles." Booklist

Spilsbury, Louise
Octopus. Heinemann Library 2011 24p il (A day in the life. sea animals) lib bdg $22; pa $6.49
Grades: 1 2 **594**
1. Octopuses
ISBN 978-1-4329-4004-1 lib bdg; 1-4329-4004-X lib bdg; 978-1-4329-4011-9 pa; 1-4329-4011-2 pa
LC 2010000922

This explores how an octopus swims, defends itself, hunts, and sleeps.

This pairs "well-chosen color photos . . . with one or two sentences of simple commentary for each. . . . [Though this title] includes references to several varieties of the chosen creature, one species in particular is highlighted. . . . [Good choice] for pleasure or purpose reading." SLJ
Includes glossary and bibliographical references

Waxman, Laura Hamilton
Let's look at snails. Lerner Publications Company 2010 32p il (Lightning bolt books: Animal close-ups) lib bdg $25.26
Grades: PreK K 1 2 **594**
1. Snails
ISBN 978-0-8225-7899-4 lib bdg; 0-8225-7899-9 lib bdg
LC 2007-29226

Introduces snails, describing their physical characteristics, life cycle, habitat, and predators

"Fresh photography, a creative use of graphics, and a collagelike layout make[s] . . . [this book] eye-catching. . . . [The] book ends with a labeled diagram of the animal, a range map, and a further-reading list that includes print and online resources in a single list, a nice way of validating both types of materials." SLJ
Includes glossary

595.3 Crustaceans

Gilpin, Daniel
Lobsters, crabs & other crustaceans; by Daniel Gilpin. Compass Point Books 2006 48 p. (Animal kingdom classification)

Grades: 4 5 6   **595.3**
1. Crabs 2. Lobsters 3. Crustacea
ISBN 0-7565-1612-9 (hard cover)

LC 2005029180

Introduces the physical characteristics and habitats of crustaceans, from lobsters and shrimps to sow bugs and barnacles.

Includes bibliographical references

Metz, Lorijo

Discovering crabs. PowerKids Press 2011 24p il (Along the shore) lib bdg $21.25
Grades: 3 4 5   **595.3**
1. Crabs
ISBN 978-1-4488-4993-2; 1-4488-4993-4

LC 2011000153

This book about crabs "briefly describes the major physical and behavioral characteristics common to all [crabs] and one or two distinctive characteristics of about a half dozen species. . . . One or two sharp color photographs of representative species, most of which are closeups, accompany the text on every page. . . . [This is] well organized and smoothly written in an engaging style." SLJ

Includes glossary

Sill, Cathryn P.

About crustaceans; a guide for children. written by Cathryn Sill; illustrated by John Sill. Peachtree Publishers 2004 un il $15.95
Grades: K 1 2 3   **595.3**
1. Crustaceans
ISBN 1-56145-301-3

LC 2003-16838

Describes the anatomy, behavior, and habitat of various crustaceans, including the lobster, crab, and shrimp

"Done in bright watercolors, the illustrations give a sense of these creatures' different habitats. . . . This is an excellent example of easy nonfiction, perfect for beginning readers or for sharing aloud with budding naturalists." SLJ

595.4   Chelicerates

Berger, Melvin

Spinning spiders; illustrated by S.D. Schindler. HarperCollins Pubs. 2003 33p il (Let's-read-and-find-out science) hardcover o.p. pa $4.99
Grades: K 1 2 3   **595.4**
1. Spiders
ISBN 0-06-445207-7 pa; 0-06-028696-2

LC 2001-39507

Describes the characteristics of spiders and the methods they use to trap their prey in webs

Written "in a clear, easy-to-read style.". . . Detailed, full-color illustrations, often on spreads, highlight the well-organized text." SLJ

Bishop, Nic

★ **Spiders**. Scholastic Nonfiction 2007 48p il $16.99
Grades: 1 2 3 4   **595.4**
1. Spiders
ISBN 0-439-87756-3; 978-0-439-87756-5

LC 2006-47179

"This photo-rich picture book is packed with astonishing facts about these highly successful predators. . . . General facts are here: the difference between spiders and insects; body parts; . . . how they eat; and more. Each double-page spread includes a dramatic, brilliantly colored close-up of a spider." Booklist

Bodden, Valerie

Ticks; Valerie Bodden. Creative Education 2013 24 p. col. ill. (Creepy creatures) (library) $25.65
Grades: 1 2 3 4   **595.4**
1. Ticks 2. Picture books for children
ISBN 1608182347; 9781608182343

LC 2011050287

This book is part of the Creepy Creatures series. The series uses "clear white backgrounds to showcase . . . magnified photos, while the simple, educational text is . . . arranged around the page." This book "features shots of the parasites feeding, and describes how some ticks balloon to 600 times their weight when bloated with blood." (Booklist)

Includes bibliographical references (p. 24) and index

Bredeson, Carmen

Tarantulas up close; [by] Carmen Bredeson. Enslow Elementary 2008 24p il (Zoom in on animals!) lib bdg $21.26
Grades: 1 2 3   **595.4**
1. Tarantulas
ISBN 978-0-7660-3076-3 lib bdg; 0-7660-3076-8 lib bdg

LC 2007025609

In this introduction to tarantulas, "short, large-print paragraphs describe key body parts . . . and how they function; . . . [the book outlines] hunting techniques, defense mechanisms, diet, and life cycle. Complementing the text is a large, usually full-page, sharp, color close-up of a representative species. . . . The text is well-organized and clearly written. . . . Bredeson's excellent illustrations and lucid text provide valuable insights into the nature of these hairy, and unjustly feared, spiders." SLJ

Camisa, Kathryn

Hairy tarantulas; by Kathryn Camisa. Bearport Pub. 2009 24p il (No backbone!: The world of invertebrates) lib bdg $21.28
Grades: 1 2 3   **595.4**
1. Tarantulas
ISBN 978-1-59716-704-8 lib bdg; 1-59716-704-5 lib bdg

LC 2008-12106

"Spreads include four or five simple sentences, each neatly spaced by a carriage return, facing a vivid, close-up view of the spider in action. Word balloon captions highlight details when needed and smaller photographs on the text pages provide further visual reference." SLJ

Includes glossary and bibliographical references

Ganeri, Anita

Scorpion. Heinemann Library 2011 24p il map (A day in the life: desert animals) $22; pa $6.49

Grades: K 1 2 **595.4**
1. Scorpions
ISBN 978-1-4329-4776-7; 1-4329-4776-1; 978-1-4329-4785-9 pa; 1-4329-4785-0 pa
LC 2010022827
"The engaging full-color photographs are key to [this] well-organized [book]. . . . Basic global maps show where the animal is found, and a diagram called a 'body map' labels its parts. The [text is] appropriate for the age group, and the pictures will draw in youngsters. [An] excellent [purchase] if material is needed on these animals." SLJ
Includes glossary and bibliographical references

Tarantula. Heinemann Library 2011 24p il map (A day in the life. Rain forest animals) lib bdg $22; pa $6.49
Grades: 1 2 **595.4**
1. Tarantulas
ISBN 978-1-4329-4109-3 lib bdg; 1-4329-4109-7 lib bdg; 978-1-4329-4120-8 pa; 1-4329-4120-8 pa
LC 2010000970
This book follows a tarantula through its day as it sleeps, eats, and moves.
"Ganeri presents information clearly and simply in large type, two-sentence comments placed below a bright, sharply reproduced color photograph of the animal in a natural setting. . . . [This is] sufficiently specific to support assignment as well as pleasure reading." SLJ
Includes glossary and bibliographical references

Gonzales, Doreen
Scorpions in the dark. PowerKids Press 2010 24p il (Creatures of the night) lib bdg $21.25; pa $8.05
Grades: 2 3 4 **595.4**
1. Scorpions
ISBN 978-1-4042-8100-4 lib bdg; 1-4042-8100-2 lib bdg; 978-1-4358-3257-2 pa; 1-4358-3257-4 pa
LC 2009-2076
A look at scorpions and their world in the dark.
"Basic details are complemented by eclectic trivia, . . . [and] each volume concludes with a defense of the animal . . . and why it is vital to humans. The layout is attractive, with easy-to-read text and eye-catching photography. Good for reports." SLJ
Includes glossary

Heos, Bridget
Stronger Than Steel; Spider Silk DNA and the Quest for Better Bulletproof Vests, Sutures, and Parachute Rope. Bridget Heos; [illustrated by] Andy Comins. Houghton Mifflin Books for Children 2013 79 p. col. ill. (hardcover) $18.99
Grades: 5 6 7 8 **595.4**
1. Silk 2. Spiders 3. Inventions 4. Scientists 5. Spider webs 6. Nephila maculata 7. Spider webs -- Therapeutic use
ISBN 0547681267; 9780547681269
LC 2012010992
This children's book, by Bridget Heos, illustrated by Andy Comis, is part of the "Scientists in the Field" series. In it "readers enter Randy Lewis' lab where they come face to face with golden orb weaver spiders, and transgenic alfalfa, silkworm silk, and goats, whose milk contains the proteins to spin spider silk--and to weave a nearly indestructible fiber." (Publisher's note)

Lasky, Kathryn
Silk & venom; searching for a dangerous spider. photographs by Christopher G. Knight. Candlewick Press 2011 57p il map
Grades: 4 5 6 7 **595.4**
1. Spiders 2. Biologists 3. Arachnologists 4. College teachers
ISBN 0-7636-4222-3; 978-0-7636-4222-8
LC 2010-41888
This book focuses on the the field work of arachnologist Greta Binford. "Binford's effort to trace the migration of Loxosceles from South American to North America . . . [led] her to field exploration in the Dominican Republic. [Glossary. Index.] Grades four to seven." (Bull Cent Child Books)
"Biology professor Greta Binford studies spiders in an Oregon lab and in the field in the Dominican Republic, where she searches for L. Taino, a Caribbean relative of the venomous brown recluse that might provide clues to how and when the recluse genus arrived in North America. . . . In leisurely, literary prose, Lasky presents the ancient class of arachnids before introducing the scientist and explaining her quest. . . . On most spreads, a full-bleed photograph is opposed by substantial text and one or two smaller pictures." Kirkus

Lunis, Natalie
Deadly black widows; by Natalie Lunis. Bearport Pub. 2009 24p il (No backbone!: The world of invertebrates) lib bdg $21.28
Grades: 1 2 3 **595.4**
1. Spiders
ISBN 978-1-59716-667-6 lib bdg; 1-59716-667-7 lib bdg
LC 2008-1997
A discussion of the black widow spider, the most dangerous kind of spider in the United States
"Spreads include four or five simple sentences, each neatly spaced by a carriage return, facing a vivid, close-up view of the spider in action. Word balloon captions highlight details when needed and smaller photographs on the text pages provide further visual reference." SLJ
Includes glossary and bibliographical references

Markle, Sandra
Black widows; deadly biters. Lerner Publications 2011 48p il (Arachnid world) lib bdg $29.27
Grades: 5 6 7 8 **595.4**
1. Spiders
ISBN 978-0-7613-5038-5; 0-7613-5038-1
This describes how black widows are similar to and different from other arachnids. Close-up photographs and diagrams reveal details about the black widow's body both inside and out. A hands-on activity compares the black widow's web to a human hair.
Markle "presents a mix of common and less-common facts . . . and her commentary accompanies a particularly strong suite of illustrations featuring large, clear, labeled outside and inside views that display body parts. Photos go beyond the standard portraits. . . . First rate." SLJ
Includes glossary and bibliographical references

Crab spiders; phantom hunters. Sandra Markle. Lerner Pub. Company 2012 48 p. col. ill. (Arachnid world)

Grades: 4 5 6 7   **595.4**
1. Spiders 2. Zoology 3. Predatory animals 4.
Arachnids 5. Crab spiders
ISBN 0761350454; 9780761350453

LC 2011020443

This book is part of Sandra Markle's "Arachnid World"
series. "In this book, you will learn how crab spiders are
similar to and different from other arachnids. Close-up photographs and diagrams reveal extraordinary details about the
crab spider's body both inside and out. A hands-on activity
illustrates how a crab spider can quickly ambush a flying
insect. . . . Enter the . . . world of the arachnid family with
award-winning science author Sandra Markle! Too often
lumped together with insects, these fascinating animals have
distinctive characteristics and habits that are all their own."
(Publisher's note)

Includes bibliographical references (p. 44-45) and index

Fishing spiders; water ninjas. Sandra Markle. Lerner Publications Company 2012 48 p. col. ill. (Arachnid
world)
Grades: 4 5 6 7   **595.4**
1. Spiders 2. Aquatic animals 3. Predatory animals 4.
Zoology -- Encyclopedias 5. Arachnids 6. Dolomedes
ISBN 9780761350446

LC 2011020442

This book is part of Sandra Markle's "Arachnid World"
series. "In this book, you will learn how fishing spiders are
similar to and different from other arachnids. Close-up photographs and diagrams reveal extraordinary details about the
fishing spider's body both inside and out. A hands-on activity shows how the fishing spider's hairy coat helps it walk
on water. . . . Enter the . . . world of the arachnid family with
award-winning science author Sandra Markle! Too often
lumped together with insects, these fascinating animals have
distinctive characteristics and habits that are all their own."
(Publisher's note)

Includes bibliographical references and index

Harvestmen; secret operatives. Lerner Publications
2011 48p il (Arachnid world) lib bdg $29.27
Grades: 5 6 7 8   **595.4**
1. Spiders
ISBN 978-0-7613-5042-2; 0-7613-5042-X

LC 2010023491

This describes how harvestmen are similar to and different from other arachnids. Close-up photographs and diagrams reveal details about the harvestmen's bodies, both
inside and out. A hands-on activity reveals how harvestmen walk on long legs using only their sense of touch to
get around.

Markle "presents a mix of common and less-common
facts . . . and her commentary accompanies a particularly
strong suite of illustrations featuring large, clear, labeled
outside and inside views that display body parts. Photos go
beyond the standard portraits. . . . First rate." SLJ

Includes glossary and bibliographical references

Jumping spiders; gold-medal stalkers. by Sandra Markle. Lerner Publications 2012 48 p. col. ill.
Grades: 4 5 6 7   **595.4**
1. Spiders 2. Animal behavior 3. Zoology --

Encyclopedias 4. Arachnids 5. Jumping spiders
ISBN 0761350470; 9780761350477

LC 2011021598

This book is part of Sandra Markle's "Arachnid World"
series. "In this book, you will learn how jumping spiders
are similar to and different from other arachnids. Close-up
photographs and diagrams reveal extraordinary details about
the jumping spider's body both inside and out. A hands-on
activity compares the reader's jumping ability with that of
a jumping spider. . . . Enter the . . . world of the arachnid
family with award-winning science author Sandra Markle!
Too often lumped together with insects, these fascinating
animals have distinctive characteristics and habits that are
all their own." (Publisher's note)

Includes bibliographical references (p. 44-45) and index

Mites; master sneaks. by Sandra Markle. Lerner Publications 2012 48 p. (Arachnid world)
Grades: 4 5 6 7   **595.4**
1. Mites 2. Animals -- Anatomy 3. Arachnids
ISBN 9780761350460

LC 2011021462

In this book, a volume of the Arachnid World series,
readers "will learn how mites are similar to and different
from other arachnids. Close-up photographs, micrographs,
and diagrams reveal . . . details about a mite's body both
inside and out. A hands-on activity shows how quickly a few
mites can multiply into hundreds." (Publisher's note) The
book "discuss[es] . . . [their] physical structure, life cycle,
and characteristic behaviors. . . . In "Mites," [author Sandra]
Markle discusses a variety of these . . . creatures." (Booklist)

Includes bibliographical references and index

Orb weavers; hungry spinners. Lerner Publications
2011 48p il (Arachnid world) lib bdg $29.27
Grades: 5 6 7 8   **595.4**
1. Spiders
ISBN 978-0-7613-5039-2; 0-7613-5039-X

LC 2010023490

This describes how orb weavers are similar to and different from other arachnids. Close-up photographs and diagrams reveal details about the spider's body both inside and
out. And a hands-on activity will give you an idea of how the
orb weaver can detect prey caught in its web.

Markle "presents a mix of common and less-common
facts . . . and her commentary accompanies a particularly
strong suite of illustrations featuring large, clear, labeled
outside and inside views that display body parts. Photos go
beyond the standard portraits. . . . First rate." SLJ

Includes glossary and bibliographical references

Scorpions; armed stingers. Lerner Publications 2011
48p il (Arachnid world) lib bdg $29.27
Grades: 5 6 7 8   **595.4**
1. Scorpions
ISBN 978-0-7613-5037-8; 0-7613-5037-3

LC 2010004275

This describes how scorpions are similar to and different
from other arachnids. Close-up photographs and diagrams
reveal details about the scorpion's body both inside and out.
And a hands-on activity reveals how a scorpion's senses
help it find its prey.

Markle "presents a mix of common and less-common facts . . . and her commentary accompanies a particularly strong suite of illustrations featuring large, clear, labeled outside and inside views that display body parts. Photos go beyond the standard portraits. . . . First rate." SLJ

Includes glossary and bibliographical references

Sneaky, spinning, baby spiders; [by] Sandra Markle. Walker & Company 2008 32p il $16.99; lib bdg $17.89
Grades: 3 4 5   **595.4**
  1. Spiders 2. Animal babies
  ISBN 978-0-8027-9697-4; 0-8027-9697-4; 978-0-8027-9698-1 lib bdg; 0-8027-9698-2 lib bdg
                                              LC 2007-49139
"Markle's intimate style beckons readers into her text and immediately immerses them in the world of spiderlings. . . . The full-color photographs are the work of many photographers and are filled with energy. . . . [Markle] introduces about 14 species (of the 30,000 spiders worldwide), but she does it in such vivid detail and with such respect and appreciation that youngsters will feel connected to these spider moms and their babies." SLJ

Tarantulas; supersized predators. by Sandra Markle. Lerner Publications Company 2012 48 p. (Arachnid world)
Grades: 4 5 6 7   **595.4**
  1. Tarantulas 2. Predatory animals 3. Arachnids 4. Tarantulas
  ISBN 9780761350439
                                              LC 2011020437
In this book, a volume of the Arachnid World series, readers "will learn how tarantulas are similar to and different from other arachnids. Close-up photographs and diagrams reveal extraordinary details about the tarantula's body both inside and out. A hands-on activity illustrates how a tarantula grows bigger and bigger by molting." (Publisher's note) The book "discuss[es] . . . [their] physical structure, life cycle, and characteristic behaviors. . . . "Tarantulas" looks at the lives of these large, hairy spiders and points out that they help control insect populations." (Booklist)

Includes bibliographical references and index

Ticks; dangerous hitchhikers. Lerner Publications 2011 48p il (Arachnid world) lib bdg $29.27
Grades: 4 5 6 7   **595.4**
  1. Ticks
  ISBN 978-0-7613-5041-5; 0-7613-5041-1
                                              LC 2010023484
This book about ticks offers "a clear, conversational text that will draw young people into the zoological facts with gripping, even gruesome examples that are well matched with unsparingly detailed photos. . . . The handsome design, featuring crisply magnified photos, and the approachable text from an experienced writer combine into a strong offering for both personal and classroom reading." Booklist

Includes bibliographical references

Wind scorpions; killer jaws. Sandra Markle. Lerner Publications 2012 48 p. (Arachnid world) (lib. bdg.: alk. paper) $30.60
Grades: 4 5 6 7   **595.4**
  1. Scorpions 2. Animals -- Anatomy 3. Arachnids 4.

Solpugida
  ISBN 0761350489; 9780761350484
                                              LC 2011021599
In this book, a volume of the Arachnid World series, readers "will learn how wind scorpions are similar to and very different from other arachnids. Close-up photographs and diagrams reveal extraordinary details about the wind scorpion's body both inside and out. A hands-on activity demonstrates how wind scorpions are able to pick up prey to eat it." (Publisher's note) The book "discuss[es] . . . [their] physical structure, life cycle, and characteristic behaviors. . . . 'Wind Scorpions' introduces a group of arachnids that use supersize jaws to defend themselves and to attack their prey." (Booklist)

Includes bibliographical references and index

Wolf spiders; mothers on guard. Lerner Publications 2010 48p il (Arachnid world) lib bdg $29.27
Grades: 5 6 7 8   **595.4**
  1. Spiders
  ISBN 978-0-7613-5040-8; 0-7613-5040-3
                                              LC 2010004273
This describes how wolf spider mothers carry their young on their backs and how wolf spiders are similar to and different from other arachnids. Close-up photographs and diagrams reveal details about the spider's body both inside and out. And hands-on activities will let you experience how a wolf spider female keeps her eggs and young safe.

Markle "presents a mix of common and less-common facts . . . and her commentary accompanies a particularly strong suite of illustrations featuring large, clear, labeled outside and inside views that display body parts. Photos go beyond the standard portraits. . . . First rate." SLJ

Includes glossary and bibliographical references

Montgomery, Sy
  ★ The **tarantula** scientist. Houghton Mifflin Co. 2004 80p il map (Scientists in the field) $18; pa $7.95
Grades: 4 5 6 7   **595.4**
  1. Tarantulas
  ISBN 0-618-14799-3; 0-618-91577-X pa
                                              LC 2003-20125
Describes the research that Samuel Marshall and his students are doing on tarantulas, including the largest spider on earth, the Goliath birdeating tarantula

"Enthusiasm for the subject and respect for both Marshall and his eight-legged subjects come through on every page of the clear, informative, and even occasionally humorous text. Bishop's full-color photos . . . are amazing." Booklist

Includes glossary and bibliographical references

Murawski, Darlyne
  Spiders and their webs; [by] Darlyne A. Murawski. National Geographic 2004 31p il $16.95
Grades: 2 3 4 5   **595.4**
  1. Spiders
  ISBN 0-7922-6979-9
                                              LC 2004-397
This describes nine species of spiders and how they make and use webs

"Even fainthearted arachnophobes will appreciate this gallery of spider profiles featuring full-color, telephoto views. . . . Murawski writes about her subjects with an awe and a reverence that will encourage reluctant children to move beyond spiders' creepy reputation to their fascinating features." Booklist

Includes bibliographical references

Otfinoski, Steven

Scorpions. Marshall Cavendish Benchmark 2011 il (Animals, animals) lib bdg $20.95

Grades: 3 4 5   595.4

1. Scorpions

ISBN 978-0-7614-4878-5; 0-7614-4878-0

LC 2010016035

Provides information on the anatomy, special skills, habitats, and diet of scorpions.

This offers "comprehensive text and striking, well-chosen photos. . . . [This is] packed with engaging facts and trivia, as well as an upbeat tone." Booklist

Includes glossary and bibliographical references

Schnell, Lisa Kahn

High tide for horseshoe crabs; Lisa Kahn Schnell; illustrated by Alan Marks. Charlesbridge 2015 40 p. (reinforced for library use) $16.95

Grades: PreK K 1 2   595.4

1. Coastal ecology 2. Horseshoe crabs 3. Animal migration 4. Limulus polyphemus

ISBN 1580896049; 9781580896047

LC 2013049024

This children's picture book, by Lisa Kahn Schnell and illustrated by Alan Marks, "describes the annual spawning of horseshoe crabs at Delaware Bay. . . . The crabs gathering on the beach to mate and lay their eggs in the sand, migratory birds arriving to feast on the eggs that haven't been buried deeply enough, scientists and volunteers coming to watch, and the baby crabs eventually hatching and making their way to the sea." (School Library Journal)

Simon, Seymour

★ Spiders; [by] Seymour Simon. updated ed.; Smithsonian 2008 31p il $16.99; pa $6.99

Grades: 3 4 5 6   595.4

1. Spiders

ISBN 978-0-06-089104-6; 0-06-089104-1; 978-0-06-089103-9 pa; 0-06-089103-3 pa

First published 2003 by HarperCollins

An introduction to the physical characteristics, behavior, and life cycle of different kinds of spiders.

"The fantastic color photos of the original edition are all here, as is Simon's crisp, informative text. . . . An attention grabber." SLJ

Wadsworth, Ginger

Up, up, and away; illustrated by Patricia J. Wynne. Charlesbridge 2009 un il lib bdg $16.95

Grades: PreK K 1 2   595.4

1. Spiders

ISBN 1-58089-221-3 lib bdg; 978-1-58089-221-6 lib bdg

LC 2008040752

This traces the life cycle of a garden spider

"Simply told with well-chosen words and phrases, the story reads aloud well. . . . Wynne uses watercolor, gouache, and colored pencil to add hue and shading to the precise ink

drawings that define the spiders and their surroundings." Booklist

595.46 Scorpions

Pringle, Laurence

Scorpions! strange and wonderful. by Laurence Pringle and illustrated by Meryl Henderson. Boyds Mills Press 2013 32 p. (Strange and wonderful) $16.95

Grades: 3 4 5   595.46

1. Scorpions

ISBN 1590784731; 9781590784730

LC 2013931088

This book, by Laurence Pringle and illustrated by Meryl Henderson, describes scorpions' "life cycle, body structure, habits, and habitat [through] realistic illustrations." (Publisher's note) "Besides briefly discussing the fossil evidence of early scorpions and the place of scorpions in ancient Greek, Mayan, and Egyptian cultures, Pringle introduces a wide variety of scorpions living around the world today." (Booklist)

595.6 Myriapods

Elkin, Matthew

20 fun facts about centipedes; by Matthew Elkin. Gareth Stevens Pub. 2013 32 p. col. ill. (Fun fact file: bugs!) (library) $25.25; (paperback) $10.50

Grades: 3 4 5   595.6

1. Centipedes 2. Centipedes -- Miscellanea

ISBN 1433982307; 9781433982309; 9781433982316

LC 2012021903

This book by Matthew Elkin is part of a series " that presents a basic bulleted list of facts [with] a few sentences of information, engaging captions, and bright photographs. The basics are covered, including anatomy, eating habits, and offspring. 'Centipedes' uncovers info on the arthropods (and uncovers is the right word, as they commonly hide in cool, dark places like under rocks and, yes, in your bathroom)." (Publisher's note)

Includes bibliographical references and index.

Povey, Karen D.

Centipede; [by] Karen Povey. KidHaven Press 2004 32p il (Bugs) $22.45

Grades: 3 4 5   595.6

1. Centipedes

ISBN 0-7377-1766-1

LC 2003-15274

Describes the physical characteristics, behavior, and habitat of centipedes.

595.7 Insects

Albee, Sarah

Bugged; How Insects Changed History. by Sarah Albee. Bloomsbury/Walker 2014 176 p. illustrations (some color) (pbk.) $17.99; (library edition) $23.89

Grades: 4 5 6 7   595.7

1. Insects 2. Human-animal relationship 3. Insects --

History 4. Human-animal relationships -- History
ISBN 0802734227; 0802734235; 9780802734228; 9780802734235

LC 2013025968

This book, by Sarah Albee, illustrated by Robert Leighton, focuses on the impact of insects on the world throughout history. According to the book, "beneficial bugs have built empires. Bad bugs have toppled them." The book is a "combination of world history, social history, natural science, epidemiology, public health, conservation, and microbiology." (Publisher's note)

"The shock value alone makes this worth the cover price, but once kids are pulled in, they will learn more than they bargained for about the impact of insects on human history... Overall, this title is astonishing, disgusting, revolting, and ultimately fascinating, making it perfect for emerging entomologists, budding historians, reluctant readers, and grossout junkies alike." SLJ

How insects have changed human history

Anderson, Margaret Jean
  Bugged-out insects; [by] Margaret J. Anderson. Enslow Publishers 2011 48p il (Bizarre science) lib bdg $23.93
  Grades: 4 5 6 7 **595.7**
    1. Insects
    ISBN 978-0-7660-3674-1; 0-7660-3674-X

LC 2010006474

First published 1996 with title: Bizarre insects

This describes insects such as cicadas, butterflies, praying mantises, walkingsticks, beetles, stinkbugs, botflies, mayflies, mosquitoes, bees, ants, and locusts.

"Aimed at reluctant readers, [this title is] sure to disgust and delight in equal measure.... [The title] will pique interest and get kids lining up at the reference desk looking for more. The text is complemented by illustrations and magnified photos of things that you would hope never to see." SLJ

Includes glossary and bibliographical references

Aronin, Miriam
  ★ The **ant's** nest; a huge, underground city. Bearport Pub. 2009 32p il (Spectacular animal towns) lib bdg $18.95
  Grades: 2 3 4 **595.7**
    1. Ants
    ISBN 978-1-59716-868-7 lib bdg; 1-59716-868-8 lib bdg

LC 2009-03065

"Through excellent photographs, high-interest texts, sidebars, maps, and other material, children learn about both the animals and their habitats. The . . . book also provides brief profiles of animals with similar habitats.... [This book is] much better than average 'report' titles." SLJ

Includes glossary and bibliographical references

Baker, Nick
  Bug zoo. DK 2010 64p il $12.99
  Grades: 2 3 4 **595.7**
    1. Insects 2. Collectors and collecting
    ISBN 978-0-7566-6166-3; 0-7566-6166-8

LC 2010-279437

Naturalist Nick Baker shows the reader how to make miniature habitats for insects, snails and worms, some interesting aspects of their lives and how to feed the contained creatures

"This is a colorful, informative, and engaging book about keeping insects-if not as pets, then as creatures worthy of intense study. . . . Baker's enthusiasm for the subject is evident throughout. Because it provides interesting facts about insects as well as how-to tips, this title will find an audience with curious readers and would-be zookeepers alike. It may even intrigue avowed entomophobes." SLJ

Beccaloni, George
  Biggest bugs life-size. Firefly Books 2010 84p il $19.95
  Grades: 4 5 6 7 **595.7**
    1. Insects
    ISBN 978-1-55407-699-4; 1-55407-699-4

"This book presents 35 of the world's biggest, longest, and heaviest bugs. . . . Double-page spreads feature each bug's statistics, a map with its area of distribution, and straightforward text that explains its living conditions, eating habits, and life cycle. . . . The highlights, of course, are the numerous life-size and up-close full-color photographs of the bugs. . . . The visual appeal alone will entice even the most reluctant readers." Booklist

Berger, Melvin
  Chirping crickets; illustrated by Megan Lloyd. HarperCollins Pubs. 1998 32p il (Let's-read-and-find-out science) lib bdg $15.89; pa $4.95
  Grades: K 1 2 3 **595.7**
    1. Crickets
    ISBN 0-06-024962-5 lib bdg; 0-06-445180-1 pa

LC 96-51661

Describes the physical characteristics, behavior, and life cycle of crickets while giving particular emphasis to how they chirp

"Clear and detailed, the ink-and-watercolor artwork is often visually striking as well as educationally sound. . . . A well-rounded introduction." Booklist

Bishop, Nic
  Butterflies; written and photographed by Nic Bishop. Scholastic Inc. 2011 31p il (Scholastic reader) pa $3.99
  Grades: 1 2 **595.7**
    1. Butterflies
    ISBN 978-0-545-28434-9 pa; 0-545-28434-1 pa

"For the first- to third-grade set, butterflies are an endless source of fascination, especially when looked at VERY close up. With breathtaking full-page images and simple, engaging text, Nic introduces young readers to the beauty and diversity of these amazing insects." Publisher's Note

  ★ **Nic** Bishop butterflies and moths. Scholastic Nonfiction 2009 48p il $17.99
  Grades: 2 3 4 **595.7**
    1. Butterflies
    ISBN 978-0-439-87757-2; 0-439-87757-1

LC 2008-15290

"The text covers the all-important topic of metamorphosis, of course, but also discusses feeding and predation, migration, and reproduction. . . . The real draw here, though, is the art; even for Bishop, the photographs are breathtaking. . . Kids will be drawn to this like Bishop's subject to flame." Bull Cent Child Books

Blobaum, Cindy

Insectigation! 40 hands-on activities to explore the insect world. [by] Cindy Blobaum. Chicago Review Press 2005 133p il pa $12.95

Grades: 3 4 5 6   **595.7**

1. Insects

ISBN 1-55652-568-0

"Raising mealworms, testing the visual acuity of bees, setting up a watering hole for butterflies—these are just a few of the 40 activities included in this earnest introduction to entomology. Each of eight chapters focuses on a different topic, such as physical and behavioral characteristics; metamorphosis; communication; methods to attract, collect and keep insects, etc. . . . Clear line drawings, diagrams of body parts and project materials, plus the occasional black-and-white photograph are found on almost every page. . . . The text is clearly written and well organized." SLJ

Includes bibliographical references

Bodden, Valerie

Cockroaches; Valerie Bodden. 1st ed. Creative Education 2013 24 p. col. ill. (Creepy creatures) (library) $25.65

Grades: 1 2 3 4   **595.7**

1. Cockroaches 2. Picture books for children

ISBN 1608182320; 9781608182329

LC 2011050277

This book is part of the Creepy Creatures series. The series uses "clear white backgrounds to showcase . . . magnified photos, while the simple, educational text is . . . arranged around the page." This book looks at "the 4,000 varieties of roach and [details] how they can hold their breath to crawl up drains into bathtubs." (Booklist)

Includes bibliographical references and index

Termites; Valerie Bodden. 1st ed. Creative Education 2013 24 p. col. ill. (Creepy creatures) (library) $25.65

Grades: 1 2 3 4   **595.7**

1. Picture books for children 2. Termites

ISBN 1608182355; 9781608182350

LC 2011050279

This children's picture book, part of the Creepy Creatures Series by Valerie Bodden, looks at termites. "Throughout most of each title, a page of large-print text, set on a plain white background, alternates with a full-page, extreme close-up photo of one or more of the featured animals. . . . Each book succinctly outlines the animals' basic structure, key body parts, distinctive characteristics of particular species, behavior, habitats, diet, natural enemies, and life cycle." (School Library Journal)

Includes bibliographical references and index

Bulion, Leslie

Hey there, stink bug! illustrated by Leslie Evans. Charlesbridge 2006 45p il lib bdg $12.95

Grades: 3 4 5 6   **595.7**

1. Insects

ISBN 9781580893046 lib bdg; 1-58089-304-X lib bdg

LC 2005-19627

This book "describes various types of insects using different poetic forms." (Publisher's note) "Grades four to seven." (Bull Cent Child Books)

"Bulion uses gory, visceral facts to pull children into both the science and the various poetic forms. . . . Striking, watercolor-washed linoleum prints and notes about poetic forms round out this title." Booklist

Catt, Thessaly

Migrating with the monarch butterfly. PowerKids Press 2011 24p il (Animal journeys) lib bdg $21.25; pa $8.25

Grades: 2 3 4   **595.7**

1. Butterflies -- Migration

ISBN 978-1-4488-2546-2 lib bdg; 978-1-4488-2676-6 pa

LC 2010030647

This describes the yearly migration of the monarch butterfly, which can travel between 50 to 100 miles a day.

Dickmann, Nancy

A **bee's** life. Heinemann Library 2010 24p il (Watch it grow) lib bdg $21.50; pa $5.99

Grades: PreK K 1   **595.7**

1. Bees

ISBN 978-1-4329-4137-6 lib bdg; 1-4329-4137-2 lib bdg; 978-1-4329-4146-8 pa; 1-4329-4146-1 pa

LC 2009-49151

"Practically unique among early introductions to life cycles because death is mentioned . . . this . . . follows [a bee] . . . from egg . . . to maturity with a set of close-up color photographs, one per page, paired to large-type, one or two-sentence captions. . . . Offers nourishing fare for young naturalists." SLJ

Includes glossary

A **butterfly's** life. Heinemann Library 2010 24p il (Watch it grow) lib bdg $21.50; pa $5.99

Grades: PreK K 1   **595.7**

1. Butterflies

ISBN 978-1-4329-4138-3 lib bdg; 1-4329-4138-0 lib bdg; 978-1-4329-4147-5 pa; 1-4329-4147-X pa

LC 2009-49152

"Practically unique among early introductions to life cycles because death is mentioned . . . this . . . follows [a butterfly] . . . from egg . . . to maturity with a set of close-up color photographs, one per page, paired to large-type, one or two-sentence captions. . . . Offers nourishing fare for young naturalists." SLJ

Dixon, Norma

Focus on flies. Fitzhenry & Whiteside 2008 32p il $18.95

Grades: 4 5 6 7   **595.7**

1. Flies

ISBN 978-1-55005-128-5; 1-55005-128-8

This "chatty, informative title, illustrated with many clear color photos and diagrams, will hook readers with its fascinating view of a fly's 'creepy cool world.' . . . The gross details will appeal to middle-grade readers, who will then go on to learn about anatomy, metamorphosis, adaptation, diversity, classification, and flies' roles in plant pollination." Booklist

Includes bibliographical references

Dorros, Arthur

Ant cities; written and illustrated by Arthur Dorros. Crowell 1987 28p il (Let's-read-and-find-out science book) hardcover o.p. lib bdg $11.89; pa $5.99

Grades: K 1 2 3   595.7

1. Ants

ISBN 0-690-04568-9; 0-690-04570-0 lib bdg; 0-06-445079-1 pa

LC 85-48244

"Using harvester ants as a basic example, Dorros shows how the insects build tunnels with rooms for different functions and how workers, queens, and males have distinct roles in the ant hill. Along the way, she works in details of food and reproduction, ending with descriptions of other kinds of ants and suggestions for ways to observe them (including instructions for making an ant farm). The text is simple without becoming choppy, the full-color illustrations are inviting as well as informative." Bull Cent Child Books

Glaser, Linda

Dazzling dragonflies; a life cycle story. illustrated by Mia Posada. Millbrook Press 2008 un il (Linda Glaser's classic creatures) lib bdg $22.60

Grades: K 1 2 3   595.7

1. Dragonflies

ISBN 0-8225-6753-9 lib bdg; 978-0-8225-6753-0 lib bdg

LC 2007-21886

This book shows how a dragonfly nymph grows, sheds its skin and then flies. "Ages five to nine." (Publisher's note)

"Clearly written text and bright-hued watercolor collage illustrations introduce the life cycle of that zip-a-dipping aerialist, the dragonfly, from newly laid eggs, through months of aquatic life as a nymph, to the final metamorphosis into a glitter-winged creature. . . . [This] is basic, attractive, and easy to read." SLJ

Not a buzz to be found; insects in winter. illustrations by Jaime Zollars. Millbrook Press 2011 31p il lib bdg $25.26

Grades: K 1 2 3   595.7

1. Winter 2. Insects

ISBN 978-0-7613-5644-8; 0-7613-5644-4

LC 2011001148

"This look at how insects survive the cold may have young naturalists scouring the winter landscape to find them for themselves. From those who migrate or hibernate to ones that hide or are still eggs, Glaser has assembled a wide variety of 12 of the more common insects, including ants, ladybugs, dragonflies, honeybees, monarchs, praying mantises and black swallowtail butterflies. Short verses present readers with how each gets through the winter. . . . Gorgeous full-bleed illustrations filled with color and detail depict the insects in winter." Kirkus

Gonzales, Doreen

Crickets in the dark. PowerKids Press 2010 24p il (Creatures of the night) lib bdg $21.25; pa $8.05

Grades: 2 3 4   595.7

1. Crickets

ISBN 978-1-4042-8098-4 lib bdg; 1-4042-8098-7 lib bdg; 978-1-4358-3253-4 pa; 1-4358-3253-1 pa

LC 2009-483

A look at crickets and their world in the dark.

"Basic details are complemented by eclectic trivia, . . . [and] each volume concludes with a defense of the animal . . . and why it is vital to humans. The layout is attractive, with easy-to-read text and eye-catching photography. Good for reports." SLJ

Includes glossary

Gray, Susan Heinrichs

Emerald ash borer; by Susan H. Gray. Cherry Lake Pub. 2008 32p il map (Animal invaders) lib bdg $27.07

Grades: 3 4 5 6   595.7

1. Emerald ash borer 2. Biological invasions

ISBN 978-1-60279-112-1 lib bdg; 1-60279-112-0 lib bdg

LC 2007-34973

This describes the Emerald ash borers' "outstanding physical and behavioral characteristics at each stage in their life cycle, diet, and natural habitat, and then [explains] how they were introduced into areas outside their natural range . . . and the nature and extent of the ecological damage they have caused, and various attempts to eradicate or at least control the animals. . . . Larvae of the emerald ash borer have infested and destroyed thousands of valuable ash trees in the Midwest. . . . Clear color photographs . . . accompany the texts on about every other page. . . . [This title is] clearly written and well organized, and [has] up-to-date information." SLJ

Includes glossary

The life cycle of insects; [by] Susan H. Gray. Heinemann Library 2011 48p il (Life cycles) lib bdg $35; pa $8.95

Grades: 3 4 5   595.7

1. Insects

ISBN 978-1-4329-4983-9 lib bdg; 978-1-4329-4990-7 pa

LC 2010038508

This describes what an incsect is, types of insects, their life cycles, habitats, foods, defenses, and relationships to humans.

Includes glossary and bibliographical references

Hamilton, Sue L.

Swarmed by bees; [by] Sue Hamilton. ABDO Pub. Co. 2010 32p il (Close encounters of the wild kind) lib bdg $27.07

Grades: 4 5 6 7   595.7

1. Bees 2. Animal attacks

ISBN 978-1-60453-933-2 lib bdg; 1-60453-933-X lib bdg

LC 2009-45598

Readers learn of actual human-bee encounters, information about bees, survival strategies, and attack statistics.

"Students will be drawn to the realistic full-color photographs, the realistic diagrams of the creatures' bodies, the real-life stories told by victims, and the interesting, attractive formatting that includes text, diagrams, photographs, and graphics on each page. . . . [This is] exciting and attractive in a 'gross' sort of way and will appeal particularly to boys for both leisure reading and research." Libr Media Connect

Includes glossary

Hansen, Amy S.

Bugs and bugsicles; insects in the winter. [by] Amy S. Hansen; illustrations by Robert C. Kray. Boyds Mills Press 2010 32p il

Grades: 3 4 5   595.7

1. Winter 2. Insects

ISBN 1590782690; 9781590782699

"This colorful book describes what happens in winter to seven different insects: a praying mantis, a field cricket, a ladybug, a honeybee, a pavement ant, a monarch butterfly, and an Arctic woolly bear caterpillar. . . . The title concludes with an author's note and two science activities related to freezing water. A typical double-page spread includes a few paragraphs of text accompanied by large-scale illustrations." Booklist

Includes glossary and bibliographical references

Himmelman, John, 1959-

Noisy bug sing-along; by John Himmelman. 1st ed. Dawn Publications 2013 32 p. (hardcover) $16.95; (paperback) $8.95

Grades: 2 3 4   595.7

1. Picture books for children 2. Insects 3. Insect sounds

ISBN 1584691913; 9781584691914; 9781584691921

LC 2012024253

This children's picture book looks at the noises made by bugs. "The opening page tells readers that bugs sing day and night, loudly and softly, and that they should sing along. . . . Each double-page spread is devoted to one insect and its sound, a sentence telling the name of the creature and what it does, followed by the sound the bug makes—in a huge display type that spreads across and fills the pages." (Kirkus)

Johnson, Jinny

Butterfly; illustrations by Michael Woods. Smart Apple Media 2010 32p il (How does it grow?) lib bdg $28.50

Grades: 1 2 3   595.7

1. Butterflies

ISBN 978-1-59920-352-2 lib bdg; 1-59920-352-9 lib bdg

LC 2009-3397

Introduces children to the lifecycle of a butterfly

"Each stage is described on a spread that features clearly written, oversized text and a caption opposite a full-page, realistic watercolor, or, occasionally, a photograph. . . . A worthwhile purchase." SLJ

Includes glossary

Insects and creepy-crawlies; Jinny Johnson. Kingfisher 2011 32 p.

Grades: 3 4 5   595.7

1. Animal behavior 2. Insects -- Pictorial works

ISBN 0753465922; 9780753465929

In this book, "readers get an up-close view of life in a wide variety of insect colonies through six illustrated story scenes that each examine a key aspect of entomological study-from insect homes, to reproduction, life in the water, hunting and gathering, and insects that fly. Once readers absorb the key elements of the story, they explore the science through photos and fact boxes on the following page." (Publisher's note) This book is "[p]art of [Kingfisher/Macmillan Children's Books]'s 'Explorer' series." (Children's Lit)

Simon & Schuster children's guide to insects and spiders. Simon & Schuster Bks. for Young Readers 1996 80p il $19.95

Grades: 4 5 6 7   595.7

1. Insects 2. Spiders

ISBN 0-689-81163-2

LC 96-27600

Provides an introduction to more than 100 insects and arachnids, giving general information about family characteristics and habits, and more specific facts about some species

"Crisp and well-designed, this is an inviting visual introduction to insects and arachnids." Booklist

Includes glossary

Knudsen, Shannon

From egg to butterfly. Lerner Publs. 2003 24p il (Start to finish) lib bdg $18.60

Grades: K 1 2   595.7

1. Butterflies

ISBN 0-8225-0713-7

LC 2001-4652

Follows the development of a butterfly from the egg its mother lays on a plant to the fully developed insect that flies away

"Readers will be transfixed by the incredibly crisp and clear photographs accompanying the text. This up-close and intimate look at the life stages of a monarch butterfly will be an asset to any young entomologist's library." Sci Teach

Koontz, Robin Michal

What's the difference between a butterfly and a moth? by Robin Koontz; illustrated by Bandelin-Dacey. Picture Window Books 2010 24p il (What's the difference) lib bdg $25.32

Grades: K 1 2   595.7

1. Moths 2. Butterflies

ISBN 978-1-4048-5543-4 lib bdg; 1-4048-5543-2 lib bdg

LC 2009-6884

"Compares and contrasts the habitats, physical characteristics, location, and lifestyles of [butterflies and moths]. The picture-book format is used to great effect as it allows the two animals to be compared side by side on each spread. The bold, expressive watercolors provide the same visual impact as photographs. . . . Short sentences and highlighted fun facts make this a . . . [book] with broad appeal for both researchers and browsers." SLJ

Includes glossary

Latimer, Jonathan P.

Caterpillars; [by] Jonathan P. Latimer, Karen Stray Nolting; illustrations by Amy Bartlett Wright; foreword by Virginia Marie Peterson. Houghton Mifflin 2000 48p il (Peterson field guides for young naturalists) pbk. $5.95

Grades: 4 5 6 7   595.7

1. Caterpillars

ISBN 9780395979457

LC 99-38944

Describes the physical characteristics, behavior, and habitat of a variety of caterpillars, arranged by the categories "Smooth," "Bumpy," "Sluglike," "Horned," "Hairy," "Bristly," and "Spiny"

Lawrence, Ellen

A **dragonfly's** life; by Ellen Lawrence. Bearport Pub. 2013 24 p. (Animal diaries: life cycles) (library binding) $23.93

Grades: 1 2 3 4   **595.7**

1. Dragonflies -- Life cycles

ISBN 1617725943; 9781617725944

LC 2012019344

This book seeks to "help children understand the amazing life cycle of dragonflies. Each page showcases stunning photographs of dragonflies from egg to adult. . . . The primary text of the book is presented as a child's diary. The diary entries are presented as though they were constructed by a young boy, Joseph, over the course of a summer when he and his grandfather observed and learned about dragonflies." (SB&F: Your Guide to Science Resources for All Ages)

"Through the eyes of a child who shares observations of animal life in ongoing journal entries, Lawrence keeps readers thoroughly engaged as they process a generous amount of information pertaining to the natural world...Memorable photos and a thoughtful narrative are perfectly organized to maximize comprehension in these outstanding titles." (School Library Journal)

Includes bibliographical references (p. 24) and index

Lockwood, Sophie

Ants; by Sophie Lockwood. Child's World 2008 40p il map (World of insects) lib bdg $29.93

Grades: 4 5 6   **595.7**

1. Ants

ISBN 978-1-59296-817-6 lib bdg; 1-59296-817-1 lib bdg

LC 2006103452

This describes ants' "basic anatomy, outstanding physical and behavioral characteristics, [diet, life cycle], roles in myths and legends, and effects on humans. . . . With [its] well-organized, succinct [text] and excellent photography, [this] solid [introduction] will be [a] valuable [resource]." SLJ

Includes glossary and bibliographical references

Dragonflies; by Sophie Lockwood. Child's World 2008 40p il map (World of insects) lib bdg $29.93

Grades: 4 5 6   **595.7**

1. Dragonflies

ISBN 978-1-59296-821-3 lib bdg; 1-59296-821-X lib bdg

LC 2006103454

This describes dragonflies' "basic anatomy, outstanding physical and behavioral characteristics, [diet, life cycle], roles in myths and legends, and effects on humans. . . . With [its] well-organized, succinct [text] and excellent photography, [this] solid [introduction] will be [a] valuable [resource]." SLJ

Includes glossary and bibliographical references

Flies; by Sophie Lockwood. Child's World 2008 40p il (World of insects) lib bdg $29.93

Grades: 4 5 6   **595.7**

1. Flies

ISBN 978-1-59296-822-0 lib bdg; 1-59296-822-8 lib bdg

LC 2007000182

This describes flies' "basic anatomy, outstanding physical and behavioral characteristics, [diet, life cycle], roles in myths and legends, and effects on humans. . . . With [its] well-organized, succinct [text] and excellent photography, [this] solid [introduction] will [a] be valuable [resource]." SLJ

Includes glossary and bibliographical references

Maley, Adrienne Houk

20 fun facts about praying mantises; by Adrienne Houk Maley. 1st ed. Gareth Stevens Pub. 2013 32 p. col. ill. (library) $25.25; (paperback) $10.50

Grades: 3 4 5   **595.7**

1. Praying mantis 2. Mantodea

ISBN 1433982404; 9781433982408; 9781433982415

LC 2012031287

This book by Adrienne Houk Maley focuses on praying mantieses and states that "female praying mantises sometimes eat the head of their mate, and then offers possible reasons for this behavior. Other entries briefly describe: key body parts, senses, defense mechanisms, hunting and/or feeding methods, diets, life cycles, etc. Captions, mounted on yellow backgrounds mimicking sticky notes, provide additional information." (Publisher's note)

Includes bibliographical references (page 31) and index.

Markle, Sandra

Hornets; incredible insect architects. by Sandra Markle. Lerner Publications Company 2008 48p il (Insect world) lib bdg $27.93

Grades: 2 3 4 5   **595.7**

1. Hornets and yellowjackets

ISBN 978-0-8225-7297-8 lib bdg; 0-8225-7297-4 lib bdg

LC 2007022290

This describes the anatomy, life cycle, and behavior of hornets

This "will please report writers, budding entomologists, and anyone who expects children's nonfiction to be as carefully documented as adult nonfiction. . . . The [book is] notable for the sharp photos placed precisely to enhance understanding. . . . The main [text is] clear and [flows] well." SLJ

Includes glossary and bibliographical references

Insects; biggest! littlest! photographs by Simon Pollard. Boyds Mills Press 2009 32p il $16.95

Grades: 2 3 4 5   **595.7**

1. Size 2. Insects

ISBN 978-1-59078-512-6; 1-59078-512-6

LC 2008-33524

"This simply written introduction examines insects from the perspective of size. Employing over a dozen kinds as examples, Markle explains why those that are unusually large, small, or equipped with extraordinary body parts have an edge over predators or competing species. . . . An amazingly detailed, closeup color photograph of one or more of the insects discussed complements the text on almost every page. . . . Well organized and clearly written in an engaging style." SLJ

Includes glossary and bibliographical references

Luna moths; masters of change. by Sandra Markle. Lerner Publications Co. 2008 48p il (Insect world) lib bdg $27.93

Grades: 2 3 4 5   **595.7**
1. Moths
ISBN 978-0-8225-7302-9 lib bdg; 0-8225-7302-4
lib bdg
LC 2007025260
This describes the anatomy, life cycle, and behavior of
luna moths

This "will please report writers, budding entomologists,
and anyone who expects children's nonfiction to be as carefully documented as adult nonfiction. . . . The [book is] notable for the sharp photos placed precisely to enhance understanding. . . . The main [text is] clear and [flows] well." SLJ

Includes glossary and bibliographical references

★ **Praying** mantises; hungry insect heroes. Lerner
Publications Company 2008 48p il (Insect world) lib
bdg $27.93
Grades: 2 3 4 5   **595.7**
1. Praying mantis
ISBN 978-0-8225-7300-5 lib bdg; 0-8225-7300-8
lib bdg
LC 2007-25961
This describes the anatomy, life cycle, and behavior of
praying mantises.

This "will please report writers, budding entomologists,
and anyone who expects children's nonfiction to be as carefully documented as adult nonfiction. . . . The [book is] notable for the sharp photos placed precisely to enhance understanding. . . . The main [text is] clear and [flows] well." SLJ

Includes glossary and bibliographical references

Termites; hard-working insect families. by Sandra
Markle. Lerner Publications Co. 2008 48p il (Insect
world) lib bdg $27.93
Grades: 2 3 4 5   **595.7**
1. Termites
ISBN 978-0-8225-7301-2 lib bdg; 0-8225-7301-6
lib bdg
LC 2007025963
This describes the anatomy, life cycle, and behavior
of termites

This "will please report writers, budding entomologists,
and anyone who expects children's nonfiction to be as carefully documented as adult nonfiction. . . . The [book is] notable for the sharp photos placed precisely to enhance understanding. . . . The main [text is] clear and [flows] well." SLJ

Includes glossary and bibliographical references

Markovics, Joyce L.
The **honey** bee's hive; a thriving city. by Joyce Mar-
kovics; consultant, Brian V. Brown. Bearport Pub. 2009
32p il map (Spectacular animal towns) lib bdg $25.27
Grades: 2 3 4   **595.7**
1. Bees
ISBN 978-1-59716-867-0 lib bdg; 1-59716-867-X
lib bdg
LC 2009-11295
Describes the activities within a honey bee hive

"Through excellent photographs, high-interest texts,
sidebars, maps, and other material, children learn about both
the animals and their habitats. The . . . book also provides
brief profiles of animals with similar habitats. . . . [This book
is] much better than average 'report' titles." SLJ

Includes glossary and bibliographical references

Marsh, Laura
Butterflies. National Geographic 2010 48p il map
(Great migrations) $11.90; pa $3.99
Grades: 1 2 3   **595.7**
1. Butterflies
ISBN 978-1-4263-0740-9; 1-4263-0740-3; 978-1-
4263-0739-3 pa; 1-4263-0739-X pa
This offers facts about monarch butterflies and their
migration from Northern United States and Canada to the
Oyamel forest of Mexico.

"Dynamic full-color photographs, informative writing,
and consistent organization work well together in [this vol-
ume]. . . . Along with the many photographs, the fascinating
details are supported by boxes of related information, helpful definitions of new terms, and a sprinkling of entertaining
jokes/riddles." SLJ

Includes glossary

Marshall, Stephen A.
Insects A to Z. Firefly 2009 32p il lib bdg $19.95;
pa $7.95
Grades: 4 5 6   **595.7**
1. Insects
ISBN 978-1-55407-555-3 lib bdg; 1-55407-555-6 lib
bdg; 978-1-55407-503-4 pa; 1-55407-503-3 pa
This is an illustrated dictionary of 26 insects which includes the Latin and common names of the order, family,
genus and species, as well as information on geographic
distribution. Fact boxes for each entry provide information
detailing each insect's scientific name, diet, average size and
the location at which each was photographed.

"The photography . . . is well composed and sharply focused, with a nicely varied layout from page to page. . . . The
[text is] clearly written." SLJ

Miller, Heather
This is your life cycle; by Heather Lynn Miller; illustrated by Michael Chesworth. Clarion Books 2008 32p
il $16
Grades: K 1 2 3   **595.7**
1. Dragonflies 2. Life cycles (Biology)
ISBN 978-0-618-72485-7; 0-618-72485-0
LC 2007-7245
Told in the form of a TV show, this describes the different stages of the life of Dahlia the dragonfly, including the
various predators she faced, what she ate, and other facts.

"Lively, vibrant watercolor illustrations supplement the
ambitious text. . . . Children will find this playful science
book memorable." Libr Media Connect

Mortensen, Lori
In the trees, honeybees! illustrated by Cris Arbo. Dawn
Publications 2009 un il $16.95; pa $8.95
Grades: PreK K 1 2 3   **595.7**
1. Bees
ISBN 978-1-58469-114-3; 1-58469-114-X; 978-1-
58469-115-0 pa; 1-58469-115-8 pa
LC 2008038513
"Short, simple rhyming words and phrases, printed in
large type on realistic illustrations, describe the amazing life
cycle of the honeybee. The vibrantly colored scenes center
on a beehive hidden in a tree trunk and the grass and gardens
surrounding it. Brief paragraphs in a smaller font provide
more information about the insect's depicted activities. . .

. A wonderful choice for sharing aloud, Mortensen's finely crafted book makes a solid addition." SLJ

Mound, L. A.
Insect; written by Laurence Mound. rev ed; DK Pub. 2007 72p il (Eyewitness books) $15.99; lib bdg $19.99
Grades: 4 5 6 7   595.7
1. Insects
ISBN 978-0-7566-3004-1; 0-7566-3004-5; 978-0-7566-0691-6 lib bdg; 0-7566-0691-8 lib bdg
LC 2007-281241
First published 1990 by Knopf
Includes glossary and bibliographical references

Munro, Roxie
Busy builders; written and illustrated by Roxie Munro. Marshall Cavendish Children 2012 40 p. (hardcover) $17.99
Grades: 3 4 5   595.7
1. Picture books for children 2. Insects 3. Arachnids 4. Insects -- Habitations
ISBN 0761461051; 9780761461050; 9780761461067
LC 2011017391
This children's book, by Roxie Munro, describes "eight insects, one spider, and [offers] an inside look at the unique structures they each build. Roxie Munro's . . . art, drawn in India ink and colored ink, brings these remarkable feats of engineering into full focus. A glossary and resources to learn more are included." (Publisher's note)

Murawski, Darlyne
Face to face with butterflies; by Darlyne A. Murawski. National Geographic 2010 31p il map (Face to face) $16.95
Grades: 3 4 5 6   595.7
1. Butterflies
ISBN 978-1-4263-0618-1; 1-4263-0618-0
The author describes the life cycle and behavior of butterflies.
Includes glossary and bibliographical references

★ Face to face with caterpillars; by Darlyne A. Murawski. National Geographic 2007 32p il (Face to face) $16.95; lib bdg $25.90
Grades: 3 4 5 6   595.7
1. Caterpillars
ISBN 978-1-4263-0052-3; 1-4263-0052-2; 978-1-4263-0053-0 lib bdg; 1-4263-0053-0 lib bdg
LC 2006-20499
"Murawski tells how to find caterpillars and discusses their developmental stages, body parts, diet problems, and self-defense mechanisms. . . . Attractive, well written, and fascinating." SLJ
Includes bibliographical references

Nelson, Maria
20 fun facts about dragonflies; by Maria Nelson. 1st ed. Gareth Stevens Pub. 2013 32 p. col. ill. (Fun fact file: bugs!) (library) $25.25; (paperback) $10.50
Grades: 3 4 5   595.7
1. Dragonflies
ISBN 1433982358; 9781433982354; 9781433982361
LC 2012021207

This book by Maria Nelson provides information on dragonflies and presents "one or two sentences per page, in large, eye-catching red print [and] offer[s] salient facts about the featured insects, usually involving an unusual physical or behavioral characteristic. Each numbered statement is followed by a short paragraph with more detail." (Publisher's note)

Niver, Heather Moore
20 fun facts about stick bugs; by Heather Moore Niver. 1st ed. Gareth Stevens Publishing 2013 32 p. col. ill. (library) $25.25; (paperback) $10.50
Grades: 3 4 5   595.7
1. Stick insects
ISBN 143398251X; 9781433982514; 9781433982521
LC 2012031356
In this book by Heather Moore Niver "readers get the . . . opportunity to [see stick bugs] blending in with their natural habitat while learning many fun facts about stick bugs—including which is the longest, which resembles a lobster, and the many devious ways they avoid being caught by predators." (Publisher's note)
Includes bibliographical references (page 31) and index.

Pringle, Laurence P.
Cicadas! strange and wonderful. [by] Laurence Pringle; illustrated by Meryl Henderson. Boyd Mills Press 2010 32p il map $16.95
Grades: 3 4 5   595.7
1. Cicadas
ISBN 978-1-59078-673-4; 1-59078-673-4
LC 2010-925563
This "provides an attractive introduction to cicadas, which typically spend 1, 13, or 17 years below ground before emerging for only a few weeks. . . . Pringle describes cicadas' physical features, behaviors, life cycle, and loss of habitat. . . . Henderson's watercolor paintings are precisely delineated, informative, and sometimes lovely as well. . . . This [is a] clearly written, informative introduction." Booklist
Includes bibliographical references

Prischmann, Deirdre A.
Poop-eaters; dung beetles in the food chain. by Deirdre A. Prischmann. Capstone Press 2008 32p il (Fact finders. Extreme life) lib bdg $23.93
Grades: 2 3 4   595.7
1. Beetles
ISBN 978-1-4296-1265-4 lib bdg; 1-4296-1265-7 lib bdg
LC 2007-20440
"The beetles' features, traits, and development are explained in breezy text, accompanied by vivid photographs and additional 'Gross!' fact boxes. . . . The volume provides an informative introduction to an underappreciated insect." Horn Book Guide
Includes glossary and bibliographical references

Rockwell, Anne F.
Bugs are insects; by Anne Rockwell; illustrated by Steve Jenkins. HarperCollins Pubs. 2001 29p il (Let's-read-and-find-out science) hardcover o.p. lib bdg $15.89; pa $4.95

Grades: K 1 2 3 **595.7**
1. Insects
ISBN 0-06-028568-0; 0-06-028569-9 lib bdg; 0-06-445203-4 pa

LC 99-39846

Introduces common backyard insects and explains the basic characteristics of these creatures

This is a "well-written and informative book. . . . The collage illustrations are beautifully rendered with layered colored papers of a variety of textures that add both depth and details to the creatures." SLJ

Honey in a hive; by Anne Rockwell; illustrated by S. D. Schindler. HarperCollinsPublishers 2005 33p il (Let's-read-and-find-out science) $15.99; lib bdg $16.89; pa $4.99
Grades: K 1 2 3 **595.7**
1. Bees 2. Honey
ISBN 0-06-028566-4; 0-06-028567-2 lib bdg; 0-06-445204-2 pa

LC 2003-10357

An introduction to the behavior and life cycle of honey-bees, with particular emphasis on the production of honey

"Schindler's realistic artwork is both colorful and nicely matched to the text. . . . This attractive introduction to honey production will serve students well." Booklist

Rodriguez, Ana Maria
Secret of the plant-killing ants . . . and more! Enslow Publishers 2008 48p il (Animal secrets revealed!) lib bdg $23.93
Grades: 5 6 7 8 **595.7**
1. Ants 2. Insects
ISBN 978-0-7660-2953-8 lib bdg; 0-7660-2953-0 lib bdg

LC 2007039494

"Explains why ants in the Amazon rainforest kill all but one species of plant and details other strange abilities of different types of animals." Publisher's note

Includes glossary and bibliographical references

Rotner, Shelley
The **buzz** on bees; why are they disappearing? by Shelley Rotner and Anne Woodhull; photographs by Shelley Rotner. Holiday House 2010 un il $16.95
Grades: 2 3 4 **595.7**
1. Bees 2. Beekeeping 3. Fertilization of plants
ISBN 978-0-8234-2247-0; 0-8234-2247-X

"Excellent color photos provide an eye-catching backdrop for a simple, readable text that explains the importance of bees as pollinators and the current mystery of CCD (Colony Collapse Disorder) as hundreds of thousands of bees vanish without a trace. . . . Rotner and Woodhull offer a look at a variety of bees and other pollinators and a sample of the many products dependent on their efforts. . . . This title is eye-catching and informative." SLJ

Includes bibliographical references

Rustad, Martha E. H.
Ants and aphids work together. Capstone Press 2011 24p il (Pebble Plus: animals working together) lib bdg $23.99; pa $6.95

Grades: K 1 2 **595.7**
1. Ants 2. Aphids 3. Symbiosis
ISBN 978-1-4296-5298-8 lib bdg; 1-4296-5298-5 lib bdg; 978-1-4296-6197-3 pa; 1-4296-6197-6 pa

LC 2010025460

Simple text and full-color photographs introduce the symbiotic relationship of ants and aphids.

In this series "the easy-to-understand examples are well selected to show of range of relationships in a variety of environments, and children will come away with some exposure to the concepts of 'parasite' and 'predator' as well." SLJ

Includes glossary and bibliographical references

Simon, Seymour
★ **Butterflies**. Collins 2011 30p il $17.99
Grades: 1 2 3 4 **595.7**
1. Butterflies
ISBN 978-0-06-191493-5; 0-06-191493-2

LC 2010032203

"Science writer Simon vividly explores the life cycles of butterflies and moths around the globe. . . . Simon's often breathtaking photographs offer closeup views of the insects, demonstrating color variations and their incredible transformations from pupa to adult moth or butterfly. Readers will be armed for the field with juicy vocabulary . . . and tantalizing anatomical descriptions to share." Publ Wkly

Singer, Marilyn, 1948-
Caterpillars. EarlyLight Books 40p il $14.95
Grades: PreK K 1 2 3 4 **595.7**
1. Caterpillars
ISBN 978-0-9797455-7-7; 0-9797455-7-8

"This basic introduction to caterpillar reproduction, development, diet, survival, habitat, and anatomy is combined with powerfully clear photography that will captivate a wide audience. The book has two levels of text: simple capitalized red letters that swirl across the pages for the youngest readers to more complicated paragraphs easy enough for third or fourth graders to enjoy." SLJ

Siy, Alexandra
Bug shots; the good, the bad, and the bugly. text and photographys by Alexandra Siy; photomicrographs by Dennis Kunkel. Holiday House 2011 il $16.95
Grades: 3 4 5 6 **595.7**
1. Insects
ISBN 978-0-8234-2286-9; 0-8234-2286-0

LC 2010024063

"Insects are virtually on trial in this unusual introduction. The book begins by suggesting that readers 'Join the FBI—become a Fellow Bug Investigator' study the insects' 'mug shots,' read their 'rap sheets,' and decide if they are good or bad. After offering general information on classification, anatomy, numbers of species, etc., successive chapters focus on the 'suspects,' comprised of five large insect groups: true bugs; beetles; butterflies and moths; bees, ants, and wasps; and true flies. Each chapter describes the group's outstanding characteristics, as well as the distinctive physical and/or behavioral characteristics of representative species, their diet, harmful or beneficial effects on humans, and so on. . . . Photomicrographs of the insects or body parts illustrate the text on every page; all are brightly colored to highlight anatomical features. . . . The text is clearly written, and the photomicrographs are remarkably detailed." SLJ

★ **Mosquito** bite; [by] Alexandra Siy & Dennis Kunkel. Charlesbridge 2005 32p il $16.95; pa $6.95
Grades: 3 4 5 **595.7**
1. Mosquitoes
ISBN 1-57091-591-1; 1-57091-592-X pa
LC 2004-18959

"Black-and-white photographs of an evening game of hide-and-seek are interspersed with stunning color-enhanced microphotographs that record the life cycle of another seeker: a female Culex pipiens mosquito looking for a meal. . . . This title is fascinating for its photography and the informative text and captions." SLJ

Stewart, Melissa
Ants. National Geographic 2010 32p il (National Geographic readers) $13.90; pa $3.99
Grades: 1 2 3 **595.7**
1. Ants
ISBN 978-1-4263-0609-9; 1-4263-0609-1; 978-1-4263-0608-2 pa; 1-4263-0608-3 pa
Describes different types of ants and their behavior.

Butterfly or moth? how do you know? Enslow Publishers 2011 24p il (Which animal is which?) lib bdg $21.26; pa $6.95
Grades: 1 2 3 **595.7**
1. Moths 2. Butterflies
ISBN 978-0-7660-3678-9 lib bdg; 0-7660-3678-2 lib bdg; 978-1-59845-235-8 pa; 1-59845-235-5 pa
LC 2010003276

"This clearly written volume lays out the differences between butterflies and moths in double-page spreads that allow readers to compare the characteristics of the two animals. . . . The precisely worded, informative text is brief but does not simplify the facts. . . . Captions identify each species shown in the highly magnified, color photos." Booklist
Includes bibliographical references

Insect or spider? how do you know? Enslow Publishers 2011 24p il (Which animal is which?) lib bdg $21.26; pa $6.95
Grades: 1 2 3 **595.7**
1. Insects 2. Spiders
ISBN 978-0-7660-3681-9 lib bdg; 0-7660-3681-2 lib bdg; 978-1-59845-237-2 pa; 1-59845-237-1 pa
LC 2010003278

This describes the differences between insects and spiders.

This "should give budding naturalists an increased understanding of how scientists use appearance and behavior of classify sometimes-similar living things. . . . Spreads feature sharply detailed paired photographs of identified specimens seen from the same angle and at roughly equal size." SLJ
Includes bibliographical references

Swanson, Diane
Bugs up close; written by Diane Swanson; photographed by Paul Davidson. Kids Can Press 2008 40p il pa $16.95

Grades: 3 4 5 6 **595.7**
1. Insects
ISBN 978-1-55453-138-7 pa; 1-55453-138-1 pa
This describes "basic insect anatomy, major body parts and how they function, special adaptations of close to three dozen kinds of insects, egg-laying, metamorphosis, defense mechanisms, etc. . . . Most of the photos are so highly magnified that individual hairs, spines, and anatennae segments are clearly visible. . . . This attractive, informative overview will appeal to both browsers and budding entomologists." SLJ

Tait, Noel
Insects & spiders. Simon & Schuster Books for Young Readers 2008 64p il map (Insiders) $16.99
Grades: 5 6 7 8 **595.7**
1. Insects 2. Spiders
ISBN 978-1-4169-3868-2; 1-4169-3868-0
LC 2008-61110

Provides an overview of insects and spiders in a book that includes detailed three-dimensional illustrations.

"Sharp, hyper-realistic, larger-than-life drawings . . . are . . . set against a plain colored background or within a natural setting. . . . [This] title succinctly describes basic anatomy; physical and behavioral characteristics common to all [insects and spiders]." SLJ
Includes glossary

Trueit, Trudi Strain
Ants; reading consultant, Nanci R. Vargus. Marshall Cavendish Benchmark 2009 23p il (Benchmark rebus. Creepy critters) lib bdg $22.79
Grades: PreK K 1 **595.7**
1. Ants
ISBN 978-0-7614-3961-5; 0-7614-3961-7
LC 2008-12152

"Brilliant close-up photos will help beginning readers make meaning and appeal to students who like these creatures. . . . Glossary, print and media resources for further learning, and an about the author section conclude . . . [the] book. Reading specialists will want to be advised about [this book] . . . as will teachers. . . . This . . . is an excellent resource for beginning research projects." Libr Media Connect
Includes glossary and bibliographical references

Beetles. Marshall Cavendish Benchmark 2010 23p il (Benchmark rebus. Creepy critters) lib bdg $22.79
Grades: PreK K 1 **595.7**
1. Beetles
ISBN 978-0-7614-3962-2; 0-7614-3962-5
LC 2008-23153

This book on beetles is part of the "Backyard Safari series," which provides "a hands-on, practical point of view on discovering local insects. . . . The first part of each book offers information on the life cycle and anatomy of the title creatures." The book also includes "three hands-on sections" offering "practical instructions and tips for finding and observing the title creatures . . . characteristics and about a dozen pictures . . . and a final section suggest[ing] additional projects." (Booklist)

"Brilliant closeup photos will help beginning readers make meaning and appeal to students who like these creatures. . . . Glossary, print and media resources for further learning, and an about the author section conclude . . . [the]

book. Reading specialists will want to be advised about [this book] . . . as will teachers. . . . This . . . is an excellent resource for beginning research projects." Libr Media Connect

Includes glossary and bibliographical references

Caterpillars. Marshall Cavendish Benchmark 2009 23p il (Benchmark rebus. Creepy critters) lib bdg $22.79
Grades: PreK K 1   **595.7**
1. Caterpillars
ISBN 978-0-7614-3963-9 lib bdg; 0-7614-3963-3 lib bdg

LC 2008-17108

"Brilliant closeup photos will help beginning readers make meaning and appeal to students who like these creatures. . . . Glossary, print and media resources for further learning, and an about the author section conclude . . . [the] book. Reading specialists will want to be advised about [this book] . . . as will teachers. . . . This . . . is an excellent resource for beginning research projects." Libr Media Connect

Includes glossary and bibliographical references

Grasshoppers. Marshall Cavendish Benchmark 2009 23p il (Benchmark rebus. Creepy critters) lib bdg $22.79
Grades: PreK K 1   **595.7**
1. Grasshoppers
ISBN 978-0-7614-3964-6 lib bdg; 0-7614-3964-1 lib bdg

LC 2008-24210

This book on grasshoppers is part of the "Backyard Safari series," which provides "a hands-on, practical point of view on discovering local insects. . . . The first part of each book offers information on the life cycle and anatomy of the title creatures." The book also includes "three hands-on sections" offering "practical instructions and tips for finding and observing the title creatures . . . characteristics and about a dozen pictures . . . and a final section suggest[ing] additional projects." (Booklist)

"Brilliant closeup photos will help beginning readers make meaning and appeal to students who like these creatures. . . . Glossary, print and media resources for further learning, and an about the author section conclude . . . [the] book. Reading specialists will want to be advised about [this book] . . . as will teachers. . . . This . . . is an excellent resource for beginning research projects." Publisher's note

Includes glossary and bibliographical references

Voake, Steve

★ **Insect** detective; illustrated by Charlotte Voake. Candlewick Press 2010 28p il $16.99; pa $6.99
Grades: K 1 2 3   **595.7**
1. Insects
ISBN 978-0-7636-4447-5; 1-4063-1051-4; 978-0-7636-5816-8 pa

LC 2009-11152

"This charming collaboration . . . gently encourages young readers to explore their natural surroundings and observe some of the more commonly found insects in it. In spare prose, brief facts about a variety of creatures, such as leaf-miner caterpillars, ground beetles, ants, earwigs, and dragonflies, are shared, as are hints on where and how to find them. . . . Simple but elegant pen and watercolor illustrations show the creatures in their habitats." SLJ

Webster, Christine

Mosquitoes. Weigl 2010 24p il (Backyard animals) $24.45; pa $8.95
Grades: 1 2 3   **595.7**
1. Mosquitoes
ISBN 978-1-60596-086-9; 1-60596-086-1; 978-1-60596-087-6 pa; 1-60596-087-X pa

LC 2009004447

This is "packed with information and [includes] fine close-up photos." Booklist

This describes "physical and behavioral characteristics [of mosquitoes]; some historical background; natural habitats and life cycle; role in the mythology of various cultures (a short myth is recounted); and tips on how to respond to (or avoid) encounters with the creatures." SLJ

Includes glossary

Werner, Sharon

Bugs by the numbers; facts and figures for multiple types of bugbeasties. by Sharon Werner and Sarah Forss. Blue Apple Books 2011 un il $19.99
Grades: 2 3 4   **595.7**
1. Insects 2. Counting
ISBN 978-1-60905-061-0; 1-60905-061-4

LC 2010046644

Provides readers with facts about bugs and other creepy-crawlers while introducing the concept of numbers and counting.

"Werner and Forss use 1s, 2s, and 3s, to distinguish between an ant's head, thorax, and abdomen; a mosquito consists of 75s . . . and a group of ladybugs are made up of numerals that correspond to the number of spots on their wings. Add in several liftable flaps and a wealth of facts about the featured species, and this duo has another winner on their hands." Publ Wkly

Wilson, J. V.

Bumblebee. Frances Lincoln 2011 il $16.95
Grades: K 1 2 3   **595.7**
1. Bees
ISBN 1847800084; 1-84780-008-4

"The pastoral life of a bumblebee queen. Her yearly cycle begins on the first day of spring, when she sleepily flies in search of food and a nest. . . . On the last day of summer, 'the old bumblebee queen flies out of her wonderful nest for the last time.' And in the autumn, all the new queens fly out to find drones to mate with before settling into another winter of sleep. Wilson's narrative is crisp and concise. . . . Kennaway's watercolors are straightforward and mostly realistic in their particulars. A valuable page about 'Helping bumblebees' and a glossary conclude the book. Informative and, in its way, lovely." Kirkus

Includes glossary

Winnick, Nick

Butterflies. Weigl Publishers 2010 24p il (World of wonder: watch them grow) lib bdg $25.70; pa $9.95
Grades: 1 2   **595.7**
1. Butterflies
ISBN 978-1-60596-928-2 lib bdg; 1-60596-928-1 lib bdg; 978-1-60596-929-9 pa; 1-60596-929-X pa

LC 2009052102

Learn about the fascinating transition these insects make from egg to caterpillar, pupa, and finally, colorful butterfly.

The text "is simple without being simplistic; it is thoughtful and comprehensive without being overwhelming. The real appeal for teachers, students, and independent young readers, however, will be the photographs that fill the facing pages. Bold, bright, and colorful, the photographs bring you marvelously close to the subject. . . . On many different levels, this is a very appealing [book]." Libr Media Connect

Includes glossary

595.76 Beetles

Burns, Loree Griffin

★ **Beetle** busters; a rogue insect and the people who track it. Loree Griffin Burns; photographs by Ellen Harasimowicz. Houghton Mifflin Harcourt 2014 64 p. color illustrations, color map (Scientists in the field) $18.99

Grades: 5 6 7 8 **595.76**

1. Nonindigenous pests 2. Beetles 3. Asian longhorned beetle

ISBN 0547792670; 9780547792675

LC 2013050160

This book, by Loree Griffin Burns, focuses on the "Asian longhorned beetle (ALB). . . . These beetles came to America from China, living in wood turned into shipping material. At first the beetles invaded urban areas, where hardwood trees were in limited supply. . . . But . . . now . . . infestations have erupted in . . . hardwood forests, and these beetles, while bad at flying, are very good at killing trees. Clint McFarland's job? Stop the ALB at any cost." (Publisher's note)

"They arrived unseen, burrowed in wooden pallets, spools, and crates, aboard ships from China. The first group spotted in the United States, in Brooklyn, NY, was contained, and quickly taken care of, but since then infestations have been discovered from Massachusetts to Illinois, and as far north as Canada. They're Asian longhorned beetles, pests with "powerful jaws and a taste for wood" and the frightening potential to eat their way through North American forests...The author lives within the quarantined area in Massachusetts and has seen firsthand areas where swatches of infested (and other) trees have been cut down. Her questions about the method employed will leave readers asking some of their own—as they should. A timely, well-told story and a call to action." SLJ

Gibbons, Gail

Ladybugs; by Gail Gibbons. Holiday House 2012 32 p. col. ill., col. map (hardcover) $17.95

Grades: K 1 2 **595.76**

1. Ladybugs 2. Beneficial insects 3. Picture books for children

ISBN 0823423689; 9780823423682

LC 2011014700

This book is about ladybugs. It features illustrations done in "watercolors, enhanced with black ink outline and detail and some crayon highlighting . . . Half of the illustrations include one or more brief notes and/or labels in addition to the oversize text. [Gail] Gibbons identifies the small beetle's body parts; shows some species of ladybugs from around the world; details the four stages of its life cycle; and discusses its usefulness to farmers and how it protects itself from predators and cold weather. Appended are some additional facts (e.g., "Ladybugs can swim") and the National

Geographic websites for the U.S. and Canada." (School Library Journal)

Jenkins, Steve

The **beetle** book; Steve Jenkins. Houghton Mifflin Books for Children 2011 31 p. $16.99

Grades: 4 5 6 7 **595.76**

1. Beetles 2. Ecology -- Encyclopedias 3. Insects -- Encyclopedias

ISBN 9780547680842

LC 2011027129

This nonfiction natural history book presents pictures and information about an "array of beetles." Author/illustrator Steve Jenkins describes "the colors and patterns of this ubiquitous insect . . . [and] the details about the various adaptations that beetles have made over millennia in response to their environment, diet, and predators." Jenkins claims that "one out of four creatures on the planet is a beetle." (Kirkus Reviews)

Smith, Siân

Ladybugs; Sian Smith. Raintree 2013 24 p. (paperback) $8.95

Grades: PreK K **595.76**

1. Ladybugs 2. Picture books for children

ISBN 1410948226; 9781410948090; 9781410948229

LC 2011041230

This children's picture book by Sian Smith "introduces readers to ladybugs. The text is presented in . . . rhyming patterns" and includes photographs. It is part of the Creepy Critters series, which "gives readers an up close and personal view of some of their favorite creepy critters." (Publisher's note)

Includes bibliographical references and index

595.77 Flies (Diptera) and fleas

Gravel, Élise, 1977-

The **fly**; Elise Gravel. Tundra Books of Northern New York 2014 32 p. color illustrations (Disgusting critters) (hardcover) $10.99

Grades: K 1 2 3 **595.77**

1. Flies 2. Insects

ISBN 177049636X; 9781770496361; 9781770496385

LC 2013940756

This children's book, part of Elise Gravel's "Disgusting Critters" series, is an "illustrated non-fiction book about the house fly. . . . It covers such topics as the hair on the fly's body (requires a lot of shaving), its ability to walk on the ceiling (it's pretty cool, but it's hard to play soccer up there), and its really disgusting food tastes (garbage juice soup followed by dirty diaper with rotten tomato sauce, for example)." (Publisher's note)

"This humorous, informative volume gives basic facts about the title creature. Cartoon illustrations and speech-bubble text play up the kid-friendly silliness: 'The housefly is a member of the Muscidae family. Mom Muscidae, Dad Muscidae . . . Teenager Muscidae: "Yo!"' The familiar subject and friendly presentation give this book broad appeal." Horn Book

Heos, Bridget

I, fly; the buzz about flies and how awesome they are. Bridget Heos; illustrated by Jennifer Plecas. Henry Holt & Co. 2015 48 p. color illustrations (hardcover) $17.99

Grades: 2 3 4 **595.77**

1. Flies 2. Housefly

ISBN 0805094695; 9780805094695

LC 2014023463

In this book, written by Bridget Heos and illustrated by Jennifer Plecas, "Fly is fed up with everyone studying butterflies. Flies are so much cooler! They flap their wings 200 times a second, compared to a butterfly's measly five to twelve times. Their babies--maggots--are much cuter than caterpillars (obviously). And when they eat solid food, they even throw up on it to turn it into a liquid. Who wouldn't want to study an insect like that?" (Publisher's note)

"The pictures incorporate chalkboard notes and charts to back up the fly's overview of muscid physiology, habits and life cycle. A breezy bucketful of buggy braggadocio, with tasty nuggets of well-digested natural history stirred in." Kirkus

Includes bibliographical references

595.78 Moths and butterflies

Aston, Dianna

A **butterfly** is patient; by Dianna Aston; illustrated by Sylvia Long. Chronicle Books 2011 40 p. col. ill., col. maps $16.99

Grades: 1 2 **595.78**

1. Butterflies 2. Insects -- Metamorphosis 3. Picture books for children

ISBN 0811864790; 9780811864794

LC 2010008548

"Aston explains the life cycle of a butterfly through a series of themed spreads on the insect's various attributes. . . . Ages five to eight." (Bull Cent Child Books)

This picture book "offers specific and accurate descriptions of metamorphosis, pollination, camouflage, migration and other butterfly features and functions, along with the differences between butterflies and moths. Imagination-stretching comparisons-"monarchs weigh only as much as a few rose petals," the wingspan of the Arian Small Blue is "about the length of a grain of rice"--lend wings to the body of facts, and though the author avoids direct mention of reproduction or death, a quick closing recapitulation that harks back to the opening page's hatching egg provides [a] . . . hint of life's cyclical pattern. . . . [Illustrator Sylvia] Long depicts dozens of caterpillars and butterflies, each one posed to best advantage, unobtrusively labeled." (Kirkus)

"Aston explores the development, habits, migration, and attributes of one of nature's flashier, yet familiar creations. Long's watercolors are precise but enchanting as ever. . . . A lovely mix of science and wonder." Publ Wkly

Burns, Loree Griffin

Handle with care; an unusual butterfly journey. Loree Griffin Burns; Photographs by Ellen Harasimowicz. Millbrook Press 2014 33 p. (lib. bdg.: alk. paper) $26.60

Grades: 1 2 3 4 **595.78**

1. Butterflies 2. Butterfly farming -- Costa Rica

ISBN 0761393420; 9780761393429

LC 2013018086

In this book, author Loree Griffin Burns "focuses first on the life of the blue morpho butterfly at the El Bosque Nuevo butterfly farm in Costa Rica and concludes with its a final destination, the Museum of Science in Boston. . . . Factual back matter further supports the story. Additional information appears in the section 'Insects and Their Life Cycles,' which discusses the process of metamorphosis." (School Library Journal)

"An explanation of the life cycle of butterflies gets an intriguing twist in this account of the work of a Costa Rican butterfly farm, where blue morpho butterflies are raised and the pupae eventually shipped to museums for display and observation. Detailed discussion of each life stage is accompanied by wonderfully sharp, close-up photographs that show intricate structural details." Horn Book

Includes bibliographical references (page 33) and index

Ehlert, Lois

★ **Waiting** for wings. Harcourt 2001 un il $17

Grades: PreK K 1 2 **595.78**

1. Butterflies 2. Stories in rhyme

ISBN 0-15-202608-8

LC 00-9765

Eggs clinging to leaves become caterpillars which become butterflies which lay their eggs

"A brief rhyming text and cheery tone invite readers to explore the full and half pages that form this brilliantly designed book-within-a book." Publ Wkly

Gibbons, Gail

Monarch butterfly. Holiday House 1989 un il $16.95; pa $6.95

Grades: K 1 2 3 **595.78**

1. Butterflies

ISBN 0-8234-0773-X; 0-8234-0909-0 pa

LC 89-1880

"Large-scale paintings, clearly detailed, and a simply written, sequential text describe the life cycle of the monarch butterfly and its migratory patterns. This is Gibbons at her best, providing information in a text that is cohesive and comprehensible." Bull Cent Child Books

Heiligman, Deborah

From caterpillar to butterfly; illustrated by Bari Weissman. HarperCollins Pubs. 1996 31p il (Let's-read-and-find-out science) $15.95; pa $4.95

Grades: K 1 **595.78**

1. Butterflies 2. Caterpillars

ISBN 0-06-024264-7; 0-06-024268-X lib bdg; 0-06-445129-1 pa

LC 93-39055

Young children observe the metamorphosis of a caterpillar into a butterfly in a jar in their classroom

"Pen-and-ink and watercolor illustrations create a cheerful setting. . . . A small collection of butterflies commonly found in most parts of the U.S. and a list of addresses of butterfly centers are appended. An inviting book that young children can relate to and one that teachers will find valuable to support nature-study projects." SLJ

Marsh, Laura
  Caterpillar to butterfly; Laura Marsh. National Geographic 2012 32 p.
Grades: K 1 2   **595.78**
  1. Butterflies 2. Caterpillars 3. Insects -- Metamorphosis
ISBN 1426309201; 142630921X; 9781426309205; 9781426309212
          LC 2011277485
  Author Laura March describes the transformation from caterpillars to butterflies, focusing on the wingspan, colors, and wing patterns of butterflies. "This level 1 Reader gives kids an up-close look at exactly how a caterpillar becomes a butterfly. . . . [The book also includes] bonus information including different types of butterflies and poisonous caterpillars." (Publisher's note)

Pasternak, Carol
  How to raise monarch butterflies; a step-by-step guide for kids. Carol Pasternak. Firefly Books 2012 48 p. col. ill. (bound) $19.95
Grades: 3 4 5 6 7   **595.78**
  1. Caterpillars 2. Insects -- Care 3. Monarch butterflies 4. Monarch butterfly -- Life cycles
ISBN 1770850015; 1770850023; 9781770850019; 9781770850026
          LC 2012419489
  This book by Carol Pasternak presents a "detailed guide to locating and hatching. . . Monarch butterflies. . . . [R]eaders will learn about the life cycle of the Monarch and how to encourage populations in their own backyards, with tips on which plants to grow, as well as the care and feeding of their pet caterpillars. 'How to Raise Monarch Butterflies' explains what threats face Monarchs and how readers can help conserve the Monarch's feeding grounds from encroachment." (Publisher's note)
  Includes bibliographical references and index.

Whalley, Paul
  Butterfly & moth; written by Paul Whalley. Revised ed. DK Pub. 2012 72 p. ill. (chiefly col.), col. map (Eyewitness books) (hardcover) $16.99; (library) $19.99
Grades: 4 5 6 7   **595.78**
  1. Moths 2. Butterflies
ISBN 0756692989; 0756692997; 9780756692988; 9780756692995
          LC 2012418030
  This book is part of the DK Eyewitness Books series and focuses on butterflies and moths. The titles in this series "focus on subjects that complement students' personal interests and areas of study to make learning simple and fun." Wall charts, clip art CDs, and photographs and illustrations are included. (Publisher's note)

595.79 Hymenoptera

Huber, Raymond
  ★ **Flight** of the honey bee; by Raymond Huber and illustrated by Brian Lovelock. Candlewick Press 2013 32 p. $16.99
Grades: PreK K 1 2   **595.79**
  1. Bees -- Fiction 2. Fertilization of plants 3. Picture books for children 4. Honeybee
ISBN 0763667609; 9780763667603
          LC 2013931462
  Author Raymond Huber presents an illustrated children's book. "A tiny honey bee emerges from the hive for the first time. Using sunlight, landmarks, and scents to remember the path, she goes in search of pollen and nectar to share with the thousands of other bees in her hive. She uses her powerful sense of smell to locate the flowers that sustain her, avoids birds that might eat her, and returns home to share her finds with her many sisters." (Publisher's note)
  "As the hive prepares for winter, worker bee Scout embarks on a food-foraging expedition, searching for enough nectar and pollen to survive. Huber's simple but dynamic language hums with an avian vibrancy. In Lovelock's watercolor, acrylic ink, and colored-pencil illustrations, splattered dots represent pollen and hailstones; textured brushstrokes convey flight patterns, vibrating wings, and pelting rain. A satisfying early science book." (Horn Book)

Markle, Sandra, 1946-
  The **case** of the vanishing honey bees; a scientific mystery. by Sandra Markle. Lerner Pub Group 2013 48 p. (lib. bdg.; alk. paper) $29.27
Grades: 4 5 6 7 8   **595.79**
  1. Insects -- Behavior 2. Honeybee 3. Honeybee -- Health
ISBN 1467705926; 9781467705929
          LC 2012046913
  This book, by Sandra Markle, "explores the world of honeybees and the mysterious malady that threatens them. After an opening in which a beekeeper discovers that most of the bees in his 400 hives are gone due to colony collapse disorder (CCD), the book describes how healthy honeybees pollinate flowering plants, gather nectar, and raise their young." (Booklist)

Micucci, Charles
  ★ The **life** and times of the ant. Houghton Mifflin 2003 32p hardcover o.p. pa $6.95
Grades: 2 3 4   **595.79**
  1. Ants
ISBN 0-618-00559-5; 0-618-68949-4 pa
          LC 2002-478
  Describes the evolution, physical characteristics, behavior, and social nature of ants
  This "offers succinct text and an impressive amount of information presented in an attractive, picture-book format." Booklist
  Includes bibliographical references

Rissman, Rebecca
  Ants; Rebecca Rissman. Raintree 2013 24 p. (lib. bdg.) $24.50
Grades: PreK K   **595.79**
  1. Ants 2. Animal behavior 3. Insects -- Behavior
ISBN 1410948013; 1410948145; 9781410948014; 9781410948144
          LC 2011038864
  This "book uses . . . rhymes and . . . images to teach readers about ants." (Publisher's note) "'Ants' begins with counting exercises that use both body segments and legs, before showing off cool photos of differently colored ants, ants marching in rows, and . . . a nest of larvae." It "concludes

with a two-page exercise involving finding the titular insects within a cartoon landscape." (Booklist)

Includes bibliographical references and index.

Bees; Rebecca Rissman. Raintree 2013 24 p. (lib. bdg.) $24.50

Grades: PreK K   **595.79**

1. Bees 2. Picture books for children

ISBN 1410948021; 1410948153; 9781410948021; 9781410948151

LC 2011038869

This book is part of the Creepy Critters series, which offers "readers an up close and personal view of some of their favorite creepy critters! This book introduces readers to bees. The text is presented in . . . rhyming patterns." A "cartoon-like design combined with . . . photos" is meant to be "visually appealing for young readers." (Publishers Weekly)

Includes bibliographical references and index.

596   Chordates

Bishop, Nic, 1955-

Spiders; written and photographed by Nic Bishop. Scholastic 2012 32 p. $3.99

Grades: K 1 2   **596**

1. Spiders

ISBN 0545237572; 9780545237574

This book by Nic Bishop adapts his 2007 book of the same title for younger readers. "Designed for independent readers in first and second grades, the current book offers a completely new text that is shorter, simpler, and printed in larger type. Like its predecessor, the book discusses spiders' physical features, behaviors, and life cycles, and it provides illustrations of different species, which are clearly identified." (Booklist)

Lord, Michelle

Animal school; what class are you? by Michelle Lord; illustrated by Michael Garland. Holiday House 2014 32 p. color illustrations (hardcover) $16.95

Grades: 1 2 3 4   **596**

1. Animals -- Classification 2. Vertebrates -- Classification

ISBN 0823430456; 9780823430451

LC 2013019680

This children's book, written by Michelle Lord and illustrated by Michael Garland, is an "exploration of the five vertebrate classifications—mammals, birds, reptiles, amphibians, and fish. . . . With a focus on trademark characteristics, such as birds' beaks or the scales of fish, the book explains the differences between the five classes. Back matter includes an index and a glossary of scientific terms." (Publisher's note)

"Lord's rhyming verse explores those different vertebrate classes (reptiles, fish, mammals, birds, amphibians) in language that is understandable, sometimes humorous and even elegant at times; always, it highlights the basic characteristics that mark the animals of each class and gives some facts about a few species. . . . Other verses describe how the animals are born, whether they are coldblooded or warm-blooded, whether they have skin, scales or fur, and what adaptations they enjoy. . . . Garland's 'digi-woodcut' illus-

trations are a highlight. His realistic animals share shadings and habitats with the natural world, while the look of the art is rustic and scratchy. The colors are particularly vivid; one undersea page about fish has the look of batik, while a group of wolves in a snowy scene uses just grays, browns and white. Backmatter includes a chart of characteristics, examples and exceptions; an afterword . . . bibliography; and websites. Both beautiful and educational." Kirkus

Includes bibliographical references

597   Cold-blooded vertebrates

Arnosky, Jim

All about sharks. Scholastic Press 2003 un il $15.95; pa $5.95

Grades: K 1 2 3   **597**

1. Sharks

ISBN 0-590-48166-5; 0-545-02600-8 pa

LC 2002-67004

Describes the physical characteristics, behavior, and survival techniques of different kinds of sharks

"Different species and families are illustrated in simple drawings, and the various parts of a shark's body are labeled and explained in a basic, easy-to-read text." SLJ

Bodden, Valerie

Sharks. Creative Education 2010 24p il (Amazing animals) lib bdg $24.25

Grades: K 1 2   **597**

1. Sharks

ISBN 978-1-58341-812-3 lib bdg; 1-58341-812-1 lib bdg

LC 2009002715

A basic exploration of the appearance, behavior, and habitat of sharks, the feared fishes of the sea. Also included is a story from folklore explaining why sharks have a bump on their heads.

This is illustrated with "dynamically colored photographs." Booklist

Includes bibliographical references

Butterworth, Christine

★ **Sea** horse; the shyest fish in the sea. [by] Chris Butterworth; illustrated by John Lawrence. Candlewick Press 2006 27p il $16.99; pa $6.99

Grades: K 1 2   **597**

1. Sea horses

ISBN 978-0-7636-2989-2; 0-7636-2989-8; 978-0-7636-4140-5 pa; 0-7636-4140-5 pa

LC 2005-50755

"Pairing a central narrative about a male Barbour's sea horse with facts in smaller type, Butterworth first pinpoints the creatures' most immediately appealing attributes . . . then goes on to discuss the males' gestational role in reproduction and survival tactics of newly independent offspring. . . . Butterworth has a flair for dynamic writing. . . . Lawrence has created vinyl engravings that masterfully capture the delicate textures of sea horses' graceful, spiny bodies and of their undersea habitats." Booklist

Catt, Thessaly

Migrating with the salmon. PowerKids Press 2011 24p il map (Animal journeys) lib bdg $21.25; pa $8.25
Grades: 2 3 4 597
1. Salmon 2. Animals -- Migration
ISBN 978-1-4488-2545-5 lib bdg; 1-4488-2545-8 lib bdg; 978-1-4488-2674-2 pa; 1-4488-2674-8 pa
LC 2010029655
Learn about the life cycle and migration patterns of the salmon.

"Keywords are bolded throughout and can be found in the glossary. The format is attractive with inset captioned photographs and page heading that seem to move across the page." Libr Media Connect

Includes glossary

Cerullo, Mary M.

The **truth** about great white sharks; written by Mary M. Cerullo; photographs by Jeffrey L. Rotman; illustrations by Michael Wertz. Chronicle Bks. 2000 48p il hardcover o.p. $14.95
Grades: 4 5 6 7 597
1. Sharks
ISBN 0-8118-2467-5; 0-8118-5759-X pa
LC 00-31506
This provides information "about shark anatomy, senses, eating habits, and their relationships with humans. ... . The book also contains unusual information such as how these fish are measured and photographed and why they are not able to survive in an aquarium. The attractive layout blends line drawings, full-color photographs, varied typefaces, and eye-catching graphics. Rotman's pictures are clear and informative. ... . This title will be accessible to reluctant readers and is a must for most collections." SLJ

Includes bibliographical references

Coldiron, Deborah

Eels; by Deborah Coldiron. ABDO Pub. 2008 32p il (Underwater world) lib bdg $24.21
Grades: 2 3 4 597
1. Eels
ISBN 978-1-59928-818-5 lib bdg; 1-59928-818-4 lib bdg
LC 2007-14850
"The captioned photographs are engaging. ... 'Fast Facts' appear on some pages. ... Provide[s] solid information for elementary school reports." Horn Book Guide

Includes glossary

Stingrays; by Deborah Coldiron. ABDO Pub. 2008 32p il (Underwater world) lib bdg $24.21
Grades: 2 3 4 597
1. Rays (Fishes)
ISBN 978-1-59928-817-8 lib bdg; 1-59928-817-6 lib bdg
LC 2007-14856
"The captioned photographs are engaging. ... 'Fast Facts' appear on some pages. ... Provide[s] solid information for elementary school reports." Horn Book Guide

Includes glossary

Curtis, Jennifer Keats

Seahorses; Jennifer Keats Curtis; illustrated by Chad Wallace. Henry Holt 2012 32 p.

Grades: 1 2 3 597
1. Sea horses
ISBN 0805092390; 9780805092394
LC 2011034059
In this children's book by Jennifer Keats Curtis, illustrated by Chad Wallace, "a baby seahorse is born, turning and tumbling as he floats through ocean currents alongside his three hundred brothers and sisters. ... . [H]e changes color to fit in with the surroundings of his spectacular coral reef and sea grass surroundings; his lizard-like eyes can look in two directions at once; and when he has grown, he -- not the female -- will give birth to the next batch of whirling seahorses." (Publisher's note)

Includes bibliographical references

Doubilet, David

★ **Face** to face with sharks; by David Doubilet and Jennifer Hayes. National Geographic 2009 31p il (Face to face) $16.95; lib bdg $25.90
Grades: 3 4 5 6 597
1. Sharks
ISBN 978-1-4263-0404-0; 1-4263-0404-8; 978-1-4263-0405-7 lib bdg; 1-4263-0405-6 lib bdg
LC 2008038244
The authors describe the life cycle and behavior of sharks and their own experiences with sharks in the wild

Includes glossary and bibliographical references

Ganeri, Anita

Piranha. Heinemann Library 2011 24p il map (A day in the life. Rain forest animals) lib bdg $22; pa $6.49
Grades: 1 2 597
1. Piranhas
ISBN 978-1-4329-4108-6 lib bdg; 1-4329-4108-9 lib bdg; 978-1-4329-4119-2 pa; 1-4329-4119-4 pa
LC 2010000969
This book follows a piranha through its day as it sleeps, eats, and moves.

"Ganeri presents information clearly and simply in large type, two-sentence comments placed below a bright, sharply reproduced color photograph of the animal in a natural setting. ... [This is] sufficiently specific to support assignment as well as pleasure reading." SLJ

Includes glossary and bibliographical references

Gibbons, Gail

Sharks. Holiday House 1992 un il $16.95; pa $6.95
Grades: K 1 2 3 597
1. Sharks
ISBN 0-8234-0960-0; 0-8234-1068-4 pa
LC 91-31524
Describes shark behavior and different kinds of sharks

The author's "bold, appealing illustrations (many of them labeled and explained) are the strength of the presentation. An excellent choice for even the youngest shark fan, this will be useful for simple reports as well." Booklist

Gray, Susan Heinrichs

Walking catfish; by Susan H. Gray. Cherry Lake Pub. 2009 32p il map (Animal invaders) lib bdg $27.07

Grades: 3 4 5   **597**

1. Catfish 2. Biological invasions
ISBN 978-1-60279-242-5 lib bdg; 1-60279-242-9
lib bdg

LC 2008000804

"Clear color photographs, most of which are closeups, accompany the [text] on about every other page. . . . [This title provides] report writers with in-depth and up-to-date information on these invaders and the serious problems they cause." SLJ

Includes glossary and bibliographical references

Green, Jen

Moray eel; by Jen Green. Bearport Publishing 2013 24 p. (library binding) $23.93

Grades: 1 2   **597**

1. Eels 2. Morays
ISBN 1617729213; 9781617729218

LC 2013010804

In this book, by Jen Green, "young readers will explore the underwater world of [moray eels] through clear text, full-color photos, and diagrams. Age-appropriate activities, such as matching descriptions of various moray eels to pictures of the fish, give readers a chance to make observations and develop key animal-science skills." (Publisher's note)

Includes bibliographical references and index

Hamilton, Sue L.

Eaten by a shark; [by] Sue Hamilton. ABDO Pub. 2010 32p il (Close encounters of the wild kind) lib bdg $22.61

Grades: 4 5 6 7   **597**

1. Sharks 2. Animal attacks
ISBN 978-1-60453-931-8 lib bdg; 1-60453-931-3 lib bdg

LC 2009-37230

In this volume, readers learn of actual human-wildlife encounters, creature information, survival strategies, and attack statistics.

"Students will be drawn to the realistic full-color photographs, the realistic diagrams of the creatures' bodies, the real-life stories told by victims, and the interesting, attractive formatting that includes text, diagrams, photographs, and graphics on each page. . . . [This is] exciting and attractive in a 'gross' sort of way and will appeal particularly to boys for both leisure reading and research." Libr Media Connect

Includes glossary

Markle, Sandra

Great white sharks; by Sandra Markle. Carolrhoda Books 2004 40p il (Animal predators) lib bdg $25.26; pa $7.95

Grades: 3 4 5 6   **597**

1. Sharks
ISBN 1-57505-731-X lib bdg; 1-57505-747-6 pa

LC 2003-23180

"The role of camouflage is aptly explained in flowing text and illustrated in clear photography. . . . The full-color photography bedazzles on almost every page." SLJ

Includes bibliographical references

Miller, Sara Swan

Seahorses, pipefishes, and their kin; Sara Swan Miller. Franklin Watts 2002 47 p. col. ill. (Animals in order) (library) $26.50; (paperback) $6.95

Grades: 4 5 6   **597**

1. Picture books for children 2. Marine biology 3. Marine animals 4. Gasterosteiformes
ISBN 9780531121719; 0531163792; 9780531163795

LC 2001003034

This book by Sara Swan Miller is part of the Animals in Order series and looks at seahorses, pipefishes, and related animals. "These colorful series entries present a wide variety of creatures that have been sorted by scientific classification into similar groupings called orders . . . . Family names, common names, genus, species, size, and/or location are given, and paragraphs describe various behaviors (food gathering, courtship, etc.)." (School Library Journal)

Includes bibliographical references (p. 46) and index.

Musgrave, Ruth

Everything sharks; all the shark facts, photos, and fun that you can sink your teeth into. National Geographic 2011 64p il (National Geographic kids) lib bdg $25.90; pa $12.95

Grades: 3 4 5 6   **597**

1. Sharks
ISBN 978-1-4263-0802-4 lib bdg; 1-4263-0802-7 lib bdg; 978-1-4263-0769-0 pa; 1-4263-0769-1 pa

LC 2010049108

This offers facts and photos of sharks, and scientists' tales about encounters with sharks.

"Exploding with astounding full-color photographs and written in an appealing conversational tone, [this book is] for every kid. . . . The [text] will keep kids interested and turning pages to discover more and more facts. . . . [This] compelling, browseable, and completely engrossing [title] will delight readers." SLJ

Includes glossary and bibliographical references

Pfeffer, Wendy

What's it like to be a fish? illustrated by Holly Keller. HarperCollins Pubs. 1996 32p il (Let's-read-and-find-out science) hardcover o.p. pa $4.95

Grades: K 1   **597**

1. Fishes 2. Goldfish
ISBN 0-06-024429-1 lib bdg; 0-06-445151-8 pa

LC 94-6543

"By comparing goldfish to wild fish and human beings, this book describes the basic physiology of fish. The colorful illustrations are done in watercolors and pastels. . . . In a very accessible narrative that flows from point to point, the basic external anatomy of fish and such behaviors as movement, breathing, eating, and maintenance of temperature are defined in terms of caring for a goldfish in a bowl." Sci Books Films

Pringle, Laurence P.

Sharks!: strange and wonderful; by Laurence Pringle; illustrated by Meryl Henderson. Boyds Mills Press 2001 32p il $15.95

Grades: 3 4 5   **597**

1. Sharks
ISBN 1-56397-863-6

"Basic information about sharks—including physical characteristics, feeding habits, and their role in the chain of ocean life—is presented in clear, accessible prose. The acrylic paintings serve as a veritable catalog showcasing the variety of known sharks." Horn Book Guide

Rockwell, Anne F.

Little shark; [by] Anne Rockwell; pictures by Megan Halsey. Walker & Co. 2005 un il $15.95; lib bdg $16.85

Grades: K 1 2 **597**

1. Sharks

ISBN 0-8027-8955-2; 0-8027-8956-0 lib bdg

LC 2004-52611

"Rockwell invites her readers to follow a newborn shark pup as it grows, explores its ocean home on its own, and develops at last into an adult blue shark. Strung throughout the narrative . . . are interesting facts about shark physiology, behaviors, and deep-sea dangers. . . . The whole is decorated with soft watercolor-and-pencil collage illustrations that are both attractive and . . . informative." SLJ

Rodriguez, Ana Maria

Secret of the suffocating slime trap . . . and more! Enslow Publishers 2008 48p il (Animal secrets revealed!) lib bdg $23.93

Grades: 5 6 7 8 **597**

1. Fishes

ISBN 978-0-7660-2954-5 lib bdg; 0-7660-2954-9 lib bdg

LC 2007039493

This book offers "fascinating accounts of how scientists systematically analyzed, tested, and proved their theories or how their findings led to other, serendipitous discoveries. . . . Science experiments are thoughtfully placed to inspire exploration, and captioned, full-color photos appear throughout." SLJ

Includes glossary and bibliographical references

Roth, Susan L.

★ **Parrots** over Puerto Rico; by Susan L. Roth and Cindy Trumbore. Lee & Low Books 2013 48 p. color illustrations (hardcover) $19.95

Grades: 2 3 4 5 **597**

1. Parrots 2. Puerto Rico -- History 3. Natural history -- Puerto Rico 4. Endangered species -- Puerto Rico 5. Puerto Rican parrot -- Conservation 6. Puerto Rico -- Environmental conditions

ISBN 9781620140048; 1620140047

LC 2012048195

Orbis Pictus Awards Honor Book (2014)

Robert F. Sibert Informational Book Award (2014)

Authors Susan L. Roth and Cindy Trumbore present "a picture book telling the intertwined histories of the Puerto Rican parrot and the island of Puerto Rico, culminating with current efforts to save the parrots from extinction. Roth and Trumbore recount the efforts of the scientists of the Puerto Rican Parrot Recovery Program to save the parrots and ensure their future. Woven into the parrots' story is a brief history of Puerto Rico itself." (Publisher's note)

"Every paper-and-fabric collage is frame-worthy, from depictions of waterfalls and rain forest to sailing ships, hazards and, of course, parrots. From the commanding cover illustration to the playful image on the back, simply spectacular." Kirkus

Includes bibliographical references

Rustad, Martha E. H.

Clown fish and sea anemones work together. Capstone Press 2011 24p il (Pebble Plus: animals working together) lib bdg $23.99; pa $6.95

Grades: K 1 2 **597**

1. Anemones 2. Clownfish 3. Symbiosis

ISBN 978-1-4296-5297-1 lib bdg; 1-4296-5297-7 lib bdg; 978-1-4296-6198-0 pa; 1-4296-6198-4 pa

LC 2010025462

Simple text and full-color photographs introduce the symbiotic relationship of clown fish and sea anemones.

In this series "the easy-to-understand examples are well selected to show of range of relationships in a variety of environments, and children will come away with some exposure to the concepts of 'parasite' and 'predator' as well." SLJ

Includes glossary and bibliographical references

Moray eels and cleaner shrimp work together. Capstone Press 2011 24p il (Pebble Plus: animals working together) lib bdg $23.99; pa $6.95

Grades: K 1 2 **597**

1. Eels 2. Shrimps 3. Symbiosis

ISBN 978-1-4296-5299-5 lib bdg; 1-4296-5299-3 lib bdg; 978-1-4296-6199-7 pa; 1-4296-6199-2 pa

This describes the lives of moray eels and cleaner shrimp and how they work together to survive.

In this series "the easy-to-understand examples are well selected to show of range of relationships in a variety of environments, and children will come away with some exposure to the concepts of 'parasite' and 'predator' as well." SLJ

Simon, Seymour

★ **Sharks**. HarperCollins Pubs. 1995 un il $16.95; pa $6.95

Grades: 2 3 4 **597**

1. Sharks

ISBN 0-06-023029-0; 0-06-446187-4 pa

LC 95-1593

The author "explores the fascinating undersea life of sharks, examining the truths and myths about these amazing creatures. Astounding close-up photographs enhance the informative and exciting text." Sci Child

Stewart, Melissa

A **place** for fish; written by Melissa Stewart; illustrated by Higgins Bond. Peachtree 2011 un il map $16.95

Grades: K 1 2 3 **597**

1. Fishes 2. Wildlife conservation

ISBN 978-1-56145-562-1; 1-56145-562-8

"Environmental threats facing fish in various habitats around the world are introduced in a picture-book, read-aloud format. . . . Sidebars briefly describe a species affected by the threat and actions that can be taken to resolve it. Each entry repeats the same phrase, 'fish can live and grow.' The information is presented in a simple and idealistic way for young readers. The full-color illustrations on every page are very detailed, but some of the fish have humanlike eyes." SLJ

Shark or dolphin? how do you know? Enslow Publishers 2011 24p il (Which animal is which?) lib bdg $21.26; pa $6.95

Grades: 1 2 3   597

1. Sharks 2. Dolphins

ISBN 978-0-7660-3680-2 lib bdg; 0-7660-3680-4 lib bdg; 978-1-59845-239-6 pa; 1-59845-239-8 pa

LC 2010003280

This describes the differences between sharks and dolphin.

This "should give budding naturalists an increased understanding of how scientists use appearance and behavior of classify sometimes-similar living things. . . . Spreads feature sharply detailed paired photographs of identified specimens seen from the same angle and at roughly equal size." SLJ

Includes bibliographical references

Stille, Darlene R.

The **life** cycle of fish. Heinemann Library 2011 48p il (Life cycles) lib bdg $35; pa $8.95

Grades: 3 4 5   597

1. Fishes

ISBN 978-1-4329-4980-8 lib bdg; 978-1-4329-4987-7 pa

LC 2010038278

This describes what a fish is, types of fishes, their life cycles, habitats, foods, defenses, and relationships to humans.

Includes glossary and bibliographical references

Stockdale, Susan

★ **Fabulous** fishes; written and illustrated by Susan Stockdale. Peachtree 2008 un il $15.95

Grades: PreK K 1 2 3   597

1. Fishes

ISBN 978-1-56145-429-7; 1-56145-429-X

LC 2007-29749

"With simple, rhyming text and full-page illustrations in acrylic and collage, this picture book introduces dramatic facts about more than 20 different fishes. . . . Young children will enjoy pointing out the various fish in the illustrations, while older children will switch back and forth from the pictures to the fascinating biological facts about fish behavior, habitat, and camouflage gathered in notes at the back." Booklist

Swinney, Geoff

Fish facts; illustrated by Janeen Mason. Pelican Pub. Co. 2011 48p il $17.99

Grades: 5 6 7 8   597

1. Fishes

ISBN 978-1-58980-908-6; 1-58980-908-4

LC 2010046220

"This comprehensive collection of facts about fish is sure to educate as well as fascinate. . . . From fish that produce light and fish that are capable of powered flight, to fish that can change sex and fish that carry their offspring in their mouths, this is chock full of both the amazing and the weird. . . . While the rather advanced vocabulary and biology that Swinney delves into mark this as a book for older readers, younger ones can certainly enjoy both the illustrations and the occasional factoid. Mason's artwork is both painstakingly detailed and realistically colored, even down to the mut-

ing effect that water has on colors. Few books come close to this one's inclusiveness." Kirkus

Turner, Pamela S.

★ **Project** Seahorse; [photographs by Scott Tuason] Houghton Mifflin Harcourt 2010 56p il (Scientists in the field) $18

Grades: 4 5 6 7   597

1. Sea horses

ISBN 978-0-547-20713-1; 0-547-20713-1

LC 2009-49707

"With striking images of coral-reef inhabitants, this photo-essay introduces Project Seahorse, an international effort to protect and rehabilitate the Danajon Bank, a double reef off a Philippine Island where seahorses once flourished . . . Tuason, a noted Asian marine photographer whose specialty is the Philippines, seems equally adept at photographing the land and people and the underwater world. This is another splendid demonstration of the work of Scientists in the Field." Kirkus

Walker, Sally M.

Rays. Carolrhoda Bks. 2003 48p il (Carolrhoda nature watch book) lib bdg $23.93

Grades: 3 4 5 6   597

1. Rays (Fishes)

ISBN 1-57505-172-9

LC 2001-6586

Describes the physical characteristics, behavior, life cycle, and endangered status of rays

"The crisp, well-captioned color photos highlight the many varieties of this unusual fish. Information is presented clearly." Horn Book Guide

Includes index

Wallace, Karen

Think of an eel; illustrated by Mike Bostock. Candlewick Press 1993 un il hardcover o.p. pa $6.99; pa with audio CD $8.99

Grades: K 1 2 3   597

1. Eels

ISBN 1-56402-180-7; 978-0-7636-1522-2 pa; 0-7636-1522-6 pa; 978-0-7636-3994-5 pa with audio CD; 0-7636-3994-X pa with audio CD

LC 92-53131

Text and illustrations discuss the characteristics and life cycle of the eel

"Bostock's watercolor paintings illustrate the places and creatures in the text without diminishing the mystery of the eel's journey. . . . The short phrases of the prose create a rhythm almost like unrhymed verse that will please readers." Booklist

Wearing, Judy

Manta rays. Weigl Publishers 2010 24p il (World of wonder: underwater life) lib bdg $24.45; pa $8.95

Grades: K 1 2   597

1. Rays (Fishes)

ISBN 978-1-60596-104-0 lib bdg; 1-60596-104-3 lib bdg; 978-1-60596-105-7 pa; 1-60596-105-1 pa

LC 2009-25988

This book about mantra rays begins "with introductory information and progress[es] to more unique details of the featured creatures. Bold photographs juxtaposed on colorful background graphic will hold the attention of even the most novice readers. . . . [This book is] sure to make a splash with budding marine biologists everywhere." SLJ

Includes glossary

Seahorses. Weigl 2010 24p il (World of wonder: underwater life) lib bdg $24.45; pa $8.95

Grades: K 1 2   **597**

1. Sea horses

ISBN 978-1-60596-102-6 lib bdg; 1-60596-102-7 lib bdg; 978-1-60596-103-3 pa; 1-60596-103-5 pa

LC 2009-4986

This book about seahorses begins "with introductory information and progress[es] to more unique details of the featured creatures. Bold photographs juxtaposed on colorful background graphic will hold the attention of even the most novice readers. . . . [This book is] sure to make a splash with budding marine biologists everywhere." SLJ

Includes glossary

597.3   Selachii, Holocephali, fleshy-finned fishes

Green, Jen

Great white shark; By Jen Green. Bearport Publishing 2013 24 p. (library binding) $23.93

Grades: 1 2   **597.3**

1. Sharks 2. Marine biology 3. White shark

ISBN 1617729183; 9781617729188

LC 2013010869

In this book, by Jen Green, "readers will explore the underwater world of [the great white shark] through clear text, full-color photos, and diagrams. Age-appropriate activities, such as describing the differences between an adult and a pup, give readers a chance to make observations and to develop animal-science skills." (Publisher's note)

Includes bibliographical references and index

Macquitty, Miranda

Shark; written by Miranda MacQuitty. DK Pub. 2008 72 p. col. ill (Eyewitness books) (hardcover) $16.99

Grades: 4 5 6 7   **597.3**

1. Sharks 2. Marine biology

ISBN 0756637783; 9780756637781

LC 2008276031

This book is part of the DK Eyewitness Books series and focuses on sharks. The titles in this series "focus on subjects that complement students' personal interests and areas of study to make learning simple and fun." Wall charts, clip art CDs, and photographs and illustrations are included. (Publisher's note)

Mallory, Kenneth

Swimming with hammerhead sharks. Houghton Mifflin 2001 48p il (Scientists in the field) pbk. $7.99

Grades: 4 5 6 7   **597.3**

1. Sharks

ISBN 9780618250790

LC 00-61401

"Mallory, editor-in-chief of publishing programs at the New England Aquarium, uses the context of an IMAX film production on hammerhead sharks to explain how scientists—in particular, marine biologist Pete Klim-

ley—are studying these {animals. Index.} Intermediate." (Horn Book)

This book follows "marine biologist Pete Klimley and an IMAX film team to seamounts off Cocos Island in the Pacific Ocean to observe and film schooling hammerhead sharks. . . . A fascinating record of research and investigation, this inviting book is larded with numerous dramatic color photos." SLJ

Includes bibliographical references

Roy, Katherine

★ **Neighborhood** sharks; hunting with the great whites of California's Farallon Islands. Katherine Roy. David Macaulay Studio, Roaring Brook Press 2014 48 p. color illustrations, color map (hardcover) $17.99

Grades: 2 3 4 5   **597.3**

1. Sharks 2. Marine biology

ISBN 1596438746; 9781596438743

LC 2014008940

Robert F. Sibert Honor Book (2015)

In this book, author Katherine Roy presents a "portrait of the life cycle, biology, and habitat of the great white shark, based on the latest research and an up-close visit with these amazing animals. In the fall of 2012 . . . Roy visited the Farallons with the scientists who study the islands' shark population. She witnessed seal attacks, observed sharks being tagged in the wild, and got an up close look at the dramatic Farallons--a wildlife refuge." (Publisher's note)

"Scientific facts and concepts mesh smoothly with sequential action scenes, making the content accessible and logical. It is difficult to talk about sharks and their feeding habits without a bit of gore, and the illustrations, though not overly sensational, do not disappoint." Booklist

Includes bibliographical references

Sharks; facts at your fingertips. DK Pub. 2012 156 p. col. ill., map (Pocket genius) (hc) $7.99

Grades: 5 6 7 8   **597.3**

1. Sharks 2. Rays (Fishes) 3. Sharks

ISBN 0756692865; 9780756692865

LC 2011277726

This book, part of the "Pocket Genius" encyclopedia series, "profiles more that 150 sharks and rays -- from the great white to the tiny dwarf lantern -- and tells what they eat, where they live and how fast they swim." It "offers a . . . catalog-style presentation, which clearly lays out individual subcategories." (Publisher's note)

Simon, Seymour

Incredible sharks; by Seymour Simon. Seastar Books 2004 32 p. (SeeMore readers) $4.99

Grades: K 1 2 3   **597.3**

1. Sharks

ISBN 1587172380; 1587172399; 9781587172397

LC 2002191194

In this book on sharks, written by Seymour Simon, readers can "find out . . . about these impressive hunters, from the tiny pygmy shark to the giant whale shark." Such facts include "sharks can bite 300 times harder than a person and can hear prey in the water from 3,000 feet away." (Publisher's note)

Walker, Sally M.

Fossil fish found alive; discovering the coelacanth. Carolrhoda Bks. 2002 72p il map lib bdg $17.95

Grades: 5 6 7 8   **597.3**

1. Coelacanth

ISBN 1-57505-536-8

LC 2001-3815

Describes the 1938 discovery of the coelacanth, a fish previously believed to be extinct, and subsequent research about it

"Walker writes well, making this relatively unknown area of science history an exciting story of exploration and discovery. Excellent, full-color photos illustrate the text." Booklist

Includes bibliographical references

597.8   Amphibians

Allen, Kathy

Deformed frogs; a cause and effect investigation. Capstone Press 2010 32p il map (Fact finders. Animals on the edge) lib bdg $25.99

Grades: 3 4 5 6   **597.8**

1. Frogs

ISBN 978-1-4296-4533-1 lib bdg; 1-4296-4533-4 lib bdg

LC 2010004412

"Excellent discussions address those who doubt the severity of the issue and those who wonder why people should care what happens to animals. The captioned photographs are timely and poignant. . . . [This] makes serious subject matter interesting and accessible." SLJ

Includes glossary and bibliographical references

Bekkering, Annalise

Frogs. Weigl 2011 24p il (World of wonder: watch them grow) lib bdg $25.70; pa $9.95

Grades: 1 2   **597.8**

1. Frogs

ISBN 978-1-60596-925-1 lib bdg; 1-60596-925-7 lib bdg; 978-1-60596-926-8 pa; 1-60596-926-5 pa

LC 2009050954

Readers will discover the world of frogs and their transition from swimming tadpoles to amphibious adults.

The text "is simple without being simplistic; it is thoughtful and comprehensive without being overwhelming. The real appeal for teachers, students, and independent young readers, however, will be the photographs that fill the facing pages. Bold, bright, and colorful, the photographs bring you marvelously close to the subject. . . . On many different levels, this is a very appealing [book]." Libr Media Connect

Includes glossary and bibliographical references

Beltz, Ellin

Frogs: inside their remarkable world. Firefly Books 2005 175p il $34.95

Grades: 5 6 7 8 9 10   **597.8**

1. Frogs 2. Toads

ISBN 1-55297-869-9

LC 2006-365517

The author gives a "picture of the history of the frog, its anatomical makeup, its place in the natural world and the

threats that are seriously reducing its numbers around the world." Publisher's note

Bishop, Nic

★ Nic Bishop frogs. Scholastic Nonfiction 2008 48p il $17.99

Grades: 2 3 4   **597.8**

1. Frogs

ISBN 978-0-439-87755-8; 0-439-87755-5

LC 2007-08699

Boston Globe-Horn Book Award honor book: Nonfiction (2008)

Bishop "presents a number of large, striking photos illustrating a clearly written discussion of the physical characteristics and habits of frogs. Dominating the book are Bishop's remarkably fine color photographs of frogs from around the world." Booklist

Includes glossary

Bluemel Oldfield, Dawn

Leaping ground frogs. Bearport 2010 24p il map (Amphibiana) lib bdg $22.61

Grades: 3 4 5 6   **597.8**

1. Frogs

ISBN 978-1-936087-35-8 lib bdg; 1-936087-35-9 lib bdg

This book about ground frogs "is informative, eye-catching, well organized, and useful for reports. . . . Large, clear color photos depict the animals in their natural habitats." SLJ

Includes glossary and bibliographical references

Bredeson, Carmen

Poison dart frogs up close; [by] Carmen Bredeson. Enslow Elementary 2008 24p il (Zoom in on animals!) lib bdg $21.26

Grades: 1 2 3   **597.8**

1. Frogs

ISBN 978-0-7660-3077-0 lib bdg; 0-7660-3077-6 lib bdg

LC 2007039467

"Short paragraphs of simply written text describe [poison dart frogs'] key body parts and how they function. . . . Behavior, diet, and care and development of the young are briefly addressed. Facing the text on each spread is a full-page, sharp, color close-up of one or more of the . . . animals in their natural habitat. . . . Bredeson's simply written and colorful [title] will provide younger readers with [a] satisfying first [introduction] to these fascinating creatures." SLJ

Includes glossary and bibliographical references

Carney, Elizabeth

Frogs! National Geographic 2009 32p il (National Geographic kids) $11.90; pa $3.99

Grades: K 1 2   **597.8**

1. Frogs

ISBN 978-1-4263-0393-7; 1-4263-0393-9; 978-1-4263-0392-0 pa; 1-4263-0392-0 pa

LC 2008014028

This "volume employs simple sentence structures to convey basic facts about frogs . . . including life cycles, habitats, and feeding information. The excellent photographs showcase a variety of species in vivid detail. Vocabulary-word text boxes and goofy jokes . . . increase accessibility." Horn Book Guide

Cowley, Joy

★ Red-eyed tree frog; story by Joy Cowley; illustrated with photographs by Nic Bishop. Scholastic Press 1999 un il $16.95

Grades: PreK K 1 2   **597.8**

1. Frogs -- Fiction 2. Rain forests -- Fiction

ISBN 0-590-87175-7

LC 98-15674

This frog found in the rain forest of Central America spends the night searching for food while also being careful not to become dinner for some other animal

"Stunning color photographs and a gripping interactive text." Booklist

Crump, Marty

The **mystery** of Darwin's frog; by Marty Crump; illustrated by Steve Jenkins and Edel Rodriquez. Boyds Mills Press 2013 40 p. ill. (reinforced) $16.95

Grades: 3 4 5 6 7   **597.8**

1. Picture books for children 2. Frogs

ISBN 1590788648; 9781590788646

LC 2012947844

In this book, Marty Crump, a researcher who has investigated the Rhinoderma darwinii, an inch-long frog discovered by Charles Darwin in Chile in 1834, "describes the earlier investigations of this intriguing frog and records her own efforts to document how it lives in the wild. She discusses her findings and goes on to present the problems facing not only Darwin's frogs, but also frogs in general-loss of habitat, pollution, and the assault of the lethal Bd fungus." (School Library Journal)

Dickmann, Nancy

A **frog's** life. Heinemann Library 2010 24p il (Watch it grow) lib bdg $21.50; pa $5.99

Grades: PreK K 1   **597.8**

1. Frogs

ISBN 978-1-4329-4140-6 lib bdg; 1-4329-4140-2 lib bdg; 978-1-4329-4149-9 pa; 1-4329-4149-6 pa

LC 2009-49156

"Practically unique among early introductions to life cycles because death is mentioned . . . this . . . follows [a frog] . . . from egg . . . to maturity with a set of close-up color photographs, one per page, paired to large-type, one or two-sentence captions. . . . Offers nourishing fare for young naturalists." SLJ

Includes glossary and bibliographical references

Firestone, Mary

What's the difference between a frog and a toad? illustrated by Bandelin-Dacey. Picture Window Books 2010 24p il (What's the difference) lib bdg $25.32

Grades: K 1 2   **597.8**

1. Frogs 2. Toads

ISBN 978-1-4048-5544-1 lib bdg; 1-4048-5544-0 lib bdg

LC 2009-6885

"Compares and contrasts the habitats, physical characteristics, location, and lifestyles of [frogs and toads]. The picture-book format is used to great effect as it allows the two animals to be compared side by side on each spread. The bold, expressive watercolors provide the same visual impact as photographs. . . . Short sentences and highlighted fun facts

make this . . . [a book] with broad appeal for both researchers and browsers." SLJ

Includes glossary

Ganeri, Anita

Poison dart frog. Heinemann Library 2011 24p il map (A day in the life. Rain forest animals) lib bdg $22; pa $6.49

Grades: 1 2   **597.8**

1. Frogs

ISBN 978-1-4329-4104-8 lib bdg; 1-4329-4104-6 lib bdg; 978-1-4329-4115-4 pa; 1-4329-4115-1 pa

LC 2010000959

This book follows a poison dart frog through its day as it sleeps, eats, and moves.

"Ganeri presents information clearly and simply in large type, two-sentence comments placed below a bright, sharply reproduced color photograph of the animal in a natural setting. . . . [This is] sufficiently specific to support assignment as well as pleasure reading." SLJ

Includes glossary and bibliographical references

Gibbons, Gail

Frogs. Holiday House 1993 un il $16.95; pa $6.95

Grades: K 1 2 3   **597.8**

1. Frogs

ISBN 0-8234-1052-8; 0-8234-1134-6 pa

LC 93-269

An introduction to frogs, discussing their tadpole beginnings, noises they make, their hibernation, body parts, and how they differ from toads

"Gibbons' distinctive, labeled drawings identify the features described in the text, and her subjects float, swim, jump, and dive in colorful, lifelike illustrations. . . . This attractive book will appeal to prereaders, beginning readers, and the adults who read to those groups." Booklist

Gilpin, Daniel

Tree frogs, mud puppies, & other amphibians; by Daniel Gilpin. Compass Point Books 2006 48 p. col. ill. (Animal kingdom classification) (library) $29.99

Grades: 5 6 7 8   **597.8**

1. Picture books for children 2. Amphibians

ISBN 0756512492; 9780756512491

LC 2005003683

This book by Daniel Gilpin is part of the Families series and looks at tree frogs, mud puppies, and other amphibians. It "discusses the large diversity of amphibians, a typical amphibian's body, ancient amphibians, and an amphibian's skin and senses. It discusses hiding and warning, movement, prey, courtship, strange breeders, and the life-cycle." (Publisher's note)

Includes bibliographical references (p. 47) and index.

Goldish, Meish

Amazing water frogs. Bearport 2010 24p il map (Amphibiana) lib bdg $22.61

Grades: 3 4 5 6   **597.8**

1. Frogs

ISBN 978-1-936087-34-1 lib bdg; 1-936087-34-0 lib bdg

This book about water frogs "is informative, eye-catching, well organized, and useful for reports. . . . Large, clear color photos depict the animals in their natural habitats." SLJ

Includes glossary and bibliographical references

Little newts. Bearport 2010 24p il map (Amphibiana) lib bdg $22.61

Grades: 3 4 5 6   **597.8**

1. Newts

ISBN 978-1-936087-38-9 lib bdg; 1-936087-38-3 lib bdg

This book about newts "is informative, eye-catching, well organized, and useful for reports. . . . Large, clear color photos depict the animals in their natural habitats." SLJ

Includes glossary and bibliographical references

Slimy salamanders. Bearport 2010 24p il map (Amphibiana) lib bdg $22.61

Grades: 3 4 5 6   **597.8**

1. Salamanders

ISBN 978-1-936087-37-2 lib bdg; 1-936087-37-5 lib bdg

This book about salamanders "is informative, eye-catching, well organized, and useful for reports. . . . Large, clear color photos depict the animals in their natural habitats." SLJ

Includes glossary and bibliographical references

Warty toads. Bearport 2010 24p il (Amphibiana) lib bdg $22.61

Grades: 3 4 5 6   **597.8**

1. Toads

ISBN 978-1-936087-36-5 lib bdg; 1-936087-36-7 lib bdg

This book about toads "is informative, eye-catching, well organized, and useful for reports. . . . Large, clear color photos depict the animals in their natural habitats." SLJ

Includes glossary and bibliographical references

Guiberson, Brenda Z., 1946-

Frog song; by Brenda Guiberson; illustrations by Gennady Spirin. Henry Holt and Company 2012 40 p. (hc) $17.99

Grades: K 1 2 3   **597.8**

1. Frogs -- Vocalization 2. Frogs 3. Frogs -- Behavior

ISBN 0805092544; 9780805092547

LC 2011041940

This children's book, by Brenda Z. Guiberson, illustrated by Gennady Spirin, profiles exotic frogs and their sounds. "Since the time of the dinosaurs, frogs have added their birrups and bellows to the music of the earth. . . . Onomatopoeic text and . . . illustrations introduce young readers to these fascinating and important creatures, from Chile to Nepal to Australia." (Publisher's note)

Kolpin, Molly

Salamanders; consulting editor, Gail Saunders-Smith. Capstone Press 2010 24p il map (Pebble plus. Amphibians) lib bdg $22.65

Grades: K 1 2   **597.8**

1. Salamanders

ISBN 978-1-4296-3990-3 lib bdg; 1-4296-3990-3 lib bdg

This "is well suited to emerging readers. Dynamic, full-page color photographs complement controlled, repetitive vocabulary, printed in a large font against solid backgrounds. . . . The information and its presentation are solid." SLJ

Includes glossary and bibliographical references

Lunis, Natalie

Tricky tree frogs. Bearport 2010 24p il map (Amphibiana) lib bdg $22.61

Grades: 3 4 5 6   **597.8**

1. Frogs

ISBN 978-1-936087-33-4 lib bdg; 1-936087-33-2 lib bdg

This book about tree frogs "is informative, eye-catching, well organized, and useful for reports. . . . Large, clear color photos depict the animals in their natural habitats." SLJ

Includes glossary and bibliographical references

Markle, Sandra

★ **Hip**-pocket papa; illustrated by Alan Marks. Charlesbridge 2010 un il lib bdg $15.95

Grades: K 1 2 3   **597.8**

1. Frogs 2. Natural history -- Australia

ISBN 978-1-57091-708-0 lib bdg; 1-57091-708-6 lib bdg

LC 2008025334

"Markle writes with clarity and precision, while Marks' evocative watercolor, ink, and pencil artwork brings the frogs' world to life." Booklist

Markle, Sandra, 1946-

★ The **case** of the vanishing golden frogs. Milbrook Press 2011 48p il

Grades: 4 5 6   **597.8**

1. Frogs 2. Endangered species 3. Wildlife conservation

ISBN 0761351086; 9780761351085

LC 2010042642

"Notable for clarity, directness, and simplicity of writing and design alike, this volume [is] both handsome and fascinating. . . . Excellent photos, microscopic views, and maps illustrate the book." Booklist

Includes glossary and bibliographical references

Moffett, Mark W.

Face to face with frogs. National Geographic 2008 31p il map (Face to face) $16.95; lib bdg $25.90

Grades: 3 4 5 6   **597.8**

1. Frogs

ISBN 978-1-4263-0205-3; 1-4263-0205-3; 978-1-4263-0206-0 lib bdg; 1-4263-0206-1 lib bdg

LC 2007-12445

This book has "personal accounts of [Moffett's] own explorations providing entertaining specifics to go with the arresting visuals, as casual sidebars offer information on random hoppy topics." Bull Cent Child Books

Includes glossary and bibliographical references

Pfeffer, Wendy

From tadpole to frog; illustrated by Holly Keller. HarperCollins Pubs. 1994 32p il (Let's-read-and-find-out science) $15.95; pa $4.95

Grades: K 1   **597.8**

1. Frogs

ISBN 0-06-023044-4; 0-06-445123-2 pa

LC 93-3135

"The illustrations are simple, interesting, and just right for young children. The science is accurate and presented in a way to excite young readers to get outside and look for some frogs and tadpoles." Sci Books Films

Pringle, Laurence

Frogs! strange and wonderful. Laurence Pringle; illustrated by Meryl Henderson. Boyds Mills Press 2012 30 p. col. ill (reinf. trade ed.) $16.95

Grades: 3 4 5 **597.8**

1. Frogs 2. Poisonous animals 3. Camouflage (Biology) 4. Picture books for children 5. Amphibians
ISBN 1590783719; 9781590783719

LC 2011928834

In this book, author Laurence P. Pringle offers a "look at the similarities and differences among the many and varied species of frogs . . . The Reinwardt's flying frog glides between trees, the mantella and poison frogs come in all the colors of the rainbow and one can guess what makes the marsupial frog stand out. Camouflage, mating, development, coloring, size, locomotion, how and what they eat and how and why they make sounds are just some of the topics." (Kirkus)

Includes bibliographical references

Salas, Laura Purdie

Amphibians; water-to-land animals. illustrated by Kristin Kest. Picture Window Books 2010 24p il (Amazing science. Animal classification) lib bdg $25.32

Grades: K 1 2 **597.8**

1. Amphibians
ISBN 978-1-4048-5521-2 lib bdg; 1-4048-5521-1 lib bdg

LC 2009-3290

"This is the way to introduce kids to science as well as lead them to a deeper level of understanding how the animal kingdom is divided into phylum, class, order, family, genus, and species. Excellent picture book-quality illustrations fill each page with a few well chosen words to extend visual understanding. . . . The writing is clear, age-appropriate science writing. Every school should purchase this book." Libr Media Connect

Includes glossary

Somervill, Barbara A.

Cane toad; by Barbara A. Somervill. Cherry Lake Pub. 2008 32p il map (Animal invaders) lib bdg $26.26

Grades: 3 4 5 6 **597.8**

1. Toads 2. Biological invasions
ISBN 978-1-60279-115-2 lib bdg; 1-60279-115-5 lib bdg

LC 2007-33510

This describes the cane toads' "outstanding physical and behavioral characteristics at each stage in their life cycle, diet, and natural habitat, and then [explains] how they were introduced into areas outside their natural range . . . and the nature and extent of the ecological damage they have caused, and various attempts to eradicate or at least control the animals. . . . The prolific cane toads, which are fast supplanting native amphibians in Australia, excrete a toxin powerful enough to kill the animals, and some humans unfortunate enough to ingest them. . . . Clear color photographs . . . accompany the [text] on about every other page. . . . [This title

is] clearly written and well organized, and [has] up-to-date information." SLJ

Includes glossary

Stewart, Melissa

Frog or toad? how do you know? Enslow Publishers 2011 24p il (Which animal is which?) lib bdg $21.26; pa $6.95

Grades: 1 2 3 **597.8**

1. Frogs 2. Toads
ISBN 978-0-7660-3682-6 lib bdg; 0-7660-3682-0 lib bdg; 978-1-59845-236-5 pa; 1-59845-236-3 pa

LC 2010003277

This describes the differences between frogs and toads.
Includes bibliographical references

A place for frogs; written by Melissa Stewart; illustrated by Higgins Bond. Peachtree Publishers 2010 un il map $16.95

Grades: K 1 2 3 **597.8**

1. Frogs 2. Wildlife conservation
ISBN 978-1-5614-5521-8; 1-5614-5521-0

LC 2009-24515

"This wide-format book shows how people's actions have endangered frogs and what has been done to reverse those environmental threats. A typical double-page spread includes a large, detailed acrylic painting showing various frogs in their habitats. . . . Written and illustrated with young children in mind, this book is a good starting place for environmental studies." Booklist

Salamander or lizard? how do you know? Enslow Publishers 2011 24p il (Which animal is which?) lib bdg $21.26; pa $6.95

Grades: 1 2 3 **597.8**

1. Lizards 2. Salamanders
ISBN 978-0-7660-3679-6 lib bdg; 0-7660-3679-0 lib bdg; 978-1-59845-238-9 pa; 1-59845-238-X pa

LC 2010003279

This describes the differences between salamanders and lizards.

This "should give budding naturalists an increased understanding of how scientists use appearance and behavior of classify sometimes-similar living things. . . . Spreads feature sharply detailed paired photographs of identified specimens seen from the same angle and at roughly equal size." SLJ

Includes bibliographical references

Stille, Darlene R.

The life cycle of amphibians. Heinemann Library 2011 48p il (Life cycles) lib bdg $32; pa $8.99

Grades: 3 4 5 **597.8**

1. Amphibians
ISBN 978-1-4329-4978-5 lib bdg; 978-1-4329-4985-3 pa

LC 2010038276

This describes how amphibians "are born or hatched, where they live, and how they grow, move, protect themselves, spend their time, and reproduce. Focusing on frogs, toads, salamanders, and caecilians, [this book] is informative."

Includes glossary and bibliographical references

Sweeney, Alyse

Toads. Capstone Press 2010 24p il map (Pebble plus. Amphibians) lib bdg $22.65

Grades: K 1 2   **597.8**

1. Toads

ISBN 978-1-4296-3991-0 lib bdg; 1-4296-3991-1 lib bdg

This "is well suited to emerging readers. Dynamic, full-page color photographs complement controlled, repetitive vocabulary, printed in a large font against solid backgrounds. . . . While the information and its presentation are solid." SLJ

Includes glossary and bibliographical references

Turner, Pamela S.

★ The frog scientist; photographs by Andy Comins. Houghton Mifflin Books for Children 2009 58p il (Scientists in the field) lib bdg $18

Grades: 5 6 7 8   **597.8**

1. Frogs 2. Biologists 3. College teachers

ISBN 978-0-618-71716-3 lib bdg; 0-618-71716-1 lib bdg

LC 2008-39770

This volume "opens with biologist Tyrone Hayes and his team collecting frogs at a pond in Wyoming. After a short chapter on Hayes' background, the discussion returns to his work: he addresses the general question of why amphibian populations world-wide are declining by studying the effects of atrizine, an agricultural pesticide, on the reproductive organs of leopard frogs from a particular pond. Well organized and clearly written. . . . Excellent color photos offer clear pictures of frogs and of this scientific team at work in the field and in the lab. . . . A vivid, realistic view of one scientist at work." Booklist

Includes glossary and bibliographical references

Winnick, Nick

Salamanders. Weigl 2010 24p il (Backyard animals) lib bdg $24.45; pa $8.95

Grades: 1 2 3   **597.8**

1. Salamanders

ISBN 978-1-60596-084-5 lib bdg; 1-60596-084-5 lib bdg; 978-1-60596-085-2 pa; 1-60596-085-3 pa

LC 2008052060

This describes the physical characteristics, natural habitats, history, and folklore of salamanders.

This is "packed with information and [includes] fine close-up photos." Booklist

Includes glossary

597.9 Reptiles

Arnosky, Jim

★ Slither and crawl; eye to eye with reptiles. Sterling Pub. 2009 31p il $14.95

Grades: 2 3 4 5   **597.9**

1. Reptiles

ISBN 978-1-4027-3986-6; 1-4027-3986-9

LC 2008022493

"Arnosky's painterly eye and personal observations match handsomely in this face-to-face experience. The slim volume presents-head-on-life-size depictions of a plethora

of scaly or otherwise armored critters, along with a nice selection of data included in the conversational text. Neat foldouts of a passel of snakes, an American crocodile, . . . a skitter of lizards, and the heads of a variety of sea turtles add an interactive touch to the artist's outstanding acrylics." SLJ

Includes bibliographical references

Hutchinson, Mark

Reptiles. Simon & Schuster Books for Young Readers 2011 64p il (Insiders) $16.99

Grades: 4 5 6 7   **597.9**

1. Reptiles

ISBN 978-1-4424-3276-5; 1-4424-3276-4

"Arranged around the digitally rendered, sharply focused central images . . . smaller inset pictures and blocks of text systematically present distinctive physical features, typical behaviors, habitats, ranges, diets, and other information about each type of reptile. . . . This book will wow casual browsers and budding herpetologists alike." Booklist

McCarthy, Colin

Reptile; written by Colin McCarthy; [special photography, Karl Shone . . . [et al.]] Dorling Kindersley 2000 63p il (DK eyewitness books) $15.99

Grades: 4 5 6 7   **597.9**

1. Reptiles

ISBN 0-7894-5786-5

First published 1991 by Knopf

Photographs and text depict the many different kinds of reptiles, their similarities and differences, habitats, and behavior

Stille, Darlene R., 1942-

The life cycle of reptiles. Heinemann Library 2011 48p il map (Life cycles)

Grades: 3 4 5   **597.9**

1. Reptiles

ISBN 9781432949822 lib bdg; 9781432949891

LC 2010038507

This describes what a reptile is, types of reptiles, their life cycles, habitats, foods, and defenses.

"The book offers a good sense of the variety of reptiles in the world. The books' colorful illustrations include many fine photos from a variety of sources as well as some clearly delineated digital drawings." Booklist

Includes glossary and bibliographical references

Wilson, Hannah

Life-size reptiles; written by Hannah Wilson. Sterling 2007 48p il $9.95

Grades: 3 4 5 6   **597.9**

1. Reptiles

ISBN 1-4027-4542-7

This "covers lizards, crocodilians, and others of their cold-blooded kin. Colorful, realistic illustrations fill the pages, depicting reptiles in all their scaly/shelled splendor, many—as promised in the title—life-sized." SLJ

597.92 Turtles

Allen, Kathy

★ Sea turtles' race to the sea; a cause and effect investigation. Capstone Press 2011 32p il map (Animals on the edge) lib bdg $25.99

Grades: K 1 2 3   **597.92**

1. Sea turtles 2. Endangered species

ISBN 978-1-4296-5402-9; 1-4296-5402-3

LC 2010033003

Describes the sea turtle and its disappearing habitat.

"The thoughtfulness with which this . . . book is arranged shows through on each page. Photos truly complement the text without overwhelming it. . . . The book merits praise for its content and its compound contribution to the environment." Sci Books Films

Includes glossary and bibliographical references

Berger, Melvin

Look out for turtles! illustrated by Megan Lloyd. HarperCollins Pubs. 1992 32p il (Let's-read-and-find-out science book) hardcover o.p. pa $4.95

Grades: K 1 2 3   **597.92**

1. Turtles

ISBN 0-06-022540-8 lib bdg; 0-06-445156-9 pa

LC 90-36894

"This simple introductory resource provides an overview of the different types of turtles and their characteristics and habits. It is a good resource for young children to use independently." Sci Child

Christopherson, Sara Cohen

Top 50 reasons to care about marine turtles; animals in peril. Enslow Publishers 2009 103p il (Top 50 reasons to care about endangered animals) lib bdg $31.93

Grades: 4 5 6 7   **597.92**

1. Sea turtles 2. Endangered species

ISBN 978-0-7660-3455-6 lib bdg; 0-7660-3455-0 lib bdg

LC 2009-10555

This describes marine turtles-their life cycles, diets, young, habitats, and reasons why they are endangered animals

"The illustrations, mostly color photographs, represent a wonderful selection of the animals and their habitats. Reluctant readers may be enticed by this . . . simply because of the great images. This . . . would make a substantial supplement to the science curriculum when studying endangered animals." Libr Media Connect

Includes glossary and bibliographical references

Davies, Nicola, 1958-

One tiny turtle; illustrated by Jane Chapman. Candlewick Press 2001 29p il hardcover o.p. pa with audio CD $9.99

Grades: K 1 2 3   **597.92**

1. Turtles

ISBN 0-7636-1549-8; 978-0-7636-4193-1 pa with audio CD

LC 00-52326

This offers "simple, lyrical words and bright, acrylic double-page pictures. . . . Without condescension, this tells a powerful nature story for a young audience." Booklist

Gibbons, Gail

Sea turtles. Holiday House 1995 un il $16.95; pa $6.95

Grades: K 1 2 3   **597.92**

1. Sea turtles

ISBN 0-8234-1191-5; 0-8234-1373-X pa

LC 94-48579

This is "a very appealing book. . . . The illustrations are lovely paintings, highlighted with black outlines and clear labels. Children should find the diagram that shows differences between sea turtles and other turtles fascinating because they are often familiar only with the latter." Sci Books Films

Guiberson, Brenda Z.

Into the sea; illustrated by Alix Berenzy. Holt & Co. 1996 un il $16.95; pa $6.95

Grades: K 1 2 3   **597.92**

1. Sea turtles

ISBN 0-8050-2263-5; 0-8050-6481-8 pa

LC 95-46757

"Guiberson uses italicized sound words such as tap, tap, and scritch to draw readers into the story. Berenzy captures the essence of the text with her colored-pencil and gouache illustrations that alternate from dark to light, reflecting the various habitats." SLJ

Hall, Kirsten

Leatherback turtle; the world's heaviest reptile. Bearport Pub. 2007 24p il map (Super sized!) lib bdg $21.28

Grades: K 1 2   **597.92**

1. Sea turtles

ISBN 978-1-59716-393-4 lib bdg; 1-59716-393-7 lib bdg

LC 2006033247

This describes the size, habitat, diet, and life cycle of the leatherback turtle

This is "attractive. . . . Most spreads include two to five large-type sentences, a boxed fact, and a large colorful photograph." SLJ

Includes glossary and bibliographical references

Jackson, Tom

Green sea turtle; by Tom Jackson. Bearport Publishing 2013 24 p. (library binding) $23.93

Grades: 1 2   **597.92**

1. Sea turtles 2. Marine biology 3. Green turtle

ISBN 1617729205; 9781617729201

LC 2013011548

In this book, by Tom Jackson, "readers will explore the underwater world of [the green sea turtle] through clear text, full-color photos, and diagrams. Age-appropriate activities, such as using tape on the floor to show how big green sea turtles can grow, give readers a chance to make observations and to develop animal-science skills." (Publisher's note)

Includes bibliographical references and index

Lockwood, Sophie

Sea turtles; by Sophie Lockwood. Child's World 2006 40p col. ill., col. maps (library) $29.93

Grades: 4 5 6   **597.92**

1. Sea turtles

ISBN 1592965504; 9781592965502

LC 2005024792

"Conservation is the dominant theme of this attractive photo-essay. . . . which has beautiful full-page color photos that bring readers close to the subject. Fast-fact boxes focus on particular species, providing spot statistics on weight, length, color, habitat, threatened or endangered status, and more." Booklist

Includes bibliographical references (p. 39) and index.

Monroe, Mary Alice

Turtle summer; a journal for my daughter. Mary Alice Monroe, Barbara J. Bergwerf. Sylvan Dell 2007 32p il $15.95

Grades: K 1 2　　　　　　　　　　　　　597.92

1. Sea turtles

ISBN 978-0-9777423-5-6; 0-9777423-5-0

LC 2006-938664

"This is a companion book to Mary Alice Monroe's novel, Swimming Lessons, the sequel to The Beach House. In the novel, the readers witness a young mother, Toy, writing a journal for her daughter, Little Lovie. This is the journal Toy is writing. Using original photographs, this scrapbook journal explains the nesting cycle of sea turtles and the natural life along the southeastern coast, including local shore birds, shells, and the sea turtle hospital." (Publisher's note) "Grades three to six." (Sci Books Films)

Spilsbury, Louise

Sea turtle. Heinemann Library 2011 24p il (A day in the life. sea animals) lib bdg $22; pa $6.49

Grades: 1 2　　　　　　　　　　　　　　597.92

1. Sea turtles

ISBN 978-1-4329-4001-0 lib bdg; 1-4329-4001-5 lib bdg; 978-1-4329-4008-9 pa; 1-4329-4008-2 pa

LC 2010000626

This pairs "well-chosen color photos . . . with one or two sentences of simple commentary for each. . . . [Though this title] includes references to several varieties of the chosen creature, one species in particular is highlighted. . . . [Good choice] for pleasure or purpose reading." SLJ

Includes glossary and bibliographical references

Swinburne, Stephen R.

Sea turtle scientist; by Stephen R. Swinburne. Houghton Mifflin Harcourt 2013 65 p. ill. (chiefly col.), col. map (Scientists in the field) $18.99

Grades: 5 6 7 8 9　　　　　　　　　　　597.92

1. Biologists 2. Sea turtles

ISBN 0547367554; 9780547367552

LC 2012034045

"Dr. Kimberly Stewart, also known as the Turtle Lady of St. Kitts, is already waiting at midnight when an 800-pound leatherback sea turtle crawls out of the Caribbean surf and onto the sandy beach. The mother turtle has a vital job to do: dig a nest in which she will lay eggs that will hatch into part of the next generation of leatherbacks." (Publisher's note)

"This refreshing journey with a dedicated woman hard at work in her chosen field will resonate with readers." SLJ

Includes bibliographical references and index

Turtle tide; the ways of sea turtles. illustrated by Bruce Hiscock. Boyds Mills Press 2005 un il $15.95

Grades: 2 3 4　　　　　　　　　　　　　597.92

1. Sea turtles

ISBN 1-59078-081-7

LC 2004-16856

"Simple, lyrical prose accompanies brilliant watercolors in this account." SLJ

Wearing, Judy

Sea turtle. Weigl 2010 24p il (World of wonder: underwater life) lib bdg $24.45; pa $8.95

Grades: K 1 2　　　　　　　　　　　　　597.92

1. Sea turtles

ISBN 978-1-60596-106-4 lib bdg; 1-60596-106-X lib bdg; 978-1-60596-107-1 pa; 1-60596-107-8 pa

LC 2009-4987

This book about sea turtles begins "with introductory information and progress[es] to more unique details of the featured creatures. Bold photographs juxtaposed on colorful background graphic will hold the attention of even the most novice readers. . . . [This book is] sure to make a splash with budding marine biologists everywhere." SLJ

Includes glossary

597.95　Lizards

Bishop, Nic

★ Lizards. Scholastic Nonfiction 2010 48p il $17.99

Grades: 2 3 4　　　　　　　　　　　　　597.95

1. Lizards

ISBN 978-0-545-20634-1; 0-545-20634-0

"Bishop introduces lizards from around the world: their habitats, egg-laying and lack of child-rearing, their specialized bodies and behaviors, their feeding and courtship. His astonishing photographs are beautifully composed and clearly reproduced. . . . The well-organized two-level text is . . . inviting." Kirkus

Includes glossary and bibliographical references

Bodden, Valerie

Komodo dragons; by Valerie Bodden. 1st ed. Creative Education 2013 24 p. col. ill. (library) $25.65

Grades: 1 2 3 4　　　　　　　　　　　597.95

1. Komodo dragon

ISBN 1608180875; 9781608180875

LC 2011050275

This book, part of the Amazing Animals series from author Valerie Bodden, is a "basic exploration of the appearance, behavior, and habitat of Komodo dragons, Earth's heaviest lizards. Also included is a story from folklore explaining why Indonesians respect Komodo dragons." (Publisher's note)

Includes bibliographical references and index

Cowley, Joy

★ Chameleon chameleon; story by Joy Cowley; illustrated with photographs by Nic Bishop. Scholastic Press 2005 un il $16.95

Grades: K 1 2　　　　　　　　　　　　　597.95

1. Chameleons

ISBN 0-439-66653-8

LC 2004-7291

A chameleon creeps through the rain forest avoiding danger and searching for food

This is a "stunning photo-essay. . . . Crisp, clear, full-color photos portray this reptile and its habitat. . . . An informative, thoughtfully produced science book that will be popular with a wide range of animal lovers. Excellent for browsing as well as learning." Booklist

Crump, Marty

Mysteries of the Komodo dragon; the biggest, deadliest lizard gives up its secrets. Boyd Mills Press 2010 40p il map $18.95

Grades: 3 4 5 6   **597.95**

1. Komodo dragon

ISBN 978-1-59078-757-1; 1-59078-757-9

"While Crump's lively text does not supply a stage-by-stage description of the animal's life cycle and physiology, it does give enough data to satisfy many readers and researchers. More importantly, it follows a long-term research project into the chemical makeup of 'dragon drool' and the possible practical applications of the chemicals in this deadly substance to human pharmacology. Clear, color photos depict dragons from hatchlings to adults, scientists hiding in blinds and weighing catches, and zookeepers cuddling dragons with 'gentle' dispositions. . . . A surefire selection in terms of appeal and information." SLJ

Includes glossary and bibliographical references

Gish, Melissa

Komodo dragons. Creative Education 2011 48p il (Living wild) lib bdg $23.95; pa $8.99

Grades: 5 6 7 8   **597.95**

1. Komodo dragon

ISBN 978-1-60818-080-6 lib bdg; 1-60818-080-8 lib bdg; 978-0-89812-672-3 pa; 0-89812-672-X pa

LC 2010028307

A look at Komodo dragons, including their habitats, physical characteristics such as their sawlike teeth, behaviors, relationships with humans, and threatened status in the world today.

"Stunning, full-page photographs create immediate visual interest. A brief narrative introduction sets the scene for the richer, more scientific information in the rest of the text." Booklist

Includes glossary and bibliographical references

Jango-Cohen, Judith

Let's look at iguanas. Lerner Publications Co. 2010 32p il map (Lightning bolt books: Animal close-ups) lib bdg $25.26; pa $7.95

Grades: PreK K 1 2   **597.95**

1. Iguanas

ISBN 978-0-7613-3888-8 lib bdg; 0-7613-3888-8 lib bdg; 978-0-7613-5005-7 pa; 0-7613-5005-5 pa

LC 2008-51857

Introduces desert iguanas, describing their physical characteristics, habitat, and predators.

"Fresh photography, a creative use of graphics, and a collagelike layout make[s] . . . [this book] eye-catching. . . . [The] book ends with a labeled diagram of the animal, a range map, and a further-reading list that includes print and online resources in a single list, a nice way of validating both types of materials." SLJ

Includes glossary

Lunis, Natalie

Black spiny-tailed iguana; lizard lightning! Bearport Pub. 2010 24p il map (Blink of an eye. Superfast animals!) lib bdg $22.61

Grades: 1 2 3   **597.95**

1. Iguanas 2. Lizards

ISBN 978-1-936087-91-4; 1-936087-91-X

LC 2010019671

This describes the black spiny-tailed iguana, including where it lives, what it eats, and the ways its body helps it reach its record-breaking speeds.

This "is sure to appeal to a wide variety of readers. Vibrant photos illustrate each animal from multiple perspectives, providing opportunity for readers to closely examine the animal. Information is organized by subject heading and branches into the animal's physical features and how they contribute to its speed, the animal's natural predators, and how the animal makes use of speed as a means of survival. . . . This . . . will be a worthwhile addition to your nonfiction collection." Libr Media Connect

Includes glossary and bibliographical references

Sneed, Collard B. III

Sneed B. Collard III's most fun book ever about lizards; Sneed B. Collard III. Charlesbridge 2012 47 p. (reinforced for library use) $16.95

Grades: 3 4 5 6 7   **597.95**

1. Lizards 2. Lizards as pets 3. Wildlife photography 4. Lizards -- Miscellanea

ISBN 9781580893244; 9781580893251

LC 2011000809

This book offers an "introduction to the world of lizards [which] describes their . . . variety and life in the wild and offers cautions from a long-time reptile fan for those who want to keep lizards as pets. [Author Sneed B.] Collard . . . turns his attention . . . to modern-day lizards. After presenting an exemplar, 'Joe Lizard,' a western fence lizard, he goes on to describe other well-known species, including Komodo dragons, Gila monsters, chameleons and iguanas, as well as some with unusual talents, including 'religious lizards' that can walk on water. He covers eating and being eaten, the ways saurians keep warm and reproduce, and threats to their survival. . . . [Photographs] show lizard characteristics. . . . Captions and sidebars add further information." (Kirkus)

Somervill, Barbara A.

Monitor lizard. Cherry Lake 2010 32p il (Animal invaders) lib bdg $27.07

Grades: 5 6 7 8   **597.95**

1. Lizards 2. Biological invasions

ISBN 978-1-60279-627-0 lib bdg; 1-60279-627-0 lib bdg

This offers "an introduction to the problems caused by [the monitor lizard], a discussion of its physical characteristics and habits, a history of how it arrived in its new habitat, and an analysis of challenges encountered by those trying to limit its spread. . . . [It] describes the threat posed by these aggressive 7-foot reptiles, sold as babies by pet vendors and now loose in Florida. . . . [This] well-focused [book is] clearly written. The uncluttered page design features at least one color photo on each page." Booklist

Includes glossary and bibliographical references

597.96 Snakes

Bishop, Nic, 1955-

★ **Nic** Bishop snakes; Nic Bishop. Scholastic Nonfiction 2012 48 p. ill. (jacketed hardcover) $17.99
Grades: 3 4 5 **597.96**
1. Snakes
ISBN 0545206383; 9780545206389
LC 2011039316

In this juvenile zoology book, "Sibert Medal-winning photographer Nic Bishop introduces the terrifying and beautiful world of snakes. The . . . text presents both basic information and . . . details about the appearance, habits, and remarkable abilities of these amazing reptiles. An index and glossary are included, along with an author's note detailing his research and the . . . stories behind the photographs." (Publisher's note)

Blobaum, Cindy

Awesome snake science; 40 activities for learning about snakes. Cindy Blobaum. 1st ed. Chicago Review Press 2012 x, 118 p.p ill. (ebook) $11.99; (prebind) $23.95; (paperback) $14.95
Grades: 4 5 6 **597.96**
1. Science projects 2. Educational games 3. Science -- Experiments 4. Snakes -- Experiments 5. Snakes -- Study and teaching (Elementary) -- Activity programs
ISBN 9781613743188; 9781451775303;
9781569768075
LC 2011050257

Author Cindy Blobaum's book includes "40 science experiments, art projects, and games . . . [about snakes] from cobras and copperheads to pythons and boas . . . Activities include making foldable fangs to learn how snakes' teeth and jaws work together . . . [and] simulating cytotoxic snake venom . . . Engaging, simple, and safe experiments teach kids about the biology of snakes, such as how they use their tongues and nostrils to detect smells, how they are cold-blooded and sensitive to subtle changes in temperature, and how they can detect the slightest vibrations or tremors." (Amazon)

Includes bibliographical references (p. 115-116) and index.

Bodden, Valerie

Snakes. Creative Education 2010 24p il (Amazing animals) lib bdg $24.25
Grades: K 1 2 **597.96**
1. Snakes
ISBN 978-1-58341-813-0 lib bdg; 1-58341-813-X lib bdg
LC 2009002717

A basic exploration of the appearance, behavior, and habitat of snakes, a family of scaly reptiles. Also included is a story from folklore explaining why snakes do not have legs.

Includes bibliographical references

Ganeri, Anita

Anaconda. Heinemann Library 2011 24p il map (A day in the life. Rain forest animals) lib bdg $22; pa $6.49

Grades: 1 2 **597.96**
1. Anacondas
ISBN 978-1-4329-4112-3 lib bdg; 1-4329-4112-7 lib bdg; 978-1-4329-4123-9 pa; 1-4329-4123-2 pa
LC 2010001135

This book follows an anaconda through its day as it sleeps, eats, and moves.

"Ganeri presents information clearly and simply in large type, two-sentence comments placed below a bright, sharply reproduced color photograph of the animal in a natural setting. . . . [This is] sufficiently specific to support assignment as well as pleasure reading." SLJ

Includes glossary and bibliographical references

Gibbons, Gail

Snakes. Holiday House 2007 32p il map $16.95
Grades: K 1 2 3 **597.96**
1. Snakes
ISBN 978-0-8234-2122-0; 0-8234-2122-8
LC 2007-24585

"Gibbons injects a healthy dose of snake basics, delivered in her customary matter-of-fact style and illustrated with watercolor portraits of dozens of different species, pictured mostly in natural settings." Booklist

Hamilton, Sue L.

Bitten by a rattlesnake; [by] Sue Hamilton. ABDO Pub. 2010 32p il (Close encounters of the wild kind) lib bdg $27.07
Grades: 4 5 6 7 **597.96**
1. Rattlesnakes 2. Animal attacks
ISBN 978-1-60453-930-1 lib bdg; 1-60453-930-5 lib bdg
LC 2009-45423

Readers learn of actual human-rattlesnake encounters, information about rattlesnakes, survival strategies, and attack statistics.

"Students will be drawn to the realistic full-color photographs, the realistic diagrams of the creatures' bodies, the real-life stories told by victims, and the interesting, attractive formatting that includes text, diagrams, photographs, and graphics on each page. . . . [This is] exciting and attractive in a 'gross' sort of way and will appeal particularly to boys for both leisure reading and research." Libr Media Connect

Includes glossary

Holub, Joan

Why do snakes hiss? and other questions about snakes, lizards, and turtles. illustrations by Anna DiVito. Dial Books for Young Readers 2004 46p il (Dial easy-to-read) hardcover o.p. pa $3.99
Grades: K 1 2 **597.96**
1. Snakes 2. Reptiles
ISBN 0-8037-3000-4; 0-14-240105-6 pa
LC 2003-64948

Questions and answers present information about the behavior and characteristics of snakes, lizards, and turtles

"The photos and attractive ink drawings with color washes that come two to three to a page result in a colorful presentation with illustrations in different styles from many sources." Booklist

Markle, Sandra

Rattlesnakes. Lerner Publications 2009 39p il (Animal predators) lib bdg $26.60

Grades: 4 5 6 **597.96**

1. Rattlesnakes

ISBN 978-1-58013-539-9 lib bdg; 1-58013-539-0 lib bdg

LC 2008-38038

Introduces the physical characteristics, habitat, and predatory behavior of rattlesnakes.

"Vivid close-up photographs accompany a narrative." Horn Book Guide

Includes glossary and bibliographical references

Montgomery, Sy

★ The **snake** scientist; photographs by Nic Bishop. Houghton Mifflin 1999 48p il map $16; pa $5.95

Grades: 4 5 6 7 **597.96**

1. Snakes

ISBN 0-395-87169-7; 0-618-11119-0 pa

LC 98-6124

Discusses the work of Bob Mason and his efforts to study and protect snakes, particularly red-sided garter snakes

"The lively text communicates both the meticulous measurements required in this kind of work and the thrill of new discoveries. Large, full-color photos of the zoologist and young students at work, and lots of wriggly snakes, pull readers into the presentation." SLJ

Includes bibliographical references

Patent, Dorothy Hinshaw

Slinky, Scaly, Slithery Snakes; by Dorothy Hinshaw Patent and illustrated by Kendahl Jan Jubb. Walker Childrens 2003 32 p. il $7.99

Grades: K 1 2 3 **597.96**

1. Snakes

ISBN 0802776523; 9780802776525

LC 0028099

In this book author Dorothy Hinshaw Patent and illustrator Kendahl Jan Jubb "combine their talents and knowledge in this scientifically accurate and . . . illustrated book [designed for] snake lovers [noting] they have many characteristics in common [and] they can range in patterns and sizes from the two-inch-long thread snake." (Publisher's note)

"Patent discusses camouflage and predatory skills as well as how snakes move, where they live, how they can devour animals larger than themselves. . . . Surrounding and sometimes underlying the text are vibrant paintings that offer close-up views of snakes in the wild. An inviting look at snakes." Booklist

Simon, Seymour

Giant snakes; [by] Seymour Simon. Chronicle Books 2006 un il (See more readers) lib bdg $14.95; pa $3.95

Grades: K 1 2 3 **597.96**

1. Snakes

ISBN 978-0-8118-5410-8 lib bdg; 0-8118-5410-8 lib bdg; 978-0-8118-5411-5 pa; 0-8118-5411-6 pa

LC 2005-25360

An easy-to-read illustrated introduction to large snakes.

"The text is lively, well organized, and clear, with the many facts it presents cleverly woven into the story. The illustrations, which are beautiful, show distinctly the intricate patterns of the snakes' skin." Sci Books Films

Stewart, Melissa

Snakes! National Geographic 2009 31p il (National Geographic kids) lib bdg $11.90; pa $3.99

Grades: K 1 2 **597.96**

1. Snakes

ISBN 978-1-4263-0429-3 lib bdg; 978-1-4263-0428-6 pa

LC 2008-47001

An introduction to the types, physical features, behavior, and pet potential of snakes.

"The excellent photographs showcase a variety of species in vivid detail. Vocabulary-word text boxes and goofy jokes . . . increase accessibility." Horn Book Guide

597.98 Crocodilians

Bodden, Valerie

Crocodiles. Creative Education 2010 24p il (Amazing animals) lib bdg $24.25; pa $5.99

Grades: K 1 2 **597.98**

1. Crocodiles

ISBN 978-1-58341-806-2 lib bdg; 1-58341-806-7 lib bdg; 978-1-926722-21-4 pa; 1-926722-21-3 pa

LC 2009002706

A basic exploration of the appearance, behavior, and habitat of crocodiles, a family of sharp-toothed reptiles. Also included is a story from folklore explaining why crocodiles have rough skin.

This is illustrated with "dynamically colored photographs . . . showcasing the animal's intricately textured scales, craggy ridges, and of course, hide-rending teeth." Booklist

Includes bibliographical references

Feigenbaum, Aaron

American alligators; freshwater survivors. Bearport Pub. Company, Inc. 2008 32p il map (America's animal comebacks) lib bdg $25.27

Grades: 2 3 4 **597.98**

1. Alligators

ISBN 978-1-59716-503-7 lib bdg; 1-59716-503-4 lib bdg

LC 2007-13160

Explains why American alligators became an endangered species, and describes the efforts of scientists to bring them back from the brink of extinction

"Closeup photos, maps, and an accessible text provide solid information for readers and report writers. Statistics and information about other endangered alligators are appended." Horn Book Guide

Includes glossary and bibliographical references

Gibbons, Gail

Alligators and crocodiles. Holiday House 2010 32p il map $17.95

Grades: K 1 2 3 **597.98**

1. Alligators 2. Crocodiles

ISBN 0-8234-2234-8; 978-0-8234-2234-0

Gibbons "draws young readers into the world of alligators and crocodiles by first asking readers to distinguish between them. She describes the physical similarities and differences between the two most common species of the world's largest reptiles, as well as their habitats, habits, prey, locomotion, senses, communication, mating and nesting behavior, and status as endangered species. The author has chosen facts that will engage her readers, organized the information logically, and presented it in straightforward exposition. Pen-and-ink and watercolor illustrations show both species in their likely environment." Booklist

Gish, Melissa

    Alligators. Creative Education 2010 46p il (Living wild) $23.95; pa $9.95

Grades: 5 6 7 8   **597.98**

    1. Alligators

    ISBN 978-1-58341-967-0; 1-58341-967-5; 978-0-89812-550-4 pa; 0-89812-550-2 pa

                               LC 2010017372

The "book lucidly discusses conservation and the animals' often tenuous relationships with humans. The layout is uniformly simple but effective, constructed with a nice balance of main text for the report writers, smaller chunks of esoterica for browsers, and . . . killer photos." Booklist

Hamilton, Sue L.

    Attacked by a crocodile; [by] Sue Hamilton. ABDO Pub. 2010 32p il (Close encounters of the wild kind) lib bdg $27.07

Grades: 4 5 6 7   **597.98**

    1. Crocodiles 2. Animal attacks

    ISBN 978-1-60453-929-5; 1-60453-929-1

                               LC 2009-45514

Readers learn of actual human-crocodile encounters, information about crocodiles, survival strategies, and attack statistics.

"Students will be drawn to the realistic full-color photographs, the realistic diagrams of the creatures' bodies, the real-life stories told by victims, and the interesting, attractive formatting that includes text, diagrams, photographs, and graphics on each page. . . . [This is] exciting and attractive in a 'gross' sort of way and will appeal particularly to boys for both leisure reading and research." Libr Media Connect

    Includes glossary

Jackson, Tom

    Saltwater crocodile; by Tom Jackson. Bearport Publishing 2013 24 p. (library binding) $23.93

Grades: 1 2   **597.98**

    1. Crocodiles 2. Crocodylus porosus

    ISBN 161772923X; 9781617729232

                               LC 2013011638

In this book, by Tom Jackson, "readers will explore the underwater world of [saltwater crocodiles] through clear text, full-color photos, and diagrams. Age-appropriate activities, such as describing the advantages of ambushing prey, give readers a chance to make observations and develop animal-science skills." (Publisher's note)

    Includes bibliographical references and index

Markle, Sandra

    ★ **Crocodiles**; by Sandra Markle. Carolrhoda Books 2004 39p il (Animal predators) lib bdg $25.26; pa $7.95

Grades: 3 4 5 6   **597.98**

    1. Crocodiles

    ISBN 1-57505-726-3 lib bdg; 1-57505-742-5 pa

                               LC 2003-15402

"The straightforward, descriptive text and superb photos give [this title] surefire appeal to middle readers." Booklist

"Markle observes Nile crocodiles' hunting techniques and includes information about their physiology, habitats, and care of young." Horn Book Guide

    Includes glossary and bibliographical references

Meinking, Mary

    Crocodile vs. wildebeest. Raintree 2011 32p il (Predator vs. prey) $29; pa $7.99

Grades: 1 2 3   **597.98**

    1. Gnus 2. Crocodiles 3. Predatory animals

    ISBN 978-1-4109-3935-7; 1-4109-3935-9; 978-1-4109-3944-9 pa; 1-4109-3944-8 pa

Explores the features of crocodiles and gnu that make them particularly suited to catch or evade.

"The struggle between predator crocodile and its wildebeest prey is described in clear language and illustrated with engaging color photographs." Horn Book Guide

Otfinoski, Steven

    ★ **Alligators**; by Steven Otfinoski. Marshall Cavendish Benchmark 2009 47p il (Animals animals) lib bdg $20.95

Grades: 3 4 5 6   **597.98**

    1. Alligators

    ISBN 978-0-7614-2930-2 lib bdg; 0-7614-2930-1 lib bdg

                               LC 2007-25448

"Provides comprehensive information on the anatomy, special skills, habitats, and diet of alligators." Publisher's note

    Includes glossary

Pringle, Laurence P.

    Alligators and crocodiles! strange and wonderful. [by] Laurence Pringle; illustrated by Meryl Henderson. Boyds Mills Press 2009 32p il $16.95

Grades: 3 4 5   **597.98**

    1. Alligators 2. Crocodiles

    ISBN 978-1-59078-256-9; 1-59078-256-9

                               LC 2008-30018

This describes alligators' and crocodiles' "habitats and nesting behavior, and explains their common anatomical features and distinguishing characteristics. . . . Henderson presents a gallery of full-body portraits of 21 crocodilian species, as well as a series of close-ups. These illustrations are drawn and colored in . . . clear, precise detail." Booklist

Riggs, Kate

    Alligators; by Kate Riggs. Creative Education 2012 24 p. (Amazing animals)

Grades: K 1 2   **597.98**

    1. Aquatic animals 2. Alligators -- Folklore 3. Alligators

    ISBN 1608181049; 9781608181049

                               LC 2010049122

This book, a volume of the Amazing Animals series, offers an "exploration of the appearance, behavior, and habitat of alligators. . . . Also included is a story from folklore explaining why alligators and dogs don't get along." (Publisher's note) "This book also shows alligator hatchlings breaking free from an egg, open-jawed waiting to feed, and clinging as it rides on its mother's back. This book also addresses the question: How do you tell the difference between an alligator and a crocodile? . . . This book shares with readers how the alligator lives in the swamplands, how it hunts, raises young, and lives mostly alone." (Children's Literature)

Includes bibliographical references (p. 24) and index

Rockwell, Anne F.

Who lives in an alligator hole? by Anne Rockwell; illustrated by Lizzy Rockwell. HarperCollins 2006 33p il (Let's-read-and-find-out science) $15.99; pa $4.99
Grades: K 1 2 3   **597.98**
    1. Ecology 2. Alligators
    ISBN 0-06-028530-3; 0-06-445200-X pa

Describes the habitats of these reptiles which scientists call a "keystone species" because they change the environment for their own use in a way that helps many other plants and animals.

"Information and illustration work well together in this picture book presentation. . . . Simplified yet not anthropomorphized, the clearly delineated paintings feature alligators and other animals as the focal points of well-composed scenes." Booklist

Simon, Seymour

Crocodiles & alligators. HarperCollins Pubs. 1999 un il hardcover o.p. pa $6.99
Grades: 4 5 6 7   **597.98**
    1. Alligators 2. Crocodiles
    ISBN 0-06-027473-5; 0-06-443829-5 pa

LC 98-34705

Describes the physical characteristics and behavior of various members of the family of animals known as crocodilians

"The book is filled with interesting information, and the vivid, well-composed, full-color photographs and entertaining text will draw in browsers." SLJ

Stewart, Melissa

Alligator or crocodile? how do you know? Enslow Publishers 2011 24p il (Which animal is which?) lib bdg $21.26
Grades: 1 2 3   **597.98**
    1. Alligators 2. Crocodiles
    ISBN 978-0-7660-3677-2; 0-7660-3677-4

LC 2010003275

This explains the differences between alligators and crocodiles.

This "should give budding naturalists an increased understanding of how scientists use appearance and behavior of classify sometimes-similar living things. . . . Spreads feature sharply detailed paired photographs of identified specimens seen from the same angle and at roughly equal size." SLJ

Includes bibliographical references

598   Birds

Alderfer, Jonathan

National Geographic kids bird guide of North America; the best birding book for kids from National Geographic's bird experts. by Jonathan Alderfer. National Geographic 2013 176 p. (paperback) $15.95; (library) $23.90

Grades: 4 5 6 7 8   **598**
    1. Birds -- North America 2. Birds -- Identification 3. Birds -- North America -- Identification
    ISBN 1426310943; 9781426310942; 9781426310959

LC 2012028615

Author "[Jonathan] Alderfer offers in-depth studies of 60 birds native to North America (plus 'mini-profiles' of another 60 specimens) in a guide for nascent birders. . . . The book is organized by region, and each bird's spread offers . . . color photographs, 'vital statistics' (including its call, diet, and habitat), maps of where it can be found, and other background." (Publishers Weekly)

Includes bibliographical references and index

Arnold, Caroline

A **bald** eagle's world; written and illustrated by Caroline Arnold. Picture Window Books 2010 24p il (Caroline Arnold's animals) lib bdg $25.32
Grades: PreK K 1 2   **598**
    1. Bald eagle
    ISBN 978-1-4048-5741-4 lib bdg; 1-4048-5741-9 lib bdg

LC 2009033358

This narrative describes the life of a bald eagle from the time it hatches until it can fly on its own.

The story "related in the present tense, [feels] immediate and engaging. . . . The plainness of the fact boxes [contrast] with Arnold's beautiful but simple artwork, which cleanly captures the essence of [the] animal. . . . [This book's] perfectly balanced mix of facts, story, and pictures will hold young readers' attention and help then learn." Booklist

Birds; nature's magnificent flying machines. illustrated by Patricia J. Wynne. Charlesbridge Pub. 2003 32p il $16.95; pa $6.95
Grades: 3 4 5 6   **598**
    1. Birds -- Flight
    ISBN 1-57091-516-4; 1-57091-572-5 pa

LC 2002-10441

An introduction to the science that explains how birds fly

"A clear, interesting book. . . . Each spread contains one or two paragraphs with a large, full-color illustration as well as smaller, captioned pictures that cover such topics as bone structure and preening. The colorful artwork consistently clarifies the concepts being discussed." SLJ

Includes glossary and bibliographical references

A **penguin's** world; written and illustrated by Caroline Arnold. Picture Window Books 2005 24p il $23.93
Grades: K 1 2 3   **598**
    1. Penguins
    ISBN 1-4048-1323-3

LC 2005023159

"This title follows an Adelie penguin family from scenes in which the parents build a nest and warm their eggs to final pages showcasing the four-month-old, newly independent chicks. The simple, well-paced text weaves basic concepts into the captivating narrative, and the artwork's strong colors and bold, uncluttered compositions capture the expression and movement of the birds." Booklist

Includes glossary and bibliographical references

Arnosky, Jim

★ **Thunder** birds; nature's flying predators. Sterling 2011 32p il $14.95

Grades: 3 4 5 6   **598**

1. Birds of prey

ISBN 978-1-4027-5661-0; 1-4027-5661-5

LC 2010019680

"Foldout pages group birds according to species and common characteristics. Lifelike owls peer at readers with deep, glassy eyes; in a section featuring birds of prey, an osprey's spectacular wing spans three panels, and journal-like passages vividly document Arnosky's observations of each bird. . . . Arnosky's enthusiasm is evident in his deftly crafted images and in the immediacy of his 'field-note' style." Publ Wkly

Bailer, Darice

Geese. Marshall Cavendish Benchmark 2010 47p il (Animals animals) lib bdg $29.93

Grades: 3 4 5   **598**

1. Geese

ISBN 978-0-7614-4840-2 lib bdg; 0-7614-4840-3 lib bdg

LC 2009019482

This offers information on the anatomy, special skills, habitats, and diet of geese.

Includes glossary and bibliographical references

Barner, Bob

Penguins, penguins, everywhere! Chronicle Books 2007 un il $14.95

Grades: PreK K 1   **598**

1. Penguins

ISBN 978-0-8118-5664-5; 0-8118-5664-X

LC 2006-20960

"Colorful collages depict plump penguins performing a plethora of penguiny pastimes. . . . Barner's simply rhyming text presents a variety of the birds. . . . A final spread proffers a parade of all 17 species, including data on global location, size, and weight." SLJ

Bash, Barbara

★ **Urban** roosts: where birds nest in the city. Sierra Club Bks. 1990 un il hardcover o.p. pa $6.95

Grades: 1 2 3 4   **598**

1. Birds -- Nests

ISBN 0-316-08312-7 pa

LC 89-70187

"Excellent treatment of an unusual subject reveals that human-made places of steel, stone, and concrete are home to a variety of birds. Includes information on sparrows, finches, barn and snowy owls, swallows, swifts, nighthawks, killdeers, pigeons, wrens, crows, starlings, and falcons that have successfully adapted to city life." Sci Child

Berendt, John

My baby blue jays. Viking 2011 un il $16.99

Grades: K 1 2 3   **598**

1. Blue jays

ISBN 978-0-670-01290-9; 0-670-01290-4

LC 2010033296

The author "delivers a warm photo-essay about a pair of blue jays that make their home on his apartment balcony in New York City. While the arc of the story—nestbuilding,

laying eggs, the first flight of a fledgling—is an old one, Berendt's telling is welcoming and personal, as if he were relating the story to a child in his lap while paging through a family photo album. . . . Set within scalloped borders against a cream backdrop, the photographs provide a remarkably intimate view of the birds' lives." Publ Wkly

Bodden, Valerie

Parrots. Creative Education 2010 24p il (Amazing animals) lib bdg $24.25

Grades: K 1 2   **598**

1. Parrots

ISBN 978-1-58341-809-3 lib bdg; 1-58341-809-1 lib bdg

LC 2009002711

A basic exploration of the appearance, behavior, and habitat of parrots, a family of colorful birds. Also included is a story from folklore explaining why parrots can imitate speech.

Includes bibliographical references

Penguins. Creative Education 2010 24p il (Amazing animals) lib bdg $24.25

Grades: K 1 2   **598**

1. Penguins

ISBN 978-1-58341-810-9 lib bdg; 1-58341-810-5 lib bdg

LC 2009002712

A basic exploration of the appearance, behavior, and habitat of penguins, a family of flightless birds. Also included is a story from folklore explaining why emperor penguins are so big.

This is illustrated with "dynamically colored photographs." Booklist

Includes bibliographical references

Bouler, Olivia

★ **Olivia's** birds; saving the Gulf. Sterling Pub. 2011 32p il $14.95

Grades: 4 5 6   **598**

1. Birds 2. Nature conservation

ISBN 978-1-4027-8665-5; 1-4027-8665-4

LC 2010046002

"Eleven-year-old Bouler, who raised more than $150,000 for the Audubon Society's Gulf Coast oil spill recovery efforts through the sale of her bird paintings, pairs her artwork with casual, informative passages to create an upbeat lesson on bird identification, habitat, and nature preservation. . . . Bouler's depictions of familiar birds like the Canada goose, bald eagle, and hummingbird are carefully observed and spirited; her vivacious attitude may inspire ecologically minded readers to get involved." Publ Wkly

Burnie, David

Bird; written by David Burnie. rev ed.; DK Pub. 2008 72p il (DK eyewitness books) $15.99

Grades: 4 5 6 7   **598**

1. Birds

ISBN 978-0-7566-3768-2; 0-7566-3768-6

First published 1988 by Knopf

A photo essay on the world of birds examining such topics as body construction, feathers and flight, the adaptation of beaks and feet, feeding habits, courtship, nests and eggs, and bird watching.

Includes glossary

Cate, Annette LeBlanc

★ **Look up!** bird-watching in your own backyard. Annette LeBlanc Cate. Candlewick Press 2013 64 p. $15.99

Grades: 2 3 4 5 **598**

1. Birds

ISBN 0763645613; 9780763645618

LC 2012942416

Robert F. Sibert Honor Book (2014)

This children's picture book puts an "emphasis on looking at the birds near home-from suburbs to inner cities." It groups "birds by colors, shapes, behaviors, feathers, calls, habitat, migration, and more" and "emphasizes the importance of observation and includes sketching instructions as a way to hone those skills on the individual aspects of a bird along with its species' characteristics." (School Library Journal)

"...Jam-packed with accurate information likely to increase any potential birder's enthusiasm and knowledge." Kirkus

Catt, Thessaly

Migrating with the Arctic tern. PowerKids Press 2011 24p il map (Animal journeys) lib bdg $21.25; pa $8.25

Grades: 2 3 4 **598**

1. Terns 2. Birds -- Migration

ISBN 978-1-4488-2542-4 lib bdg; 1-4488-2542-3 lib bdg; 978-1-4488-2668-1 pa; 1-4488-2668-3 pa

LC 2010025389

This book follows "the yearly migratory patterns of the [arctic tern] and [covers] anatomy, diet, mating, parenting, climate change as caused by people, pollution, and more. . . . [It is illustrated] with clear color photographs. . . . Go-to nonfiction for animal enthusiasts." SLJ

Includes glossary

Dunning, Joan

★ **Seabird** in the forest; the mystery of the marbled murrelet. Boyds Mills Press 2011 un il $17.95

Grades: K 1 2 3 **598**

1. Murrelets

ISBN 978-1-59078-715-1; 1-59078-715-3

"A marbled murrelet chick's early life is surprising. Most seabirds lay their eggs on the sand or high cliffs at the water's edge, but the marbled murrelet usually lays a single egg high on a branch of an old-growth tree, far from the ocean. . . . The hatched chick spends a month hunkered down on the branch, camouflaged by its own down, waiting for a parent to arrive with fish. This large-format picture book describes the life of one such chick. . . . The text runs beneath expressive illustrations, with close-ups of adult birds and their chick as well as landscapes suggesting their contrasting worlds; they support the mood of mystery and show well at a distance. Text boxes set on the illustrations add further detail. A beautiful addition." Kirkus

Evert, Laura

Birds of prey; explore the fascinating worlds of eagles, falcons, owls, vultures. by Laura Evert and Wayne Lynch; illustrations by Sherry Neidigh and John F. McGee. NorthWord 2005 191p il (Our wild world) $16.95

Grades: 3 4 5 6 **598**

1. Birds of prey

ISBN 1-55971-925-7

LC 2005000189

This "volume is divided into four sections, each addressing one of the major groups of raptors: eagles, falcons, owls, and vultures. The chapters, which have color-coded pages for quick reference, are similarly organized, making for easier reading, and deal with all aspects of the birds' life cycles and habits. Plentiful, high-quality photographs . . . and clear illustrations elucidate the narrative." SLJ

Ganeri, Anita

Macaw. Heinemann Library 2011 24p il map (A day in the life. Rain forest animals) lib bdg $22; pa $6.49

Grades: 1 2 **598**

1. Birds 2. Cage birds

ISBN 978-1-4329-4105-5 lib bdg; 1-4329-4105-4 lib bdg; 978-1-4329-4116-1 pa; 1-4329-4116-X pa

LC 2010000960

This book follows a macaw through its day as it sleeps, eats, and moves.

"Ganeri presents information clearly and simply in large type, two-sentence comments placed below a bright, sharply reproduced color photograph of the animal in a natural setting. . . . [This is] sufficiently specific to support assignment as well as pleasure reading." SLJ

Includes glossary and bibliographical references

Gibbons, Gail

Owls; [by] Gail Gibbons. Holiday House 2005 32p il $16.95; pa $6.95

Grades: K 1 2 3 **598**

1. Owls

ISBN 0-8234-1880-4; 0-8234-2014-0 pa

LC 2004-48225

A "factual look at raptors of the night, full of information tied specifically to the owls of North America. General facts on physiology, hunting tactics, digestion, habitats, and communication are offered, as is a section on mating, egg laying and incubation, and owlet development. . . . Gibbons's trademark watercolors provide lively renditions of a variety of these silent hunters. . . . This is a bright addition to owl lore for younger readers." SLJ

Gish, Melissa

★ **Eagles**. Creative Education 2010 46p il (Living wild) lib bdg $23.95; pa $9.95

Grades: 5 6 7 8 **598**

1. Eagles

ISBN 978-1-58341-968-7 lib bdg; 1-58341-968-3 lib bdg; 978-0-89812-551-1 pa; 0-89812-551-0 pa

LC 2010-17373

This "book lucidly discusses conservation and the animals' often tenuous relationship with humans. The layout is uniformly simple but effective, constructed with a nice balance of main text for the report writers, smaller chunks of esoterica for browsers, and . . . killer photos." Booklist

Hummingbirds. Creative Education 2011 46p il map (Living wild) lib bdg $23.95; pa $8.95

Grades: 5 6 7 8 **598**
1. Hummingbirds
ISBN 978-1-60818-078-3; 1-60818-078-6; 978-0-89812-670-9 pa; 0-89812-670-3 pa

LC 2010028314

A look at hummingbirds, including their habitats, physical characteristics such as their ability to hover, behaviors, relationships with humans, and admired status in the world today.

"Stunning, full-page photographs create immediate visual interest. A brief narrative introduction sets the scene for the richer, more scientific information in the rest of the text." Booklist

Includes glossary and bibliographical references

Owls. Creative Education 2011 46p il map (Living wild) lib bdg $23.95
Grades: 5 6 7 8 **598**
1. Owls
ISBN 978-1-60818-081-3; 1-60818-081-6

LC 2010028308

A look at owls, including their habitats, physical characteristics such as their large and observant eyes, behaviors, relationships with humans, and protected status in the world today.

"Stunning, full-page photographs create immediate visual interest. A brief narrative introduction sets the scene for the richer, more scientific information in the rest of the text." Booklist

Includes glossary and bibliographical references

Goldin, Augusta R.
Ducks don't get wet; by Augusta Goldin; illustrated by Helen K. Davie. newly il ed; HarperCollins Pubs. 1999 32p il (Let's-read-and-find-out science) hardcover o.p. pa $4.95
Grades: K 1 2 3 **598**
1. Ducks
ISBN 0-06-027881-1; 0-06-027882-X lib bdg; 0-06-445187-9 pa

LC 97-43597

A newly illustrated edition of the title first published 1965 by Crowell

Describes the behavior of different kinds of ducks and, in particular, discusses how all ducks use preening to keep their feathers dry

"The text is well focused throughout. . . . Notable for its clarity, subtlety, and beauty, the artwork illustrates the text with precision and imagination." Booklist

Goldish, Meish
California condors; saved by captive breeding. Bearport Pub. 2009 32p il map (America's animal comebacks) lib bdg $25.27
Grades: 2 3 4 **598**
1. Condors 2. Wildlife conservation
ISBN 978-1-59716-741-3 lib bdg; 1-59716-741-X lib bdg

LC 2008-32803

Through this true tale of wildlife survival, young readers discover the bold and creative ideas that Americans and their government have used to protect and care for the country's endangered California condors

"Crisp photos and maps on every page work well with the text and give faces to the scientists and animals. The back matter includes a facts page, information on related species, and an up-to-date reading list." SLJ

Includes glossary and bibliographical references

Gonzales, Doreen
Owls in the dark. PowerKids Press 2010 24p il (Creatures of the night) lib bdg $21.25; pa $8.05
Grades: 2 3 4 **598**
1. Owls
ISBN 978-1-4042-8097-7 lib bdg; 1-4042-8097-9 lib bdg; 978-1-4358-3251-0 pa; 1-4358-3251-5 pa

A look at owls and their world in the dark.

"Basic details are complemented by eclectic trivia, . . . [and the] volume concludes with a defense of the animal . . . and why it is vital to humans. The layout is attractive, with easy-to-read text and eye-catching photography. Good for reports." SLJ

Includes glossary

Gray, Susan H.
The **life** cycle of birds; [by] Susan H. Gray. Heinemann Library 2011 48p il (Life cycles)
Grades: 3 4 5 **598**
1. Birds
ISBN 9781432949792 lib bdg; 9781432949860

LC 2010038277

This describes how birds are "hatched, where they live, and how they grow, move, protect themselves, spend their time, and reproduce. . . . [This book] provides a well-organized account of avian creatures, including topics such as preening, digestion, and adaptations to different habitats." Booklist

Includes glossary and bibliographical references

Hanel, Rachael
Penguins. Smart Apple Media 2009 46p il (Living wild) lib bdg $32.80
Grades: 4 5 6 7 **598**
1. Penguins
ISBN 978-1-58341-658-7 lib bdg; 1-58341-658-7 lib bdg

LC 2007008503

"The 17 species of penguins . . . fill [this] slim, informative [volume]. [The] overview is divided into several chapters . . . describing the shared and distinct physical characteristics of the various species, the location of their particular habitats, life cycle, social behavior, and the history of human awareness of and impact on these animals. Fine color photographs face pages of text with smaller views placed in colored sidebars or insets. The [book concludes] with current environmental threats and conservation efforts. . . . Handsome and appealing." SLJ

Harkins, Susan Sales
Threat to the whooping crane; [by] Susan Sales Harkins and William H. Harkins. Mitchell Lane Pub. 2008 32p il map (On the verge of extinction: crisis in the environment) lib bdg $17.95

Grades: 3 4 5 **598**
1. Cranes (Birds) 2. Endangered species
ISBN 978-1-58415-685-7 lib bdg; 1-58415-685-6
lib bdg

LC 2008-08037

Describes the physical characteristics and behavior of the whooping crane, including their yearly migration patterns, and details the history of threats to the species and what steps are being made to return the crane from endangerment.

This book "provide[s] a wealth of information . . . [and is] accurate and easy for young readers to comprehend." Sci Books Films

Includes glossary and bibliographical references

Helget, Nicole Lea
Swans; by Nicole Helget. Smart Apple Media 2009 46p il (Living wild) lib bdg $32.80
Grades: 4 5 6 7 **598**
1. Swans
ISBN 978-1-58341-659-4 lib bdg; 1-58341-659-5
lib bdg

LC 2007015242

The "7 [species] of swans fill [this] slim, informative [volume]. [The] overview is divided into several chapters . . . describing the shared and distinct physical characteristics of the various species, the location of their particular habitats, life cycle, social behavior, and the history of human awareness of and impact on these animals. Fine color photographs face pages of text with smaller views placed in colored sidebars or insets. The [book concludes] with current environmental threats and conservation efforts. . . . Handsome and appealing." SLJ

Includes bibliographical references

Hiscock, Bruce
Ookpik; the travels of a snowy owl. Boyds Mills Press 2008 un il map $16.99
Grades: 2 3 4 **598**
1. Owls 2. Birds -- Migration
ISBN 978-1-59078-461-7; 1-59078-461-8

LC 2007-17327

A snowy owl hatches on Baffin Island and migrates over the taiga, past Ottawa, spends the winter in northern New York, and returns to his arctic home.

"An informative author's note comments on the range, size, food, courtship, nesting, growth, and survival of snowy owls. Varied in composition, well focused, and often panoramic in effect, the watercolor paintings depict the snowy owl's world as well as the bird himself. . . . The owl's journey becomes an involving story for children." Booklist

Holub, Joan
★ Why do birds sing? illustrations by Anna DiVito. Dial Books for Young Readers 2004 47p il (Dial easy-to-read) hardcover o.p. pa $3.99
Grades: K 1 2 **598**
1. Birds
ISBN 0-8037-2999-5; 0-14-240106-4 pa

LC 2003-64945

Questions and answers present information about the behavior and characteristics of birds

"The photos and attractive ink drawings with color washes that come two to three to a page result in a colorful presentation with illustrations in different styles from many sources." Booklist

Hudak, Heather C.
Robins; [by] Heather Hudak. Weigl Publishers Inc. 2011 24p il (World of wonder: watch them grow) lib bdg $25.70; pa $9.95
Grades: 1 2 **598**
1. Robins
ISBN 978-1-60596-922-0 lib bdg; 1-60596-922-2 lib bdg; 978-1-60596-923-7 pa; 1-60596-923-0 pa

LC 2010037947

Explore the life of a robin from egg to adult, as well as learn about the special ways robins communicate with each other.

The text is "well-written, providing examples that put a human face to each problem. Quotes and facts are clearly attributed, and their sources are noted in the extensive back matter. . . . Sidebars provide further information, or, more compellingly, offer stories about those touched by the topic. . . . [This] will be of great assistance to students writing reports." Libr Media Connect

Includes glossary

Jacquet, Luc
March of the penguins; [by] Luc Jacquet; including narration written by Jordan Roberts; photographs by Jérôme Maison; translated and adapted by Donnali Fifield. National Geographic 2006 160p il $30
Grades: K 1 2 3 **598**
1. Penguins 2. Antarctica
ISBN 0-7922-6190-9

"From summer's end in Antarctica, the book takes the reader on a journey through a year's cycle in the life of emperor penguins. . . . The quality of the photographs makes this simple story accessible to a wide audience." Sci Books Films

Johnson, Jinny
Duck; illustrations by Michael Woods. Smart Apple Media 2010 32p il (How does it grow?) lib bdg $28.50
Grades: 1 2 3 **598**
1. Ducks
ISBN 978-1-59920-353-9 lib bdg; 1-59920-353-7
lib bdg

LC 2008-53338

Introduces the life cycle of a duck and explains each stage in its development

"Each stage is described on a spread that features clearly written, oversized text and a caption opposite a full-page, realistic watercolor, or, occasionally, a photograph. . . . A worthwhile purchase." SLJ

Includes glossary

Johnson, Sylvia A.
Crows; by Sylvia A. Johnson. Carolrhoda Books 2005 48p il (Carolrhoda nature watch book) lib bdg $25.26
Grades: 3 4 5 6 **598**
1. Crows
ISBN 1-57505-628-3

LC 2004-564

This "book introduces the American crow, its broader family of corvids, and its range, habitats, cooperative breeding system, life cycle, winter migration, roosting behavior, language, and relations with people. . . . Though the clear, color photographs take up most of the space on the pages, the text offers a well-organized, informative discussion of the species." Booklist

Judge, Lita
Bird talk; what birds are saying and why. Lita Judge. Roaring Brook Press 2011 48 p.
Grades: 1 2 3 4 5　　　　　　　　　　　　　**598**
1. Birdsongs 2. Birds -- Behavior 3. Animal communication 4. Picture books for children
ISBN 1596436468; 9781596436466
LC 2010030353
In this picture book, "[a] simple ornithological discourse for very young readers offers several examples of feathered non-verbal communication. Over two dozen bird species--most, but not all, with North American ranges, and many fairly familiar--are shown communicating essential messages via calls, displays of plumage and other, less well-known behaviors. Birds from distant parts of the world may appear in the same opening describing behaviors that accomplish similar aims: wooing mates, camouflage, encouragement to fledglings, protection. . . . Further information about each of the species, including their habitats and ranges, appears on several pages at the back, along with a brief glossary and list of sources." (Kirkus)

Kalman, Bobbie
The life cycle of an emperor penguin; [by] Bobbie Kalman & Robin Johnson. Crabtree Pub. 2007 32p il lib bdg $25.27; pa $6.95
Grades: 2 3 4　　　　　　　　　　　　　　　**598**
1. Penguins
ISBN 978-0-7787-0630-4 lib bdg; 0-7787-0630-3 lib bdg; 978-0-7787-0704-2 pa; 0-7787-0704-0 pa
LC 2006018781
"The information is presented in a flowing narrative accompanied by color photographs and drawings that perfectly illustrate the [text]. . . . Facts are . . . outlined in a lively manner. [This work has] a wealth of factual information and would be excellent for reports." SLJ

Kelly, Irene
★ Even an ostrich needs a nest; where birds begin. Holiday House 2009 un il map $16.95
Grades: K 1 2 3　　　　　　　　　　　　　　**598**
1. Birds -- Nests
ISBN 978-0-8234-2102-2; 0-8234-2102-3
LC 2007-51059
"This nonfiction picture book describes materials used by 40 species of birds from all parts of the world to build their unique nests and how they go about building them. . . . The diversity of materials and designs . . . make this a topic that will appeal to many. The pleasant format features text, creatively placed with the softly colored illustrations, and makes the engaging subject matter even more accessible." Booklist

Kirby, Pamela F.
What bluebirds do. Boyds Mills Press 2009 48p il $18.95

Grades: K 1 2 3　　　　　　　　　　　　　　**598**
1. Bluebirds
ISBN 978-1-59078-614-7; 1-59078-614-9
LC 2008-34057
"Big, full-color photos provide the drama in this personal, picture-book introduction to a common North American bird. . . . The captions include some brief commentary, and kids will feel the call for conservation as they marvel, along with Kirby, at the bird behavior she sees in her yard." Booklist
Includes glossary and bibliographical references

Landau, Elaine
Emperor penguins. Enslow Elementary 2010 31p il (Animals of the snow and ice) lib bdg $22.60
Grades: 2 3 4　　　　　　　　　　　　　　　**598**
1. Penguins
ISBN 978-0-7660-3462-4 lib bdg; 0-7660-3462-3 lib bdg
LC 2009006479
This describes emperor penguins, including habitat, eating habits, mating, babies, and conservation
"Throughout most of [this] title, a full-page, or page and a quarter, sharp, color photograph . . . alternates with a page of text. An addendum of miscellaneous facts, a short list for further reading, and some websites are appended. Landau's smoothly written, well-illustrated [title is] right on target for the intended audience." SLJ
Includes glossary and bibliographical references

Larson, Jeanette C.
Hummingbirds; facts and folklore from the Americas. written by Jeanette Larson and Adrienne Yorinks; illustrated by Adrienne Yorinks. Charlesbridge 2011 64p il $16.95; pa $8.95
Grades: 5 6 7 8　　　　　　　　　　　　　　**598**
1. Hummingbirds 2. Birds -- Folklore 3. Native Americans -- Folklore
ISBN 978-1-58089-332-9; 1-58089-332-5; 978-1-58089-333-6 pa; 1-58089-333-3 pa
LC 2010-07578
"In a narrative that flows easily between fact and lore, hummingbird behavior is thoroughly described and interwoven with the folktales it generated among Native American peoples. . . . All the stories show how ancient people answered the 'how and why' questions of the behaviors they observed, and these stories beautifully echo modern-day scientific observations. The full-color photos of quilts and embroidery by Yorinks invite readers to stop and savor each one." SLJ
Includes glossary and bibliographical references

Lunis, Natalie
Peregrine falcon; dive, dive, dive! Bearport 2010 24p il (Blink of an eye: superfast animals) lib bdg $22.61
Grades: 1 2 3　　　　　　　　　　　　　　　**598**
1. Falcons
ISBN 978-1-936087-93-8 lib bdg; 1-936087-93-6 lib bdg
LC 2010008023
"In terms of pure velocity, no animal can touch a diving peregrine falcon, which this [book] . . . points out right off the bat. Subsequent spreads cover such topics as where peregrine falcons live and their nesting habits, aerial abilities,

and, best of all, hunting techniques. . . . Dynamic, sometimes exhilarating photos . . . accompany the straightforward text." Booklist

Includes glossary and bibliographical references

Lynch, Wayne

Penguins! text and photographs by Wayne Lynch. Firefly Bks. (Willowdale) 1999 64p il map $19.95; pa $9.95

Grades: 4 5 6 7   **598**

1. Penguins

ISBN 1-55209-421-9; 1-55209-424-3 pa

This "is a delightful book. . . . The beautiful color photographs and the text tell a fascinating, exciting, and revealing story." Sci Books Films

Mara, Wil

★ **Ducks**; by Wil Mara. Marshall Cavendish Benchmark 2009 47p il (Animals animals) $20.95

Grades: 3 4 5 6   **598**

1. Ducks

ISBN 978-0-7614-2927-2; 0-7614-2927-1

LC 2007-26004

"The material is well researched and would be an excellent source for reports, and the [book has] a narrative flow that makes [it] easy and enjoyable to read. [The] title includes expert full-color photography." SLJ

Includes glossary and bibliographical references

Markle, Sandra

Eagles. Lerner Publications Company 2009 39p il (Animal predators) lib bdg $26.60

Grades: 4 5 6   **598**

1. Eagles

ISBN 978-1-58013-519-1; 1-58013-519-6

LC 2008038119

Introduces the physical characteristics, habitat, and predatory behavior of different types of eagles.

"Crisp photographs illustrate the hunting activities of eagles. . . . Facts are presented in a dramatic and informational manner." Horn Book Guide

Includes glossary and bibliographical references

★ A **mother's** journey; illustrated by Alan Marks. Charlesbridge 2005 32p il $15.95; pa $6.95

Grades: K 1 2 3   **598**

1. Penguins

ISBN 1-57091-621-7; 1-57091-622-5 pa

LC 2004-18954

"A simple, lyrical text follows the fortunes of an Emperor penguin from laying her first egg through her epic journey to open sea seeking food and culminating in her timely return with a belly full to regurgitate for her newly hatched chick. The whole is perfectly accompanied by Marks's luminous blue-toned watercolors." SLJ

Marzollo, Jean

Pierre the penguin; a true story. written by Jean Marzollo; illustrated by Laura Regan. Sleeping Bear Press 2010 un il $15.95

Grades: PreK K 1 2   **598**

1. Penguins

ISBN 978-1-58536-485-5; 1-58536-485-1

LC 2009040871

Rhyming text and colorful illustrations describe the efforts of aquatic biologist Pam to help Pierre, an African penguin living at the California Academy of Sciences, when he begins to go bald.

"Stories don't come any sweeter than this. . . . Regan's realistic paintings work well with the text and enhance the drama and appeal of the storytelling." SLJ

Metz, Lorijo

Discovering seagulls. PowerKids Press 2011 24p il (Along the shore) lib bdg $21.25

Grades: 3 4 5   **598**

1. Gulls

ISBN 978-1-4488-4995-6; 1-4488-4995-0

LC 2011000154

This book about seagulls "briefly describes the major physical and behavioral characteristics common to all [seagulls] and one or two distinctive characteristics of about a half dozen species. . . . One or two sharp color photographs of representative species, most of which are closeups, accompany the text on every page. . . . [This is] well organized and smoothly written in an engaging style." SLJ

Includes glossary

Momatiuk, Yva

★ **Face** to face with penguins; by Yva Momatiuk and John Eastcott. National Geographic 2009 31p il (Face to face) $16.99; lib bdg $25.90

Grades: 3 4 5 6   **598**

1. Penguins

ISBN 978-1-4263-0561-0; 1-4263-0561-3; 978-1-4263-0562-7 lib bdg; 1-4263-0562-1 lib bdg

LC 2009011439

The authors describe the life cycle and behavior of penguins and their own experiences with penguins in the wild.

"The exquisite photos and firsthand information provide an in-depth and personal look into the lives of these animals." SLJ

Includes glossary and bibliographical references

Munro, Roxie

Hatch! Marshall Cavendish Children's 2011 un il $17.99

Grades: 1 2 3 4   **598**

1. Eggs 2. Birds

ISBN 0761458824; 9780761458821; 978-0-7614-5882-1; 0-7614-5882-4

LC 2010021297

This picture book describes and helps readers learn to identify nine birds and their eggs and nests. "For each bird, we start with a two-page spread: on one side, a close-up of eggs; . . .and on the other side, a series of clues about the producers of those eggs. . . . Primary." (Horn Book)

"Munro uses a guessing game format to deliver an impressive amount of trivia about nine types of birds. 'Can you guess whose eggs these are?' is the repeated refrain that appears above clusters of eggs against a cream-colored backdrop; opposite, a silhouette of the eggs' shape contains several sentences to aid in the guessing. . . . Straightforward, but packed with information." Publ Wkly

Peterson, Roger Tory

Peterson field guide to birds of Eastern and Central North America; [by] Roger Tory Peterson, with contributions from Michael DiGiorgio [et al.] 6th ed; Houghton Mifflin Harcourt 2010 445p il map (Peterson field guide series) $19.95

Grades: 5 6 7 8 9 10 11 12 Adult   **598**

1. Birds -- North America

ISBN 978-0-547-15246-2; 0-547-15246-9

LC 2009-37681

First published 1934 with title: A field guide to the birds

This guide to birds found east of the Rocky Mountains contains colored illustrations painted by the author, with a description of each species on the facing page. Views of young birds and seasonal variations in plumage are included.

★ **Peterson** field guide to birds of North America; with contributions from Michael DiGiorgio . . . [et al.] Houghton Mifflin Co. 2008 527p il map (Peterson field guide series) $26

Grades: 5 6 7 8 9 10 11 12 Adult   **598**

1. Birds -- North America

ISBN 0-618-96614-5; 978-0-618-96614-1

LC 2007-39803

First published 1934 with title: A field guide to the birds. Previously published in two separate parts as A field guide to western birds (1990) and A field guide to the birds of eastern and central North America (2002)

This guide to birds found in North America contains colored illustrations painted by the author, with a description of each species on the facing page. Views of young birds and seasonal variations in plumage are included. The book also includes a URL to video podcasts.

"This field guide is of high quality and should be in millions of birders' and other nature lovers' backpacks." Sci Books Films

Peterson field guide to birds of Western North America; with contributions from Michael DiGiorgio [et al.] 4th ed; Houghton Mifflin Harcourt 2010 493p il map (Peterson field guide series) pa $19.95

Grades: 5 6 7 8 9 10 11 12 Adult   **598**

1. Birds -- North America

ISBN 978-0-547-15270-7; 0-547-15270-1

LC 2009-39158

First published 1941 with title: A field guide to western birds

This guide illustrates over 600 species of birds on 176 color plates. In addition, over 588 range maps are included.

Piehl, Janet

Let's look at pigeons. Lerner Publications Co. 2010 32p il (Lightning bolt books: Animal close-ups) lib bdg $25.26; pa $7.95

Grades: PreK K 1 2   **598**

1. Pigeons

ISBN 978-0-8225-7897-0 lib bdg; 0-8225-7897-2 lib bdg; 978-1-58013-863-5 pa; 1-58013-863-2 pa

LC 2007-29224

Introduces pigeons, describing their physical characteristics, habitat, and predators

"Fresh photography, a creative use of graphics, and a collagelike layout make[s] . . . [this book] eye-catching. . . . [The] book ends with a labeled diagram of the animal, a range map, and a further-reading list that includes print and

online resources in a single list, a nice way of validating both types of materials." SLJ

Includes glossary

Post, Hans

Sparrows; [by Hans Post & Kees Heij; illustrated by Irene Goede] Lemniscaat 2008 un il $16.95

Grades: PreK K 1 2   **598**

1. Sparrows

ISBN 978-1-59078-570-6; 1-59078-570-3

LC 2008-02563

Original Dutch edition 2006

"A year in the life of the European House Sparrow is conveyed to young readers through a friendly text and beguiling illustrations. . . . The tone of the text is both playful and informative. . . . The realistic illustrations intersperse views from the birds' prespective . . . with field guide-like pages that help illustrate bird anatomy and behavior and introduce other animals in the sparrow habitat." Horn Book

Pringle, Laurence P.

Penguins! strange and wonderful; illustrated by Meryl Henderson. Boyds Mills Press 2007 un il $16.95

Grades: 3 4 5   **598**

1. Penguins

ISBN 978-1-59078-090-9; 1-59078-090-6

LC 2006000521

This "highlights the diversity among the habitats, physical traits, and behaviors of the 17 amazingly adaptable species. Pringle's succinct text provides an engaging overview of penguin life. . . . Henderson's realistic paintings vary between double-page spreads of penguins in their diverse Southern Hemisphere environments and finely detailed insets that echo the text." Booklist

Includes bibliographical references

Read, Tracy C.

Exploring the world of eagles. Firefly 2010 24p il (Exploring the world of . . .) $16.95; pa $6.95

Grades: 3 4 5   **598**

1. Eagles

ISBN 978-1-55407-647-5; 1-55407-647-1; 978-1-55407-656-7 pa; 1-55407-656-0 pa

This describes the American bald eagle and the golden eagle, including their anatomy and behavior and the ways they have been affected by the human environmental footprint.

This offers "an abundance of in-depth, intriguing information and [is] appropriate for research or pleasure reading. . . . Two- to four-page chapters mix smaller photos with full-page color photos, and the attractive format will help less-able readers navigate the sometimes dense, detailed paragraphs." Booklist

Rebman, Renee C.

Vultures. Marshall Cavendish Benchmark 2011 il (Animals, animals) lib bdg $20.95

Grades: 3 4 5   **598**

1. Vultures

ISBN 978-0-7614-4880-8; 0-7614-4880-2

LC 2010016037

Provides information on the anatomy, special skills, habitats, and diet of vultures.

This offers "comprehensive text and striking, well-chosen photos. . . . [This is] packed with engaging facts and trivia, as well as an upbeat tone." Booklist

Includes glossary and bibliographical references

Savage, Stephen

Duck. PowerKids Press 2009 32p il map (Animal neighbors) lib bdg $23.95

Grades: 3 4 5 6   598

1. Ducks

ISBN 978-1-4358-4988-4 lib bdg; 1-4358-4988-4 lib bdg

LC 2008-5401

This describes the life cycle, habitat, and behavior of ducks

This title features "beautiful, detailed, close-up photos of animals displayed on child-friendly page layouts. The information is well organized for reports." SLJ

Includes glossary and bibliographical references

Sayre, April Pulley

★ **Honk,** honk, goose! Canada geese start a family. illustrated by Huy Voun Lee. Henry Holt and Company 2009 un il $16.95

Grades: K 1 2 3   598

1. Geese

ISBN 978-0-8050-7103-0; 0-8050-7103-2

LC 2008013423

"A fun read-aloud grounded by informational back matter. . . . Lee's cut-paper collage illustrations wonderfully complement the text—they're simple yet expressive." Booklist

★ **Vulture** view; illustrated by Steve Jenkins. Henry Holt 2007 un il $16.95

Grades: K 1 2   598

1. Vultures

ISBN 978-0-8050-7557-1; 0-8050-7557-7

LC 2006-30766

"Sayre's poetic text begins with the sun rising. . . . The words, almost startling in their brevity, describe a group of turkey vultures as they soar in the sky, seeking food that reeks. . . . Jenkins . . . places the birds against strong, vivid colors—brilliant sky blues, hot desert reds—and gives them wide wingspans that make them seem to soar across the pages. . . . A final two-page spread . . . does a solid job of explaining how turkey vultures live." Booklist

Schulman, Janet

★ **Pale** Male; citizen hawk of New York City. by Janet Schulman; illustrated by Meilo So. Knopf 2008 un il $16.99; lib bdg $19.99

Grades: 3 4 5 6   598

1. Hawks 2. New York (N.Y.)

ISBN 0-375-94558-X lib bdg; 978-0-375-84558-1; 0-375-84558-5; 978-0-375-94558-8 lib bdg

LC 2007-14661

This is "about the first red-tailed hawk to take up residence in New York City's Central Park since its construction in 1857. . . . The artist's evocative watercolor and colored pencil pictures perfectly capture the power and grace of the majestic raptors. . . . Readers experience New Yorkers' excitement about Pale Male and his various mates and their

offspring and understand why his story has captured the interest of so many people." SLJ

Sill, Cathryn P.

About hummingbirds; a guide for children. [by] Cathryn Sill; illustrated by John Sill. Peachtree Publishers 2011 un il $16.95

Grades: K 1 2 3   598

1. Hummingbirds

ISBN 1561455881; 9781561455881; 978-1-56145-588-1; 1-56145-588-1

LC 2010051999

"The Sills cover the [hummingbird's] diet, size, migratory habits, anatomical features, reproduction, predators, and habitats. Of special interest are their hovering skills and aerobatic displays. Each spread consists of one large-type sentence and a large watercolor depiction with just enough information for youngsters to gain an introduction to hummingbirds. The text and art combine to make this title a useful and engaging read."

"The Sills cover the [hummingbird's] diet, size, migratory habits, anatomical features, reproduction, predators, and habitats. Of special interest are their hovering skills and aerobatic displays. Each spread consists of one large-type sentence and a large watercolor depiction with just enough information for youngsters to gain an introduction to hummingbirds. The text and art combine to make this title a useful and engaging read." SLJ

★ **About** raptors; a guide for children. [by] Cathryn Sill; illustrated by John Sill. Peachtree 2010 un il $16.95

Grades: K 1 2 3   598

1. Birds of prey

ISBN 978-1-56145-536-2; 1-56145-536-9

"One short, clearly written sentence or phrase per page communicates the basics about raptors: who they are, where they live, what they eat, and how they hunt. Their similarities, such as strong feet with sharp claws, and their differences, such as locations and kinds of nests, communicate diversity in raptors throughout the world. Eighteen quality watercolors focus on the birds in their natural habitats. . . . This book is a must-buy for all libraries interested in building a strong natural-science collection for their young patrons." SLJ

Simon, Seymour

Penguins. HarperCollins Publishers 2007 31p il (Smithsonian) $16.99; lib bdg $17.89

Grades: 2 3 4   598

1. Penguins

ISBN 978-0-06-028395-7; 0-06-028395-5; 978-0-06-028396-4 lib bdg; 0-06-028396-3 lib bdg

LC 2006-24116

This describes penguin behavior, reproduction, and feeding

This is written "in a voice perfectly attuned to the conceptual level of elementary-age readers. . . . The full-page color photographs competently capture . . . penguin appeal and are skillfully discussed in the narrative." Horn Book

Stearns, Precious McKenzie

Whooping cranes; [by] Precious McKenzie. Rourke Pub. 2010 24p il map (Eye to eye with endangered species) lib bdg $27.07

Grades: 2 3 4   **598**
  1. Cranes (Birds)
ISBN 978-1-60694-401-1 lib bdg; 1-60694-401-0
lib bdg
                                        LC 2009-5992
  Examines the issues endangered whooping cranes face
and how they can be saved
  "Sets out to introduce readers to [whooping cranes] . . . .
explain the dangers they face, and detail the efforts of biologists and conservationists to save them. . . . Serviceable and
informative." SLJ
  Includes glossary

Stewart, Melissa
  ★ **Feathers**; not just for flying. Melissa Stewart; illustrated by Sarah S. Brannen. Charlesbridge 2014 32 p.
(softcover) $7.95
Grades: K 1 2 3 4   **598**
  1. Feathers 2. Birds -- Anatomy 3. Birds -- Behavior
ISBN 1580894313; 9781580894302; 9781580894319
                                        LC 2012038694
  In this book by Melissa Stewart, readers "meet sixteen
birds in this elegant introduction to the many uses of feathers. A concise main text highlights how feathers are not just
for flying. Informative sidebars, which underscore specific
ways each bird uses its feathers for a variety of practical purposes [are included]. A scrapbook design showcases life-size
feather illustrations." (Publisher's note)
  "—Depicting birds from around the United States as
well as South America, India, Africa, and Antarctica, Stewart illuminates the various functions of feathers. Presented
in a scrapbook format with images and text that appear to be
taped, stapled, or pinned to the pages, the book explains that
feathers can provide sun protection, assist in carrying nest
materials, or attract a mate with sound or color... With its
simple text and captivating art, this title could be featured in
a group storytime or in a unit on birds." (SLJ)
  Includes bibliographical references and index

  A **place** for birds; written by Melissa Stewart; illustrated by Higgins Bond. Peachtree 2009 un il $16.95
Grades: K 1 2 3   **598**
  1. Birds
ISBN 1-56145-474-5; 978-1-56145-474-7
                                        LC 2008036744
  "This title focuses on the effects, good and bad, that human behavior has on birds, highlighting the progress that
we've made toward living in harmony with our winged
friends and acknowledging problems still not solved. The
rhythmic main text highlights birds' needs and what people
can do to see that they are met. Insets on each page then provide specific examples to drive the point home. . . . This format . . . is effective and engaging, and Bond's acrylic illustrations depict realistic scenes with a crisp vibrancy." Kirkus

Stockdale, Susan
  Bring on the birds; written and illustrated by Susan
Stockdale. Peachtree 2011 un il $15.95
Grades: PreK K 1 2   **598**
  1. Birds
ISBN 1-56145-560-1; 978-1-56145-560-7
                                        LC 2010-26893
  This book celebrates the different types of birds found
around the world, from dancing birds, to swimming birds,

to birds with bills. Bibliography. "Ages two to six." (Publisher's note)
  "This cheerful survey introduces 21 species [of birds]
from varied parts of the world in spare, rhyming text and attractive acrylic paintings. . . . Picture placement follows the
nice rhythm of the text with each two sets of facing framed
paintings followed by a double-page view for each of the
longer phrases of verse. Simple, flat stylized settings . . .
showcase the lively, colorful birds. . . . Carefully crafted in
charm and simplicity, the book offers many possibilities for
use and enjoyment in reading aloud, browsing, and teaching." SLJ

Thomson, Ruth
  The **life** cycle of an owl. PowerKids Press 2009 24p
il lib bdg $21.23; pa $8.25
Grades: K 1 2   **598**
  1. Owls
ISBN 978-1-4358-2833-9 lib bdg; 1-4358-2833-X lib
bdg; 978-1-4358-2883-4 pa; 1-4358-2883-6 pa
                                        LC 2008026176
  This introduction to the life cycle of the owl is "arranged
in a series of spreads, each of which covers a subtopic. Pages
feature one to three simple sentences of large-print text and
a clear, color photograph of one or more animals in various
stages of growth. . . . With [its] easily accessible format, and
clear [text] and photographs, [this book] will appeal to both
browsers and report writers." SLJ

Underwood, Deborah
  Colorful peacocks; by Deborah Underwood. Lerner
Publications Co. 2007 32p il (Pull ahead books) lib bdg
$22.60; pa $5.95
Grades: K 1 2 3   **598**
  1. Peacocks
ISBN 978-0-8225-5930-6 lib bdg; 0-8225-5930-7 lib
bdg; 978-0-8225-6507-9 pa; 0-8225-6507-2 pa
                                        LC 2005017977
  "This charming introduction to the peafowl family presents facts and color photographs in an easy-to-read format.
Underwood covers what they eat, where they sleep, and how
they care for their young. An outline drawing of a peafowl
with the parts labeled and a map showing countries native
to the species are included. An informative and enjoyable
book." SLJ
  Includes bibliographical references

Vande Griek, Susan
  Loon; pictures by Karen Reczuch. Groundwood Books
2011 il $18.95
Grades: K 1 2   **598**
  1. Loons
ISBN 978-1-55498-077-2; 1-55498-077-1
  "This book follows two loon chicks from birth to maturity and has a lyrical text and lush, full-color illustrations.
The acrylic-on-canvas paintings are presented from different
perspectives to engage viewers—straight on, closeup, and
far away." SLJ

Vogel, Carole Garbuny
  The **man** who flies with birds; [by] Carole G. Vogel
and Yossi Leshem. Kar-Ben Pub. 2009 64p il map lib
bdg $18.95

Grades: 5 6 7 8   **598**
1. Aircraft accidents 2. Birds -- Migration
ISBN 978-0-8225-7643-3 lib bdg; 0-8225-7643-0 lib bdg
    LC 2008-31198
Discusses the work of the bird expert whose lifelong study of the patterns of bird migration in Israel has led to a significant reduction in the number of collisions between aircraft and bird flocks.
"The book is heavily illustrated with good-quality color photos, maps, and diagrams, many of them captioned with incredible facts about wildlife and migration. This inspiring title on a most timely topic will appeal to those who are fascinated with wildlife, Earth science, and technology." SLJ
Includes bibliographical references

Webster, Christine
Ravens. Weigl Publishers 2010 24p il (Backyard animals) lib bdg $24.45; pa $8.95
Grades: 1 2 3   **598**
1. Ravens
ISBN 978-1-60596-082-1 lib bdg; 1-60596-082-9 lib bdg; 978-1-60596-083-8 pa; 1-60596-083-7 pa
    LC 2009004175
This describes the physical characteristics, natural habitats, history, and folklore of ravens
This is "packed with information and [includes] fine close-up photos." Booklist
Includes glossary

Wilcox, Charlotte
Bald eagles; photographs by Jerry Boucher. Carolrhoda Bks. 2003 48p il (Carolrhoda nature watch book) lib bdg $25.26
Grades: 3 4 5 6   **598**
1. Bald eagle
ISBN 1-57505-170-2
    LC 2001-6803
Describes the physical characteristics, life cycle, and behavior of bald eagles, as well as efforts to protect them
Includes index

Willis, Nancy Carol
Red knot; a shorebird's incredible journey. Birdsong Books 2006 un il map $15.95; pa $6.95
Grades: 2 3 4   **598**
1. Sandpipers 2. Birds -- Migration
ISBN 0-9662761-4-0; 0-9662761-5-9 pa
"This title introduces an endangered sandpiper and chronologically documents her journey from Tierra del Fuego along a 20,000-mile route to the Arctic where she has her young and then makes her way back down south for the winter. . . . The smooth, simple text is complemented with well-composed, colored-pencil drawings." SLJ

Winter, Jeanette
The **tale** of Pale Male; a true story. Harcourt, Inc. 2007 un il $16
Grades: K 1 2 3   **598**
1. Hawks 2. New York (N.Y.)
ISBN 978-0-15-205972-9; 0-15-205972-5
    LC 2006-08741
"Working with acrylics on watercolor paper, Winter uses Easter-egg colors to frame her appealing cityscapes. .

. . Winter blends the realistic with the fanciful throughout the story." Booklist
"When Pale Male and his mate built a nest high on the side of a Fifth Avenue apartment building, they attracted the attention of local bird-watchers. . . . However, some residents complained about bird droppings and animal remains falling from the hawks' living space. In December 2004, the nest was removed, generating local protests and national media attention. Eventually, the nesting spot was restored." SLJ

Wolf, Sallie
★ The **robin** makes a laughing sound; a birder's journal. designed by Micah Bornstein. Charlesbridge 2010 43p il $11.95
Grades: 5 6 7 8   **598**
1. Birds 2. Bird watching
ISBN 978-1-58089-318-3; 1-58089-318-X
    LC 2008-7248
Presents observations made through every season of the year of different birds and their behavior, from robins taking a bath, to cardinals searching for food in the snow, to an owl perched on a tree at night.
"The charming, eye-catching format includes short dated nature notes written in script, some of them on glued or taped-in torn paper pieces; other paper scraps contain short typeset poems and small, labeled watercolors. . . . Pen-and-ink sketches capture a baby house sparrow, a V-formation of geese, a downy woodpecker at a suet feeder, and more. . . . This small, instructional guide may provide the inspiration for young authors with even a bit of artistic talent to begin keeping nature journals of their own." SLJ

598.072   Bird watching

Hoose, Phillip
★ **Moonbird**; a year on the wind with the great survivor B95. Phillip Hoose. Farrar Straus Giroux 2012 148 p. col. ill. (hardcover) $21.99
Grades: 5 6 7 8   **598.072**
1. Endangered species 2. Birds -- Protection 3. Wildlife conservation 4. Red knot 5. Bird watching
ISBN 0374304688; 9780374304683
    LC 2011035612
Robert F. Sibert Honor Book (2013)
YALSA Award for Excellence in Nonfiction for Young Adults Finalist (2013)
In this book, Phillip Hoose "explores the tragedy of extinction through a single bird species, but there is hope for survival in this story, and that hope is pinned on understanding the remarkable longevity of a single bird. . . . Hoose takes readers around the hemisphere, showing them the obstacles rufa red knots face, introducing a global team of scientists and conservationists, and offering insights about what can be done to save them before it's too late." (Kirkus Reviews)

598.3   Water birds

Gibbons, Gail
Gulls--gulls--gulls. Holiday House 1997 un il $16.95; pa $6.95

Grades: K 1 2 3 **598.3**
1. Gulls
ISBN 0-8234-1323-3; 0-8234-1664-X pa

LC 97-1266

Describes the life cycle, behavior patterns, and habitat of various species of gulls, focusing on those found in North America

"Both illustration and text provide basic, easy-to-understand facts. . . . The format is attractive with framed, simply drawn watercolor illustrations showing the birds in the foreground against bright colorful seashore or seascape backgrounds of dominant blues and greens." SLJ

Markle, Sandra, 1946-
The **long,** long journey; the godwit's amazing migration. by Sandra Markle; illustrated by Mia Posada. Millbrook Press 2013 32 p. col. ill., col. map (library) $26.60
Grades: 1 2 3 **598.3**
1. Picture books for children 2. Bar-tailed godwit 3. Bar-tailed godwit -- Migration
ISBN 0761356231; 9780761356233

LC 2012020915

This children's picture book by Sandra Markle follows the migration journey of the bar-tailed godwit chick. "Migrating 7,000 miles south from their breeding grounds, bar-tailed godwits flee the Arctic winter for the Southern-Hemisphere summer, making the longest known nonstop flight of any bird." (Kirkus Reviews)

Includes bibliographical references

598.4 Miscellaneous orders of water birds

Bodden, Valerie
Swans; by Valerie Bodden. Creative Education 2009 24 p. (hardcover: alk. paper) $24.25
Grades: K 1 2 3 **598.4**
1. Swans
ISBN 1583417192; 9781583417195

LC 2007051589

In this book,by Valerie Bodden, "photos are paired with accessible text to examine the [swan's] appearance, behaviors, and life cycle. [The] book also presents a folk story that helps explain a defining feature [of the animal]." (Publisher's note)

Includes bibliographical references and index

McMillan, Bruce
Days of the ducklings; written and photo-illustrated by Bruce McMillan. Houghton Mifflin 2001 32p il hardcover o.p. pa $6.95
Grades: 2 3 4 **598.4**
1. Ducks
ISBN 0-618-04878-2; 0-618-86270-6 pa

LC 00-13258

"McMillan's photographs are of extremely high quality, a wonderful blend of artistry and emotion, and his text flows well." Booklist

Includes bibliographical references

598.47 Penguins

Gibbons, Gail
Penguins! Holiday House 1998 un il maps $16.95; pa $6.95
Grades: K 1 2 3 **598.47**
1. Penguins
ISBN 0-8234-1388-8; 0-8234-1516-3 pa

LC 98-5194

Describes the habitat, physical characteristics, and behavior of different kinds of penguins

This book has "simply written, clear text. . . . The oversized format, brightly colored illustrations, and large type font result in an eye-catching appearance that will attract young researchers and the curious minded alike." SLJ

Guiberson, Brenda Z.
★ The **emperor** lays an egg; illustrated by Joan Paley. Holt & Co. 2001 un il $16.95; pa $7.99
Grades: K 1 2 3 **598.47**
1. Penguins
ISBN 0-8050-6204-1; 0-8050-7636-3 pa

LC 00-40980

"Guiberson's vivid prose fleshes out the bare bones of the penguin's life cycle. . . . Paley's collages of painted and cut papers provide exceptionally beautiful scenes of the birds." Booklist

"Beginning with the laying of an egg, Guiberson describes the care given to a baby emperor penguin by both parents from the time it hatches until it is on its own." SLJ

Tatham, Betty
Penguin chick; illustrated by Helen K. Davie. HarperCollins Pubs. 2002 33p il (Let's-read-and-find-out science) $15.95; pa $4.95
Grades: K 1 2 3 **598.47**
1. Penguins
ISBN 0-06-028594-X; 0-06-445206-9 pa

LC 00-59696

This book "follows the growth of one penguin chick from egg to adulthood. The story has been told before, but the clear, simple text provides intriguing details and inherent drama that will keep young children involved straight through till the end." Booklist

598.7 Miscellaneous orders of land birds

Riggs, Kate
Woodpeckers; by Kate Riggs. Creative Education 2014 24 p. col ill. $7.99
Grades: K 1 2 **598.7**
1. Woodpeckers
ISBN 0898129311; 9780898129311; 9781608183524

LC 2013005401

This children's book by Kate Riggs, part of the Amazing Animals series, provides "A basic exploration of the appearance, behavior, and habitat of woodpeckers, nature's drummers. Also included is a story from folklore explaining how woodpeckers take good care of their young." (Publisher's note)

"Across from the photos, the text is laid out cleanly in a large, clear font, and the sentences are simple and easy to read. Photo captions, meanwhile, add interesting facts, while occasional vocabulary words are defined at the bottoms of pages. At the end of each book, the author retells a myth or story about that kind of animal." - Booklist

Includes bibliographical references (p. 24) and index

598.9 Falconiformes, Caprimulgiformes, owls

Bodden, Valerie
Owls; by Valerie Bodden. 1st ed. Creative Education 2013 24 p. (Amazing animals) (paperback) $25.65
Grades: 1 2 3 4   598.9
1. Owls
ISBN 1608180883; 9781608180882
LC 2011050280
This book, by Valerie Bodden, as part of the publisher's "Amazing Animals" series, presents an introduction to various species of owls. It presents "a basic exploration of the appearance, behavior, and habitat of owls, the winged nighttime hunters. Also included is a story from folklore explaining why some owls have big eyes and ears." (Publisher's note)
Includes bibliographical references and index

Harasymiw, N. D.
Condors in danger. Gareth Stevens Publishing 2013 24 p. $22.60
Grades: 2 3 4   598.9
1. Condors 2. Vultures 3. Endangered species
ISBN 1433991543; 9781433991547
This book, by N. D. Harasymiw, offers "information and ... photographs .... for kids beginning to learn about endangered species. [The book] explains that although vultures (a kind of condor) might sound like "scary birds," they perform important tasks in the food chain. Condor captivity-and-release programs have been successful, but the birds still face dangers from poisoning and hitting power lines." (Booklist)

Riggs, Kate
Eagles; by Kate Riggs. Creative Paperbacks 2012 24p. col. ill.
Grades: K 1 2   598.9
1. Eagles
ISBN 9780898126914
LC 2012008602
"A basic exploration of the appearance, behavior, and habitat of eagles, Earth's most widespread birds of prey. Also included is a story from folklore explaining why people respect eagles." (Publisher's note)
Includes bibliographical references (p. 24) and index.

Sattler, Helen Roney
The book of North American owls; illustrated by Jean Day Zallinger. Clarion Bks. 1995 64p il maps hardcover o.p. pa $7.95
Grades: 4 5 6 7   598.9
1. Owls
ISBN 0-395-60524-5; 0-395-90017-4 pa
LC 91-43626
This "is a superb ornithological primer. ... The book is lavishly illustrated." Appraisal

This volume "includes owl classification and history, hunting and habitat, courtship and nesting, and the complex relationship between owls and humans. The comprehensive glossary includes all of the 21 North American species." Sci Child
Includes bibliographical references

599 Mammals

★ Exploring the world of mammals; [edited by Nancy Simmons, Richard Beatty, Amy Jane Beer] Chelsea House 2008 6v il map set $210
Grades: 5 6 7 8   599
1. Reference books 2. Mammals -- Encyclopedias
ISBN 978-0-7910-9651-2 set; 0-7910-9651-3 set
LC 2007028223
"This colorful and appealing set offers an introduction to the world of mammals. Most of entries are 2 to 4 pages in length. Sidebars offer extra details, and bright photographs and illustrations appear on every 2-page spread." Booklist

Gray, Susan Heinrichs
The life cycle of mammals; [by] Susan H. Gray. Heinemann Library 2011 48p il (Life cycles) lib bdg $32; pa $8.95
Grades: 3 4 5   599
1. Mammals
ISBN 978-1-4329-4981-5 lib bdg; 978-1-4329-4988-4 pa
LC 2010038498
This describes what a mammal is, types of mammals, their life cycles, habitats, foods, defenses, and relationships to humans.
Includes glossary and bibliographical references

Rodriguez, Ana Maria
Secret of the singing mice ... and more! [by] Ana Maria Rodriguez. Enslow Publishers 2008 48p il (Animal secrets revealed!) lib bdg $23.93
Grades: 5 6 7 8   599
1. Mammals
ISBN 978-0-7660-2956-9 lib bdg; 0-7660-2956-5 lib bdg
LC 2007-39495
This book offers "fascinating accounts of how scientists systematically analyzed, tested and proved their theories or how their findings led to other, serendipitous discoveries. ... Science experiments are thoughtfully placed to inspire exploration, and captioned, full-color photos appear throughout." SLJ
Includes glossary and bibliographical references

599.2 Marsupials and monotremes

Arnold, Caroline
A wombat's world; written and illustrated by Caroline Arnold. Picture Window Books 2008 24p il (Caroline Arnold's animals) lib bdg $26.60

Grades: PreK K 1 2   **599.2**
1. Wombats
ISBN 978-1-4048-3986-1
                              LC 2007032891

"This introduction to wombats combines a narrative story with boxed facts about the animals. The uncluttered cut-paper collages and simple, straightforward text show and tell events in a wombat's life over a year's time.... Arnold gives a mostly clear, compelling sense of the lives and characteristics of these unique animals." Booklist

Bishop, Nic

★ Nic Bishop marsupials. Scholastic 2009 48p il $17.99

Grades: 3 4 5 6   **599.2**
1. Marsupials
ISBN 978-0-439-87758-9; 0-439-87758-X
                              LC 2008-53379

"This broad-ranging discussion includes the Virginia opossum and related animals in the Americas before turning to the main topic, the varied marsupials of Australia. Large in scale and often exceptionally clear, the many color photos will attract animal lovers to the book. . . . This inviting title pairs some remarkable photos with a wealth of intriguing facts." Booklist

Bredeson, Carmen

Kangaroos up close; [by] Carmen Bredeson. Enslow Elementary 2008 24p il (Zoom in on animals!) lib bdg $21.26

Grades: 1 2 3   **599.2**
1. Kangaroos
ISBN 978-0-7660-3079-4 lib bdg; 0-7660-3079-2 lib bdg

"Short paragraphs of simply written text describe [kangaroos'] key body parts and how they function. . . . Behavior, diet, and care and development of the young are briefly addressed. Facing the text on each spread is a full-page, sharp, color closeup. . . . Bredeson's simply written and colorful [title] will provide younger readers with [a] satisfying first [introduction] to these fascinating creatures." SLJ

Includes glossary and bibliographical references

Doudna, Kelly

It's a baby kangaroo! ABDO Pub. Co. 2009 24p il (Baby Australian animals) $13.95

Grades: K 1 2 3   **599.2**
1. Kangaroos
ISBN 978-1-60453-576-1; 1-60453-576-8
                              LC 2008055075

The "book opens with a page of vital statistics: the 'baby name,' number in litter, 'weight at birth,' 'age of independence,' 'adult weight,' and 'life expectancy.' The [book] then [goes] on to describe where the animals live and their predators and conclude with a 'Fun Fact.' The photography is excellent. Sidebars on some pages include more facts or reinforce the text." SLJ

Gish, Melissa

Kangaroos. Creative Education 2010 46p il (Living wild) $23.95; pa $9.95

Grades: 5 6 7 8   **599.2**
1. Kangaroos
ISBN 978-1-58341-970-0; 1-58341-970-5; 978-0-89812-553-5 pa; 0-89812-553-7 pa
                              LC 2010017375

"A look at kangaroos, including their habitats, physical characteristics such as the females' pouches, behaviors, relationships with humans, and valued status in the world today." Publisher's note

Heos, Bridget

What to expect when you're expecting joeys; a guide for marsupial parents (and curious kids) illustrated by Stephane Jorisch. Millbrook Press 2011 il (Expecting animal babies)

Grades: 2 3 4 5   **599.2**
1. Marsupials
ISBN 0761358595; 9780761358596
                              LC 2010051506

"Directed at marsupial parents of all kinds, from kangaroos and koalas to possums and bandicoots, this tongue-in-cheek guide to joey development takes it step by step, from the birth of your pinkie to where your baby goes after it leaves the pouch. Never once dropping the pretense that this is written for pouched mammals, this manages to be both entertaining and informative.... [The author] uses appropriate vocabulary, making meanings clear in context and also providing a glossary. Jorisch's painted pen-and-ink sketches show lively, lightly anthropomorphized animals and add considerably to the humor." Kirkus

Includes glossary and bibliographical references

Markle, Sandra

★ **Finding** home; [by] Sandra Markle; illustrated by Alan Marks. Charlesbridge 2008 un il lib bdg $15.95

Grades: K 1 2 3   **599.2**
1. Koalas
ISBN 978-1-58089-122-6
                              LC 2007-01473

"Based on the true story of a koala that survived multiple bushfires and wandered into a residential area, this picture book, narrated in dramatic free verse, tells a gripping story of animal survival. . . . Markle's smooth, elegant poetry and Marks' expressive, realistic mixed-media images give a strong sense of the animals' terror and the mother's intense bond with her child." Booklist

Includes bibliographical references

Markovics, Joyce L.

Tasmanian devil; nighttime scavenger. by Joyce L. Markovics. Bearport Pub. 2009 32p il map (Uncommon animals) lib bdg $25.27

Grades: 1 2 3   **599.2**
1. Tasmanian devils
ISBN 978-1-59716-733-8 lib bdg; 1-59716-733-9 lib bdg
                              LC 2008-9307

"The explanatory text works spendidly, with large photographs that bring readers as close as they'll ever get to such beasts." Booklist

"Describes the physical characteristics, habits, and habitat of the Tasmanian devil." Publisher's note

Includes glossary and bibliographical references

Montgomery, Sy

★ **Quest** for the tree kangaroo; an expedition to the cloud forest of New Guinea. text by Sy Montgomery; photographs by Nic Bishop. Houghton Mifflin 2006 79p il map (Scientists in the field) $18

Grades: 5 6 7 8   **599.2**

1. Zoologists 2. Tree kangaroos 3. New Guinea
ISBN 0-618-49641-6

LC 2005-34849

"The writer and photographer of this exemplary description of science field work accompanied researcher Lisa Dabek on an expedition high in New Guinea's mountains to study tree kangaroos and promote the conservation of this elusive and endangered species. . . . Montgomery . . . paces her narrative well . . . keeping the reader engaged and concerned. . . . Bishop's photographs . . . are beautifully reproduced." Publ Wkly

Racanelli, Marie

Animals with pockets. PowerKids Press 2010 24p il (Crazy nature) lib bdg $21.25; pa $8.25

Grades: 2 3 4 5   **599.2**

1. Marsupials
ISBN 978-1-4358-9385-6 lib bdg; 1-4358-9385-9 lib bdg; 978-1-4358-9862-2 pa; 1-4358-9862-1 pa

LC 2009036517

This book takes a look at different kinds of marsupials, and what makes them unique from other mammals.

This book "combines attention-grabbing information with a well-organized format. . . . [The book has] spectacular color photography and eye-popping facts. . . . Excellent for reports." SLJ

Includes glossary

Riggs, Kate

Kangaroos; by Kate Riggs. Creative Education 2012 24 p. col. ill.

Grades: K 1 2   **599.2**

1. Kangaroos 2. Animal behavior 3. Animals -- Folklore 4. Wildlife photography 5. Zoology -- Encyclopedias
ISBN 1608181081; 9781608181087

LC 2010049210

This children's book, part of Kate Riggs' "Amazing Animals" series, focuses on kangaroos. "This . . . popular series continues traveling the planet to study alligators, bats, and other fascinating animals. . . . [P]hotos are paired with . . . text to examine the featured creature's appearance, habitat, behaviors, and life cycle. . . . A basic exploration of the appearance, behavior, and habitat of kangaroos, Australia's iconic marsupials. Also included is a story from folklore explaining why kangaroos jump instead of run." (Publisher's note)

Includes bibliographical references (p. 24) and index

Saxby, Claire

Big red kangaroo; Claire Saxby, illustrated by Graham Byrne. Candlewick Press 2015 32 p. color illustrations $16.99

Grades: K 1 2 3 4   **599.2**

1. Kangaroos 2. Red kangaroo
ISBN 0763670758; 9780763670757

LC 2013955949

This juvenile book, by Claire Saxby, illustrated by Graham Byrne, follows "a dominant male kangaroo. . . . In the center of Australia, the sun is setting over the baked earth, and Red Kangaroo stirs from his rest. It's breakfast time, and Red must lead his mob of kangaroos off to find grasses for grazing. But Red is also on the watch for young male kangaroos who are ready to challenge him and try to take his place as leader." (Publisher's note)

"First-time illustrator Bryne's digitally enhanced charcoals offer haunting depictions of a male kangaroo and his mob in the Australian outback. Scraggly trees take on a charred look, while a blue-black night sky contrasts with a barren, white ground to create an almost lunar landscape... Italicized paragraphs provide further information about kangaroo behavior ("Red kangaroos are most active at dusk and dawn"), and other Australian animals make appearances, including wallaroos and thorny devils. An understated but visually arresting portrait of a species." PW

Sill, Cathryn P.

About marsupials; a guide for children. [by] Cathryn Sill; illustrated by John Sill. Peachtree 2006 un il $15.95

Grades: K 1 2 3   **599.2**

1. Marsupials
ISBN 1-56145-358-7

LC 2005-20582

This introduces the characteristics and behavior of 17 marsupials, such as the marsupial mole, the red kangaroo, the numbat, the spotted cuscus, the koala and tasmanian devil.

"Written with simplicity and dignity. . . . Well-suited to classroom sharing, the paintings are attractively composed and clearly delineated." Booklist

Includes glossary and bibliographical references

Webster, Christine

Opossums; [by] Christine Webster. Weigl Publishers Inc. 2008 24p il map (Backyard animals) lib bdg $24.45; pa $6.95

Grades: 2 3 4   **599.2**

1. Opossums
ISBN 978-1-59036-677-6 lib bdg; 978-1-59036-678-3 pa

LC 2006-102107

This describes the physical characteristics, behavior, and life cycle of the opossum.

"Large, full-color photos appear thoughout, and the [text is] clearly written and well organized." SLJ

Includes glossary and bibliographical references

599.3   Miscellaneous orders of placental mammals

Aronin, Miriam

The **prairie** dog's town; a perfect hideaway. Bearport Pub. 2009 32p il map (Spectacular animal towns) lib bdg $25.27

Grades: 2 3 4   **599.3**

1. Prairie dogs
ISBN 978-1-59716-870-0 lib bdg; 1-59716-870-X lib bdg

LC 2009-4064

"Introduces prairie dogs and how they live, covering the building of burrows and towns for families, different types of communication skills, and conservation efforts to protect them." Publisher's note

"Through excellent photographs, high-interest texts, sidebars, maps, and other material, children learn about both the animals and their habitats. The . . . book also provides brief profiles of animals with similar habitats. . . . [This book is] much better than average 'report' titles." SLJ

Includes glossary and bibliographical references

Bailer, Darice

Prairie dogs. Marshall Cavendish Benchmark 2011 il (Animals, animals) lib bdg $20.95

Grades: 3 4 5   **599.3**

1. Prairie dogs

ISBN 978-0-7614-4876-1; 0-7614-4876-4

LC 2010016033

Provides information on the anatomy, special skills, habitats, and diet of prairie dogs.

Includes glossary and bibliographical references

Cooke, Lucy

★ A **little** book of sloth; by Lucy Cooke. Margaret K. McElderry Books 2013 64 p. col. ill. (hardcover) $16.99

Grades: PreK K 1 2 3   **599.3**

1. Sloths 2. Picture books for children 3. Sloths -- Costa Rica

ISBN 1442445572; 9781442445574

LC 2012018737

In this children's picture book, author Lucy Cooke "offers an encyclopedic look at" sloths "by way of a photo-tour of their . . . sanctuary in Costa Rica. There are sloths in pajamas (which are actually necessary because they can't control their body temperature), sloths in a 'cuddle puddle,' sloths hugging stuffed animals, [and] sloths gazing into the camera with small but trusting eyes." (Publishers Weekly)

George, Lynn

Prairie dogs; tunnel diggers. PowerKids Press 2011 24p il (Animal architects) lib bdg $21.25; pa $8.25

Grades: 1 2 3   **599.3**

1. Prairie dogs 2. Animals -- Habitations

ISBN 978-1-4488-0695-9 lib bdg; 1-4488-0695-X lib bdg; 978-1-4488-1351-3 pa; 1-4488-1351-4 pa

LC 2010008867

Includes glossary

Gibbons, Gail

Rabbits, rabbits, & more rabbits! Holiday House 2000 un il $16.95; pa $6.95

Grades: K 1 2 3   **599.3**

1. Rabbits

ISBN 0-8234-1486-8; 0-8234-1660-7 pa

LC 99-16765

Describes different kinds of rabbits, their physical characteristics, behavior, where they live, and how to care for them

"Colored washes and crayon shading enliven the clearly delineated ink drawings." Booklist

Glaser, Linda

Hello, squirrels! scampering through the seasons. by Linda Glaser; illustrated by Gay W. Holland. Millbrook Press 2006 32p il lib bdg $22.60

Grades: K 1 2   **599.3**

1. Squirrels

ISBN 978-0-7613-2887-2 lib bdg; 0-7613-2887-4 lib bdg

LC 2005003692

"The book documents a year in a squirrel's life in a first-person narration that imitates a child's voice and cadences. . . . . The text is filled with the kind of natural details that a child would observe. Holland's realistic colored-pencil drawings . . . are complemented by generous white space and easy-to-read print. More scientific information is provided in the answers to four questions at the end of the book." Booklist

Kalman, Bobbie

The **life** cycle of a beaver; [by] Bobbie Kalman. Crabtree 2007 32p il lib bdg $25.27; pa $6.95

Grades: 2 3 4   **599.3**

1. Beavers

ISBN 978-0-7787-0628-1 lib bdg; 0-7787-0628-1 lib bdg; 978-0-7787-0702-8 pa; 0-7787-0702-4 pa

LC 2006023330

The beaver "is described as a mammal (a term that is explained) belonging to the rodent family. Its habitat is outlined, along with information on how it builds lodges, dams, and burrows. Diet, growth, and facts about the young are included. The information is presented in a flowing narrative accompanied by color photographs and drawings that perfectly illustrate the [text]." SLJ

Markle, Sandra

Prairie dogs. Lerner Publications Company 2007 39p il map (Animal prey) lib bdg $25.26; pa $7.95

Grades: 4 5 6   **599.3**

1. Prairie dogs

ISBN 978-0-8225-6438-6 lib bdg; 0-8225-6438-6 lib bdg; 978-0-8225-6441-6 pa; 0-8225-6441-6 pa

LC 2006-598

Describes the behavior of prairie dogs in their native habitat, where they are the prey of larger animals and birds and where they must work together as a colony to create burrows and warning systems to protect themselves and their young

Includes glossary and bibliographical references

Otfinoski, Steven

Squirrels. Marshall Cavendish Benchmark 2010 47p il (Animals, animals) lib bdg $29.93

Grades: 3 4 5   **599.3**

1. Squirrels

ISBN 978-0-7614-4843-3; 0-7614-4843-8

LC 2009022628

This offers information on the anatomy, special skills, habitats, and diet of squirrels.

Includes glossary and bibliographical references

Reingold, Adam

The **beaver's** lodge; building with leftovers. Bearport Pub. 2009 32p il map (Spectacular animal towns) lib bdg $25.27

Grades: 2 3 4   **599.3**
   1. Beavers
   ISBN 978-1-59716-872-4 lib bdg; 1-59716-872-6
   lib bdg

                           LC 2009-11723
Explores the remarkable homes built by beavers.
"Through excellent photographs, high-interest texts, sidebars, maps, and other material, children learn about both the animals and their habitats. The . . . book also provides brief profiles of animals with similar habitats. . . . [This book is] much better than average 'report' titles." SLJ
Includes glossary and bibliographical references

Swinburne, Stephen R.
   Armadillo trail; the northward journey of the armadillo. illustrated by Bruce Hiscock. Boyds Mills Press 2009 un il $16.95
Grades: K 1 2 3   **599.3**
   1. Armadillos
   ISBN 978-1-59078-463-1

                           LC 2008028774
"In a burrow beneath a Texas field, an armadillo gives birth to four pups. As the little ones grow, they venture outside with her to hunt for food. . . . This handsome picture book offers enough detail to engage them in understanding armadillos, and a refreshing lack of sensationalism and sentimentality about events in the animals' lives." Booklist

Zuchora-Walske, Christine
   Let's look at prairie dogs. Lerner Publications Co. 2010 32p il map (Lightning bolt books: Animal close-ups) lib bdg $25.26
Grades: PreK K 1 2   **599.3**
   1. Prairie dogs
   ISBN 978-0-7613-3891-8 lib bdg; 0-7613-3891-8
   lib bdg

                           LC 2008-51856
Introduces prairie dogs, describing their physical characteristics, habitat, and predators
"Fresh photography, a creative use of graphics, and a collagelike layout make[s] . . . [this book] eye-catching. . . . [The] book ends with a labeled diagram of the animal, a range map, and a further-reading list that includes print and online resources in a single list, a nice way of validating both types of materials." SLJ
   Includes glossary

599.35   Rodents

Bill, Tannis
   ★ **Pika**; life in the rocks. photographs by Jim Jacobson. Boyds Mills Press 2010 32p il $18.95
Grades: K 1 2 3   **599.35**
   1. Pikas
   ISBN 978-1-59078-803-5; 1-59078-803-6
"The pika is a cousin to the rabbit. . . . Using short, declarative sentences, Tannis follows the laborious life of a pika living in the Rocky Mountains. It is a daily grind of gathering leaves and branches for his hay pile, a massive thatch that can grow as large as a bathtub and that serves as a food reserve, particularly during winter months. . . . The photos capture the pika at his cutest. . . . Loaded with rich

back matter on the pika and its predators, this is a cycle-of-life book that satisfies to the end." Booklist
Includes glossary and bibliographical references

Ganeri, Anita
   Capybara. Heinemann Library 2011 24p il map (Day in the life. rain forest animals) lib bdg $22; pa $6.49
Grades: 1 2   **599.35**
   1. Capybara
   ISBN 978-1-4329-4110-9 lib bdg; 1-4329-4110-0 lib bdg; 978-1-4329-4121-5 pa; 1-4329-4121-6 pa

                           LC 2010001132
This book follows a capybara through its day as it sleeps, eats, and moves.
"Ganeri presents information clearly and simply in large type, two-sentence comments placed below a bright, sharply reproduced color photograph of the animal in a natural setting. . . . [This is] sufficiently specific to support assignment as well as pleasure reading." SLJ
Includes glossary and bibliographical references

Kalman, Bobbie
   Baby rodents; by Bobbie Kalman. Crabtree Publishing Company 2013 24 p. col. ill. (library) $22.60; (paperback) $6.95
Grades: 1 2 3 4   **599.35**
   1. Rodents 2. Animal babies 3. Rodents -- Infancy
   ISBN 9780778710097; 9780778710141

                           LC 2012043742
This book by Bobbie Kalman presents "photographs of different kinds of rodents from cute baby chipmunks to chubby capybaras. Easy-to-understand text explains in which habitats rodents live and how their babies are born and raised. Young readers will also learn about rodent teeth, rodent diets, how different rodents move, build their homes, and which rodents are popular pets." (Publisher's note)
Includes bibliographical references and index.

Lunde, Darrin
   Dirty rats; Darrin Lunde; illustrated by Adam Gustavson. Charlesbridge 2015 32 p. color illustrations (reinforced for library use) $16.95
Grades: K 1 2 3   **599.35**
   1. Rats
   ISBN 1580895662; 9781580895668

                           LC 2013049022
This children's book, by Darrin Lunde, illustrated by Adam Gustavson, discusses rats. "Nobody likes a rat. . . . But, hold on . . . are rats really so bad? There are hundreds of rat species all around the world that defy common stereotypes. Rats help predators survive, allow plants to spread their seeds, and even contribute to medical research that helps humans stay healthy." (Publisher's note)
"Few animals are as maligned as rats, something mammal specialist Lunde knows well. "Dirty rats. Their beady eyes and naked tails make us scream. Eek! Aargh! Yikes!" he writes as a frightened woman in hair curlers tries to sweep rats off her apartment's fire escape...Gustavson's typically lush oil paintings do their part to help sway opinions—his sewer rats come across as intelligent, curious, and even adorable." PW

Markle, Sandra

Outside and inside rats and mice. Atheneum Bks. for Young Readers 2001 39p il hardcover o.p. pa $10.99

Grades: 2 3 4   **599.35**

1. Mice 2. Rats

ISBN 0-689-82301-0; 1-4169-7571-3 pa

LC 00-29290

Describes the external and internal physical characteristics of mice and rats and their behavior

"Markle skillfully draws readers into careful observation of outstanding close-up photographs of mice and rats. . . . The friendly text maintains its scientific rigor." Horn Book

Includes glossary

★ **Porcupines**; [by] Sandra Markle. Lerner Publications Company 2007 39p il (Animal prey) lib bdg $25.26

Grades: 3 4 5   **599.35**

1. Porcupines

ISBN 978-0-8225-6439-3 lib bdg; 0-8225-6439-4 lib bdg

LC 2006000601

This describes the physical characteristics, habits, and life cycle of porcupines

"An outstanding combination of fascinating [text] and informative, appealing photos." SLJ

Includes glossary and bibliographical references

Marrin, Albert

★ **Oh,** rats! the story of rats and people. illustrated by C.B. Mordan. Dutton Children's Books 2006 48p il $16.99

Grades: 3 4 5 6   **599.35**

1. Rats

ISBN 0-525-47762-4

LC 2004-24512

This is "lively and informative. . . . The nine short chapters are set in a handsome slim book with striking black-and-white scratchboard illustrations and muted red framing on many pages." SLJ

Includes bibliographical references

Savage, Stephen

Mouse. PowerKids Press 2009 32p il (Animal neighbors) lib bdg $23.95

Grades: 3 4 5 6   **599.35**

1. Mice

ISBN 978-1-4358-4990-7 lib bdg; 1-4358-4990-6 lib bdg

LC 2008-5414

This describes the life cycle, habitat, and behavior of mice

Rat. PowerKids Press 2009 32p il (Animal neighbors) lib bdg $23.95

Grades: 3 4 5   **599.35**

1. Rats

ISBN 978-1-4358-4991-4 lib bdg; 1-4358-4991-4 lib bdg

LC 2008-5451

This describes the life cycle, habitat, and behavior of rats

This title features "beautiful, detailed, close-up photos of animals displayed on child-friendly page layouts. The information is well organized for reports." SLJ

Sill, Cathryn P.

About rodents; [by] Cathryn Sill; illustrated by John Sill. Peachtree 2008 un il $15.95

Grades: K 1 2 3   **599.35**

1. Rodents

ISBN 978-1-56145-454-9; 1-56145-454-0

Explains what rodents are, how they live, and what they do.

"Beautifully illustrated with clear, well-composed paintings of animals, this book shows respect for its audience as well as its subject." Booklist

Includes glossary and bibliographical references

Tait, Leia

Mice. Weigl 2010 24p il (Backyard animals) lib bdg $24.45; pa $8.95

Grades: 1 2 3   **599.35**

1. Mice

ISBN 978-1-60596-080-7 lib bdg; 1-60596-080-2 lib bdg; 978-1-60596-081-4 pa; 1-60596-081-0 pa

LC 2008052059

This is "packed with information and [includes] fine close-up photos. . . . [It] does a solid job of introducing the tiny animal's habits and habitats." Booklist

Includes glossary

Webster, Christine

Porcupines. Weigl 2010 24p il (Backyard animals) lib bdg $24.45; pa $8.95

Grades: 1 2 3   **599.35**

1. Porcupines

ISBN 978-1-60596-078-4 lib bdg; 1-60596-078-0 lib bdg; 978-1-60596-079-1 pa; 1-60596-079-9 pa

LC 2009004446

This describes the physical characteristics, natural habitats, history, and folklore of porcupines.

Includes glossary

599.37   Beavers

Gibbons, Gail

Beavers; by Gail Gibbons. Holiday House 2013 32 p. (hardcover) $17.95

Grades: K 1 2 3   **599.37**

1. Beavers 2. Picture books for children

ISBN 082342412X; 9780823424122

LC 2011049420

Author and illustrator Gail Gibbons features a children's picture book on beavers. "Beavers are fascinating animals. They build their own homes and live in family groups. They keep busy with their sharp teeth, powerful tails, and big webbed feet. Their work helps to preserve wetlands. Gibbons explores where they live, what they eat, how they raise their young, and much more." (Publisher's note)

599.4   Bats

Bekkering, Annalise

Bats. Weigl 2010 24p il (Backyard animals) lib bdg $24.45; pa $8.95

Grades: 1 2 3 **599.4**
1. Bats
ISBN 978-1-60596-076-0 lib bdg; 1-60596-076-4 lib bdg; 978-1-60596-077-7 pa; 1-60596-077-2 pa
LC 2008052056
This describes the "outstanding physical and behavioral characteristics [of bats]; some historical background; natural habitats and life cycle; role in the mythology of various cultures (a short myth is recounted); and tips on how to respond to (or avoid) encounters with the creatures. . . . A large, clear color photograph of one or more of the . . . animals . . . appears on about every other page." SLJ
Includes glossary

Berman, Ruth
Let's look at bats. Lerner Publications Co. 2010 32p il (Lightning bolt books: Animal close-ups) lib bdg $25.26
Grades: PreK K 1 2 **599.4**
1. Bats
ISBN 978-0-7613-3885-7 lib bdg; 0-7613-3885-3 lib bdg
LC 2008-51858
Introduces bats, describing their physical characteristics, habitat, nocturnal behavior, and feeding habits
"Fresh photography, a creative use of graphics, and a collagelike layout make[s] . . . [this book] eye-catching. . . . [The] book ends with a labeled diagram of the animal, a range map, and a further-reading list that includes print and online resources in a single list, a nice way of validating both types of materials." SLJ
Includes glossary

Carney, Elizabeth
Bats. National Geographic 2010 31p il (National Geographic readers) pa $3.99; $11.90
Grades: 1 2 3 **599.4**
1. Bats
ISBN 978-1-4263-0710-2 pa; 1-4263-0710-1 pa; 978-1-4263-0711-9; 1-4263-0711-X
LC 2010011636
"This leveled reader offers very basic information about bats. Topics range from types of bats to bat diet to behaviors such as echolocation and hanging upside down. . . . 'Bat Myths,' such as consuming human blood, are debunked. Simple sentence structures, along with corny jokes and excellent well-captioned photos, increase accessibility." Horn Book Guide
Includes glossary

Carson, Mary Kay
★ The **bat** scientists; with photographs by Tom Uhlman. Houghton Mifflin Books for Children 2010 79p il (Scientists in the field) $18
Grades: 4 5 6 7 **599.4**
1. Bats
ISBN 978-0-547-19956-6; 0-547-19956-2
LC 2010006767
This describes "patient field work, rescue and conservation efforts to save bats. . . . Woven into particular researchers' stories is an enormous amount of information about bat biology and behavior. Uhlman's photographs are clearly identified in context and the backmatter supports further research." Kirkus
Includes glossary and bibliographical references

Davies, Nicola, 1958-
★ **Bat** loves the night; illustrated by Sarah Fox-Davies. Candlewick Press 2001 28p il hardcover o.p. pa $6.99
Grades: PreK K 1 2 **599.4**
1. Bats -- Fiction
ISBN 0-7636-1202-2; 0-7636-2438-1 pa
LC 00-66681
Bat wakes up, flies into the night, uses the echoes of her voice to navigate, hunts for her supper, and returns to her roost to feed her baby
"An enticing picture book . . . that blends story with fact. . . . Lovely, atmospheric watercolor-and-pencil illustrations show surprising detail and succeed in making an oft-maligned animal appear realistically fuzzy and appealing." Booklist

Earle, Ann
Zipping, zapping, zooming bats; illustrated by Henry Cole. HarperCollins Pubs. 1995 32p il (Let's-read-and-find-out science) hardcover o.p. pa $4.95
Grades: K 1 2 3 **599.4**
1. Bats
ISBN 0-06-023480-6; 0-06-445133-X pa
LC 93-11052
"Brown bats are introduced as fliers, hunters, and contributors to good ecology in this simple discussion of the flying mammals' physical characteristics and behavior. The illustrations include realistic close-ups, informative diagrams, and scenes incorporating children. Instructions for building a bat house are included." Horn Book Guide

Gibbons, Gail
Bats. Holiday House 1999 un il $16.95; pa $6.95
Grades: K 1 2 3 **599.4**
1. Bats
ISBN 0-8234-1457-4; 0-8234-1637-2 pa
LC 99-12051
Describes different kinds of bats, their physical characteristics, habits and behavior, and efforts to protect them
"The occasional splashes of color light up brilliantly against the dark backgrounds. Well suited for classroom use, this book makes a good case for bats as an admirable part of the natural world." Booklist

Gish, Melissa
Bats. Creative Paperbacks 2010 46p il (Living wild) $23.95; pa $9.95
Grades: 5 6 7 8 **599.4**
1. Bats
ISBN 978-1-58341-966-3; 1-58341-966-7; 978-0-89812-549-8 pa; 0-89812-549-9 pa
LC 2010017371
The "book lucidly discusses conservation and the animals' often tenuous relationship with humans. The layout is uniformly simple but effective, constructed with a nice balance of main text for the report writers, smaller chunks of esoterica for browsers, and . . . killer photos." Booklist

Gonzales, Doreen
Bats in the dark. PowerKids Press 2010 24p il (Creatures of the night) lib bdg $21.25; pa $8.05

Grades: 2 3 4   **599.4**
1. Bats
ISBN 978-1-4042-8096-0 lib bdg; 1-4042-8096-0 lib bdg; 978-1-4358-3249-7 pa; 1-4358-3249-3 pa
    LC 2008-53802

A look at bats and their world in the dark

"Basic details are complemented by eclectic trivia, . . . [and] each volume concludes with a defense of the animal . . . and why it is vital to humans. The layout is attractive, with easy-to-read text and eye-catching photography. Good for reports." SLJ

Includes glossary

Lunde, Darrin P.
Hello, bumblebee bat; [by] Darrin Lunde; illustrated by Patricia J. Wynne. Charlesbridge 2007 un il lib bdg $15.95
Grades: PreK K 1 2   **599.4**
1. Bats
ISBN 978-1-57091-374-7 lib bdg; 1-57091-374-9 lib bdg
    LC 2006-20952

A Geisel Award honor book, 2008

"Meet the inch-long bumblebee bat, the smallest bat species in the world. Each left-hand page poses a question to a little bat. . . . Beginning each question with the bat's memorable name heightens the pleasing sense of pattern in the text, which offers information that children can understand, but avoids overwhelming them with too many facts. Wynne . . . contributes an appealing set of pictures that complement the text." Booklist

Markle, Sandra, 1946-
The case of the vanishing little brown bats; a scientific mystery. Sandra Markle. Millbrook Press 2014 48 p. illustrations, maps (lib. bdg.: alk. paper) $29.27
Grades: 4 5 6   **599.4**
1. Bats 2. Animals -- Diseases 3. Little brown bat
ISBN 1467714631; 9781467714631
    LC 2013030953

"This informative title sheds light on a mystery of nature: how little brown bats, nature's insect eaters, are mysteriously dying in their caves during hibernation. Each chapter takes readers into the problems that plague this endangered member of our ecosystem, describing how teams of scientists examined how 'white-nose syndrome,' caused by a fungus called Pd, is infecting the brown bat population." (School Library Journal)

"With plentiful details about the scientific work, photographs showing scientists and their tiny subjects, clear explanations, and an organization that is both topical and chronological, this title brings science to life." Kirkus

Includes bibliographical references and index

Markovics, Joyce L.
The bat's cave; a dark city. by Joyce Markovics. Bearport Pub. 2009 32p il map (Spectacular animal towns) lib bdg $25.27
Grades: 2 3 4   **599.4**
1. Bats
ISBN 978-1-59716-871-7 lib bdg; 1-59716-871-8 lib bdg
    LC 2009-8146

A look inside a bat's dark world, how bats hunt, sleep, and raise their young, and more

"Through excellent photographs, high-interest texts, sidebars, maps, and other material, children learn about both the animals and their habitats. The . . . book also provides brief profiles of animals with similar habitats. . . . [This book is] much better than average 'report' titles." SLJ

Includes glossary and bibliographical references

Riggs, Kate
Bats; by Kate Riggs. Creative Education 2012 24 p. col. ill.
Grades: K 1 2   **599.4**
1. Bats 2. Animals -- Food 3. Bats -- Folklore 4. Wildlife photography 5. Zoology -- Encyclopedias
ISBN 1608181057; 9781608181056
    LC 2010049117

This children's book is part of Kate Riggs' "Amazing Animals" series, which presents photographs and "general facts about physiology, behaviors, eating habits, habitats, and life spans" of various animals. (Booklist) ""A basic exploration of the appearance, behavior, and habitat of bats, Earth's only flying mammals. Also included is a story from folklore explaining how bats helped shape the earth." (Publisher's note)

Includes bibliographical references (p. 24) and index

Rodriguez, Cindy
Bats. Rourke Pub. 2010 24p il map (Eye to eye with endangered species) lib bdg $27.07
Grades: 2 3 4   **599.4**
1. Bats
ISBN 978-1-60694-406-6 lib bdg; 1-60694-406-1 lib bdg
    LC 2009-5997

Text examines the issues endangered bats face and how they can be saved

"Sets out to introduce readers to [bats] . . . explain the dangers they face, and detail the efforts of biologists and conservationists to save them. . . . Serviceable and informative." SLJ

Includes glossary

Stewart, Melissa
How do bats fly in the dark? Marshall Cavendish Benchmark 2009 32p il (Tell me why, tell me how) lib bdg $20.95
Grades: 3 4 5   **599.4**
1. Bats
ISBN 978-0-7614-2924-1 lib bdg; 0-7614-2924-7 lib bdg
    LC 2007023821

"Provides comprehensive information on bats and the process of how they use their sensory system to find their way in the dark" Publisher's note

Includes glossary and bibliographical references

A place for bats; written by Melissa Stewart; illustrated by Higgins Bond. 1st ed. Peachtree Publishers 2012 32 p. col. ill. (reinforced) $16.95
Grades: K 1 2   **599.4**
1. Bats 2. Habitat (Ecology) 3. Human influence on

nature

ISBN 1561456241; 9781561456246

LC 2011020468

"This book introduces 12 varieties of bats and their habitats around Canada, the United States, and Mexico, and brings to life their challenges to survive." (School Library Journal) "[Melissa] Stewart points out problems faced by bats and what specific steps people have taken . . . to help the bats, such as . . . putting up 'bat boxes' to house bats that can no longer find dead trees for shelter. The text clearly conveys the idea that people can make a difference in animal survival." (Booklist)

Includes bibliographical references.

Vogel, Julia

Bats; by Julia Vogel; illustrations by Andrew Recher. NorthWord 2007 47p il (Our wild world) $10.95; pa $7.95

Grades: 3 4 5 6   **599.4**

1. Bats

ISBN 978-1-55971-968-1; 978-1-55971-969-8 pa

LC 2006021917

The "text describes the major physical characteristics shared by all [bats], . . . behavior, distinctive characteristics of several large groups and more than two dozen species, habitats, defense mechanisms, diets, and life cycles. . . . A sharp color photograph . . . illustrates the text on most pages." Booklist

599.5   Cetaceans and sea cows

Arnosky, Jim

Jim Arnosky's All about manatees. Scholastic Nonfiction 2008 un pa $5.99

Grades: K 1 2 3   **599.5**

1. Manatees

ISBN 0-439-90361-0 pa; 978-0-439-90361-5 pa

LC 2007061717

This is an "introductory guide to manatees. . . . Artwork, captions, and paragraphs of information work together seamlessly to present the physical characteristics, behaviors, and habitats of manatees living in Florida waters, as well as the threats to their survival. Fluid paintings illustrate points in the text and depict the animals' lumbering grace." Booklist

Baker, Molly

The **secret** world of whales; illustrated by Molly Baker. Chronicle Books 2011 108p il $16.99

Grades: 4 5 6 7   **599.5**

1. Whales

ISBN 978-0-8118-7641-4; 0-8118-7641-1

LC 2010-27355

"In this small-format volume, Siebert creates a concise introduction to whales, addressing myths and stories, the history of the whaling industry, communication and intelligence, and encounters between whales and humans. With playful, anthropomorphic cartoons, striking photographs, and a discussion of the dangers facing whales—noise pollution from boats, potentially lethal sonar—readers should gain a vivid impression of their behavior in the wild, as well as an appreciation for their majesty." Publ Wkly

Catt, Thessaly

Migrating with the humpback whale. PowerKids Press 2011 24p il (Animal journeys) lib bdg $21.25; pa $8.25

Grades: 2 3 4   **599.5**

1. Whales 2. Animals -- Migration

ISBN 978-1-4488-2543-1 lib bdg; 1-4488-2543-1 lib bdg; 978-1-4488-2670-4 pa; 1-4488-2670-5 pa

LC 2010027076

This book follows "the yearly migratory patterns of the [humpback whale] and [covers] anatomy, diet, mating, parenting, climate change as caused by people, pollution, and more. . . . [It is illustrated] with clear color photographs. . . . Go-to nonfiction for animal enthusiasts." SLJ

Christopherson, Sara Cohen

Top 50 reasons to care about whales and dolphins; animals in peril. Enslow Publishers 2010 103p il (Top 50 reasons to care about endangered animals) lib bdg $31.93

Grades: 4 5 6 7   **599.5**

1. Whales 2. Dolphins 3. Endangered species

ISBN 978-0-7660-3453-2 lib bdg; 0-7660-3453-4 lib bdg

LC 2008-48695

This describes whales and dolphins—their life cycles, diets, young, habitats, and reasons why they are endangered animals

"The illustrations, mostly color photographs, represent a wonderful selection of the animals and their habitats. Reluctant readers may be enticed by this . . . simply because of the great images. This . . . would make a substantial supplement to the science curriculum when studying endangered animals." Libr Media Connect

Includes glossary and bibliographical references

Davies, Nicola, 1958-

Big blue whale; illustrated by Nick Maland. Candlewick Press 1997 27p il hardcover o.p. pa $6.99

Grades: K 1 2 3   **599.5**

1. Whales

ISBN 1-56402-895-X; 0-7636-1080-1 pa

LC 96-42327

Examines the physical characteristics, habits, and habitats of the blue whale

"Davies's brief overview offers young readers exactly what they want to know about this magnificent animal, and her judicious use of comparison makes the abstract more understandable. . . . Maland's cross-hatched pen-and-ink drawings rest on blue watercolor wash backgrounds." Horn Book Guide

Esbensen, Barbara Juster

Baby whales drink milk; illustrated by Lambert Davis. HarperCollins Pubs. 1994 32p il (Let's-read-and-find-out science) hardcover o.p. pa $4.95

Grades: K 1   **599.5**

1. Whales 2. Mammals

ISBN 0-06-445119-4 pa

LC 92-30375

Describes the behavior of the humpback whale, with an emphasis on the fact that it is a mammal and shares the characteristics of other mammals

"Full-color paintings, mainly in watery greens and blues, show the animals in their habitat, along with a scene of a whale model in a museum and a map of migration. The book's strong point, though, is Esbensen's simple, informative text, which keeps its young audience clearly in view." Booklist

Gish, Melissa

Killer whales. Creative Paperbacks 2010 46p il map (Living wild) $23.95; pa $9.95

Grades: 5 6 7 8   **599.5**

1. Whales

ISBN 978-1-58341-971-7; 1-58341-971-3; 978-0-89812-554-2 pa; 0-89812-554-5 pa

LC 2010017376

"A look at killer whales, including their habitats, physical characteristics such as their unique coloration, behaviors, relationships with humans, and protected status in the world today." Publisher's note

Whales. Creative Education 2011 46p il map (Living wild) lib bdg $23.95

Grades: 5 6 7 8   **599.5**

1. Whales

ISBN 978-1-60818-084-4

LC 2010028414

A look at whales, including their habitats, physical characteristics such as their streamlined bodies, behaviors, relationships with humans, and threatened status in the world today.

Includes glossary and bibliographical references

Goldish, Meish

Florida manatees; warm water miracles. by Meish Goldish. Bearport Pub. 2007 32p il map (America's animal comebacks) lib bdg $18.95

Grades: 2 3 4   **599.5**

1. Manatees 2. Wildlife conservation

ISBN 978-1-59716-507-5 lib bdg; 1-59716-507-7 lib bdg

LC 2007010311

"This accessible title discusses the environmental threats facing the Florida manatee and the efforts that saved this appealing sea creature from extinction. . . . Double-page spread feature attention-grabbing fact boxes and large, full-color photos." Booklist

Includes glossary and bibliographical references

Greenberg, Daniel A.

Whales; [by] Dan Greenberg, with Nina Hess. Cavendish Square Publishing 2010 24p il map (Benchmark rockets. Animals) lib bdg $16.95

Grades: 3 4 5 6   **599.5**

1. Whales

ISBN 978-0-7614-4346-9; 0-7614-4346-0

LC 2008-52110

"Describes the physical characteristics, habitat, behavior, diet, life cycle, and conservation status of whales." Publisher's note

Includes glossary

Harris, Caroline

Whales and dolphins. Kingfisher 2010 56p il (Discover science) $9.99

Grades: 1 2 3   **599.5**

1. Whales 2. Dolphins

ISBN 978-0-7534-6448-9; 0-7534-6448-9

First published in the series Kingfisher young knowledge in 2005

Introduces readers to some of the largest and most acrobatic mammals in oceans and seas. Young students will discover the many types of whales and dolphins and learn about their behavior and how they survive in their watery world

"There is enough information for basic reports, but . . . [this] will also be popular with browsers. . . . [Features] large, colorful images as well as smaller, more detailed close-up." Libr Media Connect

Includes glossary and bibliographical references

Hodgkins, Fran

★ The **whale** scientists; solving the mystery of whale strandings. Houghton Mifflin Co. 2007 63p il map (Scientists in the field) $18

Grades: 5 6 7 8   **599.5**

1. Whales

ISBN 978-0-618-55673-1; 0-618-55673-7

LC 2006-34634

This describes the evolution of whales and their relationship to humans and offers various scientific theories about their strandings.

"Hodgkins packs her text with an impressive amount of information. . . . Well-chosen color photographs amply illustrate the well-organized discussion." SLJ

Includes glossary and bibliographical references

Landau, Elaine

Beluga whales. Enslow Elementary 2010 31p il map (Animals of the snow and ice) lib bdg $22.60

Grades: 2 3 4   **599.5**

1. Whales

ISBN 978-0-7660-3459-4 lib bdg; 0-7660-3459-3 lib bdg

LC 2009006478

This describes beluga whales, including habitat, eating habits, mating, babies, and conservation

"Throughout most of [this] title, a full-page, or page and a quarter, sharp, color photograph . . . alternates with a page of text. An addendum of miscellaneous facts, a short list for further reading, and some websites are appended. Landau's smoothly written, well-illustrated titles are right on target for the intended audience." SLJ

Includes glossary and bibliographical references

Lourie, Peter

★ The **manatee** scientists; saving vulnerable species. Houghton Mifflin Books for Children 2011 80p il map (Scientists in the field) $18.99

Grades: 4 5 6 7   **599.5**

1. Manatees 2. Scientists 3. Marine biology 4. Endangered species 5. Wildlife conservation

ISBN 978-0-547-15254-7; 0-547-15254-X

This book highlights the work scientists are doing to protect the manatee, including John Reynolds, who does an aerial count of manatees from the Florida sky; Lucy Keith who spends a weekend rescuing manatees trapped in a dam in Senegal; and Fernando Rosas who takes the author on an Amazonian boat trip, looking for a young manatee he released back into the wild.

"The manatees photographed by Lourie and others add plenty of visual appeal. . . . A sturdy addition to a standard-setting nonfiction series." Booklist

★ **Whaling** season; a year in the life of an arctic whale scientist. Houghton Mifflin Books for Children 2009 80p il map (Scientists in the field) $18

Grades: 4 5 6 7 **599.5**
1. Inuit 2. Whales 3. Biologists 4. Alaska
ISBN 978-0-618-77709-9; 0-618-77709-1
LC 2009-18596

Profiles the work of John Craighead George, an Arctic whale scientist, as he studies the bowhead whale and works with the indigenous people of Alaska to better understand the history of the animal.

"Combining exemplary color photos and simple, vivid language, the chapters detail not only George's day-today methodology but also his motivation." Booklist

Includes glossary and bibliographical references

Lunde, Darrin P.
Hello, baby beluga; [by] Darrin Lunde; illustrated by Patricia J. Wynne. Charlesbridge 2011 un il $15.95; pa $6.95

Grades: PreK K 1 **599.5**
1. Whales 2. Animal babies
ISBN 978-1-57091-739-4; 1-57091-739-6; 978-1-57091-740-0 pa; 1-57091-740-X pa
LC 2010007550

"Lunde delivers facts about baby belunga whales in a simple direct-address question-and-answer format, almost as if a child is conducting a casual interview with a candid young whale. . . . Cool blues, whites, and grays dominate the illustrations, which showcase the happy calf in its arctic surroundings." Horn Book Guide

Markle, Sandra
Killer whales; [by] Sandra Markle. Carolrhoda Books 2004 39p il (Animal predators) lib bdg $25.26; pa $7.95

Grades: 3 4 5 6 **599.5**
1. Whales
ISBN 1-57505-728-X lib bdg; 1-57505-743-3 pa
LC 2003-25944

"Dramatic, large color photos keep step with informative, readable [text]." SLJ

Includes glossary and bibliographical references

Marsh, Laura
Whales. National Geographic 2010 48p il map (Great migrations) $11.90; pa $3.99

Grades: 1 2 3 **599.5**
1. Whales
ISBN 978-1-4263-0746-1; 1-4263-0746-2; 978-1-4263-0745-4 pa; 1-4263-0745-4 pa
LC 2010017959

This offers facts about sperm whales in an easy reader format.

"Dynamic full-color photographs, informative writing, and consistent organization work well together in [this volume]. . . . Along with the many photographs, the fascinating details are supported by boxes of related information, helpful definitions of new terms, and a sprinkling of entertaining jokes/riddles." SLJ

Includes glossary

Nicklin, Flip
★ **Face** to face with dolphins; by Flip and Linda Nicklin. National Geographic 2007 32p il (Face to face) $16.95; lib bdg $25.90

Grades: 3 4 5 6 **599.5**
1. Dolphins
ISBN 978-1-4263-0141-4; 1-4263-0141-3; 978-1-4263-0142-1 lib bdg; 1-4263-0142-1 lib bdg
LC 2006-36273

"The Nicklins outline the special abilities and physical features of dolphins, such as echolocation, as well as diet, reproduction, swimming habits, and threats to their existence. . . . [This] attractive, smoothly written [book], topped off with advice about self-directed research, will catch the attention of enthusiasts and motivate them toward personal investigation." SLJ

Includes glossary and bibliographical references

★ **Face** to face with whales; by Flip & Linda Nicklin. National Geographic 2008 31p il map (Face to face) $16.95; lib bdg $25.95

Grades: 3 4 5 6 **599.5**
1. Whales
ISBN 978-1-4263-0244-2; 1-4263-0244-4; 978-1-4263-0245-9 lib bdg; 1-4263-0245-2 lib bdg
LC 2007-34249

The authors describe the life cycle and behavior of whales and their own experiences with whales in the wild.

Includes glossary and bibliographical references

O'Connell, Jennifer
The **eye** of the whale; a rescue story. Jennifer O'Connell. 1st hardcover ed. Tilbury House, Publishers 2012 32 p. col. ill. (hardcover) $16.95

Grades: 5 6 7 8 **599.5**
1. Whales 2. Animal rescue 3. Humpback whale -- California -- San Francisco 4. Wildlife rescue -- California -- San Francisco
ISBN 0884483355; 9780884483359
LC 2012031165

This true children's story, by Jennifer O'Connell, begins when, "near San Francisco, a distress call was radioed to shore by a local fisherman. He had discovered a humpback whale tangled in hundreds of yards of crab-trap lines. . . . A team of volunteers answered the call, and four divers risked their lives to rescue the enormous animal." (Publisher's note)

Rake, Jody Sullivan
Blue whales up close. Capstone Press 2010 24p il (First facts. Whales and dolphins up close) lib bdg $21.32

Grades: K 1 2 3 **599.5**
1. Whales
ISBN 978-1-4296-3336-9 lib bdg; 1-4296-3336-0 lib bdg
LC 2009-6005

This "title has colorful pages and chapter heading to capture the interest of young readers as well as short, straightforward sentence structure to keep them reading. Captivating photographs of whales in the wild are present on each spread and feature up close images of body parts such as blow holes and baleen. . . . This . . . will be a fabulous addition to any elementary school library collection." Libr Media Connect

Includes glossary and bibliographical references

Humpback whales up close. Capstone Press 2010 24p il (First facts. Whales and dolphins up close) lib bdg $21.32

Grades: K 1 2   **599.5**
1. Whales
ISBN 978-1-4296-3337-6 lib bdg; 1-4296-3337-9 lib bdg
    LC 2009-6004

This "title has colorful pages and chapter heading to capture the interest of young readers as well as short, straightforward sentence structure to keep them reading. Captivating photographs of whales in the wild are present on each spread and feature up close images of body parts such as blow holes and baleen. . . . This . . . will be a fabulous addition to any elementary school library collection." Libr Media Connect

Includes glossary and bibliographical references

The **mystery** of whale strandings; a cause and effect investigation. Capstone Press 2010 32p il map (Fact finders. Animals on the edge) lib bdg $25.99

Grades: 3 4 5 6   **599.5**
1. Whales
ISBN 978-1-4296-4531-7 lib bdg; 1-4296-4531-8 lib bdg
    LC 2010008561

"Excellent discussions address those who doubt the severity of the issue and those who wonder why people should care what happens to animals. The captioned photographs are timely and piognant. . . . [This] makes serious subject matter interesting and accessible." SLJ

Includes glossary and bibliographical references

Riggs, Kate
Dolphins. Creative Education 2011 24p il (Amazing animals) $24.25; pa $5.99

Grades: K 1 2   **599.5**
1. Dolphins
ISBN 978-1-58341-989-2; 1-58341-989-6; 978-0-89812-562-7 pa; 0-89812-562-6 pa
    LC 2010019053

"The large, beautiful photos on each spread include vivid shots of animals in action as well as close-ups of their faces. Photo captions consistently add interesting animal facts. . . . The text is laid out in a large, easy-to-read font. The text, although made up of simple sentences, conveys plenty of interesting information." Booklist

Whales; Kate Riggs. Creative Education 2015 24 p. $7.99

Grades: K 1 2   **599.5**
1. Whales 2. Animals -- Folklore
ISBN 0898129303; 9780898129304; 9781608185177
    LC 2014000189

This children's book by Kate Riggs, part of the Amazing Animals series, provides "(a) basic exploration of the appearance, behavior, and habitat of whales, the large ocean animals. Also included is a story from folklore explaining why New Zealanders traditionally rode whales. " (Publisher's note)

"Across from the photos, the text is laid out cleanly in a large, clear font, and the sentences are simple and easy to read. Photo captions, meanwhile, add interesting facts, while occasional vocabulary words are defined at the bottoms of pages." - Booklist

Rockwood, Leigh
Dolphins are smart! PowerKids Press 2010 24p il (Super smart animals) lib bdg $21.25; pa $8.25

Grades: 2 3 4 5   **599.5**
1. Dolphins
ISBN 978-1-4358-9398-6 lib bdg; 1-4358-9398-0 lib bdg; 978-1-4358-9842-4 pa; 1-4358-9842-7 pa
Examines the intelligence of dolphins.

"Readers get an overview of the . . . [dolphin's] life cycle, its domestic history (where relevant), and natural habitat, and examples of how it is smart in the wild as well as when helped by human tutelage. . . . Interesting color photographs and large, easy-to-read print will attract browsers and report writers alike." SLJ

Includes glossary

Sayre, April Pulley
Here come the humpbacks! April Pulley Sayre; illustrated by Jamie Hogan. Charlesbridge 2013 40 p. (reinforced for library use) $17.95

Grades: 2 3 4   **599.5**
1. Whales 2. Whale watching 3. Humpback whale
ISBN 1580894054; 9781580894050; 9781580894067
    LC 2012000785

This children's picture book by April Pulley Sayre looks at humpback whales. The male whales' singing is described. "As mother and calf move from the shallows into the open ocean, they encounter other creatures and objects, which Sayre introduces in offset text about whale-watching tours, barnacles, suckerfish, chemical pollution, and more." (Publishers Weekly)

Simon, Seymour
Dolphins. Smithsonian/Collins 2009 32p il $17.99; lib bdg $18.89

Grades: 1 2 3 4   **599.5**
1. Dolphins
ISBN 978-0-06-028393-3; 0-06-028393-9; 978-0-06-028394-0 lib bdg; 0-06-028394-7 lib bdg
    LC 2008010654

"Simon presents fascinating facts about these playful mammals and describes the difference between dolphins, porpoises, and whales in terms that children can understand. Without being didactic, he discusses the physiology and habits of dolphins, as well as the greatest threat to the species—humans. Accompanied by full-page color photographs of dolphins, the text is presented with considerable white space in the margins." Booklist

Skerry, Brian
Face to face with manatees. National Geographic 2010 31p il map (Face to face) $16.95; lib bdg $25.90

Grades: 3 4 5 6   **599.5**
1. Manatees
ISBN 978-1-4263-0616-7; 1-4263-0616-4; 978-1-4263-0617-4 lib bdg; 1-4263-0617-2 lib bdg
    LC 2009-40783

The author describes the life cycle and behavior of the manatee and his own experiences with manatees in the wild.

"The amazing, literally face-to-face photographs dominate the book. . . . Although written for children, this colorful, informative book will appeal to adults as well." Sci Books Films

Includes glossary and bibliographical references

Spilsbury, Louise

Dolphin. Heinemann Library 2010 24p il (A day in the life: sea animals) lib bdg $22; pa $6.49

Grades: 1 2   **599.5**

1. Dolphins

ISBN 978-1-4329-3999-1 lib bdg; 1-4329-3999-8 lib bdg; 978-1-4329-4006-5 pa; 1-4329-4006-6 pa

LC 2010000485

This pairs "well-chosen color photos . . . with one or two sentences of simple commentary for each. . . . [Though this title] includes references to several varieties of the chosen creature, one species in particular is highlighted. . . . [Good choice] for pleasure or purpose reading." SLJ

Includes glossary and bibliographical references

Stearns, Precious McKenzie

Manatees; [by] Precious McKenzie. Rourke 2010 24p il map (Eye to eye with endangered species) lib bdg $27.07

Grades: 2 3 4   **599.5**

1. Manatees

ISBN 978-1-60694-403-5 lib bdg; 1-60694-403-7 lib bdg

LC 2009-6011

This describes manatees and why they are threatened with extinction

"Sets out to introduce readers to [manatees] . . . explain the dangers they face, and detail the efforts of biologists and conservationists to save them. . . . Serviceable and informative." SLJ

Includes glossary and bibliographical references

Thomson, Sarah L.

★ **Amazing** whales! written by Sarah L. Thomson; photographs provided by the Wildlife Conservation Society. HarperCollins 2004 27p il (I can read book) $15.99; lib bdg $16.89

Grades: 1 2 3   **599.5**

1. Whales

ISBN 0-06-054465-1; 0-06-054466-X lib bdg

LC 2004-2473

"Thomson's superior text sustains readers' attention with interesting facts and apt comparisons. . . . Spectacular color photographs add detail and drama." SLJ

"Thomson takes a look at blue whales, killer whales, sperm whales, dolphins, and porpoises, describing common physical characteristics of the group as well as hunting and feeding habits, methods of communication, and endangered status." Booklist

599.53   Dolphins and porpoises

Coleman, Janet Wyman

Eight Dolphins of Katrina; A True Tale of Survival. written by Janet W. Coleman; illustrated by Yan Nascimbene. Houghton Mifflin Harcourt 2013 40 p. $16.99

Grades: 2 3 4 5   **599.53**

1. Dolphins 2. Hurricane Katrina, 2005

ISBN 054771923X; 9780547719238

LC 2012024419

"This story of the rescue of eight dolphins off the coast of Mississippi after Hurricane Katrina underscores the bonds between dolphins and their trainers. . . . After a 40-foot tidal wave destroys the dolphin pool at the Marine Life Oceanarium in Gulfport, eight dolphins disappear. . . . Via helicopter and boat, the trainers set out to search for the dolphins, who were raised in captivity and thus unaccustomed to feeding or protecting themselves." (Publishers Weekly)

Riggs, Kate

Killer whales; by Kate Riggs. Creative Education 2012 24 p. (Amazing animals)

Grades: K 1 2   **599.53**

1. Killer whales 2. Marine animals 3. Marine biology

ISBN 9781608181094

LC 2010049129

This book offers a "look at killer whales, including their habitats, physical characteristics such as their unique coloration, behaviors, relationships with humans, and protected status." (Publisher's note) "This book shares with readers how the whale waits above water for food, how there is only one killer whale and it is found in the coldest oceans. The reader is then informed about the whale's ability to maintain its warmth thanks to blubber before attention turns toward how the whale moves and swims with the help of its strong tail and flukes." (Children's Literature)

Includes bibliographical references and index

Turner, Pamela S.

The **dolphins** of Shark Bay; by Pamela S. Turner. Houghton Mifflin Harcourt 2013 76 p. $18.99

Grades: 5 6 7 8   **599.53**

1. Dolphins 2. Bottlenose dolphin -- Behavior -- Australia -- Shark Bay (W.A.) 3. Bottlenose dolphin -- Research -- Australia -- Shark Bay (W.A.)

ISBN 0547716389; 9780547716381

LC 2012048463

In this book, "ride alongside the author Pamela S. Turner and her scientific team . . . as they seek to answer the question: just why are dolphins so smart? And what does their behavior tell us about human intelligence, captive animals, and the future of the ocean?" (Publisher's note)

599.6   Ungulates

Lunis, Natalie

Pronghorn; long-distance runner! Bearport Pub. 2011 24p il map (Blink of an eye. Superfast animals!) lib bdg $21.26

Grades: 1 2 3   **599.6**
1. Pronghorn antelopes
ISBN 978-1-936087-94-5; 1-936087-94-4

LC 2010011127

This decribes the pronghorn antelope, including where it lives, what it eats, and the ways its body helps it reach its record-breaking speeds.

This "is sure to appeal to a wide variety of readers. Vibrant photos illustrate each animal from multiple perspectives, providing opportunity for readers to closely examine the animal. Information is organized by subject heading and branches into the animal's physical features and how they contribute to its speed, the animal's natural predators, and how the animal makes use of speed as a means of survival. . . . This . . . will be a worthwhile addition to your nonfiction collection." Libr Media Connect

Includes glossary and bibliographical references

599.63   Even-toed ungulates

Anderson, Jill
Giraffes; by Jill Anderson. NorthWord 2005 un il (Wild ones) $12.95; pa $8.95
Grades: K 1 2   **599.63**
1. Giraffes
ISBN 978-1-55971-928-5; 1-55971-928-1; 978-1-55971-929-2 pa; 1-55971-929-X pa

LC 2004031117

This describes the physiology, habitat, and life cycle of giraffes

"With simple, direct words and clear, closeup color photo images, this . . . does an excellent job of introducing preschoolers to basic facts about giraffe physiology and habitat, and, especially, how the animals get their food and digest it, and how they care for their young." Booklist

Bredeson, Carmen
Giraffes up close. Enslow Elementary 2008 24p il (Zoom in on animals!) lib bdg $21.26
Grades: 1 2 3   **599.63**
1. Giraffes
ISBN 978-0-7660-3081-7 lib bdg; 0-7660-3081-4 lib bdg

This describes the anatomy, behavior, and life cycle of the giraffe.

Includes glossary and bibliographical references

Clarke, Penny
★ **Hippos**; written by Penny Clarke. F. Watts 2009 32p il (Scary creatures) lib bdg $26; pa $8.95
Grades: 3 4 5   **599.63**
1. Hippopotamus
ISBN 978-0-531-21671-2 lib bdg; 0-531-21671-3 lib bdg; 978-0-531-21042-0 pa; 0-531-21042-1 pa

LC 2009010798

This describes the hippo's life cycle, habitat, behavior, and relationship to humans

This title has "two-page chapters of accessible, large-type text and bright color photos and illustrations. . . . The series distinguishes itself with 'X-Ray Vision.' When readers hold the page with this prompt up to the light, an image emerges. The X-rays mostly show the skeletal structures of

the animals. Text boxes throughout add to the visual appeal. . . . [This title is an] excellent [resource for school assignments and browsing." SLJ

Includes glossary

Hatkoff, Isabella
★ **Owen** & Mzee: the language of friendship; told by Isabella Hatkoff, Craig Hatkoff, and Paula Kuhumbu; with photographs by Peter Greste. Scholastic Press 2007 un il $16.99
Grades: K 1 2 3   **599.63**
1. Turtles 2. Hippopotamus 3. Kenya
ISBN 978-0-439-89959-8; 0-439-89959-1

LC 2006015612

"Owen & Mzee: The True Story of a Remarkable Friendship (Scholastic, 2006) chronicled the fascinating story of a baby hippo who was orphaned by the December 2004 tsunami and the bond he formed with Mzee, a 130-year-old Alhambra tortoise at a wildlife sanctuary in Kenya. This sequel updates readers on the status of that friendship a year and a half later, particularly with regard to the way this unusual duo has learned to communicate with one another. . . . The text is clearly written and accompanied by numerous high-quality, full-color photos of this unique pair." SLJ

Includes bibliographical references

London, Jonathan
Hippos are huge! Jonathan London; illustrated by Matthew Trueman. Candlewick Press 2015 32 p. color illustrations $16.99
Grades: PreK K 1 2   **599.63**
1. Animals 2. Hippopotamus
ISBN 0763665924; 9780763665920

LC 2014944797

This children's book by Jonathan London, illustrated by Matthew Trueman, is designed to "spur interest in the world of hippos. Trueman's vivid images take advantage of every inch of available space to convey the size of these creatures. Two types of text appear on each page: larger print encompasses the main narrative full of fascinating facts (ideal for reading aloud), while smaller print presents drier statistics and additional facts of interest." (School Library Journal)

Tourville, Amanda Doering
A **giraffe** grows up; by Amanda Doering Tourville; illustrated by Michael Denman and William J. Huiett. Picture Window Books 2007 24p il map hardcover o.p. lib bdg $25.26
Grades: PreK K 1 2   **599.63**
1. Giraffes
ISBN 978-1-4048-3158-2 lib bdg; 1-4048-3158-4 lib bdg; 978-1-4048-3565-8 pa; 1-4048-3565-2 pa

LC 2006027307

"Each spread has an acrylic painting with a paragraph or two of text and a box of facts. . . . Easy-to-read . . . with enough information for basic reports." SLJ

Includes glossary and bibliographical references

Walden, Katherine
Warthogs. PowerKiDS Press 2009 24p il (Safari animals) lib bdg $21.25

Grades: PreK K 1 2   **599.63**

1. Warthogs
ISBN 978-1-4358-2688-5 lib bdg; 1-4358-2688-4
lib bdg

LC 2008019531

This book provides "succinctly written introductory information about [warthogs'] range, habitat, social groups,
and diet. Spreads consist of one to three short, simply constructed sentences opposite crisp, color photographs, most
of which represent the subject perfectly." SLJ

599.64 Bovids

Caper, William
American bison; a scary prediction. by William Caper.
Bearport 2007 32p il map (America's animal comebacks)
lib bdg $25.27
Grades: 2 3 4   **599.64**

1. Bison 2. Zoologists 3. Wildlife conservation 4.
Bronx Zoo 5. Zoo directors
ISBN 978-1-59716-504-4 lib bdg; 1-59716-504-2
lib bdg

LC 2007010863

This describes how the American bison was saved from
extinction by William Temple Hornaday, the American Bison Society, and the The Bronx Zoo.

This book is "well organized and [has] an easy style and
an accessible vocabulary and text size . . . [and] color photographs." SLJ

Includes glossary and bibliographical references

Catt, Thessaly
Migrating with the wildebeest. PowerKids Press 2011
24p il map (Animal journeys) lib bdg $21.25; pa $8.25
Grades: 2 3 4   **599.64**

1. Gnus 2. Animals -- Migration
ISBN 978-1-4488-2544-8 lib bdg; 1-4488-2544-X lib
bdg; 978-1-4488-2795-4 pa; 1-4488-2795-7 pa

LC 2010028194

Learn about the wildebeest and its migration patterns.

"Keywords are bolded throughout and can be found in
the glossary. The format is attractive with inset captioned
photographs and page heading that seem to move across the
page." Libr Media Connect

Includes glossary

Ganeri, Anita
Arabian oryx. Heinemann Library 2011 24p il map
(A day in the life: desert animals) $22; pa $6.49
Grades: K 1 2   **599.64**

1. Oryx
ISBN 978-1-4329-4769-9; 1-4329-4769-9; 978-1-
4329-4778-1 pa; 1-4329-4778-8 pa

LC 2010022817

"The engaging full-color photographs are key to [this]
well-organized [book]. . . . Basic global maps show where
the animal is found, and a diagram called a 'body map' labels its parts. The [text is] appropriate for the age group, and
the pictures will draw in youngsters. [An] excellent [pur-
chase] if material is needed on these animals." SLJ

Includes glossary and bibliographical references

George, Jean Craighead
The buffalo are back; paintings by Wendell Minor.
Dutton Children's Books 2010 un il $16.99
Grades: 3 4 5   **599.64**

1. Bison 2. West (U.S.) -- History
ISBN 978-0-525-42215-0; 0-525-42215-3

"This handsome book discusses the history of the buffalo on the American plains. Succintly and gracefully written,
it envisions the centuries when Indians carefully managed
the land, using the buffalo for food, shelter, and clothing. . .
. Illustrated with beautiful landscape paintings and striking
close-ups of people and animals, this book offers a very effective presentation of the buffalo's story." Booklist

Gish, Melissa
Bison. Creative Education 2011 46p il map (Living
wild) $23.95
Grades: 5 6 7 8   **599.64**

1. Bison
ISBN 978-1-60818-077-6; 1-60818-077-8

LC 2010028305

A look at bison, including their habitats, physical characteristics such as their shaggy coats, behaviors, relationships
with humans, and threatened status in the world today.

This offers "an array of interesting facts. Photography is
large and beautiful—a real draw." SLJ

Includes bibliographical references

Martin, Jacqueline Briggs
★ The chiru of high Tibet; a true story. written by
Jacqueline Briggs Martin; illustrated by Linda Wingerter.
Houghton Mifflin Harcourt 2010 un il $17.99
Grades: 1 2 3   **599.64**

1. Chirus 2. Zoologists 3. Wildlife conservation 4.
Tibet (China) 5. Nonfiction writers
ISBN 978-0-618-58130-6; 0-618-58130-8

"The antelope-like chiru of the Chang Tang in northern Tibet were a million strong before they were hunted
nearly to extinction for their marvelously soft wool. . . .
Wildlife champion George Schaller . . . hoped to save the
chiru by protecting the remote valley where females give
birth each spring. . . . The birthing ground is now protected
from poachers. Martin's account of all this is brief, dramatic,
and supplemented with boxed facts, and nicely amplified in
Wingerter's art." Horn Book

Includes bibliographical references

Walden, Katherine
Wildebeests. Rosen Pub. Group's PowerKids Press
2009 24p il (Safari animals) lib bdg $21.25; pa $8.25
Grades: PreK K 1 2   **599.64**

1. Gnus
ISBN 978-1-4358-2692-2 lib bdg; 1-4358-2692-2 lib
bdg; 978-1-4358-3066-0 pa; 1-4358-3066-0 pa

LC 2008021587

This book provides "succinctly written introductory information about [wildebeests'] range, habitat, social groups,
and diet. Spreads consist of one to three short, simply constructed sentences opposite crisp, color photographs, most
of which represent the subject perfectly." SLJ

Includes glossary

599.65 Deer

Arnold, Caroline

A **moose's** world; written and illustrated by Caroline Arnold. Picture Window Books 2010 24p il (Caroline Arnold's animals) lib bdg $25.32

Grades: PreK K 1 2 **599.65**

1. Moose

ISBN 978-1-4048-5742-1 lib bdg; 1-4048-5742-7 lib bdg

LC 2009033360

This narrative tells the story of a moose from birth until it can live on its own.

Catt, Thessaly

Migrating with the caribou. PowerKids Press 2011 24p il map (Animal journeys) lib bdg $21.25; pa $8.25

Grades: 2 3 4 **599.65**

1. Caribou 2. Animals -- Migration

ISBN 978-1-4488-2541-7 lib bdg; 1-4488-2541-5 lib bdg; 978-1-4488-2666-7 pa; 1-4488-2666-7 pa

LC 2010024146

Learn about the life cycle of the caribou and its migration patterns.

"Keywords are bolded throughout and can be found in the glossary. The format is attractive with inset captioned photographs and page heading that seem to move across the page." Libr Media Connect

Inlcudes glossary

Gish, Melissa

Moose. Creative Education 2010 46p il map (Living wild) $23.95; pa $9.95

Grades: 5 6 7 8 **599.65**

1. Moose

ISBN 978-1-58341-973-1; 1-58341-973-X; 978-0-89812-556-6 pa; 0-89812-556-1 pa

LC 2010017378

"A look at moose, including their habitats, physical characteristics such as their imposing antlers, behaviors, relationships with humans, and secure status in the world today." Publisher's note

Heuer, Karsten

★ **Being** caribou; five months on foot with a caribou herd. Walker & Co. 2007 48p il map $17.95; lib bdg $18.95

Grades: 4 5 6 7 **599.65**

1. Caribou 2. Arctic regions

ISBN 978-0-8027-9565-6; 0-8027-9565-X; 978-0-8027-9566-3 lib bdg; 0-8027-9566-8 lib bdg

LC 2006-27651

This is an adaptation of an adult title by the same name, published 2005 by Mountaineers Books

"The caribou calving grounds in the Arctic National Wildlife Refuge are being threatened by oil exploration. [This title] will help make kids aware of what is at stake and give them a glimpse of an extraordinary part of the world and the lengths the caribou go to traverse it. It is an important book." Quill Quire

Includes bibliographical references

Riggs, Kate

Moose; by Kate Riggs. Creative Education 2012 24 p. col. ill.

Grades: K 1 2 **599.65**

1. Moose 2. Animal behavior 3. Habitat (Ecology) 4. Animals -- Folklore 5. Zoology -- Encyclopedias

ISBN 9781608181117

LC 2010049131

This children's book, part of Kate Riggs' "Amazing Animals" series, focuses on moose. "This . . . popular series continues traveling the planet to study alligators, bats, and other fascinating animals. . . . [P]hotos are paired with . . . text to examine the featured creature's appearance, habitat, behaviors, and life cycle. . . . "A basic exploration of the appearance, behavior, and habitat of moose, Earth's largest deer. Also included is a story from folklore explaining how moose interact with other animals." (Publisher's note)

Includes bibliographical references (p. 24) and index

Urbigkit, Cat

★ **Path** of the pronghorn; photographs by Mark Gocke. Boyds Mills Press 2010 32p il map $17.95

Grades: 3 4 5 6 **599.65**

1. Pronghorn antelopes

ISBN 978-1-59078-756-4; 1-59078-756-0

"Large, eye-catching color photos accompany a quiet, informative text in this elegant book that celebrates an equally elegant North American mammal: Antilocapra americana—'the antelope-goat of America.' Urbigkit provides enough quality information to satisfy many young researchers, and Gocke's outstanding photos record the migratory year of Wyoming's Sublette herd." SLJ

Includes bibliographical references

599.66 Odd-toed ungulates

Carson, Mary Kay

★ **Emi** and the rhino scientist; [by] Mary Kay Carson; with photographs by Tom Uhlman. Houghton Mifflin Company 2007 57p il (Scientists in the field) $18

Grades: 5 6 7 8 **599.66**

1. Rhinoceros 2. Zoo employees 3. Animal scientists

ISBN 978-0-618-64639-5; 0-618-64639-6

LC 2006-34517

This describes "how Terri Roth, an expert in endangered-species reproduction at the Cincinnati Zoo, helped Emi to give birth to the first Sumatran rhino born in captivity in more than 100 years. . . . The text is full of important details, and the photographs are unfailingly crisp, bright, and full of variety." SLJ

Firestone, Mary

Top 50 reasons to care about rhinos; animals in peril. Enslow Publishers 2010 103p il (Top 50 reasons to care about endangered animals) lib bdg $31.93

Grades: 4 5 6 7 **599.66**

1. Rhinoceros 2. Endangered species

ISBN 978-0-7660-3457-0 lib bdg; 0-7660-3457-7 lib bdg

LC 2008048692

This describes the different types of rhino, their life cycle, diet, young, habitat, and reasons why they are endangered animals

"The illustrations, mostly color photographs, represent a wonderful selection of the animals and their habitats. Reluctant readers may be enticed by this . . . simply because of the great images. This . . . would make a substantial supplement to the science curriculum when studying endangered animals." Libr Media Connect

Includes glossary and bibliographical references

Gish, Melissa
Rhinoceroses. Creative Education 2011 46p il map (Living wild) lib bdg $23.95
Grades: 5 6 7 8   **599.66**
1. Rhinoceros
ISBN 978-1-60818-083-7; 1-60818-083-2
LC 2010028316

A look at rhinoceroses, including their habitats, physical characteristics such as their horned noses, behaviors, relationships with humans, and protected status in the world today.

Includes glossary and bibliographical references

Holmes, Mary Tavener
My travels with Clara; illustrated by Jon Cannell. J. Paul Getty Museum 2007 un il $17.95
Grades: 2 3 4   **599.66**
1. Rhinoceros
ISBN 978-0-89236-880-8
LC 2006-35719

"In the mid-eighteenth century, a Dutch sea captain bought an orphaned baby rhinoceros in India, named her Clara, and toured with her around western Europe. . . . His first-person, fictionalized narrative affectionately tells of his kindness, his bond with his extraordinary companion, and the public excitement she caused. . . . Illustrations include costumed period figures and reproductions of the art Clara inspired. . . . The facts about Clara . . . are as fascintating as the art and pet story." Booklist

Momatiuk, Yva
★ **Face** to face with wild horses; by Yva Momatiuk and John Eastcott. National Geographic 2009 31p il (Face to face) $16.95; lib bdg $25.90
Grades: 3 4 5 6   **599.66**
1. Horses
ISBN 978-1-4263-0466-8; 1-4263-0466-8; 978-1-4263-0467-5 lib bdg; 1-4263-0467-6 lib bdg
LC 2008-38247

The authors describe the behavior of wild horses and their personal encounters with them.

Includes bibliographical references

Montgomery, Sy
★ **The** tapir scientist; written by Sy Montgomery; photographed by Nic Bishop. Houghton Mifflin Harcourt 2013 80 p. $18.99
Grades: 5 6 7 8   **599.66**
1. Brazil 2. Tapirs 3. Tapirs -- Brazil 4. Tapirs -- Research -- Brazil
ISBN 0547815484; 9780547815480
LC 2012018678

In this book, author Sy Montgomery and photographer Nic Bishop "experience long, hot days, cramped conditions, nervous waiting and itchy tick bites while searching for [tapirs]. . . . In less than a week, they see tapirs in the wild, find their tracks, take photographs, locate them through radio telemetry, collect 'samples of tapir poop, skin, fur, and blood,' and capture and collar two new tapirs, with more to come. This research matters, and the author . . . explains why." (Kirkus Reviews)

Rustad, Martha E. H.
Zebras and oxpeckers work together. Capstone Press 2011 24p il (Pebble Plus: animals working together) lib bdg $23.99; pa $6.95
Grades: K 1 2   **599.66**
1. Zebras 2. Symbiosis 3. Oxpeckers (Birds)
ISBN 978-1-4296-5300-8 lib bdg; 1-4296-5300-0 lib bdg; 978-1-4296-6200-0 pa; 1-4296-6200-X pa
LC 2010025465

Simple text and full-color photographs introduce the symbiotic relationship of zebras and oxpeckers.

In this series "the easy-to-understand examples are well selected to show of range of relationships in a variety of environments, and children will come away with some exposure to the concepts of 'parasite' and 'predator' as well." SLJ

Includes glossary and bibliographical references

Walden, Katherine
Rhinoceroses. PowerKids Press 2009 24p il (Safari animals) lib bdg $21.25
Grades: PreK K 1 2   **599.66**
1. Rhinoceros
ISBN 978-1-4358-2687-8 lib bdg; 1-4358-2687-6 lib bdg
LC 2008019534

This book provides "succinctly written introductory information about [rhinoceroses'] range, habitat, social groups, and diet. Spreads consist of one to three short, simply constructed sentences opposite crisp, color photographs, most of which represent the subject perfectly." SLJ

Includes glossary and bibliographical references

599.67 Elephants

Allen, Kathy
Elephants under pressure; a cause and effect investigation. Capstone Press 2010 32p il map (Fact finders. Animals on the edge) lib bdg $25.99
Grades: 3 4 5 6   **599.67**
1. Elephants
ISBN 978-1-4296-4534-8; 1-4296-4534-2
LC 2010008562

"Excellent discussions address those who doubt the severity of the issue and those who wonder why people should care what happens to animals. The captioned photographs are timely and poignant. . . . [This] makes serious subject matter interesting and accessible." SLJ

Includes glossary and bibliographical references

Arnold, Katya

★ **Elephants** can paint, too! pictures and text by Katya Arnold. Atheneum Books for Young Readers 2005 un il $16.95
Grades: K 1 2 3 **599.67**
1. Painting 2. Elephants
ISBN 0-689-86985-1

LC 2004-17387

The author "tells how she trains elephants to paint and compares the work of her human and elephant pupils. The spare narrative is easy to understand and reads like a picture book. . . . Arnold's amusing and colorful photographs—of elephants and children at work—will have readers laughing as they view them side-by-side." SLJ

Buckley, Carol

Tarra & Bella; the elephant and dog who became best friends. text and photography by Carol Buckley. G.P. Putnam's Sons 2009 un il $16.99
Grades: K 1 2 3 4 **599.67**
1. Dogs 2. Elephants 3. Animal behavior
ISBN 978-0-399-25443-7; 0-399-25443-9

LC 2009-18888

Spotlights the true-life friendship between Tarra, a retired circus elephant, and one of the Tennessee Elephant Sanctuary's stray dogs, Bella

"Shots of Tarra petting Bella with her trunk are among the book's most endearing pictures, which range from snapshotlike to skillfully framed images; also notable are photographs that underscore the dramatic difference in the animals' sizes. . . . The animals' friendship will inspire young readers." Publ Wkly

Cowcher, Helen

Desert elephants. Farrar Straus Giroux 2011 un il $16.99
Grades: K 1 2 3 **599.67**
1. Elephants 2. Desert ecology 3. Mali
ISBN 978-0-374-31774-4; 0-374-31774-7

LC 2010019817

"In Mali, West Africa, the last remaining desert elephants migrate 300 miles in search of water in a circular route just south of the Sahara Desert. In this picture book introduction, Cowcher's beautiful watercolor-and-mixed media illustrations chart the animals' route. . . . The present-day interaction with people is a crucial part of the well-told story." Booklist

Downer, Ann

Elephant talk; the surprising science of elephant communication. Twenty-First Century Books 2011 112p il map lib bdg $33.26
Grades: 4 5 6 7 8 **599.67**
1. Elephants 2. Animal communication
ISBN 978-0-7613-5766-7 lib bdg; 0-7613-5766-1 lib bdg

LC 2010-24880

"The complex behavior of wild elephants is introduced in a flowing narrative accompanied by full-color photographs, diagrams and maps. Downer provides an overview of elephant evolution, places the creatures in their African and Asian contexts, and describes the lives of these intelligent social animals. Her narrative then focuses on the elephants' inticate verbal and nonverbal communication techniques. . .

. The illustrations and clearly labeled diagrams and maps are well placed to amplify the text. . . . Throughout this highly readable, informative title are profiles of individuals . . . who work with these animals." SLJ
Includes glossary and bibliographical references

Gibbons, Gail

Elephants of Africa. Holiday House 2008 32p il
Grades: K 1 2 3 **599.67**
1. Elephants
ISBN 0-8234-2168-6; 978-0-8234-2168-8

LC 2007051619

This book describes the habitats, physical characteristics, diet, offspring development, and behavior of the African elephant. "Grades one to four." (Sci Books Films)

"Gibbons introduces young readers to [African elephants]. Each page is filled with illustrations and a succinct but informative text that details the habitats, physical characteristics, diet, offspring development, and behavior of these dwellers of Africa's savannas and forests. . . . The text is well organized and simple to understand, enhanced by the pen-and-ink and watercolor artwork." SLJ
Includes glossary and bibliographical references

Jackson, Donna M.

★ The **elephant** scientist; by Caitlin O'Connell and Donna M. Jackson; photographs by Caitlin O'Connell and Timothy Rodwell. Houghton Mifflin Books for Children 2011 70p il map $17.99
Grades: 4 5 6 7 **599.67**
1. Elephants 2. Biologists 3. Ecologists
ISBN 978-0-547-05344-8; 0-547-05344-4

LC 2010014134

In this book, "O'Connell traveled to Africa in 1992 to observe wild animals; the trip turned into a job offer to study elephants at Etosha National Park; the text focuses on the scientists' work, findings, and problems encountered. The authors offer [a] . . . look at new discoveries about elephant communication and how this knowledge can be used to slow the animal's slump into extinction. Combined with . . . full-color photographs by the scientists, the elephants' world is brought to the forefront. Readers enter the researchers' camp to see their setup, fieldwork, and takedown in action. They will learn how elephant anatomy and hierarchy work together to aid in communication." (School Library Journal)

O'Connell "worked with other scientists to [identify] the vibration-sensitive cells in elephants' feet and trunks that enabled to them to 'hear' sounds transmitted through the ground. Illustrated with many well-captioned, color photos, this eye-catching book provides a sometimes fascinating look at O'Connell's work with elephants in America and in Namibia." Booklist

Joubert, Beverly

★ **Face** to face with elephants; by Beverly and Dereck Joubert. National Geographic 2008 31p il map (Face to face) $16.95; lib bdg $25.90
Grades: 3 4 5 6 **599.67**
1. Elephants
ISBN 978-1-4263-0325-8; 1-4263-0325-4; 978-1-4263-0326-5 lib bdg; 1-4263-0326-2 lib bdg

LC 2007-41229

The authors describe the life cycle and behavior of elephants and their own experiences with elephants in the wild

"The photographs are stunning, sometimes intimate, sometimes epic. . . . [This book] conveys [elephants'] magnificence and fascination." Bull Cent Child Books

Includes glossary and bibliographical references

Marsh, Laura

Elephants. National Geographic 2010 48p il map (Great migrations) $11.90; pa $3.99

Grades: 1 2 3   599.67

1. Elephants

ISBN 978-1-4263-0744-7; 1-4263-0744-6; 978-1-4263-0743-0 pa; 1-4263-0743-8 pa

LC 2010017961

This offers facts about elephants in an easy reader format. "Dynamic full-color photographs, informative writing, and consistent organization work well together in [this volume]. . . . Along with the many photographs, the fascinating details are supported by boxes of related information, helpful definitions of new terms, and a sprinkling of entertaining jokes/riddles." SLJ

Includes glossary

Morgan, Jody

Elephant rescue; changing the future for endangered wildlife. Firefly Books 2004 64p il $19.95; pa $9.95

Grades: 5 6 7 8   599.67

1. Elephants 2. Wildlife conservation

ISBN 1-55297-595-9; 1-55297-594-0 pa

This is "well-written. . . . Stunning, full-color photographs bring [these animals] to life." SLJ

This "photo-essay . . . combines an urgent message about conservation with a close-up view of elephant physiology, behavior, and habitat in Africa and Asia." Booklist

O'Connell, Caitlin

★ A baby elephant in the wild; by Caitlin O'Connell; with photographs by Timothy Rodwell. 1st ed. Houghton Mifflin Harcourt 2014 40 p. $16.99

Grades: K 1 2 3   599.67

1. Animal babies 2. Elephants 3. African elephant -- pictorial works 4. African elephant -- Infancy -- Namibia

ISBN 0544149440; 9780544149441

LC 2013017880

"In this account of a journey into the scrub desert of Namibia, readers meet a newborn elephant and her family. Children learn about Liza's early accomplishments: walking within hours, keeping up with the herd as they travel, and learning how to use her trunk and what is safe to eat. The animals walk 10 to 20 miles a day to find food, with the babies hidden behind their mothers or under them between their legs." (School Library Journal)

Riggs, Kate

Elephants. Creative Education 2011 24p il (Amazing animals) $24.25; pa $5.99

Grades: K 1 2   599.67

1. Elephants

ISBN 978-1-58341-990-8; 1-58341-990-X; 978-0-89812-563-4 pa; 0-89812-563-4 pa

LC 2010019054

"A basic exploration of the appearance, behavior, and habitat of elephants, Earth's biggest land animals. Also in-cluded is a story from folklore explaining why elephants' trunks are so long." Publisher's note

Schwabacher, Martin

Elephants; by Martin Schwabacher, with Lori Mortensen. Marshall Cavendish Benchmark 2010 24p il map (Animals) lib bdg $16.95

Grades: 3 4 5   599.67

1. Elephants

ISBN 978-0-7614-4343-8 lib bdg; 0-7614-4343-6 lib bdg

LC 2008-52103

"The straightforward presentation of the information and the uncluttered and attractive layout make [this] . . . good . . . for reports. Color photographs . . . are well utilized and complete a solid package." SLJ

Includes glossary and bibliographical references

599.7 Carnivores

Gonzales, Doreen

Raccoons in the dark. PowerKids Press 2010 24p il (Creatures of the night) lib bdg $21.25; pa $8.05

Grades: 2 3 4   599.7

1. Raccoons

ISBN 978-1-4042-8101-1 lib bdg; 1-4042-8101-0 lib bdg; 978-1-4358-3259-6 pa; 1-4358-3259-0 pa

LC 2009-2758

A look at raccoons and their world in the dark.

"Basic details are complemented by eclectic trivia, . . . [and] each volume concludes with a defense of the animal . . . and why it is vital to humans. The layout is attractive, with easy-to-read text and eye-catching photography. Good for reports." SLJ

Includes glossary

Skunks in the dark. PowerKids Press 2010 24p il (Creatures of the night) lib bdg $21.25; pa $8.05

Grades: 2 3 4   599.7

1. Skunks

ISBN 978-1-4042-8099-1 lib bdg; 1-4042-8099-5 lib bdg; 978-1-4358-3255-8 pa; 1-4358-3255-8 pa

LC 2009-718

A look at skunks and their world in the dark.

"Basic details are complemented by eclectic trivia, . . . [and] each volume concludes with a defense of the animal . . . and why it is vital to humans. The layout is attractive, with easy-to-read text and eye-catching photography. Good for reports." SLJ

Includes glossary

Kalman, Bobbie

Baby carnivores; by Bobbie Kalman. Crabtree Publishing Company 2013 24 p. ill. (library) $22.60; (paperback) $6.95

Grades: 1 2 3 4   599.7

1. Carnivorous animals 2. Food chains (Ecology) 3. Carnivorous animals -- Infancy

ISBN 0778710106; 9780778710103; 9780778710158

LC 2012043739

This book by Bobbie Kalman presents "images of many kinds of baby carnivores that belong to a group of mammals with sharp teeth and claws. Fascinating text explains how baby carnivores are cared for by their mothers and how they learn to hunt. Young readers will learn about the food chain and where dogs, cats, bears, seals, weasels, meerkats, and other animals live." (Publisher's note)

Includes bibliographical references and index.

Leardi, Jeanette

Southern sea otters; fur-tastrophe avoided. by Jeanette Leardi. Bearport Pub. 2008 32p il map (America's animal comebacks) lib bdg $25.27

Grades: 2 3 4   **599.7**

1. Otters 2. Wildlife conservation

ISBN 978-1-59716-534-1 lib bdg; 1-59716-534-4 lib bdg

LC 2007012593

This describes efforts by scientists and environmentalists to protect southern sea otters from hunting, pollution, and other dangers

This book is "well organized and [has] an easy style and an accessible vocabulary and text size . . . [and] color photographs." SLJ

Includes glossary and bibliographical references

Lunis, Natalie

California sea lion; fast and smart. Bearport Pub. 2011 24p il map (Blink of an eye. Superfast animals!) lib bdg $22.61

Grades: 1 2 3   **599.7**

1. Seals (Animals)

ISBN 978-1-936088-08-9; 1-936088-08-8

LC 2010017683

This describes the California sea lion, where it lives, how it hunts, and the ways its body helps it reach its record-breaking speeds.

This "is sure to appeal to a wide variety of readers. Vibrant photos illustrate each animal from multiple perspectives, providing opportunity for readers to closely examine the animal. Information is organized by subject heading and branches into the animal's physical features and how they contribute to its speed, the animal's natural predators, and how the animal makes use of speed as a means of survival. . . . This . . . will be a worthwhile addition to your nonfiction collection." Libr Media Connect

Includes glossary and bibliographical references

Mason, Adrienne

Skunks; written by Adrienne Mason; illustrated by Nancy Gray Ogle. Kids Can Press 2006 32p (Kids Can Press wildlife series) $10.95

Grades: 2 3 4   **599.7**

1. Skunks

ISBN 1-55337-733-8

"Focusing primarily on the four types of skunks found in North America, Mason has provided readers with an accurate, fun-to-read look at this sometimes misunderstood animal. She offers a straightforward description of the mammals habitat, appearance, predators, diet, reproduction, and human interaction. Realistically rendered watercolor illustrations appear on every spread." SLJ

Includes glossary

Otfinoski, Steven

★ **Skunks**; by Steven Otfinoski. Marshall Cavendish Benchmark 2009 47p il (Animals animals) lib bdg $20.95

Grades: 3 4 5 6   **599.7**

1. Skunks

ISBN 978-0-7614-2929-6 lib bdg; 0-7614-2929-8 lib bdg

LC 2007-24117

"The material is well researched and would be an excellent source for reports, and the [book has] a narrative flow that makes [it] easy and enjoyable to read. [The] title includes expert full-color photography." SLJ

Includes glossary

599.74   Land carnivores

Ganeri, Anita

Meerkat. Heinemann Library 2011 24p il map (A day in the life: desert animals) $22; pa $6.49

Grades: K 1 2   **599.74**

1. Meerkats

ISBN 978-1-4329-4773-6; 1-4329-4773-7; 978-1-4329-4782-8 pa; 1-4329-4782-6 pa

LC 2010022821

"The engaging full-color photographs are key to [this] well-organized [book]. . . . Basic global maps show where the animal is found, and a diagram called a 'body map' labels its parts. The [text is] appropriate for the age group, and the pictures will draw in youngsters. [An] excellent [purchase] if material is needed on these animals." SLJ

Includes glossary and bibliographical references

Gibbons, Gail

Wolves. Holiday House 1994 un il $16.95; pa $6.95

Grades: K 1 2 3   **599.74**

1. Wolves

ISBN 0-8234-1127-3; 0-8234-1202-4 pa

LC 94-2108

"A simply written introduction that focuses on the gray, or timber, wolf. . . . Material covered includes physical characteristics, behavior within a pack, and communication by howling and body language. . . . The format is open and spacious, the print is large, and the realistic, watercolor illustrations are set against backgrounds of white and deep blues." SLJ

Goldish, Meish

Fossa; a fearsome predator. by Meish Goldish. Bearport Pub. 2009 32p il map (Uncommon animals) lib bdg $25.27

Grades: 1 2 3   **599.74**

1. Fossa (Mammals)

ISBN 978-1-59716-732-1 lib bdg; 1-59716-732-0 lib bdg

LC 2008-4817

"The explanatory text works spendidly, with large photographs that bring readers as close as they'll ever get to such beasts." Booklist

Includes glossary and bibliographical references

Lunde, Darrin

Meet the Meerkat; by Darrin Lunde and illustrated by Patricia J. Wynne. Charlesbridge Publishing 2007 28 p. il $7.95

Grades: PreK K 1 2 **599.74**

1. Meerkats

ISBN 1580891101; 1580891543; 9781580891103; 9781580891547

LC 200621252

In this book, by Darrin Lunde and illustrated by Patricia J. Wynne, "a series of questions and answers introduce children to the life and habitat of Little Meerkat. Scientifically accurate illustrations make these exotic animals accessible to young readers. Back matter includes additional child-friendly facts." (Publisher's note)

"Addressing Little Meerkat, the author receives responses from the animal about its habitat, family structure, food, enemies, and so on. Watercolor, ink, and colored-pencil illustrations capture the activities of the meerkat family and are large enough to share with a small group." SLJ

Ryder, Joanne

Little panda; the world welcomes Hua Mei at the San Diego Zoo. Simon & Schuster 2001 un il $16.95; pa $7.99

Grades: K 1 2 3 **599.74**

1. Giant panda

ISBN 0-689-84310-0; 0-689-86616-X pa

"Ryder's photo-essay chronicles the life of Hua Mei, born at the World Famous San Diego Zoo in 1999. . . . Ryder's brief, almost haiku-like text is bolstered by informative paragraphs set in smaller type. The crisp, engaging photos were provided by the zoo." Booklist

Somervill, Barbara A.

Small Indian Mongoose. Cherry Lake Pub. 2010 32p il map (Animal invaders) lib bdg $27.07

Grades: 5 6 7 8 **599.74**

1. Mongooses 2. Biological invasions

ISBN 978-1-60279-630-0 lib bdg; 1-60279-630-0 lib bdg

LC 2009028179

This offers "an introduction to the problems caused by [the Small Indian Mongoose], a discussion of its physical characteristics and habits, a history of how it arrived in its new habitat, and an analysis of challenges encountered by those trying to limit its spread. . . . [This] considers the destructive effects of these mammals on islands (including several in Hawaii), where they were initially introduced to prey on rats. . . . [This] well-focused [book is] clearly written. The uncluttered page design features at least one color photo on each spread." Booklist

Includes glossary and bibliographical references

Walden, Katherine

Meerkats. PowerKids Press 2009 24p il (Safari animals) lib bdg $21.25

Grades: PreK K 1 2 **599.74**

1. Meerkats

ISBN 978-1-4358-2691-5 lib bdg; 1-4358-2691-4 lib bdg

LC 2008020793

This book provides "succinctly written introductory information about [meerkats'] range, habitat, social groups, and diet. Spreads consist of one to three short, simply constructed sentences opposite crisp, color photographs, most of which represent the subject perfectly." SLJ

599.75 Cat family

Becker, John E.

★ Wild cats: past & present; illustrations by Mark Hallett. Darby Creek 2008 80p il $18.95

Grades: 5 6 7 8 **599.75**

1. Wild cats

ISBN 978-1-58196-052-5; 1-58196-052-2

"Becker provides an informative introduction to wild cats, including an account of their ancient ancestors, an overview of the family Felidae and its subdivisions, accounts of wild cats alive in the world today, and woven throughout, discussions of the endangered status of many species. . . . Clearly written and well organized, the text is enhanced by many side-bars, maps, photos, and paintings." Booklist

Bodden, Valerie

Jaguars; by Valerie Bodden. 1st ed. Creative Education 2013 24 p. col. ill. (library) $25.65

Grades: 1 2 3 4 **599.75**

1. Jaguars

ISBN 1608180867; 9781608180868

LC 2011050284

This book, part of the Amazing Animals series, focuses on jaguars. "Jaguars, the third largest member of the cat family, are found in Mexico, Central and South America. They can spring as far as 6 meters to catch prey. Families, which include one to four cubs, live together, but by age two the cubs live alone and stalk their own territory. Like other books in the series, glossary words are explained on pages where they first are mentioned." (NSTA Recommends)

Includes bibliographical references and index.

Lions. Creative Education 2010 24p il map (Amazing animals) lib bdg $24.25

Grades: K 1 2 **599.75**

1. Lions

ISBN 978-1-58341-807-9 lib bdg; 1-58341-807-5 lib bdg

LC 2009002709

A basic exploration of the appearance, behavior, and habitat of lions, the majestic big cats of Africa and India. Also included is a story from folklore explaining why lions roar

Includes bibliographical references

Bredeson, Carmen

Lions up close; [by] Carmen Bredeson. Enslow Elementary 2008 24p il (Zoom in on animals!) $21.26

Grades: 1 2 3 **599.75**

1. Lions

ISBN 978-0-7660-3080-0; 0-7660-3080-6

LC 2007025610

This describes the anatomy, behavior, and life cycle of lions.

Includes glossary and bibliographical references

Carney, Elizabeth

Everything big cats. National Geographic 2011 64p il map (National Geographic kids) lib bdg $25.90; pa $12.95

Grades: 3 4 5 6   **599.75**

1. Wild cats

ISBN 978-1-4263-0806-2 lib bdg; 1-4263-0806-X lib bdg; 978-1-4263-0805-5 pa; 1-4263-0805-1 pa

LC 2010026963

This describes four big predators, the lion, leopard, jaguar, and tiger.

"Exploding with astounding full-color photographs and written in an appealing conversational tone, [this book is] for every kid. . . . The [text] will keep kids interested and turning pages to discover more and more facts. . . . [This] compelling, browseable, and completely engrossing [title] will delight readers." SLJ

Includes glossary and bibliographical references

Clutton-Brock, Juliet

Cat; written by Juliet Clutton-Brock. rev ed.; Dorling Kindersley 2004 72p il (DK eyewitness books) $15.99

Grades: 4 5 6 7   **599.75**

1. Cats 2. Wild cats

ISBN 0-7566-0662-4

First published 1991

Text and photographs present the anatomy, behavior, habitats, and other aspects of wild and domestic cats

Firestone, Mary

Top 50 reasons to care about tigers; animals in peril. Enslow Publishers 2010 103p il (Top 50 reasons to care about endangered animals) lib bdg $31.93

Grades: 4 5 6 7   **599.75**

1. Tigers 2. Endangered species

ISBN 978-0-7660-3452-5 lib bdg; 0-7660-3452-6 lib bdg

LC 2008-48689

This describes a tiger's life, how they hunt, the purpose of its stripes, caring for young, competing with people for space, and that these animals are very close to extinction

"The illustrations, mostly color photographs, represent a wonderful selection of the animals and their habitats. Reluctant readers may be enticed by this . . . simply because of the great images. This . . . would make a substantial supplement to the science curriculum when studying endangered animals." Libr Media Connect

Includes glossary and bibliographical references

Ganeri, Anita

Jaguar. Heinemann Library 2011 24p il map (A day in the life. Rain forest animals) lib bdg $22; pa $6.49

Grades: 1 2   **599.75**

1. Jaguars

ISBN 978-1-4329-4106-2 lib bdg; 1-4329-4106-2 lib bdg; 978-1-4329-4117-8 pa; 1-4329-4117-8 pa

LC 2010000962

This book follows a day in the life of a jaguar.

"Ganeri presents information clearly and simply in large type, two-sentence comments placed below a bright, sharply reproduced color photograph of the animal in a natural setting. . . . [This is] sufficiently specific to support assignment as well as pleasure reading." SLJ

Includes glossary and bibliographical references

Gish, Melissa

Jaguars. Creative Education 2011 46p il map (Living wild) lib bdg $23.95

Grades: 5 6 7   **599.75**

1. Jaguars

ISBN 978-1-60818-079-0; 1-60818-079-4

LC 2010028315

A look at jaguars, including their habitats, physical characteristics such as their powerful jaws, behaviors, relationships with humans, and threatened status in the world today.

This offers "an array of interesting facts. Photography is large and beautiful–a real draw." SLJ

Includes glossary and bibliographical references

Leopards. Creative Education 2010 46p il (Living wild) lib bdg $34.25; pa $8.99

Grades: 5 6 7 8   **599.75**

1. Leopards

ISBN 978-1-58341-972-4 lib bdg; 1-58341-972-1 lib bdg; 978-0-89812-555-9 pa; 0-89812-555-3 pa

LC 2010017377

"A look at leopards, including their habitats, physical characteristics such as their spotted fur, behaviors, relationships with humans, and threatened status in the world today." Publisher's note

Hamilton, Sue L.

Ambushed by a cougar; [by] Sue Hamilton. ABDO Pub. Co. 2010 32p il (Close encounters of the wild kind) lib bdg $27.07

Grades: 4 5 6 7   **599.75**

1. Pumas 2. Animal attacks

ISBN 978-1-60453-928-8 lib bdg; 1-60453-928-3 lib bdg

LC 2009-45521

Readers learn of actual human-cougar encounters, information about cougars, survival strategies, and attack statistics.

"Students will be drawn to the realistic full-color photographs, the realistic diagrams of the creatures' bodies, the real-life stories told by victims, and the interesting, attractive formatting that includes text, diagrams, photographs, and graphics on each page. . . . [This is] exciting and attractive in a 'gross' sort of way and will appeal particularly to boys for both leisure reading and research." Libr Media Connect

Includes glossary

Hanel, Rachael

Tigers. Creative Education 2008 46p il map (Living wild) lib bdg $22.95

Grades: 3 4 5   **599.75**

1. Tigers

ISBN 978-1-58341-660-0 lib bdg; 1-58341-660-9 lib bdg

LC 2007-08504

This describes the behavior, life cycle, and physical characteristics of tigers and their relationships to humans.

"Children will turn first to the excellent, informatively captioned photos. . . . But this . . . also has solid, informative content to accompany the captivating visuals." Booklist

Hatkoff, Juliana

★ **Leo** the snow leopard; the true story of an amazing rescue. told by Juliana Hatkoff, Isabella Hatkoff, and Craig Hatkoff. Scholastic Press 2010 un il $17.99

Grades: 3 4 5 6   **599.75**

1. Snow leopard 2. Wildlife conservation 3. New York Zoological Society

ISBN 978-0-545-22927-2; 0-545-22927-8

"This inspirational picture book conveys the importance of caring and protecting the world's wildlife. The story recounts the rescue of an orphaned snow leopard cub from Pakistan, and how the goodwill between people and nations can make a difference in the survival of endangered species. Excellent photographic detail recreates Leo's discovery by a goat herder, who in turn contacted the authorities when he got too large, and his cross-country adventure before being relocated to the Bronx Zoo in New York." SLJ

Johns, Chris

★ **Face** to face with cheetahs; by Chris Johns with Elizabeth Carney. National Geographic 2008 32p il map (Face to face) $16.95; lib bdg $25.90

Grades: 3 4 5 6   **599.75**

1. Cheetahs

ISBN 978-1-4263-0323-4; 1-4263-0323-8; 978-1-4263-0324-1 lib bdg; 1-4263-0324-6 lib bdg

LC 2007041220

Chris Johns describes the life cycle and behavior of cheetahs and his own experiences with cheetahs in the wild.

Includes glossary and bibliographical references

Joubert, Beverly

★ **Face** to face with leopards; by Beverly and Dereck Joubert. National Geographic 2009 31p il (Face to face) $16.95; lib bdg $25.90

Grades: 3 4 5 6   **599.75**

1. Leopards

ISBN 978-1-4263-0636-5; 1-4263-0636-9; 978-1-4263-0637-2 lib bdg; 1-4263-0637-7 lib bdg

LC 2009011441

The authors describe the life cycle and behavior of leopard and their own experiences with leopards in the wild.

"The exquisite photos and firsthand information provide an in-depth and personal look into the lives of these animals." SLJ

Includes glossary and bibliographical references

★ **Face** to face with lions; by Beverly and Dereck Joubert. National Geographic 2008 31p il (Face to face) $16.95; lib bdg $25.90

Grades: 3 4 5 6   **599.75**

1. Lions

ISBN 978-1-4263-0207-7; 1-4263-0207-X; 978-1-4263-0208-4 lib bdg; 1-4263-0208-8 lib bdg

LC 2007-11118

The authors describe the life cycle and behavior of lions and their own experiences with lions in the wild.

This is "well written and complete. . . . [It contains] many beautiful color photographs." Sci Books Films

Includes glossary and bibliographical references

Landau, Elaine

Big cats; hunters of the night. Enslow Publishers 2007 32p il (Animals after dark) $16.95

Grades: 1 2 3 4   **599.75**

1. Wild cats

ISBN 978-0-7660-2770-1; 0-7660-2770-8

LC 2006-16805

This "book presents basic information on the night-hunting big cats—lions, tigers, leopards, and jaguars—in an entertaining and informative format. . . . The photographs and clear text on mostly black pages add to a rewarding reading experience." Sci Books Films

Includes bibliographical references

Lunis, Natalie

Cheetah; speed demon! Bearport Pub. 2011 24p il map (Blink of an eye. Superfast animals!) lib bdg $22.61

Grades: 1 2 3   **599.75**

1. Cheetahs

ISBN 978-1-936087-89-1; 1-936087-89-8

LC 2009-53573

This describes the cheetah, including where it lives, how it hunts, and the ways its body helps it reach its record-breaking speeds.

This "is sure to appeal to a wide variety of readers. Vibrant photos illustrate each animal from multiple perspectives, providing opportunity for readers to closely examine the animal. Information is organized by subject heading and branches into the animal's physical features and how they contribute to its speed, the animal's natural predators, and how the animal makes use of speed as a means of survival. . . This . . . will be a worthwhile addition to your nonfiction collection." Libr Media Connect

Includes glossary and bibliographical references

Markle, Sandra

★ **Lions**; by Sandra Markle. Carolrhoda 2004 39p il (Animal predators) lib bdg $25.26; pa $7.95

Grades: 3 4 5 6   **599.75**

1. Lions

ISBN 1-57505-727-1 lib bdg; 1-57505-744-1 pa

LC 2003-11198

"The straightforward, descriptive text and superb photos give [this title] surefire appeal to middle readers." Booklist

The author observes lions' "hunting techniques and includes information about their physical characteristics, physiology, habitats, and care of young." Horn Book Guide

Includes glossary and bibliographical references

Marks, Jennifer L.

Bobcats. Capstone Press 2011 24p il map (Pebble plus. Wildcats) lib bdg $23.99

Grades: K 1 2   **599.75**

1. Bobcats

ISBN 978-1-4296-4480-8 lib bdg; 1-4296-4480-X lib bdg

LC 2010002795

"Plenty of full-page, close-up photos of . . . [bobcats] . . . in natural (or seemingly natural) settings will attract a broad audience. . . . [The book] covers geographical range (with a small map), average size, physical adaptations for the cat's habitat, typical prey, life cycle, threats, and average life span in the wild." SLJ

Includes glossary and bibliographical references

Clouded leopards. Capstone Press 2011 24p il map (Pebble plus. Wildcats) lib bdg $23.99

Grades: K 1 2   **599.75**
1. Leopards
ISBN 978-1-4296-4482-2 lib bdg; 1-4296-4482-6
lib bdg

LC 2010002797

"Plenty of full-page, close-up photos of . . . [clouded leopards] . . . in natural (or seemingly natural) settings will attract a broad audience. . . . [The book] covers geographical range (with a small map), average size, physical adaptations for the cat's habitat, typical prey, life cycle, threats, and average life span in the wild." SLJ

Includes glossary and bibliographical references

Jaguars. Capstone Press 2011 24p il map (Pebble plus. Wildcats) lib bdg $23.99
Grades: K 1 2   **599.75**
1. Jaguars
ISBN 978-1-4296-4481-5 lib bdg; 1-4296-4481-8
lib bdg

LC 2010002798

"Plenty of full-page, close-up photos of . . . [jaguars] . . . in natural (or seemingly natural) settings will attract a broad audience. . . . [The book] covers geographical range (with a small map), average size, physical adaptations for the cat's habitat, typical prey, life cycle, threats, and average life span in the wild." SLJ

Includes glossary and bibliographical references

Meinking, Mary
Polar bear vs. seal. Raintree 2011 32p il (Predator vs. prey) $29; pa $7.99
Grades: 1 2 3   **599.75**
1. Polar bear 2. Seals (Animals) 3. Predatory animals
ISBN 978-1-4109-3939-5; 978-1-4109-3948-7 pa

Explores the features of the polar bear and the seal that make them particularly suited to catch or evade the other.

"The struggle between polar bear and seal is described in clear language and illustrated with engaging color photographs." Horn Book Guide

Includes glossary and bibliographical references

Montgomery, Sy
★ **Chasing** cheetahs; the race to save Africa's fastest cats. written by Sy Montgomery; photographs by Nic Bishop. Houghton Mifflin Harcourt 2014 80 p. illustrations $18.99
Grades: 5 6 7 8   **599.75**
1. Cheetahs 2. Cheetah -- Africa 3. Cheetah Conservation Fund
ISBN 0547815492; 9780547815497

LC 2013017611

Scientists in the field

This book, by Sy Montgomery, focuses on cheetahs. "At the Cheetah Conservation Fund's (CCF) African headquarters in Namibia, Laurie Marker and her team save these . . . creatures from extinction. Since the organization's start in 1990, they've rescued more than 900 cheetahs. . . . But this arduous challenge continues. For most African livestock farmers, cheetahs are the last thing they want to see on their properties. In the 1980s, as many as 19 cheetahs per farmer died each year." (Publisher's note)

"Montgomery introduces readers to Laurie Marker and her team at the Cheetah Conservation Fund's site in Namibia. Scientific information about the cheetahs and profiles of

the people who study them are interspersed with in-the-moment, journal-style accounts of activities at the site. Striking photographs capture the dedication of the scientists and the awesome power of the cheetahs." Horn Book

Includes bibliographical references and index.

Saving the ghost of the mountain; an expedition among snow leopards in Mongolia. text by Sy Montgomery; photographs by Nic Bishop. Houghton Mifflin Books for Children 2009 48p il map (Scientists in the field) $18
Grades: 5 6 7 8   **599.75**
1. Biologists 2. Snow leopard 3. Conservationists 4. Mongolia
ISBN 978-0-618-91645-0; 0-618-91645-8

LC 2008-36762

Author Sy Montgomery and photographer Nic Bishop accompany conservationist Tom McCarthy and his team as they travel to Mongolia's Altai Mountains to gather data about snow leopard populations in an attempt to save this endangered species

"Montgomery's enthusiasm translates well to the page and will have readers cheering for the entourage as they attempt to spot a snow leopard. This slender book abounds with information. Bishop's trademark stunning photography fills out the book with breathtaking views of the extreme environs of Central Asia and warm portraits of the charming people who live there." SLJ

Includes glossary and bibliographical references

Person, Stephen
Cougar; a cat with many names. by Stephen Person. Bearport Pub. 2013 32 p. (America's hidden animal treasures) (library binding) $26.60
Grades: 1 2 3 4   **599.75**
1. Pumas 2. Animals -- North America
ISBN 1617725692; 9781617725692

LC 2012003342

This book by Stephen Person "opens with an intriguing introduction that shows the cougar and a housecat appearing to recognize each other. This is followed by a discussion of how the cougar adapts to a variety of habitats and its ability to swim, climb trees and jump unusual heights. . . . In their quest for survival, readers will learn how they hunt for a variety of animals and are excellent predators." (SB&F: Your Guide to Science Resources for All Ages)

Includes bibliographical references and index.

Riggs, Kate
Leopards; by Kate Riggs. Creative Education 2012 24 p. col. ill.
Grades: K 1 2   **599.75**
1. Leopards 2. Animal behavior 3. Habitat (Ecology) 4. Animals -- Folklore 5. Zoology -- Encyclopedias
ISBN 1608181103; 9781608181100

LC 2010049130

This children's book, part of Kate Riggs' "Amazing Animals" series, focuses on leopards. "This . . . popular series continues traveling the planet to study alligators, bats, and other fascinating animals. . . . [P]hotos are paired with . . . text to examine the featured creature's appearance, habitat, behaviors, and life cycle. . . . "A basic exploration of the appearance, behavior, and habitat of leopards, Earth's fourth-largest cats. Also included is a story from folklore explaining why leopards and baboons don't get along." (Publisher's note)

Includes bibliographical references and index

Rodriguez, Cindy

Cougars. Rourke Pub. 2009 24p il map (Eye to eye with endangered species) lib bdg $27.07

Grades: 2 3 4   **599.75**

1. Pumas

ISBN 978-1-60694-404-2 lib bdg; 1-60694-404-5 lib bdg

LC 2009-5995

Text examines the issues endangered cougars face and how they can be saved

"Sets out to introduce readers to [cougars] . . . explain the dangers they face, and detail the efforts of biologists and conservationists to save them. . . . Serviceable and informative." SLJ

Includes glossary

Schafer, Susan

Lions; by Susan Schafer, with Susan Markowitz Meredith. Marshall Cavendish Benchmark 2010 24p il map (Animals) lib bdg $16.95

Grades: 3 4 5   **599.75**

1. Lions

ISBN 978-0-7614-4344-5 lib bdg; 0-7614-4344-4 lib bdg

LC 2008-52104

"The straightforward presentation of the information and the uncluttered and attractive layout make [this] . . . good . . . for reports. Color photographs . . . are well utilized and complete a solid package." SLJ

Includes glossary and bibliographical references

Tigers; by Susan Schafer, with Fay Robinson. Marshall Cavendish Benchmark 2010 24p il map (Animals) lib bdg $16.95

Grades: 3 4 5   **599.75**

1. Tigers

ISBN 978-0-7614-4345-2 lib bdg; 0-7614-4345-2 lib bdg

LC 2008-52109

"The straightforward presentation of the information and the uncluttered and attractive layout make [this] . . . good . . . for reports. Color photographs . . . are well utilized and complete a solid package." SLJ

Includes glossary and bibliographical references

Shores, Erika L.

Canada lynx. Capstone Press 2011 24p il map (Pebble plus. Wildcats) lib bdg $23.99

Grades: K 1 2   **599.75**

1. Lynx

ISBN 978-1-4296-4484-6 lib bdg; 1-4296-4484-2 lib bdg

LC 2010002796

"Plenty of full-page, close-up photos of . . . [the Canada Lynx] . . . in natural (or seemingly natural) settings will attract a broad audience. . . . [The book] covers geographical range (with a small map), average size, physical adaptations

for the cat's habitat, typical prey, life cycle, threats, and average life span in the wild." SLJ

Includes glossary and bibliographical references

Mountain lions. Capstone Press 2011 24p il map (Pebble plus. Wildcats) lib bdg $23.99

Grades: K 1 2   **599.75**

1. Pumas

ISBN 978-1-4296-4485-3 lib bdg; 1-4296-4485-0 lib bdg

LC 2010002799

"Plenty of full-page, close-up photos of . . . [mountain lions] . . . in natural (or seemingly natural) settings will attract a broad audience. . . . [The book] covers geographical range (with a small map), average size, physical adaptations for the cat's habitat, typical prey, life cycle, threats, and average life span in the wild." SLJ

Includes glossary and bibliographical references

Snow leopards. Capstone Press 2011 24p il map (Pebble plus. Wildcats) lib bdg $23.99

Grades: K 1 2   **599.75**

1. Snow leopard

ISBN 978-1-4296-4483-9 lib bdg; 1-4296-4483-4 lib bdg

LC 2010002800

"Plenty of full-page, close-up photos of . . . [snow leopards] . . . in natural (or seemingly natural) settings will attract a broad audience. . . . [The book] covers geographical range (with a small map), average size, physical adaptations for the cat's habitat, typical prey, life cycle, threats, and average life span in the wild." SLJ

Includes glossary and bibliographical references

Simon, Seymour

★ Big cats. HarperCollins Pubs. 1991 un il hardcover o.p. pa $6.95

Grades: 3 4 5 6   **599.75**

1. Wild cats

ISBN 0-06-021647-6; 0-06-446119-X pa

LC 90-36374

Simon "begins with a general overview of the big cats, and then presents details on the tiger, lion, leopard, jaguar, puma, cheetah and snow leopard. . . . The author also discusses concerns about wildlife conservation." Appraisal

The author "offers a clear, succinct text illuminated with stunning, large color photographs." Booklist

Squire, Ann

Cheetahs; by Ann O. Squire. Children's Press 2005 47p il (True book) lib bdg $25; pa $6.95

Grades: 2 3 4   **599.75**

1. Cheetahs

ISBN 0-516-22792-0 lib bdg; 0-516-27932-7 pa

LC 2003-5174

"Beginning with cheetahs' best-known quality, their speed, this very readable volume goes on to discuss their prowess and limitations as hunters as well as their prey, social habits, life cycle, and use of camouflage. . . . Remarkably clear, often-dramatic color photos of cheetahs in the wild offer unusually good views of the animals." Booklist

Includes bibliographical references

Wells, Robert E.

Can we share the world with tigers? by Robert E. Wells. Albert Whitman & Company 2012 32 p. (hardcover) $16.99

Grades: 3 4 5 **599.75**

1. Ecology 2. Biodiversity conservation 3. Picture books for children 4. Bengal tiger -- India 5. Endangered species -- India 6. Wildlife conservation -- India 7. Bengal tiger -- Conservation -- India

ISBN 0807510556; 9780807510551

LC 2011038269

In this children's picture book, "using threats to endangered Bengal tigers' survival as a springboard, [Robert E.] Wells teaches young readers about the many ways humans interfere with the natural world and its biodiversity." A tigress, her cubs, and a monkey "travel through the book together, teaching readers about habitat destruction, pollution, overharvesting, invasive species, biodiversity and extinction." (Kirkus)

599.769 Otters

Green, Jen

Sea otter; by Jen Green. Bearport Publishing 2013 24 p. (library binding) $23.93

Grades: 1 2 **599.769**

1. Sea otter 2. Marine biology

ISBN 1617729221; 9781617729225

LC 2013011520

In this book, by Jen Green, "readers will explore the underwater world of this marine mammal [,the sea otter,] through clear text, full-color photos, and diagrams. Age-appropriate activities give readers a chance to make observations and develop animal-science skills." (Publisher's note)

Includes bibliographical references and index

599.77 Dog family

Brandenburg, Jim

★ Face to face with wolves; by Jim and Judy Brandenburg. National Geographic 2008 31p il map (Face to face) $16.95; lib bdg $25.90

Grades: 3 4 5 6 **599.77**

1. Wolves

ISBN 978-1-4263-0242-8; 1-4263-0242-8; 978-1-4263-0243-5 lib bdg; 1-4263-0243-6 lib bdg

LC 2007-41217

The authors describe the life cycle and behavior of wolves and their own experiences with wolves in the wild.

This is "well written and complete. . . . [It contains] many beautiful color photographs." Sci Books Films

Includes glossary and bibliographical references

Cohn, Scotti

One wolf howls; by Scotti Cohn; illustrated by Susan Detwiler. Sylvan Dell Pub. 2009 un il $16.95; pa $8.95

Grades: PreK K 1 **599.77**

1. Months 2. Wolves 3. Counting 4. Stories in rhyme

ISBN 978-1-934359-92-1; 1-934359-92-0; 978-1-607180-37-1 pa; 1-607180-37-5 pa

The months of the year and the numbers 1 through 12 are used in rhyming text to introduce children to the behavior of wolves in natural settings

"Readers should be captivated by the animals' resilient joie de vivre as well as by their habitats' seasonal glories. The educational guide offers wolf facts, activities and details about their life cycle." Publ Wkly

Ganeri, Anita

Fennec fox. Heinemann Library 2011 24p il map (A day in the life: desert animals) lib bdg $22; pa $6.49

Grades: K 1 2 **599.77**

1. Foxes

ISBN 978-1-4329-4771-2 lib bdg; 1-4329-4771-0 lib bdg; 978-1-4329-4780-4 pa; 1-4329-4780-X pa

LC 2010022819

"The engaging full-color photographs are key to [this] well-organized [book]. . . . Basic global maps show where the animal is found, and a diagram called a 'body map' labels its parts. The [text is] appropriate for the age group, and the pictures will draw in youngsters. [An] excellent [purchase] if material is needed on these animals." SLJ

Includes glossary and bibliographical references

George, Jean Craighead

★ The wolves are back; paintings by Wendell Minor. Dutton Children's Books 2008 un il lib bdg $16.99

Grades: 2 3 4 5 **599.77**

1. Wolves 2. Yellowstone National Park

ISBN 978-0-525-47947-5

LC 2007017064

"In 1995, wolves were reintroduced to Yellowstone Park. . . . The emphasis here is not as much on the wolves and their habits, but on how their presence has changed the ecosystem and returned its natural balance. . . . George writes . . . in simple, rhythmic, informative prose. Adding to the book's appeal are Minor's finely detailed illustrations, featuring spectacularly rendered animals in the foreground of the bold, western landscapes." Booklist

Goldish, Meish

Red wolves; and then there were (almost) none. Bearport Pub. 2009 32p il map (America's animal comebacks) lib bdg $25.27

Grades: 2 3 4 **599.77**

1. Wolves 2. Wildlife conservation

ISBN 978-1-59716-742-0 lib bdg; 1-59716-742-8 lib bdg

LC 2008-30831

Through this true tale of wildlife survival, young readers discover the bold and creative ideas that Americans and their government have used to protect and care for the countrys endangered red wolves

"Crisp photos and maps on every page work well with the text and give faces to the scientists and animals. The back matter includes a facts page, information on related species, and an up-to-date reading list." SLJ

Includes glossary and bibliographical references

Mara, Wil

★ Coyotes. Marshall Cavendish Benchmark 2009 48p il (Animals animals) $20.95

Grades: 3 4 5 6 **599.77**
1. Coyotes
ISBN 978-0-7614-2928-9; 0-7614-2928-X
LC 2007023411

"The material is well researched and would be an excellent source for reports, and the [book has] a narrative flow that makes [it] easy and enjoyable to read. [The] title includes expert full-color photography." SLJ

Includes glossary and bibliographical references

Markle, Sandra
★ **Wolves**; by Sandra Markle. Lerner Publications 2004 40p il (Animal predators) hardcover o.p. pa $7.95
Grades: 3 4 5 6 **599.77**
1. Wolves
ISBN 1-57505-732-8; 1-57505-748-4 pa
LC 2003-11197

"The text works well with the often striking full-color photos that illustrate the book." Booklist

Includes glossary and bibliographical references

McAllister, Ian
The **sea** wolves; living wild in the Great Bear Rainforest. written by Ian McAllister and Nicholas Read; photographs by Ian McAllister. Orca Book Publishers 2010 121p il $19.95
Grades: 5 6 7 8 **599.77**
1. Wolves 2. Rain forest ecology
ISBN 978-1-55469-206-4; 1-55469-206-7

The coastal wolf, a genetically distinct strain that swims and fishes, inhabits the Great Bear Rainforest on British Columbia's rugged west coast.

"This extensive, informative text is illustrated with remarkable photographs taken by McAllister, who has lived in and studied the area for years. They show the lush, old-growth forest and rocky shoreline and a variety of animals that share this habitat, but the wolves are the stars: at rest, at play, on the prowl and catching fish. . . . Fascinating and useful." Kirkus

Nobleman, Marc Tyler
★ **Foxes**; by Marc Tyler Nobleman. Marshall Cavendish Benchmark 2007 47p il (Animals, animals) lib bdg $19.95
Grades: 3 4 5 6 **599.77**
1. Foxes
ISBN 978-0-7614-2237-2 lib bdg; 0-7614-2237-4 lib bdg
LC 2005025608

"Describes the physical characteristics, behavior, habitat, and endangered status of foxes." Publisher's note

Includes glossary and bibliographical references

Patent, Dorothy Hinshaw
When the wolves returned; restoring nature's balance in Yellowstone. photographs by Dan Hartman and Cassie Hartman. Walker 2008 39p il $17.95; lib bdg $18.85
Grades: 3 4 5 **599.77**
1. Wolves 2. Yellowstone National Park
ISBN 978-0-8027-9686-8; 0-8027-9686-9; 978-0-8027-9687-5 lib bdg; 0-8027-9687-7 lib bdg
LC 2007-37141

NCTE Orbis Pictus Award honor book (2009)

When wolves were eliminated from Yellowstone National Park the natural system was out of balance. Shows the return of the wolves to the park and the natural balance being restored.

"Outstanding historical and present-day photographs of Yellowstone, its inhabitants, and its visitors capture the rugged natural beauty of the park." Horn Book

Includes bibliographical references

Person, Stephen
Arctic fox; very cool! by Stephen Person. Bearport Pub. 2009 32p il map (Uncommon animals) lib bdg $25.27
Grades: 1 2 3 **599.77**
1. Foxes
ISBN 978-1-59716-730-7 lib bdg; 1-59716-730-4 lib bdg
LC 2008-10637

"Easily readable sections detail the bitter natural habitat of the arctic fox and highlight the ways in which the animal is uniquely outfitted to survive such harsh conditions. The text works splendidly with the large, clear photographs on each page that will delight readers." Booklist

Includes glossary and bibliographical references

Read, Tracy C.
Exploring the world of coyotes. Firefly 2011 24p il (Exploring the world of) $16.95; pa $6.95
Grades: 4 5 6 **599.77**
1. Coyotes
ISBN 978-1-55407-795-3; 1-55407-795-8; 978-1-55407-796-0 pa; 1-55407-796-6 pa

This describes the physical features, habitat, diet, and behavior of coyotes.

A "well-organized [text] and good-quality pictures taken from photo archives provide the basics. [This book] reveals how North America's 'super dog' has had to adapt to survive humankind's continuous assault. . . . Insets of information in colorful circles add to the attractive configuration. [The book offers] simple language and good use of space." SLJ

Exploring the world of wolves. Firefly 2010 24p il (Exploring the world of . . .) $16.95; pa $6.95
Grades: 3 4 5 **599.77**
1. Wolves
ISBN 978-1-55407-646-8; 1-55407-646-3; 978-1-55407-655-0 pa; 1-55407-655-2 pa

This describes the anatomy and behavior of wolves.

This offers "an abundance of in-depth, intriguing information and [is] appropriate for research or pleasure reading. . . . Two- to four-page chapters mix smaller photos with full-page color photos, and the attractive format will help less-able readers navigate the sometimes dense, detailed paragraphs." Booklist

Riggs, Kate
Wolves. Creative Education 2011 24p il (Amazing animals) $24.25; pa $5.99
Grades: K 1 2 **599.77**
1. Wolves
ISBN 978-1-58341-991-5; 1-58341-991-8; 978-0-89812-564-1 pa; 0-89812-564-2 pa
LC 2010019055

"A basic exploration of the appearance, behavior, and habitat of wolves, a family of wild dogs. Also included is a story from folklore explaining why wolves are different from domestic dogs." Publisher's note

Swinburne, Stephen R.

Coyote; North America's dog. Boyds Mills Press 1999 32p il $16.95; pa $8.95

Grades: 4 5 6   **599.77**

1. Coyotes

ISBN 1-56397-765-6; 1-59078-485-5 pa

This book "packs a lot of information about North American coyotes into a small space. The author, a veteran park ranger, knows his subject well and succeeds in making it interesting to his audience. . . . The full-color photographs are clean and clear and enliven the text." Booklist

599.775 Foxes

Holland, Mary

Ferdinand Fox's first summer; by Mary Holland. Sylvan Dell Publishing 2013 32 p. ill. (reinforced) $17.95; (paperback) $9.95

Grades: K 1 2 3   **599.775**

1. Foxes

ISBN 1607186144; 9781607186144; 9781607186267
LC 2012030121

In this children's picture book, author "[Mary] Holland presents the first part of the red fox's life cycle with the story of Ferdinand, one fox kit she photographed throughout his first summer. Short, bland paragraphs of information describe how the five fox kits grow and learn, their mother nursing and grooming them and, when they are ready, bringing back food for them to eat." (Kirkus Reviews)

599.78 Bears

Arnold, Caroline

A polar bear's world; written and illustrated by Caroline Arnold. Picture Window Books 2010 24p il (Caroline Arnold's animals) lib bdg $25.32

Grades: PreK K 1 2   **599.78**

1. Polar bear

ISBN 978-1-4048-5743-8 lib bdg; 1-4048-5743-5 lib bdg
LC 2009033366

This narrative tells the story of a polar bear from birth until it is on its own.

The story, "related in the present tense, [feels] immediate and engaging. . . . The plainness of the fact boxes contrasts with Arnold's beautiful but simple artwork, which cleanly captures the essence of [the] animal. . . . [This book's] perfectly balanced mix of facts, story, and pictures will hold young readers' attention and help them learn." Booklist

Baines, Rebecca

A den is a bed for a bear; a book about bears. by Becky Baines. National Geographic 2008 29p il (Zig zag) $14.95; lib bdg $19.90

Grades: PreK K 1   **599.78**

1. Bears 2. Hibernation

ISBN 978-1-4263-0309-8; 1-4263-0309-2; 978-1-4263-0310-4 lib bdg; 1-4263-0310-6 lib bdg
LC 2008-07221

"Readers curiosity will be piqued by the vibrant color photographs, accommodating illustrations, large font size, and helpful captions. Special features include drawings superimposed over photographs, and a zigzag path at the end of . . . [the] book prompting readers to further explore the topic in new and fun ways." SLJ

Barner, Bob

Bears! bears! bears! Chronicle Books 2010 un il $14.99

Grades: PreK K 1   **599.78**

1. Bears -- Fiction

ISBN 978-0-8118-7057-3; 0-8118-7057-X

"Collages rendered in vibrant hues lead youngsters through a fanciful expedition. The colorful spreads and rhyming text will entertain children as they discover the variety of bears found around the world. . . . Two concluding spreads contain facts about bears and ursine habitats. . . . Beginning readers might like to attempt this one on their own." SLJ

Bekoff, Marc

Jasper's story; saving moon bears. by Jill Robinson & Marc Bekoff; illustrated by Gijsbert van Frankenhuyzen. Sleeping Bear Press 2013 40 p. (reinforced) $16.99

Grades: 1 2 3 4 5   **599.78**

1. Bears 2. Animal welfare 3. Wildlife rescue 4. Asiatic black bear

ISBN 1585367982; 9781585367986
LC 2012033687

This book by Jill Robinson was written after she encountered the practice of bear farming in China. The book "tells of one moon bear [Jasper] and how he came to symbolize the forgiveness and trust that come with love. . . . At the time of his rescue, he was both physically and emotionally battered, but through the gentle care of Robinson and her helpers, he can play and interact with other bears and humans, and seems to have forgiven the cruelties that were once inflicted upon him." (School Library Journal)

Berman, Ruth

Let's look at brown bears. Lerner Publications Co. 2010 32p il map (Lightning Bolt Books: Animal close-ups) lib bdg $25.26

Grades: PreK K 1 2   **599.78**

1. Bears

ISBN 978-0-7613-3890-1 lib bdg; 0-7613-3890-X lib bdg
LC 2008-51855

Introduces the Alaskan brown bear, describing its physical characteristics, hibernation behavior, and feeding habits

"Fresh photography, a creative use of graphics, and a collagelike layout make[s] . . . [this book] eye-catching. . . . [The] book ends with a labeled diagram of the animal, a range map, and a further-reading list that includes print and online resources in a single list, a nice way of validating both types of materials." SLJ

Includes glossary

Bodden, Valerie

Polar bears. Creative Education 2010 24p il (Amazing animals) lib bdg $24.25

Grades: K 1 2   599.78

1. Polar bear

ISBN 978-1-58341-811-6 lib bdg; 1-58341-811-3 lib bdg

LC 2009002714

A basic exploration of the appearance, behavior, and habitat of polar bears, Earth's biggest land predators. Also included is a story from folklore explaining why polar bears have short tails.

This is illustrated with "dynamically colored photographs." Booklist

Includes bibliographical references

Bortolotti, Dan

Panda rescue; changing the future for endangered wildlife. Firefly 2003 64p il map lib bdg $19.95; pa $9.95

Grades: 4 5 6 7   599.78

1. Giant panda 2. Wildlife conservation

ISBN 1-55297-598-3 lib bdg; 1-55297-557-6 pa

This describes the panda's "natural habitat, habits, physiology, and behavior in captivity. [It also includes] a time line of conservation efforts, profiles of conservationists in the field, and forecasts of the animals' future. Throughout, the author makes clear the factors that can threaten animal populations, and discusses human attitudes toward the animals throughout history. . . . Written in accessible, lively language and nicely illustrated with exciting color photos, [this] will be useful for reports and browsing." Booklist

Brett, Jeannie

Wild about bears; Jeannie Brett. Charlesbridge 2013 32 p. col. ill., col. map (softcover) $7.95

Grades: K 1 2 3   599.78

1. Bears

ISBN 1580894194; 9781580894180; 9781580894197; 9781607346364

LC 2012038700

This children's book, written and illustrated by Jeannie Brett, offers a "comprehensive look at the world's eight bear species focuses first on common physical traits and behaviors before profiling each bear. [Topics include] the habits and habitats of the polar bear, brown bear, American black bear, spectacled bear, Asiatic black bear, sloth bear, sun bear, and giant panda." (Publisher's note)

"This fact-filled guide provides an overview of each species, focusing on their physical and behavioral characteristics in relationship to their environments. After initial introductory paragraphs, Brett scatters brief, captionlike sentences throughout her warm, naturalistic watercolor scenes." Pub Wkly

Includes bibliographical references and index

Davies, Nicola, 1958-

★ Ice bear; in the steps of the polar bear. illustrated by Gary Blythe. Candlewick Press 2005 un il $16.99

Grades: K 1 2 3   599.78

1. Polar bear

ISBN 0-7636-2759-3

Describes how the polar bear, also called Nanuk, thrives in the Arctic and explains the lessons that the Inuit people have learned from watching the creature.

"This inviting picture book delivers facts about polar bears and conveys respect for their adaptive success. . . . Children will be fascinated by the impressionistic oil paintings of stunning polar settings and bears at play, tenderly nursing young, and, yes, hunting seals, an activity represented by a stark image of a bear's crimson-stained muzzle that may startle the youngest readers." Booklist

De Vries, Maggie

Fraser bear; a cub's life. illustrated by Renné Benoit. Greystone Books 2010 il $16.95

Grades: 2 3 4   599.78

1. Bears 2. Salmon

ISBN 978-1-55365-521-3; 1-55365-521-4

"Set along British Columbia's Fraser River and arranged chronologically by months of the year, this story follows a cub from his birth through his first season of independence. With each phase of his growth, the life cycle of the chinook salmon is also explained as they migrate out to the ocean then back up the river to spawn and die, providing an abundance of rich food for Fraser and other animals. . . . A good resource for any study of the life cycle of bears or salmon." SLJ

Firestone, Mary

Top 50 reasons to care about giant pandas; animals in peril. Enslow Publishers 2010 103p il (Top 50 reasons to care about endangered animals) lib bdg $31.93

Grades: 4 5 6 7   599.78

1. Giant panda 2. Endangered species

ISBN 978-0-7660-3451-8 lib bdg; 0-7660-3451-8 lib bdg

LC 2008-48953

This describes the giant panda's life cycle, habitat, young, diet, living in the wild and in captivity, and why it is endangered

"The illustrations, mostly color photographs, represent a wonderful selection of the animals and their habitats. Reluctant readers may be enticed by this . . . simply because of the great images. This . . . would make a substantial supplement to the science curriculum when studying endangered animals." Libr Media Connect

Includes glossary and bibliographical references

Gish, Melissa

Pandas. Creative Education 2011 48p il (Living wild) lib bdg $23.95; pa $8.95

Grades: 5 6 7 8   599.78

1. Giant panda

ISBN 978-1-60818-082-0 lib bdg; 1-60818-082-4 lib bdg; 978-1-60818-082-0 pa; 1-60818-082-4 pa

LC 2010028311

A look at pandas, including their habitats, physical characteristics such as their black-and-white fur, behaviors, relationships with humans, and threatened status in the world today.

Includes glossary and bibliographical references

Greene, Jacqueline Dembar

Grizzly bears; saving the silvertip. by Jacqueline Dembar Greene. Bearport Pub. 2008 32p il map (America's animal comebacks) lib bdg $25.27

Grades: 2 3 4   **599.78**
1. Grizzly bear 2. Wildlife conservation
ISBN 978-1-59716-533-4 lib bdg; 1-59716-533-6
lib bdg
                                    LC 2007012606
This describes efforts by environmentals to save the silvertip grizzly bear from extinction in the American West

This book is "well organized and [has] an easy style and an accessible vocabulary and text size . . . [and] color photographs." SLJ

Includes glossary and bibliographical references

Guiberson, Brenda Z.
Ice bears; [by] Brenda Z. Guiberson; illustrated by Ilya Spirin. Henry Holt & Co. 2008 un il $16.95
Grades: 1 2 3 4   **599.78**
1. Polar bear 2. Arctic regions
ISBN 978-0-8050-7607-3; 0-8050-7607-7
                                    LC 2007040895
"This story of the struggle of a polar bear mother and her two cubs to survive introduces both the harsh conditions of the Arctic and the challenges of global warming for polar bears in general. Guiberson uses precise verbs and onomatopoeia to paint a picture of the daily activities of the bears while gracefully weaving in facts about their weight, diet, and climate. Spirin's detailed watercolors are surprisingly varied in depicting an essentially frozen world, using interesting perspectives." SLJ

★ **Moon** bear; illustrated by Ed Young. Henry Holt & Co. 2010 un il $16.99
Grades: PreK K 1 2 3   **599.78**
1. Bears
ISBN 978-0-8050-8977-6; 0-8050-8977-2
                                    LC 2009017931
"This picture book both celebrates the endangered black moon bear in Southeast Asia and warns about the urgent threats against the species. Filled with physical details, the spare, question-and-answer text . . . is illustrated with Young's stark, large silhouette images of a beautiful, dark bear throughout the seasons." Booklist

Hamilton, Sue L.
Mauled by a bear; [by] Sue Hamilton. ABDO Pub. Co. 2010 32p il (Close encounters of the wild kind) lib bdg $27.07
Grades: 4 5 6 7   **599.78**
1. Bears 2. Animal attacks
ISBN 978-1-60453-932-5 lib bdg; 1-60453-932-1
lib bdg
                                    LC 2009-35078
Readers learn of actual human-bear encounters, information about bears, survival strategies, and attack statistics.

"Students will be drawn to the realistic full-color photographs, the realistic diagrams of the creatures' bodies, the real-life stories told by victims, and the interesting, attractive formatting that includes text, diagrams, photographs, and graphics on each page. . . . [This is] exciting and attractive in a 'gross' sort of way and will appeal particularly to boys for both leisure reading and research." Libr Media Connect
Includes glossary

Hatkoff, Juliana
Knut; how one little polar bear captivated the world. told by Juliana, Isabella, and Craig Hatkoff, and Gerald R. Uhlich. Scholastic Press 2007 un il $16.99
Grades: 2 3 4   **599.78**
1. Polar bear
ISBN 978-0-545-04716-6; 0-545-04716-1
                                    LC 2007-21379
"Knut is a German polar bear born in captivity. His story is told in simple language and accompanied by adorable, engaging close-ups of him and his primary handler, a zookeeper named Thomas Dörflein. . . . Consider this well-written, well-documented title an essential addition to every collection." SLJ

Hirsch, Rebecca E.
Top 50 reasons to care about polar bears; animals in peril. Enslow Publishers 2010 103p il (Top 50 reasons to care about endangered animals) lib bdg $31.93
Grades: 4 5 6 7   **599.78**
1. Polar bear 2. Endangered species
ISBN 978-0-7660-3458-7 lib bdg; 0-7660-3458-5
lib bdg
                                    LC 2008-48693
This describes polar bears--their life cycle, diet, young, habitat, and reasons why they are endangered animals

"The illustrations, mostly color photographs, represent a wonderful selection of the animals and their habitats. Reluctant readers may be enticed by this . . . simply because of the great images. This . . . would make a substantial supplement to the science curriculum when studying endangered animals." Libr Media Connect
Includes glossary and bibliographical references

Hirschi, Ron
Our three bears; [by] Ron Hirschi; photographs by Thomas D. Mangelsen. Boyds Mills Press 2008 32p il $16.95
Grades: 2 3 4 5   **599.78**
1. Bears
ISBN 978-1-59078-015-2
                                    LC 2007049380
"North America's bears—black, grizzly, and polar—are introduced in this attractive presentation made compelling by Mangelsen's full-color photographic delights. . . . Hirschi reveals the differences in each bear's hibernation patterns, habitats, diets, size, and population estimates. These short paragraphs are chock-full of information. Beginning researchers as well as young wildlife enthusiasts will find Our Three Bears well suited to their interests." SLJ
Includes bibliographical references

★ **Searching** for grizzlies; photographs by Thomas D. Mangelsen; drawings by Deborah Cooper. Boyds Mills Press 2005 un il $15.95
Grades: 3 4 5   **599.78**
1. Bears
ISBN 1-59078-014-0
Describes the physical characteristics, behavior, and habitat primarily of grizzly bears, with some comparisons to black bears and polar bears.

"Mangelsen's fine photos and Cooper's attractive sketches accompany Hirschi's readable text bursting with the bear facts." SLJ

Kvatum, Lia

Saving Yasha; The Incredible True Story of an Adopted Moon Bear. by Lia Kvatum; photographs by Liya Pokrovskaya. National Geographic 2012 32 p. col. ill., col. maps (hardcover) $16.95; (lib. bdg.) $25.90

Grades: 1 2 3   **599.78**

1. Bears 2. Wildlife 3. Animal behavior

ISBN 142631051X; 9781426310515; 1426310765; 9781426310768

LC 2012288404

In this book, Lia Kvatum tells the story of "Yasha, joined later by Shum and Shiksha, [who] are nurtured by" scientists after being "orphaned by poachers . . . [in] the Siberian wild. . . . Kvatum chronicles the cubs' development as they learn to forage on their own while playing together and learning to climb trees. She also notes how important it is for human observers to remain aloof . . . to prevent the animals from becoming dependent or domesticated." (Kirkus Reviews)

Leathers, Dan

Polar bears on the Hudson Bay; by Dan Leathers. Mitchell Lane Publishers 2008 32p il map (On the verge of extinction: crisis in the environment) lib bdg $17.95

Grades: 3 4 5   **599.78**

1. Polar bear

ISBN 978-1-58415-586-7

LC 2007000797

This describes the life cycle of polar bears on the Hudson Bay and how they are threatened by climate change and other environmental dangers.

"Short chapters, large font, and pronunciation guides to key words engage children doing research, but the depth of information is not compromised. . . . Colorful, up-close photographs are accompanied by satisfying explanatory captions." SLJ

Includes glossary and bibliographical references

Markle, Sandra

Grizzly bears. Lerner Publications Company 2010 39p il (Animal predators) $26.60

Grades: 4 5 6   **599.78**

1. Grizzly bear

ISBN 978-1-58013-537-5; 1-58013-537-4

LC 2008-38120

Introduces the physical characteristics, habitat, and predatory behavior of grizzly bears.

"Vivid photographs alongside Markle's narrative, which provides factual information about grizzly bears' physical characteristics and hunting behaviors, introduce readers to these majestic and dangerous creatures." Horn Book Guide

Includes glossary and bibliographical references

★ How many baby pandas? Walker 2009 23p il map $15.99; lib bdg $16.89

Grades: K 1 2 3   **599.78**

1. Giant panda 2. Animal babies

ISBN 978-0-8027-9783-4; 0-8027-9783-0; 978-0-8027-9784-1 lib bdg; 0-8027-9784-9 lib bdg

"Clear accessible text . . . and sharp photos provide an engaging, informative introduction to baby pandas, highlighting those born at China's Wolong Giant Panda Breeding

Center in 2005. . . . Scientific concepts are well explained, and pages are filled with panda facts." Booklist

Includes glossary and bibliographical references

Polar bears; [by] Sandra Markle. Carolrhoda Books 2004 40p il (Animal predators) lib bdg $25.26; pa $7.95

Grades: 3 4 5 6   **599.78**

1. Polar bear

ISBN 1-57505-730-1 lib bdg; 1-57505-746-8 pa

LC 2003-19515

The author observes polar bears' "hunting techniques and includes information about their physical characteristics, physiology, habitats and care of young." Horn Book Guide

Includes glossary and bibliographical references

Marsh, Laura

Polar bears; by Laura Marsh. National Geographic Children's Books 2013 32 p. (pbk.: alk. paper) $13.90

Grades: K 1 2   **599.78**

1. Polar bear

ISBN 1426311052; 9781426311048; 9781426311055

LC 2012039727

In this book, by Laura Marsh, readers will "learn all . . . about polar bears. With their beautiful white fur and powerful presence, polar bears rule the Arctic. These majestic giants swim from iceberg to iceberg in chilling waters, care for their adorable cubs, and are threatened by global warming. [It is] complete with fascinating facts, beautiful images." (Publisher's note)

McAllister, Ian

★ Salmon bears; giants of the Great Bear Rainforest. [by] Ian McAllister & Nicholas Read; photographs by Ian McAllister. Orca Book Publishers 2010 89p il map pa $18.95

Grades: 5 6 7 8   **599.78**

1. Bears 2. Salmon 3. Rain forest ecology

ISBN 978-1-55469-205-7 pa; 1-55469-205-9 pa

"Read's conversational text and McAllister's excellent photos provide a perfect framework for this evocative look at the big bears of the Great Bear Rainforest of British Columbia, and an intriguing investigation of its ecological pattern of dependency. The authors present a round of seasons from one winter to the next, touching upon such topics as the effects of fish farms on wild salmon populations, what happens during a salmon run, and what the future may hold for the fish, the bears, and the Great Bear Rainforest itself. . . . Superbly readable, informative, and attractive." SLJ

Includes bibliographical references

Newman, Mark

Polar bears. Henry Holt & Co. 2011 un il map $16.99

Grades: K 1 2 3   **599.78**

1. Polar bear

ISBN 978-0-8050-8999-8; 0-8050-8999-3

"Irresistibly endearing polar bear photographs are the highlight of this picture book, although each spread also includes a factual statement about polar bears . . . , accompanied by smaller additional text that goes into deeper detail." Horn Book

Includes bibliographical references

Olson, Gillia M.

Polar bears' search for ice; a cause and effect investigation. Capstone Press 2010 32p il map (Fact finders. Animals on the edge) lib bdg $25.99

Grades: 3 4 5 6   **599.78**

1. Polar bear 2. Greenhouse effect

ISBN 978-1-4296-4532-4 lib bdg; 1-4296-4532-6 lib bdg

LC 2010007719

"Excellent discussions address those who doubt the severity of the issue and those who wonder why people should care what happens to animals. The captioned photographs are timely and poignant. . . . [This] makes serious subject matter interesting and accessible." SLJ

Includes glossary and bibliographical references

Rosing, Norbert

Face to face with polar bears; by Norbert Rosing with Elizabeth Carney. National Geographic 2007 32p il (Face to face) $16.95; lib bdg $25.90

Grades: 3 4 5 6   **599.78**

1. Polar bear

ISBN 978-1-4263-0139-1; 978-1-4263-0140-7 lib bdg

LC 2006032847

"Rosing tells how he and his wife tried to fend off a polar bear 'with a toothache' and a yen for their spaghetti dinner while they waited for a helicopter rescue. The book describes the animal's diet, physical features, and habitat, and the dangers of global warming. . . . [This] attractive, smoothly written [book], topped off with advice about self-directed research, will catch the attention of enthusiasts and motivate them toward personal investigation." SLJ

Includes glossary and bibliographical references

Polar bears. Firefly Books 2010 55p il map $19.95; pa $9.95

Grades: 3 4 5   **599.78**

1. Polar bear

ISBN 978-1-55407-599-7; 1-55407-599-8; 978-1-55407-623-9 pa; 1-55407-623-4 pa

LC 2010294457

Photographs and captions present the life of polar bears across the four seasons of the year. Topics covered include habitat activities, diet, anatomy, and survival.

"The high quality of the photos and their reproduction will draw many readers to this visually appealing book, which provides plenty of worthwhile information in the captions and back matter." Booklist

Ryder, Joanne

A **pair** of polar bears; twin cubs find a home at the San Diego Zoo. photos by the world-famous San Diego Zoo. Simon & Schuster Books for Young Readers 2006 un il $16.95

Grades: K 1 2   **599.78**

1. Polar bear

ISBN 0-689-85871-X

LC 2005014013

"This photo-essay introduces children to an engaging, true story from the San Diego Zoo. . . . The stars are rescued polar bear twins Tatqiq and Kalluk, who progress through the photo-rich pages from needy, quarantined cubs to fully acclimated adults with mastery over their outdoor habitat.

The images, all provided by the zoo and most sharply focused and closeup, will elicit coos from readers." Booklist

Sartore, Joel

★ **Face** to face with grizzlies. National Geographic 2007 32p il (Face to face) $16.95; lib bdg $25.90

Grades: 3 4 5 6   **599.78**

1. Grizzly bear

ISBN 978-1-4263-0050-9; 1-4263-0050-6; 978-1-4263-0051-6 lib bdg; 1-4263-0051-4 lib bdg

LC 2006-20500

"In accessible, exciting language, Sartore . . . describes his close encounters with bears while on assignment. . . . He matches stunning photographs of bears playing, fighting, eating, and chasing prey . . . with basic information about bears' bodies, habitats, and behavior." Booklist

Includes bibliographical references

Schreiber, Anne

Pandas. National Geographic 2010 32p il (National Geographic readers) pa $3.99

Grades: 1 2 3   **599.78**

1. Giant panda

ISBN 978-1-4263-0610-5; 1-4263-0610-5

This describes pandas and their behavior.

Schwabacher, Martin

Bears; by Martin Schwabacher with Terry Miller Shannon. Marshall Cavendish Benchmark 2010 24p il map (Animals) lib bdg $16.95

Grades: 3 4 5   **599.78**

1. Bears

ISBN 978-0-7614-3820-5 lib bdg; 0-7614-3820-3 lib bdg

"The straightforward presentation of the information and the uncluttered and attractive layout make [this] . . . good . . . for reports. Color photographs . . . are well utilized and complete a solid package." SLJ

Includes glossary and bibliographical references

Sirota, Lyn A.

Giant pandas. Capstone Press 2010 24p il map (Pebble plus. Asian animals) lib bdg $22.65

Grades: PreK K 1   **599.78**

1. Giant panda

ISBN 978-1-4296-4028-2; 1-4296-4028-6

"This . . . is an excellent resource for great pictures and information to share with students in storytimes or to support other content areas. This will be an excellent addition to nonfiction collections, especially for very young readers." Libr Media Connect

Includes bibliographical references

Swinburne, Stephen R.

★ **Black** bear; North America's bear. Boyds Mills 2003 32p il map $15.95

Grades: 3 4 5   **599.78**

1. Bears

ISBN 1-59078-023-X

An examination of black bears, their behavior and habitat.

"Stunning, full-color photos and a lively text make for an intriguing introduction to these fascinating animals." SLJ

Thomson, Sarah L.

Where do polar bears live? illustrated by Jason Chin. Collins 2010 37p il (Let's-read-and-find-out science) $16.99; pa $5.99

Grades: K 1 2 3   **599.78**

1. Polar bear 2. Arctic regions

ISBN 978-0-06-157518-1; 0-06-157518-6; 978-0-06-157517-4 pa; 0-06-157517-8 pa

LC 2008056030

"This title explores a year in the life of a polar bear, focusing on facts about the animal's diet, hunting techniques, and habitat. Thomson also covers the impact of global warming on polar bears' food sources. . . . This is an affecting introduction to polar bears and their threatened existence for young children." Booklist

Walker, Sally M.

Winnie; the remarkable tale of a real bear. Sally M. Walker; illustrated by Jonathan D. Voss. Henry Holt & Co. 2015 40 p. color illustrations, portraits

Grades: PreK K 1 2 3   **599.78**

1. Bears 2. World War, 1914-1918 3. Black bear 4. Winnipeg (Bear) 5. Canada. Canadian Armed Forces -- Mascots 6. Winnie-the-Pooh (Fictitious character) -- History

ISBN 9780805097153

LC 2014028434

In this children's book, by Sally M. Walker, illustrated by Jonathan D. Voss, "Harry Colebourn saw a baby bear for sale at the train station [and] he knew he could care for it. Harry was a veterinarian. But he was also a soldier in training for World War I. Harry named the bear Winnie, short for Winnipeg, his company's home town, and he brought her along to the training camp in England. . . . But who could care for the bear when Harry had to go to the battleground in France?" (Publisher's note)

"A soldier's pet becomes famous.During a short stop on a train ride across Canada during World War I, veterinarian-turned-soldier Harry Colebourn buys an orphaned bear cub he sees at a station. He names her Winnipeg for his company's hometown; it's quickly shortened to Winnie...An author's note expands on Harry's story and adds some facts on black bears and Milne's children's books. Ideal for Winnie-the-Pooh fans, this clear, straightforward biography reveals the bear behind the tale. (sources, websites)." Kirkus

Includes bibliographical references

599.786   Polar bear

Markle, Sandra, 1946-

Waiting for ice; by Sandra Markle; illustrated by Alan Marks. Charlesbridge 2012 32 p.

Grades: 1 2 3   **599.786**

1. Polar bear 2. Arctic region 3. Global warming 4. Polar bear -- Effect of global warming on

ISBN 1580892558; 9781580892551; 9781580892568

LC 2011002113

This children's book by Sandra Markle, illustrated by Alan Marks, "provides a . . . look at polar bears, the largest hunters on land, in this narrative that follows an orphaned cub barely old enough to survive on her own. Trapped on Wrangel Island in the Arctic Sea, waiting late into the fall

for the annual floating pack ice to form, she and other polar bears subsist on the few animals they can find—typically only birds and walruses, as a note on global warming explains. . . . [The story offers a] look at how polar bears survive during so much of the year, when there's no ice to help them in their hunt for seals in the Arctic waters." (Kirkus)

599.79   Marine carnivores

Arnold, Caroline

A **walrus'** world; written and illustrated by Caroline Arnold. Picture Window Books 2010 24p il (Caroline Arnold's animals) lib bdg $25.32

Grades: PreK K 1 2   **599.79**

1. Walruses

ISBN 978-1-4048-5744-5 lib bdg; 1-4048-5744-3 lib bdg

LC 2009033380

This narrative tells the story of a walrus from birth until it can live on its own.

The story, "related in the present tense, [feels] immediate and engaging. . . . The plainness of the fact boxes contrasts with Arnold's beautiful but simple artwork, which cleanly captures the essence of [the] animal. . . . [This book's] perfectly balanced mix of facts, story, and pictures will hold young readers' attention and help them learn." Booklist

Butterworth, Chris

See what a seal can do! by Chris Butterworth and illustrated by Kate Nelms. Candlewick Press 2013 32 p. $14.99

Grades: K 1 2   **599.79**

1. Marine animals 2. Seals (Animals)

ISBN 0763665746; 9780763665746

LC 2012947729

This book, by Chris Butterworth and illustrated by Kate Nelms, features illustrations that "portray the seal's transformation from awkward land dweller to sinuous and powerful denizen of the deep. The below-water scenes . . . evoke the murky ocean habitat and the singular seal's steep descent to the bottom." (School Library Journal)

Green, Jen

California sea lion; by Jen Green. Bearport Publishing 2013 24 p. (library binding) $23.93

Grades: 1 2   **599.79**

1. Sea lions

ISBN 1617729191; 9781617729195

LC 2013011505

In this book, by Jen Green, "readers will explore the underwater world of the marine mammal [the California sea lion] through clear text, full-color photos, and diagrams. Age-appropriate activities, such as researching how California sea lions compare to other pinnipeds, [are designed to] give readers a chance to make observations and to develop animal-science skills." (Publisher's note)

Includes bibliographical references and index

Harvey, Jeanne

Astro the Steller sea lion; illustrated by Shennen Bersani. Sylvan Dell Pub. 2010 un il $16.95; pa $8.95

Grades: 1 2 3   **599.79**
1. Seals (Animals) -- Fiction
ISBN 978-1-60718-076-0; 1-60718-076-6; 978-1-60718-087-6 pa; 1-60718-087-1 pa
LC 2010-921908

"Harvey tells a gentle tale of an orphaned Steller sea lion pup whose early imprinting on his human nurturers at the Marine Mammal Center in Sausalito, CA, leaves him determinedly reluctant to live in the wild on any terms. Bersani's nearly photographic illustrations keep perfect time with the simple text." SLJ

Hengel, Katherine
It's a baby Australian fur seal! ABDO 2010 24p il (Baby Australian animals) lib bdg $19.93
Grades: K 1 2 3   **599.79**
1. Animal babies 2. Seals (Animals)
ISBN 978-1-60453-574-7 lib bdg; 1-60453-574-1 lib bdg
LC 2008-55073

This book about fur seals "is a great choice. Though the focus of . . . [the] book is the animal baby, the reader will learn a great many facts. Information includes how they are born, how they are fed, age of independence, food, habitat, predators, and features that help them find food and protect themselves. . . . This . . . is a sound addition for any school library." Libr Media Connect
Includes glossary

Malam, John
Pinnipeds; written by John Malam; created and designed by David Salariya. Franklin Watts 2009 32p il (Scary creatures) lib bdg $26; pa $8.95
Grades: 3 4 5   **599.79**
1. Walruses 2. Marine mammals 3. Seals (Animals)
ISBN 978-0-531-21672-9 lib bdg; 0-531-21672-1 lib bdg; 978-0-531-21043-7 pa; 0-531-21043-X pa
LC 2009010799

This defines pinnipeds and describes their life cycles, habitats, behavior, and relationship to humans

This title has "two-page chapters of accessible, large-type text and bright color photos and illustrations. . . . The series distinguishes itself with 'X-Ray Vision.' When readers hold the page with this prompt up to the light, an image emerges. The X-rays mostly show the skeletal structures of the animals. Text boxes throughout add to the visual appeal. . . . [This title is an] excellent [resource] for school assignments and browsing." SLJ
Includes glossary

Markovics, Joyce L.
Weddell seal; fat and happy. by Joyce L. Markovics. Bearport Pub. 2009 32p il map (Uncommon animals) lib bdg $25.27
Grades: 1 2 3   **599.79**
1. Seals (Animals)
ISBN 978-1-59716-734-5 lib bdg; 1-59716-734-7 lib bdg
LC 2008-14391

"The explanatory text works spendidly, with large photographs that bring readers as close as they'll ever get to such beasts." Booklist
Includes glossary and bibliographical references

Metz, Lorijo
Discovering sea lions. PowerKids Press 2011 24p il (Along the shore) lib bdg $21.25
Grades: 3 4 5   **599.79**
1. Seals (Animals)
ISBN 978-1-4488-4992-5; 1-4488-4992-6
LC 2010047570

This book about sea lions "briefly describes the major physical and behavioral characteristics common to all [sea lions] and one or two distinctive characteristics of about a half dozen species. . . . [The book] outlines the major physical differences between [sea lions] and seals. . . . One or two sharp color photographs of representative species, most of which are closeups, accompany the text on every page. . . . [This is] well organized and smoothly written in an engaging style." SLJ
Includes glossary

Peterson, Brenda
★ Leopard & Silkie; one boy's quest to save the seal pups. by Brenda Peterson; photographs by Robin Lindsey. 1st ed. Henry Holt and Co. (BYR) 2012 32 p. col. ill. (hardback) $16.99
Grades: 1 2 3   **599.79**
1. Compassion 2. Animal welfare 3. Seals (Animals) 4. Wildlife rescue 5. Seals (Animals) -- Conservation
ISBN 080509167X; 9780805091670
LC 2011029041

Author Brenda Peterson tells the story of "concerned volunteers [who] become seal sitters [in the Pacific Northwest], keeping vigil over the vulnerable baby seals that are left on the shore while their mothers hunt for food. . . . With its emphasis on human compassion, this true account teaches children to appreciate the natural world by helping in any way they can. The star of the book is six year old Miles, who organizes his own rescue mission to help the seals survive." (Publisher's note)
Includes bibliographical references.

Read, Tracy C.
Exploring the world of seals and walruses. Firefly 2011 24p il (Exploring the world of) $16.95; pa $6.95
Grades: 4 5 6   **599.79**
1. Walruses 2. Seals (Animals)
ISBN 978-1-55407-784-7; 1-55407-784-2; 978-1-55407-797-7 pa; 1-55407-797-4 pa

This describes the physical features, habitats, diets, and behavior of seals and walruses.

A "well-organized [text] and good-quality pictures taken from photo archives provide the basics. . . . [This focuses] on the different habitats and challenges faced by three pinniped subgroups: eared and earless seals and the walrus. Insets of information in colorful circles add to the attractive configuration. [The book offers] simple language and good use of space." SLJ

Rebman, Renee C.
Walruses. Marshall Cavendish Benchmark 2011 il (Animals, animals) lib bdg $20.95
Grades: 3 4 5   **599.79**
1. Walruses
ISBN 978-0-7614-4881-5; 0-7614-4881-0
LC 2010016036

This offers information on the anatomy, special skills, habitats, and diet of walruses.

This offers "comprehensive text and striking, well-chosen photos. . . . [This is] packed with engaging facts and trivia, as well as an upbeat tone." Booklist

Includes glossary and bibliographical references

Riggs, Kate
  Sea lions; Kate Riggs. Creative Education 2015 24 p. (Amazing Animals) $7.99
Grades: K 1 2   599.79
  1. Animals -- Folklore 2. Sea lions
  ISBN 0898129281; 9780898129281; 9781608185160
                                          LC 2013051259
"A basic exploration of the appearance, behavior, and habitat of sea lions, oceanic mammals related to seals. Also included is a story from folklore explaining why Japanese fishers respected sea lions. . . . Photos are paired with accessible text to examine the [sea lion's] appearance, habitat, behaviors, and life cycle." (Publisher's note)

" Large, appealing photos on each spread include more vivid close-ups, showing both animals' faces as well as the creatures in action. Across from the photos, the text is laid out cleanly in a large, clear font, and the sentences are simple and easy to read. Photo captions, meanwhile, add interesting facts, while occasional vocabulary words are defined at the bottoms of pages." -Booklist

Spilsbury, Louise
  Seal. Heinemann Library 2011 24p il (A day in the life. sea animals) lib bdg $22; pa $6.49
Grades: 1 2   599.79
  1. Seals (Animals)
  ISBN 978-1-4329-4002-7 lib bdg; 1-4329-4002-3 lib bdg; 978-1-4329-4009-6 pa; 1-4329-4009-0 pa
                                          LC 2010000628
This book follows a seal through its day as it sleeps, eats, and moves.

This pairs "well-chosen color photos . . . with one or two sentences of simple commentary for each. . . . [Though this title] includes references to several varieties of the chosen creature, one species in particular is highlighted. . . . [Good choice] for pleasure or purpose reading." SLJ

Includes glossary and bibliographical references

599.8 Primates

Aronin, Miriam
  Aye-aye; an evil omen. by Miriam Aronin. Bearport Pub. 2009 32p il map (Uncommon animals) lib bdg $25.27
Grades: 1 2 3   599.8
  1. Lemurs 2. Aye-aye (Animal)
  ISBN 978-1-59716-731-4 lib bdg; 1-59716-731-2 lib bdg
                                          LC 2008-15387
This describes the aye-aye, a lemur from Madagascar, believed, according to legend, to be an evil omen

"The explanatory text works splendidly, with large photographs that bring readers as close as they'll ever get to such beasts." Booklist

Includes glossary and bibliographical references

Barker, David
  Top 50 reasons to care about great apes; animals in peril. Enslow Publishers 2010 103p il (Top 50 reasons to care about endangered animals) lib bdg $31.93
Grades: 4 5 6 7   599.8
  1. Apes 2. Endangered species
  ISBN 978-0-7660-3456-3 lib bdg; 0-7660-3456-9 lib bdg
                                          LC 2008048691
This describes the great apes—their life cycle, habitats, young, and why these animals are endangered

"The illustrations, mostly color photographs, represent a wonderful selection of the animals and their habitats. Reluctant readers may be enticed by this . . . simply because of the great images." Libr Media Connect

Includes glossary and bibliographical references

Bodden, Valerie
  Monkeys. Creative Education 2010 24p il (Amazing animals) lib bdg $24.25
Grades: K 1 2   599.8
  1. Monkeys
  ISBN 978-1-58341-808-6 lib bdg; 1-58341-808-3 lib bdg
                                          LC 2009002710
A basic exploration of the appearance, behavior, and habitat of monkeys, a family of tree-climbing mammals. Also included is a story from folklore explaining why monkeys look like people.

Includes bibliographical references

Bow, Patricia
  Chimpanzee rescue; changing the future for endangered wildlife. Firefly Books 2004 64p il (Firefly animal rescue series) $19.95; pa $9.95
Grades: 5 6 7 8   599.8
  1. Chimpanzees 2. Wildlife conservation
  ISBN 1-55297-909-1; 1-55297-908-3 pa
This introduces chimpanzees, how and why they are in danger, and explains what efforts are being made to protect them.

This is "well-written. . . . Stunning, full-color photographs bring [this] species to life and depict a number of individuals in the field and laboratory working to save these animals." SLJ

Bredeson, Carmen
  Orangutans up close; [by] Carmen Bredeson. Enslow Elementary 2008 24p il (Zoom in on animals!) lib bdg $21.26
Grades: 1 2 3   599.8
  1. Orangutan
  ISBN 978-0-7660-3078-7 lib bdg; 0-7660-3078-4 lib bdg
                                          LC 2007039466
"Short paragraphs of simply written text describe [orangutans'] key body parts and how they function. . . . Behavior, diet, and care and development of the young are briefly addressed. Facing the text on each spread is a full-page, sharp, color closeup. . . . Bredeson's simply written and colorful [title] will provide younger readers with [a] satisfying first [introduction] to these fascinating creatures." SLJ

Includes glossary and bibliographical references

Bustos, Eduardo

Going ape! Eduardo Bustos. Tundra Books of Northern New York 2012 24 p. col. ill. (hardcover) $9.95

Grades: K 1 2   **599.8**

1. Apes 2. Monkeys 3. Gorillas 4. Primates

ISBN 1770492828; 9781770492820

LC 2011923289

In this book, "[Eduardo] Bustos offers simple facts about a variety of primates, from the well-known gorilla to the lesser-known De Brazza's monkey." The illustrations offer "large close-ups of face of the different apes on the recto, and one or two sentences and a smaller illustration of each one on the verso." (School Library Journal)

Coxon, Michele

Termites on a stick; a chimp learns to use a tool. by Michèle Coxon. Star Bright Books 2008 un il $17.95; pa $7.95

Grades: PreK K 1 2   **599.8**

1. Termites 2. Chimpanzees

ISBN 978-1-59572-121-1; 1-59572-121-5; 978-1-59572-183-9 pa; 1-59572-183-5 pa

"A young chimpanzee is rewarded with a tasty treat once he figures out how to fish termites out of their nest. Simple text and realistic paintings follow Little Chimp and his mother through a day in which the youngster emulates his mother's use of a handy tool. . . . Carefully crafted, this picture-book introduction to tool-using chimps could work as a read-aloud story or as independent reading." SLJ

Ganeri, Anita

Howler monkey. Heinemann Library 2011 24p il map (A day in the life. Rain forest animals) lib bdg $22; pa $6.49

Grades: 1 2   **599.8**

1. Monkeys

ISBN 978-1-4329-4113-0 lib bdg; 1-4329-4113-5 lib bdg; 978-1-4329-4124-6 pa; 1-4329-4124-0 pa

LC 2010001137

This book follows a day in the life of a howler monkey.

"Ganeri presents information clearly and simply in large type, two-sentence comments placed below a bright, sharply reproduced color photograph of the animal in a natural setting. . . . [This is] sufficiently specific to support assignment as well as pleasure reading." SLJ

Includes glossary and bibliographical references

Lemur. Heinemann Library 2011 24p il map (A day in the life. Rain forest animals) lib bdg $22; pa $6.49

Grades: 1 2   **599.8**

1. Lemurs

ISBN 978-1-4329-4111-6 lib bdg; 1-4329-4111-9 lib bdg; 978-1-4329-4122-2 pa; 1-4329-4122-4 pa

LC 2010001134

This book follows a lemur through its day as it sleeps, eats, and moves.

"Ganeri presents information clearly and simply in large type, two-sentence comments placed below a bright, sharply reproduced color photograph of the animal in a natural setting. . . . [This is] sufficiently specific to support assignment as well as pleasure reading." SLJ

Includes glossary and bibliographical references

Orangutan. Heinemann Library 2011 24p il map (A day in the life. Rain forest animals) lib bdg $22; pa $6.49

Grades: 1 2   **599.8**

1. Orangutan

ISBN 978-1-4329-4107-9 lib bdg; 1-4329-4107-0 lib bdg; 978-1-4329-4118-5 pa; 1-4329-4118-6 pa

LC 2010000966

This book follows an orangutan through its day as it sleeps, eats, and moves.

"Ganeri presents information clearly and simply in large type, two-sentence comments placed below a bright, sharply reproduced color photograph of the animal in a natural setting. . . . [This is] sufficiently specific to support assignment as well as pleasure reading." SLJ

Includes glossary and bibliographical references

Gibbons, Gail

Gorillas. Holiday House 2010 32p il map $17.95

Grades: K 1 2 3   **599.8**

1. Gorillas

ISBN 978-0-8234-2236-4; 0-8234-2236-4

LC 2010012418

"In her familiar, winning style, Gibbons introduces wild gorillas. Through detailed watercolor illustrations, she takes readers to Africa to explore the habitat and diet of the western lowland, eastern lowland, and mountain gorillas. . . . Readers will enjoy examining the many inset diagrams and maps that accompany the informational text , and they're sure to find Gibbons's 'extras,' like the skeletal view of a gorilla's jaw, fascinating." SLJ

Gish, Melissa

Gorillas. Creative Education 2010 46p il (Living wild) $23.95; pa $9.95

Grades: 5 6 7 8   **599.8**

1. Gorillas

ISBN 978-1-58341-969-4; 1-58341-969-1; 978-0-89812-552-8 pa; 0-89812-552-9 pa

LC 2010017374

This "book lucidly discusses conservation and the animals' often tenuous relationship with humans. The layout is uniformly simple but effective, constructed with a nice balance of main text for the report writers, smaller chunks of esoterica for browsers, and . . . killer photos." Booklist

Goodall, Jane, 1934-

Chimpanzee Children of Gombe; by Jane Goodall; photography by Michael Neugebauer. minedition 2014 64 p. color illustrations $19.99

Grades: K 1 2 3   **599.8**

1. Chimpanzees 2. Endangered species 3. Chimpanzees -- behavior

ISBN 9789888240838; 9888240838

This book, by Jane Goodall, with photography by Michael Neugebauer, shares "stories and photos of chimpanzee children living in the Gombe National Park. . . . Dr. Goodall has campaigned unceasingly for the protection of the chimpanzee—now an endangered species—and this moving, personal account will educate readers about the many threats to the animals in the wild and inspire readers of all ages to join in her vital work." (Publisher's note)

"Goodall introduces and reflects on the chimpanzees of the Gombe National Park that she has known and studied, describing the structure and dynamics of chimpanzee families and considering the ways human and chimpanzee social relationships are similar...Absorbing photographs from publisher Neugebauer provide intimate glimpses of baby chimps playing with family members, as well as of the other animals that populate the Gombe. A lovely look at Goodall's service to the welfare of the great apes." PW

Greenberg, Daniel A.

Chimpanzees; by Dan Greenberg, with Christina Wilsdon. Marshall Cavendish Benchmark 2010 24p il map (Benchmark rockets. Animals) lib bdg $16.95
Grades: 3 4 5   599.8
1. Chimpanzees
ISBN 978-0-7614-4341-4; 0-7614-4341-X
LC 2008-52102

"The straightforward presentation of the information and the uncluttered and attractive layout make [this title] . . . good . . . for reports. Color photographs . . . are well utilized and complete a solid package." SLJ

Includes glossary and bibliographical references

Jenkins, Martin

★ Ape; illustrated by Vicky White. Candlewick Press 2007 45p il $16.99
Grades: K 1 2 3   599.8
1. Apes
ISBN 978-0-7636-3471-1; 0-7636-3471-9
LC 2007023456

Close-up illustrations and facts about five great apes: chimps, orangutans, bonobos, gorillas, and humans.

"Working in oil and pencil, White portrays [the apes] . . . as having psychologically complex, fully realized personalities. The pictures are consistently stunning. . . . Jenkins's . . . economical, conservation-oriented text ably sets each scene . . . while occasional captions add information about the apes' habitat or behavior." Publ Wkly

Laman, Tim

★ Face to face with orangutans; by Tim Laman & Cheryl Knott. National Geographic 2009 31p il (Face to face) $16.95; lib bdg $25.90
Grades: 3 4 5 6   599.8
1. Orangutan
ISBN 978-1-4263-0464-4; 1-4263-0464-1; 978-1-4263-0465-1 lib bdg; 1-4263-0465-X lib bdg
LC 2009-00170

The authors describe orangutan behavior and their personal encounters with orangutans in Borneo.

Includes glossary and bibliographical references

Mattern, Joanne

Orangutans. Capstone Press 2010 24p il map (Pebble plus. Asian animals) lib bdg $22.65
Grades: PreK K 1   599.8
1. Orangutan
ISBN 978-1-4296-4030-5; 1-4296-4030-8

"This . . . is an excellent resource for great pictures and information to share with students in storytimes or to support other content areas. This will be an excellent addition to nonfiction collections, especially for young readers." Libr Media Connect

Includes bibliographical references (p. 23)

Nichols, Michael

★ Face to face with gorillas; by Michael "Nick" Nichols with Elizabeth Carney. National Geographic 2009 31p il map (Face to face) $16.95; lib bdg $25.90
Grades: 3 4 5 6   599.8
1. Gorillas
ISBN 978-1-4263-0406-4; 1-4263-0406-4; 978-1-4263-0407-1 lib bdg; 1-4263-0407-2 lib bdg
LC 2008023002

"Nichols has spent much of his life raising awareness about the plight of gorillas, and through brief text and accompanying photographs he shares some of his experiences as well as information about their family structure, habits, habitats, and connections to humans. . . . The attractive format will appeal to the intended audience." Booklist

Includes glossary and bibliographical references

Ottaviani, Jim

Primates; The Fearless Science of Jane Goodall, Dian Fossey, and Biruté Galdikas. Jim Ottaviani; illustrated by Maris Wicks. First edition First Second 2013 133 p. chiefly color illustrations (hardcover) $19.99
Grades: 5 6 7 8 9 10   599.8
1. Scientists -- Biography
ISBN 1596438657; 9781596438651
LC 2013427678

This nonfiction graphic novel, by Jim Ottaviani, illustrated by Maris Wicks, presents an "account of the three greatest primatologists of the last century: Jane Goodall, Dian Fossey, and Biruté Galdikas. These three ground-breaking researchers were all students of the great Louis Leakey, and each made profound contributions to primatology--and to our own understanding of ourselves." (Publisher's note)

"More story than study, the book provides an accessible introduction to Goodall's, Fossey's and Galdikas' lives and work." Kirkus

Includes bibliographical references, page 138

Rockwood, Leigh

Chimpanzees are smart! PowerKids Press 2010 24p il (Super smart animals) lib bdg $21.25; pa $8.25
Grades: 2 3 4 5   599.8
1. Chimpanzees
ISBN 978-1-4358-9375-7 lib bdg; 1-4358-9375-1 lib bdg; 978-1-4358-9840-0 pa; 1-4358-9840-0 pa
This book examines the intelligence of chimpanzees.

"Readers get an overview of the . . . [chimpanzee's] life cycle, its domestic history (where relevant), and natural habitat, and examples of how it is smart in the wild as well as when helped by human tutelage. . . . Interesting color photographs and large, easy-to-read print will attract browsers and report writers alike." SLJ

Includes glossary

Sayre, April Pulley

Meet the howlers; illustrated by Woody Miller. Charlesbridge 2010 un il lib bdg $16.95
Grades: K 1 2   599.8
1. Monkeys
ISBN 978-1-57091-733-2 lib bdg; 1-57091-733-7 lib bdg
LC 2009-3953

"Sayre's . . . latest is a rhyming introduction to the howler monkeys of Central and South America. Verses appear in a jaunty typeface atop . . . Miller's full-bleed spreads; prose paragraphs in smaller type provide additional information. . . . A solid read-aloud for young animal enthusiasts." Publ Wkly

Schindel, John

Busy gorillas; [by] John Schindel, Andy Rouse. Tricycle Press 2010 un il (A busy book) bd bk $6.99

Grades: PreK   599.8

1. Gorillas 2. Board books for children

ISBN 978-1-58246-352-0 bd bk; 1-58246-352-2 bd bk

Simple text and color photographs describe gorillas participating in various activities.

"Intimate close-ups of winsome baby faces and blurred, movement-filled action photos combine with more standard longshots of our primate cousins. Playfully active text . . . and vivid color-block backgrounds help to keep the necessarily limited palette . . . sparkling. Another standout." Kirkus

599.813   Primates – Infancy

Kalman, Bobbie

Baby primates; by Bobbie Kalman. Crabtree Publishing Company 2013 24 p. (library) $22.60; (paperback) $6.95

Grades: 1 2 3 4   599.813

1. Primates 2. Habitat (Ecology) 3. Primates -- Infancy

ISBN 0778710076; 9780778710073; 9780778710110

LC 2012043728

In this book by Bobbie Kalman "simple text and captivating photos inform young readers about [primates] and the different groups to which they belong, including monkeys, apes, humans, lemurs, and more. Children will also learn about the habitats of baby primates and why some are endangered." (Publisher's note)

Includes bibliographical references and index.

599.88   Great apes and gibbons

Antle, Bhagavan

The **tiger** cubs and the chimp; the true story of how Anjana the chimp helped raise two baby tigers. written and illustrated by Bhagavan Antle. Henry Holt and Co. 2013 32 p. (hardcover) $16.99

Grades: K 1 2   599.88

1. Tigers 2. Chimpanzees 3. Animal sanctuaries 4. Tiger cubs 5. Chimpanzees -- Behavior

ISBN 0805093192; 9780805093193

LC 2012047320

In this book by Bhagavan, "when two baby white tigers on an animal preserve get into trouble during a storm, they are taken in by a human animal worker named China and her helper, a chimpanzee named Anjana. China and Anjana soon become the tigers' mothers. Set on a preserve for endangered animals, The Institute of Greatly Endangered and Rare Species (T.I.G.E.R.S.), Anjana's amazing true story showcases her surprising love for two adorable tiger cubs." (Publisher's note)

599.884   Gorillas

Applegate, Katherine

Ivan; the remarkable true story of the shopping mall gorilla. written by Katherine Applegate; illustrated by G. Brian Karas. Clarion Books, Houghton Mifflin Harcourt 2014 40 p. illustrations (chiefly color) (hardcover) $17.99

Grades: K 1 2 3   599.884

1. Gorillas 2. Animal welfare 3. Animal rescue -- Fiction 4. Shopping centers and malls 5. Animal rescue 6. Tacoma (Wash.) 7. Shopping malls -- Washington (State) -- Tacoma

ISBN 0544252306; 9780544252301

LC 2013043952

This children's book, by Katherine Applegate and illustrated by G. Brian Karas, is the "real story of a special gorilla. Captured as a baby, Ivan was brought to a Tacoma, Washington, mall to attract shoppers. Gradually, public pressure built until a better way of life for Ivan was found at Zoo Atlanta." (Publisher's note)

"Applegate introduces picture-book readers to the true story that inspired her Newbery-winning The One and Only Ivan. In poetic prose she describes gorilla Ivan's early life in Africa; his dramatic capture; his time on display in a shopping mall; and his transition to the Atlanta Zoo. Karas's mixed-media illustrations--in his warm and unaffected style--are at once straightforward and provocative." Horn Book

Eszterhas, Suzi

Gorilla. Frances Lincoln Children's Books 2012 32 p. col. ill. (hbk.) $15.99; (hbk.) $15.99

Grades: K 1 2   599.884

1. Gorillas 2. Wildlife photography

ISBN 1847802990; 9781847802996

This book, the first in the "Eye on the Wild series . . . follows a newborn gorilla from birth to age 6, the age of maturity, although the majority focuses on her first two years of life. From nestling in her mother's arms and napping to sucking her thumb and drinking her mother's milk . . . [Suzi] Esterhas . . . slightly anthropomorphiz[es] the actions, feelings and intentions of her subjects . . . Backmatter offers children more facts about gorillas, along with a website for more information." (Kirkus Reviews)

Riggs, Kate

Gorillas; by Kate Riggs. Creative Education 2012 24 p. col. ill.

Grades: K 1 2   599.884

1. Gorillas 2. Animal behavior 3. Habitat (Ecology) 4. Animals -- Folklore 5. Zoology -- Encyclopedias

ISBN 1608181073; 9781608181070

LC 2010049121

This children's book is part of Kate Riggs' illustrated "Amazing Animals" series, which presents "general facts about physiology, behaviors, eating habits, habitats, and life spans. . . . In 'Gorillas,' an African story answers the arguably accurate question, 'Why do gorillas do nothing but eat and sleep all day long?' Legend has it that they tried to help after a flood but goofed up so badly that they quit doing just about everything ever since." (Booklist) "A basic exploration of the appearance, behavior, and habitat of gorillas, Earth's largest apes." (Publisher's note)

"The books' easy-reading text will be a boon to both beginning and struggling readers, and the beautiful photos are inviting enough to linger over." Booklist

Includes bibliographical references (p. 24) and index

599.9 Humans

Szpirglas, Jeff

You just can't help it! your guide to the wild and wacky world of human behavior. Josh Holinaty, illustrator. Owlkids Books 2011 64p il $22.95; pa $10.95

Grades: 4 5 6 7 **599.9**

1. Human behavior 2. Human biology

ISBN 1-926818-07-5; 1-926818-08-3 pa; 978-1-926818-07-8; 978-1-926818-08-5 pa

"How many times have you been frightened and felt the hairs on the back of your neck stand up? Or been unable to hold back a laugh? Or flinched when an object whizzed by, too close for comfort? . . . [This] book provides a cultural, historical, and sociobiological perspective on human behavior. . . . [It is an] exploration of the basic human biology that determines our reactions, social interactions, and the ways we communicate with one another." (Publisher's note) Index. "Ages nine to twelve." (Quill Quire)

This is a "collection of curious facts and intriguing studies about human behavior. With a breezy text supported by a lively design, the author . . . presents science in a way certain to attract middle-grade and middle-school readers. Chapters on the senses, emotions, communication, and interactions with other human beings cover a variety of topics. . . . The digital art includes bits of photographs, line drawings, the use of color and shapes to help organize the print and plenty of symbols." Kirkus

Includes index

599.93 Genetics, sex and age characteristics, evolution

Goldenberg, Linda

★ **Little** people and a lost world; an anthropological mystery. Twenty-First Century Books 2007 112p il (Discovery!) lib bdg $31.93

Grades: 5 6 7 8 **599.93**

1. Pygmies 2. Fossil hominids 3. Excavations (Archeology) -- Indonesia

ISBN 978-0-8225-5983-2 lib bdg; 0-8225-5983-8 lib bdg

LC 2005-33431

This is an account of the 2003 discovery of small fossil hominids on Flores Island, Indonesia

"This will add important insights to the study of early humans as well as, more broadly, how science and politics interact." Booklist

Includes bibliographical references

Tattersall, Ian

★ **Bones,** brains and DNA; the human genome and human evolution. by Ian Tattersall & Rob DeSalle; illustrated by Patricia J. Wynne. Bunker Hill Pub., Inc. 2007 47p il $16.95

Grades: 5 6 7 8 **599.93**

1. Genetics 2. Evolution 3. Human origins

ISBN 978-1-59373-056-7; 1-59373-056-X

LC 2006931578

The "text follows the trail of human evolution, basing its factual content on current data exhibited in the New Hall of Human Origins in New York City's American Museum of Natural History. Using the skills of anthropologists, archaeologists, and paleontologists, the authors track clues laid down in the fossil record, and, more importantly, in our DNA. . . . The very unsimple concepts are presented clearly, in an attractive format, with splashings of small photos, colorful artwork, diagrams, and maps to attract the eye and elucidate the text." SLJ

Thimmesh, Catherine

★ **Lucy** long ago; uncovering the mystery of where we came from. Houghton Mifflin Harcourt 2009 63p il $18

Grades: 4 5 6 7 **599.93**

1. Human origins 2. Fossil hominids

ISBN 978-0-547-05199-4; 0-547-05199-9

LC 2008-36761

"The 1974 discovery of the fossilized partial skeleton of a small-brained primate who apparently walked upright 3.2 million years ago in what is now Ethiopia significantly changed accepted theories about human origins. Step by step, Thimmesh presents the questions the newly discovered bones raised and how they were answered. . . . Extensive research, clear organization and writing, appropriate pacing for new ideas and intriguing graphics all contribute to this exceptionally accessible introduction to the mystery of human origins." Kirkus

600 TECHNOLOGY

600 Technology (Applied sciences)

Biskup, Agnieszka

Batman science; the real-world science behind Batman's gear. by Agnieszka Biskup and Tammy Enz; Batman created by Bob Kane. Capstone Press Inc. 2014 144 p. color illustrations (pbk.) $9.95

Grades: 4 5 6 7 **600**

1. Batman (Fictional character) 2. Technology -- Comic books, strips, etc. 3. Inventions 4. Technology 5. Batman (Comic strip) 6. Crime prevention -- Technological innovations

ISBN 1623700647; 9781623700645

LC 2013028330

This book, by Agnieszka Biskup and Tammy Enz, presents "the real-world science behind Batman's gear. . . . When it comes to fighting crime, technology is Batman's greatest weapon. From his gadget-packed Utility Belt to his high-tech Batmobile, the Dark Knight tackles Gotham's criminal underworld. But does any of his gear have a basis in reality? Or is it merely the stuff of fiction?" (Publisher's note)

Enz, Tammy

Repurpose it; invent new uses for old stuff. by Tammy Enz. Capstone Press 2012 32 p. col. ill. (Fact finders. Invent it) (library) $26.65

Grades: 3 4 5   600

1. Recycling 2. Art 3. Recycling (Waste, etc.) 4. Refuse and refuse disposal 5. Conservation of natural resources 6. Conservation projects (Natural resources)
ISBN 1429676361; 9781429676366

LC 2011028738

This book by Tammy Enz is part of the Invent It series "focuses on using basic engineering skills—and your own imagination—to repurpose garbage. After leading readers through the 'Six Steps of Inventing,' the book offers step-by-step numbered instructions for seven do-it-yourself projects." Examples of projects include plastic bag rain ponchos and out-of-date textbooks as hollowed-out hiding places. (Booklist)

Includes bibliographical references and index

Macaulay, David

The **new** way things work; [by] David Macaulay with Neil Ardley. Houghton Mifflin 1998 400p il $35
Grades: 4 5 6 7 8 9 10 11 12 Adult   600

1. Machinery 2. Inventions 3. Technology
ISBN 0-395-93847-3

LC 98-14224

First published 1988 with title: The way things work

Arranged in five sections this volume provides information on "the workings of hundreds of machines and devices—holograms, helicopters, airplanes, mobile phones, compact disks, hard disks, bits and bytes, cash machines. . . . Explanations [are also given] of the scientific principles behind each machine—how gears make work easier, why jumbo jets are able to fly, how computers actually compute." Publisher's note

Piddock, Charles

Future tech; from personal robots to motorized monocycles. by Charles Piddock; Dr. James Lee, consultant. National Geographic 2009 64p il (National Geographic investigates) $17.95
Grades: 5 6 7 8   600

1. Technology 2. Forecasting
ISBN 978-1-4263-0468-2; 1-4263-0468-4

"This effort takes an appreciative, uncritical look at robots, transportation, bionics, nanotechnology and future life in general. It concludes with ten specific predictions for 2025. . . . Interesting color photographs appear on almost every page and entertaining text boxes with additional related information add appeal." Kirkus

Includes glossary and bibliographical references

Solway, Andrew

Inventions and investigations. Raintree 2008 48p il (Sci-hi: physical science) lib bdg $22; pa $8.99
Grades: 5 6 7 8   600

1. Inventors 2. Inventions
ISBN 978-1-4109-3379-9 lib bdg; 1-4109-3379-2 lib bdg; 978-1-4109-3384-3 pa; 1-4109-3384-9 pa

LC 2009-3508

This explores the scientific processes used by inventors throughout history.

A "compelling read for both browsers and science buffs. . . . Information is clearly presented and flows smoothly. . . . A treasure trove of information." SLJ

Includes glossary and bibliographical references

Woodford, Chris

★ **Cool** Stuff 2.0 and how it works; written by Chris Woodford and Jon Woodcock. DK Pub. 2007 256p il $24.99
Grades: 5 6 7 8 9 10   600

1. Inventions 2. Technology
ISBN 978-0-7566-3207-6; 0-7566-3207-2

LC 2007-299442

"More than 100 entries present a wide variety of topics with high child appeal, from robot cars to high-tech toilets. . . . Full but uncluttered layouts mix photos, text boxes, diagrams, and captions to highlight key elements. . . . Readers should have an easy time understanding the basics of what each item does, how it is used, and how it works. Along with up-to-date scientific information on high-interest topics, this title has very strong browsing appeal and great booktalk potential." SLJ

Zuckerman, Amy

2030; a day in the life of tomorrow's kids. [by] Amy Zuckerman and James Daly; illustrated by John Manders. Dutton Children's Books 2009 un il $16.99
Grades: K 1 2 3   600

1. Technology 2. Forecasting
ISBN 978-0-525-47860-7; 0-525-47860-4

LC 2008-14606

"A talking dog, a housecleaning robot, and a three-dimensional data orb" are among the many cool features that kids might enjoy in the future, according to this lighthearted look at 2030. The breezy narrative follows one boy through a typical day, highlighting many interesting aspects of his world. Fanciful cartoon drawings show a lively and appealing world full of new and intriguing activities that correspond neatly to modern equivalents." SLJ

608 Patents

Lee, Dora

Biomimicry; Inventions inspired by nature. written by Dora Lee; illustrated by Margot Thompson. Kids Can Press 2011 40 p. $18.95
Grades: 4 5 6   608

1. Inventions 2. Nature study 3. Human ecology 4. Technological innovations
ISBN 9781554534678

This book explores "modern innovations [that] have sprung from observation and imitation of the natural world. In topically organized double-page spreads, [Dora] Lee describes shapes and structures, materials and designs, as well as systems for exploration, communication, rescue and delivery. . . . Three or four specific examples, each with illustrative vignettes, follow or sometimes precede the general explanation. These topics range widely and include medical marvels, new power sources, [and] biological computers and robots. . . . [The book] includes a strong ecological message: The most important natural model is the sustainable ecosystem. Through biomimicry, humans can learn to live in balance on the Earth as well." (Kirkus)

St. George, Judith

★ **So** you want to be an inventor? illustrated by David Small. Philomel Bks. 2002 53p il $16.99; pa $7.99

Grades: 3 4 5 6   **608**
1. Inventors 2. Inventions
ISBN 0-399-23593-0; 0-14-240460-8 pa
       LC 2001-55447
Presents some of the characteristics of inventors by describing the inventions of people such as Alexander Graham Bell, Thomas Edison, and Eli Whitney
"St. George and Small take a skewed, funny, and informative look at the history of inventions and their inventors and what it takes to become one. . . . Small's lively, fluid caricatures make for a winning collaboration." SLJ
Includes bibliographical references

609   History, geographic treatment, biography

Barretta, Gene
Neo Leo; the ageless ideas of Leonardo da Vinci. Henry Holt & Co. 2009 un il
Grades: 2 3 4 5   **609**
1. Artists 2. Painters 3. Inventors 4. Scientists 5. Writers on science 6. Inventions -- History
ISBN 0805087036; 9780805087031
       LC 2008038220
"This book focuses on sketches found in Leonardo's writings that reveal an understanding of inventions that would not come into being until hundreds of years after the death of this quintessential Renaissance man. Vivid watercolor illustrations depict more than a dozen, including the hang glider, contact lenses, the tank, and robots. . . . Barretta provides clear information without veering into scientific explanations." SLJ
Includes bibliographical references

Now & Ben; the modern inventions of Benjamin Franklin. by Gene Barretta. Henry Holt & Co. 2006 un il $16.95
Grades: 2 3 4 5   **609**
1. Authors 2. Diplomats 3. Inventors 4. Statesmen 5. Inventions 6. Scientists 7. Writers on science 8. Members of Congress
ISBN 978-0-8050-7917-3; 0-8050-7917-3
       LC 2005012491
"This humorous book covers twenty-two inventions, first by showing their use in today's world . . . and a second by explaining Franklin's role in their development. . . . Read this one aloud; the busy cartoon illustrations offer plenty for listeners to contemplate." Horn Book Guide
Includes bibliographical references

Becker, Helaine
What's the big idea? inventions that changed life on Earth forever. illustrated by Steve Attoe. Maple Tree Press 2010 96p il $27.95; pa $17.95
Grades: 3 4 5 6   **609**
1. Inventions -- History
ISBN 978-1-897349-60-1; 1-897349-60-2; 978-1-897349-61-8 pa; 1-897349-61-0 pa
This book shares the big ideas behind more than thirty of the world's greatest innovations
"Identifying significant inventions in a historic timeline, this book has wonderful kid appeal. It begins with prehistory to the Middle Ages, advancing to the 1900s, finishing with not so long ago. . . . Information is displayed in short paragraphs making it easier to read than many invention books. . . . Author Helaine Becker does an excellent job of crediting diverse cultural and female contributions known or presumed." Libr Media Connect

Bender, Lionel
Invention; written by Lionel Bender. rev ed; DK Pub. 2005 72p il (DK eyewitness books) $15.99; lib bdg $19.99
Grades: 4 5 6 7   **609**
1. Inventions
ISBN 0-7566-1076-1; 0-7566-1075-3 lib bdg
First published 1991 by Knopf
Photographs and text explore such inventions as the wheel, gears, levers, clocks, telephones, and rocket engines.

Crowther, Robert
Robert Crowther's pop-up house of inventions; hundreds of fabulous facts about your home. Candlewick Press 2009 un il $17.99
Grades: 4 5 6 7   **609**
1. Inventions 2. Pop-up books
ISBN 978-0-7636-4253-2; 0-7636-4253-3
First published 2000 with title: Robert Crowther's amazing pop-up house of inventions
"As a beautifully engineered pop-up book, it is complex, highly visual, and inviting. . . . . It is also durably manufactured. . . . The book is essentially an encyclopedic assortment of facts and anecdotes about the earliest forms of household appliances, furnishings, novelties, . . . games, clothing, and consumables such as soap, soda and candles. The author integrates history and science in a chatty, colorful, and humorous way that quickly draws readers into his subject." Sci Books Films

Harper, Charise Mericle
Imaginative inventions; the who, what, where, when, and why of roller skates, potato chips, marbles, and pie and more! Little, Brown 2001 32p il $14.95
Grades: K 1 2 3   **609**
1. Inventions
ISBN 0-316-34725-6
       LC 00-62443
This "volume explains how such everyday items as gum, roller skates and potato chips came to be, describing each item in doggerel verse. With its crazy-quilt visual patterns, bouncy stanzas and fun facts, this collection of miscellany zigzags between informational and whimsical." Publ Wkly

Jedicke, Peter
Great inventions of the 20th century; by Peter Jedicke. Chelsea House 2007 72p il (Scientific American) $30
Grades: 5 6 7 8   **609**
1. Inventions -- History 2. Technology -- History
ISBN 978-0-7910-9048-0; 0-7910-9048-5
       LC 2006014773
"The text is simple, clear, and concise. . . . [The book has] captioned color photos throughout." SLJ
This "presents a celebration of the inventors and inventions that transformed the world during the age of technology. Topics presented include cellophane, the microwave oven, liquid-filled rockets, ultrasound, and robotic machines, among many others." Publisher's note
Includes glossary and bibliographical references

Landau, Elaine

The history of everyday life. 21st Century Bks. 2005
56p il (Major inventions through history) $26.60
Grades: 5 6 7 8   **609**
1. Inventions -- History
ISBN 0-8225-3808-3

This "explores fireplaces and central heating, indoor
plumbing, the washing machine, food and clothing production, and microwave ovens. . . . [It] presents information
about daily living from ancient times to the present. . . . The
text . . . is breezy but informative. . . . Illustrations are a
mixture of period black-and-white and color photos." SLJ

Includes bibligraphical references

Lee, Richard B.

Africans thought of it! amazing innovations. [by]
Bathseba Opini [and] Richard B. Lee. Annick Press 2011
48p il (We thought of it) $21.95; pa $11.95
Grades: 3 4 5 6   **609**
1. Inventions 2. Africa -- Civilization
ISBN 978-1-55451-277-5; 1-55451-277-8; 978-1-
55451-276-8 pa; 1-55451-276-X pa

Describes the inventions created by the peoples of Africa
in hunting, agriculture, architecture, metalwork, medicine,
the arts, and other fields, and how they have spread through
the world and continue to fit into modern African civilization.

"Vivid photographs feature authentic objects used . . .
while people engaged in activities capture an enthusiastic
look at the reliance on community. Colored backgrounds
and borders present a busy, though uncluttered, dynamic
portrayal of nuanced cultures. . . . Succinct definitions and
compact descriptions provide a brief and interesting blend of
the contemporary with the traditional." SLJ

Robinson, James

Inventions; foreword by James Dyson. Kingfisher
2006 63p il (Kingfisher knowledge) $12.95
Grades: 5 6 7 8   **609**
1. Inventions -- History 2. Technology -- History
ISBN 978-0-7534-5973-7; 0-7534-5973-6

"A slim, colorful overview of inventions." Kirkus
Includes glossary

Rossi, Ann

★ Bright ideas; the age of invention in America,
1870-1910. [by] Ann Rossi. National Geographic 2005
40p il (Crossroads America) $12.95
Grades: 4 5 6   **609**
1. Inventions -- History
ISBN 0-7922-8276-0
        LC 2003-19834

This describes the history of late 19th and early 20th
century inventions such as the light bulb, the telegraph, the
telephone, and the automobile.

This "solid [title] for report writers may even pull in a
few curious browsers because of [its] plentiful, full-color
photos and reproductions. The [layout is] inviting, and the
[text is] clear, informative, and readable." SLJ
Includes glossary

Ye, Ting-xing

The Chinese thought of it; amazing inventions and innovations. Annick Press 2009 48p il map (We thought of
it) $19.95; pa $9.95

Grades: 5 6 7 8   **609**
1. China -- Civilization 2. Inventions -- History 3.
Technology -- History
ISBN 978-1-55451-196-9; 1-55451-196-8; 978-1-
55451-195-2 pa; 1-55451-195-X pa

In this survey of Chinese inventions "at least one double-
page spread is devoted to each of the eleven topics: farming,
working with metal, transportation and exploration, canals
and bridges, weapons and warfare, paper and printing, silk,
and everyday innovations. . . . The layout of the book is appealing and just right for quick reading or browsing. . . . The
author's personal story about her childhood in Shanghai effectively draws the reader in." Voice Youth Advocates

Includes bibliographical references

610   Medicine and health

Auden, Scott

Medical mysteries; science researches conditions from
bizarre to deadly. by Scott Auden; Elizabeth Brownell, consultant. National Geographic 2008 64p il (National Geographic investigates) $17.95; lib bdg $27.90
Grades: 4 5 6 7   **610**
1. Diseases 2. Medicine -- Research
ISBN 978-1-4263-0356-2; 1-4263-0356-4; 978-1-
4263-0261-9 lib bdg; 1-4263-0261-4 lib bdg

This title features "full-color photographs that readers
have come to expect from this publisher. . . . [It] focuses on
diseases that are regarded as bizarre and are often deadly,
including Creutzfeldt-Jakob, Progeria, and Morgellons. The
approach is to examine the way in which these mysterious
diseases were discovered and how they are being studied
to find a cure. . . . [This book offers] explanations simple
enough for middle school students but with enough content
to make them a useful resource for high school students as
well." Voice Youth Advocates

Includes glossary and bibliographical references

Bredeson, Carmen

Don't let the barber pull your teeth; could you survive
medieval medicine? illustrated by Gerald Kelley. Enslow
Publishers 2011 48p il (Ye yucky Middle Ages) lib bdg
$23.93
Grades: 3 4 5 6   **610**
1. Medieval civilization 2. Medicine -- History
ISBN 978-0-7660-3693-2
        LC 2010011898

This describes medieval medicine.
Includes glossary and bibliographical references

★ Encyclopedia of health; 4th ed.; Marshall Cavendish
2009 18v il set $514.21
Grades: 5 6 7 8 9 10   **610**
1. Reference books 2. Medicine -- Encyclopedias
ISBN 978-0-7614-7845-4; 0-7614-7845-0
        LC 2008033014

First published 1995 with title: The Marshall Cavendish
encyclopedia of health

This reference features alphabetically arranged entries
on body function; diet and nutrition; human behavior; illness, injury and disorders; and prevention and care

"Easy-to-understand language, an attractive design, and content that supports student research and interest lend value to the set." Booklist

Includes bibliographical references

Goldsmith, Connie
Cutting-edge medicine. Lerner Publications Co. 2008 48p il (Cool science) lib bdg $26.60
Grades: 4 5 6   610
1. Medicine
ISBN 978-0-8225-6770-7 lib bdg; 0-8225-6770-9 lib bdg

LC 2007001946

"This book explains the many amazing ways new medical techniques are helping people live longer, healthier lives." Publisher's note

Includes glossary and bibliographical references

Lew, Kristi
Bat spit, maggots, and other amazing medical wonders. Capstone Press 2010 32p il (Fact finders. Nasty (but useful!) science) lib bdg $25.99
Grades: 3 4 5   610
1. Medicine
ISBN 978-1-4296-4537-9 lib bdg; 1-4296-4537-7 lib bdg

This informative guide also explains "relevant chemical processes, medical rationales, and ecological functions in reasonably specific detail. . . . A list of relevant web resources is maintained on the publisher's page." SLJ

Includes glossary and bibliographical references

Murphy, Liz
ABC doctor. Blue Apple 2007 un il $15.95
Grades: PreK K 1   610
1. Medicine 2. Medical care
ISBN 978-1-593545-93-2; 1-593545-93-2

"The basics of seeing a doctor and/or nurse are . . . explained with clever, colorful collage illustrations setting the scene and clarifying the explanation. . . . Some medical tools are included. Physical conditions such as fever and vomit appear, and procedures such as a urine sample and X-ray take readers through the alphabet. Murphy has compiled an interesting array of terms to help children realize that medical professionals are there to help them." SLJ

Rooney, Anne
Health and medicine; the impact of science and technology. Gareth Stevens Pub. 2009 64p il (Pros and cons) lib bdg $35
Grades: 5 6 7 8   610
1. Health 2. Medicine 3. Medical technology
ISBN 978-1-4339-1988-6 lib bdg; 1-4339-1988-5 lib bdg

LC 2008-54133

An "active layout that features color photographs, maps, graphs or charts on every spread, this . . . [book] has much to offer. . . . It conveniently outlines the range of views . . . helping students to learn how to view both sides of [the] issue[s]." SLJ

Includes glossary and bibliographical references

Sandvold, Lynnette Brent
Revolution in medicine. Marshall Cavendish Benchmark 2010 32p il (It works!) lib bdg $19.95
Grades: 3 4 5   610
1. Medical technology 2. Medicine -- History
ISBN 978-0-7614-4376-6 lib bdg; 0-7614-4376-2 lib bdg

LC 2008-54364

"This interesting, information packed [book] . . . motivates students to do their own exploring. . . . The appealing cartoon-like photographs add humor. . . . This . . . just may be that spark needed to create eager budding scientists." Libr Media Connect

Includes glossary and bibliographical references

Singer, Marilyn
I'm getting a checkup; illustrated by David Milgrim. Clarion Books 2009 32p il $16
Grades: PreK K   610
1. Medicine 2. Medical care 3. Stories in rhyme
ISBN 978-0-618-99000-9; 0-618-99000-3

LC 2007034977

"Informative and fun, this rhyming picture book will help prepare preschoolers for a visit to the doctor's office. The digitally rendered oil-and-pastel pictures show three kids, each with a parent or caregiver, getting a checkup from three different doctors. . . . Each quick rhyme is followed by a long explanatory note. . . . The bright, cartoon-style pictures keep the visit playful." Booklist

Woolf, Alex, 1964-
Death and disease; [by] Alex Woolf. Lucent Books 2004 48p il map (Medieval realms) $29.95
Grades: 5 6 7 8   610
1. Medieval civilization 2. Medicine -- History
ISBN 1-59018-533-1

LC 2003-61797

"Clear, well-organized [text] along with full-color reproductions of art and artifacts and photos of period structures immerse readers in . . . medieval life and offer sufficient information for reports." SLJ

Includes glossary and bibliographical references

610.69 Medical personnel and relationships

Marsico, Katie
The doctor. Marshall Cavendish Benchmark 2011 il (Colonial people) $29.93
Grades: 3 4 5 6   610.69
1. Physicians 2. Medicine -- History 3. United States -- History -- 1600-1775, Colonial period
ISBN 978-1-60870-412-5; 1-60870-412-2

LC 2010033895

This descibes the life of a colonial doctor and his importance to the community, as well as everyday life, responsibilities, and social practices during that time.

This "lively [text] and colorful reproductions and photos will engage casual readers and researchers alike. . . . Large illustrations and thoughtful captions explain complicated scientific ideas. . . . [The] volume also includes step-by-step instructions for a related craft project. . . . [This is a] must-have." SLJ

Includes glossary and bibliographical references

610.73   Nursing and services of allied health personnel

Glasscock, Sarah

How nurses use math; math curriculum consultant: Rhea A. Stewart. Chelsea Clubhouse 2010 32p il (Math in the real world) lib bdg $28

Grades: 4 5 6   **610.73**

1. Nurses 2. Mathematics 3. Vocational guidance
ISBN 978-1-60413-607-4 lib bdg; 1-60413-607-3 lib bdg

LC 2009-20199

This describes how nurses use math in such tasks as giving eye tests, keeping records, taking the pulse, and measuring medicine and includes relevant math problems and information about how to become a nurse

Includes glossary and bibliographical references

Kenney, Karen Latchana

Nurses at work; by Karen L. Kenney; illustrated by Brian Caleb Dumm; content consultant, Judith Stepan-Norris. Magic Wagon 2010 32p il (Meet your community workers!) lib bdg $18.95

Grades: K 1 2 3   **610.73**

1. Nurses 2. Vocational guidance
ISBN 978-1-60270-651-4 lib bdg; 1-60270-651-4 lib bdg

LC 2009-2393

This book about nurses has "an uncluttered layout and consistent organization. . . . Chapter headings such as 'Problems on the Job' and 'Technology at Work,' and 'Special Skills and Training' make it easy to pinpoint specific information." SLJ

Includes glossary

610.82   Women in medicine

Harness, Cheryl

Mary Walker wears the pants; the true story of the doctor, reformer, and Civil War hero. Cheryl Harness; illustrated by Carlo Molinari. Albert Whitman & Co. 2013 32 p. (reinforced) $16.99

Grades: 2 3 4 5   **610.82**

1. Picture books for children 2. Women physicians 3. Physicians -- United States -- Biography 4. Suffragists -- United States -- Biography 5. Women physicians -- United States -- Biography 6. United States -- History -- Civil War, 1861-1865 -- Women 7. United States -- History -- Civil War, 1861-1865 -- Medical care
ISBN 0807549908; 9780807549902

LC 2012019531

This children's picture book focuses on the life of 19th-century "women's rights advocate, doctor, and abolitionist Mary Walker," who was "one of the first women doctors and the first woman to receive the Medal of Honor for her 'services and sufferings' during wartime." A "volunteer for the Union Army during the Civil War, her hard work and

determination finally led to her appointment as an assistant surgeon in 1863, the first woman doctor in the U.S. Army." (School Library Journal)

611   Human anatomy, cytology, histology

Allen, Kathy

The **human** head. Capstone Press 2010 32p il (Fact finders. Anatomy class) lib bdg $23.99; pa $7.95

Grades: 3 4 5   **611**

1. Head
ISBN 978-1-4296-3338-3 lib bdg; 1-4296-3338-7 lib bdg; 978-1-4296-3882-1 pa; 1-4296-3882-6 pa

LC 2009-2793

"The vivid scientific photographs . . . and micrographs . . . are a plus. . . . On-page definitions, current further-reading lists, and a webliography maintained at the publisher's FactHound Web site all add value." SLJ

Includes glossary and bibliographical references

Delafosse, Claude

Inside the body; created by Claude Delafosse and Gallimard Jeunesse; illustrated by Pierre-Marie Valat. Reprint Moonlight Pub. 2012 36 p. col. ill. (hardcover: spiral) $12.99

Grades: K 1 2   **611**

1. Picture books for children 2. Human body
ISBN 1851034129; 9781851034123

This children's picture book explores the human body. "This is a beginner's guide . . . with short sentences providing basic groundwork: 'You have a skeleton! This frame of bones helps you stay upright and move around.'" Some step-by-step diagrams are included that show "the process of digestion, the growth of a fetus, or the passing down of physical traits from parents and grandparents." (Booklist)

Gold, Susan Dudley

Learning about the respiratory system; Susan Dudley Gold. Enslow Publishers 2013 48 p. (library) $23.93

Grades: 5 6 7 8   **611**

1. Picture books for children 2. Respiratory system 3. Respiratory organs
ISBN 0766041611; 9780766041615

LC 2012011104

This book by Susan Dudley Gold is part of the Learning About the Human Body Systems series and looks at the respiratory system. She "discusses what this body system is and what organs are involved in its various processes. She discusses the potential health problems that can affect the respiratory system, such as cancer, pneumonia, and emphysema, as well as ways to keep healthy and problem-free." (Publisher's note)

Includes bibliographical references and index.

Lew, Kristi

Human organs. Capstone Press 2010 32p il (Fact finders. Anatomy class) lib bdg $23.99; pa $7.99

Grades: 3 4 5   **611**

1. Human body
ISBN 978-1-4296-3339-0 lib bdg; 1-4296-3339-5 lib bdg; 978-1-4296-3886-9 pa; 1-4296-3886-9 pa

LC 2009-2775

"The vivid scientific photographs . . . and micrographs . . . are a plus. . . . On-page definitions, current further-reading lists, and a webliography maintained at the publisher's FactHound Web site all add value." SLJ

Includes glossary and bibliographical references

Rake, Jody Sullivan

The **human** skeleton. Capstone Press 2010 32p il (Fact finders. Anatomy class) lib bdg $23.99; pa $7.95

Grades: 3 4 5 **611**

1. Bones 2. Skeleton

ISBN 978-1-4296-3340-6 lib bdg; 1-4296-3340-9 lib bdg; 978-1-4296-3888-3 pa; 1-4296-3888-5 pa

LC 2009-2771

"The vivid scientific photographs . . . and micrographs . . . are a plus. . . . On-page definitions, current further-reading lists, and a webliography maintained at the publisher's FactHound Web site all add value." SLJ

Includes glossary and bibliographical references

Wheeler-Toppen, Jodi

Human muscles. Capstone Press 2010 32p il (Fact finders. Anatomy class) lib bdg $23.99; pa $7.95

Grades: 3 4 5 **611**

1. Muscles

ISBN 978-1-4296-3341-3 lib bdg; 1-4296-3341-7 lib bdg; 978-1-4296-3884-5 pa; 1-4296-3884-2 pa

LC 2009-2766

"The vivid scientific photographs . . . and micrographs . . . are a plus. . . . On-page definitions, current further-reading lists, and a webliography maintained at the publisher's FactHound Web site all add value." SLJ

Includes glossary and bibliographical references

612 Human physiology

Aliki

My feet. Crowell 1990 31p il (Let's-read-and-find-out science book) hardcover o.p. pa $5.99

Grades: PreK K 1 **612**

1. Foot

ISBN 0-690-04815-7 lib bdg; 0-06-445106-2 pa

LC 89-49357

"An extensive discussion of feet, through simple text and playful illustration, demonstrates their parts, relative sizes, what they do, and what they wear in different seasons. Includes a handicapped child whose crutches supplement feet." Sci Child

My hands; rev ed; Crowell 1990 32p il (Let's-read-and-find-out science book) hardcover o.p. pa $5.99

Grades: PreK K 1 **612**

1. Hand

ISBN 0-690-04880-7 lib bdg; 0-06-445096-1 pa

LC 89-49158

First published 1962

The author "calls attention to hand structure—fingers, nails, an opposable thumb—and the special ways we use our hands to carry on everyday activities. . . . The jaunty illustrations and simple but efficient text combine for a fresh take on some very basic information." Booklist

Arnold, Caroline

Too hot? too cold? keeping body temperature just right. Caroline Arnold; Illustrated by Annie Patterson. Charlesbridge 2013 32 p. (reinforced) $17.95; (paperback) $7.95

Grades: 1 2 3 4 5 **612**

1. Body temperature 2. Biology 3. Body temperature -- Regulation

ISBN 1580892760; 9781580892766; 9781580892773

LC 2012000792

In this children's book, by Caroline Arnold and Annie Patterson, describes body heat regulation. "Have you ever wondered why you shiver when you're cold, or sweat when you're hot?" This book explores "the many different ways humans and animals adapt to heat and cold. The book includes [an] . . . explanation of cold-blooded and warm-blooded animals." (Publisher's note)

Bailey, Gerry

Body and health; discover science through facts and fun. by Gerry Bailey & Steve Way. Gareth Stevens Pub. 2009 32p il (Simply science) lib bdg $26

Grades: 3 4 5 **612**

1. Human body

ISBN 978-1-4339-0030-3 lib bdg; 1-4339-0030-0 lib bdg

LC 2008-27573

Along with facts that explore concepts across a wide range of topics, comic-strip illustrations present historical background information and foster modern-day science connections.

"The brightly colored cover with its montage of people and cartoon characters is a real eye-catcher. This is a wonderful little book that is packed with lots of information." Sci Books Films

Includes glossary and bibliographical references

Basher, Simon

Human body; a book with guts! by Simon Basher and Dan Green; illustrated by Simon Basher. Kingfisher 2011 128p il $14.95; pa $8.99

Grades: 5 6 7 8 **612**

1. Human body

ISBN 978-0-7534-6628-5; 0-7534-6628-7; 978-0-7534-6501-1 pa; 0-7534-6501-9 pa

"Basher brings his signature informative irreverence and smiley little cartoon icons to the world of human biology. Not a comprehensive resource, but supplemental science reading doesn't come much more fun." Booklist

Bruhn, Aron

Inside the human body; illustrations by Joel Ito and Kathleen Kemly. Sterling 2010 48p il (Inside) $19.95; pa $9.95

Grades: 4 5 6 **612**

1. Human body

ISBN 978-1-4027-7091-3; 1-4027-7091-X; 978-1-4027-7779-0 pa; 1-4027-7779-5 pa

LC 2010002503

"The illustrations in [this] cool . . . [title is] enhanced by 10 large gatefolds that allow kids to dig deeper into the topics and enjoy amazing illustrations. [The] title clearly defines fact and theory, leaving puzzles for the next generation of scientists to solve. . . . [The book] touches on each of the body systems and provides a highly detailed look at a human cell." SLJ

Includes glossary and bibliographical references

Calabresi, Linda

Human body. Simon & Schuster Books for Young Readers 2008 un il (Insiders) $16.99

Grades: 4 5 6 7   **612**

1. Human body

ISBN 978-1-4169-3861-3; 1-4169-3861-3

LC 2007-61744

This volume "offers excellent pictures of systems, organs, and even individual cells in the human body. . . . A visually dynamic introduction to the human package." Booklist

Cole, Joanna, 1944-

The **magic** school bus inside the human body; illustrated by Bruce Degen. Scholastic 1989 un il hardcover o.p.

Grades: 2 3 4   **612**

1. Human body 2. Physiology 3. Human anatomy 4. Metabolism

ISBN 0-590-41426-7; 0-590-41427-5 pa

LC 8803070

"Ms. Frizzle's class leaves on a trip to the science museum, but stops for a snack along the way. Arnold is left behind when his classmates reboard the bus. Meanwhile, Ms. Frizzle has miniaturized the bus and its riders. Unwittingly, Arnold swallows it. Traveling through Arnold's insides, the class visits his digestive system, arteries, lungs, heart, brain, and muscles, finally departing through his nostrils when he sneezes. . . . Grades two to five." (Booklist)

"This is an enjoyable look at factual material painlessly packaged with the ribbons and balloons of jokes and asides meant to appeal to kids. Degen's zany, busy, full-color drawings fill the pages with action and information far beyond the text." SLJ

Fromer, Liza

My achy body. Tundra Books 2011 un il (Body works) $14.99

Grades: 2 3 4 5   **612**

1. Pain 2. Human body 3. Wounds and injuries

ISBN 978-1-77049-204-2; 1-77049-204-6

This describes bruises, scrapes, scabs, broken bones, sprains, stomach aches, earaches, and sore throats.

Includes glossary

My messy body; [by] Liza Fromer and Francine Gerstein; illustrated by Joe Weissmann. Tundra Books 2011 un il (Body works) $12.95

Grades: 2 3 4 5   **612**

1. Human body

ISBN 978-1-77049-202-8; 1-77049-202-X

This describes the purpose of the body's secretions, including tears, sweat, snot, urine, excrement, earwax, vomit, pus, and mucus.

Includes glossary

My noisy body; [by] Liza Fromer and Francine Gerstein; illustrated by Joe Weissmann. Tundra Books 2011 un il (Body works) $12.95

Grades: 2 3 4 5   **612**

1. Human body

ISBN 978-1-77049-201-1; 1-77049-201-1

This describes the meaning of sounds the body creates, including the voice, burps, hiccups, stomach growls, farts, sneezes and coughs.

The authors explain noisy body functions "with a playful attitude and with that buffet a solid body of factual information. . . . Weissmann's squiggly paintings are amusing, . . . This . . . offers a fun, frank look at sometimes taboo topics." Booklist

Gardner, Robert

Ace your human biology science project; great science fair ideas. [by] Robert Gardner and Barbara Gardner Conklin. Enslow Publishers 2009 128p il (Ace your biology science project) lib bdg $31.93

Grades: 5 6 7 8   **612**

1. Biology 2. Science projects 3. Science -- Experiments

ISBN 978-0-7660-3219-4 lib bdg; 0-7660-3219-1 lib bdg

LC 2008-30799

"Dozens of . . . science activities are presented with background information, step-by-step instructions, and suggestions for extending to the science fair level. . . . Color illustrations and important safety information are included." Horn Book Guide

Includes bibliographical references

Goddard, Jolyon

Inside the human body. Marshall Cavendish Benchmark 2010 48p il (Invisible worlds) lib bdg $28.50

Grades: 4 5 6 7   **612**

1. Human body 2. Physiology

ISBN 978-0-7614-4190-8 lib bdg; 0-7614-4190-5 lib bdg

LC 2008037254

This describes the details of the human body that are too small for the unaided eye to see, and how these microscopic systems work to keep the body alive and healthy.

The narrative is "clear, well written, broken down into manageable pieces, and peppered with eye-opening facts. The numerous photographs are so phenomenal that they will inspire kids to read the text . . . so that they can wrap their minds around what they see." SLJ

Includes glossary and bibliographical references

Green, Dan

Human body factory; the nuts and bolts of your insides. Kingfisher 2012 48 p. $16.99

Grades: 1 2 3 4   **612**

1. Biology 2. Human body 3. Picture books for children

ISBN 0753468085; 9780753468081

This children's book describes human anatomy by comparing the body to a factory. From "the CEO sending out orders in the brain to 'waste' being sorted and delivered out of the body at the other end, the busy workers who keep everything running smoothly introduce each 'department.' All the major systems are covered, and the . . . illustrations are packed with . . . details . . . . All of this . . . artwork is backed up with . . . facts and . . . explanations of the body's essential processes." Images include "toxic signs and workers wearing biohazard suits in the large intestine, lab workers in dinghies mixing gastric juices in the stomach with a giant whisk, or park keepers on the skin keeping things clean among glades of gently swaying hairs and sweat-gland sprinklers." (Publisher's note)

Greenwood, Marie

Animals and me; [written by Marie Greenwood] DK Pub. 2010 48p il $12.99

Grades: 2 3 4 5   612

1. Human body 2. Physiology

ISBN 978-0-7566-6886-0; 0-7566-6886-7

Photographs and text examine different parts of the human body, explaining what they are for, and comparing them to the similar body parts of animals.

"The full-color photography is fantastic and clearly illustrates each point. Because of the wealth of information presented, this book would be enjoyed by browsers as well as students looking for report topics." SLJ

Lew, Kristi

Farts, vomit, and other functions that help your body. Capstone Press 2010 32p il (Fact finders. Nasty (but useful!) science) lib bdg $25.99

Grades: 3 4 5   612

1. Physiology

ISBN 978-1-4296-4539-3 lib bdg; 1-4296-4539-3 lib bdg

This informative guide also explains "relevant chemical processes, medical rationales, and ecological functions in reasonably specific detail. . . . A list of relevant web resources is maintained on the publisher's page." SLJ

Includes glossary and bibliographical references

Manning, Mick

Under your skin; your amazing body. [by] Mick Manning and Brita Granström. Albert Whitman 2007 23p il $16.95

Grades: 1 2 3   612

1. Human body

ISBN 978-0-8075-8313-5; 0-8075-8313-8

LC 2007-02350

"This well-designed introduction to human body parts and their functions features eight half-page flaps that lift up to reveal simple views of internal organs. The terminology allows for different levels of comprehension . . . and the cartoon illustrations in bright colors help make the science aproachable." Horn Book Guide

Nicolson, Cynthia Pratt

Totally human; why we look and act the way we do. illustrated by Dianne Eastman. Kids Can Press 2011 40p il $16.95

Grades: 3 4 5   612

1. Human body 2. Psychology

ISBN 978-1-55453-569-9; 1-55453-569-7

"This playful science book introduces the biology of human evolution and behavior with an accessible, interactive text packed with information and wry, bright computer graphics on each spread. . . . The wild images . . . and the detailed text reveal astonishing answers to questions readers might never have thought to ask." Booklist

Parker, Nancy Winslow

★ Organs! how they work, fall apart, and can be replaced (gasp!) Greenwillow Books 2009 48p il $17.99; lib bdg $18.89

Grades: 1 2 3 4   612

1. Human body

ISBN 978-0-688-15105-8; 0-688-15105-1; 978-0-688-15106-5 lib bdg; 0-688-15106-X lib bdg

LC 2008-20718

"This is an engaging children's textbook on human anatomy and functioning. . . . Spot illustrations, charmingly rendered in colored pencil, show people with their organs in action. . . . Author Nancy Winslow Parker admirably tackles the challenge of visualizing objects that are typically masked from everyday view. . . . This fun and lighthearted book is . . . recommend[ed] for every child's library and one that will easily become a go-to reference for many years." Sci Books Films

Podesto, Martine

The body; by Martine Podesto. Gareth Stevens Pub. 2009 104p il (My science notebook) lib bdg $31

Grades: 4 5 6   612

1. Human body

ISBN 978-0-8368-9212-3 lib bdg; 0-8368-9212-7 lib bdg

LC 2008-12428

This book answers questions about the human body

"Designed to resemble a notebook with illustrated paper clips, pasting, and tape appearing on most pages, this [book] . . . offers comprehensive information. . . . supplemented by colorful drawings, diagrams, and photographs." SLJ

Includes glossary and bibliographical references

Reilly, Kathleen M.

The human body; 25 fantastic projects illuminate how the body works. illustrated by Shawn Braley. Nomad Press 2008 120p il $21.95; pa $15.95

Grades: 5 6 7 8   612

1. Human body

ISBN 978-1-934670-25-5; 1-934670-25-1; 978-1-934670-24-8 pa; 1-934670-24-3 pa

"The workings of the human body are expertly summarized in 11 tidy chapters, which include experiments that explain how the body works by creating models that either imitate or test its functions. . . . Many of the activities require adult supervision due to the materials required. . . . Simple drawings and cartoons enliven and illuminate the text. . . . The scientific explanations are superb." SLJ

Rockwell, Lizzy

The busy body book; a kid's guide to fitness. Crown 2004 un il $15.95

Grades: K 1   612

1. Exercise 2. Physiology

ISBN 0-375-82203-8; 0-375-92203-2 lib bdg

An introduction to the human body, how it functions, and its need for exercise.

"The text is purposely motivating, yet easy to understand and informative. The age-appropriate artwork is colorful and lively, and provides just the right amount of detail." SLJ

Rotner, Shelley

Body actions; Shelley Rotner and David A. White. Holiday House 2012 32 p. (hardcover) $16.95
Grades: 1 2 3   612
1. Human body 2. Nervous system 3. Digestive system 4. Musculoskeletal system 5. Picture books for children
ISBN 0823423662; 9780823423668
LC 2011007268
This children's picture book is a "brief overview of the entire human body. The nervous, skeletal, muscular, respiratory, circulatory and digestive systems; the five senses; skin, and hair are all touched on. The full-color photographs . . . feature racially diverse children, and some of the photographs include an illustration of the body system superimposed on the child." (School Library Journal)

Seuling, Barbara

Your skin weighs more than your brain; and other freaky facts about your skin, skeleton, and other body parts. by Barbara Seuling; illustrated by Matthew Skeens. Picture Window Books 2008 40p il (Freaky facts) lib bdg $23.93; pa $4.95
Grades: 2 3 4 5   612
1. Human body
ISBN 978-1-4048-3751-5 lib bdg; 1-4048-3751-5 lib bdg; 978-1-4048-3756-0 pa; 1-4048-3756-6 pa
LC 2007004030
A collection of amazing facts and statistics about the human body
"This quick read is a light, fun, and at times fascinating collection of various facts about the human body. . . . The book is eye-catching—a convenient and kid-friendly small size, with illustrations on every couple of pages." Sci Books Films
Includes glossary and bibliographical references

Silverstein, Alvin

Snot, poop, vomit, and more; the yucky body book. [by] Alvin Silverstein, Virginia Silverstein, and Laura Silverstein Nunn; illustrated by Gerald Kelley. Enslow Publishers 2010 48p il (Yucky science) lib bdg $23.93
Grades: 3 4 5 6   612
1. Human body 2. Physiology
ISBN 978-0-7660-3318-4 lib bdg; 0-7660-3318-X lib bdg
LC 2009012280
"Explores 'Yucky' things about the human body, including earwax, gas, bodily wastes, and more" Publisher's note
Includes bibliographical references

Somervill, Barbara A.

★ The **human** body. Gareth Stevens Pub. 2008 48p il (Gareth Stevens vital science: life science) lib bdg $26.60; pa $11.95
Grades: 5 6 7 8   612
1. Human body
ISBN 978-0-8368-8441-8 lib bdg; 978-0-8368-8450-0 pa
LC 2007-16175
First published 2006 in the United Kingdom
This describes "human anatomy and physiology. . . . Factoids are scattered throughout the text in a fashion that captures the reader's attention and interest. . . . [The book offers] excellent graphics, namely photos and diagrams. The

artwork complements and enhances the written content." Sci Books Films
Includes glossary and bibliographical references

Stewart, David Evelyn

How your body works; a good look inside your insides. written by David Stewart; illustrated by Carolyn Franklin. Children's Press 2008 32p il (Amaze) $26; pa $8.95
Grades: K 1 2   612
1. Human body
ISBN 978-0-531-20444-3; 0-531-20444-8; 978-0-531-20455-9 pa; 0-531-20455-3 pa
This "is a bright, colorful, vivid, and easy-to-digest children's book about the basics of physiology. The book includes simple, well-illustrated chapters on the eyes, ears, intestines, cardiovascular system, liver and kidneys. . . . Organs are represented with big, colorful blocks, with very little distracting detail." Sci Books Films

Swanson, Diane

You are weird; your body's peculiar parts and funny functions. written by Diane Swanson; illustrated by Kathy Boake. Kids Can Press 2009 40p il $16.95; pa $7.95
Grades: 2 3 4 5   612
1. Human body
ISBN 978-1-55453-282-7; 1-55453-282-5; 978-1-55453-283-4 pa; 1-55453-283-3 pa
"This chatty, interactive humorous science book make[s] human physiology accessible and interesting, with lots of wild facts about hair, bacteria, sweat, skin, joints, muscles, and more. . . . The irreverence is right on . . . and the sound of words extend the fun without jargon." Booklist

VanCleave, Janice Pratt

Janice VanCleave's the human body for every kid; easy activities that make learning science fun. Wiley 1995 223p hardcover o.p. pa $12.95
Grades: 4 5 6 7   612
1. Human body 2. Science -- Experiments
ISBN 0-471-02413-9; 0-471-02408-2 pa
LC 94-20862
"The activities described are easy to follow, are inexpensive, use readily obtainable supplies, and, most importantly, make the learning of human anatomy and physiology fun and exciting. Moreover, the material is presented in an organized, clear, and accurate manner." Sci Books Films

Walker, Richard, 1951-

Dr. Frankenstein's human body book; the monstrous truth about how your body works. [author, Richard Walker; artist, Nick Abadzis] DK Pub. 2008 93p il $24.99
Grades: 4 5 6 7   612
1. Human body
ISBN 978-0-7566-4091-0; 0-7566-4091-1
"This anatomy book is as engrossing as any science fiction. Dr. Frankenstein, shown in a sepia photograph standing in a laboratory, gazing at a skull he holds in one hand, invites readers to join him as he creates a human being. . . . The story line is sustained with brief, pun-happy journal entries. . . . Gothic fonts and engraved illustrations and vignettes (in red and black and also hand-colored) blend with state-of-the-art images from MEG scans, gamma scans and other advanced technology. Clear explanations broken into

easily assimilable captions and text blocks encourage the reader." Publ Wkly

Includes glossary

Human body; written by Richard Walker. DK Pub. 2009 72 p. ill. (chiefly col.) (DK eyewitness books) (hardcover) $16.99

Grades: 4 5 6 7   **612**

1. Human body

ISBN 9780756645458; 075664545X

LC 2009419529

In this book, text and illustrations present information on the parts of the body and how they work

Includes glossary and bibliographical references

Ouch! how your body makes it through a very bad day. written by Richard Walker. DK Pub. 2007 71p il $16.99

Grades: 4 5 6 7   **612**

1. Human body

ISBN 978-0-7566-2536-8; 0-7566-2536-X

"Tag along on a rotten day as a body copes with sneezing, getting cut, being stung by a bee, and vomiting, as well as performing more mundane actions such as urinating, tapping into its melanin supply, acting reflexively, and sweating. . . . Dramatic color graphics, both large and small, are accompanied by a multitude of informative captions. Researchers who find the information on the busy pages hard to grasp can pop in the accompanying CD-ROM and catch a ride up the esophagus on a wave of vomit. . . . Eye-catching, highly pictorial, informative, and with a megadose of ick! factor." SLJ

Includes glossary

Zoehfeld, Kathleen Weidner

Human body. Scholastic Inc. 2010 32p il (Scholastic reader) pa $3.99

Grades: K 1   **612**

1. Human body

ISBN 978-0-545-23752-9 pa; 0-545-23752-1 pa

A simple explanation of how the human body works, discussing the five senses, muscles, bones, digestion, the heart, and the brain.

"With simple chatty sentences and clearly labeled images of kids in action, this . . . title packs in fascinating facts about body parts, how they work individually and together." Booklist

Includes glossary

612.1 Specific functions, systems, organs

Corcoran, Mary K.

The **circulatory** story; illustrated by Jef Czekaj. Charlesbridge 2010 41p il lib bdg $17.95

Grades: 2 3 4   **612.1**

1. Cardiovascular system 2. Blood -- Circulation

ISBN 978-1-58089-208-7 lib bdg; 1-58089-208-6 lib bdg

LC 2008025332

"The author and illustrator of The Quest to Digest (2006) take young readers on an equally engaging ride through the heart, lungs, arteries, veins, capillaries, and back again. In the big, labeled cartoon illustrations a small, green Smoo-

like creature rides a red blood cell down a river of plasma. . . . Corcoran's breezy commentary lays out the whole 60,000-mile system in easy-to-understand terms. . . . An irresistable invitation to go with the flow." Booklist

Gold, John Coopersmith

Learning about the circulatory and lymphatic systems; by John C. Gold. Enslow Publishers 2013 48 p. (library) $23.93

Grades: 5 6 7 8   **612.1**

1. Picture books for children 2. Lymphatic system 3. Cardiovascular system

ISBN 0766041565; 9780766041561

LC 2012011099

This book by John Coopersmith Gold is part of the Learning About the Human Body Systems series and looks at the circulatory and lymphatic systems. "The circulatory system runs through the body carrying oxygen and nutrients to our cells and removes waste. It's driven by the never-resting heart, which pumps blood through more than 60,000 miles of arteries and veins. The lymphatic system regulates the amount of liquid in the body among other tasks." (Publisher's note)

Includes bibliographical references and index.

Guillain, Charlotte

Our hearts. Heinemann Library 2010 24p il (Our bodies) lib bdg $20.71; pa $5.99

Grades: K 1 2 3   **612.1**

1. Heart

ISBN 978-1-4329-3590-0 lib bdg; 1-4329-3590-9 lib bdg; 978-1-4329-3599-3 pa; 1-4329-3599-2 pa

LC 2009-22294

This describes what the heart is, how it pumps blood through the body, and how to keep it healthy.

This explains "visually and verbally complicated medical information in a clear, understandable way. . . . Large, vivid photographs are placed alongside one or two sentences per page." Booklist

Includes bibliographical references

Kyi, Tanya Lloyd

Seeing red; the true story of blood. Annick Press 2012 121 p. (hardcover) $22.95

Grades: 4 5 6   **612.1**

1. Blood

ISBN 1554513855; 9781554513857

This book by Tanya Lloyd Kyi, illustrated by Steve Rolston, discusses "the symbolism and reality of blood, from its role in ancient sacrifices to its uses in modern medicine and forensics. . . . Around the world, blood has always been a symbol of both life and death: blood rites, blood oaths, and blood-soaked legends. Today, we have scientific facts about blood types, transfusions, blood-borne illnesses, and crime-scene blood spatter. Yet the fluid still holds mystery." (Publisher's note)

Includes bibliographical references (p. 112-115), Internet addresses and index.

Markle, Sandra

Faulty hearts; true survival stories. Lerner Pub. 2010 48p il (Powerful medicine) lib bdg $27.93

Grades: 5 6 7 8   **612.1**
1. Heart 2. Heart diseases 3. Cardiovascular system
ISBN 978-0-8225-8699-9 lib bdg; 0-8225-8699-1
lib bdg

LC 2009-33980

This book "is extremely well done, with a number of great examples of survival stories. The examples exemplify different and important heart diseases, symptoms, and treatments. . . . That the author is a former science teacher enables her to write clearly for the intended audience. The illustrations and photographs are perfect, adding to a full understanding of the diseases described." Sci Books & Films

Includes glossary and bibliographical references

Newquist, Hp
The **book** of blood; from legends and leeches to vampires and veins. HP Newquist. Houghton Mifflin Books for Children 2012 160 p. ill. (chiefly col.) (hardback) $17.99
Grades: 4 5 6   **612.1**
1. Blood
ISBN 0547315848; 9780547315843

LC 2011025134

In this book, "[H.P.] Newquist . . . demystifies one of the most elemental and (literally) vital components of life as we know it. After an overview of the complex makeup of blood, Newquist dives into humankind's history with, beliefs about, and study of blood, including missteps and misconceptions along the way . . . . Newquist goes into detail to explain how blood moves through the human body and the critical role it plays in keeping us alive." (Publishers Weekly)

Showers, Paul
A **drop** of blood; illustrated by Edward Miller. HarperCollins Pub. 2004 32p il (Let's-read-and-find-out science) hardcover o.p. pa $4.99
Grades: K 1 2 3   **612.1**
1. Blood
ISBN 0-06-009108-8; 0-06-009109-6 lib bdg; 0-06-009110-X pa

A newly illustrated edition of the title first published 1967 and revised in 1989

A simple introduction to the composition and functions of blood

"Showers's classic introduction to this vital fluid is cleverly updated by Miller's amusing illustrations featuring a Dracula-like vampire and his Igorish friend. . . . High-quality, closeup photographs of blood cells, platelets, and fibrin under the microscope are well placed within the illustrations, and science concepts are presented with just the right amount of detail for the intended audience." SLJ

Hear your heart; illustrated by Holly Keller. HarperCollins Pubs. 2001 33p il (Let's-read-and-find-out science) hardcover o.p. pa $4.95
Grades: K 1 2 3   **612.1**
1. Heart
ISBN 0-06-025410-6; 0-06-025411-4 lib bdg; 0-06-445139-9 pa

LC 99-41336

A revised and newly illustrated edition of the title first published 1968

A simple explanation of the structure of the heart and how it works

"This is an excellent introduction to the heart and how it works. . . . The open, informal design brings the physiology right into daily life. Factual, accurate, and fun." Booklist

Simon, Seymour
★ The **heart**; our circulatory system. [by] Seymour Simon. rev ed.; Collins 2006 30p il hardcover o.p. pa $6.99
Grades: 4 5 6 7   **612.1**
1. Heart 2. Cardiovascular system
ISBN 978-0-06-087720-0; 0-06-087720-0; 978-0-06-087721-7 pa; 0-06-087721-9 pa

LC 2006-279215

First published 1996

Describes the heart, blood, and other parts of the body's circulatory system and explains how each component functions

"The text is succinct and direct, making the details understandable without losing the sense that the whole process of circulation is 'strange and wonderful.' . . . The often striking pictures include many computer-enhanced photographs as well as diagrams and highly enlarged images made possible by electron microscopes. Handsome and well-conceived in every way." Booklist [review of 1996 edition]

Tieck, Sarah
Circulatory system. ABDO Pub. 2011 32p il (Body systems) lib bdg $27.07; e-book $27.07
Grades: 2 3 4   **612.1**
1. Cardiovascular system
ISBN 978-1-61613-497-6 lib bdg; 1-61613-497-6 lib bdg; 978-1-61613-987-4 e-book

LC 2010019665

"Double-page spreads describe the workings of the [circulatory system] . . . with simple text on left-hand pages and large, colorful photographs or diagrams on the right. The [text touches] on common disorders (e.g., high blood pressure . . .) and healthy practices. 'Brain Food' spreads pose three questions and provide answers. Ample white space, engaging images, and 'Word of Mouth' sidebars are reader-friendly." Horn Book Guide

Includes glossary

612.17 Heart

Halvorson, Karin
Inside the heart; Karin Halvorson, M.D.; consulting editor, Diane Craig, M.A./Reading Specialist. ABDO Publishing Company, a division of ABDO 2013 32 p. (Super simple body) $27.07
Grades: 2 3 4 5   **612.17**
1. Heart -- Anatomy 2. Heart -- Physiology
ISBN 1617836125; 9781617836121

LC 2012030978

Author Karin Halvorson's book "offers children an exciting voyage through the heart. Detailed illustrations, color photos, and simple text combine to make a fun and easy introduction to how the heart works. This book also includes simple activities and crafts like We've Got a Beat, Valuable Valves and how to make a Heart with how-to photos to further engage young learners." (Publisher's note)

612.2 Respiratory system

Guillain, Charlotte
Our lungs. Heinemann Library 2010 24p il (Our bodies) lib bdg $20.71; pa $5.99
Grades: K 1 2 3   **612.2**
1. Lungs
ISBN 978-1-4329-3594-8 lib bdg; 1-4329-3594-1 lib bdg; 978-1-4329-3603-7 pa; 1-4329-3603-4 pa
LC 2009-22298
This describes what lungs are, why we need lungs, and how to keep them healthy.
This explains "visually and verbally complicated medical information in a clear, understandable way. . . . Large, vivid photographs are placed alongside one or two sentences per page." Booklist
Includes bibliographical references

Korb, Rena
My nose; illustrated by Remy Simard; content consultant, Anthony J. Weinhaus. Magic Wagon 2010 32p il (My body) lib bdg $27.07
Grades: 1 2 3   **612.2**
1. Nose
ISBN 978-1-60270-808-2; 1-60270-808-8
This "volume stars a child narrator who straightforwardly describes [the nose] and how it works. A round-faced, lab-coat-wearing man appears at the bottom of every spread to provide additional details and tidbits of anatomical information. . . . Black-outlined digital-looking cartoon illustrations enliven the [text]." Horn Book Guide
Includes glossary

Simon, Seymour
Lungs; your respiratory system. [by] Seymour Simon. Smithsonian/Collins 2007 30p il hardcover o.p. $16.77; lib bdg $17.89
Grades: 3 4 5 6   **612.2**
1. Respiratory system
ISBN 978-0-06-054654-0; 978-0-06-054655-7 lib bdg; 0-06-054655-7 lib bdg; 0-06-054656-5 pa
LC 2006003768
"This straightforward overview of the respiratory system follows the journey of a breath through the body. Color diagrams, X-rays, and photos provide visual support. . . . The writing is concise and full of clear examples meaningful to kids." SLJ
Includes glossary and bibliographical references

Siy, Alexandra
★ Sneeze! [by] Alexandra Siy and Dennis Kunkel. Charlesbridge 2007 45p il lib bdg $16.95; pa $6.95
Grades: 4 5 6 7   **612.2**
1. Allergy 2. Sneezing
ISBN 978-1-57091-653-3 lib bdg; 978-1-57091-654-0 pa
LC 2005-27567
"Kunkel's big, clear, beautiful color electron micrographs on every double-page spead show everything from dust mites, mildew, and pollen to the influenza A virus." Booklist
Includes glossary and bibliographical references

Tieck, Sarah
Respiratory system. ABDO Pub. 2011 32p il (Body systems) lib bdg $27.07; e-book $27.07
Grades: 2 3 4   **612.2**
1. Respiratory system
ISBN 978-1-61613-501-0 lib bdg; 1-61613-501-8 lib bdg; 978-1-61613-991-1 e-book
LC 2010019652
"Double-page spreads describe the workings of the [respiratory system] . . . with simple text on lefthand pages and large, colorful photographs or diagrams on the right. The [text touches] on common disorders . . . and healthy practices. 'Brain Food' spreads pose three questions and provide answers. Ample white space, engaging images, and 'Word of Mouth' sidebars are reader-friendly." Horn Book Guide
Includes glossary

612.3 Digestive system

Corcoran, Mary K.
The quest to digest; illustrated by Jef Czekaj. Charlesbridge 2006 32p il lib bdg $16.95; pa $6.95
Grades: 2 3 4   **612.3**
1. Digestion
ISBN 978-1-57091-664-9 lib bdg; 978-1-57091-665-6 pa
LC 2005-19622
"This graphically appealing, colorful, and fact-rich story describes the importance of food to the body by following an apple as it goes through the human digestion system. . . . Abundant, humorous cartoons and clever text handle explanations of belching, passing gas, and diarrhea." SLJ
Includes glossary

Donovan, Sandra, 1967-
Hawk & Drool; gross stuff in your mouth. by Sandy Donovan; illustrated by Michael Slack. Millbrook Press 2010 48p il (Gross body science) lib bdg $29.27
Grades: 4 5 6   **612.3**
1. Saliva 2. Mouth -- Diseases
ISBN 978-0-8225-8966-2 lib bdg; 0-8225-8966-4 lib bdg
LC 2008-50699
Presents disgusting facts about the human mouth, how it works to aid in digestion, the organisms that live there, and ways to keep it clean and healthy
"Solid information layered between sarcastic comments and kid-friendly terminology like fart, poop, barf, and puke will keep readers engaged. . . . Labeled, captioned (and graphic) photographs, cartoon-style illustrations, and micrographs add information." SLJ
Includes glossary and bibliographical references

Rumble & spew; gross stuff in your stomach and intestines. by Sandy Donovan; illustrated by Michael Slack. Millbrook Press 2010 48p il (Gross body science) lib bdg $29.27
Grades: 4 5 6   **612.3**
1. Intestines
ISBN 978-0-8225-8899-3 lib bdg; 0-8225-8899-4 lib bdg
LC 2008-37713

Presents disgusting facts about the human digestive system and its functions

"Solid information layered between sarcastic comments and kid-friendly terminology like fart, poop, barf, and puke will keep readers engaged. . . . Labeled, captioned (and graphic) photographs, cartoon-style illustrations, and micrographs add information." SLJ

Includes glossary and bibliographical references

Gold, Susan Dudley

Learning about the digestive and excretory systems; by Susan Dudley Gold. Enslow Publishers 2013 48 p. (Learning about the human body systems) (library) $23.93

Grades: 5 6 7 8   **612.3**

1. Picture books for children 2. Digestive system 3. Urinary organs 4. Digestive organs

ISBN 0766041573; 9780766041578

LC 2012011100

This book by Susan Dudley Gold is part of the Learning About the Human Body Systems series and looks at the digestive and excretory systems. She "explains why these systems are discussed together, how they work, and ways to keep healthy." Illustrations and color photographs are included. (Publisher's note)

Includes bibliographical references and index.

Guillain, Charlotte

Our stomachs. Heinemann Library 2010 24 p. il (Our bodies) lib bdg $20.71; pa $5.99

Grades: K 1 2 3   **612.3**

1. Stomach 2. Digestion

ISBN 978-1-4329-3591-7 lib bdg; 1-4329-3591-7 lib bdg; 978-1-4329-3600-6 pa; 1-4329-3600-X pa

LC 2009-22295

This describes what the stomach is, what it does to food, and how to keep it healthy.

This explains "visually and verbally complicated medical information in a clear, understandable way. . . . Large, vivid photographs are placed alongside one or two sentences per page." Booklist

Includes bibliographical references

Jakab, Cheryl

The **digestive** system; by Cheryl Jakab. Smart Apple Media 2006 32 p. il (Our body) lib bdg $28.50

Grades: 3 4 5   **612.3**

1. Digestion

ISBN 978-1-58340-737-0 lib bdg; 1-58340-737-5 lib bdg

LC 2005057881

This "clear, approachable book contains six chapters that [describes] the [digestive] system, how it works, diseases, treatment, and more. A final chapter promotes a healthy lifestyle and educates readers on first aid and avoiding possible problems associated with the system. Health tips appear throughout, and an activity is included. [This book is] interactive in tone and [provides] plenty of sidebar material, along with color photographs, drawings, charts, and diagrams, and a fascinating 'under the microscope' look at parts of the body." SLJ

Includes glossary

Korb, Rena

My mouth. Magic Wagon 2011 32 p. il (My body) lib bdg $27.07

Grades: 1 2 3   **612.3**

1. Mouth

ISBN 978-1-60270-806-8; 1-60270-806-1

This "volume stars a child narrator who straightforwardly describes [the mouth] and how it works. A round-faced, lab-coat-wearing man appears at the bottom of every spread to provide additional details and tidbits of anatomical information. . . . Black-outlined digital-looking cartoon illustrations enliven the [text]." Horn Book Guide

Includes glossary

My stomach; illustrated by Remy Simard; content consultant, Anthony J. Weinhaus. Magic Wagon 2010 32 p. il (My body) lib bdg $27.07

Grades: 1 2 3   **612.3**

1. Stomach

ISBN 978-1-60270-810-5; 1-60270-810-X

This "volume stars a child narrator who straightforwardly describes [the stomach] and how it works. A round-faced, lab-coat-wearing man appears at the bottom of every spread to provide additional details and tidbits of anatomical information. . . . Black-outlined digital-looking cartoon illustrations enliven the [text]." Horn Book Guide

Includes glossary

Showers, Paul

What happens to a hamburger? illustrated by Edward Miller. HarperCollins Pubs. 2001 33 p. il (Let's-read-and-find-out science) hardcover o.p. pa $5.99

Grades: K 1 2 3   **612.3**

ISBN 0-06-027947-8; 0-06-027948-6 lib bdg; 0-06-445183-6 pa

LC 97-39007

A newly illustrated edition of the title first published 1970

Explains the processes by which a hamburger and other foods are used to make energy, strong bones, and solid muscles as they pass through the digestive system

This edition offers "attractive new illustrations, enhanced in a few places with photos that show body parts such as the epiglottis and the stomach lining. . . . Miller's digital artwork has a jaunty, retro look." Booklist

Simon, Seymour

★ **Guts**; our digestive system. [by] Seymour Simon. HarperCollins 2005 un il $16.99; lib bdg $17.89

Grades: 4 5 6 7   **612.3**

1. Digestion

ISBN 0-06-054651-4; 0-06-054652-2 lib bdg

LC 2004-14508

"Simon's specialty of drawing in readers through large, detailed, breathtaking photos and then entertaining them with facts is again in evidence. . . . The text is enhanced with detailed colored X rays, computer-generated pictures, and microscopic photos." SLJ

Thomas, Isabel

Why do I burp? digestion and diet. Raintree 2011 32 p. il (Inside my body) lib bdg $29; pa $7.99

Grades: 3 4 5 6 **612.3**
1. Digestion
ISBN 978-1-4109-4014-8 lib bdg; 1-4109-4014-4 lib
bdg; 978-1-4109-4025-4 pa; 1-4109-4025-X pa
LC 2010024679

"Double-page spreads begin with questions related to
the . . . digestive system. The answers, in the form of short
paragraphs, bulleted lists, labeled diagrams and schematics,
charts, and captioned photos, pack a surprising amount of
information into relatively uncluttered pages. . . . Sidebars
debunk common misconceptions, give practical advice, and
add quirky facts." Horn Book Guide
Includes glossary and bibliographical references

Tieck, Sarah
Digestive system. ABDO Pub. 2011 32p il (Body
systems) lib bdg $27.07; e-book $27.07
Grades: 2 3 4 **612.3**
1. Digestion
ISBN 978-1-61613-498-3 lib bdg; 1-61613-498-4 lib
bdg; 978-1-61758-988-1 e-book
LC 2010019663

"Double-page spreads describe the workings of the [di-
gestive system] . . . with simple text on lefthand pages and
large, colorful photographs or diagrams on the right. The
[text touches] on common disorders . . , and healthy practices. 'Brain Food' spreads pose three questions and provide
answers. Ample white space, engaging images, and 'Word
of Mouth' sidebars are reader-friendly." Horn Book Guide
Includes glossary

612.4 Hematopoietic, lymphatic, glandular, urinary systems

Kim, Melissa
Learning about the endocrine and reproductive sys-
tems; by Melissa L. Kim. Enslow Publishers 2013 48 p.
(Learning about the human body systems) (library) $23.93
Grades: 5 6 7 8 **612.4**
1. Picture books for children 2. Endocrine glands 3.
Reproductive system 4. Generative organs
ISBN 0766041581; 9780766041585
LC 2012011101

This book by Melissa L. Kim is part of the Learning
About the Human Body Systems series and looks at the endocrine and reproductive systems. "The endocrine system is
essential to human life. It enables a person to grow, respond
to change and stress, and helps turn food into energy. The
reproductive system has one crucial task: that of making the
next generation of people." (Publisher's note)
Includes bibliographical references and index.

612.6 Reproduction, development, maturation

Brown, Laurene Krasny
What's the big secret? talking about sex with girls and
boys. [by] Laurie Krasny Brown and Marc Brown. Little,
Brown 1997 31p il hardcover o.p. pa $5.95

Grades: K 1 2 3 **612.6**
1. Sex education
ISBN 0-316-10915-0; 0-316-10183-4 pa
LC 96-15521

This "picture book's subject is sex and sexuality: not
simply physical differences but also gender roles, the issue
of privacy, and reproduction. . . . The Browns do an outstanding and very responsible job of introducing a wide variety of terms (everything from the expected, umbilical cord,
to the unexpected, masturbation, which is handled with honesty but restraint), synthesizing a great deal of information
kids want to know at this age, and presenting facts in a non-
threatening but forthright context. They even manage a good
deal of humor along the way. . . . The words and illustrations
work extremely well together, with the busy, bright cartoon
art and balloon dialogue conveying as much of the information as the text." Booklist

Butler, Dori Hillestad
★ **My** mom's having a baby! illustrated by Carol
Thompson. Albert Whitman & Co. 2005 un il $15.95
Grades: 2 3 4 **612.6**
1. Pregnancy 2. Childbirth 3. Sex education
ISBN 0-8075-5344-1
LC 2004-18585

"Elizabeth describes the month-by-month development of the baby as well as the changes in Mom's body. . .
. Through very direct language and clear illustrations, children will learn about a man's testicles where sperm are made
and the fallopian tube where an egg is fertilized. . . . Mom
answers Elizabeth's big question, 'how do Dad's sperm and
your egg get together?' . . . Details are not spared when the
birth is described. The playful and colorful illustrations add
exuberance to the text, combining full-page paintings, cartoon panels, word balloons, and free-floating images. The
joy and love felt by all of the family members is palpable.
This volume is an excellent choice for those readers who
are ready to ask and be told some of life's basic facts." SLJ

Cocovini, Abby
★ **What's** inside your tummy, Mommy? [by] Abby
Cocovini. Henry Holt & Co. 2008 un il pa $8.95
Grades: PreK K **612.6**
1. Pregnancy
ISBN 978-0-8050-8760-4 pa; 0-8050-8760-5 pa

"Cocovini has designed this oversize guide so that 'if the
mommy holds the book up to her belly, you will see what
the baby looks like (actual size) inside her every month!'
. . . This book is warm and nonthreatening to the max, its
crayoned and watercolor spot illustrations and hand-drawn
timeline lending it a homey, scrapbook/journal feel. The five
or so factoids on each page are shaped around easy-to-grasp,
domestic concepts." Publ Wkly

Cole, Joanna
★ **How** you were born; photographs by Margaret Mill-
er. rev & expanded ed; Morrow Junior Bks. 1993 48p il
$15.95; pa $6.99
Grades: K 1 2 **612.6**
1. Infants 2. Pregnancy 3. Childbirth
ISBN 0-688-12059-8; 0-688-12061-X pa
LC 92-23970

A revised and newly illustrated edition of the title first
published 1984

"Illustrated with photographs of culturally diverse families, Cole's text explains conception, the development of the fetus, and the birth process. A note to parents and a suggested reading list are included." J Youth Serv Libr

When you were inside Mommy; illustrated by Maxie Chambliss. HarperCollins Pubs. 2001 un il $7.99
Grades: PreK K 1   612.6
1. Infants 2. Pregnancy 3. Childbirth
ISBN 0-688-17043-9
LC 00-40890

This "begins with a simple explanation of a baby's development in the mother's uterus. It goes on to show the baby's birth, followed by his growth to a child of perhaps three or four years old. An appended 'Note to Parents' offers a sound approach to talking with children. . . . The simplicity and sensitivity of the writing is well matched by Chambliss' line and watercolor wash illustrations." Booklist

Fromer, Liza
My stretchy body; [by] Liza Fromer and Francine Gerstein; illustrated by Joe Weissmann. Tundra Books 2011 un il (Body works) $12.95
Grades: 2 3 4 5   612.6
1. Growth
ISBN 978-1-77049-203-5; 1-77049-203-8

This describes how we grow, including hair, skin, nails, teeth, muscles, and bones, as well as growth spurts and growing pains.
Includes glossary

Gaff, Jackie
Looking at growing up; how do people change? [by] Jackie Gaff. Enslow Publishers 2008 32p il (Looking at science: how things change) lib bdg $22.60
Grades: 1 2 3   612.6
1. Growth
ISBN 978-0-7660-3090-9 lib bdg; 0-7660-3090-3 lib bdg
LC 2007-24509

"Fills a huge void in elementary science collections. . . . Text is arranged in succinct 'chunks,' giving important facts without overwhelming readers. . . . [This] is an essential addition." Libr Media Connect
Includes glossary and bibliographical references

Gravelle, Karen
The **period** book; everything you don't want to ask (but need to know) by Karen Gravelle & Jennifer Gravelle; illustrations by Debbie Palen. updated ed.; Walker & Co. 2006 126p il $16.95
Grades: 4 5 6 7   612.6
1. Menstruation
ISBN 978-0-8027-8072-0; 0-8027-8072-5
LC 2008270981
First published 1996
Explains what happens at the onset of menstruation, discussing what to wear, going to the gynecologist, and how to handle various problems
"The cartoonlike illustrations and conversational tone make this updated edition a friendly, reassuring resource as well as a thorough one." Horn Book Guide

Harris, Robie H.
★ **It's** not the stork! a book about girls, boys, babies, bodies, families, and friends. illustrated by Michael Emberley. Candlewick Press 2006 59p il $16.99
Grades: K 1 2 3   612.6
1. Pregnancy 2. Childbirth 3. Sex education
ISBN 0-7636-0047-4
LC 2005-54280

"Harris opens by introducing two cartoon characters—a green-feathered bird clad in a purple shirt and blue hightop sneakers and his spike-haired friend, a bee. They wonder, 'So where DO babies come from?' Their conversational commentary, given in word balloons, is a lighthearted supplement to a more focused narrative. Told in the second person, the text is straightforward, informative, and personable. Facts are presented step-by-step, starting from the similarities and differences between boys' and girls' bodies, moving to a baby's conception, growth in the womb, and birth, ending with an exploration of different configurations of families as well as a section on 'okay' versus 'not okay' touches." SLJ

★ **It's** so amazing! a book about eggs, sperm, birth, babies, and families. illustrated by Michael Emberley. Candlewick Press 1999 81p il $21.99; pa $10.99
Grades: 2 3 4   612.6
1. Pregnancy 2. Childbirth 3. Sex education 4. Reproduction 5. Sex instruction for children 6. Human reproduction
ISBN 0-7636-0051-2; 0-7636-1321-5 pa
LC 98-33119

Uses bird and bee cartoon characters to present straightforward explanations of topics related to sexual development, love, reproduction, adoption, sexually transmitted diseases, and more
"While the illustrations are engaging and often hilarious, factual information is effectively presented in a clear, nonjudgmental tone that will inform and assure readers." SLJ

★ **Who** has what? all about girls' bodies and boys' bodies. Candlewick Press 2011 un il $15.99
Grades: PreK K 1   612.6
1. Human body 2. Sex education
ISBN 978-0-7636-2931-1; 0-7636-2931-6
LC 2010040464

"A family outing to the beach provides the opportunity for a discussion of the similarities and differences between boys and girls. Nellie's play on the words 'everybody' and 'every body' leads Gus to wondering about body parts. Their beach visit provides an opportunity to see a variety of people and puppies, to itemize all the parts that boys and girls and dogs have in common. . . . Harris . . . matter-of-factly combines common childhood language . . . and anatomically correct terms. . . . Westcott's digital cartoonlike illustrations show different compositions of families representing a wide range of ages, races and nationalities." Kirkus

Harris, Robie H., 1940-
★ **What's** in there? all about you before you were born. by Robie H. Harris and illustrated by Nadine Bernard Westcott. Candlewick Press 2013 40 p. (All about us!) (hardback: alk. paper) $15.99
Grades: PreK K 1   612.6
1. Pregnancy 2. Childbirth 3. Human reproduction 4.

Sex instruction for children
ISBN 0763636304; 9780763636302

LC 2008025455

This book, by Robie H. Harris and illustrated by Nadine Bernard Westcott, "follows the stages of pregnancy and childbirth in a matter-of-fact and comfortable way. Gus and Nellie have some exciting news: there's going to be a baby in their family! Join them through the seasons as they watch their mother's pregnancy with fascination and curiosity while awaiting the birth of their new baby sibling." (Publisher's note)

Jukes, Mavis
★ **Growing** up: it's a girl thing; straight talk about first bras, first periods, and your changing body. illustrations by Debbie Tilley. Knopf 1998 72p il hardcover o.p. pa $10
Grades: 4 5 6 7   **612.6**
1. Girls 2. Adolescence 3. Menstruation
ISBN 0-679-89027-0 pa

LC 98-18113

This "covers body hair and shaving, perspiration and deodorant, and how to buy your first bra. The second half of the book is devoted to what to expect and how to plan for your first period. . . . The narration has an easy, comfortable voice and imparts accurate and important information." SLJ

Katz, Anne
Girl in the know; your inside-and-out guide to growing up. written by Anne Katz; illustrated by Monika Melnychuk. Kids Can Press 2010 111p il $18.95
Grades: 4 5 6 7   **612.6**
1. Puberty 2. Girls -- Health and hygiene 3. Life skills guides 4. Girls -- Psychology
ISBN 978-1-55453-303-9; 1-55453-303-1
"This reassuring title is aimed at girls who want clear facts about puberty but who may not be ready to read indepth specifics of sex and birth-control. The author . . . offers a holistic guide that covers the body changes puberty brings as well as tips about maintaining physical and emotional health. . . . The warm, straightforward, useful advice on a broad range of topics . . . will captivate both middle graders and middle-schoolers, and the frequent color drawings of stylish, diverse girls . . . reinforce the book's appeal to a wide age group." Booklist

Madaras, Lynda
★ **On** your mark, get set, grow! a what's happening to my body? book for younger boys. [by] Lynda Madaras; illustrations by Paul Gilligan. Newmarket Press 2008 123p il $22; pa $12
Grades: 3 4 5 6   **612.6**
1. Puberty 2. Boys -- Health and hygiene
ISBN 978-1-55704-780-9; 1-55704-780-4; 978-1-55704-781-6 pa; 1-55704-781-2 pa

LC 2007043095

"Madaras draws on her experience teaching sex education (called puberty classes here) to inform boys about the physical changes they will experience as they start to mature. . . . The age-appropriate presentation includes cartoon art on almost every page and a sprinkling of humor. Along with covering sex-organ growth, height, weight, and muscle gain, Madaras also discusses health and nutrition, hygiene, and 'becoming your own self.' A reassuring tone pervades

the text. . . . This is an excellent resource for both children and parents." SLJ

★ **Ready,** set, grow! a what's happening to my body? book for younger girls. illustrations by Linda Davick. Newmarket Press 2003 127p il $22; pa $12
Grades: 3 4 5 6   **612.6**
1. Puberty 2. Girls -- Health and hygiene
ISBN 1-55704-587-9; 1-55704-565-8 pa

LC 2003-9489

This "is a timely and important book. In a consistently sensitive and encouraging tone, Madaras reassures preadolescents that the changes they know are approaching or they are beginning to experience are normal, natural, and cause for celebration. Humorous sketches illustrate the emotions and stages of puberty, and keep the tone light." SLJ

★ The **what's** happening to my body? book for boys; [by] Lynda Madaras with Area Madaras; drawings by Simon Sullivan. 3rd rev ed.; Newmarket Press 2007 xx, 233p il $24.95; pa $12.95
Grades: 4 5 6 7   **612.6**
1. Puberty 2. Adolescence 3. Sex education 4. Boys -- Health and hygiene
ISBN 978-1-55704-769-4; 1-55704-769-3; 978-1-55704-765-6 pa; 1-55704-765-0 pa

LC 2007009874

First published 1984
Discusses the changes that take place in a boy's body during puberty, including information on the body's changing size and shape, the growth spurt, reproductive organs, pubic hair, beards, pimples, voice changes, wet dreams, and puberty in girls
Includes bibliographical references

★ The **what's** happening to my body? book for girls; [by] Lynda Madaras with Area Madaras; drawings by Simon Sullivan. 3rd rev ed.; Newmarket Press 2007 xxvi, 259p il $24.95; pa $12.95
Grades: 4 5 6 7   **612.6**
1. Puberty 2. Adolescence 3. Sex education 4. Girls -- Health and hygiene
ISBN 978-1-55704-768-7; 1-55704-768-5; 978-1-55704-764-9 pa; 1-55704-764-2 pa

LC 2007009862

Discusses the changes that take place in a girl's body during puberty, including information on the body's changing size and shape, pubic hair, breasts, reproductive organs, the menstrual cycle, and puberty in boys
Includes bibliographical references

Mar, Jonathan
The **body** book for boys; by Jonathan Mar and Grace Norwich. Scholastic 2010 128p il $8.99
Grades: 4 5 6   **612.6**
1. Boys 2. Puberty 3. Adolescence
ISBN 978-0-545-23751-2 pa; 0-545-23751-3 pa
"In this reassuring title aimed at boys just entering adolescence, the authors present frank information on such topics as hygiene, the changes brought on by puberty, exercise, and dealing with girls. The tone is kept light, and the many bright illustrations also have a fun, jokey quality." Booklist

Plaisted, Caroline

Boy talk; a survival guide to growing up. illustrated by Chris Dickason. QEB Pub. 2011 il (Growing up)

Grades: 4 5 6 7   **612.6**

1. Boys 2. Puberty

ISBN 1-60992-085-6; 978-1-60992-085-2

LC 2011009206

Discusses body changes that happen to boys during puberty, such as acne, body hair, body odor, mood swings, crushes, and more, and gives suggestions to teen boys for taking care of their hygiene and keeping good relationships.

"Using a colorful design featuring Dickason's wacky, mugging cartoon characters, this is about as appealing as a book on these topics can get, and it maintains a mildly funny, usually frank, and always healthy tone." Booklist

Girl talk; a survival guide to growing up. illustrated by Chris Dickason. QEB Pub. 2011 il (Growing up) lib bdg $23.95

Grades: 4 5 6 7   **612.6**

1. Girls 2. Puberty

ISBN 978-1-60992-084-5; 1-60992-084-8

LC 2011009125

Discusses body changes that happen to girls during puberty, such as acne, periods, cramps, body hair, mood swings, and more, and gives suggestions to teen girls for taking care of their health.

Pringle, Laurence P.

Everybody has a bellybutton; your life before you were born. by Laurence Pringle; illustrated by Clare Wood. Boyds Mills Press 1997 un il $14.95

Grades: PreK K 1 2 3   **612.6**

1. Fetus 2. Pregnancy 3. Childbirth

ISBN 1-56397-009-0

LC 95-83168

Pringle "offers a gently phrased, solidly scientific look at the growth of a baby. . . . The narrative gives specific, sensorial details that will keep even young children engaged, and the description of childbirth is matter-of-fact and undisturbing. . . . Illustrations are softly realistic pencil drawings on pink and blue backgrounds." Booklist

Includes bibliographical references

Rand, Casey

Human reproduction. Raintree 2009 48p il (Sci-hi: life science) lib bdg $31.43; pa $8.99

Grades: 5 6 7 8   **612.6**

1. Reproduction 2. Sex education

ISBN 978-1-4109-3327-0 lib bdg; 1-4109-3327-X lib bdg; 978-1-4109-3335-5 pa; 1-4109-3335-0 pa

LC 2009003464

In this introduction to human reproduction "clear language, embedded definitions, and interesting examples illustrate abstract concepts through both text and well-chosen photographs. . . . [It] includes suggested activities to test ideas as well as a thorough glossary and a Webliography." SLJ

Includes glossary and bibliographical references

Saltz, Gail

★ **Amazing** you; getting smart about your private parts. illustrated by Lynne Avril Cravath. Dutton Children's Books 2005 un il $15.99

Grades: PreK K 1   **612.6**

1. Growth 2. Reproduction 3. Sex education

ISBN 0-525-47389-0

LC 2004-22014

"This upbeat picture book, illustrated with sunny cartoon drawings, introduces kids to basic reproductive physiology. Saltz offers simple, accessible definitions of terms, accompanied by pictures of unclothed kids and labeled diagrams of internal organs. Subsequent drawings show three stages of body development from baby to young adult, followed by an abbreviated explanation, illustrated with a heart-shaped drawing of a smiling egg and sperm, of reproduction. . . . Saltz presents the information clearly in a cheerful, positive tone." Booklist

Changing you! a guide to body changes and sexuality. [by] Gail Saltz; illustrated by Lynne Avril Cravath. Dutton Children's Books 2007 un il $16.99

Grades: 3 4 5   **612.6**

1. Puberty 2. Sex education

ISBN 978-0-525-47817-1; 0-525-47817-5

LC 2006035593

"This is an introduction to puberty and sexual intercourse in the context of a loving relationship between a man and woman. The book covers topics that kids often inquire about, such as bodily changes and how babies are born. Bright, cartoon illustrations of the human body at different stages and ages and labeled diagrams fill the pages. The clear, straightforward text uses language that young children can easily grasp while the running commentary that accompanies the art takes a lighter, more conversational approach." SLJ

Schwartz, John

Short; walking tall when you're not tall at all. Roaring Brook Press 2010 132p il $16.99

Grades: 4 5 6 7 8   **612.6**

1. Size 2. Growth 3. Body image 4. Prejudices

ISBN 978-1-59643-323-6; 1-59643-323-X

"In a humorous, personal voice, . . . Schwartz combines his own memories of growing up short with related discussions about physiology, statistics, popular culture, and societal prejudice, always returning to his own self-image. . . . Short kids will want every word. . . . and many readers will move on to the resource list of articles, Web sites, and scientific papers in the detailed, informal back matter." Booklist

Includes bibliographical references

612.7 Musculoskeletal system, integument

Baines, Rebecca

The bones you own; a book about the human body. by Becky Baines. National Geographic 2009 27p il (Zigzag) $16.95; lib bdg $25.90

Grades: PreK K 1   **612.7**

1. Bones 2. Skeleton

ISBN 978-1-4263-0410-1; 1-4263-0410-2; 978-1-4263-0411-8 lib bdg; 1-4263-0411-0 lib bdg

LC 2008-47900

This describes functions that bones perform in a human body.

This title engages "children through humor, clear language, interesting facts, and abundant photos. . . . [An] excellent [introduction] for young science students." SLJ

Your skin holds you in; a book about your skin. by Becky Baines. National Geographic 2008 29p il (Zigzag) $14.95; lib bdg $19.90

Grades: PreK K 1 **612.7**

1. Skin

ISBN 978-1-4263-0311-1; 1-4263-0311-4; 978-1-4263-0312-8 lib bdg; 1-4263-0312-2 lib bdg

LC 2007-44156

"Thirteen short sentences describe skin . . . in all its glory. Additional facts appear in smaller print . . . on the same pages with the main idea sentences. Photographs of people, outlined in white and reproduced on brightly colored pages, serve as diagrams for important elements. . . . Exuberant double-page spreads encourage looking and talking." Horn Book

Barner, Bob

Dem bones; [illustrations and informational bone text by] Bob Barner. Chronicle Bks. 1996 un il $16.99

Grades: K 1 2 3 **612.7**

1. Bones 2. Skeleton

ISBN 0-8118-0827-0

LC 95-29

"A rollicking read-aloud, sing-along treat for children as they learn anatomy, rhyme, and language. . . . Scientific facts and names combined with lyrics make this a fascinating book." Exploring Sci in the Libr

Berger, Melvin

Why I sneeze, shiver, hiccup, and yawn; illustrated by Paul Meisel. HarperCollins Pubs. 2000 un il (Let's-read-and-find-out science) hardcover o.p. pa $4.99

Grades: K 1 2 3 **612.7**

1. Reflexes 2. Nervous system

ISBN 0-06-028144-8; 0-06-445193-3 pa

LC 98-55542

A revised and newly illustrated edition of Why I cough, sneeze, shiver, hiccup & yawn, published 1983 by Crowell

An introduction to reflex acts that explains why we sneeze, shiver, hiccup, and yawn

"The writing is simple but effective, and the charming, colorful pen-and-ink and watercolors are [detailed]. . . . Attractive introductory nonfiction." SLJ

Gold, Susan Dudley

Learning about the musculoskeletal system and the skin; Susan Dudley Gold. Enslow Publishers 2013 48 p. (Learning about the human body systems) (library) $23.93

Grades: 5 6 7 8 **612.7**

1. Picture books for children 2. Musculoskeletal system 3. Skin

ISBN 076604159X; 9780766041592

LC 2012011102

This book by Susan Dudley Gold is part of the Learning About the Human Body Systems series and looks at the musculoskeletal system. "Bone and muscles join forces to move us from one place to another. The musculoskeletal system controls our breathing, allows our eyes to focus, and shapes our smiles. It enables us to talk and to eat. Our strong bones support our weight. Skin wraps our body in a tough

layer of tissue that keeps moisture in and germs out." (Publisher's note)

Includes bibliographical references and index..

Guillain, Charlotte

Our bones. Heinemann Library 2010 24p il (Our bodies) lib bdg $20.71; pa $5.99

Grades: K 1 2 3 **612.7**

1. Bones

ISBN 978-1-4329-3596-2 lib bdg; 1-4329-3596-8 lib bdg; 978-1-4329-3605-1 pa; 1-4329-3605-0 pa

LC 2009-22300

This describes what bones are, how they support the body, and how to keep them healthy.

This explains "visually and verbally complicated medical information in a clear, understandable way. . . . Large, vivid photographs are placed alongside one or two sentences per page." Booklist

Includes bibliographical references

Our muscles. Heinemann Library 2010 24p il (Our bodies) lib bdg $20.71; pa $5.99

Grades: K 1 2 3 **612.7**

1. Muscles

ISBN 978-1-4329-3593-1 lib bdg; 1-4329-3593-3 lib bdg; 978-1-4329-3602-0 pa; 1-4329-3602-6 pa

LC 2009-22297

This describes what muscles are, how they help us move, and how to keep them healthy.

This explains "visually and verbally complicated medical information in a clear, understandable way. . . . Large, vivid photographs are placed alongside one or two sentences per page." Booklist

Includes bibliographical references

Our skin. Heinemann Library 2010 24p il (Our bodies) lib bdg $20.71; pa $5.99

Grades: K 1 2 3 **612.7**

1. Skin

ISBN 978-1-4329-3597-9 lib bdg; 1-4329-3597-6 lib bdg; 978-1-4329-3606-8 pa; 1-4329-3606-9 pa

LC 2009-22301

This describes what skin is, how it protects the body, and how to keep it healthy.

This explains "visually and verbally complicated medical information in a clear, understandable way. . . . Large, vivid photographs are placed alongside one or two sentences per page." Booklist

Includes bibliographical references

Jenkins, Steve

★ **Bones**; skeletons and how they work. Scholastic Press 2010 un il $16.99

Grades: 3 4 5 6 **612.7**

1. Bones 2. Skeleton

ISBN 978-0-545-04651-0; 0-545-04651-3

Jenkins "begins with a single human finger bone, then shows where it fits in the hand, then attaches the arm bones and sets it aside the forelimbs of a mole, spider monkey, gray whale, turtle, and fruit bat to illustrate how they all share the same basic structure. Similar comparisons take a look at feet, legs, rib cages, necks, and heads, almost always using a consistent scale to display the relative size of elephant and stork legs or a giraffe and human neck. Jenkins provides concise chunks of text alongside his always impressive cut-paper collages. . . . The clean design of the intricate skeletons set against solid background colors is striking and provides a wonderful visual introduction to what keeps us all upright." Booklist

Kaner, Etta

And the Winner Is ... Amazing Animal Athletes. by Etta Kaner; illustrated by David Anderson. Kids Can Press 2013 32 p. ill. (hardcover) $16.95

Grades: PreK K 1 2 3 **612.7**

1. Animals 2. Athletics

ISBN 1554539048; 9781554539048

This book "presents the World Animal Games, with quartets of different critters competing in a variety of Olympic-type events. A walrus and a cockatoo provide facts and color as the contestants vie for the gold in the high jump, sprinting, weight lifting, swimming, and other trials . . . . A data box for each entrant is provided, as is information on just why the winner came out on top, and how the record stands up to human athletes." (School Library Journal)

Korb, Rena

My muscles; illustrated by Remy Simard; Content Consultant; Anthony J. Weinhaus. Magic Wagon 2010 32p il (My body) lib bdg $27.07

Grades: 1 2 3 **612.7**

1. Muscles

ISBN 978-1-60270-807-5; 1-60270-807-X

This "volume stars a child narrator who straightforwardly describes [muscles] and how [they work]. A round-faced, lab-coat-wearing man appears at the bottom of every spread to provide additional details and tidbits of anatomical information. . . . Black-outlined digital-looking cartoon illustrations enliven the [text]." Horn Book Guide

Includes glossary

My spine; illustrated by Remy Simard; content consultant, Anthony J. Weinhaus. Magic Wagon 2010 32p il (My body) lib bdg $27.07

Grades: 1 2 3 **612.7**

1. Spine

ISBN 978-1-6027-0809-9; 1-60270-809-6

This "volume stars a child narrator who straightforwardly describes [the spine] and how it works. A round-faced, lab-coat-wearing man appears at the bottom of every spread to provide additional details and tidbits of anatomical information. . . . Black-outlined digital-looking cartoon illustrations enliven the [text]." Horn Book Guide

Includes glossary

Parker, Steve, 1952-

How do my muscles get strong? Raintree 2011 32p il (Inside my body) lib bdg $29; pa $7.99

Grades: 3 4 5 6 **612.7**

1. Muscles 2. Exercise

ISBN 978-1-4109-4017-9 lib bdg; 1-4109-4017-9 lib bdg; 978-1-4109-4028-5 pa; 1-4109-4028-4 pa

LC 2010024800

"Double-page spreads begin with questions related to the human muscular . . . system. The answers, in the form of short paragraphs, bulleted lists, labeled diagrams and schematics, charts, and captioned photos, pack a surprising amount of information into relatively uncluttered pages. . . .

. Sidebars debunk common misconceptions, give practical advice, and add quirky facts." Horn Book Guide

Includes glossary and bibliographical references

The **skeleton** and muscles; [by] Steve Parker. Raintree 2004 48p il (Our bodies) lib bdg $29.93

Grades: 5 6 7 8 **612.7**

1. Musculoskeletal system

ISBN 0-7398-6622-2

LC 2003-6594

This "takes a look at bones, muscles, and joints; how they are connected and function; and how to keep them healthy. The anatomy is accurate, and the format, with plenty of pictures, diagrams, and magnified photos, is very accessible. There are also lots of lively boxed facts." Booklist

Includes bibliographical references

Simon, Seymour

Bones; our skeletal system. Morrow Junior Bks. 1998 un il hardcover o.p. pa $6.99

Grades: 4 5 6 7 **612.7**

1. Bones 2. Skeleton

ISBN 0-688-14645-7 lib bdg; 0-688-17721-2 pa

LC 97-44751

Describes the skeletal system and outlines the many important roles that bones play in the healthy functioning of the human body

"Simon once again proves his remarkable facility for making complicated science clear and understandable." Booklist

Muscles; our muscular system. Morrow Junior Bks. 1998 un il hardcover o.p. pa $6.99

Grades: 4 5 6 7 **612.7**

1. Muscles

ISBN 0-688-14642-2; 0-688-14643-0 lib bdg; 0-688-17720-4 pa

LC 97-44758

Describes the nature and work of muscles, the different kinds, and the effects of exercise and other activities on them

"The full-paged illustrations are great and include full-color photographs, MRI scans, X rays, and excellent drawings." SLJ

An introduction to reflexology that explains . . .

Stewart, Melissa

Here we grow; the secrets of hair and nails. illustrated by Janet Hamlin. Marshall Cavendish Benchmark 2010 48p il (The gross and goofy body) lib bdg $20.95

Grades: 2 3 4 **612.7**

1. Hair

ISBN 978-0-7614-4172-4 lib bdg; 0-7614-4172-7 lib bdg

LC 2008033563

This provides information on the role hair and nails play in the body science of humans and animals.

This "offers detailed science facts in a fashion approachable enough to make it a welcome supplement to school textbooks. . . . The layout is fresh, clean, and colorful, sidebars keep things conversational, and the back matter is solid." Booklist

Includes glossary and bibliographical references

Moving and grooving; the secrets of muscles and bones. illustrated by Janet Hamlin. Marshall Cavendish

Benchmark 2010 48p il (The gross and goofy body) lib bdg $20.95

Grades: 2 3 4 **612.7**

1. Musculoskeletal system
ISBN 978-0-7614-4166-3 lib bdg; 0-7614-4166-2 lib bdg

LC 2008033557

This offers information on the role bones and muscles play in the body science of humans and animals

Includes glossary and bibliographical references

Tieck, Sarah

Muscular system. ABDO Pub. Co. 2011 32p il (Body systems) lib bdg $27.07; ebook $27.07

Grades: 2 3 4 **612.7**

1. Muscles 2. Musculoskeletal system
ISBN 978-1-61613-499-0; 1-61613-499-2 lib bdg; 978-1-61613-989-8 ebook

LC 2010019664

"Double-page spreads describe the workings of the [muscular system] . . . with simple text on left-hand pages and large, colorful photographs or diagrams on the right. The [text touches] on common disorders . . . and healthy practices. 'Brain Food' spreads pose three questions and provide answers. Ample white space, engaging images, and 'Word of Mouth' sidebars are reader-friendly." Horn Book Guide

Includes glossary

Skeletal system. ABDO Pub. 2011 32p il (Body systems) lib bdg $27.07; e-book $27.07

Grades: 2 3 4 **612.7**

1. Bones 2. Skeleton
ISBN 978-1-61613-502-7 lib bdg; 1-61613-502-6 lib bdg; 978-1-61613-992-8 e-book

LC 2010019651

"Double-page spreads describe the workings of the [skeletal system] . . . with simple text on left-hand pages and large, colorful photographs or diagrams on the right. The [text touches] on common disorders . . . and healthy practices. 'Brain Food' spreads pose three questions and provide answers. Ample white space, engaging images, and 'Word of Mouth' sidebars are reader-friendly." Horn Book Guide

Includes glossary

612.8 Nervous system

Aliki

My five senses; rev ed; Crowell 1989 31p il (Let's-read-and-find-out science book) $16.95; pa $4.99

Grades: PreK K 1 **612.8**

1. Senses and sensation
ISBN 0-690-04792-4; 0-06-445083-X pa

LC 88-35350

First published 1962

The faculties of touch, hearing, sight, smelling and taste are introduced in relation to everyday experiences

"Each sense is used independently to observe common phenomena. Next, the author demonstrates more than one sense being used. . . . The book effectively introduced the five senses to young people." Appraisal

Boothroyd, Jennifer

What is hearing? Lerner Publications Co. 2010 32p il (Lightning Bolt Books TM-Your amazing senses) lib bdg $25.26

Grades: K 1 2 **612.8**

1. Sound 2. Hearing
ISBN 978-0-7613-4250-2 lib bdg; 0-7613-4250-8 lib bdg

LC 2008-51848

Describes the properties of sound and hearing, including everyday examples and information on how an ear functions

"Given [its] . . . simple sentences, colorful layout, full-page photos, and well-chosen diagrams, [this title] . . . will be useful for reports." SLJ

Includes glossary and bibliographical references

What is sight? Lerner Publications Co. 2010 32p il (Lightning Bolt Books TM-Your amazing senses) lib bdg $25.26

Grades: K 1 2 **612.8**

1. Vision
ISBN 978-0-7613-4248-9 lib bdg; 0-7613-4248-6 lib bdg

LC 2008-51849

Describes the importance of the sense of sight and how the human eye works, including information on color, depth perception, and protecting sight

"Given [its] . . . simple sentences, colorful layout, full-page photos, and well-chosen diagrams, [this title] . . . will be useful for reports." SLJ

Includes glossary and bibliographical references

What is smell? Lerner Publications Co. 2010 32p il (Lightning Bolt Books TM-Your amazing senses) lib bdg $25.26

Grades: K 1 2 **612.8**

1. Smell
ISBN 978-0-7613-4253-3 lib bdg; 0-7613-4253-2 lib bdg

LC 2008-51850

Provides information on the sense of smell, including why there are good and bad smells and how noses function

"Given [its] . . . simple sentences, colorful layout, full-page photos, and well-chosen diagrams, [this title] . . . will be useful for reports." SLJ

Includes glossary and bibliographical references

What is taste? Lerner Publications Co. 2010 32p il (Lightning Bolt Books TM-Your amazing senses) lib bdg $25.26

Grades: K 1 2 **612.8**

1. Taste
ISBN 978-0-7613-4251-9 lib bdg; 0-7613-4251-6 lib bdg

LC 2008-51847

Explains how human beings use their sense of taste and illustrates good and bad tastes

"Given [its] . . . simple sentences, colorful layout, full-page photos, and well-chosen diagrams, [this title] . . . will be useful for reports." SLJ

Includes glossary and bibliographical references

What is touch? Lerner Publications Co. 2010 32p il (Lightning Bolt Books TM-Your amazing senses) lib bdg $25.26

Grades: K 1 2   **612.8**
    1. Touch
    ISBN 978-0-7613-4252-6 lib bdg; 0-7613-4252-4 lib bdg

LC 2008-51587

The book about touch has "simple sentences, colorful layout, full-page photos, and well-chosen diagrams . . . [and] will be useful for reports." SLJ

Brocket, Jane
    Spiky, slimy, smooth; what is texture? [text and photographs by Jane Brocket] Millbrook Press 2011 un il (Jane Brocket's clever concepts) lib bdg $25.26

Grades: PreK K 1 2   **612.8**
    1. Touch
    ISBN 978-0-7613-4614-2; 0-7613-4614-7

LC 2010028933

"Bright, attention-grabbing, and, in some cases, enlarged photographs of hard candies, duck slippers, stone walls, and other common objects give viewers the impression that they can reach out and touch them. That's exactly the point in this . . . book, which introduces texture to young children. It not only lets readers imagine what a woolly blanket or cactus plant might feel like but offers a host of adjectives, highlighted in color, to describe their textures. . . . Clever, indeed." Booklist

Cobb, Vicki
    Open your eyes; discover your sense of sight. illustrations by Cynthia C. Lewis. Millbrook Press 2001 un il (Five senses) lib bdg $22.90

Grades: 2 3 4   **612.8**
    1. Eye 2. Vision
    ISBN 0-7613-1705-8

LC 2001-30394

"A discussion of the science of the eye, its parts, and how it works, and easy, child-friendly experiments on sensory perception and optical illusions result in an interesting title and an amusing look at one of our five senses. The collage illustrations are done with photographs, newspapers, and drawings. Many have humorous captions." SLJ

    Your tongue can tell; discover your sense of taste. illustrations by Cynthia C. Lewis. Millbrook Press 2000 un il (Fivr senses) lib bdg $22.60; pa $7.95

Grades: 2 3 4   **612.8**
    1. Taste
    ISBN 0-7613-1473-3 lib bdg; 0-7613-1979-4 pa

LC 99-47873

Text and suggested activities explore the sense of taste, how it works, and how it can help us detect which foods are sweet, sour, salty, or spicy

Degen, Bruce
    The **magic** school bus explores the senses; illustrated by Bruce Degen. Scholastic Press 1999 47p il hardcover o.p. pa $5.99

Grades: 2 3 4   **612.8**
    1. Senses and sensation
    ISBN 0-590-44697-5; 0-590-44698-3 pa

LC 98-18662

Ms. Frizzle and her science class explore the senses by traveling on the magic school bus. "Grades two to five." (SLJ)

"Along the margins are snippets of information in the form of Frizzle Facts and excerpts from kids' school reports. Degen's clever illustrations are both humorous and informative, acting as excellent visual aids for little learners." Booklist

Funston, Sylvia
    It's all in your head; a guide to your brilliant brain. [by] Sylvia Funston, Jay Ingram; illustrated by Gary Clement. 2nd ed; Maple Tree Press 2005 64p il $16.95; pa $9.95

Grades: 3 4 5 6   **612.8**
    1. Brain 2. Psychology
    ISBN 1-897066-43-0; 1-897066-44-9 pa
    First published 1994 with title: A kid's guide to the brain

This "explains how the brain controls our senses, emotions, memory, and thinking. Each chapter includes experiments, with easy-to-find items such as buttons and jelly beans, brain teasers, . . . historical information, and current theories on brain function. . . . Color photographs and whimsical illustrations make the presentation appealing." SLJ

Ganeri, Anita
    Hearing; by Anita Ganeri. Smart Apple Media 2013 24 p. (hardcover, library bound: alk. paper) $25.65

Grades: K 1 2   **612.8**
    1. Hearing 2. Senses and sensation 3. Ear
    ISBN 1599208512; 9781599208510

LC 2012004122

This book by Anita Ganeri, part of a series on the senses, "begins with a succinct definition: 'Sounds make the air wobble.' From there, [readers] learn how our ear flaps catch sound with ear hair, why we have two ears, and other relevant stuff like ear wax, balance, and how the sense varies in other animals." (Publisher's note)

    Sight; by Anita Ganeri. Smart Apple Media 2013 24 p. (The senses) (hardcover, library bound: alk. paper) $25.65

Grades: K 1 2   **612.8**
    1. Picture books for children 2. Vision 3. Eye
    ISBN 1599208520; 9781599208527

LC 2012004123

This children's picture book by Anita Ganeri is part of the Senses series and looks at sight. At the beginning, a "diagram orients [readers] to all five senses . . . . The texts "discuss what each particular sense provides and the organs involved and how they work. . . . A final spread shares three or four facts that extend the topic." (School Library Journal)

    Smell; Anita Ganeri. A+/Smart Apple Media 2013 24 p. (Senses) (hardcover, library bound) $25.65

Grades: K 1 2   **612.8**
    1. Picture books for children 2. Smell 3. Nose
    ISBN 1599208539; 9781599208534

LC 2012004124

This children's picture book by Anita Ganeri is part of the Senses series and looks at smell. At the beginning, a "diagram orients [readers] to all five senses . . . . The texts "discuss what each particular sense provides and the organs involved and how they work. . . . A final spread shares three or four facts that extend the topic." (School Library Journal)

Taste; Anita Ganeri. A+/Smart Apple Media 2013 24 p. (Senses) (hardcover, library bound) $25.65

Grades: K 1 2   **612.8**

1. Picture books for children 2. Taste

ISBN 1599208547; 9781599208541

LC 2012008594

This children's picture book by Anita Ganeri is part of the Senses series and looks at smell. At the beginning, a "diagram orients [readers] to all five senses . . . . The texts "discuss what each particular sense provides and the organs involved and how they work. . . . A final spread shares three or four facts that extend the topic." (School Library Journal)

Gardner, Robert

Ace your science project about the senses; great science fair ideas. [by] Robert Gardner . . . [et al.] Enslow Publishers 2009 112p il (Ace your biology science project) lib bdg $31.93

Grades: 5 6 7 8   **612.8**

1. Science projects 2. Senses and sensation 3. Science -- Experiments

ISBN 978-0-7660-3217-0 lib bdg; 0-7660-3217-5 lib bdg

LC 2008-30797

"Presents several science projects and science project ideas about the senses." Publisher's note

Includes glossary and bibliographical references

Gold, Martha V.

Learning about the nervous system; by Martha V. Gold. Enslow Publishers 2013 48 p. (Learning about the human body systems) (library) $23.93

Grades: 5 6 7 8   **612.8**

1. Picture books for children 2. Nervous system

ISBN 0766041603; 9780766041608

LC 2012011103

This book by Martha V. Gold is part of the Learning About the Human Body Systems series and looks at the nervous system. "The nervous system is made up of the brain, the spinal cord and nerves. It is responsible for telling the heart to beat, the lungs to breathe, and the muscles to move. The brain—the central command center—processes everything from understanding a teacher's instructions to enjoying a piece of chocolate cake." (Publisher's note)

Includes bibliographical references and index.

Guillain, Charlotte

How do we hear? Heinemann Library 2008 24p il (Sounds all around us) lib bdg $20.71; pa $5.99

Grades: PreK K 1   **612.8**

1. Sound 2. Hearing 3. Sound waves

ISBN 978-1-4329-3201-5 lib bdg; 1-4329-3201-2 lib bdg; 978-1-4329-3207-7 pa; 1-4329-3207-1 pa

LC 2008-51738

Learn about sound waves, how the human ear works, and how animals can have a special sense of hearing.

This book "introduces the basics of sound through vibrant photographs, large text, and simple sentences. . . . [A] great introduction[s] and worthy addition[s]." SLJ

Includes glossary and bibliographical references

Our brains. Heinemann Library 2010 24p il (Our bodies) lib bdg $20.71; pa $5.99

Grades: K 1 2 3   **612.8**

1. Brain

ISBN 978-1-4329-3592-4 lib bdg; 1-4329-3592-5 lib bdg; 978-1-4329-3601-3 pa; 1-4329-3601-8 pa

LC 2009-22296

This explains what the brain is, how it controls other body parts, and how to keep it healthy.

This explains "visually and verbally complicated medical information in a clear, understandable way. . . . Large, vivid photographs are placed alongside one or two sentences per page." Booklist

Includes bibliographical references

Halvorson, Karin

Inside the brain; Karin Halvorson; consulting editor, Diane Craig. ABDO Pub. Co. 2013 32 p. (Super simple body) $27.07

Grades: 2 3 4 5   **612.8**

1. Brain 2. Brain -- Physiology

ISBN 1617836095; 9781617836091

LC 2012028763

Author Karin Halvorson's book "offers children an exciting voyage through the brain. Detailed illustrations, color photos, and simple text combine to make a fun and easy introduction to how the brain works. This book also includes simple activities and crafts like Reaction Action, Thinking Cap and how to make a Brain with how-to photos to further engage young learners." (Publisher's note)

Inside the ears; by Karin Halvorson. ABDO 2013 32 p. $27.07

Grades: 2 3 4 5   **612.8**

1. Ear 2. Human anatomy 3. Hearing

ISBN 1617836109; 9781617836107

LC 2012028770

In this book, by Karin Halvorson, readers will "find out what goes on every day inside of the human body! This title offers children [a] . . . voyage through the ears. Detailed illustrations, color photos, and simple text combine to make [an] introduction to how ears work. This book also includes simple activities and crafts like Tin Can Telephone, Music to My Ears and how to make an Ear with how-to photos." (Publisher's note)

Hewitt, Sally

Hear this! [by] Sally Hewitt. Crabtree Pub. 2008 24p il (Let's start! science) pa $6.95

Grades: PreK K 1 2   **612.8**

1. Sounds 2. Hearing

ISBN 978-0-7787-4058-2 pa; 0-7787-4058-7 pa

LC 2008-5007

First published 2005 by QEB publications

This book about hearing "will provide a good starting point for younger students to learn more about their senses. . . . Most chapters are accompanied by a related activity, none are too complex for the intended audience." Libr Media Connect

Includes glossary and bibliographical references

Look here! [by] Sally Hewitt. Crabtree 2008 24p il (Let's start! science) pa $6.95

Grades: PreK K 1 2   **612.8**
1. Vision
ISBN 978-0-7787-4059-9 pa; 0-7787-4059-5 pa
LC 2008-5008
First published 2005 by QEB publications with title:
Look out!

This book about vision "will provide a good starting
point for younger students to learn more about their senses. . . . Most chapters are accompanied by a related activity, none are too complex for the intended audience." Libr
Media Connect

Includes glossary and bibliographical references

Smell it! Crabtree Pub. Company 2008 24p il (Let's
start! science) pa $6.95
Grades: PreK K 1 2   **612.8**
1. Smell
ISBN 978-0-7787-4060-5 pa; 0-7787-4060-9 pa
LC 2008-5009
First published 2005 by QEB publications with title:
Smell that!

This book "will provide a good starting point for younger
students to learn more about their senses. . . . Most chapters
are accompanied by a related activity, none are too complex
for the intended audience." Libr Media Connect

Includes glossary and bibliographical references

Tastes good! [by] Sally Hewitt. Crabtree Pub. Com-
pany 2008 24p il (Let's start! science) pa $6.95
Grades: PreK K 1 2   **612.8**
1. Taste
ISBN 978-0-7787-4061-2 pa; 0-7787-4061-7 pa
LC 2008-5010
First published 2005 by QEB publications

This book "will provide a good starting point for younger
students to learn more about their senses. . . . Most chapters
are accompanied by a related activity, none are too complex
for the intended audience." Libr Media Connect

Includes glossary and bibliographical references

Touch that! [by] Sally Hewitt. Crabtree Pub. Co. 2008
24p il (Let's start! science) pa $6.95
Grades: PreK K 1 2   **612.8**
1. Touch
ISBN 978-0-7787-4062-9 pa; 0-7787-4062-5 pa
LC 2008-5011
First published 2005 by QEB publications

This book "will provide a good starting point for younger
students to learn more about their senses. . . . Most chapters
are accompanied by a related activity, none are too complex
for the intended audience." Libr Media Connect

Includes glossary and bibliographical references

Korb, Rena
My brain; illustrated by Remy Simard; content consultant, Anthony J. Weinhaus. Magic Wagon 2011 32p il (My
body) lib bdg $27.07
Grades: 1 2 3   **612.8**
1. Brain
ISBN 978-1-60270-805-1; 1-60270-805-3

This "volume stars a child narrator who straightforwardly describes [the brain] and how it works. A round-faced,
lab-coat-wearing man appears at the bottom of every spread
to provide additional details and tidbits of anatomical infor-

mation. . . . Black-outlined digital-looking cartoon illustrations enliven the [text]." Horn Book Guide

Includes glossary

Larsen, C. S.
Crust and spray; gross stuff in your eyes, ears, nose,
and throat. illustrated by Michael Slack. Millbrook Press
2010 48p il (Gross body science) lib bdg $29.27
Grades: 4 5 6   **612.8**
1. Ear 2. Eye 3. Nose 4. Throat
ISBN 978-0-8225-8964-8 lib bdg; 0-8225-8964-8
lib bdg
LC 2008-33777

"Solid information layered between sarcastic comments
and kid-friendly terminology like fart, poop, barf, and puke
will keep readers engaged. . . . Labeled, captioned (and
graphic) photographs, cartoon-style illustrations, and micrographs add information." SLJ

Includes glossary and bibliographical references

Macaulay, David
★ **Eye**; how it works. David Macaulay. Roaring Brook
Press 2013 28 p. (hardcover) $15.99
Grades: 1 2 3   **612.8**
1. Eye 2. Human anatomy
ISBN 1596437812; 9781596437814; 9781596437821
LC 2012951526

This children's nonfiction book discusses and illustrates
the working of the human eye, providing an anatomical perspective for young independent readers. Through both text
and drawings, author and illustrator "David Macaulay shows
how this extraordinary organ works to capture light and send
signals to our brains." (Publisher's note)

Read, Leon
My senses. Sea-to-Sea Publications 2010 23p il (Ti-
ger talk. All about me) lib bdg $24.25
Grades: PreK K   **612.8**
1. Senses and sensation
ISBN 978-1-59771-188-3 lib bdg; 1-59771-188-8
lib bdg
LC 2008-45010

This book about the senses "makes learning fun. . . .
[The] book employs a simplified game of 'Where's Waldo?'
by hiding a cartoon tiger on almost every page. This approach, combined with questions . . . will encourage discussion and involvement." SLJ

Royston, Angela
Why do I sleep? QEB Pub. 2010 24p il (QEB my
body) lib bdg $28.65
Grades: PreK K 1 2   **612.8**
1. Sleep
ISBN 978-1-59566-974-2 lib bdg; 1-59566-974-4
lib bdg
LC 2009-15226

Introduces the function and importance of sleep, and
outlines good sleeping habits

"This . . . is meant to be read to young children because it
is written at a higher reading level than its intended audience.
The information is straightforward, well presented, and easy
to understand. . . . [This] title is well designed, filled with
color photographs, and scattered with fact boxes. . . . This .

.. will be useful in preschool and primary classrooms where health and hygiene are stressed." Libr Media Connect

Includes glossary and bibliographical references

Scott, Elaine

All about sleep from A to ZZZZ; by Elaine Scott; illustrated by John O'Brien. Viking 2008 58p il $17.99

Grades: 5 6 7 8 9 10 **612.8**

1. Sleep

ISBN 978-0-670-06188-4; 0-670-06188-3

LC 2008-6074

"This excellent overview is packed with interesting tidbits. . . . Scott is careful to point out which information is factual and which is theory, an important distinction. . . . The fanciful cartoon illustrations add to the book's appeal. . . . It is interesting, highly engaging, and fun to read." SLJ

Showers, Paul

Sleep is for everyone; illustrated by Wendy Watson. HarperCollins Pubs. 1997 32p il (Let's-read-and-find-out science) hardcover o.p. pa $4.99

Grades: K 1 2 **612.8**

1. Sleep

ISBN 0-06-025392-4; 0-06-025393-s lib bdg; 0-06-445141-0 pa

LC 96-49375

A newly illustrated edition of the title first published 1974 by Crowell

This volume examines "how different animals sleep, why we sleep, and what happens while we sleep and when we don't sleep enough. Colorful paper cut-out illustrations are simple and light-hearted with mottled paper as background creating a restful, gentle feeling." Horn Book Guide

Simon, Seymour

★ The **brain**; our nervous system. [by] Seymour Simon. rev ed.; Collins 2006 30p il $17.99; pa $6.99

Grades: 4 5 6 7 **612.8**

1. Brain 2. Nervous system

ISBN 978-0-06-087718-7; 0-06-087718-9; 978-0-06-087719-4 pa; 0-06-087719-7 pa

LC 2007-272349

First published 1997

Describes the various parts of the brain and the nervous system and how they function to enable us to think, feel, move, and remember.

Simon's "clear, concise writing style is complemented by stunning color images taken with radiological scanners, such as CAT scans, MRIs, and SEMs (scanning electron microscopes.)" SLJ [review of 1997 edition]

Includes bibliographical references

★ **Eyes** and ears. HarperCollins Pubs. 2003 un il hardcover o.p. pa $6.99

Grades: 4 5 6 7 **612.8**

1. Ear 2. Eye 3. Vision 4. Hearing

ISBN 0-688-15303-8; 978-0-06-073302-5 pa; 0-06-073302-0 pa

LC 2002-19060

Describes the anatomy of the eye and ear, how those organs function and some ways in which they may malfunction, and how the brain is also involved in our seeing and hearing

"Simon is at his very best here. . . . The large, exquisitely reproduced photographs from a number of sources look like fiery planets, galaxies, and monster creatures. . . . The anatomy and physiology are detailed and accurate, with clear diagrams." Booklist

Simpson, Kathleen

The **human** brain; inside your body's control room. National Geographic 2009 64p il (National Geographic investigates) lib bdg $27.90

Grades: 5 6 7 8 **612.8**

1. Brain

ISBN 978-1-4263-0421-7 lib bdg; 1-4263-0421-8 lib bdg

"Readers will learn about . . . new brain research in this title, which includes a basic discussion of the parts of the brain, their functions, and how neurons send messages throughout the body. Information is also included about the role of the brain during sleep, dreaming, and various emotional states, as well as explanations of the various technologies available to measure brain activity. This is a well-organized, compelling introduction, sure to pique the curiosity of many children. Full-color photographs and illustrations enliven the text." SLJ

Includes bibliographical references

Stewart, Melissa

You've got nerve! the secrets of the brain and nerves. illustrated by Janet Hamlin. Marshall Cavendish Benchmark 2010 48p il (The gross and goofy body) lib bdg $20.95

Grades: 2 3 4 **612.8**

1. Nervous system

ISBN 978-0-7614-4157-1 lib bdg; 0-7614-4157-3 lib bdg

LC 2008033560

This includes information on the role the brain and nerves play in the body science of humans and animals

This "offers detailed science facts in a fashion approachable enough to make it a welcome supplement to school textbooks. . . . The layout is fresh, clean, and colorful, sidebars keep things conversational, and the back matter is solid." Booklist

Includes glossary and bibliographical references

Tieck, Sarah

Nervous system. ABDO Pub. 2011 32p il (Body systems) lib bdg $27.07; ebook $27.07

Grades: 2 3 4 **612.8**

1. Nervous system

ISBN 978-1-61613-500-3 lib bdg; 1-61613-500-X lib bdg; 978-1-61613-990-4 ebook

LC 2010019654

"Double-page spreads describe the workings of the [nervous system] . . . with simple text on left-hand pages and large, colorful photographs or diagrams on the right. The [text touches] on common disorders . . . and healthy practices. 'Brain Food' spreads pose three questions and provide answers. Ample white space, engaging images, and 'Word of Mouth' sidebars are reader-friendly." Horn Book Guide

Includes glossary

Veitch, Catherine

Sound and hearing. Heinemann Library 2009 24p il (Sounds all around us) lib bdg $20.71; pa $5.99
Grades: PreK K I   **612.8**
1. Sound 2. Hearing 3. Sound waves
ISBN 978-1-4329-3224-4 lib bdg; 1-4329-3224-1 lib bdg; 978-1-4329-3225-1 pa; 1-4329-3225-X pa
LC 2008-51741

This book "introduces the basics of sound through vibrant photographs, large text, and simple sentences. . . . [A] great introduction[s] and worthy addition[s]." SLJ

Includes glossary

Winston, Robert M. L., 1940-

What goes on in my head? how your brain works and why you do what you do. [by] Robert Winston. DK Pub. 2010 96p il $16.99
Grades: 4 5 6 7   **612.8**
1. Brain 2. Psychology
ISBN 978-0-7566-6885-3; 0-7566-6885-9

"The author presents a great deal of scientific content and supplements it with examples, anecdotes, and current findings in the field. . . . In addition, interactive brain teasers and exercises make the science come alive. . . . The book combines vibrant colors and illustrations with explanations to keep young readers engaged." Sci Books Films

613   Personal health and safety

Ajmera, Maya

Healthy kids; Maya Ajmera, Victoria Dunning, Cynthia Pon. Charlesbridge 2012 32 p. (reinforced) $17.95
Grades: PreK K 1 2   **613**
1. Everyday life 2. Children -- Health and hygiene 3. Multiculturalism
ISBN 1580894364; 9781580894364; 9781580894371
LC 2012000784

This book, by Maya Ajmera, Victoria Dunning, and Cynthia Pon, part of the "Global Fund of Children Book" series, offers photographs of children throughout the world doing about active and healthy daily life. Activities profiled include eating food, playing, and doing chores. Children from several countries are illustrated, including Argentina, Bhutan, Canada, Guatemala, Romania and Kenya.

Gardner, Robert

Ace your exercise and nutrition science project: great science fair ideas; [by] Robert Gardner, Barbara Gardner Conklin, and Salvatore Tocci. Enslow Publishers 2009 128p il (Ace your biology science project) lib bdg $31.93
Grades: 5 6 7 8   **613**
1. Exercise 2. Nutrition 3. Science projects 4. Science -- Experiments
ISBN 978-0-7660-3218-7 lib bdg; 0-7660-3218-3 lib bdg
LC 2008-30798

"Presents several science projects and science project ideas about exercise and nutrition." Publisher's note

Includes bibliographical references

Lehman, Robert

★ **Will** puberty last my whole life? real answers to real questions from preteens about body changes, sex, and other growing-up stuff. Julie Giesy Metzger and Robert Lehman; illustrated by Cerizo. Sasquatch Books 2011 90 p. col. ill. (pbk.) $16.95
Grades: 4 5 6 7 8   **613**
1. Puberty 2. Questions and answers 3. Boys -- Health and hygiene 4. Girls -- Health and hygiene 5. Teenage boys -- Physiology 6. Teenage girls -- Physiology 7. Interpersonal relations in adolescence
ISBN 1570617392; 9781570617393
LC 2011038401

This book "for boys and girls between the ages of 9 and 12 has questions asked by girls in one half of the book" and "questions asked by boys are on the other side." The book contains "answers to questions pre-adolescents have about puberty, friends, feelings, sex, pimples, babies, body hair, menstruation, bras, and much more." (Amazon.com)

Miller, Edward, 1964-

★ The **monster** health book; a guide to eating healthy, being active, & feeling great for monsters & kids! [by] Edward Miller. Holiday House 2006 40p il $16.95
Grades: 2 3 4   **613**
1. Health 2. Nutrition
ISBN 978-0-8234-1956-2; 0-8234-1956-8
LC 2005046383

"Featuring a friendly, rotund, green monster determined to make healthy choices, this book presents basic information about food, exercise, and health. . . . Subjects include food nutrients, counting calories and understanding food labels, tips for making healthy lunches and snacks, the benefits of getting enough sleep and exercise, and ways to improve self-esteem. Miller's retro-style illustrations fill the pages with color, shapes, and humorous details, and silly jokes are tucked everywhere. . . . This lively, visually appealing book . . . belongs in children's hands." SLJ

Natterson, Cara

The **care** & keeping of you 2; the body book for older girls. Dr. Cara Natterson; illustrated by Josee Masse. American Girl 2013 96 p. (paperback) $12.99
Grades: 5 6 7 8   **613**
1. Puberty 2. Life skills -- Handbooks, manuals, etc. 3. Teenage girls -- Health and hygiene4. Girls -- Life skills guides
ISBN 1609580427; 9781609580421
LC 2012045813

This book, by Cara Natterson, illustrated by Josee Masse, is a body image and physiology guide written for girls going through puberty. "This . . . advice book will guide you through the next steps of growing up. . . . This book covers new questions about periods, your growing body, peer pressure, personal care, and more." (Publisher's note)

"The friendly illustrations support the overall tone and style. . . . Its neutral, matter-of-fact approach will help show readers . . . that all the changes they may be feeling are perfectly normal." SLJ

Pfeifer, Kate Gruenwald

American Medical Assocation boy's guide to becoming a teen. Jossey-Bass 2006 128p il pa $12.95

Grades: 4 5 6 7   **613**
1. Puberty 2. Adolescence 3. Boys -- Health and hygiene
ISBN 0-7879-8343-8

"This guide addresses puberty's changes clearly. . . . The text's approach is straightforward, accessible, and nonjudgmental, whether the topic is same-sex attraction or divorcing parents. The volume closes with an extensive resource section, including hotlines." Booklist

Includes bibliographical references

American Medical Association girl's guide to becoming a teen. Jossey-Bass 2006 128p pa $12.95
Grades: 4 5 6 7   **613**
1. Puberty 2. Adolescence 3. Girls -- Health and hygiene
ISBN 0-7879-8344-6

This "covers the physical and emotional changes that puberty brings, along with solid tips about grooming, diet, exercise, and other health issues, such as eating disorders. . . . The clear text communicates concepts clearly , . . and girls will find plenty of useful information." Booklist

Includes bibliographical references

Read, Leon
Keeping well. Sea-to-Sea Publications 2010 23p il (Tiger talk. All about me) lib bdg $24.25
Grades: PreK K   **613**
1. Health 2. Hygiene
ISBN 978-1-59771-186-9 lib bdg; 1-59771-186-1 lib bdg
      LC 2008-45008

This book about keeping well "makes learning fun. . . . [The] book employs a simplified game of 'Where's Waldo?' by hiding a cartoon tiger on almost every page. This approach, combined with questions . . . will encourage discussion and involvement." SLJ

Royston, Angela
Why do I wash my hands? QEB Pub. 2010 24p il (QEB my body) lib bdg $28.65
Grades: PreK K 1 2   **613**
1. Hygiene
ISBN 978-1-59566-972-8 lib bdg; 1-59566-972-8 lib bdg
      LC 2009-15228

Introduces the effects of germs on the skin and outlines the principles of personal hygiene.

"The information is straightforward, well presented, and easy to understand. . . . [This] title is well designed, filled with color photographs, and scattered with fact boxes." Libr Media Connect

Includes glossary and bibliographical references

Schaefer, Adam
Staying healthy; [by] A. R. Schaefer. Heinemann Library 2010 32p il (Health and fitness) lib bdg $25.36; pa $7.99
Grades: PreK K 1   **613**
1. Health 2. Hygiene 3. Exercise
ISBN 978-1-4329-2769-1 lib bdg; 1-4329-2769-8 lib bdg; 978-1-4329-2774-5 pa; 1-4329-2774-4 pa
      LC 2008-52298

Find out about the importance of a good diet, exercise, staying clean, and what to do if you are injured or sick.

"Spare, declarative sentences coupled with bright, full-color photos . . . [makes this book] appropriate for reading aloud in the classroom or even during a themed story hour. . . . While each spread introduces a new topic . . . [a] solid [introduction] and [conclusion] make for [a] cohesive [package]." SLJ

Includes glossary and bibliographical references

Schaefer, Valorie
The **care** & keeping of you; the body book for younger girls. by Valorie Schaefer; Cara Natterson, MD, medical consultant; illustrated by Josee Masse. American Girl Publishing 2012 102 p. (pbk.) $12.99
Grades: 3 4 5 6   **613**
1. Puberty 2. Girls -- Health and hygiene 3. Grooming for girls 4. Preteens -- Health and hygiene
ISBN 1609580834; 9781609580834
      LC 2012045846

This book by Valorie Schaefer, illustrated by Josee Masse includes "all-new illustrations and updated content for girls ages 8 and up, it features tips, how-tos, and facts from the experts." Readers will "find answers to questions about your changing body, from hair care to healthy eating, bad breath to bras, periods to pimples, and everything in between." (Publisher's note)

"Head-to-toe advice for preteen girls. This cheerful discussion of the changes puberty brings combines friendly, conversational advice from the author with signed comments and questions, perhaps from preteens...Positive and personal, this might be an especially good choice for early bloomers." Kirkus

Companion to:
The Care and Keeping of You 2: The Body Book for Older Girls

Body book for younger girls
Care and keeping of you

Simons, Rae
At home in your body; care for the shape you're in. Mason Crest Publishers 2010 48p il (Kids & obesity) lib bdg $19.95; pa $7.95
Grades: 3 4 5   **613**
1. Obesity 2. Self-confidence 3. Health self-care 4. Personal appearance
ISBN 978-1-4222-1715-3 lib bdg; 1-4222-1715-9 lib bdg; 978-1-4222-1903-4 pa; 1-4222-1903-8 pa
      LC 2010015436

Discusses healthy body types.

This book "presents the expected information about the food pyramid, the need for physical activity, and the influence of the media on our psyches. Where the material shines is in its holistic approach. Readers are encouraged to develop their inner lives as much as their physical selves and to take responsibility for their own health and eating habits. . . . This brightly-colored, ego-boosting, responsibility-championing . . . [book] is a winner." SLJ

Includes bibliographical references

Does television make you fat? lifestyle and obesity. Mason Crest Publishers 2010 48p il (Kids & obesity) lib bdg $19.95; pa $7.95

Grades: 3 4 5   **613**
1. Obesity 2. Exercise 3. Lifestyles
ISBN 978-1-4222-1712-2 lib bdg; 1-4222-1712-4 lib
bdg; 978-1-4222-1900-3 pa; 1-4222-1900-3 pa
       LC 2010022849
This book about lifestyle and obesity "presents the expected information about the food pyramid, the need for
physical activity, and the influence of the media on our
psyches. Where the material shines is in its holistic approach. Readers are encouraged to develop their inner lives
as much as their physical selves and to take responsibility for
their own health and eating habits. . . . This brightly-colored,
ego-boosting, responsibility-championing . . . [book] is a
winner." SLJ
Includes bibliographical references

613.2   Dietetics

Currie, Stephen
Junk food. Cherry Lake Pub. 2009 32p il (Health at
risk) lib bdg $27.07
Grades: 4 5 6 7 8   **613.2**
1. Nutrition
ISBN 978-1-60279-284-5 lib bdg; 1-60279-284-4
lib bdg
       LC 2008017498
This describes what junk food is, why it's not good for
your body, and what's being done to help us control our junk
food habit.
"Great for reports or reluctant readers." Booklist
Includes bibliographical references

Doeden, Matt
Eat right! how you can make good food choices. illustrations by Jack Desrocher. Lerner Publications 2008 64p
il (Health zone) lib bdg $30.60
Grades: 4 5 6 7   **613.2**
1. Nutrition
ISBN 978-0-8225-7552-8; 0-8225-7552-3
       LC 2007043322
"This offers a highly readable, never preachy exploration into the benefits of providing quality fuel for your body.
It opens with an anecdote of a kid who snacks on soda and
chips while playing volleyball. A friend challenges him to to
eat better for a week, and he comes back with more sustained
energy and a fresh outlook. . . . The following chapters do a
great job of detailing everything from the food pyramid and
benefits of different nutrients to warnings against following
the faddish, ineffective diets." Booklist
Includes bibliographical references

Durrie, Karen
Health. Weigl 2011 il (Community helpers) $27.13
Grades: PreK K 1 2   **613.2**
1. Health 2. Nutrition
ISBN 978-1-61690-950-5; 1-61690-950-1
       LC 2011024904
"A diverse group of people represents seven occupations: doctor, nurse, optometrist, fitness teacher, nutritionist,
counselor, and dentist. A large, color photo fills each double-page spread, along with a text box carrying a sentence,
such as 'I check your teeth and gums to make sure they are

healthy.' . . . All the clearly reproduced photos provide clues
that will help children guess who is speaking." Booklist

Edwards, Hazel
Talking about your weight; by Hazel Edwards and
Goldie Alexander. Gareth Stevens 2010 32p il (Healthy
living) lib bdg $26
Grades: 4 5 6 7   **613.2**
1. Obesity 2. Nutrition 3. Weight loss
ISBN 978-1-4339-3655-5; 1-4339-3655-0
"This guidebook offers a simple look at healthy lifestyle
choices involving exercise and diet. It examines people's relationships with food, body shape and genetics, eating disorders, and ways to combat obesity." Publisher's note

Furgang, Adam
Carbonated beverages; the incredibly disgusting story.
Rosen Central 2011 48p il (Incredibly disgusting food) lib
bdg $26.50; pa $11.75
Grades: 4 5 6 7   **613.2**
1. Carbonated beverages
ISBN 978-1-4488-1266-0 lib bdg; 1-4488-1266-6 lib
bdg; 978-1-4488-2282-9 pa; 1-4488-2282-3 pa
       LC 2010023227
This presents "straightforward information about why
[carbonated beverages] are unhealthy without resorting to
extreme gross-out factors. The [book contains] a breakdown
of the foods' components . . . insight into how they are processed, and both short- and long-term effects of consumption. . . . Readers may or may not be disgusted, but they will
definitely learn a thing or two about smart eating habits."
SLJ
Includes glossary and bibliographical references

Salty and sugary snacks; the incredibly disgusting story. Rosen Central 2011 48p il (Incredibly disgusting food)
lib bdg $26.50; pa $11.75
Grades: 4 5 6 7   **613.2**
1. Salt 2. Sugar 3. Nutrition 4. Snack foods
ISBN 978-1-4488-1267-7 lib bdg; 1-4488-1267-4 lib
bdg; 978-1-4488-2283-6 pa; 1-4488-2283-1 pa
       LC 2010025751
This book describes how salty and sugary snacks put
dangerous amounts of sugar and salt into our bodies and
how these unnecessary calories can have terrible effects on
the body.
"Readers may or may not be disgusted, but they will definitely learn a thing or two about smart eating habits." SLJ
Includes glossary and bibliographical references

Harris, Robie H., 1940-
What's so yummy? all about eating well and feeling
good. Robie H. Harris, illustrated by Nadine Bernard Westcott. 1st edition Candlewick Press 2014 40 p. color illustrations (reinforced) $15.99
Grades: PreK K 1   **613.2**
1. Health 2. Nutrition
ISBN 9780763636326; 0763636320
       LC 2013955674
In this children's book by Robie H. Harris, illustrated
by Nadine Bernard Westcott, "Gus, Nellie, and baby Jake
can't wait to go on a picnic! In the morning the family heads
to their community garden, then to the farmer's market and

the grocery store to gather vegetables, fruit, meat, and other fresh and delicious foods." (Publisher's note)

"[T]he main text discusses topics related to wholesome eating and feeling good. Speech balloons on every double-page spread carry the children's dialogue. . . . Including a wide variety of people in the backgrounds, Westcott's digital line-and-wash illustrations are clearly delineated, cheerful, and appealing." Booklist

Head, Honor

Healthy eating; Honor Head. Sea to Sea Publications 2013 30 p. (alk. paper) $28.50

Grades: 2 3 4   613.2

1. Nutrition 2. Food 3. Health

ISBN 1597713945; 9781597713948

LC 2011052695

This book, by Honor Head, "asks and answers questions about healthy eating. It explores why fruit and vegetables are good for us, what are the best snacks, why we shouldn't just eat sweet foods and much more. It is part of the 'Let's read and talk about' series which includes ready-to-use questions and discussion points to help young readers gain more from their reading experience, and to give . . . teachers and parents quality extension material." (Publisher's note)

Hunt, Jamie

The truth about diets; what's right for you? Mason Crest Publishers 2011 48p il (Kids & obesity) lib bdg $19.95; pa $7.95

Grades: 3 4 5   613.2

1. Diet 2. Nutrition 3. Weight loss

ISBN 978-1-4222-1710-8 lib bdg; 1-4222-1710-8 lib bdg; 978-1-4222-1898-3 pa; 1-4222-1898-8 pa

LC 2010010014

Learn about diets and whether or not they are actually a good way to lose weight.

This "presents the expected information about the food pyramid, the need for physical activity, and the influence of the media on our psyches. Where the material shines is in its holistic approach. Readers are encouraged to develop their inner lives as much as their physical selves and to take responsibility for their own health and eating habits. . . . This brightly-colored, ego-boosting, responsibility-championing . . . [book] is a winner." SLJ

Includes bibliographical references

Johanson, Paula

Fake foods; fried, fast, and processed: the incredibly disgusting story. Rosen Central 2011 48p il (Incredibly disgusting food) lib bdg $26.50; pa $11.75

Grades: 4 5 6 7   613.2

1. Nutrition 2. Natural foods 3. Convenience foods

ISBN 978-1-4488-1269-1 lib bdg; 1-4488-1269-0 lib bdg; 978-1-4488-2285-0 pa; 1-4488-2285-8 pa

LC 2010020534

This presents "straightforward information about why various junk foods are unhealthy without resorting to extreme gross-out factors. The [book contains] a breakdown of the foods' components . . . insight into how they are processed, and both short- and long-term effects of consumption. . . . Readers may or may not be disgusted, but they will

definitely learn a thing or two about smart eating habits." SLJ

Includes glossary and bibliographical references

King, Hazel

Carbohydrates for a healthy body; 2nd ed.; Heinemann Library 2009 48p il (Body needs) $17.99; pa $8.99

Grades: 4 5 6   613.2

1. Nutrition 2. Carbohydrates

ISBN 978-1-4329-2186-6; 1-4395-3782-8; 978-1-4329-2192-7 pa; 1-4329-2192-4 pa

LC 2009290513

First published 2003

Describes what carbohydrates are, what types of foods contain them, how they are digested and used to produce energy, and their role in a healthy diet.

This is "written in a clear, organized style and the full-color illustrations and photos complement the [text]." SLJ [review of 2003 edition]

Includes bibliographical references

Leedy, Loreen

The edible pyramid; good eating every day. written and illustrated by Loreen Leedy. rev ed.; Holiday House 2007 un il $17.95; pa $6.95

Grades: K 1 2 3   613.2

1. Diet 2. Nutrition

ISBN 978-0-8234-2074-2; 0-8234-2074-4; 978-0-8234-2075-9 pa; 0-8234-2075-2 pa

LC 2006036590

First published 1994

This is a "picture-book guide to healthy, delicious eating. . . . Featuring the smart cat waiter at the Edible Pyramid restaurant who recommends the menu to stylishly dressed animal customers, the bright, clear pictures show breads and grains, pasta in amazing shapes, vegetables and fruits in delicious colors, an abundance of beans, and more." Booklist

Powell, Jillian

Fats for a healthy body; 2nd ed.; Heinemann Library 2009 48p il (Body needs) lib bdg $31.43

Grades: 4 5 6   613.2

1. Nutrition 2. Oils and fats

ISBN 978-1-4329-2187-3 lib bdg; 1-4329-2187-8 lib bdg

LC 2009290512

First published 2003

Discusses what fats are, how they are absorbed and stored in the body, how the body uses fats, and health problems caused by fats.

Includes bibliographical references

Rau, Dana Meachen, 1971-

Going vegetarian; a healthy guide to making the switch. by Dana Meachen Rau. Compass Point Books 2012 64 p. (hardcover) $33.99

Grades: 5 6 7 8 9   613.2

1. Nutrition 2. Vegetarianism 3. Vegetarian cooking 4. Vegetarian children

ISBN 0756545226; 9780756545222; 9780756545307

LC 2011040836

Author Dana Meachen Rau presents a guide to becoming a vegetarian. "Learn about the benefits and challenges of a diet that does not include red meat, poultry, or fish. Helpful tips, delicious vegetarian recipes, and how tos will make the switch so much easier." The book also offers various organic, meatless, and vegan recipes and meal ideas. (Publisher"s note)

"Whether looking to go organic, ovo-lacto vegetarian, or vegan, kids will find the information necessary to make the switch in these titles...Organic focuses on the USDA's National Organic Program (NOP) regulations, making no mention of other certification programs. It does, however, warn kids about trusting organic labels implicitly and recommends that they go straight to the source when possible by researching and even visiting companies. Serve these up to budding health foodies.." (School Library Journal)

Includes bibliographical references (p. 62) and index

Royston, Angela
Proteins for a healthy body; 2nd ed.; Heinemann Library 2009 48p il (Body needs) lib bdg $31.43; pa $8.99
Grades: 4 5 6   **613.2**
1. Proteins 2. Nutrition
ISBN 978-1-4329-2188-0; 1-4329-2188-6 lib bdg; 978-1-4329-2194-1 pa; 1-4329-2194-0 pa
LC 2009290511

First published 2003
"Royston looks at different kinds of proteins—antibodies, hormones, enzymes—and how vegetarians and vegans can get enough of them. . . . [This is] written in a clear, organized style and the full-color illustrations and photos complement the [text]." SLJ [review of 2003 edition]

Vitamins and minerals for a healthy body; 2nd ed.; Heinemann Library 2009 48p il (Body needs) lib bdg $31.43; pa $8.99
Grades: 4 5 6   **613.2**
1. Minerals 2. Vitamins 3. Nutrition
ISBN 978-1-4329-2189-7; 1-4329-2189-4 lib bdg; 978-1-4329-2195-8 pa; 1-4329-2195-9 pa
LC 2009293230

First published 2003
Discusses what vitamins and minerals are, how they are digested, absorbed, and used by the body, and the role of these substances in a healthy diet
Includes bibliographical references

Water and fiber for a healthy body; 2nd ed.; Heinemann Library 2009 48p il (Body needs) lib bdg $31.43; pa $8.99
Grades: 4 5 6   **613.2**
1. Water 2. Nutrition 3. Food -- Fiber content
ISBN 978-1-4329-2190-3 lib bdg; 1-4329-2190-8; 978-1-4329-2196-5 pa; 1-4329-2196-7 pa
LC 2009293229

First published 2003
Discusses what water and fiber are, what foods they can be found in, and how the body absorbs, digests, and uses these ingredients
Includes bibliographical references

Schaefer, Adam
Healthy food; [by] A. R. Schaefer. Heinemann Library 2010 32p il (Health and fitness) lib bdg $25.36; pa $7.99

Grades: PreK K 1   **613.2**
1. Diet 2. Nutrition
ISBN 978-1-4329-2768-4 lib bdg; 1-4329-2768-X lib bdg; 978-1-4329-2773-8 pa; 1-4329-2773-6 pa
LC 2008-52367

Find out what the main food groups are, and the best ways to eat these foods
"Spare, declarative sentences coupled with bright, full-color photos . . . [makes this book] appropriate for reading aloud in the classroom or even during a themed story hour. . . . While each spread introduces a new topic . . . [a] solid [introduction] and [conclusion] make for [a] cohesive [package]." SLJ

Includes glossary and bibliographical references

Simons, Rae
Bigger isn't always better; choosing your portions. Mason Crest Publishers 2011 48p il (Kids & obesity) lib bdg $19.95; pa $7.95
Grades: 3 4 5   **613.2**
1. Diet 2. Obesity 3. Nutrition 4. Eating customs
ISBN 978-1-4222-1706-1 lib bdg; 1-4222-1706-X lib bdg; 978-1-4222-1894-5 pa; 1-4222-1894-5 pa
LC 2010028159

Explores the contributions of increasingly larger portion sizes to the problem of obesity in America.

This book "presents the expected information about the food pyramid, the need for physical activity, and the influence of the media on our psyches. Where the material shines is in its holistic approach. Readers are encouraged to develop their inner lives as much as their physical selves and to take responsibility for their own health and eating habits. . . . This brightly-colored, ego-boosting, responsibility-championing . . . [book] is a winner." SLJ
Includes bibliographical references

Thompson, Helen
Cookies or carrots? you are what you eat. Mason Crest Publishers 2010 48p il (Kids & obesity) lib bdg $19.95; pa $7.95
Grades: 3 4 5   **613.2**
1. Diet 2. Nutrition
ISBN 978-1-4222-1707-8 lib bdg; 1-4222-1707-8 lib bdg; 978-1-4222-1895-2 pa; 1-4222-1895-3 pa
LC 2010025502

This book about nutrition and diet "presents the expected information about the food pyramid, the need for physical activity, and the influence of the media on our psyches. Where the material shines is in its holistic approach. Readers are encouraged to develop their inner lives as much as their physical selves and to take responsibility for their own health and eating habits. . . . This brightly-colored, ego-boosting, responsibility-championing . . . [book] is a winner." SLJ
Includes bibliographical references

Watson, Stephanie
Mystery meat; hot dogs, sausages, and lunch meats: the incredibly disgusting story. Rosen Pub. Group 2011 48p il (Incredibly disgusting food) lib bdg $26.50; pa $11.75
Grades: 4 5 6 7   **613.2**
1. Meat 2. Sausages 3. Nutrition 4. Frankfurters
ISBN 978-1-4488-1268-4 lib bdg; 1-4488-1268-2 lib bdg; 978-1-4488-2284-3 pa; 1-4488-2284-X pa
LC 2010013649

"The short but substantive chapters begin with a look at typical hot-dog ingredients and manufacturing practices, followed by discussions of how 'mystery meats,' including common, highly processed sandwich fillers, affect the body. A closing chapter about the components of a healthy diet widens the book into an opportunity for adults and kids to discuss general nutrition and includes useful tips on reading food labels. . . . Young readers will find plenty of browsing and report fodder in these pages." Booklist

Includes bibliographical references

Zahensky, Barbara A.
Diet fads. Rosen 2007 64p il (Danger zone: dieting and eating disorders) lib bdg $27.95
Grades: 4 5 6 7 8   613.2
 1. Obesity 2. Weight loss
 ISBN 978-1-4042-1999-1
 "This clearly written overview emphasizes the impact of super-thin celebrity images on general self-esteem. . . . Zahensky considers the reasons people overeat and walks readers through practical steps to recognizing true hunger, making a weight-loss plan, and establishing good diet and exercise habits. She examines different types of fad and crash diets, pointing out their inherent dangers." SLJ

613.4   Personal cleanliness

Head, Honor
Keeping clean; by Honor Head. Sea-to-Sea Publications 2013 30 p. (Let's read and talk about) (hdbk.: alk. paper) $28.50
Grades: 2 3 4   613.4
 1. Children -- Health and hygiene 2. Hygiene
 ISBN 1597713953; 9781597713955
                           LC 2011052696
 This book, by Honor Head, "asks and answers questions about keeping clean. It explores why you should wash, how you can stop germs spreading, how to keep hair and teeth clean and much more. It is part of the 'Let's read and talk about' series which includes ready-to-use questions and discussion points to help young readers gain more from their reading experience, and to give busy teachers and parents quality extension material." (Publisher's note)

613.6   Personal safety and special topics of health

Catel, Patrick
Surviving stunts and other amazing feats. Raintree 2011 56p il (Extreme survival)
Grades: 4 5 6 7   613.6
 1. Stunts
 ISBN 1-4109-3969-3; 978-1-4109-3969-2
                           LC 2010028690
 This book is "fun and informative. [This] well-organized title starts with an overview, offers some specific examples, and includes additional facts or tips and resources. Catel defines activities that encompass adventure and amazement and then leads readers through a discussion of sideshows, movies, and daring stunts (some of which include fire). . . . [It features] dramatic archival and full-color photos on

nearly every page. . . . [This is a book] that youngsters will enjoy and talk about." SLJ

Includes glossary and bibliographical references

Champion, Neil
Finding food and water. Amicus 2010 32p il (Survive alive) lib bdg $28.50
Grades: 4 5 6 7   613.6
 1. Wilderness survival
 ISBN 978-1-60753-037-4 lib bdg; 1-60753-037-6 lib bdg
                           LC 2009030889
 This offers survival tips for finding food and water in the wild, including how to know what is safe to eat or drink from land, plant, and animal sources.
 This "colorful [book contains] numerous photos and illustrations that effectively break the [text] into small, readable chunks. There's lots of practical, everyday information here. . . . Brief yet gripping real-life survival stories are interspersed throughout the [book]." SLJ
 Includes glossary

Finding your way. Amicus 2011 32p il (Survive alive) lib bdg $28.50
Grades: 4 5 6 7   613.6
 1. Orienteering 2. Wilderness survival
 ISBN 978-1-60753-038-1 lib bdg; 1-60753-038-4 lib bdg
                           LC 2009030888
 "With eye-catching photographs, clear explanations, a survival skills quiz, a glossary, Web sites, and 'True Survival' stories . . . this engaging text encourages readers to figure out where they are and where they want to go." Booklist
 Includes glossary

In an emergency. Amicus 2010 32p il (Survive alive) lib bdg $28.50
Grades: 4 5 6 7   613.6
 1. Survival skills
 ISBN 978-1-60753-040-4; 1-60753-040-6
                           LC 2010002517
 This offers survival tips on what to do in emergency situations. Includes scenarios about fire, bad weather, accidents, injuries, extreme conditions, and more.'
 This "colorful [book contains] numerous photos and illustrations that effectively break the [text] into small, readable chunks. There's lots of practical, everyday information here. . . . Brief yet gripping real-life survival stories are interspersed throughout the [book]." SLJ
 Includes glossary

Making shelter. Amicus 2010 32p il (Survive alive) lib bdg $28.50
Grades: 4 5 6 7   613.6
 1. Wilderness survival
 ISBN 978-1-60753-041-1 lib bdg; 1-60753-041-4 lib bdg
                           LC 2010001378
 This offers survival tips for building shelter in the wild, including using natural means in different regions such as the desert, forest, jungle, and cold areas. Also includes information on what to bring for aid when building shelters.

Hurley, Michael

Surviving the wilderness. Raintree 2011 56p il (Extreme survival) lib bdg $33.50

Grades: 4 5 6 7   **613.6**

1. Wilderness survival

ISBN 978-1-4109-3972-2; 1-4109-3972-3

LC 2010028839

This book is "fun and informative. [This] well-organized title starts with an overview [of wilderness survival], offers some specific examples, and includes additional facts or tips and resources. . . . [It features] dramatic archival and full-color photos on nearly every page. . . . [This is a book] that youngsters will enjoy and talk about." SLJ

Includes glossary and bibliographical references

Long, Denise

Survivor kid; a practical guide to wilderness survival. Chicago Review Press 2011 222p il $12.95

Grades: 4 5 6 7   **613.6**

1. Wilderness survival

ISBN 978-1-56976-708-5; 1-56976-708-4

LC 2011004952

"Long offers lessons on how to stay healthy and out of trouble while awaiting rescue. Her matter-of-fact, no-nonsense tone will play well with young readers, and the clear writing style is appropriate to the content. The engaging guide covers everything from building shelters to avoiding pigs and javelinas. . . . The volume invites browsing as much as studying. . . . An excellent bibliography will lead young readers to a host of fascinating websites, and 150 clipart-style line drawings complement the text." Kirkus

Includes bibliographical references

Miller, Edward, 1964-

Fireboy to the rescue! a fire safety book. Holiday House 2010 un il $16.95

Grades: K 1 2   **613.6**

1. Fire fighting 2. Fire prevention 3. Safety education

ISBN 978-0-8234-2222-7; 0-8234-2222-4

"Fireboy is a superhero intent on keeping the world's children safe from fire. After heralding all the great things fire can do . . . the cut paper-style artwork bursts into reds and yellows and oranges as all manners of things—including homes—catch aflame. . . . The snazzy presentation is entertaining in its own right. . . . Some of the especially vital details (fire alarms, extinguishers) are incorporated as photos." Booklist

Nelson, Sara Kirsten

Stay safe! how you can keep out of harm's way. by Sara Nelson; illustrated by Jack Desrocher. Lerner Publications 2008 64p il (Health zone) lib bdg $30.60

Grades: 4 5 6 7   **613.6**

1. Safety education 2. Children and strangers 3. Child sexual abuse -- Prevention

ISBN 978-0-8225-7551-1; 0-8225-7551-5

The offers safety education on such subjects as bullying in schools, inappropriate touching by family members, internet solicitations and threats in public places (such as attempted abductions).

"The format is beyond lively, with lots of color, cartoons, and an informal writing style, but it manages to present sometimes frightening material in a non-threatening and browsable way." Booklist

Includes glossary and bibliographical references

Schaefer, Adam

Staying safe. Heinemann Library 2009 32p il (Health and fitness) lib bdg $25.36; pa $7.99

Grades: PreK K 1   **613.6**

1. Safety education

ISBN 978-1-4329-2770-7 lib bdg; 1-4329-2770-1 lib bdg; 978-1-4329-2775-2 pa; 1-4329-2775-2 pa

LC 2008-52300

Find out what to do in a fire, how to stay safe in the street, and who to call in an emergency.

"Spare, declarative sentences coupled with bright, full-color photos . . . [makes this book] appropriate for reading aloud in the classroom or even during a themed story hour. . . . While each spread introduces a new topic . . . [a] solid [introduction] and [conclusion] make for [a] cohesive [package]." SLJ

Includes glossary and bibliographical references

613.7   Physical fitness

Aikman, Louise

Pilates step-by-step; [by] Louise Aikman and Matthew Harvey. Rosen Central 2011 93p il (Skills in motion) lib bdg $31.95

Grades: 5 6 7 8   **613.7**

1. Pilates method

ISBN 978-1-4488-1549-4; 1-4488-1549-5

LC 2010007510

Presents a general guide to the Pilates exercise system using a sequence of stop-action images and text instructions to illustrate some of the most common movements.

Includes bibliographical references

Atha, Antony

Fitness for young people; step-by-step. [by] Antony Atha and Simon Frost. Rosen Central 2010 93p il (Skills in motion) lib bdg $31.95

Grades: 5 6 7 8   **613.7**

1. Physical fitness

ISBN 978-1-4358-3364-7; 1-4358-3364-3

LC 2009-13245

Describes how to maintain physical fitness for youth, providing exercises that are both effective and fun.

"Colorful photographs show the entire movement of each skill presented, giving new meaning to the term 'step-by-step.' Progression borders at the bottom of the pages highlight the salient points to notice in performing each skill from beginning to end." SLJ

Includes bibliographical references

Birkemoe, Karen

★ **Strike** a pose; the Planet Girl guide to yoga. written by Karen Birkemoe; illustrated by Heather Collett. Kids Can Press 2007 96p il (Planet girl) spiral $12.95

Grades: 5 6 7 8   **613.7**

1. Yoga 2. Girls -- Health and hygiene

ISBN 978-1-55337-004-8

"This compact book offers a well-rounded overview of Hatha yoga. Using an easy conversational tone, Birkemoe relates the general practice and specific poses to reader's lives. The simple line drawings and color illustrations partner effectively with text to explain each move." SLJ

Includes glossary

Eason, Sarah

Free running; by Paul Mason and Sarah Eason. Lerner Publications 2011 il (On the radar: sports)

Grades: 5 6 7 8   613.7

1. Running 2. Parkour

ISBN 076137759X; 9780761377597

LC 2011000467

"Free running, also known as parkour, is a combination of speed running, gymnastics, and, in some cases, sheer fearlessness. Lovers of the sport launch over walls, clear fences in a single bound, and somersault down stairwells. This . . . captures the adrenaline-fueled energy of runners, using bold graphics, bright colors, and short interviews to showcase professionals, demonstrate moves, and trace the origins of free running." Booklist

Head, Honor

Keeping fit; by Honor Head. Sea to Sea Publications 2013 30 p. (hdbk.: alk. paper) $28.50

Grades: 2 3 4   613.7

1. Exercise 2. Physical fitness 3. Exercise -- Physiological aspects

ISBN 1597713961; 9781597713962

LC 2011052697

In this book, by Honor Head, readers can "find out all about keeping fit from how to get started, what exercise does for the body to how exercise can help you at school. Keeping Fit is part of the Let's read and talk about series. Each book has a range of questions to help children with speaking and listening skills, and 'take action' panels which give ideas for activities." (Publisher's note)

Hunt, Jamie

Getting stronger, getting fit; the importance of exercise. Mason Crest Publishers 2011 48p il (Kids & obesity) lib bdg $19.95; pa $7.95

Grades: 3 4 5   613.7

1. Exercise 2. Physical fitness

ISBN 978-1-4222-1709-2 lib bdg; 1-4222-1709-4 lib bdg; 978-1-4222-1897-6 pa; 1-4222-1897-X pa

LC 2010017921

This book about nutrition and exercise "presents the expected information about the food pyramid, the need for physical activity, and the influence of the media on our psyches. Where the material shines is in its holistic approach. Readers are encouraged to develop their inner lives as much as their physical selves and to take responsibility for their own health and eating habits. . . . This brightly-colored, ego-boosting, responsibility-championing . . . [book] is a winner." SLJ

Includes bibliographical references

Jennings, Madeleine

Tai chi step-by-step; [by] Madeleine Jennings and James Drewe. Rosen Central 2011 93p il (Skills in motion) lib bdg $31.95

Grades: 5 6 7 8   613.7

1. Tai chi

ISBN 978-1-4488-1551-7; 1-4488-1551-7

LC 2010008411

This book introduces both basic and higher level techniques of tai chi, with step-by-step instructions, illustrated by stop-motion sequential photography.

Includes bibliographical references

Kuskowski, Alex

Cool relaxing; healthy & fun ways to chill out! Alex Kuskowski. ABDO Pub. Co. 2012 32 p. col. ill. (Cool health and fitness) (library) $28.50

Grades: 4 5 6   613.7

1. Creative activities 2. Rest 3. Relaxation

ISBN 1617834289; 9781617834288

LC 2012010345

This nonfiction children's book by Alex Kuskowski presents a "hodgepodge of activities and techniques to achieve zen calm. The suggestions in this 'Cool Health and Fitness' title are all over the place--cooking, running, reading, baths, even cleaning--but that's the unspoken truth: whatever pleasantly distracts you does the trick. Eight activities are given step-by-step attention, including yoga, stretching, making a lavender pillow, and meditation." (Booklist)

Mason, Paul, 1967-

Improving endurance. PowerKids Press 2011 32p il (Training for sports) lib bdg $25.25

Grades: 5 6 7 8   613.7

1. Sports 2. Exercise

ISBN 978-1-4488-3300-9; 1-4488-3300-0

LC 2010024356

This offers "detailed tips on improving . . . endurance. All-around athletes will love this and so will kids who just want to work on getting fit." Booklist

Improving flexibility. PowerKids Press 2011 32p il (Training for sports) lib bdg $25.25

Grades: 5 6 7 8   613.7

1. Sports 2. Exercise

ISBN 978-1-4488-3299-6; 1-4488-3299-3

LC 2010024359

This offers tips on improving flexibility for sports.

"All-around athletes will love this and so will kids who just want to work on getting fit." Booklist

Improving speed. PowerKids Press 2011 32p il (Training for sports) lib bdg $25.25

Grades: 5 6 7 8   613.7

1. Speed 2. Sports 3. Exercise

ISBN 978-1-4488-3302-3; 1-4488-3302-3

LC 2010024354

This offers "detailed tips on improving speed. . . . All-around athletes will love this and so will kids who just want to work on getting fit." Booklist

Improving strength & power. PowerKids Press 2011 32p il (Training for sports) lib bdg $25.25

Grades: 5 6 7 8   613.7

1. Exercise 2. Physical fitness

ISBN 978-1-4488-3301-6; 1-4488-3301-6

LC 2010024425

This offers tips on improving strength and power for sports.

"All-around athletes will love this and so will kids who just want to work on getting fit." Booklist

Royston, Angela

Why do I run? QEB Pub. 2010 24p il (QEB my body) lib bdg $28.65

Grades: PreK K 1 2   613.7

1. Running 2. Exercise 3. Physical fitness
ISBN 978-1-59566-971-1 lib bdg; 1-59566-971-X lib bdg

LC 2009-15223

Introduces the effects of running and other exercise on the body, and outlines the principles of physical fitness and healthy, safe exercise

"The information is straightforward, well presented, and easy to understand. . . . [This] title is well designed, filled with color photographs, and scattered with fact boxes." Libr Media Connect

Includes glossary and bibliographical references

Schaefer, Adam

Exercise; [by] A. R. Schaefer. Heinemann Library 2010 32p il (Health and fitness) lib bdg $25.36; pa $7.99

Grades: PreK K 1   613.7

1. Exercise
ISBN 978-1-4329-2767-7 lib bdg; 1-4329-2767-1 lib bdg; 978-1-4329-2772-1 pa; 1-4329-2772-8 pa

LC 2008-52297

This book about exercise has "spare, declarative sentences coupled with bright, full-color photos. . . . While each spread introduces a new topic . . . [a] solid [introduction] and [conclusion] make for [a] cohesive [package]." SLJ

Includes glossary and bibliographical references

Spilling, Michael

Yoga step-by-step; [by] Michael Spilling and Liz Lark. Rosen Central 2011 95p il (Skills in motion) lib bdg $31.95

Grades: 5 6 7 8   613.7

1. Yoga
ISBN 978-1-4488-1550-0; 1-4488-1550-9

LC 2010008665

Readers are introduced to basic yoga techniques through step-by-step instructions, depicted with numerous photographs.

Includes bibliographical references

Tuminelly, Nancy

Super simple bend & stretch; healthy & fun activities to move your body. ABDO Pub. Company 2012 32p il (Super simple exercise) lib bdg $27.07

Grades: 1 2 3   613.7

1. Exercise 2. Physical fitness
ISBN 978-1-61714-959-7; 1-61714-959-4

LC 2011000963

"This volume opens with general pages on the benefits of healthy eating and physical activities as well as instructions for making a chart to track each week's efforts. Some of the book's double-page spreads explain and demonstrate several exercise ideas related to a theme. . . . Other spreads present a single activity. . . . Colorful photos show smiling children demonstrating the moves. A cheerful introduction to some basic exercises." Booklist

Includes glossary

Whitford, Rebecca

Little yoga; a toddler's first book of yoga. [by] Rebecca Whitford & Martina Selway. Holt & Co. 2005 un il $9.95

Grades: PreK K 1   613.7

1. Yoga
ISBN 0-8050-7879-7

"This small, square book offers a simple sequence of yoga poses designed especially for toddlers. On each cheerfully designed spread, a simple, black-outlined illustration shows a smiling toddler in a pose; on the opposite page, an animal mimics the same motion. . . . Appended material includes tips for adults to help guide children through the motions and photos of toddlers performing the poses." Booklist

613.9   Birth control, reproductive technology, sex hygiene, sexual techniques

Cole, Joanna

Asking about sex & growing up; a question-and-answer book for kids. illustrated by Bill Thomas. rev ed.; Collins 2009 89p il $15.99; pa $6.99

Grades: 4 5 6   613.9

1. Sex education
ISBN 978-0-06-142987-3; 0-06-142987-2; 978-0-06-142986-6 pa; 0-06-142986-4 pa

LC 2008022710

First published 1988 by Morrow Junior Books

This book "offers straightforward information about topics such as physical changes in puberty, masturbation, birth control, pregnancy, homosexuality, and STDs. . . . Libraries . . . should consider adding it as a source of basic information for curious preteens." SLJ

Harris, Robie H.

★ It's perfectly normal; changing bodies, growing up, sex and sexual health. Robie H. Harris; illustrated by Michael Emberley. 4th edition Candlewick Press 2014 98 p. color illustrations (reinforced) $22.99; (pbk) $12.99

Grades: 4 5 6 7   613.9

1. Puberty 2. Sex education
ISBN 0763668710; 0763668729; 9780763668716; 9780763668723

This provides information about sex, puberty, family relationships and reproduction, sexual decision-making and birth control, abortion laws, sexual abuse, sexual health, sexually transmitted diseases, and internet safety.

"This edition has been revised for a new generation, including updates in scientific and medical information about reproduction, birth control, abortion, sexual abuse, and sexually transmitted diseases." SLJ

614 Forensic medicine; incidence of injuries, wounds, disease; public preventive medicine

Spilsbury, Richard

Bones speak! solving crimes from the past. Enslow Publishers 2009 48p il (Solve that crime!) lib bdg $23.93
Grades: 5 6 7 8   **614**
1. Forensic sciences 2. Forensic anthropology
ISBN 978-0-7660-3377-1 lib bdg; 0-7660-3377-5
lib bdg

     LC 2008-33309

This "title boasts in-depth information, sidebars detailing events of true crime, and activities that will increase understanding. . . . Photographs are colorful, well-captioned, and related to the text." SLJ

Includes glossary and bibliographical references

614.4 Incidence of and public measures to prevent disease

Barnard, Bryn

★ **Outbreak**; plagues that changed history. written and illustrated by Bryn Barnard. Crown Publishers 2005 47p il maps $17.95
Grades: 5 6 7 8   **614.4**
1. Diseases 2. Epidemics
ISBN 0-375-82986-5

     LC 2005-15086

This "volume explores specific plagues that have impacted society. Barnard begins with an introduction to microbes and the positive and negative effects that they can have on humans. A history of the study of microorganisms follows. The bulk of the book then focuses on specific plagues with a chapter devoted to each, including the Black Death, smallpox, yellow fever, cholera, tuberculosis, and influenza. The final chapter discusses the modern struggle against disease. . . . The evocative paintings help to clarify the text. Browsers and report writers alike will find this to be a fascinating and informative resource." SLJ

Cunningham, Kevin

Pandemics. Children's Press 2011 48p il (True book: disasters) lib bdg $28; pa $6.99
Grades: 3 4 5   **614.4**
1. Epidemics 2. Communicable diseases
ISBN 978-0-531-25423-3 lib bdg; 0-531-25423-2;
978-0-531-26628-1 pa; 0-531-26628-1 pa

     LC 2011007507

This describes epidemics of smallpox, cholera, plague, influenza, and HIV/AIDS.

This is "thoughtfully designed. . . . The information . . . is right on target: concise, accurate, and thorough. . . . The photographs . . . are especially effective at putting a human face on large-scale devastation." Booklist

Includes glossary and bibliographical references

Fox, Nancy

Hide and Seek; No Ticks Please. by Nancy Fox and illustrated by Daniel Seward. Morgan James Pub 2014 42 p. $9.95

Grades: 2 3 4 5   **614.4**
1. Lyme disease 2. Tick-borne diseases
ISBN 9781614487050; 1614487057

This children's book by Nancy Fox "teaches strategies for preventing Lyme disease and tick-borne diseases. Through the story of Alex and José, children will learn about José's discovery of a hidden danger (a tick) and how their activities may put them at risk of getting a tick bite." (Publisher's note)

Gleason, Carrie

Feasting bedbugs, mites, and ticks. Crabtree Pub. Co. 2010 32p il (Creepy crawlies) lib bdg $26.60; pa $8.95
Grades: 4 5 6 7   **614.4**
1. Mites 2. Ticks 3. Bedbugs
ISBN 978-0-7787-2500-8 lib bdg; 0-7787-2500-6 lib bdg; 978-0-7787-2507-7 pa; 0-7787-2507-3 pa

     LC 2010009552

"The informational yet easy-to-read text in double-page spreads explains the classification, anatomy, life cycles, and ideal feeding and living conditions for mites, ticks, and bedbugs as well as the differences among them. . . . Children will be most interested in the long history, myths, and lore associated with these pests as well as the eye-catching layout, with numerous color photographs. . . . [This is an] equally repulsive and fascinating book." Booklist

Includes glossary and bibliographical references

Piddock, Charles

Outbreak; science seeks safeguards for global health. [Caryn Oryniak, consultant] National Geographic 2008 64p il (National Geographic investigates) $17.95; lib bdg $27.90
Grades: 4 5 6 7   **614.4**
1. Diseases 2. Epidemics 3. Medicine -- Research
ISBN 978-1-4263-0357-9; 1-4263-0357-2; 978-1-4263-0263-3 lib bdg; 1-4263-0263-0 lib bdg

     LC 2009-275290

This is an "introduction to the fight against infectious diseases, including scientists who discovered various viruses and bacteria. The text outlines how we have learned to fight nature's harmful strains and to use others to our advantage; it also provides the latest findings on bird flu and SARS, Ebola and AIDS, and highly resistant strains of tuberculosis." Publisher's note

Platt, Richard

Plagues, pox, and pestilence; written by Richard Platt; illustrated by John Kelly. Kingfisher 2011 48 p. col. ill. (hardcover) $15.99
Grades: 4 5 6   **614.4**
1. Diseases -- Causes 2. Animals -- Diseases 3. Communicable diseases -- History 4. Epidemics -- History 5. Animals as carriers of disease 6. Communicable diseases -- Transmission
ISBN 0753466872; 9780753466872

     LC 2011041641

Author Richard Platt provides a "history of disease and pestilence, told from the point of view of the bugs and pests that cause them. The book features case histories of specific epidemics, 'eyewitness' accounts from the rats, flies, ticks and creepy-crawlies who spread diseases, plus plenty of fascinating facts and figures on the biggest and worst afflictions." (Publisher's note)

614.5 Incidence of and public measures to prevent specific diseases and kinds of diseases

Ballard, Carol

AIDS and other epidemics. Gareth Stevens Pub. 2008
48p il map (What if we do nothing?) lib bdg $31
Grades: 5 6 7 8   **614.5**
1. Epidemics 2. AIDS (Disease) 3. Communicable
diseases
ISBN 978-1-4339-0085-3 lib bdg; 1-4339-0085-8
lib bdg
     LC 2008029189

"Using intelligent, focused text; an open design; vivid
photos; and excellent maps, [this] book demands attention."
Booklist

"This book looks at the causes of major infectious diseases, how they spread, and how they can be treated. It also
discusses different steps that governments and health organizations can take to handle and prevent epidemics and pandemics." (Publisher's note)

Includes bibliographical references

Murphy, Jim

★ An American plague; the true and terrifying story
of the yellow fever epidemic of 1793. Clarion Bks. 2003
165p il map $18
Grades: 5 6 7 8   **614.5**
1. Yellow fever 2. Philadelphia (Pa.) -- History
ISBN 0-395-77608-2
     LC 2002-151355

A Newbery Medal honor book, 2004

"Murphy culls from a number of historical records the
story of the yellow fever epidemic that swept Philadelphia in 1793, skillfully drawing out from these sources the
fear and drama of the time and making them immediate to
modern readers. . . . Thoroughly documented, with an annotated source list, the work is both rigorous and inviting."
Horn Book

Person, Stephen

Bubonic plague; the Black Death! Bearport Pub. 2010
32p il map (Nightmare plagues) lib bdg $25.27
Grades: 4 5 6 7   **614.5**
1. Plague
ISBN 978-1-936088-03-4; 1-936088-03-7

This describes what causes bubonic plague and how it
affects the body.

"The writing is accessible and interspersed with interesting photographs and fact boxes. . . . [The book relies] on an
honest discussion of [bubonic plague and is an] . . . effective,
easily navigated [introduction]." SLJ

Includes glossary and bibliographical references

Malaria; super killer! Bearport Pub. 2011 32p il map
(Nightmare plagues) lib bdg $25.27
Grades: 4 5 6 7   **614.5**
1. Malaria
ISBN 978-1-936088-07-2 lib bdg; 1-936088-07-X
lib bdg
     LC 2010012018

Discover what causes malaria and how it affects the body.

"The writing is accessible and interspersed with interesting photographs and fact boxes. . . . [The book relies] on an

honest discussion of [malaria and is an] . . . effective, easily
navigated [introduction]." SLJ

Includes glossary and bibliographical references

Reingold, Adam

Smallpox; is it over? Bearport Pub. 2010 32p il map
(Nightmare plagues) lib bdg $25.27
Grades: 4 5 6 7   **614.5**
1. Smallpox
ISBN 978-1-936088-02-7; 1-936088-02-9
     LC 2010009371

Discover what causes smallpox and how it affects
the body.

"The writing is accessible and interspersed with interesting photographs and fact boxes. . . . [The book relies] on an
honest discussion of [smallpox and is an] . . . effective, easily navigated [introduction]." SLJ

Includes glossary and bibliographical references

Rudolph, Jessica

The flu of 1918; millions dead worldwide! Bearport
Pub. 2011 32p il map (Nightmare plagues) lib bdg $25.27
Grades: 4 5 6 7   **614.5**
1. Influenza
ISBN 978-1-936088-05-8 lib bdg; 1-936088-05-3
lib bdg
     LC 2010004684

Discover what caused the Influenza epidemic of 1918
and how it affected the body.

"The writing is accessible and interspersed with interesting photographs and fact boxes. . . . [The book relies] on an
honest discussion of [Influenza epidemic of 1918 and is an] .
. . effective, easily navigated [introduction]." SLJ

Includes glossary and bibliographical references

615 Pharmacology and therapeutics

Hyde, Natalie

What is germ theory? Crabtree Pub. Co. 2011 64p il
(Shaping modern science) lib bdg $30.60; pa $10.95
Grades: 5 6 7 8   **615**
1. Chemists 2. Germ theory of disease 3.
Microbiologists 4. Writers on science
ISBN 978-0-7787-7201-9 lib bdg; 0-7787-7201-9 lib
bdg; 978-0-7787-7208-8 pa; 0-7787-7208-X pa
     LC 2010052631

This title is "not only written and organized well, but
[it is] also gorgeous in design. Full-color photographs and
illustrations are set over colorful backgrounds that add depth
but not distraction. [The title] includes thought-provoking
quotes from famous authors and scientists and some eyebrow-raising 'Quick Facts' throughout." SLJ

Includes glossary and bibliographical references

Petersen, Christine

The apothecary. Marshall Cavendish Benchmark
2010 48p il (Colonial people) lib bdg $29.93
Grades: 3 4 5 6   **615**
1. Pharmacy 2. United States -- History -- 1600-1775,
Colonial period
ISBN 978-0-7614-4795-5; 0-7614-4795-4
     LC 2009015274

This describes the life of a colonial apothecary and his importance to the community, as well as everyday life, responsibilities, and social practices during that time.

"The type font, just slightly larger than usual, makes the text very visually appealing. . . . [The] book is liberally illustrated with artwork dating from the colonial period . . . [and] information boxes offer supplemental material." Libr Media Connect

Includes glossary and bibliographical references

615.8 Specific therapies and kinds of therapies

Beccia, Carlyn
I feel better with a frog in my throat: history's strangest cures; written and illustrated by Carlyn Beccia. Houghton Mifflin Books for Children 2010 48p il $17.99
Grades: 2 3 4 **615.8**
1. Therapeutics 2. Medicine -- History
ISBN 978-0-547-22570-8; 0-547-22570-9
LC 2010-01138

This discusses some of history's "disgusting and futile medical practices. . . . [Characterized by] dry-witted artwork, conversational text, [and] engaging historical detective work, [this book] asks readers to guess which 'cures' may actually have helped a handful of ailments. . . . The author provides intriguing background information on the cures—where they arose, why they were thougth to be efficacious—and pulls more than one gem out of the nastiness." Kirkus

Bozzo, Linda
Therapy dog heroes. Enslow Publishers 2010 48p il (Amazing working dogs with American humane) lib bdg $23.93
Grades: 2 3 4 **615.8**
1. Working dogs
ISBN 978-0-7660-3200-2; 0-7660-3200-0
LC 2008048020

"The text opens with a true story of a therapy dog, and then it explains the history of the therapy dog and the training methods used to transform an ordinary dog into a canine hero." Publisher's note

Includes glossary and bibliographical references

615.9 Toxicology

Day, Jeff
Don't touch that! the book of gross, poisonous, and downright icky plants and critters. Chicago Review Press 2008 108p il pa $9.95
Grades: 3 4 5 6 **615.9**
1. Poisonous plants 2. Poisonous animals
ISBN 978-1-55652-711-1 pa; 1-556527-11-X pa
LC 2007027466

"Packed with potentially lifesaving information, this guide is humorous without sacrificing usefulness. The author, a medical doctor, begins with some basic plants (poison ivy, poison oak, and poison sumac) that might be encountered. Drawings of the leaves are carefully labeled and accompanied by the warning not to touch any part of the plant, and not to burn it as even the smoke can irritate. Poisonous

insects, spiders, amphibians, reptiles, and mammals are also included, and every entry explains why the creature's venom causes the bad reaction it does and how to treat it. . . . Genuinely funny, colorful drawings on every page amplify the text and make it memorable." SLJ

Jakubiak, David J.
What can we do about toxins in the environment? PowerKids Press 2011 24p il (Protecting the planet) lib bdg $21.25; pa $8.25
Grades: 2 3 4 **615.9**
1. Pollution 2. Poisons and poisoning
ISBN 978-1-4488-4987-1 lib bdg; 978-1-4488-5121-8 pa
LC 2011000151

This explains the harm that toxins do in the environment and what can be done about them.

"Every spread has a full-page, thoughtfully captioned color photograph. . . . School and public libraries will want [this title] to round out collections or as [an update] to replace older books." SLJ

Includes glossary

Owen, Ruth
Disgusting food invaders. Bearport Pub. 2011 24p il (Up close and gross) lib bdg $22.61
Grades: 3 4 5 **615.9**
1. Parasites 2. Food contamination
ISBN 978-1-61772-126-7; 1-61772-126-3
LC 2010044417

This describes impurities and parasites which can be found in food, including fruit flies, moths, cheese mites, mold, grubs, rat hairs and insect parts, maggots, and bacteria.

"Never have the wonders of electron microscopy been more thrillingly displayed. . . . These knife-sharp, all-too-explicit photos are riveting. The [text doesn't] trail far behind in appeal either." SLJ

Includes glossary and bibliographical references

616 Diseases

Calamandrei, Camilla
★ Fever. Marshall Cavendish Benchmark 2009 64p il (Health alert) $22.95
Grades: 4 5 6 7 **616**
1. Fever
ISBN 978-0-7614-2915-9; 0-7614-2915-8
LC 2007-26002

This "title features a handsome format, with well-chosen illustrations, a substantial amount of information, and some practical insights." Booklist

Includes glossary

Dendy, Leslie A.
★ Guinea pig scientists; bold self-experimenters in science and medicine. [by] Leslie Dendy and Mel Boring; with illustrations by C. B. Mordan. Henry Holt & Co. 2005 213p il $19.95
Grades: 5 6 7 8 **616**
1. Scientists 2. Medicine -- Research
ISBN 9780805073164; 0-8050-7316-7
LC 2004-52364

This is a collection of "stories of human 'guinea pigs' who have tested the limits of the human body for the sake of science. Starting with Sir Charles Blagden, M.D., and his heat experiments, the stories are chronologically ordered from the 1770s to 1989. Included are descriptions of experiments dealing with digestion, laughing gas, vaccinations, mosquitoes as vectors of yellow fever, radioactivity, [and] G-forces." (Sci Books Films) Index.

"The authors offer 10 . . . case studies of scientists from the past several centuries who became their own test subjects. . . . The accounts are lively, compelling, and not always for the squeamish. . . . The authors cogently discuss each experiment's significance in advancing our understanding of science and medicine. Illustrated with a mix of period black-and-white photos and Mordan's nineteenth-century-style portraits . . . the episodes make riveting reading." Booklist

Includes bibliographical references

Evans, Michael

The **adventures** of Medical Man; kids' illnesses and injuries explained. by Michael Evans & David Wichman; illustrated by Gareth Williams. Annick 2010 72p il $21.95; pa $12.95

Grades: 5 6 7 8   616

1. Diseases 2. Wounds and injuries

ISBN 978-1-55451-263-8; 1-55451-263-8; 978-1-55451-262-1 pa; 1-55451-262-X pa

"Using tangible experiences that kids can relate to, this book does a fantastic job of explaining common medical issues in an accessible way. A variety of heroic characters explain otherwise complicated and seemingly scary conditions and occurrences. Through the use of science fiction, adventure, and comics, the book covers nut allergies, concussions, broken bones, strep throat, ear infections, and asthma. . . . The extensive glossary is straightforward and user-friendly. The pumped-up graphic illustrations are extremely engaging and further bring these otherwise abstract concepts to life." SLJ

Murphy, Patricia J.

Illness; [by] Patricia J Murphy. Heinemann Library 2008 32p il (Tough topics) lib bdg $25.36; pa $7.99

Grades: PreK K 1 2 3   616

1. Diseases

ISBN 978-1-4034-9777-2 lib bdg; 978-1-4034-9782-6 pa

LC 2007005345

This "book talks about different kinds of illnesses, coping mechanisms, and varieties of medical treatments available. . . . Murphy gives an overview of the topic in a way that young readers can understand. . . . The two-page chapters include full-color photos and two paragraphs of text that are frank yet sensitive in their approach." SLJ

Includes glossary and bibliographical references

Nardo, Don

Cure quest; the science of stem cell research. by Don Nardo. Compass Point Books 2009 48p il (Headline science) lib bdg $27.93; pa $7.95

Grades: 5 6 7   616

1. Stem cell research

ISBN 978-0-7565-3371-7 lib bdg; 0-7565-3371-6 lib bdg; 978-0-7565-3374-8 pa; 0-7565-3374-0 pa

LC 2008-5738

Explains the science behind stem cell research.

"Color photos and graphics provide visual information; a timeline is helpful to find fast facts, and the Facthound Web site provides student with additional information." Libr Media Connect

Includes glossary and bibliographical references

Ollhoff, Jim

What are germs? ABDO Pub. Co. 2010 32p il (A history of germs) $27.07

Grades: 3 4 5 6   616

1. Bacteria 2. Germ theory of disease

ISBN 978-1-60453-502-0; 1-60453-502-4

"What Are Germs? includes kinds of germs and germ-fighting organizations. The short, informative chapters provide plenty of details for reports. The illustrations, many of which are color photos, enhance the information." SLJ

Includes glossary

Rhatigan, Joe

Ouch! the weird & wild ways your body deals with agonizing aches, ferocious fevers, lousy lumps, crummy colds, bothersome bites, breaks, bruises & burns & makes them feel better. Joe Rhatigan; original Illustrations by Anthony Owsley. Imagine! 2013 80 p. $14.95

Grades: 3 4 5 6   616

1. Wounds and injuries 2. Children -- Health and hygiene 3. Pain -- Popular works 4. Psychology, Pathological

ISBN 1623540054; 9781623540050

LC 2012048462

This book by author Joe Rhatigan is a "compendium of low-key medical information for the upper grade school set. Got a headache? A rash? A pulled muscle or a sprained ankle? Disease by disease and injury by injury, this basic medical text takes young readers through various ailments, breaking each one down into a simple explanation of the problem." (Kirkus Reviews)

Silverstein, Alvin

Tapeworms, foot fungus, lice, and more; the yucky disease book. by Alvin Silverstein, Virginia Silverstein, and Laura Silverstein Nunn; illustrated by Gerald Kelley. Enslow Publishers 2010 48p il (Yucky science) lib bdg $23.93

Grades: 3 4 5 6   616

1. Diseases 2. Medicine

ISBN 978-0-7660-3314-6 lib bdg; 0-7660-3314-7 lib bdg

LC 2009012282

"Explores 'yucky' diseases, including leprosy, plague, tapeworms, and more" Publisher's note

Includes glossary and bibliographical references

Stoyles, Pennie

The A-Z of health. Black Rabbit/Smart Apple 2010 6v il set $119.70

Grades: 5 6 7 8   616

1. Health 2. Reference books 3. Medicine -- Encyclopedias

ISBN 978-1-59920-654-7; 1-59920-654-4

"This reference set provides a simple, brief, and easy-to-read introduction to key aspects of physical and mental health, including various body processes and diseases as well as information on treatments and preventative measures. . . . The explanations are concise, clear, and easy to understand. In addition to the abundance of images, the large type and white space that is prevalent on every page will make this set accessible to a broad array of young readers." Booklist

616.027 Experimental medicine

Barber, Nicola
Cloning and genetic engineering; Nicola Barber. Rosen Pub.'s Rosen Central 2013 48 p. (Both sides of the story) (library binding) $29.25
Grades: 5 6 7 8 **616.027**
1. Cloning 2. Genetic engineering
ISBN 1448871875; 9781448871872
LC 2012013797

Author Nicola Barber's book focuses on cloning and genetic engineering. The book "offers arguments for both sides of the cloning and genetic engineering debate. Among the subjects examined are the human genome, transgenics, reproductive cloning, research cloning, stem cell therapy, genetic disease and testing, gene therapy, plant and animal pharming, genetically modified animals and crops, and gene doping." (Publisher's note)

Includes bibliographical references (p. 46) and index

616.2 Diseases of respiratory system

Chilman-Blair, Kim
Medikidz explain sleep apnea; [by] Kim Chilman-Blair and Shawn Deloache; medical content reviewed for accuracy by Paul Gringras and David Rapoport. Rosen Central 2011 40p il (Superheroes on a medical mission) lib bdg $29.25; pa $11.75
Grades: 3 4 5 6 **616.2**
1. Sleep apnea 2. Superheroes 3. Graphic novels
ISBN 978-1-4358-9459-4 lib bdg; 1-4358-9459-6 lib bdg; 978-1-4488-1841-9 pa; 1-4488-1841-9 pa
LC 2010002554

"A team of superheroes rides around on a medi-jet and whisks ill children, or their siblings, off to Mediland, a giant replica of the human body, to teach them about [sleep apnea]. . . . The comic panels are visually exciting with eye-popping colors. Inside Mediland, the science behind various conditions is expertly simplified and explained with a sometimes tongue-in-cheek repartee among the characters as well as with very basic analogies reminiscent of video games. . . . This approach makes the health issues accessible and much less scary for readers wanting to learn more for personal or academic reasons." SLJ

Includes glossary and bibliographical references

Medikidz explain swine flu; [by] Kim Chilman-Blair; medical content reviewed for accuracy by John McCauley and Calum Semple. Rosen Central 2011 40p il (Superheroes on a medical mission) lib bdg $29.25; pa $11.75

Grades: 3 4 5 6 **616.2**
1. Superheroes 2. Graphic novels 3. Swine influenza
ISBN 978-1-4358-9457-0 lib bdg; 1-4358-9457-X lib bdg; 978-1-4488-1843-3 pa; 1-4488-1843-5 pa
LC 2010003236

"A team of superheroes rides around on a medi-jet and whisks ill children, or their siblings, off to Mediland, a giant replica of the human body, to teach them about [swine flu]. . . . The comic panels are visually exciting with eye-popping colors. Inside Mediland, the science behind various conditions is expertly simplified and explained with a sometimes tongue-in-cheek repartee among the characters as well as with very basic analogies reminiscent of video games. . . . This approach makes the health issues accessible and much less scary for readers wanting to learn more for personal or academic reasons." SLJ

Includes glossary and bibliographical references

Cobb, Vicki
★ Your body battles a cold; written by Vicki Cobb; photomicrographs by Dennis Kunkel; illustrated by Andrew N. Harris. Millbrook Press 2009 32p il (Body battles) lib bdg $25.26
Grades: 3 4 5 **616.2**
1. Immune system 2. Cold (Disease)
ISBN 978-0-8225-6813-1; 0-8225-6813-6
LC 2008002839

Color illustrations and photomicrographs show what happens when a human body is attacked by a cold virus

"The body's immune system has never looked like this before with plasma cells using sling shots to fire antibodies into viruses, platelets riding inner tubes down a stream of blood, and viruses multiplying in a 'Germco' factory. [The] title introduces five or six defense cells, disguised as superheroes protecting the body from adversarial viruses. . . . The oversize text uses metaphors that readers will understand. . . . The micrographs will fascinate and compel young readers to read everything." SLJ

Includes glossary and bibliographical references

Glaser, Jason
Asthma. Capstone Press 2006 24p il (First facts: health matters) $21.26
Grades: K 1 2 3 **616.2**
1. Asthma
ISBN 978-0-7368-4287-7; 0-7368-4287-X
LC 2004031021

"Describes asthma and its causes, symptoms, and treatments." Publisher's note
Includes bibliographical references

Colds. Capstone Press 2006 24p il (First facts: health matters) $21.26
Grades: K 1 2 3 **616.2**
1. Cold (Disease)
ISBN 978-0-7368-4289-1; 0-7368-4289-6
LC 2004031051

"Introduces readers to the common cold, its symptoms, treatments, and prevention." Publisher's note
Includes bibliographical references

Flu. Capstone Press 2006 24p il (First facts: health matters) $21.26

Grades: K 1 2 3   **616.2**
1. Influenza
ISBN 978-0-7368-4290-7; 0-7368-4290-X
LC 2004031052

"Introduces the flu, its symptoms, treatments, and prevention." Publisher's note

Includes bibliographical references

Hoffmann, Gretchen
★ The **flu**. Marshall Cavendish Benchmark 2007 64p
il (Health alert) lib bdg $31.36
Grades: 4 5 6 7   **616.2**
1. Influenza
ISBN 978-0-7614-2208-2; 0-7614-2208-0 \
LC 2006011980

This "title features a handsome format, with well-chosen illustrations, a substantial amount of information, and some practical insights." Booklist

Includes glossary and bibliographical references

Landau, Elaine
★ **Asthma**. Marshall Cavendish Benchmark 2009 32p
il (Head-to-toe health) lib bdg $19.95
Grades: 2 3 4   **616.2**
1. Asthma
ISBN 978-0-7614-2845-9; 0-7614-2845-3
LC 2007-34998

"Photo illustrations are apt and age appropriate. . . . Pervading the [book] . . . is an overall sense of reassurance that even if something hurts, 'all better' is never too far away. Appealing and readable nonfiction." SLJ

Includes glossary and bibliographical references

★ The **common** cold. Marshall Cavendish Benchmark 2009 32p il (Head-to-toe health) lib bdg $19.95
Grades: 2 3 4   **616.2**
1. Cold (Disease)
ISBN 978-0-7614-2844-2; 0-7614-2844-5
LC 2007-35005

"Photo illustrations are apt and age appropriate. . . . Pervading the [book] . . . is an overall sense of reassurance that even if something hurts, 'all better' is never too far away. Appealing and readable nonfiction." SLJ

Includes glossary and bibliographical references

Moore-Mallinos, Jennifer
I have asthma; illustrated by Rosa M. Cirto. Barron's 2007 35p il (What do I know about?) pa $6.99
Grades: K 1 2 3   **616.2**
1. Asthma
ISBN 0-7641-3785-9

After a young boy has trouble breathing during soccer practice, he is taken to his doctor who says that he has asthma, but he learns that with proper treatment and medical supervision, his asthma can be kept under control.

"The easy text, combined with soft, rounded figures in the colorful illustrations, results in a sensitively told story that offers encouragement to children suffering from this condition, complete with helpful advice." SLJ

Ollhoff, Jim
The **flu**. ABDO Pub. Co. 2010 32p il (A history of germs) $27.07

Grades: 3 4 5 6   **616.2**
1. Viruses 2. Influenza
ISBN 978-1-60453-498-6; 1-60453-498-2
LC 2008055063

"Flu provides a concise look at the illness, pandemics, treatments, and recent strains, including H1N1. . . . The short, informative chapters provide plenty of details for reports. The illustrations, many of which are color photos, enhance the information." SLJ

Includes glossary

Robbins, Lynette
How to deal with asthma. PowerKids Press 2010 24p
il (Kids' health) lib bdg $21.25
Grades: 2 3 4   **616.2**
1. Asthma
ISBN 978-1-4042-8141-7 lib bdg; 1-4042-8141-X
lib bdg
LC 2009-7653

"Hypothetical situations with fictional characters put readers in the moment and provide a solid foundation for comprehending [asthma]. . . . Robbins maintains a comforting tone, reassuring readers that it is possible to lead active lives with proper attention to diet and guidance from parents and doctors." SLJ

Includes glossary

Royston, Angela
Asthma. Black Rabbit Books 2009 30p il (How's your health) lib bdg $27.10
Grades: 1 2 3   **616.2**
1. Asthma
ISBN 978-1-59920-219-8 lib bdg; 1-59920-219-0
lib bdg
LC 2007-35689

First published 2004 by Heinemann Library

"Encourages further learning with sidebars that help readers think concretely about the subject. . . . Altogether a pitch perfect presentation." SLJ

Includes glossary and bibliographical references

Explaining asthma. Smart Apple Media 2010 45p il (Explaining) lib bdg $34.25
Grades: 5 6 7 8   **616.2**
1. Asthma
ISBN 978-1-59920-315-7 lib bdg; 1-59920-315-4
lib bdg
LC 2008-49284

Describes what living with asthma is like, discussing symptoms, triggers, treatments, and lifestyle changes that may be necessary to prevent asthma attacks

The book provides a "basic [overview] of the health concerns related to the disease; information on diagnosis and treatment; and a discussion of the challenges or complications experienced by the affected person and their family/friends, and how to manage those problems. . . . The incorporation of quotes and personal accounts in 'Case Notes' sidebars adds to the sensitive tone found throughout [the title]." SLJ

Includes glossary

616.3 Diseases of digestive system

Allman, Toney
Obesity. Cherry Lake Pub. 2009 32p il (Health at risk) lib bdg $27.07
Grades: 4 5 6 7   **616.3**
1. Obesity
ISBN 978-1-60279-285-2 lib bdg; 1-60279-285-2 lib bdg
LC 2008017499

This describes the causes and dangers of obesity and the many efforts being made to help people control their weight.
"Great for reports or reluctant readers." Booklist
Includes bibliographical references

Bjorklund, Ruth
★ **Cystic** fibrosis. Marshall Cavendish Benchmark 2009 64p il (Health alert) $22.95
Grades: 4 5 6 7   **616.3**
1. Cystic fibrosis
ISBN 978-0-7614-2912-8; 0-7614-2912-3
LC 2007-46674

This "title features a handsome format, with well-chosen illustrations, a substantial amount of information, and some practical insights." Booklist

Cobb, Vicki
★ **Your** body battles a stomachache; written by Vicki Cobb; with photomicrographs by Dennis Kunkel; illustrations by Andrew N. Harris. Millbrook Press 2009 32p il (Body battles) lib bdg $25.26
Grades: 3 4 5   **616.3**
1. Stomach 2. Intestines 3. Immune system
ISBN 978-0-8225-7166-7 lib bdg; 0-8225-7166-8 lib bdg
LC 2008002852

Color illustrations and photomicrographs show what happens when a human digestive system is attacked by a rotavirus

"The body's immune system has never looked like this before with plasma cells using sling shots to fire antibodies into viruses, platelets riding inner tubes down a stream of blood, and viruses multiplying in a 'Germco' factory. [The] title introduces five or six defense cells, disguised as superheroes protecting the body from adversarial viruses. . . . The oversize text uses metaphors that readers will understand. . . . The micrographs will fascinate and compel young readers to read everything." SLJ
Includes glossary and bibliographical references

Glaser, Jason
Obesity. Capstone Press 2007 24p il (First facts: health matters) $21.26
Grades: K 1 2 3   **616.3**
1. Obesity
ISBN 978-0-7368-6331-5; 0-7368-6331-1
LC 2006002832

"Describes obesity, how and why it occurs, and how to treat and prevent it." Publisher's note
Includes bibliographical references

Hicks, Terry Allan
★ **Obesity**. Marshall Cavendish Benchmark 2009 63p il (Health alert) $22.95

Grades: 4 5 6 7   **616.3**
1. Obesity
ISBN 978-0-7614-2911-1; 0-7614-2911-5
LC 2007-31246

This "title features a handsome format, with well-chosen illustrations, a substantial amount of information, and some practical insights." Booklist
Includes glossary

Hunt, Jamie
Tired of being teased; obesity and others. Mason Crest Publishers 2010 48p il (Kids & obesity) lib bdg $19.95; pa $7.95
Grades: 3 4 5   **616.3**
1. Obesity
ISBN 978-1-4222-1711-5 lib bdg; 1-4222-1711-6 lib bdg; 978-1-4222-1899-0 pa; 1-4222-1899-6 pa
LC 2010012759

Teaches that a person is more than appearance, and discusses how to deal with being teased about one's appearance.

This book about obesity "presents the expected information about the food pyramid, the need for physical activity, and the influence of the media on our psyches. Where the material shines is in its holistic approach. Readers are encouraged to develop their inner lives as much as their physical selves and to take responsibility for their own health and eating habits. . . . This brightly-colored, ego-boosting, responsibility-championing . . . [book] is a winner." SLJ
Includes bibliographical references

Powell, Jillian
Explaining cystic fibrosis. Smart Apple Media 2010 45p il (Explaining) lib bdg $34.25
Grades: 5 6 7 8   **616.3**
1. Cystic fibrosis
ISBN 978-1-59920-312-6 lib bdg; 1-59920-312-X lib bdg
LC 2008-49288

Describes the illness, including its causes, how it is diagnosed, current treatments for the illness, and how those with cystic fibrosis lead everyday lives

The book provides a "basic [overview] of the health concerns related to the disease; information on diagnosis and treatment; and a discussion of the challenges or complications experienced by the affected person and their family/friends, and how to manage those problems. . . . The incorporation of quotes and personal accounts in 'Case Notes' sidebars adds to the sensitive tone found throughout [the title]." SLJ
Includes glossary and bibliographical references

Robbins, Lynette
How to deal with obesity. PowerKids Press 2010 24p il (Kids' health) lib bdg $21.25
Grades: 2 3 4   **616.3**
1. Obesity
ISBN 978-1-4042-8143-1 lib bdg; 1-4042-8143-6 lib bdg
LC 2009-8902

"Hypothetical situations with fictional characters put readers in the moment and provide a solid foundation for comprehending [obesity]. . . . Robbins maintains a comforting tone, reassuring readers that it is possible to lead active lives with proper attention to diet and guidance from parents and doctors." SLJ

Includes glossary

Simons, Rae

Too many Sunday dinners; family and diet. Mason Crest Publishers 2010 48p il (Kids & obesity) lib bdg $19.95; pa $7.95

Grades: 3 4 5   **616.3**

1. Obesity 2. Heredity

ISBN 978-1-4222-1713-9 lib bdg; 1-4222-1713-2 lib bdg; 978-1-4222-1901-0 pa; 1-4222-1901-1 pa

LC 2010019188

Discusses how obesity can be hereditary.

This book "presents the expected information about the food pyramid, the need for physical activity, and the influence of the media on our psyches. Where the material shines is in its holistic approach. Readers are encouraged to develop their inner lives as much as their physical selves and to take responsibility for their own health and eating habits. . . . This brightly-colored, ego-boosting, responsibility-championing . . . [book] is a winner." SLJ

Includes bibliographical references

616.39   Nutritional and metabolic diseases

Jarrow, Gail

Red madness; how a medical mystery changed what we eat. Gail Jarrow. Calkins Creek 2014 192 p. $16.95

Grades: 5 6 7 8 9   **616.39**

1. Diseases 2. Malnutrition 3. Pellagra -- History 4. Epidemics -- United States -- History 5. United States. Public Health Service -- History

ISBN 1590787323; 9781590787328

LC 2008049497

In this book, author Gail Jarrow "tracks [a] disease, commonly known as pellagra, and highlights how doctors, scientists, and public health officials finally defeated it. Illustrated with 100 archival photographs, [it] includes stories about real-life pellagra victims and accounts of scientific investigations. It concludes with a glossary, timeline, further resources, author's note, bibliography, and index." (Publisher's note)

"In 1902, a young man in Georgia displayed symptoms of a disease believed to be nonexistent in the U.S.: pellagra, a deficiency disease. Jarrow unfolds the suspenseful search for a cause of the South's epidemic, as corn fungus, insect- and bird-born parasites, and more were all blamed and rejected. Plentiful archival photos, many of victims, add emotional heft. Reading list, timeline, websites. Bib., glos., ind." Horn Book

616.4   Diseases of endocrine, hematopoietic, lymphatic, glandular systems; diseases of male breast

Glaser, Jason

Juvenile diabetes. Capstone Press 2007 24p il (First facts: health matters) $21.26

Grades: K 1 2 3   **616.4**

1. Diabetes

ISBN 978-0-7368-6392-6; 0-7368-6392-3

LC 2006002820

"Describes juvenile diabetes, why it occurs, and how it is diagnosed and treated." Publisher's note

Includes bibliographical references

Loughrey, Anita

Explaining diabetes. Smart Apple Media 2010 45p il (Explaining) lib bdg $34.25

Grades: 5 6 7 8   **616.4**

1. Diabetes

ISBN 978-1-59920-314-0 lib bdg; 1-59920-314-6 lib bdg

LC 2008-49290

Provides an overview of Type 1 and Type 2 diabetes, discussing causes and symptoms, recommended and required lifestyle changes, how the disease is managed, and possible complications that may occur

The book provides a "basic [overview] of the health concerns related to the disease; information on diagnosis and treatment; and a discussion of the challenges or complications experienced by the affected person and their family/friends, and how to manage those problems. . . . The incorporation of quotes and personal accounts in 'Case Notes' sidebars adds to the sensitive tone found throughout [the title]." SLJ

Includes glossary and bibliographical references

Pirner, Connie White

Even little kids get diabetes; pictures by Nadine Bernard Westcott. Whitman, A. 1991 un il hardcover o.p. pa $6.95

Grades: K 1   **616.4**

1. Diabetes

ISBN 0-8075-2158-2; 0-8075-2159-0 pa

LC 90-12738

A young girl who has had diabetes since she was two years old describes her adjustments to the disease

"Language is simple, age appropriate, and effectively gets the point across. The ink-and-watercolor drawings are lively and often upbeat. . . . Perhaps the most valuable part of the book is the 'note for parents,' which relates Pirner's personal experience over the last three years in caring for a diabetic child." SLJ

Robbins, Lynette

How to deal with diabetes. PowerKids Press 2010 24p il (Kids' health) lib bdg $21.25

Grades: 2 3 4   **616.4**

1. Diabetes

ISBN 978-1-4042-8144-8 lib bdg; 1-4042-8144-4 lib bdg

LC 2009-10467

"Hypothetical situations with fictional characters put readers in the moment and provide a solid foundation for comprehending [diabetes]. . . . Robbins maintains a comforting tone, reassuring readers that it is possible to lead active lives with proper attention to diet and guidance from parents and doctors." SLJ

Includes glossary

616.5   Diseases of integument

Caffey, Donna

Yikes-lice! illustrations by Patrick Girouard. Whitman,
A. 1998 un il $14.95; pa $5.95

Grades: K 1 2 3   **616.5**
1. Lice
ISBN 0-8075-9374-5; 0-8075-9375-3 pa

LC 97-30679

Rhyming text describes what happens when a family
discovers lice in the home and fights against them. Includes
factual information about how lice live, spread, and can
be eradicated

DerKazarian, Susan

You have head lice! by Susan DerKazarian. Children's
Press 2005 31p il (Rookie read-about health) $20.50;
pa $5.95

Grades: PreK K 1 2   **616.5**
1. Lice
ISBN 0-516-25879-6; 0-516-27920-3 pa

LC 2004-15308

This "approaches the sometimes-touchy subject of head
lice in a straightforward, reassuring manner. . . . Adults
wanting to explain head lice to children will find this a helpful source of basic information." Booklist

Faulk, Michelle

The **case** of the flesh-eating bacteria; Annie Biotica
solves skin disease crimes. by Michelle Faulk. Lake Book
Manufacturing, Inc. 2013 48 p. (Body system disease investigations) (library) $23.93

Grades: 5 6 7 8   **616.5**
1. Picture books for children 2. Skin -- Diseases 3.
Virus diseases 4. Skin -- Infections
ISBN 0766039455; 9780766039452

LC 2011023985

This book by Michelle Faulk "from the Body System
Disease Investigations series introduces Agent Annie Biotica, a 'Disease Scene Investigator with the Major Health
Crimes Unit'. This cartoon-style heroine is called in to solve
a series of skin-related medical cases . . . caused by flesh-
eating bacteria, pinkeye, ringworm, chicken pox, [and]
measles." (Booklist)

Includes bibliographical references (p. 47) and index

Landau, Elaine

★ **Warts**. Marshall Cavendish Benchmark 2010 32p
il (Head-to-toe health) lib bdg $28.50

Grades: 2 3 4   **616.5**
1. Warts
ISBN 978-0-7614-4836-5 lib bdg; 0-7614-4836-5
lib bdg

This provides information about warts.
This "manages to pack in surprising amount information,
including facts about good hygiene. The text addresses the
readers directly, and the photos are real grabbers." Booklist

Includes glossary and bibliographical references

Lew, Kristi

Itch & ooze; gross stuff on your skin. illustrations by
Michael Slack. Millbrook Press 2010 48p il (Gross body
science) lib bdg $29.27

Grades: 4 5 6   **616.5**
1. Skin 2. Skin -- Diseases
ISBN 978-0-8225-8963-1 lib bdg; 0-8225-8963-X
lib bdg

LC 2008-45591

Presents disgusting facts about human skin, the diseases
and parasites that can cause problems with it, and how it
functions to protect the body and itself.

"Solid information layered between sarcastic comments
and kid-friendly terminology like fart, poop, barf, and puke
will keep readers engaged. . . . Labeled, captioned (and
graphic) photographs, cartoon-style illustrations, and micrographs add information." SLJ

Includes glossary and bibliographical references

Royston, Angela

Head lice. Black Rabbit Books 2009 30p il (How's
your health) lib bdg $27.10

Grades: 1 2 3   **616.5**
1. Lice
ISBN 978-1-59920-218-1 lib bdg; 1-59920-218-2
lib bdg

First published 2001 by Heinemann Library

"Encourages further learning with sidebars that help
readers think concretely about the subject. . . . Altogether a
pitch perfect presentation." SLJ

Includes glossary

616.7   Diseases of musculoskeletal system

Gray, Susan Heinrichs

Living with juvenile rheumatoid arthritis. Child's
World 2003 32p il (Living well) lib bdg $25.64

Grades: 4 5 6   **616.7**
1. Arthritis
ISBN 1-56766-104-1

LC 2002-2870

This title "leads off with an introduction to a young
person who has [juvenile rheumatoid arthritis]. Subsequent
chapters explain the physiology of the illness, what causes
it, and what it's like to live with it. [The concluding section looks] at possible treatments and potential cures. [The
text is] clear and simple, double spaced, and punctuated by
colorful exemplary photos of kids dealing with the disease."
SLJ

Includes glossary and bibliographical references

Hoffmann, Gretchen

★ **Osteoporosis**. Marshall Cavendish Benchmark
2007 64p il (Health alert) lib bdg $21.95

Grades: 4 5 6 7   **616.7**
1. Osteoporosis
ISBN 978-0-7614-2702-5; 0-7614-2702-3

LC 2007008787

This describes what it is like to have osteoporosis, what
it is, its history and its diagnosis and treatment

This "title features a handsome format, with well-chosen
illustrations, a substantial amount of information, and some
practical insights." Booklist

Includes glossary and bibliographical references

616.8　Diseases of nervous system and mental disorders

Ali-Walsh, Rasheda

★ **I'll** hold your hand so you won't fall; a child's guide to Parkinson's disease. [by] Rasheda Ali; foreword for Muhammad Ali. Merit 2005 40p il $19.95

Grades: 2 3 4　　　　　　　　　　　　　**616.8**

1. Parkinson's disease

ISBN 1-873413-13-0

"Ali's father, Muhammad Ali, suffers from Parkinson's disease, and she answers questions children may have about the illness. . . . The text is well written and basic, without being oversimplified. . . . A short CD-ROM of the author introducing the book and its contents is included. An excellent overview written in an approachable style that will be reassuring to young readers." SLJ

Bender, Lionel

Explaining epilepsy. Smart Apple Media 2010 45p il (Explaining) lib bdg $34.25

Grades: 5 6 7 8　　　　　　　　　　　　　**616.8**

1. Epilepsy

ISBN 978-1-59920-309-6 lib bdg; 1-59920-309-X lib bdg

LC 2008-49292

Describes the nature, symptoms, and possible causes of epilepsy, gives a history of its study, and discusses its treatment

The book provides a "basic [overview] of the health concerns related to the disease; information on diagnosis and treatment; and a discussion of the challenges or complications experienced by the affected person and their family/friends, and how to manage those problems. . . . The incorporation of quotes and personal accounts in 'Case Notes' sidebars adds to the sensitive tone found throughout [the title]." SLJ

Includes glossary and bibliographical references

Bjorklund, Ruth

★ **Cerebral** palsy. Marshall Cavendish Benchmark 2007 64p il (Health alert) lib bdg $31.36

Grades: 4 5 6 7　　　　　　　　　　　　　**616.8**

1. Cerebral palsy

ISBN 978-0-7614-2209-9; 0-7614-2209-9

LC 2006-15818

This "title features a handsome format, with well-chosen illustrations, a substantial amount of information, and some practical insights." Booklist

Includes glossary and bibliographical references

★ **Epilepsy**. Marshall Cavendish Benchmark 2007 63p il (Health alert) lib bdg $21.95

Grades: 4 5 6 7　　　　　　　　　　　　　**616.8**

1. Epilepsy

ISBN 978-0-7614-2206-8; 0-7614-2206-4

LC 2006-15816

This "title features a handsome format, with well-chosen illustrations, a substantial amount of information, and some practical insights." Booklist

Includes glossary and bibliographical references

Colligan, L. H.

★ **Sleep** disorders. Marshall Cavendish Benchmark 2009 64p il (Health alert) $22.95

Grades: 4 5 6 7　　　　　　　　　　　　　**616.8**

1. Sleep disorders

ISBN 978-0-7614-2913-5; 0-7614-2913-1

This "title features a handsome format, with well-chosen illustrations, a substantial amount of information, and some practical insights." Booklist

Includes glossary

Klosterman, Lorrie

★ **Meningitis**. Marshall Cavendish Benchmark 2007 64p il (Health alert) lib bdg $31.36

Grades: 4 5 6 7　　　　　　　　　　　　　**616.8**

1. Meningitis

ISBN 978-0-7614-2211-2; 0-7614-2211-0

LC 2006015819

This "title features a handsome format, with well-chosen illustrations, a substantial amount of information, and some practical insights." Booklist

"Explores the history, causes, symptoms, treatments, and future of different types of meningitis." Publisher's note

Includes glossary and bibliographical references

Levete, Sarah

Explaining cerebral palsy. Smart Apple Media 2010 45p il (Explaining) lib bdg $34.25

Grades: 5 6 7 8　　　　　　　　　　　　　**616.8**

1. Cerebral palsy

ISBN 978-1-59920-311-9 lib bdg; 1-59920-311-1 lib bdg

LC 2008-49287

Describes the illness, including its causes, how it is diagnosed, current treatment methods, and how those with cerebral palsy live everyday lives

The book provides a "basic [overview] of the health concerns related to the disease; information on diagnosis and treatment; and a discussion of the challenges or complications experienced by the affected person and their family/friends, and how to manage those problems. . . . The incorporation of quotes and personal accounts in 'Case Notes' sidebars adds to the sensitive tone found throughout [the title]." SLJ

Includes glossary and bibliographical references

616.85　Miscellaneous diseases of nervous system and mental disorders

Amenta, Charles A.

Russell's world; a story for kids about autism. illustrated by Monika Pollak. Magination Press 2011 un il $14.95; pa $9.95

Grades: K 1 2 3　　　　　　　　　　　　　**616.85**

1. Autism

ISBN 978-1-4338-0975-0; 1-4338-0975-3; 978-1-4338-0976-7 pa; 1-4338-0976-1 pa

LC 2010048837

First published 1992 with title: Russell is extra special

"Likable young Russell puts a face on autism. Amenta's experience with his own son (now grown) shapes this heartfelt approach. This child craves routine and rituals and struggles to relate to his younger brothers. . . . Focusing on Russell's experiences, the book avoids sweeping generalizations while fairly outlining the condition's complexities. . . . Vivid mixed-media spreads include black-and-white childhood photos and display a hodgepodge of household objects and crayon scribbles. . . . Supportive without sugarcoating, this realistic account of a disorder that affects so many contains at its core a raw emotional heart." Kirkus

Andrews, Beth

Why are you so scared? a child's book about parents with PTSD. illustrated by Katherine Kirkland. Magination Press 2011 un il $14.95; pa $9.95

Grades: 1 2 3 4   **616.85**

1. Post-traumatic stress disorder

ISBN 978-1-4338-1045-9; 1-4338-1045-X; 978-1-4338-1044-2 pa; 1-4338-1044-1 pa

LC 2011011082

"This straightforward, reassuring guide strives to explain some of the causes of Posttraumatic Stress Disorder . . . while not skimping on day-to-day survival tips. . . . Kirkland uses soft, hopeful illustrations that underscore the message that kids are not alone and that their parent's tired, cranky, jumpy emotions are to be expected. . . . The material is far too useful to be ignored." Booklist

Barton, Michael

It's raining cats and dogs; an autism spectrum guide to the confusing world of idioms, metaphors, and everyday expressions. Michael Barton; foreword, Delia Barton; illustrator, Michael Barton. Jessica Kingsley Publishers 2012 95 p. (alk. paper) $15.95

Grades: 3 4 5 6   **616.85**

1. Autism 2. Metaphor 3. Figures of speech 4. English language -- Idioms 5. Autistic people -- Language 6. Autism spectrum disorders -- Patients -- Language

ISBN 1849052832; 9781849052832

LC 2011039514

This book offers "insight into the mind of someone with an ASD [autism spectrum disorder]. It . . . illustrates why people with ASDs have problems understanding common phrases and idioms that others accept unquestioningly as part of everyday speech. The . . . drawings" are meant to "entertain and inspire those on the spectrum, giving them the confidence to recognise figures of speech, feel less alienated and even use idioms themselves. The drawings" are designed to "form instantly memorable references for those with ASDs to recall whenever they need to and" should "be helpful for anyone curious to understand the ASD way of thinking." (Publisher's note)

Bennett, Howard J.

Max Archer, kid detective: the case of the wet bed; illustrated by Spike Gerrell. Magination Press 2011 48p il $14.95; pa $9.95

Grades: K 1 2 3   **616.85**

1. Enuresis

ISBN 978-1-4338-0953-8; 1-4338-0953-2; 978-1-4338-0954-5 pa; 1-4338-0954-0 pa

LC 2010051485

"Max is a detective who like to 'help kids with their problems'—this case takes on bedwetting. . . . Bennett strikes the right balance between story and self-help to provide a title whose tone and careful explanations both parents and kids

will appreciate. . . . Even if there were not an alarming dearth of titles on this subject aimed at kids, this would stand out as a most thorough, highly readable resource." Kirkus

Brill, Marlene Targ

★ Down syndrome. Marshall Cavendish Benchmark 2007 64p il (Health alert) lib bdg $31.36

Grades: 4 5 6 7   **616.85**

1. Down syndrome

ISBN 978-0-7614-2207-5 lib bdg; 0-7614-2207-2 lib bdg

LC 2006-15817

This "title features a handsome format, with well-chosen illustrations, a substantial amount of information, and some practical insights." Booklist

Includes glossary and bibliographical references

Capaccio, George

★ ADD and ADHD. Marshall Cavendish Benchmark 2007 64p il (Health alert) lib bdg $21.95

Grades: 4 5 6 7   **616.85**

1. Attention deficit disorder

ISBN 978-0-7614-2705-6; 0-7614-2705-8

LC 2007008790

This describes what it is like to have Attention Deficit Disorder or Attention Deficit Hyperactivity Disorder, what they are, their history, and living with the disorders.

This "title features a handsome format, with well-chosen illustrations, a substantial amount of information, and some practical insights." Booklist

Includes glossary and bibliographical references

Chilman-Blair, Kim

Medikidz explain ADHD; [by] Kim Chilman-Blair and John Taddeo; medical content reviewed for accuracy by Peter D. Hill. Rosen Central 2011 40p il (Superheroes on a medical mission) lib bdg $29.25; pa $11.75

Grades: 3 4 5 6   **616.85**

1. Superheroes 2. Graphic novels 3. Attention deficit disorder

ISBN 978-1-4358-9456-3 lib bdg; 1-4358-9456-1 lib bdg; 978-1-4488-1833-4 pa; 1-4488-1833-8 pa

LC 2010001063

"A team of superheroes rides around on a medi-jet and whisks ill children, or their siblings, off to Mediland, a giant replica of the human body, to teach them about [ADHD]. . . . The comic panels are visually exciting with eye-popping colors. Inside Mediland, the science behind various conditions is expertly simplified and explained with a sometimes tongue-in-cheek repartee among the characters as well as with very basic analogies reminiscent of video games. . . . This approach makes the health issues accessible and much less scary for readers wanting to learn more for personal or academic reasons." SLJ

Includes glossary and bibliographical references

Medikidz explain autism; [by] Kim Chilman-Blair and John Taddeo. Rosen Central 2011 40p il (Superheroes on a medical mission) lib bdg $29.25; pa $11.75

Grades: 3 4 5 6   **616.85**

1. Autism 2. Superheroes 3. Graphic novels

ISBN 978-1-4358-9460-0 lib bdg; 1-4358-9460-X; 978-1-4488-1835-8 pa; 1-4488-1835-4 pa

LC 2010008830

"A team of superheroes rides around on a medi-jet and whisks ill children, or their siblings, off to Mediland, a giant replica of the human body, to teach them about [autism]. . . . The comic panels are visually exciting with eye-popping colors. Inside Mediland, the science behind various conditions is expertly simplified and explained with a sometimes tongue-in-cheek repartee among the characters as well as with very basic analogies reminiscent of video games. . . . This approach makes the health issues accessible and much less scary for readers wanting to learn more for personal or academic reasons." SLJ

Includes glossary and bibliographical references

Medikidz explain depression; [by] Kim Chilman-Blair and Shawn deLoache. Rosen Central 2011 40p il (Superheroes on a medical mission) lib bdg $29.25; pa $11.75
Grades: 3 4 5 6   **616.85**
   1. Superheroes 2. Graphic novels 3. Depression (Psychology)
   ISBN 978-1-4358-9455-6 lib bdg; 1-4358-9455-3 lib bdg; 978-1-4488-1837-2 pa; 1-4488-1837-0 pa
               LC 2010008833

"A team of superheroes rides around on a medi-jet and whisks ill children, or their siblings, off to Mediland, a giant replica of the human body, to teach them about [depression]. . . . The comic panels are visually exciting with eye-popping colors. Inside Mediland, the science behind various conditions is expertly simplified and explained with a sometimes tongue-in-cheek repartee among the characters as well as with very basic analogies reminiscent of video games. . . . This approach makes the health issues accessible and much less scary for readers wanting to learn more for personal or academic reasons." SLJ

Includes glossary and bibliographical references

Donovan, Sandra, 1967-
   Keep your cool! what you should know about stress. illustrations by Jack Desrocher. Lerner Publications Co. 2009 64p il (Health zone) lib bdg $30.60
Grades: 4 5 6 7   **616.85**
   1. Stress (Psychology)
   ISBN 978-0-8225-7555-9; 0-8225-7555-8
               LC 2007038858

This describes what causes stress and what you can do to relieve it.

"The format is beyond lively, with lots of color, cartoons, and an informal writing style, but it manages to present sometimes frightening material in a non-threatening and browsable way." Booklist

Includes glossary and bibliographical references

Levy, Joel
   Phobiapedia; all the things we fear the most! Scholastic 2011 80p il pa $8.99
Grades: 4 5 6 7   **616.85**
   1. Phobias
   ISBN 978-0-545-34929-1; 0-545-34929-X

This briefly describes over 50 phobias.

"With an appealing layout, plenty of color, and enough germs, snakes, and bats to get the heart racing, this title has kid written all over it." Booklist

Quinn, Patricia O.
   Attention, girls! a guide to learn all about your AD/HD. illustrated by Carl Pearce. Magination Press 2009 119p il $16.95; pa $12.95
Grades: 4 5 6 7   **616.85**
   1. Attention deficit disorder
   ISBN 978-1-4338-0447-2; 1-4338-0447-6; 978-1-4338-0448-9 pa; 1-4338-0448-4 pa
               LC 2008054524

"Quinn has attention deficit hyperactivity disorder and is a medical doctor; she addresses the types of AD/HD; who can help; differences between girls and boys with AD/HD; making friends; talking with adults about the condition; relaxation techniques; and medication. Her aim is to give girls a variety of ways to manage their disorders. . . . The book is attractive and inviting with colorful cartoon illustrations, sidebars, and highlighted reminders." SLJ

Robbins, Lynette
   How to deal with ADHD. PowerKids Press 2010 24p il (Kids' health) lib bdg $21.25
Grades: 2 3 4   **616.85**
   1. Attention deficit disorder
   ISBN 978-1-4042-8140-0 lib bdg; 1-4042-8140-1 lib bdg
               LC 2009-6412

"Hypothetical situations with fictional characters put readers in the moment and provide a solid foundation for comprehending [ADHD]. . . . Robbins maintains a comforting tone, reassuring readers that it is possible to lead active lives with proper attention to diet and guidance from parents and doctors." SLJ

Includes glossary

   How to deal with autism. PowerKids Press 2010 24p il (Kids' health) lib bdg $21.25
Grades: 2 3 4   **616.85**
   1. Autism
   ISBN 978-1-4042-8142-4 lib bdg; 1-4042-8142-8 lib bdg
               LC 2009-7862

"Hypothetical situations with fictional characters put readers in the moment and provide a solid foundation for comprehending [autism]. . . . Robbins maintains a comforting tone, reassuring readers that it is possible to lead active lives with proper attention to diet and guidance from parents and doctors." SLJ

Includes glossary

Royston, Angela
   Explaining down syndrome. Smart Apple Media 2010 45p il (Explaining) lib bdg $34.25
Grades: 5 6 7 8   **616.85**
   1. Down syndrome
   ISBN 978-1-59920-308-9 lib bdg; 1-59920-308-1 lib bdg
               LC 2008-49291

This book about down syndrome provides a "basic [overview] of the health concerns related to the disease; information on diagnosis and treatment; and a discussion of the challenges or complications experienced by the affected person and their family/friends, and how to manage those problems. . . . The incorporation of quotes and personal accounts in 'Case Notes' sidebars adds to the sensitive tone found throughout [the title]." SLJ

Includes glossary

Shapiro, Ouisie

Autism and me; sibling stories. photographs by Steven Vote. Albert Whitman 2009 un il $16.99

Grades: 3 4 5 6   616.85

1. Autism 2. Siblings

ISBN 978-0-8075-0487-1; 0-8075-0487-4

LC 2008-31700

Children tell their stories of what it is like to live with a sibling who has autism.

"The children's emotions ring true, telling what they love about their sibling; the preaching comes from their hearts. This book would be useful in families and in classrooms to help explain both the struggles and the triumphs of living with someone who has this disorder." SLJ

Silverstein, Alvin

The **ADHD** update; understanding attention-deficit/hyperactivity disorder. [by] Alvin and Virginia Silverstein and Laura Silverstein Nunn. Enslow Publishers 2008 112p il (Disease update) lib bdg $31.93

Grades: 5 6 7 8   616.85

1. Attention deficit disorder

ISBN 978-0-7660-2800-5 lib bdg; 0-7660-2800-3 lib bdg

LC 2007-13853

This describes Attention-deficit hyperactivity disorder (ADHD) and its history, diagnosis and treatment, living with it, and its future

"This book is an excellent primer on AD/HD." Sci Books Films

Includes glossary and bibliographical references

The **eating** disorders update; understanding anorexia, bulimia, and binge eating. [by] Alvin and Virginia Silverstein and Laura Silverstein Nunn. Enslow Publishers 2008 128p il (Disease update) lib bdg $31.93

Grades: 5 6 7 8   616.85

1. Bulimia 2. Anorexia nervosa 3. Eating disorders

ISBN 978-0-7660-2802-9 lib bdg; 0-7660-2802-X lib bdg

LC 2007013985

"An introduction to the history and most up-to-date research and treatment of eating disorders." Publisher's note

Includes glossary and bibliographical references

Simons, Rae

I eat when I'm sad; food and feelings. Mason Crest Publishers 2010 48p il (Kids & obesity) lib bdg $19.95; pa $7.95

Grades: 3 4 5   616.85

1. Obesity 2. Weight loss 3. Eating disorders

ISBN 978-1-4222-1714-6 lib bdg; 1-4222-1714-0 lib bdg; 978-1-4222-1902-7 pa; 1-4222-1902-X pa

LC 2010007065

This book about childhood obesity makes "a compelling case by plainly stating the consequences of carrying around 'a little extra.' . . . The tone is highly sympathetic, capturing the vicious cycle of emotional eating and giving kids tools to combat weight gain." Booklist

Includes bibliographical references

Skotko, Brian

Fasten your seatbelt; a crash course on Down syndrome for brothers and sisters. [by] Brian G. Skotko and Susan P. Levine. Woodbine House 2009 191p il pa $18.95

Grades: 4 5 6 7   616.85

1. Siblings 2. Down syndrome

ISBN 978-1-890627-86-7 pa; 1-890627-86-0 pa

LC 2008049753

"Skotko and Levine address preteens and teenagers who have a sibling with Down syndrome, answering questions that have been generated through their work with this population. . . . With a wealth of information, numerous resources, and the reassurance that all siblings of people with disabilities sometimes go through periods of contradictory feelings, this is an excellent guide for young people who are trying to figure out how to negotiate an often-confusing relationship." SLJ

Includes bibliographical references

Snedden, Robert

Explaining autism. Smart Apple Media 2010 45p il (Explaining) lib bdg $34.25

Grades: 5 6 7 8   616.85

1. Autism 2. Asperger's syndrome

ISBN 978-1-59920-307-2 lib bdg; 1-59920-307-3 lib bdg

LC 2008-49285

Describes the illness, including its symptoms, how it affects physical and mental health, current treatments, and how people with autism live everyday lives

"The incorporation of quotes and personal accounts in 'Case Notes' sidebars adds to the sensitive tone found throughout [the title]." SLJ

Includes glossary and bibliographical references

Stefanski, Daniel, 1997-

★ **How** to talk to an autistic kid; illustrated by Hazel Mitchell. Free Spirit 2011 43p il $12.99

Grades: 3 4 5 6   616.85

1. Autism

ISBN 978-1-57542-365-4; 1-57542-365-0

"Stefanski provides clear, sometimes blunt, often humorous advice for readers on how to interact with autistic classmates. An authority on this topic—he is a 14-year-old boy with autism—he begins by describing autism. . . . He describes, using a brief paragraph or two per page, some of the traits many autistic people share. . . . For each trait, he offers down-to-earth suggestions for resolving problems. . . . His insightful, matter-of-fact presentation demystifies behaviors that might confuse or disturb non-autistic classmates. Simple cartoon illustrations in black, gray and two shades of turquoise accompany the text. . . . A thought-provoking introduction to autism . . . and an essential purchase for every primary and middle-school classroom." Kirkus

Stewart, Gail

Anorexia; [by] Gail B. Stewart. Cherry Lake Pub. 2009 32p il (Health at risk) lib bdg $27.07

Grades: 4 5 6 7   616.85

1. Anorexia nervosa

ISBN 978-1-60279-281-4 lib bdg; 1-60279-281-X lib bdg

LC 2008017496

This explains why anorexics feel the need to keep losing weight, what can happen to them as a result of their desperate struggle to be thin, and how they can get help.

"Great for reports or reluctant readers." Booklist

Includes bibliographical references

Bulimia; [by] Gail B. Stewart. Cherry Lake Pub. 2009 32p il (Health at risk) lib bdg $27.07

Grades: 4 5 6 7   **616.85**

1. Bulimia

ISBN 978-1-60279-282-1 lib bdg; 1-60279-282-8 lib bdg

LC 2008-17497

This describes the health risks of bulimia and what can be done to help people fight this disease.

"Great for reports or reluctant readers." Booklist

Includes bibliographical references

Taylor, John F.

The **survival** guide for kids with ADD or ADHD; [by] John F. Taylor. Free Spirit Pub. 2006 119p il pa $13.95

Grades: 3 4 5   **616.85**

1. Attention deficit disorder

ISBN 978-1-57542-195-7 pa; 1-57542-195-X pa

LC 2005033737

"Packed with good advice, this guide will catch readers' eyes with its bright cover, varied fonts, and cartoon-style illustrations. The writing is clear and kid-friendly." SLJ

Thomas, Pat

I see things differently a first look at autism; Pat Thomas. Barrons Educational Series, Inc. 2014 29 p. color illustrations (A first look at) $6.99

Grades: K 1 2   **616.85**

1. Autism 2. Autistic children

ISBN 1438004796; 9781438004792

LC 2013957082

This children's book on autism, by Pat Thomas, is part of the "A First Look At . . . " series. "Aimed at siblings and classmates," the book "comments on how and why kids with autism 'see things differently' and on behaviors that may seem puzzling. . . . The appended section for parents and teachers offers . . . advice as well as suggested books and online resources." (Booklist)

Part of the "First Look At..." series

Van Niekerk, Clarabelle

Understanding Sam and Asperger Syndrome; [by] Clarabelle van Niekerk and Liezl Venter; illustrated by Clarabelle van Niekerk. Skeezel Press 2008 un il $17.95

Grades: PreK K 1 2   **616.85**

1. Asperger's syndrome

ISBN 978-0-9747217-1-2; 0-9747217-1-9

"A third-person past-tense narrative tells the story of Sam, a boy with Asperger Syndrome. . . . Because of the interesting story line, the positive approach, and the notion that others can learn to help Sam instead of expecting him to change, this is an excellent introduction to the topic. The pictures are bright and lively, showing mostly happy faces. The book concludes with 10 helpful tips to remember when a friend or a classmate has Asperger's." SLJ

616.86   Substance abuse (Drug abuse)

Allman, Toney

Drugs. Cherry Lake Pub. 2009 32p il (Health at risk) lib bdg $27.07

Grades: 4 5 6 7   **616.86**

1. Drug abuse

ISBN 978-1-60279-283-8 lib bdg; 1-60279-283-6 lib bdg

LC 2008017503

This describes the dangers of drug abuse, the programs that help people get off drugs, and how to avoid drug use.

"Great for reports or reluctant readers." Booklist

Includes bibliographical references

Miller, Heather

Smoking. Cherry Lake Pub. 2009 32p il (Health at risk) lib bdg $27.07

Grades: 4 5 6 7   **616.86**

1. Smoking 2. Tobacco habit

ISBN 978-1-60279-286-9 lib bdg; 1-60279-286-0 lib bdg

LC 2008017501

This describes why smoking is dangerous, how difficult it is to stop once you start, and what efforts are underway to put the brakes on this habit.

"Great for reports or reluctant readers." Booklist

Includes bibliographical references

616.89   Mental disorders

Rashkin, Rachel

Feeling better; a kid's book about therapy. by Rachel Rashkin; illustrated by Bonnie Adamson. Magination Press 2005 48p il $14.95; pa $8.95

Grades: 4 5 6 7   **616.89**

1. Psychotherapy

ISBN 1-59147-237-7; 1-59147-238-5 pa

LC 2004022727

"Clearly written and well-organized. . . . Animated black-and-white sketches portray the girl's various emotions. This title gently encourages kids who are struggling with issues to seek help." SLJ

616.9   Other diseases

Aronin, Miriam

Tuberculosis; the white plague! Bearport Pub. 2011 32p il map (Nightmare plagues) lib bdg $25.27

Grades: 4 5 6 7   **616.9**

1. Tuberculosis

ISBN 978-1-936088-06-5; 1-936088-06-1

LC 2010010679

Discover what causes tuberculosis and how it affects the body.

"The writing is accessible and interspersed with interesting photographs and fact boxes. . . . [The book relies] on an honest discussion of [tuberculosis and is an] . . . effective, easily navigated [introduction]." SLJ

Includes glossary and bibliographical references

Berger, Melvin

Germs make me sick! illustrated by Marylin Hafner. rev ed; HarperCollins Pubs. 1995 32p il (Let's-read-and-find-out science) hardcover o.p. pa $4.99

Grades: K 1 2 3   **616.9**

1. Viruses 2. Bacteria

ISBN 0-06-024250-7 lib bdg; 0-06-445154-2 pa

LC 93-27059

First published 1985

Explains how bacteria and viruses affect the human body and how the body fights them

This features "Hafner's lively color cartoon illustrations. . . . [It offers a] lively combination of fact and narrative that has made this a great title for easy reading and for sharing aloud." Booklist

Blank, Alison

Invincible microbe; tuberculosis and the never-ending search for a cure. Jim Murphy, Alison Blank. Clarion Books 2012 149 p. (hardback) $18.99

Grades: 5 6 7 8 9   **616.9**

1. Tuberculosis 2. Lungs -- Diseases 3. Communicable diseases -- Treatment 4. Microorganisms

ISBN 0618535748; 9780618535743

LC 2011025951

This book looks at tuberculosis. It "starts with archeologists finding evidence of tuberculosis in a 500,000 year old skull and continues through to the present day. Various 'cures' such as the medieval 'king's touch' . . . , bloodletting of the 19th century, twentieth century sanatoriums and modern day drug cocktails are all discussed." Also "covered is the socioeconomic side of the disease, with a discussion of how treatment often varied depending on the race and economic status of the patient." (Children's Literature)

Includes bibliographical references

Colligan, L. H.

★ **Tick**-borne illnesses. Marshall Cavendish Benchmark 2009 64p il (Health alert) $22.95

Grades: 4 5 6 7   **616.9**

1. Tick-borne diseases

ISBN 978-0-7614-2914-2; 0-7614-2914-X

LC 2007-38517

This "title features a handsome format, with well-chosen illustrations, a substantial amount of information, and some practical insights." Booklist

Includes glossary

Duke, Shirley Smith

Infections, infestations, and disease; [by] Shirley Duke. Rourke Pub. 2010 48p il (Let's explore science) $32.79

Grades: 4 5 6 7   **616.9**

1. Communicable diseases

ISBN 978-1-61590-321-4; 1-61590-321-6

LC 2010009908

This describes communicable diseases.

Includes bibliographical references

Glaser, Jason

Chicken pox; consultant, James R. Hubbard. Capstone Press 2006 24p il (First facts: Health matters) $21.26

Grades: K 1 2 3   **616.9**

1. Chickenpox

ISBN 978-0-7368-4288-4; 0-7368-4288-8

LC 2004028549

This introduction to chicken pox is "general and straightforward. Two or three simple sentences in large font appear on each page and address the causes, symptoms, appearances, and treatments." SLJ

Includes bibliographical references

Strep throat. Capstone Press 2007 il (First facts: health matters) $21.26

Grades: K 1 2 3   **616.9**

1. Strep throat

ISBN 978-0-7368-6393-3; 0-7368-6393-1

LC 2006002821

"Describes strep throat, how people get it, and how to treat and prevent it." Publisher's note

Includes bibliographical references

Hoffmann, Gretchen

★ **Chicken** pox. Marshall Cavendish Benchmark 2009 62p il (Health alert) $22.95

Grades: 4 5 6 7   **616.9**

1. Chickenpox

ISBN 978-0-7614-2916-6; 0-7614-2916-6

This "title features a handsome format, with well-chosen illustrations, a substantial amount of information, and some practical insights." Booklist

Includes glossary

Jarrow, Gail

Chiggers; [by] Gail Jarrow. KidHaven Press 2004 32p il (Parasites) $22.45

Grades: 4 5 6   **616.9**

1. Mites

ISBN 0-7377-1778-5

LC 2003-9614

"Several short chapters briefly describe the distinctive physical and behavioral characteristics of [chiggers] and special characteristics of particular species. [The book] also [highlights] the symptoms, victims' experiences, the organisms' potential threats as disease vectors, current treatments, and prevention methods. . . . Clear, color photographs illustrate the [text]. . . . Well organized and clearly written." SLJ

Kornberg, Arthur

Germ stories; illustrations by Adam Alaniz; photography by Roberto Kolter. University Science Books 2007 70p il $22

Grades: 2 3 4   **616.9**

1. Bacteria 2. Microbiology

ISBN 978-1-891389-51-1; 1-891389-51-3

LC 2007-09960

"This book of poems is a visual and lyrical journey into the wonderful world of . . . germs. . . . Nobel Prize winner Arthur Kornberg gives readers a look at the structures, methods, and cycles of germs. . . . The poetry is easy and flowing. Cartoon germs—fanged slime bacteria and wispy penicillin—are bright additions. After each poem is an electron micrograph, plus a visual comparison to help children understand just how small germs are." Libr Media Connect

Includes glossary

Landau, Elaine

★ **Chickenpox**. Marshall Cavendish Benchmark 2010 32p il (Head-to-toe health) $28.50

Grades: 2 3 4   **616.9**

1. Chickenpox

ISBN 978-0-7614-3498-6; 0-7614-3498-4

LC 2008-10782

"The book will satisfy researchers as well as those with a personal interest in the virus. . . . [This is] well-organized, informative." SLJ

Includes glossary and bibliographical references

★ **Strep** throat. Marshall Cavendish Benchmark 2010 32p il (Head-to-toe health) lib bdg $28.50

Grades: 2 3 4   **616.9**

1. Strep throat

ISBN 978-0-7614-4834-1 lib bdg; 0-7614-4834-9 lib bdg

This provides basic information about strep throat and its prevention.

This "manages to pack in a surprising amount of information, including facts about good hygiene. The text addresses the reader directly, and the photos are real grabbers." Booklist

Includes glossary and bibliographical references

Ollhoff, Jim

The **Black** Death. ABDO Pub. Co. 2010 32p il map (A history of germs) lib bdg $27.07

Grades: 3 4 5 6   **616.9**

1. Plague

ISBN 978-1-60453-497-9 lib bdg; 1-60453-497-4 lib bdg

LC 2008-55061

This book "examines the plague's origins, causes, effects, cures, and historical legacy. . . . The short, informative chapters provide plenty of details for reports. The illustrations, many of which are color photos, enhance the information." SLJ

Includes glossary

The **germ** detectives. ABDO Pub. Co. 2010 32p il (A history of germs) lib bdg $27.07

Grades: 3 4 5 6   **616.9**

1. Bacteria 2. Chemists 3. Surgeons 4. Physicians 5. Scientists 6. Microbiology 7. Microscopists 8. Microbiologists

ISBN 978-1-60453-499-3 lib bdg; 1-60453-499-0 lib bdg

LC 2008-55062

This book "highlights the work of Antoni van Leeuwenhoek, Ignaz Semmelweis, Joseph Lister, Louis Pasteur, and Robert Koch, all of whom contributed to current knowledge about germs. . . . The short, informative chapters provide plenty of details for reports. The illustrations, many of which are color photos, enhance the information." SLJ

Includes glossary

Malaria. ABDO Pub. Co. 2010 32p il (A history of germs) lib bdg $27.07

Grades: 3 4 5 6   **616.9**

1. Malaria

ISBN 978-1-60453-500-6 lib bdg; 1-60453-500-8 lib bdg

"Malaria explains why the disease is so deadly, notes types of treatments, looks at efforts to control it, and suggests the future development of a vaccine. . . . The short, informative chapters provide plenty of details for reports. The illustrations, many of which are color photos, enhance the information." SLJ

Smallpox. ABDO Pub. Co. 2010 32p il (A history of germs) lib bdg $27.07

Grades: 3 4 5 6   **616.9**

1. Smallpox 2. Physicians 3. Writers on medicine

ISBN 978-1-60453-501-3 lib bdg; 1-60453-501-6 lib bdg

"Smallpox discusses the disease's symptoms, highlights Edward Jenner's work in developing a vaccine, and touches upon the potential use of the virus as a biological weapon. . . . The short, informative chapters provide plenty of details for reports. The illustrations, many of which are color photos, enhance the information." SLJ

Includes glossary

616.97   Diseases of immune system

Ballard, Carol

Explaining food allergies. Smart Apple Media 2010 45p il (Explaining) $23.95

Grades: 5 6 7 8   **616.97**

1. Food allergy

ISBN 978-1-59920-316-4; 1-59920-316-2

LC 2008049936

This "does an excellent job of discussing complex clinical science while showing what daily life is like for kids living with food allergies, from the signs and symptoms to the tests and treatments. . . . This blend of the technical and the personal will have wide appeal." Booklist

Chilman-Blair, Kim

Medikidz explain HIV; [by] Kim Chilman-Blair and John Taddeo; medical content reviewed for accuracy by Vas Novelli and Karyn Moshal. Rosen Central 2011 40p il (Superheroes on a medical mission) lib bdg $29.25; pa $11.75

Grades: 3 4 5 6   **616.97**

1. Superheroes 2. AIDS (Disease) 3. Graphic novels

ISBN 978-1-4358-9458-7 lib bdg; 1-4358-9458-8 lib bdg; 978-1-4488-1839-6 pa; 1-4488-1839-7 pa

LC 2010001333

"A team of superheroes rides around on a medi-jet and whisks ill children, or their siblings, off to Mediland, a giant replica of the human body, to teach them about [HIV]. . . . The comic panels are visually exciting with eye-popping colors. Inside Mediland, the science behind various conditions is expertly simplified and explained with a sometimes tongue-in-cheek repartee among the characters as well as with very basic analogies reminiscent of video games. . . . This approach makes the health issues accessible and much less scary for readers wanting to learn more for personal or academic reasons." SLJ

Includes glossary and bibliographical references

Landau, Elaine
★ **Food** allergies. Marshall Cavendish Benchmark 2010 32p il (Head-to-toe health) lib bdg $28.50
Grades: 2 3 4   **616.97**
  1. Food allergy
  ISBN 978-0-7614-3500-6; 0-7614-3500-X
                                   LC 2008-10785
"Color photographs appear throughout. . . . [This is] well-organized, informative." SLJ
Includes glossary and bibliographical references

Royston, Angela
  Allergies. Black Rabbit Books 2009 30p il (How's your health?) lib bdg $27.10
Grades: 1 2 3   **616.97**
  1. Allergy
  ISBN 978-1-59920-220-4 lib bdg; 1-59920-220-4 lib bdg
                                   LC 2007-35174
First published 2004 by Heinemann Library
"Encourages further learning with sidebars that help readers think concretely about the subject. . . . Altogether a pitch perfect presentation." SLJ
Includes glossary and bibliographical references

Thomas, Pat
  I think I am going to sneeze; a first look at allergies. [by] Pat Thomas; illustrated by Lesley Harker. Barron's Educational Series 2008 29p il pa $6.99
Grades: PreK K 1 2   **616.97**
  1. Allergy
  ISBN 978-0-7641-3900-0 pa; 0-7641-39002 pa
This "title covers the causes and effects of allergies and treatments and reassures youngsters that they don't have to be left out of school activities. Sidebars . . . ask questions about children's personal experiences and thoughts, which can be used as discussion starters. [The] title ends with an extensive note to parents, with practical advice for . . . helping children cope with allergies. [This is a] solid [addition] for most collections." SLJ

616.99   Tumors and miscellaneous communicable diseases

Markle, Sandra, 1946-
  Leukemia; true survival stories. Lerner Publications 2010 48p il (Powerful medicine) lib bdg $27.93
Grades: 5 6 7 8   **616.99**
  1. Leukemia
  ISBN 978-0-8225-8700-2 lib bdg; 0-8225-8700-9 lib bdg
                                   LC 2009-34441
This book about leukemia "will grab the attention of middle school readers. . . . The illustrations and photos are stunning with medically accurate captions. Real-life patients, whose photos are included in the text, are highlighted, with updates on their progress at the end of . . . [the] book. . . . This . . . fills the need for up-to-date books on medical topics using vocabulary that a young teenager can understand." Voice Youth Advocates
Includes glossary and bibliographical references

Silverstein, Alvin
  The **breast** cancer update; [by] Alvin and Virginia Silverstein and Laura Silverstein Nunn. Enslow Publishers 2008 128p il (Disease update) lib bdg $31.93
Grades: 5 6 7 8   **616.99**
  1. Breast cancer
  ISBN 978-0-7660-2747-3 lib bdg; 0-7660-2747-3 lib bdg
                                   LC 2006-32821
This offers a history of breast cancer, a definition of it, and describes its diagnosis and treatment, prevention, and future
Includes glossary and bibliographical references

Watters, Debbie
  Where's Mom's hair? a family's journey through cancer. by Debbie Watters; with Haydn and Emmett Watters; photographs by Sophie Hogan. Second Story Press 2005 31p il pa $10.95
Grades: 2 3 4   **616.99**
  1. Hair 2. Cancer
  ISBN 1-896764-94-0
"When the author underwent chemotherapy following cancer surgery, she faced the loss of her hair with courage and humor. Family and friends gathered for a 'haircutting party,' where her husband and two young sons . . . joined her in getting buzz cuts. . . . The gentle kindness conveyed in the often-humorous writing will reassure young children facing similar circumstances." SLJ

617   Surgery, regional medicine, dentistry, ophthalmology, otology, audiology

Markle, Sandra, 1946-
  Wounded brains; true survival stories. Lerner Publications 2011 48p il (Powerful medicine) lib bdg $27.93
Grades: 5 6 7 8   **617**
  1. Brain -- Wounds and injuries
  ISBN 978-0-8225-8704-0 lib bdg; 0-8225-8704-1 lib bdg
                                   LC 2009034440
Describes several true cases of traumatic brain injury and the medical treatment that followed.
This narrative reads "like information from the Discovery Health channel, for kids: part fascinating science, part human interest story, and part 'Eew, gross!'. . . Clear, straightforward prose is supplemented by definitions and explanations of medical techniques and jargon. The numerous color photos and medical images will satisfy readers' curiosity." SLJ
Includes glossary and bibliographical references

Mullins, Matt
  Surgical technologist. Cherry Lake Pub. 2010 32p il (Cool careers: career and technical education) lib bdg $27.07
Grades: 4 5 6 7   **617**
  1. Surgery 2. Vocational guidance 3. Medical technologists
  ISBN 978-1-60279-939-4 lib bdg; 1-60279-939-3 lib bdg
                                   LC 2010001437

This "provides an overview of the duties performed by these allied health professionals, requirements and training for the job, and the anticipated future of this occupation. . . . Full color, captioned photographs . . . appear on most spreads, clarifying the text. . . . This will make a useful addition to the career shelf." Booklist

Includes bibliographical references

Woog, Adam
The **bionic** hand. Norwood House Press 2009 48p il (A great idea) lib bdg $25.27
Grades: 3 4 5 6   **617**
1. Bionics 2. Artificial limbs
ISBN 978-1-59953-341-4 lib bdg; 1-59953-341-3 lib bdg
                                              LC 2009-15640
"Explores the development and creation of the i-LIMB which is the first commercially available bionic hand." Publisher's note

Includes glossary and bibliographical references

617.1 Injuries and wounds

Cobb, Vicki
★ **Your** body battles a broken bone; written by Vicki Cobb; photomicrographs by Dennis Kunkel; illustrations by Andrew N. Harris. Millbrook Press 2009 32p il (Body battles) lib bdg $25.26
Grades: 3 4 5   **617.1**
1. Bones 2. Fractures
ISBN 978-0-8225-7468-2; 0-8225-7468-3
                                              LC 2008002837
This book provides comic illustrations and photomicrographs that describe how the body heals a broken bone

"Many of the vibrant illustrations anthropomorphize various cells and other 'battle' participants, making the science explained approachable and easy to understand. Photomicrographs further illuminate the text. These amazing pictures, taken with a scanning electron microscope, are greatly magnified and colored to highlight certain features." SLJ

Includes glossary and bibliographical references

★ **Your** body battles a skinned knee; written by Vicki Cobb; photomicrographs by Dennis Kunkel; illustrations by Andrew N. Harris. Millbrook Press 2009 32p il (Body battles) lib bdg $25.26
Grades: 3 4 5   **617.1**
1. Skin 2. Immune system 3. Wounds and injuries
ISBN 978-0-8225-6814-8; 0-8225-6814-4
                                              LC 2008002826
"By combining simple yet engaging text; comic-like illustrations; and greatly magnified photomicrographs, this book describes the healing process of a bloodied knee in a fashion that is both entertaining and easy to understand." Booklist

Includes glossary and bibliographical references

Landau, Elaine
★ **Bites** and stings. Marshall Cavendish Benchmark 2009 32p il (Head-to-toe health) lib bdg $28.50

Grades: 2 3 4   **617.1**
1. Bites and stings
ISBN 978-0-7614-2850-3; 0-7614-2850-X
                                              LC 2007-43022
"Photo illustrations are apt and age appropriate. . . . Pervading the [book] . . . is an overall sense of reassurance that even if something hurts, 'all better' is never too far away. Appealing and readable nonfiction." SLJ

Includes glossary and bibliographical references

★ **Broken** bones. Marshall Cavendish Benchmark 2009 32p il (Head-to-toe health) lib bdg $28.50
Grades: 2 3 4   **617.1**
1. Bones 2. Fractures
ISBN 978-0-7614-2847-3; 0-7614-2847-X
                                              LC 2007-26665
"Photo illustrations are apt and age appropriate. . . . Pervading the [book] . . . is an overall sense of reassurance that even if something hurts, 'all better' is never too far away. Appealing and readable nonfiction." SLJ

Includes glossary and bibliographical references

★ **Bumps,** bruises, and scrapes. Marshall Cavendish Benchmark 2009 32p il (Head-to-toe health) lib bdg $28.50
Grades: 2 3 4   **617.1**
1. Wounds and injuries
ISBN 978-0-7614-2849-7; 0-7614-2849-6
                                              LC 2007-26959
"Photo illustrations are apt and age appropriate. . . . Pervading the [book] . . . is an overall sense of reassurance that even if something hurts, 'all better' is never too far away. Appealing and readable nonfiction." SLJ

Includes glossary and bibliographical references

★ **Burns**. Marshall Cavendish Benchmark 2010 32p il (Head-to-toe health) lib bdg $28.50
Grades: 2 3 4   **617.1**
1. Burns and scalds
ISBN 978-0-7614-4832-7 lib bdg; 0-7614-4832-2 lib bdg
This provides basic information about the different types of burns a person can get.

This "manages to pack in a surprising amount of information, including facts about good hygiene. The text addresses the reader directly, and the photos are real grabbers." Booklist

Includes glossary and bibliographical references

★ **Sprains** and strains. Marshall Cavendish Benchmark 2010 32p il (Head-to-toe health) lib bdg $28.50
Grades: 2 3 4   **617.1**
1. Wounds and injuries
ISBN 978-0-7614-4833-4 lib bdg; 0-7614-4833-0 lib bdg
This provides basic information about the different types of sprains and strains the body can get.

This "manages to pack in a surprising amount of information, including facts about good hygiene. The text addresses the reader directly, and the photos are real grabbers." Booklist

Includes glossary and bibliographical references

Lew, Kristi

Clot & scab; gross stuff about your scrapes, bumps, and bruises. illustrations by Michael Slack. Millbrook Press 2010 48p il (Gross body science) lib bdg $29.27

Grades: 4 5 6 **617.1**

1. Wounds and injuries

ISBN 978-0-8225-8965-5 lib bdg; 0-8225-8965-6 lib bdg

LC 2008-45626

"Solid information layered between sarcastic comments and kid-friendly terminology like fart, poop, barf, and puke will keep readers engaged. . . . Labeled, captioned (and graphic) photographs, cartoon-style illustrations, and micrographs add information." SLJ

Includes glossary and bibliographical references

Markle, Sandra

Bad burns; true survival stories. Lerner Publications 2010 48p il (Powerful medicine) lib bdg $27.93

Grades: 5 6 7 8 **617.1**

1. Burns and scalds

ISBN 978-0-8225-8702-6 lib bdg; 0-8225-8702-5 lib bdg

LC 2009034439

Explores how advancements in medicine and technology have helped victims of severe skin burns, and includes real-life stories of burn survivors and tips on burn prevention and treatment.

This narrative reads "like information from the Discovery Health channel, for kids: part fascinating science, part human interest story, and part 'Eew, gross!'. . . Clear, straightforward prose is supplemented by definitions and explanations of medical techniques and jargon. The numerous color photos and medical images will satisfy readers' curiosity." SLJ

Includes glossary and bibliographical references

Shattered bones; true survival stories. Lerner Publications 2010 48p il (Powerful medicine) lib bdg $27.93

Grades: 5 6 7 8 **617.1**

1. Bones 2. Fractures

ISBN 978-0-8225-8703-3 lib bdg; 0-8225-8703-3 lib bdg

LC 2009034442

Offers true stories of people who suffered broken bones, along with information on the skeleton, its structure and function, and the treatments doctors use for injuries.

This narrative reads "like information from the Discovery Health channel, for kids: part fascinating science, part human interest story, and part 'Eew, gross!'. . . Clear, straightforward prose is supplemented by definitions and explanations of medical techniques and jargon. The numerous color photos and medical images will satisfy readers' curiosity." SLJ

Includes glossary and bibliographical references

Royston, Angela

Cuts, bruises, and breaks. Black Rabbit Books 2009 30p il (How's your health) lib bdg $27.10

Grades: 1 2 3 **617.1**

1. Wounds and injuries

ISBN 978-1-59920-222-8 lib bdg; 1-59920-222-0 lib bdg

"Encourages further learning with sidebars that help readers think concretely about the subject. . . . Altogether a pitch perfect presentation." SLJ

Includes glossary

617.6 Dentistry

Cobb, Vicki

★ **Your** body battles a cavity; written by Vicki Cobb; photomicrographs by Dennis Kunkel; illustrations by Andrew N. Harris. Millbrook Press 2009 32p il (Body battles) lib bdg $25.26

Grades: 3 4 5 **617.6**

1. Teeth 2. Immune system

ISBN 978-0-8225-7469-9 lib bdg; 0-8225-7469-1 lib bdg

LC 2008002827

With comic illustrations and photomicrographs, this shows what happens when a person gets a cavity, depicting the body's defenses as superheroes

Includes glossary and bibliographical references

Guillain, Charlotte

Visiting the dentist. Heinemann Library 2011 24p il (Growing up) lib bdg $22; pa $6.49

Grades: PreK K 1 2 **617.6**

1. Dentistry

ISBN 978-1-4329-4804-7 lib bdg; 1-4329-4804-0 lib bdg; 978-1-4329-4814-6 pa; 1-4329-4814-8 pa

LC 2010024198

This book examines a "common, often scary [event] in children's lives and [guides] readers through [it] step-by-step. The [author discusses] the who, what, and why of [the] experience . . . By confronting . . . fears head-on, children will feel 'in the know' and be prepared to experience [this first]. The text—two sentences per page in a large font and placed on white space—is accompanied by large color photos of children, families, and adults of a variety of ethnic backgrounds. [The] volume includes boldface vocabulary words, a picture glossary, and dos and don'ts." SLJ

Includes glossary and bibliographical references

Landau, Elaine

★ **Cavities** and toothaches. Marshall Cavendish Benchmark 2008 32p il (Head-to-toe health) lib bdg $28.50

Grades: 2 3 4 **617.6**

1. Teeth 2. Dentistry

ISBN 978-0-7614-2848-0; 0-7614-2848-8

LC 2007-19192

"Photo illustrations are apt and age appropriate. . . . Pervading the [book] . . . is an overall sense of reassurance that even if something hurts, 'all better' is never too far away. Appealing and readable nonfiction." SLJ

Includes glossary and bibliographical references

Miller, Edward, 1964-

★ The **tooth** book; a guide to healthy teeth and gums. [by] Edward Miller. Holiday House 2008 un il $16.95

Grades: K 1 2 3 **617.6**
1. Teeth 2. Dentistry
ISBN 978-0-8234-2092-6; 0-8234-2092-2
LC 2007018302
"In this brightly illustrated picture book, Miller goes well beyond the basics of brushing, flossing, and visiting the dentist. Readers view the inside of a tooth and learn about primary and permanent teeth, decay, losing teeth, and dental first aid. Especially welcome is the emphasis on eating healthy foods and avoiding sugar. . . . The cleanly designed, computer-generated artwork is appealing, lively, and instructive." SLJ

Royston, Angela
Tooth decay. Black Rabbit Books 2009 30p il (How's your health) lib bdg $27.10
Grades: 1 2 3 **617.6**
1. Teeth
ISBN 978-1-59920-221-1 lib bdg; 1-59920-221-2 lib bdg
First published 2004 by Heinemann Library
"Encourages further learning with sidebars that help readers think concretely about the subject. . . . Altogether a pitch perfect presentation." SLJ
Includes glossary

Why do I brush my teeth? QEB Pub. 2010 24p il (QEB my body) lib bdg $28.65
Grades: PreK K 1 2 **617.6**
1. Teeth 2. Dentistry
ISBN 978-1-59566-973-5 lib bdg; 1-59566-973-6 lib bdg
LC 2009-15219
Introduces the structure and growth of the teeth, and outlines the principles of dental health and hygiene
"The information is straightforward, well presented, and easy to understand. . . . [This] title is well designed, filled with color photographs, and scattered with fact boxes." Libr Media Connect
Includes glossary and bibliographical references

Schuh, Mari C.
All about teeth; by Mari Schuh. Capstone Press 2008 24p il (Pebble plus. Healthy teeth) lib bdg $21.26; pa $5.95
Grades: K 1 2 3 **617.6**
1. Teeth
ISBN 978-1-4296-1238-8 lib bdg; 1-4296-1238-X lib bdg; 1-4296-1784-5 pa; 978-1-4296-1784-0 pa
LC 2007-27115
"Feature[s] bright close-up photographs . . . and simple vocabulary and sentences to engage pre-readers as well as new readers." Horn Book Guide
Includes glossary and bibliographical references

Thomas, Pat
Do I have to go to the dentist? a first look at healthy teeth. [by] Pat Thomas; illustrated by Lesley Harker. Barron's Educational Series 2008 29p il pa $6.99
Grades: PreK K 1 2 **617.6**
1. Teeth 2. Dentistry
ISBN 978-0-7641-3901-7 pa; 0-7641-3901-0 pa
This "book addresses the purpose of dental visits, what to expect, the dental exam and tooth cleaning, and cavities.

. . . Sidebars . . . ask questions about children's personal experiences and thoughts, which can be used as discussion starters. [The] title ends with an extensive note to parents, with practical advice for lessening anxiety about going to the dentist. . . . [This is a] solid [addition] for most collections." SLJ

617.7 Ophthalmology

Bender, Lionel
Explaining blindness. Smart Apple Media 2010 45p il (Explaining) lib bdg $34.25
Grades: 5 6 7 8 **617.7**
1. Blind
ISBN 978-1-59920-310-2 lib bdg; 1-59920-310-3 lib bdg
LC 2008-49286
Describes blindness, including its possible causes, the different types of visual impairment, current treatments and cures, and how blind and visually impaired people live everyday lives
"The incorporation of quotes and personal accounts in 'Case Notes' sidebars adds to the sensitive tone found throughout [the title]." SLJ
Includes glossary

Glaser, Jason
Pinkeye. Capstone Press 2006 24p il (First facts: health matters) $21.26
Grades: K 1 2 3 **617.7**
1. Conjunctivitis
ISBN 978-0-7368-4292-1; 0-7368-4292-6
LC 2004031054
"Introduces pinkeye, its causes, symptoms, treatments, and prevention." Publisher's note
Includes bibliographical references

Markle, Sandra
Lost sight; true survival stories. Lerner Publications 2010 48p il (Powerful medicine) lib bdg $27.93
Grades: 5 6 7 8 **617.7**
1. Eye 2. Blind 3. Vision
ISBN 978-0-8225-8701-9 lib bdg; 0-8225-8701-7 lib bdg
LC 2009-34443
This book about vision loss "will grab the attention of middle school readers. . . . The illustrations and photos are stunning with medically accurate captions. Real-life patients, whose photos are included in the text, are highlighted, with updates on their progress at the end of . . . [the] book." Voice Youth Advocates
Includes glossary and bibliographical references

Parker, Victoria
Having an eye test; [by] Vic Parker. Heinemann Library 2011 24p il (Growing up) lib bdg $22; pa $6.49
Grades: PreK K 1 2 **617.7**
1. Eye
ISBN 978-1-4329-4798-9 lib bdg; 1-4329-4798-2 lib bdg; 978-1-4329-4808-5 pa; 1-4329-4808-3 pa
LC 2010024192

This explains what to expect from an eye test.
Includes bibliographical references

617.8 Otology and audiology

Cobb, Vicki
★ **Your** body battles an earache; written by Vicki
Cobb; photomicrographs by Dennis Kunkel; illustrated by
Andrew N. Harris. Millbrook Press 2009 32p il (Body
battles) lib bdg $25.26
Grades: 3 4 5   **617.8**
    1. Immune system 2. Ear infections
    ISBN 978-0-8225-6812-4 lib bdg; 0-8225-6812-8
    lib bdg
                                      LC 2008002846
Microphotographs and comic illustrations show what
happens when a person has an earache
"Many of the vibrant illustrations anthropomorphize
various cells and other 'battle' participants, making the science explained approachable and easy to understand. Photomicrographs further illuminate the text." SLJ
Includes glossary and bibliographical references

Glaser, Jason
    Ear infections. Capstone Press 2007 24p il (First
facts: health matters) $21.26
Grades: K 1 2 3   **617.8**
    1. Ear infections
    ISBN 978-0-7368-6390-2; 0-7368-6390-7
                                      LC 2006002809
"Describes ear infections, how and why they occur, and
how to treat and prevent them." Publisher's note
Includes bibliographical references

Landau, Elaine
    ★ **Earaches**. Marshall Cavendish Benchmark 2010
32p il (Head-to-toe health) lib bdg $28.50
Grades: 2 3 4   **617.8**
    1. Ear infections
    ISBN 978-0-7614-4831-0 lib bdg; 0-7614-4831-4
    lib bdg
This provides basic information about earaches and
their prevention.
This "manages to pack in a surprising amount of infor-
mation, including facts about good hygiene. The text ad-
dresses the reader directly, and the photos are real grabbers."
Booklist
Includes glossary and bibliographical references

Levete, Sarah
    Explaining deafness. Smart Apple Media 2010 45p il
(Explaining) lib bdg $34.25
Grades: 5 6 7 8   **617.8**
    1. Deafness
    ISBN 978-1-59920-313-3 lib bdg; 1-59920-313-8
    lib bdg
                                      LC 2008-49289
Discusses the history, diagnosis, and treatment of deaf-
ness, including ways to cope with living with the condition

"The incorporation of quotes and personal accounts
in 'Case Notes' sidebars adds to the sensitive tone found
throughout [the title]." SLJ
Includes glossary, bibliographical references
and filmography

Parker, Victoria
    Having a hearing test; [by] Vic Parker. Heinmann Li-
brary 2011 24p il (Growing up) lib bdg $22; pa $6.49
Grades: PreK K 1 2   **617.8**
    1. Hearing
    ISBN 978-1-4329-4799-6 lib bdg; 1-4329-4799-0 lib
    bdg; 978-1-4329-4809-2 pa; 1-4329-4809-1 pa
                                      LC 2010024193
This explains how a hearing test works and possible next
steps for those with hearing problems.
"The text is simple, and the pictures are big and bright."
Booklist
Includes bibliographical references

617.9 Operative surgery and special fields of surgery

Fullick, Ann
    Rebuilding the body; organ transplantation. Ann Ful-
lick. Rev. and updated Heinemann Library 2002 64 p. col.
ill. (library) $34.29; (library) $35
Grades: 5 6 7 8   **617.9**
    1. Medicine 2. Medical ethics 3. Transplantation of
    organs, tissues, etc.
    ISBN 9781588107008 out of print; 1432924524;
    9781432924522
                                      LC 2001006082
This book is part of the Science at the Edge series and
looks at organ transplantation. It "begins with a survey of
the major human body organs. . . . This is followed by a
description of the failure of major organs, infections that occur within them, and gradual damage and deterioration. This
leads to a discussion about organ transplants . . . . The challenges of organ transplantation, pitfalls of rejection, and ethics of transplantation from the dead are all touched upon."
(NSTA Recommends)
Includes bibliographical references (p. 63) and index.

Jango-Cohen, Judith
    Bionics; [by] Judith Jango-Cohen. Lerner Publications
Co. 2007 48p il (Cool science) lib bdg $26.60
Grades: 4 5 6 7   **617.9**
    1. Bionics 2. Artificial organs
    ISBN 978-0-8225-5937-5 lib bdg; 0-8225-5937-4
    lib bdg
                                      LC 2005032221
This "introduction to the field of bionics is divided into
four chapters: 'Replacing Parts,' 'Fixing Malfunctions,' 'Assisting the Senses,' and 'Facing the Future.' Jango-Cohen
uses a number of personal stories and references to pop
culture to engage readers. . . . The explanations are clearly
written and easily understood. Colorful photographs and illustrations are featured throughout the text." SLJ
Includes bibliographical references

618.92   Pediatrics

Grossberg, Blythe

★ **Asperger's** rules! how to make sense of school and friends. by Blythe Grossberg. Magination Press 2012 127 p. col. ill. (paperback) $9.95; (hardcover) $14.95

Grades: 5 6 7 8   **618.92**

1. Life skills 2. Social skills 3. Asperger's syndrome 4. Autism in children 5. Autistic children -- Education 6. Asperger's syndrome -- Social aspects

ISBN 1433811286; 9781433811272; 9781433811289

LC 2011053483

This book by Blythe Grossberg presents a "guide for readers with Asperger's, covering feelings and emotions, teachers, asking for help, and dealing with bullies. Quizzes let readers reflect on their own approaches to situations like interacting with kids at school, and Grossberg also includes tips on how to interpret social situations. . . . Flowcharts illustrate how various conversations might progress, and other sections focus on dressing properly and eating healthful meals." (Publishers Weekly)

Reeve, Elizabeth

The **survival** guide for kids with autism spectrum disorders (and their parents) by Elizabeth Verdick & Elizabeth Reeve; illustrated by Nick Kobyluch. Free Spirit Pub. 2012 234 p. col. ill. (pbk.) $16.99

Grades: 5 6 7 8 Adult   **618.92**

1. Autism 2. Autistic children 3. Parents of autistic children 4. Parents of autistic children

ISBN 1575423855; 9781575423852; 9781575426747

LC 2011046520

This book "offers kids with autism spectrum disorders (ASDs) their own comprehensive resource for both understanding their condition and finding tools to cope with the challenges they face every day . . . with an emphasis on helping children gain new self-understanding and self-acceptance. Meant to be read with a parent, the book addresses questions . . . and provides strategies for communicating, making and keeping friends, and succeeding in school." (Publisher's note)

"This volume could become a treasured resource for families looking for help in successfully working through some of the problems faced by higher-functioning children with ASD." SLJ

Thomas, Pat

Don't call me fat a first look at being overweight; a first look at being overweight. Pat Thomas. Barrons Educational Series, Inc. 2014 29 p. color illustrations (A first look at) $6.99

Grades: K 1 2   **618.92**

1. Obesity 2. Obesity in children

ISBN 1438004710; 9781438004716

LC 2013957084

This children's book on being overweight by Pat Thomas is part of the "A First Look At . . . " series. It "acknowledges the difficulties faced by children who are overweight but encourages them to work with others toward healthy changes and ask for support along the way. . . . The appended section for parents and teachers offers . . . advice as well as suggested books and online resources." (Booklist)

"Though the picture books in the A First Look at . . . series deal with a wide range of conditions, they all begin with respect for children. Thomas doesn't define individuals by their differences, instead discussing their physical, mental, and emotional challenges in a straightforward, kindly manner... Some unusually positive features include apt discussion questions, illustrations showing children with autism sometimes looking happy, and even girls with autism (often only boys are depicted). A worthwhile series of helpful picture books." Booklist

Part of the "First Look At..." series

620.1   Engineering mechanics and materials

Blaxland, Wendy

Plates and mugs. Marshall Cavendish Benchmark 2009 32p il (How are they made?) $19.95

Grades: 3 4 5 6   **620.1**

1. Ceramics 2. Tableware

ISBN 978-0-7614-3809-0; 0-7614-3809-2

LC 2008026210

This describes how plates and mugs are made, including their history, raw materials, design, manufacture, and relationship to the environment.

Claybourne, Anna

Materials. QEB Pub. 2008 24p il (Why it works) $24.25

Grades: 2 3 4 5   **620.1**

1. Materials

ISBN 978-1-59566-557-7; 1-59566-557-9

LC 2008-11711

This is "colorfully illustrated and should help young students relate better to the concepts being presented. A glossary of key words and a page of suggestions for parents and teachers to extend the learning experience round out the text." Sci Books & Films

Includes glossary and bibliographical references

Hillman, Ben

How strong is it? a mighty book all about strength. [by] Ben Hillman. Scholastic Reference 2008 48p il (What's the big idea?) $14.99

Grades: 3 4 5   **620.1**

1. Power (Mechanics)

ISBN 978-0-439-91866-4; 0-439-91866-9

This describes the strength of such things as spiderwebs, bulldozers, wood, elephants, glue, lasers, hair, rope, and volcanoes.

"The conversational, fact-filled text and computer-manipulated illustrations add humor to this random sampling of awesome powers." Horn Book Guide

Langley, Andrew

Glass; [by] Andrew Langley. Crabtree Pub. Co. 2009 24p il (Everyday materials) lib bdg $21.27; pa $6.95

Grades: K 1 2 3   **620.1**

1. Glass

ISBN 978-0-7787-4126-8 lib bdg; 0-7787-4126-5 lib bdg; 978-0-7787-4134-3 pa; 0-7787-4134-6 pa

LC 2008-24157

This title "introduces [glass] in an engaging style. The text and photos work together, progressing from a definition of the material to how it is manufactured and what it is used for. . . . [It] concludes with a recycling section, a simple comprehension quiz, and a topic web that offers extension ideas. The large type, bright photos, and uncluttered layout will allow large and small group use." SLJ

Includes glossary

Metal; [by] Andrew Langley. Crabtree Pub. Co. 2009 24p il (Everyday materials) lib bdg $21.27; pa $6.95

Grades: K 1 2 3   **620.1**

1. Metals

ISBN 978-0-7787-4127-5 lib bdg; 0-7787-4127-3 lib bdg; 978-0-7787-4134-3 pa; 0-7787-4134-6 pa

       LC 2008-24036

This title "introduces [metals] in an engaging style. The text and photos work together, progressing from a definition of the material to how it is manufactured and what it is used for. . . . [It] concludes with a recycling section, a simple comprehension quiz, and a topic web that offers extension ideas. The large type, bright photos, and uncluttered layout will allow large and small group use." SLJ

Includes glossary

Wood; [by] Andrew Langley. Crabtree Pub. Co. 2009 24p il (Everyday materials) lib bdg $21.27; pa $6.95

Grades: K 1 2 3   **620.1**

1. Wood

ISBN 978-0-7787-4130-5 lib bdg; 0-7787-4130-3 lib bdg; 978-0-7787-4137-4 pa; 0-7787-4137-0 pa

       LC 2008-24037

This title "introduces [wood] in an engaging style. The text and photos work together, progressing from a definition of the material to how it is manufactured and what it is used for. . . . [It] concludes with a recycling section, a simple comprehension quiz, and a topic web that offers extension ideas. The large type, bright photos, and uncluttered layout will allow large and small group use." SLJ

Includes glossary

Morris, Neil

Glass. Amicus 2010 48p il (Materials that matter) lib bdg $28.50

Grades: 4 5 6 7   **620.1**

1. Glass

ISBN 978-1-60753-065-7 lib bdg; 1-60753-065-1 lib bdg

       LC 2009029796

"The clean layout includes photographs and occasional charts, graphs, and technical illustrations against a range of pastel backgrounds. Inset boxes provide further detail, interesting extras, and recycling information. . . . [This book offers] easily accessible background information for report writers." SLJ

Includes glossary and bibliographical references

Metals. Amicus 2010 48p il (Materials that matter) lib bdg $28.50

Grades: 4 5 6 7   **620.1**

1. Metals

ISBN 978-1-60753-066-4 lib bdg; 1-60753-066-X lib bdg

       LC 2009029797

"The clean layout includes photographs and occasional charts, graphs, and technical illustrations against a range of pastel backgrounds. Inset boxes provide further detail, in-

teresting extras, and recycling information. . . . [This book offers] easily accessible background information for report writers." SLJ

Includes glossary and bibliographical references

Oxlade, Chris

Changing shape. Heinemann Library 2008 32p il (Changing materials) lib bdg $25.36; pa $7.99

Grades: K 1 2   **620.1**

1. Materials

ISBN 978-1-4329-3271-8 lib bdg; 1-4329-3271-3 lib bdg; 978-1-4329-3276-3 pa; 1-4329-3276-4 pa

       LC 2008-54586

Discusses "the properties of materials and whether or not they can bend or twist or are brittle, or are in liquid or gas form. . . . A few simple activities provide opportunities to experiment. The color photographs are engaging." SLJ

Includes glossary and bibliographical references

Joining materials; [by] Chris Oxlade. Crabtree Pub. Company 2008 32p il (Working with materials) lib bdg $26.60; pa $7.95

Grades: 2 3 4   **620.1**

1. Materials

ISBN 978-0-7787-3639-4 lib bdg; 0-7787-3639-3 lib bdg; 978-0-7787-3649-3 pa; 0-7787-3649-0 pa

       LC 2007027420

This describes how materials are joined with nuts, bolts, and screws, glue, wood joints, welding, soldering, sewing, tape, and velcro

This "title has numerous captioned color photographs. . . . The [book offers] three simple, easy, and safe reproducible experiments. . . . Students will appreciate the pleasing design, easy-to-read font, and direct, clear writing style." Libr Media Connect

Includes glossary and bibliographical references

Shaping materials; [by] Chris Oxlade. Crabtree Pub. Company 2008 32p il (Working with materials) lib bdg $26.60; pa $7.95

Grades: 2 3 4   **620.1**

1. Materials

ISBN 978-0-7787-3641-7 lib bdg; 0-7787-3641-5 lib bdg; 978-0-7787-3651-6 pa; 0-7787-3651-2 pa

       LC 2007027422

This describes how materials are shaped with scissors, molds, hammers, saws, chisels, and machine shapers, and by folding and bending, glassblowing, and clay modeling

This "title has numerous captioned color photographs. . . . The [book offers] three simple, easy, safe reproducible experiments. . . . Students will appreciate the pleasing design, easy-to-read font, and direct, clear writing." Libr Media Connect

Includes glossary and bibliographical references

Riley, Peter D.

Materials. Sea-to-Sea Publications 2011 32p il (The real scientist investigates) lib bdg $28.50

Grades: 3 4 5   **620.1**

1. Materials

ISBN 978-1-59771-282-8; 1-59771-282-5

       LC 2010005373

In this book about materials "solid scientific material is presented in accessible language and a visually engaging, boldly colored layout. Budding scientists are encouraged to hone their skills by recording observations, making predictions, and analyzing results. Hands-on activities are included on almost every spread. . . . The many color photos feature diverse children demonstrating the activities." SLJ

Includes glossary and bibliographical references

Ward, David J.
  Materials science; by D. J. Ward. Lerner Publications 2009 47p il (Cool science) lib bdg $26.60
Grades: 4 5 6   **620.1**
  1. Materials
  ISBN 978-0-8225-7588-7 lib bdg; 0-8225-7588-4 lib bdg
                                         LC 2007042176
  This describes how scientists study the microscopic parts of materials such as plastic, glass, or stainless steel, how they learn how each part makes something hard or soft, strong or weak, or good or bad at carrying heat, and how they use that knowledge to create supermaterials to help make better sports equipment, tinier computer chips, and more.
  Includes glossary and bibliographical references

621   Applied physics

Spilsbury, Richard
  What is energy? exploring science with hands-on activities. [by] Richard and Louise Spilsbury. Enslow Elementary 2008 32p il (In touch with basic science) lib bdg $22.60
Grades: 3 4 5   **621**
  1. Energy resources 2. Force and energy 3. Power (Mechanics) 4. Science -- Experiments
  ISBN 978-0-7660-3099-2 lib bdg; 0-7660-3099-7 lib bdg
                                         LC 2007024521
  This book includes "a discussion about what energy is and then moves on to examine heat energy, chemical energy, energy for life, electrical energy, and finally, renewable energy. Energy is such a broad topic, yet this small volume masterfully provides a good basis for understanding the concept." Sci Books Films
  Includes glossary and bibliographical references

621.1   Fluid-power technologies

O'Neal, Claire
  How to use waste energy to heat and light your home. Mitchell Lane Publishers 2009 47p il (Tell your parents) lib bdg $21.50
Grades: 4 5 6 7   **621.1**
  1. Recycling 2. Waste products as fuel
  ISBN 978-1-58415-765-6 lib bdg; 1-58415-765-8 lib bdg
                                         LC 2009-4483
  Explores how to reduce the amount of trash produced and stored by reusing items and recycling materials, and describes how these efforts can help protect the environment
  This title "offers numerous facts and statistics, all of which are cited. . . . Chapters cover present-day issues and . .

. are interspersed with full-color photographs and short 'Did You Know' trivia boxes. . . . Back matter includes detailed resource lists and 'Try This!' experiments." SLJ

Includes glossary and bibliographical references

621.3   Electrical, magnetic, optical, communications, computer engineering; electronics, lighting

Price, Sean
  The **story** behind electricity; [by] Sean Stewart Price. Heinemann Library 2009 32p il (True stories) $28.21
Grades: 3 4 5   **621.3**
  1. Electricity 2. Electrical engineering
  ISBN 978-1-4329-2339-6; 1-4329-2339-0
                                         LC 2008043408
  This answers such questions as: How does a lightning rod work? What animals use electricity? Why did Thomas Edison have to build a power station?
  Includes bibliographical references

621.31   Generation, modification, storage, transmission of electric power

Bartholomew, Alan
  Electric mischief; battery-powered gadgets kids can build. written by Alan Bartholomew; illustrated by Lynn Bartholomew. Kids Can Press 2002 48p il (Kids can do it) $12.95; pa $5.95
Grades: 4 5 6   **621.31**
  1. Electricity 2. Electric apparatus and appliances
  ISBN 1-55074-923-4; 1-55074-925-0 pa
  This provides instructions for building 10 electric gadgets such as a bumper car, electric dice, and a robot hand
  "Projects are clearly explained and easy to follow; colorful illustrations aid understanding. Materials required . . . are readily available at hardware stores." SLJ

Benduhn, Tea
  Water power; by Tea Benduhn. Weekly Reader Pub. 2009 24p il (Energy for today) lib bdg $21; pa $5.95
Grades: 2 3 4   **621.31**
  1. Water power 2. Energy resources
  ISBN 978-0-8368-9264-2 lib bdg; 0-8368-9264-X lib bdg; 978-0-8368-9363-2 pa; 0-8368-9363-8 pa
                                         LC 2008012021
  This explains how flowing water is used as an energy resource, and how it may be used in the future.
  "New readers will be able to wrap their hands around the small, square size, and their minds around the clear, enlightening text. [This book has] crisp photos and strong back matter." Booklist
  Includes glossary and bibliographical references

  Wind power; by Tea Benduhn. Weekly Reader Pub. 2009 24p il (Energy for today) lib bdg $21; pa $5.95
Grades: 2 3 4   **621.31**
  1. Wind power 2. Energy resources
  ISBN 978-0-8368-9265-9 lib bdg; 0-8368-9265-8 lib bdg; 978-0-8368-9364-9 pa; 0-8368-9364-6 pa
                                         LC 2008012019

This explains how wind forms and the ways we may use it as an energy source in the future.

"New readers will be able to wrap their hands around the small, square size, and their minds around the clear enlightening text. [This book has] crisp photos and strong back matter." Booklist

Includes glossary and bibliographical references

Graf, Mike

How does a waterfall become electricity? Raintree 2008 32p il (How does it happen?) lib bdg $27.50; pa $7.99

Grades: 3 4 5   **621.31**

1. Electricity 2. Water power 3. Hydrodynamics
ISBN 978-1-4109-3448-2 lib bdg; 1-4109-3448-9 lib bdg; 978-1-4109-3456-7 pa; 1-4109-3456-X pa

LC 2008-52653

The explains the cause and effect of waterfalls, and the many ways they can be used to make electricity.

"Information is clearly presented using a large font, diagrams, and photographs formatted to resemble Polaroid pictures. . . . A first-rate job answering some important scientific questions." SLJ

Includes glossary and bibliographical references

Lew, Kristi

Goodbye, gasoline; the science of fuel cells. Compass Point Books 2009 48p il (Headline science) lib bdg $27.93

Grades: 5 6 7 8   **621.31**

1. Fuel cells
ISBN 978-0-7565-3521-6 lib bdg; 0-7565-3521-2 lib bdg

LC 2008011729

This "clearly examines the history and technology of hydrogen fuel cells, including the various types such as proton exchange membrane and alkaline cells. An excellent description of how the technology works gives readers an understanding of both the successes and problems relating to these promising energy sources. . . . The color illustrations and charts . . . are clear and helpful, and the text, although information rich, is not overly difficult." SLJ

O'Neal, Claire

How to use wind power to light and heat your home. Mitchell Lane Publishers 2009 47p il map (Tell your parents) lib bdg $21.50

Grades: 4 5 6 7   **621.31**

1. Wind power 2. Renewable energy resources
ISBN 978-1-58415-762-5 lib bdg; 1-58415-762-3 lib bdg

LC 2009-4530

Introduces wind power, including the history of harnessing the wind for work, how modern wind power generates electricity, and how to install a turbine to a home

This book "offers numerous facts and statistics, all of which are cited. . . . Chapters cover present-day issues and . . . are interspersed with full-color photographs and short 'Did You Know' trivia boxes. . . . Back matter includes detailed resource lists and 'Try This!' experiments." SLJ

Includes glossary and bibliographical references

Rusch, Elizabeth

The next wave; the quest to harness the power of the oceans. by Elizabeth Rusch. Houghton Mifflin Harcourt 2014 80 p. color illustrations (Scientists in the field) $18.99

Grades: 5 6 7 8 9   **621.31**

1. Ocean 2. Ocean energy resources 3. Renewable energy resources 4. Tidal power 5. Renewable energy sources
ISBN 0544099990; 9780544099999

LC 2013050150

In this book, by Elizabeth Rusch, part of the Scientists in the Field series, readers "journey to the wave-battered coast of the Pacific Northwest to meet some of the engineers and scientists working to harness the punishing force of our oceans. . . . With an array of amazing devices that cling to the bottom of the sea floor and surf on the crests of waves, these explorers are using a combination of science, imagination, and innovation to try to capture wave energy." (Publisher's note)

"Transferring ocean wave action into electricity (without damaging collection equipment or harming marine life) is a significant engineering challenge with a potentially big financial payoff. Rusch captures the determined, entrepreneurial spirit of the profiled engineers as well as the need for creative problem-solving and ingenuity. Photographs and illustrations feature prototypes in both small-scale laboratory and full-ocean tests. Reading list, websites. Bib., glos., ind. " Horn Book

Includes bibliographical references and index

621.319 Transmission

Cole, Joanna

The magic school bus and the electric field trip; illustrated by Bruce Degen. Scholastic 1997 48p il hardcover o.p. pa $6.99

Grades: 2 3 4   **621.319**

1. Electricity 2. Electric power
ISBN 0-590-44682-7; 0-590-44683-5 pa

LC 97-2080

Ms. Frizzle takes her class on a field trip through the town's electrical wires so they can learn how electricity is generated and how it is used

"Spiced with plenty of puns and jokes, the writing and the colorful artwork continue the series' unbeatable combination of clearly presented information and plenty of fun." Booklist

621.382 Communications engineering

Perritano, John

Revolution in communications. Marshall Cavendish Benchmark 2010 32p il (It works!) lib bdg $19.95

Grades: 3 4 5   **621.382**

1. Telecommunication
ISBN 978-0-7614-4373-5 lib bdg; 0-7614-4373-8 lib bdg

LC 2008-54347

"This interesting, information packed [book] . . . motivates students to do their own exploring. . . . The appealing cartoon-like photographs add humor. . . . This . . . just may be that spark needed to create eager budding scientists." Libr Media Connect

Includes glossary and bibliographical references

621.385 Telephony

Spilsbury, Richard

The **telephone**; [by] Richard and Louise Spilsbury. Heinemann Library 2011 32p il (Tales of invention) lib bdg $29; pa $7.99

Grades: 4 5 6 7   **621.385**

1. Telephone 2. Cellular telephones

ISBN 978-1-4329-3826-0 lib bdg; 1-4329-3826-6 lib bdg; 978-1-4329-3833-8 pa; 1-4329-3833-9 pa

LC 2009049027

"Beginning with the first telegraph, the book discusses how sound travels, how speech is transmitted by wire, and how Alexander Graham Bell's first telephones worked. Then the text quickly traces later technological developments, from transatlantic cables to early cell phones to the small, light, versatile models available today. . . . The many photographs and other illustrations include excellent labeled diagrams." Booklist

Includes bibliographical references

621.389 Security, sound recording, related systems

Gilbert, Adrian

Top technology. Firefly 2009 32p il (Spy files) pa $6.95

Grades: 3 4 5 6   **621.389**

1. Espionage 2. Electronic surveillance

ISBN 978-1-55407-576-8; 1-55407-576-9

First published 2008 in the United Kingdom

Discusses equipment and technology used by spies, including satellites, cameras, lie detectors, listening devices, and more.

The text's "short paragraphs and great pictures are combined in a collage style that will draw readers quickly through the information. Useful for reports and browsing." SLJ

Includes glossary

621.4 Prime movers and heat engineering

Cartlidge, Cherese

Home windmills; by Cherese Cartlidge. Norwood House Press 2008 48p il (A great idea) lib bdg $25.27

Grades: 3 4 5 6   **621.4**

1. Windmills

ISBN 978-1-59953-192-2 lib bdg; 1-59953-192-5 lib bdg

LC 2008-24190

"Describes the invention and development of the home windmills." Publisher's note

Includes glossary and bibliographical references

Woelfle, Gretchen

The **wind** at work; an activity guide to windmills. Gretchen Woelfle. 2nd ed. Chicago Review Press 2013 vii, 145 p.p ill. (paperback) $16.95

Grades: 4 5 6   **621.4**

1. Windmills 2. Science -- Experiments

ISBN 1613741006; 9781613741009

LC 2012046319

This introduction to windmills "discusses their history and function through modern times. . . . About one-third of the book is devoted to activities illustrating the properties of wind and the jobs performed by windmills. . . . The concluding chapters focus on windmills as a source of energy and suggest how to chart household energy use." (Booklist) Index. "Grades four to eight." (SLJ)

"The historical information is excellent, and includes Persian windmills of 1000 years ago, Dutch windmills of the 17th century, and modern wind turbines. Amusing anecdotes and intriguing facts are woven into the text, keeping it lively. . . . Black-and-white historical prints, photographs, and diagrams appear throughout." SLJ

Includes bibliographical references (pages 133-135) and index

621.43 Internal-combustion engines

Shores, Lori

How to build a fizzy rocket. Capstone Press 2011 24p il (Hands-on science fun) lib bdg $17.99; pa $6.95

Grades: PreK K 1   **621.43**

1. Science -- Experiments 2. Rockets (Aeronautics) -- Models

ISBN 978-1-4296-4491-4 lib bdg; 1-4296-4491-5 lib bdg; 978-1-4296-5573-6 pa; 1-4296-5573-9 pa

LC 2009051419

Simple text and full-color photos instruct readers how to build a fizzy rocket and explain the science behind the activity.

"Bright, glossy photos and irresistible ideas make these science lessons effortless fun." Booklist

Includes bibliographical references

621.47 Solar-energy engineering

Bang, Molly

★ **My** light. Blue Sky Press 2004 un il $16.95

Grades: 1 2 3   **621.47**

1. Electricity 2. Solar energy

ISBN 0-439-48961-X

"Bang's strong design sense comes through in compositions that gracefully incorporate diagrams and strike a balance between graphic forms and delicate, decorative patterns. A lovely and illuminating book that presents sound science while expressing the wonder of flipping a switch and flooding a room with light." Booklist

Bearce, Stephanie

How to harness solar power for your home. Mitchell Lane Publishers 2009 47p il map (Tell your parents) lib bdg $21.50

Grades: 4 5 6 7 **621.47**

1. Solar energy

ISBN 978-1-58415-761-8 lib bdg; 1-58415-761-5 lib bdg

LC 2009-4529

This title about solar power "offers numerous facts and statistics, all of which are cited. . . . Chapters cover present-day issues and . . . are interspersed with full-color photographs and short 'Did You Know' trivia boxes. . . . Back matter includes detailed resource lists and 'Try This!' experiments." SLJ

Includes glossary and bibliographical references

Benduhn, Tea

Solar power; by Tea Benduhn. Weekly Reader Pub. 2008 24p il (Energy for today) lib bdg $21; pa $5.95

Grades: 2 3 4 **621.47**

1. Solar energy

ISBN 978-0-8368-9263-5 lib bdg; 0-8368-9263-1 lib bdg; 978-0-8368-9362-5 pa; 0-8368-9362-X pa

LC 2008015515

"This title presents a surprising amount of information about solar power in brief sentences that are calibrated to newly confident readers' abilities. . . . The selection of well-chosen photos, which are crisply reproduced on each page, is particularly strong in the final chapters about solar technology. . . . The language is direct, clear, and enlightening." Booklist

Includes glossary and bibliographical references

Bright, Sandra

Examining solar energy; by Sandra Bright. Clara House Books 2013 48 p. (hardcover: alk. paper) $24.95

Grades: 5 6 7 8 **621.47**

1. Solar energy 2. Energy resources

ISBN 1934545457; 9781934545454

LC 2012035316

This book, by Sandra Bright, looks at solar energy through "fictitious research journals that examine the history, science, and future outlook of [energy resources]. Additional historical information, better scientific explanations, and extended future outlooks round-out the content." (Publisher's note)

Includes bibliographical references (pages 46-47) and index

621.48 Nuclear engineering

Benduhn, Tea

Nuclear power; by Tea Benduhn. Weekly Reader Pub. 2009 24p il (Energy for today) lib bdg $21; pa $5.95

Grades: 2 3 4 **621.48**

1. Nuclear energy

ISBN 978-0-8368-9262-8 lib bdg; 0-8368-9262-3 lib bdg; 978-0-8368-9361-8 pa; 0-8368-9361-1 pa

LC 2008012020

This describes how nuclear power works and how it may be used in the future.

"New readers will be able to wrap their hands around the small, square size, and their minds around the clear, en-lightening text. [This book has] crisp photos and strong back matter." Booklist

Includes glossary and bibliographical references

Feigenbaum, Aaron

Emergency at Three Mile Island; by Aaron Feigenbaum. Bearport Pub. 2007 32p il map (Code red) lib bdg $23.96

Grades: 3 4 5 **621.48**

1. Nuclear power plants 2. Three Mile Island Nuclear Power Plant (Pa.)

ISBN 978-1-59716-364-4 lib bdg; 1-59716-364-3 lib bdg

LC 2006031635

This "discusses the 1979 malfunction of a nuclear reactor that could have cost thousands of lives and devastated the area but, fortunately, did not. . . . The writing is clear and concise. . . . The facts are allowed to speak for themselves. The [book is] liberally laced with pertinent period photographs and numerous quotes."

Includes glossary and bibliographical references

621.5 Pneumatic, vacuum, low-temperature technologies

Pringle, Laurence

Ice! the amazing history of the ice business. Laurence Pringle. Calkins Creek 2012 74 p. $17.95

Grades: 4 5 6 7 8 **621.5**

1. Ice 2. Refrigeration 3. Food -- Preservation

ISBN 159078801X; 9781590788011

LC 2012937320

This book looks at "iceboxes, icehouses, icemen, and . . . more about the history of the harvesting, storage, and delivery of ice." Author Laurence Pringle "briefly covers early food preservation . . . before delving into the rise of the ice industry in the early 1800s, and, in particular, the harvesting of the frozen stuff at pristine Rockland Lake in New York." (School Library Journal)

Includes bibliographical references and index.

621.8 Machine engineering

Bodden, Valerie

Levers. Creative Education 2011 23p il (Simple machines) $24.25; pa $8.99

Grades: K 1 2 3 **621.8**

1. Levers

ISBN 978-1-60818-009-7; 1-60818-009-3; 978-0-89812-580-1 pa; 0-89812-580-4 pa

"The pages are uncluttered and are typeset in a large font, making the words practically pop off the [page]. Also, the author makes the definitions that are presented simple to understand with her selection of photographs. . . . [This is] outstanding and well suited to young elementary school children." Sci Books & Films

Includes glossary

Pulleys. Creative Education 2011 23p il (Simple machines) $24.25; pa $8.99

Grades: K 1 2 3 **621.8**
1. Pulleys
ISBN 978-1-60818-010-3; 1-60818-010-7; 978-0-89812-581-8 pa; 0-89812-581-2 pa
"The pages are uncluttered and are typeset in a large font, making the words practically pop off the [page]. Also, the author makes the definitions that are presented simple to understand with her selection of photographs. . . . [This is] outstanding and well suited to young elementary school children." Sci Books & Films
Includes glossary

Screws. Creative Education 2011 23p il (Simple machines) $24.25; pa $8.99
Grades: K 1 2 3 **621.8**
1. Screws
ISBN 978-1-60818-011-0; 1-60818-011-5; 978-0-89812-582-5 pa; 0-89812-582-0 pa
"The pages are uncluttered and are typeset in a large font, making the words practically pop off the [page]. Also, the author makes the definitions that are presented simple to understand with her selection of photographs. . . . [This is] outstanding and well suited to young elementary school children." Sci Books & Films
Includes glossary

Wheels and axles. Creative Education 2011 23p il (Simple machines) $24.25; pa $8.99
Grades: K 1 2 3 **621.8**
1. Axles 2. Wheels
ISBN 978-1-60818-013-4; 1-60818-013-1; 978-0-89812-584-9 pa; 0-89812-584-7 pa
"The pages are uncluttered and are typeset in a large font, making the words practically pop off the [page]. Also, the author makes the definitions that are presented simple to understand with her selection of photographs. . . . [This is] outstanding and well suited to young elementary school children." Sci Books & Films
Includes glossary

Caterpillar Inc.
My big book of trucks & diggers. Chronicle Books 2011 il bd bk $7.99
Grades: PreK K **621.8**
1. Trucks 2. Construction equipment 3. Board books for children
ISBN 978-0-8118-7892-0; 0-8118-7892-9
      LC 2010053590
An oversized board book featuring photos of 10 Caterpillar machines-a bulldozer, excavator, dump truck, skid steer loader, paver, motor grader, wheel loader, backhoe loader, material handler, and telehandler.
"This board book uses excellent photographs. . . . The bold colors and clear text enhance the presentation. Even though the terms are a bit challenging, the simplicity of the book and the sharp photographs will have youngsters very excited." SLJ

Coppendale, Jean
The **great** big book of mighty machines; [by] Jean Coppendale and Ian Graham. Firefly Books 2009 160p il $19.95

Grades: PreK K 1 2 3 **621.8**
1. Vehicles 2. Machinery
ISBN 978-1-55407-521-8; 1-55407-521-1
"A vehicle-lover's dream come true, this meaty volume focuses on cars, bikes, trains, tractors, rescue vehicles, construction trucks and monster trucks. Each section . . . ends with an activity page. . . . The text is easy to read and understand. Brightly colored page edges draw eyes inward to the exciting full-color photos that fill the pages." Kirkus
Includes glossary

De Medeiros, James, 1975-
Pulleys. Weigl Publishers 2009 24p il (Science matters: simple machines) lib bdg $24.45; pa $8.95
Grades: 2 3 4 **621.8**
1. Pulleys
ISBN 978-1-60596-041-8 lib bdg; 1-60596-041-1 lib bdg; 978-1-60596-042-5 pa; 1-60596-042-X pa
      LC 2009-1947
Discusses what a pulley is, where it can be found, and how it is used.
"The bold, large-scale, colorful photographs . . . are sure to draw in even the most reluctant readers." SLJ
Includes glossary

De Medeiros, Michael
Screws. Weigl Publishers 2009 24p il (Science matters: simple machines) lib bdg $24.45; pa $8.95
Grades: 2 3 4 **621.8**
1. Screws
ISBN 978-1-60596-039-5 lib bdg; 1-60596-039-X lib bdg; 978-1-60596-040-1 pa; 1-60596-040-3 pa
      LC 2009-1941
Discusses what a screw is, where it can be found, and how it is used.
"De Medeiros' description of the object's function is unusually elegant: Screws convert movement in a circle to movement straight ahead. . . . The back matter (including on-line suggestions, a craft, a quiz, a well-chosen glossary, and more) is strong and features what is likely the only 10-word index in existence to feature the terms nuts, bolts, and King Nebuchadnezzar." Booklist
Includes glossary

Gardner, Robert
Sensational science projects with simple machines; [by] Robert Gardner. Enslow Elementary 2006 48p il (Fantastic physical science experiments) $23.93
Grades: 4 5 6 **621.8**
1. Simple machines 2. Science -- Experiments
ISBN 0-7660-2585-3
      LC 2005008974
"The first chapter of [this book] explains force, friction, distance, and work. The book then introduces levers, inclined planes, pulleys, etc. . . . Large colorful, cartoonlike drawings complement the [text]. . . . [This offers] solid information." SLJ
Includes glossary and bibliographical references

Howse, Jennifer
Inclined planes. Weigl Publishers 2009 24p il (Science matters: simple machines) lib bdg $24.45; pa $8.95

Grades: 2 3 4 **621.8**
1. Inclined planes
ISBN 978-1-60596-035-7 lib bdg; 1-60596-035-7 lib bdg; 978-1-60596-036-4 pa; 1-60596-036-5 pa
LC 2009-25972
Discusses what an inclined plane is, where it can be found, and how it is used.
"The bold, large-scale colorful photographs . . . are sure to draw in even the most reluctant readers." SLJ
Includes glossary

Levers. Weigl Publishers 2009 24p il (Science matters: simple machines) lib bdg $24.45; pa $8.95
Grades: 2 3 4 **621.8**
1. Levers
ISBN 978-1-60596-031-9 lib bdg; 1-60596-031-4 lib bdg; 978-1-60596-032-6 pa; 1-60596-032-2 pa
LC 2009-1921
Discusses what a lever is, where it can be found, and how it is used.
"The bold, large-scale, colorful photographs . . . are sure to draw in even the most reluctant readers." SLJ
Includes glossary

Kulling, Monica
Going up! Elisha Otis's trip to the top. Monica Kulling. Tundra Books of Northern New York 2012 32 p. (hardcover) $17.95
Grades: 2 3 4 **621.8**
1. Elevators 2. Picture books for children 3. Otis, Elisha Graves, 1811-1861
ISBN 1770492402; 9781770492400
LC 2011938777
This children's book offers a biography of Elisha Otis. Fascinated by farm machines, he notes "the dangerous possibility of the hoisting platform in the factory falling if the cable breaks" and "designs a safety brake. He realizes that with this, people can also be moved up and down safely. When he gives a demonstration at the New York World's Fair, the Otis Elevator Company takes off." (Children's Literature)

Low, William
Machines go to work. Holt & Co. 2009 un il $14.95
Grades: PreK K 1 **621.8**
1. Machinery
ISBN 978-0-8050-8759-8; 0-8050-8759-1
"The realistic digital paintings will delight youngsters; spreads alternate with three-page foldouts that show the machines at work. . . . This well-constructed picture book is a surefire hit." SLJ

Solway, Andrew
Castle under siege! simple machines. [by] Andrew Solway. Raintree 2005 32p il lib bdg $28.21; pa $7.85
Grades: 3 4 5 **621.8**
1. Castles 2. Simple machines
ISBN 1-4109-1918-8 lib bdg; 1-4109-1949-8 pa
LC 2005014549
"The author leads readers through the construction of a castle, the workings of the drawbridge, the execution of a siege and how the inhabitants would protect the castle from attack, methods the invaders might use, and what would happen afterward to repair the damage. While readers are drawn into the action, they are also introduced to the simple

machines used during this period of time. . . . Detailed, easily interpreted diagrams are included for added understanding of concepts. Vivid and realistic photos add to the appeal. An excellent choice for research or for general interest." SLJ

Thales, Sharon
Inclined planes to the rescue. Capstone Press 2007 24p il (Simple machines to the rescue) lib bdg $21.26
Grades: K 1 2 3 **621.8**
1. Inclined planes 2. Simple machines
ISBN 978-0-7368-6752-8
This is "brightly colored, attractive . . . [and written] in language students can read and understand independently." SLJ
"Describes inclined planes, including what they are, how they work, and common uses of these simple machines today." Publisher's note
Includes glossary and bibliographical references

Levers to the rescue. Capstone Press 2007 24p il (Simple machines to the rescue) lib bdg $21.26
Grades: K 1 2 3 **621.8**
1. Levers 2. Simple machines
ISBN 978-0-7368-6747-4 lib bdg; 0-7368-6747-3 lib bdg
This is "brightly colored, attractive . . . [and written] in language students can read and understand independently." SLJ
Includes glossary and bibliographical references

Pulleys to the rescue; by Sharon Thales. Capstone Press 2007 24p il (Simple machines to the rescue) lib bdg $21.26
Grades: K 1 2 3 **621.8**
1. Pulleys 2. Simple machines
ISBN 978-0-7368-6748-1 lib bdg; 0-7368-6748-1 lib bdg
LC 2006021503
"The presentation of the material . . . is impressive." Sci Books Films
Includes glossary and bibliographical references

Screws to the rescue; by Sharon Thales. Capstone Press 2007 24p il (Simple machines to the rescue) lib bdg $21.26
Grades: K 1 2 3 **621.8**
1. Screws 2. Simple machines
ISBN 978-0-7368-6749-8 lib bdg; 0-7368-6749-X lib bdg
LC 2006021502
"The presentation of the material . . . is impressive." Sci Books Films
Includes glossary and bibliographical references

Wedges to the rescue; by Sharon Thales. Capstone Press 2007 24p il (Simple machines to the rescue) lib bdg $21.26
Grades: K 1 2 3 **621.8**
1. Wedges 2. Simple machines
ISBN 978-0-7368-6750-4 lib bdg; 0-7368-6750-3 lib bdg
LC 2006021495

"The presentation of the material . . . is impressive." Sci Books Films

Includes glossary and bibliographical references

Wheels and axles to the rescue. Capstone Press 2007 24p il (Simple machines to the rescue) lib bdg $21.26

Grades: K 1 2 3   **621.8**

1. Axles 2. Wheels 3. Simple machines

ISBN 978-0-7368-6751-1

This is "brightly colored, attractive. . . [and written] in language students can read and understand independently." SLJ

Includes glossary and bibliographical references

Tomljanovic, Tatiana

Wedges. Weigl Publishers 2010 24p il (Science matters: simple machines) lib bdg $24.45; pa $8.95

Grades: 2 3 4   **621.8**

1. Wedges

ISBN 978-1-60596-037-1 lib bdg; 1-60596-037-3 lib bdg; 978-1-60596-038-8 pa; 1-60596-038-1 pa

LC 2009-1936

Discusses what a wedge is, where it can be found, and how it is used.

"The bold, large-scale, colorful, photographs . . . are sure to draw in even the most reluctant readers." SLJ

Includes glossary

Walker, Sally M.

Put inclined planes to the test; by Sally M. Walker and Roseann Feldmann. Lerner Publications Co. 2012 40p il (How do simple machines work?) lib bdg $27.93

Grades: 3 4 5   **621.8**

1. Inclined planes

ISBN 978-0-7613-5324-9; 0-7613-5324-0

LC 2009032228

"Written in simple language and sentences, [this title offers a] straightforward [explanation] of how [inclined planes] work. Starting with the basics, the material gradually builds upon readers' growing understanding of the concepts presented. The experiments suggested can be performed with little assistance and with materials found in the home. Clear, distinct, color photos of children demonstrating the activities on each page help reinforce the concepts, as do the many drawings and diagrams." SLJ

Includes bibliographical references

Put levers to the test; by Sally M. Walker and Roseann Feldmann. Lerner Publications Co. 2011 40p il (How do simple machines work?) lib bdg $27.93

Grades: 3 4 5   **621.8**

1. Levers

ISBN 978-0-7613-5321-8; 0-7613-5321-6

LC 2010035551

"Written in simple language and sentences, [this title offers a] straightforward [explanation] of how [levers] work. Starting with the basics, the material gradually builds upon readers' growing understanding of the concepts presented. The experiments suggested can be performed with little assistance and with materials found in the home. Clear, distinct, color photos of children demonstrating the activities

on each page help reinforce the concepts, as do the many drawings and diagrams." SLJ

Includes bibliographical references

Put pulleys to the test; [by] Sally M. Walker and Roseann Feldmann. Lerner Publications Co. 2012 40p il (Early bird physics) lib bdg $27.93

Grades: 3 4 5   **621.8**

1. Gravity 2. Pulleys 3. Force and energy 4. Science -- Experiments

ISBN 978-0-7613-5322-5; 0-7613-5322-4

LC 2010035395

"Written in simple language and sentences, [this] slim [title offers a] straightforward [explanation] of how [pulleys] work. Starting with the basics, the material gradually builds upon readers' growing understanding. . . . The experiments suggested can be performed with little assistance and with materials found in the home. Clear, distinct, color photos of children demonstrating the activities on each page help reinforce the concepts, as do the many drawings and diagrams. Children will find [this] accessible [title] informative." SLJ

Includes bibliographical references

Put screws to the test; by Sally M. Walker and Roseann Feldmann. Lerner Publications Company 2011 40p il (How do simple machines work?) lib bdg $27.93

Grades: 3 4 5   **621.8**

1. Screws

ISBN 978-0-7613-5323-2; 0-7613-5323-2

LC 2010035552

"Written in simple language and sentences, [this title offers a] straightforward [explanation] of how [screws] work. Starting with the basics, the material gradually builds upon readers' growing understanding of the concepts presented. The experiments suggested can be performed with little assistance and with materials found in the home. Clear, distinct, color photos of children demonstrating the activities on each page help reinforce the concepts, as do the many drawings and diagrams." SLJ

Put wedges to the test; [by] Sally M. Walker and Roseann Feldmann. Lerner Publications 2012 40p il (How do simple machines work?) lib bdg $27.93

Grades: 3 4 5   **621.8**

1. Wedges

ISBN 978-0-7613-5325-6; 0-7613-5325-9

LC 2009032230

"Written in simple language and sentences, [this title offers a] straightforward [explanation] of how [wedges] work. Starting with the basics, the material gradually builds upon readers' growing understanding of the concepts presented. The experiments suggested can be performed with little assistance and with materials found in the home. Clear, distinct, color photos of children demonstrating the activities on each page help reinforce the concepts, as do the many drawings and diagrams." SLJ

Includes bibliographical references

Put wheels and axles to the test; [by] Sally M. Walker and Roseann Feldmann. Lerner Publications Co. 2011 39p il (How do simple machines work?) lib bdg $27.93

Grades: 3 4 5   **621.8**

1. Axles 2. Wheels
ISBN 978-0-7613-5326-3; 0-7613-5326-7

                   LC 2010029108

"Written in simple language and sentences, [this title offers a] straightforward [explanation] of how [wheels and axles] work. Starting with the basics, the material gradually builds upon readers' growing understanding of the concepts presented. The experiments suggested can be performed with little assistance and with materials found in the home. Clear, distinct, color photos of children demonstrating the activities on each page help reinforce the concepts, as do the many drawings and diagrams." SLJ

Includes bibliographical references

Yasuda, Anita

Explore simple machines; 25 great projects, activities, experiments. illustrated by Bryan Stone. Nomad Press 2011 il (Explore your world) pa $12.95

Grades: 2 3 4   **621.8**

1. Simple machines
ISBN 978-1-936313-82-2; 1-936313-82-0

This "introduces the six simple machines in enough detail to include worm gears, all three kinds of levers, compound pulleys, and unusual examples. . . . Yasuda writes in particularly clear simple language and intersperses her explanations with historical notes, jokes . . . and 25 easy projects or demonstrations constructed from common materials." Booklist

621.9   Tools

Blaxland, Wendy

Helmets. Marshall Cavendish Benchmark 2011 32p il map (How are they made?) lib bdg $12.99

Grades: 4 5 6   **621.9**

1. Helmets 2. Plastics
ISBN 978-0-7614-4755-9 lib bdg; 0-7614-4755-5 lib bdg

                   LC 2009039881

"The opening spread of Helmets, which shows both a football player and an astronaut, illustrates the wide range of protective headgear, which stretches back to the leather war apparel of 3,000 BCE. Shots of gleaming orbs shuttling down assembly lines accompany text on thermoplastics, testing methods, and laws." Booklist

Includes glossary

Clements, Andrew

Workshop; illustrated by David Wisniewski. Clarion Bks. 1998 un il $16

Grades: K 1 2   **621.9**

1. Tools 2. Workshops
ISBN 0-395-85579-9

                   LC 97-48534

"Wisniewski's cut-paper illustrations and collage ably illustrate Clements' spare, poetic text. . . . A unique introduction to the world of wood and art for budding artisans." Bull Cent Child Books

Tomecek, Steve

Tools and machines; by Stephen M. Tomecek. Chelsea House Publishers 2010 182p il (Experimenting with everyday science) $35

Grades: 5 6 7 8   **621.9**

1. Tools 2. Machinery 3. Science -- Experiments
ISBN 978-1-60413-171-0; 1-60413-171-3

                   LC 2009-22332

This "offers 25 easy-to-perform activities that illuminate scientific principles. . . . [This] discusses levers, pulleys, and meters and explains how people use them in their daily lives. . . . Following each experiment are additional comments on the science behind the experiment and link to the one that follows. Photographs, simple diagrams and illustrations, and sample data tables appear throughout, and the [layout is] clear and colorful." SLJ

Includes bibliographical references

622   Mining and related operations

Squire, Ann O.

Hydrofracking; the process that has changed America's energy needs. by Ann O. Squire. Children's Press, an imprint of Scholastic Inc. 2013 64 p. (Cornerstones of freedom) (library binding) $30

Grades: 4 5 6   **622**

1. Hydraulic fracturing 2. Shale gas 3. Gas well drilling
ISBN 0531236048; 9780531219621; 9780531236048

                   LC 2012034322

This book by Ann O. Squire is part of the "Cornerstones of Freedom" series, which provides "overviews of important national and global issues and their effects on current world development, especially in the United States." It "discusses the advantages and disadvantages of this method of extracting petroleum and natural gas, by pumping water and chemicals deep below the Earth's surface. Renewable energy sources are discussed as alternatives to this practice." (School Library Journal)

Includes bibliographical references (page 61) and index

623   Military and nautical engineering

Keenan, Sheila

★ **Castle**; how it works. David Macaulay with Sheila Keenan. Roaring Brook 2012 31 p. col. ill. (My readers) (hardcover) $15.99

Grades: 1 2 3   **623**

1. Picture books for children 2. Castles 3. Fortification
ISBN 1596437448; 9780395329207; 9781596437449

                   LC 2011962088

In this children's book, author David Macaulay provides "a tour of a medieval castle. . . . Walls keep the enemy out. Towers protect the lord and the soldiers. From the moat and portcullis to the great hall and dungeon . . . [readers can] see how a castle works as an enemy army tries to storm the walls." (Publisher's note)

Mooney, Carla

Becoming invisible; from camouflage to cloaks. Norwood House Press 2010 48p il (A great idea) lib bdg $25.27

Grades: 3 4 5 6   **623**

1. Optics 2. Camouflage (Military science)
ISBN 978-1-59953-378-0 lib bdg; 1-59953-378-2 lib bdg

     LC 2010016516

This "traces the history of camouflage; looks at invisibility in stealth aircraft, films, and television today; considers current research into light and light-bending materials; and imagines future uses for invisibility technology.... Presenting specific, current information, [this book] will appeal to young people intrigued by inventions." Booklist

Includes glossary and bibliographical references

623.4 Ordnance

Gurstelle, William

The **art** of the catapult; build Greek ballistae, Roman onagers, English trebuchets, and more ancient artillery. Chicago Review Press 2004 172p il map $16.95

Grades: 5 6 7 8   **623.4**

1. Catapult
ISBN 1-55652-526-5

"This collection of 10 working catapult projects offers a fascinating look at world history, military strategy, and physics, related with an engaging yet lighthearted touch... . Instructions are clear, with full materials lists, helpful diagrams, and no skipped steps. . . . There's excellent booktalk potential here, and lively reading even for those who never get around to constructing a catapult." SLJ

Includes bibliographical references

Sheinkin, Steve

★ **Bomb**; the race to build and steal the world's most dangerous weapon. Steve Sheinkin. Roaring Brook Press 2012 266 p. ill. (hc) $19.99

Grades: 5 6 7 8 9 10 11 12 Adult   **623.4**

1. Nuclear warfare 2. Nuclear weapons 3. World War, 1914-1918 -- Chemical warfare 4. Atomic bomb -- History 5. Operation Freshman, 1942 6. Atomic bomb -- Germany -- History 7. World War, 1939-1945 -- Secret service -- Soviet Union 8. World War, 1939-1945 -- Secret service -- Great Britain 9. World War, 1939-1945 -- Commando operations -- Norway -- Vemork
ISBN 1596434872; 9781596434875

     LC 2011044096

Robert F. Sibert Informational Book Medal (2013)

YALSA Award for Excellence in Nonfiction for Young Adults (2013)

John Newbery Honor Book (2013)

Author Steve Sheinkin's "story unfolds in three parts, covering American attempts to build the [atomic] bomb, how the Soviets tried to steal American designs and how the Americans tried to keep the Germans from building a bomb. It was the eve of World War II, and the fate of the world was at stake . . . all along the way spies in the United States were feeding sensitive information to the KGB." (Kirkus Reviews)

Includes bibliographical references (p. [243]-259)

and index

623.74 Vehicles

Abramson, Andra Serlin

Fighter planes up close. Sterling 2008 48p (Up close) lib bdg $9.95

Grades: 2 3 4   **623.74**

1. Fighter planes
ISBN 978-1-4027-4796-0 lib bdg; 1-4027-4796-9 lib bdg

     LC 2007008215

An introduction to fighter planes

623.82 Nautical craft

Abramson, Andra Serlin

Submarines up close. Sterling 2008 48p il (Up close) lib bdg $9.95

Grades: 2 3 4   **623.82**

1. Submarines
ISBN 978-1-4027-4797-7 lib bdg; 1-4027-4797-7 lib bdg

     LC 2006102593

An introduction to submarines

Clark, Willow

Boats on the move. PowerKids Press 2010 24p il (Transportation station) lib bdg $21.25; pa $8.25

Grades: 2 3   **623.82**

1. Boats and boating
ISBN 978-1-4358-9336-8 lib bdg; 1-4358-9336-0 lib bdg; 978-1-4358-9760-1 pa; 1-4358-9760-9 pa

     LC 2009-27410

Learn all about speedboats, military boats, boats used by the Coast Guard, and much more.

Includes glossary

Kirk, Shoshanna

T is for tugboat; navigating the seas from A to Z. [text by Shoshanna Kirk; designed by Sara Gillingham] Chronicle Books 2008 un il $15.99

Grades: 2 3 4   **623.82**

1. Ships 2. Navigation
ISBN 978-0-8118-6094-9; 0-8118-6094-9

     LC 2007018333

This is an introduction to sea-related terms such as buoy, figurehead, hornpipe, and sextant

"This attractive title is an eye-pleaser filled with a mix of photographs, illustrations, and graphic images set on textured, woodgrain backgrounds. Images are both vintage and contemporary, and range from black-and-white to full-color reproductions. . . . A spread depicting an array of sailors' knots, a page illustrating Morse code, a spread labeling the parts of a ship, and the endpapers with the international code of maritime flags will be of interest to older children." SLJ

Lindeen, Mary

Ships; by Mary Lindeen. Bellwether Media 2007 24p il (Mighty machines) lib bdg $18.95

Grades: PreK K 1 2 3 **623.82**
1. Ships
ISBN 978-1-60014-060-0 lib bdg; 1-60014-060-2
lib bdg
LC 2006035262

This explains what a ship is, describes its major parts, and what it does

The glossary features "easy-to-read-and-understand definitions. . . . With [its] exciting, full-color photos on every spread [this] colorful [title] will certainly appeal to the mighty curiosity of young readers." SLJ

Includes glossary and bibliographical references

Sutherland, Jonathan
Aircraft carriers; [by] Jonathan Sutherland and Diane Canwell. Gareth Stevens Pub. 2008 32p il (Amazing ships) lib bdg $23.93
Grades: 4 5 6 **623.82**
1. Aircraft carriers
ISBN 978-0-8368-8376-3
LC 2007017049

This is an illustrated introduction to aircraft carriers from various parts of the world

"Bright colors and eye-catching photos are an enticing invitation of younger readers. . . . Vocabulary is appropriate in both text and captions. . . . Attractive, accurate, and informative." SLJ

Includes glossary and bibliographical references

Container ships and oil tankers; [by] Jonathan Sutherland and Diane Canwell. Gareth Stevens Pub. 2008 32p il (Amazing ships) lib bdg $23.93
Grades: 4 5 6 **623.82**
1. Tankers 2. Container ships
ISBN 978-0-8368-8377-0
LC 2007020479

An illustrated introduction to container ships and oil tankers from various parts of the world

"Bright colors and eye-catching photos are an enticing invitation to younger readers. . . . Vocabulary is appropriate in both text and captions. . . . Attractive, accurate, and informative." SLJ

Includes glossary and bibliographical references

Cruise ships; [by] Jonathan Sutherland and Diane Canwell. Gareth Stevens Pub. 2008 32p il (Amazing ships) lib bdg $23.93
Grades: 4 5 6 **623.82**
1. Cruise ships 2. Ocean liners
ISBN 978-0-8368-8378-7
LC 2007017050

This is an illustrated introduction to cruise ships from various parts of the world

"Bright colors and eye-catching photos are an enticing invitation to younger readers. . . . Vocabulary is appropriate in both text and captions. . . . Attractive, accurate, and informative." SLJ

Includes glossary and bibliographical references

Submarines; [by] Jonathan Sutherland and Diane Canwell. Gareth Stevens Pub. 2008 32p il (Amazing ships) lib bdg $23.93

Grades: 4 5 6 **623.82**
1. Submarines
ISBN 978-0-8368-8379-4
LC 2007017051

This is an illustrated introduction to submarines from various parts of the world

"Bright colors and eye-catching photos are an enticing invitation to younger readers. . . . Vocabulary is appropriate in both text and captions. . . . Attractive, accurate, and informative." SLJ

Includes glossary and bibliographical references

623.88 Seamanship

Mooney, Carla
Get all tied up; tying knots. Norwood House Press 2010 48p il (Creative adventure guides) lib bdg $25.27
Grades: 3 4 5 6 **623.88**
1. Knots and splices
ISBN 978-1-59953-384-1; 1-59953-384-7
LC 2010010403

"Some historical background and scientific or cultural information places the making and use of . . . knots . . . in context for young readers. [The] book has four chapters that culminate in step-by-step projects." Horn Book Guide

Includes glossary and bibliographical references

623.89 Navigation

Morrison, Taylor
The **coast** mappers. Houghton Mifflin Co. 2004 45p il map $16
Grades: 5 6 7 8 **623.89**
1. Maps 2. Surveying 3. Astronomers 4. Geographers 5. Cartographers 6. College teachers 7. Pacific Coast (North America)
ISBN 0-618-25408-0
LC 2003-13534

Chronicles the difficulties encountered by George Davidson and others as they attempted to create nautical charts to complete the U.S. Coast Survey of the West Coast in the mid-nineteenth century

"Cartographic methods are clearly explained through both the carefully researched text and the precise illustrations. . . . The artwork clarifies the text, depicts the breathtaking beauty of the coastline, and adds a sense of adventure." SLJ

Includes glossary and bibliographical references

Young, Karen Romano
Across the wide ocean; the why, how, and where of navigation for humans and animals at sea. Greenwillow Books 2007 78p il $18.99; lib bdg $19.89
Grades: 4 5 6 7 **623.89**
1. Ocean 2. Navigation 3. Marine animals
ISBN 978-0-06-009086-9; 0-06-009086-3; 978-0-06-009087-6 lib bdg; 0-06-009087-1 lib bdg
LC 2005-46146

"Readers follow such disparate entities as a loggerhead sea turtle, a nuclear submarine, and a sailboat crew seeking scientific sightings of North Atlantic right whales as Young explores the concept of navigation. . . . Larded with photos, diagrams, and maps. . . . Deceptively simple in appearance, the informative text can push some intense mental activity." SLJ

624 Civil engineering

Caney, Steven
★ Steven Caney's ultimate building book. Running Press 2006 596p il $29.95
Grades: 4 5 6 7 8 **624**
1. Building 2. Civil engineering
ISBN 0-7624-0409-4
"Caney examines 'building' in its broadest sense, encompassing everything from skyscrapers and bridges to bird feeders and peanut-shell 'bricks.' Opening sections investigate the history and techniques of construction, with clearly written explanations supported by black-and-white photographs and diagrams. . . . The author reinforces important concepts of design in a way that is fascinating and effective." SLJ

Fantastic feats and failures; by the editors of YES magazine. Kids Can Press 2004 52p il hardcover o.p. pa $7.95
Grades: 4 5 6 7 **624**
1. Civil engineering
ISBN 1-55337-633-1; 1-55337-634-X pa
This "book spotlights 20 notable highs and lows in engineering. The 'feats' celebrated include the Sydney Opera House, the Brooklyn Bridge, and Canadarm (a huge, Canadian-built robotic arm used for repairs in space). Among the 'failures' are the space shuttle Challenger, the Tacoma Narrows Bridge, and the Chernobyl nuclear power plant. . . . Well organized and engagingly written. . . . Excellent photos . . . illustrate the places and events discussed, while colorful drawings visually represent concepts." Booklist

Macaulay, David
★ Underground. Houghton Mifflin 1976 109p il hardcover o.p. pa $9.95
Grades: 5 6 7 8 9 **624**
1. Subways 2. Building 3. Sewerage 4. Electric lines 5. Public utilities 6. Civil engineering
ISBN 0-395-24739-X; 0-395-34065-9 pa
"Introduced by a visual index—a bird's eye view of a busy, hypothetical intersection with colored indicators marking the specific locations analyzed in subsequent pages—detailed illustrations are combined with a clear, precise narrative to make the subject comprehenssible and fascinating." Horn Book
Includes glossary

Sandvold, Lynnette Brent
Revolution in construction. Marshall Cavendish Benchmark 2010 32p il (It works!) lib bdg $19.95
Grades: 3 4 5 **624**
1. Building 2. Engineering
ISBN 978-0-7614-4378-0 lib bdg; 0-7614-4378-9 lib bdg
LC 2008-54363

"This interesting, information packed [book] . . . motivates students to do their own exploring. . . . The appealing cartoon-like photographs add humor. . . . This . . . just may be that spark needed to create eager budding scientists." Libr Media Connect
Includes glossary and bibliographical references

Sullivan, George
Built to last; building America's amazing bridges, dams, tunnels, and skyscrapers. Scholastic Nonfiction 2005 128p il map $18.99
Grades: 5 6 7 8 **624**
1. Civil engineering
ISBN 0-439-51737-0
LC 2004-60996
This is a "survey of American building—from the Erie Canal to Boston's current 'Big Dig.' Chronological chapters describe the historical forces that helped drive each project as well as the specific technological feats linked to each pioneering structure. . . . The wide selection of captivating illustrations includes archival photos and engravings, architectural drawings, and color photos. . . , Sullivan's skillful integration of social and economic history distinguishes this clear, well-designed title." Booklist

624.1 Structural engineering and underground construction

Askew, Amanda
Bulldozers. QEB Pub. 2010 24p il (Mighty machines) lib bdg $25.65; pa $5.95
Grades: PreK K 1 2 **624.1**
1. Construction equipment
ISBN 978-1-59566-925-4 lib bdg; 1-59566-925-6 lib bdg; 978-1-55407-703-8 pa; 1-55407-703-6 pa
LC 2010001217
"With huge, clear color photos of machines at work, the Mighty Machines series is an exciting way to connect books with kids' vrooming play and with what they see on the road, construction sites, and farms. . . . In Bulldozers, the parts called 'blades' and 'rippers' say it all, and the pages of full-bleed photographs show the machines building roads and even clearing a path as part of an army convoy." Booklist

Cranes. QEB Pub. 2010 24p il (Mighty machines) lib bdg $25.65; pa $5.95
Grades: PreK K 1 2 **624.1**
1. Construction equipment 2. Cranes, derricks, etc.
ISBN 978-1-59566-924-7 lib bdg; 1-59566-924-8 lib bdg; 978-1-55407-704-5 pa; 1-55407-704-4 pa
LC 2010001219
"With large, clear color photos of machines at work, the Mighty Machines series is an exciting way to connect books with kids' vrooming play and with what they see on the road, construction sites, and farms. . . . The subjects of Cranes lift containers at the docks, construct bridges, and more, and the aerial photo of a tower crane high above a cityscape is dizzying." Booklist
Includes glossary

Diggers. QEB Pub. 2010 24p il (Mighty machines) lib bdg $25.65; pa $5.95

Grades: PreK K 1 2 **624.1**
1. Construction equipment
ISBN 978-1-59566-926-1 lib bdg; 1-59566-926-4 lib bdg; 978-1-55407-705-2 pa; 1-55407-705-2 pa
LC 2010001221
"With huge, clear color photos of machines at work, the Mighty Machines series is an exciting way to connect books with kids' vrooming play, and with what they see on the road, construction sites, and farms. . . . Machines shown in Diggers are made of arms, tracks, bucket attachments, and a driver's cab and perform demolition as well as breaking up ground at a building site." Booklist
Includes glossary

Loaders. QEB Pub. 2010 24p il (Mighty machines) lib bdg $25.65; pa $5.95
Grades: PreK K 1 2 **624.1**
1. Construction equipment
ISBN 978-1-59566-923-0 lib bdg; 1-59566-923-X lib bdg; 978-1-55407-706-9 pa; 1-55407-706-0 pa
LC 2010001222
"With huge, clear color photos of machines at work, the Mighty Machines series is an exciting way to connect books with kids' vrooming play and with what they see on the road, construction sites, and farms. . . . Loaders covers tractors with large buckets on the front, which are used primarily at building sites but can also be found in mines and quarries, as well as being used to clear snow, repair roads, and move bales of straw on the farm." Booklist
Includes glossary

Graham, Ian
Tremendous tunnels. Amicus 2010 32p il (Superstructures) lib bdg $28.50
Grades: 5 6 7 8 **624.1**
1. Tunnels
ISBN 978-1-60753-134-0; 1-60753-134-8
LC 2009030865
"The vivid illustrations often help clarify points made in the text. . . . [This] colorful, informative [book offers] intriguing glimpses of notable engineering feats." Booklist
Includes glossary and bibliographical references

Hill, Lee Sullivan
Earthmovers on the move. Lerner Publications 2010 32p il (Lightning bolt books. Vroom-vroom) lib bdg $25.26
Grades: K 1 2 **624.1**
1. Construction equipment
ISBN 978-0-7613-3918-2; 0-7613-3918-3
LC 2009039739
This book about earthmovers has "big, high-energy color photos. . . . [The text provides] lively commentary in a mix of declarative statements and non-rhetorical questions. . . . [The] volume closes with a labeled diagram, a page of 'fun facts,' and a short list of print and web resources. . . . [This] will make a worthwhile and popular addition." SLJ
Includes glossary and bibliographical references

Mason, Adrienne
Build it! structures, systems and you. written by Adrienne Mason; illustrated by Claudia Dávila. Kids Can Press 2006 32p il (Primary physical science) $14.95; pa $5.95

Grades: K 1 2 **624.1**
1. Building 2. Structural engineering
ISBN 978-1-55337-835-8; 1-55337-835-0; 978-1-55337-836-5 pa; 1-55337-836-9 pa
This provides "a first glimpse of how structures and structural systems exist both in nature and in human-made designs. The author makes reading this book an easy and enjoyable reading experience. The book uses carefully worded descriptions, creative and vivid colors with striking graphics representations, and clear fonts." Sci Books Films

624.2 Bridges

Curlee, Lynn
★ **Brooklyn** Bridge. Atheneum Bks. for Young Readers 2001 35p il map $18
Grades: 3 4 5 6 **624.2**
1. Bridges 2. Bridge engineers 3. Brooklyn Bridge (New York, N.Y.)
ISBN 0-689-83183-8
LC 99-43771
"Biography, social history, and introductory engineering are . . . precisely balanced, with human-interest angles. . . . This is a grand yet practical tribute to a grand yet practical edifice." Bull Cent Child Books
Includes bibliographical references

Graham, Ian
Fabulous bridges. Amicus 2010 32p il (Superstructures) lib bdg $28.50
Grades: 5 6 7 8 **624.2**
1. Bridges
ISBN 978-1-60753-132-6; 1-60753-132-1
LC 2009030864
"The vivid illustrations often help clarify points made in the text. . . . [This] colorful, informative [book offers] intriguing glimpses of notable engineering feats." Booklist
Includes glossary and bibliographical references

Johmann, Carol
Bridges! amazing structures to design, build & test. [by] Carol Johmann & Elizabeth Rieth; illustrations by Michael Kline. Williamson 1999 96p il pa $12.95
Grades: 4 5 6 7 **624.2**
1. Bridges
ISBN 1-88559-330-9
LC 98-53272
Describes different kinds of bridges, their history, design, construction, and effects on populations, environmental dilemmas, safety, and more
"Eye-catching photographs and cartoon illustrations in blue and orange tones abound; clear organization of text and unifying page borders create an attractive graphic package. The volume includes a list of notable bridges by state and country." SLJ

625.1 Railroads

Barton, Byron
★ **Trains.** Crowell 1986 un il lib bdg $16.89

Grades: PreK K 1　　　　　　　**625.1**
1. Railroads
ISBN 0-690-04534-4

LC 85-47898

Brief text and illustrations present a variety of trains and what they do

"The concepts are simple and Barton's illustrations are just enough, and no more." Publ Wkly

Clark, Willow

Trains on the move; [by] Willow Clark. PowerKids Press 2010 24p il (Transportation station) lib bdg $21.25; pa $8.025

Grades: 2 3　　　　　　　　　**625.1**
1. Railroads
ISBN 978-1-4358-9331-3 lib bdg; 1-4358-9331-X lib bdg; 978-1-4358-9750-2 pa; 1-4358-9750-1 pa

LC 2009-21776

Learn all about the different types of trains, how they work, and how important they are

"Clark has done a fine job of including meaningful content in a limited space. . . . [This book] consists of 10 two-page chapters printed in a font of an inviting size. Full-page photos–all color except one vintage photograph–with informative captions face two-paragraph text blocks. . . . Will make readers feel they have learned something" SLJ

Includes glossary

Crowther, Robert

Trains: a pop-up railroad book. Candlewick Press 2006 un il $17.99

Grades: 2 3 4 5　　　　　　　**625.1**
1. Railroads 2. Pop-up books
ISBN 978-0-7636-3082-9; 0-7636-3082-9

"With pop-up effects that, appropriately enough, tend to be long, narrow, and placed in parallel tracks, this history of railroading opens with outside and inside views of a small steam locomotive and closes with a full-spread, double-tiered train station. In between, the book covers methods of propulsion, the development of passenger cars, speed and other records, tunnels, bridges, and other engineering feats. . . . Crowther simplifies technological details in his neat, brightly colored collage illustrations." SLJ

Lindeen, Mary

Trains; by Mary Lindeen. Bellwether Media 2007 24p il (Mighty machines) lib bdg $18.50

Grades: PreK K 1 2 3　　　　　　**625.1**
ISBN 978-1-60014-062-4 lib bdg; 1-60014-062-9 lib bdg

LC 2006035264

This explains what a train is and discusses its major parts and what they do

The glossary features "easy-to-read-and-understand definitions. . . . With [its] exciting, full-color photos on every spread, [this] colorful [title] will certainly appeal to the mighty curiosity of young readers." SLJ

Includes glossary and bibliographical references

National Railway Museum (Great Britain)

Big book of trains; [by] National Railway Museum, York, England. DK Pub. 1998 32p il $14.99

Grades: 4 5 6　　　　　　　　　**625.1**
1. Railroads
ISBN 0-7894-3436-9

LC 98-18830

Describes the locomotives, cars, tunnels, stations, and functions of such trains as freight trains, channel tunnel trains, bullet trains, mountain trains, and snow trains

Includes glossary

625.26　Locomotives

Zimmermann, Karl

The **Stourbridge** Lion; America's First Locomotive. Karl Zimmermann; illustrated by Steven Walker. 1st ed. Boyds Mills Press 2012 32 p. ill., maps (hardcover) $16.95

Grades: 2 3 4　　　　　　　　　**625.26**
1. Steam locomotives 2. Railroads -- History 3. Locomotives 4. Transportation -- United States -- History 5. Stourbridge Lion (Steam locomotive) 6. Steam locomotives -- United States -- History 7. Railroads -- Pennsylvania -- Honesdale -- History 8. Railroads -- United States -- History -- 19th century
ISBN 1590788591; 9781590788592

LC 2011939995

Includes bibliographical references.

625.4　Local rail transit systems

McKendry, Joe

Beneath the streets of Boston; building America's first subway. written & illustrated by Joe McKendry. David R. Godine 2005 un il maps $19.95

Grades: 4 5 6　　　　　　　　　**625.4**
1. Subways 2. Boston (Mass.) -- History
ISBN 1-56792-284-8

LC 2004-16418

This book covers over twenty years of the early history of the Boston subway system

"The text is clear and well written. . . . The paintings convey the sense of story, while the drawings provide specific details. Both are equally well executed and contribute to the overall understanding of the text." SLJ

Weitzman, David L.

A **subway** for New York; [by] David Weitzman. Farrar, Straus and Giroux 2005 un il map $17

Grades: 4 5 6 7　　　　　　　　**625.4**
1. Subways 2. New York (N.Y.) -- History
ISBN 0-374-37284-5

LC 2004-56286

"Weitzman recounts the construction of [New York's] first subterranean train system, beginning above ground with descriptions of [the city's] crowded streets in 1904. . . . The text and captivating images convey the awe-inspiring scope of the project and the engineering feats that produced what remains the fastest method of navigating the city." Booklist

Includes bibliographical references

627 Hydraulic engineering

Mann, Elizabeth

 Hoover Dam; with illustrations by Alan Witschonke. Mikaya Press 2001 44p il (Wonders of the world) $19.95; pa $9.95

Grades: 4 5 6 7   **627**

 1. Hoover Dam (Ariz. and Nev.)

 ISBN 978-1-931414-02-9; 1-931414-02-5; 978-1-931414-13-5 pa; 1-931414-13-0 pa

LC 2001-34520

Describes the engineering, construction, and social and historical contexts of the Hoover Dam

 "A wonderfully readable, well-organized book filled with fascinating detail." SLJ

Zuehlke, Jeffrey

 The **Hoover** Dam. Lerner Publications Co. 2010 32p il map (Lightning Bolt Books. Famous places) lib bdg $25.26

Grades: 2 3 4   **627**

 1. Hoover Dam (Ariz. and Nev.)

 ISBN 978-0-8225-9408-6 lib bdg; 0-8225-9408-0 lib bdg

LC 2008-31245

Describes the Hoover Dam and includes information on its design, construction, and environmental issues

 This book uses "high-quality photos, illustrations, maps, and diagrams. . . . Readers will enjoy learning about [the Hoover Dam] . . . and the challenges of building and maintaining large structures." SLJ

 Includes glossary and bibliographical references

628 Sanitary engineering

Horn, Geoffrey

 Environmental engineer; by Geoffrey M. Horn. Gareth Stevens Pub. 2010 32p il (Cool careers: cutting edge) lib bdg $26; pa $8.95

Grades: 4 5 6   **628**

 1. Vocational guidance 2. Sanitary engineering 3. Environmental protection

 ISBN 978-1-4339-1956-5 lib bdg; 1-4339-1956-7 lib bdg; 978-1-4339-2155-1 pa; 1-4339-2155-3 pa

LC 2009004746

This introduction to environmental engineering careers offers "clear, solid information in a large font. . . . [This] short [book is] packed with relevant, current material." SLJ

 Includes glossary and bibliographical references

628.1 Water supply

Cartlidge, Cherese

 Water from air; water-harvesting machines. by Cherese Cartlidge. Norwood House Press 2008 48p il (A great idea) lib bdg $25.27

Grades: 3 4 5 6   **628.1**

 1. Humidity 2. Water supply 3. Water resources

development

 ISBN 978-1-59953-196-0 lib bdg; 1-59953-196-8 lib bdg

LC 2008-10780

 "Describes the invention and development of water harvesting machines." Publisher's note

 Includes glossary and bibliographical references

Person, Stephen

 Saving animals from oil spills. Bearport Pub. 2011 32p il map (Rescuing animals from disasters) lib bdg $25.27

Grades: 3 4 5 6   **628.1**

 1. Oil spills 2. Animal rescue

 ISBN 978-1-61772-288-2; 1-61772-288-X

LC 2011002430

 "Featuring colorful, visually packed pages and readable prose, this title . . . offers an acceessible introduction to the impact of oil spills on a variety of creatures. . . . Throughout, basic concepts are well conveyed, and inset text adds additional, useful commentary on each page." Booklist

 Includes glossary and bibliographical references

628.9 Other branches of sanitary and municipal engineering

Abramson, Andra Serlin

 Fire engines up close. Sterling 2008 48p (Up close) lib bdg $9.95

Grades: 2 3 4   **628.9**

 1. Fire engines

 ISBN 978-1-4027-4798-4 lib bdg; 1-4027-4798-5 lib bdg

LC 2007008214

An introduction to fire fighters and their equipment

Allman, Toney

 The **Jaws** of Life. Norwood House Press 2008 48p il (A great idea) lib bdg $25.27

Grades: 3 4 5 6   **628.9**

 1. Rescue work

 ISBN 978-159953-191-5 lib bdg; 1-59953-191-7 lib bdg

LC 2008007041

 "Full-color photographs and copious fun facts help make this . . . enjoyable reading, but it's really the choice of [topic] that is so enthralling." Booklist

 Includes glossary and bibliographical references

Bingham, Caroline

 Fire truck. DK Pub. 2003 29p il (Machines at work) $8.99

Grades: K 1 2 3   **628.9**

 1. Fire engines 2. Fire fighting

 ISBN 0-7894-9221-0

Introduces fire engines and the work that they help firefighters do in all kinds of settings

 "Bingham immediately grabs the reader's attention with brilliantly colored pictures. . . . An excellent stimulant for a child's imagination." Sci Books Films

 Includes glossary

Butler, Dori Hillestad

F is for firefighting; by Dori Hillestad Butler; illustrated by Joan C. Waites. Pelican 2007 un il $15.95

Grades: PreK K 1   **628.9**

1. Alphabet 2. Fire fighting

ISBN 978-1-58980-420-3; 1-58980-420-1

LC 2006031113

"From 'A is for Alarm' to 'Z is for Zones,' each page introduces a different aspect of firefighting. Crisp, colorful illustrations depict the topics, and thick borders frame the artwork as well as the text boxes at the bottom of the pages." SLJ

Demarest, Chris L.

Firefighters A to Z. Margaret K. McElderry Bks. 2000 un il lib bdg $16.95

Grades: K 1   **628.9**

1. Alphabet 2. Fire fighters

ISBN 0-689-83798-4

LC 99-56382

An alphabetic look at a firefighter's day

"There's nothing babyish or cute about the robust, action-oriented pastel artwork in Firefighters A to Z. . . . Permeated with intense primary colors, the images build on one another to convey the physical nature of this dramatic but serious job. The firefighters themselves, in their bulky yellow suits and oxygen masks, appear straight out of science fiction, but the smoothly rhyming text grounds their activities in reality." Horn Book

Jango-Cohen, Judith

Fire trucks on the move. Lerner Publications 2010 32p il (Lightning bolt books. Vroom-vroom) lib bdg $25.26

Grades: K 1 2   **628.9**

1. Fire engines

ISBN 978-0-7613-6023-0 lib bdg; 0-7613-6023-9 lib bdg

LC 2009039740

This book about fire trucks has "big, high-energy color photos. . . . [The text provides] lively commentary in a mix of declarative statements and non-rhetorical questions. . . . [The] volume closes with a labeled diagram, a page of 'fun facts,' and a short list of print and web resources. . . . [This] will make a worthwhile and popular addition." SLJ

Includes glossary and bibliographical references

Kenney, Karen Latchana

Firefighters at work; by Karen L. Kenney; illustrated by Brian Caleb Dumm. Magic Wagon 2010 32p il (Meet your community workers!) lib bdg $18.95

Grades: K 1 2 3   **628.9**

1. Fire fighters 2. Vocational guidance

ISBN 978-1-60270-648-4 lib bdg; 1-60270-648-4 lib bdg

LC 2009-2384

This book about firefighters has "an uncluttered layout and consistent organization. . . . Chapter headings such as 'Problems on the Job,' and 'Technology at Work,' and 'Special Skills and Training' make it easy to pinpoint specific information." SLJ

Includes glossary

Landau, Elaine

Smokejumpers; photographs by Ben Klaffke. Millbrook Press 2002 48p il lib bdg $23.90

Grades: 3 4 5 6   **628.9**

1. Forest fires 2. Fire fighters

ISBN 0-7613-2324-4

LC 2001-30974

"The first half explains the physical training smokejumpers undergo and the fire-fighting theory they must learn. The second half shows what happens when a fire call comes in. . . . The pictures and text work together beautifully. . . . This is a must-purchase for libraries in places where forest fires occur, and the true-life-adventure aspect will make it popular in other libraries as well." Booklist

Includes glossary and bibliographical references

629 Other branches of engineering

The amazing International Space Station; by the editors of YES Mag. Kids Can Press 2003 48p il $15.95; pa $8.95

Grades: 4 5 6   **629**

1. Space stations

ISBN 1-55337-380-4; 1-55337-523-8 pa

This describes the construction, crew, life, and work aboard the International Space Station.

"This book packs a lot of information into clear, short chapters that are chock-full of facts, action, and cool language." SLJ

Biggs, Brian

Everything goes: On land. Balzer + Bray 2011 un il (Everything goes) $14.99

Grades: PreK K 1   **629**

1. Vehicles

ISBN 0-06-195809-3; 978-0-06-195809-0

LC 2011019349

A young boy learns about land vehicles from bicycles to subways and trolleys as he and his father travel to the train station.

"Biggs has a cheery cartooning style that's reminiscent of R. Crumb and ideal for populating his oversized pages with a multitude of players and detail. With running visual jokes and mini-narratives adding to the fun, Biggs gives readers lots to take in and enjoy." Publ Wkly

Ganeri, Anita

Things that go; illustrated by Mark Bergin. Kingfisher 2010 18p il (Flip the flaps) $9.99

Grades: PreK K 1   **629**

1. Vehicles

ISBN 978-0-7534-6409-0; 0-7534-6409-8

This provides "cutaways of airplanes and trains and [shows] a fire in progress along with a spread about emergency vehicles. Some questions . . . are given suprisingly thorough answers. . . . Perfect for light, educational browsing." Booklist

Simon, Seymour

The paper airplane book; illustrated by Byron Barton. Viking 1971 48p il pa $6.99

Grades: 3 4 5 **629**
1. Paper crafts 2. Airplanes -- Models
ISBN 0-14-030925-X
Step-by-step instructions for making paper airplanes with suggestions for experimenting with them

629.04 Transportation engineering

Arlon, Penelope
Emergency vehicles; by Penelope Arlon and Tory Gordon-Harris. 1st ed. Scholastic 2013 32 p. col. ill. (Scholastic discover more) (reinforced) $7.99
Grades: PreK K 1 **629.04**
1. Vehicles 2. Fire engines 3. Rescue work 4. Emergency vehicles
ISBN 0545495636; 9780545495639
LC 2012285426
This book, written by Penelope Arlon, presents a "reference book about emergency vehicles for emergent readers. 'Emergency Vehicles' is full of facts and . . . pictures of rescue vehicles. Big, annotated photos reveal . . . details of how fire trucks, ambulances, police cars, motorbikes, and helicopters really work. Alongside are explorations of more unusual vehicles . . . from superscoopers to fireboats. (Publisher's note)

Perritano, John
Revolution in transportation. Marshall Cavendish Benchmark 2010 32p il (It works!) lib bdg $19.95
Grades: 3 4 5 **629.04**
1. Transportation
ISBN 978-0-7614-4379-7 lib bdg; 0-7614-4379-7 lib bdg
LC 2008-54366
"This interesting, information packed [book] . . . motivates students to do their own exploring. . . . The appealing cartoon-like photographs add humor. . . . This . . . just may be that spark needed to create eager budding scientists." Libr Media Connect
Includes glossary and bibliographical references

629.046 Transportation equipment

Green, Rod
Giant vehicles; Rod Green, illustrated by Stephen Biesty. Candlewick Press 2014 16 p. $15.99
Grades: K 1 2 3 **629.046**
1. Vehicles 2. Ships 3. Dump trucks 4. Flying machines 5. Railroad trains
ISBN 0763674044; 9780763674045
LC 2013953451
"[Author Rod] Green and [illustrator Stephen] Biesty explore the biggest of the big in this oversize [children's] book devoted to vehicles. ... Biesty's detailed colored-pencil illustrations demonstrate how each machine operates, with labels and captions explaining how various components work together." (Publishers Weekly)
"Known for his exceptionally fine cutaway drawings in books such as Stephen Biesty's Cross-Sections: Man-of-War (1993) and Egypt in Spectacular Cross-Section (2005), Biesty uses this new book's wide format to showcase gargan-

tuan vehicles, such as an exceptionally long train, a double-decker passenger jet, a gigantic dump truck, an enormous container ship, a jumbo Russian submarine, and (turn the book 90 degrees) the Saturn V rocket for NASA's 1969 moonshot..hildren intrigued by the subject will pore over the handsome illustrations—intricately detailed pen-and-ink drawings with colored-pencil shading. An engaging, interactive learning experience." Booklist

629.13 Aeronautics

Adler, David A.
A picture book of Amelia Earhart; illustrated by Jeff Fisher. Holiday House 1998 un il $16.95; pa $6.95
Grades: 1 2 3 **629.13**
1. Air pilots 2. Missing persons 3. Women air pilots 4. Memoirists
ISBN 0-8234-1315-2; 0-8234-1517-1 pa
LC 96-54854
Discusses the life of the pilot who was the first woman to cross the Atlantic by herself in a plane
This offers "a straightforward, informative text full of detail. The illustrations ably reflect both the humorous and more serious moments in the narrative." Horn Book Guide
Includes bibliographical references

Bailey, Gerry
Flight. Gareth Stevens Pub. 2009 32p il (Simply science) lib bdg $26
Grades: 3 4 5 **629.13**
1. Flight 2. Aeronautics
ISBN 978-1-4339-0032-7 lib bdg; 1-4339-0032-7 lib bdg
LC 2008-27569
"In this little book, various vehicles associated with human flight are introduced . . . [and] fundamental principles underlying how these various vehicles are able to travel through the air are explained in a straightfoward and understandable manner. . . . This text will provide . . . an entertaining and informative introduction to aircraft and aerodynamic vehicles." Sci Books Films
Includes glossary and bibliographical references

Borden, Louise
Touching the sky; the flying adventures of Wilbur and Orville Wright. [by] Louise Borden & Trish Marx; illustrated by Peter Fiore. Margaret K. McElderry Bks. 2003 un il map $18.95
Grades: 3 4 5 **629.13**
1. Inventors 2. Aeronautics -- History 3. New York (N.Y.) -- History 4. Aircraft industry executives
ISBN 0-689-84876-5
LC 2002-12041
A look at how the Wright Brothers became the first celebrities of the twentieth century through their 1909 public flying exhibitions in New York City and Germany
"Fiore's detailed watercolors dramatically and accurately record the two venues. The narrative, too, is laced with engaging facts that are successfully married to the pictures." SLJ

Brown, Don, 1949-

Ruth Law thrills a nation; story and pictures by Don Brown. Ticknor & Fields 1993 un il $16; pa $5.95

Grades: K 1 2 3   **629.13**

1. Air pilots 2. Women air pilots 3. Aeronautics -- Flights

ISBN 0-395-66404-7; 0-395-73517-3 pa

LC 92-45701

The author discusses the flight performed by Ruth Law, who in 1916 "tried to fly from Chicago to New York City in one day. She did not succeed (she landed outside Binghamton, New York), but she broke a nonstop cross-county flying record." (Booklist) "Kindergarten to grade three." (School Library Journal)

"Using a simple text and effective watercolors, Brown successfully re-creates the remarkable flying feat. He sets Law in her historical context with humor and precision." Booklist

Burleigh, Robert

Flight: the journey of Charles Lindbergh; illustrated by Mike Wimmer; introduction by Jean Fritz. Philomel Bks. 1991 un il hardcover o.p. pa $6.99

Grades: 2 3 4   **629.13**

1. Generals 2. Air pilots 3. Memoirists 4. Air force officers 5. Aeronautics -- Flights

ISBN 0-399-22272-3; 0-698-11425-6 pa

LC 90-35401

Describes how Charles Lindbergh achieved the remarkable feat of flying nonstop and solo from New York to Paris in 1927

"Using Charles Lindbergh's autobiography, The Spirit of St. Louis, as the basis for his text, Burleigh vividly creates that first solo flight in words, while Wimmer fashions exhilarating pictures that are, above all else, emotional. . . . This artistic emotion . . . works terrifically with the terseness of the near-poetic text." Booklist

★ **Night** flight; Amelia Earhart crosses the Atlantic. [illustrated by] Wendell Minor. Simon & Schuster Books for Young Readers 2011 un il $16.99

Grades: K 1 2   **629.13**

1. Air pilots 2. Missing persons 3. Women air pilots 4. Memoirists 5. Aeronautics -- Flights 6. Transatlantic flights

ISBN 1-4169-6733-8; 978-1-4169-6733-0

LC 2008-52269

This is an account of Amelia Earhart's 1932 flight across the Atlantic Ocean from Newfoundland to Ireland. Bibliography. "Grades three to six." (Bull Cent Child Books)

"A gripping narrative and dynamic art immediately pull readers into the story of Earhart's historic 1932 solo transatlantic flight. . . . Minor's . . . gouache and watercolor paintings easily convey the journey's intense drama, balancing lifelike closeups of Earhart with images of her imperiled plane. . . . Hearts will be racing. Back matter includes notes on Earhart's life." Publ Wkly

Includes bibliographical references

Carson, Mary Kay

★ The **Wright** Brothers for kids; how they invented the airplane: 21 activities exploring the science and history of flight. illustrations by Laura D'Argo. Chicago Review Press 2003 146p il pa $14.95

Grades: 4 5 6 7   **629.13**

1. Inventors 2. Aeronautics -- History 3. Science -- Experiments 4. Aircraft industry executives

ISBN 1-55652-477-3

LC 2002-155449

This account of the Wright brothers' invention of the airplane, explains the forces of flight-lift, thrust, gravity, and drag and includes such activities as making a Chinese flying top, building a kite, bird watching, making a paper glider and a rubber-band-powered flyer

"A treasure trove of activities awaits readers of this wonderfully executed survey of the Wright brothers and their invention. The narrative flows easily and is complemented by numerous photographs that give a sense of history and this event. . . . This is a valuable resource for student reports and projects, and for classroom units." SLJ

Includes glossary and bibliographical references

Crowther, Robert

Flight: a pop-up book of aircraft. Candlewick Press 2007 un il $17.99

Grades: 2 3 4 5   **629.13**

1. Aeronautics 2. Pop-up books

ISBN 978-0-7636-3459-9; 0-7636-3459-X

This is "a history of flight, from the ancient Chinese invention of the kite to the X-43A scramjet that NASA still has under development. Along with dozens of small, simplified but clean-lined portraits of renowned aircraft, many of which 'fly' along die-cut slots, [Crowther] includes a pop-up modern air terminal, a large two-sided globe on which famous firsts are traced, and a particularly well-designed 747 cockpit with moving control levers." SLJ

Cummins, Julie

Flying solo; how Ruth Elder soared into America's heart. Julie Cummins; illustrated by Malene Laugesen. Roaring Brook Press 2013 32 p.

Grades: K 1 2   **629.13**

1. Air pilots -- United States -- Biography 2. Women air pilots -- United States -- Biography

ISBN 9781596435094

LC 2012029743

Amelia Bloomer Project (2014)

Includes bibliographical references (p.   )

Goldish, Meish

Freaky-big airplanes. Bearport Pub. 2010 24p il (World's biggest) lib bdg $22.61

Grades: 2 3 4   **629.13**

1. Airplanes

ISBN 978-1-59716-959-2 lib bdg; 1-59716-959-5 lib bdg

LC 2009-14620

Describes different types of aircraft used around the world, including information on their history, dimensions, weight, and performance

"The simply phrased narrative and captions describe what each vehicle carries, along with top speed, full weight, and other basic facts. . . . A visual glossary and a look at four other outsize flying machines . . . cap this awe-inspiring entry in the World's Biggest series." Booklist

Includes glossary and bibliographical references

Hardesty, Von

Epic flights. Kingfisher 2011 il (Epic adventure) $19.99

Grades: 5 6 7 8   **629.13**

1. Aeronautics -- History

ISBN 978-0-7534-6669-8; 0-7534-6669-4

LC 2011041637

This describes Charles Lindbergh's transatlantic flight; the Breitling Orbiter 3 which set a record for non-stop around the world flight by balloon; the Apollo 11 flight to the moon; Amy Johnson's solo flight from England to Australia in a small bi-plane; and the Voyager, which set a record by flying non-stop around the world without refueling.

"The graphics will grab readers in [this] exciting, extra-large-size [title] . . . packed with high-quality color photos on every double-page spread. Just as gripping are the narratives, captions, and technical details of exploration, adventure, and survival." Booklist

Includes glossary

Hense, Mary

How fighter pilots use math; math curriculum consultant: Rhea A. Stewart. Chelsea Clubhouse 2010 32p il (Math in the real world) lib bdg $28

Grades: 4 5 6   **629.13**

1. Air pilots 2. Aeronautics 3. Mathematics 4. Vocational guidance

ISBN 978-1-60413-605-0 lib bdg; 1-60413-605-7 lib bdg

LC 2009-20242

This describes how fighter pilots use math to judge speed, attain altitude, and maintain safety, and includes relevant math problems and information about how to become a fighter pilot

Includes glossary and bibliographical references

Hodgkins, Fran

How people learned to fly; by Fran Hodgkins; illustrated by True Kelley. HarperCollinsPublishers 2007 33p il (Let's-read-and-find-out science) $15.99; pa $5.99

Grades: K 1 2 3   **629.13**

1. Flight 2. Aeronautics

ISBN 978-0-06-029558-5; 0-06-029558-9; 978-0-06-445221-2 pa; 0-06-445221-2 pa

LC 2006000482

"This book explains the development of aircraft and the scientific principles behind them. Complex ideas, such as gravity and lift, are made accessible through concise explanations and excellent illustrations and diagrams, which are always bright, clear, and appealing." SLJ

629.133 Aircraft types

Clark, Willow

Planes on the move. PowerKids Press 2010 24p il (Transportation station) lib bdg $21.25; pa $8.25

Grades: 2 3   **629.133**

1. Airplanes 2. Aeronautics

ISBN 978-1-4358-9332-0 lib bdg; 1-4358-9332-8 lib bdg; 978-1-4358-9752-6 pa; 1-4358-9752-8 pa

Learn about all kinds of planes, including passenger planes, seaplanes, and planes used by the military.

"Clark has done a fine job of including meaningful content in a limited space. . . . [This] title consists of 10 two-page chapters printed in a font of an inviting size. Full-page photos–all color except one vintage photograph–with informative captions face two-paragraph text blocks. . . . Will make readers feel they have learned something." SLJ

Includes glossary

Graham, Ian

Aircraft; [by] Ian Graham. Black Rabbit Books 2009 32p il (How machines work) $18.95

Grades: 3 4 5   **629.133**

1. Airplanes

ISBN 978-1-59920-292-1; 1-59920-292-1

LC 2008002399

This "uses informational drawings, cutaway diagrams, and photos—including some dazzling shots of cockpit control panels. The layout is sufficiently busy to capture interest." Booklist

Hosking, Wayne

Asian kites. Tuttle 2005 63p il (Asian arts & crafts for creative kids) $12.95

Grades: 3 4 5 6   **629.133**

1. Kites 2. Handicraft

ISBN 0-8048-3545-4

"This survey offers brief anecdotes and legends along with carefully annotated construction diagrams for 15 simple kites commonly flown in Asia. . . . Closing with notes on running a kite-making workshop for children, lists of associations and sources of supplies, and a relatively extensive bibliography, this title merits, and will find, a wide audience in libraries large or small." SLJ

Keenan, Sheila

Jet plane; how it works. David Macaulay with Sheila Keenan. 1st ed. David Macaulay Studio 2012 28 p. col. ill. (My readers) (hardcover) $15.99; (paperback) $3.99

Grades: 2 3 4   **629.133**

1. Jet planes 2. Picture books for children 3. Jet planes

ISBN 1596437642; 1596437677; 9781596437647; 9781596437678

LC 2012289085

This book is part of David Macaulay's The Way Things Work series. This installment looks at the jet plane. "It weighs as much as 100 elephants, but it can fly for hours. How does a jet do that? From the engine that provides the power and wings that lift the plane off the ground to the cockpit controls and passenger cabin, see how these modern marvels work and what makes them stay in the air." (Publisher's note)

Includes bibliographical references and index

Nahum, Andrew

Flying machine; written by Andrew Nahum. rev ed; DK Pub. 2004 72p il (DK eyewitness books) $15.99; lib bdg $19.99

Grades: 4 5 6 7   **629.133**

1. Aeronautics -- History

ISBN 0-7566-0680-2; 0-7566-0679-9 lib bdg

First published 1990 by Knopf

A photo essay tracing the history and development of aircraft from hot-air balloons to jetliners. Includes information on the principles of flight and the inner workings of various flying machines.

Oxlade, Chris

Airplanes; uncovering technology. Firefly Books 2006 52p il $16.95

Grades: 4 5 6 7   **629.133**

1. Airplanes

ISBN 1-55407-134-8

This offers "appealing visuals and plenty of well-chosen facts." SLJ

Rau, Dana Meachen

Hot air balloons. Marshall Cavendish Benchmark 2010 24p il (Surprising science) lib bdg $22.79

Grades: 2 3 4   **629.133**

1. Balloons 2. Air-cushion vehicles

ISBN 978-0-7614-4873-0; 0-7614-4873-X

"Colorfully illustrated with photographs on each page, this . . . will be well received by elementary students and educators." Libr Media Connect

Includes glossary and bibliographical references

629.2   Motor land vehicles, cycles

Cooper, Wade

On the road. Cartwheel Books 2008 30p il (Scholastic reader) pa $3.99

Grades: PreK K 1   **629.2**

1. Vehicles

ISBN 978-0-545-00720-7 pa; 0-545-00720-8 pa

"Vehicles—from lumbering tractors and cement mixers to sleek sports cars—roll across the pages of this Level One entry in the Scholastic Reader series. Each spread combines a large, crisp color photo of a vehicle, with a banner of smaller photos. The rhyming sentences are well tuned for brand-new readers." Booklist

Includes glossary

Gifford, Clive

Things that go. Kingfisher 2011 32 p. ill. $10.99

Grades: 3 4 5   **629.2**

1. Motion 2. Physics 3. Transportation 4. Science -- Encyclopedias

ISBN 0753465930; 9780753465936

This illustrated children's book "uses a series of . . . story scenes to set the stage for a[n] . . . examination of the science behind motion. From the speed of racing, to transport on the rails, the science of heavy machinery, the physics of flight, and what keeps boats afloat. After readers absorb the elements of each story, they can explore the details through photographs and explanations on the following page. If they are interested in a particular aspect of transportation they can hop through the book following one of four icons related to their interest. Back matter offers plenty of resources for further multimedia exploration." (Publisher's note)

Mara, Wil

From locusts to...automobile anti-collision systems; by Wil Mara. Cherry Lake Pub. 2012 32 p. col. ill. (Innovations from nature) (library) $28.50; (e-book) $28.50; (paperback) $14.21

Grades: 4 5 6 7   **629.2**

1. Automobiles -- Collision avoidance systems 2. Locusts 3. Biomimicry

ISBN 1610805011; 9781610805018; 9781610805889; 9781610806756

LC 2012011856

"This . . . entry in the '21st Century Skills Innovation Library: Innovations from Nature' series explores how automobile manufacturers and scientists are trying to develop . . . collision avoidance systems based on the instincts of the humble locust, which has the ability to avoid oncoming objects while in a swarm. . . . [Wil] Mara describes the science of biomimicry, or 'the practice of copying nature--plants and animals--to build or improve something.'" (Booklist)

Includes bibliographical references (p. 31) and index.

Smith, Miranda

Speed machines; and other record-breaking vehicles. Kingfisher 2009 63p il (Kingfisher knowledge) $12.95

Grades: 5 6 7 8   **629.2**

1. Speed 2. Vehicles

ISBN 978-0-7534-6287-4; 0-7534-6287-7

"This well-organized, full-color book is packed with facts, photos, and history. It covers all aspects in history dealing with humankind's quest for speed, including land, water and air. . . . There are short blocks of main text and sidebars or blurbs to add additional information. Besides the usual suspects in books that cover this topic—cars, motorcycles, and planes—this book includes boats, gliders, hot air balloons, trains, and windsurfing among other speed machines. . . . It is an essential purchase, especially where books about racing, cars, planes, trucks, motorcycles, etc. are popular." Voice Youth Advocates

Includes glossary and bibliographical references

629.222   Gasoline-powered, oil-powered, man-powered vehicles

Benjamin, Daniel

Prius. Marshall Cavendish Benchmark 2010 47p il (Green cars) $28.50

Grades: 3 4 5 6   **629.222**

1. Electric automobiles

ISBN 978-1-60870-011-0; 1-60870-011-9

"The Prius is one of the first hybrids sold in America. . . . [The] book opens with [an] . . . introduction explaining how global warming and limited oil availability are among the factors reshaping automobile design and technology. The [book provides a] clear [explanation] of how hybrid and all-electrical vehicles operate. . . . Color photos in various sizes add visual appeal." SLJ

Includes glossary and bibliographical references

Clark, Willow

Cars on the move. PowerKids Press 2010 24p il (Transportation station) lib bdg $21.25; pa $8.25

Grades: 2 3   **629.222**

1. Automobiles

ISBN 978-1-4358-9333-7 lib bdg; 1-4358-9333-6 lib bdg; 978-1-4358-9754-0 pa; 1-4358-9754-4 pa

Explains how cars work and shows the many different types of cars.

"Clark has done a fine job of including meaningful content in a limited space. . . . [This] title consists of 10 two-page chapters printed in a font of an inviting size. Full-page photos–all color except one vintage photograph–with informative captions face two-paragraph text blocks. . . . Will make readers feel they have learned something." SLJ

Includes glossary

Crowther, Robert

Cars; a pop-up book of automobiles. Candlewick Press 2009 un il $17.99

Grades: K 1 2 3   629.222

1. Automobiles 2. Pop-up books

ISBN 978-0-7636-4448-2; 0-7636-4448-X

"This introduction to all things automotive begins with the earliest examples that can be considered cars, finishes with a nifty foldout track scene that doubles as both stock car and Formula One, and features an intelligent array of information on luxury, everyday, and record-breaking cars in between. Most of the moving pieces are sturdily designed . . . and go a long way toward adding some pizzazz to the straightforward text." Booklist

Juettner, Bonnie

Hybrid cars; by Bonnie Juettner. Norwood House Press 2009 48p il (A great idea) lib bdg $25.27

Grades: 3 4 5 6   629.222

1. Electric automobiles

ISBN 978-1-59953-193-9 lib bdg; 1-59953-193-3 lib bdg

LC 2008-22970

"Full-color photographs and copious fun facts help make this . . . enjoyable reading, but it's really the choice of [topic] that is so enthralling." Booklist

Includes glossary and bibliographical references

Lew, Kristi

Volt. Marshall Cavendish Benchmark 2010 47p il (Green cars) $28.50

Grades: 3 4 5 6   629.222

1. Electric automobiles

ISBN 978-1-60870-013-4; 1-60870-013-5

"The Volt is one of the first mass-produced cars to depend heavily on battery power. . . . [The] book opens with [an] . . . introduction explaining how global warming and limited oil availability are among the factors reshaping automobile design and technology. The [book provides a] clear [explanation] of how hybrid and all-electrical vehicles operate. . . . Color photos in various sizes add visual appeal." SLJ

Includes glossary and bibliographical references

Mitchell, Joyce Slayton

Crashed, smashed, and mashed; a trip to junkyard heaven. photographs by Steven Borns. Tricycle Press 2001 un il hardcover o.p. pa $7.95

Grades: 3 4 5 6   629.222

1. Salvage 2. Automobiles

ISBN 1-58246-034-5; 1-58246-156-2 pa

LC 00-10713

This describes an automobile junkyard where old cars are salvaged for parts and scrap metal

This book offers "excellent, clear, close-up photographs and a wealth of facts." Booklist

Includes glossary

Niver, Heather Moore

Camaros. Gareth Stevens Pub. 2011 32p il (Wild wheels) lib bdg $26.60; pa $10.50

Grades: 3 4 5 6   629.222

1. Automobiles

ISBN 978-1-4339-4735-3 lib bdg; 1-4339-4735-8 lib bdg; 978-1-4339-4736-0 pa; 1-4339-4736-6 pa

LC 2010032883

This book about Camaro automobiles "is sure to be . . . popular. . . . The light, somewhat breezy [text moves] quickly, presenting the history of the cars and just the right amount of information. . . . The bright, colorful illustrations are excellent. . . . A first purchase." SLJ

Includes glossary and bibliographical references

GTOs. Gareth Stevens Pub. 2011 32p il (Wild wheels) lib bdg $26.60; pa $10.50

Grades: 3 4 5 6   629.222

1. Automobiles

ISBN 978-1-4339-4747-6 lib bdg; 1-4339-4747-1 lib bdg; 978-1-4339-4748-3 pa; 1-4339-4748-X pa

LC 2010037589

This book about GTO automobiles "is sure to be . . . popular. . . . The light, somewhat breezy [text moves] quickly, presenting the history of the cars and just the right amount of information. . . . The bright, colorful illustrations are excellent. . . . A first purchase." SLJ

Includes glossary and bibliographical references

Portman, Michael

Chargers. Gareth Stevens Pub. 2011 32p il (Wild wheels) lib bdg $26.60; pa $10.50

Grades: 3 4 5 6   629.222

1. Automobiles

ISBN 978-1-4339-4739-1 lib bdg; 1-4339-4739-0 lib bdg; 978-1-4339-4740-7 pa; 1-4339-4740-4 pa

LC 2010035555

This book about Dodge Charger automobiles "is sure to be . . . popular. . . . The light, somewhat breezy [text moves] quickly, presenting the history of the cars and just the right amount of information. . . . The bright, colorful illustrations are excellent. . . . A first purchase." SLJ

Includes glossary and bibliographical references

Chevelles. Gareth Stevens Pub. 2011 32p il (Wild wheels) lib bdg $26.60; pa $10.50

Grades: 3 4 5 6   629.222

1. Automobiles

ISBN 978-1-4339-4743-8 lib bdg; 1-4339-4743-9 lib bdg; 978-1-4339-4744-5 pa; 1-4339-4744-7 pa

LC 2010038391

This book about Chevelle automobiles "is sure to be . . . popular. . . . The light, somewhat breezy [text moves] quickly, presenting the history of the cars and just the right amount of information. . . . The bright, colorful illustrations are excellent. . . . A first purchase." SLJ

Includes glossary and bibliographical references

Mustangs. Gareth Stevens Pub. 2011 32p il (Wild wheels) lib bdg $26.60; pa $10.50

Grades: 3 4 5 6   629.222
1. Automobiles
ISBN 978-1-4339-4751-3 lib bdg; 1-4339-4751-X lib bdg; 978-1-4339-4752-0 pa; 1-4339-4752-8 pa
LC 2010037587

This book about Ford Mustang automobiles "is sure to be . . . popular. . . . The light, somewhat breezy [text moves] quickly, presenting the history of the cars and just the right amount of information. . . . The bright, colorful illustrations are excellent. . . . A first purchase." SLJ

Includes glossary and bibliographical references

Torinos. Gareth Stevens Pub. 2011 32p il (Wild wheels) lib bdg $26.60; pa $10.50
Grades: 3 4 5 6   629.222
1. Automobiles
ISBN 978-1-4339-4755-1 lib bdg; 1-4339-4755-2 lib bdg; 978-1-4339-4756-8 pa; 1-4339-4756-0 pa
LC 2010039151

This book about Torino automobiles "is sure to be . . . popular. . . . The light, somewhat breezy [text moves] quickly, presenting the history of the cars and just the right amount of information. . . . The bright, colorful illustrations are excellent. . . . A first purchase." SLJ

Includes glossary and bibliographical references

Steggall, Susan
The **life** of a car. Henry Holt & Co. 2008 un il $16.95
Grades: PreK K 1 2   629.222
1. Automobiles
ISBN 0-8050-8747-8

"With torn-paper collages in saturated color and just three words for every spread except the last, Steggall presents the life cycle of a car from its manufacture to its destruction and recycling, when the process begins anew." SLJ

Swanson, Jennifer
★ **How** hybrid cars work; illustrated by Glen Mullaly. Child's World 2011 il (How things work) lib bdg $28.50
Grades: 4 5 6   629.222
1. Electric automobiles
ISBN 1-60973-217-0; 978-1-60973-217-2
LC 2011010917

This volume "is bouncy, savvy, and, above all, clear; it is hard to come away without a working knowledge of everything from the mechanics of hybrid engines to why dependence on foreign oil is bad. Hosting the series are two cartoons—a robot and a caveman—especially apt choices for a book couched in the concept of discarding old energy sources for new. . . . This is a model of how to make science appeal to young readers."

This volume "is bouncy, savvy, and, above all, clear; it is hard to come away without a working knowledge of everything from the mechanics of hybrid engines to why dependence on foreign oil is bad. Hosting the series are two cartoons—a robot and a caveman—especially apt choices for a book couched in the concept of discarding old energy sources for new. . . . This is a model of how to make science appeal to young readers." Booklist

Includes bibliographical references

Warhol, Tom
Aptera. Marshall Cavendish Benchmark 2010 47p il (Green cars) $28.50

Grades: 3 4 5 6   629.222
1. Electric automobiles
ISBN 978-1-60870-008-0; 1-60870-008-9

"The futuristic Aptera appeared in a 'Star Trek' film. . . . [The] book opens with [an] . . . introduction explaining how global warming and limited oil availability are among the factors reshaping automobile design and technology. The [book provides a] clear [explanation] of how hybrid and all-electrical vehicles operate. . . . Color photos in various sizes add visual appeal." SLJ

Includes glossary and bibliographical references

Wheeler, Jill C.
Alternative cars; [by] Jill C. Wheeler. ABDO 2008 32p il (Eye on energy) $16.95
Grades: 3 4 5   629.222
1. Alternative fuel vehicles
ISBN 978-1-59928-803-1; 1-59928-803-6
LC 2007007107

This "begins with an explantion of the internal-combustion engine and its shortcomings. Wheeler then introduces readers to more efficient methods of powering automobiles, including electricity, a combination of gas and electricty, diesel fuel, hydrogen, natural gas, and ethanol. For each alternative she describes advantages, disadvantages, and the current availability of this technology. Captioned, full-color photographs . . . appear on nearly every page, complementing the clearly written text." Booklist

Includes glossary

Williams, Brian
Who invented the automobile? Arcturus Pub. 2010 46p il (Breakthroughs in science and technology) lib bdg $32.80
Grades: 5 6 7 8   629.222
1. Engines 2. Automobiles
ISBN 978-1-84837-681-6; 1-84837-681-2
LC 2010011019

Examines the history of the automobile.

This book is "divided into easy to read short chapters with large, colorful photographs and graphics on every page. . . . The added inserts provide additional information to engage readers and help them connect with the scientific details." Libr Media Connect

Woods, Bob
Hottest muscle cars; by Bob Woods. Enslow Publishers 2008 48p il (Wild wheels!) lib bdg $23.93; pa $7.95
Grades: 4 5 6 7   629.222
1. Automobiles
ISBN 978-0-7660-2872-2 lib bdg; 0-7660-2872-0 lib bdg; 978-0-7660-3611-6 pa; 0-7660-3611-1 pa
LC 2007007423

This focuses on "the beginning of America's love for muscle cars, and see why they are still loved today." Publisher's note

Includes glossary and bibliographical references

Hottest sports cars; by Bob Woods. Enslow Publishers 2008 48p il (Wild wheels!) lib bdg $23.93; pa $7.95

Grades: 4 5 6 7 **629.222**
1. Automobiles
ISBN 978-0-7660-2873-9 lib bdg; 0-7660-2873-9 lib bdg; 978-0-7660-3609-3 pa; 0-7660-3909-X pa
LC 2007007428

This focuses on "some of the world's most famous sports cars; how they began, and where they are going in the future." Publisher's note

Includes glossary and bibliographical references

Zabludoff, Marc
Ebox. Marshall Cavendish Benchmark 2010 47p il (Green cars) $28.50
Grades: 3 4 5 6 **629.222**
1. Electric automobiles
ISBN 978-1-60870-009-7; 1-60870-009-7

"The all-electric Ebox is a conversion of the gasoline-powered Toyota Scion XB. [The] book opens with [an] . . . introduction explaining how global warming and limited oil availability are among the factors reshaping automobile design and technology. The [book provides a] clear [explanation] of how hybrid and all-electrical vehicles operate. . . . Color photos in various sizes add visual appeal." SLJ

Includes glossary and bibliographical references

629.224 Trucks (Lorries)

Barton, Byron
★ Trucks. Crowell 1986 un il lib bdg $15.89
Grades: PreK K 1 **629.224**
1. Trucks
ISBN 0-690-04530-1
LC 85-47901

Brief text and illustrations present a variety of trucks from cement trucks to ice-cream trucks, and what they do

"A tightly focused (book) . . . featuring Barton's trademark bright, blocky graphics and spare text." Publ Wkly

Lindeen, Mary
Trucks; by Mary Lindeen. Bellwether Media 2007 24p il (Mighty machines) lib bdg $18.50
Grades: PreK K 1 2 3 **629.224**
1. Trucks
ISBN 978-1-60014-063-1 lib bdg; 1-60014-063-7 lib bdg
LC 2006035265

This explains what a truck is and describes its major parts and that they do.

The glossary features "easy-to-read-and-understand definitions. . . . With [its] exciting, full-color photos on every spread, [this] will certainly appeal to the mighty curiosity of young readers." SLJ

Includes glossary and bibliographical references

Maass, Robert
Little trucks with big jobs; [by] Robert Maass. Henry Holt & Co. 2007 un il $16.95
Grades: PreK K **629.224**
1. Trucks
ISBN 978-0-8050-7748-3; 0-8050-7748-0
LC 2006030617

"Children are introduced to 15 little rigs and the important work they do. Simple, clear explanations accompany each full-page photograph. . . . Bright, primary colored backgrounds frame the pictures, and the text appears inside road-sign shapes. This high-interest book is sure to be popular with vehicle fans." SLJ

Mara, Wil
Trucks. National Geographic 2009 32p il (National Geographic readers) $12.99; pa $3.99
Grades: K 1 2 **629.224**
1. Trucks
ISBN 978-1-4263-0527-6; 1-4263-0527-3; 978-1-4263-0526-9 pa; 1-4263-0526-5 pa
LC 2009-21037

"Mara describes truck parts and their functions in brief, simple text for early readers. Colorful close-up photographs dominate each spread, often using arrows to point to and clarify labeled parts." Horn Book Guide

Murrell, Deborah Jane
Mega trucks. Tangerine Press 2008 32p il $6.99
Grades: PreK K 1 2 **629.224**
1. Trucks
ISBN 0-439-85056-8
First published in 2005 by Scholastic

"Discusses the parts and functions of different kinds of trucks, including tractor-trailers, loaders, and monster trucks." Publisher's note

Ransom, Candice F.
Big rigs on the move; [by] Candice Ransom. Lerner Publications 2011 32p il (Lightning Bolt Books. Vroom-vroom) lib bdg $25.26
Grades: K 1 2 **629.224**
1. Trucks
ISBN 978-0-7613-3919-9 lib bdg; 0-7613-3919-1 lib bdg
LC 2009-39738

This book about big rigs has "big, high-energy color photos. . . . [The text provides] lively commentary in a mix of declarative statements and non-rhetorical questions. . . . [The] volume closes with a labeled diagram, a page of 'fun facts,' and a short list of print and web resources. . . . [This] will make a worthwhile and popular addition." SLJ

Includes glossary and bibliographical references

Stille, Darlene R.
Trucks. Children's Press 1997 47p il (True book) lib bdg $22; pa $6.95
Grades: 2 3 4 **629.224**
1. Trucks
ISBN 0-516-20343-6 lib bdg; 0-516-26179-7 pa
LC 96-25727

Describes different kinds of trucks, including tractor trailers and tank trucks, pick-ups, tow trucks, fire trucks, garbage trucks, vans, and recreational vehicles

Includes bibliographical references

Zuehlke, Jeffrey
Pickup trucks on the move. Lerner Publications 2010 32p il (Lightning bolt books. Vroom-vroom) lib bdg $25.26

Grades: K 1 2   **629.224**
1. Trucks
ISBN 978-0-7613-6024-7 lib bdg; 0-7613-6024-7
lib bdg

LC 2009039747

This book about pickup trucks has "big, high-energy
color photos. . . . [The text provides] lively commentary in a
mix of declarative statements and non-rhetorical questions.
. . . [The] volume closes with a labeled diagram, a page of
'fun facts,' and a short list of print and web resources. . . .
[This] will make a worthwhile and popular addition." SLJ

Includes glossary and bibliographical references

629.225   Work vehicles

Abramson, Andra Serlin
  ★ Heavy equipment up close; [by] Andra Serlin
Abramson. Sterling Pub. Co. 2008 47p il (Up close)
$9.95
Grades: 2 3 4   **629.225**
1. Construction equipment
ISBN 978-1-4027-4799-1; 1-4027-4799-3

LC 2007019277

This is "packed with full-color photographs on pages
measuring about 10 1/2 x 14 inches, many of which open
out into eye-popping gatefolds. This . . . title is tailor-made
for children known to gaze longingly at construction sites.
Even preschoolers will enjoy the photos . . . but children
who can read on their own, or sit still through each page's
several pages of text, will get the most out the book's terrific
mix of fun and technical vocabulary." Booklist

Lindeen, Mary
  Tractors; by Mary Lindeen. Bellwether Media 2007
24p il (Mighty machines) lib bdg $18.50
Grades: PreK K 1 2 3   **629.225**
1. Tractors
ISBN 978-1-60014-061-7 lib bdg; 1-60014-061-0
lib bdg

LC 2006035263

This explains what a tractor is and discusses its major
parts and what they do.

The glossary features "easy-to-read-and-understand
definitions. . . . With [its] exciting, full-color photos on every spread, [this] colorful [title] will certainly appeal to the
mighty curiosity of young readers." SLJ

Includes glossary and bibliographical references

629.227   Cycles

Clark, Willow
  Bikes on the move. PowerKids Press 2010 24p il
(Transportation station) lib bdg $21.25; pa $8.25
Grades: 2 3   **629.227**
1. Cycling 2. Bicycles
ISBN 978-1-4358-9334-4 lib bdg; 1-4358-9334-4 lib
bdg; 978-1-4358-9756-4 pa; 1-4358-9756-0 pa
Learn about mountain bikes, racing bikes and
lowrider bikes.

"Clark has done a fine job of including meaningful content in a limited space. . . . [This] title consists of 10 two-

page chapters printed in a font of an inviting size. Full-page
photos–all color except one vintage photograph–with informative captions face two-paragraph text blocks. . . . Will
make readers feel they have learned something." SLJ

Includes glossary

Motorcycles on the move. PowerKids Press 2010 24p
il (Transportation station) lib bdg $21.25; pa $8.25
Grades: 2 3   **629.227**
1. Motorcycles
ISBN 978-1-4358-9335-1 lib bdg; 1-4358-9335-2 lib
bdg; 978-1-4358-9758-8 pa; 1-4358-9758-7 pa
Introduces the various kinds of motorcycles and
their uses.

"Clark has done a fine job of including meaningful content in a limited space. . . . [This] title consists of 10 two-
page chapters printed in a font of an inviting size. Full-page
photos–all color except one vintage photograph–with informative captions face two-paragraph text blocks. . . . Will
make readers feel they have learned something." SLJ

Includes glossary

Gibbons, Gail
  Bicycle book. Holiday House 1995 un il $16.95;
pa $6.95
Grades: K 1 2 3   **629.227**
1. Cycling 2. Bicycles
ISBN 0-8234-1199-0; 0-8234-1408-6 pa

LC 95-5911

"The history of bicycles, the science behind their design,
descriptions of different types, their care, and safety rules are
all clearly and simply presented in Gibbons's typical, inimitable style. Lots of color, accurate explanations, and interesting facts make this a winning choice." SLJ

Haduch, Bill
  ★ Go fly a bike! the ultimate book about bicycle fun,
freedom & science. illustrated by Chris Murphy. Dutton
Children's Books 2004 83p il $16.99
Grades: 4 5 6 7   **629.227**
1. Cycling 2. Bicycles
ISBN 0-525-47024-7
Gives the history, science, types of cycles, safety and the
basics and maintenance of bicycles

"Halftone cartoonlike illustrations are scattered throughout, and a funny fact or joke appears in an inset on most
pages. . . . This is a versatile, fact-packed book that can work
for both research and recreational reading." Booklist

Smedman, Lisa
  From boneshakers to choppers; the rip-roaring history
of motorcycles. Annick Press 2007 120p il $24.95; pa
$14.95
Grades: 5 6 7 8   **629.227**
1. Motorcycles
ISBN 978-1-55451-016-0; 1-55451-016-3; 978-1-
55451-015-3 pa; 1-55451-015-5 pa
"Smedman defines 'motorcycles' broadly enough to include everything from Harleys to Vespas, and even bicycles,
in this lively, wide-ranging history. . . . Illustrated with a
generous array of action photos, historical shots, and period
advertisements." Booklist

Includes bibliographical references

Woods, Bob

Hottest motorcycles; by Bob Woods. Enslow Publishers 2008 48p il (Wild wheels!) lib bdg $23.93; pa $7.95
Grades: 4 5 6 7   **629.227**

1. Motorcycles

ISBN 978-0-7660-2874-6 lib bdg; 0-7660-2874-7 lib bdg; 978-0-7660-3608-6 pa; 0-7660-3608-1 pa

LC 2007007425

This focuses on "the motorcycle's beginning, the chopper phenomenon, and motorcycle racing." Publisher's note

Includes bibliographical references

629.228   Racing cars

Rex, Michael

My race car. Holt & Co. 2000 un il lib bdg $15.95
Grades: PreK K 1   **629.228**

1. Automobiles 2. Automobile racing

ISBN 0-8050-6101-0

LC 99-31773

"'I have a race car. I drive it all the time,' says a boy sitting on the floor with his toy cars. As the pages turn, the toy world becomes reality: the boy finds himself on the track with his crew, checking his car engine, and then driving his laps. . . . Short, simple sentences create excitement . . . and Rex's bright, thick-lined cartoon drawings are appealingly energetic and clear. A great choice for young race car enthusiasts who are beginning to read on their own." Booklist

Sandler, Michael

Dynamic drag racers. Bearport Pub. 2011 24p il (Fast rides) lib bdg $22.61
Grades: 3 4 5 6   **629.228**

1. Automobiles 2. Automobile racing

ISBN 978-1-61772-138-0; 1-61772-138-7

LC 2010041872

This describes different types of vehicles used in drag races including top fuel dragsters, pro stock motorcycles, funny cars, and exhibition wheelstanders.

"Sharp, colorful photos and [a] succinct [text provides a] brief but informative [introduction] to record-setting vehicles. . . . This [book] deserves first consideration." SLJ

Includes glossary and bibliographical references

Electrifying eco-race cars. Bearport Pub. 2011 24p il (Fast rides) lib bdg $22.61
Grades: 3 4 5 6   **629.228**

1. Automobile racing 2. Electric automobiles

ISBN 978-1-61772-137-3; 1-61772-137-9

LC 2010040095

This describes earth-friendly race cars including hydrogen-fueled cars that can reach speeds of over 300 miles per hour and wind-powered speedsters that don't use a motor.

"Sharp, colorful photos and [a] succinct [text provides a] brief but informative [introduction] to record-setting vehicles. . . . This [book] deserves first consideration." SLJ

Includes glossary and bibliographical references

Hot hot rods. Bearport Pub. 2011 24p il (Fast rides) lib bdg $22.61

Grades: 3 4 5 6   **629.228**

1. Automobiles 2. Automobile racing

ISBN 978-1-61772-139-7; 1-61772-139-5

LC 2010041875

This describes hot rods including modified 1930s Ford cars, such as the "Deuce" roadster and classic Model T, VW Bugs and pumped-up pickup trucks.

"Sharp, colorful photos and [a] succinct [text provides a] brief but informative [introduction] to record-setting vehicles. . . . This [book] deserves first consideration." SLJ

Includes glossary and bibliographical references

Jet-powered speed. Bearport Pub. 2011 24p il (Fast rides) lib bdg $22.61
Grades: 3 4 5 6   **629.228**

1. Jet propulsion 2. Automobile racing

ISBN 978-1-61772-136-6; 1-61772-136-0

LC 2010037210

This describes jet-powered cars such as the Thrust2, which broke speed records using a huge jet engine that came from a British fighter plane, and the ThrustSCC which traveled faster than the speed of sound.

"Sharp, colorful photos and [a] succinct [text provides a] brief but informative [introduction] to record-setting vehicles. . . . This [book] deserves first consideration." SLJ

Includes glossary and bibliographical references

629.4   Astronautics

Aldrin, Buzz

Look to the stars. G. P. Putnam's Sons 2009 40p il $17.99
Grades: 2 3 4   **629.4**

1. Astronautics 2. Space flight 3. Outer space

ISBN 978-0-399-24721-7; 0-399-24721-1

LC 2008018575

This is "a quick overview of the past and near future of human space flight. Paired with Minor's clean-lined, realistically detailed scenes of significant aircraft, spacecraft, and high spots, [the] narrative opens with Galileo, [and] closes with the rousing suggestion that the opportunity to venture into space lies just a tantalizing few years down the road for many young readers." SLJ

Includes glossary and bibliographical references

Barchers, Suzanne I.

Revolution in space. Marshall Cavendish Benchmark 2010 32p il (It works!) lib bdg $19.95
Grades: 3 4 5   **629.4**

1. Astronautics 2. Outer space -- Exploration

ISBN 978-0-7614-4377-3 lib bdg; 0-7614-4377-0 lib bdg

LC 2008-54365

"This interesting, information packed [book] . . . . motivates students to do their own exploring. . . . [The] book starts with an invention from long ago and gradually builds on it. The scientist famous for each invention is highlighted; the brief synopsis shares his interests growing up. The ideas that ultimately inspired the invention are shown in visual 'idea clouds' sharing the process with students. Timelines show that the inventions not only took creative thought, they also took perseverance. The appealing cartoon-like photographs add humor. . . . This . . . just may be that spark needed to create eager budding scientists." Libr Media Connection

Includes glossary and bibliographical references

Benoit, Peter

The **space** race; by Peter Benoit. Children's Press 2012 64 p. ill. (some col.) (library) $30.00; (paperback) $8.95

Grades: 4 5 6   **629.4**

1. Astronautics -- United States 2. Space flight 3. Astronautics -- Soviet Union -- History

ISBN 0531281655; 9780531230657; 9780531281659

LC 2011031454

This book by Peter Benoit is part of the "Cornerstones of Freedom" series. It "attempts to provide an historical overview of the race between the United States and Soviet Union to explore space. . . . The book ends with a map . . . a . . . list of influential individuals, a timeline, and a glossary." (Children's Literature)

Includes bibliographical references (p. 60-61) and index.

Bortz, Alfred B.

Seven wonders of space technology; by Fred Bortz. Twenty-First Century Books 2011 80p il (Seven wonders) lib bdg $33.26; ebook $24.95

Grades: 5 6 7 8   **629.4**

1. Astronautics 2. Space vehicles 3. Outer space -- Exploration

ISBN 978-0-7613-5453-6 lib bdg; 0-7613-5453-0 lib bdg; 9780761372806

LC 2010-23996

This book examines the science involved in the Great Observatories, the International Space Station, New Horizons, Moon bases and lunar water, Mars rovers, rocketry, and weather satellites. Glossary. Index. "Grades seven to twelve." (Sci Books Films)

"Highlights some of astronomy's greatest technical advancements, from land observatories to spinning satellites to moon bases. . . . [This] volume makes basic concepts clear in lively, energetic language that, along with the mesmerizing color photos and artists' renderings of space, will easily captivate a young audience, while up-to-date examples, including discoveries made in the last five years, will only increase the sense of immediacy and excitement." Booklist

Includes glossary and bibliographical references

Harris, Joseph

Space exploration; impact of science and technology. Gareth Stevens Pub. 2010 64p il map (Pros and cons) lib bdg $35

Grades: 5 6 7 8   **629.4**

1. Astronautics 2. Outer space -- Exploration

ISBN 978-1-4339-1989-3 lib bdg; 1-4339-1989-3 lib bdg

LC 2009-12436

"This book examines the politics of space—the space race, weapons in space, and international cooperation, the realities of living in space, the uses of satellites and space probes, space age technologies that changed life on Earth, the future of space exploration, from space tourism to space elevators." Publisher's note

Includes glossary and bibliographical references

Houran, Lori Haskins

A **trip** into space; An Adventure to the International Space Station. Lori Haskins Houran; illustrated by Francisca Marquez. Albert Whitman & Company 2014 24 p. $15.99

Grades: PreK K 1   **629.4**

1. Astronauts 2. Space flight 3. International Space Station

ISBN 0807580910; 9780807580912

LC 2013033073

This children's book, by Lori Haskins Houran, is a "look at life on the International Space Station. . . . It features . . . full-bleed illustrations," by Francisca Marquez, "of astronauts loading supplies, taking a space walk, eating, sleeping, etc." (School Library Journal)

"Although scientifically slight, this book adeptly captures some of the key personal experiences of astronauts on the International Space Station, from blastoff to zipping themselves into stationary sleeping bags at bedtime. Understated verse is illustrated with approachable illustrations that reinforce such details as straps to hold down food. Additional information on each rhymed heading ("Whipping through space"; "Flipping in space") is appended." Horn Book Guide Review

Jedicke, Peter

Great moments in space exploration. Chelsea House 2007 72p il (Scientific American) $30

Grades: 5 6 7 8   **629.4**

1. Astronautics 2. Outer space -- Exploration

ISBN 978-0-7910-9046-6; 0-7910-9046-9

LC 2006-14774

This "introduction to the history of space exploration is well illustrated with numerous photos, many from NASA. The history is well told, with the achievements of the Soviet Union, in particular, covered quite nicely." Sci Books Films

Includes glossary and bibliographical references

Skurzynski, Gloria

★ **This** is rocket science; true stories of the risk-taking scientists who figure out ways to explore beyond Earth. National Geographic 2010 80p il $18.95; lib bdg $28.90

Grades: 5 6 7 8   **629.4**

1. Rocketry 2. Aeronautics 3. Aerospace engineers

ISBN 978-1-4263-0597-9; 1-4263-0597-4; 978-1-4263-0598-6 lib bdg; 1-4263-0598-2 lib bdg

LC 2009-20386

"This concise book provides a historical, as well as contemporary, introduction to the field of aeronautical engineering with a decidedly human interest perspective. . . . This text will be a great introduction to many of the significant contributors to the field of rocket science." Sci Books Films

Includes glossary and bibliographical references

Stott, Carole

Space exploration; written by Carole Stott; photographed by Steve Gorton. Dorling Kindersley 2009 71p il (DK eyewitness books) $16.99

Grades: 4 5 6 7   **629.4**

1. Astronautics 2. Outer space -- Exploration

ISBN 978-0-7566-5828-1; 0-7566-5828-4

First published 1997 by Knopf

Describes rockets, exploratory vehicles, and other technological aspects of space exploration, satellites, space stations, and the life and work of astronauts.

629.43 Unmanned space flight

Jefferis, David

Space probes; exploring beyond Earth. Crabtree Pub. 2009 32p il (Exploring our solar system) lib bdg $26.60; pa $8.95

Grades: 3 4 5 **629.43**

1. Space probes

ISBN 978-0-7787-3724-7 lib bdg; 0-7787-3724-1 lib bdg; 978-0-7787-3741-4 pa; 0-7787-3741-1 pa

LC 2008-46249

"The author explains what space probes are for, names many that have visited each of the major planets, and then suggests where models and mock-ups (since they can't be observed directly) might be found. . . . [The book is] designed with easily digestible blocks of question-and-answer text sharing page space with large, sharply reproduced space photos and graphic art." SLJ

Includes glossary

Miller, Ron

Robot explorers. Twenty-First Century Books 2007 112p il (Space innovations) lib bdg $31.93

Grades: 4 5 6 **629.43**

1. Robots 2. Space probes

ISBN 978-0-8225-7152-0 lib bdg; 0-8225-7152-8 lib bdg

LC 2007002864

This describes how robots are used for space exploration

Includes bibliographical references

Siy, Alexandra

★ Cars on Mars; roving the red planet. Charlesbridge 2009 57p il $18.95

Grades: 5 6 7 8 **629.43**

1. Space vehicles 2. Mars (Planet) -- Exploration

ISBN 978-1-57091-462-1; 1-57091-462-1

LC 2008-40751

Presents an introduction to the Mars Exploration Rovers (MERS), 'Spirit' and 'Opportunity,' with photographs of the Mars landscape taken over a five-year period as the rovers searched for water on the red planet

"This title will sweep readers up in an exploratory mission that has come closer than any other so far to finding sure signs of extraterrestrial life." SLJ

Includes glossary and bibliographical references

629.44 Auxiliary spacecraft

Branley, Franklyn Mansfield

The International Space Station; by Franklyn M. Branley; illustrated by True Kelley. HarperCollins Pubs. 2000 32p il (Let's-read-and-find-out science) hardcover o.p. pa $5.95

Grades: K 1 2 3 **629.44**

1. Astronauts 2. Space stations

ISBN 0-06-028702-0; 0-06-445209-3 pa

LC 99-31897

Explains the construction and purpose of the International Space Station and the life of the astronauts on board

"The facts, including a history and background of the station and descriptions of life in space, are presented in a clear, easy-to-read manner. . . . Kelley's clearly labeled drawings and configurations reinforce the concepts presented, and the watercolor illustrations add dimension to the presentation." SLJ

Cole, Michael D.

The Columbia space shuttle disaster; from first liftoff to tragic final flight. Enslow Pubs. 2003 48p il (Countdown to space) lib bdg $18.95

Grades: 4 5 6 **629.44**

1. Space vehicle accidents 2. Columbia (Space shuttle)

ISBN 0-7660-2295-1

LC 2003-4823

First published 1995 with title: Columbia

Details the first flight of the space shuttle Columbia, as well as its tragic final flight

"The account offers a lot of information, helping to make sense of a highly complicated subject. . . . The color and b&w photographs complement the story." Libr Media Connect

Includes glossary and bibliographical references

NASA space vehicles; capsules, shuttles, and space stations. Enslow Pubs. 2000 48p il (Countdown to space) lib bdg $18.95

Grades: 4 5 6 7 **629.44**

1. Space vehicles 2. Outer space -- Exploration

ISBN 0-7660-1308-1

LC 99-35533

Describes American space vehicles and their uses, including various space probes, the Mercury, Gemini, and Apollo capsules, Skylab, the space shuttles, and the International Space Station

Includes glossary and bibliographical references

Holden, Henry M.

The coolest job in the universe; working aboard the International Space Station. Henry M. Holden. Enslow 2013 48 p. (American space missions, astronauts, exploration, and discovery) (hbk.) $23.93

Grades: 4 5 6 7 8 **629.44**

1. International Space Station 2. Space flight 3. Space sciences 4. Manned space flight 5. Space sciences -- Research

ISBN 0766040747; 9780766040748

LC 2012002222

This book, by Henry M. Holden, is part of the "American Space Missions: Astronauts, Exploration, and Discovery" series. In it the daily life of astronauts working on the International Space Station is explored. This book "focuses on the construction of the ISS, what life is like onboard, and the importance of the research projects conducted. . . . Throughout, the courage, dedication, and sacrifice of the astronauts are emphasized." (School Library Journal)

Includes bibliographical references (p. 43-45, 47) and index

Kerrod, Robin

Space stations; [by] Robin Kerrod. World Almanac Library 2005 48p il (History of space exploration) hardcover o.p. lib bdg $30

Grades: 5 6 7 8   **629.44**

1. Space stations

ISBN 0-8368-5710-0 lib bdg; 0-8368-5717-8 pa

LC 2004-49071

Explores the history of space homes such as the Soviet's Salyut 1, Mir, the United States's Skylab, and the International Space Station, a truly international venture between several countries and scheduled for completion in 2008

This "is profusely illustrated with sharply reproduced space photos and artists' conceptions. . . . [This] makes an important addition for any collection supporting avid young scientists or strong science curricula." SLJ

Includes bibliographical references

Waxman, Laura Hamilton

Exploring the International Space Station. Lerner Publications 2011 40p il (What's amazing about space?) lib bdg $27.23

Grades: 4 5 6   **629.44**

1. Astronautics 2. Space stations

ISBN 978-0-7613-5443-7; 0-7613-5443-3

LC 2010035394

This describes how the International Space Station was built and how crew members live and work there.

This book is "written in simple language, [and] illustrated nicely. . . . The information presented is factually correct. . . . Every page includes a well-chosen illustration or photograph." Sci Books Films

Includes glossary and bibliographical references

629.45   Manned space flight

Bodden, Valerie

Man walks on the Moon. Creative Education 2009 48p il map (Days of change) $32.80

Grades: 5 6 7 8   **629.45**

1. Space flight to the moon 2. Project Apollo

ISBN 978-1-58341-735-5; 1-58341-735-4

LC 2008009166

"With elegant design and mature prose, the Days of Change series is an ideal starting point for all manner of school projects. . . . The very first page of Man Walks on the Moon questions whether or not the feat was worth the resources, before reveling in the tech-heavy details of spaceflight and offering up some telling photos." Booklist

Includes bibliographical references

To the moon; by Valerie Bodden. Creative Education 2011 48 p. col. ill. (Great expeditions) (paperback) $12.00; (hardcover) $34.25

Grades: 5 6 7 8   **629.45**

1. Apollo project 2. Space flight to the moon -- History 3. Project Apollo (U.S.) -- History 4. Space flight to the moon -- History

ISBN 1608180689; 9780898126662; 9781608180684

LC 2010033549

This book by Valerie Bodden on the 1969 moon landing is part of the "Great Expeditions" series. "This factual

account is . . . accompanied with both black and white and color photographs. Profiles of four of the astronauts, reproductions of some of their significant journal entries, and inset boxes of supplemental information aid in understanding. Includes a table of contents, a timeline, end notes, a bibliography, and an index." (Children's Literature)

Includes bibliographical references (p. 46-47) and index.

Branley, Franklyn Mansfield

Floating in space; by Franklyn M. Branley; illustrated by True Kelley. HarperCollins Pubs. 1998 32p il (Let's-read-and-find-out science) hardcover o.p. pa $4.95

Grades: K 1 2 3   **629.45**

1. Astronauts 2. Space shuttles

ISBN 0-06-025433-5 lib bdg; 0-06-445142-9 pa

LC 97-13052

Examines life aboard a space shuttle, describing how astronauts deal with weightlessness, how they eat and exercise, some of the work they do, and more

"This is a beautifully illustrated children's book. . . . The textual information is clearly written, easy to read, and well organized." Sci Books Films

Mission to Mars; by Franklyn M. Branley; illustrated by True Kelley; foreword by Neil Armstrong. HarperCollins Pubs. 2002 33p il (Let's-read-and-find-out science) hardcover o.p. lib bdg $17.89; pa $4.99

Grades: K 1 2 3   **629.45**

1. Space flight to Mars 2. Mars (Planet) -- Exploration

ISBN 0-06-029807-3; 0-06-029808-1 lib bdg; 0-06-445233-6 pa

LC 00-54036

The author invites readers to envision "themselves as members of the first Mars Mission's crew. . . . Along with a sprinkling of black-and-white and full-color photos, the illustrations mix clearly drawn schematics with scenes of crew members working busily inside the Mars Station or outside in heavy protective suits. An informative, inspirational introduction." SLJ

Bredeson, Carmen

What do astronauts do. Enslow Elementary 2008 32p il (I like space!) lib bdg $22.60

Grades: K 1 2 3   **629.45**

1. Astronautics

ISBN 978-0-7660-2942-2 lib bdg; 0-7660-2942-5 lib bdg

LC 2007-02742

This book "is beautifully illustrated, with photographs from NASA and other sources, and is well organized." Sci Books Films

Includes bibliographical references

Burleigh, Robert

★ One giant leap; paintings by Mike Wimmer. Philomel Books 2009 un il $16.99

Grades: 1 2 3   **629.45**

1. Astronautics 2. Apollo project 3. Space flight to the moon 4. Project Apollo (U.S.) -- History

ISBN 978-0-399-23883-3; 0-399-23883-2

LC 2008-15695

"Distinguished language and compelling imagery make this commemoration of the first Moon landing's 40th anniversary particularly intense. . . . The sense of immediacy is irresistible." SLJ

Chaikin, Andrew

★ **Mission** control, this is Apollo; the story of the first voyages to the moon. [by] Andrew Chaikin, with Victoria Kohl; [with paintings by] Alan Bean. Penguin Group 2009 114p il $23.99

Grades: 5 6 7 8 9   **629.45**

1. Astronautics 2. Space flight to the moon 3. Project Apollo

ISBN 978-0-670-01156-8; 0-670-01156-8

LC 2009000833

"Based on interviews with 28 astronauts, this history of the Apollo program masterfully describes the missions and personalizes them with astronauts' own words. Chaikin starts with a brief overview of its origins and of the Mercury and Gemini missions. He then highlights the significance of each manned Apollo mission in chronological chapters, with full-page sidebars on such topics as food, TV coverage, space sickness and going to the bathroom in space. The handsome design has many photographs, diagrams of the rockets and modules and more than 30 well-reproduced paintings by Apollo 12 astronaut Bean." Kirkus

Includes bibliographical references

Cole, Michael D.

Space emergency; astronauts in danger. Enslow Pubs. 2000 48p il (Countdown to space) lib bdg $18.95

Grades: 4 5 6 7   **629.45**

1. Astronautics 2. Space vehicle accidents

ISBN 0-7660-1307-3

LC 99-26855

Describes emergencies that occurred during several space missions, including Apollo 13, Friendship 7, Gemini 8, and Mir

Includes glossary and bibliographical references

Dyer, Alan

Mission to the moon. Simon & Schuster Books for Young Readers 2009 80p il $19.99

Grades: 5 6 7 8   **629.45**

1. Space flight to the moon 2. Project Apollo 3. Moon -- Exploration

ISBN 978-1-4169-7935-7; 1-4169-7935-2

LC 2008-61118

"Sporting a highly visual encyclopedic format, this informative book features 200 photographs documenting early research into mankind's history with the moon, early space exploration and the space race, and the Apollo missions. Detailed cross-sections of modules, space suits and other equipment offer a sound technological overview, while information on the phases, structure and surface of the moon provides added insight. . . . A DVD and poster are included." Publ Wkly

Dyson, Marianne J.

Home on the moon; living on a space frontier. National Geographic Soc. 2003 64p il $18.95

Grades: 4 5 6 7   **629.45**

1. Moon

ISBN 0-7922-7193-9

LC 2002-5280

Considers the moon as a frontier that has been only partially explored, looking at its history, geography, and weather, as well as what people would require to live and work there. Includes activities

"Clear writing, vivid images, interesting details, and quotes from astronauts and scientists make this a lively, fact-filled introduction." Booklist

Includes glossary and bibliographical references

Floca, Brian

★ **Moonshot**; the flight of Apollo 11. written and illustrated by Brian Floca. Atheneum Books for Young Readers 2008 un il $17.99

Grades: K 1 2 3   **629.45**

1. Astronautics 2. Space flight to the moon 3. Apollo 11 (Spacecraft) 4. Project Apollo

ISBN 1-4169-5046-X; 978-1-4169-5046-2

LC 2007-52358

ALA ALSC Sibert Medal Honor Book (2010)

This is the story of the 1969 Apollo 11 mission to the Moon. "Grades two to five." (Bull Cent Child Books)

"Forty years after NASA's Apollo 11 mission first landed astronauts on the moon, this striking nonfiction picture book takes young readers along for the ride. . . . Written with quiet dignity and a minimum of fuss, the main text is beautifully illustrated with line-and-wash artwork that provides human interest, technological details, and some visually stunning scenes." Booklist

Goodman, Susan E.

How do you burp in space? and other tips every space tourist needs to know. by Susan Goodman; illustrated by Michael Slack. Bloomsbury Pub. Distributed by Macmillan Publishers 2013 80 p. (hardback) $16.99

Grades: 4 5 6   **629.45**

1. Space flight 2. Interplanetary voyages 3. Space tourism 4. Manned space flight

ISBN 1599900688; 9781599900681; 9781599909349

LC 2011035303

In this children's book, author Susan E. Goodman "gives readers who will be the first generation of true space tourists general advice about how to prepare for the trip, what to pack, what food and accommodations will be like, and recreational opportunities both in Earth's orbit and on the moon. She also highlights some hazards, such as drinking carbonated drinks: Burping in microgravity brings up more than just CO_2." (Kirkus Reviews)

Green, Carl R.

Spacewalk; the astounding Gemini 4 mission. Carl R. Green. Enslow Publishers 2013 48 p. $23.93

Grades: 4 5 6 7 8   **629.45**

1. Gemini project 2. Outer space 3. Space flight 4. Project Gemini (U.S.) -- History

ISBN 0766040755; 9780766040755

LC 2011030869

This children's book, by Carl R. Green, "explores the astounding GEMINI 4 mission. . . . Pilot Ed White could see Hawaii, California, Texas, and Florida . . . while walking in space! . . . The first American spacewalk was a monumental achievement, and it helped push the space program toward its ultimate goal of landing men on the Moon." (Publisher's note)

Includes bibliographical references and index

Hartman, Eve

Mission to Mars; [by] Eve Hartman and Wendy Meshbesher. Raintree 2010 56p il lib bdg $33.50; pa $9.49

Grades: 5 6 7 8   **629.45**

1. Space flight to Mars 2. Mars (Planet)

ISBN 9781-4109-3821-3 lib bdg; 1-4109-3821-2 lib bdg; 978-1-4109-3996-8 pa; 1-4109-3996-0 pa

LC 2009-53209

"Excellent black-and-white and color photos throughout are matched perfectly to the texts and well captioned. Good choices for reports and debates." SLJ

Hense, Mary

How astronauts use math; math curriculum consultant: Rhea A. Stewart. Chelsea Clubhouse 2010 32p il (Math in the real world) lib bdg $28

Grades: 4 5 6   **629.45**

1. Astronauts 2. Mathematics 3. Astronautics 4. Vocational guidance

ISBN 978-1-60413-610-4 lib bdg; 1-60413-610-3 lib bdg

LC 2009-23926

This describes how astronauts use math for such tasks as calculating distance, speed, and velocity, and includes relevant math problems and information about how to become an astronaut

Includes glossary and bibliographical references

Holden, Henry M.

Danger in space; surviving the Apollo 13 disaster. Henry M. Holden. Enslow Publishers 2013 48 p. $23.93

Grades: 4 5 6 7 8   **629.45**

1. Apollo project 2. Picture books for children 3. Apollo 13 (Spacecraft) 4. Project Apollo (U.S.) 5. Space vehicle accidents -- United States

ISBN 0766040720; 9780766040724

LC 2011037734

This children's picture book tells the story of the U.S. National Aerospace and Space Administration's Apollo 13 mission. "Soaring through space at twenty-five thousand miles per hour, Apollo 13 was on course for the Moon. Suddenly, the three astronauts aboard the spacecraft heard a loud bang. A strong vibration rumbled through the crew cabin. There had been an explosion in the oxygen tank! More than two hundred thousand miles from Earth, Apollo 13 was in grave danger." (Publisher's note)

Includes bibliographical references and index

McCarthy, Meghan

Astronaut handbook. Alfred A. Knopf 2008 un il $16.99; lib bdg $19.99

Grades: K 1 2 3   **629.45**

1. Astronautics

ISBN 978-0-375-84459-1; 0-375-84459-7; 978-0-375-94459-8 lib bdg; 0-375-94459-1 lib bdg

LC 2007-31951

"Readers follow four aspiring astronauts from classroom to cockpit as they focus, study, practice, and ultimately take off. McCarthy applies a light, comic tone to the subject, reflected in her simple, expressive, cartoony acrylic paintings. . . . McCarthy introduces the paraphernalia of rocket travel with direct humor that understands and respects its audience." Booklist

McNulty, Faith

★ If you decide to go to the moon; illustrated by Steven Kellogg. Scholastic Press 2005 un il $16.99

Grades: K 1 2 3   **629.45**

1. Space flight to the moon 2. Moon

ISBN 0-590-48359-5

LC 2004-27755

In this "picture book, readers accompany a boy on a fascinating excursion to the moon. The lyrical text provides tips on what to pack and describes the distance to be covered. After blastoff, facts about space travel are mingled with descriptions of what the journey might be like. . . . Rich artwork complements the strong text." SLJ

McReynolds, Linda

Eight days gone; Linda McReynolds; illustrated by Ryan O'Rourke. Charlesbridge 2012 44 p. col. ill. (reinforced for library use) $16.95

Grades: 1 2 3   **629.45**

1. Astronauts 2. Outer space -- Exploration 3. Project Apollo (U.S.) 4. Apollo 11 (Spacecraft) 5. Space flight to the moon

ISBN 1580893643; 9781580893640

LC 2011025776

In this book, Linda McReynolds tells the story of Apollo 11. "Eighteen two-page spreads illustrate the story, and McReynolds tells it in tight four-line verses using identical rhyme schemes. . . . The rocket blasts into space, begins its orbit, and, after a uniform check, the lunar module disconnects and lands safely on the moon." McReynolds looks at astronauts Michael Collins, Neil Armstrong, and Buzz Aldrin. (Kirkus Reviews)

"The bold, punchy text and vivid illustrations combine to make this a great candidate for storytime as well as exciting solo enjoyment." SLJ

Ottaviani, Jim

T-Minus: the race to the moon; [illustrated by] Zander Cannon, Kevin Cannon. Aladdin 2009 124p il $21.99; pa $12.99

Grades: 4 5 6 7 8 9 10 11 12 Adult   **629.45**

1. Graphic novels 2. Apollo project -- Graphic novels 3. Gemini project -- Graphic novels 4. Space flight to the moon -- Graphic novels

ISBN 978-1-4169-8682-9; 1-4169-8682-0; 978-1-4169-4960-2 pa; 1-4169-4960-7 pa

LC 2009-920999

Ottaviani, Zander Cannon, and Kevin Cannon show what happened when the U.S. and the U.S.S.R. started the space race in the 1950s, and how it progressed to the NASA Apollo 11 mission which landed two men on the moon in July of 1969.

"Organized as a countdown, making the outcome seem inevitable, the frequent, prominent sidebars list a type of rocket, the duration of its flight, and whether the mission was a success or a failure. There are more than 30 attempts chronicled, and the shift between Soviet and U.S. successes creates an interesting balance in the narrative. . . . Ottaviani is particular with facts and eager to inspire readers with regard to the scientific process." SLJ

Platt, Richard

★ **Moon** landing; a pop-up celebration of Apollo 11. by Richard Platt; paper engineering by David Hawcock. Candlewick Press 2008 un il $29.99

Grades: 4 5 6 7   629.45

1. Space flight to the moon 2. Pop-up books 3. Apollo 11 (Spacecraft)

ISBN 978-0-7636-4046-0; 0-7636-4046-8

"This is a handsome, carefully engineered compendium. The text begins with the so-called space race between the United States and the Soviet Union in the 1950s and '60s and then offers brief descriptions of the 17 flights that made up the Apollo program. Here the emphasis is on the famous landing of the Eagle on the Moon in July 1969. The pop-ups and foldout pages on sturdy, shiny paper demonstrate the mechanical aspects of the spacecraft and offer a bold sense of both the rocketry and the trip. Small photographs and drawings surround the larger views." SLJ

Ross, Stewart

Moon: science, history, and mystery. Scholastic 2009 128p il lib bdg $18.99

Grades: 4 5 6   629.45

1. Astronautics 2. Space flight to the moon 3. Project Apollo 4. Moon -- Exploration

ISBN 978-0-545-12732-5 lib bdg; 0-545-12732-7 lib bdg

"Jam-packed with information, this colorful oversize volume chronicles the race to land a person on the Moon. Alternating chapters describe Moon mythologies and superstitions, the history of astronomical study, and the efforts involved in launching a lunar expedition.... The photographs pop with color and action.... The invaluable contribution of Muslim scientists is included.... [The book's] multicultural history will expand any collection." SLJ

Includes glossary

Thimmesh, Catherine

★ **Team** moon; how 400,000 people landed Apollo 11 on the moon. Houghton Mifflin Company 2006 80p il $19.95

Grades: 5 6 7 8   629.45

1. Space flight to the moon 2. Apollo 11 (Spacecraft)

ISBN 0-618-50757-4

LC 2005-10755

"Thimmesh retraces the course of the space mission that landed an actual man, on the actual Moon. It's an oft-told tale, but the author tells it from the point of view not of astronauts or general observers, but of some of the 17,000 behind-the-scenes workers at Kennedy Space Center, the 7500 Grumman employees who built the lunar module, the 500 designers and seamstresses who actually constructed the space suits, and other low-profile contributors who made the historic flight possible.... This dramatic account will mesmerize even readers already familiar with the event.... This stirring, authoritative tribute to the collective effort ... belongs in every collection." SLJ

Includes glossary and bibliographical references

Vogt, Gregory

Spacewalks; the ultimate adventure in orbit. {by} Gregory L. Vogt. Enslow Pubs. 2000 48p il (Countdown to space) lib bdg $18.95

Grades: 4 5 6 7   629.45

1. Space flight 2. Extravehicular activity (Space flight)

ISBN 0-7660-1305-7

LC 99-37094

Describes the training and preparation for spacewalking, the hazards faced by astronauts, as well as the construction of spacesuits

Includes glossary and bibliographical references

Waxman, Laura Hamilton

Exploring space travel. Lerner Publications Company 2011 40p il (What's amazing about space?) lib bdg $27.93

Grades: 4 5 6   629.45

1. Astronautics 2. Space flight

ISBN 978-0-7613-5447-5; 0-7613-5447-6

LC 2010042471

This describes what it's like to be an astronaut in space.

"Readers will come away with new knowledge, such as how scientists observe the behavior of other stars to infer the presence of exoplanets." Booklist

Includes bibliographical references

629.46   Engineering of unmanned spacecraft

Johnson, Rebecca L.

Satellites. Lerner Publications Co. 2006 48p il (Cool science) lib bdg $25.26

Grades: 4 5 6   629.46

1. Artificial satellites

ISBN 978-0-8225-2908-8 lib bdg; 0-8225-2908-4 lib bdg

LC 2004-30298

This book has "an attractive, colorful layout that will appeal to readers. Each spread includes captioned, color photographs and/or illustrations; text boxes; and, often, a 'fun fact.'... [This] title explains what a satellite is and discusses many aspects of satellites, including how they pertain to television broadcasts, weather forecasting, and locating black holes. Numerous amazing facts are included to pique readers' interest." SLJ

Includes bibliographical references

Kops, Deborah

Exploring space robots. Lerner Publications 2011 40p il map (What's amazing about space?) lib bdg $27.93

Grades: 4 5 6   629.46

1. Robots 2. Outer space -- Exploration

ISBN 978-0-7613-5445-1; 0-7613-5445-X

LC 2010044213

This explains how robots help us explore space, including a probe called New Horizons which is heading toward Pluto.

This book is "written in simple language, [and] illustrated nicely.... The information presented is factually correct. ... Every page includes a well-chosen illustration or photograph." Sci Books Films

Includes bibliographical references

629.8 Automatic control engineering

Allman, Toney

The **Nexi** robot. Norwood House Press 2009 48p il
(A great idea) lib bdg $25.27
Grades: 3 4 5 6 **629.8**
1. Robots 2. Inventors 3. Electronics engineers
ISBN 978-1-59953-342-1 lib bdg; 1-59953-342-1
lib bdg

LC 2009-14714

"The real star of this title . . . is Cynthia Breazeal, the
head of the Personal Robotics Group at MIT. . . . The challenge of creating a robot with personality is understandably
complex, but Allman does a fine job of making it accessible
by offering up examples, and numerous photographs. . . . It's
all fascinating stuff, for sure, and presented in a simple yet
informative manner." Booklist

Includes glossary and bibliographical references

Chaffee, Joel

How to build a prize-winning robot. Rosen Central
2011 48p il (Robotics) lib bdg $26.50; pa $11.75
Grades: 5 6 7 8 **629.8**
1. Robots
ISBN 978-1-4488-1238-7 lib bdg; 1-4488-1238-0 lib
bdg; 978-1-4488-2252-2 pa; 1-4488-2252-1 pa

LC 2010025748

"Kids who are fascinated with robots will want [this
title] available." SLJ

Includes glossary and bibliographical references

Freedman, Jeri

Robots through history. Rosen Central 2011 48p il
(Robotics) lib bdg $26.50; pa $11.75
Grades: 5 6 7 8 **629.8**
1. Robots
ISBN 978-1-4488-1236-3 lib bdg; 1-4488-1236-4 lib
bdg; 978-1-4488-2250-8 pa; 1-4488-2250-5 pa

LC 2010024139

"Kids who are fascinated with robots will want [this
title] available." SLJ

Includes glossary and bibliographical references

Graham, Ian

Robot technology. Smart Apple Media 2012 il (New
technology)
Grades: 4 5 6 7 **629.8**
1. Robots
ISBN 1-599-20533-5; 978-1-599-20533-5

LC 2010044240

Describes current robotics technology, including the applications of robots in space, in the military, in industry, and
around the house. Discusses the pros and cons of creating
fully autonomous robots.

This "offers a fine overview for reports, and its attractive
design may also entice middle-grade readers to learn more."
Booklist

Mason, Adrienne

Robots: from everyday to out of this world; written
by the editors of Yes mag. Kids Can Press 2008 48p il
$16.95; pa $8.95

Grades: 3 4 5 6 **629.8**
1. Robots
ISBN 978-1-55453-203-2; 1-55453-203-5; 978-1-
55453-204-9 pa; 1-55453-204-3 pa

This is a history of robots from Leonardo da Vinci's "ro-
bot-knight" to those of the present and future. Index. "Ages
eight to twelve." (Quill Quire)

This "introduces robots that work (defusing bombs, assembling cars, assisting surgeons, exploring Mars) and play
(riding camels, kicking soccer balls). . . . Each section is
packed with fascinating information, entertaining cartoon
graphics, and numerous full-color photographs. The text is
hip and accessible. . . . Well-organized and engaging." Booklist

Includes glossary

Payment, Simone

Robotics careers; preparing for the future. Rosen Central 2011 48p il (Robotics) lib bdg $26.50; pa $11.75
Grades: 5 6 7 8 **629.8**
1. Robots 2. Vocational guidance
ISBN 978-1-4488-1239-4 lib bdg; 1-4488-1239-9 lib
bdg; 978-1-4488-2253-9 pa; 1-4488-2253-X pa

LC 2010024134

"Kids who are fascinated with robots will want [this
title] available." SLJ

Includes glossary and bibliographical references

Rau, Dana Meachen

Robots. Marshall Cavendish Benchmark 2010 24p il
(Surprising science) lib bdg $22.79
Grades: 2 3 4 **629.8**
1. Robots
ISBN 978-0-7614-4871-6; 0-7614-4871-3

LC 2009053764

"Colorfully illustrated with photographs on each page,
this . . . will be well received by elementary students and
educators." Libr Media Connect

Includes glossary and bibliographical references

Shea, Therese

The **robotics** club; teaming up to build robots. Rosen
Central 2011 48p il (Robotics) lib bdg $26.50; pa $11.75
Grades: 5 6 7 8 **629.8**
1. Clubs 2. Robots
ISBN 978-1-4488-1237-0 lib bdg; 1-4488-1237-2 lib
bdg; 978-1-4488-2251-5 pa; 1-4488-2251-3 pa

This title "will provide students with the information
necessary to form a club and compete at making and using
robots. Kids who are fascinated with robots will want [this
title] available." SLJ

VanVoorst, Jennifer

Rise of the thinking machines; the science of robots.
Compass Point Books 2009 48p il (Headline science) lib
bdg $27.93; pa $7.95
Grades: 5 6 7 **629.8**
1. Robots
ISBN 978-0-7565-3377-9 lib bdg; 0-7565-3377-5 lib
bdg; 978-0-7565-3518-6 pa; 0-7565-3518-2 pa

LC 2008-05732

"Describes various types of robots and their functions,
discusses technological advancements in the field of robot-

ics, and considers the ethical issues surrounding autonomous robots." Publisher's note

Includes glossary and bibliographical references

Woog, Adam

SCRATCHbot. Norwood House Press 2010 48p il (A great idea) lib bdg $25.27

Grades: 3 4 5 6   **629.8**

1. Robots

ISBN 978-1-59953-380-3 lib bdg; 1-59953-380-4 lib bdg

LC 2010008502

"Woog introduces a small, rolling robot with prominent whiskers, used to mimic a rodent's ability to sense its surroundings through touch. Discussions include how inventors are inspired by nature and how this appealing robot might be useful. Presenting specific, current information, [this book] will appeal to young people intrigued by inventions." Booklist

Includes glossary and bibliographical references

630   Agriculture and related technologies

Apte, Sunita

Eating green. Bearport Pub. 2009 32p il map (Going green) lib bdg $25.27

Grades: 4 5 6 7   **630**

1. Natural foods 2. Sustainable agriculture

ISBN 978-1-59716-965-3 lib bdg; 1-59716-965-X lib bdg

LC 2009-19183

"Color photographs (most full page) and a few diagrams accompany the informative text. . . . Overall, the [book] . . . is user-friendly and covers topics that are not easily found elsewhere." SLJ

Includes glossary and bibliographical references

Bailey, Gerry

Farming for the future. Gareth Stevens Pub. 2011 48p il (Planet SOS) lib bdg $31.95; pa $14.05

Grades: 4 5 6   **630**

1. Agriculture 2. Food supply

ISBN 978-1-4339-4966-1 lib bdg; 1-4339-4966-0 lib bdg; 978-1-4339-4967-8 pa; 1-4339-4967-9 pa

LC 2010032887

This well-designed book presents farming methods "and how they affect human beings. . . . [It] includes a chapter on new types of farms and foods. . . . The many large, colorful photos will engage readers and assist them in understanding the important concepts introduced." SLJ

Includes glossary

Hodge, Deborah

★ **Up** we grow! a year in the life of a small, local farm. written by Deborah Hodge; photographed by Brian Harris. Kids Can Press 2010 32p il $16.95

Grades: PreK K 1 2   **630**

1. Farm life 2. Agriculture 3. Organic farming

ISBN 978-1-55453-561-3; 1-55453-561-1

This is "a photo-essay about a year on a communal organic farm. Moving chronologically through the seasons, the spreads, illustrated with close-up photographs, follow a

small collective of farmers. . . . Filled with sensory descriptions, the rhythmic text gives a strong sense of life on the farm and in the field." Booklist

Watch me grow! a down-to-earth look at growing food in the city. written by Deborah Hodge; photographed by Brian Harris. Kids Can Press 2011 32p il $16.95

Grades: PreK K 1 2   **630**

1. Gardening 2. Urban agriculture

ISBN 978-1-55453-618-4; 1-55453-618-9

This "explores ways that gardeners are growing food in community gardens, on rooftops, and in backyards. Harris contributes numerous photos of children getting in on the action—watering plants, tilling soil, and enjoying the (literal) fruits of their labor. . . . Direct and informative, this should inspire many kids to test out how green their thumbs are." Publ Wkly

Michelson, Richard

Tuttle's Red Barn; the story of America's oldest family farm. illustrated by Mary Azarian. G.P. Putnam's Sons 2007 un il $17

Grades: K 1 2 3   **630**

1. Family farms

ISBN 978-0-399-24354-7; 0-399-24354-2

LC 2007-07514

Michelson and Azarian "salute 12 generations of Tuttles from Dover, N.H., operators of the longest continuously running family farm in the country. . . . Each chapter focuses on the male Tuttle who inherits the farm, and that Tuttle, glimpsed in his youth, observes some history. . . . In Azarian's tableau-like woodcuts, styles change while character endures. Her hand-crafted aesthetic enhances the story's warmth and humanity." Publ Wkly

Parker, Steve, 1952-

Food and farming. QEB Pub. 2010 32p il (QEB changes in . . .) lib bdg $28.50

Grades: 3 4 5 6   **630**

1. Farms 2. Agriculture 3. Food supply

ISBN 978-1-59566-775-5 lib bdg; 1-59566-775-X lib bdg

LC 2008-56069

"The information is presented in brief paragraphs and sidebars. Suggestions for kids to help improve the planet are sprinkled throughout. . . . Students will enjoy this appealing layout and the information can spark further research on the topic. . . . Either digitally or on paper, students could make fantastic presentations using a similar design." Libr Media Connect

Includes glossary

Rosen, Michael J.

★ **Our** farm; four seasons with five kids on one family's farm. written and photographed by Michael J. Rosen. Darby Creek Pub. 2008 144p il $18.95

Grades: 4 5 6 7 8   **630**

1. Family life 2. Ohio 3. Farm life -- United States

ISBN 978-1-58196-067-9; 1-58196-067-0

A journal of one year on the Bennett farm in central Ohio. Shows how one family, with the help of relatives and friends, creates a life and livelihood on a 150-acre farm.

"This engaging book is an unsentimental, appreciative look into the world of one farm family." SLJ

Vogel, Julia

Local farms and sustainable foods. Cherry Lake 2010 32p il (Save the planet) lib bdg $27.07

Grades: 3 4 5 6 **630**

1. Farms 2. Sustainable agriculture

ISBN 978-1-60279-660-7 lib bdg; 1-60279-660-2 lib bdg

LC 2009-38096

Teaches young readers about locally grown fruits and vegetables

"At the beginning of . . . [the] book, readers are given a mission and advised to be alert to the facts provided so that they can successfully answer the questions at the end. . . . Children are made to feel part of the process; suggestions for how they can become involved abound." SLJ

Includes glossary and bibliographical references

Watterson, Carol

The edible alphabet; 26 reasons to love the farm. illustrated by Michela Sorrentino. Tricycle Press 2011 un il $16.99; lib bdg $19.99

Grades: K 1 2 3 **630**

1. Farms 2. Alphabet 3. Farm produce 4. Domestic animals

ISBN 1-58246-421-9; 1-58246-422-7 lib bdg; 978-1-58246-421-3; 978-1-58246-422-0 lib bdg

LC 2010030478

"This informative alphabet book focuses on the importance of agricultural and animal farms. For each letter, Watterson uses bouncy alliteration to introduce her subjects. . . . Sorrentino matches Watterson's friendly prose with lively mixed-media collages that include polka-dotted fowl and cars fashioned from zucchini, while interactive prompts and intriguing facts give readers a lot to munch on." Publ Wkly

630.9 Agriculture and related technologies - Historical, geographic treatment

Richardson, Gillian

10 plants that shook the world; Gillian Richardson; illustrated by Kim Rosen. Annick Press 2013 132 p. (hardcover) $24.95

Grades: 4 5 6 7 8 **630.9**

1. Plants 2. Agriculture -- History

ISBN 1554514452; 9781554514458

This book, by Gillian Richardson, illustrated by Kim Rosen, profiles ten plants with significant histories. It describes how "countries went to war to control trade centers for pepper . . . , a grass called papyrus became the first effective tool for sharing knowledge through writing . . . , Europeans in the 1600s cut down rainforests to grow sugar, contributing to soil erosion . . . [and] dependence on the potato caused one of the greatest tragedies in history." (Publisher's note)

"With bold, lively caricatures from Rosen throughout, it's an intriguing and well-designed study of the ways plants have helped start wars, cure diseases, and advance technology." Pub Wkly

631.3 Tools, machinery, apparatus, equipment

Peterson, Cris

★ Fantastic farm machines; photographs by David R. Lundquist. Boyd Mills Press 2006 un il $17.95

Grades: K 1 2 3 **631.3**

1. Agricultural machinery

ISBN 1-59078-271-2

LC 2005-33561

"Peterson gives readers an accurate firsthand view of modern, often computerized equipment used on today's farms. Her easy-to-understand text describes both the machines and their functions. . . . The short, informative paragraphs are surrounded by excellent color photographs that extend the text." SLJ

631.4 Soil science

Bourgeois, Paulette

The dirt on dirt; by Paulette Bourgeois with Kathy Vanderlinden; illustrated by Martha Newbigging. Kids Can Press 2008 48p il $15.95; pa $7.95

Grades: 3 4 5 6 **631.4**

1. Soils 2. Soil ecology

ISBN 978-1-55453-101-1; 1-55453-101-2; 978-1-55453-1028 pa; 1-55453-102-0 pa

"From dirty toes, fossils, earthworms, and animal burrows to buried treasure, cities, and dog bones, this engaging introduction to soil touches on a wide variety of topics clearly and concisely. 'Fun with Dirt' experiments and activities demonstrate concepts and stimulate imagination. Illustrated with well-captioned photographs and cartoon-style sketches." Booklist

Gardner, Robert

Super science projects about Earth's soil and water; [by] Robert Gardner; illustrations by Tom Labaff. Enslow Elementary 2007 48p il (Rockin' earth science experiments) $17.95

Grades: 3 4 5 **631.4**

1. Soils 2. Water 3. Science projects 4. Science -- Experiments

ISBN 978-0-7660-2735-0; 0-7660-2735-X

LC 2006006680

This is a "selection of earth-science projects, all focused on soil and water concepts, such as evaporation, the water cycle, and the components of soil. Each experiment is clearly explained in step-by-step instructions, illustrated with Labaff's clean-lined diagrams and formatted on uncluttered pages." Booklist

Includes glossary and bibliographical references

Hall, Pamela

Dig in! Learn about dirt; illustrated by Jane Yamada. Child's World, Inc. 2010 24p il (Science definitions) lib bdg $22.79

Grades: PreK K 1 2 **631.4**

1. Soils

ISBN 978-1-60253-507-7 lib bdg; 1-60253-507-8 lib bdg

LC 2010010974

This book about soil is "attractive and succinct. . . . Large, eye-catching photos cover the recto of each spread. . . . Varying, jewel-toned accents are used in headings, highlighted glossary terms, and in a sidebar on each spread." SLJ

Includes glossary

Spilsbury, Richard
Soil; [by] Richard and Louise Spilsbury. Heinemann Library 2011 32p il (Let's rock) $29; pa $7.99
Grades: 4 5 6   **631.4**
1. Soils
ISBN 978-1-4329-4685-2; 1-4329-4685-4; 978-1-4329-4693-7 pa; 1-4329-4693-5 pa
LC 2010022242
"Enhanced by plenty of photos, digital paintings, and diagrams, [this examination] of [soil treats its topic] in unusual detail. [It] describes distinguishing characteristics, creation, history, . . . and human uses in [a] central [narrative] with additional notes, suggestions for activities during walks outside, and occasional thumbnail biographies of scientists in side boxes. [The] volume ends with a simple activity." SLJ

Includes bibliographical references

631.5 Cultivation and harvesting

Juettner, Bonnie
The seed vault. Norwood House Press 2009 48p il (A great idea) lib bdg $25.27
Grades: 3 4 5 6   **631.5**
1. Seeds 2. Endangered species 3. Biological diversity 4. Plants -- Collection and preservation
ISBN 978-1-59953-343-8 lib bdg; 1-59953-343-X lib bdg
LC 2009-16567
"With a mix of scientific terminology and accessible sentence structure, the [book] effectively [describes] how the [idea] took shape and were put into practice by the scientists involved. . . . Color photographs are included on every page and provide a visual complement to the [text]." SLJ

Includes glossary and bibliographical references

Rustad, Martha E. H.
Fall harvests; bringing in food. illustrated by Amanda Enright. Millbrook Press 2011 24p il (Fall's here!) lib bdg $23.95
Grades: K 1 2 3   **631.5**
1. Autumn 2. Agriculture
ISBN 978-0-7613-5067-5; 0-7613-5067-5
LC 2010053467
"This offers . . . information about planting or reaping, and directions for making a cornhusk doll. . . . Colorful illustrations fill the spreads with active, cartoonlike boys and girls surrounded by the green, brown, and orange hues of autumn." SLJ

631.8 Fertilizers, soil conditioners, growth regulators

Barker, David
Compost it. Cherry Lake Pub. 2010 32p il (Save the planet) lib bdg $27.95

Grades: 3 4 5 6   **631.8**
1. Compost
ISBN 978-1-60279-656-0 lib bdg; 1-60279-656-4 lib bdg
LC 2009038092
"Written as dispatches from an imaginary journalist, the pages follow several individuals who explain different types of composting: a soil ecologist, . . . a home owner, . . . an apartment dweller, . . . and, finally, the manager of large-scale, urban operation. The creative, uncrowded format features text printed in an old-fashioned typewriter font on a notebook-paper background, numerous color photos, and facts boxes. . . . This upbeat, lucid overview of compost and its benefits is a strong choice." Booklist

Glaser, Linda
Garbage helps our garden grow; a compost story. story by Linda Glaser; photography by Shelley Rotner. Millbrook 2010 32p il lib bdg $25.26
Grades: K 1 2 3   **631.8**
1. Compost
ISBN 978-0-7613-4911-2 lib bdg; 0-7613-4911-1 lib bdg
"Clear, vivid photos give this simple introduction to composting a realistic look that makes the process look downright doable. . . . Most of Rotner's excellent photos feature one or two children as they scrape their dinner plates into a bucket indoors, add kitchen and yard waste to the compost bin outside, observe the leaves and food rotting over time, add the compost to their vegetable garden, put new plants into the ground, and watch them grow." Booklist

632 Plant injuries, diseases, pests

Mooney, Carla
Sunscreen for plants. Norwood House Press 2009 48p il (A great idea) lib bdg $25.27
Grades: 3 4 5 6   **632**
1. Plants 2. Sun
ISBN 978-1-59953-344-5 lib bdg; 1-59953-344-8 lib bdg
LC 2009-15641
"With a mix of scientific terminology and accessible sentence structure, the [book] effectively [describes] how the [idea] took shape and were put into practice by the scientists involved. . . . Color photographs are included on every page and provide a visual complement to the [text]." SLJ

Includes glossary and bibliographical references

633.1 Cereals

Aliki
Corn is maize; the gift of the Indians. written and illustrated by Aliki. Crowell 1976 33p il (Let's-read-and-find-out science book) hardcover o.p. pa $5.99
Grades: K 1 2 3   **633.1**
1. Corn
ISBN 0-690-00975-5 lib bdg; 0-06-445026-0 pa
In this book, the author provides a history of corn, or maize, and "also the life cycle of the plant itself, its growth and reproductive patterns, and its many uses. Excellent il-

lustrations by the author help convey both cultural aspects and technological uses of corn." Sci Child

Gibbons, Gail

Corn; by Gail Gibbons. Holiday House 2008 32p il $16.95

Grades: K 1 2 3   633.1

1. Corn

ISBN 978-0-8234-2169-5; 0-8234-2169-4

LC 2007051632

"The colorful watercolors are sure to attract even the most reluctant readers. . . . A simple, yet informative and engaging look at an important food source." SLJ

Landau, Elaine

Wheat. Children's Press 1999 47p il (True book) lib bdg $22; pa $6.95

Grades: 2 3 4   633.1

1. Wheat

ISBN 0-516-21029-7 lib bdg; 0-516-26792-2 pa

LC 98-47333

Examines the history, cultivation, and uses of wheat

Includes glossary and bibliographical references

Micucci, Charles

The life and times of corn; written and illustrated by Charles Micucci. Houghton Mifflin Books for Children 2009 32p il $16

Grades: 2 3 4   633.1

1. Corn

ISBN 978-0-618-50751-1; 0-618-50751-5

LC 2008040466

This focuses on the science, uses and history of corn

This is an "entertaining and informative mix of bite-size scientific information and historical facts and mouth-watering watercolors." Booklist

Includes bibliographical references

Reynolds, Jan

★ Cycle of rice, cycle of life; a story of sustainable farming. Lee & Low Books 2009 un il map $19.95

Grades: 3 4 5   633.1

1. Rice 2. Sustainable agriculture 3. Bali Island (Indonesia)

ISBN 978-1-60060-254-2; 1-60060-254-1

LC 2008-30518

This is "filled with beautiful color images. . . . [It is written] in precise, accessible language. . . . Reynolds offers young readers a broad, deep understanding of the concept, even as she provides a fascinating introduction to a specific culture." Booklist

Includes glossary

Sobol, Richard

The life of rice; from seedling to supper. Candlewick Press 2010 36p il map (Traveling photographer) $17.99

Grades: 3 4 5 6   633.1

1. Rice 2. Thailand

ISBN 978-0-7636-3252-6; 0-7636-3252-X

LC 2009-15138

"Turning his lens to the rice fields of Thailand, Sobol begins this affectionate account with a description of the Royal Plowing Ceremony that kicks off the planting season and continues through cultivation and into the harvest. Brief

explanations of the growing stages of rice are accompanied by beautiful color photographs of the fields in their various phases. . . . Sobol offers an interesting look at a country and its people, and their relationship to the land. The writing is accessible and lively, providing a unique, specific look at one of the world's most important staples." SLJ

633.3 Legumes, forage crops other than grasses and legumes

Bial, Raymond

The super soybean. Albert Whitman & Co. 2007 40p il $16.95

Grades: 4 5 6   633.3

1. Soybean

ISBN 978-0-8075-7549-9; 0-8075-7549-6

LC 2007-14165

"Pairing a densely informational text with color photos, mostly of soybeans being grown and harvested, [the author] traces their cultivation's historical background, catalogs many of the uses to which they are put, and . . . trumpets enthusiastic appreciation for their twin roles as a major U.S. export and a renewable natural resource." Booklist

633.5 Fiber crops

Moore, Heidi

The story behind cotton. Heinemann Library 2009 32p il (True stories) $28.21

Grades: 3 4 5   633.5

1. Cotton

ISBN 978-1-4329-2341-9; 1-4329-2341-2

LC 2008043334

This offers history, ephemera, and basic facts about cotton and its production and uses.

Includes bibliographical references

633.7 Alkaloidal crops

Stewart, Melissa

No monkeys, no chocolate; Melissa Stewart and Allen Young; illustrated by Nicole Wong. Charlesbridge 2013 32 p.

Grades: K 1 2 3   633.7

1. Cocoa 2. Monkeys 3. Fertilization of plants 4. Cacao 5. Chocolate 6. Cacao beans 7. Cocoa processing 8. Cacao -- Diseases and pests

ISBN 9781580892872 (reinforced for library use); 9781580892889 (softcover)

LC 2012000789

This children's picture book explores "the rain forest microhabitat of the cocoa tree. In each spread, the authors take children backward through the life cycle of the tree: pods, flowers, leaves, stems, roots and back to beans. The interdependence of plants and animals is introduced in the process: Midges carry pollen from one flower to another; aphids destroying tender stems are kept in check by an anole." (Kirkus Reviews)

633.8　Other crops grown for industrial processing

Smith, Danna

    Balloon trees; by Danna Smith; illustrated by Laurie Allen Klein. Sylvan Dell Publishing 2013 32 p. (English hardcover) $17.95

Grades: PreK K 1 2　　　　　　　　　　　　**633.8**

    1. Rubber　2. Rubber plants

    ISBN 1607186128; 9781607186120; 9781607186243

                  LC 2012030119

In this children's book, by Danna Smith, illustrated by Laurie Allen Klein, "rhyming couplets and effective illustrations describe the general process by which latex is extracted from trees, converted into a colorful mix, shaped into forms, treated and sent to stores to be sold as balloons. Each double-page spread shows a separate step, watched over by what looks like a warbler with an observant eye." (Kirkus)

634　Orchards, fruits, forestry

Dickmann, Nancy

    An **apple's** life. Heinemann Library 2010 24p il (Watch it grow) lib bdg $21.50; pa $5.99

Grades: PreK K 1　　　　　　　　　　　　**634**

    1. Apples

    ISBN 978-1-4329-4141-3 lib bdg; 1-4329-4141-0 lib bdg; 978-1-4329-4150-5 pa; 1-4329-4150-X pa

                  LC 2009-49157

This title shows the reader how an apple begins life, grows, and reproduces.

    "Practically unique among early introductions to life cycles because death is mentioned . . . this . . . follows [an apple] . . . from . . . seed to maturity with a set of close-up color photographs, one per page, paired to large-type, one or two-sentence captions. . . . Offers nourishing fare for young naturalists." SLJ

    Includes glossary

Esbaum, Jill

    Apples for everyone. National Geographic 2009 16p il (Picture the seasons) pa $5.95

Grades: K 1 2　　　　　　　　　　　　**634**

    1. Apples

    ISBN 978-1-4263-0523-8 pa; 1-4263-0523-0 pa

                  LC 2009-12719

Discusses how apples develop from blossoms to fruit, how they are harvested, how people use them, the history of apples in the United States, and different varieties of them

    This does "a fabulous job of conjuring up the sights, smells, and sensations of a brisk autumn. Using minimal text with National Geographic's typically fine photographs, Esbaum brings out familiar, comforting details of the outdoors. . . . The writing flows with sensory details." Booklist

Farmer, Jacqueline

    Apples; illustrated by Phyllis Limbacher Tildes. Charlesbridge 2007 un il map lib bdg $16.95; pa $6.95

Grades: 1 2 3 4　　　　　　　　　　　　**634**

    1. Apples

    ISBN 978-1-57091-694-6 lib bdg; 1-57091-694-2 lib bdg; 978-1-57091-695-3 pa; 1-57091-695-0 pa

                  LC 2006-20942

"Farmer provides a wealth of information here. The process of grafting is clearly explained, as are the differences between apple juice and cider, the nutritional value of the popular fruit, and the apple in history and legend. A handy chart detailing the various kinds of apples and their appropriate uses is included, as is a page of facts and records and a recipe for apple pie. Watercolor illustrations feature a multicultural cast of smiling children. The pictures accurately reflect the text and are attractive." SLJ

Gibbons, Gail

    Apples. Holiday House 2000 un il $17.95; pa $6.95

Grades: K 1 2 3　　　　　　　　　　　　**634**

    1. Apples

    ISBN 0-8234-1497-3; 0-8234-1669-0 pa

                  LC 99-54246

Explains how apples were brought to America, how they grow, their traditional uses and cultural significance, and some of the varieties grown

    "With its cheerful, bright illustrations and clear, simple presentation, this title will be the perfect pick for the perennial fall apple-book requests." SLJ

    The **berry** book. Holiday House 2002 un il $16.95

Grades: K 1 2 3　　　　　　　　　　　　**634**

    1. Berries　2. Cooking

    ISBN 0-8234-1697-6

                  LC 2001-40602

Describes different types of berries and how they grow. Includes recipes with berry ingredients

    This is a "brief, informative account. . . . Cheerful illustrations with clear labels enliven the accessible text." Horn Book Guide

Kellogg, Steven

    ★ **Johnny** Appleseed; a tall tale retold and illustrated by Steven Kellogg. Morrow Junior Bks. 1988 un il $16.95; lib bdg $16.89

Grades: K 1 2 3　　　　　　　　　　　　**634**

    1. Frontier and pioneer life　2. Pioneers　3. Fruit growers

    ISBN 0-688-06417-5; 0-688-06418-3 lib bdg

                  LC 87-27317

"Oversize pages have given Kellogg a fine opportunity for pictures that are on a large scale, colorful and animated if often busy with details. His version of Chapman's life is more substantial than the subtitle (A TallTale) would indicate, since the text makes clear the difference between what Chapman really did and what myths grew up about his work, his life, his personality, and his achievements. There's some exaggeration, but on the whole the biography is factual and written with clarity." Bull Cent Child Books

Landau, Elaine

    Bananas. Children's Press 1999 47p il (True book) lib bdg $22; pa $6.95

Grades: 2 3 4　　　　　　　　　　　　**634**

    1. Banana

    ISBN 0-516-21025-4 lib bdg; 0-516-26574-1 pa

                  LC 98-47328

Examines the history, cultivation, and uses of bananas

Includes glossary and bibliographical references

Maestro, Betsy

How do apples grow? illustrated by Giulio Maestro. HarperCollins Pubs. 1992 32p il (Let's-read-and-find-out science book) hardcover o.p. pa $5.99

Grades: K 1 2 3   **634**

1. Apples

ISBN 0-06-020056-1 lib bdg; 0-06-445117-8 pa

LC 91-9468

Describes the life cycle of an apple from its initial appearance as a spring bud to that point in time when it becomes a fully ripe fruit

"Clear, complete. . . . Inquisitive children will find simple yet scientifically accurate answers to their questions about apple trees and their fruit. Large illustrations and limited text facilitate group-reading. The endearing, soft-toned drawings are clearly labelled, providing an excellent teaching tool or reference point for the science teacher." Sci Child

Malam, John

Grow your own smoothie. Heinemann Library 2011 32p il (Grow it yourself!) lib bdg $26; pa $7.99

Grades: K 1 2   **634**

1. Cooking 2. Strawberries 3. Vegetable gardening

ISBN 978-1-4329-5111-5 lib bdg; 978-1-4329-5118-4 pa

LC 2010049836

This describes how to grow strawberries and how to make a strawberry smoothie.

Includes glossary and bibliographical references

Moses, Will

Johnny Appleseed; the story of a legend. Philomel Bks. 2001 un il $16.99

Grades: 3 4 5 6   **634**

1. Frontier and pioneer life 2. Pioneers 3. Fruit growers

ISBN 0-399-23153-6

LC 00-44600

This is a "picture-book biography of John Chapman, aka Johnny Appleseed. . . . Starting in 1774, the year of Chapman's birth, Moses briefly covers Chapman's early childhood, and then quickly moves on to his young adult years, when he leaves home for the frontier. The bulk of the book documents Chapman's rich adult life and celebrates his odd ways. . . . The paintings . . . are filled with rich detail and are unforgettable." Booklist

Includes bibliographical references

Rustad, Martha E. H.

Fall apples; crisp and juicy. illustrated by Amanda Enright. Millbrook Press 2011 24p il (Fall's here!) lib bdg $23.93

Grades: K 1 2 3   **634**

1. Apples 2. Cooking

ISBN 978-0-7613-5064-4; 0-7613-5064-0

LC 2010051510

"In this book, the reader discovers how fall apples grow and the many things that you can make with them. . . . Colorful illustrations enhance the lively text." Sci Books Films

Includes glossary and bibliographical references

Smucker, Anna Egan

Golden delicious; a Cinderella apple story. by Anna Egan Smucker; illustrated by Kathleen Kemly. Albert Whitman & Company 2008 un il $16.99

Grades: 1 2 3   **634**

1. Apples

ISBN 978-0-8075-2987-4; 0-8075-2987-7

LC 2007052792

This is "the story of the discovery and successful marketing of the Golden Delicious apple. The narrative is simple and direct, with an occasional flair. . . . Kemly's soft pastel illustrations provide interesting historical details, including dress and transportation, and help to move the story along. An author's note gives more background, along with details about the grafting process." SLJ

Ziefert, Harriet

One red apple; paintings by Karla Gudeon. Blue Apple Books 2009 un il $16.99 **634**

1. Apples

ISBN 978-1-934706-67-1; 1-934706-67-1

LC 2009012663

This follows the life cycle of an apple: from fruit growing on the tree to market, to picnic, to seed, to sapling and tree, and finally to a new apple.

"With lyrical text and folk-style artwork, this handsome picture book celebrates the pleasures of a favorite food while accentuating nature's cycles and Earth's bounty." SLJ

634.9   Forestry

Jakubiak, David J.

What can we do about deforestation? PowerKids Press 2011 24p il (Protecting our planet) lib bdg $21.25; pa $8.25

Grades: 2 3 4   **634.9**

1. Deforestation

ISBN 978-1-4488-4986-4 lib bdg; 1-4488-4986-1 lib bdg; 978-1-4488-5119-5 pa; 1-4488-5119-X pa

LC 2011000160

This explains the importance of forests and trees in our environment, the reasons for deforestation and the damage caused by the destruction of trees.

"Every spread has a full-page, thoughtfully captioned color photograph. . . . School and public libraries will want [this title] to round out collections or as [an update] to replace older books." SLJ

Includes glossary

Morris, Neil

Wood. Amicus 2011 48p il map (Materials that matter) lib bdg $28.50

Grades: 4 5 6 7   **634.9**

1. Wood

ISBN 978-1-60753-070-1 lib bdg; 1-60753-070-8 lib bdg

LC 2010001621

"The clean layout includes photographs and occasional charts, graphs, and technical illustrations against a range of pastel backgrounds. Inset boxes provide further detail, interesting extras, and recycling information. . . . [This book offers] easily accessible background information for report writers." SLJ

Includes glossary and bibliographical references

Silverstein, Alvin

★ **Wildfires**; the science behind raging infernos. [by] Alvin and Virginia Silverstein and Laura Silverstein Nunn. Enslow Publishers 2010 48p il map (The science behind natural disasters) lib bdg $23.93

Grades: 4 5 6   **634.9**
  1. Wildfires
  ISBN 978-0-7660-2973-6 lib bdg; 0-7660-2973-5 lib bdg
                                         LC 2008-48025

"Scientific explanations are accompanied by plentiful color diagrams that will help students to grasp causes and effects. . . . Photos . . . are effective, and are sometimes turned into helpful, lively diagrams by the addition of such features as wind-direction arrows." SLJ

"Examines the science behind wildfires, including what causes them, the different types of wildfires, their devastating effects, and how to stay safe during a wildfire." Publisher's note

Includes glossary and bibliographical references

Trammel, Howard K.

Wildfires; by Howard K. Trammel. Children's Press 2009 48 p. col. ill. (A true book) (library) $29

Grades: 4 5 6   **634.9**
  ISBN 0531168875; 9780531168875
                                         LC 2008014796

This book by Howard K. Trammel is part of the True Books: Earth Science series and looks at wildfires. The series answers questions such as "what makes the earth quake, rivers flood, and volcanoes blow their tops? How do natural forces become natural disasters?" (Publisher's note)

634.11   Apples

Codell, Raji Esme

Seed by seed; the legend and legacy of Johnny "Appleseed" Chapman. by Esme Raji Codell; illustrations by Lynne Rae Perkins. Greenwillow Books 2012 32 p. (trade ed.) $16.99

Grades: K 1 2 3   **634.11**
  1. Legendary characters 2. Picture books for children 3. Frontier and pioneer life -- Middle West 4. Apple growers -- United States -- Biography
  ISBN 0061455156; 9780061455155; 9780061455162
                                         LC 2011033653

In this children's picture book, the author looks at American folk hero John Chapman, also known as Johnny Appleseed, and answers the question "Why should we remember him today, more than two hundred years later, and call him a hero?" by presenting the "five tenets Chapman lived by: 'Use what you have. Share what you have. Respect nature. Try to make peace where there is war. You can reach your destination by taking small steps.'" (Publishers Weekly)

635   Garden crops (Horticulture)

Berkes, Marianne

What's in the garden? by Marianne Berkes; illustrated by Cris Arbo. 1st ed. Dawn Publications 2013 32 p. ill. (hardcover) $16.95; (paperback) $8.95

Grades: K 1 2   **635**
  1. Gardens -- Poetry 2. Picture books for children 3. Gardening 4. Kitchen gardens 5. Vegetable gardening 6. Cooking
  ISBN 1584691891; 9781584691891; 9781584691907
                                         LC 2012024245

This children's gardening book from Marianne Berkes combines "rhyming verses with recipes celebrating the garden's bounty. . . . From the popular ants on a log to the more daring French onion soup, breakfast-y carrot muffins to a dessert of blueberry pie, young chefs are likely to get a wide introduction to both the products of the garden and the culinary arts." (Kirkus Reviews)

Cohen, Whitney

The **book** of gardening projects for kids; 101 ways to get kids outside, dirty, and having fun. Whitney Cohen and John Fisher. 1st ed. Timber Press 2012 264 p. col. ill. $29.95

Grades: Adult   **635**
  1. Gardening 2. Gardens -- Guidebooks 3. Gardens -- Activity projects 4. Gardening for children
  ISBN 1604693738; 9781604692457
                                         LC 2011036778

In this book, "Whitney Cohen and John Fisher draw on years of experience in the Life Lab Garden Classroom and gardening with their own children to teach parents how to integrate the garden into their family life, no matter its scope or scale. The book features . . . gardening advice, including how to design a play-friendly garden, ideas for fun-filled theme gardens, and how to cook and preserve the garden's bounty. 101 . . . garden activities are also featured." (Publisher's note)

Creasy, Rosalind

Blue potatoes, orange tomatoes; illustrations by Ruth Heller. Sierra Club Bks. for Children 1994 40p il hardcover o.p. pa $6.95

Grades: 3 4 5   **635**
  1. Vegetables 2. Vegetable gardening
  ISBN 0-87156-576-5; 0-87156-919-1 pa
                                         LC 92-38800

Describes how to plant and grow a variety of colorful vegetables, including red corn, yellow watermelons, and multicolored radishes, and includes recipes

"With interesting and authentic information about gardening accompanied by brilliant, life-like illustrations, this book will not only promote the delight in growing plants but enhance the wonder in the natural world right in your own backyard." Appraisal

Ehlert, Lois, 1934-

★ **Growing** vegetable soup; written and illustrated by Lois Ehlert. Harcourt Brace Jovanovich 1987 un il $17; pa $7; bd bk $6.95

Grades: PreK K 1 2   **635**
  1. Vegetable gardening -- Fiction 2. Vegetable

gardening
ISBN 0-15-232575-1; 0-15-232580-8 pa; 0-15-205055-8 bd bk

LC 86-22812

"Brightly-colored large illustrations and a boldly-worded text show how to plant and grow vegetables for Dad's soup. Shocking pinks, reds and greens give the illustrations an almost three-dimensional quality and will be good for large audiences of preschoolers." Child Book Rev Serv

Esbaum, Jill

Seed, sprout, pumpkin, pie. National Geographic 2009 16p il (Picture the seasons) pa $5.95
Grades: K 1 2   635
1. Pumpkin
ISBN 978-1-4263-0582-5 pa; 1-4263-0582-6 pa

LC 2009-12735

Discusses how pumpkins grow, the different varieties of pumpkins, and the many ways people use them

"Using minimal text with National Geographic's typically fine photographs, Esbaum brings out familiar, comforting details of the outdoors. . . . Perfect for Halloween, [this] is a veritable festival of orange featuring . . . panoramas of pumpkin fields and market stands, . . . the rarely appreciated pumpkin flower, pumpkins so big people make boats out of them, and . . . jack-'o-lanterns. . . . Fun, cozy, evocative stuff." Booklist

Fridell, Ron

Life cycle of a pumpkin; [by] Ron Fridell and Patricia Walsh. rev ed; Heinemann Library 2009 32p il (Life cycle of a) $25.36; pa $7.99
Grades: 2 3 4   635
1. Pumpkin
ISBN 978-1-4329-2527-7; 1-4329-2527-X; 978-1-4329-2544-4 pa; 1-4329-2544-X pa

LC 00011234

First published 2002

"From seed to seedling, vine, and finally full-grown fruit, the life cycle of the pumpkin is clearly and colorfully described. Bright and engaging full-color photographs amplify the text on each page." SLJ

Includes bibliographical references

Gaarder-Juntti, Oona

What in the world is a green garden? ABDO Pub. Co. 2011 24p il (Going green) lib bdg $24.21
Grades: 1 2 3 4   635
1. Sustainable agriculture
ISBN 978-1-61613-188-3; 1-61613-188-8

LC 2010004322

"The lively layout design, featuring colorful headings, short paragraphs, and attractive photographs, has a scrapbook-like quality. . . . [The title explains] how all our choices require energy and resources, and encourage readers to make changes in their lifestyles. . . . [This] . . . will inspire and empower readers to make a difference." SLJ

Includes glossary and bibliographical references

Gibbons, Gail

The pumpkin book. Holiday House 1999 un il $16.95; pa $6.95

Grades: K 1 2 3   635
1. Pumpkin
ISBN 0-8234-1465-5; 0-8234-1636-4 pa

LC 98-45267

Describes how pumpkins come in different shapes and sizes, how they grow, and their traditional uses and cultural significance. Includes instructions for carving a pumpkin and drying the seeds

"Bold, clear watercolor illustrations and a concise text work together. . . . Gibbons succeeds once again at covering a topic in a useful way at just the right level for beginning readers." SLJ

The vegetables we eat; by Gail Gibbons. Holiday House 2007 32p il $16.95
Grades: K 1 2 3   635
1. Vegetables
ISBN 0-8234-2001-9; 978-0-8234-2001-8

LC 2005052654

"A clear, informative introduction to eight groups of vegetables, categorized by the part of the plant that is eaten. For each group, Gibbons includes an illustration of one representative veggie as it grows in a garden. The rest of the page includes illustrations of related plants. . . . The author offers basic suggestions for starting a garden and shows how produce goes from large farms to processing plants and grocery stores. . . . Familiar paneled illustrations and accessible text combine to present a simple, effective approach to the topic." SLJ

Grow it, cook it. DK Pub. 2008 80p il $15.99
Grades: 3 4 5 6   635
1. Cooking 2. Vegetable gardening
ISBN 978-0-7566-3367-7; 0-7566-3367-2

This "title combines instructions for growing edible plants with recipes based on the harvest. . . . The lush photos of ripening vegetables . . . will spark children's curiosity and inspire them to learn more. . . . Most children will need help . . . as they prepare the delicious, often sophisticated culinary treats. . . . An attractive introduction to both gardening and healthy meals." Booklist

Hirsch, Rebecca E.

Growing your own garden; by Rebecca Hirsch. Cherry Lake Pub. 2010 32p il (Save the planet) lib bdg $27.07
Grades: 3 4 5 6   635
1. Vegetable gardening
ISBN 978-1-60279-657-7 lib bdg; 1-60279-657-2 lib bdg

LC 2009-38093

"At the beginning of . . . [the] book, readers are given a mission and advised to be alert to the facts provided so that they can successfully answer the questions at the end. . . . Children are made to feel part of the process; suggestions for how they can become involved abound." SLJ

Includes glossary and bibliographical references

Malam, John

Grow your own sandwich. Heinemann Library 2011 32p il (Grow it yourself!) lib bdg $26; pa $7.99

Grades: K 1 2   **635**
1. Cooking 2. Tomatoes 3. Vegetable gardening
ISBN 978-1-4329-5108-5 lib bdg; 978-1-4329-5115-3 pa

LC 2010049833

This describes how to grow tomatoes and how to make a cheese and tomato sandwich.

Includes glossary and bibliographical references

Grow your own soup. Heinemann Library 2011 32p il (Grow it yourself!) lib bdg $26; pa $7.99
Grades: 2 3 4   **635**
1. Cooking 2. Pumpkin 3. Vegetable gardening
ISBN 978-1-4329-5106-1 lib bdg; 978-1-4329-5113-9 pa

LC 2010049830

This describes how pumpkins grow, how to plant and raise your own, and how to make pumpkin soup.

Includes glossary and bibliographical references

Morris, Karyn
★ The **Kids** Can Press jumbo book of gardening; written by Karyn Morris; illustrated by Jane Kurisu. Kids Can Press 2000 240p il pa $14.95
Grades: 4 5 6 7   **635**
1. Gardening
ISBN 1-55074-690-1

"Sections cover general information; fruit, vegetable, and flower gardens; noninvasive native plants; gardens that attract wildlife; and group projects. Projects range from a few annuals in a container and thickets designed with native wildlife in mind to community gardens. Directions are clear, with plenty of diagrams and illustrations." Booklist

Ready set grow! quick and easy gardening projects. DK Pub. 2010 79p il $12.99
Grades: 3 4 5   **635**
1. Gardening
ISBN 978-0-7566-5887-8; 0-7566-5887-X

"Sunny and energetic spreads feature more than 30 garden project ideas, aimed at getting kids outdoors and in the dirt. Photographs and illustrations teach the basics about plant cultivation. . . . Recycling is a recurring theme, . . . many of the garden-related projects tend toward the whimsical, . . . and there's a strong emphasis on growing edible plants. . . . The fun, easy, and green concepts should have readers eagerly awaiting spring." Publ Wkly

Rockwell, Anne F.
One bean; pictures by Megan Halsey. Walker & Co. 1998 un il hardcover o.p. pa $6.95
Grades: K 1 2   **635**
1. Beans
ISBN 0-8027-8648-0; 0-8027-7572-1 pa

LC 97-36249

"An easy-to-read text combines with lively illustrations to create the story of what happens to one small bean when it interacts with some soil, just a little water, a lot of sunlight, and a young child's tender care." Sci Child

Rustad, Martha E. H.
Fall pumpkins; orange and plump. illustrated by Amanda Enright. Millbrook Press 2011 24p il (Fall's here) lib bdg $23.93

Grades: K 1 2 3   **635**
1. Pumpkin
ISBN 978-0-7613-5065-1; 0-7613-5065-9

LC 2010048310

The author "takes the young reader on a journey to learn how pumpkins are planted, tended, and grown. . . . The book also shows the reader how to use fully grown pumpkins: carving them for Halloween, making roasted pumpkins seeds, and us the pumpkin meat to make pumpkin pie. . . . The illustrations are very colorful." Sci Books Films

Includes glossary and bibliographical references

Sayre, April Pulley
Touch a butterfly; wildlife gardening with kids. April Pulley Sayre. 1st ed. Roost Books 2013 xiv, 207 p.p (paperback) $19.95
Grades: Adult Professional   **635**
1. Wildlife attracting 2. Gardening3. Garden animals 4. Gardening to attract wildlife
ISBN 1590309170; 9781590309179

LC 2012021579

This book, by April Pulley Sayre, offers instructions on how to "turn your garden into a hummingbird hotspot, a haven for butterflies, and a thriving ecosystem that will delight and inspire the young and young-at-heart. . . . Begin to see your yard from an animal's perspective; discover plants that attract colorful birds and bugs; embrace sensory experiences that native plants and creatures bring; and understand how your yard fits into the surrounding landscape." (Publisher's note)

635.9   Flowers and ornamental plants

Bearce, Stephanie
A **kid's** guide to container gardening. Mitchell Lane Publishers 2009 48p il (Gardening for kids) lib bdg $29.95
Grades: 3 4 5 6   **635.9**
1. Container gardening
ISBN 978-1-58415-814-1 lib bdg; 1-58415-814-X lib bdg

LC 2009001314

This is a guide to growing plants in tubs, buckets, and other containers

This book is "filled with information, which is divided into neat chapters written in a chatty, enthusiastic voice. . . . [The book features] large type, embedded with bolded vocabulary words, . . . as well as sharp color photos on every page." Booklist

Includes bibliographical references

A **kid's** guide to making a terrarium. Mitchell Lane Publishers 2009 48p il (Gardening for kids) lib bdg $29.95
Grades: 3 4 5 6   **635.9**
1. Terrariums
ISBN 978-1-58415-813-4 lib bdg; 1-58415-813-1 lib bdg

LC 2009001319

This book is "filled with information, which is divided into neat chapters written in a chatty, enthusiastic voice. . . . [The book features] large type, embedded with bolded vocabulary words, . . . as well as sharp color photos on every page." Booklist

Includes bibliographical references

636 Animal husbandry

Gunter, Veronika Alice
Pet science; 50 purr-fectly woof-worthy activities for you & your pets. by Veronika Alice Gunter and Rain Newcomb; illustrated by Tom LaBaff. Lark Books 2006 80p il $14.95
Grades: 3 4 5 6   636
1. Pets 2. Science -- Experiments
ISBN 1-57990-786-5

LC 2005-4860

This "book of 50 activities encourages budding ethnologists to investigate, explore, and record their pet's behavior. . . . Delightful four-color illustrations fill the pages. . . . This engaging book is a delightful way to bring science to young children." Sci Books Films

Includes glossary

Jones, Charlotte Foltz
The **king** who barked; real animals who ruled. illustrated by Yayo. Holiday House 2009 40p il $16.95
Grades: 3 4 5   636
1. Animals
ISBN 978-0-8234-1925-8; 0-8234-1925-8

LC 2008-25669

"The brief accounts in this whimsical collection of animal anecdotes introduce symbolic leaders such as goat mayors, dog-kings, and a rhinoceros who won a seat on the São Paulo city council in a write-in campaign. The stories, which are arranged by continent of origin, hail from legends and oral histories, though some are more recent and better documented. Yayo's acrylic-on-canvas paintings capture the topsy-turvy spirit of the tales and add playful details." SLJ

Includes bibliographical references

Keenan, Sheila
★ **Animals** in the house; a history of pets and people. Scholastic Nonfiction 2007 112p il $17.99
Grades: 4 5 6   636
1. Pets
ISBN 978-0-439-69286-1; 0-439-69286-5

"Keenan provides an overview of pets andtheir people. Beginning with statistics about pet ownership, the text goes on to describe how animals and humans came together . . . and discusses how this relationship has changed and deepened. . . . Eye-catchingly designed, the format uses Photoshop to best advantage, providing interesting graphics, popping borders, and plenty of pictures featuring adorable animals." Booklist

Includes bibliographical references

Love, Ann
Talking tails; the incredible connection between people and their pets. [by] Ann Love & Jane Drake; illustrated by Bill Slavin. Tundra Books 2010 80p il $22.95
Grades: 3 4 5 6   636
1. Pets
ISBN 978-0-88776-884-2; 0-88776-884-9

"Focusing mainly on dogs and cats but with some attention to fish, reptiles, rodents, and birds, Love and Drake celebrate the affection that connects people with their pets. Along with providing a historical overview of animal domestication, . . . the authors profile some famous real pets. . . . They run through major cat and dog breeds; discuss characteristic instincts, personalities, behavior, and body language; and explain how to plan for, choose, . . . and care for an animal. . . . Slavin skillfully captures the bountiful warmth here. . . . This will draw animal lovers like a magnet." Booklist

Martin, Claudia
Farming. Marshall Cavendish Benchmark 2010 64p il (Working animals) $28.50
Grades: 4 5 6 7   636
1. Agriculture 2. Domestic animals
ISBN 978-1-60870-162-9; 1-60870-162-X

LC 2010006895

"Attractively designed and packed with information. . . . The composition of each page is attractively set up with well-selected and reproduced stock and historical photos." SLJ

Montgomery, Sy
Temple Grandin; how the girl who loved cows embraced autism and changed the world. by Sy Montgomery. Houghton Mifflin Harcourt 2012 147 p. col. ill. $17.99
Grades: 4 5 6 7 8   636
1. Autism 2. Cattle 3. Biography 4. Women scientists -- Biography 5. Animal welfare -- United States 6. Livestock -- Housing -- United States 7. Livestock -- Handling -- United States 8. Autistic people -- United States -- Biography 9. Animal scientists -- United States -- Biography 10. Animal specialists -- United States -- Biography 11. Women animal specialists -- United States -- Biography
ISBN 0547443153; 9780547443157

LC 2011039911

AAAS/Subaru SB&F Prize for Excellence in Science Books: Middle Grade Science Book (2013)

This book by Sy Montgomery presents a biography of autistic animal scientist Temple Grandin. Sy Montgomery argues that "though one never outgrows autism, it doesn't condemn those who have it to unproductive lives, and an appendix, 'Temple's Advice for Kids on the Spectrum,' provides first-hand wisdom. Photos and diagrams depict Grandin's work as well as documenting her early life and career." (Kirkus Reviews)

Includes bibliographical references and index.

Steele, Christy
Cattle ranching in the American West; by Christy Steele. World Almanac Library 2005 48p il map (America's westward expansion) lib bdg $30; pa $11.95
Grades: 5 6 7 8   636
1. Cattle 2. Ranch life 3. West (U.S.) -- History
ISBN 0-8368-5787-9 lib bdg; 0-8368-5794-1 pa

LC 2004-56769

This volume describing Western cattle ranching is "richly illustrated with historical photographs, illustrations, maps, and quotes from primary sources presented in sidebars." SLJ

Includes bibliographical references

Tafuri, Nancy

★ **Spots,** feathers, and curly tails. Greenwillow Bks. 1988 un il $16.95

Grades: PreK K 1 2 **636**

1. Domestic animals

ISBN 0-688-07536-3; 0-688-07537-1 lib bdg

LC 87-15638

Questions and answers highlight some outstanding characteristics of farm animals, such as a chicken's feathers and a horse's mane

"In the watercolor illustrations with black pen outline, Nancy Tafuri manages in the simplest style to give energy and personality to the animals through the angle of a head or the set of a snout. The story will provide a successful experience for both child and adult reader and is an ideal book for the beginning reader to entertain a younger sibling in a game they'll both enjoy." Horn Book

Turner, Pamela S.

★ **Hachiko**; written by Pamela S. Turner; illustrated by Yan Nascimbene. Houghton Mifflin 2004 un il $15

Grades: K 1 2 3 **636**

1. Dogs -- Fiction 2. Japan -- Fiction

ISBN 0-618-14094-8

LC 2002-155546

This "picture book pays tribute to one of the world's lesser-known animal heroes: Hachiko, a dog who kept vigil for nearly 10 years at a Tokyo train station, waiting for his deceased master to return from work. Turner unfolds this poignant true story in the natural, unaffected voice of Kentaro, a fictional little boy, who wonders at the dog's unswerving devotion. Unobtrusive details evoke a sense of place . . . as does Nascimbene's spare line-and-watercolor artwork, reminiscent of Japanese woodblock prints. . . . This will resonate with any child who has loved a dog and been loved in return." Booklist

636.08 Specific topics in animal husbandry

Curtis, Jennifer Keats

Sanctuaries; by Jennifer Keats Curtis; with Karine Aigner [and nine others] Sylvan Dell Publishing 2013 32 p. (Animal helpers) (English hardcover) $17.95

Grades: K 1 2 **636.08**

1. Animal rescue 2. Animal sanctuaries 3. Wildlife refuges

ISBN 160718611X; 9781607186113; 9781607186236

LC 2012039949

In this book, "using examples from six animal-rescue organizations . . . [Jennifer Keats] Curtis describes what wild-animal sanctuaries do. Short informational paragraphs are set on . . . photographs of animals being cared for. The account begins with a series of portraits of shelter animals: several tigers, a binturong, a declawed Canadian lynx, a pair of blind bobcats and a bear. The author goes on to describe animal medical and dental treatments, training and enrichment." (Kirkus Reviews)

Doner, Kim

On a road in Africa; [by] Kim Doner; afterword by Chryssee Perry Martin. Tricycle Press 2008 un il $15.95

Grades: PreK K 1 2 **636.08**

1. Stories in rhyme 2. Wildlife conservation 3. Animals -- Africa

ISBN 978-1-58246-230-1; 1-58246-230-5

LC 2007-18199

"This is a lovely picture book to share as a rhyming story, animal book, or cultural introduction." Libr Media Connect

"Doner celebrates the work of Chryssee Perry Martin, dubbed 'Mama Orphanage' for her work as an honorary warden of the Kenya Wildlife Service." SLJ

Kehret, Peg

Animals welcome; a life of reading, writing, and rescue. Peg Kehret. W.W. Norton & Co. Inc. 2012 272 p. (hardback) $16.99

Grades: 4 5 6 7 **636.08**

1. Wildlife 2. Autobiography 3. Animal behavior 4. Animal rescue -- United States -- Anecdotes 5. Animal welfare -- United States -- Anecdotes 6. Animal shelters -- United States -- Anecdotes

ISBN 0525423990; 9780525423997

LC 2011035440

Author Peg Kehret shares "her life on a small wildlife sanctuary, . . . the tragedy of her husband's sudden death, and the pain of losing Pete, the shelter cat who co-authored three of her books." In addition to stories of animal rescue and facts about birds and animals, the book is "a personal glimpse into the life of an author who loves animals, and the philosophy by which she lives." (Publisher's note)

Larson, Kirby

Two Bobbies; a true story of Hurricane Katrina, friendship, and survival. [by] Kirby Larson and Mary Nethery; illustrations by Jean Cassels. Walker & Co. 2008 un il $16.99

Grades: K 1 2 3 **636.08**

1. Cats 2. Dogs 3. Hurricane Katrina, 2005

ISBN 978-0-8027-9754-4; 0-8027-9754-7

"Abandoned during the [Hurricane] Katrina evacuations, pets Bobbi [the dog] and Bob Cat wander dangerous, debris-strewn streets seeking food and water. Eventually taken to a rescue shelter, the Bobbies show distress when separated but remain calm when together. Workers then discover that Bob Cat is blind and that Bobbi seems to serve as his seeing-eye dog. . . . The descriptive, sometimes folksy prose and realistically rendered gouache illustrations accessibly convey the Bobbies' experiences and mutual devotion. . . . This moving story about the importance of friendship and home highlights the plight of the hurricane's lost and left-behind animals, as well as the value of animal shelters." Booklist

636.088 Animals for specific purposes

Grayson, Robert

Transportation. Marshall Cavendish Benchmark 2010 64p il (Working animals) $28.50

Grades: 4 5 6 7 **636.088**

1. Pack animals (Transportation)

ISBN 978-1-60870-167-4; 1-60870-167-0

LC 2010006899

"Describes animals that people all over the world use to transport people and goods, such as elephants, horses, yaks, water buffalo, and dogs." Publisher's note

Includes glossary and bibliographical references

Halls, Kelly Milner

Saving the Baghdad Zoo; a true story of hope and heroes. by Kelly Milner Halls, with William Sumner. Greenwillow Books 2010 64p il map $17.99

Grades: 4 5 6 7   636.088

1. Zoos 2. Wildlife conservation 3. Baghdad (Iraq) 4. Baghdad Zoo (Iraq)

ISBN 978-0-06-177202-3; 0-06-177202-X

LC 2008-52820

"This eye-opening tale of compassion and cooperation chronicles the mission of an international team of military personnel, zoo staffers, veterinarians, and relief workers to rescue neglected animals in Baghdad. . . . Sobering and uplifting photographs—many taken by Sumner—underscore both the direness of the situation and the spirit of hope that drove the project." Publ Wkly

Includes bibliographical references

Kent, Deborah

★ Animal helpers for the disabled. Watts 2003 63p il (Watts library) hardcover o.p. $25.50

Grades: 4 5 6 7   636.088

1. Guide dogs 2. Animals and people with disabilities 3. Animals -- Training

ISBN 0-531-12017-1; 0-531-16663-5 pa

LC 2002-8885

Explores the history of guide dogs, service animals, and assistance dogs, and discusses the process of training them to help people who have physical disabilities

This is an "informative, often inspirational and thought-provoking [book]." Booklist

Includes bibliographical references

Laidlaw, Rob

Wild animals in captivity; [by] Rob Laidlaw. Fitzhenry & Whiteside 2008 48p il $19.95

Grades: 4 5 6 7 8   636.088

1. Zoos 2. Animal welfare

ISBN 978-1-55455-025-8; 1-55455-025-4

"A passionate, well-written, and well-researched argument against the practices of most zoos around the world. . . . Describes the damage done when animals are unnaturally confined and moved to inhospitable climates, and compares the wild and captive lives of polar bears, orcas, elephants, and great apes—the four species most harmed by captivity. . . . The issues raised in this important and powerful book will resonate with young and old." SLJ

Markle, Sandra

Animal heroes; true rescue stories. by Sandra Markle. Millbrook Press 2009 64p il lib bdg $29.27

Grades: 4 5 6 7   636.088

1. Pets 2. Animals 3. Rescue work

ISBN 978-0-8225-7884-0 lib bdg; 0-8225-7884-0 lib bdg

LC 2007-50435

"Nine stories, based on interviews with the grateful survivors, describe how brave animals rescued people in catastrophic circumstances. Each edgy retelling reveals details

that only the participants could know, including sounds, smells, sights, and the knowledge that at any moment they could die, deepening the tension. Mixed in are Markle's broad and perfectly attuned insights about animal behavior." SLJ

Includes glossary and bibliographical references

636.089 Veterinary medicine

Jackson, Donna M.

ER vets; life in an animal emergency room. Houghton Mifflin 2005 88p il $17

Grades: 5 6 7 8   636.089

1. Veterinary medicine

ISBN 0-618-43663-4

"With plentiful, excellent-quality photographs, this highly visual book offers a behind-the-scenes look at an emergency animal hospital in Colorado. . . . A section on grief counseling for families with critically ill pets and a spread on how to put together a pet first-aid kit are included. Well-researched and well-written, ER Vets is an engaging book on a hot topic." SLJ

636.1 Horses

Barnes, Julia

Horses at work; [by] Julia Barnes. North American ed.; Gareth Stevens 2006 32p il (Animals at work) lib bdg $23.93

Grades: 3 4 5   636.1

1. Horses 2. Working animals

ISBN 0-8368-6225-2

LC 2005054066

This describes horses' uses throughout history, their relationship with humans, habitat, diet, and appearance.

This is "well-written, well-organized, . . . visually appealing and fun to read." SLJ

Includes bibliographical references

Bowers, Nathan

4-H guide to training horses. Voyageur Press 2009 176p il $18.99

Grades: 5 6 7 8   636.1

1. Horses -- Training

ISBN 978-0-7603-3627-4; 0-7603-3627-X

LC 2009015299

This provides "sound and comprehensive information. [The book] covers basic training techniques and riding skills such as mounting, saddling, reining, stopping and starting, and posture among other topics. The training techniques offer insight into equine behavior based on their history as prey animals. The authors also emphasize that horse owners' success will be determined by how much effort they are willing to expend on their relationship with their animals. The many color photographs clearly depict the methods and activities that are taking place, and the accompanying images further clarify what is happening and its significance." SLJ

Includes glossary

Bozzo, Linda

My first horse; [by] Linda Bozzo. Enslow Elementary 2007 32p il (My first pet library from the American Humane Association) lib bdg $22.60

Grades: 1 2 3   **636.1**

1. Horses

ISBN 978-0-7660-2753-4 lib bdg; 0-7660-2753-8 lib bdg

LC 2006014969

This offers brief basic advice on selecting a horse and caring for it.

Includes glossary and bibliographical references

Crosby, Jeff

Harness horses, bucking broncos & pit ponies; a history of horse breeds. written and illustrated by Jeff Crosby and Shelley Ann Jackson. Tundra Books 2011 69p il map $21.99

Grades: 4 5 6 7   **636.1**

1. Horses

ISBN 978-0-88776-986-3; 0-88776-986-1

"After a brief introduction, the animals are grouped by the roles they have played in relation to people: 'Rapid Transit,' 'Military Advantage,' 'Horsepower,' 'Equine Entertainment,' and 'Feral Horses.' The concise and interesting information on each of the 43 breeds is accompanied by an illustration of the type as well as one of the horse in action and often includes a small map showing its origins. The excellent painterly pictures clearly capture the unique life of each horse." SLJ

Includes bibliographical references

Draper, Judith

★ **My** first horse and pony care book; [by] Judith Draper. Kingfisher 2006 48p il $9.95

Grades: K 1 2 3   **636.1**

1. Horses 2. Horsemanship

ISBN 978-0-7534-5989-8; 0-7534-5989-2

LC 2006005962

"Draper focuses on pony breeds commonly used in the United Kingdom and on English-style riding and tack. The information about feeding, grooming, and riding is detailed, accurate, and accessible. . . . The photographs are beautiful and in sharp focus. . . . This book is a must-have for young horse lovers." SLJ

Includes glossary

Gibbons, Gail

Horses! Holiday House 2003 un il $17.95; pa $6.95

Grades: K 1 2 3   **636.1**

1. Horses 2. Horsemanship

ISBN 0-8234-1703-4; 0-8234-1875-8 pa

LC 2003-41683

Presents information on horses, including their physical characteristics, behavior, and how to ride a horse

"Attractive, full-color labeled illustrations fill every page, with many expanding on a particular point in the main text. . . . The book's accessible format will attract browsers as well as legions of young would-be equestrians." Booklist

Hamilton, Libby

Horse: the essential guide for young equestrians; writer, Libby Hamilton; illustrators: Sophie Allsopp . . . [et al.] Candlewick Press 2008 24p il $15.99

Grades: 2 3 4 5   **636.1**

1. Horses

ISBN 978-0-7636-3547-3; 0-7636-3547-2

"This clever and pleasing guide contains a wealth of information on horses, including history, breeds, care and grooming, equipment, riding, and shows. Facts and tips are presented in an imaginative and lively format. The excellent, realistic illustrations are colorful and accurate and even occasionally humorous." SLJ

Jeffrey, Laura S.

★ **Horses**; how to choose and care for a horse. Enslow Publishers 2004 48p il (American Humane pet care library) lib bdg $23.93

Grades: 3 4 5   **636.1**

1. Horses

ISBN 0-7660-2519-5

LC 2003-22970

Provides information on owning a horse, including how to choose among different breeds and how to groom, house, feed, and keep a horse healthy

This offers "children solid information . . . at a level they can understand. Many endearing photos . . . make [this book] fun to look at." Booklist

Includes glossary and bibliographical references

Lewin, Ted

★ **Stable**. Roaring Brook Press/Flash Point 2010 un il $17.99

Grades: K 1 2 3   **636.1**

1. Horses 2. Brooklyn (New York, N.Y.) 3. Kensington Stables (New York, N.Y.)

ISBN 978-1-59643-467-7; 1-59643-467-8

LC 2009-44431

"Lewin conveys the spirit of a Brooklyn institution through sumptuously detailed, luminous watercolors. Kensington Stables, a relic from the days when horses provided necessary transportation, shelters 37 animals, large and small. . . . The straightforward, present-tense prose conveys the central point that horses are important to the community, and they should be preserved." Kirkus

Lomberg, Michelle

Horse. Weigl Publishers 2009 32p il (My pet) lib bdg $26; pa $9.95

Grades: 3 4 5   **636.1**

1. Pets 2. Horses

ISBN 978-1-60596-092-0 lib bdg; 1-60596-092-6 lib bdg; 978-1-60596-093-7 pa; 1-60596-093-4 pa

LC 2009-25974

Information about how to house, feed, and care for horses.

"With clear, formal writing, and extensive coverage . . . [this title is] useful for reports. . . . Numerous color photographs, charts . . . and question-and-answer boxes supplement the [text]." SLJ

Includes glossary

Lunis, Natalie

Miniature horses. Bearport 2010 24p il (Peculiar pets) lib bdg $22.61

Grades: 3 4 5   **636.1**
1. Horses
ISBN 978-1-59716-861-8 lib bdg; 1-59716-861-0
lib bdg

LC 2009-10379

Introduces the miniature horse, describing its physical characteristics, history, and behavior, and discussing the care and diet that it needs

"The language . . . is lively . . . [and] the illustrations are vivid, with photos offering some amusing shots. . . . This [book] . . . will hold readers' attention, but also challenge them to consider the responsibilities required of owners of unusual creatures." SLJ

Includes glossary and bibliographical references

Mack, Gail

Horses. Marshall Cavendish Benchmark 2010 48p il (Great pets) lib bdg $29.93
Grades: 2 3 4   **636.1**
1. Horses
ISBN 978-0-7614-4147-2 lib bdg; 0-7614-4147-6
lib bdg

LC 2008037262

"Describes the characteristics and behavior of pet horses, also discussing their physical appearance and place in history." Publisher's note

Includes glossary and bibliographical references

MacLeod, Elizabeth

Why do horses have manes? Kids Can Press 2009 64p $14.95
Grades: 3 4 5 6   **636.1**
1. Horses
ISBN 978-1-55453-312-1; 1-55453-312-0

In a question and answer format "this slim volume covers standard information . . . and branches out to the more esoteric. . . . Freestanding text sections with a light and engaging tone combined with glossy photo vignettes of horses vamping for the camera make the book highly browsable." Horn Book Guide

Niven, Felicia Lowenstein

Learning to care for a horse. Enslow Publishers 2010 48p il (Beginning pet care with American Humane) lib bdg $23.93
Grades: 2 3 4   **636.1**
1. Horses
ISBN 978-0-7660-3196-8; 0-7660-3196-9

LC 2008048961

"Readers will learn how to choose a horse and care for a horse, from what kind of horse is best for them and how long they live." Publisher's note

Includes glossary and bibliographical references

Ransford, Sandy

Horse & pony breeds; written by Sandy Ransford; photographed by Bob Langrish. Kingfisher (NY) 2003 64p il (Kingfisher riding club) $14.95; pa $8.99
Grades: 4 5 6 7   **636.1**
1. Horses
ISBN 0-7534-5575-7; 0-7534-6075-0 pa

LC 2003-272944

An "overview of an international array of horse and pony breeds including many that may be unfamiliar to American children. The book covers the majority of breeds in half-page treatments that feature at least a paragraph of commentary and a captioned side body, and a full-color photograph that points out conformation differences particular to each breed. . . . An attractive, informative book that is sure to please both readers and browsers." SLJ

Includes glossary

Horse & pony care; written by Sandy Ransford; photographed by Bob Langrish. Kingfisher (NY) 2002 64p il (Kingfisher riding club) hardcover o.p. pa $8.95
Grades: 4 5 6 7   **636.1**
1. Horses
ISBN 0-7534-5439-4; 0-7534-5744-X pa

This offers instructions on such topics as washing and clipping a pony, exercise routines and caring for pastureland, and includes information about types of feed and how much feed a pony needs

"Children who have a horse or want one will find a good deal of information in this attractive, photo-rich book. There are clear instructions. . . . The full-color photos are well composed, fully captioned, and quite thorough." Booklist

★ The **Kingfisher** illustrated horse & pony encyclopedia; written by Sandy Ransford; photographed by Bob Langrish. Kingfisher 2004 224p il $24.95
Grades: 4 5 6 7   **636.1**
1. Horses 2. Horsemanship
ISBN 0-7534-5781-4

LC 2003-27293

"The first part of the book covers the life cycle, domestication, and types of horses and ponies. . . . The second part deals with how to care for these animals and discusses horsemanship from taking riding lessons to training and driving a horse. . . . Filled with appealing photos of young people interacting with their four-legged friends, this title is an extremely useful addition to any collection." SLJ

Rockwood, Leigh

Horses are smart! PowerKids Press 2010 24p il (Super smart animals) lib bdg $21.25; pa $8.25
Grades: 2 3 4 5   **636.1**
1. Horses
ISBN 978-1-4358-9399-3 lib bdg; 1-4358-9399-9 lib bdg; 978-1-4358-9838-7 pa; 1-4358-9838-9 pa

Examines the intelligence of horses.

"Bright, colorful, captioned photographs complement the text. Rockwood does an excellent job of simplifying the information without making it choppy or boring." Libr Media Connect

Includes glossary

Simon, Seymour

★ **Horses**. HarperCollins Pubs. 2006 un il $15.99; lib bdg $16.89
Grades: 2 3 4   **636.1**
1. Horses
ISBN 0-06-028944-9; 0-06-028945-7 lib bdg

LC 2004-30392

"Simon provides the basic facts, which include the importance of horses to humans throughout history, their evolution, physical traits, interactions among themselves, and the various breeds. The information is clear and accurate.

The striking color photos will capture readers attention." SLJ

Wilsdon, Christina

For horse-crazy girls only; everything you want to know about horses. illustrated by Alecia Underhill. Feiwel and Friends 2010 150p il $14.99

Grades: 4 5 6 7　　　　　　　　　　　　　**636.1**

1. Horses

ISBN 978-0-312-60323-6; 0-312-60323-1

LC 2010015677

"Filled with quizzes, trivia, top 10 lists, and information about equine behavior, history, sports, and more, this guidebook aims straight at the hearts of horse-loving tweens. . . . The book runs the gamut from how to pick a horse's name to horses in popular culture, the evolution of the species, and horse-related events nationwide. The many sidebars, tidbits, and anecdotes encourage casual browsing-horse lovers will be in heaven." Publ Wkly

636.2　Cattle and related animals

Barnes, Julia

Camels and llamas at work; [by] Julia Barnes. Gareth Stevens 2006 32p il map (Animals at work) lib bdg $23.93

Grades: 3 4 5　　　　　　　　　　　　　**636.2**

1. Camels 2. Llamas 3. Working animals

ISBN 0-8368-6222-8

LC 2005054065

This is "well-written, well-organized, . . . visually appealing and fun to read." SLJ

Includes bibliographical references

Boynton, Sandra

Amazing cows; udder absurdity for children. Workman Pub. 2010 89p il $15.99; pa $10.95

Grades: K 1 2　　　　　　　　　　　　　**636.2**

1. Cattle

ISBN 978-0-7611-6371-8; 0-7611-6371-9; 978-0-7611-6214-8 pa; 0-7611-6214-3 pa

LC 2010034583

Jokes, humorous stories and poems, a comic book and other misinformation about cows.

"Not since the heyday of Gary Larson has so much adoration been shown to bovines. With her trademark irreverence, Boynton offers an impassioned and hyperbolic ode to cows, replete with jokes, a spread devoted to cow fashion, a cow 'myth' that takes place in ancient Athens . . . , limericks, and puns aplenty. . . . It's pure fun." Publ Wkly

Diemer, Lauren

Cows. Weigl Publishers 2010 24p il (World of wonder: watch them grow) lib bdg $25.70; pa $9.95

Grades: 1 2　　　　　　　　　　　　　**636.2**

1. Cattle

ISBN 978-1-60596-919-0 lib bdg; 1-60596-919-2 lib bdg; 978-1-60596-920-6 pa; 1-60596-920-6 pa

LC 2009052101

Learn about how cows are born and grow up, as well as their role in the world.

The text "is simple without being simplistic; it is thoughtful and comprehensive without being overwhelming. The real appeal for teachers, students, and independent young readers, however, will be the photographs that fill the facing pages. Bold, bright, and colorful, the photographs bring you marvelously close to the subject. . . . On many different levels, this is a very appealing [book]." Libr Media Connect

Includes glossary

Freedman, Russell

★　In the days of the vaqueros; America's first true cowboys. Clarion Bks. 2001 70p il $18; pa $9.99

Grades: 4 5 6 7　　　　　　　　　　　　　**636.2**

1. Cowhands 2. Ranch life 3. Mexican Americans 4. Southwestern States

ISBN 0-395-96788-0; 978-0-395-96788-1; 978-0-547-13365-2 pa; 0-547-13365-0 pa

LC 2001-17357

The author "tells the story with depth, clarity, and a vigor that conveys the thrilling excitement of the work and the macho swagger of the culture. . . . The book's design is beautiful, with spacious type on thick paper, and the dazzling illustrations—prints, paintings, and photos on almost every page." Booklist

Includes glossary and bibliographical references

Peterson, Cris

Clarabelle; making milk and so much more. [by] Cris Peterson; photographs by David R. Lundquist. Boyds Mills Press 2007 un il $16.95

Grades: 1 2 3　　　　　　　　　　　　　**636.2**

1. Cattle 2. Dairying

ISBN 1-59078-310-7; 978-1-59078-310-8

This focuses on "a dairy farm in northern Wisconsin, introduced through the daily life of a single cow, Clarabelle. In describing the basics of cow physiology and care and the dairy's operations, Peterson illuminates facts with comparisons that will grab kids' attention. . . . Lundquist's sharp, close-up photographs . . . will easily draw curious kids back into the science." Booklist

Includes glossary

Pinkney, Andrea Davis

★　Bill Pickett, rodeo-ridin' cowboy; written by Andrea D. Pinkney; illustrated by Brian Pinkney. Harcourt Brace & Co. 1996 un il hardcover o.p. pa $7

Grades: K 1 2 3　　　　　　　　　　　　　**636.2**

1. Rodeos 2. Cowhands 3. Cowboys 4. African Americans -- Biography

ISBN 0-15-200100-X; 0-15-202103-5 pa

LC 95-35920

Describes the life and accomplishments of the son of a former slave whose unusual bulldogging style made him a rodeo star

"The story is told with verve, relish, and just enough of a cowboy twang, with Pinkney giving an excellent overview of the history of rodeos and black cowboys in a closing note. Husband Brian Pinkney's pictures, in his typical scratchboard technique, are well suited to the story, their lines and colors swirling with movement and excitement on the deep black surface." Booklist

Includes bibliographical references

636.3   Sheep and goats

Minden, Cecilia

Sheep. Cherry Lake Pub. 2010 24p il (21st century junior library: farm animals) lib bdg $22.80

Grades: 1 2 3   **636.3**

1. Sheep

ISBN 978-1-60279-544-0 lib bdg; 1-60279-544-4 lib bdg

LC 2009-3318

This is an introduction to sheep as farm animals

This manages "to parlay [its] low page count into surprisingly deep and wide-ranging discussions on the various aspects of [the sheep's] existence. . . . It's the text that is so impressive, with its use of simple, explanatory language to introduce unusually advanced vocabulary. . . . [The] animal is not only shown in its natural (and often adorable) state but also as meat on a plate. Info boxes called 'Think!' expand the discussion even further." Booklist

Includes glossary and bibliographical references

Urbigkit, Cat

The shepherd's trail; [by] Cat Urbigkit. Boyds Mills Press 2008 32p il $16.95

Grades: 2 3 4   **636.3**

1. Sheep 2. Shepherds

ISBN 978-1-59078-509-6

LC 2007017475

This "discusses the migration of domestic sheep in the western U.S. . . . Clear color photos offer close-ups of individual animals and long-range views of the flocks and the often striking landscapes. Topics discussed in the text include the roles of sheepherders, camptenders, herding dogs, guardian dogs, and sheepshearers, as well as details of the sheep's lives through the cycle of a year." Booklist

A young shepherd. Boyd Mills Press 2006 un il $15.95

Grades: K 1 2 3   **636.3**

1. Sheep 2. Shepherds

ISBN 1-59078-364-6

"This photo-essay features a 12-year-old 4-H member (Urbigkit's son) who tends his own flock of sheep. Urbigkit . . . communicates Cass' commitment to his task in compelling photos that showcase the gamboling baby animals. . . . The close-up look at a fascinating, animal-focused activity will appeal even to readers who rarely rub shoulders with livestock." Booklist

636.4   Swine

Gibbons, Gail

Pigs. Holiday House 1999 un il $16.95; pa $6.95

Grades: K 1 2 3   **636.4**

1. Pigs

ISBN 0-8234-1441-8; 0-8234-1554-6 pa

LC 98-28807

Examines the basic characteristics, common breeds, intelligence, behavior, life cycle, and uses of pigs

"Bright with spring greens and yellows, this attractive book introduces pigs through simple sentences and many colorful pictures." Booklist

King-Smith, Dick

★ All pigs are beautiful; illustrated by Anita Jeram. Candlewick Press 1993 un il (Read and wonder) hardcover o.p. pa $6.99; pa with audio CD $9.99

Grades: K 1 2 3   **636.4**

1. Pigs

ISBN 978-0-7636-1433-1 pa; 0-7636-1433-5 pa; 978-0-7636-4195-5 pa with audio CD; 0-7636-4195-2 pa with audio CD

LC 92-53136

The author "interlards fond reminiscences of porkers he has known with interesting facts about them that are sure to keep children absorbed. His tone is affectionate, amusing, and informative. Jeram's pen-and-ink and watercolor illustrations, done in soft, earthy colors, are a warm match for the text." SLJ

Minden, Cecilia

Pigs. Cherry Lake Pub. 2010 24p il (21st century junior library: farm animals) lib bdg $22.80

Grades: 1 2 3   **636.4**

1. Pigs

ISBN 978-1-60279-542-6 lib bdg; 1-60279-542-8 lib bdg

LC 2009-3676

This is an introduction to pigs as farm animals

This manages "to parlay [its] low page count into surprisingly deep and wide-ranging discussions on the various aspects of [the pig's] existence. . . . It's the text that is so impressive, with its use of simple, explanatory language to introduce unusually advanced vocabulary. . . . [The] animal is not only shown in its natural (and often adorable) state but also as meat on a plate. Info boxes called 'Think!' expand the discussion even further ([The book] encourages readers to ask why some of their friends may not eat pork)." Booklist

Includes glossary and bibliographical references

Rockwood, Leigh

Pigs are smart! PowerKids Press 2010 24p il (Super smart animals) lib bdg $21.25; pa $8.25

Grades: 2 3 4 5   **636.4**

1. Pigs

ISBN 978-1-4358-9373-3 lib bdg; 1-4358-9373-5 lib bdg; 978-1-4358-9834-9 pa; 1-4358-9834-6 pa

Examines the intelligence of pigs

"Readers get an overview of the . . . [pig's] life cycle, its domestic history (where relevant), and natural habitat, and examples of how it is smart in the wild as well as when helped by human tutelage. . . . Interesting color photographs and large, easy-to-read print will attract browsers and report writers alike." SLJ

Includes glossary

636.5   Chickens and other kinds of domestic birds

Dickmann, Nancy

A chicken's life. Heinemann Library 2011 24p il (Watch it grow) lib bdg $21.50; pa $5.99

Grades: PreK K 1   **636.5**
  1. Chickens
  ISBN 978-1-4329-4139-0 lib bdg; 1-4329-4139-9 lib
  bdg; 978-1-4329-4148-2 pa; 1-4329-4148-8 pa
           LC 2009-49153
"Practically unique among early introductions to life
cycles because death is mentioned . . . this . . . follows [a
chicken] . . . from egg . . . to maturity with a set of close-up
color photographs, one per page, paired to large-type, one or
two-sentence captions. . . . Offers nourishing fare for young
naturalists." SLJ

Includes glossary and bibliographical references

Gibbons, Gail
  Chicks & chickens. Holiday House 2003 un il
$17.95; pa $6.95
Grades: K 1 2 3   **636.5**
  1. Chickens
  ISBN 0-8234-1700-X; 0-8234-1939-8 pa
           LC 2002-27472
An introduction to the physical characteristics, behavior,
and life cycle of chickens, as well as a discussion of how
chickens are raised on farms

The author "offers lots of solid information as well as
bits of trivia that will be of interest to this audience. Cartoon
illustrations are large, colorful, and plentiful." SLJ

Heppermann, Christine
  City chickens; by Christine Heppermann. Houghton
Mifflin Books for Children 2012 47 p. ill. (chiefly col.)
(hardcover) $16.99; (ebook) $16.99
Grades: 4 5   **636.5**
  1. Animal housing 2. Animal behavior 3. Birds --
Protection 4. Chickens 5. Animal welfare 6. Animal
shelters 7. Chickens -- Minnesota -- Anecdotes
  ISBN 0547518307; 9780547518305; 9780547518336
           LC 2011009754
In author Christine Hepperman's book, she provides stories of adopted chickens. "Just outside of downtown Minneapolis, follow the sounds of crowing and clucking and you
will find Mary Britton Clouse's Chicken Run Rescue. Over
the years, Mary and her husband have given hundreds of
homeless birds a safe place to rest until they can be adopted
by caring families." (Publisher's note)

Includes bibliographical references.

Kindschi, Tara
  4-H guide to raising chickens. Voyageur Press 2010
176p il pa $18.99
Grades: 5 6 7 8   **636.5**
  1. Chickens
  ISBN 978-0-7603-3628-1 pa; 0-7603-3628-8 pa
           LC 2009015300
"This title has everything one ever wanted to know about
chickens but didn't know enough to ask. Eight chapters divide the text into broad topics such as getting started, choosing a breed, housing equipment, and exhibiting chickens. . .
. Line drawings and charts give additional information, and
the excellent color photography is profuse." SLJ

Includes glossary and bibliographical references

Minden, Cecilia
  Ducks. Cherry Lake Pub. 2010 24p il (21st century
junior library: farm animals) lib bdg $22.80

Grades: 1 2 3   **636.5**
  1. Ducks
  ISBN 978-1-60279-546-4 lib bdg; 1-60279-546-0
lib bdg
           LC 2009-5033
This is an introduction to ducks as farm animals

This manages "to parlay [its] low page count into surprisingly deep and wide-ranging discussions on the various
aspects of [the duck's] existence. . . . It's the text that is so
impressive, with its use of simple, explanatory language to
introduce unusually advanced vocabulary. In [this book]
readers learn such terminology as clutch, dabbling, and
gland. . . . [The] animal is not only shown in its natural (and
often adorable) state but also as meat on a plate. Info boxes
called 'Think!' expand the discussion even further." Booklist

Includes glossary and bibliographical references

Page, Robin
  A **chicken** followed me home; questions and answers
about a familiar fowl. by Robin Page. Beach Lane Books
2015 40 p. color illustrations (hardcover: alk. paper)
$17.99
Grades: PreK K 1 2 3   **636.5**
  1. Chickens 2. Children's questions and answers
  ISBN 1481410288; 9781481410281
           LC 2013041955
In this nonfiction book for children "author-illustrator
Robin Page leads a step-by-step, question-and-answer-style
journey through the world of chickens. Along the way you'll
explore different breeds, discover different types of coops,
and learn everything there is to know about chicken reproduction and hatching." (Publisher's note)

Includes bibliographical references

Sklansky, Amy E.
  Where do chicks come from? illustrated by Pam Paparone. HarperCollins Publishers 2005 un il (Let's-read-
and-find-out science) hardcover o.p. pa $4.99
Grades: K 1 2   **636.5**
  1. Eggs 2. Chickens
  ISBN 0-06-028892-2; 0-06-028893-0 lib bdg; 0-06-
445212-3 pa
           LC 2003-7711
Describes what happens day-by-day for the three weeks
from the time a hen lays an egg until the baby chick hatches

This offers "clear and accurate text. . . . The illustrations
are soft and friendly, but retain enough realism for children
to understand the subject matter. . . . This is an enjoyable
and informative introduction to scientific information." SLJ

Wearing, Judy
  Chickens. Weigl 2011 24p il (World of wonder: watch
them grow) lib bdg $25.70; pa $9.95
Grades: 1 2   **636.5**
  1. Eggs 2. Chickens
  ISBN 978-1-60596-913-8 lib bdg; 1-60596-913-3 lib
bdg; 978-1-60596-914-5 pa; 1-60596-914-1 pa
           LC 2009050943
Learn about the transition these birds make from egg to
chick, and finally, to full-grown chicken.

The text is "well-written, providing examples that put
a human face to each problem. Quotes and facts are clearly
attributed, and their sources are noted in the extensive back
matter. . . . Sidebars provide further information, or, more

compellingly, offer stories about those touched by the topic.
. . . [This] will be of great assistance to students writing reports." Libr Media Connect

Includes glossary and bibliographical references

636.6   Birds other than poultry

Altman, Linda Jacobs

Parrots. Benchmark Bks. 1999 32p il (Perfect pets)
lib bdg $28.50

Grades: 3 4 5 6   **636.6**

1. Parrots

ISBN 0-7614-1102-X

LC 99-49672

Provides information about the history, physical characteristics, choosing, and care of all kinds of parrots

"The writing is clear and informative. . . . Colorful,
nicely detailed, framed photographs and reproductions of
the animals are interspersed throughout." SLJ

Includes glossary and bibliographical references

Bozzo, Linda

My first bird; [by] Linda Bozzo. Enslow Elementary
2007 32p il (My first pet library from the American Humane Association) lib bdg $22.60

Grades: 1 2 3   **636.6**

1. Cage birds

ISBN 978-0-7660-2749-7 lib bdg; 0-7660-2749-X
lib bdg

LC 2006008405

"The material is brief, providing a general overview. .
. . [Illustrated with] attractive, heartwarming color photographs." SLJ

Includes glossary and bibliographical references

Haney, Johannah

Small birds. Marshall Cavendish Benchmark 2010
46p il (Great pets) lib bdg $29.93

Grades: 2 3 4   **636.6**

1. Cage birds

ISBN 978-0-7614-4150-2 lib bdg; 0-7614-4150-6
lib bdg

LC 2008037258

"Describes the characteristics and behavior of small pet
birds, also discussing their physical appearance and place in
history." Publisher's note

Includes glossary and bibliographical references

Mead, Wendy

Top 10 birds for kids; [by] Wendy Mead. Enslow Publishers 2008 48p il (Top pets for kids with American Humane) lib bdg $23.93

Grades: 2 3 4 5   **636.6**

1. Pets 2. Cage birds

ISBN 978-0-7660-3072-5 lib bdg; 0-7660-3072-5
lib bdg

LC 2007-38479

"Includes beautiful full-color photos showing the animals at their best. Judicious use of text boxes, crisp fonts,
and white space will make it easy for readers to follow the
flow of information." SLJ

Includes glossary and bibliographical references

Niven, Felicia Lowenstein

Learning to care for a bird. Enslow Publishers 2010
48p il (Beginning pet care with American Humane) lib
bdg $23.93

Grades: 2 3 4   **636.6**

1. Cage birds

ISBN 978-0-7660-3192-0; 0-7660-3192-6

LC 2008048964

"Readers will learn how to choose, train, and care for a
bird." Publisher's note

Includes glossary and bibliographical references

Rockwood, Leigh

Parrots are smart! PowerKids Press 2010 24p il (Super smart animals) lib bdg $21.25; pa $8.25

Grades: 2 3 4 5   **636.6**

1. Parrots

ISBN 978-1-4358-9376-4 lib bdg; 1-4358-9376-X lib
bdg; 978-1-4358-9844-8 pa; 1-4358-9844-3 pa

Examines the intelligence of parrots.

"Bright, colorful, captioned photographs complement
the text. Rockwood does an excellent job of simplifying the
information without making the text choppy or boring." Libr
Media Connect

Includes glossary and bibliographical references

Spinner, Stephanie

Alex the parrot; no ordinary bird. by Stephanie Spinner; illustrations by Meilo So. Alfred A. Knopf 2012 41
p. $17.99

Grades: 1 2 3 4   **636.6**

1. Birds 2. Parrots 3. Animal intelligence 4. African
gray parrot

ISBN 0375868461; 9780375868467; 9780375968464

LC 2011014381

In this picture-book biography, author Stephanie Spinner tells the story of how "Irene Pepperberg's African gray
parrot learned to speak and understand English so well [that]
he changed both public and scientific beliefs about animal
communication and cognition. Named Alex, for Avian
Learning Experiment, the parrot was randomly acquired
from a pet shop for graduate student Pepperberg's research."
(Kirkus Reviews)

636.7   Dogs

Altman, Linda Jacobs

Big dogs. Benchmark Bks. 2001 32p il (Perfect pets)
lib bdg $15.95

Grades: 3 4 5 6   **636.7**

1. Dogs

ISBN 0-7614-1101-1

LC 99-49674

Provides information about the history, physical characteristics, choice, training and care of various breeds of
large dogs

Includes glossary and bibliographical references

American Kennel Club

★ The **Complete** dog book for kids; official publication of the American Kennel Club. Howell Book House
1996 274p il maps hardcover o.p. pa $22.95

Grades: 4 5 6 7 **636.7**
1. Dogs
ISBN 0-87605-458-0; 0-87605-460-2 pa
LC 96-29228

This "begins with a general section that advises readers on buying a dog, responsibilities, rewards, and how to match a dog with one's situation. . . . More than 100 dogs are profiled, with information on history, appearance, health, and 'fun facts.' Crisp color photographs accompany each article. . . . A final section gives good advice about nutrition and health issues." Booklist

Arlon, Penelope

Puppies and kittens; by Penelope Arlon and Tory Gordon-Harris. Scholastic 2013 32 p. (Scholastic discover more) (hardcover) $7.99
Grades: PreK K 1 **636.7**
1. Cats 2. Dogs 3. Animals -- Infancy 4. Cats -- Habits and behavior 5. Dogs -- Habits and behavior 6. Kittens 7. Puppies
ISBN 0545495660; 9780545495660
LC 2012285421

This book by Penelope Arlon and Tory Gordon-Harris "is packed with facts about everyone's favorite pets. Each double-page spread features as aspect of the life of animal babies for children to compare with their own lives. Where to eat and sleep, learning, playing, even fighting with your brothers and sisters! Collection spreads feature many puppy and kitten breeds and there's lots of information about these mammals' wild cousins." (Publisher's note)

Baines, Becky

Everything dogs; All the canine facts, photos, and fun that you can get your paws on! by Becky Baines; with Dr. Gary Weitzman. National Geographic 2012 64 p. col. ill. (paperback) $12.95; (library) $21.90
Grades: 3 4 5 **636.7**
1. Picture books for children 2. Dogs
ISBN 1426310242; 1426310250; 9781426310249; 9781426310256
LC 2012289035

This book by Becky Baines looks at dogs. "Baines starts with the basics ('What is a dog?') and moves on to discuss small and large breeds, answer doggie-related questions ('Why do dogs roll in smelly stuff?'), and imagine your pet's daily schedule. . . . This also presents a chart for decoding canine moods and looks at the dog family, which includes coyotes, dingoes, and jackals, among others." (Booklist)

Includes bibliographical references (page 62) and index.

Barnes, Julia

Pet dogs; [by] Julia Barnes. Gareth Stevens Pub. 2007 un il (Pet pals) lib bdg $23.93
Grades: 2 3 4 5 **636.7**
1. Dogs
ISBN 0-8368-6777-7
LC 2006042378

This places dogs "within the context of [their] wild roots and [their] relationship to humans. . . . Barnes explains what makes the animal an ideal pet, recommends how to be a good caregiver, and reveals how the creature communicates (as well as how to answer). The [book mixes] practical advice with trivia in a way that children will find informative

and easy to navigate. Crisp, full-color photos enhance the [text]." SLJ

Includes glossary and bibliographical references

Bial, Raymond

Rescuing Rover; saving America's dogs. Houghton Mifflin 2011 80p il
Grades: 4 5 6 7 **636.7**
1. Dogs 2. Animal welfare
ISBN 0-547-34125-3; 978-0-547-34125-5
LC 2010025123

"This accessible, amply illustrated title offers and informative introduction to canine-rescue endeavors. After recounting his own moving story of adopting a rescue dog, Bial provides a history of human-dog relationships. . . . Bial also explores rescue organizations, such as the ASPCA. . . . Bial frankly discusses the abuse many dogs experience . . . as well as euthanasia. . . . Historical and contemporary photos; extensive book lists . . .; websites; and detailed index complete this well-presented resource." Booklist

Includes bibliographical references

Bidner, Jenni

Is my dog a wolf? how your pet compares to its wild cousin. Lark Books 2006 64p il $9.95
Grades: 3 4 5 6 **636.7**
1. Dogs 2. Wolves
ISBN 978-1-57990-732-7; 1-57990-732-6
LC 2005-34865

"This book identifies instinctual behaviors in wolves, such as pack living, licking and biting at one another, and howling, and describes how they are manifested in the common house dog, even though the species changed thousands of years ago. . . . Clear color photographs beautifully illustrate the text. This informative, entertaining title is suitable for reports and for general reading." SLJ

Biniok, Janice

The miniature schnauzer. Eldorado Ink 2010 112p il (Our best friends) lib bdg $34.95
Grades: 4 5 6 7 **636.7**
1. Dogs
ISBN 978-1-932904-61-1 lib bdg; 1-932904-61-1 lib bdg

"The Our Best Friends series continues to be an ideal resource for those kids (or even adults) looking for a cradle-to-grave primer on responsible pet ownership. . . . These [books] offer far more than the customary cursory enticements and warnings usually aimed at first-time animal caregivers, with in-depth information on health issues and extensive explanations of the various types of species. . . . This is required (if sobering) reading for the serious pet owner." Booklist

Includes bibliographical references

The rottweiler. Eldorado Ink 2010 112p il (Our best friends) lib bdg $34.95
Grades: 4 5 6 7 **636.7**
1. Dogs
ISBN 978-1-932904-64-2 lib bdg; 1-932904-64-6 lib bdg

"The Our Best Friends series continues to be an ideal resource for those kids (or even adults) looking for a cradle-to-grave primer on responsible pet ownership. . . . These

[books] offer far more than the customary cursory enticements and warnings usually aimed at first-time animal
caregivers, with in-depth information on health issues and
extensive explanations of the various types of species. . .
. This is required (if sobering) reading for the serious pet
owner." Booklist

Includes bibliographical references

Bozzo, Linda

Fire dog heroes. Enslow Publishers 2010 48p il
(Amazing working dogs with American Humane) lib bdg
$23.93
Grades: 2 3 4　　　　　　　　　　　　　**636.7**
　1. Arson 2. Working dogs 3. Fire fighting
　ISBN 978-0-7660-3202-6; 0-7660-3202-7
　　　　　　　　　　　　　　　　　LC 2008048019
"The text opens with a true story of an arson dog, and
then it explains the history of the arson K-9 team and the
training methods used to transform an ordinary dog into a
canine hero." Publisher's note
Includes glossary and bibliographical references

My first dog; [by] Linda Bozzo. Enslow Elementary
2007 32p il (My first pet library from the American Hu-
mane Association) lib bdg $22.60
Grades: 1 2 3　　　　　　　　　　　　　**636.7**
　1. Dogs
　ISBN 978-0-7660-2754-1 lib bdg; 0-7660-2754-6
lib bdg
　　　　　　　　　　　　　　　　　LC 2006008404
"The material is brief, providing a general overview. .
. [Illustrated with] attractive, heartwarming color photo-
graphs." SLJ
Includes glossary and bibliographical references

Search and rescue dog heroes. Enslow Publishers 2010
48p il (Amazing working dogs with American Humane) lib
bdg $23.93
Grades: 2 3 4　　　　　　　　　　　　　**636.7**
　1. Rescue dogs
　ISBN 978-0-7660-3201-9; 0-7660-3201-9
　　　　　　　　　　　　　　　　　LC 2008048018
"The text opens with a true story of a search and rescue
(SAR) dog, and then it explains the history of the SAR K-9
team and the training methods used to transform an ordinary
dog into a canine hero." Publisher's note
Includes glossary and bibliographical references

Calmenson, Stephanie

May I pet your dog? the how-to guide for kids meeting dogs (and dogs meeting kids) by Stephanie Calmenson;
illustrated by Jan Ormerod. Clarion Books 2007 32p il
$9.95
Grades: PreK K 1 2　　　　　　　　　　　**636.7**
　1. Dogs
　ISBN 978-0-618-51034-4; 0-618-51034-6
　　　　　　　　　　　　　　　　　LC 2005-34955
Harry the dog explains how to safely meet him and
his friends.
"Straightforward guidelines and a positive, encouraging
tone make this book appealing and practical. Young dog lovers will delight in the variety of breeds shown in the bright,
clear illustrations." SLJ

Rosie; a visiting dog's story. photographs by Justin Sutcliffe. Clarion Bks. 1994 47p il hardcover o.p. pa $6.95
Grades: K 1 2 3　　　　　　　　　　　　　**636.7**
　1. Dogs
　ISBN 0-395-65477-7; 0-395-92722-6 pa
　　　　　　　　　　　　　　　　　LC 93-21243
"Rosie is the true story of an endearing Tibetan terrier
who works as a therapy dog with Delta Society's Pet Partners Program of New York City. Rosie's tenderness and enthusiasm come through in Sutcliffe's fantastic photos that
chronicle Rosie's training and first visit to a children's hospital and a nursing home." Child Book Rev Serv

Carnesi, Monica

Little dog lost; a true story of a brave dog named Baltic.
Nancy Paulsen Books 2012 il $15.99
Grades: PreK K　　　　　　　　　　　　　**636.7**
　1. Dogs 2. Animal rescue
　ISBN 978-0-399-25666-0; 0-399-25666-0
On a cold winter day, a curious dog wandered onto a
frozen river, and before he knew it he was traveling fast on a
sheet of ice. Many people tried to help, but the dog could not
be reached. Finally, after two nights and seventy-five miles,
the little dog was saved by a ship out in the Baltic Sea.
"The story is told simply and charmingly. The author's
use of the present tense gives the narrative immediacy, and
with very brief sentences, some dialogue and questions
posed to readers, Carnesi imbues the tale with a strong sense
of drama that will captivate young listeners." Kirkus

Castaldo, Nancy F.

Sniffer dogs; how dogs (and their noses) save the
world. Nancy F. Castaldo. Houghton Mifflin Harcourt
2014 160 p. color illustrations $16.99
Grades: 4 5 6 7 8　　　　　　　　　　　**636.7**
　1. Rescue dogs 2. Search dogs 3. Smell 4. Detector
dogs 5. Dogs -- Sense organs
　ISBN 054408893X; 9780544088931
　　　　　　　　　　　　　　　　　LC 2013017612
This middle grade book by Nancy F. Castaldo describes
how "some dogs work with police officers, soldiers and
even scientists to put their 'sniffers' to work. Sniffer dogs
make use of the amazing biology behind their noses to protect people from bombs, catch criminals smuggling drugs,
or help researchers locate a hard to find snail in a forest."
(Publisher's note)
"The attractive color photos that capture many of these
canines in action and the accessible tone of the text make
this an appealing read. A well-organized, thoughtfully written title that celebrates the achievements of these great
dogs." SLJ
Includes bibliographical references and index

Coren, Stanley

Why do dogs have wet noses? Kids Can Press 2006
63p il $14.95; pa $9.95
Grades: 3 4 5 6　　　　　　　　　　　　　**636.7**
　1. Dogs
　ISBN 1-55337-657-9; 1-55337-658-7 pa
"This interesting, entertaining book has chapters on
'How Humans and Dogs Became Friends,' 'How Dogs See
the World,' 'How Dogs Talk,' and 'How Dogs Think.' The
question-and-answer format is interspersed with facts and

stories in sidebars. . . . Beautiful full-color photos show many breeds." SLJ

Crosby, Jeff

Little lions, bull baiters & hunting hounds; a history of dog breeds, written and illustrated by Jeff Crosby and Shelley Ann Jackson. Tundra Books 2008 72p il $19.95
Grades: 2 3 4 5   **636.7**
  1. Dogs
  ISBN 978-0-88776-815-6; 0-88776-815-6
                LC 2007927387

"Featuring more than breeds that are categorized as hunting, herding, working, or companion dogs, this attractive volume includes interesting and sometimes unusual facts about canines. . . . The painterly illustrations are often action-packed. . . . There is also a brief history of the origin of dogs and a succinct look at mixed breeds. . . . This is a great browsing book." SLJ

Includes bibliographical references

Dennis, Brian

★ **Nubs**; the true story of a mutt, a Marine & a miracle. by Brian Dennis, Kirby Larson, and Mary Nethery. Little, Brown Books for Young Readers 2009 un il $17.99
Grades: K 1 2 3   **636.7**
  1. Dogs 2. Iraq War, 2003- --- Personal narratives
  ISBN 978-0-316-05318-1; 0-316-05318-X
                LC 2009003808

This is a "hugely inspirational true account. . . . The gritty, low-res shots of the two companions against the bleak Iraqi horizon are married with text so gracefully that many of the compositions could be book jackets." Booklist

Gaines, Ann

Top 10 dogs for kids; [by] Ann Graham Gaines. Enslow Publishers 2008 48p il (Top pets for kids with American Humane) lib bdg $23.93
Grades: 2 3 4 5   **636.7**
  1. Dogs
  ISBN 978-0-7660-3070-1 lib bdg; 0-7660-3070-9 lib bdg
                LC 2007-24510

"Includes beautiful full-color photos showing the animals at their best. Judicious use of text boxes, crisp fonts, and white space will make it easy for readers to follow the flow of information." SLJ

Includes glossary and bibliographical references

George, Jean Craighead

★ **How** to talk to your dog; illustrated by Sue Truesdell. HarperCollins Pubs. 2000 26p il $9.95
Grades: 2 3 4   **636.7**
  1. Dogs
  ISBN 0-06-027092-6
                LC 98-41515

Describes how dogs communicate with people through their behavior and sounds and explains how to talk back to them using sounds, behavior, and body language

"The mixed photography (of George, representing the humans) and illustration (an endearingly scruffy yellow mutt is the main canine representative) is . . . effective. . . . This will be an accessible and perhaps paradigm-shifting introduction for young readers." Bull Cent Child Books

Gewirtz, Elaine Waldorf

The **bulldog**. Eldorado Ink 2010 112p il (Our best friends) lib bdg $34.95
Grades: 4 5 6 7   **636.7**
  1. Dogs
  ISBN 978-1-932904-58-1 lib bdg; 1-932904-58-1 lib bdg

"The Our Best Friends series continues to be an ideal resource for those kids (or even adults) looking for a cradle-to-grave primer on responsible pet ownership. These [books] offer far more than the customary cursory enticements and warnings usually aimed at first-time animal caregivers, with in-depth information on health issues and extensive explanations of the various types of species. . . . This is required (if sobering) reading for the serious pet owner." Booklist

Includes bibliographical references

Fetch this book. Eldorado Ink 2010 112p il (Our best friends) lib bdg $34.95
Grades: 4 5 6 7   **636.7**
  1. Dogs -- Training
  ISBN 978-1-932904-60-4 lib bdg; 1-932904-60-3 lib bdg

This "is a dog-training manual, with pet-care advice only in reference to training. [This] well-written [book provides] examples to support [its] points and solid online and text resources and feature [a] clean, uncluttered [layout]. . . . There is plenty of practical information that motivated readers can glean from [this title]." SLJ

Includes bibliographical references

Gibbons, Gail

Dogs. Holiday House 1996 32p il $16.95; pa $6.95
Grades: K 1 2 3   **636.7**
  1. Dogs
  ISBN 0-8234-1226-1; 0-8234-1335-7 pa
                LC 95-24966

An introduction to dogs including their history, types of breeds, senses, and ways of communication

"There is something for all dog enthusiasts here. A good choice for both reports and pleasure reading." SLJ

Goldish, Meish

Ground zero dogs; by Meish Goldish. Bearport Pub. 2013 32 p. col. ill. (library binding) $25.27
Grades: 2 3 4   **636.7**
  1. Search dogs 2. Picture books for children 3. September 11 terrorist attacks, 2001 4. Rescue dogs 5. World Trade Center Site (New York, N.Y.)
  ISBN 1617725765; 9781617725760
                LC 2012003341

This children's picture book is part of the Dog Heroes series. The book introduces "readers to a select few of the roughly 300 search-and-rescue dogs that used their agile feet and powerful senses of smell . . . to locate both survivors and bodies among the World Trade Center rubble. . . . Salty helped his blind owner escape alive from the seventy-first floor, and Trakr uncovered a woman who had been buried for 24 hours." (Booklist)

Includes bibliographical references and index

Goodman, Susan E.

It's a dog's life; how man's best friend sees, hears, and smells the world. written by Susan E. Goodman; illustrated

by David Slonim. 1st ed. Roaring Brook Press 2012 32
p. col. ill.
Grades: 2 3 4   **636.7**
1. Dogs 2. Dogs -- Juvenile humor 3. Dogs -- Behavior
4. Dogs -- Evolution
ISBN 9781596434486

LC 2011022965

This book by Susan E. Goodman and illustrated by David Slonim focuses on dog breeds and dog behavior. "Have you ever wondered what your dog sees when he looks at a sunset? Or what she smells when she has her nose to the ground? And what IS your pooch trying to say when he looks at you with those big puppy eyes? . . . [Goodman] answers those questions and a whole lot more." (Publisher's note)

Includes bibliographical references.

Gorrell, Gena K.

Working like a dog; the story of working dogs through history. Tundra 2003 156p il pa $16.95
Grades: 4 5 6 7   **636.7**
1. Working dogs
ISBN 0-88776-589-0

"Gorrell begins by tracing the evolution of 'household canids' from the wild into the civilized world. Other chapters delve into the many ways in which these animals have been viewed throughout history, what makes particular breeds right for certain jobs, dogs at war, famous pooches, etc. . . The well-captioned, black-and-white photographs and reproductions add greatly to a narrative that's packed with intriguing details." SLJ

Includes bibliographical references

Grogan, John

Marley; a dog like no other. Collins 2007 196p il $16.99; lib bdg $17.89
Grades: 4 5 6   **636.7**
1. Dogs
ISBN 978-0-06-124033-1; 978-0-06-124034-8 lib bdg

LC 2007-08600

"Grogan's anecdotal adaptation of his bestselling memoir, Marley & Me: Life and Love with the World's Worst Dog speaks to a middle-grade audience. . . . The narrative maintains all the energy, humor and poignancy of the adult book. . . . Grogan leaves young readers with fond memories of this exasperating yet thoroughly endearing creature." Publ Wkly

Hart, Joyce

Big dogs; by Joyce Hart. Marshall Cavendish Benchmark 2008 48p il (Great pets) lib bdg $29.93
Grades: 2 3 4   **636.7**
1. Dogs
ISBN 978-0-7614-2707-0 lib bdg; 0-7614-2707-4
lib bdg

LC 2007013042

This is an "enthusiastic, warm [introduction]. . . . [It is] clearly written and [is] the most thorough, honest [introduction] to owning [big dogs] for this audience." SLJ

Includes glossary and bibliographical references

Small dogs. Marshall Cavendish Benchmark 2008 48p
il (Great pets) lib bdg $29.93

Grades: 2 3 4   **636.7**
1. Dogs
ISBN 978-0-7614-2995-1 lib bdg; 0-7614-2995-6
lib bdg

LC 2007-36784

"Describes the characteristics and behavior of small dogs, also discussing their physical appearance and place in history." Publisher's note

Includes glossary and bibliographical references

Hoffman, Mary Ann

Guard dogs. Gareth Stevens Pub. 2011 24p il (Working dogs) lib bdg $22.60; pa $8.15
Grades: 2 3 4   **636.7**
1. Working dogs
ISBN 978-1-4339-4647-9 lib bdg; 1-4339-4647-5 lib
bdg; 978-1-4339-4648-6 pa; 1-4339-4648-3 pa

LC 2010035241

This describes guard "dogs and the training they receive. The short chapters, complemented by numerous color photographs, provide examples of particular breeds that do [this] job and show how their characteristics are suited for the tasks. The charts provided are especially helpful, covering commands and more specific tasks. There is enough information to make the [text] feel fresh. . . . A solid choice for readers looking for more than cute pictures." SLJ

Herding dogs. Gareth Stevens Pub. 2011 24p il (Working dogs) lib bdg $22.60; pa $8.15
Grades: 2 3 4   **636.7**
1. Dogs
ISBN 978-1-4339-4655-4 lib bdg; 1-4339-4655-6 lib
bdg; 978-1-4339-4656-1 pa; 1-4339-4656-4 pa

LC 2010035243

This describes herding "dogs and the training they receive. The short chapters, complemented by numerous color photographs, provide examples of particular breeds that do [this] job and show how their characteristics are suited for the tasks. The charts provided are especially helpful, covering commands and more specific tasks. There is enough information to make the [text] feel fresh. . . . A solid choice for readers looking for more than cute pictures." SLJ

Houston, Dick

Bulu, African wonder dog. Random House 2010 323p
il $15.99; lib bdg $18.99
Grades: 5 6 7 8   **636.7**
1. Dogs 2. Wildlife conservation 3. Zambia
ISBN 978-0-375-84723-3; 0-375-84723-5; 978-0-375-
94720-9 lib bdg; 0-375-94720-5 lib bdg

LC 2009015804

"In the Nyanja language, bulu means 'wild dog,' and that's what Steve and Anna Tolan named the beloved little Jack Russell mix they adopted. Disregarding warnings about the dangers of raising a dog in the bush, the Tolans moved from England to rural Zambia to fulfill their lifelong dream of setting up an animal rescue and conservation center. . . . Bulu's energy, high spirits, and loyalty to his masters make the book read like a praise song to dogs. Houston's account is an animal-lover's delight, complete with the action-adventure of surviving the bush, fighting poachers, and spreading a message of conservation." Booklist

Huneck, Stephen

Even bad dogs go to heaven; more from the dog chapel. Abrams 2010 un il $19.95

Grades: 2 3 4   636.7

1. Dogs 2. Bereavement

ISBN 978-0-8109-9629-8; 0-8109-9629-4

"After recovering from a near-fatal illness, Huneck established a chapel dedicated to the relationship between dogs and their owners on his property in Vermont. . . . The introduction is lengthy . . . but touching. It is illustrated with color photographs of the small chapel. . . . Following the introduction, the artist presents about 30 short sayings about dogs, one per spread, in large informal print and illustrates each one with his characteristic style. The sayings are clever and celebrate the richness that pets bring to life. They also offer comfort for those who might have lost a beloved canine friend. The illustrations are simple and solid, but brightly colored and have a gentle humor of their own." SLJ

Jackson, Emma

A home for Dixie; the true story of a rescued puppy. by Emma Jackson, with full-color photographs by Bob Carey. Collins 2008 un il $16.99; lib bdg $17.89

Grades: 1 2 3 4   636.7

1. Dogs

ISBN 978-0-06-144962-8; 0-06-144962-8; 978-0-06-144963-5 lib bdg; 0-06-144963-6 lib bdg

LC 2008-006049

"In this photo-essay, the author, a high school student, chronicles her quest for a puppy, her family's decision to adopt one, and their trip to Aunt Mary's Doghouse—a non-profit rescue agency—to find the right animal. . . . The book's strengths are the large, full-color, often full-page photos of the appealing pup and her new owner. The Web sites recommended for potential pet owners are regularly updated." SLJ

Jeffrey, Laura S.

Dogs; how to choose and care for a dog. Enslow Publishers 2004 48p il (American humane pet care library) lib bdg $23.93

Grades: 3 4 5   636.7

1. Dogs

ISBN 0-7660-2520-9

LC 2003-22971

Explains who to consult, where to go to pick the right dog, and how to keep them happy and healthy

Includes glossary and bibliographical references

Jenkins, Steve

★ Dogs and cats; written and illustrated by Steve Jenkins. Houghton Mifflin Co. 2007 un il $16

Grades: 1 2 3 4   636.7

1. Cats 2. Dogs

ISBN 978-0-618-50767-2; 0-618-50767-1

LC 2006-24654

"The lively narrative provides a copious amount of information, examining each species in human history, describing evolution and domestication, highlighting physical characteristics and behaviors, and finishing up with amazing facts about each animal. The layout is excellent, with images dominating the text. Jenkins's cut and torn-paper collages are stunning." SLJ

Johnson, Jinny

Dogs and puppies; [by] Jinny Johnson. Smart Apple Media 2008 32p il (Get to know your pet) $27.10

Grades: 3 4 5 6   636.7

1. Dogs

ISBN 978-1-59920-089-7; 1-59920-089-9

LC 2007-52598

"Spreads include in-depth care instruction, and 'Q & A' sidebars that answer common behavioral questions. . . . The layout is clear, with full color photos and illustrations breaking up the text." SLJ

Includes glossary

Katz, Jon

★ Meet the dogs of Bedlam Farm; a true story. Henry Holt and Company 2011 un il $16.99

Grades: K 1 2 3   636.7

1. Farm life 2. Working dogs

ISBN 978-0-8050-9219-6; 0-8050-9219-6

LC 2010011698

"Border collies Rose and Izzy; Frieda, a rottweiler/German shepherd mix; and black Lab Lenore are four dogs living on Bedlam Farm in Upstate New York. Katz lives on the farm and has written about it for older audiences. . . . The large, full-color photographs are totally engaging and capture the animals' distinct personalities. . . . The writing is crisp and clear, and the stories (each dog gets its own turn) are sweet and filled with gentle humor." SLJ

Kehret, Peg

Shelter dogs; amazing stories of adopted strays. Whitman, A. 1999 un il $14.95

Grades: 3 4 5   636.7

1. Dogs

ISBN 0-8075-7334-5

LC 98-34760

Tells the stories of eight stray dogs that were adopted from animal shelters and went on to become service dogs, actors, and heroes

"The writing is clear and straightforward, letting the drama and pathos of the dogs' triumphs, and the owners' dedication, carry the stories." SLJ

Laidlaw, Rob

No shelter here; Making the world a kinder place for dogs. Rob Laidlaw. Pajama Press 2012 63 p.

Grades: 3 4 5 6 7 8   636.7

1. Dogs 2. Animal rights 3. Animal welfare

ISBN 0986949558; 9780986949555

This book provides an "informative and visually varied introduction to problems affecting dogs worldwide. In a short, colorful volume with sidebars and photographs on nearly every page, professional dog advocate [Rob] Laidlaw . . . presents facts about how dogs live, provides an overview of the cruelty dogs face at the hands of humans and offers profiles of young activists who are working to better dogs' lives. . . . A list of animal welfare websites points interested readers toward further information." (Kirkus)

Includes bibliographical references and index.

Lunis, Natalie

Greyhound; canine blur! Bearport Pub. 2011 24p il map (Blink of an eye. Superfast animals!) lib bdg $22.61

Grades: 1 2 3   **636.7**
1. Dogs 2. Animal locomotion
ISBN 978-1-936087-90-7; 1-936087-90-1
LC 2010010576
This describes the greyhound dog, including where it
was first bred, why it was so helpful to hunters, and the ways
its body helps it reach its record-breaking speeds.

This "is sure to appeal to a wide variety of readers. Vibrant photos illustrate each animal from multiple perspectives, providing opportunity for readers to closely examine
the animal. Information is organized by subject heading and
branches into the animal's physical features and how they
contribute to its speed, the animal's natural predators, and
how the animal makes use of speed as a means of survival. .
. . This . . . will be a worthwhile addition to your nonfiction
collection." Libr Media Connect
Includes glossary and bibliographical references

McCarthy, Meghan
The **incredible** life of Balto. Alfred A. Knopf 2011 un
il $16.99; lib bdg $19.99
Grades: K 1 2   **636.7**
1. Sled dogs 2. Diphtheria 3. Nome (Alaska) 4. Balto
(Dog)
ISBN 978-0-375-84460-7; 0-375-84460-0; 978-0-375-
94460-4 lib bdg; 0-375-94460-5 lib bdg
LC 2009-52707
"After making an arduous journey to deliver medicine
to combat diphtheria in Nome, Alaska, in 1925, Balto and
his owner at first enjoy fame. But after a statue and a starring movie role, Balto's fortunes change when he's sold to a
vaudeville act. . . . Straightforward narration keeps this picture-book biography moving toward its happy conclusion. .
. . It's an accessible introduction to the story of Balto, and a
reminder of the fickle nature of fame." Publ Wkly

Mehus-Roe, Kristin
Dogs for kids! everything you need to know about
dogs. by Kristin Mehus-Roe. BowTie Press 2007 384p
il pa $14.95
Grades: 4 5 6 7   **636.7**
1. Dogs
ISBN 978-1-931993-83-8 pa; 1-931993-83-1 pa
LC 2006035434
"If you are looking for a book about canines that is entertaining as well as immensely informative, this is it. In a
lively, conversational tone, Mehus-Roe offers a vast amount
of material, from the history of dogs to vacationing with a
pet, and provides practical and upbeat explanations, ideas,
offbeat tidbits, and pertinent details." SLJ
Includes bibliographical references

Morn, September B.
The **pug**. Eldorado Ink 2010 112p il (Our best friends)
lib bdg $34.95
Grades: 4 5 6 7   **636.7**
1. Dogs
ISBN 978-1-932904-63-5 lib bdg; 1-932904-63-8
lib bdg
"The Our Best Friends series continues to be an ideal
resource for those kids (or even adults) looking for a cradle-
to-grave primer on responsible pet ownership. . . . These
[books] offer far more than the customary cursory enticements and warnings usually aimed at first-time animal

caregivers, with in-depth information on health issues and
extensive explanations of the various types of species. . .
. This is required (if sobering) reading for the serious pet
owner." Booklist
Includes bibliographical references

Niven, Felicia Lowenstein
Learning to care for a dog. Enslow Publishers 2010
48p il (Beginning pet care with American Humane) lib
bdg $23.93
Grades: 2 3 4   **636.7**
1. Dogs
ISBN 978-0-7660-3190-6; 0-7660-3190-X
LC 2008048962
"Readers will learn how to choose, train, and care for a
dog." Publisher's note
Includes glossary and bibliographical references

Patent, Dorothy Hinshaw
★ **Saving** Audie; a pit bull puppy gets a second chance.
photographs by William Muñoz. Walker & Company 2011
un il $16.99; lib bdg $17.89
Grades: 2 3 4   **636.7**
1. Dogs 2. Animal welfare 3. Football players
ISBN 978-0-8027-2272-0; 0-8027-2272-5; 978-0-
8027-2273-7 lib bdg; 0-8027-2273-3 lib bdg
LC 2010-36547
When Michael Vick's dog fighting ring was discovered,
more than forty dogs were rescued. But their struggle was
far from over. Most animal advocates believed the former
fighting dogs were too damaged to save, but Audie and his
kennel mates would prove them wrong when public outcry
and the publicity surrounding Michael Vick's punishment
won them a chance at a happy life.

"Munoz's photographs range from moody . . . . to adorable. . . . Patent wrings emotion from her understated text
and remains nonjudgmental about Vick's reemergence."
Booklist

Prap, Lila
Doggy whys. North-South Books 2011 un il $16.95
Grades: 2 3 4   **636.7**
1. Dogs
ISBN 0-7358-4014-8; 978-0-7358-4014-0
"Although this book could have coasted by entirely on
the strength of the funky, ruff-n-tuff cartoon pooches that
are the centerpiece of each spread, Prap goes one better and
provides insightful information on why dogs are so, well,
darn doggy. . . . A few of her inquiries will enlighten even
veteran fact hounds." Booklist

Rajczak, Kristen
Pulling dogs. Gareth Stevens Pub. 2011 24p il (Working dogs) lib bdg $22.60; pa $8.15
Grades: 2 3 4   **636.7**
1. Working dogs 2. Sled dog racing
ISBN 978-1-4339-4663-9 lib bdg; 1-4339-4663-7 lib
bdg; 978-1-4339-4664-6 pa; 1-4339-4664-5 pa
LC 2010037168
This describes pulling "dogs and the training they receive. The short chapters, complemented by numerous color
photographs, provide examples of particular breeds that do
[this] job and show how their characteristics are suited for
the tasks. The charts provided are especially helpful, cov-

ering commands and more specific tasks. There is enough information to make the [text] feel fresh. . . . A solid choice for readers looking for more than cute pictures." SLJ

Rescue dogs. Gareth Stevens Pub. 2011 24p il (Working dogs) lib bdg $22.60; pa $7

Grades: 2 3 4   **636.7**

1. Rescue dogs

ISBN 978-1-4339-4667-7 lib bdg; 1-4339-4667-X lib bdg; 978-1-4339-4668-4 pa; 1-4339-4668-8 pa

          LC 2010037169

This describes rescue "dogs and the training they receive. The short chapters, complemented by numerous color photographs, provide examples of particular breeds that do [this] job and show how their characteristics are suited for the tasks. The charts provided are especially helpful, covering commands and more specific tasks. There is enough information to make the [text] feel fresh. . . . A solid choice for readers looking for more than cute pictures." SLJ

Rockwood, Leigh

Dogs are smart! PowerKids Press 2010 24p il (Super smart animals) lib bdg $21.25; pa $8.25

Grades: 2 3 4 5   **636.7**

1. Dogs

ISBN 978-1-4358-9374-0 lib bdg; 1-4358-9374-3 lib bdg; 978-1-4358-9836-3 pa; 1-4358-9836-2 pa

Examines the intelligence of dogs.

"Bright, colorful, captioned photographs complement the text. Rockwood does an excellent job of simplifying the information without making the text choppy or boring." Libr Media Connect

Includes glossary

Rogers, Tammie

4-H guide to dog training and dog tricks. Voyageur Press 2009 176p il pa $18.99

Grades: 5 6 7 8 9 10   **636.7**

1. Dogs -- Training

ISBN 978-0-7603-3629-8; 0-7603-3629-6

         LC 2009-17040

"This is not simply a how-to-train book; it is also a guide to cultivating a respectful relationship with your dog. The excellent information is comprehensive, and it is presented in a clear and detailed style. The author covers different training methods, discussing the tools needed from food to collar selection. Using this manual, dog owners can move through the basics (sit, down, etc.) to obedience competition and fun tricks and activities." SLJ

Includes bibliographical references

Rutherford, Clarice

★ A **dog** is a dog; and that's why he's so special. by Clarice Rutherford. Alpine 2012 xi, 98 p.p col. ill. (paperback: alk. paper) $14.95

Grades: 4 5 6   **636.7**

1. Pets 2. Wolves 3. Animal behavior 4. Dogs -- Behavior 5. Dogs -- Training

ISBN 1577791037; 9781577791034

         LC 2009003029

"The author, Clarice Rutherford, brings her many years of experience with dogs into this book, and explains dogs, how to manage, train, as well as understand them . . . The reader will learn the basic history of dogs and their rela-

tionship to the wolf. How the dog's brain develops and the importance of early socialization and basic training is explained, as well as how the genetics and instincts of the wolf play an important role in the behavior of the dog." (Barnes & Noble)

Includes bibliographical references and index.

Schweitzer, Karen

The **beagle**. Eldorado Ink 2010 112p il (Our best friends) lib bdg $34.95

Grades: 4 5 6 7   **636.7**

1. Dogs

ISBN 978-1-932904-57-4 lib bdg; 1-932904-57-3 lib bdg

"The Our Best Friends series continues to be an ideal resource for those kids (or even adults) looking for a cradle-to-grave primer on responsible pet ownership. . . . These [books] offer far more than the customary cursory enticements and warnings usually aimed at first-time animal caregivers, with in-depth information on health issues and extensive explanations of the various types of species. . . . This is required (if sobering) reading for the serious pet owner." Booklist

Includes bibliographical references

The **dachshund**. Eldorado Ink 2010 112p il (Our best friends) lib bdg $34.95

Grades: 4 5 6 7   **636.7**

1. Dogs

ISBN 978-1-932904-59-8 lib bdg; 1-932904-59-X lib bdg

"The Our Best Friends series continues to be an ideal resource for those kids (or even adults) looking for a cradle-to-grave primer on responsible pet ownership. . . . These [books] offer far more than the customary cursory enticements and warnings usually aimed at first-time animal caregivers, with in-depth information on health issues and extensive explanations of the various types of species. . . . This is required (if sobering) reading for the serious pet owner." Booklist

Includes bibliographical references

Simon, Seymour

★ **Dogs**. HarperCollinsPublishers 2004 un il $17.99; lib bdg $18.89; pa $6.99

Grades: 1 2 3 4   **636.7**

1. Dogs

ISBN 0-06-028942-2; 0-06-028943-0 lib bdg; 978-0-06-446255-6 pa; 0-06-446255-2 pa

         LC 2003-12484

Provides a basic introduction to the physical characteristics and behavior of dogs

"The striking color photos, including many close-ups, create a feeling of intimacy. . . . Simon succeeds in addressing his topic in clear, easily understood vocabulary without writing down to children." SLJ

Singer, Marilyn

A **dog's** gotta do what a dog's gotta do; dogs at work. Holt & Co. 2000 86p il $16

Grades: 3 4 5 6   **636.7**

1. Working dogs

ISBN 0-8050-6074-X

Describes how dogs use their physical abilities, intelligence, and training by humans to perform a variety of jobs, including working in the movies, catching burglars, delivering messages, and cheering up children in hospitals

"Dog lovers will appreciate this readable, informative look at canines and the work they do." Booklist

Stamper, Judith Bauer

Eco dogs. Bearport Pub. 2011 32p il (Dog heroes) lib bdg $25.27

Grades: 3 4 5   **636.7**

1. Working dogs 2. Endangered species
ISBN 978-1-61772-152-6; 1-61772-152-2

LC 2010041191

"Eco Dogs help scientists by sniffing out scat, which is analyzed for signs of pollutants or changes in the food chain that might have harmful effects on the environment and on indigenous species. [This book is] engaging not just because the content is so compelling, but also because the [author has] highlighted specific dogs currently working in [this field]. The use of real names and full-color photographs on every page, many contributed by the individuals who work with these dogs, makes reading [this book] a personal experience. . . . [An] excellent [introduction] to [this] new [development] in service-dog training." SLJ

Includes glossary and bibliographical references

Urbigkit, Cat

Brave dogs, gentle dogs; how they guard sheep. Boyds Mills Press 2005 32p il $15.95; pa $8.95

Grades: K 1 2 3   **636.7**

1. Sheep dogs
ISBN 1-59078-317-4; 978-1-59078-674-1 pa

LC 2004-16855

A "photo-essay on guardian dogs. Accompanied by clear, full-color photos, the simple, informative text describes the raising of these sheepdogs and their natural proclivity for guarding 'their' flocks." SLJ

The guardian team; on the job with Rena and Roo. Boyds Mills Press 2011 32p il

Grades: K 1 2 3   **636.7**

1. Sheep 2. Donkeys 3. Ranch life 4. Working dogs
ISBN 1590787706; 9781590787700

"Orphaned wild burro Roo and litter-runt puppy Rena become livestock guardians and, eventually, friends on the author's ranch. They are initially paired to protect lamb orphans from predators. Youthful, mutual wariness eventually unfolds into friendship between the two. . . . Heartwarming photos and clear, accessible text combine to make this story a winner." SLJ

Includes bibliographical references

Weitzman, Gary

How to Speak Dog; A Guide to Decoding Dog Language. by Aline Alexander Newman and Gary Weitzman. Natl Geographic Soc Childrens books 2013 176 p. $12.95

Grades: 4 5 6   **636.7**

1. Dogs -- Behavior 2. Animal communication
ISBN 142631373X; 1426315597; 9781426313738; 9781426315596

Authors Aline Alexander Newman and Gary Weitzman present an "informative, and photographically driven book that helps kids understand what their dog is trying to tell

them through body language and behavior. Quick-hit tip boxes, fun facts about mankind's best friends, and informative sidebars from the experts enliven the text." (Publisher's note)

636.73   Working and herding dogs

Katz, Jon

Lenore finds a friend; a true story from Bedlam Farm. Story and photographs by Jon Katz. Henry Holt and Company 2012 32 p. (hc) $15.99

Grades: K 1 2 3   **636.73**

1. Friendship 2. Animal behavior 3. Picture books for children 4. Farm life -- Fiction 5. Animals -- Anecdotes 6. Animal communication 7. Bedlam Farm (West Hebron, N.Y.) 8. Emotions in animals -- Anecdotes 9. Social behavior in animals -- Anecdotes 10. Working dogs -- New York (State) -- Anecdotes 11. Farm life -- New York (State) -- West Hebron -- Anecdotes
ISBN 080509220X; 9780805092202

LC 2011029040

This children's picture book is based on the story of the friendship between puppy Lenore and ram Brutus at Bedlam Farm. Lenore "was lonely because the other animals . . . were not friendly towards her. Rose, the other dog at the farm, was too busy herding the sheep" to play. Lenore starts making friends with Brutus by giving him daily kisses. "Despite Rose's attempts to keep Lenore away from Brutus, Lenore does not give up and the friendship . . . grows." (Children's Literature)

Kimmel, Elizabeth Cody

Balto and the great race; illustrated by Nora Koerber. Random House 1999 99p il map (Stepping stone book) hardcover o.p. pa $3.99

Grades: 3 4 5   **636.73**

1. Diphtheria 2. Sled dog racing 3. Nome (Alaska)
ISBN 0-679-99198-0 lib bdg; 0-679-89198-6 pa

LC 98-35753

Recounts how the sled dog Balto saved Nome, Alaska, in 1925 from a diphtheria epidemic by delivering medicine through a raging snowstorm

"Kimmel's writing deftly combines geography, sled racing, and historical background with the gripping adventure of Balto's race to save lives. In many ways, the book reads like fast-paced fiction. Koerber's serviceable black-and-white illustrations appear throughout and reflect the action. Sure to appeal to beginning chapter-book readers." SLJ

636.8   Cats

Barnes, Julia

Pet cats; [by] Julia Barnes. Gareth Stevens Pub. 2007 32p il (Pet pals) lib bdg $23.93

Grades: 2 3 4 5   **636.8**

1. Cats
ISBN 0-8368-6776-9

LC 2006042377

"In spreads filled with color photographs, Barnes presents a short explanation of the feline family tree, as well as the history of cat-human relationships, before delving into cat breeds, characteristics, and behavior. Final sections offer ideas for new cat owners." Booklist

Includes glossary and bibliographical references

Bidner, Jenni

Is my cat a tiger? how your cat compares to its wild cousins. Lark Books 2006 64p il $9.95

Grades: 3 4 5 6　　　　　　　　　　　　　636.8

1. Cats 2. Wild cats

ISBN 1-57990-815-2

　　　　　　　　　　　　　　　　LC 2006023356

"This book shows how domestic cats compare with their wild cousins. Specifically, it addresses what domestic behavior reveals about wild roots. . . . The color photographs are fantastic. . . . This is a fascinating volume." SLJ

Biniok, Janice

Mixed breed cats. Eldorado Ink 2010 112p il (Our best friends) lib bdg $34.95

Grades: 4 5 6 7　　　　　　　　　　　　　636.8

1. Cats

ISBN 978-1-932904-62-8 lib bdg; 1-932904-62-X lib bdg

This "is a cradle-to-grave overview of a cat's life. . . . [This] well-written [book provides] examples to support [its] points and solid online and text resources and feature [a] clean, uncluttered [layout]. . . . There is plenty of practical information that motivated readers can glean from [this title]. [It] debunks some presumptions about domesticated felines, commenting that the 'finicky eater' tag is unwarranted, and that cats are easier to train than people think." SLJ

Includes bibliographical references

Bozzo, Linda

My first cat; [by] Linda Bozzo. Enslow Elementary 2007 32p il (My first pet library from the American Humane Association) lib bdg $22.60

Grades: 1 2 3　　　　　　　　　　　　　636.8

1. Cats

ISBN 978-0-7660-2750-3 lib bdg; 0-7660-2750-3 lib bdg

　　　　　　　　　　　　　　　　LC 2006008403

This offers brief basic advice on selecting a cat and caring for it.

Includes glossary and bibliographical references

George, Jean Craighead

How to talk to your cat; illustrated by Paul Meisel. HarperCollins Pubs. 2000 28p il $9.95

Grades: 2 3 4　　　　　　　　　　　　　636.8

1. Cats

ISBN 0-06-027968-0

　　　　　　　　　　　　　　　　LC 98-41517

Describes how cats communicate with people through their behavior and sounds and explains how to talk back to them using sounds, behavior, and body language

"The writing style is breezy, conversational, and amusing, and is helped along by the many color illustrations. The photographs of the author are cleverly combined with humorous cartoon drawings of cats that display a great deal of intelligence and comedic personality. . . . A useful and readable addition to any pet collection." SLJ

Gibbons, Gail

Cats. Holiday House 1996 un il hardcover o.p. $16.95

Grades: K 1 2 3　　　　　　　　　　　　636.8

1. Cats

ISBN 0-8234-1253-9; 0-8234-1410-8 pa

　　　　　　　　　　　　　　　　LC 96-3953

Presents information about the physical characteristics, senses, and behavior of cats, as well as how to care for these animals and some general facts about them

"This easy-to-read picture book will appeal to lovers of the popular pet. Brightly colored illustrations identify different breeds, while the informative . . . text describes physical and behavioral traits of kittens and cats." Horn Book Guide

Hart, Joyce

Cats; by Joyce Hart. Marshall Cavendish Benchmark 2008 48p il (Great pets) lib bdg $29.93

Grades: 2 3 4　　　　　　　　　　　　　636.8

1. Cats

ISBN 978-0-7614-2710-0 lib bdg; 0-7614-2710-4 lib bdg

　　　　　　　　　　　　　　　　LC 2007016462

This is an "enthusiastic, warm [introduction]. . . . [It is] clearly written and [is] the most thorough, honest [introduction] to owning [pet cats] for this audience." SLJ

Holub, Joan

Why do cats meow? illustrations by Anna DiVito. Dial Books for Young Readers 2001 46p il (Dial easy-to-read) hardcover o.p. pa $3.99

Grades: K 1 2　　　　　　　　　　　　　636.8

1. Cats

ISBN 0-8037-2503-5; 0-14-056788-7 pa

　　　　　　　　　　　　　　　　LC 00-23985

Questions and answers present information about the history, behavior, and characteristics of cats and their interaction with humans

"Packed with interesting information and illustrated with an abundance of cartoon artwork and color photographs." Horn Book Guide

Johnson, Jinny

Cats and kittens; [by] Jinny Johnson. Black Rabbit Books 2009 32p il (Get to know your pet) $27.10

Grades: 3 4 5 6　　　　　　　　　　　　636.8

1. Cats

ISBN 978-1-59920-088-0; 1-59920-088-0

　　　　　　　　　　　　　　　　LC 2007-43435

"Spreads include in-depth care instruction, and 'Q & A' sidebars that answer common behavioral questions. . . . The layout is clear, with full color photos and illustrations breaking up the text." SLJ

Includes glossary

Laidlaw, Rob

★ Cat champions; caring for our feline friends. By Rob Laidlaw. Orca Book Pub 2014 64 p. illustrations (chiefly color) $19.95

Grades: 4 5 6 7 8　　　　　　　　　　　636.8

1. Cats 2. Animal welfare 3. Voluntarism 4. Cats -- Health 5. Animal shelters

ISBN 1927485312; 9781927485316

In this book, readers "meet kids who are helping at shelters, fostering kittens, volunteering with sterilization programs and caring for abandoned cats. Animal advocate Rob Laidlaw brings readers a hopeful, inspiring look at the issues facing domesticated and feral cats, and the cat champions who are working to help them." (Publisher's note)

"Here's a book for cat lovers and those who want to know more about caring for furry friends...The format is busy, but cat lovers probably won't mind so many photos, and the sidebars are all informative. The list of organizations where kids can learn about ways they can help is extensive and useful." Booklist

MacLeod, Elizabeth

Why do cats have whiskers? Kids Can Press 2008 64p il $14.95

Grades: 3 4 5 6   **636.8**

1. Cats

ISBN 978-1-55453-196-7; 1-55453-196-9

"With its lively text and copious photographs, this title offers readers an accessible introduction to the world of felines. . . . MacLeod's interesting facts and anecdotes are sure to keep young cat owners engaged." Horn Book Guide

Malam, John

Grow your own cat toy. Heinemann Library 2011 32p il (Grow it yourself!) lib bdg $26; pa $7.99

Grades: 2 3 4   **636.8**

1. Gardening 2. Handicraft 3. Catnip

ISBN 978-1-4329-5110-8 lib bdg; 1-4329-5110-6; 978-1-4329-5117-7 pa; 1-4329-5117-3 pa

LC 2010049835

This describes the catnip plant and why cats like it, how to grow it, and how to make a catnip toy.

This book "turns the idea [of growing a catnip toy] into a fun and fascinating project. . . . A big part of the book's appeal is the crisp color photographs. . . . Simple sentences in an easily read typeface . . . are just right for the elementary-school age group. . . . A well-done package in every way." Booklist

Includes glossary and bibliographical references

Myron, Vicki

Dewey the library cat; a true story. [by] Vicki Myron with Bret Witter. Little, Brown 2010 214p $16.99

Grades: 4 5 6 7 8   **636.8**

1. Cats 2. Libraries

ISBN 978-0-316-06871-0; 0-316-06871-3

Adapted from: Dewey: the small town library cat who touched the world, published 2008 by Grand Central Publisher for adults

"From the opening chapter, when librarian Vicki Myron finds a fragile, freezing kitten in the book return, children will be hooked on her heartwarming story about Dewey Readmore Books. . . . Anecdotes such as Dewey's fascination with rubber bands, his bizarre behavior during a bat invasion, and his finicky eating habits are ideal booktalk material. So are descriptions of Dewey's tender, intuitive interactions with people of all ages and backgrounds." Booklist

Niven, Felicia Lowenstein

Learning to care for a cat. Enslow Publishers 2010 48p il (Beginning pet care with American Humane) lib bdg $23.93

Grades: 2 3 4   **636.8**

1. Cats

ISBN 978-0-7660-3191-3; 0-7660-3191-8

LC 2008048963

"Readers will learn how to choose, train, and care for a cat." Publisher's note

Includes glossary and bibliographical references

Rau, Dana Meachen

Top 10 cats for kids; [by] Dana Meachen Rau. Enslow Publishers 2008 48p il (Top pets for kids with American Humane) lib bdg $23.93

Grades: 2 3 4 5   **636.8**

1. Cats

ISBN 978-0-7660-3071-8 lib bdg; 0-7660-3071-7 lib bdg

LC 2007-24440

"Includes beautiful full-color photos showing the animals at their best. Judicious use of text boxes, crisp fonts, and white space will make it easy for readers to follow the flow of information." SLJ

Includes glossary and bibliographical references

Rebman, Renee C.

Cats. Marshall Cavendish Benchmark 2009 47p il (Animals, animals) lib bdg $20.95

Grades: 3 4 5   **636.8**

1. Cats

ISBN 978-0-7614-3975-2

LC 2008020918

Provides comprehensive information on the anatomy, special skills, habitats, and diet of cats.

Includes glossary and bibliographical references

Simon, Seymour

★ **Cats**. HarperCollins Pub. 2004 un il lib bdg $16.89; pa $6.99

Grades: 1 2 3 4   **636.8**

1. Cats

ISBN 0-06-028940-6; 0-06-028941-4 lib bdg; 0-06-446254-4 pa

LC 2003-8337

Discusses the history, physical characteristics, behavior, and various breeds of cats, and provides basic information on caring for one as a pet.

"The striking color photos, including many closeups, create a feeling of intimacy. . . . Simon succeeds in addressing his topic in clear, easily understood vocabulary without writing down to children." SLJ

Tildes, Phyllis Limbacher

Calico's cousins; cats from around the world. Charlesbridge Pub. 1999 un il lib bdg $15.95; pa $6.95

Grades: K 1 2 3   **636.8**

1. Cats

ISBN 0-88106-648-6 lib bdg; 0-88106-649-4 pa

LC 98-4011

"Calico, a domestic longhair cat, introduces various breeds by describing both their origin and common traits. Each double-page spread features realistic illustrations of several cats in an environment appropriate to their origin, and a map at the end provides geographical reference." Horn Book Guide

Whitehead, Sarah

How to speak cat. Scholastic 2009 96p il pa $6.99

Grades: 4 5 6 7 8   **636.8**

1. Cats

ISBN 978-0-545-02079-4 pa; 0-545-02079-4 pa

"This pet-care book focuses on developing a relationship with a pet. The author states that the communication process is a two-way street, and she describes how readers can translate a cat's body language and vocalizations. . . . the bright color photographs of children with their cats on every page will appeal greatly to readers. This is a fun book that offers a good understanding of its audience and subject." SLJ

636.9   Other mammals

Barnes, Julia

Elephants at work; [by] Julia Barnes. Gareth Stevens 2006 32p il map (Animals at work) lib bdg $23.93

Grades: 3 4 5   **636.9**

1. Elephants 2. Working animals

ISBN 0-8368-6224-4

LC 2005054067

This describes uses of elephants throughout history, their relationship with humans, habitat, diet, and appearance

This is "well-written, well-organized, . . . visually appealing and fun to read." SLJ

Includes bibliographical references

Pet guinea pigs; [by] Julia Barnes. Gareth Stevens Pub. 2007 32p il (Pet pals) lib bdg $23.93

Grades: 2 3 4 5   **636.9**

1. Guinea pigs

ISBN 0-8368-6779-3

LC 2006042373

This places guinea pigs "within the context of [their] wild roots and [their] relationship to humans. From there, Barnes explains what makes the animal an ideal pet, recommends how to be a good caregiver, and reveals how the creature communicates (as well as how to answer). The [book mixes] practical advice with trivia in a way that children will find informative and easy to navigate. Crisp, full-color photos enhance the [text]." SLJ

Includes glossary and bibliographical references

Pet rabbits; [by] Julia Barnes. Gareth Stevens Pub. 2007 32p il (Pet pals) lib bdg $32.92

Grades: 2 3 4 5   **636.9**

1. Rabbits

ISBN 0-8368-6781-5

LC 2006042374

This places rabbits "within the context of [their] wild roots and [their] relationship to humans. From there, Barnes explains what makes the animal an ideal pet, recommends how to be a good caregiver, and reveals how the creature communicates (as well as how to answer). The [book mixes] practical advice with trivia in a way that children will find informative and easy to navigate. Crisp, full-color photos enhance the [text]." SLJ

Includes glossary and bibliographical references

Bjorklund, Ruth

Rabbits; by Ruth Bjorklund. Marshall Cavendish Benchmark 2008 48p il (Great pets) lib bdg $28.50

Grades: 2 3 4   **636.9**

1. Rabbits

ISBN 978-0-7614-2708-7 lib bdg; 0-7614-2708-2 lib bdg

LC 2007013044

The offers an introduction to rabbits as pets and how to choose and care for them

This is an "enthusiastic, warm [introduction]. . . . [This is] clearly written and [is] the most thorough, honest [introduction] to owning a pet [rabbit] for this audience." SLJ

Includes glossary and bibliographical references

Bozzo, Linda

My first guinea pig and other small pets; [by] Linda Bozzo. Enslow Elementary 2007 32p il (My first pet library from the American Humane Association) lib bdg $22.60

Grades: 1 2 3   **636.9**

1. Mice 2. Pets 3. Rats 4. Ferrets 5. Gerbils 6. Rabbits 7. Hamsters 8. Guinea pigs

ISBN 978-0-7660-2752-7 lib bdg; 0-7660-2752-X lib bdg

LC 2006014970

This offers advice on selecting and caring for small pets including guinea pigs, hamsters, gerbils, rabbits, ferrets, rats, and mice.

Includes glossary and bibliographical references

Ellis, Carol

Hamsters and gerbils. Marshall Cavendish Benchmark 2009 46p il (Great pets) $20.95

Grades: 2 3 4   **636.9**

1. Gerbils 2. Hamsters

ISBN 978-0-7614-2999-9; 0-7614-2999-9

LC 2008-24336

"Describes the characteristics and behavior of pet hamsters and gerbils, also discussing their physical appearance and place in history." Publisher's note

Includes glossary and bibliographical references

Foran, Jill

Guinea pig. Weigl 2010 32p il (My pet) lib bdg $26; pa $9.95

Grades: 3 4 5   **636.9**

1. Pets 2. Guinea pigs

ISBN 978-1-60596-090-6 lib bdg; 1-60596-090-X lib bdg; 978-1-60596-091-3 pa; 1-60596-091-8 pa

LC 2009-5128

Information about how to house, feed, and care for guinea pigs.

"With clear, formal writing, and extensive coverage . . . [this title is] useful for reports. . . . Numerous color photographs, charts . . . and question-and-answer boxes supplement the [text]." SLJ

Includes glossary

Gaines, Ann

Top 10 small mammals for kids; [by] Ann Graham Gaines. Enslow Publishers 2008 48p il (Top pets for kids with American Humane) lib bdg $23.93

Grades: 2 3 4 5   **636.9**
1. Pets 2. Mammals
ISBN 978-0-7660-3075-6 lib bdg; 0-7660-3075-X
lib bdg

LC 2007-38480

"Includes beautiful full-color photos showing the animals at their best. Judicious use of text boxes, crisp fonts, and white space will make it easy for readers to follow the flow of information." SLJ

Includes glossary and bibliographical references

Ganeri, Anita
★ **Rabbits**. Heinemann 2009 32p il (A pet's life) $17.75
Grades: 3 4 5   **636.9**
1. Rabbits
ISBN 978-1-4329-3394-4; 1-4329-3394-9

"Pretty much everything a child needs to know about taking care of rabbits in this title. . . . The book is organized in a logical way that will keep kids focused. . . . [The book uses] a good-size typeface and clear, adorable photos. . . . Fact-filled, fun to look at, and a pleasure to read." Booklist

Hamilton, Lynn
Ferret. Weigl 2010 32p il (My pet) lib bdg $26; pa $9.95
Grades: 3 4 5   **636.9**
1. Pets 2. Ferrets
ISBN 978-1-60596-096-8 lib bdg; 1-60596-096-9 lib bdg; 978-1-60596-097-5 pa; 1-60596-097-7 pa

LC 2009-4985

Information about how to house, feed, and care for ferrets.

"With clear, formal writing, and extensive coverage . . . [this title is] useful for reports. . . . Numerous color photographs, charts . . . and question-and-answer boxes supplement the [text]." SLJ

Includes glossary

Haney, Johannah
Ferrets. Marshall Cavendish Benchmark 2010 46p il (Great pets) lib bdg $29.93
Grades: 2 3 4   **636.9**
1. Pets 2. Ferrets
ISBN 978-0-7614-4153-3 lib bdg; 0-7614-4153-0 lib bdg

LC 2009020561

"Describes the characteristics and behavior of pet ferrets, also discussing their physical appearance and place in history." Publisher's note

Includes glossary and bibliographical references

Jeffrey, Laura S.
Hamsters, gerbils, guinea pigs, rabbits, ferrets, mice, and rats; how to choose and care for a small mammal. Enslow Publishers 2004 48p il (American humane pet care library) lib bdg $23.93
Grades: 3 4 5   **636.9**
1. Mice 2. Rats 3. Ferrets 4. Rabbits 5. Hamsters 6. Guinea pigs
ISBN 0-7660-2518-7

LC 2003-22969

Explains the different personalities of several small mammals, where to go to pick the right one, and how to keep them happy and healthy

Includes glossary and bibliographical references

Johnson, Jinny
Guinea pigs; [by] Jinny Johnson. Black Rabbit Books 2009 32p il (Get to know your pet) $27.10
Grades: 3 4 5 6   **636.9**
1. Guinea pigs
ISBN 978-1-59920-211-2; 1-59920-211-5

LC 2007-43437

"Spreads include in-depth care instruction, and 'Q & A' sidebars that answer common behavioral questions. . . . The layout is clear, with full color photos and illustrations breaking up the text." SLJ

Includes glossary

Hamsters and gerbils; [by] Jinny Johnson. Black Rabbit Books 2009 32p il (Get to know your pet) $27.10
Grades: 3 4 5 6   **636.9**
1. Gerbils 2. Hamsters
ISBN 978-1-59920-092-7; 1-59920-092-9

LC 2007-52813

"Spreads include in-depth care instruction, and 'Q & A' sidebars that answer common behavioral questions. . . . The layout is clear, with full color photos and illustrations breaking up the text." SLJ

Includes glossary

Rabbits; [by] Jinny Johnson. Black Rabbit Books 2009 32p il (Get to know your pet) $27.10
Grades: 3 4 5 6   **636.9**
1. Rabbits
ISBN 978-1-59920-090-3; 1-59920-090-2

LC 2007-43436

"Spreads include in-depth care instruction, and 'Q & A' sidebars that answer common behavioral questions. . . . The layout is clear, with full color photos and illustrations breaking up the text." SLJ

Includes glossary

Rats and mice; [by] Jinny Johnson. Black Rabbit Books 2009 32p il (Get to know your pet) $27.10
Grades: 3 4 5 6   **636.9**
1. Mice 2. Rats
ISBN 978-1-59920-091-0; 1-59920-091-0

LC 2007-52815

"Spreads include in-depth care instruction, and 'Q & A' sidebars that answer common behavioral questions. . . . The layout is clear, with full color photos and illustrations breaking up the text." SLJ

Includes glossary

Lewin, Ted
★ **Balarama**; a royal elephant. [by] Ted and Betsy Lewin. Lee & Low Books 2009 un il $19.95
Grades: 3 4 5 6   **636.9**
1. Elephants 2. India
ISBN 978-1-60060-265-8; 1-60060-265-7

LC 2009-1499

"Ted Lewin's brilliant, realistic watercolors capture the sun-drenched pageantry of Mysore as well as the dusty, filtered light of the forest, while Betsy Lewin's lively cartoons aptly depict the action and personalities involved. The story has pathos and tension." SLJ

Lunis, Natalie

Furry ferrets. Bearport 2010 24p il (Peculiar pets) lib bdg $22.61

Grades: 3 4 5   **636.9**

1. Pets 2. Ferrets

ISBN 978-1-59716-860-1 lib bdg; 1-59716-860-2 lib bdg

LC 2009-10378

Introduces the furry ferret, describing its physical characteristics, habitat, and behavior, and discussing the care and diet that it needs if it is kept as a pet

"The language . . . is lively . . . [and] the illustrations are vivid, with photos offering some amusing shots. . . . This [book] . . . will hold readers' attention, but also challenge them to consider the responsibilities required of owners of unusual creatures." SLJ

Includes glossary and bibliographical references

McNicholas, June

Rats. Heinemann Lib. 2003 48p il (Keeping unusual pets) $24.22

Grades: 4 5 6 7   **636.9**

1. Rats

ISBN 1-4034-0283-3

LC 2002-3164

Describes how to select a pet rat, what to feed it, and when to take it to the vet, as well as how to keep a pet scrapbook

"A valuable, accessible resource." Booklist

Includes bibliographical references

Newcomb, Rain

Is my hamster wild? the secret lives of hamsters, gerbils & guinea pigs. by Rain Newcomb & Rose McLarney. Lark Books 2008 64p il $9.95

Grades: 2 3 4   **636.9**

1. Gerbils 2. Hamsters 3. Guinea pigs

ISBN 978-1-60059-242-3; 1-60059-242-2

LC 2007-44312

"Crisp photo album-style pictures with humorous captions reinforce the deft main text." Horn Book Guide

Niven, Felicia Lowenstein

Learning to care for small mammals. Enslow Publishers 2010 48p il (Beginning pet care with American Humane) lib bdg $23.93

Grades: 2 3 4   **636.9**

1. Ferrets 2. Rabbits 3. Rodents

ISBN 978-0-7660-3195-1; 0-7660-3195-0

This describes how to care for small mammals such as rabbits, guinea pigs, gerbils, hamsters, rats, mice, or ferrets.

"The pictures are colorful and engaging, with a no-fuss layout. The text is easy to follow, pitched at just the right level for the audience." SLJ

Includes glossary and bibliographical references

Petrylak, Ashley

Guinea pigs. Marshall Cavendish Benchmark 2009 44p il (Great pets) lib bdg $29.93

Grades: 2 3 4   **636.9**

1. Guinea pigs

ISBN 978-0-7614-4148-9 lib bdg; 0-7614-4148-4 lib bdg

LC 2008037238

"Describes the characteristics and behavior of pet guinea pigs, also discussing their physical appearance and place in history." Publisher's note

Includes glossary and bibliographical references

Richardson, Adele

Caring for your hamster; by Adele Richardson. Capstone Press 2007 24p il (Positively pets) $21.26

Grades: K 1 2 3   **636.9**

1. Hamsters

ISBN 978-0-7368-6387-2; 0-7368-6387-7

LC 2005035852

This is a "concise, competent [introduction] to the responsibility and fun of being a pet owner. . . . Attractive and well suited for young readers in both tone and content. The clear color photographs display the animals in all their glory." SLJ

Includes bibliographical references

Sobol, Richard

An elephant in the backyard; text and photographs by Richard Sobol. Dutton Children's Books 2004 un il $17.99

Grades: K 1 2 3   **636.9**

1. Elephants 2. Thailand

ISBN 0-525-47288-6

LC 2003-52492

Describes how special elephants are in the village of Tha Kleng in Thailand and looks at the life of one particular young elephant named Wan Pen.

This is an "engaging photo-essay. Large, colorful photographs enhance the text. . . . The text is packed with interesting tidbits about these large mammals." SLJ

636.935   Rodents – animal husbandry

Boruchowitz, David E.

Sugar gliders; David E. Boruchowitz; [editor, Thomas Mazorlig] T.F.H. 2012 111 p. (Animal planet. Pet care library) (pbk.: alk. paper) $10.95

Grades: 4 5 6 7   **636.935**

1. Sugar gliders as pets 2. Sugar glider

ISBN 0793837111; 9780793837113

LC 2011049947

This book on sugar gliders by David E. Boruchowitz is part of the "Animal Planet Pet Care Library" series. "According to Boruchowitz, they make excellent house pets due to their affinity for cuddling in tiny places. . . . Every aspect of ownership is covered, from basic dietary requirements to grooming and socialization." (Booklist)

Includes bibliographical references and index

637 Processing dairy and related products

Aliki

Milk from cow to carton; rev ed; HarperCollins Pubs. 1992 31p il (Let's-read-and-find-out science book) hardcover o.p. pa $5.95

Grades: K 1 2 3   637

1. Milk 2. Cattle 3. Dairying

ISBN 0-06-445111-9 pa

LC 91-23807

First published 1974 by Crowell with title: Green grass and white milk

Briefly describes how a cow produces milk, how the milk is processed in a dairy, and how various other dairy products are made from milk

This features "full-color artwork. . . . An excellent primary-level introduction to dairy science." Booklist

Gibbons, Gail

The **milk** makers. Macmillan 1985 un il hardcover o.p. pa $5.99

Grades: K 1 2 3   637

1. Milk 2. Cattle 3. Dairying

ISBN 0-02-736640-5; 0-689-71116-6 pa

LC 84-20081

Explains how cows produce milk and how it is processed before being delivered to stores

"Starting with dairy cows grazing at pasture, nothing is overlooked in the procedure, from the role of the calf to winter feed and shelter, the function of four stomachs, milking, milk handling, and the operation of a dairy. Diagrams of the cow stomachs as well as the machines used at farm and dairy leave no question unanswered, although city children will be unfamiliar with what it means to breed a cow. Finally, there is a pictorial list of the many other dairy products found in most homes." Sci Books Films

Malam, John

Journey of a glass of milk; John Malam. Heinemann Library 2013 32 p. (hb) $26.65

Grades: 1 2 3   637

1. Milk supply 2. Picture books for children 3. Milk 4. Milk trade 5. Dairy processing

ISBN 1432966030; 9781432966034; 9781432966102

LC 2011050559

This book is part of the "Journey of a . . . " series that "looks at how common products end up in our homes, starting with the raw materials and ending with the finished goods. This title looks at the journey of a glass of milk, examining how cows are milked, how the milk is treated, how it is packaged, transported and distributed to stores, and how it is sold and eventually drunk!" (Publisher's note)

Includes bibliographical references and index

Peterson, Cris

Extra cheese, please! mozzarella's journey from cow to pizza. photographs by Alvis Upitis. Boyds Mills Press 1994 un il $16.95; pa $9.95

Grades: K 1 2 3   637

1. Cheese 2. Dairying

ISBN 1-56397-177-1; 1-59078-246-1 pa

LC 93-70876

"Nicely balanced pages contain brief blocks of clearly written text and many full-color photographs." SLJ

Includes glossary and bibliographical references

638 Insect culture

Burns, Loree Griffin

★ The **hive** detectives; chronicle of a honey bee catastrophe. by Loree Griffin Burns with photographs by Ellen Harasimowicz. HMH Books for Young Readers 2010 80 p. il (Scientists in the field) $18.99

Grades: 5 6 7 8 9 10   638

1. Bees 2. Beekeeping 3. Insects -- Behavior 4. Honeybee 5. Bee culture

ISBN 0547152310; 9780547152318

LC 2009045249

A Junior Library Guild selection

In this book, author Loree Griffin Burns "profiles bee wranglers and bee scientists who have been working to understand colony collapse disorder, or CCD. In this dramatic and enlightening story, readers explore the lives of the fuzzy, buzzy insects and learn what might happen to us if they were gone." (Publisher's note)

"Not long after beekeepers encountered a devastating new problem in their hives in 2006, a team of bee scientists began working to discover the causes of colony collapse disorder (CCD), now attributed to a combination of factors possibly including pesticides, nutrition, mites and viruses. . . . Mock notebook pages break up the narrative with biographies of the individual scientists, information about who and what can be found inside the hive and the features of bee bodies. An appendix adds varied fascinating facts about bees—again using the format of an illustrated research journal. Harasimowicz's clear, beautifully reproduced photographs support and extend the text." Kirkus

Includes bibliographical references (p. 65) and index

Fujiwara, Yumiko

Honey; a gift from nature. written by Yumiko Fujiwara; illustrated by Hideko Ise. Kane/Miller 2006 un il (Nature: a child's eye view) pa $7.95

Grades: PreK K 1   638

1. Bees 2. Honey

ISBN 1-929132-94-8 pa; 978-1-929132-94-2 pa

LC 2005-930528

Original Japanese edition 1997

A young Japanese girl spends the day with her beekeeping father in the mountains where he keeps his hives. Explains how bees gather nectar, how it is turned into honey, and how the honey is collected.

Harkins, Susan Sales

Design your own butterfly garden; by Susan Sales Harkins and William H. Harkins. Mitchell Lane Publishers 2008 48p il (Gardening for kids) lib bdg $29.95

Grades: 3 4 5 6   638

1. Butterfly gardens

ISBN 978-1-58415-638-3 lib bdg; 1-58415-638-4 lib bdg

LC 2008-2245

Introduces the principles of butterfly gardening, discussing how to plan the garden, what flowers to plant there, and how to maintain it in all seasons

"All the tasks delineated are well within the scope of children's abilities, and the items needed to complete them are not hard to find. . . . [The book has] excellent full-color photography and include[s] charts and diagrams to assist in the completion of the projects." SLJ

Includes bibliographical references

Malam, John

Grow your own butterfly farm. Heinemann Library 2011 32p il (Grow it yourself!) lib bdg $26; pa $7.99

Grades: K 1 2 **638**

1. Gardening 2. Butterflies

ISBN 978-1-4329-5109-2 lib bdg; 978-1-4329-5116-0 pa

LC 2010049834

This describes how to grow a flower garden which attracts butterflies.

Includes glossary and bibliographical references

639 Hunting, fishing, conservation, related technologies

Lomberg, Michelle

Spider. Weigl Publishers 2009 32p il (My pets) lib bdg $26; pa $9.95

Grades: 3 4 5 **639**

1. Pets 2. Spiders

ISBN 978-1-60596-094-4 lib bdg; 1-60596-094-2 lib bdg; 978-1-60596-095-1 pa; 1-60596-095-0 pa

LC 2009-25979

Information about how to house, feed, and care for spiders.

"With clear, formal writing, and extensive coverage . . . [this title is] useful for reports. . . . Numerous color photographs, charts . . . and question-and-answer boxes supplement the [text]." SLJ

Includes glossary

Richardson, Adele

Caring for your hermit crab; by Adele Richardson. Capstone Press 2007 24p il (Positively pets) $21.26

Grades: K 1 2 3 **639**

1. Pets 2. Crabs

ISBN 978-0-7368-6388-9; 0-7368-6388-5

LC 2006006390

This is a "concise, competent [introduction] to the responsibility and fun of being a pet owner. . . . Attractive and well suited for young readers in both tone and content. The clear color photographs display the animals in all their glory." SLJ

Includes bibliographical references

639.2 Commercial fishing, whaling, sealing

Foster, Mark

★ Whale port; a history of Tuckanucket. written by Mark Foster; illustrated by Gerald Foster. Houghton Mifflin Company 2007 64p il $18

Grades: 4 5 6 7 **639.2**

1. Whaling

ISBN 978-0-618-54722-7; 0-618-54722-3

LC 2006018772

This describes the history of whaling in New England through the fictional village of Tuckanucket and Zachariah Taber, his family and neighbors.

The village is "depicted in precisely detailed ink and crayon pictures. . . . The Fosters . . . have elegantly synthesized a tremendous amount of information into a beguiling format." Horn Book

Kurlansky, Mark

★ The cod's tale; illustrated by S.D. Schindler. Putnam 2002 43p il map $16.99

Grades: 3 4 5 6 **639.2**

1. Codfish 2. Commercial fishing

ISBN 0-399-23476-4

LC 00-68412

"Schindler's line-and-watercolor scenes are rendered with the delicate hatching of fine engraving and suffused with gentle humor. . . . This is a classic example of an unlikely subject made not only likely but fascinating and informative through authorial and illustrative craftsmanship." Bull Cent Child Books

Includes bibliographical references

McKissack, Patricia C.

★ Black hands, white sails; the story of African-American whalers. [by] Patricia C. McKissack & Fredrick L. McKissack. Scholastic Press 1999 xxiv, 152p il $17.95

Grades: 5 6 7 8 **639.2**

1. Whaling 2. Abolitionists 3. African Americans

ISBN 0-590-48313-7

LC 99-11439

A Coretta Scott King honor book for text, 2000

A history of African-American whalers between 1730 and 1880, describing their contributions to the whaling industry and their role in the abolitionist movement

"A well-researched and detailed book." SLJ

Includes bibliographical references

McMillan, Bruce

Salmon summer; written and photo-illustrated by Bruce McMillan. Houghton Mifflin 1998 32p il $17

Grades: 2 3 4 **639.2**

1. Salmon 2. Fishing 3. Alaska

ISBN 0-395-84544-0

LC 97-29679

A photo essay describing a young native Alaskan boy fishing for salmon on Kodiak Island as his ancestors have done for generations

"McMillan documents the goings on with his trademark crystal-clear color photographs and an engaging text." Booklist

Includes glossary and bibliographical references

Sandler, Martin W.

★ Trapped in ice! an amazing true whaling adventure. Scholastic Nonfiction 2006 168p il $16.99

Grades: 5 6 7 8 **639.2**

1. Whaling

ISBN 0-439-74363-X

LC 2005-42644

"In 1871, people aboard 32 whaling ships discovered just how dangerous Arctic waters could be after they ignored warnings of an early winter. As conditions worsened, the ships were trapped by ice, forcing the 1,219 people to abandon the vessels or die. Sandler's account of this true story is both informative and absorbing. . . . Well-chosen illustrations and side notes on such topics as life aboard ship and women at sea extend readers' understanding." Booklist

Includes glossary and bibliographical references

Somervill, Barbara A.

Commercial fisher. Cherry Lake Pub. 2011 32p il (Cool careers) lib bdg $27.07

Grades: 4 5 6 7   **639.2**

1. Commercial fishing 2. Vocational guidance

ISBN 978-1-60279-986-8; 1-60279-986-5

LC 2010029123

This book begins "with a personal story of a teen and then [segues] into the occupation [of commercial fisher]. . . . [It covers] the necessary training and skills for the job (and options for obtaining them), a typical day, salary expectations, and well-known professionals in the field. The [text is] accessible and clearly written. . . . The [volume has] a generous number of clear color photographs that depict people at work." SLJ

Includes glossary and bibliographical references

639.3 Culture of cold-blooded vertebrates

Bjorklund, Ruth

Lizards. Marshall Cavendish Benchmark 2009 48p il (Great pets) $20.95

Grades: 2 3 4   **639.3**

1. Lizards

ISBN 978-0-7614-2997-5; 0-7614-2997-2

LC 2008-17560

"Describes the characteristics and behavior of pet lizards, also discussing their physical appearance and place in history." Publisher's note

Includes glossary and bibliographical references

Cone, Molly

★ **Come** back, salmon; how a group of dedicated kids adopted Pigeon Creek and brought it back to life. photographs by Sidnee Wheelright. Sierra Club Bks. for Children 1992 48p il $16.95; pa $7.95

Grades: 3 4 5 6   **639.3**

1. Salmon 2. Wildlife conservation

ISBN 0-87156-572-2; 0-87156-489-0 pa

LC 91-29023

Describes the efforts of the Jackson Elementary School in Everett, Washington, to clean up a nearby stream, stock it with salmon, and preserve it as an unpolluted place where the salmon could return to spawn

"The photographs are superb. . . . Personal and inspiring, the text alternates between descriptions of the project, background information about pollution and renewal, and dialogue of the students recorded; additional scientific information is displayed in panels set off from the main text." Horn Book

Includes glossary

Craats, Rennay

Gecko. Weigl Publishers 2009 32p il (My pet) lib bdg $26; pa $9.95

Grades: 3 4 5   **639.3**

1. Pets 2. Geckos

ISBN 978-1-60596-098-2 lib bdg; 1-60596-098-5 lib bdg; 978-1-60596-099-9 pa; 1-60596-099-3 pa

LC 2009-25985

Information about how to house, feed, and care for geckos.

"With clear, formal writing, and extensive coverage . . . [this title is] useful for reports. . . . Numerous colorful photographs, charts . . . and question-and-answer boxes supplement the [text]." SLJ

Includes glossary

Gaines, Ann

Top 10 reptiles and amphibians for kids; [by] Ann Graham Gaines. Enslow Publishers 2008 48p il (Top pets for kids with American Humane) lib bdg $23.93

Grades: 2 3 4 5   **639.3**

1. Pets 2. Reptiles 3. Amphibians

ISBN 978-0-7660-3074-9 lib bdg; 0-7660-3074-1 lib bdg

LC 2007047884

"Includes beautiful full-color photos showing the animals at their best. Judicious use of text boxes, crisp fonts, and white space will make it easy for readers to follow the flow of information." SLJ

Includes glossary and bibliographical references

Hamilton, Lynn

Turtle. Weigl Publishers 2009 32p il (My pet) lib bdg $26; pa $9.95

Grades: 3 4 5   **639.3**

1. Pets 2. Turtles

ISBN 978-1-60596-088-3 lib bdg; 1-60596-088-8 lib bdg; 978-1-60596-089-0 pa; 1-60596-089-6 pa

LC 2009-25973

Information about how to house, feed, and care for turtles.

"With clear, formal writing, and extensive coverage . . . [this title is] useful for reports. . . . Numerous color photographs, charts . . . and question-and-answer boxes supplement the [text]." SLJ

Includes glossary

Haney, Johannah

Frogs. Marshall Cavendish Benchmark 2009 48p il (Great pets) lib bdg $29.93

Grades: 2 3 4   **639.3**

1. Pets 2. Frogs

ISBN 978-0-7614-4151-9 lib bdg; 0-7614-4151-4 lib bdg

LC 2008037242

"Describes the characteristics and behavior of pet frogs, also discussing their physical appearance and place in history." Publisher's note

Includes glossary and bibliographical references

Turtles; [by] Johannah Haney. Marshall Cavendish Benchmark 2008 48p il (Great pets) lib bdg $28.50

Grades: 2 3 4   **639.3**
1. Pets 2. Turtles
ISBN 978-0-7614-2709-4 lib bdg; 0-7614-2709-0 lib bdg
LC 2006038157

The offers an introduction to turtles as pets and how to choose and care for them

This is an "enthusiastic, warm [introduction]. . . . [It is] clearly written and [is] the most thorough, honest [introduction] to owning a pet [turtle] for this audience." SLJ

Includes glossary and bibliographical references

Hart, Joyce
Snakes. Marshall Cavendish Benchmark 2008 48p il (Great pets) $20.95
Grades: 2 3 4   **639.3**
1. Pets 2. Snakes
ISBN 978-0-7614-2996-8; 0-7614-2996-4
LC 2008-24333

"Describes the characteristics and behavior of pet snakes, also discussing their physical appearance and place in history." Publisher's note

Includes glossary and bibliographical references

Hernandez-Divers, Sonia
Geckos. Heinemann Lib. 2003 48p il (Keeping unusual pets) lib bdg $24.22
Grades: 3 4 5 6   **639.3**
1. Pets 2. Geckos
ISBN 1-4034-0282-5
LC 2002-3163

This offers information about geckos and advice about keeping them as pets

"Lively and informative, with photos scattered across and around the pages . . . [this offers] a wealth of valuable advice." SLJ

Includes glossary and bibliographical references

Lunis, Natalie
Green iguanas. Bearport Pub. 2010 24p il map (Peculiar pets) lib bdg $25.26
Grades: 3 4 5   **639.3**
1. Pets 2. Iguanas
ISBN 978-1-59716-863-2 lib bdg; 1-59716-863-7 lib bdg
LC 2009-17545

Introduces the green iguana, describing its physical characteristics, habitat, and behavior, and discussing the care and diet that it needs if it is kept as a pet

"The language . . . is lively . . . [and] the illustrations are vivid, with photos offering some amusing shots. . . . This [book] . . . will hold readers' attention, but also challenge them to consider the responsibilities required of owners of unusual creatures." SLJ

Includes glossary and bibliographical references

Niven, Felicia Lowenstein
Learning to care for reptiles and amphibians. Enslow Publishers 2010 48p il (Beginning pet care with American Humane) lib bdg $23.93
Grades: 2 3 4   **639.3**
1. Reptiles 2. Amphibians
ISBN 978-0-7660-3194-4; 0-7660-3194-2

This describes how to care for pet reptiles and amphibians such as frogs, geckos, snakes, salamanders, newts, and turtles.

Includes glossary and bibliographical references

639.34   Fish culture in aquariums

Aliki
★ **My** visit to the aquarium. HarperCollins Pubs. 1993 un il $15.95; pa $6.95
Grades: K 1 2 3   **639.34**
1. Marine animals 2. Marine aquariums 3. Freshwater animals
ISBN 0-06-021458-9; 0-06-446186-6 pa
LC 92-18678

During his visit to an aquarium, a boy finds out about the characteristics and environments of many different marine and freshwater creatures

"Fish facts, selected for their child-appeal and delivered in a brisk, conversational tone, are neatly organized by marine environment. . . . The dominant blues and greens of Aliki's watercolors are not only cool and inviting; they also provide visual continuity amid the riot of brightly colored fish." Booklist

Bozzo, Linda
My first fish; [by] Linda Bozzo. Enslow Publishers 2007 32p il (My first pet library from the American Humane Association) lib bdg $22.60
Grades: 1 2 3   **639.34**
1. Fishes 2. Aquariums
ISBN 978-0-7660-2751-0 lib bdg; 0-7660-2751-1 lib bdg
LC 2006010500

"This book explores how to choose the right fish and how to care for your new pet." Publisher's note

Includes glossary and bibliographical references

Buckmaster, Marjorie L.
Freshwater fishes; [by] Marjorie L. Buckmaster. Marshall Cavendish Benchmark 2007 48p il (Great pets) $19.95
Grades: 2 3 4   **639.34**
1. Fishes 2. Aquariums
ISBN 978-0-7614-2712-4
LC 2007017809

The offers an introduction to freshwater fish as pets and how to choose and care for them.

This is an "enthusiastic, warm [introduction]. . . . [It is] clearly written and [is] the most thorough, honest [introduction] to owning [pet fish] for this audience." SLJ

Niven, Felicia Lowenstein
Learning to care for fish. Enslow Publishers 2010 48p il (Beginning pet care with American Humane) lib bdg $23.93
Grades: 2 3 4   **639.34**
1. Fishes 2. Aquariums
ISBN 978-0-7660-3193-7; 0-7660-3193-4

This describes how to care for pet fish.

"The pictures are colorful and engaging, with a no-fuss layout. The text is easy to follow, pitched at just the right level for the audience." SLJ

Includes glossary and bibliographical references

Rau, Dana Meachen

Top 10 fish for kids; [by] Dana Meachen Rau. Enslow Publishers 2008 48p il (Top pets for kids with American Humane) lib bdg $23.93

Grades: 2 3 4 5   **639.34**

1. Fishes 2. Aquariums

ISBN 978-0-7660-3073-2 lib bdg; 0-7660-3073-3 lib bdg

LC 2007-32319

"Includes beautiful full-color photos showing the animals at their best. Judicious use of text boxes, crisp fonts, and white space will make it easy for readers to follow the flow of information." SLJ

Includes glossary and bibliographical references

Richardson, Adele

Caring for your fish; by Adele Richardson. Capstone Press 2007 24p il (Positively pets) $21.26

Grades: K 1 2 3   **639.34**

1. Fishes 2. Aquariums

ISBN 978-0-7368-6386-5; 0-7368-6386-9

LC 2005035854

This is a "concise, competent [introduction] to the responsibility and fun of being a pet owner. . . . Attractive and well suited for young readers in both tone and content. The clear color photographs display the animals in all their glory." SLJ

Includes bibliographical references

639.9 Conservation of biological resources

Buckley, Carol

Just for elephants. Tilbury House 2006 un il $16.95

Grades: 3 4 5 6   **639.9**

1. Elephants 2. Wildlife conservation

ISBN 978-0-88448-283-3; 0-88448-283-9

LC 2006-22283

"This is a beautifully written, compelling story of a conscientious drive to care for these animals in a humane way." SLJ

Curtis, Jennifer Keats

Animal helpers; wildlife rehabilitators. Jennifer Keats Curtis. Sylvan Dell Pub. 2012 32 p. (hardcover) $17.95

Grades: K 1 2   **639.9**

1. Animals 2. Veterinarians 3. Wildlife rehabilitation

ISBN 1607186713; 9781607186717; 9781607186724; 9781607186731; 9781607186748

LC 2012937373

This "photographic journal takes readers 'behind the scenes' at four different wildlife rehabilitation centers" that help "wild animals when they are injured, become ill, or are orphaned." It shows "backyard animals as they are nursed back to health and released back to the wild when possible." (Publisher's note)

Fleming, Denise, 1950-

★ Where once there was a wood. Holt & Co. 1996 un il $16.95; pa $6.95

Grades: K 1 2   **639.9**

1. Habitat (Ecology) 2. Wildlife conservation 3. Wildlife conservation

ISBN 0-8050-3761-6; 0-8050-6482-6 pa

LC 95-18906

"Lush, textured collage artwork features a stunning combination and arrangement of colors with brilliant hues juxtaposed against muted earth tones. . . . The gentle, poetic narration is never overpowered by the pictures." SLJ

Includes bibliographical references

George, Jean Craighead

A tarantula in my purse; and 172 other wild pets. written and illustrated by Jean Craighead George. Harper-Collins Pubs. 1996 134p il hardcover o.p. pa $5.99

Grades: 4 5 6   **639.9**

1. Pets 2. Artists 3. Authors 4. Naturalists 5. Illustrators 6. Women authors 7. Authors, American 8. Children's authors

ISBN 0-06-023626-4; 0-06-446201-3 pa

LC 95-54151

"Brief, engaging stories about the many wild animals that lived in and around the author's home over the years are filled with humor, affection, and just enough drama." Horn Book

"George tells of the many wild pets that lived with her family, particularly while her children were growing up. Each chapter describes a different animal or incident." Booklist

Hatkoff, Juliana

Winter's tail; how one little dolphin learned to swim again. told by Juliana Hatkoff, Isabella Hatkoff, and Craig Hatkoff. Scholastic Press 2009 un il $16.99

Grades: 3 4 5 6   **639.9**

1. Dolphins 2. Artificial limbs

ISBN 978-0-545-12335-8; 0-545-12335-6

"A compassionate look at the true odyssey of an orphaned Atlantic bottlenose dolphin. Rescued from a crab trap, with severe injuries, 'Winter' was brought to the Clearwater (FL) Marine Aquarium and, despite the heroic efforts of the staff, lost her tail. . . . Winter caught the attention of a prosthetic engineer, and the Hatkoffs' clear text follows the efforts of a mixed team from the aquarium and Hanger Prosthetics & Orthotics to design a workable 'tail' to keep her healthy. Full-color photos reveal the cooperative efforts of the human team and Winter in this journey toward a more normal life." SLJ

Lasky, Kathryn

★ Interrupted journey; illustrated by Christopher Knight. Candlewick Press 2001 un il hardcover o.p. pa $6.99

Grades: 3 4 5 6   **639.9**

1. Sea turtles 2. Rare animals 3. Wildlife conservation

ISBN 0-7636-0635-9; 0-7636-2883-2 pa

LC 99-57126

Describes efforts to protect sea turtles, particularly Kemp's ridley turtles, and help them reproduce and replenish their once-dwindling numbers

"There's a sense of wonder in the simple words and the huge, thrilling color pictures in this photo-essay." Booklist

Montgomery, Sy

★ Kakapo rescue; saving the world's strangest parrot. text by Sy Montgomery; photographs by Nic Bishop. Houghton Mifflin 2010 73p il map (Scientists in the field) $18

Grades: 4 5 6 7 **639.9**
1. Parrots 2. Endangered species 3. Wildlife conservation 4. New Zealand
ISBN 978-0-618-49417-0; 0-618-49417-0
LC 2009-45250

Awarded the Robert F. Sibert Medal, 2011
Montgomery and Bishop head "to a remote island off the southern tip of New Zealand, where they join a local government-sponsored research team that is working to save the Kakapo parrot from extinction. . . . Montgomery's delight in her subject is contagious, and throughout her enthusiastic text, she nimbly blends scientific and historical facts with immediate, sensory descriptions of fieldwork. Young readers will be fascinated. . . . Bishop's photos of the creatures and their habitat are stunning." Booklist

Stetson, Emily

Kids' easy-to-create wildlife habitats; [by] Emily Stetson. Williamson Books 2004 128p il map (Quick starts for kids!) pa $12.95

Grades: 2 3 4 **639.9**
1. Habitat (Ecology) 2. Wildlife conservation
ISBN 0-8249-8665-2
LC 2004-40871

This "book shows children how to observe and support wildlife around their homes, schools, and communities. Packed with useful information. . . . With sound advice and many helpful illustrations, precisely drawn in blue and gray ink, this offers children small ways to support wildlife close to home." Booklist

640 Home and family management

Ernst, Lisa Campbell, 1957-

How things work in the house; Lisa Campbell Ernst. 1st ed. Blue Apple Books 2012 1 v. (unpaged) col. ill. (hardcover) $16.99

Grades: 1 2 3 **640**
1. Kitchen utensils 2. Questions and answers 3. Household equipment and supplies 4. Home economics -- Equipment and supplies
ISBN 1609051890; 9781609051891
LC 2011038908

In her book, author Lisa Campbell Ernst "explains what can be done with things in our houses" and how things work. "The varied uses of . . . bananas . . . and spoons" are discussed. "Similarly, popcorn, sandwiches, scissors, glue, piggy banks and kazoos are featured." The book offers a "glimpse at how things work in our houses . . . [and] everyday worlds." (Kirkus Reviews)

Gaarder-Juntti, Oona

What in the world is a green home? ABDO Pub. Co. 2010 24p il (Going green) lib bdg $24.21

Grades: 1 2 3 4 **640**
1. Housing -- Environmental aspects
ISBN 978-1-61613-189-0 lib bdg; 1-61613-189-6 lib bdg
LC 2010004340

"The lively layout design, featuring colorful headings, short paragraphs, and attractive photographs, has a scrapbook-like quality. . . . [The title explains] how all our choices require energy and resources, and encourage readers to make changes in their lifestyles. . . . [This] . . . will inspire and empower readers to make a difference." SLJ

Includes glossary and bibliographical references

641.3 Food

Butterworth, Chris

★ How Did That Get in My Lunchbox? the story of food. by Chris Butterworth and illustrated by Lucia Gaggiotti. Candlewick 2013 25 p. il $5.99

Grades: K 1 2 3 **641.3**
1. Food 2. Nutrition
ISBN 0763665037; 9780763665036
LC 2010003034

This book, by Chris Butterworth and illustrated by Lucia Gaggiotti, "look[s] at the steps involved in producing some common foods." Topics covered include "planting wheat to mixing dough, climbing trees to machine-squeezing fruit, picking cocoa pods to stirring a vat of melted bliss.Health tips and a peek at basic food groups [are included]," (Publisher's note)

"With reader-directed prose and cheerfully retro artwork, Butterworth and Gaggiotti use a balanced meal—sandwich, fruit, veggies, juice box, and cookie—to explain how foodstuffs make it from farms, dairies, and factories into kids' lunches." Publ Wkly

Chapman, Garry

Coffee; by Garry Chapman and Gary Hodges. Black Rabbit 2010 32p il (World commodities) lib bdg $28.50

Grades: 5 6 7 8 **641.3**
1. Coffee
ISBN 978-1-59920-584-7 lib bdg; 1-59920-584-X lib bdg

"The first part of the book discusses how coffee beans are grown, treated, prepared, and enjoyed around the world. . . . The second section offers an opportunity to use the commodity of coffee to understand such economics concepts as supply and demand or futures trading. . . . Finally, the book spins through a look at fair trade practices; political, environmental, and social issues surrounding coffee trade; and the sustainability and outlook of the global coffee industry. In all, the book gleans a pretty impressive and diverse array of accessible information from such a small bean." Booklist

Includes glossary

Cleary, Brian P.

Apples, cherries, red raspberries; what is in the fruits group? illustrations by Martin Goneau; consultant, Jennifer K. Nelson. Millbrook Press 2010 31p il (Food is CATegorical) lib bdg $25.26

Grades: K 1 2 3   **641.3**
1. Fruit 2. Nutrition
ISBN 978-1-58013-589-4 lib bdg; 1-58013-589-7
lib bdg

LC 2009049582

"With highly readable bits and pieces about which yum-my foods have which nutrients and vitamins [this book is] . . . just right for sharing with young kids, introducing the value of healthy foods and exercise through silly rhymes, puns, zany color cartoons of cats in wild action. The scenarios . . . range from cat characters picking apples in an orchard to a big cat that triumphs in a boxing ring after eating 'cool' bananas." Booklist

Green beans, potatoes, and even tomatoes; what is in the vegetable group? by Brian P. Cleary; illustrations by Martin Goneau; consultant, Jennifer K. Nelson. Millbrook Press 2010 31p il (Food is CATegorical) lib bdg $25.26
Grades: K 1 2 3   **641.3**
1. Nutrition 2. Vegetables
ISBN 978-1-58013-588-7 lib bdg; 1-58013-588-9
lib bdg

LC 2009-49592

"With highly readable bits and pieces about which yum-my foods have which nutrients and vitamins [this book is] . . . just right for sharing with young kids, introducing the value of healthy foods and exericse through silly rhymes, puns, and zany color cartoons of cats in wild action. . . . Sweet potatoes, carrots, and more are portrayed as both wholesome and tasty." Booklist

D'Amico, Joan
The **science** chef; 100 fun food experiments and reci-pes for kids. [by] Joan D'Amico, Karen Eich Drummond; illustrations by Tina Cash-Walsh. Wiley 1995 180p il $12.95
Grades: 4 5 6   **641.3**
1. Food 2. Cooking 3. Science -- Experiments
ISBN 0-471-31045-X

LC 94-9045

This includes facts about food, recipes, and experiments with food

"Attractively illustrated with black-and-white line draw-ings, easy and interesting to read, and filled with tidbits of information." SLJ
Includes glossary

Eamer, Claire
The **world** in your lunch box; the wacky history and weird science of everyday foods. Claire Eamer; artwork by Sa Boothroyd. Annick Press 2012 121 p.
Grades: 4 5 6   **641.3**
1. Nutrition 2. Food -- History 3. Food -- Composition
ISBN 1554513936; 9781554513932
This book by Claire Eamer presents an "exploration of food history and food science . . . "[E]verything's interest-ing if you take the time to learn about it," says the cooking teacher, who challenges his students to keep a record of their lunches and research their backgrounds. . . . . The lunches described are usually well-balanced. From each, the author has chosen a selection of ingredients, providing examples of their use in history and offering . . . science connections. Most topics are covered in a single page [along with] car-toon-styled drawings . . . [and] jokes . . . Ten favorite food

facts conclude the narrative, but there are also suggestions for further reading, an extensive bibliography and even an index." (Kirkus)
Includes bibliographical references and index.

Gaarder-Juntti, Oona
What in the world is green food? ABDO Pub. Co. 2010 24p il (Going green) lib bdg $24.21
Grades: 1 2 3 4   **641.3**
1. Food -- Environmental aspects
ISBN 978-1-61613-192-0 lib bdg; 1-61613-192-6
lib bdg

LC 2010004321

"The lively layout design, featuring colorful headings, short paragraphs, and attractive photographs, has a scrap-book-like quality. . . . [The title explains] how all our choices require energy and resources, and encourage readers to make changes in their lifestyles. . . . [This] . . . will inspire and empower readers to make a difference." SLJ
Includes glossary and bibliographical references

Hewitt, Sally
Your food. Crabtree Pub. Co. 2009 32p il (Green team) $26.60; pa $8.95
Grades: 3 4 5 6   **641.3**
1. Food
ISBN 978-0-7787-4099-5; 0-7787-4099-4; 978-0-7787-4106-0 pa; 0-7787-4106-0 pa

LC 2008023291

"The color graphics and layouts are highly appealing and will definitely be attractive to young readers. . . . This . . . is an excellent resource for school libraries, science teachers, and community sponsors." Libr Media Connect
Includes glossary

Jango-Cohen, Judith
The **history** of food; [by] Judith Jango-Cohen. Twen-ty-First Century Books 2006 56p il (Major inventions through history) lib bdg $26.60
Grades: 5 6 7 8   **641.3**
1. Food -- History
ISBN 0-8225-2484-8

LC 2004-23022

This history of food "discusses canning, pasteurization, refrigeration, supermarkets, and genetically modified foods. . . . The text . . . is breezy but informative; unfamiliar terms are defined. Illustrations are a mixture of period black-and-white and color photos." SLJ
Includes bibliographical references

Llewellyn, Claire
Cooking with fruits and vegetables; by Claire Llewellyn with recipes by Clare O'Shea. Rosen Central 2011 48p il (Cooking healthy) lib bdg $27.95
Grades: 5 6 7 8   **641.3**
1. Fruit 2. Cooking 3. Vegetables
ISBN 978-1-4488-4844-7; 1-4488-4844-X

LC 2010039333

This book pairs "facts about [fruits and vegetables], in-cluding where it is eaten, with eye-catching photos. . . . Each course (section) has an overview of the vegetable group . . . followed by recipes from all over the world. They vary in difficulty. . . . The cooking directions are clear and straight-forward. . . . [The book is] profusely illustrated with full-color photos. Students who are learning to cook will appreciate [this] excellently organized [read]." SLJ

Includes bibliographical references

Malam, John

Grow your own snack. Heinemann Library 2011 32p il (Grow it yourself!) lib bdg $26; pa $7.99

Grades: 2 3 4   **641.3**

1. Beans 2. Cooking 3. Vegetable gardening

ISBN 978-1-4329-5107-8 lib bdg; 978-1-4329-5114-6 pa

LC 2010049849

This describes how to grow broad beans, and how to fry them for a snack.

Includes glossary and bibliographical references

Menzel, Peter

★ **What** the world eats; photographed by Peter Menzel; written by Faith D'Aluisio. Tricycle Press 2008 160p il map $22.99

Grades: 4 5 6 7 8   **641.3**

1. Diet 2. Eating customs 3. Food -- Pictorial works

ISBN 978-1-58246-246-2; 1-58246-246-1

LC 2007-41439

An adaptation of Hungry Planet, published 2005 by Ten Speed Press for adults

"Stunning color photographs of mealtimes and daily activities illustrate the warm, informative, anecdotal narratives. . . . This is a fascinating, sobering, and instructive look at daily life around the world." Booklist

Includes bibliographical references

Miller, Jeanne

Food science. Lerner Publications 2009 48p il (Cool science) lib bdg $27.93

Grades: 4 5 6   **641.3**

1. Food

ISBN 978-0-8225-7589-4 lib bdg; 0-8225-7589-2 lib bdg

This describes how food scientists "explore how cooking changes food, create dishes that surprise the senses, and help farmers grow food in healthier ways." Publisher's note

Includes glossary and bibliographical references

Peterson, Cris

★ **Seed** soil sun; earth's recipe for food. photographs by David R. Lundquist. Boyd Mills Press 2010 un il $17.95

Grades: PreK K 1 2   **641.3**

1. Food 2. Seeds 3. Plants

ISBN 978-1-59078-713-7; 1-59078-713-7

The children's book discusses "[p]hotosynthesis . . . [and how] plants take our planet's basic resources (sunlight, water, and air) and generate food and oxygen. . . . Peterson's . . . text is [accompanied by David Lundquist's] . . . photography [that] illustrates her account, which features maize as an example. Lundquist shows . . . worms that till the soil as well as corn plants ranging from seedlings, through knee-highs, to full-grown harvestable stalks." (Science)

"Peterson explains how most food comes from seeds, which—thanks to nutrients from soil and energy from the sun—grow into fruits and vegetables. Lundquist's color

photographs . . . may have kids considering an attempt at growing their own food." Publ Wkly

Includes bibliographical references

Price, Sean

The **story** behind chocolate; [by] Sean Stewart Price. Heinemann Library 2009 32p il map lib bdg $28.21

Grades: 3 4 5   **641.3**

1. Chocolate

ISBN 978-1-4329-2347-1 lib bdg; 1-4329-2347-1 lib bdg

LC 2008037524

"Price explains how chocolate was discovered and became popular, its ingredients, the chocolate-making process, and how companies like Hershey and Cadbury became successful. . . . The well-organized [text is] informative and clearly written, and the numerous color photographs and drawings are eye-catching and complement the [narrative] well." SLJ

Includes bibliographical references

Reilly, Kathleen M.

Food; 25 amazing projects investigate the history and science of what we eat. illustrated by Farah Rizvi. Nomad Press 2010 124p il (Build it yourself) pa $15.95

Grades: 4 5 6   **641.3**

1. Food

ISBN 978-1-934670-59-0; 1-934670-59-6

"This broad overview of food touches on its history and future, production and packaging, social and cultural practices, and health and safety concerns. . . . The information presented and questions posed on food packaging, megafarming, locally grown vs. commercially grown foods, freerange grazing, and healthy food choices make this a particularly up-to-date survey. . . . Every chapter concludes with two to three hands-on activities that range from cooking to science and art projects. . . . This soup-to-nuts look at the business and consumption of food will make a good addition to most collections." SLJ

Includes glossary and bibliographical references

Robbins, Ken

★ **Food** for thought; the stories behind the things we eat. Roaring Brook Press 2009 45p il $17.95

Grades: 2 3 4   **641.3**

1. Food

ISBN 978-1-59643-343-4; 1-59643-343-4

LC 2007-44062

"Robbins focuses on a mouthwatering array of produce: apples, oranges, potatoes, tomatoes, grapes, bananas, mushrooms, and pomegranates. Each spacious spread combines Robbins' vibrantly hued photographs with engaging text filled with information about each food, including its nutritional content, history, current methods of cultivation, and appearance in figures of speech ('couch potato'), as well as mythology and folklore. . . . The enticing images will draw young readers into the captivating assortment of facts." Booklist

Sayre, April Pulley

★ **Go,** go, grapes! April Pulley Sayre. 1st ed. Simon & Schuster 2012 1v. (unpaged) col. ill. (hardcover) $16.99

Grades: K 1 2   **641.3**

1. Fruit 2. Children's poetry 3. Picture books for

children 4. Grapes

ISBN 1442433906; 9781442433908

LC 2011011602

In this book, April Pulley Sayre presents photographs of "the standard apple, orange, banana, grapes and berries, [and] she entices readers with such exotics as tamarillo, kiwano, guava, rambutan, currant, durian and . . . dragon fruit. . . . Sayre shows off the colors and textures. . . . Several fruits are cut to show off their insides, such as the seeds of the kiwi and pomegranate and the intriguing cross sections of a lychee and mangosteen." (Kirkus Reviews)

★ **Rah,** rah, radishes! a vegetable chant. Beach Lane Books 2011 un il $14.99

Grades: PreK K   **641.3**

1. Vegetables 2. Food -- Poetry

ISBN 978-1-4424-2141-7; 1-4424-2141-X

LC 2010034360

Photographs of vegetables and rhyming text celebrate vegetables in all their colorful and tasty variety.

"Each page calls out a cheer-worthy vegetable in two short lines of text, accompanied by a large, colorful photograph. . . . With its upbeat, easy-to-digest text and large, clear images, this book will become a go-to choice in spring-themed preschool storytimes and early elementary health or environmental units." SLJ

Sylver, Adrienne

Hot diggity dog; the history of the hot dog. illustrated by Elwood H. Smith. Dutton Children's Books 2010 un il $16.99

Grades: K 1 2 3   **641.3**

1. Frankfurters

ISBN 978-0-525-47897-3; 0-525-47897-3

"How did hot dogs become so popular? asks Sylver in this popular history of the wiener. . . . Accompanied by Smith's handsomely goofy, retro artwork, the narrative offers sidebars with factual tidbits galore." Kirkus

Thornhill, Jan

Who wants pizza? the kids' guide to the history, science & culture of food. Maple Tree Press 2010 64p il $22.95; pa $10.95

Grades: 4 5 6   **641.3**

1. Food 2. Agriculture

ISBN 978-1-897349-96-0; 1-897349-96-3; 978-1-897349-97-7 pa; 1-897349-97-1 pa

This discusses "where food comes from and if there's enough to go around. Amid color photographs and sidebars, Thornhill writes concisely about hunter-gatherers, agriculture, processed foods, globalization, and poverty, among numerous other topics, providing a straightforward and balanced overview of the modern food industry, and the choices readers have when it comes to their own meals." Publ Wkly

641.5   Cooking

Arroyo, Sheri L.

How chefs use math; math curriculum consultant, Rhea A. Stewart. Chelsea Clubhouse 2010 32p il (Math in the real world) lib bdg $28

Grades: 4 5 6   **641.5**

1. Cooks 2. Cooking 3. Mathematics 4. Vocational guidance

ISBN 978-1-60413-608-1 lib bdg; 1-60413-608-1 lib bdg

LC 2009-14180

This describes how chefs use math for such tasks as measuring ingredients, watching temperatures, buying food, setting menu prices, and managing restaurant and catering businesses, and includes relevant math problems and information about how to become a chef

Includes glossary and bibliographical references

Batmanglij, Najmieh

Happy Nowruz; cooking with children to celebrate the Persian New Year. [by] Najmieh Batmanglij. Mage Publishers 2008 119p il $40

Grades: 4 5 6 7 8   **641.5**

1. New Year 2. Eating customs 3. Middle Eastern cooking 4. Iran -- Social life and customs

ISBN 1-933823-16-X; 978-1-933823-16-4

LC 2007-036047

"Combining a cookbook format with straightforward, informational text, this amply illustrated title offers a detailed introduction to the history and customs surrounding Nowruz, the Persian New Year. . . . The covered spiral binding allows pages to remain open while cooking, and the uncluttered, attractive format, featuring color photos of kids in the kitchen and whimsical illustrations, will attract interested browsers." Booklist

Beery, Barbara

Barbara Beery's pink princess party cookbook; photography by Zac Williams. Simon & Schuster Books for Young Readers 2011 55p il spiral $15.99

Grades: 2 3 4 5   **641.5**

1. Cooking 2. Parties 3. Entertaining

ISBN 978-1-4424-1231-6; 1-4424-1231-3

LC 2010017691

"Beery offers ideas for six themed celebrations, such as a mermaid princess party, a garden fairy princess party, and a spa princess party. They all include delicate but easy-to-follow recipes for punch, cookies, cakes, sushi, and decorations, as well as themed crafts such as body lotion and floral headbands. These are well-planned ideas, with plenty of full-color photographs to support the text." SLJ

Behnke, Alison

Cooking the Central American way; [by] Alison M. Behnke, in consultation with Griselda Aracely Chacon and Kristina Anderson. Lerner Publications Co. 2005 72p il (Easy menu ethnic cookbooks) lib bdg $25.26

Grades: 5 6 7 8   **641.5**

1. Central American cooking

ISBN 978-0-8225-1236-3; 0-8225-1236-X

LC 2004-11870

An introduction to the cooking of Central America. Includes glossary

Cooking the Mediterranean way; culturally authentic foods, including low-fat and vegetarian recipes. Alison M. Behnke, in consultation with Anna and Lazaros Christoforides. Lerner Publications 2005 72p il map (Easy menu ethnic cookbooks) lib bdg $25.26

Grades: 5 6 7 8   **641.5**
   1. Mediterranean cooking
   ISBN 0-8225-1237-8; 978-0-8225-1237-0
            LC 2004-11054
An introduction to Mediterranean cooking and food habits, featuring traditional recipes and including information
on the history, geography, customs, and people of this region
of the world.
   Includes glossary

Cooking the Middle Eastern way; culturally authentic foods including low-fat and vegetarian recipes. Alison
Behnke in consultation with Vartkes Ehramjian. Lerner
Publications Co. 2005 72p il map (Easy menu ethnic cookbooks) lib bdg $25.26
Grades: 5 6 7 8   **641.5**
   1. Middle Eastern cooking
   ISBN 978-0-8225-1238-7; 0-8225-1238-6
            LC 2004-19658
"This volume begins with an introduction to the history
and varied cultures of the Middle East, followed by lists of
cooking tips, utensils, terminology, and regional ingredients
as well as a discussion of healthy, low-fat choices. . . . This
is a well-designed, attractive source of recipes for Middle
Eastern fare." Booklist
   Includes glossary

Berman, Karen
   Easy-peasy recipes; snacks and treats to make and eat.
Karen Berman; [edited by] Kirsten Hall. Running Press
Kids 2012 40 p. $14.95
Grades: 1 2 3   **641.5**
   1. Cooking 2. Cookbooks 3. Children -- Nutrition
   ISBN 0762444436; 9780762444434
            LC 2011937816
This cookbook by Karen Berman is "geared toward independent child chefs. The 13 snack and treat recipes . . . [in-
clude] a taco-salad pirate face, a breakfast buffet shaped like
a train with individual cars and a berry-and-yogurt-snow-
capped mountain. To assemble these creations, young chefs
are directed to use a pair of (washed) safety scissors instead
of knives. . . . 'Do It Another Way' sections accompanying
each recipe give readers ideas for substituting ingredients or
trying new ones." (Kirkus Reviews)

Blaxland, Wendy
   American food. Smart Apple Media 2012 32p il map
(I can cook!) lib bdg $28.50
Grades: 3 4 5 6   **641.5**
   1. Cooking
   ISBN 978-1-59920-667-7; 1-59920-667-6
            LC 2011005443
Describes historical, cultural, and geographical factors
that have influenced the cuisine of the United States. In-
cludes recipes to create American food.
   This includes "recipes with kid appeal. . . . Captioned,
full-color photographs provide step-by-step directions. . . .
[An] ideal [supplement] to culture and country studies." SLJ
   Includes glossary

   Chinese food. Smart Apple Media 2012 32p il map (I
can cook!) lib bdg $28.50

Grades: 3 4 5 6   **641.5**
   1. Chinese cooking
   ISBN 978-1-59920-671-4; 1-59920-671-4
            LC 2011005448
Describes historical, cultural, and geographical factors
that have influenced the cuisine of China. Includes recipes
to create Chinese food.
   This includes "recipes with kid appeal. . . . Captioned,
full-color photographs provide step-by-step directions. . . .
[An] ideal [supplement] to culture and country studies." SLJ
   Includes glossary

   French food. Smart Apple Media 2012 32p il map (I
can cook!) lib bdg $28.50
Grades: 3 4 5 6   **641.5**
   1. French cooking
   ISBN 978-1-59920-669-1; 1-59920-669-2
            LC 2011005445
Describes historical, cultural, and geographical factors
that have influenced the cuisine of France. Includes recipes
to create French food.
   This includes "recipes with kid appeal. . . . Captioned,
full-color photographs provide step-by-step directions. . . .
[An] ideal [supplement] to culture and country studies." SLJ
   Includes glossary

   Italian food. Smart Apple Media 2012 32p il map (I
can cook!) lib bdg $28.50
Grades: 3 4 5 6   **641.5**
   1. Italian cooking
   ISBN 978-1-59920-670-7; 1-59920-670-6
            LC 2011005446
Describes historical, cultural, and geographical factors
that have influenced the cuisine of Italy. Includes recipes to
create Italian food.
   Includes glossary

   Mexican food. Smart Apple Media 2012 32p il map
(I can cook!) lib bdg $28.50
Grades: 3 4 5 6   **641.5**
   1. Mexican cooking
   ISBN 978-1-59920-668-4; 1-59920-668-4
            LC 2011005444
Describes historical, cultural, and geographical factors
that have influenced the cuisine of Mexico. Includes recipes
to create Mexican food.
   This includes "recipes with kid appeal. . . . Captioned,
full-color photographs provide step-by-step directions. . . .
[An] ideal [supplement] to culture and country studies." SLJ
   Includes glossary

   Middle Eastern food. Smart Apple Media 2012 32p il
map (I can cook!) lib bdg $28.50
Grades: 3 4 5 6   **641.5**
   1. Middle Eastern cooking
   ISBN 978-1-59920-672-1
            LC 2011005450
Describes historical, cultural, and geographical factors
that have influenced the cuisine of the Middle East. Includes
recipes to create Middle-Eastern food.

This includes "recipes with kid appeal. . . . Captioned, full-color photographs provide step-by-step directions. . . . [An] ideal [supplement] to culture and country studies." SLJ

Includes glossary

Bloomfield, Jill

Jewish holidays cookbook; by Jill Colella Bloomfield; Janet Ozur Bass, consultant; photography by Angela Coppola. DK Pub. 2008 128p il spiral bdg $19.99

Grades: 4 5 6 7   **641.5**

1. Jewish cooking 2. Jewish holidays

ISBN 978-0-7566-4089-7 spiral bdg; 0-7566-4089-X spiral bdg

"More than 40 recipes are included for celebrations from Shabbat to Lag B'Omer. Several introductions explain cooking tools, kitchen safety, and the general principles of keeping kosher, and brief background information is given for each holiday. Simple step-by-step instructions make the recipes easy. . . . Beautiful color photographs, both full page and spot, whet the appetite." SLJ

Bowers, Sharon

Ghoulish goodies. Storey Pub. 2009 153p il pa $14.95

Grades: 3 4 5 6   **641.5**

1. Desserts 2. Halloween 3. Holiday cooking

ISBN 978-1-60342-146-1 pa; 1-60342-146-7 pa

LC 2009007802

This offers recipes for Halloween-themed desserts such as Monster Eyeballs, Chocolate Spider Clusters, Buried Alive Cupcakes, and Screaming Red Punch

"Perfect for Halloween and beyond, this conveniently organized, well-illustrated cookbook is sure to be a crowd-pleaser. . . . Most recipes are complemented by a full-color photograph of the finished product. . . . Hauntingly appetizing." SLJ

Bucholz, Dinah

The unofficial Narnia cookbook; from Turkish delight to gooseberry fool--over 150 recipes inspired by the Chronicles of Narnia. Dinah Bucholz. Sourcebooks Jabberwocky 2012 233 p. $19.99

Grades: 4 5 6   **641.5**

1. Cookbooks 2. Narnia (Imaginary place)

ISBN 1402266413; 9781402266416

In this cookbook by Dinah Bucholz "each recipe is clearly tied to particular incidents and chapters in the books of Narnia. . . . While striving to stick to the actual meals in the stories (Eel Stew! Boar's Head!), [Bucholz] creates or re-creates Beautiful Breakfasts; Snacks, Teas, and Meals on the Run; Lunch and Dinner Menus; and Fabulous Feasts in four chapters." (Kirkus)

Cornell, Kari A.

Cooking the Indonesian way; [by] Kari A. Cornell and Merry Anwar. Lerner Publications Company 2004 72p il (Easy menu ethnic cookbooks) lib bdg $25.26

Grades: 5 6 7 8   **641.5**

1. Indonesian cooking

ISBN 978-0-8225-4127-1; 0-8225-4127-0

LC 2003-11205

Introduces the land, people, and regional cooking of Indonesia and includes recipes for such dishes as pork sate, corn fritters, and chicken in coconut cream sauce.

Includes glossary

Cooking the southern African way; by Kari Cornell in consultaiton with Peter Thomas. Lerner Publications Co. 2005 72p il map (Easy menu ethnic cookbooks) lib bdg $25.26

Grades: 5 6 7 8   **641.5**

1. South African cooking

ISBN 978-0-8225-1239-4; 0-8225-1239-4

LC 2004-11869

Introduces the history, land, and food of South Africa and includes recipes.

Includes glossary

D'Amico, Joan

★ The coming to America cookbook; delicious recipes and fascinating stories from America's many cultures. [by] Joan D'Amico, Karen Eich Drummond. Wiley 2005 180p il pa $14.95

Grades: 5 6 7 8   **641.5**

1. Cooking 2. United States -- Immigration and emigration

ISBN 0-471-48335-4

LC 2004-14947

The authors "provide information about American immigrants from 18 nations as well as recipes representing each group. . . . Accompanied by line drawings of ethnic families choosing, preparing, and eating food, . . . chapters discuss each country's climate, history, major waves of emigration, and traditional foods. Typically, three recipes follow. . . . Teachers and students looking for recipes from American immigrant cultures will make good use of this handy resource." Booklist

Dodge, Abigail Johnson

★ Around the world cookbook. DK Publishing 2008 124p il map spiral bdg $19.99

Grades: 3 4 5 6   **641.5**

1. Cooking

ISBN 978-0-7566-3744-6 spiral bdg; 0-7566-3744-9 spiral bdg

"This book presents more than 50 step-by-step recipes for ethnic cuisine. Dodge opens with instructions for basic cooking skills, an illustrated list of kitchen tools, a glossary of terms used in the recipes, and tips for working with different types of ingredients. . . . Possibly tricky steps are clarified with photographs and captions." SLJ

Ejaz, Khadija

Recipe and craft guide to India. Mitchell Lane Publishers 2010 63p il map (World crafts and recipes) lib bdg $33.95

Grades: 4 5 6 7 8   **641.5**

1. Handicraft 2. Indic cooking

ISBN 978-1-58415-938-4 lib bdg; 1-58415-938-3 lib bdg

LC 2010008950

Provides recipes for several popular Indian dishes and includes instructions on creating colorful and traditional Indian crafts.

This provides "plenty of ideas for adding tasty treats and impressive visual aids to cultural reports or presentations." SLJ

Includes glossary and bibliographical references

Gerasole, Isabella

The **Spatulatta** cookbook; by Isabella and Olivia Gerasole; photographs by John Zich. Scholastic 2007 128p il spiral bdg $16.99

Grades: 3 4 5 6   **641.5**

1. Cooking

ISBN 978-0-439-02250-7 spiral bdg; 0-439-02250-9 spiral bdg

"This lively, colorful companion book to the Gerasole sisters' Web site . . . contains an enticing array of dishes both sweet and savory, easy and complicated. . . . Beautifully reproduced color photos show the completed dishes and smaller photos show some of the steps. . . . This book strikes a great balance between fun and practical." SLJ

Includes glossary

Gold, Rozanne

Kids cook 1-2-3; recipes for young chefs using only 3 ingredients. illustrated by Sara Pinto. Bloomsbury Children's Books 2006 144p il $17.95

Grades: 3 4 5 6   **641.5**

1. Cooking

ISBN 978-1-58234-735-6; 1-58234-735-2

LC 2006-00623

"This very basic cookbook offers 125 recipes for breakfast, lunch, dinner, healthy snacks, side dishes, and desserts. The recipes are clearly presented, and are broken into easy-to-follow steps." SLJ

Gregory, Josh

Chef. Cherry Lake Pub. 2011 32p il (Cool careers) lib bdg $27.07

Grades: 4 5 6 7   **641.5**

1. Cooks 2. Cooking 3. Vocational guidance

ISBN 978-1-60279-985-1; 1-60279-985-7

LC 2010029085

This book begins "with a personal story of a teen and then [segues] into the occupation [of chef]. . . . [It covers] the necessary training and skills for the job (and options for obtaining them), a typical day, salary expectations, and well-known professionals in the field. The [text is] accessible and clearly written. . . . The [volume has] a generous number of clear color photographs that depict people at work." SLJ

Includes glossary and bibliographical references

Hargittai, Magdolna

Cooking the Hungarian way; by Magdolna Hargittai. rev and expanded; Lerner Publications Co 2003 72p il map (Easy menu ethnic cookbooks) lib bdg $25.26

Grades: 5 6 7 8   **641.5**

1. Hungarian cooking

ISBN 978-0-8225-4132-5; 0-8225-4132-7

LC 2001-6612

First published 1986

An overview of Hungarian cookery, including information about the country's geography, history, holidays, and festivals. Features simple recipes, menu planning, and information about low-fat cooking and vegetarian options

Includes glossary and bibliographical references

Hughes, Helga

Cooking the Austrian way; [by] Helga Hughes. rev and expanded ed; Lerner Publications 2004 72p il map (Easy menu ethnic cookbooks) lib bdg $25.26

Grades: 5 6 7 8   **641.5**

1. Austrian cooking

ISBN 978-0-8225-4102-8; 0-8225-4102-5

LC 2002-152146

First published 1990

An introduction to the cooking of Austria including such traditional recipes as Wiener schnitzel, potato noodles, and Sacher cake. Also includes information on the geography, customs, and people of this European country

"Updated to include low-fat and vegetarian options. . . . Color photos and definitions of cooking terms and unusual ingredients will aid novice cooks." Horn Book Guide

Includes glossary

Ichord, Loretta Frances

Skillet bread, sourdough, and vinegar pie; cooking in pioneer days. illustrated by Jan Davey Ellis. Millbrook Press 2003 64p il map hardcover o.p. pa $8.95

Grades: 3 4 5   **641.5**

1. Cooking 2. Frontier and pioneer life -- West (U.S.)

ISBN 0-7613-1864-X lib bdg; 0-7613-9521-0 pa

LC 2002-8157

Presents a look at what was eaten in the American West by pioneers on the trail, cowboys on cattle drives, and gold miners in California camps, with available ingredients, cooking methods, and equipment. Includes recipes and appendix of classroom cooking directions

"This unique title effectively combines recipes with history, a must for any collection needing information on the old West." Libr Media Connect

Includes bibliographical references

Karmel, Annabel

My favorite recipes. DK Pub. 2011 96p il $14.99

Grades: 3 4 5 6   **641.5**

1. Cooking

ISBN 978-0-7566-7195-2; 0-7566-7195-7

"These recipes . . . look good enough to eat. Each one includes a full-page, full-color picture of the dish, as well as step-by-step instructions, with smaller pictures. . . . All recipes need adult assistance, and some require more than basic cooking skills. The recipes are organized in four sections: light bites, main meals, fruity treats, and cakes and cookies. They include children's favorites like spaghetti and chicken dippers . . . as well as more exotic dishes like paella and lamb tagine. Where this cookbook really shines is in the creative and fun plating. Karmel often creates faces or animals out of a dish. . . . A bright and colorful cookbook that is sure to appeal to children." SLJ

Katsoris, Nick

Loukoumi's celebrity cookbook; featuring favorite childhood recipes by over 50 celebrities. Nick Katsoris. Dream Day Press/NK Publications/Loukoumi Books 2011 87 p. (hardcover) $19.95

Grades: 4 5 6   **641.5**

1. Cookbooks

ISBN 0984161015; 9780984161010

Gourmand World Cookbook Award (2012) -"Best Charity Cookbook in the United States"

This cookbook "opens with a story about a lamb, Louk-oumi, and her friends, a dog, a monkey, and a cat, that are hungry. The cast of ... animals joins Aunt Cat Cora, who gives tips about making a cake. The recipe follows, with the table of contents finally appearing on page 22, divided into sections: 'Weekend Breakfasts,' 'Lunchtime Favorites,' 'After School Snacks,' 'Family Meals,' and 'Delicious Desserts.'" (School Library Journal)

Katzen, Mollie

★ **Salad** people and more real recipes; a new cookbook for preschoolers and up. Tricycle Press 2005 93p il $17.95

Grades: K 1 2 3   **641.5**
1. Cooking
ISBN 1-58246-141-4

"Katzen offers a range of vegetarian, kid-friendly recipes in an artistic, innovative format. Each recipe receives two spreads. The first contains detailed, step-by-step instructions for adults; the second, directed to children, illustrates stages of preparation in a series of clear, boxed drawings. Katzen's whimsical color pictures of dancing produce and animals decorate the pages. . . . These detailed, practical, and inspired ideas may extend far beyond the kitchen, helping adults approach parenting in new ways and helping kids develop a lifelong interest and confidence in healthy food." Booklist

Lagasse, Emeril

★ **Emeril's** there's a chef in my world! recipes that take you places. illustrated by Charles Yuen; photographs of Emeril Lagasse and children by Quentin Bacon. HarperCollins Publishers 2006 210p il $22.99

Grades: 5 6 7 8   **641.5**
1. Cooking
ISBN 978-0-06-073926-3; 0-06-073926-6

LC 2005-15133

"The famous chef introduces dishes from around the world, dividing the recipes into familiar food categories—sweets, snacks, sandwiches, entrees, etc. . . . The recipes, from latkes to egg-drop soup, are good choices for open-minded eaters. . . . Many children will enjoy the mix of maps, flags, cartoon drawings, and color photos . . . and the cultural facts woven into each recipe." Booklist

LaPenta, Marilyn

Way cool drinks. Bearport Pub. 2011 24p il (Yummy tummy recipes) lib bdg $22.61

Grades: 3 4 5 6   **641.5**
1. Cooking 2. Beverages
ISBN 978-1-61772-163-2; 1-61772-163-8

LC 2011017444

This offers recipes for fruit drinks such as mango tango, fruit fusion, and blueberry bash smoothie.

"All 14 recipes are easy to follow with little more than four or five listed steps, clearly defined serving sizes, and minimal prep time. A healthy tip and oather facts are included with each recipe." Booklist

Includes glossary and bibliographical references

LaRoche, Amelia

Recipe and craft guide to France. Mitchell Lane Publishers 2010 63p il map (World crafts and recipes) lib bdg $33.95

Grades: 4 5 6 7 8   **641.5**
1. Handicraft 2. French cooking
ISBN 978-1-58415-936-0 lib bdg; 1-58415-936-7 lib bdg

LC 2010008949

Provides recipes for several popular French dishes and includes instructions on creating crafts using household items.

This provides "plenty of ideas for adding tasty treats and impressive visual aids to cultural reports or presentations." SLJ

Includes glossary and bibliographical references

Larson, Jennifer S.

Delicious vegetarian main dishes; by Jennifer S. Larson; photographs by Brie Cohen. Millbrook Press 2013 32 p. col. ill. (library) $26.60

Grades: 1 2 3 4   **641.5**
1. Cooking 2. Vegetarian cooking 3. Vegetarian cooking 4. Entrées (Cooking)
ISBN 0761366350; 9780761366355

LC 2012020923

This book by Jennifer S. Larson presents "easy-to-follow recipes such as baked potato pile up, lemony couscous, crispy tofu sticks, and tasty tortilla towers. [Also included are] simple drawings of important steps as well as photographs of the finished dishes. This book also provides key information, such as an equipment list, a technique list, safety tips, notes on special ingredients, and more." (Publisher's note)

Includes bibliographical references (page 32) and index.

Lee, Frances

Fun with Chinese cooking. PowerKids Press 2009 32p il (Let's get cooking!) lib bdg $18.95; pa $11.75

Grades: 4 5 6 7   **641.5**
1. Chinese cooking
ISBN 978-1-4358-3453-8 lib bdg; 1-4358-3453-4 lib bdg; 978-1-4358-3475-0 pa; 1-4358-3475-5 pa

LC 2009010337

This includes recipes for such Chinese dishes as spring rolls and braised mushrooms, and highlights the history and dishes that surround the Chinese New Year.

"The photography is exceptional, with children engaged in the cooking process. . . . Children, and the adults who assist them, will spend hours together mastering the techniques." SLJ

Locricchio, Matthew

★ The **2nd** international cookbook for kids; photographs by Jack McConnell. Marshall Cavendish 2008 176p il $18.99

Grades: 5 6 7 8   **641.5**
1. Cooking
ISBN 978-0-7614-5513-4

LC 2008003178

The recipes are "presented in a challenging yet teen-friendly step-by-step sequence. The book is best for patient chefs with kitchen experience and adventurous appetites. Informative sidebars provide facts about the recipes and cultures." Horn Book Guide

★ The **international** cookbook for kids; by Matthew Locricchio; photographs by Jack McConnell. Reprint Marshall Cavendish 2012 175p il $12.99

Grades: 5 6 7 8 **641.5**
1. Cooking
ISBN 9780761463139

LC 2004-5894

This includes "60 classic recipes from Italy, France, China, and Mexico, . . ., chef's tips discussing ingredients, nutrition, and technique, safety section discussing basic kitchen precautions, cooking terms and definitions." Publisher's note

Mattern, Joanne

Recipe and craft guide to China. Mitchell Lane Publishers 2010 63p il map (World crafts and recipes) lib bdg $33.95

Grades: 4 5 6 7 8 **641.5**
1. Handicraft 2. Chinese cooking
ISBN 978-1-58415-937-7 lib bdg; 1-58415-937-5 lib bdg

LC 2010009242

Provides recipes for several popular Chinese dishes and includes instructions on creating crafts using household items.

This provides "plenty of ideas for adding tasty treats and impressive visual aids to cultural reports or presentations." SLJ

Includes glossary and bibliographical references

McCallum, Ann

Eat your math homework; recipes for hungry minds. illustrated by Leeza Hernandez. Charlesbridge 2011 46p il $16.95; pa $7.95

Grades: 2 3 4 **641.5**
1. Cooking 2. Mathematics
ISBN 978-1-57091-779-0; 1-57091-779-5; 978-1-57091-780-6 pa; 1-57091-780-9 pa

LC 2010033631

"McCallum combines math with cooking in this attractive book. After a brief introduction and a few basic cooking tips, she explains the Fibonacci sequence and shows how to demonstrate it using chunks of fruit on skewers. Fractions are expressed through fried flour tortillas cut into fractional portions; tessellations with two-tone brownies; tangrams with flat cookies; variables and pi with pizza and probability with trail mix. In six-page chapters, the recipe sounds good, the math is clearly explained, and there's a playfulness of presentation that makes each activity look inviting. The mixed-media illustrations feature dressed rabbits, whose zany attitudes broaden their appeal. . . . Witty and smart." Booklist

Mendez, Sean

One world kids cookbook; easy, healthy and affordable family meals. foreword by Ferran Adrià. Interlink 2011 96p il $20

Grades: 4 5 6 **641.5**
1. Cooking
ISBN 978-1-56656-866-1; 1-56656-866-8

"International recipes for families interested in cooking a variety of world cuisines together. This colorful, amply illustrated cookbook emphasizes the educational, nutritional and social benefits of cooking with children, offering 19 recipes from as many nations. The book devotes four pages to each recipe and country, along with enriching notes on food and cultural facts. The country's flag is depicted with a

map locating the country, followed by a double-page spread documenting how to create each recipe. . . . This cookbook offers complex, authentic international flavors without overcomplicating the process, and the result is something you'd really enjoy having for dinner. A deliciously engaging fusion of cookbook and cultural lesson." Kirkus

Mofford, Juliet Haines

Recipe and craft guide to Japan. Mitchell Lane Publishers 2010 63p il map (World crafts and recipes) lib bdg $33.95

Grades: 4 5 6 7 8 **641.5**
1. Handicraft 2. Japanese cooking
ISBN 978-1-58415-933-9 lib bdg; 1-58415-933-2 lib bdg

LC 2010008951

Provides recipes for several popular Japanese dishes and includes instructions on creating traditional Japanese crafts using household items.

This provides "plenty of ideas for adding tasty treats and impressive visual aids to cultural reports or presentations." SLJ

Includes glossary and bibliographical references

Recipe and craft guide to the Caribbean. Mitchell Lane Publishers 2010 64p il map (World crafts and recipes) lib bdg $33.95

Grades: 4 5 6 7 8 **641.5**
1. Handicraft 2. Caribbean cooking
ISBN 978-1-58415-935-3 lib bdg; 1-58415-935-9 lib bdg

LC 2010009240

Provides recipes for several popular Caribbean dishes and includes instructions on creating traditional Caribbean crafts using household items.

This provides "plenty of ideas for adding tasty treats and impressive visual aids to cultural reports or presentations." SLJ

Includes glossary and bibliographical references

Reusser, Kayleen

Recipe and craft guide to Indonesia. Mitchell Lane Publishers 2010 64p il map (World crafts and recipes) lib bdg $33.95

Grades: 4 5 6 7 8 **641.5**
1. Handicraft 2. Indonesian cooking
ISBN 978-1-58415-934-6 lib bdg; 1-58415-934-0 lib bdg

LC 2010009243

Provides recipes for several popular Indonesian dishes and includes instructions on creating crafts using household items.

This provides "plenty of ideas for adding tasty treats and impressive visual aids to cultural reports or presentations." SLJ

Includes glossary and bibliographical references

Seaver, Barton

National Geographic Kids Cookbook; A Year-round Fun Food Adventure. by Barton Seaver. Natl Geographic Soc Childrens books 2014 160 p. color illustrations $19.99

Grades: 3 4 5 6   **641.5**
1. Cooking 2. Cookbooks
ISBN 1426317174; 1426317182; 9781426317170;
9781426317187
LC bl2014038122
This children's cookbook, by Barton Seaver, "provides
mouthwatering recipes, the ins and outs of healthy eating,
awesome crafts and activities, and food-focused challenges,
proving once and for all that cooking can be a blast. Follow
along as he teaches you to plant a kitchen garden, host a
dinner party for your friends, and pack the perfect school
lunch." (Publisher's note)

"A month-by-month guide to seasonal cooking, green
craft projects and enjoyable challenges that has something
to offer even the most environmentally conscious kids.
Recipes include everything from novice-friendly Ants on a
Log to more challenging undertakings such as New England
Pot Roast. Even reluctant cooks will not be able to refuse
Ghoulish Guacamole, Witches' Toenail Trail Mix, or Tilly's
Gingersnaps. . . . Engaging photographs and brightly colored
layouts will entice even reluctant readers. Resources for further research as well as separate indices for the activities and
the recipes are included. Calling this a cookbook is a bit limiting; this resource is intended to engage young chefs both
inside and outside of the kitchen, connecting the world of
food with the larger world around them.Hands-on kids will
find much to appreciate in this compendium of fun and food
with an Earth-friendly focus." Kirkus

Sheen, Barbara
  Foods of Chile. KidHaven Press 2011 64p il map (A
taste of culture) $28.75
Grades: 4 5 6   **641.5**
1. Chilean cooking 2. Chile -- Social life and customs
ISBN 978-0-7377-5421-6; 0-7377-5421-4
LC 2010035995
"Demonstrating that a nation's cuisine springs from its
geography, history, and traditions, [this volume explores
Chile's background], the availability of fresh ingredients,
and recipes that followed. . . . Culturally specific foods are
described alongside some accompanying recipes and photos
of people enjoying the dishes." Horn Book Guide
  Includes glossary and bibliographical references

  Foods of Cuba. KidHaven Press 2011 64p il map (A
taste of culture) $28.75
Grades: 4 5 6   **641.5**
1. Cuban cooking 2. Cuba -- Social life and customs
ISBN 978-0-7377-5113-0; 0-7377-5113-4
LC 2010030795
"Demonstrating that a nation's cuisine springs from its
geography, history, and traditions, [this volume explores
Cuba's background], the availability of fresh ingredients,
and recipes that followed. . . . Culturally specific foods are
described alongside some accompanying recipes and photos
of people enjoying the dishes." Horn Book Guide
  Includes glossary and bibliographical references

  Foods of Egypt. KidHaven Press 2010 64p il map (A
taste of culture) $28.75
Grades: 4 5 6   **641.5**
1. Egyptian cooking 2. Egypt -- Social life and customs
ISBN 978-0-7377-4843-7; 0-7377-4843-5
LC 2009038461

"Sheen explores how different native dishes and types
of local celebrations emerge from [Egypt's] culture and surroundings. [An] introductory [map] with a [key] to areas of
food production illuminate the country's cuisine by identifying geographical landforms and climate. Traditions and
tastes are described in accessible detail; key recipes are included and unfamiliar foods are pictured." Horn Book Guide
  Includes glossary and bibliographical references

  Foods of Ireland. KidHaven Press 2011 64p il map (A
taste of culture) $28.75
Grades: 4 5 6   **641.5**
1. Irish cooking 2. Ireland -- Social life and customs
ISBN 978-0-7377-5114-7; 0-7377-5114-2
LC 2010018791
"Sheen explores how different native dishes and types
of local celebrations emerge from [Ireland's] culture and
surroundings. [An] introductory [map] with a [key] to areas
of food production illuminate the country's cuisine by identifying geographical landforms and climate. Traditions and
tastes are described in accessible detail; key recipes are included and unfamiliar foods are pictured." Horn Book Guide
  Includes glossary and bibliographical references

  Foods of Kenya. KidHaven Press 2010 64p il map (A
taste of culture) $28.75
Grades: 4 5 6   **641.5**
1. African cooking 2. Kenyan cooking 3. Kenya --
Social life and customs
ISBN 978-0-7377-4813-0; 0-7377-4813-3
LC 2009048378
"Sheen explores how different native dishes and types
of local celebrations emerge from [Kenya's] culture and surroundings. [An] introductory [map] with a [key] to areas of
food production illuminate the country's cuisine by identifying geographical landforms and climate. Traditions and
tastes are described in accessible detail; key recipes are included and unfamiliar foods are pictured." Horn Book Guide
  Includes glossary and bibliographical references

  Foods of Korea. KidHaven Press 2011 64p il map (A
taste of culture) $26.75
Grades: 4 5 6   **641.5**
1. Korean cooking 2. Korea -- Social life and customs
ISBN 978-0-7377-5115-4; 0-7377-5115-0
LC 2010018789
"Demonstrating that a nation's cuisine springs from its
geography, history, and traditions, [this volume explores
Korea's background], the availability of fresh ingredients,
and recipes that followed. . . . Culturally specific foods are
described alongside some accompanying recipes and photos
of people enjoying the dishes." Horn Book Guide
  Includes glossary and bibliographical references

  Foods of Peru. KidHaven Press 2011 64p il map (A
taste of culture) $28.75
Grades: 4 5 6   **641.5**
1. Peruvian cooking 2. Peru -- Social life and customs
ISBN 978-0-7377-5346-2; 0-7377-5346-3
LC 2010032959
"Demonstrating that a nation's cuisine springs from its
geography, history, and traditions, [this volume explores
Peru's background], the availability of fresh ingredients, and

recipes that followed. . . . Culturally specific foods are described alongside some accompanying recipes and photos of people enjoying the dishes." Horn Book Guide

Includes glossary and bibliographical references

Tuminelly, Nancy

Cool creepy food art; easy recipes that make food fun to eat! ABDO Pub. Company 2011 32p il (Cool food art) lib bdg $25.65

Grades: 3 4 5 **641.5**

1. Food 2. Cooking

ISBN 978-1-61613-363-4; 1-61613-363-5

LC 2010003286

This offers recipes for such dishes as severed finger pizza; floating head cider, to die for dip, eyeball spaghetti, gross-out pita, garbage goop, bloody hand punch, and snot stick pretzels.

"Photographs provide clear step-by-step instructions as well as images of the finished products." Horn Book Guide

Includes glossary

Cool fruit & veggie food art; easy recipes that make food fun to eat! ABDO Pub. Company 2010 32p il (Cool food art) lib bdg $25.65

Grades: 3 4 5 **641.5**

1. Food 2. Fruit 3. Cooking -- Vegetables

ISBN 978-1-61613-364-1; 1-61613-364-3

LC 2010003285

Provides step-by-step instructions for creating fruit and vegetable food art, such as a funny face salad, an apple flutterfly, and a flying cucumber; and includes tips on techniques.

"Photographs provide clear step-by-step instructions as well as images of the finished products." Horn Book Guide

Includes glossary

Cool holiday food art; easy recipes that make food fun to eat! ABDO Pub. Company 2010 32p il (Cool food art) lib bdg $25.65

Grades: 3 4 5 **641.5**

1. Food 2. Holiday cooking

ISBN 978-1-61613-365-8; 1-61613-365-1

LC 2010003476

Provides step-by-step instructions for creating holiday-themed food art, such as reindeer cookies, dreidel pretzels, and creepy popcorn balls; and includes tips on techniques.

"Photographs provide clear step-by-step instructions as well as images of the finished products." Horn Book Guide

Includes glossary

Cool meat-free recipes; delicious & fun foods without meat. Nancy Tuminelly. ABDO Pub. Co. 2013 32 p. (Checkerboard how-to library. Cool recipes for your health) $28.50

Grades: 3 4 5 6 7 8 **641.5**

1. Cooking 2. Vegetarian cooking

ISBN 161783582X; 9781617835827

LC 2012023989

Author Nancy Tuminelly's book "gives young readers the tools to make healthy, tasty--and safe--dishes for anybody, anytime. This book has kid-tested, easy meat-free recipes, perfect for those who follow a vegetarian or vegan diet. Basic baking techniques, tools, and ingredients are il-

lustrated so kids can quickly prepare each recipe, such as Breakfast Bars and Sloppy Joes." (Publisher's note)

Includes bibliographical references and index

Cool snack food art; easy recipes that make food fun to eat! ABDO Pub. Company 2010 32p il (Cool food art) lib bdg $25.65

Grades: 3 4 5 **641.5**

1. Food 2. Snack foods

ISBN 978-1-61613-367-2; 1-61613-367-8

LC 2010003573

Provides step-by-step instructions for creating snack food art, such as chili snake dogs, a peanut butter and candy pizza, and a sweet treat flowerpot; and includes tips on techniques.

Includes glossary

Walker, Barbara Muhs

The Little House cookbook; frontier foods from Laura Ingalls Wilder's classic stories. by Barbara M. Walker; illustrated by Garth Williams. Harper & Row 1979 240p il $16.95; pa $9.95

Grades: 5 6 7 8 **641.5**

1. Authors 2. Cooking 3. Novelists 4. Frontier and pioneer life 5. Western writers 6. Children's authors 7. Young adult authors

ISBN 0-06-026418-7; 0-06-446090-8 pa

LC 76-58733

Recipes based on the pioneer food written about in the "Little House" books of Laura Ingalls Wilder, along with quotes from the books and descriptions of the food and cooking of pioneer times

"Illustrated by Williams's familiar warm drawings, the adaptations of menus from pioneer days include paragaphs describing the Wilder and Ingalls families working together, preparing holiday meals, individual foods, special treats and staple fare." Publ Wkly

Includes bibliographical references

Webb, Lois Sinaiko

Holidays of the world cookbook for students; [by] Lois Sinaiko Webb and Lindsay Grace Roten. updated and rev.; Greenwood 2011 442p il map $95; pa $32.95

Grades: 5 6 7 8 9 10 **641.5**

1. Cooking 2. Holidays

ISBN 978-0-313-38393-9; 0-313-38393-6; 978-0-313-39790-5 pa; 0-313-39790-2 pa; 978-0-313-38394-6 ebook

LC 2011-8458

First published 1995 by Oryx Press

"The recipes appear with each country entry, and the countries are arranged in alphabetical order within each region: Africa, Asia and the South Pacific, the Caribbean, Europe, Latin America, the Middle East, and North America." Publisher's note

Yolen, Jane

Fairy tale feasts; a literary cookbook for young readers and eaters. [by] Jane Yolen and Heidi E. Y. Stemple; illustrated by Philippe Beha. Crocodile Books 2006 197p il $24.95

Grades: 2 3 4 5 **641.5**

1. Cooking 2. Folklore

ISBN 1-56656-543-6

This "folds fairy tales into a cookbook of kid-friendly recipes. The stories, with the exception of one original story by Yolen, represent mostly European folktales, and Yolen retells them with her usual verve and ease. . . . Each story is paired with at least one recipe that connects with the story's themes or references. . . . Stemple's recipes require adult supervision, but the resulting dishes, as well as Beha's spare, whimsical spot illustrations, will capture children's fancy." Booklist

Jewish fairy tale feasts; stories retold by Jane Yolen; recipes by Heidi E.Y. Stemple; illustrations by Sima Elizabeth Shefrin. 1st American ed. Crocodile Books, an imprint of Interlink Pub. Group, Inc. 2012 200 p. (hardcover) $25 Grades: 2 3 4 5   **641.5**
1. Fairy tales 2. Jewish cooking 3. Cooking
ISBN 1566569095; 9781566569095
                                              LC 2012016174
This children's book, by Jane Yolen, Heidi E. Y. Stemple, illustrated by Sima Elizabeth Shefrin, offers Jewish cooking recipes and fairy tales to accompany them. "Here you'll find Yolen's . . . retellings of Jewish tales from around the world paired with Stemple's recipes-for everything from challah to matzo brei to pomegranate couscous, tzimmes chicken, and rugelah, in creative versions of classic dishes that any family will delight in cooking together." (Publisher's note)
Includes bibliographical references and index

641.509   History, geographic treatment, biography

Hartland, Jessie
Bon appetit! the delicious life of Julia Child. Jessie Hartland. Schwartz & Wade Books 2012 48 p. (hbk.) $17.99
Grades: 2 3 4 5   **641.509**
1. Women cooks 2. Women -- Biography 3. Picture books for children 4. Women cooks -- United States -- Biography 5. Women cooks -- United States -- Biography
ISBN 0375869441; 0375969446; 9780375869440; 9780375969447
                                              LC 2011018658
This juvenile biography, by Jessie Hartland, follows "Julia Child--chef, author, and television personality--from her childhood in Pasadena, California, to her life as a spy in WWII, . . . to the publication of 'Mastering the Art of French Cooking,' to the funny moments of being a chef on TV. This is a comprehensive and enchanting picture book biography, told in many panels and jam-packed with lively, humorous, and child-friendly details." (Publisher's note)
Includes bibliographical references.

641.59   Cooking characteristic of specific geographic environments, ethnic cooking

Blaxland, Wendy
Chinese food; by Wendy Blaxland. Smart Apple Media 2012 32 p. (library binding) $28.50

Grades: 4 5 6 7   **641.59**
1. Food 2. Cooking, Chinese
ISBN 1599206714; 9781599206714
                                              LC 2011005448
Author Wendy Blaxland's book "offers them the tastes of foreign or favorite cuisine. Beginning with a discussion about this area's culinary roots, it shows the growing of favorite foods are grown, its purchase and preparation. Step-by-step illustrated instructions for recipes are included along with nutritional data, safety and hygiene information." (Wheelers)

Mexican food; by Wendy Blaxland. Smart Apple Media 2012 32 p. (I can cook!) (library binding) $28.50
Grades: 4 5 6 7   **641.59**
1. Cookbooks 2. Mexican cooking 3. Food -- Mexico -- History
ISBN 1599206684; 9781599206684
                                              LC 2011005444
This book, by Wendy Blaxland, "presents a good amount of information on the geography, food staples, and even culture of [Mexico]. 'Mexican Food' finds a balance of spicy and sweet flavors in dishes from huevos rancheros to pan de muertos. Each recipe features helpful digital step-by-step illustrations and ideas for variations, underlining the fact that cooking is a creative process." (Booklist)

Locricchio, Matthew
The **cooking** of France; by Matthew Locricchio. Benchmark Books 2011 96 p. (Superchef) (print) $35.64
Grades: 4 5 6 7 8   **641.59**
1. Cookbooks 2. French cooking 3. Food habits -- France
ISBN 160870551X; 9781608705511; 9781608707393
                                              LC 2010052549
Author Matthew Locricchio presents a book on French cooking. "After a shared introduction about safety, [it] introduces . . . regional cuisines, mentioning festivals, traditions, and music to give readers a broader cultural view of [France]. Recipes, divided into categories such as soups and salads, main courses, and so on, make up the bulk of [the] book." (Booklist)
Includes bibliographical references and index

The **cooking** of Greece; Matthew Locricchio. Marshall Cavendish Benchmark 2011 96 p. (print) $35.64
Grades: 4 5 6 7 8   **641.59**
1. Cookbooks 2. Greek cooking 3. Food habits -- Greece 5. Cooking, Mediterranean
ISBN 1608705528; 9781608705528; 9781608707409
                                              LC 2010052548
In this book, author Matthew Locricchio "begins with a region-by-region overview of Greece, highlighting the natural produce of each area and the resulting cuisine, then groups his recipes by type-'Pies & Pitas,' 'Entrées,' etc. A section on kitchen safety . . . gives particulars on using knives. Fresh, healthful ingredients are emphasized, and suggestions are offered for adapting the recipes for vegetarians." (School Library Journal)
Includes bibliographical references and index

The **cooking** of Italy; by Matthew Locricchio. Marshall Cavendish Benchmark 2011 96 p. (print) $35.64

Grades: 4 5 6 7 8 **641.59**

1. Cookbooks 2. Italian cooking 3. Food habits -- Italy
ISBN 1608705544; 9781608705542; 9781608707423

LC 2010051849

In this book, by Matthew Locricchio, Italian cooking recipes are presented. It also "discusses general safety rules in the kitchen as well as specific rules for using knives. Regions of Italy . . . are defined along with a description of how geography influences crops, celebrations, and traditions that flourish within each area. Cooking terms are [also] explained." (Publisher's note)

Includes bibliographical references and index

Mendez, Sean

One world kids cookbook; easy, healthy and affordable family meals. by Sean Mendez. Interlink 2011 96 p. $20
Grades: 5 6 7 8 **641.59**

1. Diet 2. Cookbooks 3. Eating habits
ISBN 1566568668; 9781566568661

Author Sean Mendez presents a cookbook "aimed at encouraging young people to think about what they eat through emphasizing the importance of a balanced diet. It contains kitchen tips and suggests vegetarian substitutes to the meat recipes. One World Kids Cookbook aims to instill a passion for good, wholesome, healthy food as well as a passion for life." (Publisher's note)

Sheen, Barbara

Foods of Australia; by Barbara Sheen. KidHaven Press 2010 64 p. (hardcover) $31.95
Grades: 4 5 6 **641.59**

1. Australian cooking 2. Australia -- Social life and customs 3. Cooking -- Australia 4. Cooking, Australian
ISBN 0737748125; 9780737748123

LC 2009032643

This book, by Barbara Sheen, "explores the foods, cooking traditions, customs, eating habits, and food sources of [Australia]. [It discusses] ingredients that form the staples of cooking . . ., the favorite dishes, the snacks and sweets, the traditional holiday meals, and the preparations and traditions associated with these foods." (Publisher's note)

Includes bibliographical references and index

641.595 Cooking – Asia

Wagner, Lisa

Cool Chinese and Japanese cooking; fun and tasty recipes for kids. by Lisa Wagner. ABDO Pub. 2011 32 p. (Cool world cooking) $28.50
Grades: 3 4 5 6 **641.595**

1. Chinese cooking 2. Japanese cooking 3. Cooking
ISBN 1617146595; 9781617146596

LC 2010022191

This book, by Lisa Wagner, "introduces readers to world geography and authentic, easy-to-make recipes [for Chinese and Japanese cuisine]. Cooking teaches kids about food, math and measuring, and following directions. Each kid-tested recipe includes step-by-step instructions and how-to photos. Tools and ingredients lists are also provided, as well as pronunciation guides when needed." (Publisher's note)

641.5944 Cooking – French

Wagner, Lisa

Cool French cooking; fun and tasty recipes for kids. by Lisa Wagner. Checkerboard Library 2011 32 p. $28.50
Grades: 3 4 5 6 **641.5944**

1. French cooking 2. Cooking
ISBN 1617146609; 9781617146602

LC 2010022192

This book, by Lisa Wagner, "introduces readers to world geography and authentic, easy-to-make recipes [for French cuisine]. Cooking teaches kids about food, math and measuring, and following directions. Each kid-tested recipe includes step-by-step instructions and how-to photos. Tools and ingredients lists are also provided, as well as pronunciation guides when needed." (Publisher's note)

641.5945 Cooking – Italian

Wagner, Lisa

Cool Italian cooking; fun and tasty recipes for kids. by Lisa Wagner. Checkerboard Library 2011 32 p. $28.50
Grades: 3 4 5 6 **641.594**

1. Italian cooking 2. Cooking
ISBN 1617146617; 9781617146619

LC 2010022193

This book, by Lisa Wagner, "introduces readers to world geography and authentic, easy-to-make recipes [for Italian cuisine}. Cooking teaches kids about food, math and measuring, and following directions. Each kid-tested recipe includes step-by-step instructions and how-to photos. Tools and ingredients lists are also provided, as well as pronunciation guides when needed." (Publisher's note)

641.5972 Cooking -- Mexican

Wagner, Lisa

Cool Mexican cooking; fun and tasty recipes for kids. by Lisa Wagner. Checkerboard Library 2011 32 p. (Cool world cooking) $28.50
Grades: 3 4 5 6 **641.5972**

1. Mexican cooking 2. Cooking 3. Cooking, Mexican
ISBN 1617146625; 9781617146626

LC 2010022194

This book, by Lisa Wagner, "introduces readers to world geography and authentic, easy-to-make recipes [for Mexican cuisine]. Cooking teaches kids about food, math and measuring, and following directions. Each kid-tested recipe includes step-by-step instructions and how-to photos. Tools and ingredients lists are also provided, as well as pronunciation guides when needed." (Publisher's note)

641.6 Cooking specific materials

Llewellyn, Claire

Cooking with meat and fish; [by] Claire Llewellyn, Clare O'Shea. Rosen Central 2011 48p il map (Cooking healthy) lib bdg $27.95

Grades: 5 6 7 8   **641.6**
1. Meat 2. Cooking 3. Seafood
ISBN 978-1-4488-4845-4; 1-4488-4845-8
           LC 2010039337

A description of each type of meat and fish, how to cook them in a healthy manner, and recipe examples of each.

This book pairs "facts about [meat and fish], including where it is eaten, with eye-catching photos. . . . Each course (section) has an overview of the . . . [meat] followed by recipes from all over the world. They vary in difficulty. . . . The cooking directions are clear and straightforward. . . . [The book is] profusely illustrated with full-color photos. Students who are learning to cook will appreciate [this] excellently organized [read]." SLJ

Includes glossary and bibliographical references

MacLeod, Elizabeth
    Chock full of chocolate; written by Elizabeth MacLeod; illustrated by June Bradford. Kids Can Press 2005 40p il (Kids can do it) hardcover o.p. pa $6.95
Grades: 4 5 6   **641.6**
1. Cooking 2. Chocolate
ISBN 1-55337-762-1; 1-55337-763-X pa
This includes recipes for chocolate cookies, cakes, and other desserts.

641.8   Cooking specific kinds of dishes and preparing beverages

DeVore, Janna
    Ballerina cookbook; photographs by Zac Williams. Gibbs Smith 2011 70p il $14.99
Grades: 2 3 4 5 6   **641.8**
1. Ballet 2. Parties 3. Desserts
ISBN 978-1-4236-0793-9; 1-4236-0793-7
           LC 2010030688

"An elegant and beautifully arranged cookbook of desserts and drinks. The recipes are organized into four sections: 'Ballerina Basics,' 'The Nutcracker,' 'Sleeping Beauty,' and 'Swan Lake.' The recipes have 'ballerina' names that for the most part describe the dish. . . . The overall layout is appealing with the recipe on one page and a luscious, full-page picture on the other. . . . The recipes are perfect for a party or a tasty treat any day of the week." SLJ

Dunnington, Rose
    Sweet eats; mmmore than just desserts. [by] Rose Dunnington. Lark Books 2008 112p $9.95
Grades: 3 4 5 6   **641.8**
1. Baking 2. Desserts
ISBN 978-1-60059-236-2; 1-60059-236-8
           LC 2007037094

This "offers mouthwatering recipes, explains how to cook safely and efficiently, and introduces basic skills. In a breezy first-person style, the author covers such useful aspects as how to organize a work space, safety tips, the tools needed, and how and why to do things. The 35 recipes include a pie crust and various frostings/toppings and are accompanied by plenty of full-color visual aids along the way." SLJ

Includes glossary

Gibbons, Gail
    Ice cream; the full scoop. by Gail Gibbons. Holiday House 2006 un il $16.95
Grades: K 1 2 3   **641.8**
1. Ice cream, ices, etc.
ISBN 978-0-8234-2000-1; 0-8234-2000-0
           LC 2005052575

"Gibbons explains how this favorite food developed from flavored ice to the creamy dessert we know today, describes the invention and workings of the ice-cream maker, follows the journey from cow to factory to grocery-store shelves, and mentions the innovative creation of the cone. . . . The narrative is simple and direct and the cartoon illustrations are colorful and cheerful." SLJ

Goodman, Susan
    All in just one cookie; by Susan E. Goodman; illustrated by Timothy Bush. Greenwillow Books 2006 un il $16.99; lib bdg $17.89
Grades: 2 3 4   **641.8**
1. Baking 2. Cookies
ISBN 978-0-06-009092-0; 0-06-009092-8; 978-0-06-009093-7 lib bdg; 0-06-009093-6 lib bdg
           LC 2005040308

"As Grandma gathers the ingredients for her chocolate-chip cookies, her cat collects facts about the process of making butter, vanilla, baking soda, and other cookie components. . . . Cartoonlike illustrations show where each ingredient comes from, along with side comments from the cat and dog." Horn Book Guide

Love, Ann
    Sweet! the delicious story of candy. [by] Ann Love & Jane Drake; illustrated by Claudia Dávila. Tundra Books 2007 64p il map $19.95
Grades: 4 5 6 7   **641.8**
1. Candy
ISBN 978-0-88776-752-4

"This history of things sweet and sugary is a yummy feast. The prose is chatty and inviting. Color cartoon illustrations show multiethnic people in the process of making or enjoying everything from honey to ice cream to cotton candy (called candy floss here) to jelly beans and chocolate." SLJ

MacLeod, Elizabeth
    Bake and make amazing cookies; written by Elizabeth MacLeod; illustrated by June Bradford. Kids Can Press 2004 40p il (Kids can do it) hardcover o.p. pa $6.95
Grades: 4 5 6   **641.8**
1. Cookies
ISBN 1-55337-631-5; 1-55337-632-3 pa

This offers "32 recipes under four headings 'Holidays,' 'For Special People,' 'Seasons,' and 'Just for Fun.' This book is sure to please bakers. The step-by-step instructions . . . are easy to follow, and the ingredients/tools listed are readily available or easily obtainable. . . . Each recipe is accompanied by precise, softly colored illustrations." SLJ

Raum, Elizabeth
    The **story** behind bread. Heinemann Library 2009 32p il (True stories) lib bdg $28.21

Grades: 3 4 5   641.8
  1. Bread
  ISBN 978-1-4329-2346-4 lib bdg; 1-4329-2346-3
  lib bdg

LC 2008037394

The story behind "bread covers the history of the staple
and its importance, the harvesting of grains, and the equipment used to bring it 'From Fields to Tables.' Readers will
learn, for example, that bagels were originally created in the
shape of a stirrup to honor the King of Poland. . . . The well-
organized [text is] informative and clearly written, and the
numerous color photographs and drawings are eye-catching
and complement the [narrative] well." SLJ

  Includes bibliographical references

Smart, Denise

The **children's** baking book; recipes & styling by Denise Smart; photography by Howard Shooter. DK 2009
128p il $17.99

Grades: 3 4 5   641.8
  1. Baking
  ISBN 0-7566-5788-1; 978-0-7566-5788-8

Instructions for making bread, pastry, muffins, cakes and
cookies. Includes more than 50 easy-to-follow recipes.

"This accessible baking book features more than 50
sweet and savory recipes . . . with full-color photographs that
show both preparations and tasty end results. Divided into
sections on cookies and baked goods, dough, cakes, and pastry, the recipes are further labeled with levels of difficulty. . .
. The sweet-toothed should find the mouthwatering pictures
and straightforward instructions hard to resist." Publ Wkly

Tuminelly, Nancy

Cool cake & cupcake food art; easy recipes that make
food fun to eat! ABDO Pub. Company 2011 32p il (Cool
food art) lib bdg $25.65

Grades: 3 4 5   641.8
  1. Cake 2. Food 3. Baking
  ISBN 978-1-61613-362-7; 1-61613-362-7

LC 2010003287

Provides step-by-step instructions for creating cake
and cupcake food art, such as a flower garden cake, a
portly panda, and a hole in one cupcake; and includes tips
on techniques.

"Photographs provide clear step-by-step instructions as
well as images of the finished products." Horn Book Guide

  Includes glossary

Cool sandwich food art; easy recipes that make food
fun to eat! ABDO Pub. Company 2011 32p il (Cool food
art) lib bdg $25.65

Grades: 3 4 5   641.8
  1. Food 2. Sandwiches
  ISBN 978-1-61613-366-5; 1-61613-366-X

LC 2010003475

Provides step-by-step instructions for creating sandwich food art, such as a peanut butter and jelly flower, a
happy hippo hoagie, and a caterpillar wrap; and includes tips
on techniques.

  Includes glossary

641.81   Side dishes, sauces, garnishes

Larson, Jennifer S.

Yummy soup and salad recipes; Jennifer S. Larson;
photographs by Brie Cohen. Millbrook Press 2013 32 p.
(You're the chef) (lib. bdg.: alk. paper) $26.60

Grades: 1 2 3 4   641.81
  1. Soups 2. Cookbooks 3. Cooking
  ISBN 0761366334; 9780761366331

LC 2012020921

This illustrated kids' cookbook by Jennifer S. Larson is
part of the You're the Chef series and offers soup and salad
recipes. It "proves that soups can include everything from
chili to chowder to fruit. Each title" includes a glossary of
technique terms, "notes about special ingredients and a website link." (Booklist)

  Includes bibliographical references and index

641.82   Main dishes

Larson, Jennifer S.

Meaty main dishes; Jennifer S. Larson; photographs by
Brie Cohen. Millbrook Press 2013 32 p. (You're the chef)
(lib. bdg.: alk. paper) $26.60

Grades: 1 2 3 4   641.82
  1. Cooking -- Meat 2. Entrées (Cooking)
  ISBN 0761366342; 9780761366348

LC 2012020922

This cookbook by Jennifer S. Larson presents "easy-to-
follow recipes for Asian shrimp stir fry, juicy chicken drum-
sticks, taco meatballs, and other tasty dishes. You'll find
simple drawings of important steps as well as photographs
of the finished dishes. This book also provides key information, such as an equipment list, a technique list, safety tips,
notes on special ingredients, and more." (Publisher's note)

  Includes bibliographical references (page 32) and index

642   Meals and table service

Duncan, Karen

The **good** fun! book; 12 months of parties that celebrate service. by Karen Duncan & Kate Hannigan Issa;
illustrated by Anthony Alex LeTourneau. Blue Marlin Publications 2010 un il $15.95

Grades: 3 4 5 6   642
  1. Cooking 2. Parties 3. Handicraft 4. Social action
  ISBN 978-0-9792918-5-2; 0-9792918-5-2

LC 2010025848

"For each month of the year, Duncan and Issa suggest a
party with a service theme. For example, they suggest making Valentines for children at a local hospital in February,
cleaning up a park for Earth Day in April, or making jacko-
lanterns for a nursing home in October. The ideas are realistic, age appropriate, and thoughtful. The authors have done
a good job mixing fun with function. . . . Each plan contains
two ideas, a treat recipe, a craft, and information about a
national charity related to the theme. The book is illustrated
with child-friendly color cartoons featuring youngsters doing good deeds." SLJ

  Includes bibliographical references

644.6   Plumbing

Macaulay, David

★ **Toilet**; how it works. David Macaulay, Sheila Keenan. Roaring Brook Press 2013 28 p. (hardcover) $15.99
Grades: K 1 2   **644.6**
1. Toilets 2. Sewage disposal 3. Water purification
ISBN 1596437790; 9781596437791; 9781596437807
                                   LC 2012947300
This book, by David Macaulay and Sheila Keenan, "takes readers on a tour of the bathroom and the sewer system, from the familiar family toilet to the mysterious municipal water treatment plant. Everyone knows what a toilet is for, right? But what exactly happens after you flush? Where does our waste go, and how is it made safe?" (Publisher's note)

"In this beginning reader/nonfiction chapter book, clear step-by-step directions and unobstructed diagrams and cross sections outline how waste is produced by the body, disposed of through a toilet, sent to either a septic tank or sewer system, and purified. Macaulay's humor is evident, as he reminds readers that the language of science can be both precise and lively." (Horn Book)

646   Sewing, clothing, management of personal and family life

Neitzel, Shirley

The **jacket** I wear in the snow; pictures by Nancy Winslow Parker. Greenwillow Bks. 1989 un il $16.99; pa $6.99
Grades: PreK K 1 2   **646**
1. Stories in rhyme 2. Snow -- Fiction 3. Clothing and dress -- Fiction
ISBN 0-688-08028-6; 0-688-04587-1 pa
                                    LC 88-18767
A young girl names all the clothes that she must wear to play in the snow

"Written in cheerful, cumulative verse that recalls the well-known favorite nursery rhyme 'The House That Jack Built,' the text, with its easy-going rhythm, will be simple for children to recite from memory. . . . The artist's drawings are executed in . . . watercolor, pencil, and pen; they combine with the large typeface and a generous amount of white space to create a tremendously appealing book." Horn Book

646.2   Sewing and related operations

Plumley, Amie Petronis

Sewing school; 21 sewing projects kids will love to make. [by] Amie Petronis Plumley & Andria Lisle; photography by Justin Fox Burks. Storey Pub. 2010 143p il $16.95
Grades: 3 4 5 6   **646.2**
1. Sewing
ISBN 978-1-60342-578-0; 1-60342-578-0
                                    LC 2010022154
"This large-format book offers appealing projects illustrated with color photos of step-by-step directions as well as kids engaged in sewing and showing off work. The opening 12 lessons begin with topics such as threading a needle, knotting the thread, and making a basic running stitch. After covering basic knowledge and skills, the presentation moves on to instructions for fun easy projects." Booklist

Sadler, Judy Ann

Simply sewing; written by Judy Ann Sadler; illustrated by Jane Kurisu. Kids Can Press 2004 48p il (Kids can do it) hardcover o.p. pa $6.95
Grades: 4 5 6   **646.2**
1. Sewing
ISBN 1-55337-659-5; 1-55337-660-9 pa
This "book opens with a section on sewing supplies. . . . Subsequent chapters discuss fabric and the basics of hand and machine stitching. . . . Each of the 12 projects is accompanied by a color photo, step-by-step color illustrations, and a list of supplies needed. . . . This attractive book has a wide assortment of ideas to spark interest." SLJ

646.4   Clothing and accessories construction

D'Cruz, Anna-Marie

Make your own masks. PowerKids Press 2009 24p il (Do it yourself projects!) lib bdg $23.95; pa $9.40
Grades: 2 3 4   **646.4**
1. Handicraft 2. Masks (Facial)
ISBN 978-1-4358-2853-7 lib bdg; 1-4358-2853-4 lib bdg; 978-1-4358-2923-7 pa; 1-4358-2923-9 pa
                                    LC 2008033677
This offers "step-by-step instructions and full-color photos to illustrate the crafts. Projects have a broad cultural representation and are not gender specific. Materials are easily obtained. [The projects include] an Aztec skull, a Bwa sun mask, a Greek Medusa, and a Viking mask." SLJ

Includes glossary and bibliographical references

Make your own purses and bags. PowerKids Press 2009 24p il (Do it yourself projects!) lib bdg $23.95; pa $9.40
Grades: 2 3 4   **646.4**
1. Bags 2. Handicraft
ISBN 978-1-4358-2856-8 lib bdg; 1-4358-2856-9 lib bdg; 978-1-4358-2929-9 pa; 1-4358-2929-8 pa
                                    LC 2008033671
This offers "step-by-step instructions and full-color photos to illustrate the crafts. Projects have a broad cultural representation and are not gender specific. Materials are easily obtained. . . . A Didgeridoo pencil case and an MP3-player case are among the projects [included]." SLJ

Includes glossary and bibliographical references

Petersen, Christine

The **tailor**. Marshall Cavendish Benchmark 2011 il (Colonial people) $29.93
Grades: 3 4 5 6   **646.4**
1. Tailoring 2. United States -- History -- 1600-1775, Colonial period
ISBN 978-1-60870-417-0; 1-60870-417-3
                                    LC 2010016864
This describes the life of a colonial tailor and his importance to the community, as well as everyday life, responsibilities, and social practices during that time.

This "lively [text] and colorful reproductions and photos will engage casual readers and researchers alike. . . . Large illustrations and thoughtful captions explain complicated scientific ideas. . . . [The] volume also includes step-by-step instructions for a related craft project. . . . [This is a] must-have." SLJ

Includes glossary and bibliographical references

Schwarz, Renee
Making masks; written and illustrated by Renée Schwarz. Kids Can Press 2002 40p il (Kids can do it) $12.95; pa $5.95
Grades: 4 5 6   **646.4**
1. Handicraft 2. Masks (Facial)
ISBN 1-55074-929-3; 1-55074-931-5 pa

This offers instructions for creating a variety of masks using such materials as cardboard, felt, paper, and pipe cleaners

This includes "appealing projects and easy-to-follow directions. . . . Schwarz does a good job constructing and illustrating a variety of masks." SLJ

Torres, Laura
Rock your wardrobe. QEB Pub. 2010 32p il (Rock your . . .) lib bdg $28.50
Grades: 4 5 6   **646.4**
1. Fashion 2. Handicraft 3. Clothing and dress
ISBN 978-1-59566-937-7; 1-59566-937-X
LC 2010010671

This book "gives kids easy step-by-step ways to . . . fashion clothes with simple, easily found scraps and a little glue and paint. Colorful photographs show youngsters crafting appealing T-shirts . . . etc., some of which are created from recycled found items. All are projects they can complete by themselves." Horn Book Guide

646.7 Management of personal and family life

Buchholz, Rachel
How to survive anything; shark attack, quicksand, embarrassing parents, pop quizzes, and other perilous situations. illustrations by Chris Philpot. National Geographic 2011 176p il (National geographic kids) pa $12.95
Grades: 5 6 7 8   **646.7**
1. Life skills 2. Survival skills
ISBN 978-1-4263-0774-4; 1-4263-0774-8
LC 2010028045

"Buchholz doles out hilarious and handy advice for suffering though both natural and manmade catastrophes. Part survival guide and part self-help book, it provides honest, tongue-in-cheek answers to questions teens may be reluctant to ask out loud, in addition to imparting disaster preparedness strategies. It's a clever, winning combination. Superb full-color digital illustrations and photographs and a lively, conversational tone will catch and keep readers' attention, and the list-heavy layout is fun to read and easy to understand." SLJ

Chancellor, Deborah
Happy and healthy. QEB Pub. 2011 32p il (For girls!) lib bdg $18.95
Grades: 2 3 4 5   **646.7**
1. Life skills 2. Personal grooming 3. Girls -- Health

and hygiene
ISBN 978-1-60992-104-0; 1-60992-104-6
LC 2011006913

This guide for girls gives advice on how to keep healthy, including exercise and keeping fit, creative cooking, skin and hair care, healthy foods, and sports.

"Each lively, readable spread is packed with color photos, computer graphics, and lots of boxes filled with facts, lists, and practical suggestions." Booklist

Heinrichs, Ann
The **barber**. Marshall Cavendish Benchmark 2010 48p il (Colonial people) lib bdg $29.93
Grades: 3 4 5 6   **646.7**
1. Barbers and barbershops 2. United States -- History -- 1600-1775, Colonial period
ISBN 978-0-7614-4800-6; 0-7614-4800-4
LC 2009018626

"The type font, just slightly larger than usual, makes the text very visually appealing. . . . [The] book is liberally illustrated with artwork dating from the colonial period . . . [and] information boxes offer supplemental material." Libr Media Connect

Includes glossary and bibliographical references

646.700 Management of personal and family life

Buchanan, Andrea J.
The **daring** book for girls; Andrea Buchanan, Miriam Peskowitz; illustrated by Alexis Seabrook. 1st ed. Collins 2007 viii, 279 p.p ill. (some col.), col. map (hardcover) $26.95
Grades: 4 5 6 7 8 9   **646.700**
1. Girls 2. Amusements 3. Recreation 4. Curiosities and wonders 5. Girls in literature 6. Girls -- Conduct of life 7. Girls -- Life skills guides
ISBN 0061472573; 9780061472572
LC 2007031986

This book is "filled with interesting activities to try and important facts [girls] may not know, but are sure to keep them busy for hours. The authors cover everything from making a lemon-powered clock to the history of writing and cursive, from how to paddle a canoe to the Periodic Table of the Elements." (School Library Journal)

Includes bibliographical references (p. 274-276).

647.9 Specific kinds of public households and institutions

Mara, Wil
The **innkeeper**. Marshall Cavendish Benchmark 2010 48p il (Colonial people) lib bdg $29.93
Grades: 3 4 5 6   **647.9**
1. Hotels and motels 2. United States -- History -- 1600-1775, Colonial period
ISBN 978-0-7614-4796-2; 0-7614-4796-2
LC 2009011873

This describes the life of a colonial innkeeper and his importance to the community, as well as everyday life, responsibilities, and social practices during that time.

"The type font, just slightly larger than usual, makes the text very visually appealing. . . . [The] book is liberally illustrated with artwork dating from the colonial period . . . [and] information boxes offer supplemental material." Libr Media Connect

Includes glossary and bibliographical references

648   Housekeeping

Barber, Nicola

Moving to a new house. PowerKids Press 2009 24p il (The big day!) lib bdg $21.25; pa $8.25

Grades: PreK K 1   **648**
  1. Moving
  ISBN 978-1-4358-2841-4 lib bdg; 978-1-4358-2897-1 pa

LC 2008026222

"Children in kindergarten will enjoy [this book] as [a read-aloud] . . . while those at the end of first grade will be able to read [it] independently. The writing is straightforward and reassuring, and the content provides a realistic view of what youngsters might experience in [a new home]. . . . [The book] mentions the possibility of feeling strange in the new environment, but also discusses how quickly the child will adjust and make new friends." SLJ

Includes bibliographical references

Parker, Victoria

Moving; [by] Vic Parker. Heinemann Library 2011 24p il (Growing up) lib bdg $22; pa $6.49

Grades: PreK K 1 2   **648**
  1. Moving
  ISBN 978-1-4329-4800-9 lib bdg; 1-4329-4800-8 lib bdg; 978-1-4329-4810-8 pa; 1-4329-4810-5 pa

LC 2010024194

This explains what to expect from a move across the street or across the country.

Includes bibliographical references

649   Child rearing; home care of people with disabilities and illnesses

Buckley, Annie

Be a better babysitter; by Annie Buckley. Child's World 2007 32p il (Girls rock!) lib bdg $24.21

Grades: 5 6 7 8   **649**
  1. Babysitting
  ISBN 1-59296-740-X

LC 2006001639

This "describes what babysitting entails, examines pros and cons, discusses safety issues, offers tips for doing a good job, and suggests saving as much as half of any money earned. . . . [This] realistic [title is] well written and [provides] excellent information." SLJ

Includes bibliographical references

Chasse, Jill D.

The babysitter's survival guide; fun games, cool crafts, and how to be the best babysitter in town. illustrated by Jessica Secheret. Sterling Pub. Co. 2010 107p il $12.95

Grades: 5 6 7 8   **649**
  1. Babysitting
  ISBN 978-1-4027-4654-3; 1-4027-4654-7

LC 2009-2538

"This useful, up-to-date handbook offers plenty of practical advice with a wise emphasis on safety, which makes it a good choice for new sitters as well as those with experience. Chassé starts with information on starting a business, including references, advertising, and interviewing. Child development is a main focus; suggested activities and tips on interaction with children at different developmental stages will be appreciated by sitters and parents alike. . . . Occasional two-color cartoons feature diverse children and sitters." SLJ

Includes bibliographical references

Danzig, Dianne

Babies don't eat pizza; the big kids' book about baby brothers and baby sisters. by Dianne Danzig; illustrated by Debbie Tilley. Dutton Children's Books 2009 un il $16.99

Grades: PreK K   **649**
  1. Infants 2. Siblings
  ISBN 978-0-525-47441-8; 0-525-47441-2

"Focusing on day-to-day living with an infant, the text adopts an unfussy tone that subtly flatters readers as being sensible and mature (relatively speaking). . . . Tilley's ink and watercolor cartoons are sunny and empathic . . . and include plenty of visual jokes to encourage anxious kids—and their parents—to bond. Headings on most spreads make this volume eminently browsable—and therefore a handy family resource." Publ Wkly

Wells, Rosemary

My shining star; raising a child who is ready to learn. [by] Rosemary Wells. Scholastic Press 2006 un il $8.99

Grades: PreK K   **649**
  1. Parenting
  ISBN 0-439-84701-X

LC 2005010481

"Young children will enjoy the adorable bunny characters and the small size that is just right for their little hands. But this gem of a picture book is directed to adults—and it belongs in the big hands of every teacher and parent. On each colorful spread, Wells expands on 10 principles to help any child succeed. The direct, simple advice is illustrated with Wells' favorite rabbits demonstrating the recommendations." Booklist

650.1   Personal success in business

Orr, Tamra

A kid's guide to earning money; by Tamra Orr. Mitchell Lane Publishers 2008 47p il (Money matters: a kid's guide to money) lib bdg $29.95

Grades: 4 5 6   **650.1**
  1. Personal finance 2. Money-making projects for children
  ISBN 978-1-58415-643-7 lib bdg; 1-58415-643-0 lib bdg

LC 2008-2253

"This chatty, interactive guide offers practical suggestions for finding jobs, from babysitting and dogwalking to delivering newspapers. . . . Also included is useful advice on setting price points, how to cut costs, and what the labor laws allow for kids under 18, as well as a frank view of the negatives associated with the working world. . . . Stress is laid on the importance of getting parental permission before setting out on the trail to riches." Booklist

Includes glossary and bibliographical references

652 Processes of written communication

Bell-Rehwoldt, Sheri

Speaking secret codes. Capstone Press 2010 32p il (Edge books: making and breaking codes) lib bdg $26.65
Grades: 4 5 6 7   652

1. Ciphers 2. Cryptography
ISBN 978-1-4296-4569-0 lib bdg; 1-4296-4569-5 lib bdg

LC 2010004163

"Spoken codes in history, including the Underground Railroad and POWs during the Vietnam War, are introduced by using various examples of word substitutions. Educators will appreciate the concise information provided by codes that have shaped world history. . . . Historical photographs, highlighted vocabulary words and definitions, and do-it-yourself suggestions will keep readers interested." SLJ

Includes glossary and bibliographical references

Blackwood, Gary L.

Mysterious messages; a history of codes and ciphers. [by] Gary Blackwood; designed and illustrated by Jason Henry. Dutton Children's Books 2009 170p il $16.99
Grades: 5 6 7 8   652

1. Ciphers 2. Cryptography
ISBN 978-0-525-47960-4; 0-525-47960-0

LC 2008-48970

"This well-written history of cryptography begins with a pottery-glaze formula encrypted in cuneiform on a clay tablet (1500 BCE) and traces the uses of secret messages in statecraft, espionage, warfare, crime, literature, and business up to the present. Along the way, Blackwood . . . discusses the historical development of coding and encryption and tells many good stories of messages ciphered and deciphered. . . . The many sidebars and illustrations, including photos, reproductions of artworks and artifacts, and the pictures demonstrating the codes themselves, contribute to the book's approachable look." Booklist

Gilbert, Adrian

Codes and ciphers. Firefly 2009 32p il (Spy files) pa $6.95
Grades: 3 4 5 6   652

1. Ciphers 2. Espionage 3. Cryptography
ISBN 978-1-55407-573-7 pa; 1-55407-573-4 pa
First published 2008 in the United Kingdom

Discusses the difference between codes and ciphers, common codes and ciphers that have been used during wars, and how to create simple ciphers

This "gives an excellent overview of the historical and practical use of codes and ciphers in spy work. . . . The [text's] short paragraphs and great pictures are combined in a collage style that will draw readers quickly through the information." SLJ

Includes glossary

Gregory, Jillian

Breaking secret codes. Capstone Press 2010 32p il (Edge books: making and breaking codes) lib bdg $26.65
Grades: 4 5 6 7   652

1. Ciphers 2. Cryptography
ISBN 978-1-4296-4568-3 lib bdg; 1-4296-4568-7 lib bdg

LC 2010004162

"Educators will appreciate the concise information provided by codes that have shaped world history. Sample cryptographs are scattered throughout the pages, along with other noteworthy facts. Historical photographs, highlighted vocabulary words and definitions, and do-it-yourself suggestions will keep readers interested." SLJ

Includes glossary and bibliographical references

Making secret codes. Capstone Press 2010 32p il (Edge books: making and breaking codes) lib bdg $26.65
Grades: 4 5 6 7   652

1. Ciphers 2. Cryptography
ISBN 978-1-4296-4567-6 lib bdg; 1-4296-4567-9 lib bdg

LC 2010004161

"Educators will appreciate the concise information provided by codes that have shaped world history. Sample cryptographs are scattered throughout the pages, along with other noteworthy facts. Historical photographs, highlighted vocabulary words and definitions, and do-it-yourself suggestions will keep readers interested." SLJ

Includes glossary and bibliographical references

Mitchell, Susan K.

Spy codes and ciphers. Enslow Publishers 2011 48p il (The secret world of spies) lib bdg $23.93
Grades: 4 5 6   652

1. Spies 2. Ciphers 3. Espionage 4. Cryptography
ISBN 978-0-7660-3709-0

LC 2010006176

Discusses different methods of secret communications used by spies, such as Morse code, the Enigma machine, the Najavo language, and digital steganography, and includes career information.

Includes glossary and bibliographical references

658 General management

Bochner, Arthur Berg

The **new** totally awesome business book for kids (and their parents) with twenty super businesses you can start right now! [by] Arthur Bochner & Rose Bochner; foreword by Andriane G. Berg. rev and updated 3rd ed.; Newmarket Press 2007 188p il pa $9.95
Grades: 4 5 6 7   658

1. Small business 2. Money-making projects for children
ISBN 978-1-55704-757-1 pa; 1-55704-757-X pa

LC 2007002637

First published 1995 with title: The totally awesome business book for kids

A comprehensive look at the basic financial and management aspects of moneymaking businesses for children

"This book can certainly be thought provoking for young people with an entrepreneurial spirit. . . . The illustrations are lively and engaging, and the text non-threatening." Voice Youth Advocates

Includes bibliographical references

Mooney, Carla

Starting a business; have fun and make money. Norwood House Press 2010 48p il (Creative adventure guides) lib bdg $25.27

Grades: 3 4 5 6 **658**

1. Business enterprises 2. Money-making projects for children

ISBN 978-1-59953-386-5; 1-59953-386-3

This book "outlines a small business plan for kids, with examples of successful young entrepreneurs." Horn Book Guide

Includes glossary and bibliographical references

662 Technology of explosives, fuels, related products

Benduhn, Tea

Ethanol and other new fuels; by Tea Benduhn. Weekly Reader Pub. 2009 24p il (Energy for today) lib bdg $21; pa $5.95

Grades: 2 3 4 **662**

1. Energy resources 2. Alcohol as fuel

ISBN 978-0-8368-9260-4 lib bdg; 0-8368-9260-7 lib bdg; 978-0-8368-9359-5 pa; 0-8368-9359-X pa

LC 2008014483

This describes how ethanol and other new fuels work and how they can be used in the future.

"New readers will be able to wrap their hands around the small, square size, and their minds around the clear, enlightening text. [This book has] crisp photos and strong back matter." Booklist

Includes glossary and bibliographical references

Cobb, Vicki

Fireworks; photographs by Michael Gold. Millbrook Press 2005 48p il (Where's the science here?) lib bdg $23.93

Grades: 3 4 5 **662**

1. Fireworks

ISBN 0-7613-2771-1

LC 2004-29823

"From pictures of different types of display formations to those of chemicals being loaded into mortar tubes, readers will find interesting illustrations that support the text in Fireworks. They will learn about the science of pyrotechnics and be exposed to words like chemical reaction, combustion, and lift charges. Sections offer a historical overview of the evolution of the study of fire, the mechanics of building fireworks . . . how explosions are timed, and how pyrotechnicians avoid nasty surprises." SLJ

Rau, Dana Meachen

Fireworks. Marshall Cavendish Benchmark 2010 24p il (Surprising science) $22.79

Grades: 2 3 4 **662**

1. Fireworks

ISBN 978-0-7614-4868-6; 0-7614-4868-3

LC 2009053723

This book "opens with the experience of watching fireworks, traces their history from China to Europe to colonial America, and discusses the rocketry and chemistry that make them possible. Although the discussions are relatively short, they provide good, basic knowledge as well as some intriguing details. . . . Rau provides information about the dangers of fireworks as well. . . . The book's paper quality and page layouts are quite good, maximizing the effectiveness of the clear, colorful photos and well-chosen period artworks that illustrate the text." Booklist

Includes glossary and bibliographical references

664 Food technology

Cobb, Vicki

Junk food; photographs by Michael Gold. Millbrook 2005 48p il (Where's the science here?) lib bdg $23.93

Grades: 3 4 5 **664**

1. Food industry 2. Food -- Composition

ISBN 0-7613-2773-8

The author "focuses on food chemistry, not nutrition, in examinations of six seductive snack foods (popcorn, corn chips, chocolate, candy, potato chips, and soda). Well-digested explanations and low-tech projects reinforce Cobb's reputation for snappy hands-on science writing for children. . . . Gold's photos stand well above those in most nonfiction science series and directly support Cobb's intentions." Booklist

Gardner, Robert

Ace your food science project; great science fair ideas. [by] Robert Gardner, Salvatore Tocci, and Thomas R. Rybolt. Enslow Publishers 2009 128p il (Ace your science project) lib bdg $31.93

Grades: 5 6 7 8 **664**

1. Food 2. Science projects 3. Science -- Experiments

ISBN 978-0-7660-3228-6 lib bdg; 0-7660-3228-0 lib bdg

LC 2008-49780

"Presents several science experiments and project ideas using food." Publisher's note

Includes bibliographical references

McCarthy, Meghan

★ **Pop!** the accidental invention of bubble gum. Simon & Schuster Books for Young Readers 2010 un il $15.99

Grades: 1 2 3 **664**

1. Bubble gum

ISBN 978-1-4169-7970-8; 1-4169-7970-0

LC 2008-49272

Traces the 1928 invention of bubble gum by a hardworking accountant at a candy company, describing how in his spare time he experimented with different recipes and ingredients to eventually create the product known today as Double Bubble.

"Kids who enjoy blowing gum bubbles may never have considered how the treat came to be, but here, in easy language and with amusing illustrations, McCarthy changes that..... The acrylic paintings portray humor throughout, in part by peopling the book with googly-eyed characters who are often chewing a wad of gum." Booklist

Petersen, Christine

The **miller**. Marshall Cavendish Benchmark 2011 il (Colonial people) $29.93

Grades: 3 4 5 6   664

1. Flour mills 2. United States -- History -- 1600-1775, Colonial period

ISBN 978-1-60870-416-3; 1-60870-416-5

LC 2010033890

This describes the life of a colonial miller and his importance to the community, as well as everyday life, responsibilities, and social practices during that time.

This "lively [text] and colorful reproductions and photos will engage casual readers and researchers alike. . . . Large illustrations and thoughtful captions explain complicated scientific ideas. . . . [The] volume also includes step-by-step instructions for a related craft project. . . . [This is a] must-have." SLJ

Includes glossary and bibliographical references

Ridley, Sarah

A **chocolate** bar; [by] Sarah Ridley. Gareth Stevens Pub. 2006 32p il (How it's made) lib bdg $23.93

Grades: 3 4 5   664

1. Chocolate

ISBN 0-8368-6293-7

LC 2005054075

First published 2005 in the United Kingdom

This presents "the origins of a chocolate bar, from a Ghana cocoa farm to a factory. The facts are clear and well organized; each spread shows a logical progression in the process, and sharp color photos and maps will help cement the concepts in readers' minds." Booklist

Rotner, Shelley

Where does food come from? by Shelley Rotner and Gary Goss; photographs by Shelley Rotner. Millbrook Press 2006 32p il lib bdg $22.60

Grades: K 1 2   664

1. Food 2. Food industry

ISBN 0-7613-2935-8

LC 2005000874

Explains where various foods originate from, how food is grown, and brought to supermarkets and other stores, in simple text with illustrations.

"Large print, a well-spaced text, varied typeface, simple explanations, and appealing color photos of children on every page make this book a pleasant reading experience. . . . This is a book that teachers, librarians, and parents will find useful, informative, and fun to share." SLJ

665 Technology of industrial oils, fats, waxes, gases

Walker, Niki

Hydrogen; running on water. [by] Niki Walker. Crabtree Pub. 2007 32p il (Energy revolution) lib bdg $25.20; pa $8.95

Grades: 5 6 7 8   665

1. Hydrogen as fuel

ISBN 978-0-7787-2915-0 lib bdg; 0-7787-2915-X lib bdg; 978-0-7787-2929-7 pa; 0-7787-2929-X pa

LC 2006014369

This describes various sources of hydrogen power, including natural gas, gasified coal, fuel from water, and biomass gas, and how it is stored and distributed, and offers energy conservation tips.

Includes glossary

665.5   Petroleum

Benduhn, Tea

Oil, gas, and coal; by Tea Benduhn. Weekly Reader Pub. 2009 24p il (Energy for today) lib bdg $21; pa $5.95

Grades: 2 3 4   665.5

1. Coal 2. Gasoline 3. Natural gas 4. Energy resources

ISBN 978-0-8368-9261-1 lib bdg; 0-8368-9261-5 lib bdg; 978-0-8368-9360-1 pa; 0-8368-9360-3 pa

LC 2008015517

This describes what fossil fuels are, how they work as energy sources, and their future.

"New readers will be able to wrap their hands around the small, square size, and their minds around the clear, enlightening text. [This book has] crisp photos and strong back matter." Booklist

Includes glossary and bibliographical references

Rockwell, Anne F.

What's so bad about gasoline? fossil fuels and what they do. by Anne Rockwell; illustrated by Paul Meisel. Collins 2009 33p il (Let's-read-and-find-out science) $16.99; pa $5.99

Grades: 1 2 3   665.5

1. Gasoline 2. Air pollution 3. Energy resources 4. Energy conservation 5. Greenhouse effect

ISBN 978-0-06-157528-0; 0-06-157528-3; 978-0-06-157527-3 pa; 0-06-157527-5 pa

LC 2007-52947

"Rockwell presents the basic facts about how gasoline is produced, how it was first discovered, and its uses. She then discusses how gasoline and other fossil fuels . . . have contributed to polluting the environment. Suggestions are offered on how to cut back our gas consumption, and alternatives such as solar power, wind power, nuclear energy, and alternative fuels are addressed. . . . Detailed pen-and-ink and watercolor drawings in shades of blue and brown appear throughout, and text balloons help provide humor to various scenarios." SLJ

666 Ceramic and allied technologies

Blaxland, Wendy

Bottles and jars. Marshall Cavendish Benchmark 2011 32p il map (How are they made?) lib bdg $28.50

Grades: 3 4 5 6   666
1. Plastics 2. Glassware 3. Glass -- History
ISBN 978-0-7614-4752-8 lib bdg; 0-7614-4752-0
lib bdg

LC 2009040080

This discusses how bottles and jars are made, including their history, raw materials, design, manufacture, packaging and distribution, marketing and advertising, and their relationship to the environment.

Includes glossary

Koscielniak, Bruce
Looking at glass through the ages; by Bruce Koscielniak. Houghton Mifflin Co. 2006 un $16
Grades: 3 4 5 6   666
1. Glass -- History
ISBN 0-618-50750-7

LC 2005003916

"A handsome book on the history of glassmaking. Starting with faience, developed in Egypt around 2500 B.C., the author's precisely worded, carefully detailed text and watercolor artwork explain the steps for producing various types of glass and glassware. . . . Much information is compacted into the smoothly written narrative. Captioned illustrations are well matched with the text and extend the information value of the book." SLJ

Petersen, Christine
The **glassblower**. Marshall Cavendish Benchmark 2011 il (Colonial people) $29.93
Grades: 3 4 5 6   666
1. Glassblowing 2. United States -- History -- 1600-1775; Colonial period
ISBN 978-1-60870-413-2; 1-60870-413-0

LC 2010033901

This describes the life of a colonial glassblower and his importance to the community, as well as everyday life, responsibilities, and social practices during that time.

This "lively [text] and colorful reproductions and photos will engage casual readers and researchers alike. . . . Large illustrations and thoughtful captions explain complicated scientific ideas. . . . [The] volume also includes step-by-step instructions for a related craft project. . . . [This is a] must-have." SLJ

Includes glossary and bibliographical references

Stewart, Melissa
How does sand become glass? Raintree 2010 32p il (How does it happen?) lib bdg $27.50; pa $7.99
Grades: 3 4 5   666
1. Sand 2. Glass 3. Erosion
ISBN 978-1-4109-3449-9 lib bdg; 1-4109-3449-7 lib bdg; 978-1-4109-3457-4 pa; 1-4109-3457-8 pa

LC 2008-52654

"Information is clearly presented using a large font, diagrams, and photographs formatted to resemble Polaroid pictures. . . . A first-rate job answering some important scientific questions." SLJ

Includes glossary and bibliographical references

668   Technology of other organic products

Wagner, Lisa, 1958-
Cool melt & pour soap; [by] Lisa Wagner. ABDO Pub. 2005 32p il (Cool crafts) lib bdg $22.78
Grades: 4 5 6   668
1. Soap 2. Handicraft
ISBN 1-59197-741-X

LC 2004-46291

This guide to soap crafting "discusses premade bases, coloring and fragrance, layered soaps, treasure-packed soaps, relief soaps, and packaging ideas." SLJ

668.4   Plastics

Langley, Andrew
Plastic; [by] Andrew Langley. Crabtree Pub. Co. 2009 24p il (Everyday materials) lib bdg $21.27; pa $6.95
Grades: K 1 2 3   668.4
1. Plastics
ISBN 978-0-7787-4129-9 lib bdg; 0-7787-4129-X lib bdg; 978-0-7787-4136-7 pa; 0-7787-4136-2 pa

LC 2008-25324

This title "introduces [plastics] in an engaging style. The text and photos work together, progressing from a definition of the material to how it is manufactured and what it is used for. . . . [It] concludes with a recycling section, a simple comprehension quiz, and a topic web that offers extension ideas. The large type, bright photos, and uncluttered layout will allow large and small group use." SLJ

Includes glossary

Morris, Neil
Plastics. Amicus 2010 48p il (Materials that matter) lib bdg $28.50
Grades: 4 5 6 7   668.4
1. Plastics
ISBN 978-1-60753-068-8 lib bdg; 1-60753-068-6 lib bdg

LC 2009051435

"The clean layout includes photographs and occasional charts, graphs, and technical illustrations against a range of pastel backgrounds. Inset boxes provide further detail, interesting extras, and recycling information. . . . [This book offers] easily accessible background information for report writers." SLJ

Includes glossary and bibliographical references

670   Manufacturing

Slavin, Bill
Transformed; how everyday things are made. written by Bill Slavin with Jim Slavin; illustrated by Bill Slavin. Kids Can Press 2005 160p il $24.95
Grades: 4 5 6 7   670
1. Manufactures
ISBN 1-55337-179-8

This describes the manufacture of such items "as baseballs, plastic dinosaurs, toothpaste, cereal, paper, and bricks. Each two-page spread covers the making of one of the 69 items in numbered paragraphs. The pictures are the best part—clear watercolor and ink images, made all the more engaging by folks in overalls directing the action." Booklist

Includes glossary and bibliographical references

671 Manufacture of products from specific materials

Blaxland, Wendy

Cans. Marshall Cavendish Benchmark 2011 32p il map (How are they made?) lib bdg $28.50

Grades: 3 4 5 6   **671**

1. Cans

ISBN 978-0-7614-4753-5 lib bdg; 0-7614-4753-9 lib bdg

LC 2009039876

This discusses how cans are made, including their history, raw materials, design, manufacture, packaging and distribution, marketing and advertising, production, and their relationship to the environment.

671.5 Joining and cutting of metals

Nelson, David Erik

Soldering; by David Erik Nelson. Cherry Lake Publishing 2015 32 p. color illustrations (21st Century skills innovation library. Makers as innovators) (lib. bdg.) $28.50

Grades: 4 5 6 7 8   **671.5**

1. Soldering 2. Metal-work

ISBN 1631377744; 9781631377747; 9781631377945

LC 2014005538

This juvenile manual, by David Erik Nelson, part of the "21st Century Skills Innovation Library: Makers As Innovators" series, teaches "how to solder electronic components together and build your own devices. Readers will learn basic soldering skills, which will be useful in pursuing a variety of engineering projects." (Publisher's note)

"Though not the most obvious fit into the 21st Century Skills Innovation Library series, this introduction to soldering provides DIYers with basic guidelines to a skill still useful for a variety of projects, from jewelry making and plumbing to creating or repairing electronic circuits. ..Color photos depict gear, a soldered electronic board, and a young solderer at work. This quick but utilitarian guide closes with leads to several more detailed print and online resources." Booklist

Includes bibliographical references and index

Other titles in the series include:

3D Modeling (2015)

3D Printing (2014)

Arduino (2014)

Digital Badges (2013)

E-textiles (2013)

Game Design (2014)

Maker Faire (2014)

Makerspaces (2014)

Raspberry Pi (2014)

Squishy Circuits (2014)

Web Design with HTML5 (2015)

674 Lumber processing, wood products, cork

Blaxland, Wendy

Pencils. Marshall Cavendish Benchmark 2009 32p il (How are they made?) $19.95

Grades: 3 4 5 6   **674**

1. Pencils

ISBN 978-0-7614-3807-6; 0-7614-3807-6

LC 2008026215

This describes how pencils are made, including raw materials, design, manufacture, and relationship to the environment.

675 Leather and fur processing

Petersen, Christine

The tanner. Marshall Cavendish Benchmark 2011 il (Colonial people) $29.93

Grades: 3 4 5 6   **675**

1. Leather industry 2. United States -- History -- 1600-1775, Colonial period

ISBN 978-1-60870-418-7; 1-60870-418-1

LC 2010033896

This describes the life of a colonial tanner and his importance to the community, as well as everyday life, responsibilities, and social practices during that time.

This "lively [text] and colorful reproductions and photos will engage casual readers and researchers alike. . . . Large illustrations and thoughtful captions explain complicated scientific ideas. . . . [The] volume also includes step-by-step instructions for a related craft project. . . . [This is a] must-have." SLJ

Includes glossary and bibliographical references

676 Pulp and paper technology

Langley, Andrew

Paper products; [by] Andrew Langley. Crabtree Pub. Co. 2009 24p il (Everyday materials) lib bdg $21.27; pa $6.95

Grades: K 1 2 3   **676**

1. Paper 2. Papermaking

ISBN 978-0-7787-4128-2 lib bdg; 0-7787-4128-1 lib bdg; 978-0-7787-4135-0 pa; 0-7787-4135-4 pa

LC 2008-24011

This title "introduces [paper products] in an engaging style. The text and photos work together, progressing from a definition of the material to how it is manufactured and what it is used for. . . . [It] concludes with a recycling section, a simple comprehension quiz, and a topic web that offers extension ideas. The large type, bright photos, and uncluttered layout will allow large and small group use." SLJ

Includes glossary

Morris, Neil

Paper. Amicus 2010 48p il (Materials that matter) lib bdg $28.50

Grades: 4 5 6 7　　　　　　　　　　　**676**
1. Paper
ISBN 978-1-60753-067-1 lib bdg; 1-60753-067-8 lib bdg

LC 2009051436

"The clean layout includes photographs and occasional charts, graphs, and technical illustrations against a range of pastel backgrounds. Inset boxes provide further detail, interesting extras, and recycling information. . . . [This book offers] easily accessible background information for report writers." SLJ

Includes glossary and bibliographical references

677　Textiles

Langley, Andrew
Wool; [by] Andrew Langley. Crabtree Pub. Co. 2009 24p il (Everyday materials) lib bdg $21.27; pa $6.95
Grades: K 1 2 3　　　　　　　　　　　**677**
1. Wool
ISBN 978-0-7787-4131-2 lib bdg; 0-7787-4131-1 lib bdg; 978-0-7787-4138-1 pa; 0-7787-4138-9 pa

LC 2008-25323

This title "introduces [wool] in an engaging style. The text and photos work together, progressing from a definition of the material to how it is manufactured and what it is used for. . . . [It] concludes with a recycling section, a simple comprehension quiz, and a topic web that offers extension ideas. The large type, bright photos, and uncluttered layout will allow large and small group use." SLJ

Includes glossary

Morris, Neil
Textiles. Amicus 2010 48p il (Materials that matter) lib bdg $28.50
Grades: 4 5 6 7　　　　　　　　　　　**677**
1. Fabrics
ISBN 978-1-60753-069-5 lib bdg; 1-60753-069-4 lib bdg

LC 2009051434

"The clean layout includes photographs and occasional charts, graphs, and technical illustrations against a range of pastel backgrounds. Inset boxes provide further detail, interesting extras, and recycling information. . . . [This book offers] easily accessible background information for report writers." SLJ

Includes glossary and bibliographical references

Sobol, Richard
★ The story of silk; from worm spit to woven scarves. Richard Sobol. Candlewick Press 2012 36 p. col. ill., col. maps (reinforced) $17.99
Grades: 2 3 4 5　　　　　　　　　　　**677**
1. Thailand 2. Silkworms 3. Silk 4. Silkworms
ISBN 0763641650; 9780763641658

LC 2012942294

This children's educational book answers the question "What does worm spit have to do with the world's most luxurious fabric? . . . Join author and photographer Richard Sobol as he picks up his camera once more and travels to a small village in Thailand for an in-depth exploration of the story of silk and the labor-intensive process of making it." (Publisher's note)

678　Elastomers and elastomer products

Allman, Toney
Recycled tires; by Toney Allman. Norwood House Press 2008 48p il (A great idea) lib bdg $25.27
Grades: 3 4 5 6　　　　　　　　　　　**678**
1. Tires 2. Recycling
ISBN 978-1-59953-197-7 lib bdg; 1-59953-197-6 lib bdg

LC 2008-15736

"'Describes the invention and development of recycled rubber tires." Publisher's note

Includes glossary and bibliographical references

680　Manufacture of products for specific uses

Tunis, Edwin
★ Colonial craftsmen and the beginnings of American industry; written and illustrated by Edwin Tunis. Johns Hopkins Univ. Press 1999 159p pa $18.95
Grades: 4 5 6 7　　　　　　　　　　　**680**
1. Handicraft 2. Decorative arts 3. United States -- Social life and customs -- 1600-1775, Colonial period
ISBN 0-8018-6228-0

LC 99-20398

The author describes the working methods and products, houses and shops, town and country trades, individual and group enterprises by which the early Americans forged the economy of the New World. He discusses such trades as papermaking, glassmaking, shipbuilding, printing, and metalworking

"An oversize book that is impressively handsome and that should be tremendously useful; well-organized and superbly illustrated, the text is comprehensive, lucid, and detailed. . . . An extensive index is appended." Chicago. Children's Book Center

681　Precision instruments and other devices

Rau, Dana Meachen
Become an explorer; make and use a compass. Norwood House Press 2010 48p il (Creative adventure guides) lib bdg $25.27
Grades: 3 4 5 6　　　　　　　　　　　**681**
1. Compass
ISBN 978-1-59953-383-4; 1-59953-383-9

LC 2010010359

"Some historical background and scientific or cultural information places the making and use of . . . compasses in context for young readers. [The] book has four chapters that culminate in step-by-step projects." Horn Book Guide

Includes glossary and bibliographical references

682 Small forge work (Blacksmithing)

Petersen, Christine
The **blacksmith**. Marshall Cavendish Benchmark 2010 48p il (Colonial people) lib bdg $29.93
Grades: 3 4 5 6 **682**
1. Blacksmithing 2. United States -- History -- 1600-1775, Colonial period
ISBN 978-0-7614-4799-3; 0-7614-4799-7

This describes the life of a colonial blacksmith and his importance to the community, as well as everyday life, responsibilities, and social practices during that time.

"The type font, just slightly larger than usual, makes the text very visually appealing. . . . [The] book is liberally illustrated with artwork dating from the colonial period . . . [and] information boxes offer supplemental material." Libr Media Connect

Includes glossary and bibliographical references

683 Hardware and household appliances

Blaxland, Wendy
Knives and forks. Marshall Cavendish Benchmark 2009 32p il (How are they made?) $19.95
Grades: 3 4 5 6 **683**
1. Cutlery 2. Tableware
ISBN 978-0-7614-3805-2; 0-7614-3805-X
LC 2008026214

This describes how knives and forks are made, including their history, raw materials, design, manufacture, and relationship to the environment.

683.4 Small firearms

Mara, Wil
The **gunsmith**; Wil Mara. Marshall Cavendish 2013 48 p.
Grades: 3 4 5 6 **683.4**
1. Guns -- United States -- History 2. United States -- History -- 1600-1775, Colonial period 3. United States -- Social life and customs -- To 1775 4. Gunsmiths -- United States -- History -- 17th century 5. Gunsmiths -- United States -- History -- 18th century 6. Gunsmithing -- United States -- History -- 17th century 7. Gunsmithing -- United States -- History -- 18th century 8. United States -- History -- Colonial period, ca. 1600-1775
ISBN 9781608704149; 9781608709854
LC 2011028342

This book on gunsmiths in colonial America, by Wil Mara, is part of the Colonial People series. It "traces the increasing use of guns and their manufacture in the colonies from the early 1600s to the late 1700s. . . . The informative text is illustrated with tinted engravings and paintings from earlier eras as well as . . . color photos of artifacts and replicas and reenactments of historical trades in Colonial Williamsburg." (Booklist)

"These excellent titles provide context about when people working during the colonial period would have first come to America and why, how they fit into the community, and the skills and tools required for their jobs...Illustrations include some period engravings and paintings, but primar-

ily use photographs from modern interpreters, such as the Colonial Williamsburg Foundation...Many libraries own Leonard Everett Fisher's "Colonial Craftsmen" titles (Cavendish Square); the intricate pictorial spreads in those titles portray craft procedures in wonderful detail, but the text is difficult for elementary students. This new series is much easier for children to navigate and understand." (School Library Journal)

Includes bibliographical references and indexes

684 Furnishings and home workshops

Robertson, J. Craig
The **kids'** building workshop; 15 woodworking projects for kids and parents to build together. [by] J. Craig and Barbara Robertson, with their daughters Camille and Allegra. Storey Kids 2004 136p il $22.96; pa $12.95
Grades: 3 4 5 6 **684**
1. Woodwork
ISBN 1-58017-572-4; 1-58017-488-4 pa
LC 2004-1521

"The first section, 'Setting Up Shop: Getting to Know Your Tools,' includes a basic introduction to hammering, sawing, drilling, block planing, and measuring. Next, 'Down to Business: Building Your Own Projects' puts these tools and techniques to work in simple, yet cleverly designed, kid-friendly projects that increase in complexity. . . . Clear instructions, black-and-white photos, and cutting diagrams are included for each one. . . . Practical and enjoyable introduction to the subject." SLJ

685 Leather and fur goods, and related products

Blaxland, Wendy
Sneakers. Marshall Cavendish Benchmark 2009 32p il (How are they made?) $19.95
Grades: 4 5 6 **685**
1. Sneakers
ISBN 978-0-7614-3810-6; 0-7614-3810-6
LC 2008026211

This is an "introduction to athletic shoes and the global trade involved in their manufacture and marketing. . . . A typical page offers a paragraph or more of informative text as well as a color photo and, perhaps, a small sidebar." Booklist

Cobb, Vicki
Sneakers; photographs by Michael Gold. Millbrook Press 2006 48p il (Where's the science here?) lib bdg $23.93
Grades: 3 4 5 **685**
1. Sneakers
ISBN 0-7613-2772-X
LC 2004-29816

"From photographs of the inside of a sneaker factory to X-rays of the foot to a picture of how rubber is extracted from a rubber tree, readers will find a new angle to spark their interest in Sneakers. They will learn about how sneakers are designed and made, and even how to test their fit. [An] attractive [choice] that [relates] science to [a topic] that fascinate kids." SLJ

D'Cruz, Anna-Marie
    Make your own slippers and shoes. PowerKids Press 2009 24p il (Do it yourself projects!) lib bdg $23.95; pa $9.40

Grades: 2 3 4   **685**
    1. Shoes 2. Handicraft
    ISBN 978-1-4358-2852-0 lib bdg; 1-4358-2852-6 lib bdg; 978-1-4358-2921-3 pa; 1-4358-2921-2 pa
                            LC 2008033669

Learn how to make different types of shoes from around the world using easy-to-find materials.
    Includes glossary and bibliographical references

Heinrichs, Ann
    The **shoemaker**. Marshall Cavendish Benchmark 2010 48p il (Colonial people) lib bdg $29.93

Grades: 3 4 5 6   **685**
    1. Shoemakers 2. United States -- History -- 1600-1775, Colonial period
    ISBN 978-0-7614-4798-6; 0-7614-4798-9
                            LC 2009007938

This describes the life of a colonial shoemaker and his importance to the community, as well as everyday life, responsibilities, and social practices during that time
    "The type font, just slightly larger than usual, makes the text very visually appealing. . . . [The] book is liberally illustrated with artwork dating from the colonial period . . . [and] information boxes offer supplemental material." Libr Media Connect
    Includes glossary and bibliographical references

686   Printing and related activities

D'Cruz, Anna-Marie
    Make your own books. PowerKids Press 2009 24p il (Do it yourself projects!) lib bdg $23.95; pa $9.40

Grades: 2 3 4   **686**
    1. Books 2. Handicraft 3. Bookbinding
    ISBN 978-1-4358-2855-1 lib bdg; 1-4358-2855-0 lib bdg; 978-1-4358-2927-5 pa; 1-4358-2927-1 pa
                            LC 2008033659

Projects for creating many different kinds of books from easy-to-find materials
    Includes glossary and bibliographical references

Petersen, Christine
    The **printer**. Marshall Cavendish Benchmark 2010 48p il (Colonial people) lib bdg $29.93

Grades: 3 4 5 6   **686**
    1. Printing -- History 2. United States -- History -- 1600-1775, Colonial period
    ISBN 978-0-7614-4802-0; 0-7614-4802-0
                            LC 2009044588

This describes the life of a colonial printer and his importance to the community, as well as everyday life, responsibilities, and social practices during that time.
    "The type font, just slightly larger than usual, makes the text very visually appealing. . . . [The] book is liberally illustrated with artwork dating from the colonial period . . . [and] information boxes offer supplemental material." Libr Media Connect
    Includes glossary and bibliographical references

686.2   Printing

Adler, David A.
    A **picture** book of Louis Braille; illustrated by John & Alexandra Wallner. Holiday House 1997 un il $16.95; pa $6.95

Grades: 1 2 3   **686.2**
    1. Blind 2. Inventors 3. Teachers of the blind 4. Blind -- Books and reading
    ISBN 0-8234-1291-1; 0-8234-1413-2 pa
                            LC 96-38453

Presents the life of the nineteenth-century Frenchman, accidentally blinded as a child, who originated the raised dot system of reading and writing used by the blind throughout the world
    "The text is simple yet informative. . . . Adler sprinkles in interesting facts about early 19th-century France that help readers better grasp Braille's world. . . . Softly colored illustrations in line and watercolor add visual clues for younger children." SLJ

Koscielniak, Bruce
    Johann Gutenberg and the amazing printing press. Houghton Mifflin Co. 2003 un il $16

Grades: 2 3 4   **686.2**
    1. Inventors 2. Printers 3. Printing -- History
    ISBN 0-618-26351-9
                            LC 2002-151176

A history of the modern printing industry, including how paper and ink are made, looking particularly at the printing press invented by Gutenberg around 1450 but also at its precursors
    "The pleasing line drawings and the subtle hues of Boscielniak's watercolors give the illustrations an informal look that makes their informative content all the more accessible." Booklist

687   Clothing and accessories

Kent, Peter
    Peter Kent's big book of armor; from armadillos to armored cars. Kingfisher 2010 64p il $16.99

Grades: 1 2 3 4   **687**
    1. Armor
    ISBN 978-0-7534-6423-6; 0-7534-6423-3

Describes the history of armor and protective clothing, from prehistoric protection and the armors of ancient Egypt and Assyria to medieval and modern armor, armored transport, and fortified buildings.
    "With its broad definition of armor and the plentiful color illustrations, this informative volume will appeal to a large audience for pleasure reading, as well as providing a solid volume for research purposes." Libr Media Connect
    Includes glossary

688.7   Recreational equipment

Bedford, Allan
    The **unofficial** LEGO builder's guide; by Allan Bedford. No Starch Press 2005 xviii, 319 p.p $24.95

Grades: 4 5 6 7 8   **688.7**
   1. LEGO toys
   ISBN 1593270542; 1593274416; 9781593274412
       LC 2005013747

This is a handbook about building LEGO structures. "Starting with the basic structure, anatomy, and flexibility of the Lego system, readers are taught different building techniques to add stability and ideas to their creations. Much of the book is devoted to the kinds of scale used in the Lego world and provides mathematical explanations for one's work. Chapters on sculpting and mosaic-making are also" offered. (School Library Journal)

Blaxland, Wendy
   Basketballs. Marshall Cavendish Benchmark 2011 32p il map (How are they made?) lib bdg $28.50
Grades: 3 4 5 6   **688.7**
   1. Basketball 2. Sporting goods
   ISBN 978-0-7614-4751-1 lib bdg; 0-7614-4751-2 lib bdg
       LC 2009039874

This book "starts out with the raw materials used to make [basketballs]. . . . Next, [a] time [line] handily [sums] up basketball from 1891 to 1992, when composite rubber balls were developed. . . . Design and stages of production are then explained. . . . Nicely designed and well executed." SLJ

Includes glossary

Fridell, Ron
   Sports technology. Lerner Publications 2009 48p il (Cool science) lib bdg $27.93
Grades: 4 5 6   **688.7**
   1. Sports 2. Technology
   ISBN 978-0-8225-7587-0 lib bdg; 0-8225-7587-6 lib bdg
       LC 2007050905

This describes "how science helps athletes stay safer, perform better, and have more fun." Publisher's notes
Includes glossary and bibliographical references

Hirschmann, Kris
   LEGO toys. Norwood House Press 2008 48p il (A great idea) lib bdg $25.27
Grades: 3 4 5 6   **688.7**
   1. Toys 2. LEGO (Firm)
   ISBN 978-1-59953-194-6 lib bdg; 1-59953-194-1 lib bdg
       LC 2008010712

Describes the invention and development of LEGO toys
"Full-color photographs and copious fun facts help make this . . . enjoyable reading, but it's really the choice of [topic] that is so enthralling." Booklist
Includes glossary and bibliographical references

Oxlade, Chris
   Gadgets and games; Chris Oxlade. Capstone Heinemann Library 2013 56 p. col. ill. (Design and engineering for STEM) (library) $33.50; (paperback) $9.49
Grades: 5 6 7   **688.7**
   1. Electronics 2. Industrial design 3. Product life cycle 4. Toys -- Design and construction 5. Household appliances -- Design and construction 6. Electronic

apparatus and appliances -- Design and construction
   ISBN 1432970364; 9781432970314; 9781432970369
       LC 2012013468

This book, part of the Design and Engineering for STEM series, looks at electronic devices and mobile games. It looks at the life cycle of these items, or "the stages from their design, manufacture, and sale to their use, maintenance, and disposal." Topics include "prototyping, the sourcing of components, the production process, the decisions made by designers and engineers, and recycling." (Publisher's note)
Includes bibliographical references (p. 54) and index.

Ross, Stewart
   Sports technology. Smart Apple Media 2011 il (New technology)
Grades: 4 5 6 7   **688.7**
   1. Sports
   ISBN 1-599-20534-3; 978-1-599-20534-2
       LC 2010044241

Describes the technological advances in the sports industry, including the technology used to create better equipment, sports wear, judging tools, and playing surfaces.
This "offers a fine overview for reports, and its attractive design may also entice middle-grade readers to learn more." Booklist

Wulffson, Don L.
   Toys! amazing stories behind some great inventions. [by] Don Wulffson; with illustrations by Laurie Keller. Holt & Co. 2000 137p il $16.95
Grades: 4 5 6 7   **688.7**
   1. Toys 2. Inventions
   ISBN 0-8050-6196-7
       LC 99-58440

Describes the creation of a variety of toys and games, from seesaws to Silly Putty and toy soldiers to Trivial Pursuit
"Each of the 25 chapters is illustrated with small, humorous drawings and discusses a particular toy or game's origin and development. The book ends with a bibliography and a list of Web sites. Good, readable fare for browsing or light research." Booklist
Includes bibliographical references

688.72   Toys

Rothrock, Megan
   The **LEGO** adventure book; cars, castles, dinosaurs & more! Megan Rothrock. No Starch Press 2013 199 p. [Vol. 1] $24.95
Grades: 4 5 6 7 8 9   **688.72**
   1. LEGO toys 2. Models and modelmaking
   ISBN 1593274424; 9781593274429
       LC 2012033902

This book on LEGO building, by Megan Rothrock, "is filled with bright visuals, step-by-step breakdowns of 25 models, and nearly 200 example models from the world's best builders. Learn to build robots, trains, medieval villages, spaceships, airplanes, and much more." (Publisher's note)
"LEGO enthusiast Megs builds an Idea Lab for creating projects and, with its completion, travels by Transport-O-lux to see what others are inspired to make...This one certainly

won't sit on shelves. A fun read for LEGO fans of all ages."
SLJ

Cars, castles, dinosaurs & more!
Cars, castles, dinosaurs and more!

Schwartz, Jordan

The **art** of LEGO design; creative ways to build amazing models. Jordan Schwartz. No Starch Press 2014 267 p. (pbk.) $24.95

Grades: 4 5 6 7 8 9   **688.72**
1. LEGO toys 2. LEGO toys -- Design and construction
ISBN 1593275536; 9781593275532

LC 2013048974

This book, by Jordan Schwartz, "explores LEGO as an artistic medium. This wide-ranging collection of creative techniques will help you craft your own amazing models as you learn to see the world through the eyes of some of the greatest LEGO builders. Each concept is presented with a collection of impressive models to spark your imagination, like fantastic dragons, futuristic spaceships, expressive characters, and elaborate dioramas." (Publisher's note)

"Part inspirational guide and part project design manual, the book encourages creativity and ingenuity while educating builders about the customs of the LEGO community (e.g., never paint LEGOs). There are helpful sections designed for novices that suggest how to organize workspace, find inspiration, select tools, and prepare for projects, while more advanced builders might embrace sections about developing personal style, sharing models publicly, and using feedback to enhance skills...The creative thinking process conveyed in the book is fascinating and could inspire non-LEGO builders (e.g., writers and painters) in their innovative efforts." VOYA

690 Construction of buildings

Barton, Byron

Building a house. Greenwillow Books 1981 un il lib bdg $17.89; pa $6.99

Grades: PreK K 1   **690**
1. House construction
ISBN 978-0-688-84291-8 lib bdg; 0-688-84291-7 lib bdg; 978-0-688-09356-3 pa; 0-688-09356-6 pa

"In the simplest possible book on building a house, a step-by-step, one-line description is given of the major factors in construction. Such workers as bricklayers, carpenters, plumbers, electricians, and painters do their own jobs until the small, bright red-and-green house is completed and a family moves in. Flat drawings in brilliant primary colors enable the very young to visualize the methods of house-building." Horn Book

★ **Machines** at work. Crowell 1987 un il $17.99; bd bk $7.99

Grades: PreK K 1   **690**
1. Building
ISBN 0-694-00190-2; 0-694-01107-X bd bk

LC 86-24221

"The short, punchy narrative reinforces the dynamics of the illustrations. . . . . This should be a popular read-aloud for preschoolers and satisfying read-alone for beginners." Publ Wkly

Byers, Ann

Jobs as green builders and planners. Rosen Pub. 2010 80p il (Green careers) lib bdg $30.60

Grades: 5 6 7 8   **690**
1. Building 2. Vocational guidance 3. Environmental science
ISBN 978-1-4358-3566-5 lib bdg; 1-4358-3566-2 lib bdg

LC 2009015517

This "well-conceived [introduction focuses] on various jobs in [building and construction planning], the education and experience required, and expected earnings. The [book is] well organized, making it easy to gain an overview of the major aspects of the work. . . . [This book] will make [a] good [addition] to career collections. Photographs from the field and website and contact information for professional organizations add value." SLJ

Includes glossary and bibliographical references

Dillon, Patrick

The **Story** of buildings; from the pyramids to the Sydney Opera House and beyond. Patrick Dillon, illustrated by Stephen Biesty. Candlewick Press 2014 96 p. $19.99

Grades: 5 6 7 8   **690**
1. Building 2. Buildings 3. Architecture 4. Architecture -- History
ISBN 0763669903; 9780763669904

LC 2013943096

This book, by Patrick Dillon and illustrated by Stephen Biesty, is a "narrative history of buildings. . . . Why and how did people start making buildings? How did they learn to make them stronger, bigger, and more comfortable? Why did they start to decorate them in different ways? . . . Dillon's stories of remarkable buildings—and the remarkable people who made them—celebrates the ingenuity of human creation." (Publisher's note)

"This large, handsome volume combines broad discussions of architectural history with exceptional drawings of significant buildings from ancient to modern times... Through his signature cross sections, details of interiors and construction can be seen as well. While the text, illustrations, and captions all provide information, it's the drawings of buildings that make this a valuable resource. " Booklist

Gibbons, Gail

How a house is built. Holiday House 1990 un il $16.95; pa $6.95

Grades: K 1 2 3   **690**
1. Houses 2. Building
ISBN 0-8234-0841-8; 0-8234-1232-6 pa

LC 90-55107

This book describes how the surveyor, heavy machinery operators, carpenter crew, plumbers, and other workers build a house

"With her customary bright illustrations, Gibbons gives a fine introduction to the construction of a wood-frame house. . . . Construction machines and materials as well as parts of the house are identified, and each stage of construction logically follows the others. Workers are drawn in both sexes and several skin tones." Booklist

Hudson, Cheryl Willis

★ **Construction** zone; photographs by Richard Sobol; text by Cheryl Willis Hudson. Candlewick Press 2006 un il $15.99

Grades: 2 3 4   690

1. Building

ISBN 0-7636-2684-8

"Large photographs of the construction of the MIT Stata Center in Cambridge, MA, are the core of this book. The simple text explains the process from the design by Frank O. Gehry to the completed building. Construction-zone activity, equipment, and jargon are pictured and explained. . . . Words in bold . . . are defined and explained at the bottom of the page on which they appear. . . . Children will be fascinated by both the picture story and the informative text." SLJ

Newhouse, Maxwell

The **house** that Max built. Tundra Books 2008 un il $18.95

Grades: K 1 2 3   690

1. House construction

ISBN 978-0-88776-774-6; 0-88776-774-5

"When Max decides to build a house beside the lake, 'he needs a lot of help.' This simple introduction takes readers through the major steps of the construction, from the architect's drawings to the completed house. In one or two sentences per page, the present-tense narrative neatly applies the personal viewpoint of the homeowner to each construction phase. . . . Warmly rendered folk-art-style oil paintings show the house coming together over time. . . . [This has] strong visual appeal and just enough detail." SLJ

Ritchie, Scot

Look at that building! a first book of structures. written and illustrated by Scot Ritchie. Kids Can Press 2011 32 p. col. ill. (hardcover) $16.95

Grades: PreK K 1 2 3 4   690

1. Houses 2. Buildings 3. Picture books for children 4. Building

ISBN 1554536960; 9781554536962

This book introduces young readers to basic construction concepts through the eyes of five friends keen on building a doghouse for their pet pooch, Max. To find out more about the task, Yulee, Martin, Nick, Sally and Pedro head to the library, where they learn about foundations, beams, frames and other building fundamentals.

"Winsome cartoon art shows a mutlicultural group of friends taking steps to tackle their project. . . . Budding architects and anyone researching the process will appreciate this colorful overview." Booklist

Schwarz, Renee

Birdfeeders. Kids Can Press 2005 40p il (Kids can do it) $12.95; pa $6.95

Grades: 4 5 6   690

1. Bird feeders

ISBN 1-55337-699-4; 1-55337-700-1 pa

This offers instructions for constructing nine types of bird feeders composed of recycled or common household materials such as flowerpots, juice cans, Frisbees and ketchup bottles.

Birdhouses. Kids Can Press 2005 40p il (Kids can do it) $12.95; pa $6.95

Grades: 4 5 6   690

1. Woodwork 2. Birdhouses

ISBN 1-55337-549-1; 1-55337-550-5 pa

This "shows and tells how to build nine birdhouses using inexpensive materials such as wood, plastic drainage pipes, flower pots, and even an old boot. . . . Small, clear pictures illustrate the step-by-step directions." Booklist

Somervill, Barbara A.

Green general contractor. Cherry Lake Pub. 2011 32p il (Cool careers) lib bdg $27.07

Grades: 4 5 6 7   690

1. Building 2. Vocational guidance 3. Sustainable architecture

ISBN 978-1-60279-987-5; 1-60279-987-3

LC 2010029535

This book begins "with a personal story of a teen and then [segues] into the occupation [of general contractor]. . . . [It covers] the necessary training and skills for the job (and options for obtaining them), a typical day, salary expectations, and well-known professionals in the field. The [text is] accessible and clearly written. . . . The [volume has] a generous number of clear color photographs that depict people at work." SLJ

Includes glossary and bibliographical references

694   Wood construction

Walker, Lester

Carpentry for children; preface by David Macaulay. Overlook Press 1982 208p il hardcover o.p. pa $14.95

Grades: 4 5 6 7   694

1. Carpentry 2. Handicraft

ISBN 0-87951-990-8 pa

LC 82-3469

A step-by-step guide to carrying out such carpentry projects as a birdhouse, candle chandelier, doll cradle, puppet theater, and coaster car

696   Utilities

Gregory, Josh

Plumber. Cherry Lake Pub. 2011 32p il (Cool careers) lib bdg $27.07

Grades: 4 5 6 7   696

1. Plumbing 2. Vocational guidance

ISBN 978-1-60279-984-4; 1-60279-984-9

LC 2010029538

This book begins "with a personal story of a teen and then [segues] into the occupation [of plumber]. . . . [It covers] the necessary training and skills for the job (and options for obtaining them), a typical day, salary expectations, and wellknown professionals in the field. The [text is] accessible and clearly written. . . . The [volume has] a generous number of clear color photographs that depict people at work." SLJ

Includes glossary and bibliographical references

Raum, Elizabeth

★ The **story** behind toilets. Heinemann Library 2009 32p il (True stories) $19.75

Grades: 2 3 4 **696**

1. Toilets

ISBN 978-1-4329-2350-1; 1-4329-2350-1

LC 2008037392

"Virtually everything related to toilets is covered, from the bodily functions that require such facilities all the way to the technology of the toilets of tomorrow. . . . 'A Short History of Toilets' is the most surprising chapter, with its running time line of toilet innovations. . . . Raum has the arcana down. . . . But there's real educational value here, too, notably in the discussion of sewage plants, the debate over pay toilets, the international scope of health problems related to poor sanitation, and the twisty time line that ends the book." Booklist

Includes bibliographical references

700 ARTS

700 The arts

Ajmera, Maya

★ To be an artist; [by] Maya Ajmera & John D. Ivanko; foreword by Jacques d'Amboise. Charlesbridge 2004 un il $15.95

Grades: K 1 2 3 **700**

1. Arts

ISBN 1-57091-503-2

LC 2003-8154

This includes "photographs of youngsters from many different countries engaged in a variety of art forms, including dancing, singing, writing, and painting. The bold text introduces each discipline and is supported with more extensive descriptions of the individual endeavors and the nature of artistic expression in general. . . . This vibrant book pulsates with the energy and sense of accomplishment that accompanies participation in the arts." SLJ

Apodaca, Blanca

Behind the canvas; an artist's life. by Blanka Apodaca and Michael Serwich. Teacher Created Materials 2012 48 p. (paperback) $8.96; (prebind) $18.99

Grades: 4 5 6 **700**

1. Artists 2. Art -- Technique

ISBN 1433348268; 145177074X; 9781433348266; 9781451770742

This book is part of the TIME for Kids Nonfiction Readers series and looks at the lives of artists. "Most of the books tie the subject to related professions, sharing ways in which students could help solve the dilemmas. . . . Colorful photographs with extensive captioning, 'Dig Deeper' sections that provide added detail and ask probing questions, diagrams, and informative maps all help guide students." (Library Media Connection)

McArthur, Meher

An ABC of what art can be; pictures by Esther Pearl Watson. J. Paul Getty Museum 2010 un il $17.95

Grades: 2 3 4 5 **700**

1. Art 2. Alphabet

ISBN 978-0-89236-999-7; 0-89236-999-X

LC 2009-15387

"This lighthearted artist's alphabet finds inspiration from many forms. . . . Each page is unique in the color and style choices enriching the text and is unified by the collage style used throughout. . . . Watson's fun-loving illustrations are a good match for McArthur's rhyming text. An enjoyable alphabet for young artists." SLJ

Speaking of art; colorful quotes by famous painters. edited by Bob Raczka. Millbrook Press 2010 31 p. col. ill.

Grades: 3 4 5 **700**

1. Art 2. Artists -- Quotations 3. Art -- Quotations, maxims, etc

ISBN 9780761350545

LC 2009023484

This book presents information about eighteen famous artists and answers questions such as "When did Vincent Van Gogh feel most alive? Why did Juan Gris always pet a dog with his left hand? . . . Art lover [and author] Bob Raczka pairs . . . quotes by famous painters with . . . examples of their best work. The result is a . . . gallery of observations about the joys and the mysteries of art. From Edgar Degas' The Rehearsal (1878-79) to Georgia O'Keeffe's Evening Star, No. III (1917) to Romare Bearden's Family (1986), you'll discover the works - and the wisdom - of eighteen artistic masters." (Publisher's note)

Includes bibliographical references

700.9 History, geographic treatment, biography of the arts

Flatt, Lizann

Arts and culture in the early Islamic world; Lizann Flatt. Crabtree Pub. Company 2012 48 p. col. ill., col. map (Life in the early Islamic world) (reinforced library binding; alk. paper) $30.60

Grades: 5 6 7 **700.9**

1. Islamic art 2. Islamic civilization 3. Islamic art

ISBN 0778721671; 9780778721673; 9780778721741; 9781427195609; 9781427198372

LC 2012000074

This book by Lizann Flatt is part of the "Life in the Early Islamic World" series. It "introduces the important roles that many of the arts, but especially calligraphy, architecture, and the decorative arts, have had in Islamic culture, in which art is meant to be 'useful as well as beautiful.'" (Booklist) "The main texts are supplemented with blue boxes of information, subsections, and many high-quality reproductions, maps, and paintings." (School Library Journal)

701 Philosophy and theory of fine and decorative arts

Benduhn, Tea

What is color? Crabtree Pub. Co. 2009 24p il (Get art smart) lib bdg $15.95; pa $6.95

Grades: K 1 2 3 **701**

1. Color in art

ISBN 978-0-7787-5123-6 lib bdg; 0-7787-5123-6 lib bdg; 978-0-7787-5137-3 pa; 0-7787-5137-6 pa

LC 2009-22914

Isolates the artistic element of color, discusses what thoughts and feelings can be conveyed by different colors, and examines how they contribute to a work of art through various examples

This book has a "first-person plural tone that uses accessible, well-thought-out phrases. Concrete visual examples are in the form of frequent and excellent reproductions of fine art in a variety of mediums. . . . [A] respectable and respectful resource[s]." SLJ

Includes glossary and bibliographical references

What is shape? Crabtree Pub. 2009 24p il (Get art smart) lib bdg $15.95; pa $6.95
Grades: K 1 2 3   **701**
  1. Shape
ISBN 978-0-7787-5139-7 lib bdg; 0-7787-5139-2 lib bdg; 978-0-7787-5125-0 pa; 0-7787-5125-2 pa

This describes how shapes of all kinds, including geometric shapes and the organic shapes found in nature, can be used in art.

This book has a "first-person plural tone that uses accessible, well-thought-out phrases. Concrete visual examples are in the form of frequent and excellent reproductions of fine art in a variety of mediums. . . . [A] respectable and respectful resource[s]." SLJ

Includes glossary and bibliographical references

Ehlert, Lois
  ★ **Color** zoo. Lippincott 1989 un il $17.99; lib bdg $17.89; bd bk $7.99
Grades: PreK K 1   **701**
  1. Color 2. Shape
ISBN 0-397-32259-3; 0-397-32260-7 lib bdg; 0-694-01067-7 bd bk

LC 87-17065

A Caldecott Medal honor book, 1990

"Not only an effective method for teaching basic concepts, the book is also a means for sharpening visual perception, which encourages children to see these shapes in other contexts." Horn Book

Fitzgerald, Stephanie
  What is texture? Crabtree Pub. Co. 2009 24p il (Get art smart) lib bdg $15.95; pa $6.95 **701**
  1. Handicraft 2. Art -- Technique
ISBN 978-0-7787-5127-4 lib bdg; 0-7787-5127-9 lib bdg; 978-0-7787-5141-0 pa; 0-7787-5141-4 pa

LC 2009-22917

Introduces different kinds of texture and how they are used in art, and includes information on making a rubbing

This book has a "first-person plural tone that uses accessible, well-thought-out phrases. Concrete visual examples are in the form of frequent and excellent reproductions of fine art in a variety of mediums. . . . [A] respectable and respectful resource[s]." SLJ

Includes glossary and bibliographical references

Gonyea, Mark
  ★ A **book** about color. Henry Holt & Co. 2010 un il $19.99
Grades: 1 2 3 4 5   **701**
  1. Color in art
ISBN 978-0-8050-9055-0; 0-8050-9055-X

"Topics presented include primary and secondary colors, warm and cool colors, saturation, and the addition of black and white. In the digital illustrations, simple forms in solid colors stand out sharply against white or other solid backgrounds. . . . This attractive volume offers plenty to observe, ponder, and discuss." Booklist

Hensley, Laura
  Art for all; what is public art? Raintree 2010 32p il (Culture in action) $29
Grades: 5 6 7 8   **701**
  1. Art
ISBN 978-1-4109-3923-4; 1-4109-3923-5

LC 2009051126

This "briefly surveys public art, from murals and graffiti to obelisks and religious statues. . . . A world map shows the locations of 16 public artworks mentioned in the text. . . . The quality of the illustrations is fine. . . . Given the book's broad scope and few pages, it accomplishes a good deal. Three activities, a time line, a glossary, and a brief bibliography round out this attractive presentation." Booklist

Includes glossary and bibliographical references

Kutschbach, Doris
  The **art** treasure hunt; I spy with my little eye. Doris Kutschbach. Prestel 2012 48 p. $14.95
Grades: 3 4 5   **701**
  1. Art 2. Painters 3. Picture books for children
ISBN 3791370979; 9783791370972

LC 2011942236

In this book, readers "are . . . challenged to find details 'hidden' in some of the world's greatest paintings. On each double-page spread, a large reproduction of a masterpiece such as Kandinsky's 'Heavenly Blue,' Seurat's 'A Sunday Afternoon on the Island of La Grande Jatte,' Rousseau's 'The Dream' or Breugel's 'Children's Games' is paired with a list of items to search for: a dog, an umbrella, or a ball, for instance." (Publisher's note)

Meredith, Susan
  What is form? by Susan Markowitz Meredith. Crabtree Pub. Co. 2009 24p il (Get art smart) lib bdg $15.95; pa $6.95
Grades: K 1 2 3   **701**
  1. Composition (Art)
ISBN 978-0-7787-5124-3 lib bdg; 0-7787-5124-4 lib bdg; 978-0-7787-5138-0 pa; 0-7787-5138-4 pa

Introduces the concept of form, demonstrates how it is used in art, and includes information on reliefs, sculpture, and identifying forms in everyday life

This book has a "first-person plural tone that uses accessible, well-thought-out phrases. Concrete visual examples are in the form of frequent and excellent reproductions of fine art in a variety of mediums. . . . [A] respectable and respectful resource[s]." SLJ

Includes glossary and bibliographical references

What is line? by Susan Markowitz Meredith. Crabtree Pub. Co. 2009 24p il (Get art smart) lib bdg $15.95; pa $6.95

Grades: K 1 2 3　　　**701**

1. Line (Art)

ISBN 978-0-7787-5122-9 lib bdg; 0-7787-5122-8 lib bdg; 978-0-7787-5136-6 pa; 0-7787-5136-8 pa

LC 2009-22912

Identifies lines in art and demonstrates how differently shaped lines are used to create texture, movement, patterns, and emotion.

This book has a "first-person plural tone that uses accessible, well-thought-out phrases. Concrete visual examples are in the form of frequent and excellent reproductions of fine art in a variety of mediums. . . . [A] respectable and respectful resource[s]." SLJ

Includes glossary and bibliographical references

What is space? by Susan Markowitz Meredith. Crabtree Pub. Co. 2009 24p il (Get art smart) lib bdg $15.95; pa $6.95

Grades: K 1 2 3　　　**701**

1. Space and time in art

ISBN 978-0-7787-5126-7 lib bdg; 0-7787-5126-0 lib bdg; 978-0-7787-5140-3 pa; 0-7787-5140-6 pa

Introduces the concept of space; how differences in space are used in art; and includes information on distance, form, and overlap.

This book has a "first-person plural tone that uses accessible, well-thought-out phrases. Concrete visual examples are in the form of frequent and excellent reproductions of fine art in a variety of mediums. . . . [A] respectable and respectful resource[s]." SLJ

Includes glossary and bibliographical references

Museum of Modern Art (New York, N.Y.)

Make art mistakes; an inspired sketchbook for everyone. Chronicle Books 2010 un il $16.99

Grades: 3 4 5 6　　　**701**

1. Art

ISBN 978-0-8118-7076-4; 0-8118-7076-6

"This lively sketchbook contains decorative graphic spreads and prompts that ask readers to integrate their own words and drawings. Quotations from artists such as O'Keeffe and Picasso invite deeper reflection on making art while loosely introducing themes on line, color, pattern, and texture. Most of the exercises emphasize free expression . . . while others introduce concepts like perspective. Young artists are likely to enjoy the balance between instruction and independent exploration." Publ Wkly

Renshaw, Amanda

★ The **art** book for children; [texts by Amanda Renshaw and Gilda Williams Ruggi] Phaidon Press 2005 79p il $19.95

Grades: 2 3 4 5　　　**701**

1. Art appreciation

ISBN 978-0-7148-4530-2

Invites the reader to take a closer look at art work while pointing out tiny details hidden in famous works of art, providing information about a work or an artist, or explaining the techniques used to create the pieces

This is "an excellent, accessible introduction to art that speaks directly to children without condescension." Booklist

★ The **art** book for children: book two; text by Amanda Renshaw. Phaidon Press 2007 79p il $19.95

Grades: 2 3 4 5　　　**701**

1. Art appreciation

ISBN 978-0-7148-4706-1

"Each double-page spread features a top-quality reproduction of an artwork, accompanied by simple text that will engage both young children and mature, independent readers. . . . The brief words . . . encourage viewers to imagine themselves in the scenes, to find objects in the compositions, or to reflect on the moods and activities depicted and in their own lives. This interactive approach creates a wonderful introduction to the history of Western art." Booklist

Tomecek, Steve

Art & architecture; by Stephen M. Tomecek. Chelsea House Publishers 2010 174p il (Experimenting with everyday science) $35

Grades: 4 5 6 7　　　**701**

1. Architecture 2. Art and science 3. Science -- Experiments 4. Art -- Study and teaching

ISBN 978-1-60413-168-0; 1-60413-168-3

LC 2009030195

"This fun and informative book features 25 simple experiments using common household items and foods such as blueberries, colored cellophane, food coloring, Magic Markers, miniature marshmallows, and wooden toothpicks to demonstrate principles and inspire creative thought about the intersection of science with the visual and mechanical arts. The six chapters include activities that illuminate certain scientific aspects of each respective subject. . . . Accessible for independent reading by children with a scientific bent or curiosity about how the world works, these experiments would also be useful for scout projects or science clubs." SLJ

Includes bibliographical references

702.8　Auxiliary techniques and procedures; apparatus, equipment, materials

Hanson, Anders

Cool collage; the art of creativity for kids! [by] Anders Hanson. ABDO Pub. Co. 2009 32p il (Cool art) lib bdg $24.21

Grades: 2 3 4　　　**702.8**

1. Collage

ISBN 978-1-60453-146-6 lib bdg; 1-60453-146-0 lib bdg

LC 2008-8641

This book about collage making is "well organized, with clearly written sections . . . and several clever projects and exercises. . . . [It] should have substantial child appeal." SLJ

Includes glossary

Luxbacher, Irene

1 2 3 I can collage! [by] Irene Luxbacher. Kids Can Press 2009 23p il (Starting art) $14.95; pa $6.95

Grades: 2 3 4　　　**702.8**

1. Collage

ISBN 978-1-55453-313-8; 1-55453-313-9; 978-1-55453-314-5 pa; 1-55453-314-7 pa

Collage activities with step-by-step instructions will help kids create a whale, a crab, a sea turtle and more.

Schwake, Susan

3-D art lab for kids; 36 hands-on adventures in sculpture and mixed media. Susan Schwake; Photogtraphy by Rainer Schwake. Quarry Books 2013 144 p. color illustrations (pbk.) $24.99

Grades: 4 5 6   **702.8**

1. Sculpture 2. Handicraft for children 3. Sculpture -- Technique 4. Mixed media (Art) -- Technique

ISBN 1592538150; 9781592538157

LC 2013012624

In this book, author Susan Schwake "combines 32 3-D art projects with interviews with four artists, each of whom is photographed. The first two chapters give general instructions for setting up for each project, providing an exhaustive list of materials needed. The subsequent five chapters each focus on a single medium: paper, clay, textiles, sculpture, and jewelry." (Booklist)

Vry, Silke

13 art illusions children should know; Silke Vry. Prestel Pub. Random House 2012 48 p. (hardcover) $14.95

Grades: 4 5 6   **702.8**

1. Optical illusions 2. Art

ISBN 379137110X; 9783791371108

LC 2012939037

This book by Silke Vry is part of the "Children Should Know" series. "This collection features artworks that incorporate a variety of methods for tricking our eyes: including trompe l'oeil, clever uses of color and perspective, Surrealism, and Photo-Realism. Arranged thematically, each work is presented in a two-page spread. . . . [T]exts explain the methods the artists employed to shape their illusions." (Publisher's note)

704   Special topics in fine and decorative arts

Barber, Nicola

★ Islamic empires; [by] Nicola Barber. Raintree 2005 48p il map (History in art) $31.43

Grades: 4 5 6 7   **704**

1. Islam 2. Islamic art

ISBN 1-4109-0522-5

LC 2004-7527

This is an introduction to the art, culture, and history of Islamic empires.

This book has "a depth of content that is unusual in art-history books for this age group. . . . [It] is amply illustrated with full-color photographs and reproductions. . . . Well-written, informative." SLJ

Includes bibliographical references

Coyne, Jennifer Tarr

Come look with me; discovering women artists for children; [by] Jennifer Tarr Coyne. Lickle 2005 32p il $15.95

Grades: 3 4 5   **704**

1. Women artists 2. Art appreciation

ISBN 1-890674-08-7

Introduces twelve women artists, including Faith Ringgold, Mary Cassatt, Frida Kahlo, and Grandma Moses, each with a short biography, a full-page color plate, a description of the image, and a set of discussion questions.

"This offering encourages children to learn biographical facts about artists and to look closely at the images and think about artistic decisions. . . . Each spread features a beautifully reproduced image." Booklist

Raczka, Bob

Before they were famous; how seven artists got their start. Millbrook Press 2010 32p il (Art adventures) $25.26

Grades: 4 5 6 7   **704**

1. Artists 2. Creative ability

ISBN 978-0-7613-6077-3; 0-7613-6077-8

LC 2009049596

"Short biographies written in conversational, jargon-free text introduce seven great artists, as young beginners and then as creators of famous works. From Dürer and Michelangelo to Picasso and Dali, the featured artists are presented chronologically on uncluttered, open spreads that include beautiful full-page reproductions. . . . Great preparation for a gallery visit, this will appeal to older readers, too, for its exciting, never-condescending talk about the pictures and the artists who created them." Booklist

Rolling, James Haywood

Come look with me: discovering African American art for children; [by] James Haywood Rolling, Jr. Lickle 2005 32p il $15.95

Grades: 3 4 5   **704**

1. Art appreciation 2. African American art

ISBN 1-890674-07-9

This volume presents 12 works of African American art "reproduced in full color and accompanied by descriptive information; the facing page contains several questions designed to engage young viewers and an adult in conversation as well as a few paragraphs of background. . . . Artists . . . include . . . Palmer Hayden and Clementine Hunter . . . Henry Ossawa Tanner, Romare Bearden, and Jacob Lawrence." SLJ

704.9   Iconography

Luxbacher, Irene

★ The jumbo book of outdoor art; written and illustrated by Irene Luxbacher. Kids Can Press 2006 144p il pa $16.95

Grades: 3 4 5 6   **704.9**

1. Art 2. Nature craft

ISBN 978-1-55337-680-4 pa; 1-55337-680-3 pa

"Four major sections (Digging Deep, Going Green, It's All Elemental, and Fertile Ground) each contain more than a dozen activities and/or experiments. Good-quality illustrations and photos bring these ideas to life. . . . Children will polish their creative skills with a wide variety of artistic experiences, such as a secret garden, silly sprouts, terrific topiaries, beautiful batik, super spider's web, weathervanes, great flowing fountain, sparkling ice chandeliers, and more." SLJ

Raczka, Bob

Action figures; paintings of fun, daring, and adventure. Millbrook Press 2010 31p il lib bdg $25.26

Grades: 1 2 3 4   **704.9**
1. Art appreciation
ISBN 978-0-7613-4140-6 lib bdg; 0-7613-4140-4
lib bdg

LC 2008053976

"Eighteen paintings, and not a bowl of fruit in sight. Whether it is the knockout punch of George Bellows's Dempsey and Firpo or the fiery blasts of Diego Rivera's The Conquest of Mexico, this art is not about sitting still. Raczka threads selections together using few words. . . . The book includes works in various styles, dating from 1450 to 1962. Rounded out with some fun facts about the selections, this enjoyable collection presents an array of action-packed art fit for independent perusal or group discussion." SLJ

The **art** of freedom; how artists see America. by Bob Raczka. Millbrook Press 2008 32p il lib bdg $25.26
Grades: 1 2 3   **704.9**
1. American art 2. Art appreciation 3. United States in art
ISBN 978-0-8225-7508-5

LC 2007023831

"The 18 beautifully reproduced works of art in this collection cut a swath across the country—including farms and cities, baseball and jazz, hard work and sacrifice, native peoples and immigrants. . . . Concise notes about each picture at the back of the book will help children and those reading to them find out more about the artists and their work." Booklist

708   Galleries, museums, private collections of fine and decorative arts

An eye for art; focusing on great artists and their work. National Gallery of Art with Chicago Review Press, Incorporated 2013 180 p. (pbk.) $19.95
Grades: 4 5 6 7 8 9 10 11 12   **708**
1. Art 2. Art appreciation 3. National Gallery of Art (U.S.)
ISBN 1613748973; 9781613748978

LC 2013009403

This book is an "introduction to the works collected in the National Gallery of Art. More than 50 great artists are highlighted, from the 13th to the 21st centuries. The artists and their works and techniques are . . . arranged stylistically in categories that include 'Studying Nature,' 'Observing Everyday Life,' 'Exploring Places,' and 'Telling Stories.'" (School Library Journal)

709   Arts -- History, geographic treatment, biography

Ayres, Charlie
Lives of the great artists. Thames & Hudson 2008 96p il $19.95
Grades: 5 6 7 8   **709**
1. Artists 2. Art -- History
ISBN 978-0-500-23853-0; 0-500-23853-7

LC 2008-91000

Presents illustrated and age-appropriate imaginary tours of the studios of famous artists from Leonardo da Vinci and

Michelangelo to Monet and van Gogh, in an anecdotal reference that is complemented by reproductions of famous works and introductory portraits

This is "brightly written and augmented with activities, Web resources, and fun facts. . . . The works of art chosen to represent each artist are heavy on the drama and detail, resulting in high kid appeal and interesting captions. . . . The layout is clean and clear." SLJ

Children's book of art; an introduction to the world's most amazing paintings and sculptures. DK Pub. 2009 139p il $24.99
Grades: 4 5 6 7   **709**
1. Art appreciation 2. Art -- History
ISBN 978-0-7566-5511-2; 0-7566-5511-0

"From prehistoric to modern times, this expertly designed survey delivers a wealth of information. Much more than a mere time line, the focus shifts from artist to movement to medium with fluidity. Gallery pages examine how particular subjects are depicted in art from a variety of cultures and time periods. Hundreds of color reproductions are sure to hold readers' interest. . . . The vast amount of information presented is neither overwhelming nor superficial." SLJ

Cocca-Leffler, Maryann
Edgar Degas: paintings that dance; written and illustrated by Maryann Cocca-Leffler. Grosset & Dunlap 2001 un il (Smart about art) hardcover o.p. pa $5.99
Grades: 2 3 4   **709**
1. Artists 2. Painters 3. Artists, French
ISBN 0-448-42520-3; 0-448-42520-3 pa

LC 2001-23149

Written in the format of a school report by a fictitious student named Kristin Cole, this recounts events in the life of the French artist Degas and offers insight into his work

Illustrated with "charming childlike drawings and reproductions of the artist's paintings in scrapbook-style layouts. . . . [This] is a successful blend of fact and humor that makes sophisticated concepts completely accessible and even entertaining." Booklist

Finger, Brad
13 American artists children should know. Prestel 2010 46p il $14.95
Grades: 4 5 6   **709**
1. American art 2. Art appreciation 3. Artists -- United States
ISBN 978-3-7913-7036-1; 3-7913-7036-7

"Beginning with Winslow Homer and ending with Andy Warhol and Jasper Johns, this picture-book overview introduces 13 well-known American artists. On each double-page spread, short biographies combine with richly reproduced images of the artists' famous works. . . . Finger . . . writes with clarity and enthusiasm." Booklist
Includes glossary

Guery, Anne
Alphab'art; by Anne Guery, Olivier Dussutour. Frances Lincoln 2009 un il $19.95
Grades: 3 4 5 6   **709**
1. Alphabet 2. Art appreciation
ISBN 978-1-84780-013-8; 1-84780-013-0

One letter of the alphabet is concealed in each of these 26 paintings by some of the masters of Western art, including Picasso, Dalí, Van Gogh, Matisse, Giotto, Chagall, Mondrian, Hopper, Kandinsky, Klee, Magritte, and Bosch.

"Readers are challenged by representational and abstract paintings spanning seven centuries, as the text encourages close inspection of the art. . . . This [is a] rich, well-thought-out book." SLJ

Johnson, Stephen

A is for art; an abstract alphabet. [by] Stephen T. Johnson. Simon & Schuster Books for Young Readers 2008 un il $16.99

Grades: K 1 2 3   **709**
  1. Alphabet 2. Abstract art
  ISBN 978-0-689-86301-1; 0-689-86301-2
                    LC 2007-30224

"This exciting alphabetic compendium began with a dictionary. Following years of study and work as a realistic painter, Johnson found himself wanting to explore abstract art. He started by collecting words for each letter of the alphabet. Then, he created a piece based on their meanings. . . . The works vary from paintings and collages to sculptures to installations, and an index reveals the locations of the hidden letters as well as dimensions and materials for the pieces. Children will enjoy seeing everyday objects like candy used in his creations, and will no doubt be inspired to come up with some abstract art of their own." SLJ

Lane, Kimberly

Come look with me: Asian art. Charlesbridge 2008 32p il $15.95

Grades: 3 4 5   **709**
  1. Asian art 2. Art appreciation
  ISBN 978-1-890674-19-9; 1-890674-19-2
                    LC 2007037926

"The book is intended to introduce children to fine art in various Asian countries in an accessible manner, and it succeeds. . . . Lane presents a dozen full-color reproductions, done in various mediums and representing different time periods, along with background information and discussion starters." SLJ

Come look with me: Latin American art; [by] Kimberly Lane. Charlesbridge 2007 32p il $15.95

Grades: 3 4 5   **709**
  1. Art appreciation 2. Latin American art
  ISBN 978-1-890674-20-5
                    LC 2006034237

This book provides an introduction to Latin American art, pairing reproductions of works of art with questions about the artists lives and work.

"The paintings are reproduced in full color on high-quality paper. The writing is lively and interesting, yet the discussions of artistic ideas and theories are concise and easy to understand." SLJ

Raczka, Bob

  ★ **Name** that style; all about isms in art. by Bob Raczka. Millbrook Press 2008 32p il (Art adventures) lib bdg $25.26; pa $9.95

Grades: 5 6 7 8   **709**
  1. Art -- History
  ISBN 978-0-8225-7586-3 lib bdg; 0-8225-7586-8 lib bdg; 978-1-58013-824-6 pa; 1-58013-824-1 pa
                    LC 2008000312

"Beginning with naturalism and ending with photorealism, with many stops along the way, this compact overview documents the shifts, both in terms of technique as well as subject matter, that differentiate each style from its predecessors. Each 'ism' gets a two-page spread, with a beautifully reproduced example. . . . This is . . . indispensible for any middle-grade classrooms introducing art history." Booklist

Schumann, Bettina

13 women artists children should know; [by] Bettina Schumann; [translated from German by Jane Michael] Prestel 2009 46p il $14.95

Grades: 5 6 7 8   **709**
  1. Women artists 2. Art appreciation
  ISBN 978-3-7913-4333-4; 3-7913-4333-5

This is profiles women artists such as Sofonisba Anguissola, Maria Sybilla Merian, Mary Cassatt, Georgia O'Keeffe, Frida Kahlo, Louise Bourgeois, and Cindy Sherma

This "large-format, brightly colored [survey proves a] solid, even inspiring [introduction] to the art world. . . . Leading questions encourage budding artists to use the featured subjects and artworks as inspiration." Horn Book Guide
  Includes glossary

Shoemaker, Marla K.

Art museum opposites; [by] Katy Friedland, Marla K. Shoemaker. Temple University Press 2010 un il $16.95

Grades: PreK K 1 2 3   **709**
  1. Opposites 2. Art appreciation
  ISBN 978-1-4399-0523-4; 1-4399-0523-1
                    LC 2010020731

This is a "collection of fine art in a child-friendly format. Each spread pairs full-color reproductions that suggest opposites. For example, Chagall's A Wheatfield on a Summer's Afternoon is juxtaposed with Miró's Dog Barking at the Moon to suggest 'day' and 'night.' Friedland and Shoemaker have chosen a wide variety of art from ancient to modern times. . . . The layouts are attractively designed. . . . Each paired entry includes a short paragraph that discusses the two pieces exhibited. The authors ask questions and suggest activities. . . . The thoughtfully written text adds interest to the illustrations." SLJ

Wenzel, Angela

13 artists children should know; [translation by Jane Michael] Prestel 2010 46p il $14.95

Grades: 4 5 6   **709**
  1. Artists 2. Art appreciation 3. Art -- History
  ISBN 978-3-7913-4173-6; 3-7913-4173-1

This profiles 13 artists such as Leonardo da Vinci, Vincent Van Gogh, Vermeer, and Henri Matisse

This "large-format, brightly colored [survey provides a] solid, even inspiring [introduction] to the art world. . . . Leading questions encourage budding artists to use the featured subjects and artworks as inspiration." Horn Book Guide
  Includes glossary

709.04   Arts -- 20th century, 1900-1999

Finger, Brad

13 modern artists children should know. Prestel 2010
il $14.95

Grades: 4 5 6   **709.04**

1. Artists 2. Art appreciation 3. Modern art
ISBN 978-3-7913-7015-6; 3-7913-7015-4

This "large-format, brightly colored [survey provides a]
well-oranized [introduction] to the [modern] art world. . . .
[It provides] short bios and reproductions of one or more
works that illustrate the artist's accomplishments. Leading
questions encourage budding artists to use the featured subjects and artworks as inspiration." Horn Book Guide

Includes glossary

Raimondo, Joyce

★ **Imagine** that! activities and adventures in surrealism. Watson-Guptill Publications 2004 48p il (Art explorers) $13.95

Grades: 2 3 4 5   **709.04**

1. Surrealism 2. Art appreciation
ISBN 0-8230-2502-0

LC 2003-19487

An introduction to Surrealism which includes guidance
for related activities as well as brief biographies of six artists: Salvador Dali, Rene Magritte, Max Ernst, Joan Mir,
Merit Oppenheim, and Frida Kahlo

"One of the strengths of this book is the inclusion of artwork produced by children. . . . It offers a wealth of intriguing and easy-to-do activities." SLJ

What's the big idea? activities and adventures in abstract art. Watson-Guptill 2008 48p il (Art explorers)
$13.95

Grades: 2 3 4 5   **709.04**

1. Abstract art 2. Art appreciation
ISBN 978-0-8230-9998-6; 0-8230-9998-9

"Using the works of famous abstract artists, Raimondo
invites readers to discover this genre. Her tone is lively and
inquisitive. . . . The activities encourage the investigation of
shapes, colors, and patterns, as well as personal creativity.
Instructions are clear and thorough. . . . The color photos are
reproductions are well chosen and the vivid layout will draw
readers to the featured works and projects." SLJ

709.2   Arts -- Biography

Bernier-Grand, Carmen T.

Pablo Picasso; I the king, yo el rey. by Carmen T.
Bernier-Grand; illustrated by David Diaz. 1st ed. Marshall
Cavendish 2012 64 p. ill. (hardcover) $19.99

Grades: 5 6 7   **709.2**

1. Art -- History
ISBN 0761461779; 9780761461777

LC 2011032177

This biography of painter Pablo Picasso is written "in
free-verse style. . . . The artist's strong will and drive are
demonstrated in his decision to wander Madrid with sketchbook in lieu of attending art school; by his insistent attempts
to develop his own style (e.g., his Blue Period; his fascination with masklike faces; his creation of Cubism); by his

move to Paris; and his insatiable desire for women." (School
Library Journal)

Krull, Kathleen

★ **Lives** of the artists; masterpieces, messes (and what
the neighbors thought) written by Kathleen Krull; illustrated
by Kathryn Hewitt. Harcourt Brace & Co. 1995 96p il $21

Grades: 4 5 6 7   **709.2**

1. Artists
ISBN 0-15-200103-4

LC 94-35357

"Krull's brief biographies provide basic facts as well
as intriguing details. The subjects chosen range from the
famous (Michelangelo Buonarroti) to the infamous (Andy
Warhol) to the less well known. Hewitt's caricaturelike illustrations reflect and extend the lively text." Horn Book Guide

Includes glossary and bibliographical references

Stanley, Diane

★ **Leonardo** da Vinci. Morrow Junior Bks. 1996 un
il $16.95; lib bdg $15.93; pa $6.95

Grades: 4 5 6 7   **709.2**

1. Artists 2. Painters 3. Scientists 4. Artists, Italian
5. Writers on science
ISBN 0-688-10437-1; 0-688-10438-X lib bdg; 0-688-
16155-3 pa

LC 95-35227

"Stanley begins with a brief introduction to the Italian
Renaissance and then looks at the life of the artist. The text
pages feature a series of sketches from Leonardo's notebooks. These vivid drawings, chosen to reflect ideas and
events in the story, juxtapose well with the large illustrations created with colored pencil, gouache, and watercolors
on the facing pages. . . . The craftsmanship that makes this
biography so solid in concept, appealing in design, and accessible in presentation extends to the scholarship behind it,
as glimpsed in the appended postscript and bibliographies."
Booklist

Winter, Jonah

Just behave, Pablo Picasso! by Jonah Winter; pictures
by Kevin Hawkes. Arthur A. Levine Books, an imprint of
Scholastic 2012 48 p.

Grades: 1 2 3 4   **709.2**

1. Conformity 2. Child artists 3. Creative ability
ISBN 9780545132916; 9780545132923

LC 2011026234

This book offers aspiring children artists encouragement through the story of artist Pablo "Picasso [who] did not
always behave. He refused to conform to popular taste or
replicate his own successes. . . . In covering his early years
(his experimentation with style, perspective, and color were
not always appreciated), the author delivers a . . . message to
today's young artists: don't be discouraged if your creative
efforts are criticized." (School Library Journal)

709.3   Specific continents, countries, localities

Campbell-Hinshaw, Kelly

Ancient Mexico; [by] Kelly Campbell-Hinshaw.
Chronicle Books 2007 32p il (Art across the ages) hardcover o.p. pa $4.95

Grades: 2 3 4   709.3

1. Mexican art 2. Mexico -- Antiquities

ISBN 0-8118-5670-4; 0-8118-5671-2 pa

"A brief text and striking photos introduce the art of ancient Mexico in this distinctive early reader, which features artifacts such as stone and clay sculptures, a jade mask, a wall painting, and a shield decorated with feathers and inlaid gold. . . . This offers a visually impressive introduction to the arts of Mexico's earliest cultures." Booklist

711   Area planning (Civic art)

Macaulay, David

★ **City**: a story of Roman planning and construction. Houghton Mifflin 1974 112p il $18; pa $10.99

Grades: 4 5 6 7 8 9 10   711

1. Civil engineering 2. Roman architecture 3. City planning -- Rome

ISBN 0-395-19492-X; 0-395-34922-2 pa

LC 74-4280

"By following the inception, construction, and development of an imaginary Roman city, the account traces the evolution of Verbonia from the selection of its site under religious auspices in 26 B.C. to its completion in 100 A.D." Horn Book

Includes glossary

Rome antics. Houghton Mifflin 1997 79p il $18

Grades: 4 5 6 7   711

1. Rome (Italy) -- Description and travel

ISBN 0-395-82279-3

LC 97-20941

"Modern Rome is seen through the skewed perspective of a homing pigeon's erratic flight through the city streets as she delivers a message to an artist in a garret. . . . Macaulay adds sly touches of humor to the pen-and-ink sketches. . . . The book includes a map of the city 'As the pigeon flies' with each structure numbered, and an addendum shows the 22 featured buildings with a paragraph or two of interesting facts about each one." SLJ

712   Landscape architecture (Landscape design)

Gourley, Robbin

★ **First** garden; the White House garden and how it grew. written and illustrated by Robbin Gourley; foreword by Alice Waters. Clarion Books 2011 36p il $16.99

Grades: 1 2 3 4   712

1. Vegetable gardening 2. White House Gardens (Washington, D.C.)

ISBN 978-0-547-48224-8; 0-547-48224-8

LC 2010024643

The White House kitchen garden, part of Michelle Obama's campaign to encourage healthful eating, was established in 2009. This book tells the story of Mrs. Obama's garden, as well as the story of the White House grounds, the other gardens that came before, the White House children who have played there, and the teamwork that led to the garden now flourishing on the South Lawn.

"In the many watercolor illustrations, splashes of color show up brilliantly against the bright, white pages. Although Gourley includes plenty of factoids for kids intrigued by past and present residents of the White House, she also makes gardening look enjoyable and rewarding. . . . Gourley's clear, focused writing and lively illustrations will keep children engaged." Booklist

Includes bibliographical references

720   Architecture

Curlee, Lynn

★ **Skyscraper**. Atheneum Books for Young Readers 2007 40p il $17.99

Grades: 3 4 5 6   720

1. Skyscrapers

ISBN 0-689-84489-1

"Dramatic paintings and lucid prose highlight this excellent history of skyscrapers." SLJ

Farrell, Courtney

Build it green. Rourke Pub. LLC 2010 48p il (Let's explore science) lib bdg $32.79

Grades: 4 5 6 7   720

1. Sustainable architecture

ISBN 978-1-61590-320-7 lib bdg; 1-61590-320-8 lib bdg

LC 2010009907

This "introduces concepts of eco-friendly architecture with specific examples, from abode houses to Earthships, while it talks about the large impact that small home energy-saving adjustments, such as water-conserving toilets, can make. . . . In [this] title, well-chosen boxed examples, abundant color photos, diagrams, and an appended glossary add interest and support the engaging [text]." Booklist

Includes glossary and bibliographical references

Hale, Christy

★ **Dreaming** up; a celebration of building. Christy Hale. Lee & Low Books, Inc. 2012 40 p. (hardcover) $18.95

Grades: K 1 2 3   720

1. Creative ability 2. Building 3. Imagination 4. Children's art 5. Architecture

ISBN 1600606512; 9781600606519

LC 2012007376

Boston Globe-Horn Book Honor: Nonfiction (2013).

Author Christy Hale presents a story about architecture and play. "Children building--Concrete poetry--Pair them with notable structures from around the world and see children's constructions taken to the level of architectural treasures. Here is a unique celebration of children's playtime explorations and the surprising ways childhood experiences find expression in the dreams and works of innovative architects. Come be inspired to play--dream--build--discover!" (Publisher's note)

Hosack, Karen

Buildings; [by] Karen Hosack. Raintree 2009 32p il map (What is art?) lib bdg $27.50

Grades: 5 6 7 8   **720**
1. Buildings 2. Architecture
ISBN 978-1-4109-3165-8 lib bdg; 1-4109-3165-X
lib bdg

LC 2008-9700

This "features public spaces and private residences created from a variety of materials. Every page includes a paragraph about the structure with glossary terms in bold type. .
. . [Title is] consistent in quality of design and content." SLJ

Includes glossary and bibliographical references

Kaner, Etta

Earth-friendly buildings, bridges, and more; the eco-
journal of Corry Lapont. written by Etta Kaner; illustrated
by Stephen MacEachern. Kids Can Press 2012 64 p. ill.
$18.95

Grades: 3 4 5   **720**
1. Urban ecology 2. English Channel Tunnel 3.
Sustainable architecture
ISBN 1554535700; 9781554535705

Author Etta Kaner addresses topics including "site selection, planning, designing, the integration of green engineering solutions (like using rainwater for cooling) and nifty details on the how-tos of constructing eco-friendly structures.
Across a series of two-page spreads, [protagonist] Corry explores not only new buildings (domes and skyscrapers) but
also such diverse projects as the Vizcaya Bridge (Spain), the
English Channel Tunnel and the locks of Ottawa's Rideau
Canal, as well as dams, dikes and levees." (Kirkus Reviews)

"Though sustainable architecture is becoming more and
more a part of school curriculum and family discussions,
there are surprisingly few books available on the topic. This
handsome, information-rich, yet brief illustrated "eco-jour-
nal" fills a gap--and more." Kirkus

Macaulay, David

★ **Building** big. Houghton Mifflin 2000 192p il $30;
pa $12.95

Grades: 5 6 7 8 9 10   **720**
1. Dams 2. Bridges 3. Tunnels 4. Engineering 5.
Skyscrapers 6. Architecture
ISBN 0-395-96331-1; 0-618-46527-8 pa

LC 00-28116

"Macaulay combines his detailed yet vaguely whimsical
illustrations with simple, straightforward prose that breaks
down complex architectural and engineering accomplishments into easily digestible tidbits that don't insult the intelligence of the reader of any age." N Y Times Book Rev

Includes glossary

Parker, Victoria

How tall is tall? comparing structures. [by] Vic Parker.
Heinemann Library 2011 32p il (Measuring and comparing) lib bdg $26; pa $7.99

Grades: 2 3 4   **720**
1. Skyscrapers 2. Weights and measures
ISBN 978-1-4329-3955-7 lib bdg; 1-4329-3955-6 lib
bdg; 978-1-4329-3963-2 pa; 1-4329-3963-7 pa

LC 2010000924

This "contains vivid photographs, charts, and diagrams
with captions, explanations, and examples. Questions are
posed throughout . . . to entice young learners to 'stop and
think' or continue reading for more information. . . . [This]

would make an excellent addition to any classroom library."
Libr Media Connect

Includes glossary and bibliographical references

Paxmann, Christine

From mud huts to skyscrapers; architecture for children. by Christine Paxmann; illustrated by Anne Ibelings.
Prestel Pub. Random House 2012 64 p. ill. (hardcover)
$19.95

Grades: 4 5 6   **720**
1. Picture books for children 2. Architecture
ISBN 3791371134; 9783791371139

LC 2012939038

This book "takes readers on a journey through time,
exploring well-known structures such as the pyramids, Ha-
gia Sophia, Versailles, and the Guggenheim Museum. Each
spread is dedicated to a single building; in addition to a detailed illustration of the structure, it also includes information about the architect, the architectural style, and/or definitions of particular details." (School Library Journal)

Price, Sean

The **story** behind skyscrapers; [by] Sean Stewart Price.
Heinemann Library 2009 32p il (True stories) $28.21

Grades: 3 4 5   **720**
1. Skyscrapers
ISBN 978-1-4329-2349-5; 1-4329-2349-8

LC 2008043411

This offers a history of skyscrapers along with miscellaneous facts about them.

Includes bibliographical references

Roeder, Annette

13 buildings children should know; [translator, Jane
Michael] Prestel 2009 46p il $14.95

Grades: 5 6 7 8   **720**
1. Architecture
ISBN 978-3-7913-4171-2; 3-7913-4171-5

"The famous buildings featured in this pictorial collection include Notre Dame cathedral in Paris, Neuschwanstein
Castle in Germany, New York City's Guggenheim Museum
and the Beijing National Stadium (built for the 2008 Olympics), each pictured in color photographs, cross-sections
and/or ground plans, with time lines tracing the buildings'
developments and changes over time. . . . A sound introduction to some impressive structures." Publ Wkly

Stern, Steven L.

Building greenscrapers; consultant, Frank Robbins.
Bearport Pub. 2009 32p il (Going green) lib bdg $25.27

Grades: 4 5 6 7   **720**
1. Skyscrapers 2. Sustainable architecture
ISBN 978-1-59716-962-2 lib bdg; 1-59716-962-5
lib bdg

LC 2009-12494

"Color photographs (most full page) and a few diagrams
accompany the informative text. . . . Overall, the [book] . .
. is user-friendly and covers topics that are not easily found
elsewhere." SLJ

Includes glossary and bibliographical references

721 Architectural materials

Knight, Margy Burns

Talking walls; illustrated by Anne Sibley O'Brien. Tilbury House 1992 un il map hardcover o.p. pa $8.95
Grades: 3 4 5 **721**

1. Walls 2. World history
ISBN 0-88448-102-6; 0-88448-154-9 pa

LC 91-67867

An illustrated description of walls around the world and their significance

"A praiseworthy celebration of similarities and differences among the world's peoples. . . . Young readers will recognize such landmarks as the Great Wall of China, the cave walls of Lascaux, the Wailing Wall and the Vietnam Memorial. More surprising selections feature the work of Australian aborigines, Indian Hindus, Islamic Egyptians, Native Americans and Africans. The narrative is respectful and egalitarian, with the clear intent of valuing no one people over another. O'Brien's . . . well-designed and affecting pastels cover each spread." Publ Wkly

725 Specific types of structures

Graham, Ian

Amazing stadiums. Amicus 2010 32p il (Superstructures) lib bdg $28.50
Grades: 5 6 7 8 **725**

1. Stadiums
ISBN 978-1-6075-3131-9; 1-6075-3131-3

LC 2009044043

"The vivid illustrations often help clarify points made in the text. . . . [This] colorful, informative [book offers] intriguing glimpses of notable engineering feats." Booklist

Includes glossary and bibliographical references

Low, William

Old Penn Station; [by] William Low. Henry Holt and Co. 2007 un il $16.95
Grades: 3 4 5 6 **725**

1. Railroad stations 2. Historic buildings 3. Pennsylvania Station (New York, N.Y.)
ISBN 978-0-8050-7925-8; 0-8050-7925-4

LC 2006015359

"Low contributes both words and pictures in this ode to New York City's Pennsylvania Station. Introductory pages describe why and how the glorious train station was erected. Later spreads focus on how the building was utilized before it fell into disuse and was finally demolished to make way for the smaller, subterranean station used today. . . . The artwork . . . is magnificent. Full-spread, oil-and-digital, mixed-media paintings depicting people moving through the beautiful structure will draw children into Low's underlying message: 'Buildings are not just concrete and steel. They are the heart and soul of all great cities.'" Booklist

Includes bibliographical references

Nardo, Don

Roman amphitheaters. Watts 2002 63p il (Watts library) lib bdg $25.50; pa $8.95

Grades: 5 6 7 8 **725**

1. Roman architecture 2. Colosseum (Rome, Italy)
ISBN 0-531-12036-8 lib bdg; 0-531-16224-9 pa

LC 2001-17769

The author discusses the Colosseum in Rome as an example of how amphitheaters were constructed and "provides a brief cultural context; a history of the development of the building type; and a history of the . . . [Colosseum] including how it was built, what it was used for, and what happened after the society that created it lost prominence. . . . The writing is informative and engaging and not oversimplified. The illustrations are mainly clear, high-quality, full-color photographs." SLJ

Includes glossary and bibliographical references

726 Buildings for religious and related purposes

Curlee, Lynn

★ Parthenon. Atheneum Books for Young Readers 2004 un il $17.95
Grades: 3 4 5 6 **726**

1. Parthenon (Athens, Greece)
ISBN 0-689-84490-5

LC 2003-2615

A detailed history of the Parthenon exploring its construction and restoration.

This is a "splendid introduction to Greece's most renowned monument. . . . [The author's] examination of the architectural details is particularly accurate and absorbing. . . . The limpid, forthright prose matches artwork of similar clarity and elegant simplicity. The acrylic paintings balance areas of flat color with finely controlled line." SLJ

Henzel, Cynthia Kennedy

Taj Mahal. ABDO Pub. Co. 2011 32p il map (Troubled treasures: world heritage sites) $25.65
Grades: 3 4 5 **726**

1. Taj Mahal (Agra, India)
ISBN 978-1-61613-568-3; 1-61613-568-9

LC 2010021306

This "book describes in general terms [the Taj Mahal's] construction, . . . distinctive features, and history, as well as threats to its continued existence and both current and past restoration intitiatives. Revealing color photos taken from different heights and angles are supplemented by maps and by graphic reconstructions. . . . Henzel's distinctive approach gives this [book] unusual value for both assignment and general reading." SLJ

Includes glossary

Hyman, Teresa L.

Pyramids; [by] Teresa Hyman. KidHaven Press 2004 48p il (Wonders of the world) lib bdg $23.70
Grades: 3 4 5 6 **726**

1. Pyramids
ISBN 0-7377-2055-7

LC 2004-12063

This "introduces structures in ancient Egypt, Africa, Cambodia, and Mexico and is full of large, colorful photos and illustrations. . . . Attractive, readable." SLJ

Includes bibliographical references

Macaulay, David

★ **Mosque**. Houghton Mifflin 2003 96p il $18

Grades: 4 5 6 7 8 9 10   **726**

1. Mosques -- Design and construction

ISBN 0-618-24034-9

LC 2003-177

"Once again Macaulay uses clear words and exemplary drawings to explore a majestic structure's design and construction. . . . In his respectful, straightforward explanation of the mosque's design, Macaulay offers an unusual, inspiring perspective into Islamic society." Booklist

Includes glossary

★ **Pyramid**. Houghton Mifflin 1975 80p il $20; pa $9.95

Grades: 4 5 6 7 8 9 10   **726**

1. Pyramids 2. Egypt -- Civilization

ISBN 0-395-21407-6; 0-395-32121-2 pa

LC 75-9964

The construction of a pyramid in 25th century B.C. Egypt is described. "Information about selection of the site, drawing of the plans, calculating compass directions, clearing and leveling the ground, and quarrying and hauling the tremendous blocks of granite and limestone is conveyed as much by pictures as by text." Horn Book

Includes glossary

Mann, Elizabeth

The **Parthenon**; illustrations by Yuan Lee. Mikaya Press 2006 47p il (Wonders of the world) $22.95

Grades: 4 5 6 7   **726**

1. Athens (Greece) -- History 2. Greece -- Civilization 3. Parthenon (Athens, Greece)

ISBN 1-931414-15-7

This "volume introduces the history of ancient Athens culminating in the building of the Parthenon. . . . [The text is] well-researched and clearly written. . . . The color illustrations include an excellent map of Greece, photos of artifacts and sculptures, and many clearly deliniated, large-scale paintings." Booklist

726.6   Cathedrals

Macaulay, David

★ **Building** the book Cathedral. Houghton Mifflin 1999 112p il $29.95

Grades: 4 5 6 7 8 9   **726.6**

1. Cathedrals 2. Gothic architecture

ISBN 0-395-92147-3

LC 99-17975

"On its twenty-fifth anniversary, the author recounts the origins of his first book and suggests revisions he'd make in light of what he's learned. . . . Most of the original Cathedral: the story of it's construction is reproduced in this oversized celebratory volume, along with lots of preliminary sketches, new commentary, and revised, or newly deployed, art. . . . Touches of informal humor further enliven a book that's already mesmerizing for both its original content and its insights into this author-illustrator's incisive, ebulliently creative mind." Horn Book

728.8   Large and elaborate private dwellings

Humphrey, Paul

Building a castle; by Paul Humphrey. Arcturus Pub. 2012 32 p. col. ill. (library) $28.50

Grades: 4 5 6   **728.8**

1. Castles -- Design and construction 2. Castles -- Europe -- Design and construction

ISBN 1848585594; 9781848585591

LC 2011051450

This book by Paul Humphrey "takes readers on a journey from the very beginnings of castles as fortresses to the lavish tourist destinations of today." The text, along with "contextual photographs, staged reenactments, and detailed diagrams offers . . . [an] overview of how an architectural structure reveals the culture, class system, and daily life of the Middle Ages. Castles from the Czech Republic, Scotland, England, Turkey, and Holland are highlighted." (Children's Literature)

729   Design and decoration of structures and accessories

Hill, Isabel (Isabel T.)

Urban animals. Star Bright Books 2009 un il $17.95; pa $7.95

Grades: K 1 2 3   **729**

1. Animals in art 2. Architectural decoration and ornament

ISBN 978-1-59572-209-6; 1-59572-209-2; 978-1-59572-210-2 pa; 1-59572-210-6 pa

LC 2009028378

"Vivid photographs invite children to look closely at a variety of city buildings to find a column adorned with a dog's face, a bronze frieze featuring flying geese, etc. On each double-page spread, lefthand pages show wide views while right-hand pages zoom in on the highlighted animal. The child-friendly topic and approach and the small trim size make this a winning introduction to architecture." Horn Book Guide

Macaulay, David

★ **Built** to last. Houghton Mifflin Harcourt 2010 272p il $24.99

Grades: 4 5 6 7 8 9 10   **729**

1. Castles 2. Cathedrals 3. Architecture 4. Mosques -- Design and construction

ISBN 978-0-547-34240-5; 0-547-34240-3

"Significantly updating the Caldecott Honor-winning Castle (1977) and Cathedral (1973) with new text and full-color illustrations, this hefty volume combines them with a very lightly revised Mosque (2003) for a three-in-one architectural spree. No mere colorization of the black-and-white originals of the first two books, . . . the all-new, often breathtaking images have been drawn by hand and then digitally colored to harmonize, beautifully with the look of Mosque. . . . Take a moment to mourn the originals, then celebrate this entirely worthy revision." Kirkus

730 Sculpture and related arts

Raczka, Bob

★ 3-D ABC; a sculptural alphabet. by Bob Raczka. Millbrook Press 2007 32p il lib bdg $23.93

Grades: K 1 2 3   **730**

    1. Alphabet 2. Sculpture

    ISBN 978-0-7613-9456-3 lib bdg; 0-7613-9456-7 lib bdg

                        LC 2005013472

"This alphabetically arranged primer on 20th-century sculpture includes Marcel Duchamp's Bicycle Wheel, Constantin Brancusi's The Kiss (paired with Robert Indiana's Love), and Claes Oldenburg's Spoonbridge and Cherry. The selections are international in scope, and the media range from scrap metal and found objects to wood and fluorescent lights." SLJ

730.9 History, geographic treatment, biography of sculpture and related arts together, of sculpture alone

Niepold, Mil

Oooh! Picasso; [by] Mil Niepold & Jeanyves Verdu. Tricycle Press 2009 un il (The Oooh! artist) $14.95

Grades: 2 3 4   **730.9**

    1. Artists 2. Painters 3. Sculpture 4. Art appreciation

    ISBN 978-1-58246-265-3; 1-58246-265-8

                        LC 2008010646

"Niepold and Verdu introduce five of Picasso's sculptures. For each one, a close-up detail of the artwork is shown first, along with the question, 'What is this?' Two more spreads present zoomed-in images with possible answers, followed by a third spread showing the entire sculpture along with a statement like, 'oooh! i am a guitar.' . . . Bold text floating on bright solid-color pages complements the pictures. A photo of the artist is appended along with reproductions of the artworks and identifying information. . . . This book will ignite readers' imaginations and is both an effective gateway to art appreciation for young children and a fun exercise for elementary students." SLJ

730.92 Sculpture, ceramics & metalwork -- Biography

Fritz, Jean

Leonardo's horse; illustrated by Hudson Talbott. Putnam 2001 un il $16.99

Grades: 4 5 6 7   **730.92**

    1. Artists 2. Bronzes 3. Painters 4. Air pilots 5. Scientists 6. Art collectors 7. Airline employees 8. Writers on science 9. Patrons of the arts

    ISBN 0-399-23576-0

                        LC 00-41550

"Combining biography, history, and art, Fritz's absorbing text is both a lively introduction to Leonardo and a tribute to Dent." Booklist

731 Sculpture

Kenney, Karen Latchana

Super simple masks; fun and easy-to-make crafts for kids. ABDO Pub. Company 2010 32p il (Super simple crafts) lib bdg $17.95

Grades: K 1 2 3 4   **731**

    1. Handicraft 2. Masks (Sculpture)

    ISBN 978-1-60453-627-0 lib bdg; 1-60453-627-6 lib bdg

                        LC 2009-357

"Colorful photos; clean layout in a bright, primary palette; and large, abundant step-by-step instructional photos give [this book] great appeal. The . . . crafts . . . are functional and attractive. . . . Readily obtainable household materials and easy-to-follow instructions mean that children can do these crafts independently." SLJ

Includes glossary

Wenzel, Angela

13 sculptures children should know. Prestel 2010 il $14.95

Grades: 4 5 6   **731**

    1. Sculpture 2. Art appreciation

    ISBN 978-3-7913-7010-1; 3-7913-7010-3

This "large-format, brightly colored [survey provides a] well-oranized [introduction] to the . . . world [of sculpture]. [It] highlights a variety of works from antiquity to modern times. . . . Leading questions encourage budding artists to use the featured subjects and artworks as inspiration." Horn Book Guide

Includes glossary

731.4 Techniques and procedures

Hanson, Anders

Cool sculpture; the art of creativity for kids. [by] Anders Hanson. ABDO Pub. Co. 2009 32p il (Cool art) lib bdg $24.21

Grades: 2 3 4   **731.4**

    1. Sculpture -- Technique

    ISBN 978-1-60453-144-2 lib bdg; 1-60453-144-4 lib bdg

                        LC 2008-22324

This book about sculpture is "well organized, with clearly written sections . . . and several clever projects and exercises. . . . [It] should have substantial child appeal." SLJ

Includes glossary

Luxbacher, Irene

1 2 3 I can build! Kids Can Press 2009 23p il (Starting art) $14.95; pa $6.95

Grades: 2 3 4   **731.4**

    1. Sculpture -- Technique

    ISBN 978-1-55453-315-2; 978-1-55453-316-9 pa

"Illustrated step-by-step projects show kids how to build small structures out of household materials, encouraging both hands-on creativity and imaginative play. Clear photos of brightly colored materials appear on spacious layouts against white backgrounds. Each project looks sharp and appealing, with sketched cartoon characters adding liveliness and humor." SLJ

1 2 3 I can sculpt! Kids Can Press 2007 23p il (Starting art) $12.95
Grades: 2 3 4 **731.4**
1. Sculpture -- Technique
ISBN 978-1-55453-038-0; 1-55453-038-5

This "introduces the various types of simple materials and techniques that can be used to create animal sculptures. This book is . . . project-oriented, although such concepts as three-dimensionality, texture, and balance are mentioned. Children can make an egg-carton crocodile, an aluminum-foil-and-clay snake, a clay-and-pipe-cleaner giraffe, a paper-bag dinosaur, and more. . . . [The book has] lively pages with color photos and easy-to-follow directions." SLJ

736 Other plastic arts

Alexander, Chris
Difficult origami; by Chris Alexander. Capstone Press 2009 32p il (Snap books) lib bdg $25.26
Grades: 3 4 5 6 **736**
1. Origami
ISBN 978-1-4296-2022-2 lib bdg; 1-4296-2022-6 lib bdg
LC 2007-52196

This book includes "clearly illustrated diagrams and attractive photos of the completed projects using different colors and textures of paper." SLJ
Includes glossary and bibliographical references

Sort-of-difficult origami; by Chris Alexander. Capstone Press 2009 32p il (Snap books) lib bdg $25.26
Grades: 3 4 5 6 **736**
1. Origami
ISBN 978-1-4296-2023-9 lib bdg; 1-4296-2023-4 lib bdg
LC 2007-52208

This book includes "clearly illustrated diagrams and attractive photos of the completed projects using different colors and textures of paper." SLJ
Includes glossary and bibliographical references

Boursin, Didier
Folding for fun; origami for ages 4 and up. Firefly Books 2007 63p il $19.95
Grades: K 1 2 3 4 5 **736**
1. Origami
ISBN 978-1-55407-253-8; 1-55407-253-0

This offers instructions for 16 origami projects including balls, boats, twirlers, boxes, hats, and airplanes.

"The pages combine a dynamic array of images, including ink illustrations of the folding steps and color photos of young people playing with their finished work. . . . This how-to will appeal to a wide range of children . . . as well as the adults and teens who work with them." Booklist

Origami for everyone; beginner-intemediate-advanced. Firefly 2011 il pa $29.95; pa $19.95

Grades: 3 4 5 6 **736**
1. Origami
ISBN 978-1-55407-958-2; 1554079586; 978-1-55407-792-2 pa; 1-55407-792-3 pa

"Though most (possibly all) of the photographs and step diagrams for these 68 paper-folding projects are recycled from Boursin's earlier collections, he has both revised the instructions and commentary and grouped the models according to estimated difficulty. After an extensive opening tutorial of folds and bases adorned with savvy general folding tips, he offers a randomly ordered assortment of aircraft, animals, stars, ornaments, and spinners. . . . The author's lighthearted, fanciful outlook gives this extensive sampler a bright and inviting tone." SLJ

Harbo, Christopher L.
Easy animal origami. Capstone Press 2011 24p (First facts: easy origami) lib bdg $23.99
Grades: 1 2 3 **736**
1. Origami 2. Animals in art
ISBN 978-1-4296-5384-8; 1-4296-5384-1
LC 2010024791

Provides instructions and photo-illustrated diagrams for making a variety of easy animal origami models.

"There is one project per brightly colored spread, with the boxed pictures of the steps large enough to see the folding process. . . . Further appeal comes from the fact that many of the origami figures do not have to remain stationary. Some can be manipulated and played with after completion. . . . There may only be seven projects in [the] book, but they are more than enough to hold the interest of young ones smitten by the idea of folding paper into shapes." SLJ
Includes bibliographical references

Easy holiday origami. Capstone Press 2011 24p il (First facts: easy origami) lib bdg $23.99
Grades: 1 2 3 **736**
1. Origami 2. Holiday decorations
ISBN 978-1-4296-5387-9; 1-4296-5387-6
LC 2010024785

Provides instructions and photo-illustrated diagrams for making a variety of easy holiday origami models.

"There is one project per brightly colored spread, with the boxed pictures of the steps large enough to see the folding process. . . . Further appeal comes from the fact that many of the origami figures do not have to remain stationary. Some can be manipulated and played with after completion. . . . There may only be seven projects in [the] book, but they are more than enough to hold the interest of young ones smitten by the idea of folding paper into shapes." SLJ
Includes bibliographical references

Easy ocean origami. Capstone Press 2011 24p il (First facts: easy origami) lib bdg $23.99
Grades: 1 2 3 **736**
1. Origami
ISBN 978-1-4296-5385-5; 1-4296-5385-X
LC 2010024786

Provides instructions and photo-illustrated diagrams for making a variety of easy water-related origami models.

"There is one project per brightly colored spread, with the boxed pictures of the steps large enough to see the folding process. . . . Further appeal comes from the fact that many of the origami figures do not have to remain stationary. Some can be manipulated and played with after completion. . . . There may only be seven projects in [the] book, but they are more than enough to hold the interest of young ones smitten by the idea of folding paper into shapes." SLJ

Includes bibliographical references

Easy origami toys. Capstone Press 2011 24p il (First facts: easy origami) lib bdg $23.99

Grades: 1 2 3 **736**

1. Toys 2. Origami

ISBN 978-1-4296-5386-2; 1-4296-5386-8

LC 2010024788

Provides instructions and photo-illustrated diagrams for making a variety of easy origami toys.

"There is one project per brightly colored spread, with the boxed pictures of the steps large enough to see the folding process. . . . Further appeal comes from the fact that many of the origami figures do not have to remain stationary. Some can be manipulated and played with after completion. . . . There may only be seven projects in [the] book, but they are more than enough to hold the interest of young ones smitten by the idea of folding paper into shapes." SLJ

Includes bibliographical references

Henry, Sally

Paper folding; [by] Sally Henry. PowerKids Press 2009 32p il (Make your own crafts) lib bdg $25.25

Grades: 3 4 5 6 **736**

1. Origami 2. Paper crafts

ISBN 978-1-4358-2507-9 lib bdg; 1-4358-2507-1 lib bdg

LC 2008-4524

"After describing different kinds of paper, Henry explains the difference between a fold, a crease, and a burnished fold, and then lists all the other supplies besides paper (glue, rubber cement) that should be on hand. The rest of the book devotes two-page spreads to each project. . . . The ideas are fantastic. . . . This will keep plenty of hands and minds busy." Booklist

Includes glossary

Jackson, Paul

Origami toys; that tumble fly and spin. Gibbs Smith 2010 127p il $19.99 **736**

1. Toys 2. Origami

ISBN 1-4236-0524-1; 978-1-4236-0524-9

"In this handsomely packaged volume, Jackson offers 29 elegantly simple toys that he has either invented or modified. The models . . . include percussive 'instruments,' a wriggling fish, dogs, . . . a spinning star, two gliders, and even a catapult. . . . The particularly clear step diagrams use standard origami notation, and the directions that accompany them are just as easy to follow. . . . [This is an] above-average offering." SLJ

Meinking, Mary

Easy origami; by Mary Meinking. Capstone Press 2009 32p il (Snap books) lib bdg $25.26

Grades: 3 4 5 6 **736**

1. Origami

ISBN 978-1-4296-2020-8 lib bdg; 1-4296-2020-X lib bdg

LC 2008-1677

This book includes "clearly illustrated diagrams and attractive photos of the completed projects using different colors and textures of paper." SLJ

Includes glossary and bibliographical references

Not-quite-so-easy origami; by Mary Meinking. Capstone Press 2009 32p il (Snap books) lib bdg $25.26

Grades: 3 4 5 6 **736**

1. Origami

ISBN 978-1-4296-2021-5 lib bdg; 1-4296-2021-8 lib bdg

LC 2008-1679

This book includes "clearly illustrated diagrams and attractive photos of the completed projects using different colors and textures of paper." SLJ

Includes glossary and bibliographical references

Nguyen, Duy

Zombigami; paper folding for the living dead. Sterling 2011 il pa $9.95

Grades: 5 6 7 8 **736**

1. Origami 2. Zombies

ISBN 978-1-4027-8646-4; 1-4027-8646-8

"Featuring both a detachable photo gallery of folded ghouls placed in atmospheric settings and a package of origami paper in suitably ominous colors and patterns, this collection of 13 undead figures may not survive intact for long but offers experienced paper folders hours of creepy fun. Nguyen opens with a tutorial of creases and folding symbology then . . . goes on to show how each figure is folded with plenty of carefully drawn and clearly labeled step diagrams. Nonetheless, most of these models are challenging projects." SLJ

Owen, Ruth

Valentine's Day origami; by Ruth Owen. PowerKids Press 2013 32 p. col. ill. (library) $26.50; (paperback) $11.75

Grades: 4 5 6 **736**

1. Origami 2. Valentine's Day 3. Valentine decorations

ISBN 1448878659; 9781448878659; 9781448879243

LC 2012009647

"This . . . title in the Holiday Origami series encourages young people to create an original I-love-you offering. . . . After a brief history of the origin and traditions of Valentine's Day, the origami instructions start off simply, with pictures and directions on exactly how and when to fold and crease. First, there are two spreads with 9 steps that show how to make an origami heart. Later, 13 steps over four pages show how to make a red rose. Nine steps make a heart box." (Booklist)

737.4 Coins

Reid, Margarette S.

Lots and lots of coins; illustrations by True Kelley. Dutton Children's Books 2010 un il $16.99

Grades: K 1 2 3 **737.4**

1. Coins

ISBN 978-0-525-47879-9; 0-525-47879-5

LC 2009053286

"In this cheerful book, a boy tells about an interest he shares with his dad: coin collecting. . . . Throughout the book, text shares the pages with brightly colored, mixed-media artwork, captions, and speech or thought balloons. Photos of common coins appear in boxes along with a little information, and the backs of the state quarters appear on one double-page spread. . . . With an upbeat tone and plenty of interesting facts, this is a fine introduction to coin collecting for young children." Booklist

Includes bibliographical references

738   Ceramic arts

Andrews-Goebel, Nancy
★ The **pot** that Juan built; pictures by David Diaz. Lee & Low Bks. 2002 un il $16.95
Grades: K 1 2 3   738
1. Artists 2. Pottery 3. Ceramists
ISBN 1-58430-038-8

LC 2001-38139

A cumulative rhyme summarizes the life's work of renowned Mexican potter, Juan Quezada. Additional information describes the process he uses to create his pots after the style of the Casas Grandes people.

"This unusual book is set up to allow for differing levels of reading expertise. . . . One page contains a catchy cumulative rhyme modeled on 'This Is the House That Jack Built,' which outlines the process of making a pot. The facing page offers a clearly written prose presentation. . . . Diaz's arresting illustrations, rendered in Adobe Photoshop, use yellows, oranges, and reds in a layered effect that seems to glow with an inward light." SLJ

738.092   Ceramic arts -- Biography

Cheng, Andrea
Etched in clay; the life of Dave, enslaved potter and poet. Andrea Cheng; with woodcuts by the author. Lee & Low Books 2012 144 p. (hardcover: alk. paper) $17.95
Grades: 4 5 6   738.092
1. Slaves 2. Potters 3. African American poets 4. African American potters 5. Slaves -- South Carolina 6. African American poet -- Biography 7. African American potters -- Biography 8. Slaves -- South Carolina -- Biography
ISBN 160060451X; 9781600604515; 9781600608933

LC 2012027280

In this children's biography in verse, Caldecott Honor-winner Andrea Cheng looks at the "life of the enslaved potter Dave," who wrote poetry. "Records indicate Dave, who was born in the United States in 1801, was most likely purchased at a slave auction at age 17 by Harvey Drake, who, with his uncles, held the Pottersville Stoneware Manufactory in South Carolina. Dave took to the wheel within weeks and went on to become one of the most accomplished potters in the region." (Kirkus Reviews)

738.1   Ceramics -- Techniques, procedures, apparatus, equipment, materials

Cuxart, Bernadette
Modeling clay animals; easy-to-follow projects in simple steps. Barron's 2010 95p il pa $9.99
Grades: 1 2 3 4   738.1
1. Clay 2. Handicraft 3. Animals in art
ISBN 978-0-7641-4579-7 pa; 0-7641-4579-7 pa

"In this well-put-together resource, Cuxart shows readers how to make more than 50 different figures using clay and other materials. The book begins with basic tips and instructions and then devotes a page or two to each of the projects. . . . For each one there are illustrated step-by-step instructions and a photo of the final product. The instructions are primarily visual and are accompanied by a sentence or two of text. They are very clear, and even fairly young children should be able to follow the directions without much adult intervention. Some of the final products are more stylized than others, but all are appealing." SLJ

Kenney, Karen Latchana
Super simple clay projects; fun and easy-to-make crafts for kids. ABDO Pub. Company 2010 32p il (Super simple crafts) lib bdg $17.95
Grades: K 1 2 3 4   738.1
1. Clay 2. Pottery 3. Handicraft
ISBN 978-1-60453-623-2 lib bdg; 1-60453-623-3 lib bdg

LC 2009-351

"Colorful photos; clean layout in a bright, primary palette; and large, abundant step-by-step instructional photos give [this book] great appeal. The . . . crafts . . . are functional and attractive. . . . [The book] shows kids how to make a pencil holder out of an empty can, for example. . . . Readily obtainable household materials and easy-to-follow instructions mean that children can do these crafts independently." SLJ

Includes glossary

Llimos, Anna
Easy clay crafts in 5 steps. Enslow Elementary 2008 31p il (Easy crafts in 5 steps) lib bdg $22.60
Grades: 2 3 4   738.1
1. Clay 2. Ceramics
ISBN 978-0-7660-3085-5 lib bdg; 0-7660-3085-7 lib bdg
Original Spanish edition 2005

The offers instructions for 14 clay craft projects, among them a pear-shaped box, a flower vase, and a paperweight

The text is "easy to read, and the results are quirky and pleasing; steps are illustrated with bright photographs." Horn Book Guide

Includes bibliographical references

739.27   Jewelry

Kenney, Karen Latchana
Super simple jewelry; fun and easy-to-make crafts for kids. ABDO Pub. Co. 2010 32p il (Super simple crafts) lib bdg $17.95

Grades: K 1 2 3 4 **739.27**
1. Jewelry 2. Handicraft
ISBN 978-1-6045-3625-6 lib bdg; 1-6045-3625-X
lib bdg

LC 2009000354

"From bright jewelry pendants made from metal washers to necklaces made from scrap-paper beads, the likable projects featured in this slim title create bright baubles from easy-to-find, inexpensive materials. Each spread combines sharp photos both during construction and then in their finished state, and the book's design makes following along easy." Booklist

740 Graphic arts

Kidd, Chip
Go; a Kidd's guide to graphic design. Chip Kidd. Workman Publishing Company, Inc. 2013 160 p. (alk. paper) $17.95
Grades: 5 6 7 8 9 10 11 12 **740**
1. Graphic design 2. Children and design 3. Graphic arts -- Technique
ISBN 076117219X; 9780761172192

LC 2013032394

YALSA Award for Excellence in Nonfiction for Young Adults: Finalist (2014)

This book is an introduction to graphic design for children. It introduces "the aspiring designer to the thought processes behind typography and visual organization. Among the topics are color, juxtaposition, typography, design history, and the use of design to convey concepts such as irony and metaphor." (Library Journal)

Includes bibliographical references and index

741 Drawing and drawings

Ames, Lee J.
Draw 50 animal 'toons; [by] Lee J. Ames and Bob Singer. Doubleday 2000 un il (Draw 50) hardcover o.p. pa $8.95
Grades: 4 5 6 7 **741**
1. Animals in art 2. Cartooning -- Technique
ISBN 978-0-385-49142-6; 0-385-49142-5; 978-0-767-90544-2 pa; 0-767-90544-X pa

LC 00020750

"Step-by-step method shows how to draw cartoon animals, including dogs, mice, and a skateboarding crocodile." Publisher's note

Artell, Mike
Funny cartooning for kids. Sterling Pub. 2007 128p il $17.95
Grades: 3 4 5 6 **741**
1. Drawing 2. Cartooning -- Technique
ISBN 978-1-4027-2260-8

"This volume approaches the basics of traditional cartooning with what is funny—what creates humor. Pointing out the difference between 'regular' illustrations and cartoons, the author divides the book into chapters that give readers instruction in six areas—exaggeration; simplification; animals and objects doing 'people' things; people

in different poses; unusual body types and gestures; and monsters, weird creatures, and aliens. . . . Black-and-white pen-and-ink drawings throughout are designed to encourage readers to add and create their own individual changes to cartoon figures." SLJ

741.2 Techniques, procedures, apparatus, equipment, materials

Emberley, Ed
Ed Emberley's big green drawing book. Little, Brown 1979 91p il hardcover o.p. pa $10.99
Grades: 2 3 4 5 **741.2**
1. Drawing
ISBN 0-316-23596-2 pa

LC 79-16247

The author "combines basic shapes (circles, triangles, lines, squiggles) to create a variety of cartoon people and animals. The crisp green-and-black illustrations on a white background are large and well spaced. . . . As in his other drawing books, Emberley's wordless step-by-step method is easy to follow; even very young children can successfully reproduce the simple but appealing figures." SLJ

Ed Emberley's big red drawing book. Little, Brown 1987 un il hardcover o.p. pa $10.99
Grades: 2 3 4 5 **741.2**
1. Drawing
ISBN 0-316-23435-4 pa

LC 87-3091

The author explains "how to create objects and figures by building up a series of simple lines and squiggles into a more complicated and complete whole. The color red suggests most of the subjects, among them a U.S. flag, a fire engine, and assorted red-and-green Christmas items." Booklist

Ed Emberley's drawing book: make a world. Little, Brown 1972 un il hardcover o.p. pa $6.99
Grades: 2 3 4 5 **741.2**
1. Drawing
ISBN 0-316-78972-0 pa

"The final three pages, which supply suggestions for making comic strips, posters, mobiles and games, help make the volume particularly appealing. For all developing artists and even plain scribblers." Horn Book

★ Ed Emberley's fingerprint drawing book. Little, Brown 2000 un il hardcover o.p. pa $7.99
Grades: 2 3 4 5 **741.2**
1. Drawing
ISBN 0-316-23215-7; 0-316-78969-0 pa

LC 00-31026

"A step-by-step approach to drawing for beginners and those who are artistically challenged. Each figure introduced can be made with a basic fingerprint or more, and then lines and dots are placed beneath the form to take budding artists to a complete picture. It is so easy to do that even very young children can enjoy a simple art adventure." SLJ

Ed Emberley's great thumbprint drawing book. Little, Brown 1977 37p il lib bdg $15.95; pa $6.95

Grades: 2 3 4 5 **741.2**
1. Drawing
ISBN 0-316-23613-6 lib bdg; 0-316-23668-3 pa
LC 76-57346

"There is little text; most of the book consists of illustrations, step-by-step, of making pictures out of thumbprints. A few Emberley embellishments and a page that suggests other ways of making prints (carrot or potato) are included." Bull Cent Child Books

Hanson, Anders
Cool drawing; the art of creativity for kids! [by] Anders Hanson. ABDO Pub. Co. 2009 32p il (Cool art) lib bdg $24.21
Grades: 2 3 4 **741.2**
1. Drawing
ISBN 978-1-60453-142-8 lib bdg; 1-60453-142-8 lib bdg
LC 2008-8642

This book about drawing is "well organized, with clearly written sections . . . and several clever projects and exercises. . . . [It] should have substantial child appeal." SLJ
Includes glossary and bibliographical references

Luxbacher, Irene
1 2 3 I can draw! Kids Can Press 2008 23p il (Starting art) $14.95; pa $5.95
Grades: 2 3 4 **741.2**
1. Drawing
ISBN 978-1-55453-039-7; 1-55453-039-3; 978-1-55453-152-3 pa; 1-55453-152-7 pa

"A creative, eye-catching illustrated cover will attract kids to this book, and the large print; softly colored, childlike drawings; and simple sentences are sure to keep them interested in pursuing art on their own. A 'self-portrait' shows how position, figure, clothing, facial expressions, and hair are combined to create a lively piece of artwork. Materials needed are clearly labeled and accompanied by sharp color photos or neat sketches. In three easy steps, children can see how to use lines and shapes to draw faces, features, expressions, a figure drawing, or an astronaut. . . . This title is sure to please beginning artists." SLJ

Temple, Kathryn
★ Drawing; the only drawing book you'll ever need to be the artist you've always wanted to be. [by] Kathryn Temple. Lark Books 2005 112p il (Art for kids) $17.95
Grades: 5 6 7 8 **741.2**
1. Drawing
ISBN 1-57990-587-0
LC 2004-17909

This "introduction to essential drawing techniques builds from the starting points of lines and simple shapes. . . . Eight concise chapters explore seeing with artist's eyes, line drawing, light and shadow, proportion and scale, perspective, drawing faces, drawing bodies, and using imagination. The succinct text reads smoothly and is written in a clear, understandable style. Sample sketches and crisp, color photographs extend the text." SLJ

741.5 Cartoons, graphic novels, caricatures, comics

Abadzis, Nick
★ Laika. First Second Books 2007 205p il
Grades: 5 6 7 8 9 10 11 12 Adult **741.5**
1. Graphic novels 2. Space flight -- Graphic novels 3. Soviet Union -- History -- 1953-1991 -- Graphic novels
ISBN 1-59643-101-6; 978-1-59643-101-0
LC 2006-51907

Laika was the abandoned puppy destined to become Earth's first space traveler. This is her journey. Along with Laika, there is Korolev, once a political prisoner and now a driven engineer at the top of the Soviet space program, and Yelena, the lab technician responsible for Laika's health and life. The book depicts the dedication and struggles of the scientists and technicians who worked in the Soviet space program, based on research Abadzis did before writing this book. The book includes a bibliography of books and websites.

"Abadzis's tear-inducing and solidly researched graphic novel treatment of Laika's surpassingly tragic story is a standout." Publ Wkly

Aguirre, Jorge
★ Giants beware! written by Jorge Aguirre; illustrated by Rafael Rosado. First Second 2012 202 p.
Grades: 3 4 5 **741.5**
1. Humorous graphic novels 2. Adventure graphic novels 3. Giants -- Graphic novels 4. Fairy tales -- Graphic novels 5. Fairy tales 6. Graphic novels
ISBN 1596435828; 9781596435827
LC 2011030471

In this children's graphic novel, "spunky Claudette is set on becoming a monster slayer like her father. . . . When she hears the story of a giant on the loose, she is determined to leave her home--accompanied by her cowardly brother, Gaston, and best friend Marie--in order to set things right. . . . When Claudette discovers that not all stories are as they seem, she and her friends must fool the adults who have come to bring them home to protect an innocent monster." (Publishers Weekly)

Arni, Samhita
★ Sita's Ramayana; Moyna Chitrakar, illustrator. Groundwood Books 2011 il $24.95
Grades: 5 6 7 8 **741.5**
1. Graphic novels 2. Ramayana 3. Hindu mythology -- Graphic novels
ISBN 978-1-55498-145-8; 1-55498-145-X

"The Ramayana is the story of the exiled prince Rama and his beautiful wife, Sita. When she is kidnapped by a love-struck demon king, her husband's efforts to rescue her result in a war that eventually involves not only demons and mortals, but also gods, monsters, and even animals. . . . Here, a Patua scroll painter has adapted it as a fast-paced, brilliantly bold graphic novel. All of the suspense, treachery, sorcery, and pathos of this epic is depicted in homemade natural dyes layered onto paper in energetic lines, rhythmic patterns, and fields of hot, bright colors. . . . This book would be a must-purchase based on the strength of its dramatic story and arresting art, enhanced by superior design and high-quality production. Brilliant and fresh." SLJ

Baltazar, Art

Billy Batson and the magic of Shazam!: Mr. Mind over matter; Art Baltazar & Franco, writers; Byron Vaughns, artist & covers; David Tanguay, colors; Steve Wands, Travis Lanham, letterers. DC Comics 2011 un il pa $12.99
Grades: 3 4 5 **741.5**
1. Graphic novels 2. Superhero graphic novels 3. Captain Marvel (Fictional character)
ISBN 978-1-4012-2993-1; 1-4012-2993-X
Eleven-year-old Billy Batson has been given an amazing gift: The magic word Shazam!, which transforms him into Captain Marvel and gives him incredible superpowers. In this volume, Billy and his superpowered sister, Mary Marvel, fight side by side (and, occasionally, with each other) in amazing adventures featuring the world's greatest villains.
"Baltazar has hit upon exactly the right note with stories that will appeal solidly to young readers. . . . He also bothers to write up to young readers rather than down, with resonant themes, strong emotional stakes, battles won through wit as well as strength, and a complex narrative that works on many levels." Booklist

Superman Family Adventures; Volume 1 by Art Baltazar and Franco Aureliani, illustrated by Art Baltazar. DC Comics 2013 128 p. chiefly color illustrations (Superman Family Adventures) pbk $12.99
Grades: 1 2 3 **741.5**
1. Superhero graphic novels 2. Superman (Fictional character) -- Graphic novels 3. Graphic novels 4. Superheroes -- Comic books, strips, etc. 5. Superman (Fictitious character) -- Comic books, strips, etc.
ISBN 140124050X; 9781401240509
LC 2013009138
This graphic novel, by Art Baltazar and Franco, features superheroes such as "Superman, Superboy, Supergirl [and] Krypto the Superdog. The entire Superman family is re-imagined here in this energetic all-ages graphic novel. Read on as the heroes of Metropolis fight foes such as Bizarro, Metallo, Lex Luthor and...giant monkeys." (Publisher's note)
"Adult readers will get a kick out of the clever homage to their favorite superhero, and kids will be powerless to resist the silly playfulness; colorful animated characters; and easy-to-follow, superpower-packed stories." Booklist
Followed by: Volume 2 (2014)

Tiny Titans: welcome to the treehouse. DC Comics 2009 144p il $12.99
Grades: K 1 2 3 **741.5**
1. Graphic novels 2. Humorous graphic novels 3. Superhero graphic novels
ISBN 978-1-4012-2078-5
Eisner Award: Best Publication for Kids (2011)
Eisner Award: Best Publication for Kids (2009)
Here are the Teen Titans as never seen before: as little kids. They all attend Sidekick City Elementary School, where their principal and teachers are supervillains, and they get into playground showdowns with the Fearsome Five. Baltazar and Franco, who have created such characters as Patrick the Wolf Boy, present a series of short stories, most one or two pages long, featuring little kid versions of Robin, Starfire, Wonder Girl, Cassie, Speedy, Kid Flash, Cyborg, Beast Boy, Raven, and more. While these stories are written

for the young readers, the humor may also appeal to teens and adults.
Other titles in this series are:
Tiny Titans: adventures in awesomeness (2009)
Tiny Titans: sidekickin' it (2010)
Tiny Titans: the first rule of pet club (2010)
Tiny Titans: field trippin' (2011)
Tiny Titans: the treehouse and beyond! (2011)
Tiny Titans: growing up tiny! (2012)
Tiny Titans: aw yeah Titans! (2013)

Bannister (Person)

The **shadow** door; art by Bannister; story by Nykko; [colors by Jaffre; translation by Carol Klio Burrell] Graphic Universe 2009 46p il (The Elsewhere chronicles) lib bdg $27.93; pa $6.95
Grades: 4 5 6 7 **741.5**
1. Graphic novels 2. Horror graphic novels
ISBN 978-0-7613-4459-9 lib bdg; 0-7613-4459-4 lib bdg; 978-0-7613-3963-2 pa; 0-7613-3963-9 pa
LC 2008-39442
Four friends discover a movie projector that opens a passageway into a world threatened by creatures of shadow, where their only weapon is light
"This is an undeniably attractive offering, as the artwork, with deep darks and effervescent lights splayed across large, glossy pages, is strikingly rendered. . . . [This] should have no problem gaining an appreciative readership." Booklist
Other titles in this series are:
The shadow spies (2009)
The master of shadows (2009)
The calling (2010)
The parting (2011)
The tower of shadows (2013)

Barba, Corey

Yam: bite-size chunks. Top Shelf Productions 2008 88p il pa $10
Grades: PreK K 1 2 3 **741.5**
1. Graphic novels 2. Stories without words 3. Humorous graphic novels 4. Friendship -- Graphic novels
ISBN 978-1-60309-014-8 pa; 1-60309-014-2 pa
Yam is a little boy who wears a hooded suit and has a magical backpack. On the island of La Leche de la Luna, Yam meets a sentient cupcake, cheers up a crying raincloud with a lollipop, plays with his friends Gato and Mary, and has a four-legged pet TV that sleeps in bed with him. Along with short stories that originally appeared as mini comics and in Nickelodeon Magazine, the book includes an original story in which Yam develops a crush on a beautiful toy seller in town. He spends so much time daydreaming about her that he neglects all his friends.
"The wordless panels are quite effective with the tenderly drawn art powerfully conveying nuanced moments." SLJ

Bell, Cece

★ **El** deafo; Cece Bell; color by David Lasky. Abrams Books 2014 233 p. color illustrations $21.95
Grades: 3 4 5 6 7 **741.5**
1. Deaf children 2. Autobiographical graphic novels 3. Schools 4. Friendship 5. Hearing aids for children
ISBN 1419710206; 9781419710209
LC 2013955590

Newbery Honor Book (2015)

"In this . . . graphic novel memoir, author/illustrator Cece Bell chronicles her hearing loss at a young age and her subsequent experiences with the Phonic Ear, a very powerful--and very awkward--hearing aid. The Phonic Ear gives Cece the ability to hear--sometimes things she shouldn't--but also isolates her from her classmates." (Publisher's note)

"Bell's bold and blocky full-color cartoons perfectly complement her childhood stories--she often struggles to fit in and sometimes experiences bullying, but the cheerful illustrations promise a sunny future." Booklist

Bendis, Brian Michael

Takio; vol. 2 Brian Michael Bendis, illustrated by Michael Avon Oeming. Marvel Enterprises 2013 96 p. col. ill. hbk $16.99

Grades: 5 6 7 8   **741.5**

1. Graphic novels 2. Sisters -- Fiction

ISBN 0785165533; 9780785165538

"Taki and Olivia are sisters with super-powers! In fact, they are the only ones in the world with super-powers! So obviously, they have to become super heroes! But is the world ready for real-life super heroes? Are the girls ready for the challenge? And will the accident that made them who they are reveal secrets that will change their lives forever?" (Publisher's note)

"Taki and Olivia face down danger in this bright, colorful, action-heavy series, which is unconventionally (and refreshingly) girl-focused." Booklist

Takio, vol. 1. Marvel Icon 2011 un il $9.95

Grades: 5 6 7 8   **741.5**

1. Graphic novels 2. Superhero graphic novels 3. Sisters -- Graphic novels

ISBN 978-0-7851-5326-9; 0-7851-5326-8

"This entertaining graphic novel features a crunchy and kinetic art style, quick pacing, realistic dialogue, and enough action to appeal to most middle-school readers." Booklist

Bliss, Harry

★ Luke on the loose; a Toon Book. TOON Books 2009 32p il map $12.95

Grades: PreK K 1 2   **741.5**

1. Graphic novels 2. Humorous graphic novels 3. New York (State) -- Graphic novels

ISBN 978-1-935179-00-9; 1-935179-00-4

                          LC 2008-35699

A young boy's fascination with pigeons soon erupts into a full-blown chase around Central Park, across the Brooklyn Bridge, through a fancy restaurant, and into the sky

"The cartoon panels are so successful at engaging readers that young children do not have to be able to read the text to enjoy the story. Each drawing is filled with humorous details." SLJ

Bouchard, Hervé

Harvey; how I became invisible. [by] Hervé Bouchard and Janice Nadeau; translated by Helen Mixter. Groundwood Books/House of Anansi Press 2010 un il $19.95

Grades: 5 6 7 8   **741.5**

1. Graphic novels 2. Death -- Fiction 3. Fathers -- Fiction 4. Bereavement -- Fiction 5. Family life -- Fiction

ISBN 978-1-55498-075-8; 1-55498-075-5

Original French edition 2009

"This open-ended book is deserving of discussion, difficult though it may be." Booklist

Brown, Jeffrey

★ Star Wars; Jedi Academy. Jeffrey Brown; [edited by] Rex Ogle. Scholastic, Inc 2013 160 p. illustrations (Star Wars: Jedi Academy) (paper over board) $12.99

Grades: 3 4 5 6 7   **741.5**

1. Outer space -- Fiction 2. Middle schools -- Fiction 3. Star Wars -- Comic books, strips, etc.

ISBN 0545505178; 9780545505178; 9780545609999

                          LC 2013931939

In this book, by Jeffrey Brown, "Roan Novachez thought he was destined to attend Pilot Academy Middle School, just as his older brother and father did. His dreams are crushed when he is rejected by Pilot Academy and accepted into a sketchy new school called Coruscant Jedi Academy. . . . Confused and struggling to keep up, Roan tries to fly under the radar and passes the time drawing comics of his daily life at his strange boarding school." (Booklist)

"While it might be disappointing for those familiar with this world to see scant representation of beloved characters, it makes the book an easy starting point for new fans. There are plenty of references to other elements (the T-16 Skyhopper and Jedi training remotes, for example) for diehards to get excited about." SLJ

Followed by: Return of the Padawan (2014)

Cammuso, Frank

Knights of the lunch table: the battling bands. Graphix 2011 127p pa $10.99

Grades: 3 4 5 6   **741.5**

1. Graphic novels 2. Humorous graphic novels 3. Schools -- Graphic novels 4. Rock music -- Graphic novels

ISBN 978-0-439-90318-9; 0-439-90318-1

Sequel to: Knights of the lunch table: the dragon players (2009)

Artie, Wayne, and Percy enter the talent show at Camelot Middle School in a rock music band.

Knights of the lunch table: the dodgeball chronicles. Graphix 2008 141p pa $9.99

Grades: 3 4 5 6   **741.5**

1. Graphic novels 2. Humorous graphic novels 3. School stories -- Graphic novels

ISBN 978-0-439-90322-6 pa; 0-439-90322-X pa

Artie King's family has moved and now he has to start at a new school, Camelot Middle School. Dodgeball is the big game at Camelot, and the Horde is a champion team; the Horde members are also the worst bullies in the school. . . . Artie immediately gets into trouble with Joe, the leader of the Horde. . . . However, he manages to open the broken old locker . . . [which] provides mysterious, useful stuff, such as a lunch. Joe challenges Artie to a dodgeball game; Artie has new friends Percy and Wayne who'll help him, and then he meets Gwen. And science teacher Mr. Merlyn is also on his side.

"Arthurian legend gets an update for young readers in this outstanding graphic novel. . . . The funny, fast-paced tale of young Arthur's quest to defeat the bullies stands well on its own. The appealing illustrations are full of color, action, and life." SLJ

Followed by: Knights of the lunch table: the dragon players (2009)

Knights of the lunch table: the dragon players. Scholastic/Graphix 2009 127p pa $9.99
Grades: 3 4 5 6   **741.5**
1. Graphic novels 2. Humorous graphic novels 3. Schools -- Graphic novels 4. Contests -- Graphic novels 5. Conduct of life -- Graphic novels 6. Arthurian romances -- Adaptations -- Graphic novels
ISBN 978-0-439-90323-3 pa; 0-439-90323-8 pa
LC 2008-51463
Sequel to: Knights of the lunch table: the dodgeball chronicles (2008)
Artie King may have won the dodgeball game against the school bullies, but life is not easy. The new challenge comes with the dueling robot tournament at school; it's all part of Dragon Day, and The Horde has won every year by cheating—they force the smartest kid in school to design and build their robot. This year, they've done it to Percy. Circumstances force Artie's hand and willy nilly, he has entered the tournament. Seeking an edge, they go to Evo, a mysterious techno wiz kid who can build any gadget; the problem for Artie is, is he cheating by getting help from Evo? Cammuso's bright, cartoony art and schoolyard version of Arthurian legend provides lots of fun action as well as making readers think about ethics
Followed by: Knights of the lunch table: the battling bands (2011)

Otto's backwards day; a Toon book. by Frank Cammuso; illustrated by Jay Lynch. Toon Books, is an imprint of Candlewick Press 2013 32 p. (reinforced) $12.95
Grades: K 1 2   **741.5**
1. Cats -- Fiction 2. Humorous fiction 3. Birthdays -- Fiction 4. Graphic novels 5. Humorous stories
ISBN 1935179330; 9781935179337
LC 2012047661
Eisner Nominee: Best Publication for Early Readers (2014)
"Someone stole Otto's birthday! When Otto and his robot sidekick, Toot, follow the crook, they discover a topsyturvy world where rats chase cats and people wear underpants over their clothes. To get his presents back, Otto needs to solve a slew of backwards puzzles--but his greatest challenge comes at the journey's very end. On this special day, will Otto discover something even better than cake or gifts?" (Publisher's note)

★ **Otto's** orange day; a Toon Book. by Frank Cammuso & Jay Lynch. TOON Books 2008 40p il $12.95
Grades: K 1 2   **741.5**
1. Graphic novels 2. Cats -- Graphic novels 3. Color -- Graphic novels 4. Magic -- Graphic novels
ISBN 978-0-9799238-2-1; 0-9799238-2-4
LC 2007040759
"This is a text-book example of how to use page composition, expanding panel size, color, and stylized figures to make sequential art fresh, energetic, and lively." Booklist

Camper, Cathy
Lowriders in space; book 1 by Cathy Camper; illustrated by Raul Gonzalez III. Chronicle Books 2014 112 p. chiefly color illustrations (Lowriders) hc $22.99

Grades: 4 5 6 7 8   **741.5**
1. Space vehicles 2. Mechanics (Persons) 3. Automobiles -- Fiction 4. Graphic novels 5. Lowriders -- Fiction 6. Friendship -- Fiction 7. Mexican Americans -- Fiction 8. Competition (Psychology) -- Fiction 9. Lowriders -- Comic books, strips, etc
ISBN 9781452121550; 1452121559
LC 2013040709
Cathy Camper "introduces readers to Lupe Impala, Flapjack Octopus, and Elirio Malaria, three friends who love working with cars and dream of having their own garage shop. One day they see an opportunity to achieve their goal--a car competition. When they start working on a lowrider to prepare it for the competition, an out-of-this world journey begins." (School Library Journal)
"Raúl's snazzy panels--impressively drawn in only red, blue, and black ballpoint pen on tea-stained paper--resemble an amped-up Mighty Mouse cartoon rendered in anarchic yet skillful doodles. It's a joyfully explosive style, and it perfectly matches the Latino characters and barrio setting. " Booklist

Casty
Walt Disney's Mickey Mouse and the world to come. Boom Kids! 2010 un il pa $9.99
Grades: 3 4 5 6   **741.5**
1. Graphic novels 2. Science fiction graphic novels 3. Mickey Mouse (Cartoon character)
ISBN 978-1-60886-562-8; 1-60886-562-2
Mickey Mouse and his friend from the future Eega Beeva take an amazing journey into the future.
"Disney fans, both children and adults, will enjoy [this] graphic [novel]." SLJ

Cavallaro, Michael
L. Frank Baum's The Wizard of Oz; the graphic novel. Puffin Books 2005 176p pa $9.99
Grades: 3 4 5 6 7 8   **741.5**
1. Oz (Imaginary place) 2. Fantasy graphic novels
ISBN 0-14-240471-3
LC 2006-273599
This graphic novel adaptation remains true to the story by Baum: Dorothy and her dog Toto are whisked to Oz, where they meet the Tin Woodsman, the Cowardly Lion, and the Scarecrow and they all journey to find the Wizard to grant their desires.
"The black-and-white illustrations are action packed, and the characters, with their Bazooka Joe eyes, combine classic comic touches with the popular manga style. Reluctant readers will gravitate toward the cartoon cover." SLJ

Chad, Jon
Leo Geo and the cosmic crisis; Matt Data and the cosmic crisis. Jon Chad. Roaring Brook Press 2013 40 p. chiefly color illustrations (hardcover) $16.99
Grades: 2 3 4 5   **741.5**
1. Astronomy 2. Graphic novels 3. Magic -- Fiction 4. Astronauts -- Fiction 5. Space flight -- Fiction 6. Adventure and adventurers -- Fiction
ISBN 1596438223; 9781596438224
LC 2013001296
Sequel to Leo Geo and His Miraculous Journey through the Center of the Earth (2012)

In this 2-in-1 book, "[Leo Geo] and his space-based scientist brother Matt Data trace looping paths through crowded spacescapes toward each other. Before they meet in the middle, both encounter black holes, white holes, wormholes, asteroids, space pirates and some distinctly more unusual 'space sights.'" (Kirkus Reviews)

"The bright, detailed, full-page panels are covered with strange creatures and planetary objects that will catch and hold young readers' attention, and the scientific information is simply presented and well-integrated into the dialogue. The varied layout of the pages, vertical and horizontal, and the 'search engine,' a hunt for specific objects throughout the book, encourage engagement with the story." SLJ

Chantler, Scott

Tower of treasure. Kids Can Press 2010 112p il (Three thieves) $17.99; pa $8.95

Grades: 3 4 5 6   **741.5**
1. Graphic novels 2. Adventure graphic novels 3. Circus -- Fiction 4. Thieves -- Fiction 5. Acrobats and acrobatics -- Fiction

ISBN 978-1-55453-414-2; 1-55453-414-3; 978-1-55453-415-9 pa; 1-55453-415-1 pa

"Young gymnast Dessa, searching for her kidnapped twin brother, joins two fellow circus performers in an attempted heist, a prison escape and a merry chase through and out of the fortress of Kingsbridge. . . . Artfully using exchanged glances and wordless panels to add both humor and emotional depth, Chantler introduces a likable trio of thieves in a medieval-ish setting. . . . The banter among the three is sharp and witty and balances the visual pacing effortlessly. Fast paced, cleanly illustrated, great fun." Kirkus

Other titles in this series are:

The sign of the black rock (2011)
The captive prince (2012)
The king's dragon (2014)
Pirates of the silver coast (2014)

Colfer, Eoin

★ Artemis Fowl: the graphic novel; adapted by Eoin Colfer and Andrew Donkin; art by Giovanni Rigano; color by Paolo Lammana. Hyperion Books for Children 2007 un il $18.99; pa $9.99

Grades: 4 5 6 7 8 9   **741.5**
1. Graphic novels 2. Fantasy graphic novels 3. Adventure graphic novels

ISBN 978-0-7868-4881-2; 0-7868-4881-2; 978-0-7868-4882-9 pa; 0-7868-4882-0 pa

Twelve-year-old genius and criminal mastermind Artemis Fowl runs his missing father's crime empire and gets his hands on a book that will give him access to the underground fairy world. This graphic novel adaptation gives the book a European look and color palette

"Excellent use of color and shading gives the panels a tremendous sense of light with enchanting effect. Characters are expressively brought to life with fun, exaggerated style." SLJ

Collar, Orpheus

The red pyramid; the graphic novel. Rick Riordan; adapted by Orpheus Collar; lettered by Jared Fletcher. Disney/Hyperion Books 2012 un chiefly color illustrations pbk $12.99; hbk $21.99

Grades: 4 5 6 7 8 9   **741.5**
1. Magic -- Fiction 2. Egyptian mythology -- Fiction 3. Brothers and sisters -- Fiction

ISBN 1423150694; 1423150686; 9781423150695; 9781423150688

LC 2012007905

The Kane chronicles

"Since their mother's death, Sadie and Carter have become near-strangers. While Sadie has lived with her grandparents in London, Carter has traveled the world with their father, the famed Egyptologist Dr. Julius Kane. One night, Dr. Kane brings the siblings to the British Museum, where he hopes to set things right for his family. Instead, he unleashes the Egyptian god Set, who banishes him to oblivion and forces the children to flee for their lives." (Publisher's note)

"Out of necessity, much of the dialogue is dedicated to explaining actions and events, but a constant stream of humor prevents the reader from getting bogged down by logistics. The colorful artwork has an almost painting-like quality, . . . and some clever visual jokes and thoughtful use of panels make good use of the format." VOYA

Collicutt, Paul

City in peril! Templar Books/Candlewick Press 2009 un il (Robot City) pa $8.99

Grades: 3 4 5   **741.5**
1. Graphic novels 2. Mystery graphic novels 3. Science fiction graphic novels 4. Robots -- Graphic novels

ISBN 978-0-7636-4120-7 pa; 0-7636-4120-0 pa

LC 2009-931660

In Robot City, a metropolis of 15 million humans and 1 million robots, Curtis, the Colossal CoastGuard Robot works as part of a team of robots and humans to keep the Robot City Bay safe. In the middle of the night, the Red Star oil rig sends out a desperate distress call when something attacks it in the middle of a storm. Curtis, who looks like a light house on huge, long legs, helps to save the crew on the oil rig, but there's something out there in the ocean, and it means to attack Robot City. He has suffered damage in one of his legs, but Curtis knows he has to stop the menace. This science fiction adventure is full of action and derring-do with colorful retro-style comic book illustrations. Young readers, as well as adults, will appreciate the twist in the story.

"Curtis is a walking, talking lighthouseheaded robot who protects the coast of Robot City with his trusty human crew, Ali and Steve. When an oil rig out at sea catches fire, Curtis rushes to the rescue and then investigates the fishy mystery of the causes of this near disaster. . . . The illustrations . . . are full of retro-comicbook-style action and classic movieserial banter." Kirkus

Comics Squad; recess! comics by Jarrett J. Krosoczka, Gene Yang, Eric Wight, Jennifer L. Holm and Matthew Holm, Ursula Vernon, Dan Santat, Raina Telgemeier and Dave Roman, Dav Pilkey; edited by Jennifer L. Holm, Matthew Holm, and Jarrett J. Krosoczka. Random House Inc. 2014 144 p. ill. (chiefly col.) (trade paperback) $7.99; (library binding) $12.99

Grades: 2 3 4 5 6   **741.5**
1. School stories 2. Comic books, strips, etc. 3. Short stories 4. Graphic novels 5. Humorous stories 6. Recess -- Fiction 7. Schools -- Fiction

ISBN 0385370032; 9780385370035; 9780385370042

LC 2013035223

"An all-star lineup of graphic novel notables contributes original works to this anthology, sharing the common thread of recess." (School Library Journal)

"[T]his lively, upbeat and all-around-awesome offering is consistently convivial and laugh-out-loud funny from cover to cover." Kirkus

Conway, Gerry

Crawling with zombies; Gerry Conway, writer; Paulo Henrique, artist; based on the series by Franklin W. Dixon. Papercutz 2010 un il (The Hardy Boys: the new case files) $10.99; pa $6.99

Grades: 4 5 6 7　　　　　　　　　　741.5

1. Graphic novels 2. Mystery graphic novels 3. Zombies -- Graphic novels 4. Brothers -- Graphic novels

ISBN 978-1-59707-219-9; 1-59707-219-2; 978-1-59707-220-5 pa; 1-59707-220-6 pa

"This mix of the Hardy Boys with zombies is . . . a fast-paced story that should entice reluctant readers. Frank and Joe race motorcycles, communicate with ATAC (American Teens Against Crime), and try to solve the mystery of why teenagers who've been participating in flash mob stunts called 'zombie crawls' (because they dress and act like zombies) have started losing control of themselves in a decidedly zombielike way. The book is a simple page-turner. . . . Henrique's artwork is colorful, shiny, and bright, a pleasing mix of traditional American cartoon and Japanese manga styles." SLJ

Coudray, Philippe

★ Benjamin Bear in "Bright ideas!" a Toon book. by Philippe Coudray. Toon Books 2013 32 p. $12.95

Grades: PreK K 1　　　　　　　　　　741.5

1. Animals -- Graphic novels 2. Picture books for children 3. Graphic novels 4. Bears -- Fiction 5. Humorous stories

ISBN 1935179225; 9781935179221

LC 2012022895

This children's picture book is part of the Benjamin Bear series, where the bear and his animal friends appear in minimalist fables drawn . . . from French cartoonist [Philippe] Coudray's original series. . . . In 'Can I Get a Ride?' [Benjamin] picks up one woodland hitchhiker after another until, in the last panel, tables turn and they have to carry him. In 'See-Saw,' he 'helps' a fox carry a log (and demonstrates a principle of physics) not by lifting the long end, but by hopping onto the short end." (Kirkus)

Benjamin Bear in Fuzzy thinking; a Toon book. Toon Books 2011 32p il $12.99

Grades: PreK K 1 2　　　　　　　　　741.5

1. Graphic novels 2. Humorous graphic novels 3. Bears -- Graphic novels

ISBN 978-1-935179-12-2; 1-935179-12-8

LC 2011000801

Although he is a very serious bear, Benjamin Bear has a funny way of doing things, like drying dishes on a rabbit's back or sharing his sweater without taking it off.

"Coudray's droll vignettes in a muted palette will be the perfect enticement for those with a visual sense of humor who are just starting to read." Kirkus

Craddock, Erik

BC mambo. Random House Children's Books 2009 95p il (Stone rabbit) lib bdg $11.99; pa $5.99

Grades: 2 3 4 5　　　　　　　　　　741.5

1. Graphic novels 2. Rabbits -- Graphic novels

ISBN 9780375939228; 9780375843600

LC 2008-00681

After Stone Rabbit is transported back to prehistoric times, his bottle of barbecue sauce becomes the key ingredient in a power-hungry Neanderthal's plan to dominate the world

Craddock "brings a brightly colored, zany cartoon quality to the story and art, with the hero rabbit falling into one peril after another. The proposed fast-food empire is just the kind of plot that young readers can follow; reading this book is just as fun as watching Saturday morning cartoons." Booklist

Other titles in this series are:

Pirate palooza (2009)
Deep-space disco (2009)
Superhero stampede (2010)
Ninja slice (2010)
Night of the living dust bunnies (2011)
Dragon boogie (2012)
Robot frenzy (2013)

Crane, Jordan

The clouds above. Fantagraphics 2005 216p il $18.95

Grades: 3 4 5 6 7 8　　　　　　　　741.5

1. Graphic novels 2. Fantasy graphic novels

ISBN 1-560976-27-6

Simon and his cat Jack embark on an adventure among the clouds one day when Simon skips school and finds a rickety stairway leading skyward. They find a friendly cloud, flee thunderstorms and trick a flock of belligerent birds, only to find themselves back at school.

"Everything's exciting . . . and the dialogue is witty and bubbly. . . . The book is a joy to look at—Crane's loose, gliding lines burst with character, and his compositional gifts make every panel worth contemplating on its own." Publ Wkly

Dauvillier, Loic

Hidden; a child's story of the Holocaust. written by Loic Dauvillier; illustrated by Marc Lizano; color by Greg Salsedo; translated by Alexis Siege. First Second 2014 80 p. chiefly color illustrations (hardback) $16.99

Grades: 1 2 3 4 5　　　　　　　　　741.5

1. Holocaust, 1939-1945 -- Fiction 2. Graphic novels 3. Grandmothers -- Fiction 4. Jews -- France -- Fiction 5. France -- History -- German occupation, 1940-1945 -- Fiction

ISBN 1596438738; 9781596438736

LC 2013023168

Mildred L. Batchelder Honor Book (2015)

In this graphic novel, by Loic Dauvillier, illustrated by Greg Salsedo and Marc Lizano, and illustrated by Alexis Siegel, "Dounia, a grandmother, tells her granddaughter the story even her son has never heard: how, as a young Jewish girl in Paris, she was hidden away from the Nazis by a series of neighbors and friends who risked their lives to keep her alive when her parents had been taken to concentration camps." (Publisher's note)

"Lizano's stylized illustrations depict characters with oversize heads, reminiscent of 'Peanuts' comics, giving this difficult subject an age-appropriate touch." SLJ

Davis, Eleanor

★ The **secret** science alliance and the copycat crook. Bloomsbury 2009 153p il $18.99; pa $10.99

Grades: 3 4 5 6 7 8   **741.5**

1. Graphic novels 2. School stories 3. Humorous graphic novels 4. Adventure graphic novels 5. Inventors -- Fiction

ISBN 978-1-59990-142-8; 1-59990-142-0; 978-1-59990-396-5 pa; 1-59990-396-2 pa

LC 2008-45399

Eleven-year-old Julian Calendar thought changing schools would mean leaving his "nerdy" persona behind, but instead he forms an alliance with fellow inventors Greta and Ben and works with them to prevent an adult from using one of their gadgets for nefarious purposes

"With its frenetically eye-catching, full-color panels chock-full of humorous and informative detail, Davis's first (of many, one hopes) graphic adventure of the SSA pumps new life into the kids' secret society formula." Kirkus

★ **Stinky**; a Toon Book. RAW Junior 2008 40p il $12.95

Grades: K 1 2 3   **741.5**

1. Graphic novels 2. Humorous graphic novels 3. Monsters -- Graphic novels 4. Friendship -- Graphic novels

ISBN 978-0-9799238-4-5; 0-9799238-4-0

LC 2007-94387

A Geisel Award honor book, 2009

Stinky the monster is sort of a young Shrek—a little grumpy, he loves pickles and likes his swamp nicely yucky and mucky, with no kids. Kids are gross, they like to take baths. When a new boy dares to build a treehouse in the middle of his swamp, Stinky takes action with all kinds of crazy plans to scare the boy away. However, every plan backfires, so what's a monster to do?

"The charming cartoon artwork, full of humorous details, complements the text, and the muted color scheme makes Stinky endearing rather than scary. The simple vocabulary and repetition of words make the text accessible for emergent readers." SLJ

Dawson, Willow

Lila & Ecco's do-it-yourself comics club. Kids Can Press 2010 112p il $16.95

Grades: 4 5 6 7   **741.5**

1. Graphic novels 2. Cartoons and caricatures

ISBN 978-1-55453-438-8; 1-55453-438-0

Twelve-year-olds Lila and Ecco are obsessed with comics. Every summer, they dress up as their favorite characters to attend the local comic book convention. This year, after they stumble into a workshop of comics creators, Lila and Ecco come to an exciting realization they can make their very own comic books!.

"Is it a story of two friends creating a comic, or a step-by-step guide to making comics? Why, it's both, actually. And what's most surprising is not that the guide is so comprehensive and easy to follow but that the framing story not only couches the lessons in comfortable language but is also diverting in its own right. . . . Dawson's savvy, sassy black-and-white art gives the static idea of instructions some pep, and the information is quite complete." Booklist

De Campi, Alex

Kat & Mouse: Teacher torture; [by] Alex de Campi; art by Frederica Manfredi. Tokyopop 2006 96p il pa $5.99

Grades: 4 5 6 7 8 9   **741.5**

1. Graphic novels 2. Mystery fiction 3. Mystery graphic novels

ISBN 1-59816-548-8

Middle schooler Kat starts at a posh school where her father has been hired as the new science teacher, but all is not well. Accidents happen in the science lab, and an anonymous student threatens worse unless Kat's dad passes all the rich, popular students. Kat decides to investigate, aided by her one new friend, Mouse, the rebellious computer nerd and would-be CSI investigator.

Other titles in this series are:

Tripped (2007)

The ice storm (2007)

The knave of diamonds (2009)

Deas, Mike

Dalen & Gole; scandal in Port Angus. Orca Book Publishers 2011 123p il pa $9.95

Grades: 4 5 6 7   **741.5**

1. Graphic novels 2. Science fiction graphic novels 3. Extraterrestrial beings -- Graphic novels

ISBN 978-1-55469-800-4; 1-55469-800-6

Dalen and Gole, refugees on Earth from the distant planet of Budap, must solve the mystery of diminishing fish stocks and save their home planet from an evil plot.

Deas "provides solid graphics, pacing, dialogue, and humor. . . . A fun mystery-adventure that's just right for young space cases." Booklist

Delporte, Yvan

The **purple** smurfs; by Yvan Delporte and Peyo. Papercutz 2010 55p chiefly color illustrations pa $5.99; hbk $10.99

Grades: 1 2 3 4   **741.5**

1. Graphic novels

ISBN 1-59707-206-0; 978-1-59707-206-9; 978-1-59707-207-6; 1-59707-207-9

"[T]his previously untranslated version of the [Smurfs'] first solo collection (1963) offers three tales: A fly's contagious bite turns nearly all of the Smurfs into aggressive purple grunters. . . one Smurf's determination to fly results in multiple crashes and calamities; another's desire to find peace and quiet away from Smurf Village runs afoul of a mosquito and other hazards. Replete with pratfalls, butt-biting and like slapstick, the neatly squared-off comic-strip–style panels look small at first glance, but coated paper and high production values make both the dialogue and the brightly colored art easy to read." (Kirkus Reviews)

Other titles in this series are:

The Smurfs and the magic flute (2010)

The Smurf king (2010)

The Smurfette (2011)

The Smurfs and the egg (2011)

The Smurfs and the howlibird (2011)

Astrosmurf (2011)

The smurf apprentice (2011)

Gargamel and the Smurfs (2011)

The return of the Smurfette (2012)
The Smurf Olympics (2012)
Smurf vs. Smurf (2012)
Smurf soup (2012)
The baby Smurf (2013)
The Smurflings (2013)
The Aerosmurf (2013)
The Smurfs Christmas (2013)

Deutsch, Barry
★ **Hereville**: how Mirka got her sword; colors by Jake Richmond. Amulet Books 2010 137p il $15.95
Grades: 4 5 6 7   **741.5**
1. Graphic novels 2. Fantasy graphic novels 3. Jews -- Graphic novels 4. Dragons -- Graphic novels
ISBN 978-0-8109-8422-6; 0-8109-8422-9
LC 2010-924236
Mirka and her family live in an Orthodox Jewish village called Hereville. All she really wants to do is fight dragons, but what she has to fight is a troublesome pig that talks. Then Mirka meets the witch who lives nearby, and then confronts a troll, and soon she finds she has much more adventure than she knows how to handle.
"Deutsch creates authentic characters spiced with just enough fantasy to surprise. . . . Details of Orthodox daily life are well blended into the art and given just the right touches of explanation to keep readers on track." Booklist

Duffy, Chris
★ **Nursery** rhyme comics; 50 timeless rhymes by 50 celebrated cartoonists. First Second 2011 il $18.99
Grades: K 1 2 3 4 5   **741.5**
1. Graphic novels 2. Nursery rhymes
ISBN 978-1-59643-600-8; 1-59643-600-X
In this anthology, "classic nursery rhymes get a contemporary spin from artists as varied as the New Yorker's Roz Chast and Hellboy creator Mike Mignola. . . . In Dave Roman's 'One, Two, Buckle My Shoe,' the numbers in the title refer to tiny clones created by a wizard inventor." In "Lucy Kinsley's . . . 'There Was an Old Woman Who Lived in a Shoe' . . . the titular woman lives in a funky boot and runs Ruth's Rock & Rock Babysitting." (Publishers Weekly)
"No fewer than 50 cartoonists and comic-book artists provide distinctive visual riffs on as many nursery rhymes in this memorable showcase. . . . Visually far more complicated than the usual toddler-friendly nursery fare, this is best saved for older children. . . . As much as the visual styles may vary, the high levels of wit and invention never falter." Kirkus

DuPrau, Jeanne, 1944-
The **city** of Ember; the graphic novel. [an abridgement of the novel by] Jeanne DuPrau; adapted by Dallas Middaugh; art by Niklas Asker; color by Niklas Asker and Bo Ashi; lettering by Chris Dickey. 1st ed. Random House 2012 144 p. col. ill. (trade) $18.99
Grades: 4 5 6 7   **741.5**
1. Graphic novels 2. Science fiction 3. Apocalyptic fiction 4. Friendship -- Fiction 5. Fantasy
ISBN 0375868216; 9780307979100; 9780375867934; 9780375868214; 9780375968211
LC 2011051619
In this graphic novel adaptation, Lina and Doon live in darkness. "A chance encounter on Assignment Day allows the two children to . . . exchange jobs"; Doon can work underground and Lina as a messenger. "They start to unearth an evil plot by the city's . . . mayor to steal away precious resources from the people who live there. Using clues left behind by Lina's late grandmother, they travel beneath Ember's tunnels in a desperate attempt to find a way out." (School Library Journal)

Eliopoulos, Chris
Okie Dokie Donuts; open for business! Top Shelf 2011 il $9.95
Grades: 1 2 3   **741.5**
1. Graphic novels 2. Baking -- Fiction 3. Robots -- Fiction
ISBN 978-1-603090-68-1; 1-603090-68-1
"Big Mama, proprietor of Okie Dokie Donuts, is so beloved and her donuts so coveted that she is regaled in rhyming song by her customers every morning. . . . Mr. Mayweather [is] a kitchen-appliance salesman. His new ware, Mr. Baker, is a doughnut-making robot that will streamline the workload and multiply the profits. . . . Young readers may well see what's coming . . . especially when Mr. Baker's ingredient slot is accidentally loaded with garbage, but that won't detract one iota from the fun. . . . Eliopoulos creates a confection of zaniness, from the breathless slapstick and the wild, blocky art right down to the childlike lettering that fills the speech balloons." Booklist

Espinosa, Rod
The **courageous** princess. Dark Horse Comics 2007 240p il pa $9.95
Grades: 3 4 5 6 7 8 9   **741.5**
1. Graphic novels 2. Fantasy graphic novels 3. Princesses -- Graphic novels
ISBN 978-1-59307-719-8
Plain Princess Mabelrose doesn't get along with the other, prettier princesses, but her intelligence helps her when a dragon kidnaps her. Instead of waiting for rescue, Mabelrose escapes, taking a friendly hedgehog and a few useful-looking items (a pouch, a length of rope) that she doesn't know are magic.

Explorer; the hidden doors. edited by Kazu Kibuishi. Abrams Books 2014 128 p. chiefly color illustrations (Explorer) (hardcover) $19.95
Grades: 4 5 6 7 8   **741.5**
1. Doors -- Fiction 2. Comic books, strips, etc. 3. Bullying -- Fiction 4. Monsters -- Fiction
ISBN 1419708821; 9781419708824; 9781419708848
LC 2014938941
In this collection of comics edited by Kazu Kibuishi, "a bullied boy discovers a door guarded by a sly monster . . . A painting of a door opens in a forgotten Egyptian tomb . . . A portal in the park promises to turn you into a much cooler version 2.0 - if you can just get the bugs out." (Publisher's note)
"Readers are once again presented with an array of stories created by a cast of comics authors and illustrators smartly assembled by Kibuishi...The range in this slim volume is expansive. From funny to deep and fantastical to refined, all of the stories have a compelling narrative arc. The colors are just as varied, and are universally dynamic and nuanced. Consider this (and previous series installments) as a necessary addition to any graphic novel collection." SLJ
Other titles in the series are:

The Mystery Boxes (2012)
The Lost Islands (2013)

Fairy Tale Comics; Classic Tales Told by Extraordinary
Cartoonists. compiled by Chris Duffy. First Second
2013 128 p. chiefly ill. (hardcover) $19.99
Grades: K 1 2 3 4 5   **741.5**
1. Dogs -- Graphic novels 2. Princesses -- Graphic
novels 3. Fairy tales -- Graphic novels
ISBN 1596438231; 9781596438231

In this book, editor Chris Duffy "has assembled a . . .
lineup of comics versions of more than a dozen fairy tales
in this . . . follow-up to 'Nursery Rhyme Comics.' Favorites like 'The Twelve Dancing Princesses' and 'Rapunzel'
(whose heroines gain significant agency) join rarities like
'The Small Tooth Dog' and 'The Boy Who Drew Cats.'"
(Publishers Weekly)

"Every artist here knows how to turn in an elegant, flowing story, and every tale is pitch-perfect for young readers and intimate read-alouds. Overall, the book is an ideal
choice for a child's first comics experience and a new way to
enjoy old favorites." Booklist

Farshtey, Greg

Bionicle #1: rise of the Toa Nuva; Greg Farshtey,
writer; Carlos D'Anda [and] Randy Elliott, artist. Papercutz
2008 un il $12.95; pa $7.95
Grades: 3 4 5 6   **741.5**
1. Graphic novels 2. Adventure graphic novels 3.
Science fiction graphic novels
ISBN 978-1-59707-110-9; 978-1-59707-109-3 pa

Six mighty heroes the Toa arrive on a tropical island
to find a land under siege. The Great Spirit Mata Nui has
been cast into an unending sleep by the evil Makuta. Now
Makuta is attacking the island's Matoran villagers with vicious Rahi beasts. The Toa must combine their skills and
elemental and mask powers to defeat Makuta and restore
peace to the island.

"The art is vivid and attention grabbing, and the story
line, which weaves in Polynesian mythology, is exciting and
action-packed." SLJ

Other titles in this series are:
Challenge of the Rahkshi (2008)
City of legends (2008)
Trial by fire (2008)
The battle of Voya Nui (2009)
The underwater city (2009)
Realm of fear (2009)
Legends of Bara Magna (2010)
The fall of Atero (2010)

Flight explorer; edited by Kazu Kibuiski. Villard 2008
112p il pa $10
Grades: 4 5 6 7   **741.5**
1. Graphic novels 2. Fantasy graphic novels 3.
Humorous graphic novels 4. Adventure graphic novels
5. Science fiction graphic novels
ISBN 978-0-345-50313-8 pa; 0-345-50313-9 pa

This anthology includes stories that Kibuishi kept from
Flight Volume 4 because they had all-ages appeal, as well as
stories submitted especially for this volume. Kibuishi's own
Copper and his talking dog cross a deep canyon by leaping
onto mushrooms, only to discover the vegetation is intelligent. Kean Soo's Jellaby and his human friends frolic in

the snow. Missile Mouse by Jake Parker defends a village on
another planet, only to discover his coming was prophesied
(this story includes two uses of the word "crap"). The other
stories will appeal to younger readers, while some of the humor will also appeal to older readers. Other than the one
bad word in "Missile Mouse" (noted above), there shouldn't
be any other content that would keep this book out of most
elementary and middle schools.

"Every story has a layout that promotes an acute sense of
pacing and showcases the crisp, defined, full-color art." SLJ

Ford, Christopher

Stickman Odyssey; an epic doodle. Philomel Books
2011 200p il $12.99
Grades: 5 6 7 8   **741.5**
1. Graphic novels 2. Humorous graphic novels 3.
Adventure graphic novels 4. Greek mythology --
Graphic novels
ISBN 978-0-399-25426-0; 0-399-25426-9
                             LC 2010-36900

In this humorous take on the Odyssey, Zozimos, banished from his country by his evil stepmother, has many adventures as he prepares to return home to reclaim the throne
that is rightfully his.

"The black-and-white illustrations are occasionally simple to the point of hilarity. . . . There is subtlety and depth
here, however, and the contrast between the intentionally
plain characters and their seemingly larger-than-life (but ultimately universal) quests . . . makes the final product both
the promised Greek epic tale and an examination of the ways
in which modern humans are isolated and lost. . . . Ford balances allegory and madcap quest so perfectly that the book
inspires reflection even while it is clearly a quick-reading,
ridiculous, often gross adventure." Bull Cent Child Books

Friesen, Ray

A **cheese** related mishap and other stories. Don't Eat
Any Bugs 92p il (LOOKIT! comedy and mayhem) pa
$8.95
Grades: 3 4 5 6   **741.5**
ISBN 0-9728177-6-X pa

"Held together by dueling narrators, this volume features
Mellville the penguin and a cast of several as they struggle to
save exploding cheese from a horde of evil chicken ninjas!
Interspersed are stories of Captain Cautious, the timid su-
per hero, and Tbyrd Fearlessness, the inept ostrich outlaw."
(Publisher's note)

Other titles in this series are:
Yarg! and other stories (2007)
Cupcakes of doom! (2009)
Piranha pancakes (2011)

Fuji, Machiko

The **big** adventures of Majoko, volume 1; illustrated
by Tomomi Mizuna. UDON Entertainment 2009 200p il
pa $7.99
Grades: 3 4 5 6 7 8   **741.5**
1. Manga 2. Graphic novels 3. Fantasy graphic novels
4. Witches -- Graphic novels
ISBN 978-1-89737-681-2 pa; 1-89737-681-2 pa

"Young witch Majoko sends her diary to the human
world to find an adventuring partner and through it finds shy,
quiet Nana. Together the two girls have a rollicking series of
escapades. . . . Characters are simply drawn, but the back-

grounds are nicely detailed and the plot elements are clearly thought out and easy to follow. . . . The content is very appropriate for the intended audience." Booklist

Volume 1 of a 5-volume series

Gagne, Michel

The **saga** of Rex. Image 2010 200p il $17.99

Grades: 4 5 6 7 8   **741.5**

1. Graphic novels 2. Foxes -- Graphic novels 3. Science fiction -- Graphic novels

ISBN 978-1-60706-322-3; 1-60706-322-0

The adorable little fox named Rex is plucked from his home world by a mysterious spaceship and transported to the arcane world of Edernia, where he meets Aven, an enigmatic biomorph with a flying saucer.

"While children may enjoy this graphic novel for its gorgeous art—especially the cute characters—its story line will more likely be appreciated by older readers. The almost wordless story isn't meant to be read on a literal level but instead on more a mystical and dreamlike level. . . . Gagné . . . offers a sensitive and intriguing graphic novel for people who like a little enigma in what they read." Publ Wkly

Gaiman, Neil, 1960-

★ The **graveyard** book graphic novel Volume 1; based on the novel by Neil Gaiman; adapted by P. Craig Russell; illustrated by Kevin Nowlan, P. Craig Russell, Tony Harris, Scott Hampton, Galen Showman, Jill Thompson, Stephen B. Scott; colorist, Lovern Kindzierski; letterer, Rick Parker. HarperCollins 2014 188 p. color illustrations $19.99

Grades: 5 6 7 8 9 10   **741.5**

1. Graphic novels 2. Orphans -- Fiction 3. Cemeteries -- Fiction

ISBN 9780062194817; 006219481X

LC 2013953799

This graphic novel is an adaptation of the "Newbery Medal-winning novel, [where] Bod is an unusual boy . . . , the only living resident of a graveyard. Raised from infancy by the ghosts, werewolves, and other cemetery denizens, Bod has learned the antiquated customs of his guardians' time as well as their ghostly teachings." (Publisher's note)

"Russell brings his decades of comics know-how to this lovely, lyrical adaptation of [Gaiman's] well-loved, Newbery Medal--winning book. Not content to rely exclusively on his own distinctive talents, Russell has enlisted some of the industry's greatest contemporary illustrators as contributors, who fill the panels with appropriately gothic tones. In order to give ample room to the novel's twists and turns, the adaptation has been divided into two parts." Booklist

The **graveyard** book graphic novel Volume 2; based on the novel by Neil Gaiman; adapted by P. Craig Russell; illustrated by David LaFuente, Scott Hampton, P. Craig Russell, Kevin Nowlan, Galen Showman; colorist, Lovern Kindzierski; letterer, Rick Parker. HarperCollins 2014 188 p. color illustrations (hardcover) $19.99

Grades: 5 6 7 8 9 10   **741.5**

1. Dead -- Fiction 2. Orphans -- Fiction 3. Cemeteries -- Fiction 4. Supernatural graphic novels 5. Graphic novels 6. Supernatural -- Fiction

ISBN 0062194836; 9780062194831

LC 2013497350

"Russell concludes the two-part adaptation of Gaiman's Newbery Medal winner, encompassing the final three chap-

ters of the novel. Bod, raised by the ghostly denizens of a graveyard, is a young adult now, yearning for knowledge of the world of the living. After a showdown with a pair of school bullies . . . Bod finally confronts the ancient order who murdered his family and overcomes them with his supernatural know-how and his innate courage and cleverness." (Booklist)

"Russell and his team of illustrators continue to do this amazing story justice with images that lead readers down a path into Bod's dark and magical graveyard world. Gaiman has the ability to weave beauty and intrigue into a story that has a strong potential to frighten." VOYA

Hansel & Gretel; a Toon graphic. Neil Gaiman, Lorenzo Mattotti. Toon Books 2014 56 p. black and white illustrations hbk $16.95

Grades: 2 3 4 5 6   **741.5**

1. Folklore -- Germany 2. Fairy tales -- Graphic novels 3. Fairy tales 4. Graphic novels

ISBN 9781935179627; 1935179624

LC 2014000694

This graphic novel offers a retelling of the Germanic folk tale of Hansel and Gretel. "Hansel overhears his mother presenting her logical argument to abandon the children in the forest so that she and her husband might have some hope of surviving the famine caused by the war. He reluctantly agrees, but he is happy when the children outsmart the plan. However, as conditions worsen, their mother persuades their father to abandon them a second time." (Bulletin of the Center for Children's Books)

"Mattotti contributes elegant b&w ink spreads that alternate with spreads of text. His artistry flows from the movement of his brush and the play of light and shadow. . . . Gaiman makes the story's horrors feel very real and very human, and Mattotti's artwork is genuinely chilling." Pub Wkly

Includes bibliographical references

Giarrusso, Chris

G-Man, volume 1: learning to fly. Image Comics 2010 un il pa $9.99

Grades: 3 4 5 6   **741.5**

1. Graphic novels 2. Humorous graphic novels 3. Superhero graphic novels

ISBN 978-1-60706-270-7 pa; 1-60706-270-4 pa

Mikey G. is G-Man, the newest superhero on the block, in a town full of superheroes (he made his cape from the family's magic blanket). His friends Billy Demon, Tan Man, Sparky, and the Suntrooper are all ready to help, but G-Man also has to deal with his older brother Great Man (aka Dave) and their superhero dad, Mr. G.

This "hits all the right notes, from its friendly cartoon figures to the occasionally hilarious one-liners." Booklist

Other titles in this series are:

Cape crisis (2010)

Coming home (2013)

Gownley, Jimmy

Amelia rules!: the whole world's crazy! Renaissance Press 2003 176p $24.95; pa $14.95

Grades: 3 4 5 6   **741.5**

1. Graphic novels 2. Humorous graphic novels 3. Friendship -- Graphic novels 4. Family life -- Graphic

novels

ISBN 0-9712169-3-2; 0-9712169-2-4 pa

Other titles in this series are:

Amelia rules!: What makes you happy? (2004);

Amelia rules! Superheroes (2005);

Amelia rules! a very ninja Christmas (2009);

Amelia rules! When the past is a present (2010);

Amelia rules! The tweenage guide to not being unpopular (2010);

Amelia rules! True things (adults don't want kids to know (2010);

Amelia rules! The meaning of life. . . and other stuff (2011);

Amelia rules! Her permanent record (2012)

"Amelia . . . is getting used to life with her newly divorced mom and her hip, young aunt Tanner; settling in at a strange new school; and finding a group of friends. Amelia is no sweet innocent, nor are her three G.A.S.P (Gathering of Awesome Superpals) buddies: Reggie, superhero in the making; Rhonda, Amelia's tough bete noire with a fourth-grade 'thing' for Reggie; and quiet, mysterious Pajamaman. Jealousy, meanness, sadness, and confusion, as well as surprising generosity, and love crisscross the pages in energetic, freewheeling, full-color cartoon art that unwraps a kid's-eye view of life honestly, poignantly, and with a hefty dollop of melodrama." Booklist

★ **Graphic** novels and comic books; edited by Kat Kan. The H.W. Wilson Co. 2010 195p il (Reference shelf) pa $35

Grades: Adult Professional   741.5

1. Graphic novels -- History and criticism

ISBN 978-0-8242-1100-4; 0-8242-1100-6

LC 2010-34209

"This collection of articles from scholarly journals, newspapers, and blogs gives a well-rounded overview of graphic novels, as well as a strong argument for their place in schools and libraries. The first section chronicles the growing mainstream acceptance of graphic novels in the United States. . . . Susequent sections look at these books as complex works of literature, as education and literacy aids, and as significant additions to library collections, with advice for librarians on how to purchase, catalog, file, and promote them. In the final section, readers hear from writers and artists . . . who clearly convey the joy they get from this medium. This is both an entertaining and highly practical read." SLJ

Includes bibliographical references

Gravel, Elise

A **day** in the office of Doctor Bugspit. Blue Apple 2011 il (Balloon toons) $10.99

Grades: K 1 2 3   741.5

1. Graphic novels 2. Physicians -- Fiction 3. Extraterrestrial beings -- Fiction

ISBN 978-1-60905-092-4; 1-60905-092-4

"Looking like a cross between a slug and a sock puppet in Gravel's crudely drawn, garishly colored cartoons, alien Doctor Bugspit plies his trade. He blithely dispenses jars of 'Fix-It-Up Syrup' (made from sock juice, dead flies, moldy meat, pickle juice and ear wax) and other nostrums to extraterrestrial patients complaining of maladies ranging from split brains . . . to an all-body outbreak of toes. . . . Presented in a loose assortment of graphic panels, page-sized or small-

er, this . . . will exert a strong draw on budding graphic-novel fans as well as children fascinated by yucky stuff." Kirkus

Guibert, Emmanuel

Ariol; Just a Donkey Like You and Me. Papercutz 2013 124 p. ill. (paperback) $12.99

Grades: 2 3 4 5   741.5

1. Animals -- Graphic novels 2. School stories -- Graphic novels

ISBN 1597073997; 9781597073998

This book follows Ariol and his ensemble, a "cast of anthropomorphized animal children," in "10 10-page stories, originally from France, which offer . . . slice-of-life vignettes. Whether Ariol is joining his father for a trip to the ATM, arguing with a friend about sneakers, accompanying his grandmother to the movies, pursuing his great crush, or emulating his favorite superhero, the author dares to depict the exclusionary, argumentative, self-centered ways children can sometimes behave." (Booklist)

Other titles in this series are:

Thunder horse (2013)

Happy as a pig (2013)

A beautiful cow (2014)

Sardine in outer space; [by] Emmanuel Guibert; illustrated by Joann Sfar; translated by Sasha Watson; colorist, Walter Pezzali. First Second 2006 128p il pa $12.95

Grades: 3 4 5 6   741.5

1. Graphic novels 2. Humorous graphic novels 3. Science fiction graphic novels

ISBN 978-1-59643-126-3 pa; 1-59643-126-1 pa

LC 2005-21790

In this volume of twelve interconnected stories, little space pirate Sardine cruises in the spaceship Huckleberry with Uncle Yellow Shoulder and Little Louie. They do battle with Supermuscleman, who runs a tough space orphanage where children are taught "good behavior"

"Sfar's off-kilter, slightly uglified art, reminiscent of a toned-down Beavis and Butthead, gives the simple fun an unusual punch." Booklist

Other titles in this series are:

Sardine in outer space 2 (2006)

Sardine in outer space 3 (2007)

Sardine in outer space 4 (2007)

Sardine in outer space 5 (2008)

Sardine in outer space 6 (2009)

Hale, Dean

★ **Rapunzel's** revenge; [by] Shannon and Dean Hale; illustrated by Nathan Hale. Bloomsbury 2008 144p il map $18.99; pa $14.99

Grades: 5 6 7 8   741.5

1. Graphic novels 2. Fantasy graphic novels 3. Humorous graphic novels 4. Fairy tales -- Graphic novels

ISBN 1-59990-070-X; 1-59990-288-5 pa; 978-1-59990-070-4; 978-1-59990-288-3 pa

LC 2007-37670

In this graphic novel, Rapunzel escapes "from the enchanted tree where Mother Gothel imprisoned her. Rapunzel sets off alone through the ghost towns and Badlands of Gothel's Reach. She is determined to find Gothel's Villa and teach Mother Gothel a long-overdue lesson for her years of treachery and lies, and help her real mother get out of the mine camps where Mother Gothel has kept her enslaved." (Publisher's note) "Grades four to seven." (Bull Cent Child Books)

"The dialogue is witty, the story is an enticing departure from the original, and the illustrations are magically fun and expressive." SLJ

Another title about these characters is:

Calamity Jack (2009)

Hale, Shannon

Calamity Jack; [by] Shannon Hale, Dean Hale, and Nathan Hale. Bloomsbury 2010 144p il $19.99; pa $14.99

Grades: 5 6 7 8   **741.5**

1. Graphic novels 2. Fairy tales -- Graphic novels

ISBN 978-1-59990-076-6; 1-59900-076-9; 978-1-59990-373-6 pa; 1-59990-373-3 pa

LC 2008-41332

In this graphic novel interpretation of "Jack and the beanstalk," Jack is a born schemer who climbs a magical beanstalk in the hope of exacting justice from a mean giant and gaining a fortune for his widowed mother, aided by some friends.

"The urban setting suits this retelling of the familiar beanstalk tale; Nathan Hale's art gives it a steampunk twist, and the addition of fairy-tale creatures like giants and pixies is natural and convincing." Booklist

Harrell, Rob

Monster on the Hill; by Rob Harrell. Top Shelf Productions 2013 192 p. color illustrations pbk $19.95

Grades: 4 5 6 7 8   **741.5**

1. Monsters -- Graphic novels 2. Friendship -- Graphic novels

ISBN 1603090754; 9781603090759

This graphic novel by Rob Harrell is set in "1860s England [where] every . . . township is terrorized by a . . . monster - much to the townsfolk's delight! Each town's . . . monster is a source of local pride [and] tourism. Unfortunately, for . . . Stoker-on-Avon, their monster isn't quite as impressive. Can the morose Rayburn get a monstrous makeover and become a proper horror? It's up to the eccentric Dr. Charles Wilkie and plucky street urchin Timothy to get him up to snuff." (Publisher's note)

Hart, Christopher

The **cartoonist's** big book of drawing animals; [by] Christopher Hart. Watson-Guptill Publications 2008 224p il pa $21.95

Grades: 3 4 5 6   **741.5**

1. Drawing 2. Animals in art 3. Cartoons and caricatures

ISBN 978-0-8230-1421-7 pa; 0-8230-1421-5 pa

LC 2007-29102

"The simple text that accompanies each drawing explains the artist's choices and focuses readers' attention on important details in each drawing. Children will love this thorough and easy-to-use how-to guide." SLJ

Drawing the new adventure cartoons; cool spies, evil guys and action heroes. Sixth & Spring Books 2008 126p il pa $19.95

Grades: 4 5 6 7   **741.5**

1. Drawing 2. Cartoons and caricatures

ISBN 978-1-933027-60-9 pa; 1-933027-60-6 pa

"This fun guide works best for those with some previous figure-drawing experience. . . . Sections on 'Drawing the Head,' 'Drawing the Teen Action Body,' and 'Using Body Language to Convey Emotion' offer detailed and, for the most part, step-by-step instructions. Subsequent sections . . . provide examples of unique and zany aspects of adventure-style characters. . . . Throughout the book, Hart also includes useful tip boxes, often demonstrating how not to draw a character. These suggestions are invaluable, providing insight into creating kinetic and expressive cartoons." SLJ

You can draw cartoon animals; a simple step-by-step drawing guide. Walter Foster 2009 120p il (Just for kids!) pa $12.99

Grades: 2 3 4 5 6   **741.5**

1. Drawing 2. Cartoons and caricatures

ISBN 978-1-60058-611-8 pa; 1-60058-611-2 pa

"Hart begins by giving some general guidelines for drawing head and body shapes, and line thickness. Then he demonstrates, step by step, how to draw a variety of animals, both wild and domesticated. He includes an informative paragraph at the beginning of each set of instructions and side notes for some of the steps. . . . The projects are simple but yield a pleasing result reminiscent of animated characters the target age group might see on TV. Colored boarders at the top and bottom of each page unify the book and add visual appeal. Sure to be a favorite." SLJ

Hatke, Ben

Legends of Zita the spacegirl; Ben Hatke. First Second 2012 205 p. col. ill. (pbk.) $12.99; (hardcover) $18.99

Grades: 4 5 6   **741.5**

1. Science fiction 2. Adventure fiction 3. Robots -- Fiction 4. Science fiction graphic novels 5. Graphic novels 6. Fame -- Fiction 7. Heroes -- Fiction

ISBN 1596434473; 9781596434479; 9781596438064

LC 2012012748

This graphic novel, by Ben Hatke, is a children's science fiction adventure story. "Zita is determined to find her way home to earth, following the events of the first book. . . . Zita's exploits from her first adventure have made her an intergalactic megastar! But she's about to find out that fame doesn't come without a price. And who can you trust when your true self is being eclipsed by your public persona, and you've got a robot doppelganger wreaking havoc . . . while wearing your face?" (Publisher's note)

"Hatke's arrestingly vibrant art commands instant adoration of its reader... Readers would be hard-pressed to not find something to like in these tales; they're a winning formula of eye-catching aesthetics, plot and creativity, adeptly executed. Imaginative and utterly bewitching." Kirkus

★ The **Return** of Zita the Spacegirl; by Ben Hatke. First edition First Second 2014 240 p. $18.99

Grades: 3 4 5 6   **741.5**

1. Science fiction 2. Prisoners -- Fiction 3. Outer space -- Fiction 4. Science fiction graphic novels 5. Graphic novels 6. Good and evil -- Fiction

ISBN 1626720584; 9781626720589

"Zita the Spacegirl has saved planets, battled monsters, and wrestled with interplanetary fame. But she faces her biggest challenge yet in the third and final installment of the Zita adventures. Wrongfully imprisoned on a penitentiary planet, Zita has to plot the galaxy's greatest jailbreak before the evil prison warden can execute his plan of interstellar domination!" (Publisher's note)

"The art is colorful, detailed, and child-friendly. Readers of all ages can relate to the themes of friendship and loyalty while enjoying the fantasy of a far-out sci-fi adventure." Horn Book

★ **Zita** the spacegirl. First Second 2011 182p il pa $10.99; $17.99

Grades: 3 4 5 6   **741.5**

1. Graphic novels 2. Science fiction graphic novels
ISBN 1-59643-446-5 pa; 1-59643-695-6; 978-1-59643-446-2 pa; 978-1-59643-695-4

When her best friend is abducted by an alien doomsday cult, Zita leaps to the rescue and finds herself a stranger on a strange planet.

Hatke "doles out an increasingly loony and charming array of aliens, robots, and unclassifiable blobs and hairy things for Zita . . . to encounter. It's fun, plenty funny, and more than a little random. Kids will love it." Booklist

Hayes, Geoffrey

★ **Benny** and Penny in just pretend; a Toon Book. [by] Geoffrey Hayes. RAW Junior 2008 32p il $12.95

Grades: PreK K 1 2   **741.5**

1. Graphic novels 2. Mice -- Graphic novels 3. Siblings -- Graphic novels
ISBN 978-0-9799238-0-7; 0-9799238-0-8

Other titles about Benny and Penny are:
Benny and Penny in the big no-no! (2009);
Benny and Penny in the toy breaker (2010);
Benny and Penny in Lights out! (2012);
Benny and Penny in Lost and found! (2014)

"The sweet, delicately colored illustrations have an old-fashioned feel that gives the familiar sibling story a timeless quality. . . . The text uses a limited vocabulary with sufficient repetition to help with word recognition. . . . A charmer that will invite repeated readings." Booklist

★ **Benny** and Penny in The big no-no! a Toon Book. RAW Junior 2009 32p il $12.95

Grades: PreK K 1 2   **741.5**

1. Graphic novels 2. Mice -- Graphic novels 3. Siblings -- Graphic novels
ISBN 978-0-9799238-9-0; 0-9799238-9-1

LC 2008-36307

ALA ALSC Geisel Award (2010)

Two mice meet their new neighbor and discover that she is not as scary as they feared

"The simple text uses basic vocabulary and repetition, making it accessible to emerging readers. Young children will love the graphic-novel format and the sweet, charming illustrations will draw them into the narrative." SLJ

★ **Patrick** in A teddy bear's picnic and other stories; a Toon book. Toon Books 2011 32p il $12.95

Grades: PreK K 1 2   **741.5**

1. Graphic novels 2. Bullies -- Fiction 3. Teddy bears -- Fiction 4. Mother-child relationship -- Fiction
ISBN 978-1-935179-09-2; 1-935179-09-8

LC 2010-40209

The adventures of Patrick the little teddy bear as he goes on a picnic with his mother, tries to avoid his nap, goes to the bakery to buy cookies, and contends with the bullying Big Bear.

"The bears have an endearing physicality . . . and Hayes displays a keen awareness of the volatility of a child's moods. . . . The rich vocabulary talks to kids on their own level but will also gently push their reading abilities." Booklist

Helfand, Lewis

Conquering Everest; the lives of Edmund Hillary and Tenzing Norgay. illustrated by Amit Tayal. Kalyani Navyug Media 2011 91p il (Campfire Graphic Novels Series) pa $12.99

Grades: 5 6 7 8   **741.5**

1. Mountaineering 2. Mountaineers 3. Nonfiction writers
ISBN 978-93-80741-24-6; 93-80741-24-3

LC 2011321480

"The exploits of two young men mad for climbing mountains are retold in graphic panels. . . . Tayal captures their likeness in flurries of small but visually varied cartoon scenes, often placing figures in front of reworked photos of forbidding ice fields and peaks. Helfand fills the dialogue-heavy narrative with specific biographical details amd exciting accounts of some of the great triumphs and tragedies of Himalayan mountaineering. . . . A vivid double character portrait, enhanced by equally sharp glimpses of climbing techniques, strategies and hazards." Kirkus

Herge

The **adventures** of Tintin, vol. 1; Tintin in America, Cigars of the Pharaoh, The Blue Lotus. Little, Brown 1994 192p il $18.99

Grades: 4 5 6 7 8 9   **741.5**

1. Graphic novels 2. Adventure graphic novels 3. Tintin (Fictional character) -- Graphic novels
ISBN 0-316-35940-8

Tintin, the heroic boy reporter from France, travels to America where he outwits gangsters in Chicago of the 1930s and adventures in the Wild West; sails the Mediterranean Sea with faithful dog Snowy and finds himself in a mystery involving a movie tycoon, drugs, and cigars in an ancient Egyptian tomb; then he travels to India to finally solve the mystery. This Little, Brown edition reprints some of the early Tintin adventures published in the 1930s in a 3-in-1 volume. This is the first in a series that reprints most of the Tintin stories by Herge. Librarians and teachers should note that the books retain some stereotypical depictions of people of other cultures and remember that these were acceptable and expected at the time of original publication.

Herrod, Mike

Doggie dreams. Blue Apple Books 2011 il (Balloon toons) $10.99

Grades: K 1 2 3   **741.5**

1. Graphic novels 2. Dogs -- Fiction 3. Dreams -- Fiction
ISBN 978-1-60905-065-8; 1-60905-065-7

LC 2010046646

Simple text and illustrations in comic book style reveal a dog's dreams, which feature abundant food, singing, and an opportunity to demonstrate courage.

"Unfussy illustrations of the ambitious pup in repose enhance the story's humor." Horn Book Guide

Hoena, B. A.

Jack and the beanstalk: the graphic novel; retold by Blake A. Hoena; illustrated by Ricardo Tercio. Stone Arch Books 2009 33p il $21.26

Grades: 2 3 4 5   **741.5**

1. Graphic novels 2. Fairy tales -- Graphic novels
ISBN 978-1-4342-0766-1

LC 2008-6722

When Jack sells the family cow for a handful of beans, his mother is not pleased. However, they are magic beans, and when Jack plants them, a giant beanstalk grows. Curious about where the beanstalk has gone, Jack climbs it, and finds a giant's home up there. As he brings back such things as a chicken that lays golden eggs, his mother exclaims that he is finding his father's old treasures. But sooner or later, the giant will catch Jack. This graphic novel adaptation includes information about the history of the tale, along with a short glossary and reading questions.

Holm, Jennifer L.

★ **Babymouse**: queen of the world. Random House Books for Young Readers 2005 91p il lib bdg $12.99; pa $5.95

Grades: 3 4 5 6   **741.5**

1. Graphic novels 2. Humorous graphic novels 3. Babymouse (Fictional character) 4. Mice -- Graphic novels 5. Friendship -- Graphic novels
ISBN 0-375-93229-1 lib bdg; 0-375-83229-7 pa

LC 2004-51166

"In this energetic comic . . . Babymouse, a wise-cracking rodent stand-in for your average, adventure-seeking nine-year-old, strives to capture popular Felicia's goodwill, finally achieving her end at the expense of Wilson Weasel, truest of friends. But, wouldn't you know it, Felicia's world has little to offer a smart, fun-loving mouse, after all." Booklist

Other titles in this series are:
Babymouse: our hero (2005)
Babymouse: beach babe (2006)
Babymouse: rock star (2006)
Babymouse: heartbreaker (2006)
Camp Babymouse (2007)
Babymouse: skater girl (2007)
Babymouse: puppy love (2007)
Babymouse: monster mash (2008)
Babymouse the musical (2009)
Babymouse: dragonslayer (2009)
Babymouse burns rubber (2010)
Babymouse: cupcake tycoon (2010)
Babymouse: mad scientist (2011)
A very Babymouse Christmas (2011)
Babymouse for president (2012)
Extreme Babymouse (2012)
Happy birthday Babymouse (2014)

Brave new pond; by Jennifer L. Holm and Matthew Holm. Random House Childrens Books 2011 90p il (Squish) lib bdg $12.99; pa $6.99

Grades: 3 4 5   **741.5**

1. Graphic novels 2. School stories 3. Amebas -- Fiction 4. Popularity -- Fiction 5. Superheroes -- Fiction
ISBN 978-0-375-93784-2 lib bdg; 0-375-93784-6 lib bdg; 978-0-375-84390-7 pa; 0-375-84390-6 pa

LC 2010028084

Starting a new school year, Squish, a meek amoeba who loves the comic book exploits of his favorite hero, "Super Amoeba," is determined to get picked for kickball and hang out with the cool kids.

★ **Squish,** Super Amoeba; by Jennifer L. Holm & Matthew Holm. Random House 2011 90p il (Squish) lib bdg $12.99; pa $6.99

Grades: 3 4 5   **741.5**

1. Graphic novels 2. School stories 3. Amebas -- Fiction 4. Bullies -- Fiction 5. Superheroes -- Fiction
ISBN 978-0-375-93783-5 lib bdg; 0-375-93783-8 lib bdg; 978-0-375-84389-1 pa; 0-375-84389-2 pa

LC 2010-08004

"The hilarious misadvantures of a hapless young every-lad who happens to be an amoeba. . . . If ever a new series deserved to go viral, this one does." Kirkus

Other titles in this series are:
Brave new pond (2011)
The power of the parasite (2012)
Captain Disaster (2012)
Game on! (2013)
Fear the amoeba (2014)

Horowitz, Anthony

Stormbreaker: the graphic novel; [by] Anthony Horowitz; adapted Antony Johnston; illustrated by Kanako Damerum & Yusuru Takasaki. Philomel Books 2006 un il (Alex Rider) pa $14.99

Grades: 5 6 7 8   **741.5**

1. Graphic novels 2. Spies -- Graphic novels
ISBN 0-399-24633-9

In this graphic novel version on Horowitz's novel, four-teen-year-old Alex Rider is coerced into continuing his uncle's dangerous work for Britain's intelligence agency, MI6.

"If it's possible, this is even more rapidly paced than the novel. Alex remains an appealing hero here, and the idea of a heroic teen up against insidious adults continues to be an extremely powerful draw for readers." Booklist

Ita, Sam

★ The **Odyssey**; a pop-up book. Sterling 2011 il $26.95

Grades: 4 5 6 7   **741.5**

1. Graphic novels 2. Adventure graphic novels 3. Pop-up books
ISBN 978-1-4027-5867-6; 1-4027-5867-7

"A highlight-reel version of Odysseus' journey home, framed as a graphic novel and plastered with fantastically dramatic pop-ups and other special effects. Opening with Penelope working on a tapestry that transforms into an entirely different scene with the drop of a step-flap, the tale plunges on into the many escapes of Odysseus and his crew. . . . Ita . . . tells the tale in balloons of colloquial dialogue. . . . Even newbies will be riveted by this nonstop, high-energy retelling. Homer himself would be agog." Kirkus

Jamieson, Victoria

★ **Roller** girl; by Victoria Jamieson. Dial Books 2015 240 p. chiefly color illustrations (paperback) $12.99

Grades: 4 5 6 7 8   **741.5**

1. Graphic novels 2. Friendship -- Fiction 3. Roller

derby -- Fiction 4. Roller skating -- Fiction
ISBN 0803740166; 9780803740167

LC 2014011310

This graphic novel, by Victoria Jamieson, is "about friendship and surviving junior high through the power of roller derby. For most of her twelve years, Astrid has done everything with her best friend Nicole. But after Astrid falls in love with roller derby and signs up for derby camp, Nicole decides to go to dance camp instead. And so begins the most difficult summer of Astrid's life as she struggles to keep up with the older girls at camp." (Publisher's note)

"Jamieson captures this snapshot of preteen angst with a keenly decisive eye, brilliantly juxtaposing the nuances of roller derby with the twists and turns of adolescent girls' friendships." Kirkus

Keenan, Sheila

Dogs of war; by Sheila Keenan and illustrated by Nathan Fox. Graphix 2013 208 p. (hardcover) $22.99

Grades: 4 5 6 7   **741.5**

1. Dogs -- Fiction 2. War -- Graphic novels 3. Graphic novels 4. Dogs -- War use -- Fiction 5. World War, 1914-1918 -- Fiction 6. World War, 1939-1945 -- Fiction 7. Vietnam War, 1961-1975 -- Fiction

ISBN 0545128870; 9780545128872; 9780545128889

LC 2011006735

This graphic novel, by Sheila Keenan, "tells the stories of the canine military heroes of World War I, World War II, and the Vietnam War. This collection of three fictional stories was inspired by historic battles and real military practice. Each story tells the remarkable adventures of a soldier and his service dog . . . bringing to life the faithful dogs who braved bombs, barrages, and battles to save the lives of countless soldiers." (Publisher's note)

Includes bibliographical references

Kibuishi, Kazu

★ **Amulet,** book one: The Stonekeeper. Graphix 2008 185p $21.99; pa $9.99

Grades: 3 4 5 6 7 8   **741.5**

1. Graphic novels 2. Fantasy graphic novels 3. Mystery graphic novels 4. Adventure graphic novels

ISBN 978-0-439-84680-6; 0-439-84680-3; 978-0-439-84681-3 pa; 0-439-84681-1 pa

After a family tragedy, Emily, Navin, and their mother move to an ancestral home to start a new life. When their mother is kidnapped by a tentacled creature, Em and Navin have to figure out how to set things straight and save their mother's life.

"Filled with excitement, monsters, robots, and mysteries, this fantasy adventure will appeal to many readers." SLJ

Other titles in this series are:

The Stonekeeper's curse (2009)
The Cloud Searchers (2010)
The Last Council (2011)
Prince of the elves (2012)
Escape from Lucien (2014)

Copper. Graphix/Scholastic 2010 94p il $21.99; pa $12.99

Grades: 5 6 7 8   **741.5**

1. Graphic novels 2. Adventure graphic novels 3. Science fiction graphic novels 4. Dogs -- Graphic novels

ISBN 978-0-545-09892-2; 0-545-09892-0; 978-0-545-09893-9 pa; 0-545-09893-9 pa

A collection of graphic novel adventures about a boy named Copper and his dog, Fred, including "navigating a dangerous forest of giant mushrooms, [and] surviving a crash landing in a homemade airplane—that run from lyrical to the downright apocalyptic. Illustrated in a deceptively simple style, its solemn tenor and deep strangeness . . . will likely inspire heavy investment from those who prefer a somewhat off-kilter read." Booklist

Kim, Susan

★ **City** of spies; [by] Susan Kim [and] Laurence Klavan; illustrated by Pascal Dizin. First Second 2010 172p il pa $17

Grades: 4 5 6 7   **741.5**

1. Graphic novels 2. Adventure graphic novels 3. Spies -- Graphic novels 4. World War, 1939-1945 -- Graphic novels

ISBN 1-59643-262-4 pa; 978-1-59643-262-8 pa

This graphic novel, set in New York City during World War II, tells the story of Kim and Klavan, who are hunting for Nazi spies. (Bull Cent Child Books)

"With her mother gone and a father who has better things to do than be bothered raising a daughter, Evelyn is sent to live with her unconventional Aunt Lia in the bohemian art world of 1942 New York City. . . . Evelyn spends much of her time in the company of imaginary superheroes, fouling up the plans of Nazi spies. Before long she finds an unlikely friend in the building superintendent's son, Tony. Together, they . . . stumble upon an actual Nazi plot. With stupefying precision, Dizin's art channels Hergé's Tintin in tone, palette, and with the remarkable expressiveness of the clean, flexible figures. . . . With villains and danger that just border on the genuinely scary, the tale is filled not only with a thrilling sense of excitement but also with a child's longing for a grown-up to believe in." Booklist

Kochalka, James

Dragon Puncher. Top Shelf 2010 36p il $9.95

Grades: PreK K 1 2   **741.5**

1. Graphic novels 2. Cats -- Graphic novels 3. Dragons -- Graphic novels

ISBN 978-1-60309-057-5; 1-60309-057-6

This is the story of The Dragon Puncher, a cute but ruthless kitty in an armored battle suit who is dedicated to defeating dangerous dragons, and his would-be sidekick Spoony-E (a fuzzy little fellow armed with a wooden spoon).

This is illustrated using Kochalka's "signature child-like figures collaged onto photographed backgrounds with the faces of himself, his son, and his cat. . . . Through Kochalka's guerilla, one-man-and-a-pen style of creation, it magically captures the exact sense of zaniness often discovered in . . . playtime. . . . Remarkably, it does this without losing coherence; and with huge panels and spare dialogue that will amuse kids and adults, it's also the rare graphic novel that makes an excellent read-aloud." Booklist

Johnny Boo: the best little ghost in the world! Top Shelf Productions 2008 40p pa $9.95

Grades: K 1 2 3   **741.5**

1. Graphic novels 2. Humorous graphic novels 3. Ghosts -- Graphic novels 4. Friendship -- Graphic

novels
ISBN 978-1-60309-013-1

"Johnny Boo may be the best little ghost in the world, with the best little ghost pet, Squiggle, but that doesn't mean he's ready to face down scary Ice Cream Monster. When the monster turns out not to be scary after all, Johnny and Squiggle take it on as a new, if unpredictable, friend. Kochalka's simple line drawings and bright crayon colors stand out in this sweet, silly graphic novel. . . . The dialogue is fairly simple but never simplistic, and the text is printed clearly enough to make the book accessible to children just beginning to pick up chapter books." Booklist

Other titles in this series are:
Johnny Boo: Twinkle power (2009)
Johnny Boo and the happy apples (2009)
Johnny Boo and the mean little boy (2010)
Johnny Boo does something! (2013)
Johnny Boo zooms to the moon! (2014)

Kovac, Tommy
Wonderland; written by Tommy Kovac; illustrated by Sonny Liew. Disney Press 2008 159p il $19.99
Grades: 4 5 6 7 8   741.5
1. Graphic novels 2. Fantasy graphic novels
ISBN 978-1-4231-0451-3; 1-4231-0451-X

First published as single-issue comics by SLG Publishing
"Ever wonder what happened in Wonderland after Alice left? Follow the quirky tale of Mary Ann, the meticulous and dutiful housekeeper for the White Rabbit, as she continues the tale. Her boss is now wanted for treason by the Queen of Hearts for allowing the Alice Monster to enter the kingdom—off with his head! On the run and fearing for their lives, Mary Ann and White Rabbit encounter the meddlesome Cheshire Cat, the ever-contentious troublemaker, sending the White Rabbit straight into the clutches of the queen and poor Mary Ann tumbling into the Treacle Well. . . . This is a terrific look at a great classic. The energetic, action-packed illustrations complement the story in Disney-cartoon style, making for a great read for all ages" SLJ

Krosoczka, Jarrett J.
Lunch Lady and the League of Librarians. Alfred A. Knopf 2009 un il lib bdg $11.99; pa $5.99
Grades: 3 4 5 6 7 8   741.5
1. Graphic novels 2. Humorous graphic novels 3. Games -- Graphic novels 4. Librarians -- Graphic novels 5. School stories -- Graphic novels 6. School children -- Food -- Graphic novels
ISBN 978-0-375-94684-4 lib bdg; 0-375-94684-5 lib bdg; 978-0-375-84684-7 pa; 0-375-84684-0 pa
LC 2008043117

The school lunch lady, a secret crime fighter, sets out to stop a group of librarians bent on destroying a shipment of video games, while a group of students known as the Breakfast Bunch provides back-up

"The black-and-white pen-and-ink illustrations have splashes of yellow in nearly every panel. The clean layout, featuring lots of open space, is well suited for the intended audience. . . . With its appealing mix of action and humor, this clever, entertaining addition to the series should have wide appeal." SLJ

Other titles about the Lunch Lady are:
Lunch lady and the cyborg substitute (2009)
Lunch Lady and the author visit vendetta (2009)

Lunch Lady and the summer camp shakedown (2010)
Lunch Lady and the bake sale bandit (2010)
Lunch Lady and the field trip fiasco (2011)
Lunch Lady and the mutant mathletes (2012)
Lunch Lady and the picture day peril (2012)
Lunch Lady and the video game villain (2013)
Lunch Lady and the schoolwide shuffle (2014)

Larson, Hope
Chiggers; [by] Hope Larson; lettered by Jason Azzopardi. Atheneum Books for Young Readers 2008 170p il $17.99; pa $9.99
Grades: 5 6 7 8 9   741.5
1. Graphic novels 2. Camps -- Fiction 3. Friendship -- Graphic novels
ISBN 978-1-4169-3584-1; 978-1-4169-3587-2 pa
LC 2008-09557

When Abby returns to the same summer camp she always goes to, she is dismayed to find that her old friends have changed, and the only person who wants to be her friend is the strange new girl, Shasta.

"Chiggers provides a ticket to summer fun. Larson delicately handles both the usual middle-school angst and the additional pressures that come with being somewhat different. . . . The content is perfect for upper elementary and middle school students." SLJ

Le Gall, Frank
Freedom! Frank Le Gall; illustrated by Flore Balthazar; coloring by Robin Doo. Graphic Universe 2012 40 p. col. ill.
Grades: 2 3 4   741.5
1. Animals -- Fiction 2. Freedom -- Fiction 3. Cats -- Graphic novels 4. Mice -- Graphic novels 5. Graphic novels
ISBN 0761378847; 9780761378846
LC 2011021726

"Miss Annie is a kitten, and she does all of the expected kitten activities--playing with pens and yarn, napping on armchairs, and begging for food. But she does the unexpected, too, like befriending a mouse she knows she's supposed to hunt. On her first adventure outside of the house, she meets two older cats, Zeno and Miss Rostropovna, who guide her through the big, new world. Annie has a wide range of expressions, from her perked ears to the tip of her pert tail." (Publishers Weekly)

"A charming balance of cartoon and natural kitty-ness in full-color, eight-panel pages, this cat's-eye view of life will induce purrs in feline fans everywhere." Kirkus

Rooftop cat; by Frank Le Gall; illustrated by Flore Balthazar; coloring by Robin Doo. 1st American ed. Lerner/Graphic Universe 2012 40 p. col. ill. (paperback) $6.95; (lib. bdg.: alk. paper) $29.27
Grades: 2 3 4   741.5
1. Graphic novels 2. Cats -- Fiction 3. Mice -- Fiction 4. Animals -- Infancy -- Fiction
ISBN 0761385479; 9780761385479; 9780761378853
LC 2011025646

The author, Frank Le Gall, presents another entry in his Miss Annie book series. "Miss Annie is just a kitten, but she loves having adventures on the rooftops outside her home. When a gang of dangerous alley cats invade her street, Miss Annie will have to prove her bravery and determination .

. . and her loyalty to her very best friend, a mouse." (Publisher's note)

Lemke, Donald

Zinc Alloy: Super Zero; illustrated by Douglas Holgate. Stone Arch Books 2009 33p il $21.26

Grades: 2 3 4 5 6 7   741.5

1. Graphic novels 2. Humorous graphic novels 3. Superhero graphic novels 4. Robots -- Graphic novels 5. Bullies -- Graphic novels

ISBN 978-1-4342-0762-3

       LC 2008-6712

Zack Allen loves to read comics, especially Robo Hero; unfortunately, he's the kind of kid that bullies like to pick on, and they have done so. Then Zack builds his own robot suit; he was just going to get the bullies to stop, but when he hears about a runaway train, he uses the suit to become a new superhero Zinc Alloy! He's going to have to work on controlling things a lot better, though how will he explain broken doors to his mom? The book includes a short history of comic books and the glossary includes definitions for "noogies" and "wet willies."

Liniers, 1973-

★ The big wet balloon; a Toon book. by Liniers. Toon Books 2013 32 p. chiefly color illustrations (Easy-to-read comics. Level 2) (alk. paper) $12.95

Grades: PreK K 1 2   741.5

1. Graphic novels 2. Sisters -- Fiction 3. Balloons -- Fiction 4. Rain and rainfall -- Fiction

ISBN 1935179322; 9781935179320

       LC 2012047662

Eisner Nominee: Best Publication for Early Readers (2014)

This book by Ricardo Liniers "shows several tableaus of two little girls who wake up in the room they share and spend the day together. The older sister suggests fun things to do, like shouting at the top of their lungs while they run through a rain shower. Though they have one small misunderstanding, these siblings are loving and thoughtful--good companions whatever the weather." (New York Times Book Review)

"An uncommonly family-friendly tale, great for parents to share with their kids." Booklist

Littlefield, Holly

The rooftop adventure of Minnie and Tessa, factory fire survivors; by Holly Littlefield; adaptation by Amanda Doering Tourville; illustrated by Ted Hammond and Richard Carbajal. Graphic Universe 2011 31p il (History's kid heroes) $26.60

Grades: 3 4 5 6   741.5

1. Graphic novels 2. Catholics -- Fiction 3. Immigrants -- Fiction 4. New York (N.Y.) -- Fiction 5. Jews -- United States -- Fiction 6. Triangle Shirtwaist Company, Inc. -- Fiction

ISBN 978-0-7613-6179-4; 0-7613-6179-0

       LC 2010028952

Adapted from the 1996 novel Fire at the Triangle Factory by Holly Littlefield

Two immigrant friends, Jewish Minnie and Catholic Tessa, work long hours at New York City's Triangle Shirtwaist Factory, and when a fire breaks out on March 25, 1911, trapping dozens of workers inside, they help one another to escape the flames. Includes facts about the factory, the fire, and its aftermath.

"Presented in graphic novel form, the dark intensity of the illustrations engages the reader." Jewish Book World

Includes bibliographical references

Liu, Na

★ Little White Duck; a childhood in China. by Andrés Vera Martínez and Na Liu; illustrated by Andrés Vera Martínez. Graphic Universe 2012 96 p. col. ill. (lib. bdg.: alk. paper) $29.27; (pbk.) $9.95

Grades: 4 5 6   741.5

1. China -- History -- 1976- 2. Biographical graphic novels 3. Graphic novels

ISBN 0761365877; 9780761365877; 9780761381150; 0761381155

       LC 2011005347

This graphic novel provides a "glimpse into Chinese girlhood during the 1970s and '80s." It begins with the 3-year-old narrator trying to understand the death of Chairman Mao. "From there, her life unfolds in short sketches. . . . She explains about the four pests that plague China . . . and her stomach-turning school assignment to catch rats and deliver the severed tails to her teacher . . . [as well as] the origins of Chinese New Year, her favorite holiday." (Kirkus Reviews)

"This picturesque treasure introduces Chinese culture through a personal perspective that is both delightful and thought-provoking." SLJ

Long, Ethan

Rick & Rack and the great outdoors. Blue Apple 2010 un il (Balloon toons) $10.99

Grades: 1 2 3   741.5

1. Graphic novels 2. Deer -- Fiction 3. Nature -- Fiction 4. Raccoons -- Fiction 5. Friendship -- Fiction

ISBN 978-1-60905-034-4; 1-60905-034-7

       LC 2010-32388

Rick the raccoon and Rack the deer spend a day fishing, tracking wild animals, and canoeing on a lake.

"This graphic novel takes beginning readers through three very short and humorous stories. . . . This . . . puts the comics medium to good use: tracking the visual elements of the story will help emerging readers decode the text with ease." Booklist

Luciani, Brigitte

The meeting; illustrated by Eve Tharlet. Graphic Universe 2010 32p il (Mr. Badger and Mrs. Fox) lib bdg $25.26; pa $6.95

Grades: 1 2 3   741.5

1. Graphic novels 2. Foxes -- Graphic novels 3. Badgers -- Graphic novels 4. Siblings -- Graphic novels

ISBN 0-7613-5625-8 lib bdg; 0-7613-5631-2 pa; 978-0-7613-5625-7 lib bdg; 978-0-7613-5631-8 pa

       LC 2009032617

Having lost their home, a fox and her daughter move in with a badger and his three children, but when the youngsters throw a big party hoping to prove that they are incompatible, their plan backfires.

"Rendered as a beginning graphic novel, the story and characters are presented with plenty of heart and soul: expressive anthropomorphic faces and postures and rich dialogue require and reward engagement. Watercolor panels vary in size on folio pages, and balloons contain an easy-to-read font." Booklist

Other titles in this series are:
A hubbub (2010)
What a team! (2011)
Peace and quiet (2012)
The carnival (2014)

Lynch, Jay

Mo and Jo: fighting together forever; a toon book. by [illustrator] Dean Haspiel & [writer] Jay Lynch. RAW Junior 2008 40p il $12.95

Grades: K 1 2 3   **741.5**
1. Graphic novels 2. Humorous graphic novels 3. Superhero graphic novels 4. Siblings -- Graphic novels
ISBN 978-0-9799238-5-2

Mona and Joey are battling twins, and everything they do turns into a fight. They both love the same superhero, the Mighty Mojo. One day he comes to their house and says he needs to retire and gives them his costume, which has all his powers

"The text is peppered with puns and some clever idiom work, reinforced by repetition as well as what's happening in the clean panels and art." Booklist

Macherot, R.

Sibyl-Anne vs. Ratticus; translated from the French by Kim Thompson. Fantagraphics 2011 64p il $16.99

Grades: 5 6 7 8   **741.5**
1. Graphic novels 2. Mice -- Graphic novels
ISBN 978-1-60699-452-8; 1-60699-452-2

"This collection of comics, originally published in Spirou magazine in 1966 and 1967, contains several stories in which the mouse Sibyl-Anne and her friends fight back the greedy villain Ratticus. This is the first time that American audiences will be able to appreciate this story arc from the golden age of Franco-Belgian comics. . . . [The stories] are lighthearted and sometimes surreal adventures that use an artistic style reminiscent of classic comics such as Blondie or Pogo. The colors are bright and the creatures are adorable. . . . An enjoyable read for kids, teens, and even adults." SLJ

Manning, Matthew K.

Ali Baba and the forty thieves; retold by Matthew K. Manning; illustrated by Ricardo Osnaya. Stone Arch Books 2010 63p il lib bdg $26.65; pa $6.95

Grades: 4 5 6   **741.5**
1. Graphic novels 2. Folklore -- Graphic novels
ISBN 978-1-4342-1988-6 lib bdg; 1-4342-1988-7 lib bdg; 978-1-4342-2776-8 pa; 1-4342-2776-6 pa
LC 2010020144

"Ali Baba is a poor man who stumbles upon a hidden cave where a band of thieves hides its loot, opening the cave with the phrase open sesame and closing it with close sesame. When he brings some of the treasure home, his greedy brother, Kasim, finds out and forces Ali Baba to tell him everything; but the thieves discover Kasim in their cave and kill him. When they hunt after Ali Baba, it takes the courage and cunning of the servant girl Marjana to save Ali Baba and his family. Osnaya's stylish art and Manning's story combine to make a dynamic comic book." Booklist

Martin, Ann M.

The **Baby**-sitter's Club: Kristy's great idea; a graphic novel. [text by Ann M. Martin; art] by Raina Telgemeier. Scholastic Graphix 2006 192p il $16.99; pa $8.99

Grades: 3 4 5 6   **741.5**
1. Graphic novels 2. Friendship -- Graphic novels 3. Babysitting -- Graphic novels
ISBN 0-439-80241-5; 0-439-73933-0 pa
LC 2005-37749

Follows the adventures of Kristy and the other members of the Baby-sitters Club as they deal with crank calls, uncontrollable two-year-olds, wild pets, and parents who do not always tell the truth. A graphic novel based on the 1988 book by the same name.

"Comics artist Telgemeier's clean-lined, black-and-white art with stark black details nicely differentiates the four personable seventh-graders who parlay their babysitting experience into a business." Booklist

Other titles about the Baby-sitters Club are:
The truth about Stacey (2006)
Mary Anne saves the day (2007)
Claudia and Mean Janine (2008)

McCann, Jim

★ **Return** of the Dapper Men; written by Jim McCann; art by Janet Lee; lettered by Dave Lanphear; edited by Stephen Christy. Archaia Comics 2010 un il $24.95

Grades: 4 5 6 7 8   **741.5**
1. Graphic novels 2. Science fiction graphic novels 3. Robots -- Graphic novels
ISBN 978-1-932386-90-5; 1-932386-90-4

"In the dreamy land of Anorev, children, all under age 11, live underground among intricate gear-work mechanisms, while elegant robots live in abandoned houses aboveground. . . . All are perpetually stuck in the same day, and time has, essentially, ceased to mean anything—until 314 Dapper Men rain from the sky and set in motion the impetus for change. . . . Where this book truly stands out is how well the story works in concert with Lee's stunning artwork, which employs an art nouveau sheen. . . . A true dazzler that speaks on multiple levels for both child and adult readers and one that gets richer with each read." Booklist

McCranie, Stephen

★ **Mal** and Chad; the biggest, bestest time ever. Philomel Books 2011 218p il pa $9.99

Grades: 2 3 4 5   **741.5**
1. Graphic novels 2. Adventure graphic novels 3. Dogs -- Graphic novels 4. Schools -- Graphic novels 5. Time travel -- Graphic novels
ISBN 978-0-399-25221-1; 0-399-25221-5
LC 2010036904

Fourth-grade genius Mal and his talking dog Chad shrink themselves to microscopic size and travel through time, but girls and the school bully present bigger challenges.

"McCranie captures both the big-eyed, round-headed cartoon adorableness of his characters and the realistic (though age-appropriate) menace of the dinosaurs with equal aplomb. . . . An unusually satisfying read." Booklist

McGuiness, Dan

Pilot & Huxley: the first adventure. Graphix 2011 62p il pa $7.99

Grades: 3 4 5   **741.5**
1. Graphic novels 2. Adventure graphic novels
ISBN 978-0-545-26504-1 pa; 0-545-26504-5 pa

"After a late video-game rental puts them on the wrong side of some aliens who want to destroy Earth, innocent boys Pilot and Huxley are transported into an alternate dimension where Huxley's name is the ultimate swear word and boats sail on bees instead of water. . . . Our heroes will see a city inside a dragon's nose and a burger made of live rat before the exciting conclusion. It's delightfully surreal and filled with imaginative dialogue. . . . McGuinness's illustrations are colorful and kinetic, fitting the tale's many humorous twists. " Publ Wkly

Pilot & Huxley: the next adventure. Graphix 2011 60p il pa $7.99
Grades: 3 4 5   **741.5**
1. Graphic novels 2. Adventure graphic novels
ISBN 978-0-545-26845-5; 0-545-26845-1

Pilot and Huxley just want to get home, but an unexpected glitch hurtles them into the holiday lands instead. Now they're stuck in a bizarre world where ghouls and zombies in Halloween Land are friendly, and Santa and his elves in Christmas Land are evil.

"The book is full of inspired nonsense." Kirkus

McLeod, Bob
★ **SuperHero** ABC. HarperCollins Pubs. 2006 40p il $15.99; lib bdg $16.89; pa $7.99
Grades: PreK K 1 2   **741.5**
1. Alphabet 2. Graphic novels 3. Superheroes -- Fiction
ISBN 0-06-074514-2; 0-06-074515-0 lib bdg; 0-06-074516-9 pa
                       LC 2004-22180

Humorous SuperHeroes such as Goo Girl and The Volcano represent the letters of the alphabet from A to Z.

"There's strong appeal here for the youngest comic-book fans, with many doses of humor along the way. Each figure has special powers, of course, which readers learn about through alliterative captions and action-packed illustrations." SLJ

Medley, Linda
★ **Castle** waiting. Fantagraphics 2006 456p il $29.95
Grades: 5 6 7 8 9 10 11 12   **741.5**
1. Graphic novels 2. Fantasy graphic novels 3. Fairy tales -- Graphic novels
ISBN 1-56097-747-7

All of Medley's previously self-published comics are collected here in one volume for the first time. The titular castle was the home of Sleeping Beauty, whose story is retold from the viewpoint of the flibbertigibbet ladies in waiting. After the flighty princess awakens with the kiss of a handsome but not too bright prince, the castle becomes a sanctuary for various misfits. Readers will find references to many fairy tales, folk tales, and nursery rhymes in Medley's book, and her clean, clear black-and-white art reflects the works of classic illustrators such as Arthur Rackham.

Meister, Cari
Clues in the attic; illustrated by Rémy Simard. Stone Arch Books 2010 25p il (My 1st graphic novel) $21.32; pa $3.95

Grades: K 1 2   **741.5**
1. Graphic novels 2. Mystery graphic novels 3. Siblings -- Graphic novels
ISBN 978-1-4342-1889-6; 1-4342-1889-9; 978-1-4342-2283-1 pa; 1-4342-2283-7 pa

"Siblings Ben and Sofia investigate strange noises that they hear coming from above them. . . . [This title provides an] effective early-reader [equivalent] to comics and graphic novels. [Its] traditional beginning-reader trim size as well as bold and brightly colored illustrations are appealing to novice readers, while the inclusion of a 'How to Read a Graphic Novel' section, a glossary, discussion questions, and writing prompts will appeal to parents and teachers. The texts include simple sentences that closely match the art, while panels are limited to a maximum of four per page. Good fun for early graphic-novel readers." SLJ

Morse, Scott
★ **Magic** Pickle; with color by Jose Garibaldi. Scholastic/Graphix 2008 un il pa $9.99
Grades: 2 3 4 5   **741.5**
1. Graphic novels 2. Humorous graphic novels 3. Superhero graphic novels
ISBN 978-0-439-87995-8 pa; 0-439-87995-7 pa

"Starting with an irresistibly goofy premise, Morse layers on sly humor, astute references, and blazing action, turning in a charming, slam-bang story." Booklist

Other titles in this series are:
Magic Pickle and the Planet of the Grapes (2008)
Magic Pickle vs. the Egg Poacher (2008)
Magic Pickle and the Garden of Evil (2009)
Magic Pickle and the Creature from the Black Legume (2009)

Mortensen, Lori
The **missing** monster card; illustrated by Rémy Simard. Stone Arch Books 2010 25p il (My 1st graphic novel) $21.32; pa $3.95
Grades: K 1 2   **741.5**
1. Graphic novels 2. Mystery graphic novels
ISBN 978-1-4342-1888-9; 1-4342-1888-0; 978-1-4342-2284-8 pa; 1-4342-2284-5 pa

"Ethan has just found a rare Monster Card in the pack he bought, and he wants to show it to his friend Zack, but when he goes to Zack's house the next day, the card isn't in his jacket pocket. The two friends search for the card to solve the mystery. . . . The book provides a short tutorial on how to navigate the panels and uses sound effects, dialogue balloons, and brief narrative text to tell the story. . . . A brief glossary, discussion questions, and writing prompts provide teachers with easy lesson plans for classroom use. The bright colors and cartoony illustrations add to the appeal for beginning readers." Booklist

Mouly, Francoise
Big fat Little Lit; [edited by] Art Spiegelman and Francoise Mouly. Puffin 2006 144p il pa $14.99
Grades: 2 3 4 5 6 7 8   **741.5**
1. Graphic novels 2. Folklore -- Graphic novels
ISBN 0-14-240706-2

This volume collects all three previously published Little Lit books: Little Lit: Once Upon a Time, Little Lit: Strange Stories for Strange Kids, and Little Lit: It Was a Dark and Silly Night. Many comics creators and children's book writers and illustrators contributed stories, including Ian Falconer, Daniel Clowes, Maurice Sendak, David Sedaris, Chris Ware, Jules Feiffer, Barbara McClintock, Crockett Johnson, J. Otto Siebold, Neil Gaiman, Art Spiegelman, and Lemony Snicket.

★ The **TOON** treasury of classic children's comics; selected and edited by Art Spiegelman and Francoise Mouly; introduction by Jon Scieszka. Abrams ComicArts 2009 350p il $40

Grades: 3 4 5 6 **741.5**

1. Comic books, strips, etc.

ISBN 978-0-8109-5730-5; 0-8109-5730-2

LC 2009009830

"These stories are terrifically funny, joltingly exuberant, bafflingly bizarre, and best of all, compiled into one hearty, hefty, handsome volume." Booklist

Naujokaitis, Pranas T.

The **totally** awesome epic quest of the brave boy knight. Blue Apple Books 2011 40p il (Balloon toons) $10.99

Grades: K 1 2 3 **741.5**

1. Graphic novels 2. Monsters -- Fiction 3. Buried treasure -- Fiction 4. Knights and knighthood -- Fiction

ISBN 978-1-60905-099-3; 1-60905-099-1

LC 2011019009

A young boy and his furry friend, Butterscotch, as brave knights, battle a green monster that is destroying a princess's kingdom, seek a hidden treasure, and patrol the kingdom.

"The tales are loopily involving, allowing both the boy and the girl to play big parts, with humor that comes in broad strokes that Naujokaitis vividly paints on the faces of the actors." Kirkus

Nobleman, Marc Tyler

★ **Boys** of Steel; The Creators of Superman. Random House Childrens Books 2013 40 p. (library) $19.99; (paperback) $7.99

Grades: 4 5 6 7 **741.5**

1. Superhero comic books, strips, etc. 2. Shuster, Joe, 1914-1992 3. Siegel, Jerry, 1914-1996 4. Superman (Fictional character)

ISBN 9780375938023; 0449810631; 9780449810637

This book by Marc Tyler Nobleman and illustrated by Ross MacDonald "tells how writer Jerry Siegel and artist Joe Shuster, two misfit teens in Depression-era Cleveland who were more like Clark Kent than his alter ego, created this superhero [Superman] and published his adventures in comic-book format." (Publishers Weekly)

Nytra, David

The **secret** of the stone frog; a Toon graphic novel. by David Nytra. Toon Books 2012 80 p. $14.95

Grades: 2 3 4 5 **741.5**

1. Siblings -- Fiction 2. Fantasy graphic novels 3. Fantasy 4. Graphic novels 5. Brothers and sisters -- Fiction

ISBN 1935179187; 9781935179184

LC 2011050431

In this children's book by David Nytra, "Leah and her younger brother, Alan, awake to find their beds relocated to the middle of a lush forest. They soon come across a stone frog that guides them toward their home. . . . Their long, strange trip is full of bees, fanciful lions, and a subway ride

. . . After they make a narrow escape when an entire town . . . comes alive, the story ends with our hero and heroine back in their beds as a new day begins." (School Library Journal)

O'Brien, Anne Sibley

★ The **legend** of Hong Kil Dong, the Robin Hood of Korea. Charlesbridge 2006 un il $14.95

Grades: 3 4 5 6 7 **741.5**

1. Graphic novels 2. Hong Kil Dong (Legendary character) 3. Korea -- Graphic novels

ISBN 978-1-58089-302-2; 1-58089-302-3

LC 2005-56941

Hong Kil Dong is the son of a powerful government minister and one of his servants; this means the father will not recognize his son as his own. The boy grows up with great intelligence and wit, and leaves home to find his fortune. He learns martial arts and magic, and when he encounters thieves who rob only because corrupt government officials have ruined them, he turns the thieves into an army to right the wrongs. This story is based on a seventeenth century Korean legend.

Includes bibliographical references

O'Connor, George

★ **Zeus**; king of the gods. Roaring Brook Press 2010 76p il (Olympians) $16.99; pa $9.99

Grades: 5 6 7 8 **741.5**

1. Graphic novels 2. Classical mythology 3. Zeus (Greek deity)

ISBN 978-1-59643-431-8; 1-59643-625-5; 978-1-59643-432-5 pa; 1-59643-431-7 pa

Retells in graphic novel format stories from Greek mythology about the exploits of the young Zeus and how he rallied an army and overthrew his father, Kronos, to become king of the gods

"It's [the] balance between respect for myth and adherence to comic-book form that works so wonderfully well here." Bull Cent Child Books

Other titles in this series are:

Athena: grey-eyed goddess (2010)

Hera: the goddess and her glory (2011)

Hades: lord of the dead (2012)

Poseidon: earth shaker (2013)

Aphrodite: goddess of love (2013)

Ares: bringer of war (2015)

O'Donnell, Liam

Power play; illustrated by Mike Deas. Orca Book Publishers 2011 64p il (Graphic guide adventure) pa $9.95

Grades: 3 4 5 6 7 8 9 **741.5**

1. Graphic novels 2. Mystery graphic novels

ISBN 978-1-55469-069-5; 1-55469-069-2

Siblings Devin and Nadia team up with their friend Marcus, Marcus' stepbrother Bounce, and Bounce's best friend Pema when they all attend the World Leaders Summit, where Marcus' father, Dr. Ashmore is scheduled to speak. The friends find themselves mixed up in a fight between some of the most powerful people in the world and those who want more equitable rights to clean water and other environmental concerns. They investigate when one of Dr. Ashmore's assistants is murdered at the summit, and Dr. Ashmore receives threats.

"An enjoyable story with educational value, this strong mystery is presented along with information about world politics, power, and the benefits of political protest for social good." Booklist

O'Malley, Kevin

Desk stories. Albert Whitman 2011 32p il

Grades: 1 2 3   **741.5**

1. Graphic novels 2. Schools -- Graphic novels

ISBN 0-8075-1562-0; 978-0-8075-1562-4

LC 2010050423

Six separate stories tell, in words and cartoons, the surprising history and activities of the ordinary school desk.

"Presented in a graphic-novel format, six fanciful, silly stories incorporate situations that any child who has endured a tedious class will appreciate. . . . This lighthearted offering will likely produce cheers rather than jeers and makes a great choice for reluctant readers." Booklist

Parker, Jake

Missile Mouse: rescue on Tankium3. Graphix 2011 146p

Grades: 3 4 5 6   **741.5**

1. Graphic novels 2. Adventure graphic novels 3. Science fiction graphic novels 4. Mice -- Graphic novels

ISBN 0545117178; 9780545117173

The daring agent Missile Mouse must help free a planet forced into slavery by evil King Bognarsh. But things get dicey when Bognarsh hires the Blazing Bat to take Missile Mouse out before he can shut the operation down.

"The crisp, vivid illustrations combine with a clear layout to create a graphic novel that works for veterans of the genre as well as newcomers. . . . Brisk and entertaining." SLJ

Missile Mouse: the star crusher. Graphix 2010 172p (Missile Mouse) $21.99; pa $10.99

Grades: 3 4 5 6   **741.5**

1. Graphic novels 2. Adventure graphic novels 3. Science fiction graphic novels 4. Mice -- Graphic novels

ISBN 978-0-545-11714-2; 0-545-11714-3; 978-0-545-11715-9 pa; 0-545-11715-1 pa

"When his mission to recover an ancient star compass goes wrong, intrepid Galactic Security Agent Missile Mouse finds himself saddled with a partner. . . . The two are to retrieve a missing scientist who holds the key to a horrible weapon, the Star Crusher, in his hereditary memory. . . . [This is] a gem in story and art. Bright, action-filled, at times wordless panels keep the pages turning. Intelligent space opera and a realistically rounded hero will have young fans of the future demanding the next volume." Kirkus

Pearson, Luke

★ **Hilda** and the troll; Luke Pearson. Flying Eye Books 2013 40 p. chiefly color illustrations (Hildafolk) $18.95

Grades: 3 4 5 6   **741.5**

1. Adventure fiction 2. Trolls -- Fiction 3. Explorers -- Fiction

ISBN 1909263141; 9781909263147

Originally appearing in print in 2010 as Hildafolk

This book, by Luke Pearson, is "about an adventurous little girl and her habit of befriending anything, no matter how curious it might seem. While on an expedition to illustrate the magical creatures of the mountains around her home, Hilda spots a mountain troll. As the blue-haired explorer sits and sketches, she slowly starts to nod off. By the

time she wakes up, the troll has totally disappeared and, even worse, Hilda is lost in a snowstorm." (Publisher's note)

"The art is as whimsical as the protagonist, and the bright colors enhance this comic book's magical-realistic effect." Horn Book

Other titles about Hilda are:

Hilda and the Midnight Giant (2012)

Hilda and the Bird Parade (2013)

Hilda and the Black Hound (2014)

Petersen, David E., 1977-

Mouse guard; volume 1 legends of the guard. Jeremy Bastian, Ted Naifeh, Alex Sheikman, et al. Archaia Entertainment 2010 144 p. col. ill. hbk $19.95

Grades: 5 6 7 8   **741.5**

1. Mice -- Fiction 2. Adventure fiction 3. Short stories -- Collections

ISBN 1932386947; 9781932386943

Eisner Award: Best Anthology (2011)

"Petersen turns to the tested and reliable bar story as a framing device to allow other writers and artists to play in his Mouse Guard universe, where heroic mice heroes are set in a world of epic fantasy. . . . One night barkeep June . . . stages a story-telling contest. What follows are thirteen tales of danger and adventure, as protagonists contend against the predators around them and the flaws that divide mouse from mouse." (Publisher's note)

"More than just supplemental material, this book broadens Petersen's magnificently imagined miniature world and is a welcome addition for any collection that values quality, all-ages graphic novels." Booklist

★ **Mouse** Guard: Fall 1152. Archaia Studios Press 2007 un il $24.95

Grades: 5 6 7 8   **741.5**

1. Graphic novels 2. Fantasy graphic novels 3. Mice -- Graphic novels

ISBN 978-1-932386-57-8; 1-932386-57-2

Eisner Award: Best Publication for Kids (2008)

In a medieval world populated by animals, mice have their own civilization but live in constant peril from predators. They live in hidden towns protected by the Guard, who also escort travelers between towns. Three young members of the Guard, Lieam, Saxon, and Kenzie, go in search of a missing grain merchant. They find him dead in the belly of a snake who tried to eat them; but they also find evidence that the dead merchant is a traitor. Now they need to find out to whom he was betraying the Guard and why. While this story features animals and is suitable for most readers who can handle some fighting action, there's nothing cute or Disneyesque in the art. Characters die, this is a serious story, but readers who have read Bone or the Harry Potter series can handle the action in this book. This is the first in a series.

Followed by: Mouse Guard: Winter 1152 (2009)

Mouse Guard: Winter 1152; story & art by David Petersen. Archaia Studios Press 2009 un il $24.95

Grades: 5 6 7 8   **741.5**

1. Graphic novels 2. Fantasy graphic novels 3. Mice -- Graphic novels

ISBN 978-1-932386-74-5; 1-932386-74-2

Sequel to: Mouse Guard: Fall 1152 (2007)

"Picking up where Fall 1152 . . . left off, Winter 1152 follows the darkening adventures of the brave troops of the

Mouse Guard as they battle the elements, predators, and even other mice in order to secure their way of life. The high-quality artwork found in the first volume carries over into this one. The narrative . . . is fast paced and compelling. . . . Combining a tale of action, romance, comedy, and tragedy with the graphic-novel format results in a topnotch work with wide appeal." SLJ

Followed by: Mouse Guard: The black axe (2013)

Petrucha, Stefan

Mickey Mouse: 300 Mickeys; writers, Stefan Petrucha . . . [et al.]; artists, Cèsar Ferioli Pelaez . . . [et al.] Boom! Kids 2011 un il pa $9.99

Grades: 3 4 5   **741.5**

1. Graphic novels 2. Mickey Mouse (Cartoon character)
ISBN 978-1-60886-627-4; 1-60886-627-0

A collection of four Mickey Mouse stories, including tales about a cloning experiment gone wrong that leads to countless copies of Mickey Mouse and an attack by an army of robot presidents during Mickey and Minnie's vacation to Mount Rushmore.

"This book combines classic comics stories with original comics from Italy and the U.S. featuring Mickey Mouse and a few of his friends. . . . The colorful art . . . is right on model with the Disney characters. Anyone who has enjoyed Mickey Mouse cartoons will have fun with these adventures, full of action and humor that is just right for younger readers." Booklist

Phelan, Matt

★ **Around** the world. Candlewick Press 2011 240p il $24.99

Grades: 4 5 6 7   **741.5**

1. Graphic novels 2. Voyages and travels
ISBN 978-0-7636-3619-7; 0-7636-3619-3

LC 2010043153

"Phelan presents three true stories of around-the-world adventures inspired by Jules Verne's Around the World in Eighty Days that, even though they were undertaken in the late 1800s, would be hardly less arduous today. Thomas Stevens, Joshua Slocum, and Nellie Bly saw the world from the seat of a bicycle, aboard a 36-foot sloop, and via trains and ships, respectively. The small, specific pleasures of Phelan's work . . . are showcased in panels laid out in horizontal bands, reinforcing the linear, ever-onward nature of each narrative. The use of limited color palettes enhances the artist's characteristic delicate, expressive pen-and-ink drawings without overpowering them, allowing each traveler's character to be the dominant story element. . . . Design elements such as borders and frames lend a jaunty festivity to a graphic novel that will appeal to aficionados of the form and any reader in search of engrossing true journeys." SLJ

★ **Bluffton**; my summers with Buster Keaton. written and illustrated by Matt Phelan. Candlewick Press 2013 240 p. chiefly color illustrations (reinforced) $22.99

Grades: 3 4 5 6   **741.5**

1. Vaudeville -- Fiction
ISBN 076365079X; 9780763650797

LC 2012947260

In this graphic novel by Matt Phelan, set "in the summer of 1908, in Muskegon, Michigan, a visiting troupe of vaudeville performers is about the most exciting thing since baseball. Henry has a few months to ogle . . . a slapstick ac-

tor his own age named Buster Keaton. Henry longs to learn to take a fall like Buster . . . but Buster just wants to play ball with Henry and his friends." (Publisher's note)

"Historical detail, a rich sense of place, expert pacing--Phelan . . . keeps all the plates in the air in this fictionalized recreation of the boyhood summers of Buster Keaton. In lightly sketched, gently tinted watercolor panels, Phelan conveys the excitement a troupe of summering vaudeville actors brings to sleepy Bluffton." Pub Wkly

★ The **storm** in the barn. Candlewick Press 2009 201p il $24.99; pa $14.99

Grades: 4 5 6 7 8 9   **741.5**

1. Graphic novels 2. Adventure graphic novels 3. Kansas -- Graphic novels 4. Monsters -- Graphic novels 5. Dust storms -- Graphic novels 6. United States -- History -- 1933-1945 -- Graphic novels
ISBN 978-0-7636-3618-0; 0-7636-3618-5; 978-0-7636-5290-6 pa; 0-7636-5290-3 pa

In Kansas of 1937, the land has been in the grip of the Dust Bowl for four years, and eleven-year-old Jack Carter has seen his family worn down by it. But the day Jack outruns a dust storm all the way home from town, he glimpses something odd in the abandoned Talbot barn, and he tries to find the courage to go into the barn and confront what is there.

"Children can read this as a work of historical fiction, a piece of folklore, a scary story, a graphic novel, or all four. Written with simple, direct language, it's an almost wordless book: the illustrations' shadowy grays and blurry lines eloquently depict the haze of the dust. A complex but accessible and fascinating book." SLJ

Pien, Lark

Long Tail Kitty. Blue Apple Books 2009 51p il $14.95

Grades: 1 2 3 4   **741.5**

1. Graphic novels 2. Humorous graphic novels 3. Cats -- Graphic novels 4. Friendship -- Graphic novels
ISBN 978-1-934706-44-2

"This collection of comics stories opens with Long Tail Kitty showing readers where he lives. He makes friends with a bee, ice-skates with Good Tall Mouse, and makes dinner with Bernice the dog. When alien friends arrive in their flying saucer, Long Tail Kitty is waiting with a whole list of fun things to do (which are depicted on a foldout page filled with little panels), including building box forts, playing ninja, reading comics, blowing bubbles, doing cartwheels, and much more." (Booklist)

"The volume's appeal lies in the tidy, thoughtfully shaded panels and the cast's playful banter and witty barbs." Horn Book

Pilkey, Dav

The **adventures** of Ook and Gluk; Kung-fu cavemen from the future. by George Beard and Harold Hutchins. Blue Sky Press 2010 175p il $9.99

Grades: 3 4 5   **741.5**

1. Graphic novels 2. Kung fu -- Graphic novels 3. Time travel -- Graphic novels
ISBN 978-0-545-17530-2; 0-545-17530-5

LC 2010-904867

Friends Ook and Gluk are always getting into trouble with their village chief until they pass through a portal into a future run by the chief's descendant, where they learn kung fu so they can return to the past and free their people.

Powell, Martin

The **tall** tale of Paul Bunyan: the graphic novel; retold by Martin Powell; illustrated by Aaron Blecha. Stone Arch Books 2010 35p il (Tall tale) $22.65

Grades: 1 2 3 4   **741.5**

1. Tall tales 2. Graphic novels 3. Bunyan, Paul (Legendary character) 4. Folklore -- Graphic novels

ISBN 978-1-4342-1897-1; 1-4342-1897-X

The legendary woodsman Paul Bunyan was the biggest man who ever lived. One day, Paul finds a big blue ox frozen in the snow. He nurses the behemoth back to health, and names his new companion Babe.

"The book is complemented by excellent design work that mixes advertising tropes with frontier photographic elements to help reinforce the legendary quality of the myth." SLJ

Pyle, Kevin C.

Take what you can carry; Kevin C. Pyle. Henry Holt and Co. 2012 176 p. chiefly ill. (some col.) (hc) $12.99

Grades: 4 5 6   **741.5**

1. Teenagers -- Graphic novels 2. Shoplifting -- Graphic novels 3. Japanese Americans -- Evacuation and relocation, 1942-1945 -- Graphic novels

ISBN 0805082867; 9780805082869

LC 2011924430

In this graphic novel, in "1977 suburban Chicago, Kyle runs wild with his friends and learns to shoplift from the local convenience store. In 1941 Berkeley, the Himitsu family is forced to leave their home for a Japanese-American internment camp, and their teenage son must decide how to deal with his new life. But though these boys are growing up in wildly different places and times, their lives intersect in more ways than one, as they discover compassion, learn loyalty, and find renewal." (Publisher's note)

Ransom, Candice F.

The **lifesaving** adventure of Sam Deal, shipwreck rescuer; adaptation by Amanda Doering Tourville; illustrated by Zachary Trover. Graphic Universe 2011 31p il (History's kid heroes) lib bdg $26.60; pa $8.95

Grades: 2 3 4   **741.5**

1. Graphic novels 2. Horses -- Graphic novels 3. Shipwrecks -- Graphic novels 4. North Carolina -- Graphic novels 5. African Americans -- Graphic novels

ISBN 978-0-7613-6177-0 lib bdg; 0-7613-6177-4 lib bdg; 978-0-7613-6196-1 pa; 0-7613-6196-0 pa

LC 2009051719

In 1896, ten-year-old Sam Deal and Ginger, the wild horse he has tamed, assist an all-Black lifesaving crew as they attempt to rescue survivors of a shipwreck off North Carolina's Outer Banks.

This book provides an "exciting [glimpse] into the past, with just the right amount of tension and intensity to capture readers' attention. . . . [It] will serve as [a] good [introduction] to graphic novels and historical fiction for early readers. Added bonuses are the brief yet informative [introduction] and [afterword] providing more facts about the [setting]." SLJ

Includes bibliographical references

Reinhart, Matthew

DC super heroes: The ultimate pop-up book. Little, Brown 2010 un il $29.99

Grades: PreK K 1 2   **741.5**

1. Pop-up books 2. Superheroes -- Fiction

ISBN 978-0-316-01998-9; 0-316-01998-4

"The illustrations in this detailed and decidedly heroic pop-up compendium of superheroes and supervillains feel ripped from the pages of classic DC comics. Favorites like Superman, Batman, and Wonder Woman get their own majestic spreads . . . while mini-booklets highlight their allies, nemeses, and histories. Each spread is dramatic and dynamic. . . . Expertly crafted and superfun." Publ Wkly

Renier, Aaron

Spiral-bound. Top Shelf Productions 2005 144p il pa $14.95

Grades: 4 5 6 7 8 9   **741.5**

1. Graphic novels 2. Mystery graphic novels

ISBN 1-891830-50-3

"Turnip the elephant is using the summer to find his artistic voice through sculpture, his friend Stucky the dog is building a submarine, and Ana the rabbit is working on the town's underground newspaper. Their stories all wind around the town's deep, dark secret about the monster that lives in the pond. . . . The characters seem like real children, wholesome without being too sweet, and Renier's art is light and fun, a sort of Babar meets underground comix." Booklist

★ The **Unsinkable** Walker Bean; written and illustrated by Aaron Renier; colored by Alec Longstreth. First Second 2010 191p il pa $13.99

Grades: 5 6 7 8   **741.5**

1. Graphic novels 2. Adventure graphic novels

ISBN 978-1-59643-453-0 pa; 1-59643-453-8 pa

The story "centers around a cursed skull stolen from the lair of two deep-sea crustacean witches. Like all who look upon the skull, Walker's beloved grandpa falls deathly ill when he finds it, and the boy sets out to return the skull from whence it came. . . . The generous page size lets [the] reader dive into Renier's quavery and painstakingly detailed cartooning, and he really shows off his stuff with a bounty of full-splash dazzlers. . . . Exciting, deep, funny, and scary, with tremendous villains and valor galore." Booklist

Reynolds, Aaron

Joey Fly, private eye in big hairy drama; written by Aaron Reynolds; illustrated by Neil Numberman. Henry Holt 2010 128p il (Joey Fly, private eye) $16.99

Grades: 3 4 5 6   **741.5**

1. Graphic novels 2. Mystery graphic novels

ISBN 978-0-8050-8243-2; 0-8050-8243-3

When Greta Divawing, butterfly star of the Scarab Beetle Theatre, goes missing a week before the opening performance of "Bugliacci," Joey Fly is called in to investigate her puzzling disappearance.

"Numberman's stripped-down art combines just the right amount of grotesquerie with lively storytelling to propel the story along." Publ Wkly

Joey Fly, private eye in Creepy crawly crime; illustrations by Neil Numberman. Henry Holt & Co. 2009 96p il (Joey Fly, private eye) $16.95; pa $9.95

Grades: 3 4 5 6   **741.5**
1. Graphic novels 2. Mystery graphic novels
ISBN 978-0-8050-8242-5; 0-8050-8242-5; 978-0-
8050-8786-4 pa; 0-8050-8786-9 pa
LC 2007-40041
"In a city inhabited by insects, Joey fly is a private eye
combating crime for a fee. . . . Young readers will be amused
by this noir-type story filled with classic detective dialogue
and swarms of insect humor." Booklist

Robbins, Trina
The **drained** brains caper; [by] Trina Robbins and Ty-
ler Page. Graphic Universe 2010 64p il (Chicagoland
Detective Agency) lib bdg $27.97; pa $6.95
Grades: 4 5 6 7   **741.5**
1. Graphic novels 2. Mystery graphic novels 3.
Humorous graphic novels 4. Brainwashing -- Fiction
5. Schools -- Graphic novels 6. Japanese Americans
-- Graphic novels
ISBN 978-0-7613-4601-2 lib bdg; 0-7613-4601-5 lib
bdg; 978-0-7613-5635-6 pa; 0-7613-5635-5 pa
LC 2009-32620
Required to attend summer school after moving to
Chicagoland, thirteen-year-old manga-love Megan Yama-
mura needs help from twelve-year-old computer genius
Raf Hernandez to escape the maniacal principal's mind
control experiment.
This tells "an entertaining story. . . . Page's black-and-
white cartooning has a loose manga slant, with peppy goofi-
ness popping out from stippled screen tones." Booklist
Other titles in this series are:
The Maltese mummy (2011)
Night of the living dogs (2012)
The big flush (2012)
The bark in space (2013)
A midterm night's scheme (2014)

Roche, Art
★ **Cartooning**; the only cartooning book you'll ever
need to be the artist you've always wanted to be. Lark
Books 2005 111p il (Art for kids) $17.95
Grades: 3 4 5 6   **741.5**
1. Drawing 2. Cartooning -- Technique
ISBN 1-57990-623-0
"This how-to guide is a step above the average cartooning instruction book. The glossy, full-color pages are visually attractive. . . . Roche's engaging writing style is informative and fun. . . . His loose, spacious cartooning style is
perfect for beginners or kids who might be intimidated by
more detail-oriented techniques." SLJ

Roman, Dave
Astronaut Academy: Zero gravity. First Second Books
2011 185p il pa $9.99; $16.99
Grades: 4 5 6 7 8   **741.5**
1. Graphic novels 2. Humorous graphic novels 3.
Science fiction graphic novels 4. School life -- Graphic
novels
ISBN 9781596436206; 9781596437562
LC 2010-941434
Hakata Soy has been the leader of a futuristic superhero
team, but he has given that up and just wants to be a normal
student at Astronaut Academy, a school on a space station,
where students take such courses as anti-gravity gymnastics

and fire-throwing. Other students include Doug Hiro, who
always wears his space helmet, rich girl Maribelle Mellonbelly, Miyumi San (Maribelle's rival), and egotistical Billy
Lee. Hakata Soy has some trouble adjusting to school life,
and things get much worse when the villainous Gotcha Birds
steal a robotic twin to Hakata Soy and reprogram it to kill
him. The comics originally appeared as web comics, then
as mini comics that Roman took to various comic cons; this
is the first trade book collection of the stories. Middle grade
students, boys and girls, will enjoy this book, which is full of
humor and action with little actual violence.
"Students like the introspective Hakata Soy, the space-
gymnastics-obsessed Doug Hiro, and the snooty rich girl
Mirabelle Mellonbelly meet up at Astronaut Academy, a
middle school where the zany mixes with the postmodern.
. . . Silliness is high on the agenda, aided by minimal, cartoonish art that plays on manga tropes but also manages to
build character into the simple lines of a face. . . . This is one
for readers looking for more involved and complex comedy
than a cursory glance at the images might lead one to expect." Booklist
Followed by: Astronaut academy: Re-entry (2013)

Roop, Peter
The **stormy** adventure of Abbie Burgess, lighthouse
keeper; by Peter Roop and Connie Roop; adapted by
Amanda Doering Tourville; illustrated by Zachary Trover.
Graphic Universe 2011 31p il (History's kid heroes) lib
bdg $26.60; pa $8.95
Grades: 3 4 5 6   **741.5**
1. Graphic novels 2. Lighthouse keepers 3. Maine --
Graphic novels 4. Lighthouses -- Graphic novels
ISBN 978-0-7613-6172-5 lib bdg; 0-7613-6172-3 lib
bdg; 978-0-7613-6191-6 pa; 0-7613-6191-X pa
LC 2010006748
Based on Peter & Connie Roop's Keep the lights burn-
ing, Abbie, published 1985 by Carolrhoda Books
In Maine in 1856 seventeen-year-old Abbie Burgess
lives with her family on a tiny island where her father is the
lighthouse keeper. A storm hits when her father is away and
Abbie must keep the lights burning until he returns.
This book provides an "exciting [glimpse] into the past,
with just the right amount of tension and intensity to capture
readers' attention. . . . [It] will serve as [a] good [introduc-
tion] to graphic novels and historical fiction for early readers. Added bonuses are the brief yet informative [introduc-
tion] and [afterword] providing more facts about the [set-
ting]." SLJ
Includes bibliographical references

Rosenstiehl, Agnes
★ **Silly** Lilly and the four seasons. Toon Books 2008
36p il $12.95
Grades: PreK K 1   **741.5**
1. Graphic novels 2. Humorous graphic novels 3.
Seasons -- Graphic novels
ISBN 978-0-9799238-1-4; 0-9799238-1-6
"Rosenstiehl follows Lilly . . . as she undertakes simple,
familiar activities through the seasons. . . . Lilly is bold and
engaging. . . . The text is very brief, . . . the colors are warm
and bright, and the panels are large enough to draw in children new to books and reading." Booklist

Rosenstiehl, Agnès

Silly Lilly in what will I be today? RAW Junior 2010 32p il $12.95

Grades: PreK K 1 **741.5**

1. Graphic novels 2. Week -- Fiction 3. Occupations -- Fiction

ISBN 978-1-935179-08-5; 1-935179-08-X

LC 2010005308

No job is too tough for Silly Lilly: first she's a cook who paints, then an acrobat who tumbles, then a vampire.

"This concept book meets comic is an excellent addition for beginning readers. . . . Almost all of the text appears in word bubbles written in very basic vocabulary level in simple sentences. The India ink and watercolor cartoon illustrations are clear, with white backgrounds to keep the scenes uncluttered. . . . A fine example of a book that knows its audience." SLJ

Rosinsky, Natalie M.

Graphic content! the culture of comic books. Compass Point Books 2010 64p il (Pop culture revolutions) lib bdg $31.99

Grades: 5 6 7 8 9 10 **741.5**

1. Comic books, strips, etc. -- History and criticism

ISBN 978-0-7565-4241-2 lib bdg; 0-7565-4241-3 lib bdg

Traces the origins of comic books and discusses the emergence of superheroes, censorship issues, their depiction of increased social diversity, and their impact on society

"This slim and splashily designed book . . . does an admirable job of keeping things succinct yet thorough. . . . [The author] maintains a nice international scope throughout. . . . This is a super resource to have on hand to give a broader context of the medium and its fascinating history." Booklist

Ruiz, Emilio

Waluk; by Emilio Ruiz; illustrated by Ana Miralles; translated and adapted by Dan Oliverio. Graphic Universe 2013 52 p. (lib. bdg.: alk. paper) $26.60; $7.95

Grades: 3 4 5 6 **741.5**

1. Friendship -- Fiction 2. Polar bear -- Fiction 3. Graphic novels 4. Bears -- Fiction 5. Tundras -- Fiction

ISBN 1467715980; 1467716065; 9781467715980; 9781467716062

LC 2012047787

"Young Waluk is all alone. His mother has abandoned him, as is the way of polar bears, and now he must fend for himself. But he doesn't know much about the world--and unfortunately, his Arctic world is changing quickly. The ice is melting, and food is hard to find." (Publisher's note)

"Marrying exemplary sequential storytelling, mythology, and science and enhanced through respectful anthropomorphizing, Waluk takes readers into a realistic world of polar bears endangered by climate change." Booklist

Runton, Andy

Owly: The way home and The bittersweet summer; [by] Andy Runton. Top Shelf 2004 160p il pa $10

Grades: K 1 2 3 4 5 6 7 8 9 10 11 12 **741.5**

1. Graphic novels 2. Owls -- Graphic novels 3. Friendship -- Graphic novels

ISBN 1-891830-62-7

LC 2005298860

Rotund little Owly befriends Wormy despite their differences, and together they help a couple of hummingbirds and learn that friendship doesn't end with separation.

"The whimsical black-and-white art is done with great facility for expressing emotion, and Runton's reliance on icons and pictures in lieu of the usual dialogue makes the story perfect for give-and-take between children and their parents." Booklist

Other titles in this series are:

Owly: Just a little blue (2005)

Owly: Flying lessons (2005)

Owly: A time to be brave (2007)

Owly: Tiny tales (2008)

Russell, P. Craig

★ Coraline; based on the novel by Neil Gaiman; adapted and illustrated by P. Craig Russell; colorist, Lovern Kindzierski; letterer, Todd Klein. HarperCollins 2008 186p il $18.99; lib bdg $19.89

Grades: 4 5 6 7 **741.5**

1. Graphic novels 2. Horror graphic novels

ISBN 978-0-06-082543-0; 978-0-06-082544-7 lib bdg

LC 2007-930658

"An adaptation of Gaiman's 2002 novel Coraline, . . . a tale of childhood nightmares. As in the original story, Coraline wanders around her new house and discovers a door leading into a mirror place, where she finds her button-eyed 'other mother,' who is determined to secure Coraline's love one way or another. This version is a virtuoso adaptation. . . . A master of fantastical landscapes, Russell sharpens the realism of his imagery, perserving the humanity of the characters and heightening the horror." Booklist

Salati, Giorgio

Race for the Ultrapods; writers, Giorgio Salati & Alessandro Ferrari; artists, Roberta Migheli & Antonello Dalena. Boom Kids! 2010 un il (Disney's Hero Squad: Ultraheroes) pa $9.99

Grades: 4 5 6 7 **741.5**

1. Graphic novels 2. Superhero graphic novels

ISBN 978-1-60886-560-4; 1-60886-560-6

It's the year 2734 and the only one standing in the way of earth's utter destruction . . . Mickey Mouse?! In this volume, the battle for the Ultrapods is reaching it's boiling point as The Duck Avenger and the Ultraheroes clash with the villainous Emil Eagle and his Sinister Seven.

"Disney fans, both children and adults, will enjoy [this] graphic [novel]." SLJ

Santat, Dan

Sidekicks. Arthur A. Levine Books 2011 215p il $24.99; pa $12.99

Grades: 3 4 5 6 **741.5**

1. Graphic novels 2. Superhero graphic novels 3. Pets -- Graphic novels

ISBN 978-0-439-29811-7; 0-439-29811-3; 978-0-439-29819-3 pa; 0-439-29819-9 pa

LC 2010034704

When Captain Amazing feels he is getting too old to be a reliable superhero, he tries to hire a new sidekick, but his pets have different ideas.

"Despite the presence of its charming animal characters, Santat produces much more of a dramatic adventure than a hilarious romp. . . . Realistic relationship dynamics come out. . . . . Well-crafted art balances the lighthearted and the rough-and-tumble art works equally well for the character moments and the epic battle at the end." Booklist

Sava, Scott Christian

★ **Hyperactive**; by Scott Christian Sava; artist, Joseph Bergin. IDW Publishing/Worthwhile Children's Books 2009 108p il pa $12.99

Grades: 3 4 5 6 7 8   741.5

1. Graphic novels 2. Humorous graphic novels 3. Adventure graphic novels 4. Superhero graphic novels

ISBN 978-1-60010-313-1; 1-60010-313-8

"Joey Johnson learns he can move at super speed and puts his power to good use doing household chores. But when word gets out, a shady executive sees the opportunity to make big bucks off of Joey's super DNA. . . . With its surprise ending, which suggests more to come, a readership of young boys will ensure that this one flies off the shelf at the speed of light." Booklist

Sfar, Joann

★ **The little prince**; adapted from the book by Antoine de Saint-Exupéry; translated by Sarah Ardizzone; colour by Brigitte Findakly. Houghton Mifflin Harcourt 2010 110p il $19.99

Grades: 5 6 7 8 9   741.5

1. Graphic novels 2. Fantasy graphic novels 3. Extraterrestrial beings -- Graphic novels

ISBN 978-0-547-33802-6; 0-547-33802-3

"On the surface, this is a straight graphic-novel retelling of the narrator pilot getting stranded in the desert, where he meets a curious little boy who claims to be from a wee planet very far away. . . . The ultimately tricky task is to honor the source but not sound like an adaptation (otherwise, why not just read the original?) and Sfar nails it on both counts. . . . Everything is handled with both reverence and ingenuity." Booklist

Little Vampire; stories and drawings by Joann Sfar; colors by Walter; translated by Alexis Siegel and Edward Gauvin. First Second 2008 92p il pa $13.95

Grades: 3 4 5 6   741.5

1. Graphic novels 2. Vampires -- Graphic novels 3. School stories -- Graphic novels

ISBN 1-59643-233-0 pa; 978-1-59643-233-8 pa

LC 2007-38498

First published in France

An unusual friendship forms between a vampire and a human, when Little Vampire leaves notes on homework Michael has left at school. (Bull Cent Child Books)

"Joann Sfar's art is surreal, with vivid colors, busy panels and fabulous monsters." KLIATT

Shiga, Jason

★ **Meanwhile**. Abrams/Amulet 2010 un il $15.95

Grades: 4 5 6 7 8 9   741.5

1. Graphic novels 2. Science fiction graphic novels

ISBN 0-8109-8423-7; 978-0-8109-8423-3

LC 2009-39844

In this choose-your-own adventure graphic novel, a boy stumbles on the laboratory of a mad scientist who asks him to choose between testing a mind-reading device, a time machine, and a doomsday machine. (Bull Cent Child Books)

"In this graphic novel mind boggler . . . readers play the role of little Jimmy and on the first page make the seemingly innocuous decision of ordering a vanilla or chocolate ice-cream cone. Tubes connect panels in all directions and veer off into tabs to other pages, creating a head-spinningly tangled web of story. . . . The crux is that Jimmy stumbles into the lab of an affable mad scientist and is allowed to tinker with three inventions: a mind reader, a time machine, and the Killitron, which obliterates all life on earth aside from the user's. . . . It's maddening and challenging, all right, but that's precisely what makes it so crazy fun." Booklist

Sias, Ryan

Zoe and Robot: let's pretend. Blue Apple 2011 un il (Balloon Toons) $10.99

Grades: K 1 2 3   741.5

1. Graphic novels 2. Humorous graphic novels 3. Robots -- Graphic novels 4. Imagination -- Graphic novels

ISBN 978-1-60905-063-4; 1-60905-063-0

LC 2010046829

A young girl named Zoe wants Robot to play pretend with her, but she has to teach Robot how to pretend, because "Robots do not know how to pretend." From imagining a pile of pillows is a mountain to feeling the wind from a whirring fan, Zoe tries to help Robot. Finally, she draws mountains on a pair of goggles that she puts on Robot.

"The colorful art and simple panel designs make it easy to follow the story. . . . Beginning readers can easily catch the visual cues that help them interpret the simple dialogue, and they will enjoy the humor. . . . This is a fun, easy-to-read graphic novel for beginning readers." Booklist

Siegel, Siena Cherson

★ **To dance**; a ballerina's graphic novel. [by] Siena Cherson Siegel; [illustrated by] Mark Siegel. Simon & Schuster 2006 un il pa $9.99

Grades: 4 5 6 7   741.5

1. Ballet 2. Ballet dancers 3. Graphic novels 4. Puerto Ricans -- Biography 5. Autobiographical graphic novels

ISBN 1-4169-2687-9 pa

In this memoir of her youth in dance from ages six to eighteen, Siegel tells what it was like to be totally involved in dance, in ballet—all the joys and the physical pain. She worked as a young dancer with George Ballanchine. Her absolute desire to be a dancer took her from her native Puerto Rico to New York City to study. Her simple but heartfelt narration is ably illustrated by her husband Mark Siegel.

Slavin, Bill

Big city Otto: elephants never forget. Kids Can Press 2011 il

Grades: 3 4 5 6   741.5

1. Graphic novels 2. Adventure graphic novels 3. Elephants -- Fiction

ISBN 1-55453-476-3; 1-55453-477-1 pa; 978-1-55453-476-0; 978-1-55453-477-7 pa

"Simpleton pachyderm Otto enlists his friend, a clever green parrot named Crackers, to help him find Otto's very best friend, Georgie, a chimpanzee who was stolen from their African jungle home by 'the man with the wooden nose.' The duo must make their way out of the jungle and soon find themselves across the pond in America, in the big city. When the pair falls in with a gang of crooked gators who take advantage of Otto's unfortunate peanut allergy (to help them steal gator-ade, of course), Otto and Crackers need to learn who is trustworthy—and who is out to take advantage of their naivete. Slavin's lush, full-color illustrations have a yesteryear feel with a dash of European influence." Kirkus

Big Top Otto; Big top otto. Bill Slavin. Kids Can Press 2013 88 p. (Elephants never forget) $7.95
Grades: 3 4 5 6   **741.5**
1. Circus -- Fiction 2. Elephants -- Fiction
ISBN 9781554538072; 9781554538065; 1554538068; 1554538076
                   LC 2013036468

"Otto the elephant continues his search for his childhood friend Georgie, a chimpanzee who was abducted from their forest home in Africa and shipped to the wilds of America by the Man with the Wooden Nose. When Otto sees a circus poster with a chimp that looks just like Georgie, he and his parrot friend, Crackers, follow the trail of the traveling circus." (Publisher's note)

"Silly text and illustrations will make readers laugh, but some jokes will likely go over their heads." Horn Book
Followed by: Big Star Otto (2015)

Smith, Jeff
Bone: out from Boneville. Scholastic Graphix 2005 144p il $18.95; pa $9.99
Grades: 4 5 6 7 8 9 10 11 12   **741.5**
1. Graphic novels 2. Fantasy graphic novels 3. Adventure graphic novels
ISBN 0-439-70623-8; 0-439-70640-8 pa

"The story follows three cousins who have been thrown out of their town for cheating the citizens. Shortly thereafter, they are separated. Each Bone stumbles into a mysterious valley full of odd creatures that reveal strange happenings. The story is well paced with smooth transitions. It is dark, witty, mysterious, and exciting. The full-color art reflects that of classic comic books." SLJ
Other titles in this series are:
Bone: the great cow race (vol. 2)
Bone: eyes of the storm (vol. 3)
Bone: the dragonslayer (vol. 4)
Bone: Rock Jaw: Master the Eastern Border (vol. 5)
Bone: old man's cave (vol. 6)
Bone: ghost circles (vol. 7)
Bone: treasure hunters (vol. 8)
Bone: crown of horns (vol. 9)

Bone: Rose; with illustrations by Charles Vess. Scholastic Graphix 2009 138p il $21.99; pa $10.99
Grades: 4 5 6 7 8   **741.5**
1. Graphic novels 2. Fantasy graphic novels 3. Adventure graphic novels
ISBN 978-0-545-13542-9; 0-545-13542-7; 978-0-545-13543-6 pa; 0-545-13543-5 pa

"When a terrifying dragon attacks the small towns of the Northern Valley, a young Princess Rose (known later as Gran'ma Ben) must defeat it. The beast is actually the ancient evil, the Lord of the Locusts, and while Rose faces danger with honor, her elder sister, Princess Briar, follows a more sinister path." Publisher's note

Bone: tall tales; by Jeff Smith with Tom Sniegoski; color by Steve Hamaker. Graphix 2010 108p il $21.99; pa $10.99
Grades: 4 5 6 7 8   **741.5**
1. Graphic novels 2. Fantasy graphic novels 3. Adventure graphic novels
ISBN 978-0-545-14095-9; 0-545-14095-1; 978-0-545-14096-6 pa; 0-545-14096-X pa

"Long before the Bone cousins were ever lost in the uncharted desert on the outskirts of the Valley, Big Johnson Bone, the discoverer of the Rolling Bone River, founded Boneville. But little is known of the mighty explorer's adventures before he started his famous trading post. So when Smiley Bone sits down with a group of young campers to retell the legendary stories of Boneville's origin and its tough, no-nonsense founder, what they hear are tall tales in typical BONE fashion." (Publisher's note)

★ **Little** Mouse gets ready. TOON Books 2009 32p il $12.95
Grades: PreK K 1   **741.5**
1. Graphic novels 2. Humorous graphic novels 3. Mice -- Graphic novels 4. Clothing and dress -- Graphic novels
ISBN 978-1-935179-01-6; 1-935179-01-2
                   LC 2008-55403

ALA ALSC Geisel Award Honor Book (2010)
"Little Mouse is eager to go to the barn with his mother. He slowly and methodically gets dressed, which is quite an accomplishment for the little guy, only to be reminded, in classic noodlehead fashion, that mice don't wear clothes. . . . . The cartoon illustrations are large and uncomplicated without being babyish, and the punch line is preceded with places for knowing giggles." SLJ

Sonishi, Kenji
Leave it to PET!: the misadventures of a recycled super robot, vol. 1; story & art by Kenji Sonishi; translation, Katherine Schilling; touch-up art & lettering, John Hunt; editor, Traci N. Todd. Viz Media/VizKids 2009 192p il $7.99
Grades: 3 4 5 6   **741.5**
1. Manga 2. Graphic novels 3. Humorous graphic novels 4. Recycling -- Graphic novels
ISBN 978-1-4215-2649-2

PET (polyethylene terephthalate, a type of recyclable plastic) was a simple plastic bottle until nine-year-old Noboru recycled him. Now PET is a super robot programmed to "repay" Noboru for recycling him by helping him. Unfortunately for Noboru, PET's help usually ends up causing even more trouble; being a super robot doesn't mean PET has a clue about what he is doing. The book includes lots of short stories that follow the formula of Noboru getting into a bit of a fix, calling for PET, then getting into more trouble as PET does the wrong thing. Some of the stories do include some information about recycling plastics and aluminum, which is done somewhat differently in Japan than in the U.S.
Volume 1 of a 4-volume series

Soo, Kean
Jellaby; Volume 1 the lost monster. by Kean Soo. Stone Arch Books 2014 160 p. color illustrations (Jellaby) (pbk.) $12.95; (library binding) $19.99
Grades: 4 5 6 7 8 9   **741.5**
1. Monsters -- Fiction 2. Friendship -- Fiction 3.

Extraterrestrial beings -- Fiction 4. Human-alien encounters -- Comic books, strips, etc
ISBN 1434291952; 9781434264206; 9781434291950

LC 2013037026

First published 2008

"Portia has just moved to a new neighborhood with her mom. Adjusting to life without a father is hard enough, but school is boring and her classmates are standoffish. . . . But things start to get better when Portia mounts a midnight excursion into the woods behind her house where she discovers a shy and sweet purple monster. Life with Jellaby is exciting, but Portia's purple friend has secrets of his own." (Publisher's note)

"Soo grounds the story in a fairly gritty contemporary reality, where kids deal with bullies and well-meaning adults try to help. Clear, clean lines and easy-to-follow panel layouts round out the package." Booklist

Jellaby: monster in the city. Hyperion Books 2009 172p il pa $9.99

Grades: 4 5 6 7 8 9   **741.5**
1. Graphic novels 2. Fantasy graphic novels 3. Monsters -- Graphic novels 4. Friendship -- Graphic novels
ISBN 1-4231-0565-6 pa; 978-1-4231-0565-7 pa

Beginning right where the first book ended, Portia, Jason, and Jellaby continue on their way to Toronto, walking after Portia panicked and they got off the train. They're searching for a way home for Jellaby, and they think a door somewhere in Exhibition Place, where the Canadian National Exhibition is taking place, holds a clue. Portia feels torn between wanting to help her friend yet not wanting to say goodbye forever, and her ambivalence causes a rift between her and Jason. When she doesn't want to trust a masked magician who seems to know too much about them and Jellaby, Portia leaves Jason. They all end up in the Automotive Building, where the masked man leads Jason and Jellaby down below the building, while Portia seems to find her long lost father. But is he really her father, and just what is waiting for Jason and Jellaby under the Automotive Building? Soo again uses a mostly purple color palette.

Spires, Ashley

★ **Binky** the space cat. Kids Can Press 2009 64p il $16.95; pa $7.95

Grades: 2 3 4 5   **741.5**
1. Graphic novels 2. Humorous graphic novels 3. Cats -- Graphic novels 4. Space flight -- Graphic novels
ISBN 978-1-55453-309-1; 1-55453-309-0; 978-1-55453-419-7 pa; 1-55453-419-4 pa

Binky the cat lives with two humans (an unnamed mother and son) in what he thinks of as a space station. He's determined to become a space cat and venture into outer space with his stuffed mousie Ted, and to that end he gets his space cat kit through the mail, complete with instructions to build a space ship.

"Spires's mix of sly, dry and slapstick humor in her first graphic novel is perfect. . . . Details in the muted watercolor illustrations, like mousie Ted covering his nose as Binky releases 'space gas,' will keep readers of all ages giggling, whether they're cat lovers or not." Kirkus

Other titles about Binky are:
Binky to the rescue (2010)
Binky under pressure (2011)

Binky takes charge (2012)
License to scratch (2013)

Steinberg, David

★ **Sound** off! by D. J. Steinberg; illustrated by Brian Smith. Grosset & Dunlap 2008 un il (Adventures of Daniel Boom AKA Loud Boy) pa $5.99

Grades: 3 4 5   **741.5**
1. Graphic novels 2. Superhero graphic novels
ISBN 978-0-448-44698-1

LC 2007019009

"Bursting with action, color, and intriguing characters . . . this works in every way. Smith's visual wit, which puts a retro gloss on cartoon art of the 1950s, is on display without sidetracking the story, and pacing and plotting are superb." Booklist

Steinke, Aron Nels

The **Super** Duper Dog Park. Blue Apple Books 2011 il (Balloon toons) $10.99

Grades: K 1 2 3   **741.5**
1. Graphic novels 2. Dogs -- Fiction 3. Amusement parks -- Fiction
ISBN 978-1-60905-093-1; 1-60905-093-2

LC 2011019077

Dog lovers and their canine friends make their way to the Super Duper Dog Park on Dog Island, where dogs ride bicycles, make music, and enjoy a perfect day.

"Steinke's text is geared to be easy reading, but it is not without cleverness: snatches of rhyme or onomatopoeic devices that give a good taste of sound. . . . The artwork follows the text's accessible engagement. . . . Both colorful and high spirited, this title will give new readers a good run for their money." Kirkus

Stevenson, Robert Louis

The **strange** case of Dr. Jekyll and Mr. Hyde; by Robert L. Stevenson; retold by Carl Bowen; illustrated by Daniel Perez. Stone Arch Books 2009 72p il $23.93

Grades: 4 5 6 7 8 9 10   **741.5**
1. Graphic novels 2. Horror graphic novels 3. Science fiction graphic novels
ISBN 978-1-4342-0754-8

LC 2008-6248

"Scientist Dr. Henry Jekyll believes every human has two minds: one good and one evil. He develops a potion to separate them from each other. Soon, his evil mind takes over, and Dr. Jekyll becomes a hideous fiend known as Mr. Hyde." (Publisher's note)

Sturm, James

★ **Adventures** in cartooning; how to turn your doodles into comics. [by] James Sturm, Andrew Arnold, Alexis Frederick-Frost. First Second 2009 109p il pa $12.95

Grades: 2 3 4 5   **741.5**
1. Drawing 2. Graphic novels 3. Graphic novels -- Authorship 4. Comic books, strips, etc. -- Authorship
ISBN 978-1-59643-369-4 pa; 1-59643-369-8 pa

"In fairy-tale fashion, the Magic Cartooning Elf helps a young princess with writer's block produce her first comic. A story-within-a-story emerges. . . . Simple cartooning basics offered after the story are quite appealing; even the most reluctant artist may be inspired to pick up a pencil and give it a shot. Entertaining and surprisingly edifying." Kirkus

Telgemeier, Raina

★ **Drama**; Raina Telgemeier; with color by Gurihiru.
1st ed. Graphix 2012 233 p. chiefly ill. $23.99

Grades: 5 6 7 8   **741.5**

1. Graphic novels 2. School stories 3. Middle schools
-- Fiction 4. Children's plays -- Fiction 5. Schools --
Fiction 6. Theater -- Fiction 7. Interpersonal relations
-- Fiction

ISBN 0545326982; 0545326990; 9780545326988;
9780545326995

LC 2011040748

Stonewall Honor Book (2013)

Author Raina Telgemeier's book focuses on a middle
school drama production. "Callie loves theater . . . [S]he's
the set designer for the stage crew, and this year she's determined to create a set worthy of Broadway on a middle-
school budget. But how can she, when she doesn't know
much about carpentry, ticket sales are down, and the crew
members are having trouble working together?" (Publisher's note)

"In this realistic and sympathetic story, feelings and
thoughts leap off the page, revealing Telgemeier's keen eye
for young teen life." Booklist

Includes bibliographical references

★ **Sisters**; Raina Telgemeier; with color by Braden
Lamb. First edition Graphix 2014 197 p. chiefly color
illustrations hbk $24.99; pbk $10.99

Grades: 5 6 7 8   **741.5**

1. Siblings 2. Family life 3. Autobiographical graphic
novels 4. Interpersonal relations

ISBN 9780545540599; 9780545540605

LC 2013008700

"Raina can't wait to be a big sister. But once Amara is
born, things aren't quite how she expected them to be. . . .
They are sisters, after all. Raina uses her signature humor .
. . in both present-day narrative and perfectly placed flashbacks to tell the story of her relationship with her sister,
which unfolds during the course of a road trip from their
home in San Francisco to a family reunion in Colorado."
(Publisher's note)

"The author's narrative style is fresh and sharp, and
the combination of well-paced and well-placed flashbacks
pull the plot together, moving the story forward and helping
readers understand the characters' point of view. The volume captures preadolescence in an effortless and uncanny
way and turns tough subjects, such as parental marriage
problems, into experiences with which readers can identify."
(School Library Journal)

★ **Smile**. Scholastic/Graphix 2010 213p il $21.99;
pa $10.99

Grades: 5 6 7 8   **741.5**

1. Graphic novels 2. Autobiographical graphic novels
3. Dentistry -- Graphic novels 4. Friendship -- Graphic
novels 5. Personal appearance -- Graphic novels

ISBN 978-0-545-13205-3; 0-545-13205-3; 978-0-545-
13206-0 pa; 0-545-13206-1 pa

LC 2008-51782

Boston Globe-Horn Book Honor: Nonfiction (2010)

Eisner Award: Best Publication for Teens (2011)

Sixth grader Raina just wants to be normal, but when she
falls down going home from a Girl Scout meeting, she se-
verely injures her two front teeth, and this starts her down a
long road with braces, surgery, retainers, embarrassing headgear—all sure to make her stand out from her middle school
classmates for all the wrong reasons. There's also a major
earthquake, then boy confusion, friends who turn out not to
be good friends, sibling jealousy, all the stuff that makes life
interesting, if not fun. Telgemeier wrote and drew the autobiographical Smile as a webcomic; this volume collects the
story in color.

"The dental case that Telgemeier documents in this
graphic memoir was extreme: a random accident led to front
tooth loss when she was 12, and over the next several years,
she suffered through surgery, implants, headgear, false teeth,
and a rearrangement of her remaining incisors. . . . Both
adults and kids . . . are vividly and rapidly portrayed. . . . Telgemeier's storytelling and full-color cartoony images form a
story that will cheer and inspire any middle-schooler dealing
with orthodontia." Booklist

Thielbar, Melinda

The **ancient** formula; a mystery with fractions. illustrated by Tintin Pantoja. Graphic Universe 2010 46p il
(Manga math mysteries) lib bdg $29.27

Grades: 1 2 3 4   **741.5**

1. Graphic novels 2. Mystery graphic novels 3. Kung
fu -- Graphic novels 4. Schools -- Graphic novels 5.
Mathematics -- Graphic novels

ISBN 978-0-7613-4907-5 lib bdg; 0-7613-4907-3
lib bdg

LC 2010001431

The students of Sifu Faiza's Kung Fu School use their
knowledge of fractions as they try to discover what happened to Leung Jan's long-lost healing formula.

"The book is a great read and provides the reader with
mathematical instruction, practice solving problems, and entertainment all at once. . . . The images and colors are exciting and vibrant." Sci Books Films

Thompson, Jill

Magic Trixie; written and illustrated by Jill Thompson;
lettered by Jason Arthur. Harper Trophy 2008 93p il pa
$7.99

Grades: 3 4 5   **741.5**

1. Graphic novels 2. Fantasy graphic novels 3.
Humorous graphic novels 4. Magic -- Graphic novels

ISBN 978-0-06-117045-4 pa

LC 2007-24298

Magic Trixie is feeling a bit put out; everything in her
house seems to revolve around her baby sister, and she
doesn't get to do anything fun. If that wasn't bad enough,
Show & Tell time is coming up at Monstersorri School, and
all her classmates have seen all her tricks too many times.
She'll have to come up with a new one that's really special.

"Bright colors and a whimsical style make everything
friendly rather than scary. Underneath the supernatural trappings lies a classical story of sibling envy to which every big
sister and big brother can relate." Booklist

Other titles in this series are:

Magic Trixie sleeps over (2008)

Magic Trixie and the dragon (2009)

★ **Scary** Godmother; written and illustrated by Jill
Thompson. Dark Horse 2010 207p il $24.99

Grades: 3 4 5   **741.5**
1. Graphic novels 2. Supernatural graphic novels 3. Halloween -- Graphic novels
ISBN 978-1-59582-589-6; 1-59582-589-4

It's Halloween night and it's up to Scary Godmother to show one little girl just how much fun spooky can be! Meet Hannah Marie, who, with the help of Scary Godmother, stands up to her mean-spirited cousin Jimmy and her fear of monsters on her first Halloween adventure with the big kids. Later, Hannah joins forces with Orson, the vampire boy, to unravel a mystery near and dear to their hearts.

This is a "collection compiling all four of Thompson's original Scary Godmother stories plus extra goodies. Told in often-rhyming prose and word balloons on vibrant pages that balance a visually lavish picture book aesthetic with sequential-art page composition, the stories burst with complex color tones and creepy cartoon figures." Booklist

Torres, J.
Into the woods; J. Torres; illustrated by Faith Erin Hicks. Kids Can Press 2012 100 p. col. ill. (Bigfoot Boy) (hardcover) $17.95
Grades: 3 4 5 6 7   **741.5**
1. Magic -- Graphic novels 2. Sasquatch -- Graphic novels 3. Totems and totemism -- Graphic novels
ISBN 1554537118; 9781554537112

In this fantasy graphic novel, "city boy Rufus is staying at his grandmother's house on the edge of a forest for a few days without his parents," and he "decides to explore the woods. He meets a girl named Penny. . . . When looking for her in the woods, Rufus finds a glowing necklace in a tree. After reading the word on the back, he turns into Bigfoot! . . . There's danger in the forest as well as magic, and when Penny disappears, Rufus . . . use[s] the totem to effect a rescue." (Kirkus Reviews)

Followed by: The unkindness of ravens (2013)

The **Sound** of Thunder; written by J. Torres; illustrated by Faith Erin Hicks. Kids Can Press 2014 100 p. chiefly color illustrations (Bigfoot boy) hbk $17.95; pbk $9.95
Grades: 3 4 5 6 7   **741.5**
1. Graphic novels 2. Adventure fiction 3. Pacific Northwest -- Fiction
ISBN 9781894786584; 9781894786591
Sequel to: The unkindness of ravens (2013)

"This conclusion to the Bigfoot Boy graphic novel trilogy adds a backdrop of Pacific Northwest mythology to the popular story about an ordinary boy who becomes a hero through the power of magic. As the book begins, Rufus, Penny and their squirrel friend, Sidney, are eager to recapture the magic totem they lost to the ravens in the previous book." (Publisher's note)

"Torres and Hicks conclude their woodsy trilogy with an exciting adventure dotted with humor. Rufus and Penny's attempts to understand Sidney's charades are a hoot. Rufus has worked a bit of his city-boy out, but his bumbles and stumbles continue to round out his character." Kirkus

The **unkindness** of ravens; by J. Torres; illustrated by Faith Erin Hicks. Kids Can Press 2013 100 p. col. ill. (Bigfoot boy) $17.95; pa $9.95

Grades: 3 4 5 6 7   **741.5**
1. Magic 2. Ravens -- Fiction
ISBN 9781554537136; 9781554537143; 1554537134; 1554537142

LC 2013040319
Sequel to: Into the woods (2012)

This book, by J. Torres and illustrated by Faith Erin Hicks, tells the story of "another weekend of Rufus using his magic totem to transform himself into Bigfoot Boy! But when you're big, hairy and loud, it's hard to keep your powers a secret, especially when there are trickster ravens that want the magic for themselves." (Publisher's note)

"Hicks's illustrations are done in bold, black lines and rich colors and are sometimes reminiscent of Native Canadian art styles. The story's adventure, magic, and characters will appeal." SLJ

Followed by: The sound of thunder (2014)

Townsend, Michael
Kit Feeny: on the move. Alfred A. Knopf 2009 un il lib bdg $12.99; pa $5.99
Grades: 3 4 5   **741.5**
1. Graphic novels 2. Moving -- Fiction 3. Bullies -- Fiction 4. Friendship -- Fiction
ISBN 978-0-375-95614-0 lib bdg; 0-375-95614-X lib bdg; 978-0-375-85614-3 pa; 0-375-85614-5 pa
LC 2008-37443

When plucky Kit Feeny moves to a new town, he immediately makes an enemy of the sadistic school bully and must struggle to find friends who share his interests.

"Kit, a mischievous, silly, ambiguous anthropomorphic animal, . . . is an easy hero to cheer for in this graphic novel, which reluctant readers will find hard to put down." Booklist

Kit Feeny: the ugly necklace. Alfred A. Knopf 2009 un lib bdg $12.99; pa $5.99
Grades: 3 4 5   **741.5**
1. Graphic novels 2. Bears -- Fiction 3. Gifts -- Fiction 4. Family life -- Fiction
ISBN 978-0-375-95615-7 lib bdg; 0-375-95615-8 lib bdg; 978-0-375-85615-0 pa; 0-375-85615-3 pa
LC 2008040155

Kit Feeny, a young bear, enters into a competition with his sisters to see who can give their mother the best birthday present

Trondheim, Lewis
Monster Christmas; [Joe Johnson, translation; Lea Hernandez, lettering] Papercutz 2011 32p il (Monster) $9.99
Grades: K 1 2 3   **741.5**
1. Graphic novels 2. Monsters -- Graphic novels 3. Christmas -- Graphic novels 4. Family life -- Graphic novels
ISBN 978-1-59707-288-5; 1-59707-288-5
Orginal French edition, 1999

"A brother, Petey, and a sister, Jean, go on a Christmas vacation to the snowy mountains with their Mom and Dad and pet monster, Kriss. On the way they encounter another monster chasing Santa Claus and have to rely on their creativity, quick thinking, and a monster of their own to save Santa and themselves. Both Trondheim's art and the English-language translation create a story that could come from the mind of a child, despite its bizarre creatures and sudden surprises. Yet it's also the work of a talented artist channeling that childish wonder into a finely crafted tale for young audiences." Publ Wkly

Tiny Tyrant; by Lewis Trondheim; translated from the French by Alexis Siegel; illustrated by Fabrice Parme. First Second Books 2007 124p il $12.95

Grades: 4 5 6 7 8 9 10 11 12 Adult   **741.5**
1. Graphic novels 2. Humorous graphic novels
ISBN 978-1-59643-094-5

LC 2006021479

"Tiny child-king Ethelbert is spoiled and difficult, expecting to have his every whim fulfilled-or else. . . . In the end, though, he becomes a hero. The dynamic cartoons are filled with details and riddled with humor; most pages have between six and eight small pictures. . . . This title will have wide appeal. It's young and accessible enough for elementary-grade kids, but teens will also be charmed by the rascally king." SLJ

Varon, Sara
Bake sale. First Second 2011 157p il $19.99; pa $16.99

Grades: 3 4 5 6   **741.5**
1. Graphic novels 2. Cupcakes -- Graphic novels 3. Bakers and bakeries -- Graphic novels
ISBN 978-1-59643-740-1; 1-59643-740-5; 978-1-59643-419-6 pa; 1-59643-419-8 pa

LC 2010051587

"The book has a mellow, easygoing feel, using soft colors and showing many yummy foods. As an added bonus, recipes for how to make the various scrumptious meals readers watch Cupcake prepare are provided. . . . Varon's art is simple and cozy, making this sweet tale a confection of its own." Publ Wkly

Venable, Colleen AF
Hamster and cheese; illustrated by Stephanie Yue. Graphic Universe 45p il (Guinea Pig, pet shop private eye) lib bdg $27.93; pa $6.95

Grades: 2 3 4   **741.5**
1. Mystery graphic novels 2. Animals -- Graphic novels 3. Hamsters -- Graphic novels 4. Guinea pigs -- Graphic novels
ISBN 978-0-7613-4598-5 lib bdg; 0-7613-4598-1 lib bdg; 978-0-7613-5479-6 pa; 0-7613-5479-4 pa

"Who is stealing Mr. Venezi's sandwiches? The befuddled pet-shop owner misidentifies the store's animals, leading the hamsters to think they're koalas. . . . Hamisher the koala-hamster thinks Sasspants the guinea pig is a private investigator because the second G on her cage's sign has fallen off, so he asks her to investigate. . . . Young readers will appreciate the zaniness of the pet shop and the fun mystery, and Yue's colorful art uses a straightforward panel design that's easy to follow." Booklist

Other titles in this series are:
And then there were gnomes (2010)
The ferret's a foot (2011)
Fish you were here (2011)
Raining cats and detectives (2012)
Going, going, dragon! (2013)

Venditti, Robert
★ The **lightning** thief: the graphic novel; by Rick Riordan; adapted by Robert Venditti; art by Attila Futaki; color by Jose Villarrubia; layouts by Orpheus Collar; lettering by Chris Dickey. Disney/Hyperion Books 2010 un il (Percy Jackson and the Olympians) $19.99; pa $9.99

Grades: 5 6 7 8   **741.5**
1. Graphic novels 2. Greek mythology -- Graphic novels
ISBN 978-1-4231-1696-7; 1-4231-1696-8; 978-1-4231-1710-0 pa; 1-4231-1710-7 pa

LC 2010035512

After learning that he is the son of a mortal woman and Poseidon, god of the sea, twelve-year-old Percy is sent to a summer camp for demigods like himself, and joins his new friends on a quest to prevent a war between the gods.

This graphic novel adaptation of Rick Riordan's novel "succeeds in spectacular fashion. . . . The book retains the excellent pacing of the original and gives a face to Riordan's vision of the mythological made modern. Futaki's artwork is exemplary but what leaves such a lasting impression is Villarrubia's coloring, which reveals both subtlety and spectacle when needed." Publ Wkly

Weigel, Jeff
★ **Thunder** from the sea; adventure on board the HMS Defender. G. P. Putnam's Sons 2010 46p il $17.99

Grades: 3 4 5 6   **741.5**
1. Graphic novels 2. Adventure graphic novels 3. Naval art and science -- Graphic novels 4. Great Britain -- Royal Navy -- Graphic novels 5. Europe -- History -- 1789-1815 -- Graphic novels
ISBN 978-0-399-25089-7

LC 2009-32801

In 1805, during the Napoleonic Wars, twelve-year-old Jack Hoyton becomes a member of the crew of HMS Defender, a midsize ship in the British Royal Navy. The Defender patrols along a portion of the French coast to block French ships, but a major gun emplacement in Dumont hampers the ship's efforts. When some of the crew land to fill their barrels with fresh water, French gunmen fire upon them, killing an officer and wounding a crewman. The Captain assigns Jack to be part of the crew that will land and take the guns; when the men arrive, they find that there is no small village, but a major shipbuilding facility, and they're captured.

"Weigel's old-fashioned comics art shows lots of authentic details of eighteenth-century shipboard life, and there is some battle violence. . . . This picture-book-size graphic novel should find a ready audience of young adventure-loving readers." Booklist

Includes bibliographical references

Wetterer, Margaret K.
The **snowshoeing** adventure of Milton Daub, blizzard trekker; by Margaret K. Wetterer and Charles M. Wetterer; adaptation by Emma Carlson Berne; illustrated by Zachary Trover. Graphic Universe 2011 31p il (History's kid heroes) lib bdg $26.60; pa $8.95

Grades: 2 3 4   **741.5**
1. Graphic novels 2. Adventure graphic novels 3. Snowshoers 4. Blizzards -- Graphic novels 5. Bronx

(New York, N.Y.) -- Graphic novels
ISBN 978-0-7613-6175-6 lib bdg; 0-7613-6175-8 lib bdg; 978-0-7613-6194-7 pa; 0-7613-6194-4 pa

LC 2009051717

An 1888 blizzard has paralyzed much of the Northeast United States, but twelve-year-old Milton Daub puts on a pair of homemade snowshoes and braves the storm to bring food and medicine to many of his neighbors in the Bronx, New York.

This book provides an "exciting [glimpse] into the past, with just the right amount of tension and intensity to capture readers' attention. . . . [It] will serve as [a] good [introduction] to graphic novels and historical fiction for early readers. Added bonuses are the brief yet informative [introduction] and [afterword] providing more facts about the [setting]." SLJ

Includes bibliographical references

White, Mike

Amity Blamity, book one. SLG 2011 un il pa $10.95
Grades: 4 5 6   **741.5**
1. Graphic novels 2. Farm life -- Graphic novels
ISBN 978-1-59362-209-1; 1-59362-209-0

"Four-year-old Gretchen doesn't speak. Thankfully, she's got her potbellied pig, Chester, who's not only something of a motormouth but an ambitious one at that. He's the founder of Pig Corp. . . . Their main threat is Gretchen's lazy ex-jailbird uncle, Downey. . . . The resulting humor is enjoyable funny-paper fare. . . . Quirky talking-animal fare with just enough edge to tickle." Booklist

Wight, Eric

★ Frankie Pickle and the closet of doom; written and illustrated by Eric Wight. Simon & Schuster Books for Young Readers 2009 79p il $9.99
Grades: 2 3 4 5   **741.5**
1. Graphic novels 2. Humorous graphic novels 3. Cleanliness -- Fiction 4. Family life -- Fiction 5. Imagination -- Fiction 6. Family life -- Graphic novels 7. Orderliness -- Graphic novels
ISBN 978-1-4169-6484-1; 1-4169-6484-3

LC 2008-30865

Fourth-grader Frankie Piccolini has a vivid imagination when it comes to cleaning his disastrously messy room, but eventually even he decides that it is just too dirty.

"Wight's hilarious twists of language are matched with a wicked sense of fun in the illustrations and frequent sequential-paneled episodes of pretend play." Kirkus

Other titles about Frankie Pickle are:
Frankie Pickle and the Pine Run 3000 (2010)
Frankie Pickle and the mathematical menace (2011)
Frankie Pickle and the land of the lost recess (2012)

Zornow, Jeff

The legend of Sleepy Hollow; adapted and illustrated by Jeff Zornow; based upon the works of Washington Irving. Magic Wagon 2007 un il (Graphic horror) $18.95
Grades: 5 6 7 8 9 10 11 12   **741.5**
1. New York (State) -- Graphic novels
ISBN 978-1-60270-060-4; 1-60270-060-5

LC 2007-9615

This "is an entertaining and faithful, if much adapted version of Irving's classic story. Zornow's illustrations are the highlight of the work, successfully bringing the characters of the story to life." Booklist

741.6 Graphic design, illustration, commercial art

★ Artist to artist; 23 major illustrators talk to children about their art. Philomel Books 2007 105p il $30
Grades: 4 5 6 7   **741.6**
1. Illustrators 2. Illustration of books 3. Picture books for children
ISBN 978-0-399-24600-5

"This anthology celebrates and elucidates contemporary picture-book art. . . . Ashley Bryan, Quentin Blake, Leo Lionni, Alice Provensen, and Gennady Spirin are among the contributors, whose comments are formatted as signed letters illustrated with childhood photographs. . . . Each artist includes glorious self-portraits and a gatefold page that reveals a marvelous array of sketches, color mixes, and studio scenes. All readers will find something that piques curiosity or provides insight." Booklist

Carle, Eric

The art of Eric Carle. Philomel Bks. 1996 125p il $35; pa $19.99
Grades: Adult Professional   **741.6**
1. Illustration of books 2. Picture books for children
ISBN 0-399-22937-X; 0-399-24002-0 pa

LC 95-24940

This is "both a textual and visual anthology: in addition to Carle's autobiographical chapter and the text of his 1990 speech at the Library of Congress, chapters include accolades from Ann Beneduce (Carle's U.S. editor) and from Dr. Viktor Christen (Carle's German editor). A photoessay on the artist's collage technique rubs shoulders with a forty-page gallery of his illustrations over the last quarter of a century, which precedes a look at some of his quick sketches and an illustrated bibliography of his oeuvre. The book's inviting layout may appeal to artistic youngsters as well as grown Carle fans, and the information about his working process, particularly the technical details, is absorbing." Bull Cent Child Books

Kushner, Tony

The art of Maurice Sendak; 1980 to present. text by Tony Kushner. Abrams 2003 223p il $60
Grades: Adult Professional   **741.6**
1. Artists 2. Authors 3. Illustrators 4. Set designers 5. Children's authors
ISBN 0-8109-4448-0

LC 2003-9293

This "collection presents 350 illustrations, many of which are drawings for set and costume design work, . . . others of which are posters for plays and for events such as the New York is Book Country fair. . . . Sendak's precise, intensely shaded yet welcoming shapes and figures have lost none of their luster. They would ordinarily be enough in themselves in a survey like this, but Kushner's lovely, funny, partisan text . . . lifts the book to another level." Publ Wkly

Includes bibliographical references

Maguire, Gregory

Making mischief; a Maurice Sendak appreciation.
William Morrow 2009 200p il $27.50

Grades: Adult Professional   **741.6**

1. Artists 2. Authors 3. Illustrators 4. Set designers
5. Children's authors

ISBN 978-0-06-168916-1; 0-06-168916-5

LC 2009017357

"Maguire constructs a thoughtful and accessible overview of Sendak's works and artistic process, making for a
tender homage to the famed artist that only a true fan could
produce. . . . He presents a series of five essays, expounding
upon the various influences seen in Sendak's work. . . as
well as an analysis of motifs and techniques. Maguire often
allows the art to speak for itself, displaying a generous selection of Sendak's illustrations, both famed and lesser known."
Bull Cent Child Books

Marcus, Leonard S., 1950-

Randolph Caldecott; the man who could not stop drawing. Leonard S. Marcus. Farrar, Straus & Giroux (BYR)
2013 64 p. (hardcover) $24.99

Grades: 5 6 7 8   **741.6**

1. Picture books for children 2. Illustrators -- England
-- Biography

ISBN 0374310254; 9780374310257

LC 2012050406

This book is a biography of Randolph Caldecott, "the
illustrator for whom the Caldecott Medal is named." Leonard S. Marcus begins by "describing the changes wrought in
19th-century Great Britain by the steam engine, which eased
travel and greatly expanded distribution of media. He details Caldecott's early days clerking in a bank and his search
for freelance illustration work, then describes how diligence
and charm lead to his first book-illustrating assignment" and
then to a career in illustration. (Publishers Weekly)

Nahson, Claudia J.

The **snowy** day and the art of Ezra Jack Keats; Claudia
J. Nahson; with an essay by Maurice Berger. Jewish Museum, under the auspices of the Jewish Theological Seminary
of America 2011 104p il $27.50

Grades: Adult Professional   **741.6**

1. Artists 2. Authors 3. Illustrators 4. Authors,
American 5. Children's authors

ISBN 978-0-300-17022-1; 0-300-17022-X

LC 2011007880

"Keats's Caldecott-winning story about a boy's wintertime exploration of his neighborhood turns 50 in 2012; this
fascinating examination of Keats and his oeuvre, complete
with 80 full-color reproductions, coincides with the first major U.S. exhibition devoted to his work. . . . Nahson, curator
at the Jewish Museum, writes that The Snowy Day reflected
Keats's interest in 'rendering visible what has hitherto been
invisible to his audience, be that an inner-city child, a message graffitied on a wall, or a dilapidated building.' Her essay joins one from historian/art critic Maurice Berger that
makes abundantly clear the book's societal importance."
Publ Wkly

Includes bibliographical references

Neuburger, Emily K.

★ A **Caldecott** celebration; seven artists and their
paths to the Caldecott medal. rev ed.; Walker & Co. 2008
55p il $19.95; lib bdg $20.85

Grades: Adult Professional   **741.6**

1. Illustrators 2. Caldecott Medal 3. Illustration of
books

ISBN 978-0-8027-9703-2; 0-8027-9703-2; 978-0-
8027-9704-9 lib bdg; 0-8027-9704-0 lib bdg

LC 2007-23132

First published 1998

Profiles seven Caldecott award winning books and their
authors, including Robert McCloskey's "Make Way for
Ducklings," Marcia Brown's "Cinderella," Maurice Sendak's "Where the Wild Things Are," William Steig's "Sylvester and the Magic Pebble," Chris Van Allsburg's "Jumanji,"
David Wiesner's "Tuesday," and Mordicai Gerstein's "The
Man Who Walked Between the Towers"

"The value of this volume is that Marcus makes these
exceptional author/illustrators, and the processes by which
they created their award-winning picture books, accessible
to children and to adults who value children's literature."
SLJ

Say, Allen

★ **Drawing** from memory; Allen Say. 1st ed. Scholastic Press 2011 63 p. il map $17.99

Grades: 3 4 5 6   **741.6**

1. Artists 2. Authors 3. Illustrators 4. Autobiography
-- Graphic novels 5. Children's authors 6. Japanese
Americans -- Biography

ISBN 9780545176866; 0545176867

LC 2011016324

Sibert Honor Book, 2012

This book "opens with a . . . watercolor map of Japan
on the left, framed in a rectangle, while on the right is a .
. . watercolor of Yokohama's seashore and fishing village,
with two black-and-white photographs pasted on: Say as a
child, and the stone beach wall. The early arc takes readers from [Allen] Say's 1937 birth, through family moves to
escape 1941 bombings and then Say's nigh-emancipation at
age 12, when his mother supported him in his own Tokyo
apartment. The one-room apartment 'was for me to study in,
but studying was far from my mind this was going to be my
art studio!' The art table's drawer handle resembles a smile. .
. . [A]pprenticing with famous cartoonist Noro Shinpei, Say
works dedicatedly on comic panels, still-lifes and life drawing. Nothing—not political unrest, not U.S. occupation, not
paternal disapproval—derails his singular goal of becoming
a cartoonist." (Kirkus)

"Say's account is complex, poignant, and unfailingly
honest. Say's fans—and those who also feel the pull of the
artist's life—will be captivated." Publ Wkly

Stevens, Janet

From pictures to words; a book about making a book.
written and illustrated by Janet Stevens. Holiday House
1995 un il $16.95

Grades: K 1 2 3   **741.6**

1. Authorship 2. Picture books for children

ISBN 0-8234-1154-0

LC 94-18976

"The straightforward text carefully presents information while maintaining the narrative flow. Dialogue balloons

and funny asides from the characters keep the presentation lively." SLJ

Tan, Shaun

★ The **bird** king; an artist's notebook. Shaun Tan. Arthur A. Levine Books 2013 128 p. (hardcover: alk. paper) $19.99

Grades: 3 4 5 6 7   **741.6**

1. Artists' notebooks

ISBN 0545465133; 9780545465137

LC 2012016625

This book by author and illustrator Shaun Tan "is a collection of sketches, random jottings, preliminary designs for book, film and theatre projects, sketchbook pages and drawings from life. Each of these represent some aspect of a working process, whereby stories generally evolve from visual research and free-wheeling doodles. They are also 'unfinished' pieces created in a single sitting, not originally intended for publication." (Publisher's note)

Under the spell of the moon; art for children from the world's great illustrators. [edited by Patricia Aldana; texts translated by Stan Dragland] Groundwood Books 2004 80p il $25

Grades: Adult Professional   **741.6**

1. Illustrators 2. Illustration of books 3. Illustrated children's books

ISBN 0888995598

This volume includes the work of thirty-three illustrators of books for children. The illustrators "each have a double page including both their illustration and a short piece of text (written either by them or another author), or a traditional verse or saying. . . . Original texts in a language other than English are included, followed by a translation by Canadian poet and editor Stan Dragland. . . . Age four and up." (Quill Quire)

This "collection features the artwork of children's book illustrators who, together, represent more than 25 countries. Each double-page spread includes a different artist's image accompanied by a poem, nursery rhyme, song, or bit of nonsense that appears in both English and the illustrator's native language. . . . Katherine Paterson offers a stirring introduction that discusses IBBY (The International Board on Books for Young People)." Booklist

741.9 Collections of drawings

Volavkova, Hana

★ --I never saw another butterfly-- children's drawings and poems from Terezin concentration camp, 1942-1944. edited by Hana Volavková; foreword by Chaim Potok; afterword by Vaclav Havel. expanded 2nd ed; Schocken Bks. 1993 xxii, 106p il hardcover o.p. pa $17.50

Grades: 4 5 6 7   **741.9**

1. Child artists 2. Children's writings 3. Holocaust, 1933-1945 4. Terezin (Czechoslovakia: Concentration camp)

ISBN 0-8052-1015-6 pa

LC 92-50477

Original Czech edition, 1959; first American edition published 1964 by McGraw-Hill

"Of the 15,000 children who passed through Terezin before going to Auschwitz, only 100 lived. This book is a collection of poems and drawings by some of them. . . . This touching book adds another facet to library collections on the Holocaust." SLJ

743 Drawing and drawings by subject

Ames, Lee J.

Draw 50 aliens, UFO's galaxy ghouls, milky way marauders, and other extra terrestrial creatures; [by] Lee J. Ames with Ric Estrada. Doubleday 1998 un il (Draw 50) hardcover o.p. pa $8.95

Grades: 4 5 6 7   **743**

1. Drawing

ISBN 978-0-385-49144-0; 0-385-49144-1; 978-0-385-49145-7 pa; 0-385-49145-X pa

LC 98-20077

A step-by-step guide to drawing outer space creatures

Draw 50 animals. Doubleday 1974 un il (Draw 50) hardcover o.p. pa $8.95

Grades: 4 5 6 7   **743**

1. Drawing 2. Animal painting and illustration

ISBN 978-0-385-07712-5; 0-385-07712-2; 978-0-385-19519-5 pa; 0-385-19519-2 pa

LC 73-13083

This book provides step-by-step instructions for drawing animals ranging from penguins and seals to elephants and monkeys

Draw 50 athletes. Doubleday 1985 un il (Draw 50) hardcover o.p. pa $8.95

Grades: 4 5 6 7   **743**

1. Drawing 2. Athletes in art

ISBN 978-0-385-19055-8; 0-385-19055-7; 978-0-385-24638-5 pa; 0-385-24638-2 pa

LC 83-45569

This book "consists of single-page spreads, each devoted to one athlete. Each figure is drawn in a series of six or more steps, starting with a basic shape and ending with a stylish, somewhat detailed india ink drawing." Booklist

Draw 50 baby animals; the step-by-step way to draw kittens, lambs, chicks, and other adorable offspring. Broadway Books 2003 un il (Draw 50) hardcover o.p. pa $8.95

Grades: 4 5 6 7   **743**

1. Drawing 2. Animals in art

ISBN 978-0-767-91283-9; 0-767-91283-7; 978-0-767-91284-6 pa; 0-767-91284-5 pa

LC 2002-33247

Step-by-step instructions for drawing fifty baby animals.

Draw 50 beasties and yugglies and turnover uglies and things that go bump in the night. Doubleday 1988 il (Draw 50) hardcover o.p. pa $8.95

Grades: 4 5 6 7   **743**

1. Drawing 2. Monsters in art

ISBN 978-0-385-24625-5; 0-385-24625-0; 978-0-385-26767-0 pa; 0-385-26767-3 pa

LC 88-16143

Provides step-by-step instructions for drawing monsters, goons, and gruesome beasts

Ames "encourages readers to take plenty of time and suggests very lightly sketching out the step-by-step drawings so that mistakes may be rectified. This one, with its popular subject of imaginative monsters and other nightmare inhabitants, will be a sure-fire circulator." SLJ

Draw 50 birds; [by] Lee J. Ames with Tony D'Adamo. Doubleday 1996 un il (Draw 50) hardcover o.p. pa $8.95
Grades: 4 5 6 7   **743**
     1. Drawing 2. Birds in art
     ISBN 978-0-385-47006-3; 0-385-47006-1; 978-0-385-47163-3 pa; 0-385-47163-7 pa

                             LC 96-27621

Draw 50 boats, ships, trucks & trains. Doubleday 1976 un il (Draw 50) hardcover o.p. pa $8.95
Grades: 4 5 6 7   **743**
     1. Drawing 2. Vehicles in art
     ISBN 978-0-385-08903-6; 0-385-08903-1; 978-0-385-23630-0 pa; 0-385-23630-1 pa

                             LC 75-19011
Step-by-step instructions for drawing fifty different ships, boats, trucks, and trains

Draw 50 buildings and other structures. Doubleday 1980 un il (Draw 50) hardcover o.p. pa $8.95
Grades: 4 5 6 7   **743**
     1. Drawing 2. Buildings in art
     ISBN 978-0-385-14401-8; 0-385-14401-6; 978-0-385-41777-8 pa; 0-385-41777-2 pa

                             LC 79-7483
This is similar in format to the author's other books. Step by step procedures enable the reader to draw houses from the U.S. and Ireland, bridges and even a torii (a Japanese gateway)

Draw 50 cats. Doubleday 1986 un il (Draw 50) hardcover o.p. pa $8.95
Grades: 4 5 6 7   **743**
     1. Drawing 2. Cats in art 3. Animal painting and illustration
     ISBN 978-0-385-23484-9; 0-385-23484-8; 978-0-385-24640-8 pa; 0-385-24640-4 pa

                             LC 86-8964
Step-by-step instructions on how to draw a variety of cats, including domestic breeds, wild cats, cuddly kittens, and celebrity cats

Draw 50 dinosaurs and other prehistoric animals; with a foreword by George Zappler. Doubleday 1977 un il (Draw 50) hardcover o.p. pa $8.95
Grades: 4 5 6 7   **743**
     1. Drawing 2. Dinosaurs in art 3. Animal painting and illustration
     ISBN 978-0-385-11134-8; 0-385-11134-7; 978-0-385-19520-1 pa; 0-385-19520-6 pa

                             LC 76-7285
Step-by-step instructions for drawing a variety of dinosaurs and other prehistoric animals

Draw 50 dogs. Doubleday 1981 un il (Draw 50) hardcover o.p. pa $8.95
Grades: 4 5 6 7   **743**
     1. Drawing 2. Dogs in art 3. Animal painting and illustration
     ISBN 978-0-385-15686-8; 0-385-15686-3; 978-0-385-23431-3 pa; 0-385-23431-7 pa

                             LC 79-6853
"Ames' six-step drawings guide youngsters along toward fashioning their own canine figures. Each species starts out with an ultrasimple shape; ovals, circles, or rectangular extensions suggest developing proportions that lead to the completed sketch." Booklist

Draw 50 endangered animals; [by] Lee J. Ames with Warren Budd. Doubleday 1992 un il (Draw 50) hardcover o.p. pa $8.95
Grades: 4 5 6 7   **743**
     1. Drawing 2. Animals in art 3. Animal painting and illustration
     ISBN 978-0-385-41191-2; 0-385-41191-X; 978-0-385-46985-2 pa; 0-385-46985-3 pa

                             LC 92-23092
Step-by-step instructions on how to draw a variety of threatened species from all over the world

Draw 50 flowers, trees, and other plants. Doubleday 1994 un il (Draw 50) hardcover o.p. pa $8.95
Grades: 4 5 6 7   **743**
     1. Drawing 2. Plants in art 3. Flowers in art 4. Botanical illustration
     ISBN 978-0-385-47004-9; 0-385-47004-5; 978-0-385-47150-3 pa; 0-385-47150-5 pa

                             LC 94-7192

Draw 50 horses. Doubleday 1984 un il (Draw 50) hardcover o.p. pa $8.95
Grades: 4 5 6 7   **743**
     1. Horses in art 2. Animal painting and illustration 3. Drawing -- Technique
     ISBN 978-0-385-17640-8; 0-385-17640-6; 978-0-385-17642-2 pa; 0-385-17642-2 pa

                             LC 81-43646
Step-by-step instructions for drawing different breeds of horses in a variety of poses

Draw 50 monsters, creeps, superheroes, demons, dragons, nerds, dirts, ghouls, giants, vampires, zombies, and other curiosa. Doubleday 1983 un il (Draw 50) hardcover o.p. pa $8.95
Grades: 4 5 6 7   **743**
     1. Drawing 2. Monsters in art
     ISBN 978-0-385-17637-8; 0-385-17637-6; 978-0-385-17639-2 pa; 0-385-17639-2 pa

                             LC 80-3006
A "demonstration of how to draw a lengthy lineup of cartoon superheroes and assorted creeps, villains, monsters, and miscellaneous odd creatures. Each page features step-by-step directions, beginning with a simple basic shape that becomes ever more elaborate until the final version sits triumphantly at the bottom right corner of each page." Booklist

Draw 50 people; [by] Lee J. Ames with Creig Flessel. Doubleday 1993 un il (Draw 50) hardcover o.p. pa $8.95
Grades: 4 5 6 7 **743**
  1. Portraits 2. Drawing -- Technique
  ISBN 978-0-385-41193-6; 0-385-41193-6; 978-0-385-41194-3 pa; 0-385-41194-4 pa
LC 93-20631

[Draw 50 series] Doubleday 1974 21v
Grades: 4 5 6 7 **743**
  1. Drawing
Each volume presents step-by-step instructions for drawing a variety of animals, people, or objects

Bergin, Mark
  How to draw pets. PowerKids Press 2011 32p il (How to draw) lib bdg $25.25; pa $11.75
Grades: 4 5 6 7 **743**
  1. Animals in art 2. Drawing -- Technique
  ISBN 978-1-4488-4511-8 lib bdg; 978-1-4488-4517-0 pa
LC 2010049184
"The cover features sketches of a cat, dog, and rabbit, allowing children to see both structure as well as finished product. Inside, the book starts by showing pictures of animals drawn with different materials such as pencils, ink, charcoals, and pastels, and explains what each medium accomplishes. Next comes an introduction to perspective and looks at different parts of animals. The familiar circle method then gets kids drawing pets from head to tails. . . . The amount of information throughout is just right: thorough but not overwhelming." Booklist
  Includes glossary

Emberley, Ed
  Ed Emberley's drawing book of faces. Little, Brown 1975 32p il hardcover o.p. pa $6.95
Grades: 2 3 4 5 **743**
  1. Drawing 2. Face in art
  ISBN 0-316-23655-1 pa
Provides step-by-step instructions for drawing a wide variety of faces reflecting various emotions and professions

Farrell, Russell
  All about drawing horses & pets. Walter Foster 2010 80p (All about drawing) $34.25; pa $9.95
Grades: K 1 2 3 **743**
  1. Horses in art 2. Animals in art 3. Drawing -- Technique
  ISBN 978-1-936309-06-1; 1-936309-06-8; 978-1-600585-80-7 pa; 1-600585-80-9 pa
LC 2010004211
First published 2008 in paperback
"Starting with simple geometric shapes, readers are led step-by-step through stages to draw [horses and pets]; close observation is presented as key to drawing lifelike forms. Photos or illustrations of the real creatures are included with 'Fun Facts' about them for readers' reference." Horn Book Guide

  All about drawing sea creatures & animals; illustrated by Russell Farrell and Diana Fisher. Walter Foster 2010 80p il (All about drawing) $34.25; pa $9.95

Grades: K 1 2 3 **743**
  1. Marine animals in art 2. Drawing -- Technique
  ISBN 978-1-936309-08-5; 1-936309-08-4; 978-1-600585-81-4 pa; 1-600585-81-7 pa
First published 2008 in paperback
"Starting with simple geometric shapes, readers are led step-by-step through stages to draw [sea creatures and animals]; close observation is presented as key to drawing lifelike forms. Photos or illustrations of the real creatures are included with 'Fun Facts' about them for readers' reference." Horn Book Guide

Fisher, Diana
  All about drawing dinosaurs & reptiles. Walter Foster 2011 80p (All about drawing) $34.25
Grades: K 1 2 3 **743**
  1. Reptiles in art 2. Dinosaurs in art 3. Drawing -- Technique
  ISBN 978-1-936309-07-8; 1-936309-07-6
LC 2010004210
"Starting with simple geometric shapes, readers are led step-by-step through stages to draw [dinosaurs and reptiles]; close observation is presented as key to drawing lifelike forms. Photos or illustrations of the real creatures are included with 'Fun Facts' about them for readers' reference." Horn Book Guide

Masiello, Ralph
  Ralph Masiello's Halloween drawing book; Ralph Masiello. Charlesbridge 2012 48 p. (softcover) $7.95
Grades: 2 3 4 **743**
  1. Halloween 2. Drawing -- Technique 3. Halloween in art
  ISBN 1570915415; 9781570915413; 9781570915420
LC 2011036736
In this book, author and illustrator Ralph Masiello "brings a haunting twist to his popular drawing series. Step-by-step diagrams show young artist how to draw ghosts, witches, jack-o'-lanterns, skeletons, a haunted house, and more. Just follow the simple steps to create creepy critters and eerie objects. Bonus challenge steps show you how to add frightfully fun details to your drawings." (Publisher's note)

  Ralph Masiello's robot drawing book. Charlesbridge 2011 un lib bdg $16.95; pa $7.95
Grades: 2 3 4 5 **743**
  1. Robots in art 2. Drawing -- Technique
  ISBN 978-1-57091-535-2 lib bdg; 1-57091-535-0 lib bdg; 978-1-57091-536-9 pa; 1-57091-536-9 pa
LC 2010033634
"Masiello begins with a discussion of how to use circles, squares, and other basic forms to draw robot parts like switches, plugs, and antennae. He includes a brief discussion of drawing and coloring tools and shows young artists how to draw eight different robots. . . . The instructions are simple enough for primary-grade students to have success without adult assistance. Masiello's creations are humorous, old-fashioned, and two dimensional." SLJ

Peffer, Jessica
  DragonArt; how to draw fantastic dragons and fantasy creatures. Impact Books 2005 127p il pa $19.99

Grades: 5 6 7 8   **743**

1. Dragons 2. Drawing 3. Mythical animals
ISBN 1-58180-657-4

           LC 2005013013

This is a guide to drawing dragons and other mythical beasts such as griffins, guardian gargoyles, and deadly basilisks.

"This book has great writing and superb illustrations and manages to do everything right from the front cover to the index." SLJ

Roza, Greg

Drawing Dracula. Windmill Books 2011 24p il (Drawing movie monsters step-by-step) lib bdg $25.65; pa $12.85

Grades: 3 4 5 6   **743**

1. Monsters in art 2. Drawing -- Technique 3. Motion pictures -- History and criticism
ISBN 978-1-61533-015-7 lib bdg; 1-61533-015-1 lib bdg; 978-1-61533-021-8 pa; 1-61533-021-6 pa

           LC 2010004901

A "surefire [hit] with movie fans and aspiring artists, [this volume traces] the cinematic history of [Dracula] and gives step-by-step instructions on how to bring [him] to life on paper. The instructions and accompanying illustrations explaining how to draw the [monster start] with basic shapes such as circles and rectangles and gradually adding more details. . . . Each pose comes from a notable cinematic depiction of the monster . . . and includes a brief description of the movie with entertaining trivia about its cultural significance, special effects, or popularity over time. The drawing poses are logically organized in chronological order. . . . With text printed in a large, clear font and simply structured sentences, [this book provides] an accessible introduction to film history, and young artists will undoubtedly enjoy trying their hand at depicting [the monster] in a variety of poses." SLJ

Includes glossary and bibliographical references

Drawing Frankenstein. Windmill Books 2011 24p il (Drawing movie monsters step-by-step) lib bdg $25.65; pa $12.85

Grades: 3 4 5 6   **743**

1. Monsters in art 2. Drawing -- Technique 3. Motion pictures -- History and criticism
ISBN 978-1-61533-014-0 lib bdg; 1-61533-014-3 lib bdg; 978-1-61533-019-5 pa; 1-61533-019-4 pa

           LC 2010004900

A "surefire [hit] with movie fans and aspiring artists, [this volume traces] the cinematic history of [Frankenstein] and gives step-by-step instructions on how to bring [him] to life on paper. The instructions and accompanying illustrations explaining how to draw the [monster start] with basic shapes such as circles and rectangles and gradually adding more details. . . . Each pose comes from a notable cinematic depiction of the monster . . . and includes a brief description of the movie with entertaining trivia about its cultural significance, special effects, or popularity over time. The drawing poses are logically organized in chronological order. . . . With text printed in a large, clear font and simply structured sentences, [this book provides] an accessible introduction to film history, and young artists will undoubtedly enjoy trying

their hand at depicting [the monster] in a variety of poses." SLJ

Includes glossary and bibliographical references

Drawing Godzilla. Windmill Books 2010 24p il (Drawing movie monsters step-by-step) lib bdg $25.65; pa $12.85

Grades: 3 4 5 6   **743**

1. Monsters in art 2. Drawing -- Technique 3. Motion pictures -- History and criticism
ISBN 978-1-61533-013-3 lib bdg; 1-61533-013-5 lib bdg; 978-1-61533-017-1 pa; 1-61533-017-8 pa

           LC 2010004899

A "surefire [hit] with movie fans and aspiring artists, [this volume traces] the cinematic history of [Godzilla] and gives step-by-step instructions on how to bring [him] to life on paper. The instructions and accompanying illustrations explaining how to draw the [monster start] with basic shapes such as circles and rectangles and gradually adding more details. . . . Each pose comes from a notable cinematic depiction of the monster . . . and includes a brief description of the movie with entertaining trivia about its cultural significance, special effects, or popularity over time. The drawing poses are logically organized in chronological order. . . . With text printed in a large, clear font and simply structured sentences, [this book provides] an accessible introduction to film history, and young artists will undoubtedly enjoy trying their hand at depicting [the monster] in a variety of poses." SLJ

Includes glossary and bibliographical references

Drawing King Kong. Windmill Books 2011 24p il (Drawing movie monsters step-by-step) lib bdg $25.65; pa $12.85

Grades: 3 4 5 6   **743**

1. Monsters in art 2. Drawing -- Technique 3. Motion pictures -- History and criticism
ISBN 978-1-61533-016-4 lib bdg; 1-61533-016-X lib bdg; 978-1-61533-023-2 pa; 1-61533-023-2 pa

           LC 2010006166

A "surefire [hit] with movie fans and aspiring artists, [this volume traces] the cinematic history of [King Kong] and gives step-by-step instructions on how to bring [him] to life on paper. The instructions and accompanying illustrations explaining how to draw the [monster start] with basic shapes such as circles and rectangles and gradually adding more details. . . . Each pose comes from a notable cinematic depiction of the monster . . . and includes a brief description of the movie with entertaining trivia about its cultural significance, special effects, or popularity over time. The drawing poses are logically organized in chronological order. . . . With text printed in a large, clear font and simply structured sentences, [this book provides] an accessible introduction to film history, and young artists will undoubtedly enjoy trying their hand at depicting [the monster] in a variety of poses." SLJ

Includes glossary and bibliographical references

Stephens, Jay

Heroes! draw your own superheroes, gadget geeks & other do-gooders. [by] Jay Stephens. Lark Books 2007 64p il $12.95; pa $5.95

Grades: 4 5 6 7 **743**
1. Drawing 2. Superheroes 3. Cartoons and caricatures
ISBN 978-1-57990-934-5; 1-57990-934-5; 978-1-60059-179-2 pa; 1-60059-179-5 pa
LC 2006101661
"Stephens shows just how to draw [superheroes]. . . . Stephens does a good job organizing his material, beginning with a bit of history, then moving quickly to hero heads, . . . and on to masks, disguises, physical features, power effects, and action moves. The brightly colored illustrations offer plenty of how-to info and lots of great heroes, male and female, to use as models." Booklist

Monsters! draw your own mutants, freaks & creeps. [by] Jay Stephens. Lark Books 2007 64p il $12.95; pa $5.95
Grades: 4 5 6 7 **743**
1. Drawing 2. Monsters in art 3. Cartoons and caricatures
ISBN 978-1-57990-935-2; 1-57990-935-3; 978-1-60059-178-5 pa; 1-60059-178-7 pa
LC 2006036104
This offers instruction in drawing such cartoon monsters as Dockula, the aquatic nibbler; Skeeterman, the campground creep; and Spook Ook, the attic thumper

Robots! draw your own androids, cyborgs & fighting bots. [by] Jay Stephens. Lark Books 2007 64p il $12.95
Grades: 4 5 6 7 **743**
1. Drawing 2. Robots in art 3. Cartoons and caricatures
ISBN 978-1-57990-937-6; 1-57990-937-X
LC 2007027637
"With simple detailed instructions, an inviting text, and entertaining cartoon scenarios, . . . Stephens explains, step by step, how to draw a variety of robots." Booklist

745 Decorative arts

Dhom, Christel
The **Advent** Craft and Activity Book; Stories, Crafts, Recipes and Poems for the Christmas Season. Christel Dhom. Floris Books 2012 144 p. $19.95
Grades: 4 5 6 **745**
1. Advent 2. Baking 3. Children's stories 4. Handicraft for children
ISBN 0863159125; 9780863159121
This book is a "compendium of old-fashioned craft projects, recipes and stories was written by a Waldorf kindergarten teacher in Germany and translated for English-speaking countries. . . . Recipes for holiday cookies and candies are included, with measurements given in both grams and ounces. Craft projects include traditional advent wreaths, beeswax candles and Nativity figures made from unspun sheep's wool." (Kirkus)

Tejubehan (Singer)
★ **Drawing** from the City; Teju Behan. Pgw 2012 28 p. $35.95
Grades: 3 4 5 6 7 8 **745**
1. India 2. Artists 3. Poverty
ISBN 9380340176; 9789380340173

This "autobiographical art book recounts self-taught artist Teju Behan's journey from an impoverished childhood in rural India, through her family's efforts to improve their lot in a tent city in Mumbai, and into her adulthood, when she lived as a singer and artist with her husband. . . . Hand-screen-printed illustrations comprised of intricate linework and patterns of dots underscore elements of the text." (Kirkus)

745.2 Industrial art and design

Arato, Rona
Design it! the ordinary things we use every day and the not-so-ordinary ways they came to be. illustrations by Claudia Newell. Tundra Books 2010 71p il pa $20.95
Grades: 4 5 6 7 **745.2**
1. Industrial design 2. Inventors 3. Inventions
ISBN 978-0-88776-846-0 pa; 0-88776-846-6 pa
"This book opens with an explanation of what industrial designers do and with whom they work to make better products. Brief chapters then cover such topics as home, communications, lighting, and toy design and include a good-design checklist that takes function, usability, ergonomics, aesthetics, and greenness into consideration. The language is chatty and inviting, and the pages are full of cartoon illustrations and text superimposed on colorful geometric backgrounds. Sidebars offer a wealth of further information." SLJ

Welsbacher, Anne
Earth-friendly design; by Anne Welsbacher. Lerner Publications Company 2009 72p il (Saving our living Earth) lib bdg $30.60
Grades: 5 6 7 8 **745.2**
1. Industrial design 2. Environmental protection
ISBN 978-0-8225-7564-1 lib bdg; 0-8225-7564-7 lib bdg
LC 2007-35925
"Provides a thorough, interesting discussion of multiple aspects of [Earth-friendly design], including historical origins, the current situation, and potential solutions. . . . Photos from around the world accompany discussions. . . . [This is a] solid choice to replace outdated books." SLJ
Includes glossary and bibliographical references

745.5 Handicrafts

Alter, Anna
What can you do with an old red shoe? a green activity book about re-use. [by] Anna Alter. Henry Holt & Co. 2009 32p il $16.95
Grades: 1 2 3 **745.5**
1. Salvage 2. Recycling 3. Handicraft
ISBN 978-0-8050-8290-6; 0-8050-8290-5
LC 2008018341
"Recycling becomes lots of fun in this sprightly activity book. Alter offers 13 projects, and . . . the finished products are usually items kids will want to use. . . . The instructions are clear and simple . . . and what really makes this a standout is Alter's adorable artwork featuring a coterie of animals at work and play. Short poems introduce each project." Booklist

Bell-Rehwoldt, Sheri

The **kids'** guide to building cool stuff; by Sheri Bell-Rehwoldt. Capstone Press 2009 32p il (Kids' guides) lib bdg $23.99

Grades: 4 5 6 7 **745.5**

1. Amusements 2. Handicraft 3. Science -- Experiments

ISBN 978-1-4296-2276-9 lib bdg; 1-4296-2276-8 lib bdg

LC 2008-29687

This provides instructions for building such items as a kite, a balloon rocket, a paper boat, a milk carton bird feeder, and a plastic plate hovercraft

Includes glossary and bibliographical references

Blake, Susannah

Crafts for pampering yourself; Susannah Blake. Enslow Publishers, Inc. 2013 32 p. color illustrations (Eco chic) $22.60

Grades: 4 5 6 7 8 **745.5**

1. Cosmetics 2. Handicraft 3. Green products

ISBN 0766043142; 9780766043145

LC 2012045280

In this book, author Susannah Blake offers suggestions on how readers can "have an eco-friendly pampering party with these . . . craft ideas. From lip balm to bath infusion, this book offers easy step-by-step instructions to upcycle, customise and add sparkle to your bathroom routines." (Publisher's note)

"Numbered step-by-step illustrations; a fresh, tween-friendly design; explanations of basic craft skills; and instructions for throwing a 'pamper party' round out the beauty-meets-responsibility fun."

Crafty activities; over 50 fun and easy things to make. by Judy Balchin . . . [et al.] Search 2007 un il pa $19.95

Grades: 4 5 6 7 **745.5**

1. Handicraft

ISBN 978-1-84448-250-4 pa; 1-84448-250-2 pa

"The book is divided into six chapters—mosaics, printing, lettering, papier-mâché, handmade cards, and origami—with projects ranging from simple leaf prints to an elaborate necklace made from dried pasta. . . . The photos of smiling kids showing off their creations, the attractive, spacious page design, and, above all the ingenious projects will attract kids—as well as teachers." Booklist

Garner, Lynne

★ **African** crafts; fun things to make and do from West Africa. Chicago Review Press 2008 48p il $12.95

Grades: 4 5 6 **745.5**

1. Handicraft 2. African art 3. Ghana -- Social life and customs

ISBN 978-1-55652-748-7; 1-55652-748-9

First published 2004 in the United Kingdom

Presents an overview of West African culture and provides step-by-step instructions for using simple household materials to make such traditional items as a mask, a coiled pot, block-printed and woven cloths, and a drum.

"Despite the generic title, the focus is on one country, Ghana, and that is the strength of this hands-on crafts book, illustrated with clear step-by-step instructions and lots of color photos. . . . Written in chatty style, the spaciously laid out chapters cover adinkra block printing, pot coiling, mask

making, music makers, and kente strip weaving. . . . An excellent source for school and home." Booklist

Hendry, Linda

Dog crafts; written and illustrated by Linda Hendry. Kids Can Press 2002 40p il (Kids can do it) $12.95; pa $5.95

Grades: 4 5 6 **745.5**

1. Dogs 2. Handicraft

ISBN 1-55074-960-9; 1-55074-962-5 pa

This includes instructions for 17 craft projects including decorated jars, picture frames, placemats, jewelry, and bookends

"Nicely designed, double-page spreads show the project step-by-step, each one clearly and succinctly described and illustrated with a color drawing." Booklist

Henry, Sandi

Making amazing art; 40 activities using the 7 elements of art design. by Sandi Henry; illustrated by Sarah Rakitin Cole. Williamsonbooks 2007 128p il (Kids can) $16.99; pa $12.99

Grades: 2 3 4 5 **745.5**

1. Art 2. Design 3. Handicraft

ISBN 978-0-8249-6794-9; 0-8249-6794-1; 978-0-8249-6795-6 pa; 0-8249-6795-X pa

LC 2006101173

"Each chapter in this well-organized, heavily illustrated book features one element—line, texture, color, etc.—with five or six projects that cleverly support it. . . . Icons display three challenge levels; step-by-step instructions help to ensure success." SLJ

Jocelyn, Marthe

Sneaky art; crafty surprises to hide in plain sight. Marthe Jocelyn. Candlewick Press 2013 64 p. $12.99

Grades: 3 4 5 **745.5**

1. Handicraft for children

ISBN 0763656488; 9780763656485

LC 2012942615

This children's craft book, by Marthe Jocelyn, is a "how-to manual for creating removable and shareable art projects from easily found materials. The sneaky part is in the installation! Each work of art is custom-created for display in public places. . . . This utterly unique guide--part craft book, part art-philosophy--offers a stylish and sweet . . . spirit of fun meant to put a smile on the faces of strangers and loved ones alike." (Publisher's note)

Kenney, Karen Latchana

Super simple art to wear; fun and easy-to-make crafts for kids. ABDO Pub. Company 2010 31p il (Super simple crafts) lib bdg $17.95

Grades: K 1 2 3 4 **745.5**

1. Handicraft

ISBN 978-1-60453-622-5 lib bdg; 1-60453-622-5 lib bdg

LC 2009-349

"Colorful photos; clean layout in a bright, primary palette; and large, abundant step-by-step instructional photos give [this book] great appeal. The . . . crafts . . . are functional and attractive. [The book] demonstrates [for instatnce] how to paint shoelaces. . . . Readily obtainable household

materials and easy-to-follow instructions mean that children can do these crafts independently." SLJ
Includes glossary

Llimos, Anna
Easy cardboard crafts in 5 steps. Enslow Elementary 2008 31p il (Easy crafts in 5 steps) lib bdg $22.60
Grades: 2 3 4   **745.5**
   1. Handicraft
   ISBN 978-0-7660-3083-1 lib bdg; 0-7660-3083-0 lib bdg
Original Spanish edition 2005
This "has instructions for 14 projects, among them a folder, drum, and hang-glider. . . . A materials list is provided for each item, with general supplies and recyclables sufficient for most crafts. The simple directions are adequately spaced on the page and accompanied by step-by-step color photos." SLJ
Includes bibliographical references

Easy cloth crafts in 5 steps. Enslow Elementary 2008 31p il (Easy crafts in 5 steps) lib bdg $22.60
Grades: 2 3 4   **745.5**
   1. Handicraft
   ISBN 978-0-7660-3084-8 lib bdg; 0-7660-3084-9 lib bdg
Original Spanish edition 2005
This "has instructions for 14 projects, among them . . . a tray, turtle, and clown. . . . A materials list is provided for each item, with general supplies and recyclables sufficient for most crafts. The simple directions are adequately spaced on the page and accompanied by step-by-step color photos." SLJ
Includes bibliographical references

Easy earth-friendly crafts in 5 steps. Enslow Elementary 2008 31p il (Easy crafts in 5 steps) lib bdg $22.60
Grades: 2 3 4   **745.5**
   1. Recycling 2. Handicraft
   ISBN 978-0-7660-3086-2 lib bdg; 0-7660-3086-5 lib bdg
Original Spanish edition 2005
This offers instructions for 14 crafts using recycled materials such as bottle caps, egg cartons, and bottles, among them a coin purse, a spinning top, and a doll
The text is "easy to read, and the results are quirky and pleasing; steps are illustrated with bright photographs." Horn Book Guide
Includes bibliographical references

Haunted house adventure crafts. Enslow Elementary 2010 32p il (Fun adventure crafts) lib bdg $22.60; pa $6.95
Grades: 1 2 3   **745.5**
   1. Halloween 2. Handicraft
   ISBN 978-0-7660-3730-4 lib bdg; 0-7660-3730-4 lib bdg; 978-0-7660-3731-1 pa; 0-7660-3731-2 pa
           LC 2009041462
Original Spanish edition 2008
"In simple language and bright pictures, 11 crafts are laid out, including the magnum opus: a cardboard haunted house. . . . Small illustrated versions of the final products cavort across the pages, and story ideas conclude." Booklist
Includes bibliographical references

Monaghan, Kimberly
Organic crafts; 75 earth-friendly art activities. [by] Kimberly Monaghan. Chicago Review Press 2007 140p pa $14.95
Grades: 2 3 4 5   **745.5**
   1. Handicraft 2. Nature craft
   ISBN 978-1-55652-640-4 pa; 1-55652-640-7 pa
           LC 2006031659
"These activities, crafts, and games are arranged by type of material used, such as rocks, pebbles, and shells; soil, clay, and sand, etc. There's a wide range of interesting projects, including clay beads, a glittering sand castle, potpourri, a sea sparkler, a wind sock, a gourd birdhouse, broken-china mosaics, homemade paper, rock sculpture, and garden chimes. Children will also learn how to make natural glue, cornstarch paint, and salt clay." SLJ
Includes bibliographical references

My art book; amazing art projects inspired by masterpieces. DK Pub. 2011 80p il $15.99
Grades: 3 4 5 6   **745.5**
   1. Art 2. Handicraft
   ISBN 978-0-7566-7582-0; 0-7566-7582-0
"Representing a variety of cultures and styles, this book highlights 14 famous artworks and offers a craft project related to each one. The arrangement is roughly chronological, beginning with the cave paintings of Lascaux, France, and ending with the Pop Art of Andy Warhol. Each work is reproduced in a high-quality color photograph and described in a few paragraphs of succinct but interesting text. The projects are varied and appealing, and no two use the same medium or technique. . . . A great resource for teaching art history though hands-on activities." SLJ

Oldham, Todd
★ Kid made modern. AMMO 2009 184p il $22.95
Grades: 3 4 5 6   **745.5**
   1. Design 2. Handicraft
   ISBN 978-1-934429-36-5; 1-934429-36-8
           LC 2009-934393
"This activity book from renowned designer Oldham uses the work of Mid-Century modern visual artists—including Isamu Noguchi, Alexander Calder, and Charles and Ray Eames—as springboards for 52 hands-on creative projects. Brief tutorials introduce skills and techniques, paired with full-color photos of kids and the various processes. . . . There's much here to capture the eye of ambitious, crafty readers." Publ Wkly

Owen, Cheryl
Gifts for kids to make. Hamlyn 2006 128p il pa $14.95
Grades: K 1 2 3 4 5   **745.5**
   1. Gifts 2. Handicraft
   ISBN 0-600-61502-2
"This useful volume is divided into six categories—bric-a-brac, stationery, scented gifts, floral garden gifts, accessories, and edible treats—with 7 to 10 projects in each. Examples are magnets, bookmarks, gift wrap, birdfeeder, glasses case, and cookies. . . . The items are appealing to children and age appropriate. Both the written and visual instructions are clear and easy to follow." SLJ

Press, Judy

The **little** hands big fun craft book; illustrated by Loretta Trezzo Braren. 2nd ed.; Williamson 2008 142p il pa $12.99

Grades: PreK K 1   **745.5**

1. Handicraft

ISBN 978-0-8249-6827-4 pa; 0-8249-6827-1 pa

First published 1996

This craft book for young children includes 70 projects

Ross, Kathy

Bedroom makeover crafts; illustrated by Nicole in den Bosch. Millbrook Press 2008 47p il (Girl crafts) lib bdg $26.60; pa $7.95

Grades: 3 4 5   **745.5**

1. Handicraft

ISBN 978-0-8225-7593-1 lib bdg; 0-8225-7593-0 lib bdg; 978-1-58013-823-9 pa; 1-58013-823-3 pa

LC 2007001894

"This title contains step-by-step directions for an array of room accessories that includes everything from earring dolls and doorknob covers to small tables and trash baskets. Materials are readily obtained and directions are clear and easy to follow." SLJ

Crafts for kids who are learning about dinosaurs; illustrated by Jan Barger. Millbrook Press 2008 48p il lib bdg $26.60

Grades: 2 3 4   **745.5**

1. Dinosaurs 2. Handicraft

ISBN 978-0-8225-6809-4 lib bdg; 0-8225-6809-8 lib bdg

LC 2006100645

"These 22 projects include a necklace, a bathtub toy, puppets, a pencil topper, a tape dispenser, and more. Brief facts about dinosaurs are matched with each craft. Each project has a list of materials needed and illustrations for the 3 to 15 steps. . . . A welcome addition for young dinosaur fans." SLJ

Earth-friendly crafts; clever ways to reuse everyday items. [by] Kathy Ross; illustrated by Celine Malepart. Millbrook Press 2009 48p il lib bdg $26.60

Grades: 3 4 5 6   **745.5**

1. Recycling 2. Handicraft

ISBN 978-0-8225-9099-6 lib bdg; 0-8225-9099-9 lib bdg

LC 2008025481

"This clear, colorful title offers a selection of environmentally focused projects that encourage kids to reduce, reuse, and recycle. Both practical and eye-catching, the projects, from pencil cups to decorative pins, rely on everyday discarded items that many kids will find around their homes. . . . [The crafts] are presented in line drawings that demonstrate the construction step by step along with color photos of the finished product." Booklist

Sadler, Judy Ann

The **new** jumbo book of easy crafts; written by Judy Ann Sadler; illustrated by Caroline Price. Kids Can Press 2009 176p il pa $18.95

Grades: PreK K 1 2   **745.5**

1. Handicraft

ISBN 978-1-55453-239-1 pa; 1-55453-239-6 pa

First published 2001 with title: The Kids Can Press jumbo book of easy crafts

This includes instructions for over 150 crafts divided into four themed sections: Imagine and Create, Wear and Use, Make and Play and Decorate and Celebrate

Sirrine, Carol

Cool crafts with old jeans; green projects for resourceful kids. Capstone Press 2010 32p il (Snap books. Green crafts) lib bdg $26.65

Grades: 3 4 5 6   **745.5**

1. Recycling 2. Handicraft 3. Jeans (Clothing)

ISBN 978-1-4296-4006-0 lib bdg; 1-4296-4006-5 lib bdg

"Steps are easy to follow and well documented, and the projects encourage experimentation and creativity. Materials are generally easy to find. . . . This . . . is original, well-presented, and bound to inspire classroom and individual projects." SLJ

Includes glossary and bibliographical references

Cool crafts with old t-shirts; green projects for resourceful kids. Capstone Press 2010 32p il (Snap Books. Green crafts) lib bg $26.65

Grades: 3 4 5 6   **745.5**

1. Salvage 2. Handicraft

ISBN 1-4296-4009-X lib bdg; 978-1-4296-4009-1 lib bdg

"Steps are easy to follow and well documented, and the projects encourage experimentation and creativity. Materials are generally easy to find. . . . This . . . is original, well-presented, and bound to inspire classroom and individual projects." SLJ

Includes glossary and bibliographical references

Cool crafts with old wrappers, cans and bottles; green projects for resourceful kids. Capstone Press 2010 32p il (Snap books. Green crafts) lib bdg $26.65

Grades: 3 4 5 6   **745.5**

1. Salvage 2. Handicraft

ISBN 978-1-4296-4008-4 lib bdg; 1-4296-4008-1 lib bdg

"Steps are easy to follow and well documented, and the projects encourage experimentation and creativity. Materials are generally easy to find. . . . This . . . is original, well-presented, and bound to inspire classroom and individual projects." SLJ

Includes glossary and bibliographical references

Torres, Laura

Rock your school stuff. QEB Pub. 2010 32p il (Rock your . . .) lib bdg $28.50

Grades: 4 5 6   **745.5**

1. Handicraft 2. Schools -- Equipment and supplies

ISBN 978-1-59566-936-0; 1-59566-936-1

LC 2010010670

This book "gives kids easy step-by-step ways to . . . personalize school supplies. . . . Colorful photographs show youngsters crafting [such items as beaded pens, recycled paperclip bookmarks, backpack zipper pulls] . . . some of which are created from recycled found items. All are projects they can complete by themselves." Horn Book Guide

Wolf, Laurie Goldrich

Recyclo-gami; 40 crafts to make your friends green with envy! Running Press Teens 2010 112p il $14.95

Grades: 4 5 6 7   **745.5**

1. Recycling 2. Handicraft

ISBN 978-0-7624-4052-8; 0-7624-4052-X

"Wolf's fun, resourceful projects offer straightforward ways to reuse common materials to make accessories, jewelry, household decorations, games, and gifts. Leftover tissue or wrapping paper can be used to create decoupage plates; old crayons are melted and baked into molds to make multicolored crayons; and unused CDs and DVDs are transformed into funky, freeform bowls when melted in the oven. . . . The ease of most of the activities should inspire readers to see the recycling bin as a potential treasure trove." Publ Wkly

745.54   Papers

Garza, Carmen Lomas

★ **Making** magic windows; creating papel picado/cut-paper art with Carmen Lomas Garza. Children's Bk. Press 1999 61p il pa $9.95

Grades: 3 4 5 6   **745.54**

1. Paper crafts

ISBN 0-89239-159-6

LC 98-38518

Provides instructions for making paper banners and more intricate cut-outs. Includes diagrams for creating specific images

"Based on workshops conducted by the artist, the step-by-step instructions and illustrations have been fine-tuned and are clear and easy to follow. . . . Multiculturally authentic and a guaranteed kid-crowd pleaser, this workbook is enthusiastically recommended for all craft collections." Booklist

Latno, Mark

The **paper** boomerang book; build them, throw them, and get them to return every time. Chicago Review Press 2010 245p il pa $12.95

Grades: 5 6 7 8   **745.54**

1. Boomerangs 2. Paper crafts

ISBN 978-1-56976-282-0 pa; 1-56976-282-1 pa

LC 2010007251

"In a unique . . . guide Latno . . . [explains] how to make, fine-tune, and decorate a type of paper boomerang that can be constructed with commonly available materials and thrown with (relative) safety indoors. The instructions and simply drawn diagrams are embedded in a history of boomerangs and throwing sticks, a challenging technical discussion of the physics of boomerangs and gyroscopes, and very detailed descriptions of the characteristics of railroad board (Latno's preferred paper) and alternatives, plus art-and-craft materials that can be used to dress up finished models." SLJ

Includes glossary and bibliographical references

Llimos, Anna

Easy paper crafts in 5 steps. Enslow Elementary 2008 31p il (Easy crafts in 5 steps) lib bdg $22.60

Grades: 2 3 4   **745.54**

1. Paper crafts

ISBN 978-0-7660-3087-9 lib bdg; 0-7660-3087-3 lib bdg

Original Spanish edition 2005

This offers instructions for 14 paper craft projects, among them a basket, a butterfly, and pop-up card

The text is "easy to read, and the results are quirky and pleasing; steps are illustrated with bright photographs." Horn Book Guide

Includes bibliographical references

Torres, Laura

Rock your party. QEB Pub. 2010 32p il (Rock your . . .) lib bdg $28.50

Grades: 4 5 6   **745.54**

1. Parties 2. Handicraft 3. Paper crafts

ISBN 978-1-59566-935-3; 1-59566-935-3

LC 2010010668

This book "gives kids easy step-by-step ways to make decorations for their . . . parties. . . . Colorful photographs show youngsters crafting appealing . . . party hats, etc. some of which are created from recycled found items. All are projects they can complete by themselves." Horn Book Guide

Walsh, Danny

The **cardboard** box book; 25 things to make and do with empty boxes. by Danny, Jake, and Niall Walsh; [photographs by Martin Norris; illustrations by Josh Halloran] Watson-Guptill 2006 112p il pa $12.95

Grades: 3 4 5   **745.54**

1. Boxes 2. Handicraft

ISBN 0-8230-0610-7

LC 2005935223

"An eye-catching cover showcases a few of these projects designed for indoor or outdoor play, and the book's lively design and layout, featuring bold colors and various fonts, will draw in young crafters. Opening chapters discuss where to find boxes of different sizes, what a basic tool kit consists of, how to use paint and glitter, when adult help is needed, and the time involved in constructing the creations." SLJ

745.58   Beads, found and other objects

Boonyadhistarn, Thiranut

Beading; bracelets, barrettes, and beyond. by Thiranut Boonyadhistarn. Capstone Press 2007 32p il (Snap books) $25.26

Grades: 4 5 6 7   **745.58**

1. Beadwork

ISBN 978-0-7368-6472-5; 0-7368-6472-5

LC 2006004102

This describes how to create such bead crafts as safety-pin bracelets and bag charms.

"Girls will appreciate these ideas for recreating fashion trends and for achieving the artistic effects that they want. . . . Page layouts are lively and attractive. The projects use easily obtainable materials, and the directions are simple and well numbered." SLJ

Includes bibliographical references

Llimos, Anna

Easy bead crafts in 5 steps. Enslow Elementary 2008 31p il (Easy crafts in 5 steps) lib bdg $22.60

Grades: 2 3 4   **745.58**

1. Beadwork

ISBN 978-0-7660-3757-1 lib bdg; 0-7660-3757-6 lib bdg

Original Spanish edition 2005

This offers instructions for 14 bead craft projects, among them a bracelet and ring, a bookmark, and a belt

The text is "easy to read, and the results are quirky and pleasing; steps are illustrated with bright photographs." Horn Book Guide

Includes bibliographical references

Ross, Kathy

Beautiful beads; illustrated by Nicole in den Bosch. Millbrook Press 2009 48p il lib bdg $26.60

Grades: 2 3 4 5   **745.58**

1. Beadwork

ISBN 978-0-8225-9214-3 lib bdg; 0-8225-9214-2 lib bdg

LC 2008044441

"A diverse collection of 21 fun and unique projects. Young readers will learn how to make different types of beads (fabric, textured, thread, ribbon, sparkle stem), two games, a felt-bead bracelet, a cluster pin, a seed-bead flower magnet, whimsical items (beaded dog, spaghetti doll, and others), a bookmark, a tissue box, and more. The colors are vivid, and the illustrations perfectly complement the text." SLJ

Scheunemann, Pam

★ **Cool** beaded jewelry; [by] Pam Scheunemann. ABDO Pub. 2005 32p il (Cool crafts) $22.78

Grades: 4 5 6   **745.58**

1. Jewelry 2. Beadwork

ISBN 1-59197-739-8

LC 2004-46292

This "has an extensive section on bead history, sizes, shapes, types, and metal findings (clasps, etc.). Projects include a memory wire bracelet, a beaded necklace and bracelet, daisy chain necklace, and beaded rings." SLJ

Sirrine, Carol

Cool crafts with old CDs; green projects for resourceful kids. Capstone Press 2010 32p il (Snap books. Green crafts) lib bdg $26.65

Grades: 3 4 5 6   **745.58**

1. Salvage 2. Compact discs 3. Plastics craft

ISBN 978-1-4296-4007-7 lib bdg; 1-4296-4006-5 lib bdg

"Steps are easy to follow and well documented, and the projects encourage experimentation and creativity. Materials are generally easy to find. . . . This . . . is original, well-presented, and bound to inspire classroom and individual projects." SLJ

Includes glossary and bibliographical references

745.59 Making specific objects

Hufford, Deborah

★ **Greeting** card making; send your personal message. by Deborah Hufford. Capstone Press 2006 32p il (Snap books crafts) lib bdg $25.26

Grades: 3 4 5   **745.59**

1. Handicraft 2. Greeting cards

ISBN 0-7368-4385-X

LC 2005006899

"A pop-up birthday cake, a dried flower-petal design, and a lacey valentine are among the homemade card ideas featured in this simple, easy-to-follow title. . . . Introductory pages cover basic paper folds and materials; later spreads present mostly clear, step-by-step instructions." Booklist

Includes glossary and bibliographical references

Kenney, Karen Latchana

Super simple magnets; fun and easy-to-make crafts for kids. ABDO Pub. Co. 2010 32p il (Super simple crafts) lib bdg $17.95

Grades: K 1 2 3 4   **745.59**

1. Magnets 2. Handicraft

ISBN 978-1-60453-626-3 lib bdg; 1-60453-626-8 lib bdg

LC 2009-355

"Colorful photos; clean layout in a bright, primary palette; and large, abundant step-by-step instructional photos give [this book] great appeal. The . . . crafts . . . are functional and attractive. . . . Readily obtainable household materials and easy-to-follow instructions mean that children can do these crafts independently." SLJ

Includes glossary

745.592 Toys, models, miniatures, related objects

Castleforte, Brian

Papertoy monsters; 50 cool papertoys you can make yourself. Workman Pub. Co. 2010 233p il pa $16.95

Grades: 4 5 6 7   **745.592**

1. Paper crafts 2. Monsters in art

ISBN 978-0-7611-5882-0 pa; 0-7611-5882-0 pa

"Twenty-five 'papertoy' artists contribute 50 original monster designs made of colorful cardstock that can be punched out and glued together to form three dimensional cartoon characters, each with its own quirky backstory. The menagerie includes the tentacled OctoPup, who devours small boats; Yucky Chuck, a serrated-toothed 'mutant lunchbox monster'; and Lester Rottenbottom, a teacher-turned-mad-scientist. The designers' enthusiasm for their subjects should inspire readers to invent their own monsters on the blank templates provided." Publ Wkly

Harbo, Christopher L.

The **kids'** guide to paper airplanes. Capstone Press 2009 32p il (Kids' guides) $23.93

Grades: 4 5 6 7   **745.592**

1. Paper crafts 2. Airplanes -- Models

ISBN 978-1-4296-2274-5; 1-4296-2274-1

LC 2008029688

"Using colorful, vivid, and clear step-by-step illustrations, Harbo demonstrates how to construct everything from the classic Dart to the circular Space Ring to the 18-step Silent Huntress." Booklist

Includes glossary and bibliographical references

Paper airplanes: Captain, level 4. Capstone Press 2010 32p il (Edge books. Paper airplanes) lib bdg $26.65
Grades: 3 4 5 6   **745.592**
1. Paper crafts 2. Airplanes -- Models
ISBN 978-1-4296-4744-1 lib bdg; 1-4296-4744-2 lib bdg

LC 2010001003

This "includes a list of basic materials and an overview of folding instructions and techniques. . . . Along with hints on how to hold the plane for take-off to maximize strengths are suggestions on conducting friendly competitions with the finished products. Sure to keep readers busy for hours." SLJ

Includes bibliographical references

Paper airplanes: Copilot, level 2. Capstone Press 2010 32p il (Edge books. Paper airplanes) lib bdg $26.65
Grades: 3 4 5 6   **745.592**
1. Paper crafts 2. Airplanes -- Models
ISBN 978-1-4296-4742-7 lib bdg; 1-4296-4742-6 lib bdg

LC 2010001004

This "includes a list of basic materials and an overview of folding instructions and techniques. . . . Along with hints on how to hold the plane for takeoff to maximize strengths are suggestions on conducting friendly competitions with the finished products. Sure to keep readers busy for hours." SLJ

Includes bibliographical references

Paper airplanes: Flight school, level 1. Capstone Press 2010 32p il (Edge books. Paper airplanes) lib bdg $26.65
Grades: 3 4 5 6   **745.592**
1. Paper crafts 2. Airplanes -- Models
ISBN 978-1-4296-4741-0 lib bdg; 1-4296-4741-8 lib bdg

LC 2010001005

This "includes a list of basic materials and an overview of folding instructions and techniques. . . . Along with hints on how to hold the plane for takeoff to maximize strengths are suggestions on conducting friendly competitions with the finished products. Sure to keep readers busy for hours." SLJ

Includes bibliographical references

Paper airplanes: Pilot, level 3. Capstone Press 2010 32p il (Edge books. Paper airplanes) lib bdg $26.65
Grades: 3 4 5 6   **745.592**
1. Paper crafts 2. Airplanes -- Models
ISBN 978-1-4296-4743-4 lib bdg; 1-4296-4743-4 lib bdg

LC 2010001006

This "includes a list of basic materials and an overview of folding instructions and techniques. . . . Along with hints on how to hold the plane for takeoff to maximize strengths are suggestions on conducting friendly competitions with

the finished products. Sure to keep readers busy for hours." SLJ

Includes bibliographical references

Mercer, Bobby

The **flying** machine book; build and launch 35 rockets, gliders, helicopters, boomerangs, and more. Bobby Mercer. Chicago Review Press 2012 ix, 197 p.p ill. (pbk.) $14.95
Grades: 4 5 6   **745.592**
1. Flight 2. Aeronautics 3. Airplanes -- Models 4. Models and modelmaking 5. Paper airplanes 6. Flying-machines -- Models
ISBN 9781613740866

LC 2011041174

This book provides "step-by-step instructions for 35 aerodynamic projects . . . Physics teacher [Bobby] Mercer . . . here provides . . . directions for building a variety of flying machines including rockets, gliders, helicopters, boomerangs and assorted launchers. An opening chapter called 'Flight School' introduces the Bernoulli principle and four forces: lift, thrust, drag and weight. . . . Each subsequent chapter begins with more flight school, repeating the relevant principles and applying them to the different forms of flying machines described. Many of the constructions use similar techniques and most are not difficult. The models are made of common materials: card stock and old folders, drinking straws, rubber bands and duct tape." (Kirkus Reviews)

Rigsby, Mike

★ **Amazing** rubber band cars; easy-to-build wind-up racers, models, and toys. [by] Mike Rigsby. Chicago Review Press 2007 121p il lib bdg $12.95
Grades: 4 5 6 7   **745.592**
1. Toys 2. Handicraft 3. Automobiles -- Models
ISBN 978-1-55652-736-4 lib bdg; 1-55652-736-5 lib bdg

LC 2007013969

This offers instructions for making toy and model cars "using mostly cardboard, glue, pencils, rubber bands, and a few other easily obtainable materials. . . . Readers will learn about corrugated and flat cardboard, and how to use glue and work with templates. Excellent instructions are accompanied by black-and-white photos every step of the way. . . . These projects are fun to construct, and inquisitive minds will be fascinated by the moving cars." SLJ

Schwarz, Renee

Wind chimes and whirligigs. Kids Can Press 2007 40p il (Kids can do it) $12.95; pa $6.95
Grades: 4 5 6   **745.592**
1. Handicraft 2. Whirligigs 3. Wind chimes
ISBN 978-1-55337-868-6; 1-55337-868-7; 978-1-55337-870-9 pa; 1-55337-870-9 pa

"A colorfully designed and artfully arranged photographic cover is the perfect introduction to the 12 unique and creative projects within. An overall neat appearance and precise, vibrant illustrations or sharp photos add to the attractive layout. . . . The techniques, using plastic, nylon fishing line, tape, glue, and screwdrivers, are carefully explained." SLJ

Thomson, Ruth

Toys and models; photography by Neil Thomson. Sea-to-Sea Publications 2010 32p il (World of design) lib bdg $28.50

Grades: 4 5 6 7 **745.592**

1. Toys 2. Handicraft 3. Models and modelmaking
ISBN 978-1-59771-209-5 lib bdg; 1-59771-209-4
lib bdg

LC 2008-43868

This "volume presents examples of crafts made around the world, then offers six simple items inspired by these goods that children can make (mostly using recycled materials). The directions allow for easy replication, while information about the crafts provides a window into world cultures. . . . The colorful close-up photographs provide . . . interesting details." Horn Book Guide

Includes glossary and bibliographical references

745.593 Useful objects

Mooney, Carla

Light your way; make a candle. Norwood House Press 2010 48p il (Creative adventure guides) lib bdg $25.27
Grades: 3 4 5 6 **745.593**

1. Candles
ISBN 978-1-59953-387-2; 1-59953-387-1

LC 2010010399

"Some historical background and scientific or cultural information places the making and use of candles . . . in context for young readers. [The] book has four chapters that culminate in step-by-step projects." Horn Book Guide

Includes glossary and bibliographical references

Price, Pamela S.

★ **Cool** scrapbooks; [by] Pam Price. ABDO Pub. 2005 32p il (Cool crafts) lib bdg $25.65
Grades: 4 5 6 **745.593**

1. Scrapbooks
ISBN 1-59197-744-4

LC 2004-46290

This guide to scrapbooks "addresses the use of photos, embellishments, adding words, computer possibilities, and more. . . . [This book lists] required materials, [has] small color photos, and [includes] clearly explained, numbered steps." SLJ

Ransom, Candice F.

Scrapbooking just for you! how to make fun, personal, save-them-forever keepsakes. [by] Candice Ransom. Sterling Pub. 2010 120p il $14.95
Grades: 4 5 6 7 **745.593**

1. Scrapbooks
ISBN 978-1-4027-4096-1; 1-4027-4096-4

LC 2008038982

"Ransom's well-organized introduction showcases her enthusiasm for scrapbooking and also includes material for more experienced crafters. . . . High-quality color photos that are a good match with the directions make the pages pop, and directions are clear." SLJ

745.594 Decorative objects

Bledsoe, Karen E.

Chinese New Year crafts; [by] Karen E. Bledsoe. Enslow Publishers 2005 32p il (Fun holiday crafts kids can do) lib bdg $22.60
Grades: 2 3 4 **745.594**

1. Handicraft 2. Chinese New Year
ISBN 0-7660-2347-8

LC 2004-9622

This includes directions for ten craft projects related to Chinese New Year including a dragon-streamer puppet, a ribbon lantern, and Chinese zodiac pictures

This is "aesthetically pleasing with . . . bright colorful pages, clear concise instructions on the left side and photographs of various stages of the final product on the right. . . . Use of everyday items such as paper cups, cupcake liners, and construction paper makes these activities practical for both students and teachers." SLJ

Includes bibliographical references

Di Salle, Rachel

Junk drawer jewelry; written by Rachel Di Salle and Ellen Warwick; illustrated by Jane Kurisu. Kids Can Press 2006 40p il (Kids can do it) hardcover o.p. pa $6.95
Grades: 4 5 6 **745.594**

1. Jewelry 2. Handicraft
ISBN 978-1-55337-965-2; 978-1-55337-966-9 pa

This introduces the "world of jewelry crafting. . . . Projects of varying difficulty include bracelets, necklaces, rings, wristbands, chokers, and earrings. Each project is accompanied by a color photo, a You Will Need list, and step-by-step instructions. This book will be a popular addition to libraries." SLJ

Fritsch, P.

Pennsylvania Dutch Halloween scherenschnitte; written and illustrated by Peter V. Fritsch. Pelican 2011 78p il $19.95
Grades: 3 4 5 6 **745.594**

1. Paper crafts 2. Pennsylvania Dutch folk art 3. Halloween -- Poetry
ISBN 978-1-58980-956-7; 1-58980-956-4

LC 2011012276

"In the tradition of Pennsylvania Dutch folk art, Fritsch arranges scherenschnitte (scissor-cut) silhouettes against flaming orange backgrounds. Short poems, which appear both in the Pennsylvania Dutch dialect and in English, mine folklore with rascally and sometimes frightening results, and are set against often symmetrical scenes of angular cats, ghosts, witches, and other devilish creatures. An elegant treat harkens back to early American celebrations of Halloween." Publ Wkly

McGee, Randel

Paper crafts for Chinese New Year; [by] Randel McGee. Enslow Elementary 2008 48p il (Paper craft fun for holidays) lib bdg $23.93
Grades: 2 3 4 **745.594**

1. Paper crafts 2. Chinese New Year
ISBN 978-0-7660-2950-7 lib bdg; 0-7660-2950-6 lib bdg

LC 2007014026

This explains the significance of Chinese New Year and offers instructions for making paper crafts including a dancing dragon puppet, a lion dancer mask, a lai see or red gift envelope, shadow puppets, a tangram, a chinese lantern, firecracker decorations, and Chinese symbols and banners.

"The crafts contain materials lists and color photos of the steps and of the finished product. The directions are easy to follow, and enlargeable patterns are provided." SLJ

Includes bibliographical references

Paper crafts for Christmas; [by] Randel McGee. Enslow Elementary 2009 48p il (Paper craft fun for holidays) lib bdg $23.93

Grades: 2 3 4   **745.594**

1. Christmas 2. Paper crafts

ISBN 978-0-7660-2952-1 lib bdg; 0-7660-2952-2 lib bdg

Provides a brief introduction to the history of Christmas, and Christmas-themed paper craft ideas

"Filled with cultural facts . . . [this book offers] much more than just basic craft ideas. . . . Kids will . . . enjoy piecing together these appealing projects. . . . A pop-up card that sends Santa down the chimney is particularly inventive." Booklist

Paper crafts for Day of the Dead; [by] Randel McGee. Enslow Elementary 2008 48p il (Paper craft fun for holidays) lib bdg $23.93

Grades: 2 3 4   **745.594**

1. Paper crafts 2. All Souls' Day

ISBN 978-0-7660-2951-4 lib bdg; 0-7660-2951-4 lib bdg

LC 2007013987

This explains the significance of the Mexican Day of the Dead, and offers instructions for paper crafts including paper marigolds, a skeleton candy basket, happy skeleton figures, skeleton pets, paper clothes for skeletons, a skull mask, papel cortado window banners, and Aztec animal decorations.

"The crafts contain materials lists and color photos of the steps and of the finished product. The directions are easy to follow, and enlargeable patterns are provided." SLJ

Includes bibliographical references

Paper crafts for Halloween; [by] Randel McGee. Enslow Elementary 2009 48p il (Paper craft fun for holidays) lib bdg $23.93

Grades: 2 3 4   **745.594**

1. Halloween 2. Paper crafts

ISBN 978-0-7660-2947-7 lib bdg; 0-7660-2947-6 lib bdg

LC 2007014048

"Filled with cultural facts, [this book offers] . . . much more than just basic craft ideas. . . . Kids will . . . enjoy piecing together these appealing projects." Booklist

Includes bibliographical references

Paper crafts for Kwanzaa; [by] Randel McGee. Enslow Elementary 2008 48p il (Paper craft fun for holidays) lib bdg $23.93

Grades: 2 3 4   **745.594**

1. Kwanzaa 2. Paper crafts

ISBN 978-0-7660-2949-1 lib bdg; 0-7660-2949-2 lib bdg

LC 2007014039

This explains the significance of Kwanzaa and offers instructions for paper crafts including a kinara pop-up card, a mkeka mat, a muhindi or ear of corn, standing Kwanzaa figures, a standing fruit tree, cut-outs of the Nguzo Saba or Seven Guiding Principles, a lion, and an African-style hat.

"The crafts are attractive and easy to make with adult help, and they use common supplies." SLJ

Includes bibliographical references

Paper crafts for Valentine's Day. Enslow Publishers 2008 48p il (Paper craft fun for holidays) lib bdg $23.93

Grades: 2 3 4   **745.594**

1. Paper crafts 2. Valentine's Day

ISBN 978-0-7660-2948-4 lib bdg; 0-7660-2948-4 lib bdg

LC 2007014041

Explains the significance of Valentine's Day and offers instructions for making paper crafts including a Cupid figure, a heart sculpture, a lacy heart card, a pop-up heart card, a valentine heart crown, heart flowers, a stick puppet, and a Danish woven heart basket.

"These eight crafts are simple to complete, with easy-to-follow instructions. A color photo of the finished piece is included." SLJ

Includes bibliographical references

Rau, Dana Meachen

Get connected; make a friendship bracelet. Norwood House Press 2010 48p il (Creative adventure guides) lib bdg $25.27

Grades: 3 4 5 6   **745.594**

1. Beadwork 2. Bracelets

ISBN 978-1-59953-385-8; 1-59953-385-5

LC 2010010404

"Some historical background and scientific or cultural information places the making and use of . . . jewelry . . . in context for young readers. [The] book has four chapters that culminate in step-by-step projects." Horn Book Guide

Includes glossary and bibliographical references

Trusty, Brad

The **kids'** guide to balloon twisting; by Brad and Cindy Trusty. Capstone Press 2011 32p il (Kids' guides) lib bdg $26.65

Grades: 4 5 6 7   **745.594**

1. Balloons 2. Handicraft

ISBN 978-1-4296-5444-9; 1-4296-5444-9

LC 2010036470

Gives kids step-by-step instructions about how to twist balloon animals and other shapes.

"Rare is the kid not dazzled by the squeaking, twisting balloon maestros out there, and this brightly illustrated, step-by-step guide makes it easy—well, easy-ish." Booklist

Includes bibliographical references

745.6   Calligraphy, heraldic design, illumination

Hanson, Anders

Cool calligraphy; the art of creativity for kids. [by] Anders Hanson. ABDO Pub. Co. 2009 32p il (Cool art) lib bdg $24.21

Grades: 2 3 4   **745.6**

1. Calligraphy

ISBN 978-1-60453-145-9 lib bdg; 1-60453-145-2 lib bdg

LC 2008-19885

This book about calligraphy is "well organized, with clearly written sections . . . and several clever projects and exercises. . . . [It] should have substantial child appeal." SLJ

Includes glossary

745.7   Decorative coloring

Wagner, Lisa, 1958-

★ Cool painted stuff; [by] Lisa Wagner. ABDO Pub. 2005 32p il (Cool crafts) $22.78

Grades: 4 5 6   **745.7**

1. Painting 2. Handicraft

ISBN 1-59197-742-8

LC 2004-53117

This guide to painted crafts "includes four projects (in six or seven steps): a flowered mini-tote, checkered frame, treasure box, and fancy flowerpot. [This book lists] required materials, [has] small color photos, and [includes] clearly explained, numbered steps." SLJ

746.1   Products and processes

Roessel, Monty

Songs from the loom; a Navajo girl learns to weave. text and photographs by Monty Roessel. Lerner Publs. 1995 48p il (We are still here) lib bdg $21.27; pa $6.95

Grades: 3 4 5 6   **746.1**

1. Weaving 2. Navajo Indians

ISBN 0-8225-2657-3 lib bdg; 0-8225-9712-8 pa

LC 94-48765

"Ten-year-old Jaclyn's grandmother teaches her the art of traditional Navajo rug-weaving. Jaclyn learns the songs and stories that invest the weaving with meaning, as well as the use of the proper tools and techniques. The color photographs of contemporary Navajo life are clear and engrossing, enhancing the solid text." Horn Book Guide

Includes glossary and bibliographical references

746.4   Needlework and handwork

Sadler, Judy Ann

★ The jumbo book of needlecrafts; written by Judy Ann Sadler . . . [et al.]; illustrated by Esperança Melo . . . [et al.] Kids Can Press 2005 208p il $16.95

Grades: 4 5 6   **746.4**

1. Needlework

ISBN 1-55337-793-1

A compilation with a new introduction of 5 books previously published: Knitting by Judy Ann Sadler (2002); Cro-

cheting by Gwen Blakely Kinsler (2003); Simply sewing by Judy Ann Sadler (2004); Embroidery by Judy Ann Sadler (2004); Quilting by Biz Storms (2001)

This is a "how-to guide to the basics of knitting, crocheting, embroidery, quilting, and sewing. . . . The volume begins with helpful suggestions on gathering supplies, measuring, selecting fabric, and stitching. The rest of the book presents detailed, step-by-step directions on basic techniques for projects that range from very simple to intricate. . . . Color drawings and photographs are appealing as well as instructive. . . . An excellent addition to needlework collections." SLJ

746.42   Nonloom weaving and related techniques

Sadler, Judy Ann

Hemp jewelry; written by Judy Ann Sadler; illustrated by June Bradford. Kids Can Press 2005 40p il (Kids can do it) hardcover o.p. pa $6.96

Grades: 4 5 6   **746.42**

1. Jewelry 2. Beadwork 3. Macramé

ISBN 1-55337-774-5; 1-55337-775-3 pa

This "provides instructions for making jewelry from strands of hemp that are woven in various patterns while incorporating beads, clasps, and other findings. . . . Attractive and easy to follow. . . . Detailed, step-by-step instructions, . . . are clearly illustrated with large-scale, colorful ink-and-wash drawings." Booklist

★ Knotting; make your own basketball nets, guitar straps, sports bags and more! written by Judy Ann Sadler; illustrated by Céleste Gagnon. Kids Can Press 2006 40p il (Kids can do it) $12.95; pa $6.99

Grades: 4 5 6   **746.42**

1. Handicraft 2. Knots and splices

ISBN 1-55337-541-6; 1-55337-834-2 pa

This describes how use rope to make various types of knots, lanyards, guitar straps, ladders, hanging holders, swings, dog leashes, and basketball nets.

746.43   Knitting, crocheting, tatting

Bradberry, Sarah

★ Kids knit! simple steps to nifty projects. [by] Sarah Bradberry. Sterling Pub. Co. 2004 96p il hardcover o.p. pa $9.95

Grades: 5 6 7 8   **746.43**

1. Knitting

ISBN 0-8069-7733-7; 978-1-4027-4057-2 pa; 1-4027-4057-3 pa

LC 2004-19375

Presents basic knitting techniques and instructions for making a backpack, pillow, doll, and other simple projects

This "book works equally well for beginners and experienced knitters. . . . Besides the requisite information on knitting and purling, there are invaluable tips about finishing garments, fixing mistakes, and adding embellishments. The projects have been chosen with an eye toward simplicity, yet they have real appeal." Booklist

Junor, Betty

Fun & funky knits; over 20 simple knit stitch projects. by Betty Junor. 1st North American ed. Barron's Educational Series, Inc. 2012 80 p. col. ill. (paperback) $7.99

Grades: 4 5 6   **746.43**

1. Knitting 2. Sewing -- Technique 3. Needlework -- Patterns 4. Knitting -- Patterns

ISBN 1438001746; 9781438001746

LC 2012932175

Author Betty Junor presents a book on knitting projects, "starting with very basic instructions and recommending the use of brilliantly colored yarns." Junor discusses slipknots, casting off, and finishing and gives directions for making headbands, belts, drawstring bags, and purses. She also shows readers how to make knitted flowers and how to incorporate pompoms into projects. (Publisher's note)

746.44   Embroidery

Sadler, Judy Ann

Embroidery; written by Judy Ann Sadler; illustrated by June Bradford. Kids Can Press 2004 40p il (Kids can do it) $12.95; pa $6.95

Grades: 4 5 6   **746.44**

1. Embroidery

ISBN 1-55337-616-1; 1-55337-617-X pa

"With an attractively designed cover featuring photos of sample projects, this book is sure to encourage interest in needlework." SLJ

746.46   Patchwork and quilting

Rau, Dana Meachen

Quilting for fun! Compass Point Books 2009 48p il (For fun) lib bdg $25.26

Grades: 3 4 5   **746.46**

1. Quilting

ISBN 978-0-7565-3860-6 lib bdg; 0-7565-3860-2 lib bdg

LC 2008008274

This covers the basics of quilting, a brief history, and instructions for five quilting projects

"Varied typefaces and colors, large print, good spacing, and lively and creative arrangement make [this book] attractive, and color photos and other illustrations throughout are easy to follow.... Materials are easily obtainable from craft stores, and some are readily available at home." SLJ

Includes glossary and bibliographical references

746.9   Other textile products

Bertoletti, John C.

How fashion designers use math; math curriculum consultant: Rhea A. Stewart. Chelsea Clubhouse 2010 32p il (Math in the real world) lib bdg $28

Grades: 4 5 6   **746.9**

1. Mathematics 2. Fashion design 3. Fashion --

Vocational guidance

ISBN 978-1-60413-606-7 lib bdg; 1-60413-606-5 lib bdg

LC 2009-22683

This describes how designers use math to measure, create, and produce their fashions, and includes problems to solve and information about how to become a fashion designer

"Color photos of designers in action combine with diagrams that further clarify the easily digestible text." Booklist

Includes glossary and bibliographical references

Spilsbury, Richard

Hi-tech clothes; Richard Spilsbury. Capstone Heinemann Library 2013 56 p. (Design and engineering for STEM) (hb) $33.50

Grades: 5 6 7   **746.9**

1. Fashion 2. Clothing and dress 3. Fashion design 4. Clothing factories -- Technological innovations

ISBN 1432970321; 9781432970321; 9781432970376

LC 2012013469

This book by Richard Spilsbury focuses on clothes, discussing "design, manufacture, and sale to their use, cleaning, and repair, and eventually their disposal. This book explains what happens during these stages, such as prototyping, the sourcing of materials and components, the manufacturing process, the decisions made by designers, and recycling." (Publisher's note)

Includes bibliographical references and index

Wooster, Patricia

So, you want to work in fashion? how to break into the world of fashion and design. Patricia Wooster. Aladdin 2014 192 p. illustrations (Be what you want series) (hardcover) $19.99

Grades: 4 5 6 7 8   **746.9**

1. Clothing industry 2. Fashion -- Vocational guidance

ISBN 1582704538; 9781582704524; 9781582704531

LC 2014005268

"In addition to tips and interviews from a variety of fashion professionals, 'So, You Want to Work in Fashion?' includes inspiring stories from young people who are in the industry right now, as well as activities, a glossary, and resources to help you on your way to a successful career in fashion." (Publisher's note)

"A wonderfully comprehensive, accessible and realistic entree into the dynamic world of fashion." Kirkus

Includes bibliographical references

747   Interior decoration

Weaver, Janice

★ It's your room; a decorating guide for real kids. [by] Janice Weaver and Frieda Wishinsky; illustrated by Claudia Dávila. Tundra Books 2006 63p il pa $14.95

Grades: 5 6 7 8   **747**

1. Interior design

ISBN 0-88776-711-7

"Budding interior designers and readers who want to personalize their rooms will appreciate this title. It is filled with step-by-step guidelines for creating a budget, selecting paint colors and fabrics, organizing closets and desks, laying everything out, and adding finishing touches. The illustrations will be a hit with first-time decorators just starting to develop their own color sense." SLJ

748.5 Stained, painted, leaded, mosaic glass

Kenney, Karen Latchana
Super simple glass jar art; fun and easy-to-make crafts for kids. ABDO Pub. Co. 2010 32p il (Super simple crafts) lib bdg $17.95
Grades: K 1 2 3 4   **748.5**
1. Glass 2. Handicraft
ISBN 978-1-60453-624-9 lib bdg; 1-60453-624-1
lib bdg
                                        LC 2009-352
"Colorful photos; clean layout in a bright, primary palette; and large, abundant step-by-step instructional photos give [this book] great appeal. The . . . crafts . . . are functional and attractive. . . . Readily obtainable household materials and easy-to-follow instructions mean that children can do these crafts independently." SLJ
Includes glossary

750 Painting and paintings

Cressy, Judith
★ **Can** you find it? Abrams 2002 40p il $15.95
Grades: 2 3 4 5   **750**
1. Painting 2. Art appreciation 3. Metropolitan Museum of Art (New York, N.Y.)
ISBN 0-8109-3279-2
                                        LC 2002-18358
"Nineteen paintings from New York City's Metropolitan Museum of Art were chosen for careful scrutiny in this book. Next to each striking, full-color reproduction is a list of items to search for: e.g., '2 cats, 6 lotus blossoms, 3 eye amulets,' etc., for a painting from ancient Egypt. The works of art are from around the globe and range from illuminated manuscripts to 20th-century canvases. Designed to encourage discovery, the tiny, sometimes indistinct details will keep children engrossed for hours." SLJ
Other titles in this series are:
Can you find it, too? by Judith Cressey (2004)
Can you find it inside? by by Jessica Schulte (2005)
Can you find it outside? by Jessice Schulte (2005)
Can you find it? America by Linda Falken (2010)

Micklethwait, Lucy
Children; a first art book. Frances Lincoln Children's 2006 un il $14.95
Grades: K 1 2 3   **750**
1. Painting 2. Children in art 3. Art appreciation
ISBN 1-84507-116-6
"This title uses works by 18 different artists to illustrate its theme. Children are shown in nine activities, from Reading and writing to Sleeping. . . . The artwork represents several cultures and ethnic groups, as well as styles and time periods. Text is minimal—just enough to encourage conversation about the reproductions. An excellent first exposure to fine art, and great preparation for museum visits." SLJ

In the picture; get looking! get thinking! Frances Lincoln 2010 un il $17.95
Grades: K 1 2 3 4   **750**
1. Painting 2. Art appreciation
ISBN 978-1-84507-636-8; 1-84507-636-2
Micklethwait "combines familiar techniques that fold a hunt-and-find game into a survey of such diverse artworks as Marc Chagall's dreamy 1911 painting I and the Village and an amazingly intricate 1590s battle scene from the Mughal Empire text The Akbarnama. Intriguing close-ups pulled from each artwork appear across from a crisp reproduction of the full image. . . . Additional activities . . . are included on each spread and an extensive, appended section." Booklist

Raczka, Bob
★ **Artful** reading; [by] Bob Raczka. Millbrook Press 2007 32p il lib bdg $25.26
Grades: 1 2 3 4   **750**
1. Painting 2. Reading in art 3. Art appreciation
ISBN 978-0-8225-6754-7
                                        LC 2006035083
"Through 23 works of art, Raczka shows the timeless appeal of reading. . . . Simple sentences serve as captions to these masterpieces. . . . Each work is clearly labelled, and endnotes provide information about the artists and their paintings, among them Edgar Degas and Dante Gabriel Rossetti." SLJ

★ **More** than meets the eye; seeing art with all five senses. by Bob Raczka. Millbrook Press 2003 32p il hardcover o.p. pa $9.95
Grades: K 1 2 3   **750**
1. Painting 2. Art appreciation
ISBN 0-7613-2797-5 lib bdg; 0-7613-1994-8 pa
                                        LC 2003-343
Provides images of paintings and new, sensory ways to experience them, such as tasting the milk in Vermeer's "The Milkmaid," hearing the music in Tanner's "The Banjo Lesson," or feeling the fur in da Vinci's "Lady with an Ermine."
"Raczka's short, rhyming text gives structure to the book, but the color reproductions of well-chosen, vivid paintings steal the show. This art book rests on a simple concept, beautifully executed." Booklist

★ **Unlikely** pairs; fun with famous works of art. [by] Bob Raczka. Millbrook Press 2006 31p il lib bdg $23.93; pa $9.95
Grades: 4 5 6 7   **750**
1. Painting 2. Art appreciation
ISBN 0-7613-2936-6 lib bdg; 0-7613-2378-3 pa
                                        LC 2003-14078
Invites the reader to discover fourteen funny stories produced by pairing twenty-eight paintings from different eras and styles
"Raczka deserves an A+ for cleverness. . . . Rodin's The Thinker is juxtaposed with Klee's modernistic painting of a chessboard so that the statue looks as if it is contemplating the next move. Siméon-Chardin's picture of a boy blowing soap bubbles seems to be creating Kandinsky's Several Circles. Each selection takes up a page and is reproduced in crisp color. . . . This book is an amusing way to introduce children to famous works of art." SLJ

Wenzel, Angela

13 paintings children should know. Prestel 2009 46p il $14.95

Grades: 5 6 7 8   **750**

1. Painting 2. Art appreciation

ISBN 978-3-7913-4323-5; 3-7913-4323-8

This book examines "Mona Lisa's beguiling smile, Van Gogh's hypnotic night sky, and Frida Kahlo's depiction of herself with a monkey. These [paintings] and ten others are featured in the book in large reproductions with accompanying details. The . . . text offers biographical information about each artist and important facts about the painting's technical and historical aspects." Publisher's note

Includes glossary

750.1   Painting -- Philosophy and theory

Richardson, Joy

Looking at pictures; an introduction to art for young people. with illustrations by Charlotte Voake. rev ed.; Abrams Books for Young Readers 2009 80p il $21.95

Grades: 4 5 6 7   **750.1**

1. Painting 2. Art appreciation 3. National Gallery (Great Britain)

ISBN 978-0-8109-8288-8; 0-8109-8288-9

LC 2008055684

First published 1997

This "exploration of thirteenth- to twentieth-century European paintings examines the subject matter and techniques used and also delves into how the pieces were restored. Other topics covered are pigments, the use of light and perspective, the depiction of special events and daily life, and painting people and nature. Occasional well-placed illustrations supplement the numerous color reproductions." Horn Book Guide

Includes bibliographical references

Wolfe, Gillian

Look! Drawing the line in art. Frances Lincoln 2008 44p il $17.95

Grades: 3 4 5   **750.1**

1. Art appreciation

ISBN 978-1-84507-824-9; 1-84507-824-1

"Each spread introduces a different technique, such as 'strong lines' and 'leafy lines' and shows a work of fine art demonstrating it, reproduced with clarity and in full color. Occasionally, the text defines artistic techniques, such as perspective and shading. Each spread has kid-friendly ideas for making one's own creations. . . . There is a wide range of dates for the art featured, beginning in the 1600s and ending in 2003. The text describes how each piece was created and includes some anecdotal stories about the artist and the work. . . . This is an accessible introduction to art history." SLJ

Look! Seeing the light in art. Frances Lincoln 2007 45p il $16.95

Grades: 3 4 5   **750.1**

1. Art appreciation

ISBN 978-1-84507-467-8; 1-84507-467-X

"Wolfe invites readers to examine how artists have tried to convey qualities of light in works that represent night, day, rainstorms, sunlight, heat, cold, and use light to create the texture and shape of objects. Each spread includes a suggestion for an art activity . . . as well as a page of accessible text, in large print, that presents questions and observations designed to draw viewers back into the well-reproduced artworks. With a few exceptions, the artists represented are well-known, male, European masters, such as Caravaggio and Renoir." Booklist

751.4   Painting - techniques and procedures

Luxbacher, Irene

1 2 3 I can paint! Kids Can Press 2007 23p il (Starting art) $14.95; pa $5.95

Grades: 2 3 4   **751.4**

1. Painting -- Technique

ISBN 978-1-55453-037-3; 978-1-55453-150-9 pa; 1-55453-150-0 pa; 1-55453-037-7

This "introduces aspiring artists to some materials and techniques that can be successfully used to create pictures with paint. Luxbacher discusses primary and secondary colors; backgrounds; color tones; cool warm, and complementary colors; perspective and line; and several brush strokes. The brief text offers clear definitions of terms and easy-to-follow instructions for projects. . . . The artwork . . . will be easy for children to replicate." Booklist

Peot, Margaret

★ Inkblot; drip, splat, and squish your way to creativity. Boyds Mills Press 2011 56p il $19.95

Grades: 4 5 6 7   **751.4**

1. Ink painting 2. Art -- Technique 3. Painting -- Technique

ISBN 1-59078-720-X; 978-1-59078-720-5

LC 22010-929541

This describes how to make inkblots and use them in art and as inspiration for writing and other forms of creativity.

"Peot's own entrancing inkblots . . . plus a few guest blots, illustrate every step, showing how the pure blot becomes a final artwork. . . . Readers get clear directions and lively encouragement." Kirkus

Includes bibliographical references

757   Human figures

Raczka, Bob

★ Here's looking at me; how artists see themselves. [by] Bob Raczka. Millbrook Press 2006 32p il lib bdg $23.93

Grades: 3 4 5 6   **757**

1. Artists 2. Self-portraits

ISBN 978-0-7613-3404-0 lib bdg; 0-7613-3404-1 lib bdg

LC 2005006144

This is a "top-notch introduction to self-portraiture." SLJ

Thomson, Ruth

Portraits. Chelsea Clubhouse 2004 32p il (First look at art) $14.95

Grades: 2 3 4 5   **757**
1. Portraits 2. Art appreciation
ISBN 0-7910-7948-1

LC 2003-14428

First published 2003 in the United Kingdom

This describes various types of portraits including profiles and silhouettes, self-portraits, depictions of royalty, multiple faces, heroic portraits, and collage portraits, and includes related art activities.

"Teachers will find easy-to-understand art lessons and projects and students will find inspiration in [this] well-organized, attractive [title]." SLJ

Includes glossary

759 Painting -- History, geographic treatment, biography

Kelley, True

Claude Monet: sunshine and waterlilies; written and illustrated by True Kelley. Grosset & Dunlap 2001 un il (Smart about art) $14.89; pa $7.50
Grades: 2 3 4   **759**
1. Artists 2. Painters 3. Artists, French
ISBN 0-448-42613-7; 0-448-42522-X pa

LC 2001-23147

Written in the format of a school report by a fictitious student named Kristin Cole, this recounts the events in the life of the French artist and offers insight into his work

Illustrated with "charming childlike drawings and reproductions of the artist's paintings in scrapbook-style layouts. . . . [This] is a successful blend of fact and humor that makes sophisticated concepts completely accessible and even entertaining." Booklist

Markel, Michelle

The **fantastic** jungles of Henri Rousseau; by Michelle Markel; illustrated by Amanda Hall. Eerdmans Books for Young Readers 2012 34 p. (alk. paper) $17.00
Grades: PreK K 1 2 3   **759**
1. Outsider art 2. Painters -- France -- Biography
ISBN 0802853641; 9780802853646

LC 2011035838

This children's picture book chronicles the life and work of "France's most celebrated naïve painter -- Henri Rousseau. . . . When was in his 40s, Rousseau . . . began to recreate himself as an artist. Though he had no formal training and few financial resources, he persevered. . . . Rousseau was ridiculed repeatedly by critics and artists, yet he continued to create his exotic, seemingly unsophisticated paintings." (Kirkus Reviews)

Serres, Alain

★ **And** Picasso painted Guernica; written and designed by Alain Serres; translated by Rosalind Price. Allen & Unwin Children's 2010 51p il $24.99
Grades: 5 6 7 8   **759**
1. Artists 2. Painters 3. War in art 4. Spain -- History -- 1936-1939, Civil War
ISBN 978-1-74175-994-5; 1-74175-994-3
Original French edition, 2007

"Serres explains the mechanics of cubism . . . , tells the story of the horrifying German bombing of the civilians of

Guernica and Picasso's reaction to it . . . , and finishes by tracing the rest of Picasso's career as he paints 'all the beauty of the world and its monstrous face as well.' The oversize pages are packed with period photographs and color reproductions of Picasso's sketches and paintings, each captioned in detail, with a double gatefold of Guernica at the center. . . . A passionate and intelligent tribute to the transformative power of art." Publ Wkly

759.05   Painting 1800-1899

Sabbeth, Carol

★ **Monet** and the impressionists for kids; their lives and ideas, 21 activities. Chicago Review Press 2002 140p il pa $17.95
Grades: 5 6 7 8   **759.05**
1. Art appreciation 2. Impressionism (Art)
ISBN 1-55652-397-1

LC 2001-47191

Discusses the nineteenth-century French art movement known as Impressionism, focusing on the works of Monet, Renoir, Degas, Cassatt, Cezanne, Gauguin, and Seurat

"A beautifully designed introduction to Impressionism. . . . Sabbeth also includes 21 appealing extension activities such as recipes, crafts, games, and writing suggestions. Quality color reproductions on glossy pages, and varied, attractive layouts add to the book." SLJ

Includes glossary and bibliographical references

Van Gogh and the Post-Impressionists for kids; their lives and ideas, 21 activities. Chicago Review Press 2011 160p il pa $17.95
Grades: 4 5 6 7   **759.05**
1. Artists 2. Painters 3. Art appreciation 4. Postimpressionism (Art)
ISBN 1-56976-275-9; 978-1-56976-275-2

LC 2010053908

"The bulk of this wonderfully thorough study of Post-Impressionist artists focuses on van Gogh, with smaller sections devoted to Paul Gauguin, Henri de Toulouse-Lautrec, Paul Signac, and Emile Bernard. The highly engaging text follows the artists' lives with crisp writing and vivid detail, delving into their family backgrounds and relationships, and doesn't sugarcoat dark and gritty incidents such as van Gogh's self-inflicted ear amputation. Information is well organized. . . . Full-color reproductions of paintings discussed in the text add visual interest, and educational sidebars expound on topics mentioned in the main narrative. . . . With its creative, hands-on ideas for teaching art technique and history, this book is an excellent resource for students and teachers." SLJ

Includes glossary and bibliographical references

Sellier, Marie

Renoir's colors. Getty 2010 il bd bk $16.95
Grades: PreK K 1 2   **759.05**
1. Artists 2. Painters 3. Color in art 4. French painting 5. Board books for children
ISBN 978-1-60606-003-2 bd bk; 1-60606-003-1 bd bk

"Lift-the-flap windows spotlight pure colors in details of the artist's work. Turn the page to see the entire work, with a few simple lines of text guiding the eye to other shades of the highlighted color or adding an anecdote about the piece or model. Well-chosen paintings of familiar subjects . . . keep this small collection of fine art accessible to even the youngest child. This fine-art concept book is simply designed and superbly printed." SLJ

759.06   Painting 1900-1999

Barsony, Piotr
The **stories** of the Mona Lisa; an imaginary museum tale about the history of modern art. Piotr Barsony; translated from the French by Joanna Oseman. Skyhorse Publishing 2012 55 p. (hardcover: alk. paper) $19.95
Grades: 5 6 7 8   759.06
1. Art -- History 2. Mona Lisa (Painting) 3. Art movements 4. Painting, Modern
ISBN 1620872285; 9781620872284
LC 2012015603
"As [this book by Pietr Barsony] begins, a little girl asks: 'Dad, will you tell me a story?' The story her painter father tells is a history of art with the Mona Lisa as its central character. . . . He takes daughter and readers both on a journey of discovery through an imaginary museum. . . . Each painting is of only the Mona Lisa. . . . They are his own responses to and interpretations of Leonardo's masterpiece as filtered through the vision of other artists and movements." (Kirkus Reviews)

Raczka, Bob
No one saw; ordinary things through the eyes of an artist. Millbrook Press 2002 32p il lib bdg $23.90; pa $9.95
Grades: K 1 2 3   759.06
1. Modern painting 2. Art appreciation
ISBN 0-7613-2370-8 lib bdg; 0-7613-1648-3 pa
LC 2001-30006
"Reproductions of sixteen famous paintings, set against complementary backgrounds, reflect their creators' unique viewpoints, while a gentle rhyming text comments on the masterpieces ('No one saw mothers like Mary Cassatt. / No one saw Sunday like Georges Seurat'). The selections serve the impressionist through modern works well and conclude that 'nobody sees the world like you.'" Horn Book Guide

759.13   Painting -- United States

Bryant, Jen
★ A **splash** of red; the life and art of Horace Pippin. by Jen Bryant; illustrated by Melissa Sweet. Alfred A. Knopf 2013 40 p. (hard cover) $17.99
Grades: K 1 2   759.13
1. Painters -- Biography 2. Veterans -- Biography 3. African American painters -- Biography 4. Painters -- United States -- Biography
ISBN 0375867120; 9780375867125; 9780375967122
LC 2012003209
Orbis Pictus Award (2014)
Schneider Family Book Award (2014)
Robert F. Sibert Honor Book (2014)
This children's picture book by Jen Bryant presents a "portrait of African-American artist Horace Pippin (1888-

1946). . . . From Pippin's young childhood . . . to his Army service in World War I, to the well-deserved fame that arrived only late in his life, he 'couldn't stop drawing.' When a military injury threatens Pippin's painting ability, he tries wood burning--'[u]sing his good arm to move the hurt one'--and works his way back to painting." (Kirkus Reviews)

Close, Chuck, 1940-
Chuck Close; face book. by Chuck Close. Abrams Books for Young Readers 2012 64 p.
Grades: 3 4 5 6 7   759.13
1. Face in art 2. Vision disorders 3. Artists -- Interviews 4. Artists -- United States -- Biography 5. Artists -- United States -- Biography
ISBN 9781419701634
LC 2011034557
In this book, "[Chuck] Close discloses struggles with childhood ill health and severe dyslexia. He tells how . . . he adjusted for his prosopagnosia (face blindness). . . . He also discloses the many 'hows' of his . . . technique: how he uses gridded photos to build his faces and how he works from his wheelchair and wields his brush with less-abled hands. . . . At the book's . . . center is the . . . opportunity to 'mix 'n' match' various eyes, noses and mouths among 14 of the artist's . . . self-portraits." (Kirkus)

Duggleby, John
★ **Story** painter: the life of Jacob Lawrence. Chronicle Bks. 1998 55p il $16.95
Grades: 4 5 6 7   759.13
1. Artists 2. Painters 3. Illustrators 4. African American artists 5. African American painters -- Biography
ISBN 0-8118-2082-3
LC 98-4513
This is a biography of the twentieth-century African American painter. Bibliography. "Grades four to eight." (SLJ)
"Lawrence's expressionistic, stark paintings, in excellent full-page color reproduction . . . nicely complement Duggleby's measured account of a materially poor but culturally rich childhood and Lawrence's subsequent struggles and successes." Publ Wkly
Includes bibliographical references

Gherman, Beverly
Norman Rockwell; storyteller with a brush. Atheneum Bks. for Young Readers 2000 57p il $19.95
Grades: 4 5 6 7   759.13
1. Artists 2. Painters 3. Illustrators 4. Artists -- United States
ISBN 0-689-82001-1
LC 98-36546
Describes the life and work of the popular American artist who depicted both traditional and contemporary subjects, including children, family scenes, astronauts, and the poor
"The format of the biography is appealing and attractive. The pages are replete with color reproductions of Rockwell's paintings as well as photographs of the man and his family. The text is well researched and authentic; the writing style is free-flowing and the words capture the naturalness of Rockwell's paintings." SLJ
Includes bibliographical references (p. {55}) and index

Honoring our ancestors; stories and pictures by fourteen artists. edited by Harriet Rohmer. Children's Bk. Press 1999 31p il $15.95

Grades: 3 4 5 6   **759.13**

1. Artists -- United States

ISBN 0-89239-158-8

LC 98-38686

Fourteen artists and picture book illustrators present paintings with descriptions of ancestors or other sources of inspiration that have inspired them

This is "rewarding in its breadth and vivacity. The portraits are thematically rich yet accessible; generally, the texts are cheerful and resist sentimentality." Horn Book Guide

Lawrence, Jacob

The **great** migration; an American story. paintings by Jacob Lawrence; with a poem in appreciation by Walter Dean Myers. HarperCollins Pubs. 1993 un il hardcover o.p. pa $8.99

Grades: 4 5 6 7   **759.13**

1. African Americans in art

ISBN 0-06-023037-1; 0-06-443428-1 pa

LC 93-16788

"Lawrence is a storyteller with words as well as pictures: his captions and his own 1992 introduction to this book are the best commentary on his work." Booklist

Lincoln, Abraham, 1809-1965

Lincoln's Gettysburg address; a pictorial interpretation painted by James Daugherty. James Daugherty. Albert Whitman & Co. 2013 48 p. $19.99

Grades: 1 2 3 4   **759.13**

1. Gettysburg (Pa.)

ISBN 0807545503; 9780807545508

LC 2012013288

This children's book, illustrated by Caldecott Honoree and Newbery Medalist James Daugherty, presents the text of U.S. President Abraham Lincoln's Gettysburg Address. "The Gettysburg Address is one of the most influential speeches in our history, written by Abraham Lincoln at a crucial period in his presidency and in United States history." (Publisher's note)

759.2   European painting

Wenzel, Angela

13 art mysteries children should know. Prestel 2011 45p il $14.95

Grades: 4 5 6   **759.2**

1. Art 2. Artists 3. Painting

ISBN 978-3-7913-7044-6; 379-1-37044-8

Presents information about thirteen mysteries from the art world, including questions about the Mona Lisa, van Gogh, and the street artist Banksy.

"Excellent-quality reproductions appear throughout. This is definitely a different approach for introducing young people to various aspects of art history. . . . The illustrations are well chosen to support these succinct inquiries into some perplexing puzzlements from the world of art." SLJ

759.4   French painting

Parker, Marjorie Blain

★ **Colorful** dreamer; the story of artist Henri Matisse. Marjorie Blain Parker; illustrated by Holly Berry. Dial Books For Young Readers 2012 32 p. (hardcover) $16.99

Grades: 3 4 5   **759.4**

1. Painters 2. Picture books for children 3. Artists -- France -- Biography

ISBN 0803737580; 9780803737587

LC 2011035446

This "picture-book biography covers [Henri] Matisse's entire life but focuses on his career aspirations and achievements." The text includes "details such as young Henri's dream of becoming a magician and his skill with a peashooter. . . . Black-and-white drawings represent the artist's dull youth and colorful paintings are introduced when his career takes off." (School Library Journal)

" Berry's illustrations are the star of the show... The style of the artwork evokes Matisse more and more as the story progresses, ending, as his career did, with paper cut-out collage... A must for art teachers, and a nice addition to history and biography collections." Kirkus

759.9   Painting -- Other geographic areas

Gogh, Vincent van

★ **Vincent's** colors; words and pictures by Vincent van Gogh. Chronicle Books 2005 un il $14.95

Grades: K 1 2 3   **759.9**

1. Color in art 2. Artists, Dutch

ISBN 0-8118-5099-4

"This text is pulled directly from the letters Van Gogh wrote about his paintings to his brother, Theo. Each line of the rhyming stanzas is accompanied by a rich, full-color reproduction of one of the artist's key works. . . . . Van Gogh's poetic descriptions will hold the attention of young readers; even preschoolers will enjoy the simple text and vibrant pictures. The brilliant colors and brush strokes are reproduced faithfully." SLJ

Raczka, Bob

The **Vermeer** interviews; conversations with seven works of art. as imagined by Bob Raczka. Millbrook Press 2009 32p il (Art adventures) lib bdg $25.27

Grades: 3 4 5 6   **759.9**

1. Artists 2. Painters 3. Artists, Dutch 4. Art appreciation

ISBN 978-0-8225-9402-4 lib bdg; 0-8225-9402-1 lib bdg

LC 2008024969

"Raczka makes Johannes Vermeer's masterpieces accessible by employing an interview format. Clearly stating that these 'conversations' are 'as imagined' by the author, 'Bob' asks the subjects of seven paintings a series of questions about themselves and their surroundings, allowing them to give details about the art techniques, historical context, and cultural elements." SLJ

Includes bibliographical references

Winter, Jonah

★ **Frida**; illustrated by Ana Juan. Levine Bks. 2002 un il $16.95; pa $5.99

Grades: K 1 2 3   **759.9**

1. Artists 2. Painters 3. Women artists 4. Artists, Mexican

ISBN 0-590-20320-7; 0-590-20321-5 pa

LC 00-51421

This "illustrated short biography argues that the seeds of iconic painter Frida Kahlo's genius were planted during her childhood. . . . Winter consistently manages to convey much with a few well-chosen words, and the illustrations are appropriately awash with traditional Mexican folk art motifs and characters. Especially pleasing are Juan's surreal, Kahlo like touches." Horn Book

759.949 Swiss painting

Vry, Silke

Paul Klee for children; Silke Vry; [translation, Jane Michael] Prestel 2011 95 p. $14.95

Grades: 4 5 6   **759.949**

1. Art -- Technique 2. Art appreciation

ISBN 3791370774; 9783791370774

LC 2011937220

This book, by Silke Vry, is about the art work of Paul Klee. "Paul Klee's playful paintings are a natural introduction for children to the world of creativity and art. . . . The German artist was fascinated by children's drawings, and incorporated their energy and simplicity into his own work. This . . . introduction to Klee's paintings focuses on the artist's love of color and symbols, his lighthearted technique, and his belief that music and painting were inextricably linked." (Publisher's note)

759.972 Mexican painting

Rubin, Susan Goldman

★ **Diego** Rivera; an artist for the people. by Susan Goldman Rubin. Abrams Books for Young Readers 2013 56 p. (reinforced) $21.95

Grades: 5 6 7 8   **759.972**

1. Mural painting and decoration 2. Painters -- Mexico -- Biography

ISBN 0810984113; 9780810984110

LC 2012010022

This book, by Susan Goldman Rubin, "offers young readers . . . insight into the life and artwork of the famous Mexican painter and muralist [Diego Rivera]. The book follows Rivera's career, looking at his influences and tracing the evolution of his style. His work often called attention to the culture and struggles of the Mexican working class. . . . The book contains a list of museums where you can see Rivera's art, a historical note, a glossary, and a bibliography." (Publisher's note)

Includes bibliographical references and index

760.2 Miscellany

Hanson, Anders

Cool printmaking; the art of creativity for kids. [by] Anders Hanson. ABDO Pub. Co. 2009 32p il (Cool art) lib bdg $24.21

Grades: 2 3 4   **760.2**

1. Prints 2. Printing

ISBN 978-1-60453-147-3 lib bdg; 1-60453-147-9 lib bdg

LC 2008-22323

This book about printmaking is "well organized, with clearly written sections . . . and several clever projects and exercises. . . . [It] should have substantial child appeal." SLJ

Includes glossary

Luxbacher, Irene

1 2 3 I can make prints! Kids Can Press 2008 24p il (Starting art) $14.95; pa $5.95

Grades: 2 3 4   **760.2**

1. Prints 2. Printing

ISBN 978-1-55453-040-3; 1-55453-040-7; 978-1-55453-153-0 pa; 1-55453-153-5 pa

"This book presents brightly colored, framed examples and ink cartoons to invite young readers to make prints. Simple stamp prints fill the pages, as well as relief, intaglio, and block prints, with examples of patterns and symmetry. . . . A child-friendly format introduces the prints: each art project entails only three easy-to-follow steps, and embellishments add creativity and instruction. . . . Luxbacher presents bold, eye-catching examples in an easy-to-understand, entertaining manner." SLJ

761 Printmaking

Price, Pamela S.

★ **Cool** rubber stamp art; [by] Pam Price. ABDO Pub. Co. 2005 32p il (Cool crafts) lib bdg $22.78

Grades: 4 5 6   **761**

1. Handicraft 2. Rubber stamp printing

ISBN 1-59197-743-6

LC 2004-53123

This describes five rubber stamp art projects: "a terracotta flowerpot, spring greeting card, wrapping paper, canvas beach bag, and homemade stamps (sponge, string, leaf). . . . [This book lists] required materials, [has] small color photos, and [includes] clearly explained, numbered steps. . . . [It will] will appeal to children." SLJ

Ross, Kathy

One-of-a-kind stamps and crafts; illustrated by Nicole in den Bosch. Millbrook Press 2010 48p il (Girl crafts) lib bdg $25.26; pa $7.95

Grades: 3 4 5 6   **761**

1. Handicraft 2. Rubber stamp printing

ISBN 978-0-8225-9216-7 lib bdg; 0-8225-9216-9 lib bdg; 978-1-58013-885-7 pa; 1-58013-885-3 pa

LC 2009020626

"This book describes how to create 20 stamps as well as an ink-pad storage shelf and a stamp storage box. . . . Decorative top borders add to the overall neat, well-spaced pages. The projects include readily available supplies, step-by-step instructions, and clear color illustrations. . . . An enhancement to craft collections." SLJ

769.92　Prints -- Biography

Ray, Deborah Kogan

Hokusai; the man who painted a mountain. Foster Bks. 2001 un il $18

Grades: 3 4 5 6　　　　　　　　　　　　　　**769.92**

1. Artists 2. Artists, Japanese

ISBN 0-374-33263-0

LC 00-50395

"The text and evocative artwork provide details and scenes of everyday Japanese life in the 19th century. The illustrations include accomplished soft watercolor and colored-pencil paintings, labeled Chinese characters, drawings from the artist's sketchbooks, and a reproduction of Hokusai's 'The Great Wave off Kanagawa.'" SLJ

Includes bibliographical references

770　Photography, computer art, cinematography, videography

Finger, Brad

13 photos children should know. Prestel 2011 45p il lib bdg $14.95

Grades: 4 5 6　　　　　　　　　　　　　　**770**

1. Modern history 2. Documentary photography

ISBN 978-3-7913-7047-7; 3-7913-7047-2

Examines the history behind thirteen popular photographs, including the moon landing, the fall of the Berlin Wall, and the wedding of Prince Charles and Princess Diana.

Partridge, Elizabeth

Restless spirit: the life and work of Dorothea Lange. Viking 1998 122p il hardcover o.p. pa $12.99

Grades: 6 7 8 9　　　　　　　　　　　　　　**770**

1. Photographers 2. Women photographers

ISBN 0-670-87888-X; 0-14-230024-1 pa

LC 98-9807

A biography of Dorothea Lange, whose photographs of migrant workers, Japanese American internees, and rural poverty helped bring about important social reforms

"Generously placed throughout this accessibly written biography are the photographic images that make Lange a pre-eminent artist of the century. The book is elegantly designed and the photographic reproductions are excellent." Bull Cent Child Books

Includes bibliographical references

775　Digital photography

Johnson, Daniel

4-H guide to digital photography. Voyageur Press 2009 176p $18.99

Grades: 5 6 7 8　　　　　　　　　　　　　　**775**

1. Digital photography

ISBN 978-0-7603-3652-6; 0-7603-3652-0

LC 2009014679

This guide to digital photography offers "sound and comprehensive information. . . . [It] features numerous excellent photos that support the text. It explores types of digital cameras, how to take good photos, the complexities of lighting, managing images . . . and the importance of just enjoying this activity. Types of photography such as landscape and macro are explained. The author does an excellent job of discussing the importance of both technological details and artistic creativity." SLJ

Includes glossary

Rabbat, Suzy

Using digital images. Cherry Lake Pub. 2010 32p il (Super smart information strategies) lib bdg $27.07

Grades: 3 4 5 6　　　　　　　　　　　　　　**775**

1. Digital photography

ISBN 978-1-60279-954-7 lib bdg; 1-60279-954-7 lib bdg

LC 2010018941

"The information on deciding between file formats and resolutions in Using Digital Images will be tremendously helpful, and some beginner techniques on taking and editing effective photos are a nice bonus." Booklist

Includes bibliographical references

778.5　Cinematography and videography

Green, Julie

Shooting video to make learning fun. Cherry Lake Pub. 2010 32p il (Super smart information strategies) lib bdg $27.07

Grades: 3 4 5 6　　　　　　　　　　　　　　**778.5**

1. Digital video recording 2. Motion pictures -- Production and direction

ISBN 978-1-60279-955-4 lib bdg; 1-60279-955-5 lib bdg

LC 2010002022

"This books helps students learn how to harness the power of video to inform and entertain. Includes background information and practical hands on activities." Publisher's note

Includes bibliographical references

779　Photographic images

Delannoy, Isabelle

★ Our living Earth; a story of people, ecology, and preservation. by Isabelle Delannoy; photographs by Yann Arthus-Bertrand. Harry N. Abrams 2008 157p il $24.95

Grades: 5 6 7 8　　　　　　　　　　　　　　**779**

1. Human geography 2. Aerial photography

ISBN 978-0-8109-7132-5; 0-8109-7132-1

LC 2008010324

"Wrapped around Arthus-Bertrand's magnificent aerial photographs from around the world, Delannoy's text is organized thematically, covering fresh water, biodiversity, oceans, land, cities, people, food, and climate. . . . Readers will find surprising information and images to ponder. Almost every page supports the overarching theme that social justice and environmental protection are inextricably related. . . . This volume raises awareness, and the striking images, astonishing statistics, and brief explanations will stimulate readers to investigate further and possibly to take action." SLJ

Haas, Robert B.

★ **I** dreamed of flying like a bird; my adventures photographing wild animals from a helicopter. National Geographic 2010 64p il $17.95; lib bdg $27.90

Grades: 2 3 4   779
1. Aerial photography 2. Photography of animals 3. Animals -- Africa
ISBN 978-1-4263-0693-8; 1-4263-0693-8; 978-1-4263-0694-5 lib bdg; 1-4263-0694-6 lib bdg
     LC 2009-52955

"Haas, a veteran wildlike photographer, proffers another set of photos from several of his albums for adults. Here he accompanies the pictures . . . with anecdotal commentary on the hazards and pleasures of viewing nature from an aerial perspective. . . . This . . . [provides] young viewers with an unusual perspective on the natural world." Booklist

Includes glossary and bibliographical references

Hoban, Tana

Shadows and reflections. Greenwillow Bks. 1990 un il $16.99

Grades: PreK K   779
1. Shades and shadows
ISBN 978-0-688-07089-2; 0-688-07089-2
     LC 89-30461

Photographs without text feature shadows and reflections of various objects, animals, and people

"This imaginative, wordless book of color photographs is a visual treat, offering witty and subtle sets of images for enriching the eyes of children and adults." SLJ

780   Music

Aliki

★ **Ah,** music! written and illustrated by Aliki. HarperCollins Pubs. 2003 47p il $17.99; pa $6.99

Grades: K 1 2 3   780
1. Music
ISBN 0-06-028719-5; 0-06-446236-6 pa
     LC 2001-26476

This introduction to music defines such terms as rhythm, melody, pitch, and volume, gives a brief description of written music, instruments of the orchestra, vocal parts, harmony, dynamics, and tempo, cultural diversity in dance and music, and gives a brief outline of musical history

"Terms are explained in an easy, child-friendly manner. . . . Aliki's love of her subject shines through. This enjoyable title is best shared one-on-one and its format makes it ideal for browsing." SLJ

Anderson, M. T., 1968-

★ **Handel,** who knew what he liked; illustrated by Kevin Hawkes. Candlewick Press 2001 un il hardcover o.p. pa $6.99

Grades: 4 5 6   780
1. Composers -- Biography
ISBN 0-7636-1046-1; 0-7636-2562-0 pa
     LC 00-57210

In this biography Handel, who would later compose some of the world's most beautiful music, is shown as a stubborn little boy with a mind of his own

The author "infuses the composer's story with warmth and color, humor and humanity. . . . Relating pithy stories with plain words and short sentences, Anderson never forgets his audience in his enthusiasm for his subject." Booklist

Lach, William

★ **Can** you hear it? Abrams Books for Young Readers 2007 39p il $18.95

Grades: 2 3 4 5   780
1. Art and music
ISBN 978-0-8109-5721-3

"This visual and aural feast invites parents, educators, and young listeners to 'listen and look' at 13 examples of pictorial music and visual masterpieces. The introduction prepares readers with an explanation of the connections between composers' notes and art images. A woodblock print by Utagawa Hiroshige, the pointillism of Seurat, and landscapes by Jacob van Ruisdael and Thomas Cole are among those included in the presentation. The paired examples invite listeners to identify solo instruments or orchestral themes that characterize an image found in the visual art." SLJ

Nathan, Amy

Meet the musicians; from prodigy (or not) to pro. Henry Holt and Co. 2006 168p il $17.95

Grades: 5 6 7 8   780
1. Music 2. Musicians
ISBN 978-0-8050-7743-8; 0-8050-7743-X
     LC 2005026508

The author "interviewed 13 of the New York Philharmonic's members, representing 11 different instruments, and spun their articulate comments into brief, readable profiles, supplemented by various sidebars—among them, an invaluable feature outlining pros and cons of individual instruments. . . . The practical advice mixed with inspirational words strikes just the right note for children at many different stages in their musical education." Booklist

Includes bibliographical references

780.2373   Music – Vocational guidance

Anniss, Matthew

Recording and promoting your music; Matthew Anniss. Capstone Raintree 2015 48 p. color illustrations (I'm in the Band)

Grades: 5 6 7 8 9 10   780.2373
1. Sound -- Recording and reproducing 2. Music industry -- Vocational guidance 3. Rock music -- Vocational guidance 4. Music trade -- Vocational guidance 5. Sound recordings -- Production and direction
ISBN 9781410967268; 9781410967312
     LC 2013042107

"Teens aiming to get their band out of the garage and onto a stage will find helpful information in this new series. Interspersed with flashy, eye-catching photos of up-to-the-minute music celebrities, the text offers a rough outline of the process from recording to release, as well as tips on inter-

acting with fans and using interpersonal skills to book gigs...
the advice in the book will lead neophyte rock stars down a
useful path." Booklist

Includes bibliographical references and index

780.89　Music -- Ethnic and national groups

Igus, Toyomi

★ **I** see the rhythm; paintings by Michele Wood; text
by Toyomi Igus. Children's Bk. Press 1998 32p il $18.95;
pa $7.95

Grades: 4 5 6 7　　　　　　　　　　　　**780.89**

1. African American music 2. African Americans --
Music -- History and criticism 3. African Americans
-- Music -- History and criticism

ISBN 0892391510; 0892392129; 0-89239-151-0;
0-89239-212-9 pa

LC 97-29310

Coretta Scott King Award for illustration

Text and illustrations combine to give an "overview of
African American music. . . . {A} time line sets the social
context, and brief paragraphs describe the various types of
music, from African origins and slave songs through rag-
time; the blues; big band, bebop, and cool jazz; gospel;
rhythm and blues; and the contemporary sounds of rock,
hip-hop, and rap." (Booklist) "Grades four to eight." (Bull
Cent Child Books)

"The text, made up of free verse and music lyrics, incorporates different font sizes, shapes, and colors to underline
the mood of each genre. . . . The colors of each full-page
scenario underline the mood. . . . This book celebrates music
with art and words and successfully blends all three." SLJ

780.9　History, geographic treatment, biography

Children's book of music; an introduction to the world's
　　most amazing music and its creators. DK Publishing
　　2010 142p il $24.99
　　Grades: 3 4 5 6　　　　　　　　　　　　**780.9**
　　1. Music -- History and criticism
　　ISBN 978-0-7566-6734-4; 0-7566-6734-8

LC 2010564872

"Concise summaries and eye-catching photography are
combined in this chronological look at music 'from the first
hum' to digital recording and reactable electronic instruments. The book explores the nature of music, its origins,
and varied sounds. The organization creates a useful resource for research as well as for casual browsing. . . . While
the information is succinct, there is enough depth for basic
information and unusual facts. . . . Thirty-five musical highlights are included on the CD . . . each tagged by an icon and
explanation within the book, provide teaching and listening
aids. A solid resource for any library." SLJ

Includes glossary

Solway, Andrew

　　Africa; [by] Andrew Solway. Heinemann Library 2008
48p il (World of music) lib bdg $22

Grades: 5 6 7 8　　　　　　　　　　　　**780.9**
1. African music
ISBN 978-1-4034-9891-5 lib bdg; 1-4034-9891-1
lib bdg

LC 2006100578

This introduction to African music discusses "instruments, dance, and vocal styles. The photographs presented
are wonderfully colorful in quality and narrative. Topics covered include history, famous players, current styles, pop-culture, politics, world-wide connections." Libr Media Connect

Includes glossary and bibliographical references

Latin America and the Caribbean; [by] Andrew Solway. Heinemann Library 2008 48p il (World of music)
lib bdg $22

Grades: 5 6 7 8　　　　　　　　　　　　**780.9**
1. Music -- Latin America 2. Music -- Caribbean region
ISBN 978-1-4034-9889-2 lib bdg; 1-4034-9889-X
lib bdg

LC 2006100579

This introduction to music of Latin America and the Caribbean discusses "instruments, dance, and vocal styles. The
photographs presented are wonderfully colorful in quality
and narrative. Topics covered include history, famous players, current styles, pop-culture, politics, and world-wide
connections." Libr Media Connect

Includes glossary and bibliographical references

Underwood, Deborah

　　Australia, Hawaii, and the Pacific; [by] Deborah Underwood. Heinemann Library 2008 48p il (World of music) lib bdg $22

Grades: 5 6 7 8　　　　　　　　　　　　**780.9**
1. Music -- Hawaii 2. Music -- Oceania 3. Music
-- Australia
ISBN 978-1-4034-9894-6 lib bdg; 1-4034-9894-6
lib bdg

LC 2006100576

This introduction to the music of Australia, Hawaii, and
the Pacific discusses "instruments, dance, and vocal styles.
The photographs presented are wonderfully colorful in quality and narrative. Topics covered include history, famous
players, current styles, pop-culture, politics, and world-wide
connections." Libr Media Connect

Includes glossary and bibliographical references

780.94　Music of Europe

Allen, Patrick

　　Europe; [by] Patrick Allen. Heinemann Library 2008
48p il (World of music) lib bdg $22

Grades: 5 6 7 8　　　　　　　　　　　　**780.94**
1. Music -- Europe
ISBN 978-1-4034-9890-8 lib bdg; 1-4034-9890-3
lib bdg

LC 2006100580

This introduction to European music discusses "instruments, dance, and vocal styles. The photographs presented
are wonderfully colorful in quality and narrative. Topics
covered include history, famous players, current styles,

pop-culture, politics, and world-wide connections." Libr Media Connect

Includes glossary and bibliographical references

781.17 Music – Artistic principles

Ajmera, Maya

Music everywhere! Maya Ajmera, Elise Hofer Derstine, and Cynthia Pon. Random House Distribution Childrens 2013 32 p. color illustrations and maps (reinforced for library use) $17.95

Grades: PreK K 1 2 3   **781.17**

1. Music -- Pictorial works 2. Musical ability in children 3. Music appreciation

ISBN 1570919364; 9781570919367; 9781570919374; 9781607346708

LC 2012027113

In this book, by Maya Ajmera, Elise Hofer Derstine, and Cynthia Pon, "photographs from around the world celebrate the universal joy that kids get from making music, whether they're playing instruments, clapping their hands, stomping their feet, or singing." According to the book "music can . . . bring a whole community together." (Publisher's note)

"The title conveys this book's straightforward message: music is a universal pleasure, from Canada to Timor-Leste. Proof is demonstrated by a simple yet energetic running text and large photos of children exuberantly making and enjoying music worldwide. Direct captions impart information uncondescendingly: 'Playing a traditional Andean zampoqa. PERU.' A world map and suggestions for homemade musical instruments are included" Horn Book

781.2 Elements of music

Tomecek, Steve

Music; [by] Stephen M. Tomecek. Chelsea House 2010 165p il (Experimenting with everyday science) $35

Grades: 5 6 7 8   **781.2**

1. Musical instruments 2. Science -- Experiments 3. Music -- Acoustics and physics

ISBN 978-1-60413-169-7; 1-60413-169-1

LC 2009-22333

This "offers 25 easy-to-perform activities that illuminate scientific principles. . . . Topics . . . include the history of music, various instruments, and how scientific principles explain the creation of sounds. . . . Following each experiment are additional comments on the science behind the experiment and link to the one that follows. Photographs, simple diagrams and illustrations, and sample data tables appear throughout, and the [layout is] clear and colorful." SLJ

Includes bibliographical references

781.49 Recording of music

Miles, Liz

Making a recording. Raintree 2009 32p il (Culture in action) $28.21; pa $7.99

Grades: 5 6 7 8   **781.49**

1. Sound recordings 2. Music industry -- Vocational

guidance

ISBN 978-1-4109-3392-8; 1-4109-3392-X; 978-1-4109-3409-3 pa; 1-4109-3409-8 pa

LC 2009000416

This "is a must-read for any aspiring musician. A brief history is followed by a discussion of modern techniques, and technical terms are explained in simple language. Fun activities include designing a label. . . . Well organized and with bright, colorful photography, [this] introductory [title gives] readers good basic knowledge." SLJ

Includes glossary and bibliographical references

781.5 Kinds of music

Stringer, Lauren

When Stravinsky met Nijinsky; two artists, their ballet, and one extraordinary riot. Lauren Stringer. Houghton Mifflin Harcourt 2013 32 p. $16.99

Grades: K 1 2   **781.5**

1. Picture books for children 2. Rite of spring (Choreographic work)

ISBN 0547907257; 9780547907253

LC 2012025330

In this children's picture book looks at the dramatic reaction to "The Rite of Spring," a collaboration between Igor Stravinsky and Vaslav Nijinsky. It "introduces the two men and how they worked alone, while noting that they both dreamed of something different. Their collaboration brought the world 'The Rite of Spring' . . . which opened to a riot in Paris during its premier[e]." (Booklist)

781.62 Folk music

Handyside, Chris

★ Folk. Heinemann Library 2006 48p il (A history of American music) lib bdg $31.43

Grades: 5 6 7 8   **781.62**

1. Folk music

ISBN 1-4034-8150-4

This history of folk music is an "excellent, clear [introduction]. . . . [It] starts with the post-Civil War era, when folklorists gathered slave songs. It describes the music's commercial success beginning with early recordings of the Carter family and Jimmie Rodgers in the 1920s and continuing with Leadbelly, Woody Guthrie, Pete Seeger, and the many musicians who became popular during the folk revival of the late 50s and early 60s. . . . It concludes with sections on folk rock, punk rock, and the future of folk music." SLJ

Includes bibliographical references

Orozco, Jose-Luis

★ De colores and other Latin-American folk songs for children; selected, arranged, and translated by José-Luis Orozco; illustrated by Eliza Kleven. Dutton Children's Bks. 1994 56p il hardcover o.p. pa $7.99

Grades: K 1 2 3   **781.62**

1. Folk songs 2. Folklore -- Latin America 3. Bilingual books -- English-Spanish

ISBN 0-525-45260-5; 0-14-056548-5 pa

"Each of the 27 songs is presented with background notes; lyrics in both Spanish and English; simple arrangements for the voice, piano, and guitar; and suggestions for group sing-alongs and musical games. . . . The book is a delight for the eyes as well as the ear. . . . Kleven provides bountiful illustrations—the endpapers are sunshine bright with a crisp quilt of yellow flowers, and playful borders that ripple with colorful patterns and miniature pictures line the edge of every page." Booklist

781.642   Country music

Bertholf, Bret

★ **Long** gone lonesome history of country music; by Bret Bertholf. Little, Brown 2007 un il $18.99

Grades: 4 5 6   **781.642**

1. Country music
ISBN 978-0-316-52393-6; 0-316-52393-3

LC 2005016036

"This tongue-in-cheek overview features a folksy narrative of how and why country music developed in the barns and back roads of rural America. The text . . . covers instruments, early recordings, yodeling, . . . the Great Depression, gospel, movie cowboys, a 'paper-doll' spoof of singers' costumes, hillbilly jazz, World War II, . . . and much more. While poking fun at itself . . . the book offers a vast amount of historical fact amid a multitude of caricatures of country stars. . . . The ever-changing backgrounds and fonts with colored-pencil and crayon illustrations carry an amazing variation of detail." SLJ

781.643   Blues

Handyside, Chris

★ **Blues**; [by] Christopher Handyside. Heinemann Library 2006 48p il (A history of American music) lib bdg $31.43

Grades: 5 6 7 8   **781.643**

1. Blues music
ISBN 1-4034-8148-2

LC 2005019280

"This book charts the development of this uniquely American Music form from the 1600s through to the present. It also shows how social, economic, and regional factors have all helped to shape the blues over time and, in turn, how this music has gone on to influence other genres." Publisher's note

Includes glossary and bibliographical references

781.644   Soul

Aretha, David

Awesome African-American rock and soul musicians; David Aretha. Enslow Publishers, Inc. 2012 112 p. ill. (African-American Collective Biographies) (library) $31.93

Grades: 6 7 8   **781.644**

1. Rock musicians 2. Soul musicians 3. African American musicians 4. African American rock musicians -- Biography 5. Soul musicians -- United

States -- Biography
ISBN 1598451405; 9781598451405

LC 2011019956

"From the African-American Collective Biographies series, this volume introduces nine significant figures in rock and soul music: Chuck Berry, Ray Charles, Little Richard, James Brown, Aretha Franklin, Jimi Hendrix, Diana Ross, Stevie Wonder, and Prince. After a general introduction to rock and soul music, each chapter looks at the individual performer's life, career, musical style, achievements, and contributions to the field." (Booklist)

Includes bibliographical references (p. 108-109) and index.

Handyside, Chris

★ **Soul** and R&B; [by] Christopher Handyside. Heinemann Library 2006 48p il (A history of American music) lib bdg $31.43

Grades: 5 6 7 8   **781.644**

1. Soul music 2. Rhythm and blues music
ISBN 1-4034-8153-9

LC 2005019324

"This book charts the development of this uniquely American music form from the 1800s through to the present. It also shows how social, economic, and regional factors have all helped to shape soul and R&B over time and, in turn, how this music has gone on to influence other genres." Publisher's note

Includes glossary and bibliographical references

781.65   Jazz

Dillon, Leo

★ **Jazz** on a Saturday night; [by] Leo & Diane Dillon. Blue Sky Press 2007 un il $16.99

Grades: PreK K 1 2   **781.65**

1. Jazz music 2. Jazz musicians
ISBN 0-590-47893-1; 978-0-590-47893-1

LC 2006-34009

This takes readers on "an imaginary Saturday night concert featuring seven . . . [jazz] greats, from Thelonius Monk to John Coltrane. Rhythmic text acts as an introduction to the legendary musicians. . . . The sophisticated illustrations . . . recall Harlem Renaissance paintings. . . . Brief biographies of the seven featured artists serve as endnotes, while a bonus CD briefly explores jazz instruments and features an original song that shares the book's title." Publ Wkly

Handyside, Chris

★ **Jazz**; [by] Christopher Handyside. Heinemann Library 2006 48p il (A history of American music) lib bdg $31.43

Grades: 5 6 7 8   **781.65**

1. Jazz music
ISBN 1-4034-8149-0

LC 2005019305

"This book charts the development of this uniquely American Music form from the 1600s through to the present. It also shows how social, economic, and regional factors have all helped to shape Jazz over time and, in turn, how this music has gone on to influence other genres." Publisher's note

Includes glossary and bibliographical references

Marsalis, Wynton

★ **Jazz** A-B-Z; [by] Wynton Marsalis and Paul Rogers; with biographical sketches by Phil Schaap. Candlewick Press 2005 un il $24.99

Grades: 5 6 7 8 9 10 **781.65**

1. Jazz music 2. Jazz musicians

ISBN 978-0-7636-3434-6

LC 2005-48448

This is an illustrated alphabetically arranged introduction to jazz musicians.

This is a "witty, stunningly designed alphabet catalog. . . . The biographical sketches and notes on poetic forms by Phil Schaap are concise and genuinely informative. . . . Rogers's pastiche full-page portraits, his use of expressive typography and the smaller vignettes he sprinkles throughout are bound to heighten any reader's appreciation of both the musicians and the music. . . . [Marsalis offers] clever . . . poems, wordplays, odes and limericks." N Y Times Book Rev

Pinkney, Andrea Davis

★ **Duke** Ellington; the piano prince and his orchestra. illustrated by Brian Pinkney. Hyperion Bks. for Children 1998 un il $15.95; pa $5.99

Grades: 2 3 4 **781.65**

1. Composers 2. Jazz musicians 3. Band leaders 4. African Americans -- Biography

ISBN 0-7868-0178-6; 0-7868-1420-9 pa

LC 96-46031

A Caldecott Medal honor book, 1999; Coretta Scott King honor book for illustration, 1999

A brief recounting of the career of this jazz musician and composer who, along with his orchestra, created music that was beyond category

This is "written in a folksy, colloquial style. . . . The warmly colored, exquisitely designed scratchboard illustrations have a grand time evoking the sounds of Ellington's music." Horn Book Guide

Includes bibliographical references

Raschka, Chris

The **Cosmobiography** of sun ra; the sound of joy is enlightening. Chris Raschka. Candlewick Press 2014 40 p. $15.99

Grades: 1 2 3 4 **781.65**

1. Jazz music 2. Jazz musicians -- Biography

ISBN 0763658065; 9780763658069

LC 2013944131

This children's book by Chris Raschka tells how "Jazz musician Sun Ra (1914-1993) always said that he came from Saturn. Being from another planet, he was naturally intrigued by everything earthly--especially music, because music is the one thing on Earth most like the stars. . . . And he traveled with other musicians and singers, calling themselves the Sun Ra Arkestra, playing, singing, and dancing for people all over the planet." (Publisher's note)

"The images themselves are dense and dynamic, painted on a variety of textured papers and musical notation sheets and full of brilliant color and heavy black. Raschka clips and arranges them in irregular, rectilinear space, attempting to capture this individual force of nature. In the end, readers

get a bright, impressionistic portrait that follows its subject's refusal to play by the rules. A brief author's note and list of selected recordings are appended." Horn Book

781.66 Rock (Rock 'n' roll)

George-Warren, Holly

Shake, rattle, & roll; the founders of rock & roll. words by Holly George-Warren; pictures by Laura Levine. Houghton Mifflin 2001 un il hardcover o.p. pa $5.95

Grades: 3 4 5 6 **781.66**

1. Musicians 2. Rock music

ISBN 0-618-05540-1; 0-618-43229-9 pa

LC 00-33480

"A wonderfully entertaining browsing book that will also fill a gap in most music collections." SLJ

"Brief profiles of 15 men and women whose music 'created a sound that changed our culture forever,' including Bill Haley, Fats Domino, Little Richard, Elvis Presley, Carl Perkins, Wanda Jackson and Ritchie Valens." N Y Times Book Rev

Guillain, Charlotte

Punk; music, fashion, attitude! Raintree 2011 32p il (Culture in action) lib bdg $29

Grades: 5 6 7 8 **781.66**

1. Punk rock music

ISBN 978-1-4109-3916-6; 1-4109-3916-2

LC 2009052585

"Guillain delves into the history of punk and follows its influence on modern art, fashion, and politics. . . . [This volume is] quick, interesting, up-to-date . . . with plenty of supportive, captioned, full-color photographs. [It] also [provides] related project suggestions." SLJ

Includes glossary and bibliographical references

Handyside, Chris

★ **Rock.** Heinemann Library 2006 48p il (A history of American music) lib bdg $31.43

Grades: 5 6 7 8 **781.66**

1. Rock music

ISBN 1-4034-8150-4

This history of rock music is an "excellent, clear [introduction]. . . . [It] opens with the mid-1950s advent of rock n roll and continues with surf music, girl groups, the British invasion, psychedelic rock, heavy metal, punk, and grunge. Featured musicians range from Elvis Presley to Kurt Cobain." SLJ

Includes bibliographical references

Stamaty, Mark Alan

★ **Shake,** rattle & turn that noise down! how Elvis shook up music, me, and mom. Alfred A. Knopf 2010 un il $17.99; lib bdg $20.99

Grades: 2 3 4 **781.66**

1. Actors 2. Singers 3. Rock music 4. Rock musicians

ISBN 978-0-375-84685-4; 0-375-84685-9; 978-0-375-94685-1 lib bdg; 0-375-94685-3 lib bdg

LC 2008-02231

"Dividing each page into multiple panels with sizable chunks of text allows Stamaty to cram a lot of information into the picture-book format. . . . [The book] makes a

convincing case that that old, dead singer really was cool."
Booklist

782.1   Vocal forms

Siberell, Anne
★ **Bravo!** brava! a night at the opera; behind the scenes
with composers, cast, and crew. introduction by Frederica
von Stade. Oxford Univ. Press 2001 64p il $19.95
Grades: 4 5 6 7   782.1
1. Opera
ISBN 0-19-513966-6
LC 2001-21206
This "book introduces all features of the opera, including stars, stagehands, set designers, conductors, and super-
numeraries. . . . Cartoon artwork illustrates the text, and a
world map highlighting the settings of well-known operas
is also included, as are curtain diagrams, plot summaries of
favorite operas, and sample costumes." Horn Book Guide
Includes glossary and bibliographical references

782.25   Small-scale vocal forms

All night, all day; a child's first book of African-American
spirituals. selected and illustrated by Ashley Bryan; musical arrangements by David Manning Thomas. Atheneum Pubs. 1991 48p il music hardcover o.p. pa $6.99
Grades: K 1 2 3 4   782.25
1. Spirituals (Songs)
ISBN 0-689-31662-3; 0-689-86786-7 pa
LC 90-753145
"An exuberance of warm color and great variety in pattern and design distinguish the illustrations. . . . Excellent
piano accompaniments and guitar chords further enrich the
beautiful, wholly gratifying book." Horn Book

Igus, Toyomi
★ **I** see the rhythm of gospel; paintings by Michele
Wood; text by Toyomi Igus. Zonderkidz 2010 40p il
$16.99
Grades: 4 5 6 7   782.25
1. Gospel music 2. African American music
ISBN 978-0-310-71819-2; 0-310-71819-8
LC 2010-08987
"Gospel music—its origins and its effects on the souls
and stories of African Americans—gets a strong, loving
treatment here. . . . Igus [provides] the stirring text and Wood
the inventive folk art. . . . Adding to the book's usefulness is
a terrific CD with five songs spanning the history of gospel
music." Booklist

★ **Let** it shine; three favorite spirituals. [illustrated by]
Ashley Bryan. Atheneum Books for Young Readers
2007 un il $16.99
Grades: K 1 2 3   782.25
1. Spirituals (Songs)
ISBN 0-689-84732-7
"The inspiring words of three well-known spirituals,
'This Little Light of Mine,' 'Oh, When the Saints Go March-
ing In,' and 'He's Got the Whole World in His Hands,' are
matched with powerful construction-paper collage illustra-

tions. Each double-page spread of this oversize picture book
is an explosion of shapes and bright colors." Booklist

Nelson, Kadir
★ **He's** got the whole world in his hands. Dial Books
for Young Readers 2005 un il $16.99
Grades: K 1 2   782.25
1. Spirituals (Songs)
ISBN 0-8037-2850-6
LC 2004-23075
An illustrated version of the well-known spiritual song
"Nelson uses pencils, oils, and watercolors to create a
series of striking, beautifully composed pictures. . . . Nelson
envisions the song in a highly personal and involving man-
ner while embodying its strength and spirit." Booklist

★ **This** little light of mine; illustrated by E. B. Lewis. Simon & Schuster Books for Young Readers 2005 32p
il $16.95
Grades: K 1 2 3   782.25
1. Spirituals (Songs)
ISBN 0-689-83179-X
"A visual interpretation of an African-American spiritual. It is morning when the book opens, and readers are
greeted by a smiling boy. Throughout the day, he spreads
his own special brand of joy wherever he goes. . . . Lewis's
watercolor illustrations across double pages effectively convey emotions of happiness and the giving and sharing of
oneself." SLJ

782.28   Carols

Spirin, Gennady
We three kings; illustrated by Gennady Spirin. Atheneum Books for Young Readers 2007 un il $16.99
Grades: K 1 2 3   782.28
1. Carols
ISBN 978-0-689-82114-1; 0-689-82114-X
"This handsome picture book illustrates the verses and
repeated choruses of the Christmas carol 'We Three Kings.'
. . . Created with watercolors and colored pencils, the formally composed and richly detailed illustrations create a distinctive world, with landscapes reminiscent of Renaissance
paintings." Booklist

782.4   Secular forms

Ho, Minfong
★ **Hush!** a Thai lullaby. pictures by Holly Meade.
Orchard Bks. 1996 un il hardcover o.p. pa $6.99
Grades: PreK K 1 2   782.4
1. Lullabies 2. Thailand -- Fiction
ISBN 0-531-07166-9 pa
LC 95-23251
A Caldecott Medal honor book, 1997
"A mother goes to each animal, from lizard to water buf-
falo to elephant, trying to quiet noises that might wake her
child. When the animals are silenced and the mother finally
falls asleep, the baby lies awake, with wide eyes and a smile.
Ho's rhythmic text is fine for reading aloud. . . . The setting,
apparently a remote Thai village, is gently evoked in cut pa-

per and ink pictures that are bold enough to be used with groups. . . . The comforting earth tones suit the quiet nature of the story." Booklist

782.42 Songs

★ The **12** days of Christmas; a pop-up celebration by Robert Sabuda. anniversary edition; Little Simon 2006 un il $26.95

Grades: K 1 2 3   **782.42**

1. Folk songs 2. Pop-up books 3. Christmas -- Songs
ISBN 978-1-4169-2792-1; 1-4169-2792-1

A reissue of the edition first published 1996

This pop-up version of the popular Christmas folk song about gift-giving features "a partridge popping, snow scattering, and lords a-leaping off the page. . . . For this . . . anniversary edition . . . paper engineer Robert Sabuda encloses . . . extra pages with a pop-up Christmas tree with real lights aglow, and a . . . pop-up ornament of two turtledoves." Publisher's note

Bates, Ivan

★ **Five** little ducks; illustrated by Ivan Bates. Scholastic 2006 un il $12.99

Grades: K 1 2   **782.42**

1. Songs 2. Counting 3. Ducks -- Songs
ISBN 0-439-74693-0

LC 2005000112

One by one, five little ducks wander away from their mother until her lonely quack brings them all waddling back

"Bates's muted watercolors bring a lively energy . . . to this beloved song. The artist's sweet and nostalgic adaptation is unique for its gentle and warm tone." SLJ

Baum, Maxie

I have a little dreidel; illustrated by Julie Paschkis. Scholastic Press 2006 un il $9.99

Grades: K 1 2   **782.42**

1. Songs 2. Hanukkah -- Songs
ISBN 0-439-64997-8; 978-0-439-64997-1

LC 2005-31318

An illustrated retelling of the classic Hannukah song, with directions for playing the dreidel game and a recipe for making latkes.

"A favorite Hanukkah song is given new life in this charmingly illustrated variation. . . . Distinctive, folk-art-style illustrations feature a mix of patterns and vibrant solids, thick lines and simple shapes, while the bottom third of each spread frames the text in a bold blue-and-white woodcutlike design." SLJ

Berkes, Marianne Collins

Over in Australia; amazing animals Down Under. by Marianne Berkes; illustrated by Jill Dubin. Dawn Publications 2011 un il $16.95; pa $8.95

Grades: PreK K 1 2   **782.42**

1. Songs 2. Counting 3. Animals -- Songs 4. Animals -- Australia
ISBN 978-1-58469-135-8; 1-58469-135-2; 978-1-58469-136-5 pa; 1-58469-136-0 pa

LC 2010031038

"Berkes incorporates some of Australia's unique animals in her latest variant of the familiar song, 'Over in the Meadow.' . . . Dubin's charming paper collages deftly use a variety of patterns plus a bonus 'hidden' animal noted on one of the informative pages after the song text. That section also includes more facts about all the mentioned animals, offers suggestions for class activities, explains Dubin's illustration process, and provides the score for those unfamiliar with the tune." SLJ

Boynton, Sandra

Blue Moo; 17 jukebox hits from way back never; deluxe illustrated songbook. lyrics and drawings by Sandra Boynton; music by Sandra Boynton & Michael Ford. Workman Pub. Co. 2007 64p il $16.95

Grades: K 1 2 3   **782.42**

1. Songs
ISBN 978-0-7611-4775-6; 0-7611-4775-6

A book and audio CD of songs in the style of 1950s pop music.

"Grandparents, parents, and children alike can enjoy this collection. . . . Boynton has combined a roster of celebrity singers, good humor, and lots of creativity for a gift of music and fun for every member of the family." SLJ

Dog train; deluxe illustrated lyrics book of the unpredictable rock-and-roll journey. music by Sandra Boynton & Michael Ford; lyrics and drawings by Sandra Boynton. Workman Pub. 2005 64p il $17.95

Grades: K 1 2 3   **782.42**

1. Songs 2. Rock music
ISBN 0-7611-3966-4

LC 2005051801

"This collection of songs erupts with energy, humor, and a strong dose of rock n roll. . . . The book has a spread for each song—a colorful, cheerful illustration and excerpts of lyrics—followed by complete lyrics and musical scores at the end. An About the Artists section includes a photo and biographical sketch of each artist who performs on the accompanying CD." SLJ

Philadelphia chickens; a too-illogical zoological musical revue: deluxe illustrated lyrics book of the original cast recording of the unforgettable (though completely imaginary) stage spectacular. music by Sandra Boynton & Michael Ford; lyrics and drawings by Sandra Boynton. Workman Pub. 2002 64p il $16.95

Grades: K 1 2 3   **782.42**

1. Songs 2. Musicals
ISBN 0-7611-2636-8

LC 2002-27049

This is "a book-and-CD package billed as an 'imaginary musical revue.' The first 32 pages contain lyrics and illustrations, the second half of the book includes musical notation and additional lyrics for each song. An all-star cast, including Meryl Streep, Laura Linney, Eric Stoltz and the Bacon Brothers, headlines the musical recording, which features a variety of original show tunes." Publ Wkly

Sandra Boynton's One shoe blues; starring B.B. King. Workman 2009 59p il $10.95

Grades: PreK K 1 2 3   **782.42**

1. Songs 2. Singers 3. Guitarists 4. Blues musicians 5. Puppets and puppet plays -- Fiction 6. Lost and

found possessions -- Fiction
ISBN 978-0-7611-5138-8; 0-7611-5138-9

LC 2009035847

"Boynton transforms a song from her 2007 book-and-CD title Blue Moo: 17 Jukebox Hits from Way Back Never into a stand-alone book-plus-DVD, starring blues legend B.B. King. Boynton weaves the lyrics of her original song into an extended tale about some colorful sock puppets who watch King perform the song in a cozy country house. . . . Still photographs from Boynton's music video and other complementary shots illustrate the story. . . . In addition to King's humorous and engaging performance (complete with sock puppet accompaniment), the DVD contains other kid-pleasing tidbits." Publ Wkly

Cabrera, Jane

Old MacDonald had a farm; [by] Jane Cabrera. Holiday House 2008 un il $16.95
Grades: PreK K　　　　　　　　　　　　　**782.42**
1. Farm life -- Songs 2. Folk songs -- United States
ISBN 978-0-8234-2141-1

LC 2007034036

First published 2007 in the United Kingdom

"A gray-haired, rosy-cheeked Old MacDonald starts off by introducing his young-looking wife, with 'a kiss kiss here, and a kiss kiss there. . . .' Then it's off to the fields, barn, and pond to meet his dog, sheep, horse, hens, goat, ducks, cow, and pig. . . . Cabrera's bright, splotchy illustrations follow the text, with full spreads devoted to each verse. Young children can read along easily enough and can probably add their own verses to the mix." SLJ

The **wheels** on the bus. Holiday House 2011 un il $16.95
Grades: PreK K　　　　　　　　　　　　　**782.42**
1. Songs 2. Animals -- Songs
ISBN 978-0-8234-2350-7; 0-8234-2350-6

LC 2011000120

In this version of the classic song, animal passengers roar, flap, and chatter while riding a bus.

"Readers will enjoy the journey Cabrera illustrates with her easily recognizable style—bright hues outlined in black, with a finger-paint–like texture." Kirkus

Carle, Eric

★ **Today** is Monday; pictures by Eric Carle. Philomel Bks. 1993 un il music hardcover o.p. pa $6.99
Grades: K 1 2 3　　　　　　　　　　　　　**782.42**
1. Songs 2. Food -- Songs 3. Animals -- Songs
ISBN 0-399-21966-8; 0-698-11563-5 pa

LC 91-45866

Each day of the week brings a new food, until on Sunday all the world's children can come and eat it up

This song "gets new life in a picture book bursting with food, animals, and lots of energy. Beginning with the grinning cat on the cover . . . a zooful of animals act out the lyrics: snakes get tangled in spaghetti, elephants use their trunks to slurp 'Zoooop,' and pelicans catch fish on Friday. With text at a minimum, Carle's always innovative artwork steps center stage in an oversize format that allows gloriously colored collages to spread over two pages." Booklist

Collins, Judy

When you wish upon a star; performed by Judy Collins; paintings by Eric Puybaret; music by Ned Washington; lyrics by Leigh Harline. Charlesbridge 2011 il $17.95
Grades: PreK K 1 2　　　　　　　　　　　　**782.42**
1. Songs 2. Wishes -- Songs
ISBN 978-1-936140-35-0; 1-936140-35-7

LC 2011004945

"A short introductory verse and the song's lyrics accompany the illustrations, glossy spreads that feature an international group of children—an Eskimo, an Asian child in a bamboo hat, a boy in a turban, and half a dozen others. All of them spot a brilliant star, smiling in the sky; soon after, a woman in a blue cape and fairy wings materializes and leads the children to a country with jaunty toy buildings and candy-cane trees. . . . There, the children's wishes are fulfilled. . . . Puybaret's polished drafting gives the spreads a compelling combination of splendor and restraint." Publ Wkly

Coots, John Frederick

Santa Claus is comin' to town; written by J. Fred Coots & Haven Gillespie; illustrated by Steven Kellogg. Harper-Collins 2004 un il hardcover o.p. pa $6.99
Grades: K 1 2 3　　　　　　　　　　　　　**782.42**
1. Songs 2. Christmas -- Songs 3. Santa Claus -- Songs
ISBN 0-688-14938-3; 0-06-443865-1 pa

LC 2003-1821

This "manages to get the rhythm of the music right onto the page. . . . The pictures are packed, and the design is witty." Horn Book

Crews, Nina

★ The **neighborhood** sing-along. Greenwillow Books 2011 63p il $17.99
Grades: K 1 2 3　　　　　　　　　　　　　**782.42**
1. Songs 2. Children's songs
ISBN 978-0-06-185063-9; 0-06-185063-2; 978-0-06-185064-6 lib bdg; 0-06-185064-0 lib bdg

LC 2010010340

A collection of songs, both familiar and lesser known, illustrated with photographs in a city setting.

"A valuable collective cultural inheritance resides in these songs, and though there are other, more comprehensive volumes available (some including the music), this bright, attractive package is a good introduction." SLJ

De colores; illustrated by David Diaz. Marshall Cavendish 2008 un il $16.99
Grades: K 1 2 3　　　　　　　　　　　　　**782.42**
1. Songs 2. Bilingual books -- English-Spanish
ISBN 978-0-7614-5431-1; 0-7614-5431-4

LC 2007022133

"This popular folk song, which is also the anthem of the United Farm Workers of America, celebrates the arrival of spring and the connectedness of humankind. Diaz's joyful pictures bring the words to life. Rendered in acrylic, colored pencil, and pencil, the vibrant, fanciful artwork features flying and floating people as well as giant-sized roosters, chickens, and birds. . . . Presented in Spanish and English, each line is illustrated on an expansive spread. Piano music and historical information about the song are included." SLJ

Deck the halls; [illustrations by] Norman Rockwell. Atheneum Books for Young Readers 2008 un il $16.99
Grades: PreK K 1 2   **782.42**
1. Songs 2. Christmas -- Songs
ISBN 978-1-4169-1771-7; 1-4169-1771-3
LC 2007037461

"The traditional Christmas carol is illustrated with Rockwell's heartwarming visions of holiday cheer. The art come[s] from a variety of sources—magazine covers, advertisements, holiday cards—and matches the lyrics surprisingly well. . . . Handsomely nostalgic." SLJ

DiPucchio, Kelly S.

Sipping spiders through a straw; campfire songs for monsters. lyrics by Kelly DiPucchio; pictures by Gris Grimly. Scholastic Press 2008 un il $15.99
Grades: 2 3 4   **782.42**
1. Songs 2. Monsters
ISBN 978-0-439-58401-2; 0-439-58401-9

"This book of eighteen clever song parodies captures exactly the type of thing kids might come up with on their own. Grisly watercolor and mixed-media illustrations awash in appropriately putrid shades of brown and gray will definitely appeal to its target readers: those with a ghoulish sense of humor who are not easily grossed out by disgusting monsters or bodily fluids." Horn Book Guide

Dylan, Bob

Man gave names to all the animals; illustrated by Jim Arnosky. Sterling 2010 un il $17.95
Grades: K 1 2 3   **782.42**
1. Songs 2. Animals -- Songs
ISBN 978-1-4027-6858-3; 1-4027-6858-3

"Through vivid paintings of a primeval planet teeming with wildlife, Arnosky translates Dylan's 1979 song about the naming of Earth's animals into a gorgeous picture book. Full lyrics and a CD of the original song are included. In Dylan's narrative, Man takes note of the characteristics of various animals, including a bear, cow, bull, pig, and sheep, and determines a name for each creature. . . . A list of 170 species appears in the back of the book, with hints on locating each creature on Arnosky's website." SLJ

Engels, Christiane

Knick knack paddy whack; illustrated by Christiane Engel; sung by SteveSongs. Barefoot Books 2008 un il $16.99
Grades: PreK K   **782.42**
1. Counting 2. Folk songs
ISBN 978-1-84686-144-4; 1-84686-144-6
LC 2007-25046

An illustrated version of the traditional counting song that tells of the ten things 'this old man' played before he came rolling home.

"This bright, lively, new interpretation of the classic children's song incorporates numbers, musical-instrument families, and a multiethnic group of adorable children who march along with the 'old man' of the song. . . . With its inventive use of numbers, music, and collage illustrations, it's a worthy addition." SLJ

The **Farmer** in the dell; illustrated by Alexandra Wallner. Holiday House 1998 un il music $15.95
Grades: K 1   **782.42**
1. Folk songs -- United States
ISBN 0-8234-1382-9
LC 97-44206

An illustrated version of the traditional game song accompanied by music

"Wallner's primitive folk art sparkles with life, action, and energy. The colored pen-and-ink illustrations are packed with details." SLJ

Fatus, Sophie

Here we go round the mulberry bush; [by] Sophie Fatus and Fred Penner. Barefoot Books 2007 un il $16.99
Grades: PreK K 1 2   **782.42**
1. Songs
ISBN 978-1-84686-035-5; 1-84686-035-0
LC 2006025656

Presents ten verses of the popular song, with illustrations of children from different cultures as they get ready for school.

"The double-page spreads, rendered in bold acrylics, are separated into fours to show the kids side by side. This artfully underscores cultural diversity while uniting the children through their similar routines. Music and a CD of the song are included." Horn Book Guide

Favorite folk songs; The Peter Yarrow songbook. [compiled by Peter Yarrow]; illustrated by Terry Widener. Sterling Pub. 2008 48p il (Peter Yarrow songbook series) $16.95
Grades: PreK K 1 2   **782.42**
1. Folk songs
ISBN 978-1-4027-5961-1; 1-4027-5961-4
LC 2008022435

An illustrated compilation of folk songs with an audio CD of the songs performed by Peter Yarrow and his daughter Bethany.

"Widener's acrylic paintings are expansive and gorgeous, but the [CD is] the real treasure here." SLJ

The **Fox** went out on a chilly night; an old song. illustrated by Peter Spier. Doubleday 1961 un il music hardcover o.p. pa $6.95
Grades: K 1 2 3   **782.42**
1. Foxes -- Songs 2. Folk songs -- United States
ISBN 0-385-07990-7; 0-440-40829-6 pa

Set in New England, this old song tells about the trip the fox father made to town to get some of the farmer's plump geese for his family's dinner, and how he manages to evade the farmer who tries to shoot him

"A true picture book in the Caldecott-Brooke tradition. Fine drawings, lovely colors, and pictures so full of amusing details that young viewers will make fresh discoveries every time they . . . scrutinize these beautiful, action-filled pages." Horn Book

Harburg, E. Y.

Over the rainbow; performed by Judy Collins; music by Harold Arlen; lyrics by E.Y. Harburg; paintings by Eric Puybaret. Imagine Pub. 2010 un il $17.95

Grades: K 1 2 3   **782.42**

1. Songs

ISBN 978-1-936140-00-8; 1-936140-00-4

Illustrates the well-known song with paintings of a young girl's search for happiness.

"A musical classic inspires the creation of new images of sweeping horizons and fanciful creatures. The book includes a CD by singer Judy Collins. Her crystal-clear voice floats seamlessly through the lyrics. . . . Two additional songs interpreted by Collins make this brief CD a treasure—'I See the Moon' . . . and 'White Coral Bells.' Readers are treated to deep jewel tones as Puybaret carefully pulls them from one image to another with a succession of dreamlike scenes. . . . The art is unique, delicate, and detailed." SLJ

Henderson, Kathy

Hush, baby, hush! lullabies from around the world. illustrated by Pam Smy. Frances Lincoln Children's Books 2011 43p il $17.95

Grades: PreK K 1   **782.42**

1. Lullabies

ISBN 978-1-84507-967-3; 1-84507-967-1

"This collection includes 29 lullabies from countries including Japan, Nigeria, Malawi and Greenland. . . . Music for about half the lullabies is provided. Most songs are printed in their original languages, but lullabies in languages such as Arabic and Korean are transliterated instead of being rendered in original scripts. Animated oil-and-colored-pencil paintings show adults and children in fully-realized landscapes, city streets, marketplaces and bedrooms. . . . This attractive presentation is appropriate as a baby gift, for daycare and preschool collections and public libraries." Kirkus

Hillenbrand, Will

★ **Down** by the station. Harcourt Brace & Co. 1999 un il music $17; pa $6.99

Grades: K 1 2   **782.42**

1. Songs 2. Animals -- Songs 3. Railroads -- Songs

ISBN 0-15-201804-2; 0-15-216790-0 pa

LC 98-41770

In this version of a familiar song, baby animals ride to the children's zoo on the zoo train

"This twist on an old favorite combines sunny illustrations, playful humor, and appealing animals." SLJ

Hinojosa, Tish

Cada nino/Every child; a bilingual songbook for kids. illustrated by Lucia Angela Perez. Cinco Puntos Press 2002 56p il music hardcover o.p. pa $9.95

Grades: K 1 2 3   **782.42**

1. Songs 2. Bilingual books -- English-Spanish

ISBN 0-9383-1760-1; 0-9383-1779-2 pa

"Hinojosa has gathered 11 traditional, original, and adapted songs to celebrate both Hispanic culture and universal experiences and feelings. A brief author's note in English and Spanish prefaces the music, with chords and melody, and verses in both languages. . . . Lovely, bright, folk-art illustrations, brimming with pattern play and whimsical details, create magical worlds of familiar objects and experiences as they incorporate cultural elements. . . . A CD is available for separate purchase." Booklist

Hoberman, Mary Ann

The **eensy**-weensy spider; adapted by Mary Ann Hoberman; illustrated by Nadine Bernard Westcott. Little, Brown 2000 un il hardcover o.p. pa $6.99

Grades: K 1 2 3   **782.42**

1. Songs 2. Finger play 3. Spiders -- Songs

ISBN 0-316-36330-8; 0-316-73412-8 pa

LC 99-25701

An expanded version of the familiar children's fingerplay rhyme describing what the little spider does after being washed out of the water-spout

"Whimsical, watercolor cartoons capture the lighthearted tone of the verse. . . . This sprightly adaptation lends itself to singing aloud and is sure to be a hit." SLJ

Mary had a little lamb; adapted by Mary Ann Hoberman; illustrated by Nadine Bernard Westcott. Little, Brown 2003 un il (Sing-along stories) $15.95

Grades: K 1 2   **782.42**

1. Songs 2. Sheep -- Songs

ISBN 0-316-60687-1

LC 2002-72478

This expanded version of the traditional rhyme shows what happens after the lamb gets to school. Includes music on the last page

"This playful extension of the original nursery rhyme adds to the nonsense with simple words and clear, slapstick watercolor-and-ink illustrations." Booklist

Hort, Lenny

★ The **seals** on the bus; illustrated by G. Brian Karas. Holt & Co. 2000 un il $17.95

Grades: K 1 2   **782.42**

1. Songs 2. Animals -- Songs

ISBN 0-8050-5952-0

LC 99-33612

Different animals—including seals, tigers, geese, rabbits, monkeys, and more—make their own sounds as they ride all around the town on a bus

"Karas' artwork combines cut paper, gouache, acrylic, and pencil to create a series of pleasingly varied scenes of cheerful chaos. A good story hour choice." Booklist

★ **I** hear America singing! folk songs for American families. collected and arranged by Kathleen Krull; illustrated by Allen Garns; introductory note by Arlo Guthrie. Knopf 2003 145p il $24.95

Grades: 3 4 5 6   **782.42**

1. Folk songs -- United States

ISBN 0-375-82527-4

First published 1992 without CD with title: Gonna sing my head off!

"Work songs, love songs, ballads and blues, lullabies, spirituals, protest songs, and sheer nonsense make up this entertaining collection of 62 traditional and contemporary favorites. For each song, Krull provides the simplest piano and guitar arrangements in a clear double-page spread design that includes the words to all the verses. . . . The exuberant illustrations, mostly in bright pastels, manage to be both familiar and dramatic. . . . Informal notes at the head of each song give something about history, origin, performance, and possibilities for variation." Booklist

In the hollow of your hand; slave lullabies. collected by Alice McGill; pictures by Michael Cummings. Houghton Mifflin 2000 un il music $18

Grades: 5 6 7 8 **782.42**

1. Lullabies 2. Slavery -- Poetry 3. African Americans -- Poetry

ISBN 0-395-85755-4

LC 97-20269

A collection of lullabies orally transmitted by African-American slaves revealing their hardships and sorrows as well as soothing notes of well-being and belief in a better time to come

"This moving collection of 13 folk lullabies is a powerful way to communicate what family life was like under slavery.... Opposite each song is a handsome full-page quilt collage contributed by Michael Cummings.... There's full musical notation at the back, and a CD of the songs, sung by McGill, is included. The people's words are achingly beautiful, and the combination with history and personal experience makes this an enduring collection." Booklist

Isadora, Rachel

★ **12** days of Christmas; [illustrated by] Rachel Isadora. G.P. Putnam's Sons 2010 un il map $16.99

Grades: PreK K 1 2 **782.42**

1. Riddles 2. Folk songs 3. Africa 4. Christmas -- Songs

ISBN 978-0-399-25073-6; 0-399-25073-5

LC 2009052862

Isadora sets the traditional English Christmas carol in Africa, using a combination of text and rebuses. The book includes an author's note about some of the African traditions depicted. "Preschool." (Horn Book)

This is "illustrated with . . . visually arresting collages that incorporate African fabrics. . . . In this interpretation, the maids milk goats and the lords are masked dancers from Mali.... This change of setting gives the old song new zest." Kirkus

Jackson, Jill

Let there be peace on earth; and let it begin with me. by Jill Jackson & Sy Miller; [illustrated by David Diaz] Tricycle Press 2009 un il $18.99

Grades: PreK K 1 2 **782.42**

1. Songs 2. Peace -- Songs

ISBN 978-1-58246-285-1; 1-58246-285-2

LC 2008043122

Illustrates the award-winning song about each person's responsibility to help bring about world peace. Includes a history of the song and biographical notes on the husband and wife songwriting team.

"Diaz's luminous artwork brings [the song] to life for picture-book audiences. . . . The CD contains 12 peace-themed, secular songs. The arrangements are airy and fun for children." SLJ

Johnson, James Weldon

★ **Lift** every voice and sing; by James Weldon Johnson; illustrated by Bryan Collier. Amistad 2007 un il $16.99; lib bdg $17.89

Grades: K 1 2 3 **782.42**

1. Songs 2. African American music

ISBN 978-0-06-054147-7; 978-0-06-145897-2 lib bdg

LC 2007008602

An illustrated version of the song that has come to be considered the African American national anthem

"Collier's stirring textured collage-and-watercolor illustrations . . . express his Christian faith and his profound sense of connection with his people's historic struggle." Booklist

Katz, Alan

Mosquitoes are ruining my summer! and other silly dilly camp songs. illustrated by David Catrow. Margaret K. McElderry Books 2011 un il $16.99

Grades: 3 4 5 **782.42**

1. Songs 2. Camps -- Songs

ISBN 978-1-4169-5568-9; 1-4169-5568-2

LC 2009021167

Familiar tunes are given new words relating to summer camp, including "Whose Idea Was This Dumb Hike" sung to the tune of "Twinkle Twinkle Little Star."

"Few elements of the camp-going experience are exempt from the tongue-in-cheek riffing, and the lively cartoon-style illustrations extend the hyperbolic humor through caricature and perspective." Booklist

On top of the potty and other get-up-and-go songs; [by] Alan Katz; [illustrations] David Catrow. Margaret K. McElderry Books 2008 un il $16.99

Grades: PreK **782.42**

1. Songs 2. Toilet training -- Songs

ISBN 978-0-689-86215-1; 0-689-86215-6

LC 2007-9004

Well-known songs with new lyrics encourage toddlers to trade in their diapers for the potty chair, including 'If You Gotta Go Do Poopy,' sung to the tune of 'If You're Happy and You Know It.'

"Great for toilet training, this picture book provides adults with a different way to sing and talk about that crucial time when toddlers move from diapers to underwear, potty chair, and toilet.... Lots of youngsters and their caregivers will have fun with this." Booklist

Smelly locker; silly dilly school songs. illustrated by David Catrow. Margaret K. McElderry Books 2008 un il $16.99

Grades: K 1 2 3 **782.42**

1. Songs 2. Schools -- Songs

ISBN 978-1-4169-0695-7; 1-4169-0695-9

LC 2006-36814

Well-known songs, including "Oh Susannah" and "Take Me Out to the Ballgame," are presented with new words and titles, such as "Heavy Backpack!" and "I Don't Want to Do Homework!"

This is "an irreverent, entertaining commentary in song about school life. . . . With exaggerated features and hilarious body language, Catrow's expressive cartoon characters capture the bizarre and ridiculous elements of the text." SLJ

Take me out of the bathtub and other silly dilly songs; illustrated by David Catrow. Margaret K. McElderry Bks. 2001 un il $15

Grades: K 1 2 3 **782.42**

1. Songs

ISBN 0-689-82903-5

LC 99-89390

Well-known songs, including "Oh Susannah" and "Row Row Row Your Boat," are presented with new words and titles, such as "I'm So Carsick" and "Go Go Go to Bed"

"Catrow's animated double-spread pictures are at least as silly as the song lyrics, offering action-filled scenes bursting with odd-looking creatures." Booklist

Katz, Karen

The **babies** on the bus. Henry Holt 2011 32p il $14.99
Grades: PreK K　　　　　　　　　　　**782.42**
1. Songs
ISBN 978-0-8050-9011-6; 0-8050-9011-8
LC 2010039229

"'The Wheels on the Bus' gets a facelift with new illustrations and a few new verses focused on babies. Each of the 13 verses is complete on a spread. Bright colors and simple patterns are eye-catching for all, but will have special appeal for babies and toddlers. Katz's familiar round-faced youngsters of different ethnicities will delight readers." SLJ

Langstaff, John M.

Frog went a-courtin' retold by John Langstaff; with pictures by Feodor Rojankovsky. Harcourt Brace Jovanovich 1955 un il music $16; pa $7
Grades: K 1 2 3　　　　　　　　　　**782.42**
1. Folk songs 2. Mice -- Songs 3. Frogs -- Songs
ISBN 0-15-230214-X; 0-15-633900-5 pa
Awarded the Caldecott Medal, 1956

"Retelling of a merry old Scottish ballad with many-colored illustrations about the marriage between Mr. Frog and Miss Mouse. A composite American version set to Appalachian mountain music." Chicago Public Libr

Oh, a-hunting we will go; [by] John Langstaff; pictures by Nancy Winslow Parker. Atheneum Pubs. 1974 un il music hardcover o.p. pa $6.99
Grades: K 1 2　　　　　　　　　　　**782.42**
1. Folk songs 2. Animals -- Songs
ISBN 0-689-71503-X pa

The nonsense verses of this folk song trace the hunt for such animals as an armadillo, a fox, and a snake, and describe the imagined treatment of each animal once it is caught

"The 12 stanzas are complemented by Parker's droll crayon illustrations (the fox caught in the box is watching TV), and a score for guitar and piano is appended. An amusing addition to 'song' picture books." SLJ

★ **Over** in the meadow; with pictures by Feodor Rojankovsky. Harcourt Brace & Co. 1957 un il music hardcover o.p. pa $7
Grades: K 1 2　　　　　　　　　　　**782.42**
1. Counting 2. Folk songs 3. Animals -- Songs
ISBN 0-15-258854-X; 0-15-670500-1 pa

"This old counting rhyme tells of ten meadow families whose mothers advise them to dig, run, sing, play, hum, build, swim, wink, spin and hop. The illustrations, half in full color, show the combination of realism and imagination which little children like best. The tune, arranged simply, is on the last page, and children will have fun acting the whole thing out." Horn Book

Leodhas, Sorche Nic

Always room for one more; illustrated by Nonny Hogrogian. Holt & Co. 1965 un il music $14.95; pa $5.95

Grades: K 1 2 3　　　　　　　　　　**782.42**
1. Folk songs
ISBN 0-8050-0331-2; 0-8050-0330-4 pa
Awarded the Caldecott Medal, 1966

"A picture book based on an old Scottish folk song about hospitable Lachie MacLachlan, who invited in so many guests that his little house finally burst. Rhymed text . . . a glossary of Scottish words, and music for the tune are combined into an effective whole." Hodges. Books for Elem Sch Libr

Let's sing together; The Peter Yarrow songbook. [selected by Peter Yarrow]; illustrated by Terry Widener. Sterling Pub. 2009 48p il (Peter Yarrow songbook series) $16.95
Grades: PreK K 1 2　　　　　　　　**782.42**
1. Folk songs
ISBN 978-1-4027-5963-5; 1-4027-5963-0

"The lyrics of 12 folk songs, rooted in several cultural traditions, are illustrated in Widener's simple yet resonant folk art style, which creatively mingles conventional, earth-toned scenarios . . . with images featuring vividly hued, fanciful flourishes. . . . The author provides guitar chords, historical notes and personal anecdotes for each song. On the included CD, Yarrow sings each song, accompanied by his talented daughter Bethany Yarrow and a quartet of children. An energetic and uplifting package." Publ Wkly

Lightfoot, Gordon

★ **Canadian** railroad trilogy; art by Ian Wallace. Groundwood Books/House of Anansi Press 2010 un il
Grades: 2 3 4 5　　　　　　　　　　**782.42**
1. Children's songs 2. Canada -- History 3. Railroads -- Songs 4. Railroads -- History 5. Canadian Pacific Railway Ltd. 6. Railroads -- History
ISBN 0888999534; 9780888999535

This is an illustrated version of Gordon Lightfoot's song written in Canadia's centennial year, 1967, to commemorate the building of the Canadian Pacific Railroad. "Age four and up." (Quill Quire)

"Wallace's . . . sprawling, dreamlike paintings pay homage to the Canadian landscape; they accompany the lyrics of Lightfoot's 1967 song. . . . Mountains, forests, coastline, and plains roll past as on a railway journey—miles of lonely wilderness the Canadian Pacific Railway was built to span. . . . Wallace doesn't avoid showing the realities of the railway workers lives. . . . It's a huge and unusual project, and Wallace has executed it with admirable care." Publ Wkly

Long, Laurel

★ The **twelve** days of Christmas; illustrated by Laurel Long. Dial Books for Young Readers 2011 il $16.99
Grades: PreK K　　　　　　　　　　**782.42**
1. Songs 2. Folk songs 3. Christmas -- Songs
ISBN 978-0-8037-3357-2; 0-8037-3357-7
LC 2008015774

An illustrated version of the traditional song.

"Long's lyrical and lush oil paintings, reminiscent of Russian icon art, combined with a tricky interactive element, make this version of the traditional carol special." SLJ

Lyon, George Ella

Which side are you on? the story of a song. artwork by Christopher Cardinale. Cinco Puntos Press 2011 un il $17.95

Grades: 3 4 5   782.42

1. Miners 2. Labor unions 3. Coal mines and mining -- Songs

ISBN 978-1-933693-96-5; 1-933693-96-7

LC 2010037398

This tells the story of a song which was written in 1931 by Florence Reece in a rain of bullets. Florence's husband Sam was a coal miner in Kentucky. Miners went on strike until they could get better pay, safer working conditions, and health care. The company hired thugs to attack the organizers like Sam Reece. George Ella Lyon tells this story through the eyes of one of Florence's daughters.

"Ribbons of song lyrics weave across scenes of the miners' tools of their trade and the guns of hired company toughs. A thorough author's note follows the text, ending with the song's musical notation and one version of the words on the back cover. The use of music as a protest element makes an interesting addendum to resources on union history or the time period." SLJ

Mallett, David

★ **Inch** by inch; the garden song. pictures by Ora Eitan. HarperCollins Pubs. 1995 un il music hardcover o.p. pa $5.95

Grades: K 1 2   782.42

1. Songs 2. Gardens -- Songs

ISBN 0-06-443481-8 pa

LC 93-38352

"In this picture-book version of the song first published in 1975 . . . a young child plants seeds . . . weeds and tends them, and finally, gleans a bountiful harvest. . . . Employing a variety of media including cut paper, Eitan uses color and space to create a striking effect." SLJ

Martin, Steve

Late for school; illustrated by C. F. Payne. Grand Central 2010 un il $17.95

Grades: PreK K 1 2   782.42

1. Songs 2. Schools -- Songs

ISBN 978-0-446-55702-3; 0-446-55702-1

An illustrated song about the difficulties of getting to school on time, with an audio CD of the author singing the song with banjo accompaniment.

"In Payne's . . . hands, Martin's goofy verse achieves its comic impact on a cinematic scale. . . . Kids will relish Martin's subversive madness." Publ Wkly

★ **National** anthems of the world; edited by Michael Jamieson Bristow. 11th ed.; Weidenfeld & Nicolson 2006 629p $90

Grades: 5 6 7 8 9 10 11 12 Adult   782.42

1. National songs

ISBN 0-304-36826-1

First published 1943 in the United Kingdom with title: National anthems of the United Nations and France

This volume contains national anthems of about 198 nations, including melody and accompaniment. Words are presented in the native language with transliteration provided where necessary. English translations follow. Brief historical notes on the adoption of each anthem are included

"An essential reference resource for all libraries." Libr J

Norworth, Jack

Take me out to the ball game; performed by Carly Simon; written by Jack Norworth; illustrated by Amiko Hirao. Imagine 2011 un il $17.95

Grades: PreK K 1 2   782.42

1. Songs 2. Baseball -- Songs

ISBN 978-1-936140-26-8; 1-936140-26-8

LC 2010035438

Text and illustrations present the well-known song about baseball games, with the ball players depicted as animals.

"It's a visual tour de force, with double-page spreads of large, action-packe, brilliantly colored scenes in startlingly off-center perspective. A Carly Simon CD accompanies the book, and youngsters will have a wonderful time reading and singing along." Kirkus

Orozco, Jose-Luis

★ **Diez** deditos. Ten little fingers & other play rhymes and action songs from Latin America; selected, arranged, and translated by José-Luis Orozco; illustrated by Elisa Kleven. Dutton Children's Bks. 1997 56p il music $19.99; pa $7.99

Grades: K 1 2 3   782.42

1. Songs 2. Finger play 3. Folklore -- Latin America 4. Bilingual books -- English-Spanish

ISBN 0-525-45736-4; 0-14-230087-9 pa

"This collection of fingerplays and action songs in Spanish and English comes with clear instructions for physical movements and simple musical notation. A brief sentence or paragraph introduces each entry. . . . Orozco's selections, some traditional, some written by himself, include versifications on such child-appealing subjects as dancing, singing, animals, weather, and food. . . . Kleven's collage illustrations practically pop off the pages with flashy colors and rich details that make each bustling composition a viewer's delight." Bull Cent Child Books

★ **Fiestas**: a year of Latin American songs of celebration; selected, arranged, and translated by José-Luis Orozco; illustrated by Elisa Kleven. Dutton Children's Bks. 2002 48p il music $17.99

Grades: K 1 2 3   782.42

1. Songs 2. Festivals 3. Bilingual books -- English-Spanish 4. Latin America -- Social life and customs

ISBN 0-525-45937-5

"Orozco presents 22 songs that center around holidays. . . . Arranged by month, each song is presented with a paragraph of background, the music for the melody (with guitar chords), and the lyrics in both Spanish and English. . . . Kleven's bright borders and busy illustrations . . . make this not only an exemplary songbook, but also a stunning visual experience." SLJ

Paxton, Tom

The marvelous toy; words and music by Tom Paxton; illustrated by Steve Cox. Imagine Publishing 2009 un il $17.95

Grades: PreK K 1 2   782.42

1. Songs 2. Toys -- Songs

ISBN 978-0-9822939-2-8; 0-9822939-2-5

In this picture book adaptation of Paxton's song, a "boy receives [a] toy from his father, they enjoy it together, and the boy passes it on to his own son with similar enthusiasm. . . . Although the spindly, alien-looking toy is never completely visible, the rainbow-colored protrusions that are shown emit airbrushed beams, while sparks zoom and zip behind it, illuminating the night and leaving a trail of magic in its wake. . . . Four Paxton songs are enclosed on a CD." Publ Wkly

Pinkney, Brian

★ **Hush,** little baby; adapted and illustrated by Brian Pinkney. Greenwillow Books 2006 un il $15.99; lib bdg $17.89

Grades: K 1 2   **782.42**

1. Lullabies 2. Folk songs -- United States
ISBN 978-0-06-055993-9; 0-06-055993-4; 978-0-06-055994-6 lib bdg; 0-06-055994-2 lib bdg
LC 2005-08216

"Pinkney sets his version of the traditional Appalachian folksong in an African American household of the early 1900s. . . . Ink-on-clayboard scenes show a distraught toddler girl comforted by a playful father and older brother, who sing, dance, and, of course, offer a series of whimsical gifts. . . . An appended musical arrangement gives the tune a jazzy beat to match the wheeling, undulating figures in the story." Booklist

Raffi

Baby Beluga; illustrated by Ashley Wolff. Crown 1990 un il music (Raffi songs to read) hardcover o.p. pa $5.99; bd bk $6.99

Grades: K 1 2   **782.42**

1. Songs 2. Whales -- Songs
ISBN 0-517-58362-3 pa; 0-517-70977-5 bd bk
LC 89-49367

Presents the illustrated text to the song about the little white whale who swims wild and free

"Wolff's striking double-page spreads show the young whale among its fellow Arctic Sea inhabitants. Diversifying her views, the illustrator eyes Baby Beluga and mother swimming together underwater; takes an aerial angle, looking down on the whales from a puffin's perspective; and observes the icy yet welcoming formations where seals, polar bears, and an Eskimo find shelter. . . . An inviting approach to reading encouragement." Booklist

Down by the bay; illustrated by Nadine Bernard Westcott. Crown 1987 un il music (Raffi songs to read) hardcover o.p. pa $5.99; bd bk $6.99

Grades: K 1 2   **782.42**

1. Songs
ISBN 0-517-56645-1 pa; 0-517-80058-6 bd bk
LC 87-750291

This illustrated version of one of Raffi's songs depicts a variety of unusual sights to be seen "down by the bay"

The "cheerful nonsense verses are illustrated with equal cheer. Westcott's scraggly lines and bright, clear colors humorously portray the busy children, jolly animals, and frantic mothers that populate the song." SLJ

Five little ducks; illustrated by Jose Aruego and Ariane Dewey. Crown 1989 un il (Raffi songs to read) hardcover o.p. pa $5.99; bd bk $6.99

Grades: K 1 2   **782.42**

1. Songs 2. Ducks -- Songs
ISBN 0-517-58360-7; 0-517-56945-0 pa; 0-517-80057-8 bd bk
LC 88-3752

When her five little ducks disappear one by one, Mother Duck sets out to find them

Raven, Margot

Happy birthday to you! the mystery behind the most famous song in the world. by Margot Theis Raven; paintings by Chris K. Soentpiet. Sleeping Bear Press 2008 un il $17.95

Grades: 1 2 3 4   **782.42**

1. Songs 2. Pianists 3. Educators 4. Songwriters
ISBN 978-1-58536-169-4; 1-58536-169-0
LC 2007037438

"A lovely succession of watercolor paintings depicts the latter half of the 19th century in Louisville and illuminates the thoughtful expressions and joyful faces of the Hill family. . . . [This is] an eye-opener for history and trivia lovers in all libraries." SLJ

Ray, Jane

★ **The twelve** days of Christmas. Candlewick Press 2011 un il $16.99

Grades: PreK K 1   **782.42**

1. Songs 2. Folk songs 3. Christmas -- Songs
ISBN 978-0-7636-5735-2; 0-7636-5735-2
LC 2010052222

On each of the twelve days of Christmas, more and more gifts arrive from the recipient's true love.

"Ray's intricate illustrations offer a wealth of details to explore up close. The images are slightly busy for sharing with a large group, but irresistible for a smaller group or one-on-one. A very nice version indeed." SLJ

Reid, Rob

Children's jukebox; the select subject guide to children's musical recordings. 2nd ed; American Library Association 2007 284p pa $55

Grades: Adult Professional   **782.42**

1. Reference books 2. Children's libraries 3. Songs -- Indexes
ISBN 0-8389-0940-X pa; 978-0-8389-0940-9 pa
LC 2006103175

First published 1995

This is an index to 548 recordings for children with 147 subject headings, plus subcategories

Includes discography

Roslonek, Steve

The **shape** song swingalong; written and sung by SteveSongs; illustrated by David Sim. Barefoot 2011 il $16.99; pa $9.99

Grades: PreK K 1 2   **782.42**

1. Shape 2. Songs
ISBN 978-1-84686-671-5; 1-84686-671-5; 978-1-84686-679-1 pa; 1-84686-679-0 pa

"Children in primary colored, mixed-media spreads create the very scenes that they inhabit, using large crayons to draw various shapes that form everything from a city of brick skyscrapers to a sunny beach where Sim's naïf figures ride a purple waterslide. A jazzy song by the children's musical group SteveSongs describes the children's drawings and the shapes that they use to create specific images. . . . The shape-focused chorus, bouncy verses, and whimsical storytelling should have kids singing along with the included CD recording, which also features a video animation of the story." Publ Wkly

Roth, Susan L.
★ **Hanukkah,** oh Hanukkah; [by] Susan L. Roth. Dial Books for Young Readers 2004 un il $10.99; pa $5.99
Grades: K 1 2   782.42
  1. Songs 2. Hanukkah -- Songs
  ISBN 0-8037-2843-3; 0-14-240701-1 pa
                                                  LC 2003-13165
A family of mice celebrates the eight days of Hannukah with friends in this illustrated version of the holiday song
  "Cloth and paper collages done in many different patterns and textures add interest to the cozy tableaux. . . . The lovely colors and the appealing tune make this a good holiday choice." SLJ

Rueda, Claudia
  Let's play in the forest while the wolf is not around; by Claudia Rueda. Scholastic Press 2006 un il $16.99
Grades: PreK K 1   782.42
  1. Folk songs 2. Singing games 3. Wolves -- Songs 4. Animals -- Songs
  ISBN 0-439-82323-4
                                                  LC 2005030531
  In this adaptation of the traditional French and Latin American song, animals play in the forest while a scary wolf slowly dresses and becomes hungrier and hungrier
  "On flat backgrounds, the angular, minimally detailed but colorful digital images, enhanced with a few light pencil strokes, show the animals at play in the forest, always chanting the same line. . . . This is a great song for toddlers to act out as they are getting dressed." Booklist

Sedaka, Neil
  Waking up is hard to do; illustrated by Daniel Miyares. Imagine 2010 un il $17.95
Grades: PreK K 1 2 3   782.42
  1. Songs
  ISBN 978-1-936140-13-8; 1-936140-13-6
                                                  LC 2010001402
  "Sedaka has rewritten the lyrics of his 1962 and 1975 chart-topping tune to create this child-pleasing book. The alarm clock is ringing, birds are singing, breakfast is warming, and school is calling. The repeated chorus, 'Wakin' up is hard to do,' will allow children to chime in. . . . The charming art has fun details and an adorable cast of animal characters. . . . A CD includes the title track as well as two new songs: 'Lightnin' Jim' and 'Sing.'" SLJ

Seeger, Ruth Crawford
  ★ **American** folk songs for children in home, school, and nursery school; a book for children, parents, and teachers. by Ruth Crawford Seeger; illustrated by Barbara Cooney. Oak Publications 2002 190p il pa $24.95
Grades: PreK K 1 2 3 4 Adult Professional   782.42
  1. Songs 2. Folk music -- United States
  ISBN 978-0-8256-0346-4 pa; 0-8256-0346-3 pa
  First published 1948 by Doubleday

"This is a unique collection. It will probably be the authoritative source for American folk songs for children for many, many years." Saturday Review of Books

Seskin, Steve
  Sing my song; a kid's guide to songwriting. starring Steve Seskin and a chorus of creative kids; illustrated by Eve Aldridge . . . [et al.] Tricycle Press 2008 32p il $18.99
Grades: 1 2 3 4 5   782.42
  1. Songwriters and songwriting
  ISBN 978-1-58246-266-0; 1-58246-266-6
                                                  LC 2007046966
  "Seskin has tapped a mother lode of musical enthusiasm in this book by showing young readers the 'how to' necessary to create songs and set them to music. Following 12 excellent examples and step-by-step instructions, readers discover how to put together the parts of a song. Musical terms are defined, song forms are suggested, and a CD of tunes provides sample accompaniment as Seskin backs up his relaxed vocals on guitar and with choruses from various schools." SLJ

Sleepytime songs; The Peter Yarrow songbook. [compiled by] Peter Yarrow; illustrated by Terry Widener. Sterling Pub. 2008 48p il (Peter Yarrow songbook series) $16.95
Grades: PreK K 1 2   782.42
  1. Lullabies 2. Folk songs -- United States
  ISBN 978-1-4027-5962-8; 1-4027-5962-2
                                                  LC 2008022530
  "Yarrow, best known as the Peter of Peter, Paul, and Mary, here offers a wonderful compilation of bedtime songs, complete with CD. Beginning with a warm introduction from Yarrow about singing to children, the book continues with two-page spreads containing the lyrics of the songs, set against Widener's imaginative art." Booklist

Spirin, Gennady
  ★ **The twelve** days of Christmas; illustrated by Gennady Spirin. Marshall Cavendish 2009 un il $16.99
Grades: K 1 2 3   782.42
  1. Songs 2. Folk songs 3. Christmas -- Songs
  ISBN 978-0-7614-5551-6; 0-7614-5551-5
                                                  LC 2008-06476
  On each of the twelve days of Christmas, unusual and fanciful gifts arrive to celebrate the season.
  "This holiday favorite is brought to life through Spirin's gorgeous illustrations. . . . The elaborately detailed and exquisitely executed artwork, rendered in watercolor and colored pencil, has a Renaissance feel. Roman numerals are placed on the tree or the base of the tree planter to indicate which day is being celebrated. As the oval inset fills with calling birds, golden rings, swans-a-swimming, etc., readers will enjoy trying to count all the gifts. A must-have." SLJ

Staines, Bill
  ★ **All** God's critters; song by Bill Staines; pictures by Kadir Nelson. Simon & Schuster Books for Young Readers 2009 un il $16.99
Grades: PreK K 1   782.42
  1. Songs 2. Animals -- Songs
  ISBN 978-0-689-86959-4; 0-689-86959-2
                                                  LC 2008-23624

Celebrates how all the animals in the world make their own music in their own way, some singing low, some singing higher.

The song "is brought to rollicking life by Nelson's artwork. . . . Each delightful spread [is] full-to-bursting with . . . critters' energy. . . . The oversize type of the lyrics nearly shouts off the page." Booklist

Stotts, Stuart

★ We shall overcome; a song that changed the world. by Stuart Stotts; foreword by Pete Seeger; with illustrations by Terrance Cummings. Clarion Books 2009 72p il $18
Grades: 5 6 7 8　　　　　　　　　　　　782.42
　1. African Americans -- Civil rights -- Songs
　ISBN 978-0-547-18210-0; 0-547-18210-4
　　　　　　　　　　　　　　　　LC 2009022578

"This smart, effective telling has few missteps. From the informative black-and-white photographs to the solid back matter to the CD sung by Pete Seeger, it is a complete package." Booklist

Taback, Simms

★ There was an old lady who swallowed a fly. Viking 1997 un il $16.99
Grades: K 1 2 3　　　　　　　　　　　　782.42
　1. Folk songs 2. Animals -- Songs
　ISBN 0-670-86939-2
A Caldecott Medal honor book, 1998

Simms Taback's illustrated version of the folk song in which an old lady swallows a variety of progressively larger animals

"Each page is full of details and humorous asides. . . . A die-cut hole allows readers to see inside [the old lady's] belly, first the critters already devoured and, with the turn of the page, the new animal that will join the crowd in her ever-expanding stomach. . . . The text is handwritten on vivid strips of paper that are loosely placed on the patterned page, thus creating a lively interplay between the meaning of the words and their visual power." SLJ

They Might Be Giants (Musical group)

Kids go! [by] They Might Be Giants; illustrations by Pascal Campion. Simon & Schuster 2009 un il $19.99
Grades: K 1 2 3　　　　　　　　　　　　782.42
　1. Songs
　ISBN 978-0-7432-7275-9; 0-7432-7275-7
　　　　　　　　　　　　　　　　LC 2009019668

An illustrated version of the song 'Go, Kid, Go,' exhorting the reader to get up and move around

"With just a hint of retro style about them, Campion's thick and loose black ink lines provide a sense of fluidity in riotous scenes that use a limited but appealing palette of green, gray, and peach, splashed over lots of white space. Befitting the action words in the text, the font size bounces from small to large, adding to the energetic tone. . . . An accompanying DVD features an animated video of the song." Publ Wkly

Vetter, Jennifer Riggs

Down by the station; illustrations by Frank Remkiewicz. Tricycle Press 2009 un il $15.99

Grades: PreK K　　　　　　　　　　　　782.42
　1. Songs 2. Vehicles
　ISBN 978-1-58246-243-1; 1-58246-243-7
　　　　　　　　　　　　　　　　LC 2008011308

This illustrated version of the traditional song expands and describes more vehicles, different locations, and their unique sounds, from puffer-billies to racecars and rockets

"Remkiewicz uses candy-bright colors and a hint of goofy elasticity in his slightly busy watercolor art. With enough repetition to tempt early readers to try the text on their own, the book will also attract the lap-sit crowd." SLJ

Voake, Charlotte

★ Tweedle dee dee; [by] Charlotte Voake. Candlewick Press 2008 un il $16.99
Grades: PreK K 1 2　　　　　　　　　　782.42
　1. Folk songs -- United States
　ISBN 978-0-7636-3797-2; 0-7636-3797-1
　　　　　　　　　　　　　　　　LC 2007040414

Illustrations of a forest in spring and simple text provide a variation on the traditional folk song, "The green leaves grew around"

The pages are "washed with pale green and covered with squiggly line drawings and watercolors. . . . The minimal text invites a read-aloud—and even before arriving at the musical score on the final spread, readers are likely to find themselves singing." Publ Wkly

Weave little stars into my sleep; Native American lullabies. edited by Neil Philip; photographs by Edward S. Curtis. Clarion Bks. 2001 un il $16
Grades: 2 3 4　　　　　　　　　　　　782.42
　1. Lullabies 2. Native American literature
　ISBN 0-618-08856-3
　　　　　　　　　　　　　　　　LC 00-60324

Published in the United Kingdom with title: Where did you fall from?

This is a "book of 15 lullabies, selected, adapted, and, in some cases, reworked from original Native American material. Striking, carefully chosen photographs, originally published in the early 1900s, portray the spirit of the words." Booklist

Includes bibliographical references

Yolen, Jane

★ Apple for the teacher; thirty songs for singing while you work. collected and introduced by Jane Yolen; music arranged by Adam Stemple; art edited by Eileen Michaelis Smiles. Harry N. Abrams 2005 117p il $24.95
Grades: 4 5 6 7　　　　　　　　　　　　782.42
　1. Songs 2. Work -- Songs
　ISBN 0-8109-4825-7
　　　　　　　　　　　　　　　　LC 2004-24404

"Yolen has brought together a collection of 30 work songs . . . which represent a wide variety of occupations. . . . She introduces each job, explaining unusual vocabulary and references in the songs. . . . The artwork . . . is elegant. Ranging from sculpture to paintings to needlework, each selection of Americana has been carefully matched to the occupation, beautifully reproduced on high-quality paper, and meticulously identified." Booklist

Zelinsky, Paul O.

★ Knick-knack paddywhack! a moving parts book. adapted from the counting song and illustrated by Paul O. Zelinsky; paper engineering by Andrew Baron. Dutton 2002 un il $18.99

Grades: K 1 2 3 **782.42**

1. Songs 2. Counting

ISBN 0-525-46908-7

A young boy sets out on a walk—pull the tabs and tiny old men from One to Ten act out the familiar refrain of the traditional counting song on and all around him.

"This glorious title is a paper-engineering and bookmaking marvel as well as a freewheeling romp." SLJ

782.42162 Folk music

Christensen, Bonnie

★ Woody Guthrie, poet of the people. Knopf 2001 un il hardcover o.p. pa $7.99

Grades: 3 4 5 6 **782.42162**

1. Singers 2. Folk musicians 3. Memoirists 4. Songwriters 5. Folk singers -- United States -- Biography

ISBN 0-553-11203-1; 0375811133; 0375911138 lib bdg

LC 00-65504

This book tells "the life story of American songwriter Woody Guthrie. . . . Grades three to six." (Bull Cent Child Books)

"Christensen makes a fine union of a spirited, vibrant text and hand-colored woodcuts that are sinewy and emotionally compelling." Booklist

Hush, little baby; a folk song. with pictures by Marla Frazee. Harcourt Brace & Co. 1999 un il hardcover o.p. pa $7

Grades: K 1 2 **782.42162**

1. Lullabies 2. Folk songs -- United States

ISBN 0-15-201429-2; 0-15-204761-1 pa

LC 98-9608

In an old lullaby a baby is promised an assortment of presents from its adoring parent

"True to the song's Appalachian roots, Frazee sets the traditional lullaby in the hills of West Virginia, with big, detailed pictures that add character and exaggerated sibling rivalry to the nonsense story. . . . The music is on the last page, and Frazee's clear narrative pictures in acrylics and pencil capture the rhythm of the words, the historic particulars of the place, the nighttime farce, and the universal family scenarios of jealousy and love." Booklist

782.421649 Rap

Hill, Laban Carrick

When the beat was born; DJ Kool Herc and the creation of hip hop. Laban Carrick Hill; illustrated by Theodore Taylor III. Roaring Brook Press 2013 32 p. (hardcover) $17.99

Grades: 1 2 3 4 5 **782.421649**

1. Picture books for children 2. Hip-hop culture -- Juvenile literature 3. Disc jockeys -- United States

-- Biography 4. Rap musicians -- United States -- Biography

ISBN 1596435402; 9781596435407

LC 2012029746

Coretta Scott King/John Steptoe New Talent Award (2014)

This children's picture book discusses the origin of hip-hop through the story of DJ Kool Herc. "Young Clive fell in love with music as a child in Jamaica. . . . When he moved to the Bronx, Clive became Kool Herc, and when he had the opportunity to throw his own dance parties, he became DJ Kool Herc. Herc's innovative style as a DJ, stretching the breaks in songs from seconds into minutes, allowed the creativity of others to erupt, such as break dancers, rappers and MCs. Hip-hop was born." (Kirkus Reviews)

782.42165 Jazz

Schroeder, Alan, 1961-

Baby Flo; Florence Mills lights up the stage. by Alan Schroeder; illustrated by Cornelius Van Wright & Ying-Hwa Hu. Lee & Low Books 2012 40 p. (hardcover: alk. paper) $18.95

Grades: 1 2 3 **782.42165**

1. Biography 2. African American singers -- Biography

ISBN 1600604102; 9781600604102

LC 2011036553

This book, by Alan Schroeder, tells the story of "'Baby Florence' Mills [who] was singing and dancing just about as soon as she could talk and walk. . . . Baby Flo went on to become an international superstar during the Harlem Renaissance—but first she had to overcome a case of stage fright and discover that winning wasn't everything. Here is the spirited story of that spunky young girl learning to chase her dreams with confidence." (Publisher's note)

Watson, Renée

★ Harlem's little blackbird; Renee Watson; illustrated by Christian Robinson. 1st ed. Random House Children's Books 2012 1 v. (unpaged) (trade) $17.99

Grades: 2 3 4 **782.42165**

1. African American singers 2. Picture books for children 3. Singers -- New York (State) -- New York -- Biography 4. African American singers -- New York (State) -- New York -- Biography

ISBN 0375869735; 9780375869730; 9780375969737; 9780375985379

LC 2011043314

Author Renée Watson tells the story of "Florence Mills, [who] knew that she was blessed with a gift--a sweet, bird-like singing voice that everyone loved. But she also knew firsthand the profound ache of racism. When she moved to New York City, the stages got bigger, the lights grew brighter, and offers that could make her an international star were hers for the taking. Instead, Florence chose shows that helped promote other black performers. And she sang songs that heralded the call for civil rights." (reneewatson.net)

782.42166   Rock (Rock 'n' roll) songs

Behnke, Alison Marie

Death of a dreamer; the assassination of John Lennon. Alison Marie Behnke. Twenty-First Century Books 2012 96 p.

Grades: 5 6 7 8   782.42166

1. Assassination 2. Rock musicians -- Political activity 3. Rock musicians -- England -- Biography 4. Rock musicians 5. Murder -- New York (State) -- New York 6. Rock musicians -- England -- Biography 7. Murderers -- New York (State) -- Biography

ISBN 0822590360; 9780822590361

LC 2010005550

"Twin narratives converge in New York City on December 8, 1980, when John Lennon was murdered by Mark David Chapman. [Alison Marie] Behnke calls the murder an assassination, and by the general definition of the word—to murder (a usually prominent person) by sudden or secret attack, often for political reasons—the murder of John Lennon might qualify. Lennon was political by the end of his life, writing "Give Peace a Chance," which became the anthem of the peace movement, but he was hardly a revolutionary, as Behnke terms him. Chapman was not especially political, and he didn't really seem to know why he attacked Lennon; it was certainly not from any well-thought-out political motives, as the author herself describes." (Kirkus)

Includes bibliographical references (p. 92), discography (p. 93), filmography (p. 93), and index

Brewer, Paul

The Beatles were fab (and they were funny) by Kathleen Krull and Paul Brewer; illustrated by Stacy Innerst. Harcourt Children's Books 2013 40 p. col. ill. (reinforced) $16.99

Grades: 2 3 4   782.42166

1. Wit and humor 2. Rock musicians -- England -- Biography 3. Beatles -- Juvenile humor 4. Rock musicians -- England -- Juvenile humor

ISBN 054750991X; 9780547509914

LC 2012025483

This book, by Kathleen Krull, Paul Brewer, and illustrated by Stacy Innerst, explores when "the Beatles burst onto the music scene in the early 1960s, . . . their off-the-charts talent and offbeat humor made them the most famous band on both sides of the Atlantic. . . . [This] text and expressive, quirky paintings chronicle the phenomenal rise of Beatlemania, showing how the Fab Four's sense of humor helped the lads weather everything that was thrown their way." (Publisher's note)

783   Music for single voices

Fishkin, Rebecca Love

Singing; a practical guide to pursuing the art. Compass Point Books 2010 48p il (Performing arts) lib bdg $28.65

Grades: 5 6 7 8   783

1. Singing 2. Vocational guidance

ISBN 978-0-7565-4362-4 lib bdg; 0-7565-4362-2 lib bdg

LC 2010012607

This guide on a singing career includes tips on education, technique, and more.

"Meant for students contemplating a career in the field . . . [this book goes] beyond basic introductions and into more detail about what it takes to make it as a professional. . . . [The author maintains] . . . a frank, realistic tone, stressing the importance of hard work and dedication. Great [resource] . . . for those wanting to make their passions more than just a hobby." SLJ

Includes glossary and bibliographical references

Landau, Elaine

Is singing for you? Lerner Publications 2011 40p il (Ready to make music) lib bdg $27.93

Grades: 4 5 6 7   783

1. Singing

ISBN 978-0-7613-5427-7 lib bdg; 0-7613-5427-1 lib bdg

LC 2009052350

Helps readers explore the art of singing. This book covers the basics, including tips for getting started and info on vocal technique.

"Landau covers all the bases so that prospective musicians have the information they need. . . . Kids thinking about taking up an instrument will find . . . [this book] helpful in their decision-making process." SLJ

Includes glossary and bibliographical references

784.19   Instruments

D'Cruz, Anna-Marie

Make your own musical instruments. PowerKids Press 2009 24p il (Do it yourself projects!) lib bdg $23.95; pa $9.40

Grades: 2 3 4   784.19

1. Handicraft 2. Musical instruments

ISBN 978-1-4358-2854-4 lib bdg; 1-4358-2854-2 lib bdg; 978-1-4358-2925-1 pa; 1-4358-2925-5 pa

LC 2008033667

This offers "step-by-step instructions and full-color photos to illustrate the crafts. Projects have a broad cultural representation and are not gender specific. Materials are easily obtained. . . . [Projects include] castanets, bongo drums, and a jazz washboard." SLJ

Includes glossary and bibliographical references

Helsby, Genevieve

★ Those amazing musical instruments; [by] Genevieve Helsby; with Marin Alsop as your guide. Sourcebooks Jabberwocky 2007 176p il $19.95

Grades: 4 5 6 7 8 9   784.19

1. Musical instruments

ISBN 978-1-4022-0825-6; 1-4022-0825-1

LC 2007013821

This is "a guide to instruments commonly found in an orchestra. . . . Utilizing large print; ample, colorful illustrations; and an open format, the book is logically organized into chapters about each of the musical instrument families, including keyboards, the voice, and modern electronic instruments. Throughout, readers are prompted to listen to the accompanying CD-ROM, which features more than 100 musical samples. Information is clearly presented, and the author's enthusiasm for her subject is contagious." SLJ

VanHecke, Susan

★ **Raggin',** jazzin', rockin' a history of American musical instrument makers. Boyds Mills Press 2011 136p il $17.95

Grades: 5 6 7 8 9   **784.19**

1. Musical instruments 2. C. G. Conn Ltd. 3. C. F. Martin & Co. 4. Manufacturing executives 5. Musical instrument makers

ISBN 1-59078-574-6; 978-1-59078-574-4

LC 2010-04877

This is a history of American musical instrument making, including the stories of the Zildjian family's cymbals, Steinway's pianos, Charles Gerard Conn's brass instruments, C. F. Martin's guitars, William F. Ludwig's drums, Hammond keyboards, Fender electric guitars, and Moog synthesizers.

"Musicians and music lovers look no further. [This] is a book for everyone. . . . This is an interesting book." Voice Youth Advocates

Includes bibliographical references

Wiseman, Ann Sayre

Making music; [by] Ann Sayre Wiseman and John Langstaff; illustrations by Ann Sayre Wiseman. Storey Bks. 2003 96p il hardcover o.p. pa $9.95

Grades: 3 4 5 6   **784.19**

1. Handicraft 2. Musical instruments

ISBN 1-58017-513-9; 1-58017-512-0 pa

LC 2003-54218

First published 1979 by Scribner with title: Making musical things

Includes instructions for making a variety of simple musical instruments from ordinary household items

Includes glossary and bibliographical references

784.2 Full orchestra (Symphony orchestra)

Celenza, Anna Harwell

Saint-Saens's Danse Macabre; Anna Harwell Celenza; illustrated by JoAnn E. Kitchel. Charlesbridge 2013 32 p. (reinforced for library use) $19.95

Grades: 2 3 4 5   **784.2**

1. Music 2. Composition (Music) 3. Saint-Saëns, Camille, 1835-1921. Danse Macabre (Symphonic poem) 4. Composers -- France

ISBN 157091348X; 9781570913488

LC 2012024575

This book is the "eighth in [Anna Harwell] Celenza's series of biographies of famous pieces of music, this account opens with an unsettling scene in which composer Camille Saint-Saëns (1835-1921) and his poet friend Henri Cazalis visit the catacombs of Paris at midnight. . . . Inspired by the visit, Saint-Saëns returns home and writes the famous piece." (Publishers Weekly)

Other biographies by this author include:
Bach's Goldberg Variations (2005)
Duke Ellington's Nutcracker Suite (2011)
The Farewell Symphony (2000)
Gershwin's Rhapsody in Blue (2006)
The Heroic Symphony (2004)

Pictures at an Exhibition (2003)
Vivaldi's Four Seasons (2012)

Ganeri, Anita

★ The **young** person's guide to the orchestra; Benjamin Britten's composition on CD narrated by Ben Kingsley. book written by Anita Ganeri. Harcourt Brace & Co. 1996 56p il $25

Grades: 4 5 6 7   **784.2**

1. Orchestra 2. Music appreciation 3. Musical instruments

ISBN 0-15-201304-0

LC 95-41478

"Accompanying this book on orchestral music is a CD featuring Britten's A Young Person's Guide to the Orchestra . . . as well as Dukas' The Sorcerer's Apprentice. The book begins with an overview of the orchestra and then centers around groups of instruments, explaining a bit of their history and their sound's distinctive quality. . . . The book also introduces eight famous composers, world music, Benjamin Britten, and the background of The YoungPerson's Guide to the Orchestra. . . . Handsome and useful." Booklist

Includes glossary

Koscielniak, Bruce

★ The **story** of the incredible orchestra; an introduction to musical instruments and the symphony orchestra. Houghton Mifflin 2000 un il $16; pa $6.95

Grades: 2 3 4   **784.2**

1. Orchestra 2. Musical instruments

ISBN 0-395-96052-5; 0-618-31112-2 pa

LC 98-43933

Describes the orchestra, the families of instruments of which it is made, and the individual instruments in each family

"The illustrations are dense with gentle color and filled with scenes of musicians at play and pictures of instruments, with banner labels adding more information. . . . A lot of information about who invented what and how it's played is packed into these engaging pages." Booklist

784.4 Light orchestra

Brown, Monica

Tito Puente, Mambo King; Tito Puente, Rey del Mambo. by Monica Brown; illustrated by Rafael Lopez; translated by Adriana Dominguez. HarperCollins 2013 32 p. col. ill. (hardcover) $17.99

Grades: 2 3 4   **784.4**

1. Puente, Tito, 1923-2000 2. Salsa musicians -- United States -- Biography

ISBN 0061227838; 9780061227837

LC 2012025493

Pura Belpre Illustrator Honor Book (2014)

This children's picture-book biography of Tito Puente presents a "bilingual tribute to the salsa drummer and band leader extraordinaire. [Monica] Brown's narrative . . . takes her preschool and primary audience from Tito's toddlerhood . . . through childhood loves: drum lessons, dancing and stickball on the streets of Harlem. Bouncing through the musician's adulthood, Brown highlights early gigs, a Navy stint . . . and regular shows at the Palladium in New York City." (Kirkus Reviews)

786.2　Keyboard instruments

Ganeri, Anita
    Pianos and Keyboards. Smart Apple Media 2011 il (How the world makes music)
Grades: 4 5 6　　　　　　　　　　　　　　　　**786.2**
    1. Keyboard instruments
    ISBN 1-599-20479-7; 978-1-599-20479-6
LC 2010052912

Describes various keyboard instruments from around the world, such as the familiar piano and organ, along with other keyboard instruments such as the accordian, harpsichord, and the hurdy-gurdy.

"The text reads smoothly, the layout is attractive. . . . This will be useful for collections serving schools, especially those assigning instrument reports." Booklist

Includes glossary and bibliographical references

Reich, Susanna
    ★ Clara Schumann; piano virtuoso. Clarion Bks. 1999 118p il $18; pa $9.95
Grades: 5 6 7 8　　　　　　　　　　　　　　　**786.2**
    1. Pianists 2. Women composers
    ISBN 0-395-89119-1; 0-618-55160-3 pa
LC 98-24510

Describes the life of the German pianist and composer who made her professional debut at age nine and who devoted her life to music and to her family

"This thoroughly researched book draws on primary sources, both Clara's own diaries and her voluminous correspondence with her husband. . . . Reich's lucid, quietly passionate biography is liberally illustrated with photographs and reproductions." Horn Book Guide

786.8　Percussion instruments

Ganeri, Anita
    Drums and percussion instruments. Smart Apple Media 2011 il (How the world makes music) lib bdg $28.50
Grades: 4 5 6　　　　　　　　　　　　　　　　**786.8**
    1. Percussion instruments
    ISBN 978-1-599-20478-9
LC 2010043356

Describes various percussion instruments from around the world, including current drum kits, orchestral instruments such as the xylophone, and more traditional drums from Africa and Asia.

Includes glossary and bibliographical references

786.9　Drums and devices used for percussive effects

Greenwood, Mark
    Drummer boy of John John; by Mark Greenwood; illustrations by Frané Lessac. Lee & Low 2012 40 p. (hardcover: alk. paper) $18.95

Grades: PreK K 1 2 3　　　　　　　　　　　　**786.9**
    1. Music 2. Biography 3. Musical instruments 4. Steel drum (Musical instrument) 5. Musicians -- Trinidad and Tobago -- Biography
    ISBN 1600606520; 9781600606526
LC 2011045370

In author Mark Greenwood's book, "Carnival is coming, and the villagers of John John, Trinidad, are getting ready to jump up and celebrate with music, dancing, and a parade. Best of all, the Roti King has promised free rotis--tasty fried pancakes filled with chicken, herbs, and spices--for the best band in the parade. . . . With ingenuity and the help of his friends, Winston takes on the Carnival bands, drumming his way to victory--and to the Roti King's prized treat." (Publisher's note)

Landau, Elaine
    Are the drums for you? Lerner Publications 2011 40p il (Ready to make music) lib bdg $27.93
Grades: 4 5 6 7　　　　　　　　　　　　　　**786.9**
    1. Drums 2. Percussion instruments
    ISBN 978-0-7613-5426-0 lib bdg; 0-7613-5426-3 lib bdg
LC 2009-48971

Hear what professional drummers like about their instrument, and learn what skills a good drummer needs.

"Landau covers all the bases so that prospective musicians have the information they need. . . . Kids thinking about taking up an instrument will find . . . [this book] helpful in their decision-making process." SLJ

Includes glossary and bibliographical references

787　Stringed instruments (Chordophones)

Ganeri, Anita
    Stringed instruments. Smart Apple Media 2011 32p il (How the world makes music) lib bdg $28.50
Grades: 4 5 6　　　　　　　　　　　　　　　　**787**
    1. Stringed instruments
    ISBN 978-1-599-20480-2
LC 2010042418

Describes various stringed instruments from around the world including familiar instruments such as the guitar and violin, along with other traditional instruments such as the Japanese Koto and Indian lutes.

787.2　Violins

Landau, Elaine
    Is the violin for you? Lerner Publications 2011 40p il (Ready to make music) lib bdg $27.93
Grades: 4 5 6 7　　　　　　　　　　　　　　**787.2**
    1. Violins
    ISBN 978-0-7613-5423-9 lib bdg; 0-7613-5423-9 lib bdg
LC 2009045609

Hear what professional violinists like about their instrument, and learn what skills a good violinist needs.

"Landau covers all the bases so that prospective musicians have the information they need. . . . Kids thinking about taking up an instrument will find . . . [this book] helpful in their decision-making process." SLJ

Includes glossary and bibliographical references

787.87 Guitars

Blaxland, Wendy

Guitars. Marshall Cavendish Benchmark 2011 32p il map (How are they made?) lib bdg $12.99

Grades: 4 5 6   787.87

1. Guitars

ISBN 978-0-7614-4754-2 lib bdg; 0-7614-4754-7 lib bdg

LC 2009039880

This describes how guitars are made including their history, parts, materials, design, manufacture, packaging and distribution, marketing and advertising, and affect on the environment

"There is a bounty of color photos, including fascinating contructiion shots as well as pics of axe-wielding notables Les Paul, Bruce Springsteen, and Prince." Booklist

Includes glossary

Landau, Elaine

Is the guitar for you? Lerner Publications 2011 40p il (Ready to make music) lib bdg $27.93

Grades: 4 5 6 7   787.87

1. Guitars

ISBN 978-0-7613-5424-6 lib bdg; 0-7613-5424-7 lib bdg

LC 2009-48750

Hear what professional guitarists like about their instrument, and learn what skills a good guitarist needs.

"Landau covers all the bases so that prospective musicians have the information they need. . . . Kids thinking about taking up an instrument will find . . . [this book] helpful in their decision-making process." SLJ

Includes glossary and bibliographical references

788 Wind instruments (Aerophones)

Ganeri, Anita

Brass instruments. Smart Apple Media 2011 il (How the world makes music) lib bdg 28.50

Grades: 4 5 6   788

1. Wind instruments

ISBN 978-1-599-20477-2

LC 2010053889

Describes various brass instruments from around the world, such as the familiar trumpet and trombone, along with historical instruments such as the Alphorn, serpent, and traditional instruments still played today, including the didgeridoo and the dung-chen.

Includes glossary and bibliographical references

Wind instruments. Smart Apple Media 2011 il (How the world makes music) lib bdg $28.50

Grades: 4 5 6   788

1. Wind instruments

ISBN 978-1-599-20482-6

LC 2010042423

Describes various wind instruments from around the world, such as the familiar clarinet, saxophone, and flute, along with other traditional instruments such as the Chinese flute, nose flute, and pan pipes.

Landau, Elaine

Is the flute for you? Lerner Publications 2011 40p il (Ready to make music) lib bdg $27.93

Grades: 4 5 6 7   788

1. Flutes

ISBN 978-0-7613-5420-8 lib bdg; 0-7613-5420-4 lib bdg

LC 2009048970

Hear what professional flutists like about their instrument, and learn what skills a good flutist needs.

"Landau covers all the bases so that prospective musicians have the information they need. . . . Kids thinking about taking up an instrument will find . . . [this book] helpful in their decision-making process." SLJ

Includes glossary and bibliographical references

Is the trumpet for you? Lerner Publications 2011 40p il (Ready to make music) lib bdg $27.93

Grades: 4 5 6 7   788

1. Trumpet

ISBN 978-0-7613-5422-2 lib bdg; 0-7613-5422-0 lib bdg

LC 2009048280

Hear what professional trumpeters like about their instrument, and learn what skills a good trumpeter needs.

"Landau covers all the bases so that prospective musicians have the information they need. . . . Kids thinking about taking up an instrument will find . . . [this book] helpful in their decision-making process." SLJ

Includes glossary and bibliographical references

788.7 Saxophones

Golio, Gary

Spirit seeker; John Coltrane's musical journey. by Gary Golio; paintings by Rudy Gutierrez. Clarion Books 2012 48 p. (hardcover) $17.99

Grades: 3 4 5 6 7   788.7

1. Music and religion 2. Creation (Literary, artistic, etc.) 3. Saxophonists -- United States -- Biography 4. Jazz musicians -- United States -- Biography

ISBN 0547239947; 9780547239941

LC 2011045948

Includes bibliographical references and discography.

This book, by Gary Golio, illustrated by Rudy Gutierrez, explores the musical career of Jazz saxophonist John Coltrane. "Growing up, John was a seeker. He wondered about spirit, and the meaning of life. And whether music could be a key to unlocking those mysteries. . . . This is the story of a shy, curious boy from a deeply religious family who grew up to find solace and inspiration in his own unique approach to both spirituality and music." (Publisher's note)

788.9   Brass instruments (Lip-reed instruments)

Lynette, Rachel

Miles Davis; legendary jazz musician. by Rachel Lynette. KidHaven Press 2010 48 p. ill. (some col.) (hardcover) $29.95

Grades: 5 6 7 8   **788.9**

1. Jazz music   2. Jazz musicians -- United States -- Biography

ISBN 0737750340; 9780737750348

LC 2009045056

This biography of Miles Davis by Rachel Lynette is part of the Innovators series. Lynette "pinpoints the many works in which Davis pushed musical boundaries." She "refrains from mentioning the album Bitches Brew by name, instead offering . . . 'Davis and his band made an album that sold more than . . . any other jazz record ever.'" (Booklist)

Includes bibliographical references and index.

790   Recreational and performing arts

Glenn, Joshua

Unbored; the essential field guide to serious fun. [compiled by] Joshua Glenn & Elizabeth Foy Larsen; design by Tony Leone. Bloomsbury USA 2012 352 p. (hardback) $25

Grades: 5 6 7   **790**

1. Games 2. Amusements 3. Handicraft 4. Recreation

ISBN 1608196410; 9781608196418

LC 2012012368

This activity book by Elizabeth Foy Larsen and Joshua Glen, illustrated by Heather Kasunick and Mister Reusch, "provides kids with information to round out their world view and inspire them to learn more. From how-tos on using the library or writing your representative to a graphic history of video games, the book isn't shy about teaching. Yet the bulk of the 350-page mega-resource presents hands-on activities." (Publisher's note)

790.06   Organizations and management of recreation

Rosen, Michael J.

Let's build a playground; Michael J. Rosen. Candlewick Press 2013 32 p. (reinforced) $15.99

Grades: 2 3 4 5   **790.06**

1. Playgrounds 2. Community development

ISBN 0763655325; 9780763655327

LC 2012943649

This book, by Michael J. Rosen, illustrated by Ellen Kelson and Jennifer Cecil, is part of the "Kaboom! Books" series. It describes how "two hundred kids and grown-ups in an Indianapolis community got together to build the playground in this book--one of over two thousand that KaBOOM! has helped create." (Publisher's note)

790.1   General kinds of recreational activities

Ball, Jacqueline A.

Traveling green. Bearport Pub. 2009 32p il (Going green) lib bdg $25.27

Grades: 4 5 6 7   **790.1**

1. Travel -- Environmental aspects

ISBN 978-1-59716-964-6 lib bdg; 1-59716-964-1 lib bdg

LC 2009-19836

"Color photographs (most full page) and a few diagrams accompany the informative text[s]. . . . Overall, the [book] . . . is user-friendly and covers topics that are not easily found elsewhere." SLJ

Includes glossary and bibliographical references

Bell-Rehwoldt, Sheri

The kids' guide to classic games. Capstone Press 2009 32p il (Kids' guides) lib bdg $23.99

Grades: 4 5 6 7   **790.1**

1. Games

ISBN 978-1-4296-2273-8 lib bdg; 1-4296-2273-3 lib bdg

LC 2008-29686

This provides instructions and rules for indoor and outdoor games such as ping-pong soccer, ringer, paper football, spiderweb, tug-of-war, and pipeline

Includes glossary and bibliographical references

Conner, Bobbi

Unplugged play; no batteries, no plugs, pure fun. illustrations by Amy Patacchiola. Workman Pub. 2007 xxv, 401p il $27.95; pa $16.95

Grades: Adult Professional   **790.1**

1. Play 2. Games

ISBN 978-0-7611-4114-3; 978-0-7611-4390-1 pa

LC 2007-23999

"Conner has compiled more than 710 games and activities sorted by age level. Good old-fashioned play and fun are the motto here with simple props from around the house or just an imagination. The book is separated into three major parts: 'Toddler Play,' 'Preschool Play,' and 'Grade School Play.' Each has a section on solo play, ideas for parent and child, playing with others, and birthday-party activities. Each chapter and section is loaded with ideas and suggestions for simple crafts. There is such a wealth of information in this book." SLJ

Danks, Fiona

Run wild! outdoor games and adventures. [by] Fiona Danks and [phototgraphy by] Jo Schofield. Frances Lincoln 2011 159p il pa $24.95

Grades: 5 6 7 8   **790.1**

1. Games 2. Parties 3. Handicraft 4. Nature study 5. Outdoor life 6. Storytelling

ISBN 978-0-7112-3172-6; 0-7112-3172-9

"This large-format book introduces a cornucopia of ideas for outdoor activities, along with mesmerizing color photos of children and teens creatively enjoying themselves in fields, woods, backyards, and at rivers and beaches. . . . From skimming stones to making leaf masks to whittling walking sticks to following treasure trails, here's an enticing array of ideas for outdoor fun and wilderness discovery." Booklist

Davies, Huw

The **games** book; written by Huw Davies; illustrated by Lisa Jackson. Scholastic 2009 118p il pa $9.99

Grades: 1 2 3 4 5 6   **790.1**

1. Games

ISBN 978-0-545-13403-3 pa; 0-545-13403-X pa

LC 2009004292

"This small book takes a look at the games in simpler times. There are no electronics, batteries, cell phones, or videos involved. They mostly require physical and/or mental action along with the use of an imagination and some sweat, and maybe a little dirt. There are old favorites such as Red Rover and Simon Says as well as Rummy, Hangman, and I Spy. The clear instructions are easy for early readers to follow." SLJ

Ferrer, J. J.

The **art** of stone skipping and other fun old-time games; stoopball, jacks, string games, coin flipping, line baseball, jump rope, and more. by J.J. Ferrer; illustrated by Todd Dakins. Charlesbridge Pub., Inc. 2012 192 p. (paperback) $14.95

Grades: K 1 2 3 4 5 6 7 8 9 10 11 12 Adult   **790.1**

1. Games

ISBN 1936140748; 9781936140749

LC 2012015052

This book, by J. J. Ferrer, offers a "collection of timeless games that guarantees kids a good time- by themselves, with a group of friends, or with family. Includes ball games . . . , card games . . . , sack races, and old favorites such as Duck, Duck, Goose and Red Rover. There is also a chapter for car games. Simple instructions explain the rules, how many people can play, the object of the game, and what you need." (Publisher's note)

Includes bibliographical references and index.

Gillman, Claire

The **kids'** summer fun book; great games, activities, and adventures for the entire family. [by] Claire Gillman & Sam Martin. Barron's 2011 128p il pa $12.99

Grades: 3 4 5 6   **790.1**

1. Games 2. Sports 3. Summer 4. Cooking 5. Handicraft 6. Recreation

ISBN 978-0-7641-4581-0; 0-7641-4581-9

This offers ideas for summer activities such as beach parties, sand castle building, hiking and camping trips, kite flying, snorkeling, croquet, fishing, games, water sports, handicrafts, and cooking.

The **kids'** winter fun book; homespun adventures for family fun. [by] Claire Gillman & Sam Martin. Barron's 2011 128p il pa $12.99

Grades: 3 4 5 6   **790.1**

1. Sports 2. Winter 3. Cooking 4. Amusements 5. Handicraft 6. Recreation 7. Indoor games

ISBN 978-0-7641-4726-5; 0-7641-4726-9

This book "offers a variety of activities, games, crafts, and opportunities for family bonding throughout the winter. Indoor projects include knitting scarves, making a snow globe, and creating an obstacle course. Among the outdoor activities are hiking, winter photography, ice skating, and making a sled; more than a dozen recipes for items like caramel apples and winter stew are also included." Publ Wkly

Goldstone, Bruce

100 ways to celebrate 100 days. Henry Holt and Company 2010 un il $16.99

Grades: K 1 2 3   **790.1**

1. Amusements 2. Recreation

ISBN 978-0-8050-8997-4; 0-8050-8997-7

"Bright color photographs that pop from white backgrounds invite youngsters to celebrate the first 100 days of school by doing things: 'Recycle 100 cans'; 'Walk 100 steps in any direction.' 'Make a snake with 100 beads'; and even mop. Highlighting the ideas shown on each spread is a number line in 100 hues, which are also backgrounds for saying hello in 100 languages. . . . A more clever collection of 100 ideas is hard to imagine. A must-have for schools." SLJ

Hines-Stephens, Sarah

Show off; how to do absolutely everything one step at a time. [by] Sarah Hines Stephens and Bethany Mann. Candlewick Press 2009 224p il $18.99

Grades: 5 6 7 8   **790.1**

1. Amusements 2. Handicraft 3. Recreation

ISBN 978-0-7636-4599-1; 0-7636-4599-0

LC 2009015847

"This lively illustrated activity book delivers concise instructions for a variety of indoor and outdoor activities. Projects include crafts, pranks and magic tricks; ideas for nature exploration; and other purely entertaining feats. . . . The instructions are heavy on graphics and light on detail, making for an eye-catching but potentially frustrating experience. But readers should enjoy the irreverence and variety." Publ Wkly

Regan, Lisa

Games on the move! QEB Pub. 2011 32p il (Games handbook) lib bdg $27.10

Grades: 3 4 5   **790.1**

1. Games

ISBN 978-1-59566-933-9; 1-59566-933-7

LC 2010018098

First published 2010 in the United Kingdom

These travel games "will keep kids occupied and engaged. . . . The games are formatted by degree of difficulty with easier activities at the beginning; almost all of them take up a single page and can be learned by following the three-step directions. Surrounding these explanations are bright illustrations, suggestions for altering the game if there is a solo player or to make it more challenging, and an occasional fact related to the activity." SLJ

Outdoor games! QEB Pub. 2011 32p il (Games handbook) lib bdg $27.10

Grades: 3 4 5   **790.1**

1. Games

ISBN 978-1-59566-934-6; 1-59566-934-5

LC 2010014187

First published 2010 in the United Kingdom

These games "will keep kids occupied and engaged. . . . The games are formatted by degree of difficulty with easier activities at the beginning; almost all of them take up a single page and can be learned by following the three-step directions. Surrounding these explanations are bright illustrations, suggestions for altering the game if there is a solo player or to make it more challenging, and an occasional fact related to the activity." SLJ

Party games. QEB Pub. 2011 32p il (Games handbook) lib bdg $27.10
Grades: 3 4 5   **790.1**
  1. Games 2. Parties
  ISBN 978-1-59566-932-2; 1-59566-932-9
           LC 2010014188
First published 2010 in the United Kingdom
These party games "will keep kids occupied and engaged. . . . The games are formatted by degree of difficulty with easier activities at the beginning; almost all of them take up a single page and can be learned by following the three-step directions. Surrounding these explanations are bright illustrations, suggestions for altering the game if there is a solo player or to make it more challenging, and an occasional fact related to the activity." SLJ

Rowell, Victoria
  Tag, toss & run; 40 classic lawn games. Paul Tukey & Victoria Rowell. Storey Pub. 2012 207 p. (pbk.; alk. paper) $14.95
Grades: Adult Professional   **790.1**
  1. Games 2. Outdoor recreation
  ISBN 1603425608; 9781603425605
           LC 2011049410
This book on "family lawn games" presents a "guide to 40 time-tested favorites -- from classics like capture the flag, croquet, badminton, and bocce to the lesser-known Cherokee marbles, cornhole, and Kubb. The authors offer a quick overview of the basic structure of each game, as well as strategies for playing and tips for creating fun variations." (Publisher's note)
Includes bibliographical references and index.

791   Public performances

Gerstein, Mordicai, 1935-
  ★ The **man** who walked between the towers. Roaring Brook Press 2003 un il $17.95; lib bdg $24.90
Grades: PreK K 1 2 3   **791**
  1. Tightrope walking 2. Aerialists 3. World Trade Center (New York, N.Y.) 4. Biography, Individual 5. World Trade Center (New York, N.Y.)
  ISBN 0-7613-1791-0; 0-7613-2868-8 lib bdg
           LC 2003-9040
Awarded the Caldecott Medal, 2004
A lyrical evocation of Philippe Petit's 1974 tightrope walk between the World Trade Center towers
"The pacing of the narrative is as masterful as the placement and quality of the oil-and-ink paintings. . . . Gerstein captures his subject's incredible determination, profound skill, and sheer joy." SLJ

Lusted, Marcia Amidon
  Entertainment. ABDO Pub. Company 2011 112p il (Inside the industry) $23.95
Grades: 5 6 7 8   **791**
  1. Performing arts -- Vocational guidance
  ISBN 978-1-61714-799-9; 1-61714-799-0
           LC 2010041255

This "well-designed [book describes] a variety of careers in [entertainment]. Because [it helps] readers assess if these positions are suitable for their personality types and backgrounds, the [title is a] good [choice] for career exploration and self-discovery. [It is] also useful for research and reports. . . . Sidebars and full-color photos appear throughout." SLJ
  Includes bibliographical references

791.068   Amusement parks

Rau, Dana Meachen
  Roller coasters. Marshall Cavendish Benchmark 2010 24p il (Surprising science) lib bdg $22.79
Grades: 2 3 4   **791.068**
  1. Roller coasters
  ISBN 978-0-7614-4872-3; 0-7614-4872-1
           LC 2009053722
"Colorfully illustrated with photographs on each page, this . . . will be well received by elementary students and educators." Libr Media Connect
  Includes glossary and bibliographical references

791.3   Circuses

Helfer, Ralph
  The **world's** greatest elephant; illustrated by Ted Lewin. Philomel Books 2006 un il $16.99
Grades: 1 2 3   **791.3**
  1. Circus 2. Elephants
  ISBN 0-399-24190-6
           LC 2005-06490
The true story of the lives and travels of the circus elephant Modoc who travelled widely and experienced dangerous adventures with his owner and trainer Bram Gunterstein.
"The large picture-book format is the typical choice for Lewin's fine watercolors, boldly portraying the dramatic episodes of the elephants life and the story of friendship, separation, and reunion. This bold and heartwarming adventure tale should have wide appeal." SLJ

791.43   Motion pictures

Bliss, John
  Art that moves; animation around the world. Raintree 2011 32p il (Culture in action) lib bdg $29
Grades: 5 6 7 8   **791.43**
  1. Animated films
  ISBN 978-1-4109-3922-7; 1-4109-3922-7
           LC 2009051125
This "is a good choice for children interested in animated movies. Bliss looks at techniques from the early beginnings to modern times and mentions recent film releases such as Cars (2006) and Where the Wild Things Are (2010). . . . [This volume is] quick, interesting, up-to-date . . . with plenty of supportive, captioned, full-color photographs. [It] also [provides] related project suggestions." SLJ
  Includes bibliographical references

Brown, Don

Mack made movies. Roaring Brook Press 2003 un il
$16.95; lib bdg $23.90

Grades: 2 3 4   **791.43**

1. Actors 2. Motion picture directors 3. Motion picture
producers

ISBN 0-7613-1538-1; 0-7613-2504-2 lib bdg

LC 2002-6357

A simple biography of the director whose silent films
immortalized such slapstick clowns as the Keystone Kops,
Charlie Chaplin, Fatty Arbuckle, Mabel Normand, and
Ben Turpin

"sing his inimitable picture-book-biography style,
Brown turns a camera's eye on film pioneer Mack Sennett.
The opening line sets the stage for this witty, fascinating profile of the King of Comedy: "In 1900, twenty-year-old Mack
Sennett was a horse's rear end.""... Especially fine in conveying facial expression, Brown's spare, fluid sketches, softly
washed in sepia and butterscotch tones, cunningly capture
the look of the times...Ingeniously staged and picture perfect, it's Brown's best book yet." Booklist

Cech, John

Imagination and innovation; the story of Weston
Woods. with a foreword by Maurice Sendak. Scholastic
Press 2009 175p il $29.99

Grades: Adult Professional   **791.43**

1. Animated films 2. Weston Woods, Inc. 3. Motion
picture executives

ISBN 978-0-545-08922-7; 0-545-08922-0

LC 2009014207

"This is a fascinating look at Weston Woods and its creator, Morton Schindel. Rich with full-color archival photographs, detailed production notes, animation cels, and first-
person accounts, the book gives readers a personal, behind-
the-scenes look at the man and the studio that has animated
most of the great works of children's literature from the mid-
20th century to the present." SLJ

Cohn, Jessica

Animator. Gareth Stevens Pub. 2010 32p il (Cool
careers: cutting edge) lib bdg $26; pa $8.95

Grades: 4 5 6   **791.43**

1. Vocational guidance 2. Animation (Cinematography)
ISBN 978-1-4339-1953-4 lib bdg; 1-4339-1953-2 lib
bdg; 978-1-4339-2152-0 pa; 1-4339-2152-9 pa

LC 2009002006

Describes the work of an animator.

This title offers "clear, solid information in a large font. .
. . [This] short [book is] packed with relevant, current material." SLJ

Includes glossary and bibliographical references

Hill, Z. B.

Filmmaking & documentaries; Z.B. Hill. Mason
Crest, an imprint of National Highlights 2014 64 p. (Art
today!) (hardback) $23.95

Grades: 5 6 7 8   **791.43**

1. Vocational guidance 2. Motion pictures -- Production
and direction 3. Documentary films -- Production and
direction

ISBN 1422231712; 9781422231678; 9781422231715;
9781422287088

LC 2014011828

In this book, by Z. B. Hill, "[d]iscover the world of filmmaking, including the business behind both Hollywood hits
and small films. Learn how you can get started on a career
behind the camera!" (Publisher's note)

"This entry in the Art Today! series provides students
interested in filmmaking with a solid introductory survey,
including basic definitions of jobs and elements of the industry, a brief history of filmmaking and documentaries, the
all-important business of profitability and funding, and realistic ways to get involved at a beginner's level...Though this
offers more of a broad overview than detailed instruction,
tweens who want to know where to start with filmmaking
will find enough direction here. A "Find Out More" section,
further reading, and a glossary append the text." Booklist

Filmmaking and documentaries

Kinney, Jeff

The wimpy kid movie diary; how Greg Heffley went
Hollywood. Amulet Books 2010 199p il $14.95

Grades: 4 5 6 7   **791.43**

1. Diary of a wimpy kid (Motion picture) 2. Motion
pictures -- Production and direction

ISBN 978-0-8109-9616-8; 0-8109-9616-2

LC 2010001859

"Diary of a Wimpy Kid was made into a movie in 2010.
The process is here chronicled, through text, photos, and illustrations. Many details are included, from the way the actors were chosen to how the moldy cheese was filmed. The
process is explained clearly and will be interesting to new
and seasoned Kid fans and future filmmakers alike." Horn
Book Guide

McDonald, Megan

Judy Moody goes to Hollywood; behind the scenes
with Judy Moody and friends. by Megan McDonald with
Richard Haynes; set photography by Suzanne Tenner. Candlewick Press 2011 144p il map $14.99

Grades: 2 3 4   **791.43**

1. Motion pictures -- Production and direction 2. Judy
Moody and the not bummer summer (Motion picture)

ISBN 978-0-7636-5551-8; 0-7636-5551-1

LC 2011283432

"This behind the scenes look to the 2011 movie Judy
Moody and the NOT Bummer Summer is filled with facts
about the characters and the actors who play them. It also
gives a surprisingly detailed yet accessible view of movie-
making, explaining key elements of everything from set design to lighting." Horn Book Guide

O'Brien, Lisa

Lights, camera, action! making movies and TV from
the inside out. [by] Lisa O'Brien; illustrated by Stephen
MacEachern. 2nd ed.; Maple Tree Press 2007 64p il
$21.95; pa $12.95

Grades: 4 5 6 7   **791.43**

1. Acting 2. Motion pictures -- Production and direction
ISBN 978-1-897066-88-1; 1-897066-88-0; 978-1-
897066-89-8 pa; 1-897066-89-9 pa

First published 1998 by Firefly Books

This book "follows Johnny, a young aspiring actor, as he
auditions for and gets a part in a new movie called The Mists
of Time. Author Lisa O'Brien examines the development
and production of movies from early concept through final
production. Along the way, readers get a guided tour of the

world of acting, from finding an agent, through to 'acting' an audition, to handling the media." Publisher's note

Reynolds, David West

Star wars: incredible cross sections; illustrated by Hans Jenssen & Richard Chasemore. DK Pub. 1998 32p il $19.95

Grades: 4 5 6 7 **791.43**

1. Star Wars films

ISBN 0-7894-3480-6

LC 98-22878

This book "includes diagrams for the Millennium Falcon, T-65 X-wing, Blockade Runner, Tie Fighters, Sandcrawler, and BLT-A4 Y-wing, among others. An elaborate four-page fold-out analyzes the Death Star in minute detail. . . . AT-AT Walkers, AT-STs, snowspeeders, and speeder bikes are also included. Diagrams are surrounded by inserts of fascinating trivia, history, and technical notes." Voice Youth Advocates

791.44 Radio

McCarthy, Meghan

★ **Aliens** are coming! the true account of the 1938 War of the worlds radio broadcast. Knopf 2006 un il $16.95; lib bdg $18.99

Grades: 1 2 3 **791.44**

1. War of the worlds (Radio program)

ISBN 0-375-83518-0; 0-375-93518-5 lib bdg

LC 2005-08941

"In an average American living room of 1938, folks gather around the radio for a night's entertainment, when there's a new bulletin: 'Aliens are coming!' Orson Welles' infamous Halloween trick, his October 30 broadcast of H. G. Wells' War of the Worlds, is greatly excerpted and put together with quirky, imaginative artwork that reinforces the fantasy. . . . Using a 1930's art style, and a palette comprising mostly muted grays and reds, McCarthy evokes an era gone by. . . . This is packed with age-appropriate thrills and scares." Booklist

791.5 Puppetry and toy theaters

D'Cruz, Anna-Marie

Make your own puppets. PowerKids Press 2009 24p il (Do it yourself projects!) lib bdg $23.95; pa $9.40

Grades: 2 3 4 **791.5**

1. Handicraft 2. Puppets and puppet plays

ISBN 978-1-4358-2851-3 lib bdg; 1-4358-2851-8 lib bdg; 978-1-4358-2919-0 pa; 1-4358-2919-0 pa

LC 2008033661

This offers "step-by-step instructions and full-color photos to illustrate the crafts. Projects have a broad cultural representation and are not gender specific. Materials are easily obtained. . . . [Projects include] a Venus flytrap and a Chinese dragon." SLJ

Includes glossary and bibliographical references

Exner, Carol R.

Practical puppetry A-Z; a guide for librarians and teachers. [by] Carol R. Exner. McFarland 2005 267p il pa $39.95

Grades: Adult Professional **791.5**

1. Puppets and puppet plays

ISBN 0-7864-1516-9

LC 2005010590

"Exner presents the art of puppetry as a creative and engaging way to snag the interests of both adults and children. Presented in alphabetical order, approximately 135 entries cover everything from starting a puppetry business to puppetry history to creating numerous kinds of puppets: glove, sponge, life-size, even marionettes. . . . This is an excellent resource for school or public libraries." Booklist

Includes bibliographical references

Kennedy, John E.

★ **Puppet** planet. North Light Books 2006 79p il $16.99

Grades: 4 5 6 7 **791.5**

1. Puppets and puppet plays

ISBN 978-1-58180-794-3; 1-58180-794-5

LC 2005033711

This book offers twelve "puppet projects, each using a variety of techniques, [and] features 'action panels' so readers can see how each puppet comes to life. [It also] Includes staging ideas to play up each project's uniqueness." Publisher's note

Minkel, Walter

★ **How** to do The three bears with two hands; performing with puppets. American Lib. Assn. 2000 154p il pa $28

Grades: Adult Professional **791.5**

1. Children's libraries 2. Puppets and puppet plays

ISBN 0-8389-0756-3

LC 99-28228

This guide to performing puppet plays in libraries offers advice on such topics as voice control and manipulation technique, script writing and adaptation, puppets, stages, scenery and props, and includes five puppet show scripts and stage-building plans

Includes bibliographical references

791.8 Animal performances

Collard III, Sneed B.

The **world** famous Miles City Bucking Horse Sale. Bucking Horse Books 2010 64p il $18

Grades: 5 6 7 8 **791.8**

1. Horses 2. Rodeos 3. Montana

ISBN 0984446001; 9780984446001; 978-0-9844460-0-1; 0-9844460-0-1

"Collard takes readers inside the Miles City [Montana] Bucking Horse Sale, a four-day event that draws visitors from across the country. Started in 1951 as a sale of wild horses, it's evolved into a jamboree of music, rodeo, food, contests, and a parade. . . . Plenty of action-filled color photographs break up the narrative. . . . Handsomely designed, . . . this is a fascinating look at a fresh topic."

"Collard takes readers inside the Miles City [Montana] Bucking Horse Sale, a four-day event that draws visitors from across the country. Started in 1951 as a sale of wild horses, it's evolved into a jamboree of music, rodeo, food, contests, and a parade. . . . Plenty of action-filled color photographs break up the narrative. . . . Handsomely designed, . . . this is a fascinating look at a fresh topic." Booklist

Includes glossary

Grayson, Robert

Performers. Marshall Cavendish Benchmark 2010 64p il (Working animals) lib bdg $28.50

Grades: 4 5 6 7 **791.8**

1. Animals in entertainment
ISBN 978-1-60870-165-0 lib bdg; 1-60870-165-4 lib bdg

LC 2010006893

"Describes the role of animals in movies, sporting events, and various competitions." Publisher's note

Includes glossary and bibliographical references

Laidlaw, Rob

On parade; the hidden world of animals in entertainment. Fitzhenry & Whiteside 2010 55p il $19.95

Grades: 4 5 6 **791.8**

1. Zoos 2. Circus 3. Animal welfare 4. Animals in entertainment
ISBN 978-1-55455-143-9; 1-55455-143-9

This book examines animals at the zoo and circus, animals working in movies and television, violence in the world of performing animals and offers ways to improve conditions and prevent animal abuse.

The author's "clearly argued text; crisp, captioned color photos; and appended list of organizations make this an important source for animal advocates." Booklist

Munro, Roxie

Rodeo; by Roxie Munro. Bright Sky Press 2007 un il $15.95

Grades: PreK K 1 2 **791.8**

1. Rodeos
ISBN 978-1-933979-03-8

LC 2007015245

"Clear, concise text and clever lift-the-flap illustrations capture the action and excitement of a rodeo." SLJ

Schubert, Leda

★ **Ballet** of the elephants; illustrated by Robert Andrew Parker. Roaring Brook Press 2006 un il $17.95

Grades: K 1 2 3 **791.8**

1. Ballet 2. Circus 3. Dancers 4. Composers 5. Elephants 6. Choreographers 7. Circus executives
ISBN 1-59643-075-3

LC 2005-02670

The story of how "Circus polka" a dance of 50 elephants and 50 ballerinas, conceived by John Ringling North, choreographed by George Balanchine to music written by Igor Stravinsky, was created

"Schubert's book tells an astonishing true story. . . . The words are simple and lyrical . . . and the beautiful, freely sketched double-page ink-and-watercolor art celebrates the excitement of the animals' dance." Booklist

792   Stage presentations

Chrisp, Peter

Welcome to the Globe; the story of Shakespeare's theater. written by Peter Chrisp. Dorling Kindersley 2000 48p il (Dorling Kindersley readers) $12.95; pa $3.95

Grades: 1 2 3 **792**

1. Poets 2. Authors 3. Dramatists 4. Globe Theatre (London, England)
ISBN 0-7894-6641-4; 0-7894-6640-6 pa

LC 00-21931

Various characters, including a waterman, an actor, a gallant, and an apple seller, from Shakespeare's London describe the Globe Theatre from their own perspective

"Illustrations and photographs are excellent, showing details of the building and the people." SLJ

Includes glossary

Jacobs, Paul DuBois

★ **Putting** on a play; drama activities for kids. [by] Paul DuBois Jacobs and Jennifer Swender; illustrated by Debra Spina Dixon. Gibbs Smith 2005 64p il pa $9.95

Grades: 2 3 4 **792**

1. Theater -- Production and direction
ISBN 1-58685-767-3

LC 2005011249

"This little book is a powerhouse of information. . . . An excellent beginning resource for any child or group of children interested in theater." SLJ

Kenney, Karen Latchana

Cool costumes; how to stage your very own show. ABDO Pub. Company 2010 32p il (Cool performances) lib bdg $17.95

Grades: 4 5 6 **792**

1. Costume 2. Theater
ISBN 978-1-60453-714-7 lib bdg; 1-60453-714-0 lib bdg

LC 2009-1751

Includes step-by-step instructions on how to create royalty robes, animal ears, baseball T-Shirts and more

"Simple language, colorful page design, and detailed step-by-step photos invite children to gather some easily available household items, apply paint and some imagination, and put on a play—or just play." SLJ

Includes glossary and webliography

Cool makeup; how to stage your very own show. ABDO Pub. Company 2010 32p il (Cool performances) lib bdg $17.95

Grades: 4 5 6 **792**

1. Theatrical makeup
ISBN 978-1-60453-715-4 lib bdg; 1-60453-715-9 lib bdg

LC 2009-1752

Offers instructions and step-by-step pictures to reveal how theatrical makeup can create the illusion of facial hair, bruises and wounds, animals, skeletons, or old age.

"Simple language, colorful page design, and detailed step-by-step photos invite children to gather some easily available household items, apply paint and some imagination, and put on a play—or just play." SLJ

Includes glossary and webliography

Cool productions; how to stage your very own show. ABDO Pub. Co. 2010 32p il (Cool performances) lib bdg $17.95

Grades: 4 5 6 **792**

1. Theater -- Production and direction

ISBN 978-1-60453-716-1 lib bdg; 1-60453-716-7 lib bdg

LC 2009-405

Includes step-by-step instructions on how to make flyers, tickets, programs and more

"Simple language, colorful page design, and detailed step-by-step photos invite children to gather some easily available household items, apply paint and some imagination, and put on a play—or just play." SLJ

Includes glossary

Cool scripts & acting; how to stage your very own show. ABDO Pub. Company 2010 32p il (Cool performances) lib bdg $17.95

Grades: 4 5 6 **792**

1. Acting 2. Drama -- Technique 3. Theater -- Production and direction

ISBN 978-1-60453-717-8 lib bdg; 1-60453-717-5 lib bdg

LC 2009-406

Includes step-by-step instructions on how to write a script, use stage directions, play acting games and more

"Simple language, colorful page design, and detailed step-by-step photos invite children to gather some easily available household items, apply paint and some imagination, and put on a play." SLJ

Includes glossary

Cool sets & props; how to stage your very own show. ABDO Pub. Company 2010 32p il (Cool performances) lib bdg $17.95

Grades: 4 5 6 **792**

1. Theaters -- Stage setting and scenery

ISBN 978-1-60453-718-5 lib bdg; 1-60453-718-3 lib bdg

LC 2009-408

"This volume focuses on the primarily cardboard and paper objects that motivated youngsters can turn into backdrops, set pieces, and props. Photo examples set the bar high (though many are achievable), and the text breaks down the creation process into bite-size chunks. It's fairly challenging stuff, but the information is metered out so efficiently that patience, not artistic ability, will be the key to success." Booklist

Includes glossary and webliography

Cool special effects; how to stage your very own show. ABDO Pub. Company 2010 32p il (Cool performances) lib bdg $17.95

Grades: 4 5 6 **792**

1. Stage lighting 2. Theaters -- Stage setting and scenery

ISBN 978-1-60453-719-2 lib bdg; 1-60453-719-1 lib bdg

LC 2009-1753

Offers instructions on creating special effects for a theatrical production, including information on different light effects, keeping a prompt book, and recording your own sound effects

"Simple language, colorful page design, and detailed step-by-step photos invite children to gather some easily available household items, apply paint and some imagination, and put on a play—or just play." SLJ

Includes glossary and webliography

McLean, Dirk

Curtain up! a book for young performers. illustrated by France Brassard. Tundra Books 2010 un il $17.95

Grades: K 1 2 3 **792**

1. Theater -- Fiction

ISBN 978-0-88776-899-6; 0-88776-899-7

"This brief, straightforward depiction of a young girl's theatrical experiences provides a realistic and accurate glimpse into the art. Amaya's dream is to be on the stage, and her mother has been helping her with her memorization and articulation. She auditions for a musical and is chosen to play the lead in a professional play. . . . The realistic illustrations are done in a pastel palette and bring the personalities of the characters to life." SLJ

Schumacher, Thomas L.

How does the show go on? an introduction to the theater. by Thomas Schumacher with Jeff Kurtti. 2nd ed; Disney 2008 128p il $22.95

Grades: 4 5 6 7 **792**

1. Theater

ISBN 978-1-4231-2031-5; 1-4231-2031-0

"Filled with lavish color photos of Disney theater productions, this eye-catching volume has clever chapter titles, beginning with 'Overture,' which tells about 'styles of theaters' and 'kinds of shows.' In 'Act One' and 'Act Two,' aspects of the front and back of the house are discussed, including the marquee, the box office, props, special effects, and so on. Interspersed throughout the facts and photos are 'Stage Notes,' where bits of trivia are doled out." SLJ

Skog, Jason

Acting; a practical guide to pursuing the art. Compass Point Books 2010 48p il (Performing arts) lib bdg $28.65

Grades: 5 6 7 8 **792**

1. Acting 2. Vocational guidance

ISBN 978-0-7565-4364-8 lib bdg; 0-7565-4364-9 lib bdg

LC 2010012604

A guide for those interested in a career in acting, and includes tips on education, technique, and more.

"Meant for students contemplating a career in the field . . . [this book goes] beyond basic introductions and into more detail about what it takes to make it as a professional. . . . [The author maintains] . . . a frank, realistic tone, stressing the importance of hard work and dedication. Great [resource] . . . for those wanting to make their passions more than just a hobby." SLJ

Includes glossary and bibliographical references

Underwood, Deborah

Staging a play. Raintree 2009 32p il (Culture in action) $28.21; pa $7.99

Grades: 5 6 7 8　　　　　**792**
1. Theater -- Production and direction
ISBN 978-1-4109-3396-6; 1-4109-3396-2; 978-1-4109-3413-0 pa; 1-4109-3413-6 pa
　　　　　LC 2009000417
This "discusses the various professionals involved in a production, such as actors, costume designers, prop masters, and stage handlers. Well organized and with bright, colorful photography, [this] introductory [title gives] readers good basic knowledge." SLJ
Includes glossary and bibliographical references

792.09　Stage presentations -- History, geographic treatment, biography

Aliki
　★ **William** Shakespeare & the Globe; written & illustrated by Aliki. HarperCollins Pubs. 1999 48p il hardcover o.p. pa $6.99
Grades: 4 5 6 7 8 9　　　　　**792.09**
1. Poets 2. Authors 3. Dramatists 4. Globe Theatre (London, England) 5. Shakespeare's Globe (London, England)
ISBN 0-06-027820-X; 0-06-443722-1 pa
　　　　　LC 98-7903
"A logically organized and engaging text, plenty of detailed illustrations with informative captions, and a clean design provide a fine introduction to both bard and theater." Horn Book Guide

792.6　Musical plays

Amendola, Dana
　A **day** at the New Amsterdam Theatre; photos by Gino Domenico; written by Dana Amendola. Disney Editions 2004 125p il $24.95
Grades: 4 5 6 7　　　　　**792.6**
1. Theater 2. New Amsterdam Theatre (New York, N.Y.)
ISBN 0-7868-5438-3
"This title covers a day in the life of Disney's The Lion King, the long-running Broadway musical. . . . A clock in a corner of each spread guides readers through the day as box-office personnel, makeup designers, dancers, actors, cleaning staff, and others do their jobs. Each spread includes several full-color photos that are often gritty, sometimes glamorous. . . . This unique volume provides an honest, realistic, eye-opening look at the behind-the-scenes work that goes into the running of a Broadway show." SLJ

792.7　Variety shows and theatrical dancing

Dillon, Leo
　★ **Rap** a tap tap; here's Bojangles--think of that! [by] Leo & Diane Dillon. Blue Sky Press (NY) 2002 un il $15.95
Grades: PreK K 1 2 3　　　　　**792.7**
1. Actors 2. Tap dancing 3. Stories in rhyme 4.

African Americans 5. Tap dancers
ISBN 0-590-47883-4
　　　　　LC 2001-43896
In illustrations and rhyme describes the dancing of Bill "Bojangles" Robinson, one of the most famous tap dancers of all time
　"The spreads feature a bouncy text and eye-catching art. . . . The paintings have the effect of collage and employ strong city shapes, with bridges, buildings, and park benches pressed against feather-white backgrounds." Booklist

792.8　Ballet and modern dance

Augustyn, Frank
　★ **Footnotes**; dancing the world's best-loved ballets. [by] Frank Augustyn and Shelley Tanaka. Millbrook Press 2001 94p il $17.95
Grades: 5 6 7 8　　　　　**792.8**
1. Ballet
ISBN 0-7613-1646-9
　　　　　LC 00-50075
"Footnotes uses seven classical ballets as a jumping-off point to talk about the evolution of this unique art form, partnering, dancer as actor, training, costumes, choreography, and some of the world's most well-known performers." SLJ

Collins, Pat Lowery
　I am a dancer; by Pat Lowery Collins; illustrated by Mark Graham. Millbrook Press 2008 un il lib bdg $22.60
Grades: PreK K 1 2 3　　　　　**792.8**
1. Dance
ISBN 978-0-8225-6369-3 lib bdg; 0-8225-6369-X lib bdg
　　　　　LC 2007021885
"This book shows girls and boys in various movements that can be defined as dance steps. . . . Graham's beautiful oil paintings are filled with solidly built children on the move, while some of the backgrounds are almost ethereal. Even the brushstrokes convey action. This book is a lovely merging of art and poetry and gives a delightful sense of joyful motion." SLJ

Friedman, Lise
　Becoming a ballerina; a nutcracker story. by Lise Friedman; photographs by Mary Dowdle. Penguin Group 2012 44 p. (hardcover) $18.99
Grades: 4 5 6　　　　　**792.8**
1. Ballet 2. Athletes 3. Picture books for children 4. Ballerinas
ISBN 0670013927; 9780670013920
　　　　　LC 2012000867
This book follows "13-year-old Fiona, a real-life fledgling ballerina, on her journey from hopeful auditionee to starring performer as Clara in the Boston Ballet's production of 'The Nutcracker.' . . . Fiona talks about her aches and pains ('Sometimes hurt so much that I want to cry'), her sacrifices ('I miss going to birthday parties and the movies, being in school talent shows, sleepovers--normal stuff'), [and] the fierce competition." (Publishers Weekly)

Gladstone, Valerie

A **young** dancer; the life of an Ailey student. photographs by Jose Ivey. Henry Holt and Co. 2009 un il $18.95

Grades: 1 2 3 4   **792.8**

1. Ballet 2. African American dancers 3. Alvin Ailey American Dance Theater

ISBN 978-0-8050-8233-3; 0-8050-8233-6

LC 2008-18343

"This book about a 13-year-old African American dancer . . . combines strong color photos and lively first-person text. Iman Bright is a student at New York City's Ailey School, founded by the late Alvin Ailey. . . . A wide range of readers will find inspiration in Iman's dedication and in her joyful approach to her discipline." Booklist

Goodman, Joan E.

Ballet bunnies; written and illustrated by Joan Elizabeth Goodman. Marshall Cavendish 2008 un il $14.99

Grades: K 1 2   **792.8**

1. Ballet

ISBN 978-0-7614-5392-5; 0-7614-5392-X

LC 2007-11907

This ballet primer demonstrates basic technique in ballet, from warm-ups to the barre to the hop, skip, twirl, and wiggle fun of centerwork.

"The simply drawn acrylic illustrations show the boys and girls demonstrating positions, and the easy-to-understand text gives further guidance. . . . This is a gentle introduction." SLJ

Includes glossary

Greenberg, Jan

★ **Ballet** for Martha; making Appalachian Spring. [by] Jan Greenberg and Sandra Jordan; illustrated by Brian Floca. Flash Point 2010 48p il $17.99

Grades: 2 3 4   **792.8**

1. Ballet 2. Artists 3. Dancers 4. Composers 5. Sculptors 6. American music 7. Choreographers

ISBN 978-1-59643-338-0; 1-59643-338-8

Robert F. Sibert Medal honor book, 2011

Tells the story behind the creation of "Appalachian Spring," describing Aaron Copland's composition and Martha Graham's intense choreography.

"Matching the mood of Graham's moves, the writing is pared down but full of possibilities. Floca's ink-and-watercolor artwork nimbly shifts from the prosaic . . . to the visionary . . . to the several-spread finale of the ballet itself. The book as a whole beautifully captures the process of artistic creation." Booklist

Isadora, Rachel

★ **Lili** at ballet. Putnam 1993 un il hardcover o.p. pa $6.99

Grades: PreK K 1 2   **792.8**

1. Ballet -- Fiction

ISBN 0-399-22423-8; 0-698-11408-6 pa

LC 92-8429

Lili dreams of becoming a ballerina and goes to her ballet lessons four afternoons a week

"Isadora uses pastel shades of purple, pink, green, and blue with bold splashes of black. This is a prettily illustrated book that captures the magic and hard work involved in ballet." SLJ

Other titles about Lili are:

Lili backstage (1997)

Lili on stage (1995)

Kupesic, Rajka

The **white** ballets. Tundra Books 2011 40p il $19.95

Grades: 4 5 6 7   **792.8**

1. Ballet -- Stories, plots, etc.

ISBN 978-0-88776-923-8; 0-88776-923-3

This retells the stories of Swan Lake, Giselle, and La Bayadère and includes information and comments on the three ballets.

"The tales are well told, and the author, a former ballerina, provides information on the history of the ballet. Each painting in gold leaf and oil represents a scene from one of the ballets. The richly colored illustrations are very stylized with graceful figures dressed in flowing, romantic costumes, and Kupesic elaborates on the details, symbols, and characters in her artwork. . . . For ballet enthusiasts this is a unique look at these classics." SLJ

Marsico, Katie

Choreographer. Cherry Lake Pub. 2011 32p il (Cool arts careers) lib bdg $18.95

Grades: 4 5 6 7   **792.8**

1. Dance 2. Choreographers 3. Vocational guidance

ISBN 978-1-61080-136-2; 1-61080-136-9

LC 2011001170

"Illustrated with color photos of the famous, the young, and the fabulously festooned, this is a sturdy presentation of facts and case studies that will bring the process of professional choreography home to those students considering such a competitive and demanding career." Booklist

Includes bibliographical references

Mellow, Mary Kate

Ballet for beginners; featuring the School of American Ballet. by Mary Kate Mellow and Stephanie Troeller. Imagine! 2010 80p il $14.95

Grades: 3 4 5 6   **792.8**

1. Ballet

ISBN 978-1-936140-01-5; 1-936140-01-2

"The education of a dancer's body and mind is a long and complicated process, and this book tells that story with a lighthearted grace and brio." SLJ

Miles, Lisa

Ballet spectacular; a young ballet lover's guide and an insight into a magical world. Lisa Miles. Barrons Educational Series, Inc. 2014 80 p. color illustrations $18.99

Grades: 4 5 6 7 8   **792.8**

1. Ballet 2. Ballet dancers 3. Royal Ballet

ISBN 0764167456; 9780764167454

LC 2014940905

Author Lisa Miles presents this "reference volume for children who love ballet. Featuring stunning full-color photos from The Royal Ballet's own collections and informative, fact-filled entries, it covers all things dance. Most intriguing to passionate young lovers of dance will be the exploration of a day in the life of a professional ballet dancer, images of beloved performers such as Margot Fonteyn, Darcey Bussell, and Carlos Acosta, detailed close-ups of costumes, and photos." (Publisher's note)

"Combining aspects of a coffee-table book and an introductory handbook, it provides a hodgepodge of basic information about ballet history, famous ballets, life in a major company, and the elements involved in a performance, such as choreography, music, sets, and costumes, while Britain's Royal Ballet Company and School are referenced throughout the book." Booklist

Nelson, Marilyn

Beautiful ballerina; photographs by Susan Kuklin. Scholastic Press 2009 un il $17.99

Grades: PreK K 1 2   **792.8**

    1. Ballet 2. African American dancers

    ISBN 978-0-545-08920-3; 0-545-08920-4

LC 2009009135

"The description 'poetry in motion' may be taken quite literally in this paean to the young dancers who train at the Dance Theatre of Harlem. The heartfelt poem's playful words could make a lively read-aloud dance-along, and young balletomanes will be intrigued by the girls in the photographs. The phrase 'Beautiful ballerina, you are the dance' is repeated throughout and invites audience participation." SLJ

Relota, Agatha

Carla and Leo's world of dance; illustrations by Thierry Perez. Thames & Hudson 2011 il $19.95

Grades: 3 4 5 6   **792.8**

    1. Dance

    ISBN 978-0-500-51560-0; 0-500-51560-3

"Ten-year-old Carla and her friend, Leo, sign up for ballroom-dance classes. As they learn the Viennese waltz, foxtrot, swing, merengue, mambo, cha-cha, rumba, salsa, and tango, their teacher offers information on the history and culture of these dances. The format has a comic-book, poster-art style with the print highlighted in rectangular colored shapes. The bold, linear illustrations of the dancers fill the pages as Carla and Leo demonstrate the steps with grace and zest. . . . This is not a how-to manual but a celebration and introduction to the diverse dances. The enthusiasm of these two characters is infectious, and the slick artwork captures the elegance and drama of these movements and makes them look like lots of fun." SLJ

Thompson, Lauren

★ Ballerina dreams; a true story. by Lauren Thompson; photographs by James Estrin. Feiwel & Friends 2007 un il $16.95

Grades: PreK K 1 2   **792.8**

    1. Ballet 2. Cerebral palsy

    ISBN 978-0-312-37029-6; 0-312-37029-6

LC 2006036338

"Five adorable little girls are given the opportunity to learn to dance like ballerinas and eventually perform on stage. This is no small accomplishment since the girls have cerebral palsy and other muscle disorders and several wear leg braces. . . . This is an inspiring portrayal of determination and love that will foster empathy among young readers. The colorful photographs of this dancing community working toward a common goal accurately and sensitively capture the struggles and joyful enthusiasm of all of the participants." SLJ

Troupe, Thomas Kingsley

If I were a ballerina; illustrated by Heather Heyworth. Picture Window Books 2010 24p il (Dream big) lib bdg $25.32; pa $7.95

Grades: K 1 2 3   **792.8**

    1. Ballet

    ISBN 978-1-4048-5532-8 lib bdg; 1-4048-5532-7 lib bdg; 978-1-4048-5706-3 pa; 1-4048-5706-0 pa

LC 2009-3295

This "begins with a small girl who imagines herself as a star onstage, dancing to beautiful music played by a glorious orchestra. Then the story tracks back to imagined ballet classes, where she envisions the pointed shoes she would wear and the barre exercises she would do with the other dancers before practicing at home. The simple, first-person narrative and clear, digitally enhanced color drawings partner well together, and even young preschoolers will enjoy the fun blend of the fantasy . . . and facts, including ballet's five basic positions." Booklist

Includes glossary

Vaughan, Carolyn

Invitation to ballet; by Carolyn Vaughan; works of art by Edgar Degas; illustrated by Rachel Isadora. Abrams Books for Young Readers 2012 31 p. col. ill. $16.95

Grades: 2 3 4   **792.8**

    1. Dance in art 2. Ballet dancers 3. Artists -- Biography 4. Ballet 5. Ballet in art

    ISBN 1419702602; 9781419702600

LC 2011019046

The author Carolyn Vaughan presents provides a book "with a brief history of ballet and a biography of . . . French impressionist Edgar Degas. . . . [Vaughan explains] what happens in ballet class [to young children]. . . . [Illustrations show] modern-day girls and boys practicing ballet positions, [dances,] and steps . . . [and] works of art by . . . Degas." (Publisher's note)

792.9 Stage productions

Cox, Carole

Shakespeare kids; performing his plays, speaking his words. Libraries Unlimited 2010 xx, 126p il pa $30

Grades: Adult Professional   **792.9**

    1. Poets 2. Authors 3. Dramatists 4. Theater -- Production and direction

    ISBN 978-1-59158-838-2 pa; 1-59158-838-3 pa

LC 2009041731

This is a "a practical guide for performing Shakespeare's plays, albeit in condensed form, without changing his poetic dialogue. . . . Cox gears her work to teachers of students in grades 3-8, librarians, or adults leading recreational programs, providing precise, detailed instructions on all facets of youth-oriented Shakespearean play production. . . . The text is clear and concise . . . Black-and-white photos capture specific moments that illustrate the performers' enthusiasm." SLJ

Includes bibliographical references

793   Indoor games and amusements

Gunter, Veronika Alice

★ The **ultimate** indoor games book; the 200 best boredom busters ever! [by] Veronika Alice Gunter. Lark Books 2005 128p il hardcover o.p. pa $7.95

Grades: 3 4 5 6   **793**

1. Indoor games

ISBN 1-57990-625-7; 1-60059-198-1 pa

LC 2005006054

"This compilation of brain games, ball games, pen-and-paper games, etc., provides a good supply of ideas that will appeal to most any player in a variety of circumstances. The activities are suitable for individuals or two or more players. Most of the suggestions require little or no equipment." SLJ

King, Bart

Bart's king-sized book of fun. Gibbs Smith 2010 304p pa $19.99

Grades: 4 5 6   **793**

1. Amusements

ISBN 978-1-4236-0641-3; 1-4236-0641-8

LC 2010011438

"This is a lively and entertaining collection of tricks, jokes, facts, recipes, games, pranks, wordplay, and all-around fun. Inventions include airbag pants, a disco ball made from old CDs, and a remote-control pumpkin. Creative costume ideas include a piñata, an alien, chewed gum, a shooting star, and more. . . . An activity book extraordinaire for cool kids everywhere." SLJ

Includes bibliographical references

Regan, Lisa

Indoor games! QEB Pub. 2011 32p il (Games handbook) lib bdg $27.10

Grades: 3 4 5   **793**

1. Indoor games

ISBN 978-1-59566-931-5; 1-59566-931-0

LC 2010014139

First published 2010 in the United Kingdom

These indoor games "will keep kids occupied and engaged. . . . The games are formatted by degree of difficulty with easier activities at the beginning; almost all of them take up a single page and can be learned by following the three-step directions. Surrounding these explanations are bright illustrations, suggestions for altering the game if there is a solo player or to make it more challenging, and an occasional fact related to the activity." SLJ

793.2   Parties and entertainments

Guillain, Charlotte

My first sleepover. Heinemann Library 2011 24p il (Growing up) lib bdg $22; pa $6.49

Grades: PreK K 1 2   **793.2**

1. Sleepovers

ISBN 978-1-4329-4802-3 lib bdg; 1-4329-4802-4 lib bdg; 978-1-4329-4812-2 pa; 1-4329-4812-1 pa

LC 2010024196

This book examines a "common, often scary [event] in children's lives and [guides] readers through [it] step-by-step. The [author discusses] the who, what, and why of [the]

experience . . . . By confronting . . . fears head-on, children will feel 'in the know' and be prepared to experience [this first]. The text—two sentences per page in a large font and placed on white space—is accompanied by large color photos of children, families, and adults of a variety of ethnic backgrounds. [The] volume includes boldface vocabulary words, a picture glossary, and dos and don'ts." SLJ

Includes glossary and bibliographical references

Kenney, Karen Latchana

Cool family parties; perfect party planning for kids. Abdo Pub. 2011 il (Cool parties) lib bdg $27.07

Grades: 3 4 5 6   **793.2**

1. Parties

ISBN 978-1-61714-973-3; 1-61714-973-X

LC 2011003503

This book about family parties "has a lot of child appeal. The vivid photos and well-organized and readable content provide great springboards for party ideas. . . . Step-by-step crafts, sample menus, and easy-to-replicate games and activities add to the fun." SLJ

Cool holiday parties; perfect party planning for kids. Abdo Pub. Co. 2011 il (Cool parties) lib bdg $27.07

Grades: 3 4 5 6   **793.2**

1. Parties 2. Holidays

ISBN 978-1-61714-974-0; 1-61714-974-8

LC 2011003504

This book about holiday parties "has a lot of child appeal. The vivid photos and well-organized and readable content provide great springboards for party ideas. . . . Step-by-step crafts, sample menus, and easy-to-replicate games and activities add to the fun." SLJ

Cool international parties; perfect party planning for kids. ABDO Pub. Co. 2011 il (Cool parties) lib bdg $27.07

Grades: 3 4 5 6   **793.2**

1. Parties

ISBN 978-1-61714-975-7

LC 2011003498

This book about international parties "has a lot of child appeal. The vivid photos and well-organized and readable content provide great springboards for party ideas. . . . Step-by-step crafts, sample menus, and easy-to-replicate games and activities add to the fun." SLJ

Includes glossary and bibliographical references

Cool slumber parties; perfect party planning for kids. ABDO Pub. Co. 2011 il (Cool parties) lib bdg $27.07

Grades: 3 4 5 6   **793.2**

1. Parties 2. Sleepovers

ISBN 978-1-61714-976-4; 1-61714-976-4

LC 2011004213

This book about slumber parties "has a lot of child appeal. The vivid photos and well-organized and readable content provide great springboards for party ideas. . . . Step-by-step crafts, sample menus, and easy-to-replicate games and activities add to the fun." SLJ

Cool sports parties; perfect party planning for kids. Abdo Pub. Co. 2012 il (Cool parties) lib bdg $27.07

Grades: 3 4 5 6 **793.2**
1. Sports 2. Parties
ISBN 978-1-61714-977-1; 1-61714-977-2
LC 2011004214

This book about sports parties "has a lot of child appeal. The vivid photos and well-organized and readable content provide great springboards for party ideas. . . . Step-by-step crafts, sample menus, and easy-to-replicate games and activities add to the fun." SLJ

Cool theme parties; perfect party planning for kids. ABDO Pub. Co. 2011 il (Cool parties) lib bdg $27.07
Grades: 3 4 5 6 **793.2**
1. Parties
ISBN 978-1-61714-978-8; 1-61714-978-0
LC 2011004215

This book about theme parties "has a lot of child appeal. The vivid photos and well-organized and readable content provide great springboards for party ideas. . . . Step-by-step crafts, sample menus, and easy-to-replicate games and activities add to the fun." SLJ

McGillian, Jamie Kyle
Sleepover party! games and giggles for a fun night. [by] Jamie Kyle McGillian. Sterling Pub. 2007 95p il $14.95
Grades: 3 4 5 6 **793.2**
1. Parties
ISBN 978-1-4027-2978-2; 1-4027-2978-2
LC 2006029509

"An attractive, girl-friendly compendium of party-planning ideas. All of the basics are covered, such as house rules, what to make/buy, 'Top 10 Things to Get Straight before the Party,' invitations, menus, music, and more. . . . Dozens of indoor and outdoor games . . . and craft ideas are briefly described. The chapter on food includes snacks, dinners, desserts, breakfasts, and goodie-bag ideas." SLJ

Ross, Kathy
The **best** birthday parties ever! a kid's do-it-yourself guide. art by Sharon Lane Holm. Millbrook Press 1999 78p il lib bdg $24.90; pa $9.95
Grades: 2 3 4 **793.2**
1. Games 2. Parties 3. Birthdays 4. Handicraft
ISBN 0-7613-1410-5 lib bdg; 0-7613-0989-6 pa
LC 98-27503

Provides instructions for the invitations, games, crafts, table decorations, and cakes for a dozen birthday parties based on such themes as outer space, puppets, and dinosaurs

"The book is appealing. The illustrations are colorful and plentiful." SLJ

793.3 Social, folk, national dancing

Ancona, George
★ **Capoeira**; game! dance! martial art! [by] George Ancona. Lee & Low Books 2007 un il $18.95
Grades: 3 4 5 6 **793.3**
1. Capoeira (Dance)
ISBN 978-1-58430-268-1
LC 2006028866

This offers "uncomplicated words and engaging, step-by-step photographs of young capoeristas in action. . . . Ancona's . . . enthusiasm and awe for his subject is contagious." Booklist

Includes glossary and bibliographical references

★ **Ole!** Flamenco. Lee & Low 2010 un il map $19.95
Grades: 5 6 7 8 **793.3**
1. Flamenco
ISBN 978-1-60060-361-7; 1-60060-361-0
LC 2010-22272

Ancona tells "the story of flamenco, an art form that's more than dancing and has been around for hundreds of years. He begins with a short introduction that chronicles his visit to Spain. . . . He then returns readers to Santa Fe, New Mexico, where a group of young people are learning flamenco. A helpful map traces the art form's roots, while the text explains both the history of the Gypsies and flamenco. Full-color photographs capture the excitement and dazzle. . . . All aspects of flamenco are explored, including movements, facial expressions, and sound effects." Booklist

Includes glossary and bibliographical references

Fishkin, Rebecca Love
Dance; a practical guide to pursuing the art. content adviser, Hannah Seidel and Chris Ferris and dancers; reading adviser, Alexa L. Sandmann. Compass Point Books 2011 48p il (Performing arts) lib bdg $28.65
Grades: 5 6 7 8 **793.3**
1. Dance 2. Vocational guidance
ISBN 978-0-7565-4363-1 lib bdg; 0-7565-4363-0 lib bdg
LC 2010012605

This guide about a career in dance includes tips on education, technique, and more.

"Meant for students contemplating a career in the field . . . [this book goes] beyond basic introductions and into more detail about what it takes to make it as a professional. . . . [The author maintains] . . . a frank, realistic tone, stressing the importance of hard work and dedication. Great [resource] . . . for those wanting to make their passions more than just a hobby." SLJ

Includes glossary and bibliographical references

Garofoli, Wendy
Hip-hop dancing. Capstone Press 2011 4v il lib bdg ea $30.65
Grades: 4 5 6 **793.3**
1. Dance 2. Hip-hop
ISBN 978-1-4296-5484-5 v1; 1-4296-5484-5 v1; 978-1-4296-5485-2 v2; 1-4296-5485-6 v2; 978-1-4296-5486-9 v3; 1-4296-5486-9 v3; 978-1-4296-5487-6 v4; 1-4296-5487-2 v4
LC 2010030394

Provides instructions for joining or starting a hip-hop dance crew, and includes information about real-life crews.

"These volumes cover the basic moves as well as more detailed movements often seen on television programs. . . . Everything about the set is jazzy and current. Sentences are short and direct, with a small-sized font detailing step-by-step instructions and fact boxes extending the information." Booklist

Includes bibliographical references

Haney, Johannah

Capoeira. Marshall Cavendish Benchmark 2011 47p il (Martial arts in action) $29.93

Grades: 4 5 6 7　　　　　　　　　　**793.3**

1. Capoeira (Dance)

ISBN 978-0-7614-4932-4; 978-1-6087-0362-3 e-book

LC 2010013829

This describes the history, equipment, and technique of capoeira.

This treats "martial arts with the dignity that serious enthusiasts bring to the sport. . . . Illustrations include not only photos of modern gear and from films but also historical images." Booklist

Keeler, Patricia A.

★ **Drumbeat** in our feet. Lee & Low 2006 un il $16.95

Grades: 3 4 5　　　　　　　　　　**793.3**

1. Dance -- Africa

ISBN 1-58430-264-X

This "book opens with a concise overview of the origins of African dance traditions that highlights the diversity of African peoples, cultures, and landscapes. Other two-page chapters cover how dances are passed on to children, different types of dances, image dances (those that mimic animal movements), costumes and body painting, honoring spirits and ancestors, musical instruments, drums, call-and-response songs, masked dancers, and performance. Keeler's watercolor-and-pencil illustrations impart a sense of vibrancy, movement, and joy. . . . A fresh, uplifting, and captivating offering." SLJ

793.7　Games not characterized by action

Macaulay, David

★ **Black** and white. Houghton Mifflin 1990 un il hardcover o.p. pa $7.99

Grades: 1 2 3　　　　　　　　　　**793.7**

1. Cattle -- Fiction 2. Railroads -- Fiction

ISBN 0-395-52151-3; 0-618-63687-0 pa

LC 89-28888

Awarded the Caldecott Medal, 1990

Four brief "stories" about parents, trains, and cows, or is it really all one story? The author recommends careful inspection of words and pictures to both minimize and enhance confusion

"The magic of Black and White comes not from each story, . . . but from the mysterious interactions between them that creates a fifth story. . . . Eventually, the stories begin to merge into a surrealistic tale spanning several levels of reality. . . . Black and White challenges the reader to use text and pictures in unexpected ways." Publ Wkly

Shortcut. Houghton Mifflin 1995 un il $15.95; pa $7.95

Grades: 1 2 3　　　　　　　　　　**793.7**

ISBN 0-395-52436-9; 0-618-00607-9 pa

LC 95-2542

"This picture book concerns six humans whose paths cross and recross in the eight chapters of brief text and distinctive artwork. Albert and his horse, June, take their wagon of melons to market, sell them, and go home. . . . Patty's pet

pig, Pearl, wanders onto an abandoned railroad line. . . . Professor Tweet is studying birds when suddenly his hot air balloon breaks free and heads toward a nearby cathedral spire. . . . Seemingly inconsequential details in one story become the moving forces in another." Booklist

Scieszka, Jon

★ **Math** curse; illustrated by Lane Smith. Viking 1995 un il $16.99

Grades: 2 3 4 5　　　　　　　　　　**793.7**

1. Mathematics -- Fiction

ISBN 0-670-86194-4

LC 95-12341

When the teacher tells her class that they can think of almost everything as a math problem, one student acquires a math anxiety which becomes a real curse

"Bold in design and often bizarre in expression, Smith's paintings clearly express the child's feelings of bemusement, frustration, and panic as well as her eventual joy when she overcomes the math curse. . . . A child-centered, witty picture book." Booklist

793.73　Puzzles and puzzle games

Agee, Jon

Smart feller fart smeller & other Spoonerisms. Hyperion Books 2006 un il $14.95

Grades: 3 4 5 6　　　　　　　　　　**793.73**

1. Spoonerisms

ISBN 0-7868-3692-X

LC 2005-929187

"Using full-page black-and-white cartoons that play with the mixed-up words, Agee captures the fun of spoonerisms. The farce of the verbal puns is extended by pictures that caricature everyone. . . . A brief introduction explains what a spoonerism is, and the last page summarizes 'what they said' with 'what they meant to say.'" Booklist

Chedru, Delphine

Spot it again! find more hidden creatures. translated from French by Scott Auerbach. Abrams Books for Young Readers 2011 un il $14.95

Grades: PreK K 1　　　　　　　　　　**793.73**

1. Picture puzzles

ISBN 978-0-8109-9736-3; 0-8109-9736-3

LC 2010020924

Original French edition 2009

This "conceals 16 more small creatures within its modish patterns. The simple and lively text prompts readers to poke among the flaps, die cuts, and vibrant lines and shapes to find snails, hungry earthworms, crying crocodiles, and more. . . . Beautifully designed from its large size to its rounded corners and heavy stock, this interactive adventure concludes with a search for sleepwalking sheep on a nighttime spread. Children will enjoy this striking volume." SLJ

Spot it! find the hidden creatures. Abrams Books for Young Readers 2009 un il $14.95

Grades: PreK K 1　　　　　　　　　　**793.73**

1. Picture puzzles

ISBN 978-0-8109-0632-7; 0-8109-0632-5

LC 2008032549

"This rounded-corner volume employs op-art designs to hide 15 creatures, and a farm girl, for viewers to find. The searches vary in difficulty. . . . The bright patterns vary from packed geometrics to a gathering of flowers, mushrooms, or trees. . . . Great for one-on-one lap sharing." SLJ

Cole, Joanna

Why did the chicken cross the road? and other riddles, old and new; compiled by Joanna Cole and Stephanie Calmenson; illustrated by Alan Tiegreen. Morrow Junior Bks. 1994 64p il hardcover o.p. pa $7.95

Grades: 3 4 5   **793.73**

1. Riddles

ISBN 0-688-12204-3

LC 94-2582

The authors "begin with a brief explanation about the origin of riddles and proceed with a collection of over two hundred, classic and new. Though many of the riddles appear in other collections, the book, illustrated with black-and-white line drawings, will be useful for its short bibliography and subject index." Horn Book Guide

Hall, Katy

★ Creepy riddles; [by] Katy Hall and Lisa Eisenberg; pictures by S.D. Schindler. Dial Bks. for Young Readers 1998 48p il (Dial easy-to-read) hardcover o.p. pa $3.99

Grades: K 1 2   **793.73**

1. Riddles

ISBN 0-8037-1684-2; 0-14-130988-1 pa

LC 94-37524

"A collection of riddles about vampires, ghosts, ghouls, and assorted monsters. . . . The illustrations are a scream. Schindler uses a find-nibbed pen to include lots of subtle details before adding vivid watercolor washes. . . . A superior choice for most joke or beginning-to-read collections." SLJ

★ Dino riddles; by Katy Hall and Lisa Eisenberg; pictures by Nicole Rubel. Dial Bks. for Young Readers 2002 40p il (Dial easy-to-read) hardcover o.p. pa $3.99

Grades: K 1 2   **793.73**

1. Riddles

ISBN 0-8037-2239-7; 0-14-250179-4 pa

LC 97-49947

A collection of riddles relating to dinosaurs, such as "What do you get if you cross a dinosaur with a rabbit? Tricerahops!" and "What did dinosaur campers cook over the fire? Dino-s'mores!"

"Rubel's informal ink-and-marker illustrations are suitably silly. . . . This will be just right for joke-book junkies, beginning readers, and teachers looking to breathe new life into staid dinosaur units." Bull Cent Child Books

Ribbit riddles; by Katy Hall and Lisa Eisenberg; pictures by Robert Bender. Dial Bks. for Young Readers 2001 40p il (Dial easy-to-read) hardcover o.p. pa $3.99

Grades: K 1 2   **793.73**

1. Jokes 2. Riddles

ISBN 0-8037-2525-6; 0-14-240056-4 pa

LC 99-89174

A collection of riddles and jokes about frogs. Example: What do little frogs like to eat on a hot summer day? Hopsicles!

"The distinctive art, cell-vinyl on layers of acetate, has a shimmery, almost fuzzy look that catches the eye—and the jokes." Booklist

★ Simms Taback's great big book of spacey, snakey, buggy riddles; riddles by Katy Hall and Lisa Eisenberg; [illustrated by Simms Taback] Viking 2008 un il $17.99

Grades: K 1 2 3   **793.73**

1. Riddles

ISBN 978-0-670-01121-6; 0-670-01121-5

"Taback brings his vibrant trademark exuberance to this picture-book riddle collection, which fairly hums with fun. Rainbow-bright colors pop off black backgrounds, making the riddles bigger than life. As the title suggests, space, snakes, and bugs dominate the subject matter." Booklist

Snakey riddles; by Katy Hall and Lisa Eisenberg; pictures by Simms Taback. Dial Bks. for Young Readers 1990 48p il (Dial easy-to-read) hardcover o.p. pa $3.99

Grades: K 1 2   **793.73**

1. Riddles

ISBN 0-14-037141-9 pa

LC 88-23687

An illustrated collection of riddles about snakes

"Riddle lovers will groan with delight at some of these riddles. . . . The best thing about the book is the cleverly drawn, lively cartoon illustrations. Long, colorful snakes form borders framing the text and picture for each riddle." SLJ

Turkey riddles; by Katy Hall and Lisa Eisenberg; pictures by Kristin Sorra. Dial Bks. for Young Readers 2002 40p il (Dial easy-to-read) hardcover o.p. pa $3.99

Grades: K 1 2   **793.73**

1. Riddles

ISBN 0-8037-2530-2; 0-14-240369-5 pa

LC 2001-47475

A collection of nearly three dozen riddles featuring turkeys, such as "What happened when Tom Turkey stepped up to the plate? He hit a fowl ball!"

"The art, with cross-hatched details, is bright and appealing. . . . Great for a good time alone, with friends, or even in a classroom." Booklist

Kalz, Jill

An A-MAZE-ing amusement park adventure; illustrated by Mattia Cerato. Picture Window Books 2010 32p il (A-MAZE-ing adventures) lib bdg $25.99

Grades: K 1 2 3   **793.73**

1. Maps 2. Maze puzzles 3. Amusement parks

ISBN 978-1-4048-6023-0 lib bdg; 1-4048-6023-1 lib bdg

LC 2010009865

"Fantastically illustrated, the adventures take the form of overhead maps, which allow Cerato to give in to her every twisty, turny impulse. . . . The first maze is a view of an entire amusement park, while subsequent mazes zero in on individual areas. . . . It's impressively orchestrated and enjoyable. . . . Navigating maps is an important real-world skill and is rarely—let's face it, never—this much fun." Booklist

Kidslabel (Firm)

Spot 7 animals; by KIDSLABEL. Chronicle Books 2007 un il (Seek & find) $12.95

Grades: K 1 2 3 4   **793.73**
1. Puzzles
ISBN 978-0-8118-5722-2; 0-8118-5722-0
      LC 2006018069
"The creative, colorful pictures and the challenge of finding differences and particular items make this book constructive fun." SLJ

Spot 7 Christmas; by KIDSLABEL. Chronicle Books 2006 un il (Seek & find) $12.95
Grades: K 1 2 3 4   **793.73**
1. Puzzles 2. Christmas
ISBN 978-0-8118-5323-1; 0-8118-5323-3
      LC 2005028795
"This bright, spot-the-difference book features 13 (if you count the front and back covers) photo spreads of wreaths, Santa-filled dioramas, and Christmas cards, asking readers to find seven oddities and solve a riddle for each one." SLJ

Spot 7 School; by KIDSLABEL. Chronicle Books 2006 un il (Seek & find) $12.95
Grades: K 1 2 3 4   **793.73**
1. Puzzles
ISBN 978-0-8118-5324-8; 0-8118-5324-1
      LC 2005026114
Original Japanese edition 2003
"This book has colorful, busy photos of objects and lists of items associated with school for readers to locate. . . . It also offers viewers some additional tasks: the two pages of each spread are identical except for seven differences, and each left-hand page contains a riddle, the answer to which is found on the page. . . . The clear images depict imaginative groupings. . . . It offers entertainment and an opportunity to hone observational skills rolled into one." SLJ

Other titles in this series are:
Spot 7 Christmas (2006)
Spot 7 Animals (2007)
Spot 7 Spooky (2007)
Spot 7 Toys (2008)

Spot 7 spooky. Chronicle Books 2007 un il (Seek & find) $12.95
Grades: K 1 2 3 4   **793.73**
1. Puzzles
ISBN 978-0-8118-5723-9; 0-8118-5723-9
      LC 2006032422
Original Japanese edition 2004
"Each spread of this Halloween-themed activity book features two spooky photographs that appear identical. Eagle-eyed readers, however, will spot seven things that have changed from one photo to the other. . . . [There is] a riddle on each spread and [there are] extra things to look for throughout the book." Publisher's note

Spot 7 Toys; by KIDSLABEL. Chronicle Books 2008 un il $12.99
Grades: K 1 2 3 4   **793.73**
1. Puzzles
ISBN 978-0-8118-6563-0; 0-8118-6563-0
"This collection of 12 riddles accompanied by collage-style photos will keep children entertained. Each selection is paired with two full-color photos filled with tiny toys. Upon first glance the paired pictures appear identical. However,

close inspection reveals many differences, some of which are more obvious than others. The riddles range in difficulty, and their solutions can be found within the illustrations. . . . The book follows the successful format of other 'Spot 7' titles." SLJ

Lankford, Mary D.
    Mazes around the world; by Mary D. Lankford; illustrated by Karen Dugan. Collins 2008 26p il $16.99; lib bdg $17.89
Grades: 3 4 5   **793.73**
1. Maze puzzles
ISBN 978-0-688-16519-2; 0-688-16519-2; 978-0-688-16520-8 lib bdg; 0-688-16520-6 lib bdg
      LC 2007008580
"Lankford traces the history of mazes from the ancient Egyptian Labyrinth . . . to today's mazes in North America's corn fields. . . . Each left-hand page offers an engaging account of a particular maze or type of maze, depicted on the facing page in a charming painting by Dugan. . . . Drawing from many cultures and historical periods, this well-researched, accessible book explores a topic with inherent child appeal." Booklist
Includes bibliographical references

Maestro, Giulio
    Riddle roundup; a wild bunch to beef up your word power. Clarion Bks. 1989 64p il hardcover o.p. pa $7.95
Grades: 2 3 4   **793.73**
1. Riddles 2. Word games
ISBN 0-89919-537-7 pa
      LC 86-33403
A collection of sixty-one riddles based on different kinds of word play such as puns, homonyms, and homographs

Maestro, Marco
    What do you hear when cows sing? and other silly riddles. by Marco and Giulio Maestro; pictures by Giulio Maestro. HarperCollins Pubs. 1996 48p il (I can read book) hardcover o.p. pa $3.95
Grades: K 1 2   **793.73**
1. Riddles
ISBN 0-06-444227-6 pa
      LC 94-18686
"The subjects of the riddles will be familiar to most readers—trains, bugs, mice, fish, boats. . . . Most of the selections involve plays on words, but some are relatively straightforward. . . . Children will love the silly pictures, laugh at the riddles, enjoy sharing them with others, and expand their vocabularies all at the same time." SLJ

Marzollo, Jean
    I spy a Christmas tree; riddles by Jean Marzollo; photographs by Walter Wick. Scholastic 2010 un il $9.99
Grades: PreK K 1 2   **793.73**
1. Christmas 2. Picture puzzles
ISBN 978-0-545-22092-7; 0-545-22092-0
Rhyming verses ask readers to find hidden objects in the photographs of Christmas tree ornaments and toys.

    I spy an egg in a nest; riddles by Jean Marzollo; photographs by Walter Wick. Scholastic 2011 un il (Scholastic reader) pa $3.99

Grades: PreK K 1 2 **793.73**
1. Picture puzzles
ISBN 978-0-545-22093-4 pa; 0-545-22093-9 pa
LC 2009051611
This visual game book consists of a series of rhymed riddles listing objects that children must locate in the accompanying photographs of subjects relating to spring.

"Sharpening children's visual discrimination and concentration, this colorful book offers a fun approach to reading skills." Booklist

I spy school days; a book of picture riddles. photographs by Walter Wick; riddles by Jean Marzollo. Scholastic 1995 33p il $18.95
Grades: K 1 2 3 4 **793.73**
1. Puzzles
ISBN 0-590-48135-5
LC 94-43629
"This riddle book in verse follows the . . . format of large, oversized pages chock-full of objects and realia. This time, the double-page spreads are devoted to unifying activities or themes associated with school, chalkboard, a puppet show, art or science classrooms, a playground, etc. The full-color photographs are sharp, bright, and busy." SLJ

Munro, Roxie
Amazement park; by Roxie Munro. Chronicle Books 2005 37p il $16.95
Grades: K 1 2 3 **793.73**
1. Maze puzzles
ISBN 0-8118-4581-8
LC 2004-8482
This book includes "12 . . . mazes to navigate. . . . All mazes lead from one page to the next and then back again to the first one. . . . The mazes do get tricky and sometimes completely confusing, but an answer key is included for those who get stuck. The cartoon art is eye-catching and colorful." SLJ

Another book of maze puzzles by this author is:
Mazescapes (2001)

Mazeways: A to Z; by Roxie Munro. Sterling Pub. Co., Inc. 2007 un il $12.95
Grades: K 1 2 3 **793.73**
1. Alphabet 2. Maze puzzles
ISBN 978-1-4027-3774-9; 1-4027-3774--2
LC 2007001586
"Each letter is featured on a spread or a page with directions for traveling through the maze and finding different objects along the way. . . . Back pages provide solutions. This engaging title works as an interactive alphabet book, an introduction to mapping skills, or to sharpen visual discrimination skills." SLJ

Nickle, John
Alphabet explosion! search and count from alien to zebra. [by] John Nickle. Schwartz & Wade Books 2006 un il $16.95
Grades: K 1 2 3 **793.73**
1. Puzzles 2. Alphabet
ISBN 0-375-83598-9
LC 2005024372
"Each wordless page features animals and objects whose names begin with a featured letter. A number indicates how many items are buried within the picture. . . . Nickle's finely rendered scenes are imaginative, humorous, and sophisticated, and he incorporates a free-flowing range of artistic styles that adds energy to the pages.." Booklist

Rosenthal, Amy Krouse
Wumbers; it's a word cr8ed with a number! wri10 by Amy Krouse Rosenthal; illustr8ed by Tom Lichtenheld. Chronicle Books 2012 40 p. col. ill. (alk. paper) $16.99
Grades: K 1 2 3 **793.73**
1. Word games
ISBN 1452110220; 9781452110226
LC 2011041591
This children's picture book by Amy Krouse Rosenthal "combines words and numbers ('wumbers') that challenge readers to use their number recognition and phonological skills. . . . From a boy and girl enjoying their '10ts' to the smiling child who is 'el8ed' because he lost his first '2th,' [Tom] Lichenheld's ink and pastel coloring-book-style drawings supply visual clues to decoding the text." (School Library Journal)

Schnur, Steven
Autumn; an alphabet acrostic. illustrated by Leslie Evans. Clarion Bks. 1997 un il $16
Grades: K 1 2 3 **793.73**
1. Autumn 2. Alphabet 3. Acrostics
ISBN 0-395-77043-2
LC 96-50219
"A fall riddle is presented for each letter of the alphabet. The answer is spelled out in the first letter of each line. The riddles are spare with striking images. . . . Evans's stunning hand-colored linoleum block prints are clear, bright, and provide sharp clues for the riddles. . . . This delightful alphabet book with a new twist will provide inspiration and challenges for a wide audience." SLJ

Summer; an alphabet acrostic. illustrated by Leslie Evans. Clarion Books 2001 un il $16
Grades: K 1 2 3 **793.73**
1. Summer 2. Alphabet 3. Acrostics
ISBN 0-618-02372-0
LC 00-31674
"This concept book features a short poem in which the first letter of each line spells out the word it represents. 'Daisy' becomes 'Dragonflies dart/And hover,/Inspecting white flowers with/Sunlike/Yellow centers.' The sheer inventiveness of each poem is impressive. . . . Neatly framed linoleum-block illustrations feature rich colors and bold lines that capture the brightness of the days." SLJ

Sirett, Dawn
Hide and seek first words; [written by Dawn Sirett; photography by Dave King]. DK Publishing 2010 48p il $12.99
Grades: PreK **793.73**
1. Vocabulary 2. Picture puzzles
ISBN 978-0-7566-6300-1; 0-7566-6300-8
LC 2010280415
"This seek-and-find, with its colorful collection of photographic puzzles, will capture the attention of young children and draw them into the book. Working with an adult to locate the brightly colored objects hidden throughout loosely themed spreads . . . preschoolers will also be helping

build reading readiness and verbal skills through short rhyming text and object labeling." Horn Book Guide

Steig, William

★ C D B. Simon & Schuster Bks. for Young Readers 2000 47p il $16; pa $4.99

Grades: 2 3 4 5   **793.73**

1. Word games

ISBN 0-689-83160-9; 0-671-66689-4 pa

LC 99-32720

First published 1968 by Windmill Bks.

Letters and numbers are used to create the sounds of words and simple sentences 4 u 2 figure out with the aid of illustrations

Readers "will delight in puzzling out the letter-and-number messages, aided by the simple, thickly outlined drawings and an answer key." Booklist

C D C? Farrar, Straus & Giroux 2003 57p il $16

Grades: 2 3 4 5   **793.73**

1. Word games

ISBN 0-374-31233-8

LC 2002-111704

A color illustrated edition of the title first published 1984

Letters, numbers, and symbols are used to create the sounds of words and simple sentences which U R expected to figure out with the aid of illustrations. Includes an answer key

"Flawlessly executed, purely pleasurable, the book is definitely 'D-Q-R' for doldrums at any season." Horn Book

Steiner, Joan

Look-alikes; photography by Thomas Lindley. Little, Brown 1998 un il $13.95

Grades: K 1 2 3 4   **793.73**

1. Puzzles

ISBN 0-316-81255-2

LC 97-32795

"Bursting with creativity, this work of visual genius will set imaginations soaring." Publ Wkly

Look-alikes around the world; concept, constructions & text by Joan Steiner; design by Stephen Blauweiss; photography by Ogden Gigli. Little, Brown and Company 2007 un il $15.99

Grades: K 1 2 3 4   **793.73**

1. Puzzles

ISBN 978-0-316-81172-9; 0-316-81172-6

LC 2007012332

"Using everyday objects . . . artist Joan Steiner has created three-dimensional scenes of more than 40 famous landmarks and familiar vacation locales. . . . Complete with photographs of the actual sites, . . . facts, and more than 500 look-alikes to search for, this [is in the format of a] postcard album." Publisher's note

Other titles in this series are:

Look-alikes (1998)

Look-alikes Jr (1999)

Look-alikes Christmas (2003)

Look-alikes Christmas; [by] Joan Steiner; photography by Ogden Gigli. Little, Brown 2003 un il lib bdg $14.95

Grades: K 1 2 3 4   **793.73**

1. Puzzles 2. Christmas

ISBN 0-316-81187-4

LC 2003-47406

Simple verses challenge readers to identify the everyday objects used to construct nine three-dimensional Christmas scenes, including a cathedral, Nutcracker ballet, and Santa's workshop.

"In both presentation and delivery, this is clever, ingenious, and fun both for readers and nonreaders." SLJ

Look-alikes, jr. photography by Thomas Lindley. Little, Brown 1999 un il $13.95

Grades: K 1 2 3   **793.73**

1. Puzzles

ISBN 0-316-81307-9

LC 99-11683

Simple verses challenge readers to identify the everyday objects used to construct eleven three-dimensional scenes, including a house, kitchen, bedroom, school bus, train, farm, and rocket

"The design is both witty and cunning, offering lots of just-hard-enough opportunities for looking and finding." Horn Book

Wick, Walter

★ Can you see what I see? picture puzzles to search and solve. Scholastic 2002 35p il $13.95

Grades: PreK K 1 2   **793.73**

1. Puzzles

ISBN 0-439-16391-9

LC 2001-49032

Presents twelve brain-teasing hidden picture puzzles to solve

"With its range of activities and perspective-shifting challenges, this is sure to appeal to a wide age group of children, who won't be satisfied until they've solved the last puzzle." Booklist

Other titles in this series are:

Can you see what I see?: Cool collections (2004)

Can you see what I see?: Dream machine (2003)

Can you see what I see?: On a scary scary night (2008)

Can you see what I see?: Once upon a time (2006)

Can you see what I see?: Seymour and the juice box boat (2004)

Can you see what I see: Seymour makes new friends (2006)

Can you see what I see?: The night before Christmas (2005)

Can you see what I see?: Treasure ship (2010)

Can you see what I see? Cool collections; picture puzzles to search and solve. Scholastic 2004 35p il $13.95

Grades: PreK K 1 2   **793.73**

1. Puzzles

ISBN 0-439-61772-3

Readers search for objects hidden in photographs of buttons, dinosaurs, robots, shells, cars, animals, leaves, beads, game pieces, and the contents of a junk drawer.

"Wick offers pleasing rhymes that clearly direct readers to retrieve a requisite number of objects. Once again, his photography engages, even mesmerizes viewers." SLJ

Can you see what I see? Dream machine; a picture adventure to search and solve. Scholastic 2003 35p il $13.95
Grades: PreK K 1 2   **793.73**
1. Puzzles
ISBN 0-439-39950-5

LC 2003-3547
A child enters a dream machine and encounters hidden picture puzzles intended for the reader to solve
"Wick uses homonyms and visual tricks, giving children more to see and look for than what may appear at first glance. . . . A wonderful addition to any collection." SLJ

Can you see what I see? On a scary, scary night; by Walter Wick. Scholastic 2008 35p il $13.99
Grades: PreK K 1 2   **793.73**
1. Puzzles
ISBN 0-439-70870-2; 978-0-439-70870-8
LC 2007029839
Picture puzzles in which the reader is invited to search for hidden objects in scary settings.

Can you see what I see? Seymour and the juice box boat. Scholastic 2004 29p il $8.99
Grades: PreK K 1 2   **793.73**
1. Puzzles
ISBN 0-439-61778-2
The reader is asked to find various animals and objects and a boy named Seymour in the photographs.
"Just right for the youngest seek-and-find aficionados, this engaging offering will sail right off of the shelves." SLJ

Can you see what I see? toyland express. Scholastic 2011 35p il $13.99
Grades: PreK K 1 2   **793.73**
1. Puzzles
ISBN 978-0-545-24483-1; 0-545-24483-8
"Complex seek-and-find images provide an intriguing backdrop for the story of a tenacious toy train. This latest collection of picture puzzles in the Can You See What I See? series provides a nostalgic glimpse into the life, death and resurrection of a wooden train. . . . Wick plays with similar colors to enhance these expressive camouflaged spreads. Digitally processed photographs capture crisp dimensions with remarkable clarity. No puzzle here—these well-designed scenes are another success from the picture-challenge master." Kirkus

Can you see what I see?: once upon a time; picture puzzles to search and solve. by Walter Wick. Scholastic 2006 35p il $13.99
Grades: K 1 2 3   **793.73**
1. Puzzles
ISBN 0-439-61777-4
LC 2006005853
"Each scene is crammed with delightful details that will be a pleasure to examine while hunting for the specified items." SLJ

Can you see what I see?: Treasure ship; picture puzzles to search and solve. Scholastic Inc. 2010 34p $13.99
Grades: PreK K 1 2   **793.73**
1. Puzzles
ISBN 978-0-439-02643-7; 0-439-02643-1

Readers are challenged to find objects in photographic scenes related to treasure ships.

★ I spy; a book of picture riddles. photographs by Walter Wick; riddles by Jean Marzollo; design by Carol Devine Carson. Scholastic 1992 33p il $13.95
Grades: K 1 2 3 4   **793.73**
1. Puzzles
ISBN 0-590-45087-5
LC 91-28268
This visual game book consists of "a series of rhymed riddles listing objects that children must locate in the accompanying photographs. Each double-page spread features crisp, full-color shots featuring an abundance of familiar items. The objects range from large and easy-to-spot to tiny and partially hidden. . . . An appealing book for children and adults to share and enjoy together." SLJ
Other titles in this series are:
I spy a Christmas tree (2010)
I spy Christmas (1992)
I spy extreme challenger! (2000)
I spy fantasy (1994)
I spy fun house (1993)
I spy gold challenger! (1998)
I spy mystery (1993)
I spy school days (1995)
I spy spooky night (1996)
I spy super challenger! (1997)
I spy treasure hunt (1999)
I spy ultimate challenger! (2003)
I spy year-round challenger! (2003)

I spy extreme challenger! a book of picture riddles. photographs by Walter Wick; riddles by Jean Marzollo. Scholastic 2000 31p il $13.95
Grades: K 1 2 3 4   **793.73**
1. Puzzles
ISBN 0-439-19900-X
LC 00-27910
This features a collection of favorite I Spy riddles that send readers searching 12 photographs for hidden objects.

I spy fantasy; a book of picture riddles. photographs by Walter Wick; riddles by Jean Marzollo. Scholastic 1994 37p il $13.95
Grades: K 1 2 3 4   **793.73**
1. Puzzles
ISBN 0-590-46295-4
LC 93-44814
"Rhyming riddles direct a hunt for a series of objects in each of 13 sumptuously styled photographs." Publ Wkly

I spy gold challenger! a book of picture riddles. photographs by Walter Wick; riddles by Jean Marzollo. Scholastic 1998 31p il $18.95
Grades: K 1 2 3 4   **793.73**
1. Puzzles
ISBN 0-590-04296-3
LC 98-13982
This "presents photographed setups of carefully arranged objects with riddles underneath each picture that encourage children to find particular objects in the photo. This series entry includes photographs that the author and pho-

tographer decided were their favorites from previous books, and substitutes more difficult riddles for the original ones, challenging children who like a truly vigorous search. As in earlier books, a list of riddles at the end gives young seekers the opportunity to work backwards and find the picture that matches the riddle." Booklist

I spy spooky night; a book of picture riddles. photographs by Walter Wick; riddles by Jean Marzollo. Scholastic 1996 31p il $13.99

Grades: K 1 2 3 4   **793.73**
1. Puzzles
ISBN 0-590-48137-1

                   LC 95-50528

"The puzzles take place in and around a haunted house (an altered Victorian dollhouse). Readers are invited to search for mice, spiders, candles, bats, jacko-lanterns, and bones among other creepy things found in the hallway, library, fireplace, and laboratory of the house, as well as in the graveyard and a garden of ghoulies outside. . . . Wick achieves a definite dramatic effect. Marzollo's clever rhyming puzzles add great flair." SLJ

I spy super challenger! a book of picture riddles. photographs by Walter Wick; riddles by Jean Marzollo. Scholastic 1997 31p il $18.95

Grades: K 1 2 3 4   **793.73**
1. Puzzles
ISBN 0-590-34128-6

                   LC 97-6864

"Wick's spectacularly photographed, double-page spreads are taken from favorites such as I Spy Funhouse (1993) and I Spy School Days (1995, both Scholastic), Marzollo's cleverly written new rhyming couplets encourage readers to seek a new batch of items. Playing cards, beads, dominos, blocks, and other trinkets are all arranged attractively and with wit, yet this does not lessen the difficulty of locating the sought-after objects." SLJ

I spy treasure hunt; a book of picture riddles. photographs by Walter Wick; riddles by Jean Marzollo. Scholastic 1999 36p il $13.95

Grades: K 1 2 3 4   **793.73**
1. Puzzles
ISBN 0-439-04244-5

                   LC 99-30581

"On oversize pages, brightly colored photographs are crammed with small objects; each double-page spread is organized by theme. . . . The rhyming captions at the foot of each page suggest objects to be found. . . . While the pages are very busy, it's the sort of crowding many young children enjoy, and it certainly fosters observation of detail." Bull Cent Child Books

I spy ultimate challenger! a book of picture riddles. photographs by Walter Wick; riddles by Jean Marzollo. Scholastic 2003 31p il $13.99

Grades: K 1 2 3 4   **793.73**
1. Puzzles
ISBN 0-439-45401-8

                   LC 2002-8196

Rhyming text leads the reader to find objects hidden in the photographs, selected from previously published volumes in the series

793.74   Mathematical games and recreations

Ball, Johnny
Go figure! DK Pub. 2005 96p il map $15.99
Grades: 4 5 6 7   **793.74**
1. Mathematics 2. Mathematical recreations
ISBN 0-7566-1374-4
A collection of math activities that include brainteasers, magic tricks, and mind-reading games

"A dynamic book. . . . Blocks of color, diagrams, and photo collages contribute to the exciting layout. . . . A fun romp for number and puzzle lovers." SLJ

Polonsky, Lydia
Math for the very young; a handbook of activities for parents and teachers. [by] Lydia Plonsky . . . [et al.]; illustrated by Marcia Miller. Wiley 1995 210p il hardcover o.p. pa $14.95
Grades: Adult Professional   **793.74**
1. Mathematical recreations
ISBN 0-471-01671-3; 0-471-01647-0 pa

                   LC 94-20861

"This guide suggests ways to introduce math to children through everyday activities. Sections include making a record book about the child and the family as well as activities for each month of the year, geometric crafts, math games, counting rhymes and stories, and ways to use math in the home and on the road." Booklist
Includes bibliographical references

Tang, Greg
The **grapes** of math; mind-stretching math riddles. illustrated by Harry Briggs. Scholastic Press 2001 un il $16.95
Grades: 2 3 4   **793.74**
1. Mathematical recreations
ISBN 0-439-21033-X

                   LC 00-30062

Illustrated riddles introduce strategies for solving a variety of math problems in using visual clues

"This clever collection of puzzles could spark the interest of even the mathematically challenged. . . . The simple, staccato rhymes and crisp lines of the artwork keep attention focused, while those who find themselves stumped can consult the 'Answers' section at the back of the book." Publ Wkly

Math appeal; mind-stretching math riddles. illustrated by Harry Briggs. Scholastic Press 2003 un il $16.95
Grades: 2 3 4   **793.74**
1. Mathematical recreations
ISBN 0-439-21046-1

                   LC 2002-5354

Rhyming anecdotes present opportunities for simple math activities and hints for solving

"Bright, whimsical illustrations and clever rhymes introduce challenging exercises. . . . In a note, Tang states that his goal is 'to encourage clever, creative thinking,' and the questions posed do that." SLJ

★ **Math** potatoes; mind-stretching brain food. illustrated by Harry Briggs. Scholastic Press 2005 un il $16.95
Grades: 2 3 4 **793.74**
1. Mathematical recreations
ISBN 0-439-44390-3
LC 2004-16638

"This picture book uses all kinds of visual tricks to demonstrate how to make arithmetic faster and easier. On each double-page spread, a rhyming verse has fun with a variety of subjects. Most rhymes are about foods . . . and the bright, computer-generated pictures are as playful as the words. . . . The games are complex, the visuals are tricky, and although the rhyme seems straightforward . . . readers must think carefully about adding, subtracting, and multiplying." Booklist

793.8   Magic and related activities

Barnhart, Norm
Amazing magic tricks: a beginner level; by Norm Barnhart. Capstone Press 2009 32p il (Magic Tricks) lib bdg $23.93
Grades: 4 5 6 **793.8**
1. Magic tricks
ISBN 978-1-4296-1942-4 lib bdg; 1-4296-1942-2 lib bdg
LC 2008-2572

"Numbered steps, clearly illustrated by crisp photographs, guide students through the preparation and performance of such classic magician's fare as 'The Magical Sailor's Knot.'. . . The books' design, with the text neatly packaged in boxes, will attract reluctant readers." SLJ
Includes glossary and bibliographical references

Amazing magic tricks: apprentice level; by Norm Barnhart. Capstone Press 2009 32p il (Magic Tricks) lib bdg $23.93
Grades: 4 5 6 **793.8**
1. Magic tricks
ISBN 978-1-4296-1943-1 lib bdg; 1-4296-1943-0 lib bdg
LC 2008-2573

"Numbered steps, clearly illustrated by crisp photographs, guide students through the preparation and performance of such classic magician's fare as 'The Magical Sailor's Knot.'. . . The books' design, with the text neatly packaged in boxes, will attract reluctant readers." SLJ
Includes glossary and bibliographical references

Amazing magic tricks: expert level; by Norm Barnhart. Capstone Press 2009 32p il (Magic Tricks) lib bdg $23.93
Grades: 4 5 6 **793.8**
1. Magic tricks
ISBN 978-1-4296-1945-5 lib bdg; 1-4296-1945-7 lib bdg
LC 2008-2574

"Numbered steps, clearly illustrated by crisp photographs, guide students through the preparation and performance of such classic magician's fare as 'The Magical

Sailor's Knot.'. . . The books' design, with the text neatly packaged in boxes, will attract reluctant readers." SLJ
Includes glossary and bibliographical references

Amazing magic tricks: master level; by Norm Barnhart. Capstone Press 2009 32p il (Magic Tricks) lib bdg $23.93
Grades: 4 5 6 **793.8**
1. Magic tricks
ISBN 978-1-4296-1944-8 lib bdg; 1-4296-1944-9 lib bdg
LC 2008-2575

"Numbered steps, clearly illustrated by crisp photographs, guide students through the preparation and performance of such classic magician's fare as 'The Magical Sailor's Knot.'. . . The books' design, with the text neatly packaged in boxes, will attract reluctant readers." SLJ
Includes glossary and bibliographical references

Becker, Helaine
Magic up your sleeve; amazing illusions, tricks, and science facts you'll never believe. illustrated by Claudia Dávila. Maple Tree Press 2010 64p il $22.95; pa $10.95
Grades: 3 4 5 6 **793.8**
1. Science 2. Magic tricks
ISBN 978-1-897349-75-5; 1-897349-75-0; 978-1-897349-76-2 pa; 1-8973497-6-9 pa

"Thirty tricks are presented covering optical illusions, mind reading, 'math magic,' chemistry, and physics. All directions are clear and easy to follow. . . . The digital cartoon illustrations are nicely executed and add flashes of humor to the scenarios. . . . A welcome addition that should vanish off library shelves." SLJ

Colgan, Lynda
Mathemagic! number tricks. written by Lynda Colgan; illustrated by Jane Kurisu. Kids Can Press 2011 40p il $16.95
Grades: 3 4 5 **793.8**
1. Magic tricks 2. Mathematical recreations
ISBN 978-1-55453-425-8; 1-55453-425-9

"Colgan introduces 10 magic tricks that are accomplished using mathematical principles. The directions are clear and easy to follow, and each trick is followed by an explanation of how it actually works, as well as suggestions for performing it effectively for an audience. Interesting historical tidbits occasionally appear in sidebars. The simple cartoon illustrations add interest and clarify how the tricks are accomplished." SLJ
Includes glossary

Jennings, Madeleine
Magic step-by-step; [by] Madeleine Jennings and Colin Francome. Rosen Central 2010 89p il (Skills in motion) lib bdg $31.95
Grades: 5 6 7 8 **793.8**
1. Magic tricks
ISBN 978-1-4358-3363-0; 1-4358-3363-5
LC 2009-13221

Presents step-by-step instructions on performing magic tricks, including card tricks, rope tricks, and sleight of hand.
"Colorful photographs show the entire movement of each skill presented, giving new meaning to the term 'step-by-step.' Progression borders at the bottom of the pages

highlight the salient points to notice in performing each skill from beginning to end." SLJ

Includes bibliographical references

Tremaine, Jon

Magic with numbers. QEB Pub. 2010 32p il (Magic handbook) lib bdg $28.50

Grades: 4 5 6   **793.8**

1. Numbers 2. Magic tricks 3. Mathematical recreations

ISBN 978-1-59566-945-2; 1-59566-945-0

LC 2010014138

Provides step-by-step instructions for fifteen magic tricks using numbers, including profiles of famous magicians.

This "is uncommonly good. . . . [The book] uses sharp, comprehensible illustrations set up on old-fashioned marbled backdrops. . . . Best of all, the friendly, crystal-clear [text] makes this one of the most coherent [books] in the genre." Booklist

Magical illusions. QEB Pub. 2010 32p il (Magic handbook) lib bdg $28.50

Grades: 4 5 6   **793.8**

1. Magic tricks

ISBN 978-1-59566-944-5; 1-59566-944-2

LC 2010008525

This volume explains how to perform magic tricks that involve creating illusions.

This "is uncommonly good. . . . [The book] uses sharp, comprehensible illustrations set up on old-fashioned marbled backdrops. . . . Best of all, the friendly, crystal-clear [text] makes this one of the most coherent [books] in the genre." Booklist

Paper tricks. QEB Pub. 2010 32p il (Magic handbook) lib bdg $28.50

Grades: 4 5 6   **793.8**

1. Magic tricks 2. Paper crafts

ISBN 978-1-59566-852-3; 1-59566-852-7

LC 2010017910

This offers instructions for magic tricks using paper.

This "is uncommonly good. . . . [The book] uses sharp, comprehensible illustrations set up on old-fashioned marbled backdrops. . . . Best of all, the friendly, crystal-clear [text] makes this one of the most coherent [books] in the genre." Booklist

Pocket tricks. QEB Pub. 2010 32p il (Magic handbook) lib bdg $28.50; pa $13.50

Grades: 4 5 6   **793.8**

1. Magic tricks

ISBN 978-1-59566-853-0 lib bdg; 1-59566-853-5 lib bdg; 978-1-84835-443-2 pa; 1-84835-443-6 pa

LC 2010008526

This volume explains how to perform simple magic tricks using items that are commonly in a person's pocket.

This "is uncommonly good. . . . [The book] uses sharp, comprehensible illustrations set up on old-fashioned marbled backdrops. . . . Best of all, the friendly, crystal-clear [text] makes this one of the most coherent [books] in the genre." Booklist

Includes bibliographical references

Wyler, Rose

Magic secrets; by Rose Wyler and Gerald Ames; pictures by Arthur Dorros. rev ed.; Harper & Row 1990 63p il (I can read book) hardcover o.p. pa $3.99

Grades: K 1 2   **793.8**

1. Magic tricks

ISBN 0-06-444153-9 pa

LC 89-35841

A revised and newly illustrated edition of the title first published 1967

Easy magic tricks for the aspiring young magician

"Most of the magic tricks presented here are easily understood and appear to be simple to learn and to execute with ample practice." SLJ

793.809   Magicians (Performers)

Jarrow, Gail

★ The amazing Harry Kellar; great American magician. Gail G. Jarrow. Calkins Creek 2012 96 p. col. ill. $17.95

Grades: 3 4 5 6 7 8   **793.809**

1. Magicians 2. Optical illusions

ISBN 1590788656; 9781590788653

LC 2011940465

This book is a biography of Harry Keller (later Kellar), "the first dean of the Society of American Magicians, a man [magician Harry] Houdini regarded as a mentor. . . . Few secrets of the illusions are revealed here, but [Gail] Jarrow makes it clear that it was Kellar's art that made them seem like real magic." The book also includes "[d]ozens of . . . Kellar posters" and a "timeline, bibliography, [and] annotated sources." (Kirkus)

Includes glossary and bibliographical references

794.1   Chess

Basman, Michael

Chess for kids; written by Michael Basman. Dorling Kindersley 2001 45p il $12.99; pa $6.99

Grades: 4 5 6 7   **794.1**

1. Chess

ISBN 0-7894-6540-X; 0-7566-1807-X pa

LC 00-59018

This guide to chess explains the rudiments of the game, techniques and winning strategies

"A solid introduction for novices and good for skilled players wanting to develop their strategies and find out about chess clubs and tournaments." Booklist

King, Daniel

★ Chess; from first moves to checkmate. New ed.; Kingfisher 2010 64p il pa $8.99

Grades: 5 6 7 8 9 10 11 12   **794.1**

1. Chess

ISBN 978-0-7534-1930-4

First published 2000

Introduces the rules and strategies of chess, as well as its history and some of the great players and matches.

794.8   Electronic games

Egan, Jill

How video game designers use math; math curriculum consultant: Rhea A. Stewart. Chelsea Clubhouse 2010 32p il (Math in the real world) lib bdg $28

Grades: 4 5 6   **794.8**

1. Mathematics 2. Video games 3. Computer games 4. Computer animation 5. Vocational guidance

ISBN 978-1-60413-603-6 lib bdg; 1-60413-603-0 lib bdg

LC 2009-24173

This describes how video game designers use math to create and produce their games and includes relevant math problems and information about how to become a video game designer

Includes glossary and bibliographical references

Jozefowicz, Chris

Video game developer. Gareth Stevens Pub. 2010 32p il (Cool careers: cutting edge) lib bdg $26; pa $8.95

Grades: 4 5 6   **794.8**

1. Video games 2. Computer games 3. Vocational guidance

ISBN 978-1-4339-1958-9 lib bdg; 1-4339-1958-3 lib bdg; 978-1-4339-2157-5 pa; 1-4339-2157-X pa

LC 2008053549

This introduction to video game developer careers offers "clear, solid information in a large font. . . . [This] short [book is] packed with relevant, current material." SLJ

Includes glossary and bibliographical references

Oxlade, Chris

Gaming technology. Smart Apple Media 2011 46p il (New technology) lib bdg $34.25

Grades: 4 5 6 7   **794.8**

1. Video games 2. Computer games

ISBN 9781599205311

LC 2010044239

Describes the technology used for creating and playing video games. Includes information on how different platforms work and the direction video game technology may be going.

This "offers a fine overview for reports, and its attractive design may also entice middle-grade readers to learn more." Booklist

Includes glossary and bibliographical references

Schrier, Allyson Valentine

Gaming safely; by Allyson Valentine Schrier; [Jennifer Besel, editor] Capstone Press 2013 32 p. col. ill. (Fact finders. Tech safety smarts) (library binding) $26.65

Grades: 4 5 6 7   **794.8**

1. Internet games 2. Internet -- Safety measures

ISBN 9781429699464; 9781476515748; 9781620658000

LC 2012029268

"This pertinent, practical series clearly explains safety protocols students should follow while online. The content includes how to create strong passwords, which information to share, and how to protect yourself from a cyberbully. The authors are respectful of the tween reader's ability to understand difficult realities and to put preventative measures into action." Lib Med Con

Includes bibliographical references and index

796   Athletic and outdoor sports and games

Berman, Len

The greatest moments in sports. Sourcebooks 2009 136p il $16.99

Grades: 5 6 7 8   **796**

1. Sports

ISBN 978-1-4022-2099-9; 1-4022-2099-5

LC 2009023686

"Forty years as a sportscaster gives Berman plenty of experience to choose the 25 greatest sports moments. His writing is lively, humorous, and informative—just right to sustain kids' (or adults') interest. Quality photos throughout are another plus. . . . An audio CD that includes many of the moments as they were broadcast live is part of the package." SLJ

Includes bibliographical references

Blumenthal, Karen

Let me play; the story of Title IX, the law that changed the future of girls in America. Atheneum Books for Young Readers 2005 152p il $19.95

Grades: 6 7 8 9 10   **796**

1. Women athletes 2. Sex discrimination 3. Education Amendments of 1972 -- Title IX

ISBN 0-689-85957-0

LC 2004-1450

Title IX legislation assured "that 'no one could be closed out of any educational program or activity receiving federal money simply because of sex.' After explaining the genesis of the legislation, . . . Blumenthal discusses how evolving guidelines and interpretations brought girls' school athletic programs into its purview. [Bibliography. Index.] Grades nine to twelve." (Bull Cent Child Books)

"The author looks at American women's evolving rights by focusing on the history and future of Title IX, which bans sex discrimination in U.S. education. . . . The images are . . . gripping, and relevant political cartoons and fact boxes add further interest. Few books cover the last few decades of American women's history with such clarity and detail." Booklist

Includes bibliographical references

Hile, Lori

Surviving extreme sports. Raintree 2011 56p il (Extreme survival) lib bdg $33.50

Grades: 4 5 6 7   **796**

1. Extreme sports 2. Wilderness survival

ISBN 978-1-4109-3968-5; 1-4109-3968-5

LC 2010028689

This book is "fun and informative. [This] well-organized title starts with an overview [of extreme sports], offers some specific examples, and includes additional facts or tips and resources. . . . [It features] dramatic archival and full-color photos on nearly every page. . . . [This is a book] that youngsters will enjoy and talk about." SLJ

Includes glossary and bibliographical references

Howell, Brian

Sports. ABDO Pub. Co. 2011 112p il (Inside the industry) lib bdg $23.95

Grades: 5 6 7 8   **796**

1. Sports -- Vocational guidance

ISBN 978-1-61714-804-0; 1-61714-804-0

LC 2010042558

This " well-designed [book describes] a variety of careers in [sports]. Because [it helps] readers assess if these positions are suitable for their personality types and backgrounds, the [title is a] good [choice] for career exploration and self-discovery. [It is] also useful for research and reports. . . . Sidebars and full-color photos appear throughout." SLJ

Includes bibliographical references

Kelley, K. C.

Weird races. Child's World 2011 24p il (Weird sports) lib bdg $25.64

Grades: 3 4 5 6   **796**

1. Racing

ISBN 978-1-60954-376-1; 1-60954-376-1

LC 2010042898

This describes sports such as lawnmower racing, bed racing, wife carrying, street luge, cheese rolling, and toilet racing.

"Both the writing and the visual style are exuberant-without relying too much on exclamation points." Booklist

Weird sports moments. Child's World 2011 24p il (Weird sports) lib bdg $25.64

Grades: 3 4 5 6   **796**

1. Sports 2. Curiosities and wonders

ISBN 978-1-60954-377-8; 1-60954-377-7

LC 2010042899

This describes weird moments in sports such as the outfield bonfire, football vs. the band, celebrating too early, and run the other way.

"Both the writing and the visual style are exuberant-without relying too much on exclamation points." Booklist

Krull, Kathleen

★ Lives of the athletes; thrills, spills (and what the neighbors thought) written by Kathleen Krull; illustrated by Kathryn Hewitt. Harcourt Brace & Co. 1997 96p il $21

Grades: 4 5 6 7   **796**

1. Actors 2. Athletes 3. Baseball players 4. Football players 5. Golfers 6. Surfers 7. Hurdlers 8. Swimmers 9. Decathletes 10. Ice skaters 11. High jumpers 12. Mountaineers 13. Pentathletes 14. Army officers 15. Hockey players 16. Soccer players 17. Tennis players 18. Martial artists 19. Javelin throwers 20. Olympic athletes 21. Basketball players 22. Nonfiction writers 23. Runners (Athletes) 24. Volleyball players

ISBN 0-15-200806-3

LC 95-50702

"Krull profiles twenty legendary athletes of the twentieth century who broke new ground in their sports and often broke through racial or gender barriers as well. . . . The brief biographies are enhanced by unusual details of personality and Hewitt's lively caricatures of the subjects." Horn Book

Includes bibliographical references

Mattern, Joanne

So, you want to work in sports? the ultimate guide to exploring the sports industry. Joanne Mattern. Aladdin/Beyond Words 2014 224 p. illustrations (Be what you want) (paperback) $9.99; (hardback) $18.99

Grades: 4 5 6 7 8   **796**

1. Sports 2. Vocational guidance

ISBN 1582704481; 158270449X; 9781582704487; 9781582704494

LC 2013025469

This book, by Joanne Mattern, is a "guide that can help you score a career in the sports industry. . . . From the popular careers of professional athlete, coach, sports broadcaster, and photographer, to the lesser-known professions of sports agent, statistician, sports therapist, and scout, [this book] delves into a wide variety of possible futures that are exciting and rewarding." (Publisher's note)

"Information is presented dynamically, with numerous sidebars ("Did you know "), graphs, lists, a career quiz, and hand-drawn illustrations. There are no photos. One of the book's strongest assets is its excellent resource section, including a six-page list of websites for professional organizations . . . and two pages of books and online documents." SLJ

Includes bibliographical references and index

Ralston, Birgitta

Snow play; how to make forts & slides & winter campfires plus the coolest Loch Ness monster and 23 other brrriliant [i.e. brilliant] project in the snow. Artisan 2010 111p il $14.95

Grades: 4 5 6 7 8 9 10 11 12 Adult   **796**

1. Snow 2. Outdoor recreation

ISBN 978-1-57965-405-4; 1-57965-405-3

"Opening with explanations of different types of snow and the various tools needed to work with it, this how-to book describes more than two dozen projects, most of which will require adult help and supervision. . . . Ratings of difficulty, the number of people and tools needed, the type of snow required, and the time frame are included with each project. Short snow-related facts appear throughout. . . . A brief listing of worldwide snow festivals, snow hotels and igloos, and an ice museum completes the package. While kids can certainly use this book to inspire ideas for winter fun, adults will find it equally useful, especially for generating ideas for family projects." SLJ

Rand, Casey

Graphing sports. Heinemann Library 2009 32p il (Real world data) $28.21; pa $7.99

Grades: 5 6 7 8   **796**

1. Graphic methods 2. Sports -- Statistics

ISBN 978-1-4329-2621-2; 1-4329-2621-7; 978-1-4329-2630-4 pa; 1-4329-2630-6 pa

LC 2009001189

This explains sports related concepts through charts and graphs.

"The writing is spot-on for the audience. Most importantly, the statistics used are well chosen and instantly understandable, and the text clearly explains how each type of graph can be used to best display different types of data." SLJ

Includes glossary and bibliographical references

Rose, Julianna

Go out and play! favorite outdoor games from Ka-boom! 1st ed. Candlewick Press 2011 vii, 96 p.p col. ill. (paperback) $11.99

Grades: 3 4 5   **796**

1. Games 2. Recreation

ISBN 0763655309; 9780763655303

LC 2011046634

This resource book is a "collection of 69 group games . . . to encourage children to engage in outdoor play. . . . Organized according to game type, the book focuses on versions of tag, hide-and-seek, ball games, team games, sidewalk games, circle games and races. . . . Sections at the beginning and end tell adults how to best be partners in children's play and how to create safe play spaces that will get kids outdoors." (Kirkus Reviews)

"This lively offering describes and outlines simple games that center on physical activity, including multiple versions of tag, hide-and-seek, ball games, race games, and 'no-rules games.' Each game is introduced in basic language, with a brief sidebar highlighting the number of players, recommended ages, space required, and suggested materials. Enlivened with cartoon spot art and photographs of children at play, the book should give readers plenty of activity options come spring." Publ Wkly

Includes bibliographical references.

Strother, Scott

★ The **adventurous** book of outdoor games; classic fun for daring boys and girls. [by] Scott Strother. Source-books 2008 293p il pa $14.99

Grades: 4 5 6 7 Adult Professional   **796**

1. Games

ISBN 978-1-4022-1443-1 pa; 1-4022-1443-X pa

This book "outlines more than 100 games, each at different activity levels set by the amount of physical exertion required. . . . Each game discusses the number of players, ages, time allotted, and type of playing field, followed by a brief description of equipment, startup, object of the game, and how to play. . . . The easy-to-read, easy-to-follow format will provide hours of imaginative play for all of those who are willing to try. An excellent resource for parents, teachers, and activity directors and even for children themselves." SLJ

Watson, S. B.

Weird animal sports. Child's World 2011 24p il (Weird sports) lib bdg $25.64

Grades: 3 4 5 6   **796**

1. Sports 2. Animals 3. Curiosities and wonders

ISBN 978-1-60954-3754; 1-60954-375-0

LC 2010042897

This describes sports such as turkey bowling, frog jumping, race car hamsters, camel racing, and elephant soccer.

"Both the writing and the visual style are exuberant—without relying too much on exclamation points." Booklist

Weird sports of the world. Child's World 2011 24p il (Weird sports) lib bdg $25.64

Grades: 3 4 5 6   **796**

1. Sports 2. Curiosities and wonders

ISBN 978-1-60954-378-5; 1-60954-378-5

LC 2010042901

This describes sports such as parkour, tough guy, unicycle hockey, mountain boarding, chess boxing, and waterfall kayaking.

"Both the writing and the visual style are exuberant-without relying too much on exclamation points." Booklist

Weird throwing and kicking sports. Child's World 2011 24p il (Weird sports) lib bdg $25.64

Grades: 3 4 5 6   **796**

1. Sports 2. Curiosities and wonders

ISBN 978-1-6095-4379-2; 1-6095-4379-3

LC 2010044026

This describes sports such as fish flinging, toe wrestling, stone tossing, stick kicking, and blanket riding.

"Both the writing and the visual style are exuberant-without relying too much on exclamation points." Booklist

Includes bibliographical references

Woods, Mark

Xtreme! Extreme sports facts and stats; [by] Mark Woods and Ruth Owen. Gareth Stevens Pub. 2011 32p il (Top score math) lib bdg $26.60

Grades: 4 5 6   **796**

1. Extreme sports

ISBN 978-1-4339-5020-9; 1-4339-5020-9

LC 2010029612

This book, "chock-full of numbers, presents 'facts and stats' associated with [extreme sports]. Figures include sports records, players' heights, jersey numbers, and surfing speeds. . . . [The book succeeds] at entertaining and instructing fans through engaging text and quiz challenges." Horn Book Guide

796.1 Miscellaneous games

Birmingham, Maria

Weird zone; sports. Maria Birmingham. Owlkids Books Inc. 2013 128 p. (Weird zone) $22.95

Grades: 4 5 6 7   **796.1**

1. Sports

ISBN 1926973607; 9781926973609

LC 2012948714

This book on unusual sports by Maria Birmingham is part of the "Weird Zone" book series. It includes such sports as "rolling down a hill in a plastic ball (aka 'zorbing') . . . professional-grade pillow fighting . . . lawn-mower racing . . . [and] extreme ironing. . . . Each sport gets a two-page spread." (Kirkus Reviews)

★ The **Eentsy**, weentsy spider: fingerplays and action rhymes; compiled by Joanna Cole and Stephanie Calmenson; illustrated by Alan Tiegreen. Morrow Junior Bks. 1991 64p il music hardcover o.p. pa $8.99

Grades: K 1 2 3   **796.1**

1. Songs 2. Finger play

ISBN 0-688-10805-9 pa

LC 90-44594

"Tiegreen uses a few simple lines to create a cast of multicultural characters whose enthusiasm is infectious. . . . An attractive, upbeat addition to the finger-play collection." Booklist

Includes bibliographical references

★ **Miss** Mary Mack and other children's street rhymes; compiled by Joanna Cole and Stephanie Calmenson; illustrated by Alan Tiegreen. Morrow Junior Bks. 1990 64p hardcover o.p. pa $7.95

Grades: K 1 2 3   **796.1**
1. Games 2. Nursery rhymes
ISBN 0-688-09749-9 pa
LC 89-37266

This is a collection of over 100 traditional childhood hand-clapping and street rhymes

"Tiegreen's lighthearted pen-and-ink illustrations are sure to tickle the fancy of young readers. . . . A book that's sure to produce smiles in any story hour or program." SLJ

796.2 Activities and games requiring equipment

Bell-Rehwoldt, Sheri
The **kids'** guide to jumping rope. Capstone Press 2011 32p il (Kids' guides) lib bdg $26.65

Grades: 4 5 6 7   **796.2**
1. Rope skipping
ISBN 978-1-4296-5443-2; 1-4296-5443-0
LC 2010035018

Describes the sport of jumping rope, including how-to information on jumps and tricks.

This includes "plentiful photos of giddy girls (and a few guys) madly skipping rope. . . . This makes jumping rope look like the best time in the world." Booklist

Includes bibliographical references

796.22 Skateboarding

Fitzpatrick, Jim
Skateboarding. Cherry Lake Pub. 2009 32p il (Innovation in sports) lib bdg $27.07

Grades: 4 5 6 7   **796.22**
1. Skateboarding
ISBN 978-1-60279-259-3 lib bdg; 1-60279-259-3 lib bdg
LC 2008007548

This describes skateboarding history, equipment, safety, and health benefits

This "stands out by emphasizing monumental shifts and advances in the events themselves. . . . Concise and occasionally revelatory." Booklist

Includes glossary and bibliographical references

Spencer, Russ
Skateboarding; by Russ Spencer. Child's World 2005 32p il (Kids' guides) lib bdg $24.21

Grades: 4 5 6   **796.22**
1. Skateboarding
ISBN 1-59296-210-6
LC 2003-27370

This "opens with an explanation of the sport and gives reasons why people enjoy it. The four chapters that follow cover background and development, equipment, technique, and stars and competitions. The excellent color photos are clear and exciting." SLJ

Includes bibliographical references

Stock, Charlotte
Skateboarding step-by-step; [by] Charlotte Stock and Ben Powell. Rosen Central 2010 91p il (Skills in motion) lib bdg $31.95

Grades: 5 6 7 8   **796.22**
1. Skateboarding
ISBN 978-1-4358-3365-4; 1-4358-3365-1
LC 2009-11414

Presents instructions on skateboarding from learning to skateboard to executing jumps, flips, and tricks.

"Colorful photographs show the entire movement of each skill presented, giving new meaning to the term 'step-by-step.' Progression borders at the bottom of the pages highlight the salient points to notice in performing each skill from beginning to end." SLJ

Includes bibliographical references

796.3 Ball games

Rosen, Michael J.
Balls!: round 2; illustrations by John Margeson. Darby Creek Pub. 2008 80p il $18.95

Grades: 3 4 5 6   **796.3**
1. Sports 2. Sporting goods
ISBN 978-1-58196-066-2; 1-58196-066-2

"Rosen offers a lighthearted look at a variety of balls, covering their production and history, and how they're used in sports. . . . The author highlights balls used in baseball, softball, bowling, bocce, croquet, shot put, billiards, and lacrosse. Each sport receives a brief introduction . . . complemented by color photographs, cartoons, and graphics. There's an emphasis on fun science, with simple puzzles and experiments. . . . Rosen serves up a feast of whimsical trivia and wordplay, and he rounds out this collection with sections on marbles and extreme goofballs." SLJ

Includes bibliographical references

796.323 Basketball

Bekkering, Annalise
NCAA Basketball. Weigl Publishers 2010 32p il map (Sporting championships) lib bdg $26; pa $9.95

Grades: 3 4 5   **796.323**
1. Basketball 2. Women's National Basketball Association 3. National Collegiate Athletic Association
ISBN 978-1-60596-634-2 lib bdg; 1-60596-634-7 lib bdg; 978-1-60596-635-9 pa; 1-60596-635-5 pa
LC 2009-8366

This sets the NCAA Basketball championship "within the context of the sport and explains what you need to know when watching the big [event]." Booklist

Includes glossary and bibliographical references

Burns, Brian
Basketball step-by-step; [by] Brian Burns and Mark Dunning. Rosen Central 2010 95p il (Skills in motion) lib bdg $31.95

Grades: 5 6 7 8   **796.323**
1. Basketball
ISBN 978-1-4358-3360-9; 1-4358-3360-0
LC 2009-14417

An introduction to the skills needed to play basketball uses a sequence of stop-action images and text instructions to illustrate such offensive and defensive moves as inside pivot and shoot, blocking out, and overhead pass.

"Colorful photographs show the entire movement of each skill presented, giving new meaning to the term 'step-by-step.' Progression borders at the bottom of the pages highlight the salient points to notice in performing each skill from beginning to end." SLJ

Includes bibliographical references

Doeden, Matt

The **greatest** basketball records; by Matt Doeden. Capstone Press 2009 32p il (Sports records) lib bdg $17.95

Grades: 4 5 6 7 8 **796.323**

1. Basketball 2. National Basketball Association

ISBN 978-1-4296-2006-2 lib bdg; 1-4296-2006-4 lib bdg

LC 2008-2033

This "has enough historical insight and trivia to remain appealing over time. . . . Brief, lively sentences sum up individual feats and set them in context. . . . [This] should appeal to a wide audience." SLJ

Includes glossary and bibliographical references

Gibbons, Gail

My basketball book. HarperCollins Pubs. 2000 un il $6.99

Grades: K 1 2 **796.323**

1. Basketball

ISBN 0-688-17140-0

LC 99-87902

Introduces the basics of the game of basketball, describing the players, court, techniques, and rules of play

Includes glossary

Gifford, Clive

Basketball; [by] Clive Gifford. PowerKids Press 2009 32p il (Personal best) lib bdg $25.25

Grades: 4 5 6 7 8 **796.323**

1. Basketball

ISBN 978-1-4042-4444-3 lib bdg; 1-4042-4444-1 lib bdg

LC 2007-42989

This guide to basketball "offers well-organized and easy-to-follow instructions, focusing on rules, clothing, specific skills, and competitions. . . . Informative, readable." SLJ

Includes bibliographical references

Labrecque, Ellen

Basketball; by Ellen Labrecque. Cherry Lake Pub. 2009 32p il (Innovation in sports) lib bdg $27.07

Grades: 4 5 6 7 **796.323**

1. Basketball

ISBN 978-1-60279-256-2 lib bdg; 1-60279-256-9 lib bdg

LC 2008002044

This describes basketball history, rules, equipment, training, and great players

This "stands out by emphasizing monumental shifts and advances in the events themselves. . . . Concise and occasionally revelatory." Booklist

Includes glossary and bibliographical references

Macy, Sue, 1954-

Basketball belles; how two teams and one scrappy player put women's hoops on the map. illustrated by Matt Collins. Holiday House 2010 un il $16.95

Grades: 1 2 3 4 **796.323**

1. Women athletes 2. Basketball players 3. Basketball -- Biography 4. Women basketball players

ISBN 0-8234-2163-5; 978-0-8234-2163-3

LC 2009-42498

This book is told from the perspective of Agnes Morley, who played on Stanford University's women's basketball team. It is a play-by-play account of an 1896 game played between Morley's team and the University of California at Berkeley team. "Ages six to nine." (Bull Cent Child Books)

"In this rousing picture book, Macy and Collins take readers to the (very) early days of women's basketball through the eyes of Agnes Morley, who offers a play-by-play account of an 1896 game between Stanford and Berkeley—the first ever between two women's basketball teams. . . . Whether Agnes is wrangling with a calf on her family's ranch or diving for a loose ball, her determination shines through in Collins's dynamic, painterly digital spreads." Publ Wkly

McClellan, Ray

Basketball. Bellwether Media 2010 24p il (Blastoff! readers. My first sports) $19.95

Grades: K 1 2 3 **796.323**

1. Basketball

ISBN 978-1-60014-279-6; 1-60014-279-6

LC 2009-8186

Simple text and full color photographs introduce beginning readers to the sport of basketball.

Includes glossary and bibliographical references

Robinson, Tom

Basketball. Norwood House Press 2010 64p il (Girls play to win) lib bdg $26.60

Grades: 4 5 6 7 **796.323**

1. Basketball

ISBN 978-1-59953-388-9; 1-59953-388-X

LC 2010009814

Covers the history, rules, fundamentals and significant personalities of the sport of women's basketball. Topics include: techniques, strategies, competitive events, and equipment.

"With an easy design and format, the [text is] highly accessible to even the most reluctant readers and [provides] great exposure and insight into the world of female professional sports." Horn Book Guide

Includes glossary and bibliographical references

Slade, Suzanne

Basketball; how it works. Capstone Press 2010 48p il (Science of sports) lib bdg $29.32; pa $7.95

Grades: 4 5 6 7 **796.323**

1. Basketball

ISBN 978-1-4296-4021-3 lib bdg; 1-4296-4021-9 lib bdg; 978-1-4296-4873-8 pa; 1-4296-4873-2 pa

The book's "photograph-heavy design works to engage its audience, while the easy-to-read [text explains] the science." Horn Book Guide

Includes glossary

Stewart, Mark

Swish; the quest for basketball's perfect shot. by Mark Stewart and Mike Kennedy. Millbrook Press 2009 64p il lib bdg $25.26

Grades: 5 6 7 8   **796.323**

1. Basketball

ISBN 978-0-8225-8752-1 lib bdg; 0-8225-8752-1 lib bdg

LC 2008-24958

"The wide pages offer plenty of room for well-spaced text, sidebars, and illustrations. Each page has at least one picture, with mostly color photos, and the many action shots make the book more exciting. With information on women's and men's basketball at both collegiate and professional levels, this is a nice addition to sports collections." Booklist

Includes bibliographical references

Thomas, Keltie

★ How basketball works. Maple Tree Press 2005 64p il hardcover o.p. $16.95

Grades: 5 6 7 8   **796.323**

1. Basketball

ISBN 1-89706-618-X; 1-89706-619-8 pa

This guide to basketball offers information about the game's origins, history, and equipment as well as positions, training, skills, stats, & rules of the game. It also offers tips and fascinating factoids.

"The writing style is razzle-dazzle energetic. . . . The layout features numerous sidebars and brightly colored photos and digital drawings. Even longtime fans will learn something from this engaging, enthusiastic book." Booklist

Thornley, Stew

Kevin Garnett; champion basketball star. by Stew Thornley. Enslow Publishers 2013 48 p. col. ill. (library) $23.93

Grades: 4 5 6 7   **796.323**

1. Picture books for children 2. Basketball players -- United States -- Biography

ISBN 0766040283; 9780766040281

LC 2011031517

This book by Stew Thornley is a children's picture book biography of professional basketball player Kevin Garnett. In his "career, Garnett has won MVP trophies and other individual awards, but his NBA championship ring is most important to him. The team has always come first for KG." (Publisher's note)

Includes bibliographical references (p. 47) and index.

Kobe Bryant; champion basketball star. by Stew Thornley. Enslow Publishers 2013 48 p. col. ill. (library) $23.93

Grades: 4 5 6 7   **796.323**

1. Picture books for children 2. Bryant, Kobe, 1978- 3. Basketball players -- United States -- Biography

ISBN 0766040291; 9780766040298

LC 2011038174

This picture book by Stew Thornley is a biography of professional basketball player Kobe Bryant. "He can swish shots from long range or drive to the basket for a vicious dunk. Bryant once scored 81 points in a single game! He can also dish it to his teammates and play lockdown defense. . . . The Los Angeles Lakers superstar has won five NBA titles

since coming out of high school, and he has earned many individual awards." (Publisher's note)

Tim Duncan; champion basketball star. by Stew Thornley. Enslow Publishers 2013 48 p. col. ill. (Sports Star Champions) (library) $23.93

Grades: 4 5 6 7   **796.323**

1. Basketball players -- United States -- Biography

ISBN 0766040305; 9780766040304

LC 2011050440

This book by Stew Thornley is part of the Sports Star Champions series and looks at basketball player Tim Duncan. The texts "focus on the athletes' professional careers, with very little information about their personal lives. . . . Each book ends with career statistics, the player's address, and a brief list for further reading." (School Library Journal)

Includes bibliographical references (p. 47) and index.

Yancey, Diane

Basketball. Lucent Books 2011 112p il (Science behind sports) lib bdg $33.45

Grades: 5 6 7 8   **796.323**

1. Basketball

ISBN 978-1-4205-0293-0; 1-4205-0293-X

LC 2010035239

This "explores the scientific principles such as momentum, gravity, friction, and aerodynamics, plus many more, behind [basketball]. . . . [The author discusses the sport's] origins, history, and changes, . . . the biomechanics and physiology of playing, related health and medical concerns, and the causes and treatment of sports-related injuries. Additional information tells how exercise, diet and nutrition, warming up, and training relate to peak performance and enjoyment of the sport. . . . [The book] has features on possible side effects of anabolic steroid use; how MRIs work; and how various improvements to the courts, basketballs, shoes, and uniforms have affected the game. The action photography . . . is fantastic. . . . [A must-have] for sports fans, athletes, science students, and even anyone considering a career in sports-related medicine, coaching, or other connected fields." SLJ

Includes glossary and bibliographical references

796.325 Volleyball

Crossingham, John

Spike it volleyball; [by] John Crossingham. Crabtree Pub. Co. 2008 32p il (Sports starters) lib bdg $18.95; pa $6.95

Grades: 2 3 4   **796.325**

1. Volleyball

ISBN 978-0-7787-3143-6 lib bdg; 0-7787-3143-X lib bdg; 978-0-7787-3175-7 pa; 0-7787-3175-8 pa

LC 2008004853

This "offers a sturdy overview of volleyball, from rules and scoring to basic moves. The accessible text lays out clear explanations of terms and concepts. . . . The eye-catching design combines large color photos of athletes in action with smaller inset pictures." Booklist

McDougall, Chros

Volleyball. Norwood House Press 2010 64p il (Girls play to win) lib bdg $26.60

Grades: 4 5 6 7 **796.325**

1. Volleyball

ISBN 978-1-59953-392-6; 1-59953-392-8

LC 2010009810

Covers the history, rules, fundamentals and significant personalities of the sport of women's volleyball. Topics include: techniques, strategies, competitive events, and equipment.

"With an easy design and format, the [text is] highly accessible to even the most reluctant readers and [provides] great exposure and insight into the world of female professional sports." Horn Book Guide

Includes glossary and bibliographical references

796.332 American football

Buckley, James

The **Child's** World encyclopedia of the NFL; by James Buckley, Jr. . . . [et al.] Child's World 2007 4v il

Grades: 3 4 5 6 7 **796.332**

1. Reference books 2. National Football League 3. Football -- Encyclopedias

ISBN 978-1-59296-922-7 v1; 978-1-59296-923-4 v2; 978-1-59296-924-1 v3; 978-1-59296-925-8 v4

LC 2007005662

This encyclopedia of the National Football League is "full of color photos; significant names, terms, and events; and plenty of popular football figures. The authors are all experienced sportswriters and editors." Booklist

Ultimate guide to football; by James Buckley, Jr. Franklin Watts 2010 160p il $30; pa $7.99

Grades: 4 5 6 7 **796.332**

1. Football

ISBN 978-0-531-20752-9; 0-531-20752-8; 978-0-531-21023-9 pa; 0-531-21023-5 pa

LC 2009011003

This guide to football covers "historical highlights and delectable ephemera . . . with spreads covering each NFL team interspersed among chatty tales. . . . The highlighter-green color scheme matches the loud, vibrant layout and heightens the contrasting black-and-white player photos, while sporadic cartoons add some pep to the presentation." Booklist

Includes bibliographical references

Diemer, Lauren

Rose Bowl. Weigl Publishers 2010 32p il map (Sporting championships) lib bdg $26; pa $9.95

Grades: 3 4 5 **796.332**

1. Football 2. Rose Bowl (Pasadena, Calif.)

ISBN 978-1-60596-638-0 lib bdg; 1-60596-638-X lib bdg; 978-1-60596-639-7 pa; 1-60596-639-8 pa

LC 2009-8362

This sets the Rose Bowl "within the context of the sport and explains what you need to know when watching the [event]." Booklist

Includes glossary and bibliographical references

Doeden, Matt

Play football like a pro; key skills and tips. Capstone Press 2011 32p il (Play like the pros) lib bdg $25.32; pa $6.95

Grades: 3 4 5 **796.332**

1. Football

ISBN 978-1-4296-4825-7 lib bdg; 1-4296-4825-2 lib bdg; 978-1-4296-5646-7 pa; 1-4296-5646-8 pa

LC 2010007243

"Provides instructional tips on how to improve one's football skills, including quotes and advice from professional coaches and athletes." Publisher's note

Includes glossary and bibliographical references

Dougherty, Terri

The **greatest** football records; by Terri Dougherty. Capstone Press 2009 32p il (Sports records) lib bdg $17.95

Grades: 4 5 6 7 8 **796.332**

1. Football 2. National Football League

ISBN 978-1-4296-2007-9 lib bdg; 1-4296-2007-2 lib bdg

LC 2008-2035

This "has enough historical insight and trivia to remain appealing over time. . . . Brief, lively sentences sum up individual feats and set them in context. . . . [This] should appeal to a wide audience." SLJ

Includes glossary and bibliographical references

Gibbons, Gail

My football book. HarperCollins Pubs. 2000 un il $6.99

Grades: K 1 2 **796.332**

1. Football

ISBN 0-688-17139-7

LC 99-87202

Introduces the basics of the game of football, describing the players, field, and how the game is played

"What shines through [in this book] is Gibbons's dedication to presenting the game as fun. . . . The illustrations, especially those of the players, clearly reflect the action." SLJ

Includes glossary

Gifford, Clive

Football. Marshall Cavendish Benchmark 2009 30p il (Tell me about sports) $19.95

Grades: 3 4 5 **796.332**

1. Football

ISBN 978-0-7614-4456-5; 0-7614-4456-4

LC 2009-4828

"An introduction to football, including techniques, rules, and the training regimen of professional athletes in the sport." Publisher's note

Includes glossary and bibliographical references

Gigliotti, Jim

Defensive backs. Gareth Stevens Pub. 2010 48p il (Game day. Football) lib bdg $31

Grades: 3 4 5 **796.332**

1. Football

ISBN 978-1-4339-1964-0 lib bdg; 1-4339-1964-8 lib bdg

LC 2009-6801

"The attractive page design showcases a mix of colorful photographs along with some vintage black-and-white shots, all within an attractive green border that shows yardage marks on a field. . . . This [book] . . . will generate discussion and sharing of opinions about favorite players and record book statistics." SLJ

Includes glossary and bibliographical references

Football. Cherry Lake Pub. 2009 32p il (Innovation in sports) lib bdg $27.07
Grades: 4 5 6 7   **796.332**
1. Football
ISBN 978-1-60279-257-9 lib bdg; 1-60279-257-7 lib bdg

LC 2008002305

This describes football history, rules, equipment, training and strategy, and innovators

This "stands out by emphasizing monumental shifts and advances in the events themselves. . . . Concise and occasionally revelatory." Booklist

Includes glossary and bibliographical references

Linebackers. Gareth Stevens Pub. 2010 48p il (Game day. Football) lib bdg $31
Grades: 3 4 5   **796.332**
1. Football
ISBN 978-1-4339-1959-6 lib bdg; 1-4339-1959-1 lib bdg

LC 2009-6802

"The attractive page design showcases a mix of colorful photographs along with some vintage black-and-white shots, all within an attractive green border that shows yardage marks on a field. . . . This [book] . . . will generate discussion and sharing of opinions about favorite players and record book statistics." SLJ

Includes glossary and bibliographical references

Linemen. Gareth Stevens Pub. 2010 48p il (Game day. Football) lib bdg $31
Grades: 3 4 5   **796.332**
1. Football
ISBN 978-1-4339-1960-2 lib bdg; 1-4339-1960-5 lib bdg

LC 2009-2272

"The attractive page design showcases a mix of colorful photographs along with some vintage black-and-white shots, all within an attractive green border that shows yardage marks on a field. . . . This [book] . . . will generate discussion and sharing of opinions about favorite players and record book statistics." SLJ

Includes glossary and bibliographical references

Receivers. Gareth Stevens Pub. 2010 48p il (Game day. Football) lib bdg $31
Grades: 3 4 5   **796.332**
1. Football
ISBN 978-1-4339-1962-6 lib bdg; 1-4339-1962-1 lib bdg

LC 2008-55595

"The attractive page design showcases a mix of colorful photographs along with some vintage black-and-white shots, all within an attractive green border that shows yardage marks on a field. . . . This [book] . . . will generate dis-

cussion and sharing of opinions about favorite players and record book statistics." SLJ

Includes glossary and bibliographical references

Kelley, K. C.
Quarterbacks. Gareth Stevens Pub. 2010 48p il (Game day. Football) lib bdg $31
Grades: 3 4 5   **796.332**
1. Football
ISBN 978-1-4339-1961-9 lib bdg; 1-4339-1961-3 lib bdg

LC 2008-55596

"The attractive page design showcases a mix of colorful photographs along with some vintage black-and-white shots, all within an attractive green border that shows yardage marks on a field. . . . This [book] . . . will generate discussion and sharing of opinions about favorite players and record book statistics." SLJ

Includes glossary and bibliographical references

Running backs. Gareth Stevens Pub. 2010 48p il (Game day. Football) lib bdg $31
Grades: 3 4 5   **796.332**
1. Football
ISBN 978-1-4339-1963-3 lib bdg; 1-4339-1963-X lib bdg

LC 2009-2277

"The attractive page design showcases a mix of colorful photographs along with some vintage black-and-white shots, all within an attractive green border that shows yardage marks on a field. . . . This [book] . . . will generate discussion and sharing of opinions about favorite players and record book statistics." SLJ

Includes glossary and bibliographical references

Marsico, Katie
Football; by Katie Marsico and Cecilia Minden. Cherry Lake Pub. 2009 32p il (Real world math: Sports) lib bdg $27.07
Grades: 4 5 6   **796.332**
1. Football 2. Arithmetic
ISBN 978-1-60279-247-0 lib bdg; 1-60279-247-X lib bdg

LC 2008-1165

This book "starts with a short story on the history of [football], fundamental rules, and a math challenge in every chapter. . . . [This book] will pique your imagination." Sci Books Films

Includes glossary and bibliographical references

McClellan, Ray
Football. Bellwether Media 2010 24p il (Blastoff! readers. My first sports) $19.95
Grades: K 1 2 3   **796.332**
1. Football
ISBN 978-1-60014-194-2; 1-60014-194-3

LC 2009-8187

"Simple text and full color photographs introduce beginning readers to the sport of football." Publisher's note

Includes glossary and bibliographical references

Rappoport, Ken

Peyton Manning; champion football star. by Ken Rappoport. Enslow Publishers 2013 48 p. col. ill. (Sports Star Champions) (library) $23.93

Grades: 4 5 6 7 **796.332**

1. Quarterbacks (Football) 2. Football players -- United States -- Biography 3. Quarterbacks (Football) -- United States -- Biography

ISBN 0766040275; 9780766040274

LC 2011052759

This book is part of the Sports Star Champion series and looks at quarterback Peyton Manning. The "texts focus on the athletes' professional careers, with very little information about their personal lives. Occasional sidebars add additional interest, and each book ends with career statistics, the player's address, and a brief list for further reading." (School Library Journal)

Includes bibliographical references (p. 47) and index.

Stewart, Mark

Touchdown; the power and precision of football's perfect play. by Mark Stewart and Mike Kennedy. Millbrook Press 2009 64p il lib bdg $27.93

Grades: 5 6 7 8 **796.332**

1. Football

ISBN 978-0-8225-8751-4 lib bdg; 0-8225-8751-3 lib bdg

LC 2008044295

"This attractive book opens with an intriguing history of American football. . . . Next, 10 double-page spreads feature 'Ten Unforgettable Touchdowns' in both professional and collegiate games from 1913 to 2006. After a chapter on 'touchdown makers,' spotlighting outstanding players . . . comes a short section on notable touchdown bloopers and another on trick plays and the element of surprise. . . . Photos, period prints, and reproductions of trading cards illustrate the text while adding color to the pages. . . . This nicely designed book provides plenty of on-the-field drama as well as pertinent information in a smoothly written overview of the touchdown." Booklist

Thomas, Keltie

How football works; illustrated by Stephen MacEachern. Owlkids 2010 64p il (How sports work) $22.95; pa $12.95

Grades: 3 4 5 **796.332**

1. Football

ISBN 978-1-897349-87-8; 1-897349-87-4; 978-1-897349-88-5 pa; 1-897349-88-2 pa

"A wide range of football facts are packed into every double-page spread of this picture-book overview of the sport. The covered topics include the history of the game, the changing turf of the NFL, equipment, and some of the most memorable clashes and players. Each short chapter is laid out with boxes containing a few paragraphs of information, along with color photos and illustrations. Young readers are bound to enjoy this browser-friendly approach, which presents an array of facts that can be absorbed quickly." Booklist

796.334 Soccer (Association football)

Bazemore, Suzanne

Soccer: how it works. Capstone Press 2010 48p il (Science of sports) lib bdg $29.32; pa $7.95

Grades: 4 5 6 7 **796.334**

1. Soccer

ISBN 978-1-4296-4025-1 lib bdg; 1-4296-4025-1 lib bdg; 978-1-4296-4876-9 pa; 1-4296-4876-7 pa

"Describes the science behind the sport of soccer, including kicking, ball control, and goalkeeping." Publisher's note

Includes glossary

Forest, Christopher

Play soccer like a pro; key skills and tips. Capstone Press 2011 32p il (Play like the pros) lib bdg $25.32; pa $6.95

Grades: 3 4 5 **796.334**

1. Soccer

ISBN 978-1-4296-4827-1 lib bdg; 1-4296-4827-9 lib bdg; 978-1-4296-5647-4 pa; 1-4296-5647-6 pa

LC 2010007244

"Provides instructional tips on how to improve one's soccer skills, including quotes and advice from professional coaches and athletes." Publisher's note

Includes glossary and bibliographical references

Gibbons, Gail

My soccer book. HarperCollins Pubs. 2000 un il $6.99

Grades: K 1 2 **796.334**

1. Soccer

ISBN 0-688-17138-9

LC 99-34514

Briefly describes the equipment, terminology, rules, positions, and plays of one of the world's most popular games

This "small, snappily designed book [is] attractive, accessible. . . . Diverse groups of children, drawn in Gibbons' typically bright colors and cheery style, demonstrate sports equipment and game plays." Booklist

Includes glossary

Gifford, Clive

The Kingfisher soccer encyclopedia. Kingfisher 2010 144p il $19.99

Grades: 5 6 7 8 **796.334**

1. Reference books 2. Soccer -- Encyclopedias

ISBN 978-0-7534-6397-0; 0-7534-6397-0

First published 2006

"Gifford does an excellent job of covering most aspects of the game from its history of a hundred-plus years to its current rules and tactics, teams, competitions, and famous players. Each section is clearly identified and provides additional information about the game. . . . Students involved in the sport or interested in specific teams or players will appreciate this book." Voice Youth Advocates

Includes glossary and bibliographical references

My first soccer book; Clive Gifford. Kingfisher 2012 48 p. col. ill. (hardcover) $12.99

Grades: 2 3 4 **796.334**

1. Soccer 2. Soccer -- Training

ISBN 0753467836; 9780753467831

LC 2012036444

In this children's picture book about soccer, "[Clive] Gifford discusses the field, positions, gear, and basic rules, then moves on to warm-ups and stretching. The book's main section offers double-page spreads on topics such as ball control, passing, shooting, goalkeeping, tackling, and paying attention to the referee." (Booklist)

Soccer; Clive Gifford. 1st ed. PowerKids Press 2009 32 p. col. ill. (Personal best) (library) $26.50
Grades: 4 5 6 7 8   **796.334**
  1. Soccer
  ISBN 9781404244412; 1404244417
                        LC 2007042997
This guide to soccer "offers well-organized and easy-to-follow instructions, focusing on rules, clothing, specific skills, and competitions. . . . Informative, readable." SLJ

Soccer skills; Clive Gifford. Kingfisher 2005 48 p. col. ill. (paperback) $6.99
Grades: 4 5 6   **796.334**
  1. Soccer -- Training
  ISBN 0753459329; 9780753459324
                        LC 2005006232
This book presents an "overview of tactics and moves for beginning soccer players by a well-known expert in the field. After an initial chapter on referees and rules, [Clive] Gifford goes on to ball control, various passing techniques, and shooting and tacking skills. Four pages are devoted to goaltending. The text consists of brief paragraphs of information placed around the illustrations rather than a flowing narrative." (School Library Journal)
Includes bibliographical references (p. 47) and index.

Guillain, Charlotte
  Soccer. Heinemann Library 2009 24p il (Sports and my body) lib bdg $21.36; pa $6.49
Grades: 1 2   **796.334**
  1. Soccer
  ISBN 978-1-4329-3456-9 lib bdg; 1-4329-3456-2 lib bdg; 978-1-4329-3461-3 pa; 1-4329-3461-9 pa
                        LC 2009-7082
Learn what soccer is, how it can help them stay healthy, and how they can play soccer safely.
This book relates "activity to health . . . [and] explains that in order to stay healthy, children should get plenty of rest, eat healthy food, and drink plenty of water." SLJ
Includes glossary

Hornby, Hugh
  Soccer; written by Hugh Hornby; photographed by Andy Crawford. DK Pub. 2008 70p il (DK eyewitness books) $15.99
Grades: 4 5 6 7   **796.334**
  1. Soccer
  ISBN 978-0-7566-3779-8; 0-7566-3779-1
                        LC 2008276290
First published 2000
Examines all aspects of the game of soccer: its history, rules, techniques, tactics, equipment, playing fields, competitive play, and more.

Hyde, Natalie
  Soccer science. Crabtree Pub. Co. 2009 32p il (Sports science) lib bdg $26.60; pa $8.95

Grades: 3 4 5 6   **796.334**
  1. Soccer
  ISBN 978-0-7787-4537-2 lib bdg; 0-7787-4537-6 lib bdg; 978-0-7787-4554-9 pa; 0-7787-4554-6 pa
                        LC 2008-46276
This book approachs soccer "from a scientific angle, describing some of the physics behind [the] pursuit and how athletes can use this knowledge to improve performance. . . . Fascinating facts . . . [such as] information about the soccer robots in the RoboCup, are presented in a captivating, lively manner. . . . The layout features colorful text boxes interspersed among photographs." SLJ
Includes glossary

Jennings, Madeleine
  Soccer step-by-step; [by] Madeleine Jennings and Ian Howe. Rosen Central 2010 95p il (Skills in motion) lib bdg $31.95
Grades: 5 6 7 8   **796.334**
  1. Soccer
  ISBN 978-1-4358-3362-3; 1-4358-3362-7
                        LC 2009-12538
Presents instructions on the basic movements of soccer, including passing, shooting, and goalkeeping.
"Colorful photographs show the entire movement of each skill presented, giving new meaning to the term 'step-by-step.' Progression borders at the bottom of the pages highlight the salient points to notice in performing each skill from beginning to end." SLJ
Includes bibliographical references

Kassouf, Jeff
  Soccer. Norwood House Press 2011 64p il (Girls play to win) lib bdg $26.60
Grades: 4 5 6 7   **796.334**
  1. Soccer
  ISBN 978-1-59953-464-0; 1-59953-464-9
                        LC 2011011037
Covers the history, rules, fundamentals, and significant personalities of the sport of women's soccer. Topics include: techniques, strategies, competitive events, and equipment.
Includes glossary and bibliographical references

Kelley, K. C.
  Soccer. Cherry Lake Pub. 2008 32p il (Innovation in sports) lib bdg $27.07
Grades: 4 5 6 7   **796.334**
  1. Soccer
  ISBN 978-1-60279-261-6 lib bdg; 1-60279-261-5 lib bdg
                        LC 2008006749
This describes soccer history, rules, styles of play, equipment, and innovators
This "stands out by emphasizing monumental shifts and advances in the events themselves. . . . Concise and occasionally revelatory." Booklist
Includes glossary and bibliographical references

Stewart, Mark
  ★ **Goal!**: the fire and fury of soccer's greatest moment; [by] Mark Stewart and Mike Kennedy. Millbrook Press 2010 64p il lib bdg $27.93

Grades: 5 6 7 8   **796.334**

1. Soccer

ISBN 978-0-8225-8754-5 lib bdg; 0-8225-8754-8 lib bdg

LC 2009014098

"This well-written book explores the nuances of scoring in the world's most popular sport. A quick history of the game lays the groundwork with details that may be new to even hard-core fans. The second chapter jumps right into the good stuff with descriptions of 10 of the most famous goals. . . . Also included is a rundown of the best male and female scorers from the early twentieth century to the present and weird anomalies and amusing anecdotes from soccer lore." Booklist

Wendorff, Anne

Soccer. Bellwether Media 2010 24p il (Blastoff! readers. My first sports) $19.95

Grades: K 1 2 3   **796.334**

1. Soccer

ISBN 978-1-60014-329-8; 1-60014-329-6

LC 2009-8183

"Simple text and full color photographs introduce beginning readers to the sport of soccer." Publisher's note

Includes glossary and bibliographical references

Woods, Mark

Goal! soccer facts and stats. [by] Mark Woods and Ruth Owen. Gareth Stevens Pub. 2011 32p il (Top score math) lib bdg $26.60

Grades: 4 5 6   **796.334**

1. Soccer

ISBN 978-1-4339-5015-5; 1-4339-501505

LC 2010029686

This book, "chock-full of numbers, presents 'facts and stats' associated with [soccer]. Figures include sports records, players' heights, jersey numbers, and surfing speeds. . . . [The book succeeds] at entertaining and instructing fans through engaging text and quiz challenges." Horn Book Guide

Includes glossary

796.34   Racket games

Smolka, Bo

Lacrosse. Norwood House Press 2011 64p il (Girls play to win) lib bdg $26.60

Grades: 4 5 6 7   **796.34**

1. Lacrosse

ISBN 978-1-59953-463-3; 1-59953-463-0

LC 2011011050

Covers the history, rules, fundamentals, and significant personalities of the sport of women's lacrosse. Topics include: techniques, strategies, competitive events, and equipment.

Includes glossary and bibliographical references

796.342   Tennis (Lawn tennis)

Bow, Patricia

Tennis science. Crabtree Pub. Co. 2009 32p il (Sports science) lib bdg $26.60; pa $8.95

Grades: 3 4 5 6   **796.342**

1. Tennis

ISBN 978-0-7787-4539-6 lib bdg; 0-7787-4539-2 lib bdg; 978-0-7787-4556-3 pa; 0-7787-4556-2 pa

LC 2008-48874

This book approachs tennis "from a scientific angle, describing some of the physics behind [the] pursuit and how athletes can use this knowledge to improve performance. . . . Fascinating facts . . . are presented in a captivating, lively manner. . . . The layout features colorful text boxes interspersed among photographs." SLJ

Includes glossary and bibliographical references

Gifford, Clive

Tennis; [by] Clive Gifford. Sea-to-Sea Publications 2009 30p il (Know your sport) lib bdg $27.10

Grades: 5 6 7 8   **796.342**

1. Tennis

ISBN 978-1-59771-153-1 lib bdg; 1-59771-153-5 lib bdg

LC 2008-7322

"Describes the equipment, courts, training, moves, and competitions of tennis. Includes step-by-step descriptions of moves." Publisher's note

Includes glossary

Marsico, Katie

Tennis; [by] Katie Marsico and Cecilia Minden. Cherry Lake Pub. 2009 32p il (Real world math: Sports) lib bdg $27.07

Grades: 4 5 6   **796.342**

1. Tennis 2. Arithmetic

ISBN 978-1-60279-248-7 lib bdg; 1-60279-248-8 lib bdg

LC 2008-1179

This book "starts with a short story on the history of [tennis], fundamental rules, and a math challenge in every chapter. . . . [This book] will pique your imagination." Sci Books Films

Includes glossary and bibliographical references

Wendorff, Anne

Tennis. Bellwether Media 2010 24p il (Blastoff! readers. My first sports) $19.95

Grades: K 1 2 3   **796.342**

1. Tennis

ISBN 978-1-60014-328-1; 1-60014-328-8

LC 2009-8188

"Simple text and full color photographs introduce beginning readers to the sport of tennis." Publisher's note

Includes glossary and bibliographical references

Woods, Mark

Ace! tennis facts and stats. [by] Mark Woods and Ruth Owen. Gareth Stevens Pub. 2011 32p il (Top score math) lib bdg $26.60

Grades: 4 5 6   **796.342**
1. Tennis
ISBN 978-1-4339-4986-9; 1-4339-4986-9
LC 2010025704

This book, "chock-full of numbers, presents 'facts and stats' associated with [tennis]. Figures include sports records, players' heights, jersey numbers, and surfing speeds. . . . [The book succeeds] at entertaining and instructing fans through engaging text and quiz challenges." Horn Book Guide

796.35   Ball driven by club, mallet, bat

Rosenstock, Barb
The **Streak**; how Joe Dimaggio became America's hero. Barb Rosenstock; illustrated by Terry Widener. Calkins Creek 2014 32 p. $16.95
Grades: 2 3 4 5   **796.35**
1. Baseball 2. New York Yankees (Baseball team) 3. Baseball bats 4. Baseball players
ISBN 159078992X; 9781590789926
LC 2013947717

"In the summer of 1941, Yankee center fielder Joe DiMaggio and his favorite bat, Betsy Ann, begin the longest hitting streak in baseball history. But when Betsy Ann goes missing, will DiMaggio keep hitting? Set on the brink of World War II," this book, by Barb Rosenstock and illustrated by Terry Widener, is a "sports story that united the country and made DiMaggio a hero." (Publisher's note)

"Placed within the historical context of the last perfect baseball summer before America's involvement in World War II, Joe DiMaggio's 56-game hitting streak of 1941 becomes even more impressive. Rosenstock also captures the drama surrounding the feat: how a player from humble beginnings with hands that were used to hard work now held a bat, how DiMaggio named his bat "Betsy Ann" and only used it for games, and how the bat was stolen on the very day he was to break the previously held record...Detailed source notes, a lengthy bibliography, and lots of stats round out the presentation." SLJ

796.352   Golf

Gifford, Clive
Golf: from tee to green; the essential guide for young golfers. Sea-to-Sea Publications 2010 64p il (Know your sport) $16.99
Grades: 5 6 7 8   **796.352**
1. Golf
ISBN 978-1-59771-217-0; 1-59771-217-5
LC 2008045861

Presents an instructional guide to the sport of golf, with information on different aspects of play and the equipment used.

"This book will be welcomed by young golf enthusiasts, whether they're beginners or experienced players. . . . A useful and attractive guide." Horn Book Guide

Includes bibliographical references

Kelley, K. C.
Golf. Cherry Lake Pub. 2009 32p il (Innovation in sports) lib bdg $27.07
Grades: 4 5 6 7   **796.352**
1. Golf
ISBN 978-1-60279-262-3 lib bdg; 1-60279-262-3 lib bdg
LC 2008002045

This describes golf history, rules, balls, and club technology, and innovators

This "stands out by emphasizing monumental shifts and advances in the events themselves. . . . Concise and occasionally revelatory." Booklist

Includes bibliographical references

Michelson, Richard
Twice as good; the story of William Powell and clearview, the only golf course designed, built and owned by an African-American. written by Richard Michelson; illlustrated by Eric Velasquez. Sleeping Bear Press 2011 32 p. col. ill. $16.95
Grades: 2 3 4   **796.352**
1. African American businesspeople 2. Golfers -- United States -- Biography 3. Discrimination in sports 4. Golf course architects -- United States -- Biography 5. Golf courses -- United States -- Design and construction -- History
ISBN 1585364665; 9781585364664
LC 2011029114

This children's picture book tells the story of "Willie Powell . . . [who] dreamed of becoming a professional golfer, but his accomplishments went far beyond playing the game of golf. Willie was often denied the opportunity to play golf because he was African American. Determined, he decided to build his own course, and welcome people of all color to play golf." (Publisher's note)

"An inspirational story, suitable for Black History Month and for children interested in the game of golf." LJ

Webster, Christine
Masters Golf Tournament. Weigl Publishers 2009 32p il map (Sporting championships) lib bdg $26; pa $9.95
Grades: 3 4 5   **796.352**
1. Golf
ISBN 978-1-60596-640-3 lib bdg; 1-60596-640-1 lib bdg; 978-1-60596-641-0 pa; 1-60596-641-X pa
LC 2009-12346

This sets the Masters Golf Tournament "within the context of the sport and explains what you need to know when watching the big [event]." Booklist

Includes glossary and bibliographical references

796.357   Baseball

Adler, David A.
Lou Gehrig; the luckiest man. illustrated by Terry Widener. Harcourt Brace & Co. 1997 un il $17; pa $7
Grades: 2 3 4   **796.357**
1. Baseball players 2. Baseball -- Biography
ISBN 0-15-200523-4; 0-15-202483-3 pa
LC 95-7997

Traces the life of the Yankees' star ballplayer, focusing on his character and his struggle with the terminal disease amyotrophic lateral sclerosis

"Adler's restrained tone makes his description of Gehrig's stoic and uncomplaining struggle all the more moving. The illustrations, meticulously detailed . . . also pack an emotional wallop." Horn Book Guide

A **picture** book of Jackie Robinson; illustrated by Robert Casilla. Holiday House 1994 un il $17.95; pa $6.95
Grades: 1 2 3   **796.357**
1. Baseball players 2. African American athletes 3. Army officers 4. Baseball -- Biography
ISBN 0-8234-1122-2; 0-8234-1304-7 pa

LC 93-27224

"A brief look at the life of baseball great Jackie Robinson. The subject's childhood, sporting accomplishments, and later endeavors are touched upon, as are the bigotry and prejudice he faced as the first African American to play in the major leagues. . . . Casilla's full-and double-page watercolors provide attractive backgrounds for the text. A sound introduction to a significant figure." SLJ

Bertoletti, John C.
How baseball managers use math; math curriculum consultant: Rhea A. Stewart. Chelsea Clubhouse 2010 32p il (Math in the real world) lib bdg $28
Grades: 4 5 6   **796.357**
1. Baseball 2. Mathematics 3. Vocational guidance
ISBN 978-1-60413-604-3 lib bdg; 1-60413-604-9 lib bdg

LC 2009-16265

"The layout for [this] slim [title] is bright and colorful with a photograph and a 'You Do the Math' problem to solve and large, easy-to-read text on every spread. An answer key is included in the back matter, along with a page detailing the career choices and the educational requirements. . . . [It] includes such topics as how managers rely on player statistics to make decisions and why the pitch count is important to monitor. [This title] would be useful to supplement lessons on mathematics. [It] will also appeal to students wanting to learn more about math as it relates to specific careers." SLJ
Includes glossary and bibliographical references

Bildner, Phil
★ The **unforgettable** season; the story of Joe DiMaggio, Ted Williams and the record-setting summer of '41. illustrated by S. D. Schindler. G. P. Putnam's Sons 2011 un il $16.99
Grades: 1 2 3   **796.357**
1. Baseball 2. Baseball players 3. Baseball managers 4. Baseball -- History
ISBN 978-0-399-25501-4; 0-399-25501-X

LC 2010007382

"In a narrative that's conversational yet informative, Bildner dives into the baseball season of 1941, alternately focusing on Yankee slugger DiMaggio, who had a 56-game hitting streak, and Red Sox star Williams, who ended the season with a batting average of .406. Bildner builds suspense with taut descriptions of critical on-field moments . . . while Schindler's paintings capture the ballpark energy." Publ Wkly

Bow, James
Baseball science. Crabtree Pub. 2009 32p il (Sports science) lib bdg $26.60; pa $8.95
Grades: 3 4 5 6   **796.357**
1. Baseball
ISBN 978-0-7787-4534-1 lib bdg; 0-7787-4534-1 lib bdg; 978-0-7787-4551-8 pa; 0-7787-4551-1 pa

LC 2008-46274

This describes baseball skills and techniques from a scientific point of view.
Includes glossary and bibliographical references

Buckley, James
Ultimate guide to baseball. Shoreline Pub. 2010 160p il $30; pa $7.99
Grades: 4 5 6 7   **796.357**
1. Baseball
ISBN 978-0-531-20750-5; 0-531-20750-1; 978-0-531-21021-5 pa; 0-531-21021-9 pa

LC 2009043684

"This is a wide-ranging, brisk overview of the game. Sections briefly skim baseball history, hitting, pitching, defense and baserunning, and the World Series. Each major league team is introduced in a thumbnail sketch. . . . Other topics include baseball slang and nicknames, the 11 ways to get on base, and the author's choices for the best defensive players of all time. . . . Buckley writes with a lightly humorous touch that should appeal to fans and browsers." SLJ
Includes bibliographical references

Child's World (Firm)
The **Child's** World encyclopedia of baseball; by James Buckley, Jr. . . . [et al.] Child's World 2009 5v il set $247.75
Grades: 4 5 6 7 8   **796.357**
1. Baseball -- Encyclopedias
ISBN 978-1-60253-175-8 set; 1-60253-175-7 set

LC 2008039461

In this baseball encyclopedia, the authors "definitely convey an enthusiasm for their subject." Booklist

Coleman, Janet Wyman
Baseball for everyone; stories from the great game. by Janet Wyman Coleman with Elizabeth V. Warren. Abrams 2003 48p il $16.95
Grades: 4 5 6   **796.357**
1. Baseball
ISBN 0-8109-4580-0

LC 2002-155971

An illustrated history of baseball, covering the origins of the game, some of its best-known players, and significant changes in rules and practices throughout the nineteenth and twentieth centuries

"Drawing on The Perfect Game, Warren's adult book and exhibit of the same name at New York's American Folk Art Museum, . . . this elegant volume may well be irresistible to fans of America's favorite pastime. . . . [This offers] lively, informative text . . . enticingly packaged with a plethora of photographs, memorabilia and often astonishing folk art." Publ Wkly

Cook, Sally
Hey batta batta swing! the wild old days of baseball. [by] Sally Cook & James Charlton; illustrated by Ross

MacDonald. Margaret K. McElderry Books 2007 48p il
$17.99
Grades: 3 4 5 6   **796.357**
1. Baseball
ISBN 978-1-4169-1207-1; 1-4169-1207-X
LC 2006-08132
"The authors present a lively, puckish history of base-
ball's earliest years, relating what young readers actually
want to know. . . . Boldface words in the text identify jar-
gon, most of which is still used today, and definitions stud
the page borders. The jaunty tone is flawlessly matched by
MacDonald's illustrations, with their wriggling lines and
Katzenjammer Kids colors." Booklist

Curlee, Lynn
★ **Ballpark**; the story of America's baseball fields.
Atheneum Books for Young Readers 2005 41p il $17.95
Grades: 3 4 5 6   **796.357**
1. Baseball 2. Stadiums
ISBN 0-689-86742-5
LC 2003-23144
This is a "succinct and thoughtful overview. . . . Stylized,
full-page acrylic paintings add to the nostalgic tone of the
book." SLJ

Doeden, Matt
The **World** Series; baseball's biggest stage. by Matt
Doeden. Millbrook Press, A division of Lerner Publishing
Group, Inc. 2014 64 p. (lib. bdg.: alk. paper) $33.27
Grades: 4 5 6 7   **796.357**
1. Baseball 2. World Series (Baseball) 3. World Series
(Baseball) -- History
ISBN 1467718963; 9781467718967
LC 2013018082
This book describes how "when the top teams face off in
the World Series each season, team legacies and fans' hearts
are on the line. Author Matt Doeden covers the century-long
history of the World Series, from its humble beginnings to
becoming a worldwide sensation. Discover the drama behind the statistics and record books that keeps the crowd
enthralled!" (Publisher's note)
"This valentine to the Fall Classic opens with a quick
history - —though only through the 2012 series - —then
goes on in separate chapters to highlight renowned games,
awesome individual performances, and memorable plays
or incidents...The color photos on every spread are almost
all action shots and capture the excitement of each feat or
moment. An adequate set of recommended print and web
resources follows a closing won-lost chart. A fine commemoration of the World Series' first century." Booklist
Includes bibliographical references (p. 62) and index

Dreier, David
Baseball; how it works. Capstone Press 2010 48p il
(Science of sports) lib bdg $29.32; pa $7.95
Grades: 4 5 6 7   **796.357**
1. Baseball
ISBN 978-1-4296-4020-6 lib bdg; 1-4296-4020-0 lib
bdg; 978-1-4296-4872-1 pa; 1-4296-4872-4 pa
"The well-designed layout, featuring glossy color visu-
als, is stimulating, and the concepts are further reinforced in
brief definitions that appear at the bottom of many pages and

in an appended glossary. . . . The clever approach will help
draw interest and build understanding." Booklist
Includes glossary

Frager, Ray
Baltimore Orioles. ABDO Pub. Co. 2011 48p il (Inside MLB) $31.35
Grades: 4 5 6   **796.357**
1. Baseball 2. Baltimore Orioles (Baseball team)
ISBN 978-1-61714-036-5; 1-61714-036-8
LC 2010036557
"Written by [a] professional [sportswriter], peppered
with well-chosen quotations and illustrated with photos on
every page turn, this [book about the Baltimore Orioles] will
interest die-hard baseball fans and is likely to engage reluctant readers." Horn Book Guide
Includes glossary and bibliographical references

Freedman, Lew
Boston Red Sox. ABDO Pub. Co. 2011 48p il (Inside
MLB) $31.35
Grades: 4 5 6   **796.357**
1. Baseball 2. Boston Red Sox (Baseball team)
ISBN 9781617140372; 1617140376
LC 2010036554
"Written by [a] professional [sportswriter], peppered
with well-chosen quotations and illustrated with photos on
every page turn, this [book about the Boston Red Sox] will
interest diehard baseball fans and is likely to engage reluc-
tant readers." Horn Book Guide
Includes glossary and bibliographical references

Gibbons, Gail
My baseball book. HarperCollins Pubs. 2000 un il
$6.99
Grades: K 1 2   **796.357**
1. Baseball
ISBN 0-688-17137-0
LC 99-32945
An introduction to baseball, describing the equipment,
playing field, rules, players, and process of the game
"The information is well augmented by clearly labeled,
colorful drawings." SLJ
Includes glossary

Gitlin, Marty
Softball. Norwood House Press 2011 64p il (Girls
play to win) lib bdg $26.60
Grades: 4 5 6 7   **796.357**
1. Softball
ISBN 978-1-59953-465-7; 1-59953-465-7
LC 2011011051
Covers the history, rules, fundamentals, and signifi-
cant personalities of the sport of women's softball. Top-
ics include: techniques, strategies, competitive events,
and equipment.
Includes glossary and bibliographical references

Glaser, Jason
Batter. Gareth Stevens 2011 48p il (Play ball: baseball) lib bdg $31.95; pa $14.05; ebook $31.95

Grades: K 1 2 3 **796.357**
1. Baseball
ISBN 978-1-4339-4619-6 lib bdg; 1-4339-4619-X lib bdg; 978-1-4339-4620-2 pa; 1-4339-4620-2 pa; 978-1-4339-4622-6 ebook

LC 2010039132

"A well-conceived, up-to-date look at the particular skills needed to play [batter] in baseball. [This] volume discusses the [batter's] evolution through baseball history, describes the player's responsibilities during games, and highlights famous players. Clearly written and amply illustrated with photos of recent and current stars, [this book offers] solid information for young baseballers and casual fans alike." Horn Book Guide

Includes glossary and bibliographical references

Catcher. Gareth Stevens Pub. 2011 48p il (Play ball: baseball) lib bdg $31.95
Grades: K 1 2 3 **796.357**
1. Baseball
ISBN 9781433944840 pa; 9781433944833 lib bdg

LC 2010035720

"A well-conceived, up-to-date look at the particular skills needed to play [catcher] in baseball. [This] volume discusses the [catcher's] evolution through baseball history, describes the player's responsibilities during games, and highlights famous players. Clearly written and amply illustrated with photos of recent and current stars, [this book offers] solid information for young baseballers and casual fans alike." Horn Book Guide

Includes glossary and bibliographical references

Infielders. Gareth Stevens 2011 48p il (Play ball: baseball) lib bdg $31.95; pa $14.05; e-book $31.95
Grades: K 1 2 3 **796.357**
1. Baseball
ISBN 978-1-4339-4487-1 lib bdg; 1-4339-4487-1 lib bdg; 978-1-4339-4488-8 pa; 1-4339-4488-X pa; 987-1-4339-4490-1 e-book

LC 2010026667

"A well-conceived, up-to-date look at the particular skills needed to play [infield] in baseball. [This] volume discusses the [infielder's] evolution through baseball history, describes the player's responsibilities during games, and highlights famous players. Clearly written and amply illustrated with photos of recent and current stars, [this book offers] solid information for young baseballers and casual fans alike." Horn Book Guide

Outfielders. Gareth Stevens 2011 48p il (Play ball: baseball) lib bdg $31.95; pa $14.05; e-book $31.95
Grades: K 1 2 3 **796.357**
1. Baseball
ISBN 978-1-4339-4491-8 lib bdg; 1-4339-4491-8 lib bdg; 978-1-4339-4492-5 pa; 1-4339-4492-5 pa; 978-1-4339-4494-9 e-book

LC 2010030690

"A well-conceived, up-to-date look at the particular skills needed to play [outfield] in baseball. [This] volume discusses the [outfielder's] evolution through baseball history, describes the player's responsibilities during games, and highlights famous players. Clearly written and amply illustrated with photos of recent and current stars, [this book

offers] solid information for young baseballers and casual fans alike." Horn Book Guide

Includes glossary and bibliographical references

Pitcher. Gareth Stevens 2011 48p il (Play ball: baseball) lib bdg $31.95; pa $14.05; ebook $31.95
Grades: K 1 2 3 **796.357**
1. Baseball
ISBN 978-1-4339-4495-6 lib bdg; 1-4339-4495-2 lib bdg; 978-1-4339-4496-3 pa; 1-4339-4496-3 pa; 978-1-4339-4498-7 ebook

LC 2010039136

"A well-conceived, up-to-date look at the particular skills needed to play [pitcher] in baseball. [This] volume discusses the [pitcher's] evolution through baseball history, describes the player's responsibilities during games, and highlights famous players. Clearly written and amply illustrated with photos of recent and current stars, [this book offers] solid information for young baseballers and casual fans alike." Horn Book Guide

Includes glossary and bibliographical references

Golenbock, Peter
★ **Hank** Aaron; brave in every way. illustrated by Paul Lee. Harcourt 2001 un il $16
Grades: 1 2 3 **796.357**
1. Baseball players 2. African American athletes 3. Baseball -- Biography
ISBN 0-15-202093-4

LC 00-8855

A biography of the Hall of Fame baseball player who broke Babe Ruth's career home run record

"This richly illustrated biography . . . deftly tells the athlete's story. . . . Lee's strong, full-page acrylic illustrations in rich tones and textures work well and give the story depth and intensity." SLJ

Teammates; written by Peter Golenbock; designed and illustrated by Paul Bacon. Harcourt Brace Jovanovich 1990 un il $16; pa $7
Grades: 1 2 3 4 **796.357**
1. Baseball players 2. African American athletes 3. Army officers 4. Baseball -- Biography 5. Brooklyn Dodgers (Baseball team)
ISBN 0-15-200603-6; 0-15-284286-1 pa

LC 89-38166

Describes the racial prejudice experienced by Jackie Robinson when he joined the Brooklyn Dodgers and became the first black player in Major League baseball and depicts the acceptance and support he received from his white teammate Pee Wee Reese

"Golenbock's bold and lucid style distills this difficult issue, and brings a dramatic tale vividly to life. Bacon's spare, nostalgic watercolors, in addition to providing fond glimpses of baseball lore, present a haunting portrait of one man's isolation. Historic photographs of the major characters add interest and a touch of stark reality to an unusual story, beautifully rendered." Publ Wkly

Hetrick, Hans
Play baseball like a pro; key skills and tips. Capstone Press 2011 32p il (Play like the pros) lib bdg $25.32; pa $6.95

Grades: 3 4 5   796.357
  1. Baseball
  ISBN 978-1-4296-4824-0 lib bdg; 1-4296-4824-4 lib
  bdg; 978-1-4296-5644-3 pa; 1-4296-5644-1 pa
                                        LC 2010007241
"Provides instructional tips on how to improve one's
baseball skills, including quotes and advice from professional coaches and athletes." Publisher's note
  Includes glossary and bibliographical references

Jennings, Madeleine
  Baseball step-by-step; [by] Madeleine Jennings, Alan
Smith, and Alan Bloomfield. Rosen Central 2009 95p il
(Skills in motion) lib bdg $31.95
Grades: 5 6 7 8   796.357
  1. Baseball
  ISBN 978-1-4358-3361-6; 1-4358-3361-9
                                        LC 2009-13246
  An introduction to the skills needed to play baseball
uses a sequence of stop-action images and text instructions
to illustrate the moves needed to pitch, catch, field, hit, and
run bases.
  "Colorful photographs show the entire movement of
each skill presented, giving new meaning to the term 'step-
by-step.' Progression borders at the bottom of the pages
highlight the salient points to notice in performing each skill
from beginning to end." SLJ
  Includes bibliographical references

Kelly, David A.
  Miracle mud; Lena Blackburne and the secret mud that
changed baseball. by David A. Kelly; illustrated by Oliver
Dominguez. Millbrook Press 2013 32 p. (lib. bdg.: alk.
paper) $16.95
Grades: 3 4 5   796.357
  1. Baseball -- History 2. Picture books for children
  3. Sports -- United States -- Marketing 4. Inventors
  -- United States -- Biography 5. Baseball players --
  United States -- Biography 6. Baseball -- United States
  -- Equipment and supplies
  ISBN 0761380922; 9780761380924
                                        LC 2012020917
  This children's picture book is a biography of baseball
player Lena Blackburne. "Blackburne was never an outstanding player, but he will go down in history for developing a solution to the wet, soggy baseballs that could be
difficult to throw during a game. One day after fishing, he
stepped in some soft, gooey mud and an idea was born. Because the mud took the shine off any new white baseball, he
began to sell it." (School Library Journal)

Kisseloff, Jeff
  Who is baseball's greatest pitcher? Cricket Bks. 2003
181p il $15.95
Grades: 5 6 7 8   796.357
  1. Baseball
  ISBN 0-8126-2685-0
                                        LC 2003-1245
  Asks the reader to compare the statistics for thirty-three
of baseball's greatest starting pitchers and decide who is
the best
  "Accomplishments and anecdotes are related in an informative and entertaining manner. . . . Anyone who enjoys

baseball will be delighted with this information-packed, informal book." SLJ
  Includes bibliographical references

Lipsyte, Robert
  ★ **Heroes** of baseball; the men who made it America's
favorite game. [by] Robert Lipsyte. Atheneum Books for
Young Readers 2006 92p il $19.95
Grades: 4 5 6 7   796.357
  1. Baseball -- Biography
  ISBN 0-689-86741-7; 978-0-689-86741-5
                                        LC 2005010841
  "Using as a focus some of baseball's greats—Big Al
Spalding, Babe Ruth, Mickey Mantle, Jackie Robinson, Curt
Flood . . . —Lipsyte offers a strong history of the game and
its place in American culture. . . . Although much of this
material, including the pictures, might be familiar to young
readers already absorbed in the game, it is nicely laid out
and colorfully formatted. Lipsyte has a clear, vivid style."
Booklist
  Includes glossary and bibliographical references

McClellan, Ray
  Baseball. Bellwether media 2010 24p il (Blastoff!
readers. My first sports) $19.95
Grades: K 1 2 3   796.357
  1. Baseball
  ISBN 978-1-60014-277-2; 1-60014-277-X
                                        LC 2009-8157
  "Simple text and full color photographs introduce begin-
ning readers to the sport of baseball." Publisher's note
  Includes glossary and bibliographical references

Moss, Marissa
  Barbed wire baseball; by Marissa Moss; illustrated by
Yuko Shimizu. Abrams Books for Young Readers 2013 48
p. (reinforced) $18.95
Grades: 3 4 5   796.357
  1. Baseball -- History 2. Japanese Americans --
  Evacuation and relocation, 1942-1945 3. World War,
  1939-1945 4. Baseball -- United States -- History --
  20th century
  ISBN 1419705210; 9781419705212
                                        LC 2012010021
  Asian/Pacific American Awards for Literature: Picture
Book Honor (2014)
  This children's book, by Marissa Moss, illustrated by
Yuko Shimizu, profiles a 1940s Japanese American baseball
player. "Kenichi 'Zeni' Zenimura dreams of playing profes-
sional baseball, . . . [and] he grows up to be a successful
player, playing with Babe Ruth and Lou Gehrig! When the
Japanese attack Pearl Harbor in 1941, Zeni and his family
are sent to one of ten internment camps. . . . Zeni brings the
game of baseball to the camp, along with a sense of hope."
(Publisher's note)

Nelson, Kadir
  ★ **We** are the ship; the story of Negro League baseball.
words and paintings by Kadir Nelson; forward by Hank
Aaron. Jump at the Sun 2008 88p il $18.99
Grades: 2 3 4   796.357
  1. Baseball 2. Negro leagues 3. African American
  athletes 4. Negro leagues -- History 6. African
  American baseball players 7. Baseball -- United States

-- History

ISBN 978-0-7868-0832-8; 0-7868-0832-2

Awarded the Sibert Medal, 2009

The author "delivers a history of the Negro Leagues in a sumptuous volume that no baseball fan should be without. Using a folksy vernacular, a fictional player gives an insider account of segregated baseball. . . . As illuminating as the text is, Nelson's muscular paintings serve as the true draw. His larger-than-life players have oversized hands, elongated bodies and near-impossible athleticism." Publ Wkly

Nevius, Carol

Baseball hour; illustrated by Bill Thomson. Marshall Cavendish 2008 un il $16.99

Grades: 1 2 3   **796.357**

1. Baseball

ISBN 978-0-7614-5380-2; 0-7614-5380-6

LC 2007014254

This "picture book follows a multicultural group of boys and girls through their team's baseball practice. . . . The rhyming, rhythmic text works well enough, but . . . the photorealistic artwork, which a note describes as 'rendered in mixed media,' steal the show. Technically impressive, the black, white, and sepia illustrations capture form, details, action, and gesture well." Booklist

Rappaport, Doreen

Dirt on their skirts; the story of the young women who won the world championship. [by] Doreen Rappaport, Lyndall Callan; pictures by E.B. Lewis. Dial Bks. for Young Readers 1999 un il $16.99

Grades: K 1 2 3   **796.357**

1. Baseball -- Fiction 2. All-American Girls Professional Baseball League -- Fiction

ISBN 0-8037-2042-4

LC 98-47080

Margaret experiences the excitement of watching the 1946 championship game of the All-American Girls Professional Baseball League as it goes into extra innings.

"With its economy of language and telling period details, this book provides an exciting slice of sports history and an appealing bit of Americana. . . . Lewis's finely wrought watercolor paintings deftly capture the crowd and the action on the field." SLJ

Rappoport, Ken

Alex Rodriguez; champion baseball star. by Ken Rappoport. Enslow Publishers 2013 48 p. col. ill. (Sports star champions) (library) $23.93

Grades: 4 5 6 7   **796.357**

1. Baseball players -- Biography 2. Baseball players -- United States -- Biography

ISBN 0766040267; 9780766040267

LC 2011043754

"Of the forty-three glossy story pages in the book, fifteen describe . . . [baseball player Alex Rodriguez's] career from 2004 forward. A Career Statistics Chart follows his performance through 2011. Color photos include A-Rod's early baseball career through 2011. Many of his impressive stats are discussed, including being the only major league player to hit thirty home runs and drive in one hundred runs in thirteen consecutive seasons." (Children's Literature)

Derek Jeter; champion baseball star. by Ken Rappoport. Enslow Publishers 2013 48 p. col. ill. (Sports star champions) (library) $23.93

Grades: 4 5 6 7   **796.357**

1. Baseball players -- Biography 2. Baseball players -- United States -- Biography

ISBN 0766040259; 9780766040250

LC 2011033514

This book by Ken Rappoport, part of the Sports Star Champions series, presents a biography of "New York Yankees shortstop" Derek Jeter, who "has led the Yankees to five World Series titles and has won several individual awards." (Publisher's note) The "book ends with career statistics, the player's address, and a brief list for further reading." (School Library Journal)

Robinson, Sharon, 1950-

Jackie Robinson; American hero. by Sharon Robinson. Scholastic, Inc. 2013 48 p. $16.99

Grades: 3 4 5   **796.357**

1. Picture books for children 2. African American baseball players -- Biography 3. Baseball players -- United States -- Biography

ISBN 054556915X; 9780545569156

LC 2012046058

This book by Jackie Robinson's daughter Sharon Robinson is a biography of "the famous African American baseball player" that looks at "the significance of how a young black ballplayer broke the racial barrier and helped desegregate Major League Baseball. . . . The author gives a brief overview from childhood, to marriage, to death while showcasing myriad black-and-white family photos." (School Library Journal)

Skead, Robert

Something to prove; the great Satchel Paige vs. rookie Joe DiMaggio. by Robert Skead; illustrated by Floyd Cooper. Carolrhoda Books 2013 32 p. ill. (library) $16.95

Grades: 2 3 4 5   **796.357**

1. Baseball 2. Baseball players -- United States -- Social conditions 3. Discrimination in baseball -- United States -- History

ISBN 0761366199; 9780761366195

LC 2012019709

This children's book, by Robert Skead, tells how "in 1936, the New York Yankees wanted to test a hot prospect named Joe DiMaggio to see if he was ready for the big leagues. They knew just the ballplayer to call: Satchel Paige, the best pitcher anywhere, black or white. For the game, Paige joined a group of amateur African American players, and they faced off against a team of white major leaguers plus young DiMaggio." (Publisher's note)

Smith, Charles R., 1969-

Diamond life; baseball sights, sounds, and swings. Orchard Bks. 2004 28p il $15.95

Grades: 2 3 4   **796.357**

1. Baseball

ISBN 0-439-43180-8

"Smith captures the colorful language and vivid images of the game. . . . The energetic, playful language begs to be read aloud. Combined with bright colors, bold print in a variety of fonts, and exceptional photography, this book is a winner." SLJ

Stars in the shadows; the Negro league all-star game of 1934. Charles R. Smith Jr.; illustrated by Frank Morrison. Atheneum 2012 106 p. ill. (hardcover) $14.99

Grades: 2 3 4   **796.357**

1. Negro leagues   2. African American athletes   3. Radio broadcasting of sports   4. Baseball -- History

ISBN 0689866380; 9780689866388

LC 2011017469

In this chapter book, "[Charles R.] Smith uses a fictional radio sports announcer to introduce the players on both Negro League East-West Classic teams. . . . The story takes place during a time when baseball was segregated and fans voted for their favorite players to make the All-Star roster. Within a basic organization plan of nine innings, or chapters, the author writes in a poetic narrative style." (School Library Journal)

"Some of the best-ever baseball players face off in 1934 at the second annual Negro League All-Star game in Chicago. . . . Cool Papa Bell, Josh Gibson, Willie Wells, Satchel Paige and Oscar Charleston are legendary names despite the segregation that kept them from competing in one integrated league for their entire careers. The concept behind this slim volume is excellent—a story in poems told in nine innings, each inning properly divided into the top of the inning and bottom. Graphite illustrations lend an old-timey feel to the text, and various advertisements, fan comments and even a performance by the Jubilee Singers complete the event." Kirkus

Includes bibliographical references

Stewart, Mark

Long ball; the legend and lore of the home run. [by] Mark Stewart and Mike Kennedy. Millbrook Press 2006 64p il lib bdg $22.60

Grades: 4 5 6 7   **796.357**

1. Baseball

ISBN 978-0-7613-2779-0 lib bdg; 0-7613-2779-7 lib bdg

LC 2005015041

"The highly readable text is extended by excellent graphics, photographs, and reproductions of baseball cards and magazine covers." Booklist

Includes bibliographical references

Stout, Glenn

Baseball heroes. Houghton Mifflin Harcourt 2011 121p il (Good sports) pa $5.99

Grades: 3 4 5 6   **796.357**

1. Baseball players   2. Army officers   3. Baseball -- Biography

ISBN 978-0-547-41708-0 pa; 0-547-41708-X pa

LC 2010006760

"This strong title . . . focuses on the careers of four trailblazing ballplayers: Hank Aaron, Jackie Robinson, Fernando Valenzuela, and Ila Borders. . . . Stout writes with conviction and does not sugar-coat the hateful, sometimes racially motivated comments these players endured. . . . Stout's action-packed, suspenseful descriptions of milestone games will easily draw young people's interest." Booklist

Tavares, Matt

Becoming Babe Ruth; Matt Tavares. Candlewick Pr 2013 40 p. $16.99

Grades: K 1 2 3   **796.357**

1. Baseball players -- Biography

ISBN 0763656461; 9780763656461

LC 2012942357

Author Matt Tavares presents a biography of George Herman Ruth, more commonly known as Babe Ruth. At "Saint Mary's Industrial School for Boys," George is "expected to study hard and follow a lot of rules. But there is one good thing about Saint Mary's: almost every day, George gets to play baseball. Here, under the watchful eye of Brother Matthias, George evolves as a player and as a man." (Publisher's note)

Teitelbaum, Michael

Baseball; by Michael Teitelbaum. Cherry Lake Pub. 2009 32p il (Innovation in sports) lib bdg $18.95

Grades: 5 6 7 8   **796.357**

1. Baseball

ISBN 978-1-60279-255-5 lib bdg; 1-60279-255-0 lib bdg

LC 2008-2310

This title "traces the many leaps forward in the history of baseball. [It] chronicles innovations that changed the game. . . . Nice-sized color photographs and sidebars . . . accompany the concise and easy-to-follow text." Booklist

Includes glossary and bibliographical references

Thorn, John

First pitch; how baseball began. Beach Ball Books 2011 40p il pa $14.99

Grades: 4 5 6 7   **796.357**

1. Baseball -- History

ISBN 978-1-936310-04-3; 1-936310-04-X

"Packed with vintage images and photographs, this history of baseball takes readers from the origins of the sport to the present day. . . . Thorn . . . writes clearly and eloquently. . . . Fans who think they know baseball may discover they have much to learn." Publ Wkly

Tocher, Timothy

Odd ball; hilarious, unusual, and bizarre baseball moments. illustrated by Stacy Curtis. Marshall Cavendish 2011 64p il $15.99

Grades: 3 4 5   **796.357**

1. Baseball

ISBN 978-0-7614-5813-5; 0-7614-5813-1

LC 2010013847

"Tocher and Curtis serve up an enjoyable, offbeat collection of trivia. . . . Tocher's deftly limned accounts are broadly humorous and supplemented by Curtis's giggle-inducing cartoons. . . . Ranging from baseball's early days to the present, this collection offers an appealing selection of entertaining baseball facts." SLJ

Vernick, Audrey

★ **Brothers** at bat; the true story of an amazing all-brother baseball team. by Audrey Vernick; Illustrated by Steven Salerno. Clarion Books 2012 39 p.

Grades: 3 4 5   **796.357**

1. Brothers   2. Baseball -- History   3. Picture books for children   4. Baseball players -- Biography   5. Baseball

teams -- New Jersey -- History 6. Acerras (Baseball team) 7. Baseball teams -- United States -- History 8. Brothers -- New Jersey -- Biography

ISBN 9780547385570

LC 2011025645

This biographical picture book depicts "a time when local baseball was part of the American landscape, one family fielded its own team. The Acerra family numbered 16 children, 12 of whom were brothers who all loved to play baseball. The boys played in high school and later formed their own semi-pro team. They played wherever they could get a good game and were known as highly skilled players and crowd pleasers. They shared a special closeness and loyalty. . . . That loyalty extended to a love of country as six of them fought in World War II. . . . After the war they continued to play in local leagues, with younger brothers taking over when big brothers aged out. In 1997 they were recognized by the Baseball Hall of Fame as the all-time longest playing all-brother team." (Kirkus)

Weatherford, Carole Boston

★ A **Negro** league scrapbook; foreword by Buck O'Neil. Boyds Mills Press 2005 48p il $19.95

Grades: 4 5 6 7   796.357

1. Baseball 2. Negro leagues 3. African American athletes

ISBN 1-59078-091-4

LC 2004-19324

"Weatherford's text covers . . . a summation of the history of the Negro Leagues and sections on the pitchers, hitters, utility men, various teams, and so forth. Each topic is briefly covered on a spread of text with black-and-white photos and full-color realia designed to look like a scrapbook. Topics are introduced with a few lines of verse. . . . The book is especially successful in conveying the significance of the Negro Leagues to the black community, and in detailing the realities of segregation. . . . This title succeeds as a thoughtful introduction." SLJ

Winter, Jonah

★ **You** never heard of Willie Mays?! by Jonah Winter; illustrations by Terry Widener. Schwartz & Wade Books 2013 40 p. (trade) $17.99

Grades: K 1 2 3   796.357

1. Baseball -- History 2. Baseball players -- United States -- Biography

ISBN 0375868445; 9780375868443; 9780375968440

LC 2011047347

This children's book, by Jonah Winter, profiles the baseball star Willy Mays. "Many believe him to be the best baseball player that ever lived. . . . In . . . [this] picture book biography, young readers can follow Mays's unparalleled career from growing up in Birmingham, Alabama, to playing awe-inspiring ball in the Negro Leagues and then the Majors, where he was center fielder for the New York (later San Francisco) Giants." (Publisher's note)

Wise, Bill

Silent star; the story of deaf major leaguer William Hoy. by Bill Wise; illustrated by Adam Gustavson. Lee & Low Books 2012 40 p. col. ill. (hardcover: alk. paper) $18.95; (ebook) $18.95

Grades: 3 4 5   796.357

1. Deaf athletes -- Biography 2. Baseball players --

Biography 3. Deaf athletes -- United States -- Biography 4. Baseball players -- United States -- Biography

ISBN 1600604110; 9781600604119; 9781600609763

LC 2011036827

This "picture-book biography of William Ellsworth Hoy (1862-1961), one of the first deaf players in major league baseball . . . follows Hoy from his childhood . . . through his chance discovery by in amateur league coach and his ascent into the minor leagues and beyond. [Bill] Wise outlines the hardships and prejudices Hoy encountered at every turn . . . but Hoy's determination cuts through all the doubt he faced, and some of the records he set stand to this day." (Publishers Weekly)

Wong, Stephen

Baseball treasures; by Stephen Wong; photographs by Susan Einstein. Collins 2007 58p il $16.99; lib bdg $17.89

Grades: 5 6 7 8   796.357

1. Baseball -- History 2. Baseball -- Collectibles

ISBN 978-0-06-114464-6; 0-06-114464-9; 978-0-06-114473-8 lib bdg; 0-06-114473-8 lib bdg

LC 2006036069

This describes collectibles connected with the history of baseball, including balls, gloves and bats, jerseys, baseball cards, World Series memorabilia, and trophies.

This is "a well-designed, well-illustrated book for kids. . . . The text manages to impart the essential information without becoming bogged down in too much detail." Booklist

796.4   Weight lifting, track and field, gymnastics

Bobrick, Benson

A **passion** for victory: the story of the Olympics in ancient and early modern times; the story of the Olympics in ancient and early modern times. Benson Bobrick. Alfred A. Knopf 2012 xvi, 143 p.p ill. (hardback) $19.99

Grades: 4 5 6 7   796.4

1. Olympic games 2. Sports tournaments 3. Olympics

ISBN 9780375868696; 9780375968693

LC 2011016036

The book offers an "account of the Olympic Games and their place in history. . . . [Athletes] Milo of Croton, Jim Thorpe, Johnny Weissmuller and Jesse Owens are given their due here. The photo-essay format conveys their stories . . . as well as the glory, shenanigans and pettiness of the Olympics throughout history. Almost every full-page spread includes at least one photograph, and the text . . . addresses the cultural context of the games." (Kirkus Reviews)

Includes bibliographical references.

Schwartz, Heather E.

Gymnastics. Lucent Books 2011 96p il (Science behind sports) lib bdg $33.45

Grades: 5 6 7 8   796.4

1. Gymnastics

ISBN 978-1-4205-0277-0; 1-4205-0277-8

LC 2010033544

This "explores the scientific principles such as momentum, gravity, friction, and aerodynamics, plus many more, behind [gymnastics]. . . . [The author discusses the sport's] origins, history, and changes, . . . the biomechanics and physiology of playing, related health and medical concerns, and the causes and treatment of sports-related injuries. Additional information tells how exercise, diet and nutrition, warming up, and training relate to peak performance and enjoyment of the sport. . . . One of the most interesting chapters . . . is 'The Psychology of Gymnastics,' which discusses fears, force of will, honing the competitive edge, and the pressure to succeed. . . . [This volume is] jam-packed full of information. [A must-have] for sports fans, athletes, science students, and even anyone considering a career in sports-related medicine, coaching, or other connected fields." SLJ

Includes glossary and bibliographical references

796.42   Track and field

Adler, David A.
A **picture** book of Jesse Owens; [by] David Adler; illustrated by Robert Casilla. Holiday House 1992 un il lib bdg $16.95; pa $6.95
Grades: 1 2 3   **796.42**
1. Track athletics 2. African American athletes 3. Olympic athletes 4. Runners (Athletes)
ISBN 0-8234-0966-X lib bdg; 0-8234-1066-8 pa
LC 91-44735
A simple biography of the noted black track star who competed in the 1936 Berlin Olympics

"The portrait presented, although brief, is accurate and touches on the major events of the track-and-field champion's life. . . . Casilla contributes full-page watercolor paintings that nicely complement and expand the writing." SLJ

Gifford, Clive
Track and field; [by] Clive Gifford. PowerKids Press 2009 32p il (Personal best) lib bdg $25.25
Grades: 4 5 6 7 8   **796.42**
1. Track athletics
ISBN 978-1-4042-4442-9 lib bdg; 1-4042-4442-5 lib bdg
LC 2007-42984
This guide to track and field "offers well-organized and easy-to-follow instructions, focusing on rules, clothing, specific skills, and competitions. . . . Informative, readable." SLJ

Includes bibliographical references

Track athletics; [by] Clive Gifford. Sea-to-Sea Publications 2009 30p il (Know your sport) lib bdg $27.10
Grades: 5 6 7 8   **796.42**
1. Track athletics
ISBN 978-1-59771-154-8 lib bdg; 1-59771-154-3 lib bdg
LC 2008-7323
"Describes the equipment, training, moves, and running events of track competitions. Includes step-by-step descriptions of moves." Publisher's note

Includes glossary

Lang, Heather
Queen of the track; Alice Coach, olympic high-jump champion. Heather Lang; illustrated by Floyd Cooper. 1st ed. Boyds Mills Press 2012 40 p. col. ill. (reinforced trade ed.) $16.95

Grades: 3 4 5   **796.42**
1. Olympic games 2. Black athletes 3. Olympic athletes
ISBN 1590788508; 9781590788509
LC 2011939994
Author Heather Lang tells the story of "the 1948 Olympics in London, [where] members of the U.S. Women's Track and Field team went down to defeat one by one. Any hope of winning rested on Alice Coachman. . . . She became the first African American woman to win an Olympic gold medal. . . . This book follows Coachman on her journey from rural Georgia, where she overcame adversity both as a woman and as a black athlete, to her triumph in Wembly Stadium." (Publisher's note)

Includes bibliographical references.

Malaspina, Ann
Touch the sky; Alice Coachman, Olympic high jumper. by Ann Malaspina; illustrated by Eric Velasquez. Albert Whitman 2012 32 p.
Grades: 2 3 4   **796.42**
1. Picture books for children 2. Women athletes 3. Track athletics 4. African American athletes 5. Jumping -- United States
ISBN 080758035X; 9780807580356
LC 2011008564
This children's picture book by Ann Malaspina tells the story of the African American Olympic high jumper Alice Coachman. "In Alice's Georgia hometown, there was no track where an African-American girl could practice, so she made her own crossbar with sticks and rags. . . . Her dream to compete at the Olympics came true in 1948. This is a . . . free-verse story of the first African-American woman to win an Olympic gold medal. Photos . . . are also included." (Publisher's note)

Includes bibliographical references.

Marsico, Katie
Running; [by] Katie Marsico and Cecilia Minden. Cherry Lake Pub. 2009 32p il (Real world math: Sports) lib bdg $27.07
Grades: 4 5 6   **796.42**
1. Running 2. Arithmetic 3. Track athletics
ISBN 978-1-60279-249-4 lib bdg; 1-60279-249-6 lib bdg
LC 2008-1167
This book "starts with a short story on the history of [running], fundamental rules, and a math challenge in every chapter. . . . [This book] will pique your imagination." Sci Books Films

Includes glossary and bibliographical references

McDougall, Chros
Track & field. Norwood House Press 2011 64p il (Girls play to win) lib bdg $26.60
Grades: 4 5 6 7   **796.42**
1. Track athletics
ISBN 978-1-59953-467-1; 1-59953-467-3
LC 2011011053
Covers the history, rules, fundamentals, and significant personalities of the sport of women's track and field. Topics include: techniques, strategies, competitive events, and equipment.

Includes glossary and bibliographical references

Wiseman, Blaine

Boston Marathon. Weigl Publishing 2011 32p il (Sporting championships) lib bdg $26; pa $10.95
Grades: 3 4 5 **796.42**
1. Boston Marathon 2. Marathon running
ISBN 978-1-61690-124-0 lib bdg; 1-61690-124-1 lib bdg; 978-1-61690-125-7 pa; 1-61690-125-X pa
This sets the Boston Marathon "within the context of the sport and explains what you need to know when watching the [event]." Booklist
Includes bibliographical references

796.44   Gymnastics

Veitch, Catherine

Gymnastics. Heinemann Library 2009 24p il (Sports and my body) lib bdg $21.36; pa $6.49
Grades: 1 2 **796.44**
1. Gymnastics
ISBN 978-1-4329-3454-5 lib bdg; 1-4329-3454-6 lib bdg; 978-1-4329-3459-0 pa; 1-4329-3459-7 pa
LC 2009-7084
Readers learn what gymnastics is, how it can help them stay healthy, and how they can do gymnastics safely.
This book relates "activity to health . . . [and] explains that in order to stay healthy, children should get plenty of rest, eat healthy food, and drink plenty of water." SLJ
Includes glossary

Wendorff, Anne

Gymnastics. Bellwether Media 2010 24p il (Blastoff! readers. My first sports) $19.95
Grades: K 1 2 3 **796.44**
1. Gymnastics
ISBN 9781600143274; 160014327X
LC 2009-8181
Simple text and full color photographs introduce beginning readers to the sport of gymnastics.
Includes glossary and bibliographical references

796.44092   Gymnastics -- Biography

Burford, Michelle

Grace, gold and glory; my leap of faith: the Gabrielle Douglas story. by Gabrielle Douglas; with Michelle Burford. Zondervan 2012 222 p. ill. (hardcover) $24.99
Grades: 4 5 6 7 8 **796.44092**
1. Gymnastics 2. Olympic athletes 3. Women gymnasts -- United States -- Biography 4. Women Olympic athletes -- United States -- Biography
ISBN 0310740614; 9780310740612
LC 2012042389
This book is a "first-person account of 2012 Olympic gold medalist [Gabrielle] Douglas's life from birth to the Olympics written in collaboration with [Michelle] Burford. . . . Douglas mentions the lows—her family lived in their van for months when she was an infant—and bullying, but never dwells on them. . . . Supported by her mother and siblings, and by her strong faith in God, she sees herself as capable of achieving greatness 'because God has equipped me with all I need to succeed.'" (Publishers Weekly)

Washburn, Kim

Heart of a champion; the Dominique Dawes story. Kim Washburn. Zonderkidz 2012 123 p. ill. (softcover) $6.99
Grades: 4 5 6 **796.44092**
1. Olympic games 2. Blacks -- Biography 3. African American women 4. African American athletes 5. Christian biography 6. Gymnasts -- United States -- Biography
ISBN 0310722683; 9780310722687
LC 2012008588
Author Kim Washburn tells the story of gymnast Dominique Dawes, who "competed in three Olympic games and was one of two women to be the first African American to medal in gymnastics. She was also a member of the celebrated Magnificent Seven, the team that won the gold medal in Atlanta in 1996 over the dominant Russian and Romanian squads. . . . Washburn offers up many of Dawes' less illustrious moments, . . . including disappointing performances at World Championships, a brief stint on Broadway, and her search for a lasting and fulfilling career." (Booklist)

796.48   Olympic games

Butterfield, Moira

Events. Sea-to-Sea Publications 2011 32p il (The Olympics) lib bdg $19.95
Grades: 4 5 6 7 **796.48**
1. Olympic games
ISBN 978-1-5977-1321-4; 1-5977-1321-X
LC 2011006465
This describes events of the Olympics.
Includes glossary and bibliographical references

History. Sea-to-Sea Publications 2011 32p il (The Olympics) lib bdg $28.50
Grades: 4 5 6 7 **796.48**
1. Olympic games
ISBN 978-1-5977-1319-1; 1-5977-1319-8
LC 2011006470
This is a history of the Olympics.
Includes glossary and bibliographical references

Scandals. Sea-to-Sea Publications 2011 32p il (The Olympics) lib bdg $28.50
Grades: 4 5 6 7 **796.48**
1. Olympic games 2. Sports -- Corrupt practices
ISBN 978-1-5977-1320-7; 1-5977-1320-1
LC 2011006473
"The book is divided into chapters that cover such topics as bribes, doping, and political problems. Along with famous events, such as the tragedy at the Munich Olympics, in which Israeli athletes were murdered, and the Marion Jones running scandal, in which she was stripped of her medals, there are other shocking and suprising moments. . . . This . . . volume, full of historical and contemporary photos, gives readers a lot to think about." Booklist

Macy, Sue

★ Swifter, higher, stronger; a photographic history of the Summer Olympics. by Sue Macy; foreword by Bob

Costas. updated for the 2008 Summer Olympics; National Geographic 2008 96p il $18.95; lib bdg $27.90

Grades: 4 5 6 7 **796.48**

1. Olympic games

ISBN 978-1-4263-0290-9; 1-4263-0290-8; 978-1-4263-0302-9 lib bdg; 1-4263-0302-5 lib bdg

First published 2004

A detailed look at the history of the Olympic Games, from their origins in Ancient Greece, through their rebirth in nineteenth century France, to the present, highlighting the contributions of individuals to the Games' success and popularity.

"While other books on the topic go into more depth on specific sports, athletes, or historical events, none are as enthusiastically broad or as enjoyable to read as this one. And, it's superbly illustrated with colorful, well-chosen, and enticing photographs." SLJ [review of 2004 ed.]

Includes bibliographical references

796.5   Outdoor life

George, Jean Craighead

★ **Pocket** guide to the outdoors; [by] Jean Craighead George; with Twig C. George . . . [et al.] Dutton Children's Books 2009 138p il pa $9.99

Grades: 5 6 7 8 **796.5**

1. Camping 2. Outdoor life 3. Wilderness survival

ISBN 978-0-525-42163-4 pa; 0-525-42163-7 pa

"This survival guide is the book to read before a wilderness adventure. In short, clearly written chapters, it provides practical tips about ways to enjoy nature and includes information about building shelters, starting fires, making a fishing line and cleaning a fish, outdoor cooking, identifying animal tracks and edible and poisonous plants, and the basics of orienteering. Safety is always considered. Drawings and clearly labeled sketches help with identification." SLJ

Includes bibliographical references

Schofield, Jo

Make it wild; 101 things to make and do outdoors. [by] Jo Schofield and Fiona Danks. Frances Lincoln 2010 159p il pa $24.95

Grades: 4 5 6 7 8 **796.5**

1. Nature craft 2. Outdoor life

ISBN 978-0-7112-2885-6; 0-7112-2885-X

"Using the raw materials nature has to offer, the authors offer clear, concise instructions on how to create ephemeral art, outdoor toys, jewelry, sculptures, and dozens of other things using materials like clay, ice, leaves, sand, and wood. The instructions offer good guidance but also encourage children to use their own creativity and imagination to craft the final product. The projects range in level of difficulty and, depending on the age of the child, can be done individually or in collaboration with siblings, peers, or parents. The authors include safety instructions and recommendations for further resources on outdoor creative exercises. The activities will teach problem solving and commonsense, useful skills; instill a deeper appreciation of nature; and encourage creativity and ingenuity. An excellent choice for any library collection." Booklist

796.52   Walking and exploring by kind of terrain

Athans, Sandra K.

Tales from the top of the world; climbing Mount Everest with Pete Athans. by Sandra K. Athans. Millbrook Press 2013 64 p. ill. (lib. bdg.: alk. paper) $31.93

Grades: 4 5 6 **796.52**

1. Mountaineering 2. Mount Everest (China and Nepal) 3. Mountaineers -- Biography 4. Everest, Mount (China and Nepal)

ISBN 0761365060; 9780761365068

LC 2011045834

In this book by Sandra K. Athans and Pete Athans, "readers are invited to accompany Pete Athans (who has climbed Everest some 14 times and stood on top of the world on 7 different occasions) on the arduous journey from below base camp to the summit. The matter-of-fact text is broken by tales of Athans's personal adventures . . . and all are decorated with a plethora of color photos." (School Library Journal)

Includes bibliographical references (p. 61) and index

Bodden, Valerie

To the top of Mount Everest; by Valerie Bodden. 1st ed. Creative Education 2012 48 p. ill. (some col.) (Great Expeditions) (paperback) $12.00; (library) $34.25

Grades: 5 6 7 8 **796.52**

1. Exploration 2. Mount Everest (China and Nepal) 3. Mountaineering -- Everest, Mount (China and Nepal) -- History 4. Mountaineers -- Everest, Mount (China and Nepal) -- Biography

ISBN 1608180700; 9780898126686; 9781608180707

LC 2010033553

This book by Valerie Bodden is part of the Great Expeditions series and looks at expeditions to the top of Mount Everest. "Bodden includes brief biographies of major people involved in each expedition, interspersed with the text. There are also numerous photographs or reproductions of paintings and woodcuts from the time of the expeditions." (Library Media Connection)

Includes bibliographical references and index.

Cleare, John

Epic climbs. Kingfisher 2011 64p il (Epic adventure) $19.95

Grades: 5 6 7 8 **796.52**

1. Mountaineering

ISBN 978-0-7534-6573-8; 0-7534-6573-6

"Cleare gives the history of five of the most famous and dangerous mountains to climb: Eiger, K2, Everest, McKinley, and Matterhorn. Each section has a short, easy-to-read summary that gives the history of climbers who have conquered these peaks. Full-color photos include the view from the top and historical and contemporary climbing equipment." SLJ

Jenkins, Steve

★ **The** top of the world; climbing Mount Everest. Houghton Mifflin 1999 un il $16; pa $6.95

Grades: 2 3 4 **796.52**

1. Mountaineering 2. Mount Everest (China and Nepal)

ISBN 0-395-94218-7; 0-618-19676-5 pa

LC 98-42748

"Jenkins' papercut illustrations are extraordinary—feathery light to catch the effect of fog radiating off the mountains, mottled and striated to replicate rocky plateaus, pebbled to look like ice flowers. . . . A very attractive book, with plenty of substance for curious children." Booklist

Includes bibliographical references

Skreslet, Laurie

To the top of Everest; [by] Laurie Skreslet with Elizabeth MacLeod. Kids Can Press 2001 56p il hardcover o.p. pa $9.95

Grades: 4 5 6 7 **796.52**

1. Mountaineering 2. Mount Everest (China and Nepal)
ISBN 1-55074-721-5; 1-55074-814-9 pa

This is an account of Skreslet's "1982 trek up Everest when he became one of the first Canadians to make it to the top. Skreslet takes readers through every exciting, excruciating element of the climb. Beautiful color photographs abound." Booklist

Includes glossary

796.522 Mountains, hills, rocks

Athans, Sandra K.

Secrets of the sky caves; danger and discovery on Nepal's Mustang Cliffs. Sandra K. Athans. Millbrook Press 2014 64 p. color illustrations (lib. bdg.: alk. paper) $33.27

Grades: 4 5 6 7 **796.522**

1. Mountaineering 2. Nepal -- Description and travel 3. Caves -- Nepal -- Mustang (District) 4. Mustang (Nepal: District) -- Antiquities 5. Mountaineering -- Nepal -- Mustang (District) 6. Mustang (Nepal: District) -- Discovery and exploration
ISBN 1467700169; 9781467700160

LC 2013017736

"What's more dangerous than scaling Mount Everest? For mountaineer Pete Athans, the answer lies in the ancient kingdom of Mustang, a remote part of the Asian nation of Nepal. . . From 2007 to 2012, Pete explored Mustang's sky caves with a team that included scientists, mountain climbers, and even two children. They found mummies, murals, manuscripts, and other priceless artifacts." (Publisher's note)

"The author, sister of expedition leader Pete Athans, offers a wealth of information about this little-known archaeological wonder. Color photographs provide stunning visuals. Reading list, timeline, websites. Bib., glos., ind." Horn

Includes bibliographical references (pages 61-62) and index

Berne, Emma Carlson

Summiting Everest; how a photograph celebrates teamwork at the top of the world. by Emma Carlson Berne. Capstone Compass Point Books 2014 64 p. (Compass point books. Captured history.) (library binding) $33.99

Grades: 5 6 7 8 9 **796.522**

1. Mountaineering 2. Mount Everest (China and Nepal) 3. Portrait photography -- Everest, Mount (China and Nepal) 4. Mountaineering expeditions -- Everest, Mount (China and Nepal) -- Pictorial works
ISBN 0756547342; 9780756547349; 9780756547905

LC 2013027843

This middle grades book by Emma Carlson Berne describes how "Not far from the top, before their final hours of climbing, team photographer Alfred Gregory snapped a picture of [Edmund] Hillary and [Tenzing] Norgay, with the imposing Himalayas spread out behind them. It was the highest photograph anyone in human history had ever taken. With a click of his camera shutter in May 1953, Gregory opened up a hidden world for the rest of humanity to share." (Publisher's note)

"This outstanding follow-up to Capstone's "Captured History" series continues the same format, focusing on a single, emblematic photograph that defines an era or event... This set will show students how a single image can "capture" history and influence the perceptions and actions of those who see it. The books will certainly draw a large readership and are must-buys for all middle-level and secondary collections." SLJ

Includes bibliographical references and index
Other titles in the series include:
Assassination and its Aftermath (2014)
The Blue Marble (2014)
Breaker Boys (2012)
Civil War Witness (2014)
Hitler in Paris (2014)
Little Rock Girl 1957 (2012)
Man on the Moon (2011)
Migrant Mother (2011)
Raising the Flag (2011)
Tank Man (2014)

796.54 Camping

Champion, Neil

Fire and cooking. Amicus 2010 32p il (Survive alive) lib bdg $19.95

Grades: 4 5 6 7 **796.54**

1. Fires 2. Camping 3. Wilderness survival
ISBN 978-1-60753-039-8 lib bdg; 1-60753-039-2 lib bdg

LC 2010001626

This offers survival tips for building a fire and cooking in the wild, including information on different kinds of fires. Also discusses how to know what to cook and utensils to use.

This "colorful [book contains] numerous photos and illustrations that effectively break the [text] into small, readable chucks. There's lots of practical, everyday information here. . . . Brief yet gripping real-life survival stories are interspersed throughout the [book]." SLJ

796.6 Cycling and related activities

Bow, James

Cycling science. Crabtree Pub. Co. 2009 32p il (Sports science) lib bdg $26.60; pa $8.95

Grades: 4 5 6 **796.6**

1. Cycling
ISBN 978-0-7787-4535-8 lib bdg; 0-77874535-X lib bdg; 978-0-7787-4552-5 pa; 0-7787-4552-X pa

LC 2008-46275

This book approachs cycling "from a scientific angle, describing some of the physics behind [the] pursuit and how athletes can use this knowledge to improve performance. . . . Fascinating facts . . . . are presented in a captivating, lively manner. . . . The layout features colorful text boxes interspersed among photographs." SLJ

Includes glossary and bibliographical references

Guillain, Charlotte

Cycling. Heinemann Library 2009 24p il (Sports and my body) lib bdg $21.36; pa $6.49

Grades: 1 2　　　　　　　　　　　　　　　**796.6**

1. Cycling

ISBN 978-1-4329-3457-6 lib bdg; 1-4329-3457-0 lib bdg; 978-1-4329-3462-0 pa; 1-4329-3462-7 pa

LC 2009-7085

Readers learn what cycling is, how it can help them stay healthy, and how they can cycle safely.

This book relates "activity to health . . . . [and] explains that in order to stay healthy, children should get plenty of rest, eat healthy food, and drink plenty of water." SLJ

Includes glossary

Macy, Sue, 1954-

★ **Wheels** of change; how women rode the bicycle to freedom (with a few flat tires along the way) National Geographic 2011 96p il map $18.95; lib bdg $27.90

Grades: 4 5 6 7 8　　　　　　　　　　　　**796.6**

1. Cycling 2. Bicycles 3. Gender role 4. Women athletes 5. Sex role 6. Feminism 7. Women -- United States -- History 8. Cycling for women

ISBN 978-1-4263-0761-4; 1-4263-0761-6; 978-1-4263-0762-1 lib bdg; 1-4263-0762-4 lib bdg

LC 2010-27141

This is an "engaging look at the emancipating impact that bikes had on late-nineteenth-century U.S. women. The eye-catching chapters, filled with archival images . . . zero in on the profound ways that bicycles subverted traditional notions of femininity. . . . Macy seamlessly weaves together research, direct quotes . . . and historical overviews that put the facts into context, while sidebars expand on related topics. . . . A strong, high-interest choice for both classroom and personal reading." Booklist

Robinson, Laura

★ **Cyclist** bikelist; a book for every rider. illustrated by Ramón K. Pérez. Tundra Books 2010 55p il pa $17.95

Grades: 4 5 6 7　　　　　　　　　　　　　**796.6**

1. Cycling 2. Bicycles

ISBN 978-0-88776-784-5; 0-88776-784-2

The author "covers a broad range of topics, from choosing and caring for a bike to differences in tires, how gear ratios work, and even proper dress and nutrition. She also provides a quick overview of the bicycle's history and inspiring sketches of several renowned racers. . . . Supplemented by photos of different types of bikes, Pérez's bright, cartoon-style pictures add both humor and . . . sharply drawn details. A first-rate guide." Booklist

Schoenherr, Alicia

Mountain biking; by Alicia and Rusty Schoenherr. Child's World 2005 32p il (Kids' guides) lib bdg $24.21

Grades: 4 5 6　　　　　　　　　　　　　　**796.6**

1. Mountain biking

ISBN 1-59296-209-2

LC 2003-27371

This "opens with an explanation of the sport and gives reasons why people enjoy it. The four chapters that follow

cover background and development, equipment, technique, and stars and competitions. The excellent color photos are clear and exciting." SLJ

Includes bibliographical references

796.7　Driving motor vehicles

Nelson, Kristin L.

Monster trucks on the move. Lerner Publications 2011 32p il (Lightning bolt books. Vroom-vroom) lib bdg $25.26

Grades: K 1 2　　　　　　　　　　　　　**796.7**

1. Trucks

ISBN 978-0-7613-6022-3 lib bdg; 0-7613-6022-0 lib bdg

LC 2009038530

This book about monster trucks has "big, high-energy color photos. . . . [The text provides] lively commentary in a mix of declarative statements and non-rhetorical questions. . . . [The] volume closes with a labeled diagram, a page of 'fun facts,' and a short list of print and web resources. . . . [This] will make a worthwhile and popular addition." SLJ

Includes glossary and bibliographical references

796.72　Automobile racing

Arroyo, Sheri L.

How race car drivers use math; math curriculum consultant: Rhea A. Stewart. Chelsea Clubhouse 2010 32p il (Math in the real world) lib bdg $28

Grades: 4 5 6　　　　　　　　　　　　　　**796.72**

1. Mathematics 2. Automobile racing 3. Vocational guidance

ISBN 978-1-60413-609-8 lib bdg; 1-60413-609-X lib bdg

LC 2009-21476

"The layout for [this slim [title] is bright and colorful with a photograph and a 'You Do the Math' problem to solve and large, easy-to-read text on every spread. An answer key is included in the back matter, along with a page detailing the career choices and the educational requirements. . . . In [this title], readers learn about qualifying times, track designs, and tracking fuel. . . . [This title] would be useful to supplement lessons on mathematics. [It] will also appeal to students wanting to learn more about math as it relates to specific careers." SLJ

Includes glossary and bibliographical references

Eagen, Rachel

NASCAR; written by Rachel Eagen. Crabtree Pub. Co. 2007 32p il (Automania!) lib bdg $25.20; pa $8.95

Grades: 4 5 6　　　　　　　　　　　　　　**796.72**

1. Automobile racing 2. National Association for Stock Car Auto Racing

ISBN 978-0-7787-3007-1 lib bdg; 0-7787-3007-7 lib bdg; 978-0-7787-3029-3 pa; 0-7787-3029-8 pa

LC 2006012406

"Eagen has done an excellent job explaining the National Association of Stock Car Automobile Racing—the history, the modification of the cars, the drivers, and the competitions—while conveying a sense of the magnitude of the sport's current fan base. Her lucid, interesting text gets a lift from plenty of high-energy photos." Booklist

Egan, Erin

★ **Hottest** race cars; by Erin Egan. Enslow Publishers 2007 48p il (Wild wheels!) $17.95
Grades: 4 5 6   796.72
1. Automobile racing
ISBN 978-0-7660-2871-5; 0-7660-2871-2
LC 2007007427

"Along with presenting a bit of racing's history, Egan unravels confusion about the three kinds of open-wheel competitions (Formula One, Indy, and Champ). Then she takes a quick but revealing look at major car components. . . . Information on driver's gear, race strategy, and more, along with a sprinkling of anecdotes . . . fill the rest of the pages, which are loaded with color photos." Booklist

Includes glossary and bibliographical references

Howse, Jennifer

NASCAR Sprint Cup. Weigl Publishers 2009 32p il map (Sporting championships) lib bdg $26; pa $9.95
Grades: 3 4 5   796.72
1. Automobile racing 2. National Association for Stock Car Auto Racing
ISBN 978-1-60596-636-6 lib bdg; 1-60596-636-3 lib bdg; 978-1-60596-637-3 pa; 1-60596-637-1 pa
LC 2009-12344

This sets the NASCAR Sprint Cup "within the context of the sport and explains what you need to know when watching the big [event]." Booklist

Includes glossary and bibliographical references

Kelley, K. C.

Hottest NASCAR machines; by K. C. Kelley. Enslow Publishers 2008 48p il (Wild wheels!) lib bdg $23.93
Grades: 4 5 6 7   796.72
1. Automobile racing 2. National Association for Stock Car Auto Racing
ISBN 978-0-7660-2869-2 lib bdg; 0-7660-2869-0 lib bdg
LC 2007007426

"Experience the thrill of a NASCAR race, and learn about the cars, personalities, and races associated with this sport." Publisher's note

Includes glossary and bibliographical references

Piehl, Janet

Formula one race cars on the move. Lerner Publications 2010 32p il (Lightning bolt books. Vroom-vroom) lib bdg $25.26
Grades: K 1 2   796.72
1. Automobile racing
ISBN 978-0-7613-3920-5 lib bdg; 0-7613-3920-5 lib bdg
LC 2009039745

This book about race cars has "big, high-energy color photos. . . . [The text provides] lively commentary in a mix of declarative statements and non-rhetorical questions. . . . [The] volume closes with a labeled diagram, a page of 'fun facts,' and a short list of print and web resources. . . . [This] will make a worthwhile and popular addition." SLJ

Includes glossary and bibliographical references

Pimm, Nancy Roe

The **Daytona** 500; the thrill and thunder of the great American race. Milbrook Press 2011 64p il (Spectacular sports) lib bdg $29.27
Grades: 5 6 7 8   796.72
1. Automobile racing
ISBN 978-0-7613-6677-5; 0-7613-6677-6
LC 2010027263

"Pimm, who worked in the pit box during her husband Ed Pimm's NASCAR racing days, offers an informative introduction to the Daytona 500. Beginning in 1903 . . . this traces the event's history and discusses the cars, drivers, strategies, and memorable moments. Colorful photos illustrate the clear text, while the many sidebars spotlight related facts." Booklist

Includes bibliographical references

796.8 Combat sports

Bjorklund, Ruth

Aikido. Marshall Cavendish Benchmark 2011 47p il (Martial arts in action) $29.93
Grades: 4 5 6 7   796.8
1. Aikido
ISBN 978-0-7614-4931-7; 978-1-6087-0361-6 e-book
LC 2010013820

This describes the history, equipment, and technique of aikido.

This treats "martial arts with the dignity that serious enthusiasts bring to the sport. . . . Illustrations include not only photos of modern gear and from films but also historical images." Booklist

Ditchfield, Christin

Wrestling. Children's Press 2000 47p il (True book) hardcover o.p. lib bdg $25
Grades: 2 3 4   796.8
1. Wrestling
ISBN 0-516-21611-2 lib bdg; 0-516-27033-8 pa
LC 99-28191

Describes the history, rules, and styles of wrestling
Includes bibliographical references

Ellis, Carol

Judo and jujitsu. Marshall Cavendish Benchmark 2011 47p il (Martial arts in action) $29.93
Grades: 4 5 6 7   796.8
1. Judo 2. Jiu-jitsu
ISBN 978-0-7614-4933-1; 978-1-6087-0363-0 e-book
LC 2010013821

This describes the history, equipment, and technique of judo and jujitsu.

This treats "martial arts with the dignity that serious enthusiasts bring to the sport. . . . Illustrations include not only photos of modern gear and from films but also historical images." Booklist

Kendo. Marshall Cavendish Benchmark 2010 47p il (Martial arts in action) $29.93

Grades: 4 5 6 7   **796.8**
1. Kendo
ISBN 978-0-7614-4935-5; 0-7614-4935-3
LC 2010013827

This book about kendo offers "an introduction, a brief history, and expectations for students who begin taking classes. . . . [This title is] outstanding, using an approachable voice without fictionalizing and presenting the history of [kendo] in a way that makes it feel relevant." SLJ

Includes glossary and bibliographical references

Wrestling. Marshall Cavendish Benchmark 2010 47p il (Martial arts in action) $29.93
Grades: 4 5 6 7   **796.8**
1. Wrestling
ISBN 978-0-7614-4941-6; 0-7614-4941-8
LC 2010013819

This book about wrestling offers "an introduction, a brief history, and expectations for students who begin taking classes. . . . [This title is] outstanding, using an approachable voice without fictionalizing and presenting the history of [wrestling] in a way that makes it feel relevant." SLJ

Includes glossary and bibliographical references

Gifford, Clive
Martial arts. Marshall Cavendish Benchmark 2009 30p il (Tell me about sports) $19.95
Grades: 3 4 5   **796.8**
1. Martial arts
ISBN 978-0-7614-4457-2; 0-7614-4457-2
LC 2008-55993

"An introduction to martial arts, including techniques, rules, and the training regimen of professional athletes in the sport." Publisher's note

Includes glossary and bibliographical references

Haney-Withrow, Anna
Tae kwon do. Marshall Cavendish Benchmark 2011 47p il (Martial arts in action) $29.93
Grades: 4 5 6 7   **796.8**
1. Tae kwon do
ISBN 978-0-7614-4940-9; 978-1-6087-0368-5 e-book
LC 2010013828

This describes the history, equipment, and technique of tae kwon do.

This treats "martial arts with the dignity that serious enthusiasts bring to the sport. . . . Illustrations include not only photos of modern gear and from films but also historical images." Booklist

Hicks, Terry Allan
Karate. Marshall Cavendish Benchmark 2010 47p il (Martial arts in action) $29.93
Grades: 4 5 6   **796.8**
1. Karate
ISBN 978-0-7614-4934-8; 0-7614-4934-5
LC 2010013818

This books looks at karate including its history, fighting techniques, training methods, and the values of respect and discipline.

This treats "martial arts with the dignity that serious enthusiasts bring to the sport. . . . Illustrations include not only

photos of modern gear and from films but also historical images." Booklist

Includes glossary

Lewin, Ted
★ **At** Gleason's gym. Roaring Brook Press 2007 un il $17.95
Grades: 2 3 4 5   **796.8**
1. Boxing 2. Gleason's Gyms
ISBN 978-1-59643-231-4; 1-59643-231-4
LC 2006-32176

"Gleason's gym in Brooklyn is where 'the world works out.' . . . Nine-year-old Sugar Boy Younan, National Silver Gloves Champion, 110-pound division, goes there to shadow box and spar with partners. This glorious tribute to Gleason's . . . packs a punch of its own, with a text that is both moving and informative and with vibrant artwork so realistic that readers can practically smell the sweat." Booklist

Mack, Gail
Kickboxing. Marshall Cavendish Benchmark 2011 47p il lib bdg $29.93
Grades: 4 5 6 7   **796.8**
1. Kickboxing
ISBN 978-0-7614-4936-2; 978-1-6087-0366-1 e-book
LC 2010014798

This describes the history, equipment, and technique of kickboxing.

This treats "martial arts with the dignity that serious enthusiasts bring to the sport. . . . Illustrations include not only photos of modern gear and from films but also historical images." Booklist

Mason, Paul, 1967-
Boxing. Sea-to-Sea Publications 2011 32p il (Combat sports) lib bdg $28.50
Grades: 4 5 6   **796.8**
1. Boxing
ISBN 978-1-59771-273-6; 1-59771-273-6

"...[Provides] an inviting look for students who are learning about techniques and for examining records and statistics... Use to refresh an older collection." SLJ

Includes glossary and bibliographical references

Watkins, Richard Ross
Gladiator; by Richard Watkins. Houghton Mifflin 1997 80p il map hardcover o.p. pa $8.95
Grades: 4 5 6 7   **796.8**
1. Gladiators 2. Rome -- Social life and customs
ISBN 0-395-82656-X; 0-618-07032-X pa
LC 96-21107

Describes the history of gladiators, including types of armor, use of animals, amphitheaters, and how the practice fit into Roman society for almost 700 years

"In a balanced treatment of a potentially sensational topic, Watkins provides colorfully written, detailed accounts of the fights as well as pithy discussions of what gladiators meant to the Romans and what they tell us about Roman society. . . . The solid gray-and-white drawings illustrate the text effectively." Booklist

Includes glossary and bibliographical references

Wiseman, Blaine

Ultimate fighting. Weigl Publishers 2011 il (Sporting championships) lib bdg $26; pa 10.95

Grades: 3 4 5 **796.8**

1. Martial arts 2. Ultimate Fighting Championship (Organization)

ISBN 978-1-61690-130-1 lib bdg; 1-61690-130-6 lib bdg; 978-1-61690-131-8 pa; 1-61690-131-4 pa

LC 2010038886

This sets the ultimate fighting championship "within the context of the sport and explains what you need to know when watching the [event]." Booklist

Wouk, Henry

Kung fu. Marshall Cavendish Benchmark 2010 47p il (Martial arts in action) $29.93

Grades: 4 5 6 **796.8**

1. Kung fu

ISBN 978-0-7614-4937-9; 0-7614-4937-X

LC 2010013842

Centuries ago a small band of warrior monks living in the remote forests of ancient China created a mysterious and unique style of fighting that used no weapons. It is known today as kung fu. This is the story of how that once secret martial art has become one of the most famous in the world

This treats "martial arts with the dignity that serious enthusiasts bring to the sport. . . . Illustrations include not only photos of modern gear and from films but also historical images." Booklist

Includes glossary

796.812 Wrestling

Jones, Patrick

The **main** event; the moves and muscle of pro wrestling. Patrick Jones. Millbrook Press 2013 64 p. (lib. bdg.: alk. paper) $31.93

Grades: 4 5 6 **796.812**

1. Wrestling 2. Wrestling -- History

ISBN 0761386351; 9780761386353

LC 2011046180

This book is a "history of wrestling as 'sports entertainment'—read that as meaning staged—from [Patrick] Jones. This is . . . the art of making the blows and throws look like the real thing while the outcome has been predetermined." He tracks "the evolution of the various professional circuits and the shenanigans of the promoter Vince McMahon" and tells stories of wrestlers like "Gorgeous George, Strangler Lewis, Andre the Giant, Hulk Hogan, The Undertaker, [and] The Rock." (Kirkus)

796.815 Oriental martial arts forms

Mason, Paul, 1967-

Judo; [by] Paul Mason. Sea-to-Sea Publications 2009 30 p. col. ill. (Know your sport) (library) $27.10

Grades: 5 6 7 8 **796.815**

1. Judo

ISBN 978-1-59771-151-7; 1-59771-151-9

LC 2008007318

"Describes the equipment, training, moves, and competitions of judo. Includes step-by-step descriptions of moves." Publisher's note

Includes index

796.9 Ice and snow sports

Woods, Bob

Snowboarding; by Bob Woods. Child's World 2005 32p il (Kids' guides) lib bdg $24.21

Grades: 4 5 6 **796.9**

1. Snowboarding

ISBN 1-59296-211-4

LC 2003-27365

This "opens with an explanation of the sport and gives reasons why people enjoy it. The four chapters that follow cover background and development, equipment, technique, and stars and competitions. The excellent color photos are clear and exciting." SLJ

Includes bibliographical references

796.91 Ice skating

Marsico, Katie

Speed skating; [by] Katie Marsico and Cecilia Minden. Cherry Lake Pub. 2009 32p il (Real world math: Sports) lib bdg $27.07

Grades: 4 5 6 **796.91**

1. Arithmetic 2. Ice skating

ISBN 978-1-60279-250-0 lib bdg; 1-60279-250-X lib bdg

LC 2008-806

This book "starts with a short story on the history of [speed skating], fundamental rules, and a math challenge in every chapter. . . . [This book] will pique your imagination." Sci Books Films

McDougall, Chros

Figure skating. Norwood House Press 2010 64p il (Girls play to win) lib bdg $26.60

Grades: 4 5 6 7 **796.91**

1. Ice skating

ISBN 978-1-59953-389-6; 1-59953-389-8

LC 2010009809

"This begins with a look back at the origin of [figure skating] and the traces the young women who played a role in skating from the olden days to today. The first of six chapters describes skating basics . . . and then the progression of stars begins. . . . Color photos, sidebars, and boxed explanations break up the text. . . . A nicely compact history." Booklist

Includes glossary and bibliographical references

Thomas, Keltie

How figure skating works; illustrated by Stephen MacEachern. OwlKids 2009 64p il $22.95; pa $10.95

Grades: 3 4 5 6 **796.91**

1. Ice skating

ISBN 978-1-897349-58-8; 1-897349-58-0; 978-1-897349-59-5 pa; 1-897349-59-9 pa

"This lively overview features clear, well-written explanations of the technical elements of figure skating and anecdotes from skating history. The readable text is supplemented with eye-catching photos, cartoon illustrations, and simple diagrams and charts." SLJ

Includes glossary

796.93   Skiing and snowboarding

Kenney, Karen Latchana

Skiing & snowboarding. Norwood House Press 2010 64p il (Girls play to win) lib bdg $26.60

Grades: 4 5 6 7   **796.93**

1. Skiing 2. Snowboarding

ISBN 978-1-59953-391-9; 1-59953-391-X

LC 2010009808

Covers the history, rules, fundamentals and significant personalities of the sports of women's skiing and snowboarding. Topics include: techniques, strategies, competitive events, and equipment.

"With an easy design and format, the [text is] highly accessible to even the most reluctant readers and [provides] great exposure and insight into the world of female professional sports." Horn Book Guide

Includes glossary and bibliographical references

Schwartz, Heather E.

Snowboarding. Lucent Books 2011 104p il (Science behind sports) $33.45

Grades: 5 6 7 8   **796.93**

1. Snowboarding

ISBN 978-1-4205-0322-7; 1-4205-0322-7

LC 2010033274

This "explores the scientific principles such as momentum, gravity, friction, and aerodynamics, plus many more, behind [snowbarding]. . . . [The author discusses the sport's] origins, history, and changes, . . . the biomechanics and physiology of playing, related health and medical concerns, and the causes and treatment of sports-related injuries. Additional information tells how exercise, diet and nutrition, warming up, and training relate to peak performance and enjoyment of the sport. . . . The action photography . . . is fantastic. . . . [This volume is] jam-packed full of information. [A must-have] for sports fans, athletes, science students, and even anyone considering a career in sports-related medicine, coaching, or other connected fields." SLJ

Includes glossary and bibliographical references

796.94   Snowmobiling

Woods, Bob

Snowmobile racers. Enslow Publishers 2010 48p il (Kid racers) lib bdg $23.93

Grades: 5 6 7 8   **796.94**

1. Snowmobiles

ISBN 978-0-7660-3487-7 lib bdg; 0-7660-3487-9 lib bdg

LC 2009020784

This describes snowmobiles and races for kids, discussing which snowmobiles qualify, how they are built and raced, who the best drivers are, what to look for in a snow-

mobile, safety, good sportsmanship, and how racing activities can be a good part of family life.

"The easily digestible text gets more visual weight on the page, but there are plenty of captioned color photos depicting different sorts of races as well as recreational snowmobiling." Booklist

Includes glossary and bibliographical references

796.96   Ice games

Wiseman, Blaine

Stanley Cup. Weigl Publishers 2011 32p il map (Sporting championships) lib bdg $26; pa $10.95

Grades: 3 4 5   **796.96**

1. Hockey

ISBN 978-1-61690-127-1 lib bdg; 1-61690-127-6 lib bdg; 978-1-61690-128-8 pa; 1-61690-128-4 pa

LC 2010006164

This sets the Stanley Cup "within the context of the sport and explains what you need to know when watching the [event]." Booklist

796.962   Ice hockey

Adams, Carly

Queens of the ice; they were fast, they were fierce, they were teenage girls. Lorimer 2011 131p il (Record books) $16.95; pa $9.95

Grades: 5 6 7 8   **796.962**

1. Hockey 2. Women athletes

ISBN 978-1-55277-721-3; 1-55277-721-9; 978-1-55277-720-6 pa; 1-55277-720-0 pa

"Filled with exciting action, this . . . title . . . showcases the history of the Preston Rivulettes, a Canadian hockey team of teenage girls who played together for 10 seasons, from 1931 until 1940, without losing a game and at a time when many believed that girls could not play the sport and needed chaperones. . . . Adams deepens the story with the historical background of the Great Depression and the team's struggle to find money. Occasional achival photos and boxed inserts add to the clear, readable account." Booklist

Johnstone, Robb

Hockey; rev ed.; Weigl Publishers 2009 24p il (In the zone) $24.45; pa $8.95

Grades: 4 5 6 7   **796.962**

1. Hockey

ISBN 978-1-6059-6130-9; 1-6059-6130-2; 978-1-6059-6131-6 pa; 1-6059-6131-0 pa

LC 2009005607

First published 2001

"Colorful, informative. . . . For those just showing an interest in the bone-crushing sport, [this is] an excellent place to get their bearings. Using short, mostly two-page chapters, Johnstone explains the genesis of the sport, the gear needed, the rules, the positions, and the leagues, before concluding with biographies of eight legendary NHL players." Booklist

McClellan, Ray

Hockey. Bellwether Media 2010 24p il (Blastoff! readers. My first sports) $19.95

Grades: K 1 2 3   **796.962**
1. Hockey
ISBN 978-1-60014-330-4; 1-60014-330-X
LC 2009-8180
"Simple text and full color photographs introduce beginning readers to the sport of hockey." Publisher's note
Includes bibliographical references

McKinley, Michael
Ice time; the story of hockey. Tundra Books 2006
80p il $18.95
Grades: 5 6 7 8   **796.962**
1. Hockey
ISBN 978-0-88776-762-3; 0-88776-762-1
"This straightforward history of hockey emphasizes the professional game and Canadian players.... Hockey enthusiasts will find this a welcome arrival." Booklist

McMahon, Dave
Hockey. Norwood House Press 2010 64p il (Girls play to win) lib bdg $26.60
Grades: 4 5 6 7   **796.962**
1. Hockey
ISBN 978-1-59953-390-2; 1-59953-390-1
LC 2010009811
Covers the history, rules, fundamentals and significant personalities of the sport of women's hockey. Topics include: techniques, strategies, competitive events, and equipment.
"With an easy design and format, the [text is] highly accessible to even the most reluctant readers and [provides] great exposure and insight into the world of female professional sports." Horn Book Guide
Includes glossary and bibliographical references

Sharp, Anne Wallace
Ice hockey. Lucent Books 2011 112p il map (Science behind sports) lib bdg $33.45
Grades: 5 6 7 8   **796.962**
1. Hockey
ISBN 978-1-4205-0281-7; 1-4205-0281-6
LC 2010025670
This book about ice hockey highlights "performance; chapter headings include topics such as 'Training and Nutrition,' 'High-Tech Equipment,' and 'Injuries and Treatments.' Physics, biology, and psychology concepts related to the [sport] are . . . wrapped into technical discussions of moves and techniques. Many photographs of pros and novices in action add interest." Horn Book Guide
Includes glossary and bibliographical references

Stewart, Mark
Score! the action and artistry of hockey's magnificent moment. Millbrook Press 2010 64p il $29.27
Grades: 5 6 7 8   **796.962**
1. Hockey
ISBN 978-0-8225-8753-8; 0-8225-8753-X
"Stewart and Kennedy take readers on a chatty, photo-studded tour of the art of scoring in the rink. This intermediate-level hockey book definitely isn't for beginners. . . . What savvy readers will get, however, is a bounty of information on the game's defining goals, goal scorers, and goal-scoring techniques. . . . This makes a worthy addition to any sports shelf." Booklist

796.98   Winter Olympic games

Macy, Sue
★ Freeze frame; a photographic history of the Winter Olympics. National Geographic 2006 96p il map $18.95
Grades: 5 6 7 8 9 10   **796.98**
1. Olympic games 2. Winter sports
ISBN 0-7922-7887-9; 978-0-7922-7887-0
Highlights in the history of the Winter Olympics from their inception in 1924 to today, including profiles of the Olympic athletes and information on the lesser-known winter sports. Also includes an Olympic almanac with information about each Olympiad.
This book "has spectacular photographs and clear, captivating prose." SLJ
Includes bibliographical references

797   Aquatic and air sports

Kelley, K. C.
Weird water sports. Child's World 2011 24p il (Weird sports) lib bdg $25.64
Grades: 3 4 5 6   **797**
1. Water sports
ISBN 978-1-60954-380-8; 1-60954-380-8
LC 2010044028
This describes sports such as noodling, bog bike racing, concrete canoeing, underwater hockey, and river surfing.
"Both the writing and the visual style are exuberant-without relying too much on exclamation points." Booklist

797.1   Aquatic sports

Bass, Scott
Kayaking; by Scott Bass. Child's World 2005 32p il (Kids' guides) lib bdg $24.21
Grades: 4 5 6   **797.1**
1. Kayaks and kayaking
ISBN 1-59296-208-4
LC 2003-27372
This "opens with an explanation of the sport and gives reasons why people enjoy it. The four chapters that follow cover background and development, equipment, technique, and stars and competitions. The excellent color photos are clear and exciting." SLJ
Includes bibliographical references

Storey, Rita
Sailing. Sea-to-Sea Publications 2011 30p il (Know your sport) lib bdg $28.50
Grades: 4 5 6   **797.1**
1. Sailing
ISBN 978-1-59771-286-6
LC 2010003439
This "volume provides an introduction to the equipment, techniques, and safety measures for [sailing]. . . . Instructive photographs help illustrate such concepts as [tacking a sailboat], . . . while engaging stock images capture the excitement on the water. The [volume concludes] with racing

information, profiling top racers, rules, and tactics." Horn Book Guide

Includes glossary

Thorpe, Yvonne

Canoeing and kayaking. Sea-to-Sea Publications 2011 30p il (Know your sport) $28.50

Grades: 4 5 6   **797.1**

1. Canoes and canoeing 2. Kayaks and kayaking

ISBN 9781597712859

LC 2010003438

This "volume provides an introduction to the equipment, techniques, and safety measures for [canoeing and kayaking]. . . . Instructive photographs help illustrate such concepts as . . . paddling a kayak, while engaging stock images capture the excitement on the water. The [volume concludes] with racing information, profiling top racers, rules, and tactics." Horn Book Guide

Includes glossary

Wurdinger, Scott D.

Kayaking; by Scott Wurdinger and Leslie Rapparlie. Creative Education 2006 48p il (Adventure sports) $21.95

Grades: 5 6 7 8   **797.1**

1. Kayaks and kayaking

ISBN 978-1-58341-397-5

LC 2005051057

"Strong, full-page color photographs illustrate this overview of kayaking. . . . Tracing the use of kayaks back thousands of years, the authors touch on the history of the boats before moving on to contemporary usage for sports and recreation. . . . The exciting views . . . will instantly draw browsers and serious readers alike." Booklist

Includes bibliographical references

797.2 Swimming and diving

Arroyo, Sheri L.

How deep sea divers use math; math curriculum consultant: Rhea A. Stewart. Chelsea Clubhouse 2010 32p il (Math in the real world) lib bdg $28

Grades: 4 5 6   **797.2**

1. Mathematics 2. Scuba diving 3. Vocational guidance

ISBN 978-1-60413-611-1 lib bdg; 1-60413-611-1 lib bdg

LC 2009-18413

"The layout for [this] slim [title] is bright and colorful with a photograph and a 'You Do the Math' problem to solve and large, easy-to-read text on every spread. An answer key is included in the back matter, along with a page detailing the career choices and the educational requirements. . . . [It] discusses how divers use math to determine how much air they will need in their tanks and use grids to map underwater shipwrecks. The mathematical topics covered include measurement, estimation, data analysis, and problem solving. . . . [This title] would be useful to supplement lessons on mathematics. [It] will also appeal to students wanting to learn more about math as it relates to specific careers." SLJ

Includes glossary and bibliographical references

Boudreau, Helene

Swimming science. Crabtree Pub. Co. 2009 32p il (Sports science) lib bdg $26.60; pa $8.95

Grades: 3 4 5 6   **797.2**

1. Swimming

ISBN 978-0-7787-4538-9 lib bdg; 0-7787-4538-4 lib bdg; 978-0-7787-4555-6 pa; 0-7787-4555-4 pa

LC 2008-48870

This book approachs swimming "from a scientific angle, describing some of the physics behind [the] pursuit and how athletes can use this knowledge to improve performance. . . . Fascinating facts . . . [such as] a discussion of the swimmer who covered 3,270 miles down the Amazon River . . . are presented in a captivating, lively manner. . . . The layout features colorful text boxes interspersed among photographs." SLJ

Includes glossary and bibliographical references

Gifford, Clive

Swimming; [by] Clive Gifford. PowerKids Press 2009 32p il (Personal best) lib bdg $25.25

Grades: 4 5 6 7 8   **797.2**

1. Swimming

ISBN 978-1-4042-4443-6 lib bdg; 1-4042-4443-3 lib bdg

LC 2007-43003

This guide to swimming "offers well-organized and easy-to-follow instructions, focusing on rules, clothing, specific skills, and competitions. . . . Informative, readable." SLJ

Guillain, Charlotte

Swimming. Heinemann Library 2009 24p il (Sports and my body) lib bdg $21.36; pa $6.49

Grades: 1 2   **797.2**

1. Swimming

ISBN 978-1-4329-3455-2 lib bdg; 1-4329-3455-4 lib bdg; 978-1-4329-3460-6 pa; 1-4329-3460-0 pa

LC 2009-7083

Learn what swimming is, how it can help them stay healthy, and how they can swim safely.

This book relates "activity to health . . . [and] explains that in order to stay healthy, children should get plenty of rest, eat healthy food, and drink plenty of water." SLJ

Includes glossary and bibliographical references

Hoblin, Paul

Swimming & diving. Norwood House Press 2011 64p il (Girls play to win) lib bdg $26.60

Grades: 4 5 6 7   **797.2**

1. Diving 2. Swimming

ISBN 978-1-59953-466-4; 1-59953-466-5

LC 2011011038

Covers the history, rules, fundamentals, and significant personalities of the sport of women's swimming and diving. Topics include: techniques, strategies, competitive events, and equipment.

Includes glossary and bibliographical references

Lourie, Peter

First dive to shark dive. Boyds Mills Press 2006 48p il $17.95 **797.2**

1. Scuba diving 2. Bahamas
ISBN 1-59078-068-X

LC 2005-24987

"In this photo-essay, a father and his 12-year-old daughter, Suzanna, fly to Andros, in the Bahamas, so Suzanna can learn to scuba dive. During an intense seven days, she becomes certified and makes four dives. The narrative . . . also covers information about the island . . . the ocean and its inhabitants . . . and the old Andros traditions. . . . Stunning color photographs . . . reveal why Suzanna wanted to be certified to dive." Booklist

Minden, Cecilia

Swimming; [by] Cecilia Minden and Katie Marsico. Cherry Lake Pub. 2009 32p il (Real world math: Sports) lib bdg $27.07

Grades: 4 5 6 **797.2**

1. Swimming 2. Arithmetic
ISBN 978-1-60279-246-3 lib bdg; 1-60279-246-1 lib bdg

LC 2008-1198

This book "starts with a short story on the history of [swimming], fundamental rules, and a math challenge in every chapter. . . . [This book] will pique your imagination." Sci Books Films

Includes glossary and bibliographical references

Timblin, Stephen

Swimming. Cherry Lake Pub. 2009 32p il (Innovation in sports) lib bdg $27.07

Grades: 4 5 6 7 **797.2**

1. Swimming
ISBN 978-1-60279-258-6 lib bdg; 1-60279-258-5 lib bdg

LC 2008002046

This describes swimming history, rules, equipment, training, and swimming stars

This "stands out by emphasizing monumental shifts and advances in the events themselves. . . . Concise and occasionally revelatory." Booklist

Includes glossary and bibliographical references

Wendorff, Anne

Swimming. Bellwether Media 2010 24p il (Blastoff! readers. My first sports) $19.95

Grades: K 1 2 3 **797.2**

1. Swimming
ISBN 978-1-60014-326-7; 1-60014-326-1

LC 2009-8182

Simple text and full color photographs introduce beginning readers to the sport of swimming.

Includes glossary and bibliographical references

798.4 Horse racing

Joyce, Gare

Northern Dancer; king of the racetrack. Gare Joyce. Fitzhenry & Whiteside 2011 72 p.

Grades: 4 5 6 **798.4**

1. Northern Dancer (Race horse)
ISBN 1554551633; 9781554551637

This book by Gare Joyce focuses on the racing horse Northern Dancer. "As a colt, he was unimpressive. . . . Eventually, the colt that nobody wanted took the racing world by storm. Northern Dancer won the Kentucky Derby, and went on to win the Preakness Stakes of Baltimore, and nearly won the Belmont of New York. On retirement, Northern Dancer became the greatest horse stud in history, worth over $40 million by 1981." (Publisher's note)

McCarthy, Meghan

★ Seabiscuit; the wonder horse. Simon & Schuster Books for Young Readers 2008 un il $15.99

Grades: K 1 2 3 **798.4**

1. Horse racing 2. Seabiscuit (Race horse)
ISBN 978-1-4169-3360-1; 1-4169-3360-3

LC 2008-06729

"The book covers Seabiscuit's transformation from scruffy loser to—well, scruffy winner, his loyal team of owner, trainer, and jockey, and his appeal to the economically pinched crowds; the saga here culminates in Seabiscuit's famous match with War Admiral. . . . The account is simplified for the youngest audiences, and they'll get the high points of the story . . . without getting lost in detail. . . . The cartooning is genuinely comic at times; the acrylic paintings are subtly toned, though, with gray touches muting the colors slightly." Bull Cent Child Books

Scanlan, Lawrence

The big red horse; the story of Secretariat and the loyal groom who loved him. with photos by Raymond Woolfe. Harper Trophy 2011 166p il pa $7.99

Grades: 4 5 6 7 **798.4**

1. Horse racing 2. Stablehands
ISBN 978-0-06-202669-9; 0-06-202669-0

"This biography of the legendary racehorse provides many intimate details about his daily life and incredible prowess. . . . His good looks and tremendous athletic ability enabled him to win the Triple Crown at a record-breaking pace and the hearts of the American people. Scanlan focuses on the special relationship between Secretariat and his groom, Eddie Sweat. . . . Black-and-white photos are scattered throughout. . . . This solid book will have special appeal for horse lovers." SLJ

Tate, Nikki

Behind the scenes; the racehorse. Fitzhenry & Whiteside 2008 72p il $22.95; pa $18.95

Grades: 5 6 7 8 **798.4**

1. Horse racing
ISBN 978-1-55455-018-0; 1-55455-018-1; 978-1-55455-032-6 pa; 1-55455-032-7 pa

"A short history of horse racing opens this attractive and informative book. Tate discusses the breeding, training, and care of the horses but devotes plenty of space to the people who are involved in the sport. . . . The many color photos . . . are quite clear and well matched to the text." Booklist

Wiseman, Blaine

Kentucky Derby. Weigl Publishers 2010 32p il (Sporting championships) lib bdg $26; pa $10.95

Grades: 3 4 5　　　　　　　　　　　　798.4
1. Horse racing 2. Kentucky Derby
ISBN 978-1-61690-121-9 lib bdg; 1-61690-121-7 lib
bdg; 978-1-61690-122-6 pa; 1-61690-122-5 pa
This sets the Kentucky Derby "within the context of the
sport and explains what you need to know when watching
the [event]." Booklist
Includes bibliographical references

798.8　Dog racing

Blake, Robert J.
★ Togo. Philomel Bks. 2002 un il $16.99
Grades: K 1 2 3　　　　　　　　　　798.8
1. Dogs -- Fiction 2. Alaska -- Fiction
ISBN 0-399-23381-4

LC 2001-45926

In 1925, Togo, a Siberian husky who loves being a sled
dog, leads a team that rushes to bring diphtheria antitoxin
from Anchorage to Nome, Alaska
The author "paints a vivid word-picture of bitter, deadly conditions and the grueling effort required to surmount
them, reinforcing it with dramatic art." Booklist

Miller, Debbie S.
The **great** serum race; blazing the Iditarod Trail. illustrations by Jon van Zyle. Walker & Co. 2002 un il map
hardcover o.p. pa $8.95
Grades: 3 4 5　　　　　　　　　　　798.8
1. Dogs 2. Iditarod Trail Sled Dog Race, Alaska 3.
Alaska
ISBN 0-8027-8811-4; 0-8027-8812-2 lib bdg; 0-8027-
7723-2 pa

LC 2001-56777

The story of the heroic role played by sled dogs, including the Siberian husky Togo, in the delivery of antitoxin
serum to those stricken with diphtheria in 1925 Nome. Includes historical notes about the event as well as about the
Iditarod Sled Dog Race which commemorates it
"Zyle, official artist of the Iditarod and a musher himself,
has created vivid, full-spread paintings to bring the story to
life. . . . This is an excellent account told with lots of detail
and drama." SLJ
Includes bibliographical references

799.1　Fishing

Lindeen, Carol
Freshwater fishing; by Carol K. Lindeen. Capstone
Press 2011 32p il (Blazers. Wild outdoors) lib bdg $25.32
Grades: 2 3 4　　　　　　　　　　　799.1
1. Fishing
ISBN 978-1-4296-4810-3 lib bdg; 1-4296-4810-4
lib bdg

LC 2010001015

This "will fill a gap in many rural communities. . . .
Blocks of text or 'Wild Facts' are scattered among the pages
providing humorous or memorable trivia. . . . Close-up photography fills the pages and shows safe hunting attire." SLJ
Includes glossary and bibliographical references

799.2　Hunting

Adamson, Thomas K.
Bowhunting. Capstone Press 2011 32p il (Blazers.
Wild outdoors) lib bdg $25.32
Grades: 2 3 4　　　　　　　　　　　799.2
1. Hunting 2. Bow and arrow
ISBN 978-1-4296-4808-0 lib bdg; 1-4296-4808-2
lib bdg

LC 2009053410

This "will fill a gap in many rural communities. . . .
Blocks of text or 'Wild Facts' are scattered among the pages
providing humorous or memorable trivia. . . . Close-up photography fills the pages and shows safe hunting attire." SLJ
Includes glossary and bibliographical references

Deer hunting. Capstone Press 2011 32p il (Blazers.
Wild outdoors) lib bdg $25.32
Grades: 2 3 4　　　　　　　　　　　799.2
1. Deer hunting
ISBN 978-1-4296-4807-3 lib bdg; 1-4296-4807-4
lib bdg

LC 2009053412

Describes how to hunt deer, including the skills and patience required for the hunt, the proper guns and ammunition
needed, and the safety skills every hunter should follow.
This "will fill a gap in many rural communities. . . .
Blocks of text or 'Wild Facts' are scattered among the pages
providing humorous or memorable trivia. . . . Close-up photography fills the pages and shows safe hunting attire." SLJ
Includes glossary and bibliographical references

Duck hunting. Capstone Press 2011 32p il (Blazers.
Wild outdoors) lib bdg $25.32
Grades: 2 3 4　　　　　　　　　　　799.2
1. Ducks 2. Hunting
ISBN 978-1-4296-4809-7 lib bdg; 1-4296-4809-0
lib bdg

LC 2010001097

This "will fill a gap in many rural communities. . . .
Blocks of text or 'Wild Facts' are scattered among the pages
providing humorous or memorable trivia. . . . Close-up photography fills the pages and shows safe hunting attire." SLJ
Includes glossary and bibliographical references

Peterson, Judy Monroe
Big game hunting. Rosen Central 2011 64p il map
(Hunting: pursuing wild game!)) lib bdg $29.25; pa $12.95
Grades: 5 6 7 8　　　　　　　　　　799.2
1. Hunting
ISBN 978-1-4488-1240-0 lib bdg; 1-4488-1240-2 lib
bdg; 978-1-4488-2270-6 pa; 1-4488-2270-X pa

LC 2010006859

In this introduction to big game hunting "Peterson displays an impressive grasp of the pastime by throwing in
almost everything: types of guns and bows, safety laws, licenses, land access, animal behavior, clothing, methods of
hunting, and preparing harvested meat. . . . [The book] is
jam-packed with info. . . . A green-heavy design, bright pho-
toss of hunters . . . and prey, and above average back matter
close out this solid entry." Booklist
Includes bibliographical references

Wolny, Philip

Waterfowl. Rosen Central 2011 64p il (Hunting: pursuing wild game!) lib bdg $29.25; pa $12.95

Grades: 4 5 6 7   **799.2**

1. Hunting 2. Water birds

ISBN 978-1-4488-1243-1 lib bdg; 1-4488-1243-7 lib bdg; 978-1-4488-2273-7 pa; 1-4488-2273-4 pa

LC 2010017396

This guide to waterfowl hunting covers what to wear and pack, shooting strategies, the construction of duck blinds, gun safety, hunting permits and licenses, and other laws relating to hunting limits, seasons, and private and public property.

Includes bibliographical references

800 LITERATURE, RHETORIC & CRITICISM

808 Rhetoric and collections of literary texts from more than two literatures

Children's writer's & illustrator's market; edited by Alice Pope. Writer's Digest Books il

Grades: Adult Professional   **808**

1. Publishers and publishing 2. Authorship -- Handbooks, manuals, etc.

Annual. First published 1998

This reference includes listings of children's book publishers, magazines, agents, art reps, contests, clubs, conferences, awards, and grants with contact information, along with articles and interviews on a variety of subjects relating to children's writing, illustrating, and publishing

Includes bibliographical references

Christelow, Eileen

★ What do authors do? Clarion Bks. 1995 32p il hardcover o.p. pa $5.95

Grades: 1 2 3   **808**

1. Authors 2. Authorship 3. Illustrators 4. Publishers and publishing

ISBN 0-395-71124-X; 0-395-86621-9 pa

LC 94-19725

"Christelow packs a great deal of humor as well as information into her attractive pages. Best of all, she infuses the whole with a sense of the zest and love that writers feel for their work." Booklist

Cleary, Brian P., 1959-

Skin like milk, hair of silk; what are similes and metaphors? illustrated by Brian Gable. Millbrook Press 2009 il (Words are categorical) lib bdg $15.95

Grades: 2 3 4   **808**

1. Simile 2. Metaphor

ISBN 978-0-8225-9151-1; 0-8225-9151-0

LC 2008049643

"Cleary provides brief definitions of similes and metaphors, offers roughly 15 examples of each one, and explains how they are used. Large pen-and-ink illustrations feature cartoon cats rendered in bold, vibrant colors. The style is fun and inviting." SLJ

Cornwall, Phyllis

Put it all together. Cherry Lake Pub. 2010 32p il (Super smart information strategies) lib bdg $27.97

Grades: 3 4 5 6   **808**

1. Report writing

ISBN 978-1-60279-643-0 lib bdg; 1-60279-643-2 lib bdg

LC 2009027806

"The appealing layout includes manageable paragraphs, a variety of engaging illustrations, and examples that clearly guide readers through each topic. In [this book], strategies include gathering resources, organizing information, and ways of presenting discoveries." SLJ

Includes glossary and bibliographical references

Fox, Kathleen

Plagiarism! Plagiarism! 25 fun games and activities to teach documenting and sourcing skills to students. Upstart Books 2011 56p il pa $14.95

Grades: Adult Professional   **808**

1. Authorship 2. Plagiarism

ISBN 978-1-60213-050-0; 1-60213-050-7

"This handy book is aimed at teaching a tricky concept to primary and elementary grade children. The author provides a discussion of sources, rewording, when to use quotation marks, etc. Each activity is written in the style of a lesson plan." SLJ

Greenwood, Cathleen

So, you wanna be a writer? how to write, get published, and maybe even make it big! Vicki Hambleton, Cathleen Greenwood. Aladdin/Beyond Words 2012 186 p. ill. (So, you wanna be ..) (pbk.) $9.99

Grades: 4 5 6   **808**

1. Vocational guidance 2. Authorship -- Handbooks, manuals, etc.

ISBN 9781582700434 2001 edition.; 1582700435 2001 edition; 9781582703534 2012 edition; 1582703590 2012 edition; 9781582703596 2012 edition; 9781442452916 2012 edition

LC 2011046252

This book presents a "[s]oup-to-nuts overview on all aspects of developing a writing career, from picking a genre to publicizing a finished work." It includes "myriad interviews, not only of established professionals such as Wendelin Van Draanen and Todd Strasser, but of young writers who may not be as familiar. Additionally, the authors sample some of these young wordsmiths' work . . . It includes quizzes, writing exercises to loosen up the brain and a handy section on further resources as well as a . . . short glossary of terms that all professional writers should know." (Kirkus Reviews)

It rained all day that night; autographs, rhymes & inscriptions. compiled by Lillian Morrison; illustrated by Christy Hale. August House 2003 80p il $16.95; pa $9.95

Grades: 3 4 5 6   **808**

1. American poetry -- Collections

ISBN 0-87483-735-9; 0-87483-726-X pa

LC 2003-51987

An illustrated compilation of short poems and other inscriptions from autograph albums, arranged by such themes as friendship, school, and nonsense.

"Morrison has created a stunning collection of autograph verses. . . . Hale's ink-and-watercolor paintings dance across each page, extending the sentiment . . . implicit in each verse." SLJ

Leedy, Loreen
★ **Look** at my book; how kids can write & illustrate terrific books. written and illustrated by Loreen Leedy. Holiday House 2004 32p il $16.95
Grades: K 1 2 3   **808**
1. Authorship 2. Bookbinding 3. Illustration of books
ISBN 0-8234-1590-2
LC 2003-41713

Provides ideas and simple directions for writing, illustrating, designing, and binding books.
"Following the writing process fairly closely . . . [the author] takes readers through a step-by-step formula that almost guarantees a successful product. . . . Lively, colorful illustrations expand and interpret the text." SLJ

Mack, James
Journals and blogging; [by] Jim Mack. Raintree 2009 32p il (Culture in action) $28.21; pa $7.99
Grades: 5 6 7 8   **808**
1. Diaries 2. Weblogs
ISBN 978-1-4109-3406-2; 1-4109-3406-3; 978-1-4109-3423-9 pa; 1-4109-3423-3 pa
LC 2009000490

This "encourages readers to write as a way to express their feelings. It describes different types of journals and blogs. A page on Internet safety and the danger of downloading material encourages adult supervision. . . . Well organized and with bright, colorful photography, [this] introductory [title gives] readers good basic knowledge." SLJ
Includes glossary and bibliographical references

Miles, Liz
Writing a screenplay. Raintree 2009 32p il (Culture in action) $28.21; pa $7.99
Grades: 5 6 7 8   **808**
1. Drama -- Technique
ISBN 978-1-4109-3407-9; 1-4109-3407-1; 978-1-4109-3424-6 pa; 1-4109-3424-1 pa

This covers writing for "film and television. Plot, location, characters, dialogue, and mood are a few of the components discussed. . . . Well organized and with bright, colorful photography, [this] introductory [title gives] readers good basic knowledge." SLJ
Includes glossary and bibliographical references

Rau, Dana Meachen
Ace your creative writing project. Enslow Elementary 2009 48p il (Ace it! information literacy) lib bdg $23.93
Grades: 3 4 5   **808**
1. Creative writing
ISBN 978-0-7660-3395-5 lib bdg; 0-7660-3395-3 lib bdg
LC 2008024888

This describes where writers get their ideas, your story's characters and setting, writing, revising, and presenting your writing
Includes bibliographical references

Ace your writing assignment. Enslow Elementary 2009 48p il (Ace it! information literacy) lib bdg $23.93
Grades: 3 4 5   **808**
1. English language -- Composition and exercises
ISBN 978-0-7660-3394-8 lib bdg; 0-7660-3394-5 lib bdg
LC 2008024887

This describes how to make writing better and more interesting
Includes bibliographical references

Rosinsky, Natalie M.
Write your own biography; by Natalie M. Rosinsky. Compass Point Books 2008 64p il (Write your own) lib bdg $31.93
Grades: 5 6 7 8   **808**
1. Biography -- Authorship
ISBN 978-0-7565-3366-3 lib bdg; 0-7565-3366-X lib bdg
LC 2007011471

"Rosinsky adroitly leads readers through the challenging process of researching and writing a biography. Chapters include helpful suggestions, excerpts from published works, and writing exercises. Full-color photos, charts, and graphics break up the text." SLJ
Includes glossary and bibliographical references

Writing and publishing; the librarian's handbook. edited by Carol Smallwood. American Library Association 2010 189p (ALA guides for the busy librarian) pa $65
Grades: Adult Professional   **808**
1. Authorship 2. Library science
ISBN 978-0-8389-0996-6; 0-8389-0996-5
LC 2009-25047

"This important writer's guide is readable from cover to cover or by bits and pieces and is a helpful and handy read for every librarian." Libr Media Connect
Includes bibliographical references

808.02   Authorship techniques, plagiarism, editorial techniques

Levine, Gail Carson, 1947-
Writer to writer; from think to ink. Gail Carson Levine. HarperCollins 2014 304 p. (hardback) $16.99
Grades: 5 6 7 8   **808.02**
1. Authorship 2. Creative writing
ISBN 0062275305; 9780062275301
LC 2014005858

In this book, author Gail Carson Levine "offers a behind-the-scenes take on writing and teaches you how to become a world-class author. Drawing from her popular blog, Gail answers readers' fiction- and poetry-writing questions and dives into how to make a story come alive. If you're interested in writing prose and poetry or just want to be a better and more rounded writer, this book will help you on your creative journey." (Publisher's note)
"Ella Enchanted author Levine offers writing advice and prompts, primarily for fiction writers. The chapters, mostly expanded from her blog, look in-depth at aspects of writing including large-scale character and plot concerns and more specific matters of style. A lengthy section focuses on po-

etry and its role in fiction. Levine's second book on writing (Writing Magic) takes budding authors' craft questions seriously." Horn Book

808.042 Rhetoric in English

Gutman, Dan

My weird writing tips; by Dan Gutman and illustrated by Jim Paillot. HarperCollins Publishers 2013 160 p. $5.99
Grades: 3 4 5 6 7 **808.042**
1. Language arts 2. English language -- Composition and exercises
ISBN 0062091069; 9780062091062; 9780062091079
LC 2012029985

This book by Dan Gutman "offers tricks for spelling hard words, understanding the difference between similar words like "its" and "it's," and conquering grammar stumbling blocks like commas and apostrophes. He also teaches readers how to write an engaging story, in line with the grades 2-5 Common Core goals for writing a narrative." (Publisher's note)

808.06 Rhetoric of specific kinds of writing

Fletcher, Ralph

Guy-write; what every guy writer needs to know. by Ralph Fletcher. 1st ed. Christy Ottaviano Books/Henry Holt and Co. 2012 166 p. ill. (hardcover) $15.99
Grades: 4 5 6 **808.06**
1. Writing & handwriting 2. Boys -- Books and reading 3. Authors 4. Authorship 5. Illustrators 6. Children's literature -- Authorship
ISBN 0805094040; 9780805094046
LC 2011033487

Author Ralph "Fletcher offers a new writing guide with advice aimed squarely at boys. . . . He lets guy writers know it's OK to write what they love: humor, grossness, battles, fantasy and horror. And he counsels guy writers on how to talk with their teachers about writing what they love to satisfy assignments. Along the way Fletcher peppers the text with general writing tips and suggestions for ways to make all types of writing stronger and more enjoyable." (Kirkus Reviews)

808.1 Rhetoric in specific literary forms

Prelutsky, Jack

★ Pizza, pigs, and poetry; how to write a poem. Greenwillow Books 2008 191p il $16.99; pa $5.99
Grades: 4 5 6 **808.1**
1. Poetics
ISBN 978-0-06-143449-5; 0-06-143449-3; 978-0-06-143448-8 pa; 0-06-143448-5 pa
LC 2007-36738

"Along with easy-to-follow tips for creating verse, haiku, and concrete poetry, the reigning Children's Poet Laureate offers insights into his own thought processes, . . . glimpses of his childhood, and personal anecdotes. . . . Prelutsky tucks in more than a dozen examples of his own work, plus 10 two-and-part-of-a-third line 'poem starts.'" Booklist

808.3 Rhetoric of fiction

Bullard, Lisa

You can write a story! a story-writing recipe for kids. by Lisa Bullard; illustrated by Deborah Haley Melmon. Two-Can 2007 47p il $16.95
Grades: 2 3 4 **808.3**
1. Authorship 2. Creative writing 3. Fiction -- Technique
ISBN 978-1-58728-587-5; 1-58728-587-8
LC 2006016771

"Bullard takes a clever approach to teaching children the basic steps in story composition by treating the process as a cooking exercise. She begins with the basic ingredients of character, setting, and action, and then takes readers through the various ways they can add flavorings to their stories, including spicy settings, tempting titles, and the all-important taste test (revising). . . . The clear, engaging text speaks directly to a child. . . . Melmon's cartoon illustrations are bright, amusing, and strategically placed to add interest." Booklist

Includes bibliographical references

Hershenhorn, Esther

S is for story; a writer's alphabet. written by Esther Hershenhorn; illustrated by Zachary Pullen. Sleeping Bear Press 2009 un il $17.95; lib bdg $7.95
Grades: 3 4 5 6 **808.3**
1. Alphabet 2. Authorship 3. Fiction -- Technique
ISBN 978-1-58536-439-8; 1-58536-439-8; 978-1-58536-511-1 lib bdg; 1-58536-511-4 lib bdg
LC 2009005433

"This engaging, instructive introduction to writing stands out. The concepts paired with each letter cover elements of story (plot, characters); technique (revision, journaling); and basic practices for fostering creativity (observe). Short poems; clear, enthusiastic explanations; tips; and quotes from well-known children's authors appear on each page." Booklist

Levine, Gail Carson

★ Writing magic; creating stories that fly. Collins 2006 167p $16.99; pa $5.99
Grades: 5 6 7 8 **808.3**
1. Authorship 2. Creative writing 3. Fiction -- Technique
ISBN 978-0-06-051961-2; 0-06-051969-4; 978-0-06-051960-5 pa; 0-06-051960-6 pa
LC 2006-00481

"Levine, best known for Ella Enchanted (1997), offers middle-graders ideas about making their own writing take flight. . . . Among the topics she covers are shaping character, beginnings and endings, revising, and finding ideas. . . . Each chapter concludes with writing exercises. . . . A terrific item to have on hand for writing groups or for individual young writers who want to improve." Booklist

Litwin, Laura Baskes

Write horror fiction in 5 simple steps; Laura Baskes Litwin. Enslow Publishers 2013 48 p. (Creative Writing in 5 Simple Steps) $23.93
Grades: 4 5 6 **808.3**
1. Horror fiction -- Authorship 2. Horror tales --

Technique 3. Horror tales -- Authorship
ISBN 076603836X; 9780766038363

LC 2010038776

This book by Laura Baskes Litwin, part of the Creative Writing in 5 Simple Steps series, "shows aspiring writers how to write a terrifying tale of horror. . . . A good horror story is like a good ride at an amusement park. Feeling scared without having to face real danger is exhilarating. The story builds with tantalizing ideas. The reader inches out on the coaster track, knowing the precarious drop is seconds away." (Publisher's note)

Includes bibliographical references, filmography and index

Mazer, Anne

★ **Spilling** ink; a young writer's handbook. by Anne Mazer and Ellen Potter; illustrated by Matt Phelan. Flash Point 2010 275p il $17.99; pa $9.99

Grades: 5 6 7 8   **808.3**
1. Authorship 2. Creative writing 3. Fiction -- Technique 4. Authorship 5. Fiction -- Authorship
ISBN 978-1-59643-514-8; 1-59643-514-3; 978-1-59643-628-2 pa; 1-59643-628-X pa

"Two fine writers put their heads together and come up with an equally fine guide to their craft for beginners. . . . Mazer speaks to beginnings . . . while Potter tackles endings; and both have diverting things to say about everything that happens in between, whether it's the narrative voice or (eek) writer's block. [They are] always agreeable, practical, and commonsensical in their approach. . . . Their text is enlivened with sidebar features, personal anecdotes, and suggestions to readers for exercising their new skills. . . . Such devices, along with the authors' unfailing good humor, will go a long way to convincing their audience that writing can actually be fun! A notion that is nicely underscored by Phelan's engaging and always appealing illustrations." Booklist

808.5   Rhetoric of speech

Bullard, Lisa
Ace your oral or multimedia presentation. Enslow Elementary 2009 48p il (Ace it! information literacy) lib bdg $23.93

Grades: 3 4 5   **808.5**
1. Multimedia 2. Public speaking
ISBN 978-0-7660-3391-7 lib bdg; 0-7660-3391-0 lib bdg

LC 2008024885

"Learn how to research, write, practice, and present an oral or multimedia presentation with confidence" Publisher's note

Includes bibliographical references

808.8   Collections of literary texts from more than two literatures

The **big** book for toddlers; edited by Alice Wong & Lena Tabori. Welcome Books 2009 219p il $24.95

Grades: PreK K   **808.8**
1. Games 2. Handicraft 3. Fairy tales 4. Nursery

rhymes
ISBN 978-1-59962-071-8; 1-59962-071-5

"Full-bleed vintage illustrations by Jessie Willcox Smith, Maxfield Parrish, Margaret Evans Price and others grace the pages of this cheerful . . . hardcover book, divided into five sections: arts and crafts activities, condensed fairy tales, songs, games and nursery rhymes. The projects are simple and have buoyant instructions, . . . songs such as 'Old MacDonald' and 'Ants Go Marching' include musical notation; and familiar stories and rhymes appear as well. The lively assemblage will appeal to toddlers, and the heirloom images should captivate them as well as nostalgic adults." Publ Wkly

Classic horse stories; compiled by Christina Rossetti Darling and Blue Lantern Studio. Chronicle Books 2010 144p $19.99

Grades: 4 5 6   **808.8**
1. Horses 2. Literature -- Collections
ISBN 978-0-8118-6569-2; 0-8118-6569-X

LC 2010008550

"This compilation of stories, poems, and artwork celebrates the relationship between horses and their devotees. Darling pulls from a wide range of familiar, beloved material: excerpts from Steinbeck's The Red Pony, Farley's The Black Stallion, and Lewis's The Horse and His Boy join poetry from Shakespeare, Farjeon, and Stevenson. Varied paintings and illustrations from throughout the 20th century underscore the point that the book offers something for all tastes." Publ Wkly

DePaola, Tomie, 1934-
Joy to the world; Christmas stories and songs. G.P. Putnam's Sons 2010 111p il lib bdg $24.99

Grades: K 1 2 3   **808.8**
1. Carols 2. Christmas 3. Literature -- Collections
ISBN 978-0-399-25536-6; 0-399-25536-2

LC 2010284499

"This handsome omnibus includes three of dePaola's adaptations of traditional Christmas legends—The Night of Las Posadas, The Story of the Three Wise Kings, and The Legend of the Poinsettia—in addition to five selections from Tomie dePaola's Book of Christmas Carols. The distinctions of tone and style reveal a versitility with which this illustrator is not always credited." Horn Book Guide

Everything I need to know I learned from a children's book. Roaring Brook 2009 233p $29.99

Grades: Adult Professional   **808.8**
1. Children's literature -- History and criticism
ISBN 978-1-59643-395-3; 1-59643-395-7

"Over 100 noteworthy figures, from Ursula K. Le Guin to Jay Leno, convey lessons learned from specific children's books in this affirming collaboration, which is divided into six thematic sections and features full-color images. For each selection, a contributor provides a brief essay about how the book influenced him or her, accompanied by an excerpt. . . . A moving patchwork message about the transformative powers of reading." Publ Wkly

Griffiths, Andy
Killer koalas from outer space; and lots of other very bad stuff that will make your brain explode! illustrations by Terry Denton. Feiwel and Friends 2011 172p il $12.99

Grades: 3 4 5 6 **808.8**

1. Literature -- Collections

ISBN 978-0-312-36789-3; 0-312-36789-9

Portions of this book were originally published in Australia as "The Bad Book" and "The Very Bad Book" copyright page

"Sometimes bad can be very, very good indeed. Griffiths proves this time and again in this hilarious collection of rude, lewd and crude poems, jokes and cautionary tales. Deliciously revolting characters in stories . . . are sure to leave young, potty-humor-loving readers in stitches. Denton's edgy, stick-figure illustrations only add to the fun, upping the gross-out ante and giving the collection a frenetic energy that makes the book nearly impossible to put down. . . . The genius of this subversive little tome lies in its perfect combination of zany subject matter that will appeal to a broad spectrum of readers and a format that make it easily accessible to beginning and struggling readers." Kirkus

Julie Andrews' collection of poems, songs, and lullabies; edited by Julie Andrews and Emma Walton Hamilton; paintings by James McMullan. Little, Brown Books for Young Readers 2009 192p il $24.99

Grades: K 1 2 3 **808.8**

1. Songs 2. Lullabies 3. Poetry -- Collections

ISBN 978-0-316-04049-5; 0-316-04049-5

LC 2009-5121

"Julie Andrews and her daughter's selection of material for children contains works by figures as diverse as Emily Dickinson, Langston Hughes, Rodgers and Hammerstein, A.A. Milne and Shel Silverstein, as well as offerings by Andrews and Hamilton. McMullan's paintings express the sometimes silly, sometimes melancholic temperaments of the pieces, which together form a tapestry of human emotions and experiences, grand and small. The broad potpourri of voices, given a modern yet comforting flair by the artwork, is bound to become a favorite. An audio CD with poems read by Andrews and Hamilton is included." Publ Wkly

The **Norton** anthology of children's literature; the traditions in English. Jack Zipes, general editor . . . [et al.] W.W. Norton 2005 xxxviii, 2471p il pa $65

Grades: Adult Professional **808.8**

1. Literature -- Collections 2. Children's literature -- History and criticism

ISBN 0-393-97538-X

LC 2004-54172

A collection of fairy tales, picture books, nursery rhymes, fantasy, alphabets, chapbooks, and comics published in English since 1659, representing 170 authors and illustrators, and including more than ninety complete works and excerpts from others

"The delights are abundant. . . . A mile wide and very deep, this is an invaluable resource for professionals, but fun for casual perusing, too." Publ Wkly

Includes bibliographical references

808.81 Collections in specific forms

All the wild wonders; poems of our Earth. edited by Wendy Cooling; illustrated by Piet Grobler. Frances Lincoln 2010 42p il $19.95

Grades: 2 3 4 5 **808.81**

1. Nature poetry 2. Poetry -- Collections

ISBN 978-1-84780-073-2; 1-84780-073-4

"The selections from more than 30 poets in this anthology celebrate the beauty of the wild and warn of the danger that threatens the environment. . . . With a multiracial cast, Grobler's moving, pencil-and-watercolor illustrations extend the global, environmental connections. . . . Great for sharing, this will grab conservationists with both the warnings and the hope." Booklist

Carle, Eric

Eric Carle's animals, animals. Philomel Bks. 1989 87p $21.99; pa $7.99

Grades: 2 3 4 5 **808.81**

1. Animals -- Poetry 2. Poetry -- Collections

ISBN 0-399-21744-4; 0-698-11855-3 pa

LC 88-31646

"Illustrations take center stage in Eric Carle's Animals Animals . . . compiled by Laura Whipple. The well-chosen poems are from a variety of sources—the Bible, Shakespeare, Japanese Haiku, Pawnee Indian, weather sayings and contemporary poets like Judith Viorst, Ogden Nash, and Jack Prelutsky. On many pages the poem may be only two or three lines but the pictures are full-page spreads in Mr. Carle's familiar vividly colored, collage style." Kobrin Letter

Eric Carle's dragons dragons and other creatures that never were. Philomel Bks. 1991 69p il $21.99; pa $12.99

Grades: 2 3 4 5 **808.81**

1. Poetry -- Collections 2. Mythical animals -- Poetry

ISBN 0-399-22105-0; 0-399-22837-3 pa

LC 91-11986

An illustrated collection of poems about dragons and other fantastic creatures by a variety of authors

"The collection offers a sumptuous viewing of Carle's rich blend of tissue-paper and paint collages and a grand introduction to the imaginary beasts. Laura Whipple concludes this adroit compilation with a brief commentary on the fabulous animals as 'a magical part of our human heritage.'" Horn Book

Includes glossary

A **children's** treasury of poems; illustrations by Linda Bleck. Sterling 2008 un il $12.95

Grades: PreK K 1 2 **808.81**

1. Poetry -- Collections

ISBN 978-1-4027-4498-3; 1-4027-4498-6

"This collection of 19 humorous poems includes Robert Louis Stevenson's 'Bed in Summer,' Vachel Lindsay's 'The Little Turtle,' Edward Lear's 'The Owl and the Pussycat,' and Gelett Burgess's 'The Purple Cow,' among other familiar verses. Playful, cartoonlike illustrations with cutout characters and details superimposed on sturdy pages give the book texture and help create a novel effect. Different ethnicities are represented in the illustrations, although most are of fanciful animals and fairies. Young children should find the childlike format appealing." SLJ

Collins-Philippe, Jane

Sail away with me; old and new poems. selected and written by Jane Collins-Philippe; illustrated by Laura Beingessner. Tundra Books 2010 un il $15.95

    Grades: K 1 2 3   **808.81**

    1. Sea poetry 2. Poetry -- Collections

    ISBN 978-0-88776-842-2; 0-88776-842-3

"Starting off with 'My Bonnie Lies Over the Ocean' and other folk-song favorites, this picture-book poetry collection celebrates the sea and sailing traditions. . . . The lively watercolor illustrations extend the images i the words. . . . Ranging in theme from adventure to nonsense, these poems will be fun for reading aloud." Booklist

★ The **Death** of the Hat; A Brief History of Poetry in 50 Objects. selected by Paul B. Janeczko; illustrated by Chris Raschka. Candlewick Press 2015 80 p. color illustrations $17.99

    Grades: 3 4 5 6 7   **808.81**

    1. Poetry -- Collections 2. Creation (Literary, artistic, etc.)

    ISBN 0763669636; 9780763669638

                            LC 2013957308

This children's book, by Paul B. Janeczko, illustrated by Chris Raschka, focuses on "poems through history inspired by objects. . . . A book-eating moth in the early Middle Ages. A peach blossom during the Renaissance. A haunted palace in the Victorian era. A lament for the hat in contemporary times. Poetry has been a living form of artistic expression for thousands of years, and throughout that time poets have found inspiration in everything." (Publisher's note)

"Janeczko and Raschka's stellar fourth poetry collaboration, following A Poke in the I and other acclaimed titles, presents a chronological 'history' of the development of poetry, from the Middle Ages to the present. The highlighted poems are, ostensibly, about objects, but a cigar is rarely just a cigar. . . . Janeczko's substantial introduction gives an overview of poetry's evolution over the centuries, yet works like Lord Byron's 'A Riddle, on the Letter E' resonate powerfully on their own." Pub Wkly

Driscoll, Michael

★ A **child's** introduction to poetry; listen while you learn about the magic words that have moved mountains, won battles and made us laugh and cry. illustrated by Meredith Hamilton. Black Dog & Leventhal 2003 90p il $19.95
Grades: 4 5 6 7   **808.81**

    1. Poetry -- Collections 2. Poetry -- History and criticism

    ISBN 1-57912-282-5

"The first section discusses the different forms the genre takes: nursery rhyme, narrative verse, ballad, free verse, pastoral, etc. Driscoll offers a clear explanation of each type and defines any difficult, associated vocabulary. Commentary on each example and a note on where to find the recording on the accompanying CD is provided for each selection. The second section covers individual poets from Homer to Maya Angelou and offers at least one example or excerpt from each writer's work. The brief introductions to the forms and poets are lively and often amusing. Readers will find the varied layouts and warm cartoon watercolors inviting." SLJ

    Includes glossary and bibliographical references

A **family** of poems; my favorite poetry for children. [selected by] Caroline Kennedy; paintings by Jon J. Muth. Hyperion Books for Children 2005 143p il $19.95

    Grades: 3 4 5 6   **808.81**

    1. Poetry -- Collections

    ISBN 0-7868-5111-2

An anthology of over 100 poems divided into categories such as "About Me," "Animals," "Adventure" and "Bedtime," including works by such poets as A.A. Milne, Robert Louis Stevenson, Jack Prelutsky, Edward Lear, Robert Frost, William Wordsworth, T.S. Eliot, Carl Sandberg, William Shakespeare.

"From the cover photograph of Kennedy as a toddler reading to her teddy to the red linen-textured endpapers; from her thoughtful introduction and words of encouragement to children at the beginning of each section of carefully chosen poems to Muth's beautifully executed watercolors, this volume is a treasure." SLJ

★ A **foot** in the mouth; poems to speak, sing, and shout. [edited by Paul B. Janeczko; illustrated by Chris Raschka] Candlewick Press 2009 64p il $17.99

    Grades: 4 5 6 7   **808.81**

    1. Poetry -- Collections

    ISBN 978-0-7636-0663-3; 0-7636-0663-4

                            LC 2008-935581

"The poems in Janeczko and Raschka's collection . . . are not complacent, although plenty are funny and some are familiar. . . . Punchy collages flutter across airy white pages in loose visual arrangements; torn scraps of origami paper layer with fluid lines in tart color. Janeczko introduces the collection with the idea that 'Poetry is sound,' a pleasure to vocalize and memorize. . . . Readers will be emboldened to join in the 'song.'" Publ Wkly

Julie Andrews' treasury for all seasons; poems and songs to celebrate the year. selected by Julie Andrews & Emma Walton Hamilton; paintings by Marjorie Priceman. Little, Brown and Company 2012 192 p. $19.99

    Grades: K 1 2 3   **808.81**

    1. Songbooks 2. Children's poetry 3. Seasons -- Poetry

    ISBN 0316040517; 9780316040518

                            LC 2011053202

This book is a "compilation of poems and songs (including some of [Julie] Andrews and [Emma Walton] Hamilton's own) from more than 75 writers, organized by month. Summer sees . . . poems about discovery and outdoor activity, with works by Billy Collins, Joy Harjo, and E.B. White; fall poems include nature, back-to-school, and Thanksgiving themes, with pieces by Emily Dickinson, Sandra Cisneros, and others. Caldecott Honor artist [Marjorie] Priceman" illustrates. (Publishers Weekly)

Leave your sleep; selected by Natalie Merchant; pictures by Barbara McClintock. Frances Foster Books 2012 48 p. (hardcover) $24.99

    Grades: K 1 2 3   **808.81**

    1. Songbooks 2. Children's poetry 3. Poetry -- Collections

    ISBN 0374343683; 9780374343682

                            LC 2011047064

This book is a children's poetry collection. "For her 2010 hit album with the same title, [Natalie] Merchant composed music for 30 19th- and 20th-century British and American poems, some written for children and some written about childhood. For this volume, she's selected 19 of those poems (18 from the CD set and one other), describing them as 'representing the long conversation I had with my daughter during the first six years of her life.'" (Kirkus Reviews)

My village; rhymes from around the world. collected by by Danielle Wright; illustrated by Mique Moriuchi; introduction by Michael Rosen. Frances Lincoln Children's 2010 53p il $19.95
    Grades: PreK K 1 2   **808.81**
    1. Nursery rhymes 2. Poetry -- Collections
    ISBN 978-1-84780-086-2; 1-84780-086-6
"A sunny cover invites readers into this collection of nursery rhymes from around the world. Selections from 22 countries presented in both English and the original language are included as well as the original script/alphabet when appropriate. . . . The rhymes are well chosen and range from funny and bouncy to quiet and thoughtful. The brightly colored collage illustrations complement them well." SLJ

★ **National** Geographic book of animal poetry; 200 poems that squeak, soar, and roar. [edited by] J. Patrick Lewis. National Geographic 2012 183 p.
    Grades: 2 3 4 5   **808.81**
    1. Animals -- Poetry -- Collections 2. Animals -- Poetry
    ISBN 1426310099; 9781426310096; 9781426310546
    LC 2012010404
This collection of poetry about animals, edited by J. Patrick Lewis, features "lighthearted poems from the likes of Basho and Ben Franklin, Leadbelly, Jack Prelutsky and Joyce Sidman . . . [and] animal photographs. Lewis adds advice for budding animal poets to the . . . bibliography and multiple indexes at the end." (Kirkus)
    Includes bibliographical references and index

The **Oxford** book of story poems; [compiled by] Michael Harrison and Christopher Stuart-Clark. Oxford University Press 2006 175p il pa $18.95
    Grades: 5 6 7 8   **808.81**
    1. Poetry -- Collections
    ISBN 978-0-19-276344-0 pa; 0-19-276344-X pa
    LC 2007282711
First published 1990
This anthology contains "narrative verse by British and American poets, from traditional ballads such as 'Sir Patrick Spens' to contemporary poems such as Judith Nicholls' 'Storytime.' . . . The poets include Carroll, Keats, de la Mare, Kennedy, Lear, Lindsay, Longfellow, Noyes, Poe, Southey, and Tolkien. . . . A handy collection of story poems for reading aloud or alone." Booklist [review of 1990 edition]

★ **Poetry** speaks: who I am; poems of discovery, inspiration, independence, and everything else. Sourcebooks Jabberwocky 2010 136p $19.99
    Grades: 5 6 7 8 9 10   **808.81**
    1. Poetry -- Collections
    ISBN 978-1-4022-1074-7; 1-4022-1074-4
This collection "aims at middle-grade readers with more than 100 strikingly diverse poems by writers including Poe, Frost, Nikki Giovanni, and Sandra Cisneros. The works are slotted together in mindful thematic order, beside occasional spot art. . . . Pairing a contemporary poem like Toi Derricotte's 'Fears of the Eighth Grade' alongside Keats's 'When

I Have Fears That I May Cease to Be,' results in a refreshing lack of literary hierarchy that enables disparate works to build and reflect upon one another. An accompanying CD features recordings of 44 of the poems. . . . A sound and rewarding introduction to the joys of poetry." Publ Wkly

Rhymes round the world; [compiled by] Kay Chorao, Dutton Children's Books 2009 40p il $17.99
    Grades: PreK K 1   **808.81**
    1. Poetry -- Collections
    ISBN 978-0-525-47875-1; 0-525-47875-2
    LC 2008013887
"These 40 poems and songs offer children a taste of many different cultures. Most are anonymous or traditional nursery rhymes; a few are by English or American poets. The tone is light and joyous. Sweet illustrations of babies and toddlers engaged in playful activities depict the universality of children everywhere." SLJ

★ **River** of words; young poets and artists on the nature of things. edited by Pamela Michael; introduced by Robert Hass. Milkweed Editions 2008 298p il hardcover o.p. pa $18
    Grades: 4 5 6 7 8 9   **808.81**
    1. Nature poetry 2. Children's art 3. Children's writings 4. Teenagers' writings 5. Poetry -- Collections
    ISBN 978-1-57131-685-1; 1-57131-685-X; 978-1-57131-680-6 pa; 1-57131-680-9 pa
"In 1995 Michael and Hass . . . cofounded the River of Words project, designed to connect students' art and poetry education to the natural world immediately around them. . . . The poems and pictures in this handsomely designed volume have been culled from yearly contests. . . . The works are startling, many of them dislocating and highly complex." Publ Wkly

The **tree** that time built; a celebration of nature, science, and imagination. selected by Mary Ann Hoberman and Linda Winston; [illustrations by Barbara Fortin] Sourcebooks Jabberwocky 2009 209p il $19.99
    Grades: 5 6 7 8   **808.81**
    1. Nature poetry 2. Science -- Poetry 3. Poetry -- Collections
    ISBN 978-1-4022-2517-8; 1-4022-2517-2
    LC 2009032608
An anthology of more than 100 poems celebrating the wonders of the natural world and encouraging environmental awareness. Includes an audio CD that comprises readings of 44 of the poems, many performed by the poets themselves.
"Classic works by Walt Whitman, Emily Dickinson, Christina Rossetti, and the like, and selections from contemporary poets are included. . . . This handsome collection is especially appropriate for classroom use and instruction. . . . From the playful to the profound, the poems invite reflection and inspire further investigation." SLJ
    Includes glossary and bibliographical references

808.88 Collections of miscellaneous writings

Alcorn, Stephen
    A **gift** of days; the greatest words to live by. Atheneum Books for Young Readers 2009 115p il $21.99

Grades: 5 6 7 8 **808.88**

1. Quotations 2. Celebrities

ISBN 978-1-4169-6776-7; 1-4169-6776-1

LC 2007-48766

"Beautifully designed and imaginatively conceptualized, this volume presents 366 days and 366 quotations from famous people, tagged to the days they were born. Alcorn lays this out on each double-page spread with a stunning polychrome-relief block-print bordered with pattern on one leaf and, facing, a week of birthdays and quotes. These images are often brilliantly inventive. . . . Librarians, educators and historically minded kids will take much pleasure from looking up birthdays to see the associated wisdom from women and men across the ages." Kirkus

809 History, description, critical appraisal of more than two literatures

Carpenter, Humphrey

The **Oxford** companion to children's literature; [by] Humphrey Carpenter and Mari Prichard. Oxford Univ. Press 1984 586p il hardcover o.p. pa $70

Grades: Adult Professional **809**

1. Reference books 2. Children's literature -- Dictionaries

ISBN 0-19-211582-0; 0-19-860228-6 pa

LC 83-15130

"One volume work with brief critiques of authors, illustrators, books, characters, and radio and television programs. Largely British in coverage of materials but does include most Newbery winners as well as well-known American, Australian and Canadian authors. Contemporary and historical subjects related to children's literature are examined." N Y Public Libr. Ref Books for Child Collect. 2d edition

Krull, Kathleen

★ **Lives** of the writers; comedies, tragedies (and what the neighbors thought) written by Kathleen Krull; illustrated by Kathryn Hewitt. 1st ed. Harcourt Brace & Co. 1994 96 p. col. ill. (reinforced) $21

Grades: 4 5 6 7 **809**

1. Poets 2. Authors 3. Humorists 4. Novelists 5. Dramatists 6. Historians 7. Journalists

ISBN 0152480099; 9780152480097

LC 93032436

This volume presents biographical sketches of writers. Arranged "in chronological order by date of birth, the selection of writers begins with Murasaki Shikibu, the first-century Japanese author of 'The Tale of Genji' . . . and concludes with Isaac Bashevis Singer, the Jewish American storyteller who died in 1991." (Horn Book Magazine)

This offers "views of twenty writers . . . from various countries and historical periods. Included are William Shakespeare, Edgar Allan Poe, Mark Twain, Zora Neale Hurston, Isaac Bashevis Singer, and many others." Publisher's note

Includes bibliographical references (p. 96) and index.

The **Oxford** encyclopedia of children's literature; Jack Zipes, editor in chief. Oxford University Press 2006 4v il set $495

Grades: Adult Professional **809**

1. Reference books 2. Children's literature --

Encyclopedias

ISBN 978-0-19-514656-1; 0-19-514656-5

LC 2005-34390

"The 3200 signed articles in this set include brief discussions of the work of major writers, important trends, genres, characters, organizations, and noteworthy publications and people in the field. All of the alphabetical articles are clearly written and most include cross-references. . . . There is no comparable single work that brings together all aspects of the topic, making this a valuable resource." SLJ

Includes bibliographical references

Sutton, Roger

A **family** of readers; the book lover's guide to children's and young adult literature. [by] Roger Sutton and Martha V. Parravano; foreword by Gregory Maguire. Candlewick Press 2010 350p il $22; pa $14.99

Grades: Adult Professional **809**

1. Children -- Books and reading 2. Teenagers -- Books and reading 3. Children's literature -- History and criticism

ISBN 978-0-7636-3280-9; 0-7636-3280-5; 978-0-7636-5755-0 pa; 0-7636-5755-7 pa

"This collection of essays from editors, reviewers, and authors emanates enthusiasm for books and reading. . . . Each section begins with an overview, followed by a selection of essays. The first chapter addresses the very smallest book lovers, and the last tackles the needs of young adults. Each chapter is followed by an annotated list of books. A complete bibliography and biographical sketches of the contributors are included in the end. . . . It should be required reading for every youth services librarian." Voice Youth Advocates

809.1 Literature in specific forms other than miscellaneous writings

Bodden, Valerie

Concrete poetry. Creative Education 2010 32p il (Poetry basics) $28.50

Grades: 5 6 7 8 **809.1**

1. Poetry -- History and criticism

ISBN 978-1-58341-775-1; 1-58341-775-3

LC 2008009156

This book describes concrete poetry's "history, characteristics, and variations. Many examples are provided as well as ideas for how children can write their own pieces. The information is accessible, and the writing is sufficiently lively to engage readers. The well-designed pages feature a variety of art reproductions from different literary eras and some photographs." Horn Book Guide

Includes glossary and bibliographical references

Haiku. Creative Education 2010 32p il (Poetry basics) $19.95

Grades: 5 6 7 8 **809.1**

1. Haiku

ISBN 978-1-58341-776-8; 1-58341-776-1

LC 2008-9158

Presents history and examples of the Japanese form of poetry called haiku.

"The information is accessible, and the writing is sufficiently lively to engage readers. The well-designed pages feature a variety of art reproductions from different literary eras and some photographs." Horn Book Guide

Includes glossary and bibliographical references

Limericks. Creative Education 2010 32p il (Poetry basics) $19.95
Grades: 5 6 7 8   809.1
1. Limericks
ISBN 978-1-58341-777-5; 1-58341-777-X
LC 2008-9159
This describes limericks' "history, characteristics, and variations. Many examples are provided as well as ideas for how children can write their own pieces. The information is accessible, and the writing is sufficiently lively to engage readers. The well-designed pages feature a variety of art reproductions from different literary eras and some photographs." Horn Book Guide

Includes glossary and bibliographical references

810 Literatures of specific languages and language families

Wilkin, Binnie Tate
African and African American images in Newbery Award winning titles; progress in portrayals. Scarecrow Press 2009 195p pa $40
Grades: Adult Professional   810
1. Newbery Medal 2. African Americans in literature 3. Children's literature -- History and criticism
ISBN 978-0-8108-6959-2 pa; 0-8108-6959-4 pa
LC 2009017726
"The author has exhaustively examined all books that have won the Newbery Medal and been cited as honor books since the award's creation in 1922. Her purpose is to evaluate the representation of Africans and African Americans, and to describe how these groups are portrayed in each title's historical context. . . . Books with the most positive images are awarded three pluses, while books with marginal African-American characters are indicated with an 'M.' . . . An essential volume for scholars, teachers, and librarians." SLJ

Includes bibliographical references

811 American poetry

★ The **20th** century children's poetry treasury; selected by Jack Prelutsky; illustrated by Meilo So. Knopf 1999 87p il $19.95
Grades: 3 4 5 6   811
1. American poetry -- Collections
ISBN 0-679-89314-8; 0-679-99314-2 lib bdg
LC 99-23988
A collection of more than 200 poems by such modern poets as Nikki Grimes, John Ciardi, Karla Kuskin, Ted Hughes, e.e. cummings, Eve Merriam, Deborah Chandra, Arnold Adoff, and more than 100 others

"While all of these selections have been published elsewhere, the format and illustrations in this collection give them new life. . . . So's watercolor illustrations are, by turn, impressionistic, childlike, silly, and serious, as called for by the tone of the poems featured. . . . A splendid collection." SLJ

Ada, Alma Flor, 1938-
★ **Gathering** the sun; an alphabet in Spanish and English. English translation by Rosa Zubizarreta; illustrated by Simón Silva. Lothrop, Lee & Shepard Bks. 1997 un il $16.95; pa $6.99
Grades: 2 3 4   811
1. Alphabet 2. Mexican Americans -- Poetry 3. Poetry -- By individual authors 4. Bilingual books -- English-Spanish
ISBN 0-688-13903-5; 0-688-17067-7 pa
"Using the Spanish alphabet as a template, Ada has written 27 poems that celebrate both the bounty of the harvest and the Mexican heritage of the farmworkers and their families. The poems, presented in both Spanish and English, are short and simple bursts of flavor. . . . Silva's sun-drenched gouache paintings are robust, with images sculpted in paint." Booklist

Adoff, Arnold
★ **Roots** and blues; a celebration. paintings by R. Gregory Christie. Clarion Books 2011 88p il
Grades: 4 5 6   811
1. Children's poetry 2. Blues music -- Poetry 3. African Americans -- Poetry 4. Poetry -- By individual authors 5. Blues (Music) -- History and criticism
ISBN 0547235542; 9780547235547
LC 2009-26625
Adoff tells the story of the blues in this collection of sixty poems and prose pieces. "Grades eight to twelve." (Bull Cent Child Books)

"In this visceral collaboration, Adoff and Christie honor the enduring legacy of blues music. Vibrant, haunting acrylic paintings portray crowded slave ships, chain gang labor, and the crackling energy of juke joints. . . . Several poems titled 'Listening' capture the sounds of the decades in which they're set . . . and mimic the rhythms and repetitions of the blues. . . . This is a challenging, openhearted collection with images and poems that bleed into one another, but also stand powerfully alone." Publ Wkly

African American Poetry; edited by Arnold Rampersad and Marcellus Blount; illustrated by Karen Barbour. Sterling Pub Co Inc. 2013 48 p. ill. (hardcover) $14.95
Grades: 3 4 5 6 7   811
1. American poetry -- Asian American authors
ISBN 1402716893; 9781402716898
This book of poetry by African American authors"introduces 27 poets from the days of Phillis Wheatley to well-established poets writing in the 21st century. A four-page introduction outlines historical periods and influences. Presented chronologically, the entries begin with a paragraph describing the poet's life and work. Paul Laurence Dunbar, Countee Cullen, Langston Hughes, Lucille Clifton, Maya Angelou, and others are joined by George Moses Horton . . . and others." (School Library Journal)

Ahlberg, Allan
Everybody was a baby once, and other poems; illustrator Bruce Ingman. Candlewick Press 2010 63p il $15.99
Grades: PreK K 1   811
1. Infants -- Poetry 2. Poetry -- By individual authors
ISBN 978-0-7636-4682-0; 0-7636-4682-2
"From the creators of The Pencil, these 19 poems cover whimsical territory and feature kids, angels, sausages, and

monsters, rendered in kinetic, childlike sketches. A few poems strike nostalgic, melancholy notes . . . but most are upbeat, with gently jazzy rhythms. . . . The Lilliputian cast and memorable verse could make this a dog-eared favorite." Publ Wkly

Alarcon, Francisco X.

  Iguanas in the snow and other winter poems; poems, Francisco X. Alarcón; illustrations, Maya Christina Gonzalez. Children's Bk. Press 2001 31p il hardcover o.p. pa $7.95

Grades: 2 3 4   **811**

  1. Winter -- Poetry 2. Poetry -- By individual authors 3. Bilingual books -- English-Spanish

  ISBN 0-89239-168-5; 0-89239-202-9 pa

                        LC 00-65667

  "Brief, zippy verses express delight in such simple things as a family frolic in the snow and the wonder of giant redwoods. . . . The selections are short of line and long on meter, with a rhythmic roll that begs reading aloud. . . . Gonzalez's illustrations are bright and busy, catching the playful cadence of the words." SLJ

Amazing faces; edited by Lee Bennett Hopkins; illustrated by Chris Soentpiet. Lee & Low 2010 un il $18.95

  Grades: 2 3 4 5   **811**

  1. American poetry -- Collections

  ISBN 978-1-60060-334-1; 1-60060-334-3

  "Illustrated with large, handsome watercolor portraits, the 16 poems in this anthology celebrate the rich diversity of American kids—what makes each one special and the connections between them. . . . A great collection for sharing at home and in the classroom." Booklist

★ **America** at war; poems. selected by Lee Bennett Hopkins; illlustrated by Stephen Alcorn. Margaret K. McElderry Books 2008 84p il $21.99

  Grades: 5 6 7 8   **811**

  1. War poetry 2. American poetry -- Collections 3. United States -- History -- Poetry

  ISBN 978-1-4169-1832-5; 1-4169-1832-9

                    LC 2006-08723

  "This handsome anthology, expressing Americans' varied experience during wartime, is a fine selection of poems accessible to children. . . . The poems will touch readers with their sharp poignancy and undeniable power. Throughout the well-designed book, the expressive watercolor artwork enhances the poetry." Booklist

Angelou, Maya

  Amazing peace; a Christmas poem. by Maya Angelou; paintings by Steve Johnson and Lou Fancher. Schwartz & Wade Books 2008 un il $17.99; lib bdg $20.99

  Grades: 3 4 5   **811**

  1. Christmas -- Poetry 2. Poetry -- By individual authors

  ISBN 978-0-375-84150-7; 0-375-84150-4; 978-0-375-94327-0 lib bdg; 0-375-94327-7 lib bdg

  "This poem was largely inspired by the terrible natural disasters occurring throughout the world. When Angelou was invited to read at the 2005 White House tree-lighting ceremony. Thus, the opening lines rumble and roil almost menacingly to illustrate the climate of doubt and anxiety into which the spirit of Christmas arrives. Hope enters as a whisper and grows until it is 'louder than the explosion of

bombs.' . . . Johnson and Fancher's paintings, rendered in oil, acrylic, and fabric on canvas, elegantly depict a calm, snow-blanketed village where children play, families shop, and artisans ply their crafts. . . . This is a comforting book that gets to the heart of what Christmas should mean. As an added treat, Angelou reads the poem on the accompanying CD." SLJ

Archer, Peggy

  From dawn to dreams; poems for busy babies. illustrated by Hanako Wakiyama. Candlewick Press 2007 un il $15.99

  Grades: PreK   **811**

  1. Infants -- Poetry 2. Poetry -- By individual authors

  ISBN 978-0-7636-2467-5; 0-7636-2467-5

                    LC 2006051832

  "15 poems cover the gamut of activities in which babies and toddlers participate: a first step, clomping around in adult shoes, exploring faces in a mirror, introducing oneself to the family cat, and so on. . . . The oil-on-paper illustrations are in a style reminiscent of art in the 1950s. On various pages, the text is surrounded by a zigzag frame that adds to the old-fashioned feel." SLJ

  Name that dog! puppy poems from A to Z. illustrations by Stephanie Buscema. Dial Books for Young Readers 2010 un il $16.99

  Grades: PreK K 1 2 3   **811**

  1. Dogs -- Poetry 2. Poetry -- By individual authors

  ISBN 978-0-8037-3322-0; 0-8037-3322-4

                    LC 2009009286

  "This picture book poetry collection presents a rogue's gallery of pooches in selections designed to help an unidentified dog owner name his or her new pet. . . . The poems, representing a variety of styles, read smoothly and are complemented by Buscema's energetic, stylized illustrations." Booklist

Argueta, Jorge

  Talking with Mother Earth; poems. illustrated by Lucia Angela Perez. Groundwood Books 2006 un il $15.95

  Grades: 3 4 5 6   **811**

  1. Nature poetry 2. Racism -- Poetry 3. Pipil Indians -- Poetry 4. Poetry -- By individual authors 5. Bilingual books -- English-Spanish

  ISBN 0-88899-626-8

  This presents poems which explore a Pipil Nahua Indian boy's connection to Mother Earth and how it heals the wounds of racism.

  "This literary offering stands out for its beauty and depth of expression. . . . Pérez's illustrations are colorful, detailed, and appealing, incorporating many indigenous icons." SLJ

Aronica-Buck, Barbara

  Over the moon; the Broadway lullaby project. Easton Studio Press 2012 46 p.

  Grades: 3 4 5   **811**

  1. Lullabies

  ISBN 1935212702; 9781935212706

  This book compiled by Kate Dawson and Jodi Glucksman presents a "collection of original lullabies and illustrations featuring music by some of Broadway's biggest stars and brightest composers with illustrations by acclaimed Children's artists and Broadway set designers. . . . each offering a . . . visual interpretation of a song from the CD bound in the book." (Publisher's note)

The **arrow** finds its mark; a book of found poems. edited by Georgia Heard; illustrated by Antoine Guilloppé. Roaring Brook Press 2012 38 p.
Grades: 3 4 5   **811**
1. American poetry 2. Children's poetry 3. Poetry -- Collections 4. Children's poetry, American
ISBN 1596436654; 9781596436657
LC 2011017180
This poetry collection, edited by Georgia Heard with illustrations by Antoine Guillope, features material from Twitter feeds, school notes, advertisements, street signs. . . .poetry in . . . unlikely places [by] thirty contemporary poets. Imagine picking up a scrap of paper off the floor or reading a sign at a gas station or looking at graffiti on the subway and finding poetry in these words. The literary equivalent of a collage, found poems take existing text, reorder and refashion it, and present it as a poem. (Publisher's note)

★ **Ashley** Bryan's ABC of African-American poetry. Atheneum Bks. for Young Readers 1997 un il hardcover o.p. pa $7.99
Grades: K 1 2 3   **811**
1. Alphabet 2. African Americans -- Poetry 3. American poetry -- African American authors -- Collections
ISBN 0-689-81209-4; 0-689-84045-4 pa
LC 96-25148
Each letter of the alphabet is represented by a line from a poem by a different African American poet, describing an aspect of the black experience
This book is illustrated "by Bryan's vivid tempera and gouache paintings. . . . The selections . . . display a loving acquaintance with poets from James Weldon Johnson to Rita Dove. While there is a full range of emotions, joy and pride predominate." SLJ

Bagert, Brod
School fever; by Brod Bagert; pictures by Robert Neubecker. Dial Books for Young Readers 2008 un il $16.99
Grades: 1 2 3   **811**
1. Schools -- Poetry 2. Poetry -- By individual authors
ISBN 978-0-8037-3201-8; 0-8037-3201-5
LC 2007-9324
This is a book of "poems, most of which follow a basic rhyming pattern, [and] touch on a number subjects and school situations near and dear to children. . . . The fun illustrations, completed with ink and a computer, really capture the essence of the poems." Libr Media Connect

Bates, Katharine Lee
★ **America** the beautiful; illustrated by Chris Gall. Little, Brown 2004 un il $16.95
Grades: K 1 2 3   **811**
1. Songs -- United States 2. United States -- Poetry
ISBN 0-316-73743-7
LC 2003-54552
Four verses of the nineteenth-century poem later set to music, illustrated by the author's great-great-grandnephew
"Children will be stirred by Gall's pictures. Using hand engraving on clay-covered board and enhancing elements such as color with a computer, he offers a series of pictures

resembling woodcuts in form and WPA paintings in style." Booklist

★ **Behind** the museum door; poems to celebrate the wonders of museums. selected by Lee Bennett Hopkins; illustrated by Stacey Dressen-McQueen. Abrams Books for Young Readers 2007 un il $16.95
Grades: 3 4 5   **811**
1. Art -- Poetry 2. Museums -- Poetry 3. American poetry -- Collections
ISBN 978-0-8109-1204-5; 0-8109-1204-X
LC 2006013576
"This collection of poems touches on the sights and sensations a group of children experience on a field trip. . . . Selections are by such poets as Lilian Moore, Jane Yolen, Alice Schertle, and Myra Cohn Livingston. . . . Each of Dressen-McQueen's folk-art-style 'exhibits,' carefully crafted in acrylic paint, oil pastel, and colored pencil, successfully captures and reinforces the mood of its accompanying poem." SLJ

Bernier-Grand, Carmen T.
Cesar; si, se puede! yes, we can! illustrated by David Diaz. Marshall Cavendish 2004 48p il $16.95
Grades: 3 4 5 6   **811**
1. Agricultural laborers 2. Labor leaders 3. Mexican Americans -- Poetry 4. Poetry -- By individual authors
ISBN 0-7614-5172-2
LC 2003-26866
"The lyrical language describes events and paints evocative pictures to which children will relate. Diaz's stylized, computer-drawn, folk-art illustrations capture the subject's private and public life." SLJ
Inlcudes glossary and bibliographical references

★ The **Bill** Martin Jr. Big book of poetry; edited by Bill Martin Jr., with Michael Sampson; foreword by Eric Carle; afterword Steven Kellogg. Simon & Schuster Books for Young Readers 2008 175p $21
Grades: PreK K 1 2 3   **811**
1. American poetry -- Collections
ISBN 978-1-4169-3971-9; 1-4169-3971-7
"The almost 200 selections in this big handsome anthology . . . have a singing beat. . . . The collection brings together poems from Robert Frost, Christina Rossetti, Langston Hughes, Nikki Grimes, Aliki, Jack Prelutsky, and many other well-known poets. Accompanying the poems are pictures from many of the best picture-book illustrators whose work . . . extends the words' lyrical rhythms and playfulness." Booklist

Blackaby, Susan
★ **Nest,** nook & cranny; poems by Susan Blackaby; illustrated by Jamie Hogan. Charlesbridge 2010 48p il $15.95
Grades: 3 4 5 6   **811**
1. Habitat (Ecology) 2. Animals -- Poetry 3. Poetry -- By individual authors
ISBN 978-1-58089-350-3; 1-58089-350-3
LC 2009004302
"This lively poetry collection pairs verse about animals with black-and-white drawings of creatures in their natural habitats. . . . The various settings, accompanied by notes on nature, will grab young conservationists. . . . Teachers will

welcome the extensive final notes on animal habitats and poetic forms for science and creative-writing classes." Booklist

Blackall, Sophie

★ **Spinster** Goose; twisted rhymes for naughty children. [by] Lisa Wheeler & Sophie Blackall. Atheneum Books for Young Readers 2011 41p il $16.99

Grades: 3 4 5   **811**

1. Parodies 2. Nursery rhymes 3. Children's poetry 4. Poetry -- By individual authors

ISBN 978-1-4169-2541-5; 1-4169-2541-4

"This collection of Mother Goose parodies . . . is as elegant as it is, like Mary, 'quite contrary.' The no-nonsense Spinster Goose oversees a reform school. . . . Blackall's pallid vignettes balance chilly poise and mordant humor. . . . Wheeler adds some intellectual depth to the original nursery rhymes while grossifying them. . . . Though some may shrink from its clever ghastliness, kids with twisted senses of humor will feel right at home." Publ Wkly

Brooks, Gwendolyn

★ **Bronzeville** boys and girls; illustrated by Faith Ringgold. newly illustrated ed.; Amistad/HarperCollins Publishers 2007 41p il $16.99; lib bdg $18.89

Grades: K 1 2 3   **811**

1. African Americans -- Poetry 2. Poetry -- By individual authors

ISBN 978-0-06-029505-9; 0-06-029505-8; 978-0-06-029506-6 lib bdg; 0-06-029506-6 lib bdg

LC 2006-01947

A newly illustrated edition of the title first published 1956

"Brooks's deceptively simple poems for children combined with Ringgold's vibrant illustrations help to rejuvenate this collection first published in 1956. . . . Each poem is tightly constructed, rhythmic and distinctive. . . . Ringgold's bold illustrations, outlined with her signature thick black lines, are among some of her best and most narrative works since Tar Beach." Publ Wkly

Brown, Calef

★ **Flamingoes** on the roof; poems and paintings by Calef Brown. Houghton Mifflin 2006 un il $16

Grades: 3 4 5 6   **811**

1. Humorous poetry 2. Poetry -- By individual authors

ISBN 0-618-56298-2

LC 2004-25125

"These 29 nonsense poems, written in a variety of rhymed meters, are deliciously loaded with alliterative and assonant sounds and filled with delightful doggerel. . . . Full-page, flat acrylic illustrations, most painted in harmonious jewel tones, face single-toned pages of text in a variety of colors." SLJ

★ **Hallowilloween**; nefarious silliness. Houghton Mifflin Books for Children 2010 un il $16.99

Grades: 2 3 4 5   **811**

1. Humorous poetry 2. Monsters -- Poetry 3. Poetry -- By individual authors

ISBN 978-0-547-21540-2; 0-547-21540-1

"Brown's playful collection of poems and paintings is likely to inspire as many giggles as it does shivers. Readers meet a werewolf named Jack, Duncan the shrunken head, and an unhappy mummy. . . . Brown's acrylic illustrations add to the creepy silliness: an artful mix of naive and styl-

ized, whimsical details and vibrant color. Young readers will relish the wordplay and find themselves torn to choose a favorite among this wacky menagerie." SLJ

Soup for breakfast; poems and pictures. Houghton Mifflin Co. 2008 un il $16

Grades: K 1 2 3   **811**

1. Humorous poetry 2. Poetry -- By individual authors

ISBN 978-0-618-91641-2; 0-618-91641-5

LC 2007047734

Brown's "fun-filled poems feature an unpredictable range of topics and imagery. . . . He offsets each poem with one of his flat, idiosyncratic paintings; with their oddball beasts and improbable color combinations, his pictures are somewhere between surreal and folk art." Publ Wkly

Brown, Margaret Wise

Nibble nibble; [by] Margaret Wise Brown; paintings by Wendell Minor. HarperCollins 2007 un il $16.99; lib bdg $17.89

Grades: PreK K 1   **811**

1. Rabbits -- Poetry 2. Poetry -- By individual authors

ISBN 978-0-06-059208-0; 0-06-059208-7; 978-0-06-059209-7 lib bdg; 0-06-059209-5 lib bdg

LC 2006029869

A collection of poetry about rabbits

"Large, almost tactile paintings of birds, butterflies, and bunnies combine well with the flow of Brown's charming poems, originally published in 1959. . . . Onomatopoeic and motion words are reflected in the pictures with their ground-level perspective. These five beautifully and newly illustrated poems will enchant another generation of children." SLJ

Bryan, Ashley

★ **Ashley** Bryan's Puppets; Making Something from Everything. Ashley Bryan. Simon & Schuster 2014 80 p. $19.99

Grades: PreK K 1 2 3 4 5 6   **811**

1. Poetry 2. Waste products 3. Puppets and puppet plays 4. Children's poetry 5. Puppets -- Poetry 6. Found objects -- Poetry

ISBN 1442487283; 9781442487284

In this book, "storyteller and creator Ashley Bryan reveals the vibrant spirit of found objects in this . . . treasury of poetry and puppets. . . . For decades, Ashley has walked up and down the beach, stopping to pick up sea glass, weathered bones, a tangle of fishing net, an empty bottle, a doorknob. Treasure. And then, with glue and thread and paint and a sprinkling of African folklore, Ashley breathes new life into these materials." (Publisher's note)

"Award-winning author and illustrator Bryan has combined his love of art and poetry in this captivating and beautifully designed book...Traditional African themes abound as the characters introduce themselves through their poems, and readers are invited into the world of puppets and poetry. Bryan has truly created a book for all to treasure." SLJ

Bulion, Leslie

At the sea floor cafe; odd ocean critter poems. written by Leslie Bulion; illustrated by Leslie Evans. Peachtree Publishers 2011 45p il $14.95

Grades: 5 6 7 8   **811**

1. Marine animals -- Poetry 2. Poetry -- By individual

authors

ISBN 978-1-56145-565-2; 1-56145-565-2

LC 2010026691

"Using complex poetry forms and cleverly constructed lines, Bulion plays tribute to sea creatures. . . . Evans's spare, well-placed hand-colored linoleum block prints hold their own without overwhelming the text." Horn Book Guide

Burleigh, Robert

★ **Home** run; the story of Babe Ruth. illustrated by Mike Wimmer. Harcourt Brace & Co. 1998 un il hardcover o.p. pa $7

Grades: K 1 2 3   **811**

1. Baseball players 2. Baseball -- Fiction

ISBN 0-15-200970-1; 0-15-204599-6 pa

LC 95-10038

A poetic account of the legendary Babe Ruth as he prepares to make a home run

"With a flowing minimal text, Burleigh brings the Babe to life through the moment of one at bat. . . . Wimmer's sprawling, photorealistic oil paintings depict the larger-than-life figure and his surroundings with folksy Norman Rockwell-like charm." SLJ

★ **Hoops**; illustrated by Stephen T. Johnson. Harcourt Brace & Co. 1997 un il hardcover o.p. pa $6

Grades: 6 7 8 9   **811**

1. Basketball -- Poetry 2. Poetry -- By individual authors

ISBN 0-15-201450-0; 0-15-216380-8 pa

LC 96-18440

Illustrations and poetic text describe the movement and feel of the game of basketball

"Burleigh's staccato text is well matched by Johnson's dynamic pastels. Muted colors and a strong sense of motion as bodies leap and lift, pounce and poke, aptly complement the words." SLJ

Child, Lydia Maria Francis

Over the river and through the wood; the New England boy's song about Thanksgiving day. [by] L. Maria Child; illustrated by Matt Tavares. Candlewick Press 2011 un il $16.99

Grades: 2 3 4   **811**

1. Thanksgiving Day -- Poetry 2. Poetry -- By individual authors

ISBN 978-0-7636-2790-4; 0-7636-2790-9

LC 2010038878

"A charming and dynamic rendition of the song about Thanksgiving Day, originally published in 1844. All 12 original verses are included, each old-fashioned scene appropriately matching the text. Tavares's watercolor, ink, and pencil illustrations are crisp and bright, expertly capturing the wind-whipped outdoor scenes of the sleigh moving from page to page and ultimately to grandfather's house for a feast." SLJ

Ciardi, John

★ **You** read to me, I'll read to you; drawings by Edward Gorey. Lippincott 1962 64p il hardcover o.p. pa $7.95

Grades: 1 2 3 4   **811**

1. Humorous poetry 2. Poetry -- By individual authors

ISBN 0-06-446060-6 pa

Thirty-five "imaginative and humorous poems for an adult and a child to read aloud together. Written in a basic first-grade vocabulary, the poems to be read by the child alternate with poems to be read by the adult." Booklist

Clayton, Dallas

Make magic! do good! Dallas Clayton. Candlewick Press 2012 112 p. $17.99

Grades: 3 4 5   **811**

1. Children's poetry 2. Friendship -- Poetry

ISBN 0763657468; 9780763657468

LC 2012942305

This is a poetry collection for children by Dallas Clayton. "Recurring themes in the nearly 50 poems include seizing the day, making friends of enemies, being kind, and blazing one's own trail. 'You won't be fast forever/ so the clever thing to do/ is to stop and help the others keep up/ because someday/ they'll be you,' writes Clayton in 'Running!'" (Publishers Weekly)

Clements, Andrew

Dogku; [by] Andrew Clements; illustrations by Tim Bowers. Simon & Schuster Books for Young Readers 2007 un il $16.99

Grades: 1 2 3 4   **811**

1. Haiku 2. Dogs -- Poetry 3. Poetry -- By individual authors

ISBN 978-0-689-85823-9; 0-689-85823-X

LC 2006003691

"A stray dog's first day in a family's home is more or less a test of whether he'll get to stay. . . . [The author] tells the entire tale in haiku, a remarkably effective vehicle for delivering such a sweet and simple story. . . . While each haiku is typically spare, Bowers's vibrant illustrations are busy and bright, filling the pages with the same unbounded energy as the lovable pooch." SLJ

Coombs, Kate

Water sings blue; ocean poems. by Kate Coombs; illustrated by Meilo So. Chronicle Books 2012 36 p.

Grades: PreK K 1 2 3   **811**

1. Sea poetry 2. Ocean -- Poetry 3. Children's poetry 4. Poetry -- Collections 5. Picture books for children

ISBN 9780811872843

LC 2010030163

This picture book presents "twenty-three poems and . . . watercolor paintings [that] pay tribute to the wonders of the ocean world. . . . [Kate Coombs] invites young readers into her celebration with an opening 'Song of the Boat' and ends with the message of the 'Tideline'. . . . [In another poem] Gulper Eel's 'astronomical maw' is compared to a black hole." (Kirkus Reviews)

Crawley, Dave

Reading, rhyming, and 'rithmetic; poems by Dave Crawley; illustrations by Liz Callen. Wordsong 2010 31p il $17.95

Grades: 3 4 5   **811**

1. Schools -- Poetry 2. Poetry -- By individual authors

ISBN 978-1-59078-565-2; 1-59078-565-7

LC 2009019917

This anthology focuses on school-themed poems.

"The verses flow easily and the rhymes are engaging and well done. Each one lends itself to being read aloud. Kids will love this collection. The illustrations are pleasant, humorous, and just enough to complement the verses." Libr Media Connect

Dakos, Kalli

A **funeral** in the bathroom; and other school bathroom poems. illustrated by Mark Beech. Albert Whitman & Co. 2011 47p il

Grades: 3 4 5   **811**

1. Schools -- Poetry 2. Bathrooms -- Poetry 3. Poetry -- By individual authors

ISBN 0-8075-2675-4; 978-0-8075-2675-0

LC 2010045591

"Dakos's humorous, bittersweet poems and Beech's mischievous illustrations center on the school bathroom as a place of refuge, camaraderie, and, of course, necessity. . . . A heartfelt collage of relatable moments." Publ Wkly

Dant, Traci

Some kind of love; a family reunion in poems. illustrated by Eric Velasquez. Marshall Cavendish Children 2010 un il $17.99

Grades: K 1 2 3   **811**

1. Family reunions -- Poetry 2. African Americans -- Poetry 3. Poetry -- By individual authors

ISBN 978-0-7614-5559-2; 0-7614-5559-0

LC 2008-20878

"'Must be some kind of love.' That is the refrain that starts off each moving poem in this picture book about an annual African American family reunion, told in free verse from the viewpoint of a nine-year-old boy. Handsome oil paintings show the 'giant sleepover,' with group pictures of multiple generations, as well as closeups of cousins sharing bikes, eating fried chicken, and sleeping four boys to a bed." Booklist

Dizzy dinosaurs; silly dino poems. edited by Lee Bennett Hopkins; illustrated by Barry Gott. Harper 2011 44p il (I can read!) $16.99; pa $3.99

Grades: K 1 2 3   **811**

1. Dinosaurs -- Poetry 2. American poetry -- Collections

ISBN 978-0-06-135839-5; 0-06-135839-8; 978-0-06-135841-8 pa; 0-06-135841-X pa

"Nineteen dinosaur poems plus a pronunciation guide to dinosaur names make up this easy reader collection. . . . The poets do surprisingly well at writing poems using the short words and easy vocabulary of an I Can Read book. . . . Gott's paintings exaggeate the dinosaurs comically, giving the prehistoric critters a variety of bright colors and showing their disparate sizes by including other animals. . . . Even non-dino-fans will enjoy the humor of these dinosaurs set amidst ordinary modern life." Horn Book

Durango, Julia

★ **Under** the mambo moon; illustrated by Fabricio Vanden Broeck. Charlesbridge Pub. 2011 un il lib bdg $12.95

Grades: 3 4 5   **811**

1. Music -- Poetry 2. Latin Americans -- Poetry 3. Poetry -- By individual authors

ISBN 157091723X; 9781570917233; 1-57091-723-X; 978-1-57091-723-3

LC 2008007255

"In understated verse, a girl named Marisol explores the role that music plays in her Latino community, introducing the people who visit her father's music store. . . . Grainy grayscale scenes inside the store alternate with kinetic acrylic and colored-pencil tableaus, placed opposite the visitors' monologues. . . . A vivid mingling of poetry, narrative, and art."

"In understated verse, a girl named Marisol explores the role that music plays in her Latino community, introducing the people who visit her father's music store. . . . Grainy grayscale scenes inside the store alternate with kinetic acrylic and colored-pencil tableaus, placed opposite the visitors' monologues. . . . A vivid mingling of poetry, narrative, and art." Publ Wkly

Eliot, T. S.

★ **Old** Possum's book of practical cats; illustrated by Axel Scheffler. Harcourt Children's Books 2009 64p il $16

Grades: 3 4 5 6   **811**

1. Cats -- Poetry 2. Poetry -- By individual authors

ISBN 978-0-547-24827-1; 0-547-24827-X

"Scheffler brings his considerable illustrative talents to this new edition of Eliot's much-loved collection of cat whimsy, first published in 1939. Scheffler's cartoon felines, with their expressive eyes, are a deliciously animated cast. . . . These cats by turns baffle and delight the humans around them." SLJ

Elliott, David

In the sea; David Elliott; illustrated by Holly Meade. 1st U.S. ed. Candlewick Press 2012 32 p. col. ill.

Grades: 1 2 3   **811**

1. Children's poetry 2. American poetry -- Collections 3. Marine animals -- Poetry 4. Poetry -- By individual authors

ISBN 9780763644987; 0763644986

LC 2010047666

This book of poems for children by David Elliot and illustrated by Holly Meade presents an "exploration of life in the sea. From the tiny sea horse 'dainty as a wish,' to the clown fish, which is 'not an enemy / of anemone,' to the blue whale who sings 'of shipwrecked sailors down below,' 20 creatures are celebrated with rhymes that accentuate their quirks and charm." (Booklist)

★ **In** the wild; illustrated by Holly Meade. Candlewick Press 2010 un il

Grades: 1 2 3   **811**

1. Animals -- Poetry 2. Children's poetry 3. Poetry -- By individual authors

ISBN 0-7636-4497-8; 978-0-7636-4497-0

LC 2009008244

A woodcut-illustrated collection of poems that celebrates wild animals. "Preschool, primary." (Horn Book)

"A lion standing alone on a grassy plain leads off the assortment of 14 mammals introduced in short, reflective poems and bold, energetic woodblock scenes. . . . Mead's woodblock prints . . . have just a hint of humor and capture the powerful wild nature of the creatures. . . . The poems are read-aloud gems." SLJ

Esbensen, Barbara Juster

★ **Swing** around the sun; poems. art by Cheng-Khee Chee . . . [et al.] Carolrhoda Bks. 2003 un il lib bdg $16.95

Grades: 2 3 4 **811**

1. Seasons -- Poetry 2. Poetry -- By individual authors ISBN 0-87614-143-2

LC 2002-7980

A newly illustrated edition of the title first published 1965 by Lerner

A collection of poems that celebrates the seasons, with illustrations for each season by a different Minnesota artist

"A rich, vibrant reading and viewing experience. . . . The poetry's impact is heightened by masterful new illustrations from four distinguished artists. . . . Cheng-Khee Chee's textured watercolors sprout and bloom across the pages of 'Spring.' Janice Lee Porter's 'Summer' oil pastels hum with energetic color and sinuous shapes. Mary GrandPré ushers in fall with a warmer palette of pastels. . . . Finally, Stephen Gammell's snowscapes, spattered in icy grays and blue capture winter's wild spirit." SLJ

An eyeball in my garden; and other spine-tingling poems. selected and edited by Jennifer Cole Judd and Laura Wynkoop; with illustrations by Johan Olander. Marshall Cavendish Childrens 2010 64p il $15.99

Grades: 3 4 5 6 **811**

1. Monsters -- Poetry 2. Supernatural -- Poetry 3. American poetry -- Collections ISBN 978-0-7614-5655-1; 0-7614-5655-4

LC 2010008081

"This compilation of new poems covers scary as well as silly Halloween territory. For every truly chilling ghost train, there's a witch's shopping list or a monster that turns out to be the speaker's own reflection. Easily flowing meter in most of the pieces makes for smooth read-alouds. Black-and-white ink illustratiions are appropriately spooky." Horn Book Guide

Falling down the page; [compiled] by Georgia Heard. Roaring Brook Press 2009 47p il $16.95

Grades: 3 4 5 6 **811**

1. American poetry -- Collections ISBN 978-1-59643-220-8; 1-59643-220-9

LC 2007-38870

"Thirty-two 'list' poems are presented in a dynamic design and trim size. . . . The accessible yet thought-provoking selections are from mostly well-known poets such as Marilyn Singer, Lee Bennett Hopkins and Rebecca Kai Dotlich, and include a couple from Heard. . . . The poems will spark imagination." Kirkus

Farrar, Sid

The **year** comes round; haiku through the seasons. Sid Farrar; illustrated by Ilse Plume. Albert Whitman & Co. 2012 32 p. $16.99

Grades: K 1 2 3 **811**

1. Haiku 2. Nature poetry 3. Children's poetry 4. Seasons -- Poetry 5. Haiku, American 6. Months ISBN 0807581291; 9780807581292

LC 2011015478

This book, by Sid Farrar, illustrated by Ilse Plume, offers "[t]welve nature-themed haiku accompanied by lush illustrations [that] take the reader from January to December."

Describing natural elements such as fireflies and frost on windowpanes, this collection seeks "to introduce children to the traditional Japanese poetry form." (Publisher's note)

Field, Eugene

Wynken, Blynken, and Nod; written by Eugene Field; illustrated by Giselle Potter. Schwartz & Wade Books 2008 un il $16.99; lib bdg $19.99

Grades: PreK K 1 2 **811**

1. Sleep -- Poetry 2. Poetry -- By individual authors ISBN 978-0-375-84196-5; 0-375-84196-2; 978-0-375-94596-0 lib bdg; 0-375-94596-2 lib bdg

LC 2007-09568

"Field's soothing lullaby of a poem (1889) is handsomely visualized via the classic device of translating the contents of a child's own room into the stuff of dreams. Potter's appealing dreamlike art features a moon-faced child and the three eponymous figures who are as like him . . . as peas in a pod. . . . An idyllic and imaginative new look at an old favorite." Horn Book

Fisher, Aileen Lucia

Do rabbits have Christmas? poems. by Aileen Fisher; illustrated by Sarah Fox-Davies. Henry Holt 2007 un il $16.95

Grades: PreK K 1 2 **811**

1. Nature poetry 2. Winter -- Poetry 3. Christmas -- Poetry 4. Poetry -- By individual authors ISBN 978-0-8050-7491-8; 0-8050-7491-0

LC 2006030504

"This well-chosen verse collection features 15 short poems culled from eight of Fisher's books. . . . Clean and precise, the poems create indeliable but often delicate images. Fox-Davies' endearing paintings reflect the childlike tone and quiet appreciation of nature inherent in the verse." Booklist

Fitch, Sheree

★ **Night** Sky Wheel Ride; Sheree Fitch; illustrated by Yayo. Tradewind 2012 32 p. $16.95

Grades: PreK K 1 2 **811**

1. Fairs -- Poetry 2. Stories in rhyme ISBN 189658067X; 9781896580678

This illustrated narrative children's poem, by Sheree Fitch and illustrated by the artist Yayo, "take[s] . . . a spectacular ride through the imagination. We fly past illustrations displaying a [kaleidoscope] of colors. Magical, fun fair creatures appear and disappear in a jungle of cotton-candy trees." (Publisher's note)

Fleischman, Paul

★ **Big** talk; poems for four voices. illustrated by Beppe Giacobbe. Candlewick Press 2000 44p il $17.99; pa $7.99

Grades: 4 5 6 7 **811**

1. Poetry -- By individual authors ISBN 0-7636-0636-7; 0-7636-3805-6 pa

LC 99-46882

A collection of poems to be read aloud by four people, with color-coded text to indicate which lines are read by which readers

"Each poem is more demanding, and more rewarding, than the last. Giacobbe highlights the humor in strips of vignettes that run along the bottom of the page. This is 'toe-tapping, tongue-flapping fun.'" Horn Book Guide

★ **I** am phoenix: poems for two voices; illustrated by Ken Nutt. Harper & Row 1985 51p il hardcover o.p. pa $5.99

Grades: 4 5 6 7   **811**

1. Birds -- Poetry 2. Poetry -- By individual authors
ISBN 0-06-446092-4 pa

LC 85-42615

A collection of poems about birds to be read aloud by two voices

"Devotés of the almost lost art of choral reading should be among the first to appreciate this collection. . . . Printed in script form, the selections . . . have a cadenced pace and dignified flow; their combination of imaginative imagery and realistic detail is echoed by the combination of stylized fantasy and representational drawings in the black and white pictures, all soft line and strong nuance." Bull Cent Child Books

★ **Joyful** noise: poems for two voices; illustrated by Eric Beddows. Harper & Row 1988 44p il $15.99; lib bdg $16.89; pa $5.99

Grades: 4 5 6 7   **811**

1. Insects -- Poetry 2. Poetry -- By individual authors
ISBN 0-06-021852-5; 0-06-021853-3 lib bdg; 0-06-446093-2 pa

LC 87-45280

Awarded the Newbery Medal, 1989

"There are fourteen poems in the handsomely designed volume, with stylish endpapers and wonderfully interpretive black-and-white illustrations. Each selection is a gem, polished perfection." Horn Book

Fletcher, Ralph

A **writing** kind of day; poems for young poets. illustrations by April Ward. Wordsong/Boyds Mills Press 2005 32p il $17.95; pa $9.95

Grades: 3 4 5   **811**

ISBN 1-59078-276-3; 1-59078-353-0 pa

"A young writer's daily experiences and concerns are folded into poems to which many readers can relate. . . . Varied in mood and tone, the offerings entertain as they celebrate words and language. . . . Ward's black-and-white illustrations use a variety of mediums, including pencil, photography, computer-generated images, and ink. " SLJ

Florian, Douglas

★ **Autumnblings**; poems and paintings by Douglas Florian. Greenwillow Bks. 2003 48p il $15.99; lib bdg $16.89

Grades: 2 3 4 5   **811**

1. Autumn -- Poetry 2. Poetry -- By individual authors
ISBN 0-06-009278-5; 0-06-009279-3 lib bdg

LC 2002-29780

A collection of poems that portray the essence of the season between summer and winter

"Short verse lines make the entries particularly suitable for reading aloud or reciting. . . . The illustrations, luminous watercolors touched with colored pencils, often move beyond the decorative to witty visual commentary or elegant, streamlined scenes." Bull Cent Child Books

★ **Bing** bang boing; poems and drawings by Douglas Florian. Harcourt Brace & Co. 1994 144p il hardcover o.p. pa $8

Grades: 2 3 4 5   **811**

1. Nonsense verses 2. Poetry -- By individual authors
ISBN 0-15-233770-9; 0-15-205860-9 pa

LC 94-3894

An illustrated collection of more than 150 nonsense verses

"The author's spare, pen-and-ink drawings, like the poems themselves, deftly explore the comic potential in each combination of words. With a few clean lines, he creates an original, funny vision." SLJ

★ **Comets,** stars, the Moon, and Mars; space poems and paintings. Harcourt 2007 45p il $16

Grades: 2 3 4 5   **811**

1. Children's poetry 2. Astronomy -- Poetry 3. Poetry -- By individual authors
ISBN 0-15-205372-7; 978-0-15-205372-7

LC 2006-08274

The subjects of these twenty poems include the planets as well as "other heavenly bodies and phenomena. . . . Grades three to seven." (Bull Cent Child Books)

This "book looks at astronomy through the magnifying, clarifying lens of poetry. Each double-page spread features a short, accessible poem about a subject such as the sun, each of its planets, a comet, a constellation, or the universe, set with an impressive painting." Booklist

★ **Dinothesaurus**; prehistoric poems and paintings. by Douglas Florian. Atheneum 2009 43p il $17.99

Grades: 2 3 4 5   **811**

1. Dinosaurs -- Poetry 2. Poetry -- By individual authors
ISBN 978-1-4169-7978-4; 1-4169-7978-6

"Florian's freeflowing, witty collection of poems and collages about dinosaurs is a giganotosaurus delight. . . . The poems marry facts with a poet's eye for detail. . . . The heart of the book is in its humor, the spontaneity of both illustrations and poems, and Florian's slightly askew view of the Mesozoic creatures." Publ Wkly

Includes glossary and bibliographical references

★ **For** laughing out loud; poems to tickle your funnybone. selected by Jack Prelutsky; illustrated by Marjorie Priceman. Knopf 1991 84p il $17

Grades: 3 4 5 6   **811**

1. Humorous poetry 2. American poetry -- Collections
ISBN 0-394-82144-0

LC 90-33010

A collection of humorous poems by writers including Ellen Raskin, Karla Kuskin, Ogden Nash, and Arnold Lobel

"These nonsense verses by a wide variety of poets combine the domestic and the gross, deadpan and slapstick, with a lilting rhythm and satisfying rhyme. . . . The design is ebullient, often with several poems appearing on a double-page spread surrounded by wildly energetic wash-and-line illustrations." Booklist

★ **Laugh**-eteria; poems and drawings by Douglas Florian. Harcourt Brace & Co. 1999 157p $17; pa $8

Grades: 2 3 4 5   **811**
1. Humorous poetry 2. Poetry -- By individual authors
ISBN 0-15-202084-5; 0-15-206148-7 pa

LC 98-20047

A collection of more than 100 humorous poems on such topics as ogres, pizza, fear, school, dragons, trees, and hair

"Florian's pithy poems echo playground chants (and sometimes, better yet, jeers) in their rhythmic recitability . . . and his focus on orality and absurdity makes them thematically irresistible. The line drawings have a sophisticated quirkiness." Bull Cent Child Books

Poem-mobiles; crazy car poems. by J. Patrick Lewis and Douglas Florian; illustrated by Jeremy Holmes. 1st ed. Schwartz & Wade Books 2014 40 p. $17.99
Grades: K 1 2 3 4   **811**
1. Automobiles 2. Children's poetry 3. Automobiles -- Poetry
ISBN 0375866906; 9780375866906; 9780375966903

LC 2011011023

In this book, authors J. Patrick Lewis and Douglas Florian present "poems packed with wordplay, puns, and double entendre. An impish array of people, monsters, and animals inhabit a loony, on-the-go world with such exotic vehicular mashups as the Fish Car, High-Heel Car, Balloon Car, and Caterpillar Cab." (Publishers Weekly)

★ **Poetrees.** Beach Lane Books 2010 45p il $16.99
Grades: 3 4 5 6   **811**
1. Trees -- Poetry 2. Poetry -- By individual authors
ISBN 978-1-4169-8672-0; 1-4169-8672-3

LC 2009-03025

"Florian focuses on trees (seeds, bark, leaves, roots, and tree rings) and introduces readers to 13 species from around the world. An oversize, double-page illustration accompanies each poem. . . . The selections are accessible and concise, with child-friendly wordplay and artful design. . . . The primitive illustrations—crafted on 'primed paper bags' using mixed media including gouache watercolor paints, colored pencils, rubber stamps, oil pastels, and collage—range in nuance from whimsy to mystery and reverence." SLJ

★ **UnBEElievables**; honeybee poems and paintings. Douglas Florian. Beach Lane Books 2012 32 p. col. ill. (hardcover) $16.99
Grades: 1 2 3 4 5   **811**
1. Beehives 2. Children's poetry 3. Bees 4. Bees -- Juvenile poetry 5. Children's poetry, American 6. Honeybee -- poetry 7. Bees -- Ecology -- poetry
ISBN 1442426527; 9781442426528

LC 2011005613

This children's picture book presents a collection of poetry about bees. "The 14 poems introduce the roles of the queen, drones and workers and touch on such matters as anatomy, development from egg to bee, and even Colony Collapse Disorder." (Kirkus Reviews)

"Florian bestows yet another pleasing mix of punny poems and colorful collages that blend whimsy and fact... Spreads like "Swarm" epitomize Florian's skill at combining pithy rhymes, well-chosen facts and playfully tongue-in-cheek pictures." Kirkus

Includes bibliographical references

★ **Winter** eyes; poems & paintings by Douglas Florian. Greenwillow Bks. 1999 48p il $16
Grades: 2 3 4 5   **811**
1. Winter -- Poetry 2. Poetry -- By individual authors
ISBN 0-688-16458-7

LC 98-19483

A collection of poems about winter, including "Sled," "Icicles," and "Ice Fishing"

"The short rhyming lines are clear and will be easy to read aloud, and the softly toned watercolor-and-colored-pencil pictures show snowy winter scenes, some realistic, some playful." Booklist

★ **Zoo's** who; poems and paintings by Douglas Florian. Harcourt 2005 47p il $17
Grades: K 1 2 3   **811**
1. Animals -- Poetry 2. Poetry -- By individual authors
ISBN 0-15-204639-9

LC 2004-4576

A collection of short poems about animals

"There's plenty of humor throughout. . . . The artwork . . . always has unexpected bits. . . . The more astute the reader, the better the time he or she will have with this." Booklist

Forbes, Robert L.

Beast Friends Forever; by Robert L. Forbes; illustrated by Ronald Searle. Penguin Group USA 2013 80 p. (hardcover) $19.95
Grades: 4 5 6 7   **811**
1. Animal courtship 2. Animals -- Poetry 3. Animals
ISBN 1590208080; 9781590208083

In this book of children's poetry by Robert Forbes, "animal courtship is infused with quirky human characteristics and some sneaky social commentary. Readers meet Lancelot the Ocelot, doing time for 'his romance turned to tragedy,' ending in a crime.' And Babette the Skunk, having studied with 'Parisian perfumers,' has fashioned a new scent, 'packaged in black and called "In-d-scent,"/It's sure to enflame any white-striped gent.'" (School Library Journal)

Forler, Nan

Winterberries and apple blossoms; reflections and flavors of a Mennonite year. paintings by Peter Etril Snyder. Tundra Books 2011 39p il $22.95
Grades: 4 5 6 7   **811**
1. Cooking 2. Months -- Poetry 3. Mennonites -- Poetry 4. Poetry -- By individual authors
ISBN 978-1-77049-254-7; 1-77049-254-2

With a poem for every month of the year, young Naomi introduces us to her family and hosts a journey through the seasonal rhythms of her rural Mennonite community. Includes a recipe for each month of the year.

This includes "12 evocative poems. . . . Snyder . . . contributes smudgy, sunlit acrylic scenes that convey a close-knit family that works, plays, and prays together. Along with Forler's graceful verse, and recipes for every season, it all adds up to a warm portrait of a community seldom found in the spotlight." Publ Wkly

Franco, Betsy

★ **Bees,** snails, and peacock tails shapes--naturally; [by] Betsy Franco; illustrated by Steve Jenkins. Margaret K. McElderry Books 2008 un il $16.99

Grades: PreK K 1 2   **811**

1. Nature poetry 2. Shape -- Poetry 3. Poetry -- By individual authors

ISBN 978-1-4169-0386-4; 1-4169-0386-0

LC 2006-12094

"The pair behind Birdsongs tackles another science topic—geometry in the animal world. Whether addressing hexagonal beehive cells or a snail's spiral shell, brisk rhymes draw attention to nature's math. ... . Striking color combinations make the illustrations pop. This inviting book is bound to spark more careful observation of the shapes and colors in the reader's natural world." Publ Wkly

A **curious** collection of cats; concrete poems. illustrations by Michael Wertz. Tricycle Press 2009 un il $16.99
Grades: PreK K 1 2 3   **811**

1. Cats -- Poetry 2. Poetry -- By individual authors

ISBN 978-1-58246-248-6; 1-58246-248-8

LC 2008-11359

"Thirty-two unusual, concrete poems, one per page with a single exception, are matched by Wertz's monoprints. The words move in several directions and sometimes inhabit multiple objects. The poems are so embedded within the illustrations that it is hard to imagine them without the artwork. . . . Cat lovers will recognize their felines stretching, purring, and napping." SLJ

Messing around on the monkey bars; illustrated by Jessie Hartland. Candlewick Press 2009 45p il $17.99
Grades: 3 4 5   **811**

1. Schools -- Poetry 2. Poetry -- By individual authors

ISBN 978-0-7636-3174-1; 0-7636-3174-4

"A cheeky romp through elementary schoolchildren's academic and social lives. Though readers could tackle the poems alone, differences in typeface cue the possibility for two readers to share the poems aloud. . . . Hartland's energetic gouache illustrations adopt a naive style that matches the playful spirit of the text while serving as a splendid complement to its evocation of children's voices." Kirkus

Frost, Robert

Birches; illustrated by Ed Young. Holt & Co. 1988 un il hardcover o.p. pa $8.95
Grades: 3 4 5   **811**

1. Trees -- Poetry 2. Poetry -- By individual authors

ISBN 0-8050-7230-6 pa

LC 86-4787

An illustrated version of the well-known poem written in 1916, about birch trees and the pleasures of climbing them

"The freedom called for in the sweep and depth of Frost's words should not be hemmed in by rigidly defined illustrations, and Young allows this license, giving the viewer ample opportunity to absorb and be absorbed by the imagery. The text is set two to three lines to a page, with the poem repeated in its entirety at the end." Booklist

★ **Robert** Frost; edited by Gary D. Schmidt; illustrated by Henri Sorensen. Sterling 1994 48p il (Poetry for young people) $14.95; pa $6.95
Grades: 4 5 6 7   **811**

1. Poetry -- By individual authors

ISBN 0-8069-0633-2; 1-4027-5475-2 pa

LC 94-11161

This volume "contains a three-page overview of the poet's life, 29 poems selected and arranged around the seasons of the year, brief and apt commentaries on each, and a useful index of titles and subject matter. The realistic watercolor illustrations capture the delicate beauty of a New England spring and the glory of fall while still suggesting the around-the-corner chill of winter, a disquiet echoing throughout much of Frost's poetry." SLJ

George, Kristine O'Connell

★ **Emma** Dilemma: big sister poems. Clarion Books 2011 47p il $16.99
Grades: K 1 2 3   **811**

1. Children's poetry 2. Sisters -- Poetry 3. Poetry -- By individual authors

ISBN 0618428429; 9780618428427; 978-0-618-42842-7; 0-618-42842-9

LC 2008-50647

"A likable fourth-grader shares her frustrations about her preschool-age sister, Emma, in candid narrative poems. . . . There are tender moments, genuinely conveyed in Carpenter's expressive pen-and-ink illustrations. ... . The vignettes form such a vivid portrait of Emma and Jessica that readers may feel as if they personally know them." Publ Wkly

★ The **great** frog race and other poems; pictures by Kate Kiesler; with an introduction by Myra Cohn Livingston. Clarion Bks. 1997 40p il $15; pa $5.95
Grades: 3 4 5   **811**

1. Poetry -- By individual authors

ISBN 0-395-77607-4; 0-618-60478-2 pa

LC 95-51090

A collection of poems about frogs and dragonflies, wind and rain, a visit to the tree farm, the garden hose, and other aspects of country life

"George's astute imagery pairs beautifully with Kiesler's rich, warm-toned oil paintings to impart a strong sense of the pleasures of rural landscape." Booklist

★ **Old** Elm speaks; tree poems. illustrated by Kate Kiesler. Clarion Bks. 1998 48p il $15; pa $5.95
Grades: 2 3 4   **811**

1. Trees -- Poetry 2. Poetry -- By individual authors

ISBN 0-395-87611-7; 0-618-75242-0 pa

LC 97-49333

A collection of short, simple poems which present images relating to trees in various circumstances and throughout the seasons

"George conveys a deep understanding of nature, here particularly of trees, in a way that is readily accessible to children. Kiesler's warm oil paintings beautifully complement the poems." Booklist

Toasting marshmallows; camping poems. illustrated by Kate Kiesler. Clarion Bks. 2001 48p il $15
Grades: 3 4 5   **811**

1. Camping -- Poetry 2. Poetry -- By individual authors

ISBN 0-618-04597-X

LC 00-56984

"All of the selections convey a child-focused sense of wonder. ... . The poems are varied and inventive, replete with marvelous images and universal truths. ... . Each one is accompanied by a well-executed and evocative acrylic painting." SLJ

Gerstein, Mordicai, 1935-
Dear hot dog; poems about everyday stuff. Abrams 2011 un il
Grades: PreK K 1 2 **811**
1. Poetry -- By individual authors
ISBN 0810997320; 9780810997325

This collection of poems follows three friends from the time they wake up and brush their teeth to when they snuggle up for bed with their favorite stuffed animal.

This is "lyrical yet accessible. . . . Gerstein infuses humanity into a toothbrush, shoes, a bowl, a kite, leaves and an ice-cream cone. His acrylic illustrations are in harmony with his verses; sharp black lines and rich colors that spread outside their outlines, giving a dreamy yet vivid effect." Kirkus

Gibson, Amy
Around the world on eighty legs; illustrated by Daniel Salmieri. Scholastic Press 2010 un il $18.99
Grades: K 1 2 **811**
1. Children's poetry 2. Animals -- Poetry 3. Poetry -- By individual authors
ISBN 978-0-439-58755-6; 0-439-58755-7
LC 2009007160

"Gibson's collection of poems cleverly presents creatures from all across the globe in witty, rhythmic, and well-crafted verse. Instructional and entertaining, the poems nicely balance information with humor and wordplay. . . . Emphasizing humor over naturalism, Salmieri's . . . illustrations match the playfulness of Gibson's verse point for point." Publ Wkly

Giovanni, Nikki
★ **Spin** a soft black song; poems for children; illustrated by George Martins. rev ed; Hill & Wang 1985 57p il hardcover o.p. pa $4.95
Grades: 3 4 5 6 **811**
1. African Americans -- Poetry 2. Poetry -- By individual authors
ISBN 0-374-46469-3 pa
LC 84-19287

First published 1971

A poetry collection which recounts the feelings of black children about their neighborhoods, American society, and themselves

"A beautifully illustrated book of poems about black children for children of all ages. . . . Simple in theme but a very moving collection nonetheless." Read Ladders for Hum Relat. 5th edition

★ **The sun** is so quiet; poems. illustrations by Ashley Bryan. Holt & Co. 1996 31p il $14.95
Grades: K 1 2 3 **811**
1. Nature poetry 2. Poetry -- By individual authors
ISBN 0-8050-4119-2
LC 95-39357

A collection of poems primarily about nature and the seasons but also concerned with chocolate and scary movies

"Of the 13 poems presented here, 12 appeared in books published between 1973 and 1993. The new poem, entitled 'Connie,' represents the best of Giovanni: a series of quick-silver images that capture a mood to perfection. Painted in Bryan's signature style, the illustrations fill the pages with sunny colors and bold patterns." Booklist

Got geography! poems. selected by Lee Bennett Hopkins; pictures by Philip Stanton. Greenwillow Books 2006 32p il $15.99; lib bdg $16.89
Grades: 3 4 5 **811**
1. Geography -- Poetry 2. American poetry -- Collections
ISBN 0-06-055601-3; 0-06-055602-1 lib bdg
LC 2004-59662

"Sixteen selections from a variety of poets explore the curiosity piqued by maps, globes, the land we live on, and places far away. The gentle, often-moving verses cover a wide spectrum of ways to explore the Earth from mapping the world to examining its surface to finding one's place within it. . . . The bright acrylic-and-watercolor illustrations bring energy to the pages and set the mood for each poem." SLJ

Gottfried, Maya
★ **Our** farm; by the animals of Farm Sanctuary. [by] Maya Gottfried [and] Robert Rahway Zakanitch. Alfred A. Knopf 2010 un il $17.99; lib bdg $20.99
Grades: PreK K 1 2 3 **811**
1. Animals -- Poetry 2. Farm Sanctuary Inc. 3. Farm life -- Poetry 4. Poetry -- By individual authors
ISBN 978-0-375-86118-5; 0-375-86118-1; 978-0-375-96118-2 lib bdg; 0-375-96118-6 lib bdg
LC 2009-14885

"This homage to the shelter for neglected and abused farm animals where Gottfried served as a volunteer is a book of poems and accompanying paintings that will raise awareness both of the Sanctuary and the sad reasons for which such a place exists. But it has more to recommend it. The poems are 'narrated' by some of the shelter's inhabitants. . . . There's a disarming innocence throughout, and the best of the selections are enchanting. Zakanitch's illustrations are superb. Each one is a collectible work of art, exhibiting a masterful technique, tenderness, subtlety, and humor." SLJ

Graham, Joan Bransfield
★ **Flicker** flash; poems by Joan Bransfield Graham; illustrated by Nancy Davis. Houghton Mifflin 1999 un il $15; pa $6.95
Grades: K 1 2 3 **811**
1. Light -- Poetry 2. Poetry -- By individual authors
ISBN 0-395-90501-X; 0-618-31102-5 pa
LC 98-12956

A collection of poems celebrating light in its various forms, from candles and lamps to lightning and fireflies

"A vivid fusion of ingenious concrete poetry and boldly colored graphics." SLJ

Grandits, John
★ **Blue** lipstick; concrete poems. Clarion Books 2007 un il $15; pa $5.95
Grades: 5 6 7 8 9 10 **811**
1. Poetry -- By individual authors
ISBN 978-0-618-56860-4; 0-618-56860-3; 978-0-618-85132-4 pa; 0-618-85132-1 pa
LC 2006-23332

"This selection introduces readers to Jessie, who impulsively purchases blue lipstick, but later, regretfully decides to give it 'the kiss-off.' Jessie is big sister to Robert, who was featured in Grandits's Technically, It's Not My Fault (Clarion, 2004). As he did in that terrific collection, the author uses artful arrangements of text on the page, along with 54 different typefaces, to bring his images and ideas to life. . . . This irreverent, witty collection should resonate with a wide audience." SLJ

★ **Technically,** it's not my fault; concrete poems. by John Grandits. Clarion Books 2004 un il $15; pa $5.95
Grades: 5 6 7 8   **811**
1. Poetry -- By individual authors
ISBN 0-618-42833-X; 0-618-50361-7 pa
LC 2004-231
A collection of concrete poems on such topics as roller coasters, linguini, basketball, and sisters

"Grandits combines technical brilliance and goofy good humor to provide an accessible, fun-filled collection of poems, dramatically brought to life through a brilliant book design." SLJ

Grant, Shauntay
Up home; artwork by Susan Tooke; story by Shauntay Grant. Nimbus Publishing 2009 un il $19.95
Grades: K 1 2 3   **811**
1. Nova Scotia -- Poetry 2. African Americans -- Poetry
ISBN 978-1-55109-660-5; 1-55109-660-9
This illustrated poem evokes the author's memories of growing up in the Canadian town of Preston, Nova Scotia.

"Deceptively simple, the poetic narrative vividly conveys an array of remembered images, sights, sounds, and emotions, all of which are brought to life in Tooke's realistic acrylic images." SLJ

Gray, Rita
One big rain; poems for rainy days. compiled by Rita Gray; illustrated by Ryan O'Rourke. Charlesbridge 2010 30 p. $9.95
Grades: 2 3 4   **811**
1. Children's poetry 2. Rain -- Poetry 3. Seasons -- poetry 5. American poetry -- Collections 6. Children's poetry, American 7. Haiku -- Translations into English 8. Rain and rainfall
ISBN 1570917167; 9781570917165; 978-1-57091-716-5; 1-57091-716-7
LC 2009026748
"With five short poems for each season of the year, this unassuming anthology offers a sampling of poems about rain. . . . Gray's collection of poems, nicely balanced in tone, style, and origin, includes eight Japanese haiku in translation and short works by a number of American poets, some renowned and others little known. Understated in color and somewhat stylized in form, the oil-on-paper illustrations capture the seasons of the year as well as the moods of the verse."

"With five short poems for each season of the year, this unassuming anthology offers a sampling of poems about rain. . . . Gray's collection of poems, nicely balanced in tone, style, and origin, includes eight Japanese haiku in translation and short works by a number of American poets, some renowned and others little known. Understated in color and somewhat stylized in form, the oil-on-paper illustrations capture the seasons of the year as well as the moods of the verse." Booklist

Includes bibliographical references and index

Greenfield, Eloise
Brothers & sisters; family poems. illustrated by Jan Spivey Gilchrist. Amistad 2009 32p il $17.99; lib bdg $18.89
Grades: K 1 2 3   **811**
1. Siblings -- Poetry 2. African Americans -- Poetry 3. Poetry -- By individual authors
ISBN 978-0-06-056284-7; 0-06-056284-6; 978-0-06-056285-4 lib bdg; 0-06-056285-4 lib bdg
LC 2008020209
"Greenfield's poetic observations and commentaries succinctly capture siblings at various ages and stages. . . . With only a few lines, the author grasps the love and admiration, the frustration and hurt, the fun and aggravation that they can engender. . . . The illustrator is equally as skillful in depicting the wide range of emotions and ages in the faces of the individual African Americans peopling the paintings. The realistic watercolors fit around and beside the poems, using the white space to highlight the art and give balance to the pages." SLJ

★ The **Great** Migration; journey to the North. HarperCollins Children's Books 2010 un il $16.99
Grades: K 1 2 3   **811**
1. African Americans -- Poetry 2. Poetry -- By individual authors 3. United States -- History -- Poetry
ISBN 978-0-06-125921-0; 0-06-125921-7
LC 2008-43821
"Collaborators Greenfield and Gilchrist . . . shape an evocative portrait of African-Americans who moved North during the Great Migration between 1915 and 1930 to escape Ku Klux Klan fueled racism and to secure better lives. . . . Chronicling the journey by train, lilting poetry and pictures capture a sense of both apprehension and hope. . . . Making intriguing use of photographs of people, news headlines, maps, and painted elements, each of Gilchrist's collages has a distinctive look and lighting, ranging from conventional portraits of the travelers to more abstract images." Publ Wkly

★ **Honey,** I love, and other love poems; pictures by Diane and Leo Dillon. Crowell 1978 un il $14.95; pa $5.95
Grades: 2 3 4   **811**
1. Love poetry 2. African Americans -- Poetry 3. Poetry -- By individual authors
ISBN 0-690-01334-5; 0-06-443097-9 pa
LC 77-2845
"These 16 poems explore facets of warm, loving relationships with family, friends and schoolmates as experienced by a young Black girl. Central to the theme of the book is the idea that the child loves herself and is very confident in expressing that love." Interracial Books Child Bull

When the horses ride by; children in the times of war. poems by Eloise Greenfield; illustrations by Jan Spivey Gilchrist. Lee & Low Books 2006 un il $17.95
Grades: 2 3 4   **811**
1. War poetry 2. Poetry -- By individual authors
ISBN 978-1-58430-249-0; 1-58430-249-6
LC 2005015393
Collection of poems about children around the world, focusing on the children's perceptions of war and how the turmoil of war affects their lives.

"Combining 17 rhythmic poems with dramatic illustrations, this title addresses a complex topic. Greenfield's deceptively simple verses express universal truths about both conflict and childhood." SLJ

Grimes, Nikki

At Jerusalem's gate; poems of Easter. with woodcuts by David Frampton. Eerdmans Books for Young Readers 2005 un il $20

Grades: 5 6 7 8 **811**

1. American poetry 2. Easter -- Poetry 3. Children's poetry, American 4. Poetry -- By individual authors
ISBN 0-8028-5183-5

LC 2003-1089

"Twenty-two poems trace the events celebrated by Christians as Easter Week, from Jesus' entry into Jerusalem through his appearance to disciples after the Resurrection... . Grades five to eight." (Bull Cent Child Books)

"Each poem is preceded by a brief synopsis of the event, often accompanied by the author's own musings and queries, which prompt readers to think and ask questions of their own.... Bold, handsome woodcuts reinforce the powerful drama depicted in poetry. An outstanding effort." SLJ

★ **Meet** Danitra Brown; illustrated by Floyd Cooper. Lothrop, Lee & Shepard Bks. 1994 un il hardcover o.p. pa $6.99

Grades: 2 3 4 **811**

1. Friendship -- Poetry 2. African Americans -- Poetry 3. Poetry -- By individual authors
ISBN 0-688-15471-9 pa

LC 92-43707

"A collection of 13 original poems that stand individually and also blend together to tell a story of feelings and friendship between two African-American girls.... Cooper's distinguished illustrations in warm dusty tones convey the feeling of closeness. The poignant text and lovely pictures are an excellent collaboration." SLJ

Other titles about Danitra Brown are:

Danitra Brown, class clown (2005)
Danitra Brown leaves town (2002)

Thanks a million; poems by Nikki Grimes; pictures by Cozbi A. Cabrera. Greenwillow Books 2006 31p il $15.99; lib bdg $16.89

Grades: K 1 2 3 **811**

1. Poetry -- By individual authors
ISBN 0-688-17292-X; 0-688-17293-8 lib bdg

LC 2004-54158

"Sixteen thoughtful poems about being thankful for everyday things. Grimes uses a variety of forms that include haiku, a riddle, and a rebus in selections that speak directly to the experiences of young children.... Cabreras acrylic illustrations are distinctive, folksy, and effective." SLJ

★ **When** Gorilla goes walking; by Nikki Grimes; illustrated by Shane Evans. Orchard Books 2007 un il $16.99

Grades: PreK K 1 2 **811**

1. Cats -- Poetry 2. African Americans -- Poetry 3. Poetry -- By individual authors
ISBN 978-0-439-31770-2

LC 2006017194

"In interlinked poems, Cecilia, a young African American girl, introduces her 'cool cat'—a fierce, tailless, gray

shorthair named Gorilla.... In spare, expressive lines and bold colors, Evans' dynamic paintings capture the messy intimacy of the cat and human bond." Booklist

Gutman, Dan

★ **Casey** back at bat; paintings by Steve Johnson and Lou Fancher. HarperCollins 2007 un il $16.99; lib bdg $17.89

Grades: K 1 2 3 4 **811**

1. Baseball -- Poetry 2. Poetry -- By individual authors
ISBN 978-0-06-056025-6; 0-06-056025-8; 978-0-06-056026-3 lib bdg; 0-06-056026-6 lib bdg

LC 2006029468

Sequel to Ernest Lawrence Thayer's Casey at the bat

"Gutman revisits and updates Thayer's classic baseball poem. This time around ... Casey hits a fly ball that soars out of the park and keeps on going. It crosses the Atlantic Ocean and has an unfortunate encounter with a tower in Pisa before continuing on to the Sphinx in Egypt.... It passes dinosaurs ... and astronauts before heading back to Earth. The ride is uproarious from start to finish, and Gutman's broadly humorous verse hits all the right notes.... Johnson and Fancher's paintings have a playfully nostalgic look, with a mix of textured papers and newsprint splashed across the surfaces of uniforms." SLJ

Hale, Sarah Josepha

Mary had a little lamb; by Sarah Josepha Hale; illustrated by Laura Beith. Marshall Cavendish 2011 il $12.99

Grades: PreK K 1 2 **811**

1. Nursery rhymes 2. Sheep -- Poetry 3. Poetry -- By individual authors
ISBN 978-0-7614-5824-1; 0-7614-5824-7

LC 2010012807

"Though Mary Had a Little Lamb was published in 1830, it seems anything but old-fashioned in this jaunty picture book.... The characters clothing and the many touches of fantasy and humor lift the poem out of its historical period and into some timeless, lighthearted landscape of the imagination. All six verses appear, from the very familiar to the nearly forgotten, and each illustrated with one or more double-page pictures that magnify the hilarity.... Even the potentially unctuous-sounding ending verse is lightened by the joyous spirit and amusing details in the accompanying illustrations, digital collages combining fabric elements with acrylic and gouache painting. A child-pleasing version of the well-known poem." Booklist

Hamsters, shells, and spelling bees; school poems. edited by Lee Bennett Hopkins; pictures by Sachiko Yoshikawa. HarperCollins 2008 46p il (I can read!) $16.99; lib bdg $17.89

Grades: PreK K 1 2 **811**

1. Schools -- Poetry 2. American poetry -- Collections
ISBN 978-0-06-074112-9; 0-06-074112-0; 978-0-06-074113-6 lib bdg; 0-06-074113-9 lib bdg

LC 2007020881

"Contributed by well-known poets for young people (Jane Yolen, J. Patrick Lewis, Alice Schertle, among others), the poems in this bright compilation ... describe a wide range of school experiences.... The selections range in style from haikus to free verse, although many poems follow a bouncy, rhyming structure. All are written in accessible words targeted straight to emerging readers. . . . [Illustrated with] jellybean-bright cartoon-style illustrations." Booklist

★ **Hanukkah** lights; holiday poetry. selected by Lee Bennett Hopkins; pictures by Melanie Hall. HarperCollins 2004 28p il (I can read book) $15.99; lib bdg $16.89
Grades: K 1 2 3   **811**
1. Hanukkah -- Poetry 2. American poetry -- Collections
ISBN 0-06-008051-5; 0-06-008052-3 lib bdg
LC 2003-18901

A collection of poems that celebrate the activities and experiences of Hanukkah

"The poems are simple, evocative, and rhythmic without lapsing into a singsong cadence. Hall's expressive artwork creates an appealing contemporary tone with vivid pastels and a smattering of collage." SLJ

Harley, Avis

★ **African** acrostics; a word in edgeways. poems by Avis Harley; photographs by Deborah Noyes. Candlewick Press 2009 un il $17.99; pa $6.99
Grades: 4 5 6 7   **811**
1. Acrostics 2. Children's poetry 3. Animals -- Africa 4. Animals -- Poetry 5. Poetry -- By individual authors
ISBN 978-0-7636-3621-0; 0-7636-3621-5; 978-0-7636-5818-2 pa
LC 2008017916

This volume depicts "such wild animals as giraffes, zebras, and lions, in poems written to contain acrostics, in which beginning or ending letters from the poetry lines can be used to spell other words." (Publisher's note) "Grades four to six." (Bull Cent Child Books)

"Harley has written 18 poems, each one featuring a different animal. All are written as acrostics, with most of them based on the first letter of each line, but several with more unusual patterns. . . . Much of Harley's poetry consists of carefully crafted descriptive word imagery that is right on target. . . . Most of the full-page, full-color photos of the animals are perfect companions to the facing selections." SLJ

The **monarch's** progress; poems with wings. written and illustrated by Avis Harley. Wordsong 2008 32p il $16.95
Grades: 3 4 5   **811**
1. Butterflies -- Poetry 2. Poetry -- By individual authors
ISBN 978-1-59078-558-4

"This collection of 18 illustrated poems celebrates butterflies in general and monarchs in particular. Cleverly written with obvious attention to craft, the poetry varies in form from rhymed couplets to acrostic verse to haiku and explores topics such as the physical differences between the larval and adult stages, the way monarch wings look when magnified, and the usefulness of having taste sensors in one's feet. Accompanying each poem is a color-pencil drawing, often featuring precise lines and intense hues." Booklist

★ **Sea** stars; saltwater poems. [by] Avis Harley; photographs by Margaret Butschler. Wordsong 2006 35p il $16.95
Grades: 3 4 5   **811**
1. Marine animals -- Poetry 2. Poetry -- By individual

authors
ISBN 978-1-59078-429-7; 1-59078-429-4
LC 2006000931

"Butschler's beautiful color photographs came first, and her visual images of creatures on the seashore and in the aquarium inspired Harley's brief, concrete poems—from haiku and tanka to rhyming couplets and nursery rhyme parody. The wordplay will grab readers . . . and so will the exquisite images in both words and pictures." Booklist

Harrison, David L.

Vacation; we're going to the ocean. poems by David Harrison; illustrations by Rob Shepperson. Wordsong 2009 62p il $16.95
Grades: 2 3 4   **811**
1. Ocean -- Poetry 2. Vacations -- Poetry 3. Family life -- Poetry 4. Poetry -- By individual authors
ISBN 978-1-59078-568-3; 1-59078-568-1
LC 2008017718

"These delightful poems center on a family's trip to the ocean and are told from the perspective of young Sam. . . . This book, with its expressive art that expands on the humor in each poem, should have wide appeal." SLJ

Hauth, Katherine B.

What's for dinner? quirky, squirmy poems from the animal world. illustrated by David Clark. Charlesbridge 2011 48p il lib bdg $16.95; pa $7.95
Grades: 3 4 5   **811**
1. Children's poetry 2. Animals -- Poetry 3. Poetry -- By individual authors 4. Animals -- Food
ISBN 978-1-57091-471-3 lib bdg; 1-5709-1471-0 lib bdg; 978-1-57091-472-0 pa; 1-57091-472-9 pa
LC 2010-07588

"Hauth's funny, eloquent poems celebrate the often-grisly realities of the food chain, depicted in Clark's scraggly ink and watercolor illustrations. A mole gags on a banana slug, a rat 'gets a hug' from a boa constrictor, and a flattened toad becomes a roadkill restaurant. . . . Appended notes provide additional animal facts. A satisfying mix of tutelage and repartee." Publ Wkly

★ **Heart** to heart; new poems inspired by twentieth-century American art. edited by Jan Greenberg. Abrams 2001 80p il map $19.95
Grades: 5 6 7 8 9 10   **811**
1. American art 2. Art -- 20th century 3. American poetry -- Collections
ISBN 0-8109-4386-7
LC 99-462335

Michael L. Printz Award honor book, 2002

A compilation of poems by Americans writing about American art in the twentieth century, including such writers as Nancy Willard, Jane Yolen, and X. J. Kennedy.

"From a tight diamante and pantoum to lyrical free verse, the range of poetic styles will speak to a wide age group. . . . Concluding with biographical notes on each poet and artist, this rich resource is an obvious choice for teachers, and the exciting interplay between art and the written word will encourage many readers to return again and again to the book." Booklist

Heidbreder, Robert

  Noisy poems for a busy day. Kids Can Press 2012 40 p. col. ill. (hardcover) $16.95

Grades: K 1 2   **811**

  1. Day 2. Children 3. Poetry -- Collections

  ISBN 1554537061; 9781554537068

  This children's picture book by Robert Heibreder presents "a collection of (mostly) five-line poems that recreate the sounds and actions of a prechooler's day. . . . The collection is structured in the shape of a day, and Lori Joy Smith's child-like illustrations introduce us to five children whose lives involve toast and jam, goofing around, playing tag, kissing dogs, turning somersaults, going down the slide, and watching clouds." (Quill and Quire)

★ **Here's** a little poem; a very first book of poetry. collected by Jane Yolen and Andrew Fusek Peters; illustrated by Polly Dunbar. Candlewick Press 2007 104p il $21.99

Grades: PreK   **811**

  1. American poetry -- Collections

  ISBN 978-0-7636-3141-3; 0-7636-3141-8

LC 2006-40621

  "This big, spacious anthology of more than 60 poems is a wonderful first book to read with babies and toddlers over and over again. . . . The clear, active, mixed-media illustrations show very young children outdoors and in; morning to bedtime; loving, teary, absurd, furious." Booklist

Herrera, Juan Felipe

★ **Laughing** out loud, I fly; poems in English and Spanish. drawings by Karen Barbour. HarperCollins Pubs. 1998 un il $15.99

Grades: 6 7 8 9   **811**

  1. Mexican Americans -- Poetry 2. Poetry -- By individual authors 3. Bilingual books -- English-Spanish

  ISBN 0-06-027604-5

LC 96-45476

  A collection of poems in Spanish and English about childhood, place, and identity

  "Barbour's black-and-white drawings accompany each poem, delicately underlining its images but allowing the strong sensuality of the words to seep into readers' minds." SLJ

Hines, Anna Grossnickle, 1946-

★ **Peaceful** pieces; poems and quilts about peace. Henry Holt 2011 32p il

Grades: PreK K 1 2   **811**

  1. Peace -- Poetry 2. Poetry -- By individual authors

  ISBN 0805089969; 9780805089967

LC 2010011697

  "Hines pairs poems with images of her handmade quilts to reflect on the theme of peace. Several works focus on individual relationships: when two sisters fight, their mother makes them face each other at close range, which diffuses their anger into laughter. . . . Poems like 'Soldier Daddy' are socially resonant. . . . Often Hines needs just a few words to convey oceans of meaning. . . . The beauty and painstaking detail evident in each quilt brings the book's vision a stitch closer." Publ Wkly

Pieces; a year in poems & quilts. Greenwillow Bks. 2001 un il $15.95; lib bdg $15.89

Grades: K 1 2 3   **811**

  1. Quilts 2. Nature poetry 3. Poetry -- By individual authors

  ISBN 0-688-16963-5; 0-688-16964-3 lib bdg

LC 99-86463

  Poems about the four seasons, as reflected in the natural world, are accompanied by photographs of quilts made by the author

  "An appendix explains Hines's meticulous quilting process. . . . Hines takes her quilter's stash of fabric swatches and her wordsmith's metaphors for memories of the seasons, and pieces together a unified, artistic whole. An outstanding book for aspiring quilters or anyone at all." Publ Wkly

  Includes bibliographical references

★ **Winter** lights; a season in poems & quilts. Greenwillow Bks. 2005 un il $16.99; lib bdg $17.89

Grades: K 1 2 3   **811**

  1. Quilts 2. Winter -- Poetry 3. Holidays -- Poetry 4. Poetry -- By individual authors

  ISBN 0-06-000817-2; 0-06-000818-0 lib bdg

  "Winter is the time of lights, and Hines celebrates the season in thoughtful poems and pictures of gorgeous quilts full of bright, beautiful colors. Christmas is only one of the light-producing celebrations that Hines illuminates. The feast of Santa Lucia, Hanukkah, Kwanzaa, and the Chinese New Year are spectacularly introduced with short bursts of poetry and quilts that capture the spirit of the day." Booklist

★ **Hip** hop speaks to children; a celebration of poetry with a beat. editor, Nikki Giovanni; advisory editors, Tony Medina, Willie Perdomo, Michele Scott; series editor, Dominique Raccah; illustrators, Kristen Balouch, Michele Noiset, Jeremy Tugeau, Alicia Vergel de Dios, and Damian Ward. Sourcebooks Jabberwocky 2008 72p il $19.99

Grades: 3 4 5 6   **811**

  1. American poetry -- Collections 2. American poetry -- African American authors -- Collections

  ISBN 978-1-4022-1048-8; 1-4022-1048-5

LC 2008004627

  "Editor Giovanni states, 'Poetry with a beat. That's hip hop in a flash,' and she goes on to link hip-hop to grand opera and present a capsule history of African American vernacular music. This features a wide-ranging selection of 51 entries, plus a CD with new or previously released recorded versions of 29, some with music. The poets range from Langston Hughes and W.E.B. DuBois to Kanye West, Mos Def, and Queen Latifah. . . . Although created by five illustrators, the art shares both vibrant colors and a dancing free-spirited look that matches the general tone of the poetry." Booklist

Hoberman, Mary Ann

  Forget-me-nots; poems to learn by heart. selected by Mary Ann Hoberman; illustrated by Michael Emberley. Megan Tingley Books 2012 143 p.

Grades: PreK K   **811**

  1. Children's poetry 2. Poetry -- Memorizing 3. Poetry -- Collections 4. Children's poetry, American

  ISBN 031612947X; 9780316129473

LC 2011025119

This poetry collection is a "compendium of verse . . . chosen with children in mind. The Children's Poet Laureate from 2008 to 2010, [Mary Ann] Hoberman chose 123 poems that are memorable in both senses of the word. They're 'easy to remember' (though she concedes that the longer ones will take more time) and 'worth remembering.' In an appended section, she discusses an approach to learning poems by heart, making the process a game with a specific prize." (Booklist)

★ **You** read to me, I'll read to you: very short scary tales to read together; illustrated by Michael Emberley. Little, Brown 2007 32p il $16.99

Grades: K 1 2 3   **811**
1. Monsters -- Poetry 2. Poetry -- By individual authors
ISBN 978-0-316-01733-6

"The fourth uproarious poetry picture book in Hoberman and Emberley's popular You Read to Me, I'll Read to You series continues the pattern of simple, rhyming, illustrated stories for two voices. . . . The clear words with gorgeously gruesome, comic-style pictures tell of wild action and monster characters as lurid as they come." Booklist

★ **You** read to me, I'll read to you; very short stories to read together. illustrated by Michael Emberley. Little, Brown 2001 un il $15.95

Grades: K 1 2 3   **811**
1. American poetry 2. Books and reading 3. Children's poetry, American 4. Poetry -- By individual authors
ISBN 0-316-36350-2

LC 00-35230

"These rhyming short stories are written in three columns: a left and right-hand column for each of the two readers meant to alternate in the reading of most of the text, and a middle italicized column indicating that the two readers should read those lines together. . . . Each short story covers a two-page spread and features . . . two characters, one for each reader; story subjects range from animals to friendship. . . . Grades two to three." (Bull Cent Child Books)

"Hoberman offers 13 rhymed variations on the theme of getting together to read. The short poems are designed to be read aloud by two voices, with occasional parts to share. . . . The energy never flags, neither in Hoberman's trademark bouncy rhythms nor in Emberley's exuberant illustrations, which picture a wonderful array of children and animals tumbling across the pages." Booklist

Holbrook, Sara

Zombies! evacuate the school! illustrations by Karen Sandstrom. Wongsong 2010 56p il $16.95

Grades: 2 3 4 5   **811**
1. Schools -- Poetry 2. Poetry -- By individual authors
ISBN 978-1-59078-820-2; 1-59078-820-6

"With a breezy and comedic touch, Holbrook shines a light on school experiences, from academic pursuits to classroom rivalries to gym-class exploits. Humor reigns, and readers will identify with themes and emotions. . . . Many of the poems utilize an inner voice and encourage self-reflection. They are brief and accessible. . . . Sandstrom's pen-and-ink illustrations provide additional humor." SLJ

Hopkins, Lee Bennett, 1938-

★ **City** I love; by Lee Bennett Hopkins; illustrated by Marcellus Hall. Abrams Books for Young Readers 2009 un il $16.95

Grades: K 1 2 3 4   **811**
1. City and town life -- Poetry 2. Poetry -- By individual authors
ISBN 978-0-8109-8327-4; 0-8109-8327-3

LC 2008008226

"A backpack-toting, humble hound with wanderlust and a winged companion tour several of the world's cities. Hopkins's 18 poems observe skyscrapers, hot-dog vendors, subways, taxis, bridges, bright lights, and the diversity of people and pigeons. . . . These polished poems are equally matched by Hall's graphic-style cartoons, which offer many added layers of narrative delight as well as beautiful colors and an eye-catching sense of design." SLJ

I am the book; poems selected by Lee Bennett Hopkins; illustrated by Yayo. Holiday House 2010 un il $16.95

Grades: K 1 2   **811**
1. Books and reading -- Poetry 2. American poetry -- Collections
ISBN 0823421198; 9780823421190

LC 2009014743

"This collection of poems by contemporary writers celebrates the joys of reading. . . . In Yayo's acrylic spreads, an open book becomes a whale's tail, a treasure box, and a drifting raft, emphasizing the transformative potential of words." Publ Wly

Hughes, Langston, 1902-1967

★ **The dream** keeper and other poems; including seven additional poems. [by] Langston Hughes; illustrated by Brian Pinkney. 75th anniversary ed.; Alfred A. Knopf 2007 83p il $16.99

Grades: 4 5 6 7   **811**
1. African Americans -- Poetry 2. Poetry -- By individual authors
ISBN 978-0-679-84421-1

First published 1932; this is a reissue of the 1994 edition

A collection of sixty-six poems, selected by the author for young readers, including lyrical poems, songs, and blues, many exploring the black experience

"Black-and-white scratchboard illustrations in Pinkney's signature style express the emotion and beat of the poetry. . . . The poems are . . . colloquial and direct yet mysterious and complex." Booklist

★ **I,** too, am America; Langston Hughes; illustrated by Bryan Collier. Simon & Schuster Books for Young Readers 2012 40 p.

Grades: K 1 2 3   **811**
1. Railroads -- Fiction 2. Picture books for children 3. African Americans -- Poetry 4. United States -- History -- Poetry
ISBN 1442420081; 9781442420083

LC 2011002879

Coretta Scott King Illustrator Book Award (2013)

In this picture book, a "celebration of Pullman porters is the focus of this . . . edition of Langston Hughes' classic poem. . . . [It] begin[s] with . . . a speeding train before moving on to large portraits of African American porters serving white passengers aboard a luxury train. . . . [T]he porters gather left-behind items--newspapers, blues and jazz albums--and toss them from the train. . . . [T]he words and music fall into the hands of African Americans across the country." (Booklist)

★ **Langston** Hughes; edited by Arnold Rampersad & David Roessel; illustrations by Benny Andrews. Sterling Pub. 2006 48p il (Poetry for young people) $14.95
Grades: 5 6 7 8   **811**
1. African Americans -- Poetry 2. Poetry -- By individual authors
ISBN 1-4027-1845-4; 978-1-4027-1845-8
LC 2005025369
A brief profile of African American poet Langston Hughes accompanies some of his better known poems for children.
"This charming collection of 26 poems is vibrantly illustrated with depictions of African Americans in varied settings. . . . This will be a welcome introduction to Hughes's poetry for elementary students, and it includes sufficient detail to make it useful and enjoyable for older students." SLJ

Lullaby (for a Black mother) a poem. Langston Hughes; illustrated by Sean Qualls. Houghton Mifflin Harcourt 2012 32 p. $16.99
Grades: PreK K   **811**
1. Lullabies 2. Children's poetry 3. Mother-child relationship 4. American poetry -- African American authors 5. Infants 6. Mother and child 7. African Americans 8. Lullabies, English 9. Children's poetry, American
ISBN 054736265X; 9780547362656
LC 2012025484
This book, written by poet Langston Hughes and illustrated by Sean Qualls, "celebrates the love between an African American mother and her baby. . . . In the end, readers will find a rare photo of baby Hughes and his mother, a biographical note, further reading, and the complete lullaby." (Publisher's note)
"The poem's images of night and innocence are well suited for a picture book, too. Qualls (Freedom Song) keeps his artwork simple, painting a series of spreads that hew closely to the words. He renders "A necklace of stars" with a bird flying around mother and child, leaving a trail of stars around the woman's neck. "Moon,/ Moon,/ Great diamond moon" shows the white-gowned, long-haired mother floating among the clouds, holding her son up so he can see the shining disk in a dark, gray-blue sky. Swirls of grass and celestial orbs embellish daytime scenes, while the lights of tall buildings join with the stars above to form a backdrop for several nocturnal spreads." Kirkus
Includes bibliographical references (p.   )

★ **My** people; photographs by Charles R. Smith Jr. Atheneum Books for Young Readers 2009 un il $17.99
Grades: K 1 2 3   **811**
1. African Americans -- Poetry 2. Poetry -- By individual authors
ISBN 978-1-4169-3540-7; 1-4169-3540-1
LC 2008025604
ALA EMIERT Coretta Scott King Illustrator Award (2010)

"Introducing the poem two or three words at a time, Smith pairs each phrase with a portrait of one or more African Americans; printed in sepia, the faces of his subjects materialize on black pages. . . . Smith's faces emerge into the light, displaying the best that humanity has to offer—intelligence, wisdom, curiosity, love and joy." Publ Wkly

★ **I** am the darker brother; an anthology of modern poems by African Americans. edited and with an afterword by Arnold Adoff; drawings by Benny Andrews; introduction by Rudine Sims Bishop; foreword by Nikki Giovanni. rev ed; Simon & Schuster Bks. for Young Readers 1997 208p il hardcover o.p. pa $5.99
Grades: 6 7 8 9 10   **811**
1. American poetry -- African American authors -- Collections
ISBN 0-689-81241-8; 0-689-80869-0 pa
LC 97-144181
First published 1968
This anthology presents "the African-American experience through poetry that speaks for itself. . . . Because of the historical context of many of the poems, the book will be much in demand during Black History Month, but it should be used and treasured as part of the larger canon of literature to be enjoyed by all Americans at all times of the year. An indispensable addition to library collections." SLJ

★ **I,** too, sing America; three centuries of African American poetry. [selected and annotated by] Catherine Clinton; illustrated by Stephen Alcorn. Houghton Mifflin 1998 128p il $21
Grades: 6 7 8 9   **811**
1. African Americans -- Poetry 2. American poetry -- African American authors -- Collections
ISBN 0-395-89599-5
LC 97-46137
"For each poet, Clinton provides a biography and a brief, insightful commentary on the poem(s) she has chosen, including a discussion of political as well as literary connections. Alcorn's dramatic, full-page, full-color illustrations opposite each poem evoke the quiltlike patterns and rhythmic figures of folk art." Booklist

★ **In** daddy's arms I am tall; African Americans celebrating fathers. illustrated by Javaka Steptoe. Lee & Low Bks. 1997 un il pa $6.95; $15.95
Grades: K 1 2 3   **811**
1. Children's poetry 2. Fathers -- Poetry 3. African Americans -- Poetry 4. American poetry -- Collections
ISBN 1-58430-016-7 pa; 1-880000-31-8
LC 97-7311
Coretta Scott King Award for illustration
This "picture book celebrates the role of fathers in the African-American experience. The artist illustrates 13 poems with collages. . . . {The poems were} written by Angela Johnson, Davida Adedjouma, Carole Boston Weatherford, and others. . . . Grade three and up." (SLJ)
"Certain poems . . . elevate this collection above the mundane, but it is the illustrations that set this volume apart. Steptoe uses a variety of materials and techniques and art forms to enhance the language of the poems, including torn paper, collages, realia, paintings, and drawings." Horn Book

Incredible inventions; poems selected by Lee Bennett Hopkins; illustrations by Julia Sarcone-Roach. Greenwillow Books 2009 27p il $17.99; lib bdg $18.89
Grades: 1 2 3 4   811
1. Inventions -- Poetry 2. American poetry -- Collections
ISBN 978-0-06-087245-8; 0-06-087245-4; 978-0-06-087246-5 lib bdg; 0-06-087246-2 lib bdg
LC 2008003830

"Ingenious inventions are the focus of this lively picture-book poetry collection. Contributed by both well-known and emerging poets, the selections represent a wide range of styles. . . . The subjects, drawn from a young person's everyday world, add to the poems' accessiblity. . . . The mixed-media artwork's well-designed compositions add energy without overwhelming the words." Booklist

Iyengar, Malathi Michelle

Tan to tamarind; poems about the color brown. poems by Malathi Michelle Iyengar; illustrations by Jamel Akib. Children's Book Press 2009 30p il $16.95
Grades: K 1 2 3   811
1. Color -- Poetry 2. Poetry -- By individual authors
ISBN 978-0-89239-227-8; 0-89239-227-4
LC 2008022225

"Illustrated with pastel pictures in warm autumn colors, both dark and light, the simple poems celebrate the diversity and the connections in nature, culture, place, and language among blacks, Latinos, Indians, Native Americans, and many mixed-race kids. All the names for brown—from tan to honey, beige, and ocher—show the wonder of the senses." Booklist

Janeczko, Paul B., 1945-

★ **Firefly** July and other very short poems; Paul B. Janeczko, illustrated by Melissa Sweet. First edition Candlewick Press 2014 48 p. $16.99
Grades: K 1 2 3 4   811
1. Children's poetry 2. Seasons -- Poetry 3. American Poetry
ISBN 0763648426; 9780763648428
LC 2013943087

This collection of poems, by Paul B. Janeczko, is "organized by the seasons, beginning with spring. . . . The poems range from work by William Carlos Williams, Emily Dickinson, and Langston Hughes to that of James Stevenson, Joyce Sidman, and Ralph Fletcher. The first verse opens the book with daybreak, and after exploring the whole year, the final selection sends readers off to sleep." (School Library Journal)

"Sweet's child-friendly mixed-media illustrations--loosely rendered, collage-like assemblages in seasonal palettes--enhance the thirty-six excellent poems showcased on the book's ample spreads. As brief as three lines or a dozen words, most of the verses are by familiar poets (Carl Sandburg, Langston Hughes), including those known for their children s verse (Alice Schertle, Charlotte Zolotow). A fine addition to the seasonal poetry shelf." Horn Book

Katz, Alan

Oops! poems by Alan Katz; drawings by Edward Koren. Margaret K. McElderry Books 2008 132p il $17.99

Grades: 3 4 5 6   811
1. Humorous poetry 2. Poetry -- By individual authors
ISBN 978-1-4169-0204-1; 1-4169-0204-X
LC 2005-32439

"This collection of more than 100 short, funny, rhyming poems never lags. It includes occasional (rather funny) potty humor. . . . Puns and other groaners abound and are sure to delight young readers, especially boys. . . . Koren's pen-and-ink cartoons resemble the art in Shel Silverstein's collections. The illustrations match the tone of the book and sometimes add extra interpretations of the poems. This is a great choice for reluctant poetry readers and aspiring class clowns." SLJ

Poems I wrote when no one was looking; drawings by Edward Koren. Margaret K. McElderry Books 2011 153p il $17.99
Grades: 3 4 5   811
1. Humorous poetry 2. Poetry -- By individual authors
ISBN 978-1-4169-3518-6; 1-4169-3518-5
LC 2007052523

"Accompanied by Koren's impish, characteristically furry caricatures, Katz's comedic poems take aim at familiar experiences like family squabbling and avoiding homework, while offering child-centric observations about the world. . . . Kids will revel in the gently wicked jokes . . . and mild gross-out gags . . . that run throughout the collection." Publ Wkly

Kennedy, X. J.

City kids; street and skyscraper rhymes. illustrated by Philippe Béha. Tradewind Books 2010 104p il $17.95
Grades: 3 4 5   811
1. City and town life -- Poetry 2. Poetry -- By individual authors
ISBN 978-1-896580-44-9; 1-896580-44-0

"The urban world is examined from every angle in this lively collection of verse about city life. Most can apply to cities generally, though there are specific poems about Toronto, San Francisco, London, and others. . . . Béha's illustrations have a naïf, crayon-scrawled exuberance, and most match the upbeat tone of Kennedy's verse." Publ Wkly

★ **A kick** in the head; selected by Paul B. Janeczko; illustrated by Chris Raschka. Candlewick Press 2005 61p il $17.99; pa $9.99
Grades: 4 5 6 7   811
1. American poetry -- Collections
ISBN 978-0-7636-0662-6; 0-7636-0662-6; 978-0-7636-4132-0 pa; 0-7636-4132-4 pa
LC 2004-48508

"Raschka's high-spirited, spare torn-paper-and-paint collages ingeniously broaden the poems' wide-ranging emotional tones. . . . Clear, very brief explanations of poetic forms . . . accompany each entry; a fine introduction and appended notes offer further information. . . . This is the introduction that will ignite enthusiasm." Booklist

Kinerk, Robert

Oh, how Sylvester can pester! and other poems more or less about manners. pictures by Drazen Kozjan. Simon & Schuster Books for Young Readers 2011 28p il $16.99
Grades: K 1 2 3   811
1. Children's poetry 2. Etiquette -- Poetry 3. Poetry

-- By individual authors 4. Etiquette for children and teenagers

ISBN 1-4169-3362-X; 978-1-4169-3362-5

LC 2010000771

In these illustrated poems "Kinerk pokes fun at what can happen when good manners are neglected." (Publisher's note) "Primary." (Horn Book)

"The rhymes in this picture book about manners have fun with names and with nonsense. . . . The clear, bright digital pictures extend the farce." Booklist

Knock at a star; a child's introduction to poetry. [compiled by] X. J. Kennedy and Dorothy M. Kennedy; illustrated by Karen Lee Baker. rev ed; Little, Brown 1999 180p il hardcover o.p. pa $12.99

Grades: 3 4 5 6   **811**

1. English poetry -- Collections 2. American poetry -- Collections

ISBN 0-316-48436-9; 0-316-48800-3 pa

LC 98-21572

A revised and newly illustrated edition of the title first published 1982

An anthology of mostly very short poems by standard, contemporary, and anonymous poets, intended to stimulate interest in reading and writing poetry

"Karen Lee Baker's small, shaded-pencil drawings capture the many moods of the verse." Booklist

Lang, Diane

Vulture verses; love poems for the unloved. written by Diane Lang; illustrated by Lauren Gallegos. Prospect Park Media 2012 32 p.

Grades: 2 3 4   **811**

1. Didactic poetry 2. Animals -- Poetry 3. Children's poetry

ISBN 0983459452; 9780983459453

LC 2012002823

Latham, Irene

★ **Dear** Wandering Wildebeest; And Other Poems from the Water Hole. By Irene Latham; Illustrated by Anna Wadham. Millbrook Press 2014 33 p. (lib. bdg.: alk. paper) $17.95

Grades: 2 3 4 5   **811**

1. Animals -- Africa 2. Children's poetry 3. Poems. Selections.

ISBN 1467712329; 9781467712323

LC 2013030195

In this children's poetry book, written by Irene Latham and illustrated by Anna Wadham, readers will "Spend a day at a water hole on the African grasslands. From dawn to nightfall, animals come and go. Giraffes gulp, wildebeest graze, impalas leap, vultures squabble, and elephants wallow." (Publisher's note)

"This will be a much-sought-after book for teaching reading and inquiry skills...Charming illustrations in dusty colors convey the habitat of the African grasslands while portraying the passing of a day. A strong choice." SLJ

Lawrence, Jacob

★ **Harriet** and the Promised Land. Simon & Schuster Bks. for Young Readers 1993 un il $18; pa $6.99

Grades: 2 3 4 5   **811**

1. Abolitionists 2. Underground railroad -- Poetry 3.

Poetry -- By individual authors

ISBN 0-671-86673-7; 0-689-80965-4 pa

LC 92-33740

A newly illustrated edition of the title first published 1968 by Windmill Books

"The strength of this volume is in the forceful, stylized paintings by the famous black artist, which capture the degradation of slavery." Brooklyn. Art Books for Child

Lesynski, Loris

Crazy about soccer. Annick Press 2012 47 p. $22.95

Grades: 3 4 5   **811**

1. Soccer -- Poetry 2. Children's poetry 3. Picture books for children

ISBN 1554514223; 9781554514229

This poetry collection "celebrates the sport of soccer... . From the commiseration offered to players who must persevere through squalls in 'Rain Game' to . . . 'Turf Burn,' which . . . describes the perils of artificial grass, [Loris] Lesynski's verse explores the gamut of soccer experiences. The format varies, with verses that range from brief . . . , such as the sole line comprising 'The Concussion Discussion,' to the lengthier 'How to Be a Referee,' which pays homage to . . . game officials." (Kirkus)

Levy, Debbie

Maybe I'll sleep in the bathtub tonight; and other funny bedtime poems. illustrated by Stephanie Buscema. Sterling Pub. 2010 24p il $14.95

Grades: PreK K 1 2   **811**

1. Humorous poetry 2. Bedtime -- Poetry 3. Poetry -- By individual authors

ISBN 978-1-4027-4944-5; 1-4027-4944-9

LC 2008-48826

"These cozy rhymes for sharing at bedtime have a lot of fun with wordplay, from the literal interpretations of sleepover, showing kids on a roof, and sleep tight (I unkinked myself and vowed: / Tonight I will sleep loose!), to a familiar nursery lullaby. . . . Young children with their caregivers will giggle at the humorous scenes, illustrated with colorful gouache pictures, which could make a good prelude to the usual soothing lullabies." Booklist

★ The **year** of goodbyes; a true story of friendship, family and farewells. Disney-Hyperion Books 2010 136p il $16.99

Grades: 5 6 7 8   **811**

1. Jews -- Poetry 2. Holocaust, 1933-1945 -- Poetry 3. Poetry -- By individual authors

ISBN 1-4231-2901-6; 978-1-4231-2901-1

LC 2009-18671

"In 1930s Germany, it was common for young girls to keep poesiealbums, or autograph books, in which friends could write poems, draw pictures, or offer wishes to the owner. Levy has based this novel in verse on the actual poesiealbum kept by her mother, Jutta Salzberg, when she was twelve years old. . . . Grades four to seven." (Bull Cent Child Books)

"Artfully weaving together her mother's poesiealbum (autograph/poetry album), diary, and her own verse, Levy crafts a poignant portrait of her Jewish mother's life in 1938 Nazi Germany that crackles with adolescent vitality." Publ Wkly

Lewis, J. Patrick

★ **Blackbeard**, the pirate king; several yarns detailing the legends, myths, and real-life adventures of history's most notorious seaman. told in verse by J. Patrick Lewis. National Geographic Society 2006 un il map $16.95; lib bdg $25.90

Grades: 3 4 5   **811**

1. Pirates -- Poetry 2. Poetry -- By individual authors
ISBN 0-7922-5585-2; 0-7922-5586-0 lib bdg
LC 2005-29514

"Lewis crafts sophisticated verse around the few facts and many fictions told of Edward Teach, otherwise known as Blackbeard, the seventeenth century pirate king. In antique type, the poems are either set against parchment-style backgrounds or against one of the book's diverse images, which include paintings by N. C. Wyeth, and Caspar David Friedrich, as well as archival prints and striking modern paintings. Despite the broad range of art styles, the story flows cohesively throughout, vividly evoking the buccaneer's adventures in swashbuckling lines that read aloud well." Booklist

Countdown to summer; a poems for every day of the school year. illustrations by Ethan Long. Little, Brown and Co. 2009 un il $15.99

Grades: 4 5 6   **811**

1. Schools -- Poetry 2. Poetry -- By individual authors
ISBN 978-0-316-02089-3; 0-316-02089-3
LC 2008016772

"180 poems are here gathered to be enjoyed on a vitamin-like one-a-day basis. . . . Some verses are long, some short, some thought-provoking, some laugh-provoking. Long's penciled spot art provides an agreeable visual accompaniment." Kirkus

★ **Doodle** dandies; poems that take shape. J. Patrick Lewis, words; Lisa Desimini, images; with design and typography by Ann Bobco and Lisa Desimini. Atheneum Bks. for Young Readers 1998 un il hardcover o.p. pa $7.99

Grades: 1 2 3 4   **811**

1. American poetry 2. Visual poetry 3. Visual poetry, American 4. Poetry -- By individual authors
ISBN 0-689-81075-X; 0-689-84889-7 pa
LC 9601920

This is a collection of poems each of which appears on the page in the shape of its subject so that the poem looks like whatever it's about. "Grades three to six." (SLJ)

"Every page of this book is well designed, creating words and images that work together in harmony. . . . Doodle Dandies captures the joy that wordplay can bring." SLJ

Edgar Allan Poe's apple pie; math puzzlers in classic poems. written by J. Patrick Lewis; illustrated by Michael H. Slack. Harcourt 2012 37 p.

Grades: 4 5 6   **811**

1. Children's poetry 2. Mathematics -- Poetry 3. Mathematical recreations 4. Word problems (Mathematics) 5. Poetry -- Parodies, imitations, etc. 6. English poetry -- Adaptations 7. American poetry -- Adaptations 8. Mathematics -- poetry 9. Mathematical recreations
ISBN 9780547513386
LC 2011025735

The author J. Patrick Lewis "combines math and language arts with this collection of humorous poetry parodies that present readers with math word problems to solve. Fourteen famous poets and some of their more prominent works are the basis for Lewis' parodies, which . . . retain the structure, rhyme and rhythm of the originals." The book presents challenges based on works by poets including Walt Whitman, Emily Dickinson, and Shel Silverstein on mathematics concepts such as fractions, decimals, and perimeter. (Kirkus)

★ **The house**; illustrated by Roberto Innocenti. Creative Editions 2009 un il $19.95

Grades: 4 5 6 7   **811**

1. Houses -- Poetry 2. Poetry -- By individual authors
ISBN 978-1-56846-201-1; 1-56846-201-8

"The walls in a stone farmhouse literally talk in this first-person narrative that deals with the ravages of time and their effects on the structure and its inhabitants. After a brief history, the house (constructed in 1656, 'a plague year') fast forwards to the dawn of the 20th century, when children discover its ruins. The quatrains, one to a spread, alternate between an AABB and ABBA rhyme scheme, thus avoiding singsong predictability. . . . Children will pore over Innocenti's marvelously detailed spreads, composed in an oversize, vertical format and set in an Italian hill town. . . . In the subset of books dealing intelligently with the effects of time on a single location, this is a provocative choice." SLJ

If you were a chocolate mustache; J. Patrick Lewis. WordSong 2012 159 p. $18.95

Grades: 3 4 5   **811**

1. Children's poetry 2. Dragons -- Poetry 3. Turtles -- Poetry
ISBN 159078927X; 9781590789278
LC 2012939794

For this book, "in offbeat poems that include haikus, limericks, riddles, and wordplay of every kind, current children's poet laureate [J. Patrick] Lewis offers quirky contemplations, silly vignettes, and improbable events." Here, "a dragon serves as a clothes dryer, Bigfoot laments that he can't find stylish shoes in his size, and an old turtle complains to the sky that there is 'nothing new under the sun,' only to have his claim challenged by a snowflake." (Publishers Weekly)

★ **Monumental** verses. National Geographic 2005 31p il $16.95; lib bdg $25.90

Grades: 5 6 7 8   **811**

1. Monuments -- Poetry 2. Poetry -- By individual authors
ISBN 0-7922-7135-1; 0-7922-7139-4 lib bdg

"Lewis offers 14 poems celebrating monumental structures. From the remnants of civilizations at Stonehenge, Easter Island, and Machu Picchu to the more modern achievements of the Taj Mahal, the Eiffel Tower, and the Statue of Liberty, the subjects are varied and the accompanying photos are striking." Booklist

★ **Once** upon a tomb; gravely humorous verses. illustrated by Simon Bartram. Candlewick 2006 un il $16.99

Grades: 3 4 5   **811**

1. Death -- Poetry 2. Poetry -- By individual authors
ISBN 0-7636-1837-3

"Proving himself to be anything but a grave man, Lewis offers 22 irreverent epitaphs and other mortuary verses, each of which is paired with a large, polished portrait or burial scene created in richly hued acrylics.... This rare look at the lighter side of death should elicit plenty of surprised giggles from young audiences." Booklist

Please bury me in the library; illustrated by Kyle M. Stone. Harcourt 2005 32p il $16

Grades: 3 4 5 **811**

1. Books and reading -- Poetry 2. Poetry -- By individual authors

ISBN 0-15-216387-5

LC 2003-26983

A "collection of 16 poems celebrating books, reading, language, and libraries.... The brief selections encompass various forms, from an eight-word acrostic to haiku to rhyming quatrains and couplets.... The poems are accompanied by richly dark artwork. The thickly applied acrylic paint and mixed-media illustrations ... [have] a comically grotesque air, and add comprehension to the verses." SLJ

★ **Self**-portrait with seven fingers; the life of Marc Chagall in verse. [by] J. Patrick Lewis &Jane Yolen. Creative Editions 2011 38p il $18.99

Grades: 5 6 7 8 **811**

1. Artists 2. Painters 3. Jews -- Poetry 4. Artists -- Poetry 5. Jews -- Biography

ISBN 978-1-56846-211-0; 1-56846-211-5

LC 2009034767

"Lewis and Yolen pair 14 poems about Marc Chagall (1887–1985) with reproductions of more than a dozen of his paintings (as well as vintage photographs) in this moving account of the artist's Jewish upbringing in what is now Belarus, ... his ascent in the art world, and his loves and losses, including arrest by the Nazis while living in Paris.... The duo's emphatic and empathetic verse is put into context by informative biographical sidebars that appear beneath each poem. A study in resilience, dedication, and wide-ranging talent." Publ Wkly

Includes bibliographical references

Skywriting; poems to fly. illustrated by Laszlo Kubinyi. Creative Editions 2010 32p il $25.65

Grades: 3 4 5 6 **811**

1. Flight -- Poetry 2. Poetry -- By individual authors

ISBN 978-1-56846-203-5; 1-56846-203-4

LC 2008014229

"Tracing the history of flight, this collection of poems celebrates the daring dreams of humans, from Icarus's doomed journey ... to modern space shuttles.... Kubinyi's precise linework and sense of movement are well-matched to the mechanical subject matter and capture the spirit of flight across the ages." Publ Wkly

Spot the plot; a riddle book of book riddles. illustrated by Lynn Munsinger. Chronicle Books 2009 un il $15.99

Grades: K 1 2 3 **811**

1. Riddles 2. Books and reading -- Poetry 3. Poetry -- By individual authors

ISBN 978-0-8118-4668-4; 0-8118-4668-7

LC 2008-03206

"Short poetic riddles are presented on spreads, each providing the clues in both text and illustrations of the plot of a well-known children's story. Two young detectives and their dog are looking at such activities as farm animals typing letters in a field (Click, Clack, Moo), a train running along snowy railway tracks (The Polar Express), or a pumpkin coach careening along as it's drawn by a bunch of rats (Cinderella).... This book is perfect for an interactive readaloud." SLJ

Under the kissletoe; Christmastime poems. [by] J. Patrick Lewis; illustrations by Rob Shepperson. Wordsong 2007 32p il $16.95

Grades: 2 3 4 **811**

1. Christmas -- Poetry 2. Poetry -- By individual authors

ISBN 978-1-59078-438-9; 1-59078-438-3

LC 2006038984

"In Lewis's collection of poems ... affable wit and infectious cadence bring fresh energy to traditional yuletide images.... Shepperson's brightly shaded, borderline cartoon-y illustrations balance humor with warmth." Horn Book

The **underwear** salesman; and other jobs for better or verse. [by] J. Patrick Lewis; illustrated by Serge Bloch. Atheneum Books for Young Readers 2009 un il $16.99

Grades: 3 4 5 **811**

1. Work -- Poetry 2. Occupations -- Poetry 3. Poetry -- By individual authors

ISBN 978-0-689-85325-8; 0-689-85325-4

LC 2008025884

"Puns are everywhere in this playful, rhyming survey of jobs, and the collage illustrations extend the verbal fun with wry, literal images." Booklist

★ **When** thunder comes; poems for civil rights leaders. by J. Patrick Lewis, 2011-2013 Children's Poet Laureate; illustrated by R. Gregory Christie. Chronicle Books 2012 44 p. (alk. paper) $16.99

Grades: 4 5 6 **811**

1. Children's poetry 2. Civil rights 3. Children's poetry, American

ISBN 1452101191; 9781452101194

LC 2011045938

In this collection, "Children's Poet Laureate J. Patrick Lewis gives ... voice to seventeen heroes of civil rights.... Illustrated by five ... artists, this ... collection of poems invites the reader to hear in each verse the thunder that lies in every voice, no matter how small." Civil rights figures profiled include "Coretta Scott King, Harvey Milk, Mohandas Gandhi, Nelson Mandela, Sylvia Mendez, Aung San Suu Kyi, ... Andrew Goodman, and Michael Schwerner." (Publisher's note)

The **World's** Greatest; poems. [written by] J. Patrick Lewis; [illustrated by Keith Graves] Chronicle Books 2008 33p il $16.99

Grades: K 1 2 3 **811**

1. World records -- Poetry 2. Poetry -- By individual authors

ISBN 978-0-8118-5130-5; 0-8118-5130-3

LC 2007-14717

"This sprightly, clever collection centers on facts found in various editions of the 'Guinness Book of Records.' ...

. The droll, distinct illustrations created using acrylic paint and colored pencils capture perfectly the humor and vigor of the text. This attractive book is saturated with color and will charm children who understand its adroit wordplay." SLJ

★ **Lives**: poems about famous Americans; selected by Lee Bennett Hopkins; illustrated by Leslie Staub. Harper-Collins Pubs. 1999 31p il $15.99

Grades: 4 5 6 7   **811**

1. American poetry -- Collections 2. United States -- Biography -- Poetry

ISBN 0-06-027767-X; 0-06-027768-8 lib bdg

LC 98-29851

A collection of poetic portraits of sixteen famous Americans from Paul Revere to Neil Armstrong, by such authors as Jane Yolen, Nikki Grimes, and X. J. Kennedy

"Hopkins's eloquent introduction praises the power of poetry. Concluding 'Notes on the Lives' give readers useful biographical information. Full-page portraits feature Staub's distinctive, flat, primitive style, and their backgrounds have details particular to the subject. . . . A winning combination of poems and illustrations." SLJ

Lobel, Arnold

★ The **frogs** and toads all sang; color by Adrianne Lobel. HarperCollinsPublishers 2009 29p il $16.99; lib bdg $17.89

Grades: PreK K 1 2   **811**

1. Frogs -- Poetry 2. Toads -- Poetry 3. Poetry -- By individual authors

ISBN 978-0-06-180022-1; 978-0-06-180023-8 lib bdg

LC 2008051768

A collection of poems featuring frogs, toads, and polliwogs

"Originally created by the late Lobel as a handmade book for a fellow author, these poems and pencil sketches (skillfully given washes of color by his daughter, Adrianne) are the progenitors of Lobel's classic Frog and Toad series. But even kids who haven't spent much time with those amphibious friends will find plenty to enjoy. . . . The drawings of genteelly domesticated amphibians large and small bring to mind the spontaneity, intimacy and exuberance of the sketchpad." Publ Wkly

Odd owls & stout pigs; a book of nonsense. color by Adrianne Lobel. Harper 2009 31p il $15.99; lib bdg $16.89

Grades: PreK K 1 2   **811**

1. Humorous poetry 2. Owls -- Poetry 3. Pigs -- Poetry 4. Poetry -- By individual authors

ISBN 978-0-06-180054-2; 0-06-180054-6; 978-0-06-180055-9 lib bdg; 0-06-180055-4 lib bdg

LC 2009001406

Presents a linked collection of brief rhymes featuring owls and pigs

"This collection of nonsense rhymes and poems explodes with fun and frivolity. . . . The verses cover a wide variety of topics, and the words create sound patterns that will engage listeners. . . . Original illustrations were scanned and enhanced with oil pastels and colored pencils. They play buoyantly off Mr. Lobel's clever text and provide a breezy feel." SLJ

Longfellow, Henry Wadsworth

Hiawatha; pictures by Susan Jeffers. Dial Bks. for Young Readers 1983 un il hardcover o.p. pa $6.99 **811**

1. Native Americans -- Poetry 2. Native Americans -- Folklore 3. Poetry -- By individual authors

ISBN 0-14-055882-9 pa

LC 83-7225

Verses excerpted from the poem first published 1855 with title: Song of Hiawatha

"Jeffers has captured the essence of this brief section from the classic poem. . . . The pale tints of the pictures are in complete harmony with nature and with the text and show in detail how Hiawatha might have seen his world. A fine first exposure to the poem for children and a beautiful artistic experience." SLJ

Low, Alice

The **fastest** game on two feet and other poems about how sports began; illustrated by John O'Brien. Holiday House 2009 40p il $17.95

Grades: 3 4 5 6   **811**

1. Sports -- Poetry 2. Poetry -- By individual authors

ISBN 978-0-8234-1905-0; 0-8234-1905-3

LC 2007013441

"These 19 poems, each for a different sport, score a goal. Under the title, a short paragraph establishes a context for the origin of the sport. . . . The poems are tightly phrased and put a spin on the historical information of how the sport has evolved. O'Brien's signature style of dappled watercolors-over-ink comically underscores the theme that sports are fun." Kirkus

Luján, Jorge

Doggy slippers; poems by Jorge Luján (with the contribution of Latin American children); translated by Elisa Amado; pictures by Isol. Groundwood Books/House of Anansi Press 2010 un il $18.95

Grades: PreK K 1   **811**

1. Pets -- Poetry 2. Poetry -- By individual authors

ISBN 978-0-88899-983-2; 0-88899-983-6

"Using suggestions from kids in Mexico and Argentina, Luján crafts this refreshing collection of 12 free-verse poems about children's pets. . . . Abstract, whimsical illustrations in a retro palette of brown, gold, olive and aqua rely on squiggly pencil outlines to economically define details and highlight sublime and ridiculous aspects from each poem. . . . Poetic pet snapshots packaged with panache and translated with aplomb." Kirkus

MacLachlan, Patricia

I didn't do it; [by] Patricia MacLachlan and Emily MacLachlan Charest; illustrated by Katy Schneider. Katherine Tegan Books 2010 un il $16.99

Grades: PreK K 1 2   **811**

1. Dogs -- Poetry 2. Poetry -- By individual authors

ISBN 978-0-06-135833-3; 0-06-135833-9

LC 2009-27541

This is a "charming volume of verses showing the thoughts of puppies of many breeds. . . . The verses are short, and the authors seem to understand canines and their likes, dislikes and self discipline (or lack thereof). Humor abounds, as do the activities, and illustrated in lively, tex-

tured oil paintings that make breeds clearly recognizable."
Kirkus

★ **Once** I ate a pie; by Patricia MacLachlan and Emily
MacLachlan Charest; illustrated by Katy Schneider. Joanna
Cotler Books 2006 un il $15.99; lib bdg $16.89; pa
$6.99
Grades: K 1 2 3   **811**
1. Dogs -- Poetry 2. Poetry -- By individual authors
ISBN 978-0-06-073531-9; 0-06-073531-7; 978-0-06-
073532-6 lib bdg; 0-06-073532-5 lib bdg; 978-0-06-
073533-3 pa; 0-06-073533-3 pa
LC 2004-22225
"Free-verse poems about 14 individual dogs sprawl
across oversize spreads accompanied by large oil illustrations. The poems and paintings together delightfully capture each distinct personality in few words and with broad
strokes of the brush." SLJ

★ **Marvelous** math; a book of poems. selected by Lee
Bennett Hopkins; illustrated by Karen Barbour. Simon
& Schuster Bks. for Young Readers 1997 31p il hard-
cover o.p. pa $6.99
Grades: 3 4 5   **811**
1. Mathematics -- Poetry 2. American poetry --
Collections
ISBN 0-689-80658-2; 0-689-84442-5 pa
LC 96-21597
Presents such poems as "Math Makes Me Feel Safe,"
"Fractions," "Pythagoras," and "Time Passes," by such writ-
ers as Janet S. Wong, Lee Bennett Hopkins, and Ilo Orleans
"Rhymed and open verse styles are represented, as are a
variety of tones. . . . Barbour's lively illustrations dance and
play around the poems. Her boldly outlined watercolor figures, often wearing ill-fitting hats, fill the pages with child-
like whimsy." SLJ

Moore, Clement C.
★ The **night** before Christmas; [illustrated by] Charles
Santore. Applesauce 2011 il $18.95
Grades: PreK K 1   **811**
1. Christmas -- Poetry 2. Santa Claus -- Poetry 3.
Poetry -- By individual authors
ISBN 978-1-60433-237-7; 1-60433-237-9
Santore "brings to life Moore's 'A Visit from St. Nicho-
las' in characteristically elegant and detail-rich paintings.
His is a very traditional vision, as he brings readers inside
a stately colonial home, tastefully appointed with wreaths,
garlands, and stockings. . . . It's a gorgeous interpretation of
a beloved holiday classic." Publ Wkly

★ The **night** before Christmas; by Clement C. Moore
and illustrated by Holly Hobbie. Little, Brown & Co. 2013
40 p. $18
Grades: PreK K 1 2   **811**
1. Watercolor painting 2. Christmas -- Fiction 3.
Christmas poetry 4. Children's poetry, American 5.
Santa Claus -- poetry
ISBN 0316070181; 9780316070188
LC 2012049185
In this book, by Clement C. Moore and illustrated by
Holly Hobbie, "a toddler awakens, looks out the window,
and sees a flying sleigh. He makes his way downstairs,
where he peeks around a chair to watch St. Nicholas at work.

. . . An appended section offers some historical background
on Moore and the poem, first published in 1823, while an
artist's note comments on Hobbie's technique and her approach to the work." (Booklist)

The **night** before Christmas; retold and illustrated by
Rachel Isadora. G. P. Putnam's Sons 2009 un il $16.99
Grades: PreK K 1 2   **811**
1. Christmas -- Poetry 2. Santa Claus -- Poetry 3.
Poetry -- By individual authors
ISBN 978-0-399-25408-6; 0-399-25408-0
LC 2008053359
"Santa's Christmas Eve journey takes him to Africa in
this charming version of the poem. Isadora uses collaged papers and oil paints to create a vibrant African village, dusted
by snow. . . . Full of details, rich color, and an exuberant spirit, this book will provide opportunities for discussion as well
as a new cultural landscape for the 'right jolly old elf.'" SLJ

'**Twas** the night before Christmas; illustrated by Chris-
topher Wormell. Running Press Kids 2010 un il $16.95
Grades: PreK K 1   **811**
1. Christmas -- Poetry 2. Santa Claus -- Poetry 3.
Poetry -- By individual authors
ISBN 978-0-7624-2717-8; 0-7624-2717-5
The well-known poem about an important
Christmas visitor.
"With their strong black lines and deep colors, Wormell's
signature block prints are a fittingly iconic pairing for
Moore's holiday classic. . . . This is an enchanting and el-
egant adaptation." Publ Wkly

Moore, Lilian
★ **Beware,** take care; fun and spooky poems. by Lil-
ian Moore; illustrated by Howard Fine. Henry Holt and Co.
2006 un il $16.95
Grades: PreK K 1 2   **811**
1. Fear -- Poetry 2. Monsters -- Poetry 3. Supernatural
-- Poetry 4. Poetry -- By individual authors
ISBN 978-0-8050-6917-4; 0-8050-6917-8
LC 2005020257
Poems first published in the author's Spooky Rhymes
and Riddles (1973) and See My Lovely Poison Ivy (1975)
"The ghosts, monsters, and dragons are amusing and not
the least bit scary in this congenial picture-book gathering of
short verses. . . . Illustrated with humor and warmth, these
poems are simple enough for independent readers and silly
enough to evoke chuckles and giggles during read-aloud
sharing." SLJ

Mural on Second Avenue, and other city poems; il-
lustrated by Roma Karas. Candlewick Press 2005 un il
$16.99
Grades: K 1 2 3   **811**
1. City and town life -- Poetry 2. Poetry -- By individual
authors
ISBN 0-7636-1987-6
LC 2002-73702
"These 17 poems, all but one of which were chosen from
Moore's previous collections, celebrate life in the city. . . .
The poems appear on pages covered in bright oil paintings. .
. . These poems speak loudly to children." SLJ

Mora, Pat

★ **Yum! mmmm! que rico!** Americas' sproutings: haiku. illustrated by Rafael López. Lee & Low 2007 un il map lib bdg $16.95

Grades: 1 2 3 4   **811**

1. Fruit 2. Haiku 3. Vegetables 4. Food -- Poetry 5. Children's poetry

ISBN 1-58430-271-2 lib bdg; 978-1-58430-271-1 lib bdg

LC 2006-38199

"From blueberries to vanilla, indigenous foods of the Americas are celebrated in this collection of haiku, which also includes information about each food's origins." (Publisher's note) "Grades three to five." (Bull Cent Child Books)

"This inventive stew of food haiku celebrates indigenous foods of the Americas. Each of the 13 poems appears on a gloriously colorful double-page spread, accompanied by a sidebar that presents information about the origin of the food. . . . The acrylic-on-wood-panel illustrations burst with vivid colors and stylized Mexican flair." Booklist

Includes bibliographical references

Mordhorst, Heidi

Pumpkin butterfly; poems from the other side of nature. illustrations by Jenny Reynish. Wordsong 2009 32p il $16.95

Grades: 3 4 5 6   **811**

1. Nature poetry 2. Poetry -- By individual authors

ISBN 978-1-59078-620-8; 1-59078-620-3

LC 2009019918

"A collection of 23 nature poems cycles through the seasons, emphasizing the play between the outward and the hidden realms. The vocabulary and imagery stretch the maturing apprehension of young readers. . . . The use of contrasts . . . vividly convey an observant look at what is often overlooked. . . . Reynish's decorative illustrations reflect a thoughtful and purposeful artistic hand." Kirkus

Muth, Jon J., 1960-

★ **Hi, Koo!** a year of seasons. presented by Koo and Jon J. Muth. Scholastic Press 2013 32 p. (hardcover) $17.99

Grades: PreK K 1 2 3   **811**

1. Children's poetry 2. Seasons -- Poetry 3. Pandas 4. Seasons

ISBN 0545166683; 9780545166683

LC 2012040378

In this book of children's poems, author "Jon J. Muth--and his delightful little panda bear, Koo--challenge readers to stretch their minds and imaginations with twenty-six haikus about the four seasons." This book uses the haiku form to take children through the seasons with watercolored images. (Publisher's note)

"Twenty-six haiku are presented by young panda Koo, eventually joined by two human children. The story told through the haiku follows the cycle of the seasons (a note explains Muth's choice to forgo the traditional five-seven-five syllable pattern). Each haiku contains just one capital letter, in order from A to Z. Muth's watercolors are as clear and translucent as the child-friendly, easily understood haiku." (Horn Book)

★ **My** America; a poetry atlas of the United States. selected by Lee Bennett Hopkins; illustrated by Stephen Alcorn. Simon & Schuster Bks. for Young Readers 2000 83p il $21.95

Grades: 4 5 6 7   **811**

1. United States -- Poetry 2. American poetry -- Collections

ISBN 0-689-81247-7

LC 98-47402

A collection of poems evocative of seven geographical regions of the United States, including the Northeast, Southeast, Great Lakes, Plains, Mountain, Southwest, and Pacific Coast States.

"Some poems are purposive, but the best . . . capture places and people in all their diversity. Stephen Alcorn's handsome, multi-textured pictures . . . avoid literal interpretation and capture the sweep of the land and the rhythm of the words." Booklist

Myers, Christopher

★ **We** are America; a tribute from the heart. Walter Dean Myers, Christopher Myers. HarperCollins Children's Books 2011 1 v. (unpaged) $16.99; lib bdg $17.89

Grades: 3 4 5 6   **811**

1. United States -- poetry 2. Children's poetry, American

ISBN 978-0-06-052308-4; 0-06-052308-5; 978-0-06-052309-1 lib bdg; 0-06-052309-3 lib bdg; 0060523085; 0060523093; 9780060523084; 9780060523091

LC 2007011852

Walter Dean and Christopher Myers pay "homage to the entire United States in a soul-searching, free-verse poem examining the people, ideals, and promise of America. The verse journeys along a rough historical chronology. . . . Christopher Myers's evocative paintings often juxtapose different eras. . . . Closing notes explicate quotations that lace the pages and identify figures shown in the artwork. . . . Few will be unmoved by this stirring and provocative collaboration." Publ Wkly

Myers, Walter Dean, 1937-2014

★ **Blues** journey; illustrated by Christopher Myers. Holiday House 2003 un il $18.95; pa $8.95

Grades: 4 5 6   **811**

1. Blues music -- Poetry 2. African Americans -- Poetry 3. Poetry -- By individual authors

ISBN 978-0-8234-1613-4; 0-8234-1613-5; 978-0-8234-2079-7 pa; 0-8234-2079-5 pa

LC 2001-16645

"In this picture book for older readers, Myers offers blues-inspired verse that touches on the black-and-blue moments of individual lives. . . . Much of Myers' poetry here is terrific, by turn, sweet, sharp, ironic, but it's the memorable collage artwork, executed in the bluest of blue ink and brown paper, that will draw readers first." Booklist

★ **Harlem**; a poem. pictures by Christopher Myers. Scholastic 1997 un il $16.95

Grades: 5 6 7 8 9 10   **811**

1. African Americans -- Poetry 2. Poetry -- By individual authors 3. Harlem (New York, N.Y.) -- Poetry

ISBN 0-590-54340-7

LC 96-8108

A Caldecott Medal honor book, 1998

A poem celebrating the people, sights, and sounds of Harlem

"Myers's paean to Harlem sings, dances, and swaggers across the pages, conveying the myriad sounds on the streets. . . . Christopher Myers's collages add an edge to his father's words, vividly bringing to life the sights and scenes of Lenox Avenue." Horn Book Guide

★ **Jazz**; illustrated by Christopher Myers. Holiday House 2006 un il $18.95; pa $8.95
Grades: 4 5 6 7   **811**
1. Children's poetry 2. Jazz music -- Poetry 3. Jazz 4. Poetry -- By individual authors
ISBN 0-8234-1545-7; 0-8234-2173-2 pa; 978-0-8234-1545-8; 978-0-8234-2134-2 pa
LC 2005-52639
In poems amd illustrations, this volume depicts "a variety of jazz forms, from New Orleans funerals to bebop, from stride piano to blues. . . . Grades five to eight." (Bull Cent Child Books)

"Walter Dean Myers infuses his lines . . . with so much savvy syncopation that readers can't help but be swept up in the rhythms. . . . Christopher Myers lays black-inked acetate over brilliant, saturated acrylics. The resulting chiaroscuro conjures the deep shadows and lurid reflections of low-lit after-dark jazz clubs." Publ Wkly

Nash, Ogden
★ **Lineup** for yesterday; illustrated by C. F. Payne. Creative Editions 2011 55p il $19.99
Grades: 3 4 5 6   **811**
1. Alphabet 2. Baseball -- Poetry 3. Poetry -- By individual authors
ISBN 978-1-56846-212-7; 1-56846-212-3
LC 2010040121
"Baseball legends of yesteryear come alive more or less alphabetically in Nash's pithy verses. Twenty-four players of the first half of the 20th century are profiled in playful, humorous short poems with an ABCB rhyme scheme. . . . The verses are accompanied by statistical information and delightful, large-scale, closeup depictions of the players in action, rendered by Payne in layers of colored pencil, acrylics, water colors and a variety of other media. . . . Following each group of three or four verses, and headed by a diminutive version of the appropriate illustration, Nash's daughter Linell Nash Smith provides more detailed information about each player. She also contributes a charming introduction." Kirkus

Nelson, Marilyn, 1946-
★ **Sweethearts** of rhythm; the story of the greatest all-girl swing band in the world. written by Marilyn Nelson; illustrated by Jerry Pinkney. Dial Books 2009 un il $21.99
Grades: 4 5 6 7   **811**
1. Women musicians 2. Jazz music -- Poetry 3. Jazz 4. Poetry -- By individual authors 5. Young adult 6. International Sweethearts of Rhythm
ISBN 0-8037-3187-6; 978-0-8037-3187-5
LC 2008-46255
This is a study of the racially mixed group the International Sweethearts of Rhythm. Bibliography. "Grades six to nine." (Bull Cent Child Books)
"On all fronts, a resonant performance." Publ Wkly

Nesbitt, Kenn
My hippo has the hiccups; and other poems I totally made up. illustrated by Ethan Long. Sourcebooks Jabberwocky 2009 155p il $17.99
Grades: 2 3 4   **811**
1. Poetry -- By individual authors
ISBN 978-1-4022-1809-5; 1-4022-1809-5
LC 2008-48478
"This is a zany and at times challenging volume of more than 100 poems, 39 of which are read by the author on an accompanying CD. Nesbitt's consistent rhythms and unforced rhymes make these poems readable . . . [and] Long's spare line illustrations add humorous touches. This will be a popular addition to most collections." SLJ

Nye, Naomi Shihab
Come with me; poems for a journey. images by Dan Yaccarino. Greenwillow Bks. 2000 32p il $15.95; lib bdg $15.89
Grades: 3 4 5 6   **811**
1. Poetry -- By individual authors
ISBN 0-688-15946-X; 0-688-15947-8 lib bdg
LC 99-34164
"Sixteen poems depict different aspects of going places: subjects include imaginary voyages, the pace of travel, arrival in new places, the trajectory of words, and personal journeys of growth. . . . Nye uses sophisticated metaphor and oblique evocations of emotion in simple and concrete phraseology, making the poems conceptually challenging yet literarily accessible. The visuals are bold and dramatic, making excellent use of collage and mixed media." Bull Cent Child Books

O'Neill, Mary Le Duc
Hailstones and halibut bones; adventures in color. newly illustrated by John Wallner. Doubleday 1989 un il $15.95; pa $9.95
Grades: K 1 2 3   **811**
1. Color -- Poetry 2. Poetry -- By individual authors
ISBN 978-0-385-24484-8; 0-385-24484-3; 978-0-385-41078-6 pa; 0-385-41078-6 pa
LC 88-484
A newly illustrated edition of the title first published 1961
Twelve poems reflect the author's feelings about various colors
"Wallner has created montages of each poem's images and colored them with various hues of the featured color. The results do complement the moods of the poems." SLJ

Ode, Eric
When you're a pirate dog and other pirate poems; Eric Ode, Jim Harris. Pelican Pub. 2012 40 p.
Grades: 1 2 3   **811**
1. Humorous poetry 2. Children's poetry 3. Pirates -- Poetry 4. Children's poetry, American
ISBN 1455614939; 9781455614936; 9781455614943
LC 2011036785
This children's poetry collection by Eric Ode, illustrated by Jim Harris, is centered on pirates. "Pirates find their literary voices in this rollicking romp on the salty seas. Hilarity ensues as they go about their tasks narrated in poetry and song. The jolly illustrations bring their adventures, above and below decks, to life. See all their silly exploits in this swashbuckling adventure!" (Publisher's note)

Paolilli, Paul

Silver seeds; a book of nature poems. by Paul Paolilli and Dan Brewer; paintings by Steve Johnson and Lou Fancher. Viking 2001 un il $15.99; pa $6.99

Grades: K 1 2 3   **811**

1. Nature poetry 2. Poetry -- By individual authors

ISBN 0-670-88941-5; 0-14-250010-0 pa

LC 00-9469

"Paolilli and Brewer have selected 15 . . . words on which to build nature poems. The first letter of the first word in each line of a poem is part of another word that is the title (or subject) of the poem." Booklist

Park, Linda Sue

★ **Tap** dancing on the roof; sijo (poems) illustrated by Istvan Banyai. Clarion Books 2007 un il $16

Grades: 4 5 6   **811**

1. Sijo 2. Poetry -- By individual authors

ISBN 978-0-618-23483-7; 0-618-23483-7

LC 2006-24901

Park's "sijo skip lightly from breakfast . . . to bedtime . . . with excursions to the backyard, the classroom, and the beach. . . . The sijo's contours are clean and spare, qualities echoed in the blue-gray, black and white architecture and crisp shadows of Banyai's . . . digital illustrations." Publ Wkly

Peters, Lisa Westberg

★ **Earthshake**; poems from the ground up. pictures by Cathie Felstead. Greenwillow Bks. 2003 32p il $16.99; lib bdg $17.89

Grades: 3 4 5   **811**

1. Geology -- Poetry 2. Poetry -- By individual authors

ISBN 0-06-029265-2; 0-06-029266-0 lib bdg

LC 2002-32177

Presents twenty-two poems about geology. End notes provide information about the earth's surface and interior, types of rocks, and how volcanoes, glaciers, and erosion modify the landscape

"Exuberant, silly, and serious by turns, the selections engage imagination with often-humorous wordplay. The simple yet clever collages, many of which incorporate clip-art elements, deepen the intellectual and emotional content, yet keep a light tone." SLJ

Volcano wakes up! illustrated by Steve Jenkins. Henry Holt and Company 2010 un il $16.99

Grades: 2 3 4   **811**

1. Hawaii -- Poetry 2. Volcanoes -- Poetry 3. Poetry -- By individual authors

ISBN 0805082875; 9780805082876; 978-0-8050-8287-6; 0-8050-8287-5

LC 2008-38225

"Personified features of a Hawaiian landscape speak in verse during a day in the life of a waking volcano, rendered in Jenkins's atmospheric trademark cut-paper collages. . . . A humorous, imaginative, and artful concept."

"Personified features of a Hawaiian landscape speak in verse during a day in the life of a waking volcano, rendered in Jenkins's atmospheric trademark cut-paper collages. . . . A humorous, imaginative, and artful concept." Publ Wkly

★ The **Place** my words are looking for; what poets say about and through their work. selected by Paul B. Janeczko. Bradbury Press 1990 150p il $17.95

Grades: 4 5 6 7   **811**

1. Poetics 2. American poetry -- Collections

ISBN 0-02-747671-5

LC 89-39331

"More than forty contemporary poets are included: Eve Merriam, X. J. Kennedy, Felice Holman, Gary Soto, Mark Vinz, Karla Kuskin, and John Updike, among others. Their contributions vary widely in theme and mood and style, though the preponderance of the pieces are written in modern idiom and unrhymed meter. The accompanying comments frequently are as insightful and eloquent as the poems themselves." Horn Book

Poetry speaks to children; editor, Elise Paschen; illustrators, Judy Love, Wendy Rasmussen, Paula Zinngrabe Wendland. Sourcebooks 2005 104p il $19.95

Grades: 3 4 5 6   **811**

1. American poetry -- Collections

ISBN 1-4022-0329-2; 978-1-4022-0329-9

"A fine, basic collection. Approximately half of the 97 selections are read or performed on the accompanying CD. The book provides a mix of adult writers (Rita Dove, Seamus Heaney, and Billy Collins, among others) and those whose work is specifically for children, such as X. J. Kennedy and Mary Ann Hoberman. Topics include childhood, animals, nonsense poems, and humor. . . . The three illustrators have captured the different tones of the selections." SLJ

★ A **Poke** in the I; [selected by] Paul Janeczko; illustrated by Chris Raschka. Candlewick Press 2001 35p il hardcover o.p. pa $7.99

Grades: 4 5 6 7 8 9 10   **811**

1. American poetry -- Collections

ISBN 0-7636-0661-8; 0-7636-2376-8 pa

LC 00-33675

"Thirty concrete poems of all shapes and sizes are carefully laid on large white spreads, extended by Raschka's quirky watercolor and paper-collage illustrations. . . . Beautiful and playful, this title should find use in storytimes, in the classroom, and just for pleasure anywhere." SLJ

Prelutsky, Jack, 1940-

Be glad your nose is on your face and other poems; some of the best of Jack Prelutsky. illustrated by Brandon Dorman. Greenwillow Books 2008 194p il $22.99

Grades: PreK K 1 2 3   **811**

1. Poetry -- By individual authors

ISBN 978-0-06-157653-9; 0-06-157653-0

LC 2008013371

"This fat, sunny volume brings together 112 of Prelutsky's poems. Most are old favorites from the past four decades, but 15 of them have never been published before. Kicking off with a letter from the poet, the book contains five sections, each concluding with a page of activities such as word games and drawing prompts. Digital illustrations with lavish details and colors stand out nicely from the ample white space. . . . A CD features the author reading 30 of the poems to a . . . musical accompaniment." SLJ

★ **Behold** the bold umbrellaphant; and other poems. illustrations by Carin Berger. Greenwillow Books 2006 31p il $16.99; lib bdg $17.89

Grades: 3 4 5 6 **811**

1. Humorous poetry 2. Poetry -- By individual authors
ISBN 978-0-06-054317-4; 0-06-054317-5; 978-0-06-054318-1 lib bdg; 0-06-054318-3 lib bdg

LC 2005-22185

Each poem in this collection "is about a creature that is part animal and part inanimate object. For instance, the Alarmadillos have alarm clocks for bodies, and the Ballpoint Penguins can write with their beaks. The poems are full of fun and wit, with wordplay and meter that never miss a beat. The whimsical illustrations use cut-print media, old-fashioned print images, and a variety of paper textures to create a rich visual treat well suited to the poetry." SLJ

★ The **carnival** of the animals; music by Camille Saint-Saëns; new verses by Jack Prelutsky; illustrated by Mary GrandPré; with a fully orchestrated CD of the Camille Saint-Saëns music. Alfred A. Knopf 2010 un $19.99; lib bdg $22.99

Grades: 2 3 4 5 **811**

1. Animals -- Poetry 2. Poetry -- By individual authors
ISBN 978-0-375-86458-2; 0-375-86458-X; 978-0-375-96458-9 lib bdg; 0-375-96458-4 lib bdg

LC 2009008734

This is an illustrated collection of verses inspired by Camille Saint-Saens' musical suite The carnival of the animals.

"This delightful collection of new poems . . . serves as both helpful libretto and stand-alone treasure. The poems correlate to the animal-themed movements and neatly capture each creature's essence. . . . GrandPré's . . . vibrant acrylic and paper collage scenes exude the same imaginative insight. . . . An accompanying CD contains music performed by the Württemberg Chamber Orchestra and poems read by Prelutsky." Publ Wkly

★ The **dragons** are singing tonight; pictures by Peter Sis. Greenwillow Bks. 1993 39p il $16; pa $6.95

Grades: 2 3 4 5 **811**

1. Dragons -- Poetry 2. Poetry -- By individual authors
ISBN 0-688-09645-X; 0-688-12511-5 lib bdg; 0-688-16162-6 pa

LC 92-29013

"Dragons are verbally and visually portrayed in this collection with wonder, whimsy, and a touch of wistfulness. . . . The oil and gouache paintings on a gesso background have marvelous details and unexpected bursts of humor." SLJ

★ The **frogs** wore red suspenders; rhymes by Jack Prelutsky; pictures by Petra Mathers. Greenwillow Bks. 2002 63p il $16.95; lib bdg $16.89; pa $6.99

Grades: K 1 2 3 **811**

1. Nursery rhymes 2. Nonsense verses 3. Poetry -- By individual authors
ISBN 0-688-16719-5; 0-688-16720-9 lib bdg; 0-06-073776-X pa

LC 00-68128

A collection of 28 "lighthearted poems, many of which invoke place names in the United States. . . . The mild humor lies not in the action but in Prelutsky's deft use of language, particularly effective shared aloud. The result is enjoyable, but it is Petra Mathers's illustrations that make the book memorable. Demurely naive, her cheerful, delicately delineated human and animal characters focus on their activities with becoming modesty and grace." Horn Book

★ **Good** sports; illustrated by Chris Raschka. Alfred A. Knopf 2007 un il $16.99; lib bdg $19.99

Grades: 2 3 4 5 **811**

1. Sports -- Poetry 2. Poetry -- By individual authors
ISBN 978-0-375-83700-5; 978-0-375-93700-2 lib bdg

LC 2006-05092

"This picture book uses poetry to express the physical sensations and wide-ranging emotions of participating in sports. Prelutsky's smoothly rhyming quatrains, ideal for recitation, cover team sports . . . as well as several individual ones and celebrate disciplined efforts as exuberantly as noncompetitive play. . . . Raschka's watercolors extend the high-energy verses without overwhelming them." Booklist

Includes bibliographical references

★ The **Headless** Horseman rides tonight; more poems to trouble your sleep. illustrated by Arnold Lobel. Greenwillow Bks. 1980 38p il hardcover o.p. pa $6.99

Grades: 2 3 4 5 **811**

1. Monsters -- Poetry 2. Poetry -- By individual authors
ISBN 0-688-11705-8 pa

LC 80-10372

The author's "rhymes are as lethal, lithe, and literate as ever and Lobel wrings every atmospheric ounce out of them." SLJ

★ **I've** lost my hippopotamus; Jack Prelutsky; illustrations by Jackie Urbanovic. 1st ed. Greenwillow Books 2012 143 p. ill. (trade bdg.) $18.99; (lib. bdg.) $19.89

Grades: K 1 2 3 4 5 **811**

1. Humorous poetry 2. Animals -- Poetry 3. Children's poetry 4. Humorous poetry, American 5. Children's poetry, American
ISBN 0062014579; 9780062014573; 9780062014580

LC 2011002636

This children's book by Jack Prelutsky, illustrated by Jackie Urbanovic, offers "more than 100 . . . poems that poke holes in the serious facade of the adult world. A snake performs arithmetic, a boy is puzzled by the rainstorm in his bedroom, . . . and a thirsty centipede drinks too much water." (Publishers Weekly)

If not for the cat; haiku by Jack Prelutsky; paintings by Ted Rand. Greenwillow Books 2004 40p il $16.99; lib bdg $17.89

Grades: 1 2 3 4 **811**

1. Haiku 2. Animals -- Poetry 3. Poetry -- By individual authors
ISBN 0-06-059677-5; 0-06-059678-3 lib bdg

LC 2003-17064

"Each of the 17 haiku in this collection explores the essence of an animal, the words forming a sort of riddle answered in Rand's accompanying double-page illustration. . . . Prelutsky shows his command of word choice through a minimalist form that is perfectly matched by Rand's control of his mixed-media artwork to create a wonderful celebration of the art of haiku." SLJ

★ **It's** Christmas! by Jack Prelutsky; pictures by Marylin Hafner. HarperCollins Publishers 2008 46p il (I can read!) $16.99

Grades: K 1 2 3 **811**

1. Christmas -- Poetry 2. Poetry -- By individual authors
ISBN 978-0-06-053706-7; 0-06-053706-X

LC 2007040112

A newly illustrated edition of the title first published 1981 by Greenwillow Books

This collection of Christmas poems covers such topics as Christmas trees, mistletoe, Santa Claus, a Christmas play, and gifts.

"Hafner's line-and-watercolor pictures illustrate the bouncing, rhyming words in clear, playful holiday scenes." Booklist

★ **It's** snowing! it's snowing! winter poems. illustrated by Yossi Abolafia. HarperCollins Pubs. 2006 48p il (I can read book) $15.99; lib bdg $16.89

Grades: 1 2 3 **811**

1. Winter -- Poetry 2. Poetry -- By individual authors
ISBN 0-06-053715-9; 0-06-053716-7 lib bdg

A newly illustrated edition of the title first published 1984 by Greenwillow Bks.

A collection of short poems about winter

"The sounds of the rhyming words are as much fun as the snow action in these 16 poems . . . accompanied by exuberant line-and-watercolor illustrations that capture all the play in the cold." Booklist

★ **It's** Thanksgiving! by Jack Prelutsky; pictures by Marylin Hafner. HarperCollins 2007 44p il (I can read!) $15.99; lib bdg $16.89

Grades: 1 2 3 **811**

1. Thanksgiving Day -- Poetry 2. Poetry -- By individual authors
ISBN 978-0-06-053710-4; 978-0-06-053709-8 lib bdg

LC 2007014465

First published 1982 by Greenwillow Books

A collection of twelve Thanksgiving Day poems

★ **It's** Valentine's Day; pictures by Yossi Abolafia. Greenwillow Bks. 1983 47p il (Greenwillow read-alone books) hardcover o.p. pa $5.95

Grades: 1 2 3 **811**

1. Valentine's Day -- Poetry 2. Poetry -- By individual authors
ISBN 0-688-14652-X pa

LC 83-1449

"The 14 poems here range from the genuine joy of 'It's Valentine's Day' . . , to the giddy goofiness of 'I love you more than applesauce' or 'Jelly Jill loves Weasel Will'. . . . The rhymes are generally simple but clever and the line drawings in red and blue, with their expressive faces and explanatory vignettes, add tremendously to the enjoyment of the poetry." SLJ

★ **My** dog may be a genius; poems. [drawings by James Stevenson] Greenwillow Books 2008 159p il $18.99; lib bdg $19.89

Grades: 2 3 4 5 **811**

1. Children's poetry, American. 2. Poetry -- By

individual authors
ISBN 978-0-06-623862-3; 978-0-06-623863-0 lib bdg

LC 2007-19462

"Prelutsky has created yet another volume of short poems with guaranteed child appeal. Again he has assembled a zany cast of imaginary creatures and machines. . . . Prelutsky plays with language and does not shy away from challenging vocabulary. . . . Stevenson's simple signature drawings capture the spirit of each poem with just the right amount of illustration." SLJ

★ The **new** kid on the block: poems; drawings by James Stevenson. Greenwillow Bks. 1984 159p il $17.95; lib bdg $17.93

Grades: 3 4 5 6 **811**

1. Humorous poetry 2. Poetry -- By individual authors
ISBN 0-688-02271-5; 0-688-02272-3 lib bdg

LC 83-20621

"The author's rollicking, silly poems bounce and romp with fun; Stevenson's cartoon-like sketches capture the hilarity with equal skill. A book everyone will enjoy dipping into." Child Book Rev Serv

★ **Nightmares**: poems to trouble your sleep; illustrated by Arnold Lobel. Greenwillow Bks. 1976 38p il lib bdg $17.89

Grades: 2 3 4 5 **811**

1. Monsters -- Poetry 2. Poetry -- By individual authors
ISBN 0-688-84053-1

LC 76-4820

This "collection of poems is calculated to evoke icy apprehension, and the poems about wizards, bogeymen, ghouls, ogres (well, one poem apiece to each or to others of their ilk) are exaggerated just enough to bring simultaneous grins and shudders. Prelutsky uses words with relish and his rhyme and rhythm are, as usual, deft. Lobel's illustrations are equally adroit, macabre yet elegant." Bull Cent Child Books

★ A **pizza** the size of the sun; poems by Jack Prelutsky; drawings by James Stevenson. Greenwillow Bks. 1996 159p il $18; lib bdg $17.93

Grades: 3 4 5 6 **811**

1. Humorous poetry 2. Poetry -- By individual authors
ISBN 0-688-13235-9; 0-688-13236-7 lib bdg

LC 95-35930

This collection of humorous poems is "filled with zany people, improbable creatures, and rhythm and rhyme galore, all combining to celebrate the unusual, the mundane, and the slightly gruesome. . . . Each page is brimming with Stevenson's complementary, droll watercolors, reproduced here in black and white." SLJ

★ **Ride** a purple pelican; pictures by Garth Williams. Greenwillow Bks. 1986 64p il $17.95; pa $7.95

Grades: K 1 2 3 **811**

1. Nursery rhymes 2. Nonsense verses 3. Poetry -- By individual authors
ISBN 0-688-04031-4; 0-688-15625-8 pa

LC 84-6024

A collection of short nonsense verses and nursery rhymes

"Prelutsky has caught the rhythm and spirit of nursery rhymes in 29 short poems about drum-beating bunnies, bullfrogs on parade, Chicago winds, giant sequoias and other wondrous things. Many of these easy-to-remember poems are filled with delicious sounding American and Canadian place names. Garth Williams' full-color, full-page illustrations are good complements to the poems. Highly recommended." Child Book Rev Serv

Scranimals; poems by Jack Prelutsky; pictures by Peter Sis. Greenwillow Bks. 2002 40p il $16.99; lib bdg $18.89

Grades: 2 3 4 5   811
1. Nonsense verses 2. Poetry -- By individual authors
ISBN 0-688-17819-7; 0-688-17820-0 lib bdg
LC 2001-23620

"The verse sparkles with wit and mad invention. . . . Sis' art picks up on the strange and otherworldly aspects of the poems, evincing a surreal and haunting edge to its intricately lined visions." Bull Cent Child Books

★ **Something** big has been here; drawings by James Stevenson. Greenwillow Bks. 1990 160p il $17.95

Grades: 3 4 5   811
1. Humorous poetry 2. Poetry -- By individual authors
ISBN 0-688-06434-5
LC 89-34773

An illustrated collection of humorous poems on a variety of topics

"Puns and verbal surprises abound. Clever use of alliteration and abundant variety in the sound and texture of words add to the pleasure. . . . Stevenson's small cartoons of snaggle-toothed animals and deadpan children extend and expand the mad humor of the poems, supporting but never overwhelming their good-natured fun. A fine prescription against the blues at any time of year." Horn Book

★ **Stardines** swim high across the sky and other poems; by Jack Prelutsky; illustrations by Carin Berger. Greenwillow Books 2012 40 p.

Grades: K 1 2 3   811
1. Children's poetry, American 2. Imaginary creatures
ISBN 9780062014641; 9780062014658
LC 2011025993

This children's poetry collection, by Jack Prelutsky, illustrated by Carin Berger, presents lyric descriptions of two dozen imaginary "creatures of animal and inanimate origin. . . . Procrastinating pandas, self-adhering geese and cacophonous magpies are a few of the carefully selected creatures on display . . . ," embellished by multi-media dioramas by Berger. (Kirkus Reviews)

The **swamps** of Sleethe; poems from beyond the solar system. illustrated by Jimmy Pickering. Alfred A. Knopf 2009 un il $16.99; lib bdg $19.99

Grades: 3 4 5 6   811
1. Extrasolar planets -- Poetry 2. Poetry -- By individual authors 3. Extraterrestrial beings -- Poetry
ISBN 978-0-375-84674-8; 0-375-84674-3; 978-0-375-94674-5 lib bdg; 0-375-94674-8 lib bdg
LC 2008006530

"Nineteen poems with jaunty rhythms lure readers to some very menacing planets. Almost all tell of the horrors to be found in worlds beyond our solar system. . . . Dark colors with sharp contrasts help define these worlds in mixed-

media illustrations. Some of the unusual planet names are anagrams to solve with answers in the back of the book. Science-fiction and poetry lovers should unite over this slim and entertaining volume." SLJ

★ **Tyrannosaurus** was a beast; illustrated by Arnold Lobel. Greenwillow Bks. 1988 31p il hardcover o.p. pa $6.99

Grades: 2 3 4 5   811
1. Dinosaurs -- Poetry 2. Poetry -- By individual authors
ISBN 0-688-06443-4 lib bdg; 0-688-11569-1 pa
LC 87-25131

A collection of humorous poems about dinosaurs

"Fourteen dinosaurs meet their match in this outstanding author/illustrator team. While Prelutsky's short, pithy, often witty verses sum up their essential characters, Lobel's line and watercolor portraits bring the beasts to life, enormous yet endearingly vulnerable." Booklist

★ **What** a day it was at school! poems by Jack Prelutsky; pictures by Doug Cushman. Greenwillow Books 2006 39p il $15.99; lib bdg $16.89

Grades: K 1 2 3   811
1. Schools -- Poetry 2. Poetry -- By individual authors
ISBN 978-0-06-082336-8; 0-06-082336-4; 978-0-06-082335-1 lib bdg; 0-06-082335-6 lib bdg
LC 2005-48968

"Cushman has interpreted Prelutsky's school-aged protagonist as a cat. The feline's journal contains 17 poems about everyday joys and predicaments. . . . Lively and fun, with perfect meter and an abundance of interesting word choices, these poems beg to be read aloud. And they will be. Cushman has created an appealing school environment with a variety of colorful cartoon animal characters that are happily compatible with Prelutsky's silly and energetic verse." SLJ

Raczka, Bob
★ **Guyku**; a year of haiku for boys. illustrated by Peter H. Reynolds. Houghton 2010 un il

Grades: 1 2 3   811
1. Haiku 2. Children's poetry 3. Boys -- Poetry 4. Seasons -- Poetry 5. Poetry -- By individual authors
ISBN 0547240031; 9780547240039
Claudia Lewis Award for Poetry, 2011

This is a collection of seventeen-syllable poems about a boy's life. "Primary." (Horn Book)

"The poems in this picture-book collection capture natural moments that boys, and many girls, have while playing outdoors. Each season is addressed, and moments like riding bikes in the spring with baseball cards attached to the wheels to mimic the sound of a motorcycle almost define spring. . . . The artwork and the text dovetail beautifully and help set the inquisitive and playful intent of the poems. . . . This wonderful collection will resonate with all children. . . . The pen, ink, and watercolor illustrations mirror the simplicity of each entry and capture the expressions of the boys and their adventures honestly." SLJ

★ **Lemonade**, and other poems squeezed from a single word; illustrations by Nancy Doniger. Roaring Brook Press 2011 43p il

Grades: 2 3 4 5 **811**

1. Children's poetry 2. Poetry -- By individual authors
ISBN 1596435410; 9781596435414

LC 2010-24807

"Each poem is displayed in two formats, first a patterned visual that . . . aligns the letters in each word under the relevant titular letter, . . . and then a simple one-word-per-line arrangement. . . . Grades three to seven." (Bull Cent Child Books)

"Raczka offers an accessible, playful poetry collection. . . . Doniger's spare illustrations add quirky appeal without distracting from the inventive formations of type." Booklist

★ The **Random** House book of poetry for children; selected and introduced by Jack Prelutsky; illustrated by Arnold Lobel. Random House 1983 248p il $19.95; lib bdg $21.99

Grades: 3 4 5 6 **811**

1. English poetry -- Collections 2. American poetry -- Collections
ISBN 0-394-85010-6; 0-394-95010-0 lib bdg

LC 83-2990

In this anthology emphasis "is placed on humor and light verse; but serious and thoughtful poems are also included. . . . Approximately two thirds of the selections were written within the past forty years—the splendid contributions of such writers as John Ciardi, Aileen Fisher, Dennis Lee, Myra Cohn Livingston, David McCord, Eve Merriam, and Lilian Moore. [There are] . . . samplings of earlier poets from Shakespeare and Blake to Emily Dickinson and Walter de la Mare." Horn Book

★ **Read** a rhyme, write a rhyme; poems selected by Jack Prelutsky; illustrated by Meilo So. Alfred A. Knopf 2005 23p il $16.95

Grades: 2 3 4 **811**

1. Poetics 2. American poetry -- Collections
ISBN 0-375-82286-0

LC 2004-26501

"Prelutsky designed this collection to jumpstart children's creative juices. Three short poems were chosen for each theme: dogs, food, birthdays, bugs, cows, friends, snow, turtles, rain, and self. He also includes a poemstart: an unfinished verse, along with advice and lists of rhyming words, so that readers can complete the poem on their own. The compiler displays a fine sense for lighthearted, kid-friendly poetry. . . . So's watercolor-and-ink illustrations add playfully jumbled perspectives." SLJ

★ **Read**-aloud rhymes for the very young; selected by Jack Prelutsky; illustrated by Marc Brown; with an introduction by Jim Trelease. Knopf 1986 98p il $19.95; lib bdg $21.99

Grades: K 1 2 **811**

1. Nursery rhymes 2. English poetry -- Collections 3. American poetry -- Collections
ISBN 0-394-87218-5; 0-394-97218-X lib bdg

LC 86-7147

"Prelutsky has selected and combined joyous, sensitive poems . . . by such traditional poets as Dorothy Aldis and A. A. Milne, as well as by more contemporary poets such as Karla Kuskin, Dennis Lee, and Prelutsky himself. All are lively, rhythmic poems that young children will enjoy. . . . Brown's bright pastel illustrations effectively use fram-

ing, action, and cheerful creatures to echo the light tone of the book. The poems are arranged with others of the same topic and include popular concerns of small children such as animals, bath time, dragons, and play. Teachers and librarians will appreciate poems about seasons, months, holidays, and special events that can be easily incorporated into story hours and classroom life." SLJ

Rex, Adam

★ **Frankenstein** makes a sandwich. Harcourt 2006 40p il $16

Grades: 2 3 4 5 **811**

1. Monsters -- Poetry 2. Poetry -- By individual authors
ISBN 0-15-205766-8

LC 2005-13678

A collection of humorous poems about monsters such as Frankenstein, The Creature from the Black Lagoon, Count Dracula, The Invisible Man, Godzilla, and The Phantom of the Opera

"Told with smooth, unstrained rhymes, each selection captures its subject's voice. Rex uses an impressive variety of techniques and media in the artwork while paying homage to famed illustrators. . . . The book is fresh, creative, and funny, with just enough gory detail to cause a few gasps." SLJ

★ **Frankenstein** takes the cake. Harcourt 2008 39p il lib bdg $16

Grades: 2 3 4 5 **811**

1. Monsters -- Poetry 2. Poetry -- By individual authors
ISBN 978-0-15-206235-4 lib bdg; 0-15-206235-1 lib bdg

LC 2007-44634

Frankenstein wants to marry his undead bride in peace, but his best man, Dracula, is freaking out about the garlic bread, and the Headless Horseman wishes everyone would stop drooling over his pumpkin head.

"With maniacal glee, Rex . . . delivers spot-on rhymes about B-movie monsters, loosely organized around the nuptials of Frankenstein and his bride. . . . Rex's eclectic imagery and freewheeling verse will have readers going back for seconds." Publ Wkly

Rockwell, Thomas

Emily Stew; with some side dishes. illustrated by David McPhail. Roaring Brook Press 2010 43p il $16.99

Grades: 2 3 4 5 **811**

1. Poetry -- By individual authors
ISBN 978-1-59643-336-6; 1-59643-336-1

This is "a wildly inventive poetic portrait of a riveting character who's made up—rather literally—of a stew of contradictions. Moody and prone to the most erratic behavior, Emily is depicted in these playful rhymed vignettes as an eccentric yet eminently recognizable and likable young creature. . . . McPhail's pen-and-ink spot art helps capture the defiant Emily as she asserts her individuality in scenes ranging from dancing with a fish to being eaten by a tiger." Kirkus

Rosen, Michael J.

★ The **cuckoo's** haiku; and other birding poems. illustrated by Stan Fellows. Candlewick Press 2009 un il $17.99

Grades: 2 3 4 **811**

1. Haiku 2. Birds -- Poetry 3. Poetry -- By individual

authors
ISBN 978-0-7636-3049-2; 0-7636-3049-7

LC 2008-21417

"A rare gift for young and old alike, this exquisite book about birds combines delicate verses and stunning watercolors that celebrate the natural world. Designed as if it were a birder's notebook, the book provides an intriguing haiku for each bird, dazzling paintings of the species in their habitats, as well as notes about their behaviors and traits." Publ Wkly

★ The **Hound** dog's haiku; and other poems for dog lovers. [illustrated by] Mary Azarian. Candlewick Press 2011 56p il

Grades: 2 3 4   **811**
1. Haiku 2. Dogs -- Poetry 3. Poetry -- By individual authors
ISBN 0-7636-4499-4; 978-0-7636-4499-4

"These delightful selections will engage haiku composers and dog lovers. . . . Twenty canines are represented, with each dog given a fully illustrated spread; the breed's name is in large letters and the haiku on the opposing page is in a smaller font. Endnotes take the form of visual avatars culled from the illustrations, with a short paragraph about the breed. Fetch this title full of wordplay, creative romps, and pet prompts for a fun read." SLJ

Ruddell, Deborah
The **popcorn** astronauts; and other biteable rhymes. Deborah Ruddell; illustrated by Joan Rankin. Margaret K. McElderry Books 2015 40 p. (hardcover) $17.99

Grades: PreK K 1 2 3 4   **811.6**
1. Food -- Poetry 2. Children's poetry
ISBN 1442465557; 9781442465558

LC 2013037332

In this children's book, author Deborah Ruddell presents a "cheerful collection of delicious seasonal poems, each one an ode to a favorite food! . . . In spring, bow to the 'Strawberry Queen' and eat 'Only Guacamole.' In summer you'll meet Bob the Ogre, who only eats corn on the cob, and in fall, you can learn '21 Things to Do with an Apple.' And then in winter, retreat from the cold at 'The Cocoa Cabana!'" (Publisher's note)

★ A **whiff** of pine, a hint of skunk; a forest of poems. illustrated by Joan Rankin. Margaret K. McElderry Books 2009 un il $16.99

Grades: 3 4 5   **811**
1. Nature poetry 2. Forest animals -- Poetry 3. Poetry -- By individual authors
ISBN 978-1-4169-4211-5; 1-4169-4211-4

LC 2007-38023

"Twenty-three evocative poems about forest animals, beautifully illustrated. Literary variety serves this collection well, with many different lengths, rhyme schemes and moods. The common elements in Ruddell's verse are economy and an observer's respect for her subjects. . . . Similarly, Rankin's watercolors show respect via their accuracy and detail, while still capturing the various flavors of the poems." Kirkus

Salas, Laura Purdie
Bookspeak! poems about books. written by Laura Purdie Salas; illustrated by Josée Bisaillon. Clarion Books 2011 un il $16.99

Grades: PreK K 1 2   **811**
1. Books and reading -- Poetry 2. Poetry -- By individual authors
ISBN 978-0-547-22300-1; 0-547-22300-5

LC 2010043173

"This collection of poems makes its message clear: books are where it's at. Sala's polished verse demonstrates a deep love for all aspects of books. . . . Bisaillon's mixed media illustrations are dizzyingly inventive, their bright colors, sampling of typography, and whimsical details underscoring the idea of the potential that awaits between the covers." Publ Wkly

San Jose, Christine
Every second something happens; poems for the mind and senses. selected by Christine San José and Bill Johnson; illustrations by Melanie Hall. Wordsong 2009 48p il $17.95

Grades: PreK K 1 2   **811**
1. American poetry -- Collections
ISBN 978-1-59078-622-2; 1-59078-622-X

LC 2008024115

"Fun for reading aloud, the very short verses in this collection are easy, rhythmic, and immediate. Some are written by young kids and some by children's poets, and there are even a few lines from Shakespeare. . . . Hall's clear colorful illustrations never overwhelm the words as they show kids in action." Booklist

Scanlon, Liz Garton
★ **All** the world; illustrated by Marla Frazee. Beach Lane Books 2009 un il $17.99

Grades: PreK K 1   **811**
1. Beaches -- Poetry 2. Family life -- Poetry 3. Poetry -- By individual authors
ISBN 978-1-4169-8580-8; 1-4169-8580-8

LC 2008-51057

ALA ALSC Caldecott Medal Honor Book (2010)

"Charming illustrations and lyrical rhyming couplets speak volumes in celebration of the world and humankind, combining to create a lovely book that will be appreciated by a wide audience. The pictures, made with black Prismacolor pencil and watercolors, primarily follow a multicultural family from a summer morning on the beach through a busy day and night." SLJ

Schertle, Alice
★ **Button** up! [illustrations by] Petra Mathers. Harcourt 2009 33p il $16

Grades: PreK K 1 2   **811**
1. Animals -- Poetry 2. Clothing and dress -- Poetry 3. Poetry -- By individual authors
ISBN 978-0-15-205050-4; 0-15-205050-7

LC 2007-42839

An illustrated collection of poetry features animals wearing an array of shoes, jackets, hats, and other fun attire to demonstrate their unique personalities.

"Mathers' charming watercolors show a variety of decked out animals in vignettes and double-page spreads that add to the humor. . . . The whimsical illustrations pair perfectly with the wittiness of the text, and the whole is a clever and original poetic treat." Booklist

Scieszka, Jon

Truckery rhymes; written by Jon Scieszka; characters and environments developed by the Design Garage David Shannon, Loren Long, David Gordon. Simon & Schuster Books for Young Readers 2009 57p il $17.99

Grades: PreK K 1 2 3 **811**

1. Nursery rhymes 2. Trucks -- Poetry 3. Poetry -- By individual authors

ISBN 978-1-4169-4135-4; 1-4169-4135-5

LC 2007037439

"This collection of lively truck-themed 'Mother Goose' rhymes is filled with humor. . . . The digital illustrations are colorful, energetic, and playful: the vehicles have personality plus. . . . This effervescent picture book will zoom off your shelves." SLJ

Sendak, Maurice, 1928-2012

★ **My** brother's book; Maurice Sendak; [edited by] Michael di Capua. HarperCollins 2013 32 p. (hardcover bdg.) $18.95

Grades: 4 5 6 7 8 **811**

1. Poetry 2. Poetry -- Collections

ISBN 0062234897; 9780062234896

LC 2012942549

In this book, "with influences from Shakespeare and William Blake, [Maurice] Sendak pays homage to his late brother, Jack, whom he credited for his passion for writing and drawing. Pairing Sendak's . . . poetry with his . . . artwork, . . . Sendak's tribute to his brother is an expression of both grief and love. . . . Pulitzer Prize--winning literary critic and Shakespearean scholar Stephen Greenblatt contributes a[n] . . . introduction." (Publisher's note)

Service, Robert W.

★ **The** cremation of Sam McGee; by Robert W. Service; paintings by Ted Harrison; introduction by Pierre Berton. 20th anniversary ed.; Kids Can Press 2006 un il $17.95

Grades: 4 5 6 7 **811**

1. Yukon Territory -- Poetry 2. Poetry -- By individual authors

ISBN 978-1-55453-092-2; 1-55453-092-X

Text first published 1907. This is a reissue of the edition first published 1986 in Canada and 1987 in the United States by Greenwillow Bks.

This poem "has gripped readers and listeners for decades. . . . [The illustrator] obviously appreciates the humor inherent in the text. . . . As Pierre Berton observes in his introduction, [Harrison's] 'style is unique: part Oriental, part native American, part Ted Harrison.'" Horn Book

Shange, Ntozake

★ **Freedom's** a-callin' me; poems by Ntozake Shange; paintings by Rod Brown. Amistad/Collins 2012 il $16.99

Grades: 4 5 6 7 **811**

1. Slavery -- Poetry 2. African Americans -- Poetry 3. Underground railroad -- Poetry

ISBN 978-0-06-133741-3; 0-06-133741-2

LC 2010050515

The author and illustrator present "a series of poems and paintings that express the hope and frustration of enslaved people trying to navigate the Underground Railroad. Using dialect to convey a Southern cadence, Shange's poems communicate powerful emotions. . . . These poems are a cry

from the heart. . . . The expressive, impressionistic paintings capture attention with their bold strokes and vivid coloring." SLJ

★ **We** troubled the waters; poems by Ntozake Shange; paintings by Rod Brown. Amistad/Collins 2009 un il $16.99; lib bdg $17.89

Grades: 4 5 6 7 8 9 10 **811**

1. Poetry -- By individual authors 2. African Americans -- Civil rights -- Poetry

ISBN 978-0-06-133735-2; 0-06-133735-8; 978-0-06-133737-6 lib bdg; 0-06-133737-4 lib bdg

LC 2008025360

"Each spread pairs a poem with blurred, expressive acrylic paintings, and the pages feature both well-known civil rights leaders and ordinary people who endured oppression. . . . The messages are haunting. . . . The colloquial lines, indelible images, and comparisons between then and now will keep readers talking." Booklist

Shannon, George

Chicken scratches; Grade A poultry poetry and rooster rhymes. by George Shannon & Lynn Brunelle; illustrated by Scott Menchin. Chronicle Books 2010 un il $14.99

Grades: K 1 2 3 **811**

1. Chickens -- Poetry

ISBN 978-0-8118-6648-4; 0-8118-6648-3

"This attractive volume features 16 wacky rhyming verses. The somewhat irreverent poems include odes to imagined daily lives of opera-singing and sumo-wrestling chickens to complex egg laying and eating. . . . Rendered in pen and colored digitally, the simple yet expressive cartoon illustrations really bring out the fun of the poetry." SLJ

Shapiro, Karen Jo

I must go down to the beach again; [by] Karen Jo Shapiro; illustrated by Judy Love. Charlesbridge 2007 48p il lib bdg $14.95; pa $5.95

Grades: 4 5 6 7 **811**

1. Parodies 2. Humorous poetry 3. Poetry -- By individual authors

ISBN 978-158089-143-1 lib bdg; 1-58089-143-8 lib bdg; 978-158089-144-8 pa; 1-58089-144-6 pa

LC 2006009029

"Shapiro offers parodies of 23 classic British and American poems. . . . It is clear in reading her selections that the author knows the sources through and through and that she is quite a good poet in her own right. . . . Love's black-and-white pen-and-ink drawings underscore the humor in each selection." SLJ

★ **Sharing** the seasons; a book of poems. selected by Lee Bennett Hopkins; illustrated by David Diaz. Margaret K. McElderry Books 2010 83p il $21.99

Grades: 3 4 5 **811**

1. Seasons -- Poetry 2. American poetry -- Collections

ISBN 978-1-4169-0210-2; 1-4169-0210-4

LC 2009-19297

"This dynamic collection features 48 poems—12 for each of the seasons—mingling previously published poems by Carl Sandburg, Karla Kuskin, and others, with new works by several poets, including Hopkins. The diverse, accessible selections create a mosaic that stirs the senses. Diaz's ethereal silhouettes of animals and people, which resemble layered, cut-paper shadows, are ornately inlaid with nature motifs." Publ Wkly

Shields, Carol Diggory

★ **English,** fresh squeezed! 40 thirst-for-knowledge-quenching poems. by Carol Diggory Shields; illustrations by Tony Ross. Handprint Books 2004 80p il $14.95

Grades: 4 5 6 7   **811**

1. English language -- Poetry 2. Poetry -- By individual authors

ISBN 1-59354-053-1

LC 2004-53905

"Shields presents humorous poems both celebrating and bemoaning parts of speech, grammatical rules, and other annoyances of English class. Her rhyming verse is generally snappy and pointed. . . . Ross's spot illustrations in black and white with a blue tone add visual amusement without overwhelming." SLJ

Shore, Diane ZuHone

★ **This** is the dream; by Diane Z. Shore and Jessica Alexander; illustrated by James Ransome. HarperCollinsPublishers 2006 un il $15.99; lib bdg $16.89

Grades: 2 3 4   **811**

1. Poetry -- By individual authors 2. African Americans -- Civil rights -- Poetry

ISBN 0-06-055519-X; 0-06-055520-3 lib bdg

LC 2003-26554

"A chronicle of the Civil Rights movement presented through lyrical verses and distinguished illustrations. Ransome juxtaposes collaged archival photographs and newspaper clippings with his paintings. . . . Each succinct and evocative verse is accompanied by a double-page image." SLJ

This is the game; by Diane Z. Shore; illustrated by Owen Smith. HarperCollinsPublishers 2011 32p il $16.99

Grades: K 1 2 3   **811**

1. Baseball -- Poetry 2. Poetry -- By individual authors

ISBN 978-0-06-055522-1; 0-06-055522-X

LC 2008047700

"In this picture-book celebration of baseball, aspects of the game are described in verse and illustrated with, bold double-page spreads." Booklist

Sidman, Joyce

Butterfly eyes and other secrets of the meadow; written by Joyce Sidman; illustrated by Beth Krommes. Houghton Mifflin Co. 2006 un il $16

Grades: 3 4 5 6   **811**

1. Animals -- Poetry 2. Meadows -- Poetry 3. Poetry -- By individual authors

ISBN 0-618-56313-X

LC 2005-03921

"Eight pairs of 'poetry riddles' present such related elements as the spittlebug . . . and the xylem sap it sucks from its host plant. A spread giving answers to the riddle and adding specific details . . . follows each pair of poems. . . . Krommes's scratchboard illustrations are splendid. . . . An elegantly conceived, beautifully integrated volume." Horn Book

★ **Dark** Emperor and other poems of the night; written by Joyce Sidman; illustrated by Rick Allen. Houghton Mifflin Harcourt 2010 29p il $16.99

Grades: 3 4 5 6   **811**

1. Children's poetry 2. Night -- Poetry 3. Forest animals -- Poetry 4. Poetry -- By individual authors

ISBN 978-0-547-15228-8; 0-547-15228-0

A Newbery Medal honor book, 2011

"This picture book combines lyrical poetry and compelling art with science concepts. . . . Poems about the woods at night reveal exciting biology facts that are explained in long notes on each double-page spread. . . . In an opening note, Allen explains his elaborate, linoleum-block printmaking technique, and each atmospheric image shows the creatures and the dense, dark forest with astonishing clarity." Booklist

★ **Meow** ruff; a story in concrete poetry. written by Joyce Sidman; illustrated by Michelle Berg. Houghton Mifflin 2006 un il $16

Grades: 1 2 3   **811**

1. Cats -- Poetry 2. Dogs -- Poetry 3. Rain -- Poetry 4. Poetry -- By individual authors

ISBN 0-618-44894-2

"Sidman develops a simple tale about a cat and dog trapped in a rainstorm, coding much of the substance right into the physical landscape. . . . Berg, who created the pictures digitally and is also the book's graphic designer, intelligently showcases the concept of words as building blocks in a stylized landscape of flat colors, two-dimensional forms, and wildly mutating typefaces." Booklist

★ **Song** of the water boatman; & other pond poems. written by Joyce Sidman; illustrated by Beckie Prange. Houghton Mifflin 2005 un il $16

Grades: 3 4 5   **811**

1. Ponds -- Poetry 2. Poetry -- By individual authors

ISBN 0-618-13547-2

A Caldecott Medal honor book, 2006

A collection of poems that provide a look at some of the animals, insects, and plants that are found in ponds, with accompanying information about each.

"In this strikingly illustrated collection, science facts combine with vivid poems about pond life through the seasons. . . . Throughout, plants and animals come alive in the bold woodcut prints." Booklist

★ **Swirl** by swirl; spirals in nature. Houghton Mifflin Harcourt 2011 40p il $16.99

Grades: PreK K 1 2   **811**

1. Nature poetry 2. Shape -- Poetry 3. Poetry -- By individual authors

ISBN 978-0-547-31583-6; 0-547-31583-X

LC 2010040724

"Krommes's scratchboard illustrations suffuse every spread with color, shape, and movement, vividly depicting spirals in nature. . . . Sidman's very simple text provides the perfect backdrop: powerful, poetic, good for reading aloud and reading again. . . . This book is elegantly constructed, and as poetry, picture book, or nonfiction, a success in every way." Horn Book

This is just to say; poems of apology and forgiveness. by Joyce Sidman; illustrated by Pamela Zagarenski. Houghton Mifflin Co. 2007 47p il $16

Grades: 4 5 6   **811**

1. Children's poetry, American. 2. Apologizing --

Juvenile poetry. 3. Poetry -- By individual authors
ISBN 978-0-618-61680-0; 0-618-61680-2

LC 2006009820

"Mrs. Merz assigns her sixth-grade students to write poems of apology, and what emerges is a surprising array of emotions, poetic forms, and subjects. . . . Sidman's ear is keen, capturing many voices. Her skill as a poet accessible to young people is unmatched. Zagarenski's delicately outlined collage drawings and paintings are created on mixed backgrounds—notebook paper, paper bags, newspaper, graph paper, school supplies." SLJ

★ **Ubiquitous**; celebrating nature's survivors. poetry by Joyce Sidman; illustrated by Beckie Prange. Houghton Mifflin 2010 un il $17
Grades: 2 3 4 5   **811**
1. Children's poetry 2. Animals -- Poetry 3. Poetry -- By individual authors
ISBN 978-0-618-71719-4; 0-618-71719-6

Sidman and Prange "offer another winning blend of poetry, science, and art in this picture-book collection that celebrates the earth's most resilient and long-lived species. . . Each dynamic spread features a poem, a prose paragraph, and a captivating illustration that work together to reinforce both the science concepts and the awe they inspire. Prange's watercolor-tinted linocut illustrations beautifully expand both the information and imagery in the words." Booklist

Sierra, Judy
★ **Monster** Goose; illustrated by Jack E. Davis. Harcourt 2001 un il $17; pa $7
Grades: 2 3 4 5   **811**
1. Monsters -- Poetry 2. Poetry -- By individual authors
ISBN 0-15-202034-9; 0-15-205417-0 pa

LC 00-8808

A collection of parodies of Mother Goose rhymes featuring monsters

"Davis, working in acrylics and colored pencil, crowds his illustrations with monsters, vermin and gross gags. . . . This volume strikes a nice balance between goofy and ghastly." Publ Wkly

Silverstein, Shel
★ **Don't** bump the glump and other fantasies; [by] Shel Silverstein. HarperCollins Publishers 2008 un il $17.99; lib bdg $18.89
Grades: 3 4 5 6   **811**
1. Humorous poetry 2. Poetry -- By individual authors
ISBN 978-0-06-149338-6; 978-0-06-149619-6 lib bdg

LC 2007036737

First published 1964 by Simon & Schuster with title: Uncle Shelby's zoo: don't bump the glump!

"This collection of 45 poems tours readers past imaginary creatures. . . . There's no question that the intensity of Silverstein's watercolor palette adds to the fun." Publ Wkly

★ **Every** thing on it; poems and drawings by Shel Silverstein. Harper 2011 194p il $19.99; lib bdg $20.89
Grades: 3 4 5 6   **811**
1. Humorous poetry 2. Nonsense verses 3. Poetry -- By individual authors
ISBN 978-0-06-199816-4; 0-06-199816-8; 978-0-06-199817-1 lib bdg; 0-06-199817-6 lib bdg

The second original book to be published since Silverstein's passing in 1999, this poetry collection includes more than one hundred and thirty never-before-seen poems and drawings completed by the cherished American artist and selected by his family from his archives.

"Silverstein's inspired word play and impish sense of humor are in abundant evidence. His signature line drawings accompany many of the poems and complete the jokes of some. . . . Adults who grew up with Uncle Shelby will find themselves wiping their eyes by the time they get to the end of this collection; children new to the master will find themselves hooked." Kirkus

★ **Falling** up; poems and drawings by Shel Silverstein. HarperCollins Pubs. 1996 171p il $17.99; lib bdg $18.89
Grades: 3 4 5 6   **811**
1. Humorous poetry 2. Nonsense verses 3. Poetry -- By individual authors
ISBN 0-06-024802-5; 0-06-024803-3 lib bdg

LC 96-75736

This "collection includes more than 150 poems. . . . As always, Silverstein has a direct line to what kids like, and he gives them poems celebrating the gross, the scary, the absurd, and the comical. The drawings are much more than decoration. They often extend a poem's meaning and, in many cases, add some great comedy." Booklist

★ **A light** in the attic; Special edition; Harper 2009 185p il $18.99
Grades: 3 4 5 6   **811**
1. Humorous poetry 2. Nonsense verses 3. Poetry -- By individual authors
ISBN 978-0-06-190585-8; 0-06-190585-2
First published 1981

This collection of more than one hundred poems "will delight lovers of Silverstein's raucous, rollicking verse and his often tender, whimsical, philosophical advice. . . . The poems are tuned in to kids' most hidden feelings, dark wishes and enjoyment of the silly. . . . The witty line drawings are a full half of the treat of this wholly satisfying anthology by the modern successor to Edward Lear and Hilaire Belloc." SLJ [review of 1981 edition]

★ **Runny** Babbit; a billy sook. HarperCollins Pub. 2005 89p il $17.99; lib bdg $18.89
Grades: 3 4 5 6   **811**
1. Humorous poetry 2. Poetry -- By individual authors
ISBN 0-06-025653-2; 0-06-028404-8 lib bdg

In this book "readers are introduced to Runny Babbit and his friends . . . and are encouraged to plunge headlong into this phonemic flipflop world of funny poems. . . . Complete with signature comical bold line drawings that provide visual clues, the poems require concentration to translate the silly phrases. . . . Children will love these clever poems and without prompting will probably create their own." SLJ

★ **Where** the sidewalk ends; the poems & drawings of Shel Silverstein. 30th anniversary special ed; HarperCollins 2004 183p il $17.99; lib bdg $18.89
Grades: 3 4 5 6 7 8 9 10   **811**
1. Humorous poetry 2. Nonsense verses 3. Poetry --

By individual authors
ISBN 0-06-057234-5; 0-06-058653-2 lib bdg
LC 2004-269335
First published 1974
"There are skillful, sometimes grotesque line drawings with each of the 127 poems, which run in length from a few lines to a couple of pages. The poems are tender, funny, sentimental, philosophical, and ridiculous in turn, and they're for all ages." Sat Rev

Singer, Marilyn, 1948-
★ **Follow** follow; a book of reverso poems. by Marilyn Singer; illustrated by Josée Masse. Dial Books for Young Readers 2013 32 p. (hardcover: acid-free paper) $16.99
Grades: 1 2 3 4   **811**
1. Children's poetry 2. Fairy tales -- Poetry 3. Children's poetry, American 4. Characters and characteristics in literature -- Juvenile poetry
ISBN 0803737696; 9780803737693
LC 2012014359
This children's book, by Marilyn Singer, illustrated by Josee Masse, offers several fairy tales in the form of "reversos--a poetic form in which the poem is presented forward and then backward. . . . Read these . . . poems from top to bottom and they mean one thing. Then reverse the lines and read from bottom to top and they mean something else--it is almost like magic!" (Publisher's note)

A **full** moon is rising; poems. pictures by Julia Cairns. Lee & Low Books 2011 48p il $19.95
Grades: 1 2 3 4   **811**
1. Moon -- Poetry 2. Poetry -- By individual authors
ISBN 978-1-60060-364-8; 1-60060-364-5
LC 2010034693
"Singer's sparkling verses celebrate the majesty of the moon as experienced in settings around the world, each distinctly conveyed in Cairns's perceptive watercolors. . . . The lunar celebration even extends beyond Earth, with a scientist in the International Space Station contemplating both Earth's moon and the Martian moon, Phobos. The breadth of perspectives creates a stirring portrait of a familiar but no less marvelous sight." Publ Wkly

★ **Mirror** mirror; illustrated by Josée Masse. Dutton Children's Books 2010 un il $16.99
Grades: 3 4 5 6   **811**
1. Children's poetry 2. Fairy tales -- Poetry 3. Poetry -- By individual authors
ISBN 978-0-525-47901-7; 0-525-47901-5; 0525479015; 9780525479017
LC 2009017917
A collection of short poems which, when reversed, provide new perspectives on the fairy tale characters they feature.
"This appealing collection . . . is a marvel to read. . . . The vibrant artwork is painterly yet unfussy and offers hints to the characters who are narrating the poems. An endnote shows children how to create a 'reverse' poem. This is a remarkably clever and versatile book." SLJ

★ A **stick** is an excellent thing; poems celebrating outdoor play. illustrated by LeUyen Pham. Clarion Books 2012 il $16.99

Grades: PreK K 1 2   **811**
1. Imagination -- Poetry 2. Outdoor recreation -- Poetry 3. Poetry -- By individual authors
ISBN 978-0-547-12493-3; 0-547-12493-7
LC 2011009848
"Singer presents the full spectrum of outdoor activities in rhymed poems consummately animated by Pham's vibrant drawings. . . . While many of the snappy lyrics show off the pleasures of moving . . . a real strength of the collection is its engagement of the imagination. . . . Pham's evocative artwork heightens the imagination's importance in play, with her digitally colored pencil-and-ink renderings so finely textured that they radiate a warmth as arresting as Ezra Jack Keats'. A thrilling integration of verse and image." Kirkus

The **superheroes'** employment agency; by Marilyn Singer; illustrated by Noah Z. Jones. Clarion Books 2012 39 p. col. ill. (hardcover) $16.99
Grades: 1 2 3   **811**
1. Magic -- Fiction 2. Superheroes -- Fiction 3. Supernatural -- Fiction 4. Superheroes -- Juvenile poetry
ISBN 0547435592; 9780547435596
LC 2011025722
Author Marilyn Singer's book features "underemployed B-list superheroes. . . . Got rats and mice? Call on the . . . Verminator! Supernatural foes will flee from the garlic foam wielded by Muffy the Vampire Sprayer. . . . Along with having distinct individual powers and abilities, several of these eager job seekers combine to offer enhanced services. Armored Sir Knightly and The Masked Man, both aging veterans, can team up to entertain at children's parties, for instance." (Kirkus Reviews)

Sklansky, Amy E.
Out of this world; poems and facts about space. by Amy E. Sklansky; illustrated by Stacey Schuett. Alfred A. Knopf 2012 40 p.
Grades: 3 4 5   **811**
1. Outer space -- Poetry 2. Space sciences
ISBN 0375857915; 0375864598; 0375964592; 0375987339; 9780375857911; 9780375864599; 9780375964596; 9780375987335
LC 2011032506
This children's book combines astronomy and other space science facts, space-themed poetry by Amy Sklansky, and illustrations and supplemental educational diagrams by Stacey Schuett. "The mysteries of the universe and the science of space exploration are perennially popular subjects, . . . Amy Sklansky has written . . . poems about planets and stars and rockets and moon landings and satellites. Each poem is supported by additional facts and explanations in the margins." Schuett's illustrations depict various subjects such as the Earth's atmospheric layers, star systems and other planets. (Publisher's note)

Smith, Hope Anita
★ **Mother** poems; words and pictures by Hope Anita Smith. Henry Holt and Co. 2009 72p il $16.95
Grades: 4 5 6 7   **811**
1. Death -- Poetry 2. Mothers -- Poetry 3. Bereavement -- Poetry 4. African Americans -- Poetry 5. Poetry --

By individual authors
ISBN 978-0-8050-8231-9; 0-8050-8231-X

LC 2008-18342

"Smith writes about an African American child's grief at the sudden death of her mother. . . . Like the poetry, Smith's simple, torn-paper collages in a folk-art style show the close embraces and vignettes without overwhelming the words." Booklist

Snyder, Betsy

I haiku you; Betsy Snyder. Random House Childrens Books 2012 32 p. (trade) $9.99

Grades: PreK K 1   811

1. Haiku 2. American poetry 3. Children's poetry 4. Haiku, American 5. Children's poetry, American
ISBN 0375867503; 9780375867507; 9780375967504; 9780375981265

LC 2012008884

Author Betsy Snyder presents a "collection of haiku [that] captures special moments of friendship and appreciation from a child's point of view. Love is explored in its broadest sense as a cast of winsome, ethnically diverse children are featured in everyday activities such as making snow angels, riding a bicycle and sharing a purple Popsicle." (Kirkus Reviews)

Soto, Gary

Canto familiar; [illustrated by Annika Nelson] Harcourt Brace & Co. 1995 79p il $18; pa $5.95

Grades: 4 5 6   811

1. Mexican Americans -- Poetry 2. Poetry -- By individual authors
ISBN 978-0-15-200067-7; 0-15-200067-4; 978-0-15-205885-2 pa; 0-15-205885-0 pa

LC 94-24218

"This collection of simple free verse captures common childhood moments at home, at school, and in the street. Many of the experiences are Mexican American . . . and occasional Spanish words are part of the easy, colloquial, short lines. . . . The occasional full-page, richly colored woodcuts by Annika Nelson capture the child's imaginative take on ordinary things." Booklist

★ Neighborhood odes; illustrated by David Diaz. Harcourt Brace Jovanovich 1992 68p il hardcover o.p. pa $5.95

Grades: 4 5 6   811

1. Hispanic Americans -- Poetry 2. Poetry -- By individual authors
ISBN 0-15-256879-4; 0-15-205364-6 pa

LC 91-20710

"Twenty-one poems, all odes, celebrate life in a Hispanic neighborhood. Other than the small details of daily life— peoples' names or the foods they eat—these poems could be about any neighborhood. With humor, sensitivity, and insight, Soto explores the lives of children. . . . David Diaz's contemporary black-and-white illustrations, which often resemble cut paper, effortlessly capture the varied moods— happiness, fear, longing, shame, and greed—of this remarkable collection. With a glossary of thirty Spanish words and phrases." Horn Book

★ Soul looks back in wonder; [illustrated by] Tom Feelings. Dial Bks. 1993 un il hardcover o.p. pa $7.99

Grades: 4 5 6 7   811

1. African Americans -- Poetry 2. American poetry -- African American authors -- Collections
ISBN 0-8037-1001-1; 0-14-056501-9 pa

LC 93-824

Coretta Scott King Award for illustration

Artwork and poems by such writers as Maya Angelou, Langston Hughes, and Askia Toure portray the creativity, strength, and beauty of their African American heritage

"This thoughtful collection of poetry is unique. . . . Feelings selected sketches done while he was in West Africa, South America, and at home in America. The original drawings were enhanced with colored pencils, colored papers, stencil cut-outs, and other techniques to give a collage effect. Marbled textures bring vibrancy to the work." Horn Book

Swaim, Jessica

Scarum fair; poems by Jessica Swaim; illustrations by Carol Ashley. Wordsong 2010 31p il $17.95

Grades: 3 4 5   811

1. Monsters -- Poetry 2. Poetry -- By individual authors
ISBN 978-1-59078-590-4; 1-59078-590-4

LC 2008040336

"Clever writing pulls children into a creepy carnival of 29 humorous poems. . . . Dark background colors add a sense of foreboding as the cartoon children meet the ghouls illustrated in acrylics, graphite, and pen and ink." SLJ

★ Switching on the moon; a very first book of bedtime poems. collected by Jane Yolen and Andrew Fusek Peters; illustrated by G. Brian Karas. Candlewick Press 2010 95p il $21.99

Grades: PreK K   811

1. Lullabies 2. Children's poetry 3. Night -- Poetry 4. Sleep -- Poetry 5. Bedtime -- Poetry 6. American poetry -- Collections
ISBN 0763642495; 9780763642495; 978-0-7636-4249-5; 0-7636-4249-5

LC 2008025442

This is an anthology of sixty poems for bedtime reading by authors from Britain, Canada and the United States. Subjects include "the moon, dreams, lullabies, stars, bathtime, bedtime, the dark, night sounds, toothbrushes. [Indexes.] Preschool." (Horn Book)

"Yolen and Peters's 60-poem anthology reveals the many faces of nighttime through the words of these collaborators as well as poets that include Tennyson, Plath, Lee Bennett Hopkins, and Mary Ann Hoberman. . . . With Kara's mixed-media illustrations creating a chalky, dreamlike atmosphere, this book is made for bedtime." Publ Wkly

Thayer, Ernest Lawrence

★ Casey at the bat; a ballad of the republic sung in the year 1888. [by] Ernest L. Thayer; illlustrated by C.F. Payne. Simon & Schuster Bks. for Young Readers 2003 un il lib bdg $16.95

Grades: K 1 2 3   811

1. Baseball -- Poetry 2. Poetry -- By individual authors
ISBN 0-689-85494-3

LC 2002-3472

Poem first published 1888

A narrative poem about the celebrated baseball player who strikes out at the crucial moment of the game

"Payne's caricatures, rendered in a mix of acrylics, watercolor ink, oils, and colored pencils, are a marvel of texture and personality." SLJ

Ernest L. Thayer's Casey at the bat; a ballad of the Republic sung in the year 1888. reported by Ernest L. Thayer; illustrated by Christopher Bing. Handprint Books 2000 un il $17.95

Grades: 3 4 5 6   **811**

  1. Baseball -- Poetry 2. Poetry -- By individual authors

  ISBN 1-929766-00-9

               LC 00-37010

A Caldecott Medal honor book, 2001

"Thayer's classic poem of the 19th-century baseball legend has been revived for a new generation in this creatively designed package. . . . Bing has orchestrated every detail to great effect. Each double spread, rendered in ink and brush on scratchboard, is a scene from the poem. The multitude of lines adds energy; the multiple perspectives create interest." SLJ

There's no place like school; classroom poems. selected by Jack Prelutsky; illustrations by Jane Manning. Greenwillow Books 2010 32p il $16.99; lib bdg $17.89

  Grades: K 1 2 3   **811**

  1. Schools -- Poetry 2. American poetry -- Collections

  ISBN 978-0-06-082338-2; 0-06-082338-0; 978-0-06-082339-9 lib bdg; 0-06-082339-9 lib bdg

               LC 2009020373

This is a "picture-book collection of poems that range from the classroom to the cafeteria to the playground. Contributed by well-known poets, including Carol Diggory Shields and Lee Bennett Hopkins, the mostly rhyming, lighthearted selections hit familiar targets. . . . The energetic, fruit-juice-hued watercolor scenes hum with cheerful energy and subversive humor and, like the poems, capture the chaotic intensity and fun of a typical school day." Booklist

Thomas, Joyce Carol

  ★ The **blacker** the berry; poems. illustrated by Floyd Cooper. HarperCollins 2008 un il $16.99; lib bdg $17.89

Grades: PreK K 1 2   **811**

  1. African Americans -- Poetry 2. Poetry -- By individual authors

  ISBN 978-0-06-025375-2; 0-06-025375-4; 978-0-06-025376-9 lib bdg; 0-06-025376-2 lib bdg

  Coretta Scott King honor book for text, 2009

  Coretta Scott King Award for illustration, 2009

"Black comes in all shades from dark to light, and each is rich and beautiful in this collection of simple, joyful poems and glowing portraits that show African American diversity and connections." Booklist

  ★ **Brown** honey in broomwheat tea; poems by Joyce Carol Thomas; illustrated by Floyd Cooper. HarperCollins Pubs. 1993 un il $16.95; pa $6.99

Grades: K 1 2 3   **811**

  1. African Americans -- Poetry 2. Poetry -- By individual authors

  ISBN 0-06-021087-7; 0-06-443439-7 pa

               LC 91-46043

"A dozen poems rooted in home, family, and the African American experience combine with a series of warm and evocative watercolors in this highly readable and attractive picture book." Booklist

Thomas, Patricia

  Nature's paintbox; a seasonal gallery of art and verse. [by] Patricia Thomas; illustrated by Craig Orback. Millbrook Press, Inc. 2007 un il lib bdg $16.95

Grades: 2 3 4   **811**

  1. Seasons -- Poetry 2. Poetry -- By individual authors

  ISBN 978-0-8225-6807-0

               LC 2006035079

"The verse connects each season with the artist's medium, beginning with pen and ink for winter, then cycling through pastel chalk for springs, watercolor for summer, and oils for fall. . . . This picture book is both intriguing to look at and excellent for reading aloud." Booklist

Updike, John, 1932-2009

  ★ A **child's** calendar; illustrations by Trina Schart Hyman. Holiday House 1999 un il $16.95

Grades: K 1 2 3   **811**

  1. American poetry 2. Months -- Poetry 3. Months -- Juvenile poetry 4. Children's poetry, American 5. Poetry -- By individual authors

  ISBN 0-8234-1445-0

               LC 98-46166

A newly illustrated edition of the title first published 1965 by Knopf

A Caldecott Medal honor book, 2000

A collection of twelve poems describing the activities in a child's life and the changes in the weather as the year moves from January to December. "Grades three to five." (Booklist)

"Hyman's colorful illustrations portray a multiracial family living in rural New Hampshire. . . . Each evocative illustration has its own story to tell, celebrating the small moments in children's lives with clarity and sensitivity, with empathy and joy." Booklist

Van Wassenhove, Sue

  The **seldom**-ever-shady glades; poems and quilts by Sue Van Wassenhove. Wordsong 2008 32p il $17.95

Grades: 3 4 5 6   **811**

  1. Nature poetry 2. Birds -- Poetry 3. Everglades (Fla.) -- Poetry 4. Poetry -- By individual authors

  ISBN 978-1-59078-352-8

               LC 2007018099

"Through exuberant poems and quilted illustrations . . . Van Wassenhove offers an unusual tour of the delicate Everglades habitat. . . . Van Wassenhove's creative application of quilting techniques to depict the rippled surfaces and shifting hues of a wetland environment will draw fascinated gazes." Booklist

Vardell, Sylvia M.

  Poetry people; a practical guide to children's poets. Libraries Unlimited 2007 170p $50

Grades: Adult Professional   **811**

  1. Poets 2. Reference books 3. Children's poetry 4. Poetry -- By individual authors 5. Children's literature

-- Bio-bibliography
ISBN 978-1-59158-443-8; 1-59158-443-4
LC 2007003329

This is "a comprehensive survey of 62 contemporary children's poets. Each of the one- to two-page entries begins with a brief biography and includes Web sites, bibliographies, suggestions for use and reading of specific poems, plus connections to other children's literature. . . . This book will be welcomed by all adults interested in connecting children with poetry." SLJ

Includes bibliographical references

Viorst, Judith

If I were in charge of the world and other worries; poems for children and their parents. illustrated by Lynne Cherry. Atheneum Pubs. 1981 56p il lib bdg $16.95; pa $4.95

Grades: 3 4 5 6 **811**

1. Humorous poetry 2. Poetry -- By individual authors
ISBN 0-689-30863-9 lib bdg; 0-689-70770-3 pa
LC 81-2342

"Forty-one lively, funny poems written from a wry, self-deprecating point of view. Some poems verge on adult feelings—such as a broken heart or a lyrical appreciation of spring—but most of them deal with children's worries, to which the author seems to be specially attuned." Horn Book

Walker, Alice

There is a flower at the tip of my nose smelling me; by Alice Walker; illustrated by Stefano Vitale. HarperCollinsPublishers 2006 un il $16.99; lib bdg $17.89

Grades: 2 3 4 **811**

1. Senses and sensation -- Poetry 2. Poetry -- By individual authors
ISBN 978-0-06-057080-4; 0-06-057080-6; 978-0-06-057081-1 lib bdg; 0-06-057081-4 lib bdg
LC 2005014517

"Walker celebrates the beauty of the world and our connection to it through a series of short verses that praise the senses. . . . Vitale's vibrant, jewel-toned illustrations embolden the folk-art simplicity of each verse." SLJ

Why war is never a good idea; illustrations by Stefano Vitale. HarperCollins Publishers 2007 un il $16.99; lib bdg $17.89

Grades: 3 4 5 **811**

1. War poetry 2. Poetry -- By individual authors
ISBN 978-0-06-075385-6; 0-06-075385-4; 978-0-06-075386-3 lib bdg; 0-06-075386-2 lib bdg
LC 2006036255

Simple, rhythmic text explores the wanton destructiveness of War, which has grown old but not wise, as it demolishes nice people and beautiful things with no consideration for the consequences

"A thought-provoking, eloquent poem and brilliant art combine to bring the abstract concept of war to a personal, immediate level." SLJ

Weatherford, Carole Boston, 1956-

★ **Birmingham,** 1963. Wordsong 2007 39p il $17.95

Grades: 3 4 5 6 **811**

1. Bombings -- Poetry 2. Poetry -- By individual authors 3. African Americans -- Civil rights -- Poetry

4. Birmingham (Ala.) -- Race relations -- Poetry
ISBN 978-1-59078-440-2; 1-59078-440-5
LC 2006038105

"In free verse, a fictional 10-year-old tells of actual events leading up to the Ku Klux Klan bombing of the Sixteenth Street Baptist Church on September 15, 1963, and of the four young girls who died in the explosion. On each double-page spread, a few lines of spare poetry . . . are placed opposite a stirring, unframed archival photograph. . . . The quiet yet arresting book design will inspire readers." Booklist

Remember the bridge; poems of a people. designed by Semador Megged. Philomel Bks. 2002 53p il $17.99

Grades: 5 6 7 8 **811**

1. African Americans -- Poetry 2. Poetry -- By individual authors
ISBN 0-399-23726-7
LC 2001-36161

"The author evokes imagined and actual individual experiences of the people . . . in the historical black-and-white photos, drawings, and etchings. . . . This celebratory, visually striking book will be appreciated in most collections." SLJ

Wilbur, Richard

The disappearing alphabet; illustrated by David Diaz. Harcourt Brace & Co. 1998 un il hardcover o.p. pa $7

Grades: 3 4 5 **811**

1. Alphabet 2. Poetry -- By individual authors
ISBN 0-15-201470-5; 0-15-216362-X pa
LC 97-24617

A collection of twenty-six short poems pondering what the world would be like if any letters of the alphabet should disappear

"The poems presented here were first printed in The Atlantic Monthly magazine. A series of rhyming couplets of varying lengths, they range from the innocently whimsical to the cleverly sophisticated. Diaz uses computer-generated illustrations to add just the right touches to the verses; the images are lush and playful at the same time." SLJ

Willard, Nancy

★ A **visit** to William Blake's inn; poems for innocent and experienced travelers. illustrated by Alice and Martin Provensen. Harcourt Brace Jovanovich 1981 44p il $16; pa $7

Grades: 2 3 4 5 **811**

1. Nonsense verses 2. Poetry -- By individual authors
ISBN 0-15-293822-2; 0-15-293823-0 pa
LC 80-27403

Awarded the Newbery Medal, 1982; A Caldecott Medal honor book, 1982

"Nancy Willard's fantasy is pure pleasure, and her joy is expressed in the juxtaposition of sense and nonsense. . . . Done chiefly in glowing tawny colors, the pictures are highly decorative, and the whole book, printed on buff paper speckled to simulate an antique look, presents an elegant appearance." Horn Book

Williams, Vera B.

Amber was brave, Essie was smart; the story of Amber and Essie told here in poems and pictures by Vera B.

Williams. Greenwillow Bks. 2001 un il $15.95; lib bdg $15.89; pa $7.99

Grades: 3 4 5 **811**

1. Sisters -- Poetry 2. Poetry -- By individual authors
ISBN 0-06-029460-4; 0-06-029461-2 lib bdg; 0-06-057182-9 pa

LC 00-48438

Two sisters help each other deal with life while their mother is working and their father has been sent to jail

"An engaging, affecting view of the bonds between sisters, this balances reality with hope and love as it shows how small moments tell a big story." Booklist

Wilson, Karma

What's the weather inside? poems by Karma Wilson; drawings by Barry Blitt. Margaret McElderry Books 2009 170p il $17.99

Grades: 2 3 4 **811**

1. Humorous poetry 2. Poetry -- By individual authors
ISBN 978-1-4169-0092-4; 1-4169-0092-6

LC 2006-23623

"This collection of more than 100 poems features comical wordplay . . . as well as lots of fun riffs on Mother Goose rhymes and fairy tales. Many are about family, friends, and school. . . . Blitt's line drawings are a great match for the verses. They are funny, dynamic, and full of personality." SLJ

Wong, Janet S.

Knock on wood; poems about superstitions. written by Janet S. Wong; illustrated by Julie Paschkis. Margaret K. McElderry Bks. 2003 33p il $17.95

Grades: 3 4 5 **811**

1. Superstition -- Poetry 2. Poetry -- By individual authors
ISBN 0-689-85512-5

LC 2002-8319

A collection of seventeen original poems about superstitions, including walking under a ladder, breaking a mirror, and knocking on wood. Includes notes about the superstitions

"Some selections are haunting, and some humorous. . . . Paschkis creates an exquisite backdrop for the verses. Presented on a panoramic spread, each poem and facing watercolor scene have matching frames, anchoring them as reflections of one another. . . . There is much to ponder in both words and pictures." SLJ

Twist; yoga poems. written by Janet S. Wong; illustrated by Julie Paschkis. Margaret K. McElderry Books 2007 39p il $17.99

Grades: 2 3 4 5 **811**

1. Yoga -- Poetry 2. Poetry -- By individual authors
ISBN 0-689-87394-8; 978-0-689-87394-2

LC 2005-15888

"This collection of 16 poems touches on the uplifting and emotional aspects of yoga, putting words to the spirit of the poses and evoking the energy and feelings of the practice. . . . Paschkis's watercolor paintings frame both the poem and a child performing the pose with colorful fauna, flora, and people that suggest India as well as that particular exercise." SLJ

★ **Words** with wings; a treasury of African-American poetry and art. selected by Belinda Rochelle. HarperCollins Pubs. 2001 un il lib bdg $18.99

Grades: 4 5 6 7 **811**

1. African Americans in art 2. African Americans -- Poetry 3. American poetry -- African American authors -- Collections
ISBN 0-688-16415-3

LC 00-26864

Pairs twenty works of art by African-American artists such as Horace Pippin and Jacob Lawrence with twenty poems by African-American poets such as Langston Hughes, Countee Cullen, and Lucille Clifton

"Most of the combinations are stunning. . . . Short biographical paragraphs on each poet and artist round out this moving presentation." SLJ

Worth, Valerie

★ **All** the small poems and fourteen more; pictures by Natalie Babbitt. Farrar, Straus & Giroux 1994 194p il hardcover o.p. pa $6.95

Grades: 2 3 4 5 **811**

1. Poetry -- By individual authors
ISBN 0-374-40345-7 pa

LC 94-8810

"As the title implies, all the original collaborations between this poet and artist are collected in this volume, which includes ninety-nine poems and an additional fourteen new ones. The earlier works have been widely praised, for good reason, and the new verses are every bit as worthy as their predecessors." Horn Book

★ **Animal** poems; pictures by Steve Jenkins. Farrar, Straus & Giroux 2007 un il $17

Grades: 4 5 6 **811**

1. Animals -- Poetry 2. Poetry -- By individual authors
ISBN 0-374-38057-0; 978-0-374-38057-1

LC 2005-56812

A collection of twenty-three illustrated poems about animals

"This pairing of . . . Worth's exquisite poems with Jenkins's . . . extraordinary, cut-paper illustrations make this a volume to treasure. . . . Each poem in this handsome volume is a gem—full of crisp language, vivid images and thoughtful ideas." Publ Wkly

Pug and other animal poems; Valerie Worth; pictures by Steve Jenkins. Margaret Ferguson Books, Farrar Straus Giroux 2012 40 p. $16.99

Grades: 2 3 4 5 **811**

1. Animals -- Poetry 2. Children's poetry 3. Children's poetry, American
ISBN 0374350248; 9780374350246

LC 2010034300

This juvenile poetry collection, by Valerie Worth, illustrated by Steve Jenkins, "examines a wide range of animal behavior, from the fleetingness of a fly sipping spilled milk to the constant steely presence of a powerful bull; the greedy meal of a street rat to a cat's quiet gift of a dead mouse on the doorstep." (Publisher's note)

Yolen, Jane

★ **Birds** of a feather; poems by Jane Yolen; photographs by Jason Stemple; foreword by Donald Kroodsma. Wordsong 2011 32p il $17.95

Grades: 3 4 5   **811**

1. Birds -- Poetry 2. Poetry -- By individual authors

ISBN 978-1-59078-830-1; 1-59078-830-3

"Striking photographs of birds that might be seen in the eastern United States illustrate this . . . collection of 14 poems in varied forms. . . . Semple's splendid photographs show birds in the wild. . . . The colors are true, and the details sharp; careful focus and composition make the birds the center of attention. . . . Short sidebars add interesting, informative details about each species." Kirkus

Bug off! creepy, crawly poems. by Jane Yolen; photographs by Jason Stemple. 1st ed. Wordsong 2012 30 p. col. ill. (reinforced) $16.95

Grades: 3 4 5   **811**

1. Children's poetry 2. Insects -- Poetry 3. Spiders -- Poetry

ISBN 1590788621; 9781590788622

LC 2011939947

Author Jane Yolen presents a book of poetry for children. In the collection, "[f]ly, praying mantis, butterfly, ants, honey bee, lovebug, daddy longlegs, spider, dragonfly, tick, ladybug and grasshopper each take a spread, the photo opposite a page of text that includes the poem and a paragraph of facts. Most of Yolen's poems rhyme, and an author's note encourages readers to create their own poems." (Kirkus)

The **Emily** sonnets; the life of Emily Dickinson. by Jane Yolen; illustrations by Gary Kelley. 1st ed. Creative Editions 2012 40 p. col. ill. (reinforced) $19.99

Grades: 5 6 7   **811**

1. Dickinson, Emily, 1830-1886 -- Poetry

ISBN 1568462158; 9781568462158

LC 2011040841

This book by Jane Yolen presents 15 sonnets about poet Emily Dickinson. "The selections are constructed in various voices. . . . In the first five pieces, Emily speaks of the family's brick house, her close relationship with her sister Vinnie, her schooling, her variance with her family's religious beliefs, and the companionship of her dog. . . . The other speakers . . . tell of her always dressing in white, her life as a recluse, and her work." (School Library Journal)

A **mirror** to nature; poems about reflection. [by] Jane Yolen; photographs by Jason Stemple. Wordsong 2009 31p il $17.95

Grades: 3 4 5   **811**

1. Nature poetry 2. Poetry -- By individual authors

ISBN 978-1-59078-624-6

LC 2008031760

"Water acts as a mirror in this picture book that combines short poems with full-page color photographs of animals in the wild. . . . The poetic forms are well matched to the mood in the pictures. . . . Drawn by the rich play in words and pictures, kids will see reflections, strange and beautiful, in the the natural world." Booklist

Zimmer, Tracie Vaughn

Cousins of clouds; elephant poems. illustrated by Megan Halsey and Sean Addy. Clarion Books 2011 31p il $16.99

Grades: 3 4 5   **811**

1. Children's poetry 2. Elephants -- Poetry 3. Poetry -- By individual authors

ISBN 978-0-618-90349-8; 0-618-90349-6

This "collection of poems and factoids celebrates the 'wonders of elephants,' from glorious winged creatures of myth to the realities of their precarious modern existence. With a wide-ranging stock of lore and fact, Vaughn limns the complex relationship between humans and the largest land animals. In 'Inspiration,' she observes that their image is 'etched in the imagination/of all mankind,/a behemoth of hope.' Poems like 'Ivory' and 'Grace,' however, remind readers that elephants have been hunted and used for hard labor and public performance. . . . 'Fortress' graphically depicts the protective instincts of female elephants, while 'Elephant Blues' places cartoon drawings and verses atop colored sheets of music." (School Library Journal)

"Against fanciful collage backdrops portraying pachyderms in an array of styles and arrangements, Zimmer pairs prose and mostly free-verse tributes to elephants and those who care for them. . . . She writes with passion and sympathy. . . . Along with giving each spread a different look and palette, the illustrators inject dashes of visual wit. . . . Both informative and heartfelt." Kirkus

★ **Steady** hands; poems about work. by Tracie Vaughn Zimmer; illustrated by Megan Halsey and Sean Addy. Clarion Books 2009 48p il $16

Grades: 4 5 6   **811**

1. Work -- Poetry 2. Occupations -- Poetry 3. Poetry -- By individual authors

ISBN 978-0-618-90351-1; 0-618-90351-8

LC 2007038848

"Inventive, complicated collages and well-crafted poems focus on the activities of working people in this eye-catching book. With an observant eye, Zimmer . . . captures different individuals performing work with 'steady hands.' . . . Halsey and Addy's . . . hip collages combine individual cut-outs of people along with drawings, photos, textured backgrounds and designs." Publ Wkly

811.5   American poetry -- 20th century

Cleary, Brian P., 1959-

If It Rains Pancakes; Haiku and Lantern Poems. Brian P. Cleary; illustrations by Andy Rowland. Millbrook Press 2014 32 p. (Poetry Adventures) (lib. bdg.: alk. paper) $26.60

Grades: 2 3 4   **811.5**

1. Haiku 2. Poetry -- Authorship 3. Poetry

ISBN 146771609X; 9781467716093

LC 2013018079

This children's book, written by Brian P. Cleary and illustrated by Andy Rowland, is about ancient Japanese poetry known as haiku and lanterns. "Cleary explains how each form works--and shows how these little poems can contain big surprises[.] . . . When you've finished reading, you can try your hand at writing your own haiku and lanterns[.]" (Publisher's note)

"Cleary introduces two traditional Japanese poetic forms, the well-known haiku and the less-familiar lantern. The thirty-five verses and accompanying illustrations feature good-natured, kid-pleasing fun (e.g., "Yummy": "When something's so good / you want to taste it again, / that's what burps are for"; and "Sneeze": "Sneeze-- / ah-CHOOOO-- / hurricane / out of my nose / blows"). This amusing collection can't miss with kids or teachers. Reading list, websites." Horn Book

Other titles include:

Ode to a comode: concrete poems (2015)

811.54 American poetry -- 1945-1999

Rogers, Stan
Northwest Passage. Groundwood Books 2013 56 p. $24.95
Grades: 3 4 5 **811.54**
1. Picture books for children 2. Northwest Passage
ISBN 1554981530; 9781554981533

This book is an illustrated version of Canadian folk musician Stan Rogers' song "Northwest Passage." The song "describes Stan's own journey overland as he contemplates the arduous journeys of some of the explorers, including Kelsey, Mackenzie, Thompson and Franklin." Along with the illustrations, the book "contains the music for the song, a note on the Northwest Passage, maps, information about Stan Rogers . . . and notes on the illustrations." (Publisher's note)

Rosen, Michael
★ The Maine coon's haiku; and other poems for cat lovers. Michael J. Rosen, illustrated by Lee White. Candlewick Press 2015 56 p. color illustrations $17.99
Grades: 2 3 4 **811.54**
1. Haiku 2. Cats -- Poetry
ISBN 0763664928; 9780763664923
LC 2013957344

"Set against Lee White's graceful illustrations, with intriguing facts about each of twenty breeds at the end, this [book] for lovers of America's most popular house pet provides the purr-fect book to curl up with." (Publisher's note)

"The brevity and poignancy of the haiku format perfectly capture the feline essence in this book of verse. Each spread defines an individual breed, some familiar and others less so, with a deft haiku and an inviting illustration about a brief moment." SLJ

Sidman, Joyce
★ Winter Bees & Other Poems of the Cold; Written by Joyce Sidman and illustrated by Rick Allen. Houghton Mifflin Books for Children, Houghton Mifflin Harcourt 2014 32 p. colored illustrations $17.99
811.54
1. Children's poetry 2. Winter -- Poetry 3. Animals -- Poetry
ISBN 0547906501; 9780547906508
LC 2013039007

This book by Joyce Sidman, with illustrations by Rick Allen, offers "a new poetic treatment of natural history.

Twelve poems treat subjects ranging from moose and snakes to snowflakes and skunk cabbage, each entry partnered with a prose paragraph giving more factual detail behind the subject of the verse." (Bulletin of the Center for Children's Books)

"Sidman exemplifies winter survival strategies of a well-chosen sample of species. Her poems are precise, evocative, lyrical, varied in tone; facts in succinct (separate) prose illuminate the imagery of each. It's as beautiful visually as it is verbally: winter's browns, blues, and whites are warmed with glowing honey tones; a note describes Allen's "unlikely marriage" of hand-colored linoleum blocks with computer techniques. Glos." Horn Book

Winter Bees and Other Poems of the Cold

Singer, Marilyn, 1948-
Rutherford B., who was he? poems about our presidents. Marilyn Singer; John Hendrix. 1st ed. Disney-Hyperion Books 2013 56 p. $17.99
Grades: 3 4 5 6 7 **811.54**
1. Children's poetry 2. Presidents -- United States 3. Children's poetry, American 4. Historical poetry, American 5. Presidents -- United States -- Biography
ISBN 1423171004; 9781423171003
LC 2013010690

In this collection of children's poetry, author Marilyn Singer and illustrator John Hendrix bring "the presidents of the United States to life--from [George] Washington to [Barack] Obama and contextualizes them in their time. Backmatter enriches the experience with short biographies, quotes by each president, and more." (Publisher's note)

VanHecke, Susan
Under the freedom tree; Susan Vanhecke; Illustrated by London Ladd. Charlesbridge 2013 32 p. (reinforced for library use) $16.95
Grades: 1 2 3 4 **811.54**
1. Poetry 2. Fugitive slaves 3. United States -- History -- 1861-1865, Civil War -- Poetry 4. Fugitive slaves -- Poetry
ISBN 1580895506; 9781580895507; 9781607346340
LC 2012038698

This book, by Susan Vanhecke and illustrated by London Ladd, "illuminates . . . [a] slice of Civil War history: runaway slaves' establishment of a settlement in newly seceded Virginia. In 1861, three slaves--Frank Baker, James Townsend, and Shepard Mallory--escape by boat from a Confederate camp. . . . The three men land at a Union camp whose commander declares them 'contraband of war' and refuses to return them to the Confederates." (Publishers Weekly)

"In 1861, when a Union general refused to return three escaped slaves to their owners, he set off a little-known episode in American history in which more than nine hundred slaves ended up in Hampton, Virginia, working for the Union army. The brief, spare verse is accompanied by realistic acrylic paintings depicting everyday life as the growing community builds a new town." Horn Book

Includes bibliographical references and index

811.6

Raczka, Bob

★ **Santa** Clauses; short poems from the North Pole. By Bob Raczka; Illustrated by Chuck Groenink. Carolrhoda Books 2014 32 p. (lib. bdg.: alk. paper) $16.95

Grades: K 1 2 3 4 5   **811.6**

  1. Poetry 2. Christmas -- Poetry 3. Santa Claus -- Fiction 4. Christmas poetry

  ISBN 146771805X; 9781467718059

                       LC 2013030819

In this children's book, by Bob Raczka, "you know that Santa can fly a sleigh, squeeze down chimneys, and circle the globe in a night. But did you know that another of his talents is writing haiku? These twenty-five short poems--composed by Santa himself--give you a peek into life at the North Pole as the December days tick down to Christmas." (Publisher's note)

"Readers are offered a day-by-day "glimpse of life at the North Pole" in twenty-five festive haiku "penned" by Santa himself. The poems are rich with tender emotions and crisp imagery, all reflected affectionately and vividly in Groenink's art. A warm seasonal collection notable for its clever, gently comical visual details (note St. Nick's adult beverage as he relaxes on December 26th)." Horn Book

Wilson, Karma

Outside the box; Karma Wilson; illustrated by Diane Goode. Margaret K. McElderry Books 2013 176 p. $17.99

Grades: 3 4 5 6   **811.6**

  1. American poetry -- Collections

  ISBN 1416980059; 9781416980056

                       LC 2011049239

This book, by Karma Wilson and illustrated by Diane Goode, is a "collection of more than 100 poems that touch on everything from creativity and luck to animals, siblings, and holidays. The narrator of 'My Pet Robot' stares glumly at her creation. . . . Elsewhere, a boy reflects on the duality of oatmeal . . . and a girl shouts her head off as she's about to be devoured by a monster." (Publishers Weekly)

"Wilson's mostly humorous poems cover the usual ground, touching on imagination, family relationships, and food preferences. The rhyme and meter are often forced, and the poems with messages are heavy-handed. In most cases, the concrete poems are stronger than those in rhyming verse. The calligraphic feel of Goode's line drawings distinguishes them from illustrations in similar collections. Ind." Horn Book

812   American drama in English

Black, Ann N.

Readers theatre for middle school boys; investigating the strange and mysterious. illustrated by Cody Rust. Teachers Idea Press 2008 190p il (Readers theatre) pa $30

Grades: Adult Professional   **812**

  1. Readers' theater 2. Drama -- Collections

  ISBN 978-1-59158-535-0 pa; 1-59158-535-X pa

                       LC 2007034923

"This book provides solid offerings of Readers Theater scripts for educators working with middle school boys. Selections include adaptations of such creepy classics as 'The Legend of Sleepy Hollow,' 'The Masque of the Red Death,' . . . and 'The Monkey's Paw.' The scripts have a new, fresh feel, and contain plenty of elements to capture and maintain adolescent males' attention." Libr Media Connect

Includes bibliographical references

Bruchac, Joseph

Pushing up the sky: seven Native American plays for children; illustrated by Teresa Flavin. Dial Bks. for Young Readers 2000 94p il hardcover o.p. $21.99

Grades: 3 4 5   **812**

  1. Native American drama 2. Drama -- Collections

  ISBN 0-8037-2168-4; 0-8037-2535-3 pa

                       LC 98-20483

Uses drama to tell seven different stories from Native American traditions including the Abenaki, Ojibway, Cherokee, Cheyenne, Snohomish, Tlingit, and Zuni

"The short, simple scripts are accessible to young, inexperienced actors. . . . Suggestions are given for easy-to-make costumes, props, and scenery. A variety of pen-and-ink drawings illustrate the plays, as well as one lively gouache illustration per selection." SLJ

Includes bibliographical references

Dabrowski, Kristen

My first monologue book; 100 monologues for young children. by Kristen Dabrowski. Smith and Kraus 2006 112p (Young actors series) pa $11.95

Grades: 2 3 4 5 6   **812**

  1. Acting 2. Monologues

  ISBN 1-57525-533-2 pa; 978-1-57525-533-0 pa

                       LC 2006938162

"Dabrowski offers short, accessible selections on common topics such as games, families, food, friends, school, and wishes. The true-to-life experiences and emotions are delivered in a child's voice and run the gamut from funny to serious." SLJ

My second monologue book; famous and historical people: 101 monologues for young children. Smith and Kraus 2008 115p il (My first acting series) pa $11.95

Grades: 2 3 4 5 6   **812**

  1. Acting 2. Monologues

  ISBN 978-1-57525-601-6 pa; 1-57525-601-0 pa

                       LC 2008927862

Presents over a hundred monologues focusing on ordinary and famous people designed for use by children who are just starting with acting

"The monologues and activities will fire the imaginations of young students." SLJ

My third monologue book; places near and far: 102 monologues for young children. Smith and Kraus Publishers 2008 116p il (My first acting series) pa $11.95

Grades: 2 3 4 5 6   **812**

  1. Acting 2. Monologues

  ISBN 978-1-57525-602-3

                       LC 2008927864

This collection of monologues is "divided into four parts: places you know (the woods, grandma's house), places in the United States (Laredo, TX; Flagstaff, AZ), foreign countries (Italy, Morocco), and imaginary and far-out places (Hogwarts, an alien world). . . . Concluding activities range from figuring out where the character is, to circling or underlining grammar clues, to completing a travel journal. [This is a] good [addition] as [it suggests] well-rounded activities for students to practice reading, writing, speaking, and both critical and imaginative thinking." SLJ

Fredericks, Anthony D.

African legends, myths, and folktales for readers theatre; illustrated by Bongaman. Teachers Ideas Press 2008 xxiii, 166p il map (Readers theatre) pa $25

Grades: Adult Professional   812

1. Readers' theater 2. Folklore -- Africa 3. Drama -- Collections

ISBN 978-1-59158-633-3 pa; 1-59158-633-X pa

LC 2007-44594

Author Tony Fredericks and illustrator, Bongaman, present readers theatre scripts based on traditional African folklore. Includes background information for teachers on each African country, as well as instruction and presentation suggestions, and additional resources for studies of African folklore

"For the most part, the stories . . . are short, lively, and often humorous. . . . A valuable volume." SLJ

Includes bibliographical references

Levine, Karen

★ Hana's suitcase on stage; original story by Karen Levine; play by Emil Sher. Second Story 2007 171p il (Holocaust remembrance book for young readers) pa $18.95

Grades: 5 6 7 8   812

1. Holocaust victims 2. Holocaust, 1933-1945 -- Drama

ISBN 978-1-89718-705-0 pa; 1-89718-705-X pa

"Set in the Tokyo Holocaust Center, the two-act play opens with the woman and two of her student helpers questioning and searching for answers to the suitcase's history. . . . Act II blends characters of Ishioka and her students with Hana and her family, each group individually recounting their stories in alternating voices. As with the original book, this title succeeds in recreating a striking representation of one child's tragic and beautiful life in a terrifying world of hate and prejudice. This volume will serve as one of the most effective teaching models for Holocaust curriculums available. Photographs and facsimiles of Nazi documents are included." SLJ

Shepard, Aaron

Stories on stage; children's plays for reader's theater (or readers theatre), with 15 Play scripts from 15 authors. 2nd ed; Shepard 2005 160p pa $15

Grades: Adult Professional   812

1. Readers' theater 2. Drama -- Collections

ISBN 0-938497-22-7

First published 1993 in H. W. Wilson Co.

A collection of twenty-two plays adapted from folk tales, short stories, myths, and novels and intended for use in reader's theater programs

"With its mix of humor, fantasy, and multicultural tales . . . this book gives teachers both a fun and useful tool for bringing reading and literature to their students." SLJ

813   American fiction in English

Ada, Alma Flor

Under the royal palms; a childhood in Cuba. Atheneum Bks. for Young Readers 1998 85p il $15

Grades: 4 5 6 7   813

1. Authors 2. Educators 3. Dramatists 4. Women authors 5. Authors, American 6. Children's authors 7. Cuba -- Social life and customs

ISBN 0-689-80631-0

LC 97-48887

Companion volume to Where the flame trees bloom (1994)

The author recalls her life and impressions growing up in Cuba

"The attention paid to small daily things as well as the occasional awareness of historical events will encourage readers to look for their own family stories." Booklist

Fleischman, Sid

★ The abracadabra kid; a writer's life. Greenwillow Bks. 1996 198p il hardcover o.p. $16.99

Grades: 5 6 7 8   813

1. Authors 2. Magicians 3. Magazine editors 4. Authors, American 5. Children's authors 6. Young adult authors

ISBN 0-688-14859-X; 0-688-15855-2 pa

LC 95-47382

This autobiography, "turns real life into a story complete with cliffhangers. And it's a classic boy's story, from card tricks and traveling magic shows to World War II naval experiences and screen-writing gigs for John Wayne movies. En route, we learn how Fleischman learned the craft of writing." Bull Cent Child Books

Includes bibliographical references

Fradin, Dennis Brindell

Zora! the life of Zora Neal Hurston. Judith Bloom Fradin and Dennis Brindell Fradin. Clarion Books 2012 xi, 180 p.p ill. $17.99

Grades: 5 6 7 8   813

1. African American authors -- Biography 2. African American women -- Biography 3. African American authors -- Biography 4. Folklorists -- United States -- Biography 5. Authors, American -- 20th century -- Biography

ISBN 0547006950; 9780547006956

LC 2011025949

This book by Dennis Brindell Fradin and Judith Bloom Fradin presents a "biography of . . . African-American author . . . [Zora Neale] Hurston. . . . Beginning with a . . . scene of the 59-year-old Hurston, already a well-known author, working as a white family's domestic helper because she needed a paycheck, the Fradins . . . establish the complexities of Zora's inner and external worlds, before offering highlights of her life in chronological order." (Publishers Weekly)

Includes bibliographical references and index.

Fritz, Jean

Harriet Beecher Stowe and the Beecher preachers. Putnam 1994 144p il $15.99; pa $5.99

Grades: 5 6 7 8   813

1. Authors 2. Novelists 3. Abolitionists 4. Women authors 5. Authors, American 6. Children's authors 7.

Nonfiction writers 8. Short story writers
ISBN 0-399-22666-4; 0-698-11660-7 pa

LC 93-6408

This is a biography of the abolitionist author of "Uncle Tom's Cabin" with an emphasis on the influence of her preacher father and her family on her life and work.

"Written with vivacity and insight, this readable and engrossing biography is an important contribution to women's history as well as to the history of American letters." Horn Book

Includes bibliographical references

Hamilton, Virginia

★ **Virginia** Hamilton: speeches, essays, and conversations; edited by Arnold Adoff & Kacy Cook. Blue Sky Press 2010 368p $29.99

Grades: 8 9 10 11 12 Adult Professional   813
1. Authorship 2. Children's literature -- History and criticism
ISBN 978-0-439-27193-6; 0-439-27193-2

LC 2009031676

"A groundbreaking writer of children's fiction, folktales, biography, and picture books, Hamilton won every major award, and much of this book is made up of her acceptance speeches, including those for the Newbery, Hans Christian Andersen, and Coretta Scott King awards, as well as her Arbuthnot and Zena Sutherland lectures. Aimed at a general audience, the book employs a tone both scholarly and informal, as Hamilton talks about her career as a woman and a black writer in America and about the form and content of her work in general and with particular titles. . . . Many speeches include introductions by children's literature scholars and editors, who add perspective on Hamilton's lasting influence, while family members fill in biographical details. A must for YAs who love her books, this will also appeal to librarians, teachers, and children's literature students." Booklist

Includes bibliographical references

Juster, Norton

The **annotated** Phantom tollbooth; by Norton Juster; illustrations by Jules Feiffer; introduction and notes by Leonard Marcus. Alfred A. Knopf 2011 284p il $29.99; lib bdg $32.22

Grades: Adult Professional   813
1. Authors 2. Architects 3. Children's authors
ISBN 978-0-375-85715-7; 0-375-85715-X; 978-0-375-95715-4 lib bdg; 0-375-95715-4 lib bdg

LC 2011013174

"Still ferrying dazzled readers to Dictionopolis and beyond 50 years after his first appearance, young Milo is accompanied this time through by encyclopedic commentary from our generation's leading (and most readable) expert on the history of children's literature and publishing. . . . Leonard opens with typically lucid and well-organized pictures of both Juster's and Feiffer's formative years and later careers, interwoven with accounts of the book's conception, publication and critical response. In notes running alongside the ensuing facsimile, he puts on an intellectual show. . . . he delivers notes on topics as diverse as the etymological origins of "BALDERDASH!" and mimetic architecture to textual parallels with the Wizard of Oz and echoes of Winsor McKay and George Grosz in the art. Family photos, scrawled notes and images of handwritten and typescript manuscript pages further gloss a work that never ages nor fails to astonish." Kirkus

Lester, Helen

Author; a true story. Houghton Mifflin 1997 32p il $11

Grades: K 1 2 3   813
1. Authors 2. Authorship 3. Women authors 4. Children's authors 5. Elementary school teachers
ISBN 0-395-82744-2

LC 96-9645

An "autobiographical look at the evolution of a writer describes Lester's experiences—including her earliest three-year-old scribbles and the acceptance of her first manuscript (on the seventh try). Illustrated with Lester's own rather childlike illustrations, this lighthearted but realistic (and helpful) guide for the writer has lots of fresh tips for young authors-in-the-making." Horn Book Guide

Lowry, Lois

Looking back; a book of memories. Houghton Mifflin 1998 181p il $17

Grades: 5 6 7 8   813
1. Authors 2. Novelists 3. Women authors 4. Authors, American 5. Young adult authors
ISBN 0-395-89543-X

LC 98-11376

Using family photographs and quotes from her books, the author provides glimpses into her life

"A compelling and inspirational portrait of the author emerges from these vivid snapshots of life's joyful, sad and surprising moments." Publ Wkly

Miller, William

Zora Hurston and the chinaberry tree; illustrated by Cornelius Van Wright and Ying-hwa Hu. Lee & Low Bks. 1994 un il $15.95; pa $6.95

Grades: K 1 2 3   813
1. Authors 2. Novelists 3. Dramatists 4. Women authors 5. African American authors 6. Memoirists 7. Folklorists 8. Short story writers
ISBN 1-880000-14-8; 1-880000-33-4 pa

LC 94-1291

"Conveying the changing expressions on the face of the young Hurston as easily as they show the grandeur of the sky at nightfall, the versatile artists neatly capture the emotions in this lucidly told story." Publ Wkly

"This biography, which covers a brief period in Zora Neale Hurston's childhood, ends with the young girl grieving over her mother's death but finding inner power and strength from her mother's life." Horn Book

Paulsen, Gary

★ **How** Angel Peterson got his name; and other outrageous tales about extreme sports. Wendy Lamb Bks. 2003 111p hardcover o.p. pa $5.99

Grades: 5 6 7 8   813
1. Authors 2. Sled dog racers 3. Authors, American 4. Children's authors 5. Short story writers 6. Young adult authors
ISBN 0-385-72949-9; 0-385-90090-2 lib bdg; 978-0-440-22935-3 pa; 0-440-22935-9 pa

LC 2002-7668

Author Gary Paulsen relates tales from his youth in a small town in northwestern Minnesota in the late 1940s and early 1950s, such as skiing behind a souped-up car and imitating daredevil Evel Knievel

"Writing with humor and sensitivity, Paulsen shows boys moving into adolescence believing they can do anything... . None of them dies (amazingly), and even if Paulsen exaggerates the teensiest bit, his tales are side-splittingly funny and more than a little frightening." Booklist

★ **My** life in dog years; with drawings by Ruth Wright Paulsen. Delacorte Press 1998 137p il $15.95; pa $6.50
Grades: 4 5 6 7   **813**
1. Dogs 2. Authors 3. Sled dog racers 4. Authors, American 5. Children's authors 6. Short story writers 7. Young adult authors
ISBN 0-385-32570-3; 0-440-41471-7 pa
LC 97-40254

The author describes some of the dogs that have had special places in his life, including his first dog, Snowball, in the Philippines; Dirk, who protected him from bullies; and Cookie, who saved his life

"Paulsen differentiates his canine friends beautifully, as only a keen observer and lover of dogs can. At the same time, he presents an intimate glimpse of himself, a lonely child of alcoholic parents, who drew strength and solace from his four-legged companions and a love of the great outdoors. Poignant but never saccharine, honest, and open." Booklist

Peet, Bill
★ **Bill** Peet: an autobiography. Houghton Mifflin 1989 190p il hardcover o.p. pa $15
Grades: 4 5 6 7   **813**
1. Artists 2. Authors 3. Illustrators 4. Authors, American 5. Children's authors 6. Walt Disney Productions
ISBN 0-395-50932-7; 0-395-68982-1 pa
LC 88-37067

A Caldecott Medal honor book, 1990

"Every page of this oversized book is illustrated with Peet's unmistakable black-and-white drawings of himself and the people, places, and events described in the text. Familiar characters from his books and movies appear often." SLJ

Spinelli, Jerry
★ **Knots** in my yo-yo string; the autobiography of a kid. Knopf 1998 148p il hardcover o.p. pa $10.95
Grades: 4 5 6 7   **813**
1. Authors 2. Magazine editors 3. Authors, American 4. Children's authors
ISBN 0-679-98791-6; 0-679-88791-1 pa
LC 97-30827

This Italian-American Newbery Medalist presents a humorous account of his childhood and youth in Norristown, Pennsylvania

"There is an 'everyboy' universality to Spinelli's experiences, but his keen powers of observation and recall turn the story into a richly rewarding personal history." Horn Book Guide

817   American humor and satire in English

Brewer, Paul
You must be joking, two! even cooler jokes, plus 11 1/2 tips for laughing yourself into your own stand-up comedy routine. written and illustrated by Paul Brewer. Cricket Books 2007 92p il $16.95
Grades: 3 4 5 6   **817**
1. Jokes 2. Riddles 3. Wit and humor
ISBN 978-0-8126-2752-7; 0-8126-2752-0
LC 2007014450

Includes riddles, jokes, and knock-knocks about monsters, aliens, cyberspace, school, pirates, animals, birds, and bugs

"An introduction plus the 11 ½ Tips will inspire readers to look at everyday events with an eye for humor and offer some suggestions on keeping children's attention, jokes to avoid, stage fright, and more. Black-and-white drawings introduce each chapter and spot art is sprinkled throughout the book. Most collections should make room for this one." SLJ

Freymann, Saxton
Knock, knock! [by] Saxton Freymann . . . [et al.] Dial Books for Young Readers 2007 un il $16.99
Grades: K 1 2   **817**
1. Jokes
ISBN 978-0-8037-3152-3; 0-8037-3152-3
LC 2006-39463

"14 children's book artists . . . . illustrate a different groan-inducing knock-knock joke in signature style. Saxton Freymann uses photos of lettuce ('Lettuce who?' 'Lettuce in!') made to look like pigs. Tomie de Paola creates two love-struck gorillas to illustrate 'Gorilla who?' 'Gorilla my dreams, I love you!' and so on. . . . The artwork is . . . just great and varied enough to keep children turning the pages." Booklist

Rosenthal, Amy Krouse
The **wonder** book; drawings by Paul Schmid. Harper 2010 79p il $17.99
Grades: 2 3 4   **817**
1. Wit and humor
ISBN 978-0-06-142974-3; 0-06-142974-0
LC 2008-939052

"Here is a joyous, totally original potpourri of stories, poems, lists, palindromes, visual jokes, and random observations about the universal delights and conundrums of childhood. Set squarely in the world of the 21st-century child . . . these varied musings nonetheless speak to everyone's inner child, young or old. . . . Simple, evocative, and childlike black-and-white line drawings, in concert with judicious and varied use of white space, perfectly capture the happy/sad/serious/silly moods of the selections." SLJ

818   American miscellaneous writings in English

Cooper, Floyd
★ **Coming** home; from the life of Langston Hughes. Philomel Bks. 1994 un il lib bdg $16.95; pa $6.99
Grades: K 1 2 3   **818**
1. Poets 2. Authors 3. Novelists 4. Dramatists 5. African American authors 6. Poets, American 7. Short

story writers 8. Young adult authors
ISBN 0-399-22682-6 lib bdg; 0-698-11612-7 pa
LC 93-36332

This "biography highlights pivotal events in Hughes's life, emphasizing his loneliness as a child and his development as a poet. . . . Cooper's hazy illustrations in gold, brown, and sepia tones reveal keen observations of people and neighborhood. The text and art combine to create a fine tribute and introduction to the writer's life." Horn Book

Includes bibliographical references

★ **Guys** read; true stories. edited and with an introduction by Jon Scieszka; stories by Candace Fleming, Douglas Florian, Nathan Hale, Thanhha Lai, Sy Montgomery, Jim Murphy, T. Edward Nickens, Elizabeth Partridge, Steve Sheinkin, and James Sturm; with illustrations by Brian Floca. Walden Pond Press 2014 272 p. (Guys read) (hardback) $16.99
Grades: 4 5 6 7 8   **818**
1. Essays 2. Short stories 3. American prose literature 4. American prose literature -- 21st century
ISBN 0061963828; 9780061963810; 9780061963827
LC 2014010024

Part of the Guys Read series, edited by Jon Scieszka, this book "features ten stories that are 100% amazing, 100% adventurous, 100% unbelievable--and 100% true. A star-studded group of award-winning nonfiction authors and journalists provides something for every reader, all aligned with the Common Core State Standards." (Publisher's note)

"Ten terrifically told true stories demonstrate the wide range of subjects and formats available for young readers of nonfiction. This fifth anthology in the Guys Read series stars some of the best-known names in informational writing today. . . . Selected, edited, and neatly introduced by Scieszka, National Ambassador for Young People's Literature emeritus, these appetite-whetting accounts are accompanied by occasional illustrations by Floca (not seen). You certainly don't have to be a guy to appreciate these morsels of fact-based storytelling and then beg for more." Booklist

Lewis, J. Patrick

Last laughs; animal epitaphs. J. Patrick Lewis and Jane Yolen; illustrated by Jeffrey Stewart Timmins. Charlesbridge 2012 48 p. ill. (reinforced for library use) $16.95
Grades: 3 4 5 6   **818**
1. Obituaries 2. Death in literature 3. Animals in literature 4. Animals -- humor 5. Animals -- poetry
ISBN 1580892604; 9781580892605
LC 2011025702

Author J. Patrick Lewis provides "30 tombstone remembrances [for a variety of animals]. . . . Sometimes they are gruesome, as with the newt, 'so small, / so fine, / so squashed / beneath / the crossing / sign.' There are the macabre and the simply passing: 'In his pond, / he peacefully soaked, / then, ever so quietly / croaked.' [Other animals include] . . . the eel . . . [and] the piranha." (Kirkus Reviews)

McCurdy, Michael

Walden then & now; an alphabetical tour of Henry Thoreau's pond. Charlesbridge 2010 un il lib bdg $16.95
Grades: 4 5 6 7   **818**
1. Authors 2. Alphabet 3. Naturalists 4. Essayists 5. Pacifists 6. Writers on nature 7. Nonfiction writers 8.

Natural history -- Massachusetts
ISBN 978-1-58089-253-7 lib bdg; 1-58089-253-1 lib bdg
LC 2009-26645

"Elegiac woodcarvings evoke the setting of Henry Thoreau's Walden Pond as the text weaves past and present in this lengthy alphabet poem. On each spread, consecutive letters face one another, making a couplet of the lines. A dark, but not somber, woodcarving illustrates each letter, and an explanatory paragraph expands upon the information in the verse. . . . The book ends with entries from Thoreau's diary and McCurdy's inspiration and starting point for this book. Purchase as an introduction to Thoreau and for poetry shelves." SLJ

Paulsen, Gary

★ **Caught** by the sea; my life on boats. Delacorte Press 2001 103p maps $15.95; pa $5.50
Grades: 5 6 7 8   **818**
1. Authors 2. Ocean travel 3. Boats and boating 4. Sled dog racers 5. Authors, American 6. Children's authors 7. Short story writers 8. Young adult authors
ISBN 0-385-32645-9; 0-440-40716-8 pa
LC 2001-17336

"Paulsen traces his life at sea, from buying his first sailboat to getting lost in the Pacific to encountering sharks. . . . His sometimes comic, sometimes near-fatal sea-going errors make for absorbing, captivating reading." Booklist

Sandburg, Carl

The **Sandburg** treasury; prose and poetry for young people. introduction by Paula Sandburg; illustrated by Paul Bacon. Harcourt Brace Jovanovich 1970 480p il hardcover o.p. pa $24
Grades: 5 6 7 8   **818**
1. American literature
ISBN 0-15-202678-9 pa

This volume brings together all of Sandburg's books for young people; his whimsical stories, two books of poetry, a version of his biography of Abraham Lincoln, and portions of his autobiography specially edited for children

818.602   Jokes – American literature – 2001-

Griffiths, Andy

What Body Part Is That? A Wacky Guide to the Funniest, Weirdest, and Most Disgustingest Parts of Your Body. by Andy Griffiths; illustrated by Terry Denton. 1st U.S. ed. Feiwel & Friends 2012 ix, 180 p.p ill. (hardcover) $12.99
Grades: 3 4 5   **818.602**
1. Human anatomy 2. Wit and humor, Juvenile 3. Human body -- humor 4. Human anatomy -- humor
ISBN 0312367902; 9780312367909
LC 2012288587

"This humorous book is about every body part and then some -- from your head to your toes and everything in-between that you can and can't see." (Library Media Connection) Author "[Andy] Griffiths' anatomical tour in general steers clear of anything that would be marked as correct on a test. From 'Ears can be big or small, depending on their size' to 'Capillaries are the larval form of butterflies,' he

offers . . . inanities about 68 mostly real body features."
(Kirkus Reviews)

821 English poetry

Cohen, Barbara
★ **Canterbury** tales; [by] Geoffrey Chaucer; selected,
translated, and adapted by Barbara Cohen; illustrated by
Trina Schart Hyman. Lothrop, Lee & Shepard Bks. 1988
87p il $24.99
Grades: 4 5 6 7   **821**
1. Poets 2. Authors 3. Middle Ages 4. Poetry -- By
individual authors
ISBN 0-688-06201-6
LC 86-21045

"Cohen's evident love and respect for Chaucer's writing
keep her close to the text. Her writing retains the flavor of
the times and the spirit of Chaucer's words while her prose
retelling, enriched by Hyman's lively full-color paintings,
enhances the book's appeal to young people. . . . An excellent introduction to The Canterbury Tales for young readers." Booklist

Howitt, Mary Botham
The **spider** and the fly; based on the poem by Mary
Howitt; with illustrations by Tony DiTerlizzi. Simon &
Schuster Bks. for Young Readers 2002 un il $16.95
Grades: K 1 2 3   **821**
1. Flies -- Poetry 2. Spiders -- Poetry 3. Poetry -- By
individual authors
ISBN 0-689-85289-4
LC 2002-5760

An illustrated version of the well-known poem about
a wily spider who preys on the vanity and innocence of a
little fly

"Rendered in black-and-white gouache and pencil, then
reproduced in silver-and-black duotone, the paintings have a
spooky quality perfectly suited to retelling this melancholy
tale. Ms. Fly, with her whimsical flower umbrella and Roaring '20s attire, captures the flavor of an old-time Hollywood
heroine." SLJ

Hughes, Ted, 1930-1998
Collected poems for children; pictures by Raymond
Briggs. Farrar, Straus and Giroux 2007 259p il $18
Grades: 3 4 5 6   **821**
1. Poetry. 2. Children's poetry, English. 3. Poetry --
By individual authors
ISBN 978-0-374-31429-3; 0-374-31429-2
LC 2006-37437

First published 2005 in the United Kingdom

This is a "collection of 250 poems by the late English
poet laureate Ted Hughes. . . . Children will love the sounds
of the rhythmic lines, and Briggs' scattering of small black-
and-white drawings perfectly captures the tiny details in the
words." Booklist

Includes bibliographical references

Kipling, Rudyard, 1865-1936
If; a father's advice to his son. [by] Rudyard Kipling;
photographs by Charles R. Smith. Atheneum Books for
Young Readers 2007 un il $14.99

Grades: 4 5 6   **821**
1. Poetry -- By individual authors
ISBN 978-0-689-87799-5; 0-689-87799-4
LC 2006005312

"Kipling's powerful poem comes to life for a contemporary audience in atmospheric photographs that use the
metaphor of sports. A lovely shot of a boy heading a soccer ball accompanies the opening couplet: 'If you can keep
your head/when all about you/are losing theirs/and blaming
it on you.' The mood and actions in most of the illustrations
clearly invoke the verse." SLJ

Lear, Edward
The **complete** verse and other nonsense; compiled and
edited with an introduction and notes by Vivien Noakes.
Penguin Bks. 2002 566p il pa $18
Grades: 4 5 6 7 8 9 10 11 12 Adult   **821**
1. Nonsense verses 2. Poetry -- By individual authors
ISBN 0-14-200227-5
LC 2002-28998

This volume "presents all of Lear's verse and other
nonsense writings, including stories, letters, and illustrated
alphabets, as well as previously unpublished material, line
drawings, and . . . [an] introduction by scholar Vivien Noakes." Publisher's note

Includes bibliographical references

★ **Edward** Lear; edited by Edward Mendelson; il-
lustrated by Laura Huliska-Beith. Sterling 2002 48p il
(Poetry for young people) $14.95; pa $6.95
Grades: 4 5 6 7   **821**
1. Limericks 2. Nonsense verses 3. Poetry -- By
individual authors
ISBN 0-8069-3077-2; 1-4027-7294-7 pa
LC 2001-20112

"In an analytical introduction, Mendelson looks at Lear's
serious and silly sides before selecting 15 limericks and 18
longer poems, all of which feature odd creatures adapting to,
or reveling in, their differences. Sporting conical noses or
other physical peculiarities, Huliska-Beit's smiling, rubber-
limbed figures dance through vertiginously tilted, brightly
colored minimalist settings. . . . Thought- and laugh-provoking." Booklist

★ **Edward** Lear's The duck & the kangaroo; illus-
trated by Jane Wattenberg. Greenwillow Books 2009 un
il $17.99
Grades: PreK K 1 2   **821**
1. Nonsense verses 2. Ducks -- Poetry 3. Kangaroos
-- Poetry 4. Poetry -- By individual authors
ISBN 0-06-136683-8; 978-0-06-136683-3
LC 2008024126

"Duck, envious of Kangaroo's hop . . . asks to ride upon
the larger animal's back. Upon reflection, Kangaroo expresses his concern that Duck's wet and cold feet will give him
rheumatism. Duck solves the problem by wearing beautifully knitted socks. . . . Wattenberg's quirky photo collages .
. . are perfectly suited for Lear's nonsensical text." Booklist

His shoes were far too tight; poems. by Edward Lear;
selected and introduced by Daniel Pinkwater and illustrated
by Calef Brown. Chronicle Books 2010 un il $16.99

Grades: K 1 2 3 **821**

1. Nonsense verses 2. Poetry -- By individual authors
ISBN 978-0-8118-6792-4; 0-8118-6792-7;
0811867927; 9780811867924

LC 2010008549

"Pinkwater and Brown honor a fellow champion of absurdity, Edward Lear, in this frisky collection. Even before readers get to the poems, a cartoon self-portrait of Lear in the introduction . . . hints at the revelry that's to follow. Brown's elegantly quirky collages convey the gentle lunacy of the Owl and the Pussycat . . . and lesser-known characters. . . . These seasoned collaborators provide an assuring nudge for readers to embrace Lear's sumptuously silly verse." Publ Wkly

★ The **owl** and the pussycat; by Edward Lear; illustrated by Anne Mortimer. Katherine Tegen Books 2006 un il $15.99; lib bdg $16.89
Grades: K 1 2 3 **821**

1. Nonsense verses 2. Cats -- Poetry 3. Owls -- Poetry 4. Poetry -- By individual authors
ISBN 0-06-027228-7; 0-06-027229-5 lib bdg

LC 2003015476

After a courtship voyage of a year and a day, Owl and Pussy finally buy a ring from Piggy and are blissfully married

"Lear's poem is beautifully illustrated with a mixture of elaborate, stylized borders and sumptuous portrayals of natural elements like verdant plant and tree leaves and colorful tropical flowers." SLJ

Milne, A. A.

★ **Now** we are six; with decorations by Ernest H. Shepard. Dutton 1961 104p il $22.99; pa $4.99
Grades: K 1 2 3 **821**

1. Poetry -- By individual authors
ISBN 0-525-44960-4; 0-14-0361234-3 pa

First published 1927. Reprinted September 1961 in this completely new format designed by Warren Chappell. Verso of title page

"The boy or girl who has liked 'When were were very young' and 'Winnie-the-Pooh' will enjoy reading about Alexander Beetle who was mistaken for a match, the knight whose armor didn't squeak, and the old sailor who had so many things which he wanted to do. There are other entertaining poems, also, and many pictures as delightful as the verses." Pittsburgh

★ **When** we were very young; with decorations by Ernest H. Shepard. Dutton 1961 102p il $11.99; pa $6.99
Grades: K 1 2 3 **821**

1. Poetry -- By individual authors
ISBN 0-525-44445-9; 0-14-036123-5 pa

First published 1924. Reprinted September 1961 in this completely new format designed by Warren Chappell. Verso of title page

"Mr. Milne's gay jingles have found a worthy accompaniment in the charming illustrations of Mr. Shepard." Saturday Rev

Morpurgo, Clare

Where my wellies take me; Michael Morpurgo, Clare Morpurgo, illustrated by Olivia Lomenech Gill. Candlewick Press 2013 110 p. $29.99

Grades: 2 3 4 5 **821**

1. English poetry 2. Vacations
ISBN 0763666297; 9780763666293

LC 2012954328

In this book, "a young English girl explores the Devon countryside." The book is formatted as a scrapbook "as Pippa, on a visit to her aunt, shares her favorite pastimes: walking, horseback riding and poetry. Her first-person narration is on notebook paper in cursive writing, while the poetry selections are in old-fashioned Times New Roman. These range from traditional rhymes to a medley of English-language poets writing about cows, lambs and meadow mice, among other topics." (Kirkus Reviews)

Stevenson, Robert Louis

★ A **child's** garden of verses; pictures by Barbara McClintock. Harper 2011 80p il $17.99
Grades: K 1 2 3 **821**

1. Poetry -- By individual authors
ISBN 978-0-06-028228-8; 0-06-028228-2

LC 2010007031

"McClintock offers a complete edition of these old favorites in a format generous with white space and spot art as well as illustrative fantasies. . . . McClintock's blend of old and new should attract a new generation." Horn Book

821.008   English poetry -- collections

★ **Poems** to learn by heart; [selected by] Caroline Kennedy; paintings by Jon J Muth. Disney Hyperion Books 2012 192 p. (hardcover) $19.99
Grades: 2 3 4 5 6 7 8 **821.008**

1. Poetry -- Collections 2. English poetry 3. American poetry
ISBN 1423108051; 9781423108054

LC 2011022651

This anthology, by Caroline Kennedy, illustrated by John J. Muth, offers "more than a hundred poems that speak to all of us: the young and young at heart, readers new to poetry and devoted fans. These poems explore deep emotions, as well as ordinary experiences. They cover the range of human experience and imagination. Divided into sections about nature, sports, monsters and fairies, friendship and family." (Publisher's note)

822.3   Drama of Elizabethan period, 1558-1625

Coville, Bruce

William Shakespeare's A midsummer night's dream. Dial Bks. 1996 un $17.95; pa $7.99
Grades: 5 6 7 8 9 **822.3**

1. Poets 2. Authors 3. Audiobooks 4. Dramatists
ISBN 0-8037-1784-9; 0-14-250168-9 pa

LC 94-12600

A simplified prose retelling of Shakespeare's play about the strange events that take place in a forest inhabited by fairies who magically transform the romantic fate of two young couples.

"Coville introduces the story and also conveys something of the poetry and drama. Nolan's framed graphite and watercolor paintings express the dreaminess and absurdity of the play, and the pictures have a theatrical flair." Booklist

William Shakespeare's Twelfth night; retold by Bruce Coville; illustrated by Tim Raglin. Dial Bks. 2003 un il $16.99
Grades: 5 6 7 8 9   **822.3**
  1. Poets 2. Authors 3. Dramatists
  ISBN 0-8037-2318-0
                          LC 2001-28252
This "provides a short, prose version of Shakespeare's Twelfth Night. . . . Though simplified, the story is intact and bits of the original language are preserved. Large-scale ink drawings, warmed with tints of color and shaded with cross-hatching, clearly depict the action." Booklist

Nettleton, Pamela Hill
  William Shakespeare; playwright and poet. by Pamela Hill Nettleton. Compass Point Books 2005 112p il map (Signature lives) lib bdg $30.60
Grades: 5 6 7 8   **822.3**
  1. Poets 2. Authors 3. Dramatists
  ISBN 0-7565-0816-9
                          LC 2004-23081
Profiles the life and work of William Shakespeare
"This biography is one of the best available for younger students. Nettleton supplements what little is actually known about the bard's life with detailed and accurate information about everyday life in England during the period, the theater, and publishing practices of the time. The text is enhanced by full-color illustrations and black-and-white reproductions." SLJ
  Includes bibliographical references

Raum, Elizabeth
  Twenty-first-century Shakespeare. Raintree 2011 32p il (Culture in action) lib bdg $29
Grades: 5 6 7 8   **822.3**
  1. Poets 2. Authors 3. Dramatists 4. Dramatists, English 5. Authors, English
  ISBN 978-1-4109-3920-3; 1-4109-3920-0
                          LC 2009050693
This "discusses modern adaptations of the Bard's classic works; teachers may find this a useful resource to help students see how Shakespeare remains a part of today's culture. [This volume is] quick, interesting, up-to-date . . . with plenty of supportive, captioned, full-color photographs. [It] also [provides] related project suggestions." SLJ
  Includes glossary and bibliographical references

Stanley, Diane
  ★ **Bard** of Avon: the story of William Shakespeare; by Diane Stanley and Peter Vennema; illustrated by Diane Stanley. Morrow Junior Bks. 1992 un il hardcover o.p. pa $6.99
Grades: 4 5 6 7   **822.3**
  1. Poets 2. Authors 3. Dramatists
  ISBN 0-688-09108-3; 0-688-09109-1 lib bdg; 0-688-16294-0 pa
                          LC 90-46564
A brief biography of the world's most famous playwright, using only historically correct information
"A remarkably rounded picture of Shakespeare's life and the period in which he lived is presented . . . together with

a thoughtful attempt to relate circumstances in his personal life to the content of his plays. . . . The text is splendidly supported by the illustrations, which are stylized, yet recognizable, and present a clear view of life in the late sixteenth century. A discerning, knowledgeable biography, rising far above the ordinary." Horn Book
  Includes bibliographical references

Weiner, Miriam
  Shakespeare's Seasons; created by Miriam Weiner; illustrations by Shannon Whitt; edited by Miriam Weiner & Shannon Whitt. Downtown Bookworks 2012 1 v. (unpaged) col. ill. (hardcover) $16.99
Grades: K 1 2 3   **822.3**
  1. Seasons
  ISBN 1935703579; 9781935703570
In this book by author Miriam Weiner, "tiny snippets of Shakespeare form the text for an illustrated almanac. . . . Readers see children on the beach flying kites and building sandcastles, watched by a woman with a book. The beachscape is visually anchored by the head of a woman with long hair, hinting that this may be a memory. . . . The longest quote is eight lines but most are four or less. . . . [Weiner incorporates] The Winter's Tale, The Tempest . . . [and] As You Like It." (Kirkus Reviews)

823   English fiction

Bannerman, Helen
  ★ The **story** of Little Babaji; illustrated by Fred Marcellino. HarperCollins Pubs. 1996 un il $16.99; pa $7.95
Grades: PreK K 1 2   **823**
  1. India -- Fiction 2. Tigers -- Fiction
  ISBN 0-06-205064-8; 0-06-008093-0 pa
In this edition of the Story of Little Black Sambo, originally published 1899, the characters have been given Indian names
Babaji gives his new clothing to tigers who threaten to eat him, but they chase one another around a tree until they turn to butter
  "Marcellino has set the story of Little Black Sambo in India. . . . Except for a change of names . . . Bannerman's text is essentially unaltered, retaining the narrative rhythm that has always paced a tightly patterned plot. Marcellino's watercolor paintings project a toy-like quality that emphasizes humor over suspense." Bull Cent Child Books

Colbert, David
  The **magical** worlds of Harry Potter; David Colbert. Updated and complete ed. Berkley Books 2008 xi, 209 p.p ill. (paperback) $14.00
Grades: 5 6 7 8   **823**
  1. Authors 2. Novelists 3. Fantasy writers 4. Children's authors 5. Young adult authors 6. Fantasy fiction -- History and criticism
  ISBN 0425223183; 9780425223185
                          LC 2008274096
First published 2001 in the United Kingdom; first United States edition 2002
Explores the sources and meanings of aspects of the literary world of Harry Potter within myths, legends, and history.

"Long after the enthusiasm for Harry and friends has abated, this small volume will serve as a resource to answer questions that may result from reading other stories in the genre." SLJ [review of 2002 edition]

Includes bibliographical references (p. 317-318) and index.

Mahy, Margaret

17 kings and 42 elephants; pictures by Patricia Mac-Carthy. Dial Bks. for Young Readers 1987 26p il $16.99

Grades: K 1 2 3　　**823**

1. Stories in rhyme　2. Animals -- Fiction

ISBN 0-8037-0458-5

LC 87-5311

A newly illustrated edition of the title first published 1972 in the United Kingdom

Seventeen kings and forty-two elephants romp with a variety of jungle animals during their mysterious journey through a wild, wet night

"This book takes you on a jungle journey you will never forget. . . . The text is lyrical, humorous, and full of nonsense and fantasy. Children and adults will be charmed by the melodic use of language and the beautiful batik illustrations." Child Book Rev Serv

Wells-Cole, Catherine

Charles Dickens; England's most captivating storyteller. written by Catherine Wells-Cole; including extracts from the works of Charles Dickens. 1st U.S. ed. Candlewick/Templar Books 2011 28 p. ill., maps (some col.) (Historical notebook) (hardcover) $19.99

Grades: 7 8 9 10 11 12　　**823**

1. Authors　2. Novelists　3. Authors, English　4. London (England) -- Social life and customs -- 19th century　5. London (England) -- Social life and customs -- 19th century

ISBN 0763655678; 9780763655679

LC 2011013677

This book by Catherine Wells-Cole "provides a . . . glimpse into the life" of author Charles Dickens. "Like a scrapbook, the book includes excerpts from Dickens' personal letters, illustrations from his original books, family photos, and other images from the Victorian age. . . . Double-page spreads focus on Dickens' childhood, family life, and fame. Other spreads focus on topics that influenced his writing, including schools, prisons, and workhouses." (Library Media Connection)

"In this scrapbook homage to Dickens, each page teems with images and reproductions, from letters to book excerpts to maps, all pertaining to a different area of Dickens's life and work. The topics range widely, skimming the surface of both the esteemed author's life and the subjects that interested him most. . . . The gorgeous, high-quality reproductions make a strong visual impact, and while the flaps, folds, and envelopes make readers work to uncover information, most will be quickly drawn into the hunt for more treasured tidbits about Dickens and his time." SLJ

828　English miscellaneous writings

Thomas, Dylan

★ A **child's** Christmas in Wales; illustrated by Chris Raschka. Candlewick Press 2004 un il $17.99

Grades: 2 3 4 5 6 7 8 9　　**828**

1. Christmas -- Wales

ISBN 0-7636-2161-7

LC 2003-65274

The Welsh poet Dylan Thomas recalls the celebration of Christmas with his family and the feelings it evoked in him as a child.

"Applied to torn paper, the ink and watercolors spread through the fibers, freely forming soft outlines and shadows. The result is an intriguing contemporary take on a story that is by now part of the rather staid canon of Christmas classics." N Y Times Book Rev

831　German poetry

Rasmussen, Halfdan

★ A **little** bitty man and other poems for the very young; Halfdan Rasmussen; translated by Marilyn Nelson and Pamela Espeland; illustrated by Kevin Hawkes. Candlewick Press 2011 29 p.

Grades: PreK K 1　　**831**

1. Children's poetry, Danish -- Translations into English

ISBN 9780763623791

LC 2009007515

"A charming collection of poems finds an American audience in a splendid translation. . . . Rasmussen (1915-2002) was a beloved Danish poet, known both for his human-rights writings as well as nonsense verse for children. A sweet compendium of the latter is translated here . . . and animated by Hawkes' dynamic, colorful acrylic-and-pencil renderings, effectively capturing the playfulness of Rasmussen's verse in both sound and image." Kirkus

839.31　Dutch literature

Schmidt, Annie M. G.

A **pond** full of ink; By Annie M. G. Schmidt; Illustrated by Sieb Posthuma; translated by David Colmer. Eerdmans Books for Young Readers 2014 34 p. $16

Grades: 1 2 3 4 5 6　　**839.31**

1. Children's poetry　2. Children's poetry, Dutch -- Translations into English

ISBN 0802854338; 9780802854339

LC 2013030888

Originally published in Dutch with the title Een vijver vol inkt

This collection of children's poems, by Annie M. G. Schmidt, "tell the stories of such intriguing characters as three elderly otters who long to go boating but find themselves biking instead, animated furniture that comes to life when no one is home, and Aunt Sue and Uncle Steve who nest up in a tree!" (Publisher's note)

"Fans of Shel Silverstein will love this collection of light, humorous poems that is full of fantastical characters. The titular pond features in the first selection about a prolific fairy-tale writer who refills his pen at the giant inkwell...The drawings and collage images are colorful and quirky, full of patterns and details that add depth. Illustrated spreads follow some of the poems, providing a closer look at the situation or characters introduced in the preceding poem. This book is a kid-pleasing must-have for any poetry collection." SLJ

841 French poetry

Cendrars, Blaise

★ **Shadow**; translated and illustrated by Marcia Brown from the French of Blaise Cendrars. Scribner 1982 un il $17; pa $6.99

Grades: 1 2 3 **841**

1. French poetry 2. Africa -- Poetry 3. Shades and shadows -- Poetry 4. Poetry -- By individual authors
ISBN 0-684-17226-7; 0-689-71875-6 pa

LC 81-9424

Original text first published in France

Awarded the Caldecott Medal, 1983

"Inspired by the exotic atmosphere and the dramatic possibilities of the text, Brown has choreographed a sequence of almost theatrical illustrations, placing human and animal figures—and their shadows—against brilliant, contrasting, always changing settings. Resplendent—yet controlled—in color, texture, and form, the work is an impressive, sophisticated example of the art of the picture book." Horn Book

861 Spanish poetry

Argueta, Jorge

★ A **movie** in my pillow; story by Jorge Argueta; illustrations by Elizabeth Gómez. Children's Bk. Press 2001 31p il $15.95

Grades: 3 4 5 6 **861**

1. Immigrants -- Poetry 2. Hispanic Americans -- Poetry 3. Poetry -- By individual authors 4. Bilingual books -- English-Spanish
ISBN 0-89239-165-0

LC 00-55582

"Gómez's rich and bright paintings fill every spread with . . . joy and literal humor. . . . An excellent addition to any poetry collection." SLJ

Lujan, Jorge

Colors! Colores! by Jorge Luján; illustrated by Piet Grobler; translated by John Oliver Simon and Rebecca Parfitt. Groundwood Books 2008 36p il $17.95

Grades: K 1 2 **861**

1. Color -- Poetry 2. Poetry -- By individual authors 3. Bilingual books -- English-Spanish
ISBN 978-0-88899-863-7; 0-88899-863-5

This is "a fully illustrated collection of 11 brief, free-verse poems linked by a common theme: colors. Each poem appears in English and then in Spanish on a double-page spread surrounded by white space and accompanied by an eye-catching watercolor painting. . . . Gobler . . . interprets the verse through watercolor paintings that are as spare and fanciful as the writing." Booklist

Messengers of rain and other poems from Latin America; edited by Claudia M. Lee; illustrated by Rafael Yock-

teng; translations by Andrew C. Leone . . . [et al.] Douglas & McIntyre 2002 80p il $18.95

Grades: 3 4 5 6 **861**

1. Spanish poetry -- Collections
ISBN 0-88899-470-2

"The 64 poems from 19 countries include 20th-century classics and more recent selections, and represent women, indigenous writers, and widely published names such as Octavio Paz and Rafael Pombo. . . . Yockteng's fanciful watercolors head each section with a full-page spread, and spots brighten the pages between, here and there, without distracting from the poems." SLJ

883 Classical Greek epic poetry and fiction

Landmann, Bimba

★ The **fate** of Achilles. Getty 2011 36p il $19.95

Grades: 4 5 6 7 **883**

1. Poets 2. Authors
ISBN 978-1-60606-085-8; 1-60606-085-6

"Landmann (The Incredible Voyage of Ulysses) continues her retelling of Homer's epics with this haunting version of the Iliad. Ghostly, Giacometti-style figures accompany the story of Achilles's life, from his baptism in the river Styx . . . to his departure for Troy, . . . the death of his dearest friend, . . . and his reconciliation with the father of the enemy he has slain. . . . Readers with the patience to sit through saga-length narratives will be fascinated by her prose, which moves easily through the sprawling epic without feeling ponderous or hurried. These kinds of retellings are few and far between, and hers are magic." Publ Wkly

★ The **incredible** voyage of Ulysses; text and illustrations by Bimba Landmann. Getty Publications 2010 un il $19.95

Grades: 4 5 6 7 **883**

1. Poets 2. Authors
ISBN 978-1-60606-012-4; 1-60606-012-0

"With narrative restraint and illustrative power, Landmann's . . . retelling of Homer's Odyssey follows Ulysses as he battles frightening creatures and endures the treachery of the gods while sailing home to Ithaca. . . . The paintings, worked with swift, bold strokes, combine the solemn stiffness of Greek statuary with the prophetic sweep of William Blake's imaginings." Publ Wkly

891 East Indo-European and Celtic literatures

Laird, Elizabeth

Shahnameh; the Persian book of kings. Retold by Elizabeth Laird; illustrated by Shirin Adl. Frances Lincoln Children's Books 2012 129 p.

Grades: 2 3 4 5 **891**

1. Epic poetry 2. Persian legends 3. Persian mythology
ISBN 1847802532; 9781847802538

This children's book, by Elizabeth Laird, illustrated by Shirin Adl, is a "collection of stories and myths from ancient Persia, written into an epic poem by . . . Firdousi in the 10th century. . . . The tales describe the beginning of the world, and include amazing birds who bring up orphaned Kings, . . . a feisty princess who goes to war incognito, and above all the great hero Rostam, who tragically kills his own son Sohrab, not knowing his identity." (Publisher's note)

895.6   Japanese literature

Kobayashi, Issa

★ **Today** and today; by Kobayashi Issa; pictures by G. Brian Karas. Scholastic Press 2007 un il $16.99

Grades: K 1 2 3   **895.6**

1. Haiku

ISBN 0-4395-9078-7

LC 2003-26684

"Karas uses the haiku of the eighteenth-century Japanese poet Issa to limn a gentle, understated tale of one family over a year. . . . The translations . . . are simply and clearly crafted. . . . Kara's art, using rice paper, paint, and pencil, is precise, enticing, and evocative." Booklist

897   Literatures of North American native languages

★ **Dancing** teepees: poems of American Indian youth; selected by Virginia Driving Hawk Sneve, with art by Stephen Gammell. Holiday House 1989 32p il $17.95; pa $8.95

Grades: 4 5 6   **897**

1. Native Americans -- Poetry

ISBN 0-8234-0724-1; 0-8234-0879-5 pa

LC 88-11075

An illustrated collection of poems from the oral tradition of Native Americans

This is an "eclectic collection, drawn from a variety of tribal traditions. Printed on heavy paper, the book is illustrated with a catalogue of marvelously rendered designs and motifs, ranging from those of the Northwest Coast to the intricate beadwork patterns of the Great Lakes and the zigzag geometric borders of Southwestern pottery." N Y Times Book Rev

900   HISTORY

904   Collected accounts of events

Blackwood, Gary L.

Enigmatic events. Marshall Cavendish Benchmark 2005 72p il (Unsolved history) lib bdg $29.93

Grades: 4 5 6 7   **904**

1. Disasters 2. Curiosities and wonders 3. History -- Miscellanea

ISBN 0-7614-1889-X

LC 2004-23755

Explores several events that have baffled scientists and historians for years, such as the demise of the dinosaurs, the "lost colony" of Roanoke, the sinking of the Main, and the Hindenberg disaster

This collection of "tidbits about lingering mysteries of the past . . . [offers] more substance than most. . . . [This of-

fers] a full-page illustration opening each chapter; reproductions, many in color; and a generously spaced format." SLJ

Includes glossary and bibliographical references

Guiberson, Brenda Z.

★ **Disasters**; natural and man-made catastrophes through the centuries. Henry Holt and Company 2010 228p il $18.99

Grades: 5 6 7 8 9   **904**

1. Disasters 2. Natural disasters

ISBN 978-0-8050-8170-1; 0-8050-8170-4

LC 2009018908

"The subtitle provides an accurate outline of the contents of this lively treatment of disasters from smallpox to Hurricane Katrina. In each chapter, Guiberson outlines the sources of the disaster, the results, and means of obviating the problems that caused these tragedies. For example, the chapter on the Great Chicago Fire begins with the construction of the city over unstable marshland. . . . This kind of exhaustive background serves to create an understanding of the contributory issues and demonstrates possible preventive steps. Guiberson's compellingly written exegesis is equally good in the other nine chapters. Well-placed, black-and-white reproductions and photos extend the text. A perfect example of solid historical research coupled with engaging writing." SLJ

Includes bibliographical references

909   World history

Adams, Simon

★ The **Kingfisher** atlas of world history; a pictorial guide to the world's people and events, 10,000 BCE-present. Kingfisher 2010 181p il map $24.99

Grades: 4 5 6 7   **909**

1. World history 2. Historical geography

ISBN 978-0-7534-6388-8; 0-7534-6388-1

"This colorful and fact-packed book is not only informative but well organized. Sections cover 'The Ancient World,' 'The Medieval World,' 'Exploration and Empire,' and 'The Modern World,' and each section contains 15 or 16 thematic maps presented in chronological order. . . . It is very useful and entertaining as well as data-filled." Booklist

Chrisp, Peter

History year by year; written by Peter Chrisp, Joe Fullman, and Susan Kennedy; consultant, Philip Parker. DK Publishing 2013 320 p. col. ill., col. maps $24.99

Grades: 4 5 6 7 8 9   **909**

1. Anthropology 2. World history 3. Chronology, Historical

ISBN 1465414185; 9781465414182

LC 2012286068

Learning Magazine Teacher's Choice Awards for the Classroom (2015)

This book "presents the world through a detailed timeline, letting children follow the influences, patterns, and connections between historical events.Beginning with prehistory and running up to the Arab Spring, budding historians will learn about the history of humans across the world. Spreads highlight major historical eras . . . while quotations from primary and secondary sources alongside insight from experts give proper historical context." (Publisher's note)

"...Every few pages, a particular subtopic gets extra attention. For instance, in the "700 BCE-500 CE" section, there is a two-page discussion, replete with a color picture of Chinese emperor Qin Shi Huangdi's terra-cotta army. Features such as these make this an excellent browsing book, but students can still pull information from the text. A brief history of both the United States and Canada is appended. A good addition to most collections, both for the information it offers and for its appealing format." SLJ

Smithsonian history year by year

910 Geography and travel

Goodman, Joan E.

A long and uncertain journey: the 27,000 mile voyage of Vasco da Gama; by Joan Elizabeth Goodman; illustrated by Tom McNeely. Mikaya Press 2001 47p il map (Great explorers book) $22.95

Grades: 4 5 6 7   **910**

1. Explorers

ISBN 0-9650493-7-X

    LC 00-63795

"McNeely's full-page illustrations, which vibrate with life and action, lighten the format, and quotations from the diary of an anonymous sailor on the voyage add fascinating detail and vivid description. . . . A good resource for reports, but the book is also intelligently written and exciting." Booklist

Jenkins, Steve

★ Hottest, coldest, highest, deepest. Houghton Mifflin 1998 un il $16

Grades: K 1 2   **910**

1. Geography

ISBN 0-395-89999-0

    LC 97-53080

Describes some of the remarkable places on earth, including the hottest, coldest, windiest, snowiest, highest, and deepest

This book "uses striking colorful paper collage illustrations. . . . This eye-catching introduction to geography will find a lot of use in libraries and classrooms." SLJ

Includes bibliographical references

Jennings, Ken

Maps and geography; by Ken Jennings; illustrated by TK. Little Simon, an imprint of Simon & Schuster Children's Pub. Division 2014 160 p. (The junior genius guide) $18.99

Grades: 3 4 5 6   **910**

1. Maps 2. Geography

ISBN 144249848X; 9781442473287; 9781442498488

    LC 2012050862

This book, by Ken Jennings and illustrated by Mike Lowery, is part of the "Junior Genius Guides" series. "With this . . . guide to maps and geography, you'll become an expert and wow your friends and teachers with clever facts. . . . With great illustrations, cool trivia, and fun quizzes to test your knowledge, this guide will have you on your way to whiz-kid status in no time!" (Publisher's note)

"The new line of Junior Genius Guide books kicks off with a stellar collection of facts about climate, national flags, maps, and more, all in an engaging, arch tone. Jeopardy! champ and author Jennings, making his first foray into books for children, arranges the trivia in chapters that lightly satirize a school-day schedule, including a lunch period offering an ingenious and easy recipe for an edible map, a craft project in art class, and an official certification exam before the dismissal bell... Lowery's black-and-white spot illustrations help explain concepts, such as cartographic projections, and add the overall levity, making this a successful nonfiction package as well as pure reading fun. Published simultaneously with the second in the series, Greek Mythology." Booklist

Includes bibliographical references and index

Other titles include:

Greek Mythology

Outer Space

U.S. Presidents

Kerley, Barbara

★ The world is waiting for you; by Barbara Kerley. National Geographic 2013 48 p. (hardcover: alk. paper) $17.95

Grades: 1 2 3 4 5 6   **910**

1. Vocational guidance 2. Discoveries in geography

ISBN 1426311141; 9781426311147; 9781426311154

    LC 2012026526

This book, by Barbara Kerley, "shows kids a pathway from their current interests and talents to a future career or interest. And in so doing, it also encourages adventure, exploration, and discovery, three core principles of National Geographic's mission. Selected photos make the connections compelling and the future real for kids, then rich back matter brings the message home with inspirational quotes from the real-life adventurers pictured in the images." (Publisher's note)

Richards, Jon

Planet Earth; by Jon Richards and illustrated by Ed Simkins. Owl Kids 2013 32 p. $15.95

Grades: 3 4 5 6   **910**

1. Graphic design 2. Signs and symbols

ISBN 1926973755; 9781926973753

In this book by Jon Richards "explores planet Earth using a wide variety of icons, graphics, and pictograms." Readers can "compare the tallest mountains from each continent, see the entire volume of water on the Earth poured into one glass, stack up Eiffel Towers and compare the height of the world's tallest waterfall." (Publisher's note)

Rockwell, Anne F.

★ Our earth; written and illustrated by Anne Rockwell. Harcourt Brace & Co. 1998 un il hardcover o.p. pa $6

Grades: K 1 2   **910**

1. Geography

ISBN 0-15-201679-1; 0-15-202383-6 pa

    LC 97-1247

A simple introduction to geography which explains such things as how the earth was shaped, how islands are born from volcanoes, and how gushing springs affect rivers

"The watercolor-and-gouache illustrations are very accessible. The pictures should provoke questions; parents and teachers can use the answers to provide kids with more information." Booklist

Rumford, James

Traveling man: the journey of Ibn Battuta, 1325-1354; written, illustrated, and illuminated by James Rumford. Houghton Mifflin 2001 un il map hardcover o.p. pa $7.99
Grades: 3 4 5 6   **910**
   1. Travelers 2. Voyages and travels 3. Travel writers 4. Asia -- Description
   ISBN 0-618-08366-9; 0-618-43233-7 pa
                         LC 00-57257
"Rumford's presentation is lavish and undeniably impressive. Ibn Battuta's route snakes across the spreads to create an extended map, with text boxes serving as stopping points along the way. Lush watercolor scenes, awash in gold highlights, are frequently borded by equally lush calligraphy quotes, rendered in Arabic, Persian, or Chinese." Bull Cent Child Books

Includes glossary

Wojtanik, Andrew, 1989-

The **National** Geographic Bee ultimate fact book; countries A to Z. Andrew Wojtanik. National Geographic 2012 384 p. maps (pbk.) $21.90; (reinforced library binding) $21.90
Grades: 5 6 7 8 9 10   **910**
   1. Atlases 2. Nations 3. Geography -- Encyclopedias
   ISBN 1426309473; 1426309635; 9781426309472; 9781426309632
                      LC 2011282873
This book "provides statistical information for the world's 195 countries at a glance. The book starts off with a world map and full-page continental maps. Individual entries for countries are listed alphabetically. . . . A glossary explains terms that may be unfamiliar to students . . . . Each country entry includes a map with longitude and latitude and basic facts: continent, size, population, and capital." (Voice of Youth Advocates)

Includes bibliographical references (p. 382)

910.2   Geography--Miscellany; world travel guides

Ching, Jacqueline

Jobs in green travel and tourism. Rosen Pub. 2010 80p il (Green careers) lib bdg $30.60
Grades: 5 6 7 8   **910.2**
   1. Tourist trade 2. Vocational guidance 3. Environmental movement 4. Environmental protection 5. Travel -- Environmental aspects
   ISBN 978-1-4358-3571-9 lib bdg; 1-4358-3571-9 lib bdg
                      LC 2009016587
This "well-conceived [introduction focuses] on various jobs in [travel and tourism], the education and experience required, and expected earnings. The [book is] well organized, making it easy to gain an overview of the major aspects of the work. . . . [This book] will make [a] good [addition] to career collections. Photographs from the field and website

and contact information for professional organizations add value." SLJ

Includes glossary and bibliographical references

910.3   Geography--Dictionaries, encyclopedias, concordances, gazetteers

Gifford, Clive

The **Kingfisher** geography encyclopedia; 2nd ed., rev. and updated ed.; Kingfisher 2011 487p il map $34.99
Grades: 4 5 6 7   **910.3**
   1. Reference books 2. Geography -- Encyclopedias
   ISBN 978-0-7534-6575-2; 0-7534-6575-2
Statistics, text, and color maps reveal the physical geography, peoples, politics, governments, languages, religions, and currencies of each nation of the world.

"The geographical descriptions are well written and include striking photos. The text is large and easy to read. . . . It is a great book to keep around the library for students to browse and dream about their next journey." Voice Youth Advocates

★ **Junior** worldmark encyclopedia of the nations; Timothy L. Gall, Susan Bevan Gall, and Derek M. Gleason, editors. 6th ed; Gale, Cengage Learning 2012 3200 p. 10v col. ill. (set: alk. paper) $677
Grades: 5 6 7 8   **910.3**
   1. Geography -- Encyclopedias 2. World history -- Encyclopedias 3. Political science -- Encyclopedias 4. History -- Encyclopedias, Juvenile 5. Geography -- Encyclopedias, Juvenile 6. United Nations -- Encyclopedias, Juvenile 7. Political science -- Encyclopedias, Juvenile
   ISBN 1414463138; 9781414463131; 9781414463148; 9781414463155; 9781414463162; 9781414463179; 9781414463186; 9781414463193; 9781414463209; 9781414463216; 9781414463223; 9781414463230; 9781414490861
                      LC 2011050016
First published 1996

This book series, edited by Timothy L. Gall, Susan Bevan Gall, and Derek M. Gleason, is a juvenile national encyclopedia. "Each volume . . . starts with a table of contents for the specific volume and a guide to country articles. Each country profile, organized alphabetically, begins with . . ., capital, flag, anthem, monetary unit, weights and measures. . . . Thirty-five color-coded subheadings and their corresponding numbers, as well as geographical profiles, complete each section." (Booklist)

"This new edition contains 196 countries of the world and the Palestinian Territories. Color maps... photos, and charts enhance the overall attractiveness of this updated set... This well-written encyclopedia would be a valuable resource for elementary, middle-school, and public libraries." Booklist

Includes bibliographical references and index

910.4 Accounts of travel and facilities for travelers

Aronson, Marc

★ The **world** made new; why the Age of Exploration happened & how it changed the world. [by] Marc Aronson & John W. Glenn. National Geographic 2007 64p il map $17.95; lib bdg $27.90

Grades: 4 5 6 7   **910.4**

   1. Explorers 2. Exploration

   ISBN 978-0-7922-6454-5; 978-0-7922-6978-6 lib bdg

                                   LC 2006022091

"This highly pictorial, readable overview provides significant depth of coverage. . . . The illustrations, most in full color, make ample and appropriate use of period prints as well as contemporary illustrations and photographs. The result is a visual feast that fleshes out the . . . remarkably evenhanded narrative." SLJ

Includes glossary and bibliographical references

Benoit, Peter

The **Titanic** disaster. Children's Press 2011 il (True book: disasters) lib bdg $26; pa $6.95

Grades: 3 4 5   **910.4**

   1. Shipwrecks 2. Titanic (Steamship)

   ISBN 978-0-531-20627-0 lib bdg; 0-531-20627-0 lib lib; 978-0-531-29026-2 pa; 0-531-29026-3 pa

                                 LC 2010045932

This describes the sinking of the Titanic in 1912.

"Benoit provides unbiased information that is on target for the intended audience. . . . The photographs and reproductions enhance the [text]. . . . [This book is] well-conceived." SLJ

Includes bibliographical references

Bristow, David

★ **Sky** sailors; true stories of the balloon era. [by] David L. Bristow. Farrar Straus Giroux 2010 134p il $18.99

Grades: 4 5 6 7   **910.4**

   1. Balloons

   ISBN 978-0-374-37014-5; 0-374-37014-1

                                 LC 2009037285

"This lively look at escapades of daring men—and a surprising number of women—who risked their lives flying in balloons will appeal to adventure, history and science buffs—and perhaps steampunk fans as well. Each of the nine chapters, which are chronologically arranged, focuses on an exciting story, starting with the first confirmed human balloon flight in 1783 . . . and ending with Dolly Shepherd, a young British woman in the early 1900s who parachuted out of balloons, hanging onto a trapeze. . . . Useful captions accompany many full-color illustrations of artwork and photographs." Kirkus

Includes bibliographical references

Brown, Don

★ **All** stations! distress! April 15, 1912, the day the Titanic sank. Roaring Brook Press 2008 un il (Actual times) $17.95

Grades: 2 3 4   **910.4**

   1. Shipwrecks 2. Titanic (Steamship)

   ISBN 978-1-59643-222-2; 1-59643-222-5

                                 LC 2008-08934

"Don Brown recounts the complicated, compact last moments of the [Titanic's] only voyage. . . . The tale ends with something of the later lives of the survivors. . . . The glory of All Stations! Distress! is in Brown's moody watercolors done with a brush dipped in stardust and frozen mist." Horn Book

Cerullo, Mary M.

★ **Shipwrecks**; exploring sunken cities beneath the sea. [by] Mary M. Cerullo. Dutton Children's Books 2009 64p il $18.99

Grades: 5 6 7 8   **910.4**

   1. Shipwrecks 2. Portland (Steamer) 3. Henrietta Marie (Ship)

   ISBN 978-0-525-47968-0; 0-525-47968-6

                                 LC 2008-48967

This focuses "on two wrecks: the Henrietta Marie, sunk in 1700 near the Florida Keys, and the Portland, sunk in 1898 off the coast of Massachusetts. The book makes the convincing case that these wrecks are important not only for historical reasons but also for the underwater ecosystems their structures now host. . . . This delivers both education and shivers." Booklist

Clifford, Barry

Real pirates; the untold story of the Whydah from slave ship to pirate ship. by Barry Clifford and Kenneth J. Kinkor with Sharon Simpson; photography by Kenneth Garrett. National Geographic 2008 175p il map $16.95

Grades: 4 5 6 7   **910.4**

   1. Pirates 2. Archeology 3. Shipwrecks 4. Slave trade 5. Whidah (Ship) 6. Cape Cod (Mass.)

   ISBN 978-1-4263-0279-4; 1-4263-0279-7

                                 LC 2008299778

"Clifford, an underwater archaeological explorer, used research and the artifacts recovered from the Whydah to tell the story of its life as a slave galley and pirate ship. In the process, he dispels many myths about buccaneers. . . . Photographs of artifacts . . . and the recovery crew at work combine with large visually appealing paintings of dramatic battle, storm, and courtroom scenes. . . . The book is a fascinating blend of history, ocean-diving recovery, and archaeology, and demonstrates archaeology in action and the role artifacts play in informing us about the past." SLJ

Includes bibliographical references

Denenberg, Barry

★ **Titanic** sinks! Viking 2011 72p il $19.99

Grades: 5 6 7 8   **910.4**

   1. Shipwrecks 2. Titanic (Steamship)

   ISBN 0670012432; 9780670012435

                                 LC 2011012040

This is a "gripping recounting of the Titanic's doomed maiden voyage, chronicled in the tabloid-style pages of a fictional magazine. . . . Melding fact and fiction, the book compiles dramatic headlines, articles that range from news bulletins about the building of the ship to a chatty tour of its lavish interior, and an array of stunning period photographs." Publ Wkly

Emery, William

Kodoku; William Emery; illustrations by Hanae Rivera. Heyday 2012 32 p. col. ill. (hardcover: alk. paper) $16.95

Grades: 4 5 6 **910.4**

1. Ocean travel -- Fiction 2. Voyages around the world -- Fiction 3. Mermaid (Boat)

ISBN 1597141739; 9781597141734

LC 2011032355

This children's picture book by William Emery presents a "recreation of the voyage of Kenichi Horie, the first (recorded) sailor to cross the Pacific solo. . . . Emery places the young mariner aboard a custom-built sailboat and sends him out for intense mid-ocean encounters with a typhoon, whales, sharks, jellyfish and a towering passenger ship before journey's end beneath the Golden Gate Bridge." (Kirkus Reviews)

Gibbons, Gail

★ **Sunken** treasure. Crowell 1988 32p il hardcover o.p. pa $6.95

Grades: K 1 2 3 **910.4**

1. Shipwrecks 2. Buried treasure 3. Nuestra Señora de Atocha (Ship)

ISBN 0-690-04736-3 lib bdg; 0-06-446097-5 pa

LC 87-30114

"Gibbons concentrates on the ancient Spanish galleon, the Atocha, which sank off the coast of Florida in 1662, describing under labeled headings the sinking, the search, the find, recording, salvage, restoration and preservation, cataloguing, and eventual distribution of the treasure. . . . A handsomely designed book, well organized, and easily accessible to younger readers." Horn Book

Grove, Tim

First flight around the world; the adventures of the American fliers who won the race. by Tim Grove. Abrams Books for Young Readers, in assoc. w/Smithsonian Ntl. Air & Space Museum 2015 96 p. col. ill.; maps (hardcover) $21.95

Grades: 5 6 7 8 **910.4**

1. Aeronautics -- Flights 2. Voyages around the world 3. World records 4. Flights around the world 5. United States. Army. Air Corps

ISBN 1419714821; 9781419714825

LC 2014024665

This children's book, by Tim Grove, "documents the exciting journey of four American planes--the Chicago, Boston, New Orleans, and Seattle--and their crews on a race around the world. The trip held many challenges: extreme weather, tricky navigation, unfamiliar cultures, fragile planes, and few airfields. The world fliers risked their lives for the sake of national pride." (Publisher's note)

"This gripping, well-designed title details the United States' 1924 successful attempt to become the first nation to circumnavigate the globe by flight...Offering a look at a lesser-known historical event, this beautiful, well-written book is an essential addition for all collections." SLJ

Includes bibliographical references

Hagglund, Betty

Epic treks. Kingfisher 2011 64p il (Epic adventure) $19.99

Grades: 5 6 7 8 **910.4**

1. Explorers 2. Voyages and travels

ISBN 978-0-7534-6668-1; 0-7534-6668-6

LC 2011041638

"The graphics will grab readers in [this] exciting, extra-large-size [title] . . . packed with high-quality color photos on every double-page spread. Just as gripping are the narratives, captions, and technical details of exploration, adventure, and survival. . . . Epic Treks covers Lewis and Clark, Livingston and Stanley, Burk and Wells, and Amundsen and Scott, each journey an exciting adventure filled with details about what they endured and what they found, as well as their failures and shortcomings." Booklist

Includes glossary

Hopkinson, Deborah

★ **Titanic**; voices from the disaster. by Deborah Hopkinson. Scholastic Press 2012 289 p. (hardcover) $17.99

Grades: 5 6 7 8 **910.4**

1. Titanic (Steamship) 2. Shipwrecks

ISBN 0545116740; 9780545116749

LC 2011006695

Robert F. Sibert Honor Book (2013)

YALSA Award for Excellence in Nonfiction for Young Adults Finalist (2013)

In this book about the sinking of the Titanic, author Deborah "Hopkinson begins with a description of the ship . . . and introduces some of the passengers who embarked on its maiden voyage. The narrative shifts . . . to the disaster itself with a litany of things gone wrong. . . . [M]emoirs . . . are interlaced throughout the text, as survivors testified . . . on the relative chaos or calm, heroism or cowardice, of passengers and crew." (Bulletin of the Center for Children's Books)

Includes bibliographical references

Hunter, Nick

Pirate treasure; by Nick Hunter. Raintree 2013 48 p. (hb) $29.33

Grades: 5 6 7 8 **910.4**

1. Pirates 2. Buried treasure

ISBN 1410949532; 9781410949530; 9781410949608

LC 2012012890

This book, by Nick Hunter, "examines the hunt for treasures lost or hidden by pirates, and examines whether any of the legends of buried treasure could really be true. Part of the Treasure Hunters series, 'Pirate Treasure' offers a crosscurricular mix of science & technology and history & civilizations. Pirate treasures covered in the book include those of the famous Blackbeard and Captain Kidd, the pirate shipwreck the Whydah, and the mysterious Oak Island Money Pit." (Publisher's note)

Includes bibliographical references and index

Jenson-Elliott, Cindy

Life under the pirate code; by Cindy Jenson-Elliott. Capstone Press 2013 32 p. (Blazers. Pirates) (library binding) $25.99

Grades: 2 3 4 **910.4**

1. Pirates

ISBN 1429686111; 1620652013; 9781429686112; 9781620652015

LC 2011048907

In this book, by Cindy Jenson-Elliott, readers will "look inside to learn about the pirate code and how it guided everyday life on a pirate ship. Pirates were thieves and murderers. But even these criminals had to follow certain rules. And if they broke the rules, they faced severe punishments." (Publisher's note)

Includes bibliographical references (p. 31) and index

The **most** famous pirates; by Cindy Jenson-Elliott. Capstone Press 2012 32 p. (library binding) $25.99
Grades: 2 3 4   **910.4**
1. Pirates
ISBN; 142968609X; 9781429686099
LC 2011048910

This book, by Cindy Jenson-Elliott, provides an introduction to pirate life for young readers. Pages contain "information about tools, weaponry, the pirate code, life on a ship, and famous buccaneers. The books are . . . organized into short chapters, and some paragraphs have their own simple subtitles." Well-known pirates discussed include Frances Drake, William Kidd, and Blackbeard. (School Library Journa)

Includes bibliographical references (p. 31) and index

Pirate ships ahoy! by Cindy Jenson-Elliott. Capstone Press 2013 32 p. (library binding) $25.99
Grades: 2 3 4   **910.4**
1. Ships 2. Pirates 3. Sailing ships
ISBN 1429686103; 9781429686105
LC 2011048909

This book, by Cindy Jenson-Elliott, examines "how pirates lived, worked, and fought on their ships, [noting that] a ship was more to a pirate than just a place to make a living. Ships often provided more freedom than pirates could get in most places." (Publisher's note)

Includes bibliographical references and index

Pirates' tools for life at sea; by Cindy Jenson-Elliott. Capstone Press 2012 32 p. (library binding) $25.99
Grades: 2 3 4   **910.4**
1. Pirates 2. Weapons
ISBN 142968612X; 9781429686129; 9781620652046
LC 2011048906

This book, by Cindy Jenson-Elliott, looks at "pirates most important gear. From swords and cannons to maps and carpentry tools . . . weapons and tools were as important to pirates as the ships they sailed on. [It examines how] to succeed at sea, pirates kept their gear clean and ready for action." (Publisher's note)

Includes bibliographical references (p. 31) and index

Marschall, Ken
★ **Inside** the Titanic; illustrated by Ken Marschall; text by Hugh Brewster. Little, Brown 1997 32p il $19.95
Grades: 4 5 6 7   **910.4**
1. Shipwrecks 2. Titanic (Steamship)
ISBN 0-316-55716-1
LC 97-382

"Color cutaway paintings of the Titanic in this oversize book allow readers to view every deck as they follow two 12-year-old boys exploring the vessel, and to see how the liner struck the iceberg and sank." Booklist

Includes glossary and bibliographical references

McPherson, Stephanie Sammartino
★ **Iceberg** right ahead! the tragedy of the Titanic. Twenty-First Century Books 2011 112p il lib bdg $33.26

Grades: 4 5 6 7 8   **910.4**
1. Shipwrecks 2. Titanic (Steamship)
ISBN 9780761367567
LC 2011002352

"With innumerable books, movies, documentaries, novels, and biographies all telling versions of the Titanic story, it would seem that there is little more to learn, yet by providing more details and some of the most up-to-date research, McPherson's compelling, thoughtful narrative proves otherwise. . . . The layout includes plenty of period photographs, diagrams, artwork, and sidebars with interesting tangential tidbits, making for a thorough resource. . . . A comprehensive, well-written, thoroughly researched title." SLJ

Includes bibliographical references

Mundy, Robyn
Epic voyages. Kingfisher 2011 64p il (Epic adventure) $19.99
Grades: 5 6 7 8   **910.4**
1. Explorers
ISBN 978-0-7534-6574-5; 0-7534-6574-4

"The graphics will grab readers in [this] exciting, extra-large-size [title] . . . packed with high-quality color photos on every double-page spread. Just as gripping are the narratives, captions, and technical details of exploration, adventure, and survival. . . . [This] book covers Magellan, Cook, Shackleton, Heyedahl and also Chichester, who, in 1966, sailed alone around the world." Booklist

Riggs, Kate
Pirates. Creative Education 2010 24p il (Great warriors) $24.25; pa $8.99
Grades: K 1 2   **910.4**
1. Pirates
ISBN 978-1-60818-002-8; 1-60818-002-6; 978-0-89812-573-3 pa; 0-89812-573-1 pa
LC 2010019611

A introduction to the roving warriors known as pirates, including their history, lifestyle, weapons, and how they remain a part of today's culture by their continued existence.

This title makes pirates "accessible to students just beginning to read on their own. The text and design of the [book is] spare, and vocabulary words are introduced unobtrusively. . . . The concepts are simple, but introduced without oversimplification that might lead to misunderstandings. [This is an] excellent [introduction] and fun to read aloud." SLJ

Includes glossary and bibliographical references

Ross, Stewart
★ **Into** the unknown; how great explorers found their way by land, sea, and air. Candlewick Press 2011 un il map $19.99
Grades: 4 5 6 7   **910.4**
1. Explorers 2. Discoveries in geography
ISBN 978-0-7636-4948-7; 0-7636-4948-1
LC 2010038720

"Biesty's trademark amusing, informatively detailed illustrations are a highlight of this entertaining examination of several voyages of exploration. . . . Chapters cover an impressive range of exploration. In addition to the usual suspects, they include a 340 B.C.E. Greek voyage to the Arctic Circle; Chinese Admiral Zheng He to India; [and] David Livingston and Mary Kingsley into the African interior. . . .

Each chapter includes a fold-out section of illustrations with a map of the journey and a cross-section of the method of transportation. . . . An altogether agreeable package for armchair explorers." Kirkus

910.91634   Shipwrecks

Sherman, Casey

The **finest** hours; the true story of a heroic sea rescue. Michael J. Tougias and Casey Sherman. Christy Ottaviano Books 2014 176 p. illustrations (hardback) $17.99

Grades: 4 5 6 7 8   **910.91634**

1. Shipwrecks   2. Survival after airplane accidents, shipwrecks, etc.   3. CG36500 (Lifeboat)   4. Pendleton (Tanker)   5. Shipwrecks -- Massachusetts   6. Shipwreck survival -- History

ISBN 0805097643; 9780805097641; 9781250044235
                             LC 2013030661

This book by Michael J. Tougias and Casey Sherman "tells the story of a harrowing Coast Guard rescue when four men in a tiny lifeboat overcame insurmountable odds and saved more than 30 stranded sailors." In this book, the events of the February 18, 1952 wreck of two oil tankers near Cape Cod are adapted for middle-grade readers. (Publisher's note)

"The accounts of each rescue's logistics—for example, sailors trying to time their leaps from their destroyed tanker to the rescue boat amid rocking waves—are nail-biting, and they are relayed by the authors with an effectively sober, just-the-facts terseness." Booklist

Includes bibliographical references

910.92   Geographers, travelers, explorers regardless of country of origin

Fritz, Jean

Around the world in a hundred years; from Henry the Navigator to Magellan. illustrated by Anthony Bacon Venti. Putnam 1994 128p il map hardcover o.p. pa $8.99

Grades: 4 5 6 7   **910.92**

1. Princes   2. Explorers   3. Colonial administrators

ISBN 0-399-22527-7; 0-698-11638-0 pa
                            LC 92-27042

"Fritz examines the voyages of ten explorers, acknowledging that their contributions, though deserving of recognition, were dearly bought. Opening and closing chapters summarize the fourteenth-century world view and indicate later expansion of geographic understanding. As always, Fritz tempers scholarship with humor in this brief volume—illustrated with drawings in pencil—which reads like an adventure story." Horn Book Guide

Includes bibliographical references

911   Historical geography

Chrisp, Peter

Atlas of ancient worlds; author, Peter Chrisp; consultant, Philip Parker. DK Pub. 2009 96p il map $21.99

Grades: 4 5 6 7 8   **911**

1. Reference books   2. Historical atlases   3. Ancient

civilization

ISBN 978-0-7566-4512-0; 0-7566-4512-3

This atlas consists "of maps and illustrations accompanied by extensive captions outlining the cultures of many civilizations. Each section begins with a map of a continent and a table of contents detailing which peoples will be discussed in it. Each civilization is covered in a chapter spread that includes a small map of the extent of each empire and many photos, pictures, and captioned drawings. . . . The accompanying clip art CD contains images of many of the artifacts as well as of the maps found in the book. . . . This atlas offers a wonderful introduction to [ancient civilizations] as well as solid geography basics." SLJ

Includes glossary

Leacock, Elspeth

★ **Places** in time; a new atlas of American history. [by] Elspeth Leacock and Susan Buckley; illustrations by Randy Jones. Houghton Mifflin 2001 48p il $15; pa $6.95

Grades: 4 5 6 7   **911**

1. Reference books   2. United States -- Historical geography

ISBN 0-395-97958-7; 0-618-3113-0 pa
                            LC 00-59741

This book presents "20 sites in American history at the moment of their historical significance, beginning in 1200 (Cahokia) and ending in 1953. Places and times include New Plymouth—1627, Charlestown—1739, Saratoga—1777, Philadelphia—1787, Abilene—1871, and Chicago—1893. The detailed cutaway views of homes, forts, and mills are impressive enough to keep readers looking again and again. These fascinating slices of life stir the imagination and lead to questions and further research." SLJ

Includes bibliographical references

Todras, Ellen H.

Explorers, trappers, and pioneers; by Ellen H. Todras. Kingfisher 2012 32 p. ill. (All About America) (paperback) $9.99

Grades: 4 5 6   **911**

1. America -- Exploration   2. Frontier and pioneer life -- United States

ISBN 0753465159; 9780753465158

This book by Ellen H. Todras is part of the "All About America" series. It "begins with the Vikings landing in Newfoundland 1,000 years ago and concludes with the Oklahoma Land Rush in 1889." It "offers 13 highly illustrated double-page spreads that present topics using a few paragraphs of information, related text boxes, and several color illustrations and five or more captioned illustrations." (Booklist)

912   Graphic representations of surface of earth and of extraterrestrial worlds

★ **Beginner's** United States atlas; a it's your country, be a part of it! National Geographic 2009 128p il map $18.95

Grades: 1 2 3 4   **912**

1. Atlases   2. Reference books   3. United States -- Maps

ISBN 978-1-4263-0512-2; 1-4263-0512-5

Provides information about the United States, including state flags, birds, flowers, and capitals, as well as key points about the water, people, and physical features of each state

Boyer, Crispin

National Geographic kids ultimate U.S. road trip atlas; maps, games, activities, and more for hours of backseat fun. by Crispin Boyer. 1st ed. National Geographic 2012 128 p. col. ill., col. maps (pbk.: alk. paper) $5.99; (lib. bdg.: alk. paper) $14.90

Grades: 4 5 6   **912**

1. Atlases 2. Road maps 3. United States -- Historical geography -- Maps 4. United States -- Maps 5. United States -- Description and travel 6. Recreation areas -- United States -- Maps 7. Outdoor recreation -- United States -- Maps

ISBN 1426309333; 1426309341; 9781426309335; 9781426309342

LC 2011034647

This book, by author Crispin Boyer, "includes . . . road maps of each state and Washington, D.C., and a map of the United States. State symbols, cool things to do, boredom busters, fun facts, wacky roadside attractions, and games accompany the maps. . . . In the back matter [there is] a comprehensive index . . . for kids to look up names and places." (Publisher's note)

Includes bibliographical references and index.

Crane, Nick

Barefoot Books world atlas. Barefoot Books 2011 56p

Grades: 3 4 5   **912**

1. Maps 2. Atlases 3. Geography

ISBN 1-84686-333-3; 978-1-84686-333-2

"This fresh and informative atlas offers engaging, fact-filled overviews of Earth's oceans and continents. Mini-books, flaps, and sidebars address topics ranging from 'People and Places' to 'Transport.' Dean's maps are crowded with warmly illustrated people, animals, places, and objects that represent particular areas of the world. . . . With its emphasis on sustainability, interconnectedness, and diversity, the book offers young armchair travelers and globe-trotters much to discover. Includes a removable world map. An app is also available." Publ Wkly

Leedy, Loreen

★ Mapping Penny's world. Holt & Co. 2000 un il map $17; pa $7.95

Grades: 1 2 3   **912**

1. Maps

ISBN 0-8050-6178-9; 0-8050-7262-4 pa

LC 99-48327

After learning about maps in school, Lisa maps all the favorite places of her dog Penny

"The concepts are clear, and the digital-painting and photo-collage illustrations are uncluttered and ably clarify the text." SLJ

★ National Geographic atlas of the world; 9th ed.; National Geographic Society 2010 153p il $175

Grades: 5 6 7 8 9 10   **912**

1. Atlases 2. Reference books

ISBN 978-1-4262-0634-4

First published 1963

"The National Geographic Society presents more than 80 large-format color maps grouped by continent portraying the world with detailed, digitally painted terrain modeling. Each continent is introduced by satellite, political, and physical maps. Political maps for regions and specific countries follow." Libr J

★ National Geographic Kids beginner's world atlas; 3rd ed.; National Geographic 2011 il map $27.90

Grades: K 1 2 3   **912**

1. Atlases 2. Reference books

ISBN 978-1-4263-0839-0; 1-4263-0839-6

First published 1999 with title: National Geographic beginner's world atlas

This is an "eye-catching atlas for the child who is ready to learn about the world beyond his or her own community. Enticing panoramic photographs introduce each continent, and easy-to-decipher maps make this oversize volume one that will fascinate inquisitive young children given to browsing." Booklist

★ National Geographic United States atlas for young explorers; 3rd ed.; National Geographic 2008 175p il map $24.95

Grades: 4 5 6 7   **912**

1. Atlases 2. Reference books 3. United States -- Maps

ISBN 978-1-4263-0255-8; 1-4263-0255-X

First published 1999

This atlas offers maps of each of the states in the United States, divided into five geographical regions, plus U.S. territories. Each state map indicates physical features such as mountains and rivers, national forests, cities, major interstate roads, and industries, and is accompanied by color photos and facts about the state. An introductory section describes how to use the companion web site for more information, maps of the United States biomes, climates, natural hazards, political states, population, ethnic diversity, and energy use.

★ National Geographic world atlas for young explorers; 3rd ed.; National Geographic 2007 191p il map $24.95

Grades: 3 4 5 6   **912**

1. Atlases 2. Reference books

ISBN 978-1-4263-0088-2

First published 1998

This atlas includes photographs taken from space, political and physical maps, flags and statistics, and links to additional images and information on a companion website.

Parker, Victoria

How far is far? comparing geographical distances. [by] Vic Parker. Heinemann Library 2011 32p il (Measuring and comparing) lib bdg $26; pa $7.99

Grades: 2 3 4   **912**

1. Maps 2. Measurement

ISBN 978-1-4329-3956-4 lib bdg; 1-4329-3956-4 lib bdg; 978-1-4329-3964-9 pa; 1-4329-3964-5 pa

LC 2010000926

This "contains vivid photographs, charts, and diagrams with captions, explanations, and examples. Questions are posed throughout . . . to entice young learners to 'stop and think' or continue reading for more information. . . . [This]

would make an excellent addition to any classroom library."
Libr Media Connect

Includes glossary and bibliographical references

Rand McNally Goodes World Atlas; edited by Howard
Veregin. Rand McNally 2009 400 p. $45

Grades: 4 5 6 7 8 9 10 11 12 Adult 912

1. Maps 2. Atlases

ISBN 0528877542; 9780528877544

This book, edited by Howard Veregin, "features over
250 pages of maps, from definitive physical and political
maps to important thematic maps that illustrate the spatial
aspects of many important topics. [It] includes 160 pages
of new, digitally produced reference maps, as well as new
thematic maps on global climate change, sea level rise, $CO2$
emissions, polar ice fluctuations, deforestation, extreme
weather events, infectious diseases, water resources, and energy production." (Publisher's note)

Student atlas; Dorling Kindersley, Inc. 6th ed. DK Pub.
2013 176 p. ill. (hardcover) $14.99

Grades: 5 6 7 8 912

1. Atlases 2. Geography

ISBN 0756663199; 9780756663193

This book from DK Publishing is part of the Student
Atlas series. It is a "single-volume guide to the nations of
the world. [It's] fully revised and updated, and packed with
clear, detailed maps highlighting landscape, industry, land
use, population, climate and environmental issues." (Publisher's note)

912.01 Maps -- Philosophy and theory

Waldron, Melanie

How to read a map; Melanie Waldron. Capstone Raintree 2013 32 p. (Let's get mapping!) (pb) $7.99

Grades: 2 3 4 5 912.01

1. Maps 2. Atlases 3. Map reading

ISBN 1410949060; 9781410948991; 9781410949066
LC 2012008416

Author Melanie Waldron's book offers a guide to map-
reading. "Maps are essential tools for understanding the
world around us. Learning to read maps - both printed and
online - is a core skill that forms the basis of social studies.
This book explores the different types of features used on
maps, explaining what they can show us and how to make
sense of them." (Publisher's note)

Includes bibliographical references and index

916 Geography of and travel in Africa

Bodden, Valerie

To the heart of Africa; by Valerie Bodden. Creative
Education 2011 48 p. col. ill. (Great Expeditions) (library)
$34.25

Grades: 5 6 7 8 916

1. Exploration 2. Africa -- Exploration 3. Explorers --
Scotland -- Biography 4. Explorers -- Africa, Southern
-- Biography 5. Africa, Sub-Saharan -- Discovery
and exploration 6. Missionaries, Medical -- Africa,

Southern -- Biography

ISBN 1608180662; 9781608180660
LC 2010033414

This book by Valerie Bodden is part of the Great Expeditions series and looks at expeditions into Africa. "Bodden includes brief biographies of major people involved
in each expedition, interspersed with the text. There are
also numerous photographs or reproductions of paintings
and woodcuts from the time of the expeditions." (Library
Media Connection)

Includes bibliographical references (p. 46-47) and index.

917 Geography of and travel in North America

Butts, Edward

Shipwrecks, monsters, and mysteries of the Great
Lakes; [by] Ed Butts. Tundra Books 2010 80p il pa
$14.95

Grades: 4 5 6 7 917

1. Shipwrecks 2. Great Lakes

ISBN 978-1-77049-206-6 pa; 1-77049-206-2 pa

"In 1679, a French ship called the Griffon left Green Bay
on Lake Michigan, bound for Niagara with a cargo of furs.
Neither the Griffon nor the five-man crew was ever seen
again. . . . Its disappearance was probably the result of the
first shipwreck on a Great Lake. Since then, more than six
thousand vessels, large and small, have met tragic ends. . . .
Shoals and reefs, uncharted rocks, and sandbars could snare
a ship or rip open a hull. Unpredictable winds could capsize
a vessel at any moment. . . . The wreckage of ships and the
bones of the people who sail them litter the bottoms of the
five lakes: Ontario, Erie, Huron, Michigan, and Superior. Ed
Butts has gathered stories and lake lore in this [volume]."
(Publisher's note) "Ages nine to twelve." (Quill Quire)

Clark, Diane C.

★ A kid's guide to Washington, D.C. [written by Diane C. Clark; illustrations and maps by Richard E. Brown]
rev and updated ed.; Harcourt, Inc. 2008 154p il map pa
$14

Grades: 3 4 5 6 917

1. Puzzles 2. Washington (D.C.) 3. Children -- Travel

ISBN 978-0-15-206125-8 pa; 0-15-206125-8 pa
LC 2007-015509

First published 1989

"Brimming with useful information in both text and
sidebars, this sturdy, large-format guidebook covers a broad
array of topics, everything from a brief history of Washington, D.C., to practical advice on how to get around the city.
. . . The extensive appendix now lists 128 places to see and
gives their locations in the city and online. Shades of blue
and red add color to the pages, which usually include graphic elements such as photos and line drawings. An attractive,
practical guide for young visitors to Washington." Booklist

Koehler-Pentacoff, Elizabeth

Jackson and Bud's bumpy ride; America's first cross-
country automobile trip. by Elizabeth Koehler-Pentacoff;
illustrated by Wes Hargis. Millbrook Press 2009 un il

Grades: 1 2 3 917

1. Physicians 2. Automobile travel 3. United States

-- Description and travel
ISBN 0822578859; 9780822578857

LC 2008012752

An account of the first cross-country automobile trip in the United States made in 1903 by Dr. Horatio Jackson, mechanic Sewall J. Crocker, and bulldog Bud

"Short sentences and readable prose capture much of the triumph and challenge of the 63-day trip. . . . The animated, cartoon illustrations are lighthearted and detailed, and add much to the narrative." SLJ

Includes bibliographical references

Rubbino, Salvatore

★ A walk in New York. Candlewick Press 2009 37p il map $16.99

Grades: PreK K 1 2 3 4   **917**

1. New York (N.Y.) -- Description and travel
ISBN 978-0-7636-3855-9; 0-7636-3855-2

LC 2008-20787

This follows a wide-eyed boy and his dad on their walk around Manhattan, from Grand Central Terminal to the top of the Empire State Building, from Greenwich Village to the Statute of Liberty. Includes lots of facts and trivia and a gatefold of the Empire State Building.

"The book's large trim size and the illustrator's perspective provide an entertaining and palpable sense of scale as the small boy marvels at skyscrapers and landmarks. . . . Neophytes and jaded residents alike will embrace this vibrant and enticing slice of the Big Apple." Pub Wkly

Schanzer, Rosalyn

★ How we crossed the West; the adventures of Lewis & Clark. National Geographic Soc. 1997 un il hardcover o.p. pa $7.95

Grades: 3 4 5   **917**

1. Explorers 2. Lewis and Clark Expedition (1804-1806) 3. Territorial governors 4. West (U.S.) -- Exploration
ISBN 0-7922-3738-2; 0-7922-6726-5 pa

LC 96-6585

"Pithy and sometimes humorous, the text tells of contacts with Native Americans, encounters with wildlife . . . and the hardships of the trail. Warm in color and accessible in style, the acrylic paintings have a folk-art inspiration." Booklist

917.3   Geography of and travel in United States

National Geographic kids national parks guide U.S.A. the most amazing sights, scenes, and cool activities from coast to coast. National Geographic. National Geographic Society 2012 160 p.

Grades: 4 5 6   **917.3**

1. National parks and reserves -- United States -- Guidebooks 2. United States -- Description and travel -- Guidebooks
ISBN 9781426309311; 9781426309328

LC 2011034235

This children's guidebook of America's National Parks, by Sarah Wassner Flynn, features "tips on exploration, information about animals, sidebars, checklists, fun facts, maps, cool things to do, and much more. Conservation informa-

tion, a 'find out more' section, glossary, and index add ample back matter to round out this book." (Publisher's note)

Includes bibliographical references and index

917.804   West (U.S.) -- travel

Bodden, Valerie

Through the American West; by Valerie Bodden. Creative Education 2011 48 p. col. ill. (Great Expeditions) (library) $34.25

Grades: 5 6 7 8   **917.804**

1. Lewis and Clark Expedition (1804-1806) 2. West (U.S.) -- Discovery and exploration
ISBN 1608180654; 9781608180653

LC 2010033413

This book by Valerie Bodden is part of the "Great Expeditions" series. It describes an expedition "led by William Clark and Meriwether Lewis to explore the wilderness to the west and look for an all water route to the Pacific Ocean. They were aided by Sacagawea, a Shoshone Indian. The adventures and hardships of the arduous three-year journey include both the achievements and the disappointments encountered along the way". (Children's Literature)

Includes bibliographical references (p. 46-47) and index.

919   Geography of and travel in Australasia, Pacific Ocean islands, Atlantic Ocean islands, Arctic islands, Antarctica and on extraterrestrial worlds

Martin, Jacqueline Briggs

★ The lamp, the ice, and the boat called Fish; based on a true story. pictures by Beth Krommes. Houghton Mifflin 2001 un il $15

Grades: 3 4 5 6   **919**

1. Inuit 2. Karluk (Ship) 3. Arctic regions 4. Canadian Arctic Expedition (1913-1918)
ISBN 0-618-00341-X

LC 99-35303

"The quiet, intriguing language, with a poet's attention to sound, will lull young ones into the story's drama, as will Beth Krommes' captivating scratchboard illustrations." Booklist

O'Brien, Patrick

★ You are the first kid on Mars. G.P. Putnam's Sons 2009 un il $16.99

Grades: K 1 2 3   **919**

1. Life on other planets 2. Mars (Planet) -- Exploration
ISBN 978-0-399-24634-0; 0-399-24634-7

LC 2008-29486

"This intriguing vision of space exploration should set imaginations soaring." Publ Wkly

919.89   Antarctica - Geography

Bodden, Valerie

To the South Pole; by Valerie Bodden. Creative Education 2011 48 p. col. ill. (Great Expeditions) (library) $34.25

Grades: 5 6 7 8   **919.89**

1. South Pole -- Exploration 2. Amundsen, Roald, 1872-1928 3. Explorers -- Norway -- Biography

ISBN 1608180697; 9781608180691

LC 2010033552

This book by Valerie Bodden, part of the "Great Expeditions" series, presents "a history of Roald Amundsen's . . . 1911 trip to the South Pole, detailing the challenges encountered, the individuals involved, the discoveries made, and how the expedition left its mark upon the world." (Publisher's note) . Major historical milestones and details about the search for the southernmost tip of the world are related in" addition to "profiles of four of the major explorers". (Children's Literature)

Includes bibliographical references (p. 46-47) and index.

Dowdeswell, Evelyn

Scott of the Antarctic; Evelyn Dowdeswell, Julian Dowdeswell, and Angela Seddon. Heinemann Library 2013 32 p. (hb) $26.65

Grades: 2 3 4   **919.89**

1. Explorers 2. South Pole 3. Antarctica -- Discovery and exploration -- British

ISBN 1432968904; 9781432968908; 9781432968915

LC 2011037936

This book "[e]xamines Antarctica and [explorer] Robert Scott's epic expedition to the South Pole." (WorldCat) To "commemorate the 100th anniversary of Scott[']s Antarctic trek, and his tragic death before returning home, this book charts the epic race to the South Pole." (Google Books)

Includes bibliographical references and index

92   Individual biography

Aaron, Hank, 1934-

★ Tavares, Matt. **Henry** Aaron's dream. Candlewick Press 2010 un il $16.99; pa $6.99

Grades: 3 4 5   **92**

1. Baseball players 2. African American athletes 3. Baseball -- Biography

ISBN 978-0-7636-3224-3; 0-7636-3224-4; 978-07636-6129-8 pa

LC 2008037417

"Well-written text and brilliantly composed art highlight the poignancy and triumph in Aaron's story. This rousing tribute should resonate with a wide audience." SLJ

"This is a biography of Henry Aaron's young life — from his sandlot days through his time in the Negro Leagues to the day he played his first spring training game for the Braves." Publisher's note

Ada, Alma Flor, 1938-

Parker-Rock, Michelle. **Alma** Flor Ada; an author kids love. Enslow Publishers 2008 48p bibl il por (Authors kids love) lib bdg $23.93

Grades: 3 4 5   **92**

1. Authors 2. Educators 3. Dramatists 4. Women authors 5. Cuban Americans 6. Authors, American 7. Children's authors

ISBN 978-0-7660-2760-2 lib bdg; 0-7660-2760-0 lib bdg

LC 2008004641

"The frequent use of direct quotes makes the [text] particularly enjoyable. . . . Kids will be fascinated with Ada's childhood home in Cuba. . . . Well written, interesting, and useful for reports." SLJ

Includes bibliographical references

Adams, Abigail, 1744-1818

Adler, David A. A **picture** book of John and Abigail Adams; by David A. Adler and Michael S. Adler; illustrated by Ronald Himler. Holiday House 2010 un il $17.95

Grades: 1 2 3   **92**

1. Presidents 2. Vice-presidents 3. Parents of presidents 4. Spouses of presidents 5. Presidents -- United States 6. Presidents' spouses -- United States

ISBN 978-0-8234-2007-0; 0-8234-2007-8

LC 2006050069

"This excellent picture-book biography introduces the childhoods, courtship, and family life of John and Abigail Adams as well as their years in public service. . . . Himler's graceful and well-composed drawings are brightened with luminous washes." Booklist

Includes bibliographical references

Adams, John, 1735-1826

Adler, David A. A **picture** book of John and Abigail Adams; by David A. Adler and Michael S. Adler; illustrated by Ronald Himler. Holiday House 2010 un il $17.95

Grades: 1 2 3   **92**

1. Presidents 2. Vice-presidents 3. Parents of presidents 4. Presidents -- United States 5. Presidents' spouses -- United States

ISBN 978-0-8234-2007-0; 0-8234-2007-8

LC 2006050069

"This excellent picture-book biography introduces the childhoods, courtship, and family life of John and Abigail Adams as well as their years in public service. . . . Himler's graceful and well-composed drawings are brightened with luminous washes." Booklist

Includes bibliographical references

Adams, Samuel, 1722-1803

★ Fritz, Jean. **Why** don't you get a horse, Sam Adams? illustrated by Trina Schart Hyman. 1974 47p il $15.99; pa $5.99

Grades: 2 3 4   **92**

1. Statesmen 2. Members of Congress 3. Writers on politics 4. United States -- History -- 1775-1783, Revolution

ISBN 0-399-23401-2; 0-698-11416-7 pa

"A piece of history far more entertaining and readable than most fiction. . . . The author has humanized a figure of the Revolution: Adams emerges a marvelously funny and believable man. The illustrations play upon his foibles; they are, in fact, even more outrageously mocking than the text. A tour de force, for both author and illustrator." Horn Book

Albers, Josef, 1888-1976

★ Wing, Natasha. An **eye** for color: the story of Josef Albers; illustrated by Julia Breckenreid. Holt & Co. 2009 un il $16.99

Grades: 3 4 5 6   92

1. Artists 2. Painters 3. Color in art 4. Artists, German 5. Printmakers 6. Art teachers

ISBN 978-0-8050-8072-8; 0-8050-8072-4

LC 2008038214

"This creative biography explores how Albers, perhaps best known for his paintings of squares in different color combinations, 'saw art in the simplest things.' . . . . After visiting Mexico—Albers is shown climbing an abstract templelike structure of colorful rectangles—he reflects on the effects of combining different colors. . . . An accessible and lively introduction to this artist and to color theory." Publ Wkly

Includes glossary and bibliographical references

Alcott, Louisa May, 1832-1888

McDonough, Yona Zeldis. **Louisa**; the life of Louisa May Alcott. illustrated by Bethanne Andersen. Henry Holt and Co. 2009 un il $17.99

Grades: 2 3 4   92

1. Authors 2. Novelists 3. Women authors 4. Authors, American 5. Young adult authors

ISBN 978-0-8050-8192-3; 0-8050-8192-5

LC 2008-38222

"McDonough clearly lays out the essentials of Alcott's life story. Often striking and occasionally memorable, Andersen's gouache-and-pastel illustrations use strong shapes and rich colors to create iconic images." Booklist

Includes bibliographical references

Aldrin, Buzz, 1930-

★ Aldrin, Buzz, 1930- **Reaching** for the moon; paintings by Wendell Minor. HarperCollins Children's Books 2005 un il $16.99; lib bdg $17.89; pa $6.99

Grades: 2 3 4   92

1. Astronauts 2. Air force officers 3. Nonfiction writers 4. Biography, Individual

ISBN 0-06-055445-2; 0-06-055446-0 lib bdg; 0-06-055447-7 pa

LC 2004-6247

Aldrin "discusses his childhood interest in flight, his military training and academic preparation for a career as an astronaut, and . . . his pride and excitement in both his Gemini 12 extravehicular activity and his moon walk. . . . Ages five to nine." (Bull Cent Child Books)

"In this picture book, Aldrin, the second man to step foot on the moon, relates the life events that led him to the space program and his assignment on Apollo 11. . . . Minor's colorful and precisely rendered illustrations help this effort really take off, especially in the images of Aldrin's space journeys." Booklist

Alexander, the Great, 356-323 B.C.

Adams, Simon. **Alexander**; the boy soldier who conquered the world. National Geographic 2005 64p il map (World history biographies) $17.95; lib bdg $27.90

Grades: 4 5 6 7   92

1. Ancient civilization 2. Kings

ISBN 0-7922-3660-2; 0-7922-3661-0 lib bdg

This describes the life and times of Alexander the Great.

This is a "handsomely designed [book]. . . . illustrated with maps and many color photographs of art and sculpture that give substance to [the era]. . . . Adams does not downplay Alexander's brutality or all-consuming ambition and includes examples of both." SLJ

Includes bibliographical references

Demi. **Alexander** the Great; written and illustrated by Demi. Marshall Cavendish 2010 59p il $19.99

Grades: 4 5 6 7   92

1. Kings and rulers 2. Greece -- History -- 323-1453

ISBN 978-0-7614-5700-8; 0-7614-5700-3

"Demi's meticulous, expansive story highlights the achievements of Alexander the Great, who conquered much of the known world (to the Greeks) in only 12 years. . . . Illustrated with Demi's customary skill, . . . Alexander's conflicts and victories will delight young history lovers with their daring." Publ Wkly

Ali, Muhammad, 1942-

★ Bolden, Tonya. The **champ!** the story of Muhammad Ali. illustrated by R. Gregory Christie. Alfred A. Knopf 2004 un il $17.95; lib bdg $19.99; pa $6.99

Grades: 2 3 4 5   92

1. African American athletes 2. Boxers (Persons) 3. Boxing -- Biography

ISBN 0-375-82401-4; 0-375-92401-9 lib bdg; 0-440-41782-1 pa

LC 2004-10082

A biography of the African American boxer

"In simple, clear, and lively text, Bolden introduces both Ali the fighter and Ali the activist. . . . The words interact well with Christie's sturdy acrylic paintings." Booklist

Myers, Walter Dean, 1937- **Muhammad** Ali; the people's champion. illustrated by Alix Delinois. Collins Amistad 2010 un il $16.99; lib bdg $17.89

Grades: 1 2 3   92

1. African American athletes 2. Boxers (Persons) 3. Boxing -- Biography

ISBN 978-0-06-029131-0; 0-06-029131-1; 978-0-06-029132-7 lib bdg; 0-06-029132-X lib bdg

LC 2009-05326

"The curious mix of bravado and humility constituting the life of Muhammad Ali receives a sensitive exploration in this vibrantly illustrated biography. . . . Delinois is with Myers every step, using wild splotches of paint and scribbles of chalk not only to capture the velocity of a punch but also fill in contexual blanks. . . . Unexpectedly far reaching, this is a Muhammed Ali for the thinking child." Booklist

★ Smith, Charles R., 1969- **Twelve** rounds to glory: the story of Muhammad Ali; illustrated by Bryan Collier. Candlewick Press 2007 80p il $19.99

Grades: 5 6 7 8   92

1. African American athletes 2. Boxers (Persons) 3. Boxing -- Biography

ISBN 978-0-7636-1692-2; 0-7636-1692-3

LC 2007-25998

"Rap-style cadences perfectly capture the drama that has always surrounded the boxer's life. . . . Collier's compelling watercolor collages with their brown overtones beautifully portray Ali's determination and strength." SLJ

Ali, Rubina

Ali, Rubina. **Slumgirl** dreaming; Rubina's journey to the stars. [by] Rubina Ali in collaboration with Anne Berthod and Divya Dugar. Delacorte Press 2009 187p il pa $9.99

Grades: 5 6 7 8 **92**

1. Actors 2. Children 3. India 4. Slumdog millionaire (Motion picture)

ISBN 978-0-385-73908-5 pa; 0-385-73908-7 pa

LC 2009029305

The young actress describes her life growing up in the slums of Mumbai, her experiences on the set of the film "Slumdog Millionaire," and how her life has changed as a result of her role in the film

"The writing here has a journalistic feel. It is not poetic or especially nuanced. But in a sea of cookie-cutter biography series, this book stands out. It has heart, and is aimed at an age group that will identify with Ali in essential ways." SLJ

Allen, Will

★ Martin, Jacqueline Briggs, 1945- **Farmer** Will Allen and the growing table; Jacqueline Briggs Martin, Eric Larkin. Readers to Eaters 2013 32 p. $17.95

Grades: K 1 2 3 4 5 **92**

1. Urban agriculture 2. Picture books for children

ISBN 0983661537; 9780983661535

LC 2013937817

In this book, Jacqueline Briggs Martin "shares the real-life story of Will Allen, innovative farmer and founder of Growing Power, an urban farm in Milwaukee. 'Will Allen can see / what others can't see. / When he sees kids, he sees farmers.' Martin begins and ends with this positive premise. In between, she sketches salient events that stoked Allen's commitment to empowering people to grow their own food." (Kirkus Reviews)

Alonso, Alicia

★ Bernier-Grand, Carmen T. **Alicia** Alonso; prima ballerina. illustrated by Raúl Colón. Marshall Cavendish Children's 2011 64p il $19.99

Grades: 4 5 6 7 **92**

1. Cubans 2. Ballet dancers 3. Choreographers 4. Dance directors

ISBN 978-0-7614-5562-2; 0-7614-5562-0

LC 2010018269

"An informative, beautifully illustrated introduction to the world-renowned dancer. Alonso's focused life and illustrious career are made even more remarkable by the fact that she lost her peripheral vision at age 19 and had to learn to visualize both the stage set and the dance itself in order to execute spins and lifts, and to choreograph ballets. Each one is presented as a titled one-page piece in abbreviated poetic prose; many face full-page textured paintings rendered in Colón's distinctive mix of watercolor, colored, and lithograph pencils." SLJ

Includes bibliographical references

Alvarez, Luis W., 1911-1988

Venezia, Mike. **Luis** Alvarez; wild idea man. written and illustrated by Mike Venezia. Children's Press 2010 32p il (Getting to know the world's greatest inventors & scientists) lib bdg $28; pa $6.95

Grades: 2 3 4 **92**

1. Physicists 2. Nobel laureates for physics

ISBN 978-0-531-23703-8 lib bdg; 0-531-23703-6 lib bdg; 978-0-531-20777-2 pa; 0-531-20777-3 pa

LC 2009-356

"Employing oversized font, judicious use of white space, and appealing illustrations . . . readers learn about physicist Luis Alvarez and his numerous contributions to early 20th-century science. . . . Student researchers will appreciate the glossary and index, since there are no chapter headings or subheadings. This title, . . . serves equally well for research assignments, biography units, or as engaging leisure reading for aspiring scientists." Libr Media Connect

Includes glossary

Andersen, Hans Christian, 1805-1875

★ Varmer, Hjordis. **Hans** Christian Andersen; his fairy tale life. illustrated by Lilian Brogger; translated by Tiina Nunnally. Groundwood Books 2005 111p il $19.95

Grades: 5 6 7 8 **92**

1. Authors 2. Novelists 3. Dramatists 4. Authors, Danish 5. Children's authors 6. Short story writers

ISBN 0-88899-690-X

"Most of this book describes Andersen's childhood and belated schooling, showing his poverty and the grief he experienced over the death of his beloved father, as well as several horrifying events such as being forced by a teacher to witness the beheading of three young people. . . . The biography is divided into 11 chapters, set up as if they were stories. . . . The writing flows smoothly, with many details provided to help students picture the places and events. Brøgger's haunting, mixed-media illustrations add to the somber and at times surreal feeling of the text." SLJ

Anderson, Marian, 1897-1993

★ Freedman, Russell. The **voice** that challenged a nation; Marian Anderson and the struggle for equal rights. Clarion Books 2004 114p il $18

Grades: 5 6 7 8 **92**

1. African American singers 2. Opera singers 3. African Americans -- Civil rights 4. African American women -- Biography

ISBN 0-618-15976-2

LC 2003-19558

A Newbery Medal honor book, 2005

In the mid-1930s, Marian Anderson was a famed vocalist who had been applauded by European royalty and welcomed at the White House. But, because of her race, she was denied the right to sing at Constitution Hall in Washington, D.C. This is the story of her resulting involvement in the civil rights movement of the time.

"In his signature prose, plain yet eloquent, Freedman tells Anderson's triumphant story, with numerous black-and-white photos and prints that convey her personal struggle, professional artistry, and landmark civil rights role." Booklist

Includes bibliographical references

★ Ryan, Pam Munoz. **When** Marian sang; the true recital of Marian Anderson, the voice of a century; libretto by Pam Muñoz Ryan; staging by Brian Selznick. Scholastic Press 2002 un il $16.95

Grades: 2 3 4 **92**

1. African American singers 2. Opera singers 3.

African American women -- Biography
ISBN 0-439-26967-9

LC 2001-49508

An introduction to the life of Marian Anderson, extraordinary singer and civil rights activist, who was the first African American to perform at the Metropolitan Opera, whose life and career encouraged social change

"This book masterfully distills the events in the life of an extraordinary musician. . . . Working with a sepia-toned palette, Selznick's paintings shimmer with emotion." Publ Wkly

Anderson, Tillie

★ Stauffacher, Sue. **Tillie** the terrible Swede; how one woman, a sewing needle, and a bicycle changed history. Alfred A. Knopf 2011 un il $17.99; lib bdg $20.99
Grades: K 1 2   92
1. Cycling 2. Women athletes 3. Biography, Individual
ISBN 978-0-375-84442-3; 0-375-84442-2; 978-0-375-94442-0 lib bdg; 0-375-94442-7 lib bdg

LC 2010-07083

"Reaching back more than a century, Stauffacher and McMenemy resurrect the story of pioneering woman cyclist Tillie Anderson. . . . Racing in a self-created aerodynamic outfit . . . Anderson both scandalized and thrilled 1890s America as she shattered records for speed and endurance, leaving competitors and conventional wisdom in the dust. . . . Stauffacher's . . . writing is as sprightly and heartfelt as ever, and to her credit, she connects Tillie's accomplishments to the building women's rights movement. An excellent afterword, tucked on the inside back cover, provides fascinating historical context for Anderson's story." Publ Wkly

Anderson, Walter Inglis, 1903-1965

★ Bass, Hester. The **secret** world of Walter Anderson; illustrated by E.B. Lewis. Candlewick Press 2009 un il $17.99
Grades: 2 3 4 5   92
1. Artists 2. Artists -- United States
ISBN 978-0-7636-3583-1; 0-7636-3583-9

LC 2008029674

"This sensitive portrait of Anderson—'the most famous American artist you've never heard of'—paints him as a solitary man who kept a private room hidden from his wife and children and often took his rowboat to the Mississippi Gulf Coast's isolated Horn Island to glean inspiration. Subdued watercolors evoke the artist's love of the natural world. . . . A powerful tribute to the lengths artists will go for their passions." Publ Wkly

Andrews, Benny, 1930-2006

Benson, Kathleen, 1947- **Draw** what you see; the life and art of Benny Andrews. by Kathleen Benson; illustrated with paintings by Benny Andrews. Clarion Books 2015 32 p. color illustrations (hardcover) $16.99
Grades: K 1 2 3   92
1. African American artists 2. Andrews, Benny, 1930-2006 3. African American artists -- Biography 4. Artists -- United States -- Biography
ISBN 0544104870; 9780544104877

LC 2013046203

This biography, by Kathleen Benson, focuses on artist Benny Andrews. "Benny Andrews loved to draw. . . . And he dreamed of a better life - something beyond the segregation,

the backbreaking labor, and the limited opportunities of his world. Benny's dreams took him far from the rural Georgia of his childhood. He became one of the most important African American painters of the twentieth century, and he opened doors for other artists of color." (Publisher's note)

"Benny Andrews began drawing when he was able to hold pencil in his hands and "once he started, he never stopped...Whether two or three dimensional, existing on a shallow stage or in an expansive landscape, Andrews's often elongated, stylized figures carry weight and their postures tell stories of oppression, of joy, of curiosity, and of pride...A powerful work about an influential artist and activist." SLJ

Andrews, Roy Chapman, 1884-1960

★ Bausum, Ann. **Dragon** bones and dinosaur eggs: a photobiography of Roy Chapman Andrews. National Geographic Soc. 2000 64p il map $17.95
Grades: 5 6 7 8   92
1. Fossils 2. Dinosaurs 3. Explorers 4. Zoologists 5. Naturalists 6. Travel writers 7. Writers on nature 8. Writers on science 9. Museum administrators
ISBN 0-7922-7123-8

LC 99-38363

A biography of the great explorer-adventurer, who discovered huge finds of dinosaur bones in Mongolia, pioneered modern paleontology field research, and became the director of the American Museum of Natural History

"Bausum's account reads smoothly, and a layout dense with captioned sepia photographs and quotes from Andrews provides plenty of oases for readers as they follow him through the desert." Bull Cent Child Books

Includes bibliographical references

Andrews, Troy

Trombone Shorty; by Troy Andrews and Bill Taylor; illustrated by Bryan Collier. Abrams Books for Young Readers 2015 40 p. (hardcover) $17.95
Grades: PreK K 1 2 3   92
1. Jazz musicians -- Biography 2. Trombonists -- United States 3. Jazz musicians -- United States
ISBN 1419714651; 9781419714658

LC 2014016106

This book, written by Troy Andrews and Bill Taylor, and illustrated by Bryan Collier, is "a lively picture book autobiography about how [Troy "Trombone Shorty" Andrews] followed his dream of becoming a musician, despite the odds, until he reached international stardom." (Publisher's note)

Appleseed, Johnny, 1774-1845

Worth, Richard. **Johnny** Appleseed; select good seeds and plant them in good ground. Enslow Publishers 2010 128p il map (Americans: the spirit of a nation) $23.95
Grades: 4 5 6 7   92
1. Apples 2. Frontier and pioneer life 3. Pioneers 4. Fruit growers
ISBN 978-0-7660-3352-8; 0-7660-3352-X

LC 2008048701

"This nicely illustrated and sourced [biography] . . . includes full-page sidebars." Booklist

"Discusses the life of Johnny Appleseed, including his childhood in colonial America, his moveable nursery, the real stories behind his folk legend, and the legacy he left on American history." Publisher's note

Includes glossary and bibliographical references

Yolen, Jane. **Johnny** Appleseed; the legend and the truth. by Jane Yolen; illustrated by Jim Burke. HarperCollinsPublishers 2008 un il $16.99; lib bdg $17.89

Grades: K 1 2 3   **92**

1. Apples 2. Frontier and pioneer life 3. Pioneers 4. Fruit growers

ISBN 978-0-06-059135-9; 0-06-059135-8; 978-0-06-059136-6 lib bdg; 0-06-059136-6 lib bdg

LC 2005017789

"In this comely, homespun picture-book biography, Yolen assembles the fact and fiction surrounding America's favorite orchardist into a tale both substantive and lyrical. . . . Burke's striking paintings conform to a natural, yarn-dyed palette of apple reds, forest greens, meadow golds, and midnight blues." Booklist

Archimedes, ca. 287-212 B.C.

Hightower, Paul. The **greatest** mathematician; Archimedes and his eureka! moment. Enslow Publishers 2010 128p il (Great minds of ancient science and math) lib bdg $31.93

Grades: 5 6 7 8   **92**

1. Mathematicians 2. Greece -- History 3. Writers on science

ISBN 978-0-7660-3408-2 lib bdg; 0-7660-3408-9 lib bdg

LC 2008051818

This biography is a "solid [choice], as . . . [it provides] a good overview of the cultural and political landscape of the times, as well as pictures." SLJ

"A biography of ancient Greek mathematician Archimedes, who invented the compound pulley and other machines. His contributions to mathematics included devising the formulas for the surface and volume of a sphere" Publisher's note

Includes glossary and bibliographical references

Armstrong, John Barclay, 1850-1913

Alter, Judy. **John** Barclay Armstrong; Texas Ranger. by Judy Alter. Bright Sky Press 2007 59p il $14.95

Grades: 4 5 6 7   **92**

1. Sheriffs 2. Texas Rangers 3. West (U.S.) -- History

ISBN 978-1-931721-86-8

"Born in 1850 and raised in Tennessee, Armstrong went west to seek his fortune. At 25, he joined the Texas Rangers and soon came to embody the legendary qualities of these remarkable lawmen. He is an interesting character, and the author aptly tells his tale. The archival black-and-white photos add authenticity and help bring the man to life." SLJ

Armstrong, Louis, 1900-1971

★ Kimmel, Eric A. A **horn** for Louis; by Eric A. Kimmel; illustrated by James Bernardin. Random House 2005 86p il $11.95; lib bdg $13.99; pa $3.99

Grades: 2 3 4   **92**

1. Singers 2. Jazz musicians 3. African American musicians 4. Band leaders 5. Trumpet players

ISBN 0-375-83252-1; 0-375-93252-6 lib bdg; 978-0-375-84005-0 pa

LC 2005004151

"Adapted from an unpublished memoir, this beginning chapter book is an account of [Louis] Armstrong's youthful acquisition of his first true horn. . . . Kimmel's skilled narrative accentuates the diversity of the boys surroundings and the early influence of local music upon his innate gift. Bernardins dynamic black-and-white artwork captures the vivacious subject well and includes many period and cultural details." SLJ

Weinstein, Muriel Harris. **Play,** Louis, play! the true story of a boy and his horn. illustrated by Frank Morrison. Bloomsbury Books for Young Readers 2010 99p il $15.99

Grades: 3 4 5   **92**

1. Singers 2. Jazz musicians 3. African American musicians 4. Band leaders 5. Trumpet players

ISBN 978-1-59990-375-0; 1-59990-375-X

LC 2010025974

"With a bouncy, freewheeling tone that would make her subject proud, Weinstein tells the story of Louis Armstrong's childhood from the point of view of his first cornet. . . . Morrison's sketchy black-and-white spot art livens up an already ebullient chapter-book biography of a true artistic pioneer." Booklist

Arn Chorn-Pond

Lord, Michelle. A **song** for Cambodia; by Michelle Lord; illustrated by Shino Arihara. Lee & Low 2008 un il $16.95

Grades: 3 4 5   **92**

1. Musicians 2. Cambodia 3. Flutists 4. Human rights activists

ISBN 978-1-60060-139-2; 1-60060-139-1

LC 2007026248

A biography of Arn Chorn-Pond who, as a young boy in 1970s Cambodia, survived the Khmer Rouge killing fields because of his skill on the khim, a traditional instrument, and later went on to help heal others and revive Cambodian music and culture.

"Filled with drama and tragedy, this picture-book biography skillfully telescopes Arn's tumultuous boyhood. Realistic gouache illustrations depict the terrors of war but refrain from showing graphic violence. Amazing and inspiring." Booklist

Ashe, Arthur, 1943-1993

Hubbard, Crystal. **Game,** set, match, champion Arthur Ashe; illustrated by Kevin Belford. Lee & Low Books 2010 un il $19.95

Grades: 3 4 5 6   **92**

1. African American athletes 2. Tennis players 3. Nonfiction writers 4. Tennis -- Biography

ISBN 978-1-60060-366-2; 1-60060-366-1

LC 2010013304

"Tennis legend Ashe's life, on and off the court, is the focus of this stirring picture-book biography . . . which combines a detailed narrative with powerful acrylic paintings." Booklist

Astaire, Adele, 1896-1981

Orgill, Roxane. **Footwork**; the story of Fred and Adele Astaire. illustrated by Stephane Jorisch. Candlewick Press 2007 un il $17.99

Grades: 2 3 4 5 **92**
1. Actors 2. Dancers 3. Singers
ISBN 978-0-7636-2121-6; 0-7636-2121-8

LC 2006-40068

The biography of Fred and Adele Astaire, from their humble beginnings to Broadway stars.

Orgill's text "brims with well-chosen biographical and period details, and . . . Jorisch's whisper-weight, line-and-watercolor drawings convey the fizz of the footwork and the gritty backdrop of steam trains and stage doors." Booklist

Includes bibliographical references

Astaire, Fred

Orgill, Roxane. **Footwork**; the story of Fred and Adele Astaire. illustrated by Stephane Jorisch. Candlewick Press 2007 un il $17.99

Grades: 2 3 4 5 **92**
1. Actors 2. Dancers 3. Singers
ISBN 978-0-7636-2121-6; 0-7636-2121-8

LC 2006-40068

The biography of Fred and Adele Astaire, from their humble beginnings to Broadway stars.

Orgill's text "brims with well-chosen biographical and period details, and . . . Jorisch's whisper-weight, line-and-watercolor drawings convey the fizz of the footwork and the gritty backdrop of steam trains and stage doors." Booklist

Includes bibliographical references

Audubon, John James, 1785-1851

★ Davies, Jacqueline. The **boy** who drew birds: a story of John James Audubon; illustrated by Melissa Sweet. Houghton Mifflin Co. 2004 un il map $15

Grades: 2 3 4 **92**
1. Birds 2. Artists 3. Painters 4. Naturalists 5. Ornithologists 6. Writers on science 7. Artists -- United States 8. Biography, Individual
ISBN 0-618-24343-7

LC 2004-971

This describes how John James Audubon studied and painted birds

"Sweet's mixed-media collage artwork includes sensitive pencil sketches and ink drawings washed with watercolors and gouache, as well as elements such as photos of bird nests and bones. . . . This handsome book makes a beguiling introduction to the painter." Booklist

Includes bibliographical references

Aung San Suu Kyi

Rose, Simon. **Aung** San Suu Kyi. 2011 24p il por (Remarkable people) $27.13; pa $12.95

Grades: 4 5 6 7 **92**
1. Political prisoners 2. Women political activists 3. Dissenters 4. Political leaders 5. Nonfiction writers 6. Human rights activists 7. Nobel laureates for peace 8. Myanmar -- Politics and government
ISBN 978-1-61690-833-1; 1-61690-833-5; 978-1-61690-834-8 pa; 1-61690-834-3 pa

LC 2011011584

This looks at Aung San Suu Kyi's "life, accomplishments, and challenges while including a page of quotes, an annotated list of contemporaries and influences, starter suggestions for writing a paper, and a time line and glossary. [The book] looks into the Nobel Peace Prize–winning

Myanmar activist, whose struggle for democracy has landed her under house arrest multiple times." Booklist

Baker, Alia Muhammad

★ Winter, Jeanette. The **librarian** of Basra; a true story from Iraq. Harcourt, Inc. 2004 32p il $16

Grades: PreK K 1 2 3 **92**
1. Books 2. Libraries 3. Librarians 4. Iraq War, 2003
ISBN 0-15-205445-6

LC 2004-12969

The story of Alia Muhammad Baker, a librarian in Basra, Iraq, who managed to rescue seventy percent of the library's collection before the library burned in the Iraq War in 2003

"Winter's bright, folk-art style does much to mute the horrific realties of war. . . . The librarian's quiet bravery serves as a point of entry into a freighted topic." Booklist

Baker, Josephine, 1906-1975

★ Powell, Patricia Hruby. **Josephine**; the dazzling life of Josephine Baker. By Patricia Hruby Powell and illustrated by Christian Robinson. Chronicle Books Llc 2014 104 p. color illustrations (alk. paper) $17.99

Grades: 2 3 4 5 **92**
1. Dancers 2. African Americans 3. Dancers -- France -- Biography 4. African American entertainers -- France -- Biography
ISBN 1452103143; 9781452103143

LC 2012030440

Boston Globe-Horn Book Nonfiction Award (2014)
Coretta Scott King (Illustrator) Honor Book (2015)
Robert F. Sibert Honor Book (2015)

In this picture book, author Patricia Hruby Powell presents a biography of Josephine Baker, who "rose from a childhood of poverty and race riots in St. Louis, Mo., to dance in New York and Paris, the city where she finally achieved fame and escaped American segregation and racism. Grateful to the French, she worked as a spy during World War II and later adopted 12 children from around the world." (Kirkus Reviews)

"This incomparable biography conveys dancer Josephine Baker's passion, exuberance, dignity, and eccentricity through words and pictures that nearly jump off the page. Powell doesn't shy away from the challenges (including racism) Baker faced but emphasizes that Baker never let them overwhelm her joy from performing. Robinson's highly stylized, boldly colored illustrations are at once sophisticated and inviting to young readers." (Horn Book)

★ Winter, Jonah. **Jazz** age Josephine; illustrated by Marjorie Priceman. Atheneum 2012 il $16.99

Grades: K 1 2 3 **92**
1. Actors 2. Dancers 3. Singers 4. Jazz music 5. African American singers 6. African American women -- Biography
ISBN 978-1-4169-6123-9; 1-4169-6123-2

"Even though the ranks of picture-book biographies of significant artists (many of whom kids have likely never heard of) have swollen considerably in recent years, this one about the singer, dancer, and all-around entertainer Josephine Baker still manages to dazzle. . . . The biographical details . . . are covered in broad strokes, with more attention given to recreating the style and swagger of her onstage performances. . . . Winter's syncopated language dances nearly as much as the energized, loose-limbed figures in Priceman's kinetic artwork to convey the spirit, as much as the life, of the subject." Booklist

Banneker, Benjamin, 1731-1806

Maupin, Melissa. **Benjamin** Banneker. Child's World 2010 39p il map (Journey to freedom) lib bdg $20.92

Grades: 3 4 5 6   **92**

1. Astronomers 2. Mathematicians 3. Nonfiction writers 4. Clock and watch makers 5. African Americans -- Biography

ISBN 978-1-60253-117-8 lib bdg; 1-60253-117-X lib bdg

LC 2009003639

A biography of the African American scientist and mathematician

"Maupin has created an accessible account of Banneker's like and accomplishments. Short, uncomplicated text is interspersed with sepia-tone primary source photographs and documents." Booklist

Includes bibliographical references

Barnum, P. T. (Phineas Taylor), 1810-1891

★ Fleming, Candace. The **great** and only Barnum; the tremendous, stupendous life of showman P.T. Barnum. illustrated by Ray Fenwick. Schwartz & Wade Books 2009 151p il $18.99; lib bdg $21.99

Grades: 5 6 7 8   **92**

1. Circus 2. Circus executives

ISBN 978-0-375-84197-2; 0-375-84197-0; 978-0-375-94597-7 lib bdg; 0-375-94597-0 lib bdg

LC 2008-45847

"In this sweeping yet cohesive biography, Fleming so finely tunes Barnum's legendary ballyhoo that you can practically hear the hucksterism and smell the sawdust. . . . The material is inherently juicy, but credit Fleming's vivacious prose, bountiful period illustrations, and copious source notes for fashioning a full picture on one of the forebearers of modern celebrity." Booklist

Includes bibliographical references

Barrie, J. M. (James Matthew), 1860-1937

★ Yolen, Jane. **Lost** boy; the story of the man who created Peter Pan. illustrated by Steve Adams. Dutton Children's Books 2010 un il $17.99

Grades: 2 3 4   **92**

1. Authors 2. Novelists 3. Dramatists 4. Authors, Scottish 5. Essayists 6. Satirists

ISBN 978-0-525-47886-7; 0-525-47886-8

LC 2009-24697

"This handsome picture-book biography presents the life of James Barrie, the creator of Peter Pan. . . . Adams' paintings provide evocative views of Barrie and his world. Yolen smoothly relates intriguing incidents from Barrie's childhood and adult life without making comments or drawing conclusions." Booklist

Includes bibliographical references

Barton, Clara, 1821-1912

Krensky, Stephen. **Clara** Barton. DK Pub. 2011 128p il (DK biography) $14.99; pa $5.99

Grades: 5 6 7 8   **92**

1. Nurses 2. American Red Cross 3. Red Cross

officials 4. Social welfare leaders

ISBN 978-0-7566-7279-9; 0-7566-7279-1; 978-0-7566-7278-2 pa; 0-7566-7278-3 pa

Describes the life and accomplishments of Clara Barton, a teacher who organized efforts to bring nursing care to wounded soldiers during the Civil War and who went on to become the founder of the American Red Cross.

"Barton is placed in historical context, and key concepts, such as the causes of the Civil War, the struggle for women's suffrage, and the importance of the Geneva Convention, are explained. Compact in form, the text is complemented by full-color and archival photographs and reproductions on every spread. . . . An excellent resource for reports that will also appeal to fans of biography." SLJ

Includes bibliographical references

Somervill, Barbara A. **Clara** Barton; founder of the American Red Cross. Compass Point Books 2007 112p bibl il por lib bdg $23.95

Grades: 5 6 7 8   **92**

1. Nurses 2. American Red Cross 3. Red Cross officials 4. Social welfare leaders

ISBN 978-0-7565-1888-2 lib bdg; 0-7565-1888-1 lib bdg

LC 2006027071

"With an open design, clear type, and period prints and photos on every double-page spread, this highly readable biography . . . does a great job of setting Barton's personal story within the history of her time." Booklist

Includes bibliographical references

Wade, Mary Dodson. **Amazing** civil war nurse Clara Barton. Enslow Publishers 2009 24p il (Amazing Americans) lib bdg $21.26

Grades: 1 2 3   **92**

1. Nurses 2. American Red Cross 3. Red Cross officials 4. Social welfare leaders

ISBN 978-0-7660-3281-1 lib bdg; 0-7660-3281-7 lib bdg

LC 2008-24889

"Colorful photos are found throughout, with a timeline, dictionary, websites concerning the topic, as well as an index making . . . [this] book a wonderful introduction to nonfiction features." Libr Media Connect

Includes glossary

Bates, Peg Leg

★ Barasch, Lynne. **Knockin'** on wood; starring Peg Leg Bates. by Lynne Barasch. Lee & Low Books 2004 un il $16.95

Grades: 2 3 4   **92**

1. Dancers 2. Tap dancing 3. African American dancers 4. People with disabilities 5. Hotel executives 6. Dancers with disabilities 7. Tap dancers -- United States -- Biography

ISBN 1-58430-170-8

LC 2003-22905

A picture book biography of Clayton "Peg Leg" Bates, an African American who lost his leg in a factory accident at the age of twelve and went on to become a world-famous tap dancer

"Sprightly ink-and-watercolor art ably depicts both the poverty of Bates' early life and the colorful world of entertainment. . . . Barasch subtly sets the story against American racism." Booklist

Baum, L. Frank, 1856-1919

Krull, Kathleen. The **road** to Oz; twists, turns, bumps, and triumphs in the life of L. Frank Baum. illustrated by Kevin Hawkes. Alfred A. Knopf 2008 un il $17.99; lib bdg $20.99

Grades: 2 3 4 5   92

1. Authors 2. Dramatists 3. Journalists 4. Authors, American 5. Children's authors

ISBN 978-0-375-83216-1; 0-375-83216-5; 978-0-375-93216-8 lib bdg; 0-375-93216-X lib bdg

LC 2007-41526

This picture-book biography of the author of The Wonderful Wizard of Oz "displays Krull's usual stylistic strengths: a conversational tone, well-integrated facts, vivid anecdotes, and sly asides. . . . Hawkes' ink-and-acrylic illustrations . . . support the sense of Baum as a multifaceted, fascinating individual." Booklist

Beatles

Manning, Mick. The **Beatles**; Mick Manning, Brita Granström. Pgw 2014 48 p. $18.99

Grades: 4 5 6   92

1. Beatles 2. Rock musicians -- England -- Biography

ISBN 1847804519; 9781847804518

Mick Manning and Brita Granström "tell the story of the Beatles. . . . This illustrated story covers John Lennon's Liverpool childhood, . . . the friendship between Paul McCartney and George Harrison, . . . the arrival of Brian Epstein as manager, . . . record label boss George Martin's influence, Ringo Starr joining the group, fame and screaming fans, the famous tour to the USA, the making of the albums, . . . and finally the breakup of the band and the beginning of solo careers." (Publisher's note)

"This slim, cheeky book is a delightful introduction to the Beatles, and the fresh, lively art will draw kids right in. The book is arranged chronologically, beginning in 1940... This is clearly an import (references to the Just William stories and jelly babies aren't really explained), but readers will make connections through context. A bouncy way to meet the Beatles. " Booklist

Beebe, William, 1877-1962

Sheldon, David. **Into** the deep; the life of naturalist and explorer William Beebe. Charlesbridge 2009 un il lib bdg $16.95

Grades: 2 3 4   92

1. Authors 2. Explorers 3. Zoologists 4. Naturalists 5. Memoirists 6. Writers on nature 7. Writers on science 8. Deep diving 9. Biography, Individual

ISBN 1-58089-341-4 lib bdg; 978-1-58089-341-1 lib bdg

LC 2008-25341

This is a biography of the American "naturalist from his childhood studying animals in New Jersey through his later years studying birds at the research station he started in Trinidad. [Glossary.] Ages five to eight." (Publisher's note)

"This colorful introduction to Beebe's life for younger readers opens with his parents' encouragement of his interests in the natural world and his early work as a curator and collector of birds before he developed the idea of observing animals in their native habitat and began to focus on

undersea life. . . . Sheldon's lush double-page paintings, in acrylic, gouache and India ink, show young Will surrounded by animals, alive and stuffed, and the older man at work in a variety of settings. . . . A fine offering for would-be explorers." Kirkus

Includes bibliographical references

Beethoven, Ludwig van, 1770-1827

Bauer, Helen. **Beethoven** for kids; his life and music with 21 activities. Chicago Review Press 2011 129p il pa $16.95

Grades: 4 5 6 7   92

1. Composers 2. Composers, Austrian

ISBN 1-56976-711-4; 978-1-56976-711-5

LC 2011018131

"This introduction to the towering classical composer sets the story of his life and work in the context of the revolutionary events of early-19th-century Europe. . . . The author's own extensive musical experience contributes to the breadth of this title. Sidebars and historical prints add further information about musical forms and instruments, historical events and people mentioned. . . . This will be particularly useful for parents and classroom teachers hoping to make the study of great music more interesting." Kirkus

Includes bibliographical references

Martin, Russell. The **mysteries** of Beethoven's hair; [by Russell Martin and Lydia Nibley] Charlesbridge 2009 120p il lib bdg $15.95

Grades: 5 6 7 8   92

1. Composers

ISBN 978-1-57091-714-1 lib bdg; 1-57091-714-0 lib bdg

LC 2008-07257

"Based on Martin's adult book Beethoven's Hair: An Extraordinary Historical Odyssey and Scientific Mystery Solved (Broadway, 2000), this reworking for a young audience presents an intriguing interdisciplinary story. Martin and Nibley trace the labyrinthine journey of a lock of Beethoven's hair encased in a glass and wooden locket from the 18th century to the present. . . . This is a most unusual, thoroughly researched detective story written in a clearly accessible and lively tone. Black-and-white photos and reproductions appear throughout. . . . It is . . . an incredibly readable and absorbing selection that demonstrates the multidimensional nature of true scholarship." SLJ

Viegas, Jennifer. **Beethoven's** world; [by] Jennifer Viegas. Rosen Pub. Group 2008 64p il (Music throughout history) lib bdg $29.25

Grades: 5 6 7 8   92

1. Composers

ISBN 1-4042-0724-4 lib bdg; 978-1-4042-0724-0 lib bdg

LC 2005028917

This "book begins with an introduction briefly addressing social issues of the day, historical background, or other significant information. . . . Successive chapters discuss the [man's] early [life], family background, social status, personality characteristics, musical training and education, obstacles or challenges, and influences. A chapter . . . focuses on the musician's well-known compositions, describing through lively and colorful language some of the musical elements employed ... The format and layout are appealing and uncluttered." SLJ

Includes glossary and bibliographical references

Bell, Alexander Graham, 1847-1922

Garmon, Anita. **Alexander** Graham Bell invents; by Anita Garmon. National Geographic 2007 40p il (National Geographic history chapters) lib bdg $17.90

Grades: 2 3 4   92

1. Inventors 2. Teachers of the deaf 3. Telecommunications executives

ISBN 978-1-4263-0189-6

LC 2007007828

This biography of the inventor is "nicely illustrated with photos, paintings, engravings, and facsimiles. [It is] just right for emerging chapter-book readers. . . . Useful for reports . . . and interesting pleasure reading." SLJ

Includes glossary and bibliographical references

Bernstein, Leonard, 1918-1990

★ Rubin, Susan Goldman. **Music** was IT: young Leonard Bernstein. Charlesbridge 2011 178p il lib bdg $19.95

Grades: 5 6 7 8   92

1. Composers 2. Conductors (Music) 3. Jews -- Biography 4. Biography, Individual

ISBN 1-58089-344-9 lib bdg; 978-1-58089-344-2 lib bdg; 978-1-60734-276-2 e-book

LC 2010-07584

This is a biography of composer and conductor Leonard Bernstein. Bibliography. Index. "Grades five to nine." (Bull Cent Child Books)

"An impeccably researched and told biography of Leonard Bernstein's musical apprenticeship, from toddlerhood to his conducting debut with the New York Philharmonic at age 25. . . . Drawn from interviews, family memoirs and other print resources, quotations are well-integrated and assiduously attributed. Photos, concert programs, early doodles and letters, excerpts from musical scores and other primary documentation enhance the text. Excellent bookmaking— from type to trim size—complements a remarkable celebration of a uniquely American musical genius." Kirkus

Bhutto, Benazir

Naden, Corinne J. **Benazir** Bhutto. Marshall Cavendish Benchmark 2010 96p il (Leading women) $39.93

Grades: 5 6 7 8   92

1. Prime ministers 2. Women politicians 3. Political leaders 4. Pakistan -- Politics and government

ISBN 978-0-7614-4952-2; 0-7614-4952-3

In this biography "readers learn about Bhutto's student years at Radcliffe College and her rise to prime minister of Pakistan, the first woman to lead a Muslim state. . . . The [woman's life is] revealed within the political and historical context of [her] times and [includes] quotes from autobiographical material. . . . Color and black-and-white photos are included. . . . The compact size, chronological organization, and accessible writing [style makes this biography a] good [resource] for reports." SLJ

Includes bibliographical references

Bieber, Justin, 1994-

Bieber, Justin. **Justin** Bieber: first step 2 forever; my story. HarperCollins Children's Books 2010 236p il $21.99

Grades: 4 5 6 7   92

1. Singers 2. Pop musicians

ISBN 978-0-06-203974-3; 0-06-203974-1

"Bieber, the platinum-selling singer/songwriter . . . debuts with an account of his 16-year-old life that's cheeky yet entirely in line with his safe and wholesome image. . . . The book covers his upbringing in Ontario, his early introduction to music, YouTube stardom, his love of pranks, and the stratospheric success he now enjoys—all interspersed with lyrics, tweets, and numerous full-bleed photographs of Bieber." Publ Wkly

Yasuda, Anita. **Justin** Bieber. 2011 24p il (Remarkable people) lib bdg $27.13; pa $12.95

Grades: 4 5 6 7   92

1. Singers 2. Pop musicians

ISBN 978-1-61690-667-2 lib bdg; 1-61690-667-7 lib bdg; 978-1-61690-672-6 pa; 1-61690-672-3 pa

LC 2010051002

This looks at Justin Bieber's "life, accomplishments, and challenges while including a page of quotes, an annotated list of contemporaries and influences, starter suggestions for writing a paper, and a time line and glossary. . . . [This book] tracks the music sensation from 12-year-old YouTube phenom to the kind of celebrity who's earned such numbing fun facts as 'Justin has a dog named Sam.'" Booklist

Black Elk, 1863-1950

★ Nelson, S. D. **Black** Elk's vision; a Lakota story. Abrams Books for Young Readers 2010 47p il $19.95

Grades: 5 6 7 8   92

1. Shamans 2. Oglala Indians 3. Indian leaders 4. Native Americans -- Biography

ISBN 978-0-8109-8399-1; 0-8109-8399-0

LC 2009-9392

"This handsomely designed, large-format book tells the story of Black Elk (1863-1950), a Lakota man who saw many changes come to his people. . . . Often quoting from Black Elk Speaks (1932), Nelson makes vivid the painful ways life changed for the Lakotain in the 1800s. . . . Colorful, imaginative artwork, created using pencils and acrylic paints, is interspersed with nineteenth-century photos, underscoring that this dramatic account reflects the experiences of a man who witnessed history." Booklist

Bly, Nellie, 1864-1922

★ Macy, Sue. **Bylines**: a photobiography of Nellie Bly; foreword by Linda Ellerbee. National Geographic 2009 64p il map $19.95; lib bdg $28.90

Grades: 5 6 7 8   92

1. Authors 2. Journalists 3. Women journalists 4. Nonfiction writers

ISBN 978-1-4263-0513-9; 1-4263-0513-3; 978-1-4263-0514-6 lib bdg; 1-4263-0514-1 lib bdg

LC 2008-52329

This is a biography of the American reporter. Index. "Grades five to nine." (Bull Cent Child Books)

"This detailed biography of the trailblazing 19th-century journalist incorporates photographs of Bly and her subjects. The extensive text explores the details of a life spent seeking justice. . . . A thorough introduction to the life of a fascinating figure." Publ Wkly

Blériot, Louis, 1872-1936

★ Provensen, Alice. The **glorious** flight: across the Channel with Louis Bleriot, July 25, 1909; [by] Alice and Martin Provensen. Viking 1983 39p il $17.99; pa $6.99

Grades: 1 2 3 4   **92**

1. Air pilots 2. Aeronautical engineers 3. Airplanes -- Design and construction

ISBN 978-0-670-34259-4; 0-670-34259-9; 978-0-14-050729-4; 0-14-050729-9 pa

LC 82-7034

Awarded the Caldecott Medal, 1984

"A pleasing text recounts Bleriot's adventures with gentle humor and admiration for his earnest, if accident-prone, determination. Best of all, the pictures shine with the illustrator's delight in the wondrous flying machines themselves." Horn Book

Boone, Daniel, 1734-1820

Spradlin, Michael P. **Daniel** Boone's great escape; [by] Michael P. Spradlin; illustrated by Ard Hoyt. Walker & Co. 2008 un il $16.95; lib bdg $17.85

Grades: K 1 2 3   **92**

1. Escapes 2. Explorers 3. Shawnee Indians 4. Frontier and pioneer life 5. Scouts 6. Pioneers

ISBN 978-0-8027-9581-6; 0-8027-9581-1; 978-0-8027-9582-3 lib bdg; 0-8027-9582-X lib bdg

LC 2007-50382

"Spradlin . . . and Hoyt . . . deliver a thrilling adventure about famed 18th-century frontiersman Daniel Boone. The storytelling is immediate and swift. . . . Gripping prose relates Boone's experiences as the Shawnee hold him captive from February to June in 1778, until he makes a daring escape to warn fellow settlers of an impending attack. Hoyt's skillful blend of closeups and eye-level perspectives pulls readers right into the action. Maintaining the tight-as-a drum tension, the watercolor-and-ink scenes show the escapee hightailing it through thick forests." Publ Wkly

Brady, Tom

Wilner, Barry. **Tom** Brady; a football star who cares. Enslow Publsihers, Inc. 2011 48p il (Sport stars who care) lib bdg $23.93; pa $7.95

Grades: 3 4 5   **92**

1. Football players 2. Football -- Biography

ISBN 978-0-7660-3773-1 lib bdg; 0-7660-3773-8 lib bdg; 978-1-59845-233-4 pa; 1-59845-233-9 pa

LC 2010041784

A biography of the quarterback for the New England Patriots who also works for charities.

This is "especially good for book reports." Booklist

Includes glossary and bibliographical references

Braille, Louis, 1809-1852

★ Freedman, Russell. **Out** of darkness: the story of Louis Braille; illustrated by Kate Kiesler. Clarion Bks. 1997 81p il $16.95; pa $7.95

Grades: 4 5 6 7   **92**

1. Blind 2. Inventors 3. Teachers of the blind 4. Blind -- Books and reading

ISBN 0-395-77516-7; 0-395-96888-7 pa

LC 95-52353

"Without melodrama, Freedman tells the momentous story in quiet chapters in his best plain style, making the facts immediate and personal. . . . A diagram explains how the Braille alphabet works, and Kate Kessler's full-page shaded pencil illustrations are part of the understated poignant drama." Booklist

Branson, Richard

Goldsworthy, Steve. **Richard** Branson. 2011 il (Remarkable people) $27.13; pa $12.95

Grades: 4 5 6 7   **92**

1. Businessmen 2. Financiers 3. Virgin Group plc 4. Retail executives 5. Airline executives 6. Telecommunications executives

ISBN 978-1-61690-671-9; 978-1-61690-676-4 pa

LC 2010051145

A biography of British financier Richard Branson.

Breckinridge, Mary, 1881-1965

★ Wells, Rosemary. **Mary** on horseback; three mountain stories. pictures by Peter McCarty. Dial Bks. for Young Readers 1998 53p il $16.99; pa $4.99

Grades: 4 5 6 7   **92**

1. Nurses 2. Midwives

ISBN 0-670-88923-7; 0-14-130815-X pa

LC 97-43409

Tells the stories of three families who were helped by the work of Mary Breckinridge, the first nurse to go into the Appalachian Mountains and give medical care to the isolated inhabitants. Includes an afterword with facts about Breckinridge and the Frontier Nursing Service she founded

"These beautifully written stories will remain with the reader long after the book is closed." Booklist

Breitbart, Siegmund, 1883-1925

Rubinstein, Robert E. **Zishe** the strongman; by Robert Rubinstein; illustrations by Woody Miller. Kar-Ben Pub. 2010 un il lib bdg $17.95; pa $7.95

Grades: K 1 2 3   **92**

1. Strong men 2. Bodybuilders 3. Jews -- Poland 4. Circus performers 5. Jews -- Biography 6. New York (N.Y.) -- History

ISBN 978-0-7613-3958-8 lib bdg; 0-7613-3958-2 lib bdg; 978-0-7613-3960-1 pa; 0-7613-3960-4 pa

LC 2009001875

"This picture book in warm sepia tones tells of a Polish Jew who emigrated to the U.S. in the early twentieth century and became a famous circus strongman. . . . This title makes a lively addition to other stories of Yiddish immigration." Booklist

Bridges, Ruby

★ Bridges, Ruby. **Through** my eyes: the autobiography of Ruby Bridges; articles and interviews compiled and edited by Margo Lundell. Scholastic Press 1999 63p il $16.95

Grades: 4 5 6   **92**

1. Travel agents 2. Civil rights activists 3. African Americans -- Civil rights 4. New Orleans (La.) -- Race relations

ISBN 0-590-18923-9

LC 98-49242

Ruby Bridges recounts the story of her involvement, as a six-year-old, in the integration of her school in New Orleans in 1960

"Profusely illustrated with sepia photos—including many gritty journalistic reproductions—this memoir brings some of the raw emotions of a tumultuous period into sharp focus. . . . A powerful personal narrative that every collection will want to own." SLJ

Donaldson, Madeline. **Ruby** Bridges. Lerner Publications 2009 48p il (History maker bios) $27.93

Grades: 3 4 5   92

1. School integration 2. Travel agents 3. Civil rights activists 4. African Americans -- Civil rights 5. New Orleans (La.) -- Race relations

ISBN 978-0-7613-4220-5; 0-7613-4220-6

LC 2008046526

"Donaldson recounts the story of this young African American girl who, in 1960 at the age of six, integrated New Orleans' William Franz Elementary School. . . . Donaldson's book is illustrated will fill-color drawings and carefully chosen period photos. . . . The book . . . makes a good introduction for report writers too young for Bridges' own memoir, Through My Eyes (1999)." Booklist

Includes bibliographical references

Bridgman, Laura Dewey, 1829-1889

Alexander, Sally Hobart. **She** touched the world: Laura Bridgman, deaf-blind pioneer; by Sally Hobart Alexander and Robert Alexander. Clarion Books 2008 100p il $18

Grades: 5 6 7 8   92

1. Deaf 2. Blind 3. Students 4. Physicians 5. Philanthropists 6. Humanitarians 7. Teachers of the blind

ISBN 978-0-618-85299-4; 0-618-85299-9

"At the age of three, in 1832, Laura Bridgman contracted scarlet fever and lost her sight, her hearing, her sense of smell, and much of her sense of taste. Her family sent her to Dr. Samuel [Gridley] Howe at the New England Institute for the Education of the Blind, and by the age of 10, Laura was world-famous for her accomplishments. . . . Alexander . . . presents a well-written and thoroughly researched biography of this remarkable woman, with numerous black-and-white photos." Booklist

Includes bibliographical references

Brown, John, 1800-1859

★ Hendrix, John. **John** Brown; his fight for freedom. written and illustrated by John Hendrix. Abrams Books for Young Readers 2009 39p il $18.95

Grades: 4 5 6 7   92

1. Abolitionists 2. Slavery -- United States

ISBN 978-0-8109-3798-7; 0-8109-3798-0

LC 2008-45969

The author "traces how John Brown went from conducting slaves along the Underground Railroad to espousing violent insurrection as a means to end slavery. . . . Reinforcing Brown as a larger-than-life folk hero, the pictures are exhilarating. . . . By embracing Brown's complexity, especially in the well-argued afterword, Hendrix sows acres of fertile ground for discussion." Booklist

Bruchac, Joseph, 1942-

Parker-Rock, Michelle. **Joseph** Bruchac; an author kids love. Enslow Publishers, Inc. 2009 48p il (Authors kids love) lib bdg $23.93

Grades: 3 4 5   92

1. Poets 2. Authors 3. Storytellers 4. College teachers 5. Magazine editors 6. Authors, American 7.

Children's authors 8. Nonfiction writers

ISBN 978-0-7660-3160-9 lib bdg; 0-7660-3160-8 lib bdg

LC 2008-33051

"Clearly written, [this] outstanding [biography provides] many interesting details about the [subject's] personal [life] and [includes] photos that enhance the [text]." SLJ

Includes glossary and bibliographical references

Bryan, Ashley, 1923-

★ Bryan, Ashley. **Ashley** Bryan; words to my life's song. with photographs by Bill McGuinness. Atheneum Books for Young Readers 2009 58p il $18.99

Grades: 3 4 5 6   92

1. Artists 2. Authors 3. Illustrators 4. African American artists 5. African American authors 6. College teachers 7. Authors, American 8. Children's authors

ISBN 978-1-4169-0541-7; 1-4169-0541-3

LC 2008-14369

"In rich collages of words and pictures, this highly visual autobiography introduces artist Ashley Bryan's life and his vision of the world around him. . . . Photos of Bryan's world and reproductions of his often bright-hued and inherently vibrant artworks appear on every page. . . . They infuse the entire presentation with energy, color, and joy. . . . Beautifully designed, the book creates an original, stimulating, and inspiring portrait of the artist . . . as well as a celebration of his vision." Booklist

Buchanan, James, 1791-1868

Burgan, Michael. **James** Buchanan. Marshall Cavendish Benchmark 2011 112p il (Presidents and their times) lib bdg $23.95

Grades: 5 6 7 8   92

1. Presidents 2. Senators 3. Members of Congress 4. Secretaries of state 5. Presidents -- United States

ISBN 978-0-7614-4810-5; 0-7614-4810-1

LC 2009025933

This offers information on President James Buchanan and places him within his historical and cultural context. Also explored are the formative events of his times and how he responded.

"The abundant sidebars provide a good deal of background information that will be helpful to students. . . . Attractive . . . as well as useful." Booklist

Includes glossary and bibliographical references

Burningham, John, 1936-

Burningham, John. **John** Burningham; preface by Maurice Sendak; commentary by Brian Alderson. Candlewick Press 2009 223p il $70

Grades: Adult Professional   92

1. Artists 2. Authors 3. Illustrators 4. Authors, English 5. Children's authors

ISBN 978-0-7636-4434-5; 0-7636-4434-X

"The British author and illustrator has garnered an international reputation for combining imaginative, offbeat illustrations with highly funny, original stories for children. In this oversize, lavishly illustrated volume, Burningham relates his life story from his nonconformist schooling and his early meanderings around the world to his various artistic ventures, picture books being only one of his endeavors. . . . Students of children's literature will be intrigued by Maurice Sendak's short preface and by the six-page opening commentary by children's literature scholar Brian Alderson. A fascinating and insightful treat for Burningham aficionados." SLJ

Caesar, Julius, 100-44 B.C.

Galford, Ellen. **Julius** Caesar; the boy who conquered an empire. [by] Ellen Galford. National Geographic 2007 64p il map (World history biographies) $17.95; lib bdg $27.90

Grades: 5 6 7 8   92

1. Statesmen 2. Historians 3. Rome -- History 4. Emperors -- Rome

ISBN 978-1-4263-0064-6; 978-1-4263-0065-3 lib bdg

LC 2006020777

A biography of the Roman emperor

This "visually appealing [title is] packed with excellent photographs and reproductions, interesting sidebars, and [has] a time line running along the bottom of every page. . . . [This book is] useful, well-written." SLJ

Includes glossary and bibliographical references

Calder, Alexander, 1898-1976

★ Stone, Tanya Lee. **Sandy's** circus; a story about Alexander Calder. illustrated by Boris Kulikov. Viking 2008 un il $16.99

Grades: 1 2 3   92

1. Artists 2. Sculptors 3. Circus in art 4. Artists -- United States

ISBN 978-0-670-06268-3; 0-670-06268-5

LC 2008-08380

"This beautifully illustrated picture-book biography . . . [offers a] spare, direct story that focuses on Calder's youth and what are, perhaps, his most kid-accessible artworks: his wire sculptures of circus performers. . . . Kulikov's elegant, fanciful, multimedia collages extend the story." Booklist

Includes bibliographical references

Campanella, Roy, 1921-1993

Adler, David A. **Campy**; the Roy Campanella story. by David A. Adler; illustrated by Gordon C. James. Viking Penguin 2007 un il $15.99

Grades: 2 3 4   92

1. Baseball players 2. African American athletes 3. Baseball -- Biography

ISBN 0-670-06041-0

LC 2005023314

"Roy Campanella . . . was the second African American signed by Branch Rickey to play for the Brooklyn Dodgers. . . . Adler . . . capably reprises Campy's on-field triumphs . . . and off-field tragedy (he was paralyzed in a car accident in 1958), while James delivers evocative illustrations in the soft-focus, pastel-heavy style that has become standard for baseball." nostalgia. Booklist

Includes bibliographical references

Cannon, Annie Jump, 1863-1941

Gerber, Carole. **Annie** Jump Cannon, astronomer; illustrated by Christina Wald. Pelican Pub. 2011 un il $16.99

Grades: 2 3 4 5   92

1. Deaf 2. Astronomers 3. Women astronomers 4. Curators

ISBN 9781589809116; 1589809114

LC 2011012147

"This inspiring picture-book biography of a trailblazer in the field presents insight into the challenges of women interested in science during the late 19th and early 20th centuries. Cannon was born in 1863 and as a young girl her mother nurtured her interest in the night sky. . . . When her father learned that Wellesley College was the only women's college offering physics classes, he enrolled her. She graduated with a degree in physics and had a successful career in astronomy. . . . The realistic illustrations capture the time period and complement the text. They're scientifically accurate. . . . A solid resource." SLJ

Carson, Rachel, 1907-1964

★ Ehrlich, Amy. **Rachel**; the story of Rachel Carson. illustrated by Wendell Minor. Silver Whistle/Harcourt 2003 un il $16

Grades: 2 3 4   92

1. Authors 2. Conservationists 3. Women scientists 4. College teachers 5. Marine biologists 6. Writers on nature 7. Writers on science

ISBN 0-15-216227-5

LC 00-13115

This "anecdotal biography of nature writer and environmentalist Carson focuses on incidents that influenced Carson's thinking and career aspirations. . . . Minor's . . . impressively realistic watercolor and gouache paintings lend a pleasing cohesiveness to the volume." Publ Wkly

Scherer, Glenn. **Who** on earth is Rachel Carson? mother of the environmental movement. [by] Glenn Scherer and Marty Fletcher. Enslow Publishers 2009 112p il (Scientists saving the earth) lib bdg $31.93

Grades: 5 6 7 8   92

1. Authors 2. Biologists 3. Conservationists 4. Women scientists 5. Environmentalists 6. College teachers 7. Marine biologists 8. Writers on nature 9. Writers on science

ISBN 978-1-59845-116-0 lib bdg; 1-59845-116-2 lib bdg

LC 2008028498

"The writing is clear and informative. . . . Color photographs are relevant and of good quality." SLJ

Includes bibliographical references

Carver, George Washington, 1864?-1943

★ Bolden, Tonya. **George** Washington Carver. Abrams Books for Young Readers 2008 41p il $18.95

Grades: 3 4 5 6   92

1. Botanists 2. Scientists 3. African Americans -- Biography

ISBN 978-0-8109-9366-2; 0-8109-9366-X

LC 2007-28069

NCTE Orbis Pictus Award honor book (2009)

This is a biography of "the slave-born black scientist. . . . Offering sourced quotations throughout, Bolden covers subtleties that simpler treatments tend to bypass. . . . Photos and reproductions, many of Carver's own paintings, are exceptional, and their arrangement in the style of an old-fashioned album lends the book a suitable gravitas. . . . [The book is] absorbing." Booklist

Includes bibliographical references

Harness, Cheryl. The **groundbreaking,** chance-taking life of George Washington Carver and science & invention in America; by Cheryl Harness. National Geographic 2008 143p il map (Cherly Harness histories) $16.95; lib bdg $25.90

Grades: 4 5 6 7   **92**

1. Botanists 2. Scientists 3. African Americans -- Biography

ISBN 978-1-4263-0196-4; 1-4263-0196-0; 978-1-4263-0197-1 lib bdg; 1-4263-0197-9 lib bdg

LC 2007029316

"Harness presents Carver as a man who, regardless of constant hardship and racial prejudice, persevered to become a beloved teacher and devoted scientist. . . . The author raises challenging questions throughout. . . . The lively prose style conveys his sense of passion and adventure about the man and his intellectual pursuits, and the simple black-and-white drawings add a further sense of drama." SLJ

Includes bibliographical references

Cassatt, Mary, 1844-1926

Harris, Lois V. **Mary** Cassatt; impressionist painter. [by] Lois V. Harris. Pelican 2007 32p il $15.95

Grades: 2 3 4   **92**

1. Artists 2. Painters 3. Women artists 4. Artists -- United States

ISBN 978-1-58980-452-4

LC 2007011755

"With large, crisply reproduced, color artwork on nearly every page, this picture-book biography of American Impressionist Mary Cassatt will appeal to a broad age-range of readers." Booklist

Cezanne, Paul, 1839-1906

Burleigh, Robert. **Paul** Cezanne; a painter's journey. H.N. Abrams 2006 31p il $17.95

Grades: 4 5 6 7   **92**

1. Artists 2. Painters 3. Artists, French

ISBN 0-8109-5784-1

LC 2005011779

"Burleigh offers brief insights into Cézanne's personal life, such as his relationship with his father, who did not support his sons interest in art. However, the emphasis is on interpreting some individual paintings and understanding the artist's various styles, including the impact of the Impressionists and his evolution to a freer and simpler manner of expression in his later years. . . . The high-quality reproductions demonstrate Burleigh's points. . . . A solid, lively introduction." SLJ

Champlain, Samuel de, 1567-1635

MacLeod, Elizabeth. **Samuel** de Champlain; written by Elizabeth MacLeod; illustrated by John Mantha. Kids Can Press 2008 32p il (Kids Can Read) $14.95; pa $3.95

Grades: 1 2 3   **92**

1. Explorers 2. America -- Exploration

ISBN 978-1-55453-049-6; 1-55453-049-0; 978-1-55453-050-2 pa; 1-55453-050-4 pa

A biography of the French explorer of Canada

This is a "fresh, short [biography] for newly independent readers. . . . The writing is clear if sedate, and the type is large. Abundant pen-and-ink illustrations are finely rendered and enhance [the] text." SLJ

Champollion, Jean Francois, 1790-1832

Rumford, James. **Seeker** of knowledge; the man who deciphered Egyptian hieroglyphs. Houghton Mifflin 2000 un il $15; pa $6.95

Grades: 3 4 5   **92**

1. Hieroglyphics 2. Archaeologists

ISBN 0-395-97934-X; 0-618-33345-2 pa

LC 99-37254

A biography of the French scholar whose decipherment of the Egyptian hieroglyphic language made the study of ancient Egypt possible

"Despite the book's traditional picture-book appearance, with a short text and nicely rendered watercolor art, the topic requires and gets sturdy treatment. . . . Those intrigued by hieroglyphs . . . will find this a useful introduction." Booklist

Chanel, Coco, 1883-1971

★ Matthews, Elizabeth. **Different** like Coco. Candlewick Press 2007 un il $16.99

Grades: 2 3 4   **92**

1. Fashion designers 2. Perfumers 3. Cosmetics industry executives

ISBN 978-0-7636-2548-1; 0-7636-2548-5

LC 2006-40622

"A celebration of the life of a major fashion designer and independent spirit. . . . The story is accompanied, appropriately, by elegant pen-and-ink and watercolor cartoons that capture her struggles as a young woman, as well as her innate sense of style." SLJ

Chaplin, Charlie, 1889-1977

★ Fleischman, Sid. **Sir** Charlie; Chaplin, the funniest man in the world. Greenwillow Books 2010 268p il $19.99; lib bdg $20.89

Grades: 5 6 7 8 9   **92**

1. Actors 2. Comedians 3. Motion pictures 4. Motion picture directors 5. Motion picture producers 6

ISBN 0-06-189640-3; 0-06-189641-1 lib bdg; 978-0-06-189640-8; 978-0-06-189641-5 lib bdg

LC 2009019689

This is a biography of the actor and director who starred in such films as City Lights (1931), Modern Times (1940), The Great Dictator (1947) and Limelight (1952). Chronology. Bibliography. Index. "Grades six to ten." (Bull Cent Child Books)

"This lively and engaging account of a poor Cockney boy who became the world's greatest silent-movie comedian is a must for biography collections. . . . Brief, easily digestible chapters, an extensive time line, and plenty of photos make the book's well-researched content accessible and appealing." SLJ

Chapman, Oscar L., 1896-1978

★ Hopkinson, Deborah. **Sweet** land of liberty; written by Deborah Hopkinson; illustrated by Leonard Jenkins. Peachtree 2007 un il $16.95

Grades: K 1 2 3 4   **92**

1. Lawyers 2. African Americans -- Biography 3. United States -- Race relations 4. African Americans -- Civil rights

ISBN 1-56145-395-1; 978-1-56145-395-5

LC 2006024331

"Jenkins' powerful, bright, mixed-media collages show and tell the connections, past, present, and future." SLJ

Chavez, Cesar, 1927-1993

Adler, David A. A **picture** book of Cesar Chavez; by David A. Adler and Michael S. Adler; illustrated by Marie Olofsdotter. Holiday House 2010 un il $17.95

Grades: 1 2 3 4   **92**

1. Migrant labor 2. Agricultural laborers 3. Labor leaders 4. Mexican Americans -- Biography

ISBN 978-0-8234-2202-9; 0-8234-2202-X

LC 2009039319

"The selfless struggles of labor leader Chávez are given a tempered and lucid treatment in this educational overview. . . . Olofsdotter keeps her illustrations gentle and ennobling. The characters are drawn in the intentionally stiff style that fits with the depth-challenged folk art backgrounds, most of which are dominated by the color of sand. . . . An elegant introduction to a man who inspired thousands." Booklist

Includes bibliographical references

★ Krull, Kathleen. **Harvesting** hope; the story of Cesar Chavez. illustrated by Yuyi Morales. Harcourt 2003 un il $17

Grades: 2 3 4   **92**

1. Migrant labor 2. Agricultural laborers 3. Labor leaders 4. Mexican Americans -- Biography

ISBN 0-15-201437-3

LC 2002-5096

A biography of Cesar Chavez, from age ten when he and his family lived happily on their Arizona ranch, to age thirty-eight when he led a peaceful protest against California migrant workers' miserable working conditions

"The brief text creates a remarkably complex view of Chavez—his experiences and feelings. Krull's empathetic words are well paired with artist Yuyi Morales's mixed-media acrylic paintings, which are suffused with a variety of emotions. . . . The pictures glow with intense shades of gold, green, pink, and orange." Horn Book

Chisholm, Shirley, 1924-2005

Raatma, Lucia. **Shirley** Chisholm. Marshall Cavendish Benchmark 2010 96p il (Leading women) $39.93

Grades: 4 5 6 7   **92**

1. Women politicians 2. Members of Congress 3. Presidential candidates 4. African American women -- Biography

ISBN 978-0-7614-4953-9; 0-7614-4953-1

"The arresting portrait on the cover will guide readers right into this well-written [biography of] . . . the first African American woman to enter Congress. . . . Raatma vividly explains what was happening in the country at the time and uses those events effectively as a backdrop. The many photos, both black and white and color, are good choices for the well-designed book." Booklist

Includes bibliographical references

Clemens, Susy, 1872-1894

★ Kerley, Barbara. The **extraordinary** Mark Twain (according to Susy) illustrated by Edwin Fotheringam. Scholastic Press 2010 un il $17.99

Grades: 2 3 4 5   **92**

1. Authors 2. Biography 3. Humorists 4. Novelists 5. Authorship 6. Essayists 7. Satirists 8. Memoirists 9. Travel writers 10. Authors, American 11. Short story writers

ISBN 978-0-545-12508-6; 0-545-12508-1

LC 2009-04752

"Wanting to present a portrait of her papa beyond that of just humorist and author, Mark Twain's 13-year-old daughter Susy spent a year chronicling her observations and reflections. . . . Kerley contextualizes the teenager's admiring musings with vivid familial backdrops. . . . Minibooklets titled 'Journal' appear in the fold of many spreads, containing excerpts from Susy's notebook. . . . Adding dynamic flair to the limited palettes of each digitally created scene are curlicues representing words, which emanate wildly from pen tips, pages, and mouths. Author notes about Susy and her father, a time line of Twain's life, and tips for writing an 'extraordinary biography' complete this accessible and inventive vision of a American legend." Publ Wkly

Clemente, Roberto, 1934-1972

★ Perdomo, Willie. **Clemente!** illustrated by Bryan Collier. Henry Holt & Co. 2010 un il $16.99

Grades: 1 2 3   **92**

1. Baseball players 2. Baseball -- Biography

ISBN 978-0-8050-8224-1; 0-8050-8224-7

"Perdomo's witty, passionate account of the beloved Puerto Rican baseball pioneer takes an unusual approach. The child narrator, whose father is president of the Roberto Clemente fan club, was named in honor of the great player, and little Clemente can tell you just about everything there is to know about the man. . . . Collier's kinetic artwork uses collage to explosive effect. . . . More than just a biography, this book warmly illustrates the parent-child bond that is one of the finer by-products of sports fandom." Booklist

★ Winter, Jonah. **Roberto** Clemente; pride of the Pittsburgh Pirates. illustrated by Raul Colón. Atheneum Books for Young Readers 2005 un il $16.95

Grades: 2 3 4   **92**

1. Baseball players 2. Baseball -- Biography 3. Puerto Ricans -- Biography 4. Biography, Individual

ISBN 0-689-85643-1

LC 2003-25546

This picture-book biography by Jonah Winter "shows how [Roberto] Clemente went from a boy with a guava tree bat, coffee-bean sack glove and soup can baseballs to a man who lifted the down-trodden Pittsburgh Pirates to victory, brought respect to Hispanic peoples, and fought to relieve his country's poverty until his death." (Children's Literature)

"Winter tells the . . . story of how Clemente's passionate love of the game and unrivaled work ethic took him from poverty in Puerto Rico . . . to World Series triumph with the Pittsburgh Pirates and, later . . . to near-mythic status as a role model for young Latino ballplayers. Soaked in pastoral greens and browns, Colon's evocatively grainy, soft-focus illustrations, rendered with a mix of watercolors, colored pencils, and litho pencils, capture perfectly the worlds in which Clemente was most at home. . . . Baseball history brought vividly to life for a younger audience." Booklist

Cleopatra, Queen of Egypt, d. 30 B.C.

Blackaby, Susan. **Cleopatra**; Egypt's last and greatest queen. Sterling Pub. 2009 124p il (Sterling biographies) $12.95; pa $5.95

Grades: 5 6 7 8   92
1. Queens 2. Egypt -- History
ISBN 978-1-4027-6540-7; 1-4027-6540-1; 978-1-
4027-5710-5 pa; 1-4027-5710-7 pa
LC 2008030146
"Villainess or goddess, a great queen or a selfish and
overly ambitious woman—readers get to decide. They will
be drawn into this biography by a description of a legendary
magnificent banquet given by Mark Antony for Cleopatra.
The lively narrative maintains interest from her birth in 69
BCE to her death in 31 BCE. . . . Sidebars, color photographs, and reproductions appear throughout. . . . This book
leaves readers fascinated and eager to learn more about her
time in history." SLJ
Includes glossary and bibliographical references

Shecter, Vicky Alvear. **Cleopatra** rules! the amazing
life of the original teen queen. Boyds Mills Press 2010
128p il map $17.95
Grades: 5 6 7 8   92
1. Queens 2. Egypt -- History 3. Biography, Individual
ISBN 1590787188; 9781590787182
LC 2009-26737
This is a biography of "Cleopatra VII, the last pharaoh of
Egypt." (Publisher's note) Bibliography. Index. "Grades six
to ten." (Bull Cent Child Books)
"This attractive book presents Cleopatra's story through
an unusual text, informative sidebars, and excellent color
illustrations. . . . Calling attention to the writing as much
as its story, the text includes puns, informal language, and
contemporary metaphors. . . . Shecter's solid research is evident." Booklist
Includes glossary and bibliographical references

Cleveland, Grover, 1837-1908
Otfinoski, Steven. **Grover** Cleveland. Marshall Caven-
dish Benchmark 2011 112p il (Presidents and their times)
lib bdg $23.95
Grades: 5 6 7 8   92
1. Mayors 2. Governors 3. Presidents 4. District
attorneys 5. Presidents -- United States
ISBN 978-0-7614-4811-2; 0-7614-4811-X
LC 2009029689
This offers information on President Grover Cleveland
and places him within his historical and cultural context.
Also explored are the formative events of his times and how
he responded.
"The abundant sidebars provide a good deal of background information that will be helpful to students. . . . At-
tractive . . . as well as useful." Booklist
Includes glossary and bibliographical references

Clinton, Hillary Rodham, 1947-
Blashfield, Jean F. **Hillary** Clinton. Marshall Caven-
dish Benchmark 2010 112p il (Leading women) $39.93
Grades: 4 5 6 7   92
1. Lawyers 2. Women politicians 3. Senators 4.
Secretaries of state 5. Spouses of presidents 6.
Presidential candidates 7. Presidents' spouses -- United
States
ISBN 978-0-7614-4954-6; 0-7614-4954-X
A biography of the Secretary of State and former Sena-
tor, presidential candidate, and First Lady.
Includes bibliographical references

Cogswell, Alice
★ McCully, Emily Arnold. **My** heart glow: Alice Cogswell, Thomas Gallaudet and the birth of American sign language. Hyperion Books for Children 2008 un il $15.99
Grades: 2 3 4   92
1. Deaf 2. Sign language 3. Teachers of the deaf
ISBN 978-1-4231-0028-7; 1-4231-0028-X
This is the story of Thomas Gallaudet and his deaf neighbor, Alice Cogswell, and how Gallaudet established a school
for the deaf in the United States and developed American
Sign Language.
"Emily Arnold McCully's watercolor illustrations are
beautifully rendered. . . . Not only does this book accurately
present the engrossing story of Alice and Gallaudet, it is also
an excellent resource for teaching diversity and encouraging
empathy for others." Libr Media Connect

Coleman, Bessie, 1896?-1926
★ Grimes, Nikki. **Talkin'** about Bessie: the story of
aviator Elizabeth Coleman; illustrated by E. B. Lewis. Orchard Bks. 2002 un il $16.95
Grades: 3 4 5   92
1. Air pilots 2. Women air pilots 3. African American
pilots
ISBN 0-439-35243-6
Coretta Scott King Award for illustration, 2003
"Following a brief introduction to Coleman's life, the
story, couched in a fictional framework, opens in the parlor
of a house in Chicago, where friends and relatives gather
to mourn Bessie's death. Each spread features one person
speaking about Bessie. . . . Lewis' paintings, subdued in tone
and color, reflect the spirit of the verse through telling details
and sensitive, impressionistic portrayals." Booklist
Includes bibliographical references

Colt, Samuel, 1814-1862
Wyckoff, Edwin Brit. The **man** behind the gun: Samuel
Colt and his revolver. Enslow Publishers 2010 32p il (Ge-
nius at work! Great inventor biographies) lib bdg $22.60
Grades: 4 5 6   92
1. Inventors 2. Firearms industry 3. Gunsmiths 4.
Manufacturing executives
ISBN 978-0-7660-3446-4 lib bdg; 0-7660-3446-1
lib bdg
LC 2009-28129
"Readers will learn about Samuel Colt, the revolver, and
mass production." Publisher's note
Includes glossary and bibliographical references

Coltrane, John, 1926-1967
Weatherford, Carole Boston, 1956- **Before** John was
a jazz giant: a song of John Coltrane; [illustrated by] Sean
Qualls. Henry Holt & Co. 2008 un il $16.95
Grades: K 1 2 3   92
1. Jazz musicians 2. African American musicians 3.
Saxophonists 4. Biography, Individual
ISBN 0-8050-7994-7; 978-0-8050-7994-4
LC 2007-07196
Coretta Scott King honor book for illustration, 2009
This is an account of John Coltrane's childhood in the
1930s. "Ages five to eight." (Bull Cent Child Books)
"The beat of lyrical words and the rhythm of the beauti-
ful illustrations express how, as a child, jazz-musician Col-
trane heard music in the world around him. Vibrant with

color and movement, double-page spreads in acrylic, collage, and pencil extend the images about the magical sounds of everyday things." Booklist

Columbus, Christopher

Fritz, Jean. **Where** do you think you're going, Christopher Columbus? pictures by Margot Tomes. Putnam 1980 80p il maps $15.99; pa $5.99

Grades: 2 3 4   **92**

1. Explorers 2. America -- Exploration

ISBN 0-399-20723-6; 0-698-11580-5 pa

LC 80-11377

Discusses the voyages of Christopher Columbus who was determined to beat everyone in the race to the Indies

"Reducing a life as well-documented as Columbus's to 80 pages must result in some simplifications of fact or context, but in this case they are not readily apparent. Mrs. Fritz's breezy narrative gives us a highly individual Columbus. . . . Margot Tomes's three-color illustrations are attractive, amusing and informative." N Y Times Book Rev

Cone, Claribel, 1864-1929

★ Fillion, Susan. **Miss** Etta and Dr. Claribel; Bringing Matisse to America. David R. Godine 2011 83p il $18.95

Grades: 4 5 6 7   **92**

1. Artists 2. Painters 3. Physicians 4. Art collectors 5. Art -- Collectors and collecting

ISBN 978-1-56792-434-3; 1-56792-434-4

LC 2010048937

"An affectionate, lively examination of the reciprocal relationship between a great artist and two great art lovers. Etta and Claribel Cone, unmarried sisters from a wealthy Baltimore family . . . [were] discerning collectors of modern art, particularly that of Henri Matisse. . . . Their account is lavishly illustrated in full color by reproductions from the Cone Collection at the Baltimore Museum of Art and Matisse-inflected paintings by the author, who drew extensively on the Cone archive that is also housed at the museum. . . . This appealing work stands as both a portrait of two unconventional women and a celebration of the possibilties of arts patronage." Kirkus

Cone, Etta, 1870-1949

★ Fillion, Susan. **Miss** Etta and Dr. Claribel; Bringing Matisse to America. David R. Godine 2011 83p il $18.95

Grades: 4 5 6 7   **92**

1. Artists 2. Painters 3. Physicians 4. Art collectors 5. Art -- Collectors and collecting

ISBN 978-1-56792-434-3; 1-56792-434-4

LC 2010048937

"An affectionate, lively examination of the reciprocal relationship between a great artist and two great art lovers. Etta and Claribel Cone, unmarried sisters from a wealthy Baltimore family . . . [were] discerning collectors of modern art, particularly that of Henri Matisse. . . . Their account is lavishly illustrated in full color by reproductions from the Cone Collection at the Baltimore Museum of Art and Matisse-inflected paintings by the author, who drew extensively on the Cone archive that is also housed at the museum. . . . This appealing work stands as both a portrait of two unconventional women and a celebration of the possibilties of arts patronage." Kirkus

Copernicus, Nicolaus, 1473-1543

Andronik, Catherine M. **Copernicus**; founder of modern astronomy. rev ed; Enslow Publishers 2009 128p bibl il (Great minds of science) lib bdg $31.93

Grades: 5 6 7 8   **92**

1. Astronomers

ISBN 978-0-7660-3013-8 lib bdg; 0-7660-3013-X lib bdg

LC 2008-23940

First published 2002

"A highly readable book that presents a good balance between the biographical information needed to understand Copernicus as a man and the scientific explanations necessary to understand his work. . . . Good-quality, black-and-white reproductions, illustrations, and photographs add interest to the clearly written text." SLJ [review of 2002 edition]

Includes glossary and bibliographical references

Corwin, Jeff

Corwin, Jeff. **Jeff** Corwin: a wild life; the authorized biography. Penguin Group 2009 100p il pa $6.99

Grades: 4 5 6 7   **92**

1. Biologists 2. Naturalists 3. Conservationists 4. Television personalities

ISBN 978-0-14-241403-3 pa; 0-14-241403-4 pa

LC 2009008092

"The host of Animal Planet . . . and other popular TV programs blends his exciting adventure in the wild with his passionate call for conservation. . . . An insert of beautifully reproduced color photos from his global travels show him with a giraffe in Kenya, a moose in Alaska, and more. . . . The adventures are thrilling, and the messages are urgent." Booklist

Cosgrove, Miranda, 1993-

Yasuda, Anita. **Miranda** Cosgrove. Weigl 2011 24p il (Remarkable people) $27.13; pa $12.95

Grades: 4 5 6 7   **92**

1. Actors 2. Singers

ISBN 978-1-6169-0668-9; 1-6169-0668-5; 978-1-6169-0673-3 pa; 1-6169-0673-1 pa

LC 2010051144

A biography of actress and singer Miranda Cosgrove

Coup, W. C., 1857-1895

Covert, Ralph. **Sawdust** and spangles: the amazing life of W.C. Coup; [by] Ralph Covert, G. Riley Mills; illustrated by Giselle Potter. Abrams Books for Young Readers 2007 un il $16.95

Grades: K 1 2 3   **92**

1. Circus 2. Circus executives

ISBN 978-0-8109-9351-8; 0-8109-9351-1

LC 2006031981

"As a boy, William Cameron Coup left home to run away with the circus. . . . He eventually became one of the industry's most successful and inventive entrepeneurs. This picture book biography relates Coup's story in an accessible . . . way. Potter's illustrations are beautifully rendered, interpreting Coup's life and world with quirky energy and imaginative color." Horn Book Guide

Cousteau, Jacques Yves, 1910-1997

Berne, Jennifer. **Manfish**: a story of Jacques Cousteau; illustrated by Eric Puybaret. Chronicle Books 2008 un il $16.99

Grades: K 1 2 3   **92**

1. Ocean 2. Authors 3. Scientists 4. Skin diving 5. Divers 6. Naval officers 7. Oceanographers 8. Nonfiction writers 9. Biography, Individual -- literature 10. Underwater exploration

ISBN 0-8118-6063-9; 978-0-8118-6063-5

LC 2007-30513

This is a biography of the underwater explorer and marine naturalist. "Ages six to nine." (Bull Cent Child Books)

"Writing in simple poetic language, both lyrical and concise. . . . Berne offers a luminous picture-book biography of about Jacques Cousteau. . . . Puybaret's smooth-looking acrylic paintings extend the words' elegant simplicity and beautifully convey the sense of infinite, underwater space." Booklist

★ Yaccarino, Dan. The **fantastic** undersea life of Jacques Cousteau. Knopf 2009 un il $16.99; lib bdg $19.99

Grades: K 1 2 3   **92**

1. Ocean 2. Authors 3. Scientists 4. Skin diving 5. Divers 6. Naval officers 7. Oceanographers

ISBN 978-0-375-85573-3; 978-0-375-95573-0 lib bdg

LC 2008-04581

This is a picture-book biography of the oceanographer and environmentalist. Chronology. "Grades two to four." (Bull Cent Child Books)

"Yaccarino deftly provides information about important events in Cousteau's life while conveying the excitement and wonder that the ocean explorer experienced. . . . Effective layout and page design plus colorful gouache illustrations result in a striking visual presentation." SLJ

Coville, Bruce

Parker-Rock, Michelle. **Bruce** Coville; by Michelle Parker-Rock. Enslow Publishers 2008 48p bibl il por (Authors kids love) lib bdg $23.93

Grades: 3 4 5   **92**

1. Authors 2. Authors, American 3. Children's authors

ISBN 978-0-7660-2755-8 lib bdg; 0-7660-2755-4 lib bdg

LC 2006015873

A biography of the popular children's author, Bruce Coville, based on a interview.

The text is "interesting and conversational throughout. . . . [A] colorful [cover], family photos, and a font size that's not too intimidating all contribute to the [book's] appeal. . . . Suitable for reports or for pleasure reading." SLJ

Includes glossary and bibliographical references

Crandall, Prudence, 1803-1890

★ Jurmain, Suzanne. The **forbidden** schoolhouse; the true and dramatic story of Prudence Crandall and her students. Houghton Mifflin 2005 150p il $18

Grades: 5 6 7 8   **92**

1. Teachers 2. Educators 3. Abolitionists 4. African Americans -- Education

ISBN 0-618-47302-5

This is the story of Prudence Crandall, who, in 1831, opened a school for African American girls in Canterbury, Connecticut.

"A compelling, highly readable book. . . . Writing with a sense of drama that propels readers forward . . . Jurmain makes painfully clear what Crandall and her students faced. . . . Including a number of sepia-toned and color photographs as well as historical engravings, the book's look will draw in readers." Booklist

Includes bibliographical references

Crazy Horse, Sioux Chief, ca. 1842-1877

Brimner, Larry Dane. **Chief** Crazy Horse; following a vision. Marshall Cavendish Benchmark 2009 41p il (American heroes) lib bdg $20.95

Grades: 2 3 4   **92**

1. Indian chiefs 2. Native Americans -- Biography

ISBN 978-0-7614-3061-2

LC 2008002868

A biography of Crazy Horse, warrior chief of the Oglala tribe of the Sioux nation

This "concise and well-written [title covers] key biographical facts without overwhelming young readers, and [includes] captioned illustrations and reproductions, most of which are in color. Text is large, and the layout is age-appropriate and attractive, with wide margins." SLJ

Includes glossary and bibliographical references

Creesy, Eleanor, 1814-1900

Fern, Tracey. **Dare** the wind; Tracey Fern; pictures by Emily Arnold McCully. Farrar, Straus and Giroux 2014 40 p. color illustrations, map (hard) $17.99

Grades: K 1 2 3 4   **92**

1. Sailing 2. Navigation 3. Women sailors -- Biography 4. Flying Cloud (Clipper-ship)

ISBN 0374316996; 9780374316990

LC 2013007868

Author Tracey Fern presents a biography of Ellen Prentiss. "As soon as she met a man who loved sailing like she did, she married him. When her husband was given command of a clipper ship custom-made to travel quickly, she knew that they would need every bit of its speed for their maiden voyage: out of New York City, down around the tip of Cape Horn, and into San Francisco, where the Gold Rush was well under way." (Publisher's note)

"McCully's expertly rendered watercolor illustrations evoke, in double-page spreads, the rich atmosphere of the sea in all its moods, while many events are shown as round vignettes--as though seen through a spyglass." Kirkus

Crews, Donald

Crews, Donald. **Bigmama's**. Greenwillow Bks. 1991 un il $16; lib bdg $15.93; pa $5.95

Grades: K 1 2 3   **92**

1. Artists 2. Authors 3. Country life 4. Illustrators 5. Photographers 6. Authors, American 7. Children's authors 8. African Americans -- Biography

ISBN 0-688-09950-5; 0-688-09951-3 lib bdg; 0-688-15842-0 pa

LC 90-33142

Visiting Bigmama's house in the country, young Donald Crews finds his relatives full of news and the old place and its surroundings just the same as the year before

"This is an evocative celebration of the joy and wonder of childhood; would that every child had such a summer. The last page is a hauntingly lovely remembrance. The illustrations are perfect and make this a truly beautiful book." Child Book Rev Serv

Crum, George, fl. 1853

Taylor, Gaylia. **George** Crum and the Saratoga chip; illustrated by Frank Morrison. Lee & Low Books 2006 32p il $16.95

Grades: 2 3 4   **92**

1. Cooks 2. Cooking 3. Racially mixed people 4. United States -- Race relations

ISBN 978-1-58430-255-1; 1-58430-255-0

LC 2005015313

"Part Native American, part African American, George Crum coped with prejudice as a boy in New York State during the 1830s. As a young man, he became an excellent cook and was hired as a chef at a renowned restaurant in Saratoga Springs. . . . Once . . . Crum retrieved [a] dish of French fries, whittled them into very thin slices, and cooked them in hot oil, creating the forerunner of the potato chip. . . . This picture-book biography describes dramatic moments that reveal Crum's creativity, artistic temperament, and relentless pursuit of perfection. Buoyant acrylic illustrations accentuate the absurdity of situations, depicting the jaunty chef, all angles and energy." Booklist

Includes bibliographical references

Cummings, E. E.

Enormous smallness; the story of E. E. Cummings. Matthew Burgess; illustrations by Kris DiGiacomo. Enchanted Lion Books 2015 64 p. (alk. paper) $17.95

Grades: 1 2 3 4   **92**

1. Biography 2. American poets 3. American authors -- Biography

ISBN 159270171X; 9781592701711

LC 2015005781

This juvenile book, by Matthew Burgess with illustrations by Kris DiGiacomo, "is a nonfiction picture book about the poet E.E. cummings. Here E.E.'s life is presented in a way that will make children curious about him and will lead them to play with words and ask plenty of questions as well." (Publisher's note)

Curie, Marie, 1867-1934

Cregan, Elizabeth R. **Marie** Curie; pioneering physicist. Compass Point Books 2009 40p il map (Mission: Science) lib bdg $26.60

Grades: 4 5 6   **92**

1. Chemists 2. Physicists 3. Women scientists 4. Nobel laureates for physics

ISBN 978-0-7565-3960-3

This biography of the discoverer of radium "does a good job of connecting the scientist's work to our lives today. . . . [The] book has a variety of graphics including diagrams, photos, and reproductions of paintings and sketches. [This volume is] a definite plus for a school library or the juvenile collection in a public library." Libr Media Connect

★ Krull, Kathleen. **Marie** Curie; [illustrations by] Boris Kulikov. Viking 2007 128p il (Giants of science) $15.99

Grades: 5 6 7 8   **92**

1. Chemists 2. Physicists 3. Women scientists 4. Nobel laureates for physics

ISBN 978-0-670-05894-5; 0-670-05894-7

LC 2007-24251

"The compelling and conversational narrative (ably assisted by Kulikov's black-and-white drawings) portrays a brilliant . . . woman with plenty of idiosyncrasies, and the story of her discovery of radium . . . is as engaging as any of her personal dramas and challenges." Horn Book

Curtis, Christopher Paul

Parker-Rock, Michelle. **Christopher** Paul Curtis; an author kids love. Enslow Publishers 2009 48p il (Authors kids love) lib bdg $23.93

Grades: 1 2 3   **92**

1. Authors 2. African American authors 3. Authors, American 4. Children's authors 5. Government employees

ISBN 978-0-7660-3161-6 lib bdg; 0-7660-3161-6 lib bdg

LC 2009022379

A biography of the author of the Newbery honor book The Watsons Go to Birmingham—1963 and the Newbery winner Bud, not Buddy

Includes glossary and bibliographical references

Custer, George Armstrong, 1839-1876

Anderson, Paul Christopher. **George** Armstrong Custer; the Indian Wars and the Battle of the Little Bighorn. [by] Paul Christopher Anderson. PowerPlus Books 2004 112p il (Library of American lives and times) lib bdg $31.95

Grades: 4 5 6 7   **92**

1. Generals 2. Little Bighorn, Battle of the, 1876 3. Army officers 4. Native Americans -- Wars

ISBN 0-8239-6631-3

LC 2002-153404

A biography of the Civil War general who died at the Battle of the Little Bighorn

This "is not an apologia but a carefully measured analysis. . . . Stunning reproductions and photos provide a clear sense of the times and settings." SLJ

Includes bibliographical references

Dahl, Roald

Dahl, Roald. The **missing** golden ticket and other splendiferous secrets; illustrated by Quentin Blake. Puffin Books 2010 115p il pa $4.99

Grades: 3 4 5 6   **92**

1. Authors 2. Authors, English 3. Children's authors 4. Short story writers

ISBN 978-0-14-241742-3 pa; 0-14-241742-4 pa

LC 2010021712

"Containing excerpts from earlier tributes to Dahl's work and wit, this is an eclectic and funny collection of tidbits by and about the late author. The kernel of the book is 'Spotty Powder,' a characteristically droll chapter from an early draft of Charlie and the Chocolate Factory. . . . Highly entertaining, it's a sparkling window into Dahl's vivid personality and oeuvre." Publ Wkly

Dahl, Roald. **More** about Boy; Roald Dahl's tales from childhood. Farrar, Straus, and Giroux 2009 229p il $16.99

Grades: 5 6 7 8   **92**
1. Authors 2. Authors, English 3. Children's authors
4. Short story writers
ISBN 978-0-374-35055-0; 0-374-35055-8
                                   LC 2009016118
First published 2008 in the United Kingdom
"Containing the entire text and artwork from Dahl's 1984 autobiography Boy, this reworked and expanded version also incorporates previously unpublished materials from the Roald Dahl Museum and Story Centre in England, as well as excerpts that have appeared in earlier books. . . . Dahl's revealing writing, open and full of wicked humor, is certain to endear the beloved writer . . . to a new generation." Publ Wkly

Dalai Lama XIV, 1935-
Kimmel, Elizabeth Cody. **Boy** on the lion throne; the childhood of the 14th Dalai Lama. with a foreword by His Holiness the Dalai Lama. Roaring Brook Press 2009 146p il map $18.95
Grades: 4 5 6 7   **92**
1. Buddhism 2. Tibet (China) 3. Buddhist leaders 4. Political leaders 5. Nobel laureates for peace
ISBN 978-1-59643-394-6; 1-59643-394-9
Follows the childhood of Lhamo Thondup, who was identified at the age of two as the fourteenth reincarnation of the Dalai Lama, describing the humble life he was born into and how his life changed after he was recognized
"Kimmel is reverent without being adulatory, and her explanation of the Dalai Lama's relationship with Maoist China is presented in simple, clear language. This is a strange and fascinating story told in an engaging style, and young readers will find lots to keep them turning the pages." Bull Cent Child Books
Includes bibliographical references

Darwin, Charles, 1809-1882
Ashby, Ruth. **Young** Charles Darwin and the voyage of the Beagle; written by Ruth Ashby. Peachtree 2009 116p il map $12.95
Grades: 4 5 6   **92**
1. Evolution 2. Naturalists 3. Travel writers 4. Writers on science 5. Beagle Expedition (1831-1836)
ISBN 978-1-56145-478-5; 1-56145-478-8
                                   LC 2008-36747
"Beginning with the letter inviting him to sail aboard the Beagle, this traditional biography relates Darwin's life with an emphasis on the trip that led him to forge his theory about natural selection. Ashby makes good use of Darwin's own writing, sprinkling quotes throughout the text, which allow his adventures and opinions to come to life. . . . This biography will work well for book reports . . . providing accurate and readable information about the scientist and his journey." Booklist
Includes bibliographical references

★ Krull, Kathleen. **Charles** Darwin; illustrated by Boris Kulikov. Viking 2010 144p il (Giants of science) $15.99
Grades: 5 6 7 8   **92**
1. Evolution 2. Naturalists 3. Travel writers 4. Writers on science
ISBN 978-0-670-06335-2; 0-670-06335-5
                                   LC 2010-07315

"Krull once again offers an illuminating, humanizing portrait of a famous scientist. . . . Krull . . . writes in easily paced, lively, conversational prose, knitting together interesting facts, anecdotes, and historical overviews into a fascinating whole. She offers clear definitions of not only Darwin's theories but also how his discoveries built on previous scientists' work. . . . Kulikov's whimsical ink drawings and well-culled list of resources round out this strong entry in the series." Booklist

Lasky, Kathryn. **One** beetle too many: the extraordinary adventures of Charles Darwin. Candlewick Press 2009 un il $17.99; pa $6.99
Grades: 3 4 5 6   **92**
1. Evolution 2. Naturalists 3. Travel writers 4. Writers on science 5. Beagle Expedition (1831-1836)
ISBN 0-7636-1436-X; 978-0-7636-1436-2; 978-0-7636-5821-2 pa
                                   LC 2002-71254
Describes the life and work of the renowned nineteenth-century biologist who transformed conventional Western thought with his theory of natural evolution.
"Distilling tough concepts into light, conversational prose, Lasky . . . gives middle-graders a just-right introduction to Charles Darwin. . . . Trueman . . . up-ends perspective with multilayed mixed-media illustrations; mostly paint, these also incorporate bits of flowers and weeds as well as string, paper, and fabric. . . . Highly accessible." Publ Wkly

Markle, Sandra. **Animals** Charles Darwin saw; an around-the-world adventure. illustrated by Zina Saunders. Chronicle Books 2009 45p il $16.99
Grades: 2 3 4 5   **92**
1. Animals 2. Evolution 3. Naturalists 4. Travel writers 5. Writers on science 6. Beagle Expedition (1831-1836)
ISBN 978-0-8118-5049-0; 0-8118-5049-8
                                   LC 2007-53058
Looks at the animals that Charles Darwin saw throughout his life, from his early explorations in local woods and fields to his travels on the HMS Beagle, and how they influenced his later thought.
"Sandra Markle tells Darwin's story in clear prose spiced with interesting vignettes, . . . and Zina Saunders brings the scenes alive with colorful woodcut illustrations." NY Times Book Rev

McGinty, Alice B. **Darwin**; illustrated by Mary Azarian. Houghton Mifflin Books for Children 2009 un il $18
Grades: 1 2 3 4   **92**
1. Evolution 2. Naturalists 3. Travel writers 4. Writers on science 5. Beagle Expedition (1831-1836)
ISBN 978-0-618-99531-8; 0-618-99531-5
                                   LC 2008-33930
"After tracing Charles Darwin's youth and education, this fully illustrated biography focuses on his five-year voyage about the HMS Beagle. . . . Azarian . . . illustrates the book using handsome woodcut prints painted with watercolors. . . . The interplay of the clearly written third-person text with Darwin's own words and occasional quotes from his contemporaries creates a multifaceted view that leads to a broader understanding." Booklist

★ Schanzer, Rosalyn. **What** Darwin saw; the journey that changed the world. National Geographic 2009 47p il map $17.95; lib bdg $26.90

Grades: 3 4 5 6 **92**

1. Evolution 2. Naturalists 3. Travel writers 4. Writers on science 5. Beagle Expedition (1831-1836)
ISBN 978-1-4263-0396-8; 1-4263-0396-3; 978-1-4263-0397-5 lib bdg; 1-4263-0397-1 lib bdg

LC 2008-39809

"Schanzer uses Darwin's own words, taken from his journals, books, and letters, in the speech balloons of her graphic depiction of the voyage of the Beagle. This is not a full biography, but begins with Darwin's acceptance of the offer to sail on the expedition and ends with the presentation of his theory of evolution in 1860. Bright, watercolor cartoons accurately portray landscapes and specimens while also creating a vivid sense of adventure." SLJ

Includes bibligraphical references

Sis, Peter. The **tree** of life: a book depicting the life of Charles Darwin, naturalist, geologist & thinker. Frances Foster Bks./Farrar, Straus & Giroux 2003 un il map $18

Grades: 4 5 6 7 **92**

1. Naturalists 2. Travel writers 3. Writers on science
ISBN 0-374-45628-3

LC 2002-40706

Presents the life of the famous nineteenth-century naturalist using text from Darwin's writings and detailed drawings by Sis

"Muted tones of blue, green, and tan, and finely hatched drawings in the manner of old prints lend a period look to the pages. Beautifully conceived and executed, the presentation is a humorous and informative tour de force that will absorb and challenge readers." SLJ

Dave, ca. 1800-ca. 1870

★ Hill, Laban Carrick. **Dave**, the potter; artist, poet, slave. illustrated by Bryan Collier. Little, Brown Books for Young Readers 2010 un il $16.99

Grades: K 1 2 3 4 **92**

1. Slaves 2. Artists 3. American pottery 4. African American artists 5. African American authors 6. Ceramists 7. Poets, American 8. Slavery -- United States 9. Biography, Individual
ISBN 0-316-10731-X; 978-0-316-10731-0

LC 2010-06382

A Caldecott Medal honor book, 2011

This is a biography of the artist known as Dave, who "spent most of his life in a rural South Carolina district famed for its stoneware. . . . [Dave's] creations included mammoth storage pots. . . . Sometimes he signed his name and put the date. Other times he wrote verse [on the pot], usually a short rhyme. . . . Ages three to six." (N Y Times Book Rev)

"The life of an astonishingly prolific and skilled potter who lived and died a slave in 19th-century South Carolina is related in simple, powerful sentences that outline the making of a pot. The movements of Dave's hands are described using familiar, solid verbs: pulling, pinching, squeezing, pounding. . . . The pithy lines themselves recall the short poems that Dave inscribed on his pots. Collier's earth-toned watercolor and collage art extends the story, showing the landscape, materials, and architecture of a South Carolina

farm. . . . A lengthy author's note fleshes out what is known of the man's life story and reproduces several of his two-line poems." SLJ

David-Neel, Alexandra, 1868-1969

★ Brown, Don. **Far** beyond the garden gate: Alexandra David-Neel's journey to Lhasa. Houghton Mifflin 2002 un il $16

Grades: 3 4 5 **92**

1. Authors 2. Buddhism 3. Explorers 4. Travelers 5. Centenarians 6. Tibet (China) 7. Travel writers 8. Religious scholars 9. Asian studies specialists
ISBN 0-618-08364-2

LC 2002-222

Describes the life and travels of Alexandra David-Neel, who became a scholar of Buddhism and Tibet in the early twentieth century and trekked thousands of miles to reach Llasa, the Tibetan capital.

This "tells a fascinating tale. . . . David-Neel's vivid quotes are interspersed throughout the story. . . . The beiges, grays, and whites of Brown's palette capture the feeling of the unfamiliar world into which the woman and her companion ventured." SLJ

Includes bibliographical references

DePaola, Tomie, 1934-

★ DePaola, Tomie, 1934- **26** Fairmount Avenue; written and illustrated by Tomie dePaola. Putnam 1999 56p il $14.99; pa $6.99

Grades: 2 3 4 **92**

1. Artists 2. Authors 3. Painters 4. Illustrators 5. Authors, American 6. Children's authors
ISBN 0-399-23246-X; 0-698-11864-2 pa

LC 98-12918

A Newbery Medal honor book, 2000

Children's author-illustrator Tomie De Paola describes his experiences at home and in school when he was a boy. "Age four and up." (Commonweal)

"A disarmingly unselfconscious reminiscence. . . . The immediacy of detail resists nostalgia, and dePaola is wise to what recent graduates of his picture books will find interesting. Neat sketches and silhouettes will draw browsers in to this satisfying easy chapter book." Horn Book Guide

Followed by Here we all are

DePaola, Tomie, 1934- **Christmas** remembered; [by] Tomie dePaola. G. P. Putnam's Sons 2006 86p il $19.99; pa $9.99

Grades: 5 6 7 8 **92**

1. Artists 2. Authors 3. Painters 4. Christmas 5. Illustrators 6. Authors, American 7. Children's authors
ISBN 0-399-24622-3; 0-14-241481-6 pa

LC 2005032658

The children's author and artist shares his love of Christmas in 15 memories, which span six decades

"Brightening the pages are illustrations in varied styles and media, from an intriguing portrait of dePaola's Italian grandmother to decorative paper collages to iconic paintings of great stillness and beauty. . . . Written with dialogue and humor as well as reflection." Booklist

DePaola, Tomie, 1934- **For** the duration; a 26 Fairmount Avenue book; the war years. written and illustrated by Tomie dePaola. Putnam's Sons 2009 99p il $15.99

Grades: 2 3 4   92
1. Artists 2. Authors 3. Painters 4. Illustrators 5.
World War, 1939-1945 6. Authors, American 7.
Children's authors
ISBN 978-0-399-25209-9; 0-399-25209-6

From gas rationing to air-raid drills, as long as the war
lasts, life is going to be different for Tomie. And sometimes
different is hard. Fortunately, Tomie still has school, his family, and the things he's good at to carry him through.

"DePaola's style and word choices are just right for his
audience, and the point of view is consistently that of a second grader. Full-page and spot art black-and-white pencil
drawings and silhouette art by the author illustrate this must-
read title for fans of the series." SLJ

DePaola, Tomie, 1934- **I'm** still scared; a 26 Fairmount
Avenue book, book 6. written and illustrated by Tomie de-
Paola. G. P. Putnam's Sons 2006 83p il $13.99; pa $5.99
Grades: 2 3 4   92
1. Artists 2. Authors 3. Painters 4. Illustrators 5.
Authors, American 6. Children's authors 7. World War,
1939-1945 -- United States
ISBN 0-399-24502-2; 0-14-240826-3 pa
LC 2005-13500

"DePaola picks up his autobiographical series right
where his last title, Things Will Never Be the Same (2003),
left off: December, 7, 1941. Now in second grade, little Tomie describes the reactions to the Pearl Harbor bombings,
first at home, then at church, and finally at school. . . . Once
again, the warm, childlike narration captures both the specifics of the time and universal experiences that will connect
with most children. The shaded, black-and-white sketches
on each page extend the story's small, revealing moments."
Booklist

Followed by Why?

DePaola, Tomie, 1934- **On** my way; a 26 Fairmount
Avenue book. written and illustrated by Tomie dePaola.
Putnam 2001 73p il $13.99; pa $6.99
Grades: 2 3 4   92
1. Artists 2. Authors 3. Painters 4. Illustrators 5.
Authors, American 6. Children's authors
ISBN 0-399-23583-3; 0-698-11948-7 pa
LC 00-38229

This is the third installment of De Paola's memoirs of
childhood. It "culminates with the artist entering first grade
and finally . . . getting to learn to read. . . . The memoir
begins in the previous spring, with the crisis of baby sister
Maureen's pneumonia. . . . There are happier times as well. .
. . Primary." (Horn Book)

"The saga of dePaola's early life related in 26 Fairmount
Avenue . . . and Here We All Are . . . continues with this reminiscence of kindergarten and first grade. dePaola describes
his baby sister Maureen's recovery from pneumonia, a family trip to the 1939 World's Fair, and his theatrical debut as
the blushing bride in a 'Tiny Tot Bridal Party.' . . . The humor
is clear and the selection of incidents indicates the author has
a comfortable familiarity with the concerns of his audience."
Bull Cent Child Books

Followed by What a year!

DePaola, Tomie, 1934- **Why?** a 26 Fairmount Avenue
book. written and illustrated by Tomie dePaola. G. P. Put-
nam's Sons 2007 85p il $14.99
Grades: 2 3 4   92
1. Artists 2. Authors 3. Painters 4. Illustrators 5.
Authors, American 6. Children's authors
ISBN 978-0-399-24692-0
LC 2006011911

"This seventh installment in dePaola's autobiography
covers New Year's Day through April 20, 1942. . . . . Tomie
overhears talk of rationing and hoarding, peeks out from behind blackout curtains, and notes that, due to the war, Fleer
bubblegum will no longer be available. As ever, the author
fills the story with authentically childlike details. . . . The
black-and-white full-page and spot pictures convey emotions effectively." SLJ

Followed by For the duration

DePrince, Michaela

DePrince, Elaine. **Ballerina** dreams; from orphan to
ballerina. by Michaela DePrince; illustrated by James Bernardin. Random House Inc 2014 48 p. color illustrations
(lib. bdg.) $12.99
Grades: 1 2 3   92
1. Ballet dancers 2. Orphans -- Sierra Leone -- Biography
3. Ballet dancers -- United States -- Biography
ISBN 0385755163; 9780385755153; 9780385755160
LC 2014013111

This children's book, by Michaela and Elaine DePrince,
illustrated by James Bernardin, tells the "true story of Michaela DePrince, one of America's top ballerinas. At the age
of three, Michaela DePrince found a photo of a ballerina that
changed her life. . . . Michaela never forgot the photo of the
dancer she once saw, and quickly decided to make her dream
of becoming a ballerina come true. She has been dancing
ever since and is now a principal dancer in New York City."
(Publisher's note)

"This autobiographical title for newly independent readers will reward efforts with an inspiring story about ballerina
Michaela DePrince's life and passion for dance. Orphaned as
a young child in Sierra Leone, Michaela is a shy girl whose
vitiligo causes a loss of pigmentation on parts of her body...
At its heart is the core message that hard work and determination are the keys to making any dream come true. A
title sure to attract ballet aficionados, with added appeal for
its depiction of an adoptive family and a ballerina who just
happens to be black." Kirkus

Desmond, Viola Irene

Warner, Jody. **Viola** Desmond won't be budged! pic-
tures by Richard Rudnicki. Groundwood Books/House of
Anansi Press 2010 un il $18.95
Grades: K 1 2 3   92
1. Hairstylists 2. Race discrimination 3. Blacks --
Canada 4. Civil rights activists 5. Canada -- Race
relations
ISBN 978-0-88899-779-1; 0-88899-779-5

"Using a cadenced style that echoes the oral tradition of
African-Canadians, Warner recounts the story simply, al-
lowing children to see raw discrimination for what it was.
Rudnicki uses bold acrylics in vivid colors to tell the story.
He captures the style, dress and look of the period." Kirkus

Devi, Dulari

Devi, Dulari. **Following** my paint brush; text by Gita Wolf. Tara Books 2011 un il $17.50

Grades: 3 4 5 6   92

1. Artists 2. Painters 3. Women artists 4. Artists, Indian

ISBN 978-93-80340-11-1; 93-80340-11-7

This is the story of Dulari Devi, a domestic helper who went on to become an artist in the Mithila style of folk painting from Bihar, eastern India.

"Set against plain white backgrounds, Devi's artwork . . . vibrates with bold reds, yellows, and greens. The focus of Devi's artwork is her immediate environment—religious imagery, trees, pottery, fish, and children at play—her delicate linework adding complexity and texture to the mural-like tableaus." Publ Wkly

DiMaggio, Joe, 1914-1999

Winter, Jonah. **Joltin'** Joe DiMaggio; Jonah Winter; illustrated by James E. Ransome. Atheneum Books for Young Readers 2014 48 p. (hardback) $17.99

Grades: 1 2 3 4   92

1. Baseball 2. Baseball players -- Biography 3. Baseball players -- United States -- Biography

ISBN 1416940804; 9781416940807

LC 2014009584

This children's book by Jonah Winter, illustrated by James E. Ransome, tells how "In the golden age of baseball, sports announcers ruled the radio, winning and losing was front-page news, and just about every young boy wanted to grow up to wear Yankee pinstripes, including Giuseppe Paolo DiMaggio, Jr., a first generation Italian from San Francisco. 'Baseball is not a job,' said young Joe's dad, but . . . Joe grew up to make headlines as a top centerfielder and ace hitter." (Publisher's note)

""Joltin' Joe" made headlines wherever he played, especially during his amazing fifty-six-game hitting streak. With a near tall-tale tone, Winter paints baseball as the bright spot in the Depression and DiMaggio as one of the biggest stars of the day. Ransome's warm watercolors capture the emotions of DiMaggio but also life's small moments. An author's note fills in blanks. Bib." Horn Book

Includes bibliographical references and index

Dickens, Charles, 1812-1870

Manning, Mick. **Charles** Dickens; scenes from an extraordinary life. [illustrated by] Brita Granström. Frances Lincoln 2011 un il $18.95

Grades: 2 3 4 5   92

1. Authors 2. Novelists 3. Authors, English

ISBN 978-1-84780-187-6; 1-84780-187-0

"Dickens narrates his own life story in this biography. . . . Loosely rendered pencil-and-watercolor scenes with speech-bubble interjections from characters take center stage, while small illustrated sidebars provide additional context. . . . A bonus: tidy comic strip panels provide quick summaries of several Dickens novels, which may whet readers' appetite to further explore his writing." Publ Wkly

Rosen, Michael, 1946- **Dickens**; his work and his world. illustrated by Robert Ingpen. Candlewick Press 2005 95p il $19.99

Grades: 5 6 7 8   92

1. Authors 2. Novelists 3. Authors, English

ISBN 0-7636-2752-6

LC 2004-61847

"The art adds to the richness of a volume designed and written with care." Booklist

Drew, Charles Richard, 1904-1950

Venezia, Mike. **Charles** Drew; doctor who got the world pumped up to donate blood. written and illustrated by Mike Venezia. Children's Press 2009 32p il (Getting to know the world's greatest inventors & scientists) $28

Grades: 2 3 4   92

1. Blood 2. Surgeons 3. Inventors 4. Physicians 5. College teachers 6. African Americans -- Biography

ISBN 978-0-531-23725-0; 0-531-23725-7

LC 2008-27648

Charles Drew "is the individual credited with discovering how to extract plasma from whole blood and store it for long periods. . . . The book . . . is written in simple terms for children and focuses on the barriers [Drew] faced as an African-American in a pre-civil-rights-era United States. . . . . There are interesting pictures of Drew's life, as well as other pictures of blood plasma being used to save the lives of soldiers on the battlefield. . . . [This] is a biography that is outside of the ordinary." Sci Books Films

Du Bois, W. E. B. (William Edward Burghardt), 1868-1963

Whiting, Jim. **W.E.B.** Du Bois; civil rights activist, author, historian. Mason Crest Publishers 2010 64p il (Transcending race in America: biographies of biracial achievers) $22.95; pa $9.95

Grades: 5 6 7 8   92

1. Authors 2. Novelists 3. Historians 4. Editors 5. Essayists 6. Sociologists 7. Nonfiction writers 8. Civil rights activists 9. African Americans -- Biography 10. African Americans -- Civil rights

ISBN 978-1-4222-1618-7; 1-4222-1618-7; 978-1-4222-1632-3 pa; 1-4222-1632-2 pa

LC 2009022049

"The author openly discusses Du Bois' political and ideological struggles, which concluded with his move to Ghana and admittance into the Communist Party. . . . The book . . . provides solid information about Du Bois." Booklist

Includes glossary and bibliographical references

Dylan, Bob, 1941-

Burckhardt, Marc. **When** Bob met Woody; the story of the young Bob Dylan. illustrated by Marc Burckhardt. Little, Brown 2011 40p il $17.99

Grades: 3 4 5   92

1. Rock musicians 2. Biography, Individual

ISBN 978-0-316-11299-4; 0-316-11299-2

LC 2010-43030

This picture book biography follows Bob Zimmerman as he renames himself after his favorite poet, Dylan Thomas, and leaves his mining town to pursue his love of music in New York City. There, he meets his folk music hero and future mentor, Woody Guthrie.

"Golio excels at portraying Zimmerman's angst as he flounders for meaning and even invents for himself a more colorful backstory. Burckhardt's acrylics have the fractured look of damaged paintings, and . . . [convey] gravity and emotion. Back matter, including quotation sources, is superb. A stirring introduction to two musical legends." Booklist

Includes bibliographical references

Earhart, Amelia, 1898-1937

★ Fleming, Candace. **Amelia** lost: the life and disappearance of Amelia Earhart. Schwartz & Wade Books 2011 118p il map

Grades: 4 5 6 7   92

1. Air pilots 2. Missing persons 3. Women air pilots 4. Memoirists 5. Biography, Individual
ISBN 0-375-84198-9; 0-375-94598-9 lib bdg; 978-0-375-84198-9; 978-0-375-94598-4 lib bdg

LC 2010-05279

Fleming "offers a fresh look at this famous aviatrix. Employing dual narratives—straightforward biographical chapters alternating with a chilling recounting of Earhart's final flight and the search that followed—Fleming seeks to uncover the 'history of the hype,' pointing out numerous examples in which Earhart took an active role in mythologizing her own life.... Frequent sidebars, well-chosen maps, archival documents, and photos further clarify textual references without disturbing the overall narrative flow." Booklist

Tanaka, Shelley. **Amelia** Earhart; the legend of the lost aviator. by Shelley Tanaka; illustrated by David Craig. Abrams Books for Young Readers 2008 48p il map $18.95

Grades: 3 4 5 6   92

1. Air pilots 2. Missing persons 3. Women air pilots 4. Memoirists
ISBN 978-0-8109-7095-3; 0-8109-7095-3

LC 2007-39749

NCTE Orbis Pictus Award (2009)

This is an account of the life of aviator Amelia Earhart from her childhood up to the time she disappeared on a flight in 1937.

"This title is notable ... for its smooth, powerful storytelling, ample gallery of well-chosen photographs, and nicely placed sidebar information on such topics as flight delays, navigation, and around-the-world flight records." Bull Cent Child Books

Includes bibliographical references

Earle, Sylvia A., 1935-

Reichard, Susan E. **Who** on earth is Sylvia Earle? undersea explorer of the ocean. Enslow Publishers 2009 112p il (Scientists saving the earth) lib bdg $31.93

Grades: 5 6 7 8   92

1. Botanists 2. Marine biology 3. Women scientists 4. Underwater exploration 5. Divers 6. Marine biologists
ISBN 978-1-59845-118-4 lib bdg; 1-59845-118-9 lib bdg

LC 2008032014

"The writing is clear and informative.... Color photographs are relevant and of good quality." SLJ

Includes glossary and bibliographical references

Earnhardt, Dale, Jr.

Rappoport, Ken. **Dale** Earnhardt, Jr. a car racer who cares. Enslow Publishers, Inc. 2011 48p il (Sports stars who care) lib bdg $23.93; pa $7.95

Grades: 3 4 5   92

1. Automobile racing 2. Automobile racing drivers
ISBN 978-0-7660-3777-9 lib bdg; 0-7660-3777-0 lib bdg; 978-1-59845-228-0 pa; 1-59845-228-2 pa

LC 2010014947

This is a biography of race car driver Dale Earnhardt Jr. and founder of the Dale Jr. Foundation.

This is "especially good for book reports." Booklist

Includes glossary and bibliographical references

Eastman, George, 1854-1932

Kulling, Monica. **It's** a snap! George Eastman's first photograph. illustrated by Bill Slavin. Tundra Books 2009 un il (Great idea) $17.95

Grades: 2 3 4   92

1. Inventors 2. Philanthropists 3. Photography -- History 4. Manufacturing executives
ISBN 978-0-88776-881-1; 0-88776-881-4

"This picture-book biography begins in 1877, in Rochester, NY, with Eastman buying his first camera.... The picture-taking process took too long and the bored townspeople headed home before he could develop the wet plate. Eastman was determined to make photography easier and more affordable for everyone. During the next eight years, he invented the dry plate, the first roll of film, and the Kodak camera, and started the Eastman Kodak Company. The book will entertain and inform readers.... Slavin's pen-and-ink and watercolor illustrations ... complement the text." SLJ

Ederle, Gertrude, 1905-2003

Adler, David A. **America's** champion swimmer: Gertrude Ederle; written by David A. Adler; illustrated by Terry Widener. Harcourt 2000 un il $16; pa $7

Grades: 2 3 4   92

1. Swimming 2. Women athletes 3. Swimmers 4. Olympic athletes
ISBN 0-15-201969-3; 0-15-205251-8 pa

LC 98-54954

Describes the life and accomplishments of Gertrude Ederle, the first woman to swim the English Channel and a figure in the early women's rights movement

This book "illustrated with richly colored acrylic paintings ... captures the highlights of Ederle's life in evocative images and telling details that will appeal to children." N Y Times Book Rev

Edison, Thomas A. (Thomas Alva), 1847-1931

★ Brown, Don. A **wizard** from the start: the incredible boyhood & amazing inventions of Thomas Edison. Houghton Mifflin Books for Children 2010 un il $16

Grades: 2 3 4   92

1. Inventors
ISBN 978-0-547-19487-5; 0-547-19487-0

"Focusing on the great inventor's youth, roughly from age eight to mid-20s, this anecdotal picture-book biography is both engaging and accessible.... Youngsters will find much to relate to.... Brown's signature sketches combine digital imagery and watercolors and reflect the period costume and key moments in Edison's early life." SLJ

★ Carlson, Laurie M. **Thomas** Edison for kids; his life and ideas: 21 activities. [by] Laurie Carlson. Chicago Review Press 2006 147p il $14.95

Grades: 5 6 7 8   **92**
  1. Inventors 2. Science -- Experiments
  ISBN 1-55652-584-2

LC 2005025659

"Part biography, part science activity book, this resource will appeal to casual researchers and novice inventors. It contains a wealth of full-page primary source archival photographs, sidebars, and short biographical profiles of Edison's contemporaries, in addition to short and straight-forward experiments." Voice Youth Advocates
  Includes bibliographical references

Kesselring, Susan. **Thomas** Edison. Child's World 2010 24p il (Basic biographies) lib bdg $22.79
Grades: PreK K 1   **92**
  1. Inventors
  ISBN 978-1-60253-345-5; 1-60253-345-8

LC 2009029374

This biography of Thomas Edison "pairs intelligent, brief text with abundant photos. Simple but never basic." Booklist

Venezia, Mike. **Thomas** Edison; inventor with a lot of bright ideas. written and illustrated by Mike Venezia. Children's Press 2008 32p il (Getting to know the world's greatest inventors & scientists) lib bdg $28; pa $6.95
Grades: 2 3 4   **92**
  1. Inventors
  ISBN 0-531-14978-1 lib bdg; 978-0-531-14978-2 lib bdg; 0-531-22209-8 pa; 978-0-531-22209-6 pa

LC 2008002306

In this biography of inventor Thomas Edison "the humor and silly scenarios depicted in the cartoon drawings will draw readers back into the smooth, straightforward language." Booklist

Edmonds, S. Emma E. (Sarah Emma Evelyn), 1841-1898
  Hendrix, John. **Nurse,** soldier, spy: the story of Sarah Edmonds, a Civil War hero; [illustrated by] John Hendrix. Abrams Books for Young Readers 2011 47p il $18.95
Grades: 2 3 4   **92**
  1. Spies 2. Nurses 3. Women soldiers 4. Soldiers -- United States 5. Biography, Individual 6. United States -- History -- 1861-1865, Civil War -- Women
  ISBN 978-0-8109-9735-6; 0-8109-9735-5

LC 2010-23171

A story of a nineteen-year-old woman who disguised herself as a man to avoid an unwanted marriage and who distinguished herself as a male nurse during the Civil War, and later as a spy for the Union Army.
  "In ink-and-wash illustrations Hendrix . . . displays his knack for visual narrative. . . . This large-format picture book illustrates Edmonds' courage and determination while conveying a good deal of information in a highly readable way." Booklist

Jones, Carrie. **Sarah** Emma Edmonds was a great pretender; the true story of a Civil War spy. illustrations by Mark Oldroyd. Carolrhoda Books 2011 un il $17.95
Grades: 2 3 4   **92**
  1. Spies 2. Nurses 3. Women soldiers 4. Soldiers -- United States 5. Biography, Individual 6. United States -- History -- 1861-1865, Civil War -- Women
  ISBN 978-0-7613-5399-7; 0-7613-5399-2

This is "an entertaining and powerful Civil War era story about living by one's own rules. Realizing she would never satisfy her father's desire for a son, teenage Sarah Emma Edmonds fled from Canada to America where she assumed the identity of Frank Thompson. Edwards then joined the Union Army, first as a male nurse, then as a spy, passing herself off as a slave and, later, as an Irish peddler. . . . In Oldroyd's full-bleed spreads, characterized by strong cross-hatching and angular shapes, Edmonds's eyes twinkle with her secret knowledge, while Jones delivers her story with the assuredness of a natural storyteller." Publ Wkly

Einstein, Albert, 1879-1955
  ★ Berne, Jennifer. **On** a beam of light; a story of Albert Einstein. by Jennifer Berne; illustrated by Vladimir Radunsky. Chronicle Books 2013 56 p. ill. (alk. paper) $17.99
Grades: 2 3 4 5   **92**
  1. Physicists -- Biography
  ISBN 0811872351; 9780811872355

LC 2011004026

In this children's biographical story, by Jennifer Berne, illustrated by Vladimir Radunsky, "a boy rides a bicycle down a dusty road. But in his mind, he envisions himself traveling at a speed beyond imagining, on a beam of light. . . . From a boy endlessly fascinated by the wonders around him, Albert Einstein ultimately grows into a man of genius recognized the world over for profoundly illuminating our understanding of the universe." (Publisher's note)
  "Radunsky's humorous, childlike drawings convey Einstein's personality as well as the important ideas in the text... provide[s] a splendid introduction to a man who never stopped questioning." Kirkus

★ Brown, Don. **Odd** boy out: young Albert Einstein. Houghton Mifflin 2004 un il $16
Grades: 2 3 4   **92**
  1. Physicists 2. Nobel laureates for physics
  ISBN 0-618-49298-4

LC 2003-17701

An introduction to the work and early life of the twentieth-century physicist whose theory of relativity revolutionized scientific thinking.
  "Brown's pen-and-ink and watercolor illustrations [are] rendered in a palette of dusky mauve and earthy brown. . . . Through eloquent narrative and illustration, Brown offers a thoughtful introduction to an enigmatic man." SLJ

★ Delano, Marfe Ferguson. **Genius**; a photobiography of Albert Einstein. National Geographic 2005 64p il $17.95; lib bdg $27.90; pa $7.95
Grades: 5 6 7 8   **92**
  1. Physicists 2. Nobel laureates for physics
  ISBN 0-7922-9544-7; 0-7922-9545-5 lib bdg; 1-4263-0294-0 pa

LC 2004-15001

A biography of the German American physicist.
  This "combines a solid text with a particularly attractive format. . . . Delano offers just enough information about Einstein's theories to give a sense of his work. . . . Oversize and filled with well-selected photographs, the book is very handsome." Booklist

Kesselring, Susan. **Albert** Einstein. Child's World 2010 24p il (Basic biographies) lib bdg $22.79

Grades: PreK K 1　　　　　　　　　　　　**92**

1. Physicists 2. Nobel laureates for physics

ISBN 978-1-60253-338-7; 1-60253-338-5

LC 2009029363

This "pairs intelligent, brief text with abundant photos. Simple but never basic." Booklist

★ Krull, Kathleen. **Albert** Einstein; illustrated by Boris Kulikov. Viking 2009 141p il (Giants of science) $15.99

Grades: 5 6 7 8　　　　　　　　　　　　**92**

1. Physicists 2. Nobel laureates for physics

ISBN 978-0-670-06332-1; 0-670-06332-0

LC 2009-16037

"Krull delivers a splendidly humane biography of that gold standard of brilliance, Albert Einstein. . . . Drawing extensively on Einstein's writings, she presents a fully rounded portrait of a man whose genius combined with a bad temper and arrogance, to the detriment of his own professional advancement, not to mention his relationships with women and his children. Using concrete examples, the author brings such mind-bending notions as his General Theory of Relativity within the grasp of child readers." Kirkus

Meltzer, Milton. **Albert** Einstein. Holiday House 2008 32p il $16.95

Grades: 3 4 5　　　　　　　　　　　　**92**

1. Physicists 2. Scientists 3. Nobel laureates for physics

ISBN 978-0-8234-1966-1; 0-8234-1966-5

LC 2006-43676

"Meltzer offers a sound, cogent introduction to Einstein in this attractive volume, which discusses the scientist's work and its significance within a lively account of his life. . . . Well-chosen black-and-white photos and a few documents illustrate the narrative that takes both its subject and its audience seriously." Booklist

Includes bibliographical references

Eisenhower, Dwight D. (Dwight David), 1890-1969

Mara, Wil. **Dwight** Eisenhower. Marshall Cavendish Benchmark 2011 112p il (Presidents and their times) lib bdg $34.21

Grades: 5 6 7 8　　　　　　　　　　　　**92**

1. Generals 2. Presidents 3. College presidents 4. Presidents -- United States

ISBN 978-0-7614-4812-9; 0-7614-4812-8

LC 2009033042

"The size makes it ideal for that one-hundred page biography assignment; the readability makes the titles accessible to reluctant readers in high school; the succinct, well-presented information makes the volumes fitting for initial research at both the middle and high school level." Voice Youth Advocates

Includes glossary and bibliographical references

Elder, Ruth, 1902-1977

Cummins, Julie. **Flying** solo; how Ruth Elder soared into America's heart. Julie Cummins; illustrated by Malene Laugesen. Roaring Brook Press 2013 32 p. ill. (chiefly col.) (hardcover) $17.99

Grades: K 1 2　　　　　　　　　　　　**92**

1. Women air pilots 2. Air pilots -- United States -- Biography 3. Women air pilots -- United States -- Biography

ISBN 1596435097; 9781596435094

LC 2012029743

Amelia Bloomer Project (2014)

Written by Julie Cummins and illustrated by Malene R. Laugesen, this book describes how "Ruth Elder, a contemporary of Amelia Earhart, set her sights on becoming the first woman to fly across the Atlantic. At age 23, and after only a few flying lessons, she and her copilot set forth. Two-thirds of the way into their flight, the gas line sprung a leak, and they were forced to abandon the plane. Fortunately, they were rescued by a nearby ship." (Booklist)

"The clever, anecdotal text and vibrant spreads of the colorful planes and period costumes transport readers to another era, glamorous, yet restrictive toward the 'fairer sex.'" SLJ

Includes bibliographical references

Eleanor, of Aquitaine, Queen, consort of Henry II, King of England, 1122?-1204

Kramer, Ann. **Eleanor** of Aquitaine; the queen who rode off to battle. National Geographic 2006 64p il map (World history biographies) $17.95; lib bdg $27.90

Grades: 5 6 7 8　　　　　　　　　　　　**92**

1. Queens 2. France -- History -- 0-1328 3. Great Britain -- History -- 1154-1399, Plantagenets

ISBN 0-7922-5895-9; 0-7922-5896-7 lib bdg

An illustrated biography of the medieval queen who traveled to the Crusades with her first husband King Louis VII of France and later married King Henry II of England.

Includes glossary and bibliographical references

Elizabeth I, Queen of England, 1533-1603

★ Adams, Simon. **Elizabeth** I; the outcast who became England's queen. [by] Simon Adams. National Geographic 2005 64p il map (World history biographies) $17.95; lib bdg $27.90

Grades: 4 5 6 7　　　　　　　　　　　　**92**

1. Queens 2. Great Britain -- Kings and rulers 3. Great Britain -- History -- 1485-1603, Tudors

ISBN 0-7922-3649-1; 0-7922-3654-8 lib bdg

LC 2005001359

An illustrated introduction to the life and times of the 16th century queen of England

"Accomplishments and hardships are clearly explained with supporting quotes and facts. . . . Beautifully illustrated and visually appealing." SLJ

Includes glossary and bibliographical references

Stanley, Diane. **Good** Queen Bess: the story of Elizabeth I of England; by Diane Stanley and Peter Vennema; illustrated by Diane Stanley. HarperCollins Pubs. 2001 un il $16.99

Grades: 4 5 6 7　　　　　　　　　　　　**92**

1. Queens 2. Great Britain -- Kings and rulers 3. Great Britain -- History -- 1485-1603, Tudors

ISBN 0-688-17961-4

LC 00-47267

A reissue of the title first published 1990 by Four Winds Press

Follows the life of the strong-willed queen who ruled England in the time of Shakespeare and the defeat of the Spanish Armada

"The handsome illustrations . . . are worthy of their subject. Although the format suggests a picture-book audience, this biography needs to be introduced to older readers who have the background to appreciate and understand this woman who dominated and named an age." SLJ

Includes bibliographical references

Ellington, Duke, 1899-1974

Stein, Stephanie. **Duke** Ellington; his life in jazz with 21 activities. [by] Stephanie Stein Crease. Chicago Review Press 2009 148p il (For kids) pa $16.95

Grades: 5 6 7 8   92

1. Composers 2. Jazz musicians 3. Band leaders

ISBN 978-1-55652-724-1; 1-55652-724-1

LC 2008-23742

"This large-format book combines an illustrated biography of Duke Ellington with activities designed to offer insights into Ellington s era and his music. An informative account in an attractive...format." Booklist

Includes bibliographical references, discography, and filmography

Emerson, Ralph Waldo, 1803-1882

A **Home** for Mr. Emerson; by Barbara Kerley; illustrated by Edwin Fotheringham. Scholastic Press 2013 48 p. $18.99

Grades: 3 4 5   92

1. American authors 2. Authors, American -- 19th century -- Biography

ISBN 0545350883; 9780545350884

LC 2013007482

This children's book presents an "introduction to the life of Ralph Waldo Emerson. . . . Emerson grows up in Boston, but yearns to make a life closer to nature where he can surround himself with books and friends. He finds a perfect home in Concord, Massachusetts, where he and his wife raise a family. . . . A house fire later in his life devastates Emerson, but allows the town to demonstrate their affection for him as they rebuild his home." (School Library Journal)

Farnsworth, Philo T.

★ Krull, Kathleen. The **boy** who invented TV; the story of Philo Farnsworth. illustrated by Greg Couch. Alfred A. Knopf 2009 40 p. il $16.99

Grades: 3 4 5   92

1. Inventors 2. Television

ISBN 0375845615; 037594561X; 9780375845611; 9780375945618

LC 2008035500

"Plowing a potato field in 1920, a 14-year-old farm boy from Idaho [named Philo Farnsworth] saw in the parallel rows of overturned earth a way to 'make pictures fly through the air.' This boy was not a magician; he was a scientific genius and just eight years later he made his brainstorm in the potato field a reality by transmitting the world's first television image." (Publisher's note)

"This entertaining book explores the life of inventor Philo Farnsworth, who discovered how to transmit images electronically, leading to the first television. . . . Krull's

substantial, captivating text is balanced by Couch's warm, mixed-media illustrations." Publ Wkly

Includes bibliographical references

Farris, Christine

★ Farris, Christine King. **March** on! the day my brother Martin changed the world. [by] Christine King Farris; illustrated by London Ladd. Scholastic Press 2008 un il $17.99

Grades: 2 3 4   92

1. Clergy 2. Civil rights demonstrations 3. College teachers 4. Nonfiction writers 5. Civil rights activists 6. Nobel laureates for peace 7. African Americans -- Civil rights

ISBN 0-545-03537-6; 978-0-545-03537-8

LC 2007038620

"Describing the 1963 March on Washington, Farris, the older sister of Martin Luther King Jr., maintains the deft touch that made My Brother Martin so moving. . . . Farris . . . effectively uses plain language and well-chosen facts to explain her brother's extraordinary achievements. . . . Ladd . . . demonstrates a rare talent for portraiture. . . . His King looks human—in other words, capable of inspiring the reader." Publ Wkly

Ferris, George Washington Gale, 1859-1896

Sneed, Dani. The **man** who invented the ferris wheel; the genius of George Ferris. by Dani Sneed. Enslow Publishers 2013 48 p. ill. (some col.) (Genius inventors and their great ideas) $23.93

Grades: 2 3 4   92

1. Ferris wheels 2. Inventors 3. Civil engineers 4. Structural engineers

ISBN 0766041360; 9780766041363

LC 2012013976

This book, by Dani Sneed, focuses on George Washington Gale Ferris, Jr., "an American engineer. . . . He is most famous for creating the original Ferris Wheel for the 1893 Chicago World's Columbian Exposition." (Publisher's note)

"Each book features five chapters of text, laid out in wide-spaced lines of fairly large type. Illustrations include contemporary color photos as well as period photos of the inventor from childhood through adulthood." Booklist

Includes bibliographical references and index

Davis, Kathryn Gibbs. **Mr.** Ferris and his wheel; by Kathryn G. Davis. Houghton Mifflin Harcourt 2014 40 p. $17.99

Grades: K 1 2 3   92

1. Inventors 2. Inventors -- United States -- Biography 3. Ferris wheels -- History 4. Civil engineers -- United States -- Biography 5. Structural engineers -- United States -- Biography

ISBN 0547959222; 9780547959221

LC 2013050147

Written by Kathryn Gibbs Davis and illustrated by Gilbert Ford, "Capturing an engineer's creative vision and mind for detail, this fully illustrated picture book biography sheds light on how the American inventor George Ferris defied gravity and seemingly impossible odds to invent the world's most iconic amusement park attraction, the Ferris wheel." (Publisher's note)

"It's almost time for the 1893 Chicago World's Fair, and American architects are hoping to design a star attraction to rival the French Eiffel Tower. Mechanical engineer George Washington Gale Ferris Jr. has a daring idea: a huge, round, moving structure made from steel, a new metal unrivaled in both lightness and strength...Overall, the modernist look, inherently interesting topic, and strong documentation (including quotations from primary sources) make this title a positive addition, especially those looking to enhance their nonfiction offerings in view of new Common Core standards." SLJ

Fibonacci, Leonardo, ca. 1170-ca. 1240

★ D'Agnese, Joseph. **Blockhead**; the life of Fibonacci. illustrated by John O'Brien. Henry Holt and Company 2010 40p il $16.99

Grades: 2 3 4 5   **92**
1. Numbers 2. Mathematicians 3. Fibonacci numbers
ISBN 0-8050-6305-6; 978-0-8050-6305-9

LC 2009005264

This is a biography of Leonardo Fibonacci, the twelfth-century mathematician who discovered the numerical sequence named for him. "Intermediate." (Horn Book)

"D'Agnese's introduction to medieval Europe's greatest mathematician offers both a coherent biographical account—spun, with some invented details, from very sketchy historical records—and the clearest explanation to date for younger readers of the numerical sequence that is found throughout nature and still bears his name. O'Brien's illustrations place the prosperously dressed, woolly headed savant in his native Pisa and other settings." Booklist

Fillmore, Millard, 1800-1874

Gottfried, Ted. **Millard** Fillmore; by Ted Gottfried. Marshall Cavendish Benchmark 2007 96p il (Presidents and their times) lib bdg $22.95

Grades: 5 6 7 8   **92**
1. Presidents 2. Vice-presidents 3. Members of Congress 4. Presidents -- United States
ISBN 978-0-7614-2431-4

LC 2006019707

"Primary-source materials and quotes, helpful insets, and carefully selected . . . reproductions bring history to life and help make [this] clearly written [biography] highly readable." SLJ

Includes glossary and bibliographical references

Fitzgerald, Ella

★ Orgill, Roxane. **Skit**-scat raggedy cat: Ella Fitzgerald; written by Roxane Orgill; illustrated by Sean Qualls. Candlewick Press 2010 un il $17.99

Grades: 2 3 4   **92**
1. Singers 2. African American singers 3. Pop musicians 4. African American women -- Biography
ISBN 978-0-7636-1733-2; 0-7636-1733-4

LC 2009-47407

This is "a stylish portrayal of Ella Fitzgerald. . . . There's no question that Orgill and Qualls know what makes [jazz] so catchy: it's slinky, rhythmic, and joyful and on full display in both the lively text and swinging artwork." Booklist

★ Pinkney, Andrea Davis. **Ella** Fitzgerald; the tale of a vocal virtuosa. by Andrea Davis Pinkney with Scat Cat Monroe; illustrated by Brian Pinkney. Hyperion 2002 un il $16.99

Grades: 2 3 4   **92**
1. Singers 2. African American singers 3. Pop musicians 4. African American women -- Biography
ISBN 0-7868-0568-4; 0-7868-2493-X lib bdg

"Scat Cat Monroe, a jazzy feline in a zoot suit, tells Fitzgerald's life story. . . . The general details of an extraordinary life—when, what, where, and how—are related in rhythmic, vivid language that matches the verve of the hand-colored scratchboard illustrations." Bull Cent Child Books

Fitzgerald, Larry, 1983-

Sandler, Michael. **Larry** Fitzgerald. Bearport Pub. 2010 24p il map (Football heroes making a difference) lib bdg $22.61

Grades: 2 3 4   **92**
1. Football players 2. Football -- Biography
ISBN 978-1-936087-58-7; 1-936087-58-8

LC 2009028305

A look at the life and career of the famous football player. Includes glossary and bibliographical references

Ford, Henry, 1863-1947

★ Mitchell, Don. **Driven**; a photobiography of Henry Ford. foreword by Lee Iacocca. National Geographic 2010 64p il map $18.95; lib bdg $27.90

Grades: 5 6 7 8   **92**
1. Businessmen 2. Philanthropists 3. Automobile industry 4. Automobile executives
ISBN 978-1-4263-0155-1; 1-4263-0155-3; 978-1-4263-0156-8 lib bdg; 1-4263-0156-1 lib bdg

LC 2009-07136

"Mitchell introduces readers to the founder of the auto company. . . . Thoughts, feelings, and quotes abound, and they are well sourced. . . . The writing is clear, and the organization is chronological. . . . Driven combines fine photography and an inviting text to depict Ford's life and his impact on the world." SLJ

Includes bibliographical references

Forten, James, 1766-1842

Figley, Marty Rhodes. **Prisoner** for liberty; by Marty Rhodes Figley; illustrations by Craig Orback. Millbrook Press 2008 48p il (On my own history) lib bdg $25.26

Grades: 2 3 4   **92**
1. Abolitionists 2. Philanthropists 3. Sailmakers 4. African Americans -- Biography 5. United States -- History -- 1775-1783, Revolution
ISBN 978-0-8225-7280-0 lib bdg; 0-8225-7280-X lib bdg

LC 2006028582

"In dramatic words and vivid paintings, this [book] . . . celebrates the heroism of an African American teen in the Revolutionary War. Born free, 15-year-old James Forten joined the crew of the Royal Louis as a sailor. When the British captured the ship, he refused the chance to escape to help a sickly white friend. . . . This inspiring, personal story will help draw early readers into U.S. history." Booklist

Includes bibliographical references

Fossey, Dian

Kushner, Jill Menkes. **Who** on earth is Dian Fossey? defender of the mountain gorillas. Enslow Publishers 2009 112p il (Scientists saving the earth) lib bdg $31.93

Grades: 5 6 7 8 **92**

1. Authors 2. Gorillas 3. Women scientists 4. Murder victims 5. Primatologists 6. Writers on science
ISBN 1-59845-117-0 lib bdg; 978-1-59845-117-7 lib bdg

LC 2008029376

"The book is filled with factual information, yet is written in a manner that makes both Fossey and her gorillas come to life for the reader." Sci Books Films

Includes glossary and bibliographical references

Foucault, Jean Bernard Léon, 1819-1868

Mortensen, Lori. **Come** see the Earth turn: the story of Leon Foucault; illustrations by Raúl Allén. Tricycle Press 2010 un il $17.99

Grades: 3 4 5 **92**

1. Physicists 2. Scientists
ISBN 978-1-58246-284-4; 1-58246-284-4

A biography of the scientist who proved that the Earth spins on its axis.

"Mortensen's prose infuses this small scientific drama with remarkable tension, while Allén's dramatically lit paintings, often organized into elegant panels, have a cinematic quality and amplify the action even further." Publ Wkly

Frank, Anne, 1929-1945

★ Frank, Anne. The **diary** of a young girl: the definitive edition; edited by Otto H. Frank and Mirjam Pressler; translated by Susan Massotty. Doubleday 1995 340p $29.95; pa $6.99

Grades: 6 7 8 9 **92**

1. Children 2. Diarists 3. Holocaust victims 4. Jews -- Netherlands 5. Holocaust, 1933-1945 6. World War, 1939-1945 -- Jews 7. Netherlands -- History -- 1940-1945, German occupation
ISBN 0-385-47378-8; 0-553-57712-3 pa

LC 94-41379

"This new translation of Frank's famous diary includes material about her emerging sexuality and her relationship with her mother that was originally excised by Frank's father, the only family member to survive the Holocaust." Libr J

★ Metselaar, Menno. **Anne** Frank: her life in words and pictures; from the archives of The Anne Frank House. [by] Menno Metselaar and Ruud van der Rol; translated by Arnold J. Pomerans. Roaring Brook Press 2009 215p il map pa $12.99

Grades: 5 6 7 8 **92**

1. Children 2. Diarists 3. Holocaust victims 4. Jews -- Netherlands 5. Holocaust, 1933-1945 6. World War, 1939-1945 -- Jews 7. Netherlands -- History -- 1940-1945, German occupation
ISBN 978-1-59643-546-9; 1-59643-546-1; 978-1-59643-547-6 pa; 1-59643-547-X pa

First published 2004 in the Netherlands with title: The story of Anne Frank

Boston Globe-Horn Book Award honor book: Nonfiction (2010)

"Beginning with a single photograph of the cover of Anne Frank's diary and the quote, 'One of my nicest presents,' this small, beautifully formatted book is accessible, compelling, and richly pictorial. . . . The book immediately immerses readers in the girl's life via a series of family photographs, many previously unpublished. Divided chronologically, the accompanying text is enhanced by diary entries, resulting in a historically succinct yet descriptive presentation. . . . Even for those collections where Anne Frank is well represented, this is a moving and valuable book." SLJ

Franklin, Benjamin, 1706-1790

★ Byrd, Robert. **Electric** Ben; the amazing life and times of Benjamin Franklin. by Robert Byrd. Penguin Group 2012 40 p. (hardcover) $17.99

Grades: 3 4 5 **92**

1. Biography 2. Inventions -- History 3. United States -- History 4. Printers -- United States -- Biography 5. Inventors -- United States -- Biography 6. Statesmen -- United States -- Biography 7. Scientists -- United States -- Biography
ISBN 0803737491; 9780803737495

LC 2011050493

Boston Globe-Horn Book Award: Nonfiction (2013).
Robert F. Sibert Honor Book (2013)

This book by Robert Byrd presents a biography of Benjamin Franklin. "A true Renaissance man, Benjamin Franklin was the first American celebrity. In pictures and text, master artist Robert Byrd documents Franklin's numerous and diverse accomplishments, from framing the Constitution to creating bifocals." The book contains "facts, quotes, and captions, while the . . . illustrations make a . . . tribute to the brilliant American." (Publisher's note)

Fleming, Candace. **Ben** Franklin's almanac; being a true account of the good gentleman's life. Atheneum Bks. for Young Readers 2003 120p il $19.95

Grades: 5 6 7 8 **92**

1. Authors 2. Diplomats 3. Inventors 4. Statesmen 5. Scientists 6. Writers on science 7. Members of Congress 8. Statesmen -- United States
ISBN 0-689-83549-3

LC 2002-6136

Brings together eighteenth century etchings, artifacts, and quotations to create the effect of a scrapbook of the life of Benjamin Franklin

"An authoritative work of depth, humor, and interest, presenting Franklin in all his complexity, ranging from the heroic to the vulgar, the saintly to the callous." SLJ

★ Freedman, Russell, 1929- **Becoming** Ben Franklin; how a candle-maker's son helped light the flame of liberty. Russell Freedman. 1st ed. Holiday House 2013 86 p. col. ill. (hardcover) $24.95

Grades: 5 6 7 8 **92**

1. Franklin, Benjamin, 1706-1790 2. Founding Fathers of the United States 3. Printers -- United States -- Biography 4. Inventors -- United States -- Biography 5. Statesmen -- United States -- Biography 6. Scientists -- United States -- Biography
ISBN 0823423743; 9780823423743

LC 2012002971

This book is a biography of Ben Franklin. Russell Freedman "chose episodes that reflect how the young man, disgruntled with being his brother's apprentice, made a life for himself . . . . By describing the obstacles Franklin overcame in establishing his print shop in Philadelphia, Freedman delineates a . . . path between his subject's early ambition and his ease with people to his success in business and then to his later roles as a diplomat, revolutionary, and public servant." (School Library Journal)

Includes bibliographical references (p. 78-82) and index.

★ Fritz, Jean. **What's** the big idea, Ben Franklin? illustrated by Margot Tomes. Putnam Pub. Group 1976 46p il $15.99; pa $5.99

Grades: 2 3 4   92

1. Authors 2. Diplomats 3. Inventors 4. Statesmen 5. Scientists 6. Writers on science 7. Members of Congress 8. Statesmen -- United States

ISBN 0-399-23487-X; 0-698-11372-1 pa

The text "focuses on Franklin's multifaceted career but also gives personal details and quotes some of his pithy sayings. Enough background information about colonial affairs is given to enable readers to understand the importance of Franklin's contributions to the public good but not so much that it obtrudes on his life story. Although the text is not punctuated by references or footnotes, a page of notes (with numbers for pages referred to) is appended." Bull Cent Child Books

★ Harness, Cheryl. The **remarkable** Benjamin Franklin; written & illustrated by Cheryl Harness. National Geographic Society 2005 47p il $17.95

Grades: 2 3 4   92

1. Authors 2. Diplomats 3. Inventors 4. Statesmen 5. Scientists 6. Writers on science 7. Members of Congress 8. Statesmen -- United States

ISBN 0-7922-7882-8

LC 2004-20504

"Beginning with Franklin's birth, Harness explores the activities that filled his days from his quest to open his own print shop to his role in the American Revolution to his personal intrigues and inventions. Her conversational writing style and vivid illustrations will appeal to readers just becoming acquainted with this important figure." SLJ

Includes bibliographical references

Krull, Kathleen. **Benjamin** Franklin; by Kathleen Krull; illustrated by Boris Kulikov. Viking 2013 121 p. (Giants of science) (hardcover) $15.99

Grades: 5 6 7 8   92

1. Inventors 2. Scientists 3. Franklin, Benjamin, 1706-1790 4. Inventors -- United States -- Biography 5. Scientists -- United States -- Biography

ISBN 0670012874; 9780670012879

LC 2013018404

This book, by Kathleen Krull, part of the Giants of Science series, "explains the many ways that Franklin was the American manifestation of the European Enlightenment, putting his discoveries in clear historical context. Known as 'natural philosophers' in the eighteenth century, scientists like Franklin specialized in the kind of theoretical thinking that could result in inventions to make life better, from lightning rods to efficient heating stoves." (Booklist)

"The majority of this helpful book deals with Franklin's innovative scientific processes and his reasoning behind such inventions as the Franklin stove and the lightning rod; he coined words (still in use today) with definitions specific to the field, such as positive, negative, and charge. Kulikov's

occasional black-and-white illustrations add sly humor to the account." (Horn Book)

Includes bibliographical references and index

Miller, Brandon Marie. **Benjamin** Franklin, American genius; his life and ideas, with 21 activities. Chicago Review Press 2009 125p il pa $16.95

Grades: 4 5 6 7   92

1. Authors 2. Diplomats 3. Inventors 4. Statesmen 5. Scientists 6. Writers on science 7. Members of Congress

ISBN 978-1-55652-757-9 pa; 1-55652-757-8 pa

LC 2009012456

"Miller does an excellent job of presenting a synopsis of Franklin's life in a highly readable manner. . . . Imbedded in each chapter are asides that further elaborate on Franklin's life and times and activities that coordinate with the text or the historical facts presented. The directions are easy to follow and enhance the overall presentation, especially in terms of classroom connections. Illustrations accompany each project and reproductions of primary documents, renderings, and paintings provide added value." SLJ

Includes glossary and bibliographical references

Rosenstock, Barb. **Ben** Franklin's big splash; the mostly true story of his first invention. Barb Rosenstock. Calkins Creek 2014 32 p. $16.95

Grades: K 1 2 3 4   92

1. Inventors -- Fiction 2. Swimming -- Fiction

ISBN 1620914468; 9781620914465

LC 2014931339

This middle grades book by Barb Rosenstock, illustrated by S. D. Schindler, tells how "Ben Franklin loved to swim and, at the age of eleven, he was determined to swim like a fish--fins and all! This . . . account of young Ben's earliest invention follows the budding scientist's journey as he tests and retests his swim fins. That first big splash led Ben to even more innovations and inventions." (Publisher's note)

"Statesman and inventor Benjamin Franklin got an early start on the creative portion of his résumé. As an 11-year-old swimming fan, he was not content to idly paddle Boston's Charles River. Instead, he pondered important questions such as, "Why can't I swim like a fish?" which led him to his first inventions: swim fins and sandals. ..Schindler's ink-and-watercolor illustrations pick up the comical nuances of the text (especially Rosenstock's penchant for vivid alliterative verbs) and convey the imagination required for invention. Appended with a list of Franklin's inventions, source notes, and time line." Booklist

Rushby, Pamela. **Ben** Franklin; printer, author, inventor, politician. by Pamela Rushby. National Geographic 2007 40p il (National Geographic history chapters) lib bdg $17.90

Grades: 2 3 4   92

1. Authors 2. Diplomats 3. Inventors 4. Statesmen 5. Scientists 6. Writers on science 7. Members of Congress 8. Statesmen -- United States

ISBN 978-1-4263-0191-9

LC 2007007896

This biography of Benjamin Franklin is "nicely illustrated with . . . paintings, engravings, and facsimiles. . . . [It is]

just right for emerging chapter-book readers. . . . Useful . . . for reports . . . and interesting pleasure reading." SLJ

Includes glossary and bibliographical references

★ Schroeder, Alan. **Ben** Franklin; his wit and wisdom from A to Z. illustrated by John O'Brien. Holiday House 2011 un il $16.95

Grades: 2 3 4   92

1. Authors 2. Alphabet 3. Diplomats 4. Inventors 5. Statesmen 6. Scientists 7. Writers on science 8. Members of Congress 9. Statesmen -- United States ISBN 978-0-8234-1950-0; 0-8234-1950-9

LC 2010024062

"Alphabetically arranged, but far more than just an alphabet book, this guide to the life of Ben Franklin covers his upbringing, his prominence in early America, his many inventions, and his beliefs and writings. Given the breadth of Franklin's accomplishments, it shouldn't be surprising that each letter gets more than one word. . . . O'Brien's ink and watercolor images contribute ample humor, and Schroeder creates a well-rounded, fascinating portrait of an iconic American." Publ Wkly

Freeman, Elizabeth, 1744?-1829

Woelfle, Gretchen. **Mumbet's** Declaration of Independence; by Gretchen Woelfle; Illustrated by Alix Delinois. Carolrhoda Books 2014 32 p. color illustrations (lib. bdg.: alk. paper) $17.95

Grades: 1 2 3 4   92

1. Slaves -- Emancipation 2. United States -- History -- 1775-1783, Revolution 3. Slavery -- Massachusetts -- History 4. Slaves -- Massachusetts -- Biography 5. African American women -- Massachusetts -- Biography ISBN 0761365893; 9780761365891

LC 2013018620

This book, written by Gretchen Woelfle and illustrated by Alix Delinois, describes how "the founders weren't the only ones who believed that everyone had a right to freedom. Mumbet, a Massachusetts slave, believed it too. She longed to be free, but how? Would anyone help her in her fight for freedom? Could she win against her owner, the richest man in town?" (Publisher's note)

"Delinois's thick layers of paint and vibrant palette infuse even the story's upsetting moments with hopefulness, and Mumbet herself glows with determination and integrity. An author's note addresses how many details of Mumbet's life were lost to history, yet her story stands as a potent reminder that the freedoms that accompanied the American Revolution left many behind." Pub Wkly

Fritz, Jean

★ Fritz, Jean. **Homesick**: my own story; illustrated with drawings by Margot Tomes and photographs. Putnam 1982 163p il $16.99; pa $5.99

Grades: 5 6 7 8   92

1. Authors 2. Women authors 3. China 4. Children's authors ISBN 0-399-20933-6; 0-698-11782-4 pa

LC 82-7646

Companion volume to China homecoming

A Newbery Medal honor book, 1983

"The descriptions of places and the times are vivid in a book that brings to the reader, with sharp clarity and candor, the yearnings and fears and ambivalent loyalties of a young girl." Bull Cent Child Books

Fulton, Robert, 1765-1815

Herweck, Don. **Robert** Fulton; engineer of the steamboat. Compass Point Books 2009 40p il (Mission: Science) lib bdg $26.60

Grades: 4 5 6 7   92

1. Engineers 2. Inventors 3. Steamboats ISBN 978-0-7565-3961-0 lib bdg; 0-7565-3961-7 lib bdg

LC 2008007728

Covers the life and accomplishments of American inventor and mechanic, Robert Fulton, who is best known for building the first successful steamboat

Galilei, Galileo, 1564-1642

★ Panchyk, Richard. **Galileo** for kids; his life and ideas: 25 activities. foreword by Buzz Aldrin. Chicago Review Press 2005 166p il map pa $16.95

Grades: 5 6 7 8   92

1. Astronomers 2. Writers on science ISBN 1-55652-566-4

LC 2004-22936

A biography of the Renaissance scientist and his times with related activities

"Clear . . . writing places Galileo squarely within the historical context of the turbulent Italian Renaissance. . . . Panchyk's title is a good choice for those interested in integrating history and science curriculums." SLJ

Includes bibliographical references

★ Steele, Philip. **Galileo**; the genius who faced the Inquisition. National Geographic 2005 64p il (World history biographies) $17.95; lib bdg $27.90

Grades: 4 5 6 7   92

1. Astronomers 2. Writers on science ISBN 0-7922-3656-4; 0-7922-3657-2 lib bdg

LC 2005-01357

An illustrated introduction to the 16th century astronomer and his times

"Accomplishments and hardships are clearly explained with supporting quotes and facts. . . . Beautifully illustrated and visually appealing." SLJ

Gallaudet, T. H. (Thomas Hopkins), 1787-1851

★ McCully, Emily Arnold. **My** heart glow: Alice Cogswell, Thomas Gallaudet and the birth of American sign language. Hyperion Books for Children 2008 un il $15.99

Grades: 2 3 4   92

1. Deaf 2. Sign language 3. Teachers of the deaf ISBN 978-1-4231-0028-7; 1-4231-0028-X

This is the story of Thomas Gallaudet and his deaf neighbor, Alice Cogswell, and how Gallaudet established a school for the deaf in the United States and developed American Sign Language.

"Emily Arnold McCully's watercolor illustrations are beautifully rendered. . . . Not only does this book accurately present the engrossing story of Alice and Gallaudet, it is also an excellent resource for teaching diversity and encouraging empathy for others." Libr Media Connect

Wyckoff, Edwin Brit. **Sign** language man: Thomas H. Gallaudet and his incredible work. Enslow Elementary

2010 32p il (Genius at work! Great inventor biographies) lib bdg $22.60

Grades: 4 5 6   92

1. Sign language 2. Deaf -- Education 3. Teachers of the deaf 4. Deaf -- Means of communication

ISBN 978-0-7660-3447-1 lib bdg; 0-7660-3447-X lib bdg

LC 2010005359

"Read about Thomas H. Gallaudet, who helped develop and teach American Sign Language." Publisher's note

Includes glossary and bibliographical references

Gama, Vasco da, 1469-1524

★ Calvert, Patricia. **Vasco** da Gama; so strong a spirit. [by] Patricia Calvert. Benchmark Books 2005 96p il map (Great explorations) lib bdg $29.93

Grades: 5 6 7 8   92

1. Explorers

ISBN 0-7614-1611-0

LC 2003-22946

Recounts the voyages undertaken by fifteenth-century Portuguese explorer Vasco da Gama to strengthen his nation's power by establishing a sea trade route to India.

Includes bibliographical references

Gandhi, Arun

★ Gandhi, Arun. **Grandfather** Gandhi; Arun Gandhi and Bethany Hegedus; illustrated by Evan Turk. Atheneum Books for Young Readers 2012 48 p. (hardcover) $17.99

Grades: K 1 2 3   92

1. Grandfathers 2. Pacifists -- India -- Biography 3. Statesmen -- India -- Biography

ISBN 144242365X; 9781442423657

LC 2011033058

In this book, by Arun Gandhi and Bethany Hegedus, illustrated by Evan Turk, "Mahatma Gandhi's grandson tells the story of how his grandfather taught him to turn darkness into light. . . . When an older boy pushes him on the soccer field, his anger fills him in a way that surely a true Gandhi could never imagine. Can Arun ever live up to the Mahatma? Will he ever make his grandfather proud?" (Publisher's note)

"Mahatma Gandhi's grandson, Arun, who angers easily, feels he will never live up to the Gandhi name. Gandhi explains that he, too, feels anger but has learned to channel it for good. Unusual for its child-centered portrait of Gandhi, the graceful narrative is matched by vivid mixed-media illustrations, rendered in watercolor, paper collage, cotton fabric, yarn, gouache, pencil, tea, and tinfoil." (Horn Book)

Gandhi, Mahatma, 1869-1948

★ Wilkinson, Philip. **Gandhi**; the young protester who founded a nation. National Geographic 2005 64p il (World history biographies) $17.95; lib bdg $27.90

Grades: 4 5 6 7   92

1. Authors 2. Journalists 3. Passive resistance 4. Essayists 5. Pacifists 6. Memoirists 7. Political leaders 8. Writers on politics 9. India -- Politics and government

ISBN 0-7922-3647-5; 0-7922-3648-3 lib bdg

"Double-page spreads describe phases in Gandhi's life, from childhood to his tragic death, detailed in Wilkinson's straightforward, succinct language and in anecdotes, which will capture young people's attention and also humanize the great leader." Booklist

Includes glossary and bibliographical references

Garnett, Kevin, 1976-

Wilner, Barry. **Kevin** Garnett; a basketball star who cares. Enslow 2011 48p il (Sports stars who care) $23.93

Grades: 3 4 5   92

1. Basketball players 2. Basketball -- Biography

ISBN 978-0-7660-3772-4; 0-7660-3772-X

This is a biography of the forward for the Boston Celtics who, through his 4XL Foundation, helps teens prepare for careers in business and who donated more than $1 million to help rebuild areas devastated by Hurricane Katrina.

This is "especially good for book reports." Booklist

Gaudí, Antoni, 1852-1926

★ Rodriguez, Rachel. **Building** on nature; the life of Antoni Gaudí. illustrated by Julie Paschkis. Henry Holt & Co. 2009 un il $16.99

Grades: 1 2 3   92

1. Architects

ISBN 978-0-8050-8745-1; 0-8050-8745-1

LC 2008-38213

This is a biography of "the Catalonian architect Antoni Gaudí. The immediacy of the present-tense narrative is simple, direct, and at times piercingly poetic. . . . Paschkis doesn't try to reproduce the delicate exoticism of Gaudí's buildings in a line-for-line manner but rather soaks up the wondrous strange oozing from his designs and renders their dreamlike qualities in pointed details and large-scale impressions." Booklist

Gee, Maggie

★ Moss, Marissa. **Sky** high: the true story of Maggie Gee; illustrated by Carl Angel. Tricycle Press 2009 un il $16.99

Grades: 3 4 5   92

1. Authors 2. Novelists 3. Women air pilots 4. World War, 1939-1945 -- Aerial operations

ISBN 978-1-58246-280-6; 1-58246-280-1

LC 2008042387

This is a biography of the Asian American World War II air pilot, Maggie Gee

"Based on interviews with Gee, this has a lovely, personal feel to it. And while some of the faces in the acrylic and colored-pencil illustrations are a bit stiff, the scenes themselves exude a panoramic joy." Booklist

Gehry, Frank

Bodden, Valerie. **Frank** Gehry. Creative Education 2009 48p il (Xtraordinary artists) lib bdg $32.80

Grades: 4 5 6 7   92

1. Architects

ISBN 978-1-58341-662-4 lib bdg; 1-58341-662-5 lib bdg

LC 2007004201

This is a biography of architect Frank Gehry

This offers an "interesting [layout]; big, high-quality reproductions and photographs on heavy paper; insightful quotes from diverse sources; and . . . an excerpt from an essay about [Gehry] at the end of the book. Readers get a strong sense of [the] artist's personality along with an excellent survey of his work." SLJ

Includes bibliographical references

Genghis Khan, 1162-1227

★ Demi. **Genghis** Khan. Marshall Cavendish Children 2009 un il $19.99

Grades: 4 5 6 7   **92**

1. Mongols 2. Kings and rulers 3. Kings

ISBN 978-0-7614-5547-9; 0-7614-5547-7

LC 2008006001

A reissue of Chingis Khan, published 1991 by Henry Holt & Co.

A biography of the Mongol leader and military-strategist who, at the height of his power, was supreme master of the largest empire ever created in the lifetime of one man.

"Demi has managed to portray a fierce conqueror as a sympathetic character who follows a strict code that places loyalty, obedience, and discipline above all else. . . . The artist achieves a clever grandeur with the liberal use of iridescent gold and detailed scenes that spill out of their gilded borders and nearly off the pages. . . . This handsome biography is a feast for the eyes from cover to cover." Booklist

George III, King of Great Britain, 1738-1820

★ Fritz, Jean. **Can't** you make them behave, King George? pictures by Tomie de Paola. Putnam 1977 45p il $16.99; pa $6.99

Grades: 2 3 4   **92**

1. Kings 2. Great Britain -- Kings and rulers

ISBN 0-399-23304-0; 0-698-11402-7 pa

LC 75-33722

"As a boy, George is seen to have had struggles in deportment; as King George III, he is mystified that the colonists refuse to be taught. Bits of history, a sense of George's personality, and the loneliness of being king are all conveyed with good humor. The artist's drawings evoke more chuckles." LC. Child Books, 1977

Gibson, Althea, 1927-2003

Deans, Karen. **Playing** to win: the story of Althea Gibson; by Karen Deans; illustrated by Elbrite Brown. Holiday House 2007 un il $16.95

Grades: 1 2 3 4   **92**

1. Women athletes 2. African American athletes 3. Tennis players 4. Tennis -- Biography

ISBN 0-8234-1926-6

LC 2004052275

"Not only was Gibson a record-breaking tennis player, but she also played an important role in breaking down racial barriers. . . . The multimedia illustrations are well matched to the power and fluidity of the text, particularly in capturing the champion in action. . . . This well-written and attractive biography will be a popular addition to most collections." SLJ

Includes bibliographical references

★ Stauffacher, Sue. **Nothing** but trouble; the story of Althea Gibson. illustrated by Greg Couch. Alfred A. Knopf 2007 un il $16.99; lib bdg $19.99

Grades: 2 3 4 5   **92**

1. Women athletes 2. African American athletes 3.

Tennis players 4. Tennis -- Biography

ISBN 978-0-375-83408-0; 978-0-375-93408-7 lib bdg

LC 2006-12605

A biography of the first African American tennis player to win at Wimbleton and Forest Hills in 1957 and 1958

"Couch's kinetic illustrations done in acrylic with digital imaging wonderfully enhance the text. Althea stands out in a blur of color against somber sepia, blue, and olive-drab backgrounds. The prose is rhythmic and has the cadence of the street, and it's a treat to read aloud." SLJ

Giff, Patricia Reilly

Giff, Patricia Reilly. **Don't** tell the girls; a family memoir. by Patricia Reilly Giff. Holiday House 2005 131p il $16.95

Grades: 4 5 6 7   **92**

1. Authors 2. Teachers 3. Women authors 4. Authors, American 5. Children's authors

ISBN 0-8234-1813-8

LC 2004-47452

"Giff reflects on her childhood and her family, going back through several generations. Spotlighting her two grandmothers, she lovingly relates remembered conversations and incidents involving the one she knew well before turning to the other grandmother, whom she never met. . . . This little book has much to offer thoughtful children. . . . With . . . sharply reproduced family photos and documents, this handsome book's small format reflects its intimate, conversational style." Booklist

Gilbreth, Lillian

Kulling, Monica. **Spic-and-span!** Lillian Gilbreth's wonder kitchen. Monica Kulling. Tundra Books of Northern New York 2014 32 p. color illustrations

Grades: K 1 2 3   **92**

1. Women engineers 2. Women inventors

ISBN 9781770493803; 9781770493810

LC 2013943889

This book, by Monica Kulling, focuses on Lillian Moller Gilbreth. "She and her husband, Frank, became efficiency experts by studying the actions of factory workers. . . . When Frank suddenly died, Lillian was left to her own devices to raise their eleven children. Eventually, she was hired by the Brooklyn Borough Gas Company to improve kitchen design, which was only the beginning. . . . [She] the first woman elected to the National Academy of Engineering." (Publisher's note)

"This engaging picture-book biography details the many accomplishments of Lillian Gilbreth, the first woman elected to the National Academy of Engineering...Parkins' rich, cartoon-like illustrations provide clear period detail, and his characters' faces portray an extensive range of emotions, adding interest and emphasizing Gilbreth's primary commitment to her family. Student researchers might also enjoy other titles in the Great Idea series, such as Kulling's In the Bag!: Margaret Knight Wraps It Up (2011)." Booklist

Gilmore, P. S. (Patrick Sarsfield), 1829-1892

Potter, Alicia. **Jubilee!** Patrick S. Gilmore's very, very loud idea. Alicia Potter, illustrated by Matt Tavares. Candlewick Press 2014 40 p. $16.99

Grades: 2 3 4 5   **92**

1. Concerts 2. Music -- United States -- History 3. United States -- History -- 1861-1865, Civil War -- Peace

4. Bands (Music) 5. Music festivals -- Massachusetts --
Boston 6. National Peace Jubilee and Musical Festival
(1869: Boston, Mass.)
ISBN 0763658561; 9780763658564

LC 2013943992

This book, by Alicia Potter, focuses on the "man behind
the 1869 National Peace Jubilee. . . . As a young boy growing up in Ireland, Patrick Sarsfield Gilmore loved music. . .
. This love of music followed him to Boston in 1849, where
he became a bandleader. During the brutal Civil War, it was
music that kept up his spirits and those of his fellow soldiers.
So when the war ended, . . . [he] create the biggest, boldest, loudest concert the world had ever known to celebrate."
(Publisher's note)

"After experiencing the horrors of the Civil War firsthand, one man was determined to celebrate the beauty of
life through music...his is both a tribute to one man's talent
and an insightful look at a different period of history." SLJ

Glenn, John, 1921-

Mitchell, Don. **Liftoff**; a photobiography of John
Glenn. National Geographic Society 2006 64p il $17.95;
lib bdg $27.90
Grades: 5 6 7 8   92

1. Astronauts 2. Senators 3. Statesmen -- United States
ISBN 0-7922-5899-1; 0-7922-5900-9 lib bdg

LC 2005-30916

This is a biography of the American astronaut, pilot, and
U.S. Senator from Ohio.

This is "well-written and well-illustrated." Sci
Books Films

Includes bibliographical references

Gogh, Vincent van, 1853-1890

Bodden, Valerie. **Vincent** van Gogh. Creative Education 2009 48p il (Xtraordinary artists) lib bdg $32.80
Grades: 4 5 6 7   92

1. Artists 2. Painters 3. Artists, Dutch
ISBN 978-1-58341-663-1 lib bdg; 1-58341-663-3
lib bdg

LC 2007002118

This biography of the artist offers an "interesting [lay-
out]; big, high-quality reproductions and photographs on
heavy paper; insightful quotes from diverse sources; and
meaty selections of the artist's own writing . . . at the end of
the book. Readers get a strong sense of [the] artist's personality along with an excellent survey of his work." SLJ

Includes bibliographical references

Goodall, Jane, 1934-

★ McDonnell, Patrick. **Me** . . . Jane. Little, Brown
2011 $15.99
Grades: PreK K 1 2   92

1. Chimpanzees 2. Women scientists 3. Primatologists
4. Writers on nature 5. Nonfiction writers 6. Biography,
Individual
ISBN 978-0-316-04546-9; 0-316-04546-2;
0316045462; 9780316045469

LC 2010019756

This book is "inspirational. . . . McDonnell's homey,
earth-toned pen and watercolor pictures give way to that
most famous of all Goodall photographs, where the young
scientist and an even younger chimp reach across their
worlds to touch hands. The simple and intimate paintings

are accented with casually arrayed stamped motifs and some
of Goodall's childhood drawings." Horn Book

★ Winter, Jeanette. The **watcher**: Jane Goodall's life
with the chimps. Schwartz & Wade Books 2011 un il
$17.99; lib bdg $20.99
Grades: PreK K 1 2   92

1. Chimpanzees 2. Women scientists 3. Primatologists
4. Writers on nature 5. Nonfiction writers
ISBN 978-0-375-86774-3; 0-375-86774-0; 978-0-375-
96774-0 lib bdg; 0-375-96774-5 lib bdg

LC 2010005280

"This tranquil picture-book biography establishes from
the beginning that Jane Goodall has always had the right
temperament for the work that made her famous. . . . The
theme of persistence, particularly in relation to observing
animals, shapes the spare, inviting text, which takes Goodall
from backyard observations to scientific study of chimpanzees in Tanzania. In Winter's signature stylized paintings,
the jungle is rendered in cool blues and greens." Horn Book

Goodman, Benny, 1909-1986

Cline-Ransome, Lesa. **Benny** Goodman & Teddy Wilson; taking the stage as the first black and white jazz band
in history. by Lesa Cline-Ransome; illustrated by James E.
Ransome. Holiday House 2014 32 p. (hardcover) $16.95
Grades: 2 3 4 5   92

1. Jazz musicians -- Biography 2. Race relations --
History -- 20th century 3. Jazz musicians -- United
States -- Biography
ISBN 082342362X; 9780823423620

LC 2010048154

"In 1936, the Benny Goodman Trio became the first interracial band to perform in public, with Benny Goodman
(the son of Jewish immigrants) on clarinet and African-
American Teddy Wilson on piano (Gene Krupa, on drums,
completed the trio). Writing in punchy free verse that echoes
the bounce of both men's music," author Lesa Cline-Ransome, "traces Goodman and Wilson's parallel--but separate-
-paths to jazz fame, before eventually meeting in 1935."
(Publishers Weekly)

"Goodman grew up in Chicago, a working-class Jewish boy; Wilson lived in Tuskegee, Alabama, a middle-class
African American boy. The story of how the two jazz musicians met and formed the Benny Goodman Trio (the "first
interracial band to perform publicly") is recounted in short
bursts of text, almost like jazz riffs, accompanied by pencil and watercolor illustrations that capture distinctive moments. Timeline." Horn Book

Greenberg, Hank, 1911-1986

Sommer, Shelley. **Hammerin'** Hank Greenberg; baseball pioneer. Calkins Creek 2011 135p il $17.95
Grades: 5 6 7 8   92

1. Baseball players 2. Jews -- Biography 3. Baseball
-- Biography
ISBN 1-59078-452-9; 978-1-59078-452-5

"Greenberg grew up in an Orthodox Jewish family in
New York and went on to be a Hall-of-Fame first baseman
and left fielder, playing most of his career with the Detroit
Tigers in the 1930s and 1940s. . . . Sommer presents a fast-
moving, straightforward biography. . . . Numerous black-
and-white photos enhance the text. . . . An excellent choice
for kids who enjoy delving into baseball history." Booklist

Greene, Nathanael, 1742-1786

Mierka, Gregg A. **Nathanael** Greene; the general who saved the Revolution. [by] Gregg A. Mierka. OTTN Pub. 2007 88p il map (Forgotten heroes of the American Revolution) $23.95; pa $12.95

Grades: 5 6 7 8   **92**

1. Generals 2. Society of Friends 3. United States -- History -- 1775-1783, Revolution

ISBN 978-1-59556-012-4; 1-59556-012-2; 978-1-59556-017-9 pa; 1-59556-017-3 pa

LC 2006021044

"This lively profile combines an engrossing account of the Revolutionary War with healthy measures of images and passages drawn from primary—and sometimes previously unpublished—sources." Booklist

Includes bibliographical references

Greenwood, Chester, 1858-1937

★ McCarthy, Meghan. **Earmuffs** for everyone! how Chester Greenwood became known as the inventor of earmuffs. Meghan McCarthy. Simon & Schuster Books for Young Readers 2015 48 p. illustrations (chiefly color) (hardback) $17.99

Grades: K 1 2 3 4   **92**

1. Patents 2. Inventors 3. Earmuffs 4. Patents 5. Inventors -- Maine -- Farmington

ISBN 148140637X; 9781481406376

LC 2014020159

In this picture book, by Meghan McCarthy, "Chester Greenwood went from having cold ears to becoming a great inventor. . . . When your ears are cold, you can wear earmuffs, but that wasn't true for Chester Greenwood back in 1873. Earmuffs didn't exist yet! But during yet another long and cold Maine winter, Chester decided to do something about his freezing ears, and he designed the first pair of ear protectors (a.k.a. earmuffs) out of wire, beaver fur, and cloth." (Publisher's note)

"Chester Greenwood Day is celebrated annually in Maine to honor a man credited with inventing earmuffs. But did he? The creator of books such as Pop! The Invention of Bubble Gum (2010) and Seabiscuit the Wonder Horse (2008), McCarthy leads off this picture-book biography with an illustrated discussion of earmuffs developed before or soon after Greenwood's birth...This unusual book also offers insight into the process of invention and how the muddling of fact, memory, and legend can result in popular history." Booklist

Gross, Elly Berkovits, 1929-

Gross, Elly Berkovits. **Elly;** my true story of the Holocaust. [by] Elly Berkovits Gross. Scholastic Press 2009 125p il $14.99

Grades: 4 5 6 7   **92**

1. Poets 2. Authors 3. Holocaust survivors 4. Memoirists 5. Jews -- Romania 6. Holocaust, 1933-1945 -- Personal narratives

ISBN 978-0-545-07494-0; 0-545-07494-0

Relates how the author was torn from her happy home and sent to Birkenau by the Nazis, describing how she worked long hours and fought for survival before being set free at the end of the war and beginning a new life in America.

"As a powerful reminder of man's capacity for inhumanity, this memoir is essential reading." Booklist

Guthrie, Woody, 1912-1967

Burckhardt, Marc. **When** Bob met Woody; the story of the young Bob Dylan. illustrated by Marc Burckhardt. Little, Brown 2011 40p il $17.99

Grades: 3 4 5   **92**

1. Rock musicians 2. Biography, Individual

ISBN 978-0-316-11299-4; 0-316-11299-2

LC 2010-43030

This picture book biography follows Bob Zimmerman as he renames himself after his favorite poet, Dylan Thomas, and leaves his mining town to pursue his love of music in New York City. There, he meets his folk music hero and future mentor, Woody Guthrie.

"Golio excels at portraying Zimmerman's angst as he flounders for meaning and even invents for himself a more colorful backstory. Burckhardt's acrylics have the fractured look of damaged paintings, and . . . [convey] gravity and emotion. Back matter, including quotation sources, is superb. A stirring introduction to two musical legends." Booklist

Includes bibliographical references

Guyton, Tyree

Shapiro, J. H. **Magic** trash; a story of Tyree Guyton and his art. [by] J.H. Shapiro; illustrated by Vanessa Newton. Charlesbridge 2011 32p il

Grades: K 1 3 4   **92**

1. Artists

ISBN 1580893856 lib bdg; 9781580893855 1

LC 2010023524

"Multicolored, multilayered, multimedia illustrations trace the life of Tyree Guyton and his visionary artwork, which used reclaimed trash to turn a derelict Detroit street into community-activist art. . . . Readers whiz through Tyree's story, propelled by his energy and zinging, trippy triplets that cap each significant event in his life. . . . An inspiring, exciting introduction to avant-garde art and social commentary, this biography convinces young readers that art can exist, thrive and effect change outside in the real world." Kirkus

Gág, Wanda, 1893-1946

Ray, Deborah Kogan. **Wanda** Gag; the girl who lived to draw. [by] Deborah Kogan Ray. Viking Childrens Books 2008 un il $16.99

Grades: 2 3 4   **92**

1. Artists 2. Authors 3. Illustrators 4. Women authors 5. Authors, American 6. Children's authors

ISBN 978-0-670-06292-8; 0-670-06292-8

LC 2008-13132

"This charming biography of the creator of Millions of Cats . . . shows how Gág's family and childhood inspired her lifelong pursuit of art. . . . Each page of text is introduced with a quote from the subject's diaries and letters, and faces a white-framed illustration reflecting the Old World charm of her childhood, which comes to life with Ray's evocative paintings." SLJ

Hale, Bruce, 1957-

Parker-Rock, Michelle. **Bruce** Hale; an author kids love. Enslow Publishers 2008 48p bibl il por (Authors kids love) lib bdg $23.93

Grades: 3 4 5   **92**

1. Artists 2. Authors 3. Illustrators 4. Storytellers 5.

Authors, American 6. Children's authors
ISBN 978-0-7660-2758-9 lib bdg; 0-7660-2758-9
lib bdg

LC 2007029319

A biography of the author of the Chet Gecko mystery
series for children, based on an interview

"The frequent use of direct quotes makes the [text]
particularly enjoyable. . . . Kids will be fascinated with . .
. Hale's hat collection and love of surfing. . . . Well written,
interesting, and useful for reports." SLJ

Halvorsen, Gail

★ Tunnell, Michael. **Candy** bomber; the story of the
Berlin airlift's chocolate pilot. Charlesbridge 2010 110p il
$18.95; pa $9.95
Grades: 4 5 6 7   92
1. Air pilots 2. Air force officers 3. Biography,
Individual 4. Berlin (Germany) -- History -- Blockade,
1948-1949
ISBN 1-58089-336-8; 1-58089-337-6 pa; 978-1-
58089-336-7; 978-1-58089-337-4 pa

This book takes place "[i]n 1948, after World War II,
[in] Berlin, . . . [where Michael] Tunnell tells us that pilot
Gail Halvorsen spent a night in the city, noticing kids behind a fence watching the planes land. He offered sticks
of Doublemint gum to two of the kids, who passed them
around so their pals could get a whiff. . . . Soon people all
over began sending candy-and-handkerchief parachutes to
Halvorsen and other pilots to drop over Berlin." (School
Library Journal)

"Curious about the city into which he ferried goods during the Berlin Airlift in 1948, pilot Gail Halvorsen stayed
over to visit, met some children, and offered to drop candy
and gum when he next flew over. This simple idea grew into
a massive project with reverberations today. Tunnell tell this
appealing story . . . clearly and chronologically, weaving
just enough background for twenty-first century readers and
illustrating almost every page with black-and-white photographs, many from Halvorsen's own collection." Booklist

Includes bibliographical references

Hamilton, Alexander, 1757-1804

★ Fritz, Jean. **Alexander** Hamilton; the outsider. illustrations by Ian Schoenherr. G.P. Putnam's Sons 2011
144p il $16.99
Grades: 5 6 7 8   92
1. Statesmen 2. Statesmen -- United States 3.
Secretaries of the treasury 4. United States -- History --
1775-1783, Revolution 5. United States -- Politics and
government -- 1783-1809
ISBN 039925546X; 9780399255465

LC 2010006008

Fritz "provides a brisk, well-written account introducing Founding Father Alexander Hamilton as an outsider to
America. . . . Fast moving and engaging, this straightforward
biography acknowledges Hamilton's flaws while portraying
him as an intelligent, energetic man who rose to the challenge of his times. . . . In addition to the black-and-white
reproductions of period paintings and prints that illustrate
the text, Schoenherr's striking, engraving-like images of
Hamilton as scholar, soldier, aide-decamp, statesman, and
duelist introduce each section." Booklist

Includes bibliographical references

Hancock, John, 1737-1793

Adler, David A. A **picture** book of John Hancock; by
David A. Adler and Michael S. Adler; illustrated by Ronald
Himler. Holiday House 2007 un il $16.95
Grades: 1 2 3   92
1. Governors 2. Statesmen 3. Colonial leaders 4.
Members of Congress 5. United States -- History --
1775-1783, Revolution
ISBN 978-0-8234-2005-6; 0-8234-2005-1

LC 2005052649

"This biography begins with what is probably Hancock's
most famous act, the signing of the Declaration of Independence. It then takes readers back to the beginning of his life
to tell how he became such an important and influential part
of America's Revolutionary War. . . . Himler's watercolors in
muted tones offer visual guides to historical events. This title
. . . is a solid addition to biography collections." SLJ

Includes bibliographical references

★ Fritz, Jean. **Will** you sign here, John Hancock? pictures by Trina Schart Hyman. Putnam Pub. Group 1976
47p il hardcover o.p. pa $5.99
Grades: 2 3 4   92
1. Governors 2. Statesmen 3. Colonial leaders 4.
Members of Congress 5. United States -- History --
1775-1783, Revolution
ISBN 0-399-23306-7; 0-698-11440-X pa

"An affectionate look at a flamboyant, egocentric, but
kindly, patriot, the book is a most enjoyable view of history.
. . . The delightful illustrations exactly suit the times and the
extraordinary character of John Hancock." Horn Book

Harvey, William, 1578-1657

Yount, Lisa. **William** Harvey; discoverer of how blood
circulates. [by] Lisa Yount. rev ed.; Enslow Publishers
2008 128p il map (Great minds of science) lib bdg $31.93
Grades: 5 6 7 8   92
1. Biologists 2. Physicians 3. Physiologists 4.
Writers on science 5. Writers on medicine 6. Blood
-- Circulation
ISBN 978-0-7660-3010-7 lib bdg; 0-7660-3010-5
lib bdg

LC 2007020301

First published 1994

"A biography of the seventeenth-century English physician William Harvey and includes related activities for readers." Publisher's note

Includes glossary and bibliographical references

Hatshepsut, Queen of Egypt

★ Galford, Ellen. **Hatshepsut**; the princess who became king. National Geographic 2005 64p il map (World
history biographies) $17.95; lib bdg $27.90
Grades: 4 5 6 7   92
1. Queens 2. Kings and rulers 3. Egypt -- History 4.
Egypt -- Civilization
ISBN 0-7922-3645-9; 0-7922-3646-7 lib bdg

This "presents the life of Queen Hatshepsut, who ruled
Egypt as pharaoh during the New Kingdom, around 3500
years ago. Illustrated with clear, color photos of artifacts and
sites as well as colorful maps, the text discusses aspects of
Egyptian life such as education and religion in Hatshepsut's
life. . . . With a clearly written text and many handsome pho-

tos, this provides an accessible introduction to Hatshepsut and her times." Booklist

Hawking, Stephen W., 1942-

Venezia, Mike. **Stephen** Hawking; cosmologist who gets a big bang out of the universe. written and illustrated by Mike Venezia. Children's Press 2009 32p il (Getting to know the world's greatest inventors & scientists) $28

Grades: 2 3 4   92

1. Cosmology 2. Physicists 3. Black holes (Astronomy) 4. People with disabilities 5. College teachers 6. Writers on science

ISBN 978-0-531-23728-1; 0-531-23728-1

LC 2008-27650

"This exemplary . . . biography will inform and motivate young readers. It introduces Stephen Hawking as a physicist and cosmologist. . . . [The author] introduces a few of Hawking's cosmological ideas in clear, but simple, ways that communicate the nature of the ideas and how scientific understanding is developed by a community of scientists. There are colorful telescopic photographs, entertaining cartoons, and numerous photographs of Hawking's professional and personal life." Sci Books Films

Henry, John William, 1847?-ca. 1875

★ Nelson, Scott Reynolds. **Ain't** nothing but a man; my quest to find the real John Henry. [by] Scott Reynolds Nelson with Marc Aronson. National Geographic 2008 64p il $18.95; lib bdg $27.90

Grades: 4 5 6 7 8   92

1. John Henry (Legendary character) 2. Railroad workers 3. Railroads -- History 4. African Americans -- Biography

ISBN 978-1-4263-0000-4; 1-4263-0000-X; 978-1-4263-0001-1 lib bdg; 1-4263-0001-8 lib bdg

LC 2007-12446

This describes the author's research to find the real man who inspired the songs and legends about the African American steel-driving hero.

"The layout is attractive, with a sepia and beige background for the text and sepia-toned photographs. . . . This is an excellent example of how much detective work is needed for original research." SLJ

Includes bibliographical references

Henry, Patrick, 1736-1799

★ Fritz, Jean. **Where** was Patrick Henry on the 29th of May? illustrated by Margot Tomes. Putnam Pub. Group 1975 47p il $16.99; pa $6.99

Grades: 2 3 4   92

1. Statesmen 2. Colonial leaders 3. United States -- History -- 1600-1775, Colonial period

ISBN 0-399-23305-9; 0-698-11439-6 pa

"The color pictures are artful evocations of the [18th] century in America and the text presents Patrick Henry as a human being—not a sterilized historic 'figure.'" Publ Wkly

Henson, Jim

Krull, Kathleen. **Jim** Henson; the guy who played with puppets. paintings by Steve Johnson and Lou Fancher. Random House 2011 35p il $16.99; lib bdg $19.99

Grades: K 1 2 3   92

1. Television programs 2. Puppets and puppet plays 3.

Puppeteers 4. Muppet show (Television program)

ISBN 978-0-375-85721-8; 0-375-85721-4; 978-0-375-95721-5 lib bdg; 0-375-95721-9 lib bdg

LC 2010043837

"Krull, Johnson, and Fancher offer an inspiring and timely portrait of the late Henson. The book covers Henson's upbringing, experimentation with and study of puppetry, and the creation and success of his beloved Muppets on TV and on the big screen. . . . Johnson and Fancher's paintings exude a warm, nostalgic glow as they show the early roots of Henson's creativity and behind-the-scenes images of him at work." Publ Wkly

Includes bibliographical references

Henson, Matthew Alexander, 1866-1955

Hopkinson, Deborah. **Keep** on! the story of Matthew Henson, co-discoverer of the North Pole. written by Deborah Hopkinson; illustrated by Stephen Alcorn. Peachtree Publishers 2009 un il $17.95

Grades: 2 3 4   92

1. Explorers 2. North Pole 3. African Americans -- Biography

ISBN 978-1-56145-473-0; 1-56145-473-7

LC 2008031118

"Written in articulate and straightforward prose, and accompanied by quotes from Henson, Keep On! tells the story of an inspiring and courageous figure and is enhanced by Alcorn's dramatic, sweeping scenes." SLJ

★ Johnson, Dolores. **Onward**; a photobiography of African-American polar explorer Matthew Henson. National Geographic 2006 64p il $17.95

Grades: 5 6 7 8   92

1. Explorers 2. North Pole 3. African Americans -- Biography

ISBN 0-7922-7914-X

LC 2005-05837

"The quest to be the first to reach the North Pole is an exciting adventure story, and Henson got there first, as part of the ninth expedition led by Robert Peary in 1909. But Henson was African American, labeled as Peary's 'Negro manservant,' and he did not get full recognition until 2001. This . . . focuses on the physical details of the dangerous Arctic journeys . . . the repeated failures and the teamwork, as well as Henson's skills, stamina, and essential role in forging relationships with the Inuit. . . . The book design is beautiful: thick paper, spacious type, and stirring photos that capture the icy storms as well as the people involved in the history." Booklist

Hepburn, Audrey, 1929-1993

Cardillo, Margaret. **Just** being Audrey; illustrated By Julia Denos. Balzer + Bray 2011 un il

Grades: 1 2 3   92

1. Actors

ISBN 006185283X; 9780061852831

LC 2010003982

"Growing up in WW II-era Europe, Audrey wanted only to be a dancer, but the other girls made fun of her physical hurdles. . . . She was spotted by entertainment heavyweights . . . and quickly catapulted to fame. Denos' soft pastel illustrations cut just the right Audrey outline . . . and fans will especially enjoy picking out the movie roles depicted in a two-page spread of costumes. Her later humanitarian deeds are given their due, but it is Audrey's simple kindness that is emphasized throughout." Booklist

Includes bibliographical references

Herrera, Juan Felipe, 1948-

Herrera, Juan Felipe. The **upside** down boy; story by Juan Felipe Herrera; illustrations by Elizabeth Gómez. Children's Bk. Press 2000 31p il $15.95

Grades: K 1 2 3   92

1. Poets 2. Authors 3. Children's authors 4. Young adult authors 5. Mexican Americans -- Biography 6. Bilingual books -- English-Spanish

ISBN 0-89239-162-6

LC 99-49113

The author recalls the year when his farm worker parents settled down in the city so that he could go to school for the first time

"Herrera's poetic prose sings with a unique voice in both languages, and Gómez's illustrations are colorful and ethereal." Horn book guide

Heschel, Abraham Joshua, 1907-1972

★ Michelson, Richard. **As** good as anybody: Martin Luther King Jr. and Abraham Joshua Heschel's amazing march toward freedom; by Richard Michelson; illustrated by Raul Colón. Knopf 2008 un il $16.99; lib bdg $19.99

Grades: 2 3 4   92

1. Clergy 2. Rabbis 3. Theologians 4. Jews -- Biography 5. Nonfiction writers 6. Civil rights activists 7. Nobel laureates for peace 8. African Americans -- Biography 9. African Americans -- Civil rights

ISBN 978-0-375-83335-9; 0-375-83335-8; 978-0-375-93335-6 lib bdg; 0-375-93335-2 lib bdg

This is the story of how Abraham Joshua Heschel, a Polish rabbi who escaped the Holocaust, and Martin Luther King worked together for African American civil rights.

"Michelson writes in poetic language. . . . Also admirable is Michelson's ability to convey complex historical concepts . . . in clear, potent terms that will speak directly to readers. . . . In both palette and style, Colón's colored-pencil and watercolor art . . . suggests the past, but his themes carry into today's headlines." Booklist

Higgins, Nadia

Jennifer Lawrence; The hunger games' girl on fire. by Nadia Higgins. Lerner Publications Company 2013 32 p. col. ill. (Pop culture bios: action movie stars) (library) $26.60

Grades: 4 5 6   92

1. Hunger games (Motion picture) 2. Actors -- United States -- Biography

ISBN 1467707430; 9781467707435

LC 2012031010

This book is part of the Pop Culture Bios: Action Movie Stars series. It "features 22-year-old Jennifer Lawrence, best known to young people as the actress who played Katniss in 'The Hunger Games.' [Nadia] Higgins describes how Lawrence grew up in Kentucky and then, at age 14, left school and took up acting in New York. After a few television and movie roles, she received a Best Actress Oscar nomination for 'Winter's Bone.'" (Booklist)

Includes bibliographical references and index

Hillary, Edmund Sir

Coburn, Broughton. **Triumph** on Everest: a photobiography of Sir Edmund Hillary. National Geographic Soc. 2000 64p il map $17.95; pa $7.95

Grades: 4 5 6 7   92

1. Mountaineering 2. Mountaineers 3. Nonfiction writers 4. Mount Everest (China and Nepal)

ISBN 0-7922-7114-9; 0-7922-7932-8 pa

LC 00-27009

A biography of Edmund Hillary, whose love of snow, mountains, and the outdoor life culminated in his conquering the highest peak in the world

"Threaded with quotes from Hillary's own writings, and full of fine, blue-toned photographs, the engrossing text presents the life of a reticent but world-renowned mountaineer, adventurer, and philanthropist." SLJ

Includes bibliographical references

Hodgman, Ann

Hodgman, Ann. The **house** of a million pets; with illustrations by Eugene Yelchin. Henry Holt & Co. 2007 263p il $16.95

Grades: 3 4 5 6   92

1. Pets 2. Authors 3. Cookbook writers 4. Children's authors

ISBN 978-0-8050-7974-6; 0-8050-7974-2

LC 2006-36447

This is a "witty and personable narrative. . . . Yelchin's inky animal vignettes are inviting, with a cheerful impudence in their scrawled lines that perfectly matches the text." Bull Cent Child Books

Hodgman, Ann. **How** to die of embarrassment every day. Henry Holt and Co. 2011 208p il $16.99

Grades: 5 6 7 8   92

1. Authors 2. Women authors 3. Cookbook writers 4. Authors, American 5. Children's authors

ISBN 978-0-8050-8705-5; 0-8050-8705-2

LC 2010-49004

Hodgman offers a "chatty personal narrative . . . focusing on her childhood years and her tendency to land herself into humiliating situations. . . . The generous supply of spot art and relevant images from Hodgman's childhood adds to the browsibility. . . . There's . . . plenty of humor . . . but more importantly there's a tacit message about the survivability of embarrassment and the fact that we all, even seemingly perfect and polished adults, spend our lives goofing up." Bull Cent Child Books

Honda, Soichiro, 1906-1991

Weston, Mark. **Honda**; the boy who dreamed of cars. illustrated by Katie Yamasaki. Lee & Low Books 2008 un il $17.95

Grades: 3 4 5   92

1. Executives 2. Businesspeople 3. Automobile industry 4. Automobile executives

ISBN 978-1-60060-246-7; 1-60060-246-0

LC 2007049040

"Weston's writing is clear and accessible. . . . The book reads like a story, with fictionalization of Honda's thoughts and dialogue. . . . Yamasaki's acrylic illustrations dominate each page. At first glance they seem representational, but on closer inspection readers will find little men climbing on the engine parts, . . . [and] miniature cars going around a globe and down Honda's arm. . . . Yamasaki's creative composition makes the pictures interesting and dynamic." SLJ

Hopkins, Sarah Winnemucca, 1844?-1891

Ray, Deborah Kogan. **Paiute** princess; the story of Sarah Winnemucca. Deborah Kogan Ray. Frances Foster Books, Farrar Straus Giroux 2011 48 p. col. ill., col. map $17.99

Grades: 3 4 5   92

1. Paiute Indians 2. Native American women 3. Paiute Indians -- Biography 4. Women political activists -- West (U.S.) -- Biography 5. Indians of North America -- Civil rights -- History -- 19th century 6. American literature -- Indian authors -- Biography

ISBN 0374398976; 9780374398972

LC 2009046090

This book is a biography of Sarah Winnemucca, who was "[b]orn into the Northern Paiute tribe of Nevada in 1844" and who "straddled two cultures: the traditional life of her people, and the modern ways of her grandfather's white friends." Her skill with languages "made her a great leader." The book includes "illustrations and . . . backmatter, including hand-drawn maps, a chronology, archival photographs, an author's notes, and additional resource information." (Publisher's note)

Includes bibliographical references

Hopper, Edward, 1882-1967

Burleigh, Robert. **Edward** Hopper paints his world; Robert Burleigh; paintings by Wendell Minor. Henry Holt & Co. 2014 40 p. color illustrations (hardback) $17.99

Grades: K 1 2 3 4   92

1. Artists -- United States -- Biography 2. Painters

ISBN 0805087524; 9780805087529

LC 2013037068

This children's book by Robert Burleigh, illustrated by Wendell Minor, describes how "as a boy, Edward Hopper knew exactly what he wanted to be when he grew up. . . . And even though no one wanted to buy his paintings for a long time, he never stopped believing in his dream to be an artist. He was fascinated with painting light and shadow and his works explore this challenge." (Publisher's note)

Burleigh and Minor "help readers comprehend Hopper from the inside out: from the actual motifs, to the edited and combined studies, to the familiar, finished and admired paintings on the museum walls. Backmatter is particularly well-organized and inclusive." Kirkus

Includes bibliographical references

★ Rubin, Susan Goldman. **Edward** Hopper; painter of light and shadow. Abrams Books for Young Readers 2007 47p il $18.95

Grades: 5 6 7 8   92

1. Artists 2. Painters 3. Artists -- United States

ISBN 978-0-8109-9347-1; 0-8109-9347-3

LC 2006-31978

"On every page of this beautifully designed biography, readers will find a reproduction of Hopper's work, matched to clear, eloquent commentary. . . . Readers . . . will come back to read about the man and look at his art again and again." Booklist

Includes bibliographical references

Houdini, Harry, 1874-1926

Biskup, Agnieszka. **Houdini**; the life of the great escape artist. illustrated by Pat Kinsella. Capstone Press 2011 32p il (Graphic library: American graphic) lib bdg $29.32; pa $7.95

Grades: 4 5 6 7   92

1. Magicians 2. Biographical graphic novels 3. Nonfiction writers

ISBN 978-1-4296-5474-6 lib bdg; 1-4296-5474-0 lib bdg; 978-1-4296-6268-0 pa; 1-4296-6268-9 pa

LC 2010024848

In graphic novel format, explores the life of Harry Houdini and describes some of his most daring escapes.

"The illustrations are eye-catching and the narration is presented simply, yet compellingly. . . . Fact-filled, entertaining, and accessible." SLJ

Includes bibliographical references

Carlson, Laurie M. **Harry** Houdini for kids; his life and adventures with 21 magic tricks and illusions. Chicago Review Press 2009 136p il pa $16.95

Grades: 4 5 6 7   92

1. Magicians 2. Magic tricks 3. Nonfiction writers

ISBN 978-1-55652-782-1 pa; 1-55652-782-9 pa

LC 2008021404

"Reluctant readers (as well as budding troublemakers) will flock to this biography/handbook hybrid about one of the most famous magicians who ever lived. Even for those familiar with Houdini's fascinating story, Carlson's snappy writing gives it new life. . . . Nearly every page is enlivened with period photographs, boxed sections containing biographies and definitions, and, most important, 21 magic tricks that will have readers breaking out their deck of cards and practicing their sleight of hand." Booklist

★ Fleischman, Sid. **Escape!** the story of the great Houdini. Greenwillow Books 2006 210p il $18.99; lib bdg $19.89

Grades: 5 6 7 8   92

1. Magicians 2. Nonfiction writers

ISBN 978-0-06-085094-4; 0-06-085094-9; 978-0-06-085095-1 lib bdg; 0-06-0850957-1 lib bdg

LC 2005052631

"Fleischman looks at Houdini's life through his own eyes, as a fellow magician. . . . Fleischman's tone is lively and he develops a relationship with readers by revealing just enough truth behind Houdini's razzle-dazzle to keep the legend alive. . . . Engaging and fascinating." SLJ

Includes bibliographical references

Krull, Kathleen. **Houdini**; the world's greatest mystery man and escape king. in a production written by Kathleen Krull; and illustrated by Eric Velasquez. Walker & Co. 2005 un il hardcover o.p. pa $6.95

Grades: 2 3 4   92

1. Magicians 2. Nonfiction writers

ISBN 0-8027-8953-6; 0-8027-8954-4 lib bdg; 0-8027-9646-X pa

LC 2004-49493

"Framed descriptions of some of Houdini's most famous stunts are interspersed within the overview of his life. The author's crisp narrative style and careful choice of detail are evident here. . . . Velasquez's impressive framed, posed oil paintings portray the magician's intensity and sense of showmanship." SLJ

Includes bibliographical references

Houston, Samuel, 1793-1863

★ Fritz, Jean. **Make** way for Sam Houston; illustrations by Elise Primavera. Putnam 1986 109p il map hardcover o.p. pa $5.99

Grades: 4 5 6   92

1. Governors 2. Statesmen 3. Senators 4. Army officers

ISBN 0-399-21303-1; 0-698-11646-1 pa

LC 85-25601

"Artfully weaving the threads of fact, Fritz creates a biography that is both interesting and informative. Developing Houston as a human character that readers can identify with as well as admire, and drawing him against the scene of America's own political turmoil, Fritz gives us a book to be read and to be felt." Voice Youth Advocates

Includes bibliographical references

Howe, Samuel Gridley, 1801-1876

Alexander, Sally Hobart. **She** touched the world: Laura Bridgman, deaf-blind pioneer; by Sally Hobart Alexander and Robert Alexander. Clarion Books 2008 100p il $18

Grades: 5 6 7 8   92

1. Deaf 2. Blind 3. Students 4. Physicians 5. Philanthropists 6. Humanitarians 7. Teachers of the blind

ISBN 978-0-618-85299-4; 0-618-85299-9

"At the age of three, in 1832, Laura Bridgman contracted scarlet fever and lost her sight, her hearing, her sense of smell, and much of her sense of taste. Her family sent her to Dr. Samuel [Gridley] Howe at the New England Institute for the Education of the Blind, and by the age of 10, Laura was world-famous for her accomplishments. . . . Alexander . . . presents a well-written and thoroughly researched biography of this remarkable woman, with numerous black-and-white photos." Booklist

Includes bibliographical references

Hudson, Henry, d. 1611

★ Weaver, Janice. **Hudson**; written by Janice Weaver; illustrated by David Craig. Tundra Books 2010 47p il map $22.95

Grades: 3 4 5 6   92

1. Explorers 2. Biography, Individual 3. America -- Exploration 4. Canada -- Discovery and exploration -- British

ISBN 978-0-88776-814-9; 0-88776-814-8

This is a biography of the explorer. "The grandson of a trader, Hudson sailed under both British and Dutch flags, looking for a northern route to China. Although none of his voyages led to the discovery of a northwest passage, he did explore what is now Hudson's Bay and what is now New York City." (Publisher's note) Index. "Ages eight to twelve." (Quill Quire)

"This dramatic picture-book biography about Henry Hudson, who discovered neither the new land nor the passage to Asia he sought, makes the explorer's lack of success a gripping read. . . . Weaver is clear about what is fact and what is supposition, and the tumultuous early-seventeenth-century history is meticulously documented. . . . Craig's glowing period portraits, landscapes, and watercolors of

the ship in dangerous seas intensify the drama, and archival prints and maps add interest." Booklist

Includes bibliographical references

Hunter, Clementine, 1886?-1988

★ Whitehead, Kathy. **Art** from her heart: folk artist Clementine Hunter; [illustrated by] Shane Evans. G.P. Putnam's Sons 2008 un il $16.99

Grades: 4 5 6 7   92

1. Artists 2. Folk art 3. Painters 4. Women artists 5. African American artists 6. Centenarians 7. Biography, Individual

ISBN 0-399-24219-8; 978-0-399-24219-9

LC 2006-34458

This is a biography of Louisiana artist Clementine Hunter, who depicted life on a plantation. Bibliography. "Ages five to eight." (Bull Cent Child Books) "In the 1950s, segregation laws

denied artist Clementine Hunter admission to the gallery that exhibited her work. . . . Hunter was not stopped by self-pity, and she did not wait for 'the perfect time to paint.' She had no canvas, so she made art with whatever she could find--window shades, glass bottles, old boards." (Booklist)

"Whitehead's lyrical text speaks of Hunter's perseverance and talent as well as of the simplicity, love of nature, and caring of friends and family that informed her work. Evans bolsters Whitehead's words with bold mixed-media illustrations that portray Hunter in hard times and in good." SLJ

Hutchinson, Anne Marbury, 1591-1643

Atkins, Jeannine. **Anne** Hutchinson's way; [by] Jeannine Atkins; pictures by Michael Dooling. Farrar, Straus and Giroux 2007 un il $17

Grades: 2 3 4   92

1. Colonists 2. Dissenters 3. Religious leaders 4. Massachusetts -- History -- 1600-1775, Colonial period

ISBN 0-374-30365-7

"Anne Hutchinson arrives with her family in Massachusetts colony in 1634 and begins preaching scripture from her home after finding herself in disagreement with the minister's beliefs. . . . Atkins is able to take the issue of religious freedom and make it personal by telling the story through the eyes of Hutchinson's young daughter, Susanna. . . . A sense of sturdiness is everywhere here: in the story . . . and in Dooling's impressive artwork, plain in color but rugged in its portrayal of the demands of colony life. Illustrated in a photo-realistic style that makes the long-ago events seem close." Booklist

Hypatia, ca. 370-415

★ Love, D. Anne. **Of** numbers and stars; the story of Hypatia. by D. Anne Love; illustrated by Pam Paparone. Holiday House 2006 un il $16.95

Grades: 2 3 4   92

1. Philosophers 2. Mathematicians 3. Women mathematicians

ISBN 0-8234-1621-6

LC 2003064725

"In fourth-century C.E. Egypt, women had few opportunities. How Hypatia, daughter of mathematician Theon, became one of the greatest philosophers of her day makes fascinating reading. . . . Attractive paintings add life to a clear and captivating text that offers a unique contribution to units about Egypt, philosophers, or women in history." SLJ

Includes bibliographical references

Irving, Washington, 1783-1859

★ Harness, Cheryl. The **literary** adventures of Washington Irving; American storyteller. by Cheryl Harness. National Geographic Society 2008 43p il $17.95; lib bdg $27.90

Grades: 2 3 4 5   **92**

1. Authors 2. Historians 3. Essayists 4. Biographers 5. Authors, American 6. Children's authors

ISBN 978-1-4263-0438-5; 1-4263-0438-2; 978-1-4263-0439-2 lib bdg; 1-4263-0439-0 lib bdg

LC 2008024975

A biography of the American author of The adventures of Rip Van Winkle and The Legend of Sleepy Hollow.

"Pairing insightful text with paintings organized into comic-book-style frames, Harness captures with exuberance everything that made Irving's life so exciting." Booklist

Includes bibliographical references

Jalāl al-Dīn Rūmī, Maulana, 1207-1273

★ Demi. **Rumi**; whirling dervish. written and illustrated by Demi. Marshall Cavendish Children 2009 31p il $19.99

Grades: 4 5 6 7   **92**

1. Poets 2. Persian poetry

ISBN 978-0-7614-5527-1; 0-7614-5527-2

LC 2008012920

"Demi presents this picture-book introduction to the thirteenth-century mystical poet. . . . Demi condenses her famous subject's life into a brief but substantive text. . . . She adds frequent excerpts from Rumi's poems and writings. . . . In an introductory note, Demi cites Turkish miniatures as her inspiration for the small-scale, elaborately patterned pictures, rendered in Turkish and Chinese inks with gold overlay. . . . The gilded, celebratory pictures create shimmering beauty from the smallest details." Booklist

James, LeBron

Gatto, Kimberly. **Lebron** James; a basketball star who cares. [by] Kimberly A. Gatto. Enslow Publishers, Inc. 2011 48p il (Sport stars who care) lib bdg $23.93; pa $7.95

Grades: 3 4 5   **92**

1. Basketball players 2. Basketball -- Biography

ISBN 978-0-7660-3776-2 lib bdg; 0-7660-3776-2 lib bdg; 978-1-59845-231-0 pa; 1-59845-231-2 pa

LC 2010014921

A biography of basketball star Lebron James, who helps those in need through several charities, from the Boys and Girls Clubs of America to his own LeBron James Family Foundation.

This is "especially good for book reports." Booklist

Includes glossary and bibliographical references

Yasuda, Anita. **Lebron** James. 2011 24p il (Remarkable people) $27.13; pa $12.95

Grades: 4 5 6 7   **92**

1. Basketball players 2. Basketball -- Biography

ISBN 978-1-6169-0669-6; 1-6169-0669-3; 978-1-6169-0674-0 pa; 1-6169-0674-X pa

LC 2010051003

This looks at Lebron James' "life, accomplishments, and challenges while including a page of quotes, an annotated list of contemporaries and influences, starter suggestions for writing a paper, and a time line and glossary. . . . [This book] follows basketball's 'King James' from his early life with a single teen mother to his splashy entry into the NBA at age 19." Booklist

Jay-Z, 1969-

Spilsbury, Richard. **Jay-Z**; Richard Spilsbury. Heinemann Library 2013 48 p. (Titans of business) (pbk.) $8.99

Grades: 4 5 6 7   **92**

1. Businessmen 2. Rap musicians 3. Success in business

ISBN 1432964305; 1432964372; 9781432964306; 9781432964375

LC 2011050758

This book, part of the Titans of Business series, looks at rapper and entrepreneur Jay-Z. "Starting with Jay-Z's early life as Shawn Corey Carter in a poor Brooklyn neighborhood, the biography recounts how he overcame his difficult adolescence as a drug dealer with his desire to be a musician." (Booklist)

Includes bibliographical references and index

Jefferson, Thomas, 1743-1826

Kalman, Maira. **Thomas** Jefferson; life, liberty and the pursuit of everything. Maira Kalman. 1st ed. Nancy Paulsen Books 2014 40 p. (hardback) $17.99

Grades: 3 4 5   **92**

1. Presidents -- United States -- Biography

ISBN 0399240403; 9780399240409

LC 2013034625

In this biography of Thomas Jefferson, author "Maira Kalman sheds light on the fascinating life and interests of the Renaissance man who was [the United States'] third president. He played violin, spoke seven languages and was a scientist, naturalist, botanist, mathematician and architect. He doubled the size of the United States and sent Lewis and Clark to explore it." (Publisher's note)

Miller, Brandon Marie. **Thomas** Jefferson for kids; his life and times, with 21 activities. Chicago Review Press 2011 ix, 132p il $16.95

Grades: 4 5 6 7   **92**

1. Vice-presidents 2. Essayists 3. Presidents -- United States

ISBN 978-1-56976-348-3; 1-56976-348-8

LC 2011019318

"Miller offers a thorough and methodical overview of Jefferson's life and political career. . . . The presentation is especially forthright about Jefferson's ownership of slaves and his fathering of children with Sally Hemmings. . . . The volume offers the chance to delve into Jefferson's life and be inspired by the range of his interests." Kirkus

Includes bibliographical references

Jemison, Mae C.

Jemison, Mae C. **Find** where the wind goes; moments from my life. [by] Mae Jemison. Scholastic Press 2001 196p il hardcover o.p. $16.95

Grades: 5 6 7 8   **92**

1. Astronauts 2. Physicians 3. African American

women -- Biography

ISBN 0-439-13195-2; 0-439-13196-0 pa

LC 00-41008

"Mae Jemson, doctor, scientist, astronaut, and professor, here tells of the formative incidents of her life. . . . The author discusses her youth—her days in the South, her family's move to Chicago's South Side, school experiences, and growing up—as well as her later life and her place in the space program. . . . Grades five to eight." (Bull Cent Child Books)

"Dr. Jemison, the first woman of color to travel in space, shares her life story in this autobiographical selection." Book Rep

Joan, of Arc, Saint, 1412-1431

Demi, 1942- **Joan** of Arc. Marshall Cavendish Children 2011 un il $19.99

Grades: 3 4 5   92

1. Saints 2. Christian saints 3. France -- History -- 1328-1589, House of Valois

ISBN 978-0-7614-5953-8; 0-7614-5953-7

LC 2011001123

"Joan of Arc's story told in the ravishing line and color of Demi's art. . . . The text unequivocally treats the 15th-century Joan as a saint, casting the craven King Charles VII as the villain he was. Joan's life is recounted with a strong emphasis on prayer and the will of God, from her beginnings as a devout peasant girl who heeded angelic and saintly voices through her victories and defeats to her imprisonment, trial and martyrdom at the stake. . . . A young female hero par excellence." Kirkus

Jobs, Steven, 1955-2011

Goldsworthy, Steve. **Steve** Jobs. Weigl 2011 24p il (Remarkable people) $27.13; pa $12.95 92

1. Entrepreneurs 2. Businesspeople 3. Computer industry 4. Computer scientists 5. Apple Computer Inc. 6. Computer industry executives 7. Electronics industry executives

ISBN 978-1-6169-0670-2; 1-6169-0670-7; 978-1-6169-0675-7 pa; 1-6169-0675-8 pa

LC 2010050999

This looks at Steve Jobs' "life, accomplishments, and challenges while including a page of quotes, an annotated list of contemporaries and influences, starter suggestions for writing a paper, and a time line and glossary. . . . [This book] kicks off as current as possible with a picture of the bearded Apple CEO displaying an iPad, before getting into the ups (he became a multimillionaire in just two years) and downs (his struggle with cancer)." Booklist

Venezia, Mike. **Steve** Jobs & Steve Wozniak; geek heroes who put the personal in computers. written and illustrated by Mike Venezia. Children's Press 2010 32p il (Getting to know the world's greatest inventors & scientists) lib bdg $28

Grades: 2 3 4   92

1. Entrepreneurs 2. Businesspeople 3. Computer industry 4. Computer scientists 5. Electronics engineers 6. Computer industry executives 7. Electronics industry executives

ISBN 978-0-531-23730-4 lib bdg; 0-531-23730-3 lib bdg

Venezia "describes the extraordinary childhoods of Jobs and Wozniak. . . . Imperceptibly, Venezia brings a broad history of computers into the picture by demonstrating simultaneously how Jobs and Wozniak were influenced by early computer pioneers and how they then made their mark on the world. . . . Venezia's thoughtful writing style and carefully chosen photos and graphics allows children to use their imagination and see part of themselves in the two 'heroes' of the title." Sci Books Films

Johnson, Jack, 1878-1946

★ Smith, Charles R., 1969- **Black** Jack: the ballad of Jack Johnson; [by] Charles R. Smith Jr.; illustrated by Shane W. Evans. Roaring Brook Press 2010 un il $16.99

Grades: K 1 2 3   92

1. African American athletes 2. Boxers (Persons) 3. Boxing -- Biography

ISBN 978-1-59643-473-8; 1-59643-473-2

A picture book biography in verse of boxer Jack Jackson, the first African American heavyweight champion of the world

"The elegant simplicity and rat-a-tat rhythms land some stunners. . . . [The book is] enhanced by Evans' lithe and swaggering artwork, which lends a tremendous visual charisma, grace, and grandeur to the man." Booklist

Includes bibliographical references

Johnson, Lyndon B. (Lyndon Baines), 1908-1973

Gold, Susan Dudley. **Lyndon** B. Johnson. Marshall Cavendish Benchmark 2009 112p il (Presidents and their times) lib bdg $34.21

Grades: 5 6 7 8   92

1. Presidents 2. Vice-presidents 3. Senators 4. Members of Congress 5. Presidents -- United States

ISBN 978-0-7614-2837-4 lib bdg; 0-7614-2837-2 lib bdg

LC 2007038518

A biography of the thirty-sixth president of the United States discusses his personal life, education, and political career and covers the formative events of his time

Includes glossary and bibliographical references

Johnson, Mamie, 1935-

★ Green, Michelle Y. A **strong** right arm: the story of Mamie Peanut Johnson; introduction by Mamie Johnson. Dial Bks. for Young Readers 2002 111p il $15.99; pa $5.99

Grades: 4 5 6 7   92

1. Women athletes 2. Baseball players 3. African American athletes 4. Collectibles dealers 5. Baseball -- Biography

ISBN 0-8037-2661-9; 0-14-240072-6 pa

LC 2001-28616

"Johnson was a pitcher with the Negro Leagues' Indianapolis Clowns from 1953 to 1955. In the introduction, Johnson speaks directly and movingly to the reader about her meeting with author Green, who then lets the famous ballplayer tell her own story in a lively first-person narrative. Johnson's ebullient personality and determination fairly leap off the page." Booklist

Includes bibliographical references

Jones, John Paul, 1747-1792

Cooper, Michael L. **Hero** of the high seas; John Paul Jones and the American Revolution. National Geographic 2006 128p il map $21.95; lib bdg $32.90

Grades: 5 6 7 8   **92**

1. Admirals 2. Naval officers 3. United States -- History -- 1775-1783, Revolution

ISBN 0-7922-5547-X; 0-7922-5548-8 lib bdg

LC 2005-36256

"Cooper charts his subject's life from a scandal-ridden Scottish captain on a trading ship to a man of self-invention who came to the American colonies to start a new life and became a naval hero. Jones is presented as a loyal captain, an arrogant leader, a determined sailor, and a flagrant social climber. The narrative style will appeal to reluctant readers, for it reads like a chronicle of thrilling naval adventures. . . . The text is clear and understandable." SLJ

Includes bibliographical references

Jordan, Michael, 1963-

Cooper, Floyd. **Jump!** from the life of Michael Jordan. Philomel Books 2004 un il $15.99

Grades: K 1 2 3   **92**

1. Basketball 2. Baseball players 3. African American athletes 4. Olympic athletes 5. Basketball players

ISBN 0-399-24230-9

LC 2003-25071

This is a "childhood profile of basketball legend Michael Jordan. Each double-page spread features powerful portraits of Jordan. . . . Children who view Jordan as a deity on the court will take comfort in Cooper's stories, written in casual, colloquial language." Booklist

Includes bibliographical references

Joseph, Nez Percé Chief, 1840-1904

Biskup, Agnieszka. **Thunder** rolling down the mountain; the story of Chief Joseph and the Nez Perce. illustrated by Rusty Zimmerman. Capstone Press 2011 32p il (Graphic library: American graphic) lib bdg $29.32; pa $7.95

Grades: 4 5 6 7   **92**

1. Biographical graphic novels 2. Indian chiefs 3. Nez Percé Indians

ISBN 978-1-4296-5472-2 lib bdg; 1-4296-5472-4 lib bdg; 978-1-4296-6270-3 pa; 1-4296-6270-0 pa

LC 2010027914

In graphic novel format, explores the battles and hardships faced by Chief Joseph and the Nez Perce when they were forced to leave their homelands.

"The illustrations are eye-catching and the narration is presented simply, yet compellingly. . . . Fact-filled, entertaining, and accessible." SLJ

Includes bibliographical references

Englar, Mary. **Chief** Joseph, 1840-1904. Blue Earth Books 2004 32p (American Indian biographies) lib bdg $23.93

Grades: 3 4 5   **92**

1. Indian chiefs 2. Nez Percé Indians 3. Native Americans -- Biography

ISBN 0-7368-2444-8

LC 2003-11071

A biography of the peace chief who ended the Nez Percé War by surrendering to United States soldiers in 1877, believing that he would be permitted lead his people back to their ancestral lands in Idaho. Includes a recipe for berry fritters and directions for "the stick game."

This "very accessible [title is] well illustrated with maps, photographs, and paintings, and [it offers] an introduction to American Indian history as well as specific information for reports." Booklist

Jumper, Betty Mae, 1923-

★ Annino, Jan Godown. **She** sang promise: the story of Betty Mae Jumper, Seminole tribal leader; illustrated by Lisa Desimini; afterword by Moses Jumper, Jr. National Geographic 2010 33p il map lib bdg $26.90

Grades: 1 2 3   **92**

1. Nurses 2. Seminole Indians 3. Storytellers 4. Indian leaders

ISBN 978-1-4263-0592-4 lib bdg; 1-4263-0592-3 lib bdg

LC 2009-16066

"Elected in 1967 as one of the first women tribal leaders in modern times, Seminole Betty Mae Tiger Jumper overcame oppression and prejudice, starting in her childhood. This picture-book biography tells her story in a dramatic present-tense narrative that blends details of her life with the historical struggle of her people. . . . The large collage paintings in bright colors blend old and new traditions, the natural world, and Seminole artwork." Booklist

Includes glossary and bibliographical references

Kahanamoku, Duke, 1890-1968

Crowe, Ellie. **Surfer** of the century; the life of Duke Kahanamoku. illustrations by Richard Waldrep. Lee & Low Books 2007 un il map $18.95

Grades: 3 4 5 6   **92**

1. Actors 2. Surfing 3. Swimming 4. Surfers 5. Swimmers 6. Olympic athletes

ISBN 978-1-58430-276-6

LC 2006036562

"The text is concise and readable, ably supported by Waldrep's full-page color art on every spread. These vibrant, action-filled illustrations . . . add much to the book's overall appeal. Well researched and fact-filled." SLJ

"A biography of Hawaiian Duke Kahanamoku, five-time Olympic swimming champion from the early 1900s who is also considered worldwide as the 'father of modern surfing.'" Publisher's note

Kahlo, Frida, 1907-1954

★ Frith, Margaret. **Frida** Kahlo; the artist who painted herself. written by Margaret Frith; illustrated by Tomie DePaola. Grosset & Dunlap 2003 un il (Smart about art) hardcover o.p. pa $5.99

Grades: 2 3 4   **92**

1. Artists 2. Painters 3. Women artists 4. Artists, Mexican

ISBN 0-448-43239-0; 0-448-42677-3 pa

LC 2003-5221

Biography of Mexican artist Frida Kahlo, written as a child's school report

"Kahlo's story is clear, concise, and accessible. All of the basic facts are here, along with many personal details that enliven the narrative. . . . The well-written prose is beautifully complemented both by photos of Kahlo and of some of her best-known paintings and by dePaola's splendid trademark illustrations, all set against vividly colored backgrounds." SLJ

Kamkwamba, William, 1987-

★ Kamkwamba, William. The **boy** who harnessed the wind; Creating Currents of Electricity and Hope. William Kamkwamba and Bryan Mealer; pictures by Elizabeth Zunon. Dial Press 2012 32 p. illustrations (chiefly color) $17.99; $16.99

Grades: 4 5 6 7 8 9 10   **92**

1. Malawi 2. Windmills 3. Irrigation 4. Electric power 5. Mechanical engineering 6. Irrigation -- Malawi 7. Windmills -- Malawi 8. Electric power production -- Malawi 9. Mechanical engineers -- Malawi -- Biography

ISBN 0803735111; 0803740808; 9780803735118; 9780803740808

LC 2011021536

In this memoir, "when fourteen-year-old William Kamkwamba's Malawi village was hit by a drought, everyone's crops began to fail. Without enough money for food, let alone school, William spent his days in the library . . . and figured out how to bring electricity to his village. Persevering against the odds, William built a functioning windmill out of junkyard scraps, and thus became the local hero who harnessed the wind." (Publisher's note)

"This youth edition of the original adult book of the same title has been skillfully adapted for middle grade readers. Kamkwamba recounts a period from his childhood living in a small Malawi village. His family was poor, but they got by working as farmers. Kamkwamba was in elementary school, about to graduate to secondary school, when the drought and famine of the mid-2000s upset the patterns of local life...This is a fascinating, well-told account that will intrigue curious minds, even the somewhat anticlimactic closing chapters describing Kamkwamba's education. There is also a picture book version of this tale (Dial, 2012), making it of interest to all-school reading programs. An inspiring, incredible story." SLJ

Kandinsky, Wassily, 1866-1944

★ Rosenstock, Barb. The **noisy** paint box; the colors and sounds of Kandinsky's abstract art. by Barb Rosenstock; illustrated by Mary GrandPre. 1st ed. Alfred A. Knopf 2014 40 p. (hard cover) $17.99

Grades: K 1 2 3 4   **92**

1. Artists, Russian 2. Artists -- Russia (Federation) -- Biography

ISBN 0307978486; 9780307978486; 9780307978493

LC 2012032800

Caldecott Honor Book (2015)

In this book, author Barb Rosenstock and illustrator Mary GrandPré "tell the fascinating story of Vasily Kandinsky, one of the very first painters of abstract art. Throughout his life, Kandinsky experienced colors as sounds, and sounds as colors. Backmatter includes four paintings by Kandinsky, an author's note, sources, links to websites on synesthesia and abstract art." (Publisher's note)

Kearton, Cherry

Bond, Rebecca. In the belly of an ox: the unexpected photographic adventures of Richard and Cherry Kearton; written and illustrated by Rebecca Bond. Houghton Mifflin Books for Children 2009 un il $16

Grades: K 1 2 3   **92**

1. Naturalists 2. Photographers 3. Photography of birds 4. Birds -- Nests

ISBN 978-0-547-07675-1; 0-547-07675-4

"In the late 19th century, these nature-loving brothers spent their youth navigating the British countryside. . . . When they were older, the boys devised a method to photograph wild birds in their nests. . . . Bond's graceful watercolors depict the brothers as they piece together their disguises and gain recognition for their innovative approach to photography. The brothers' dedication and ingenuity are especially resonant, and their elaborate costumes will amuse but also inspire." Publ Wkly

Kearton, Richard, 1862-1928

Bond, Rebecca. In the belly of an ox: the unexpected photographic adventures of Richard and Cherry Kearton; written and illustrated by Rebecca Bond. Houghton Mifflin Books for Children 2009 un il $16

Grades: K 1 2 3   **92**

1. Naturalists 2. Photographers 3. Photography of birds 4. Birds -- Nests

ISBN 978-0-547-07675-1; 0-547-07675-4

"In the late 19th century, these nature-loving brothers spent their youth navigating the British countryside. . . . When they were older, the boys devised a method to photograph wild birds in their nests. . . . Bond's graceful watercolors depict the brothers as they piece together their disguises and gain recognition for their innovative approach to photography. The brothers' dedication and ingenuity are especially resonant, and their elaborate costumes will amuse but also inspire." Publ Wkly

Keaton, Buster, 1895-1966

★ Brighton, Catherine. **Keep** your eye on the kid; the early years of Buster Keaton. Roaring Brook Press 2008 un il $16.95

Grades: 3 4 5   **92**

1. Actors 2. Motion picture producers and directors 3. Motion picture directors

ISBN 978-1-59643-158-4; 1-59643-158-X

LC 2007-16534

This is a first-person account of the early years of Buster Keaton, who started performing as a child with his parents in vaudeville and "grew up to become a famous movie producer and performer. . . . Brighton's cartoon drawings shaded in umber and gray tones have a graphic look quite appropriate to the comic subject. The account ends with a brief look at the elaborate stage falls typical of Keaton's movie humor, and a full-page author's note gives added information on his career." SLJ

Includes bibliographical references.

Keckley, Elizabeth, ca. 1818-1907

★ Jones, Lynda. **Mrs.** Lincoln's dressmaker: the unlikely friendship of Elizabeth Keckley and Mary Todd Lincoln; by Lynda D. Jones. National Geographic 2009 80p il $18.95; lib bdg $27.90

Grades: 5 6 7 8   **92**

1. Memoirists 2. Dressmakers 3. Spouses of presidents 4. Slavery -- United States 5. United States -- Race relations 6. African American women -- Biography 7. Presidents' spouses -- United States 8. Washington

(D.C.) -- Social life and customs
ISBN 978-1-4263-0377-7; 1-4263-0377-7; 978-1-4263-0378-4 lib bdg; 1-4263-0378-5 lib bdg

LC 2008-29314

"Readers may be familiar with the ups and downs of Lincoln's life, but details of Keckley's story . . . will give them new insights into the life of a slave, in this case, one who was educated and had a profession." Booklist

Includes bibliographical references

Kehret, Peg, 1936-
Kehret, Peg. **Small** steps; the year I got polio. Anniversary ed; Albert Whitman 2006 205p il $15.95; pa $6.99
Grades: 4 5 6 **92**
1. Authors 2. Poliomyelitis 3. Women authors 4. Authors, American 5. Children's authors
ISBN 978-0-8075-7459-1; 0-8075-7459-7; 978-0-8075-7458-4 pa; 0-8075-7458-9 pa

LC 2006005136

First published 1996

Kehret "writes in an approachable, familiar way, and readers will be hooked from the first page on." SLJ

This "memoir takes readers back to 1949 when the author, at age 12, contracted polio. . . . She describes her seven-month ordeal—her diagnosis and quarantine, her terrifying paralysis, her slow and difficult recuperation—and the people she encountered along the way." Booklist

Includes bibliographical references

Keller, Helen, 1880-1968
Amoroso, Cynthia. **Helen** Keller; by Cynthia Amoroso and Robert B. Noyed. Child's World 2010 24p il (Basic biographies) lib bdg $22.79
Grades: PreK K 1 **92**
1. Deaf 2. Blind 3. Authors 4. Memoirists 5. Humanitarians 6. Inspirational writers 7. Social welfare leaders
ISBN 978-1-60253-341-7; 1-60253-341-5

LC 2009029369

This biography of Helen Keller "pairs intelligent, brief text with abundant photos. Simple but never basic." Booklist

Includes bibliographical references

Delano, Marfe Ferguson. **Helen's** eyes; a photobiography of Annie Sullivan, Helen Keller's teacher. [foreword by Keller Johnson Thompson] National Geographic 2008 63p il map $17.95; lib bdg $27.90
Grades: 4 5 6 7 **92**
1. Deaf 2. Blind 3. Authors 4. Teachers 5. Memoirists 6. Humanitarians 7. Teachers of the deaf 8. Inspirational writers 9. Teachers of the blind 10. Social welfare leaders
ISBN 978-1-4263-02-9-1; 1-4263-0209-6; 978-1-4263-0210-7 lib bdg; 1-4263-0210-X lib bdg

"There are many biographies of Helen Keller and Annie Sullivan, but this one is very nicely done. . . . The book is honest in its portrayals, especially of Sullivan. . . . What makes this oversize book so appealing is the clean design, with large typeface. The many fascinating photographs are sometimes placed over historical documents." Booklist

Includes bibliographical references

Lawlor, Laurie. **Helen** Keller: rebellious spirit. Holiday House 2001 168p il $22.95

Grades: 5 6 7 8 **92**
1. Deaf 2. Blind 3. Authors 4. Memoirists 5. Humanitarians 6. Inspirational writers 7. Social welfare leaders
ISBN 0-8234-1588-0

LC 00-36950

A "biography of the most famous deaf and blind person in history. Drawing on social and scientific studies of deafness and blindness as well as on American history texts, Lawlor puts Keller's experiences in context. . . . At the same time, readers get a strong feel for Keller's personality and for the personalities of Annie Sullivan, Alexander Graham Bell, and other major figures in her life. Aided by numerous well-chosen photographs and excerpts from Keller's writings." Horn Book

Includes bibliographical references

Sullivan, George. **Helen** Keller; her life in pictures. foreword by Keller Johnson Thompson. Scholastic Nonfiction 2007 80p il $17.99
Grades: 4 5 6 7 **92**
1. Deaf 2. Blind 3. Authors 4. Memoirists 5. Humanitarians 6. Inspirational writers 7. Social welfare leaders
ISBN 0-439-91815-4; 978-0-439-91815-2

LC 2006-51401

"Accompanied by brief, simply phrased commentary from Sullivan, this suite of photos portrays Keller from early childhood into her 80s. . . . This profile will serve equally well as an introduction, or as supplementary reading for confirmed admirers." Booklist

Includes bibliographical references

Kellerman, Annette, 1888-1975
Corey, Shana. **Mermaid** Queen; the spectacular true story of Annette Kellerman, who swam her way to fame, fortune, & swimsuit history! illustrated by Edwin Fotheringham. Scholastic Press 2008 un il $17.99
Grades: K 1 2 3 **92**
1. Actors 2. Swimming 3. Women athletes 4. Swimmers
ISBN 978-0-439-69835-1; 0-439-69835-9

LC 2007-52664

"Fotheringham's glorious artwork is filled with period details and dress, high-dives and stunts, and priceless expressions on the faces of amazed audiences. . . . This well-written and brightly illustrated account is a perfect pearl." SLJ

Kennally, James
Sheinkin, Steve. **Lincoln's** Grave Robbers. Scholastic 2013 224 p. $16.99
Grades: 5 6 7 8 **92**
1. Grave robbing 2. Counterfeits and counterfeiting
ISBN 0545405726; 9780545405720

This book is an "account of the attempted heist of Abraham Lincoln's body in 1876." Steve Sheinkin first "delv[es] into the history of counterfeiting. . . . James Kennally, leader of one of the largest counterfeiting rings in the Midwest, masterminded the plot to steal the late president's body from the Lincoln Monument," intending "to ransom the purloined corpse" and extort "the government for a tidy sum of money and the freedom of his jailed, top-notch engraver." (Publishers Weekly)

Kennedy, John F. (John Fitzgerald), 1917-1963

★ Heiligman, Deborah. **High** hopes; a photobiography of John F. Kennedy. National Geographic 2003 63p il map $17.95

Grades: 4 5 6 7   **92**

1. Presidents 2. Senators 3. Members of Congress 4. Presidents -- United States

ISBN 0-7922-6141-0

LC 2003-7819

Photographs and text trace the life of President John F. Kennedy.

The text "successfully captures the spirit that makes Kennedy an enduring figure in our history. . . . This well-designed book features large, well-chosen, black-and-white photographs." SLJ

Includes bibliographical references

Rappaport, Doreen. **Jack's** path of courage; the life of John F. Kennedy. written by Doreen Rappaport; illustrated by Matt Tavares. Hyperion Books for Children 2010 un il $17.99

Grades: 2 3 4 5   **92**

1. Presidents 2. Senators 3. Members of Congress 4. Presidents -- United States

ISBN 978-1-4231-2272-2; 1-4231-2272-0

"In her signature succinct style, Rappaport fuses facts about Kennedy's personal and public lives with quotations from his writings and speeches. . . . Tavares's light and shadow-infused paintings balance lifelike portrayals of Kennedy with renderings of dramatic events. . . . An evenhanded, graphically stirring biography." Publ Wkly

Includes bibliographical references

King, Coretta Scott, 1927-2006

★ Shange, Ntozake, 1948- **Coretta** Scott; poetry by Ntozake Shange; paintings by Kadir Nelson. Amistad/Katherine Tegen Books 2009 un il $17.99; lib bdg $18.89

Grades: K 1 2 3   **92**

1. Clergy 2. Singers 3. Civil rights activists 4. Nobel laureates for peace 5. African Americans -- Civil rights 6. African American women -- Biography

ISBN 0-06-125364-2; 0-06-125365-0 lib bdg; 978-0-06-125364-5; 978-0-06-125365-2 lib bdg

LC 2008-10486

This introduction to Coretta Scott King looks at her civil rights work within the context of 1950s and 1960s activism. (Bull Cent Child Books)

Nelson's "jacket portrait of Coretta Scott, monumental and tender at the same time, sets the tone for this intimate picture biography. The artist's full-bleed paintings, powerfully molded and saturated with color, depict crucial moments in Scott's life. . . . Shange's . . . rhythmic lines and format syntax roll like waves . . . carrying readers on a soul-stirring ride." Publ Wkly

King, Martin Luther, III, 1957-

My daddy, Dr. Martin Luther King, Jr. by Martin Luther King III; illustrated by AG Ford. Amistad 2013 32 p. (hardcover bdg) $17.99

Grades: K 1 2   **92**

1. African Americans -- Civil rights 2. African Americans -- Civil rights -- History -- 20th century

ISBN 0060280751; 9780060280758; 9780060280765

LC 2012030586

This book presents a picture-book biography of Martin Luther King, Jr., written by his eldest son. "Martin Luther King III spent his childhood learning difficult lessons about segregation, jail and protest marches. . . . When he and his brother received toy guns for Christmas, they were told that guns are destructive weapons and watched as their parents burnt them in a bonfire. In the third grade, the author reluctantly integrated a school." (Kirkus Reviews)

King, Martin Luther, Jr., 1929-1968

I have a dream; Martin Luther King, Jr.; illustrated by Kadir Nelson. 1st ed. Schwartz & Wade Books 2012 40 p. ill. (some col.) $18.99

Grades: K 1 2 3 4 5   **92**

1. Freedom 2. Equality 3. Speeches 4. Picture books for children 5. African Americans -- Civil rights 6. Civil rights movements -- United States -- History

ISBN 0375858873; 9780375858871; 9780375958878

LC 2011044259

Coretta Scott King Illustrator Honor Book (2013)

This children's book celebrates Civil Rights activist Martin Luther King, Jr. "On August 28, 1963, on the steps of the Lincoln Memorial during the March on Washington, Martin Luther King [Jr.] gave one of the most powerful and memorable speeches in our nation's history. His words [are] paired with Caldecott Honor winner Kadir Nelson's . . . paintings" for this book. (Publisher's note)

★ Farris, Christine. **My** brother Martin; a sister remembers growing up with the Rev. Dr. Martin Luther King Jr. by Christine King Farris; illustrated by Chris Soentpiet. Simon & Schuster Bks. for Young Readers 2003 35p il $17.95

Grades: K 1 2 3   **92**

1. Clergy 2. Nonfiction writers 3. Civil rights activists 4. Nobel laureates for peace 5. African Americans -- Biography 6. African Americans -- Civil rights

ISBN 0-689-84387-9

LC 2001-44681

Looks at the early life of Martin Luther King, Jr., as seen through the eyes of his older sister.

"The warmth of the text is exquisitely echoed in Soentpiet's realistic, light-filled watercolor portraits. . . . This outstanding book belongs in every collection." SLJ

★ Farris, Christine King. **March** on! the day my brother Martin changed the world. [by] Christine King Farris; illustrated by London Ladd. Scholastic Press 2008 un il $17.99

Grades: 2 3 4   **92**

1. Clergy 2. Civil rights demonstrations 3. College teachers 4. Nonfiction writers 5. Civil rights activists 6. Nobel laureates for peace 7. African Americans -- Civil rights

ISBN 0-545-03537-6; 978-0-545-03537-8

LC 2007038620

"Describing the 1963 March on Washington, Farris, the older sister of Martin Luther King Jr., maintains the deft touch that made My Brother Martin so moving. . . . Farris . . . effectively uses plain language and well-chosen facts to explain her brother's extraordinary achievements. . . . Ladd . . . demonstrates a rare talent for portraiture. . . . His

King looks human—in other words, capable of inspiring the reader." Publ Wkly

★ Michelson, Richard. **As** good as anybody: Martin Luther King Jr. and Abraham Joshua Heschel's amazing march toward freedom; by Richard Michelson; illustrated by Raul Colón. Knopf 2008 un il $16.99; lib bdg $19.99
Grades: 2 3 4   92
1. Clergy 2. Rabbis 3. Theologians 4. Jews -- Biography 5. Nonfiction writers 6. Civil rights activists 7. Nobel laureates for peace 8. African Americans -- Biography 9. African Americans -- Civil rights
ISBN 978-0-375-83335-9; 0-375-83335-8; 978-0-375-93335-6 lib bdg; 0-375-93335-2 lib bdg

This is the story of how Abraham Joshua Heschel, a Polish rabbi who escaped the Holocaust, and Martin Luther King worked together for African American civil rights.

"Michelson writes in poetic language. . . . Also admirable is Michelson's ability to convey complex historical concepts . . . in clear, potent terms that will speak directly to readers. . . . In both palette and style, Colón's colored-pencil and watercolor art . . . suggests the past, but his themes carry into today's headlines." Booklist

★ Myers, Walter Dean, 1937-2014 **I've** seen the promised land; the life of Dr. Martin Luther King, Jr. illustrated by Leonard Jenkins. HarperCollins Publishers 2004 un il $15.99; lib bdg $16.89
Grades: K 1 2 3   92
1. Clergy 2. Nonfiction writers 3. Civil rights activists 4. Nobel laureates for peace 5. African Americans -- Biography 6. African Americans -- Civil rights
ISBN 0-06-027703-3; 0-06-027704-1 lib bdg
LC 2003-4098

Pictures and easy-to-read text introduce the life of civil rights leader Dr. Martin Luther King, Jr.

"This eloquent picture book presents a brief overview of King's life and accomplishments. . . . Jenkins's stunning collage artwork dramatically reflects the events described in the narrative." SLJ

★ Rappaport, Doreen. **Martin's** big words: the life of Dr. Martin Luther King, Jr. illustrated by Bryan Collier. Hyperion Bks. for Children 2001 un il $15.99; pa $6.99
Grades: K 1 2 3   92
1. Clergy 2. Nonfiction writers 3. Civil rights activists 4. Nobel laureates for peace 5. African Americans -- Biography 6. African Americans -- Civil rights
ISBN 0-7868-0714-8; 1-4231-0635-0 pa
LC 00-40957

A Caldecott Medal honor book, 2002; A Coretta Scott King honor book for illustration, 2002

"Rappaport's spare narrative captures the essentials of the man, the movement he led, and his policy of nonviolence. . . . Collier's collage art is glorious. Combining cutpaper, photographs, and watercolor he expresses his own Christian faith and King's power 'to make many different things one.'" Booklist

Watkins, Angela Farris. **My** Uncle Martin's big heart; illustrated by Eric Velasquez. Abrams 2010 un il $18.95
Grades: PreK K 1 2   92
1. Clergy 2. Nonfiction writers 3. Civil rights activists 4. Nobel laureates for peace 5. African Americans -- Civil rights
ISBN 978-0-8109-8975-7; 0-8109-8975-1

"In this warm, handsome picture book, Watkins celebrates her loving relationship as a small preschooler with 'Uncle M. L.' . . . The girl speaks about taking pride in her uncle's political role as a civil rights leader and national hero. Even more, though, she focuses on personal moments. . . . Velasquez is at his best here. . . . He shows the affection that the child and her uncle share." Booklist

Knight, Margaret, 1838-1914

McCully, Emily Arnold. **Marvelous** Mattie; how Margaret E. Knight became an inventor. Farrar, Straus & Giroux 2006 un il $16
Grades: K 1 2 3   92
1. Inventors 2. Women inventors
ISBN 0-374-34810-3
LC 2004-56415

Margaret (or Mattie) "Knight's design for a safer loom saved textile workers from injuries and death. . . . She fought in court and won the right to patent her most famous invention, a machine that would make paper bags. Mattie's story is told in a style that is not only easy to understand, but that is also a good read-aloud. The watercolor-and-ink illustrations capture the spirited inventor and support the text in style and design." SLJ

Knox, Henry, 1750-1806

★ Silvey, Anita. **Henry** Knox; bookseller, soldier, patriot. pictures by Wendell Minor. Clarion Books 2010 40p il $17.99
Grades: 2 3 4 5   92
1. Generals 2. Boston (Mass.) -- History 3. United States -- History -- 1775-1783, Revolution
ISBN 978-0-618-27485-7; 0-618-27485-5
LC 2009045353

"When the first shots were fired at Lexington and Concord, Henry Knox was a portly young bookseller who avidly read books on military science and discussed them with the British officers who frequented his Boston shop. He would soon put his theoretical knowledge to practical use, for he was placed in charge of the Continental Army's artillery. . . . The first half of this fully illustrated book deftly portrays Knox as a likable, optimistic youth, while the second half shows him as a determined 25-year-old officer leading the expedition that freed Boston in 1776. . . . Painted on wooden panels, Minor's acrylic art creates a vivid sense of the period in varied scenes crafted with a fine grasp of composition, texture, and color." Booklist

Kobayashi, Issa, 1763-1827

★ Gollub, Matthew. **Cool** melons--turn to frogs!: the life and poems of Issa; story and Haiku translations by Matthew Gollub; illustrations by Kazuko G. Stone; calligraphy by Keiko Smith. Lee & Low Bks. 1998 un il $16.95; pa $9.95
Grades: 3 4 5 6   92
1. Haiku 2. Poets 3. Authors 4. Japanese poetry
ISBN 1-880000-71-7; 1-58430-241-0 pa
LC 98-13087

A biography and introduction to the work of the Japanese haiku poet whose love for nature finds expression in the more than thirty poems included in this book

This contains the life of the poet "told in simple language; lots of his exquisite and accessible haiku; limpid watercolor and colored pencil illustrations reminiscent of Japanese prints and drawings; and beautiful Japanese calligraphy." Booklist

Korczak, Janusz, 1878-1942

Bogacki, Tomek. The **champion** of children; the story of Janusz Korczak. Farrar Straus Giroux 2009 un il $17.99
Grades: 1 2 3 4   92
   1. Authors 2. Pediatricians 3. Jews -- Poland 4. Holocaust victims 5. Children's authors 6. Holocaust, 1933-1945
   ISBN 978-0-374-34136-7; 0-374-34136-2
                      LC 2008-16188
This is a "picture-book biography of the Holocaust-era children's advocate and doctor. Early Polish childhood life and interests quickly move into the doctor's student days and expand to his renowned, democratically run orphanage. . . . He steadfastly stayed with his children during the Nazi invasion and deportation and ultimately perished with them at Treblinka. . . . Though this is a story that ends in dark despair, the author succeeds in creating a positive, upbeat atmosphere with his palette of muted reds, blues and greens." Kirkus

Kouanchao, Malichansouk, 1971-

Youme. **Mali** under the night sky; a Lao story of home. written and illustrated by Youme. Cinco Puntos Press 2010 un il $17.95
Grades: K 1 2   92
   1. Artists 2. Women artists 3. Laos
   ISBN 978-1-933693-68-2; 1-933693-68-1
Relates the true story of Laotian American artist Malichansouk Kouanchao, who enjoyed her early childhood playing in the wilderness until civil war forced her family to leave for another country, allowing her to bring only her memories of her homeland.
This story "is told in a simple, straightforward manner, from a child's point of view. . . . The focus remains tightly on Mali's experiences and feelings, keeping it accessible to young readers. . . . The watercolor illustrations, while naive in style, convey a real sense of place." SLJ

Koufax, Sandy, 1935-

★ Winter, Jonah. **You** never heard of Sandy Koufax!? illustrations by Andre Carrilho. Schwartz & Wade Books 2009 un il $17.99; lib bdg $20.99 **92**
   1. Baseball players 2. Jews -- Biography 3. Baseball -- Biography 4. Los Angeles Dodgers (Baseball team)
   ISBN 978-0-375-83738-8; 0-375-83738-8; 978-0-375-93738-5 lib bdg; 0-375-93738-2 lib bdg
                      LC 2007-41860
The author relates "the story of arguably the greatest left-handed pitcher in baseball history as if he were an unnamed teammate along for the ride. . . . Winter makes a point to emphasize that at the time, . . . Koufax was one of very few Jewish players, and he encountered his share of prejudice. . . . Carrilho's digitally enhanced graphite artwork, which resembles highly expressionistic cartoons, emphasizes movement, . . . with touches of deep gold and swift strokes of red against Dodger blue." Booklist
Includes glossary

Kublai Khan, 1216-1294

★ Krull, Kathleen. **Kubla** Khan; the emperor of everything. illustrated by Robert Byrd. Viking Children's Books 2010 un il $17.99
Grades: 2 3 4   92
   1. Mongols 2. Kings 3. China -- History
   ISBN 978-0-670-01114-8; 0-670-01114-2
                      LC 2010007322
"Krull assembles a convincingly grand impression of Kubla Khan and his vast accomplishments. . . . The grandiosity of his reign is well depicted in Bryd's Eastern-style artwork, which provides a subtle buttress to the narrative arc. . . . A solid choice for reports that is also scintillating enough for pleasure reading." Booklist
Includes bibliographical references

La Salle, Robert Cavelier, sieur de, 1643-1687

Goodman, Joan E. **Despite** all obstacles: La Salle and the conquest of the Mississippi; by Joan Elizabeth Goodman; illustrated by Tom McNeely. Mikaya Press 2001 47p il map (Great explorers book) $19.95
Grades: 4 5 6 7   92
   1. Explorers 2. Mississippi River valley
   ISBN 1-931414-01-7
                      LC 2001-31732
A biography of the man who explored the St. Lawrence, Ohio, Illinois, and Mississippi rivers, and who claimed America's heartland for King Louis XIV and France
"Vivid color illustrations and Goodman's exciting writing style will attract both researchers and pleasure readers." Voice Youth Advocates

Law, Westley Wallace, 1923-2002

Haskins, James. **Delivering** justice; W.W. Law and the fight for civil rights. [by] Jim Haskins; illustrated by Benny Andrews. Candlewick Press 2005 un il $16.99
Grades: 2 3 4   92
   1. Postal employees 2. Civil rights activists 3. African Americans -- Civil rights
   ISBN 0-7636-2592-2
                      LC 2005-47114
A biography of Westley (W. W.) Law, a mail carrier who played a leading role in the civil rights movement
"With handsome, full-page illustrations in oil and collage, this picture-book biography tells the stirring story of a quiet hero." Booklist

Lawrence, Jacob, 1917-2000

Collard, Sneed B. **Jacob** Lawrence; a painter's story. Marshall Cavendish Benchmark 2009 41p bibl il por (American heroes) lib bdg $20.95
Grades: 2 3 4   92
   1. Artists 2. Painters 3. Illustrators 4. African American artists 5. Artists -- United States
   ISBN 978-0-7614-4058-1 lib bdg; 0-7614-4058-5 lib bdg
                      LC 2008034819
This introduces "young readers to one of the preeminent twentieth-century African American artists. Collard recounts a few important touchstones of Lawrence's life . . . but mostly frames the narrative around his works. . . . The narrative is concise, but not to the point of simplicity. . . . Reproduc-

tions of paintings and period photos alternate each page of the text." Booklist

Includes glossary and bibliographical references

Lazarus, Emma, 1849-1887

★ Silverman, Erica. **Liberty's** voice: the story of Emma Lazarus; illustrated by Stacey Schuett. Dutton Children's Books 2011 un il $17.99

Grades: 2 3 4 5   **92**

1. Poets 2. Authors 3. Novelists 4. Women poets 5. Philanthropists 6. Poets, American 7. Social reformers 8. Jews -- Biography 9. Biography, Individual

ISBN 0-525-47859-0; 978-0-525-47859-1

LC 2010-13186

This is a biography of the American poet whose lines are inscribed on the Statue of Liberty. "Grades three to five." (Bull Cent Child Books)

"A well-known poet in her day, Emma Lazarus was initially hesitant to pen the poem that would make her famous, 'The New Colossus,' which is engraved on the base of the Statue of Liberty. . . . But her dedication to the plight of immigrant Russian Jews . . . ultimately inspired her message to the 'huddled masses yearning to breathe free.' In a straightforward and smooth narrative style, Silverman . . . tells the story of Lazarus' life and work. The accompanying ink-and-watercolor illustrations serve the historical setting, characters, and plot well." Booklist

Includes bibliographical references

Ledger, Heath, 1979-2008

Watson, Stephanie. **Heath** Ledger; talented actor. ABDO Pub. Company 2010 112p il (Lives cut short) lib bdg $32.79

Grades: 5 6 7 8   **92**

1. Actors

ISBN 978-1-60453-789-5 lib bdg; 1-60453-789-2 lib bdg

LC 2009034353

This discusses Heath Ledger's "early life, providing details that give insight into later success and troubles and maintaining a laudatory tone that focuses on the individual's artistic achievements and hard work to achieve fame. Details [such as] explaining that Jack Nicholson warned Heath Ledger about the Joker role . . . are bound to resonate with readers. Numerous photos and sidebars appear throughout. [A] worthwhile [resource] for reports as well as popular reading." SLJ

Includes bibliographical references

Lee, Bruce, 1940-1973

Mochizuki, Ken. **Be** water, my friend; the early years of Bruce Lee. illustrated by Dom Lee. Lee & Low Books 2006 un il $16.95

Grades: K 1 2 3   **92**

1. Actors 2. Martial arts 3. Martial artists

ISBN 1-58430-265-0

"This distinctive-looking book offers a smoothly written text and many handsome, textured acrylic paintings done in tones of brown and cream." Booklist

Lee, Sammy, 1920-

★ Yoo, Paula. **Sixteen** years in sixteen seconds; the Sammy Lee story. illustrations by Dom Lee. Lee & Low Books 2005 un il $16.95

Grades: 2 3 4   **92**

1. Diving 2. Physicians 3. Korean Americans 4. Divers 5. Olympic athletes

ISBN 1-58430-247-X

LC 2004-20962

"Yoo introduces Sammy Lee, the son of Korean immigrants who overcame formidable odds to become an Olympic diving champion as well as a doctor. . . . Washed in nostalgic sepia tones, Dom Lee's acrylic-and-wax textured illustrations are reminiscent of his fine work in Ken Mochizuki's watershed Baseball Saved Us (1993) and like Yoo's understated words, the uncluttered images leave a deep impression." Booklist

Lennon, John, 1940-1980

Anderson, Jennifer Joline. **John** Lennon; legendary musician & Beatle. ABDO 2010 112p il (Lives cut short) lib bdg $32.79

Grades: 5 6 7 8   **92**

1. Singers 2. Rock musicians 3. Songwriters

ISBN 978-1-60453-790-1 lib bdg; 1-60453-790-6 lib bdg

LC 2009034354

This discusses the John Lennon's "early life, providing details that give insight into later success and troubles and maintaining a laudatory tone that focuses on the individual's artistic achievements and hard work to achieve fame. Details [such as] explaining that . . . John Lennon had no musical training . . . are bound to resonate with readers. Numerous photos and sidebars appear throughout. [A] worthwhile [resource] for reports as well as popular reading." SLJ

Includes glossary and bibliographical references

Rappaport, Doreen. **John's** secret dreams; the life of John Lennon. written by Doreen Rappaport; illustrated by Bryan Collier. Hyperion Books for Children 2004 un il $16.99

Grades: 4 5 6 7   **92**

1. Singers 2. Rock musicians 3. Beatles 4. Songwriters

ISBN 0-7868-0817-9

LC 2003-57116

"Using a combination of simple prose, song lyrics, and illustration, this heartfelt picture-book biography traces Lennon's life from his childhood to his death. Striking in both its simplicity and complexity, it captures this enigmatic singer, artist, songwriter, and folk hero in a way that will move and fascinate those too young to remember the man but are surrounded by his music and myth." SLJ

Leonardo, da Vinci, 1452-1519

★ Krull, Kathleen. **Leonardo** da Vinci; illustrated by Boris Kulikov. Viking 2005 128p il (Giants of science) $15.99

Grades: 5 6 7 8   **92**

1. Artists 2. Painters 3. Scientists 4. Renaissance 5. Artists, Italian 6. Writers on science

ISBN 0-670-05920-X

This is a "biography of Leonardo da Vinci that highlights his scientific approach to understanding the physical world. The first half of the book describes Leonardo's apprenticeship and his work as an artist in Milan. The second half relates events in his later life, emphasizing his observation and investigation of the human body and nature. . . . Six excellent ink drawings illustrate this attractive volume. A very readable, vivid portrait set against the backdrop of remarkable times." Booklist

Includes bibliographical references

Phillips, John. **Leonardo** da Vinci; the genius who defined the Renaissance. National Geographic 2006 64p bibl il (World history biographies) $17.95; lib bdg $27.90; pa $6.95

Grades: 5 6 7 8   92

1. Artists 2. Painters 3. Scientists 4. Renaissance 5. Artists, Italian 6. Writers on science

ISBN 978-0-7922-5385-3; 0-7922-5385-X; 978-0-7922-5386-0 lib bdg; 0-7922-5386-8 lib bdg; 978-1-4263-0248-0 pa; 1-4263-0249-7 pa

Examines the life of Renaissance genius Leonardo da Vinci, discussing his inquiries and accomplishments in art and various fields of science

Includes bibliographical references

Lewis, Ida, 1842-1911

Moss, Marissa. The **bravest** woman in America; illustrations by Andrea U'Ren. Tricycle Press 2011 un il $16.99

Grades: K 1 2 3   92

1. Lighthouses 2. Rhode Island 3. Lighthouse keepers 4. Biography, Individual

ISBN 1-58246-369-7; 978-1-58246-369-8

LC 2010008917

This picture book tells the story of Ida Lewis. "In 1857, when she was fifteen, the family moved to the lighthouse at Lime Rock (which guards Rhode Island's Newport Harbor), where Mr. Lewis was lighthouse keeper. Soon after, illness disabled him; Ida took over his duties and, at sixteen, . . . rescued four boys whose boat had capsized. . . . It was the first of many rescues during a lifelong career for which she received a Congressional Lifesaving Medal. . . . Preschool, primary." (Horn Book)

"Moss's . . . short, stirring biography of 19th-century lighthouse keeper Ida Lewis centers on Lewis's first rescue, at age 16, off the coast of Rhode Island. . . . U'Ren's . . . bold, mixed-media illustrations capture the power and many moods of the sea, from calm ultramarine to the foam-topped dark slate and deep green of stormy waters. Heavy brushstrokes and black outlines . . . suggest the deliberate strength with which Ida carried out her vocation." Publ Wkly

Lewis, John, 1940-

★ Haskins, James. **John** Lewis in the lead; a story of the civil rights movement. [by] Jim Haskins and Kathleen Benson; illustrations by Benny Andrews. Lee & Low 2006 un il $17.95

Grades: 3 4 5   92

1. Members of Congress 2. Civil rights activists 3. African Americans -- Civil rights

ISBN 1-58430-250-X

LC 2005-35472

"Born in a sharecropper family in the segregated South in 1940, John Lewis grew up to lead many protests for civil rights, and he has served in Congress for the last 20 years. In this handsome picture book for older readers, the authors blend information on Lewis' political contributions with the history of the civil rights struggle. . . . Andrews' dramatic, folk-art-style, color-saturated illustrations combine handsome individual portraits of Lewis with overviews of

the horrific street violence by mobs, police, and troopers." Booklist

Li Cunxin

Li Cunxin. **Dancing** to freedom; the true story of Mao's last dancer. illustrated by Anne Spudvilas. Walker & Co. 2008 un il $16.95; lib bdg $17.85

Grades: K 1 2 3   92

1. Ballet 2. Ballet dancers 3. China 4. Securities brokers

ISBN 978-0-8027-9777-3; 0-8027-9777-6; 978-0-8027-9778-0 lib bdg; 0-8027-9778-4 lib bdg

LC 2007-37150

"A poignant memoir of a boy caught in the difficulties of life in Maoist China, this is the author's own story of how he was given a chance to break the bonds of his bleak life and become an international star. . . . [Li] was offered the chance to dance with the Houston Ballet, and his greatest dream was realized when his parents were finally able to come to the U.S. to see him perform. This fascinating, heartfelt story is perfectly matched by Spudvilas's masterful paintings." SLJ

Lichtenstein, Roy, 1923-1997

★ Rubin, Susan Goldman. **Whaam!**: the art & life of Roy Lichtenstein. Abrams 2008 47p il $18.95

Grades: 4 5 6 7   92

1. Artists 2. Pop art 3. Painters 4. Sculptors 5. Printmakers 6. Artists -- United States

ISBN 978-0-8109-9492-8; 0-8109-9492-5

LC 2007-42048

"Rubin presents an overview of a modern master with clear writing and an abundance of his eye-popping works, all framed on pages that mirror the artist's signature use of primary colors and Benday dots." Booklist

Lincoln family

★ Rabin, Staton. **Mr.** Lincoln's boys; being the mostly true adventures of Abraham Lincoln's trouble-making sons, Tad and Willie. by Staton Rabin; illustrated by Bagram Ibatoulline. Penguin Group 2008 un il $16.99

Grades: 1 2 3   92

1. Presidents 2. Pioneers 3. State legislators 4. Members of Congress 5. Children of presidents 6. Presidents -- United States

ISBN 978-0-670-06169-3; 0-670-06169-7

LC 2008-1774

"Tad and Willie, the mischievous sons of President Abraham Lincoln, scampered around the White House surprising and irritating almost everyone. Their pranks, however, delighted their father, who was faced with the grim realities of the Civil War. . . . Fictionalized dialogue throughout is believable. A large part of the appeal of this book can be credited to Ibatoulline's masterful illustrations. Evocative and detailed, they fill the pages with visual information and emotion. Readers will be intrigued by the antics of these famous children." SLJ

Includes bibliographical references

Aylesworth, Jim. **Our** Abe Lincoln; an old tune with new lyrics. adapted by Jim Aylesworth; illustrated by Barbara McClintock. Scholastic Press 2009 un il $16.99

Grades: PreK K 1 2   92

1. Songs 2. Presidents 3. State legislators 4. Members

of Congress 5. Presidents -- United States
ISBN 978-0-439-92548-8; 0-439-92548-7

LC 2007-31060

"With a fresh approach to Lincoln that is both delightful and accurate, Aylesworth sets history to the tune of 'The Old Gray Mare' and the derivative song 'Our Abe Lincoln Came Out of the Wilderness,' which was popular during the 16th president's campaign. . . . McClintock captures the exuberance with charming visuals that outline significant aspects of the leader's life and lore. Scenes rendered in watercolor and pen and ink feature a multicultural cast." SLJ

★ Brewer, Paul. **Lincoln** tells a joke; how laughter saved the President (and the country) [by] Kathleen Krull & Paul Brewer; illustrated by Stacy Innerst. Harcourt 2010 un il $16

Grades: 2 3 4   92

1. Lawyers 2. Presidents 3. Wit and humor 4. State legislators 5. Members of Congress 6. Presidents -- United States 7. Biography, Individual
ISBN 0-15-206639-X; 978-0-15-206639-0

LC 2009-24197

This biography of the American president focuses on his use of wit and humor, and his love of language. "Ages seven to ten." (Bull Cent Child Books)

"Moving through the sixteenth president's many challenges, from family deaths to lost elections to fighting slavery, the text emphasizes how Lincoln coped with a joke on his tongue and a smile on his lips. . . . Innerst's acrylic artwork feels homey and humorous." Booklist

Burleigh, Robert. **Abraham** Lincoln comes home; [by] Robert Burleigh; paintings by Wendell Minor. Henry Holt and Co. 2008 un il $16.95

Grades: 2 3 4   92

1. Presidents 2. State legislators 3. Members of Congress 4. Presidents -- United States
ISBN 978-0-8050-7529-8; 0-8050-7529-1

LC 2007040030

"Following Lincoln's death, his body was taken back to Illinois for burial. Burleigh focuses on one boy's perceptions as he and his father travel through the night by horse-drawn carriage to see the funeral train pass. . . . Minor's gouache watercolors capture the prairie as well as multiple perspectives of the train, while Burleigh's prose is almost poetic." SLJ

Denenberg, Barry. **Lincoln** shot! a president's life remembered. chief writer, Barry Denenberg; artist, Christopher Bing. Feiwel and Friends 2008 40p il $24.95

Grades: 5 6 7 8   92

1. Presidents 2. State legislators 3. Members of Congress 4. Presidents -- United States 5. United States -- History -- 1861-1865, Civil War
ISBN 978-0-312-37013-8; 0-312-37013-X

LC 2007-48851

"The concept is that this is a commemorative edition of 'The National News' published one year after Lincoln's death . . . Also included is an engaging, readable yet detailed account of Lincoln's life. . . . [This book] is an example of how high-quality bookmaking can turn a history lesson into an authentic experience." Booklist

★ Freedman, Russell. **Abraham** Lincoln and Frederick Douglass; the story behind an American friendship. by Russell Freedman. Houghton Mifflin Harcourt 2012 119 p. $18.99

Grades: 4 5 6 7 8   92

1. Friendship 2. Abolitionists -- United States 3. United States -- History -- 1861-1865, Civil War -- Biography 4. Friendship -- United States 5. Presidents -- United States -- Biography 6. African American abolitionists -- Biography
ISBN 9780547385624

LC 2011025953

This book tells the story of Abraham Lincoln, "the 16th president, . . . [along] with his friend and ally, abolitionist Frederick Douglass. The story opens with Douglass anxiously waiting to meet Lincoln for the first time to air grievances about the treatment of African-American soldiers during the Civil War. . . . Subsequent chapters detail the leaders' often parallel biographies. Both were self-made and shared a passion for reading, rising from poverty to prominence." (Publishers Weekly)

Includes bibliographical references (p. [108]-109) and index

★ Freedman, Russell. **Lincoln**: a photobiography. Clarion Bks. 1987 149p il $18; pa $7.95

Grades: 5 6 7 8 9 10   92

1. Presidents 2. State legislators 3. Members of Congress 4. Presidents -- United States 5. United States -- History -- 1861-1865, Civil War
ISBN 0-89919-380-3; 0-395-51848-2 pa

LC 86-33379

Awarded the Newbery Medal, 1988

This is "a balanced work, elegantly designed and enhanced by dozens of period photographs and drawings, some familiar, some refreshingly unfamiliar." Publ Wkly

Includes bibliographical references

Giblin, James. **Good** brother, bad brother; the story of Edwin Booth and John Wilkes Booth. Clarion Books 2005 244p il $22

Grades: 5 6 7 8   92

1. United States -- History -- 1861-1865, Civil War
ISBN 0-618-09642-6

LC 2004-21260

This is a dual biography of John Wilkes Booth, who assassinated Abraham Lincoln, and his brother, Edwin, an actor. (Horn Book)

Giblin "frames the intertwined tale of two brothers with accounts of their families, friends, the Civil War, and nineteenth-century theater. . . . Alcoholism and depression afflicted the family, but Giblin is brilliant at showing that darkness was only one part of a life. . . . Giblin's book will engross readers until the very last footnote." Booklist

Includes bibliographical references

Harness, Cheryl. **Abe** Lincoln goes to Washington, 1837-1865; written and illustrated by Cheryl Harness. National Geographic Soc. 1997 un il maps $18

Grades: 2 3 4   92

1. Lawyers 2. Presidents 3. State legislators 4.

Members of Congress 5. Presidents -- United States
ISBN 0-7922-3736-6

LC 96-9587

Companion volume to Young Abe Lincoln: the frontier
days, 1809-1837 (1996)

Portrays Lincoln's life as a lawyer in Springfield, a devoted husband and father, and president during the Civil
War years

"The text gallops through years of history, with sudden
stops for surprisingly vivid little scenes. . . . Filled with color
and action, Harness' paintings and maps dominate the pages
and provide a wealth of historical detail as well as a humanizing view of the Lincolns." Booklist

Includes bibliographical references

Herbert, Janis. **Abraham** Lincoln for kids; his life and
times with 21 activities. [by] Janis Herbert. Chicago Review Press 2007 149p il pa $14.95
Grades: 4 5 6 7   **92**
1. Lawyers 2. Presidents 3. State legislators 4.
Members of Congress 5. Presidents -- United States
ISBN 978-1-55652-656-5 pa; 1-55652-656-3 pa

LC 2007009052

"This attractive biographical guide offers a good mixture
of information, anecdotes, and activities, balancing facts
about Lincoln's personal and family life with the record of
his accomplishments as president and a broader view of his
times." Booklist

Includes glossary and bibliographical references

Kalman, Maira. **Looking** at Lincoln; Maira Kalman.
Nancy Paulsen Books 2012 1 v.
Grades: K 1 2 3 4 5   **92**
1. Picture books for children 2. Presidents -- United
States -- Biography 3. United States -- History -- Civil
War, 1861-1865
ISBN 9780399240393

LC 2011046953

'This children's book offers an account of former U.S.
President "Abraham Lincoln [who] is one of the first giants
of history children are introduced to. . . . Lincoln's legacy is
everywhere - there he is on your penny and five-dollar bill.
And we are still the United States because Lincoln helped
hold them together. But who was he, really? The little girl in
this book wants to find out. Among the many other things,
she discovers our sixteenth president was a man who believed in freedom for all, had a dog named Fido, loved Mozart, apples, and his wife's vanilla cake, and kept his notes
in his hat. From his boyhood in a log cabin to his famous
presidency and untimely death, Kalman shares Lincoln's . . .
life with young readers." (Publisher's note)

Includes bibliographical references

★ Rabin, Staton. **Mr.** Lincoln's boys; being the mostly
true adventures of Abraham Lincoln's trouble-making sons,
Tad and Willie. by Staton Rabin; illustrated by Bagram Iba-
toulline. Penguin Group 2008 un il $16.99
Grades: 1 2 3   **92**
1. Presidents 2. Pioneers 3. State legislators 4.
Members of Congress 5. Children of presidents 6.
Presidents -- United States
ISBN 978-0-670-06169-3; 0-670-06169-7

LC 2008-1774

"Tad and Willie, the mischievous sons of President Abraham Lincoln, scampered around the White House surprising
and irritating almost everyone. Their pranks, however, delighted their father, who was faced with the grim realities
of the Civil War. . . . Fictionalized dialogue throughout is
believable. A large part of the appeal of this book can be
credited to Ibatoulline's masterful illustrations. Evocative
and detailed, they fill the pages with visual information and
emotion. Readers will be intrigued by the antics of these famous children." SLJ

Includes bibliographical references

★ Rappaport, Doreen. **Abe's** honest words; the life of
Abraham Lincoln. [illustrated by] Kadir Nelson. Hyperion
Books for Children 2008 44p il $16.99
Grades: 2 3 4   **92**
1. Presidents 2. State legislators 3. Members of
Congress 4. Presidents -- United States
ISBN 1-4231-0408-0; 978-1-4231-0408-7

LC 2006-43608

"This collaboration between Rappaport and Nelson provides a sweeping arc of Lincoln's life. . . . Rappaport writes
in the very free verse and on each page echoes her narrative
with prescient samplings of Lincoln's words. In generously
sized artwork . . . Nelson makes the familiar face . . . exciting
again. . . . The exceptional art, along with Rappaport's and
Lincoln's words, makes this a fine celebration of a man who
needs little introduction." Booklist

Includes bibliographical references

Schroeder, Alan

Abe Lincoln; his wit and wisdom from A to Z. by Alan
Schroeder; illustrated by John O'Brien. Holiday House
2015 32 p. color illustrations (hardcover) $17.95
Grades: K 1 2 3 4   **92**
1. Quotations 2. Alphabet books 3. Presidents --
United States -- Biography
ISBN 0823424200; 9780823424207

LC 2013038989

This children's book, by Alan Schroeder, illustrated by
John O'Brien, presents a collection of sayings from U.S.
President Abraham Lincoln. This "nontraditional tribute
to the president who brought the homespun humor of his
humble beginnings to the White House uses the alphabet to
organize a wealth of information about his life and accomplishments." (Publisher's note)

"Schroeder provides an overview of the 16th president's
legacy, his predilections, and some significant events of his
era. Each letter introduces several ideas. . . . O'Brien's ink-
and-watercolor art has a farcical sensibility that plays on the
mythology surrounding Lincoln." Pub Wkly

St. George, Judith. **Stand** tall, Abe Lincoln; [by] Judith
St. George; illustrated by Matt Faulkner. Philomel Books
2007 un il $16.99
Grades: 2 3 4   **92**
1. Presidents 2. State legislators 43 Members of
Congress 4. Presidents -- United States
ISBN 978-0-399-24174-1

LC 2006024877

"This account of Lincoln's childhood is written in fast-
paced short sentences. St. George . . . uses a folksy, conversational style. . . . Faulkner's humorous illustrations are
a perfect match for the text. . . . The expressive images are

done in a caricature style, with slightly exaggerated hands, feet, and heads." SLJ

Includes bibliographical references

Thomson, Sarah L. **What** Lincoln said; by Sarah L. Thomson; art by James Ransome. Collins 2009 un il $17.99; lib bdg $18.89

Grades: K 1 2 3   **92**

1. Presidents 2. State legislators 3. Members of Congress 4. Presidents -- United States
ISBN 978-0-06-084819-4; 0-06-084819-7; 978-0-06-084820-0 lib bdg; 0-06-084820-0 lib bdg
LC 2008020095

"By using Lincoln's own words, Thomson builds a portrait that relates his statements to significant events in his life. . . . Short descriptions of the circumstances and a related quote are set on bold, colorful spreads. Ransome delivers a larger-than-life portrait of this homely president with acrylic, almost cartoonlike paintings. . . . An engaging overview, this is a worthy introduction to this famous president." SLJ

Lincoln, Abraham

Gilpin, Caroline Crosson. **Abraham** Lincoln; by Caroline Gilpin. National Geographic 2013 31 p. (paperback) $3.99; (library) $13.90

Grades: 1 2 3   **92**

1. Slaves -- Emancipation 2. Presidents -- United States -- Biography 3. United States -- History -- Civil War, 1861-1865
ISBN 1426310854; 9781426310850; 9781426310867
LC 2012031885

In this book, "readers will learn about the . . . life and legacy of our 16th President of the United States, Abraham Lincoln and his historic decision to abolish slavery. Readers will also learn why this decision impacted the United States, as well as the extent of Lincoln's impact as a fearless leader of the Civil War." (Publisher's note)

Lincoln, Mary Todd, 1818-1882

★ Jones, Lynda. **Mrs.** Lincoln's dressmaker: the unlikely friendship of Elizabeth Keckley and Mary Todd Lincoln; by Lynda D. Jones. National Geographic 2009 80p il $18.95; lib bdg $27.90

Grades: 5 6 7 8   **92**

1. Memoirists 2. Dressmakers 3. Spouses of presidents 4. Slavery -- United States 5. United States -- Race relations 6. African American women -- Biography 7. Presidents' spouses -- United States 8. Washington (D.C.) -- Social life and customs
ISBN 978-1-4263-0377-7; 1-4263-0377-7; 978-1-4263-0378-4 lib bdg; 1-4263-0378-5 lib bdg
LC 2008-29314

"Readers may be familiar with the ups and downs of Lincoln's life, but details of Keckley's story . . . will give them new insights into the life of a slave, in this case, one who was educated and had a profession." Booklist

Includes bibliographical references

Linné, Carl von, 1707-1778

Anderson, Margaret Jean. **Carl** Linnaeus; father of classification. [by] Margaret J. Anderson. rev ed; Enslow Publishers 2009 128p il (Great minds of science) lib bdg $31.93

Grades: 5 6 7 8 9   **92**

1. Botanists 2. Naturalists 3. Writers on science
ISBN 978-0-7660-3009-1 lib bdg; 0-7660-3009-1 lib bdg
LC 2008-23941

First published 1997

"Budding scientists will surely draw inspiration from this biography of Linnaeus. . . . Anderson creates a dramatic narrative fully capable of keeping readers enthralled." Kirkus

Includes glossary and bibliographical references

Liston, Melba

★ Russell-Brown, Katheryn. **Little** Melba and her big trombone; by Katheryn Russell-Brown; illustrations by Frank Morrison. First edition Lee & Low Books, Inc. 2014 40 p. (hardcover: alk. paper) $18.95

Grades: K 1 2 3 4   **92**

1. Jazz musicians -- Biography 2. Jazz music 3. Jazz musicians 4. African American jazz musicians
ISBN 1600608981; 9781600608988
LC 2013033662

Coretta Scott King (Illustrator) Honor Book (2015)

This children's book by Katheryn Russell-Brown, illustrated by Frank Morrison, tells how "Melba Doretta Liston loved the sounds of music. . . . As a child, she daydreamed about beats and lyrics, and hummed along with the music from her family's Majestic radio. . . . Overcoming obstacles of race and gender, Melba went on to become a famed trombone player and arranger, spinning rhythms, harmonies, and melodies into gorgeous songs for all the jazz greats of the twentieth century." (Publisher's note)

"Music lovers will enjoy this picture-book biography of Melba Liston (1926 - 99), child prodigy and virtuoso trombonist who collaborated with most 20th century jazz greats... Russell-Brown's text engages the senses ("[Melba] especially loved Fats Waller, with his growly voice and booming piano"), while Morrison's distinctive illustrations, stretched out like a slide trombone, draw the eye across each spread to the page turn..." SLJ

Lockwood, Belva Ann, 1830-1917

Bardhan-Quallen, Sudipta. **Ballots** for Belva; the true story of a woman's race for the presidency. by Sudipta Bardhan-Quallen; illustrated by Courtney A. Martin. Abrams Books for Young Readers 2008 un il $16.95

Grades: 2 3 4 5   **92**

1. Lawyers 2. Feminism 3. Suffragists 4. Women lawyers 5. Women politicians 6. Lecturers 7. Presidential candidates
ISBN 978-0-8109-7110-3; 0-8109-7110-0
LC 2007049842

"This picture-book biography introduces [Belva Ann Lockwood], the woman who ran for president more than a century ago. . . . She obtained a law degree, fought for equal rights, and ultimately became the first woman to receive certified votes during her 1884 presidential campaign. . . . Quotes from Lockwood and others enliven the text. . . . Handsome illustrations clearly set the time and place, and Lockwood's fortitude comes through in her posture and facial expressions." SLJ

Lomax, John Avery, 1867-1948

Hopkinson, Deborah. **Home** on the range; John A. Lomax and his cowboy songs. illustrated by S. D. Schindler. G. P. Putnam's Sons 2009 un il $16.99

Grades: 2 3 4   **92**

1. Ethnomusicologists 2. Folklorists 3. Musicologists 4. Folk songs -- United States

ISBN 978-0-399-23996-0; 0-399-23996-0

LC 2008-16802

This traces the early career of John A Lomax, the collector and recorder of American folk songs.

This a "colorful narrative. . . . Glimpses of his thoughts and emotions . . . as well as dialogue help personalize the story. . . . Schindler's . . . realistic illustrations, painted with a light touch in muted hues, ably capture the expressions of skeptical cowboys . . . or the eagerness with which Lomax goes about his work." Publ Wkly

Longworth, Alice Roosevelt, 1884-1980

★ Kerley, Barbara. **What** to do about Alice? how Alice Roosevelt broke the rules, charmed the world, and drove her father Teddy crazy! illustrated by Edwin Fotheringham. Scholastic Press 2008 un il $16.99

Grades: K 1 2 3   **92**

1. Presidents -- United States -- Family 2. Biography, Individual 3. White House (Washington, D.C.)

ISBN 978-0-439-92231-9; 0-439-92231-3

LC 2006-38372

Boston Globe-Horn Book Award honor book: Nonfiction (2008)

"The daughter of Theodore Roosevelt, . . . Alice had a joie de vivre that she called 'eating up the world.' . . . Kerley's text has the same rambunctious spirit as its subject. . . . The large format gives Fotheringhame . . . plenty of room for spectacular art, which includes use of digital media." Booklist

Lorenz, Konrad

Greenstein, Elaine. The **goose** man; the story of Konrad Lorenz. Clarion Books 2009 32p il $16

Grades: K 1 2 3   **92**

1. Geese 2. Scientists 3. Ethologists 4. Writers on nature 5. Writers on science 6. Nobel laureates for physiology or medicine

ISBN 978-0-547-08459-6; 0-547-08459-5

LC 2008-44618

"From childhood, Konrad Lorenz was fascinated by ducks and geese, growing up to become a prizewinning scientist who offered new insights into animal behavior. This picture-book biography . . . summarizes his life's work with geese. . . . The pastel illustrations, in gouache, ink and colored pencil, use a technique that includes scratchboard effects and is childlike in style. . . . These pictures tell the story as clearly as the simple text, whose language and frequent repetition make this scientific biography easily accessible to beginning readers." Kirkus

Includes bibliographical references

Louis, Joe, 1914-1981

Adler, David A. **Joe** Louis; America's fighter. written by David A. Adler; illustrated by Terry Widener. Harcourt 2005 un il $16

Grades: 2 3 4   **92**

1. Soldiers 2. African American athletes 3. Boxers (Persons) 4. Boxing -- Biography

ISBN 0-15-216480-4

LC 2003-12817

The life story of Joe Louis, heavyweight champion boxer, with the complete history of his career in the ring.

"This creative team's collaboration packs a powerful punch. . . . The action-packed acrylics capture the setting and emotions—Widener's signature muscular figures are particularly apt here." SLJ

Includes bibliographical references

★ De la Peña, Matt. A **nation's** hope; the story of boxing legend Joe Louis. illustrated by Kadir Nelson. Dial Books for Young Readers 2011 un il $17.99

Grades: 1 2 3   **92**

1. Soldiers 2. African American athletes 3. Boxers (Persons) 4. Boxing -- Biography 5. Boxing 6. Biography, Individual

ISBN 0-8037-3167-1; 978-0-8037-3167-7

LC 2010-13477

This biography focuses on the "1938 rematch between African-American Joe Louis and German Max Schmeling. . . . Ages five to eight." (Bull Cent Child Books)

"Nelson's . . . photographically realistic, luminescent oil paintings bring to life this lyrical tribute to boxing legend Joe Louis. Focusing on Louis's 1938 rematch against German Max Schmeling . . . de la Peña . . . in his first picture book, shows how the event unified a racially divided country for one evening. . . . Spare, evocative verse melds with the eloquent illustrations to create palpable energy around the fight and Louis's struggle to the top. . . . A dramatic introduction to a pugilist who symbolized many things for an entire country." Publ Wkly

Ludwick, Christopher, 1720-1801

Rockliff, Mara. **Gingerbread** for liberty! how a German baker helped win the American Revolution. Mara Rockliff; illustrated by Vincent X. Kirsch. HMH Books for Young Readers 2014 32 p. color illustrations (hardback) $17.99

Grades: 1 2 3 4   **92**

1. Bakers and bakeries 2. United States -- History -- 1775-1783, Revolution 3. United States -- History -- Revolution, 1775-1783 -- Biography 4. United States -- History -- Revolution, 1775-1783 -- Participation, German American

ISBN 0544130014; 9780544130012

LC 2013036934

This children's book by Mara Rockliff tells "the story of an unsung hero of the Revolutionary War who changed the course of history one loaf at a time. Christopher Ludwick was a German-born American patriot with a big heart and a talent for baking. When cries of 'Revolution!' began, Christopher was determined to help General George Washington and his hungry troops. Not with muskets or cannons, but with gingerbread!" (Publisher's note)

"A little-known figure from the American Revolution era is given a fresh look for another generation of history lovers. This book relates the tale of a generous, beloved, and industrious member of the Philadelphia community, originally from Germany, referred to as "the baker.". . .The simple recipe on the end pages offers options for different skill levels. Back matter, including a list of sources, provides fuller detail and context as well as the baker's name: Christopher Ludwick. A sweet addition to Revolutionary War units where a more behind-the-scenes look is desired and a nonfiction twist on gingerbread-themed storytimes." SLJ

Lynch, John Roy

The amazing age of John Roy Lynch; written by Chris Barton; illustrated by Don Tate. Eerdmans Books for Young Readers 2015 50 p. (hardcover) $17

    Grades: 2 3 4 5   92
    1. African Americans -- Biography 2. Reconstruction (U.S. history, 1865-1877) 3. African American legislators -- Biography 4. Legislators -- United States -- Biography 5. United States. Congress. House -- Biography 6. Mississippi -- Politics and government -- 1865-1950 7. United States -- Politics and government -- 1865-1900 8. African American politicians -- Mississippi -- Biography
    ISBN 080285379X; 9780802853790
                          LC 2014018586

This picture book, by Chris Barton, illustrated by Don Tate, tells the story of how "John Roy Lynch spent most of his childhood as a slave in Mississippi, but all of that changed with the Emancipation Proclamation. . . . While many people in the South were unhappy with the social change, John Roy thrived in the new era. He was appointed to serve as justice of the peace and was eventually elected into the United States Congress." (Publisher's note)

Includes bibliographical references

Lyons, Maritcha Rémond, 1848-1929

    ★ Bolden, Tonya. **Maritcha**; a nineteenth-century American girl. Abrams 2005 47p il $17.95

    Grades: 4 5 6 7 8 9 10   92
    1. Teachers 2. Civic leaders 3. New York (N.Y.) -- Race relations 4. African American women -- Biography 5. African Americans -- New York (N.Y.)
    ISBN 0-8109-5045-6
                          LC 2004-05849

"The high quality of writing and the excellent documentation make this a first choice for all collections." SLJ

This is a "life history of Maritcha Rémond Lyons, born a free black in 1848 in lower Manhattan. The author draws her biographical sketch primarily from Lyons's unpublished memoir, dated one year before her death in 1929. . . . One of the . . . sections of the book documents the Draft Riots . . . of July 1868, and the impact of them on Maritcha and other citizens." Publ Wkly

Maathai, Wangari, 1940-2001

    ★ Johnson, Jen Cullerton. **Seeds** of change; planting a path to peace. illustrated by Sonia Lynn Sadler. Lee & Low 2010 un il $18.95

    Grades: 2 3 4   92
    1. Biologists 2. Conservationists 3. Environmentalists 4. Kenya 5. Nobel laureates for peace 6. Green Belt Movement (Kenya)
    ISBN 978-1-60060-367-9; 1-60060-367-X
    Coretta Scott King/John Steptoe New Talent Award (Illustrator), 2011

This picture biography "draws on Wangari Maathai's autobiographical writing to present an overview of the activist's life from childhood to the present. . . . Richer than other treatments of Maathai for children and more grounded in her work's implicit feminism, this details her education in Nai-

robi and the United States, her imprisonment for activism and her scientific and environmental work, resulting in the planting of 30,000,000 trees and economic empowerment for Kenyan women. Sadler's beautiful scratchboard illustrations incise white contoured line into saturated landscapes of lush green leaf patterns, brilliant-hued textiles and undulating, stylized hills. . . . Vibrant and accomplished." Kirkus

    ★ Napoli, Donna Jo. **Mama** Miti: Wangari Maathai and the trees of Kenya; illustrated by Kadir Nelson. Simon & Schuster Books for Young Readers 2010 un il $16.99

    Grades: K 1 2 3   92
    1. Biologists 2. Conservationists 3. Environmentalists 4. Kenya 5. Nobel laureates for peace 6. Green Belt Movement (Kenya)
    ISBN 978-1-4169-3505-6; 1-4169-3505-3
                          LC 2008-23604

"Napoli adopts a folkloric narrative technique to showcase the life work of Wangari Maathai, whose seminal role in Kenya's reforestation earned her the Nobel Peace Prize in 2004. When, one after the other, women journey to Maathai to seek counsel about scarce food, disappearing firewood and ailing animals, she tells them, 'Plant a tree.' . . . Nelson's pictures, a jaw-dropping union of African textiles collaged with oil paintings, brilliantly capture the villagers' clothing and the greening landscape. The richly modulated oils portray the dignified, intent gazes of Maathai and other Kenyans. . . . This is, in a word, stunning." Kirkus

Includes bibliographical references

Winter, Jeanette. **Wangari's** trees of peace; a true story from Africa. Harcourt 2008 un il $17

    Grades: K 1 2 3   92
    1. Biologists 2. Conservationists 3. Environmentalists 4. Kenya 5. Nobel laureates for peace 6. Green Belt Movement (Kenya)
    ISBN 978-0-15-206545-4; 0-15-206545-8
                          LC 2007-34810

"Wangari Maathai, the 2004 Nobel Peace Prize winner whose Green Belt Movement has planted 30 million trees in Kenya, is the subject of Winter's . . . eloquent picture biography. . . . The tightly focused text moves quickly without sacrificing impact. . . . Winter's images appear in framed, same-size squares on each page, creating a flat, frieze-like effect." Publ Wkly

Madison, Dolley, 1768-1849

Adler, David A. A **picture** book of Dolley and James Madison; by David A. Adler and Michael S. Adler; illustrated by Ronald Himler. Holiday House 2009 un il $17.95

    Grades: 1 2 3   92
    1. Presidents 2. Members of Congress 3. Secretaries of state 4. Spouses of presidents 5. Presidents -- United States 6. Presidents' spouses -- United States
    ISBN 978-0-8234-2009-4; 0-8234-2009-4
                          LC 2007041178

"Adler's picture-book biography focuses mainly on the War of 1812, but also mentions Madison's contributions to the Constitution and the creation of the three branches of government. Although this is a biography of the couple, there is more specific information on James Madison than on Dolley. Still, readers do learn some interesting facts about her. . . . Adler's writing is clear yet not oversimplified, and is without fictionalization." SLJ

Includes bibliographical references

★ Brown, Don. **Dolley** Madison saves George Washington; written and illustrated by Don Brown. Houghton Mifflin Co. 2007 un il $16

Grades: 1 2 3   **92**

  1. War of 1812 2. Washington (D.C.) 3. Spouses of presidents 4. Presidents' spouses -- United States

  ISBN 978-0-618-41199-3; 0-618-41199-2

                 LC 2006-09813

"While First Lady, [Dolley Madison] redecorated the President's Mansion, ensuring that Gilbert Stuart's portrait of George Washington was prominently displayed. However, it was during the War of 1812 that she earned the gratitude of her nation when, despite the fact that the 100 soldiers assigned to protect the mansion ran off, she bravely remained behind to make sure that the painting as well as important government documents were saved from otherwise certain destruction by British forces. Pen and ink and watercolors effectively depict the simplicity and roughness of Colonial life and convey with humor the spirit of the time and characters." SLJ

Madison, James, 1751-1836

Adler, David A. A **picture** book of Dolley and James Madison; by David A. Adler and Michael S. Adler; illustrated by Ronald Himler. Holiday House 2009 un il $17.95

Grades: 1 2 3   **92**

  1. Presidents 2. Members of Congress 3. Secretaries of state 4. Spouses of presidents 5. Presidents -- United States 6. Presidents' spouses -- United States

  ISBN 978-0-8234-2009-4; 0-8234-2009-4

                 LC 2007041178

"Adler's picture-book biography focuses mainly on the War of 1812, but also mentions Madison's contributions to the Constitution and the creation of the three branches of government. Although this is a biography of the couple, there is more specific information on James Madison than on Dolley. Still, readers do learn some interesting facts about her. . . . Adler's writing is clear yet not oversimplified, and is without fictionalization." SLJ

Includes bibliographical references

Elish, Dan. **James** Madison; [by] Dan Elish. Marshall Cavendish Benchmark 2007 96p il (Presidents and their times) lib bdg $22.95

Grades: 5 6 7 8   **92**

  1. Presidents 2. Members of Congress 3. Secretaries of state 4. Presidents -- United States

  ISBN 978-0-7614-2432-1

                 LC 2006036856

A biography of the fourth president of the United States.

"Primary-source materials and quotes, helpful insets, and carefully selected . . . reproductions bring history to life and help make [this] clearly written [biography] highly readable." SLJ

Includes glossary and bibliographical references

Maiman, Theodore Harold, 1927-2007

Wyckoff, Edwin Brit. **Laser** man; Theodore H. Maiman and his brilliant invention. [by] Edwin Brit Wyck-

off. Enslow Elementary 2008 32p il (Genius at work!: great inventor biographies) lib bdg $20.60

Grades: 4 5 6   **92**

  1. Lasers 2. Engineers 3. Physicists

  ISBN 978-0-7660-2848-7 lib bdg; 0-7660-2848-8 lib bdg

                 LC 2006034680

A biography of Theodore H. Maiman, the engineer who invented the laser

Includes glossary and bibliographical references

Wyckoff, Edwin Brit. The **man** who invented the laser; the genius of Theodore H. Maiman. Edwin Brit Wyckoff. Enslow Elementary 2013 48 p. ill. (some col.) (Genius inventors and their great ideas) (alk. paper) $23.93

Grades: 2 3 4   **92**

  1. Lasers 2. Physicists

  ISBN 0766041387; 9780766041387

                 LC 2012013979

This book, by Edwin Brit Wyckoff, focuses on physicist Theodore H. Maiman, "Maiman . . . found that the accepted calculations of the fluorescence quantum efficiency of ruby were wrong and that the material could be used for his research. His persistence with ruby eventually paid off, for on May 16, 1960, the device he built using it became the world's first operable laser (acronym for light amplification by stimulated emission of radiation)." (Publisher's note)

Includes bibliographical references and index

Malcolm X, 1925-1965

Gunderson, Jessica. **X**: the biography of Malcolm X; illustrated by Seitu Hayden. Graphic Library 2011 32p il (Graphic library: American graphic) lib bdg $29.32; pa $7.95

Grades: 4 5 6 7   **92**

  1. Black Muslims 2. Biographical graphic novels 3. Black Muslim leaders 4. Civil rights activists 5. African Americans -- Biography

  ISBN 978-1-4296-5471-5 lib bdg; 1-4296-5471-6 lib bdg; 978-1-4296-6267-3 pa; 1-4296-6267-0 pa

                 LC 2010037029

In graphic novel format, explores the life and death of Malcolm X.

"The illustrations are eye-catching and the narration is presented simply, yet compellingly. . . . Fact-filled, entertaining, and accessible." SLJ

Includes glossary and bibliographical references

★ Myers, Walter Dean, 1937-2014 **Malcolm** X; a fire burning brightly. illustrated by Leonard Jenkins. HarperCollins Pubs. 2000 un il $15.95

Grades: 3 4 5 6   **92**

  1. Black Muslim leaders 2. Civil rights activists 3. African Americans -- Biography

  ISBN 0-06-027707-6

                 LC 99-21527

"Myers's spare and eloquent narrative makes the complexities of Malcolm X's story accessible without compromising its integrity. The book has appeal for reluctant teen readers as well as younger readers. The sophisticated paintings blend realism with abstraction to heighten the underlying emotional drama of scenes." Horn Book Guide

Mandela, Nelson

Gormley, Beatrice **Nelson** Mandela; South African revolutionary. by Beatrice Gormley. Aladdin 2014 256 p. illustrations (Real-life story) (hardback) $17.99

    Grades: 5 6 7 8   **92**

    1. Presidents -- South Africa -- Biography

    ISBN 1481420593; 9781481420594; 9781481420600

                         LC 2014019020

This book, by Beatrice Gormley, is a "comprehensive biography that tells the complete life story of internationally renowned peacemaker Nelson Mandela. . . . Born in 1918 in South Africa, he grew up in a culture of government-enforced racism and became involved in the anti-apartheid movement at a young age. Deeply committed to nonviolent activism, Mandela directed a peaceful campaign against the racist policies of his South African government, and spent 27 years in prison as a result." (Publisher's note)

"More than a year after his death, the influence of Nelson Mandela is still felt keenly by people around the world. This timely biography provides a complete picture of a complex man...This book is an understandable and multifaceted tribute to an icon of defiance and optimism in the face of tribulation." Booklist

Includes bibliographical references and index

★ Kramer, Ann. **Mandela**; the rebel who led his nation to freedom. National Geographic 2005 63p il (World history biographies) $17.95; lib bdg $27.90

Grades: 4 5 6 7   **92**

    1. Presidents 2. Political prisoners 3. Political leaders 4. Human rights activists 5. Nobel laureates for peace 6. South Africa -- Race relations 7. South Africa -- Politics and government

    ISBN 0-7922-3658-0; 0-7922-3659-9 lib bdg

"This biography introduces readers not only to Mandela, but also to the political turmoil that affected South Africa for over a century. It begins with his birth, and covers his school years, his political ventures, imprisonment, release, presidency, Nobel Peace Prize, and retirement. Full-color photographs appear throughout and a time line runs along the bottom of each spread. . . . the book is well worth purchasing." SLJ

Includes glossary and bibliographical references

★ Mandela, Nelson. **Nelson** Mandela: long walk to freedom; abridged by Chris van Wyk; illustrated by Paddy Bouma. Roaring Book Press 2009 un il $16

Grades: 2 3 4 5   **92**

    1. Presidents 2. Political prisoners 3. Political leaders 4. Human rights activists 5. Nobel laureates for peace 6. South Africa -- Race relations 7. South Africa -- Politics and government

    ISBN 978-1-59643-566-7; 1-59643-566-6

"Abridged from Mandela's 1994 autobiography, this picture book distills the basic facts of his childhood, his education, and the influences that led him to become one of the world's most renowned political activists. In a simple, yet effective manner, he describes the growing system of apartheid, and the unjust treatment of blacks in South Africa is made clear without horrifying details. . . . The writing is clear, providing chronological detail for even young students new to the concept and history of apartheid. Full-page, color paintings accompany the text on every spread and depict crucial moments from the narrative in a way that both complements and enhances the story." SLJ

Mankiller, Wilma

Sonneborn, Liz. **Wilma** Mankiller. Marshall Cavendish Benchmark 2010 112p il (Leading women) $39.93

Grades: 5 6 7 8   **92**

    1. Cherokee Indians 2. Indian chiefs

    ISBN 978-0-7614-4959-1; 0-7614-4959-0

                         LC 2009029399

"The story of Mankiller's lifelong work for the Cherokee Nation and her role as its first female principal chief will absorb readers. The [woman's life is] revealed within the political and historical context of [her] times and [includes] quotes from autobiographical material. . . . Color and black-and-white photos are included. . . . The compact size, chronological organization, and accessible writing [style makes this biography a] good [resource] for reports." SLJ

Manley, Effa, 1900-1981

★ Vernick, Audrey. **She** loved baseball: the Effa Manley story; written by Audrey Vernick; illustrated by Don Tate. Collins 2010 un il

Grades: 1 2 3   **92**

    1. African American athletes 2. Baseball executives 3. Baseball -- Biography 4. African American women -- Biography

    ISBN 0061349208; 9780061349201

This is a picture book biography of Effa Manley, the African American baseball team owner and first and only woman ever inducted into the Baseball Hall of Fame.

"Tate's energetic illustrations harmonize well with Vernick's fresh and engaging text. History favors the individuals in the spotlight: here's an entertaining portrait of a woman who made significant strides behind the scenes." Publ Wkly

Manning, Peyton, 1976-

Wilner, Barry. **Peyton** Manning; a football star who cares. Enslow Publishers, Inc. 2011 48p il (Sport stars who care) lib bdg $23.93; pa $7.95

Grades: 3 4 5   **92**

    1. Football players 2. Football -- Biography

    ISBN 978-0-7660-3774-8 lib bdg; 0-7660-3774-6 lib bdg; 978-1-59845-232-7 pa; 1059845-232-0 pa

                         LC 2010014946

"The text traces Manning's athletic prowess from his playing days in elementary and high school, his successful college career, and, of course, his outstanding professional play, with Manning winning MVP four times. . . . A large typeface, a striking design, and plenty of color photographs will entice readers, even reluctant ones. Stats, a glossary, and suggested resources for learning more complete this attractive package." Booklist

Includes glossary and bibliographical references

Marceau, Marcel, 1923-2007

★ **Monsieur** Marceau; Leda Schubert; illustrated by Gérard DuBois. Roaring Brook Press 2012 p. cm. (reinforced; alk. paper) $17.99

Grades: 2 3 4   **92**

    1. Marceau, Marcel, 1923-2007 2. Mimes -- France

    ISBN 1596435291; 9781596435292

                         LC 2011033798

This book by Leda Schubert, illustrated by Gérard Du-Bois, provides a "picture book biography [of] . . . Marcel Marceau, the world's most famous mime. . . . [Marceau] enthralled audiences around the world for more than fifty years. When he waved his hand or lifted his eyebrow he was able to speak volumes without ever saying a word. But few know the story of the man behind those gestures" (Publisher's note)

Includes bibliographical references and index

Spielman, Gloria. **Marcel** Marceau; master of mime. illustrated by Manon Gauthier. Kar-Ben Pub. 2011 un il lib bdg $17.95
Grades: 3 4 5	92
1. Mime 2. Actors 3. Mimes 4. Jews -- Biography 5. World War, 1939-1945 -- France
ISBN 978-0-7613-3961-8; 0-7613-3961-2
LC 2010027787

"Readers are introduced to the world-famous reviver of the lost art of mime in this attractive and accessible picture-book biography. Melding Marceau's childhood and evolution as an artist with world events, Spielman reveals how the young son of a kosher butcher in Strasbourg, France, pursued his dream, despite the Nazi invasion in 1939. . . . Gauthier's childlike mixed-media illustrations feature myriad rosy-cheeked characters and capture both the whimsy of Marceau's performances and the more somber conditions of war-torn France." SLJ

Marley, Bob
★ Medina, Tony. **I** and I; Bob Marley. illustrated by Jesse Joshua Watson. Lee & Low Books 2009 un il $19.95
Grades: 4 5 6	92
1. Singers 2. Jamaica 3. Reggae musicians
ISBN 978-1-60060-257-3; 1-60060-257-6
LC 2008-33485

"In the words and rhythms of Jamaican patois, Medina's lyrical, direct lines make the most sense when read in tandem with the extensive appended notes. . . . Like the words, Watson's beautifully expressive acrylic paintings evoke a strong sense of Marley's remarkable life and his Caribbean homeland." Booklist

Includes bibliographical references

Martini, Helen, 1912-1994
Lyon, George Ella. **Mother** to tigers; illustrations by Peter Catalanotto. Atheneum Bks. for Young Readers 2003 un il $16.95
Grades: K 1 2 3	92
1. Zoos 2. Zoo directors
ISBN 0-689-84221-X
LC 00-45375

"Lyon's succinct, yet elegant, prose emphasizes Martini's dedication to the animals in her care. . . . Catalanotto's watercolor, charcoal, and torn-paper art is particularly effective here." Booklist

Martínez, Pedro, 1971-
Tavares, Matt. **Growing** up Pedro; Candlewick Press 2015 40 p. illustrations reinforced $16.99
Grades: 2 3 4 5	92
1. Baseball players
ISBN 0763668249; 9780763668242
LC 2014944675

This book, written and illustrated by Matt Tavares, offers the "tale of Dominican pitcher Pedro Martínez, from his days of throwing rocks at mangoes to his years as a major-league star. . . . Pedro loved baseball more than anything, and his older brother Ramon was the best pitcher he'd ever seen. He'd dream of the day he and his brother could play together in the major leagues--and here, Matt Tavares tells the story of how that dream came true." (Publisher's note)

"Tavares traces the career of Pedro Martínez, beginning with his childhood in the Dominican Republic, where he idolized his older brother, Ramón. After Ramón was drafted to play with the Dodgers, Pedro joined the team soon after. Tavares emphasizes how the brothers' careers often ran in concert—both eventually played for the Red Sox and found time to celebrate their team's success back on their childhood turf." Pub Wkly

Includes bibliographical references

Matisse, Henri, 1869-1954
Anholt, Laurence. **Matisse**; the king of color. Barron's 2007 un il $14.99
Grades: 2 3 4 5	92
1. Artists 2. Painters 3. Artists, French
ISBN 0-7641-6047-8

"Anholt tells the story behind Matisse's final masterpiece—Chapelle du Rosaire. During a serious illness, the artist becomes friends with his nurse, Monique, and he draws and paints several pictures of her. When his health improves, she leaves the man who has been like a grandfather to her and joins a strict religious order. Years later, the two friends are reunited when Matisse moves into a villa close to the nunnery. As a final gift for Monique, now Sister Jacques-Marie, he designs a simple chapel for the nuns. . . . The bright and cheerful illustrations draw heavily on Matisse's drawings, paintings, and collages. Facts about the artist's life and style are also skillfully woven into the story and illustrations." SLJ

★ Fillion, Susan. **Miss** Etta and Dr. Claribel; Bringing Matisse to America. David R. Godine 2011 83p il $18.95
Grades: 4 5 6 7	92
1. Artists 2. Painters 3. Physicians 4. Art collectors 5. Art -- Collectors and collecting
ISBN 978-1-56792-434-3; 1-56792-434-4
LC 2010048937

"An affectionate, lively examination of the reciprocal relationship between a great artist and two great art lovers. Etta and Claribel Cone, unmarried sisters from a wealthy Baltimore family . . . [were] discerning collectors of modern art, particularly that of Henri Matisse. . . . Their account is lavishly illustrated in full color by reproductions from the Cone Collection at the Baltimore Museum of Art and Matisse-inflected paintings by the author, who drew extensively on the Cone archive that is also housed at the museum. . . . This appealing work stands as both a portrait of two unconventional women and a celebration of the possibilties of arts patronage." Kirkus

MacLachlan, Patricia, 1938- The **iridescence** of birds; a book about Henri Matisse. Patricia MacLachlan; illustrated by Hadley Hooper. Roaring Brook Press 2014 40 p. color illustrations (hardcover) $17.99

Grades: K 1 2 3 4 **92**
1. Painters -- France -- Biography
ISBN 1596439483; 9781596439481
LC 2013044238

"In two long, lyrical sentences, MacLachlan wonders about the early years of Henri Matisse, who grew up in a cold, gray city in northern France and was warmed by the colors of the paints, fabrics, and birds that surrounded him. Posing her thoughts as questions, MacLachlan distills Matisse's first experiences, assembling them in rough detail to communicate their emotional impact." (Booklist)

"Using relief prints and digital techniques with a decisive and economical rough-edged black line and colors that echo Matisse's evolving palette, Hooper sets the happily involved small boy amongst images that become bolder and brighter as the book progresses while fluidly incorporating the painter's own imagery. It's a spacious and beautiful book." Horn Book

Welton, Jude. **Henri** Matisse. Watts 2002 46p il (Artists in their time) $22; pa $6.95
Grades: 5 6 7 8 **92**
1. Artists 2. Painters 3. Artists, French
ISBN 0-531-12228-X; 0-531-16621-X pa
LC 2002-69106
Discusses the life and career of this French artist, describing and giving examples of his work

This offers a "clear and lively [text]. . . . Captioned, full-color and black-and-white photographs and art reproductions are liberally scattered throughout." SLJ

★ Winter, Jeanette. **Henri's** scissors; by Jeanette Winter. Beach Lane Books 2013 40 p. (hardcover) $16.99
Grades: K 1 2 3 **92**
1. Picture books for children 2. Art -- Technique 3. Matisse, Henri, 1869-1954 4. Artists -- France -- Biography
ISBN 1442464844; 9781442464841; 9781442464858
LC 2012033171
In this children's picture book, after "quickly tracing French painter [Henri] Matisse's journey to becoming an artist ('He was happy, and his paintings made people happy') and explaining how illness left him unable to paint at the end of his life, [Jeanette] Winter . . . describes his discovery of a medium less physically demanding than painting but just as expressive: painted paper and scissors. 'Why didn't I think of it earlier?' he asks delightedly." (Publishers Weekly)

Matzeliger, Jan, 1852-1889
Mitchell, Barbara. **Shoes** for everyone: a story about Jan Matzeliger; illustrations by Hetty Mitchell. Carolrhoda Bks. 1986 63p il (Carolrhoda creative minds book) hardcover o.p. pa $8.95
Grades: 3 4 5 **92**
1. Inventors 2. Shoe industry 3. African American inventors 4. Clothing industry executives
ISBN 0-87614-290-0; 0-87614-473-3 pa
LC 86-4157
A biography of the half-Dutch half-black Surinamese man who, despite the hardships and prejudice he found in his new Massachusetts home, invented a shoe-lasting machine that revolutionized the shoe industry in the late nineteenth century

This is "a compelling story of human endeavor. A clear text blessedly allows the extraordinary individual in focus, Jan Matzeliger, . . . to emerge without undue exclamatory adulation." Bull Cent Child Books

McCloskey, Robert, 1914-2003
McCloskey, Jane. **Robert** McCloskey; a private life in words and pictures. Seapoint Books 2011 il $24.95
Grades: Adult Professional **92**
1. Artists 2. Authors 3. Illustrators 4. Authors, American 5. Children's authors
ISBN 978-0-9786899-6-4; 0-9786899-6-8
In this "biography of the great author/illustrator, his younger daughter reconstructs his life, her recollections nicely complemented by scores of beautifully reproduced illustrations from her father's books as well as photos and never-before-published sketches and paintings. The text is artless in the best sense, not a formal biography but a sequence of significant circumstances and events as Jane observed them." Horn Book

McCoy, Elijah, 1844-1929
Kulling, Monica. **All** aboard!: Elijah McCoy's steam engine; illustrated by Bill Slavin. Tundra Books 2010 un il (Great idea) $17.95
Grades: K 1 2 3 **92**
1. Inventors 2. Railroads 3. African American inventors
ISBN 978-0-88776-945-0; 0-88776-945-4
A picture book biography of the African American inventor of the oil cup, patented in 1872, which continuously greased the engines of steam locomotives.

This is "an engaging biography. . . . Expressive watercolors . . . capture the time period, allowing readers to imagine what life was like in this era, and add energy and touches of humor." SLJ

Meir, Golda, 1898-1978
Blashfield, Jean F. **Golda** Meir. Marshall Cavendish Benchmark 2010 112p il (Leading women) $39.93
Grades: 5 6 7 8 **92**
1. Diplomats 2. Prime ministers 3. Women politicians 4. Cabinet members 5. Israel -- History 6. Jews -- Biography
ISBN 978-0-7614-4960-7; 0-7614-4960-4
"Meir survived pogroms in Russia as a child and became prime minister of Israel. . . . The [woman's life is] revealed within the political and historical context of [her] times and [includes] quotes from autobiographical material. . . . Color and black-and-white photos are included. . . . The compact size, chronological organization, and accessible writing [style makes this biography a] good [resource] for reports." SLJ
Includes bibliographical references

Menchú, Rigoberta
Menchu, Rigoberta. The **girl** from Chimel; [by] Rigoberta Menchú with Dante Liano; pictures by Domi; translated by David Unger. House of Anansi Press 2005 54p il $16.95
Grades: 4 5 6 7 **92**
1. Mayas 2. Guatemala 3. Memoirists 4. Indian leaders 5. Human rights activists 6. Nobel laureates

for peace
ISBN 0-88899-666-7

This is "Menchú's account of her childhood in the small village of Chimel, Guatamala. . . . Short sketches provide glimpses of Menchú's early years; lyrical language and repeated phrases such as 'when I was a girl in Chimel' link the text to oral storytelling. . . . Each chapter sports a vivid oil painting by Domi, featuring thick strokes of bright oranges, purples, greens, and reds and a naive approach that lends a folk-art feel, effectively capturing the action and emotion of the stories." Bull Cent Child Books

Mendel, Gregor, 1822-1884
Bardoe, Cheryl. **Gregor** Mendel; the friar who grew peas. illustrated by Jos. A. Smith. Abrams Books for Young Readers 2006 un il $18.95
Grades: 2 3 4   92
1. Genetics 2. Scientists 3. Geneticists
ISBN 0-8109-5475-3
LC 2005-22957
A picture book biography of the scientist who became known as the father of genetics

"This slim, oversize volume is as much a treat for the eye as it is for the curious mind. Smith's crisp, realistic paintings, often flooded with the bright green of pea plants, accompany Bardoe's readable text." SLJ
Includes bibliographical references

Van Gorp, Lynn. **Gregor** Mendel; genetics pioneer. science contributor, Sally Ride Science. Compass Point Books 2008 40p il (Mission: Science) lib bdg $26.60
Grades: 4 5 6   92
1. Genetics 2. Scientists 3. Geneticists
ISBN 978-0-7565-3963-4 lib bdg; 0-7565-3963-3 lib bdg
LC 2008-07725
A biography of scientist Gregor Mendel, with an introduction to the principles of genetics

This "will entice students to become excited about an assignment or just satisfy their own curiosity. . . . The text . . . does a good job of connecting the scientist's work to our lives today. . . . [The] book has a variety of graphics including diagrams, [and] photos." Libr Media Connect

Merian, Maria Sibylla, 1647-1717
★ Engle, Margarita. **Summer** birds: the butterflies of Maria Merian; pictures by Julie Paschkis. Henry Holt & Co. 2010 un il $16.99
Grades: K 1 2 3   92
1. Artists 2. Painters 3. Zoologists 4. Butterflies 5. Naturalists 6. Caterpillars 7. Illustrators 8. Women artists 9. Women scientists
ISBN 978-0-8050-8937-0; 0-8050-8937-3
LC 2009-05267
"Born in Frankfurt in 1647, Maria Sibylla Merian disagreed with the conventional wisdom . . . that 'summer birds,' or butterflies, were 'beasts of the devil' that sprang alive from the mud . . . . Engle writes in the voice of Maria as a young teen, who carefully watches the slow transformation of caterpillars to winged adults, painting everything that she sees. . . . In expertly pared-down language, the poetic lines deftly fold in basic science concepts about life cycles, along with biographical details that are further developed in an appended historical note. Paschkis' brilliantly colored

and patterned paintings are an exuberant counterpoint to the minimal words." Booklist

Michelangelo Buonarroti, 1475-1564
★ Stanley, Diane. **Michelangelo**. HarperCollins Pubs. 2000 un il $18.99; pa $6.99
Grades: 4 5 6 7   92
1. Artists 2. Painters 3. Sculptors 4. Architects 5. Renaissance 6. Artists, Italian
ISBN 0-688-15085-3; 0-06-052113-9 pa
A biography of the Renaissance sculptor, painter, architect, and poet, well known for his work on the Sistine Chapel in Rome's St. Peter's Cathedral

This is "as readable as it is useful. . . . Integrating Michelangelo's art with Stanley's watercolor, gouache, and colored-pencil figures and settings has the desired effect: readers will be dazzled with the master's ability, while at the same time pulled into his daily life and struggles." SLJ
Includes bibliographical references

Miller, Norma, 1919-
Stompin' at the Savoy; the story of Norma Miller. collected and edited by Alan Govenar; illustrated by Martin French. Candlewick Press 2006 54p il $15.99
Grades: 3 4 5 6   92
1. Dancers 2. African American dancers 3. African American women 4. African American women -- Biography 6. Biography, Individual
ISBN 0-7636-2244-3
LC 2004-57916
This is an autobiography of the African American jazz dancer of the Harlem Renaissance

This "sizzles with spirit and swings with vitality. . . . Miller tells her story with humor and candor. . . . Stylized black-and-white illustrations, produced digitally and in mixed media, nearly swing right off the pages." SLJ

Mohapatra, Jyotirmayee, 1978-
Woog, Adam. **Jyotirmayee** Mohapatra; by Adam Woog. KidHaven Press 2006 48p il $24.95
Grades: 4 5 6 7   92
1. Social action 2. Feminists 3. Women -- India 4. Children's rights advocates
ISBN 0-7377-3611-9
LC 2006009121
"Mohapatra grew up in a rural village in India and became a leader in the fight for the rights of girls and women. . . . The power of one individual to inspire others to action is clearly expressed in this well-written profile. Full-color photos and a map enhance the presentation." SLJ
Includes bibliographical references

Monet, Claude, 1840-1926
Maltbie, P. I. **Claude** Monet; the painter who stopped the trains. illustrated by Jos. A. Smith. Abrams Books for Young Readers 2010 32p il $18.95
Grades: K 1 2 3   92
1. Artists 2. Painters 3. Artists, French 4. Railroads in art
ISBN 978-0-8109-8961-0; 0-8109-8961-1
LC 2009039459
"Inspired by his son's love of trains, Monet decided to show art critics that impressionism could be more than just seascapes. For three months in 1877, he painted on the plat-

form of the Saint-Lazare train station in Paris. . . . Smith expertly illuminates the changing landscape of an evolving world, as Maltbie's thoughtful story of inspiration and imagination highlights a less remembered portion of Monet's work." Publ Wkly

Includes bibliographical references

Monroe, James, 1758-1831

Naden, Corinne J. **James** Monroe; [by] Corinne J. Naden and Rose Blue. Marshall Cavendish Benchmark 2009 96p il map (Presidents and their times) lib bdg $34.21

Grades: 5 6 7 8   **92**

1. Presidents 2. Secretaries of state 3. Presidents -- United States

ISBN 978-0-7614-2838-1 lib bdg; 0-7614-2838-0 lib bdg

LC 2007-29480

"Provides comprehensive information on President James Monroe and places him within his historical and cultural context. Also explored are the formative events of his times and how he responded." Publisher's note

Includes glossary and bibliographical references

Montezuma, Carlos, 1866?-1923

Capaldi, Gina. A **boy** named Beckoning: the true story of Dr. Carlos Montezuma, Native American hero; adapted and illustrated by Gina Capaldi. Carolrhoda Books 2008 32p il lib bdg $16.95

Grades: 2 3 4   **92**

1. Physicians 2. Physicists 3. Indian leaders 4. Native Americans -- Biography

ISBN 978-0-8225-7644-0

LC 2007021745

"Capaldi uses Montezuma's own words to tell this gripping story of a Yavapai boy who was captured by the Pima in 1871 and grew up to become a prominent doctor and Native American spokesperson. Solidly researched, the well-written text follows Wassaja (later renamed Carlos Montezuma) as he was sold into slavery and purchased by a kind Italian photographer. . . . The illustrations are stunning, with multiple perspectives and rich gold and brown tones." SLJ

Includes bibliographical references

Moran, Thomas, 1837-1926

Judge, Lita. **Yellowstone** Moran; painting the American West. Viking 2009 un il $16.99

Grades: K 1 2 3   **92**

1. Artists 2. Painters 3. Engravers 4. West (U.S.) in art 5. Artists -- United States 6. Yellowstone National Park

ISBN 978-0-670-01132-2; 0-670-01132-0

LC 2008049879

"In 1871, American artist Thomas Moran journeyed with a team of geologists through the Rocky Mountains to 'the land called the Yellowstone,' observing and sketching the landscape around him. Judge's watercolor illustrations capture the movement and pristine energy of the wilderness along with the team's arduous journey over rocks, ravines and woods." Publ Wkly

Includes bibliographical references

Morgan, Julia

★ Mannis, Celeste Davidson. **Julia** Morgan built a castle; by Celeste Mannis; illustrated by Miles Hyman. Viking 2006 un il $17.99

Grades: 1 2 3 4   **92**

1. Architects 2. Women architects

ISBN 0-670-05964-1

LC 2004-17401

A picture book biography of "a groundbreaking female architect. Luminescent illustrations, created using soft pastels and pencils in a golden-peach palette, appear to glow with the light of California and France, both seminal locations in Morgan's life. . . . Filled with rich vocabulary, the narrative employs scrumptious architectural terms such as Baroque, flying buttresses, and teakwood cornice." SLJ

Morris, Esther Hobart, 1814-1902

White, Linda. **I** could do that! Esther Morris gets women the vote. [by] Linda Arms White; pictures by Nancy Carpenter. 1st ed; Farrar, Straus and Giroux 2005 32p il

Grades: 2 3 4   **92**

1. Suffragists 2. Women -- Suffrage 3. Justices of the peace

ISBN 0-374-33527-3

LC 2003-51417

In 1869, a woman whose "can-do" attitude had shaped her life was instrumental in making Wyoming the first state to allow women to vote, then became the first woman to hold public office in the United States.

"White's carefully shaped text is amplified by Carpenter's folksy oils, which combine prim, period details and witty exaggerations." Booklist

Includes bibliographical references

Mozart, Maria Anna, 1751-1829

★ Fancher, Lou. **For** the love of music; the remarkable story of Maria Anna Mozart. paintings by Steve Johnson and Lou Fancher. Tricycle Press 2011 un il $16.99; lib bdg $19.99

Grades: 1 2 3   **92**

1. Composers 2. Musicians 3. Music 4. Biography, Individual

ISBN 978-1-58246-326-1; 1-58246-326-3; 978-1-58246-391-9 lib bdg; 1-58246-391-3 lib bdg

"In an intimate tribute to musical prodigy Maria Anna Mozart (sister of Wolfgang Amadeus), Rusch organizes biographical passages into sonata movements, with musical terms used to mark events in Maria's life. . . . Rusch's rich prose and Johnson and Fancher's lavishly detailed collages—melding paint, paper, fabrics, and weathered musical notation—seamlessly blend to form a moving portrait of an unsung musician." Publ Wkly

Includes bibliographical references

Mozart, Wolfgang Amadeus, 1756-1791

★ Fancher, Lou. **For** the love of music; the remarkable story of Maria Anna Mozart. paintings by Steve Johnson and Lou Fancher. Tricycle Press 2011 un il $16.99; lib bdg $19.99

Grades: 1 2 3   **92**

1. Composers 2. Musicians 3. Music 4. Biography, Individual

ISBN 978-1-58246-326-1; 1-58246-326-3; 978-1-58246-391-9 lib bdg; 1-58246-391-3 lib bdg

"In an intimate tribute to musical prodigy Maria Anna Mozart (sister of Wolfgang Amadeus), Rusch organizes biographical passages into sonata movements, with musical terms used to mark events in Maria's life. . . . Rusch's rich prose and Johnson and Fancher's lavishly detailed collages—melding paint, paper, fabrics, and weathered musical notation—seamlessly blend to form a moving portrait of an unsung musician." Publ Wkly

Includes bibliographical references

Riggs, Kate. **Wolfgang** Amadeus Mozart. Creative Education 2009 48p il (Xtraordinary artists) lib bdg $32.80
Grades: 4 5 6 7   92
1. Composers
ISBN 978-1-58341-664-8 lib bdg; 1-58341-664-1 lib bdg
LC 2007008963
This biography of the composer offers an "interesting [layout]; big, high-quality reproductions and photographs on heavy paper; insightful quotes from diverse sources; and meaty selections of the artist's own writing . . . at the end of the book. Readers get a strong sense of [Mozart's] personality along with an excellent survey of his work." SLJ

Includes bibliographical references

Stanley, Diane. **Mozart**, the wonder child; a puppet play in three acts. Collins 2009 un il $17.99; lib bdg $18.89
Grades: 3 4 5   92
1. Composers 2. Puppets and puppet plays
ISBN 978-0-06-072674-4; 0-06-072674-1; 978-0-06-072676-8 lib bdg; 0-06-072676-8 lib bdg
LC 2008-10487
"Stanley takes a look at one of the Western world's most celebrated prodigies, wee Wolfgang Mozart. . . . [Stanley] manages a neat overview of her subject's life in surprisingly few pages. . . . The illustrations treat the proceedings as a marionette show performed by the famous Salzberg Marionettes." Bull Cent Child Books

Includes bibliographical references

Weeks, Marcus. **Mozart**; the boy who changed the world with his music. [by] Marcus Weeks. National Geographic 2007 64p il map (World history biographies) $17.95; lib bdg $27.90
Grades: 5 6 7 8   92
1. Composers
ISBN 978-1-4263-0002-8; 1-4263-0002-6; 978-1-4263-0003-5 lib bdg; 1-4263-0003-4 lib bdg
LC 2006020783
An introduction to the life and music of the composer and musician Mozart.
This "visually appealing [title is] packed with excellent photographs and reproductions, interesting sidebars, and have a time line running along the bottom of every page. . . . [The book is] useful, well-written." SLJ

Includes bibliographical references

Muir, John, 1838-1914

Lasky, Kathryn. **John** Muir; America's first environmentalist. illustrated by Stan Fellows. Candlewick Press 2006 41p il $16.99

Grades: 3 4 5   92
1. Authors 2. Naturalists 3. Writers on nature
ISBN 0-7636-1957-4
This is a biography of the naturalist and author of Stickeen (1909), My First Summer in the Sierra (1911), and The Yosemite (1912). Bibliography. "Intermediate." (Horn Book)
"Lasky's clear prose quotes liberally from diary entries Muir recorded. . . . True to Muir's vision, Fellows' spacious double-page watercolors show the beauty of the wide landscapes in storm and sunshine as well as the tiny details in a single meadow." Booklist

Includes bibliographical references

Wadsworth, Ginger. **Camping** with the president; illustrated by Karen Dugan. Calkins Creek 2009 32p il $16.95
Grades: 3 4 5   92
1. Authors 2. Governors 3. Presidents 4. Naturalists 5. Vice-presidents 6. Environmental movement 7. National parks and reserves 8. Writers on nature 9. Nobel laureates for peace 10. Presidents -- United States 11. Yosemite National Park (Calif.)
ISBN 978-1-59078-497-6; 1-59078-497-9
LC 2008024155
"Inspired by conservationist John Muir's nature essays, President Theodore Roosevelt traveled west, visiting national parks and learing more about their resources. Wadsworth's well written, lively account highlights the pair's 1903 exploration of the Yosemite wilderness, as well as America's early conservation movement, in an accessible and engaging picture book for older readers. Dugan's abundant, intricately rendered watercolors portray the stunning vistas and wildlife and are set against white backgrounds." Booklist

Includes bibliographical references

Murphy, Lizzie, 1894-1964

Queen of the diamond; the Lizzie Murphy story. Emily Arnold McCully. Farrar, Straus & Giroux 2015 32 p. color illustrations (hardback) $17.99
Grades: K 1 2 3 4   92
1. Baseball players 2. Women baseball players -- United States 3. Baseball players -- United States -- Biography
ISBN 0374300070; 9780374300074
LC 2014010987
"Lizzie Murphy was good at baseball. In fact, she was better than most of the boys. But she was born in 1900, and back then baseball was not a game for girls. Lizzie practiced with her brother anyway, and then she talked her way onto the local boys' team, first as a batboy, then as a player." (Publisher's note)
"Realistic drawings in acrylic ink reflect the attire of the times, particularly Murphy in her feminine dresses. The scenes that show her being shunned and then gradually accepted by the boys are particularly well done. The dialogue-heavy narrative and subject matter will easily appeal to readers." SLJ

Includes bibliographical references

Naismith, James, 1861-1939

Wyckoff, Edwin Brit. The **man** who invented basketball; the genius of James Naismith. Edwin Brit Wyckoff. Enslow Elementary 2014 48 p. ill. (some col.), col. map (alk. paper) $23.93

Grades: 2 3 4 **92**

1. Basketball -- History 2. Physicians 3. Game inventors 4. College teachers 5. Basketball coaches

ISBN 0766041425; 9780766041424; 978-0-7660-2846-3 lib bdg; 0-7660-2846-1 lib bdg

LC 2006018655

Genius inventors and their great ideas

This "introduces the man behind one of today's most high-profile sports. . . . Young hoops devotees will enjoy the details of a favorite sport's infancy. . . . Crisp photos, illustrations, and a sidebar featuring Naismith's original 13 rules break up the accessible text." Booklist

Includes glossary and bibliographical references

This book, by Edwin Brit Wyckoff, focuses on James Naismith, a "Canadian-American sports coach and innovator. He invented the sport of basketball in 1891 and is often credited with introducing the first football helmet. He wrote the original basketball rulebook, founded the University of Kansas basketball program, and lived to see basketball adopted as an Olympic . . . sport." (Publisher's note)

Includes bibliographical references and index

Nakahama, Manjirō, 1827-1898

★ Blumberg, Rhoda. **Shipwrecked!**: the true adventures of a Japanese boy. HarperCollins Pubs. 2000 80p il map hardcover o.p. pa $7.99

Grades: 5 6 7 8 **92**

1. Survival after airplane accidents, shipwrecks, etc. 2. Interpreters 3. Japan -- History 4. Japan -- Foreign relations -- United States 5. United States -- Foreign relations -- Japan

ISBN 0-688-17484-1; 0-688-17485-X pa

LC 99-86664

In 1841, rescued by an American whaler after a terrible shipwreck leaves him and his four companions castaways on a remote island, fourteen-year-old Manjiro learns new laws and customs as he becomes the first Japanese person to set foot in the United States

"Exemplary in both her research and writing, Blumberg hooks readers with anecdotes that astonish without sensationalizing, and she uses language that's elegant and challenging, yet always clear. Particularly notable is the well-chosen reproductions of original artwork." Booklist

Includes bibliographical references

Napoleon I, Emperor of the French, 1769-1821

Burleigh, Robert. **Napoleon**; the story of the little corporal. Abrams Books for Young Readers 2007 43p il map $18.95

Grades: 4 5 6 7 **92**

1. Emperors 2. France -- Kings and rulers 3. France -- History -- 1799-1815

ISBN 978-0-8109-1378-3; 0-8109-1378-X

LC 2006-23610

"Burleigh's straightforward style and clear focus make accessible this account of the rapid rise and fall of the skilled military leader and emperor of France. The period artwork, accompanied by helpful captions, enhances the cleanly designed presentation." Horn Book Guide

Neruda, Pablo, 1904-1973

★ Brown, Monica. **Pablo** Neruda; poet of the people. illustrations by Julie Paschkis. Henry Holt and Co. 2011 un il

Grades: PreK **92**

1. Poets 2. Authors 3. Diplomats 4. Novelists 5. Poets, Chilean 6. Nobel laureates for peace 7. Nobel laureates for literature 8. Biography, Individual

ISBN 080509198X; 9780805091984

LC 2010025320

This is a picture-book introduction to the Chilean poet. "Primary, intermediate." (Horn Book)

"This gentle tribute to Chilean poet Neruda explores his formative experiences, from searching for 'beetles and birds' eggs' in the forest to discovering his love for books. . . . Brown and Paschkis paint a compelling portrait of a man who saw the world as a joyful, complex, and beautiful poem waiting to be unveiled." Publ Wkly

Includes bibliographical references

Newton, Isaac Sir, 1642-1727

Hollihan, Kerrie Logan. **Isaac** Newton and physics for kids; his life and ideas with 21 activities. Chicago Review Press 2009 131p il map pa $16.95

Grades: 4 5 6 7 **92**

1. Physicists 2. Scientists 3. Mathematicians 4. Writers on science

ISBN 978-1-55652-778-4 pa; 1-55652-778-0 pa

LC 2008048635

"Hollihan introduces readers to the scientific brilliance, as well as the social isolation, of this giant figure, blending a readable narrative with an attractive format that incorporates maps, diagrams, historical photographs, and physics activities." Booklist

Includes bibliographical references

★ Krull, Kathleen. **Isaac** Newton; illustrated by Boris Kulikov. Viking 2006 126p il (Giants of science) $15.99

Grades: 5 6 7 8 **92**

1. Physicists 2. Scientists 3. Mathematicians 4. Writers on science

ISBN 0-670-05921-8

LC 2005017741

This "profiles Sir Isaac Newton, the secretive, obsessive, and brilliant English scientist who invented calculus, built the first reflecting telescope, developed the modern scientific method, and discerned many of our laws of physics and optics. . . . The lively, conversational style will appeal to readers. . . . Kulikov's humorous pen-and-ink drawings complement the lighthearted text of this fascinating introduction." Booklist

Steele, Philip. **Isaac** Newton; the scientist who changed everything. [by] Philip Steele. National Geographic Society 2007 64p il map (World history biographies) $17.95; lib bdg $27.90

Grades: 4 5 6 7 **92**

1. Physicists 2. Scientists 3. Mathematicians 4. Writers on science

ISBN 978-1-4263-0114-8; 978-1-4263-0115-5 lib bdg

LC 2006020772

"The cradle-to-grave text includes vivid descriptions of Newton's youth. . . . The dynamic format is a draw; numerous mostly archival images . . . and a time-line border add interest and cultural context on each spacious page." Booklist

Includes bibliographical references

Nezahualcóyotl, King of Texcoco, 1402-1472

★ Serrano, Francisco. The **poet** king of Tezcoco; a great leader of Ancient Mexico. illustrated by Pablo Serrano; biography translated and adapted by Trudy Balch; poetry translated by Jo Anne Engelbert. Groundwood Books/House of Anansi Press 2007 35p il $18.95

Grades: 4 5 6 7   92

1. Aztecs 2. Kings 3. Mexico -- History

ISBN 978-0-88899-787-6; 0-88899-787-6

"In the fifteenth century, the land where Mexico City now sprawls was a vast, green kingdom called Tezcoco. This . . . introduces one of Tezcoco's greatest rulers, a Toltec royal named Nezahualcoyotl. . . . The folk-art inspired illustrations echo the area's artistic traditions with beautiful patterning and symbolic imagery and flat , simplified characters reminiscent of hieroglyphics. Groundbreaking in its coverage of exciting history, this book offers details that are rarely presented to young people." Booklist

Nightingale, Florence, 1820-1910

Demi, 1942- **Florence** Nightingale; Demi. Henry Holt and Co 2014 40 p. color illustrations (hardback) $17.99

Grades: 2 3 4 5   92

1. Nurses 2. Nurses -- England -- Biography

ISBN 0805097295; 9780805097290

LC 2013030801

Author Demi presents a "picture book biography of Florence Nightingale [which] portrays the story of Florence's life and explores the long-lasting effects of her career. Nightingale revolutionized the world of medicine by emphasizing cleanliness, food that was hot and nutritious, and organization in hospitals. What began as an attempt to make army hospitals safer and more effective became a lifelong mission, and remains relevant today." (Publisher's note)

"This biography offers a clear, concise telling of Nightingale's story, illustrated with Demi's spare, appealing artwork. Graceful fine-line drawings are warmed with tints of color and graced with patterns where appropriate." Booklist

Includes bibliographical references

Gorrell, Gena K. **Heart** and soul: the story of Florence Nightingale. Tundra Bks. 2000 146p il map hardcover o.p. pa $11.95

Grades: 5 6 7 8   92

1. Nurses 2. Nonfiction writers

ISBN 0-88776-494-0; 0-88776-703-6 pa

A biography of the 19th century English woman known as the founder of modern nursing

"This highly readable and well-researched biography does an excellent job of integrating the social and medical conditions of Nightingale's time. . . . Enlivening the narrative are black-and-white reproductions of drawings . . . and period photographs." SLJ

Includes bibliographical references

Nixon, Richard M. (Richard Milhous), 1913-1994

★ Aronson, Billy. **Richard** M. Nixon; [by] Billy Aronson. Marshall Cavendish Benchmark 2007 96p il (Presidents and their times) lib bdg $22.95

Grades: 5 6 7 8   92

1. Presidents 2. Vice-presidents 3. Senators 4. Nonfiction writers 5. Members of Congress 6.

Presidents -- United States

ISBN 978-0-7614-2428-4

LC 2006013839

Aronson "is able to paint a picture so full that readers will come away feeling that they know the man and understand at least some of the forces that shaped him. . . . The narrative moves chronologically, marching through the war years, Nixon's tenure in Congress and as vice-president, his presidential loss to JFK, his successful efforts to remake himself as a politician, and his years as president. . . . The typeface is clear, the photographs are well chosen." Booklist

Includes glossary and bibliographical references

Noguchi, Isamu, 1904-1988

Hale, Christy. The **East**-West house; Noguchi's childhood in Japan. Lee & Low Books 2009 un il $17.95

Grades: 3 4 5 6   92

1. Artists 2. Sculptors 3. Japanese Americans 4. Industrial designers

ISBN 978-1-60060-363-1; 1-60060-363-7

LC 2008053728

"The mixed-media collage illustrations reflect the blend of East and West. . . . Thoroughly documented and heavily reliant on primary sources. . . . An original and thought-provoking addition to biography or art collections." SLJ

"A biography of Isamu Noguchi, Japanese American artist, sculptor, and landscape architect, focusing on his boyhood in Japan, his mixed heritage, and his participation in designing and building a home that fused Eastern and Western influences. Includes an afterword about Noguchi's adult life and works, plus photographs." Publisher's note

Nuñez Cabeza de Vaca, Alvar, 16th cent.

Lourie, Peter. **On** the Texas trail of Cabeza de Vaca; 1st ed.; Boyds Mills Press 2008 48p il map $17.95

Grades: 4 5 6 7   92

1. Explorers 2. Historians 3. Travel writers 4. Texas -- History 5. Mexico -- History 6. Government officials 7. America -- Exploration 8. Colonial administrators

ISBN 978-1-59078-492-1; 1-59078-492-8

LC 2007049180

"In 1527, Governor Pánfilo de Narváez sailed westward from Spain to explore the land that stretched between present-day Florida and Mexico, colonizing and conquering. With him, as his treasurer and sheriff, was Cabeza de Vaca. . . . He [returned] with a wealth of information, codified in La Relación , his account of his experience. Then, 475 years later, Lourie set out to follow Cabeza de Vaca's trail through Texas. . . . This well-researched, beautifully composed book is the result. Using primary sources and period reproductions as well as the author's experiences and contemporary pictures, it highlights historical information within the context of current circumstances. Beautifully placed photos, reproductions, maps, and sidebars enhance the fluid text." SLJ

Includes bibliographical references

O'Keeffe, Georgia, 1887-1986

Bryant, Jennifer. **Georgia's** bones; [illustrated by] Bethanne Anderson. Eerdmans Books for Young Readers 2005 32p il $16

Grades: K 1 2 3   92

1. Artists 2. Painters 3. Women artists 4. Artists

-- United States
ISBN 0-8028-5217-3

LC 2004-6800

Artist Georgia O'Keeffe was interested in the shapes she saw around her, from her childhood on a Wisconsin farm to her adult life in New York City and New Mexico

"Bryant writes in spare, lyrical verse, honoring her subject's idiosyncratic impressions and precise observation of the natural world. . . . Cow skulls, southwestern landscapes, and oversize flowers are present and accounted for, but the swooping brushstrokes and earthy textures are unmistakably Andersen's own." Booklist

Rodriguez, Rachel. **Through** Georgia's eyes; illustrated by Julie Paschkis. Henry Holt and Co. 2006 un il $16.95
Grades: K 1 2 3   **92**
1. Artists 2. Painters 3. Women artists 4. Artists -- United States
ISBN 978-0-8050-7740-7; 0-8050-7740-5

LC 2005012479

"Rodríguez gently tells this inspirational artist's story . . . with quiet simplicity. . . . Using short, strong sentences and phrases, the author emphasizes the artist's creative force. Paschkis extends the words with the visual simplicity of colorful, cut-paper collages." SLJ

Winter, Jeanette. **My** name is Georgia; a portrait. Harcourt Brace & Co. 1998 un il $16; pa $7
Grades: K 1 2 3   **92**
1. Artists 2. Painters 3. Women artists 4. Artists -- United States
ISBN 0-15-201649-X; 0-15-204597-X pa

LC 97-7087

This book on Georgia O'Keeffe "follows the artist's journey from home to school in Chicago, to New York, to Texas, and back to New York, . . . and finally to New Mexico. . . . Ages nine to twelve." (Horn Book)

"Winter mirrors the artist's stark imagery and strong personality in spare, poetic text and folk art—inspired illustrations." Publ Wkly

Includes bibliographical references

Oakley, Annie, 1860-1926

Wills, Charles A. **Annie** Oakley; a photographic story of a life; [by] Chuck Wills. DK Pub. 2007 128p il (DK biography) $14.99
Grades: 4 5 6 7   **92**
1. Entertainers 2. Marksmen
ISBN 978-0-7566-2986-1

A biography of the sharp-shooter in Buffalo Bill's Wild West Show, from her humble Quaker heritage, her childhood filled with poverty and abuse, to her rise to international fame.

"This highly readable book has a rich layout of photographs and illustrations on every spread." SLJ

Obama, Barack, 1961-

Abramson, Jill. **Obama**; the historic journey. Young reader's ed.; Callaway 2009 94p il map $24.95
Grades: 5 6 7 8   **92**
1. Lawyers 2. Presidents 3. Racially mixed people 4. Senators 5. State legislators 6. Nobel laureates for peace 7. Presidents -- United States 8. African

Americans -- Biography
ISBN 978-0-670-01208-4; 0-670-01208-4

LC 2009-5051

"This scaled down, teen-friendly version of The New York Times's adult biography is geared for middle school students. Containing many of the same photos, it provides a brief overview of the President's life, information that has been revealed over the election year and during his administration. . . . Its allure is in the many photographs with captions, sidebars, speech quotes, and charts. The book is nicely organized. The writing is direct and simple, explaining things such as convention delegates. . . . The book should entice young readers to explore his life further." Voice Youth Advocates

Feinstein, Stephen. **Barack** Obama. Enslow Publishers 2008 24p il map por (African-American heroes) lib bdg $21.26
Grades: K 1 2 3   **92**
1. Lawyers 2. Presidents 3. Racially mixed people 4. Senators 5. State legislators 6. Nobel laureates for peace 7. Presidents -- United States 8. African Americans -- Biography
ISBN 978-0-7660-2893-7 lib bdg; 0-7660-2893-3 lib bdg

LC 2007036363

This is a "slim introduction to the [president] that begins with his childhood in Hawaii and Indonesia. Feinstein's upbeat text, divided into very short chapters, focuses on details that will capture kids' interest." Booklist

Includes bibliographical references

Grimes, Nikki. **Barack** Obama; son of promise, child of hope. illustrated by Bryan Collier. Simon & Schuster Books for Young Readers 2008 un il $16.99
Grades: 1 2 3 4   **92**
1. Lawyers 2. Presidents 3. Racially mixed people 4. Senators 5. State legislators 6. Nobel laureates for peace 7. Presidents -- United States 8. African Americans -- Biography
ISBN 978-1-4169-7144-3; 1-4169-7144-0

LC 2008-06245

Who Obama "is and where he comes from is conveyed in beautifully poetic language [and] . . . the illustrator's impressive interpretation of the author's text takes the story to a more meaningful visual level for younger readers." Libr Media Connect

Includes bibliographical references

Kesselring, Susan. **Barack** Obama. Child's World 2010 24p il (Basic biographies) lib bdg $22.79
Grades: K 1 2   **92**
1. Lawyers 2. Presidents 3. Racially mixed people 4. Senators 5. State legislators 6. Nobel laureates for peace 7. Presidents -- United States 8. African Americans -- Biography
ISBN 978-1-60253-339-4; 1-60253-339-3

LC 2009029365

This "provides a clear description of the man's life before and during his presidency and outlines some of his duties, without delving into politics. The books' clear and relevant black-and-white and color photographs sport captions that aid understanding of the subject matter." SLJ

Includes bibliographical references

Weatherford, Carole Boston. **Obama**; only in America. illustrated by Robert Barrett. Marshall Cavendish Children 2010 un il $17.99

Grades: 2 3 4 5 **92**

1. Lawyers 2. Presidents 3. Racially mixed people 4. Senators 5. State legislators 6. Nobel laureates for peace 7. Presidents -- United States 8. African Americans -- Biography

ISBN 978-0-7614-5641-4; 0-7614-5641-4

LC 2009006338

"Weatherford puts an amazing amount of information about Barack Obama into a rhythmic text that is also wonderfully concise. Most of the major moments of Obama's life are here, both personal and professional. . . . The book makes Obama seem both larger than life yet also someone beset with struggles with which readers can identify. . . . Barrett's illustrations, oils on canvas, add a soft focus to the events." Booklist

Obama, Michelle

Brophy, David. **Michelle** Obama; meet the First Lady. by David Bergen Brophy. HarperCollins 2009 114p il $16.99; pa $6.99

Grades: 5 6 7 8 **92**

1. Lawyers 2. Spouses of presidents 3. Hospital administrators 4. African American women -- Biography 5. Presidents' spouses -- United States

ISBN 978-0-06-177991-6; 0-06-177991-1; 978-0-06-177990-9 pa; 0-06-177990-3 pa

A brief biography of Michelle Obama, wife of President Barack Obama

"The author . . . mixes personal data with information about the political process that brought the Obamas to the White House. . . . This biography is a must-have for all school libraries." Voice Youth Advocates

Includes glossary

Colbert, David. **Michelle** Obama; an American story. Houghton Mifflin Harcourt 2009 151p il $16

Grades: 5 6 7 8 **92**

1. Lawyers 2. Spouses of presidents 3. Hospital administrators 4. African American women -- Biography 5. Presidents' spouses -- United States

ISBN 978-0-547-24941-4; 0-547-24941-1

This biography delves into "the subject of The First Lady's family roots. . . . It offers a strong sense of who Obama was as a child, her solid upbringing, and her adult choices, all bolstered with numerous quotes from Obama and those who know her best. . . . Two sections of color photos and appended source notes for direct quotes complete this timely, highly readable biography." Booklist

Hopkinson, Deborah. **Michelle**; illustrated by A.G. Ford. Katherine Tegen Books 2009 un il $17.99; lib bdg $18.89

Grades: K 1 2 3 **92**

1. Lawyers 2. Spouses of presidents 3. Hospital administrators 4. African American women --

Biography 5. Presidents' spouses -- United States

ISBN 978-0-06-182739-6; 0-06-182739-8; 978-0-06-182743-3 lib bdg; 0-06-182743-6 lib bdg

LC 2009014551

This biography of the First Lady "touches on Michelle's childhood years in a loving working-class family, her academic accomplishments, courtship, marriage, careers and role as devoted mother and active supporter of her husband's presidential campaign. The straightforward, accessible text at times assumes dramatic overtones. . . . Ford's paintings offer likenesses of Michelle and her family, often capturing facial expressions and nuances of posture and gesture with uncanny realism. This warm, respectful portrait succeeds in presenting its subject as both inspirational and relatable." Publ Wkly

Kesselring, Susan. **Michelle** Obama. Child's World 2010 24p il (Basic biographies) lib bdg $22.79

Grades: PreK K 1 **92**

1. Lawyers 2. Spouses of presidents 3. Hospital administrators 4. African American women -- Biography 5. Presidents' spouses -- United States

ISBN 978-1-60253-343-1; 1-60253-343-1

LC 2009029597

This biography of the First Lady "pairs intelligent, brief text with abundant photos. Simple but never basic." Booklist

Includes bibliographical references

Odetta, 1930-2008

Alcorn, Stephen. **Odetta,** the queen of folk; poem by Samantha Thornhill; conceived and illustrated by Stephen Alcorn. Scholastic Press 2010 un il

Grades: K 1 2 3 **92**

1. Singers 2. Folk music 3. Folk musicians 4. African American women -- Biography

ISBN 0-439-92818-4; 978-0-439-92818-2

LC 2009-5104

"Thornhill's poem pays powerful tribute to the folk-singing legend, beginning with early experiences that shaped her music . . . and her first exposure to segregation when her family moved to Los Angeles. . . . Filled with stars, candles, lightning bolts, music notes, and angels, Alcorn's rousing compositions borrow from folk art traditions, religious imagery, graphic design, and 1960s album cover art, creating a rich tapestry that trumpets the power of this singular figure." Publ Wkly

Ohr, George E.

Greenberg, Jan. The **mad** potter; George E. Ohr, eccentric genius. Jan Greenberg and Sandra Jordan. Roaring Brook Press 2013 56 p. (hardcover: alk. paper) $17.99

Grades: 4 5 6 7 8 **92**

1. American pottery 2. Potters -- United States -- Biography 3. Art pottery, American -- Mississippi -- Biloxi

ISBN 159643810X; 9781596438101

LC 2012047601

Robert F. Sibert Honor Book (2014)

This children's book is a biography of American potter George E. Ohr. "Ohr's eccentricities and his penchant for self-promotion are clearly presented. . . . What makes a George E. Ohr vase sell at auction nowadays for $84,000, and is he really America's greatest art potter? Certainly his work is whimsical . . . vases tilting like leaning towers, a teapot with a spout like an open-mouthed serpent, and all manner of wrinkled, twisted and squashed vessels." (Kirkus Reviews)

Includes bibliographical references and index

Paganini, Nicolò, 1782-1840

Frisch, Aaron. **Dark** fiddler: the life and legend of Nicolo Paganini; [by] Aaron Frisch; illustrated by Gary Kelley. Creative Editions 2008 un il lib bdg $17.95

Grades: 3 4 5 6   92

1. Composers 2. Violinists

ISBN 978-1-56846-200-4 lib bdg; 1-56846-200-X lib bdg

"Readers may not be familiar with the name Paganini, but after one look at the dramatic cover, with the spectral violinist staring back, a slight smile on his lips, they will want to find out more. . . . The folksy tone of the narrative will draw kids close as the story of Paganini's life unfolds. All this is set against breathtaking, chalklike art." Booklist

Paige, Satchel, 1906-1982

★ Adler, David A. **Satchel** Paige; don't look back. written by David A. Adler; illustrated by Terry Widener. Harcourt 2006 un il $16

Grades: K 1 2 3   92

1. Baseball players 2. African American athletes 3. Baseball -- Biography

ISBN 978-0-15-205585-1; 0-15-205585-1

LC 2005026354

A brief illustrated biography of the baseball player who, after a long career in the Negro Leagues, joined the Cleveland Indians and became the first African American to pitch in the World Series.

"Widener's acrylic paintings elongate and exaggerate the figures, using a rubbery perspective and old-fashioned hues to great effect." Booklist

Includes bibliographical references

Palmer, Joseph, 1791-1875

Hyatt, Patricia Rusch. The **quite** contrary man; a true American tale. illustrated by Kathryn Brown. Abrams Books for Young Readers 2010 un il $16.95

Grades: K 1 2 3   92

1. Beards 2. Social reformers 3. New England -- History

ISBN 978-0-8109-4065-9; 0-8109-4065-5

LC 2009052211

In nineteenth century New England, Joseph Palmer flouts the law against wearing a beard and is accused by his fellow citizens of being unpatriotic and sinful, stubbornly refusing to shave even when he is sent to jail.

"Although these are serious themes, this picture book offers a positive story with a happy ending, and much of the tone is due to Brown's pleasant and well-designed illustrations in pen and ink and watercolor, which set the scenes helpfully and support the folksy language." Booklist

Park, Linda Sue, 1960-

Parker-Rock, Michelle. **Linda** Sue Park; an author kids love. Enslow Publishers 2009 48p il (Authors kids love) lib bdg $23.93

Grades: 3 4 5   92

1. Authors 2. Authors, American 3. Children's authors

ISBN 978-0-7660-3158-6 lib bdg; 0-7660-3158-6 lib bdg

LC 2008-44549

"Clearly written, [this] outstanding [biography provides] many interesting details about the [subject's] personal [life] and [includes] photos that enhance the [text]." SLJ

Includes glossary and bibliographical references

Parkhurst, Charley, 1812-1879

Kay, Verla. **Rough,** tough Charley; by Verla Kay; illustrated by Adam Gustavson. Tricycle Press 2007 un il $15.95

Grades: K 1 2 3   92

1. Male impersonators 2. Coach drivers 3. Women -- West (U.S.) 4. Frontier and pioneer life -- California

ISBN 978-1-58246-184-7; 1-58246-184-8

LC 2006026611

"Many folks thought they knew the real Charley Parkhurst (1812-1879): a scrappy orphan . . . who became one of the bravest, fastest, saltiest and most respected stagecoach drivers in Gold Country. . . . But everybody had Charley wrong, for . . . Charley had successfully disguised the fact that he was actually a woman. . . . Gustavson's . . . lush, realistic oil illustrations are a lavish counterpoint to Kay's spare verse, [and] are suffused with the romance and roughness of a bygone era." Publ Wkly

Parks, Gordon, 1912-2006

★ Weatherford, Carole Boston; **Gordon** Parks; how the photographer captured black and white America. illustrations by Jamey Christoph. Albert Whitman & Co. 2015 32 p. color illustrations $16.99

Grades: 1 2 3 4   92

1. Photography 2. African Americans -- Civil rights 3. African American photographers -- Biography 4. Photographers -- United States -- Biography

ISBN 0807530174; 9780807530177

LC 2014034300

This book by Carole Boston Weatherford, illustrated by Jamey Christoph, profiles "Gordon Parks . . . , most famous for being the first black director in Hollywood. But before he made movies and wrote books, he was a poor African American looking for work. When he bought a camera, his life changed forever. . . . Gordon wanted to take a stand against the racism he observed. With his camera in hand, he found a way." (Publisher's note)

"Weatherford writes in the present tense with intensity, carefully choosing words that concisely evoke the man. Christoph's digitally rendered illustrations brilliantly present Parks' world thr ough strong linear images and montages of his photographs." Kirkus

Parks, Rosa, 1913-2005

Amoroso, Cynthia. **Rosa** Parks; by Cynthia Amoroso and Robert B. Noyed. Child's World 2010 24p il (Basic biographies) lib bdg $22.79

Grades: PreK K 1   92

1. Civil rights activists 2. African Americans -- Civil rights 3. African American women -- Biography 4. Montgomery (Ala.) -- Race relations

ISBN 978-1-60253-344-8; 1-60253-344-X

LC 2009029372

This biography of Rosa Parks "pairs intelligent, brief text with adundant photos. Simple but never basic." Booklist

Includes bibliographical references

★ Giovanni, Nikki, 1943- Rosa; illustrated by Bryan Collier. Henry Holt 2005 32p il $16.95

Grades: 3 4 5   92

1. African American women 2. Civil rights activists 3. African Americans -- Civil rights 4. African American

ISBN 0-8050-7106-7

A Caldecott Medal honor book, 2006

This book tells the story of Rosa Parks's "refusal to yield her seat to a white bus rider and that act's direct connection with the Montgomery bus boycott. . . . Ages six to nine." (Bull Cent Child Books)

"Paired very effectively with Giovanni's passionate, direct words, Collier's large watercolor-and-collage illustrations depict Parks as an inspiring force that radiates golden light, and also as part of a dynamic activist community." Booklist

Pasteur, Louis, 1822-1895

Zamosky, Lisa. Louis Pasteur; founder of microbiology. Compass Point Books 2009 40p il map (Mission: Science) lib bdg $26.60

Grades: 4 5 6   92

1. Chemists 2. Scientists 3. Microbiologists 4. Writers on science

ISBN 978-0-7565-3962-7

LC 2008007726

This biography of the father of microbiology "does a good job of connecting the scientist's work to our lives today. . . . [The] book has a variety of graphics including diagrams, photos, and reproductions of paintings and sketches. [This volume is] a definite plus for a school library or the juvenile collection in a public library." Libr Media Connect

Includes glossary and bibliographical references

Patch, Sam, 1807-1829

Cummins, Julie. Sam Patch; daredevil jumper. [illustrated by Michael Allen Austin] Holiday House 2009 un il $16.95

Grades: PreK K 1 2   92

1. Stunt performers 2. Factory workers

ISBN 978-0-8234-1741-4; 0-8234-1741-7

LC 2007-34624

This "chronicles the short life of early-19th-century stuntman Sam Patch. . . . The conversational style briskly moves the tale from Sam's childhood jumping exploits to the showstopping stunts of his brief but world-famous career. . . . Austin's . . . . sepia-infused acrylics set a tone alternating between whimsical and haunting. The dynamic illustrations make exaggerated use of light and perspective." Publ Wkly

Patrick, Saint, 373?-463?

DePaola, Tomie, 1934- Patrick: patron saint of Ireland. Holiday House 1992 un il lib bdg $16.95; pa $6.95

Grades: K 1 2 3   92

1. Saints 2. Christian saints 3. Missionaries

ISBN 0-8234-0924-4 lib bdg; 0-8234-1077-3 pa

LC 91-19417

Relates the life and legends of Patrick, the patron saint of Ireland

"The combination of book design, text, and illustration is suitably reverent but never saccharine; the whole is a well-executed treatment of an appealing subject." Horn Book

Paul, Les, 1915-2009

Wyckoff, Edwin Brit. Electric guitar man: the genius of Les Paul; [by] Edwin Brit Wyckoff. Enslow Elementary 2008 32p il (Genius at work!: great inventor biographies) lib bdg $22.60

Grades: 4 5 6   92

1. Inventors 2. Guitarists

ISBN 978-0-7660-2847-0 lib bdg; 0-7660-2847-X lib bdg

LC 2006034681

"Without the electronic guitar invented by Les Paul, music would never have been the same. In this biography of Paul's life and career, Edwin Brit Wyckoff shares how the rambunctious boy from Waukesha, Wisconsin, was propelled to stardom by his unrivaled playing ability and technological prowess." Publisher's note

Includes glossary and bibliographical references

Pavlov, Ivan Petrovich, 1849-1936

Saunders, Barbara R. Ivan Pavlov; exploring the mysteries of behavior. Enslow Publishers 2006 112p il por (Great minds of science) lib bdg $31.93

Grades: 5 6 7 8   92

1. Scientists 2. Behaviorism 3. Physiologists 4. Writers on medicine 5. Nobel laureates for physiology or medicine

ISBN 0-7660-2506-3

LC 2005031648

This is a biography of Russian scientist Ivan Pavlov, best known for his experiments with dogs, which were key to the development of behaviorism, and who won the 1904 Nobel Prize for his research on digestion

"The accessible [text has] an inviting, open format and [offers] many anecdotes. . . . Good-quality photos and illustrations complement the [narrative]." SLJ

Includes glossary and bibliographical references

Peary, Marie Ahnighito, 1893-1978

Kirkpatrick, Katherine A. Snow baby; the Arctic childhood of Admiral Robert E. Peary's daring daughter. [by] Katherine Kirkpatrick. Holiday House 2007 50p il map $16.95

Grades: 5 6 7 8   92

1. Admirals 2. Explorers 3. Arctic regions 4. Children of prominent persons

ISBN 978-0-8234-1973-9; 0-8234-1973-8

LC 2006-02016

"Born north of the Arctic Circle in 1893, Marie Ahnighito Peary published her own version of her youth in 1934 (The Snowbaby's Own Story), on which this book is based. Kirkpatrick's engaging text captures the girl's adventurous spirit and the opportunities that her father's life as an explorer presented, as well as her love of the North and her Inuit friends." SLJ

Peary, Robert Edwin, 1856-1920

Kirkpatrick, Katherine A. Snow baby; the Arctic childhood of Admiral Robert E. Peary's daring daughter. [by] Katherine Kirkpatrick. Holiday House 2007 50p il map $16.95

Grades: 5 6 7 8 **92**

1. Admirals 2. Explorers 3. Arctic regions 4. Children of prominent persons

ISBN 978-0-8234-1973-9; 0-8234-1973-8

LC 2006-02016

"Born north of the Arctic Circle in 1893, Marie Ahnighito Peary published her own version of her youth in 1934 (The Snowbaby's Own Story), on which this book is based. Kirkpatrick's engaging text captures the girl's adventurous spirit and the opportunities that her father's life as an explorer presented, as well as her love of the North and her Inuit friends." SLJ

Pelé, 1940-

★ Cline-Ransome, Lesa. **Young** Pele; soccer's first star. illustrated by James E. Ransome. Schwartz & Wade Bks. 2007 un il

Grades: K 1 2 3 **92**

1. Soccer players 2. Soccer -- Biography 3. Soccer 4. Biography, Individual

ISBN 0-375-83599-7; 0-375-93599-1 lib bdg; 978-0-375-83599-5; 978-0-375-93599-2 lib bdg

This is a biography of the soccer player and author of My Life and the Beautiful Game (1977). "Primary." (Horn Book)

"With handsome oil paintings and a stirring story, this picture-book biography will first grab children with its action. Just as exciting, though, is the account of Brazilian-born Pelé's personal struggle—his amazing rise from poverty to international soccer stardom." Booklist

Pele. **For** the love of soccer! illustrated by Frank Morrison. Disney-Hyperion Books 2010 un il $16.99

Grades: K 1 2 3 **92**

1. Soccer 2. Athletes 3. Soccer players

ISBN 978-1-4231-1538-0; 1-4231-1538-4

LC 2009-15890

"In a spare narrative enlivened by typography of various sizes and colors, soccer legend Pele underscores his lifelong passion for soccer. . . . Following two time lines simultaneously, Morrison's . . . energetic, fluid paintings spotlight Pele's soccer moves beside those of a young player today. . . . Though the narrative links the two players throughout, a warmhearted ending ties their stories together visually, as Pele signs a ball for the boy." Publ Wkly

Penrose, Antony

Penrose, Antony. The **boy** who bit Picasso. Abrams Books for Young Readers 2011 47p il $16.95

Grades: 3 4 5 **92**

1. Artists 2. Painters 3. Artists, French 4. Archivists 5. Children of prominent persons

ISBN 978-0-8109-9728-8; 0-8109-9728-2

LC 2010009444

Presents a story of Tony, the son of photographer Lee Miller and painter-writer Sir Roland Penrose, who shares his childhood memories of his special friend—a world-famous artist by the name of Pablo Picasso.

"Numerous b&w photographs appear, along with original drawings by contemporary children. Reproductions of Picasso's works demonstrate the influence Penrose's family had on Picasso's art. . . . It's a fascinating and highly personal vision of the artist." Publ Wkly

Perón, Eva, 1919-1952

Favor, Lesli J. **Eva** Peron. Marshall Cavendish Benchmark 2010 112p il (Leading women) $39.93

Grades: 5 6 7 8 **92**

1. Women politicians 2. Argentina -- History 3. Spouses of presidents

ISBN 978-0-7614-4962-1; 0-7614-4962-0

A biography of the influential and admired First Lady of Argentina.

Includes bibliographical references

Peterson, Adrian

Sandler, Michael. **Adrian** Peterson. Bearport Pub. 2010 24p il map (Football heroes making a difference) lib bdg $22.61

Grades: 2 3 4 **92**

1. Football players 2. Football -- Biography

ISBN 978-1-936087-59-4 lib bdg; 1-936087-59-6 lib bdg

LC 2009033352

Looks at the life and accomplishments of the star running back of the Minnesota Vikings.

Includes glossary and bibliographical references

Peterson, Roger Tory, 1908-1996

Thomas, Peggy. **For** the birds: the life of Roger Tory Peterson; illustrated by Laura Jacques. Calkins Creek 2011 il $16.95

Grades: 2 3 4 5 **92**

1. Birds 2. Artists 3. Naturalists 4. Illustrators 5. Ornithologists 6. Writers on nature 7. Artists -- United States

ISBN 978-1-59078-764-9; 1-59078-764-1

"Intrigued from childhood by the wildlife around him, Roger Tory Peterson grew up to publish, in 1934, the first pocket-sized bird guide. . . . Using language and imagery relevant to her topic, Thomas . . . provides a lively chronological narrative. . . . Jacques' hyper-realistic mixed-media paintings have sharp edges and blended shadows, giving the appearance of acylics and collage digitally combined. . . . An excellent addition to the 'sense of wonder' shelf." Kirkus

Phelps, Michael, 1985-

Torsiello, David P. **Michael** Phelps; swimming for Olympic gold. Enslow Publishers 2009 48p il (Hot celebrity biographies) lib bdg $23.93

Grades: 2 3 4 **92**

1. Athletes 2. Swimming 3. Swimmers 4. Olympic athletes

ISBN 978-0-7660-3591-1 lib bdg; 0-7660-3591-3 lib bdg

LC 2008-48700

"Quality design, including an interesting color palette, distinguishes [this profile] . . . [which] is illustrated with large, recent color photos. The tone is light but not breathless; the writing is solid." SLJ

Includes glossary

Picasso, Pablo, 1881-1973

Jacobson, Rick. **Picasso**; soul on fire. [by] Rick Jacobson; illustrated by Laura Fernandez & Rick Jacobson. Tundra Books 2004 un il $15.95; pa $8.95

Grades: 3 4 5   **92**
1. Artists 2. Painters 3. Artists, French
ISBN 978-0-88776-599-5; 0-88776-599-8; 978-1-
77049-263-9 pa; 1-77049-263-1 pa
This is an introduction the life of the artist, exploring his
influences, selected works, and his creative processes.
"Written in simple, clear language.... The softly radiant
oil paintings are mostly full page and enhance the enjoyment of the book. . . . This eloquent tribute will serve as an
introduction to Picasso and to an artist's inspirations." SLJ

Penrose, Antony. The **boy** who bit Picasso. Abrams
Books for Young Readers 2011 47p il $16.95
Grades: 3 4 5   **92**
1. Artists 2. Painters 3. Artists, French 4. Archivists
5. Children of prominent persons
ISBN 978-0-8109-9728-8; 0-8109-9728-2
LC 2010009444
Presents a story of Tony, the son of photographer Lee
Miller and painter-writer Sir Roland Penrose, who shares his
childhood memories of his special friend—a world-famous
artist by the name of Pablo Picasso.
"Numerous b&w photographs appear, along with origi-
nal drawings by contemporary children. Reproductions of
Picasso's works demonstrate the influence Penrose's family
had on Picasso's art. . . . It's a fascinating and highly per-
sonal vision of the artist." Publ Wkly

Pike, Lip, 1845-1893
Michelson, Richard. **Lipman** Pike; America's first
home run king. written by Richard Michelson; illustrated
by Zachary Pullen. Sleeping Bear Press 2011 un il $16.95
Grades: 2 3 4   **92**
1. Baseball players 2. Jews -- Biography 3. Baseball
-- Biography
ISBN 978-1-58536-465-7; 1-58536-465-7
LC 2010032367
This is a picture book biography of Lipman Pike, the
son of Jewish immigrants from Holland, who became, in the
1850s, one of America's first professional baseball players.
"Michelson effortlessly hurtles the story through Lip's
career . . . and baseball fans will be fascinated by the details.
. . . Pullen's unmistakable, big-headed caricatures make this
an ideal companion to Jonah Winter's You Never Heard of
Sandy Koufax?! (2009)." Booklist

Pinchot, Gifford, 1865-1946
Hines, Gary. **Midnight** forests; a story of Gifford Pin-
chot and our national forests. illustrated by Robert Casilla.
Boyds Mills Press 2005 un il $16.95
Grades: 3 4 5   **92**
1. Governors 2. Conservationists 3. Forests and
forestry 4. Foresters
ISBN 1-56397-148-8
LC 2003-26876
"This picture-book biography introduces Gifford Pinchot, a wealthy young American who studied forestry in
France and returned home to put his knowledge to good use
in his own country. Appointed Secretary of Agriculture in
1898, he later joined forces with Theodore Roosevelt to turn
16 million acres into national forests. . . . Mirroring the quiet
prose, the dignified pencil-and-watercolor illustrations depict Pinchot at work and in quiet contemplation." Booklist
Includes bibliographical references

Pippin, Horace, 1888-1946
Venezia, Mike. **Horace** Pippin; written and illustrated
by Mike Venezia. Children's Press 2008 32p il (Getting to
know the world's greatest artists) lib bdg $28
Grades: 3 4 5   **92**
1. Artists 2. Painters 3. African American artists 4.
Artists -- United States
ISBN 978-0-531-18527-8 lib bdg; 0-531-18527-3
lib bdg
LC 2007016127
A biography of the African American artist best known
for his paintings of life in America during slavery and the
years of segregation.
"Though the [text is] simply written, [this title contains]
a wealth of information. . . . [The book has] many reproductions of the [artist's] works as well as those of the masters
who influenced [him]. To help illustrate his points, Venezia
has incorporated his own cartoon-style illustrations." SLJ

Plain, Nancy
This strange wilderness; the life and art of John James
Audubon. Nancy Plain. University of Nebraska Press 2015
136 p. illustrations (chiefly color) (pbk.: alk. paper) $19.95
Grades: 4 5 6 7 8   **92**
1. Bird watching 2. Naturalists -- Biography
3. Naturalists -- United States -- Biography 4.
Ornithologists -- United States -- Biography
ISBN 0803248849; 9780803248847; 9780803284012;
9780803284029; 9780803284036
LC 2014020552
This book, by Nancy Plain, focuses on the founder of
modern ornithology John James Audubon. "His masterpiece, 'The Birds of America' depicts almost five hundred
North American bird species, each image - lifelike and life
size - rendered in vibrant color. . . . Plain brings together the
amazing story of this American icon's career and the beautiful images that are his legacy." (Publisher's note)
"In this insightful biography, Plain demonstrates how
naturalist and artist John James Audubon's groundbreaking
The Birds of America, published in England in 1827, rocked
the art and science worlds through its depictions of birds in
naturalistic poses and in their own habitats...This narrative
of the life of a dedicated and hard-working figure is the story
of an amazing individual and a glimpse into the natural history of the early United States. An excellent addition to science and biography collections." SLJ
Includes bibliographical references and index
Life and art of John James Audubon

Planck, Max, 1858-1947
Weir, Jane. **Max** Planck; revolutionary physicist.
Compass Point Books 2009 40p il (Mission: science) lib
bdg $26.60
Grades: 4 5 6   **92**
1. Physicists 2. Nobel laureates for physics
ISBN 978-0-7565-4073-9 lib bdg; 0-7565-4073-9
lib bdg
LC 2008-37622
Biography of the physicist Max Planck
Includes glossary and bibliographical references

Pocahontas, d. 1617

Brimner, Larry Dane. **Pocahontas**; bridging two worlds. Marshall Cavendish Benchmark 2009 41p il (American heroes) lib bdg $20.95

Grades: 2 3 4 **92**

1. Princesses 2. Powhatan Indians 3. Indian leaders 4. Virginia -- History 5. United States -- History -- 1600-1775, Colonial period

ISBN 978-0-7614-3065-0

This traces the life of Pocahontas from her birth in about 1595 to her death and considers the impact her life had on American history

This "concise and well-written [title covers] key biographical facts without overwhelming young readers, and [includes] captioned illustrations and reproductions, most of which are in color. Text is large, and the layout is age-appropriate and attractive, with wide margins." SLJ

Krull, Kathleen. **Pocahontas**; princess of the New World. [by] Kathleen Krull; pictures by David Diaz. Walker 2007 un il $16.95; lib bdg $17.85

Grades: K 1 2 3 **92**

1. Princesses 2. Powhatan Indians 3. Indian leaders 4. Virginia -- History 5. United States -- History -- 1600-1775, Colonial period

ISBN 978-0-8027-9554-0; 0-8027-9554-4; 978-0-8027-9555-7 lib bdg; 0-8027-9555-2 lib bdg

LC 2006025723

This focuses on "the mischievous girl Matoaka, affectionately nicknamed Pocahontas. Primary sources provide the basic facts. . . . Diaz's cut-paper collage illustrations literally glow with vibrancy. He uses a palette of tropical colors—lemon yellow, lime green, ocean blue, and orange." SLJ

Pokiak-Fenton, Margaret

Jordan-Fenton, Christy. **Fatty** legs; a true story. [by] Christy Jordan-Fenton and Margaret Pokiak-Fenton; artwork by Liz Amini-Holmes. Annick Press 2010 104p il $21.95; pa $12.95

Grades: 3 4 5 6 **92**

1. Inuit 2. Authors 3. Artisans 4. Children's authors 5. Native Americans -- Canada 6. Inuit -- Canada 7. Biography, Individual

ISBN 978-1-55451-247-8; 1-55451-247-6; 978-1-55451-246-1 pa; 1-55451-246-8 pa

This book chronicles the unbreakable spirit of an Inuit girl while attending an Arctic residential school.

"Dark, expressive original paintings are dotted throughout the story and complement the serious tone of the narrative. . . . An excellent addition to any biography collection, the book is fascinating and unique, and yet universal in its message." SLJ

Followed by: A stranger at home (2011)

Jordan-Fenton, Christy. A **stranger** at home; a true story. [by] Christy Jordan-Fenton and Margaret Pokiak-Fenton; artwork by Liz Amini-Holmes. Annick Press 2011 124p il $21.95; pa $12.95

Grades: 3 4 5 6 **92**

1. Inuit 2. Authors 3. Artisans 4. Children's authors 5. Native Americans -- Canada

ISBN 978-1-55451-362-8; 1-55451-362-6; 978-1-55451-361-1 pa; 1-55451-361-8 pa

Sequel to: Fatty legs (2010)

"After two years in Catholic residential school, 10-year-old Olemaun returns to Tuktoyaktuk on Canada's Arctic coast, a stranger to her friends and family, unaccustomed to the food and clothing and unable to speak or understand her native language. Margaret Pokiak's story continues after the events of Fatty Legs (2010), which described her boarding-school experience. In this stand-alone sequel, she describes a year of reintegration into her Inuvialuit world. . . . Olemaun's spirit and determination shine through this moving memoir." Kirkus

Pollock, Jackson, 1912-1956

★ Greenberg, Jan. **Action** Jackson; [by] Jan Greenberg and Sandra Jordan; illustrated by Robert Andrew Parker. Roaring Brook Press 2002 32p il hardcover o.p. pa $6.95

Grades: 3 4 5 6 **92**

1. Artists 2. Painters 3. Artists -- United States

ISBN 0-7613-1682-5; 0-7613-2770-3 lib bdg; 0-312-36751-1 pa

LC 2002-6211

Imagines Jackson Pollock at work during the creation of one of his paint-swirled and splattered canvasses

"Using spare, lyrical words, the authors layer the exciting story with deep observations about what art is and how it is made. . . . Parker's scribbly pen-and-watercolor illustrations get the mood just right; the loose lines have an improvised, energetic quality that echoes Pollock's painting." Booklist

Includes bibliographical references

Polo, Marco, 1254-1323?

Demi. **Marco** Polo; written and illustrated by Demi. Marshall Cavendish 2008 un il map $19.99

Grades: 4 5 6 7 **92**

1. Explorers 2. Travelers 3. Voyages and travels 4. Travel writers

ISBN 978-0-7614-5433-5; 0-7614-5433-0

"This elegant, scholarly picture-book biography brings the explorer's fantastic journey to life. . . . Demi weaves her subject's own accounts into a seamless tale of wonder. . . . The delicately rendered illustrations, painted with Chinese inks and gold overlays . . . capture the exotic beauty of 13th-century China." SLJ

Markle, Sandra. **Animals** Marco Polo saw; an adventure on the Silk Road. illustrated by Daniela Jaglenka Terrazzini. Chronicle Books 2009 45p il $16.99

Grades: 3 4 5 6 **92**

1. Explorers 2. Travelers 3. Voyages and travels 4. Travel writers 5. Animals -- Asia 6. Asia -- Description and travel

ISBN 978-0-8118-5051-3; 0-8118-5051-X

LC 2007053057

"This intriguing book discusses generally agreed-upon details of Marco Polo's explorations in Mongolia and the Far East, and speculates about the moths, jackals, van cats, zebu, oxen, Persian lions, snow cats, and camels he may have met along the way. . . . The text is enhanced by color, mixed-media illustrations that occupy one page or the top half of each spread. . . . A useful introduction to 13th-century history." SLJ

McCarty, Nick. **Marco** Polo; the boy who traveled the medieval world. National Geographic 2006 64p il map (World history biographies) $17.95; lib bdg $27.90
Grades: 5 6 7 8   **92**
1. Explorers 2. Travelers 3. Voyages and travels 4. Travel writers
ISBN 0-7922-5893-2; 0-7922-5894-0 lib bdg

A biography of the Italian explorer who became famous for his travels in Asia

Includes glossary and bibliographical references

Twist, Clint. **Marco** Polo; history's great adventurer. Candlewick Press 2011 un il (Historical notebooks) $19.99
Grades: 5 6 7 8   **92**
1. Explorers 2. Travelers 3. Voyages and travels 4. Travel writers
ISBN 978-0-7636-5286-9; 0-7636-5286-5
LC 2010040131

First published 2010 in the United Kingdom with title: Marco Polo; geographer of distant lands

"In this sumptuous scrapbook, excerpts from Marco Polo's own account of his travels are paired with beautiful maps, drawings, and illustrations. . . . This volume is well suited to browsing, and many readers will want to spend time poring over the many details." SLJ

Powell, Barbara Johns, 1935-1991

Kanefield, Teri, 1960- The **girl** from the tar paper school; Barbara Rose Johns and the advent of the civil rights movement. by Teri Kanefield. Abrams Books for Young Readers 2013 56 p. (alk. paper) $19.95
Grades: 5 6 7 8   **92**
1. Segregation in education 2. African Americans -- Civil rights 3. Civil rights -- United States -- History 4. Civil rights workers -- United States -- Biography 5. Virginia -- Race relations -- History -- 20th century 6. Women civil rights workers -- United States -- Biography 7. Segregation in education -- Virginia -- History -- 20th century 8. Civil rights movements -- United States -- History -- 20th century
ISBN 1419707965; 9781419707964
LC 2012040990

This book, by Teri Kanefield, focuses on "Barbara Rose Johns. . . . In 1951, witnessing the unfair conditions in her racially segregated high school, Barbara Johns led a walkout . . . jumpstarting the American civil rights movement. Ridiculed by the white superintendent and school board . . . Barbara and her classmates held firm and did not give up. Her school's case went all the way to the Supreme Court and helped end segregation as part of Brown v. Board of Education." (Publisher's note)

"A heartfelt tribute to Barbara Rose Johns, a lesser-known heroine of the early civil rights movement. In 1951 Virginia, black Robert R. Moton High School and white Farmville High were separate but definitely not equal, and quiet Barbara and her classmates decided to strike. Profuse details, some extraneous, threaten to overtake the inspiring story of bravery." (Horn Book)

Includes bibliographical references and index

Powell, John Wesley, 1834-1902

★ Ray, Deborah Kogan. **Down** the Colorado; John Wesley Powell, the one-armed explorer. Frances Foster Books/Farrar, Straus & Giroux 2007 un il $17
Grades: 3 4 5   **92**
1. Explorers 2. Geologists 3. West (U.S.) -- Exploration 4. Colorado River (Colo.-Mexico)
ISBN 0-374-31838-7; 978-0-374-31838-3
LC 2006-43994

"This picture-book biography traces the life of explorer John Wesley Powell, whose landmark journey in 1869 down the Colorado River made him a national hero. Each double-page spread combines text on one side describing an episode from Powell's life with a stunning, full-page illustration on the opposite side.. . . An exciting adventure story and an instructive account of the exploration of the West." Booklist

Presley, Elvis, 1935-1977

Christensen, Bonnie. **Elvis**; the story of the rock and roll King. Christy Ottaviano Books 2015 32 p. color illustrations (hardcover) $17.99
Grades: 1 2 3   **92**
1. Singers -- Biography 2. Rock musicians -- United States -- Biography
ISBN 0805094474; 9780805094473
LC 2014024990

"Elvis [Presley] was a shy kid who struggled to make friends and found comfort singing in church and learning guitar. While in high school, he continued his music but was often ridiculed by students. On a whim, he recorded a song for his mom's birthday at Sun Record Studios as part of a customer promotion. The studio loved it so much that they sent it to local record stations . . . and the rest is history." (Publisher's note)

"The inspired choice to use photocollage for the backgrounds imbues the singer's hardscrabble early years with tenderness, suggesting the nostalgia-tinged look of a 1940s postcard. Written in verse, the text is stripped down; refreshingly free of artifice, it's as soulful as one of the many songs the singer performed." SLJ

Includes bibliographical references

Collins, Terry. **Elvis**; a graphic novel. illustrated by Michele Melcher. Capstone Press 2011 32p il (Graphic library: American graphic) lib bdg $29.32; pa $7.95
Grades: 4 5 6 7   **92**
1. Actors 2. Singers 3. Rock musicians 4. Biographical graphic novels
ISBN 978-1-4296-5476-0 lib bdg; 1-4296-5476-7 lib bdg; 978-1-4296-6266-6 pa; 1-4296-6266-2 pa
LC 2010024847

In graphic novel format, explores the life of Elvis Presley and describes his return to stardom through his '68 Comeback Special.

"The illustrations are eye-catching and the narration is presented simply, yet compellingly. . . . Fact-filled, entertaining, and accessible." SLJ

Includes glossary and bibliographical references

Price, Leontyne

Weatherford, Carole Boston. **Leontyne** Price; voice of a century. by Carole Boston Weatherford; illustrated by Raul Colon. Alfred A. Knopf 2014 40 p. color illustrations (hard cover) $17.99

Grades: K 1 2 3   **92**
1. Opera 2. African American singers 3. Sopranos (Singers) -- United States -- Biography
ISBN 0375856064; 9780375856068; 9780375956065; 9780385392464

LC 2013048068

Author Carole Boston Weatherford presents a "picturebook biography of iconic African American opera star Leontyne Price. While racism made it unlikely that a poor black girl from the South would pursue an opera career, Leontyne's wondrous voice and unconquerable spirit prevailed. Leontyne was soon recognized and celebrated for her leading roles at the Metropolitan Opera and around the world." (Publisher's note)

"Weatherford continues to showcase groundbreaking African Americans often overlooked by history books and popular culture. World-famous opera singer Leontyne Price gets her due in this luscious picture book biography... A gorgeous book in the ranks of the author's I, Matthew Henson: Polar Explorer (Walker, 2007) and Becoming Billie Holliday (Boyds Mills, 2008)." SLJ

Quimby, Harriet, 1875-1912

Moss, Marissa. **Brave** Harriet; the first woman to fly the English Channel. illustrated by C.F. Payne. Silver Whistle Bks. 2001 un il $16
Grades: K 1 2 3   **92**
1. Air pilots 2. Women air pilots
ISBN 0-15-202380-1

LC 99-50463

Harriet Quimby, the first American woman to have received a pilot's license, describes her April 1912 solo flight across the English Channel, the first such flight by any woman

"Moss writes effectively in first person, putting readers in touch with Quimby's dreams and determination through direct, vivid language. The mixed media artwork combines paints and pastels in a series of beautiful scenes." Booklist

Whitaker, Suzanne. The **daring** Miss Quimby; by Suzanne George Whitaker; illustrated by Catherine Stock. Holiday House 2009 un il $16.95
Grades: 1 2 3   **92**
1. Air pilots 2. Women air pilots
ISBN 978-0-8234-1996-8; 0-8234-1996-7

LC 2008022569

A biography of Harriet Quimby, who, in 1911 "became the first American woman to earn a pilot's license. . . . Whitaker's spare, engaging narrative and Stock's lively watercolors bring this little-known female adventurer to life." Booklist

Reagan, Ronald, 1911-2004

Burgan, Michael. **Ronald** Reagan; a photographic story of a life. DK Pub. 2011 128p il (DK biography) $14.99; pa $5.99
Grades: 5 6 7 8   **92**
1. Actors 2. Governors 3. Presidents 4. Presidents -- United States
ISBN 978-0-7566-7075-7; 0-7566-7075-6; 978-0-7566-7074-0 pa; 0-7566-7074-8 pa

"Burgan's survey covers the basic facts in a positive but not propagandistic introduction. . . . Featuring small but clear photos or boxed commentary on every page and capped with

a substantial . . . multimedia resource list, this compact volume . . . gives readers a broad picture of his achievements and a sense of his compelling personal style." Booklist
Includes bibliographical references

Marsico, Katie. **Ronald** Reagan. Marshall Cavendish Benchmark 2011 112p il (Presidents and their times) lib bdg $23.95
Grades: 5 6 7 8   **92**
1. Actors 2. Governors 3. Presidents 4. Presidents -- United States
ISBN 978-0-7614-4814-3; 0-7614-4814-4

LC 2009044590

This offers information on President Ronald Reagan and places him within his historical and cultural context. Also explored are the formative events of his times and how he responded.

"The abundant sidebars provide a good deal of background information that will be helpful to students. . . . Attractive . . . as well as useful." Booklist

Includes glossary and bibliographical references

Ream, Vinnie, 1847-1914

★ Fitzgerald, Dawn. **Vinnie** and Abraham; [by] Dawn Fitzgerald; illustrated by Catherine Stock. Charlesbridge 2007 un il lib bdg $15.95
Grades: 2 3 4   **92**
1. Artists 2. Sculptors 3. Women artists
ISBN 978-1-57091-658-8 lib bdg; 1-57091-658-6 lib bdg

LC 2006009033

"This picture-book biography presents Vinnie Ream as a young woman who transcended the conventions of her time through determination and a remarkable talent for sculpture. . . . After Lincoln's assassination, Congress commissioned her to sculpt a marble statue of the late president, which is still on display in the Capital rotunda. Fitzgerald's clearly written narrative portrays Vinnie as a hardworking, resolute person who succeeded through her own gifts and the help of others who believed in her. Stock's watercolor paintings light up the pages." Booklist

Rector, Sarah

Bolden, Tonya. **Searching** for Sarah Rector; the richest black girl in America. Tonya Bolden. Abrams Books for Young Readers 2014 80 p. $21.95
Grades: 4 5 6 7 8   **92**
1. Rich 2. African American women 3. Creek County (Okla.) -- Biography 4. Creek Indians -- Oklahoma -- Creek County -- Biography 5. Women millionaires -- Oklahoma -- Creek County -- Biography 6. Petroleum industry and trade -- Oklahoma -- History -- 20th century 7. African American women -- Oklahoma -- Creek County -- Biography
ISBN 1419708465; 9781419708466

LC 2012039254

Author Tonya Bolden presents a biography of Sarah Rector, who "turned 18 in 1920, [and] the young black woman had amassed a fortune estimated at $1 million. In telling her story, Bolden makes a largely unknown portion of American history accessible to young readers. Rector and her family were 'Creek freedmen,' black citizens of the Creek Indian nation." (School Library Journal)

Includes bibliographical references and index

Reeves, Bass, 1838-1910

★ Nelson, Vaunda Micheaux. **Bad** news for outlaws; the remarkable life of Bass Reeves, deputy U.S. Marshal. illustrations by R. Gregory Christie. Carolrhoda Books 2009 un il lib bdg $17.95

Grades: 3 4 5   92

1. Law enforcement 2. Frontier and pioneer life 3. Oklahoma 4. Sheriffs 5. West (U.S.) -- History 6. African Americans -- Biography 7. Biography, Individual 8. Western States -- History

ISBN 978-0-8225-6764-6 lib bdg; 0-8225-6764-4 lib bdg

LC 2008001188

ALA EMIERT Coretta Scott King Author Award (2010)

This is a biography of Bass Reeves, a former slave who was recruited as a deputy United States Marshal in the area that was to become Oklahoma. Chronology. Glossary. Bibliography. "Grades three to six." (Bull Cent Child Books)

"Kids will have no trouble loping into this picture-book biography. Born a slave, Reeves became one of the most feared and respected Deputy U.S. Marshals to tame the West. . . . The text, especially, gets into the tall-tale spirit of things. . . . An exciting subject captured with narrative panache and visual swagger." Booklist

Reinhardt, Django, 1910-1953

★ Christensen, Bonnie. **Django**. Roaring Brook Press 2009 un il $17.99

Grades: 1 2 3 4   92

1. Guitarists 2. Jazz musicians

ISBN 978-1-59643-422-6; 1-59643-422-8

ALA Schneider Family Book Award (2010)

"Richly expressive paint and ink illustrations portray the hard-earned successes of Django Reinhardt, whose childhood was spent traveling with his impoverished gypsy family, where music was a constant and illuminating presence. . . . Christensen's soft, rhythmic prose echoes her evocative images as Django explores the music scene of 1920s Paris, before suffering serious burns on his hands and leg when his wagon catches fire. Despite his injuries, Reinhardt teaches himself to play again. . . . A sensuous tribute to an illustrious musician." Publ Wkly

Reiss, Johanna

★ Reiss, Johanna. The **upstairs** room. Crowell 1972 273p hardcover o.p. pa $5.99

Grades: 5 6 7 8 9 10   92

1. Authors 2. Holocaust survivors 3. Children's authors 4. Jews -- Netherlands 5. World War, 1939-1945 -- Jews 6. Holocaust, 1933-1945 -- Personal narratives 7. Netherlands -- History -- 1940-1945, German occupation

ISBN 0-690-85127-8; 0-06-440370-X pa

A Newbery Medal honor book, 1973

"In a vital, moving account the author recalls her experiences as a Jewish child hiding from the Germans occupying her native Holland during World War II. . . . Ten-year-old Annie and her twenty-year-old sister Sini, . . . are taken in by a Dutch farmer, his wife, and mother who hide the girls in an upstairs room of the farm house. Written from the perspective of a child the story affords a child's-eye-view of the war." Booklist

Followed by The journey back

Renoir, Auguste, 1841-1919

Somervill, Barbara A. **Pierre**-Auguste Renoir; [by] Barbara Somervill. Mitchell Lane 2007 48p il (Art profiles for kids) lib bdg $29.95

Grades: 5 6 7 8   92

1. Artists 2. Painters 3. Artists, French

ISBN 978-1-58415-566-9 lib bdg; 1-58415-566-3 lib bdg

LC 2007000661

Profiles the famous French artist best known for his portraits and his paintings such as "The Luncheon of the Boating Party" that depict people enjoying themselves

"The glossy pages allow for good reproductions of paintings as well as a few photos. . . . Back matter includes a glossary, chronology, chapter notes for quotes, lists of books and Internet sites, and a Timeline in History . . . offers a concise, readable account of the artist's life." Booklist

Includes glossary and bibliographical references

Revere, Paul, 1735-1818

★ Fritz, Jean. **And** then what happened, Paul Revere? pictures by Margot Tomes. Coward, McCann & Geoghegan 1973 45p il $16.99; pa $5.99

Grades: 2 3 4   92

1. Artisans 2. Metalworkers 3. Revolutionaries 4. United States -- History -- 1775-1783, Revolution

ISBN 0-399-23337-7; 0-698-11351-9 pa

This "description of Paul Revere's ride to Lexington is funny, fast-paced, and historically accurate; it is given added interest by the establishment of Revere's character: busy, bustling, versatile, and patriotic, a man who loved people and excitement. The account of his ride is preceded by a description of his life and the political situation in Boston, and it concludes with Revere's adventures after reaching Lexington." Bull Cent Child Books

Giblin, James. The **many** rides of Paul Revere; by James Cross Giblin. Scholastic Press 2007 85p il map $17.99

Grades: 4 5 6 7   92

1. Artisans 2. Metalworkers 3. Revolutionaries 4. United States -- History -- 1775-1783, Revolution

ISBN 978-0-439-57290-3; 0-439-57290-8

LC 2006-38369

"This well-organized biography presents a lucid account of Revere's childhood, his limited education, his training in his father's workshop, his brief military career, and his adult life as a silversmith, family man, and Revolutionary War leader. . . . Giblin presents salient facts and intriguing details to create a well-rounded and credible image of the man. Among the many illustrations are period portraits, narrative paintings, engravings, drawings, and maps as well as photos of significant sites and artifacts." Booklist

Includes bibliographical references

Mortensen, Lori. **Paul** Revere's ride; illustrated by Craig Orback. Picture Window Books 2010 32p il map (Our American story) lib bdg $23.99

Grades: 2 3 4   92

1. Artisans 2. Metalworkers 3. Revolutionaries 4. Statesmen -- United States 5. United States -- History -- 1775-1783, Revolution

ISBN 978-1-4048-5537-3; 1-4048-5537-8

LC 2009-6893

Highlights the life and accomplishments of Paul Revere, including the events leading up to his famous ride to warn of the British attack on Concord.

This book is "illustrated with well-executed, full-page, color illustrations, maps, and photos. . . . [It has] accurate, clearly written information that students can use for either leisure reading or reports." SLJ

Includes glossary and bibliographical references

Rey, H. A. (Hans Augusto), 1898-1977

★ Borden, Louise. The **journey** that saved Curious George; the true wartime escape of Margret and H. A. Rey. illustrated by Allan Drummond. Houghton Mifflin 2005 72p il $17

Grades: 3 4 5 6   92

1. Artists 2. Authors 3. Illustrators 4. Jewish refugees 5. Authors, American 6. Children's authors
ISBN 0-618-33924-8

LC 2004-01015

This "book tells the story of Margret and H. A. Rey. Part 1 concerns their childhoods in Germany, their lives together in Rio de Janeiro and Paris in the 1920s and 1930s, and the growing menace after war broke out in 1939. As German-born Jews, they were suspect in many quarters. Part 2 recalls the Reys' flight from Paris and the couple's escape to Lisbon, Rio, and finally New York. They were carrying several illustrated manuscripts, including The Adventures of FiFi, later retitled Curious George. Photos, reproductions of documents, and artwork appear throughout the book, as do Drummond's spirited ink-and-watercolor illustrations, brimming with action and details. The text . . . reads well." Booklist

Rey, Margret

★ Borden, Louise. The **journey** that saved Curious George; the true wartime escape of Margret and H. A. Rey. illustrated by Allan Drummond. Houghton Mifflin 2005 72p il $17

Grades: 3 4 5 6   92

1. Artists 2. Authors 3. Illustrators 4. Jewish refugees 5. Authors, American 6. Children's authors
ISBN 0-618-33924-8

LC 2004-01015

This "book tells the story of Margret and H. A. Rey. Part 1 concerns their childhoods in Germany, their lives together in Rio de Janeiro and Paris in the 1920s and 1930s, and the growing menace after war broke out in 1939. As German-born Jews, they were suspect in many quarters. Part 2 recalls the Reys' flight from Paris and the couple's escape to Lisbon, Rio, and finally New York. They were carrying several illustrated manuscripts, including The Adventures of FiFi, later retitled Curious George. Photos, reproductions of documents, and artwork appear throughout the book, as do Drummond's spirited ink-and-watercolor illustrations, brimming with action and details. The text . . . reads well." Booklist

Ride, Sally

Macy, Sue, 1954- **Sally** Ride; life on a mission. by Sue Macy. Aladdin 2014 160 p. illustrations (Real-life story) (hardback) $17.99

Grades: 4 5 6 7 8   92

1. Astronauts 2. Women astronauts 3. Physicists
ISBN 1442488549; 9781442488540; 9781442488557

LC 2014016685

"Sally Ride was more than the first woman in space--she was a real-life explorer and adventurer whose life story is a true inspiration for all those who dream big. . . . She was also a nationally ranked tennis player, a physicist who enjoyed reading Shakespeare, a university professor, the founder of a company that helped inspire girls . . . , and a recipient of the Presidential Medal of Freedom." (Publisher's note)

"The extensive backmatter provides scholarly data, while the writing imparts the drive and character of this famous woman. Macy's slim, empathetic account makes readers see the woman behind the achievement." Kirkus

Includes bibliographical references and index

Ringgold, Faith

Venezia, Mike. **Faith** Ringgold; written and illustrated by Mike Venezia. Children's Press 2008 32p il (Getting to know the world's greatest artists) lib bdg $28

Grades: 3 4 5   92

1. Artists 2. Authors 3. Illustrators 4. Women artists 5. African American artists 6. Children's authors 7. Artists -- United States
ISBN 978-0-531-18526-1 lib bdg; 0-531-18526-5 lib bdg

LC 2007016125

This examines the work and life of Faith Ringgold, an African American artist who works in a variety of mediums including textiles, paintings, and prints, and is best known for her story quilts.

"Though the [text is] simply written, [this title contains] a wealth of information. . . . [The book has] many reproductions of the [artist's] works as well as those of the masters who influenced [her]. To help illustrate his points, Venezia has incorporated his own cartoon-style illustrations." SLJ

Rivera, Diego, 1886-1957

★ Tonatiuh, Duncan. **Diego** Rivera; his world and ours. Abrams Books for Young Readers 2011 32p il $15.95

Grades: K 1 2 3   92

1. Artists 2. Painters 3. Artists, Mexican
ISBN 978-0-8109-9731-8; 0-8109-9731-2

LC 2010032618

"Tonatiuh relates key moments in the famous muralist's life and ponders what would capture his interest if he were alive today. The stylized brown figures are shown in profile with open mouths, exaggerated features, and heads that seem hinged to the bodies. . . . In scenes both thoughtful and humorous, Tonatiuh contrasts interpretations of Rivera's work with renderings of imagined work today. . . . An inspired approach that combines child appeal, cultural anthropology, and art history." SLJ

Robeson, Paul, 1898-1976

Greenfield, Eloise. **Paul** Robeson; illustrated by George Ford. Lee & Low Books 2009 un il $18.95; pa $9.95

Grades: 2 3 4 5   92

1. Actors 2. Singers 3. Football players 4. Political activists 5. Civil rights activists 6. African Americans

-- Biography

ISBN 978-1-60060-256-6; 1-60060-256-8; 978-1-60060-262-7 pa; 1-60060-262-2 pa

LC 2008030420

First published 1975 by HarperCollins

"Vibrant, monochromatic acrylic illustrations . . . use shading and depth to convey tremendous emotion. Powerful movements and vivid expressions enhance the narrative. . . . This book offers a fully developed portrayal of the man." SLJ

Robinson, Jackie, 1919-1972

Amoroso, Cynthia. **Jackie** Robinson; by Cynthia Amoroso and Robert B. Noyed. Child's World 2010 24p il (Basic biographies) lib bdg $22.79

Grades: PreK K 1   **92**

   1. Baseball players 2. African American athletes 3. Army officers 4. Baseball -- Biography

ISBN 978-1-60253-342-4; 1-60253-342-3

LC 2009029371

This biography of Jackie Robinson "pairs intelligent, brief text with abundant photos. Simple but never basic." Booklist

Includes bibliographical references

★ Burleigh, Robert. **Stealing** home; written by Robert Burleigh; illustrated by Mike Wimmer. Simon & Schuster Books for Young Readers 2007 un il $16.99

Grades: 1 2 3 4   **92**

   1. Baseball players 2. African American athletes 3. Army officers 4. Baseball -- Biography

ISBN 978-0-689-86276-2; 0-689-86276-8

LC 2006-01048

"Burleigh employs two narrative voices, one a spare, lyrical moment-by-moment replay of [Jackie] Robinson's bold steal home from third base in the first game of the 1955 World Series against the New York Yankees. . . . Historical sidebars on each spread supplement this dramatic, immediate account, providing anecdotes about the era, Robinson's struggles . . . plus highlights of his baseball career . . . and personal life. Wimmer's textured, animated oil paintings depict the game action at close range and with lifelike clarity." Publ Wkly

O'Sullivan, Robyn. **Jackie** Robinson plays ball; by Robyn O'Sullivan. National Geographic 2007 40p il (National Geographic history chapters) lib bdg $17.90

Grades: 2 3 4   **92**

   1. Baseball players 2. African American athletes 3. Army officers 4. Baseball -- Biography

ISBN 978-1-4263-0190-2

LC 2007007893

This biography of Jackie Robinson is "nicely illustrated with photos. . . . [It is] just right for emerging chapter-book readers. . . . Useful . . . for reports . . . and interesting pleasure reading." SLJ

Includes glossary and bibliographical references

Robinson, Sharon. **Promises** to keep: how Jackie Robinson changed America. Scholastic 2004 64p il $16.95

Grades: 4 5 6 7   **92**

   1. Baseball players 2. African American athletes 3.

Army officers 4. Baseball -- Biography

ISBN 0-439-42592-1

LC 2003-42709

"Robinson's daughter, Sharon, describes her father's youth, his rise to become major-league baseball's first African American player, and his involvement in the civil rights movement. . . . Her private view of her father's accomplishments, placed within the context of American sports and social history, makes for absorbing reading. An excellent selection of family and team photographs and other materials . . . illustrate this fine tribute." Booklist

Robinson, Sharon, 1950- **Testing** the ice: a true story about Jackie Robinson; illustrated by Kadir Nelson. Scholastic Press 2009 un il $16.99

Grades: 1 2 3 4   **92**

   1. Baseball players 2. African American athletes 3. Army officers 4. Baseball -- Biography

ISBN 0-545-05251-3; 978-0-545-05251-1

LC 2008-38838

Jackie Robinson's daughter shares memories of him, from his baseball career to the day he tests the ice for her, her brothers, and their friends. "Ages seven to ten." (N Y Times Book Rev)

"Robinson neatly sums up the significance of her father's achievements while depicting him as a loving family man. Nelson's large paintings, done in pencil, watercolor, and oils, dramatically convey Robinson's public persona, the intensely competitive athlete, and contrasts that with the relaxed, yet commanding father Sharon and her brothers knew." SLJ

Roget, Peter Mark, 1779-1869

★ Bryant, Jen. The **right** word; Roget and his thesaurus. by Jen Bryant; illustrated by Melissa Sweet. Eerdmans Books for Young Readers 2014 42 p. color illustrations $17.50

Grades: 1 2 3 4   **92**

   1. Authors 2. Reference books 3. Philologists -- Great Britain -- Biography 4. Lexicographers -- Great Britain -- Biography

ISBN 0802853854; 9780802853851

LC 2013044348

Robert F. Sibert Informational Book Award (2015)

Kirkus Prize Finalist (2014)

Caldecott Honor Book (2015)

Written by Jen Bryant and illustrated by Melissa Sweet, this children's book tells how "for shy young Peter Mark Roget, books were the best companions--and it wasn't long before Peter began writing his own book. But he didn't write stories; he wrote lists. Peter took his love for words and turned it to organizing ideas and finding exactly the right word to express just what he thought. His lists grew . . . turning into one of the most important reference books of all time." (Publisher's note)

"Bryant's and Sweet's talents combine to make the lowly thesaurus fascinating in this beautifully illustrated picture-book biography of Peter Mark Roget. . . . In brilliant pages teeming with enthusiasm for language and learning, Bryant and Sweet . . . joyfully celebrate curiosity, the love of knowledge, and the power of words." (Booklist)

includes bibliographical references

Romo, Tony, 1980-

Sandler, Michael. **Tony** Romo. Bearport Pub. 2010 24p il (Football heroes making a difference) lib bdg $22.61

Grades: 2 3 4   92

1. Football players 2. Football -- Biography

ISBN 978-1-936087-60-0 lib bdg; 1-936087-60-X lib bdg

LC 2009031216

A look at the life and career of the football star.

Includes bibliographical references

Roosevelt, Eleanor, 1884-1962

Fleming, Candace. **Our** Eleanor; a scrapbook look at Eleanor Roosevelt's remarkable life. Atheneum Books for Young Readers 2005 176p il $19.95

Grades: 5 6 7 8   92

1. Diplomats 2. Columnists 3. Humanitarians 4. Social activists 5. Spouses of presidents 6. United Nations officials 7. Presidents' spouses -- United States

ISBN 0-689-86544-9

LC 2004-22825

Told in scrapbook style, this biography looks behind the politics to present First Lady Eleanor Roosevelt in her many roles: wife and mother, United Nations delegate, popular columnist, civil rights crusader, and champion of the underprivileged.

"Each of the seven chapters leads readers through the subject's busy life with short sections of text filled with well-documented first-person accounts and direct quotes. . . . Not a spread goes by without incredible archival photographs or reproductions, newspaper and magazine clippings, handwritten letters, and diary entries. . . . They all provide relevant and fascinating insight." SLJ

★ Rappaport, Doreen. **Eleanor,** quiet no more; written by Doreen Rappaport; illustrated by Gary Kelley. Hyperion 2009 un il $16.99

Grades: 2 3 4 5   92

1. Diplomats 2. Columnists 3. Humanitarians 4. Social activists 5. Spouses of presidents 6. United Nations officials 7. Presidents' spouses -- United States

ISBN 978-0-7868-5141-6; 0-7868-5141-4

"The narrative moves swiftly through the important moments in [Eleanor] Roosevelt's life . . . but along with accomplishments, Rappaport does something more subtle— she shows the way Eleanor grew into herself. Crisp sentences focus the narrative and are bolstered by the quotes that end each page. . . . The accompanying art is composed of rich, beautifully crafted paintings that also catch Roosevelt's growing sense of purpose." Booklist

Roosevelt, Franklin D. (Franklin Delano), 1882-1945

Krull, Kathleen. A **boy** named FDR; how Franklin D. Roosevelt grew up to change America. illustrated by Steve Johnson & Lou Fancher. Alfred A. Knopf 2010 un il $17.99; lib bdg $20.99

Grades: 3 4 5   92

1. Governors 2. Presidents 3. People with disabilities 4. Philatelists 5. Presidents -- United States

ISBN 978-0-375-85716-4; 0-375-85716-8; 978-0-375-95716-1 lib bdg; 0-375-95716-2 lib bdg

LC 2009-22089

Focuses on Franklin D. Roosevelt's childhood years and summarizes his achievements as president.

"Full-page, painterly artwork evokes the times and the determination of FDR, and Krull has a knack for ferreting out interesting anecdotes that humanize the facts. Informative backmatter provides a dated list of his life and famous words and sources. Well done." Kirkus

Panchyk, Richard. **Franklin** Delano Roosevelt for kids; his life and times with 21 activities. [by] Richard Panchyk. Chicago Review Press 2007 147p il pa $14.95

Grades: 4 5 6 7   92

1. Governors 2. Presidents 3. People with disabilities 4. Philatelists 5. Presidents -- United States 6. United States -- Politics and government -- 1933-1945

ISBN 978-1-55652-657-2 pa; 1-55652-657-1 pa

LC 2007003484

"There are many interesting photos . . . and they are all sufficiently captioned. . . . Information about the Roosevelts [is] presented in a lively, engaging manner." SLJ

Includes bibliographical references

St. George, Judith. **Make** your mark, Franklin Roosevelt; [by] Judith St. George; illustrated by Britt Spencer. Philomel Books 2007 un il $16.99

Grades: 2 3 4   92

1. Governors 2. Presidents 3. People with disabilities 4. Presidents -- United States

ISBN 978-0-399-24175-8; 0-399-24175-2

LC 2006008921

"This illustrated biography . . . explores . . . the influences that shaped Roosevelt's life with stories that will delight young readers. . . . Throughout, Spencer's spirited watercolor, gouache, and ink illustrations bring to life the culture and background of this American icon." SLJ

Includes bibliographical references

Roosevelt, Theodore, 1858-1919

★ Brown, Don. **Teedie;** the story of young Teddy Roosevelt. Houghton Mifflin Books for Children 2009 un il $16

Grades: 2 3 4   92

1. Governors 2. Presidents 3. Vice-presidents 4. Nobel laureates for peace 5. Presidents -- United States

ISBN 978-0-618-17999-2; 0-618-17999-2

LC 2008033879

"Teedie led a privileged life in one of New York City's wealthiest households, but was a sickly child. His asthma didn't stop him from being curious or from reading widely. . . . Teedie became Teddy when he entered Harvard University in 1876. After graduation, Roosevelt sought his own way. . . . He traveled, became an outdoorsman, a politician, and ultimately the youngest president of the United States. Line and wash illustrations add movement and a playful tone to the serious text, which generously incorporates quotes from Roosevelt." SLJ

Includes bibliographical references

Elish, Dan. **Theodore** Roosevelt; by Dan Elish. Marshall Cavendish Benchmark 2008 96p il (Presidents and their times) lib bdg $22.95

Grades: 5 6 7 8   92

1. Governors 2. Presidents 3. Vice-presidents 4. Nobel laureates for peace 5. Presidents -- United States

ISBN 978-0-7614-2429-1

LC 2006012987

A biography of the president

"Primary-source materials and quotes, helpful insets, and carefully selected photographs and/or reproductions bring history to life and help make [this] clearly written [biography] highly readable." SLJ

Includes glossary and bibliographical references

Fritz, Jean. **Bully** for you, Teddy Roosevelt! illustrations by Mike Wimmer. Putnam 1991 127p il hardcover o.p. pa $5.99

Grades: 5 6 7 8   92

1. Governors 2. Presidents 3. Vice-presidents 4. Nobel laureates for peace 5. Presidents -- United States
ISBN 0-399-21769-X; 0-698-11609-7 pa

LC 90-8142

Follows the life of the twenty-sixth president, discussing his conservation work, hunting expeditions, family life, and political career

"Jean Fritz gives a rounded picture of her subject and deftly blends the story of a person and a picture of an era." Bull Cent Child Books

Includes bibliographical references

Harness, Cheryl. The **remarkable,** rough-riding life of Theodore Roosevelt and the rise of empire America; painstakingly written and illustrated by Cheryl Harness. National Geographic 2007 144p il map $16.95; lib bdg $25.90

Grades: 4 5 6 7   92

1. Governors 2. Presidents 3. Vice-presidents 4. Nobel laureates for peace 5. Presidents -- United States
ISBN 978-1-4263-0008-0; 1-4263-0008-5; 978-1-4263-0009-7 lib bdg; 1-4263-0009-3 lib bdg

LC 2006029039

"Animated writing and intricate black-and-white illustrations drive this biography of the ever-enthusiastic twenty-sixth president of the United States. An extensive running timeline at the bottom of the pages emphasizes the dramatic changes that occurred during Roosevelt's life. The book is jam-packed with information." Horn Book Guide

Includes bibliographical references

Hollihan, Kerrie Logan. **Theodore** Roosevelt for kids; his life and times + 21 activities. Chicago Review Press 2010 133p il pa $16.95

Grades: 5 6 7 8   92

1. Governors 2. Handicraft 3. Presidents 4. Vice-presidents 5. Nobel laureates for peace 6. Presidents -- United States 7. United States -- Politics and government -- 1898-1919
ISBN 978-1-55652-955-9 pa; 1-55652-955-4 pa

"What stands out in this volume is the writing, which presents history as an engaging and informative story. . . . The projects are interesting and accessible. . . . Both useful and entertaining, this is a worthy addition to most collections." SLJ

Keating, Frank. **Theodore**; illustrated by Mike Wimmer. Simon & Schuster Books for Young Readers 2006 un il $16.95

Grades: K 1 2 3   92

1. Governors 2. Presidents 3. Vice-presidents 4. Nobel laureates for peace 5. Presidents -- United States
ISBN 0-689-86532-5

LC 2003-17046

A picture book biography of the 26th president of the United States

"This handsome, well-researched biography is as dignified as its subject. Using a spare, readable style, the author captures Roosevelt's spirit and determination." SLJ

★ Kerley, Barbara. **What** to do about Alice? how Alice Roosevelt broke the rules, charmed the world, and drove her father Teddy crazy! illustrated by Edwin Fotheringham. Scholastic Press 2008 un il $16.99

Grades: K 1 2 3   92

1. Presidents -- United States -- Family 2. Biography, Individual 3. White House (Washington, D.C.)
ISBN 978-0-439-92231-9; 0-439-92231-3

LC 2006-38372

Boston Globe-Horn Book Award honor book: Nonfiction (2008)

"The daughter of Theodore Roosevelt, . . . Alice had a joie de vivre that she called 'eating up the world.' . . . Kerley's text has the same rambunctious spirit as its subject. . . . The large format gives Fotheringhame . . . plenty of room for spectacular art, which includes use of digital media." Booklist

★ Rappaport, Doreen, 1939- **To** dare mighty things; the life of Theodore Roosevelt. written by Doreen Rappaport; illustrated by C. F. Payne. Disney-Hyperion 2013 48 p. (hardback) $17.99

Grades: 2 3 4 5 6   92

1. Presidents -- United States 2. Presidents -- United States -- Biography
ISBN 142312488X; 9781423124887

LC 2013010691

This picture book, by Doreen Rappaport and illustrated by C. F. Payne, is a biography of American president Theodore Roosevelt. "As an American president, he left [a] . . . mark upon his country. He promised a 'square deal' to all citizens, he tamed big businesses, and protected the nation's wildlife and natural beauty. His . . . leadership assured that he would always be remembered." (Publisher's note).

St. George, Judith. **You're** on your way, Teddy Roosevelt! illustrated by Matt Faulkner. Philomel Books 2004 un il $16.99

Grades: 2 3 4   92

1. Governors 2. Presidents 3. Vice-presidents 4. Nobel laureates for peace 5. Presidents -- United States
ISBN 0-399-23888-3

LC 2003-21534

"St. George's skill in presenting information with a light touch keeps the pace lively, while Faulkner's gouache illustrations . . . further animate the narrative." Horn Book Guide

Includes bibliographical references

Wade, Mary Dodson. **Amazing** president Theodore Roosevelt. Enslow Publishers 2009 24p il (Amazing Americans) lib bdg $21.26

Grades: 1 2 3   92

1. Governors 2. Presidents 3. Vice-presidents 4.

Nobel laureates for peace 5. Presidents -- United States
ISBN 978-0-7660-3284-2 lib bdg; 0-7660-3284-1
lib bdg

LC 2008-24892

"Colorful photos are found throughout, with a timeline, dictionary, websites concerning the topic, as well as an index making . . . [this] book a wonderful introduction to nonfiction features." Libr Media Connect

Includes glossary

Wadsworth, Ginger. **Camping** with the president; illustrated by Karen Dugan. Calkins Creek 2009 32p il $16.95
Grades: 3 4 5   92

1. Authors 2. Governors 3. Presidents 4. Naturalists 5. Vice-presidents 6. Environmental movement 7. National parks and reserves 8. Writers on nature 9. Nobel laureates for peace 10. Presidents -- United States 11. Yosemite National Park (Calif.)
ISBN 978-1-59078-497-6; 1-59078-497-9

LC 2008024155

"Inspired by conservationist John Muir's nature essays, President Theodore Roosevelt traveled west, visiting national parks and learing more about their resources. Wadsworth's well written, lively account highlights the pair's 1903 exploration of the Yosemite wilderness, as well as America's early conservation movement, in an accessible and engaging picture book for older readers. Dugan's abundant, intricately rendered watercolors portray the stunning vistas and wildlife and are set against white backgrounds." Booklist

Includes bibliographical references

Ross, Betsy, 1752-1836
White, Becky. **Betsy** Ross; illustrated by Megan Lloyd. Holiday House 2011 il $16.95
Grades: K 1 2   92

1. Generals 2. Presidents 3. Dressmakers 4. Needleworkers 5. Flags -- United States 6. United States -- History -- 1775-1783, Revolution
ISBN 978-0-8234-1908-1; 0-8234-1908-8

LC 2009054296

"Fourteen spreads with four to six rhythmic words on each one tell the story of the first American flag. . . . The large, simple text, paired with the irresistible appliqué art, makes this a perfect introduction to the Stars and Stripes. Using cotton fabric, embroidery thread, dye, paint, and linoleum-block prints, Lloyd captures the period, hard work, and ingenuity of this favorite colonial figure." SLJ

Rothschild, Lionel Walter Rothschild, Baron, 1868-1937
Judge, Lita. **Strange** creatures; the story of Walter Rothschild and his museum. Hyperion 2011 un il $17.99
Grades: 1 2 3   92

1. Zoology 2. Zoologists 3. Members of Parliament 4. Biography, Individual 5. Natural History Museum at Tring (England)
ISBN 1-4231-1389-6; 978-1-4231-1389-8

This is a biography of the British zoologist and banker. Rothschild "used his own income to finance [zoological] expeditions and ultimately built a museum to house his collection on the family's grounds. . . . Ages five to eight." (Bull Cent Child Books)

"Walter Rothschild, the shy eldest son of Lord Nathan Rothschild, never took an interest in the family banking business, instead developing an all-consuming veneration

for the wild; at age seven, he began collecting living animals like kangaroos and kiwi birds for his 'museum.' Judge's expressive watercolors convey Rothschild's inquisitiveness and his parents' angst over such mishaps as a giant lizard escape. . . . Children should get a kick out of this 19th-century misfit who relentlessly pursued his unconventional passion." Publ Wkly

Rowling, J. K.
Peterson-Hilleque, Victoria. **J.K.** Rowling, extraordinary author. ABDO Pub. Company 2010 112p il (Essential lives) $32.79
Grades: 5 6 7 8   92

1. Authors 2. Novelists 3. Women authors 4. Fantasy writers 5. Authors, English 6. Children's authors 7. Young adult authors
ISBN 978-1-61613-517-1; 1-61613-517-4

LC 2010000503

This biography of author J. K. Rowling "toggles between the subject's personal and professional life. . . . [The book] offers sidebar . . . definitions of particular characters or events in the 'Harry Potter' series. The writing is accessible, the format is open, and full-color photos appear throughout." SLJ

Includes glossary and bibliographical references

Rudolph, Wilma, 1940-1994
★ Krull, Kathleen. **Wilma** unlimited: how Wilma Rudolph became the world's fastest woman; illustrated by David Diaz. Harcourt Brace & Co. 1996 un il $17; pa $7
Grades: 2 3 4   92

1. Women athletes 2. African American athletes 3. Olympic athletes 4. Runners (Athletes) 5. Track athletics -- Biography
ISBN 0-15-201267-2; 0-15-202098-5 pa

LC 95-32105

A biography of the African-American woman who overcame crippling polio as a child to become the first woman to win three gold medals in track in a single Olympics

"Brightly colored paintings contrast with sepia-toned photographic backgrounds, creating juxtapositions that extend both the text and the pictures in the foreground. Krull's understated conversational style is perfectly suited to Rudolph's remarkable and inspiring story." Horn Book Guide

Wade, Mary Dodson. **Amazing** Olympic athlete Wilma Rudolph. Enslow Publishers 2009 24p il (Amazing Americans) lib bdg $21.26
Grades: 1 2 3   92

1. Women athletes 2. Track athletics 3. African American athletes 4. Olympic athletes 5. Runners (Athletes)
ISBN 978-0-7660-3282-8 lib bdg; 0-7660-3282-5
lib bdg

LC 2008-24890

"The book features a design that is clear and inviting with a full-page photo on every double-page spread." Booklist

This brief "biography describes how Wilma Rudolph overcame childhood polio and competed in the Olympics." Publisher's note

Includes glossary and bibliographical references

Rustin, Bayard, 1910-1987

★ Brimner, Larry Dane. **We** are one: the story of Bayard Rustin. Calkins Creek 2007 48p il $17.95

Grades: 5 6 7 8 **92**

1. Civil rights activists 2. African Americans -- Biography 3. African Americans -- Civil rights

ISBN 1-59078-498-7

"Brimner sets Rustin's personal story against the history of segregation in his time and focuses on his leadership role . . . in the struggle for civil rights. On each page, the clearly written, informal text is accompanied by eloquently captioned archival photos." Booklist

Includes bibliographical references

Ruth, Babe, 1895-1948

Yomtov, Nelson. The **Bambino**: the story of Babe Ruth's legendary 1927 season; illustrated by Tim Foley. Capstone Press 2011 32p il (Graphic library: American graphic) lib bdg $29.32; pa $7.95

Grades: 4 5 6 7 **92**

1. Baseball players 2. Biographical graphic novels 3. Baseball -- Biography

ISBN 978-1-4296-5473-9 lib bdg; 1-4296-5473-2 lib bdg; 978-1-4296-6265-9 pa; 1-4296-6265-4 pa

LC 2010024764

In graphic novel format, follows Babe Ruth through the 1927 season and describes his attempt to break his own home run record.

"The illustrations are eye-catching and the narration is presented simply, yet compellingly. . . . Fact-filled, entertaining, and accessible." SLJ

Includes glossary and bibliographical references

Sís, Peter, 1949-

★ Sis, Peter, 1949- The **wall**; growing up behind the Iron Curtain. Farrar, Straus and Giroux 2007 un il $18

Grades: 4 5 6 7 8 9 10 **92**

1. Artists 2. Authors 3. Cold war 4. Animators 5. Illustrators 6. Set designers 7. Children's authors 8. Prague (Czech Republic) 9. Biography, Individual

ISBN 978-0-374-34701-7; 0-374-34701-8

LC 2006-49149

Boston Globe-Horn Book Award: Nonfiction (2008)

"The author pairs his remarkable artistry with journal entries, historical context and period photography to create a powerful account of his childhood in Cold War-era Prague." Publ Wkly

Sagan, Carl, 1934-1996

★ Sisson, Stephanie Roth. **Star** stuff; Carl Sagan and the mysteries of the cosmos. Stephanie Roth Sisson. Roaring Brook Press 2014 40 p. color illustrations (hardcover) $17.99

Grades: K 1 2 3 **92**

1. Astronomers -- Biography 2. Astronomers -- United States -- Biography

ISBN 1596439602; 9781596439603

LC 2013048396

Orbis Pictus Award for Outstanding Nonfiction for Children Honor Book (2014)

This children's book, by Stephanie Roth Sisson, is "the story of a curious boy who never stopped wondering: Carl Sagan. . . . [This book] follows Carl from his days star gazing from the bedroom window of his Brooklyn apartment,

through his love of speculative science fiction novels, to his work as an internationally renowned scientist who worked on the Voyager missions exploring the farthest reaches of space." (Publisher's note)

"Told in narrative format, this beautifully designed and illustrated picture book gives readers a glimpse into the childhood wonderings Sagan experienced as he looked at the night sky and imagined the possibilities...Children will easily relate to and may even see themselves in Sagan's youthful exuberance. Detailed notes illustrate the solid research and facts behind the narrative. A gorgeous, informative offering for biography and science collections." SLJ

Includes bibliographical references

Saint-Exupery, Antoine de

★ Sis, Peter, 1949- The **Pilot** and the Little Prince; the Life of Antoine de Saint-Exupery. Peter Sís. Frances Foster Books, Farrar Straus Giroux 2014 48 p. (hardcover) $18.99

Grades: 1 2 3 4 5 6 **92**

1. Air pilots -- Biography 2. Air travel 3. Air pilots -- France -- Biography 4. Authors, French -- 20th century -- Biography

ISBN 0374380694; 9780374380694

LC 2013027732

"Antoine de Saint-Exupéry was born in France in 1900, when airplanes were just being invented. Antoine dreamed of flying and grew up to be a pilot--and that was when his adventures began. . . . From his plane, Antoine looked down on the earth and was inspired to write about his life and his pilot-hero friends in memoirs and in fiction. Peter Sís's . . . biography celebrates the author of 'The Little Prince,' one of the most beloved books in the world." (Publisher's note)

"Sís' works are less picture books than little miracles of design, a craft he now devotes to a biography of Antoine de Saint-Exupéry, author of The Little Prince... Sís (The Wall, 2007) never misses an opportunity to hit readers with the power of pure image, as in a two-page spread of a plane flying over a geography of faces, sure to live on in many a child's imagination. Sís' masterful and moving sense of design never fails." Booklist

Saint-Georges, Joseph Boulogne, chevalier de, 1745-1799

Brewster, Hugh. The **other** Mozart; the life of the famous Chevalier de Saint George. [by] Hugh Brewster; illustrated by Eric Velasquez. Abrams Books for Young Readers 2007 48p il $18.95

Grades: 4 5 6 7 **92**

1. Nobility 2. Composers 3. Violinists 4. Racially mixed people

ISBN 978-0-8109-5720-6; 0-8109-5720-5

LC 2006-07488

"Born to a white plantation owner and a black slave in eighteenth-century Guadeloupe, Joseph Bologne grew up to become the Chevalier de Saint-George, one of France's most accomplished composers. In this picture-book biography for middle-graders, Brewster introduces his subject's fascinating life. . . . Archival images and Velasquez's arresting full-page portraits will captivate many young readers." Booklist

★ Cline-Ransome, Lesa. **Before** there was Mozart: the story of Joseph Boulogne, Chevalier de Saint-George; illustrated by James Ransome. Schwartz & Wade Books 2011 un il $17.99; lib bdg $20.99

Grades: 1 2 3 4 **92**

1. Nobility 2. Composers 3. Violinists 4. Racially mixed people

ISBN 978-0-375-83600-8; 0-375-83600-4; 978-0-375-93621-0 lib bdg; 0-375-93621-1 lib bdg

LC 2008-48825

"Born in Guadeloupe, Joseph Boulogne was the son of a black slave and a white plantation owner of French nobility. When Joseph's family moved to France, he enrolled in school and, despite facing racial prejudice, devoted himself to mastering the violin. . . . Joseph composed six operas (as well as other pieces of music), stood before audiences on the same stages as Mozart, and performed before Louis XVI and Marie Antoinette. Ransome's mixed-media paintings join tropical motifs with the sumptuous colors and prints of affluent Paris society, and his faces glow with vitality. Readers will likely marvel at why such a compelling figure has not received more attention." Publ Wkly

Santos-Dumont, Alberto, 1873-1932

Griffith, Victoria. The **fabulous** flying machines of Alberto Santos-Dumont; illustrated by Eva Montanari. Abrams Books for Young Readers 2011 il $16.95

Grades: 1 2 3 4 **92**

1. Airships 2. Engineers 3. Inventors 4. Air pilots 5. Aeronautics -- History

ISBN 978-1-4197-0011-8; 1-4197-0011-1

LC 2010048781

"Dumont is credited as being the first one to get an airplane off the ground under its own power, in 1906. In this fictionalized account, readers learn of the man's idiosyncratic and highly inventive nature. Although he was born in Brazil, he later made Paris his home where he became a larger-than-life personality, partly because of his reputation for—and the spectacle of—his chosen mode of transportation to run everyday errands: a dirigible. His quest to move through the air at a faster pace and for greater distances led to his invention of a biplane. . . . Montanari captures the look, dress, and formality of the era in her splendid, impressionistic pastel, chalk, and oil paintings. The endnotes add details and facts about the life of this charismatic, adventurous man and mark his place in aviation history." SLJ

Includes bibliographical references

Sarg, Tony, 1882-1942

★ Sweet, Melissa. **Balloons** over Broadway; the true story of the puppeteer of Macy's Parade. Houghton Mifflin Books for Children 2011 40p il $16.99

Grades: K 1 2 **92**

1. Artists 2. Parades 3. Illustrators 4. Thanksgiving Day 5. Puppets and puppet plays 6. Puppeteers

ISBN 978-0-547-19945-0; 0-547-19945-7

LC 2010044181

Flora Stieglitz Straus Award (2012); Golden Kite Award: Picture Book Illustration (2011); Lupine Award (Maine): Picture Book (2011); Robert F. Sibert Informational Book Medal (2012)

"Tony Sarg . . . the man who invented the giant balloons of the Macy's Thanksgiving Day Parade, has found a worthy biographer in . . . Sweet. . . . With lighthearted watercolors, fanciful scrapbooking, and collaged typography, Sweet shows how Sarg, a self-taught immigrant, combined an indomitable curiosity with an engineer's know-how and a forever-young imagination. The story walks readers through each stage of Sarg's development as a master of puppetry—his childhood fascination with mechanics and marionettes, his first big break as a developer of window displays for Macy's, and his early earthbound parade creations (essentially air-filled rubber bags that were steered down the street). . . . Sweet captures it all in what is truly a story for all ages." Publ Wkly

Sasaki, Sadako, 1943-1955

Coerr, Eleanor. **Sadako**; illustrated by Ed Young. Putnam 1993 un il $17.95; pa $6.99

Grades: 1 2 3 4 **92**

1. Children 2. Leukemia 3. Leukemia patients 4. Atomic bomb -- Physiological effect 5. Hiroshima (Japan) -- Bombardment, 1945

ISBN 0-399-21771-1; 0-698-11588-0 pa

LC 92-41483

"This is the same story as the author's Sadako and the Thousand Paper Cranes, told through an entirely new text. In this abbreviated version, the beautiful, limpid prose and crisp dialogue further telescope Sadako's fight with leukemia. . . . Young's pastels vividly capture all the moods of the narrative, place, and characters. . . . A masterful collaboration." SLJ

★ Coerr, Eleanor. **Sadako** and the thousand paper cranes; paintings by Ronald Himler. Putnam 1977 64p il $16.99; pa $5.99

Grades: 3 4 5 6 **92**

1. Children 2. Leukemia 3. Leukemia patients 4. Atomic bomb -- Physiological effect 5. Hiroshima (Japan) -- Bombardment, 1945

ISBN 0-399-20520-9; 0-698-11802-2 pa

LC 76-9872

"A story about a young girl of Hiroshima who died from leukemia ten years after the dropping of the atom bomb. Her dreams of being an outstanding runner are dimmed when she learns she has the fatal disease. But her spunk and bravery, symbolized in her efforts to have faith in the story of the golden crane, are beautifully portrayed by the author." Babbling Bookworm

Savage, Augusta Christine, 1892-1962

Schroeder, Alan. **In** her hands; the story of sculptor Augusta Savage. illustrated by JaeMe Bereal. Lee & Low Books 2009 un il $19.95

Grades: 3 4 5 6 **92**

1. Artists 2. Sculptors 3. Women artists 4. Harlem Renaissance 5. African American artists

ISBN 978-1-60060-332-7; 1-60060-332-7

LC 2009003859

"Young readers will . . . find this a solid introduction to the art world and a daring but lesser-known African American artist. Bereal's . . . expansive, richly hued one and two-page spreads fit nicely with the text and deftly capture the emotions of the story." Booklist

Schaller, George B.

Turner, Pamela S. A **life** in the wild; George Schaller's struggle to save the last great beasts. Farrar, Straus and Giroux 2008 103p il map $21.95

Grades: 5 6 7 8 **92**

1. Zoologists 2. Wildlife conservation 3. Nonfiction writers

ISBN 978-0-374-34578-5; 0-374-34578-3

LC 2007-42844

"The author interviewed Schaller and had access to his photos, which allowed her to capture beautifully the spirit of Schaller's work. The book is organized chronologically, and each chapter covers a geographic area and the principal animals that Schaller studied there. . . . Animal lovers and conservation-minded students will enjoy this excellent introduction to Schaller and his ideals." Voice Youth Advocates

Includes bibliographical references

Schliemann, Heinrich, 1822-1890

★ Schlitz, Laura Amy. The **hero** Schliemann; the dreamer who dug for Troy. illustrated by Robert Byrd. Candlewick Press 2006 72p il $12.23

Grades: 4 5 6 **92**

1. Archeologists 2. Excavations (Archeology) 3. Archaeologists 4. Troy (Extinct city)

ISBN 0-7636-2283-4

LC 2005046916

This is a biography of the archaeologist who rediscovered ancient Troy. "Intermediate." (Horn Book)

"In this slim biography, Schlitz introduces Heinrich Schliemann, a nineteenth-century 'storyteller, archaeologist, and crook,' who led a search for the lost cities of Homer's epic poems." Booklist

Includes bibliographical references

Schulz, Charles M.

Amoroso, Cynthia. **Charles** Schulz; by Cynthia Amoroso and Robert B. Noyed. Child's World 2010 24p il (Basic biographies) lib bdg $22.79

Grades: PreK K 1 **92**

1. Cartoonists

ISBN 978-1-60253-340-0; 1-60253-340-7

LC 2009029366

A biography of the cartoonist who created Charlie Brown in the strip "Peanuts."

This "pairs intelligent, brief text with abundant photos. Simple but never basic." Booklist

Includes bibliographical references

★ Gherman, Beverly. **Sparky**: the life and art of Charles Schulz. Chronicle Books 2010 125p il $16.99

Grades: 5 6 7 8 **92**

1. Cartoonists

ISBN 978-0-8118-6790-0; 0-8118-6790-0

A look at the life and influences of Charles Schulz, creator of the beloved comic strip Peanuts.

"Gherman's clear and direct prose is just right for portraying the life of the famous cartoonist for young readers. The splashy, bright design, with multicolored pages and several of Schulz's cartoons included, makes this a cheery read that may well introduce the Peanuts comic strip to a new generation, who likely know Charlie Brown mostly through the holiday TV specials. An informative yet lighthearted look at the life of an American icon." Kirkus

Scidmore, Eliza Ruhamah, 1856-1928

Zimmerman, Andrea. **Eliza's** cherry trees; Japan's gift to America. illustrated by Ju Hong Chen. Pelican Pub. Co. 2011 un il $16.99

Grades: 3 4 5 6 **92**

1. Photographers 2. Cherry trees 3. Travel writers 4. Washington (D.C.)

ISBN 1-58980-954-8; 978-1-58980-954-3

LC 2010046163

"This is an inspiring, heartwarming story of determination and spirit. The writing flows well, and the lush illustrations are reminiscent of Impressionist paintings." SLJ

Scieszka, Jon, 1954-

Scieszka, Jon. **Knucklehead**; tall tales and mostly true stories of growing up Scieszka. Viking 2008 106p il $16.99; pa $12.99

Grades: 4 5 6 7 **92**

1. Authors 2. Authors, American 3. Children's authors

ISBN 978-0-670-01106-3; 0-670-01106-1; 978-0-670-01138-4 pa; 0-670-01138-X pa

LC 2008-16870

"Scieszka . . . has written an autobiography about boys, for boys and anyone else interested in baseball, fire and peeing on stuff. . . . The text is divided into two- to three-page nonsequential chapters and peppered with scrapbook snapshots and comic-book-ad reproductions. . . . By themselves, the chapters entertain with abrupt, vulgar fun. Taken together, they offer a look at the makings of one very funny author." Booklist

Scott, Wendell, 1921-1990

Weatherford, Carole Boston. **Racing** against the odds; the story of Wendell Scott, stock car racing's African-American champion. illustrated by Eric A. Velasquez. Marshall Cavendish Children 2009 un il $17.99

Grades: 3 4 5 **92**

1. Automobile racing 2. African American athletes 3. Automobile racing drivers

ISBN 978-0-76145-465-6; 0-76145-465-9

LC 2008010711

"In this stirring biography of Scott, the only black race car driver to win a NASCAR race, Velasquez's expressive pastels showcase the driver's determination and resourcefulness. . . . With as much attention paid to Scott's life off the track as on, readers won't need to be racing fans to be drawn in." Publ Wkly

Selkirk, Alexander, 1676-1721

★ Kraske, Robert. **Marooned**; the strange but true adventures of Alexander Selkirk, the real Robinson Crusoe. illustrated by Robert Andrew Parker. Clarion Books 2005 120p il map $15

Grades: 5 6 7 8 **92**

1. Sailors 2. Survival after airplane accidents, shipwrecks, etc.

ISBN 0-618-56843-3

LC 2004-28769

"In 1704, English sailing master Alexander Selkirk was marooned on Juan Fernandez, an isolated Pacific island. . . . In 1709, two English ships rescued him, hired him as a second mate, and later captured a Spanish treasure ship. . . . Kraske offers a well-focused look at life in several quite different settings during the early eighteenth century as well as an absorbing telling of Selkirk's story." Booklist

Includes glossary and bibliographical references

Sendler, Irena, 1910-2008

★ Rubin, Susan Goldman. **Irena** Sendler and the children of the Warsaw Ghetto; illustrated by Bill Farnsworth. Holiday House 2011 40p il $18.95

Grades: 3 4 5 6 **92**

1. Jews -- Poland 2. Warsaw (Poland) 3. Holocaust, 1933-1945 4. World War, 1939-1945 -- Poland 5. World War, 1939-1945 -- Jews -- Rescue 6. Biography, Individual

ISBN 978-0-8234-2251-7; 0-8234-2251-8

LC 2010-23667

"Irena Sendler stands out on the list of righteous Gentiles for her incredibly daring methods of hiding and transporting nearly 400 babies and children out of Nazi-occupied Poland. . . . Rubin's documentary-style narrative is smoothly interspersed with dialogue taken from interviews conducted with many of the now-adult survivors. . . . Farnsworth's moody oil renditions authentically capture the tension, fear, despair and darkness of the period." Kirkus

Vaughan, Marcia. **Irena's** jars of secrets; illustrated by Ron Mazellan. Lee & Low Books 2011 il $18.95

Grades: 3 4 5 **92**

1. Humanitarians 2. Jews -- Poland 3. Warsaw (Poland) 4. Holocaust, 1933-1945 5. World War, 1939-1945 -- Children 6. World War, 1939-1945 -- Jews -- Rescue

ISBN 978-1-60060-439-3; 1-60060-439-0

LC 2011016386

"Vaughan tells the true story without embellishment, employing stark, unadorned syntax that never wavers into pathos, sentiment or myth. It is a definition of quiet heroism. Mazellan's very dark, deeply shadowed oil paintings capture the unabated terror and sorrow. Children should read this work with an adult who is armed with some knowledge of the material. Powerful." Kirkus

Sequoyah, 1770?-1843

★ Rumford, James. **Sequoyah**; the Cherokee man who gave his people writing. Houghton Mifflin 2004 un il $16

Grades: 1 2 3 4 **92**

1. Cherokee Indians 2. Artisans 3. Metalworkers 4. Indian leaders

ISBN 0-618-36947-3

LC 2004-00980

"Rumford presents the seminal events in Sequoyah's life, culminating in his invention of the Cherokee syllabary. The author writes with a concise eloquence that echoes the oral tradition and makes this one of those rare gems of readaloud nonfiction. . . . Done in ink, watercolor, pastel, and pencil, the illustrations were adhered to a rough piece of wood, and its textures were highlighted through the use of chalk and colored pencil. . . . The parallel text in Cherokee . . . makes this beautiful book readily accessible to Cherokee children in their own language." SLJ

Wade, Mary Dodson. **Amazing** Cherokee writer Sequoyah. Enslow Publishers 2009 24p il (Amazing Americans) lib bdg $21.26

Grades: 1 2 3 **92**

1. Cherokee Indians 2. Artisans 3. Metalworkers 4.

Indian leaders

ISBN 978-0-7660-3285-9 lib bdg; 0-7660-3285-X lib bdg

LC 2008-24893

"Colorful photos are found throughout, with a timeline, dictionary, websites concerning the topic, as well as an index making . . . [this] book a wonderful introduction to nonfiction features." Libr Media Connect

Includes glossary

Sessions, Kate

Hopkins, H. Joseph. The **tree** lady; H. Joseph Hopkins; illustrated by Jill McElmurry. Beach Lane Books 2013 32 p. (hardcover) $16.99

Grades: 2 3 4 **92**

1. Picture books for children 2. Horticulturists -- California -- San Diego -- Biography

ISBN 1442414022; 9781442414020

LC 2012032903

This "picture book biography recalls the life and contributions of a horticulturist in the late 19th century. Kate Sessions populated San Diego's landscape with not lupines but trees. Her love for nature dated back to her childhood, where, in school, 'she liked studying wind and rain, muscles and bones, plants and trees. Especially trees.'" (Publishers Weekly)

Seuss, Dr., 1904-1991

Cohen, Charles D. The **Seuss**, the whole Seuss, and nothing but the Seuss; a visual biography of Theodor Seuss Geisel. Random House 2004 390p il $35; lib bdg $36.99

Grades: Adult Professional **92**

1. Artists 2. Authors 3. Humorists 4. Illustrators 5. Authors, American 6. Children's authors

ISBN 0-375-82248-8; 0-375-92248-2 lib bdg

LC 2003-20526

This is a "profile of the creator of Horton, the Grinch, and the Cat in the Hat. . . . Crisp full-color illustrations on every page of the coffee-table volume will pull readers into Cohen's accessible recap of Theodore Geisel's career, which is enhanced with just enough personal information to bring everything together. . . . [The volume includes] clear reproductions of posters, book illustrations, newspaper cartoons, and book pages, with intriguing background information." Booklist

★ Krull, Kathleen. The **boy** on Fairfield Street: how Ted Geisel grew up to become Dr. Seuss; paintings by Steve Johnson and Lou Fancher; with decorative illustrations by Dr. Seuss. Random House 2004 43p il $16.95; lib bdg $18.99

Grades: K 1 2 3 **92**

1. Artists 2. Authors 3. Humorists 4. Illustrators 5. Authors, American 6. Children's authors

ISBN 0-375-82298-4; 0-375-92298-9 lib bdg

LC 2003-1754

Introduces the life of renowned children's author and illustrator Ted Geisel, popularly known as Dr. Seuss, focusing on his childhood and youth in Springfield, Massachusetts

"Johnson and Fancher's lovely, full-page illustrations are supplemented by samples of Dr. Seuss's artwork. . . . Krull's work is a terrific look at the boyhood of one of the most beloved author/illustrators of the 20th century." SLJ

Sewall, May Wright, 1844-1920

Boomhower, Ray E. **Fighting** for equality; a life of May Wright Sewall. [by] Ray E. Boomhower. Indiana Historical Society Press 2007 160p il $17.95

Grades: 4 5 6   **92**

1. Feminism 2. Educators 3. Reformers 4. Suffragists 5. Lecturers 6. Pacifists

ISBN 978-0-87195-253-0; 0-87195-253-X

LC 2007008517

"This accessible volume tells of the life and work of suffragist and educator [May] Wright Sewall. . . . Archival black-and-white photos enhance the text." Horn Book Guide

Includes bibliographical references

Shakur, Tupac

Harris, Ashley Rae. **Tupac** Shakur; multi-platinum rapper. ABDO Pub. Co. 2010 112p il (Lives cut short) lib bdg $32.79

Grades: 5 6 7 8   **92**

1. Poets 2. Actors 3. Hip-hop 4. Rap music 5. African American musicians 6. Rap musicians

ISBN 978-1-60453-791-8; 1-60453-791-4

This discusses Tupac Shakur's early life, "providing details that give insight into later success and troubles and maintaining a laudatory tone that focuses on the individual's artistic achievements and hard work to achieve fame. Details [such as] explaining . . . that Tupac Shakur was a standout student in high school are bound to resonate with readers. Numerous photos and sidebars appear throughout. [A] worthwhile [resource] for reports as well as popular reading." SLJ

Shiner, Michael

Capital days; Michael Shiner's journal and the growth of our nation's capital. by Tonya Bolden. Abrams Books for Young Readers 2015 90 p. (hardback) $21.95

Grades: 4 5 6   **92**

1. Washington (D.C.) -- History 2. African Americans -- Biography 3. Washington (D.C.) -- Biography 4. Slaves -- Maryland -- Biography 5. Freedmen -- Washington (D.C.) -- Biography 6. Washington (D.C.) -- History -- 19th century 7. African Americans -- Washington (D.C.) -- Biography 8. Washington (D.C.) -- Race relations -- History -- 19th century

ISBN 1419707337; 9781419707339

LC 2014024668

This book, by Tonya Bolden, "introduces young readers to Washington, D.C., during the early to mid-19th century. Spanning more than 60 years, the story of Michael Shiner (c. 1804–1880) highlights a period of immense change in our country and its capital." Topics include the burning of the city during the War of 1812, the rebuilding of the Capitol and White House, the raising of the Washington Monument . . . the Civil War, [and] the end of slavery." (Publisher's note)

Includes bibliographical references and index

Shuster, Joe, 1914-1992

★ Nobleman, Marc Tyler. **Boys** of steel; the creators of Superman. illustrated by Ross MacDonald. Knopf 2008 un il $16.99; lib bdg $19.99

Grades: 1 2 3   **92**

1. Artists 2. Cartoonists 3. Illustrators 4. Comic book writers 5. Superman (Fictional character)

ISBN 978-0-375-83802-6; 0-375-83802-3; 978-0-375-93802-3 lib bdg; 0-375-93802-8 lib bdg

LC 2007041606

"This book brings the young men behind the Man of Steel to a picture-book audience. Along with the compressed account of the partnership between nerdy high-school outcasts Joe Shuster and Jerry Siegel, Nobleman includes insights about superheroes' cultural significance and the chord struck by Superman. . . . It's hard to imagine a better sidekick for the text than MacDonald's illustrations, which capture the look of 1930s comics with their sepia-toned, stylized imagery." Booklist

Sikorsky, Igor

Wyckoff, Edwin Brit. **Helicopter** man; Igor Sikorsky and his amazing invention. Enslow 2010 32p il (Genius at work! Great inventor biographies) lib bdg $22.60

Grades: 4 5 6   **92**

1. Helicopters 2. Aeronautical engineers 3. Aeronautics -- History 4. Aircraft industry executives

ISBN 978-0-7660-3445-7; 0-7660-3445-3

LC 2009-15881

This is the story of Igor Sikorsky's life, and how he built the first successful helicopter.

Includes glossary and bibliographical references

Sitting Bull, Dakota Chief, 1831-1890

Bruchac, Joseph. A **boy** called Slow; the true story of Sitting Bull; illustrated by Rocco Baviera. Philomel Bks. 1994 un il $16.99; pa $6.99

Grades: 1 2 3   **92**

1. Dakota Indians 2. Indian chiefs

ISBN 0-399-22692-3; 0-698-11616-X pa

LC 93-21233

The author "recounts the early years of the young Lakota boy who grows from an unprepossessing child named 'Slow,' to a youth whose careful and deliberate actions bring honor to the name, to a young warrior whose courage in defeating the Crow earns him his father's vision name Tatan'ka Iyota'ke—Sitting Bull." Bull Cent Child Books

Turner, Ann Warren. **Sitting** Bull remembers; paintings by Wendell Minor. HarperCollinsPublishers 2007 un il $16.99; lib bdg $17.89

Grades: 3 4 5 6   **92**

1. Dakota Indians 2. Little Bighorn, Battle of the, 1876 3. Indian chiefs

ISBN 978-0-06-051399-3; 0-06-051399-3; 978-0-06-051400-6 lib bdg; 0-06-051400-0 lib bdg

LC 2006-29870

"In this first-person, fictionalized account, Sitting Bull is living in captivity near the end of his life and remembering his past. . . . Turner's writing is lyrical, almost poetic. The story is poignant and sympathetic to the plight of the Native peoples who were driven from their land and forced to live on tiny reservations. . . . The well-crafted art adds drama and depth to the story." SLJ

Smalls, Robert, 1839-1915

Halfmann, Janet. **Seven** miles to freedom; the Robert Smalls story. by Janet Halfmann; illustrated by Duane Smith. Lee & Low Books 2008 un il $17.95

Grades: 3 4 5   **92**

1. Slaves 2. State legislators 3. Members of Congress 4. Planter (Steamship) 5. Slavery -- United States 6. African Americans -- Biography 7. African Americans -- Civil rights 8. United States -- History -- 1861-1865, Civil War

ISBN 978-1-60060-232-0; 1-60060-232-0

LC 2007029274

This "will grab readers with exciting action. . . . Spacious, impressionistic oil paintings accompany [the] text." Booklist

This brief "biography describes how Wilma Rudolph overcame childhood polio and competed in the Olympics." Publisher's note

Smith, Elinor, 1911-2010

★ Brown, Tami Lewis. **Soar,** Elinor! pictures by François Roca. Farrar Straus Giroux 2010 un il $16.99

Grades: 2 3 4 5   **92**

1. Air pilots 2. Women air pilots 3. New York (N.Y.) -- History

ISBN 978-0-374-37115-9; 0-374-37115-6

LC 2008-30405

"Elinor Smith began talking flying lessons in 1921 when she was only 10 years old. At 16, she was the youngest person in the U.S., man or woman, to earn a pilot's license. The climax of this picture-book biography is when Smith achieved acclaim as the first person to fly a plane under . . . four of New York City's bridges. . . . Brown's narration is fluent, engaging, and full of dialogue. . . . [The book features] realistic oil illustrations. . . . Roca uses minimal background detail and skillfully arranges scenes to focus attention on the emotions and faces of the characters while still maintaining historical and geographical accuracy." SLJ

Includes bibliographical references

Smith, Louise, 1916-2006

★ Rosenstock, Barbara. **Fearless**; the story of racing legend Louise Smith. [by] Barb Rosenstock; illustrated by Scott Dawson. Dutton Children's Books 2010 un il $16.99

Grades: K 1 2   **92**

1. Automobile racing 2. Automobile drivers 3. Automobile racing drivers

ISBN 978-0-525-42173-3; 0-525-42173-4

LC 2009-53252

"Dawson's gorgeous, light-infused acrylics convey Louise's self-assured nature, while race scenes capture the rush of adrenaline in a blur of glinting metal. Rosenstock's upbeat prose finishes on a high note, with aging Louise flying down a country road. . . . This debut for both author and illustrator is a winner." Publ Wkly

Sneve, Virginia Driving Hawk

Sneve, Virginia Driving Hawk. The **Christmas** coat; memories of my Sioux childhood. illustrated by Ellen Beier. Holiday House 2011 un il $16.95

Grades: K 1 2 3   **92**

1. Authors 2. Christmas 3. Novelists 4. Dakota Indians 5. Clothing and dress 6. Christmas stories 7. Children's authors 8. Young adult authors 9. Native Americans -- Biography

ISBN 978-0-8234-2134-3; 0-8234-2134-1

LC 2010029562

Virginia's coat is too small and hardly protects her from the frigid South Dakota winter. As Christmas approaches, all the children on the Sioux reservation look forward to receiving boxes full of clothing sent by congregations in the East. Virginia spots a beautiful gray fur coat but holds back tears as it is claimed by one of her classmates. Later, Virginia can't believe what Mama brings home. Based on an event from the author's childhood.

"Virginia's personality shines through in this poignant story that entertains and informs without recourse to sterotypes." Kirkus

Snyder, Grace, 1882-1982

Warren, Andrea. **Pioneer** girl; a true story of growing up on the prairie. with a new afterword by the author. University of Nebraska Press 2009 104p il map pa $14.95

Grades: 5 6 7 8   **92**

1. Frontier and pioneer life 2. Quiltmakers 3. Centenarians

ISBN 978-0-8032-2526-8 pa; 0-8032-2526-1 pa

LC 2009-20883

First published 1998 by Morrow Junior Books

Biography of Nebraska homesteader, Grace McCance Snyder

"This new edition offers an afterword that includes information about black homesteaders, Native Americans, and the specific tasks of women, especially quilting. . . . Although it is written for younger readers than a teen audience, readability and intense subject matter should make the book popular with those readers." Voice Youth Advocates

Includes bibliographical references

Sockalexis, Louis, 1871-1913

Wise, Bill. **Louis** Sockalexis; Native American baseball pioneer. by Bill Wise; illustrated by Bill Farnsworth. Lee & Low Books 2007 un il $16.95

Grades: 2 3 4 5   **92**

1. Baseball players 2. Baseball -- Biography 3. Native Americans -- Biography

ISBN 978-1-58430-269-8

LC 2006017730

"This picture book offers a rousing introduction to the life of the first Native American to play major league baseball. . . . Wise and Farnsworth collaborate to great effect in rendering this story both informative and poignant. The color-drenched paintings do an excellent job of bringing this period to life and capturing the intense emotion of the ballpark drama." SLJ

Includes bibliographical references

Soto, Gary

Abrams, Dennis. **Gary** Soto; foreword by Kyle Zimmer. Chelsea House Pubs. 2008 120p bibl il por (Who wrote that?) $30

Grades: 5 6 7 8   **92**

1. Poets 2. Authors 3. Novelists 4. Mexican American authors 5. Essayists 6. College teachers 7. Authors, American 8. Children's authors 9. Young adult authors 10. Mexican Americans -- Biography

ISBN 978-0-7910-9529-4; 0-7910-9529-0

LC 2007045509

A biography of the popular Mexican American author for children and young adults.

Includes bibliographical references

Sotomayor, Sonia, 1954-

Gitlin, Marty. **Sonia** Sotomayor; Supreme Court justice. by Martin Gitlin. ABDO Pub. Co. 2011 112p il (Essential lives) $32.79

Grades: 5 6 7 8   92

1. Judges 2. Women judges 3. District attorneys
4. Supreme Court justices 5. Hispanic Americans --
Biography

ISBN 978-1-61613-518-8; 1-61613-518-2

LC 2010000499

This biography of Supreme Court Justice Sonia Sotomayor "toggles between the subject's personal and professional life; [it] offers sidebar explanations of legal issues. . . . The writing is accessible, the format is open, and full-color photos appear throughout." SLJ

Includes glossary and bibliographical references

McElroy, Lisa Tucker. **Sonia** Sotomayor; first Hispanic U.S. Supreme Court justice. Lerner Publications 2010 48p il lib bdg $26.60

Grades: 5 6 7 8   92

1. Judges 2. Women judges 3. District attorneys
4. Supreme Court justices 5. Hispanic Americans --
Biography

ISBN 978-0-7613-5861-9 lib bdg; 0-7613-5861-7 lib bdg

LC 2009037703

"Well organized and straightforward, this biography is appealing with its bright photographs and bold, easy-to-read font. Starting with Sotomayor's childhood in the Bronx, the author covers the justice's life and career up to her nomination to the Supreme Court. . . . An informative, interesting, and, most of all, inspiring read." SLJ

Includes bibliographical references

Winter, Jonah. **Sonia** Sotomayor; a judge grows in the Bronx. illustrated by Edel Rodriguez. Atheneum Books for Young Readers 2009 un il $16.99

Grades: K 1 2 3   92

1. Judges 2. Women judges 3. District attorneys
4. Supreme Court justices 5. Hispanic Americans --
Biography 6. Bilingual books -- English-Spanish

ISBN 978-1-4424-0303-1; 1-4424-0303-9

LC 2009031659

A biography of the Bronx-born Latina Supreme Court justice.

"This timely, accessible picture-book biography, which features both English and Spanish text on every page, brings Sotomayer's exciting rags-to-riches story to young readers. . . . Winter lets the small details convey the drama, which is amplified in the mixed-media illustrations in warm shades of red and brown." Booklist

Squires, Emily Swain, 19th cent.

Hailstone, Ruth. The **white** ox; the journey of Emily Swain Squires. [illustrations by] Dan Burr; [written by] Ruth Hailstone. Calkins Creek 2009 un il $18.95

Grades: 2 3 4   92

1. Mormons 2. Immigrants 3. Frontier and pioneer life 4. Pioneers

ISBN 978-1-59078-555-3; 1-59078-555-X

LC 2008024154

Hailstone's "narrative describes the real-life journey of ten-year-old Emily Swain Squires (her great-great grand-mother), who traveled ahead of her family from England to Salt Lake City around 1863. During the hardest part of the journey, walking across the plains, she befriended a weary white ox, which gave her enough strength to complete the long trek. Burr uses a digital version of oil painting in Photoshop, applied to a traditional surface, to create 15 stunning and dramatic spreads that appear historically accurate in every detail. Children will be swept up by the lovely art and the tale of Emily's remarkable journey." Kirkus

Standish, Myles, 1584?-1656

Harness, Cheryl. The **adventurous** life of Myles Standish; and the amazing-but-true survival story of Plymouth Colony. painstakingly written and illustrated by Cheryl Harness. National Geographic 2006 144p il map (Cheryl Harness history) $16.95; lib bdg $25.90

Grades: 4 5 6 7   92

1. Pilgrims (New England colonists) 2. Colonists 3. Pilgrim fathers 4. Colonial leaders 5. Massachusetts -- History -- 1600-1775, Colonial period

ISBN 978-0-7922-5918-3; 0-7922-5918-1; 978-0-7922-5919-0 lib bdg; 0-7922-5919-X lib bdg

"Harness chronicles the history of the Plymouth Pilgrims from their troubles in England to their first years in North America, with the focus on Standish. Separating documented history from speculation, the narrative explains religious movements, introduces key figures, and gives a balanced account of Pilgrim-Indian relationships. . . . The tone is casual. . . . A reader-friendly approach to history." Booklist

Includes bibliographical references

Stanton, Elizabeth Cady, 1815-1902

★ Stone, Tanya Lee. **Elizabeth** leads the way: Elizabeth Cady Stanton and the right to vote; illustrations by Rebecca Gibbon. Henry Holt & Co. 2008 un il $16.95

Grades: 1 2 3   92

1. Feminism 2. Suffragists 3. Women -- Suffrage

ISBN 978-0-8050-7903-6; 0-8050-7903-3

LC 2007002833

This is "a short, incisive biography covering some of the high points of Stanton's life, beginning with her shocking realization about how unfairly the law treated women, which translated into Stanton's work for women's suffrage. . . . The child-pleasing artwork features characters a bit reminiscent of clothespin dolls, but the cameos of action, matched by full-page pictures, make the history accessible." Booklist

Stein, Gertrude, 1874-1946

Winter, Jonah. **Gertrude** is Gertrude is Gertrude is Gertrude; written by Jonah Winter; illustrated by Calef Brown. Atheneum Books for Young Readers 2009 un il $16.99

Grades: K 1 2 3   92

1. Poets 2. Authors 3. Novelists 4. Women authors 5. Essayists 6. Memoirists 7. Literary critics 8. Authors, American

ISBN 978-1-4169-4088-3; 1-4169-4088-X

LC 2007-01447

Winter "crafts a Steinesque 'word portrait' of the modernist author. Stein wears a serene smile in Brown's . . . patchy acrylic images, and by her side is an enigmatic Alice B. Toklas. . . . Winter's nonlinear prose echoes The Autobiography of Alice B. Toklas, and his fugues suit a poet fond of repetition (and babble). Brown's idiosyncratic visuals and complementary palette . . . befit this impresario of experimental artists and writers on the Rive Gauche." Publ Wkly

Stowe, Harriet Beecher, 1811-1896

Adler, David A. A **picture** book of Harriet Beecher Stowe; illustrated by Colin Bootman. Holiday House 2003 un il $17.95; pa $6.95

Grades: K 1 2 3 **92**

1. Authors 2. Novelists 3. Abolitionists 4. Women authors 5. Authors, American 6. Children's authors 7. Nonfiction writers 8. Short story writers

ISBN 0-8234-1646-1; 0-8234-1878-2 pa

LC 2002-27626

Details the life and achievements of abolitionist Harriet Beecher Stowe whose book, Uncle Tom's Cabin, is said to have started the Civil War

"This biography offers easily accessible information supported by realistic, evocative oil paintings." SLJ

Includes bibliographical references

Su, Shih, 1036 or 7-1101

Demi. **Su** Dongpo; Chinese genius. Lee & Low Books 2006 un il map $24

Grades: 3 4 5 6 **92**

1. Poets 2. Authors 3. Authors, Chinese 4. Calligraphers

ISBN 978-1-58430-256-8; 1-58430-256-9

LC 2005030437

"Beautifully designed and produced, the book features delicately limned, brilliantly colored paintings of scenes from Su Dongpo's life, outlined in scarlet and bordered with thin bands of gold. A visually striking introduction to the man sometimes referred to as Su Shi or Su Tung-po." Booklist

Sullivan, Anne, 1866-1936

Amoroso, Cynthia. **Helen** Keller; by Cynthia Amoroso and Robert B. Noyed. Child's World 2010 24p il (Basic biographies) lib bdg $22.79

Grades: PreK K 1 **92**

1. Deaf 2. Blind 3. Authors 4. Memoirists 5. Humanitarians 6. Teachers of the deaf 7. Inspirational writers 8. Teachers of the blind 9. Social welfare leaders

ISBN 978-1-60253-341-7; 1-60253-341-5

LC 2009029369

This biography of Helen Keller "pairs intelligent, brief text with abundant photos. Simple but never basic." Booklist

Includes bibliographical references

Delano, Marfe Ferguson. **Helen's** eyes; a photobiography of Annie Sullivan, Helen Keller's teacher. [foreword by Keller Johnson Thompson] National Geographic 2008 63p il map $17.95; lib bdg $27.90

Grades: 4 5 6 7 **92**

1. Deaf 2. Blind 3. Authors 4. Teachers 5. Memoirists 6. Humanitarians 7. Teachers of the deaf 8. Inspirational writers 9. Teachers of the blind 10. Social welfare leaders

ISBN 978-1-4263-02-9-1; 1-4263-0209-6; 978-1-4263-0210-7 lib bdg; 1-4263-0210-X lib bdg

"There are many biographies of Helen Keller and Annie Sullivan, but this one is very nicely done. . . . The book is honest in its portrayals, especially of Sullivan. . . . What

makes this oversize book so appealing is the clean design, with large typeface. The many fascinating photographs are sometimes placed over historical documents." Booklist

Includes bibliographical references

Suzuki, Hiromi

★ Barasch, Lynne. **Hiromi's** hands. Lee & Low Books 2007 un il $17.95

Grades: K 1 2 3 **92**

1. Cooks 2. Cooking 3. Gender role 4. Japanese Americans 5. Sex role 6. Japanese Americans 7. Biography, Individual

ISBN 978-1-58430-275-9

LC 2006017283

This picture book biography tells the story of sushi chef Hiromi Suzuki. "Primary." (Horn Book)

"Ink-and-watercolor scenes are rendered in salmon and grays; each childhood is captured in black-and-white snapshots. . . . An inspiring story." SLJ

Tallchief, Maria

Tallchief, Maria. **Tallchief**; America's prima ballerina. by Maria Tallchief with Rosemary Wells; illustrations by Gary Kelley. Viking 1999 un il $15.99

Grades: 3 4 5 **92**

1. Ballet 2. Ballet dancers 3. Native American women 4. Dance teachers

ISBN 0-670-88756-0

LC 98-35783

Ballerina Maria Tallchief describes her childhood on an Osage reservation, the development of her love of dance, and her rise to success in that field

"Through eloquent words, readers are immediately drawn into the first-person narrative. . . . As beautiful as the text is, so too are Kelley's pictures. The large illustrations, several covering double-page spreads, are rendered in soft pastels." SLJ

Tatum, Art, 1910-1956

★ Parker, Robert Andrew. **Piano** starts here: the young Art Tatum. Schwartz & Wade Books 2008 un il $16.99; lib bdg $19.99

Grades: K 1 2 3 **92**

1. Pianists 2. Jazz musicians 3. African American musicians

ISBN 978-0-375-83965-8; 0-375-83965-8; 978-0-375-93965-5 lib bdg; 0-375-93965-5 lib bdg

LC 2006-102105

This is a "a biography of famed jazz pianist Art Tatum. . . . A subtle sophistication shines through Parker's easygoing yet dynamic watercolors. . . . Parker's unhurried account could inspire visions of jazz greatness among young musicians." Publ Wkly

Includes bibliographical references

Taylor, Annie Edson, 1838-1921

★ Van Allsburg, Chris, 1949- **Queen** of the Falls. Houghton Mifflin Harcourt 2011 un il $18.99

Grades: 3 4 5 **92**

1. Teachers 2. Stunt performers 3. Niagara Falls (N.Y. and Ont.) 4. Biography, Individual

ISBN 0-547-31581-3; 978-0-547-31581-2

LC 2010006780

This picture book tells the story of how "a retired sixty-two-year-old charm school instructor named Annie Edson Taylor, seeking fame and fortune, decided to . . . go over Niagara Falls in a wooden barrel." (Publisher's note) "Primary, intermediate." (Horn Book)

"Any kid who has beheld Niagara Falls—or even taken a good look at pictures of it—will be suitably gobsmacked by the true story of charm-school teacher Annie Edson Taylor, who, at age 62, decided on a whim to fund her golden years by being the first person over the falls. . . . On October 24, 1901, [a] reinforced and padded 160-pound [barrel] was dropped into the water in front of thousands of nervous spectators. Van Allsburg's trademark framed illustrations have the unnerving stillness of old-timey photos." Booklist

Taylor, Major, 1878-1932

Brill, Marlene Targ. **Marshall** Major Taylor; world champion bicyclist, 1899-1901. by Marlene Targ Brill. Twenty-First Century Books 2008 112p il (Trailblazer biography) lib bdg $31.93

Grades: 5 6 7 8   92

1. Bicycle racing 2. African American athletes 3. Cyclists

ISBN 978-0-8225-6610-6 lib bdg; 0-8225-6610-9 lib bdg

LC 2006003883

"Marshall Taylor, an African American bicyclist who, despite facing prejudice in racing and in life, achieved world renown at the turn of the last century. . . . Brill's accessible, personable prose vividly relates Taylor's experiences." Booklist

Includes bibliographical references

Tenzing Norgay, 1914-1986

Burleigh, Robert. **Tiger** of the snows; Tenzing Norgay; the boy whose dream was Everest. [by] Robert Burleigh and [illustrated by] Ed Young. Simon & Schuster 2006 un il $16.95

Grades: 3 4 5 6   92

1. Mountaineering 2. Mountaineers 3. Mount Everest (China and Nepal)

ISBN 0-689-83042-4

LC 2005-00469

Presents the true story of Nepalese Sherpa Tenzing Norgay who, realizing his own dreams, helped Sir Edmund Hillary reach the summit of Mount Everest.

"Young's hauntingly beautiful illustrations capture the mystery and grandeur of these dangerously high peaks with somber-hued pastels, predominantly blues and purples, set against black backgrounds. . . . A stunning and lyrical ode to a contemplative man and his amazing achievement." SLJ

Thurman, Howard, 1900-1981

Jackson Issa, Kai. **Howard** Thurman's great hope; by Kai Jackson Issa; illustrated by Arthur L. Dawson. Lee & Low Books 2008 un il $16.95

Grades: 2 3 4 5   92

1. Clergy 2. Theologians 3. College teachers 4. Inspirational writers

ISBN 978-1-60060-249-8; 1-60060-249-5

LC 2007050093

"Reds, blues, and yellows pop against brown wood desks or whitewashed walls in vivid, realistic oil paintings.

The author drew from Thurman's memoir and papers to create this accessible, engaging biography." SLJ

Tillage, Leon, 1936-

★ Tillage, Leon. **Leon's** story; [by] Leon Walter Tillage; collage art by Susan L. Roth. Farrar, Straus & Giroux 1997 107p il hardcover o.p. pa $6.95

Grades: 4 5 6 7 8 9 10   92

1. African Americans -- Biography 2. North Carolina -- Race relations

ISBN 0-374-34379-9; 0-374-44330-0 pa

LC 96-43544

The son of a North Carolina sharecropper recalls the hard times faced by his family and other African Americans in the first half of the twentieth century and the changes that the civil rights movement helped bring about

The author's "voice is direct, the words are simple. There is no rhetoric, no commentary, no bitterness. . . . This quiet drama will move readers of all ages . . . and may encourage them to record their own family stories." Booklist

Tingle, Tim

★ Tingle, Tim. **Saltypie**; a Choctaw journey from darkness into light. with illustrations by Karen Clarkson. Cinco Puntos Press 2010 40p il

Grades: 2 3 4 5   92

1. Blind 2. Grandmothers 3. Choctaw Indians 4. Storytellers

ISBN 1933693673; 9781933693675

"Tingle tells his family's story from their origins in Oklahoma Choctaw country to their life in Texas. The account spans generations and weaves in ghosts from the past to the present day. . . . The author was six when he learned that his grandmother was blind. Tingle was a junior in college when he got word that Mawmaw was having surgery. As the family gathered at the hospital, they told stories about their past, and he heard about her days as an orphan at an Indian boarding school and the discrimination she encountered living in Texas. . . . The large, full-spread illustrations are vibrant and vital in moving the story along. A lovely piece of family history." SLJ

Toulouse-Lautrec, Henri de, 1864-1901

Burleigh, Robert. **Toulouse**-Lautrec; the Moulin Rouge and the City of Light. Abrams 2005 32p il $17.95

Grades: 3 4 5   92

1. Artists 2. Painters 3. Lithographers 4. Artists, French

ISBN 0-8109-5867-8

This "volume introduces the life and art of Toulouse-Lautrec. . . . Burleigh relates the facts in a way that is comprehensible to children, without talking down to them. . . . The book's format allows for many illustrations, including period photos and paintings of Paris by artists such as Pissarro and Renoir, which are cleverly mingled with reproductions of Toulouse-Lautrec's arresting drawings, paintings, and lithographs, many in color. . . . A beautifully designed book that provides a lively, accessible introduction to the artist's life and work." Booklist

Toussaint Louverture, 1743?-1803

★ Rockwell, Anne F. **Open** the door to liberty!: a biography of Toussaint L'Ouverture; illustrated by R. Gregory

Christie. Houghton Mifflin Books for Children 2009 64p il $18
Grades: 5 6 7 8 **92**
  1. Generals 2. Revolutionaries 3. Haiti -- History 4. Blacks -- Biography 5. Slavery -- West Indies
  ISBN 978-0-618-60570-5; 0-618-60570-3
                  LC 2007-25746
"In this eye-opening biography, Rockwell makes a strong case that Toussaint L'Ouverture is one of the most overlooked heroes of the eighteenth century. A freed slave of the French colony of St. Domingue (what we now know as Haiti), L'Ouverture was 48 when he was so inspired by his people's uprising against the French that he joined them and, through his oratory and strategical skills, became their leader. In 1793, he led history's first triumphant slave rebellion, but the resulting freedom would not last long. . . . Evocative paintings in primary colors help tell the story." Booklist
  Includes bibliographical references

Truth, Sojourner, d. 1883
Clinton, Catherine. **When** Harriet met Sojourner; illustrated by Shane W. Evans. Katherine Tegen Books 2008 un il $16.99; lib bdg $17.89
Grades: K 1 2 3 **92**
  1. Abolitionists 2. Memoirists 3. Slavery -- United States 4. African American women -- Biography
  ISBN 978-0-06-050425-0; 0-06-050425-0; 978-0-06-050426-7 lib bdg; 0-06-050426-9 lib bdg
                  LC 2006-19099
"Clinton imagines what might have been said during a meeting between Harriet Tubman and Sojourner Truth, who both found themselves in Boston one day in October 1864. Their meeting is the climax of this picture book, which tells the stories of the two heroes in clear, simple words on alternating double-page spreads. Evans' dramatic collage-style illustrations evoke the quilts the women worked on, piecing together their history." Booklist

★ Pinkney, Andrea Davis. **Sojourner** Truth's step-stomp stride; [by] Andrea Davis Pinkney & Brian Pinkney. Disney Jump at the Sun Books 2009 un il $16.99
Grades: K 1 2 3 **92**
  1. Feminism 2. Abolitionists 3. Memoirists 4. African American women -- Biography
  ISBN 978-0-7868-0767-3; 0-7868-0767-9
The Pinkneys "collaborate on an upbeat yet nuanced picture biography of Sojourner Truth, whose slave name was Isabella. . . . Andrea Davis Pinkney's narrative adopts a confidential, admiring tone, tracing Truth's years of enslaved toil, her subsequent escape, deep religious faith and narration of her life story to abolitionist Olive Gilbert. . . . Brian Pinkney's watercolors, in washes of ochre and slate blue contoured in inky black, utilize a dry-brush technique well suited for depicting Truth's hardscrabble youth and unyielding commitment to justice." Kirkus

Rockwell, Anne F. **Only** passing through: the story of Sojourner Truth; by Anne Rockwell; illustrated by Gregory Christie. Knopf 2000 un il $16.95; lib bdg $18.99
Grades: 3 4 5 **92**
  1. Feminism 2. Abolitionists 3. Memoirists 4. African American women -- Biography
  ISBN 0-679-89186-2; 0-679-99186-7 lib bdg
                  LC 00-35736

Rockwell's narrative "is both conversational and immediately riveting. . . . The semi-abstract paintings are inspirational rather than representational, their authority residing in the presence Christie imparts to this heroine." Bull Cent Child Books

Turner, Ann. **My** Name Is Truth; The Life of Sojourner Truth. Ann Turner; illustrated by James Ransome. Harpercollins Childrens Books 2015 40 p. color illustrations $17.99
Grades: 1 2 3 4 **92**
  1. Civil rights 2. African American women 3. African American -- Biography 4. African American abolitionists -- Biography 5. Social reformers -- United States -- Biography
  ISBN 0060758988; 9780060758981
Author Ann Turner presents the "true story of how former slave Isabella Baumfree transformed herself into the preacher and orator Sojourner Truth. An iconic figure of the abolitionist and women's rights movements, Sojourner Truth famously spoke out for equal rights roughly one hundred years before the civil rights movement." (Publisher's note)
"This picture book biography tackles the life of former slave and abolitionist Isabella Baumfree, better known as Sojourner Truth. Turner details the life of this pivotal figure, who was born into slavery in the late-18th century in New York, along with 11 siblings, all of whom were sold off... Those who are already somewhat familiar with Truth will get the most out of this book, and educators will find the author's note helpful in explaining this historical figure to students. A wonderful addition to collections of African American history that will also work well as a read-aloud." SLJ

Tubman, Harriet, 1820?-1913
Clinton, Catherine. **When** Harriet met Sojourner; illustrated by Shane W. Evans. Katherine Tegen Books 2008 un il $16.99; lib bdg $17.89
Grades: K 1 2 3 **92**
  1. Abolitionists 2. Memoirists 3. Slavery -- United States 4. African American women -- Biography
  ISBN 978-0-06-050425-0; 0-06-050425-0; 978-0-06-050426-7 lib bdg; 0-06-050426-9 lib bdg
                  LC 2006-19099
"Clinton imagines what might have been said during a meeting between Harriet Tubman and Sojourner Truth, who both found themselves in Boston one day in October 1864. Their meeting is the climax of this picture book, which tells the stories of the two heroes in clear, simple words on alternating double-page spreads. Evans' dramatic collage-style illustrations evoke the quilts the women worked on, piecing together their history." Booklist

Turner, Glennette Tilley. An **apple** for Harriet Tubman; [by] Glennette Tilley Turner; illustrated by Susan Keeter. Albert Whitman & Co. 2006 un il $15.95
Grades: 2 3 4 **92**
  1. Apples 2. Abolitionists 3. Slavery -- United States 4. African American women -- Biography
  ISBN 978-0-8075-0395-9; 0-8075-0395-9
                  LC 2005037360
"At age seven, Tubman's job was to care for the baby of an unkind white woman, who whipped her. Later, the overseer of an orchard lashes her for eating an apple. . . . Ketter's unframed, thickly painted pictures depict the slave child's

cruel working conditions and her brave escape and rescue, culminating as Tubman buys a house and plants apple trees, which produce fruit for everyone to share. The story, with its concrete details, works as both fact and metaphor, bringing the transformation full circle—from the scars of suffering to the fruit of freedom." Booklist

Includes bibliographical references

★ Weatherford, Carole Boston. **Moses**; when Harriet Tubman led her people to freedom. illustrated by Kadir Nelson. Hyperion 2006 un il $15.99
Grades: 2 3 4   92
1. Abolitionists 2. Underground railroad 3. African American women -- Biography
ISBN 0-7868-5175-9
A Caldecott Medal honor book, 2007
Describes Tubman's spiritual journey as she hears the voice of God guiding her north to freedom on that very first trip to escape the brutal practice of forced servitude.
This is a "handsome, poetic account. . . . Shifting perspectives and subtle details . . . . underscore the narrative's spirituality. . . . Tubman's beautifully furrowed face is expressive and entrancing." SLJ

Tutankhamen, King of Egypt
Demi. **Tutankhamun**; written and illustrated by Demi. Marshall Cavendish Children 2009 un il map $19.99
Grades: 4 5 6 7   92
1. Kings and rulers 2. Kings 3. Egypt -- History
ISBN 978-0-7614-5558-5; 0-7614-5558-2
LC 2008029313
"The unmistakable designs and opulent glitter of ancient Egyptian art gleam on every page of Demi's picture-book introduction to Tutankhamun. Beginning with King Tut's great-grandfather, Demi presents the broad historical context surrounding the young monarch's reign. . . . Demi's language, organized into brief but pithy paragraphs, is clear. . . . It's the beautiful illustrations that will attract and hold a young audience most, and as usual, Demi incorporates artistic motifs and materials appropriate to her subject." Booklist

Twain, Mark, 1835-1910
★ Burleigh, Robert. The **adventures** of Mark Twain by Huckleberry Finn; with considerable help from Robert Burleigh and [illustrated by] Barry Blitt. Atheneum Books for Young Readers 2011 un il
Grades: 2 3 4   92
1. Authors 2. Humorists 3. Novelists 4. Essayists 5. Satirists 6. Memoirists 7. Travel writers 8. Authors, American 9. Short story writers 10. Biography, Individual
ISBN 0689830416; 9780689830419
LC 2010006512
This is a biography of Mark Twain told from the perspective of one of his characters. "Grades two to five." (Bull Cent Child Books)
"The neat switcheroo in this picture-book biography has the story of Mark Twain's life told by one of his most endearing characters, Huck Finn. . . . Although Huck's narration is almost overwhelmingly folksy, his undeniably cheery tone is infectious. . . . Blitt . . . provides jaunty, cartoony pen-and-watercolor artwork, with exaggerated, tall-tale figures and period charm aplenty." Booklist

★ Fleischman, Sid. The **trouble** begins at 8; a life of Mark Twain in the wild, wild West. Greenwillow Books 2008 224p il $18.99; lib bdg $19.89
Grades: 5 6 7 8   92
1. Authors 2. Humorists 3. Novelists 4. Essayists 5. Satirists 6. Memoirists 7. Travel writers 8. Authors, American 9. Short story writers 10. Biography, Individual
ISBN 0-06-134431-1; 0-06-134432-X lib bdg; 978-0-06-134431-2; 978-0-06-134432-9 lib bdg
LC 2007-37891
This biography of Mark Twain focuses on his travels. Chronology. Index. "Grades five to nine." (Bull Cent Child Books)
"Fleischman writes a charming biography of Samuel Clemens before he became Mark Twain, the great American novelist. . . . Written with a sense of humor and wit that honors Twain, this book is sprinkled with famous Twain quotes, excerpts of his writing, and pictures of Twain and other primary documents from the era Clemens spent both on the Mississippi River and in the West." Voice Youth Advocates
Includes bibliographical references

★ Kerley, Barbara. The **extraordinary** Mark Twain (according to Susy) illustrated by Edwin Fotheringam. Scholastic Press 2010 un il $17.99
Grades: 2 3 4 5   92
1. Authors 2. Biography 3. Humorists 4. Novelists 5. Authorship 6. Essayists 7. Satirists 8. Memoirists 9. Travel writers 10. Authors, American 11. Short story writers
ISBN 978-0-545-12508-6; 0-545-12508-1
LC 2009-04752
"Wanting to present a portrait of her papa beyond that of just humorist and author, Mark Twain's 13-year-old daughter Susy spent a year chronicling her observations and reflections. . . . Kerley contextualizes the teenager's admiring musings with vivid familial backdrops. . . . Minibooklets titled 'Journal' appear in the fold of many spreads, containing excerpts from Susy's notebook. . . . Adding dynamic flair to the limited palettes of each digitally created scene are curlicues representing words, which emanate wildly from pen tips, pages, and mouths. Author notes about Susy and her father, a time line of Twain's life, and tips for writing an 'extraordinary biography' complete this accessible and inventive vision of a American legend." Publ Wkly

Velázquez, Diego, 1599-1660
Venezia, Mike. **Diego** Velázquez; written and illustrated by Mike Venezia. Children's Press 2004 32p il (Getting to know the world's greatest artists) lib bdg $26; pa $6.95
Grades: K 1 2 3   92
1. Artists 2. Painters 3. Artists, Spanish
ISBN 0-516-22580-4 lib bdg; 0-516-26980-1 pa
LC 2003-4590
Describes the life and career of the seventeenth-century Spanish artist famous for his portraits of royalty.
"The unusually abundant full-color reproductions more than justify this series' longevity, as do Venezia's lighthearted cartoons, which foster welcome associations between 'art appreciation' and 'fun.'" Booklist

Vivaldi, Antonio, 1678-1741

Shefelman, Janice Jordan. **I,** Vivaldi; written by Janice Shefelman; illustrated by Tom Shefelman. William B. Eerdmans Pub. Co. 2007 un il $18

Grades: 3 4 5   **92**

1. Composers 2. Violinists

ISBN 978-0-8028-5318-9; 0-8028-5318-8

LC 2006-20120

This is a picture book "biography of composer Antonio Vivaldi. . . . The first-person narration offers an accessible and personable view of Vivaldi's intense passion for music. . . . Stunning ink-and-watercolor scenes evoke the ornate, shadowy church interiors and gilded ornamentation of 17th century Venice." Publ Wkly

Wagner, Honus, 1874-1955

★ Yolen, Jane. **All** star! Honus Wagner and the most famous baseball card ever. illustrated by Jim Burke. Philomel Books 2010 un il $17.99

Grades: 2 3 4   **92**

1. Baseball cards 2. Baseball players 3. Baseball coaches 4. Baseball managers 5. Baseball -- Biography 6. Pittsburgh Pirates (Baseball team)

ISBN 978-0-399-24661-6; 0-399-24661-4

LC 2009-15066

Biography of Honus Wagner and an explanation of why his baseball card is worth almost $3 million.

"The treatment of Wagner's hardscrabble early years . . . is particularly masterful. . . . An eloquently understated tribute to that archetypal American combination of stoicism, decency, drive, and sheer talent." Publ Wkly

Wague Diakite, Baba

A **gift** from childhood; memories of an African boyhood. Groundwood Books 2010 134p il $18.95

Grades: 5 6 7 8   **92**

1. Artists 2. Authors 3. Illustrators 4. Mali 5. Children's authors 6. Africa

ISBN 0-88899-931-3; 978-0-88899-931-3

This is a memoir about growing up in a small village in Mali. "Age ten and up." (N Y Times Book Rev)

"Diakite's . . . illustrated memoir focuses on his childhood in a small Malian village. . . . Interspersed with Diakite's recounting of his youth . . . are stories about his grandfather's brokering peaceful relations with the French, a blacksmith who stymies Death, and others. . . . Diakite's precise language and vibrant illustrations, created on earthenware tiles, form an engrossing story of community life. Studded with Malian proverbs, metaphors, and morals . . . it's a memoir alive with far more voices than just that of the author." Publ Wkly

Waldman, Neil, 1947-

Waldman, Neil. **Out** of the shadows; an artist's journey. Boyds Mills Press 2006 144p il $21.95

Grades: 5 6 7 8   **92**

1. Artists 2. Authors 3. Illustrators 4. Jews -- Biography 5. Children's authors 6. Artists -- United States

ISBN 1-59078-411-1

Neil Waldman reveals how his passion for art emerged in the kitchen of his family's apartment, where he discovered the work of Vincent Van Gogh and the ability to use illustration as a means to escape the sadness that plagued his home.

"Young artists, as well as readers who wonder about the person behind the pictures they have seen, will appreciate every element of this book: well-constructed story, visual richness, and uncompromising honesty." Booklist

Walker, C. J., Madame, 1867-1919

Lasky, Kathryn. **Vision** of beauty: the story of Sarah Breedlove Walker; illustrated by Nneka Bennett. Candlewick Press 2000 un il $14.99

Grades: 3 4 5   **92**

1. Philanthropists 2. African American businesspeople 3. Cosmeticians 4. Cosmetics industry executives 5. African American women -- Biography

ISBN 9780763664282

LC 99-19594

This is a biography of the African American entrepreneur who founded a cosmetics company and became a millionaire. "Grades three to five." (Bull Cent Child Books)

"Lasky's engaging account moves smoothly through events in Walker's life. . . . The illustrations . . . are attractive and rich in historical detail." Booklist

Walking Coyote

Bruchac, Joseph, 1942- **Buffalo** song; by Joseph Bruchac; illustrated by Bill Farnsworth. Lee & Low Books 2008 un il $17.95

Grades: 1 2 3   **92**

1. Bison 2. Kalispel Indians 3. Wildlife conservation 4. Animal rescue workers 5. Native Americans -- Biography

ISBN 978-1-58430-280-3; 1-58430-280-1

LC 2007024912

This biography is "partly fictionalized. . . . Bruchac's long, eloquent afterword fills in the facts. . . . [It is illustrated with] Farnsworth's beautiful, full-bleed oil paintings." Booklist

"The story of the first efforts to save the vanishing bison (buffalo) herds from extinction in the United States in the 1870s and 1880s. Based on the true story of Samuel Walking Coyote, a Salish (Kalispel) Indian who rescued and raised orphaned buffalo calves." Publisher's note

Walton, Sam

Blumenthal, Karen. **Mr.** Sam; how Sam Walton built Wal-Mart and became America's richest man. Penguin Group 2011 183p il $17.99

Grades: 5 6 7 8   **92**

1. Businessmen 2. Discount stores 3. Retail executives 4. Wal-Mart Stores, Inc. 5. Biography, Individual

ISBN 978-0-670-01177-3; 0-670-01177-0

LC 2010049520

"This spectacular success story tracks Walton's rise from lower-middle-class origins to, by the mid-1980s, the top of the 'America's Richest' list. . . . Written in a fluid, journalistic style and enhanced by photos, boxed-out 'Sam stories,' charts tracking changes in Americans' spending habits, and a lavish source list, this account of the man who created what is today the world's largest company makes compelling reading." Booklist

Warhol, Andy, 1928?-1987

★ Christensen, Bonnie. **Fabulous!** a portrait of Andy Warhol. Henry Holt and Co. 2011 un il $16.99

Grades: 3 4 5 6   **92**

   1. Artists -- United States   2. Pop art   3. Biography, Individual

ISBN 978-0-8050-8753-6; 0-8050-8753-2

LC 2010027840

"Spanning Warhol's rise to fame, this thoughtful account begins and ends with brief, fictionalized scenes that take place in 1966, illuminating the pop artist's popularity and success in contrast to the challenges he overcame to achieve recognition. The bulk of the narrative is fact-based, tracing major milestones in Warhol's personal and professional life through well-organized chronological flashbacks. . . . The differences between fine and commercial art, and Warhol's success in melding the two styles, are addressed in a way that is easy to understand even for someone with no background in art history. Christensen skillfully conveys emotion and mood through vivid, bold collage illustrations." SLJ

Includes bibliographical references

★ Rubin, Susan Goldman. **Andy** Warhol; pop art painter. H.N. Abrams 2006 48p il $18.95

Grades: 4 5 6 7   **92**

   1. Artists   2. Pop art   3. Artists -- United States   4. Motion picture directors

ISBN 0-8109-5477-X

LC 2005-13238

"Andy Warhol was a colorful figure who revolutionized how the world looks at art. Rubin's coherent and interesting narrative is filled with quotes by the artist and people who knew him. . . . Excellent-quality black-and-white and full-color photographs of Warhol and his family and reproductions of his paintings and those of others who influenced him appear throughout." SLJ

Washington, Booker T., 1856-1915

Brimner, Larry Dane. **Booker** T. Washington; getting into the schoolhouse. Marshall Cavendish Benchmark 2009 41p il (American heroes) lib bdg $20.95

Grades: 2 3 4   **92**

   1. Slaves   2. Authors   3. Educators   4. African American educators   5. Memoirists   6. Nonfiction writers   7. Tuskegee Institute   8. Civil rights activists   9. African Americans -- Biography

ISBN 978-0-7614-3063-6

LC 2008002870

A biography of Booker T. Washington, who rose from slavery to become a great African-American leader and educator

This "concise and well-written [title covers] key biographical facts without overwhelming young readers, and [includes] captioned illustrations and reproductions, most of which are in color. Text is large, and the layout is age-appropriate and attractive, with wide margins." SLJ

Includes glossary and bibliographical references

Washington, George, 1732-1799

Adler, David A. **George** Washington; an illustrated biography. by David A. Adler. Holiday House 2004 274p il map $24.95

Grades: 5 6 7 8   **92**

   1. Generals   2. Presidents   3. Presidents -- United States

ISBN 0-8234-1838-3

LC 2003-67606

This "look at America's premier founding father literally spans his lifetime and attempts to focus . . . on how Washington's early character formation impacted his decisions as a military officer and later as president. . . . The illustrations are largely engravings from the late 19th century. . . . The writing style is accessible without ever falling prey to oversimplification." SLJ

Allen, Kathy. **President** George Washington; illustrated by Len Ebert. Picture Window Books 2010 32p il (Our American story) lib bdg $23.99

Grades: 2 3 4   **92**

   1. Generals   2. Presidents   3. Presidents -- United States

ISBN 978-1-4048-5539-7; 1-4048-5539-4

LC 2009-6894

Highlights the life and accomplishments of the Commander in Chief of the Continental Army and first president of the United States.

This title is "illustrated with well-executed, full-page, color illustrations, maps, and photos. . . . [It has] accurate, clearly written information that students can use for either leisure reading or reports." SLJ

Includes glossary and bibliographical references

Dolan, Edward F. **George** Washington; [by] Edward F. Dolan. Marshall Cavendish Benchmark 2008 96p il (Presidents and their times) lib bdg $32.79

Grades: 5 6 7 8   **92**

   1. Generals   2. Presidents   3. Presidents -- United States

ISBN 978-0-7614-2427-7 lib bdg; 0-7614-2427-X lib bdg

LC 2006037802

This biography of the first president of the United States "is illustrated with color photos and contains boxed descriptions of key historical events, artwork, and political concepts experienced during the time period. . . . This . . . will be of great use both for biographical research and for enriching the curriculum." Libr Media Connect

Includes glossary and bibliographical references

Malaspina, Ann. **Phillis** sings out freedom; the story of George Washington and Phillis Wheatley. illustrated by Susan Keeter. Albert Whitman 2010 un il $16.99

Grades: 2 3 4   **92**

   1. Poets   2. Slaves   3. Authors   4. Generals   5. Presidents   6. Women poets   7. African American authors   8. Poets, American   9. Presidents -- United States   10. African American women -- Biography   11. United States -- History -- 1775-1783, Revolution

ISBN 978-0-8075-6545-2; 0-8075-6545-8

"Camped in Cambridge in the fall of 1775, General Washington despairs that his soldiers won't ever be able to defeat the British. In Providence, freed slave Phillis Wheatley pens a poem of encouragement to Washington. Malaspina intertwines information about Wheatley's early life with wartime events. . . . Keeter's rich oil paintings are full of period details that help to clarify both the war scenes and Wheatley's life." Booklist

Miller, Brandon Marie. **George** Washington for kids; his life and times with 21 activities. [by] Brandon Marie Miller. Chicago Review Press 2007 130p il pa $14.95

Grades: 4 5 6 7 **92**

1. Generals 2. Presidents 3. Presidents -- United States

ISBN 1-55652-655-5 pa; 978-1-55652-655-8 pa

This book covers Washington's life and includes 21 hands-on projects based on his experiences and the times in which he lived.

This is "accessible and absorbing . . . clearly written and informative. . . . Primary quotes are interposed throughout, and illustrations, photographs, and visual aids are plentiful and well placed." SLJ

Mooney, Carla. **George** Washington; 25 great projects you can build yourself. illustrated by Samuel Carbaugh. Nomad 2011 121p il (Build it yourself) $21.95; pa $15.95

Grades: 4 5 6 7 **92**

1. Generals 2. Handicraft 3. Presidents 4. Presidents -- United States

ISBN 978-1-934670-64-4; 1-934670-64-2; 978-1-934670-63-7 pa pa; 1-934670-63-4 pa

"The life of George Washington lends itself remarkably well to a variety of kid-friendly crafts that don't require old-fashioned materials or 18th-century skills. . . . The projects separate biographical chapters that are thorough and clear. . . . Sidebars with vocabulary words, quotes, interesting facts about the man and his time, and 'What if?' questions regarding pivotal moments in Washington's life add to the text. These sidebars, as well as amusing cartoon illustrations, make the subject light and approachable." SLJ

Includes glossary and bibliographical references

★ Rockwell, Anne F. **Big** George: how a shy boy became President Washington; [by] Anne Rockwell; illustrated by Matt Phelan. Harcourt 2009 un il $17

Grades: K 1 2 3 **92**

1. Generals 2. Presidents 3. Presidents -- United States

ISBN 0-15-216583-5; 978-0-15-216583-3

LC 2002-4984

Portrays George Washington as a shy boy who wasn't afraid of anything except talking to people, but who grew up to lead an army against the British and serve as president of the new nation

This "adulatory biography offers plenty for contemporary kids to connect with. . . . But it's Phelan's . . . extraordinary artwork that cements the bond with readers. As his pencil-and-gouache scenes review Washington's life up to the presidency, his scenes bristle with immediacy, dramatic tension and emotional insight." Publ Wkly

White, Becky. **Betsy** Ross; illustrated by Megan Lloyd. Holiday House 2011 il $16.95

Grades: K 1 2 **92**

1. Generals 2. Presidents 3. Dressmakers 4. Needleworkers 5. Flags -- United States 6. United States -- History -- 1775-1783, Revolution

ISBN 978-0-8234-1908-1; 0-8234-1908-8

LC 2009054296

"Fourteen spreads with four to six rhythmic words on each one tell the story of the first American flag. . . . The large, simple text, paired with the irresistible appliqué art, makes this a perfect introduction to the Stars and Stripes. Using cotton fabric, embroidery thread, dye, paint, and linoleum-block prints, Lloyd captures the period, hard work, and ingenuity of this favorite colonial figure." SLJ

Weber, EdNah New Rider

Weber, EdNah New Rider. **Rattlesnake** Mesa; stories from a native American childhood. by EdNah New Rider Weber; photographs by Richela Renkun. Lee & Low Books 2004 132p il $18.95

Grades: 4 5 6 7 **92**

1. Artisans 2. Memoirists 3. Storytellers 4. Native Americans -- Biography

ISBN 1-58430-231-3

LC 2004-2385

"Weber describes her experiences with warmth and affection in this unusually compelling memoir. Striking black-and-white photos . . . add to the book's appeal." Horn Book Guide

Wells-Barnett, Ida B., 1862-1931

Dray, Philip. **Yours** for justice, Ida B. Wells; the daring life of crusading journalist. written by Philip Dray; illustrated by Stephen Alcorn. Peachtree Publishers 2008 un il $18.95

Grades: 2 3 4 **92**

1. Authors 2. Journalists 3. Essayists 4. Nonfiction writers 5. Newspaper executives 6. Civil rights activists 7. United States -- Race relations 8. African Americans -- Civil rights 9. African American women -- Biography

ISBN 978-1-56145-417-4; 1-56145-417-6

LC 2007-4016

"Dray introduces this civil rights crusader and journalist who campaigned tirelessly to end the practice of lynching. . . . Alcorn's ink-and-watercolor illustrations have a fluid quality, conveying both action within the story and movement from one scene to the next. . . . This makes a good choice for middle-grade readers." Booklist

Includes bibliographical references

★ Myers, Walter Dean, 1937-2014 **Ida** B. Wells; let the truth be told. illustrated by Bonnie Christensen. HarperCollinsPublishers 2008 37p il $16.99; lib bdg $17.89

Grades: 2 3 4 5 **92**

1. Authors 2. Journalists 3. Essayists 4. Nonfiction writers 5. Newspaper executives 6. Civil rights activists 7. United States -- Race relations 8. African Americans -- Civil rights 9. African American women -- Biography

ISBN 978-0-06-027705-5; 0-06-027705-X; 978-0-06-027706-2 lib bdg; 0-06-027706-8 lib bdg

LC 2007-40107

"Myers deals with Wells-Barnett's career—from child of slaves, to teacher, to writer and organizer in the causes of anti-lynching and women's suffrage—in a style accessible to younger elementary audiences. . . . Each spread features a limited amount of text, and sourced quotations from Well-Barnett are frequently appended in red. Christensen's shaggy line and watercolor illustrations soften the rougher edges of the drama without straying into cartoonishness." Bull Cent Child Books

West, Benjamin, 1738-1820

Brenner, Barbara. The **boy** who loved to draw: Benjamin West; illustrated by Olivier Dunrea. Houghton Mifflin 1999 un il $15; pa $6.99

Grades: K 1 2 3 **92**

1. Artists 2. Painters 3. Artists -- United States 4.

United States -- History -- 1600-1775, Colonial period
ISBN 0-395-85080-0; 0-618-31089-4 pa
LC 97-5183

Recounts the life story of the Pennsylvania artist who began drawing as a boy and eventually became well known on both sides of the Atlantic

"Naive in style and reminiscent of some colonial art, the illustrations present clear visual expressions of the activities and emotions related in the story. . . . A fascinating look at art in colonial times, and a likable portrait of the artist as a young boy." Booklist

Wheatley, Phillis, 1753-1784

Clinton, Catherine. **Phillis's** big test; written by Catherine Clinton; illustrated by Sean Qualls. Houghton Mifflin 2008 un il $16
Grades: 1 2 3 4   92
1. Poets 2. Slaves 3. Authors 4. Women poets 5. African American authors 6. Poets, American 7. Slavery -- United States
ISBN 978-0-618-73739-0; 0-618-73739-1
LC 2007-13241

"This picture-book biography deals with a transformative moment in the life of Phillis Wheatley, the first African American to publish a book of poetry. In 1772, 18 members of the intelligentsia from the Massachusetts Bay Colony . . . gathered to question the 17-year-old slave to ascertain the authorship of the poems she claimed were her own. . . . Qualls's uncluttered acrylic and collage compositions employ strong diagonal lines, swirling ribbons of thought, and a combination of opaque images and outlined, transparent figures over washes of color to create visual interest. . . . A formal tone, an occasional quaint turn of phrase, and a typeface with an irregular impression create the flavor of a time past. Clinton and Qualls offer an elegant introduction to an important individual." SLJ

Lasky, Kathryn. A **voice** of her own: the story of Phillis Wheatley, slave poet; illustrated by Paul Lee. Candlewick Press 2003 un il $17.99; pa $7.99
Grades: 3 4 5   92
1. Poets 2. Slaves 3. Authors 4. Women poets 5. African American authors 6. Poets, American 7. Slavery -- United States
ISBN 0-7636-0252-3; 0-7636-2878-6 pa
LC 2001-47139

A biography of an African girl brought to New England as a slave in 1761 who became famous on both sides of the Atlantic as the first Black poet in America

Written "in evocative language that's rich with historical detail. . . . This will serve as a good introduction to Wheatley's life and times for young children, who will appreciate Lee's full-page, historically accurate acrylics." Booklist

Malaspina, Ann. **Phillis** sings out freedom; the story of George Washington and Phillis Wheatley. illustrated by Susan Keeter. Albert Whitman 2010 un il $16.99
Grades: 2 3 4   92
1. Poets 2. Slaves 3. Authors 4. Generals 5. Presidents 6. Women poets 7. African American authors 8. Poets, American 9. Presidents -- United States 10. African American women -- Biography 11. United States -- History -- 1775-1783, Revolution
ISBN 978-0-8075-6545-2; 0-8075-6545-8

"Camped in Cambridge in the fall of 1775, General Washington despairs that his soldiers won't ever be able to defeat the British. In Providence, freed slave Phillis Wheatley pens a poem of encouragement to Washington. Malaspina intertwines information about Wheatley's early life with wartime events. . . . Keeter's rich oil paintings are full of period details that help to clarify both the war scenes and Wheatley's life." Booklist

Whitfield, Simon, 1975-

Whitfield, Simon. **Simon** says gold: Simon Whitfield's pursuit of athletic excellence; by Simon Whitfield with Cleve Dheensaw. Orca Publishers 2009 118p il pa $14
Grades: 5 6 7 8   92
1. Athletes 2. Track athletics 3. Triathletes
ISBN 978-1-55469-141-8 pa; 1-55469-141-9 pa

"In 2000, Whitfield won a gold medal in the inaugural triathlon race held in the Sydney Summer Olympics. . . . He tells his story with candor, and he sheds light on the dark side of early success and the pressures athletes face. Sidebars offer more information on the sport of triathlon, and scrapbook-style color photographs enliven the tale." SLJ

Whitman, Narcissa Prentiss, 1808-1847

Harness, Cheryl. The **tragic** tale of Narcissa Whitman and a faithful history of the Oregon Trail; written and illustrated by Cheryl Harness. National Geographic Society 2006 144p il map (Cheryl Harness history) $16.95; lib bdg $25.90
Grades: 4 5 6 7   92
1. Frontier and pioneer life 2. Overland journeys to the Pacific 3. Pioneers 4. Missionaries
ISBN 0-7922-5920-3; 0-7922-7890-9 lib bdg
LC 2005-30930

This "introduces a nineteenth-century pioneer and missionary. . . . [She and her husband Marcus Whitman] journeyed along the Oregon Trail to the Waiilatpu Mission, where they ministered to the Cayuse. . . . Harness' chatty, conversational style makes the pair accessible to modern readers, and frequent quotes from Narcissa's diaries and letters and a time line help to frame the story in light of world and national events. Harness' black-line illustrations . . . help to break up the text for younger readers." Booklist

Includes bibliographical references

Whitman, Walt, 1819-1892

★ Kerley, Barbara. **Walt** Whitman; words for America. illustrated by Brian Selznick. Scholastic Press 2004 un il $16.95
Grades: 4 5 6 7   92
1. Poets 2. Authors 3. Essayists 4. Poets, American
ISBN 0-439-35791-8
LC 2003-20085

A biography of the American poet whose compassion led him to nurse soldiers during the Civil War, to give voice to the nation's grief at Lincoln's assassination, and to capture the true American spirit in verse

"Delightfully old-fashioned in design, [the book's] oversized pages are replete with graceful illustrations and snippets of poetry. The brilliantly inventive paintings add vibrant testimonial to the nuanced text." SLJ

Wiesenthal, Simon

★ Rubin, Susan Goldman. The **Anne** Frank Case: Simon Wiesenthal's search for the truth; illustrated by Bill Farnsworth. Holiday House 2009 40p il $18.95

Grades: 4 5 6 7   **92**

1. Authors 2. Architects 3. Holocaust survivors 4. Essayists 5. Memoirists 6. Nazi hunters 7. Jewish leaders 8. Jews -- Biography 9. Holocaust, 1933-1945
ISBN 978-0-8234-2109-1; 0-8234-2109-0

LC 2007-28396

"In 1958, Holocaust deniers disrupted a theater performance of The Diary of Anne Frank. In response, the well-known Nazi hunter Simon Wiesenthal vowed to prove Anne's story true. . . . This 'hook' is the framing story for a picture-book biography chronicling Wiesenthal's experiences during World War II and illustrating the development of his unusual career." SLJ

Includes glossary and bibliographical references

Wilder, Laura Ingalls, 1867-1957

Anderson, William T. **Pioneer** girl: the story of Laura Ingalls Wilder; by William Anderson; illustrated by Dan Andreasen. HarperCollins Pubs. 1998 un il hardcover o.p. pa $6.99

Grades: 2 3 4   **92**

1. Authors 2. Novelists 3. Women authors 4. Frontier and pioneer life 5. Western writers 6. Authors, American 7. Children's authors 8. Young adult authors
ISBN 0-06-027243-0; 0-06-027244-9 lib bdg; 0-06-446234-X pa

LC 96-31203

Recounts the life story of the author of the "Little House" books, from her childhood in Wisconsin to her old age at Rocky Ridge Farm

"Laura Ingalls Wilder's many fans will delight in this inviting biographical overview in a picture-book format, graced by Andreasen's dreamy landscapes, glowing prairie skies and warm character portraits." Publ Wkly

Berne, Emma Carlson. **Laura** Ingalls Wilder; by Emma Carlson Berne. ABDO Pub. 2008 112p il map $22.95

Grades: 4 5 6 7   **92**

1. Authors 2. Novelists 3. Women authors 4. Frontier and pioneer life 5. Western writers 6. Authors, American 7. Children's authors 8. Young adult authors
ISBN 978-1-59928-843-7; 1-59928-843-5

LC 2007012513

"Beginning in 1929 with the events that led up to the publication of Little House in the Big Woods , this readable biography further amplifies Wilder's life and correlates it with her books. . . . This volume is packed with relevant material, a time line, archival photographs, quotes from primary sources, and an official Web site." SLJ

Includes glossary and bibliographical references

Wilder, Laura Ingalls. A **Little** House traveler; writings from Laura Ingalls Wilder's journeys across America. by Laura Ingalls Wilder. HarperCollins 2006 344p il $16.99; pa $7.99

Grades: 5 6 7 8   **92**

1. Authors 2. Novelists 3. Women authors 4. Western writers 5. Authors, American 6. Children's authors 7. Young adult authors 8. United States -- Description

and travel
ISBN 978-0-06-072491-7; 0-06-072491-9; 978-0-06-072492-4 pa; 0-06-072492-7 pa

LC 2005014975

"This volume combines three Wilder travel diaries: On the Way Home, recounting the 1894 trip from South Dakota to Missouri, with husband Almanzo and daughter Rose; West from Home, featuring letters written by Laura to Almanzo during her 1915 solo visit to Rose in San Francisco; and The Road Back, highlighting Laura's previously unpublished record of a 1931 trip with Almanzo to De Smet, South Dakota, and the Black Hills. . . . This offers an amazing look at a beloved author, as well as a fascinating account of travel before interstate highways and air-conditioning." Booklist

Wilder, Laura Ingalls. **West** from home; letters of Laura Ingalls Wilder to Almanzo Wilder, San Francisco, 1915. edited by Roger Lea MacBride; historical setting by Margot Patterson Doss. Harper & Row 1974 124p il hardcover o.p. pa $5.99

Grades: 6 7 8 9   **92**

1. Authors 2. Novelists 3. Women authors 4. Western writers 5. Authors, American 6. Children's authors 7. Young adult authors
ISBN 0-06-024110-1; 0-06-440081-6 pa

LC 73-14342

This collection is "edited from letters sent to her beloved husband while Laura spent two months in late 1915 visiting their daughter and immersing herself in the sights of bustling San Francisco and the exciting Panama-Pacific Exposition. Wilder readers of all ages will lose themselves in this trip— the adults with nostalgia and wholesome pleasure, the youth with wonder and awe over the sights vividly described in her inimitable combination of homespun literary and journalistic styles." Child Book Rev Serv

Williams, Daniel Hale, 1856-1931

Venezia, Mike, 1945- **Daniel** Hale Williams; surgeon who opened hearts and minds. written and illustrated by Mike Venezia. Children's Press 2010 32p il (Getting to know the world's greatest inventors & scientists) lib bdg $28

Grades: 2 3 4   **92**

1. Surgeons 2. Physicians 3. Writers on medicine 4. African Americans -- Biography
ISBN 0-531-23729-X lib bdg; 978-0-531-23729-8 lib bdg

This book by Mike Venezia, part of the "Getting to Know the World's Greatest Inventors and Scientists" series, looks at "Daniel Hale Williams, founder of the first non-segregated hospital in the United States. . . . One of Williams' most significant contributions to the field of medicine was being one of the first surgeons to operate on the area around the heart." (Children's Literature)

Venezia "describes the life of Daniel Hale Williams, a pioneering physician working during the late 19th and early 20th centuries who achieved fame as one of the first open-heart surgeons. The book tells an inspiring story. . . . The colorful cartoons and historical photographs . . . complement the text well." Sci Books Films

Williams, J. W., 1929-

Barbour, Karen. **Mr.** Williams. Henry Holt and Co. 2005 29p il $16.95

Grades: K 1 2 3   **92**
1. Farmers 2. Country life 3. African Americans 4. Louisiana
ISBN 0-8050-6773-6

LC 2004-22182

"Recounting stories told by J. W. Williams, a friend of her mother's, Barbour captures the essence of a black Louisiana farmer's life in the early 20th century. . . . The words are succinct but evocative of a larger picture. . . . The ink-and-gouache illustrations, punctuated with well-placed bits of fabric collage, are perfect." SLJ

Williams, Lindsey, 1987-

Houle, Michelle E. **Lindsey** Williams; gardening for impoverished families. [by] Michelle Houle. KidHaven Press 2008 48p il (Young heroes) lib bdg $27.45
Grades: 4 5 6 7   **92**
1. Gardening 2. Food relief 3. Social action 4. Gardeners 5. Humanitarians
ISBN 978-0-7377-3867-4 lib bdg; 0-7377-3867-7 lib bdg

LC 2007022923

This "introduces 20-year-old Lindsey Williams, who has won numerous awards, including the International Eco-Hero Award, for her groundbreaking work with agriculture and hunger issues. . . . Williams has developed growing techniques that produce more food using fewer natural resources. . . . The straightforward text, with many quotes from Williams, will draw children into the science and environmental issues." Booklist

Includes glossary and bibliographical references

Williams, Roger, 1604?-1683

Avi. **Finding** Providence: the story of Roger Williams; story by Avi; illustrations by James Watling. HarperCollins Pubs. 1997 46p il (I can read chapter book) hardcover o.p. pa $3.99
Grades: 2 3 4   **92**
1. Clergy 2. Colonial leaders 3. Writers on religion 4. Rhode Island -- History 5. United States -- History -- 1600-1775, Colonial period
ISBN 0-06-025179-4; 0-06-444216-0 pa

LC 95-46360

After being forced to leave the Massachusetts Bay Colony, Roger Williams travels south and, with the help of the Narragansett Indians, founds Providence, Rhode Island

"Plentiful dialogue speeds the action along, and even the philosophical issues are cogently presented for young readers in the form of Williams' interrogation at the trial. Watling's watercolors have a roughhewn quality appropriate to the early colonies, and his grave figures are charged with tension." Bull Cent Child Books

Williams, Ted, 1918-2002

Bowen, Fred. **No** easy way; the story of Ted Williams and the last .400 season. illustrations by Charles S. Pyle. Dutton Children's Books 2010 un il lib bdg $16.99
Grades: 1 2 3   **92**
1. Baseball players 2. Baseball managers 3. Baseball -- Biography
ISBN 978-0-525-47877-5 lib bdg; 0-525-47877-9 lib bdg

LC 2009-17920

This recounts the 1941 baseball season in which Ted Williams hit .406 for the Boston Red Sox.

"Unlike many decades-old baseball stories, this one hasn't lost its appeal over the years, and Bowen makes the most of it in terms kids will understand. Pyle's illustrations, combined with vintage photographs, capture the drama of Williams at bat." Booklist

Williams, William Carlos, 1883-1963

★ Bryant, Jennifer. A **river** of words: the story of William Carlos Williams; written by Jen Bryant; illustrated by Melissa Sweet. Eerdmans Books for Young Readers 2008 un il $17
Grades: 1 2 3 4   **92**
1. Poets 2. Authors 3. Physicians 4. Essayists 5. Poets, American 6. Short story writers
ISBN 978-0-8028-5302-8; 0-8028-5302-1

LC 2007-49347

A Caldecott Medal honor book, 2009

This picture book biography of William Carlos Williams traces childhood events that lead him to become a doctor and a poet.

Bryant's "simple, spare language matches her subject well. Sweet's mixed-media collages will draw varying age groups. . . . [This is an] inspiring title." Booklist

Wilson, Teddy, 1912-1986

Cline-Ransome, Lesa. **Benny** Goodman & Teddy Wilson; taking the stage as the first black and white jazz band in history. by Lesa Cline-Ransome; illustrated by James E. Ransome. Holiday House 2014 32 p. (hardcover) $16.95
Grades: 2 3 4 5   **92**
1. Jazz musicians -- Biography 2. Race relations -- History -- 20th century 3. Jazz musicians -- United States -- Biography
ISBN 082342362X; 9780823423620

LC 2010048154

"In 1936, the Benny Goodman Trio became the first interracial band to perform in public, with Benny Goodman (the son of Jewish immigrants) on clarinet and African-American Teddy Wilson on piano (Gene Krupa, on drums, completed the trio). Writing in punchy free verse that echoes the bounce of both men's music," author Lesa Cline-Ransome, "traces Goodman and Wilson's parallel--but separate--paths to jazz fame, before eventually meeting in 1935." (Publishers Weekly)

"Goodman grew up in Chicago, a working-class Jewish boy; Wilson lived in Tuskegee, Alabama, a middle-class African American boy. The story of how the two jazz musicians met and formed the Benny Goodman Trio (the "first interracial band to perform publicly") is recounted in short bursts of text, almost like jazz riffs, accompanied by pencil and watercolor illustrations that capture distinctive moments. Timeline." Horn Book

Wilson, Woodrow, 1856-1924

Marsico, Katie. **Woodrow** Wilson. Marshall Cavendish Benchmark 2011 112p il (Presidents and their times) $23.95
Grades: 5 6 7 8   **92**
1. Governors 2. Presidents 3. College presidents 4. Nobel laureates for peace 5. Presidents -- United States
ISBN 978-0-7614-4815-0; 0-7614-4815-2

LC 2009041116

This offers information on President Woodrow Wilson and places him within his historical and cultural context. Also explored are the formative events of his times and how he responded.

"The abundant sidebars provide a good deal of background information that will be helpful to students. . . . Attractive . . . as well as useful." Booklist

Includes glossary and bibliographical references

Winfrey, Oprah

Weatherford, Carole Boston. **Oprah**; the little speaker. illustrated by London Ladd. Marshall Cavendish Children 2010 un il $17.99

Grades: K 1 2 3   **92**

1. Entertainers 2. Philanthropists 3. Television personalities 4. Talk show hosts 5. Television producers 6. African American women -- Biography

ISBN 978-0-7614-5632-2; 0-7614-5632-5

LC 2009006339

This picture book biography of Oprah Winfrey "focuses solely on her childhood. An author's note at the beginning sets the stage for the true rags-to-riches story about a poor girl on a Mississippi pig farm who became an entertainer, entrepreneur, and philanthropist. . . . The narrative portrays a bright, spunky child . . . while the soft-edged, acrylic illustrations paint a determined, sober-faced girl." Booklist

Wong, Anna May, 1905-1961

Yoo, Paula. **Shining** star: the Anna May Wong story; by Paula Yoo; illustrated by Lin Wang. Lee & Low Books 2009 un il $17.95

Grades: 2 3 4 5   **92**

1. Actors 2. Chinese Americans -- Biography

ISBN 978-1-60060-259-7; 1-60060-259-2

LC 2008042673

"Lin Wang's . . . elegant paintings in muted hues capture the actress's emotions in her expressive eyes framed by dark bangs. . . . The conversational narrative uses many descriptive vignettes. . . . A fascinating account of the life of a determined actress." Publ Wkly

Woodhull, Victoria C., 1838-1927

Krull, Kathleen. A **woman** for president; the story of Victoria Woodhull. illustrations by Jane Dyer. Walker & Co 2004 un il $16.95; lib bdg $17.85

Grades: 3 4 5   **92**

1. Feminism 2. Suffragists 3. Women in politics 4. Feminists 5. Presidential candidates

ISBN 0-8027-8908-0; 0-8027-8909-9 lib bdg

LC 2004-49483

"Woodhull is a fascinating figure, and Krull's lively and astute writing does her justice. . . . The watercolors, cast with a golden glow, are handsome." Booklist

Includes bibliographical references

Woodson, Jacqueline

★ Woodson, Jacqueline. **Brown** girl dreaming; Jacqueline Woodson. Nancy Paulsen Books 2014 336 p. illustrations, photographs (hardback) $16.99

Grades: 4 5 6 7 8   **92**

1. African American women -- Biography 2. American poetry -- African American authors 3. African American women authors -- Biography -- Poetry 4. Authors,

American -- 20th century -- Biography -- Poetry

ISBN 0399252517; 9780399252518

LC 2014021346

Newbery Honor Book (2015)

Robert F. Sibert Honor Book (2015)

National Book Award: Young People's Literature (2014)

Coretta Scott King Author Award (2015)

"Raised in South Carolina and New York, [author Jacqueline] Woodson always felt halfway home in each place. In vivid poems, she shares what it was like to grow up as an African American in the 1960s and 1970s, living with the remnants of Jim Crow and her growing awareness of the Civil Rights movement." (Publisher's note)

"Here is a memoir-in-verse so immediate that readers will feel they are experiencing the author's childhood right along with her." Horn Book

Wozniak, Stephen, 1950-

Venezia, Mike. **Steve** Jobs & Steve Wozniak; geek heroes who put the personal in computers. written and illustrated by Mike Venezia. Children's Press 2010 32p il (Getting to know the world's greatest inventors & scientists) lib bdg $28

Grades: 2 3 4   **92**

1. Entrepreneurs 2. Businesspeople 3. Computer industry 4. Computer scientists 5. Electronics engineers 6. Computer industry executives 7. Electronics industry executives

ISBN 978-0-531-23730-4 lib bdg; 0-531-23730-3 lib bdg

Venezia "describes the extraordinary childhoods of Jobs and Wozniak. . . . Imperceptibly, Venezia brings a broad history of computers into the picture by demonstrating simultaneously how Jobs and Wozniak were influenced by early computer pioneers and how they then made their mark on the world. . . . Venezia's thoughtful writing style and carefully chosen photos and graphics allows children to use their imagination and see part of themselves in the two 'heroes' of the title." Sci Books Films

Wright, David, 1982-

Rappoport, Ken. **David** Wright; a baseball star who cares. Enslow 2011 il (Sports stars who care) $23.93

Grades: 3 4 5   **92**

1. Baseball players 2. Baseball -- Biography

ISBN 978-0-7660-3775-5; 0-7660-3775-4

A biography of the all-star third baseman for the New York Mets who has worked with charities and who established the David Wright Foundation.

This is "especially good for book reports." Booklist

Wright, Orville, 1871-1948

Collins, Mary. **Airborne**: a photobiography of Wilbur and Orville Wright. National Geographic Soc. 2003 63p il maps $18.95

Grades: 4 5 6 7   **92**

1. Inventors 2. Aeronautics -- History 3. Aircraft industry executives

ISBN 0-7922-6957-8

LC 2002-5279

Examines the lives of the Wright brothers and discusses their experiments and triumphs in the field of flight

"The well-chosen photos give readers a feel for Kitty Hawk—windy, sandy, solitary. This is an exceptionally well-informed picture of the Wright brothers and what their 100-year-old achievement really meant." SLJ

★ Freedman, Russell. The **Wright** brothers: how they invented the airplane; with original photographs by Wilbur and Orville Wright. Holiday House 1991 129p il hardcover o.p. pa $14.95

Grades: 5 6 7 8 9 10   **92**

1. Inventors 2. Aeronautics -- History 3. Aircraft industry executives

ISBN 0-8234-0875-2; 0-8234-1082-X pa

LC 90-48440

A Newbery Medal honor book, 1992

In this "combination of photography and text, Freedman reveals the frustrating, exciting, and ultimately successful journey of these two brothers from their bicycle shop in Dayton, Ohio, to their Kitty Hawk flights and beyond.... An essential purchase for younger YAs." Voice Youth Advocates

Includes bibliographical references

O'Sullivan, Robyn. The **Wright** brothers fly; by Robyn O'Sullivan. National Geographic 2007 40p il (National Geographic history chapters) lib bdg $17.90

Grades: 2 3 4   **92**

1. Inventors 2. Aeronautics -- History 3. Aircraft industry executives

ISBN 978-1-4263-0188-9

LC 2007007895

This history of the Wright brothers is "nicely illustrated with photos.... [It is] just right for emerging chapter-book readers.... Useful ... for reports ... and interesting pleasure reading." SLJ

Includes glossary and bibliographical references

Venezia, Mike. The **Wright** brothers; inventors whose ideas really took flight. written and illustrated by Mike Venezia. Children's Press 2010 32p il (Getting to know the world's greatest inventors & scientists) lib bdg $28

Grades: 2 3 4   **92**

1. Inventors 2. Aeronautics 3. Aircraft industry executives

ISBN 978-0-531-23732-8 lib bdg; 0-531-23732-X lib bdg

LC 2009030222

This "explores the development of the Wright brothers by way of their early childhood environment and interests, which ultimately contributed to their successful attainment of the first powered aircraft.... Young readers will gain insights into the brothers' inventive and entrepreneurial lives from a humanistic perspective, as well as developing a sense of the qualities that are associated with contributors to advancements in technology." Sci Books Films

Wright, Patience Lovell, 1725-1786

★ Shea, Pegi Deitz. **Patience** Wright; America's first sculptor, and revolutionary spy. [by] Pegi Deitz Shea; illustrated by Bethanne Andersen. Henry Holt 2007 un il $17.95

Grades: 4 5 6   **92**

1. Spies 2. Artists 3. Sculptors 4. Women artists 5. United States -- History -- 1775-1783, Revolution

ISBN 978-0-8050-6770-5; 0-8050-6770-1

LC 2005021696

A biography of Patience Wright, born in 1725, who became a sculptor and a spy for the American colonies

"Shea writes with a dynamic simplicity that brings Wright to life. At the same time, she seamlessly incorporates information about the war and events leading up to it into her text." Booklist

Wright, Richard, 1908-1960

★ Miller, William. **Richard** Wright and the library card; illustrated by Gregory Christie. Lee & Low Bks. 1997 un il hardcover o.p. pa $6.95

Grades: K 1 2 3   **92**

1. Authors 2. Novelists 3. Dramatists 4. Essayists 5. Nonfiction writers 6. Short story writers 7. Libraries -- Fiction 8. African Americans -- Fiction 9. Books and reading -- Fiction

ISBN 1-880000-57-1; 1-880000-88-1 pa

LC 97-6847

Based on a scene from Wright's autobiography, Black boy, in which the seventeen-year-old African-American borrows a white man's library card and devours every book as a ticket to freedom

"Christie's powerful impressionistic paintings in acrylic and colored pencil show the harsh racism in the Jim Crow South. . . . Words and pictures express the young man's loneliness and confinement and, then, the power he found in books." Booklist

Wright, Wilbur, 1867-1912

Collins, Mary. **Airborne**: a photobiography of Wilbur and Orville Wright. National Geographic Soc. 2003 63p il maps $18.95

Grades: 4 5 6 7   **92**

1. Inventors 2. Aeronautics -- History 3. Aircraft industry executives

ISBN 0-7922-6957-8

LC 2002-5279

Examines the lives of the Wright brothers and discusses their experiments and triumphs in the field of flight

"The well-chosen photos give readers a feel for Kitty Hawk—windy, sandy, solitary. This is an exceptionally well-informed picture of the Wright brothers and what their 100-year-old achievement really meant." SLJ

★ Freedman, Russell. The **Wright** brothers: how they invented the airplane; with original photographs by Wilbur and Orville Wright. Holiday House 1991 129p il hardcover o.p. pa $14.95

Grades: 5 6 7 8 9 10   **92**

1. Inventors 2. Aeronautics -- History 3. Aircraft industry executives

ISBN 0-8234-0875-2; 0-8234-1082-X pa

LC 90-48440

A Newbery Medal honor book, 1992

In this "combination of photography and text, Freedman reveals the frustrating, exciting, and ultimately successful journey of these two brothers from their bicycle shop in Dayton, Ohio, to their Kitty Hawk flights and beyond.... An essential purchase for younger YAs." Voice Youth Advocates

Includes bibliographical references

O'Sullivan, Robyn. The **Wright** brothers fly; by Robyn O'Sullivan. National Geographic 2007 40p il (National Geographic history chapters) lib bdg $17.90

Grades: 2 3 4 **92**
1. Inventors 2. Aeronautics -- History 3. Aircraft industry executives
ISBN 978-1-4263-0188-9

LC 2007007895

This history of the Wright brothers is "nicely illustrated with photos. . . . [It is] just right for emerging chapter-book readers. . . . Useful . . . for reports . . . and interesting pleasure reading." SLJ
Includes glossary and bibliographical references

Venezia, Mike. The **Wright** brothers; inventors whose ideas really took flight. written and illustrated by Mike Venezia. Children's Press 2010 32p il (Getting to know the world's greatest inventors & scientists) lib bdg $28
Grades: 2 3 4 **92**
1. Inventors 2. Aeronautics 3. Aircraft industry executives
ISBN 978-0-531-23732-8 lib bdg; 0-531-23732-X lib bdg

LC 2009030222

This "explores the development of the Wright brothers by way of their early childhood environment and interests, which ultimately contributed to their successful attainment of the first powered aircraft. . . . Young readers will gain insights into the brothers' inventive and entrepreneurial lives from a humanistic perspective, as well as developing a sense of the qualities that are associated with contributors to advancements in technology." Sci Books Films

Yaccarino, Dan
★ Yaccarino, Dan. **All** the way to America; the story of a big Italian family and a little shovel. Alfred A. Knopf 2011 un il $16.99; lib bdg $19.99
Grades: K 1 2 3 **92**
1. Artists 2. Authors 3. Genealogy 4. Illustrators 5. Italian Americans 6. Authors, American 7. Children's authors 8. United States -- Immigration and emigration
ISBN 0-375-86642-6; 0-375-96642-0 lib bdg; 978-0-375-86642-5; 978-0-375-96642-2 lib bdg

LC 2010017549

"In this picture book, Yaccarino shares his family history. Starting with his great-grandfather Michele Iaccarino's immigration to America, he gives a simplified rundown of each generation's career and family life. Advice passed from parent to child creates a narrative connection among generations. . . . The text is clear and simple . . . [and] readers' interest will be held fast by the bright illustrations. In his typical retro style, Yaccarino creates a world of friendly, rounded people set against stylized background scenery. . . . The story will make an excellent family-history discussion starter." SLJ

Yeboah, Emmanuel Ofosu
Emmanuel's dream; the true story of Emmanuel Ofosu Yeboah. by Laurie Ann Thompson; illustrated by Sean Qualls. Schwartz & Wade Books 2015 40 p. (glb) $20.99
Grades: PreK K 1 2 3 **92**
1. People with mental disabilities 2. Ghana -- Biography 3. Cyclists -- Ghana -- Biography 4. People with disabilities -- Ghana -- Biography
ISBN 0449817458; 9780449817445; 9780449817452

LC 2014005767

This children's book, written by Laurie Ann Thompson and illustrated by Sean Qualls, describes a boy who was "Born in Ghana, West Africa, with one deformed leg, he was dismissed by most people--but not by his mother, who taught him to reach for his dreams. As a boy, Emmanuel hopped to school more than two miles each way, learned to play soccer, left home at age thirteen to provide for his family, and, eventually, became a cyclist." (Publisher's note)

York, ca. 1775-ca. 1815
★ Pringle, Laurence P. **American** slave, American hero; York of the Lewis and Clark Expedition. [by] Laurence Pringle; illustrations by Cornelius Van Wright and Ying-Hwa Hu. Calkins Creek Books 2005 40p il $17.95
Grades: 3 4 5 **92**
1. Slaves 2. Explorers 3. Lewis and Clark Expedition (1804-1806) 4. Slavery -- United States 5. West (U.S.) -- Exploration
ISBN 978-1-59078-282-8; 1-59078-282-8

LC 2005037352

"With a detailed text and handsome watercolor paintings, this illustrated biography celebrates the heroic role of Clark's personal slave on the famous expedition out west in 1804, with the horror of slavery in the background." Booklist
Includes bibliographical references

Young, Ed
★ Young, Ed. The **house** Baba built; an artist's childhood in China. Little, Brown and Co. 2011 48p il $17.99
Grades: 2 3 4 5 **92**
1. Artists 2. Authors 3. Illustrators 4. Authors, American 5. Children's authors 6. Artists -- United States 7. Chinese Americans -- Biography
ISBN 978-0-316-07628-9; 0-316-07628-7

LC 2011005396

"In this picture book memoir by the Caldecott Medalist, which opens in 1931 (the year he was born), the stock market has crashed, and China is in turmoil. Young's father, Baba, persuades a landowner in Shanghai to let him construct a huge brick house on his land; Baba promises to return the house after 20 years, long enough to keep his family safe until WWII ends. Young's creation, shaped with help from author Libby Koponen, is as complex and labyrinthine as Baba's house, with foldout pages that open to reveal drawings, photos, maps, and memories. Tender portraits of his siblings, torn-paper collages showing tiny figures at play, and old photos of stylish adults intermingle, as if they'd been found forgotten in a drawer." Publ Wkly

I am Malala; how one girl stood up for education and changed the world. Malala Yousafzai with Patricia McCormick. Young readers edition Little Brown & Co 2014 230 p. illustrations, map (hardback) $17
Grades: 5 6 7 8 **92**
1. Women -- Education 2. Children's rights -- Pakistan 3. Young women -- Education -- Pakistan -- Biography
ISBN 031632793X; 9780316327930

LC 2014015881

"Malala Yousafzai was only ten years old when the Taliban took control of her region. . . . They said girls couldn't go to school. Raised in a once-peaceful area of Pakistan transformed by terrorism, Malala was taught to stand up for what she believes. So she fought for her right to be educated." (Publisher's note)

"Young education activist and Taliban victim Malala Yousafzai recounts her Pakistani childhood in this deftly adapted memoir. Domestic and academic tales illustrate her unusual maturity and resilience in the face of increasing Taliban threats. Yousafzai's moving narrative and engaging, sincere voice may provide an entryway to international awareness for middle-grade readers; a map and a thorough timeline provide additional political context." Horn Book

Yunus, Muhammad, 1940-

Yoo, Paula. **Twenty**-two cents; Muhammad Yunus and the Village Bank. by Paula Yoo; illustrated by Jamel Akib. First edition Lee & Low Books Inc. 2014 40 p. color illustrations (hardcover) $18.95

Grades: 3 4 5 6   92

1. Microfinance 2. Bankers 3. Economists 4. Grameen Bank 5. Microfinance -- Developing countries
ISBN 9781600606588; 160060658X

LC 2013041045

"Growing up in Bangladesh, Muhammad Yunus witnessed extreme poverty all around and was determined to eradicate it. . . . Muhammad founded Grameen Bank where people could borrow small amounts of money to start a job. . . . Over the next few years, Muhammad's compassion and determination changed the lives of millions of people by loaning the equivalent of more than ten billion US dollars in micro-credit." (Publisher's note)

"Akib's grainy, jewel-toned chalk pastels contrast a sense of scarcity and deprivation with one of warmth and humanity. Yoo makes the significance of Yunus's contributions understandable, relevant, and immediate." Pub Wkly

Includes bibliographical references

Zaharias, Babe Didrikson, 1911-1956

Freedman, Russell. **Babe** Didrikson Zaharias; the making of a champion. Clarion Bks. 1999 192p il hardcover o.p.; pbk $10.99

Grades: 5 6 7 8 9 10   92

1. Women athletes 2. Golfers 3. Hurdlers 4. High jumpers 5. Javelin throwers 6. Olympic athletes
ISBN 0-395-63367-2; 9780544104914

LC 98-50208

A biography of Babe Didrikson, who broke records in golf, track and field, and other sports, at a time when there were few opportunities for female athletes

"Freedman's measured yet lively style captures the spirit of the great athlete. . . . Plenty of black-and-white photos capture Babe's spirit and dashing good looks; the documentation . . . is impeccable." Horn Book

Includes bibliographical references

Van Natta, Don, 1964- **Wonder** girl; the magnificent sporting life of Babe Didrikson Zaharias. Little, Brown and Co. 2011 403p il $27.99

Grades: 5 6 7 8   92

1. Women athletes 2. Golfers 3. Hurdlers 4. High jumpers 5. Javelin throwers 6. Olympic athletes
ISBN 978-0-316-05699-1; 0-316-05699-5

LC 2010041794

Describes the life and times of LPGA founder Didrikson, the Texas woman who achieved All-American status in basketball, won gold medals in track and field in the 1932

Olympics, and became the first woman to play against men in a PGA tournament.

This is an "engaging biography. . . . Van Natta marvelously narrates the forgotten life of the 'greatest all-around athlete of all time,' a story that every American sport fan should relish." Publ Wkly

Includes bibliographical references

Wallace, Rich. **Babe** conquers the world; the legendary life of Babe Didrikson Zaharias. Rich Wallace, Sandra Neil Wallace. Calkins Creek 2014 272 p. (Includes bibliographical references (page 266-268) and index.) $16.95

Grades: 4 5 6 7 8   92

1. Women athletes -- Biography
ISBN 1590789814; 9781590789810

LC 2013953471

This book, by Rich Wallace and Sandra Neil Wallace, is a biography of Babe Didrikson Zaharias. "A champion basketball player, an Olympic track-and-field star, and a career golfer, Babe didn't let obstacles stand in the way of her success. The authors detail her trajectory from the daughter of a Norwegian immigrant born in a working-class Texas neighborhood to record wins at the 1932 Olympics (still not broken to this day) to her last days as she fought cancer." (School Library Journal)

"Babe Didrikson Zaharias is perhaps the most accomplished athlete that young people have never heard of. She was an Olympic track star in the 1932 games, a noted professional basketball player, and a formative member of the LPGA...This is part sports journalism, part narrative nonfiction, and part proof that professional athletes can be exemplary role models for young people." Booklist

Zhu, Xiao-Mei

LeBlanc, Andre. The **red** piano; [illustrated by] Barroux; translated by Justine French. Wilkins Farago 2010 40p il $16.99

Grades: 2 3 4 5   92

1. Pianists 2. Music teachers 3. China -- History -- 1949-1976
ISBN 978-0-9806070-1-7; 0-9806070-1-9

"The experiences of Chinese-born French pianist Khu Xiao-Mei inspire this poignant, picture-book biography set during the Cultural Revolution. Separated from her family and forbidden to pursue classical music studies, a young girl in exile clandestinely collects Bach preludes and practices the piano in a hut on the outskirts of her rural village. When she and her accomplice, an elderly villager who hides the piano, are discovered, they are tortured and ridiculed, and the piano is destroyed. An ambiguous ending sends the girl from the camp into a murky sunset with her secreted music notebooks in tow. Leblanc's clipped, elegant phrases tell a woeful, abstracted story that is well-matched with Barroux's arresting paintings in inky brown and shocking red. . . . The dramatic imagery offers an accessible, vivid picture of life during the time of Chairman Mao." Booklist

Zitkala-Sa, 1876-1938

★ Pearce, Q. L. **Red** Bird sings: the story of Zitkala-Sa; by Gina Capaldi & Q.L. Pearce; illustrated by Gina Capaldi. Carolrhoda Books 2011 32p il lib bdg $17.95

Grades: 3 4 5 6   92

1. Authors 2. Women authors 3. Women musicians 4. Yankton Indians 5. Political activists 6. Essayists

7. Indian leaders 8. Authors, American 9. Short story writers 10. Native Americans -- Biography

ISBN 978-0-7613-5257-0; 0-7613-5257-0

LC 2011003014

This children's biography describes the life of "Gertrude Simmons Bonnin of the Yankton Sioux, later known as Zitkala-Sa [who] bridged the nineteenth and twentieth centuries, and the white and Indian cultures . . . readers follow her school days, her later career as a political advocate for Indian rights, and her struggle to reconcile her determination for personal advancement with feelings of guilt for abandoning her family." The book includes "[f]irst-person narration adapted from Zitkala-Sa's own writings and supplemented with 'additional primary and secondary sources'". (Bulletin of the Center for Children's Books)

"Capaldi and Pearce document the life of Gertrude Simmons, an author, musician, and activist best known by her pen name, Zitkala-Sa (Red Bird). Drawing from semiautobiographical stories that Zitkala-Sa wrote for the Atlantic Monthly in the early 1900s, Capaldi and Pearce eloquently describe her experience at a Quaker boarding school, where she laments the loss of her culture, but also develops passions for violin and women's suffrage. . . . Capaldi's understated illustrations integrate solid colors and doll-like characterizations with reproductions of period materials, while appended information on Sitkala-Sa rounds out this fascinating portrait." Publ Wkly

Includes bibliographical references

Zuckerberg, Mark

Woog, Adam. **Mark** Zuckerberg, Facebook creator. KidHaven Press 2009 48p il map (Innovators) $28.25

Grades: 4 5 6 7   92

1. Businesspeople 2. Facebook Inc. 3. Internet executives

ISBN 978-0-7377-4566-5; 0-7377-4566-5

LC 2009013458

"This brisk, readable [biography the creator of Facebook] . . . presents an appealing picture of the shy, lonely future billionaire . . . This is fascinating and relevant stuff." Booklist

Includes bibliographical references

920 Biography, genealogy, insignia

Adler, David A.

Heroes for civil rights; by David A. Adler; illustrated by Bill Farnsworth. Holiday House 2007 32p il $16.95

Grades: 3 4 5   920

1. African Americans -- Biography 2. African Americans -- Civil rights

ISBN 978-0-8234-2008-7

LC 2006038185

"Adler presents biographical sketches of several individuals and the defining actions or events in their lives as they relate to the roles they played during the Civil Rights Movement. . . . The format is attractive, with the easy-to-read text facing a full-page illustration. Farnsworth's oil paintings complement the simple presentations by featuring a large portrait of each individual, with one or more smaller pictures of a significant moment superimposed on it." SLJ

Includes bibliographical references

Bausum, Ann

★ **Our** country's first ladies; [by] Ann Bausum; with a foreword by First Lady Laura Bush. National Geographic 2007 127p il $19.95; lib bdg $28.90

Grades: 5 6 7 8   920

1. Presidents' spouses -- United States

ISBN 978-1-4263-0006-6; 978-1-4263-0007-3 lib bdg

LC 2006021284

"A well-researched, thoughtfully written, attractive account. Fact boxes provide basic information such as birth and death dates, marriage dates, and children's names; a 'Did You Know' section shares interesting personal tidbits. Periodic time lines help to place the women's lives within the broader events of history. There is enough information here for simple reports. Interesting facts and anecdotes will hold readers' attention. . . . An excellent layout and clear, colorful photographs and reproductions will further entice readers." SLJ

Includes bibliographical references

Beccia, Carlyn

The **raucous** royals; test your royal wits: crack codes, solve mysteries, and deduce which royal rumors are true. Houghton Mifflin 2008 64p il $17

Grades: 4 5 6 7   920

1. Nobility 2. Historiography 3. Kings and rulers

ISBN 978-0-618-89130-6; 0-618-89130-7

LC 2008-298419

"Thirteen beliefs about rulers receive an acerbic and irreverent interrogation in this blend of royal-watching and skeptical investigation. The royal rumors, arranged chronologically, start with the real story behind Prince Dracula and Richard III's murderous ways, stopping en route at Napoleon's short stature and Marie Antoinette's 'let them eat cake' utterance, and finish up with Catherine the Great's death and King George's madness. . . . The energy and gleefully gossipy nature makes this a fine companion for Krull's Lives of . . . series, while its verve particularly recommends it as an entreé into historiography and critical thinking." Bull Cent Child Books

Includes bibliographical references

Bolden, Tonya

Portraits of African-American heroes; paintings by Ansel Pitcairn. Dutton Children's Books 2003 88p il $18.99; pa $11.99

Grades: 4 5 6 7   920

1. African Americans -- Biography

ISBN 0-525-47043-3; 0-14-240473-X pa

LC 2002-75911

"Each profile lists expected biographical information, but offers even more by way of keen insights into a subject's personality based on interviews and information drawn from personal memoirs. . . . Pitcairn's beautifully rendered sepiatoned portraits make each subject jump from the page, beckoning children to come ever closer and learn." Booklist

Bragg, Georgia

How they choked; failures, flops, and flaws of the awfully famous. by Georgia Bragg; illustrated by Kevin O'Malley. Bloomsbury/Walker 2014 208 p. (pbk.) $18.89

Grades: 5 6 7 8   920

1. Inventions 2. Celebrities 3. Decision making 4. Celebrities -- Conduct of life 5. History -- Errors,

inventions, etc.

ISBN 0802734898; 9780802734884; 9780802734891

LC 2013039127

This book, by Georgia Bragg, "knocks fourteen famous achievers off their pedestals to reveal the human side of history. Successful 'failures' include: Marco Polo, Queen Isabella of Spain, Montezuma II, Ferdinand Magellan, Anne Boleyn, Isaac Newton, Benedict Arnold, Susan B. Anthony, George Armstrong Custer, Thomas Alva Edison, Vincent Van Gogh, J. Bruce Ismay, 'Shoeless Joe' Jackson, [and] Amelia M. Earhart." (Publisher's note)

"On the heels of How They Croaked: The Awful Ends of the Awfully Famous (2011), Bragg seeks to reconcile what she sees as a major flaw of the biography genre—that authors ignore the human potential for error. Her compendium is unapologetically full of bad news, criticism, and belly flops...The snarkily entertaining narratives are illustrated with caricatures of each subject. For better or worse, subjects are rarely as one-dimensional as most biographies paint them, and this book proves that nobody is perfect." Booklist

★ **How** they croaked; the awful ends of the awfully famous. Walker & Co. 2011 178p il $17.99; lib bdg $18.89
Grades: 5 6 7 8   920
1. Death 2. Biography
ISBN 978-0-8027-9817-6; 0-8027-9817-9; 978-0-8027-9818-3 lib bdg; 0-8027-9818-7 lib bdg

LC 2010-08659

"Bragg chronicles with ghoulish glee the chronic or fatal maladies that afflicted 19 historical figures. Nonsqueamish readers will by entranced by her riveting descriptions. . . . The author tucks quick notes on at least marginally relevant topics, such as leeching, scurvy, presidential assassins, and mummy eyes . . . between the chapters. . . . O'Malley's cartoon portraits and spot art add just the right notes of humor to keep the contents from becoming too gross." Booklist

Cook, Michelle
★ **Our** children can soar; a celebration of Rosa, Barack, and the pioneers of change. illustrations by Cozbi A. Cabrera . . . [et al.]; foreword by Marian Wright Edelman. Bloomsbury 2009 un il $16.99; lib bdg $17.89
Grades: K 1 2   920
1. African Americans -- History 2. African Americans -- Biography
ISBN 978-1-59990-418-4; 1-59990-418-7; 978-1-59990-419-1 lib bdg; 1-59990-419-5 lib bdg

LC 2009-1730

"The spreads understandably represent an array of artistic styles and media, yet they form a cohesive and affecting collective portrait. . . . Additional images from Leo and Diane Dillon, James Ransome, E.B. Lewis, Eric Velasquez and others, corroborate Children's Defense Fund founder Marian Wright Edelman's assertion, in the book's foreword, that African-American history is 'the story of hope.'" Publ Wkly

Cotter, Charis
Born to write; the remarkable lives of six famous authors. Annick Press 2009 167p il $24.95; pa $14.95
Grades: 5 6 7 8   920
1. Authors
ISBN 978-1-55451-192-1; 1-55451-192-5; 978-1-55451-191-4 pa; 1-55451-191-7 pa

A collective biography of authors Lucy Maud Montgomery, Christopher Paul Curtis, C. S. Lewis, E.B. White, Madeleine L'Engle, and Philip Pullman

"Younger readers will find the presentation of the book appealing, with many colorful photographs and illustrations; however, more mature readers will gain the most enjoyment as they discover the backgrounds and inspirations of some of their favorite writers. . . . An excellent resource for reports and pleasure reading." SLJ

Kids who rule; the remarkable lives of five child monarchs. Annick Press 2007 120p il map $24.95; pa $14.95
Grades: 5 6 7 8   920
1. Queens 2. Emperors 3. Kings and rulers 4. Kings 5. Buddhist leaders 6. Political leaders 7. Nobel laureates for peace
ISBN 978-1-55451-062-7; 1-55451-062-7; 978-1-55451-061-0 pa; 1-55451-061-9 pa

This "book discusses five people who became monarchs as children: Tutankhamen of Egypt, Mary Queen of Scots, Queen Christina of Sweden, China's Emperor Puyi, and the fourteenth Dalai Lama. . . . The illustrations, many in color, include portrait paintings, engravings, and maps as well as photos of people, places, and artifacts. . . . This appealing collective biography presents five unusual children whose stories are well worth reading." Booklist

Cummins, Julie
★ **Women** daredevils; thrills, chills, and frills. illustrated by Cheryl Harness. Dutton Children's Books 2008 48p il $17.99
Grades: 3 4 5 6   920
1. Stunt performers 2. Women -- Biography
ISBN 978-0-525-47948-2; 0-525-47948-1

LC 2007-18102

"Cummins introduces 10 women stunt performers, active from 1880 to 1929. . . . Each story includes broad historical context with facts about women's status and societal expectations. . . . Cummins' lively text provides a sense of each individual by including quotes and physical descriptions. . . . Harness' richly colored, detailed illustrations . . . are expressive, realistic, and filled with action." Booklist

Drucker, Malka
Portraits of Jewish American heroes; by Malka Drucker; illustrated by Elizabeth Rosen. Dutton Children's Books 2008 96p il $22.99
Grades: 4 5 6   920
1. Jews -- United States -- Biography
ISBN 978-0-525-47771-6; 0-525-47771-3

LC 2007-028481

"From Albert Einstein and Bella Abzug to Ruth Bader Ginsburg, Hank Greenberg, and Steven Spielberg, this invitingly illustrated collective biography celebrates 20 Jewish American heroes in all their diversity. . . . The nicely designed volume includes full-page portraits of the subjects in various media. . . . Drucker's eloquent, chatty style opens up big issues about Judaism as a source of idealism and for a just, compassionate society." Booklist

Includes bibliographical references

Fortey, Jacqueline
Great scientists; written by Jacqueline Fortey. DK Pub. 2007 72p il map (DK eyewitness books) $15.99

Grades: 5 6 7 8 **920**
1. Scientists
ISBN 978-0-7566-2974-8; 0-7566-2974-8
LC 2007-298205
This introduces readers to the great scientists and their discoveries from ancient history to modern times.

"An accompanying CD provides clip art taken from the book; this art can prove invaluable to both teachers and students. . . . A very fine book for elementary and middle school students and those who teach them." Sci Books and Films

Fradin, Dennis B.
The **founders**; the 39 stories behind the U.S. Constitution. [by] Dennis Brindell Fradin; illustrated by Michael McCurdy. Walker & Co. 2005 162p il map $22.95; lib bdg $23.95
Grades: 4 5 6 7 **920**
1. Statesmen -- United States 2. United States -- Constitution 3. United States -- Politics and government -- 1783-1809
ISBN 0-8027-8972-2; 0-8027-8973-0 lib bdg
"The makers of the U.S. Constitution are profiled in two or three pages each, in sections introduced by a brief note about their home states. McCurdy's black-and-white scratchboard illustrations are properly stately and engaging. Readers will find great nuggets of fact." Booklist
Includes bibliographical references

★ **Funny** business; conversations with writers of comedy. compiled and edited by Leonard S. Marcus. Candlewick Press 2009 214p il $21.99
Grades: 5 6 7 8 9 10 **920**
1. Authors 2. Authorship 3. Wit and humor
ISBN 978-0-7636-3254-0; 0-7636-3254-6
This book comprises interviews with writers of humorous books for young people: Judy Blume, Beverly Cleary, Sharon Creech, Christopher Paul Curtis, Anne Fine, Daniel Handler, Carl Hiaasen, Norton Juster, Dick King-Smith, Hilary McKay, Daniel Pinkwater, Louis Sachar, and Jon Scieszka. Index. "Intermediate, middle school." (Horn Book)

"In 12 entertaining interviews . . . Marcus's compilation explores the childhoods, writing processes and senses of humor of well-known writers for children, including Judy Blume, Beverly Cleary, Daniel Handler, Norton Juster and Jon Scieszka. Marcus's evident knowledge of his subjects' writing makes for some intriguing questions and answers. . . . Photographs, manuscript pages and even e-mail chains between the writers and their editors add fascinating tidbits." Publ Wkly

George-Warren, Holly
Honky-tonk heroes & hillbilly angels; the pioneers of country & western music. words by Holly George-Warren; pictures by Laura Levine. Houghton Mifflin 2006 32p il $16
Grades: 3 4 5 6 **920**
1. Musicians 2. Country music
ISBN 0-618-19100-3
LC 2003-5364
Profiles important and influential performers of country and western music, including the Carter Family, Roy Acuff, Gene Autry, Bill Monroe, Patsy Cline, and Loretta Lynn.
"Concise but thorough. . . . Colorful, stylized, folk art of the performers and/or their instruments is included." SLJ

Gifford, Clive
10 inventors who changed the world; written by Clive Gifford; illustrated by David Cousens. Kingfisher 2009 63p il $14.99
Grades: 4 5 6 7 **920**
1. Inventors 2. Inventions
ISBN 978-0-7534-6259-1; 0-7534-6259-1
"The innovative efforts of nine men and one woman are presented here. Some of the names will be familiar (Galileo, Franklin, Edison, Curie) while others will prove less so (Isambard Kindgom Brunel, Glenn Curtiss, Sergei Korolev). Starting in ancient times with Archimedes, the chronology ends in modern times with Korolev, a Soviet-era rocket designer. Each section offers a succinct yet thorough biography of the inventors. Striking graphic-novel-style art is a visual aid to draw readers into each setting and era." SLJ

10 kings & queens who changed the world; written by Clive Gifford; illustrated by David Cousens. Kingfisher 2009 63p il map $14.99
Grades: 4 5 6 7 **920**
1. Kings and rulers
ISBN 978-0-7534-6252-2; 0-7534-6252-4
"Cousens' bright graphic novel-style artwork is the grabber here; he uses theatrical angles to portray each historical figure as a chiseled or beautiful adventurer. . . . The writing is clear, packed with information, and presented in agile paragraphs that twist around the scenes of war, plotting, and murder." Booklist

Haven, Kendall F.
Reluctant heroes; true five-minute-read adventure stories for boys. Libraries Unlimited 2008 169p pa $30
Grades: Adult Professional **920**
1. Heroes and heroines
ISBN 978-1-59158-749-1 pa; 1-59158-749-2 pa
LC 2008014017
"These 25 true stories are divided into three sections: 'Stories from History,' 'Stories from the Modern World,' and 'Stories from the Natural World.' Each one offers a short history or explanation to place events in context and concludes with suggestions for further reading. . . . Appropriate as partnered works to nonfiction topics, these brief entries create useful classroom writing prompts or simply entertaining read-alouds. Quick-moving action and dialogue place readers squarely in the midst of dangerous, momentous events." SLJ
Includes bibliographical references

Herrera, Juan Felipe, 1948-
★ **Portraits** of Hispanic American heroes; by Juan Felipe Herrera; pictures by Raul Colon. Dial Books for Young Readers 2014 96 p. color illustrations (hardback) $19.99
Grades: 4 5 6 7 8 **920**
1. Biography 2. Latinos (U.S.) 3. Hispanic Americans -- Biography
ISBN 0803738099; 9780803738096
LC 2013044661
Pura Belpré (Author) Honor Book (2015)
This book by Juan Felipe Herrera "showcases twenty Hispanic and Latino American men and women who have made outstanding contributions to the arts, politics, science, humanitarianism, and athletics. Biographies of Cesar

Chavez, Sonia Sotomayor, Ellen Ochoa, Roberto Clemente, and many more [are included]." (Publisher's note)

"Herrera packs relevant info and kid-appropriate details . . . without overwhelming the work, infusing the narratives with engaging text. Colon's portraits are luminous." SLJ

Includes bibliographical references

Hodgkins, Fran

Champions of the ocean; illustrations by Cris Arbo. Dawn Publications 2009 144p il (Earth heroes) pa $11.95
Grades: 5 6 7 8   **920**

1. Scientists 2. Oceanography 3. Environmentalists
ISBN 978-1-58469-119-8 pa; 1-58469-119-0 pa
LC 2009-17926

This is a collective biography of oceanographers William Beebe, Archie Carr, Jacques-Yves Cousteau, Margaret Wentworth Owings, Eugenie Clark, Roger Payne, Sylvia Earle, and Tierney Thys.

This is illustrated with "black-and-white photographs and illustrations. [The book] provides young readers with fascinating facts and insights. . . . This volume is an excellent introduction to the biography genre, as well as a terrific research book." Sci Books Films

Includes bibliographical references

Housel, Debra J.

Ecologists; from Woodward to Miranda. Compass Point Books 2009 40p il (Mission: science) lib bdg $26.60
Grades: 4 5 6   **920**

1. Ecology 2. Environmentalists
ISBN 978-0-7565-4076-0 lib bdg; 0-7565-4076-3 lib bdg
LC 2008-35733

Profiles ecologists John Woodward, Aldo Leopold, Rachel Carson, Ruth Patrick, Eugene Odum, Lan Lubchenco, and Neo Martinez

Includes glossary and bibliographical references

Jankowski, Connie

Astronomers; from Copernicus to Crisp. Compass Point Books 2009 40p il (Mission: science) lib bdg $26.60
Grades: 4 5 6   **920**

1. Astronomers
ISBN 978-0-7565-3965-8 lib bdg; 0-7565-3965-X lib bdg
LC 2008-8325

Explores the lives and discoveries of noted astronomers from the fifteenth to the twenty-first century.

Includes glossary and bibliographical references

Jokulsson, Illugi

Stars of the World Cup; Illugi Jökulsson. Abbeville Kids 2014 63 p. (World soccer legends) (hardback) $12.95
Grades: 5 6 7 8   **920**

1. Soccer 2. Soccer teams 3. World Cup (Soccer) 4. Soccer players -- Biography
ISBN 0789212110; 9780789212115
LC 2014014490

In this book, by Illugi Jokulsson, "learn all about twenty-eight of the best players competing for the 2014 FIFA World Cup, from unstoppable scorers like Messi and Ronaldo to crafty playmakers like Iniesta and Modric, and ironclad defenders like Philipp Lahm and Thiago Silva." (Publisher's note)

"Young soccer fans will find plenty to enjoy in this visually dynamic introduction to 28 world-class soccer players... Readers will enjoy the information-packed text, but it's the eye-catching color photos (usually action shots) that will draw them to this attractive sports book." Booklist

Includes bibliographical references and index

Kiernan, Denise

★ **Signing** our lives away; the fame and misfortune of the men who signed the Declaration of Independence. by Denise Kiernan & Joseph D'Agnese. Quirk 2009 255p $19.95
Grades: 5 6 7 8   **920**

1. Statesmen -- United States 2. United States. Declaration of Independence 3. United States -- Politics and government -- 1775-1783, Revolution
ISBN 978-1-59474-330-6; 1-59474-330-4

"Kiernan and D'Agnese present readers with astonishing individual portraits of all the signers [of the Declaration of Independence] in an attempt both to dispel some of the mythology surrounding the document as well as to establish a place in the historical discourse for those men not named Jefferson, Hancock, Franklin, or Adams. The marvelously arranged work lends itself to either straightforward reading or skipping around. . . . An entertaining and effective narrative of about three to five pages per individual is presented." SLJ

Includes bibliographical references

Kimmel, Elizabeth Cody

Ladies first; 40 daring American women who were second to none. [by] Elizabeth Cody Kimmel; foreword by Stacy Allison. National Geographic 2006 192p il $18.95
Grades: 5 6 7 8   **920**

1. Women -- Biography 2. United States -- Biography
ISBN 0-7922-5393-0
LC 2005005113

This offers "introductions to forty of America's most brilliant and courageous women. Each essay is three pages in length and includes a fourth full-page portrait of the woman being introduced. . . . The women chosen achieved greatness in a wide range of endeavors, from athletics to the arts to politics. . . . Students will find these excellent essays useful as an introduction to the women portrayed and as a good jumping off point for further research." Voice Youth Advocates

Includes bibliographical references

Krull, Kathleen

The **brothers** Kennedy; John, Robert, Edward. illustrated by Amy June Bates. Simon & Schuster Books for Young Readers 2010 40p il $16.99
Grades: 2 3 4   **920**

1. Brothers 2. Statesmen 3. Presidents 4. Senators 5. Attorneys general 6. Political leaders 7. Members of Congress 8. Siblings of presidents 9. Presidential candidates
ISBN 978-1-4169-9158-8; 1-4169-9158-1

"Focusing on John, Robert, and Edward, the book describes the Kennedys' early family life and highlights a pivotal event for each featured sibling. . . . The stylized artwork [is] rendered in pencil, watercolor, and gouache. . . . The likenesses are strong, and the images set a historic tone." Booklist

Includes bibliographical references

★ **Lives** of extraordinary women; rulers, rebels (and what the neighbors thought) written by Kathleen Krull; illustrated by Kathryn Hewitt. Harcourt 2000 95p il $21

Grades: 4 5 6 7   **920**

1. Queens 2. Saints 3. Diplomats 4. Empresses 5. Explorers 6. Travelers 7. Suffragists 8. Abolitionists 9. Prime ministers 10. Women in politics 11. Regents 12. Feminists 13. Pacifists 14. Columnists 15. Dissenters 16. Memoirists 17. Humanitarians 18. Indian chiefs 19. Archaeologists 20. Indian leaders 21. Cabinet members 22. Social activists 23. Political leaders 24. Nonfiction writers 25. Women -- Biography 26. Members of Congress 27. Spouses of presidents 28. Human rights activists 29. United Nations officials 30. Nobel laureates for peace

ISBN 0-15-200807-1

LC 99-6840

"Each entry offers a tightly written biography, often filled with delicious anecdote. . . . Each biographical essay is accompanied by one of Hewitt's full-page, full-color caricatures. Both artful and witty, the illustrations provide perfect accompaniments to the often breezy and accessible text." N Y Times Book Rev

Includes bibliographical references

Lives of the explorers; discoveries, disasters (and what the neighbors thought) Kathleen Krull; illustrated by Kathryn Hewitt. HMH Books for Young Readers 2014 96 p. col. ill., col. maps (hardback) $20.99

Grades: 4 5 6 7   **920**

1. Explorers 2. Exploration 3. United States -- Exploration 4. Discoveries in geography 5. Adventure and adventurers

ISBN 0152059105; 9780152059101

LC 2013037697

"Krull introduces middle-grade readers to a diverse cast of 17 explorers in this latest offering from her series. A short, two-to five page chapter is devoted to each explorer, incorporating a biographical sketch and a short discussion of the explorer's contributions. The subjects are presented chronologically, beginning in the medieval period with the Norseman Leif Ericson and finishing with the astronaut Sally Ride." (School Library Journal)

"The straightforward, accessible prose makes for fast reading, and Krull doesn't shy away from some deplorable, stomach-turning facts, which kids will devour and use to spice up staid homework assignments." Kirkus

Includes bibliographical references

★ **Lives** of the musicians; good times, bad times (and what the neighbors thought) written by Kathleen Krull; illustrated by Kathryn Hewitt. Harcourt Brace Jovanovich 1993 96p il $21; pa $12; pa $8.99

Grades: 4 5 6 7   **920**

1. Authors 2. Singers 3. Pianists 4. Composers 5. Dramatists 6. Violinists 7. Librettists 8. Folk musicians 9. Jazz musicians 10. Conductors (Music) 11. Memoirists 12. Songwriters 13. Music teachers

14. Classical musicians 15. Theatrical directors

ISBN 0-15-248010-2; 0-15-216436-7 pa; 9780544238060

LC 91-33497

"Twenty (including both Gilbert and Sullivan) composers, from Vivaldi to Gershwin, are here profiled in a series of irreverent, anecdotal vignettes, each stylishly illustrated with an elegant caricature." Bull Cent Child Books

Includes glossary and bibliographical references

★ **Lives** of the presidents; fame, shame (and what the neighbors thought) written by Kathleen Krull; illustrated by Kathryn Hewitt. updated ed.; Harcourt Children's Books 2011 104p il $21

Grades: 4 5 6 7   **920**

1. Presidents -- United States

ISBN 978-0-547-49809-6; 0-547-49809-8

First published 1998

"This new edition is sure to be even more popular than the original title (Harcourt, 1998) as it includes Presidents George W. Bush and Barack Obama, who are given the same cheeky-but-respectful treatment as their predecessors. . . . [Krull] provides further information on ex-Presidential activity since 1998, such as Jimmy Carter's Nobel Prize, Ronald Reagan's passing, and the Clintons' post-White House work. All other entries and art are virtually unaltered. Guaranteed to inject some levity into the ubiquitous presidential biography assignment, the 2011 Lives of the Presidents is a must-have for elementary schools and public libraries." SLJ

Includes bibliographical references

Malnor, Bruce

Champions of the wilderness; by Bruce and Carol L. Malnor; illustrated by Anisa Claire Hovemann. Dawn Publications 2009 143p il (Earth heroes) pa $11.95

Grades: 5 6 7 8   **920**

1. Environmentalists

ISBN 978-1-58469-116-7 pa; 1-58469-116-6 pa

LC 2008-53670

"This is a short gem of a book that includes short biographies of eight 'heroes' who have championed the preservation and/or conservation of wilderness areas around the world over the past two centuries. Henry David Thoreau, John Muir, Teddy Roosevelt, Aldo Leopold, Richard St. Barbe Baker, Mardy Murie, David Suzuki, and Wangari Maathai are the heroes in question. The storytelling is fluent and engaging." Sci Books Films

Includes bibliographical references

Malnor, Carol

Champions of wild animals; by Carol L. and Bruce Malnor; illustrations by Anisa Claire Hovemann. Dawn Publications 2010 144p il (Earth heroes) pa $11.95

Grades: 5 6 7 8   **920**

1. Naturalists 2. Endangered species 3. Wildlife conservation

ISBN 978-1-58469-123-5 pa; 1-58469-123-9 pa

LC 2010-16030

This describes "the youth and careers of eight of the world's greatest environmentalists who championed the protection of wildlife, including William Hornaday (saved the bison from extinction), Ding Darling (A Duck's Best Friend), Rachel Carson (author of Silent Spring), Roger Tory Peterson (Inventor of the Modern Field Guide), R.D.

Lawrence (Storyteller for Wolves), E.O. Wilson (Lord of the Ants), Jane Goodall (Champion for Chimps), and Ian and Saba Douglas-Hamilton (Saving the Elephants)." Publisher's note

Includes bibliographical references

Nathan, Amy

Meet the dancers; from ballet, broadway, and beyond. Henry Holt 2008 231p il $18.95

Grades: 5 6 7 8 **920**

1. Dance 2. Dancers

ISBN 978-0-8050-8071-1; 0-8050-8071-6

LC 2007-27589

"This collective biography reveals the paths that 16 diverse dancers followed to become professionals and to join prestigious companies. . . . The tone of the text is conversational. . . . The pictures dramatically capture how talented these performers are. Anyone, whether considering a career in dance or not, will be inspired and educated by these up-close-and-personal accounts." SLJ

Pinkney, Andrea Davis

★ Let it shine; stories of Black women freedom fighters. illustrated by Stephen Alcorn. Harcourt 2000 107p il $20

Grades: 4 5 6 7 **920**

1. Slaves 2. Authors 3. Midwives 4. Educators 5. Journalists 6. Abolitionists 7. Philanthropists 8. Essayists 9. Memoirists 10. Political leaders 11. Nonfiction writers 12. Members of Congress 13. Newspaper executives 14. Presidential advisers 15. African American women 16. Civil rights activists 17. Organization officials 18. Political party leaders 19. Presidential candidates 20. United States -- Race relations 21. African Americans -- Civil rights 22. African American women -- Biography 23. African Americans -- Civil rights -- History 24. African American women civil rights workers -- Biography

ISBN 0-15-201005-X

LC 99-42806

This is a collection of "sketches celebrating the contributions of 10 women who moved forward the cause of civil rights in America. . . . They include Harriet Tubman, Mary McLeod Bethune and Rosa Parks, as well as Biddy Mason, Ida B. Wells-Barnett, Ella Josephine Baker, Dorothy Irene Height and Fannie Lou Hamer." (SLJ) Bibliography. "Grades three to six." (Bull Cent Child Books)

This "collective biography tells of 10 extraordinary black women. From Sojourner Truth to Shirley Chisholm, this is also a view of African American history through individual lives. . . . Stephen Alcorn's allegorical oil portraits are dramatic and beautiful. . . . The immediacy of the text and the spacious design of the large volume make this a natural for reading aloud." Booklist

Includes bibliographical references

Rappaport, Doreen

★ We are the many; a picture book of American Indians. illustrated by Cornelius Van Wright and Ying-Hwa Hu. HarperCollins Pubs. 2002 28p il hardcover o.p. lib bdg $17.89

Grades: 2 3 4 **920**

1. Native Americans -- Biography

ISBN 0-688-16559-1; 0-06-001139-4 lib bdg

LC 2001-39820

"One incident from each person's life is re-created, giving a quick, snapshot-style view of the individual's contribution to the world. . . . . The text is large, and sentences are accessible to emerging readers. . . . There is some fictionalizing . . . but it is limited and does not detract from the overall worth of the title." SLJ

Rivera, Raquel

Arctic adventures; tales from the lives of Inuit artists. pictures by Jirina Marton. Groundwood Books/House of Anansi Press 2007 47p il $18.95

Grades: 3 4 5 6 **920**

1. Artists 2. Sculptors 3. Artists, Inuit 4. Printmakers 5. Inuit -- Art

ISBN 978-0-88899-714-2; 0-88899-714-0

"This dynamic picture book draws on memoir, legend, art, and history to tell true dramatized events in the lives of four modern Inuit artists. . . . Beautiful illustrations in colored pencil and mixed media show the individual people and creatures in the Arctic landscape. . . . After each story, there is a brief, straightforward biography of the artist, a photo, and a reproduction of his or her work." Booklist

Includes glossary and bibliographical references

Roberts, Cokie

Founding mothers; remembering the ladies. by Cokie Roberts and illustrated by Diane Goode and edited by Alyson Day. HarperCollins 2014 40 p. (hardcover bdg.) $17.99

Grades: 3 4 5 6 7 **920**

1. Women -- United States -- History 2. United States -- History -- 1775-1783, Revolution

ISBN 0060780029; 9780060780029; 9780060780036

LC 2013936887

This book, by Cokie Roberts and illustrated by Diane Goode, "reveals the incredible accomplishments of the women who orchestrated the American Revolution behind the scenes. Roberts traces the stories of heroic, patriotic women such as Abigail Adams, Martha Washington, Phillis Wheatley, Mercy Otis Warren, Sarah Livingston Jay, and others. Details are gleaned from their letters, private journals, lists, and ledgers." (Publisher's note)

"Most children know that the "Founding Fathers" are the men who helped the 13 colonies develop into the United States. What about the women of the time period?...Grammarians may not appreciate the author's colloquial style, but the conversational tone is appealing. Beautifully intricate illustrations, rendered with antique pens, sepia ink, and watercolors, suit the text well. Thoughtful design, well-chosen facts, and an approachable format combine to make a book readers will enjoy and appreciate." (SLJ)

Roop, Peter

Tales of famous heroes; by Peter and Connie Roop; illustrated by Rebecca Zomchek. Scholastic 2010 106p il $17.99

Grades: 3 4 5 6 **920**

1. Heroes and heroines

ISBN 978-0-545-23750-5; 0-545-23750-5

"The lives of inspirational figures are presented in such an engaging manner that readers will not be able to stop after reading just one. The 17 profiles highlight important events from the individual's childhood, demonstrating how each was set on course for greatness. Current famous people, such as Sonia Sotomayor, Barack Obama, and Nelson Mandela, are included, as well as historical figures like Winston Churchill and Sojourner Truth. . . . The book is illustrated with caricature-type portraits superimposed on archival photographs. Each biography is made up of easy-to-read paragraphs designed for beginners or less capable older readers. An engaging collective biography." SLJ

Rosenberg, Aaron

The **Civil** War; one event, six people. Scholastic 2011 160p il map (Profiles) $14.99

Grades: 5 6 7 8   **920**

1. Nurses 2. Slaves 3. Authors 4. Lawyers 5. Generals 6. Presidents 7. Abolitionists 8. Photographers 9. Memoirists 10. Police officials 11. State legislators 12. College presidents 13. Members of Congress 14. Red Cross officials 15. Social welfare leaders 16. United States -- History -- 1861-1865, Civil War -- Biography

ISBN 978-0-545-28926-9; 0-545-28926-2

"This collective biography . . . introduces Abraham Lincoln, Frederick Douglass, Clara Barton, George McClellan, Robert E. Lee, and Matthew Brady. Single paragraph summaries of each subject's historical relevance are followed by resumes of their lives that focus on how each affected and was affected by the Civil War and that point out connections between them all. . . . Archival photographs are instuctive." Booklist

Includes bibliographical references

Stout, Glenn

Yes she can! women's sports pioneers. Houghton Mifflin Harcourt 2011 117p il (Good sports) pa $5.99

Grades: 4 5 6 7   **920**

1. Women athletes

ISBN 978-0-547-41725-7; 0-547-41725-X

"In chapters devoted to swimmer Trudy Ederle, runners Louise Stokes and Tidye Pickett, jockey Julie Krone, and Indy car driver Danica Patrick, Stout covers each woman's hard work, setbacks, and triumphs without minimizing the challenges and disappointments along the way. . . . Accessible and inspirational." Publ Wkly

Thimmesh, Catherine

★ **Girls** think of everything; illustrated by Melissa Sweet. Houghton Mifflin 2000 57p $16; pa $6.95

Grades: 5 6 7 8   **920**

1. Admirals 2. Chemists 3. Students 4. Inventors 5. Inventions 6. Physicists 7. Women inventors 8. Computer scientists 9. Home economists 10. Clothing industry executives 11. Office supply industry executives

ISBN 0-395-93744-2; 0-618-19563-7 pa

LC 99-36270

"Ten women and two girls are given a few pages each. Included are Mary Anderson, who invented the windshield wiper (after she was told it wouldn't work); Ruth Wakefield, who, by throwing chunks of chocolate in her cookie batter, gave Toll House cookies to the world; and young Becky Schroeder, who invented Glo-paper because she wanted to write in the dark. The text is written in a fresh, breezy manner, but it is the artwork that is really outstanding." Booklist

Waldman, Neil

A **land** of big dreamers; voices of courage in America. selected and illustrated by Neil Waldman. Millbrook Press 2010 32p il lib bdg $16.95

Grades: 3 4 5   **920**

1. Courage 2. American national characteristics 3. United States -- Biography

ISBN 978-0-8225-6810-0; 0-8225-6810-1

LC 2010001185

"Thirteen prominent American men and women are briefly profiled in this collection. Chronologically ranging from Thomas Jefferson to Barack Obama, each entry features an inspiring quote from its subject and a concise explanation of his or her context in history. Opposite each page of text is a watercolor painting by the author depicting an image or montage of the notable individual and illustrating the work they achieved or how they lived. Each one evokes the emotions the book is meant to inspire: courage, strength and determination." Kirkus

Winter, Jeanette

Malala, a brave girl from Pakistan/Iqbal, a brave boy from Pakistan; by Jeanette Winter. Beach Lane Books 2014 40 p. color illustrations (hardback) $17.99

Grades: 1 2 3 4   **920**

1. Pakistanis 2. Boys -- Pakistan -- Biography 3. Girls -- Education -- Pakistan 4. Girls -- Pakistan -- Biography 5. Heroes -- Pakistan -- Biography 6. Child slaves -- Pakistan -- Biography

ISBN 1481422944; 9781481422949

LC 2014009720

Author Jeanette Winter's children's book tells the true stories of "two heroes of Pakistan who stood up for the rights to freedom and education. Iqbal Masih and Malala Yousafzai. Each was unafraid to speak out. He, against inhumane child slavery in the carpet trade. She, for the right of girls to attend school. Both were shot by those who disagreed with them. Iqbal was killed instantly; Malala miraculously survived and continues to speak out around the world." (Publisher's note)

"This picture book introduces two Pakistani children who fought for peace and justice and suffered violence: one side is Malala Yousafzai's story; flip it for Iqbal Masih's. Iqbal was killed in 1995; Malala was shot by the Taliban (but survived) in 2012 "for speaking out for the right of girls to attend school." A great place to begin a young activist's education." Horn Book

Malala, a brave girl from Pakistan

Iqbal, a brave boy from Pakistan

Winter, Jonah

The **Founding** Fathers; Jonah Winter; illustrated by Barry Blitt. Atheneum Books for Young Readers 2014 48 p. color illustrations (hardcover) $17.99

Grades: 2 3 4 5   **920**

1. Founding Fathers of the United States 2. Constitutional history -- United States 3. United States -- History -- 1775-1783, Revolution

ISBN 1442442743; 9781442442740; 9781442442757

LC 2012030311

This children's book by Jonah Winter is a "look at our Founding Fathers. . . . It seems that Ben Franklin, Thomas Jefferson, and their cohorts sometimes agreed on NOTHING . . . except the thing that mattered most: creating the finest constitution in world history, for the brand-new United

States of America. The men we now call America's Founding Fathers were a motley bunch of characters who fought a lot and made mistakes and just happened to invent a whole new kind of nation." (Publisher's note)

"Pointing out that the expression "Founding Fathers" sounds like the name of a rock band or baseball team, Winter looks into who 14 of these men really were, warts and all: "Thomas Jefferson was sort of a mixed bag. Dude wrote that 'all men are created equal.' But then he also wrote that blacks were inferior humans!" Winter includes quotations from each man, as well as lists of stats with categories including their wealth, political party, "Stance on France," and "Opinion on Boston Tea Party" (Benjamin Rush was a "huge fan"). Blitt's pen-and-ink caricatures are right in line with Winter's playful tone, as he pokes fun at Washington, Franklin, Paine, and others, while giving readers a strong understanding of why these figures' contributions to the developing nation were so significant." PW

Peaceful heroes; illustrated by Sean Addy. Arthur A. Levine Books 2009 56p il $17.99

Grades: 4 5 6 7   **920**

1. Peace 2. Heroes and heroines

ISBN 978-0-439-62307-0; 0-439-62307-3

            LC 2008-48311

"Starting off with Jesus, Gandhi, King, and Sojourner Truth, this collective biography goes on to profile many less well-known peace activists across the world. . . . The detailed portraits never deny the horrifying realities that the peace-seeking leaders are fighting against. With the chatty interactive text, there are handsome full-page pictures of each activist, rendered in oil, acrylic, and collage in shades of red and brown." Booklist

Wild women of the Wild West; illustrated by Susan Guevara. Holiday House 2011 il $16.95

Grades: 2 3 4   **920**

1. Women -- Biography 2. West (U.S.) -- History 3. Frontier and pioneer life -- West (U.S.)

ISBN 978-0-8234-1601-1; 0-8234-1601-1

            LC 2010030911

"This book introduces 16 figures who made their mark between the California Gold Rush and the end of the 19th century. . . . Each page-long biographical sketch is written in a delightful colloquial style that gives the text verve and sparkle. Each biography is accompanied by a full-page, watercolor and ink portrait of the subject. All are based on historical photos and show the women as strong and powerful." SLJ

Includes bibliographical references

Wishinsky, Frieda

Freedom heroines; Susan B. Anthony, Elizabeth Cady Stanton, Jane Addams, Ida B. Wells, Alice Paul, Rosa Parks. by Frieda Wishinsky. Scholastic Inc. 2012 144 p. ill. (some col.) (Profiles) (pbk.) $6.99

Grades: 4 5 6   **920**

1. Women's rights -- History 2. African Americans -- Civil rights 3. Women -- United States -- Biography 4. Civil rights workers -- United States 5. Feminists -- United States -- Biography 6. Suffragists -- United States -- Biography 7. African American women civil

rights workers -- Biography

ISBN 0545425182; 9780545425186

            LC 2012285016

Amelia Bloomer Project (2014)

Written by Frieda Wishinsky and part of the Profiles series, this book focuses "on Civil Champions--some of the incredible women who worked tirelessly to ensure equal rights for all." Women discussed include "Susan B. Anthony, Elizabeth Cady Stanton, Ida B. Wells, Alice Paul, Rosa Parks, and Jane Addams." (Publisher's note)

"The writing is matter-of-fact, with the design shouldering a lot of the load to distinguish each woman. Photos and reproductions of printed items, mostly black-and-white, lend context." Booklist

Includes bibliographical references and index

Yolen, Jane

Sea queens; women pirates around the world. illustrated by Christine Joy Pratt. Charlesbridge 2008 103p il $18.95

Grades: 4 5 6 7   **920**

1. Women pirates 2. Women -- Biography

ISBN 978-1-58089-131-8; 1-58089-131-4

            LC 2007026983

This offers "12 portraits of sword-swinging, seafaring women throughout history, from Artemisia, in 500 B.C.E. Persia, to Madame Ching, an early nineteenth-century Chinese woman and named here as 'the most successful pirate in the world.' . . . The scratchboard illustrations work well as portraits. . . . The book is filled with fascinating, dramatically told stories and sidebars." Booklist

Includes bibliographical references

920.003 Dictionaries, encyclopedias, concordances of biography as a discipline

Biography for beginners: women who made a difference. Favorable Impressions 2011 $49

Grades: 3 4 5 6   **920.003**

1. Reference books 2. Women -- Biography

ISBN 978-1-931360-43-2

            LC 2011017258

This is a "collection of 60 biographies of women who made an impact in their fields. . . . Each 6- to 10-page article is accompanied by well-chosen illustrations of the women. . . . The articles . . . are written at the appropriate level for elementary-school to middle-grade students and divided into sections that use bold type for the first few words to catch the reader's eye. The use of quotes from the subjects and others enhances the biographies and makes them more personal. . . . The biographies . . . serve as solid resources for young readers." Booklist

Includes glossary and bibliographical references

Rockman, Connie C.

Tenth book of junior authors and illustrators; edited by Connie C. Rockman. Wilson, H.W. 2008 803p autog il por (Junior authors & illustrators series) hardcover o.p. $120

Grades: Adult Professional   **920.003**

1. Reference books 2. Authors -- Dictionaries 3. Illustrators -- Dictionaries 4. Children's literature --

Bio-bibliography

ISBN 978-0-8242-1066-3; 0-8242-1066-2

LC 2008043312

This volume covers some 200 authors and illustrators of books for children and young adults including David Almond, Blue Balliett, Terry Pratchett, and Laura Vaccaro Seeger. For 17 authors and artists whose careers include significant new works and honors since their profile in earlier editions of the series, newly written entries are featured

"Standard resource for libraries serving young readers and students studying children's and young adult literature." Booklist

Includes bibliographical references

Something about the author; facts and pictures about authors and illustrators of books for young people. Gale Res. il

Grades: Adult Professional   **920.003**

1. Reference books 2. Authors -- Dictionaries 3. Illustrators -- Dictionaries 4. Children's literature -- Bio-bibliography

First published 1971. Frequency varies

"This important series gives comprehensive coverage of the individuals who write and illustrate books for children. Each new volume adds about 100 profiles. Entries include career and personal data, a bibliography of the author's works, information on works in progress and references to further information." Safford. Guide to Ref Materials for Sch Libr Media Cent. 5th edition

Something about the author: autobiography series. Gale Res. il

Grades: Adult Professional   **920.003**

1. Reference books 2. Authors -- Dictionaries 3. Illustrators -- Dictionaries 4. Children's literature -- Bio-bibliography

First published 1986

An "ongoing series in which juvenile authors discuss their lives, careers, and published works. Each volume contains essays by 20 established writers or illustrators (e.g., Evaline Ness, Nonny Hogrogian, Betsy Byars, Jean Fritz) who represent all types of literature, preschool to young adult. . . . Some articles focus on biographical information, while others emphasize the writing career. Most, however, address young readers and provide family background, discuss the writing experience, and cite some factors that influenced it. Illustrations include portraits of the authors as children and more recent action pictures and portraits. There are cumulative indexes by authors, important published works, and geographical locations mentioned in the essays." Safford. Guide to Ref Books for Sch Libr Media Cent. 5th edition

920.02   General collections of biography

Donovan, Sandy

Lethal leaders and military madmen; by Sandy Donovan. Lerner Publications Company 2013 32 p. col. ill. (library) $26.60

Grades: 5 6 7 8   **920.02**

1. Picture books for children 2. Kings and rulers 3.

Dictators 4. Dictatorship 5. Military government

ISBN 1467706094; 9781467706094

LC 2012018444

This book by Sandy Donovan is part of the Shockzone Villains series and looks at political and military leaders. "Some of history's most ruthless leaders are headed your way. Some of these rulers schemed their way to the top. Others just conquered everything around them." (Publisher's note)

920.72   Women -- Collective biography

Branzei, Sylvia

Adventurers; Sylvia Branzei; illustrated by Melissa Sweet. Running Press 2011 96 p. ill., maps (ebook) $10.95; (paperback) $10.95

Grades: 3 4 5 6 7   **920.72**

1. Women 2. Adventure and adventurers 3. Women -- Biography 4. Women adventurers -- Biography 5. Adventure and adventurers -- Biography

ISBN 9780762443857; 0762436964; 9780762436965

LC 2009923889

This book "provides 6- to 8-page biographical sketches of 12 women who are 'the stuff of legends.' Each one is identified with a character trait, e.g. balloonist Sophie Blanchard is 'Intrepid' and Margaret Bourke-White is 'Relentless,' although most of the adjectives could apply to every subject, as [Sylvia] Branzei makes plain." Among those included are Amelia Earhart, Nellie Bly, Susan Butcher, and Kit Deslauriers. (School Library Journal)

Cowgirls; by Sylvia Branzei; illustratrated by Melissa Sweet. Running Press Kids 2011 96 p. ill. (some col.), map (paperback) $10.95

Grades: 3 4 5 6 7   **920.72**

1. Picture books for children 2. Cowgirls 3. Ranch life -- West (U.S.) 4. Cowgirls -- West (U.S.) -- History 5. Cowgirls -- West (U.S.) -- Biography

ISBN 0762436956; 9780762436958

LC 2009923890

This book "profiles 12 sketches of working cowgirls and rodeo riders from the 19th century through the present day. The term 'cowgirl' also covers other Western types: stagecoach driver Mary Fields is here, along with outlaw Sally Skull and 'Little Sure-Shot' Annie Oakley. 'Lady cowboy poet' Georgie Sicking will probably be new to most readers; one of her poems is included." (School Library Journal)

Includes bibliographical references (p. 92-96)

León, Vicki

★ **Outrageous** women of the Middle Ages; by Vicki Leon. Wiley 1998 ix, 118 p.p ill., maps hardcover o.p. (paperback) $14.95; (prebind) $23.95

Grades: 4 5 6 7 8   **920.72**

1. Middle Ages 2. Women -- History 3. Women -- Biography 4. Women -- History 5. Women -- Biography 6. Women -- History -- Middle Ages, 500-1500 7. Civilization, Medieval 8. Biography -- Middle Ages, 500-1500

ISBN 9780471170044; 9781435280090

LC 97030307

In this book, Vicki Leon looks at women of the Middle Ages. She "tells of a Viking killed by a severed head, a queen who knew the meaning of congregating frogs, and much more. The stories and sidebars provide a detailed picture of the times. . . . The women profiled lived in the 6th through 14th centuries in Europe, Asia, and Africa. Their spheres included everything from astronomy to warfare. They were nomads and empresses." (School Library Journal)

Includes bibliographical references (p. 115-117).

McCann, Michelle Roehm

Girls who rocked the world; heroines from Sacagawea to Natalie Portman. Michelle Roehm McCann and Amelie Welden. Simon & Schuster 2012 p. cm. (hardcover: alk. paper) $18.99

Grades: 5 6 7 8   920.72

1. Feminism 2. Women -- History 3. Women -- Biography 4. Girls -- Biography 5. Heros -- Biography 6. Women heros -- Biography

ISBN 9781582703022; 9781582703619

LC 2011050502

Author Michelle Roehm McCann presents "examples of strong, independent female role models, all of whom first impacted the world as teenagers or younger." The book "spans a variety of achievements, interests, and backgrounds, from Harriet Tubman and Coco Chanel to S.E. Hinton and Maya Lin--each with her own incredible story of how she created life-changing opportunities for herself and the world." (Publisher's note)

Includes bibliographical references and index.

929   Genealogy, names, insignia

Johnson, Mary J.

Your fascinating family history; super smart information strategies. by Mary J. Johnson. Cherry Lake Publishing 2011 32 p. (lib. bdg.) $28.50

Grades: 3 4 5 6   929

1. Family 2. Genealogy

ISBN 1610801229; 9781610801225

LC 2011000641

In this book, by Mary J. Johnson, readers can "learn how to research, understand, and arrange information about [their] ancestors." (Publisher's note) The book "provides ideas for beginning a genealogy search, explaining how to get started, where to find family information, and the value of oral histories and suggests creative ideas for putting everything together and sharing." (School Library Journal)

Includes bibliographical references and index

Ollhoff, Jim

Beginning genealogy; expert tips to help you trace your own ancestors. ABDO Pub. Co. 2011 32p il (Your family tree) $18.95

Grades: 4 5 6 7   929

1. Research 2. Genealogy

ISBN 978-1-61613-460-0; 1-61613-460-7

LC 2009050812

This is "great . . . for kids interested in genealogy. . . . [It does] a wonderful job of presenting the fundamentals of genealogical research in a clear and exciting manner. . . . Understanding and properly using primary documents is stressed throughout. . . . [An] attractive, spacious [layout]; full-color, sharp images; clearly labeled diagrams; and scattered maps add information and appeal." SLJ

Includes glossary

Collecting primary records. ABDO Pub. Co. 2011 32p il (Your family tree) $18.95

Grades: 4 5 6 7   929

1. Research 2. Genealogy

ISBN 978-1-61613-461-7; 1-61613-461-5

LC 2009050811

This describes how to collect primary records for geneological research.

This is "great . . . for kids interested in genealogy. . . . [It does] a wonderful job of presenting the fundamentals of genealogical research in a clear and exciting manner. . . . Understanding and properly using primary documents is stressed throughout. . . . [An] attractive, spacious [layout]; full-color, sharp images; clearly labeled diagrams; and scattered maps add information and appeal." SLJ

Includes glossary

DNA; window to the past: how science can help untangle your family roots. ABDO Pub. Co. 2011 32p il map (Your family tree) $18.95

Grades: 4 5 6 7   929

1. Genetics 2. Genealogy

ISBN 978-1-61613-462-4; 1-61613-462-3

LC 2009050808

This explains how DNA is used in geneology.

This is "great . . . for kids interested in genealogy. . . . [It does] a wonderful job of presenting the fundamentals of genealogical research in a clear and exciting manner. . . . Understanding and properly using primary documents is stressed throughout. . . . [An] attractive, spacious [layout]; full-color, sharp images; clearly labeled diagrams; and scattered maps add information and appeal." SLJ

Includes glossary

Filling the family tree. ABDO Pub. Co. 2011 32p il (Your family tree) lib bdg $18.95

Grades: 4 5 6 7   929

1. Research 2. Genealogy

ISBN 978-1-61613-464-8; 1-61613-464-X

LC 2009050806

This is "great . . . for kids interested in genealogy. . . . [It does] a wonderful job of presenting the fundamentals of genealogical research in a clear and exciting manner. . . . Understanding and properly using primary documents is stressed throughout. . . . [An] attractive, spacious [layout]; full-color, sharp images; clearly labeled diagrams; and scattered maps add information and appeal." SLJ

Using your research; how to check your facts and use your information. ABDO Pub. Co. 2011 32p il (Your family tree) lib bdg $18.95

Grades: 4 5 6 7   929

1. Research 2. Genealogy

ISBN 978-1-61613-465-5; 1-61613-465-8

LC 2009050805

Presents a brief guide on how to check facts and use other information in genealogical research.

This is "great . . . for kids interested in genealogy. . . . [It does] a wonderful job of presenting the fundamentals of genealogical research in a clear and exciting manner. . . . Understanding and properly using primary documents is stressed throughout. . . . [An] attractive, spacious [layout]; full-color, sharp images; clearly labeled diagrams; and scattered maps add information and appeal." SLJ

Includes glossary

Waddell, Dan

Who do you think you are? be a family tree detective. Candlewick Press 2011 24p il $19.99

Grades: 2 3 4 5   929

1. Genealogy

ISBN 978-0-7636-5547-1; 0-7636-5547-3

LC 2010050054

"This guide to genealogy . . . takes readers through the steps of tracing their origins, starting with a who's who of possible extended family members and an explanation of genes. Waddell provides oral history interview tips, Internet search guidelines, and suggestions such as consulting censuses for clues about deceased relatives. Flaps and other interactive features hold additional information. . . . Those with an interest in the topic should discover useful insights, ideas, and tips for conducting research." Publ Wkly

929.9   Forms of insignia and identification

Allen, Kathy

The first American flag; illustrated by Siri Weber Feeney. Picture Window Books 2010 32p il map (Our American story) lib bdg $23.99

Grades: 2 3 4   929.9

1. Flags -- United States

ISBN 978-1-4048-5541-0 lib bdg; 1-4048-5541-6 lib bdg

LC 2009-6892

An introduction to the American flag and its symbolism discusses the features and history of early American flags

This title is "illustrated with well-executed, full-page, color illustrations, maps, and photos. . . . [It has] clearly written information that students can use for either leisure reading or reports." SLJ

Includes glossary and bibliographical references

Bateman, Teresa

★ Red, white, blue, and Uncle who? the stories behind some of America's patriotic symbols. illustrated by John O'Brien. Holiday House 2001 64p il $16.95; pa $6.95

Grades: 4 5 6 7   929.9

1. National emblems 2. National monuments

ISBN 0-8234-1285-7; 0-8234-1784-0 pa

LC 00-57258

This "volume presents 17 'patriotic symbols,' an umbrella term that encompasses everything from the flag to Uncle Sam, from Mount Rushmore to the Korean War Memorial. Bateman finds plenty of interesting information to share about each symbol or site, and browsers will be entertained by the many stories of origination, construction, and history." Booklist

Includes bibliographical references

Jackson, Donna M.

The name game; a look behind the labels. illustrated by Ted Stearn. Viking 2009 64p il $16.99

Grades: 4 5 6 7 8   929.9

1. Names

ISBN 978-0-670-01197-1; 0-670-01197-5

LC 2008-37705

"All kinds of entertaining and random facts are found in this quirky book. Tips for naming pets and companies are given, in a chapter each, along with hints for remembering people's names, explanations of conventions in other countries, and the system of choosing hurricane monikers. Sports, people, and geographic locations all have different sections. Black-and-white cartoons add a bit of humor. Students will navigate this book with ease." SLJ

Znamierowski, Alfred, 1940-

The World Encyclopedia of Flags; The definitive guide to international, flags, banners, standards and ensigns, with over 1400 illustration. by Alfred Znamierowski. Lorenz Books 2013 256 p. $16.99

Grades: 5 6 7 8 9 10 11 12 Adult   929.9

1. Flags

ISBN 0754826295; 9780754826293

This book, by Alred Znamierowski, presents "a directory of flags and a fascinating history of their development and usage, featuring over 600 flags including military signs, royal standards, civic flags, ensigns and national flags, expertly illustrated throughout." (Publisher's note)

930   History of ancient world (to ca. 499)

Adams, Simon

The Kingfisher atlas of the ancient world; illustrated by Katherine Baxter. Kingfisher 2006 44p il $15.95

Grades: 4 5 6 7   930

1. Reference books 2. Ancient civilization 3. Historical geography

ISBN 978-0-7534-5914-0; 0-7534-5914-0

"Featuring seventeen . . . hand-illustrated maps and . . . with . . . information about ancient civilizations and peoples, this is [a] . . . pictorial guide to what the world was like between 10,000 B.C. and A.D. 1000. Each . . . map shows the major sites from a particular civilization or group of civilizations. . . . Feature spreads use photographs of cultural and architectural artifacts, as well as additional information, to focus in greater depth on the key cultures of Egypt, Greece, and Rome." Publisher's note

930.1   Archaeology

Barber, Nicola

Lost cities; by Nicola Barber. Capstone Raintree 2013 48 p. col. ill. (Treasure hunters) (hardcover) $29.33; (paperback) $8.99

Grades: 5 6 7 8   930.1

1. Picture books for children 2. Extinct cities 3. Legends 4. Civilization, Ancient 5. Archaeology

ISBN 1410949524; 1410949591; 9781410949523; 9781410949592

LC 2012012891

This book by Nicola Barber is part of the Treasure Hunters series and looks at lost cities. This entry "examines the search for lost cities and the important artefacts within them that can offer us an extraordinary window on to the past. . . . Cities covered in the book include Pompeii, Troy, the desert city of Ubar, and the Inca city of Machu Picchu." (Publisher's note)

Includes bibliographical references (p. 46-47) and index.

Tomb explorers; by Nicola Barber. Capstone Raintree 2013 48 p. ill. (mostly col.) (Treasure hunters) (library) $29.33; (paperback) $8.99

Grades: 5 6 7 8   **930.1**
1. Tombs 2. Archeology 3. Antiquities 4. Treasure troves 5. Civilization, Ancient
ISBN 1410949559; 9781410949554; 9781410949622
LC 2012012894

This book by Nicola Barber "examines the hunt for and discovery of ancient tombs, and the valuable treasures they hold. . . . Part of the Treasure Hunters series, 'Tomb Explorers' offers a crosscurricular mix of science & technology and history & civilizations. . . .Tombs covered in the book include that of Tutankhamun, the Sumerian royal tombs of Ur, the Terracotta Army of ancient China, and the Mayan tombs of Palanque in the Mexican Rainforest, and the Oseberg ship burial." (Publisher's note)

Includes bibliographical references and index.

Compoint, Stephane
Buried treasures; uncovering secrets of the past. Abrams Books for Young Readers 2011 72p il $19.95

Grades: 5 6 7 8   **930.1**
1. Archeology 2. Antiquities 3. Ancient civilization
ISBN 978-0-8109-9781-3; 0-8109-9781-9
LC 2010021626

"Showcasing the work of a specialist in archaeological photography, this loosely themed album offers a broad range of eye candy for fans of ancient artifacts, fossils, remote natural locales, and rare animals. . . . Confined to captions and a few introductory paragraphs, the text supplies useful background. . . . The photos are . . . dramatically lit, sharply reproduced, and tellingly angled. . . . Casual browsers will consider this book a real find." Booklist

Croy, Anita
Exploring the past. Marshall Cavendish Benchmark 2010 48p il (Invisible worlds) $28.50

Grades: 4 5 6 7   **930.1**
1. Fossils 2. Archeology 3. Human origins 4. Prehistoric peoples 5. Ancient civilization
ISBN 978-0-7614-4194-6; 0-7614-4194-8

The narrative is "clear, well written, broken down into manageable pieces, and peppered with eye-opening facts. The numerous photographs are so phenomenal that they will inspire kids to read the text . . . so that they can wrap their minds around what they see." SLJ

Includes glossary and bibliographical references

Hunter, Nick
Ancient treasures; by Nick Hunter; edited by Laura Knowles ... [et al.]; illustrated by Martin Bustamante. Raintree 2013 48 p. col. ill., col. maps (Treasure hunters) (hardcover) $29.33; (paperback) $8.99

Grades: 5 6 7 8   **930.1**
1. Archeology 2. Buried treasure 3. Ancient civilization 4. Treasure troves 5. Civilization, Ancient
ISBN 1410949508; 9781410949509; 9781410949578
LC 2012012757

"Part of the Treasure Hunters series, 'Ancient Treasures' offers a crosscurricular mix of science & technology and history. . . .Treasures covered in the book include the Roman Hoxne Hoard, the Anglo-Saxon Staffordshire Hoard, the extraordinary discoveries of the Rosetta Stone and Dead Sea Scrolls, and the South American treasures of Lake Guatavita. The book also looks at the motives for these searches, and the importance of responsible archaeology." (Publisher's note)

Includes bibliographical references (p. 46-47) and index.

Matthews, Rupert
Ancient mysteries. QEB Pub. 2011 32p il (Unexplained) lib bdg $28.50

Grades: 4 5 6 7   **930.1**
1. Legends 2. Ancient civilization 3. Curiosities and wonders
ISBN 978-1-59566-854-7; 1-59566-854-3
LC 2010014189

This discusses mysteries in the ancient world.

"This well-written and thoughtfully designed [book] features [an] engrossing [topic]. . . . Though the pages are profusely illustrated with large, well-reproduced photographs and drawings, the layout is not cluttered. This [book] just might inspire kids to seek out more in-depth materials." SLJ

Panchyk, Richard
Archaeology for kids; uncovering the mysteries of our past: 25 activities. Chicago Review Press 2001 146p il map pa $14.95

Grades: 5 6 7 8   **930.1**
1. Archeology 2. Antiquities 3. Ancient civilization
ISBN 1-55652-395-5
LC 2001-42134

Twenty five activities support an overview of the science of archaeology as well as some of the secrets it has revealed from ancient civilizations throughout the world

"Panchyk explains things clearly and vividly. . . . Illustrations are plentiful, and suggested activities are practical and illuminate the subject matter well." Booklist

Includes bibliographical references

931   China to 420

Ball, Jacqueline A.
★ **Ancient** China; archaeology unlocks the secrets of China's past. by Jacqueline Ball and Richard Levey, Robert Murowchick, consultant. National Geographic 2006 64p il (National Geographic investigates) hardcover o.p. lib bdg $27.90; $17.95

Grades: 5 6 7 8   **931**
1. China -- Antiquities 2. China -- Civilization
ISBN 9780792278566 lib bdg; 9780792277835

"This volume spotlights archaeological finds from Ancient China. . . . While the discussions of archaeology will hold readers' interest, the accompanying illustrations steal the show." Booklist

Liu-Perkins, Christine

At home in her tomb; Lady Dai and the ancient Chinese treasures of Mawangdui. Christine Liu-Perkins; illustrated by Sarah Brannen. Charlesbridge 2013 80 p. (reinforced for library use) $19.95

Grades: 5 6 7 8 **931**

1. Tombs 2. Excavations (Archeology) -- China 3. China -- History -- Han dynasty, 202 B.C.-220 A.D. 4. Treasure troves -- China -- Changsha (Hunan Sheng) 5. Material culture -- China -- Changsha (Hunan Sheng) 6. Excavations (Archaeology) -- China -- Changsha (Hunan Sheng) 7. Human remains (Archaeology) -- China -- Changsha (Hunan Sheng)

ISBN 1580893708; 9781580893701; 9781607346159

LC 2012024630

This book, by Christine Liu-Perkins, "unearths the mysteries of the Mawangdui tombs, one of China's top archaeological finds of the last century. Miniature servants, mysterious silk paintings, scrolls of long-lost secrets, and the best preserved mummy in the world (the body of Lady Dai) are just some of the artifacts that shed light upon life in China during the Han dynasty." (Publisher's note)

"In 1971, the tomb of "Lady Dai" was discovered, virtually intact and of enormous archaeological significance. Here, buried in 158 BCE, was her still-soft body and more than a thousand artifacts. Liu-Perkins describes the discovery in fascinating detail; brief imagined scenes supplement the evidence. Illustrative materials include maps and well-captioned photos as well as Brannen's watercolors of the fictionalized scenes. Timeline. Bib., glos., ind." Horn Book

Includes bibliographical references and index

O'Connor, Jane

★ The **emperor's** silent army; terracotta warriors of Ancient China. Viking 2002 48p il $17.99

Grades: 4 5 6 7 **931**

1. Emperors 2. China -- Antiquities

ISBN 0-670-03512-2

LC 2001-46900

Describes the archaeological discovery of thousands of life-sized terracotta warrior statues in northern China in 1974, and discusses the emperor who had them created and placed near his tomb

"This intriguing book is enhanced by beautiful illustrations—pictures of stone engravings, colorful paintings, drawings, and maps—while numerous photographs show the clay soldiers from different perspectives. . . . The author's writing style is entertaining, yet informative." Book Rep

Includes bibliographical references

Shuter, Jane

Ancient China; [by] Jane Shuter. Heinemann Library 2006 48p il map (Excavating the past) lib bdg $31.43

Grades: 4 5 6 **931**

1. China -- Antiquities 2. China -- Civilization 3. Excavations (Archeology) -- China

ISBN 1-4034-5995-9

LC 2005009178

"Ancient China covers the region's history from the first single kingdom dynasty, Xia (2205 B.C.E. to 1700 B.C.E), to the conquering of China by Mongols in C.E.1279. Shuter includes a history of archaeology conducted by Westerners and by the Chinese government. Artifacts and a few well-preserved burial sites reveal lifestyles of the powerful and

wealthy. Short chapters describe living conditions of the poor and of skilled workers as well." SLJ

Includes bibliographical references

932 Egypt to 640

Ancient Egypt; edited by Sherman Hollar. Britannica Educational Pub. in association with Rosen Educational Services 2011 87p il map (Ancient civilizations) lib bdg $31.70

Grades: 5 6 7 8 **932**

1. Egypt -- History 2. Egypt -- Civilization

ISBN 978-1-61530-523-0; 1-61530-523-8

LC 2011004714

This book provides "enough information about the development, way of life, accomplishments, and decline of [Ancient Egypt] without overwhelming readers. Maps; full-color illustrations and photographs, many full page; and sidebars provide additional focus. . . . The use of the Nile and its influence on the development of this civilization is emphasized. . . . The building of the great pyramids and the art of mummification are also mentioned. A detailed discussion of the everyday lives of the rich and the poor provide valuable insight." SLJ

Includes glossary and bibliographical references

Bolton, Anne

Pyramids and mummies. Simon & Schuster 2008 un il map $21.99

Grades: 3 4 5 6 **932**

1. Mummies 2. Pyramids 3. Egypt

ISBN 978-1-4169-5873-4; 1-4169-5873-8

LC 2008-299284

"The illustrations are an alluring mix of gold, images from ancient walls, cutaway views, and dried-out bodies. Almost hidden beneath all the visual glamour is a . . . text that begins with the death(s) of Osiris, ends with a game of 'Asps and Ladders,' and in between touches on the preparation of mummies, the history and purposes of Egyptian pyramids, animal mummies, sphinxes, King Tut, and other related topics. All in all, an ephemeral but artfully designed showstopper." SLJ

Hartland, Jessie

★ **How** the sphinx got to the museum. Blue Apple Books 2010 un il $17.99

Grades: 1 2 3 4 **932**

1. Queens 2. Museums 3. Sphinxes (Mythology) 4. Egypt -- Antiquities 5. Metropolitan Museum of Art (New York, N.Y.)

ISBN 978-1-609050-32-0; 1-609050-32-0

LC 2010-31603

How the seven-ton sphinx of the Pharaoh Hatshepsut got to the Metropolitan Museum of Art in New York City is described "with exhaustive, dizzying, yet crystal clear detail. . . . Before it's over we'll meet art movers, curators, conservators, riggers, registrars, retouchers, and more . . . Eye-openers abound." Booklist

Hawass, Zahi A.

★ **Tutankhamun**; the mystery of the boy king. by Zahi Hawass. National Geographic 2005 64p il $17.95; lib bdg $27.90

Grades: 3 4 5 6   932

1. Kings 2. Egypt -- History 3. Egypt -- Civilization

ISBN 0-7922-8354-6; 0-7922-8355-4 lib bdg

LC 2004-15002

"Hawass, director of excavations at the Giza pyramids and head of Egypt's archaeological council, . . . offers a solid summary . . . of the complex and controversial 18th dynasty in which Tut lived. . . . Black-and-white shots from the past join rich color photographs that almost glow. Especially marvelous is a stunning recreation, employing current reconstructive techniques, of what Tut might have looked like. . . . A first-rate investigation enriched by beautiful artwork." SLJ

Includes bibliographical references

Henzel, Cynthia Kennedy

Pyramids of Egypt. ABDO Pub. Co. 2011 32p il (Troubled treasures: world heritage sites) $25.65

Grades: 3 4 5   932

1. Pyramids 2. Egypt -- Antiquities

ISBN 978-1-61613-566-9; 1-61613-566-2

LC 2010021308

This "book describes in general terms [the Egyptian pyramids'] construction, . . . distinctive features, and history, as well as threats to its continued existence and both current and past restoration intitiatives. Revealing color photos taken from different heights and angles are supplemented by maps and by graphic reconstructions. . . . Henzel's distinctive approach gives this [book] unusual value for both assignment and general reading." SLJ

Includes glossary

Jestice, Phyllis G.

Ancient Egyptian warfare. Gareth Stevens 2010 32p il map (Ancient warfare) lib bdg $26

Grades: 3 4 5 6   932

1. Egypt -- History 2. Military art and science -- History

ISBN 978-1-4339-1971-8 lib bdg; 1-4339-1971-0 lib bdg

LC 2009006189

Ancient Egyptian warfare "is presented in a well-organized, contextualized manner. The [author discusses] the overarching history of the times and then [gets] to specifics about weapons and military tactics. . . . A strong purchase for reports and pleasure reading." SLJ

Includes glossary and bibliographical references

Kennett, David

★ **Pharaoh**; life and afterlife of a God. Walker & Company 2008 48p il map $18.95; lib bdg $19.85

Grades: 3 4 5 6   932

1. Egypt -- Religion 2. Egypt -- Civilization

ISBN 978-0-8027-9567-0; 0-8027-9567-6; 978-0-8027-9568-7 lib bdg; 0-8027-9568-4 lib bdg

LC 2007-24236

"This extraordinarily handsome [book] delves deeply into the various roles of the pharoah, and, in the process, gives readers a much fuller understanding of Egyptian life. . . . One of the best things about this is the way the narrative moves simply and logically from topics such as flooding to

farming and trading. But as fine as the text is, it more than meets its match in the masterful artwork. . . . There is much to see here, and children will want to look at the book again and again." Booklist

Kerrigan, Michael

Egyptians. Marshall Cavendish Benchmark 2010 64p il (Ancients in their own words) $32.79

Grades: 5 6 7 8   932

1. Egypt -- Civilization

ISBN 978-1-60870-064-6; 1-60870-064-X

Features "Numerous photographs provide visual interest, with text describing the images to give details and background. Translations of the writings offer primary sources to accompany the secondary material presented. . . . The text is interesting enough to read cover to cover while the table of contents' descriptive chapter titles and the comprehensive index enable the . . . [book] to be used for specific research." Libr Media Connect

Includes bibliographical references

Logan, Claudia

★ The **5,000**-year-old puzzle; solving a mystery of Ancient Egypt. illustrated by Melissa Sweet. Farrar, Straus & Giroux 2001 41p il $17

Grades: 2 3 4   932

1. Curators 2. Archaeologists 3. Egypt -- Civilization 4. Excavations (Archeology) -- Egypt

ISBN 0-374-32335-6

LC 00-60243

An account of Dr. George Reisner's 1925 discovery and excavation of a secret tomb in Giza, Egypt, based on archival documents and records, but told through the fictionalized experiences of a young boy named Will who accompanies his father on the dig.

"There's considerable value to the sidebar information . . . and the journal-style exposition of the excavation's painstaking pace. Snapshots and photographed artifacts from the expedition mingle with Sweet's golden acrylic and watercolor scenes, and readers who patiently sift through the fictional bits will be rewarded with an intriguing glimpse of an important excavation." Bull Cent Child Books

Malam, John

The **Egyptians**. PowerKids Press 2011 30p il map (Dig it: history from objects) lib bdg $25.25

Grades: 3 4 5   932

1. Egypt -- Antiquities 2. Egypt -- Civilization

ISBN 978-1-4488-3283-5; 1-4488-3283-7

LC 2010023834

Uses artifacts and other archaeological evidence to describe daily life in ancient Egypt, including their homes and towns, clothes, rulers, religion, and how they fought in war.

"The information is well-written and easily understood, well suited to the curriculum and national standards. Website links are intriguing and students will enjoy adding this piece to their research." Libr Media Connect

Includes glossary and bibliographical references

Rubalcaba, Jill

★ **Ancient** Egypt; archaeology unlocks the secrets of Egypt's past. by Jill Rubalcaba. National Geographic 2007 64p il map (National Geographic investigates) $17.95; lib bdg $27.90

Grades: 5 6 7 8 **932**
1. Egypt -- Antiquities 2. Egypt -- Civilization 3. Excavations (Archeology) -- Egypt
ISBN 0-7922-7784-8; 978-0-7922-7784-2; 0-7922-7857-7 lib bdg; 978-0-7922-7857-3 lib bdg
LC 2006032111
This describes how archeologists have learned about Ancient Egypt.
This offers "the beautiful photography and illustrations characteristic of the National Geographic Society, [a] well-written [text] and sidebars, and information on recent archaeological finds." SLJ
Includes bibliographical references

Sabuda, Robert
Tutankhamen's gift; written and illustrated by Robert Sabuda. Atheneum Pubs. 1994 un il $17; pa $6.99
Grades: K 1 2 3 **932**
1. Kings 2. Egypt -- Antiquities
ISBN 0-689-31818-9; 0-689-81730-4 pa
LC 93-5401
"His tutor foresees that little Tutankhamen's 'gift for the gods' will someday be revealed. That day comes sooner than expected, when the young boy becomes pharaoh after his brother's death and rebuilds the beautiful temples created by his father and destroyed by his brother. Bold pictures outlined in black against a background of painted, handmade Egyptian papyrus illustrate the book, and an afterword provides historical details." Horn Book Guide

Smith, Miranda
Ancient Egypt. Kingfisher 2010 48p (Navigators) $12.99
Grades: 4 5 6 7 **932**
1. Egypt -- Civilization
ISBN 978-0-7534-6429-8; 0-7534-6429-2
"Ancient Egypt opens with prominent pharaohs and continues with life at home, within a palace, and amidst the construction of a pyramid. Although it includes such typical subjects as religion, mummification, and tomb raiders, it also comprises female rulers, taxes, and extensive trading expeditions... a good first stop in the research process." Booklist

Stanley, Diane
★ **Cleopatra**; [by] Diane Stanley, Peter Vennema; illustrated by Diane Stanley. Morrow Junior Bks. 1994 un il map hardcover o.p. pa $7.99
Grades: 4 5 6 7 **932**
1. Queens 2. Egypt -- History
ISBN 0-688-10413-4; 0-688-10414-2 lib bdg; 0-688-15480-8 pa
LC 93-27032
This is a biography of the ancient Egyptian queen
"Lucid writing combines with carefully selected anecdotes, often attributed to the Greek historian Plutarch to create an engaging narrative. . . . Stanley's stunning, full-color gouache artwork is arresting in its large, well-composed images executed in flat Greek style." SLJ
Includes bibliographical references

Twist, Clint
Cleopatra; Queen of Egypt. by Clint Twist and Ian Andrew. Candlewick Press 2012 30 p. (reinforced) $19.99

Grades: 4 5 6 **932**
1. Queens 2. Queens -- Egypt 3. Egypt -- Civilization
ISBN 0763660957; 9780763660956
LC 2012942304
This book by Clint Twist presents a biography of Egyptian ruler Cleopatra. It covers topics "such as her complicated relationships with both Julius Caesar and, later, Mark Antony. Her role in the Ptolemy family is described. . . . Illustrated flaps to lift and explore and sidebars offer up . . . details about hairstyles, jewelry, battles, and religion." (School Library Journal)

Van Vleet, Carmella
Great Ancient Egypt projects you can build yourself. Nomad 2006 122p il (Build it yourself series) pa $14.95
Grades: 4 5 6 **932**
1. Handicraft 2. Egypt -- Civilization
ISBN 0-9771294-5-4
"The fascinating text in this collection of 30 projects is supplemented by sepia-colored illustrations or photos on each page. . . . The projects are tied to many aspects of this civilization, including the Nile River, agriculture, craftsmanship, pyramids, mummies, family, farming, bartering, the Egyptian calendar, Royal Library of Alexandria, temples, hieroglyphs, and more." SLJ
Includes bibliographical references

Weitzman, David L.
★ **Pharaoh's** boat; written and illustrated by David Weitzman. Houghton Mifflin Harcourt 2009 un il map $17
Grades: 4 5 6 7 **932**
1. Ships 2. Kings 3. Egypt -- Civilization
ISBN 978-0-547-05341-7; 0-547-05341-X
LC 2008036081
"Weitzman recounts the construction of a boat made for the Pharaoh Cheops and discusses its rediscovery and restoration in the 20th century. He weaves the history, texts, mythology, and customs of ancient Egypt into an effective narrative. . . . The volume's stylized illustrations are inspired by the two-dimensional depictions from ancient Egyptian art. The paintings' earth tones, accentuated by bright greens and blues, are both appropriate for the subject matter and pleasing to the eye." SLJ

Whiting, Jim
Threat to ancient Egyptian treasures; by Jim Whiting. Mitchell Lane Publishers 2007 32p il (On the verge of extinction: crisis in the environment) lib bdg $25.70
Grades: 3 4 5 **932**
1. Egypt -- Antiquities
ISBN 978-1-58415-588-1
LC 2007000817
This describes dangers to ancient Egyptian archeological sites and artifacts, including sand storms, air pollution, flooding, and human activity.
"Short chapters, large font, and pronunciation guides to key words engage children doing research, but the depth of information is not compromised. . . . Colorful, up-close photographs are accompanied by satisfying explanatory captions." SLJ
Includes glossary and bibliographical references

935 Mesopotamia to 637 and Iranian Plateau to 637

Gruber, Beth

★ **Ancient** Iraq; archaeology unlocks the secrets of Iraq's past. by Beth Gruber; Tony Wilkinson, consultant. National Geographic 2007 64p il map (National Geographic investigates) $17.95; lib bdg $27.90

Grades: 5 6 7 8 **935**

1. Iraq -- Antiquities 2. Iraq -- Civilization 3. Excavations (Archeology) -- Iraq
ISBN 978-0-7922-5382-2; 978-0-7922-5383-9 lib bdg
LC 2006032109

This explores the "world of ancient Iraq, in the region once known as Mesopotamia, the cradle of civilization. Join scientists as they study the Citadel in northern Iraq; explore the ancient city of Nineveh; and see how ancient treasures help scientists reassemble the mosaic-like puzzle of Iraq's past." Publisher's note

Includes bibliographical references

Jestice, Phyllis G.

Ancient Persian warfare. Gareth Stevens 2010 32p il map (Ancient warfare) lib bdg $26

Grades: 3 4 5 6 **935**

1. Iran -- History 2. Military art and science -- History
ISBN 978-1-4339-1973-2 lib bdg; 1-4339-1973-7 lib bdg
LC 2009006199

Ancient Persian warfare "is presented in a well-organized, contextualized manner. The [author discusses] the overarching history of the times and then [gets] into specifics about weapons and military tactics. . . . A strong purchase for reports and pleasure reading." SLJ

Includes glossary and bibliographical references

Kerrigan, Michael

Mesopotamians. Marshall Cavendish Benchmark 2010 64p il (Ancients in their own words) lib bdg $32.79

Grades: 5 6 7 8 **935**

1. Iraq -- Civilization
ISBN 978-1-60870-066-0; 1-60870-066-6

"Numerous photographs provide visual interest, with text describing the images to give details and background. Translations of the writings offer primary sources to accompany the secondary material presented. . . . The text is interesting enough to read cover to cover while the table of contents' descriptive chapter titles and the comprehensive index enable the . . . [book] to be used for specific research." Libr Media Connect

Includes bibliographical references

936 Europe north and west of Italian Peninsula to ca. 499

Aronson, Marc

★ **If** stones could speak; unlocking the secrets of Stonehenge. by Marc Aronson; with Mike Parker Pearson and the Riverside Project. National Geographic 2010 64p il map $17.95; lib bdg $26.90

Grades: 4 5 6 7 **936**

1. Archeology 2. Archaeologists 3. College teachers 4. Stonehenge (England) 5. Excavations (Archeology) -- England
ISBN 978-1-4263-0599-3; 1-4263-0599-0; 978-1-4263-0600-6 lib bdg; 1-4263-0600-8 lib bdg

"Aronson investigates the work of archaeologist Mike Parker Pearson and his controversial theory that Stonehenge is but one end of a memorial ritual pathway that would have had an equivalent wood structure at the other end. . . . Time lines, resource lists, and photos of researchers at work add even more value to this informative, thought-provoking study. A uniquely perceptive look at how real science works." Booklist

Includes bibliographical references

Green, Jen

★ **Ancient** Celts; archaeology unlocks the secrets of the Celts' past. by Jen Green; Bettina Arnold, consultant. National Geographic 2008 64p il map (National Geographic investigates) $17.95; lib bdg $27.90

Grades: 4 5 6 7 **936**

1. Celts 2. Celtic civilization 3. Ireland -- Antiquities 4. Great Britain -- Antiquities 5. Excavations (Archeology) -- Europe
ISBN 978-1-4263-0225-1; 1-4263-0225-8; 978-1-4263-0226-8 lib bdg; 1-4263-0226-6 lib bdg
LC 2007047836

This describes ancient Celtic civilization and how archeologists have found out about it.

"With excellent-quality photographs and a well-written text, this is a thorough presentation of the most up-to-date knowledge about this ancient European culture." SLJ

Includes glossary and bibliographical references

Millard, Anne

A **street** through time; written by Anne Millard; illustrated by Steve Noon. Revised ed. DK Pub. 2012 32p col il $17.99

Grades: 4 5 6 7 **936**

1. Cities and towns
ISBN 0-7894-3426-1
LC 98-3226

"The time-line construct is a useful demonstration for children, and the busy vistas would make a fine spring-board for encouraging students to create scenes of local history." Horn Book Guide

936.2 England to 410 and Wales to 410

Henzel, Cynthia Kennedy

Stonehenge. ABDO Pub. Co. 2011 32p il (Troubled treasures: world heritage sites) lib bdg $25.65

Grades: 3 4 5 **936.2**

1. Megalithic monuments 2. Stonehenge (England) 3. Great Britain -- Antiquities
ISBN 978-1-61613-567-6; 1-61613-567-0
LC 2010021307

This "book describes in general terms [Stonehenge's] construction, . . . distinctive features, and history, as well as threats to its continued existence and both current and past restoration intitiatives. Revealing color photos taken from different heights and angles are supplemented by maps and by graphic reconstructions. . . . Henzel's distinctive approach gives this [book] unusual value for both assignment and general reading." SLJ

Includes glossary

937 Italian Peninsula to 476 and adjacent territories to 476

Ancient Rome; edited by Michael Anderson. Britannica Educational Pub. in association with Rosen Educational Services 2011 88p il map (Ancient civilizations) lib bdg $31.70

Grades: 5 6 7 8   937

1. Rome -- History 2. Rome -- Civilization

ISBN 978-1-61530-522-3; 1-61530-522-X

LC 2011004749

This book provides "enough information about the development, way of life, accomplishments, and decline of [Ancient Rome] without overwhelming readers. Maps; full-color illustrations and photographs, many full page; and sidebars provide additional focus. . . . [The book] discusses the military expertise of Caesar and Pompey and the winning of the Punic Wars that led to world domination. The Romans' genius in engineering is highlighted." SLJ

Includes glossary and bibliographical references

Beller, Susan Provost

Roman legions on the march; soldiering in the ancient Roman Army. by Susan Provost Beller. Twenty-First Century Books 2008 112p il map (Soldiers on the battlefront) lib bdg $33.26

Grades: 5 6 7 8   937

1. Soldiers -- Rome 2. Rome -- Civilization

ISBN 978-0-8225-6781-3

LC 2006037829

"The format is inviting with a variety of fonts at the beginning of each chapter, quotations, and a multitude of illustrations. . . . The text is clear and to the point, and chapters are divided into short topics." SLJ

Includes bibliographical references

Bingham, Jane

How people lived in ancient Rome. PowerKids Press 2009 30p il map (How people lived) lib bdg $25.25; pa $10.60

Grades: 4 5 6 7   937

1. Rome -- Social life and customs

ISBN 978-1-4042-4432-0 lib bdg; 1-4042-4432-8 lib bdg; 978-1-4358-2622-9 pa; 1-4358-2622-1 pa

LC 2007-40221

Describes everyday life among the ancient Romans, covering family life, marriage, leisure, education, clothing, food and drink, warfare, religion, and funerals

"Clear, readable narrative is supplemented by large color and b&w reproductions of Roman art and artifacts. . . . It will hold the attention of both readers and reasearchers, and is a good choice for collections that serve elementary and younger middle level students." Libr Media Connect

Includes bibliographical references

Deckker, Zilah

★ **Ancient** Rome; archaeology unlocks the secrets of Rome's past. by Zilah Deckker; Robert Lindley Vann, Con-

sultant. National Geographic 2007 64p il map (National Geographic investigates) $17.95; lib bdg $27.90

Grades: 4 5 6 7   937

1. Archeology 2. Rome -- Antiquities 3. Rome -- Civilization

ISBN 978-1-4263-0128-5; 978-1-4263-0129-2 lib bdg

LC 2007024795

This describes what archeologists have learned about Ancient Rome

Includes glossary and bibliographical references

Deem, James M.

★ **Bodies** from the ash. Houghton Mifflin 2005 50p il $16

Grades: 4 5 6 7   937

1. Pompeii (Extinct city)

ISBN 0-618-47308-4

LC 2004-26553

"On August 24, 79 C.E., the long-silent Mt. Vesuvius erupted, and volcanic ash rained down on the 20,000 residents of Pompeii. This photo-essay explains what happened when the volcano exploded—and how the results of this disaster were discovered hundreds of years later. . . . [This offers an] enormous amount of information. . . . But the jewels here are the numerous . . . photographs, especially those featuring the plaster casts and skeletons of people in their death throes. . . . Excellent for browsers as well as researchers." Booklist

James, Simon

Ancient Rome; written by Simon James. rev ed.; DK Pub. 2008 72p il map (DK eyewitness books) $15.99

Grades: 4 5 6 7   937

1. Rome -- Antiquities 2. Rome -- Civilization

ISBN 978-0-7566-3766-8; 0-7566-3766-X

LC 2008-276034

First published 1990 by Knopf

A photo essay documenting ancient Rome and the people who lived there as revealed through the many artifacts they left behind, including shields, swords, tools, toys, cosmetics, and jewelry

Includes glossary

Kerrigan, Michael

Romans. Marshall Cavendish Benchmark 2010 64p il (Ancients in their own words) lib bdg $32.79

Grades: 5 6 7 8   937

1. Rome -- Civilization

ISBN 978-1-60870-067-7; 1-60870-067-4

"Numerous photographs provide visual interest, with text describing the images to give details and background. Translations of the writings offer primary sources to accompany the secondary material presented. . . . The text is interesting enough to read cover to cover while the table of contents' descriptive chapter titles and the comprehensive index enable the . . . [book] to be used for specific research." Libr Media Connect

Includes bibliographical references

Lassieur, Allison

★ The **ancient** Romans; written by Allison Lassieur. Franklin Watts 2004 112p il map (People of the ancient world) lib bdg $30.50; pa $9.95

Grades: 5 6 7 8 **937**

1. Rome -- Civilization
ISBN 0-531-12338-3 lib bdg; 0-531-16742-9 pa
LC 2004-1955

"This attractive, thorough, and comprehensible book . . . offers a stellar introduction to life in ancient Rome." Booklist

Includes bibliographical references

Malam, John

The **Romans**. PowerKids Press 2011 30p il map (Dig it: history from objects) lib bdg $25.25

Grades: 3 4 5 **937**

1. Rome -- Antiquities 2. Rome -- Civilization
ISBN 978-1-4488-3285-9; 1-4488-3285-3
LC 2010023832

This book about the Romans includes information about "homes and towns, daily life, clothing, religion, and entertainment. . . . The layout is crisp and the object illustrations and photographs, plus the 'What does it tell us' section provide visual understanding. These qualities will assist the teacher who needs to differentiate instruction. The information is well-written and easily understood, well suited to the curriculum and national standards. Website links are intriguing and students will enjoy adding this piece to their research." Libr Media Connect

Includes glossary and bibliographical references

Mann, Elizabeth

★ The **Roman** Colosseum; with illustrations by Michael Racz. Mikaya Press 1998 45p il (Wonders of the world) $19.95

Grades: 4 5 6 **937**

1. Rome -- Antiquities 2. Colosseum (Rome, Italy)
ISBN 0-9650493-3-7
LC 98-20060

Describes the building of the Colosseum in ancient Rome, and tells how it was used

This offers "a clear, well-written text and full-color drawings and paintings." SLJ

Includes glossary

Murrell, Deborah Jane

Gladiator; written by Deborah Murrell. QEB Pub. 2010 32p il map (QEB warriors) lib bdg $28.50

Grades: 4 5 6 7 **937**

1. Gladiators
ISBN 978-1-59566-736-6 lib bdg; 1-59566-736-9 lib bdg
LC 2009-3540

"Bold, comprehensible type and full-color and black-and-white illustrations; reproductions; and photographs will make this offering a hit with its target audience, including reluctant readers." SLJ

Includes glossary

Park, Louise

The **Roman** gladiators; by Louise Park and Timothy Love. Marshall Cavendish Benchmark 2009 32p il (Ancient and medieval people) $19.95

Grades: 4 5 6 **937**

1. Gladiators 2. Rome -- History 3. Rome -- Social life and customs
ISBN 978-0-7614-4443-5; 0-7614-4443-2

This title has "a simple and elegant design with the proper balance of quality writing and quantity of information. . . . Handy time lines, well-chosen photos of ruins and artifacts, quality illustrations, inset 'Quick Facts,' and 'What You Should Know About' features will grab reluctant readers and captivate even those with short attention spans." SLJ

Includes glossary

Rice, Rob S.

Ancient Roman warfare. Gareth Stevens 2010 32p il map (Ancient warfare) lib bdg $26

Grades: 3 4 5 6 **937**

1. Rome -- History 2. Military art and science -- History
ISBN 978-1-4339-1974-9 lib bdg; 1-4339-1974-5 lib bdg
LC 2009006201

Ancient Roman warfare "is presented in a well-organized, contextualized manner. The [author discusses] the overarching history of the times and then [gets] into specifics about weapons and military tactics. . . . A strong purchase for reports and pleasure reading." SLJ

Includes glossary and bibliographical references

Riggs, Kate

Gladiators. Creative Education 2011 24p il (Great warriors) $24.25; pa $8.99

Grades: K 1 2 **937**

1. Gladiators
ISBN 978-1-60818-000-4; 1-60818-000-X; 978-0-89812-571-9 pa; 0-89812-571-5 pa
LC 2010019599

An introduction to the Roman warriors known as gladiators, including their history, lifestyle, weapons, and how they remain a part of today's culture through sports such as wrestling.

This title makes gladiators "accessible to students just beginning to read on their own. The text and design of the [book is] spare, and vocabulary words are introduced unobtrusively. . . . The concepts are simple, but introduced without oversimplification that might lead to misunderstandings. [This is an] excellent [introduction]—and fun to read aloud." SLJ

Includes glossary and bibliographical references

Sonneborn, Liz

Pompeii; by Liz Sonneborn. Twenty-First Century Books 2008 80p il map (Unearthing ancient worlds) lib bdg $30.60

Grades: 5 6 7 8 **937**

1. Pompeii (Extinct city) 2. Rome (Italy) -- Antiquities 3. Excavations (Archeology) -- Italy
ISBN 978-0-8225-7505-4 lib bdg; 0-8225-7505-1 lib bdg
LC 2007022058

This describes the excavation of the Roman city buried in lava and ash when the volcano Mount Vesuvius erupted in A.D. 79.

This "clearly written [title is] illustrated with large photographs and period artwork, and the pages are broken up with text boxes featuring quotes and interesting anecdotes." SLJ

Includes glossary and bibliographical references

938 Greece to 323

Ancient Greece; edited by Michael Anderson. Britannica Educational Pub. in association with Rosen Educational Services 2012 88p il (Ancient civilizations) lib bdg $31.70

Grades: 5 6 7 8 **938**

1. Greece -- Civilization

ISBN 978-1-61530-513-1; 1-61530-513-0

LC 2011000086

This book provides "enough information about the development, way of life, accomplishments, and decline of [Ancient Greece] without overwhelming readers. Maps; full-color illustrations and photographs, many full page; and sidebars provide additional focus. . . . The system of city-states is explained. Literature, art, and architecture and their lasting influence are described in detail." SLJ

Includes glossary and bibliographical references

Kerrigan, Michael

Greeks. Marshall Cavendish Benchmark 2010 64p il (Ancients in their own words) lib bdg $32.79

Grades: 5 6 7 8 **938**

1. Greece -- Civilization

ISBN 978-1-60870-065-3; 1-60870-065-8

"Numerous photographs provide visual interest, with text describing the images to give details and background. Translations of the writings offer primary sources to accompany the secondary material presented. . . . The text is interesting enough to read cover to cover while the table of contents' descriptive chapter titles and the comprehensive index enable the . . . [book] to be used for specific research." Libr Media Connect

Includes bibliographical references

Malam, John

The **Greeks**. PowerKids Press 2011 30p il map (Dig it: history from objects) lib bdg $25.25

Grades: 3 4 5 **938**

1. Greece -- Antiquities 2. Greece -- Civilization

ISBN 978-1-4488-3284-2; 1-4488-3284-5

LC 2010023833

This book about the ancient Greeks includes information about "homes and towns, daily life, clothing, religion, and entertainment. . . . The layout is crisp and the object illustrations and photographs, plus the 'What does it tell us' section provide visual understanding. These qualities will assist the teacher who needs to differentiate instruction. The information is well-written and easily understood, well suited to the curriculum and national standards. Website links are intriguing and students will enjoy adding this piece to their research." Libr Media Connect

Includes glossary and bibliographical references

McGee, Marni

★ **Ancient** Greece; archaeology unlocks the secrets of Greece's past. by Marni McGee; Michael Shanks, consultant. National Geographic 2007 64p il map (National Geographic investigates) $17.95; lib bdg $27.90

Grades: 5 6 7 8 **938**

1. Greece -- Antiquities 2. Greece -- Civilization 3. Excavations (Archeology) -- Greece

ISBN 978-0-7922-7826-9; 0-7922-7826-7; 978-0-7922-7872-6 lib bdg; 0-7922-7872-0 lib bdg

LC 2006032108

This describes how archeologists have found out about Ancient Greek civilization

This offers "the beautiful photography and illustrations characteristic of the National Geographic Society, [a] well-written [text] and sidebars, and information on recent archaeological finds." SLJ

Includes bibliographical references

Park, Louise

The **Spartan** hoplites; by Louise Park and Timothy Love. Marshall Cavendish Benchmark 2009 32p il map (Ancient and medieval people) $19.95

Grades: 4 5 6 **938**

1. Soldiers 2. Sparta (Extinct city) 3. Athens (Greece) -- History

ISBN 978-0-7614-4449-7; 0-7614-4449-1

LC 2008-55779

This title has "a simple and elegant design with the proper balance of quality writing and quantity of information. . . . Handy time lines, well-chosen photos of ruins and artifacts, quality illustrations, inset 'Quick Facts', and 'What You Should Know About' features will grab reluctant readers and captivate even those with short attention spans." SLJ

Includes glossary

Reynolds, Susan

The **first** marathon: the legend of Pheidippides; by Susan Reynolds; illustrated by Daniel Minter. Albert Whitman & Company 2006 un il $16.95

Grades: 2 3 4 **938**

1. Marathon running 2. Marathon, Battle of, 490 B.C. 3. Runners (Athletes)

ISBN 978-0-8075-0867-1; 0-8075-0867-5

LC 2005024618

The author tells the "story of how the Greeks fought off the mighty Persian army on the plains of Marathon, and how the young long-distance runner Pheidippides ran 140 miles in 36 hours to Sparta to ask for help, then ran back without stopping, fought in the battle, ran to tell Athens of the victory, and died. Now marathons are named for his heroic run. The dramatic, full-color, double-page illustrations, with heavy black accents, show the strong, rhythmic movement of the brave young athlete, the battle scenes, and then runners across the world today." Booklist

Rice, Rob S.

Ancient Greek warfare. Gareth Stevens 2010 32p il map (Ancient warfare) lib bdg $26

Grades: 3 4 5 6 **938**

1. Greece -- History 2. Military art and science -- History

ISBN 978-1-4339-1972-5 lib bdg; 1-4339-1972-9 lib bdg

LC 2009006198

Ancient Greek warfare "is presented in a well-organized, contextualized manner. The [author discusses] the overarching history of the times and then [gets] into specifics about weapons and military tactics. . . . A strong purchase for reports and pleasure reading." SLJ

Includes glossary and bibliographical references

Steele, Phillip

   Ancient Greece; by Philip Steele. Kingfisher 2011 48 p. ill. (hardcover) $12.99

Grades: 4 5 6 7   **938**

   1. Greece -- History 2. Greece -- Civilization

   ISBN 0753465795; 9780753465790

   In this "look at ancient Greece," author Philip Steele "offers young readers insight into the origins of all things Greek. Two page spreads cover Minoan civilization, the rise of the Mycenaean, war with Troy, the establishment of city-states, and the spread of the Hellenistic empire in a somewhat chronological order. Digital illustrations merge with historical artifacts, maps, works of art, and photographs." (Children's Literature)

939   Other parts of ancient world

Cline, Eric H., 1960-

   ★ **Digging** for Troy; from Homer to Hisarlik. [by] Jill Rubalcaba and Eric H. Cline; with illustrations by Sarah S. Brannen. Charlesbridge 2011 74p il map $17.95; pa $9.95

Grades: 5 6 7 8   **939**

   1. Trojan War 2. Troy (Extinct city) 3. Greece -- Civilization 4. Archaeologists

   ISBN 978-1-58089-326-8; 1-58089-326-0; 978-1-58089-327-5 pa; 1-58089-327-9 pa

                   LC 2010-07586

   "Rubalcaba teams up with a noted archaeologist to make sense of the complicated, controversial, contradictory history and remains of the Turkish site called Hisarlik, better known as Troy. . . . The book begins with a brief but exciting retelling of the Trojan War . . . and goes on to profile Heinrich Schliemann. . . . After Schliemann, generations of archaeologists have excavated Hisarlik: along with the history of the excavations, readers are given an overview of technological developments in the field. . . . Source notes and an impressive bibliography attest to meticulous research and guide readers to journal articles, books, and online museum exhibits. Elegant illustrations mimicking Greek red-figure pottery are lovely and appropriate. Extraordinarily readable, gracefully laid out, and speckled with lines from The Iliad, this book will inspire young people interested in solving the mysteries of the past." SLJ

   Includes bibliographical references

Sherrow, Victoria

   ★ **Ancient** Africa; archaeology unlocks the secrets of Africa's past. by Victoria Sherrow; James Denbow, consultant. National Geographic Society 2007 64p il map (National Geographic investigates) $17.95

Grades: 4 5 6 7   **939**

   1. Africa -- Antiquities 2. Africa -- Civilization

   ISBN 978-0-7922-5384-6; 0-7922-5384-1

                   LC 2007277594

   This describes archeological discoveries about ancient peoples of Africa including the Dogon people of Mali, the ancient city of Jenne-jeno, and the Kushite temples at Jebel Barkal.

   Includes bibliographical references

940   History of Europe

Feed the children first; Irish memories of the Great Hunger. edited by Mary E. Lyons. Atheneum Bks. for Young Readers 2002 43p il pbk. $22.99

Grades: 5 6 7 8   **940**

   1. Famines 2. Ireland -- History

   ISBN 9781442482920

                   LC 00-49606

   The editor presents extracts from memoirs of the Irish famine period. Bibliography. "Intermediate, middle school." (Horn Book)

   Lyons "compiles quotations from Irish citizens on the devastating effects of the potato famine that ravaged Ireland between 1845 and 1852." Publ Wkly

Foster, Karen

   Atlas of Europe. Picture Window Books 2008 32p il map (Picture Window Books world atlases) lib bdg $27.93

Grades: 2 3 4   **940**

   1. Europe

   ISBN 978-1-4048-3882-6 lib bdg; 1-4048-3882-1 lib bdg

   This introduction to the geography of Europe offers maps and information about countries, landforms, bodies of water, climate, plants, animals, population, people and customs, places of interest, industries, transportation, and the Orient Express.

   Includes glossary

940.1   Europe--Early history to 1453

Adkins, Jan

   ★ **What** if you met a knight? [by] Jan Adkins, scribe and illuminator. Roaring Brook Press 2006 32p il $16.95

Grades: 3 4 5 6   **940.1**

   1. Medieval civilization 2. Knights and knighthood

   ISBN 1-59643-148-2; 978-1-59643-148-5

                   LC 2005-29163

   "Adkins sets out to debunk some common misconceptions about knights, and he does so with style and wit. . . . Light in approach but quite informative, the text ably explains the feudal system, the business of knighthood, and the origins of legends such as King Arthur and dragons, and also discusses castles, arms, and the Crusades. Throughout the book, colorful, detailed illustrations and captions provide information even as they open windows on the medieval world." Booklist

Aliki

   ★ **A medieval** feast; written and illustrated by Aliki. Crowell 1983 un il hardcover o.p. pa $6.95

Grades: 2 3 4 5   **940.1**

   1. Courts and courtiers 2. Medieval civilization 3. Dining -- History 4. Festivals -- History

   ISBN 0-690-04246-9 lib bdg; 0-06-446050-9 pa

                   LC 82-45923

   "In pictures of minute, charming detail and vibrant, translucent colors, Aliki takes us through the ritual of preparation and the enthusiastic consumption of a medieval feast served to a king and his retinue when they stop for a few days at Camdenton Manor. Not to be outdone by the art, the text has its own various facets. There is the fictional story set in type outside the art and there is within the paintings a collection of delightful historical, gastronomical, agricultural, and zoological facts printed by hand. And throughout the spendid whole are border decorations worthy of the great illuminated manuscripts." Child Book Rev Serv

Ashman, Linda
★ **Come** to the castle! a visit to a castle in thirteenth-century England. illuminated by S.D. Schindler. Roaring Brook Press 2009 un il $17.95
Grades: 3 4 5   **940.1**
1. Castles 2. Stories in rhyme 3. Medieval civilization
ISBN 978-1-59643-155-3; 1-59643-155-5
"Wit meets historical accuracy in a pitch-perfect mix of laugh-out-loud text and entertaining image." Kirkus

Boyer, Crispin
Everything castles; capture these facts, photos, and fun to be king of the castle! 2011 64p il (National Geographic kids) lib bdg $25.90; pa $12.95
Grades: 3 4 5 6   **940.1**
1. Castles 2. Medieval civilization
ISBN 978-1-4263-0804-8 lib bdg; 1-4263-0804-3 lib bdg; 978-1-4263-0803-1 pa; 1-4263-0803-5 pa
This describes the history of medieval castles and their inhabitants.
"Exploding with astounding full-color photographs and written in an appealing conversational tone, [this book is] for every kid. . . . The [text] will keep kids interested and turning pages to discover more and more facts. . . . [This] compelling, browseable, and completely engrossing [title] will delight readers." SLJ
Includes glossary and bibliographical references

Corbishley, Mike
The **Middle** Ages; 3rd ed.; Chelsea House 2007 96p il map (Cultural atlas for young people) $35
Grades: 5 6 7 8   **940.1**
1. Middle Ages 2. Medieval civilization
ISBN 978-0-8160-6825-8; 0-8160-6825-9
First published 1989
Maps, charts, illustrations, and text explore the history and culture of the Middle Ages.
"The maps are excellent, precise, clear, and easy to read and understand, and the illustrations, particularly those of works of art, are wonderful. . . . This attractive volume provides an intriguing cross-cultural look at the medieval world. An excellent addition." SLJ
Includes glossary and bibliographical references

Durman, Laura
Castle life; by Laura Durman. Arcturus Pub. 2013 32 p. col. ill. (library) $28.50
Grades: 4 5 6   **940.1**
1. Castles 2. Medieval civilization 3. Civilization, Medieval
ISBN 1848585608; 9781848585607
LC 2011051440
In this book, author "[Laura] Durman presents young readers with a . . . view of what life was really like for everyday people in the Middle Ages. Bound by the strict societal system known as feudalism, peasants, knights, and nobles shared space . . . in castles. Readers take a room by room

tour, learning how castles functioned both day-to-day, when under siege, and at times of feasting and banqueting." (Children's Literature)

Knights; by Laura Durman. Arcturus Pub. 2012 32 p. col. ill. (Knights and castles) (library) $28.50
Grades: 4 5 6   **940.1**
1. Picture books for children 2. Knights and knighthood 3. Civilization, Medieval
ISBN 1848585616; 9781848585614
LC 2011051452
This book by Laura Durman is part of the Knights and Castles series and looks at knights. The "books cover a wide range of topics such as weapons, castle construction, food, religion, and the structure and hierarchy of society." Full-color photographs and illustrations are included. (School Library Journal)
Includes bibliographical references (p. 31) and index.

Galloway, Priscilla
★ **Archers**, alchemists, and 98 other medieval jobs you might have loved or loathed; art by Martha Newbigging. Annick Press 2003 96p il lib bdg $24.95; pa $14.95
Grades: 3 4 5 6   **940.1**
1. Medieval civilization
ISBN 1-55037-811-2 lib bdg; 1-55037-810-4 pa
"Galloway introduces medieval Europe from 1000 to 1500 not by recounting dates, wars, and rulers but by discussing the occupations available in the society. . . . The jaunty, cartoonlike ink drawings, brightened with color washes, heighten the informal, upbeat tone of the informative text." Booklist
Includes bibliographical references

Helget, Nicole
Barbarians; Nicole Helget. Creative Education 2012 48 p. (alk. paper) $35.65
Grades: 5 6 7 8   **940.1**
1. Huns 2. Nomads 3. Vikings 4. Teutonic peoples 5. Classical civilization 6. Middle Ages 7. Migrations of nations 8. Europe -- History -- 392-814
ISBN 1608181820; 9781608181827
LC 2011035798
This book by Nicole Lea Helget "focuses on the transient, adaptable Gelts, Franks, Goths, Huns, and Vikings, collectively known as 'barbarians,' and their differing warring skills against the Greek and Roman Empires." (Booklist) "Viewed as threats by the Romans in particular, the barbarian people were often co-opted or conquered and then integrated into the Empire. Eventually, as the Roman Empire waned, the pressure of nomadic barbarians proved too much to withstand and Rome fell." (Children's Literature)
Includes bibliographical references and index

Kroll, Steven
★ **Barbarians!** illustrated by Robert Byrd. Dutton Children's Books 2009 48p il $18.99
Grades: 3 4 5   **940.1**
1. Huns 2. Goths 3. Mongols 4. Vikings 5. Middle Ages
ISBN 978-0-525-47958-1; 0-525-47958-9
LC 2008-39210
"Kroll introduces four notable groups referred to by their enemies as barbarians: the Goths, the Huns, the Vikings,

and the Mongols. . . . Showing clear differences among the four groups, the many detailed, energetic ink-and-watercolor illustrations show the barbarians at home and at war. . . . This handsome volume will fill a collection gap while providing warrior-loving browsers with an informative and brightly illustrated book to enjoy." Booklist

Langley, Andrew

Medieval life; written by Andrew Langley; photographed by Geoff Brightling. rev ed; DK Pub. 2011 72p il (DK eyewitness books) lib bdg $19.99

Grades: 4 5 6 7　　　　　　　　　　　　**940.1**

1. Medieval civilization

ISBN 9780756682828 lib bdg

First published 1996 by Knopf

An illustrated look at various aspects of life in medieval Europe, covering everyday life, religion, royalty, and more.

Park, Louise

The medieval knights; by Louise Park and Timothy Love. Marshall Cavendish Benchmark 2009 32p il map (Ancient and medieval people) $19.95

Grades: 4 5 6　　　　　　　　　　　　**940.1**

1. Medieval civilization 2. Knights and knighthood

ISBN 978-0-7614-4444-2; 0-7614-4444-0

LC 2008-55777

This title has "a simple and elegant design with the proper balance of quality writing and quantity of information. . . . Handy time lines, well-chosen photos of ruins and artifacts, quality illustrations, inset 'Quick Facts', and 'What You Should Know About' features will grab reluctant readers and captivate even those with short attention spans." SLJ

Includes glossary

Riggs, Kate

Knights. Creative Education 2011 24p il (Great warriors) $16.98; pa $8.99

Grades: K 1 2　　　　　　　　　　　　**940.1**

1. Medieval civilization 2. Knights and knighthood

ISBN 978-1-60818-001-1; 1-60818-001-8; 978-0-89812-572-6 pa; 0-89812-572-3 pa

LC 2010019604

An introduction to the European warriors known as knights, including their history, lifestyle, weapons, and how they remain a part of today's culture through books and films.

This title makes knights "accessible to students just beginning to read on their own. The text and design of the [book is] spare, and vocabulary words are introduced unobtrusively. . . . The concepts are simple, but introduced without oversimplification that might lead to misunderstandings. [This is an] excellent [introduction] and fun to read aloud." SLJ

Includes glossary and bibliographical references

Schlitz, Laura Amy

★ Good masters! Sweet ladies! voices from a medieval village. [by] Laura Amy Schlitz; illustrated by Robert Byrd. Candlewick Press 2007 85p il $19.99; pa $9.99

Grades: 5 6 7 8　　　　　　　　　　　　**940.1**

1. Monologues 2. Middle Ages -- Drama

ISBN 978-0-7636-1578-9; 0-7636-1578-1; 978-0-7636-4332-4 pa; 0-7636-4332-7 pa

Awarded the Newbery Medal, 2008

A collection of short one-person plays featuring characters, between ten and fifteen years old, who live in or near a thirteenth-century English manor

"Designed for performance and excellent for use in interdisciplinary history classrooms, the book offers students an incredibly approachable format for learning about the Middle Ages that makes the period both realistic and relevant. . . . Byrd's illustrations evoke the era and give dramatists ideas for appropriate costuming and props." SLJ

940.3　World War I, 1914-1918

Adams, Simon

World War I; written by Simon Adams; photographed by Andy Crawford. rev ed.; DK Pub. 2007 72p il (DK eyewitness books) $15.99

Grades: 4 5 6 7　　　　　　　　　　　　**940.3**

1. World War, 1914-1918

ISBN 978-0-7566-3007-2; 0-7566-3007-X

LC 2007279476

First published 2001

This look at World War I examines life in the trenches and the devastation of Europe by the Great War

Swain, Gwenyth

World War I; an interactive history adventure. by Gwenyth Swain; consultant: Timothy Solie. Capstone Press 2012 112 p. ill. (some col.) (library) $31.32; (paperback) $6.95

Grades: 3 4 5 6　　　　　　　　　　　　**940.3**

1. World War, 1914-1918

ISBN 1429679972; 9781429660204; 9781429679978

LC 2011033624

This book by Gwenyth Swain is part of the You Choose series. "At the bottom of many pages, you are asked to make a decision about what to do or where to go. Subsequent decisions take you to the adventure's end, at which point readers may choose to go back and begin again and find out where an alternate path might have led. . . . [In] Belgium . . . student nurses must decide whether to stay at their hospital or flee. Later, a British teen has to choose whether to enlist or wait." (Booklist)

Includes bibliographical references (p. 111) and index.

World War I; written by Simon Adams; photographed by Andy Crawford. DK Publishing 2014 72 p. color illustrations, color map (paperback) $9.99

Grades: 4 5 6 7　　　　　　　　　　　　**940.3**

1. World War, 1914-1918

ISBN 1465420584; 9781465420589; 9781465421005

LC 2013362556

This book, by Simon Adams, part of the Eyewitness series, "provides a quick, informative overview of WWI; how it started; who fought and why; the equipment used; what it was like in the trenches and at home; the horrific final cost. . . . It's the dramatic photos (many from London's Imperial War Museum) that will make readers pause and bring them close to the soldiers' experiences." (Booklist)

"The DK Eyewitness series exemplifies what the publisher does best: taking a broad topic and slicing it into two-page chapters that, while they contain no narrative thread, make for excellent museum-type browsing... Each book rounds out the guided tour with an FAQ of sorts, profiles, and plenty of places for interested readers to keep looking. Just the thing to whet appetites before trucking down to the local real-life museum." Booklist

Part of the "Eyewitness" series

World War One

940.4 Military history of World War I

Bausum, Ann

Stubby the War Dog; The True Story of World War I's Bravest Dog. by Ann Bausum. Natl Geographic Soc Childrens books 2014 80 p. $26.90

Grades: 4 5 6 7   **940.4**

1. Dogs -- War use 2. World War, 1914-1918 -- United States 3. Stubby (Dog) 4. Dogs -- War use -- United States 5. United States. Army. Infantry Regiment, 102nd -- Mascots

ISBN 1426314868; 1426314876; 9781426314865; 9781426314872

This book, by Ann Bausum, is the story of "Stubby, a terrier of unknown origin, [who] found his way to the training grounds in New Haven, CT, as recruits were preparing to ship off to . . . World War I. . . . He attached himself to J. Robert Conroy, one of the recruits, and they became an inseparable team for the rest of Stubby's life. . . . [T]he dog lived the life of any soldier: sleeping in trenches, dodging bullets in the heat of battle, and ferreting out enemy combatants." (School Library Journal)

"The popularity of tales about dogs in war stems from the inherent poignancy—sweet, loyal, sad-eyed canines entered into the mad chaos of man-made destruction. But enter they occasionally do, and none more famously than Stubby... The speedy story is surrounded by evocative period photos, including plenty of the goofy-faced Stubby, and leads up to his later careers as a vaudeville star and a football mascot, and his eventual taxidermied inclusion in the Smithsonian. A triumph on three fronts: educational, emotional, and inspirational. For older teens, suggest Bausman's adult title, Sergeant Stubby." Booklist

Beller, Susan Provost

The doughboys over there; soldiering in World War I. by Susan Provost Beller. Twenty-First Century Books 2008 112p il map (Soldiers on the battlefront) lib bdg $33.26

Grades: 5 6 7 8   **940.4**

1. World War, 1914-1918 2. Soldiers -- United States

ISBN 978-0-8225-6295-5 lib bdg; 0-8225-6295-2 lib bdg

LC 2006026249

The is an account of the U.S. soldiers who fought in Europe in the First World War.

"The format is inviting with a variety of fonts at the beginning of each chapter, quotations, and a multitude of illustrations. . . . The text is clear and to the point, and chapters are divided into short topics." SLJ

Includes bibliographical references

Burleigh, Robert

Fly, Cher Ami, fly! the pigeon who saved the lost battalion. by Robert Burleigh; illustrated by Robert MacKenzie. Abrams Books for Young Readers 2008 un il $16.95

Grades: K 1 2 3   **940.4**

1. Pigeons 2. World War, 1914-1918

ISBN 978-0-8109-7097-7; 0-8109-7097-X

"Burleigh tells the true story of the last flight of a U.S. Army Signal Corps carrier pigeon, which took place in France during World War I. Cher Ami was the last hope for the 'Lost Battalion' of the 77th Division in the Battle of Argonne. . . . Burleigh's short text clearly depicts the story's action, while MacKenzie's full-page-hued yet somber illustrations add to the account by showing the drama from a variety of perspectives." Booklist

Greenwood, Mark

The donkey of Gallipoli; a true story of courage in World War I. [by] Mark Greenwood; illustrated by Frane Lessac. Candlewick Press 2008 un il map $16.99

Grades: 2 3 4   **940.4**

1. Donkeys 2. Sailors 3. Soldiers 4. World War, 1914-1918 5. Gallipoli campaign, 1915

ISBN 978-0-7636-3913-6; 0-7636-3913-3

LC 2007032525

This is a "stirring picture book. . . . In folk-art style, the paintings, in shades that reflect the heat of a sandy landscape, show the heroic soldier and the gentle animal amid the slaughter of war." Booklist

Murphy, Jim

★ Truce; the day the soldiers stopped fighting. Scholastic Press 2009 116p il map $19.99

Grades: 5 6 7 8   **940.4**

1. World War, 1914-1918

ISBN 978-0-545-13049-3; 0-545-13049-2

LC 2008-40500

"By December 1918, the western front of World War I featured two parallel trenches stretching from the North Sea to the Alps. . . . On Christmas Day, an informal peace broke out in many locations along the front. . . . Murphy's excellent telling of this unusual war story begins with an account of the events that led to WWI and follows the shift in the soldiers' mind-sets. . . . Printed in tones of sepia, the illustrations in this handsome volume include many period photos as well as paintings and maps. . . . Well organized and clearly written, this presentation vividly portrays the context and events of the Christmas Truce." Booklist

Includes bibliographical references

940.53 World War II, 1939-1945

Adams, Simon

World War II; written by Simon Adams; photographed by Andy Crawford. rev ed.; DK Pub. 2007 72p il (DK eyewitness books) $16.99

Grades: 4 5 6 7   **940.53**

1. World War, 1939-1945

ISBN 978-0-7566-3008-9; 0-7566-3008-8

LC 2008273315

First published 2000

Provides a concise history of World War II including information about the Holocaust, the code-breaking Enigma, and the deadly V2 rocket

Adler, David A.

Hiding from the Nazis; illustrated by Karen Ritz. Holiday House 1997 un il $15.95; pa $6.95

Grades: 2 3 4 **940.53**

1. Holocaust survivors 2. Jews -- Netherlands 3. Holocaust, 1933-1945 4. World War, 1939-1945 -- Jews

ISBN 0-8234-1288-1; 0-8234-1666-6 pa

LC 96-38451

The true story of Lore Baer who as a four-year-old Jewish child was placed with a Christian family in the Dutch farm country to avoid persecution by the Nazis

"Adler includes a lot of factual information about the history of the time and about the people in the story, before and after the war. Ritz's realistic watercolors in warm shades of brown focus on the small girl whose childhood games of hide-and-seek become a terrifying reality." Booklist

Ambrose, Stephen E.

★ The **good** fight; how World War II was won. Atheneum Bks. for Young Readers 2001 96p il maps $19.95

Grades: 5 6 7 8 **940.53**

1. World War, 1939-1945

ISBN 0-689-84361-5

LC 00-49600

"An excellent balance between the big picture and the humanizing details, well supported by fact boxes, tinted photographs, and battlefield maps that are both simple and clear. . . . Ambrose's style is authoritative and warm." Booklist

Includes glossary and bibliographical references

Bachrach, Susan D.

★ **Tell** them we remember; the story of the Holocaust. Little, Brown 1994 109p il maps pa $15.99

Grades: 5 6 7 8 **940.53**

1. Holocaust, 1933-1945 2. United States Holocaust Memorial Museum

ISBN 0-316-69264-6; 0-316-07484-5 pa

LC 93-40090

"Intended to extend the experience of the United States Holocaust Memorial Museum beyond its walls, this book reproduces some of its artifacts, photographs, maps, and taped oral and video histories. . . . Bachrach makes the victims of Hitler's cruelty immediate to readers, showing that, like readers, they were individuals with hobbies and desires, friends and families. . . . This is a very personal approach to Holocaust history and a very effective one." SLJ

Includes glossary and bibliographical references

Callery, Sean

★ **World** War II; Visual history of the world's darkest days. by Sean Callery. 1st ed. Scholastic 2013 105 p. ill. (some col.), col. maps (paperback) $15.99

Grades: 5 6 7 8 **940.53**

1. Military history 2. World War, 1939-1945

ISBN 0545479754; 9780545479752

LC 2012285678

This book presents "World War II in a nutshell. The text is divided into five chapters: 'The Path to War,' 'Europe & the Atlantic War,' the Pacific theater, Africa & the Middle East, and the end of the war. Each section is divided into several two-page topics. The title page of each chapter asks three questions that are answered in the text. It is followed by a two-page time line with boxed information and vintage photos." (School Library Journal)

Finkelstein, Norman H.

Remember not to forget; a memory of the Holocaust. [by] Norman H. Finkelstein; illustrated by Lois and Lars Hokanson. Jewish Publication Society 2004 31p il pa $9.95

Grades: 4 5 6 7 **940.53**

1. Jews -- History 2. Holocaust, 1933-1945

ISBN 0-82760-770-9

LC 2004556462

A reissue of the title first published 1985 by Watts

"This spare, starkly illustrated book explains what the Holocaust was and how it is remembered on Yom Hashoa, Holocaust Remembrance Day. The explanation reaches back to the explusion of the Jews from Jerusalem in A.D. 70 and describes how Jews . . . became targets of anti-Semitism, which culminated in the systematic murder of six million by the Nazis in World War II. The tone is straightforward and matter-of-fact. Black-and-white woodcuts accompany the text with somber scenes reflective of the narrative." Booklist [review of 1985 edition]

Greenfeld, Howard

★ The **hidden** children. Ticknor & Fields Bks. for Young Readers 1993 118p il hardcover o.p. pa $9.99

Grades: 4 5 6 7 **940.53**

1. Jews -- Europe 2. Holocaust, 1933-1945 -- Personal narratives

ISBN 0-395-66074-2; 0-395-86138-1 pa

LC 93-20326

Describes the experiences of those Jewish children who were forced to go into hiding during the Holocaust and survived to tell about it

"Illustrated with black-and-white photographs, the moving stories and dramatic facts make inspiring, and often troubling, reading. A lovely, important book about heroism and survival." Horn Book Guide

Includes bibliographical references

Hodge, Deborah

Rescuing the children; the story of the kindertransport. Deborah Hodge. Tundra Books of Northern New York 2012 60 p. (hardcover) $17.95

Grades: 4 5 6 **940.53**

1. Holocaust, 1939-1945 2. Jewish children in the Holocaust 3. World War, 1939-1945 -- Children 4. World War, 1939-1945 -- Refugees 5. Child refugees -- Great Britain -- History

ISBN 1770492569; 9781770492561

LC 2011938776

This children's book, by Deborah Hodge, "tells the story of how ten thousand Jewish children were rescued out of Nazi Europe just before the outbreak of World War 2. They were saved by the Kindertransport--a rescue mission that transported the children (or Kinder) from Nazi-ruled countries to safety in Britain. The book includes real-life accounts of the children and is illustrated with archival photographs . . . and original art by the Kinder commemorating their rescue." (Publisher's note)

Hurwitz, Johanna

Anne Frank: life in hiding; illustrated by Vera Rosenberry. Jewish Publ. Soc. 1988 62p il map $13.95

Grades: 3 4 5 **940.53**

1. Children 2. Diarists 3. Holocaust victims 4. Jews -- Netherlands 5. Holocaust, 1933-1945 6. World War, 1939-1945 -- Jews 7. Netherlands -- History -- 1940-1945, German occupation

ISBN 0-8276-0311-8

LC 87-35263

The author "gives a concise explanation of the political and economic background to the Holocaust and provides a map of Europe and a chronology. She ably covers the events of Anne's life before, during, and after the period covered by the 'Diary of Anne Frank,' explaining the significance and importance of the 'Diary' throughout the world." SLJ

Kacer, Kathy

Hiding Edith; a true story. Second Story 2006 120p (Holocaust remembrance book for young readers) pa $10.95

Grades: 4 5 6 7 **940.53**

1. Holocaust survivors 2. Jews -- France 3. Holocaust, 1933-1945

ISBN 1-897187-06-8

"Kacer recounts some extraordinary history: in Moissac, France, under Nazi occupation, a French Jewish couple hid 100 Jewish refugee children—with the support of the townspeople. Kacer, who based her account on interviews, tells the story of one child, Edith Schwalb. Captioned black-and-white photos on almost every page show Edith at home in Vienna before the war, then in Belgium, and then, separated from her parents, living with the rescuers." Booklist

Levine, Karen

Hana's suitcase; a true story. Whitman, A. 2003 111p il lib bdg $15.95

Grades: 4 5 6 7 **940.53**

1. Holocaust victims 2. Holocaust, 1933-1945

ISBN 0-8075-3148-0

LC 2002-27439

First published 2002 in Canada

A biography of a Czech girl who died in the Holocaust, told in alternating chapters with an account of how the curator of a Japanese Holocaust center learned about her life after Hana's suitcase was sent to her

"The account, based on a radio documentary Levine did in Canada . . . is part history, part suspenseful mystery, and always anguished family drama, with an incredible climactic revelation." Booklist

Meltzer, Milton

★ Never to forget: the Jews of the Holocaust. Harper & Row 1976 217p maps hardcover o.p. pa $9.99

Grades: 6 7 8 9 **940.53**

1. Holocaust, 1933-1945

ISBN 0-06-446118-1 pa

"The mass murder of six million Jews by the Nazis during World War II is the subject of this compelling history. Interweaving background information, chilling statistics, individual accounts and newspaper reports, it provides an excellent introduction to its subject." Interracial Books Child Bull

Includes bibliographical references

★ Rescue: the story of how Gentiles saved Jews in the Holocaust. Harper & Row 1988 168p maps hardcover o.p. pa $9.99

Grades: 6 7 8 9 **940.53**

1. Holocaust, 1933-1945 2. World War, 1939-1945 -- Jews -- Rescue

ISBN 0-06-024210-8; 0-06-446117-3 pa

LC 87-47816

A recounting drawn from historic source material of the many individual acts of heroism performed by righteous gentiles who sought to thwart the extermination of the Jews during the Holocaust

"This is an excellent portrayal of a difficult topic. Meltzer manages to both explain without accusing, and to laud without glorifying. . . . The discussion of the complicated relations between countries are clear, but not simplistic. An impressive aspect of this book is its lack of didacticism." Voice Youth Advocates

Includes bibliographical references

Mochizuki, Ken

★ Passage to freedom; the Sugihara story. written by Ken Mochizuki; illustrated by Dom Lee; afterword by Hiroki Sugihara. Lee & Low Bks. 1997 un il $15.95

Grades: 3 4 5 6 **940.53**

1. Diplomats 2. Humanitarians 3. Holocaust, 1933-1945 4. World War, 1939-1945 -- Jews -- Rescue

ISBN 1-880000-49-0

LC 96-35359

"Lee's stirring mixed-media illustrations in sepia shades are humane and beautiful. . . . The immediacy of the narrative will grab kids' interest and make them think." Booklist

Robbins, Trina

Lily Renée, escape artist; illustrated by Anne Timmons and Mo Oh. Graphic Universe 2011 96p. chiefly col. ill. $7.95

Grades: 4 5 6 7 8 **940.53**

1. Artists 2. Illustrators 3. Graphic novels 4. Jews -- Biography 5. Holocaust, 1933-1945 -- Graphic novels

ISBN 978-0-7613-6010-0; 0-7613-6010-7

LC 2011001084

Presents the story of Lily Renée Wilheim, the Jewish girl who escaped from the Nazis through the Kindertransport operation, leaving her parents behind and traveling alone to England, later becoming a comic book artist in New York.

"This comic-book biography of a Jewish girl's life under the Nazi jackboot and then as a refugee is low key and that much more profound for it. The panels are brightly lit, and the narrative is crisp, both of which serve to chillingly amplify the everyday banality of evil. . . . A fitting tribute." Kirkus

Rol, Ruud van der

Anne Frank, beyond the diary; a photographic remembrance. by Ruud van der Rol and Rian Verhoeven; in association with the Anne Frank House; translated by Tony Langham and Plym Peters; with an introduction by Anna Quindlen. Viking 1993 113p il map hardcover o.p. pa $10.99

Grades: 5 6 7 8 **940.53**

1. Children 2. Diarists 3. Holocaust victims 4. Jews -- Netherlands 5. Holocaust, 1933-1945 6. World War, 1939-1945 -- Jews 7. Netherlands -- History -- 1940-1945, German occupation

ISBN 0-670-84932-4; 0-14-036926-0 pa

LC 92-41528

Original Dutch edition, 1992

Photographs, illustrations, and maps accompany historical essays, diary excerpts, and interviews, providing an insight to Anne Frank and the massive upheaval which tore apart her world

"Readers will become absorbed in the richness of the detail and careful explanation which revisit and expand the familiar, well-loved story." Horn Book

Rubin, Susan Goldman

The **flag** with fifty-six stars; a gift from the survivors of Mauthausen. illustrated by Bill Farnsworth. Holiday House 2005 39p il $16.95

Grades: 3 4 5   **940.53**

1. Jews -- Germany 2. Holocaust, 1933-1945 3. Flags -- United States 4. World War, 1939-1945 -- Germany
ISBN 0-8234-1653-4

LC 2004-47457

"In the spring of 1945, U.S. troops marched into the Mauthausen concentration camp in Austria to liberate surviving prisoners and were given an American flag that had been secretly made by a group of detainees there. This is an inspiring account of the camp, its survivors, and its liberators. . . . Nazi atrocities are muted here, but the sorrow, hunger, hopelessness, and, finally, optimism shine through in the pictures and in the text." SLJ

Includes bibliographical references

Ruelle, Karen Gray

★ The **grand** mosque of Paris; a story of how Muslims saved Jews during the Holocaust. by Karen Gray Ruelle and Deborah Durland DeSaix. Holiday House 2009 40p il $17.95

Grades: 3 4 5 6   **940.53**

1. Muslims 2. Jewish-Arab relations 3. Holocaust, 1933-1945 4. World War, 1939-1945 -- France 5. World War, 1939-1945 -- Jews -- Rescue 6. France -- History -- 1940-1945, German occupation
ISBN 978-0-8234-2159-6; 0-8234-2159-7

LC 2008-17209

"Although few documents remain, substantial evidence supports this fascinating and courageous story. . . . Realistic oil paintings complement the lengthy text. . . . A must read." Kirkus

Russo, Marisabina

★ **Always** remember me; how one family survived World War II. [by] Marisabina Russo. Atheneum Books for Young Readers 2005 un il $16.95

Grades: 3 4 5   **940.53**

1. Jews -- Germany 2. Holocaust, 1933-1945
ISBN 0-689-86920-7

LC 2004-4228

"Russo tells her Jewish family's story of Holocaust survival. She remembers herself as a small child visiting her grandmother, Oma, who tells Russo the family history with photos stretching back to Oma's youth and marriage before World War I. . . . Russo personalizes the history with photo-album entries printed on the endpapers, and her gouache illustrations, framed like photos, show the individuality and strength of family members." Booklist

Includes glossary

Samuels, Charlie

Home front; by Charlie Samuels. Brown Bear Books 2012 48 p. ill. (some col.) (World War II sourcebook) (library) $35.65

Grades: 5 6 7 8   **940.53**

1. Military history 2. World War, 1939-1945 3. World War, 1939-1945 -- Social aspects 4. World War, 1939-1945 -- Economic aspects
ISBN 1936333228; 9781936333226

LC 2011007054

This book by Charlie Samuels is part of the World War II Sourcebook series and focuses on the home front. "Each page is illustrated. Little-known facts and, sometimes, direct narratives are presented with the information given to the reader. . . . Each book has the same timeline of World War II, maps of both the European and Pacific theaters, interesting biographical snapshots of people involved, and a list of websites that students may use to further explore World War II." (Library Media Connection)

Life under occupation; by Charlie Samuels. Brown Bear Books 2011 48 p. ill. (chiefly col.), col. maps (World War II sourcebook) (library) $35.65

Grades: 5 6 7 8   **940.53**

1. World War, 1939-1945 -- Occupied territories 3. World War, 1939-1945 -- Europe 4. World War, 1939-1945 -- Atrocities 5. World War, 1939-1945 -- Pacific Area
ISBN 1936333260; 9781936333264

LC 2011007055

This book by Charlie Samuels, part of the World War II Sourcebook series, and focuses on life under occupation. "Each page is illustrated. Little-known facts and, sometimes, direct narratives are presented with the information given to the reader. . . . Each book has the same timeline of World War II, maps of both the European and Pacific theaters, . . . biographical snapshots of people involved, and a list of websites." (Library Media Connection)

Includes bibliographical references and index.

Taylor, Peter Lane

The **secret** of Priest's Grotto; a Holocaust survival story. [by] Peter Lane Taylor with Christos Nicola. Kar-Ben Pub. 2007 64p il map lib bdg $10.95; pa $8.95

Grades: 5 6 7 8 9 10 11 12   **940.53**

1. Caves 2. Jews -- Ukraine 3. Holocaust, 1933-1945
ISBN 978-1-58013-260-2 lib bdg; 1-58013-260-X lib bdg; 978-1-58013-261-9 pa; 1-58013-261-8 pa

LC 2006-21709

"This volume relays the tale of 38 Ukrainian Jews who sought refuge in a local cave to escape the invading Nazis in fall of 1942 and remained there for 344 days. . . . At once sobering and uplifting, this is an astounding story of survival, powerfully told." Publ Wkly

Thomson, Ruth

★ **Terezin**; voices from the Holocaust. Candlewick Press 2011 64p il $18.99

Grades: 5 6 7 8   **940.53**

1. Jews -- Czechoslovakia 2. Holocaust, 1933-1945 3. Holocaust, Jewish (1939-1945) 4. Terezín (Czech Republic: Concentration camp)
ISBN 0-7636-4963-5; 978-0-7636-4963-0

LC 2010-39164

"Between 1941 and 1945, Nazi Germany turned the small town of Terezín, Czechoslovakia, into a ghetto, and then into a transit camp for thousands of Jewish people. It was a 'show' camp, where inmates were forced to use their artistic talents to fool the world about the truth of gas chambers and horrific living conditions for imprisoned Jews. Here is their story, told through the firsthand accounts of those who were there." (Publisher's note) Index. "Grades five to eight." (Bull Cent Child Books)

"Two years after the Nazi invasion of Czechoslovakia, the small fortress village of Terezin was converted into a Jewish ghetto, and over the next four years, ten of thousands of Jews were transported there while in transit to death camps in the east. The history of Terezin is fascinating: the camp housed many noted artists. . . . Much of the art created at Terezin survived the Holocaust, and a generous sampling is included in this volume. Thomson opts to tell the story of Terezin almost entirely in the voices of those who lived there. . . . This is an accessible, carefully researched work that effectively uses primary-source material to make the experience of the Jews of Terezin come alive for today's students." Bull Cent Child Books

Includes glossary and bibliographical references

Warren, Andrea
★ **Surviving** Hitler; a boy in the Nazi death camps. HarperCollins Pubs. 2001 146p il hardcover o.p. pa $6.99
Grades: 5 6 7 8   **940.53**
  1. Holocaust, 1933-1945
  ISBN 0-688-17497-3; 0-06-029218-0 lib bdg; 0-06-000767-2 pa

LC 00-38899

"Simply told, Warren's powerful story blends the personal testimony of Holocaust survivor Jack Mandelbaum with the history of his time, documented by stirring photos from the archives of the U.S. Holocaust Memorial Museum. . . . An excellent introduction for readers who don't know much about the history." Booklist

Includes bibliographical references

Wood, Douglas
★ **Franklin** and Winston; a Christmas that changed the world. illustrated by Barry Moser. Candlewick Press 2011 un il $16.99
Grades: 3 4 5   **940.53**
  1. Governors 2. Statesmen 3. Historians 4. Presidents 5. Prime ministers 6. People with disabilities 7. Memoirists 8. Philatelists 9. Cabinet members 10. Members of Parliament 11. Children of presidents 12. Nobel laureates for literature 13. World War, 1939-1945 -- Diplomatic history
  ISBN 978-0-7636-3383-7; 0-7636-3383-6

LC 2008025456

"An engaging chronicle of the month that Roosevelt and Churchill spent together at the White House, forging an affectionate friendship as well as a world-changing alliance. . . . Wood's narrative effectively captures both the desperation of the times and how much Churchill and Roosevelt genuinely enjoyed each other's company. Moser's detailed watercolor illustrations likewise capture their robust personalities." Kirkus

Includes bibliographical references

940.54 Military history of World War II

Allen, Thomas B.
★ **Remember** Pearl Harbor; American and Japanese survivors tell their stories. foreword by Robert D. Ballard. National Geographic Soc. 2001 57p il maps $17.95
Grades: 5 6 7 8   **940.54**
  1. Pearl Harbor (Oahu, Hawaii), Attack on, 1941 2. World War, 1939-1945 -- Personal narratives
  ISBN 0-7922-6690-0

LC 2001-796

Personal accounts of the Japanese attack on Pearl Harbor, with background information.

"Eyewitness testimony of Japanese and American men and women from various backgrounds enriches this balanced treatment of World War II. . . . The first-person voices along with dozens of black-and-white photos and several full-color maps make this a draw for both browsers and World War II buffs." Booklist

Includes bibliographical references

Chrisp, Peter
World War II: fighting for freedom; the story of the conflict that changed the world 1939-1945. Scholastic 2010 63p il map $12.99
Grades: 4 5 6 7   **940.54**
  1. World War, 1939-1945
  ISBN 978-0-545-24984-3; 0-545-24984-8

Provides information and facts on events leading up to the war, important battles and campaigns, political and military leaders, and life on the home fronts.

"Fascinating photographs dominate each spread, but there are also maps, quotations, diagrams, and interesting text box features. . . . This book provides a solid overview of World War II, but it is the visual aspect that makes it stand out." Libr Media Connect

Includes glossary

De Capua, Sarah
The **Tuskegee** airmen; by Sarah E. De Capua. Child's World 2009 32p il map (Journey to freedom) lib bdg $28.50
Grades: 4 5 6   **940.54**
  1. African American pilots 2. World War, 1939-1945 -- Aerial operations
  ISBN 978-1-60253-138-3 lib bdg; 1-60253-138-2 lib bdg

LC 2008031939

Tuskegee "Airmen celebrates the pilots' extraordinary achievements by placing them within the context of their time, when segregation was common. . . . Personal accounts, historical photographs of training, news stories about the men's fighting ability, and records of successful missions help to explain the squadron's determination not only to fly but also to prove its proficiency and bravery. . . . The [book is] concise and direct, yet the writing remains sophisticated. Vibrant personal stories accompanied by striking photographs of historical figures and artifacts provide a sense of the subjects' hopes and dreams." SLJ

Includes glossary and bibliographical references

Drez, Ronald J.

★ **Remember** D-day; the plan, the invasion, survivor stories. National Geographic Books 2004 61p il map $17.95; lib bdg $27.90

Grades: 5 6 7 8   **940.54**

1. World War, 1939-1945 -- Campaigns -- France

ISBN 0-7922-6666-8; 0-7922-6965-9 lib bdg

LC 2003-17733

Discusses the events and personalities involved in the momentous Allied invasion of France on June 6, 1944

"This well-organized, clearly written account provides a solid overview for readers unfamiliar with the subject. A first-rate purchase." SLJ

Includes bibliographical references

Hama, Larry

★ The **battle** of Iwo Jima; guerilla warfare in the Pacific. by Larry Hama; illustrated by Anthony Williams. Rosen Pub. 2007 48p il map (Graphic battles of World War II) lib bdg $29.25

Grades: 5 6 7 8 9   **940.54**

1. Graphic novels 2. World War, 1939-1945 -- Graphic novels 3. Iwo Jima, Battle of, 1945 -- Graphic novels

ISBN 978-1-4042-0781-3 lib bdg; 1-4042-0781-3 lib bdg

LC 2006007645

"Using a graphic novel to introduce the battle for Iwo Jima makes it very accessible. Before the graphic-novel section of the book begins, Hama provides a short, informative background piece describing the run-up to World War II, the significance of the Japanese war machine, and the importance of the tiny island of Iwo Jima. Then the graphic novel, illustrated by Williams in camouflage colors, does a terrific job of examining the ups and downs of the battle as well as the horror of so many losses—on both sides." Booklist

Includes bibliographical references

Lawton, Clive

Hiroshima; the story of the first atom bomb. [by] Clive A. Lawton. Candlewick Press 2004 48p il map $18.99

Grades: 5 6 7 8   **940.54**

1. Atomic bomb 2. World War, 1939-1945 -- Japan 3. Hiroshima (Japan) -- Bombardment, 1945

ISBN 0-7636-2271-0

LC 2004-45166

"Engaging text and powerful photographs are intricately woven together to make a long-lasting impact on readers." Libr Media Connect

Manning, Mick

Tail-end Charlie; [by] Mick Manning and Brita Granström. Frances Lincoln Children's Books 2009 un il $16.95

Grades: 3 4 5   **940.54**

1. World War, 1939-1945 -- Aerial operations

ISBN 978-1-84507-651-1; 1-84507-651-6

"The remembrances of Manning's father, a British Air Force gunner during World War II, are vividly presented through comic strips, watercolor-and-ink illustrations, and memorabilia such as ration books, postcards, and photographs. . . . Reluctant readers will be drawn to the graphic format and quickly engaged by the authentic voice." SLJ

Samuels, Charlie

Propaganda; by Charlie Samuels. Brown Bear Books 2011 48 p. ill. (chiefly col.), col. maps (World War II sourcebook) (library) $35.65

Grades: 5 6 7 8   **940.54**

1. World War, 1939-1945 -- Propaganda 2. World War, 1939-1945 -- Propaganda

ISBN 1936333236; 9781936333233

LC 2011010241

This book by Charlie Samuels on propaganda is part of the World War II Sourcebook series. "Each page is illustrated. Little-known facts and, sometimes, direct narratives are presented with the information given to the reader. . . . Each book has the same timeline of World War II, maps of both the European and Pacific theaters, interesting biographical snapshots of people involved, and a list of websites that students may use to further explore World War II." (Library Media Connection)

Includes bibliographical references and index.

Soldiers; [Charlie Samuels] Brown Bear Books 2011 48 p. ill. (some col.), maps (col.) (World War II sourcebook) (library binding) $35.65

Grades: 5 6 7 8   **940.54**

1. Soldiers 2. Soldiers -- History -- 20th century

ISBN 1936333244; 9781936333240

LC 2011007057

This book by Charlie Samuels, part of the World War II Sourcebook series, "Describes the life of a soldier in World War II, from recruitment efforts around the world, to the daily life during the fighting." (Publisher's note)

Includes bibliographical references (p. 47) and index

Spying and security; by Charlie Samuels. Brown Bear Books 2012 48 p. ill. (some col.) (World War II Sourcebook) (library binding) $35.65

Grades: 5 6 7 8   **940.54**

1. Police -- History -- 20th century 2. World War, 1939-1945 -- Secret service 3. Spies -- History -- 20th century 4. Espionage -- History -- 20th century 5. World War, 1939-1945 -- Cryptography

ISBN 1936333252; 9781936333257

LC 2011007058

This book by Charlie Samuels, part of the World War II Sourcebook, provides a history of spying and security for young readers. It "Describes the role spies and police played around the world during World War II, from controlling riots to gathering intelligence from the enemy." (Publisher's note)

Seiple, Samantha

Ghosts in the fog; the untold story of Alaska's WWII invasion. Scholastic 2011 221p il map $16.99

Grades: 5 6 7 8   **940.54**

1. Alaska 2. World War, 1939-1945 -- Campaigns 3. Japan. -- Kaigun -- History -- World War, 1939-1945

ISBN 978-0-545-29654-0; 0-545-29654-4

LC 2011027821

"A little-known story from World War II shows the unique role played by a small group of military personal and native civilians in a remote region of the county. The role of Alaska in World War II following the attack on Pearl Harbor is not often told. . . . The story illuminates the cultural differences between the American and Japanese cultures at that time as well as the reluctance of the U.S. government to treat the native Alaskans as full citizens. The narrative is full of details, and . . . the text is supported by many photographs of those involved. Maps, including a strategic military map, increase the level of specificity." Kirkus

Includes bibliographical references

Sheinkin, Steve

★ The **Port** Chicago 50; disaster, mutiny, and the fight for civil rights. Steve Sheinkin. Roaring Brook Press 2014 208 p. illustrations (hardcover: alk. paper) $19.99

Grades: 5 6 7 8 9   **940.54**

1. United States. Navy 2. African American sailors 3. African Americans -- Civil rights 4. World War, 1939-1945 5. Port Chicago Mutiny, Port Chicago, Calif., 1944

ISBN 1596437960; 9781596437968

        LC 2013013452

Boston Globe-Horn Book Award: Nonfiction (2014)

National Book Award Shortlist: Young People's Literature (2014)

YALSA Award for Excellence in Nonfiction for Young Adults: Finalist (2015)

Author Steve Sheinkin tells how "on July 17, 1944, a massive explosion rocked the segregated Navy base at Port Chicago, California. On August 9th, 244 men refused to go back to work until unsafe and unfair conditions at the docks were addressed. Fifty were charged with mutiny." (Publisher's note)

"An unusual entry point for the study of WWII and the nascent civil rights movement. Photographs are helpful, and documentation is thorough." (Horn Book)

Includes bibliographical references and index

Stone, Tanya Lee

★ **Courage** has no color, the true story of the Triple Nickles; America's first black paratroopers. Tanya Lee Stone. Candlewick Press 2013 160 p. $24.99

Grades: 5 6 7 8   **940.54**

1. Parachute troops 2. United States. Army 3. World War, 1939-1945 4. African American soldiers

ISBN 0763651176; 9780763651176

        LC 2012942315

Orbis Pictus Awards Honor Book (2014)

YALSA Award for Excellence in Nonfiction for Young Adults: Finalist (2014)

This book tells the "untold story of the 555th Parachute Infantry Battalion, America's first black paratroopers." Enlisted black men "faced the tyranny of racial discrimination on the homefront. . . . When 1st Sgt. Walter Morris, whose men served as guards at The Parachute School at Fort Benning, saw white soldiers training to be paratroopers, he knew his men would have to train and act like them to be treated like soldiers." (Kirkus Reviews)

941 British Isles

Bean, Rachel

★ **United** Kingdom; [by] Rachel Bean; Robert Bennett and Michael Dunford, consultants. National Geographic 2007 64p il map (Countries of the world) lib bdg $28.50

Grades: 4 5 6 7   **941**

1. Great Britain 2. Northern Ireland

ISBN 978-1-4263-0126-1 lib bdg; 1-4263-0126-X lib bdg

        LC 2007024750

This describes the geography, nature, history, people and culture, government and economy of the United Kingdom

"What helps [this book] stand out from the pack is [its] high-quality, rich photography. . . . The photos provide as much information as the [text]. . . . The writing is straightforward and solid." SLJ

Includes glossary and bibliographical references

Dillon, Patrick

The **story** of Britain from the Norman Conquest to the European Union; illustrated by P.J. Lynch. Candlewick Press 2011 341p il map $21.99

Grades: 5 6 7 8   **941**

1. Great Britain -- History

ISBN 978-0-7636-5122-0; 0-7636-5122-2

        LC 2010038883

"This well-written, thoughtfully illustrated volume [is] an indispensible tool for European history buffs." Horn Book Guide

Dunn, James

ABC UK; illustrated by Helen Bate. Frances Lincoln 2009 un il $16.95

Grades: K 1 2 3   **941**

1. Alphabet 2. Great Britain

ISBN 978-1-84507-696-2; 1-84507-696-6

"Featuring historical and cultural highlights of Great Britain (Giant's Causeway, punk music, vindaloo), each letter of the alphabet gets a uniquely stylized treatment in Bate's mixed media art. . . . The diversity of subjects makes it a prime pick for Anglophiles of all ages." Publ Wkly

Indovino, Shaina C.

United Kingdom; by Rae Simons and Shaina C. Indovino. Mason Crest Publishers 2012 64 p. col. ill., col. maps (library) $22.95

Grades: 5 6 7 8   **941**

1. Great Britain 2. Northern Ireland 3. European Union -- Great Britain 4. European Union -- Northern Ireland

ISBN 1422222616; 9781422222614; 9781422222928

        LC 2010051852

This book on the United Kingdom by Rae Simons and Shaina Carmel Indovino "covers Modern Issues, History and Government, The Economy, People and Culture, and Looking to the Future. . . Identical information on "The Formation of the European Union" appears in every book" in the series. (Library Media Connection) Also covered are "issues like immigration and the global financial crisis". (Publisher's note)

Includes bibliographical references (p. 60) and index.

941.5 Ireland

McQuinn, Colm

★ **Ireland**; [by] Anna and Colm McQuinn; Elizabeth Malcolm and John McDonagh, consultants. National Geo-

graphic 2008 64p il map (Countries of the world) lib bdg
$27.90

Grades: 4 5 6 7   **941.5**

1. Ireland

ISBN 978-1-4263-0299-2 lib bdg; 1-4263-0299-1
lib bdg

This describes the geography, nature, history, people and
culture, government, and economy of Ireland.

Includes glossary and bibliographical references

941.508   Ireland 1800-1899

Fradin, Dennis Brindell

The **Irish** potato famine; by Dennis Fradin. Marshall
Cavendish Benchmark 2012 32 p. (Great escapes) (library) $34.21

Grades: 5 6 7 8   **941.508**

1. Famines 2. Ireland -- History -- Famine, 1845-1852
3. Escapes -- Ireland -- History -- 19th century 5. Irish
-- Migrations -- History -- 19th century 6. Disaster
victims -- Ireland -- History -- 19th century 7. Ireland
-- Emigration and immigration -- History -- 19th century

ISBN 1608704734; 9781608704736

LC 2010018788

This book, part of the Great Escapes series, focuses
on the Irish Potato Famine. "Each book begins with an introduction to an individual who escaped, followed by the
history of the precipitating events, the escape itself, and a
follow-up on what happened after the escape. Each title includes a timeline, notes, and additional information on the
topic." (Library Media Connection)

Includes bibliographical references and index.

941.7   Republic of Ireland

Blashfield, Jean F.

Ireland; Enchantment of the World. by Jean F. Blashfield. Children's Press; an imprint of Scholastic Inc. 2014
144 p. (Enchantment of the world--second series) (library
binding) $40

Grades: 5 6 7 8   **941.7**

1. Ireland

ISBN 0531236765; 9780531236765

LC 2013002015

This book, by Jean F. Blashfield, focuses on Ireland. The
book focuses on "country's culture, history, and geography
are explored in detail. . . . Sidebars highlight especially interesting people, places, and events. . . . Recipes give readers the opportunity to experience foreign cuisine." (Publisher's note)

"Many students turn to the Internet for writing reports,
but for reliably accurate, attractively presented and well-
calibrated information, the long-standing Enchantment of
the World series remains a superior choice. Each volume
has been completely rewritten from a previous edition—in
many cases to startling effect given recent political events.
Although the basic structure holds true to past versions, the
updated photographs are truly eye-popping and take care to
portray the countries as modern often opting for showing,
say, a surgeon at work rather than a rural farmer. It might not
be necessary for libraries to replace Ireland, since it hasn't

changed radically, but this is a solid offering with updated
statistics. Each volume in this reliable series includes extensive back matter with a detailed index." Booklist.

Includes bibliographical references and index

942   England and Wales

Banting, Erinn

England; by Erinn Banting; edited by Sarah Cairns;
illustrated by Jeff Crosby, Dianne Eastman, and David
Wysotski. Revised ed. Crabtree Pub. Co. 2012 32 p. ill.
(some col.) (Lands, peoples, and cultures) (library) $26.60;
(paperback) $8.95; (ebook) $26.60.

Grades: 4 5 6   **942**

1. Culture 2. England 3. England -- Civilization 4.
England -- Social life and customs

ISBN 0778798283; 9780778798286; 9780778798316;
9781427180056 pdf

LC 2012013776

This book by Erinn Banting is part of the Lands, Peoples and Cultural Series and looks at the culture of England. The books offer information about "folktales, sports,
and history." Also included are "a table of contents, short
glossary (words highlighted in test) and index." (Catholic
Library World)

Includes index

Blashfield, Jean F.

England; by Jean F. Blashfield. Children's Press 2013
144 p. ill. (some col.), col. maps (Enchantment of the
world) (library) $40.00

Grades: 4 5 6 7   **942**

1. England

ISBN 9780531275429

LC 2012000503

This book by Jean F. Blashfield, part of the "Enchantment of the World" series, "describes the geography, history,
economy, language, religions, culture, people, plants, and
animals of England." (Publisher's note) It includes "topics
as recent as the 2012 Olympics and 2012 Grammy winners,
as well as the latest royal wedding." (Children's Literature)

Includes bibliographical references (p. 134-135)
and index.

Platt, Richard

★ **London**; illustrated by Manuela Cappon. Kingfisher
2009 45p il (Through time) $16.95

Grades: 3 4 5   **942**

1. London (England) -- History

ISBN 978-0-7534-6255-3; 0-7534-6255-9

This "book explores the history of London from 'Neo-
lithic camp' to the modern city it is today. . . . Cutaway views
of various structures and concise but engaging text effectively capture the changing face of a city over time." Publ Wkly

Rubbino, Salvatore

★ **A walk** in London. Candlewick Press 2011 40p
il $16.99

Grades: PreK K 1 2 3 4   **942**

1. London (England)

ISBN 978-0-7636-5272-2; 0-7636-5272-5

LC 2010038769

"A mother and daughter get off a double-decker bus in central London for a day of sightseeing. . . . Playful yet realistic mixed-media illustrations, drawn from different perspectives, give the reader a real sense of what it's like to visit London. . . . Highly informative, visually stunning, and jampacked with things for young readers to look at." Horn Book

942.05 England--Period of House of Tudor, 1485-1603

Hollihan, Kerrie Logan

Elizabeth I--the people's queen; her life and times: 21 activities. Chicago Review Press 2011 129p il (For kids) pa $16.95

Grades: 4 5 6 7 8 **942.05**

1. Queens 2. Great Britain -- History -- 1485-1603, Tudors

ISBN 978-1-56976-349-0; 1-56976-349-6

LC 2010047647

This is an interactive biography of Queen Elizabeth I.

"The writing is clear and suited to readers with no previous knowledge of the topic. The activities vary in difficulty, from reading The Faerie Queen, to creating a family coat of arms, to growing a knot garden. The book is well illustrated with black-and-white reproductions of portraits, engravings, and paintings depicting major events in the Tudors' lives. . . . This well-organized book succeeds at being interesting and scholarly at the same time." SLJ

Includes bibliographical references

942.9 Wales

Hestler, Anna

Wales; [by] Anna Hestler and Jo-Ann Spilling. 2nd ed.; Marshall Cavendish Benchmark 2011 144p il map (Cultures of the world) lib bdg $42.79

Grades: 5 6 7 8 **942.9**

1. Wales

ISBN 978-1-6087-0457-6; 1-6087-0457-2

LC 2010030339

First published 2001

Provides information on the geography, history, wildlife, governmental structure, economy, cultural diversity, peoples, religion, and culture of Wales.

"Plentiful color photographs accompany substantial amounts of information." Booklist

Includes glossary and bibliographical references

943 Germany and neighboring central European countries

Indovino, Shaina C.

Germany; by Ida Walker and Shaina C. Indovino. Mason Crest Publishers 2013 64 p. ill. (some col.), col. maps (Major European nations) (library) $22.95

Grades: 5 6 7 8 **943**

1. Germany -- Politics and government 3. Germany -- History 4. European Union -- Germany 5. Germany -- Description and travel 6. Germany -- Social life and customs

ISBN 1422222438; 9781422222430

LC 2010051291

This book on Germany by Ida Walker and Shaina Carmel Indovino is part of the "Major European Nations" series, which "stresses the modern relationships, goals, and problems of the European Union. . . . Chapters begin with 'Modern Issues' and a brief summary of the country's history and government, followed by chapters on economy, people and culture, and 'Looking to the Future.' In addition, there is a time line and a few suggestions for finding out more." (School Library Journal)

Russell, Henry

★ Germany; [by] Henry Russell; Benedict Kork and Antje Schlottmann, consultants. National Geographic 2007 64p il map (Countries of the world) lib bdg $27.90

Grades: 4 5 6 7 **943**

1. Germany

ISBN 978-1-4263-0059-2

LC 2007024677

Describes the geography, nature, history, people and culture, government and economy of Germany.

This "appealing [title has] wonderful photographs and maps. . . . The [book offers] reliable sources for country research, and the interesting and current material holds browsing potential as well." SLJ

Includes glossary and bibliographical references

943.6 Austria and Liechtenstein

Grahame, Deborah A.

Austria; [by] Deborah Grahame. Marshall Cavendish Benchmark 2007 48p il map (Discovering cultures) lib bdg $28.50

Grades: 2 3 4 **943.6**

1. Austria

ISBN 978-0-7614-1984-6 lib bdg; 0-7614-1984-5 lib bdg

LC 2006011471

An introduction to the geography, history, people, and culture of Austria

Includes glossary and bibliographical references

Indovino, Shaina C.

Austria; by Jeanine Sanna and Shaina C. Indovino. Mason Crest Publishers 2012 64 p. col. ill., col. maps (library) $22.95

Grades: 5 6 7 8 **943.6**

1. Austria -- History 2. Austria 3. European Union -- Austria

ISBN 1422222322; 9781422222324

LC 2010051075

This book, part of the Major European Union Nations series, focuses on Austria. In "addition to history, the book details government, economy, culture, and prospects for the future. There is a glossary and an index and a nice chronology in the back of the book as well as a brief bibliography and a list of photo credits." (Children's Literature)

Includes bibliographical references (p. 57) and index.

943.7   Czech Republic and Slovakia

Sioras, Efstathia

Czech Republic; [by] Efstathia Sioras and Michael Spilling. Marshall Cavendish Benchmark 2010 144p il map (Cultures of the world) lib bdg $42.79

Grades: 5 6 7 8   **943.7**

1. Czech Republic

ISBN 978-0-7614-4476-3 lib bdg; 0-7614-4476-9 lib bdg

LC 2009003185

This describes the geography, history, wildlife, governmental structure, economy, cultural diversity, peoples, religion, and culture of the Czech Republic

Includes glossary and bibliographical references

943.710   Czech Republic -- Period of Republic, 1993-

Docalavich, Heather

Czech Republic; by Heather Docalavich and Shaina C. Indovino. Mason Crest Publishers 2013 64 p. col. ill, col. maps (library) $22.95; (ebook) $28.95

Grades: 5 6 7 8   **943.710**

1. Czech Republic 2. European Union -- Czech Republic

ISBN 1422222373; 9781422222379; 9781422222683; 9781422292648

LC 2010051083

This book by Heather Docalavich is part of the Major European Union Nations series and focuses on the Czech Republic. "The Czech Republic is one of the newest countries in the world. It's also new to the EU—it joined in 2004. People have lived in what we now call the Czech Republic for thousands of years, however. This land has a long history and is moving forward while dealing with challenges like the recent global recession." (Publisher's note)

Includes bibliographical references (p. 57-58, 63) and index.

943.8   Poland

Deckker, Zilah

★ Poland; [by] Zilah Deckker; Richard Butterwick and Iwona Sagan, consultants. National Geographic 2008 64p il map (Countries of the world) lib bdg $27.90

Grades: 4 5 6 7   **943.8**

1. Poland

ISBN 978-1-4263-0201-5

LC 2007047823

This describes the geography, nature, history, people and culture, government, and economy of Poland.

Includes glossary and bibliographical references

Docalavich, Heather

Poland; by Healther Docalavich and Shaina C. Indovino. Mason Crest Publishers 2013 64 p. col. ill., col. maps (library) $22.95

Grades: 5 6 7 8   **943.8**

1. Poland 2. European Union -- Poland

ISBN 1422222543; 9781422222546

LC 2010051465

This book by Heather Docalavich and Shaina C. Indovino is part of the Major European Union Nations series and looks at Poland. "It joined the EU in 2004 .... For long time, Poland has been home to scientific thinkers, artists, and musicians. Today, it is one of the countries that have weathered the global recession the best, proving this nation's strength." (Publisher's note)

Includes bibliographical references and index

Mara, Wil

Poland; by Wil Mara. Children's Press, an imprint of Scholastic Inc. 2014 144 p. illustrations and maps (library binding) $40

Grades: 5 6 7 8   **943.8**

1. Poland

ISBN 0531220168; 9780531220160

LC 2013026061

This book, by Wil Mara, focuses on Poland. The book discusses the "country's culture, history, and geography are explored in detail, allowing readers a chance to see how people live. . . . Sidebars highlight especially interesting people, places, and events . . . [and] easy recipes give readers the opportunity to experience foreign cuisine first-hand." (Publisher's note)

Includes bibliographical references and index

944   France and Monaco

Dubowski, Mark

Discovery in the cave; by Mark Dubowski; illustrated by Bryn Barnard. Random House 2010 48 p. col. ill.

Grades: 1 2 3   **944**

1. Caves 2. Prehistoric art 3. Cave drawings and paintings 4. Lascaux Cave (France) 5. Montignac (Dordogne, France) -- Antiquities 6. Cave paintings -- France -- Montignac (Dordogne) 7. Art, Prehistoric -- France -- Montignac (Dordogne) 8. Magdalenian culture -- France -- Montignac (Dordogne)

ISBN 0375858938; 0375958932; 9780375858932; 9780375958939

LC 2009007099

This book tells the "true adventure story about the discovery of the Lascaux Cave. . . . In 1940, four teenage boys and a dog dropped themselves into a hole in the forest floor. Using a flaming grease gun as a torch, they ventured deep underground, eventually coming to a huge cave, the walls of which were covered with life-size paintings of animals. Whole herds of horses! Deer with horns as big as tree branches! Giant bison! The boys were amazed by their discovery. They'd stumbled upon the world's finest examples of prehistoric painting!" (Publisher's note)

Indovino, Shaina C.

France; by Jeanine Sanna and Shaina C. Indovino. Mason Crest Publishers 2013 64 p. col. ill., col. maps (hardcover) $22.95

Grades: 5 6 7 8   **944**
1. France
ISBN 142222242X; 9781422222423
                                    LC 2010051290

This book by Liz Sonneborn is part of the Enchantment of the World series and looks at France. It covers "history, government, geography, natural resources, economics, the arts, and culture. . . . Maps, charts, sidebars highlighting items of interest, a time line, and a 'Fast Facts' section add to the presentation." (School Library Journal)

Includes bibliographical references (p. 59) and index.

King, David C.
  Monaco; [by] David C. King. Marshall Cavendish Benchmark 2008 144p il map (Cultures of the world) lib bdg $42.79
Grades: 5 6 7 8   **944**
  1. Monaco
  ISBN 978-0-7614-2567-0
                                    LC 2006030238

This describes the geography, history, government, economy, environment, people, and culture of Monaco
  Includes glossary and bibliographical references

Sonneborn, Liz
  France; by Liz Sonneborn. Children's Press 2013 144 p. ill., maps (library) $40
Grades: 5 6 7 8   **944**
  1. France
  ISBN 0531256006; 9780531256008
                                    LC 2012047113
  Includes bibliographical references (page 134) and index

Tidmarsh, Celia
  France. Sea-to-sea Publications 2009 32p il map (Facts about countries) lib bdg $28.50
Grades: 3 4 5   **944**
  1. France
  ISBN 978-1-59771-115-9 lib bdg; 1-59771-115-2 lib bdg
  Describes the geography, history, industries, education, government, and cultures of France

  "The attractive layout includes color photographs and charts of current statistics as well as maps illustrating main farming regions, natural resources, or the literacy rates of girls and boys. The [text is] clear and succinct." SLJ

944.04   France since 1789

Riggs, Kate
  The **French** Revolution. Creative Education 2009 48p il map (Days of change) lib bdg $32.80
Grades: 5 6 7 8   **944.04**
  1. France -- History -- 1789-1799, Revolution
  ISBN 978-1-58341-734-8 lib bdg; 1-58341-734-6 lib bdg
                                    LC 2008009728
  "With elegant design and mature prose, the Days of Change series is an ideal starting point for all manner of school projects. . . . The political pressures at the center of The French Revolution are difficult to dramatize, but Riggs carefully lays out the factions and civil disobedience that led

to the Declaration of the Rights of Man and of The Citizen—and then the emperor's reign that overthrew everything." Booklist
  Includes bibliographical references

944.36   Paris

Rubbino, Salvatore
  A **Walk** in Paris; Salvatore Rubbino. Candlewick Press 2014 40 p. color illustrations $16.99
Grades: PreK K 1 2 3 4   **944.36**
  1. Paris (France) 2. Paris
  ISBN 0763669849; 9780763669843
                                    LC 2013943083

This children's book, by Salvatore Rubbino, "follows a girl and her grandfather through the streets of Paris. . . . The girl narrates excitedly while her grandfather offers occasional details about the Place Saint-Michel, the Louvre, and more. Brief informational captions about Parisian landmarks, cuisine, and language are tucked throughout the mixed-media illustrations." (Publishers Weekly)

  "A girl and her grandpa tour Parisian sites old and new. They finally arrive, in a foldout, at the Eiffel Tower, "fizzing with lights!" It's an amiable amble, the child's travelogue nicely extended with extra facts in discreetly tiny type. The evocative art features gentle tones enlivened with verdant greens and inviting raspberry-reds. An endpaper map details the route." Horn Book

945   Italy, San Marino, Vatican City, Malta

Blashfield, Jean F.
  Italy; by Jean F. Blashfield. Children's Press, an imprint of Scholastic Inc. 2014 144 p. (library binding) $40
Grades: 5 6 7 8   **945**
  1. Italy 2. Italy -- History 3. Italy -- Civilization 4. Italy -- Economic conditions 5. Italy -- Politics and government 6. Italy -- Social life and customs
  ISBN 0531236773; 9780531236772
                                    LC 2013000087

This book, by Jean F. Blashfield, focuses on Italy. The book discusses the "country's culture, history, and geography are explored in detail, allowing readers a chance to see how people live. . . . Sidebars highlight especially interesting people, places, and events . . . [and] recipes give readers the opportunity to experience foreign cuisine firsthand." (Publisher's note)

  "Many students turn to the Internet for writing reports, but for reliably accurate, attractively presented and well-calibrated information, the long-standing Enchantment of the World series remains a superior choice. Each volume has been completely rewritten from a previous edition—in many cases to startling effect given recent political events. Although the basic structure holds true to past versions, the updated photographs are truly eye-popping and take care to portray the countries as modern often opting for showing, say, a surgeon at work rather than a rural farmer. It might not be necessary for libraries to replace [this title], since it hasn't changed radically, but this is a solid offering with updated statistics. Each volume in this reliable series includes extensive back matter with a detailed index." Booklist.

Includes bibliographical references and index

Indovino, Shaina C.

Italy; by Ademola O. Sadik and Shaina C. Indovino. Mason Crest Publishers 2013 64 p. ill. (col. ill.), maps (library) $22.95

Grades: 5 6 7 8 **945**

1. Italy 2. European Union -- Italy
ISBN 1422222489; 9781422222485

LC 2010051333

This book by Ademola O. Sadek and Shaina C. Indovino is part of the Major European Nations series and looks at Italy. "Chapters begin with "Modem Issues" and a brief summary of the country's history and government, followed by chapters on economy, people and culture, and 'Looking to the Future.'" The texts "liken Italy's treatment of the "Roma" (Gypsies) to the U.S. treatment of the American Indian; the social standing of Italy's women is examined." (School Library Journal)

Nivola, Claire A.

★ Orani; my father's village. Farrar Straus Giroux 2011 un il $16.99

Grades: 2 3 4 **945**

1. Artists 2. Illustrators 3. Italy
ISBN 978-0-374-35657-6; 0-374-35657-2

LC 2009047598

"Nivola's charming primitive-style art works well in both the upclose images as well as in the broad landscape scenes that she loving captures. A book to inspire young writers and artists to interview and write about their own parents' (or grandparents') lives." SLJ

945.8 Sicily and adjacent islands

Sheehan, Sean

Malta; by Sean Sheehan and Yong Jui Lin. 2nd ed. Marshall Cavendish Benchmark 2010 144 p. col. ill. (library) $47.07

Grades: 5 6 7 8 **945.8**

1. Malta 2. Culture 3. Malta -- Social life and customs
ISBN 1608700240; 9781608700240

LC 2010000733

This book by Sean Sheehan is part of the Cultures of the World series and looks at Malta. The books in the series provide "broad overviews of each country's culture, geography, and history. The . . . texts discuss government, economy, people, lifestyles, religion, language, arts and leisure, festivals, and food." (School Library Journal)

Includes bibliographical references (p. 142) and index.

946 Spain, Andorra, Gibraltar, Portugal

Augustin, Byron

Andorra; by Byron D. Augustin. Marshall Cavendish Benchmark 2009 144p il map (Cultures of the world) lib bdg $42.79

Grades: 5 6 7 8 **946**

1. Andorra
ISBN 978-0-7614-3122-0 lib bdg; 0-7614-3122-5 lib bdg

LC 2007040356

"Provides comprehensive information on the geography, history, governmental structure, economy, cultural diversity, peoples, religion, and culture of Andorra." Publisher's note

Includes glossary and bibliographical references

Croy, Anita

Spain. National Geographic 2010 64p il map (Countries of the world) lib bdg $27.90

Grades: 4 5 6 7 **946**

1. Spain
ISBN 978-1-4263-0633-4 lib bdg; 1-4263-0633-4 lib bdg

This describes the geography, nature, history, people and culture, government and economy of Spain

"The information is substantial but not overwhelming. The [text is] clear, and the discussion points are well chosen. . . . [The text is] complemented with stunning photographs." SLJ

Includes glossary and bibliographical references

Hanks, Reuel R.

Spain; by Zoran Pavlovic and Reuel Hanks. Chelsea House 2006 104 p. col. ill., col. maps (library) $35.00; (hardcover) $35

Grades: 5 6 7 8 **946**

1. Spain
ISBN 9780791066973 out of print; 1617530476; 9781617530470

LC 2006002218

This book by Zoran Pavlovic is part of the Modern World Nations series and looks at Spain. "Although Spain is now part of a unified Europe, . . . it is also a land divided by a combination of its own history, ethnicity, and geography." This entry "offers readers a wealth of information about this nation, touching on a variety of topics such as Spanish geography, history, political evolution, and ethnic issues." (Publisher's note)

Includes bibliographical references (p. 96) and index.

Indovino, Shaina C.

Spain; by Rae Simons and Shaina C. Indovino. Mason Crest Publishers 2013 64 p. col. ill., col. maps (library) $22.95

Grades: 5 6 7 8 **946**

1. Spain 2. European Union -- Spain
ISBN 9781422222904; 1422222594; 9781422222591

LC 2010051847

This book by Rae Simons is part of the Major European Union Nations series and looks at Spain. "Spain has it all: beaches, modern cities, soaring architecture, mountains, and more. It has been a member of the EU since 1986. From the ancient Celts to the Moors to the Christian kings and queens, many people have influenced Spain. It has recently taken a step back in the current financial crisis, but this proud nation is slowly getting back on its feet." (Publisher's note)

946.9 Portugal

Deckker, Zilah
★ **Portugal**. National Geographic 2009 64p il map (Countries of the world) lib bdg $27.90
Grades: 4 5 6 7   **946.9**
1. Portugal
ISBN 978-1-4263-0390-6 lib bdg; 1-4263-0390-4 lib bdg

LC 2009275584

This describes the geography, nature, history, people and culture, government and economy of Portugal

Includes glossary and bibliographical references

Etingoff, Kim
Portugal; by Kim Etingoff and Shaina C. Indovino. Mason Crest Publishers 2013 64 p. col. ill. (library) $22.95
Grades: 5 6 7 8   **946.9**
1. Portugal
ISBN 1422222551; 9781422222553

LC 2010051466

This book by Kim Etingoff and Shaina C. Indovino is part of the Major European Union Nations series and looks at Portugal. "Long ago, Portugal was one of the world's most powerful countries, as it explored and conquered places far from home. Today, it is a nation that has had some economic and social struggles, but also some triumphs. It joined the EU in 1986." (Publisher's note)

947 Russia and neighboring east European countries

Robinson, Anthony
Hamzat's journey; a refugee diary. by Anthony Robinson and AnneMarie Robinson; illustrated by June Allan. Frances Lincoln Books 2010 un il (Refugee diary) $17.95
Grades: 3 4 5   **947**
1. Refugees 2. Children with physical disabilities 3. Chechnya (Russia)
ISBN 978-1-84780-030-5; 1-84780-030-0

"In 2001, eight-year-old Hamzat stepped on a land mine on the way to school with two friends in Grozny, Chechnya. His friends died, but Hamzat survived with a shattered leg. In his spare, quiet first-person narrative, Hamzat describes the horrific struggle of civilians in wartime. . . . Clear, detailed back matter offers more facts about Chechnya's geography and long, troubled history, while occasional small, color family photos add even more immediacy." Booklist

Stanley, Diane
★ **Peter** the Great. Morrow Junior Bks. 1999 32p il $16
Grades: 4 5 6 7   **947**
1. Emperors 2. Russia -- Kings and rulers
ISBN 0-688-16708-X

LC 98-45250

A reissue of the title first published 1986 by Four Winds Press

A biography of the tsar who began the transformation of Russia into a modern state in the late seventeenth-early eighteenth centuries

The author's "material is presented with a modicum of oversimplification and a plethora of details that are sure to fascinate children. But what really makes this biography shine are its breathtaking illustrations. The meticulously researched, vivid scenes of Russian life during Peter's reign—courts, countryside, architecture, costumes—are beautifully rendered." Publ Wkly

Yomtov, Nel
Russia; by Nel Yomtov. Children's Press 2012 144 p. col. ill., col. maps (library) $40
Grades: 5 6 7 8   **947**
1. Russia 2. Russia (Federation)
ISBN 0531275450; 9780531275450

LC 2012000520

This children's book, by Nel Yomtov, describes the geography and culture of Russia as part of the "Enchantment of the World" series. The book includes "colourful photos . . . [with] views of foreign cities and landscapes," facts and statistics on "interesting people, places, and events" in Russian history, and "delicious, easy recipes [to] give readers the opportunity to experience foreign cuisine firsthand." (Publisher's note)

Includes bibliographical references and index

947.5 Caucasus

Dhilawala, Sakina
Armenia; [by] Sakina Dhilawala. 2nd ed.; Marshall Cavendish Benchmark 2008 144p il map (Cultures of the world) lib bdg $39.93
Grades: 5 6 7 8   **947.5**
1. Armenia
ISBN 978-0-7614-2029-3

LC 2007014890

First published 1997

"Provides comprehensive information on the geography, history, wildlife, governmental structure, economy, cultural diversity, peoples, religion, and culture of Armenia." Publisher's note

Includes glossary and bibliographical references

947.7 Ukraine

Bassis, Volodymyr
Ukraine; [by] Volodymyr Bassis & Sakina Dhilawala. 2nd ed.; Marshall Cavendish Benchmark 2008 144p il map (Cultures of the world) lib bdg $42.79
Grades: 5 6 7 8   **947.7**
1. Ukraine
ISBN 978-0-7614-2090-3

LC 2007019179

First published 1997

"Provides comprehensive information on the geography, history, wildlife, governmental structure, economy, cultural diversity, peoples, religion, and culture of Ukraine." Publisher's note

Includes glossary and bibliographical references

947.93   Lithuania

Kagda, Sakina

Lithuania; [by] Sakina Kagda & Zawiah Abdul Latif.
2nd ed.; Marshall Cavendish Benchmark 2008 144p il
map (Cultures of the world) lib bdg $42.79

Grades: 5 6 7 8   **947.93**

1. Lithuania

ISBN 978-0-7614-2087-3

LC 2007016290

First published 1997

"Provides comprehensive information on the geography,
history, wildlife, governmental structure, economy, cultural
diversity, peoples, religion, and culture of Lithuania." Publisher's note

Includes glossary and bibliographical references

947.96   Latvia

Barlas, Robert

Latvia; [by] Robert Barlas and Winnie Wong. 2nd ed.;
Marshall Cavendish Benchmark 2010 144p il map (Cultures of the world) lib bdg $42.79

Grades: 5 6 7 8   **947.96**

1. Latvia

ISBN 978-0-7614-4857-0 lib bdg; 0-7614-4857-8
lib bdg

LC 2009046001

First published 2000

This offers information on the geography, history, wildlife, governmental structure, economy, cultural diversity,
peoples, religion, and culture of Latvia

Includes glossary and bibliographical references

947.98   Estonia

Spilling, Michael

Estonia; 2nd ed.; Marshall Cavendish Benchmark
2010 142p il map (Cultures of the world) lib bdg $42.79

Grades: 5 6 7 8   **947.98**

1. Estonia

ISBN 978-0-7614-4846-4 lib bdg; 0-7614-4846-2
lib bdg

LC 2009021201

First published 1999

This describes the geography, history, wildlife, governmental structure, economy, cultural diversity, peoples, religion, and culture of Estonia

Includes glossary and bibliographical references

948   Scandinavia

Malam, John

The **Vikings**. PowerKids Press 2011 30p il (Dig it:
History from objects) lib bdg $25.25

Grades: 3 4 5   **948**

1. Vikings

ISBN 978-1-4488-3286-6; 1-4488-3286-1

LC 2010023867

This book about the Vikings includes information about
"homes and towns, daily life, clothing, religion, and entertainment. . . . The layout is crisp and the object illustrations
and photographs, plus the 'What does it tell us' section
provide visual understanding. These qualities will assist
the teacher who needs to differentiate instruction. The information is well-written and easily understood, well suited
to the curriculum and national standards. Website links are
intriguing and students will enjoy adding this piece to their
research." Libr Media Connect

Includes glossary and bibliographical references

Park, Louise

The **Scandinavian** Vikings; by Louise Park and Timothy Love. Marshall Cavendish Benchmark 2009 32p il
map (Ancient and medieval people) $19.95

Grades: 4 5 6   **948**

1. Vikings 2. Scandinavia -- Civilization

ISBN 978-0-7614-4445-9; 0-7614-4445-9

This title has "a simple and elegant design with the
proper balance of quality writing and quantity of information. . . . Handy time lines, well-chosen photos of ruins and
artifacts, quality illustrations, inset 'Quick Facts', and 'What
You Should Know About' features will grab reluctant readers and captivate even those with short attention spans." SLJ

Includes glossary

Raum, Elizabeth

What did the Vikings do for me? Heinemann Library
2010 32p il map (Heinemann infosearch: linking past to
present) lib bdg $29; pa $7.99

Grades: 3 4 5   **948**

1. Vikings

ISBN 978-1-4329-3745-4 lib bdg; 1-4329-3745-6 lib
bdg; 978-1-4329-3752-2 pa; 1-4329-3752-9 pa

LC 2009039662

"Children will likely know the Vikings primarily as marauding warriors, and although they won't stop thinking that
after reading this title, . . . they will also have a nicely balanced understanding of the other significant aspects and lasting impact of their civilization. Small chunks of text . . . sit
alongside a grab bag of digital illustrations, maps, paintings,
and photographs." Booklist

Includes glossary and bibliographical references

948.5   Sweden

Docalavich, Heather

Sweden; by Heather Docalavich and Shaina C. Indovino. Mason Crest Publishers 2013 64 p. col. ill., col. maps
(library) $22.95

Grades: 5 6 7 8   **948.5**

1. Sweden 2. European Union -- Sweden

ISBN 1422222608; 9781422222607; 9781422222911

LC 2010051848

This book by Heather Docalavich is part of the Major
European Union Nations series and looks at Sweden. "A
member of the EU since 1995, Sweden is one of the most
stable and [peaceful] countries in the world. It takes caring for its people and the environment very seriously." The
2008-2009 financial crisis is discussed. (Publisher's note)

Includes bibliographical references (p. 57-58) and index

Grahame, Deborah A.

Sweden; [by] Deborah Grahame. Marshall Cavendish Benchmark 2007 48p il map (Discovering cultures) lib bdg $28.50

Grades: 2 3 4   **948.5**

1. Sweden

ISBN 978-0-7614-1985-3 lib bdg; 0-7614-1985-3 lib bdg

LC 2006011474

An introduction to geography, history, government, and culture of Sweden

Includes glossary and bibliographical references

Heinrichs, Ann

Sweden; by Ann Heinrichs. Children's Press, an Imprint of Scholastic Inc. 2014 144 p. color illustrations (library binding) $40

Grades: 5 6 7 8   **948.5**

1. Sweden

ISBN 0531220176; 9780531220177

LC 2013022562

This book, by Ann Heinrichs, focuses on Sweden. The "country's culture, history, and geography are explored in detail, allowing readers a chance to see how people live. . . . Sidebars highlight especially interesting people, places, and events [and] recipes give readers the opportunity to experience foreign cuisine first-hand." (Publisher's note)

"Introduces Sweden, describing its geography, history, animals, government, economy, food, religion, cities, culture, and family life." Baker & Taylor

Includes bibliographical references and index

Phillips, Charles

★ Sweden; [by] Charles Phillips; Susan C. Brantly and Eric Clark consultants. National Geographic 2009 64p il map (Countries of the world) lib bdg $27.90

Grades: 4 5 6 7   **948.5**

1. Sweden

ISBN 978-1-4263-0389-0 lib bdg; 1-4263-0389-0 lib bdg

LC 2009275585

This describes the geography, nature, history, people & culture, and government & economy of Sweden

Includes glossary and bibliographical references

948.9   Denmark and Finland

Docalavich, Heather

Denmark; by Heather Docalavich and Shaina C. Indovino. Mason Crest Publishers 2013 64 p. col. ill., col. maps (hardcover) $22.95

Grades: 5 6 7 8   **948.9**

1. Denmark 2. European Union -- Denmark

ISBN 1422222381; 9781422222386

LC 2010051090

This book by Heather Docalavich and Shaina Carmel Indovino is part of the Major European Union Nations series and focuses on Denmark. "Denmark is a peaceful northern country that joined the EU in 1973. From the Vikings to the modern day, Denmark has a long [history]. Today, Denmark is a very environmentally conscious nation with a lot going on. It also must figure out how to deal with issues of im-

migration and the global recession as it looks to the future." (Publisher's note)

Includes bibliographical references (p. 57) and index

948.97   Finland

Tan, Chung Lee

★ Finland; [by] Tan Chung Lee. 2nd ed.; Marshall Cavendish Benchmark 2007 144p il map (Cultures of the world) lib bdg $39.93

Grades: 5 6 7 8   **948.97**

1. Finland

ISBN 978-0-7614-2073-6 lib bdg; 0-7614-2073-8 lib bdg

LC 2006015897

First published 1996

This provides "information on the geography, history, governmental structure, economy, cultural diversity, peoples, religion, and culture of Finland." Publisher's note

Includes glossary and bibliographical references

949.12   Iceland

McMillan, Bruce

Going fishing; written and photo-illustrated by Bruce McMillan. Houghton Mifflin Co. 2005 32p il $16

Grades: 2 3 4   **949.12**

1. Fishing 2. Iceland

ISBN 0-618-47201-0

LC 2004-15506

"This narrative photo-essay follows a young boy from Reykjavik to the fishing village where his two grandfathers live. Each takes his grandson out on his own boat to catch a type of fish important to Iceland. . . . The clarity of the color photos brings the people, their surroundings, and the process of fishing sharply into focus. . . . A delightfully illustrated presentation of fishing, family, and, of course, Iceland." Booklist

Somervill, Barbara A.

Iceland; by Barbara A. Somervill. Children's Press 2013 144 p. ill., maps (library) $40

Grades: 5 6 7 8   **949.12**

1. Iceland 2. Icelandic language

ISBN 0531256022; 9780531256022

LC 2012047117

This book by Barbara A. Somervill is part of the Enchantment of the World series and looks at Iceland. A discussion is offered of "how this land near the Arctic Circle came to be. . . . Maps and illustrations show the variety in the terrain and the areas of major geological activity. . . . Chapters [are] devoted to history, the economy, the government and the flora and fauna." (Children's Literature)

Includes bibliographical references (page 134) and index.

949.2 Netherlands

Docalavich, Heather

The **Netherlands**; by Heather Docalavich and Shaina Carmel Indovino. Mason Crest Publishers 2013 64 p. col. ill. (library) $22.95; (ebook) $28.95

Grades: 5 6 7 8   **949.2**

1. Netherlands

ISBN 9781422222539; 9781422222843; 9781422292716

LC 2010051464

This book on the Netherlands by Heather Docalvich and Shaina Carmel Indovino is part of the "Major European Union Nations" series. It presents an "overview of some of the successes and challenges that the Netherlands has faced and continues to face." Topics include "history, one on government, the economy, people and culture, and . . . . global climate change." (Children's Literature)

Includes bibliographical references (p. 57-58, 63) and index.

949.304 Belgium 1909-

Indovino, Shaina C.

Belgium; by Ida Walker and Shaina C. Indovino. Mason Crest Publishers 2012 64 p. col. ill., col. maps (library) $22.95

Grades: 5 6 7 8   **949.304**

1. Belgium 2. European Union -- Belgium

ISBN 1422222330; 9781422222331

LC 2010051078

This book, "part of the 'Modern World Nations' series, is an . . . introduction to the kingdom of Belgium. For middle school and high school readers, the chapters are descriptive of the physical features, the history, people, government, and economy. There is a chapter about the future of the nation as well as a description of life in the country today." (Children's Literature)

Includes bibliographical references and index.

949.35 Luxembourg

Sheehan, Patricia

Luxembourg; by Patricia Sheehan & Sakina Dhilawala. 2nd ed.; Marshall Cavendish Benchmark 2008 144p il map (Cultures of the world) lib bdg $42.79

Grades: 5 6 7 8   **949.35**

1. Luxembourg

ISBN 978-0-7614-2088-0

LC 2007014891

First published 1997

Discusses the geography, history, government, economy, and customs of the smallest of the Benelux countries

Includes glossary and bibliographical references

949.4 Switzerland

Harris, Pamela K.

Welcome to Switzerland; by Pamela K. Harris and Brad Clemmons. Child's World 2008 32p il map (Welcome to the world) lib bdg $27.07

Grades: 1 2 3 4   **949.4**

1. Switzerland

ISBN 978-1-59296-980-7 lib bdg; 1-59296-980-1 lib bdg

LC 2007038146

This briefly describes the geography, history, people, and culture of Switzerland.

"Report writers and browsers will appreciate [this book]. . . . The captioned, color photographs have a balanced gender representation. Maps, fast facts, and recipes round out excellent offerings." SLJ

Includes glossary and bibliographical references

949.5 Greece

Etingoff, Kim

Greece; by Kim Etingoff and Shaina C. Indovino. Mason Crest Publishers 2013 64 p. ill. (library) $22.95

Grades: 5 6 7 8   **949.5**

1. Greece

ISBN 1422222446; 9781422222447; 9781422222751

LC 2010051304

This book by Kim Etingoff and Shaina C. Indovino is part of the Major European Union Nations series and looks at Greece. The series "stresses the modern relationships, goals, and problems of the European Union. . . . Chapters begin with 'Modem Issues' and a brief summary of the country's history and government, followed by chapters on economy, people and culture, and 'Looking to the Future.'" (School Library Journal)

Green, Jen

★ **Greece**; [by] Greg Anderson and Kostas Vlassopoulos, consultants. National Geographic 2009 64p il map (Countries of the world) lib bdg $27.90

Grades: 4 5 6 7   **949.5**

1. Greece

ISBN 978-1-4263-0470-5 lib bdg; 1-4263-0470-6 lib bdg

This describes the geography, nature, history, people and culture, government and economy of Greece

Includes glossary and bibliographical references

Heinrichs, Ann

Greece; by Ann Heinrichs. Children's Press 2012 144 p. col. ill., col. maps (library) $40

Grades: 5 6 7 8   **949.5**

1. Greece -- History 2. Greece -- Civilization

ISBN 0531275434; 9780531275436

LC 2012000519

This book, part of the Enchantment of the World series, focuses on Greece. The books in the series each feature 10 "chapters, several maps, a fast-facts section, and a few references to other sources, including a referral to a Scholastic website . . . . The chapters cover geography, natural environment, history, politics, people and culture." (School Library Journal)

Includes bibliographical references and index.

Vanvoorst, Jennifer Fretland

The **Byzantine** Empire; by Jenny Fretland VanVoorst. Compass Point Books 2013 48 p. ill. (chiefly col.), col. map (library) $28.65; (paperback) $8.95

Grades: 6 7 8   **949.5**

1. Byzantine Empire -- Civilization

ISBN 075654565X; 0756545862; 9780756545659; 9780756545864

       LC 2012001994

This children's nonfiction book, by Jennifer Fretland VanVoorst, profiles the Byzantine Empire as part of the "Exploring the Ancient World" series. "The Byzantine Empire, which thrived from 395 to 1453, was a fascinating place. Its people thought of themselves as Romans, spoke Greek, and hailed from all across Europe and Asia. . . . It was a Christian empire that preserved and developed Europe's intellectual heritage at a time when western Europe was in decline." (Publisher's note)

Includes bibliographical references (p. 46-47) and index.

949.65 Albania

Knowlton, MaryLee

Albania; by MaryLee Knowlton. Marshall Cavendish Benchmark 2005 144p il map (Cultures of the world) lib bdg $42.79

Grades: 5 6 7 8   **949.65**

1. Albania

ISBN 0-7614-1852-0

       LC 2004-22236

An overview of the history, culture, peoples, religion, government, and geography of Albania

Includes glossary and bibliographical references

949.7 Serbia, Croatia, Slovenia, Bosnia and Hercegovina, Montenegro, Macedonia

Cooper, Robert

Croatia; [by] Robert Cooper and Michael Spilling. 2nd ed; Marshall Cavendish Benchmark 2011 144p il map (Cultures of the world) lib bdg $42.79

Grades: 5 6 7 8   **949.7**

1. Croatia

ISBN 978-1-6087-0215-2; 1-6087-0215-4

       LC 2010019626

First published 2001

Provides information on the geography, history, wildlife, governmental structure, economy, cultural diversity, peoples, religion, and culture of Croatia.

"Plentiful color photographs accompany substantial amounts of information." SLJ

Includes glossary and bibliographical references

Halilbegovich, Nadja

My childhood under fire; a Sarajevo diary. Kids Can Press 2006 120p il $14.95

Grades: 5 6 7 8   **949.7**

1. Yugoslav War, 1991-1995 2. Sarajevo (Bosnia and Hercegovina)

ISBN 1-55337-797-4

"In 1992, when the bombing started in Sarajevo, Halilbegovich, 12, kept a diary of her terrifying daily life under siege. Her terse vignettes replay the horror of her comfortable home torn apart." Booklist

Knowlton, MaryLee

Macedonia; by MaryLee Knowlton. Benchmark Books 2005 144p il map (Cultures of the world) lib bdg $42.79

Grades: 5 6 7 8   **949.7**

1. Macedonia (Republic)

ISBN 0-7614-1854-7

       LC 2004-22735

Describes the geography, history, government, economy, people, and culture of Macedonia

Includes glossary and bibliographical references

950 History of Asia

Law, Felicia

Atlas of Southwest and Central Asia. Picture Window Books 2008 32p il map (Picture Window Books world atlases) lib bdg $27.93; pa $7.95

Grades: 2 3 4   **950**

1. Asia 2. Middle East

ISBN 978-1-4048-3884-0 lib bdg; 1-4048-3884-8 lib bdg; 978-1-4048-3892-5 pa; 1-4048-3892-9 pa

This introduction to the geography of Southwest and Central Asia offers maps and information about countries, landforms, bodies of water, climate, plants, animals, population, people and customs, places of interest, industries, transportation, and Mount Everest

Includes glossary

Atlas of the Far East and Southeast Asia. Picture Window Books 2008 32p il map (Picture Window Books world atlases) lib bdg $27.93; pa $7.95

Grades: 2 3 4   **950**

1. Asia

ISBN 978-1-4048-3883-3 lib bdg; 1-4048-3883-X lib bdg; 978-1-4048-3891-8 pa; 1-4048-3891-0 pa

This introduction to the geography of the Far East and Southeast Asia offers maps and information about countries, landforms, bodies of water, climate, plants, animals, population, people and customs, places of interest, industries, transportation, and the Pacific Islands

Includes glossary

951 China and adjacent areas

Demi, 1942-

The **great** voyages of Zheng He; by Demi. Shen's Books 2012 64 p. col. ill., col. map (hardcover) $21.95

Grades: 3 4 5   **951**

1. China -- History 2. Explorers -- China -- Biography

ISBN 1885008457; 9781885008459

       LC 2012000934

This book is "Demi's account of 15th-century Chinese explorer Zheng He," demonstrating the "dazzling wealth his fleet carried back to China: 'Precious ambergris used for medicine, cowrie shells, sapphires, rubies, oriental topaz, and Persian carpers filled the Forbidden City.' His 62 'Treasure Ships' were the largest the world had ever seen, but Zheng He also displayed a wealth of intellect and imagination that allowed him to embrace religious tolerance and open-mindedness." (Publishers Weekly)

Henzel, Cynthia Kennedy

Great Wall of China. ABDO Pub. Co. 2011 32p il (Troubled treasures: world heritage sites) $25.65

Grades: 3 4 5   951

1. Great Wall of China

ISBN 978-1-61613-565-2; 1-61613-565-4

LC 2010021309

This "book describes in general terms [the Great Wall of China's] construction, . . . distinctive features, and history, as well as threats to its continued existence and both current and past restoration intitiatives. Revealing color photos taken from different heights and angles are supplemented by maps and by graphic reconstructions. . . . Henzel's distinctive approach gives this [book] unusual value for both assignment and general reading." SLJ

Includes glossary

Keister, Douglas

To grandmother's house; a visit to old-town Beijing. Gibbs Smith, Publisher 2008 un $15.95

Grades: K 1 2 3 4   951

1. China 2. Beijing (China) 3. Bilingual books -- English-Chinese

ISBN 978-1-4236-0283-5; 1-4236-0283-8

LC 2007033167

"Through an engaging bilingual narrative and lovely, full-color photos, Zhang Yue gives readers a tour of her hometown, beautiful and historic Beijing. She starts the day with a visit to her grandmother in a hutong , or neighborhood, in the old part of the city. Along the way she introduces the sights and shops in a voice that is natural and interesting, inviting readers to experience all of the little details that make Beijing unique. The photographs wonderfully capture the splendor of the major monuments as well as the fascinating bustle of the outdoor markets." SLJ

Levy, Patricia

Tibet; [by] Patricia Levy & Don Bosco. 2nd ed.; Marshall Cavendish Benchmark 2007 144p il map (Cultures of the world) lib bdg $42.79

Grades: 5 6 7 8   951

1. Tibet (China)

ISBN 978-0-7614-2076-7 lib bdg; 0-7614-2076-2 lib bdg

LC 2006015826

First published 1996

This provides "information on the geography, history, wildlife, governmental structure, economy, diversity, peoples, religion, and culture of Tibet." Publisher's note

Includes glossary and bibliographical references

Lewin, Betsy, 1937-

★ Horse song; the Naadam of Mongolia. [by] Ted and Betsy Lewin. Lee & Low Books 2008 un il $19.95

Grades: 2 3 4 5   951

1. Nomads 2. Festivals 3. Horse racing 4. Mongolia 5. Festivals

ISBN 978-1-58430-277-3; 1-58430-277-1

LC 2007025899

"In simple, captivating language, the Lewins describe their long journey. . . . Throughout, clearly presented cultural specifics mix with vivid sensory perceptions . . . but it's the color-washed sketches and beautiful full-page spreads . . . that will truly capture readers' attention." Booklist

Mara, Wil

People's Republic of China; by Wil Mara. Children's Press 2012 144 p. ill., maps (library) $40

Grades: 5 6 7 8   951

1. China -- Economic conditions

ISBN 053125352X; 9780531253526

LC 2011011308

This book, part of the Enchantment of the World, offers an "introduction to China. The book covers geography, climate, history, language, different ethnic groups, religion, government structure, and the arts. Frequent text boxes and large, bright photographs add extra information and deeper context. There is a heavy focus on the Chinese economy and recent strides made in human rights." (School Library Journal)

Includes bibliographical references and index.

Marx, Trish

Elephants and golden thrones; inside China's Forbidden City. written by Trish Marx; photographs and photograph selection by Ellen B. Senisi; foreword by Li Ji. Abrams Books for Young Readers 2008 48p il $18.95

Grades: 4 5 6 7   951

1. China 2. Forbidden City (Beijing, China)

ISBN 978-0-8109-9485-0; 0-8109-9485-2

LC 2007-022413

Introduces Beijing's Forbidden City, recounting some of the most famous incidents from its past, and describing its rooms, their function, and some of the daily rituals of palace life.

The author "brings the Forbidden City to life by telling stories about six different royal inhabitants from Zhengde, 'one of the worst emperors in Chinese history,' to Puyi, who became a pawn of the invading Japanese. . . . Beautiful drawings and photographs, some provided by the Palace Museum and some taken for this book, lend color and provide additional information. Of particular note are the photos of the interiors of buildings, a number of which are not regularly open to the public." Booklist

Includes bibliographical references

Riehecky, Janet

China; by Janet Riehecky. Lerner Publications Company 2008 48p il (Country explorers) lib bdg $27.93

Grades: 2 3 4   951

1. China

ISBN 978-0-8225-7129-2

LC 2006036731

This introduction to China covers "all of the areas of interest to students, including animals, sports, foods, celebrations, storytime, and even a few words in the country's native language. Small amounts of information are surrounded by current photographs, maps, charts, and illustrations. . . . Sure to grab the attention of even reluctant readers." SLJ

Includes glossary and bibliographical references

Sis, Peter

★ Tibet; through the red box. Farrar, Straus & Giroux 1998 un il maps $25

Grades: 4 5 6 7   951

1. Tibet (China)

ISBN 0-374-37552-6

LC 97-50175

A Caldecott Medal honor book, 1999

"When Sis opens the red lacquered box that has sat on his father's table for decades, he finds the diary his father kept when he was lost in Tibet in the mid-1950s. The text replicates the diary's spidery handwriting, while the illustrations depict elaborate mazes and mandalas, along with dreamlike spreads that are filled with fragmented details of the father's and son's lives. . . . Impeccably designed and beautifully made, the book has a dreamlike quality that will keep readers of many ages coming back to find more in its pages." Booklist

951.05   China--Period of People's Republic, 1949-

Chen, Jiang Hong

Mao and me; the Little Red Guard. [by] Chen Jiang Hong; [translated by Claudia Zoe Bedrick] Enchanted Lion Books 2008 77p il $19.95

Grades: 3 4 5   951.05

1. Children -- China 2. China -- History -- 1949-1976 -- Personal narratives

ISBN 978-1-59270-079-0; 1-59270-079-9

LC 2008037650

Originally published in French

Chen's "picture book memoir of growing up during the Cultural Revolution is not easy to read, but stands out for its epic sweep and unflinching honesty. Rendered in large panels, his ink and wash paintings document everything from the making of dumplings to the public humiliation of cherished neighbors. . . . [This shows] excellence in representing political upheaval." Publ Wkly

Jiang, Ji-li

Red scarf girl; a memoir of the Cultural Revolution. foreword by David Henry Hwang. HarperCollins Pubs. 1997 285p $16.99; pa $6.99

Grades: 6 7 8 9 10   951.05

1. Communism -- China 2. China -- History -- 1949-1976 -- Personal narratives

ISBN 0-06-027585-5; 0-06-446208-0 pa

LC 97-5089

"This is an autobiographical account of growing up during Mao's Cultural Revolution in China in 1966. . . . Jiang describes in terrifying detail the ordeals of her family and those like them, including unauthorized search and seizure, persecution, arrest and torture, hunger, and public humiliation. . . . Her voice is that of an intelligent, confused adolescent, and her focus is on the effects of the revolution on herself, her family, and her friends provides an emotional focal point for the book, and will allow even those with limited

knowledge of Chinese history to access the text." Bull Cent Child Books

951.25   Hong Kong

Kagda, Falaq

Hong Kong; [by] Falaq Kagda & Magdalene Koh. 2nd ed.; Marshall Cavendish Benchmark 2008 144p il map (Cultures of the world) lib bdg $42.79

Grades: 5 6 7 8   951.25

1. Hong Kong (China)

ISBN 978-0-7614-3034-6 lib bdg; 0-7614-3034-2 lib bdg

LC 2007048285

First published 1998

Surveys the geography, history, government, economy, and culture of Hong Kong

Includes glossary and bibliographical references

951.7   Mongolia

Pang, Guek-Cheng, 1950-

Mongolia; Pang Guek Cheng. Marshall Cavendish Benchmark 2010 144 p. col. ill., col. maps (Cultures of the world) (library) $42.79

Grades: 5 6 7 8   951.7

1. Mongolia

ISBN 9780761448495; 0761448497

LC 2009022643

This describes the geography, history, wildlife, governmental structure, economy, cultural diversity, peoples, religion, and culture of Mongolia

Includes bibliographical references and index.

951.9   Korea

Bowler, Ann Martin

All about Korea; stories, songs, crafts, and more. illustrated by Soosoonam Barg. Periplus Editions 2011 64p il $16.95

Grades: 3 4 5 6   951.9

1. Korea

ISBN 978-0-8048-4012-5; 0-8048-4012-1 (hardcover)

LC 2010040845

Introduces Korea, describing its history, culture, everyday life, food, sports, and holidays, as well as providing examples of Korean poems, songs, handicrafts, writing, legends, and folkore.

Includes bibliographical references

Cheung, Hyechong

K is for Korea; [by] Hyechong Chung, Prodeepta Das. Frances Lincoln 2008 un il $16.95

Grades: K 1 2 3   951.9

1. Alphabet 2. Korea

ISBN 978-1-84507-789-1; 1-84507-789-X

"This attractive book presents several aspects of Korea: its culture, traditional practices, national treasures, wildlife, food, and dress. Nicely designed pages showcase the excellent color photos. . . . Although other books speak more precisely of South Korea, North Korea, and the Korean peninsula, few are as accessible to primary-grade children as this one." Booklist

Santella, Andrew

The **Korean** War; by Andrew Santella. Compass Point Books 2007 48p il map (We the people) lib bdg $25.26; pa $8.95

Grades: 4 5 6 7　　　　　　　　　**951.9**

1. Korean War, 1950-1953

ISBN 978-0-7565-2027-4 lib bdg; 0-7565-2027-4 lib bdg; 978-0-7565-2039-7 pa; 0-7565-2039-8 pa

LC 2006006767

This "begins by explaining how North and South Korea became divided; the involvement of the United Nations and the United States; conflict between President Harry Truman and General Douglas MacArthur; eventual peace talks; and the division still occurring today. Accessible and straightforward, this book is an excellent one for the intended audience." SLJ

Includes bibliographical references

951.93　North Korea (People's Democratic Republic of Korea)

Kummer, Patricia K.

North Korea; by Patricia K. Kummer. Children's Press 2008 144p il map (Enchantment of the world, second series) lib bdg $38

Grades: 5 6 7 8 9　　　　　　　**951.93**

1. Korea (North)

ISBN 978-0-531-18485-1 lib bdg; 0-531-18485-4 lib bdg

LC 2007025693

In this introduction to North Korea "geography is the focus, but Kummer also discusses ancient and recent history, . . . the economy, religion, sports, education, and more. Without discounting the rich culture, the book doesn't shy away from more sensitive issues. . . . The open design will draw readers, with clear type on thick, high-quality paper; numerous maps and color photos and spacious back matter are also included." Booklist

Includes bibliographical references

Sonneborn, Liz

North Korea; by Liz Sonneborn. Children's Press; an imprint of Scholastic Inc. 2014 144 p. illustrations. maps (Enchantment of the world. Second series) (library binding) $40

Grades: 5 6 7 8　　　　　　　**951.93**

1. Korea (North)

ISBN 0531236781; 9780531236789

LC 2013003650

This book, by Liz Sonneborn, is part of the Enchantment of the World Series. "Each volume has been completely rewritten from a previous edition. . . . 'North Korea' has a new author and a strong political focus, discussing life under the new leader, Kim Jong-un. . . . Each volume in this . . . series includes extensive back matter with a detailed index." (Booklist)

Includes bibliographical references and index

951.95　South Korea (Republic of Korea)

Ryan, Patrick

Welcome to South Korea; by Patrick Ryan. The Child's World 2008 32p il map (Welcome to the world) lib bdg $27.07

Grades: 1 2 3 4　　　　　　　**951.95**

1. Korea (South)

ISBN 978-1-59296-978-4 lib bdg; 1-59296-978-X lib bdg

LC 2007036354

This briefly describes the geography, history, people, and culture of South Korea.

"Report writers and browsers will appreciate [this book]. . . . The captioned, color photographs have a balanced gender representation. Maps, fast facts, and recipes round out excellent offerings." SLJ

Includes glossary and bibliographical references

952　Japan

★ **Art** and life in rural Japan; Toho village through the eyes of its youth. Rolbin, Cyrus, editor. Next Generation Press 2011 176p il map $29.95; pa $24.95

Grades: 3 4 5 6　　　　　　　**952**

1. Japan 2. Country life -- Japan 3. Bilingual books -- English-Japanese

ISBN 978-0-9815595-4-4; 978-0-9815595-3-7 pa

"This gem of a book takes readers . . . into a small mountain community. . . . Simple, often poignant sentences in English and Japanese tell Toho's story, rich in history and culture. Stunning, full-color pictures capture verdant rice fields, jubilant school scenes, a lively festival, and expressive portraits of Toho's citizens. . . . A fascinating window into a vanishing way of life, this book holds appeal for both pleasure reading and reports." SLJ

Blumberg, Rhoda

★ **Commodore** Perry in the land of the Shogun. Lothrop, Lee & Shepard Bks. 1985 144p il map $21.99; pa $8.99

Grades: 5 6 7 8　　　　　　　**952**

1. Naval officers 2. Japan -- History 3. Japan -- Foreign relations -- United States 4. United States -- Foreign relations -- Japan 5. United States Naval Expedition to Japan (1852-1854)

ISBN 0-688-03723-2; 0-06-008625-4 pa

LC 84-21800

A Newbery Medal honor book, 1986

This "is a well-written story of Matthew Perry's expedition to open Japan to American trade and whaling ports. The account is sensitive to the extreme cultural differences that both the Japanese and Americans had to overcome. Especially good are the chapters and paragraphs explaining Japanese feudal society and culture. The text is marvelously complemented by the illustrations, almost all reproductions of contemporary Japanese art." SLJ

Includes bibliographical references

Moore, Willamarie

All about Japan; stories, songs, crafts, and more. illustrated by Kazumi Wilds. Tuttle Pub. 2011 63p il $16.95

Grades: 3 4 5 6   **952**
1. Japan
ISBN 978-4-8053-1077-9; 4-8053-1077-4
LC 2010040843

"In this treasure-trove of information, two children, one a Tokyo urbanite and the other from a rural village, introduce readers to their country and its culture, including geography, language, traditional arts, costume, etiquette, sports, and festivals. The dual narrators' conversational descriptions of their homes and daily routines will engage young readers while highlighting the differences between the Westernized big-city existence and the traditional way of life in Japan's countryside, deftly demonstrating the rich variety of lifestyles within this island nation. The scope of this book is remarkably comprehensive, covering almost anything a child would want to know." SLJ

Includes bibliographical references

Phillips, Charles
   ★ **Japan**; [by] Charles Phillips; Gil Latz and Kyohei Shibata, consultants. National Geographic 2007 64p il map (Countries on the world) lib bdg $27.90
Grades: 4 5 6 7   **952**
1. Japan
ISBN 1-4263-0029-8 lib bdg; 978-1-4263-0029-5 lib bdg
LC 2007296571

A basic overview of the history, geography, climate and culture of Japan.

This "clear, succinct [overview] will support assignments without overwhelming casual readers. . . . A good selection of recent, high quality color photographs gives the [book] visual appeal." SLJ

Includes glossary and bibliographical references

Riggs, Kate
   Samurai. Creative Education 2011 24p il (Great warriors) $16.95; pa $8.99
Grades: K 1 2   **952**
1. Samurai
ISBN 978-1-60818-003-5; 1-60818-003-4; 978-0-89812-574-0 pa; 0-89812-574-X pa
LC 2010019612

A simple introduction to the Japanese warriors known as samurai, including their history, lifestyle, weapons, and how they remain a part of today's culture through the martial arts

This title makes samurai "accessible to students just beginning to read on their own. The text and design of the [book is] spare, and vocabulary words are introduced unobtrusively. . . . The concepts are simple, but introduced without oversimplification that might lead to misunderstandings. [This is an] excellent [introduction] and fun to read aloud." SLJ

Includes glossary and bibliographical references

Somervill, Barbara A.
   Japan; by Barbara A. Somervill. Children's Press 2012 144 p. ill., maps (library) $40
Grades: 5 6 7 8   **952**
1. Japan 2. Japan -- Social life and customs
ISBN 0531253546; 9780531253540
LC 2011009503

This book is part of the Enchantment of the World series and focuses on Japan. "Topics such as climate, wildlife, history, government, pop culture, and the arts are all addressed, providing a . . . look at Japan's past and present. With content revised considerably from previous editions, this book goes beyond facts and statistics to give readers an intimate glimpse at typical Japanese youth through fictionalized anecdotes detailing moments in their daily lives." (School Library Journal)

Includes bibliographical references and index.

Takabayashi, Mari
   ★ **I live in Tokyo**; written & illustrated by Mari Takabayashi. Houghton Mifflin 2001 un il map $16
Grades: K 1 2 3   **952**
1. Tokyo (Japan) 2. Japan -- Social life and customs
ISBN 0-618-07702-2
LC 00-5964

"Seven-year-old narrator Mimiko takes readers on a month-by-month tour of contemporary Tokyo, briefly describing one or two festivals, customs, or facets of life each month. The narrative remains consistently childlike throughout. . . . This book is a model of efficiency and elegance, cramming numerous details into a small space in a compact and attractive manner." Horn Book

953 Arabian Peninsula and adjacent areas

King, David C.
   ★ **The United Arab Emirates**; [by] David C. King. 2nd ed; Marshall Cavendish Benchmark 2008 144p il map (Cultures of the world) lib bdg $42.79
Grades: 5 6 7 8   **953**
1. United Arab Emirates
ISBN 978-0-7614-2565-6
LC 2006030237

This describes the geography, history, government, economy, environment, people, and culture of the United Arab Emirates.

Includes glossary and bibliographical references

953.3 Yemen (Republic)

Hestler, Anna
   Yemen; by Anna Hestler and Jo-Ann Spilling. 2nd ed.; Marshall Cavendish Benchmark 2010 144p il map (Cultures of the world) lib bdg $42.79
Grades: 5 6 7 8   **953.3**
1. Yemen (Republic)
ISBN 978-0-7614-4850-1 lib bdg; 0-7614-4850-0 lib bdg
LC 2009021200

First published 1999

This describes the geography, history, wildlife, governmental structure, economy, cultural diversity, peoples, religion, and culture of Yemen

Includes glossary and bibliographical references

O'Neal, Claire
   We visit Yemen; by Claire O'Neal. Mitchell Lane Publishers 2012 63 p. ill. (chiefly col.), col. maps (library) $33.95; (ebook) $33.95

Grades: 4 5 6 7 8   **953.3**
1. Yemen (Republic) -- Description and travel 2.
Yemen (Republic)
ISBN 1584159618; 1612281060; 9781584159612;
9781612281063

         LC 2011016773

This book on Yemen by Claire O'Neal is part of the
"Your Land and My Land: The Middle East" series, which
"provides an . . . introduction to the history and geography
of several Middle Eastern and Southeast Asian countries
from a tourist's perspective." Also included are a "recipe
and a . . . craft project representing the country." (Booklist)
Includes bibliographical references and index.

953.53   Oman

Ejaz, Khadija
We visit Oman; by Khadija Ejaz. Mitchell Lane Publishers 2012 63 p. col. ill., col. maps (library) $33.95;
(ebook) $33.95
Grades: 4 5 6 7 8   **953.53**
1. Oman -- Description and travel 2. Oman
ISBN 1584159626; 1612281044; 9781584159629;
9781612281049

         LC 2011000724

This book on Oman by Khadija Ejaz is part of the "Your
Land and My Land: The Middle East" series, which "provides an . . . introduction to the history and geography of
several Middle Eastern and Southeast Asian countries from
a tourist's perspective." Also included are a "recipe and a . . .
craft project representing the country." (Booklist)
Includes bibliographical references (p. 59-61) and index.

953.6   Persian Gulf States

Cooper, Robert
Bahrain; [by] Robert Cooper and Jo-Ann Spilling. 2nd
ed.; Marshall Cavendish Benchmark 2011 144p il map
(Cultures of the world) lib bdg $42.79
Grades: 5 6 7 8   **953.6**
1. Bahrain
ISBN 978-1-6087-0213-8; 1-6087-0213-8

         LC 2010019621

First published 2000
Provides information on the geography, history, wildlife, governmental structure, economy, cultural diversity,
peoples, religion, and culture of Bahrain.
Includes glossary and bibliographical references

Orr, Tamra
Qatar; [by] Tamra Orr. Marshall Cavendish Bench-
mark 2008 144p il map (Cultures of the world) lib bdg
$42.79
Grades: 5 6 7 8   **953.6**
1. Qatar
ISBN 978-0-7614-2566-3; 0-7614-2566-7

         LC 2006033626

This describes the geography, history, government,
economy, environment, people, and culture of Qatar
Includes glossary and bibliographical references

953.67   Kuwait

O'Shea, Maria
Kuwait; by Maria O'Shea and Michael Spilling. 2nd
ed.; Marshall Cavendish Benchmark 2010 144p il map
(Cultures of the world) lib bdg $42.79
Grades: 5 6 7 8   **953.67**
1. Kuwait
ISBN 978-0-7614-4479-4 lib bdg; 0-7614-4479-3
lib bdg

         LC 2009007069

First published 1999
Provides information on the geography, history, wildlife, governmental structure, economy, cultural diversity,
peoples, religion, and culture of Kuwait
Includes glossary and bibliographical references

Sonneborn, Liz
Kuwait; Enchantment of the World. by Liz Sonneborn.
Children's Press, an imprint of Scholastic Inc. 2014 144 p.
ill., maps. (library binding) $40
Grades: 5 6 7 8   **953.67**
1. Kuwait 2. Kuwait -- Fiction
ISBN 053122015X; 9780531220153

         LC 2013026062

This book, by Liz Sonneborn, focuses on Kuwait. The
book discusses the "country's culture, history, and geography are explored in detail, allowing readers a chance to see
how people live. . . . Sidebars highlight especially interesting
people, places, and events . . . [and] easy recipes give readers the opportunity to experience foreign cuisine first-hand."
(Publisher's note)

"Many students turn to the Internet for writing reports,
but for reliably accurate, attractively presented and well-
calibrated information, the long-standing Enchantment of
the World series remains a superior choice. Each volume
has been completely rewritten from a previous edition—in
many cases to startling effect given recent political events.
Although the basic structure holds true to past versions, the
updated photographs are truly eye-popping and take care to
portray the countries as modern often opting for showing,
say, a surgeon at work rather than a rural farmer. It might not
be necessary for libraries to replace [this title], since it hasn't
changed radically, but this is a solid offering with updated
statistics. Each volume in this reliable series includes extensive back matter with a detailed index." Booklist
Includes bibliographical references and index

Tracy, Kathleen
We visit Kuwait; by Kathleen Tracy. Mitchell Lane
Publishers 2012 63 p. ill. (chiefly col.), col. maps (Your
land and my land. The Middle East) (library bound) $33.95;
(ebook) $33.95
Grades: 4 5 6 7 8   **953.67**
1. Kuwait -- Description and travel 2. Kuwait
ISBN 1584159588; 1612281001; 9781584159582;
9781612281001

         LC 2011002756

This book on Kuwait by Kathleen Tracy is part of the
"Your Land and My Land: The Middle East" series, which
"provides an . . . introduction to the history and geography
of several Middle Eastern and Southeast Asian countries

from a tourist's perspective." Also included are a "recipe and a . . . craft project representing the country." (Booklist)

Includes bibliographical references (p. 58-61) and index.

953.8   Saudi Arabia

Tracy, Kathleen

We visit Saudi Arabia; by Kathleen Tracy. Mitchell Lane Publishers 2011 63 p. col. ill., map (library) $33.95

Grades: 4 5 6 7 8   **953.8**

1. Persian Gulf region 2. Saudi Arabia

ISBN 1584159634; 9781584159636

LC 2011000728

This book by Kathleen Tracy is part of the Social Studies series and looks at Saudi Arabia. "One of the most socially conservative countries on earth, Saudi Arabia is defined by Islam and ancient traditions. At the same time, its vast oil fields have helped build glistening, modern cities filled with world-class restaurants and designer shops." (Publisher's note)

Includes bibliographical references and index.

954   India and neighboring south Asian countries

Apte, Sunita

India. Children's Press 2009 48p il map (True book) lib bdg $26

Grades: 3 4 5   **954**

1. India

ISBN 978-0-531-16890-5 lib bdg; 0-531-16890-5 lib bdg

LC 2008014786

This "attractive [work covers] the geography, history, people, customs, and economy of [India]. . . . [The book has] large-size print and colorful pictures. [It] contains a section about current political challenges such as the recent terrorist attacks in Mumbai, India." SLJ

Includes glossary and bibliographical references

Arnold, Caroline

★ Taj Mahal; by Caroline Arnold and Madeleine Comora; illustrated by Rahul Bhushan. Carolrhoda Books 2007 un il lib bdg $17.95

Grades: 4 5 6 7   **954**

1. Mogul Empire 2. Taj Mahal (Agra, India)

ISBN 978-0-7613-2609-0 lib bdg; 0-7613-2609-X lib bdg

LC 2001006685

Recounts the love story behind the building of the Taj Mahal in India, discussing how it was constructed and providing information on Indian culture.

"The small, detailed paintings are . . . set on beautifully constructed pages resembling those of illuminated manuscripts. . . . The book is sumptuous in appearance and presents a bit of history not often told for children." SLJ

Dalal, A. Kamala

★ India; [by] A. Kamala Dalal; Ramesh C. Dhussa and Pradyumna P. Karan, consultants. National Geographic 2007 64p il map (Countries of the world) lib bdg $27.90

Grades: 4 5 6 7   **954**

1. India

ISBN 978-1-4263-0127-8 lib bdg; 1-4263-0127-8 lib bdg

LC 2007039552

This describes the geography, nature, history, people and culture, government and economy of India

"What helps [this book] stand out from the pack is [its] high-quality, rich photography. . . . The photos provide as much information as the [text]. . . . The writing is straightforward and solid." SLJ

Includes glossary and bibliographical references

Mann, Elizabeth

★ Taj Mahal; a story of love and empire. by Elizabeth Mann; with illustrations by Alan Witschonke. Mikaya 2008 47p il (Wonders of the world) $22.95

Grades: 4 5 6 7   **954**

1. Mogul Empire 2. Taj Mahal (Agra, India)

ISBN 1-931414-20-3; 978-1-931414-20-3

LC 2008060054

This is a "dramatic retelling of the construction of the Taj Mahal. Mann begins with two pages of prose that relay the commonly told legend, but then proceeds to explode that legend with descriptive writing, colorful illustrations, ancient paintings, maps, and photographs." Booklist

Includes bibliographical references

954.03   India--Period of British rule, 1785-1947

Demi

★ Gandhi. Margaret K. McElderry Bks. 2001 un il $19.95

Grades: 3 4 5 6   **954.03**

1. Authors 2. Journalists 3. Passive resistance 4. Essayists 5. Pacifists 6. Memoirists 7. Political leaders 8. Writers on politics 9. India -- History -- 1765-1947, British occupation

ISBN 0-689-84149-3

LC 00-32911

"Beginning with Gandhi's failure as a student in India, this . . . biography traces Gandhi's life, from his first rallies against prejudice in South Africa to his remarkable victory over colonialism in India. . . . With extraordinarily detailed illustrations, decorated with gold leaf . . . and accessible, flowing text, veteran artist-author Demi reveals how a simple man who spun his own cloth became one of history's most important political and spiritual leaders." Booklist

McGinty, Alice B.

Gandhi. Amazon Childrens Pub 2013 40 p. (hardcover) $17.99

Grades: 1 2 3 4 5   **954.03**

1. Civil disobedience 2. India -- History -- 1765-1947, British occupation

ISBN 1477816445; 9781477816448

This children's picture book by Alice B. McGinty "tells . . . [the] present-tense story of Mohandas Gandhi's 24-day march to the sea in 1930 in search of freedom and peaceful change for the people of India. . . . His goal is to challenge 200 years of British rule by breaking the law prohibiting Indians from collecting salt from the sea." (Kirkus Reviews)

954.9　Other jurisdictions

NgCheong-Lum, Roseline, 1962-
Maldives; 2nd ed.; Marshall Cavendish Benchmark 2011 144p il map (Cultures of the world) lib bdg $42.79
Grades: 5 6 7 8　　　　　　　　　　　　954.9
1. Maldives
ISBN 978-1-6087-0217-6; 1-6087-0217-0
LC 2010019746
First published 2001
Provides information on the geography, history, wildlife, governmental structure, economy, cultural diversity, peoples, religion, and culture of Maldives.
Includes glossary and bibliographical references

Taylor-Butler, Christine
Sacred mountain; Everest. Lee & Low Books 2009 48p il $19.95
Grades: 5 6 7 8　　　　　　　　　　　　954.9
1. Mount Everest (China and Nepal)
ISBN 978-1-60060-255-9; 1-60060-255-X
LC 2008-30423
"The informative text is amply illustrated with well-chosen black-and-white and color photographs." SLJ
Includes glossary

954.91　Pakistan

Hinman, Bonnie
We visit Pakistan; by Bonnie Hinman. Mitchell Lane Publishers 2012 63 p. ill. (chiefly col.), col. maps (Your land and my land. The Middle East) (library) $33.95
Grades: 4 5 6 7 8　　　　　　　　　　954.91
1. Pakistan
ISBN 158415960X; 9781584159605
LC 2011030763
This book on Pakistan by Bonnie Hinman is part of the "Your Land and My Land: The Middle East" series, which "provides an . . . . introduction to the history and geography of several Middle Eastern and Southeast Asian countries from a tourist's perspective." Topics such as "terrorism and al-Qaeda" are covered along with "descriptions of the country's history and attractions." Also included are a "recipe and a . . . . craft project representing the country." (Booklist)
Includes bibliographical references (p. 59-61) and index.

Kwek, Karen
Pakistan; [written by Karen Kwek and Jameel Haque] Marshall Cavendish Benchmark 2010 48p il map (Welcome to my country) $19.95
Grades: 2 3 4 5　　　　　　　　　　　954.91
1. Pakistan
ISBN 978-1-60870-158-2; 1-60870-158-1
This is an introduction to Pakistan's culture, history, sports, religions, and foods.
"Beautifully illustrated. . . . The writing is clear. . . . [This title] will work well for reports and will be enjoyed by browsers." SLJ
Includes glossary and bibliographical references

Sonneborn, Liz
Pakistan; by Liz Sonneborn. Children's Press 2013 144 p. ill. (mostly col.), col. maps. (Enchantment of the world, second series) (library) $40
Grades: 5 6 7 8　　　　　　　　　　　954.91
1. Pakistan 2. Pakistan -- Description and travel
ISBN 0531275442; 9780531275443
LC 2012000505
This book, by Liz Sonneborn, is part of the "Enchantment of the World" series. In it the author provides information and photographs showcasing the people, places and events surrounding the South Asian country of Pakistan. Contents include photographs of Pakistani cities and landscapes, statistics describing the nation's features, and traditional Pakistani recipes.
Includes bibliographical references and index

954.92　Bangladesh

March, Michael
Bangladesh. Sea-to-sea Publications 2009 32p il map (Facts about countries) $28.50
Grades: 3 4 5　　　　　　　　　　　　954.92
1. Bangladesh
ISBN 978-1-59771-113-5; 1-59771-113-6
Describes the geography, history, industries, education, government, and cultures of Bangladesh
"The attractive layout includes color photographs and charts of current statistics as well as maps illustrating main farming regions, natural resources, or the literacy rates of girls and boys. The [text is] clear and succinct." SLJ
Includes glossary

955　Iran

DiPrimio, Pete
We visit Iran; by Pete DiPrimio. Mitchell Lane Publishers 2012 63 p. col. ill., maps (library) $33.95
Grades: 4 5 6 7 8　　　　　　　　　　　955
1. Iran -- History
ISBN 1584159545; 9781584159544
LC 2011016765
This book by Pete DiPrimio looks at Iran. "It is a Middle Eastern country with European (not Arabian) founders. It was the home of one of the ancient world's greatest empires, the Persian Empire. Its many ancient ruins include the palace complex of Persepolis, which was so big it took 150 years to finish. While the nation develops nuclear technology, its government—called an Islamic Republic—dictates people's lives, from the clothing they wear to the news they hear." (Publisher's note)
Includes bibliographical references and index.

Mara, Wil
Iran; [by] Wil Mara. Marshall Cavendish Benchmark 2007 48p il map (Discovering cultures) lib bdg $28.50
Grades: 2 3 4　　　　　　　　　　　　955
1. Iran
ISBN 978-0-7614-1986-0 lib bdg; 0-7614-1986-1 lib bdg
LC 2006011476

An introduction to the geography, history, people, and culture of Iran

Includes glossary and bibliographical references

956.04   Middle East--1945-1980

Marx, Trish

★ **Sharing** our homeland; Palestinian and Jewish Children at summer Peace Camp. photographs by Cindy Karp. Lee & Low Books 2010 47p il $19.95

Grades: 3 4 5 6   **956.04**

1. Palestinian Arabs 2. Jewish-Arab relations 3. Israel
ISBN 978-158430-260-5; 1-58430-260-7

"Alya, an Israeli Palestinian girl in a Muslim family, chooses to wear a hijab. Yuval, an Israeli Jewish boy, lives in a moshav farming community. In this picture-book photo-essay, crisp color images show the kids at home and then having fun at Peace Camp, where they swim, make arts and crafts, and do other universal summer-camp activities. Field trips introduce some kids to places they've never been, including a museum, a kibbutz, and an Arab village. . . . Marx weaves in detailed history of the Holy Land, from ancient times to 1948 and the establishment of the Jewish state and then the 1967 War. Throughout, she is frank about the continuing violence and conflict, and a contemporary image shows that the tall West Bank safety wall is also a divider between cultures. Realistic and upbeat, this moves beyond stereotypes and notions of the 'other.'" Booklist

Senker, Cath

The **Arab**-Israeli conflict; [by] Cath Senker. new ed.; Arcturus Pub. 2008 48p il map (Timelines) lib bdg $32.80

Grades: 5 6 7 8   **956.04**

1. Israel-Arab conflicts
ISBN 978-1-84193-725-0 lib bdg; 1-84193-725-8 lib bdg

LC 2007-7547

First published 2005 by Smart Apple Media

This describes current conditions in Israel and the occupied territories and includes a history of major events and political developments.

"A complex situation is clearly explained. . . . [This is] well-illustrated. . . . Throughout, the tone is nonjudgmental." SLJ [review of 2005 edition]

Includes bibliographical references

956.1   Turkey

LaRoche, Amelia

We visit Turkey; by Amelia LaRoche. Mitchell Lane Publishers 2012 63 p. ill. (chiefly col.), col. maps (library) $33.95

Grades: 4 5 6 7 8   **956.1**

1. Turkey -- Description and travel 2. Turkey
ISBN 1584159561; 9781584159568

LC 2011030765

This book on Turkey by Amelia Laroche is part of the "Your Land and My Land: The Middle East" series, which "provides an . . . . introduction to the history and geography of several Middle Eastern and Southeast Asian countries from a tourist's perspective." It "similarly mentions but does not dwell upon the rise of Islam and the hijab controversy." Also included are a "recipe and a . . . craft project representing the country." (Booklist)

Includes bibliographical references (p, 59-61) and index.

Shields, Sarah D.

★ **Turkey**; [by] Sarah Shields. National Geographic 2009 64p il map (Countries of the world) lib bdg $27.90

Grades: 4 5 6 7   **956.1**

1. Turkey
ISBN 978-1-4263-0387-6 lib bdg; 1-4263-0387-4 lib bdg

LC 2009275583

This describes the geography, nature, history, people and culture, government and economy of Turkey

Includes glossary and bibliographical references

956.7   Iraq

Falvey, David

Letters to a soldier; by First Lieutenant David Falvey and Mrs. Julie Hutt's fourth-grade class. Marshall Cavendish Children 2009 un il $16.99

Grades: 3 4 5   **956.7**

1. Soldiers 2. Children's writings 3. Contractors 4. Army officers 5. Iraq War, 2003- -- Personal narratives
ISBN 978-0-7614-5637-7; 0-7614-5637-6

LC 2008050268

"While serving in Iraq in 2008, First Lieutenant David Falvey received a packet of letters from Julie Hutt's fourth-grade class in Roslyn, NY. The children's correspondences and drawings, paired with Falvey's thoughtful answers and photographs from his deployment, are reproduced in an inviting, child-friendly format." SLJ

Goldish, Meish

Baghdad pups. Bearport Pub. 2011 32p il (Dog heroes) lib bdg $25.27

Grades: 3 4 5   **956.7**

1. Dogs 2. Iraq War, 2003- -- Personal narratives
ISBN 978-1-6177-2150-2; 1-6177-2150-6

LC 2010035187

This book "explores how a special division of the Society for the Prevention of Cruelty to Animals International (SPCAI) has been rescuing dogs who have befriended service people in Iraq, despite the clear disapproval of the United States military, which has strict laws about removing property, including animals, from war zones. . . . [This book is] engaging not just because the content is so compelling, but also because the [author has] highlighted specific dogs currently working in [this field]. The use of real names and full-color photographs on every page, many contributed by the individuals who work with these dogs, makes reading [this book] a personal experience. . . . [An] excellent [introduction] to [this] new [development] in service-dog training." SLJ

Includes bibliographical references

Malhotra, Sonali

Iraq. Marshall Cavendish Benchmark 2010 48p il map (Welcome to my country) $19.99

Grades: 2 3 4 5   **956.7**
1. Iraq
ISBN 978-1-60870-155-1; 1-60870-155-7

LC 2010006405

An overview of the history, geography, government, economy, language, people, and culture of Iraq.

"Beautifully illustrated. . . . The writing is clear. . . . [This title] will work well for reports and will be enjoyed by browsers." SLJ

Includes glossary and bibliographical references

O'Neal, Claire

We visit Iraq; by Claire O'Neal. Mitchell Lane Publishers 2012 63 p. ill. (chiefly col.), col. maps (library bound) $33.95

Grades: 4 5 6 7 8   **956.7**
1. Persian Gulf region 2. Iraq
ISBN 1584159553; 9781584159551

LC 2011016771

This book by Claire O'Neal is part of the Social Studies series and looks at Iraq. "Iraq's Tigris and Euphrates rivers turned this Middle Eastern desert into the world's first farmland. Over six millenia, Iraq's civilizations have laid foundations for the rest of the world. They built great stone ziggurats and soaring mosques. They invented the wheel, the calendar, and the written word. With their riches, they also attracted war." (Publisher's note)

Includes bibliographical references (p. 59-61) and index.

Samuels, Charlie

★ Iraq; [by] Charlie Samuels; Sarah Shields and Shakir Mustafa, consultants. National Geographic 2007 64p il map (Countries of the world) lib bdg $27.90

Grades: 4 5 6 7   **956.7**
1. Iraq
ISBN 978-1-4263-0061-5

LC 2007024675

This describes the geography, nature, history, people and culture, government and economy of Iraq.

Includes glossary and bibliographical references

Wilkes, Sybella

Out of Iraq; refugees' stories in words, paintings and music. Evans 2010 70p il map $17.99

Grades: 4 5 6 7   **956.7**
1. Refugees 2. Iraq
ISBN 978-0-237-53930-6; 0-237-53930-6

"Provides an concise overview of events before and during the invasion, interspersed with first-person narratives of Iraqi refugees, gathered while Wilkes worked with the United Nations Refugee Agency in Syria. . . . Moving photographs and artwork, quotations from political figures, and accessible language form a harrowing window into lives rarely paid witness." Publ Wkly

956.91   Syria

Yomtov, Nel

Syria; Nel Yomtov. Children's Press, an imprint of Scholastic Inc. 2013 144 p. color illustrations (library binding) $40

Grades: 5 6 7 8   **956.91**
1. Syria
ISBN 053123679X; 9780531236796

LC 2013000088

This book, by Nel Yomtov, focuses on Syria. The "country's culture, history, and geography are explored in detail, allowing readers a chance to see how people live. . . . Sidebars highlight especially interesting people, places, and events [and] recipes give readers the opportunity to experience foreign cuisine first-hand." (Publisher's note)

"Many students turn to the Internet for writing reports, but for reliably accurate, attractively presented and well-calibrated information, the long-standing Enchantment of the World series remains a superior choice. Each volume has been completely rewritten from a previous edition—in many cases to startling effect given recent political events. Although the basic structure holds true to past versions, the updated photographs are truly eye-popping and take care to portray the countries as modern—often opting for showing, say, a surgeon at work rather than a rural farmer. Syria obviously can't be completely up-to-date because of the ongoing rebellion, but it does a good job of explaining the roots of the unrest, along with the usual topics of food, religion, and customs. Each volume in this reliable series includes extensive back matter with a detailed index." Booklist

Includes bibliographical references and index

956.92   Lebanon

Sheehan, Sean

Lebanon; [by] Sean Sheehan & Zawiah Abdul Latif. 2nd ed.; Marshall Cavendish Benchmark 2008 144p il map (Cultures of the world) lib bdg $42.79

Grades: 5 6 7 8   **956.92**
1. Lebanon
ISBN 978-0-7614-2081-1 lib bdg; 0-7614-2081-9 lib bdg

LC 2006101735

First published 1997

"Provides comprehensive information on the geography, history, wildlife, governmental structure, economy, cultural diversity, peoples, religion, and culture of Lebanon." Publisher's note

Includes bibliographical references

956.93   Cyprus

Spilling, Michael

Cyprus; [by] Michael Spilling and Jo-Ann Spilling. 2nd ed.; Marshall Cavendish Benchmark 2010 144p il map (Cultures of the world) lib bdg $42.79

Grades: 5 6 7 8   **956.93**
1. Cyprus
ISBN 978-0-7614-4855-6 lib bdg; 0-7614-4855-1 lib bdg

LC 2009045689

First published 2000

This offers information on the geography, history, wildlife, governmental structure, economy, cultural diversity, peoples, religion, and culture of Cyprus

Includes glossary and bibliographical references

956.94 Palestine; Israel

Bowden, Rob, 1973-

Jerusalem; [by] Rob Bowden. World Almanac Library 2006 48p il map (Great cities of the world) lib bdg $31

Grades: 3 4 5 6   956.94

1. Jerusalem

ISBN 0-8368-5051-3

LC 2005043586

This describes the geography, cultures, work, play, history, and religions of Jerusalem

This is "attractive, informative . . . straightforward and objective." SLJ

Includes bibliographical references

Ellis, Deborah

Three wishes; Palestinian and Israeli children speak. Groundwood Bks. 2004 110p il map hardcover o.p. pa $9.99

Grades: 5 6 7 8   956.94

1. Palestinian Arabs 2. Israel-Arab conflicts

ISBN 0-88899-608-X; 0-88899-645-4 pa

"An excellent presentation of a confusing historic struggle, told within a palpable, perceptive and empathetic format." SLJ

Includes bibliographical references

Saul, Laya

We visit Israel; by Laya Saul. Mitchell Lane Publishers 2012 63 p. ill., maps (library) $33.95

Grades: 4 5 6 7 8   956.94

1. Israel -- Description and travel 2. Israel

ISBN 158415957X; 9781584159575

LC 2011024706

This book on Israel by Laya Saul is part of the "Your Land and My Land: The Middle East" series, which "provides an . . . introduction to the history and geography of several Middle Eastern and Southeast Asian countries from a tourist's perspective. . . . 'We Visit Israel' is clearly written from a Jewish Israeli perspective, but Saul makes sure to mention areas of conflict and controversy." Also included are a "recipe and a . . . craft project representing the country." (Booklist)

Includes bibliographical references (p. 60-61) and index.

Young, Emma

★ **Israel**; [by] Emma Young; Zvi Ben-Dor Benite, George Kanazi, and Aviva Halamish, consultants. National Geographic 2008 64p il map (Countries of the world) lib bdg $27.90

Grades: 4 5 6 7   956.94

1. Israel

ISBN 978-1-4263-0258-9 lib bdg; 1-4263-0258-4 lib bdg

This describes the geography, nature, history, people and culture, government, and economy of Israel.

Includes glossary and bibliographical references

956.95 Jordan and West Bank

Perdew, Laura

Understanding Jordan today; by Laura Perdew. Mitchell Lane Publishers 2014 63 p. (A kid's guide to the Middle East) $33.95

Grades: 4 5 6 7   956.95

1. Jordan

ISBN 1612286542; 9781612286549

LC 2014020462

This children's book, by Laura Perdew, part of the "Kid's Guide to the Middle East" series, "is an accurate and contemporary presentation that explores the Middle Eastern nation of Jordan with a focus on the country as it is today: current issues, culture, and lifestyle. The book is written in an easy-to-read enjoyable narrative form for elementary readers grades 3-6." (Publisher's note)

"Trying to sort through the Middle East can be difficult for even the most educated adults, but the titles in A Kid's Guide to the Middle East series breaks down the culture and ongoing conflict into manageable portions...Extensive back matter includes a recipe, craft, time line, glossary, and area facts. An essential series to help children appreciate and understand the rich diversity of this region." Booklist

Includes bibliographical references and index

Other recommended titles in the series are:

Understanding Afghanistan Today (2014)
Understanding Iran Today (2014)
Understanding Iraq Today (2014)
Understanding Israel Today (2014)
Understanding Lebanon Today (2015)
Understanding Palestine Today (2015)
Understanding Saudi Arabia Today (2014)
Understanding Syria Today (2014)
Understanding Turkey Today (2015)

958.1 Afghanistan

Ali, Sharifah Enayat

Afghanistan; by Sharifah Enayat Ali. 2nd ed.; Marshall Cavendish Benchmark 2006 144p il map (Cultures of the world) lib bdg $42.79

Grades: 5 6 7 8   958.1

1. Afghanistan

ISBN 978-0-7614-2064-4 lib bdg; 0-7614-2064-9 lib bdg

LC 2005034789

First published 1995

This is "well organized, informative, and entertaining. . . . Excellent-quality full-color photographs and reproductions show the people, landforms, buildings, and everyday activities of [Afghanistan]." SLJ [review of 1995 edtion]

Includes glossary and bibliographical references

Bjorklund, Ruth

Afghanistan; by Ruth Bjorklund. Children's Press 2012 144 p. col. ill., col. maps (library) $40

Grades: 5 6 7 8   958.1

1. Afghanistan 2. Afghanistan -- Description and travel

ISBN 0531253503; 9780531253502

LC 2011013627

This book by Ruth Bjorklund is part of the Enchantment of the World series and looks at Afghanistan. In each book, "colourful photos provide . . . views of foreign cities and landscapes," "sidebars highlight especially interesting people, places, and events," and "recipes give readers the opportunity to experience foreign cuisine firsthand." (Publisher's note)

Includes bibliographical references (p. 134-135) and index.

Fordyce, Deborah

Afghanistan; [written by Deborah Fordyce] Marshall Cavendish Benchmark 2010 48p il map (Welcome to my country) $19.95

Grades: 2 3 4 5   **958.1**

1. Afghanistan

ISBN 978-1-60870-149-0; 1-60870-149-2

This is an introduction to Afghanistan's culture, history, sports, religions, and foods.

"Beautifully illustrated. . . . The writing is clear. . . . [This title] will work well for reports and will be enjoyed by browsers." SLJ

Includes glossary and bibliographical references

O'Brien, Tony

★ Afghan dreams; young voices of Afghanistan. by Tony O'Brien and Mike Sullivan; photographs by Tony O'Brien. Bloomsbury Children's Books 2008 69p il map $18.99; lib bdg $19.89

Grades: 3 4 5 6   **958.1**

1. Afghanistan 2. Children -- Afghanistan 3. Teenagers -- Afghanistan

ISBN 978-1-59990-287-6; 1-59990-287-7; 978-1-59990-321-7 lib bdg; 1-59990-321-0 lib bdg

LC 2008-07004

"This handsome photo-essay features contemporary Afghan children ranging in age from 8 to 18 years. They were asked about their families, lives, and hopes for the future. The young people's straightforward statements tell much about the devastating effects of decades of war." SLJ

Whitfield, Susan

Afghanistan; [by] Susan Whitfield; Thomas Barfield and Maliha Zulfacar, consultants. National Geographic 2008 64p il map (Countries of the world) lib bdg $27.90

Grades: 4 5 6 7   **958.1**

1. Afghanistan

ISBN 978-1-4263-0256-5 lib bdg; 1-4263-0256-8 lib bdg

This describes the geography, nature, history, people and culture, government, and economy of Afghanistan.

Includes glossary and bibliographical references

958.104   Afghanistan--1919-

Lunis, Natalie

The takedown of Osama bin Laden; by Natalie Lunis. Bearport Publishing 2012 32 p. (Special ops) (lib. bdg.) $25.27

Grades: 4 5 6 7   **958.104**

1. United States. Navy 2. Terrorism 3. Terrorists -- Biography 4. United States. Navy. SEALs 5. Terrorism

6. Terrorists -- Biography

ISBN 1617724599; 9781617724596

LC 2011040472

In this book by Natalie Lunis on U.S. Navy SEALs "young readers will follow this elite group of soldiers on their raid and explore the context for their mission, from the 9/11 attacks by Al Qaeda to the war against terrorists in Afghanistan. Large, full-color photos, grade-appropriate text, and a narrative format [are designed to] keep kids turning the pages as they learn about [the U.S.] military." (Publisher's note)

Includes bibliographical references (p. 31) and index

958.4   Turkestan

King, David C.

Kyrgyzstan; [by] David C. King. Marshall Cavendish Benchmark 2005 144p il map (Cultures of the world) lib bdg $42.79

Grades: 5 6 7 8   **958.4**

1. Kyrgyzstan

ISBN 0-7614-2013-4

LC 2005001314

Describes the geography, history, government, economy, people, and culture of Kyrgyzstan

Includes glossary and bibliographical references

Pang, Guek-Cheng, 1950-

Kazakhstan; 2nd ed.; Marshall Cavendish Benchmark 2011 144p il map (Cultures of the world) lib bdg $42.79

Grades: 5 6 7 8   **958.4**

1. Kazakhstan

ISBN 978-1-6087-0455-2; 1-6087-0455-6

First published 2001

This offers information on the geography, history, wildlife, governmental structure, economy, cultural diversity, peoples, religion, and culture of Kazakhstan.

958.5   Turkmenistan

Knowlton, MaryLee

Turkmenistan; [by] MaryLee Knowlton. Marshall Cavendish Benchmark 2006 144p il map (Cultures of the world) lib bdg $42.79

Grades: 5 6 7 8   **958.5**

1. Turkmenistan

ISBN 0-7614-2014-2

LC 2005006455

Describes the geography, history, government, economy, people, and culture of Turkmenistan

Includes glossary and bibliographical references

958.6   Tajikistan

Abazov, Rafis

Tajikistan; [by] Rafis Abazov. Marshall Cavendish Benchmark 2006 144p il map (Cultures of the world) lib bdg $42.79

Grades: 5 6 7 8 **958.6**
1. Tajikistan
ISBN 0-7614-2012-6

LC 2005001166

Describes the geography, history, government, economy, people, and culture of the former Soviet republic of Tajikistan

Includes glossary and bibliographical references

959.3 Thailand

Morris, Ann

★ **Tsunami**; helping each other. by Ann Morris & Heidi Larson. Millbrook Press 2005 32p il map $15.95
Grades: 3 4 5 **959.3**
1. Tsunamis 2. Indian Ocean earthquake and tsunami, 2004 3. Thailand
ISBN 0-7613-9501-6

LC 2005-13616

The story of how one family in Thailand survived the tsunami of December 26, 2004, and, with the help of others, began to rebuild their lives.

"The brisk and straightforward text is enhanced by many excellent well-captioned color photos." Horn Book Guide

Rau, Dana Meachen

Thailand; [by] Dana Meachen Rau. Marshall Cavendish Benchmark 2007 48p il map (Discovering cultures) lib bdg $28.50
Grades: 2 3 4 **959.3**
1. Thailand
ISBN 978-0-7614-1989-1 lib bdg; 0-7614-1989-6 lib bdg

LC 2006011475

An introduction to the geography, history, people, and culture of Thailand

Includes glossary and bibliographical references

959.4 Laos

Dalal, A. Kamala

★ **Laos**; [by] A. Kamala Dalal. National Geographic 2009 64p il (Countries of the world) lib bdg $27.90
Grades: 4 5 6 7 **959.4**
1. Laos
ISBN 978-1-4263-0388-3 lib bdg; 1-4263-0388-2 lib bdg

This describes the geography, nature, history, people and culture, and govenment and economy of Laos

Includes glossary and bibliographical references

959.5 Malaysia, Brunei, Singapore

Foo Yuk Yee

Malaysia; by Heidi Munan, Foo Yuk Yee, and Jo-Ann Spilling. 3rd ed. Marshall Cavendish Benchmark 2012 144 p. col. ill., col. maps (library) $47.07

Grades: 5 6 7 8 **959.5**
1. Culture 2. Malaysia
ISBN 1608707857; 9781608707850

LC 2011004468

This book by Heidi Munan is part of the Cultures of the World series and looks at Malaysia. The "geography, history, economy and culture are all covered . . . . An entire chapter is devoted to the festivals, which are many because of the ethnic diversity of Malaysia. This is also made apparent in the section about food and manners, as the Muslims do not eat pork and the Hindus and Sikhs cannot eat beef, making it necessary to prepare various dishes for parties." (Children's Literature)

Includes bibliographical references and index.

959.57 Singapore

Layton, Leslie

Singapore; by Lesley Layton, Pang Guek Cheng, and Jo-Ann Spilling. 3rd ed. Marshall Cavendish Benchmark 2012 144 p. (library) $47.07
Grades: 5 6 7 8 **959.57**
1. Singapore
ISBN 1608707873; 9781608707874

LC 2011004479

This book is part of the Cultures of the World series and looks at Singapore. "Singapore is a small but mighty nation. Thanks to its strategic position and the energy of its people—the Malays, and migrant Chinese, Indians, and Eurasians—it is now the world's number one airport and sea port, a regional financial center, a telecommunications hub, and a favored tourist destination." (Publisher's note)

Includes bibliographical references and index.

959.6 Cambodia

Sobol, Richard

The **mysteries** of Angkor Wat; exploring Cambodia's ancient temple. Candlewick Press 2011 42p il map (Traveling photographer) $17.99
Grades: 3 4 5 6 **959.6**
1. Temples 2. Angkor (City) 3. Cambodia -- Antiquities 4. Angkor Wat (Angkor: Ancient city)
ISBN 978-0-7636-4166-5; 0-7636-4166-9

LC 2010041479

"This ancient temple, located in the jungles of Cambodia, has long been a source of mystery, reverence, and wonder. Sobol takes readers on a journey into the heart of the 1000-year-old ruins and presents a fascinating look at the history of the temple, the people who built it and worshipped there, and the current culture surrounding it. A good amount of information is presented while keeping the text conversational and accessible for young people. . . . The handsome book contains captioned color photographs on each page; they give interesting glimpses into the modern lives of the people living around this ancient site and a fascinating look at the ruins themselves. " SLJ

Includes glossary

959.604   Cambodia 1949-

Sonneborn, Liz

The **Khmer** Rouge; by Liz Sonneborn. Marshall Cavendish Benchmark 2012 80 p. ill. (some col.), col. map (library) $34.21; (ebook) $34.21

Grades: 5 6 7 8   **959.604**

1. Dith Pran, 1942-2008   2. Genocide -- Cambodia 3. Cambodia -- History -- 1975-   4. Parti communiste du Kampuchea   5. Cambodia -- History -- 1975-1979 6. Political atrocities -- Cambodia   7. Journalists -- Cambodia -- Biography   8. Political refugees -- Cambodia -- Biography

ISBN 1608704742; 9781608704743; 9781608706952 pdf

LC 2011005595

This book "tells the story of Dith Pran, a Cambodian journalist and translator who provided support to Sydney Schanberg, a New York Times correspondent. . . . Sadly, when Schanberg evacuated, Pran was forced to remain behind where he fell into captivity. Over a three year time period Dith Pran survived horrendous conditions but ultimately escaped and fled to Thailand. There, in a refugee camp, Pran was rescued by Schanberg and relocated to the United States." (Children's Literature)

Includes bibliographical references and index.

959.7   Vietnam

Green, Jen

Vietnam; [by] Jen Green. National Geographic 2008 64p il map (Countries of the world) lib bdg $27.90

Grades: 4 5 6 7   **959.7**

1. Vietnam

ISBN 978-1-4263-0202-2

LC 2007047832

This describes the geography, nature, history, people and culture, government, and economy of Vietnam.

Includes glossary and bibliographical references

Guile, Melanie

Culture in Vietnam; [by] Melanie Guile. Raintree 2005 32p il map lib bdg $29.29

Grades: 4 5 6 7   **959.7**

1. Vietnam

ISBN 1-4109-1135-7

LC 2004-16651

This "title includes a map and picture of the nation's flag as well as color photographs that bring to life the wide range of topics addressed. Two to four-page chapters briefly cover languages, history, people, religions, holidays and festivals, customs, minority groups, costumes and clothing, food, and arts and crafts, providing students with lots of cultural information. Text is well spaced in an overall neat and pleasing manner." SLJ

Includes bibliographical references

959.704   Vietnam--1945-

Skrypuch, Marsha Forchuk

Last airlift; a Vietnamese orphan's rescue from war. Marsha Forchuk Skrypuch. Pajama Press 2012 120 p. $17.95

Grades: 3 4 5 6   **959.704**

1. Orphans   2. Aeronautics -- Flights   3. International adoption   4. Evacuation of civilians -- Vietnam   5. Vietnam War, 1961-1975 -- Children

ISBN 098694954X; 9780986949548

This book "tells the story of the last Canadian airlift [from Vietnam] through the memories of one child, Son Thi Anh Tuyet. Nearly 8 years old, the sad-eyed girl . . . had lived nearly all her life in a Catholic orphanage." When "she and a number of the institution babies were taken away, placed on an airplane and flown to a new world. . . . she assumed that John and Dorothy Morris had chosen her to help with their three children; instead, she had acquired a family." (Kirkus Reviews)

959.8   Indonesia and East Timor

Cooper, Robert

Indonesia; by Gouri Mirpuri and Robert Cooper. 3rd ed. Marshall Cavendish Benchmark 2012 144 p. ill., maps (library) $47.07

Grades: 5 6 7 8   **959.8**

1. Indonesia -- History   2. Indonesia

ISBN 1608707830; 9781608707836

LC 200128607

First published 1990

This "nonfiction book in the 'Cultures of the World' series presents a . . . story of the physical, social and historical characteristics of Indonesia. . . . Throughout the book, also, there are textboxes that add . . . information to the subject matter and include . . . drawings of native musical instruments, weapons, foods and other" things. (Children's Literature)

"The pictures are lush, with captions in tiny print offering much additional information. The text is written smoothly and readably, and it contains a substantial amount of information." Booklist

Includes bibliographical references and index.

960   History of Africa

Bowden, Rob, 1973-

★ **African** culture; [by] Rob Bowden and Rosie Wilson. Heinemann Library 2009 48p il map (Africa focus) $30; pa $8.99

Grades: 4 5 6   **960**

1. Africa -- Civilization   2. Africa -- Social life and customs

ISBN 978-1-4329-2440-9; 1-4329-2440-0; 978-1-4329-2445-4 pa; 1-4329-2445-1 pa

LC 2008-48310

This book "presents a clear and timely overview of the diverse and complex continent. The full-color photographs are of exceptional quality. [The] book also includes interesting fact boxes, sidebars, maps, and a time line. [It] focuses on traditions and how they are relevant for today. Highlights include family and daily life; religion, beliefs, and customs; and the performing and visual arts." SLJ

Includes bibliographical references

★ **Ancient** Africa; [by] Rob Bowden and Rosie Wilson. Heinemann Library 2008 48p il map (Africa focus) $30; pa $8.99

Grades: 4 5 6   **960**

1. Africa -- History

ISBN 978-1-4329-2439-3; 1-4329-2439-7; 978-1-4329-2444-7 pa; 1-4329-2444-3 pa

LC 2008-48306

This book "presents a clear and timely overview of the diverse and complex continent. The full-color photographs are of exceptional quality. [The] book also includes interesting fact boxes, sidebars, maps, and a time line. . . . [It] begins with the origin of humankind and continues through the beginning of the slave trade in Europe and America. Early civilizations such as Egypt, ancient Ghana, the Mali Empire, Great Zimbabwe, and Kongo are represented. Invasions and explorations are discussed, as is slavery and colonialism." SLJ

Includes bibliographical references

★ **Changing** Africa; [by] Rob Bowden and Rosie Wilson. Heinemann Library 2009 48p il map (Africa focus) $30; pa $8.99

Grades: 4 5 6   **960**

1. Africa -- Social conditions 2. Africa -- Economic conditions

ISBN 978-1-4329-2437-9; 1-4329-2437-0; 978-1-4329-2442-3 pa; 1-4329-2442-7 pa

LC 2008-48277

This book "presents a clear and timely overview of the diverse and complex continent. The full-color photographs are of exceptional quality. [The] book also includes interesting fact boxes, sidebars, maps, and a time line. . . . [It] presents recent positive and negative changes. The rise of poverty and slums is explored, as is the lowered life expectancy due to the spread of malaria and HIV/AIDS. Positive changes include the freedom that voting has brought." SLJ

Includes bibliographical references

★ **Modern** Africa; [by] Rosie Wilson and Rob Bowden. Heinemann Library 2009 48p il map (Africa focus) $30; pa $8.99

Grades: 4 5 6   **960**

1. Africa

ISBN 978-1-4329-2438-6; 1-4329-2438-9; 978-1-4329-2443-0 pa; 1-4329-2443-5 pa

This book "presents a clear and timely overview of the diverse and complex continent. The full-color photographs are of exceptional quality. [The] book also includes interesting fact boxes, sidebars, maps, and a time line. . . . [It] chronicles the history of colonial Africa to independence, and the changes that have arisen and continue to manifest themselves. Topics include apartheid and recent and ongoing violence in Rwanda, Darfur, and the Congo. While corrupt leaders continue to hamper Africa's attempts at advancement, the exportation of oil as well as aid from missionaries and international organizations are presented as hopes for the future." SLJ

Mooney, Carla

Amazing Africa; projects you can build yourself. illustrated by Megan Stearns. Nomad Press 2010 122p il (Build it yourself) pa $15.95

Grades: 4 5 6 7   **960**

1. Handicraft 2. Africa

ISBN 978-1-934670-41-5; 1-934670-41-3

"Casual and informative, this large, attractive, browsable paperback . . . offers a view of contemporary African life that reaches far beyond the usual scenery-and-wildlife tourists' perspective. Blending history, culture, and tradition with politics and life in both cities and rural areas, the chapters begin with a look at natural wonders and dangerous wildlife that will grab readers, then move on to historical discussions of humankind's birthplace and early civilizations. . . . The open design includes sketches on every page. . . . The craft projects [include making] your own Maasai beaded necklace, kente cloth, woven basket, galimoto doll, and . . . more." Booklist

Murray, Jocelyn

Africa; updated by Brian A. Stewart. 3rd ed.; Chelsea House 2007 96p il map (Cultural atlas for young people) $35

Grades: 5 6 7 8   **960**

1. Africa -- History 2. Africa -- Civilization

ISBN 978-0-8160-6826-5; 0-8160-6826-7

First published 1990

Presents information on the history and various regions and cultures of Africa.

Includes glossary and bibliographical references

Musgrove, Margaret

★ **Ashanti** to Zulu: African traditions; pictures by Leo and Diane Dillon. Dial Bks. for Young Readers 1976 un il $21.99; pa $6.99

Grades: 3 4 5 6   **960**

1. Ethnology -- Africa 2. Africa -- Social life and customs

ISBN 0-8037-0357-0; 0-14-054604-9 pa

Awarded the Caldecott Medal, 1977

"In brief texts arranged in alphabetical order, each accompanied by a large framed illustration, the author introduces 'the reader to twenty-six African peoples by depicting a custom important to each.' . . . In most of the paintings the artists 'have included a man, a woman, a child, their living quarters, an artifact, and a local animal' and have, in this way, stressed the human and the natural ambience of the various peoples depicted." Horn Book

961.1 Tunisia

Brown, Roslind Varghese

Tunisia; [by] Roslind Varghese Brown & Michael Spilling. 2nd ed.; Marshall Cavendish Benchmark 2008 144p il map (Cultures of the world) lib bdg $42.79

Grades: 5 6 7 8   **961.1**

1. Tunisia

ISBN 978-0-7614-3037-7 lib bdg; 0-7614-3037-7 lib bdg

LC 2007050798

First published 1998

"Provides comprehensive information on the geography, history, wildlife, governmental structure, economy, cultural diversity, peoples, religion, and culture of Tunisia." Publisher note

Includes glossary and bibliographical references

962   Egypt, Sudan, South Sudan

Heinrichs, Ann
    The **Nile**. Marshall Cavendish Benchmark 2008 96p il map (Nature's wonders) lib bdg $24.95

Grades: 5 6 7 8   **962**
    1. Nile River   2. Nile River valley
    ISBN 978-0-7614-2854-1

                       LC 2007019187
    "It's tough to make a river interesting, but this . . . does an admirable job of it. . . . Crisp, full-color photos and original artwork decorate nearly every page. . . . [This is a] well-thought-out natural history." Booklist

Includes glossary and bibliographical references

962.055   Egypt

Abouraya, Karen Leggett
    ★ **Hands** around the library; protecting Egypt's treasured books. by Susan L. Roth and Karen Leggett Abouraya; collages by Susan L. Roth. Dial Books for Young Readers 2012 40 p. (hardcover) $16.99

Grades: 1 2 3   **962.055**
    1. Libraries   2. Arab Spring, 2010-   3. Picture books for children   4. Cultural property -- Protection   5. Egypt -- History -- 21st century   6. Libraries -- Egypt -- Alexandria   7. Aliksandrina; (Library) -- History   8. Libraries -- Destruction and pillage -- Egypt -- Alexandria
    ISBN 0803737475; 9780803737471

                       LC 2011038198
    Author Susan L. Roth's book shows the "days of the Arab Spring when Egyptians marched to bring down their government, [and] youthful demonstrators and library staff stood together to protect the Bibliotheca Alexandrina, contemporary counterpart to the Great Library of Alexandria, from vandalism. Roth's . . . collages capture these heady moments, blending photos, papers and fabrics to bring the people's positive actions and the building's intriguing facade together in a celebration of patriotism and libraries." (Kirkus Reviews)

962.4   Sudan and South Sudan

Brownlie, Ali
    Sudan in our world; by Ali Brownlie Bojang. Smart Apple Media 2010 32p il (Countries in our world) lib bdg $28.50

Grades: 5 6 7 8   **962.4**
    1. Sudan
    ISBN 978-1-59920-434-5 lib bdg; 1-59920-434-7 lib bdg

                       LC 2009052421

"Issues such as Civil War, fighting in Darfur, the government, and millions of displaced refugees continue to cripple the country and impede its advancement. While Sudan is rich in resources, its future remains uncertain. [This title] will appeal to children interested in learning more about Africa and those needing factual information for reports." SLJ

Includes glossary and bibliographical references

Levy, Patricia
    Sudan; [by] Patricia Levy and Zawiah Abdul Latif. 2nd ed.; Marshall Cavendish Benchmark 2008 144p il map (Cultures of the world) lib bdg $42.79

Grades: 5 6 7 8   **962.4**
    1. Sudan
    ISBN 978-0-7614-2083-5 lib bdg; 0-7614-2083-5 lib bdg

                       LC 2006101725
    Describes the geography, history, government, economy, people, lifestyle, religion, language, arts, leisure, festivals, and food of Sudan

Includes bibliographical references

963   Ethiopia and Eritrea

Gish, Steven
    Ethiopia; [by] Steven Gish & Winnie Thay & Zawiah Abdul Latif. 2nd ed.; Marshall Cavendish Benchmark 2007 144p il map (Cultures of the world) lib bdg $42.79

Grades: 5 6 7 8   **963**
    1. Ethiopia
    ISBN 978-0-7614-2025-5 lib bdg; 0-7614-2025-8 lib bdg

                       LC 2006020819
    First published 1996
    This provides "information on the geography, history, governmental structure, economy, cultural diversity, peoples, religion, and culture of Ethiopia." Publisher's note

Includes glossary and bibliographical references

963.5   Eritrea

NgCheong-Lum, Roseline, 1962-
    Eritrea; 2nd ed.; Marshall Cavendish Benchmark 2011 144p il map (Cultures of the world) lib bdg $42.79

Grades: 5 6 7 8   **963.5**
    1. Eritrea
    ISBN 978-1-6087-0454-5; 1-6087-0454-8

                       LC 2010035973
    First published 2001
    Provides information on the geography, history, wildlife, governmental structure, economy, cultural diversity, peoples, religion, and culture of Eritea.
    "Plentiful color photographs accompany substantial amounts of information." SLJ

Includes glossary and bibliographical references

964 Morocco, Ceuta, Melilla, Western Sahara, Canary Islands

Seward, Pat
Morocco; [by] Pat Seward & Orin Hargraves. 2nd ed.; Marshall Cavendish Benchmark 2006 144p il map (Cultures of the world) lib bdg $42.79
Grades: 5 6 7 8   **964**
1. Morocco
ISBN 0-7614-2051-7
     LC 2005020782
First published 1995
Describes the geography, history, government, economy, people, and culture of Morocco
Includes glossary and bibliographical references

965 Algeria

Kagda, Falaq
Algeria; [by] Falaq Kagda & Zawiah Abdul Latif. 2nd ed.; Marshall Cavendish Benchmark 2008 144p il map (Cultures of the world) lib bdg $42.79
Grades: 5 6 7 8   **965**
1. Algeria
ISBN 978-0-7614-2085-9 lib bdg; 0-7614-2085-1 lib bdg
     LC 2007014888
First published 1997
"Provides comprehensive information on the geography, history, wildlife, governmental structure, economy, cultural diversity, peoples, religion, and culture of Algeria." Publisher's note
Includes glossary and bibliographical references

966.1 Mauritania

Blauer, Ettagale
Mauritania; [by] Ettagale Blauer & Jason Lauré. Marshall Cavendish Benchmark 2009 144p il map (Cultures of the world) lib bdg $42.79
Grades: 5 6 7 8   **966.1**
1. Mauritania
ISBN 978-0-7614-3116-9
This describes the geography, history, government, economy, environment, people, and culture of Mauritania

966.2 Mali, Burkina Faso, Niger

Blauer, Ettagale
Mali; [by] Ettagale Blauer & Jason Lauré. 2nd ed.; Marshall Cavendish Benchmark 2008 144p il map (Cultures of the world) lib bdg $42.79
Grades: 5 6 7 8   **966.2**
1. Mali
ISBN 978-0-7614-2568-7
First published 1997
This describes the geography, history, government, economy, environment, people, and culture of Mali
Includes glossary and bibliographical references

McKissack, Patricia C.
The royal kingdoms of Ghana, Mali, and Songhay; life in medieval Africa. [by] Patricia and Fredrick McKissack. Holt & Co. 1993 142p il maps hardcover o.p. pa $12.99
Grades: 5 6 7 8   **966.2**
1. Ghana Empire 2. Songhai Empire 3. Mali -- History
ISBN 0-8050-4259-8 pa
     LC 93-4838
Examines the civilizations of the Western Sudan which flourished from 700 to 1700 A.D., acquiring such vast wealth that they became centers of trade and culture for a continent
"The McKissacks are careful to distinguish what is known from what is surmised; they draw on the oral tradition, eyewitness accounts, and contemporary scholarship; and chapter source notes discuss various conflicting views of events." Booklist
Includes bibliographical references

966.3 Senegal

Berg, Elizabeth
Senegal; by Elizabeth L. Berg and Ruth Lau. 2nd ed.; Marshall Cavendish Benchmark 2009 144p il map (Cultures of the world) lib bdg $42.79
Grades: 5 6 7 8   **966.3**
1. Senegal
ISBN 978-0-7614-4481-7 lib bdg; 0-7614-4481-5 lib bdg
     LC 2009007067
First published 1999
Describes the geography, history, wildlife, governmental structure, economy, cultural diversity, peoples, religion, and culture of Senegal
Includes glossary and bibliographical references

966.4 Sierra Leone

LeVert, Suzanne
Sierra Leone; [by] Suzanne LeVert. Marshall Cavendish Benchmark 2007 144p il map (Cultures of the world) lib bdg $42.79
Grades: 5 6 7 8   **966.4**
1. Sierra Leone
ISBN 978-0-7614-2334-8 lib bdg; 0-7614-2334-6 lib bdg
     LC 2005035964
This provides "information on the geography, history, governmental structure, economy, cultural diversity, peoples, religion, and culture of Sierra Leone." Publisher's note
Includes glossary and bibliographical references

966.68 Cote d'Ivoire (Ivory Coast)

Sheehan, Patricia
Cote d'Ivoire; [by] Patricia Sheehan and Jacqueline Ong. 2nd ed.; Marshall Cavendish Benchmark 2010 144p il map (Cultures of the world) lib bdg $42.79

Grades: 5 6 7 8   966.68
1. Ivory Coast
ISBN 978-0-7614-4854-9 lib bdg; 0-7614-4854-3
lib bdg

LC 2009045688

First published 2000
This offers information on the geography, history, wildlife, governmental structure, economy, cultural diversity,
peoples, religion, and culture of Cote d'Ivoire
Includes glossary and bibliographical references

966.7   Ghana

Levy, Patricia
Ghana; [by] Patricia Levy and Winnie Wong. 2nd ed.;
Marshall Cavendish Benchmark 2010 144p il map (Cul-
tures of the world) lib bdg $42.79
Grades: 5 6 7 8   966.7
1. Ghana
ISBN 978-0-7614-4847-1 lib bdg; 0-7614-4847-0
lib bdg
First published 1999
Introduces the geography, history, government, econo-
my, culture, and people of Ghana
Includes glossary and bibliographical references

966.9   Nigeria

Giles, Bridget
★ Nigeria; [by] Bridget Giles. National Geographic
2007 64p il map (Countries of the world) lib bdg $27.90
Grades: 4 5 6 7   966.9
1. Nigeria
ISBN 978-1-4263-0124-7

LC 2007024729

This describes the geography, nature, history, people and
culture, government, and economy of Nigeria
"What helps [this book] stand out from the pack is [its]
high-quality, rich photography. . . . The photos provide as
much information as the [text]. . . . The writing is straightforward and solid." SLJ
Includes glossary and bibliographical references

Oluonye, Mary N.
Nigeria; by Mary N. Oluonye. Lerner Publications
Company 2007 48p il map (Country explorers) lib bdg
$27.93; pa $8.95
Grades: 2 3 4   966.9
1. Nigeria
ISBN 978-0-8225-7131-5 lib bdg; 978-0-8225-8509-
1 pa

LC 2006035846

"With short, chatty sentences and a lively, contemporary
color photo on every page, this title . . . gives a brief overview of the history, geography, and culture of Nigeria. . . .
The current information is not oversimplified." Booklist

Onyefulu, Ifeoma
Ikenna goes to Nigeria. Frances Lincoln 2007 33p il
map hardcover o.p. $16.95

Grades: K 1 2 3   966.9
1. Nigeria
ISBN 978-1-84507-585-9; 1-84507-585-4; 978-1-
84507-960-4 pa; 1-84507-960-4 pa
"Onyefulu delivers another photo-essay filled with vivid, colorful photographs, accompanied by brief, clear text
about the land, people, and culture of her native Nigeria. The
text is narrated by the author's son. . . . An outline map of
the country shows the location of the cities/towns/villages
that Ikenna will visit during the course of his trip. . . . The
clear images contain a wealth of detail and provide valuable
visual insight into the people and culture." SLJ

967.11   Cameroon

Sheehan, Sean
Cameroon; [by] Sean Sheehan and Josie Elias. 2nd
ed.; Marshall Cavendish Benchmark 2011 144p il map
(Cultures of the world) lib bdg $42.79
Grades: 5 6 7 8   967.11
1. Cameroon
ISBN 978-1-6087-0214-5; 1-6087-0214-6

LC 2010019623

First published 2001
Provides information on the geography, history, wildlife, governmental structure, economy, cultural diversity,
peoples, religion, and culture of Cameroon.
Includes glossary and bibliographical references

967.3   Angola

Sheehan, Sean
Angola; [by] Sean Sheehan and Jui Lin Yong. 2nd ed.;
Marshall Cavendish Benchmark 2010 144p il map (Cul-
tures of the world) lib bdg $42.79
Grades: 5 6 7 8   967.3
1. Angola
ISBN 978-0-7614-4845-7 lib bdg; 0-7614-4845-4
lib bdg

LC 2009021203

"Provides comprehensive information on the geography,
history, wildlife, governmental structure, economy, cultural
diversity, peoples, religion, and culture of Angola." Publisher's note
Includes glossary and bibliographical references

967.43   Chad

Kneib, Martha
Chad; [by] Martha Kneib. Marshall Cavendish Benchmark 2007 144p il map (Cultures of the world) lib bdg
$42.79
Grades: 5 6 7 8   967.43
1. Chad
ISBN 978-0-7614-2327-0 lib bdg; 0-7614-2327-3
lib bdg

LC 2005027079

This provides "information on the geography, history, governmental structure, economy, cultural diversity, peoples, religion, and culture of Chad." Publisher's note

Includes glossary and bibliographical references

967.51 Democratic Republic of the Congo

Heale, Jay

Democratic Republic of the Congo; by Jay Heale and Yong Jui Lin. 2nd ed.; Marshall Cavendish Benchmark 2009 144p il map (Cultures of the world) lib bdg $42.79

Grades: 5 6 7 8 **967.51**

1. Congo (Republic)
ISBN 978-0-7614-4478-7 lib bdg; 0-7614-4478-5 lib bdg

LC 2009003195

First published 1999

Describes the geography, history, government, economy, people, lifestyle, religion, languages, arts, leisure, festivals, and food of The Democratic Republic of the Congo

Includes glossary and bibliographical references

967.571 Rwanda

King, David C.

Rwanda; [by] David C. King. Marshall Cavendish Benchmark 2007 144p il map (Cultures of the world) lib bdg $42.79

Grades: 5 6 7 8 **967.571**

1. Rwanda
ISBN 978-0-7614-2333-1 lib bdg; 0-7614-2333-8 lib bdg

LC 2005031817

This provides "information on the geography, history, governmental structure, economy, cultural diversity, peoples, religion, and culture of Rwanda." Publisher's note

Includes glossary and bibliographical references

967.61 Uganda

Barlas, Robert

Uganda; [by] Robert Barlas and Yong Jui Lin. 2nd ed.; Marshall Cavendish Benchmark 2010 144p il map (Cultures of the world) lib bdg $42.79

Grades: 5 6 7 8 **967.61**

1. Uganda
ISBN 978-0-7614-4859-4 lib bdg; 0-7614-4859-4 lib bdg

LC 2009046002

First published 2000

This offers information on the geography, history, wildlife, governmental structure, economy, cultural diversity, peoples, religion, and culture of Uganda

Includes glossary and bibliographical references

967.62 Kenya

Tanguay, Bridget

Kenya; Bridget Tanguay; Chege Githiora and Tabitha Otieno, consultants. National Geographic 2006 p. cm. **967.62**

1. Kenya
ISBN 978-0-7922-7628-9 (hardcover: alk. paper); 978-0-7922-7668-5 (lib bdg: alk. paper)

LC 2006029047

Includes bibliographical references

Williams, Karen Lynn

Beatrice's dream; a story of Kibera slum. photographs by Wendy Stone. Frances Lincoln 2011 il $17.95

Grades: 3 4 5 6 **967.62**

1. Kenya
ISBN 978-1-84780-019-0; 1-84780-019-X

"Beatrice, a 13-year-old orphan who lives with her brother and his wife in a Kenyan slum, describes her current life and her hopes for the future. She touches on her 30-minute walks to school, her classes, and helping her brother in his shop. Vivid color photographs give readers a firsthand glimpse into a world about which they are likely to know nothing. . . . Although the book deals with difficult subject matter, it does so in an upbeat and positive way. . . . A unique and important addition." SLJ

967.73 Somalia

Hassig, Susan M.

Somalia; by Susan M. Hassig & Zawiah Abdul Latif. 2nd ed.; Marshall Cavendish Benchmark 2008 144p il map (Cultures of the world) lib bdg $42.79

Grades: 5 6 7 8 **967.73**

1. Somalia
ISBN 978-0-7614-2082-8 lib bdg; 0-7614-2082-7 lib bdg

LC 2006102270

First published 1997

"Provides comprehensive information on the geography, history, wildlife, governmental structure, economy, cultural diversity, peoples, religion, and culture of Somalia." Publisher's note

Includes glossary and bibliographical references

967.8 Tanzania

Heale, Jay

Tanzania; by Jay Heale & Winnie Wong. 2nd ed.; Marshall Cavendish Benchmark 2009 144p il map (Cultures of the world) lib bdg $42.79

Grades: 5 6 7 8 **967.8**

1. Tanzania
ISBN 978-0-7614-3417-7 lib bdg; 0-7614-3417-8 lib bdg

LC 2008028802

First published 1998

"Provides comprehensive information on the geography, history, wildlife, governmental structure, economy, cultural diversity, peoples, religion, and culture of Tanzania." Publisher's note

Includes glossary and bibliographical references

967.9   Mozambique

King, David C.

Mozambique; [by] David C. King. Marshall Cavendish Benchmark 2007 144p il map (Cultures of the world) lib bdg $42.79

Grades: 5 6 7 8   **967.9**

1. Mozambique

ISBN 978-0-7614-2331-7 lib bdg; 0-7614-2331-1 lib bdg

            LC 2006002302

This provides "information on the geography, history, wildlife, governmental structure, economy, cultural diversity, peoples, religion, and culture of Mozambique." Publisher's note

Includes glossary and bibliographical references

968   Republic of South Africa and neighboring southern African countries

Mace, Virginia

★ South Africa; [by] Virginia Mace; Kate Rowntree and Vukile Khumalo, consultants. National Geographic 2008 64p il map (Countries of the world) lib bdg $27.90

Grades: 4 5 6 7   **968**

1. South Africa

ISBN 978-1-4263-0203-9

            LC 2007047835

This describes the geography, nature, history, people and culture, government, and economy of South Africa.

"Through its numerous maps and standout photographs, this book provides a general overview of South Africa that will satisfy the basic needs of upper-elementary research paper writers." Horn Book Guide

Includes glossary and bibliographical references

968.06   South Africa--Period as Republic, 1961-

Brownlie, Ali

South Africa in our world; [by] Ali Brownlie Bojang. Smart Apple Media 2010 32p il (Countries in our world) lib bdg $28.50

Grades: 5 6 7 8   **968.06**

1. South Africa

ISBN 978-1-59920-444-4 lib bdg; 1-59920-444-4 lib bdg

            LC 2009043163

This "contains relevant information presented in a visually appealing layout. Large colorful photographs inform readers about the past, present, and future of the country... . The book gives an honest view of apartheid, poverty, and government conflicts. At the same time, it is hopeful about recent changes, such as the hosting of the World Cup and the growing economy." SLJ

Includes glossary and bibliographical references

Cooper, Floyd

Mandela; from the life of the South African statesman. written and illustrated by Floyd Cooper. Philomel Bks. 1996 un il hardcover o.p. pa $6.99

Grades: 2 3 4   **968.06**

1. Presidents 2. Political prisoners 3. Political leaders 4. Human rights activists 5. Nobel laureates for peace 6. South Africa -- Race relations 7. South Africa -- Politics and government

ISBN 0-399-22942-6; 0-698-11816-2 pa

            LC 95-19639

"Cooper's oil paintings are infused with golden light. Elegant composition and subtle shifts in perspective add emotional value to the carefully focused account." SLJ

Includes bibliographical references

McDonough, Yona Zeldis

★ Peaceful protest: the life of Nelson Mandela; illustrations by Malcah Zeldis. Walker & Co. 2002 un il hardcover o.p. pa $8.95

Grades: 2 3 4 5   **968.06**

1. Presidents 2. Political prisoners 3. Political leaders 4. Human rights activists 5. Nobel laureates for peace 6. South Africa -- Race relations 7. South Africa -- Politics and government

ISBN 0-8027-8821-1; 0-8027-8823-8 lib bdg; 0-8027-8948-X pa

            LC 2002-23462

A biography of the black South African leader who became a civil rights activist, political prisoner, and president of South Africa

This is an "easy-to-read but engaging biography. . . . Zeldis's brightly colored folk-art illustrations reflect her subject's life and struggle with candid simplicity." SLJ

Includes bibliographical references

Nelson, Kadir

★ Nelson Mandela; Kadir Nelson. Katherine Tegen Books 2013 40 p. (hardcover bdg.) $17.99

Grades: 1 2 3   **968.06**

1. Stories in rhyme 2. South Africa -- History 3. Mandela, Nelson, 1918-

ISBN 0061783749; 9780061783746; 9780061783760

            LC 2012025492

Coretta Scott King Honor Book: Illustrator (2014)

This illustrated children's book by illustrator Kadir Nelson is a biography in verse of Nelson Mandela. "It is the story of a young boy's determination to change South Africa and of the struggles of a man who eventually became the president of his country by believing in equality for people of all colors." (Publisher's note)

968.94   Zambia

Holmes, Timothy

Zambia; by Timothy Holmes & Winnie Wong. rev ed.; Marshall Cavendish Benchmark 2008 144p il map (Cultures of the world) lib bdg $42.79

Grades: 5 6 7 8 **968.94**
1. Zambia
ISBN 978-0-7614-3039-1 lib bdg; 0-7614-3039-3
lib bdg

LC 2007050794
First published 1998
Describes the geography, history, government, economy, people, lifestyle, religion, language, arts, leisure, festivals, and food of Zambia
Includes glossary and bibliographical references

969.1 Madagascar

Heale, Jay
Madagascar; [by] Jay Heale & Zawiah Abdul Latif. 2nd ed.; Marshall Cavendish Benchmark 2008 144p il map (Cultures of the world) lib bdg $42.79
Grades: 5 6 7 8 **969.1**
1. Madagascar
ISBN 978-0-7614-3036-0 lib bdg; 0-7614-3036-9
lib bdg

LC 2007048288
First published 1998
"Provides comprehensive information on the geography, history, wildlife, governmental structure, economy, cultural diversity, peoples, religion, and culture of Madagascar." Publisher's note
Includes glossary and bibliographical references

970 History of North America

Foster, Karen
Atlas of North America. Picture Window Books 2008 32p il map (Picture Window Books world atlases) lib bdg $27.93; pa $7.95
Grades: 2 3 4 **970**
1. North America
ISBN 978-1-4048-3885-7 lib bdg; 1-4048-3885-6 lib bdg; 978-1-4048-3893-2 pa; 1-4048-3893-7 pa
This introduction to the geography of North America offers maps and information about countries, landforms, bodies of water, climate, plants, animals, population, people and customs, places of interest, industries, transportation, and the Mississippi River
This book offers "well-organized, easy-to-access information. . . . Small photographs or colorful text boxes draw readers' attention to points of interest or fun facts. Maps and legends are simple, yet disseminate information clearly." SLJ
Includes glossary

970.004 North American native peoples

Andre, Julie-Ann
We feel good out here; by Julie-Ann Andre and Mindy Willett; photographs by Tessa Macintosh. Fitzhenry & Whiteside 2008 32p il (The land is our storybook) $16.95
Grades: 3 4 5 6 **970.004**
1. Northwest Territories 2. Native Americans -- Canada
ISBN 978-1-89725-233-8; 1-89725-233-1

This title focuses on the land and culture "of Canada's Northwest Territories and is replete with sharp and attractive full-color photographs. In [this book] a local woman describes her life with her husband and two daughters. Julie-Ann is a Canadian Ranger who studies business management but, more importantly, she is a student of Gwich'in language and culture. She was sent to a residential school at age seven and has spent the last 10 years reestablishing her people's traditional practices and beliefs. A boxed area, 'Our Words,' gives a few words in English and in Gwichya Gwich'in. . . . [This title provides] some useful information for reports and [is an] interesting [addition] for general reading." SLJ

Arnold, Caroline
★ The ancient cliff dwellers of Mesa Verde; photographs by Richard Hewett. Clarion Bks. 1992 64p il hardcover o.p. pa $7.95
Grades: 4 5 6 7 **970.004**
1. Pueblo Indians
ISBN 0-395-56241-4; 0-618-05149-X pa

LC 91-8145
Discusses the native Americans known as the Anasazi, who migrated to southwestern Colorado in the first century A.D. and mysteriously disappeared in 1300 A.D. after constructing extensive dwellings in the cliffs of the steep canyon walls
"A thorough and attractive introduction to the Anasazi people with outstanding photographs of the dramatic vistas and ceremonial chambers within this national park." SLJ
Includes glossary

Baylor, Byrd
★ When clay sings; illustrated by Tom Bahti. Scribner 1972 un il hardcover o.p. pa $6.99
Grades: 1 2 3 4 **970.004**
1. Pottery 2. Native American art 3. Native Americans -- Southwestern States
ISBN 0-684-18829-5; 0-689-71106-9 pa
A Caldecott Medal honor book, 1973
"A lyrical tribute to an almost forgotten time of the prehistoric Indian of the desert West presents broken bits of pottery from this ancient time. The designs and drawings, done in rich earth tones, are derived from prehistoric pottery found in the American Southwest." Read Ladders for Hum Relat. 6th edition

Bealer, Alex W.
Only the names remain; the Cherokees and the Trail of Tears. illustrated by Kristina Rodanas. Little, Brown 1996 79p il hardcover o.p. pa $6.99
Grades: 4 5 6 **970.004**
1. Cherokee Indians
ISBN 0-316-08519-7
A reissue with new illustrations of the title first published 1972
The author describes "the rise of the Cherokee Nation, with its written language, constitution, and republican form of government, and its tragic betrayal in the 1830s." Chicago Public Libr

Bjorklund, Ruth
The Hopi; by Ruth Bjorklund. Marshall Cavendish Benchmark 2009 48p il (First Americans) lib bdg $31.36

Grades: 2 3 4 970.004

1. Hopi Indians

ISBN 978-0-7614-3021-6 lib bdg; 0-7614-3021-0 lib bdg

LC 2007-33676

"Provides comprehensive information on the background, lifestyle, beliefs, and present-day lives of the Hopi people." Publisher's note

Includes glossary and bibliographical references

Bjornlund, Lydia D.

The **Trail** of Tears; the relocation of the Cherokee Nation. Lucent Books 2010 104p il map (American history) lib bdg $33.45

Grades: 5 6 7 8 970.004

1. Cherokee Indians 2. Native Americans -- Relocation

ISBN 978-1-4205-0211-4; 1-4205-0211-5

LC 2010001549

Describes the Federal government's seizure of Cherokee lands in Georgia and the forced migration of the Cherokee Nation to Oklahoma along the route that came to be known as the Trail of Tears.

This is "well written and [includes] primary sources, photographs, reproductions, and maps." SLJ

Includes bibliographical references

★ A **Braid** of lives; Native American childhood. edited by Neil Philip. Clarion Bks. 2000 81p il $20

Grades: 4 5 6 7 970.004

1. Native Americans

ISBN 0-395-64528-X

LC 00-21343

"This is an excellent choice for curriculum support and brief read-aloud material." Booklist

Includes bibliographical references

Bruchac, Joseph

★ The **Trail** of Tears; illustrated by Diana Magnuson. Random House 1999 46p il (Step into reading) hardcover o.p. pa $3.99

Grades: 2 3 4 970.004

1. Cherokee Indians 2. Native Americans -- Relocation

ISBN 0-679-99052-6 lib bdg; 0-679-89052-1 pa

LC 98-36199

Recounts how the Cherokees, after fighting to keep their land in the nineteenth century, were forced to leave and travel 1200 miles to a new settlement in Oklahoma, a terrible journey known as the Trail of Tears

"Magnuson's colorful pictures, packed with people and action, are a little bright for the subject, but strong new readers will find that nonfiction can tell a powerful story." Booklist

Connolly, Sean

★ The **Americas** and the Pacific. Zak Books 2009 48p il map (History of the world) lib bdg $34.25

Grades: 4 5 6 7 8 970.004

1. Maoris 2. Aboriginal Australians 3. Native Americans -- History

ISBN 978-88-60981-61-5 lib bdg; 88-60981-61-1 lib bdg

LC 2008008404

"Artists' renderings show groups of people engaged in representative activities, but it's the reproductions of arti-

facts . . . that will pull readers and browsers most. . . . [This is an] engaging overview." Booklist

Includes bibliographical references

Cunningham, Kevin

The **Cheyenne**; [by] Kevin Cunningham and Peter Benoit. Children's Press 2011 48p il map (True books: American Indians) lib bdg $28; pa $6.95

Grades: 3 4 5 970.004

1. Cheyenne Indians

ISBN 978-0-531-20759-8 lib bdg; 0-531-20759-5 lib bdg; 978-0-531-29301-0 pa; 0-531-29301-7 pa

LC 2010049082

An introduction to the Cheyenne people, explaining who they are, reviewing the history of the Cheyenne, looking at how the Cheyenne lived, their beliefs, and rituals, and discussing the Council of Forty-Four.

Includes bibliographical references

The **Comanche**; [by] Kevin Cunningham and Peter Benoit. Children's Press 2011 48p il (True book: American Indians) lib bdg $28; pa $6.95

Grades: 3 4 5 970.004

1. Comanche Indians

ISBN 978-0-531-20770-3 lib bdg; 0-531-20770-6 lib bdg; 978-0-531-29312-6 pa; 0-531-29312-2 pa

LC 2010049081

This book "covers cultural basics such as diet, clothing, lifestyle, and child rearing for [the Comanche]. Relevant historical events are also covered simply and clearly, including a time line of highlights in each group's history. This balance between history and culture keeps the series dynamic and interesting. Photos, paintings, and drawings—as well as occasional contemporary illustrations—add visual interest to the well-designed package and keep the [title] from feeling formulaic. The [book] traces the historical changes in Comanche life and their causes, from the 1600s to the twentieth century." Booklist

Includes bibliographical references

The **Inuit**; [by] Kevin Cunningham and Peter Benoit. Children's Press 2011 48p il (True book: American Indians) lib bdg $28; pa $6.95

Grades: 3 4 5 970.004

1. Inuit

ISBN 978-0-531-20760-4 lib bdg; 978-0-531-29302-7 pa

LC 2010049080

This book "covers cultural basics such as diet, clothing, lifestyle, and child rearing for [the Inuit]. Relevant historical events are also covered simply and clearly, including a time line of highlights in each group's history. This balance between history and culture keeps the series dynamic and interesting. Photos, paintings, and drawings-as well as occasional contemporary illustrations-add visual interest to the well-designed package and keep the [title] from feeling formulaic." Booklist

Includes bibliographical references

The **Navajo**; [by] Kevin Cunningham and Peter Benoit. Children's Press 2011 48p il map (True book: American Indians) lib bdg $28; pa $6.95

Grades: 3 4 5 **970.004**
1. Navajo Indians
ISBN 978-0-531-20762-8 lib bdg; 0-531-20762-5 lib bdg; 978-0-531-29304-1 pa; 0-531-29304-1 pa
LC 2010050837
An exploration of the Navajo Indians, discussing the nation's relationship with Spaniards and settlers, culture, crafts, and more.

The "balance between history and culture keeps the [book] dynamic and interesting. Photos, paintings, and drawings—as well as occasional contemporary illustrations—add visual interest to the well-designed package and keep the [title] from feeling formulaic." Booklist

Includes bibliographical references

The **Pueblo**; [by] Kevin Cunningham and Peter Benoit. Children's Press 2011 48p il map (True book: American Indians) lib bdg $28; pa $6.95
Grades: 3 4 5 **970.004**
1. Pueblo Indians
ISBN 978-0-531-20763-5 lib bdg; 0-531-20763-3 lib bdg; 978-0-531-29305-8 pa; 0-531-29305-X pa
LC 2010050838
An introduction to the Pueblo people, explaining who they are, reviewing the history of the Pueblo, examining key aspects of Pueblo culture, and looking at Pueblo traditions that continue into the twenty-first century.

Includes bibliographical references

The **Sioux**; [by] Kevin Cunningham and Peter Benoit. Children's Press 2011 48p il map (True book: American Indians) lib bdg $28; pa $6.95
Grades: 3 4 5 **970.004**
1. Teton Indians
ISBN 978-0-531-20768-0 lib bdg; 0-531-207684- lib bdg; 978-0-531-29310-2 pa; 0-531-29310-6 pa
LC 2010049083
An introduction to the Sioux people, explaining who they are, reviewing the history of the Sioux, telling the story of Little Bighorn, and examining key parts of Sioux culture.

Includes bibliographical references

The **Zuni**; [by] Kevin Cunningham and Peter Benoit. Children's Press 2011 48p il map (True book: American Indians) $28; pa $6.95
Grades: 3 4 5 **970.004**
1. Zuni Indians
ISBN 978-0-531-20761-1; 978-0-531-29303-4 pa
LC 2010050846
This book "covers cultural basics such as diet, clothing, lifestyle, and child rearing for [the Zuni]. Relevant historical events are also covered simply and clearly, including a time line of highlights in each group's history. This balance between history and culture keeps the [book] dynamic and interesting. Photos, paintings, and drawings-as well as occasional contemporary illustrations-add visual interest to the well-designed package and keep the [title] from feeling formulaic." Booklist

Includes bibliographical references

De Capua, Sarah
The **Cheyenne**. Marshall Cavendish Benchmark 2007 47p il (First Americans) lib bdg $31.36

Grades: 2 3 4 **970.004**
1. Cheyenne Indians
ISBN 978-0-7614-2248-8 lib bdg; 0-7614-2248-X lib bdg
LC 2006011967
Provides information on the background, lifestyle, beliefs, and present-day lives of the Cheyenne people

Includes glossary and bibliographical references

The **Choctaw**; by Sarah De Capua. Marshall Cavendish Benchmark 2009 48p il (First Americans) lib bdg $31.36
Grades: 2 3 4 **970.004**
1. Choctaw Indians
ISBN 978-0-7614-3018-6 lib bdg; 0-7614-3018-0 lib bdg
LC 2007-33727
"Provides comprehensive information on the background, lifestyle, beliefs, and present-day lives of the Choctaw people." Publisher's note

Includes glossary and bibliographical references

The **Comanche**. Marshall Cavendish Benchmark 2007 47p il (First Americans) lib bdg $31.36
Grades: 2 3 4 **970.004**
1. Comanche Indians
ISBN 978-0-7614-2249-5 lib bdg; 0-7614-2249-8 lib bdg
LC 2006011975
Provides information on the background, lifestyle, beliefs, and present-day lives of the Comanche people

Includes glossary and bibliographical references

The **Menominee**. Marshall Cavendish Benchmark 2009 48p il (First Americans) lib bdg $31.36
Grades: 2 3 4 **970.004**
1. Menominee Indians
ISBN 978-0-7614-4131-1 lib bdg; 0-7614-4131-X lib bdg
LC 2008041999
Provides information on the background, lifestyle, beliefs, and present-day lives of the Menominee people

The **Shawnee**. Marshall Cavendish Benchmark 2007 48p il (First Americans) lib bdg $31.36
Grades: 2 3 4 **970.004**
1. Shawnee Indians
ISBN 978-0-7614-2682-0 lib bdg; 0-7614-2682-5 lib bdg
LC 2006034117
Provides information on the background, lifestyle, beliefs, and present-day lives of the Shawnee people

Includes glossary and bibliographical references

The **Shoshone**. Marshall Cavendish Benchmark 2007 48p il (First Americans) lib bdg $31.36
Grades: 2 3 4 **970.004**
1. Shoshoni Indians 2. Shoshone Indians
ISBN 978-0-7614-2683-7 lib bdg; 0-7614-2683-3 lib bdg
LC 2006034113

Provides information on the background, lifestyle, beliefs, and present-day lives of the Shoshone people

Includes glossary and bibliographical references

Dennis, Yvonne Wakim

★ **Children** of native America today; [by] Yvonne Wakim Dennis & Arlene Hirschfelder; with a foreword by Buffy Sainte-Marie. Charlesbridge Pub. 2003 64p il map lib bdg $19.95

Grades: 3 4 5 6   **970.004**

1. Native Americans

ISBN 1-57091-499-0

LC 2002-2272

"This photo-essay features 25 of the more than 500 native cultures of the U.S. as well as a section on urban Indians. In this 'book of few words and many pictures,' the clear, captioned photographs speak eloquently of contemporary Native American young people. . . . An excellent resource for multicultural studies, this handsome album will also attract browsers." Booklist

Includes glossary and bibliographical references

★ **A kid's** guide to native American history; more than 50 activities. by Yvonne Wakim Dennis and Arlene Hirschfelder. Chicago Review Press 2009 226p il pa $16.95

Grades: 3 4 5 6   **970.004**

1. Games 2. Cooking 3. Handicraft 4. Native Americans -- History

ISBN 978-1-55652-802-6 pa; 1-55652-802-7 pa

LC 2009015832

"This two-in-one history and activity book does an excellent job of explaining Native American history in easy-to-understand language while stressing the differences between and diversity among tribes. The book is divided by region. . . . Activities are kid-friendly . . . and encourage exploration of the text. . . . Clear illustrations accompany each activity." SLJ

Includes glossary and bibliographical references

Dolbear, Emily J.

The **Iroquois**; [by] Emily J. Dolbear and Peter Benoit. Children's Press 2011 48p il map (True book: American Indians) lib bdg $28; pa $6.95

Grades: 3 4 5   **970.004**

1. Iroquois Indians

ISBN 978-0-531-20771-0 lib bdg; 0-531-20771-4 lib bdg; 978-0-531-29313-3 pa; 0-531-29313-0 pa

LC 2010049079

This covers cultural basics of the Iroquois such as diet, clothing, lifestyle, and child rearing as well as relevant historical events.

Includes bibliographical references

Ehrlich, Amy

Wounded Knee: an Indian history of the American West; adapted for young readers by Amy Ehrlich from Dee Brown's Bury my heart at Wounded Knee. Holt & Co. 1974 202p il maps hardcover o.p. pa $13.95

Grades: 6 7 8 9   **970.004**

1. Generals 2. Ghost dance 3. Apache Indians 4. Dakota Indians 5. Navajo Indians 6. Arapaho Indians 7. Cheyenne Indians 8. Sand Creek, Battle of, 1864 9. Indian chiefs 10. Civil engineers 11. Government

officials 12. West (U.S.) -- History 13. Native Americans -- Wars 14. Native Americans -- West (U.S.)

ISBN 0-8050-2700-9 pa

This book traces the plight of the Navaho, Apache, Cheyenne and Sioux Indians in their struggles against the white man in the West between 1860 and 1890. It recounts battles and their causes, participants, and consequences during this era

"Some chapters [of the original] have been deleted, others condensed, and in some instances sentence structure and language have been simplified. The editing is good, and this version is interesting, readable, and smooth." SLJ

Includes bibliographical references

Enzoe, Pete

The **caribou** feed our soul; [by] Pete Enzoe and Mindy Willett; photographs by Tessa Macintosh. Fitzhenry & Whiteside 2011 26p il (The land is our storybook) $16.95

Grades: 3 4 5 6   **970.004**

1. Caribou 2. Chipewyan Indians 3. Wildlife conservation

ISBN 978-1-89725-267-3; 1-89725-267-6

LC 2010-9045793

"This informative first-person narrative cleanly captures the Dénésôliné (Chipewyan) culture's dependence on and reverence for the caribou, the predominant symbol of the tribe's existence. . . . Enzoe, a Native spokesperson, teacher, and hunter, explains aspects of his tribe's daily life in the Northwest Territories. He speaks of the mysticism of the caribou and illustrates its importance in feeding and clothing the tribe. . . . The book is thoughtfully illustrated with a variety of engaging photographs of the area and its people, immersed in the daily goings-on of their lives. The aerial photography gives readers a grand view of the stunning geography." SLJ

Includes glossary and bibliographical references

Freedman, Russell

Indian chiefs. Holiday House 1987 151p il $24.95; pa $14.95

Grades: 6 7 8 9 10   **970.004**

1. Kiowa Indians 2. Dakota Indians 3. Oglala Indians 4. Comanche Indians 5. Shoshoni Indians 6. Centenarians 7. Indian chiefs 8. Shoshone Indians 9. Nez Percé Indians 10. Native Americans -- Biography

ISBN 0-8234-0625-3; 0-8234-0971-6 pa

LC 86-46198

This "book chronicles the lives of six renowned Indian chiefs, each of whom served as a leader during a critical period in his tribe's history. . . . The text relates information about the lives of each chief and aspects of Indian/white relationships that illuminate his actions. Interesting vignettes and quotations are well integrated into the narrative as are dramatic accounts of battles. While the tone of the text is nonjudgmental, an underlying sympathy for the Indians' situation is apparent." Horn Book

Includes bibliographical references

Goble, Paul

All our relatives; traditional Native American thoughts about nature. compiled and illustrated by Paul Goble. World Wisdom 2005 un il $15.95

Grades: 5 6 7 8   970.004
  1. Native Americans 2. Philosophy of nature
  ISBN 0-941532-77-1; 978-0-941532-77-8

LC 2005004285

"The pages of this book are chock-full of quotations, songs, and brief stories that exemplify Native American attitudes toward nature. . . . Black Elk, Standing Bear, Brave Buffalo, and others observe the importance of various animals and the sacred qualities of all living things. . . . The spaces between text blocks are filled with Goble's familiar illustrations based on traditional Native American designs and colors." SLJ

  Includes bibliographical references

Hicks, Terry Allan

  The **Chumash**; by Terry Allan Hicks. Marshall Cavendish Benchmark 2008 48p il map (First Americans) lib bdg $29.93
Grades: 2 3 4   970.004
  1. Chumash Indians
  ISBN 978-0-7614-2678-3 lib bdg; 0-7614-2678-7 lib bdg

LC 2006034101

This describes Chumash "history and culture, way of life, beliefs, present status, and future outlook. Colorful modern photographs appear throughout, as do paintings, photos, and maps. [The] volume includes a simple craft . . . as well as a Native recipe. . . . [The] book has a helpful, easy-to-read graphical time line. Clear writing and attractive [layout makes this book] accessible and appealing." SLJ

  Includes glossary and bibliographical references

King, David C.

  First people; an illustrated history of American Indians. DK Pub. 2008 192p il map $19.99
Grades: 5 6 7 8   970.004
  1. Native Americans
  ISBN 978-0-7566-4092-7; 0-7566-4092-X

"This rich pictorial work serves as an entertaining, informative, and visually appealing introduction to American Indian culture and history. Each of the seven chapters covers a different time period in chronological order. . . . The glossy photographs, colorful drawings, and easily accessible paragraphs . . . make for an easy-to-use overall package." SLJ

  The **Haida**. Marshall Cavendish Benchmark 2007 48p il (First Americans) lib bdg $31.36
Grades: 2 3 4   970.004
  1. Haida Indians
  ISBN 978-0-7614-2250-1 lib bdg; 0-7614-2250-1 lib bdg

LC 2006011969

Provides information on the background, lifestyle, beliefs, and present-day lives of the Haida people
  Includes glossary and bibliographical references

  The **Huron**. Marshall Cavendish Benchmark 2007 48p il (First Americans) lib bdg $31.36
Grades: 2 3 4   970.004
  1. Huron Indians
  ISBN 978-0-7614-2251-8 lib bdg; 0-7614-2251-X lib bdg

LC 2006011970

Provides information on the background, lifestyle, beliefs, and present-day lives of the Huron people
  Includes glossary and bibliographical references

  The **Inuit**; [by] David C. King. Marshall Cavendish Benchmark 2008 48p il map (First Americans) lib bdg $31.36
Grades: 2 3 4   970.004
  1. Inuit
  ISBN 978-0-7614-2679-0 lib bdg; 0-7614-2679-5 lib bdg

LC 2006034111

This describes Inuit "history and culture, way of life, beliefs, present status, and future outlook. Colorful modern photographs appear throughout, as do paintings, photos, and maps. . . . [It] includes a simple craft . . . (soapstone carving) as well as a Native recipe . . . (fish soup). . . . [It] has a helpful, easy-to-read graphical time line. Clear writing and attractive [layout makes this book] accessible and appealing." SLJ

  Includes glossary and bibliographical references

  The **Mohawk**. Marshall Cavendish Benchmark 2009 48p il (First Americans) lib bdg $31.36
Grades: 2 3 4   970.004
  1. Mohawk Indians
  ISBN 978-0-7614-4132-8 lib bdg; 0-7614-4132-8 lib bdg

LC 2008042000

Provides information on the background, lifestyle, beliefs, and present-day lives of the Mohawk people.
  Includes glossary and bibliographical references

  The **Nez Perce**; by David C. King. Marshall Cavendish Benchmark 2008 48p il map (First Americans) lib bdg $31.36
Grades: 2 3 4   970.004
  1. Nez Percé Indians
  ISBN 978-0-7614-2680-6 lib bdg; 0-7614-2678-7 lib bdg

LC 2006034114

This describes Nez Perce "history and culture, way of life, beliefs, present status, and future outlook. Colorful modern photographs appear throughout, as do paintings, photos, and maps. [The] volume includes a simple craft . . . as well as a Native recipe. . . . [The] book has a helpful, easy-to-read graphical time line. Clear writing and attractive [layout makes this book] accessible and appealing." SLJ

  Includes glossary and bibliographical references

  The **Ojibwe**. Marshall Cavendish Benchmark 2007 45p il (First Americans) lib bdg $31.36
Grades: 2 3 4   970.004
  1. Ojibwa Indians
  ISBN 978-0-7614-2252-5 lib bdg; 0-7614-2252-8 lib bdg

LC 2006011971

Provides information on the background, lifestyle, beliefs, and present-day lives of the Ojibwe people
  Includes glossary and bibliographical references

  The **Powhatan**. Marshall Cavendish Benchmark 2007 48p il (First Americans) lib bdg $31.36

Grades: 2 3 4   **970.004**
1. Powhatan Indians
ISBN 978-0-7614-2681-3 lib bdg; 0-7614-2681-7
lib bdg
LC 2006034115
Provides information on the background, lifestyle, beliefs, and present-day lives of the Powhatan people
Includes glossary and bibliographical references

The **Seminole**. Marshall Cavendish Benchmark 2007
48p il (First Americans) lib bdg $31.36
Grades: 2 3 4   **970.004**
1. Seminole Indians
ISBN 978-0-7614-2253-2 lib bdg; 0-7614-2253-6
lib bdg
LC 2006011977
Provides information on the background, lifestyle, beliefs, and present-day lives of the Seminole people
Includes glossary and bibliographical references

Kissock, Heather
  Apache; American Indian art and culture. [by] Heather
Kissock and Jordan McGill. Weigl Publishers Inc. 2010
24p il (American Indian art and culture) lib bdg $25.70;
pa $9.95
Grades: 2 3 4   **970.004**
1. Apache Indians
ISBN 978-1-60596-991-6 lib bdg; 1-60596-991-5 lib
bdg; 978-1-60596-992-3 pa; 1-60596-992-3 pa
LC 2010005331
Introduces the history, housing, clothing, agriculture, culture, art, and recipes of the Apache Indians.
This "provides early elementary students with an outstanding overview of the art and culture of [the Apache]. . . . Perfect for beginning readers, the content is straightforward and concise. Full-color up close photographs are integral to . . . [the] book, visually clarifying each idea and extending the text to aid in the student's understanding."
Libr Media Connect
Includes glossary

  Caddo; [by] Heather Kissock and Rachel Small. Weigl
Publishers Inc. 2011 24p il (American Indian art and culture) lib bdg $25.70; pa $9.95
Grades: 2 3 4   **970.004**
1. Caddo Indians
ISBN 978-1-60596-979-4 lib bdg; 1-60596-979-6 lib
bdg; 978-1-60596-980-0 pa; 1-60596-980-X pa
LC 2010005334
Highlights the traditional ways of the Caddo.
This "provides early elementary students with an outstanding overview of the art and culture of [the Caddo]. . . . Perfect for beginning readers, the content is straightforward and concise. Full-color up close photographs are integral to . . . [the] book, visually clarifying each idea and extending the text to aid in the student's understanding."
Libr Media Connect
Includes glossary

  Cherokee; American Indian art and culture. [by]
Heather Kissock and Rachel Small. Weigl Publishers Inc.
2011 24p il (American Indian art and culture) lib bdg
$25.70; pa $9.95

Grades: 2 3 4   **970.004**
1. Cherokee Indians
ISBN 978-1-60596-994-7 lib bdg; 1-60596-994-X lib
bdg; 978-1-60596-995-4 pa; 1-60596-995-8 pa
LC 2010005335
Introduces the history, housing, clothing, agriculture, culture, art, and recipes of the Cherokee Indians
This "provides early elementary students with an outstanding overview of the art and culture of [the Cherokee Indians]. . . . Perfect for beginning readers, the content is straightforward and concise. Full-color up close photographs are integral to . . . [the] book, visually clarifying each idea and extending the text to aid in the student's understanding."
Libr Media Connect
Includes glossary

  Comanche; American Indian art and culture. Weigl
Publishers Inc. 2011 24p il (American Indian art and culture) lib bdg $25.70; pa $9.95
Grades: 2 3 4   **970.004**
1. Comanche Indians
ISBN 978-1-60596-988-6 lib bdg; 1-60596-988-5 lib
bdg; 978-1-60596-989-3 pa; 1-60596-989-3 pa
LC 2010005336
Introduces the history, housing, clothing, agriculture, culture, art, and recipes of the Comanche Indians
This "provides early elementary students with an outstanding overview of the art and culture of [the Comanche]. . . . Perfect for beginning readers, the content is straightforward and concise. Full-color up close photographs are integral to . . . [the] book, visually clarifying each idea and extending the text to aid in the student's understanding."
Libr Media Connect
Includes glossary

  Tigua; [by] Heather Kissock and Jordan McGill. Weigl
Publishers Inc. 2011 24p il (American Indian art and culture) lib bdg $25.70; pa $9.95
Grades: 2 3 4   **970.004**
1. Tigua Indians
ISBN 978-1-60596-982-4 lib bdg; 1-60596-982-6 lib
bdg; 978-1-60596-983-1 pa; 1-60596-983-4 pa
LC 2010005355
Introduces the history, housing, clothing, agriculture, culture, art, and recipes of the Tigua Indians.
This "provides early elementary students with an outstanding overview of the art and culture of [the Tigua Indians]. . . . Perfect for beginning readers, the content is straightforward and concise. Full-color up close photographs are integral to . . . [the] book, visually clarifying each idea and extending the text to aid in the student's understanding."
Libr Media Connect
Includes glossary

McLeod, Tom
  The **Delta** is my home; by Tom McLeod and Mindy
Willett; photographs by Tessa Macintosh. Fitzhenry & Whiteside 2008 26p il (The land is our storybook) $16.95
Grades: 4 5 6 7   **970.004**
1. Northwest Territories 2. Mackenzie River (N.W.T.)
3. Native Americans -- Canada
ISBN 978-1-8972-5232-1; 1-8972-5232-3
"An 11-year-old boy who lives in the Mackenzie Delta region with his family tells about life there. His father is a

renewable resource officer and has taught him how to hunt, fish, trap, and drive a boat. Readers also learn about his language, schooling, and clothing as well as the important role that storytelling plays in the culture. [This title provides] some useful information for reports and [is an] interesting [addition] for general reading." SLJ

McNeese, Tim

The **fascinating** history of American Indians; the age before Columbus. Enslow Publishers 2009 128p il map (America's living history) lib bdg $31.93

Grades: 5 6 7 8   **970.004**
1. Native Americans
ISBN 978-0-7660-2938-5 lib bdg; 0-7660-2938-7 lib bdg

"This thorough discussion of Native American life prior to Columbus's arrival combines theories of archaeologists, anthropologists, historians, and scientists to provide an engaging portrayal of the daily experiences of regional tribes. Based mostly on archaeological discoveries, the accessible text is supported by archival photographs, maps, and sidebars." Horn Book Guide

Includes glossary and bibliographical references

Molin, Paulette Fairbanks

American Indian stereotypes in the world of children; a reader and bibliography. 2nd ed; Scarecrow Press 1999 343p il hardcover o.p. pa $40.50

Grades: Adult Professional   **970.004**
1. Race awareness 2. Native Americans
ISBN 0-8108-3612-2; 0-8108-3613-0 pa
                                        LC 98-49654
First published 1982

"This volume presents a collection of . . . articles detailing uses and abuses of Native American symbols, images, ideas, and stories that are directed at youth in the mass media. Toys, cartoons, textbooks, general reading, media portrayals, sports, logos, nicknames and more are discussed in stand-alone articles." Voice Youth Advocates

Includes bibliographical references

Murdoch, David Hamilton

North American Indian; written by David Murdoch; chief consultant, Stanley A. Freed; photographed by Lynton Gardiner. rev ed; DK Pubs. 2005 72p il (DK eyewitness books) $16.99; lib bdg $19.99

Grades: 4 5 6 7   **970.004**
1. Native Americans
ISBN 0-7566-1081-8; 0-7566-1082-6 lib bdg
First published 1995 by Knopf

This is a guide to the civilizations of North American Indians including full-color photographs of artifacts and descriptions ceremonies and customs.

Pokiak, James

Proud to be Inuvialuit; by James Pokiak and Mindy Willett; illustrated by Tessa Macintosh. Fitzhenry & Whiteside 2010 26p il pa $16.95

Grades: 3 4 5   **970.004**
1. Inuit 2. Native Americans -- Northwest Coast of North America
ISBN 1-89725-259-5; 978-1-89725-259-8

"Pokiak introduces his people, the Inuvialuit . . . to readers by having them meet his own family and their commu-

nity of 900 people on the Arctic coast of Canada's Northwest Territories. Though they live in modern houses, have cell phones, and enjoy an indoor swimming pool, the people of Tuktoyaktuk still hunt beluga whales for subsistence as their ancestors did. . . . Text, illustrations, and captions work together well to present the Inuvialuit way of life. Illustrations include a large map and small paintings as well as many clear, color photos. . . . An informative introduction to an Inuit community today." Booklist

Terry, Michael Bad Hand

Daily life in a Plains Indian village, 1868. Clarion Bks. 1999 48p il map hardcover o.p. pa $9.95

Grades: 4 5 6 7   **970.004**
1. Native Americans -- Great Plains
ISBN 0-395-94542-9; 0-395-97499-2 pa
                                        LC 98-32382
Depicts the historical background, social organization, and daily life of a Plains Indian village in 1868, presenting interiors, landscapes, clothing, and everyday objects

"The author presents short paragraphs of fascinating information accompanied by visuals that explain even more than the text." SLJ

Includes glossary

Zimmerman, Dwight Jon

Saga of the Sioux; an adaptation of Dee Brown's Bury My Heart at Wounded Knee. [adapted] by Dwight Jon Zimmerman. Henry Holt and Company 2011 208p il map $18.99

Grades: 5 6 7 8   **970.004**
1. Dakota Indians 2. West (U.S.) -- History 3. Native Americans -- Wars
ISBN 978-0-8050-9364-3; 0-8050-9364-8
                                        LC 2011004792
"Dwight Jon Zimmerman has created a masterful adaptation of Dee Brown's Bury My Heart at Wounded Knee, presenting late nineteenth century history from a Native American viewpoint. While Brown's book traces the fates of several Native American tribes in the western United States, Zimmerman's adaptation focuses solely on the Sioux. . . . Historical figures central to the narrative, both Native American and white, are portrayed as real people, rather than caricatures. Rather than simply describing what happened, the book looks at why it happened. Individuals' motivations, strengths, and flaws are all explored in relation to how historical events unfolded. The book includes numerous photographs, illustrations, and maps that aid understanding and create visual appeal. . . . This is a must-have addition to any United States history collection serving teens." Voice Youth Advocates

Includes glossary and bibliographical references

Zoe, Therese

Living stories; [by] Therese Zoe, Philip Zoe and Mindy Willett; photographs by Tessa Macintosh. Fitzhenry & Whiteside 2009 32p il (The land is our storybook) $16.95

Grades: 3 4 5 6   **970.004**
1. Northwest Territories 2. Native Americans -- Canada 3. Native Americans -- Folklore
ISBN 978-1-89725-244-4; 1-89725-244-7

"Therese Zoe is a Tlicho woman from Gamèti in the Northwest Territories. . . . [In this book she] shares her love for her community and translates the sacred stories and traditional wisdom of her brother-in-law, Philip Zoe, and his sister, Elizabeth Chocolate. . . . Join Tlicho young people, Shelinda, Forest, and Bradley, as they learn about making dry-fish, bows and arrows, and birchbark baskets; the practices of old-time healers; as well as the sacred stories that tell the history of the Tlicho people." Publisher's note

970.01   North America--Early history to 1599

Bodden, Valerie
  Columbus reaches the New World. Creative Education 2009 48p il (Days of change) lib bdg $32.80
  Grades: 5 6 7 8   **970.01**
    1. Explorers 2. America -- Exploration
  ISBN 978-158341-732-4; 1-58341-732-X
                                          LC 2008009163
  "With elegant design and mature prose, the Days of Change series is an ideal starting point for all manner of school projects. . . . Columbus Reaches the New World intelligently explains the famous sailor's motivations for forging a new trade route. . . . Anti-Columbus Day sentiments are mostly relegated to sidebars, but Bodden doesn't surgarcoat the enslavement and death that followed discovery." Booklist
  Includes bibliographical references

Demi, 1942-
  Columbus; by Demi. Marshall Cavendish 2012 64 p. ill. (hardcover) $19.99
  Grades: 3 4 5 6   **970.01**
    1. America -- Exploration 2. Columbus, Christopher, 1451-1506 3. Explorers -- Spain -- Biography 4. Explorers -- America -- Biography 5. America -- Discovery and exploration -- Spanish
  ISBN 0761461671; 9780761461678
                                          LC 2011036019
  This book on Christopher Columbus was written and illustrated by the children's book author Demi. "From his childhood in Italy to his death in Spain, this biography presents a detailed view of the explorer's life. . . .Columbus's faults and accomplishments are both presented, acknowledging that his drive to explore furthered Europeans' knowledge of other lands, but that his mistreatment of Native peoples devastated their lives and culture." (School Library Journal)

Englar, Mary
  French colonies in America. Compass Point Books 2009 48p il (We the people) lib bdg $26.60
  Grades: 4 5 6   **970.01**
    1. French Americans 2. French Canadians 3. France -- Colonies 4. America -- Exploration
  ISBN 978-0-7565-3839-2
                                          LC 2008007209
  This is a history of French exploration and colonization in North America.
  This provides "solid background matter and [introduces] key people and vocabulary." SLJ

Gunderson, Jessica
  Conquistadors; by Jessica Gunderson. Creative Education 2011 48 p. (alk. paper) $35.65

Grades: 5 6 7 8   **970.01**
    1. United States -- History 2. Soldiers 3. Military art and science -- History 4. Soldiers -- Spain -- History 5. Military art and science -- History 6. America -- Discovery and exploration -- Spanish
  ISBN 1608181839; 9781608181834
                                          LC 2011035799
  Author Jessica Gunderson's book "covers the beginnings of the people, weaponry, war tactics, and famous leaders, and examines the current perception of the group in popular culture in an appealing, detailed, and evenhanded manner. Historical reproductions, primary documents, photographs, maps, and film stills appear throughout" the "explorations of history." (Publisher's note)
  Includes bibliographical references and index

Harrison, David L.
  Mammoth bones and broken stones; the mystery of North America's first people. with illustrations by Richard Hilliard and archaeological photographs. Boyds Mills Press 2010 48p il map $18.95
  Grades: 4 5 6 7   **970.01**
    1. Prehistoric peoples 2. North America -- Antiquities
  ISBN 978-1-59078-561-4; 1-59078-561-4
                                          LC 2009020247
  "How and when the Western Hemisphere . . . came to be populated continues to be both mysterious and controversial for scientists. . . . Harrison does a good job setting the issue in context. He describes the earliest efforts to identify the original inhabitants of the continents, exploring the Clovis culture. . . . After clearly explaining how scholars decided that they were the first, he then lists the arguments against this hypothesis. . . . The narrative is aided by both photographs and original illustrations that imagine scenes from both the distant past and the field experiences." Kirkus
  Includes glossary and bibliographical references

Hernandez, Roger E.
  Early explorations: the 1500s. Marshall Cavendish Benchmark 2009 79p il map (Hispanic America) lib bdg $34.21
  Grades: 4 5 6 7   **970.01**
    1. Explorers 2. Spain -- Colonies 3. America -- Exploration 4. Southern States -- History 5. Southwestern States -- History
  ISBN 978-0-7614-2937-1 lib bdg; 0-7614-2937-9 lib bdg
  "Provides comprehensive information on the history of Spanish exploration in the United States." Publisher's note
  Includes glossary and bibliographical references

Huey, Lois Miner
  American archaeology uncovers the Vikings. Marshall Cavendish Benchmark 2009 64p il map (American archaeology) lib bdg $21.95
  Grades: 4 5 6 7   **970.01**
    1. America -- Antiquities 2. America -- Exploration 3. Vikings -- North America 4. Excavations (Archeology) -- Canada 5. Excavations (Archeology) -- United States
  ISBN 978-0-7614-4270-7 lib bdg; 0-7614-4270-7 lib bdg
                                          LC 2008050266
  This describes how archeologists have learned about the Vikings in America.

This is "both intriguing and engaging for young readers. . . . A welcomed addition to classroom and school libraries." Libr Media Connect

Includes glossary and bibliographical references

Lilly, Alexandra

Spanish colonies in America. Compass Point Books 2009 48p il map (We the people) lib bdg $26.60

Grades: 4 5 6   970.01

1. Explorers 2. Spain -- Colonies 3. America -- Exploration 4. Spaniards -- United States

ISBN 978-0-7565-3840-8 lib bdg; 0-7565-3840-8 lib bdg

LC 2008011727

This is a history Spanish exploration, conquest, and colonization in North America.

This provides "solid background matter and [introduces] key people and vocabulary." SLJ

Maestro, Betsy

★ The **discovery** of the Americas; by Betsy and Giulio Maestro. Lothrop, Lee & Shepard Bks. 1990 48p il maps hardcover o.p. pa $6.95

Grades: 2 3 4   970.01

1. America -- Exploration

ISBN 0-688-06837-5; 0-688-11512-8 pa

LC 89-32375

Discusses both hypothetical and historical voyages of discovery to America by the Phoenicians, Saint Brendan of Ireland, the Vikings, and such later European navigators as Columbus, Cabot, and Magellan

"The dazzlingly clean and accurate prose and the exhilarating beauty of the pictures combine for an extraordinary achievement in both history and art." SLJ

★ **Exploration** and conquest; the Americas after Columbus, 1500-1620. [by] Betsy & Giulio Maestro. Lothrop, Lee & Shepard Bks. 1994 48p il maps hardcover o.p. pa $6.95

Grades: 2 3 4   970.01

1. America -- Exploration

ISBN 0-688-09268-3 lib bdg; 0-688-15474-3 pa

LC 93-48618

"The book's most outstanding feature is its full-color artwork. Large, double-page spreads give scope to dramatic landscapes, while smaller pictures on every page show events, places, and maps pertinent to the text. . . . This book provides a useful overview of the period." Booklist

Mann, Charles C.

★ **Before** Columbus; the Americas of 1491. Atheneum Books for Young Readers 2009 117p il map $24.99

Grades: 5 6 7 8 9 10   970.01

1. America -- Antiquities 2. Native Americans -- Origin 3. Native Americans -- History

ISBN 978-1-4169-4900-8; 1-4169-4900-3

LC 2009007691

Adapted from 1491, published 2006 by Knopf for adults

"Mann paints a superb picture of pre-Columbian America. In the process, he overturns the misconceived image of Natives as simple, widely scattered savages with minimal impact on their surroundings. Well-chosen, vividly colored graphics and photographs of mummies, pyramids, artifacts, and landscapes as well as the author's skillful storytelling

will command the attention of even the most reluctant readers." SLJ

Includes glossary and bibliographical references

Markle, Sandra

Animals Christopher Columbus saw; an adventure in the New World. by Sandra Markle; illustrations by Jamel Akib. Chronicle Books 2008 46p il $16.99

Grades: 2 3 4   970.01

1. Explorers 2. America -- Exploration 3. Animals -- North America

ISBN 978-0-8118-4916-6; 0-8118-4916-3

LC 2006033623

This "concentrates less on Christopher Columbus and more on the location, habitat, and fauna found during his discovery of the Americas." Publisher's note

Includes glossary and bibliographical references

Mooney, Carla

Explorers of the New World; discover the golden age of exploration; with 22 projects. illustrated by Tom Casteel. Nomad 2011 120p il map (Build it yourself) pa $15.95 970.01

1. Explorers 2. America -- Exploration

ISBN 978-1-936313-44-0; 1-936313-44-8

Provides twenty-two step-by-step projects to help readers learn about the explorers that discovered America and their voyages.

"This informative, entertaining activity book takes readers on a fascinating voyage of their own. . . . Each chapter concludes with 'Make Your Own' activities that bring life to the history with instructions for the construction of a logbook, clay activities, recipes, games, etc. Some may require the assistance of an adult but are not complicated or time consuming." SLJ

Includes glossary and bibliographical references

Wyatt, Valerie

★ **Who** discovered America? with illustrations by Howie Woo. Kids Can Press 2008 40p il map $17.95; pa $8.95

Grades: 4 5 6   970.01

1. America -- Antiquities 2. America -- Exploration

ISBN 978-1-55453-128-8; 1-55453-128-4; 978-1-55453-129-5 pa; 1-55453-129-2 pa

"With interesting sidebars and engaging illustrations and photos, this 'whodunit' of sorts describes, on a spread each, evidence for the journeys of various groups who discovered, or claimed to have discovered, [the North American] continent. . . . Wyatt writes clearly about how scientists unlock clues to how and when various groups could have made landfall. . . . Raising perhaps more questions than it answers, this book leaves it to readers to decide the solution to the mystery." SLJ

Includes glossary

970.02 North America 1600-1699

Maestro, Betsy

★ The **new** Americans; colonial times, 1620-1689. illustrated by Giulio Maestro. Lothrop, Lee & Shepard Bks. 1998 48p il map hardcover o.p. pa $7.99

Grades: 2 3 4   **970.02**

1. Canada -- History -- 0-1763 (New France) 2. United States -- History -- 1600-1775, Colonial period
ISBN 0-688-13448-3; 0-06-57572-7 pa

LC 95-19636

Traces the competition among the American Indians, French, English, Spanish, and Dutch for land, furs, timber, and other resources of North America

This is "accessibly written and meticulously illustrated. . . . Giulio Maestro's carefully detailed watercolor and color-pencil art includes maps, closely focused spot illustrations and dramatic spreads, which together provide a vivid picture of the century's pivotal events." Publ Wkly

971   Canada

Baker, Stuart

In the Arctic. Marshall Cavendish Benchmark 2010 32p il map (Climate change) lib bdg $19.95
Grades: 5 6 7 8   **971**

1. Arctic regions 2. Greenhouse effect
ISBN 978-0-7614-4437-4 lib bdg; 0-7614-4437-8 lib bdg

LC 2009-5767

The book about climate change in the Arctic "is perfectly organized for students. . . . Unique layout features serve as signposts and will help focus readers' attention. . . . [The book] features an outstanding chart of possible effects of global warming on the area in question, listing 'Possible Event,' 'Predicted Result,' and 'Impact' in short, bulleted statements." SLJ

Includes glossary

Bowers, Vivien

Hey Canada! by Vivien Bowers; illustrated by Milan Pavlovic. Tundra Books of Northern New York 2012 72 p. ill. (chiefly col.), maps (hardcover) $19.95
Grades: 3 4 5   **971**

1. Canada 2. Travelers 3. Voyages and travels
ISBN 1770492550; 9781770492554

LC 2011923470

This children's picture book by Vivien Bowers presents "a young traveler's . . . account of a quick province-by-province drive across Canada." The "9-year-old narrator [travels] to cities, roadside attractions and natural wonders from Cape Spear to Iqaluit." The book also provides information "about regional foods . . . and other artifacts of European settlement." (Kirkus Reviews)

Coulter, Laurie

★ Ballplayers and bonesetters; one hundred ancient Aztec and Maya jobs you might have adored or abhorred. [written] by Laurie Coulter; illustrated by Martha Newbigging. Annick Press 2008 96p il $25.95; pa $16.95
Grades: 4 5 6   **971**

1. Mayas 2. Aztecs
ISBN 978-1-55451-141-9; 1-55451-141-0; 978-1-55451-140-2 pa; 1-55451-140-2 pa

"Following a readable and humorous overview of the highly developed Aztec and Maya civilizations, this lively text lists 100 jobs that a young person might have held or aspired to during the Late Postclassic period in Mesoamerica

(1350 to 1521). . . . Taken as a whole, the descriptions of the vocations yield a rich view of the culture, and the breezy text makes this as much a browsing as a reference title. The colorful cartoon illustrations enhance the text, adding just the right artistic complement." SLJ

Greenwood, Barbara

★ A pioneer sampler; the daily life of a pioneer family in 1840. illustrated by Heather Collins. Ticknor & Fields Bks. for Young Readers 1995 240p il hardcover o.p. pa $15
Grades: 4 5 6 7   **971**

1. Frontier and pioneer life 2. Ontario
ISBN 0-395-71540-7; 0-395-88393-8 pa

LC 94-12829

First published 1994 in Canada with title: A pioneer story

"Using a combination of fiction and fact-filled supplementary commentary, with illustrations inspired by Garth Williams, the author tells the story of the Robertsons, a large, hardworking farm family. Good projects for school or home." N Y Times Book Rev

★ Junior Worldmark encyclopedia of the Canadian provinces; [Timothy L. Gall and Susan Bevan Gall, editors] 5th ed.; U.X.L 2007 294p il map $70
Grades: 5 6 7 8 9 10   **971**

1. Reference books 2. Canada
ISBN 978-1-4144-1060-9; 1-4144-1060-3

LC 2007003908

First published 1997

"Arranged by 40 . . . subheadings . . . this . . . resource provides . . . information on all of Canada's provinces and territories. [It includes] details on Canada's arts, climate, government, health, languages, notable persons, ethnic groups and . . . more." Publisher's note

Includes bibliographical references

Penn, Briony

The kids book of Canadian geography; written and illustrated by Briony Penn. Kids Can Press 2008 56p il map $19.95
Grades: 3 4 5 6   **971**

1. Canada
ISBN 978-1-55074-890-1; 1-55074-890-4

This "traces the continents' formation, touching on Canada's ancient landscapes, evolving climate, continent shaping and life on the land including human settlement, plus a geographical coast to coast tour and much more." Publisher's note

Sonneborn, Liz

Canada; by Liz Sonneborn. Children's Press 2012 144 p. col. ill.. col. maps (library) $40
Grades: 5 6 7 8   **971**

1. Canada 2. Canada -- Social life and customs
ISBN 0531253511; 9780531253519

LC 2011011970

This book by Liz Sonneborn is part of the Enchantment of the World series and looks at Canada. The introduction focuses on Canadian Terry Fox. Sonneborn "covers geography, natural resources, environment, history, government, diversity, religions, culture, and everyday life. She includes details like 'poutine' (fries, cheese curds, and gravy) and 'Timmies' (a coffee and doughnut chain)." (School Library Journal)

Includes bibliographical references (p. 134) and index.

Walker, Sally M.

★ **Blizzard** of glass; the Halifax explosion of 1917. Henry Holt 2011 xii, 145p il $18.99

Grades: 5 6 7 8   **971**

1. World War, 1914-1918 -- Naval operations 2. Halifax (N.S.) -- History -- Explosion, 1917

ISBN 978-0-8050-8945-5; 0-8050-8945-4

LC 2011005914

"The text reads smoothly with unfamiliar words defined in the text. Illustrations consist of two full-page maps and numerous black-and-white photos. The final chapter revisits the featured families and their descendants, thus tying up the loose ends. . . . This tragic, but well-told story belongs in most collections." SLJ

Includes bibliographical references

Williams, Brian

★ **Canada**; [by] Brian Williams; Tom Carter and Ben Cecil, consultants. National Geographic 2007 64p il map (Countries of the world) lib bdg $27.90; pa $12.95

Grades: 4 5 6 7   **971**

1. Canada

ISBN 978-1-4263-0025-7 lib bdg; 978-1-4263-0573-3 pa

LC 2007296572

A basic overview of the history, geography, climate and culture of Canada

This "clear, succinct [overview] will support assignments without overwhelming casual readers. . . . A good selection of recent, high-quality color photographs gives the [book] visual appeal." SLJ

Includes glossary and bibliographical references

971.01   Canada -- Early history to 1763

Worth, Richard

New France, 1534-1763; featuring the region that now includes all or parts of Michigan, Minnesota, Wisconsin, Illinois, Indiana, Ohio, Pennsylvania, Vermont, Maine, and Canada from Manitoba to Newfoundland. by Richard Worth. National Geographic Society 2007 109p il map (Voices from colonial America) $21.95; lib bdg $32.90

Grades: 5 6 7 8   **971.01**

1. Mississippi River valley -- History 2. Canada -- History -- 0-1763 (New France)

ISBN 978-1-4263-0147-6; 1-4263-0147-2; 978-1-4263-0148-3 lib bdg; 1-4263-0148-0 lib bdg

LC 2007-29544

"Worth presents the history of the vast French colony known as New France. Clearly written, the book is studded with quotes from people living in the colony and illustrated with colorful paintings, prints, and maps from a variety of periods. . . . This nicely designed introduction to a historically significant area fills a gap in many colonial history series and library collections." Booklist

Includes bibliographical references

972   Mexico, Central America, West Indies, Bermuda

Apte, Sunita

The **Aztec** empire. Children's Press 2009 48p il map (True book) lib bdg $26; pa $6.95

Grades: 3 4 5   **972**

1. Aztecs

ISBN 978-0-531-25227-7 lib bdg; 0-531-25227-2 lib bdg; 978-0-531-24108-0 pa; 0-531-24108-4 pa

LC 2009000299

In this book the Aztec empire is "outlined for young readers with care and precision. . . . Loaded with access points such as captions, pull-outs, a time line, and a map, and with better-than-usual reproductions of well-chosen primary sources and art, the [book sports] a bright, peppy design. . . . [This book is] rigorous in distinguishing fact from theory, and conscientious about presenting competing theories where they exist." SLJ

Includes glossary and bibliographical references

Cooke, Tim

★ **Ancient** Aztec; archaeology unlocks the secrets of Mexico's past. National Geographic 2007 64p il map (National Geographic investigates) $17.95; lib bdg $27.90

Grades: 4 5 6 7   **972**

1. Aztecs 2. Mexico -- Antiquities 3. Excavations (Archeology) -- Mexico

ISBN 978-1-4263-0072-1; 1-4263-0072-7; 978-1-4263-0073-8 lib bdg; 1-4263-0073-5 lib bdg

LC 2007024813

This describes ancient Aztec origins, technology, major archeological sites, civilization, and connections to the present

"Pithy and appealing. . . . Aerial photos, time [line], informative sidebars, an interview with an archaeologist, and excellent maps augment rigorously supported [text] that [asks] and [answers] interesting questions." SLJ

Gruber, Beth

★ **Mexico**; [by] Beth Gruber; Gary S. Elbow and Jorge Zamora, consultants. National Geographic 2007 64p il map (Countries of the world) lib bdg $27.90; pa $12.95

Grades: 4 5 6 7   **972**

1. Mexico

ISBN 0-7922-7669-8 lib bdg; 1-4263-0566-4 pa

LC 2004026452

"This volume introduces Mexico's geography, history, wildlife, culture, and government. The many excellent color photos and maps are a striking feature of the series. . . . This will be a useful addition to many libraries." Booklist

Includes glossary and bibliographical references

Harris, Nathaniel

★ **Ancient** Maya; archaeology unlocks the secrets to the Maya's past. by Nathaniel Harris; Elizabeth Graham, consultant. National Geographic 2008 64p il map (National Geographic investigates) $17.95; lib bdg $27.90

Grades: 4 5 6 7   **972**

1. Mayas 2. Mexico -- Antiquities 3. Excavations (Archeology) -- Mexico

ISBN 978-1-4263-0227-5; 1-4263-0227-4; 978-1-4263-0228-2 lib bdg; 1-4263-0228-2 lib bdg

LC 2007047837

This describes ancient Mayan civilization and how archeologists found out about it.

Includes glossary and bibliographical references

Heinrichs, Ann

The **Aztecs**; by Ann Heinrichs. Benchmark Books 2011 64 p. (Technology of the ancients) (print) $32.79
Grades: 4 5 6 7   972

1. Aztecs 2. Technological innovations -- History
ISBN 1608707652; 9781608707539; 9781608707652
                                LC 2011018348

This book, by Ann Heinrichs, includes "presentations of [the Aztec's] ancient cultures, emphasiz[ing] governance and material culture (clothing, crafts, architecture). The book [does] not cover the origins of the empires or try to explain how they became so powerful." (School Library Journal)

★ Junior Worldmark encyclopedia of the Mexican states; [Timothy L. Gall and Susan Bevan Gall, editors] 2nd ed.; U.X.L,Thomson/Gale 2007 423p il map $70
Grades: 5 6 7 8 9 10   972

1. Reference books 2. Mexico
ISBN 978-1-4144-1112-5
                                LC 2007003906

First published 2004

"Arranged by 28 . . . subheadings . . . Junior Worldmark Encyclopedia of the Mexican States provides . . . information on each of Mexico's 31 states. Topics covered include climate, plants and animals, population and ethnic groups, religions, transportation, history, state and local governments, political parties, judicial system, economy, education, arts, media, tourism, sports, famous people and . . . more." Publisher's note

Includes bibliographical references

Kent, Deborah

Mexico; by Deborah Kent. Children's Press 2012 144 p. cil. ill., photographs (library) $40
Grades: 5 6 7 8   972

1. Mexico 2. Culture 3. Mexico -- History
ISBN 0531253554; 9780531253557
                              LC 2011010812

This book by Deborah Kent is part of the Enchantment of the World series and looks at Mexico. The books in the series offer 10 "chapters, several maps, a fast-facts section, and a few references to other sources, including a referral to a Scholastic website (new). The chapters cover geography, natural environment, history, politics, people and culture." (School Library Journal)

Includes bibliographical references and index.

Kops, Deborah

Palenque; by Deborah Kops. Twenty-First Century Books 2008 80p il (Unearthing ancient worlds) lib bdg $30.60
Grades: 5 6 7 8   972

1. Mayas 2. Mexico -- Antiquities 3. Palenque site (Mexico) 4. Excavations (Archeology) -- Mexico
ISBN 978-0-8225-7504-7 lib bdg; 0-8225-7504-3 lib bdg
                                LC 2007021323

This describes the discovery of the ancient Mayan site of Palenque in 1840 by John Stephens and Frederick Catherwood, and the mid-20th century excavations of the site by Alberto Ruz Lhuillier, who discovered the tomb of the Mayan king Pakal, who died in 683 A.D., inside a pyramid

This "clearly written [title is] illustrated with large photographs and period artwork, and the pages are broken up with text boxes featuring quotes and interesting anecdotes." SLJ

Includes glossary and bibliographical references

Lourie, Peter

Hidden world of the Aztec. Boyds Mills Press 2006 48p il map $17.95
Grades: 4 5 6 7   972

1. Aztecs 2. Excavations (Archeology) -- Mexico
ISBN 978-1-59078-069-5; 1-59078-069-8

The author takes a "look at the Aztecs from the perspective of archaeological digs at the Great Temple in modern-day Mexico City and at the Pyramid of the Moon in Teotihuacan. . . . The writing style is clear, informative, and interesting." SLJ

Includes glossary and bibliographical references

McDaniel, Melissa

New Mexico; [by] Melissa McDaniel, Ettagale Blauer, and Jason Laure. 2nd ed.; Marshall Cavendish Benchmark 2008 144p il map (Celebrate the states) lib bdg $39.93
Grades: 4 5 6 7   972

1. New Mexico
ISBN 978-0-7614-2719-3; 0-7614-2719-8
                                LC 2007-9273

First published 1999

"Provides comprehensive information on the geography, history, wildlife, governmental structure, economy, cultural diversity, peoples, religion, and landmarks of New Mexico." Publisher's note

Includes bibliographical references

Streissguth, Thomas

Mexico; by Tom Streissguth. Lerner Publications Company 2008 48p il map (Country explorers) lib bdg $27.93; pa $8.95
Grades: 2 3 4   972

1. Mexico
ISBN 978-0-8225-7130-8 lib bdg; 978-0-8225-8508-4 pa
                                LC 2006036726

This introduction to Mexico covers "all of the areas of interest to students, including animals, sports, foods, celebrations, storytime, and even a few words in the country's native language. Small amounts of information are surrounded by current photographs, maps, charts, and illustrations. . . . Sure to grab the attention of even reluctant readers." SLJ

Includes glossary and bibliographical references

972.81   Guatemala

Croy, Anita

★ **Guatemala**. National Geographic 2009 64p il map (Countries of the world) lib bdg $27.90
Grades: 4 5 6 7   972.81

1. Guatemala
ISBN 978-1-4263-0471-2 lib bdg; 1-4263-0471-4 lib bdg

This describes the geography, nature, history, people and culture, government and economy of Guatemala

Includes glossary and bibliographical references

Mann, Elizabeth

★ Tikal; the center of the Maya world. with illustrations by Tom McNeely. Mikaya Press 2002 47p il map (Wonders of the world) $19.95

Grades: 4 5 6 7   **972.81**

1. Mayas -- Antiquities

ISBN 1-931414-05-X

LC 2002-29599

A history of the Maya Indians in the city of Tikal, founded in 800 B.C.

"Mann's narrative flows smoothly, and frequent, full-color illustrations . . . help to clarify the details mentioned in the text." Booklist

Includes glossary

Ollhoff, Jim

Mayan and Aztec mythology; by Jim Ollhoff. ABDO Publishing Company 2011 32p. ill. (The world of mythology) lib bdg $27.07

Grades: 5 6 7 8   **972.81**

1. Mythology 2. Mayas -- Folklore 3. Aztecs -- Folklore 4. Mayas -- Religion 5. Aztecs -- Religion

ISBN 1617147249; 9781617147241

LC 2010042976

This describes the history of myths of the Maya and Aztecs, their meaning, and their gods and goddesses including Itzamna, Xolotl, the Aztec feathered serpent god Quetzalcoatl,and the Mayan rain god Chac.

"Ollhoff writes in a clear and engaging fashion, presenting complex issues in a way that will be easy for youngsters to grasp. . . . The photographs and reproductions of art tie directly to the [text]." SLJ

972.82   Belize

Jermyn, Leslie

Belize; [by] Leslie Jermyn and Yong Jui Lin. 2nd ed.; Marshall Cavendish Benchmark 2012 144p il map (Cultures of the world) lib bdg $42.79

Grades: 5 6 7 8   **972.82**

1. Belize

ISBN 978-1-60870-452-1; 1-60870-452-1

LC 2010035966

Provides information on the geography, history, wildlife, governmental structure, economy, cultural diversity, peoples, religion, and culture of Belize.

"The concise writing offers enough material for report writers without overwhelming them. Numerous full-color and black-and-white photos of interest, a clean layout, and use of pastels to highlight headings and sidebars contribute to the attractiveness of . . . [this presentation]." SLJ

Includes glossary and bibliographical references

972.83   Honduras

McGaffey, Leta

Honduras; [by] Leta McGaffey and Michael Spilling. 2nd ed.; Marshall Cavendish Benchmark 2010 144p il map (Cultures of the world) lib bdg $42.79

Grades: 5 6 7 8   **972.83**

1. Honduras

ISBN 978-0-7614-4848-8 lib bdg; 0-7614-4848-9 lib bdg

LC 2009022642

First published 1999

"Provides comprehensive information on the geography, history, wildlife, governmental structure, economy, cultural diversity, peoples, religion, and culture of Honduras." Publisher's note

Includes glossary and bibliographical references

Shields, Charles J.

Honduras. Mason Crest Pubs. 2003 63p il map (Discovering Central America) lib bdg $19.95

Grades: 4 5 6 7   **972.83**

1. Honduras

ISBN 1-59084-096-8

LC 2002-9089

This describes the history, geography, and culture of Honduras

This is "jam-packed with useful information. . . . [It contains] straightforward writing, clearly titled chapters, high quality color, and well-captioned photographs and graphics." Libr Media Connect

Includes glossary and bibliographical references

972.84   El Salvador

Foley, Erin

El Salvador; [by] Erin Foley, Rafiz Hapipi. 2nd ed.; Benchmark Bks. 2005 144p il map (Cultures of the world) lib bdg $42.79

Grades: 5 6 7 8   **972.84**

1. El Salvador

ISBN 0-7614-1967-5

LC 2005009360

First published 1994

This describes the geography, history, government, economy, environment, people, lifestyle, religion, language, arts, leisure, festivals, and food of El Salvador

Includes glossary and bibliographical references

972.85   Nicaragua

Kott, Jennifer

★ Nicaragua; [by] Jennifer Kott, Kristi Streiffert. 2nd ed.; Benchmark Bks. 2005 144p il map (Cultures of the world) lib bdg $42.79

Grades: 5 6 7 8   **972.85**

1. Nicaragua

ISBN 0-7614-1969-1

LC 2005009240

First published 1994

An illustrated overview of the geography, economy, history, government, politics, and culture of Nicaragua

Includes glossary and bibliographical references

972.86   Costa Rica

Foley, Erin

Costa Rica; [by] Erin Foley and Barbara Cooke. 2nd ed.; Marshall Cavendish Benchmark 2008 144p il map (Cultures of the world) lib bdg $42.79

Grades: 5 6 7 8   **972.86**

1. Costa Rica

ISBN 978-0-7614-2079-8 lib bdg; 0-7614-2079-7 lib bdg

LC 2006101736

First published 1997

This offers "information on the geography, history, wildlife, governmental structure, economy, cultural diversity, peoples, religion, and culture of Costa Rica." Publisher's note

Includes glossary and bibliographical references

Yomtov, Nel

★ Costa Rica; by Nel Yomtov. Scholastic Library Pub 2014 144 p. illustrations, color maps (library binding) $40

Grades: 5 6 7 8   **972.86**

1. Costa Rica 2. Costa Rica

ISBN 0531220141; 9780531220146

LC 2013022563

This book, by Nel Yomtov, focuses on Costa Rica. The "country's culture, history, and geography are explored in detail, allowing readers a chance to see how people live in faraway nations. . . . Sidebars highlight especially interesting people, places, and events . . . [and] easy recipes give readers the opportunity to experience foreign cuisine first-hand." (Publisher's note)

Includes bibliographical references and index

972.87   Panama

Hassig, Susan M.

Panama; [by] Susan Hassig & Lynette Quek. 2nd ed.; Marshall Cavendish Benchmark 2007 144p il map (Cultures of the world) lib bdg $42.79

Grades: 5 6 7 8   **972.87**

1. Panama

ISBN 978-0-7614-2028-6 lib bdg; 0-7614-2028-2 lib bdg

LC 2006020824

First published 1996

This provides "information on the geography, history, wildlife, governmental structure, economy, cultural diversity, peoples, religion, and culture of Panama." Publisher's note

Includes glossary and bibliographical references

972.9   West Indies (Antilles) and Bermuda

Kras, Sara Louise

Antigua and Barbuda; [by] Sara Louise Kras. Marshall Cavendish Benchmark 2008 144p il map (Cultures of the world) lib bdg $42.79

Grades: 5 6 7 8   **972.9**

1. Antigua and Barbuda

ISBN 978-0-7614-2570-0

LC 2006031537

This describes the geography, history, government, economy, environment, people, and culture of Antigua and Barbuda

Includes glossary and bibliographical references

972.91   Cuba

Green, Jen

★ Cuba; [by] Jen Green; Damián Fernández and Alejandro de la Fuente, consultants. National Geographic 2007 64p il map (Countries of the world) lib bdg $27.90

Grades: 4 5 6 7   **972.91**

1. Cuba

ISBN 978-1-4263-0057-8

LC 2007026468

This describes the geography, nature, history, people & culture, government & economy of Cuba.

Includes glossary and bibliographical references

Sheehan, Sean

Cuba; [by] Sean Sheehan, Leslie Jermyn. 2nd ed.; Benchmark Bks. 2005 144p il map (Cultures of the world) lib bdg $42.79

Grades: 5 6 7 8   **972.91**

1. Cuba

ISBN 0-7614-1965-9

LC 2005009362

First published 1994

This describes the geography, history, government, economy, population, lifestyle, religion, language, arts, leisure, festivals, and food of Cuba

Includes glossary and bibliographical references

Stein, R. Conrad

Cuban Missile Crisis; in the shadow of nuclear war. Enslow Publishers 2009 128p il map (America's living history) lib bdg $31.93

Grades: 5 6 7 8   **972.91**

1. Cuban Missile Crisis, 1962 2. Soviet Union -- Foreign relations -- United States 3. United States -- Foreign relations -- Soviet Union

ISBN 978-0-7660-2905-7 lib bdg; 0-7660-2905-0 lib bdg

LC 2008-4703

"Discusses the Cuban missile crisis, a thirteen-day struggle between the United States and the Soviet Union, including the causes of the conflict, the leaders faced with important decisions, and the final resolution to avoid nuclear war." Publisher's note

Includes glossary and bibliographical references

Tracy, Kathleen

We visit Cuba. Mitchell Lane Publishers 2010 63p il (Your land and my land) lib bdg $33.95

Grades: 4 5 6 7   **972.91**

1. Cuba

ISBN 978-1-58415-890-5 lib bdg; 1-58415-890-5 lib bdg

LC 2010006558

"With an inviting format that includes bright color photos on every spread, this title . . . offers an appealing overview of Cuba's history, geography, culture and lifestyle, politics, economics, and more. . . . A good starting point for research as well as for personal interest." Booklist

Includes glossary and bibliographical references

972.92   Jamaica and Cayman Islands

Green, Jen

★ Jamaica; [by] Jen Green; David J. Howard and Joel Frater, consultants. National Geographic 2008 64p il map (Countries of the world) lib bdg $27.90

Grades: 4 5 6 7   **972.92**

1. Jamaica

ISBN 978-1-4263-0300-5 lib bdg; 1-4263-0300-9 lib bdg

This describes the geography, nature, history, people and culture, government, and economy of Jamaica.

Includes glossary and bibligraphical references

Sheehan, Sean

Jamaica; [by] Sean Sheehan & Angela Black. 2nd ed; Benchmark Books 2004 144p il map (Cultures of the world) lib bdg $42.79

Grades: 5 6 7 8   **972.92**

1. Jamaica

ISBN 0-7614-1785-0

LC 2004-7676

First published 1996

Introduces the geography, history, religion, government, economy, and culture of Jamaica

"An informative book with captivating pictures, a visually attractive layout, and flowing text. . . . A well-balanced and interesting look at one country's culture." SLJ

Includes glossary and bibliographical references

972.93   Dominican Republic

Foley, Erin

Dominican Republic; [by] Erin Foley & Leslie Jermyn. 2nd ed; Marshall Cavendish Benchmark 2005 144p (Cultures of the world) lib bdg $42.79

Grades: 5 6 7 8   **972.93**

1. Dominican Republic

ISBN 0-7614-1966-7

First published 1995

"The material is well organized in easily readable sections, accurately illustrated with well-placed, full-color photographs on every page." SLJ

972.94   Haiti

Aronin, Miriam

Earthquake in Haiti. Bearport Pub. 2011 32p il map (Code red) lib bdg $25.27

Grades: 4 5 6 7   **972.94**

1. Earthquakes 2. Haiti

ISBN 978-1-936088-66-9; 1-936088-66-5

LC 2010011126

Describes the devastating earthquake that occurred in Haiti on January 12, 2010.

"The text is written from the points of view of some of the people involved, including primary source direct quotes. Some of the pictures are necessarily graphic, which adds to the authenticity. . . . This title will be used for browsing as well as for reports." Libr Media Connect

Includes glossary and bibliographical references

Benoit, Peter

The Haitian earthquake of 2010. Children's Press 2011 48p il (True book: disasters) lib bdg $28; pa $6.95

Grades: 3 4 5   **972.94**

1. Earthquakes 2. Haiti

ISBN 978-0-531-25420-2 lib bdg; 0-531-25420-8; 978-0-531-26625-0 pa; 0-531-26625-7 pa

LC 2011007912

This book about the earthquake in Haiti in 2010 and its aftermath is "thoughtfully designed. . . . The information . . . is right on target: concise, accurate, and thorough. . . . The photographs . . . are especially effective at putting a human face on large-scale devastation." Booklist

Includes glossary and bibliographical references

Mara, Wil

Haiti; [by] Wil Mara. Marshall Cavendish Benchmark 2007 48p il map (Discovering cultures) lib bdg $28.50

Grades: 2 3 4   **972.94**

1. Haiti

ISBN 978-0-7614-1987-7 lib bdg; 0-7614-1987-X lib bdg

LC 2006011473

An introduction to the geography, history, people, and culture of Haiti

Includes glossary and bibliographical references

NgCheong-Lum, Roseline, 1962-

Haiti; [by] Roseline Ng Cheong-Lum & Leslie Jermyn. 2nd ed; Marshall Cavendish Benchmark 2005 144p il map (Cultures of the world) lib bdg $42.79

Grades: 5 6 7 8   **972.94**

1. Haiti

ISBN 0-7614-1968-3

First published 1995

Describes the geography, history, government, economy, culture, peoples, and religion of Haiti

Includes glossary and bibliographical references

Yomtov, Nel

Haiti; by Nel Yomtov. Children's Press 2012 144 p. col. ill. (library) $40

Grades: 5 6 7 8   **972.94**

1. Haiti

ISBN 0531253538; 9780531253533

LC 2011010048

This book is part of the Enchantment of the World series and focuses on Haiti. This series presents "factual information against a backdrop of brightly colored pictures and maps. . . . Each book provides a timeline, Fast Facts, and embassies." The books also include "brief chapters that follow real people in their daily lives." (Library Media Connection)

Includes bibliographical references and index.

972.9407   Haiti 1957-

Oelschlager, Vanita

I came from the water; one Haitian boy's incredible tale of survival. VanitaBooks 2012 $8.95

Grades: K 1 2   **972.9407**

1. Haiti 2. Orphans 3. Picture books for children

ISBN 0983290458; 9780983290452

In this book, Vanita Oelschlager "shares the real-life story of an eight-year-old Haitian boy who, as an infant, was packed into a basket during a catastrophic flood, rescued, and sent to a children's village, where he was named Moses. . . . Moses describes the priest who runs the village . . . and the new children who arrived after the great earthquake of 2012" 'I am one of the strong ones,' he says. 'I must help those who are not as strong.'" (Publishers Weekly)

972.95   Puerto Rico

DaSilva-Gordon, Maria

Puerto Rico; past and present. Rosen Central 2011 48p il map (The United States: past and present) lib bdg $26.50; pa $11.75

Grades: 3 4 5 6   **972.95**

1. Puerto Rico

ISBN 978-1-4358-9502-7 lib bdg; 1-4358-9502-9 lib bdg; 978-1-4358-9529-4 pa; 1-4358-9529-0 pa

LC 2010005891

This describes the history, culture, economy, and geography of the island of Puerto Rico.

Includes bibliographical references

Schwabacher, Martin

Puerto Rico; by Martin Schwabacher and Steve Otfinoski. 2nd ed.; Marshall Cavendish Benchmark 2010 144p il map (Celebrate the states) $42.79

Grades: 5 6 7 8   **972.95**

1. Puerto Rico

ISBN 978-0-7614-4734-4; 0-7614-4734-2

LC 2009007066

First published 2001

This offers information on the geography, history, wildlife, governmental structure, economy, cultural diversity, peoples, religion, and landmarks of Puerto Rico.

Includes bibliographical references

Stille, Darlene R.

Puerto Rico. Children's Press 2009 144p il map (America the beautiful, third series) lib bdg $39

Grades: 4 5 6 7   **972.95**

1. Puerto Rico

ISBN 978-0-531-18589-6; 0-531-18589-3

LC 2008000819

An introduction to the land, history, and people of Puerto Rico.

Includes glossary and bibliographical references

972.96   Bahama Islands

Hintz, Martin

The Bahamas; by Martin Hintz. Children's Press 2013 144 p. col. ill., col. maps (Enchantment of the world. Second series) (library) $40

Grades: 5 6 7 8   **972.96**

1. Bahamas 2. Bahamas -- Description and travel

ISBN 0531275418; 9780531275412

LC 2012000513

This book, by Martin Hintz, is part of the "Enchantment of the World" series. In it the author provides information and photographs showcasing the people, places and events surrounding the Caribbean island chain of the Bahamas. Contents include photographs of Bahaman cities and landscapes, statistics describing the islands' features, and traditional Bahaman recipes.

Includes bibliographical references and index

972.98   Windward and other southern islands

Elias, Marie Louise

Barbados; [by] Marie Louise Elias and Josie Elias. 2nd ed.; Marshall Cavendish Benchmark 2010 144p il map (Cultures of the world) lib bdg $42.79

Grades: 5 6 7 8   **972.98**

1. Barbados

ISBN 978-0-7614-4853-2 lib bdg; 0-7614-4853-5 lib bdg

LC 2009044592

First published 2000

This offers information on the geography, history, wildlife, governmental structure, economy, cultural diversity, peoples, religion, and culture of Barbados

Includes glossary and bibliographical references

Orr, Tamra

Saint Lucia; [by] Tamra Orr. 2nd ed.; Marshall Cavendish Benchmark 2008 144p il map (Cultures of the world) lib bdg $42.79

Grades: 5 6 7 8   **972.98**

1. Saint Lucia

ISBN 978-0-7614-2569-4

First published 1997

This describes the geography, history, government, economy, environment, people, and culture of Saint Lucia

Includes glossary and bibliographical references

Pang, Guek-Cheng, 1950-

Grenada; 2nd ed.; Marshall Cavendish Benchmark 2011 144p il map (Cultures of the world) lib bdg $42.79

Grades: 5 6 7 8   **972.98**

1. Grenada

ISBN 978-1-6087-0216-9; 1-6087-0216-2

LC 2010019807

First published 2001

Provides information on the geography, history, wild-life, governmental structure, economy, cultural diversity, peoples, religion, and culture of Grenada.

Includes glossary and bibliographical references

973   United States

Addasi, Maha

A **kid's** guide to Arab American history; more than 50 activities. by Yvonne Wakim Dennis and Maha Addasi. 1st ed. Chicago Review Press 2013 xx, 204 p.p ill. (paperback) $16.95

Grades: 4 5 6 7   **973**

1. Arab Americans -- History 2. Arab Americans -- Social life and customs 3. Arab Americans -- History 4. Arab Americans -- History -- Study and teaching -- Activity programs

ISBN 1613740174; 9781613740170

LC 2012035758

This book by Yvonne Wakim Dennis and Maha Addasi "provides a contemporary as well as historical look at the people and experiences that have shaped Arab American culture. Each chapter focuses on a different group of Arab Americans including those of Lebanese, Syrian, Palestinian, Jordanian, Egyptian, Iraqi, and Yemeni descent and features more than 50 fun activities that highlight their distinct arts, games, clothing, and food." (Publisher's note)

America the Beautiful, third series. Children's Press 2007 52v il map lib bdg set $851.20

Grades: 4 5 6 7   **973**

1. United States

ISBN 978-0-531-20407-8 lib bdg; 0-531-20407-3 lib bdg

Replaces America the Beautiful, second series, published 1998-2001; Original series published 1987-1992

This series describes the geography, history, people, economy, and government of each state

"Most students should be able to satisfy their information needs with these polished new editions, and the copious extras and lively presentation will help keep them interested too." Booklist

Armstrong, Jennifer

★ The **American** story; 100 true tales from American history. illustrated by Roger Roth. Alfred A. Knopf 2006 358p il map $34.95; lib bdg $39.99

Grades: 4 5 6 7   **973**

1. United States -- History

ISBN 0-375-81256-3; 0-375-91256-8 lib bdg

LC 2005-34822

"This large, fully illustrated compendium features 100 stories, familiar and lesser known, drawn from America's past and arranged in chronological order.... Thanks to writing that is consistently good and sometimes excellent, the tales will certainly hold readers' attention, and brightening nearly every page are lively drawings enhanced by water-color washes." Booklist

Includes bibliographical references

Bockenhauer, Mark H.

★ **Our** fifty states; by Mark H. Bockenhauer and Stephen F. Cunha; foreword by former president Jimmy Carter. National Geographic Society 2004 239p il map $25.95; lib bdg $45.90

Grades: 4 5 6 7   **973**

1. Reference books 2. United States

ISBN 0-7922-6402-9; 0-7922-6992-6 lib bdg

LC 2004-1190

This "book is organized by regions: the Northeast, Southeast, Midwest, Southwest, and West, with a map of each region and a short history. Four pages are devoted to each state and include basic facts and a map. The full-color photographs are outstanding. Reproductions of archival illustrations depict four important events from each state's history. The final sections offer a paragraph about each of the territories and a page of facts and figures about the United States." SLJ

Includes bibliographical references

Buckley, Susan

★ **Journeys** for freedom; a new look at America's story. [by] Susan Buckley and Elspeth Leacock; illustrations by Rodica Prato. Houghton Mifflin Co. 2006 48p il map $17

Grades: 4 5 6 7   **973**

1. United States -- History

ISBN 978-0-618-22323-7; 0-618-22323-1

LC 2004000974

This "history focuses on 20 individuals' quest for freedom across U.S. history. Some . . . will be familiar, but most will not. The stories, both varied and fascinating, often go beyond the personal. . . . Running along the bottom of each double-page spread is a pictorial map keyed to the text. . . . The authors make excellent use of primary sources. . . . As powerful as it is useful." Booklist

Kids make history; a new look at America's story. [by] Susan Buckley and Elspeth Leacock; Illustrations by Randy Jones. Houghton Mifflin 2006 48p il $17

Grades: 4 5 6 7   **973**

1. United States -- History

ISBN 978-0-618-22329-9; 0-618-22329-0

LC 2005036309

"This book introduces 20 children in extraordinary times, starting in 1607 with Pocahontas and ending in 2001 with 9/11 as experienced by high school senior Jukay Hsu. Laura Ingalls Wilder; John Rankin, Jr.; and Susie Baker, a young slave celebrating her independence in 1863, are among those included. The text and the highly detailed watercolor illustrations are married with numbers in small red boxes keyed to both elements for clarification. . . . A good browsing choice for children interested in American history." SLJ

Cooper, Ilene

★ **Jack**; the early years of John F. Kennedy. by Ilene Cooper. 1st ed. Penguin Group USA 2013 168 p. ill. (paperback) $12.99

Grades: 5 6 7 8 9 10 11 12   **973**

1. Presidents 2. Presidents -- United States

ISBN 0147510317; 9780147510310

LC 2002075912

This book by Ilene Cooper offers a "portrait of [John F.] Kennedy's "youth and the forces that shaped it. . . . Readers discover what it was like for Jack to grow up under the paradoxical influences of privilege and prejudice. His father's wealth . . . couldn't remove the perceived taint of the family's Irish Catholic heritage . . . . To compensate, Joseph and Rose Kennedy pushed their children to excel at everything they did," leading to rivalry between Jack and his brother Joe. (Horn Book Magazine)

"Intelligent design and numerous fabulous, well-placed, and well-captioned black-and-white photographs enrich Cooper's clear prose. . . . This sensitive, well-researched biography will enhance any collection." Voice Youth Advocates

Includes bibliographical references and index.

Croy, Elden

United States. National Geographic 2010 64p il map (Countries of the world) lib bdg $27.90

Grades: 4 5 6 7　　　　　　　　　　　　　　　973

1. United States

ISBN 978-1-4263-0632-7 lib bdg; 1-4263-0632-6 lib bdg

This describes the geography, nature, history, people and culture, government and economy of the United States.

"The information is substantial but not overwhelming. The [text is] clear, and the discussion points are well chosen. . . . [The text is] complemented with stunning photographs." SLJ

Hoose, Phillip M.

★ We were there, too! young people in U.S. history. [by] Phillip Hoose. Farrar, Straus & Giroux 2001 264p il $28

Grades: 5 6 7 8　　　　　　　　　　　　　　　973

1. Youth 2. Children 3. United States -- History

ISBN 0-374-38252-2

LC 99-89052

Biographies of dozens of young people who made a mark in American history, including explorers, planters, spies, cowpunchers, sweatshop workers, and civil rights workers

"A treasure chest of history come to life, this is an inspired collection. . . . Because the book is packed with historical documents, evocatively illustrated . . . and full of eyewitness quotations, it should prove valuable to young historians and researchers." SLJ

Includes bibliographical references

Isaacs, Sally Senzell

Colonists and independence. Kingfisher 2011 32p il map (All about America)

Grades: 3 4 5 6　　　　　　　　　　　　　　　973

1. United States -- History -- 1783-1809 2. United States -- History -- 1775-1783, Revolution 3. United States -- History -- 1600-1775, Colonial period

ISBN 0-7534-6513-2 pa; 0-7534-6581-7; 978-0-7534-6513-4 pa; 978-0-7534-6581-3

This book covers U.S. history from 1600 to 1800.

This "visually appealing [title] effectively [combines] paintings, engravings, primary documents, and photographs with cartoon illustrations. The eye-catching [layout includes] different font sizes, bold type, and text boxes to highlight different pieces of information. The content is interesting and pithy." SLJ

Includes glossary and bibliographical references

★ It's my state [series]　Second ed.; Marshall Cavendish Benchmark 2010 18v il map lib bdg set $564.43

Grades: 3 4 5　　　　　　　　　　　　　　　973

1. United States

ISBN 978-1-60870-044-8 group 1

Series first published 2003-2007

"These information-packed updates will be great resources both for kids doing reports as well as for families who are planning a trip. . . . Each chapter is full of interesting facts, entertaining details, and fun quotes. The texts are accessible, straightforward, and clear, and are broken up on each page by a colorful photo, graph, time line, or map." SLJ

Johnston, Robert D.

★ The making of America; the history of the United States from 1492 to the present. Robert D. Johnston; with a foreword by Douglas Brinkley. Revised ed. National Geographic 2010 240 p. ill. (chiefly col.), col. maps (hardcover) $29.95; (library) $38.90

Grades: 5 6 7 8　　　　　　　　　　　　　　　973

1. United States -- History

ISBN 9781426306631; 1426306636; 9781426306655; 1426306652

LC 2011401219

First published 2002

Includes bibliographical references (p. 226-234) and index.

"This energetically written and profusely illustrated history remains one of the top-drawer single-volume accounts of the founding and growth of the U.S. for middle grade students. The previous edition ended with 9/11; here, into the same page count, Johnston fits Hurricane Katrina, the wars in Iraq and Afghanistan, Barack Obama's election, and other major events." Booklist

★ Junior Worldmark encyclopedia of the states; [Timothy L. Gall and Susan Bevan Gall, editors] 5th ed.; Thomson Gale 2007 4v il map set $235

Grades: 5 6 7 8 9 10　　　　　　　　　　　　　973

1. Reference books 2. United States -- Encyclopedias

ISBN 978-1-4144-1106-4 set; 1-4144-1106-5 set

LC 2007003910

First published 1996

This reference "includes facts and details on every state in the U.S., including the District of Columbia and U.S. dependencies. Entries cover the geography, history, politics, economy and other facts about each state. Alphabetically arranged entries feature . . . subheadings for each state. . . . An index of people, places and subjects [is included]." Publisher's note

Includes bibliographical references

King, David C.

★ Children's encyclopedia of American history. DK Pub. 2003 304p il map $29.99

Grades: 5 6 7 8　　　　　　　　　　　　　　　973

1. Reference books 2. United States -- History -- Encyclopedias

ISBN 0-7894-8330-0

LC 2002-73388

Full-color maps, photographs, and paintings illustrate a comprehensive reference guide to American history

"A visually enticing and textually fascinating survey." SLJ

Kuntz, Lynn

★ **Celebrate** the USA; hands-on history activities for kids. [by] Lynn Kuntz; illustrated by Mark A. Hicks. Gibbs Smith, Publisher 2007 80p il map pa $7.95

Grades: 3 4 5   **973**

1. United States -- History

ISBN 978-1-58685-846-9 pa; 1-58685-846-7 pa

LC 2006021953

This is a "fact-filled, fun-to-read compendium of American history and 25 related activities. . . . Many topics and fascinating facts are covered in brief, sometimes humorous explanations. Coverage includes the early immigrants, how America got its name, Native Americans, the 13 colonies, currency, songs, and holidays." SLJ

Lapham, Steven Sellers

Philip Reid saves the statue of freedom; Written by Steven Sellers Lapham and Dr. Eugene Walton; Illustrated by R. Gregory Christie. Sleeping Bear Press 2013 40 p. color illustrations $16.99

Grades: 2 3 4   **973**

1. Slaves -- United States -- 19th century 2. United States Capitol (Washington, D.C.) 3. African Americans 4. Foundry workers -- United States

ISBN 1585368199; 9781585368198

LC 2013002586

"Born into slavery, Philip Reid grew up on a South Carolina farm, helping various craftsmen such as the blacksmith and the potter. Eventually, he was sold to a man named Clark Mills, who was opening a foundry in Washington, D.C. Mr. Mills's foundry is contracted to cast the Freedom statue but the project is jeopardized when a seemingly unsolvable puzzle arises." (Publisher's note)

"Acrylic gouache artwork adds a visual richness to the story, and endpapers include primary source documents. Only the addition of a source list could have strengthened this already strong book." Lib Med Con

Leacock, Elspeth

★ **Journeys** in time; a new atlas of American history. [by] Elspeth Leacock and Susan Buckley; illustrations by Rodica Prato. Houghton Mifflin 2001 48p il maps $15; pa $6.95

Grades: 4 5 6 7   **973**

1. United States -- History 2. United States -- Historical geography

ISBN 0-395-97956-0; 0-618-31114-9 pa

LC 00-40803

Each double-page spread of this book "takes an individual who was part of a historic movement (such as the Underground Railroad or immigration) and gives a brief narrative outlining his or her circumstances. Added to the text are sequential numbers that indicate major events in each of the twenty journeys. A double-page location map traces the routes each took, using illustrative vignettes marked with corresponding numbers that reference the text." Horn Book

Leedy, Loreen

Celebrate the 50 states; written and illustrated by Loreen Leedy. Holiday House 1999 32p il maps hardcover o.p. pa $6.95

Grades: K 1 2 3   **973**

1. United States

ISBN 0-8234-1431-0; 0-8234-1631-3 pa

LC 99-10986

Introduces statistics, emblems, notable cities, products, and other facts about the fifty states, United States territories, and Washington, D.C.

"Brightly colored and amusingly designed, this is a simple yet winning introduction to the U.S." Booklist

Moberg, Julia

Presidential pets; by Julia Moberg; illustrated by Jeff Albrecht. Charlesbridge Pub. 2012 95 p. col. ill. (reinforced) $14.95

Grades: 3 4 5   **973**

1. Presidents -- United States 2. Presidents' pets -- United States 3. Pets -- United States 4. Presidents -- United States -- Biography

ISBN 9781936140794

LC 2011047785

In this book by Julia Moberg readers "will discover that all our chief executives but one, from Washington to Obama, have owned a variety of pets -- and, in some cases, been owned by them. In addition to the familiar dogs, cats and birds, some unusual First Animals have included goats, mice, bears, zebras, hyenas, lions, snakes, rats and tigers. . . Brief details about each president's life and term [and] a 'Tell Me More!' feature with tidbits of trivia . . . supplement the pet facts." (Kirkus)

Pinkney, Andrea Davis

Hand in hand; ten Black men who changed America. by Andrea Davis Pinkney; paintings by Brian Pinkney. Disney/Jump at the Sun 2012 243 p. $19.99

Grades: 4 5 6 7   **973**

1. Biography 2. United States -- History 3. African Americans -- Biography

ISBN 1423142578; 9781423142577

LC 2011051348

Coretta Scott King Author Book Award (2013)

Boston Globe-Horn Book Honor: Nonfiction (2013).

In this book, Andrea Davis Pinkney profiles "ten influential black men--including Frederick Douglass, W.E.B. Du Bois, Thurgood Marshall, Jackie Robinson, and Martin Luther King Jr.". She presents "descriptions of each man's influence on civil rights, culture, art, or politics. . . . An examination of Barack Obama's life and presidential election carries readers into the present day, placing the achievements of those who came before him into perspective." (Publishers Weekly)

Includes bibliographical references and index.

Provensen, Alice

The **buck** stops here; the presidents of the United States. 20th anniversary ed.; Viking 2010 un il $18.99

Grades: 2 3 4   **973**

1. United States -- History 2. Presidents -- United States

ISBN 978-0-670-01252-7; 0-670-01252-1

First published 1990

"Provensen updates her compendium of presidential portraits to include Clinton, Bush, and Obama. Rhyming couplets serve as footers beneath detailed earth-toned watercolor illustrations that fill each page with miniature scenes featuring campaign slogans, historical events with time line dates, and major accomplishments and inopportune failures. . . . This is an excellent introduction to America's leaders." SLJ

Rubel, David

★ **Scholastic** encyclopedia of the presidents and their times; by David Rubel. Scholastic 1994 vii, 216 p.p ill. (some col.), col. maps (hardcover) $24.99

Grades: 5 6 7 8   973

1. Presidents -- United States -- Encyclopedias 2. United States -- History 3. United States -- Biography -- Dictionaries

ISBN 0545499852; 9780545499859

LC 93011810

Includes index.

This book is an encyclopedia of the U.S. presidency. It "begins each president's entry with a list including birth and death dates, party, vice president, and nickname, and then describes key elements of each man's presidency. Short sidebars discuss famous people and events of the time." (Cobblestone Magazine)

An "examination of the political and personal lives of U.S. Presidents that begins with George Washington and ends halfway through Bill Clinton's current term in office." SLJ

Smith, David J.

★ **If** America were a village; a book about the people of the United States. written by David J. Smith; illustrated by Shelagh Armstrong. Kids Can Press 2009 32p il $18.95

Grades: 3 4 5   973

1. United States

ISBN 978-1-55453-344-2; 1-55453-344-9

This "offers a thought-provoking perspective on the people who make up America. Organized by overarching questions such as 'Where do we come from?' and 'What do we use?' the text illustrates the ethnic divisions, income levels and material consumption (among other categories) of Americans—were a theoretical village containing only 100 people. . . . Armstrong's cheerful, smudgy paintings balance the text's heaviness." Publ Wkly

Talbott, Hudson

★ **United** tweets of America; 50 state birds; their stories, their glories. [by] Hudson Talbott. G.P. Putnam's Sons 2008 un il $17.99

Grades: 3 4 5   973

1. State birds 2. United States

ISBN 978-0-399-24520-6; 0-399-24520-0

LC 2007019419

"In this sly, comic, and irreverent book, loaded with hilarious puns and parodies about our 50 state birds, words and images deliver bits of history, folklore, and geography about each state. . . . Talbott's colored pencil and mixed-media illustrations ably combine the cartoon uproar with a sense of the individuality of the feathered creatures. . . . Clever, refeshing, and fun." Booklist

Tarrant-Reid, Linda

★ **Discovering** Black America; from the age of exploration to the twenty-first century. Linda Tarrant-Reid. Abrams Books for Young Readers 2012 xi, 244 p.p ill. (some col.), col. maps (hardcover) $29.95

Grades: 4 5 6   973

1. Blacks -- History 2. United States -- History -- 1861-1865, Civil War 4. African Americans -- History 5. African Americans -- Biography

ISBN 0810970988; 9780810970984

LC 2011052201

Author Linda Tarrant-Reid presents a book on "African-American history, beginning with accounts of black explorers before the settlement of North America . . . [The book] includes major historical events . . . [such as] the American Revolution . . . [and] the period following the Civil War and Reconstruction . . . The societal changes brought on by World War II and the civil rights movement [are presented] . . . [E]xchanges between Malcolm X and Martin Luther King . . . [and] the election of President Barack Obama and the challenges facing the first black president" are also described. (Kirkus)

Includes bibliographical references and index.

The **United** States: past and present [series] Rosen Central 2010 52v il map set $1,378

Grades: 3 4 5 6   973

1. United States

ISBN 978-1-4358-9573-7

"These attractive overviews cover the geography, history, government, economy, and famous people in each state. . . . The writing is clear, and facts are plainly stated. . . . Good-quality photos, portraits and relevant paintings illustrate the texts." SLJ

Yaccarino, Dan

Go, go America. Scholastic Press 2008 71p il map $17.99

Grades: 1 2 3 4   973

1. United States

ISBN 0-439-70338-7; 978-0-439-70338-3

LC 2007-05733

"Readers accompany the fabulous Farley Family on their circuitous car and plane trip across the U.S., from Maine to Hawaii. Mom, Dad, Freddie, Fran, and Fido appear on each pastel-colored page chronicling the fun-filled activities available in each state and learning unusual facts. . . . Each fact is presented in a separate area of the page, with accompanying cartoon art, resulting in a busy but energetic layout. . . . The concluding pages list the states in alphabetical order and give their capitals, dates of statehood, rank in entering the Union, area, bird, flower, insect, tree, motto, and nickname. This book is loads of fun and is certain to stimulate interest in the U.S." SLJ

Yorinks, Adrienne

Quilt of states; quilts by Adrienne Yorinks; written by Adrienne Yorinks and 50 librarians from across the nation; librarian contributions compiled and edited by Jeanette Larson. National Geographic 2005 122p il $19.95

Grades: 5 6 7 8   973

1. United States -- History

ISBN 0-7922-7285-4

LC 2004-17796

"The United States is stitched together chronologically in this stunning book that features a quilted spread for each state. Yorinks enlisted a librarian from each state to contribute a short entry to point up a few significant facts that add to the tapestry of the emerging nation. . . . The quilted representations are not only artistically intricate and beautiful, but also informative. A handsome book to linger over and learn from." SLJ

973.0496073　African Americans -- History

28 days; moments in Black history that changed the world. Charles Smith, Shane Evans. Roaring Brook Press 2015 56 p. color illustrations

Grades: K 1 2 3 4 5　　　　　**973.0496073**

1. African Americans　2.　Heroes and heroines　3. African Americans -- History　4. African Americans -- Biography　5.　Heroes -- United States -- Biography　6. Successful people -- United States -- Biography

ISBN 9781596438200

LC 2014009898

In this illustrated children's book, by Charles Smith, illustrated by Shane Evans, "each day features a different influential figure in African-American history, from Crispus Attucks, the first man shot in the Boston Massacre, sparking the Revolutionary War, to Madame C. J. Walker, who after years of adversity became the wealthiest black woman in the country, as well as one of the wealthiest black Americans, to Barack Obama, the country's first African-American president." (Publisher's note)

"Fueled by childhood memories of hearing the same Black History Month stories about the same people and events told the same way over and over, Smith sought to convey the importance and relevance of African American contributions and milestones in a fresh, engaging manner... Evans' buoyant and colorful illustrations have the look of cut-paper collage, and their expressive movement and joyfulness only add to the overall feeling of celebration. The book ends with the final day's exhortation: words of inspiration for young readers to make the most of every day. An inspiring, fresh take on a perennial topic." Booklist

Twenty-eight days

973.09　Presidents--United States

Bausum, Ann

★　**Our** Country's Presidents; All You Need to Know About the Presidents, From George Washington to Barack Obama. by Ann Bausum; foreword by President Barack Obama. 4th ed. National Geographic 2013 223 p. ill., maps (hardcover) $24.95

Grades: 5 6 7 8　　　　　**973.09**

1. Presidents -- United States -- Encyclopedias

ISBN 1426310897; 9781426310898

LC 2009290293

First published 2001

This book by Ann Bausum looks at U.S. presidents. The text shares "facts about the men's personal lives, humorous incidents, political backgrounds, records, struggles, battles,

successes, what they are most famous for, events that occurred during their administrations, and memorable quotes." (School Library Journal)

"This exceedingly attractive offering is . . . chock-full of information, presented . . . in such an inviting manner that children will enjoy paging through, even if there's no school report looming. . . . Full of interesting tidbits as well as solid information." Booklist

Includes bibliographical references

Gherman, Beverly

First mothers; written by Beverly Gherman; illustrated by Julie Downing. Clarion Books 2012 60 p. col. ill. (hardcover) $17.99

Grades: 3 4 5　　　　　**973.09**

1. Biography　2. Mother-child relationship　3. Presidents -- United States

ISBN 0547223013; 9780547223018

LC 2012930747

Author Beverly Gherman presents information on the mothers of past U.S. presidents. "Franklin Pierce's mother loved to shock her Puritan neighbors in New Hampshire . . . William McKinley's mother snatched roses from a train car to carry to her son's inauguration. The mother of five-star general Dwight Eisenhower was a pacifist. These are among the details Gherman . . . unearths in this collection of profiles of the mothers of each of the U.S. presidents." (Publishers Weekly)

Rhatigan, Joe

White House kids; the perks, pleasures, problems, and pratfalls of the Presidents' children. Joe Rhatigan; with illustrations by Jay Shin. Charlesbridge Pub. 2012 96 p. ill. (chiefly col.) $14.95

Grades: 5 6 7 8　　　　　**973.09**

1. United States. White House Office　2. Presidents -- United States -- Family　3. Presidents -- United States -- Children　4. Children of presidents -- United States　5. Children of presidents -- United States -- Biography

ISBN 1936140802; 9781936140800

LC 2011045090

This book presents "an overview of the young occupants of the White House . . . [and] details the perks and downfalls of being a president's child. Information on pets, favorite games and activities . . . and education of presidential offspring is . . . presented. [Joe] Rhatigan explores the press's and the public's fascination with the children . . . as well as the scrutiny and negative press endured by Amy Carter and Chelsea Clinton." (School Library Journal)

"An inviting collection of insightful, interesting and often wacky and weird facts and stories about U.S. presidents and their families." Kirkus

Includes bibliographical references and index

973.1　Early history to 1607

Hernandez, Roger E.

New Spain: 1600-1760s. Marshall Cavendish Benchmark 2009 79p il map (Hispanic America) lib bdg $34.21

Grades: 4 5 6 7　　　　　**973.1**

1. Southern States -- History　2. Spaniards -- United

States 3. Southwestern States -- History
ISBN 978-0-7614-2936-4 lib bdg; 0-7614-2936-0
lib bdg
"Provides comprehensive information on the history of
Spanish exploration in the United States." Publisher's note
Includes glossary and bibliographical references

973.2   United States--Colonial period, 1607-1775

★ **Colonial** America and the Revolutionary War; the story
of the people of the colonies, from early settlers to revolutionary leaders. Laurie Lanzen Harris, editor. Favorable Impressions 2009 399p il map (Biography for
beginners) $49
Grades: 2 3 4 5   **973.2**
1. Reference books 2. United States -- Biography 3.
United States -- History -- 1775-1783, Revolution 4.
United States -- History -- 1600-1775, Colonial period
ISBN 978-1-931360-34-0; 1-931360-34-0
                          LC 2008-49193
"This volume is highly recommended for public and
school library collections. The affordable price, well-organized basic information, and user-friendly format make it a
valuable resource for young researchers." Booklist
Includes glossary

Fishkin, Rebecca Love
English colonies in America. Compass Point Books
2009 48p il map (We the people) lib bdg $26.60
Grades: 4 5 6   **973.2**
1. United States -- History -- 1600-1775, Colonial period
ISBN 978-0-7565-3838-5
                          LC 2008007210
This is a history of English colonies in North America.
This provides "solid background matter and introduce
key people and vocabulary." SLJ
Includes glossary and bibliographical references

Heinrichs, Ann
The **Shipbuilder**; Ann Heinrichs. Marshall Cavendish
2013 48 p. (Colonial people) (print) $29.93
Grades: 3 4 5 6   **973.2**
1. Shipbuilding -- United States -- History 2. United
States -- History -- 1600-1775, Colonial period 3.
Shipwrights -- United States
ISBN 0761400052; 9780761400059; 9781608709878
                          LC 2011028344
This book on shipbuilders and shipbuilding in colonial
America, by Christine Petersen, is part of the Colonial Peo-
ple series. It "introduces the master shipbuilder as well as the
many skilled tradespeople needed to make a sailing ship."
It includes "a description of the craftsman's process" and is
"illustrated with tinted engravings and paintings from earlier
eras as well as . . . color photos of artifacts and replicas."
(Booklist)
"These excellent titles provide context about when
people working during the colonial period would have first
come to America and why, how they fit into the community,
and the skills and tools required for their jobs. The authors
emphasize various aspects related specifically to each spotlighted role...Many libraries own Leonard Everett Fisher's
"Colonial Craftsmen" titles (Cavendish Square); the intri-

cate pictorial spreads in those titles portray craft procedures
in wonderful detail, but the text is difficult for elementary
students. This new series is much easier for children to navigate and understand." (School Library Journal)
Includes bibliographical references and index

Huey, Lois Miner
American archaeology uncovers the earliest English
colonies. Marshall Cavendish Benchmark 2009 64p il
map (American archaeology) lib bdg $31.36
Grades: 4 5 6 7   **973.2**
1. America -- Antiquities 2. America -- Exploration 3.
Jamestown (Va.) -- History 4. Roanoke Island (N.C.)
-- History 5. Great Britain -- Colonies -- America 6.
Excavations (Archeology) -- United States
ISBN 978-0-7614-4264-6 lib bdg; 0-7614-4264-2
lib bdg
                          LC 2008050259
This describes how archeologists have learned about the
history of early English colonists in America at Jamestown,
Popham Colony, and Roanoke
"Huey enthusiastically brings . . . [this era] to life
through artifacts and field research. . . . [The volume begins
with an] introduction that defines 'historical archaeology'
and explains its value in terms simple enough for lower-
elementary readers to comprehend, yet detailed enough for
older children to enjoy, an approach followed in the remaining chapters. . . . Huey's focus on American history, which
is broken down into small, manageable chunks, is sure to
entice budding historians." SLJ
Includes glossary and bibliographical references

Mara, Wil
The **farmer**. Marshall Cavendish Benchmark 2010
48p il (Colonial people) lib bdg $29.93
Grades: 3 4 5 6   **973.2**
1. Farm life -- United States 2. United States -- History
-- 1600-1775, Colonial period
ISBN 978-0-7614-4797-9; 0-7614-4797-0
                          LC 2009019580
This describes the life of a colonial farmer and his importance to the community, as well as everyday life, responsibilities, and social practices during that time.
"The type font, just slightly larger than usual, makes the
text very visually appealing. . . . [The] book is liberally illustrated with artwork dating from the colonial period . . .
[and] information boxes offer supplemental material." Libr
Media Connect
Includes glossary and bibliographical references

McNeese, Tim
Colonial America, 1543-1763. Chelsea House 2010
136p il map (Discovering U.S. history) $35
Grades: 5 6 7 8   **973.2**
1. United States -- History -- 1600-1775, Colonial period
ISBN 978-1-60413-349-3; 1-60413-349-X
                          LC 2008055170
This history of Colonial America "begins with a chapter
on 'Rivals for North America' and ends with 'The Fight for
the Ohio Country.' . . . [The] book has an excellent chronology; rich sidebars; and numerous well-captioned illustrations, maps, and photos that enhance the texts. [This book

provides a] satisfying [introduction] to American history for students." SLJ

Includes glossary and bibliographical references

The **Merchant**; Wendy Mead. Marshall Cavendish 2013 48 p.

Grades: 3 4 5 6 **973.2**
1. Merchants 2. United States -- History -- 1600-1775, Colonial period 3. United States -- Social life and customs -- To 1775 4. Merchants -- United States -- History -- 17th century 5. Merchants -- United States -- History -- 18th century 6. United States -- History -- Colonial period, ca. 1600-1775

ISBN 9781608704156; 9781608709861
LC 2011028343

This book on merchants in colonial America, by Wendy Mead, is part of the Colonial People series. It "looks at the varied roles of colonial merchants, who dealt in imports, exports, and banking, as well as sales. The role of women as merchants is also discussed." The book "is illustrated with tinted engravings and paintings from earlier eras as well as . . . color photos of artifacts and replicas." (Booklist)

"—These excellent titles provide context about when people working during the colonial period would have first come to America and why, how they fit into the community, and the skills and tools required for their jobs...Many libraries own Leonard Everett Fisher's "Colonial Craftsmen" titles (Cavendish Square); the intricate pictorial spreads in those titles portray craft procedures in wonderful detail, but the text is difficult for elementary students. This new series is much easier for children to navigate and understand." (School Library Journal)

Includes bibliographical references and index

Petersen, Christine
The **wheelwright**; Christine Petersen. 1st ed. Benchmark Books 2013 48 p. (Colonial people) (print) $29.93
Grades: 3 4 5 6 **973.2**
1. United States -- History 2. United States -- Social life and customs -- 1600-1775, Colonial period 3. United States -- Social life and customs -- To 1775 4. Wheelwrights -- United States -- History -- 17th century 5. United States -- History -- Colonial period, ca. 1600-1775 6. Carriage and wagon making -- United States -- History -- 18th century

ISBN 160870419X; 9781608704194; 9781608709885
LC 2011028345

This book, by Christine Petersen, is part of the Colonial People series. "Besides explaining the uses and the construction of wheels in colonial times, 'The Wheelwright' includes instructions for making a replica wheel using Styrofoam and craft sticks. In each book, the informative text is illustrated with tinted engravings and paintings from earlier eras as well as excellent color photos of artifacts and replicas and reenactments of historical trades in Colonial Williamsburg." (Booklist)

Includes bibliographical references and index

Tunis, Edwin
★ **Colonial** living; written and illustrated by Edwin Tunis. Johns Hopkins Univ. Press 1999 155p il pa $18.95
Grades: 5 6 7 8 **973.2**
1. United States -- Social life and customs -- 1600-1775,

Colonial period
ISBN 0-8018-6227-2
LC 99-22591
A reprint of the title first published 1957 by World Pub. Co.

"Common everyday aspects of colonial living from 1564-1770 are highlighted by the detailed descriptions and numerous black and white illustrations of items such as tools, home furnishings, clothing, etc." N Y Public Libr. Ref Books for Child Collect

Voices from colonial America [series] National Geographic 2005 18v il map
Grades: 5 6 7 8 **973.2**
1. United States -- History -- 1600-1775, Colonial period

Each volume in this series describes the colonial history of a state illustrated with historical maps and reprints of period artwork, and includes excerpts from first-person accounts.

"Presented in clear, succinct text . . . this resource, containing a great deal of information, will be a welcome addition to history classes and a great source for report writers." Booklist [review of New Jersey volume]

Includes bibliographical references

973.3 United States--Periods of Revolution and Confederation, 1775-1789

Adler, David A.
★ **B.** Franklin, printer. Holiday House 2001 126p il lib bdg $19.95
Grades: 4 5 6 7 **973.3**
1. Authors 2. Diplomats 3. Inventors 4. Statesmen 5. Scientists 6. Writers on science 7. Statesmen -- United States

ISBN 0-8234-1675-5
LC 2001-24535

This "surveys Benjamin Franklin's life as a printer, a scientist, an inventor, a writer, and a statesman. . . . Throughout the book, details, anecdotes, and quotations bring the man's portrait into clearer focus, while period illustrations . . . help readers envision the background of his times." Booklist

Includes bibliographical references

Allen, Thomas B.
Remember Valley Forge; patriots, Tories, and Redcoats tell their stories. [by] Thomas B. Allen. National Geographic 2007 61p il map $17.95; lib bdg $27.90
Grades: 5 6 7 8 **973.3**
1. Generals 2. Presidents 3. Valley Forge (Pa.) -- History 4. United States -- History -- 1775-1783, Revolution

ISBN 978-1-4263-0149-0; 978-1-4263-0150-6 lib bdg
LC 2007024821

The author "recounts here the activities of Washington and his soldiers during the winter of 1777-8, spent regrouping at Valley Forge, Pennsylvania. . . . Allen's strength is his attention to military details and strategies, but his account is clearly presented and succinctly written as well. . . . Illustrated with reproductions of period artwork, drawings, maps, and a few contemporary photographs." Booklist

Anderson, Laurie Halse

★ **Independent** dames; what you never knew about the women and girls of the American Revolution. by Laurie Halse Anderson; illustrated by Matt Faulkner. Simon & Schuster Books for Young Readers 2008 37p il $16.99

Grades: 3 4 5   **973.3**

1. Women -- United States -- History 2. United States -- History -- 1775-1783, Revolution

ISBN 978-0-689-85808-6; 0-689-85808-6

LC 2007042643

"The stories of 22 'Revolutionary Grandmothers' take center stage in this well-illustrated volume. . . . Faulkner's ink-and-watercolor illustrations are exuberant, often amusing, and filled with crosshatching and dialogue balloons. The spreads are busy and information-packed, and readers will be both engaged by and educated about this critical period." SLJ

Includes bibliographical references

Blair, Margaret Whitman

Liberty or death; the surprising story of runaway slaves who sided with the British during the American Revolution. National Geographic 2010 64p il map lib bdg $27.90

Grades: 5 6 7 8   **973.3**

1. African American soldiers 2. Slavery -- United States 3. United States -- History -- 1775-1783, Revolution

ISBN 978-1-4263-0590-0 lib bdg; 1-4263-0590-7 lib bdg

LC 2009-26853

"Blair provides a well-researched account of slaves in Virginia who, beginning in 1775, fled to the British. . . . Though told in a matter-of-fact tone, the story is often heart-wrenching. . . . Colorful reproductions of period paintings, prints, and documents illustrate the clearly written text. . . . A fine and singular addition to American history collections." Booklist

Includes bibliographical references

Bobrick, Benson

★ **Fight** for freedom; the American Revolutionary War. Atheneum Books for Young Readers 2004 96p il map $22.95

Grades: 5 6 7 8   **973.3**

1. United States -- History -- 1775-1783, Revolution

ISBN 0-689-86422-1

LC 2003-25548

"This large-format volume profiles significant individuals and discusses the progress of the Revolutionary War. . . . Printed in color, most of the illustrations are period paintings and prints. . . . Students will find the book a well-organized and clearly written introduction to the war." Booklist

Includes glossary and bibliographical references

Brenner, Barbara

★ **If** you were there in 1776. Bradbury Press 1994 136p il $17.95

Grades: 3 4 5 6   **973.3**

1. United States -- Social life and customs 2. United States -- Declaration of Independence

ISBN 0-02-712322-7

LC 93-24060

Demonstrates how the concepts and principles expressed in the Declaration of Independence were drawn from the experiences of living in America in the late eighteenth century,

with emphasis given to how children lived on a New England farm, a Southern plantation, and the frontier

"The author's inclusion of details of how peoples' lives began to change as a result of the Revolution and her accessible style are the selling points here. Both budding historians and report writers will find this title worth their time." SLJ

Includes bibliographical references

Brown, Don

★ **Henry** and the cannons; an extraordinary true story of the American Revolution. Don Brown. Roaring Brook Press 2013 32 p. (hardcover) $16.99

Grades: K 1 2 3 4   **973.3**

1. Picture books for children 2. United States -- History -- 1775-1783, Revolution 3. Military roads -- Massachusetts -- History -- 18th century 4. Massachusetts -- History -- Revolution, 1775-1783 -- Campaigns 5. United States -- History -- Revolution, 1775-1783 -- Campaigns 6. Massachusetts -- History -- Revolution, 1775-1783 -- Artillery operations 7. United States -- History -- Revolution, 1775-1783 -- Artillery operations

ISBN 1596432667; 9781596432666

LC 2012013450

This children's picture book recounts the difficulties faced by the American armies in the winter of 1775. "British soldiers occupy Boston, and the Americans have no way to dislodge them. Despite the seeming impossibility of transporting heavy cannons over snowy roads, across icy lakes and through forbidding forests, young Henry Knox, a bookseller and militia member, volunteered to get the job done." (Kirkus)

★ **Let** it begin here! April 19, 1775, the day the American Revolution began. Roaring Brook Press 2008 un il (Actual times) $17.95

Grades: 2 3 4   **973.3**

1. Concord (Mass.), Battle of, 1775 2. Lexington (Mass.), Battle of, 1775 3. United States -- History -- 1775-1783, Revolution

ISBN 978-1-59643-221-5; 1-59643-221-7

LC 2008-11221

"Brown distills the fairly complex story of the beginning of the American Revolution in a manner that deftly balances information and intrigue. . . . Equally impressive and vital to the success of this picture book are Brown's compositions which sometimes dramatically, sometimes whimsically intersect with the text. . . . [This is] rousing, accessible, and splendidly executed." Booklist

Carson, Mary Kay

Did it all start with a snowball fight? and other questions about the American Revolution. by Mary Kay Carson. Sterling Pub. Co., Inc. 2012 31 p. $12.95

Grades: 3 4 5   **973.3**

1. Boston Massacre, 1770 2. Picture books for children 3. United States -- History -- 1775-1783, Revolution

ISBN 1402796269; 9781402787348; 9781402796265

LC 2011019963

This children's book offers information about the American Revolution. "Starting with the Boston Massacre (the snowball fight in question) and ending with the Treaty of Paris, the facts are related in a question-and-answer format, in an arrangement that's more topical than chronological (though there is a . . . time line at the end). Each spread has one or two questions and answers on one side and a captioned, colorful full-page painting or cartoon on the other." (School Library Journal)

Includes bibliographical references and index

Crompton, Samuel Willard

The **Boston** Tea Party; colonists protest the British government. by Russell Freeman; illustrated by Peter Malone. Holiday House 2011 39 p. (hardcover) $17.95
Grades: 3 4 5   **973.3**
1. Boston (Mass.) -- History 2. Boston Tea Party, 1773
3. United States -- History -- 1775-1783, Revolution
ISBN 9780823422661; 0823422666

LC 2010028726

This children's book, by Russell Freedman, illustrated by Peter Malone, tells the story of the Boston Tea Party. "[T]he Boston Tea Party of 1773 has come to stand for the determination of American colonists to control their own destinies." The book tells the events from "the arrival of the ships full of controversial taxed tea in Boston Harbor, through the . . . protest meetings at the Old South Church, to the . . . dumping 226 chests of fine tea into the harbor on December 16." (Publisher's note)

Includes bibliographical references and index.

Decker, Timothy

For liberty; the story of the Boston Massacre. Calkins Creek 2009 un il $17.95
Grades: 4 5 6   **973.3**
1. Boston Massacre, 1770
ISBN 978-1-59078-608-6; 1-59078-608-4

"This handsomely designed picture book begins the story of the Boston Massacre by filling in the background. . . . The book concludes with the soldiers' trial and their lawyer, John Adams, reflecting on the protection of liberty. . . . The book does quite a good job of conveying how the actions and emotions of those on both sides escalated toward violence and death. Using parallel lines, crosshatching, and other texturing effects, the black-and-white drawings hold attention. . . . A fine, balanced look at an important event." Booklist

Figley, Marty Rhodes

John Greenwood's journey to Bunker Hill; illustrated by Craig Orback. Millbrook Press 2010 48p il (History speaks: picture books plus reader's theater) lib bdg $27.93
Grades: 2 3 4   **973.3**
1. Readers' theater 2. Bunker Hill (Boston, Mass.), Battle of, 1775 3. United States -- History -- 1775-1783, Revolution
ISBN 978-1-58013-673-0 lib bdg; 1-58013-673-7 lib bdg

LC 2009050063

This tells the story of fifteen-year-old John Greenwood, who fought at the Battle of Bunker Hill.

This "title begins with a well-illustrated narrative and concludes with a tip sheet for performing Reader's Theater as well as a list of characters, a script, and a pronunciation guide. . . . [This book will] make history come alive in a unique and interesting way." Libr Media Connect

Includes bibliographical references

Fleming, Thomas J.

Everybody's revolution; a new look at the people who won America's freedom. [by] Thomas Fleming. Scholastic Nonfiction 2006 96p il $19.99
Grades: 4 5 6 7   **973.3**
1. United States -- History -- 1775-1783, Revolution
ISBN 0-439-63404-0

LC 2005051814

A history of the American Revolution, focusing on the roles played by women, young people, and various ethnic groups.

"With an open layout and clean typeface, this clearly written title is attractive and inviting. . . . Fleming's sound offering is an excellent starting point for discussions of the implications of the Revolutionary War in terms of freedom for all people." SLJ

Includes glossary and bibliographical references

Fradin, Dennis B.

The **Boston** Tea Party; [by] Dennis Brindell Fradin. Marshall Cavendish Benchmark 2007 45p il map (Turning points in U.S. history) lib bdg $31.36
Grades: 3 4 5   **973.3**
1. Boston Tea Party, 1773
ISBN 978-0-7614-2035-4

LC 2006025344

Beginning with British debt for its colonial wars and ending with the battles of Lexington and Concord, this is an account of the American colonists' rebellion against taxes on British tea

Includes glossary and bibliographical references

The **Declaration** of Independence; [by] Dennis Brindell Fradin. Marshall Cavendish Benchmark 2007 45p il map (Turning points in U.S. history) lib bdg $31.36
Grades: 3 4 5   **973.3**
1. United States -- Declaration of Independence 2. United States -- Politics and government -- 1775-1783, Revolution
ISBN 978-0-7614-2129-0 lib bdg; 0-7614-2129-7 lib bdg

LC 2005016023

This "describes the unrest that led up to the signing of the famous document, how Jefferson composed it, and the uncertainty surrounding the vote for independence. . . . The clear, concise, and dynamic style of writing simplifies the information without dumbing it down. . . . The photos, paintings, and maps . . . add a wealth of information." SLJ

Includes glossary and bibliographical references

Let it begin here! Lexington & Concord; first battles of the American Revolution. [by] Dennis Brindell Fradin; illustrations by Larry Day. Walker & Co. 2005 un il maps $16.95; lib bdg $17.85
Grades: 2 3 4   **973.3**
1. Concord (Mass.), Battle of, 1775 2. Lexington (Mass.), Battle of, 1775
ISBN 0-8027-8945-5; 0-8027-8946-3 lib bdg

LC 2004-49473

This is an "account of Paul Revere's actions on the night of April 18, 1775, and the battles in Lexington and Concord on the following day. . . . Well-composed double-page illustrations, ink drawings with watercolor and gouache, high-light the human drama implicit in the text." Booklist

Includes bibliographical references

★ The **signers**; the fifty-six stories behind the Declaration of Independence. [by] Dennis Brindell Fradin; illustrations by Michael McCurdy. Walker & Co. 2002 164p il map $22.95; lib bdg $23.85

Grades: 4 5 6 7   **973.3**

1. Statesmen -- United States 2. United States -- Declaration of Independence 3. United States -- Politics and government -- 1775-1783, Revolution

ISBN 0-8027-8849-1; 0-8027-8850-5 lib bdg

LC 2002-66364

Profiles each of the fifty-six men who signed the Declaration of Independence, giving historical information about the colonies they represented. Includes the text of the Declaration and its history

"Fradin gives brief, fascinating glimpses into the people who have been overlooked as well as those with whom readers might be familiar. . . . An excellent resource for report writing." SLJ

Includes bibliographical references

Freedman, Russell, 1929-

★ **Give** me liberty! the story of the Declaration of Independence. Holiday House 2000 90p il $24.95; pa $14.95

Grades: 5 6 7 8 9 10   **973.3**

1. United States 2. United States -- Declaration of Independence 3. United States -- Politics and government -- 1775-1783, Revolution 4. United States -- Politics and government -- 1775-1783

ISBN 0-8234-1448-5; 0-8234-1753-0 pa

LC 99-57513

This book describes the events leading up to the Declaration of Independence as well as the personalities and politics behind its framing. Chronology. Annotated bibliography. Index. "Grades five to eight." (Bull Cent Child Books)

"Handsomely designed with a generous and thoughtful selection of period art, the book is dramatic and inspiring." Horn Book

Includes bibliographical references

★ **Washington** at Valley Forge. Holiday House 2008 100p il map $24.95

Grades: 5 6 7 8 9   **973.3**

1. Generals 2. Presidents 3. Pennsylvania -- History 4. Valley Forge (Pa.) -- History 5. United States -- History -- 1775-1783, Revolution

ISBN 978-0-8234-2069-8; 0-8234-2069-8

LC 2007-52467

NCTE Orbis Pictus Award honor book (2009)

"With his usual clarity of focus and keen eye for telling quotations, Freedman documents how Washington struggled to maintain morale despite hunger, near-nakedness, and freezing conditions. . . . Throughout, high-quality reproductions depict Washington among the men, and with the numerous other influential people who played crucial roles." Booklist

Fritz, Jean

★ **Why** not, Lafayette? illustrated by Ronald Himler. Putnam 1999 87p il $16.99; pa $5.99

Grades: 5 6 7 8   **973.3**

1. Generals 2. Statesmen 3. United States -- History -- 1775-1783, Revolution

ISBN 0-399-23411-X; 0-698-11882-0 pa

LC 98-31417

Traces the life of the French nobleman who fought for democracy in revolutions in both the United States and France

This biography is "chock-full of quotes, anecdotes, and wry humor." Booklist

Includes bibliographical references

Harness, Cheryl

The **revolutionary** John Adams; written and illustrated by Cheryl Harness. National Geographic Soc. 2003 39p il map $17.95; pa $7.95

Grades: 3 4 5 6   **973.3**

1. Presidents 2. Vice-presidents 3. Presidents -- United States 4. United States -- History -- 1775-1783, Revolution

ISBN 0-7922-6970-5; 0-7922-5491-0 pa

LC 2002-11271

A biography of John Adams with emphasis on his role in the American Revolution

"Harness' warm, friendly, mixed-media illustrations, which range from full-color, double-page spreads to labeled diagrams to black-line silhouettes, will delight children, and quotes from Adams' letters, including many letters to his wife, Abigail, are a bonus. A fascinating book for young history buffs." Booklist

Includes bibliographical references

Herbert, Janis

★ The **American** Revolution for kids; a history with 21 activities. Chicago Review Press 2002 139p il pa $14.95

Grades: 4 5 6   **973.3**

1. United States -- History -- 1775-1783, Revolution

ISBN 1-55652-456-0

LC 2002-7938

Discusses the events of the American Revolution, from the hated Stamp Act and the Boston Tea Party to the British surrender at Yorktown and the writing of the Constitution. Activities include making a tricorn hat and discovering local history

"Achieving a good balance between textual material, illustration, and projects, the book immerses children in the milieu of these years. . . . The directions are detailed enough and adequately illustrated with pencil drawings to make them exciting and easy to follow." SLJ

Includes glossary and bibliographical references

Jules, Jacqueline

Unite or die; how thirteen states became a nation. illustrated by Jef Czekaj. Charlesbridge 2009 48p il $16.95; pa $7.95

Grades: 2 3 4 5   **973.3**

1. United States -- History -- 1783-1809 2. United States -- Constitution 3. United States -- History -- 1783-1815 4. Constitutional history -- United States 5. United States -- Politics and government -- 1783-1789

ISBN 1-58089-189-6; 1-58089-190-X pa; 978-1-58089-189-9; 978-1-58089-190-5 pa

LC 2008-07229

"Using the conceit of a school play, Unite or Die traces the challenges, conflicts, and compromises that shaped the United States Constitution and brought unity to the states. [Bibliography.] Ages nine to twelve." (Publisher's note)

"This presentation is written as if it were a school play about the 13 colonies becoming a nation. Told through colorful comic-book illustrations, it stars students dressed as states humorously explaining the path to the writing of the Constitution. The brief text is accompanied by speech balloons expressing the states' multiple, often competing, views. . . . The vividly colored spreads will hold the interest of even middle school students and would be useful to introduce how our form of government was created." SLJ

Includes bibliographical references

Kostyal, K. M.
1776; a new look at revolutionary Williamsburg. by K.M. Kostyal with the Colonial Williamsburg Foundation; photographs by Lori Epstein. National Geographic 2009 48p il $17.95; lib bdg $27.90
Grades: 4 5 6   **973.3**
   1. Williamsburg (Va.) -- History 2. United States -- History -- 1775-1783, Revolution
   ISBN 978-1-4263-0517-7; 1-4263-0517-6; 978-1-4263-0518-4 lib bdg; 1-4263-0518-4 lib bdg
            LC 2009-18002

"Clear, distinctive photos add visual appeal to this short history of the American Revolution, written from the point of view of those living in Williamsburg, Virginia's capital in 1776. Kostyal blends political and social history into a readable account of the period, bolstered by informative sidebars, a chronology, and a closing note about the restoration of colonial Williamsburg. . . . The increasing inclusion of nonwhite colonists in the illustrations as well as the text is a welcome trend." Booklist

Includes bibliographical references

Leavitt, Amie Jane
The **Declaration** of Independence in translation; what it really means. by Amie Jane Leavitt. Capstone Press 2009 32p il (Fact finders. Kids' translations) lib bdg $23.93; pa $7.95
Grades: 3 4 5   **973.3**
   1. United States -- Declaration of Independence 2. United States -- Politics and government -- 1775-1783, Revolution
   ISBN 978-1-4296-1929-5 lib bdg; 1-4296-1929-5 lib bdg; 978-1-4296-2844-0 pa; 1-4296-2844-8 pa
            LC 2008-3229

Provides "a nearly line-by-line translation that makes . . . the written word accessible and meaningful." SLJ

Includes glossary and bibliographical references

Maestro, Betsy
Liberty or death; the American Revolution, 1763-1783. illustrated by Giulio Maestro. HarperCollins 2005 64p il map (American story series) $15.99; lib bdg $16.89
Grades: 3 4 5 6   **973.3**
   1. United States -- History -- 1775-1783, Revolution
   ISBN 0-688-08802-3; 0-688-08803-1 lib bdg
            LC 00-54042

The author and illustrator describe "the 20 years leading up to, and fighting, the American Revolution. A simple narrative, largely from the Colonists' perspective, touches on the major events, players, and ideas of the times, beginning with the Stamp Act and ending with Yorktown and the subsequent peace treaty. . . . Full-color ink, colored-pencil, and watercolor illustrations . . . grace the page in a pleasing, uncluttered way. . . . This book serves as a good introductory overview." SLJ

A **new** nation; the United States, 1783-1815. illustrated by Giulio Maestro. HarperCollins Publishers 2009 64p il map (American story series) $17.99; lib bdg $18.89
Grades: 3 4 5 6   **973.3**
   1. United States -- History -- 1783-1865
   ISBN 978-0-688-16015-9; 0-688-16015-8; 978-0-688-16016-6 lib bdg; 0-688-16016-6 lib bdg
            LC 2008-26947

"The Maestros . . . cover a jam-packed 32 years that saw the country more than double in population and, with the Lousiana Purchase, double in size. . . . The abundant pastel artwork breaks up the pages and provides nifty images of the times. . . . Interesting for history buffs, useful for researchers." Booklist

McNeese, Tim
Revolutionary America, 1764-1789; consulting editor, Richard Jensen. Chelsea House 2010 128p il map (Discovering U.S. history) $35
Grades: 5 6 7 8   **973.3**
   1. United States -- History -- 1775-1783, Revolution
   ISBN 978-1-60413-350-9; 1-60413-350-3
            LC 2008-55179

"The information is accurate and easy to understand. Pictures are well placed, and primary sources are included. . . . The maps are well done and there are sidebars with additional information. . . . [This would be good] to have on hand for reports as it is well laid out and easy to use." Libr Media Connect

Includes glossary and bibliographical references

Micklos, John
The **brave** women and children of the American Revolution; [by] John Micklos, Jr. Enslow Publishers 2008 48p il (The Revolutionary War library) lib bdg $17.95
Grades: 3 4 5 6   **973.3**
   1. Children -- United States 2. Women -- United States -- History 3. United States -- History -- 1775-1783, Revolution
   ISBN 978-0-7660-3019-0 lib bdg; 0-7660-3019-9 lib bdg
            LC 2007048510

This describes the roles of women and children in the American Revolution, at home, in business, as spies and messengers, and on the battlefield.

This is "illustrated with historical engravings and photographs. . . . The many sidebars are informative. . . . The well-written text is studded with footnotes, and the appended time line is helpful." Booklist

Includes glossary and bibliographical references

Miller, Brandon Marie
Declaring independence; life during the American Revolution. by Brandon Marie Miller. Lerner Publications Co. 2005 112p il map (People's history) lib bdg $31.93
Grades: 5 6 7 8   **973.3**
   1. United States -- Social conditions 2. United States

-- History -- 1775-1783, Revolution

ISBN 0-8225-1275-0

LC 2004-17917

This describes the lives of American colonists in the late 1700s and the fight for independence from Great Britain with emphasis on "firsthand accounts, contemporary writings, and official documents. Miller does a good job of chronicling the history, presenting the information in a clear, concise, and well-organized manner." SLJ

Includes bibliographical references

Minor, Wendell

Yankee Doodle America; the spirit of 1776 from A to Z. [by] Wendell Minor. G.P. Putnam's Sons 2006 un il $16.99

Grades: 2 3 4   **973.3**

1. Alphabet 2. United States -- History -- 1775-1783, Revolution

ISBN 0-399-24003-9

LC 2005025174

"In colonial America, the public houses served as the news hubs of their surrounding areas. . . . Using hand-carved replicas of the signs for these inns and taverns to share facts about the American Revolution, Minor, in concert with master woodworker John Reichling, has created an unusual alphabet book. . . . The factual material is correct, clearly stated, and intriguing." SLJ

Includes bibliographical references

Murphy, Jim

★ The **crossing**; how George Washington saved the American Revolution. Scholastic Press 2010 96p il map $21.99

Grades: 5 6 7 8   **973.3**

1. Generals 2. Presidents 3. Trenton (N.J.), Battle of, 1776 4. United States -- History -- 1775-1783, Revolution

ISBN 978-0-439-69186-4; 0-439-69186-9

LC 2009-11561

Murphy "again digs into the well of history, this time emerging with a well-researched, absorbing account of the early battles of the Revolutionary War with General George Washington at their center. Enhanced by numerous sepia maps of troop movements, prints, paintings, and portraits of prominent figures, the blow-by-blow narrative begins with the shots fired at Lexington and Concord in 1775 and continues until the tide-turning battles at Trenton and Princeton in early 1777." Publ Wkly

Includes bibliographical references

★ A **young** patriot; the American Revolution as experienced by one boy. Clarion Bks. 1996 101p il maps $16; pa $7.95

Grades: 5 6 7 8   **973.3**

1. Soldiers 2. United States -- History -- 1775-1783, Revolution

ISBN 0-395-60523-7; 0-395-90019-0 pa

LC 93-38789

"Using Joseph Plumb Martin's first person account of his participation in the Revolutionary War as primary source material, Murphy intertwines this story of one teenager's life as a soldier with broader information about the Revolution, to put Martin's story in context. The handsome, informative,

and fascinating look at American history is illustrated with many period reproductions." Horn Book Guide

Includes bibliographical references

Otfinoski, Steven

The **new** republic: 1760-1840s. Marshall Cavendish Benchmark 2009 79p il map (Hispanic America) lib bdg $23.95

Grades: 4 5 6 7   **973.3**

1. Latinos (U.S.) 2. Mexico -- History 3. Florida -- History 4. Hispanic Americans 5. Spaniards -- United States 6. United States -- History -- 1775-1783, Revolution

ISBN 978-0-7614-2938-8 lib bdg; 0-7614-2938-7 lib bdg

LC 2007-45958

"Provides comprehensive information on the history of the Spanish exploring the United States." Publisher's note

Includes glossary and bibliographical references

Rockwell, Anne F.

They called her Molly Pitcher; by Anne Rockwell; illustrated by Cynthia von Buhler. Knopf 2002 un il $16.95; lib bdg $17.99

Grades: 3 4 5   **973.3**

1. Soldiers 2. Revolutionaries 3. United States -- History -- 1775-1783, Revolution

ISBN 0-679-89187-0; 0-679-99187-5 lib bdg

LC 2001-29422

A biography of the woman who was named a sergeant in the Continental Army by George Washington for her bravery in the Battle of Monmouth

"The language is inviting, the story, exciting. Von Buhler's illustrations, which appear crackled, as if they were painted during this period, make the book shine." SLJ

Sanders, Nancy I.

America's black founders; revolutionary heroes & early leaders with 21 activities. Chicago Review Press 2010 150p il $16.95

Grades: 4 5 6 7   **973.3**

1. African Americans -- History 2. United States -- History -- 1775-1783, Revolution

ISBN 978-1-55652-811-8; 1-55652-811-6

"This activity-based guide reveals how African Americans played crucial roles in helping the United States gain its independence. Sanders includes well-known figures such as Phillis Wheatley, Crispus Attucks, and James Forten in her narrative, but also enriches traditional accounts of the period by explaining the contributions of lesser-known patriots. . . . Most of the activities help make this period real to young people. . . . Sanders makes excellent use of primary sources." SLJ

Schanzer, Rosalyn

★ **George** vs. George; the American Revolution as seen from both sides. National Geographic 2004 60p il maps $16.95

Grades: 3 4 5 6   **973.3**

1. Generals 2. Presidents 3. Kings 4. United States -- History -- 1775-1783, Revolution

ISBN 0-7922-7349-4

LC 2003-20843

This book explores how the characters and lives of King George III of England and George Washington affected he progress and outcome of the American Revolution. Bibliography. Index. "Grades four to six." (Bull Cent Child Books)

"A carefully researched, evenhanded narrative with well-crafted, vibrant, watercolor illustrations. . . . This is a lovely book, showing historical inquiry at its best." SLJ

Includes bibliographical references

Sheinkin, Steve

★ **King** George: what was his problem? everything your schoolbooks didn't tell you about the American Revolution. Roaring Brook Press 2008 195p il map $19.95
Grades: 4 5 6   **973.3**
1. United States -- History -- 1775-1783, Revolution
ISBN 978-1-59643-319-9; 1-59643-319-1
LC 2007-39999

First published 2005 in paperback by Summer Street Press, in series Storyteller's History, with title: The American Revolution

This history of the American Revolution "features many droll line drawings that suit the tone of the writing and source notes for the extensive quotes. Sheinkin clearly conveys the gravity of events during the Revolutionary period, but he also has the knack of bringing historical people to life and showing what was at stake for them as individuals as well as for the new nation. . . . Vivid storytelling makes this an unusually readable history book." Booklist

Includes bibliographical references

St. George, Judith

★ The **journey** of the one and only Declaration of Independence; illustrated by Will Hillenbrand. Philomel Books 2005 un il $16.99
Grades: 2 3 4   **973.3**
1. United States -- Declaration of Independence 2. United States -- Politics and government -- 1775-1783, Revolution
ISBN 0-399-23738-0
LC 2004-13567

This decribes how the Declaration of Independence was written and how the document was preserved and displayed throughout American history

"Readers will learn fascinating details. . . . Hillenbrand's lively mixed-media illustrations are a perfect match for the text, filling the pages with visual energy and humor. . . . This well-researched, readable, and well-illustrated book belongs on the shelves of all public and school libraries." SLJ

Includes bibliographical references

Winters, Kay

★ **Colonial** voices; hear them speak. [by] Kay Winters; illustrated by Larry Day. Dutton Children's Books 2008 un il map $17.99
Grades: 3 4 5 6   **973.3**
1. Boston Tea Party, 1773 2. Boston (Mass.) -- History 3. United States -- History -- 1775-1783, Revolution
ISBN 978-0-525-47872-0; 0-525-47872-8
LC 2007-28480

"Colonial Bostonians introduce themselves through free-verse vignettes that describe their work and their feelings about the current political situation. As errand boy Ethan moves about the city, he links the people together. . . . The watercolor and ink illustrations add humor and drama

through shifting perspectives and well-detailed settings full of period details. . . . A unique presentation for all libraries." SLJ

Includes bibliographical references

973.4 United States--Constitutional period, 1789-1809

Adler, David A.

A **picture** book of Thomas Jefferson; illustrated by John & Alexandra Wallner. Holiday House 1990 un il lib bdg $17.95; pa $6.95
Grades: 1 2 3   **973.4**
1. Architects 2. Presidents 3. Vice-presidents 4. Essayists 5. Presidents -- United States
ISBN 0-8234-0791-8 lib bdg; 0-8234-0881-7 pa
LC 89-20076

Traces the life and achievements of the architect, bibliophile, president, and author of the Declaration of Independence

"The book includes an amazing amount of material. An appealing package with simple language and detailed drawings." Horn Book

Delano, Marfé Ferguson

Master George's people; George Washington, his slaves, and his revolutionary transformation. By Marfe Ferguson Delano. National Geographic 2013 64 p. (hardcover: alk. paper) $18.95
Grades: 4 5 6   **973.4**
1. Slaves -- Virginia -- Mount Vernon (Estate) 2. Slavery -- Virginia -- Mount Vernon (Estate) 3. Mount Vernon (Va.: Estate) -- Race relations
ISBN 1426307594; 9781426307591; 9781426307607
LC 2012024295

This book, by Marfé Ferguson Delano, explores the lives of the slaves owned by U.S. President George Washington at "his Virginia plantation, Mount Vernon. . . . [The book] gives us . . . portraits of cooks, overseers, valets, farm hands, and more . . . interwoven with an extraordinary examination of the conscience of the Father of Our Country." (Publisher's note)

Includes bibliographical references and index

Fradin, Dennis B.

★ **Duel!** Burr and Hamilton's deadly war of words. by Dennis Brindell Fradin; illustrated by Larry Day. Walker & Co. 2008 un il $16.95; lib bdg $17.85
Grades: 3 4 5 6   **973.4**
1. Statesmen 2. Vice-presidents 3. Secretaries of the treasury
ISBN 978-0-8027-9583-0; 0-8027-9583-8; 978-0-8027-9584-7 lib bdg; 0-8027-9584-6 lib bdg
LC 2007-37994

"Even children who don't know much about Aaron Burr . . . and Alexander Hamilton . . . will be hooked by this dramatic picture-book account of their deadly quarrel. . . . When Fradin deals with the divisive politics, Day's ink, watercolor, and gouache illustrations ably show the body language as the enemies furiously confront one another. . . . The words and art humanize the history for children." Booklist

Harness, Cheryl

George Washington. National Geographic Soc. 2000
48p il $17.95

Grades: 3 4 5   973.4

1. Generals 2. Presidents 3. Presidents -- United States
ISBN 0-7922-7096-7

LC 99-29920

Presents the life of George Washington, focusing on the
Revolutionary War years and his presidency

"Detailed paintings, full of action and rich with color,
portray Washington as well as important moments in American history. . . . This heavily illustrated biography serves as
a good introduction to Washington." Booklist

Includes bibliographical references

Jurmain, Suzanne

★ The **worst** of friends; Thomas Jefferson, John Adams, and the true story of an American feud. illustrated by
Larry Day. Dutton Children's Books 2011 32p il $16.99

Grades: 1 2 3   973.4

1. Architects 2. Presidents 3. Vice-presidents 4.
Essayists 5. Presidents -- United States 6. United States
-- History -- 1783-1809 7. United States -- History --
1775-1783, Revolution -- Biography
ISBN 978-0-525-47903-1; 0-525-47903-1

LC 2011005190

"In zingy prose, Jurmain tells how Thomas Jefferson and
John Adams 'were as different as pickles and ice cream.' .
. . Yet she emphasizes that the two were best friends who
worked together to shape America before parting ways when
Jefferson backed the Republicans and Adams the Federalists. Entertaining anecdotes about both presidents' personal
and political lives are energized by Day's lightly caricatured
watercolor cartoons, which flesh out their personalities. . . .
This entertaining and character-driven slice of history also
offers a clear message about friendship." Publ Wkly

Includes bibliographical references

Kerley, Barbara

★ **Those** rebels, John and Tom; illustrated by Edwin
Fotheringham. Scholastic Press 2012 il $17.99

Grades: 3 4 5   973.4

1. Architects 2. Presidents 3. Vice-presidents 4.
Essayists 5. Presidents -- United States 6. United States
-- History -- 1783-1809 7. United States -- History --
1775-1783, Revolution
ISBN 978-0-545-22268-6; 0-545-22268-0

LC 2011002131

"Kerley and Fotheringham . . . cleverly contrast two
diverse founding fathers and early presidents, Thomas Jefferson and John Adams. Entertaining verse and droll illustrations parlay their differences and similarities into a lens
through which to view the start of the American Revolution. . . . A playful tone also is reflected in the typeface, with
certain phrases enlarged for shout-out emphasis, and in the
caricatured artwork. Skillfully rendered and decidedly modern in a patriotic palette of red, white, blue, and brown, the
digitally created scenes mirror and enhance the text's wit."
Publ Wkly

Includes bibliographical references

McNeese, Tim

Early national America, 1790-1850. Chelsea House
2010 136p il map (Discovering U.S. history) $35

Grades: 5 6 7 8   973.4

1. United States -- History -- 1783-1865
ISBN 978-1-60413-351-6; 1-60413-351-1

LC 2009003679

McNeese "discusses the people, politics, economic
conditions, and foreign affairs of [the U.S. from 1790 to
1850], objectively explaining how the attitudes, perceptions,
and expectations of the American people and their leaders
shaped the development of the country. . . . Color period
art and photos, maps, and cutaway drawings supplement the
[text]." SLJ

Includes glossary and bibliographical references

Wallner, Alexandra

Abigail Adams; written and illustrated by Alexandra
Wallner. Holiday House 2001 un il $17.95; pa $6.95

Grades: 1 2 3   973.4

1. Parents of presidents 2. Spouses of presidents 3.
Presidents' spouses -- United States
ISBN 0-8234-1442-6; 0-8234-1942-8 pa

LC 00-23149

A biography of Abigail Adams, wife of second United
States President John Adams, and a dedicated wife and
mother who spoke up against slavery and for women's rights

"Full-page, colorful pictures in a folk-art style contribute greatly to the text, capturing the daily life, clothing, and
household routines of the times." SLJ

Includes bibliographical references

973.5   United States--1809-1845

Fritz, Jean

The **great** little Madison. Putnam 1989 159p il hardcover o.p. pa $6.99

Grades: 5 6 7 8   973.5

1. Presidents 2. Members of Congress 3. Secretaries
of state 4. Presidents -- United States
ISBN 0-399-21768-1; 0-698-11621-6 pa

LC 88-31584

"Small, soft-spoken, and by nature diffident, James
Madison found it difficult to speak in the midst of controversy, but his zeal and his convictions in the struggle between
Republicans and Federalists gave him confidence, and his
successes brought him to the presidency. Fritz has given a
vivid picture of the man and an equally vivid picture of the
problems—especially the internal dissension—that faced
the leaders of the new nation. . . . Notes by the author and a
bibliography are appended." Bull Cent Child Books

973.7   Administration of Abraham Lincoln, 1861-1865

Adler, David A., 1947-

Harriet Tubman and the Underground Railroad; by
David A. Adler. Holiday House 2013 140 p. ill. (hardcover) $18.95

Grades: 5 6 7 8   973.7

1. Underground Railroad 2. African American women
-- Biography 3. Slaves -- United States -- Biography
ISBN 0823423654; 9780823423651

LC 2012006582

This book, by David A. Adler, gives a biography of the ex-slave Harriet Tubman. "She escaped from her owners in Maryland on the Underground Railroad in 1849 and then fearlessly returned . . . to help guide . . . others to freedom as the most famous conductor of the Underground Railroad. . . . During and after the war, she helped hundreds of freed slaves begin new lives, and she later founded a home for elderly former slaves and became active in the women's suffrage movement." (Publisher's note)

Includes bibliographical references

Beller, Susan Provost

Billy Yank and Johnny Reb; soldiering in the Civil War. Twenty-First Century Books 2008 112p il map (Soldiers on the battlefront) lib bdg $33.26

Grades: 5 6 7 8 **973.7**

1. Soldiers -- United States 2. United States -- History -- 1861-1865, Civil War

ISBN 978-0-8225-6803-2 lib bdg; 0-8225-6803-9 lib bdg

LC 2006010240

First published 2000

Describes military life for the average soldier in the Civil War, including camp life, diseases, and conditions for the wounded and prisoners of war. Includes excerpts from first-person accounts, letters, and diaries

The author "presents a good deal of solid information in an interesting manner. . . . Good black-and-white reproductions, mainly of photographs from the 1860s, appear throughout the book." Booklist [review of 2000 ed]

Includes bibliographical references

Benoit, Peter

The **surrender** at Appomattox; by Peter Benoit. Children's Press 2012 64 p. chiefly col. ill., col. map (library) $30.00; (paperback) $8.95

Grades: 4 5 6 **973.7**

1. Appomattox Campaign, 1865 2. United States -- History -- 1861-1865, Civil War -- Peace 3. United States -- History -- Civil War, 1861-1865 -- Peace

ISBN 0531250415; 9780531250419; 9780531265666

LC 2011011967

This book by Peter Benoit, part of the "Cornerstones of Freedom" series, describes the events leading up to the end of the U.S. Civil War. It "sketches the events of the Battle of the Wilderness and the capture of Richmond as well as the meeting between [Ulysses S.] Grant and [Robert E.] Lee on April 9, 1865." (School Library Journal)

Includes bibliographical references (p. 61) and index.

Brown, Don, 1949-

★ **He** has shot the president! April 14, 1865: the day John Wilkes Booth killed President Lincoln. By Don Brown. First edition Roaring Brook Press 2014 64 p. (Actual times) (hardcover) $17.99

Grades: 2 3 4 **973.7**

ISBN 1596432241; 9781596432246

LC 2013016334

This book, by Don Brown, "is . . . [an] account of the assassination of President Lincoln. [John Wilkes] Booth 'believed that robbing the Union of the president's leadership would cripple the North and save the South.' . . . The assassination takes place early on, and the brunt of the book follows Booth's attempted flight, Lincoln's death, and the

'relentless, sweeping investigation' to find Booth and his conspirators." (Publishers Weekly)

"Brown introduces both major actors, Lincoln and Booth, and then begins the tricky task of chronologically following each man to his death. He does so successfully, switching back and forth with impeccable transitions. The text is matter-of-fact and detailed, and the illustrations, in Brown's slightly impressionistic style and rendered in somber shades of brown, blue, and gray, create drama. Bib."

A **Civil** War scrapbook; I was there too! History Colorado. Fulcrum Pub. 2012 64 p. ill. (some col.), maps (paperback) $14.95

Grades: 4 5 6 7 8 **973.7**

1. United States -- History -- 1861-1865, Civil War

ISBN 1555916686; 9781555916688

LC 2011042043

This book is "a multicultural Civil War history for children. The book . . . feature[es] chronological information" and "focus[es] on the different types of people and their place in the war. This . . . book emphasizes the roles of the children, women, minorities, and even pets that became mascots in the war." Also included are "historical photographs, drawings, maps, games, and primary quotes from children." (Publisher's Note)

Includes bibliographical references (p. 62-63) and index.

★ The **Civil** War: a visual history. DK Pub. 2011 360p il map $40

Grades: 5 6 7 8 **973.7**

1. United States -- History -- 1815-1861 2. United States -- History -- 1865-1898 3. United States -- History -- 1861-1865, Civil War -- Pictorial works

ISBN 978-0-7566-7185-3; 0-7566-7185-X

"A stunning, large-format pictorial history. The seven chapters are arranged chronologically, beginning with an overview of slavery in the United States, 1815 to 1860, and ending with a survey of the legacies of the conflict during the period 1865 to 1877. . . . Chapter introductions are followed by illustrated time lines and by short topical divisions that include biographies, maps, original documents or eyewitness accounts, illustrations, historical photographs, artifacts, and reproductions of paintings. Page layouts and the use of color are superb, and sidebars abound, adding to this extraordinary book." SLJ

Clinton, Catherine

★ **Hold** the flag high; illustrated by Shane W. Evans. Katherine Tegen Books 2005 un il $15.99; lib bdg $16.89

Grades: 2 3 4 **973.7**

1. Soldiers 2. African American soldiers 3. Postal employees 4. United States -- History -- 1861-1865, Civil War

ISBN 0-06-050428-5; 0-06-050429-3 lib bdg

LC 2003-11956

Describes the Civil War battle of Morris Island, South Carolina, during which Sargeant William H. Carney became the first African American to earn a Congressional Medal of Honor

"The story captures the fear and horror of battle as well as the bravery of the soldiers. . . . Evans' paintings convey the emotions of the characters as well as their actions." Booklist

Includes bibliographical references

Evans, Shane W.

★ Underground; [by] Shane W. Evans. Roaring Brook Press 2010 1 v. col. ill. $16.99

Grades: K 1 2 **973.7**

1. Abolitionists 2. Underground railroad 3. Slavery -- United States 4. Fugitive slaves

ISBN 1596435380; 9781596435384

LC 2010007735

Coretta Scott King Award (Illustrators) (2012)

This picture book portrays fugitive slaves escaping to freedom through the Underground Railroad. "Preschool, primary." (Horn Book)

"Powerfully expressive imagery will sweep young viewers into this suspenseful journey along the Underground Railroad. Accompanied by a commentary of, usually, just two or three words per spread, the scenes track a small group of escapees stealing through darkness beneath a thin crescent moon. . . . Underscoring the sense of fear and urgency with broad, slanted strokes of thinly applied paint, Evans limns his hunched, indistinct figures in dark lines and adds weight with scribbled fill and jagged bits of paper or cloth. . . . Lengthier accounts of travel on the Underground Railroad abound, but few if any portray the experience with such compelling immediacy." Kirkus

Fradin, Dennis Brindell

★ The price of freedom; how one town stood up to slavery. by Judith Bloom Fradin & Dennis Brindell Fradin; illustrated by Eric Velasquez. Walker & Co. 2013 48 p. (hardback) $16.99

Grades: 1 2 3 **973.7**

1. Fugitive slaves 2. Oberlin-Wellington Rescue, 1858 3. Underground railroad -- Ohio -- History 4. Quakers -- Ohio -- History -- 19th century 5. Fugitive slaves -- Ohio -- History -- 19th century

ISBN 0802721664; 9780802721662; 9780802721679

LC 2012015781

This juvenile history book, by Dennis Brindell Fradin and Judith Bloom Fradin, with illustrations by Eric Velasquez, describes how "an Ohio community successfully defied the 1850 Fugitive Slave Act. In 1856, John Price and two other Kentucky slaves crossed the Ohio River to freedom in Oberlin. . . . Two years later, when slave hunters tracked him down and captured him, the citizens of the town banded together to defend him." (Kirkus Reviews)

Friedman, Robin

The silent witness; a true story of the Civil War. illustrated by Claire A. Nivola. Houghton Mifflin Co. 2005 un il $16

Grades: K 1 2 3 **973.7**

1. Virginia -- History 2. United States -- History -- 1861-1865, Civil War

ISBN 0-618-44230-8

LC 2004-1013

"Young Lula McLean watched the Civil War begin and end: General Beauregard used her family's Virginia home as his headquarters, and Lee surrendered at their second home. The finely executed, primitive-like paintings accentuate the idea that this war was an intimate part of everyday life in the South, and the small telling details show a personal side of the war." Horn Book Guide

Gregory, Josh

Gettysburg; by Josh Gregory. Children's Press 2012 64 p. chiefly col. ill. (library) $30.00; (paperback) $8.95

Grades: 4 5 6 **973.7**

1. Gettysburg (Pa.), Battle of, 1863

ISBN 0531250342; 9780531250341; 9780531265598

LC 2011010751

In this book on the 1863 Battle of Gettysburg, "[Josh] Gregory takes his readers back to the precursor events that set the stage for this meeting engagement pitting General [Robert E.] Lee's Army of Northern Virginia against General [George] Meade's oft times defeated Union Army of the Potomac. In the end the efforts of Lee's seemingly indomitable veterans were not enough to overcome the forces of fate and tactics." (Children's Literature)

Includes bibliographical references (p. 61) and index.

Hernandez, Roger E.

The Civil War, 1840s-1890s. Marshall Cavendish Benchmark 2008 80p il map (Hispanic America) lib bdg $34.21

Grades: 4 5 6 7 **973.7**

1. Latinos (U.S.) 2. Hispanic Americans 3. United States -- Ethnic relations 4. United States -- History -- 1861-1865, Civil War

ISBN 978-0-7614-2939-5 lib bdg; 0-7614-2939-5 lib bdg

LC 2007049525

Discusses Hispanic participation during the Civil War

Includes glossary and bibliographical references

Holzer, Harold

The president is shot! the assassination of Abraham Lincoln. Boyds Mills Press 2004 181p il $17.95

Grades: 5 6 7 8 **973.7**

1. Lawyers 2. Presidents 3. State legislators 4. Members of Congress

ISBN 1-56397-985-3

"A page-turner of a text, a fascinating array of photos and archival illustrations, and an event that changed the course of history: all these elements combine in this strong, highly readable book." Booklist

Includes bibliographical references

Huey, Lois Miner

American archaeology uncovers the Underground Railroad. Marshall Cavendish Benchmark 2009 64p il map (American archaeology) lib bdg $21.95

Grades: 4 5 6 7 **973.7**

1. Abolitionists 2. Underground railroad 3. Slavery -- United States 4. Excavations (Archeology) -- United States

ISBN 978-0-7614-4267-7 lib bdg; 0-7614-4267-7 lib bdg

LC 2009003168

This describes how archeologists have learned about the history of the Underground Railroad.

This is "both intriguing and engaging for young readers. . . . A welcomed addition to classroom and school libraries." Libr Media Connect

Includes glossary and bibliographical references

Isaacs, Sally Senzell

The **Civil** War; Sally Senzell Isaacs. Kingfisher 2011 32 p. ill., map (hardcover) $19.89

Grades: 3 4 5 6 **973.7**

1. United States -- History -- 1861-1865, Civil War

ISBN 0753466937; 9780753466933

LC 2011049248

This book is part of the "All About America" series which "covers the most important periods in the history of a burgeoning nation, from Colonists and Independence to The Civil War, and from Cowboys and the Wild West to the early inhabitants, the Native Americans." In this volume, readers learn about the American Civil War. (Publisher's note)

Jordan, Anne Devereaux

The **Civil** War; by Anne Devereaux Jordan; with Virginia Schomp. Marshall Cavendish Benchmark 2007 72p il (Drama of African-American history) lib bdg $34.21

Grades: 5 6 7 8 **973.7**

1. African Americans -- History 2. United States -- History -- 1861-1865, Civil War

ISBN 978-0-7614-2179-5 lib bdg; 0-7614-2179-3 lib bdg

LC 2006012472

Describes the role of African Americans during the Civil War (1861-1865)

Includes glossary and bibliographical references

Kostyal, K. M.

1862, Fredericksburg; a new look at a bitter Civil War battle. National Geographic 2011 48p (National Geographic kids)

Grades: 3 4 5 6 **973.7**

1. United States -- History -- 1861-1865, Civil War -- Campaigns

ISBN 1-4263-0835-3; 1-4263-0836-1 lib bdg; 978-1-4263-0835-2; 978-1-4263-0836-9 lib bdg

LC 2011011798

Details the Civil War battle of Fredericksburg, Virginia, and profiles some of the key figures involved in what was a decisive victory for the Confederacy.

"Realistic, full-color pictures of modern-day re-enactors mix with clear language to bring the action to life. The text is interspersed with personal accounts. . . . Brief chapters tell the war's story from the perspective of what happened at Fredericksburg in a concise manner. . . . A valuable resource for classrooms, libraries, and travelers to Fredericksburg and the surrounding area." SLJ

Landau, Elaine

Fleeing to freedom on the Underground Railroad; the courageous slaves, agents, and conductors. Twenty-First Century Books 2006 88p il map (People's history) lib bdg $26.60

Grades: 5 6 7 8 **973.7**

1. Abolitionists 2. Underground railroad 3. Slavery -- United States

ISBN 978-0-8225-3490-7 lib bdg; 0-8225-3490-8 lib bdg

LC 2005020358

"Landau discusses the history of slavery in the United States, slave life, the Underground Railroad, and the leaders, both black and white, of antislavery organizations. Three chapters outline specifics of slaves' escapes. . . . An out-

standing feature of this book is the use of primary sources and quotes from former slaves, contemporary newspaper accounts, and reminiscences of escaped slaves. . . . Excellent historical photographs and illustrations enhance the text." SLJ

Includes bibliographical references

McNeese, Tim

The **Civil** War era, 1851-1865; consulting editor, Richard Jensen. Chelsea House 2010 144p il map (Discovering U.S. history) $35

Grades: 5 6 7 8 **973.7**

1. United States -- History -- 1861-1865, Civil War

ISBN 978-1-60413-352-3; 1-60413-352-X

LC 2009-3660

"The information is accurate and easy to understand. Pictures are well placed, and primary sources are included. . . . The maps are well done and there are sidebars with additional information. . . . [This would be good] to have on hand for reports as it is well laid out and easy to use." Libr Media Connect

Includes glossary and bibliographical references

McPherson, James M.

★ **Fields** of fury; the American Civil War. Atheneum Bks. for Young Readers 2002 96p il map $22.95

Grades: 5 6 7 8 **973.7**

1. United States -- History -- 1861-1865, Civil War

ISBN 0-689-84833-1

LC 2001-46048

Examines the events and effects of the American Civil War

"McPherson writes with authority, offering a broad overview as well as many details and anecdotes that give his account a human dimension. . . . The many fine illustrations include period photographs, paintings, prints, some excellent maps." Booklist

Includes glossary and bibliographical references

Murphy, Jim

★ The **boys'** war; Confederate and Union soldiers talk about the Civil War. Clarion Bks. 1990 110p il hardcover o.p. pa $8.95

Grades: 5 6 7 8 9 10 **973.7**

1. United States -- History -- 1861-1865, Civil War

ISBN 0-89919-893-7; 0-395-66412-8 pa

LC 89-23959

This book includes diary entries, personal letters, and archival photographs to describe the experiences of boys, sixteen years old or younger, who fought in the Civil War.

"An excellent selection of more than 45 sepia-toned contemporary photographs augment the text of this informative, moving work." SLJ

Includes bibliographical references

★ The **long** road to Gettysburg. Clarion Bks. 1992 116p il maps $17; pa $7.95

Grades: 5 6 7 8 9 10 **973.7**

1. Gettysburg (Pa.), Battle of, 1863

ISBN 0-395-55965-0; 0-618-05157-0 pa

LC 90-21881

Describes the events of the Battle of Gettysburg in 1863 as seen through the eyes of two actual participants, nineteen-year-old Confederate lieutenant John Dooley and seventeen-year-old Union soldier Thomas Galway. Also discusses Lincoln's famous speech delivered at the dedication of the National Cemetery at Gettysburg

The author "uses all of his fine skills as an information writer—clarity of detail, conciseness, understanding of his age group, and ability to find the drama appealing to readers—to frame a well-crafted account of a single battle in the war." Horn Book

Includes bibliographical references

★ A **savage** thunder; Antietam and the bloody road to freedom. Margaret K. McElderry Books 2009 103p il map $17.99

Grades: 5 6 7 8 9   **973.7**

1. Generals 2. Governors 3. Antietam (Md.), Battle of, 1862 4. College presidents 5. Presidential candidates 6. United States -- History -- 1861-1865, Civil War

ISBN 978-0-689-87633-2; 0-689-87633-5

LC 2008-32738

"Murphy provides readers with a lucid and compelling narrative, drawn mainly from firsthand accounts. . . . Replete with excellent-quality archival photos, reproductions, and maps, this is an outstanding account of a battle." SLJ

Includes bibliographical references

Norwich, Grace

I am Harriet Tubman; by Grace Norwich; illustrated by Ute Simon. Scholastic 2013 127 p. ill. (paperback) $5.99

Grades: 3 4 5   **973.7**

1. Slavery -- United States

ISBN 0545484367; 9780545484367

This book is part of the I Am series and focuses on Harriet Tubman, "the legendary Underground Railroad conductor. Prefaced by a time line and a page introducing important individuals to the story, [Grace] Norwich's narrative provides information as well as insight into how that information has come down to us. . . . Tubman's early life in slavery is . . . described, as are her brave efforts to escape." (Booklist)

O'Connor, Jim

What was the Battle of Gettysburg? by Jim O'Connor; illustrated by John Mantha. Grosset & Dunlap 2013 106 p. (hc) $15.99

Grades: 3 4 5 6   **973.7**

1. Gettysburg (Pa.), Battle of, 1863 2. United States -- History -- 1861-1865, Civil War

ISBN 0448465752; 9780448462868; 9780448465753

LC 2012027557

This book, by Jim O'Connor, John Mantha, and James Bennett, "offers a strongly contextualized account of the bloodiest engagement of the Civil War and a mostly chronological discussion of the battle. Chapters, each beginning with a historical date, tell the story in a narrative format, but the story is effectively broken up with boxed biographies of such figures as Mathew Brady, Jeb Stuart, and Abraham Lincoln." (Booklist)

Includes bibliographical references (p. 106)

Raatma, Lucia

The **Underground** Railroad; by Lucia Raatma. Children's Press 2011 64 p. col. ill. (library) $30.00; (paperback) $8.95

Grades: 4 5 6   **973.7**

1. Fugitive slaves 2. Underground Railroad 3.

Fugitive slaves -- United States -- History -- 19th century 4. Antislavery movements -- United States -- History -- 19th century

ISBN 0531250431; 9780531250433; 9780531265680

LC 2011009493

This book by Lucia Raatma is part of the Cornerstones of Freedom series and looks at the Underground Railroad. The entry "explains how the system worked, the journey, and important people who guided slaves such as Harriet Tubman and Levi and Catherine White Coffin of Indiana, who helped about 2,000 slaves reach freedom." (School Library Journal)

Includes bibliographical references (p. 61) and index.

Rossi, Ann

Freedom struggle; the anti-slavery movement in America 1830-1865. National Geographic 2005 40p il (Crossroads America) $12.95; lib bdg $21.90

Grades: 4 5 6   **973.7**

1. Abolitionists 2. Slavery -- United States

ISBN 0-7922-7828-3; 0-7922-8061-X lib bdg

LC 2003-19824

This discusses the Abolitionist Movement in the United States, profiling some of its leaders and its role in the Civil War.

"Period photographs, drawings, and cartoons; primary-source material; and biographical content make [this] introductory [title] interesting and accessible." SLJ

Includes glossary

Sheinkin, Steve

★ **Two** miserable presidents; everything your schoolbooks didn't tell you about the Civil War. illustrated by Tim Robinson. Roaring Brook Press 2008 246p il $19.95

Grades: 4 5 6 7   **973.7**

1. United States -- History -- 1861-1865, Civil War

ISBN 978-1-59643-320-5; 1-59643-320-5

LC 2007-33115

"Chatty and accessible, this book does double duty: it introduces Civil War history for readers who don't know much about it and supplies browsable commentary for those familiar with the big picture. . . . [Sheinkin's] fast-paced narrative is broken into short, tersely titled vignettes." Booklist

Includes bibliographical references

Stark, Ken

Marching to Appomattox; the footrace that ended the Civil War. [by] Ken Stark. G.P. Putnam's Sons 2009 un il $17.99

Grades: 3 4 5   **973.7**

1. Generals 2. Presidents 3. Appomattox Campaign, 1865 4. College presidents 5. United States -- History -- 1861-1865, Civil War

ISBN 978-0-399-24212-0; 0-399-24212-0

LC 2008012551

"The beginning of April 1865 was a pivotal time in the Civil War. Following a defeat at Richmond, VA, the Confederate forces tried to outrun the Union troops and get to waiting reinforcements in North Carolina. Instead, Lee's men ended up trapped by General Grant's army. The week culminated with Lee's surrender at Appomattox Court House. Stark frames this war vignette effectively for young readers. . . . The illustrations are a great strength. Rendered in watercolor, the inclusion of gouache and casein gives the hues a vividness and depth not always associated with the medium." SLJ

Includes bibliographical references

Turner, Ann Warren

Abe Lincoln remembers; [by] Ann Turner; pictures by Wendell Minor. HarperCollins Pubs. 2001 un il hardcover o.p. pa $6.99

Grades: K 1 2 3   **973.7**

1. Lawyers 2. Presidents 3. State legislators 4. Members of Congress 5. Presidents -- United States 6. United States -- History -- 1861-1865, Civil War

ISBN 0-06-027577-4; 0-06-027578-2 lib bdg; 0-06-051107-9 pa

LC 98-50937

A simple description of the life of Abraham Lincoln, presented from his point of view

"Turner's free-verse reminiscence gracefully ties images and themes from Lincoln's youth to those of his adult years. . . . Minor's well-composed paintings, best seen from a little distance, effectively portray the man as he ages." Booklist

Weber, Jennifer L.

Summer's bloodiest days; the Battle of Gettysburg as told from all sides. foreword by James M. McPherson. National Geographic 2010 61p il map $17.95; lib bdg $27.90

Grades: 5 6 7 8   **973.7**

1. Gettysburg (Pa.), Battle of, 1863 2. United States -- History -- 1861-1865, Civil War

ISBN 978-1-4263-0706-5; 1-4263-0706-3; 978-1-4263-0707-2 lib bdg; 1-4263-0707-1 lib bdg

"This colorful book tells of the Battle of Gettysburg, a dramatic event that becomes even more compelling because the text is laced with pertinent quotes from those who were there. Weber's vivid, pithy writing packs a great deal of information and many anecdotes into a relatively short account. . . . Many battle maps, short, informative sidebars, and the use of modern realistic paintings and photos of artifacts as well as period photographs . . . illustrate the book." Booklist

Includes bibliographical references

Williams, Carla

The Underground Railroad. Child's World 2009 32p il (Journey to freedom) lib bdg $28.50

Grades: 4 5 6   **973.7**

1. Underground railroad 2. Slavery -- United States

ISBN 978-1-60253-139-0 lib bdg; 1-60253-139-0 lib bdg

LC 2008031946

"Underground Railroad describes how this secret system worked and introduces key figures. Williams discusses relevant laws and amendments as well as the advent and conclusion of the Civil War. The facts, presented through stories, historical news accounts, and biographical sketches of Harriet Tubman and Levi Weeks, capture the desperation of the enslaved as well as the abolitionists' commitment to them. The [book is] concise and direct, yet the writing remains sophisticated. Vibrant personal stories accompanied by striking photographs of historical figures and artifacts provide a sense of the subjects' hopes and dreams." SLJ

Includes glossary and bibliographical references

973.8   United States--Reconstruction period, 1865-1901

Howell, Brian

The US Civil War and Reconstruction. Cherry Lake Pub. 2011 il (Language arts explorer: history digs) $18.95; pa $14.95

Grades: 3 4 5 6   **973.8**

1. Reconstruction (1865-1876) 2. United States -- History -- 1861-1865, Civil War

ISBN 978-1-61080-201-7; 978-1-61080-289-5 pa

LC 2011015126

"This compact volume is narrated by an unnamed child, who is helping a museum curator set up a Civil War museum. The first boxes that the narrator unpacks hold documents and exhibits about slavery. Each day, the child learns more about the origins of the war, its battles, and Reconstruction. Through simply told prose in first person, the book provides a great deal of information presented in ways that kids can understand. It also gives solid background in how research is done. . . . Photographs and numerous reproductions of historical documents add to the usefulness of this slim book." Booklist

McNeese, Tim

The Gilded Age and Progressivism, 1891-1913; Tim McNeese; consulting editor, Richard Jensen. Chelsea House 2010 136 p. ill. (some col.) (Discovering U.S. history) (library) $35.00

Grades: 5 6 7 8   **973.8**

1. Progressivism (United States politics) 2. United States -- History -- 1865-1921

ISBN 1604133554; 9781604133554

LC 2009015012

McNeese "discusses the people, politics, economic conditions, and foreign affairs of [the U.S. from 1891 to 1913], objectively explaining how the attitudes, perceptions, and expectations of the American people and their leaders shaped the development of the country. . . . Color period art and photos, maps, and cutaway drawings supplement the [text]." SLJ

Includes bibliographical references and index.

Stroud, Bettye

The Reconstruction era; by Bettye M. Stroud with Virginia Schomp. Marshall Cavendish Benchmark 2007 70p il (Drama of African-American history) lib bdg $34.21

Grades: 5 6 7 8   **973.8**

1. Reconstruction (1865-1876) 2. African Americans -- History

ISBN 978-0-7614-2181-8 lib bdg; 0-7614-2181-5 lib bdg

LC 2006012149

"Traces the history of Reconstruction, from the end of the Civil War in 1865 to 1877, when federal troops were removed from the South." Publisher's note

Includes glossary and bibliographical references

Todras, Ellen H.

Wagon trains and settlers. Kingfisher 2011 32p il (All about America) pa $9.99; $19.89

Grades: 3 4 5 6   **973.8**

1. Frontier and pioneer life 2. Overland journeys to the

Pacific 3. West (U.S.) -- History

ISBN 0-7534-6511-6 pa; 0-7534-6583-3; 978-0-7534-6511-0 pa; 978-0-7534-6583-7

This describes westward migration and pioneer life in the United States in the 19th century.

This "visually appealing [title] effectively [combines] paintings, engravings, primary documents, and photographs with cartoon illustrations. The eye-catching [layout includes] different font sizes, bold type, and text boxes to highlight different pieces of information. The content is interesting and pithy." SLJ

Includes glossary and bibliographical references

Walker, Paul Robert

★ **Remember** Little Bighorn; Indians, soldiers, and scouts tell their stories. [by] Paul Robert Walker; [foreword by John A. Doerner] National Geographic Society 2006 61p il map $17.95; lib bdg $27.90

Grades: 5 6 7 8   **973.8**

1. Little Bighorn, Battle of the, 1876

ISBN 0-7922-5521-6; 0-7922-5522-4 lib bdg

LC 2005030929

This "volume gives an almost blow-by-blow account of the famous battle that came to be known as Custer's Last Stand. Walker concentrates on the battle itself, fought on the Great Plains in 1876, and the book includes diagrams of each side's tactics. . . . Walker's exhaustive research . . . [brings] together the conflicting viewpoints of the whites and the Lakota Sioux, Cheyenne, and Arapaho fighters, documenting everything in source notes. The handsome book design, with thick paper, clear type, maps, stirring photos, and archival images, will attract readers to the battle story and then start them thinking about lasting historical issues." Booklist

Includes bibliographical references

973.9   United States--1901-

Sandler, Martin W.

★ The **Dust** Bowl through the lens; how photography revealed and helped remedy a national disaster. Walker & Co. 2008 96p il map $15.99; lib bdg $20.89

Grades: 5 6 7 8   **973.9**

1. Dust storms 2. Documentary photography 3. Great Plains -- History

ISBN 978-0-8027-9547-2; 0-8027-9547-1; 978-0-8027-9548-9 lib bdg; 0-8027-9548-X lib bdg

LC 2008-55979

"This excellent photo-essay traces the history of the Dust Bowl from its causes to its resolution. In tandem, Sandler treats the role of the budding field of photojournalism. Forty-four spreads feature a page of clear, direct text with a large, well-reproduced image, many of which are set on color pages. . . . Seldom has the connection between the arts and the general quality of life been made so clear. The text deals equally with those who fled the decimated Bread Basket for California and those who waited out the devastation and dust. Throughout, the use of primary sources is superb, with quotations from affected citizens, the photojournalists themselves, political and entertainment figures, and writers, giving a multifaceted picture of a seminal time in United States history." SLJ

973.91   United States--1901-1953

Bingham, Jane

The **Great** Depression; the Jazz Age, Prohibition, and the Great Depression, 1921-1937. Chelsea House 2011 64p il (A cultural history of women in America) $35

Grades: 5 6 7 8   **973.91**

1. Great Depression, 1929-1939 2. Women -- United States 3. Women -- United States -- History

ISBN 978-1-60413-933-4; 1-60413-933-1

LC 2010044889

An "eye-catching [layout] with good use of color, photographs, and informative sidebars, many of which use primary-source quotations, are the highlights of [this] appealing [volume]. . . . After a succinct overview of contemporary events, the chapters describe women's lives at home, at work, in education, in politics, in the arts, and their role in the general culture. . . . [This book] surveys an era after women won the right to vote and when the nation's economic crash placed new hardships on families." SLJ

Includes glossary and bibliographical references

Corrigan, Jim

The **1900s** decade in photos; a decade of discovery. Enslow Publishers 2010 64p il (Amazing decades in photos) lib bdg $27.93

Grades: 4 5 6 7   **973.91**

1. United States -- History -- 20th century

ISBN 978-0-7660-3129-6 lib bdg; 0-7660-3129-2 lib bdg

LC 2008042900

This highlights the important world, national, and cultural developments of the 1900s.

This is illustrated with "large, well-chosen black-and-white and color photos. . . . Captions provide specific information about the photos and supplement, rather than repeat, information in the [narrative]. Attractive and readable, this . . . will be popular with browsers and beginning researchers." SLJ

Includes glossary and bibliographical references

The **1910s** decade in photos; a decade that shook the world. Enslow Publishers 2010 64p il (Amazing decades in photos) lib bdg $27.93

Grades: 4 5 6 7   **973.91**

1. United States -- History -- 20th century

ISBN 978-0-7660-3130-2 lib bdg; 0-7660-3130-6 lib bdg

LC 2008042902

This highlights the important world, national, and cultural developments of the decade 1910-1919, including the sinking of the Titanic, the establishment of the Boy Scouts and Girl Scouts, immigration, income tax, Hollywood feature films, World War I, the Lusitania sinking, and more.

Includes glossary and bibliographical references

The **1920s** decade in photos; the Roaring Twenties. Enslow Publishers 2010 64p il (Amazing decades in photos) lib bdg $27.93

Grades: 4 5 6 7   **973.91**

1. United States -- History -- 1919-1933

ISBN 978-0-7660-3131-9 lib bdg; 0-7660-3131-4 lib bdg

LC 2008042903

This highlights the important world, national, and cultural developments of the decade 1920-1929, including Prohibition, jazz music, women's suffrage, the rise of Mussolini, flappers fashions, the KKK, U.S. Presidents Harding and Coolidge, the Teapot Dome Scandal, the rise of the Nazi Party, and more.

Includes glossary and bibliographical references

Kimmelman, Leslie

Hot dog! Eleanor Roosevelt throws a picnic. written by Leslie Kimmelman; illustrated by Victor Juhasz. Sleeping Bear Press 2014 40 p. color illustrations $16.99

Grades: 2 3 4 5   **973.91**

1. World history 2. Royal visitors -- United States 3. Royal visitors -- Great Britain 4. Visits of state -- United States 5. Presidents' spouses -- United States

ISBN 158536830X; 9781585368303

LC 2013024897

In this illustrated history book for children, "when King George and Queen Elizabeth decided to visit the U.S.--the first time a British monarch had set foot on U.S. shores-- Mrs. Roosevelt decided that, among other entertainments, a picnic in Hyde Park was in order. But when she said that she wanted to serve that quintessential American food, hot dogs, her menu choice became a subject of national discussion." (Booklist)

"Kimmelman's straightforward storytelling incorporates some basic explanatory facts and deftly brings this bit of Americana to life. An author's note provides further context along with a statement that quoted correspondence can be found at Hyde Park; it is silent, however, on the authenticity of the Roosevelts' dialogue. A captivating introductory piece for budding history buffs." Kirkus

Stanley, George Edward

An emerging world power (1900-1929) [by] George E. Stanley. World Almanac Library 2005 48p il (Primary source history of the United States) lib bdg $30

Grades: 5 6 7 8   **973.91**

1. United States -- Foreign relations 2. United States -- History -- 1919-1933 3. United States -- Politics and government -- 1919-1933

ISBN 0-8368-5828-X

LC 2004-61501

The author describes United States politics and foreign relations in the 1920s.

"Stanley explains and connects events utilizing clear language and a blending of text, images, and primary accounts. . . . Well-organized, highly attractive." SLJ

Includes bibliographical references

973.917 Administration of Franklin Delano Roosevelt, 1933-1945

Cooney, Barbara

★ Eleanor. Viking 1996 un il $15.99; pa $6.99

Grades: K 1 2 3   **973.917**

1. Diplomats 2. Columnists 3. Humanitarians 4. Social activists 5. Spouses of presidents 6. United Nations officials 7. Presidents' spouses -- United States

ISBN 0-670-86159-6; 0-14-055583-8 pa

LC 96-7723

"There are many biographies of Eleanor Roosevelt but this one is special. Not only does it boast Cooney's artwork, but it also gets to the heart of a young girl, which in many ways is as interesting as Roosevelt's later, well-known accomplishments." Booklist

Cooper, Michael L.

★ Dust to eat; drought and depression in the 1930's. Clarion Books 2004 81p il map hardcover o.p. $15

Grades: 4 5 6 7   **973.917**

1. Droughts 2. Migrant labor 3. Great Depression, 1929-1939

ISBN 0-618-15449-3

LC 2003-17807

This book begins "with the 1929 stock market crash that ushered in the Great Depression and {continues} with the severe drought in the Midwest, known as the Dust Bowl." (Publisher's note) Index. "Grades six to nine." (Bull Cent Child Books)

This includes "lots of stunning black-and-white archival photos and a clear, spacious text that draws on eloquent eyewitness reports—including comments from John Steinbeck and Woody Guthrie. . . . This is an excellent historical account." Booklist

Includes bibliographical references

Corrigan, Jim

The 1930s decade in photos; Depression and hope. Enslow Publishers 2010 64p il (Amazing decades in photos) lib bdg $27.93

Grades: 4 5 6 7   **973.917**

1. Great Depression, 1929-1939 2. United States -- History -- 1919-1933 3. United States -- History -- 1933-1945

ISBN 978-0-7660-3132-6 lib bdg; 0-7660-3132-2 lib bdg

LC 2008042904

This highlights the important world, national, and cultural developments of the decade 1930-1939, including the Great Depression, the Lindbergh kidnapping, the administration of FDR, the New Deal, jazz and swing music, the rise of Nazism, the repeal of Prohibition and more.

Includes glossary and bibliographical references

The 1940s decade in photos; a world at war. Enslow Publishers 2010 64p il (Amazing decades in photos) lib bdg $27.93

Grades: 4 5 6 7   **973.917**

1. World War, 1939-1945 2. United States -- History -- 1933-1945 3. United States -- History -- 1945-1953

ISBN 978-0-7660-3133-3 lib bdg; 0-7660-3133-0 lib bdg

LC 2008042910

This covers the important world, national, and cultural developments of the decade 1940-1949, focusing on World War II.

This is illustrated with "large, well-chosen black-and-white and color photos. . . . Captions provide specific information about the photos and supplement, rather than repeat, information in the [narrative]. Attractive and readable, this . . . will be popular with browsers and beginning researchers." SLJ

Includes glossary and bibliographical references

Freedman, Russell

★ **Eleanor** Roosevelt; a life of discovery. Clarion Bks.
1993 198p il hardcover o.p. pa $11.95

Grades: 5 6 7 8 9 10   **973.917**

1. Diplomats 2. Columnists 3. Humanitarians 4.
Social activists 5. Spouses of presidents 6. United
Nations officials 7. Presidents' spouses -- United States
ISBN 0-89919-862-7; 0-395-84520-3 pa

LC 92-25024

A Newbery Medal honor book, 1994

"This impeccably researched, highly readable study of
one of this country's greatest First Ladies is nonfiction at its
best. . . . Approximately 140 well-chosen black-and-white
photos amplify the text." Publ Wkly

Includes bibliographical references

★ **Franklin** Delano Roosevelt. Clarion Bks. 1990
200p il hardcover o.p. pa $9.95

Grades: 5 6 7 8 9 10   **973.917**

1. Governors 2. Presidents 3. Presidents -- United
States 4. United States -- Politics and government --
1933-1945
ISBN 0-89919-379-X; 0-395-62978-0 pa

LC 89-34986

The author "traces the personal and public events in a
life that led to the formation of one of the most influential
and magnetic leaders of the twentieth century." Horn Book

Includes bibliographical references

Garland, Sherry

Voices of the dust bowl; by Sherry Garland; illustrated
by Judith Hierstein. Pelican Pub. Co. 2011 p. cm.

Grades: 4 5 6   **973.917**

1. Great Plains -- History 2. Droughts -- United States
3. Dust Bowl Era, 1931-1939 4. Middle West -- History
-- 20th century 5. Great Plains -- History -- 20th century
6. Farmers -- Great Plains -- History -- 20th century 7.
Droughts -- Great Plains -- History -- 20th century
ISBN 9781589809642

LC 2011002670

This book, by Sherry Garland, presents "[v]oices from
those who lived through the largest environmental catastrophe in American history. From 1931 to 1940, a combination
of drought and soil erosion destroyed the fragile ecology and
economy of the Great Plains." Illustrations are given along
with accounts such as "a farmer's wife, a banker, and a child
who had never seen rain." (Publisher's note)

Includes bibliographical references

McNeese, Tim

The **Great** Depression, 1929-1940; consulting editor
Richard Jensen. Chelsea House 2010 136p il map (Discovering U.S. history) $35

Grades: 5 6 7 8   **973.917**

1. Economic conditions 2. Great Depression, 1929-
1939 3. United States -- History -- 1933-1945
ISBN 978-1-60413-357-8; 1-60413-357-0

LC 2009-22090

"The information is accurate and easy to understand.
Pictures are well placed, and primary sources are included.
. . . The maps are well done and there are sidebars with ad-
ditional information. . . . [This would be good] to have on

hand for reports as it is well laid out and easy to use." Libr
Media Connect

Includes glossary and bibliographical references

973.92   United States--1953-2001

Corrigan, Jim

The **1990s** decade in photos; the rise of technology.
Enslow Publishers 2010 64p il (Amazing decades in photos) lib bdg $27.93

Grades: 4 5 6 7   **973.92**

1. World history -- 20th century 2. United States --
History -- 1989-
ISBN 978-0-7660-3138-8 lib bdg; 0-7660-3138-1
lib bdg

LC 2008054648

This highlights the important world, national, and cul-
tural developments of the decade 1990-1999, including
Operation Desert Storm in 1991, race riots in Los Angeles,
the election of President Clinton, the 1993 bombing of the
World Trade Center, the Human Genome Project, the end of
Apartheid, massacres in Bosnia and Rwanda, the Oklahoma
City bombing, the O.J. Simpson murder trial, the Columbine
High School shootings, and more

Includes glossary and bibliographical references

McNeese, Tim

Modern America, 1964-present; consulting editor,
Richard Jensen. Chelsea House 2010 144p il map (Discovering U.S. history) $35

Grades: 5 6 7 8   **973.92**

1. United States -- History -- 1989- 2. United States
-- History -- 1961-1974 3. United States -- History --
1974-1989
ISBN 978-1-60413-361-5; 1-60413-361-9

"Through a good balance of social and political topics,
McNeese capably covers a diverse range of subjects in [this]
volume. . . . Modern America discusses civil rights, terrorism, and Barack Obama's first year as president. [The] book
has an excellent chronology; rich sidebars; and numerous
well-captioned illustrations, maps, and photos that enhance
the [text]. [This book provides a] satisfying [introduction] to
American history for students." SLJ

Includes glossary and bibliographical references

Nardo, Don

Assassination and its aftermath; how a photograph reassured a shocked nation. by Don Nardo. Compass Point
Books, a Capstone imprint 2013 64 p. (Captured history)
(library binding) $33.99

Grades: 6 7 8 9   **973.92**

1. Presidents -- United States -- Pictorial works 2.
Kennedy, John F. (John Fitzgerald), 1917-1963 --
Assassination 3. Photojournalists -- United States
-- History -- 20th century 4. Presidents -- Succession
-- United States -- History -- 20th century
ISBN 0756546923; 9780756546922; 9780756546984

LC 2012051716

In this book, by Don Nardo, "vice president, Lyndon
Baines Johnson, took the presidential oath of office on Air
Force One just hours after the assassination [of U.S. Presi-
dent John F. Kennedy] . . . Cecil Stoughton's iconic photo

[of this moment] showed the world that the smooth and orderly transfer of power called for in the U.S. Constitution had occurred." According to the book, "his photo helped ease the shock, tension, and fear in an anxious country." (Publisher's note)

Includes bibliographical references and index

973.921 Administration of Dwight David Eisenhower, 1953-1961

Corrigan, Jim
The **1950s** decade in photos; the American decade. Enslow Publishers 2010 64p il (Amazing decades in photos) lib bdg $27.93
Grades: 4 5 6 7 **973.921**
1. United States -- History -- 1945-1953 2. United States -- History -- 1953-1961
ISBN 978-0-7660-3134-0 lib bdg; 0-7660-3134-9 lib bdg
LC 2008042994

This highlights the important world, national, and cultural developments of the decade 1950-1959, including the Korean War, McCarthyism, the Baby Boom generation, the execution of the Rosenbergs, the Beat Generation, the polio epidemic and vaccine, the Montgomery Bus Boycott, the Suez Crisis, the beginning of rock music, the launching of Sputnik, and the Cuban Revolution

Includes glossary and bibliographical references

973.922 Administration of John Fitzgerald Kennedy, 1961-1963

Adler, David A.
A **picture** book of John F. Kennedy; illustrated by Robert Casilla. Holiday House 1991 un il $16.95; pa $6.95
Grades: 1 2 3 **973.922**
1. Presidents 2. Senators 3. Members of Congress 4. Presidents -- United States
ISBN 0-8234-0884-1; 0-8234-0976-7 pa
LC 90-23589

Depicts the life and career of John F. Kennedy

"Adler presents a brief, clearly written text that provides basic information about his subject in an appealing format. . . . Casilla's watercolors are full-color copies of famous photographs." SLJ

973.923 Administration of Lyndon Baines Johnson, 1963-1969

Corrigan, Jim
The **1960s** decade in photos; love, freedom, and flower power. Enslow Publishers 2010 64p il (Amazing decades in photos) lib bdg $27.93
Grades: 4 5 6 7 **973.923**
1. United States -- History -- 1961-1974
ISBN 978-0-7660-3135-7 lib bdg; 0-7660-3135-7 lib bdg
LC 2008042996

This highlights the important world, national, and cultural developments of the decade 1960-1969, including the U-2 spy plane, the election and assassination of JFK, the beginnings of manned space exploration, the Bay of Pigs invasion, the Vietnam War, the Cuban Missile Crisis, the British invasion in rock music, the Civil Rights movement, the Six-Day War in the Middle East, the assassinations of RFK and Martin Luther King, and Hippie culture

Includes glossary and bibliographical references

973.924 Administration of Richard Milhous Nixon, 1969-1974

Corrigan, Jim
The **1970s** decade in photos; protest and change. Enslow Publishers 2010 64p il (Amazing decades in photos) lib bdg $27.93
Grades: 4 5 6 7 **973.924**
1. United States -- History -- 1961-1974 2. United States -- History -- 1974-1989
ISBN 978-0-7660-3136-4 lib bdg; 0-7660-3136-5 lib bdg
LC 2008042998

This highlights the important world, national, and cultural developments of the decade 1970-1979, including protests against the Vietnam War, terrorist airplane hijackings, the thawing of the Cold War, the deaths of rock musicians Jimi Hendrix, Janice Joplin, and Jim Morrison, the attack at the Munich Olympics, Watergate and the resignation of President Nixon, Three Mile Island, and more.

Includes glossary and bibliographical references

973.927 Administration of Ronald Reagan, 1981-1989

Corrigan, Jim
The **1980s** decade in photos; the triumph of democracy. Enslow Publishers 2010 64p il (Amazing decades in photos) lib bdg $27.93
Grades: 4 5 6 7 **973.927**
1. World history -- 20th century 2. United States -- History -- 1974-1989
ISBN 978-0-7660-3137-1 lib bdg; 0-7660-3137-3 lib bdg
LC 2008052627

This highlights the important world, national, and cultural developments of the decade 1980-1989, including the 1980 Winter Olympics, the presidency of Ronald Reagan, the Iran hostage crisis, the Space Shuttle, MTV, the War on Drugs, AIDS, the rise of the computer, fashion, the Chernobyl nuclear disaster, the Iran-Contra Affair, the massacre in Tiananmen Square, the fall of the Berlin Wall, and the U.S. invasion of Panama

Includes glossary and bibliographical references

973.93   United States--2001-

Corrigan, Jim

The **2000s** decade in photos; a new millennium. Enslow Publishers 2010 64p il (Amazing decades in photos) lib bdg $27.93

Grades: 4 5 6 7   **973.93**

1. World history -- 21st century   2. United States -- History -- 21st century

ISBN 978-0-7660-3139-5 lib bdg; 0-7660-3139-X lib bdg

LC 2008054644

This highlights the important world, national, and cultural developments of the first decade of the 21st century, including the disputed presidential election of 2000, the attacks of September 11, 2001, the Iraq War, digital technology and gadgets, the drop in stock market prices of internet companies, steroid use in sports, the Space Shuttle disaster of 2003, the tsunami of 2004, Hurricane Katrina, the massacre at Virginia Tech, the energy crisis, and the 2008 presidential election

Includes glossary and bibliographical references

973.931   Administration of George W. Bush, 2001-2009

Benoit, Peter

September 11 we will never forget; by Peter Benoit. Children's Press 2012 64 p. col. ill., col. map (ornerstones of freedom) (library) $30.00; (paperback) $8.95

Grades: 4 5 6 7   **973.931**

1. September 11 terrorist attacks, 2001   2. Terrorism -- United States

ISBN 0531250407; 9780531250402; 9780531265659

LC 2011009586

This book presents an "overview of the events of September 11, 2001 and the impact the day continues to have on present day life.... Boxed text adds information about international reaction, and the life of Osama Bin Laden, and other topics throughout the book. . . . .The immediate emergency responses at each site are described as well as government actions such as immediate grounding of planes . . . and military initiatives in the Middle East." (Children's Literature)

Includes bibliographical references (p. 61) and index.

Brown, Don

★ **America** is under attack; September 11, 2001: the day the towers fell. Roaring Brook Press 2011 un il $16.99

Grades: 2 3 4   **973.931**

1. Terrorism   2. September 11 terrorist attacks, 2001   3. War on terrorism

ISBN 978-1-5964-3694-7; 1-5964-3694-8

LC 2010045417

"Brown's compelling narrative chronologically recounts the morning's events in a tone both straightforward and compassionate, without resorting to sensationalism. Brown's watercolor illustrations, covering most of each spread, mirror this voice, conveying the day's chaos and despair without unnecessarily frightening readers." SLJ

Burgan, Michael

George W. Bush; Michael Burgan. Marshall Cavendish Benchmark 2012 112 p. $34.21

Grades: 5 6 7 8   **973.931**

1. Terrorism   2. Presidents -- United States   3. Presidents -- United States -- Biography

ISBN 1608701840; 9781608701841

LC 2010014801

This book "in the 'Presidents and Their Times' series provides . . . information about George W. Bush and how he handled critical situations (e.g., domestic spying vis-a-vis telephone records to highlight the difficulty battling terrorism and the effect of Bush's response to Hurricane Katrina). . . . Personal information is also provided about his early years, including his marriage to Laura, entry into politics, relationships with other family members, a decision to stop drinking, and his choice to become a Christian fundamentalist." Also included are "color and older black and white photos" and back matter such as "a timeline, chapter notes with complete citations, a glossary, books and websites for additional information, bibliography (books, articles, media), and index." (Children's Literature)

Includes bibliographical references and index

Fradin, Dennis B.

September 11, 2001; by Dennis Brindell Fradin. Marshall Cavendish Benchmark 2009 47p il map (Turning points in U.S. history) lib bdg $21.95

Grades: 3 4 5   **973.931**

1. September 11 terrorist attacks, 2001   2. War on terrorism   3. United States -- Social conditions   4. United States -- Politics and government -- 2001-

ISBN 978-0-7614-4259-2 lib bdg; 0-7614-4259-6 lib bdg

LC 2008038267

This book provides "accurate, nonsensationalized information in [a] well-organized, clearly written, and politically neutral [text]. The photos are crisp, and, due to the subject matter, heartrending." SLJ

Includes glossary and bibliographical references

973.932   Administration of Barack Obama, 2009-

Staake, Bob

The **First** Pup; the real story of how Bo got to the White House. Feiwel and Friends 2010 un il $16.99

Grades: 1 2 3   **973.932**

1. Dogs   2. Lawyers   3. Presidents   4. Senators   5. State legislators   6. Nobel laureates for peace   7. Presidents -- United States -- Family

ISBN 978-0-312-61346-4; 0-312-61346-6

Weatherford, Carole Boston

First pooch; the Obamas pick a pet. Illustrated by Amy Bates. Marshall Cavendish 2009 un il $16.99

Grades: PreK K 1 2   **973.932**

1. Dogs   2. Lawyers   3. Presidents   4. Senators   5. State legislators   6. Nobel laureates for peace   7. Presidents -- United States -- Family

ISBN 978-0-7614-5636-0; 0-7614-5636-8

LC 2009006117

"This brief, lighthearted chronicle of the Obama family's search for a suitable puppy to fulfill candidate Obama's promise to his daughters focuses on Malia and Sasha. But it also brings in information about promises made by previous presidents, various breeds of dogs that lived in the White House, whimsical duties of a first dog. . . . Lively watercolor, pencil, and gouache illustrations featuring a smiling Obama family happy in their endeavors, portraits of select past presidents, and a lineup of adorable potential first pooches add to the telling." Booklist

Zeiger, Jennifer

Barack Obama; by Jennifer Zeiger. Children's Press 2012 64 p. ill. (chiefly col.), col. map (library binding) $30.00; (paperback) $8.95

Grades: 4 5 6   **973.932**

1. Presidents -- United States -- Biography 2. Racially mixed people -- United States -- Biography

ISBN 0531230503; 0531281507; 9780531230503; 9780531281505

LC 2011031124

This book presents a "nonfiction account of President [Barack]Obama's life for middle school students. . . . The book includes many color photographs of the President as a young boy and young adult. It gives the details of his life in Indonesia and Hawaii and traces his career up to the 2012 re-election campaign. His education is a focus of the biography and there is ample discussion of his educational career and how it has helped to shape him into the man he is today." (Children's Literature)

Includes bibliographical references (p. 61) and index.

974 Specific states of United States

Rylant, Cynthia

★ **Appalachia**; the voices of sleeping birds. illustrated by Barry Moser. Harcourt Brace Jovanovich 1991 21p il $17; pa $6

Grades: 4 5 6 7   **974**

1. Appalachian region

ISBN 0-15-201605-8; 0-15-201893-X pa

LC 90-36798

"Taking her subtitle from a passage by James Agee, the author conveys with a marvelous economy of words the essence of the very special part of America where she was raised. A poetic text projects emotion as well as information. . . . Moser's watercolors capture the scene perfectly. . . . The book is a treasure—simply a beautiful combination of text and art." Horn Book

974.1 Maine

Dornfeld, Margaret

Maine; by Margaret Dornfeld and Joyce Hart. 2nd ed.; Marshall Cavendish Benchmark 2010 144p il map (Celebrate the states) lib bdg $42.79

Grades: 5 6 7 8   **974.1**

1. Maine

ISBN 978-0-7614-4726-9; 0-7614-4726-1

LC 2009002583

This offers information on the geography, history, wildlife, governmental structure, economy, cultural diversity, peoples, religion, and landmarks of Maine.

Includes bibliographical references

Heinrichs, Ann

Maine; by Ann Heinrichs. Children's Press 2008 144p il map (America the beautiful, third series) lib bdg $38

Grades: 4 5 6 7   **974.1**

1. Maine

ISBN 978-0-531-18575-9; 0-531-18575-3

LC 2007-302

Describes the history, geography, ecology, people, economy, cities, and sights of the state of Maine.

Includes glossary and bibliographical references

Peterson, Judy Monroe

Maine; past and present. Rosen Central 2011 48p il map (The United States: past and present) lib bdg $26.50; pa $11.75

Grades: 3 4 5 6   **974.1**

1. Maine

ISBN 978-1-4358-9484-6 lib bdg; 1-4358-9484-7 lib bdg; 978-1-4358-9511-9 pa; 1-4358-9511-8 pa

LC 2009048769

Presents the history, geography, government, economy, and people of Maine, as well as general facts about the state.

Includes glossary and bibliographical references

974.2 New Hampshire

Auden, Scott

New Hampshire, 1603-1776; [by] Scott Auden; with Alan Taylor, consultant. National Geographic Society 2007 109p il map (Voices from colonial America) $21.95; lib bdg $32.90

Grades: 5 6 7 8   **974.2**

1. New Hampshire -- History

ISBN 978-1-4263-0034-9; 1-4263-0034-4; 978-1-4263-0035-6 lib bdg; 1-4263-0035-2 lib bdg

LC 2006-36055

Provides a look at the long and changing colonial history of the state of New Hampshire through a review of its borders, founding fathers, motto, and more, complete with archival images, period maps, and various first-person accounts.

Offers " thorough, well-documented information about the struggles and successes of early non-native settlers [in New Hampshire]. . . . Many reproductions of period illustrations (both color and sepia) and some photos of archival documents and maps enhance the text." Horn Book Guide

Includes bibliographical references

Ciarleglio, Lauren

New Hampshire; past and present. Rosen Central 2011 48p il map (The United States: past and present) lib bdg $26.50; pa $11.75

Grades: 3 4 5 6   **974.2**

1. New Hampshire

ISBN 978-1-4358-9489-1 lib bdg; 1-4358-9489-8 lib bdg; 978-1-4358-9516-4 pa; 1-4358-9516-9 pa

LC 2009053334

Presents the history, geography, government, economy, and people of New Hampshire, as well as general facts about the state.

Includes bibliographical references

Kent, Deborah

New Hampshire. Children's Press 2010 144p il map (America the beautiful, third series) lib bdg $39

Grades: 4 5 6 7 **974.2**

1. New Hampshire

ISBN 978-0-531-18501-8; 0-531-18501-X

LC 2008048940

Takes readers on a tour of New Hampshire, describing the state's history, culture, land, economy, government, and sights, and including unique facts, color maps and photos, the state song, suggested activities, lists of famous people, cultural institutions, and annual events, and other resources.

Includes glossary and bibliographical references

Otfinoski, Steven

New Hampshire; [by] Steve Otfinoski. 2nd ed.; Marshall Cavendish Benchmark 2008 144p il map (Celebrate the states) lib bdg $39.93

Grades: 4 5 6 7 **974.2**

1. New Hampshire

ISBN 978-0-7614-2718-6; 0-7614-2718-X

LC 2007-9944

First published 1999

"Provides comprehensive information on the geography, history, wildlife, governmental structure, economy, cultural diversity, peoples, religion, and landmarks of New Hampshire." Publisher's note

Includes bibliographical references

974.3 Vermont

Heinrichs, Ann

Vermont. Children's Press 2010 144p il map (America the beautiful, third series) lib bdg $39

Grades: 4 5 6 7 **974.3**

1. Vermont

ISBN 978-0-531-18506-3; 0-531-18506-0

LC 2008007241

Presents an introduction to the geography, natural resources, history, economy, important sites, daily life, and people of Vermont.

Includes glossary and bibliographical references

Sommers, Michael

Vermont; past and present. Rosen Central 2011 48p il map (The United States: past and present) lib bdg $26.50; pa $11.75

Grades: 3 4 5 6 **974.3**

1. Vermont

ISBN 978-1-4358-9498-3 lib bdg; 1-4358-9498-7 lib bdg; 978-1-4358-9525-6 pa; 1-4358-9525-8 pa

LC 2009053185

Presents the history, geography, government, economy, and people of Vermont, as well as general facts about the state.

Includes bibliographical references

974.4 Massachusetts

Bjorklund, Ruth

Massachusetts; [by] Ruth Bjorklund, Stephanie Fitzgerald. 2nd ed.; Marshall Cavendish Benchmark 2010 90p il map (It's my state!) lib bdg $31.36

Grades: 3 4 5 **974.4**

1. Massachusetts

ISBN 978-1-6087-0053-0; 1-6087-0053-4

LC 2010003927

First published 2003

Surveys the history, geography, government, and economy of the state of Massachusetts as well as the diverse ways of life of its people

Freedman, Jeri

Massachusetts; past and present. Rosen Central 2010 48p il map (The United States: past and present) lib bdg $26.50; pa $11.50

Grades: 3 4 5 6 **974.4**

1. Massachusetts

ISBN 978-1-4358-5294-5 lib bdg; 1-4358-5294-X lib bdg; 978-1-4358-5586-1 pa; 1-4358-5586-8 pa

LC 2008-54229

Presents the history, geography, government, economy, and people of Massachusetts, as well as general facts about the state.

Includes glossary and bibliographical references

Fritz, Jean

★ Who's that stepping on Plymouth Rock? illustrated by J. B. Handelsman. Coward, McCann & Geoghegan 1975 30p il hardcover o.p. pa $6.99

Grades: 2 3 4 **974.4**

1. Plymouth Rock

ISBN 0-698-20325-9; 0-698-11681-X pa

"Both a delightful story and a perceptive commentary on how the mythmaking process works in American history." N Y Times Book Rev

Greenwood, Mark

The Mayflower; by Mark Greenwood; illustrated by Frane Lessac. Holiday House 2014 38 p. color illustrations (hardcover) $16.95

Grades: PreK K 1 2 3 **974.4**

1. Pilgrims (New England colonists) 2. Massachusetts -- History -- 1600-1775, Colonial period 3. Mayflower (Ship) 4. Mayflower Compact (1620 5. Massachusetts -- History -- New Plymouth, 1620-1691

ISBN 0823429431; 9780823429431

LC 2013011144

This picture book, by Mark Greenwood and illustrated by Frane Lessac, "narrates the historic journey of the one hundred and two passengers aboard the Mayflower and their settlement at Plymouth Harbor. The three-thousand-mile trip was crowded and dangerous, with families cramped next to animals and stormy seas along the way. Trouble continued when the passengers settled in Plymouth for a bitter, cold winter. However, their determination was ultimately rewarded." (Publisher's note)

"Clear text describes the famous 1620 journey from England to what is now Massachusetts, as well as the difficulties of establishing a new home in the New World. Gouache paintings in deep hues interpret the oft-told story with a folk-art feel; images capturing the ocean voyage, especially one depicting a small ship in the desolate nighttime sea, are particularly arresting. Timeline. Bib." Horn Book

Krensky, Stephen

What's the big idea? four centuries of innovation in Boston. [by] Stephen Krensky. Charlesbridge 2008 64p il lib bdg $18.95; pa $9.95

Grades: 4 5 6 **974.4**

1. Boston (Mass.) -- History

ISBN 978-1-58089-310-7 lib bdg; 1-58089-310-4 lib bdg; 978-1-58089-311-4 pa; 1-58089-311-2 pa

LC 2006021255

This "title combines a short history of Boston with brief biographies of some of the city's major figures in diverse fields. . . . Each page includes a well-captioned illustration, many in color, and the book is effectively laid out, making for pleasant browsing. . . . Teachers and students . . . will find some well-presented and useful information here." Booklist

Includes bibliographical references

LeVert, Suzanne

Massachusetts; by Suzanne LeVert and Tamra B. Orr. 2nd ed.; Marshall Cavendish Benchmark 2009 144p il map (Celebrate the states) lib bdg $42.79

Grades: 4 5 6 7 **974.4**

1. Massachusetts

ISBN 978-0-7614-3005-6; 0-7614-3005-9

First published 2000

"Provides comprehensive information on the geography, history, wildlife, governmental structure, economy, cultural diversity, peoples, religion, and landmarks of Massachusetts." Publisher's note

Includes glossary and bibliographical references

Sewall, Marcia

★ The **pilgrims** of Plimoth; written and illustrated by Marcia Sewall. Atheneum Pubs. 1986 48p il hardcover o.p. pa $6.99

Grades: 3 4 5 6 **974.4**

1. Pilgrims (New England colonists) 2. Massachusetts -- History -- 1600-1775, Colonial period

ISBN 0-689-31250-4; 0-689-80861-5 pa

LC 86-3362

"Translating narrative and descriptive details into visual images, the illustrations accompany every page of text, occasionally overspreading double pages for panoramic effects. Combining subtle, modulating color with a spiritual as well as an actual luminosity, the paintings—done in gouache—are vibrant with the daily pulse of life among an energetic, enterprising people." Horn Book

Trueit, Trudi Strain

Massachusetts; by Trudi Strain Trueit. Children's Press 2008 144p il map (America the beautiful, third series) lib bdg $38

Grades: 4 5 6 7 **974.4**

1. Massachusetts

ISBN 978-0-531-18561-2; 0-531-18561-3

LC 2006-39235

Describes the history, geography, ecology, people, economy, cities, and sights of the state of Massachusetts.

Includes glossary and bibliographical references

Waters, Kate

Sarah Morton's day; a day in the life of a pilgrim girl. photographs by Russ Kendall. Scholastic 1989 32p il hardcover o.p. pa $5.99

Grades: 2 3 4 **974.4**

1. Pilgrims (New England colonists) 2. Massachusetts -- History -- 1600-1775, Colonial period

ISBN 0-590-42634-6; 0-590-47400-6 pa

LC 88-35581

Text and photographs of Plimouth Plantation follow a pilgrim girl through a typical day as she milks the goats, cooks and serves meals, learns her letters, and adjusts to her new stepfather

Includes glossary

974.5 Rhode Island

Burgan, Michael

Rhode Island. Children's Press 2009 144p il map (America the beautiful, third series) $39

Grades: 4 5 6 7 **974.5**

1. Rhode Island

ISBN 978-0-531-18590-2; 0-531-18590-7

LC 2007037178

Presents an introduction to the geography, natural resources, history, economy, important sites, daily life, and people of Rhode Island.

Includes glossary and bibliographical references

Furgang, Adam

Rhode Island; past and present. Rosen Central 2011 48p il map (The United States: past and present) lib bdg $26.50; pa $11.95

Grades: 3 4 5 6 **974.5**

1. Rhode Island

ISBN 978-1-4358-9494-5 lib bdg; 1-4358-9494-4 lib bdg; 978-1-4358-9521-8 pa; 1-4358-9521-5 pa

LC 2010001451

Presents the history, geography, government, economy, and people of Rhode Island, as well as general facts about the state.

Includes bibliographical references

Klein, Ted

Rhode Island; by Ted Klein. 2nd ed.; Marshall Cavendish Benchmark 2008 144p il map (Celebrate the states) lib bdg $39.93

Grades: 4 5 6 7 **974.5**

1. Rhode Island

ISBN 978-0-7614-2560-1; 0-7614-2560-8

LC 2006-36490

First published 1999

"Provides comprehensive information on the geography, history, wildlife, governmental structure, economy, cultural diversity, peoples, religion, and landmarks of Rhode Island." Publisher's note

Includes bibliographical references

974.6   Connecticut

Burgan, Michael
Connecticut; [by] Michael Burgan, Stephanie Fitzgerald. 2nd ed.; Marshall Cavendish Benchmark 2010 90p il map (It's my state) lib bdg $31.36
Grades: 3 4 5   **974.6**
1. Connecticut
ISBN 978-1-6087-0047-9; 1-6087-0047-X
LC 2010003917
First published 2003
Surveys the history, geography, government, economy, and people of Connecticut.

Connecticut, 1614-1776. National Geographic Society 2007 109p il map (Voices from colonial America) $21.95; lib bdg $32.90
Grades: 5 6 7 8   **974.6**
1. Connecticut -- History -- 1600-1775, Colonial period
ISBN 978-1-4263-0068-4; 1-4263-0068-9; 978-1-4263-0069-1 lib bdg; 1-4263-0069-7 lib bdg
LC 2007-3123
A history of Connecticut from its beginning as an English colony to 1788 when it became the fifth state.
Offers " thorough, well-documented information about the struggles and successes of early colonial settlers and settlements. . . . Many reproductions of period illustrations and some photographs of period documents and maps with relevant captions are included." Horn Book Guide
Includes bibliographical references

Kent, Zachary
Connecticut; by Zachary Kent. Children's Press 2008 144p il map (America the beautiful, third series) lib bdg $38
Grades: 4 5 6 7   **974.6**
1. Connecticut
ISBN 978-0-531-18571-1; 0-531-18571-0
LC 2007-2328
Describes the history, geography, ecology, people, economy, cities, and sights of the state of Connecticut.
Includes glossary and bibliographical references

La Bella, Laura
Connecticut; past and present. Rosen Central 2011 48p il map (The United States: past and present) lib bdg $26.50; pa $11.75
Grades: 3 4 5 6   **974.6**
1. Connecticut
ISBN 978-1-4358-9478-5 lib bdg; 1-4358-9478-2 lib bdg; 978-1-4358-9505-8 pa; 1-4358-9505-3 pa
LC 2010000401
Presents the history, geography, government, economy, and people of Connecticut, as well as general facts about the state.
Includes glossary and bibliographical references

974.7   New York

Bial, Raymond
★ Tenement; immigrant life on the Lower East Side. Houghton Mifflin 2002 48p il $16

Grades: 4 5 6 7   **974.7**
1. Poor 2. Immigrants -- United States 3. Lower East Side (New York, N.Y.)
ISBN 0-618-13849-8
LC 2002-00407
Presents a view of New York City's tenements during the peak years of foreign immigration, discussing living conditions, laws pertaining to tenements, and the occupations of their residents
"The writing is particularly clear and sharp. Calling upon and quoting the writing of reformer Jacob Riis (and featuring his compelling photographs), Bial explains simply, yet engagingly, what tenement life was like. . . . Along with Riis' photographs, Bial provides some of his own, taken at the Lower East Side Tenement Museum in New York City." Booklist
Includes bibliographical references

Burgan, Michael
New York, 1609-1776; [by] Michael Burgan; with Timothy J. Shannon, consultant. National Geographic Society 2006 109p il map (Voices from colonial America) $21.95; lib bdg $32.90
Grades: 5 6 7 8   **974.7**
1. New York (State) -- History
ISBN 978-0-7922-6390-6; 0-7922-6390-1; 978-0-7922-6860-4 lib bdg; 0-7922-6860-1 lib bdg
LC 2005-22033
Presents a brief history of colonial New York, from 1609 to 1776, and contains illustrations, historical maps, and first-person accounts from explorers, Native Americans, and colonists on early settlements.
Includes bibliographical references

Elish, Dan
New York; [by] Dan Elish and Stephanie Fitzgerald. 2nd ed.; Marshall Cavendish Benchmark 2010 90p il map (It's my state!) lib bdg $31.36
Grades: 3 4 5   **974.7**
1. New York (State)
ISBN 978-1-6087-0056-1; 1-6087-0056-9
LC 2010003916
First published 2003
Surveys the history, geography, and economy of New York State, as well as the diverse ways of life of its people.

Englar, Mary
Dutch colonies in America. Compass Point Books 2009 48p il map (We the people) lib bdg $26.60
Grades: 4 5 6   **974.7**
1. Dutch Americans 2. New York (State) -- History -- 1600-1775, Colonial period
ISBN 978-0-7565-3837-8
LC 2008007211
This is a history of Dutch exploration and colonization in North America.
This provides "solid background matter and [introduces] key people and vocabulary." SLJ
Includes glossary and bibliographical references

Glaser, Linda
★ Emma's poem; the voice of the Statue of Liberty. with paintings by Claire A. Nivola. Houghton Mifflin Books for Children 2010 un il $17

Grades: K 1 2 3 **974.7**

1. Poets 2. Authors 3. Novelists 4. Philanthropists 5. Social reformers 6. Immigrants -- United States 7. Statue of Liberty (New York, N.Y.) 8. Biography, Individual 9. United States -- Emigration and immigration -- History

ISBN 0-547-17184-6; 978-0-547-17184-5

LC 2009026924

This is an account of how the poet and social reformer Emma Lazarus came to write the sonnet, 'The New Colossus,' now on the pedestal of The Statue of Liberty. The text of the poem is appended. "Primary." (Horn Book)

"The art and words are moving in this picture book, which pairs free verse with detailed, full-page paintings in watercolor, ink, and gouache to tell the history behind Lazarus' famous inscription on the Statue of Liberty." Booklist

Huey, Lois Miner

American archaeology uncovers the Dutch colonies. Marshall Cavendish Benchmark 2009 64p il map (American archaeology) lib bdg $21.95

Grades: 4 5 6 7 **974.7**

1. Dutch Americans 2. America -- Antiquities 3. Netherlands -- Colonies -- America 4. Excavations (Archeology) -- United States

ISBN 978-0-7614-4263-9 lib bdg; 0-7614-4263-4 lib bdg

LC 2008050187

This describes how archeologists have learned about the history of Dutch settlers in America

"The text is quite chatty in this attractive title. . . . An inviting design with clear type includes several paintings of the period by a modern artist as well as maps and photos of excavation sites." Booklist

Includes glossary and bibliographical references

Maestro, Betsy

The **story** of the Statue of Liberty; [by] Betsy & Giulio Maestro. Lothrop, Lee & Shepard Bks. 1986 39p il hardcover o.p. pa $5.95

Grades: K 1 2 3 **974.7**

1. Artists 2. Sculptors 3. Statue of Liberty (New York, N.Y.)

ISBN 0-688-08746-9 pa

LC 85-11324

"Although Maestro simplifies the story—including only the most important people's names, for example—she still presents an accurate account of what happened. The exceptional drawings are visually delightful—primarily in the blue-green range, although they are in full color—and cover most of every page. Human figures—workers, tourists—are included in many drawings, indicating the statue's tremendous scale. Further, the drawings involve viewers through the use of unusual perspectives and angles and by placing the statue in scenes of city life." SLJ

Includes bibliographical references

Mann, Elizabeth

Statue of Liberty; a tale of two countries. with illustrations by Alan Witschonke. Mikaya Press 2011 47p il map (Wonders of the world) $22.95

Grades: 4 5 6 7 **974.7**

1. Artists 2. Authors 3. Lawyers 4. Sculptors 5. National monuments 6. Children's authors 7. Fairy tale

writers 8. Members of Parliament 9. Statue of Liberty (New York, N.Y.)

ISBN 978-1-931414-43-2; 1-931414-43-2

"The story of how Lady Liberty was conceived, constructed and bestowed makes a compelling tale. Pointing to the disparate long-term outcomes of the American and French revolutions to explain why the U.S. system of government became so admired in France, Mann takes the statue from Edouard Laboulaye's pie-in-the-sky proposal at a dinner party in 1865 to the massive opening ceremonies in 1886. . . . Witschonke supplements an array of period photos and prints with full-page or larger painted reconstructions of Bartholdi's studio and workshop, of the statue's piecemeal creation and finally of the Lady herself, properly copper colored as she initially was, presiding of New York's crowded harbor. As she still does." Kirkus

Includes bibliographical references

Marrin, Albert, 1936-

★ **Flesh** & blood so cheap; the Triangle fire and its legacy. Alfred A. Knopf 2011 182p il map $19.99; lib bdg $22.99

Grades: 5 6 7 8 **974.7**

1. Fires 2. Italian Americans 3. Jews -- United States 4. Labor -- United States 5. New York (N.Y.) -- History 6. Triangle Shirtwaist Company, Inc. 7. Industrial safety 8. United States -- Immigration and emigration

ISBN 978-0-375-86889-4; 0-375-86889-5; 978-0-375-96889-1 lib bdg; 0-375-96889-X lib bdg

LC 2010-21533

"Published to coincide with the centennial anniversary of the 1911 fire that erupted in the Triangle Shirtwaist Factory, this powerful chronicle examines the circumstances surrounding the disaster, which resulted in the deaths of 146 workers, mostly young Italian and Jewish women. . . . B&W photographs and illustrations reveal immigrant families' impoverished living environments, while testimonials describe the 'humiliating' work rules and unsafe conditions of factories like Triangle. . . . A concluding description of a Bangladeshi garment factory fire in 2010 offers contemporary parallels. Marrin's message that protecting human dignity is our shared responsibility is vitally resonant." Publ Wkly

Includes bibliographical references

McKendry, Joe

One Times Square; a century of change at the crossroads of the world. written & illustrated by Joe McKendry. David R. Godine 2011 64 p. ill. (chiefly col.), col. maps (hardcover: alk. paper) $19.95

Grades: 4 5 6 **974.7**

1. Times Square (New York, N.Y.) -- History 2. New York (N.Y.) -- History

ISBN 156792364X; 9781567923643

LC 2011027379

This children's book by Joe McKendry "takes readers on a journey through 100 years of shifts and changes to . . . Times Square. . . . Beginning in 1904 when the "New York Times" headquarters was built and forever changed the name of this small plot of land, McKendry accompanies the text with a . . . painting of the Square from a specific point of view. . . . as buildings and technology sprout and change." (Kirkus)

Includes bibliographical references and index.

Melmed, Laura Krauss

New York, New York; the Big Apple from A to Z. illustrated by Frané Lessac. HarperCollins Pub. 2005 un il $16.99; lib bdg $17.89; pa $6.99

Grades: K 1 2 3   **974.7**

1. Alphabet 2. New York (N.Y.)

ISBN 0-06-054674-6; 0-06-054876-2 lib bdg; 0-06-054877-0 pa

"From the American Museum of Natural History to the Bronx Zoo, each letter is accompanied by a peppy eight-line poem as well as multiple sidebars, factoids, and tidbits about the sights described. Melmed brilliantly touches on all the major sights of NYC." SLJ

Mills, J. Elizabeth

New York; past and present. Rosen Central 2010 48p il map (The United States: past and present) lib bdg $26.50; pa $11.75

Grades: 3 4 5 6   **974.7**

1. New York (State)

ISBN 978-1-4358-5285-3 lib bdg; 1-4358-5285-0 lib bdg; 978-1-4358-5568-7 pa; 1-4358-5568-X pa

LC 2008054256

Presents the history, geography, government, economy, and people of New York, as well as general facts about the state.

Includes bibliographical references

Murphy, Jim

The **giant** and how he humbugged America; by Jim Murphy. Scholastic Press 2012 112 p. (hardcover: alk. paper) $19.99

Grades: 5 6 7 8   **974.7**

1. Relics 2. Sculpture 3. Impostors and imposture 4. Cardiff giant 5. Cardiff (N.Y.) -- Antiquities 6. New York (State) -- Antiquities 7. Forgery of antiquities -- New York (State) -- Cardiff

ISBN 0439691842; 9780439691840

LC 2011036798

In this book, "[Jim] Murphy traces the checkered career of the 'Cardiff Giant,' a 10-foot-long stone figure unearthed in 1869 in an upstate New York farmyard. The giant was a national sensation until its unmasking as a hoax a few months later. Almost from the outset, both educated and popular opinion was divided over whether the figure was a fossilized human or a carving, an ancient relic or a modern 'humbug.' Murphy shows how the controversy itself fueled the giant's notoriety." (Booklist)

Includes bibliographical references and index

Platt, Richard

New York City; an illustrated history of the Big Apple. illustrated by Manuela Cappon. Kingfisher 2010 45p il map (Through time) $16.99

Grades: 4 5 6 7   **974.7**

1. New York (N.Y.) -- History

ISBN 978-0-7534-6416-8; 0-7534-6416-0

This is a history of New York City from its Native American origins to the present.

"In this magnificently illustrated work, historical happenings and intriguing offshoots are showcased like stars on Broadway. . . . A wealth of information in an engaging format." Booklist

Rappaport, Doreen

★ **Lady** Liberty; a biography. illustrated by Matt Tavares. Candlewick Press 2008 un il $17.99

Grades: 2 3 4 5   **974.7**

1. Statue of Liberty (New York, N.Y.)

ISBN 978-0-7636-2530-6; 0-7636-2530-2

LC 2007-40723

This presents the story of the Statue of Liberty including "its conception and construction in France, the efforts to raise funds on both sides of the Atlantic, preparations for her arrival in New York, and the celebration culminating in her unveiling in 1886. Rappaport tells the story in a series of free-verse poems representing the reflections of individuals. . . . The first-person narratives effectively convey the personal significance the statue has had for many people. Large in scale and monumental in effect, the watercolor, ink, and pencil illustrations . . . offer often beautiful views of her many-faceted story." Booklist

Includes bibliographical references

Schomp, Virginia

New York; [by] Virginia Schomp. 2nd ed.; Benchmark Books 2006 144p il map (Celebrate the states) lib bdg $39.93

Grades: 4 5 6 7   **974.7**

1. New York (State)

ISBN 978-0-7614-1738-5; 0-7614-1738-9

LC 2004-853

First published 1997

This book about New York covers "standard facts: geography, history, government, economy, landmarks, and regions. . . . [It is] attractively illustrated with clear maps, charts, and pie graphs. Photos and reproductions of original documents add to overall effectiveness. . . . Excellent additions for reports or general interest." SLJ

Includes bibliographical references

Shea, Pegi Deitz

★ **Liberty** rising; the story of the Statue of Liberty. illustrated by Wade Zahares. Henry Holt 2005 un il $17.95

Grades: 2 3 4   **974.7**

1. Artists 2. Sculptors 3. Statue of Liberty (New York, N.Y.)

ISBN 0-8050-7220-9

LC 2004-24279

In this account of the building of the Statue of Liberty "Shea introduces the size and scale of creating such a large object. . . . Each step in the process . . . is told in simple text. . . . The book is easy to read, with three-quarter spreads of illustration and single columns of text. The stylized graphic art is fairly realistic with bold colors and unusual angles to create a sense of excitement." SLJ

Includes bibliographical references

Somervill, Barbara A.

New York; by Barbara A. Somervill. Children's Press 2008 144p il map (America the beautiful, third series) lib bdg $38

Grades: 4 5 6 7   **974.7**

1. New York (State)

ISBN 978-0-531-18565-0; 0-531-18565-6

LC 2006101742

Describes the history, geography, ecology, famous people, economy, cities, and sights of the state of New York.

Includes glossary and bibliographical references

Talbott, Hudson

★ **River** of dreams; the story of the Hudson River. G. P. Putnam's Sons 2009 un il map $17.99

Grades: 4 5 6 7 **974.7**

1. Hudson River (N.Y. and N.J.)

ISBN 978-0-399-24521-3; 0-399-24521-9

Talbott offers a "compelling blend of political and natural history in this beautifully illustrated celebration of the Hudson River. Combining delicate watercolor-and-pencil illustrations with accessible text, the spreads move briskly through the Hudson's River's history." Booklist

Vila, Laura

★ **Building** Manhattan. Viking 2008 un il $16.99

Grades: K 1 2 3 **974.7**

1. Manhattan (New York, N.Y.) 2. New York (N.Y.) -- History

ISBN 978-0-670-06284-3; 0-670-06284-7

LC 2007-38119

"Tracing the growth of Manhattan from a time 'before maps or words were used' to the present day, . . . author/artist Vila employs many lenses—geography, sociology, politics, ethnography. Likewise, her radiantly dramatic mural-like paintings present a wide range of visual styles and approaches. . . . While her paintings are lavish, it takes her only one pithy sentence on each spread to convey both a specific moment and a sense of history and human ambitions." Publ Wkly

974.8 Pennsylvania

Hart, Joyce

Pennsylvania; [by] Joyce Hart and Richard Hantula. 2nd ed.; Marshall Cavendish Benchmark 2010 90p il map (It's my state!) lib bdg $31.36

Grades: 3 4 5 **974.8**

1. Pennsylvania

ISBN 978-1-6087-0058-5; 1-6087-0058-5

LC 2010003931

First published 2004

Surveys the history, geography, government, and economy of Pennsylvania, as well as the diverse ways of life of its people

Hasan, Heather

Pennsylvania; past and present. Rosen Central 2010 48p il map (The United States: past and present) lib bdg $26.50; pa $11.50

Grades: 3 4 5 6 **974.8**

1. Pennsylvania

ISBN 978-1-4358-5291-4 lib bdg; 1-4358-5291-5 lib bdg; 978-1-4358-5580-9 pa; 1-4358-5580-9 pa

LC 2008-54214

Presents the history, geography, government, economy, and people of Pennsylvania, as well as general facts about the state.

Includes glossary and bibliographical references

Magaziner, Henry J.

★ **Our** Liberty Bell; by Henry Jonas Magaziner; illustrated by John O'Brien. Holiday House 2007 32p il $15.95; pa $5.95

Grades: 2 3 4 **974.8**

1. Liberty Bell

ISBN 978-0-8234-1892-3; 0-8234-1892-8; 978-0-8234-2081-0 pa; 0-8234-2081-7 pa

LC 2004054196

"Written with clarity and verve. . . . O'Brien's imaginative and sometimes witty ink drawings illustrate with finesse." Booklist

Includes glossary and bibliographical references

Peters, Stephen

Pennsylvania; by Stephen Peters and Joyce Hart. 2nd ed.; Marshall Cavendish Benchmark 2009 144p il map (Celebrate the states) lib bdg $42.79

Grades: 4 5 6 7 **974.8**

1. Pennsylvania

ISBN 978-0-7614-3403-0; 0-7614-3403-8

LC 2008-8032

First published 2000

"Provides comprehensive information on the geography, history, wildlife, governmental structure, economy, cultural diversity, peoples, religion, and landmarks of Pennsylvania." Publisher's note

Includes bibliographical references

Somervill, Barbara A.

Pennsylvania. Children's Press 2009 144p il map (America the beautiful, third series) lib bdg $39

Grades: 4 5 6 7 **974.8**

1. Pennsylvania

ISBN 978-0-531-18588-9; 0-531-18588-5

LC 2007031121

Presents an introduction to the geography, natural resources, history, economy, important sites, daily life, and people of Pennsylvania.

Includes glossary and bibliographical references

Staton, Hilarie

Independence Hall. Chelsea Clubhouse 2010 48p il (Symbols of American freedom) $30

Grades: 3 4 5 **974.8**

1. Philadelphia (Pa.) 2. Independence Hall (Philadelphia, Pa.) 3. United States -- Politics and government -- 1783-1809 4. United States -- Politics and government -- 1775-1783, Revolution

ISBN 978-1-60413-521-3; 1-60413-521-2

LC 2009-12824

This book about Independence Hall in Phildelphia "provides nearly as much information as a guided tour by a park ranger. [It begins] with the story of how the place came to be, and where it fits into U.S. history. Information boxes offer additional background and some surprising facts. . . . The final chapter shows the landmark today and includes maps and photographs of the visitors' center and some of the things individuals might see or do while visiting the site. Much information is packed into [this] slim [book]. Excellent . . . for state reports or to complement U.S. history units." SLJ

Includes glossary

974.9   New Jersey

Doak, Robin S.

New Jersey 1609-1776; y. [by] Robin Doak with Brendan McConville. National Geographic 2005 109p il map (Voices from colonial America) $21.95; lib bdg $32.90

Grades: 5 6 7 8   **974.9**

1. New Jersey -- History

ISBN 978-0-7922-6385-2; 0-7922-6385-5; 978-0-7922-6680-8 lib bdg; 0-7922-6680-3 lib bdg

LC 2004-26242

"This book gives detailed descriptions of family life and working in a Colonial village and the fight for independence. It also includes information about the Native people, early settlers, and first developments. . . . Paintings, maps, woodcuts, portraits, and reproductions accompany the well-written text. . . . An excellent resource." SLJ

Includes bibliographical references

Kent, Deborah

New Jersey; by Deborah Kent. Children's Press 2008 144p il map (America the beautiful, third series) lib bdg $38

Grades: 4 5 6 7   **974.9**

1. New Jersey

ISBN 978-0-531-18564-3; 0-531-18564-8

LC 2006100058

Describes the history, geography, ecology, people, economy, cities, and sights of the state of New Jersey.

Includes glossary and bibliographical references

King, David C.

New Jersey; [by] David C. King and William A. McGeveran, Jr. 2nd ed.; Marshall Cavendish Benchmark 2010 90p il map (It's my state!) lib bdg $31.36

Grades: 3 4 5   **974.9**

1. New Jersey

ISBN 978-1-6087-0055-4; 1-6087-0055-0

LC 2010003910

First published 2004

Surveys the history, geography, government, and economy of New Jersey as well as the diverse ways of life of its people

Mattern, Joanne

New Jersey; past and present. Rosen Central 2010 48p il map (The United States: past and present) lib bdg $26.50; pa $11.75

Grades: 3 4 5 6   **974.9**

1. New Jersey

ISBN 978-1-4358-3525-2 lib bdg; 1-4358-3525-5 lib bdg; 978-1-4358-8500-4 pa; 1-4358-8500-7 pa

LC 2009026985

Presents the history, geography, government, economy, and people of New Jersey, as well as general facts about the state.

Includes bibliographical references

Moragne, Wendy

New Jersey; by Wendy Moragne and Tamra B. Orr. 2nd ed.; Marshall Cavendish Benchmark 2009 144p il map (Celebrate the states) lib bdg $39.93

Grades: 4 5 6 7   **974.9**

1. New Jersey

ISBN 978-0-7614-3006-3; 0-7614-3006-7

LC 2007-38642

First published 2000

"Provides comprehensive information on the geography, history, wildlife, governmental structure, economy, cultural diversity, peoples, religion, and landmarks of New Jersey." Publisher's note

Includes bibliographical references

975.1   Delaware

King, David C.

Delaware; [by] David C. King, Brian Fitzgerald. 2nd ed.; Marshall Cavendish Benchmark 2010 90p il map (It's my state) lib bdg $31.36

Grades: 3 4 5   **975.1**

1. Delaware

ISBN 978-1-6087-0048-6; 1-6087-0048-8

LC 2010003920

Surveys the history, geography, government, and economy of Delaware as well as the diverse ways of life of its people.

Price, Karen

Delaware, 1638-1776; [by] Karen Hossell, with Karin Wulf, consultant. National Geographic Society 2006 109p il map (Voices from colonial America) $21.95; lib bdg $32.90

Grades: 5 6 7 8   **975.1**

1. Delaware -- History

ISBN 978-0-7922-6408-8; 0-7922-6408-8; 978-0-7922-6864-2 lib bdg; 0-7922-6864-4 lib bdg

LC 2006-13444

"The text is . . . written in full paragraphs, making up chronological chapters. These are divided into topical sections, which are clearly marked by large headings. This lovely, calm layout is liberally sprinkled with primary source illustrations, including reproductions of period maps, pamphlets, paintings, and drawings. . . . An essential purchase for schools with a colonies research project . . . and for the public libraries that support their communities." Voice Youth Advocates

Includes bibliographical references

Schuman, Michael

Delaware; by Michael Schuman and Marlee Richards. 2nd ed.; Marshall Cavendish Benchmark 2009 144p il map (Celebrate the states) lib bdg $42.79

Grades: 4 5 6 7   **975.1**

1. Delaware

ISBN 978-0-7614-3399-6; 0-7614-3399-6

LC 2008-5369

First published 2000

"Provides comprehensive information on the geography, history, wildlife, governmental structure, economy, cultural diversity, peoples, religion, and landmarks of Delaware." Publisher's note

Includes bibliographical references

Wolny, Philip
  Delaware; past and present. Rosen Central 2010 48p il map (The United States: past and present) lib bdg $26.50; pa $11.75
  Grades: 3 4 5 6   **975.1**
    1. Delaware
    ISBN 978-1-4358-3526-9 lib bdg; 1-4358-3526-3 lib bdg; 978-1-4358-8502-8 pa; 1-4358-8502-3 pa
                            LC 2009024554
  Presents the history, geography, government, economy, and people of Delaware, as well as general facts about the state.
  Includes glossary and bibliographical references

975.2   Maryland

Blashfield, Jean F.
  Maryland; by Jean F. Blashfield. Children's Press 2008 144p il map (America the beautiful, third series) lib bdg $38
  Grades: 5 6 7 8   **975.2**
    1. Maryland
    ISBN 978-0-531-18576-6; 0-531-18576-1
                            LC 2007-12699
  Describes the history, geography, ecology, people, economy, cities, and sights of the state of Maryland.
  Includes glossary and bibliographical references

Doak, Robin S.
  Maryland, 1634-1776. National Geographic 2007 105p il map (Voices from colonial America) $21.95; lib bdg $32.90
  Grades: 5 6 7 8   **975.2**
    1. Maryland -- History
    ISBN 978-1-4263-0143-8; 1-4263-0143-x; 978-1-4263-0144-5 lib bdg; 1-4263-0144-8 lib bdg
                            LC 2007-27886
  Offers "thorough, well-documented information about the struggles and successes of early colonial settlers and settlements. . . . Many reproductions of period illustrations and some photographs of period documents and maps with relevant captions are included." Horn Book Guide
  Includes bibliographical references

Friddell, Claudia
  ★ Goliath; hero of the great Baltimore fire. illustrated by Troy Howell. Sleeping Bear Press 2010 un il (True stories) $17.95
  Grades: K 1 2 3 4 5   **975.2**
    1. Fire 2. Horses 3. Fire fighting 4. Working animals 5. Baltimore (Md.) -- History
    ISBN 978-1-58536-455-8; 1-58536-455-X
                            LC 2009036941
  "The Great Baltimore Fire of 1904 was one of the most destructive in U.S. history. Friddell brings the event to life through the true story of a huge horse from Engine Company 15. Goliath bore the full brunt of an explosion and then heroically pulled an entire fire rig to safety by himself. The text builds suspense. . . . Howell's expressive, sepia-toned illustrations interplay with the text to keep readers in the

moment. Exciting, historically accurate, and visually appealing." SLJ
  Includes glossary and bibliographical references

Mattern, Joanne
  Maryland; past and present. Rosen Central 2010 48p il map (The United States: past and present) lib bdg $26.50; pa $11.75
  Grades: 3 4 5 6   **975.2**
    1. Maryland
    ISBN 978-1-4358-3519-1 lib bdg; 1-4358-3519-0 lib bdg; 978-1-4358-8488-5 pa; 1-4358-8488-4 pa
                            LC 2009025517
  Presents the history, geography, government, economy, and people of Maryland, as well as general facts about the state.
  Includes glossary and bibliographical references

Otfinoski, Steven
  Maryland; [by] Steven Otfinoski, Andy Steinitz. 2nd ed.; Marshall Cavendish Benchmark 2010 90p il map (It's my state) lib bdg $31.36
  Grades: 3 4 5   **975.2**
    1. Maryland
    ISBN 978-1-6087-0052-3; 1-6087-0052-6
                            LC 2010003929
  First published 2003
  Surveys the history, geography, government, and economy of Maryland as well as the diverse ways of life of its people

Pietrzyk, Leslie
  Maryland; by Leslie Rauth and Martha Kneib. 2nd ed.; Marshall Cavendish Benchmark 2008 144p il map (Celebrate the states) lib bdg $39.93
  Grades: 4 5 6 7   **975.2**
    1. Maryland
    ISBN 978-0-7614-3004-9; 0-7614-3004-0
                            LC 2007-29497
  First published 2000
  "Provides comprehensive information on the geography, history, wildlife, governmental structure, economy, cultural diversity, peoples, religion, and landmarks of Maryland." Publisher's note
  Includes bibliographical references

975.3   District of Columbia (Washington)

Aretha, David
  The story of the civil rights march on Washington for jobs and freedom in photographs; David Aretha. Enslow Publishers, Inc. 2014 48 p. library $25.27
  Grades: 5 6 7 8   **975.3**
    1. March on Washington for Jobs and Freedom (1963: Washington, D.C.) 2. African Americans -- Civil rights 3. Civil rights demonstrations -- Washington (D.C.)
    ISBN 9780766042384
                            LC 2013004860
  "This series explores key events of the Civil Rights Movement through historical primary source pictures and documents. The books dramatically carry the reader from early 1963 Birmingham to sit-ins, marches, and protests.

Through dramatic photographs along with descriptive captions, the reader feels the raw emotions of the times." Lib Med Con

Elish, Dan

Washington, D.C. by Dan Elish. 2nd ed.; Marshall Cavendish Benchmark 2007 144p il map (Celebrate the states) lib bdg $39.93

Grades: 4 5 6 7   **975.3**

1. Washington (D.C.)

ISBN 978-0-7614-2352-2; 0-7614-2352-4

       LC 2006-13838

First published 1998

"Provides comprehensive information on the geography, history, wildlife, governmental structure, economy, cultural diversity, peoples, religion, and landmarks of Washington, D.C." Publisher's note

Includes bibliographical references

House, Katherine L.

The **White** House for kids; a history of a home, office, and national symbol: with 21 activities. Katherine L. House. Chicago Review Press 2014 144 p. illustrations, plans (For kids series) (pbk.) $16.95

Grades: 4 5 6 7   **975.3**

1. Presidents -- United States   2. White House (Washington, D.C.)   3. Washington (D.C.) -- Buildings, structures, etc.

ISBN 1613744617; 9781613744611

       LC 2013038108

This children's book, by Katherine L. House, offers an "educates young readers on the White House. Blending facts from numerous primary sources with engaging anecdotes . . . , this book provides the complete story of the presidents' home. Details on the many changes, updates, renovations, and redecorations that have occurred over the years are featured as well as a look at the daily lives of the White House's inhabitants." (Publisher's note)

"Chapter organization enhances interest by covering seven subjects and including examples from multiple historical periods. From the purposes and architecture of the building to the nature of multiple jobs performed, this book shows the varied functions of the White House." VOYA

Includes bibliographical references and index

Kenney, Karen Latchana

The **White** House; illustrated by Judith A. Hunt. Magic Wagon 2011 32p il (Our nation's pride) lib bdg $28.50

Grades: 2 3 4   **975.3**

1. White House (Washington, D.C.)

ISBN 978-1-61641-154-1; 1-61641-154-6

       LC 2010014010

In this title about the White House "the author describes how the land was chosen, how the White House was built, the fact in burned down in 1814 and was rebuilt in 1817, and that it takes 570 buckets of white paint to cover the outside. . . . The full-color artwork not only explains the text but also gives the most photographic renderings of the [topic]." SLJ

Kent, Deborah

Washington, D.C. Children's Press 2010 144p il map (America the beautiful, third series) lib bdg $39

Grades: 4 5 6 7   **975.3**

1. Washington (D.C.)

ISBN 978-0-531-18593-3; 0-531-18593-1

       LC 2008019546

Discusses the geography, history, people, government, economy, and recreation of Washington, D.C.

Includes glossary and bibliographical references

★ **Our** White House; looking in, looking out. created by The National Children's Book and Literacy Alliance; introduction by David McCullough. Candlewick Press 2008 241p il $29.99

Grades: 5 6 7 8   **975.3**

1. White House (Washington, D.C.)   2. Washington (D.C.)   3. Short stories -- Collections   4. United States -- Politics and government

ISBN 0-7636-2067-X; 978-0-7636-2067-7

This is a collection of essays, personal accounts, historical fiction, and poetry devoted to the history of the White House. Index. "Age ten and up." (N Y Times Book Rev)

"The White House is the focus of this handsome, large-format compendium of writings, both factual and fictional, and illustrations. . . . Poems and essays, stories and memoirs—all combine to create a mosaic of impressions of the house's residents and visitors and of the important events that occurred there. . . . The often-spectacular, beautifully reproduced on glossy paper, is particularly striking." Booklist

Rinaldo, Denise

White House Q & A. Smithsonian/Collins 2008 47p il (Smithsonian Q & A) lib bdg $16.99; pa $7.99

Grades: 3 4 5   **975.3**

1. Washington (D.C.)   2. Presidents -- United States   3. White House (Washington, D.C.)

ISBN 978-0-06-089966-0 lib bdg; 0-06-089966-2 lib bdg; 978-0-06-089965-3 pa; 0-06-089965-4 pa

       LC 2006102994

"The history and functions of the presidential residence are unveiled in the typical series format. The questions are organized so that the story of the White House unfolds logically—first with a definition of what it is, how it came to be, some of its history, how to visit, special rooms, and, of course, a look at how the first families live. Anecdotes are plentiful and child-centered. . . . The elegant page layout includes full-color, full-bleed illustrations from Smithsonian archives and some presidential libraries." SLJ

Includes glossary and bibliographical references

Slade, Suzanne

The **house** that George built; Suzanne Slade; illustrated by Rebecca Bond. Charlesbridge 2012 48 p. col. ill. (reinforced for library use) $16.95

Grades: 1 2 3   **975.3**

1. White House (Washington, D.C.)   2. Presidents -- United States -- Homes   3. Presidents -- United States -- History   5. Washington (D.C.) -- Buildings, structures, etc.

ISBN 1580892620; 9781580892629

       LC 2011025781

This book by Suzanne Slade "describes how George Washington chose the design for what would become the White House and supervised its construction. Rhyming verses, interspersed with background paragraphs to fill out the narrative, describe how Washington found the site and held a contest to get design submissions. African American and white surveyors and laborers are included in the pictures." (School Library Journal)

This is a "look at the classic era of American popular song from the 'piano era' of Irving Berlin and George Gershwin to the post-World War II era." Libr J

Sonneborn, Liz

District of Columbia; past and present. Rosen Central 2011 48p il map (The United States: past and present) lib bdg $26.50; pa $11.75

Grades: 3 4 5 6 **975.3**

1. Washington (D.C.)

ISBN 978-1-4358-9501-0 lib bdg; 1-4358-9501-0 lib bdg; 978-1-4358-9528-7 pa; 1-4358-9528-2 pa

LC 2009053986

This describes life in the U.S. capitol city, Washington D.C.

Includes glossary and bibliographical references

975.4   West Virginia

Byers, Ann

West Virginia; past and present. Rosen Central 2011 48p il map (The United States: past and present) lib bdg $26.50; pa $11.75

Grades: 3 4 5 6 **975.4**

1. West Virginia

ISBN 978-1-4358-9499-0 lib bdg; 1-4358-9499-5 lib bdg; 978-1-4358-9526-3 pa; 1-4358-9526-6 pa

LC 2010002514

Presents the history, geography, government, economy, and people of West Virginia, as well as general facts about the state.

Includes bibliographical references

Hoffman, Nancy

West Virginia; [by] Nancy Hoffman and Joyce Hart. 2nd ed.; Marshall Cavendish Benchmark 2007 144p il map (Celebrate the states) lib bdg $39.93

Grades: 4 5 6 7 **975.4**

1. West Virginia

ISBN 978-0-7614-2562-5; 0-7614-2562-4

LC 2006-29393

First published 1999

Relates the history and describes the geographic features, places of interest, government, industry, environmental concerns, and life of the people of West Virginia.

Includes bibliographical references

975.5   Virginia

Chorao, Kay

D is for drums; a Colonial Williamsburg ABC. [by] Kay Chorao. Harry N. Abrams 2004 un il $16.95

Grades: K 1 2 3 **975.5**

1. Alphabet 2. Colonial Williamsburg (Williamsburg, Va.)

ISBN 0-8109-4927-X

LC 2003-25793

"Chorao has created a large, visually charming, and fact-rich look at Colonial Williamsburg. Endpaper maps of the city's streets show everything from a shoemaker's shop to the Governor's Palace. Each page in between displays a huge capital letter decorated with drawings that showcase an alliterative list of words. . . . Chorao selected items to foster chuckles and amazement. Her pen-and-ink and watercolor drawings of children and animals add energy to the stunning layouts." SLJ

Demarest, Chris L.

Arlington; the story of our nation's cemetery. written and illustrated by Chris Demarest. Roaring Brook Press/ Flash Point 2010 un il $17.99

Grades: 3 4 5 6 **975.5**

1. Arlington National Cemetery (Va.)

ISBN 978-1-59643-517-9; 1-59643-517-8

"This handsome volume presents the history of Arlington National Cemetery. [It tells and illustrates] the story with quiet dignity. . . . Demarest writes clearly, organizes the information well, and illustrates the story in nicely composed, sometimes luminous paintings." Booklist

Kent, Deborah

Virginia. Children's Press 2008 144p il map (America the beautiful, third series) lib bdg $39

Grades: 4 5 6 7 **975.5**

1. Virginia

ISBN 978-0-531-18581-0; 0-531-18581-8

LC 2007028463

Presents an introduction to the geography, natural resources, history, economy, important sites, daily life, and people of Virginia.

Includes glossary and bibliographical references

King, David C.

Virginia; [by] David C. King and Stephanie Fitzgerald. 2nd ed.; Marshall Cavendish Benchmark 2010 90p il map (It's my state!) lib bdg $31.36

Grades: 3 4 5 **975.5**

1. Virginia

ISBN 978-1-6087-0060-8; 1-6087-0060-7

LC 2010003933

First published 2005

Surveys the history, geography, economy, and people of Virginia

Lange, Karen E.

★ **1607**; a new look at Jamestown. photography by Ira Block. National Geographic 2007 48p il $17.95; lib bdg $27.90

Grades: 3 4 5 6 **975.5**

1. Virginia -- History 2. Jamestown (Va.) -- History 3. United States -- History -- 1600-1775, Colonial period

ISBN 1-4263-0012-3; 1-4263-0013-1 lib bdg

LC 2006-05824

"In 1994, scientists unearthed important new evidence about the original Jamestown fort. The work . . . has changed many established ideas about the early settlers. 1607 incorporates these findings and offers a fascinating look at archaeology in action. Color photographs of costumed interpreters and recreated buildings from the Jamestown Settlement living-history museum depict both English and Native American ways of life." SLJ

Pobst, Sandy

Virginia, 1607-1776; [by] Sandy Pobst with Kevin D. Roberts, consultant. National Geographic Society 2005 109p il map (Voices from colonial America) $21.95; lib bdg $32.90

Grades: 5 6 7 8   **975.5**

1. Virginia -- History

ISBN 978-0-7922-6388-3; 0-7922-6388-X; 978-0-7922-6771-3 lib bdg; 0-7922-6771-0 lib bdg

LC 2005-8885

"This title discusses the colony's founding, life on the Tidewater plantations, the struggles to survive, and the desire for independence. Full of period maps; portraits; photographs; and first-person accounts from masters and slaves, explorers, Native Americans, servants, and other residents, this is narrative nonfiction at its best. . . . An excellent resource." SLJ

Includes bibliographical references

Porterfield, Jason

Virginia; past and present. Rosen Central 2009 48p il map (The United States: past and present) lib bdg $26.50; pa $11.50

Grades: 3 4 5 6   **975.5**

1. Virginia

ISBN 978-1-4358-5289-1 lib bdg; 1-4358-5289-3 lib bdg; 978-1-4358-5576-2 pa; 1-4358-5576-0 pa

LC 2008-54403

Presents the history, geography, government, economy, and people of Virginia, as well as general facts about the state.

Includes glossary and bibliographical references

975.6   North Carolina

Cannavale, Matthew C.

North Carolina, 1524-1776; by Matthew C. Cannavale; with Patrick Griffith, consultant. National Geographic Society 2007 109p il map (Voices from colonial America) $21.95; lib bdg $32.90

Grades: 5 6 7 8   **975.6**

1. North Carolina -- History

ISBN 978-1-4263-0032-5; 1-4263-0032-8; 978-1-4263-0033-2 lib bdg; 1-4263-0033-6 lib bdg

LC 2006-36004

A history of colonial North Carolina.

Includes bibliographical references

Fritz, Jean

★ The Lost Colony of Roanoke; illustrated by Hudson Talbott. G.P. Putnam's Sons 2004 58p il map $16.99

Grades: 3 4 5 6   **975.6**

1. Roanoke Island (N.C.) -- History

ISBN 0-399-24027-6

LC 2002-152000

Describes the English colony of Roanoke, which was founded in 1585, and discusses the mystery of its disappearance.

"Talbott's softly colored watercolor illustrations . . . are at once detailed and impressionistic. Clever touches of humor abound. . . . Fritz has scored again, making history

breathe while showing both historians and archaeologists at their reconstructive best." SLJ

Gaines, Ann

North Carolina; [by] Ann Graham Gaines and Andy Steinitz. 2nd ed.; Marshall Cavendish Benchmark 2010 90p il map (It's my state!) lib bdg $31.36

Grades: 3 4 5   **975.6**

1. North Carolina

ISBN 978-1-6087-0057-8; 1-6087-0057-7

LC 2010003930

First published 2003

Surveys the history, geography, government, and economy of North Carolina as well as the diverse ways of life of its people

Heinrichs, Ann

North Carolina. Children's Press 2009 144p il map (America the beautiful, third series) lib bdg $39

Grades: 4 5 6 7   **975.6**

1. North Carolina

ISBN 978-0-531-18566-7; 0-531-18566-4

LC 2007039773

Presents an introduction to the geography, natural resources, history, economy, important sites, daily life, and people of North Carolina.

Includes glossary and bibliographical references

Lew, Kristi

North Carolina; past and present. Rosen Central 2011 48p il map (The United States: past and present) lib bdg $26.50; pa $11.75

Grades: 3 4 5 6   **975.6**

1. North Carolina

ISBN 978-1-4358-9491-4 lib bdg; 1-4358-9491-X lib bdg; 978-1-4358-9518-8 pa; 1-4358-9518-5 pa

LC 2009054264

Presents the history, geography, government, economy, and people of North Carolina, as well as general facts about the state.

Includes glossary and bibliographical references

Miller, Lee

Roanoke; the mystery of the Lost Colony. Scholastic Nonfiction 2007 112p il map $18.99

Grades: 4 5 6 7   **975.6**

1. Roanoke Island (N.C.) -- History 2. United States -- History -- 1600-1775, Colonial period

ISBN 0-439-71266-1; 978-0-439-71266-8

LC 2005-51820

"Miller, author of Roanoke: solving the mystery of the Lost Colony (2001), here reprises for a young audience her historical theory that a certain man sabotaged the expedition eventually known as the Lost Colony. . . . Miller does an exceptional job of preseneting the Native American culture and viewpoint. . . . This handsomely designed book features one or two illustrations on each spread, many in color, including reproductions or period drawings, paintings, and maps, as well as modern photos of sites and wildlife." Booklist

Includes bibliographical references

Reed, Jennifer

Cape Hatteras National Seashore; adventure, explore, discover. [by] Jennifer Reed. MyReportLinks.com Books

2008 128p il map (America's national parks) lib bdg $33.27

Grades: 5 6 7 8 **975.6**

1. Cape Hatteras National Seashore (N.C.) 2. National parks and reserves -- United States

ISBN 978-1-59845-086-6 lib bdg; 1-59845-086-7 lib bdg

LC 2006102321

This "informative, well-written book contains a physical description of the park; a summary of its history including the Native peoples of the area; activities such as hiking trails, campsites, and visitor centers; information about the park's plants, animals, and weather; full-color photographs; and numerous approved links available through the publisher's Web page. . . . Thorough, useful, and appealing, this . . . is a great update for collections." SLJ

Includes glossary and bibliographical references

Shirley, David

North Carolina; by David Shirley and Joyce Hart. 2nd ed.; Marshall Cavendish Benchmark 2010 144p il map (Celebrate the states) lib bdg $43.79

Grades: 5 6 7 8 **975.6**

1. North Carolina

ISBN 978-0-7614-4729-0; 0-7614-4729-6

LC 2009007139

First published 2001

This offers information on the geography, history, wildlife, governmental structure, economy, cultural diversity, peoples, religion, and landmarks of North Carolina.

Includes bibliographical references

975.7 South Carolina

Doak, Robin S.

South Carolina, 1540-1776; by Robin Doak with Robert Olwell. National Geographic Society 2007 109p il map (Voices from colonial America) $21.95; lib bdg $32.90

Grades: 5 6 7 8 **975.7**

1. South Carolina -- History

ISBN 978-1-4263-0066-0; 1-4263-0066-2; 978-1-4263-0067-7 lib bdg; 1-4263-0067-0 lib bdg

LC 2007-3120

A history of South Carolina from its beginning as an English colony to 1788 when it became the eighth state.

Offers "thorough, well-documented information about the struggles and successes of early colonial settlers and settlements. . . . Many reproductions of period illustrations and some photographs of period documents and maps with relevant captions are included" Horn Book Guide

Includes bibliographical references

Harmon, Dan

South Carolina; past and present. [by] Daniel E. Harmon. Rosen Central 2011 48p il (The United States: past and present) lib bdg $26.50; pa $11.75

Grades: 3 4 5 6 **975.7**

1. South Carolina

ISBN 978-1-4358-9495-2 lib bdg; 1-4358-9495-2 lib bdg; 978-1-4358-9522-5 pa; 1-4358-9522-3 pa

LC 2010002586

Presents the history, geography, government, economy, and people of South Carolina, as well as general facts about the state.

Includes bibliographical references

Hoffman, Nancy

South Carolina; by Nancy Hoffman and Joyce Hart. 2nd ed.; Marshall Cavendish Benchmark 2010 144p il map (Celebrate the states) lib bdg $42.79

Grades: 5 6 7 8 **975.7**

1. South Carolina

ISBN 978-0-7614-4034-5; 0-7614-4034-8

LC 2008038266

First published 2001

This offers information on the geography, history, wildlife, governmental structure, economy, cultural diversity, peoples, religion, and landmarks of South Carolina.

Includes bibliographical references

Somervill, Barbara A.

South Carolina. Children's Press 2009 144p il map (America the beautiful, third series) lib bdg $39

Grades: 4 5 6 7 **975.7**

1. South Carolina

ISBN 978-0-531-18591-9; 0-531-18591-5

LC 2007031030

Presents an introduction to the geography, natural resources, history, economy, important sites, daily life, and people of South Carolina.

Includes glossary and bibliographical references

975.8 Georgia

Doak, Robin S.

Georgia, 1521-1776. National Geographic Society 2006 109p il map (Voices from colonial America) $21.95; lib bdg $32.90

Grades: 5 6 7 8 **975.8**

1. Georgia -- History

ISBN 978-0-7922-6389-0; 0-7922-6389-8; 978-0-7922-6858-1 lib bdg; 0-7922-6858-X lib bdg

LC 2005-22141

Provides a history of Georgia from the arrival of European explorers in the sixteenth century to its becoming a state in 1788.

Includes bibliographical references

Otfinoski, Steven

Georgia; 2nd ed.; Marshall Cavendish Benchmark 2010 144p il map (Celebrate the states) lib bdg $42.79

Grades: 5 6 7 8 **975.8**

1. Georgia

ISBN 978-0-7614-4031-4; 0-7614-4031-3

LC 2008041711

First published 2001

This offers information on the geography, history, wildlife, governmental structure, economy, cultural diversity, peoples, religion, and landmarks of Georgia.

Includes bibliographical references

Prentzas, G. S.

Georgia; by G.S. Prentzas. Children's Press 2008 144p
il map (America the beautiful, third series) lib bdg $38
Grades: 4 5 6 7 **975.8**

1. Georgia

ISBN 978-0-531-18572-8; 0-531-18572-9

LC 2007-8256

Describes the history, geography, ecology, people, economy, cities, and sights of the state of Georgia.

Includes glossary and bibliographical references

Watson, Stephanie

Georgia; past and present. Rosen Central 2010 48p il
map (The United States: past and present) lib bdg $26.50;
pa $11.50
Grades: 3 4 5 6 **975.8**

1. Georgia

ISBN 978-1-4358-5292-1 lib bdg; 1-4358-5292-3 lib
bdg; 978-1-4358-5582-3 pa; 1-4358-5582-5 pa

LC 2008-54225

Presents the history, geography, government, economy, and people of Georgia, as well as general facts about
the state.

Includes glossary and bibliographical references

975.9 Florida

Cannavale, Matthew C.

Florida, 1513-1821; [by] Matthew C. Cannavale with
Robert Olwell, consultant. National Geographic 2006 109p
il map (Voices from colonial America) $21.95; lib bdg
$32.90
Grades: 5 6 7 8 **975.9**

1. Florida -- History

ISBN 978-0-7922-6409-5; 0-7922-6409-6; 978-0-
7922-6866-6 lib bdg; 0-7922-6866-0 lib bdg

LC 2006-20505

Offers "thorough, well-documented information about
the struggles and successes of early nonnative settlers [in
Florida]. . . . Many reproductions of period illustrations
(both color and sepia) and some photos of archival documents and maps enhance the text." Horn Book Guide

Includes bibliographical references

George, Jean Craighead

★ Everglades; paintings by Wendell Minor. Harper-
Collins Pubs. 1995 un il hardcover o.p. pa $6.95
Grades: 2 3 4 **975.9**

1. Everglades (Fla.)

ISBN 0-06-021228-4; 0-06-446194-7 pa

LC 92-9517

"The story and the art create a mystical tale that flows
from a serene start to a powerful conclusion." SLJ

"Though structured as a tale told to five children whom
a storyteller has poled into the Everglades, the narrative focuses on the history of that unusual ecosystem. The narrator
tells how the Everglades became 'a living kaleidoscope of
color and beauty,' filled with plants and animals, and how
human involvement has changed the ecology, devastating
the area. . . . When the children ask about what happened
to the orchids, egrets, and alligators, the storyteller suggests

that they can make a happy ending to the story when they
grow up." Booklist

Hart, Joyce

Florida; [by] Perry Chang and Joyce Hart. 2nd ed.;
Marshall Cavendish Benchmark 2007 144p il map (Cel-
ebrate the states) lib bdg $39.93
Grades: 4 5 6 7 **975.9**

1. Florida

ISBN 978-0-7614-2348-5; 0-7614-2348-6

LC 2006-8174

First published 1998

"Provides comprehensive information on the geography,
history, wildlife, governmental structure, economy, cultural
diversity, peoples, religion, and landmarks of Florida." Publisher's note

Includes bibliographical references

Hess, Debra

Florida; [by] Debra Hess, Lori P. Wiesenfeld. 2nd ed.;
Marshall Cavendish Benchmark 2010 90p il map (It's my
state) lib bdg $31.36
Grades: 3 4 5 **975.9**

1. Florida

ISBN 978-1-6087-0049-3; 1-6087-0049-6

LC 2010003922

First published 2003

Surveys the history, geography, government, and economy of Florida as well as the diverse ways of life of its people

Jankowski, Susan

Everglades National Park; adventure, explore, discover. [by] Susan Jankowski. MyReportLinks.com Books
2009 128p il map (America's national parks) lib bdg
$33.27
Grades: 5 6 7 8 **975.9**

1. Everglades National Park (Fla.) 2. National parks
and reserves -- United States

ISBN 978-1-59845-091-0 lib bdg; 1-59845-091-3
lib bdg

LC 2007-38262

This "informative, well-written book contains a physical description of the park; a summary of its history including the Native peoples of the area; activities such as hiking
trails, campsites, and visitor centers; information about the
park's plants, animals, and weather; full-color photographs;
and numerous approved links available through the publisher's Web page. . . . Thorough, useful, and appealing, this . . .
is a great update for collections." SLJ

Includes glossary and bibliographical references

Marsico, Katie

★ The Everglades; by Katie Marsico. Cherry Lake
Pub. 2013 32 p. (It's cool to learn about America's water-
ways) (lib. bdg.) $28.50
Grades: 3 4 5 **975.9**

1. Picture books for children 2. Everglades (Fla.) 3.
Everglades National Park (Fla.)

ISBN 1624310176; 9781624310171; 9781624310416;
9781624310652

LC 2012034738

This book by Katie Marsico is part of the Social Studies
Explorer: It's Cool to Learn About America's Water-Ways
series and looks at the Everglades. In the books, the "first

chapter introduces the waterway and provides basic geographic information about the surrounding area; the second chapter discusses the wildlife; the third chapter supplies a history, including today's tourism and agriculture; and the final chapter moves on to conservation and environmental activism." (Booklist)

Includes bibliographical references and index

Orr, Tamra

Florida; by Tamra B. Orr. Children's Press 2008 144p il map (America the beautiful, third series) lib bdg $38

Grades: 4 5 6 7   **975.9**

1. Florida

ISBN 0-531-18558-3; 978-0-531-18558-2

LC 2006100102

Describes the history, geography, ecology, people, economy, cities, and sights of the state of Florida.

Includes glossary and bibliographical references

Sawyer, Sarah

Florida; past and present. Rosen Central 2010 48p il map (The United States: past and present) lib bdg $26.50; pa $11.50

Grades: 3 4 5 6   **975.9**

1. Florida

ISBN 978-1-4358-5288-4 lib bdg; 1-4358-5288-5 lib bdg; 978-1-4358-5574-8 pa; 1-4358-5574-4 pa

LC 2008-54223

Presents the history, geography, government, economy, and people of Florida, as well as general facts about the state.

Includes glossary and bibliographical references

Turner, Glennette Tilley

★ Fort Mose; and the story of the man who built the first free black settlement in Colonial America. Abrams Books for Young Readers 2010 42p il map $18.95

Grades: 5 6 7 8   **975.9**

1. Army officers 2. Florida -- History 3. Fort Mose site (Fla.) 4. Slavery -- United States 5. African Americans -- History 6. United States -- History -- 1600-1775, Colonial period

ISBN 978-0-8109-4056-7; 0-8109-4056-6

LC 2009-52205

"In the 18th century, some Africans escaped slavery in England's southern colonies to find freedom in the Spanish colony of Florida. As a leader of St. Augustine's community, African-born Francisco Menendez helped establish Fort Mose, the first free black community on North American soil. Turner does an excellent job of explaining how the residents of Fort Mose probably blended African, English, and Spanish traditions to create a unique—and uniquely American—culture." SLJ

Includes glossary and bibliographical references

976.1   Alabama

Heos, Bridget

Alabama; past and present. Rosen Central 2010 48p il map (The United States: past and present) lib bdg $26.50; pa $11.75

Grades: 3 4 5 6   **976.1**

1. Alabama

ISBN 978-1-4358-3518-4 lib bdg; 1-4358-3518-2; 978-1-4358-8486-1 pa; 1-4358-8486-8 pa

LC 2009021850

Presents the history, geography, government, economy, and people of Alabama, as well as general facts about the state.

Includes bibliographical references

Parks, Rosa

★ Rosa Parks: my story; by Rosa Parks with Jim Haskins. Dial Bks. 1992 192p il $17.99; pa $6.99

Grades: 5 6 7 8   **976.1**

1. Civil rights activists 2. African Americans -- Civil rights 3. African American women -- Biography 4. Montgomery (Ala.) -- Race relations

ISBN 0-8037-0673-1; 0-14-130120-1 pa

LC 89-1124

Rosa Parks describes her early life and experiences with race discrimination, and her participation in the Montgomery bus boycott and the civil rights movement

"A remarkable story, a record of quiet bravery and modesty, a document of social significance, a taut drama told with candor." Bull Cent Child Books

Shirley, David

Alabama; by David Shirley and Joyce Hart. 2nd ed.; Marshall Cavendish Benchmark 2009 144p il map (Celebrate the states) lib bdg $39.93

Grades: 4 5 6 7   **976.1**

1. Alabama

ISBN 978-0-7614-3397-2; 0-7614-3397-X

LC 2008-4601

First published 2000

"Provides comprehensive information on the geography, history, wildlife, governmental structure, economy, cultural diversity, peoples, religion, and landmarks of Alabama." Publisher's note

Includes bibliographical references

Somervill, Barbara A.

Alabama; by Barbara A. Somervill. Children's Press 2008 144p il map (America the beautiful, third series) lib bdg $38

Grades: 4 5 6 7   **976.1**

1. Alabama

ISBN 978-0-531-18556-8; 0-531-18556-7

LC 2006-37697

Describes the history, geography, ecology, people, economy, cities, and sights of the state of Alabama.

Includes glossary and bibliographical references

976.2   Mississippi

Casil, Amy Sterling

Mississippi; past and present. Rosen Central 2011 48p il map (The United States: past and present) lib bdg $26.50; pa $11.75

Grades: 3 4 5 6   **976.2**
1. Mississippi
ISBN 978-1-4358-9485-3 lib bdg; 1-4358-9485-5;
978-1-4358-9512-6 pa; 1-4358-9512-6 pa
     LC 2009054262
Presents the history, geography, government, economy,
and people of Mississippi, as well as general facts about
the state.
Includes glossary and bibliographical references

Dell, Pamela
Mississippi. Children's Press 2008 144p il map
(America the beautiful, third series) lib bdg $39
Grades: 4 5 6 7   **976.2**
1. Mississippi
ISBN 978-0-531-18563-6; 0-531-18563-X
     LC 2006101965
Presents an introduction to the geography, natural re-
sources, history, economy, important sites, daily life, and
people of Mississippi.
Includes glossary and bibliographical references

Shirley, David
Mississippi; [by] David Shirley and Patricia K. Kum-
mer. Marshall Cavendish Benchmark 2008 144p il map
(Celebrate the states) lib bdg $39.93
Grades: 4 5 6 7   **976.2**
1. Mississippi
ISBN 978-0-7614-2717-9; 0-7614-2717-1
     LC 2007-7868
First published 1999
"Provides comprehensive information on the geography,
history, wildlife, governmental structure, economy, cultural
diversity, peoples, religion, and landmarks of Mississippi."
Publisher's note
Includes bibliographical references

976.3   Louisiana

Benoit, Peter
Hurricane Katrina. Children's Press 2011 48p il
(True book: disasters) lib bdg $28; pa $6.95
Grades: 3 4 5   **976.3**
1. Hurricane Katrina, 2005
ISBN 978-0-531-25421-9 lib bdg; 0-531-25421-6;
978-0-531-26626-7 pa; 0-531-26626-5 pa
     LC 2011007145
This book about Hurricane Katrina in 2005 and its aftermath is "thoughtfully designed. . . . The information . . .
is right on target: concise, accurate, and thorough. . . . The
photographs . . . are especially effective at putting a human
face on large-scale devastation." Booklist
Includes glossary and bibliographical references

Bjorklund, Ruth
Louisiana; [by] Ruth Bjorklund, Andy Steinitz. 2nd
ed.; Marshall Cavendish Benchmark 2010 90p il map (It's
my state) lib bdg $31.36
Grades: 3 4 5   **976.3**
1. Louisiana
ISBN 978-1-6087-0051-6; 1-6087-0051-8
     LC 2010003925

Surveys the history, geography, government, and economy of Louisiana, as well as the diverse ways of life of
its people.

Freedman, Jeri
Louisiana; past and present. Rosen Central 2011
48p il map (The United States: past and present) lib bdg
$26.50; pa $11.75
Grades: 3 4 5 6   **976.3**
1. Louisiana
ISBN 978-1-4358-9483-9 lib bdg; 1-4358-9483-9 lib
bdg; 978-1-4358-9510-2 pa; 1-4358-9510-X pa
     LC 2010001616
Presents the history, geography, government, economy,
and people of Louisiana, as well as general facts about
the state.
Includes glossary and bibliographical references

Lassieur, Allison
Louisiana; by Allison Lassieur. Children's Press 2008
144p il map (America the beautiful, third series) lib bdg
$38
Grades: 4 5 6 7   **976.3**
1. Louisiana
ISBN 978-0-531-18560-5; 0-531-18560-5
     LC 2007-300
Describes the history, geography, ecology, people, econ-
omy, cities, and sights of the state of Louisiana.
Includes glossary and bibliographical references

Worth, Richard
Louisiana, 1682-1803. National Geographic Society
2005 109p il map (Voices from colonial America) $21.95;
lib bdg $32.90
Grades: 5 6 7 8   **976.3**
1. Louisiana -- History
ISBN 978-0-7922-6544-3; 0-7922-6544-0; 978-0-
7922-6850-5 lib bdg; 0-7922-6850-4 lib bdg
     LC 2005-16225
This "history of Louisiana begins in 1682 when Sieur
de La Salle claimed the region for France. After that time,
the region was governed under several different flags, including France, Spain, and Great Britain. . . . Thomas Jefferson purchased the land for the United States in 1803."
Publisher's note
Includes bibliographical references

976.4   Texas

Altman, Linda Jacobs
Texas; [by] Linda Jacobs Altman and Tea Benduhn.
2nd ed.; Marshall Cavendish Benchmark 2010 80p il map
(It's my state) $31.36
Grades: 3 4 5   **976.4**
1. Texas
ISBN 978-1-6087-0059-2; 1-6087-0045-3
     LC 2010003932
First published 2003
This provides a broad overview of the state of Texas,
from a concise geography and detailed history to a discus-
sion of its government and economy. Also provided are many
key facts, figures, people, and dates; information about state

symbols, plants, animals, products, and resources; a calendar of state events; and a historical time line.

Chemerka, William R.

Juan Seguin; Tejano leader. William R. Chemerka; illustrations by Don Collins. Bright Sky Press 2012 64 p. ill. $16.95

Grades: 3 4 5 6 **976.4**

1. Texas -- History 2. Political activists 3. Soldiers -- Texas -- Biography 4. Politicians -- Texas -- Biography 5. Texas -- History -- Republic, 1836-1846 6. Alamo (San Antonio, Tex.) -- Siege, 1836 7. Texas -- History -- Revolution, 1835-1836 -- Biography

ISBN 1933979798; 9781933979793

LC 2011052720

This book is a biography of Texan Juan Seguin by William R. Chemerka. Despite "having been forced to flee to Mexico and die in obscurity, Tejano Juan Seguin is recognised as a Texas hero. From his family's early support of settlers such as Stephen F. Austin to his years in the Texas Senate and as mayor of Bexar, this biography celebrates the life of Juan Seguin and his . . . efforts in securing Texas' independence." (WorldCat)

Fradin, Dennis B.

The Alamo; [by] Dennis Brindell Fradin. Marshall Cavendish Benchmark 2007 45p il map (Turning points in U.S. history) lib bdg $29.93

Grades: 3 4 5 **976.4**

1. Texas -- History 2. Alamo (San Antonio, Tex.)

ISBN 978-0-7614-2127-6 lib bdg; 0-7614-2127-0 lib bdg

LC 2005016022

This "includes the background to the battle, as well as an account of its aftermath and some information on famous combatants. . . . The clear, concise, and dynamic style of writing simplifies the information without dumbing it down. . . . The photos, paintings, and maps . . . add a wealth of information." SLJ

Includes glossary and bibliographical references

Green, Carl R.

Sam Houston; courageous Texas hero. by William R. Sanford and Carl R. Green. Enslow Publishers 2013 48 p. ill., map (library) $21.26; (paperback) $7.95

Grades: 5 6 7 8 **976.4**

1. Picture books for children 2. Governors -- Texas -- Biography 3. Legislators -- United States -- Biography 4. United States. Congress. Senate -- Biography

ISBN 0766040097; 9780766040090; 9781464400926

LC 2011051265

This book, part of the Courageous Heroes of the American West series, looks at Sam Houston. "One of the founders of Texas, Sam Houston served the state as governor and senator—but he is most remembered as an American hero" for defeating the Mexican army. "Surprising the Mexican troops with their bold attack, . . . the fiery Texans rallied to an overwhelming victory, claiming their independence." (Publisher's note)

Includes bibliographical references (p. 47) and index.

Melmed, Laura Krauss

Heart of Texas; a Lone Star ABC. Illustrated by Frané Lessac. Collins 2009 un il $17.99; lib bdg $18.89

Grades: 1 2 3 4 **976.4**

1. Alphabet 2. Texas

ISBN 978-0-06-114283-3; 0-06-114283-2; 978-0-06-114285-7 lib bdg; 0-06-114285-9 lib bdg

LC 2008026948

"From Alamo to Ziller Park, Melmed and Lessac provide a tour of places to visit, people to know, and historic events to remember about Texas. Each entry begins with an eight-line poem with an impeccable rhythmic beat that slips off the tongue for reading aloud. . . . [Lessac's] detailed and colorful folk art perfectly conveys the multicultural panorama of the second-largest state." Booklist

Nagle, Jeanne

Texas; past and present. [by] Jeanne Nagle. Rosen Central 2010 48p il map (The United States: past and present) lib bdg $26.50; pa $11.50

Grades: 3 4 5 6 **976.4**

1. Texas

ISBN 978-1-4358-5287-7 lib bdg; 1-4358-5287-7 lib bdg; 978-1-4358-5572-4 pa; 1-4358-5572-8 pa

LC 2008-50962

Presents the history, geography, government, economy, and people of Texas, as well as general facts about the state.

Includes glossary and bibliographical references

Somervill, Barbara A.

Texas. Children's Press 2009 144p il map (America the beautiful, third series) lib bdg $39

Grades: 4 5 6 7 **976.4**

1. Texas

ISBN 978-0-531-18580-3; 0-531-18580-X

LC 2007017787

Presents an introduction to the geography, natural resources, history, economy, important sites, daily life, and people of Texas.

Includes glossary and bibliographical references

Spradlin, Michael P.

Texas Rangers; legendary lawmen. [by] Michael P. Spradlin; illustrations by Roxie Munro. Walker & Co. 2008 un il $16.95; lib bdg $17.85

Grades: 2 3 4 **976.4**

1. Frontier and pioneer life 2. Texas Rangers 3. Texas -- History 4. West (U.S.) -- History

ISBN 978-0-8027-8096-6; 0-8027-8096-2; 978-0-8027-8097-3 lib bdg; 0-8027-8097-0 lib bdg

LC 2007020139

"This picture-book account of the nearly 200-year history of the Texas Rangers begins in 1823. . . . The bulk of the book covers the 1800s, when the Rangers fought Indian tribes; participated in the war against Mexico; and defended settlers from bank robbers, cattle rustlers, and horse thieves. . . . There is a brief section on modern Rangers. . . . Munro's colorful illustrations provide a look at the lawmen, depict the action and locales, and portray the changing times. They're sure to entice youngsters and keep them turning the pages." SLJ

Teitelbaum, Michael

Texas, 1527-1836. National Geographic Society 2005 109p il map (Voices from colonial America) $21.95; lib bdg $32.90

Grades: 5 6 7 8   **976.4**

1. Texas -- History

ISBN 978-0-7922-6387-6; 0-7922-6387-1; 978-0-7922-6682-2 lib bdg; 0-7922-6682-X lib bdg

LC 2005-11450

"Presents the history of Texas, including life in Spanish Texas, the arrival of American settlers, and The Texas Republic and statehood." Publisher's note

Includes bibliographical references

Wade, Mary Dodson

Henrietta King, la patrona; by Mary Dodson Wade; illustrated by Bill Farnsworth. Bright Sky Press 2012 23 p. $16.95

Grades: 4 5 6 7   **976.4**

1. Women ranchers -- Biography 2. Women philanthropists -- Biography 3. King Ranch (Tex.) 4. Texas -- Biography

ISBN 1933979631; 9781933979632

LC 2011052721

This book by Mary Dodson Wade "examines the . . . life of one of Texas's foremost frontier women and philanthropists, Henrietta Maria Morse Chamberlain King. . . . Henrietta accompanied her missionary father on his travels and later settled with her husband Richard King in the untamed frontiers of the south Texas gulf coast. . . . Under her stewardship, the family ranch went from . . . $500,000 in debt at her husband's death to a debt-free enterprise of more than one million acres." (Publisher's note)

Walker, Paul Robert

★ **Remember** the Alamo; Texians, Tejanos, and Mexicans tell their stories. by Paul Robert Walker. National Geographic 2007 61p il map $17.95; lib bdg $27.90

Grades: 5 6 7 8   **976.4**

1. Texas -- History 2. Alamo (San Antonio, Tex.)

ISBN 978-1-4263-0010-3; 978-1-4263-0011-0 lib bdg

LC 2006034497

"Opening with clear context about why tensions between Texas residents and the Mexican government were brought to a head, the book then chronicles events directly leading to the siege of the Alamo and its immediate aftermath, following up with an epilogue on the decisive battle of San Jacinto 10 months later. Bringing the history to life is a healthy selection of dramatic, modern paintings along with plenty of archival drawings, maps, and old photos." Booklist

Includes bibliographical references

Winter, Jonah

Born and bred in the Great Depression. Schwartz & Wade Books 2011 un il $17.99 **976.4**

1. Great Depression, 1929-1939 2. Texas

ISBN 978-0-375-86197-0; 0-375-86197-1

Jonah Winter offers an "account of his father's hardscrabble Depression-era childhood. He softens the rough edges and sees the beauty of the East Texas country where Grandpa Winter lives with his wife and eight children. Directly addressing his father in second-person narration, Winter pulls no punches about the humiliation Grandpa Winter faced to keep his family fed. . . . Winters writing is thoughtful and deeply felt. Root's portraits of the boy's solitary exploration convey the force of Winter's message about 'learning to love those things/ that didn't cost a single penny.'" Publ Wkly

976.6   Oklahoma

Baldwin, Guy

Oklahoma; by Guy Baldwin and Joyce Hart. 2nd ed.; Marshall Cavendish Benchmark 2009 144p il map (Celebrate the states) lib bdg $42.79

Grades: 5 6 7 8   **976.6**

1. Oklahoma

ISBN 978-0-7614-4032-1; 0-7614-4032-1

LC 2008044261

First published 2001

This offers information on the geography, history, wildlife, governmental structure, economy, cultural diversity, peoples, religion, and landmarks of Oklahoma.

Includes bibliographical references

Dorman, Robert L.

Oklahoma; past and present. Rosen Central 2011 48p il map (The United States: past and present) lib bdg $26.50; pa $11.75

Grades: 3 4 5 6   **976.6**

1. Oklahoma

ISBN 978-1-4358-9493-8 lib bdg; 1-4358-9493-6 lib bdg; 978-1-4358-9520-1 pa; 1-4358-9520-7 pa

LC 2010002591

Presents the history, geography, government, economy, and people of Oklahoma, as well as general facts about the state.

Includes bibliographical references

Orr, Tamra

Oklahoma; by Tamra B. Orr. Children's Press 2008 144p il map (America the beautiful, third series) lib bdg $38

Grades: 4 5 6 7   **976.6**

1. Oklahoma

ISBN 978-0-531-18567-4; 0-531-18567-2

LC 2007-4774

Describes the history, geography, ecology, people, economy, cities and sights of the state of Oklahoma.

Includes glossary and bibliographical references

976.7   Arkansas

Altman, Linda Jacobs

Arkansas; [by] Linda Jacobs Altman, Ettagale Blauer, and Jason Laure. 2nd ed.; Marshall Cavendish Benchmark 2009 144p il map (Celebrate the states) lib bdg $42.79

Grades: 4 5 6 7   **976.7**

1. Arkansas

ISBN 978-0-7614-3001-8; 0-7614-3001-6

First published 2000

"Provides comprehensive information on the geography, history, wildlife, governmental structure, economy, cultural diversity, peoples, religion, and landmarks of Arkansas." Publisher's note

Includes bibliographical references

Levy, Janey

Arkansas; past and present. Rosen Central 2011 48p il map (The United States: past and present) lib bdg $26.50; pa $11.75

Grades: 3 4 5 6 **976.7**
1. Arkansas
ISBN 978-1-4358-9476-1 lib bdg; 1-4358-9476-6 lib
bdg; 978-1-4358-9504-1 pa; 1-4358-9504-5 pa
LC 2009052310

Presents the history, geography, government, economy,
and people of Arkansas, as well as general facts about
the state.

Includes glossary and bibliographical references

Prentzas, G. S.
Arkansas. Children's Press 2009 144p il map (America the beautiful, third series) lib bdg $39
Grades: 4 5 6 7 **976.7**
1. Arkansas
ISBN 978-0-531-18596-4; 0-531-18596-6
LC 2007044423

Presents an introduction to the geography, natural resources, history, economy, important sites, daily life, and
people Arkansas.

Includes glossary and bibliographical references

976.8 Tennessee

Barrett, Tracy
Tennessee; by Tracy Barrett. 2nd ed.; Marshall Cavendish Benchmark 2006 144p il map (Celebrate the states)
lib bdg $39.93
Grades: 4 5 6 7 **976.8**
1. Tennessee
ISBN 978-0-7614-2151-1; 0-7614-2151-3
LC 2005-24055

First published 1998

"Provides comprehensive information on the geography,
history, wildlife, governmental structure, economy, cultural
diversity, peoples, religion, and landmarks of Tennessee."
Publisher's note

Includes bibliographical references

Graham, Amy
Great Smoky Mountains National Park; adventure, explore, discover. [by] Amy Graham. MyReportLinks.com
Books 2009 128p il map (America's national parks) lib
bdg $33.27
Grades: 5 6 7 8 **976.8**
1. Great Smoky Mountains National Park (N.C. and
Tenn.) 2. National parks and reserves -- United States
ISBN 978-1-59845-093-4 lib bdg; 1-59845-093-X
lib bdg
LC 2007-13456

This "informative, well-written book contains a physical description of the park; a summary of its history including the Native peoples of the area; activities such as hiking
trails, campsites, and visitor centers; information about the
park's plants, animals, and weather; full-color photographs;
and numerous approved links available through the publisher's Web page. . . . Thorough, useful, and appealing, this . . .
is a great update for collections." SLJ

Includes glossary and bibliographical references

Green, Carl R.
Davy Crockett; courageous hero of the Alamo. by
William R. Sanford and Carl R. Green. Rev. ed. Enslow
Publishers 2013 48 p. col. ill., map (library) $21.26;
(paperback) $7.95
Grades: 5 6 7 8 **976.8**
1. Alamo (San Antonio, Tex.) -- History -- Siege, 1836
2. Pioneers -- Tennessee -- Biography 4. Legislators --
United States -- Biography 5. United States. Congress.
House -- Biography
ISBN 0766040054; 9780766040052; 9781464400865
LC 2011037749

This book by William Sanford is part of the Courageous
Heroes of the American West series and focuses on Davy
Crockett. "The courageous Texans chose to defend the fort
in San Antonio against more than two thousands Mexican
soldiers. . . . Although his brave deeds at the Alamo made
him legendary, Crockett had already gained fame as a hunter, soldier, and U.S. Congressman." (Publisher's note)

Includes bibliographical references (p. 47) and index.

Somervill, Barbara A.
Tennessee. Children's Press/Scholastic 2010 144p il
map (America the beautiful, third series) lib bdg $39 **976.8**
1. Tennessee
ISBN 978-0-531-18504-9; 0-531-18504-4
LC 2008000505

Presents an introduction to the geography, natural resources, history, economy, important sites, daily life, and
people of Tennessee.

Includes glossary and bibliographical references

976.9 Kentucky

Barrett, Tracy
Kentucky; [by] Tracy Barrett. 2nd ed.; Marshall Cavendish Benchmark 2008 144p il map (Celebrate the states)
lib bdg $39.93
Grades: 4 5 6 7 **976.9**
1. Kentucky
ISBN 978-0-7614-2715-5; 0-7614-2715-5
LC 2007-6388

First published 1999

"Provides comprehensive information on the geography,
history, wildlife, governmental structure, economy, cultural
diversity, peoples, religion, and landmarks of Kentucky."
Publisher's note

Includes bibliographical references

Cook, C.
Kentucky; past and present. [by] Colleen Ryckert
Cook. Rosen Central 2011 48p il map (The United States:
past and present) lib bdg $26.50; pa $11.95
Grades: 3 4 5 6 **976.9**
1. Kentucky
ISBN 978-1-4358-9482-2 lib bdg; 1-4358-9482-0 lib
bdg; 978-1-4358-9509-6 pa; 1-4358-9509-6 pa
LC 2010002507

Presents the history, geography, government, economy,
and people of Kentucky, as well as general facts about
the state.

Includes bibliographical references

Green, Carl R.

Daniel Boone; courageous frontiersman. by William R. Sanford and Carl R. Green. Enslow Publishers 2013 48 p. col. ill., map (library) $21.26; (paperback) $7.95

Grades: 5 6 7 8   **976.9**

1. Frontier and pioneer life -- United States 2. Kentucky -- Biography 3. Pioneers -- Kentucky -- Biography 4. Frontier and pioneer life -- Kentucky

ISBN 076604002X; 9780766040021; 9781464400858; 9781464509926; 9781464609923

LC 2011037736

This book by William Sanford is part of the Courageous Heroes of the American West series and focuses on Daniel Boone. "Through the untamed wilderness, Daniel Boone marched forward. He was leading a group of workers to carve out the Wilderness Road. Over hills, through dense forests, along stony paths, and fending off American Indian attacks, Boone never quit. He opened the way for thousands of settlers to move west, establishing the settlement of Boonesborough in 1775." (Publisher's note)

Includes bibliographical references (p. 47) and index.

Santella, Andrew

Kentucky; by Andrew Santella. Children's Press 2008 144p il map (America the beautiful, third series) lib bdg $38

Grades: 4 5 6 7   **976.9**

1. Kentucky

ISBN 978-0-531-18574-2; 0-531-18574-5

LC 2007-4803

Describes the history, geography, ecology, people, economy, cities, and sights of the state of Kentucky.

Includes glossary and bibliographical references

977 North central United States

Kummer, Patricia K.

The **Great** Lakes; [by] Patricia K. Kummer. Marshall Cavendish Benchmark 2008 96p il map (Nature's wonders) lib bdg $35.64

Grades: 5 6 7 8   **977**

1. Great Lakes

ISBN 978-0-7614-2853-4 lib bdg; 0-7614-2853-4 lib bdg

LC 2007019728

"Provides comprehensive information on the geography, history, wildlife, peoples, and environmental issues of the Great Lakes." Publisher's note

Includes glossary and bibliographical references

Marsico, Katie

★ The **Mississippi** River; by Katie Marsico. Cherry Lake Pub. 2013 32 p. (It's cool to learn about America's waterways) (lib. bdg.) $28.50

Grades: 3 4 5   **977**

1. Picture books for children 2. Mississippi River

ISBN 1624310117; 9781624310119; 9781624310355; 9781624310591

LC 2012037581

This book by Katie Marisco is part of the Social Studies Explorer: It's Cool to Learn About America's Water-Ways series and looks at the Everglades. In the books, the "first chapter introduces the waterway and provides basic geographic information about the surrounding area; the second chapter discusses the wildlife; the third chapter supplies a history, including today's tourism and agriculture; and the final chapter moves on to conservation and environmental activism." (Booklist)

977.1 Ohio

Lew, Kristi

Ohio; past and present. Rosen Central 2010 48p il map (The United States: past and present) lib bdg $26.50; pa $11.50

Grades: 3 4 5 6   **977.1**

1. Ohio

ISBN 978-1-4358-5286-0 lib bdg; 1-4358-5286-9 lib bdg; 978-1-4358-5570-0 pa; 1-4358-5570-1 pa

LC 2008-54234

Presents the history, geography, government, economy, and people of Ohio, as well as general facts about the state.

Includes glossary and bibliographical references

Sherrow, Victoria

Ohio; [by] Victoria Sherrow. 2nd. ed.; Marshall Cavendish Benchmark 2008 144p il map (Celebrate the states) lib bdg $39.93

Grades: 4 5 6 7   **977.1**

1. Ohio

ISBN 978-0-7614-2558-8; 0-7614-2558-6

LC 2006-34103

First published 1999

"Provides comprehensive information on the geography, history, wildlife, governmental structure, economy, cultural diversity, peoples, religion, and landmarks of Ohio." Publisher's note

Includes bibliographical references

Stille, Darlene R.

Ohio. Children's Press 2009 144p il map (America the beautiful, third series) lib bdg $39

Grades: 4 5 6 7   **977.1**

1. Ohio

ISBN 978-0-531-18579-7; 0-531-18579-6

LC 2007037177

Presents an introduction to the geography, natural resources, history, economy, important sites, daily life, and people of Ohio.

Includes glossary and bibliographical references

977.2 Indiana

Brezina, Corona

Indiana; past and present. Rosen Central 2010 48p il map (The United States: past and present) lib bdg $26.50; pa $11.75

Grades: 3 4 5 6   **977.2**

1. Indiana

ISBN 978-1-4358-3521-4 lib bdg; 1-4358-3521-2; 978-1-4358-8492-2 pa; 1-4358-8492-2 pa

LC 2009023685

Presents the history, geography, government, economy, and people of Indiana, as well as general facts about the state.
Includes bibliographical references

Stille, Darlene R.
Indiana. Children's Press 2009 144p il map (America the beautiful, third series) lib bdg $39
Grades: 4 5 6 7   977.2
1. Indiana
ISBN 978-0-531-18582-7; 0-531-18582-6
LC 2007043670
Presents an introduction to the geography, natural resources, history, economy, important sites, daily life, and people of Indiana.
Includes glossary and bibliographical references

977.3   Illinois

Burgan, Michael
Illinois; by Michael Burgan. Children's Press 2008 144p il map (America the beautiful, third series) lib bdg $38
Grades: 4 5 6 7   977.3
1. Illinois
ISBN 978-0-531-18559-9; 0-531-18559-1
LC 2006-36020
Describes the history, geography, ecology, people, economy, cities, and sights of the state of Illinois.
Includes glossary and bibliographical references

Hurd, Owen
Chicago history for kids; triumphs and tragedies of the Windy city, includes 21 activities. [by] Owen Hurd. Chicago Review Press 2007 182p il map $14.95
Grades: 5 6 7 8   977.3
1. Chicago (Ill.) -- History
ISBN 978-1-55652-654-1; 1-55652-654-7
LC 2006031807
"This attractive overview begins with geography and moves to the colorful stories that characterize the city. Hurd tapped local experts and collections, using primary and secondary sources and the responses of young readers to craft this engaging resource. . . . Excellent-quality photos, maps, illustrations, or boxed facts appear on every page." SLJ
Includes bibliographical references

Mattern, Joanne
Illinois; past and present. Rosen Central 2010 48p il map (The United States: past and present) lib bdg $26.50; pa $11.50
Grades: 4 5 6   977.3
1. Illinois
ISBN 978-1-4358-5284-6 lib bdg; 1-4358-5284-2 lib bdg; 978-1-4358-5566-3 pa; 1-4358-5566-3 pa
LC 2008-50577
Presents the history, geography, government, economy, and people of Illinois, as well as general facts about the state.
Includes glossary and bibliographical references

Murphy, Jim
★ The great fire. Scholastic 1995 144p il maps $16.95; pa $12.99

Grades: 5 6 7 8 9 10   977.3
1. Fires -- Chicago (Ill.)
ISBN 0-590-47267-4; 0-439-20307-4 pa
LC 94-9963
Newbery honor book, 1996
"Firsthand descriptions by persons who lived through the 1871 Chicago fire are woven into a gripping account of this famous disaster. Murphy also examines the origins of the fire, the errors of judgment that delayed the effective response, the organizational problems of the city's firefighters, and the postfire efforts to rebuild the city. Newspaper lithographs and a few historical photographs convey the magnitude of human suffering and confusion." Horn Book Guide
Includes bibliographical references

Price-Groff, Claire
Illinois; [by] Claire Price-Groff, Elizabeth Kaplan. 2nd ed.; Marshall Cavendish Benchmark 2010 90p il map (It's my state) lib bdg $31.36
Grades: 3 4 5   977.3
1. Illinois
ISBN 978-1-6087-0050-9; 1-6087-0050-X
LC 2010003923
First published 2003
Surveys the history, geography, government, and economy of Illinois as well as the diverse ways of life of its people

977.4   Michigan

Brill, Marlene Targ
Michigan; by Marlene Targ Brill. 2d ed.; Marshall Cavendish Benchmark 2007 144p il map (Celebrate the states) lib bdg $39.93
Grades: 4 5 6 7   977.4
1. Michigan
ISBN 978-0-7614-2351-5; 0-7614-2351-6
LC 2006-8181
First published 1998
"Provides comprehensive information on the geography, history, wildlife, governmental structure, economy, cultural diversity, peoples, religion, and landmarks of Michigan." Publisher's note
Includes bibliographical references

Levy, Janey
Michigan; past and present. Rosen Central 2010 48p il map (The United States: past and present) lib bdg $26.50; pa $11.75
Grades: 3 4 5 6   977.4
1. Michigan
ISBN 978-1-4358-3523-8 lib bdg; 1-4358-3523-9 lib bdg; 978-1-4358-8496-0 pa; 1-4358-8496-5 pa
LC 2009028025
Presents the history, geography, government, economy, and people of Michigan, as well as general facts about the state.
Includes glossary and bibliographical references

Raatma, Lucia
Michigan; by Lucia Raatma. Children's Press 2008 144p il map (America the beautiful, third series) lib bdg $38

Grades: 4 5 6 7　　　　　　　　　　977.4
1. Michigan
ISBN 978-0-531-18562-9; 0-531-18562-1
　　　　　　　　　　　LC 2006100708
Describes the history, geography, ecology, people, economy, cities, and sights of the state of Michigan.
Includes glossary, filmography and bibliographical references

977.5　Wisconsin

Blashfield, Jean F.
Wisconsin; by Jean F. Blashfield. Children's Press 2008 144p il map (America the beautiful, third series) lib bdg $38
Grades: 4 5 6 7　　　　　　　　　　977.5
1. Wisconsin
ISBN 978-0-531-18568-1; 0-531-18568-0
　　　　　　　　　　　LC 2006102490
Describes the history, geography, ecology, famous people, economy, cities and sights of the state of Wisconsin.
Includes glossary and bibliographical references

Dornfeld, Margaret
Wisconsin; [by] Margaret Dornfeld and Richard Hantula. 2nd ed.; Marshall Cavendish Benchmark 2010 90p il map (It's my state!) lib bdg $31.36
Grades: 3 4 5　　　　　　　　　　　977.5
1. Wisconsin
ISBN 978-1-6087-0062-2; 1-6087-0062-3
　　　　　　　　　　　LC 2010003937
First published 2003
Surveys the history, geography, economy, and people of Wisconsin.

Heos, Bridget
Wisconsin; past and present. Rosen Central 2010 48p il map (The United States: past and present) lib bdg $26.50; pa $11.50
Grades: 3 4 5 6　　　　　　　　　　977.5
1. Wisconsin
ISBN 978-1-4358-5293-8 lib bdg; 1-4358-5293-1 lib bdg; 978-1-4358-5584-7 pa; 1-4358-5584-1 pa
　　　　　　　　　　　LC 2009-3906
Includes glossary and bibliographical references

977.6　Minnesota

Brill, Marlene Targ
Minnesota; [by] Marlene Targ Brill and Elizabeth Kaplan. 2nd ed.; Marshall Cavendish Benchmark 2010 90p il map (It's my state!) lib bdg $31.36
Grades: 3 4 5　　　　　　　　　　　977.6
1. Minnesota
ISBN 978-1-6087-0054-7; 1-6087-0054-2
　　　　　　　　　　　LC 2010003909
First published 2004
Surveys the history, geography, government, and economy of Minnesota as well as the diverse ways of life of its people

Harmon, Dan
Minnesota; past and present. [by] Daniel E. Harmon. Rosen Central 2010 48p il map (The United States: past and present) lib bdg $26.50; pa $11.75
Grades: 3 4 5 6　　　　　　　　　　977.6
1. Minnesota
ISBN 978-1-4358-3524-5 lib bdg; 1-4358-3524-7 lib bdg; 978-1-4358-8498-4 pa; 1-4358-8498-1 pa
　　　　　　　　　　　LC 2009028024
Presents the history, geography, government, economy, and people of Minnesota, as well as general facts about the state.
Includes glossary and bibliographical references

Schwabacher, Martin
Minnesota; [by] Martin Schwabacher and Patricia K. Kummer. 2nd ed.; Marshall Cavendish Benchmark 2008 144p il map (Celebrate the states) lib bdg $39.93
Grades: 4 5 6 7　　　　　　　　　　977.6
1. Minnesota
ISBN 978-0-7614-2716-2; 0-7614-2716-3
　　　　　　　　　　　LC 2007-2895
First published 1999
"Provides comprehensive information on the geography, history, wildlife, governmental structure, economy, cultural diversity, peoples, religion, and landmarks of Minnesota." Publisher's note
Includes bibliographical references

977.7　Iowa

Blashfield, Jean F.
Iowa. Children's Press 2010 144p il map (America the beautiful, third series) lib bdg $39
Grades: 4 5 6 7　　　　　　　　　　977.7
1. Iowa
ISBN 978-0-531-18599-5; 0-531-18599-0
　　　　　　　　　　　LC 2008004841
Presents an introduction to the geography, natural resources, history, economy, important sites, daily life, and people of Iowa.
Includes glossary and bibliographical references

Freedman, Jeri
Iowa; past and present. Rosen Central 2010 48p il map (The United States: past and present) lib bdg $26.50; pa $11.75
Grades: 3 4 5 6　　　　　　　　　　977.7
1. Iowa
ISBN 978-1-4358-3517-7 lib bdg; 1-4358-3517-4 lib bdg; 978-1-4358-8485-4 pa; 1-4358-8485-X pa
　　　　　　　　　　　LC 2009024564
Presents the history, geography, government, economy, and people of Iowa, as well as general facts about the state.
Includes bibliographical references

Morrice, Polly Alison
Iowa; by Polly Morrice and Joyce Hart. 2nd ed.; Marshall Cavendish Benchmark 2007 144p il map (Celebrate the states) lib bdg $39.93

Grades: 4 5 6 7   **977.7**
1. Iowa
ISBN 978-0-7614-2350-8; 0-7614-2350-8
LC 2006-13620
First published 1998
"Provides comprehensive information on the geography,
history, wildlife, governmental structure, economy, cultural
diversity, peoples, religion, and landmarks of Iowa." Pub-
lisher's note
Includes bibliographical references

977.8 Missouri

Bennett, Michelle
Missouri; by Michelle Bennett and Joyce Hart. 2nd
ed.; Marshall Cavendish Benchmark 2010 144p il map
(Celebrate the states) lib bdg $42.79 **977.8**
1. Missouri
ISBN 978-0-7614-4727-6; 0-7614-4727-X
LC 2009005754
First published 2001
This offers information on the geography, history, wild-
life, governmental structure, economy, cultural diversity,
peoples, religion, and landmarks of Missouri.
Includes bibliographical references

Blashfield, Jean F.
Missouri. Children's Press 2009 144p il map (Amer-
ica the beautiful, third series) lib bdg $39
Grades: 4 5 6 7   **977.8**
1. Missouri
ISBN 978-0-531-18585-8; 0-531-18585-0
LC 2007035320
Presents an introduction to the geography, natural re-
sources, history, economy, important sites, daily life, and
people of Missouri.
Includes glossary and bibliographical references

Bullard, Lisa
The Gateway Arch. Lerner Publications 2010 32p il
map (Lightning Bolt Books. Famous places) lib bdg $25.26
Grades: 2 3 4   **977.8**
1. Monuments 2. Gateway Arch (Saint Louis, Mo.)
ISBN 978-0-8225-9406-2; 0-8225-9406-4
LC 2008-30640
Discusses the history, design, and construction of the
Gateway Arch in Saint Louis, Missouri.
This book uses "high-quality photos, illustrations, maps,
and diagrams. . . . Readers will enjoy learning about [the
Gateway Arch] . . . and the challenges of building and main-
taining large structures." SLJ
Includes glossary and bibliographical references

Roza, Greg
Missouri; past and present. Rosen Central 2010 48p il
map (The United States: past and present) lib bdg $26.50;
pa $11.75
Grades: 3 4 5 6   **977.8**
1. Missouri
ISBN 978-1-4358-3520-7 lib bdg; 1-4358-3520-4;
978-1-4358-8490-8 pa; 1-4358-8490-6 pa
LC 2009025520

Presents the history, geography, government, economy, and people of Missouri, as well as general facts about
the state.
Includes bibliographical references

978 Western United States

Adler, David A.
A picture book of Sacagawea; illustrated by Dan
Brown. Holiday House 2000 un il $16.95; pa $6.95
Grades: 1 2 3   **978**
1. Shoshoni Indians 2. Lewis and Clark Expedition
(1804-1806) 3. Interpreters 4. Guides (Persons) 5.
West (U.S.) -- Exploration 6. Native Americans --
Biography
ISBN 0-8234-1485-X; 0-8234-1665-8 pa
LC 99-37135
A biography of the Shoshone woman who joined the
Lewis and Clark Expedition
"The narrative is clear, direct, and never fictionalized.
. . . The soft watercolor art is more successful in depicting
landscapes than human figures." Booklist
Includes bibliographical references

Burgan, Michael
The Arapaho. Marshall Cavendish Benchmark 2009
48p il map (First Americans) lib bdg $31.36
Grades: 2 3 4   **978**
1. Arapaho Indians
ISBN 978-0-7614-3017-9 lib bdg; 0-7614-3017-2
lib bdg
LC 2007-33675
Provides information on the background, lifestyle, be-
liefs, and present-day lives of the Arapaho people
Includes glossary and bibliographical references

Croy, Anita
Ancient Pueblo; archaeology unlocks the secrets of
America's past. by Anita Croy; J. Jefferson Reid, consul-
tant. National Geographic 2007 64p il map (National
Geographic investigates) $17.95; lib bdg $27.90
Grades: 4 5 6 7   **978**
1. Archeology 2. Pueblo Indians 3. Southwestern
States -- Antiquities
ISBN 978-1-4263-0130-8; 978-1-4263-0131-5 lib bdg
LC 2007024800
This describes the prehistoric sites of the American
Southwest, and what archeologists have learned from them
about the lives of ancient Pueblo peoples.
Includes glossary and bibliographical references

Freedman, Russell
★ The life and death of Crazy Horse; drawings by
Amos Bad Heart Bull. Holiday House 1996 166p il maps
$22.95
Grades: 5 6 7 8 9 10   **978**
1. Oglala Indians 2. Indian chiefs 3. Native Americans
-- Biography
ISBN 0-8234-1219-9
LC 95-33303
A biography of the Oglala Indian leader who relentlessly
resisted the white man's attempt to take over Indian lands.

This is "a compelling biography that is based on primary source documents and illustrated with pictographs by a Sioux band historian." Voice Youth Advocates

Includes bibliographical references

Friedman, Mel

The **Oregon** Trail. Children's Press 2010 il map (True book) lib bdg $26; pa $6.95

Grades: 3 4 5   978

1. Oregon Trail 2. Frontier and pioneer life 3. Overland journeys to the Pacific

ISBN 978-0-531-20584-6; 0-531-20584-3; 978-0-531-21247-9 pa; 0-531-21247-5 pa

LC 2009014186

This introduction to the Oregon Trail provides "readers with clear explanations, maps, illustrations, time lines, and engaging reproductions of primary resources. [This] volume contains eye-catching quick facts; illustrations and photographs are representational of regional Native Americans, pioneers, and explorers. This is ideal material for reports on the Westward expansion." SLJ

Includes bibliographical references

George-Warren, Holly

The **cowgirl** way; hats off to America's women of the West. Houghton Mifflin Books for Children 2010 112p il $18

Grades: 4 5 6 7   978

1. Cowhands 2. Women -- West (U.S.)

ISBN 978-0-618-73738-3; 0-618-73738-3

"With ample dynamic photos and lively quotes throughout, George-Warren presents a thoroughly absorbing overview of the history of cowgirls up to the present. . . . Famous figures such as Belle Starr, Calamity Jane, and Annie Oakley are discussed in brief, but the real delights here are the anecdotes on lesser-known figures such as Lucille Mulhall, the first woman to be dubbed a cowgirl in print. . . . The introduction of women as rodeo and trick riders and their contributions to the sports in the 1920s and '30s are covered in fascinating detail, as are the film and singing sensations of the 1940s and '50s." SLJ

Green, Carl R.

Buffalo Bill Cody; courageous wild west showman. by William R. Sanford and Carl R. Green. Enslow Publishers 2013 48 p. ill., map (library) $21.26; (paperback) $7.95

Grades: 5 6 7 8   978

1. Buffalo Bill's Wild West Show 2. Frontier and pioneer life -- West (U.S.) 3. West (U.S.) -- Biography 4. Pioneers -- West (U.S.) -- Biography 5. Entertainers -- United States -- Biography

ISBN 0766040070; 9780766040076; 9781464400902

LC 2011031052

This book by William Sanford and Carl R. Green is part of the "Courageious Heroes of the American West" series. It presents a biography of Buffalo Bill Cody, who "had many jobs--Pony Express rider, scout, soldier, buffalo hunter. But he was most famous for entertaining audiences with his Wild West show. Many Americans and others around the world could not travel to see the real Wild West, so Buffalo Bill Brought it to them." (Publisher's note)

Includes bibliographical references (p. 47) and index.

Calamity Jane; courageous wild west woman. by William R. Sanford and Carl R. Green. Enslow Publishers 2013 48 p. ill., map (library) $21.26; (paperback) $7.95

Grades: 5 6 7 8   978

1. Cowgirls 2. West (U.S.) -- Biography 3. Pioneers -- West (U.S.) -- Biography 4. Women pioneers -- West (U.S.) -- Biography

ISBN 0766040100; 9780766040106; 9781464400933

LC 2011033840

This book by William Sanford is part of the Courageous Heroes of the American West series and focuses on Calamity Jane. "The truth and myth are difficult to separate in the wild life of Calamity Jane. An independent spirit, she never stayed in one place for long. She worked as a gold prospector, bullwhacker, nurse, and had many other jobs, Calamity Jane refused to conform to the typical roles of a nineteenth-century woman." (Publisher's note)

Includes bibliographical references (p. 47) and index.

Zebulon Pike; courageous Rocky Mountain explorer. by William R. Sanford and Carl R. Green. Enslow Publishers 2013 48 p. ill. (library) $21.26; (paperback) $7.95

Grades: 5 6 7 8   978

1. Exploration 2. West (U.S.) -- Biography 3. West (U.S.) -- History -- To 1848 4. Explorers -- West (U.S.) -- Biography 5. West (U.S.) -- Discovery and exploration

ISBN 1464400954; 9780766040120; 9781464400957

LC 2011051629

This book by William R. Sanford is part of the Courageous Heroes of the American West series and looks at Zebulon Pike. "After the United States purchased the Louisiana Territory in 1803, the young nation needed brave pioneers to explore this vast uncharted land. Zebulon Pike . . . led an expedition across rolling prairies before arriving at the towering mountains" and being the first to explore the southern Rocky Mountains. (Publisher's note)

Includes bibliographical references (p. 47) and index.

Grupper, Jonathan

Destination: Rocky Mountains. National Geographic Soc. 2001 31p il $16.95

Grades: 3 4 5 6   978

1. Rocky Mountains 2. Natural history -- West (U.S.)

ISBN 0-7922-7722-8

LC 00-55926

"A hypothetical trek up the Rocky Mountains provides the framework for . . . information about its animals and the vegetation that sustains them at elevations beyond fourteen thousand feet. Each animal—from huge grizzly bear to tiny pika—has a double-page spread, lavishly illustrated with well-chosen color photographs. The text and graphics work well together." Horn Book Guide

Huey, Lois Miner

American archaeology uncovers the westward movement. Marshall Cavendish Benchmark 2009 64p il map (American archaeology) lib bdg $21.95

Grades: 4 5 6 7   978

1. Historical geography 2. West (U.S.) -- History 3. United States -- Territorial expansion 4. Frontier and pioneer life -- West (U.S.) 5. Excavations (Archeology)

-- United States
ISBN 978-0-7614-4265-3 lib bdg; 0-7614-4265-0
lib bdg

LC 2009003167

This describes how archeologists have learned about the history of the American West.

"The visually pleasing . . . [book is] replete with maps, paintings, and photographs, all appropriately placed and thoughtfully captioned. . . . Huey's focus on American history, which is broken down into small, manageable chunks, is sure to entice budding historians." SLJ

Includes glossary and bibliographical references

King, David C.

★ **Pioneer** days; discover the past with fun projects, games, activities, and recipes. Wiley 1997 118p il (American kids in history) pa $12.95

Grades: 3 4 5 6   **978**

1. Cooking 2. Handicraft 3. West (U.S.) -- Social life and customs 4. Frontier and pioneer life -- West (U.S.)
ISBN 0-471-16169-1

LC 96-37495

This book is an "assortment of history, culture, crafts, and stories to teach about the daily life of the pioneers. . . . [Crafts and recipes include] air-dried flowers, toys and games, homemade soda pop, johnny-cakes, and various holiday ornaments. The author's research is evident, and the presentation of the activities and recipes is so engaging that the book will appeal to a wide audience." SLJ

Includes glossary and bibliographical references

Nelson, Maria

The **life** of Sacagawea; Maria Nelson. Gareth Stevens Pub. 2012 24 p. ill. (chiefly col.) (library binding) $22.60; (paperback) $8.15

Grades: 2 3 4   **978**

1. Native American women 2. United States -- History 3. Native Americans -- Biography 4. Shoshoni women -- Biography 5. Shoshoni Indians -- Biography
ISBN 9781433963575; 9781433963599

LC 2011035145

Author Maria Nelson presents information on "one of the most famous Native Americans in US history--Sacagawea. Though much of her life remains a mystery, this book will explore the story of the . . . woman who helped Lewis and Clark explore the American West. . . . [Nelson also includes] a timeline of important events [for children.]" (Publisher's note)

Includes bibliographical references (p. 23) and index.

Olson, Tod

How to get rich on a Texas cattle drive; afterword by Marc Aronson; illustrations by Scott Allred & Gregory Proch. National Geographic 2010 47p il map $18.95

Grades: 4 5 6 7   **978**

1. Cowhands 2. West (U.S.) -- History 3. Frontier and pioneer life -- West (U.S.)
ISBN 978-1-4263-0524-5; 1-4263-0524-9

"This book provides one of the better true-to-life insider accounts of what happens on a cattle drive: why the cattle are being driven, where they're being driven to and from, and the multitude of daily chores and unforeseen obstacles along the way. Period photos and artwork, as well as original drawings, make for a lively design, and an ongoing ledger

keeps track of the main character's mostly modest finances." Booklist

★ **How** to get rich on the Oregon Trail; my adventures among cows, crooks & heroes on the road to fame and fortune. [illustrations by Scott Allred & Gregory Proch; afterword by Marc Anonson] National Geographic 2009 47p il (How to get rich) $18.95; lib bdg $27.90

Grades: 4 5 6 7   **978**

1. Oregon Trail 2. Frontier and pioneer life 3. Overland journeys to the Pacific 4. West (U.S.) -- History
ISBN 978-1-4263-0412-5; 1-4263-0412-9; 978-1-4263-0413-2 lib bdg; 1-4263-0413-7 lib bdg

"The action follows young Will Reed and his family as they set off from Illinois to find their fortune along the 2,000-mile Oregon Trail. . . . Informing Will's impish sketches and wry journal entries is a wealth of information about life along the trail. . . . An ongoing ledger calculates the family's balance as it fluctuates from $10.70 to $3,021.70, but it's clear that this journey is more about survival than riches. The illustrations, historical anecdotes, and run-ins with everyone from the Mormons to escaped slaves to Abraham Lincoln form a perfect blend of history and humbuggery." Booklist

Patent, Dorothy Hinshaw

The **horse** and the Plains Indians; a powerful partnership. Dorothy Hinshaw Patent; photographs by William Munoz. Clarion Books 2012 xiii, 98 p.p ill. (chiefly col.) $17.99

Grades: 4 5 6 7 8   **978**

1. Horses 2. Domestic animals 3. Native Americans -- Great Plains 4. Horses -- Great Plains -- History 5. Human-animal relationships -- Great Plains -- History 6. Indians of North America -- Domestic animals -- Great Plains
ISBN 9780547125510

LC 2011025954

This book explores the relationship between Plains Indians and horses. The "Plains Indians and the horse were not always inseparable. Once, Native Americans used dogs to help carry their goods, and even after the Spaniards introduced the horse to the Americas," the Spanish hoarded the valuable animals. But "soon horses escaped from Spanish settlements, and Native Americans quickly learned how valuable the horse could be as a hunting mount, beast of burden, and military steed." (Publisher's note)

Includes bibliographical references and index

Perritano, John

The **Lewis** and Clark Expedition. Children's Press 2010 48p il (True book) lib bdg $26; pa $6.95

Grades: 3 4 5   **978**

1. Explorers 2. Lewis and Clark Expedition (1804-1806) 3. Territorial governors 4. West (U.S.) -- Exploration
ISBN 978-0-531-20582-2 lib bdg; 0-531-20582-7 lib bdg; 978-0-531-21245-5 pa; 0-531-21245-9 pa

LC 2009014183

This introduction to the Lewis and Clark Expedition provides "elementary readers with clear explanations, maps, illustrations, time lines, and engaging reproductions of primary resources. [This] volume contains eye-catching quick facts; illustrations and photographs are representational of regional Native Americans, pioneers, and explorers. This is ideal material for reports on the Westward expansion." SLJ

Includes bibliographical references

Scott, Ann Herbert

★ Cowboy country; pictures by Ted Lewin. Clarion Bks. 1993 un il hardcover o.p. pa $6.95
Grades: K 1 2 3   **978**
1. Cowhands 2. West (U.S.)
ISBN 0-395-57561-3; 0-395-76482-3 pa
         LC 92-24499

An "old buckaroo" tells how he became a cowboy, what the work was like in the past, and how this life has changed

The author "succinctly captures the laconic speaking rhythms and distinctive jargon of her subject. . . . Lewin's . . . well-lit watercolors suggest the affability of the weathered narrator and the awe of the boy with him." Publ Wkly

Sheinkin, Steve

★ Which way to the wild West? everything your schoolbooks didn't tell you about America's westward expansion. illustrated by Tim Robinson. Roaring Brook Press 2009 260p il map $19.95
Grades: 5 6 7 8   **978**
1. West (U.S.) -- History 2. United States -- Territorial expansion 3. Frontier and pioneer life -- West (U.S.)
ISBN 978-1-59643-321-2; 1-59643-321-3

Presents the greatest adventures of America's Westward expansion, from the Louisiana Purchase and the gold rush to the Indian wars and life of the cowboy, as well as the everyday happenings that defined living on the frontier

"An engaging storyteller, the author uses humor and little-known anecdotes to make such subjects as Manifest Destiny, the Mexican-American War, the Gold Rush and Custer's Last Stand entertaining for readers. His chatty, informal style . . . will appeal to young readers turned off to history by stale textbooks. Robinson's cartoons complement the text. . . . An accessible and engaging historical overview." Kirkus

Includes bibliographical references

Staton, Hilarie

Cowboys and the wild West. Kingfisher 2011 32p il map (All about America)
Grades: 3 4 5 6   **978**
1. Cowhands 2. West (U.S.) -- History 3. Frontier and pioneer life -- West (U.S.)
ISBN 0-7534-6510-8 pa; 0-7534-6582-5; 978-0-7534-6510-3 pa; 978-0-7534-6582-0

This is a history of cowboys and the American West from the early 1800s to around 1890.

This "visually appealing [title] effectively [combines] paintings, engravings, primary documents, and photographs with cartoon illustrations. The eye-catching [layout includes] different font sizes, bold type, and text boxes to highlight different pieces of information. The content is interesting and pithy." SLJ

Includes glossary and bibliographical references

Waldman, Stuart

The last river; John Wesley Powell & the Colorado River Exploration Expedition. by Stuart Waldman; illustrated by Gregory Manchess. Mikaya Press 2005 47p il map (Great explorers book) $19.95

Grades: 3 4 5 6   **978**
1. Explorers 2. Geologists 3. West (U.S.) -- Exploration 4. Colorado River (Colo.-Mexico)
ISBN 1-931414-09-2
         LC 2005041580

"In 1869 the Colorado River Exploring Expedition set forth from Green River City led by John Wesley Powell, a one-armed explorer who was determined to reach the Colorado's canyons to study their geology. . . . Waldman relates their story clearly in the main text, while occasional sidebars carry short excerpts from the men's journals and letters. Illustrations include clear nineteenth-century photos as well as handsome full and double-page paintings. . . . Rich in color, strong in composition, and beautifully executed, these often-dramatic paintings bring the story to life." Booklist

Includes bibliographical references

Yasuda, Anita

Explore the wild west! Anita Yasuda; illustrated by Alex Kim. Nomad Press 2012 92 p. ill. (paperback) $12.95; (prebind) $21.95; (ebook) $9.99
Grades: 3 4 5   **978**
1. West (U.S.) -- History 2. Frontier and pioneer life -- West (U.S.) 3. United States -- History -- 19th century
ISBN 1936749718; 9781936749713; 9781451777307; 9781936749720

Author Anita Yasuda presents "a fun and educational journey through time [that] invites young readers to experience the spirit of the Wild West . . . [Yasuda provides a history of] Wild West legends, gold miners, settlers and frontier towns, Native American and cowboy cultures, cattle drives, and the peacekeepers and lawbreakers . . . [The book also includes f]un facts, trivia, jokes, and riddles." (Publisher's note)

978.004   Western United States--American native peoples

Green, Carl R.

Sacagawea; courageous American Indian guide. by William R. Sanford and Carl R. Green. Enslow Publishers 2013 48 p. ill., map (library) $21.26
Grades: 5 6 7 8   **978.004**
1. Native Americans -- United States 2. Shoshoni women -- Biography 3. Shoshoni Indians -- Biography
ISBN 0766040062; 9780766040069
         LC 2011048291

This book, part of the Courageous Heroes of the American West series, looks at Sacagawea. "Throughout Lewis and Clark's journey in the uncharted American West, this young America Indian woman proved to be an invaluable member of the expedition. Sacagawea served as translator and guide, all while caring for her infant son." (Publisher's note)

Includes bibliographical references (p. 47) and index.

Norwich, Grace

I am Sacagawea. Scholastic 2012 128 p. ill., map
Grades: 2 3 4   **978.004**
ISBN 0545405742; 9780545405744

Author Grace Norwich's biography of "Shoshoni Indian Sacagawea, known for guiding the Lewis and Clark expedition across the western half of the United States from 1804 to 1806," discusses "her childhood and kidnapping by the Hidatsa tribe, her marriage to Toussaint Charbonneau, and the mystery surrounding her death." (yabookscentral.com)

Includes bibliographical references (pages 124-125) and index.

978.1   Kansas

Bailey, Diane
    Kansas; past and present. Rosen Central 2011 48p il map (The United States: past and present) lib bdg $26.50; pa $11.75
    Grades: 3 4 5 6   **978.1**
        1. Kansas
        ISBN 9781435894815 lib bdg; 1-4358-9481-2 lib bdg; 978-1-4358-9508-9 pa; 1-4358-9508-8 pa
                                                        LC 2010000816
    Presents the history, geography, government, economy, and people of Kansas, as well as general facts about the state.
    Includes bibliographical references

Bjorklund, Ruth
    Kansas;   by Ruth Bjorklund and Trudi Strain Trueit. 2nd ed.;   Marshall Cavendish Benchmark 2009 144p il map (Celebrate the states) lib bdg $42.79
    Grades: 4 5 6 7   **978.1**
        1. Kansas
        ISBN 978-0-7614-3400-9; 0-7614-3400-3
                                                        LC 2008-5537
    "Provides comprehensive information on the geography, history, wildlife, governmental structure, economy, cultural diversity, peoples, religion, and landmarks of Kansas." Publisher's note
    Includes bibliographical references

Cannarella, Deborah
    Kansas. Children's Press 2009 144p il map (America the beautiful, third series) lib bdg $39
    Grades: 4 5 6 7   **978.1**
        1. Kansas
        ISBN 978-0-531-18583-4; 0-531-18583-4
                                                        LC 2007028461
    Presents an introduction to the geography, natural resources, history, economy, important sites, daily life, and people of Kansas.
    Includes glossary and bibliographical references

978.2   Nebraska

Bjorklund, Ruth
    Nebraska;   [by] Ruth Bjorklund and Marlee Richards. 2nd ed.;   Marshall Cavendish Benchmark 2010 144p il map (Celebrate the states) $42.79
    Grades: 5 6 7 8   **978.2**
        1. Nebraska
        ISBN 978-0-7614-4732-0; 0-7614-4732-6
    "Every school library should purchase this." Voice Youth Advocates

Bringle, Jennifer
    Nebraska; past and present. Rosen Central 2011 48p il map (The United States: past and present) lib bdg $26.50; pa $11.75
    Grades: 3 4 5 6   **978.2**
        1. Nebraska
        ISBN 978-1-4358-9487-7 lib bdg; 1-4358-9487-1 lib bdg; 978-1-4358-9514-0 pa; 1-4358-9514-2 pa
                                                        LC 2010002545
    Presents the history, geography, government, economy, and people of Nebraska, as well as general facts about the state.
    Includes bibliographical references

Heinrichs, Ann
    Nebraska; by Ann Heinrichs. Children's Press 2008 144p il map (America the beautiful, third series) lib bdg $38
    Grades: 4 5 6 7   **978.2**
        1. Nebraska
        ISBN 978-0-531-18577-3; 0-531-18577-X
                                                        LC 2007-6720
    Describes the history, geography, ecology, people, economy, cities, and sights of the state of Nebraska.
    Includes glossary and bibliographical references

978.3   South Dakota

Burgan, Michael
    South Dakota. Children's Press 2010 144p il map (America the beautiful, third series) lib bdg $39
    Grades: 4 5 6 7   **978.3**
        1. South Dakota
        ISBN 978-0-531-18503-2; 0-531-18503-6
                                                        LC 2008002299
    Takes readers on a tour of South Dakota, describing the state's history, culture, land, economy, government, and sights, and including unique facts, color maps and photos, the state song, suggested activities, lists of famous people, cultural institutions, and annual events, and other resources.
    Includes glossary and bibliographical references

Kenney, Karen Latchana
    Mount Rushmore; illustrated by Judith A. Hunt. Magic Wagon 2011 32p il (Our nation's pride) lib bdg $28.50
    Grades: 2 3 4   **978.3**
        1. Mount Rushmore National Memorial (S.D.)
        ISBN 978-1-61641-153-4; 1-61641-153-8
                                                        LC 2010014009
    This book "tells of the sculptor who came to work on the carving, how men were lowered on special harnesses to do the work, and how dynamite specialists and drillers prepared the mountain. . . . The full-color artwork not only explains the text but also gives almost photographic renderings of the [topic]." SLJ

Petersen, Christine
    South Dakota; past and present. Rosen Central 2011 48p il (The United States: past and present) lib bdg $26.50; pa $11.75

Grades: 3 4 5 6	978.3
1. South Dakota
ISBN 978-1-4358-9496-9 lib bdg; 1-4358-9496-0 lib bdg; 978-1-4358-9523-2 pa; 1-4358-9523-1 pa
LC 2010002584

Presents the history, geography, government, economy, and people of South Dakota, as well as general facts about the state.

Includes glossary and bibliographical references

Thomas, William

Mount Rushmore; by William David Thomas. Chelsea Clubhouse 2010 48p il (Symbols of American freedom) $30

Grades: 3 4 5	978.3
1. Mount Rushmore National Memorial (S.D.)
ISBN 978-1-60413-515-2; 1-60413-515-8
LC 2009-13027

This book about Mount Rushmore "provides nearly as much information as a guided tour by a park ranger. [It begins] with the story of how the place came to be, and where it fits into U.S. history. Information boxes offer additional background and some surprising facts, such as . . . the origin of the name of Mount Rushmore. The final chapter shows the landmark today and includes maps and photographs of the visitors' center and some of the things individuals might see or do while visiting the site. Much information is packed into [this] slim [book]. Excellent . . . for state reports or to complement U.S. history units." SLJ

Includes glossary

978.4   North Dakota

Lewis, Mark J.

North Dakota; past and present. Rosen Central 2011 48p il map (United States: past and present) lib bdg $26.50; pa $11.75

Grades: 3 4 5 6	978.4
1. North Dakota
ISBN 978-1-4358-9492-1 lib bdg; 1-4358-9492-8 lib bdg; 978-1-4358-9519-5 pa; 1-4358-9519-3 pa
LC 2010002697

This describes the geography, history, government, economy, and famous people of North Dakota.

Includes bibliographical references

McDaniel, Melissa

North Dakota; by Melissa McDaniel and Sara Louise Kras. 2nd ed.; Marshall Cavendish Benchmark 2010 144p il map (Celebrate the states) lib bdg $42.79

Grades: 5 6 7 8	978.4
1. North Dakota
ISBN 978-0-7614-4733-7; 0-7614-4733-4
LC 2009002584

First published 2001

This offers information on the geography, history, wildlife, governmental structure, economy, cultural diversity, peoples, religion, and landmarks of North Dakota.

Includes bibliographical references

Stille, Darlene R.

North Dakota. Children's Press 2010 144p il map (America the beautiful, third series) lib bdg $39

Grades: 4 5 6 7	978.4
1. North Dakota
ISBN 978-0-531-18502-5; 0-531-18502-8
LC 2008011282

Presents an introduction to the geography, natural resources, history, economy, important sites, daily life, and people of North Dakota.

Includes glossary and bibliographical references

978.6   Montana

Bennett, Clayton

Montana; by Clayton Bennett and Wendy Mead. 2nd ed.; Marshall Cavendish Benchmark 2010 144p il map (Celebrate the states) $42.79

Grades: 5 6 7 8	978.6
1. Montana
ISBN 978-0-7614-4731-3; 0-7614-4731-8
LC 2009007939

First published 2001

This offers information on the geography, history, wildlife, governmental structure, economy, cultural diversity, peoples, religion, and landmarks of Montana.

Includes bibliographical references

Porterfield, Jason

Montana; past and present. Rosen Central 2011 48p il map (The United States: past and present) lib bdg $26.50; pa $11.75

Grades: 3 4 5 6	978.6
1. Montana
ISBN 978-1-4358-9486-0 lib bdg; 1-4358-9486-3 lib bdg; 978-1-4358-9513-3 pa; 1-4358-9513-4 pa
LC 2010000415

Presents the history, geography, government, economy, and people of Montana, as well as general facts about the state.

Includes bibliographical references

Stein, R. Conrad

Montana. Children's Press 2010 144p il map (America the beautiful, third series) lib bdg $39

Grades: 4 5 6 7	978.6
1. Montana
ISBN 978-0-531-18500-1; 0-531-18500-1
LC 2008000823

Takes readers on a tour of Montana, describing the state's history, culture, land, economy, government, and sights, and including unique facts, color maps and photos, the state song, suggested activities, lists of famous people, cultural institutions, and annual events, and other resources.

Includes glossary and bibliographical references

978.7 Wyoming

Baldwin, Guy

Wyoming; [by] Guy Baldwin and Joyce Hart. 2nd ed.; Marshall Cavendish Benchmark 2008 144p il map (Celebrate the states) lib bdg $39.93

Grades: 4 5 6 7 **978.7**

1. Wyoming

ISBN 978-0-7614-2563-2; 0-7614-2563-2

LC 2007-19560

First publsihed 1999

"Provides comprehensive information on the geography, history, wildlife, governmental structure, economy, cultural diversity, peoples, religion, and landmarks of Wyoming." Publisher's note

Includes bibliographical references

Byers, Ann

Wyoming; past and present. Rosen Central 2011 48p il map (The United States: past and present) lib bdg $26.50; pa $11.75

Grades: 3 4 5 6 **978.7**

1. Wyoming

ISBN 978-1-4358-9500-3 lib bdg; 1-4358-9500-2 lib bdg; 978-1-4358-9527-0 pa; 1-4358-9527-4 pa

LC 2010002519

Presents the history, geography, government, economy, and people of Wyoming, as well as general facts about the state.

Includes glossary and bibliographical references

Prentzas, G. S.

Wyoming. Children's Press 2010 144p il map (America the beautiful, third series) lib bdg $39

Grades: 4 5 6 7 **978.7**

1. Wyoming

ISBN 978-0-531-18508-7; 0-531-18508-7

LC 2008016789

Takes readers on a tour of Wyoming, describing the state's history, culture, land, economy, government, and sights, and including unique facts, color maps and photos, the state song, suggested activities, lists of famous people, cultural institutions, and annual events, and other resources.

Includes glossary and bibliographical references

978.8 Colorado

Altman, Linda Jacobs

Colorado; [by] Linda Jacobs Altman, Stephanie Fitzgerald. 2nd ed.; Marshall Cavendish Benchmark 2010 90p il map (It's my state) $31.36

Grades: 3 4 5 **978.8**

1. Colorado

ISBN 978-1-6087-0046-2; 1-6087-0046-1

LC 2010003903

Surveys the history, geography, government, and economy of Colorado as well as the diverse ways of life of its people.

Heos, Bridget

Colorado; past and present. Rosen Central 2011 48p il map (The United States: past and present) lib bdg $26.50; pa $11.75

Grades: 3 4 5 6 **978.8**

1. Colorado

ISBN 978-1-4358-9477-8 lib bdg; 1-4358-9477-4 lib bdg; 978-1-4358-9530-0 pa; 1-4358-9530-4 pa

LC 2010000419

Presents the history, geography, government, economy, and people of Colorado, as well as general facts about the state.

Includes glossary and bibliographical references

Lowery, Linda

★ Aunt Clara Brown; official pioneer. illustrations by Janice Lee Porter. Carolrhoda Bks. 1999 48p il (On my own biography) lib bdg $19.93; pa $5.95

Grades: 2 3 4 **978.8**

1. Slaves 2. Frontier and pioneer life 3. Pioneers 4. African American women -- Biography

ISBN 1-57505-045-5 lib bdg; 1-57505-416-7 pa

LC 98-24259

A biography of the freed slave who made her fortune in Colorado and used her money to bring other former slaves there to begin new lives

"The well-defined primitivist shapes, canvas-y textures, and muted earth tones of the illustrations perfectly evoke the roughness of the terrain and the historical period, as well as the powerful basic emotions motivating the characters. The straightforward text allows the facts speak for themselves... . A good story and a solid resource." Bull Cent Child Books

Marsico, Katie

★ The Rio Grande; by Katie Marsico. Cherry Lake Publishing 2013 32 p. (lib. bdg.) $28.50

Grades: 3 4 5 **978.8**

1. Rivers 2. Rio Grande valley 3. Rio Grande (Colo.-Mexico and Tex.) 4. Rio Grande Valley (Colo.-Mexico and Tex.)

ISBN 1624310125; 9781624310126; 9781624310362; 9781624310607

LC 2012035444

This book by Katie Marsico presents "a tour of the Rio Grande and its surrounding area." It is part of a series that provides "information regarding each waterway's history, geographical characteristics, wildlife, and influence on the development of nearby towns and cities. Conservation is emphasized in all the titles. The importance of each waterway commercially and recreationally is also discussed. Vocabulary words are set apart in bold font and defined in the glossary." (Publisher's note)

Includes bibliographical references and index

Quigley, Mary

Mesa Verde; [by] Mary Quigley. Heinemann Library 2006 48p il (Excavating the past) lib bdg $31.43

Grades: 4 5 6 **978.8**

1. Native Americans -- Antiquities 2. Mesa Verde National Park (Colo.) 3. Excavations (Archeology) -- United States

ISBN 1-4034-5997-5

LC 2005009179

"Mesa Verde explains how these ancient people reached North and South America using the land bridge and settled down to farm in the Four Corners area. Quigley uses the term Ancestral Puebloans rather than the sometimes derogatory Anasazi and explains why. She describes the daily lives of the people and includes current theories about why they may have abandoned this site. Activities and discoveries by the Wetherill brothers and other archaeologists as well as cultural information from modern-day people bring knowledge about the ancients up to date. This [is an] excellent title." SLJ

Includes bibliographical references

Somervill, Barbara A.

Colorado; by Barbara A. Somervill. Children's Press 2008 144p il map (America the beautiful, third series) lib bdg $38

Grades: 4 5 6 7 **978.8**

1. Colorado

ISBN 978-0-531-18570-4; 0-531-18570-2

LC 2007-301

Describes the history, geography, ecology, people, economy, cities, and sights of the state of Colorado.

Includes glossary and bibliographical references

978.9   New Mexico

Brezina, Corona

New Mexico; past and present. Rosen Central 2011 48p il map (The United States: past and present) lib bdg $26.50; pa $11.75

Grades: 3 4 5 6 **978.9**

1. New Mexico

ISBN 978-1-4358-9490-7 lib bdg; 1-4358-9490-1; 978-1-4358-9517-1 pa; 1-4358-9517-7 pa

LC 2010003059

Presents the history, geography, government, economy, and people of New Mexico, as well as general facts about the state.

Includes bibliographical references

Burgan, Michael

New Mexico; land of enchantment. World Almanac Library 2003 48p il map (World Almanac Library of the states) $31; pa $14.05

Grades: 4 5 6 7 **978.9**

1. New Mexico

ISBN 978-0-8368-5156-4; 0-8368-5156-0; 978-0-8368-5327-8 pa; 0-8368-5327-X pa

LC 2002-191008

Text and illustrations present the history, geography, people, politics and government, economy, customs, and attractions of New Mexico

Includes bibliographical references

979.1   Arizona

Brezina, Corona

Arizona; past and present. Rosen Central 2010 48p il map (The United States: past and present) lib bdg $26.50; pa $11.75

Grades: 3 4 5 6 **979.1**

1. Arizona

ISBN 978-1-4358-3516-0 lib bdg; 1-4358-3516-6 lib bdg; 978-1-4358-8483-0 pa; 1-4358-8483-3 pa

LC 2009017004

Presents the history, geography, government, economy, and people of Arizona, as well as general facts about the state.

Includes glossary and bibliographical references

McDaniel, Melissa

Arizona; by Melissa McDaniel and Wendy Mead. 2nd ed.; Marshall Cavendish Benchmark 2009 144p il map (Celebrate the states) lib bdg $39.93

Grades: 4 5 6 7 **979.1**

1. Arizona

ISBN 978-0-7614-3398-9; 0-7614-3398-8

LC 2008-6212

First published 2000

"Provides comprehensive information on the geography, history, wildlife, governmental structure, economy, cultural diversity, peoples, religion, and landmarks of Arizona." Publisher's note

Includes bibliographical references

Somervill, Barbara A.

Arizona; by Barbara A. Somervill. Children's Press 2008 144p il map (America the beautiful, third series) lib bdg $38

Grades: 4 5 6 7 **979.1**

1. Arizona

ISBN 978-0-531-18595-7; 0-531-18595-8

LC 2007-37923

Presents an introduction to the geography, natural resources, history, economy, important sites, daily life, and people of Arizona.

"This title in the America the Beautiful series is also a fun read, with a chatty style, open design, and color photos, maps, screens, and charts on just about every spread." Booklist

Includes glossary and bibliographical references

979.2   Utah

Ching, Jacqueline

Utah; past and present. Rosen Central 2011 48p il map (The United States: past and present) lib bdg $26.50; pa $11.75

Grades: 3 4 5 6 **979.2**

1. Utah

ISBN 978-1-4358-9497-6 lib bdg; 1-4358-9497-9 lib bdg; 978-1-4358-9524-9 pa; 1-4358-9524-X pa

LC 2010002493

Presents the history, geography, government, economy, and people of Utah, as well as general facts about the state.

Includes bibliographical references

Kent, Deborah

Utah. Children's Press 2009 144p il map (America the beautiful, third series) $39

Grades: 4 5 6 7   **979.2**
   1. Utah
   ISBN 978-0-531-18592-6; 0-531-18592-3
                                    LC 2007051225

Presents an introduction to the geography, natural resources, history, economy, important sites, daily life, and people of Utah.
   Includes glossary and bibliographical references

Stefoff, Rebecca
   Utah; by Rebecca Stefoff and Wendy Mead. 2nd ed.; Marshall Cavendish Benchmark 2010 144p il map (Celebrate the states) lib bdg $42.79
Grades: 5 6 7 8   **979.2**
   1. Utah
   ISBN 978-0-7614-4035-2; 0-7614-4035-6
                                    LC 2008040026

This offers information on the geography, history, wildlife, governmental structure, economy, cultural diversity, peoples, religion, and landmarks of Utah.
   Includes bibliographical references

979.3   Nevada

Heinrichs, Ann
   Nevada; by Ann Heinrichs. Children's Press 2008 144p il map (America the beautiful, third series) lib bdg $38
Grades: 4 5 6 7   **979.3**
   1. Nevada
   ISBN 978-0-531-18586-5; 0-531-18586-9
                                    LC 2006-39526

Describes the history, geography, ecology, people, economy, cities, and sights of the state of Nevada.
   Includes glossary and bibliographical references

Roza, Greg
   Nevada; past and present. Rosen Central 2011 48p il map (The United States: past and present) lib bdg $26.50; pa $11.75
Grades: 3 4 5 6   **979.3**
   1. Nevada
   ISBN 978-1-4358-9488-4 lib bdg; 1-4358-9488-X; 978-1-4358-9515-7 pa; 1-4358-9515-0 pa
                                    LC 2010001980

Presents the history, geography, government, economy, and people of Nevada, as well as general facts about the state.
   Includes bibliographical references

Stefoff, Rebecca
   Nevada; 2nd ed.; Marshall Cavendish Benchmark 2010 144p il map (Celebrate the states) lib bdg $42.79
Grades: 5 6 7 8   **979.3**
   1. Nevada
   ISBN 978-0-7614-4728-3; 0-7614-4728-8
                                    LC 2009007137

This offers information on the geography, history, wildlife, governmental structure, economy, cultural diversity, peoples, religion, and landmarks of Nevada.
   Includes bibliographical references

979.4   California

Brown, Don
   ★ **Gold!** Gold from the American River! Roaring Brook Press 2011 un il map (Actual times) $17.99
Grades: 2 3 4   **979.4**
   1. California -- History 2. California -- Gold discoveries 3. Frontier and pioneer life -- California
   ISBN 978-1-59643-223-9; 1-59643-223-3
                                    LC 2010-14375

"Brown here takes a look at the 1849 California gold rush. [This is written] with easygoing prose and revealing quotes from forty-niners and historians alike. . . . The inventive page compositions and scratchy watercolor cartoon figures carry small, telling dramas . . . and sweeping landscapes come into full relief, bringing not only visual context but a sense of playfulness to the book." Booklist
   Includes bibliographical references

Burgan, Michael
   California; [by] Michael Burgan, William McGeveran. 2nd ed.; Marshall Cavendish Benchmark 2010 80p il map (It's my state) lib bdg $31.36
Grades: 3 4 5   **979.4**
   1. California
   ISBN 978-1-6087-0045-5; 1-6087-0045-3
                                    LC 2010003902

Surveys the history, geography, government, and economy of California as well as the diverse ways of life of its people.

Calabro, Marian
   ★ The **perilous** journey of the Donner Party. Clarion Bks. 1999 192p il maps $20
Grades: 5 6 7 8   **979.4**
   1. Donner party 2. Overland journeys to the Pacific 3. Frontier and pioneer life -- West (U.S.)
   ISBN 0-395-86610-3
                                    LC 98-29610

Uses materials from letters and diaries written by survivors of the Donner Party to relate the experiences of that ill-fated group as they endured horrific circumstances on their way to California in 1846-47
   "Calabro's offering is a fine addition to the Donner Party canon and particularly well suited to its young audience, for whom the story of hardship and survival will be nothing short of riveting. . . . From the haunting cover with its lonely campfire to the recounting of a survivors' reunion, this is a page-turner." Booklist
   Includes bibliographical references

Doak, Robin S.
   California, 1542-1850; by Robin Doak; Andres Resendez, consultant. National Geographic Society 2006 109p map il (Voices from colonial America) $21.95; lib bdg $32.90
Grades: 5 6 7 8   **979.4**
   1. California -- History
   ISBN 978-0-7922-6391-3; 0-7922-6391-X; 978-0-7922-6861-1 lib bdg; 0-7922-6861-X lib bdg
                                    LC 2005-30920

"The text is not written in sound bites but in full paragraphs, making up chronological chapters. These are divided into topical sections, which are clearly marked by large headings. This lovely, calm layout is liberally sprinkled with primary source illustrations, including reproductions of period maps, pamphlets, paintings, and drawings. . . . An essential purchase for schools with a colonies research project . . . and for the public libraries that support their communities." Voice Youth Advocates

Includes bibliograhical references

Freedman, Russell, 1929-

★ Angel Island; gateway to Gold Mountain. Russell Freedman; Chinese poems translated by Evans Chan. Clarion Books 2013 96 p. (hardcover) $17.99

Grades: 4 5 6 7 8   979.4

1. Immigrants -- United States 2. Angel Island Immigration Station (San Francisco, Calif.) 3. Angel Island (Calif.) -- History 4. Asia -- Emigration and immigration -- History 5. Angel Island Immigration Station (Calif.) -- History 6. United States -- Emigration and immigration -- History 7. San Francisco Bay Area (Calif.) -- Emigration and immigration -- History

ISBN 0547903782; 9780547903781

LC 2012036532

This book is a "history of Angel Island and its legacy in the American immigration narrative. Detailed descriptions of the island, the actual building, the events that took place there, and the people who passed through its doors are sprinkled with the emotional poems, quotes, and other writings that were discovered covering the walls of the areas where the detainees were housed." (School Library Journal)

Includes bibliographical references

Krensky, Stephen

Lizzie Newton and the San Francisco earthquake; illustrated by Jeremy Tugeau. Millbrook Press 2010 48p il (History speaks: picture books plus reader's theater) lib bdg $27.93

Grades: 2 3 4   979.4

1. Earthquakes 2. Readers' theater 3. San Francisco (Calif.) -- History

ISBN 978-0-8225-9031-6 lib bdg; 0-8225-9031-X lib bdg

LC 2009049597

Ten-year-old Lizzie Newton, having helped take her grandmother to the hospital after the 1906 San Francisco earthquake, sets off on her own to find her parents. Includes a readers' theater script and performance tips.

This "title begins with a well-illustrated narrative and concludes with a tip sheet for performing Reader's Theater as well as a list of characters, a script, and a pronunciation guide. . . . [This book will] make history come alive in a unique and interesting way." Libr Media Connect

Includes bibliographical references

La Bella, Laura

California; past and present. Rosen Central 2010 48p il map (The United States: past and present) lib bdg $26.50; pa $11.50

Grades: 3 4 5 6   979.4

1. California

ISBN 978-1-4358-5290-7 lib bdg; 1-4358-5290-7 lib bdg; 978-1-4358-5578-6 pa; 1-4358-5578-7 pa

LC 2008-55151

Presents the history, geography, government, economy, and people of California, as well as general facts about the state.

Includes glossary and bibliographical references

Olson, Tod

★ How to get rich in the California Gold Rush; an adventurer's guide to the fabulous riches discovered in 1848 . . . illustrations by Scott Allred; afterword by Marc Aronson. National Geographic 2008 47p il map (How to get rich) $16.95; lib bdg $25.90

Grades: 4 5 6 7   979.4

1. Gold mines and mining 2. California -- Gold discoveries 3. Prospecting 4. Frontier and pioneer life -- California 5. California -- History 6. California -- Gold discoveries

ISBN 1-4263-0315-7; 1-4263-0316-5 lib bdg; 978-1-4263-0315-9; 978-1-4263-0316-6 lib bdg

LC 2008-19601

This is a personal account of the California Gold Rush from the point-of-view of the fictitious character Thomas Hartley. "Grades four to seven." (Bull Cent Child Books)

This "deftly blends story with history to not only give readers an understanding of a gold rush but also to provide a lighthearted and engaging entry point into frontier life. . . . Period lithographs are reproduced alongside original illustrations. . . . A ledger on each page tracks the young men's finances in a genuinely exciting way, adding a sly element of math to this well-conceived and compulsively appealing book." Booklist

Includes bibliographical references

Orr, Tamra

California; by Tamra B. Orr. Children's Press 2008 144p il map (America the beautiful, third series) lib bdg $38

Grades: 4 5 6 7   979.4

1. California

ISBN 978-0-531-18557-5; 0-531-18557-5

LC 2006-36021

Describes the history, geography, ecology, people, economy, cities, and sights of the state of California.

Includes glossary and bibliographical references

Rosenstock, Barb

The camping trip that changed America; Theodore Roosevelt, John Muir, and our national parks. by Barbara Rosenstock; illustrated by Mordicai Gerstein. Dial Books for Young Readers 2012 32 p. col. ill. (hardcover) $16.99

Grades: 1 2 3 4   979.4

1. Picture books for children 2. National parks and reserves -- United States 3. Yosemite National Park (Calif.) -- History 4. Environmentalism -- United States 5. National parks and reserves -- United States -- History

ISBN 0803737106; 9780803737105

LC 2011021927

This children's picture book, by Barb Rosenstock and illustrated by Mordicai Gerstein, "captures the majestic redwoods of Yosemite in this little-known but important story from our nation's history. In 1903, President Theodore Roosevelt joined naturalist John Muir on a trip to Yosemite. Camping by themselves in the uncharted woods, the two men saw sights and held discussions that would ultimately lead to the establishment of our National Parks." (Publisher's note)

"Brimming with fun and fact, this book recounts a 1903 camping trip in which Roosevelt asked Muir to convince him that conservation mattered. Soon after the trip, Roosevelt enacted legislation that marked the nascency of America's national park system. Ink and watercolor illustrations, with a studied messiness, match the folksy tone of the text. " SLJ

Includes bibliographical references.

Ryan, Pam Munoz

Our California; by Pam Munoz Ryan; illustrated by Rafael Lopez. Charlesbridge 2008 un il $17.95; pa $7.95

Grades: PreK K 1 2   **979.4**

1. California

ISBN 978-1-58089-116-5; 978-1-58089-117-2 pa

"A whirlwind loop tour whisks readers through the Golden State, starting with the beaches of San Diego, heading up to L.A. and beyond to Gold Country, then swinging down through Yosemite (depicted in a stunning nighttime vertical spread) and Death Valley before ending up poolside at Palm Springs. . . . López's illustrations, paintings rendered on wood and sometimes distressed, remain fresh and surprising as he finds ways to express wonder and affection. . . . This title is virtually certain to inspire California dreamin' in readers of all ages." Publ Wkly

Walker, Paul Robert

Gold rush and riches. Kingfisher 2011 32p il map (All about America)

Grades: 3 4 5 6   **979.4**

1. California -- History 2. California -- Gold discoveries 3. Frontier and pioneer life -- California

ISBN 0-7534-6512-4 pa; 0-7534-6584-1; 978-0-7534-6512-7 pa; 978-0-7534-6584-4

This book looks at California and its neighboring states starting in 1848, with the discovery of gold and other precious metals.

This "visually appealing [title] effectively [combines] paintings, engravings, primary documents, and photographs with cartoon illustrations. The eye-catching [layout includes] different font sizes, bold type, and text boxes to highlight different pieces of information. The content is interesting and pithy." SLJ

Includes glossary and bibliographical references

Yep, Laurence, 1948-

The lost garden; Laurence Yep. 1st Beech Tree ed. Beech Tree Books 1996 xi, 116 p.p ill. (paperback) $6.99

Grades: 5 6 7 8   **979.4**

1. Authors 2. Novelists 3. College teachers 4. Authors, American 5. Children's authors 6. Young adult authors 7. Chinese Americans -- Biography

ISBN 9780688137014 reprint; 0688137016

LC 95053801

First published 1991 by Julian Messner

The author describes how he grew up as a Chinese American in San Francisco and how he came to use his writing to celebrate his family and his ethnic heritage

"The writing is warm, wry, and humorous. . . . The Lost Garden will be welcomed as a literary autobiography for children and, more, a thoughtful probing into what it means to be an American." SLJ

Zuehlke, Jeffrey

The Golden Gate Bridge. Lerner Publications 2010 32p il map (Lightning bolt books. Famous places) lib bdg $25.26

Grades: 2 3 4   **979.4**

1. Golden Gate Bridge (San Francisco, Calif.)

ISBN 978-0-8225-9407-9; 0-8225-9407-2

LC 2008-30641

Describes the Golden Gate Bridge that connects Marin County to the city of San Francisco, including information about its history, design, and construction.

This book uses "high-quality photos, illustrations, maps, and diagrams. . . . Readers will enjoy learning about [the Golden Gate Bridge] . . . and the challenges of building and maintaining large structures." SLJ

Includes glossary and bibliographical references

979.5   Oregon

Kent, Deborah

Oregon. Children's Press 2008 144p il map (America the beautiful, third series) lib bdg $39

Grades: 4 5 6 7   **979.5**

1. Oregon

ISBN 978-0-531-18587-2; 0-531-18587-7

LC 2007038691

Presents an introduction to the geography, natural resources, history, economy, important sites, daily life, and people of Oregon.

Includes glossary and bibliographical references

Roza, Greg

Oregon; past and present. Rosen Central 2010 48p il map (The United States: past and present) lib bdg $26.50; pa $11.75

Grades: 3 4 5 6   **979.5**

1. Oregon

ISBN 978-1-4358-3515-3 lib bdg; 1-4358-3515-8 lib bdg; 978-1-4358-8480-9 pa; 1-4358-8480-9 pa

LC 2009016193

Presents the history, geography, government, economy, and people of Oregon, as well as general facts about the state.

Includes bibliographical references

979.6   Idaho

Kent, Deborah

Idaho. Children's Press 2010 144p il map (America the beautiful, third series) lib bdg $39

Grades: 4 5 6 7   **979.6**

1. Idaho

ISBN 978-0-531-18598-8; 0-531-18598-2

LC 2008005647

Takes readers on a tour of Idaho, describing the state's history, culture, land, economy, government, and sights, and including unique facts, color maps and photos, the state song, suggested activities, lists of famous people, cultural institutions, and annual events, and other resources.

Includes glossary and bibliographical references

Stanley, John

Idaho; past and present. Rosen Central 2011 48p il map (The United States: past and present) lib bdg $26.50; pa $11.75

Grades: 3 4 5 6 **979.6**

1. Idaho

ISBN 978-1-4358-9480-8 lib bdg; 1-4358-9480-4 lib bdg; 978-1-4358-9507-2 pa; 1-4358-9507-X pa

LC 2009049391

Presents the history, geography, government, economy, and people of Idaho, as well as general facts about the state.

Includes glossary and bibliographical references

Stefoff, Rebecca

Idaho; by Rebecca Stefoff. 2nd ed.; Marshall Cavendish Benchmark 2008 144p il map (Celebrate the states) lib bdg $39.93

Grades: 4 5 6 7 **979.6**

1. Idaho

ISBN 978-0-7614-3003-2; 0-7614-3003-2

LC 2007-29496

First published 2000

"Provides comprehensive information on the geography, history, wildlife, governmental structure, economy, cultural diversity, peoples, religion, and landmarks of Idaho." Publisher's note

Includes bibliographical references

979.7 Washington

Harmon, Dan

Washington; past and present. [by] Daniel E. Harmon. Rosen Central 2010 48p il map (The United States: past and present) lib bdg $26.50; pa $11.50

Grades: 3 4 5 6 **979.7**

1. Washington (State)

ISBN 978-1-4358-5295-2 lib bdg; 1-4358-5295-8 lib bdg; 978-1-4358-5588-5 pa; 1-4358-5588-4 pa

LC 2008-54236

Presents the history, geography, government, economy, and people of Washington, as well as general facts about the state.

Includes glossary and bibliographical references

Jankowski, Susan

Olympic National Park; adventure, explore, discover. [by] Susan Jankowski. MyReportLinks.com Books 2009 128p il map (America's national parks) lib bdg $33.27

Grades: 5 6 7 8 **979.7**

1. Olympic National Park (Wash.) 2. National parks and reserves -- United States

ISBN 978-1-59845-092-7 lib bdg; 1-59845-092-1 lib bdg

LC 2007-17341

This "informative, well-written book contains a physical description of the park; a summary of its history including the Native peoples of the area; activities such as hiking trails, campsites, and visitor centers; information about the park's plants, animals, and weather; full-color photographs; and numerous approved links available through the publish-

er's Web page. . . . Thorough, useful, and appealing, this . . . is a great update for collections." SLJ

Includes glossary and bibliographical references

Otfinoski, Steven

Washington; [by] Steven Otfinoski and Tea Benduhn. 2nd ed.; Marshall Cavendish Benchmark 2010 90p il map (It's my state!) lib bdg $31.93

Grades: 3 4 5 **979.7**

1. Washington (State)

ISBN 978-1-6087-0061-5; 1-6087-0061-5

LC 2010003935

First published 2003

Surveys the history, geography, economy, and people of the state of Washington.

Stefoff, Rebecca

Washington; [by] Rebecca Stefoff. 2nd ed.; Marshall Cavendish Benchmark 2008 144p il map (Celebrate the states) lib bdg $39.93

Grades: 4 5 6 7 **979.7**

1. Washington (State)

ISBN 978-0-7614-2561-8; 0-7614-2561-6

LC 2006-32436

First published 1999

"Provides comprehensive information on the geography, history, wildlife, governmental structure, economy, cultural diversity, peoples, religion, and landmarks of Washington." Publisher's note

Includes bibliographical references

979.8 Alaska

Mattern, Joanne

Alaska; past and present. Rosen Central 2011 48p il map (The United States: past and present) lib bdg $26.50; pa $11.75

Grades: 3 4 5 6 **979.8**

1. Alaska

ISBN 978-1-4358-9475-4 lib bdg; 1-4358-9475-8 lib bdg; 978-1-4358-9503-4 pa; 1-4358-9503-7 pa

LC 2009046615

This describes the history, culture, geography and people of Alaska.

Includes bibliographical references

Miller, Debbie S.

Big Alaska; journey across America's most amazing state. illustrations by Jon Van Zyle. Walker 2006 un il map $17.95; lib bdg $18.85

Grades: 2 3 4 **979.8**

1. Alaska

ISBN 978-0-8027-8069-0; 0-8027-8069-5; 978-0-8027-8070-6 lib bdg; 0-8027-8070-9 lib bdg

LC 2005-24086

"Miller's text follows a bald eagle's flight across Alaska, beginning with Admiralty Island and circling back to the Chilkat Bald Eagle Preserve. . . . Zyle's acrylic paintings perfectly suit the grandeur of the subject. . . . Back matter includes Alaska Facts, State Symbols, Climate Records, and Alaska's Special Places, which has additional information on the locations described in the text. . . . The book . . . is a special treasure both for readers already interested in the subject and newcomers." SLJ

Includes bibliographical references

Orr, Tamra

Alaska; by Tamra B. Orr. Children's Press 2008 144p il map (America the beautiful, third series) lib bdg $38

Grades: 4 5 6 7   **979.8**

1. Alaska

ISBN 978-0-531-18569-8; 0-531-18569-9

LC 2007-22220

Describes the history, geography, ecology, people, economy, cities, and sights of the state of Alaska.

Includes glossary and bibliographical references

980   History of South America

Foster, Karen

Atlas of South America. Picture Window books 2008 32p il map (Picture Window Books world atlases) lib bdg $27.93

Grades: 2 3 4   **980**

1. South America

ISBN 978-1-4048-3887-1 lib bdg; 1-4048-3887-2 lib bdg

This introduction to the geography of South America offers maps and information about countries, landforms, bodies of water, climate, plants, animals, population, people and customs, places of interest, industries, transportation, and Lake Titicaca.

Includes glossary

Gorrell, Gena K.

★ In the land of the jaguar; South America and its people. illustrated by Andrej Krystoforski. Tundra Books 2007 149p il $22.95

Grades: 5 6 7 8 9   **980**

1. South America

ISBN 978-0-88776-756-2

"This beautifully designed volume, with an engaging narrative, combines a highly informative overview of the continent with country-by-country detail. . . . The spacious design includes big maps, clear type on thick paper, and small, beautiful, fully captioned illustrations." Booklist

981   Brazil

Berkenkamp, Lauri

Discover the Amazon; the world's largest rainforest. illustrated by Blair Shedd. Nomad Press 2008 90p il map pa $16.95

Grades: 4 5 6 7   **981**

1. Amazon River valley

ISBN 978-1-9346702-7-9 pa; 1-9346702-7-8 pa

"Berkenkamp's introduction to the [Amazon] river basin incorporates maps, drawings, and photos in various shades of green and brown on recycled paper. . . . The conversational style provides a 'you are there' feeling, conveying information and anecdotes while stressing outdoor survival skills. . . . Even readers who never travel to Amazonia will

appreciate the region's complexity and significance after perusing this book." SLJ

Deckker, Zilah

★ Brazil; [by] Zilah Deckker; David Robinson and Joao Cezar de Castro Rocha, consultants. National Geographic 2008 64p il (Countries of the world) lib bdg $27.90

Grades: 4 5 6 7   **981**

1. Brazil

ISBN 978-1-4263-0298-5 lib bdg; 1-4263-0298-3 lib bdg

This describes the geography, nature, history, people and culture, government, and economy of Brazil.

Includes glossary and bibliographical references

Heinrichs, Ann

★ Brazil; by Ann Heinrichs. Children's Press, an imprint of Scholastic Inc. 2013 144 p. illustrations, color maps (library binding) $40

Grades: 5 6 7 8   **981**

1. Brazil

ISBN 0531236757; 9780531236758

LC 2013000089

This book, by Ann Heinrichs, focuses on Brazil. The "country's culture, history, and geography are explored in detail, allowing readers a chance to see how people live. . . . Sidebars highlight especially interesting people, places, and events . . . [and] recipes give readers the opportunity to experience foreign cuisine first-hand." (Publisher's note)

"Many students turn to the Internet for writing reports, but for reliably accurate, attractively presented and well-calibrated information, the long-standing Enchantment of the World series remains a superior choice...Each volume in this reliable series includes extensive back matter with a detailed index." Booklist

Includes bibliographical references (page 134), filmography (page 134), and index.

982   Argentina

Lourie, Peter

Tierra del Fuego; a journey to the end of the earth. Boyds Mills Press 2002 47p il map $19.95

Grades: 4 5 6 7   **982**

1. Tierra del Fuego (Argentina and Chile)

ISBN 1-56397-973-X

LC 2001-96395

The author describes his travels in Tierra del Fuego and provides historical background on the area

"Lourie's smooth, first-person narrative mixes history, adventure, and personal insights, while glorious photographs of the remarkable land at the southernmost point of the world enhance his travelogue. . . . Highly informative for reports, this fascinating account will also appeal to young readers with wanderlust." SLJ

983   Chile

Rau, Dana Meachen

Chile. Marshall Cavendish Benchmark 2007 48p il map (Discovering cultures) lib bdg $28.50

Grades: 2 3 4   **983**

1. Chile

ISBN 978-0-7614-1988-4 lib bdg; 0-7614-1988-8 lib bdg

An introduction to the geography, history, people, and culture of Chile

Includes glossary and bibliographical references

984   Bolivia

Pateman, Robert

Bolivia; [by] Robert Pateman & Marcus Cramer. 2nd ed.; Marshall Cavendish Benchmark 2006 144p il map (Cultures of the world) lib bdg $42.79

Grades: 5 6 7 8   **984**

1. Bolivia

ISBN 978-0-7614-2066-8 lib bdg; 0-7614-2066-5 lib bdg

LC 2006002425

First published 1995

This is "well organized, informative, and entertaining. . . . Excellent-quality full-color photographs and reproductions show the people, landforms, buildings, and everyday activities." SLJ

Includes bibliographical references

985   Peru

Calvert, Patricia

★ The **ancient** Inca; written by Patricia Calvert. Franklin Watts 2004 128p il (People of the ancient world) lib bdg $30.50; pa $9.95

Grades: 5 6 7 8   **985**

1. Incas

ISBN 0-531-12358-8 lib bdg; 0-531-16740-2 pa

LC 2004-1956

This "well-written, attractive [title has] extensive collections of quality color photographs of ruins and artifacts." SLJ

Includes bibliographical references

Gruber, Beth

★ **Ancient** Inca; archaeology unlocks the secrets of the Inca's past. by Beth Gruber; Johan Reinhard, consultant. National Geographic 2007 64p il map (National Geographic investigates) $17.95; lib bdg $27.90

Grades: 5 6 7 8   **985**

1. Incas 2. Peru -- Antiquities 3. Excavations (Archeology) -- Peru

ISBN 978-0-7922-7827-6; 978-0-7922-7873-3 lib bdg

LC 2006032104

This describes how archeologists have found out about ancient Incan civilization.

This offers "the beautiful photography and illustrations characteristic of the National Geographic Society, [a] well-

written [text] and sidebars, and information on recent archaeological finds." SLJ

Includes bibliographical references

Krebs, Laurie

Up and down the Andes; a Peruvian festival tale. [by] Laurie Krebs, Aurelia Fronty. Barefoot Books 2008 un il $16.99

Grades: K 1 2 3   **985**

1. Inti Raymi Festival 2. Andes 3. Festivals -- Peru 4. Native Americans -- Peru 5. Peru -- Social life and customs

ISBN 978-1-84686-203-8; 1-84686-203-5

LC 2008020722

This is a "picture book about the Peruvian Inti Raymi Festival as children travel from all over southern Peru, by bus, train, boat, mule, and truck, to the city of Cusco to celebrate with feasting and fun in their traditional costumes. The simply rhyming text and the bright, clear, beautiful unframed acrylic paintings express a strong sense of the rich traditions that are still part of contemporary life." Booklist

Lewin, Ted

★ **Lost** city; the discovery of Machu Picchu. Philomel Bks. 2003 un il $16.99

Grades: 2 3 4   **985**

1. Machu Picchu (Peru)

ISBN 0-399-23302-4

LC 2002-4461

In 1911, Yale professor Hiram Bingham discovers a lost Incan city with the help of a young Peruvian boy

"The language is graceful and uncomplicated, weaving in bits of background history along the way. . . . Full-page watercolors spreads of the stunning vistas and thick forests contrast with dark, intimate views of Bingham inside homes and walking along walled city streets. . . . An exciting, eye-catching story." Booklist

Newman, Sandra

The **Inca** empire. Children's Press 2009 48p il map (True book) lib bdg $26; pa $6.95

Grades: 3 4 5   **985**

1. Incas

ISBN 978-0-531-25228-4 lib bdg; 0-531-25228-0 lib bdg; 978-0-531-24109-7 pa; 0-531-24109-2 pa

LC 2009000293

In this book the Inca civilization is "outlined for young readers with care and precision. . . . Loaded with access points such as captions, pull-outs, a time line, and a map, and with better-than-usual reproductions of well-chosen primary sources and art, the [book sports] a bright, peppy design. . . . [This book is] rigorous in distinguishing fact from theory, and conscientious about presenting competing theories where they exist." SLJ

986.1   Colombia

Croy, Anita

★ **Colombia**; [by] Anita Croy; Ulrich Oslender and Mauricio Pardo, consultants. National Geographic 2008 64p il map (Countries of the world) lib bdg $27.90

Grades: 4 5 6 7 **986.1**
1. Colombia
ISBN 978-1-4263-0257-2 lib bdg; 1-4263-0257-6
lib bdg
This describes the geography, nature, history, people and
culture, government, and economy of Colombia
Includes glossary and bibliographical references

De Capua, Sarah
Colombia. Benchmark Bks. 2004 48p il maps (Dis-
covering cultures) lib bdg $28.50
Grades: 2 3 4 **986.1**
1. Colombia
ISBN 0-7614-1715-X

LC 2003-8128
Highlights the geography, people, food, schools, recre-
ation, celebrations, and language of Colombia
Includes glossary and bibliographical references

Yomtov, Nel
★ Colombia; by Nel Yomtov. Children's Press, an
imprint of Scholastic Inc. 2014 144 p. illustrations, color
maps (library binding) $40
Grades: 5 6 7 8 **986.1**
1. Colombia
ISBN 0531220133; 9780531220139

LC 2013026060
This book, by Nel Yomtov, focuses on Colombia. The
"country's culture, history, and geography are explored in
detail, allowing readers a chance to see how people live in
faraway nations. . . . Sidebars highlight especially interesting
people, places, and events . . . [and] easy recipes give readers the opportunity to experience foreign cuisine first-hand."
(Publisher's note)
Includes bibliographical references and index

986.6 Ecuador

Foley, Erin
Ecuador; [by] Erin L. Foley & Leslie Jermyn. 2nd ed.;
Marshall Cavendish Benchmark 2006 144p il map (Cul-
tures of the world) lib bdg $42.79
Grades: 5 6 7 8 **986.6**
1. Ecuador
ISBN 0-7614-2050-9

LC 2005022671
First published 1995
This briefly describes Ecuador's "history, government,
economy, and geography. . . . Particularly useful is the information on religion, the arts, food, leisure activities, and
social roles. The [book has] great visual appeal with excellent full-color photographs on every page. [It] is especially
successful in explaining social and economic hierarchies
within the country." SLJ
Includes glossary and bibliographical references

Henzel, Cynthia Kennedy
Galapagos Islands. ABDO Pub. Co. 2011 32p il
(Troubled treasures: world heritage sites) $25.65

Grades: 3 4 5 **986.6**
1. Galapagos Islands
ISBN 978-1-61613-563-8; 1-61613-563-8

LC 2010021311
This "book describes in general terms [the Galapagos
Islands'] . . . creation, distinctive features, and history, as
well as threats to its continued existence and both current
and past restoration initiatives. Revealing color photos taken
from different heights and angles are supplemented by maps
and by graphic reconstructions. . . . Henzel's distinctive approach gives this [book] unusual value for both assignment
and general reading." SLJ
Includes glossary

Kras, Sara Louise
The Galapagos Islands; [by] Sara Louise Kras. Marshall Cavendish Benchmark 2008 96p il map (Nature's
wonders) lib bdg $35.64
Grades: 5 6 7 8 **986.6**
1. Galapagos Islands
ISBN 978-0-7614-2856-5 lib bdg; 0-7614-2856-9
lib bdg

LC 2007020416
"Provides comprehensive information on the geography,
history, wildlife, peoples, and environmental issues of the
Galapagos Islands." Publisher's note
Includes glossary and bibliographical references

988.1 Guyana

Jermyn, Leslie
Guyana; by Leslie Jermyn and Winnie Wong. Marshall
Cavendish Benchmark 2010 144 p. col. ill., col. maps (li-
brary) $47.07
Grades: 5 6 7 8 **988.1**
1. Guyana
ISBN 1608700232; 9781608700233

LC 2010000724
This book by Leslie Jermyn is part of the Cultures of
the World series and looks at the South American nation of
Guyana. "Touching upon everything from its history to religion to architecture, this book . . . highlights the country's
rich diversity and unique qualities. With a population that
includes many different ethnic groups, the author . . . examines the contributions of each to Guyana's development and
to its present culture." (Children's Literature)
Includes bibliographical references (p.142) and index.

989.2 Paraguay

Jermyn, Leslie
Paraguay; [by] Leslie Jermyn and Yong Jui Lin. 2nd
ed.; Marshall Cavendish Benchmark 2010 144p il map
(Cultures of the world) lib bdg $42.79
Grades: 5 6 7 8 **989.2**
1. Paraguay
ISBN 978-0-7614-4858-7 lib bdg; 0-7614-4858-6
lib bdg

LC 2009046495
First published 2000

This offers information on the geography, history, wildlife, governmental structure, economy, cultural diversity, peoples, religion, and culture of Paraguay

Includes glossary and bibliographical references

989.5   Uruguay

Jermyn, Leslie

Uruguay; by Leslie Jermyn and Winnie Wong. 2nd ed.; Marshall Cavendish Benchmark 2009 144p il map (Cultures of the world) lib bdg $42.79

Grades: 5 6 7 8   **989.5**

1. Uruguay

ISBN 978-0-7614-4482-4 lib bdg; 0-7614-4482-3 lib bdg

LC 2009007127

First published 1999

Provides information on the geography, history, wildlife, governmental structure, economy, cultural diversity, peoples, religion, and culture of Uruguay

Includes glossary and bibliographical references

993   New Zealand

Jackson, Barbara

★ New Zealand; [by] Barbara Jackson; Vaughan Wood and Simon Milne, consultants. National Geographic 2008 64p il map (Countries of the world) lib bdg $27.90

Grades: 4 5 6 7   **993**

1. New Zealand

ISBN 978-1-4263-0301-2 lib bdg; 1-4263-0301-7 lib bdg

This describes the geography, nature, history, people and culture, government, and economy of New Zealand.

Smelt, Roselynn

New Zealand; by Roselynn Smelt. 2nd ed.; Marshall Cavendish Benchmark 2009 128p il map (Cultures of the world) lib bdg $42.79

Grades: 5 6 7 8   **993**

1. New Zealand

ISBN 978-0-7614-3415-3 lib bdg; 0-7614-3415-1 lib bdg

LC 2008028792

First published 1998

"Provides comprehensive information on the geography, history, wildlife, governmental structure, economy, cultural diversity, peoples, religion, and culture of New Zealand." Publisher's note

Includes glossary and bibliographical references

994   Australia

Arnold, Caroline

★ Uluru, Australia's Aboriginal heart; photographs by Arthur Arnold. Clarion Books 2003 64p il $16

Grades: 5 6 7 8   **994**

1. Aboriginal Australians 2. Australia 3. Uluru-Kata

Tjuta National Park (Australia)

ISBN 0-618-18181-4

LC 2002-15542

Describes Uluru, formerly known as Ayers Rock, in Australia's Uluru-Kata Tjuta National Park, its plant and animal life, and the country's Aboriginal people for whom the site is sacred

"The book's greatest accomplishment . . . is to give readers a sense of the ongoing spiritual importance of Uluru to the Anangu, who have lived around it for 10,000 years. Clear, colorful photos of Uluru and its surroundings appear on nearly every page, illustrating the text with beauty and finesse." Booklist

Foster, Karen

Atlas of Australia. Picture Window Books 2008 32p il map (Picture Window Books world atlases) lib bdg $27.93

Grades: 2 3 4   **994**

1. Australia

ISBN 978-1-4048-3881-9 lib bdg; 1-4048-3881-3 lib bdg

This introduction to the geography of Australia offers maps and information about landforms, bodies of water, climate, plants, animals, population, people and customs, places of interest, industries, transportation, and the Great Barrier Reef.

This book offers "well-organized, easy-to-access information. . . . Small photographs or colorful text boxes draw readers' attention to points of interest or fun facts. Maps and legends are simple, yet disseminate information clearly." SLJ

Includes glossary

Rau, Dana Meachen

Australia. Sea-to-Sea Publications 2009 32p il map (Facts about countries) lib bdg $28.50

Grades: 3 4 5   **994**

1. Australia

ISBN 978-1-59771-112-8 lib bdg; 1-59771-112-8 lib bdg

LC 2008004630

Describes the geography, history, industries, education, government, and cultures of Australia

"The attractive layout includes color photographs and charts of current statistics as well as maps illustrating main farming regions, natural resources, or the literacy rates of girls and boys. The [text is] clear and succinct." SLJ

Includes glossary

Turner, Kate

★ Australia; [by] Kate Turner; Elaine Stratford and Joseph Powell, consultants. National Geographic 2007 64p il map (Countries of the world) lib bdg $27.90

Grades: 4 5 6 7   **994**

1. Australia

ISBN 978-1-4263-0055-4

Describes the geography, nature, history, people and culture, government and economy of Australia

This "appealing [title has] wonderful photographs and maps. . . . [This book is a] reliable [source] for country research, and the interesting current material hold browsing potential as well." SLJ

Includes glossary and bibliographical references

995.3 Papua New Guinea

Gascoigne, Ingrid

Papua New Guinea; [by] Ingrid Gascoigne. 2nd ed.; Marshall Cavendish Benchmark 2009 144p il map (Cultures of the world) lib bdg $42.79

Grades: 5 6 7 8 **995.3**

1. Papua New Guinea

ISBN 978-0-7614-3416-0 lib bdg; 0-7614-3416-X lib bdg

LC 2008028794

First published 1998

"Provides comprehensive information on the geography, history, wildlife, governmental structure, economy, cultural diversity, peoples, religion, and culture of Papua New Guinea." Publisher's note

Includes glossary and bibliographical references

996 Polynesia and other Pacific Ocean islands

NgCheong-Lum, Roseline, 1962-

Tahiti; [by] Roseline NgCheong-Lum. 2nd ed.; Marshall Cavendish Benchmark 2008 144p il map (Cultures of the world) lib bdg $42.79

Grades: 5 6 7 8 **996**

1. Tahiti (French Polynesia)

ISBN 978-0-7614-2089-7

LC 2007014901

"Provides comprehensive information on the geography, history, wildlife, governmental structure, economy, cultural diversity, peoples, religion, and culture of Tahiti." Publisher's note

Includes glossary and bibliographical references

996.9 Hawaii and neighboring north central Pacific Ocean islands

Feeney, Stephanie

Sun and rain; exploring seasons in Hawaii. University of Hawaii Press 2008 un il $13.95

Grades: K 1 2 3 **996.9**

1. Rain 2. Seasons 3. Sun 4. Hawaii

ISBN 978-0-8248-3088-5; 0-8248-3088-1

LC 2008272547

"Readers learn that Hawaii has only two seasons: wet and dry. Easy-to-read text and large, inviting photographs show the changing seasons and explain how humans, animals, and plants are affected. . . . Back matter includes additional information for adults." Horn Book Guide

Kent, Deborah

Hawaii; by Deborah Kent. Children's Press 2008 144p il map (America the beautiful, third series) lib bdg $38

Grades: 4 5 6 7 **996.9**

1. Hawaii

ISBN 978-0-531-18573-5; 0-531-18573-7

LC 2007-5705

Describes the history, geography, ecology, people, economy, cities, and sights of the state of Hawaii.

Includes glossary and bibliographical references

Mattern, Joanne

Hawaii; past and present. Rosen Central 2011 48p il map (The United States: past and present) lib bdg $26.50; pa $11.75

Grades: 3 4 5 6 **996.9**

1. Hawaii

ISBN 978-1-4358-9479-2 lib bdg; 1-4358-9479-0 lib bdg; 978-1-4358-9506-5 pa; 1-4358-9506-1 pa

LC 2009050544

Presents the history, geography, government, economy, and people of Hawaii, as well as general facts about the state.

Includes glossary and bibliographical references

998 Arctic islands and Antarctica

Bledsoe, Lucy Jane

★ **How** to survive in Antarctica; written and photographed by Lucy Jane Bledsoe. Holiday House 2006 101p il map $16.95

Grades: 5 6 7 8 **998**

1. Antarctica

ISBN 0-8234-1890-1

LC 2004-60639

"Bledsoe, who made three trips to study Antarctica, bases her informal, chatty narrative on her thrilling adventure, bringing close the amazing science and geography as well as the gritty facts of human survival in the frigid environment. . . . Bledsoe's own black-and-white photos . . . will grab students across the curriculum." Booklist

Includes glossary

Foster, Karen

Atlas of the Poles and Oceans. Picture Window Books 2008 32p il map (Picture Window Books world atlases) lib bdg $27.93

Grades: 2 3 4 **998**

1. Ocean 2. Antarctica 3. Arctic regions

ISBN 978-1-4048-3886-4 lib bdg; 1-4048-3886-4 lib bdg

This introduction to the geography of the Arctic, Antarctic, and the oceans offers maps and information about plants, animals, people, and protecting the environment.

Includes glossary

Goodman, Susan

★ **Life** on the ice; [by] Susan E. Goodman; with photographs by Michael J. Doolittle. Millbrook Press 2006 32p il lib bdg $22.60

Grades: 3 4 5 **998**

1. Arctic regions 2. Polar regions

ISBN 978-0-7613-2775-2 lib bdg; 0-7613-2775-4 lib bdg

LC 2005-06141

This book is "about the ice caps of both the North and South Poles. [Index.] Grades five to six." (Sci Books Films)

"This fully illustrated book introduces a few aspects of the Earth's polar regions. Topics presented include the difficulties of flying to and landing at the poles, scientific research done at each pole, and the challenge of human survival in the extreme cold." Booklist

Lourie, Peter

Arctic thaw; the people of the whale in a changing climate. Boyds Mills Press 2007 47p il map $17.95
Grades: 5 6 7 8 **998**
1. Inupiat 2. Whaling 3. Human ecology 4. Alaska 5. Greenhouse effect
ISBN 978-1-59078-436-5; 1-59078-436-7
LC 2006-20045

"A somewhat sobering, yet upbeat examination of the probable effects of global warming on the culture of the Iñupiaq whale hunters of Alaska's North Slope..... [Lourie's] lively, straightforward text describes the mixture of traditional and modern ways of the present-day Iñupiaq, as well as the work of [Paul] Shepson and his team to record weather and climate changes and to predict what effect they will have locally and globally." SLJ

Includes bibliographical references

Markle, Sandra

Animals Robert Scott saw; an adventure in Antarctica. Chronicle Books 2008 45p il (Explorers) $16.99
Grades: 2 3 4 5 **998**
1. Explorers 2. Animals -- Antarctica 3. Antarctica -- Exploration
ISBN 978-0-8118-4918-0; 0-8118-4918-X
LC 2006-20920

"Well illustrated with acrylic paintings and archival photos, this volume . . . traces the two Antarctic expeditions of English explorer Robert Falcon Scott, who reached the South Pole with his companions in 1912, 35 days after Amundsen's Norwegian expedition. The story may be Scott's, but the focus continually turns to animals. . . . Children fascinated by both explorers and animals are the natural audience for this." Booklist

Includes glossary and bibliographical references

Thompson, Gare

Roald Amundsen and Robert Scott race to the South Pole; by Gare Thompson. National Geographic 2007 48p il (National Geographic history chapters) lib bdg $17.90
Grades: 2 3 4 **998**
1. Explorers 2. South Pole 3. Antarctica -- Exploration
ISBN 978-1-4263-0187-2
LC 2007007898

This "presents the dramatic, tragic story of the South Pole's dueling explorers. . . . Crisp, informatively captioned photographs, some presumably taken by the doomed men, lend immediacy to the facts." Booklist

Wade, Rosalyn

Polar worlds. Simon & Schuster Books for Young Readers 2011 64p il (Insiders) $16.99
Grades: 4 5 6 7 **998**
1. Antarctica 2. Arctic regions
ISBN 978-1-4424-3275-8; 1-4424-3275-6

This "takes a look at the nether regions of the globe in this browser-friendly resource. . . . 'Introducing' opens with a geographic look at the Arctic and Antarctic regions, then moves on to the related topics of icebergs, plant and animal life, exploration, survival measures, and environmental threats. The 'In Focus' section zeroes in on 12 specific animals found in polar regions. . . . Each spread is dominated by a sharply rendered, often dramatic digital illustration. . . . A fine introduction to the world's deep freezers." Booklist

E EASY BOOKS

Ackerman, Karen

Song and dance man; illustrated by Stephen Gammell. Knopf 1988 un il lib bdg $17.99; pa $6.99
Grades: K 1 2 3 **E**
1. Entertainers -- Fiction 2. Grandfathers -- Fiction
ISBN 0-394-99330-6 lib bdg; 0-679-81995-9 pa
LC 87-3200

Awarded the Caldecott Medal, 1989

The illustrator "captures all the story's inherent joie de vivre with color pencil renderings that fairly leap off the pages." Booklist

Ada, Alma Flor, 1938-

I love Saturdays y domingos; by Alma Flor Ada; illustrated by Elivia. 1st ed; Atheneum Books for Young Readers 1998 32 p. $18.99
Grades: PreK K 1 2 **E**
1. Family life 2. Grandparent-grandchild relationship 3. Grandparents -- Fiction 4. Mexican Americans -- Fiction
ISBN 0689318197; 9780689318191
LC 94003362

Americas Award for Children's and Young Adult Literature. Commended

In this children's book by Alama Flor Ada and illustrated by Elivia Salvadier, "Saturdays and Sundays are very special days for the child in this story. On Saturdays, she visits Grandma and Grandpa, who come from a European-American background, and on Sundays -- los domingos -- she visits Abuelito y Abuelita, who are Mexican-American. This affirmation of both heritages [is designed to] speak to all children who want to know more about their own families and ethnic backgrounds." (Publisher's note)

"A little girl visits her Grandpa and Grandma, her father's parents, on Saturdays and her "abuelito y abuelita," her mother's parents, on "los domingos." Dearly cherished by both sets of grandparents, the little girl delights in the unique differences of the two households and moves with ease between the two cultures...Together, Ada and Savadier have created a picture book that gracefully embraces and celebrates a young child's involvement in her dual heritages. Especially recommended for libraries serving Latino and multicultural communities." Booklist

With love, Little Red Hen; illustrated by Leslie Tryon. Atheneum Books for Young Readers 2001 40 p. col il $17.99
Grades: PreK K 1 2 3 **E**
1. Chickens -- Fiction 2. Neighbors -- Fiction 3. Letters 4. Characters in literature
ISBN 0689825811; 9780689825811
LC 00042021

In this children's book by Alma Flor Ada and illustrated by Leslie Tryon "Hidden Forest has a new resident. Little Red Hen and her seven little chicks have moved into a cottage and plan to grow a bountiful crop of corn in the nearby field. The problem is that none of the Red Hen's neighbors are willing to help with the hard work. So Goldilocks . . . comes up with a neighborly idea: Why don't all the residents of Hidden Forest chip in and work on the garden? Why not make it a surprise?" (Publisher's note)

"In this third collection of letters back and forth between the storybook residents of Hidden Forest, the wolf bad guys are turning their attention to poultry. The format is the same as the first two books: each double-page spread comprises a personal letter and a lively pen-and-ink and watercolor illustration. In addition to being a creative letter-writing lesson, this book offers readers a chance to spend some time with old friends." Horn Book

Adams, Diane

I can do it myself! written by Diane Adams; illustrated by Nancy Hayashi. Peachtree Publishers 2009 un il $15.95
Grades: PreK K   E
1. Stories in rhyme 2. Bedtime -- Fiction
ISBN 978-1-56145-471-6; 1-56145-471-0
LC 2008031117

Emily Pearl is a big girl who insists on doing everything for herself until evening, when having someone help her get ready for bed is nice

"Hayashi's cheerful watercolors vary in size from spreads to small vignettes and help give the story just the right pace. . . . This tale is told in a fresh, yet familiar way." SLJ

Adams, Sarah

Dave & Violet. Frances Lincoln 2011 il $17.95
Grades: PreK K 1 2   E
1. Dragons -- Fiction 2. Friendship -- Fiction
ISBN 978-1-84780-052-7; 1-84780-052-1

"Violet's best friend Dave has a hard time fitting in. Not only is he a dragon, Dave is also shy. Violet, a little girl, takes him to the park to meet her friends, who have never seen a dragon before. They approach him amiably, but Dave gets very nervous. He turns bright orange, and a huge flame gushes from his mouth. . . . Adams' illustrations, like her story, are simple and direct; the lino prints have bold outlines and bright colors, and eggplant-shaped, mop-topped Dave has a goofy appeal. A fitting fable for the very young about friendship and diversity." Kirkus

Addasi, Maha

Time to pray; Arabic translation by Nuha Albitar; illustrated by Ned Gannon. Boyds Mills Press 2010 un il $17.95
Grades: 1 2 3 4   E
1. Islam -- Fiction 2. Prayer -- Fiction 3. Muslims -- Fiction 4. Grandmothers -- Fiction 5. Bilingual books -- English-Arabic
ISBN 978-1-59078-611-6; 1-59078-611-4
LC 2010005090

When young Yasmin goes for a visit, her grandmother teaches her a Muslim's daily prayers, makes special prayer clothes, and gives a gift that will help Yasmin remember when to pray. Includes facts about prayer customs.

"This is a beautifully woven tale of grandparent affection and spiritual development. Gannon's illustrations present a warm and authentic balance of Islamic geometric designs and Arab architecture and culture. . . . Familiarizing Islamic prayer through realistic fiction makes this a fine choice for most collections." SLJ

The white nights of Ramadan; [by] Maha Addasi; illustrated by Ned Gannon. Boyds Mills Press 2008 un il $16.95

Grades: 1 2 3 4   E
1. Kuwait -- Fiction 2. Muslims -- Fiction 3. Ramadan -- Fiction
ISBN 978-1-59078-523-2; 1-59078-523-1
LC 2008002637

"This story is centered around Girgian, a Muslim celebration observed mostly in the Arabian Gulf states during the middle of the month of Ramadan. When Noor, who lives in Kuwait, sees the almost-full moon rise, she knows it's time to prepare for the festival. The family makes candy from honey, sugar, and nuts to share with the children in the neighborhood, wrapping it with cellophane and colorful bows. . . . Shimmering with moonlit hues, the attractive illustrations are done in a style that reflects one of many Muslim cultures. A helpful author's note and glossary are appended. An excellent choice for units on diversity and multiculturalism." SLJ

Adderson, Caroline

Jasper John Dooley; Left Behind. By Caroline Adderson, illustrated by Ben Clanton. Kids Can Press 2013 132 p. (Jasper John Dooley) (hardcover) $15.95
Grades: 1 2 3   E
1. Grandmothers -- Fiction 2. Grandparent-grandchild relationship -- Fiction
ISBN 1554535794; 9781554535798

In this book, "one of Jasper's favorite things to do is to spend Wednesdays with his Nan, riding the elevator up and down, playing Go Fish, and eating jujubes. When he learns that his grandmother is going on an Alaskan cruise for a week, he is worried that she might never come back. . . . It's a busy week while Nan is gone, though, as Jasper accidentally staples his stomach, attempts to build a cruise ship with a friend, and takes the class hamster home for the weekend." (School Library Journal)

Addy, Sharon

Lucky Jake; illustrated by Wade Zahares. Houghton Mifflin 2006 un il $17
Grades: PreK K 1 2   E
1. Pigs -- Fiction 2. Gold mines and mining -- Fiction
ISBN 0-618-47286-X; 978-0-618-47286-4
LC 2005-03917

While panning for gold with his Pa, Jake adopts a pig that he names Dog.

"Using pastels in deep and heavy hues, solid shapes, and unusual perspectives, he provides images that roll breathtakingly across the pages. . . . An intriguing mix of old-fashioned storytelling and cutting-edge art." Booklist

Adler, David A., 1947-

The Babe & I; written by David A. Adler; illustrated by Terry Widener. Harcourt Brace & Co. 1999 un il $17; pa $7
Grades: K 1 2 3   E
1. Baseball players 2. Great Depression, 1929-1939 -- Fiction
ISBN 0-15-201378-4; 0-15-205026-4 pa
LC 97-37580

While helping his family make ends meet during the Depression by selling newspapers, a boy meets Babe Ruth

"Widener's illustrations evoke the ambiance of the period in this book that is carefully paced and remarkable for its unified focus." Horn Book Guide

It's time to sleep, it's time to dream; illustrated by Kay Chorao. Holiday House 2009 un il $16.95
Grades: PreK K   E
    1. Bedtime -- Fiction 2. Seasons -- Fiction
    ISBN 978-0-8234-1924-1; 0-8234-1924-X
                                        LC 2008022570
A parent lulls a child to sleep with visions of soft spring breezes, lazy summer days, cool autumn winds, and moonlit winter nights

"Chorao's gouache-and-watercolor illustrations lend a new-fashioned slant to a bedtime book. . . . The softly infused color pictures pair well with the spare text. . . . Kids will be drawn to the comforting cover image of a cute tyke cuddling his toy bunny." Booklist

Millions, billions & trillions; understanding big numbers. by David A. Adler; illustrated by Edward Miller. 1st ed. Holiday House 2012 32 p. col. ill. (hardcover) $17.95
Grades: 2 3 4   E
    1. Counting 2. Picture books for children 3. Number concept 4. Billion (The number) 5. Million (The number) 6. Trillion (The number)
    ISBN 0823424030; 9780823424030
                                        LC 2011044752
In this book, David A. Adler and Edward Miller "put giant numbers into perspective by using familiar frames of reference and by appealing to readers' imaginations: 'How many ice cream sundaes would one billion dollars buy? At five dollars a sundae, you could buy one thousand sundaes every day for more than five hundred years.' Real-world examples (New York City has a population of over eight million people) combine with more fanciful ways to conceptualize these quantities.'" (Publishers Weekly)

Young Cam Jansen and the 100th day of school mystery; illustrated by Susanna Natti. Viking 2009 31p il (Viking easy-to-read) $13.99
Grades: K 1 2   E
    1. School stories 2. Mystery fiction
    ISBN 978-0-670-06172-3; 0-670-06172-7
To celebrate their 100th day of school, Cam and Eric's class party will have snacks that start with "P"-pretzels, popcorn, pineapple juice, and pizza. But when the pizza disappears from the kitchen, it's up to Cam and her photographic memory to solve this delicious mystery.

"Colorful, small-scale line-and-wash illustrations brighten the pages of this entertaining . . . book." Booklist

★ **Young** Cam Jansen and the dinosaur game; illustrated by Susanna Natti. Viking 1996 32p il (Viking easy-to-read) $13.99; pa $3.99
Grades: K 1 2 3   E
    1. Mystery fiction
    ISBN 0-670-86399-8; 0-14-037779-4 pa
                                        LC 95-46463
"At Jane's birthday party, everyone guesses the number of toy dinosaurs in a big jar. Jennifer 'the Camera' Jansen's photographic memory helps her nab Robert, who has cheated in order to win all the dinosaurs. Observant readers can

follow Cam's reasoning and solve the mystery, too." Horn Book Guide

Other easy-to-read titles about Cam Jansen are:
Young Cam Jansen and the 100th day of school mystery (2009)
Young Cam Jansen and the baseball mystery (1999)
Young Cam Jansen and the double beach mystery (2002)
Young Cam Jansen and the ice skate mystery (1998)
Young Cam Jansen and the library mystery (2001)
Young Cam Jansen and the lions' lunch mystery (2007)
Young Cam Jansen and the lost tooth (1997)
Young Cam Jansen and the Molly shoe mystery (2008)
Young Cam Jansen and the missing cookie (1996)
Young Cam Jansen and the new girl mystery (2004)
Young Cam Jansen and the pizza shop mystery (2000)
Young Cam Jansen and the speedy car mystery (2010)
Young Cam Jansen and the substitute mystery (2005)
Young Cam Jansen and the zoo note mystery (2003)

Adler, Victoria
    ★ **All** of baby, nose to toes; pictures by Hiroe Nakata. Dial Books for Young Readers 2009 un il $14.99
Grades: PreK   E
    1. Stories in rhyme 2. Infants -- Fiction
    ISBN 978-0-8037-3217-9; 0-8037-3217-1
                                        LC 2008-30971
Rhyming text celebrates everything about a beloved baby, from eyes to toes

"Adler's sunny poem and Nakata's ebullient watercolors demonstrate not only a baby's exploratory joy but also the palpable delight a baby brings to a family." Publ Wkly

Baby, come away; pictures by David Walker. Farrar Straus Giroux 2011 un il $16.99
Grades: PreK K 1   E
    1. Stories in rhyme 2. Animals -- Fiction 3. Infants -- Fiction
    ISBN 978-0-374-30480-5; 0-374-30480-7
                                        LC 2010036234
A bird, a cat, a dog, and a fish each imagines an ideal day spent with a baby.

"This offering is destined to become a cherished favorite. [It has] utterly charming paintings. . . . Full of rhyme, alliteration, and playful wording, the text lends itself to group reading or one-on-one sharing equally well." SLJ

Adoff, Arnold
    ★ **Black** is brown is tan; pictures by Emily Arnold McCully. HarperCollins Pubs. 2002 un il $17.99; pa $6.99
Grades: PreK K 1 2   E
    1. Family life -- Fiction 2. Racially mixed people -- Fiction
    ISBN 0-06-028776-4; 0-06-443644-6 pa
                                        LC 00-44864
A newly illustrated edition of the title first published 1973
Describes in verse a family with a brown-skinned mother, white-skinned father, two children, and their various relatives

"Children everywhere will love the simple, joyful rhythmic words in Adoff's signature 'shaped speech' style, with McCully's beautiful dancing watercolors." Booklist

Agee, Jon

★ **Little** Santa; Jon Agee. Dial Books for Young Readers, an imprint of Penguin Group (USA) Inc. 2013 40 p. (hardcover) $17.99

Grades: PreK K 1   E

1. Picture books for children 2. Santa Claus -- Fiction
ISBN 0803739060; 9780803739062

LC 2012031855

In this children's picture book, "Little Santa is the youngest child of a hardworking family eking out a hardscrabble existence at the North Pole. The whole family, except for Santa, hates their hard life, and they decide they will relocate to Florida. When a major blizzard buries everyone inside, brave Santa takes his snowshoes and a sack of food and goes up the chimney to seek help." He finds flying reindeer and magic elves, and soon the reader understands Santa's origins. (Kirkus Reviews)

Milo's hat trick; story and pictures by Jon Agee. Hyperion Bks. for Children 2001 un il $15.95

Grades: PreK K 1 2   E

1. Bears -- Fiction 2. Magicians -- Fiction
ISBN 0-7868-0902-7

In the busy city, there are lots of people with hats. But there is only one guy with a bear in his hat. That's Milo The Magician

"Agee's bold, angular pencil-and-paint illustrations drive this warm story about perseverance, luck, and courage." Booklist

Mr. Putney's quacking dog. Michael Di Capua Books 2010 un il $16.95

Grades: PreK K 1   E

1. Puns -- Fiction
ISBN 978-0-545-16203-6; 0-545-16203-3

"Clue-packed pictures add to the fun. Agee fills out the spreads with thick-lined, soft-colored, comedic pictures. A great choice for fans of punnery." SLJ

My rhinoceros. Scholastic 2011 un il $16.95

Grades: PreK K 1   E

1. Pets -- Fiction 2. Rhinoceros -- Fiction
ISBN 978-0-545-29441-6; 0-545-29441-X

"Adopting a rhinoceros, in and of itself, would be absurd enough for most storytellers. For Agee, . . , it is simply the first in a series of weird narrative curveballs. . . . When two bank robbers attempt a getaway, using a hot-air balloon and a hang-glider, does the rhinoceros prove its mettle, springing into superheroic action and demonstrating a third, even more surprising ability. Agee's deadpan voice and blocky, India-ink-and-watercolor pictures play into the inherent oddity of the story." Publ Wkly

Nothing. Hyperion Books for Children 2007 un il $16.99

Grades: K 1 2 3   E

ISBN 978-0-7868-3694-9; 0-7868-3694-6

LC 2007-25191

When Suzie Gump, the richest lady in town, walks into Otis's empty antique shop and insists on buying nothing, she starts a fad that has everyone buying nothing and emptying their homes and stores to make room for it—until Suzie realizes things have gone too far.

"In illustrations that possess a timeless air, Agee contrasts cluttered, patterned spaces with airy rooms, outlines chunky, geometric areas with firm charcoal lines and tints broad surfaces with transparent watercolor wash. . . . This timely parable is certainly something worth having." Publ Wkly

The **retired** kid. Hyperion Books for Children 2008 un il $16.99

Grades: K 1 2 3   E

1. Florida -- Fiction 2. Old age -- Fiction 3. Retirement -- Fiction
ISBN 978-1-4231-0314-1; 1-4231-0314-9

LC 2007-41998

Although he enjoys some aspects of his retirement, eight-year-old Brian gains a new perspective on his job of being a child after spending time in Florida's Happy Sunset Retirement Community

"Agee's gentle story about juvenile job dissatisfaction is filled with witty verbal and visual flourishes . . . that will have kids—and their grandparents—chuckling from start to finish." Booklist

★ **Terrific;** story and pictures by Jon Agee. Hyperion Books for Children 2005 un il $15.95

Grades: PreK K 1 2   E

1. Parrots -- Fiction 2. Shipwrecks -- Fiction
ISBN 0-7868-5184-8

LC 2004-117133

"Terrific," says Eugene when he wins an all-expenses-paid cruise to Bermuda. "I'll probably get a really nasty sunburn." But Eugene's luck is much worse than that. His ship sinks, and he ends up stranded on a tiny island. "Preschool." (Publisher's note)

"With pithy humor and a knack for comic timing, Agee has created a character who will endear himself to readers despite his curmudgeonly exterior and posturing. . . . The cartoon illustrations feature strong lines and soft colors that contrast wonderfully with the story line." SLJ

★ **Why** did the chicken cross the road? [by] Jon Agee . . . [et al.] Dial Books for Young Readers 2006 un il $16.99

Grades: 1 2 3 4   E

1. Chickens -- Fiction
ISBN 0-8037-3094-2

LC 2005-16196

"What is perhaps the world's most tired joke becomes fresh and inspired in this lively collection of work by well-known contemporary children's book artists. On each double-page spread, a different contributor offers a new, illustrated punch line to the title question. . . . Lots of fun for young children, this collection, which demonstrates the impressive artistic range and talent featured in today's picture books, will also attract older art students and children's book enthusiasts." Booklist

Ahlberg, Allan, 1938-

★ The **baby** in the hat; written by Allan Ahlberg; illustrations by Andre Amstutz. Candlewick Press 2008 un il $16.99

Grades: K 1 2   E

1. Seafaring life -- Fiction 2. Great Britain -- History

-- 19th century -- Fiction
ISBN 978-0-7636-3958-7; 0-7636-3958-3
LC 2007-52029

Catching a baby in his hat sets off a series of adventures for a young nineteenth-century English boy as he becomes a sea captain and finds a surprising mate.

"Ahlberg and Amstutz . . . overlook few opportunities for humor in this tall tale. . . . Witty, detailed gouaches dotted with dialogue balloons lend a theatricality to the picaresque tale." Publ Wkly

Hooray for bread; Allan Ahlberg, illustrated by Bruce Ingman. Candlewick Press 2013 32 p. ill. (reinforced) $15.99
Grades: PreK K 1   E
1. Bread -- Fiction
ISBN 0763663115; 9780763663117
LC 2012942661

In this children's story, by Allan Ahlberg, illustrated by Bruce Ingman, "early in the morning the baker bakes a delicious loaf of bread. So delicious, in fact, that by the time the sun goes down it has been gobbled up! Who eats it all? . . . The baker's wife eats some toast for breakfast, and the baker's son gets a cheese and ham sandwich for lunch. And let's not forget the dog! As the loaf gets smaller, slice by slice and crumb by crumb, everyone eats their fill." (Publisher's note)

★ The **pencil**; [illustrated by] Bruce Ingman. Candlewick Press 2008 un il $16.99
Grades: PreK K 1 2   E
1. Drawing -- Fiction
ISBN 978-0-7636-3894-8; 0-7636-3894-3
LC 2007-51885

A lonely pencil timidly draws a boy, a dog, and other items but soon faces a problem as his creations begin demanding changes, and when he draws an eraser to make them happy, the real trouble begins.

"Both clever and suspenseful, this surefire delight tells the story of a pencil who must deal with the consequences of his inventions. . . . The book's comical, unexpected plot and wry narrator keep the story fresh throughout." Publ Wkly

Previously; [by] Allan Ahlberg; [illustrated by] Bruce Ingman. Candlewick Press 2007 un il $16.99
Grades: PreK K 1 2   E
1. Fairy tales
ISBN 978-0-7636-3542-8; 0-7636-3542-1
LC 2006-51831

The adventures of various nursery rhyme and fairy tale characters are retold in backward sequence with each tale interrelated to the other. Includes Goldilocks, Jack and the beanstalk, Jack and Jill, the frog prince, Cinderella, and the gingerbread man.

"The jazzy, colorful pictures display substantive variety. . . . Children will delight in this energetic, amusing, and very approachable tale." SLJ

The **runaway** dinner; [by] Allan Ahlberg and [illustrated by] Bruce Ingman. Candlewick Press 2006 un il $15.99; pa $6.99

Grades: PreK K 1 2   E
1. Dining -- Fiction
ISBN 978-0-7636-3142-0; 0-7636-3142-6; 978-0-7636-3893-1 pa; 0-7636-3893-5 pa
LC 2005058126

A young boy named Banjo Cannon always eats a sausage for dinner, until the night that his sausage—and the rest of his meal—runs away

"With a plot timed faster than fast food and illustrations that keep pace, this picture book about a dinner that literally runs away is a comic treat." Publ Wkly

The **shopping** expedition; illustrated by André Amstutz. Candlewick Press 2005 un il $16.99
Grades: PreK K 1   E
1. Shopping -- Fiction 2. Imagination -- Fiction
ISBN 0-7636-2586-8
LC 2003-69674

A routine shopping trip becomes a grand adventure in the eyes of a little girl

"Amstutz's richly colored illustrations have a painterly look, often with visible brush strokes, that really suits the imaginative subject matter. The repetitive phrase keeps the pace of the story going and works well for reading aloud." SLJ

Ahlberg, Janet

The **jolly** postman; or other people's letters. [by] Janet and Allan Ahlberg. Little, Brown Books for Young Readers 2001 un il $17.99
Grades: PreK K 1 2   E
1. Fairy tales 2. Stories in rhyme 3. Letters -- Fiction 4. Postal service -- Fiction
ISBN 978-0-316-12644-1; 0-316-12644-6
A reissue of the title first published 1986

A Jolly Postman delivers letters to several famous fairy-tale characters such as the Big Bad Wolf, Cinderella, and the Three Bears. Each letter may be removed from its envelope page and read separately.

"The story of the postman's travels is told in charming verse; the pictures are delightful, full of clever detail; and the results are frequently hilarious." Publ Wkly

Aigner-Clark, Julie

You are the best medicine; [by] Julie Aigner Clark; illustrated by Jana Christy. Balzer + Bray 2010 un il $16.99
Grades: PreK K 1 2   E
1. Sick -- Fiction 2. Cancer -- Fiction 3. Mother-child relationship -- Fiction
ISBN 978-0-06-195644-7; 0-06-195644-9

A mother who has cancer gently informs her child of what the effects will be, and reminds her little one of all the special times they have shared, and will continue to share, even while she undergoes treatment.

"Here's a much-needed book, and one that's done with lots of love. . . . Soft-edge illustrations, tender in feel and comforting in color, add sweetness." Booklist

Ain, Beth

★ **Starring** Jules (as herself) Beth Ain; illustrated by Anne Keenan Higgins. Scholastic Press 2013 160 p. (hardcover) $14.99
Grades: 2 3 4 5   E
1. Acting 2. Acting -- Fiction 3. Schools -- Fiction

4. Auditions -- Fiction 5. Friendship -- Fiction 6. Elementary schools -- Fiction
ISBN 0545443520; 9780545443524

LC 2012017678

This children's story, by Beth Ain, is the first book in the "Starring Jules" series. "Seven-year-old Jules has been asked to audition for a television commercial. But she needs help. . . . But Jules is in the middle of a mean fight with her former best friend, Charlotte. . . . But with the opportunity of a lifetime four days away, Jules doesn't have the time to stay angry with Charlotte." (Kirkus Reviews)

Ainsworth, Kimberly

Hootenanny! a festive counting book. illustrated by Jo Brown. Little Simon 2011 un il $12.99
Grades: PreK K   E
1. Counting 2. Owls -- Fiction 3. Parties -- Fiction
ISBN 978-1-4424-2273-5; 1-4424-2273-4; 978-1-4424-3490-5 e-book; 1-4424-3490-2 e-book

LC 2011006557

"Five owls help youngsters learn to count from one to five as they get ready for a party at the top of an old oak tree. . . . The text is printed in a large, easy-to-read font with each numeral highlighted in a different color. The bright spreads feature a rainbow of colors, smiling characters, and some humorous details. With its jazzy vocabulary and cheerful illustrations, the book lives up to its title." SLJ

Akbarpour, Ahmad

Good night, Commander; pictures by Morteza Zahedi; translated by Shadi Eskandani and Helen Mixter. Groundwood Books 2010 un il $17.95
Grades: 3 4 5   E
1. Iran-Iraq War, 1980-1988 -- Fiction 2. Physically disabled children -- Fiction
ISBN 978-0-88899-989-4; 0-88899-989-5

"This picture book with difficult concepts could possibly be used with younger students who need a fiction bridge to their own reality. This is a brief and powerful story about the impact of war on the youngest inhabitants of the country." Libr Media Connect

Alalou, Ali

The **butter** man; [by] Elizabeth Alalou and Ali Alalou; illustrated by Julie Klear Essakalli. Charlesbridge 2008 un il lib bdg $14.95
Grades: K 1 2 3   E
1. Morocco -- Fiction
ISBN 978-1-58089-127-1 lib bdg; 1-58089-127-6 lib bdg

LC 2007-02278

While Nora waits for the couscous her father is cooking to be finished, he tells her a story about his youth in the High Atlas Mountains of Morocco. "Ages seven to ten." (Bull Cent Child Books)

The authors "write in descriptive language that speaks directly to children. . . . The folk-art paintings, created by a textile designer, feature whimsical characters and cozy domestic scenes, while the ochre, gold, and rust palette evokes the feeling of the dusty, sunlit landscape." Booklist

Alborough, Jez

★ **Duck** in the truck. HarperCollins Pubs. 2000 un il hardcover o.p. pa $7.95; bd bk $8.99

Grades: PreK K 1   E
1. Stories in rhyme 2. Ducks -- Fiction 3. Animals -- Fiction
ISBN 0-06-028685-7; 1-933605-76-6 pa; 978-1-929132-83-6 bd bk; 1-929132-83-2 bd bk

LC 99-60934

"A rhyming text relates the troubles of a duck whose truck gets stuck in the muck. . . . The art makes the most of the story's physical comedy, with exaggerated humor and an engaging animal cast, including a frog, a sheep, and a goat who all come to help out." Horn Book Guide
Other titles about Duck are:
Captain Duck (2003)
Duck's key, where can it be (2005)
Fix-it Duck (2002)
Hit the ball Duck (2006)
Super Duck (2009)

Some dogs do. Candlewick Press 2003 un il $15.99
Grades: PreK K 1 2   E
1. Stories in rhyme 2. Dogs -- Fiction
ISBN 0-7636-2201-X

LC 2002-41760

When Sid tries to convince his doggy classmates that he flew to school, they do not believe him.
"Done in gouache, the illustrations glow with bright colors. . . . A wonderful addition to any library and a great choice for storytime." SLJ

Tall. Candlewick Press 2005 un il $15.99
Grades: PreK K 1 2   E
1. Size -- Fiction 2. Chimpanzees -- Fiction
ISBN 0-7634-2784-4

LC 2004-062941

Illustrations and just a few words depict how various jungle animals help Bobo the chimp to feel that he is tall.
"Bobo embodies an impressive range of identifiable emotions. Alborough's adept pen-and-gouache illustrations make each feeling and point of view crystal clear. . . . A must-have title for any children who have ever felt less than enchanted with their diminutive status." SLJ
Other titles about Bobo the chimp are:
Hug (2000)
Yes (2006)

Where's my teddy? Candlewick Press 1992 un il hardcover o.p. pa $6.99
Grades: PreK K   E
1. Stories in rhyme 2. Bears -- Fiction 3. Teddy bears -- Fiction
ISBN 1-5640-2048-7; 1-5640-2280-3 pa

When a small boy named Eddie goes searching for his lost teddy in the dark woods, he comes across a gigantic bear with a similar problem.
"Alborough's verse adroitly employs kid-pleasing rhythms and repetitions, while his watercolor, crayon and pencil drawings underscore the broad comedy of this perfectly satisfying scenario of scary fun." Publ Wkly

Alda, Arlene

Did you say pears? Tundra Books 2006 31p il $16.95
Grades: K 1 2 3   E
1. English language -- Homonyms
ISBN 0-88776-739-7

"A marvelously imaginative pairing (sorry) of homonyms (words that sound alike but have different meanings and the same spelling) and homophones (words that sound alike but have different meanings and different spellings), wrapped up in a rhyme of amazingly few words and terrific offbeat photographs." Booklist

Hello, good-bye. Tundra Books 2009 un il $16.95
Grades: PreK K   **E**
   1. Opposites
   ISBN 978-0-88776-900-9; 0-88776-900-4

"Exceptionally fine color photographs bring clarity as well as beauty to this book of opposites. Alda . . . creates images that are striking in themselves and meaningful when paired with their opposites. . . . This offers plenty of opportunities for interaction between young children and those reading to them." Booklist

Alderson, Brian
   Thumbelina; [by] Hans Christian Andersen; retold by Brian Alderson; illustrated by Bagram Ibatoulline. Candlewick Press 2009 un il $17.99
Grades: 1 2 3 4   **E**
   1. Fairy tales
   ISBN 978-0-7636-2079-0; 0-7636-2079-3
              LC 2008-27721

A tiny girl no bigger than a thumb is stolen by a great ugly toad and subsequently has many adventures and makes many animal friends, before finding the perfect mate in a warm and beautiful southern land.

"This retelling of Andersen's classic tale remains close to the original. . . . Alderson retells these adventures and misadventures with a wry wit, moving the plot quickly through each scene. . . . Ibatoulline's illustrations are lavishly composed in watercolor and gouache." Bull Cent Child Books

Alexander, Claire
   ★ **Lucy** and the bully; by Claire Alexander. Albert Whitman & Co. 2008 un il $16.99
Grades: PreK K 1 2   **E**
   1. School stories 2. Animals -- Fiction 3. Bullies -- Fiction
   ISBN 978-0-8075-4786-1; 0-8075-4786-7
              LC 2008001340

When a mean classmate in preschool wrecks Lucy's artwork, she discovers that they can be friends once he stops being jealous of her.

"Alexander's child-friendly watercolors beautifully convey a range of emotions. An excellent note to parents and teachers discusses bullying and ways to combat it." Booklist

Alexander, Kwame
   Acoustic Rooster and his barnyard band; written by Kwame Alexander; illustrated by Tim Bowers. Sleeping Bear Press 2011 il $15.95
Grades: K 1 2 3   **E**
   1. Stories in rhyme 2. Contests -- Fiction 3. Musicians -- Fiction 4. Jazz music -- Fiction 5. Domestic animals -- Fiction
   ISBN 978-1-58536-688-0; 1-58536-688-9
              LC 2010053709

Acoustic Rooster forms a jazz band with Duck Ellington, Bee Holliday, and Pepe Ernesto Cruz to compete in the annual Barnyard Talent Show against such greats as Thelonius

Steer, Mules Davis, and Ella Finchgerald. Includes glossary, notes on the characters and songs, and jazz timeline.

This is a "delightful picture book. . . . The large illustrations are done in bold colors and have humorous, jazzy details." SLJ

Alexander, Lloyd
   The **fortune-**tellers; illustrated by Trina Schart Hyman. Dutton Children's Bks. 1992 un il hardcover o.p. pa $6.99
Grades: K 1 2 3   **E**
   1. Cameroon -- Fiction 2. Fortune telling -- Fiction
   ISBN 0-525-44849-7; 0-14-056233-8 pa
              LC 91-30684

A carpenter goes to a fortune teller and finds the predictions about his future coming true in an unusual way

"Alexander's rags-to-riches story combines universal elements of the trickster character and the cumulative disaster tale. Hyman's pictures set it all in a vibrant community in Cameroon, West Africa. . . . The energetic, brilliantly colored paintings are packed with people and objects that swirl around the main characters. . . . With its ups and downs, this is a funny, playful story that evokes the irony of the human condition." Booklist

Alexander, Martha G.
   Max and the dumb flower picture; [by] Martha Alexander with James Rumford. Charlesbridge 2009 un il $9.95
Grades: PreK K 1 2   **E**
   1. School stories 2. Artists -- Fiction 3. Mother's Day -- Fiction
   ISBN 978-1-58089-156-1; 1-58089-156-X
              LC 2008007251

Despite his teacher's entreaties that it would be perfect for Mother's Day, Max refuses to color in the same flower picture as the rest of the class

"Before her death in 2006, Alexander . . . left her manuscript and sketches in the hands of James Rumford. . . . The tender result honors both Alexander and the children for whom she wrote for 40 years. . . . The soft sketches are color washed digitally and by hand, and with Rumford's collaboration, still bear Alexander's simple, expressive style." Publ Wkly

Aliki
   All by myself! written and illustrated by Aliki. HarperCollins Pubs. 2000 un il $14.95; lib bdg $14.89; pa $6.99
Grades: K 1 2 3   **E**
   1. Self-reliance -- Fiction
   ISBN 0-06-028929-5; 0-06-028930-9 lib bdg; 0-06-446253-2 pa
              LC 99-51672

A child shows all the things he has learned to do all on his own

"Aliki's colorful illustrations closely match the moods and energy levels of a five- or six-year-old. . . . The text has a hand-printed appearance, large and easy to read. . . . A good choice for story-hours and beginning readers." SLJ

   ★ **Painted** words: Marianthe's story one. Greenwillow Bks. 1998 un il $16.99; lib bdg $17.89

Grades: K 1 2 3   **E**
> 1. School stories 2. Immigrants -- Fiction
> ISBN 0-688-15661-4; 0-688-15662-2 lib bdg
>
> LC 97-34653

Two separate stories, the first telling of Mari's starting school in a new land, and the second describing village life in her country before she and her family left in search of a better life

"In simple, understated language, Aliki has captured the emotions and experiences of many of today's children. Colored-pencil and crayon illustrations in soft primary and secondary colors reinforce the mood of the text." SLJ

★ A **play's** the thing; written and illustrated by Aliki. HarperCollins 2005 32p il $16.99; lib bdg $17.89
Grades: K 1 2 3   **E**
> 1. School stories 2. Theater -- Fiction
> ISBN 0-06-074355-7; 0-06-074356-5 lib bdg
>
> LC 2004-22101

When Miss Brilliant's class puts on a performance of "Mary had a little lamb," all the children are eager to participate except for the uncooperative José—until Miss Brilliant assigns him the role of teacher. "Primary." (Horn Book)

"When Miss Brilliant's class decides to put on a fractured version of [Mary Had a Little Lamb], José must learn to work with his classmates and overcome his antisocial tendencies. . . . This is . . . the type of work that children will be drawn to again and again because they recognize their world so aptly captured in both word and art. Each time they revisit, they will find something new in the colorful cartoon illustrations." SLJ

★ **Push** button. Greenwillow Books 2010 un il $16.99; lib bdg $17.89
Grades: PreK   **E**
> 1. Stories in rhyme 2. Play -- Fiction
> ISBN 978-0-06-167308-5; 0-06-167308-0; 978-0-06-167309-2 lib bdg; 0-06-167309-9 lib bdg
>
> LC 2008047690

A little boy who loves pushing buttons of all kinds ends up with such a sore finger that he must play with other things.

"Against the clean white backgrounds, Aliki's familiar style of mixing pencils, watercolors, ink, and markers give the tousle-headed protagonist a vivid, crayon-colored expressiveness. . . . Rhyming text and sound effects add wry touches." Booklist

Quiet in the garden; written and illustrated by Aliki. Greenwillow Books 2009 un il lib bdg $18.89
Grades: PreK K   **E**
> 1. Animals -- Fiction 2. Gardens -- Fiction
> ISBN 978-0-06-155207-6; 0-06-155207-0; 978-0-06-155208-3 lib bdg; 0-06-155208-9 lib bdg
>
> LC 2008-12641

Sitting quietly in his garden, a little boy observes the eating habits of birds, bugs, butterflies, and other small animals. Includes instructions on how to make your own garden and a detailed illustration of plants typically found in a garden.

"With spare words and a balance of line and color against white backgrounds framed with lacey branches, Aliki deftly portrays the benefits of observing nature." SLJ

The **two** of them; written and illustrated by Aliki. Greenwillow Bks. 1979 un il hardcover o.p. pa $6.99
Grades: PreK K 1 2   **E**
> 1. Death -- Fiction 2. Grandfathers -- Fiction
> ISBN 0-688-07337-9 pa
>
> LC 79-10161

Describes the relationship of a grandfather and his granddaughter from her birth to his death

"The eloquent illustrations in muted full color and the smaller soft-pencil drawings show the life the two shared as well as the tenderness and pure pleasure implicit in their relationship." Horn Book

We are best friends. Greenwillow Bks. 1982 un il hardcover o.p. $16.99; pa $5.99
Grades: PreK K 1 2   **E**
> 1. Friendship -- Fiction
> ISBN 0-688-00822-4; 0-688-07037-X pa
>
> LC 81-6549

When Robert's best friend Peter moves away, both are unhappy, but they learn that they can make new friends and still remain best friends

"Brightly lit pictures in cheerful primary colors portray with just a stroke of the pen the misery of losing a friend who must move away and the tentative beginnings of a new companionship. . . . Details of school and home abound in the lively pictures." Horn Book

Alko, Selina

Every-day dress-up. Alfred A. Knopf 2011 un il $16.99; lib bdg $19.99
Grades: PreK K 1   **E**
> 1. Week -- Fiction 2. Women -- Fiction 3. Costume -- Fiction 4. Imagination -- Fiction
> ISBN 978-0-375-86092-8; 0-375-86092-4; 978-0-375-96092-5 lib bdg; 0-375-96092-9 lib bdg
>
> LC 2010001604

A young girl imagines her own future as she puts on costumes and pretends to be great women from history, including Amelia Earhart, Lucille Ball, and Eleanor Roosevelt.

All the great women "are introduced in a fun way with minimal text. Humorous, detailed gouache and collage illustrations will hold children's attention and spark their imagination." SLJ

Allard, Harry

★ **Miss** Nelson is missing! [by] Harry Allard, James Marshall. Houghton Mifflin 1977 32p il $16; pa $5.95
Grades: PreK K 1 2   **E**
> 1. School stories 2. Teachers -- Fiction
> ISBN 0-395-25296-2; 0-395-40146-1 pa
>
> LC 76-55918

"Humor and suspense fill the pages of [this book]." Christ Sci Monit

Other titles about Miss Nelson are:
Miss Nelson has a field day (1985)
Miss Nelson is back (1982)

Allegra, Mike

Sarah gives thanks; how Thanksgiving became a national holiday. by Mike Allegra; illustrated by David Gardner. Albert Whitman & Co. 2012 32 p. col. ill.

Grades: 2 3 4 E

1. Thanksgiving Day -- History

ISBN 080757239X; 9780807572399

LC 2011034161

This book by Mike Allegra, illustrated by David Gardner, tells the story of Sarah Josepha Hale, who "dedicated her life to making Thanksgiving a national holiday, all while raising a family and becoming a groundbreaking writer and women's magazine editor . . . [d]uring the nineteenth century. . . . Sarah Hale's . . . story, accompanied by . . . watercolor illustrations, tells the tale of one woman who wouldn't take no for an answer." (Publisher's note)

Allen, Debbie

Dancing in the wings; pictures by Kadir Nelson. Dial Bks. for Young Readers 2000 un il $16.99; pa $6.99

Grades: PreK K 1 2 E

1. Ballet -- Fiction 2. African Americans -- Fiction

ISBN 0-8037-2501-9; 0-14-250141-7 pa

LC 99-462181

Sassy tries out for a summer dance festival in Washington, D.C., despite the other girls' taunts that she is much too tall

"Allen's dialogue is realistic, and Nelson's illustrations of the predominantly African-American cast ably capture Sassy's love of dance and her lively personality." Horn Book Guide

Allen, Elanna

★ **Itsy** Mitsy runs away. Atheneum Books for Young Readers 2011 un il $16.99

Grades: PreK K 1 2 E

1. Runaway children -- Fiction 2. Father-daughter relationship -- Fiction

ISBN 978-1-4424-0671-1; 1-4424-0671-2

LC 2010004418

When Mitsy decides to run away, her father helps her pack.

"Mitsy may be itsy, but she has no shortage of energy or determination. She's also a sartorial standout, wearing lime green, dinosaur-style footie/hoodie pajamas and bright orange goggles. . . . Allen . . . has a breezy drawing style and a cheery disdain for logic reminiscent of 1950s-era cartoons. . . . Yet the freewheeling art stays anchored by Allen's very funny text, which combines rhythmic, cumulative passages with Mitsy's irreverent, precocious voice." Publ Wkly

Allen, Jonathan

I'm not Santa! Hyperion Books for Children 2008 un il $14.99

Grades: PreK K E

1. Owls -- Fiction 2. Rabbits -- Fiction 3. Christmas -- Fiction 4. Santa Claus -- Fiction

ISBN 978-1-4231-1300-3; 1-4231-1300-4

When Baby Hare mistakes Baby Owl for Santa Claus, it takes a visit from St. Nick himself to straighten things out.

"With almost no background illustration, the two cartoon-style characters face off from opposite pages, their growing frustration evident in their body language. . . . This will . . . have appeal for children at the stage where Christmas is all about Santa sightings." Booklist

I'm not scared! Hyperion Books for Children 2007 un il $14.99

Grades: PreK K E

1. Fear -- Fiction 2. Owls -- Fiction 3. Animals -- Fiction

ISBN 978-0-7868-3722-9

When Baby Owl takes his stuffed Owly out for a walk in the moonlit woods, he insists that he is not afraid of the other animals that keep popping up and making them jump.

"The cartoon illustrations are painted in dusky hues with black outlines, and the glossy quality of the light-infused colors makes the art look like animation cels. . . . The expressive visuals, brief text, and protagonist's believably childlike behavior are just right for young audiences." SLJ

The **little** rabbit who liked to say moo. Boxer Books 2008 un il $14.95

Grades: PreK K 1 E

1. Sound -- Fiction 2. Animals -- Fiction 3. Rabbits -- Fiction

ISBN 978-1-905417-78-0; 1-905417-78-0

"Little Rabbit likes to say 'moo,' because rabbits don't have a big noise. The little creature also likes to say 'baa,' 'oink,' 'heehaw,' and 'quack,' and gets the other young farm animals to join the refrain until a surprise ending reveals the bunny's favorite sound. The illustrations are large, uncluttered, simple, and bold, made of black lines and computer air-brushed color. . . . With its large print and natural repetition, this cumulative tale will be useful for building early literacy skills." SLJ

Alsdurf, Phyllis

★ **It's** milking time; by Phyllis Alsdurf; illustrations by Steve Johnson & Lou Fancher. Random House 2012 40 p. col. ill. (hardcover) $16.99

Grades: K 1 2 3 E

1. Milk -- Fiction 2. Farms -- Fiction 3. Milk supply -- Fiction 4. Cows -- Fiction 5. Milking -- Fiction 6. Farm life -- Fiction 7. Fathers and daughters -- Fiction

ISBN 0375869115; 9780375869112; 9780375899935; 9780375969119

LC 2010047772

In this children's book by Phyllis Alsdurf, illustrated by Steve Johnson and Lou Fancher, "a little girl and her father begin the evening milking. They work side by side, fanning out beds of straw, bringing in the cows, and hooking up the milkers. . . . The fresh dairy product isn't just for them--other families will buy their milk, butter, and cheese at stores and farmers' markets near and far, connecting the little girl's farm to the world beyond." (Publisher's note)

Alter, Anna

Abigail spells. Alfred A. Knopf 2009 un il $16.99; lib bdg $19.99

Grades: K 1 2 E

1. Friendship -- Fiction 2. Spelling bees -- Fiction

ISBN 978-0-375-85617-4; 0-375-85617-X; 978-0-375-95617-1 lib bdg; 0-375-95617-4 lib bdg

LC 2008024529

George helps his best friend Abigail practice for the city spelling bee, then cheers her up when she makes a mistake.

"Alter's folk-style acrylics done in warm, muted shades beautifully complement this steady-paced, conversational story." SLJ

A **photo** for Greta. Alfred A. Knopf 2011 un il $16.99; lib bdg $19.99

Grades: PreK K 1   **E**

    1. Rabbits -- Fiction 2. Photographers -- Fiction 3. Father-daughter relationship -- Fiction

    ISBN 978-0-375-85618-1; 0-375-85618-8; 978-0-375-95618-8 lib bdg; 0-375-95618-2 lib bdg

                                  LC 2010036001

"Greta, a young rabbit, loves her father, a photographer who 'travels all around the world taking pictures of very important people.' Admiring the framed pictures he's taken . . . she wishes to be famous and photo-ready herself. . . . Alter displays notable sensitivity to children's insecurities and doubts, while providing reassurance of their worth. Her acrylics have a comforting sturdiness, and readers who similarly take pride in their parents' professions, even as they miss them in their absence, will relate both to Greta's role-playing when her father is away and their tender time together when he comes home." Publ Wkly

Altes, Marta

My grandpa; by Marta Altes. Abrams Books for Young Readers 2013 32 p. ill. (reinforced) $15.95

Grades: PreK K 1   **E**

    1. Picture books for children 2. Senile dementia -- Fiction 3. Bears -- Fiction 4. Old age -- Fiction 5. Grandfathers -- Fiction

    ISBN 1419705881; 9781419705885

                                  LC 2012015616

This children's picture book is "narrated by a young bear whose grandfather is exhibiting signs of advanced age and dementia. The simple text uses single sentences that vacillate between the joy of the pair's loving bond and the young bear's honest look at Grandpa's decline." (School Library Journal)

Alvarez, Julia

A **gift** of gracias; the legend of Altagracia. written by Julia Alvarez; illustrated by Beatriz Vidal. Knopf 2005 un il $15.95; lib bdg $17.99

Grades: K 1 2 3   **E**

    1. Saints -- Fiction 2. Oranges -- Fiction 3. Dominican Republic -- Fiction

    ISBN 0-375-82425-1; 0-375-92425-6 lib bdg

Maria's family is almost forced to leave their farm on the new island colony, until a mysterious lady appears in Maria's dream

"Rich in cultural authenticity and brimming with the magical realism that is characteristic of Hispanic literature, this elegantly woven tale introduces the legend of Our Lady of Altagracia, the patron saint of the Dominican Republic. . . . With an exquisite use of watercolor and gouache, Vidal has painted colorful, yet warm illustrations that add depth to the story." SLJ

Amado, Elisa

Tricycle; [by] Elisa Amado; [illustrated by] Alfonso Ruano. Groundwood Books/House of Anansi Press 2007 un il $17.95

Grades: 1 2 3 4   **E**

    1. Theft -- Fiction 2. Friendship -- Fiction 3. Social classes -- Fiction 4. Truthfulness and falsehood -- Fiction

    ISBN 978-0-88899-614-5; 0-88899-614-4

"This book tells of rich and poor from the viewpoint of young Margarita, who climbs a tree on her rich family's estate and sees the shacks on the other side of the hedge, where her friend Rosario lives. Margarita watches as Rosario and her brother take her tricycle, but she doesn't say anything about it, even when her mother's lunch guests spew prejudice. . . . The text is spare, and the richly colored acrylic art . . . is just on the edge of magical realism. Although there is no overt message, there is much to talk about." Booklist

What are you doing? pictures by Manuel Monroy. Groundwood Books/House of Anansi Press 2011 un il $16.95

Grades: PreK K 1 2   **E**

    1. Books and reading -- Fiction 2. Books and reading

    ISBN 978-1-55498-070-3; 1-55498-070-4

"Everywhere Chepito goes in his little village, there are people reading. He questions the readers on their motives . . . and receives a variety of responses. . . . When he starts school, he's drawn to the classroom's big shelf of books. . . . He takes one home to share with his sister, who then asks him why he wants to read to her. . . . Monroy's digitally enhanced colored pencil and watercolor illustrations offer simple renderings of Chepito's conversations around town. . . . This is a thoughtful offering for soon-to-be literates that just may get them thinking about the power of reading." Bull Cent Child Books

Amato, Mary

The **chicken** of the family; illustrated by Delphine Durand. G.P. Putnam's Sons 2007 un il $16.99

Grades: PreK K 1 2   **E**

    1. Sisters -- Fiction 2. Chickens -- Fiction

    ISBN 0-399-24196-5; 978-0-399-24196-3

                                  LC 2006-03606

When her older sisters tease her into believing that she is actually a chicken, Henrietta runs off to a farm to be among her own kind.

The "storytelling is set off brilliantly by Durand's . . . off-kilter, kid-like cartooning. Packed with funny details and small plots . . . the art, like the story, delivers grade-AA comedy." Publ Wkly

Ander

Me and my bike; [written & illustrated by] Ander. Heryin Books 2008 un il $16.95

Grades: 2 3 4 5   **E**

    1. Wishes -- Fiction 2. Bicycles -- Fiction

    ISBN 978-0-9787550-2-7; 0-9787550-2-2

                                  LC 2007005817

A child wants nothing more than a new bicycle, and it seems the wish might come true with some help from the magic lamp that once made Grandpa grow up really fast

"The book has the feel of a graphic novel. The sketchy cartoon illustrations done on heavy stock are full of movement and changes in perspective, and they carry much of the storytelling and humor. This is a beautifully understated, often amusing meditation on being resilient, appreciating what you have, and still sustaining hope for something better." SLJ

Andersen, Hans Christian, 1805-1875

The **emperor's** new clothes; designed and illustrated by Virginia Lee Burton. Houghton Mifflin 2004 44p il $16

Grades: K 1 2 3   E
1. Fairy tales
ISBN 0-618-34421-7
A reissue of the edition first published 1949
Weavers convince the vain emperor that the clothing they make for him can only be seen by those who are not fools, but only the child recognizes the truth

"Burton's sense of pageantry sets forth in beautiful colors the magnificence of the Emperor's domain and entourage; her sense of humor brings out rightly the ridiculous situation with all its implications." Horn Book Guide

The **nightingale**; illustrated by Pirkko Vainio. North South Books 2011 un il $16.95
Grades: K 1 2 3   E
1. China -- Fiction 2. Nightingales -- Fiction
ISBN 978-0-7358-4029-4; 0-7358-4029-6
Though the emperor banishes the nightingale in preference of a jeweled mechanical imitation, the little bird remains faithful and returns years later when the emperor is near death and no one else can help him.

"A fresh version of Andersen's tender tale is illustrated with delicate watercolors. . . . This retelling, first published in Switzerland . . . is straightforward, allowing the soft, muted artwork to accent the details and ambiance." Kirkus

★ The **Snow** Queen; a retelling of the fairy tale. by Hans Christian Andersen; illustrated by Bagram Ibatoulline. HarperCollins 2013 40 p. (hardcover) $17.99
Grades: K 1 2   E
1. Friendship -- Fiction 2. Blessing and cursing -- Fiction 3. Fairy tales
ISBN 0062209507; 9780062209504
LC 2012011533
Author Hans Christian Andersen and illustrator Bagram Ibatoulline present a story of "friendship, love, and bravery. Best friends Kai and Gerda would do anything for each other. When Kai starts to behave cruelly and disappears, Gerda sets out on an epic quest to save Kai from the evil Snow Queen. But can Gerda break the Snow Queen's enchantment and complete the final task?" (Publisher's note)

★ **Thumbeline**; illustrated by Lisbeth Zwerger; translated by Anthea Bell. North-South Bks. 2000 un il hardcover o.p. pa $6.95
Grades: K 1 2 3   E
1. Fairy tales
ISBN 0-7358-1213-6; 0-7358-2236-0 pa
LC 99-57073
A reissue of 1985 edition published by Picture Book Studio
The adventures of a tiny girl no bigger than a thumb and her many animal friends

"The book's squarish design . . . draws the reader's attention to the exceptional art. Lovely, lean, lithe lines combine with a palette of tawny earth tones to create a minimalist world redolent with grace and rich with imagination." Horn Book Guide

The **ugly** duckling; [illustrated by] Pirkko Vainio. NorthSouth 2009 un il $16.95

Grades: PreK K 1 2   E
1. Fairy tales 2. Ducks -- Fiction 3. Swans -- Fiction
ISBN 978-0-7358-2226-9; 0-7358-2226-3
"Andersen's timeless story is lovingly revisited in this modest yet engaging retelling. With the sound and feel of a classic in the very best sense, the familiar tale has been reworked but not oversimplified, making it particularly appealing for children who might be too young for some of the harsher elements of the original. But what makes this version particularly appealing is the lovely watercolor artwork, which, like the text, exudes a feeling of tradition and familiarity." SLJ

Anderson, AnnMarie

★ The **Nutcracker**; pictures by Alison Jay. Dial Books for Young Readers 2010 un il $16.99
Grades: K 1 2 3   E
1. Fairy tales 2. Nutcracker (Ballet) 3. Christmas -- Fiction 4. Ballet -- Stories, plots, etc.
ISBN 978-0-8037-3285-8; 0-8037-3285-6
LC 2009051657
After rescuing her Christmas nutcracker from an army of angry toys, Marie and her brother are rewarded by the nutcracker, now a prince, with a fantastic nighttime journey to a realm of dancing fairies, beautiful palaces, and wonderful things to eat.

"Jay's delicate crackle-varnish oil paintings—equal parts elegant and whimsical-distinguish this edition of Hoffman's Nutcracker, based on Balanchine's staging of the ballet. . . . Jay's gleaming marzipan palace, pink spun-sugar trees, and peppermint-stick gates are the stuff of holiday visions, indeed" Publ Wkly

Anderson, Brian, 1974-
Monster chefs; Brian and Liam Anderson. Roaring Brook Press 2014 32 p. (hardcover: alk. paper) $16.99
Grades: PreK K 1 2   E
1. Humorous fiction 2. Monsters -- Fiction 3. Kings and rulers -- Fiction 4. Diet -- Fiction 5. Cooks -- Fiction 6. Humorous stories 7. Kings, queens, rulers, etc. -- Fiction
ISBN 1596438088; 9781596438088
LC 2012046930
In this book, by Brian and Liam Anderson, "the horribly horrible monster king summoned his four equally horrible chefs. . . . Trembling with fear, they each set off in a different direction to look for something truly scrumptious. But what, besides eyeballs and ketchup, could a monster king possibly want to eat? A rabbit? A fish? A snake? What one finally brings back may change dinnertime in the kingdom forever." (Publisher's note)

"A monster king tells his monster chefs that he wants to eat more than eyeballs and ketchup, so they set off in search of alternatives. Only one finds a solution, via a pastry chef: eyeball cupcakes (recipe included). Several layouts are cramped, and the backgrounds could be more interesting, but the setup is fresh and the execution riotous." Horn Book

The **Prince's** new pet. Roaring Brook Press 2011 il $16.99
Grades: K 1 2 3   E
1. Pets -- Fiction 2. Color -- Fiction 3. Princes --

Fiction
ISBN 978-1-59643-357-1; 1-59643-357-4

LC 2010036798

In a gray and colorless kingdom, the Prince receives an unusual, colorful new pet called a wooglefoof for his birthday.

"Fans of Tim Burton's films will love the stylized artwork and the oh-so-dreary palette. To keep it visually interesting, Anderson plays with the design by adding insets that pop off the page despite the shared palette. . . . Careful readers will chuckle at the wordplay." SLJ

Anderson, Derek

Story County; here we come! Orchard Books 2011 un il $16.99
Grades: PreK K   E
1. Farms -- Fiction 2. Domestic animals -- Fiction
ISBN 978-0-545-16844-1; 0-545-16844-9

LC 2010-12094

A farmer and his animal friends—Dog, Pig, Chicken, and Miss Cow—join forces to build a farm that they can all enjoy.

"This book's loose aesthetic features characters composed of boldly outlined geometric shapes, splashy colors, and confident brushwork. Chronicled in punchy, dialogue-driven prose, the friends' slapdash process lends itself to amusing scenes." Publ Wkly

Anderson, Laurie Halse

The **hair** of Zoe Fleefenbacher goes to school; illustrated by Ard Hoyt. Simon & Schuster Books for Young Readers 2009 un il $16.99
Grades: K 1 2   E
1. School stories 2. Hair -- Fiction
ISBN 978-0-689-85809-3; 0-689-85809-4

LC 2007045161

A young girl's talented but untamed tresses do not impress her strict first-grade teacher, who has rules for everything, including hair.

"Anderson's narrative sparkles with exuberant language and exaggerated humor. Hoyt's buoyant cartoons, done in pen and ink and watercolors, are filled with flowing lines and comical touches." SLJ

Anderson, Peggy Perry

Chuck's truck; by Peggy Perry Anderson. Houghton Mifflin 2006 un il $16
Grades: PreK K 1 2   E
1. Stories in rhyme 2. Trucks -- Fiction 3. Domestic animals -- Fiction
ISBN 0-618-66836-5; 978-0-618-66836-6

LC 2005020870

When too many barnyard friends climb in to go to town, Chuck's truck breaks down, but Handyman Hugh knows just what to do.

"Filled with rhyming language, this story will be a boon for beginning readers who will easily identify the rhyming words. . . . Anderson uses a crayon-resist technique to great effect, and the pictures are filled with dimension and texture. The bright colors are vibrant and energetic." SLJ

Another title about Chuck is:
Chuck's band (2008)

Joe on the go; [by] Peggy Perry Anderson. Houghton Mifflin 2007 32p il $16
Grades: PreK K 1 2   E
1. Stories in rhyme 2. Play -- Fiction 3. Frogs -- Fiction 4. Family reunions -- Fiction
ISBN 978-0-618-77331-2; 0-618-77331-2

LC 2006009771

Joe the frog wants to be on the go, but even at a family reunion he is out of luck, as everyone says they are too busy, or he is too fast, too slow, too big, or too small to go with them, until Grandma invites him to go with her on a special outing.

"Illustrated with bright, boisterous line-and-watercolor pictures, the simple rhyming text . . . will draw story hour listeners as well as beginning readers to a scenario they may recognize." Booklist

Other titles about Joe the frog are:
Time for bed, the babysitter said (1987)
To the tub (1996)
Out to lunch (1998)
Let's clean up (2002)

Andreae, Giles, 1966-

I love my mommy; [by] Giles Andreae and [illustrated by] Emma Dodd. Hyperion/Disney 2011 un il $12.99
Grades: PreK   E
1. Mother-child relationship -- Fiction
ISBN 978-1-4231-4327-7; 1-4231-4327-2

First published 2010 in the United Kingdom with title: I love my mummy

"This appealing oversize book has a rhyming text and a huggable-looking toddler who clutches a purple toy duck. He lists some of the reasons he loves his mother. . . . The bright illustrations are set against pastel backgrounds with close-ups of the child and Mom outlined in black. . . . This is a tale oft told, but with its cheerful, familiar scenarios, it will be a hit at storytimes." SLJ

Andreasen, Dan

The **baker's** dozen; [by] Dan Andreasen. Henry Holt 2007 un il $16.95
Grades: PreK K   E
1. Counting 2. Stories in rhyme 3. Baking -- Fiction
ISBN 978-0-8050-7809-1; 0-8050-7809-6

LC 2006031372

The reader is invited to count from one to thirteen as a jolly baker makes delectable treats from one mouthwatering eclair to twelve luscious cupcakes, and serves them to invited guests

This offers "a simple rhyme and clear, mouthwatering illustrations." Booklist

The **giant** of Seville; a tall tale based on a true story. Abrams Books for Young Readers 2007 un il $15.95
Grades: K 1 2 3   E
1. Giants 2. Army officers 3. Circus performers
ISBN 978-0-8109-0988-5; 0-8109-0988-X

LC 2006-13579

"Seville, Ohio, is so quiet that you can 'hear the corn grow' until a giant comes to town. Nearly eight feet tall, Captain Martin Van Buren is searching for a friendly community in which to settle down. Seville's residents welcome him, but accommodating a guest of his stature proves difficult. . . . An endnote introduces the historical people and events that inspired the story, and Andreasen extends the tale's old-fashioned feel in detailed, color-washed ink drawings of townspeople in nineteenth-century dress." Booklist

The **treasure** bath. Henry Holt and Co. 2009 un il $16.99

Grades: PreK   E
   1. Stories without words 2. Baths -- Fiction 3. Imagination -- Fiction
   ISBN 978-0-8050-8686-7; 0-8050-8686-2
LC 2008-38224

A wordless picture book in which a young boy explores a creature-filled world beneath the bubbles in his bathtub

"Andreasen borrows motifs from comic-book art—extra gleam on objects, squared-off, blunt-cut hair and the humans' doll-like postures—and combines them with Disneyesque cheer to create amiable scenarios with just a hint of irony." Publ Wkly

Andrews, Julie
   The **very** fairy princess; graduation girl. by Julie Andrews & Emma Walton Hamilton; illustrated by Christine Davenier. Little, Brown & Co. 2014 32 p. color illustrations (The very fairy princess) (reinforced) $18

Grades: PreK K 1 2   E
   1. School stories 2. Princesses -- Fiction 3. Change -- Fiction 4. Schools -- Fiction 5. Teachers -- Fiction
   ISBN 0316219606; 9780316219600
LC 2013014112

In this story, "the end of the school year is here, and Very Fairy Princess Gerry is getting ready to graduate! She always loves a celebration, but can't help but feel a little sad as she empties her cubby, takes down her art projects, and says goodbye to her class pet, Houdini the hamster." (Publisher's note)

"Davenier's ink-and-colored-pencil illustrations neatly capture Gerry's feelings, making them stand out against the rest of her class' more joyful faces.Though the cover is bedecked in sparkles, Gerry's sparkle is just as internal as it is external—her essential self-confidence shines." Kirkus

Angleberger, Tom
   ★ **Crankee** Doodle; by Tom Angleberger; illustrations by Cece Bell. Clarion Books 2013 32 p. ill. (hardcover) $16.99

Grades: PreK K 1   E
   1. Picture books for children 2. Historical fiction 3. Humorous stories 4. Ponies -- Fiction 5. Mood (Psychology) -- Fiction
   ISBN 0547818548; 9780547818542
LC 2012001346

In this children's picture book, "when a colonial-era Yankee announces that he's bored, his pony suggests the pair could go to town. 'Town?' replies the man. 'No way. I hate going to town. There are too many people in town.' For each subsequent nudge from the pony . . ., the Yankee has a long-winded and highly opinionated rant against the idea." (Publishers Weekly)

Anholt, Laurence
   Cezanne and the apple boy. Barron's 2009 un il

Grades: PreK K 1   E
   1. Artists 2. Painters 3. Artists -- Fiction 4. Father-son

relationship -- Fiction
   ISBN 0-7641-6282-9; 978-0-7641-6282-4

Paul's father, the artist Paul Cézanne has been away from home for so long that the boy hardly recognizes his father when he returns. But the two soon become fast friends. The local townspeople laugh at the artist's pictures. But young Paul likes the art. An influential art dealer comes from Paris the lives of the artist and his son change dramatically.

"Evocative, realistic illustrations mix with reproductions of Cézanne works and, along with the young character, will draw kids into this enjoyable, informative portrayal of Cézanne as both a father and an influential artist." Booklist

Anno, Mitsumasa
   ★ **Anno's** counting book. Crowell 1977 un il $17.99; lib bdg $18.89; pa $6.99

Grades: PreK K 1   E
   1. Counting 2. Stories without words 3. Seasons -- Fiction
   ISBN 0-690-01287-X; 0-690-01288-8 lib bdg; 0-06-443123-1 pa
LC 76-28977

Original Japanese edition, 1975

"A distinctive, beautifully conceived counting book in which twelve full-color doublespreads show the same village and surrounding countryside during different hours (by the church clock) and months. Both the seasons and community changes are studied, as such components of the scene as flowers, trees, animals, people, and buildings increase from one to twelve." LC. Child Books, 1977

Antle, Bhagavan
   Suryia swims!: the true story of how an orangutan learned to swim; Bhagavan "Doc" Antle, with Thea Feldman; photographs by Barry Bland. Henry Holt 2012 32 p. (hc) $16.99

Grades: 1 2 3   E
   1. Swimming 2. Orangutan 3. Animal behavior 4. Swimming -- Fiction 5. Orangutan -- Fiction 6. Wildlife refuges -- Fiction
   ISBN 0805093176; 9780805093179
LC 2011029047

This book, by Bhagavan Antle, illustrated by Barry Bland, narrated by Thea Feldman, describes an episode in the life of the orangutan Suryia. "Suryia is not your average orangutan. In the first book about him, . . . Suryia found an unusual best friend: a dog named Roscoe. Now Suryia jumps into an unusual new hobby: swimming! Orangutans don't swim; it doesn't come naturally to them. But Suryia shows that adventures await those who are willing to try something new." (Publisher's note)

Appelt, Kathi
   ★ **Bats** around the clock; illustrated by Melissa Sweet. HarperCollins Pubs. 2000 un il $15.99; lib bdg $16.89

Grades: PreK K 1 2   E
   1. Stories in rhyme 2. Bats -- Fiction 3. Rock music -- Fiction
   ISBN 0-688-16469-2; 0-688-16470-6 lib bdg
LC 99-15502

Click Dark hosts a special twelve-hour program of American Bat Stand where the bats rock and roll until the midnight hour ends.

"The rhymes are delightful and the narrative jives right along." SLJ

Other titles about the bats are:

The bat jamboree (1996)

Bats on parade (1999)

Brand-new baby blues; words by Kathi Appelt; illustrations by Kelly Murphy. HarperCollins Publishers 2010 un il $16.99

Grades: PreK K 1 2   **E**

1. Stories in rhyme 2. Infants -- Fiction 3. Siblings -- Fiction

ISBN 978-0-06-053233-8; 0-06-053233-5; 978-0-06-053234-5 lib bdg; 0-06-053234-3 lib bdg

LC 2008-05796

The arrival of a new little brother has his big sister singing the blues.

"Funny and concise, the rollicking rhyme bounces along, accepting the frustration natural to the situation, while gently allowing the girl's love of and appreciation for her brother. . . . The process is complemented by the illustrations, which modulate in palette from angry blues and greens to sunny yellows, while serene compositions replace off-kilter ones. Older brothers and sisters will easily identify with this jaunty heroine and profit from her realizations—an excellent choice for a new older sibling." Kirkus

Counting crows; Kathi Appelt; illustrated by Rob Dunlavey. Atheneum Books for Young Readers 2015 40 p. color illustrations (hardcover) $17.99

Grades: PreK K 1   **E**

1. Counting 2. Crows -- Fiction 3. Stories in rhyme

ISBN 1442423277; 9781442423275

LC 2014002094

In this story by Kathi Appelt, illustrated by Rob Dunlavey, "hungry crows avoid a feline foe. . . . Crows in a tree . . . fly out of their nest with snacking in mind . . . , but before they have time to complain about bellyaches, they have a bigger problem: a cat has been eyeing them as potential snacks! Can these well-fed crows become well-FLED crows?" (Publisher's note)

"Writing a fresh counting rhyme calls for the poet to hear the numbers in a new way, and that's just what Appelt . . . has done. She tweaks sequences, varies rhythms, and punctuates her lines with piquant sound words." Pub Wkly

★ **Mogie**; the heart of the house. Kathi Appelt; illustrated by Marc Rosenthal. Atheneum Books for Young Readers 2014 40 p. (hardcover) $17.99

Grades: PreK K 1 2 3   **E**

1. Sick -- Fiction 2. Charities -- Fiction 3. Dogs -- Fiction 4. Animals -- Infancy -- Fiction 5. Ronald McDonald House Charities -- Fiction

ISBN 1442480548; 9781442480544

LC 2013018100

In this children's book, written by Kathi Appelt and illustrated by Marc Rosenthal, "Mogie, a labradoodle with a trademarked name who lives at the Ronald McDonald House in Houston, has his story fictionally told. . . . While seemingly not cut out for other canine careers, [he] bonds instantly with Gage, a . . . boy at the house who has lost his 'mojo.' The two become fast friends, and once Gage finally recovers from his unstated illness and moves out, Mogie turns his affection to Antonia." (Booklist)

"In this touching story, rambunctious Mogie fails as a service dog, at search-and-rescue work, and in the show ring, but when he wanders into a Ronald McDonald House (unnamed in the main text), he discovers his true calling as a comfort dog. Colored-in pencil and charcoal illustrations depict Mogie's exuberance and affection as he helps once-energetic young patients get their "mojo" back." Horn Book

Oh my baby, little one; pictures by Jane Dyer. Harcourt Brace & Co. 2000 un il $16; pa $3.99

Grades: PreK K   **E**

1. Stories in rhyme 2. Mother-child relationship -- Fiction

ISBN 0-15-200041-0; 0-15-206031-6 pa

LC 99-6363

"The light, bright pictures will charm young listeners, who will find this book best enjoyed while cuddled up next to Mama." Booklist

"An exploration of the love that exists between mother and child, even when Mama Bird must leave her baby at nursery school. Told in rhyming verse, each four-line stanza is a reassurance that mama's love will permeate all areas of Baby Bird's day." SLJ

★ **When** Otis courted Mama; Kathi Appelt; illustrated by Jill McElmurry. Houghton Mifflin Harcourt 2014 40 p. col. ill. $16.99

Grades: PreK K 1 2 3   **E**

1. Single mothers -- Fiction 2. Children of divorced parents 3. Coyote -- Fiction 4. Stepfathers -- Fiction 5. Fathers and sons -- Fiction 6. Mothers and sons -- Fiction

ISBN 0152166882; 9780152166885

LC 2007029880

In this children's book by Kathi Appelt and illustrated by Jill McElmurry "Cardell's life is mostly wonderful. He knows he's loved . . . by his perfectly good mama and his perfectly good daddy. They live in different parts of the desert, but that's okay--Cardell is mostly used to it. Then Otis comes calling, and Cardell feels a grrr form in his throat. Otis can't make jalapeño flapjacks or play Zig-the-Zag anything like Cardell's daddy. And so Cardell waits for Mama to say "Adiós, Otis." But what will happen if she doesn't?" (Publisher's note)

"Aside from a few sticker burrs and occasional sand fleas, Cardell, a little coyote, has a mostly wonderful life. He has a perfectly good mama and a perfectly good daddy, and even though his daddy lives in a different part of the desert, Cardell still gets to see him... And gradually, Cardell's "grrrs" get softer until they stop altogether. Like Otis, Appelt is a gifted storyteller, and families whose circumstances echo Cardell's will welcome this gentle story, which is nicely augmented by illustrator McElmurry's gouache pictures, with their vivid desert colors. " Booklist

Applegate, Katherine

The **buffalo** storm; illustrated by Jan Ormerod. Clarion Books 2007 32p il $16

Grades: 2 3 4   **E**

1. Fear -- Fiction 2. Grandmothers -- Fiction 3. Frontier and pioneer life -- Fiction 4. Overland journeys

to the Pacific -- Fiction

ISBN 978-0-618-53597-2; 0-618-53597-7

LC 2006-15661

When Hallie and her parents join a wagon train to Oregon and leave her grandmother behind, Hallie must learn to face the storms that frighten her so, as well as other, newer fears, with just her grandmother's quilt to comfort her.

"Ormerod's . . . textured watercolors and pastels employ billowy swaths of color to suggest the vastness of the setting. . . . Vivid imagery makes this lyrical tale an accessible, fresh addition to the children's pioneer genre as it tackles themes of change, courage and home." Publ Wkly

Archer, Dosh

Big Bad Wolf; Dosh Archer. Albert Whitman & Company 2013 48 p. color illustrations (Urgency emergency!) (hardback) 48 p.

Grades: K 1 2 3   E

1. Wolves -- Fiction 2. Hospitals -- Fiction 3. Humorous stories 4. Animals -- Fiction 5. Asphyxia -- Fiction 6. Medical care -- Fiction 7. Characters in literature -- Fiction

ISBN 0807583529; 9780807583524

LC 2013005440

Cybil Award: Early Reader (2013)

In this children's book, written and illustrated by Dosh Archer, "A choking wolf is rushed to City Hospital, and a lost little girl in a red coat has been found, looking for her missing granny. What on earth did the wolf eat?" The book is an "animal hospital adventure story" for "young readers." (Publisher's note)

"New readers are in for a treat with these British imports. Both are set in an emergency room where Doctor Glenda (a dog) and Nurse Percy (a rooster) assist their nursery-rhyme- and fairy-tale-character patients. Muted colors and droll cartoon-style illustrations keep the action light and to the point. Limited, easy-to-decode vocabulary in a large typeface will support emerging readers." Horn Book

Urgency emergency! Itsy bitsy spider; written and illustrated by Dosh Archer. Albert Whitman & Company 2013 48 p. (hardback) $12.99

Grades: K 1 2   E

1. Hospitals -- Fiction 2. Spiders -- Fiction 3. Humorous stories 4. Animals -- Fiction 5. Medical care -- Fiction 6. Wounds and injuries -- Fiction

ISBN 0807583588; 9780807583586

LC 2013005442

In this book by Dosh Archer "a spider arrives at City Hospital with some strange head injuries. How did this happen? And does it have anything to do with all the water rushing down the water spout? This animal hospital adventure story [includes] bright color illustrations on every page, minimal easy-to-read text and a . . . fast-paced plot." (Publisher's note)

Armand, Glenda

Love twelve miles long; illustrated by Colin Bootman. Lee & Low Books 2011 il $17.95

Grades: K 1 2   E

1. Slaves 2. Authors 3. Abolitionists 4. Memoirists 5. Slavery -- Fiction 6. Mother-son relationship -- Fiction

ISBN 978-1-60060-245-0; 1-60060-245-2

LC 2011014275

In 1820s Maryland, Frederick's mother, who is a slave on a different plantation, walks twelve miles each way for a nighttime visit with her son, during which she recounts what each mile of the journey represents. Based on the childhood of Frederick Douglass.

"Armand's debut reveals a poignant conversation between young Frederick and his mother, paired with Bootman's arresting and emotive paintings. . . . Bootman . . . deftly uses candlelight and moonlight to give his art a lovely iridescence, and presents intimate portraits of mother and son." Pub Wkly

Armstrong, Jennifer

Magnus at the fire; illustrated by Owen Smith. Simon & Schuster Books for Young Readers 2005 un il $15.95

Grades: PreK K 1 2   E

1. Horses -- Fiction 2. Fire fighting -- Fiction

ISBN 0-689-83922-7

LC 2004-11487

When the Broadway Fire House acquires a motorized fire engine, Magnus the fire horse is not ready to retire.

A "stirring historical story. . . . Impressive oil paintings in vibrant colors capture the drama of firefighting in the 1800s." SLJ

★ **Once** upon a banana; illustrated by David Small. Simon & Schuster Books for Young Readers 2006 un il $16.95

Grades: PreK K 1 2   E

1. Stories without words 2. City and town life -- Fiction

ISBN 0-689-84251-1; 978-0-689-84251-1

LC 2005-08567

"A street juggler's pet monkey runs off and steals a deli's outdoor stall. . . . The monkey tosses the banana peel on the sidewalk, thus triggering a book-long, slapstick-rich chase that covers an entire city center and ensnares a cavalcade of characters. . . . Small's loose yet precise ink lines and watercolor wash seem ideal for these crowded streets where anarchy abounds. . . . The pages overflow with enough pratfalls and comic asides to reward many readings." Publ Wkly

Armstrong, Matthew S.

Jane and Mizmow; by Matthew S. Armstrong. Harper 2011 il

Grades: PreK K 1   E

1. Monsters -- Fiction 2. Friendship -- Fiction

ISBN 0061177199; 9780061177194

LC 2010012628

Jane and her best friend, a monster named Mizmow, are best friends in spite of their differences, and nothing can keep them apart.

"A palette of fall colors mirrors the warmth of their friendship, while the expressive faces of the two characters reinforce both mood and action. Emerging readers will be able to read much of the simple text, but the illustrations really tell the tale. . . . A solid choice that youngsters will enjoy time and time again." SLJ

Arndt, Michael

Cat says meow; and other animalopoeia. by Michael Arndt. Chronicle Books LLC 2014 36 p. col. ill. (alk. paper) $12.99

Grades: PreK K   E

1. Animal sounds 2. English language -- Terms and

phrases 3. Animal sounds -- Fiction
ISBN 1452112347; 9781452112343

LC 2013003270

In this book by Michael Arndt, "animals and the sounds they make are paired up in playfully compelling ways . . . featuring bold colors and an engaging use of onomatopoeia. Kids and parents [can discover] the ways in which the letters that spell out each animal's sound are key elements of that animal's illustration." (Publisher's note)

"Each page turn reveals a new graphic in a bold color, with a pleasing variety of single- and double-page spreads, as well as subtle changes in composition. This is one of those rare picture books with something for everyone to enjoy, beginning with colors, sounds and shapes for the youngest." Kirkus

Arnold, Tedd

Dirty Gert; by Tedd Arnold. Holiday House 2013 40 p. (hardcover) $16.95
Grades: K 1 2 3   E
1. Stories in rhyme 2. Trees -- Fiction 3. Humorous stories 5. Trees -- Fiction
ISBN 0823424049; 9780823424047

LC 2012006578

This children's story, by Tedd Arnold, follows a girl who becomes a tree. "Gert loves dirt. . . . Then one day while making mud pies in the rain, Gert becomes reorganized: she grows branches, leaves and roots. Gert is delighted . . . until camera crews televise her, botanists analyze her, and Hollywood tries to immortalize her. The child is traumatized! But Mom and Dad know what to do to protect their offbeat plant-child." (Publisher's note)

Fix this mess! Tedd Arnold. Holiday House 2014 32 p. color illustrations (I like to read) (hardcover) $14.95
Grades: PreK K 1 2   E
1. Cleaning 2. Robots -- Fiction 3. Orderliness -- Fiction
ISBN 0823429423; 9780823429424

LC 2013009565

In this children's book, part of the I Like to Read series, written and illustrated by Tedd Arnold, "Robug [the robot] tries to obey when Jake instructs it to 'fix this mess' but somehow manages to make things worse. . . . Robug comes up with a solution: Jake can fix his own mess." (Publisher's note)

"Jake turns Robug ("Remote Operating Basic Utility Gizmo") on and commands it to 'fix this mess.' Robug energetically fires into action, but things don't quite turn out right. Funny details in Arnold's characteristic cartoon-style illustrations build momentum from page to page, and the vocabulary is simple enough to allow the newest readers to enjoy it all on their own." Horn Book

Fly Guy presents; space. by Tedd Arnold. Scholastic 2013 32 p. $3.99
Grades: PreK K 1 2   E
1. Comets 2. Space vehicles 3. Outer space
ISBN 0545564921; 9780545564922

In this book, author Tedd Arnold "brings nonfiction to life. . . . During a visit to a space museum, Fly Guy and Buzz learn all about planets, space crafts, space suits, and even dirty snowballs (i.e. comets!)! With straightforward .

. . facts, . . . illustrations of Fly Guy and Buzz, and vivid photographs throughout." (Publisher's note)

Green Wilma, frog in space. Dial Books for Young Readers 2009 un il $16.99
Grades: K 1 2   E
1. Stories in rhyme 2. Frogs -- Fiction 3. Space flight -- Fiction 4. Extraterrestrial beings -- Fiction
ISBN 978-0-8037-2698-7; 0-8037-2698-8

LC 2008039497

Green Wilma the frog is mistaken for an alien child and taken on a trip through space.

This is written "in perfect rhyme. . . . The illustrations explode across the pages with frantic innocence. . . . To say that the pictures complement the text is like declaring that the Sun complements the Earth. Children will adore Wilma." SLJ

Another title about Green Wilma is:
Green Wilma (1993)

Hi, Fly Guy! Scholastic 2005 30p il $5.99; pa $3.99
Grades: PreK K 1 2   E
1. Pets -- Fiction 2. Flies -- Fiction
ISBN 0-439-63903-4; 0-439-85311-7 pa; 978-0-439-63903-3; 978-0-439-85311-8 pa

LC 2004-20553

When Buzz captures a fly to enter in The Amazing Pet Show, his parents and the judges tell him that a fly cannot be a pet, but Fly Guy proves them wrong. "Grades one to three." (Bull Cent Child Books)

"Suitably wacky cartoon art accompanies the text, which is simple enough for beginning readers." Publ Wkly

Other titles in this series are:
Super Fly Guy (2006)
Shoo Fly Guy (2006)
There was an old lady who swallowed Fly Guy (2007)
Fly high, Fly Guy (2008)
Hooray for Fly Guy! (2008)
I spy Fly Guy! (2009)
Fly Guy meets Fly Girl! (2010)
Buzz Boy and Fly Guy (2010)
Fly Guy vs. the flyswatter! (2011)

A **pet** for Fly Guy; Tedd Arnold. Orchard Books 2014 32 p. $16.99
Grades: PreK K 1 2   E
1. Pets -- Fiction 2. Flies -- Fiction 3. Humorous fiction 4. Humorous stories
ISBN 0545316154; 9780545316156

LC 2013035044

In this children's book, by Tedd Arnold, "Buzz tries to help Fly Guy find the right pet. It seems that everyone else at the park has a pet, so Fly Guy wants one, too. A dog licked Fly Guy. A frog chased Fly Guy. A cricket was too jumpy. Who will be the best pet for Fly Guy?" (Publisher's note)

"Fly Guy's latest adventure is in picture-book format. While on a picnic at the park, Buzz and Fly Guy watch people playing with their zany pets...This humorous selection is fun to read aloud but is also well designed for new readers. The simple text is well placed on each page, including occasional thought and speech bubbles that are easy to follow. Children who have enjoyed other books about Buzz and Fly Guy will love this one, too." SLJ

Arnosky, Jim

At this very moment. Dutton Children's Books 2011 un il $16.99

Grades: K 1 2   E

1. Stories in rhyme 2. Nature -- Fiction 3. Animals -- Fiction

ISBN 978-0-525-42252-5; 0-525-42252-8

LC 2010037711

Identifies some of the things happening in nature while one goes about an ordinary day, such as a shark circling a reef while one brushes one's teeth, or puffins eating fresh-caught fish while one eats dinner.

"With a gentle rhythm, unforced rhymes and near rhymes and perfect pacing, this bedtime story encourages children to think, dream and wonder about the lives of animals in the wild." Kirkus

★ **Babies** in the bayou; [by] Jim Arnosky. G. P. Putnam's Sons 2007 un il $16.99

Grades: PreK K   E

1. Wetlands 2. Animal babies

ISBN 978-0-399-22653-3; 0-399-22653-2

LC 2006011910

There are many babies in the bayou, and even though they might have sharp white teeth, hard shells, webbed feet, or quick claws, their mothers still need to protect them.

"This is a wonderful resource to use with children to illuminate the ways of nature; it's economical and rhythmic in text, and beautifully and clearly illustrated. Arnosky uses simple language and a repeated refrain to describe the animals that live in a lush Southern environment." SLJ

Dolphins on the sand; by Jim Arnosky. G.P. Putnam's Sons 2008 un il $16.99

Grades: PreK K 1 2   E

1. Dolphins -- Fiction 2. Wildlife conservation -- Fiction

ISBN 978-0-399-24606-7; 0-399-24606-1

LC 2007045384

A dozen dolphins, led by their eldest member and her youngster, become stranded on a sandbar and must be helped to safety by humans.

This "juxtaposes a straightforward narrative with particularly colorful paintings. . . . Arnosky reflects the simple beauty of the dolphins of the dolphins' happy existence in tropical pinks, oranges, and aquas, moving to a more somber palette of grays and blacks as danger sets in. He includes all manner of flora and fauna in his illustrative arc." Booklist

Gobble it up! a fun song about eating. Scholastic Press 2008 un il $16.99

Grades: PreK K 1 2   E

1. Stories in rhyme 2. Food -- Songs 3. Food -- Fiction 4. Animals -- Songs 5. Animals -- Fiction

ISBN 978-0-439-90362-2; 0-439-90362-9

LC 2007-29510

"This book takes a direct look at different animals and what they eat. It works well as a picture book, telling readers that if they were wild raccoons, or crocodiles, or great white sharks, they would 'gobble up' crawdads, or ducklings, or fishes. The catchy song sung by the author on the accompanying CD adds the element of fun that's advertised. Recog-

nizable, true-to-life acrylic illustrations . . . fill the spreads." SLJ

Grandfather Buffalo; [by] Jim Arnosky. G.P. Putnam's Sons 2006 un il $16.99

Grades: PreK K 1 2   E

1. Bison -- Fiction 2. Old age -- Fiction

ISBN 0-399-24169-8

LC 2005003535

When Grandfather Buffalo, the oldest bull of the herd, trails behind the group, he finds that he is joined by a newborn calf.

"Arnosky's signature artwork, which beautifully evokes the western landscape, is especially effective showing the buffalo closeup, and the writer-artist's respect for nature is clearly reflected in the simple, poignant story." Booklist

I'm a turkey! Scholastic Press 2009 un il $16.99

Grades: PreK K 1   E

1. Stories in rhyme 2. Turkeys -- Fiction

ISBN 978-0-439-90364-6; 0-439-90364-5

LC 2008-38335

"Arnosky's illustrations manage to be both autumnal and bright. . . . Arnosky gives [the birds] personality and charm." Booklist

Aronson, Billy

The **chicken** problem; Jennifer Oxley & Billy Aronson. Random House 2012 25 p. col. ill. (hardcover) $16.99; (library) $16.99

Grades: PreK K   E

1. Picture books for children 2. Chickens -- Fiction 3. Counting -- Fiction 4. Farm life -- Fiction 5. Problem solving -- Fiction

ISBN 0375869891; 9780375869891; 9780375969898

LC 2011031249

In this children's picture book by Jennifer Oxley, "Peg (a girl) and her pal Cat (a cat) are getting ready 'to have a perfect picnic with a pig' when they realize that they've cut one too many pieces of pie. Cat retrieves a little chicken (for the little piece of pie) from the nearby chicken coop, but she leaves the door to the coop wide open. . . . Peg and Cat eventually manage to return the errant poultry to the coop." (Bulletin of the Center for Children's Books)

Arree Chung

Ninja! Arree Chung. Henry Holt & Co. 2014 40 p. color illustrations (hardback) $16.99

Grades: PreK K 1 2   E

1. Ninja -- Fiction 2. Comic books, strips, etc. 3. Play -- Fiction 4. Brothers and sisters -- Fiction

ISBN 0805099115; 9780805099119

LC 2013043353

"Readers follow the main character through comic-book-style panels as he moves with stealthlike precision, covertly navigating each room and the furniture, to fulfill his mission of capturing his prize: his sister's snack. Silent as a spider, this cartoonish little guy is regaled in makeshift black ninja fashion (where is Dad's necktie?), with only his wide eyes (and several teeth) visible to his enemies." (School Library Journal)

"Told through a blend of traditional picture-book illustrations and comic-book-style panels, this seamlessly hybridizes the two forms, creating the perfect jumping-in point for readers interested in ninjas and comics." Kirkus

Arrigan, Mary

★ **Mario's** Angels; a story about the artist Giotto. written by Mary Arrigan; illustrated by Gillian McClure. Frances Lincoln 2006 un il $15.95

Grades: PreK K 1 2   E

  1. Artists 2. Painters 3. Sculptors 4. Architects 5. Italy -- Fiction 6. Angels -- Fiction 7. Artists -- Fiction

ISBN 1-84507-404-1

LC 2001-5260

"Mario, an exuberant boy, visits the artist [Giotto] as he works on his fresco Nativity in Padua. . . . When the artist is at a loss about how to fill the sky, Mario suggests angels. . . . The gentle text is matched by light, airy colors and feathery movement in the art. The cherubic Mario is full of life and will seem very real to readers." SLJ

Aruego, Jose

★ The **last** laugh; [by] Jose Aruego & Ariane Dewey. Dial Books for Young Readers 2006 un il $12.99

Grades: PreK K 1 2   E

  1. Stories without words 2. Ducks -- Fiction 3. Snakes -- Fiction

ISBN 0-8037-3093-4

LC 2005-48461

A wordless tale in which a clever duck outwits a bullying snake

"In comic-strip panels, Aruego and Deweys signature pen-and-ink and gouache art is droll and accessible. . . . Young readers will find the format and the karmic justice of this story appealing." SLJ

Asch, Frank

The **Daily** Comet; boy saves Earth from giant octopus. written by Frank Asch; illustrated by Devin Asch. Kids Can Press 2010 un il $16.95

Grades: K 1 2 3   E

  1. Octopuses -- Fiction 2. Journalists -- Fiction 3. Father-son relationship -- Fiction

ISBN 978-1-55453-281-0; 1-55453-281-7

When Hayward Palmer accompanies his father, a reporter for the sensationalistic Daily Comet, on a "Go to Work with a Parent Day," he has a rational explanation for all the weird and wacky things they encounter until he finally comes face to face with an enormous octopus.

"The dialogue is brisk, and visual quotes from Hollywood abound; Devin Asch's digital illustrations portray Hayward's father as a Gregory Peck look-alike and his photographer sidekick is an Elvis clone; dozens of other retro elements whirl at high speed. . . . It's a strangely believable tall tale." Publ Wkly

Happy birthday, Moon. Simon & Schuster Books for Young Readers 2000 un il pa $6.99

Grades: PreK K 1   E

  1. Moon -- Fiction 2. Bears -- Fiction 3. Birthdays -- Fiction

ISBN 978-0-689-83544-5; 0-689-83544-2

First published 1982 by Prentice Hall

Bear travels to the highest mountaintop to find out what to give the Moon for its birthday and discovers a delightful surprise—the Moon has the same birthday as Bear. Or so it seems.

Other titles in this series are:

Mooncake (1983)

Moongame (1984)

Moonbear's shadow (1985)

Like a windy day; [by] Frank Asch & Devin Asch. Harcourt 2002 un il $16; pa $7

Grades: PreK K   E

  1. Winds -- Fiction

ISBN 0-15-216376-X; 0-15-206403-6 pa

LC 2001-5260

A young girl discovers all the things the wind can do, by playing and dancing along with it

Written "in a poetic text. . . . The brief story is filled with action verbs. . . . The exciting pen-and-ink illustrations were colorized in Adobe Photoshop. Broad and sweeping spreads are filled with movement." SLJ

The **sun** is my favorite star. Harcourt 2001 un il $15; pa $7

Grades: PreK K 1   E

  1. Sun -- Fiction

ISBN 0-15-202127-2; 0-15-206397-8 pa

LC 98-46383

Celebrates a child's love of the sun and the wondrous ways in which it helps the earth and the life upon it

"Asch strikes just the right tone for his audience. . . . With colors as warm as a summer day, he creates a series of large-scale illustrations that reflect the direct unaffected tone of the writing." Booklist

Ashburn, Boni

I had a favorite dress; pictures by Julia Denos. Abrams 2011 un il $16.95

Grades: PreK K 1 2   E

  1. Clothing and dress -- Fiction

ISBN 978-1-4197-0016-3; 1-4197-0016-2

"When the unnamed narrator's favorite dress is suddenly a size too small, she is not a happy camper; she wears that dress every Tuesday, which is her favorite day of the week. Then her mother transforms the too-small dress into the perfect shirt. As the child's favorite day of the week changes so does her garment as she grows out of it. It becomes a tank top . . . a skirt . . . a scarf . . . socks . . . a hair bow . . . and, finally, a picture of the original dress by the narrator herself. . . . Some of Ashburn's text is playfully placed in and around the art to good effect. . . . Denos's multimedia illustrations, a combination of collages, watercolors, and graphite and colored pencil artwork, reinforce the narrator's vibrant personality and the amazing transformations of the dress while capturing the action and emotion of the story." SLJ

Over at the castle; illustrated by Kelly Murphy. Abrams 2010 un il $15.95

Grades: PreK K 1 2   E

  1. Counting 2. Stories in rhyme 3. Castles -- Fiction 4. Dragons -- Fiction 5. Middle Ages -- Fiction

ISBN 978-0-8109-8414-1; 0-8109-8414-8

"The familiar rhythm of the folk song Over in the Meadow finds a new setting as over at the castle, on the hill in the sun, an old mother dragon tries to teach her little dragon patience as they laze about near a castle. . . . Richly textured paintings in subtle hues that fit the medieval period convey the chores of the occupants of the castle, and comedic touches throughout . . . deepen the story and will have children flipping back through the pages." Booklist

Ashman, Linda

★ **Babies** on the go; illustrated by Jane Dyer. Harcourt 2003 un il $16

Grades: PreK K 1   E

1. Animal babies 2. Animal locomotion
ISBN 0-15-201894-8

LC 2002-6310

Illustrations and rhyming text show how different animals carry their babies when they are on the move

"The large, soft watercolor illustrations and rhyming text make this celebration of parent/child love a natural for toddler storytime, and it's also perfect for one-on-one sharing." SLJ

Castles, caves, and honeycombs; illustrated by Lauren Stringer. Harcourt 2001 un il $16

Grades: PreK K 1   E

1. Home 2. Stories in rhyme 3. Animals -- Habitations
ISBN 0-15-202211-2

LC 99-50801

Describes some of the unique places where animals build their homes such as in a heap of twigs, on a castle tower, in a cave, or in the hollow space inside a tree

"The concise text and womb-like illustrations convey the feelings of love, safety, and security that a home should have." Horn Book Guide

Creaky old house; A topsy-turvy tale of a real fixer-upper. illustrated by Michael Chesworth. Sterling 2009 un il $14.95

Grades: K 1   E

1. Stories in rhyme 2. Houses -- Fiction 3. Family life -- Fiction
ISBN 978-1-4027-4461-7; 1-4027-4461-7

LC 2008037836

A large family gets into an increasingly complicated home repair situation when the doorknob falls off a door

"The clever, rhyming text bounces along with a perfect cadence. The ink, watercolor, and pencil illustrations enhance the telling, and readers will take great pleasure in poring over the many amusing details." SLJ

M is for mischief; an A to Z of naughty children. illustrated by Nancy Carpenter. Dutton Children's Books 2008 un il $16.99

Grades: K 1 2   E

1. Alphabet 2. Stories in rhyme 3. Children's poetry
ISBN 0-525-47564-8; 978-0-525-47564-4

LC 2007-28491

A rhyme for each letter of the alphabet describes the misbehavior of a child, from Angry Abby to Zany Zelda. "Grades three to five." (Bull Cent Child Books)

"Each eight-line rhyme in this energetic title has fun with the sounds of words, as well as their slapstick meaning. . . . Though the words are the wonderful winners here, Carpenter's rambunctious watercolor-and-collage pictures provide excellent comedic support." Booklist

★ **Mama's** day; [illustrated by] Jan Ormerod. Simon & Schuster Books for Young Readers 2006 un il $15.95

Grades: PreK K 1   E

1. Stories in rhyme 2. Mother-child relationship -- Fiction
ISBN 0-689-83475-6

LC 00-45063

In rhyming text, mothers and their babies are described sharing in a variety of activities, from playing at the ocean to reading books and taking a bath

"Ashman's skillful verse and Ormerod's cozy ink-and-gouache artwork improve upon many other picture-book fulminations on mother love. A lilting line of verse appears on each spread, illustrated by a neatly framed scene of a different mother-child pair (including a demure image of breastfeeding) as well as a crew of charming, multicultural babies." Booklist

No dogs allowed! [illustrated by] Kristin Sorra. Sterling 2011 un il $14.95

Grades: PreK K 1   E

1. Dogs -- Fiction 2. Pets -- Fiction 3. Animals -- Fiction 4. Restaurants -- Fiction
ISBN 978-1-4027-5837-9; 1-4027-5837-5

When Alberto turns away people with pets from his restaurant, they gather in the street and buy treats from a street vendor.

"Digital artwork with plenty of captivating details essentially tells this story; the only text appears in speech bubbles and changing restaurant signage. . . . This lively picture book is a good choice for one-on-one sharing; the details in the art could serve as a visual stimulus to initiate conversations about what is happening." SLJ

Rain! written by Linda Ashman; illustrated by Christian Robinson. Houghton Mifflin Books for Children 2013 32 p. col. ill. (reinforced) $16.99

Grades: PreK K 1   E

1. Rain -- Fiction 2. Picture books for children 3. Neighbors -- Fiction 4. Mood (Psychology) -- Fiction 5. Rain and rainfall -- Fiction
ISBN 054773395X; 9780547733951

LC 2011042039

This children's picture book is set on a rainy day. "Two strangers have very different views about the weather: one is an elderly man who grumbles and complains throughout the day, and the other is a little boy who makes the most of the puddles on the sidewalk. When they meet at the Rain or Shine Café, the child finds himself momentarily brought down by the man's sullen demeanor until a mix-up with their hats brings out the old man's smile and optimism." (School Library Journal)

★ **Samantha** on a roll; pictures by Christine Davenier. Farrar, Straus & Giroux 2011 un il $16.99

Grades: K 1 2   E

1. Stories in rhyme 2. Roller skating -- Fiction
ISBN 978-0-374-36399-4; 0-374-36399-4

"Samantha decides to try out her roller skates for the first time, despite her mother's admonition to wait. She likes skating so much in the house that she hungers for the wide open spaces of the great outdoors. She sneaks outside, and the fun begins. . . . The rhyming text makes this delightful story tons of fun to read aloud. Davenier's illustrations aptly capture the action with bold colors and plenty of lines indicating motion." SLJ

Stella, unleashed; notes from the doghouse. illustrated by Paul Meisel. Sterling Pub. Co. 2008 40p il $14.95
Grades: K 1 2   **E**
1. Stories in rhyme 2. Dogs -- Fiction 3. Family life -- Fiction
ISBN 978-1-4027-3987-3; 1-4027-3987-7
        LC 2007036499
The family dog describes her life in a series of rhymes.
"Ashman aptly captures life with a pup, balancing the sweet (lap naps) with the sour (shedding). . . . Meisel's realistic acrylic, gouache, and pencil illustrations are filled with a variety of people and pups. . . . This collection of rhymes is ideal for family read-alouds." SLJ

To the beach! illustrated by Nadine Bernard Westcott. Harcourt 2005 un il $16
Grades: PreK K 1 2   **E**
1. Beaches -- Fiction 2. Family life -- Fiction
ISBN 0-15-216490-1
        LC 2003-19444
A family keeps forgetting the things they need to take to the beach
"Rhyming text and bouncy and boldly colored illustrations in acrylic on watercolor paper capture the frenzy surrounding this hilarious . . . family. A rip-roaring fun read-aloud." SLJ

When I was king; by Linda Ashman; illustrated by David McPhail. HarperCollins 2008 un il $16.99; lib bdg $17.89
Grades: PreK K 1   **E**
1. Stories in rhyme 2. Infants -- Fiction 3. Brothers -- Fiction
ISBN 978-0-06-029051-1; 0-06-029051-X; 978-0-06-029052-8 lib bdg; 0-06-029052-8 lib bdg
        LC 2005017868
A young boy describes how he is no longer "king" now that there is a new baby in the house, but then his family helps him enjoy the change
This is an "expertly rhymed story. . . . McPhail's charming illustrations perfectly capture the narrator's mood in his facial expressions and body language. Ashman's verses, lettered in a child-friendly font that varies in size, are perfect for reading aloud." SLJ

Asper-Smith, Sarah
Have you ever seen a smack of jellyfish? an alphabet book. Sasquatch Books 2010 un il $16.95
Grades: PreK K   **E**
1. Animals 2. Alphabet
ISBN 978-1-57061-687-7; 1-57061-687-6
"Asper-Smith's background in graphic design is evident in this ABC book devoted to collective nouns. Crisp, eye-popping silhouettes put the animals' shapes . . . in high relief. A murder of crows perches on a tree's spindly blue branches against a neon green sky . . . while the yellow-on-pink victim of a 'scourge of mosquitoes' makes their descriptor feel all the more apt. Clean design, attention to detail, and intriguing animal selections . . . make this an elegant primer." Publ Wkly

I would tuck you in; Sarah Asper-Smith. Sasquatch Books 2012 32 p. $16.99
Grades: K 1 2   **E**
1. Picture books for children 2. Bedtime -- Fiction 3. Animal behavior 4. Love -- Fiction 5. Mother and child -- Fiction 6. Animals -- Alaska -- Fiction 7. Animals -- Infancy -- Fiction
ISBN 1570618445; 9781570618444
        LC 2012032054
This children's picture book features drowsy animals alongside scientific explanations of animal behavior. "Each two-page spread features an illustration of an adult/child animal pair and a sweet, nonrhyming promise . . . . The feel-good sentiment is then explained in scientific terms via smaller text at the bottom of the page." (Booklist)

Aston, Dianna Hutts
★ **Dream** something big; the story of the Watts Towers. Dial Books for Young Readers 2011 un il $16.99
Grades: K 1 2 3   **E**
1. Artists 2. Folk artists 3. Watts Towers Arts Center (Los Angeles, Calif.)
ISBN 978-0-8037-3245-2; 0-8037-3245-7
        LC 2010028797
"Aston pays tribute to the creative genius of an Italian immigrant and tile worker who, in the 1920s, begins a unique project on his Watts, Calif., property that takes 34 years to complete. Simon Rodia uses only rebar, cement, broken tiles, shells, and other found items to build towering spires, some almost a hundred feet tall, decorated with mosaic designs. A fictional neighbor girl, Marguerite, provides lyrical first-person narration as she watches the towers take shape throughout her childhood. The subject lends itself perfectly to the collage illustrations. Employing mostly paper, but also bits of pottery, cloth, clay and string, Roth stunningly recreates bold, stylized versions of the towers. This book beautifully illuminates a little-known story of imagination and perseverance that resulted in a national landmark." Publ Wkly

★ **Moon** over Star; pictures by Jerry Pinkney. Dial Books for Young Readers 2008 un il $17.99
Grades: PreK K 1 2 3   **E**
1. Farm life -- Fiction 2. African Americans -- Fiction 3. Apollo 11 (Spacecraft) -- Fiction 4. Space flight to the moon -- Fiction
ISBN 978-0-8037-3107-3; 0-8037-3107-8
        LC 2007050703
Coretta Scott King honor book for illustration, 2009
On her family's farm in the town of Star, eight-year-old Mae eagerly follows the progress of the 1969 Apollo 11 flight and moon landing and dreams that she might one day be an astronaut, too.
"Spaced vertically in phrases like free verse alongside the large illustrations, the text combines dignity and immediacy in a clean, spare telling of events. Pinkney's evocative artwork, created using graphite, ink, and watercolor, depicts a black family captivated, and perhaps subtly changed, by the moon landing in 1969." Booklist

An **orange** in January; [by] Dianna Hutts Aston; illustrated by Julie Maren. Dial Books for Young Readers 2007 un il $16.99

Grades: PreK K 1   E
1. Oranges -- Fiction
ISBN 978-0-8037-3146-2

LC 2006014488

An orange begins its life as a blossom where bees feast on the nectar, and reaches the end of its journey, bursting with the seasons inside it, in the hands of a child.

This is a "poetic tale. . . . Like the text, the glowing acrylic paintings are artfully simple and make beautiful use of color." SLJ

Atinuke (Author)

Splash! Anna hibiscus; Atinuke. Kane Miller, A Division of EDC Pub. 2013 32 p. (hardcover) $17.95
Grades: 1 2 3 4   E
1. Ocean waves 2. Beaches -- Fiction
ISBN 1610671732; 9781610671736

LC 2012954083

In this picture book, by Atinuke and illustrated by Lauren Tobia, "Anna Hibiscus is at the beach and all she wants to do is SPLASH! . . . But everyone, including Grandmother and Grandfather, Chocolate, Benz, Wonderful, Joy, Clarity and Common Sense, is much too busy to wave-jump! So, it's just Anna Hibiscus and the white waves." (Publisher's note)

Auch, Mary Jane

Beauty and the beaks; a Turkey's cautionary tale. [by] Mary Jane and Herm Auch. Holiday House 2007 un il $16.95; pa $6.95
Grades: K 1 2 3   E
1. Turkeys -- Fiction 2. Chickens -- Fiction 3. Thanksgiving Day -- Fiction
ISBN 978-0-8234-1990-6; 0-8234-1990-8; 978-0-8234-2164-0 pa; 0-8234-2164-3 pa

LC 2006049468

When Lance, a very pretentious turkey, arrives on the farm and boasts that he is the only bird invited to a special feast, no hen is impressed, but when Beauty learns that Lance is the main course, she convinces the others to save him

"Wonderfully creative handmade characters and sets are the highlight of this over-the-top chicken tale. . . . The author made chicken mannequins with polymer eyes, beaks, and shoes, as well as wool wings and yarn feathers. Her husband designed the sets, built them, and photographed the images, adjusting their size. A humorous story about dressing a turkey, but not in the usual manner." SLJ

The **plot** chickens; by Mary Jane and Herm Auch. Holiday House 2009 un il $16.95
Grades: PreK K 1 2   E
1. Chickens -- Fiction 2. Authorship -- Fiction 3. Books and reading -- Fiction
ISBN 978-0-8234-2087-2; 0-8234-2087-6

LC 2007011234

Henrietta the chicken loves to read so much that she decides to write a book herself, but first no one will publish a book written by a chicken, and then, when she publishes it herself and it gets a terrible review in "The Corn Book," Henrietta is devastated

"The illustrations, a combination of oil paints and digital technology, are bold and colorful. . . . A droll chicken with a repeating line adds to the humor. This offering works on two levels. It's a funny picture book that could be used as a manual on writing." SLJ

Averbeck, Jim

Except if. Atheneum Books for Young Readers 2011 un il $12.99
Grades: PreK K 1   E
1. Eggs -- Fiction 2. Animals -- Fiction
ISBN 978-1-4169-9544-9; 1-4169-9544-7

LC 2009-52489

An egg is just an egg, except if, after hatching it becomes something else.

"Averbeck's simple shapes are outlined in pastel, a coloring-book style nicely suited to the deadpan narration. . . . It's a book in which the action unfolds in the mind as much as it does on the page." Publ Wkly

★ **In** a blue room; [by] Jim Averbeck; illustrated by Trica Tusa. Harcourt 2008 un il $16
Grades: PreK K 1 2   E
1. Color -- Fiction 2. Bedtime -- Fiction 3. Mother-daughter relationship -- Fiction
ISBN 978-0-15-205992-7; 0-15-205992-X

LC 2006034453

Alice wants everything in her bedroom to be blue before she falls asleep

"Prose and pictures partner each other effortlessly all the way to the last page." Publ Wkly

Avi

Silent movie; Avi, the author; C.B. Mordan, the illustrator. Atheneum Bks. for Young Readers 2002 un il $16.95
Grades: K 1 2 3   E
1. Immigrants -- Fiction 2. Silent films -- Fiction
ISBN 0-689-84145-0

LC 2001-33025

In the early years of the twentieth century, a Swedish family encounters separation and other hardships upon immigrating to New York City until the son is cast in a silent movie, in a picture book that evokes an actual silent movie

"Clear, beautiful ink-on-clayboard illustrations; white type on thick, glossy black paper; and cinematic lighting effects combine to evoke the historical period." Booklist

Avraham, Kate Aver

What will you be, Sara Mee? illustrated by Anne Sibley O'Brien. Charlesbridge 2010 un il $16.95; pa $7.95
Grades: PreK K 1   E
1. Parties -- Fiction 2. Siblings -- Fiction 3. Birthdays -- Fiction 4. Korean Americans -- Fiction
ISBN 978-1-58089-210-0; 1-58089-210-8; 978-1-58089-211-7 pa; 1-58089-211-6 pa

LC 2009-1708

At her Tol, the first birthday party, Sara Mee plays the traditional Korean prophecy game—Toljabee—while her extended family and friends watch.

"The illustrations are ink brush line with watercolor and done in vibrant colors. The love among family and friends is evident in these pictures, depicting their joy about this important event." SLJ

Axtell, David

We're going on a lion hunt; [illustrated by] David Axtell. Holt & Co. 2000 un il $15.95

Grades: PreK K 1 2   **E**
  1. Lions -- Fiction 2. Africa -- Fiction
  ISBN 0-8050-6159-2

                   LC 98-47507
First published 1999 in the United Kingdom
Two girls set out bravely in search of a lion, going
through long grass, a swamp, and a cave before they find
what they're looking for
"Axtell takes a storytime classic to the African savanna. .
. . [His] sun-soaked, impressionistic oil paintings offer beautiful landscapes and engaging details. . . . Large figures on
the page make this a good choice for storytimes as well as
lap times." SLJ

Aylesworth, Jim
  ★ The **full** belly bowl; illustrated by Wendy Halperin.
Atheneum Bks. for Young Readers 1998 un il $16.95
Grades: K 1 2 3   **E**
  1. Fairy tales
  ISBN 0-689-81033-4
                   LC 98-14052
In return for the kindness he showed a wee small man, a
very old man is given a magical bowl that causes problems
when it is not used properly
"From the dainty pictures on the endpapers to the stun-
ning artwork inside, this book is a feast for the eyes. The
story . . . is just as good, smoothly blending folktale conventions with touches of magic and a dusting of comedy."
Booklist

  Little Bitty Mousie; [by] Jim Aylesworth; illustrated
by Michael Hague. Walker 2007 un il $16.95; lib bdg
$17.85
Grades: PreK K 1   **E**
  1. Alphabet 2. Stories in rhyme 3. Mice -- Fiction
  ISBN 978-0-8027-9637-0; 0-8027-9637-0; 978-0-
  8027-9638-7 lib bdg; 0-8027-9638-9 lib bdg
               LC 2007002366
Little Bitty Mousie sneaks into a house one night and
discovers many tantalizing new things, as well as one very
scary thing.
  "The alphabet-related words are in boldface, the bouncy
rhymes are fun, and the cute periodic refrain . . . will encourage listener participation. . . . Enchanting, vividly colored
pictures, created in pencil and then digitally colored, set the
sweet miss mouse in the middle of realistic, detailed close-
ups of familiar household objects." Booklist

  My grandfather's coat; retold by Jim Aylesworth; illustrated by Barbara McClintock. Scholastic Press 2012 32
p. col. ill. (hardcover: alk. paper) $17.99
                       E
  1. Coats 2. Folklore 3. Grandfathers 4. Coats --
  Folklore 5. Folklore -- Europe, Eastern
  ISBN 0439925452; 9780439925457
                LC 2011012226
  This children's book, written by Jim Aylesworth and illustrated by Barbara McClintock, "chronicles four generations . . . from a boy's arrival at Ellis Island . . . to his story
being shared with a great-grandson." (Publishers Weekly)
"He made a coat for his wedding and wore it for years until
it was ragged and torn, at which point he cut it down to make
a jacket. The pattern continues, with each item becoming
smaller." (Kirkus Reviews)

"Aylesworth extends the Yiddish folksong's events over
four generations. "My grandfather," a tailor, made his own
blue wedding coat; while his daughter's a baby, it serves for
a jacket. Soon it's reduced to a vest, then a tie, then a toy for
"you" (his great-grandchild). The old-timey, inviting book
has well-paced pages, spreads, and vignettes that nicely
celebrate one family's ongoing affection and continuity."
Horn Book

  Old black fly; illustrations by Stephen Gammell. Holt
& Co. 1992 un il $16.95; pa $6.95
Grades: K 1 2 3   **E**
  1. Alphabet 2. Stories in rhyme 3. Flies -- Fiction
  ISBN 0-8050-1401-2; 0-8050-3924-4 pa
                  LC 91-26825
Rhyming text and illustrations follow a mischievous old
black fly through the alphabet as he has a very busy bad day
landing where he should not be
Aylesworth's "snappy couplets constitute a waggish
presentation of a basic concept. . . . Gammell's paintings
are exuberant splashes of mayhem—rainbows of splattered
hues from which truly memorable characters emerge. His
appropriately bug-eyed (and cross-eyed) fly and gap-toothed
humans sporting crazy hairdos provide a level of dementia
that children will relish." Publ Wkly

Baasansuren, Bolormaa
  My little round house; adapted by Helen Mixter.
Groundwood Books 2009 un il $18.95
Grades: K 1 2 3   **E**
  1. Infants -- Fiction 2. Mongolia -- Fiction 3. Family
  life -- Fiction
  ISBN 978-0-88899-934-4; 0-88899-934-8
"The little round house of the title is a large tent, or ger,
home to the nomadic people of Mongolia. In a spare first-
person narrative, baby Jilu recounts his first year and introduces readers to the rhythm of his loving family's nomadic
life. . . . Attractive full-page gouache illustrations by the
Mongolian writer/illustrator Baasansuren show the round
house's interior as well as the characters' clothes, including
elaborate details such as painted woodwork, embroidery,
and the texture of fabrics." SLJ

Bachelet, Gilles
  My cat, the silliest cat in the world; written and illustrated by Gilles Bachelet. Abrams 2006 un il $16.95
Grades: PreK K 1 2   **E**
  1. Cats -- Fiction 2. Elephants -- Fiction
  ISBN 0-8109-4913-X; 978-0-8109-4913-3
                LC 2005-27837
"While the text is a completely conventional list of a
cat's habits, the very, very, large cat in the pictures is, in fact,
an elephant. The straight-faced humor becomes all the fun-
nier because Bachelet captures a cat's peculiar postures and
behavior exactly. The paintings are filled with visual wit."
Horn Book Guide
  Another title about the silliest cat is:
  When the silliest cat was small (2007)

Badescu, Ramona
  Pomelo begins to grow; illustrated by Benjamin Chaud;
translated from French by Claudia Bedrick. Enchanted
Lion Books 2011 un il $16.95

Grades: 1 2 3   E
  1. Growth -- Fiction 2. Elephants -- Fiction
  ISBN 978-1-59270-111-7; 1-59270-111-6
                     LC 2010053472
  When his favorite dandelion looks surprisingly small, Pomelo the garden elephant discovers that he is growing and then wonders about the mysterious process called growth.

  "The author and illustrator demonstrate a brilliant marriage of text and illustration. Chaud's charming paintings of Pomelo in his landscape of dandelions, strawberries, and smiling potatoes—set simply against oversize white pages—breathe life and humor into Badescu's big-picture questions, while playing with scale." SLJ

  Pomelo explores color; Ramona Badescu; [illustrated by] Benjamin Chaud. Enchanted Lion Books 2012 120 p.
Grades: K 1 2   E
  1. Color -- Fiction 2. Elephants -- Fiction
  ISBN 1592701264; 9781592701261
                     LC 2012022766
  This children's book by Ramona Badescu and illustrated by Benjamin Chaud "is all about exploration and the experience of seeing color anew. . . . Pomelo discovers colors in all their nuance. He encounters the infinite white of falling snow, the hypnotizing red of love, and the shadowy blue of the unknown. The colors describe our concrete world, but also reflect emotional states, as well as the curious, oddball sensibility of our dear Pomelo." (Publisher's note)

  Pomelo's Opposites; by Ramona Badescu and illustrated by Benjamin Chaud. Enchanted Lion Books 2013 120 p. $15.95
Grades: K 1 2   E
  ISBN 1592701329; 9781592701322
  In this book, written by Ramona Badescu and illustrated by Benjamin Chaud, "Pomelo . . . is here again in a surprisingly comic and playful book of opposites. True to the concept, there are classic oppositions such as left/right, thin/fat, up/down. There are also philosophical opposites, such as with/without, dream/reality, and possible/impossible. And then there are silly, surreal, and laugh-out-loud opposites for the reader to discover on his or her own!" (Publisher's note)

Bae, Hyun-Joo
  ★ **New** clothes for New Year's Day. Kane/Miller 2007 un il $15.95
Grades: K 1 2 3   E
  1. Korea -- Fiction 2. New Year -- Fiction 3. Clothing and dress -- Fiction
  ISBN 978-1-933605-29-6
  A young Korean girl describes the new clothes that she will be wearing to celebrate the new year.

  "Simple words and inventively composed pictures depict each step in donning the elaborate, traditional costume. . . . Bae's delicate illustrations move smoothly between depictions of mishaps as the child wrestles with troublesome accessories and grand, wordless portraits." Booklist

Baeten, Lieve
  The **curious** Little Witch. North-South 2010 un il $16.95
Grades: PreK K 1 2   E
  1. Witches -- Fiction
  ISBN 978-0-7358-2305-1; 0-7358-2305-7

First published 1992
  "A young blonde witch and her cat decide to investigate a house, but the witch's broomstick breaks. As she explores the house, flaps reveal each of the residents: the Music Witch, who creates 'sublime' sounds; the Kitchen Witch, who prepares delicious food; and the Bedroom Witch, with soporific powers. Luckily, the Tinkering Witch is able to fix her broom-while adding rocket power. The cozy, cluttered details on every floor lend the book warmth and charm." Publ Wkly

  Other titles about Little Witch are:
  Up and away with the Little Witch (2011)
  Happy Birthday, Little Witch (2011)

Baker, Barbara
  ★ **Digby** and Kate and the beautiful day; pictures by Marsha Winborn. Dutton Children's Bks. 1998 48p il hardcover o.p. pa $3.99
Grades: PreK K 1 2   E
  1. Cats -- Fiction 2. Dogs -- Fiction
  ISBN 0-525-45855-7; 0-14-240035-4 pa
  Digby the dog and Kate the cat disagree about many things but they remain best friends

  "The artwork . . . together with the cheerful stories make up good, light fare for beginning readers." Horn Book Guide
  Other titles about Digby and Kate are:
  Digby and Kate (1988)
  Digby and Kate 1 2 3 (2004)
  Digby and Kate again (1989)

  One Saturday evening; pictures by Kate Duke. Dutton Children's Books 2007 48p il hardcover o.p. $13.99
Grades: K 1 2 3   E
  1. Bears -- Fiction 2. Family life -- Fiction
  ISBN 978-0-525-47103-5; 0-525-47103-0
                     LC 2006-24785
  On a Saturday evening, the members of a bear family busy themselves with cleaning up the kitchen, taking baths, and reading.

  "The chapter structure and short, basic sentences are well tuned to newly confident readers, and the reassuringly familiar scenarios, nicely extended in Duke's expressive ink-and-watercolor pictures, will draw children into the cozy nighttime mayhem." Booklist

  Another title about the bear family is:
  One Saturday morning (1994)

Baker, Jeannie
  Home. Greenwillow Books 2004 un il $15.99
Grades: PreK K 1 2   E
  1. City and town life 2. Stories without words
  ISBN 0-06-623935-4
                     LC 2003-49287
  A wordless picture book that observes the changes in a neighborhood from before a girl is born until she is an adult, as it first decays and then is renewed by the efforts of the residents

  "Baker uses natural materials to create detailed, arresting collages that tell a story in which words are superfluous. Children can pore over these pages again and again and make fresh discoveries with each perusal." SLJ

  ★ **Mirror**. Candlewick Press 2010 un il $18.99

Grades: PreK K 1 2   E
1. Stories without words 2. Markets -- Fiction 3. Morocco -- Fiction 4. Australia -- Fiction
ISBN 978-0-7636-4848-0; 0-7636-4848-5

LC 2009-50391

In Sydney, Australia, and in Morocco, two boys and their families have a day of shopping. Readers are invited to compare illustrations in two wordless stories that are intended to be read one from left to right and the other from right to left.

"Baker's entrancing collages, packed with visual information and created with fabric, sand, vegetation, and other unusual materials, have the power to bring back child and adult viewers for infinite 'readings.' Perfectly spectacular." Kirkus

Where the forest meets the sea; story and pictures by Jeannie Baker. Greenwillow Bks. 1988 un il $16
Grades: PreK K 1 2   E
1. Australia -- Fiction 2. Rain forests -- Fiction
ISBN 0-688-06363-2

LC 87-7551

First published 1987 in the United Kingdom
On a camping trip in an Australian rain forest with his father, a young boy thinks about the history of the plant and animal life around him and wonders about their future

The illustrations "are relief collages 'constructed from a multitude of materials, including modeling clay, papers, textured materials, preserved natural materials, and paints.' Integrated by the artist's vision, the collages create three-dimensional effects on two-dimensional pages drawing the reader into each scene as willing observer and explorer." Horn Book

Window. Greenwillow Bks. 1991 un il lib bdg $17.89
Grades: PreK K 1 2   E
1. Stories without words 2. Australia -- Fiction 3. Human ecology -- Fiction
ISBN 0-688-08918-6

LC 90-3922

"Filled with marvelous detail, the textured collages make an affecting statement about the erosion of the planet Earth." SLJ

Baker, Keith
Hickory dickory dock; [by] Keith Baker. Harcourt 2007 un il $16
Grades: PreK K 1 2   E
1. Stories in rhyme 2. Animals -- Fiction 3. Clocks and watches -- Fiction
ISBN 978-0-15-205818-0; 0-15-205818-4

LC 2006003257

"The nursery rhyme 'Hickory Dickory Dock' gets new life as it goes through 12 hours of the day. . . . As each hour chimes, another creature appears, often completing an action initiated in the previous spread. . . . With a bouncy, easy-to-enjoy text and child-appealing collage-style pictures, this is a book that will work well one-on-one or with groups." Booklist

Just how long can a long string be!? Arthur A. Levine Books 2009 un il hardcover o.p. $16.99

Grades: PreK K 1 2   E
1. Stories in rhyme 2. Ants -- Fiction 3. Birds -- Fiction
ISBN 978-0-545-08661-5; 0-545-08661-2; 978-0-545-08662-2 pa; 0-545-08662-0 pa

LC 2008027344

Be it tied to a balloon, or kite, or hanging a picture, or stringing a banjo or a mop, a bird explains to an ant how long a string needs to be

"By using pale overlapping images, Baker creates a sense of movement in many of the illustrations. A palette of pastels captures the beauty of spring. . . . [This is a] lovely book . . . for a fine spring storytime." SLJ

★ **LMNO** peas. Beach Lane Books 2010 un il $16.99
Grades: PreK K 1 2   E
1. Alphabet 2. Stories in rhyme 3. Occupations -- Fiction
ISBN 978-1-4169-9141-0; 1-4169-9141-7

LC 2009012672

Busy little peas introduce their favorite occupations, from astronaut to zoologist.

"With its digital illustrations' luminous colors, buoyant spirit, and engaging characters, this handsome picture book is definitely worth a second look, even in the overcrowded field of alphabet books." Booklist

★ **Meet** Mr. and Mrs. Green. Harcourt 2004 71p il hardcover o.p. pa $5.95
Grades: K 1 2   E
1. Alligators -- Fiction
ISBN 0-15-204954-1; 0-15-204955-X pa

LC 2001-1955

First published 2002
A loving alligator couple enjoy going camping, eating pancakes, and visiting the county fair

"The acrylic illustrations have a loud, oversized presence that is complemented by the strong text." SLJ

Other titles about Mr. and Mrs. Green are:
Lucky days with Mr. and Mrs. Green (2005)
More Mr. and Mrs. Green (2004)
On the go with Mr. and Mrs. Green (2006)

★ **No** two alike. Beach Lane Books 2011 un il $16.99
Grades: PreK K 1   E
1. Stories in rhyme 2. Birds -- Fiction 3. Winter -- Fiction
ISBN 978-1-4424-1742-7; 1-4424-1742-0

LC 2010044659

Follows a pair of birds on a snowflake-filled journey through a winter landscape, where everything everywhere, from branches and leaves to forests full of trees, is unique.

"Brief rhyming couplets, printed in large type and each requiring a page turn for completion, describe the birds' discoveries. . . . The engaging, digitally rendered avian characters stand out against the wintry landscape, and their many antics as they navigate their surroundings will sustain readers' interest." SLJ

Potato Joe; [by] Keith Baker. Harcourt 2008 un il $16

Grades: PreK K 1   E

1. Nursery rhymes 2. Counting -- Fiction

ISBN 978-0-15-206230-9; 0-15-206230-0

LC 2007005930

Potato Joe leads the other spuds from the familiar nursery rhyme, "One Potato, Two Potato," in various activities, from a game of tic-tac-toe to a rodeo.

"The fuzzy-edged, childlike illustrations were done in Adobe Photoshop and complement the bouncy tone of the text. This will be fun to share, and even young children will soon have the rhyme committed to memory." SLJ

Baldacchino, Christine

★ **Morris** Micklewhite and the Tangerine Dress; by Christine Baldacchino; illustrated by Isabelle Malenfant. Pgw 2014 32 p. color illustrations $16.95

Grades: PreK K 1 2   E

1. School stories 2. Imagination -- Fiction 3. Outer space -- Fiction 4. Clothing and dress -- Fiction

ISBN 1554983479; 9781554983476

Stonewall Honor Book: Children's & Young Adult Literature (2015)

In this book by Christine Baldacchino, "Morris is a little boy who loves using his imagination. But most of all, Morris loves wearing the tangerine dress in his classroom's dress-up center. The children in Morris's class don't understand. Dresses, they say, are for girls. . . . One day when Morris feels all alone and sick from their taunts, his mother lets him stay home from school. Morris dreams of a fantastic space adventure with his cat, Moo." (Publisher's note)

"Baldacchino's gentle story sensitively depicts gender nonconforming children, offering them reassurance and, one hopes, acceptance by introducing other children to the concept. An excellent book for discussion." Booklist

Balian, Lorna

Humbug witch; [by] Lorna Balian. Star Bright Books 2003 un il $12.95

Grades: PreK K 1 2   E

1. Witches -- Fiction

ISBN 1-932065-32-6

LC 2003-16979

A reissue of the title first published 1965 by Abingdon Press

Despite looking the part, a little witch cannot seem to do the things that witches are supposed to do.

This is a "warm-hearted, conversational story. . . . [Illustrated with] friendly ink drawings in black, red, and yellow." Horn Book Guide

Balouch, Kristen

Feelings. Little Simon 2011 un il bd bk $6.99

Grades: PreK   E

1. Board books for children 2. Animals -- Fiction 3. Emotions -- Fiction

ISBN 978-1-4424-1199-9; 1-4424-1199-6

"Familiar animals convey common emotions through body language and facial expressions. A lion's frown, curled-in tail, and droopy mane communicate his sadness, . . . while a crocodile with a sly smile is feeling sneaky about planning a surprise. . . . Vivid colors, relatable examples, and a compact trim size should appeal to toddlers." Publ Wkly

★ The **little** little girl with the big big voice. Little Simon 2011 un il $12.99

Grades: PreK K 1   E

1. Play -- Fiction 2. Voice -- Fiction 3. Friendship -- Fiction

ISBN 1-4424-0808-1; 978-1-4424-0808-1

A loud little girl has trouble finding a jungle friend to play with because of her booming voice, until at last, she meets the one jungle animal whose roar is louder than hers. "Preschool." (Horn Book)

"Exuberant, stylized illustrations in bright pink, peach, coral, lime, orange and lemon effectively portray this girl and her energy. . . . Young readers can practically hear this little, little girl's big, big voice from where they're sitting, and most pre-schoolers will know exactly how she feels." Kirkus

Bancroft, Bronwyn

Kangaroo and crocodile; my big book of Australian animals. Bronwyn Bancroft. Little Hare Books 2011 48 p. (hbk) $19.99

Grades: 1 2 3   E

1. Australia 2. Animals -- Australia 3. Picture books for children

ISBN 1921714255; 9781921714252

LC 2012405708

This children's picture book looks at Australian animals. "Most of the double-page spreads feature two often-related animals (bottlenose dolphin and great white shark, for instance), although a few . . . concentrate on one animal. There are also several spreads with four different animals." (Kirkus)

W is for wombat; my first Australian word book. Little Hare 2010 un il bd bk $8.99

Grades: PreK   E

1. Alphabet 2. Board books for children 3. Animals -- Australia

ISBN 978-1-921541-17-9 bd bk; 1-921541-17-2 bd bk

"This ABC book features Australian Aboriginal motifs. Creatures like a koala, platypus, and quokka are thickly outlined in paint and decorated with multicolored dots, making them resemble ornate masks, while a river, sun, and tree take on an elemental quality. It's an aesthetically striking guide to Australian wildlife." Publ Wkly

Bandy, Michael S.

White water; [by] Michael S. Bandy and Eric Stein; illustrated by Shadra Strickland. Candlewick Press 2011 40p il $16.99

Grades: K 1 2 3   E

1. Segregation -- Fiction 2. African Americans -- Fiction

ISBN 978-0-7636-3678-4; 0-7636-3678-9

LC 2010040343

After tasting the warm, rusty water from the fountain designated for African Americans, a young boy questions why he cannot drink the cool, refreshing water from the 'Whites Only' fountain. Based on a true experience co-author Michael S. Bandy had as a boy.

"Strickland's watercolor-and-ink illustrations extend the story. . . . Inspirational in tone, this is a strong introduction for young listeners and readers to the American Civil Rights movement." Kirkus

Bang, Molly

All of me! a book of thanks. Blue Sky Press 2009 un il $16.99
Grades: PreK K   E
1. Human body -- Fiction
ISBN 978-0-545-04424-0; 0-545-04424-3
LC 2008-49692

A celebration of how the body's parts work together, from hands and eyes to lips and heart, allowing one to exist in the wondrous universe. Includes instructions for making a book.

"Bang's artwork incorporates cut paper and fabric, photographed elements, red crayon, and paints. . . . Unusual, uneven, creative, and challenging." Booklist

★ The **paper** crane. Greenwillow Bks. 1985 un il $16.99; pa $6.99
Grades: K 1 2 3   E
ISBN 0-688-04108-6; 0-688-07333-6 pa
LC 84-13546

"Every detail of the restaurant interior, from the strawberries on the cake to the floral centerpieces, is a delight to the eye and imagination. . . . The book successfully blends Asian folklore themes with contemporary Western characterization." Horn Book

★ **When** Sophie gets angry--really, really angry. Blue Sky Press (NY) 1999 un il $16.99; pa $6.99
Grades: PreK K 1   E
1. Anger -- Fiction
ISBN 0-590-18979-4; 0-439-59845-1 pa
LC 97-42209

A Caldecott Medal honor book, 2000

"The text is appropriately brief, for it is Bang's double-page illustrations, vibrating with saturated colors, that reveal the drama of the child's emotions." SLJ

Bang-Campbell, Monika

Little Rat makes music; [by] Monika Bang-Campbell; illustrated by Molly Bang. Harcourt 2007 un il $15
Grades: 1 2 3   E
1. Rats -- Fiction 2. Music -- Fiction 3. Violins -- Fiction
ISBN 978-0-15-205305-5; 0-15-205305-0
LC 2005-27536

Little Rat loves the violin but hates to practice, until her teacher suggests she perform a duet with one of the advanced students at the holiday concert.

"The jewel-toned watercolor-and-gouache artwork will help keep readers engaged. A realistic and meaningful look at the satisfying results of hard work and perseverance." SLJ

Banks, Kate

★ **And** if the moon could talk; pictures by Georg Hallensleben. Foster Bks. 1998 un il $15
Grades: PreK K 1 2   E
1. Moon -- Fiction 2. Night -- Fiction 3. Bedtime -- Fiction
ISBN 0-374-30299-5
LC 97-29770

As evening progresses into nighttime, the moon looks down on a variety of nocturnal scenes, including a child getting ready for bed

"The deeply saturated tones of the lovely, impressionistic oil paintings perfectly match the somnolent feeling of the text." SLJ

Baboon; pictures by Georg Hallensleben. Farrar, Straus & Giroux 1997 un il $14
Grades: PreK K 1 2   E
1. Baboons -- Fiction
ISBN 0-374-30474-2
LC 96-20888

Original French edition, 1994

"Visible brush-strokes give texture to the impressionistic paintings, and adept lighting evokes sunlight and shadow. The simple, eloquent text is as subtly understated." Horn Book Guide

The **bear** in the book; Kate Banks; pictures by Georg Hallensleben. Frances Foster Books 2012 36 p. $16.99
Grades: PreK K 1 2   E
1. Bears -- Fiction 2. Bedtime -- Fiction 3. Reading -- Fiction 4. Hibernation -- Fiction
ISBN 0374305919; 9780374305918
LC 2011036691

In this children's book by Kate Banks, illustrated by Georg Hallensleben, "it's time for bed, and a little boy chooses his favorite book for his mother to read to him. The bear in the book is preparing for his own deep slumber, hibernating through the winter while humans and other animals explore the snowy landscape around him. Just when the bear wakes up to greet the spring, the boy drifts off to sleep. . . . This bedtime read . . . will carry young readers through the seasons." (Publisher's note)

The **cat** who walked across France; pictures by Georg Hallensleben. Farrar, Straus and Giroux 2004 un il $16
Grades: PreK K 1 2   E
1. Cats -- Fiction 2. France -- Fiction
ISBN 0-374-39968-9
LC 2002-25091

After his owner dies, a cat wanders across the countryside of France, unable to forget the home he had in the stone house by the edge of the sea

"Banks uses simple, lovely words to tell the elemental story of an outcast's journey home. . . . The paintings are exquisite . . . but what kids will like best is the cat's adventure and the loving welcome he receives." Booklist

★ **Close** your eyes; pictures by Georg Hallensleben. Foster Bks. 2002 un il $16
Grades: PreK K 1   E
1. Sleep -- Fiction 2. Dreams -- Fiction 3. Tigers -- Fiction
ISBN 0-374-31382-2
LC 99-46430

A mother tiger entices her child to sleep by telling of all that can been seen with one's eyes closed

"Banks' language will delight young children with its delicious rhythms, patterned sounds, and the mystery in the poetic imagery. . . . Hallensleben's thick, expressive brush strokes occasionally blur shapes and details, but the vividly colored dreamscapes . . . will capture young imaginations and reassure children who . . . harbor secret fears of falling asleep." Booklist

The **eraserheads**; pictures by Boris Kulikov. Farrar, Straus and Giroux 2010 un il $16.99
Grades: PreK K 1 2   E
1. Adventure fiction 2. Drawing -- Fiction
ISBN 978-0-374-39920-7; 0-374-39920-4
LC 2008024144

Three eraserheads that live with a boy in the land of pencils, paper, rulers, numbers, letters, and drawings become trapped in one of his pictures while trying to correct mistakes

"Kulikov combines loving attention to detail . . . with beguiling portraits of the erasers in various attitudes of dismay and distress. In the story's dueling realities, the 'real life' sections of the spreads feature three-dimensional figures, while the boy's drawings are done in gawky crayon." Publ Wkly

Max's math; Kate Banks; pictures by Boris Kulikov. Frances Foster Books, Farrar Straus Giroux 2015 40 p. color illustrations (Max's Words) (hardcover) $17.99
Grades: PreK K 1 2   E
1. Shape -- Fiction 2. Mathematics -- Fiction 3. Numbers -- Fiction 4. Arithmetic -- Fiction
ISBN 0374348758; 9780374348755
LC 2014015873

In this book by Kate Banks, illustrated by Boris Kulikov, part of the Max's Words series, "Max and his two brothers hop into a car and go looking for problems they can solve. They cruise down highway number 4 on their way to Shapeville, but they see an abandoned number along the way. Is it a 6? Is it a 9? And what's it doing on the side of the road? Once the trio reach Shapeville, there's another problem: a flood washed away all of the squares." (Publisher's note)

"All too often, math content in books for children feels contrived or tacked on, or it smacks of reconstituted textbook material--and didacticism reigns. Here, Banks's characters experience math more organically; the boys play with numbers and shapes--encouraging readers to do likewise." Horn Book

★ **Max's** words; pictures by Boris Kulikov. Farrar, Straus and Giroux 2006 un il $16
Grades: PreK K 1 2   E
1. Storytelling -- Fiction 2. English language -- Fiction 3. Collectors and collecting -- Fiction
ISBN 978-0-374-39949-8; 0-374-39949-2

When Max cuts out words from magazines and newspapers, collecting them the way his brothers collect stamps and coins, they all learn about words, sentences, and storytelling

"Imaginative, softly colored illustrations reveal the gathered words scattered all over the pages. . . . This tale pays homage to the written word and may get children thinking about cutting and pasting their own stories or creating concrete poetry." SLJ

Other titles about Max are:
Max's dragon (2008)
Max's castle (2011)

Monkeys and dog days; pictures by Tomek Bogacki. Farrar, Straus and Giroux 2008 48p il $14.95

Grades: 1 2 3   E
1. Dogs -- Fiction 2. Pets -- Fiction 3. Brothers -- Fiction 4. Chimpanzees -- Fiction
ISBN 0-374-35029-9; 978-0-374-35029-1
LC 2007060726

When Max and Pete get a new dog, they learn that taking care of a pet is not as easy as they thought.

"The story, divided into four chapters, includes a sprinkling of fun facts about dogs and emphasizes important lessons about responsibility, loyalty, and cooperation. Muted pastel illustrations show the brothers and their new pet." SLJ

★ The **night** worker; pictures by Georg Hallensleben. Farrar, Straus & Giroux 2000 un il $16
Grades: PreK K 1 2   E
1. Work -- Fiction 2. Night -- Fiction 3. Building -- Fiction
ISBN 0-374-35520-7
LC 99-27595

Alex wants to be a "night worker" like his father who goes to work at a construction site after Alex goes to bed

"Banks' elegant, simple words and poetic images and rhythms evoke the book's exciting activity and the secure comfort Alex feels with his father. With thick brush strokes and deep, satisfying primary and earth colors, Hallensleben's paintings extend the story's balance of exhilarating intensity and reassuring calm." Booklist

This baby; pictures by Gabi Swiatkowska. Farrar, Straus and Giroux 2010 il $16.99
Grades: PreK K 1 2   E
1. Infants -- Fiction 2. Siblings -- Fiction
ISBN 978-0-374-37514-0; 0-374-37514-3
LC 2009009299

While waiting for it to be born, a young child wonders what its new sibling will be like.

"Swiatkowska . . . pivots easily between the real and the magical . . . [and] Banks . . . acknowledges the gravity of children's thoughts and the depth of their love; it's a quiet, idiosyncratic celebration of new life." Publ Wkly

What's coming for Christmas? pictures by Georg Hallensleben. Farrar, Straus and Giroux 2009 un il $15.99
Grades: PreK K 1   E
1. Christmas -- Fiction 2. Domestic animals -- Fiction
ISBN 978-0-374-39948-1; 0-374-39948-4
LC 2008-20753

While a farm family bustles about, preparing for the arrival of Christmas, they do not notice the great anticipation spreading among the animals, who know that something very special is on its way.

"The muted colors and quality of Hallensleben's illustrations create a dreamlike feeling, matched by the quiet, lyrical text, with its simple, repeated refrains that create a mounting sense of mysterious expectation." Kirkus

Bansch, Helga
Brava, mimi! NorthSouth 2010 un il $16.95
Grades: PreK K 1 2   E
1. Mice -- Fiction 2. Acting -- Fiction 3. Dancers -- Fiction 4. Singing -- Fiction 5. Theater -- Fiction
ISBN 978-0-7358-2322-8; 0-7358-2322-7

"Mimi the mouse wants to be on stage, but she doesn't think she is talented or beautiful enough. As she seeks advice and lessons from friends, she prepares herself for an audition. . . . The scale of the illustrations portray the size of Mimi in comparison to her environment. Budding ballerinas will recognize the tutus on the cover; this is sure to delight all who love to read about performing in theater." Libr Media Connect

I want a dog! North-South 2009 un il $16.95
Grades: K 1 2   E
   1. Dogs -- Fiction
   ISBN 978-0-7358-2255-9; 0-7358-2255-7
"A dog is all young Lisa yearns for, but whether wheedles or tantrums, the parental answer is the same; 'Our apartment is still too small for a dog.' Finally, the clever girl puts up signs in the park asking for a dog to borrow, whereupon Mr. Lewis shows up at her door with sausagy hound Rollo. . . . Bausch writes with a dry humor even as the text effectively conveys Lisa's longing, and the solution is both a reasonable and creative one." Bull Cent Child Books

Odd bird out; translated from the German by Monika Smith. Gecko Press 2011 il $17.95
Grades: K 1 2   E
   1. Ravens -- Fiction
   ISBN 978-1-8774-6708-0; 1-8774-6708-1
Robert is different from all other ravens. He is a happy bird. But when he laughs and tells jokes, the other birds don't like it at all. Nor do they like his colorful clothes and they hold their ears when he tries to sing.
"The conversational text is paired with paintings that perfectly capture the raven's nature. Who knew birds could have so many facial expressions and disapproving postures? In his wildly colored outfits and high-heeled shoes, Robert shines amid the status quo." SLJ

Banyai, Istvan
  The **other** side. Chronicle Books 2005 un il $15.95
Grades: K 1 2 3   E
   1. Stories without words
   ISBN 0-8118-4608-3
                  LC 2004-63448
"This is a challenging book, one that allows for creative speculation. The graphite-rendered artwork is quirky as well as infinitely interesting." SLJ

Baram, Gilad
  Wall; Tom Clohosy Cole. Candlewick Press 2014 32 p. color illustrations $16.99
Grades: K 1 2 3 4   E
   1. Family life -- Fiction 2. Berlin Wall (1961-1989) -- Fiction 3. Cold War -- Fiction
   ISBN 0763675601; 9780763675608
                  LC 2013957276
This children's story, written and illustrated by Tom Clohosy Cole, is being released "on the 25th anniversary of the fall of the Berlin Wall. A young boy and his mother and sister were separated from their father when the Berlin Wall was built between East and West Germany. This story shows the family's struggle as they try to cross the wall so they can be together again." (Publisher's note)
"When a wall divides their city, a boy searches for a way to reunite his now-separated family members. Although the jacket calls it a story about the Berlin Wall, the book proper does not provide any such identification (probably wise, giv-

en its ahistorical conclusion). Digital illustrations reinforce the story's fabular nature, with tenderly cartooned characters set against ominous silhouettes and the monumental wall." Horn Book

Barclay, Jane
  Proud as a peacock, brave as a lion; illustrated by Renné Benoit. Tundra Books 2009 un il $18.95
Grades: PreK K 1 2   E
   1. Memory -- Fiction 2. Veterans -- Fiction 3. Grandfathers -- Fiction 4. World War, 1939-1945 -- Fiction
   ISBN 978-0-88776-951-1; 0-88776-951-9
"A small boy has fun with his grandfather as they page through an old photo album, and Poppa tells how, at age 17, he lied about his age so that he could join the army. Small photos in sepia shades evoke the past. . . . Opposite the wartime photos, large, bright, unframed pictures in watercolor and gouache show the boy and Poppa in the present, talking about the soldier's feelings—proud as a peacock, pretending to be brave as a lion—and the lively animal images in the words are also part of the pictures. . . . The blend of grim reality, heroic battle, and playful fantasy will speak to kids." Booklist

Bardhan-Quallen, Sudipta
  Chicks run wild; [by] Sudipta Bardhan; illustrated by Ward Jenkins. Simon & Schuster Books for Young Readers 2011 un il
Grades: PreK K 1   E
   1. Stories in rhyme 2. Bedtime -- Fiction 3. Chickens -- Fiction 4. Mother-child relationship -- Fiction
   ISBN 1-4424-0673-9; 978-1-4424-0673-5
When her little chicks refuse to settle down for the night, Mama decides to surprise them with an unusual request.
"The pencil and digitally painted illustrations carry the folksy tale in an able fashion. An entertaining selection for bedtime." SLJ

  Duck, Duck, Moose! by Sudipta Bardhan-Quallen; illustrated by Noah Z. Jones. Disney-Hyperion Books 2014 32 p. color illustrations $16.99
Grades: PreK K 1   E
   1. Ducks -- Fiction 2. Moose -- Fiction 3. Parties -- Fiction 4. Humorous stories 5. Surprise -- Fiction 6. Roommates -- Fiction
   ISBN 1423171101; 9781423171102
                  LC 2013012211
In this children's book by Sudipta Bardhan-Quallen, "Duck and Duck are preparing for a party, and each step of the way, Moose inadvertently messes things up. When he disappears in shame, Duck and Duck must go find him so he can join in the party-which was for him!" (Publisher's note)
"Jones' cartoon artwork tells the story with detailed, precise drawings of the ducks outlined in black against a clean white background. The moose's antics, in contrast, are chaotic, with colors and spillage abounding. All three faces are wonderfully expressive." Kirkus

  Tyrannosaurus wrecks! by Sudipta Bardhan-Quallen; illustrated by Zachariah OHora. Abrams Books for Young Readers 2014 32 p. $14.95
Grades: PreK K 1   E
   1. Tyrannosaurus rex 2. Dinosaurs -- Fiction 3. Stories

in rhyme 4. Behavior -- Fiction 5. Tyrannosaurus rex
-- Fiction
ISBN 1419710354; 9781419710353

LC 2013022197

Written by Sudipta Bardhan-Quallen and illustrated
by Zachariah O'Hora, "in this read-along picture book,
a classroom full of young dinosaurs plays with toys, does
art projects, and reads books. But each activity is another
opportunity for the over-enthusiastic Tyrannosaurus Rex to
wreak havoc. . . . The format is extra vertical in order to
accommodate T. Rex's biggest messes." (Publisher's note)

"All is harmony in the dinosaur classroom, except for
one member with a self-control issue: "Apatosaurus colors.
Pteranodon inspects. Velociraptor glitters. Tyrannosaurus...
WRECKS!" Naively drawn dinosaurs with bold outlines
and flat, digitally added colors pop from white pages. A text
consisting primarily of simple subjects and verbs builds tension until the students band together to reform the disrup-
tive dino. A satisfyingly high-energy, primal read-aloud."
Horn Book

Bardoe, Cheryl

The **ugly** dinosaur; a prehistoric tale. illustrated by
Doug Kennedy. Abrams Books for Young Readers 2011
un il $16.95
Grades: PreK K 1   **E**
1. Ducks -- Fiction 2. Dinosaurs -- Fiction
ISBN 978-0-8109-9739-4; 0-8109-9739-8

LC 2010021624

In this take on "The Ugly Duckling," a tyrannosaurus rex is hatched in a nest of ducklings. Includes facts
about dinosaurs.

"Kennedy's cartoonish watercolors nicely balance the
ugly 'duckling's' good intentions with his slightly threatening appearance and clumsiness, helping readers empathize
with him. . . . A sure winner for those dino-hungry readers."
Kirkus

Includes bibliographical references

Bardos, Magali

★ **100** Bears. Flying Eye Books 2014 104 p. $19.95
Grades: K 1 2 3   **E**
1. Counting 2. Bears -- Fiction
ISBN 190926315X; 9781909263154

This illustrated children's counting book, written and illustrated by Magali Bardos is a "real bear caper." The book
presents "a a wacky, . . . anarchic tale of hunters, feasts, and
marauding beasts, [in which] we chase the numbers 1-100
through mountains, forests, and cities." (Publisher's note)

Barner, Bob

★ **Bug** safari. Holiday House 2004 un il $16.95
Grades: PreK K 1 2   **E**
1. Ants -- Fiction 2. Insects -- Fiction
ISBN 0-8234-1707-7

LC 2003-56619

"The bright, cut-paper collages will appeal to the youngest bug lovers, but the funny, dramatically told story is tailored to a more sophisticated young entomologist." Booklist

"A young explorer describes his experiences as he tracks
an army of ants through 'a bug-infested jungle,' observing
their progress through a magnifying glass." SLJ

Barnett, Mac

Billy Twitters and his big blue whale problem; Mac
Barnett, author; Adam Rex, illustrator. Disney/Hyperion
Books 2009 un il $16.99
Grades: PreK K 1 2   **E**
1. School stories 2. Whales -- Fiction 3. Family life
-- Fiction
ISBN 978-0-7868-4958-1; 0-7868-4958-4

LC 2009-11203

When Billy Twitters' mother follows through on her
threat to buy him a blue whale if he refuses to obey, he finds
himself the owner of an enormous pet that he must take
with him everywhere, which does not make him popular
at school.

"Young readers will likely enjoy the ridiculous premise,
and the many whale facts worked seamlessly into the tale."
SLJ

★ **Extra** yarn; written by Mac Barnett; illustrated by
Jon Klassen. Balzer & Bray 2012 il $16.99
Grades: PreK K 1 2   **E**
1. Yarn -- Fiction 2. Magic -- Fiction 3. Knitting
-- Fiction
ISBN 978-0-06-195338-5; 0-06-195338-5

LC 2010015945

Caldecott Honor Book (2013)

With a supply of yarn that never runs out, Annabelle
knits for everyone and everything in town until an evil arch-
duke decides he wants the yarn for himself.

"Klassen . . . uses inks, gouache and colorized scans of a
sweater to create a stylized, linear design of dark geometric
shapes against a white background. . . . Barnett . . . maintains a folkloric narrative that results in a traditional story arc
complete with repetition, drama and a satisfying conclusion.
A quiet story of sharing with no strings attached." Kirkus

Guess again! illustrated by Adam Rex. Simon &
Schuster Books for Young Readers 2009 un il $16.99
Grades: 1 2 3 4   **E**
1. Stories in rhyme
ISBN 978-1-4169-5566-5; 1-4169-5566-6

LC 2008-12882

"A rhymed text joins with hinting illustrations to encourage readers to fill in the last word of the verse. A page
turn, however, unveils an answer that's an absurd breach of
expectation. . . . The confounding of expectations is pleasingly goofy. . . . Rex partners the rhyme with robust and solid
gouache scenes that are comedic in their own right. . . . This
would be particularly useful as a quick pick for reluctant
readers, who'll warm to the combination of corniness and
sophistication in the satirically unguessable guessing game."
Bull Cent Child Books

Oh no! Not again! (or how I built a time machine to
save history) (or at least my history grade) written by Mac
Barnett; illustrated by Dan Santat. Disney-Hyperion 2012
40 p. col. ill. $17.99
Grades: K 1 2 3   **E**
1. Belgium -- Fiction 2. Time travel -- Fiction 3.
Picture books for children 4. Humorous stories 5. Cave
dwellers -- Fiction 6. Cave paintings -- Fiction
ISBN 1423149122; 9781423149125

LC 2011011111

In this book, part of the "Oh No!" series "[Mac] Barnett's overachiever has a new dilemma: Her history test is returned with one point off for an incorrect answer. Noting that 'Belgium' is not the country where the oldest prehistoric cave paintings exist . . . she builds a time machine to alter history. After a few glitches . . . she finds her Belgian cavemen. . . . The duo gives the transporter a spin while the frustrated scholar decorates the cave herself." (Kirkus Reviews)

★ Oh no!, or, How my science project destroyed the world; written by Mac Barnett; illustrated by Dan Santat. Disney Hyperion Books 2010 un il $16.99
Grades: K 1 2   E
1. Robots -- Fiction 2. Science projects -- Fiction
ISBN 978-1-4231-2312-5; 1-4231-2312-3
                                        LC 2010004516
After winning the science fair with the giant robot she has built, a little girl realizes that there is a major problem.
"Santat's brilliantly hued digital illustrations are the perfect foil for Barnett's almost-wordless tale of a science project gone awry. . . . Comic-book, picture-book and movie styles come together in a well-designed package that includes a movie poster on the reverse side of the jacket, an old-time computation book as the inside cover and detailed scientific drawings on the endpapers. . . . A must-have." Kirkus

President taft is stuck in the bath; Mac Barnett, illustrated by Chris Van Dusen. Candlewick Press 2014 32 p. color illustrations $16.99
Grades: 1 2 3 4   E
1. Presidents -- United States
ISBN 0763663174; 9780763663179
                                        LC 2013943103
"Mac Barnett begins with a historically unconfirmed rumor that President Taft once got stuck in his bathtub. While President Taft gets increasingly louder and more frustrated, the First Lady remains calm. He calls on the vice-president and his Cabinet members, each of them offering a self-serving or unworkable solution. Finally, his wife suggests that they use their muscle to get the President out and he is quickly freed." (Library Media Connection)
"The combination of Barnett's repetitive assonance . . . and Van Dusen's gouache caricature illustrations (with strategically placed water and bubbles) sets the hilarious tone." Booklist

★ Sam and Dave dig a hole; Mac Barnett, illustrated by Jon Klassen. First edition Candlewick Press 2014 40 p. $16.99
Grades: PreK K 1 2   E
1. Humorous fiction 2. Adventure and adventurers 3. Holes 4. Imagination
ISBN 0763662291; 9780763662295
                                        LC 2013955959
Caldecott Honor Book (2015)
In this children's book, by Mac Barnett and illustrated by Jon Klassen, "Sam and Dave are on a mission. A mission to find something spectacular. So they dig a hole. And they keep digging. And they find . . . nothing. Yet the day turns out to be pretty spectacular after all." (Publisher's note)
"Sam and Dave, each wearing baseball caps and wielding long-handled shovels, set out to dig a hole. How big

a hole? "We won't stop digging until we find something spectacular," says Dave, so off they go, digging ever deeper while their little dog follows their progress. A cross section of their dig reveals that Sam and Dave come awfully close to their prize, but they keep digging and missing treasure until they decide to take a nap, during which they tumble right through the earth..." Booklist

Barracca, Debra
★ The adventures of Taxi Dog; by Debra and Sal Barracca; pictures by Mark Buehner. Dial Bks. for Young Readers 1990 30p il $16.99; pa $5.99
Grades: PreK K 1 2   E
1. Stories in rhyme 2. Dogs -- Fiction 3. Taxicabs -- Fiction
ISBN 0-8037-0671-5; 0-14-056665-1 pa
                                        LC 89-1056
"In snappy, rhymed lines, Maxi recalls his days as a stray and his adoption by taxi-driving Jim. Applying oil paint over acrylics, Buehner creates color with lush character. The hues' intense depth, coupled with the artist's finesse with perspective, will draw readers into the action." Booklist
Other titles about Maxi, the Taxi Dog are:
Maxi, the hero (1991)
Maxi, the star (1993)
A Taxi Dog Christmas (1994)

Barrett, Judi
Cloudy with a chance of meatballs; written by Judi Barrett and drawn by Ron Barrett. Aladdin Paperbacks 1982 un il pa $6.99
Grades: PreK K 1 2   E
1. Food -- Fiction 2. Weather -- Fiction
ISBN 0-689-70749-5
                                        LC 87-29643
First published 1978
Life is delicious in the town of Chewandswallow where it rains soup and juice, snows mashed potatoes, and blows storms of hamburgers—until the weather takes a turn for the worse.

★ Never take a shark to the dentist and other things not to do; [by] Judi Barrett; illustrated by John Nickle. Atheneum Books for Young Readers 2007 un il $16.99
Grades: PreK K 1 2   E
1. Animals -- Fiction
ISBN 978-1-4169-0724-4; 1-4169-0724-6
                                        LC 2006000153
A list of things one should not do with various animals, such as "hold hands with a lobster"
"Nickle, working in hyper-detailed acrylics, enhances the comical phrases with surreal imagery. . . . Kids will revel in the absurd humor." Publ Wkly

Santa from Cincinnati; How a Little Boy Named Santa Grew up to Become the Real Thing. Judi Barrett; illustrated by Kevin Hawks. Atheneum Books for Young Readers 2012 48 p. (hardcover) $16.99
Grades: K 1 2 3   E
1. Humorous fiction 2. Christmas -- Fiction 3. Santa Claus -- Fiction
ISBN 9781442429932; 9781442429949; 1442429933
                                        LC 2011050810

This children's book, by Judi Barrett, illustrated by Kevin Hawkes, tells the story of Santa Claus' childhood. "His first words were 'ho ho ho!' By five he was wearing a fake beard and mustache, and could rarely be found without his favorite stuffed reindeer. . . . Despite this, his parents went to great lengths to keep the normalcy in his life. . . . But there was no stopping Santa from being Santa, and one winter, he began to make his lists." (Publisher's note)

Barrett, Mary Brigid

 Shoebox Sam; illustrated by Frank Morrison. Zonderkidz 2011 un il $15.99

Grades: K 1 2   E
 1. Shoes -- Fiction 2. Christian life -- Fiction 3. Homeless persons -- Fiction

 ISBN 978-0-310-71549-8; 0-310-71549-0

On Saturdays, Delia and Jesse help Shoebox Sam, who teaches them about charity and love by not only repairing shoes for paying customers, but also giving poor and homeless people the dignity—and footwear—they need.

"Even in quieter poses, Morrison's bright-eyed, rubber-limbed figures look like they are dancing, and they perfectly reflect the lively sounds and rhythms of Barrett's language." Booklist

Barretta, Gene

 Timeless Thomas; how Thomas Edison changed our lives. Gene Barretta. Henry Holt 2012 37 p.

Grades: 2 3 4   E
 1. Inventions -- History 2. Inventions

 ISBN 0805091084; 9780805091083

                                          LC 2011034057

In this children's book, by Gene Barretta, the life and inventions of Thomas Edison are described. "Edison is most famous for inventing the incandescent lightbulb, but at his landmark laboratories in Menlo Park & West Orange, New Jersey, he also developed many other staples of modern technology. Despite many failures, Edison persevered. And good for that, because it would be very difficult to go through a day without using one of his life-changing inventions." (Publisher's note)

 Includes bibliographical references

 Zoola Palooza; a book of homographs. Henry Holt 2011 un il $16.99

Grades: K 1 2   E
 1. Animals -- Fiction 2. Concerts -- Fiction 3. Musicians -- Fiction 4. English language -- Homonyms

 ISBN 0-8050-9107-6; 978-0-8050-9107-6

                                          LC 2010025833

Playing a variety of musical instruments, an all-animal touring concert group introduces words that are spelled the same but sound differently and have different meanings, such as tear (to cry) and tear (to rip).

"While teachers are sure to reach for this entertaining resource again and again, the humor, illustrations, wordplay and story are strong enough that casual readers will pick this up, chuckle and even . . . learn." Kirkus

Barron, T. A.

 Ghost hands; a story inspired by Patagonia's Cave of the Hands. illustrated by William Low. Philomel Books 2011 un il $18.99

Grades: PreK K 1   E
 1. Courage -- Fiction 2. Native Americans -- Fiction 3. Cave drawings and paintings -- Fiction 4. Patagonia (Argentina and Chile) -- Fiction

 ISBN 978-0-399-25083-5; 0-399-25083-2

                                          LC 2010010648

Auki, a young member of the Tehuelche tribe in Patagonia, wants to prove himself as a hunter but when he sets out on his own to face the puma, he stumbles upon a sacred cave and its guardian.

"As in Barron and Low's previous collaboration . . . tightly connected visuals and text provoke curiosity and awe about a phenomenon at once mysterious and accessible." Kirkus

Bartlett, T. C.

 Tuba lessons; illustrated by Monique Felix. Creative Editions 2009 un il $25.65

Grades: PreK K 1   E
 1. Stories without words 2. Animals -- Fiction 3. Musical instruments -- Fiction

 ISBN 978-1-56846-209-7; 1-56846-209-3

                                          LC 2009-3834

 First published 1997 by Harcourt, Brace and Company

While walking through the woods on his way to his tuba lesson, a boy becomes sidetracked by all the animals that want to hear him play.

"This text is not only for storytimes, but can be used as a catalyst to get young readers and writers to create their own words to enhance the imaginative, playful illustrations. Friendship, music and the journey are the themes in this picture tale." Libr Media Connect

Bartoletti, Susan Campbell

 ★ **Naamah** and the ark at night. Candlewick Press 2011 un il $16.99

Grades: PreK K 1 2   E
 1. Lullabies 2. Stories in rhyme 3. Children's poetry 4. Night -- Fiction 5. Animals -- Fiction 6. Noah's ark -- Fiction

 ISBN 978-0-7636-4242-6; 0-7636-4242-8

                                          LC 2010040398

"Bartoletti shapes his verse form into a gentle litany . . . centerd on Naamah's lulling song. . . . Meade's watercolor collages are a fine complement. . . . A lovely lullaby, in a beautiful, masterfully integrated book." Horn Book

Barton, Byron

 ★ **Dinosaurs,** dinosaurs. Crowell 1989 un il $16.99; lib bdg $17.89; pa $6.99; bd bk $7.99

Grades: PreK K   E
 1. Dinosaurs -- Fiction

 ISBN 0-694-00269-0; 0-690-04768-1 lib bdg; 0-06-443298-X pa; 0-694-400625-4 bd bk

                                          LC 88-22938

This book examines the many different kinds of dinosaurs, big and small, those with spikes and those with long, sharp teeth

"Barton conveys the primordial sense of excitement that draws children to these beasts. . . . The endpapers identify the creatures by scientific name and pronunciation. Barton wisely keeps his text simple, describing dinosaurs only by size and physical features." SLJ

My bike; Byron Barton. Greenwillow Books, an imprint of HarperCollinsPublishers 2015 40 p. color illustrations hbk $16.99

Grades: PreK K 1   E

1. Circus -- Fiction 2. Bicycles -- Fiction 3. Bicycles and bicycling -- Fiction

ISBN 0062336991; 9780062336996

LC 2014013919

In this picture book by Byron Barton, "Tom . . . is the proud owner of a bright green bicycle. After Tom describes all the parts of his bike, he rides the bike to work. He rides along busy roads and bustling streets, past cars and buses and animals and people, until he arrives at the circus, changes into his work clothes, and goes to work. It turns out that Tom is a clown, and his job is to ride a unicycle on a high wire under the big top!" (Publisher's note)

★ **My** bus; Byron Barton. First edition Greenwillow Books, an imprint of HarperCollinsPublishers 2014 40 p. (trade ed.) $16.99

Grades: PreK K   E

1. Pets -- Fiction 2. Buses -- Fiction 3. Mathematics -- Fiction 4. Transportation -- Fiction

ISBN 0062287362; 9780062287366

LC 2013007869

This book, by Byron Barton, "is a lively celebration of vehicles and transportation, occupations, pets, and basic math concepts. The busy bus driver . . . has a job to do. He drives his bus along his route, picks up the cat and dog passengers waiting at the bus stops, and delivers them to their destinations--which in this case include the airport, the harbor, and the train station. Along the way, children are introduced to the concepts of addition, subtraction, and sets." (Publisher's note)

"In a companion volume to My Car, Joe drives Bus #123 across a bold-hued landscape populated with feline and canine passengers. The book ingeniously and subtly introduces the basic concepts of cardinal and ordinal numbers, addition, subtraction, and sets. Illustrated in Barton's signature style, with bold, flat colors and with only the most important visual details included, there are sure to be re-readings." Horn Book

★ **My** car. Greenwillow Bks. 2001 un il $14.95; pa $6.99; bd bk $7.99

Grades: PreK K   E

1. Automobiles -- Fiction

ISBN 0-06-029624-0; 0-06-029625-9 lib bdg; 0-06-058940-X pa; 0-06-056045-2 bd bk

LC 00-50334

Sam describes in loving detail his car and how he drives it

"The chunky blocks of color and minimalist text will withstand countless readings." Publ Wkly

Barton, Chris

★ **Shark** vs. train; by Chris Barton & [illustrated by] Tom Lichtenheld. Little, Brown 2010 un il $16.99

Grades: PreK K 1   E

1. Sharks -- Fiction 2. Railroads -- Fiction

ISBN 978-0-316-00762-7; 0-316-00762-5

LC 2009-17961

A shark and a train compete in a series of contests on a seesaw, in hot air balloons, bowling, shooting baskets, playing hide-and-seek, and more.

"This is a genius concept. . . . Lichtenheld's . . . watercolor cartoons have a fluidity and goofy intensity that recalls Mad magazine, while Barton . . . gives the characters snappy dialogue throughout." Publ Wkly

Bartone, Elisa

★ **Peppe** the lamplighter; illustrations by Ted Lewin. Lothrop, Lee & Shepard Bks. 1993 un il $17.99; pa $6.99

Grades: K 1 2 3   E

1. New York (N.Y.) -- Fiction 2. Italian Americans -- Fiction

ISBN 0-688-10268-9; 0-688-15469-7 pa

LC 92-1397

A Caldecott Medal honor book, 1994

Peppe's father is upset when he learns that Peppe has taken a job lighting the gas street lamps in his New York City neighborhood

"Peppe's quiet quest for familial respect and pleasure in his work is touching and rhythmically written. The early-American city scenes are dark but have a nice period luminescence in the myriad street and table lamps, and the earth-toned watercolors lend the bustling streets and interiors of Little Italy an air both somber and lively." Bull Cent Child Books

Bartram, Simon

Bob's best ever friend. Templar Books 2009 un il $16.99

Grades: K 1 2   E

1. Dogs -- Fiction 2. Moon -- Fiction 3. Astronauts -- Fiction 4. Friendship -- Fiction

ISBN 978-0-7636-4425-3; 0-7636-4425-0

"Bob, an astronaut who travels daily from Earth to the Moon to entertain tourists, is lonely: there are no visitors this Tuesday and his friends have gone off to Pluto. The next day, he begins to look for a 'best-ever friend' and decides that it could be a pet. One day he sees something amazing pop out of a crater: a dog. Bartram's detailed acrylics give readers comic relief while Bob is on his quest. . . . The artwork is reminiscent of books from the 1950s and is done in electric blues, yellows, and reds." SLJ

Another title about Bob is:

Man on the moon (2002)

Baruzzi, Agnese

The **true** story of Little Red Riding Hood; [by] Agnese Baruzzi and Sandro Natalini. Templar Books 2009 un il $14.99

Grades: K 1 2 3   E

1. Fairy tales 2. Pop-up books

ISBN 978-0-7636-4427-7

"In this fractured fairy tale, the wolf asks for help rehabilitating his reputation. Little Red Riding Hood's advice (become a vegetarian) works—for a while. The book overflows with lift-the-flaps; envelopes with tiny letters inside and a fabric shower curtain and apron are also included. The boldly colored naive-style paintings are enhanced by collage elements, including rickrack borders." Horn Book Guide

Base, Graeme

★ **Animalia**; Graeme Base. H.N. Abrams 1993 32 p. $12.95

Grades: PreK K 1 2 3   E

1. Animals -- Fiction 2. Alphabet -- Fiction 3. Animals -- Pictorial works 4. English language -- Alphabet

ISBN 0810919397; 9780810919396

In this children's book, author Graeme Base "has created an ABC book that goes far beyond a simple listing of items in alphabetical order. There are captions or headlines accompanying each letter's scene, such as 'Eight Enormous Elephants Expertly Eating Easter Eggs,' or 'Two Tigers Taking the 10:20 Train to Timbuktu.' Each picture is replete with an apparently random choice of objects that have in common (on every page but the one for the letter X) their first letters." (Publishers Weekly)

★ The **Jewel** Fish of Karnak. Abrams Books for Young Readers 2011 un il

Grades: K 1 2 3   E

1. Magic -- Fiction 2. Thieves -- Fiction 3. Egypt -- History -- Fiction 4. Kings and rulers -- Fiction

ISBN 1-4197-0086-3; 978-1-4197-0086-6

LC 2010050080

Two thieves, caught stealing from an Egyptian market, are brought before the Cat Pharaoh, who agrees to pardon them if they bring back a treasure that was stolen from her, without taking anything else and without getting the precious Jewel Fish wet.

Base "doesn't disappoint his sleuthing fans, providing decodable hieroglyphic messages on painted stone tablets across the bottom of each spread. This tale packs in plenty of puzzle solving and Egyptology amid the boldly animated scenes; the illustrations' exquisite details—right down to the comical facial expressions of the bumbling thieves—tell much of the story." Publ Wkly

The **water** hole; Graeme Base. Harry N. Abrams 2001 32 p. col. ill. $19.95

Grades: PreK K 1 2 3   E

1. Counting 2. Habitat (Ecology)

ISBN 0810945681; 9780810945685

LC 00066378

In this children's book, author Graeme Base "takes the reader on a journey of discovery, from the plains of Africa and the jungles of the Amazon to the woodlands of North America and the deserts of the Australian outback. . . . Page by page the numbers increase as the animals come to their water hole to drink. But at the same time, the cast of frogs frolicking by the water hole is diminishing. What is going on?" (Publisher's note)

"One rhino, two tigers, and other animals up to ten kangaroos come to drink from a water hole, a die-cut hole that shrinks through successive pages. Why are animals on different continents shown drinking from the same water hole? Why is the water hole shrinking? Don't ask--just enjoy searching the detailed paintings for hidden animal images and a family of sartorially savvy frogs." Horn Book

Basher, Simon

★ **ABC** Kids. Kingfisher Books 2011 un il $17.99

Grades: PreK K   E

1. Alphabet

ISBN 978-0-7534-6495-3; 0-7534-6495-0

"This ABC book provides a stylish introduction to the alphabet while building vocabularies. [Basher's] chunky cartoon illustrations are front and center, joined by heavily alliterative sentences. . . . Full-bleed pastel backdrops give the book the feel of a cheerily illustrated sheaf of construction paper; with inventive vocab on left-hand pages opposite pages focusing on one stand-alone image, . . . the book is appropriate for both beginning and developing readers. Smart fun." Publ Wkly

Go! go! Bobo: colors. Kingfisher 2011 un il bd bk $6.99

Grades: PreK   E

1. Color 2. Board books for children

ISBN 978-0-7534-6493-9; 0-7534-6493-4

Bouncy Bobo can't sit still. He just has to bounce his way across the pages of this book, painting everything he sees. From yellow ducks, to blue butterflies, orange carrots, pink piggies, red roses, and green apples.

"A great title in encourage toddlers' interactive play. . . . Kids will want to move from the book to the real world and name the colors all around them." Booklist

Bass, L. G.

Boom boom go away! by Laura Geringer; illustrated by Bagram Ibatoulline. Atheneum 2010 un il $15.99

Grades: PreK K 1   E

1. Toys -- Fiction 2. Music -- Fiction 3. Bedtime -- Fiction

ISBN 978-0-689-85093-6; 0-689-85093-X

"Each time a parent tells a boy to go to bed, the toys in his room delay the process by playing their instruments and saying they can't be disturbed. . . . The rhythmical text has an appealing cadence and a catchy refrain. Ibatoulline's watercolor and acrylic-gouache spreads of the child's room are wonderfully designed." SLJ

Bastedo, Jamie

Free as the wind; saving the horses of Sable Island. illustrated by Susan Tooke. Red Deer Press 2007 32p il (Northern lights books for children) hardcover o.p. pa $10.95

Grades: K 1 2   E

1. Horses -- Fiction 2. Islands -- Fiction 3. Nova Scotia -- Fiction

ISBN 978-0-88995-350-5; 0-88995-350-3; 978-0-88995-446-5 pa; 0-88995-446-1 pa

In the 1960s, the wild horses of Sable Island in Nova Scotia were to be sold and auctioned off, many of them to be slaughtered for dog meat. School children from across Canada wrote to the Prime Minister pleading with him to have the horses returned and to save them from certain death. This fictional account follows young Lucas Beauregard, son of the retiring superintendent of Sable Island, as he befriends and then plots to save Gem, one of the horses.

"The writing style of this well-told story draws readers into the urgency of the horses' situation. The plot develops quickly. Tooke's realistic, painterly artwork follows the story line well and places readers on the island." SLJ

Bastianich, Lidia

Nonna's birthday surprise; Lidia Bastianich. Running Press Kids 2013 60 p. (hardcover) $16.95

Grades: K 1 2 3   E
    1. Birthdays -- Fiction 2. Farm life -- Fiction
    ISBN 0762446552; 9780762446551

                 LC 2012944237

In this children's story, by Lidia Bastianich, illustrated by Renée Graef, "It's Nonna Mima's birthday, and Nonna Lidia and her grandkids are determined to throw her a surprise feast! While planning the evening's menu, Nonna Lidia shares her memories of growing up on the farm during each season of the year, gardening her own fruits and vegetables, and being surrounded by animals of all kinds." (Publisher's note)

Bataille, Marion
    10. Roaring Brook Press 2011 un il $14.99
Grades: 1 2 3 4 5   E
    1. Numbers 2. Pop-up books
    ISBN 978-1-59643-682-4; 1-59643-682-4

"Housed within a shiny red slipcase, this minimalist counting book can be viewed in multiple ways. By turning the pages once from left to right, readers can count from '01' to '10,' the black numerals appearing on the left side of each white spread. By proceeding through the book and unfolding each page twice, however, the numbers transform—the top of the '2' swivels, losing its base to become a '9,' for example—so readers can count down to '01.' . . . the sleek construction should appeal to pop-up fans of any age." Publ Wkly

    ★ **ABC3D**. Roaring Brook Press 2008 un il $19.95
Grades: 1 2 3 4 5   E
    1. Alphabet 2. Pop-up books
    ISBN 978-1-59643-425-7; 1-59643-425-2

                 LC 2008-08933

"From the lenticular cover to the jazzy use of a red, white and black color scheme, this hand-size French alphabet book is as stylish as a pop-up can be. Letters here not only pop up, they move and transform. . . . Many letters are three-dimensional (i.e., the legs of H are hollow paper rectangles), and gain extra glamour from high-contrast backgrounds (white on black; red or black on white). A-plus for drama and innovation." Publ Wkly

Bateman, Teresa
    April foolishness; illustrated by Nadine Bernard Westcott. Albert Whitman & Co. 2004 un il $15.95
Grades: PreK K 1 2   E
    1. Stories in rhyme 2. Farm life -- Fiction 3. April Fools' Day -- Fiction
    ISBN 0-8075-0404-1

                 LC 2004-825

"Bateman's verse prances along in a pleasing way, never sounding a false note or tripping over its metric feet. Bright with colorful washes, Westcott's ink drawings illustrate the action with equal lightness and grace. . . . Zany and inventive, the artwork amplifies the story's humor." Booklist

    ★ **Keeper** of soles; illustrated by Yayo. Holiday House 2006 un il $16.95
Grades: K 1 2 3   E
    1. Death -- Fiction 2. Shoes -- Fiction 3. Shoemakers -- Fiction
    ISBN 0-8234-1734-4

                 LC 2004-52297

When Death comes for a shoemaker's soul, he outwits him by making shoes for him, giving him soles instead of souls.

"Bateman pairs the cadences of a traditional folktale with contemporary humor. The scenes are imbued with suspense without being macabre. Yayo's full-bleed acrylics provide large expanses of rich, layered colors as foils for the smaller, whimsical details." SLJ

Bates, Janet Costa
    Seaside dream; illustrated by Lambert Davis. Lee & Low Books 2010 un il $17.95
Grades: K 1 2   E
    1. Gifts -- Fiction 2. Birthdays -- Fiction 3. Cape Verde -- Fiction 4. Grandmothers -- Fiction
    ISBN 978-1-60060-347-1; 1-60060-347-5

                 LC 2009-17049

At a birthday celebration on the beach, Cora gives her grandmother a special gift and encourages her to make a trip back to her home country, Cape Verde.

"This poignant tale of a special relationship between a young girl and her grandmother showcases the joy of gift giving as well as the importance of family connections. . . . Color-drenched illustrations in deep-blue tones effectively evoke the summery coastal setting." Booklist

Battersby, Katherine
    Squish Rabbit. Viking 2011 un il $12.99
Grades: PreK K   E
    1. Size -- Fiction 2. Rabbits -- Fiction 3. Friendship -- Fiction 4. Loneliness -- Fiction
    ISBN 978-0-670-01267-1; 0-670-01267-X

                 LC 2010042227

A lonely little rabbit wants to make a friend.

"Battersby's expert, ample distribution of white space provides room on each page for readers to luxuriate in her impressive, evocative ink, watercolor and collage illustrations—and to absorb a small rabbit's feelings. Rough papers and textured fabrics add depth, creating an almost tactile reading experience. . . . Minimal, moving and adorable, little Squish makes a big impression." Kirkus

Battut, Eric
    ★ **The fox** and the hen. Boxer 2010 un il $16.95
Grades: PreK K   E
    1. Eggs -- Fiction 2. Foxes -- Fiction 3. Domestic animals -- Fiction
    ISBN 978-1-907152-02-3; 1-907152-02-4

"Henrietta Hen lays her first egg and innocently trades it to Red Fox for a worm. The other farm animals quickly tell her that she must get her precious egg back and go with her to make the trade. . . . Each time Red Fox refuses and thinks of a new way to eat the egg. . . . Henrietta finds an enormous stone that her friends paint white, and Red Fox eagerly trades her egg for this bigger one. . . . The animals are outlined in thick, black line and dabs of white highlight the vibrant red and orange palette. . . . With great economy, Battut gives each animal an expressive face and moves the story to a satisfying conclusion." SLJ

    Little Mouse's big secret. Sterling 2011 un il $12.95
Grades: PreK K   E
    1. Mice -- Fiction 2. Trees -- Fiction 3. Apples --

Fiction 4. Animals -- Fiction
ISBN 978-1-4027-7462-1; 1-4027-7462-1
LC 2010019689

Little Mouse refuses to reveal his secret despite being questioned by his friends.

"The urge to hoard treats is a common one, and Battut's . . . brisk, spare treatment of the problem has the feel of a classic. . . . Elemental text and artwork effectively convey the lesson about Mouse's best-laid plans, while his obliviousness to the tree's growth provides suspense and satisfaction." Publ Wkly

Bauer, Marion Dane

In like a lion, out like a lamb; illustrated by Emily Arnold McCully. Holiday House 2011 un il $16.95
Grades: PreK K 1 2   E
  1. Stories in rhyme 2. Lions -- Fiction 3. Sheep -- Fiction 4. Spring -- Fiction
  ISBN 0-8234-2238-0; 978-0-8234-2238-8
LC 2010007892

"In Bauer's capable hands, the age-old simile of March coming in like a lion and going out like a lamb is made quite literal. . . . While the text provides the skeleton, McCully's pen, ink and watercolor illustrations truly bring the old song to life. Her lion is a wonderful cross between a fierce foe . . . and a party pooper. . . . Meanwhile, the lamb is a perfect ball of fluff. . . . A good addition to the spring shelf, it is sure to find its way, roaring and bleating, to classrooms studying similes." Kirkus

The **longest** night; illustrated by Ted Lewin. Holiday House 2009 un il $17.95
Grades: K 1 2 3   E
  1. Night -- Fiction 2. Winter -- Fiction 3. Animals -- Fiction
  ISBN 978-0-8234-2054-4; 0-8234-2054-X
LC 2008022575

One very long night, a crow, a moose, and a fox all claim they can bring back the sun, but the wind knows that only one little creature has what is needed to end the darkness.

"This stunningly crafted tale, written in the language of the storyteller, realistically pictures, in both words and paintings, the phenomenon that is the winter solstice. . . . There is plenty of moonlight in Lewin's watercolor paintings created with just blue, brown, and green." SLJ

Thank you for me! illustrated by Kristina Stephenson. Simon & Schuster Books for Young Readers 2010 un il $14.99
Grades: PreK K 1   E
  1. Human body -- Fiction
  ISBN 978-0-689-85788-1; 0-689-85788-8
LC 2006023872

Rhythmic text enumerates what various body parts can do, including hands to clap and a body to twirl, then expresses thanks for each of those parts—and for the whole.

"Bauer's lilting text matches the jubilant energy in Stephenson's watercolor rainbow palette." SLJ

Bean, Jonathan

  ★ **At** night. Farrar, Straus and Giroux 2007 un il $15
Grades: PreK K 1   E
  1. Night -- Fiction 2. Sleep -- Fiction 3. City and town

life -- Fiction
ISBN 0-374-30446-7; 978-0-374-30446-1
LC 2006-48403

Boston Globe-Horn Book Award: Picture Book (2008)

A sleepless city girl imagines what it would be like to get away from snoring family members and curl up alone with one's thoughts in the cool night air under wide-open skies.

"The artist supplies luminous aerial scenes of the roof garden amid a friendly, well-lit cityscape. . . . The story breathes reassurance and adventure at the same time." Publ Wkly

  ★ **Building** our house; Jonathan Bean. Farrar, Straus and Giroux 2013 48 p. (reinforced) $17.99
Grades: 1 2 3   E
  1. Houses 2. House construction 3. Picture books for children 4. Building -- Fiction 5. Dwellings -- Design and construction -- Fiction
  ISBN 0374380236; 9780374380236
LC 2007027681

Boston Globe-Horn Book Award: Picture Book (2013).

In this children's picture book, Jonathan Bean tells the story of his "back-to-the-land parents, who built his childhood home in the 1970s. . . . Frontmatter depicts [the family] packing and leaving the city, Ensuing spreads detail how they live in a trailer on their new property while slowly building the house: setting the corners of the foundation; digging out the basement; gathering rocks and using them in the foundation; measuring, marking and cutting timber for the frame; and so on." (Kirkus)

"The watercolor-and-ink illustrations invite close examination for narrative details such as these while also providing ample visual information about construction." Kirkus

Beard, Alex

  The **jungle** grapevine. Abrams Books for Young Readers 2009 un il $16.95
Grades: K 1 2 3   E
  1. Africa -- Fiction 2. Animals -- Fiction 3. Communication -- Fiction
  ISBN 978-0-8109-8001-3; 0-8109-8001-0
LC 2008046197

When Turtle makes an off-hand remark to Bird at the watering hole one day, Bird's misunderstanding starts a series of rumors that stirs up the other animals.

"Young children will easily understand the moral of the story. This book will be constantly circulating, thanks to the dialogue, storyline, and artwork." Libr Media Connect

Monkey see monkey draw. Abrams Books for Young Readers 2010 un il $16.95
Grades: PreK K 1   E
  1. Play -- Fiction 2. Africa -- Fiction 3. Monkeys -- Fiction 4. Elephants -- Fiction
  ISBN 978-0-8109-8970-2; 0-8109-8970-0

Elephant leads a troupe of monkeys into a cave they have been afraid to explore, and after admiring the paintings found on the walls they make their own art with mud, squabbling over whose painting is best until Elephant explains that this is not a game to win or lose.

"Bold, imaginative and very comical pen, ink and watercolor illustrations rely on line, color, pattern and thumbprints to produce surreal, gangly blue monkeys frenetically cavorting and clambering across the pages. . . . Beard aptly conjures the look and feel of prehistoric cave paintings, inspiring readers to create their own. Wild and wonderful." Kirkus

Beaty, Andrea

Doctor Ted; [illustrated by] Pascal Lemaitre. Atheneum Books for Young Readers 2008 32p il $14.99

Grades: PreK K 1   E

1. Bears -- Fiction 2. Physicians -- Fiction 3. Imagination -- Fiction

ISBN 978-1-4169-2820-1; 1-4169-2820-0

LC 2006-03191

After bumping his knee one morning, Ted the bear cub decides to become a doctor, but he has only one problem—he has no patients!

This is "a breezy story about pretend play that's laugh-out-loud funny. . . . The pictures' chunky ink lines and almost neon-like digital colors give every page plenty of punch." Publ Wkly

Other titles about Ted are:

Firefighter Ted (2009)

Artist Ted (2012)

Happy Birthday, Madame Chapeau; by Andrea Beaty; illustrated by David Roberts. Harry N Abrams Inc 2014 32 p. color illustrations $16.95

Grades: K 1 2 3   E

1. Hats -- Fiction 2. Birthdays -- Fiction 3. Paris (France) -- Fiction 4. Millinery -- fiction 5. Friendship -- fiction

ISBN 1419712195; 9781419712197

LC bl2014037828

This children's book, by Andrea Beaty and illustrated by David Roberts, tells "the tale of a lonely hat maker who matches customers to the perfect hat but lacks her own perfect match in life. Once a year, on her birthday, Madame Chapeau ventures out in her favorite bonnet to dinner. This time, a crow snatches her hat and flies away." (Publisher's note)

"Madame Chapeau is the world's finest hat maker. She's also lonely. Once a year, she treats herself to a posh birthday dinner, wearing her finest gown and a beloved hat made especially for her. When a crow steals it from her head, Madame Chapeau endures the loss of her treasured hat but then enjoys the misguided generosity of so many—presumably satisfied customers—who offer her their own lids. . . . Although there are some abrupt shifts in the storytelling, the effervescent cadence of Beaty's rhyming text compensates, as do Roberts' quirky, doll-like characters. An artist's note reveals that Roberts, who worked as a milliner himself, has included many famous hats and styles among Chapeau's repertoire. Hats off to a story brimming with charm and panache." Booklist

Rosie Revere, engineer; by Andrea Beaty; illustrated by David Roberts. Abrams Books for Young Readers 2013 32 p. (alk. paper) $16.95

Grades: K 1 2   E

1. Picture books for children 2. Women engineers -- Fiction 3. Stories in rhyme 4. Engineers -- Fiction 5. Inventions -- Fiction 6. Failure (Psychology) -- Fiction 7. Perseverance (Ethics) -- Fiction

ISBN 1419708457; 9781419708459

LC 2012048268

This children's picture book conveys "the story of a girl who likes to build things but is shy about it. . . . Rosie picks up trash and oddments where she finds them, stashing them in her attic room to work on at night. Once, she made a hat for her favorite zookeeper uncle to keep pythons away, and he laughed so hard that she never made anything publicly again. But when her great-great-aunt Rose comes to visit and reminds Rosie of her own past building airplanes," Rosie is inspired. (Kirkus Reviews)

Beaty, Daniel

★ **Knock** knock; my dad's dream for me. by Daniel Beaty; illustrated by Bryan Collier. Little, Brown and Company 2014 40 p. $18

Grades: K 1 2 3   E

1. Father-son relationship -- Fiction 2. Fathers and sons -- Fiction 3. African Americans -- Fiction 4. Separation (Psychology) -- Fiction

ISBN 0316209171; 9780316209175

LC 2012043088

Boston Globe-Horn Book Honor: Picture Book (2014)

Coretta Scott King Book Award: Illustrator (2014)

In this book, by Daniel Beaty, a father and son play knock knock every morning. "But what happens when, one day, that 'knock knock' doesn't come? This . . . book shows the love that an absent parent can leave behind, and the strength that children find in themselves as they grow up and follow their dreams." (Publisher's note)

Beaumont, Karen

★ **Baby** danced the polka; pictures by Jennifer Plecas. Dial Books for Young Readers 2004 un il $12.99

Grades: PreK K 1 2   E

1. Infants -- Fiction

ISBN 0-8037-2587-6

"What a happy, rollicking baby. And what a rolling, rhythmic text. . . . The sprightly pen-and-watercolor artwork bears a very strong resemblance to the work of Helen Oxenbury." Booklist

Doggone dogs! pictures by David Catrow. Dial Books for Young Readers 2008 un il $16.99

Grades: PreK K   E

1. Counting 2. Stories in rhyme 3. Dogs -- Fiction

ISBN 978-0-8037-3157-8; 0-8037-3157-4

LC 2007008620

Ten unruly dogs get loose at obedience school, and when they are captured by the dog-catcher, they work together to effect their escape and return home.

"The minimal rhyming text is paired with Catrow's exuberant, comic, pencil and watercolor illustrations. The frenetic, goofy-looking dogs of various sizes and breeds romping through the park are sure to bring smiles to young faces." SLJ

Duck, duck, goose! a coyote's on the loose! illustrated by Jose Aruego and Ariane Dewey. HarperCollins Pubs. 2004 un il $15.95; lib bdg $16.89

Grades: PreK K 1 2   E

1. Stories in rhyme 2. Animals -- Fiction

ISBN 0-06-050802-7; 0-06-050804-3 lib bdg

LC 2003-8734

Several farm animals try to evade a coyote that they think is dangerous

"Aruego and Dewey use bold paints as varied as a child's imagination to color their comically rendered farmyard animals. A suspenseful romp that will strike a chord with children." SLJ

★ **I** ain't gonna paint no more! illustrated by David Catrow. Harcourt 2005 un il $16
Grades: PreK K 1 2   E
     1. Stories in rhyme 2. Painting -- Fiction
     ISBN 0-15-202488-3
                       LC 2003-27739
"Catrow splashes color all over, uses white space cleverly, and includes playful flourishes. . . . Elongated figures and exaggerated expressions match the silly tone of the story. . . . With rhymes that invite audience participation and scenes that draw the eye, this is a strong storytime choice." SLJ

Move over, Rover; [by] Karen Beaumont; illustrated by Jane Dyer. Harcourt 2006 un il $16
Grades: PreK K 1 2   E
     1. Stories in rhyme 2. Dogs -- Fiction 3. Rain -- Fiction 4. Animals -- Fiction
     ISBN 978-0-15-201979-2; 0-15-201979-0
                       LC 2005014557
When a storm comes, Rover expects to have his doghouse all to himself but finds that various other animals, including a skunk, come to join him.
This offers "marvelously textured watercolor-and-acrylic illustrations. . . . The repetition of key phrases, the rhythmic text, and the cumulative structure of the narrative make this book an ideal read-aloud." SLJ

★ **No** sleep for the sheep! illustrated by Jackie Urbanovic. Houghton Mifflin Harcourt 2011 un il $16.99
Grades: PreK K 1   E
     1. Stories in rhyme 2. Sleep -- Fiction 3. Sounds -- Fiction 4. Domestic animals -- Fiction
     ISBN 978-0-15-204969-0; 0-15-204969-X
                       LC 2009007978
A sheep wants nothing but to go to sleep in the big red barn on the farm, but each time he closes his eyes, another animal moos or neighs or peeps to come in.
"Beaumont's playful, repetitive text, with its loud animal sounds, will have children chanting along to the beat." Kirkus

Shoe-la-la! illustrated by Leuyen Pham. Scholastic Press 2011 un il $16.99
Grades: PreK K   E
     1. Stories in rhyme 2. Shoes -- Fiction
     ISBN 978-0-545-06705-8; 0-545-06705-7
                       LC 2010007848
Four girls go in search of the perfect pair of party shoes.
"The sparkly jacket is an irresistible draw, depicting the girls vamping in dress-up clothes and high heels, as are the humorously expressive, cartoonlike illustrations rendered in full-color with lots of girl-pleasing pink and purple. Pure fun." SLJ

Where's my t-r-u-c-k? pictures by David Catrow. Dial Books for Young Readers 2011 un il $16.99
Grades: PreK K 1   E
     1. Stories in rhyme 2. Dogs -- Fiction 3. Toys -- Fiction

     4. Trucks -- Fiction 5. Lost and found possessions -- Fiction
     ISBN 978-0-8037-3222-3; 0-8037-3222-8
                       LC 2010045689
"This peppy picture book relates in rhyming verse the story of a boy's expansive search for his favorite toy—a riding truck. . . . A raucous and rotund dog finally digs a huge hole and reveals the treasure, which lies amid other items, including an iPod and a set of false teeth. Beaumont's refrain promises that listeners will know how to spell 'truck' by tale's end and is perfectly paced for expressive pauses and exclamations. Catrow's jam-packed pencil and watercolor scenes are masterworks of detail and humor." SLJ

Who ate all the cookie dough? [by] Karen Beaumont; illustrated by Eugene Yelchin. Henry Holt and Company 2008 un il $16.95
Grades: PreK K 1   E
     1. Stories in rhyme 2. Animals -- Fiction 3. Lost and found possessions -- Fiction
     ISBN 978-0-8050-8267-8; 0-8050-8267-0
                       LC 2007012733
Kanga and her friends try to discover who ate all of her cookie dough
"Infectious repetitive rhyming verse, eye-catching gouache illustrations with ample white space, and a lift-the-flap surprise combine to create a joyful tale." Horn Book Guide

Bechtold, Lisze
Sally and the purple socks; [by] Lisze Bechtold. Philomel Books 2008 un il $15.99
Grades: PreK K 1   E
     1. Size -- Fiction 2. Clothing and dress -- Fiction
     ISBN 978-0-399-24734-7; 0-399-24734-3
                       LC 2007023649
When her tiny purple socks start to expand, Sally turns them into a scarf and then curtains, but things soon get out of hand.
"The quirky, playful, and ultimately warm illustrations, coupled with the simple text and a plot with just the right amount of suspense, make the book spot-on for sharing with young audiences." Booklist

Beck, Andrea
Pierre Le Poof! written and illustrated by Andrea Beck. Orca Book Publishers 2009 un il $19.95
Grades: PreK K 1 2   E
     1. Dogs -- Fiction
     ISBN 978-1-55469-028-2; 1-55469-028-5
"Lapdog Pierre Le Poof, 'a pedigreed pooch,' lives a pampered life with Miss Murphy but longs to frolic with the dogs in the park. At a practice session for a dog championship, Pierre makes his escape . . . but soon longs for the comforts of home. . . . Dog and owner bear a strong resemblance to each other in airy ink-and-watercolor pictures that delightfully go for the laughs." Booklist
Other titles about Pierre are:
Pierre's friends (2010)
Pierre in the air! (2011)

Becker, Aaron
★ **Journey**; Aaron Becker. Candlewick Press 2013 40 p. color illustrations hbk $15.99

Grades: K 1 2 3   **E**
1. Magic -- Fiction 2. Drawing -- Fiction 3. Stories
without words 4. Picture books for children
ISBN 9780763660536; 0763660531

LC 2012947264

Caldecott Honor Book (2014)

In this book by Aaron Becker "a lonely girl draws a
magic door on her bedroom wall and through it escapes into
a world where wonder, adventure, and danger abound. Red
marker in hand, she creates a boat, a balloon, and a flying
carpet that carry her on a spectacular journey toward an uncertain destiny. When she is captured by a sinister emperor,
only an act of tremendous courage and kindness can set her
free." (Publisher's note)

"An imaginative adventure story whose elaborate illustrations inspire wonder, careful examination and multiple
reads." Kirkus

★ **Quest**; Aaron Becker. First edition Candlewick
Press 2014 40 p. color illustrations $15.99
Grades: K 1 2 3   **E**
1. Adventure and adventurers 2. Kings and rulers
-- Fiction 3. Maps -- Fiction 4. Magic -- Fiction 5.
Drawing -- Fiction
ISBN 0763665959; 9780763665951

LC 2013952837

Sequel to: Journey (2013)

"A king emerges from a hidden door in a city park, startling two children sheltering from the rain. No sooner does
he push a map and some strange objects into their hands than
he is captured by hostile forces that whisk him back through
the enchanted door. Just like that, the children are caught up
in a quest to rescue the king and his kingdom from darkness,
while illuminating the farthest reaches of their imagination.
Colored markers in hand, they make their own way through
the portal, under the sea, through a tropical paradise, over a
perilous bridge, and high in the air with the help of a winged
friend." (Publisher's note)

"In addition to the winning adventure of the silent story,
Becker manages to evolve his imagery with more sophisticated designs and ideas that draw readers into the narrative
ever more deeply, proving once again that lush details, a meticulous sense of motion and action, and a boundless love of
fun are worth all the words in the world." Booklist

Becker, Bonny

A **Library** book for bear; Bonny Becker, illustrated by
Kady MacDonald Denton. Candlewick Press 2014 32 p.
color illustrations $16.99
Grades: PreK K 1 2   **E**
1. Mice -- Fiction 2. Bears -- Fiction 3. Libraries
-- Fiction
ISBN 0763649244; 9780763649241

LC 2013952827

In this children's book, by Bonny Becker, "Bear does
not want to go to the library. He is quite sure he already has
all the books he will ever need. Yet the relentlessly cheery
Mouse, small and gray and bright-eyed, thinks different.
When Bear reluctantly agrees to go with his friend to the big
library, neither rocket ships nor wooden canoes are enough
for Bear's picky tastes. How will Mouse ever find the perfect
book for Bear?" (Publisher's note)

"Reclusive Bear reluctantly accompanies extrovert
Mouse on a library visit. Mouse's reminders about us-

ing one's 'library voice' go unheeded, and Bear is hushed
by another patron. He prepares to leave, but he's stopped
in his huffy tracks when he overhears a librarian reading a
story. The hooray-for-books message is served subtly. Bear's
grouchiness and Mouse's joie de vivre come through in Denton's expressive lines." Horn Book

A **visitor** for Bear; illustrated by Kady MacDonald
Denton. Candlewick Press 2008 un il $16.99
Grades: PreK K 1 2   **E**
1. Mice -- Fiction 2. Bears -- Fiction 3. Friendship
-- Fiction
ISBN 978-0-7636-2807-9; 0-7636-2807-7

LC 2006-51850

Bear's efforts to keep out visitors to his house are undermined by a very persistent mouse.

This offers "watercolor, ink and gouache illustrations in
a soft color palette. . . . The characters are highly expressive
. . . and the dramatic text will lend itself to reading aloud."
Booklist

Other titles about Bear are:
A birthday for Bear (2009)
A bedtime for Bear (2010)
The sniffles for Bear (2011)

Becker, Helaine

Juba this, juba that; illustrated by Ron Lightburn. Tundra 2011 il $17.95
Grades: PreK K   **E**
1. Cats -- Fiction 2. Fairs -- Fiction
ISBN 978-0-88776-975-7; 0-88776-975-6

"This modern-day version of a traditional African chant
imagines an adventure that happens one evening when a
dark-skinned boy follows a yellow cat to the fair. They laugh
at their reflections in the House of Mirrors, take a spooky
fun-house ride, and generally have a wonderful time before
returning home to bed. Becker's simple rhyme plays with
opposites and is just right for clapping and bouncing along.
Lightburn's lively illustrations perfectly capture the joy of
the nighttime escapade and extend the story." SLJ

Becker, Suzy

★ **Manny's** cows; the Niagara Falls tale. written and
illustrated by Suzy Becker. HarperCollins 2006 un il lib
bdg $16.89
Grades: PreK K 1 2   **E**
1. Cattle -- Fiction 2. Vacations -- Fiction 3. Niagara
Falls (N.Y. and Ont.) -- Fiction
ISBN 978-0-06-054152-1; 0-06-054152-0; 978-0-06-
054153-8 lib bdg; 0-06-054153-9 lib bdg

LC 2005-14508

For his summer vacation, Manny takes his five hundred
cows to Niagara Falls.

"The over-the-top story, full of fun and laced with amusing visual and verbal details, . . . is accompanied by occasional sidebar facts about dairy cattle. The cows' outrageous
comments and antics are bolstered by free-spirited ink drawings brightened with color." Booklist

Bedford, David, 1969-

The **way** I love you. Simon & Schuster Books for
Young Readers 2005 un il $12.95

Grades: PreK K   E
1. Dogs -- Fiction
ISBN 0-689-87625-4

LC 2004-3964

First published 2004 in Australia with title: I love

A little girl celebrates all of the ways she loves her puppy.

"Loose charcoal lines provide texture and motion, while splashes of pastel-hued watercolors keep the pictures warm and cozy. . . . The simple language and clean, colorful artwork make this book just right for the youngest pet lovers." SLJ

Bee, William

And the cars go... William Bee. First U.S. edition Candlewick Press 2013 32 p. $15.99

Grades: PreK K   E
1. City traffic 2. Automobile travel -- Fiction 3. Automobiles -- fiction
ISBN 0763665800; 9780763665807

LC 2012947829

This children's book by William Bee centers around a traffic jam where "everyone's in a hurry! There's the family in the paneled station wagon . . . packed to the roof rack with gear for the beach. There's the be-hatted Duke and Duchess, out for a drive in their ornate Rolls Royce. Not to mention a yellow school bus . . . an overheating race car . . . and other vehicles revving to go." (Publisher's note)

""Here is the traffic, all ground to a halt, / and the policeman calls out... / 'What's causing this holdup?'" The vehicles may be at a standstill, but the rhythmic text motors along as the officer investigates the problem. Bee's stylish compositions have a distinctly sixties vibe; the pages practically vibrate with eye-popping colors held in place with a lively, sure-handed line." Horn Book

And the train goes. . . Candlewick Press 2007 un il $15.99

Grades: PreK K   E
1. Sounds -- Fiction 2. Parrots -- Fiction 3. Railroads -- Fiction
ISBN 978-0-7636-3248-9; 0-7636-3248-1

LC 2006-43857

As assorted passengers comment on their train ride, and the train itself goes "Clickerty click, clickerty clack," the station parrot is carefully listening to every sound

"Filled with sound effects galore, this rollicking read-aloud is perfect for transportation storytimes. . . . The train and the characters' clothing are depicted in glossy colors and covered with flat floral patterns and other graphic designs. . . . There are many details for children to pore over." SLJ

Beebe, Katy

Brother Hugo and the bear; by Katy Beebe; illustrated by S.D. Schindler. Eerdmans Books for Young Readers 2014 34 p. $17

Grades: 1 2 3 4   E
1. Bears -- Fiction 2. Monks -- Fiction 3. Middle Ages -- Fiction 4. Books and reading -- Fiction 5. Manuscripts -- Fiction
ISBN 0802854079; 9780802854070

LC 2013031001

In this book, by Kathryne Beebe, "Brother Hugo can't return his library book - the letters of St. Augustine - because, it turns out, the precious book has been devoured by a bear! Instructed by the abbot to borrow another monastery's copy and create a replacement, the hapless monk painstakingly crafts a new book, copying it letter by letter and line by line. But when he sets off to return the borrowed copy, he finds himself trailed by his hungry new friend." (Publisher's note)

"According to detailed back matter, the author learned of a documented incident involving a book-eating bear and the subsequent letter written by Peter the Venerable to a neighboring French monastery requesting St. Augustine's letters...Arches and columns cleverly frame the monk, creating sequential panels to portray his painstaking progress on what becomes, alas, another "choice morsel" for the insatiable beast. Combine this with C. M. Millen's The Ink Garden of Brother Theophane (Charlesbridge, 2010) and Jan Pancheri's Brother William's Year (Frances Lincoln, 2010) for further insights into how monasteries nourish bodies and souls." SLJ

Beil, Karen Magnuson

Jack's house; illustrated by Mike Wohnoutka. Holiday House 2008 un il $16.95

Grades: PreK K 1 2   E
1. Dogs -- Fiction 2. House construction -- Fiction
ISBN 978-0-8234-1913-5; 0-8234-1913-4

LC 2007014978

Cumulative text reveals who was really responsible for the house that Jack claims to have built, and all of the trucks involved, from the bulldozer used to clear the land to the van that brought a hammock for the back yard

"A wonderful twist on an age-old rhyme. . . . Wohnoutka's full-page acrylic paintings are large scale, but are also full of small details for readers to enjoy. . . . This beguiling book will be a hit both at storytimes and in circulating collections." SLJ

Bell, Cece

Itty bitty. Candlewick Press 2009 un il $9.99

Grades: PreK K 1   E
1. Dogs -- Fiction 2. Size -- Fiction
ISBN 978-0-7636-3616-6; 0-7636-3616-9

"Where does a tiny dog find just the right decor for his hollowed-out-bone house? Why, the 'teeny-weeny department' at a huge store downtown, of course! Such is the premise of this sweet and silly picture book that introduces a sunny pup of small size but big personality. . . . Bell's . . . crisp acrylic and ink artwork features blocks of color and simple stylized shapes on grainy, speckled backgrounds." Publ Wkly

Rabbit and Robot; the sleepover. Cece Bell. Candlewick 2012 56 p. (hardback) $14.99

Grades: K 1 2   E
1. Children's stories 2. Negotiation -- Fiction 3. Friendship -- Fiction 4. Humorous stories 5. Robots -- Fiction 6. Rabbits -- Fiction 7. Friendship -- Fiction 8. Sleepovers -- Fiction
ISBN 0763654752; 9780763654757

LC 2011048365

Theodor Seuss Geisel Honor Book (2013)

This "book's four chapters . . . correspond to the plan for [Rabbit and Robot's] eagerly anticipated sleepover: make pizza, watch TV, play Go Fish, go to bed. But it's a list Rabbit generated without consulting his friend, so negotiations .

.. are the order of the day. . . . Robot wants to play Old Maid in addition to Go Fish; Rabbit insists it's 'not on the list.' Robot . . . insists on taking apart Rabbit's furniture to get his favorite topping, nuts and bolts." (Publishers Weekly)

Belloc, Hilaire

Jim who ran away from his nurse and was eaten by a lion; a cautionary tale. pictures by Mini Grey. Alfred A. Knopf 2010 un il $19.99

Grades: 2 3 4   **E**

1. Stories in rhyme 2. Pop-up books 3. Zoos -- Fiction 4. Lions -- Fiction

ISBN 978-0-375-85970-0; 0-375-85970-5

Text originally published 1907; A newly illustrated edition of the title first published 1987 by Little Brown; this edition first published 2009 in the United Kingdom

Jim runs away from his nurse at the zoo and he is eaten by a lion.

"Grey's artwork is gorgeous and bold. . . . Fold-outs, pop-ups and lift-up flaps contribute to the over-the-top element that makes even little Jim's bloody, chewed-off head seem not as horrific as it might. . . . All but the most sensitive children (over eight) will laugh . . . especially if the book is read aloud with an English accent." Kirkus

Belton, Robyn

Herbert; the true story of a brave sea dog. Candlewick Press 2010 un il $15.99

Grades: PreK K 1 2   **E**

1. Sea stories 2. Dogs -- Fiction

ISBN 978-0-7636-4741-4; 0-7636-4741-1

LC 2009-46538

Herbert, a beloved, small dog who lives near the sea in New Zealand, sets out one fine day with his boy Tim's father on a boat that is beset by a sudden storm, which washes Herbert overboard.

"Belton's beautiful watercolor illustrations bring to life the dangerously changeable weather at sea without making it too scary. Reproductions of newspaper articles and letters about the incident, as well as Herbert's 'Iron Dog' medal, appear on the endpapers. These real-life documents give readers a fascinating taste of the true story behind the book and provide a nice balance to Belton's dreamy illustrations." Booklist

Bemelmans, Ludwig

★ **Madeline**; story and pictures by Ludwig Bemelmans. Viking 1985 un il $17.99; pa $7.99

Grades: PreK K 1 2   **E**

1. Stories in rhyme 2. Paris (France) -- Fiction

ISBN 0-670-44580-0; 0-14-056439-X pa

A reissue of the title first published 1939 by Simon & Schuster

A Caldecott Medal honor book, 1940

"Madeline is a nonconformist in a regimented world—a Paris convent school. This rhymed story tells how she made an adventure out of having appendicitis." Hodges. Books for Elem Sch Libr

Other titles about Madeline are:

Madeline and the bad hat (1957)

Madeline and the gypsies (1959)

Madeline in London (1961)

Madeline's Christmas (1985)

Madeline's rescue (1985)

Ben draws trouble; Matt Davies. Roaring Brook Press 2015 32 p. color illustrations (hardback) $17.99

Grades: PreK K 1 2 3   **E**

1. Drawing -- Fiction 2. Lost and found possessions -- Fiction 3. Ability -- Fiction 4. Schools -- Fiction

ISBN 1596437952; 9781596437951

LC 2014009905

In this children's story, by Matt Davies, "Ben loved drawing more than anything else in the world (with the possible exception of riding his bicycle). He drew boats as well as bicycles, sharks and spaceships. But most of all he loved drawing people. When Ben loses his sketchbook his world is turned upside down. Who will find it? And how will they react?" (Publisher's note)

"Through the succinct text and emotionally charged illustrations, children will feel Ben's panic and anguish over losing his sketchbook, his fear of punishment for the caricatures, and his satisfaction at the happy ending." Booklist

Another book about Ben is:

Ben Rides On (2013)

Benchley, Nathaniel

★ **A ghost** named Fred; pictures by Ben Shecter. Harper & Row 1968 un il (I can read mystery book) lib bdg $17.89

Grades: K 1 2   **E**

1. Ghost stories

ISBN 0-06-020474-5

"More humorous than scary . . . this is a pleasing and acceptable ghost story for beginning readers." Booklist

Bennett, Kelly

Dad and Pop; an ode to fathers & stepfathers. illustrated by Paul Meisel. Candlewick Press 2010 un il $15.99

Grades: PreK K 1 2   **E**

1. Fathers -- Fiction 2. Stepfathers -- Fiction 3. Father-daughter relationship -- Fiction

ISBN 978-0-7636-3379-0; 0-7636-3379-8

"A cheerful girl explains that Dad and Pop are different in many ways, but the same in their love for her. . . . Dad is the girl's biological father and . . . Pop is her step-father. . . . This is a positive and playful portrayal of a blended family. . . . Expressive faces and gentle humor add charm to the pictures." SLJ

Your daddy was just like you; illustrated by David Walker. G. P. Putnam's Sons 2010 un il $16.99

Grades: PreK K 1   **E**

1. Fathers -- Fiction 2. Grandmothers -- Fiction

ISBN 978-0-399-24798-9; 0-399-24798-X

LC 2008053644

A grandmother describes to her grandson how his father was just like him when he was a child, never wanting to take a bath, fearing the dark, and swooping through the house in a cape and mask.

"Characters' facial expressions and body language successfully capture emotions, actions, and reactions. . . . The humorous text is in perfect sync with the simple illustrations." SLJ

Your mommy was just like you; illustrated by David Walker. G. P. Putnam's Sons 2011 un il $16.99
Grades: PreK K **E**
1. Mothers -- Fiction 2. Grandmothers -- Fiction
ISBN 978-0-399-24798-9; 0-399-24798-X

"A grandmother looks at an old photo album with her granddaughter, telling her stories about her mother when she was little. . . . The illustrations are soft and gentle, complementing each milestone mentioned in the story. Perfect for intergenerational sharing." SLJ

Bently, Peter
★ **King** Jack and the dragon. Dial Books for Young Readers 2011 un il $17.99
Grades: PreK K **E**
1. Stories in rhyme 2. Play -- Fiction 3. Imagination -- Fiction
ISBN 978-0-8037-3698-6; 0-8037-3698-3
LC 2011001273

"Bently's verse never misses a beat, and Oxenbury shifts between monochromatic, engraving-like drawings and pale watercolors; the images feel as if they were drawn from a classic fairy tale book and contemporary life simultaneously. It's an enchanting tribute to both full-throttle pretend play and the reassurance of a parent's embrace." Publ Wkly

Berger, Carin
Forever friends. Greenwillow Books 2010 un il $16.99; lib bdg $17.89
Grades: PreK K **E**
1. Birds -- Fiction 2. Rabbits -- Fiction 3. Seasons -- Fiction 4. Friendship -- Fiction
ISBN 978-0-06-191528-4; 0-06-191528-9; 978-0-06-191529-1 lib bdg; 0-06-191529-7 lib bdg
LC 2009-18758

In the spring, a blue bird awakens a rabbit and invites him to play, and they enjoy every day together until it is time for the bird to fly south for the winter, with a promise to return again next spring.

"Berger's superb, stylized cut-paper collage illustrations, constructed from lined and graph paper and magazines, depict sylvan landscapes with graceful curves and airy compositions that echo the simplicity and gentleness of the tale. A reassuring, poetic story that will give young children much to ponder any time of the year." Booklist

Finding spring; Carin Berger. Greenwillow Books, an imprint of HarperCollinsPublishers 2015 40 p. color illustrations (hardcover) $17.99
Grades: PreK K 1 **E**
1. Bears -- Fiction 2. Spring -- Fiction 3. Winter -- Fiction 4. Seasons -- Fiction
ISBN 0062250191; 9780062250193
LC 2014003155

"Instead of hibernating as he should, a little bear cub goes out in search of spring—and he thinks he's found it! Gloriously illustrated with dioramas and cut-paper collages by the award-winning designer and illustrator Carin Berger, this stunning picture book celebrates the changing of the seasons." (Publisher's Note)

"Winter is coming, but little bear Maurice, excited about his first spring, imagines springtime flowers. Instead of sleeping, he leaves his den to look for spring... Eager to share his discovery, Maurice takes his mother and friends back over his path, this time passing blooming trees and green buds. "Everything had changed." They do, indeed, find spring—and spring flowers. Chock-full of visual cues and information, this is a charming exploration of seasonal changes." Booklist

The **little** yellow leaf. Greenwillow Books 2008 un il $16.99; lib bdg $17.89
Grades: PreK K 1 2 **E**
1. Trees -- Fiction 2. Autumn -- Fiction 3. Leaves -- Fiction
ISBN 978-0-06-145223-9; 0-06-145223-8; 978-0-06-145224-6 lib bdg; 0-06-145224-6 lib bdg
LC 2007-39191

A yellow leaf is not ready to fall from the tree when autumn comes, but finally, after finding another leaf still on the tree, the two let go together.

"In Berger's eye-catching collage illustrations, pieced background papers in shades of yellow, green, blue, and beige show off stylized forms of naked tree branches, leaves, and sun created by clipping and pasting (sometimes tiny) segments of various papers—faded, lined ledger, and graph paper; colored and printed magazine pages—and adding touches of paint." SLJ

★ **OK** go. Greenwillow Books 2009 un il $17.99; lib bdg $18.89
Grades: K 1 2 3 **E**
1. Automobiles -- Fiction 2. Environmental protection -- Fiction
ISBN 978-0-06-157666-9; 0-06-157666-2; 978-0-06-157669-0 lib bdg; 0-06-157669-7 lib bdg
LC 2008-14681

In this almost wordless picture book, car drivers stuck in traffic under smoggy skies seek "greener" alternatives to driving, including riding bicycles, walking, and playing

"Berger's simple environmental message is delivered through clever, innovative illustrations that make her point without being didactic. Idiosyncratic creatures decked out in fabric pieces, buttons, and tall imaginative hats sail along in even more idiosyncratic vehicles that are variously colored and decorated with stickers and decals." SLJ

Berger, Lou
Dream dog; by Lou Berger; illustrated by David J. Catrow. 1st ed. Schwartz & Wade Books 2013 40 p. ill. (hardcover) $17.99; (library) $20.99
Grades: PreK K 1 2 **E**
1. Picture books for children 2. Imaginary playmates -- Fiction 3. Dogs -- Fiction 4. Imagination -- Fiction 5. Fathers and sons -- Fiction
ISBN 0375866558; 9780375866555; 9780375966552
LC 2011048582

In this children's picture book, "Harry wants a dog, but Dad has allergies. So Harry puts on his X-35 Infra-Rocket Imagination Helmet and conjures up his own perfect pet, a dream dog named Waffle. This new pet is huge and fuzzy, all light blue and white like cumulous clouds, and only Harry can see him. Waffle and Harry become best pals, with Harry's dad playing along with the idea of the imaginary dog. . . . When Dad's allergies suddenly improve, he brings home a real dog." (Kirkus Reviews)

Berger, Samantha

Crankenstein; by Samantha Berger; illustrated by Dan Santat. 1st ed. Little, Brown and Co. 2013 40 p. ill. (reinforced) $16.99

Grades: PreK K   E

1. Anger -- Fiction 2. Bad behavior -- Fiction. 3. Behavior -- Fiction

ISBN 031612656X; 9780316126564

LC 2012029480

This book, written by Samantha Berger and illustrated by Dan Santat, features Crankenstein, "a monster of grumpiness. He may look like any ordinary boy, but when faced with a rainy day, a melting popsicle, or an early bedtime, one little boy transforms into a mumbling, grumbling Crankenstein! When Crankenstein meets his match in a fellow Crankenstein, the results could be catastrophic--or they could be just what he needs to brighten his day." (Publisher's note)

Martha doesn't say sorry! illustrated by Bruce Whatley. Little, Brown and Co. 2009 un il $15.99

Grades: PreK K 1 2   E

1. Otters -- Fiction

ISBN 978-0-316-06682-2; 0-316-06682-6

LC 2008-16769

Young Martha learns that she must apologize for her bad behavior if she wants people to cooperate with her.

"The watercolor and colored pencil artwork encapsulates Martha's girliness, her better-than-thou attitude and her internal struggle with her conscience. Whatley's representation of body language and facial expression powerfully complement the text. An enjoyable introduction to what could be a new beloved character." Kirkus

Another title about Martha is:

Martha doesn't share (2010)

Bergman, Mara

Lively Elizabeth! what happens when you push; illustrated by Cassia Thomas. Albert Whitman 2010 un il

Grades: PreK K 1 2   E

1. School stories

ISBN 0807547026; 9780807547021

Describes a chain reaction that is caused by Elizabeth pushing her classmate Joe.

"The text is placed in and around the illustrations for maximum effect. . . . Thomas's illustrations make the whole thing work. The action is clear, as are the consequences of that ill-fated push. The myriad children wear wacky costumes, have expressive faces, and are awash in detail that makes multiple readings a joy." SLJ

Bergstein, Rita M.

Your own big bed; by Rita M. Bergstein; illustrated by Susan Kathleen Hartung. Viking 2008 un il $15.99

Grades: PreK K 1   E

1. Beds -- Fiction 2. Growth -- Fiction

ISBN 978-0-670-06079-5; 0-670-06079-8

LC 2007-17902

Introduces how different animals and even human babies grow from being newly-hatched or born, through being carried everywhere, to having their own special place to sleep.

"The absence of the anxiety, whining, or excuses common to books of this ilk is refreshing. . . . This sweet book provides a gentle, matter-of-fact introduction to a sometimes-difficult transition." SLJ

Berk, Ari

Nightsong; by Ari Berk and illustrated by Loren Long. Simon & Schuster Books for Young Readers 2012 48 p. (hardcover: alk. paper) $17.99

Grades: 1 2 3   E

1. Bats -- Fiction 2. Senses and sensation in animals 3. Mother-son relationship -- Fiction 4. Echolocation (Physiology) -- Fiction

ISBN 1416978860; 9781416978862

LC 2009026608

Author Ari Berk and illustrator Loren Long present a picture book "about a young bat setting off into the world using only his good sense! Chiro's mother sends him off into the night for the first time alone. It's an adventure, but how will he find his way? And how will he find his way home? As the young bat discovers, navigating the world around him is easy as long as he uses his good sense." (Publisher's note)

Berkes, Marianne

Over in the forest; come and take a peek. by Marianne Berkes; illustrated by Jill Dubin. Dawn Publications 2012 32 p. (hardback) $16.95

Grades: PreK K 1 2   E

1. Counting 2. Stories in rhyme 3. Forest animals -- Poetry 4. Nature 5. Forest animals -- Fiction 6. Animals -- Infancy -- Fiction

ISBN 9781584691624; 9781584691631; 158469162X

LC 2011030879

This nature book by Marianne Berkes allows children to "follow the tracks of ten woodland animals. . . . Children learn the ways of forest animals to the rhythm of 'Over in the Meadow' as they leap like a squirrel, dunk like a raccoon, and pounce like a fox. They . . . also count the babies and search for ten hidden forest animals. . . . Marianne [also] provides [multiple] ideas for activities and curriculum extensions about forest animals, literature, and writing." (Publisher's note)

Berne, Jennifer

Calvin can't fly; the story of a bookworm birdie. illustrated by Keith Bendis. Sterling 2010 un il $14.95

Grades: PreK K 1 2   E

1. Birds -- Fiction 2. Books and reading -- Fiction

ISBN 978-1-4027-7323-5; 1-4027-7323-4

LC 2009050797

A young starling chooses to read books when his cousins are learning to fly, and the knowledge he acquires comes in handy when a hurricane threatens the flock's migration.

"The irresistible story of a proud bookworm will put smiles on the faces of readers of all ages. . . . The illustrations are wildly original and full of funny details." Kirkus

Bernheimer, Kate

The girl in the castle inside the museum; [illustrated by] Nicoletta Ceccoli. Schwartz & Wade Books 2008 un il $16.99; lib bdg $19.99

Grades: K 1 2 3   E

1. Castles -- Fiction 2. Museums -- Fiction

ISBN 978-0-375-83606-0; 978-0-375-83606-7 lib bdg

LC 2006-101854

"In an eclectic toy museum, children are drawn to a snow globe where it is said that, if they look hard enough, they can see the little girl who lives in the castle therein. To their delight, she is visible, as is her entire enchanted world.

The girl is lonely when the museum empties, and she dreams of other children visiting her. . . . Using media as varied as clay sculpture and photography, Ceccoli has created a world that beckons young readers inside. . . . This unusual book will jump-start the imaginations of all who are lucky enough to enter it." SLJ

Berry, Lynne

★ **Duck** skates; illustrated by Hiroe Nakata. Henry Holt and Co. 2005 un il $15.95

Grades: PreK K   **E**

1. Stories in rhyme 2. Snow -- Fiction 3. Ducks -- Fiction

ISBN 978-0-8050-7219-8; 0-8050-7219-5

LC 2004-22176

Five little ducks skate, romp, and play in the snow.

"The illustrations follow the text exactly, allowing children to count the ducks engaged in each activity. The water-color-and-ink pictures convey the playfulness in warm, cozy tones, and a surprising amount of expression is conveyed in simple lines." SLJ

Other titles about these ducks are:

Duck dunks (2008)

Duck tents (2009)

Ducking for apples (2010)

What floats in a moat? by Lynne Berry; illustrated by Matthew Cordell. 1st ed. Simon & Schuster Books for Young Readers 2013 48 p. col. ill. (hardcover) $17.99

Grades: K 1 2 3   **E**

1. Floating bodies 2. Science -- Experiments 3. Goats -- Fiction 4. Stories in rhyme 5. Chickens -- Fiction 6. Floating bodies -- Fiction

ISBN 1416997636; 9781416997634

LC 2010002844

This children's book by Lynne Berry is "inspired by Archimedes' principle. "Archie . . . the goat and Skinny the hen need to deliver three barrels of buttermilk to the queen . . . in her moated castle. Rejecting the drawbridge in the name of 'Science!' they embark on a process of trial and error to float the barrels across the moat." (Kirkus Reviews)

Berry, Matt

Up on Daddy's shoulders; by Matt Berry; illustrated by Lucy Corvino. Scholastic 2006 un il $6.99

Grades: PreK K 1 2   **E**

1. Size -- Fiction 2. Father-son relationship -- Fiction

ISBN 0-439-67045-4

LC 2005023626

While riding on his father's shoulders, a young boy feels taller than everything in his house, his neighborhood, and the world.

"Corvino's sunny paintings fill each double-page spread. . . . Easy on the eyes and ears, this title's rhythm and attractiveness make it a fine read-aloud choice." Booklist

Bertrand, Diane Gonzales

Adelita and the veggie cousins; illustrations by Christina Rodriguez; Spanish translation by Gabriela Baeza Ventura. Pinata Books/Arte Publico Press 2011 il

Grades: PreK K 1   **E**

1. School stories 2. Vegetables -- Fiction 3. Bilingual books -- English-Spanish

ISBN 1-55885-699-4; 978-1-55885-699-8

LC 2010054521

On her first day at a new school, Adelita makes new friends through a lesson on vegetables, including how some vegetables are 'cousins' because they share certain characteristics.

"The dual message of nutrition and diversity will probably find its place in today's curriculum and can certainly augment units on food, language and culture." Kirkus

Bertrand, Lynne

★ **Granite** baby; pictures by Kevin Hawkes. Farrar, Straus and Giroux 2005 un il $16

Grades: PreK K 1 2   **E**

1. Tall tales 2. Infants -- Fiction 3. New Hampshire -- Fiction

ISBN 0-374-32761-0

LC 2002-192882

Five talented New Hampshire sisters try to care for a baby that one of them has carved out of granite.

"Together with Bertrand's rollicking text, Hawkes' broad double-page paintings make this ideal for sharing with groups." Booklist

Beskow, Elsa

Princess Sylvie. 2011 il $17.95

Grades: PreK K 1   **E**

1. Dogs -- Fiction 2. Rabbits -- Fiction 3. Princesses -- Fiction 4. Father-daughter relationship -- Fiction

ISBN 978-086315-813-1; 0-86315-813-7

First published 1934

Princess Sylvie persuades her father, the king, to leave the palace gardens and walk in the woods. The king is unsure. What might be in the woods? Then Sylvie's dog Oskar runs off after a long-eared hare and Sylvie's adventures begin.

"The bear looks like a very large teddy, the 'wild' wood is spacious and airy and Sylvie never loses her tiny crown or musses her dress. . . . Old-fashioned in all the senses of the word, but quite charming in its art-deco shapes and vintage colors." Kirkus

Best, Cari

Goose's story; pictures by Holly Meade. Farrar, Straus & Giroux 2002 un il hardcover o.p. pa $6.99

Grades: PreK K 1 2   **E**

1. Geese -- Fiction

ISBN 0-374-32750-5; 0-374-40032-6 pa

LC 2001-27285

A young girl finds a Canada goose with a badly injured foot and looks for her each day to see how she is doing

"Holly Meade's animated paper collage enhances Best's poignant story. . . . Best tells the story from the girl's point of view, and her language is appropriately childlike and empathetic." Horn Book

★ **Sally** Jean, the Bicycle Queen; pictures by Christine Davenier. Farrar, Straus and Giroux 2005 un il $16

Grades: PreK K 1 2   **E**

1. Cycling -- Fiction 2. Bicycles -- Fiction

ISBN 0-374-36386-2

LC 2004-40461

When Sally Jean outgrows her beloved bicycle, Flash, she experiments with various ideas for acquiring a new, bigger one.

"Davenier's ink-and-watercolor illustrations are light and airy and convey a variety of emotions and delightful details. Sally Jean is a real charmer, and children will appreciate her resourcefulness and tenacity." SLJ

★ **Three** cheers for Catherine the Great! illustrated by Giselle Potter. Sunburst ed.; Farrar, Straus and Giroux 2003 un il pa $7.99
Grades: PreK K 1 2   **E**
   1. Gifts -- Fiction 2. Parties -- Fiction 3. Birthdays -- Fiction 4. Grandmothers -- Fiction 5. Russian Americans -- Fiction
   ISBN 0-374-47551-2

                 LC 2002040804
First published 1999 by DK Pub.
Sara's Russian grandmother has requested that there be no presents at her seventy-eighth birthday party so Sara must think of a gift from her heart.

"In lively, lyrical prose, Best celebrates a special family relationship, and conveys the unique challenges and joys of an immigrant's new life. . . . Potter's festive, whimsical artwork is an irresistible play of vibrant colors and patterns, filled with rich detail and diverse, expressive characters." Booklist

Another title about Sara and her grandmother is:
When Catherine the Great and I were eight! (2003)

What's so bad about being an only child? [by] Cari Best; pictures by Sophie Blackall. Farrar, Straus and Giroux 2007 un il $16
Grades: PreK K 1 2   **E**
   1. Pets -- Fiction 2. Only child -- Fiction
   ISBN 0-374-39943-3; 978-0-374-39943-6

                 LC 2005-51232
Rosemary Emma Angela Lynette Isabel Iris Malone grows tired of being an only child, but eventually finds a way to feel less alone.

"Kids should applaud this self-reliant, spunky heroine." Publ Wkly

Best, Cari, 1951-
   Beatrice spells some lulus and learns to write a letter; by Cari Best; illustrated by Giselle Potter. Margaret Ferguson Books 2013 40 p. ill. (reinforced) $16.99
Grades: K 1 2 3   **E**
   1. Grandparent-grandchild relationship -- Fiction 2. Schools -- Fiction 3. Show-and-tell presentations -- Fiction 4. English language -- Spelling -- Fiction
   ISBN 0374399042; 9780374399047

                 LC 2012015337
This children's picture book by Cari Best "tell[s] the story of a girl named Beatrice whose initially rocky relationship with spelling (she spells her name ABCTERIE) turns into a full-fledged romance. Although Beatrice's family doesn't share her interest in spelling ('Leo had his ant farm, June had gymnastics, and her parents had their music'), she discovers a fellow word lover in her grandmother." (Publishers Weekly)

   Easy as pie; [pictures by Melissa Sweet] Farrar, Straus and Giroux 2010 un il $16.99

Grades: K 1 2 3   **E**
   1. Pies -- Fiction 2. Baking -- Fiction
   ISBN 0-374-39929-8; 978-0-374-39929-0

                 LC 2008-16803
Jacob watches his favorite television show, Baking with Chef Monty, and bakes a beautiful peach pie, which he gives to his parents on their anniversary. "Ages six to nine." (Bull Cent Child Books)

"With pencil and watercolor illustrations done in a palette of soft colors, Sweet captures the warmth and security Jacob feels in the kitchen. . . . Important themes abound— love, security, cooperation, warmth, respect—and somehow all are tied to the simple acts of cooking and eating together. A delicious book for all collections." SLJ

★ **My** three best friends and me, Zulay; Cari Best; illustrated by Vanessa Newton. Farrar Straus & Giroux 2015 40 p. color illustrations (hardback) $17.99
Grades: K 1 2 3   **E**
   1. Blind 2. Running 3. Friendship -- Fiction 4. Blind -- Fiction 5. Schools -- Fiction 6. People with disabilities -- Fiction
   ISBN 0374388199; 9780374388195

                 LC 2014021833
In this children's book by Cari Best "Zulay and her three best friends are all in the same first grade class and study the same things, even though Zulay is blind. When their teacher asks her students what activity they want to do on Field Day, Zulay surprises everyone when she says she wants to run a race. With the help of a special aide and the support of her friends, Zulay does just that." (Publisher's note)

"Best friends Maya, Nancy, Chyng, and Zulay laugh and sing and help one another with homework. When their first-grade teacher, Ms. Seeger, surprises them with an announcement about an upcoming field day, excitement fills the air... This story is a great read-aloud for younger students due to the length of the text, but just right as independent reading for second and third graders. This picture book is a great way to continue building diverse library collections for all readers." SLJ

Bevis, Mary Elizabeth
   Wolf song; [by] Mary Bevis; illustrated by Consie Powell. Raven Productions 2007 un il $18.95; pa $12.95
Grades: K 1 2 3   **E**
   1. Uncles -- Fiction 2. Wolves -- Fiction
   ISBN 978-0-9794202-0-7; 978-0-9794202-1-4 pa

                 LC 2007027953
At twilight, Nell and her Uncle Walter go into the north woods, hoping to hear—and join—the howling of the wolves. Includes facts about wolves and howling expeditions.

"The text and illustrations both convey the wonder and mystery of nature." SLJ

Biddulph, Rob
   Blown away; written and illustrated by Rob Biddulph. Harper, an imprint of HarperCollinsPublishers 2015 40 p. color illustrations (hardback) $17.99
Grades: PreK K 1 2   **E**
   1. Home -- Fiction 2. Flight -- Fiction 3. Penguins -- Fiction 4. Tropics -- Fiction 5. Arctic regions -- Fiction 6. Voyages and travels -- Fiction 7. Animals -- Arctic

regions -- Fiction
ISBN 0062367242; 9780062367242

LC 2014022227

In this book, "when Penguin Blue flies his kite, it ends up flying him, along with some penguin pals who try to help. Then Wilbur, a seal, and Clive, a polar bear in a fishing raft, also find themselves towed along by the kite until it runs out of wind power over a remote, shark-encircled jungle island. Fortunately, Penguin Blue rigs up a parasaillike contraption from leaves and vines and attaches it to Clive's raft, and the wayward group makes it home." (Bulletin of the Center for Children's Books)

"Crisp, formal, and understated, newcomer Biddulph's images give evidence of his training as a graphic designer (as well as his sense of humor). He begins with a simple idea—a kite that carries its owner into the sky—and develops it with tongue-in-cheek charm...With the book's gentle ending and the kind of narrative voice that gives readers the sense that everything's well in hand, children will demand repeat reads." PW

Biedrzycki, David

Ace Lacewing, bug detective: the big swat. Charlesbridge 2010 un $16.95
Grades: K 1 2   E
  1. Mystery fiction 2. Insects -- Fiction
ISBN 978-1-57091-747-9; 1-57091-747-7

Me and my dragon. Charlesbridge 2011 un il $16.95; pa $7.95
Grades: PreK K   E
  1. Pets -- Fiction 2. Dragons -- Fiction
ISBN 1-58089-278-7; 1-58089-279-5 pa; 978-1-58089-278-0; 978-1-58089-279-7 pa

A child tells all the reasons a small, fire-breathing dragon would make an excellent pet, and the ways to take proper care of it.

"The Adobe Photoshop artwork abounds with expressions of surprise and alarm when others see the dragon. . . . While the brief text is a boon for early readers, this clever, funny book will delight young dragon lovers at storytimes." SLJ

Biggs, Brian

By sea; by Brian Biggs. Balzer + Bray 2013 56 p. color illustrations (Everything goes) (hardcover) $14.99
Grades: PreK K 1   E
  1. Sailing -- Fiction 2. Vehicles -- Fiction 3. Boats and boating -- Fiction 4. Ships -- Fiction
ISBN 9780061958113; 0061958115

LC 2012051820

Author and illustrator Brian Biggs presents "the third picture book in the Everything Goes series of picture books, board books, and I Can Reads, [which] is a wonderful celebration of sailboats, submarines, and many other interesting sea vehicles. Featuring . . . mini-story lines, seek-and-find activities, tons of . . . details, and . . . cutaways, 'Everything Goes: By Sea' is an interactive book." (Publisher's note)

"The pleasingly busy cartoon illustrations are packed with details and visual jokes, including some comedic bits from the earlier books, which should delight the series' frequent visitors. . . . Biggs navigates this nautical lesson with a steady hand." Horn Book

Everything goes in the air; Brian Biggs; edited by Donna Bray. 1st ed. Balzer + Bray 2012 56 p. col. ill. (hardcover) $14.99
Grades: PreK K 1   E
  1. Air travel -- Fiction 2. Transportation -- Fiction 3. Voyages and travels -- Fiction
ISBN 0061958107; 9780061958106

LC 2012942240

Author Brian Biggs presents an interactive book about things that fly. "Jets and blimps and helicopters and gliders! Balloons and biplanes too! Everything goes! Zoom along with Henry and his parents as they take off on an airborne journey and learn about all kinds of flying vehicles. . . . [The book includes] mini-story lines, seek-and-find activities, . . . [and] cutaways." (Publisher's note)

Bildner, Phil

The **greatest** game ever played; a football story. by Phil Bildner; illustrated by Zachary Pullen. Putnam's Sons 2006 un il $16.99
Grades: K 1 2 3   E
  1. Football -- Fiction 2. Father-son relationship -- Fiction
ISBN 0-399-24171-X

LC 2005025177

"The New York Giants are Sam and his father's favorite baseball team until they move west. Sam misses the team, but most of all he misses spending time with Pop, who has forsaken sports—despite Sam's breathless discovery of a football team with the same name. When Sam is given tickets to the 1958 NFL championship game, he and Pop go together. . . . The father-son relationship . . . is realistically portrayed. . . . The energy of the paintings perfectly matches Bildner's lively text." Booklist

★ The **Hallelujah** Flight; illustrated by John Holyfield. G.P. Putnam's Sons 2010 un il $16.99
Grades: K 1 2 3   E
  1. Air pilots 2. Mechanics (Persons) 3. Flight -- Fiction 4. Air pilots -- Fiction 5. African Americans -- Fiction
ISBN 978-0-399-24789-7; 0-399-24789-0

LC 2009-10362

In 1932, James Banning, along with his co-pilot Thomas Allen, make history by becoming the first African Americans to fly across the United States, relying on the generosity of people they meet in the towns along the way who help keep their 'flying jalopy' going.

"Based on both fictional and nonfiction sources, the story is briskly told in Allen's voice, with plenty of imagined dialogue. Holyfield's gorgeous . . . paintings are done on textured backgrounds in a palette of blues and browns." Kirkus

★ **Shoeless** Joe & Black Betsy; illustrated by C.F. Payne. Simon & Schuster Bks. for Young Readers 2002 un il $17
Grades: K 1 2 3   E
  1. Baseball players 2. Baseball -- Fiction
ISBN 0-689-82913-2

LC 99-40563

Shoeless Joe Jackson, said by some to be the greatest baseball player ever, goes into a hitting slump just before he is to start his minor league career, so he asks his friend to make him a special bat to help him hit

This is "told in a folksy, Southern voice, with many of the stylistic elements of a tall tale. . . . The mixed-media illustrations are layered and rich in texture, qualities that add depth and drama." SLJ

The **soccer** fence; a story of friendship, hope, and apartheid in South Africa. by Phil Bildner; illustrated by Jesse Joshua Watson. G. P. Putnam's Sons 2014 40 p. color illustrations $16.99

Grades: K 1 2 3   E
   1. Soccer -- Fiction 2. Apartheid -- Fiction 3. South Africa -- History 4. Race relations -- Fiction 5. Johannesburg (South Africa) 6. Blacks -- South Africa -- Fiction

ISBN 0399247904; 9780399247903

LC 2013014675

"Hector loved playing soccer in his small Johannesburg township. He dreamed of playing on a real pitch with the boys from another part of the city, but apartheid made that impossible. Then, in 1990, Nelson Mandela was released from prison, and apartheid began to crumble. . . When the beloved Bafana Bafana national soccer team won the African Cup of Nations, Hector realized that dreams once impossible could now come true." (Publisher's note)

"Bildner and Watson offer young readers an informative snapshot of a divided land through the lens of boys who just want to play." Kirkus

Includes bibliographical references

Turkey Bowl; [by] Phil Bildner; illustrated by C.F. Payne. Simon & Schuster Books for Young Readers 2008 un il $15.99

Grades: 1 2 3   E
   1. Snow -- Fiction 2. Football -- Fiction 3. Family life -- Fiction 4. Thanksgiving Day -- Fiction

ISBN 9780-689-87896-1; 0-689-87896-6

LC 2005020139

Ethan looks forward to the Thanksgiving Day when he and his friends are finally old enough to play in the annual family football game, but that day arrives full of snow and icy roads

"Payne's muted, full-color illustrations capture the disappointment and joy the characters experience and feature plenty of gridiron action. Perfect for reading aloud at holiday time, this lively story will resonate year-round with sports fans." SLJ

Billingsley, Franny

★ **Big** Bad Bunny; story by Franny Billingsley; art by G. Brian Karas. Atheneum Books for Young Readers 2008 un il $16.99

Grades: PreK K 1   E
   1. Mice -- Fiction 2. Mother-child relationship -- Fiction

ISBN 978-1-4169-0601-8; 1-4169-0601-0

LC 2006-32754

When Baby Boo-Boo, a mouse dressed in a bunny suit, becomes lost in the forest, his mother follows the sound of his cries to locate him.

Billingsley "extends her plot with satisfying onomatopoeia; the oversize format, too, marks this for a readaloud. Karas . . . strategically deploys mixed-media to render the id-gone-wild scenes with comic abandon." Publ Wkly

Bingham, Kelly

Circle, square, Moose; by Kelly Bingham; pictures by Paul O. Zelinsky. First edition. Greenwillow Books, an imprint of HarperCollinsPublishers 2014 48 p. color illustrations (trade ed.) $17.99

Grades: PreK K 1 2   E
   1. Humorous fiction 2. Moose -- Fiction 3. Shape -- Fiction 4. Zebras -- Fiction 5. Friendship -- Fiction 6. Humorous stories 7. Behavior -- Fiction

ISBN 0062290037; 9780062290038; 9780062290045

LC 2013019534

In this children's book, by Kelly Bingham & illustrated by Paul O. Zelinsky, "Moose infiltrates a book about shapes (because he loves shapes, naturally) and it is up to his best friend, Zebra, to restore order and save the day." (Publisher's note)

"Moose is back! Hooray—unless you are a book about circles and squares. The simple concept book starts off well enough with a button representing a circle and a sandwich representing a square. And then mischief and mayhem erupt as Moose takes an enormous bite out of the sandwich. Admonitions from the book follow, and then it attempts to continue with a wedge of cheese and a slice of pie to illustrate triangles. Alas, Moose interrupts again, presenting a cat with triangular ears. Leave the book, they are told. More Moose antics ensue with rectangles and diamonds. . . . It is a great joy to watch Bingham and Zelinsky, who brilliantly collaborated on Z Is for Moose (2012), once more let Moose loose to naughtily and enthusiastically disrupt reading. . . . Hilarious fun." Kirkus

★ **Z** is for Moose; by Kelly Bingham; illustrations by Paul O. Zelinsky. Greenwillow Books 2012 32 p.

Grades: PreK K 1 2   E
   1. Moose -- Fiction 2. Zebras -- Fiction 3. Children's stories 4. Alphabet -- Fiction 5. Books and reading -- Fiction 6. Humorous stories 7. Behavior -- Fiction

ISBN 9780060799847; 9780060799854

LC 2011002148

In this illustrated children's book, "[c]lipboard-bearing Zebra is in charge of getting the players on and off the stage in an item-by-item alphabetical pageant. . . . [Then] the excited Moose . . . pops onto the stage for D, leaving the distressed Duck fluttering in frustration. . . . Moose then tantrums through the rest of the book, . . . defacing other subjects with crayoned-on antlers and claiming . . . that R and S are also for Moose." (Bulletin of the Center for Children's Books)

Birdsall, Jeanne

★ **Flora's** very windy day; illustrated by Matt Phelan. Clarion Books 2010 un il $16

Grades: K 1 2   E
   1. Winds -- Fiction 2. Siblings -- Fiction

ISBN 978-0-618-98676-7; 0-618-98676-6

LC 2008-56061

When a big wind blows her annoying little brother away, Flora decides to save him despite the many tempting offers she gets for him from, among others, a cloud, an eagle, the man in the moon, and the wind itself.

"This is a gem of a book that will resonate with older siblings everywhere." SLJ

Birtha, Becky

★ **Grandmama's** pride; illustrated by Colin Bootman. Albert Whitman 2005 un il $16.95

Grades: K 1 2 3   E

1. Segregation -- Fiction 2. Grandmothers -- Fiction 3. African Americans -- Fiction

ISBN 0-8075-3028-X

LC 2005003991

While on a trip in 1956 to visit her grandmother in the South, six-year-old Sarah Marie experiences segregation for the first time, but discovers that things have changed by the time she returns the following year.

"The strong, sensitive writing is enhanced by beautiful watercolor paintings filled with chips of light." SLJ

★ **Lucky** beans; illustrated by Nicole Tadgell. Albert Whitman 2010 un il $16.99

Grades: 1 2 3   E

1. Beans -- Fiction 2. Mathematics -- Fiction 3. African Americans -- Fiction 4. Great Depression, 1929-1939 -- Fiction

ISBN 978-0-8075-4782-3; 0-8075-4782-4

During the Great Depression, an African American boy named Marshall uses lessons learned in arithmetic class to figure out how many beans are in a jar to win his mother a sewing machine.

"Math and wry comedy mix in this lively historical story. . . . The expressive watercolor paintings show both the racism that Marshall and his family endure as well as his final triumph, and Tadgell folds in humor." Booklist

Bitterman, Albert

Fortune cookies; illustrated by Chris Raschka. Beach Lane Books 2011 un il $14.99

Grades: PreK K   E

1. Fortune telling -- Fiction

ISBN 978-1-4169-6814-6; 1-4169-6814-8

LC 2008-20158

Seven fortune cookies foretell a child's fortunes for each day of the week.

"A tidy, perfectly paced story with subtle grace and a kernel of wisdom." Publ Wkly

Bjorkman, Steve

Dinosaurs don't, dinosaurs do. Holiday House 2011 un il (I like to read) $14.95

Grades: PreK K 1   E

1. Dinosaurs -- Fiction 2. Etiquette -- Fiction

ISBN 978-0-8234-2355-2; 0-8234-2355-7

LC 2010032832

This book "deftly [combines] text and art to create a positive experience for new readers. [It is] larger than typical easy readers, leaving plenty of room for uncluttered, colorful cartoon illustrations and clear, large fonts. . . . Björkman uses repetitive text and playful pictures to introduce appropriate behavior. 'Dinosaurs don't run here' is demonstrated by a dismayed dinosaur in front of glassware falling from a china cabinet; opposite, 'Dinosaurs do run here' shows two smiling creatures running through a playground. . . . [This title has] similar-sounding vowels and consonants, popular sight words, and short, simple sentences with clear punctuation, making [it a] successful [entry] in the beginning-reader canon." SLJ

Black, Michael Ian

Chicken cheeks; illustrated by Kevin Hawkes. Simon & Schuster Books for Young Readers 2009 un il $15.99

Grades: PreK K 1 2   E

1. Stories in rhyme 2. Animals -- Fiction

ISBN 1-4169-4864-3; 978-1-4169-4864-3

LC 2007-16872

Illustrations and text describe the back ends of various animals. "Ages five to seven." (Bull Cent Child Books)

This "features the hind quarters of animals, complete with silly names for them. . . . The closeup, color-saturated illustrations—which are at the same time obviously hilarious and sneakily deadpan—tell a story. A brown bear stands poised atop a ladder, gazing thoughtfully up the skinny trunk of a tall, branch-free tree. He grabs a duck and sets it on his head. . . . Sixteen animals later, children can only laugh helplessly at the absurd ladder of animals balanced parallel to the tree trunk. . . . Filled with visual jokes and amusing details, ChickenCheeks is a lot more than a list of words for kids to snicker at." SLJ

★ A **pig** parade is a terrible idea; illustrated by Kevin Hawkes. Simon & Schuster Books for Young Readers 2010 un il $16.99

Grades: PreK K 1 2   E

1. Pigs -- Fiction 2. Parades -- Fiction

ISBN 978-1-4169-7922-7; 1-4169-7922-0

LC 2008-51562

Explains precisely why, although it may sound like a good idea, gathering hundreds of pigs to march in a parade through one's hometown is inadvisable.

"If this book's arch-toned text wasn't flat-out funny enough, Hawkes' deliciously down-and-dirty art takes the concept to a whole other level." Booklist

Blackaby, Susan

★ **Brownie** Groundhog and the February fox; illustrated by Carmen Segovia. Sterling 2010 un il $16.99

Grades: PreK K 1   E

1. Foxes -- Fiction 2. Winter -- Fiction 3. Marmots -- Fiction

ISBN 978-1-4027-4336-8; 1-4027-4336-X

Brownie the groundhog encounters a fox while waiting for winter to be over, and through clever maneuvering—and tasty snacks—the two become friends.

"Segovia's acrylic paints and inks elevate the simple-seeming story, truly driving home the bone-penetrating chill of a typical February day. Blackaby is as tricky as her heroine, economically developing two distinct and likable characters and delivering plenty of chuckles and wordplay. Elegant." Kirkus

Followed by: Brownie Groundhog and the wintry surprise (2013)

Blackall, Sophie

★ **Are** you awake? Henry Holt 2011 un il $12.99

Grades: PreK K 1   E

1. Night -- Fiction 2. Bedtime -- Fiction 3. Mother-son relationship -- Fiction

ISBN 978-0-8050-7858-9; 0-8050-7858-4

LC 2010026946

Persistent young Edward has many questions for his sleepy mother, many of which are answered, "Because it's night time."

Blackall's "palette starts out gray, warming to sunlit yellow as the bedside clock hands rotate and dawn breaks. Dialogue moves from speech balloons to type and back again, while watercolor panels offer affectionate closeups of Edward, his mother, and night scenes from their apartment window. Edward's antics hit the mark. . . . while Blackall's arch voice . . . makes this a solid candidate for the favorites pile." Publ Wkly

★ The **baby** tree; Sophie Blackall. Nancy Paulsen Books, an imprint of Penguin Group (USA) Inc. 2014 40 p. $17.99

Grades: PreK K 1 2   E
1. Children's stories 2. Reproduction 3. Humorous stories 4. Babies -- Fiction 5. Pregnancy -- Fiction 6. Questions and answers -- Fiction 7. Sex instruction for children -- Fiction
ISBN 0399257187; 9780399257186
LC 2013036309
"Revealing the basics of reproduction in an age-appropriate way, award-winning Sophie Blackall has created a beautiful picture book full of playful details to amuse and engage readers. . . . Join a curious little boy who asks everyone from his babysitter to the mailman, getting all sorts of funny answers along the way, before his parents gently set him straight." (Publisher's note)

"After learning he's going to be a big brother, a boy asks various grownups (babysitter, teacher, grandfather) where babies come from. At bedtime, Mom and Dad provide a very basic, concise explanation. Blackall's text is straightforward, calm, and reassuring. Her Chinese-ink and watercolor illustrations feature cherubic, rosy-cheeked, cute-as-a-button babies of different ethnicities. An appended page provides suggestions for adults addressing the same question." Horn Book

Blackford, Andy
Bill's bike; illustrated by Hannah Wood. Crabtree Pub. Co. 2011 21p il (Tadpoles) lib bdg $21.27; pa $6.95
Grades: PreK K 1   E
1. Wheels -- Fiction 2. Bicycles -- Fiction
ISBN 978-0-7787-0575-8 lib bdg; 0-7787-0575-7 lib bdg; 978-0-7787-0586-4 pa; 0-7787-0586-2 pa
LC 2010052360
"Bill starts off with four wheels on his bike but finds that he only needs two. . . . The [story is] gently funny with supportive illustrations that offer a solid structure within which kids can begin to read on their own. . . . [This book offers] characters with personality and scenes full of action." SLJ

The **hungry** little monkey; illustrated by Gabriele Antonini. Crabtree Pub. Co. 2011 21p il (Tadpoles) lib bdg $21.27; pa $6.95
Grades: PreK K 1   E
1. Animals -- Fiction 2. Monkeys -- Fiction
ISBN 978-0-7787-0581-9 lib bdg; 0-7787-0581-1 lib bdg; 978-0-7787-0592-5 pa; 0-7787-0592-7 pa
LC 2010052367
"A little monkey gets advice from the other animals on how to eat his banana, . . . but the right answer eventually comes from his mother. The [story is] gently funny with supportive illustrations that offer a solid structure within which kids can begin to read on their own. . . . [This book offers] characters with personality and scenes full of action." SLJ

Blackstone, Stella
My granny went to market; a round-the-world counting rhyme. written by Stella Blackstone; illustrated by Christopher Corr. Barefoot Books 2005 un il $16.99
Grades: PreK K 1 2   E
1. Counting 2. Stories in rhyme 3. Grandmothers -- Fiction 4. Voyages and travels -- Fiction
ISBN 1-84148-792-9
LC 2004-17394
A child's grandmother travels around the world, buying things in quantities that illustrate counting from one to ten.
"The brightly colored gouache illustrations have the feel of Mexican folk art, and endpaper maps route Granny's travels, with a one-page legend showing her purchases—from one carpet to 10 llamas. A cheery, global shopping trip, fun to read alone and also useful in the classroom." Booklist

Blackwood, Freya
★ **Ivy** loves to give. Arthur A. Levine Books 2010 un il $15.99
Grades: PreK K 1   E
1. Gifts -- Fiction
ISBN 978-0-545-23467-2; 0-545-23467-0
First published 2009 in Australia
Ivy loves to give presents, and although they are not always appropriate, they are always given with enthusiasm and generosity.
Blackwood's "text—five sentences total—is brilliant in its economy, empathy, and pacing; the same can be said for the subtle and slyly funny family characterizations of her delicate pencil and watercolor drawings, rendered on a creamy white backdrop with minimal propping." Publ Wkly

Blake, Robert J.
Painter and Ugly. Philomel Books 2011 un il $16.99
Grades: K 1 2 3   E
1. Dogs -- Fiction 2. Alaska -- Fiction 3. Friendship -- Fiction 4. Sled dog racing -- Fiction
ISBN 978-0-399-24323-3; 0-399-24323-2
LC 2010005395
Painter and Ugly, two sled dogs who are inseparable best friends, are put on different teams for the Junior Iditarod, but they manage to find their way back to one another for the big race.
"Blake paints the dogs' heavy coats and eager faces in painstaking detail, and does a notably good job of narrating from a dog's point of view. His portrait of this specialized world will lure even those who have never been part of it." Publ Wkly

Blake, Stephanie
I don't want to go to school! written and illustrated by Stephanie Blake. Random House 2009 un il $12.99; lib bdg $15.99
Grades: PreK K   E
1. School stories 2. Rabbits -- Fiction
ISBN 0-375-85688-9; 0-375-95688-3 lib bdg; 978-0-375-85688-4; 978-0-375-95688-1 lib bdg
LC 2008011256
Original French edition 2007
Simon the rabbit does not want to go to his first day of school, but by the time his mother comes to take him home, he is having such a good time that he does not want to leave

"This title has a standard premise that is instantly understandable and reassuring, and the naive-style art, rendered in bold outlines and primary colors, is appealing and expressive." Booklist

Another title about Simon the Rabbit is:

A deal's a deal (2011)

Blechman, Nicholas

Night light; Nicholas Blechman. Scholastic 2013 48 p. ill. (reinforced) $16.99

Grades: PreK K 1   E

1. Counting 2. Picture books for children 3. Light -- Fiction 4. Stories in rhyme 5. Counting -- Fiction 6. Vehicles -- Fiction

ISBN 0545462630; 9780545462631

LC 2012024221

This children's picture book is "a counting book about big vehicles . . . with an extra . . . twist. [Nicholas Btechman] invites readers to identify the vehicles with a turn-the-page guessing game. First, spreads of pure black show only the vehicles' distinctive signature of lights. '1 light, shining bright?' reads the first black spread, a small, die-cut circle on the right side creating a single white dot. A page turn uncovers the answer: 'train.'" (Publishers Weekly)

Blessing, Charlotte

New old shoes; written by Charlotte Blessing; illustrated by Gary R. Phillips. Pleasant St. Press 2009 un il $16.95

Grades: K 1 2   E

1. Shoes -- Fiction 2. Africa -- Fiction

ISBN 978-0-9792035-6-5; 0-9792035-6-2

"This story is narrated by a pair of red sneakers and follows their journey from their first home with a young boy in America to children in Africa. . . . The color-saturated illustrations provide a vibrant background to this touching story." SLJ

Blexbolex

★ People; [translated by Claudia Bedrick] Enchanted Lion Books 2011 il $19.95

Grades: K 1 2   E

1. Occupations -- Fiction

ISBN 978-1-59270-110-0; 1-59270-110-8

LC 2011001132

Explores, through brief text and illustrations, various sorts of people, the jobs they do, and the connections among them.

"German artist Blexbolex's captivating silk-screens explore human archetypes using a 1960s-era design aesthetic. Powder-blue type identifies each figure. As with its predecessor, the book's brilliance lies in the intriguing ways in which the images mimic, challenge, and inform one another. . . . Readers will form new associations and make new discoveries upon each revisiting." Publ Wkly

★ Seasons; translated by Claudia Bedrick. Enchanted Lion Books 2010 un il $19.95

Grades: K 1 2   E

1. Seasons -- Fiction

ISBN 978-1-59270-095-0; 1-59270-095-0

LC 2010001114

Original French edition, 2009

Explores, through brief text and illustrations, various aspects of each season of the year.

"This thick volume is both beautiful and intriguing—artist's portfolio, concept book, and word book rolled into one. The words, in huge, vividly pink block capitals, caption full pages and spreads for which seasons are the organizing principle. . . . These sophisticated images are sure to stimulate creative thought." Horn Book

Bley, Anette

And what comes after a thousand? Kane/Miller 2007 un il $15.95

Grades: PreK K 1 2   E

1. Death -- Fiction 2. Friendship -- Fiction 3. Bereavement -- Fiction

ISBN 978-1-933605-27-2

"This tender tale about intergenerational friendship, love, and loss tells of the cozy relationship between a young girl and an old, hard-of-hearing man. . . . After he dies, she must learn to deal with her pain and feelings of abandonment. The closeness of the characters is portrayed in heartwarming illustrations. . . . This universal story will speak to many readers." SLJ

Bliss, Harry

★ Bailey. Scholastic 2011 un il $16.99

Grades: PreK K 1 2   E

1. School stories 2. Dogs -- Fiction

ISBN 978-0-545-23344-6; 0-545-23344-5

LC 2010045096

Although he is a dog, Bailey goes to school where his canine abilities enliven an ordinary day.

"Deceptively simple cartoon illustrations belie the brilliance of the story. . . . From the facial expressions to the titles of the books Bailey reads, no opportunity is lost for fleshing out this character; and laughs abound on every page." SLJ

Bloch, Serge

Butterflies in my stomach and other school hazards; by Serge Bloch. Sterling Pub. Co. 2008 un il $12.95

Grades: PreK K 1 2   E

1. School stories 2. English language -- Idioms -- Fiction

ISBN 978-1-4027-4158-6; 1-4027-4158-8

LC 2007-43372

On the first day of school, a student is confused by many of the phrases that are used, such as when the librarian says not to open a can of worms, or when the teacher says he expects the class to be busy bees doing their homework.

"Bloch's simple though imaginative pictures and clean visual style invite discussion of the deeper meanings of these oft-used phrases, making this an ideal book for the classroom or for one-on-one sharing." SLJ

Snowed under and other Christmas confusions. Sterling 2011 il $12.95

Grades: PreK K 1   E

1. Christmas -- Fiction

ISBN 978-1-4027-7131-6; 1-4027-7131-2

LC 2010037056

A snow storm the day before Christmas causes a boy many worries, which are not helped by such confusing phrases as "Don't be a wet blanket" and "That's the way the cookie crumbles."

"The illustrations are creatively composed with effective use of white space, shadows and perspective along with motion and sight gags. As all kids know, 'time flies when you're having fun,' even on Christmas Eve. This is more fun than a barrel of monkeys." Kirkus

Blomgren, Jennifer

Where do I sleep? a Pacific Northwest lullabye. illustrated by Andrea Gabriel. Sasquatch Bks. 2001 un il $15.95

Grades: PreK K 12   E

1. Stories in rhyme 2. Sleep -- Fiction 3. Animals -- Fiction 4. Pacific Northwest -- Fiction

ISBN 1-57061-258-7

LC 2001-20940

Rhyming text describes some of the young animals—from a gray wolf pup and a horned puffin to a cougar kit and a small brown bat—as they settle down to sleep

"Kids get an opportunity to practice map skills, learn about new animals, find out why Alaska's summer days are so long, and add such unfamiliar words as tundra to their vocabulary. . . . Gabriel's gorgeous artwork reflects the beauty and diversity of the wildlife and landscape." Booklist

Bloom, Suzanne

Alone together; Suzanne Bloom. Boyds Mills Press 2014 32 p. color illustrations (Goose and bear books) $16.95

Grades: PreK K   E

1. Bears -- Fiction 2. Foxes -- Fiction 3. Friendship -- Fiction 4. Geese -- fiction

ISBN 162091736X; 9781620917367

LC 2014931586

In this children's book, author Suzanne Bloom "crafts a story about her beloved Goose, Bear, and Fox that focuses on the simple emotional truths of childhood. Bear is quietly sitting by himself so Fox wonders if Bear is sad or mad or lonely. But no, Bear just occasionally enjoys a little quiet time alone. Not to be outdone, Fox decides that she would like quiet time alone, too—with Bear! Needless to say, Fox's version of quiet time is very different from Bear's." (Publisher's note)

"Big, white, cuddly Bear tries to have quiet time alone. Large white lettering over a deep blue background presents the sparse text, perfectly worded for a beginning reader to figure out or for a preschooler to memorize. . . . As Fox tries to join Bear's quiet time, the small red critter's idiosyncratic interpretation of 'quiet' leads to paws on the head, rolled eyes and other hints of ursine distress. Eventually, Bear is moved to firmer, although never intimidating tactics. By the time Goose rejoins the trio, Bear and Fox have attained agreement or have they? Short on words and long on expressive artwork—a charming addition to a winning series for little ones." Kirkus

Feeding friendsies. Boyds Mills Press 2011 un il $16.95

Grades: PreK K   E

1. Play -- Fiction 2. Gardens -- Fiction

ISBN 978-1-59078-529-4; 1-59078-529-0

Baby and friends are busy in the garden making lunch that includes puddle-water soup, mud pie, and dandelion-and-dirt dessert.

"Bloom's sunny, naive watercolor illustrations show the children joyfully playing in the dirt while a shaggy dog and a black cat watch with curiosity. . . . This celebration of imaginative, outdoor fun is a tasty treat." SLJ

★ A **splendid** friend, indeed; written and illustrated by Suzanne Bloom. Boyds Mills Press 2005 un il $15.95

Grades: PreK K 1   E

1. Geese -- Fiction 2. Friendship -- Fiction 3. Polar bear -- Fiction

ISBN 1-59078-286-0

LC 2004-10780

Other titles about Bear and Goose are:

Treasure (2007);

What about Bear? (2010);

Oh! What a surprise! (2012);

Fox forgets (2013);

Alone together (2014)

When a studious polar bear meets an inquisitive goose, they learn to be friends.

"The cool palette of the pastel illustrations, consisting of shades of blue and white and touches of violet, sets a quiet, friendly tone, and the animals' priceless expressions tell all. The gentle humor will elicit giggles." SLJ

Blue, Rose

Ron's big mission; [by] Rose Blue and Corinne J. Naden; illustrated by Don Tate. Dutton Childrens Books 2009 un il $16.99

Grades: K 1 2 3   E

1. Astronauts 2. Physicists 3. Libraries -- Fiction 4. Segregation -- Fiction 5. South Carolina -- Fiction 6. African Americans -- Fiction 7. Books and reading -- Fiction

ISBN 978-0-525-47849-2; 0-525-47849-3

LC 2007050563

One summer day in 1959, nine-year-old Ron McNair, who dreams of becoming a pilot, walks into the Lake City, South Carolina, public library and insists on checking out some books, despite the rule that only white people can have library cards. Includes facts about McNair, who grew up to be an astronaut

"Vibrant illustrations portray a cozy small town. . . . Tate's figures feature oversized heads with very expressive faces that vividly convey well-meant kindness and the frustrations of injustice. . . . This will make a good choice for reading aloud and discussing." Booklist

Bluemle, Elizabeth

★ **How** do you wokka-wokka? illustrated by Randy Cecil. Candlewick Press 2009 un il $15.99

Grades: PreK K 1   E

1. Stories in rhyme 2. Dance -- Fiction

ISBN 978-0-7636-3228-1; 0-7636-3228-7

LC 2008-27715

A young boy who likes to "wokka-wokka, shimmy-shake, and shocka-shocka" gathers his neighbors together for a surprise celebration.

"The sketchy, full-color oil illustrations in muted colors feature cartoon children cavorting alternately against stark white backgrounds or cityscapes as they join a giant block party. This bouncy book is a joy as a read-aloud." SLJ

Tap tap boom boom; Elizabeth Bluemle, illustrated by G. Brian Karas. Candlewick Press 2014 32 p. color illustrations $16.99
Grades: PreK K 1   E
1. Thunderstorms 2. City and town life 3. Picture books for children
ISBN 0763656968; 9780763656966
LC 2013943093
In this children's picture book, by Elizabeth Bluemle and illustrated by G. Brian Karas, "as a thunderstorm rolls in, people of all stripes race down to the subway to get away from the crackling rain and wind. With quirky wordplay and . . . rhymes, Elizabeth Bluemle crystallizes an unexpected moment of community." (Publisher's note)
"The poetic rhythm of the language mimics the stages of the storm and the tempo of the citizens' footsteps. Though minimal, the text is powerful, and works well with the illustrations to create positive feelings about the weather." Lib Med Con

Blume, Judy
★ The **Pain** and the Great One; illustrations by Irene Trivas. rev format ed; Atheneum Books for Young Readers 2002 un il $17.95; pa $6.99
Grades: K 1 2 3   E
1. Siblings -- Fiction
ISBN 0-689-85507-9; 0-440-40967-5 pa
First published 1984 by Bradbury Press
A six-year-old (The Pain) and his eight-year-old sister (The Great One) see each other as troublemakers and the best-loved in the family
"Young readers, depending on their position within the family, will readily identify with either character and may learn empathy for the other. Used in a group, this will provide much healthy discussion. . . . Trivas' vibrant colors add depth and humor to a valuable book on sibling relationships." SLJ

Blumenthal, Deborah
The **blue** house dog; illustrated by Adam Gustavson. Peachtree 2010 un il $15.95
Grades: K 1 2 3   E
1. Dogs -- Fiction
ISBN 978-1-56145-537-9; 1-56145-537-7
"After his owner dies, Bones [a dog] roams the streets until young Cody acknowledges his grief over losing his own pet and persuades Bones to trust him. Perceptive art and emotive, free verse-style text work well together." Booklist

Bodeen, S. A.
★ **Elizabeti's** doll; illustrated by Christy Hale. Lee & Low Bks. 1998 un il $15.95
Grades: K 1 2 3   E
1. Siblings -- Fiction 2. Tanzania -- Fiction
ISBN 1-880000-70-9
LC 98-13086
When a young Tanzanian girl gets a new baby brother, she finds a rock, which she names Eva, and makes it her baby doll
"Vibrant patterns and soft watercolor backgrounds evoke a sense of place and familial love." SLJ

Other titles about Elizabeti are:
Elizabeti's school (2002)
Mama Elizabeti (2000)

A **small,** brown dog with a wet, pink nose; by Stephanie Stuve-Bodeen; [illustrations by Linzie Hunter] Little Brown Books for Young Readers 2009 un il $16.99
Grades: K 1 2   E
1. Dogs -- Fiction 2. Parent-child relationship -- Fiction
ISBN 978-0-316-05830-8; 0-316-05830-0
LC 2008039298
Amelia will stop at nothing to convince her parents to let her adopt a very special dog.
"The concepts are complicated but clear, and Hunter's patterned illustrations are appropriately unpredictable, with nearly every page design different from the last. Plenty for kids to pore over." Booklist

Boelts, Maribeth
Before you were mine; story by Maribeth Boelts; pictures by David Walker. Putnam 2007 un il $15.99
Grades: PreK K 1 2   E
1. Dogs -- Fiction
ISBN 978-0-399-24526-8; 0-399-24526-X
LC 2006-20525
A young boy imagines what his rescued dog's life might have been like before he adopted him.
"Cozy, soft-edged pictures of an adorable dog characterize this warmhearted book. . . . The pastel illustrations use a variety of layouts to infuse the story with emotion." Booklist

Dogerella; illustrated by Donald Wu. Random House 2008 48p il (Step into reading) lib bdg $11.99; pa $3.99
Grades: 1 2 3   E
1. Fairy tales 2. Dogs -- Fiction
ISBN 978-0-375-93393-6 lib bdg; 0-375-93393-X lib bdg; 978-0-375-83393-9 pa; 0-375-83393-5 pa
LC 2007-15229
With the help of her fairy dogmother, Dogerella attends Princess Bea's ball where she competes with other dogs to become the princess's royal pet
"The combination of dozens of dogs, an earnest princess and a touch of magic add up to a charming whole." Kirkus

Those shoes; [by] Maribeth Boelts; illustrated by Noah Z. Jones. Candlewick Press 2007 un il $15.99; pa $6.99
Grades: K 1 2 3   E
1. Shoes -- Fiction 2. Grandmothers -- Fiction
ISBN 978-0-7636-2499-6; 0-7636-2499-3; 978-0-7636-4284-6 pa; 0-7636-4284-3 pa
LC 2006-51839
Jeremy, who longs to have the black high tops that everyone at school seems to have but his grandmother cannot afford, is excited when he sees them for sale in a thrift shop and decides to buy them even though they are the wrong size.
"Jones mixed-media, digitally assembled pictures cleverly capture how thoroughly the shoe craze permeates every aspect of Jeremy's life. . . . Boelts and Jones create a work with broad appeal." Bull Cent Child Books

Bogan, Paulette
★ **Goodnight** Lulu. Bloomsbury Children's Bk. 2003 un il hardcover o.p. pa $6.95

Grades: PreK K 1 2   E
    1. Bedtime -- Fiction 2. Chickens -- Fiction
    ISBN 1-58234-803-0; 1-58234-983-5 pa
           LC 2002-27825

When her mother tucks her in for the night, Lulu the chicken worries what would happen if a bear or a tiger or an alligator should come in during the night

This is a "funny, original, and reassuring tale. . . . The saturated watercolor and ink spreads deftly capture the night's ominous as well as cozy qualities." Horn Book Guide

Another title about Lulu is:

Lulu the big little chick (2009)

Bogart, Jo Ellen

Big and small, room for all; illustrated by Gillian Newland. Tundra Books 2009 un il $18.95
Grades: PreK K 1 2   E
    1. Size -- Fiction
    ISBN 978-0-88776-891-0; 0-88776-891-1

"A young girl sitting on a low tree branch views the vast mountains, sky, and fields around her. As the book progresses, realistic watercolor illustrations show the universe, the solar system, and a mountain range, as the spare text labels each concept in comparison to the size of the one before it. . . . Youngsters will delight in the awe-inspiring illustrations. . . . Word choice is highly suitable for the earliest independent readers." SLJ

Boisrobert, Anouck

Popville; [by] Anouck Boisrobert & Louis Rigaud. Roaring Brook Press 2010 un il lib bdg $16.99
Grades: K 1 2 3   E
    1. Stories without words 2. Pop-up books 3. City and town life -- Fiction
    ISBN 1-59643-593-3 lib bdg; 978-1-59643-593-3 lib bdg

Successive pop-up scenes show the progress as a rural area is built up into a busy city. "Ages four to eight." (N Y Times Book Rev)

"Using crisp, appealing pop-ups in a long, thin binding, [this book] chronicles a city's evolution from a bucolic, perhaps lonely, country church to an urban landscape. . . . 'Popville' has a clever central mechanism that tells the story quietly: a window cut out right through the book allows all the successive buildings to stay popped up even when the pages turn. The artwork is uncluttered and stylized, using muted, solid colors with a fabric-like texture to create clean geometric shapes." New York Times

Bolden, Tonya

Beautiful moon; a child's prayer. by Tonya Bolden; illustrated by Eric Velasquez. Abrams Books for Young Readers 2014 32 p. color illustrations $16.95
Grades: K 1 2 3   E
    1. Prayer -- Fiction 2. Bedtime -- Fiction 3. Moon -- Fiction 4. City and town life -- Fiction
    ISBN 1419707922; 9781419707926
           LC 2013031976

In this children's book, by Tonya Bolden, illustrated by Eric Velasquez, "a young boy wakes. He has forgotten to say his prayers. Outside his window, a beautiful harvest moon illuminates the city around him and its many inhabitants. As the moon slowly makes its way across the heavens, the boy offers a simple prayer for the homeless, the hungry, and others." (Publisher's note)

"Bolden (Maritcha: A 19th Century American Girl) expands a pleasingly simple premise into a depiction of the profound possibility of prayer. It's night. An 'amber orb' — the moon—floats above the city, and a boy startles awake in bed, having forgotten to say his nightly prayers. Velasquez (My Uncle Martin's Big Heart) shows the subjects of the boy's prayers: 'people with no homes,' the hungry, the lonely, 'for wars to end.' . . . Velasquez's illustrations, done in mixed media and oil on watercolor paper, convey mostly urban scenes in dark blues and browns, each illuminated by moonlight, which are both peaceful and full of detail. The book offers young readers plenty to look at, along with a simple message about the way prayer unites everyone, as the multicultural subjects in Velasquez's gorgeous illustrations make clear." Pub Wkly

Boldt, Mike

123 versus ABC; by Mike Boldt. Harper, an imprint of HarperCollinsPublishers 2013 32 p. (hardcover) $17.99
Grades: K 1 2 3   E
    1. Alphabet 2. Counting 3. Humorous stories 4. Alphabet -- Fiction 5. Numbers, Natural -- Fiction
    ISBN 0062102990; 9780062102997
           LC 2012025494

This book, written by Mike Boldt, asks "which is more important, numbers or letters? Numbers and letters, the colorful characters in this story, compete to be the stars of this book. Their debate escalates when funny animals and props arrive—starting with 1 alligator, 2 bears, and 3 cars." (Publisher's note)

Bond, Felicia

Big hugs, little hugs. Philomel Books 2012 un il $16.99
Grades: PreK K   E
    1. Animals -- Fiction 2. Hugging -- Fiction
    ISBN 978-0-399-25614-1; 0-399-25614-8
           LC 2010053139

"This jubilant ode to the joys of hugging boldly announces its message on the first page: 'Everyone hugs all over the world.' What follows are tidy snippets of text that declare what animals like to hug, . . . as well as where, how, and when this hugging takes place. Bond . . . works in torn and cut-paper collage, her cheerful animal families showing various happy emotions. . . . The book's many whimsical touches should prove both comforting and entertaining." Publ Wkly

Bonsall, Crosby Newell

★ The **case** of the hungry stranger; by Crosby Bonsall. HarperCollins Pubs. 1992 64p il (I can read book) hardcover o.p. pa $3.99
Grades: K 1 2 3   E
    1. Mystery fiction
    ISBN 0-06-020571-7 lib bdg; 0-06-444026-5 pa
           LC 91-13345

A reissue of the title first published 1963. This edition has full color illustrations

Wizard and his friends are clueless when they are sent on the trail of a blueberry pie thief, until Wizard hits on a plan that is sure to nab the sweet-toothed pilferer

This offers "suspense and humor." Horn Book

Other titles in this series are:
The case of the cat's meow (1965)
The case of the double cross (1980)
The case of the dumb bells (1966)
The case of the scaredy cats (1971)

★ The **day** I had to play with my sister; story and pictures by Crosby Bonsall. newly il ed; HarperCollins Pubs. 1999 32p il (My first I can read book) hardcover o.p. pa $3.99
Grades: K 1 2   E
1. Siblings -- Fiction
ISBN 0-06-028181-2; 0-06-444253-5 pa
LC 98-20342
A newly illustrated edition of the title first published 1972
A young boy becomes very frustrated when he tries to teach his little sister to play hide-and-seek
"The extremely simple text . . . is one with which children can readily identify. . . . The realistic atmosphere makes Bonsall's book an excellent addition to the very early reading shelves." SLJ

★ **Mine's** the best; newly il ed; HarperCollins Pubs. 1996 32p il (My first I can read book) lib bdg $16.89; pa $3.99
Grades: K 1 2   E
1. Balloons -- Fiction 2. Friendship -- Fiction
ISBN 0-06-027091-8 lib bdg; 0-06-444213-6 pa
LC 95-12405
A newly illustrated edition of the title first published 1973
Two little boys meet at the beach, each sure that his balloon is better
"The playful illustrations tell their own story; the extremely brief text (not to mention the head start provided by the two initial wordless spreads) will give new readers a sense of accomplishment." Horn Book Guide

★ **Who's** afraid of the dark? by Crosby Bonsall. Harper & Row 1980 32p il (Early I can read book) lib bdg $16.89; pa $3.99
Grades: K 1 2   E
1. Fear -- Fiction 2. Night -- Fiction
ISBN 0-06-020599-7 lib bdg; 0-06-444071-0 pa
LC 79-2700
"A little boy describes to a friend the nighttime fears of his dog Stella. Stella shivers in the dark, he claims; she sees shapes and hears scary sounds. The doubting but sympathetic friend offers a suggestion—hug Stella in the night and comfort her until her fears go away. . . . The illustrations in shades of light blue and brown are filled with as much life and warmth as ever." Horn Book

Bootman, Colin
Steel pan man of Harlem. Carolrhoda Books 2009 un il lib bdg $16.95
Grades: K 1 2 3   E
1. Rats -- Fiction 2. Harlem (New York, N.Y.) -- Fiction 3. Steel drum (Musical instrument) -- Fiction
ISBN 978-0-8225-9026-2 lib bdg; 0-8225-9026-3 lib bdg
LC 2008039654
A mysterious man appears in Harlem and promises to rid the city of its rats by playing the steel pan drum

Bootman "triumphs with this gorgeously moody, thoroughly cinematic retelling of the Pied Piper of Hamelin. . . . The oil paintings conjure up a gritty, workaday world where magic has taken hold." Publ Wkly

Borden, Louise, 1949-
The **A** + custodian; illustrated by Adam Gustavson. Margaret K. McElderry Books 2004 un il $15.95
Grades: K 1 2 3   E
1. School stories 2. Janitors -- Fiction
ISBN 0-689-84995-8
LC 2002-12029
The students and teachers at Dublin Elementary School make banners, posters, and signs for their school custodian to show how much they appreciate him and all the work he does
"The simple, unrhymed poetic words and the realistic oil paintings create a strong sense of a diverse school community and a man in flannel shirt and worn leather shoes." Booklist

A. Lincoln and me; illustrated by Ted Lewin. Scholastic 1999 un il hardcover o.p. pa $5.99
Grades: K 1 2 3   E
1. Lawyers 2. Presidents 3. State legislators 4. Members of Congress
ISBN 0-590-45714-4 pa
LC 98-51921
With the help of his teacher, a young boy realizes that he not only shares his birthday and similar physical appearance with Abraham Lincoln, but that he is like him in other ways as well
"Borden's text flows nicely, creating imagery of the physical presence of the man. Lewin's distinctive watercolors lend style and substance to the book, producing a treat for the eyes." SLJ

Baseball is... Louise Borden; illustrated by Raul Colon. Margaret K. McElderry Books, an imprint of Simon & Schuster Children's Pub. Division 2013 48 p. (hardcover) $17.99
Grades: 2 3 4 5   E
1. Baseball
ISBN 141695502X; 9781416955023
LC 2013008621
This picture book presents a free-verse tribute to baseball. Author Louise Borden "enumerates the elements of the game, including ballparks and fans, plays and players. . . . A fold-out page gives special attention to Babe Ruth, Jackie Robinson, and Roberto Clemente. The author also mentions the 'long ago' Negro leagues and the women's league; and notes baseball's ability to bring diverse people together. Emphasis is placed on patriotic elements." (School Library Journal)
"America's national pastime gets a treatment that is both lively and knowledgeable in this oversize, fact-filled volume...This is due in no small part to Colón's signature colored-pencil artwork, which impressively captures baseball moments big and small. A neat vehicle for getting an intergenerational conversation going over a shared passion." Booklist

Big brothers don't take naps; art by Emma Dodd. Margaret K. McElderry Books 2011 un il $16.99

Grades: PreK K 1   **E**
1. Infants -- Fiction 2. Brothers -- Fiction 3. Siblings -- Fiction
ISBN 978-1-4169-5503-0; 1-4169-5503-8

"Nicholas admires and pays great attention to everything his big brother does. . . . James is a patient teacher and role model for his younger sibling. . . . When the two boys work together on a list of names for a 'special event' to take place in June, the older boy lets his brother make the definitive choice. Of course, the surprise is a baby sister, which makes Nicholas a big brother himself. Bright pastel, digitally rendered illustrations span autumn, winter, and spring and show the brothers and their ever-present dogs in a loving, noncompetitive relationship." SLJ

The **little** ships; the heroic rescue at Dunkirk in World War II. illustrated by Michael Foreman. Margaret K. McElderry Bks. 1997 un il hardcover o.p. pa $6.99
Grades: K 1 2 3   **E**
1. World War, 1939-1945 -- Fiction 2. Dunkerque (France), Battle of, 1940 -- Fiction
ISBN 0-689-80827-5; 0-689-85396-3 pa
    LC 95-52557

A young English girl and her father take their sturdy fishing boat and join the scores of other civilian vessels crossing the English Channel in a daring attempt to rescue Allied and British troops trapped by Nazi soldiers at Dunkirk

"Borden's descriptive style is potent, and Foreman's watercolors perfectly express the dulled and watery scenes of devastation, the exhausted and hopeful soldiers awaiting rescue." Horn Book Guide

Off to first grade; illustrated by Joan Rankin. Margaret K. McElderry Books 2008 un il $16.99
Grades: PreK K 1   **E**
1. School stories
ISBN 978-0-689-87395-9; 0-689-87395-6
    LC 2005-02320

Each member of a first grade class, as well as their teacher, principal, and a bus driver, expresses excitement, worry, or hope as the first day of school begins.

"The sequence is gentle yet genuinely perceptive in its documentation of the varying responses to the dramatic transition from home to school." Bull Cent Child Books

Boswell, Addie K.
The **rain** stomper. Marshall Cavendish 2008 un il $16.99
Grades: PreK K 1 2   **E**
1. Rain -- Fiction 2. Parades -- Fiction
ISBN 978-0-7614-5393-2; 0-7614-5393-8

When it begins to rain and storm on the day of her big parade, Jazmin stomps, shouts, and does all she can think of to drive the rain away.

"Velasquez's large oils impart a sense of the girl's disappointment as well as the feel of a driving rain and eventual pleasure. Large letters in white, black, or red and in different sizes emphasize the sounds and rhythm of the rain and thunder. . . . A delightful read-aloud that deals with making the best of a disappointing situation." SLJ

Bottner, Barbara
★ An **annoying** ABC; illustrated by Michael Emberley. Alfred A. Knopf 2011 un il $17.99; lib bdg $20.99

Grades: PreK K 1 2   **E**
1. Alphabet 2. School stories
ISBN 978-0-375-86708-8; 0-375-86708-2; 978-0-375-96708-5 lib bdg; 0-375-96708-7 lib bdg; 978-0-375-98469-3 e-book
    LC 2011011843

"Adelaide annoys Bailey when she runs at him wearing her tiger costume, scaring him and causing him to let the gerbil out of its cage. So begins a rollicking preschool/early elementary romp featuring kids who appear in alphabetical order with a corresponding action. . . . The hilarity lies in the illustrations, typical Emberley style, done in mechanical pencil and watercolors. . . . One read-through will simply not be enough to enjoy all the fun." Kirkus

Bootsie Barker bites; illustrated by Peggy Rathmann. Putnam 1992 un il $17.99; pa $5.99
Grades: K 1 2 3   **E**
1. Bullies -- Fiction
ISBN 0-399-22125-5; 0-698-11427-2 pa
    LC 91-12182

"Bottner's tone is a model of simplicity and matter-of-factness, sometimes droll but never coy. Rathmann's neon-bright, full-color artwork extends the emotional tenor and the humor of the text." Booklist
Another title about Bootsie is:
Bootsie Barker ballerina (1997)

★ **Miss** Brooks loves books (and I don't) story by Barbara Bottner; illustrations by Michael Emberley. Alfred A. Knopf 2010 un il $17.99; lib bdg $20.99
Grades: PreK K 1 2   **E**
1. School stories 2. Librarians -- Fiction 3. Books and reading -- Fiction
ISBN 978-0-375-84682-3; 0-375-84682-4; 978-0-375-94682-0 lib bdg; 0-375-94682-9 lib bdg
    LC 2009-02305

A first-grade girl who does not like to read stubbornly resists her school librarian's efforts to convince her to love books until she finds one that might change her mind.

"Children will delight in Emberley's spirited watercolor and ink renderings of literary favorites. . . . Bottner's deadpan humor and delicious prose combine with Emberley's droll caricatures to create a story sure to please those who celebrate books—and one that may give pause to those who don't (or who work with the latter)." SLJ

Miss Brooks' Story Nook; (where tales are told and ogres are welcome) by Barbara Bottner; illustrated by Michael Emberley. Alfred A. Knopf 2014 40 p. color illustrations (trade) $16.99
Grades: PreK K 1 2   **E**
1. Bullies -- Fiction 2. Librarians -- Fiction 3. Storytelling -- Fiction
ISBN 0449813282; 9780449813287; 9780449813294
    LC 2013013799

Companion to: Miss Brooks loves books! (and I don't)
In this book by Barbara Bottner, illustrated by Michael Emberley, "Missy loves her librarian, Miss Brooks. And she loves to go to Miss Brooks' before-school story time. But to get to Story Nook, she has to pass Billy Toomey's house-- and she does not love Billy Toomey. . . . And that's when

Missy has a brainstorm. She sees a way to use her made-up story to deal with her real-life bully." (Publisher's note)

"Capably constructed and full of lively dialogue, the story is well served by Emberley's many expressive drawings of the characters, including a sympathetic, symbolic portrayal of Missy burdened by her nemesis." Booklist

Boudreau, Helene

 I dare you not to yawn; Helene Boudreau, illustrated by Serge Bloch. Candlewick Press 2013 32 p. (reinforced) $15.99

Grades: PreK K 1   E
 ISBN 9780763650704

           LC 2012942415

Bourguignon, Laurence

 Heart in the pocket; by Laurence Bourguignon; illustrated by Valerie d'Heur. Eerdmans Books for Young Readers 2008 un il $16.50

Grades: PreK K 1 2   E
 1. Kangaroos -- Fiction 2. Mother-child relationship -- Fiction
 ISBN 978-0-8028-5343-1; 0-8028-5343-9

           LC 2007049348

A baby kangaroo is reluctant to leave the comfort of his mother's pocket, where he is safe and warm and can always hear her heartbeat, until he finds out that her heart is not actually in her pocket.

"The gentle, well-crafted text is sweet, but not overly so. The watercolor illustrations have a soft palette dominated by yellowish tans and light blues, and expressively portray a wise and loving mother with her shy, slightly fearful child." SLJ

Boyd, Lizi

 Flashlight; by Lizi Boyd. Chronicle Books 2014 40 p. color illustrations (reinforced) $16.99

Grades: PreK K 1   E
 1. Boys -- Fiction 2. Night -- Fiction 3. Stories without words 4. Flashlights -- Fiction
 ISBN 9781452118949; 1452118949

           LC 2013029635

"In this wordless picture book" by Lizi Boyd, "a child camping at night in a forest uses a flashlight to explore the flora and fauna of the area; when he trips over a rock and drops the flashlight, the animals take their turn with the light, highlighting various parts of the child and eventually helping him find his way to his tent." (Bulletin of the Center for Children's Books)

"With each successive page, more color appears, even outside of the beam of light, as knowledge of and comfort with the woodland surroundings grows, and the final endpapers feature bits of color, whereas the opening endpapers had none. Children will enjoy repeatedly poring over the many details and creating their own nighttime narratives." Booklist

Boyer, Cecile

 Woof, meow, tweet-tweet. Seven Footer Kids 2011 un il $15.95

Grades: PreK K 1   E
 1. Cats -- Fiction 2. Dogs -- Fiction 3. Birds -- Fiction
 ISBN 978-1-934734-60-5; 1-934734-60-8

Presents a humorous account of the differences between dogs, cats, and birds, from the sounds they make, how they behave, and what happens when they all meet.

"The book's unique juxtaposition of text, clean graphic images, and font changes might also encourage older readers, noting its text-as-art or perhaps a few new vocabulary words. . . . This simple yet cleverly executed story can be used in multiple ways in various classes and individual settings." SLJ

Boyle, Bob

 Hugo and the really, really, really long string. Random House 2010 un il $15.99; lib bdg $18.99

Grades: PreK K 1 2   E
 1. Stories in rhyme 2. Animals -- Fiction
 ISBN 978-0-375-83423-3; 0-375-83423-0; 978-0-375-93423-0 lib bdg; 0-375-93423-5 lib bdg

           LC 2006016303

Hugo follows a mysterious red string through his town, collecting a series of new friends along the way, all of them knowing that something special must be at the end of the string.

"This is a great story that can lead to a discussion of friends and neighborhoods. Written in rhyme, it is an entertaining story. The geometric style used in the artwork will be familiar to students as Boyle is the author/illustrator who created the Nick Jr. television show, WOW! WOW! Wubbzy!" Libr Media Connect

Boynton, Sandra

 ★ Happy Hippo, angry Duck; a book of moods. Little Simon 2011 un il $5.99

Grades: PreK K   E
 1. Board books for children 2. Animals -- Fiction 3. Emotions -- Fiction
 ISBN 978-1-4424-1731-1; 1-4424-1731-5

"With her familiar brand of gentle absurdity, Boynton creates similes that ascribe moods to various animals. . . . Part of the book's pleasure is that Boynton doesn't rely on clichéd animal personifications. . . . Even kids in the stoniest of moods will feel the effect of this pick-me-up." Publ Wkly

Bradby, Marie

 ★ Momma, where are you from? illustrated by Chris K. Soentpiet. Orchard Bks. 2000 un il $16.95

Grades: K 1 2 3   E
 1. African Americans -- Fiction 2. Mother-daughter relationship -- Fiction
 ISBN 0-531-30105-2

           LC 99-23068

Momma describes the special people and surroundings of her childhood, in a place where the edge of town met the countryside, in a time when all the children at school were brown.

"Soentpiet's detailed, beautifully lit paintings freeze the mother's vivid memories, culminating in a dreamy, gray-toned montage of all the previous scenes. Children will be inspired by the mother's eloquent, proud answer to her daughter's essential question." Booklist

 ★ More than anything else; story by Marie Bradby; pictures by Chris K. Soentpiet. Orchard Bks. 1995 un il $15.95

Grades: K 1 2 3   **E**

1. Slaves 2. Authors 3. Educators 4. Memoirists 5. Nonfiction writers 6. Civil rights activists 7. African Americans -- Fiction 8. Books and reading -- Fiction
ISBN 0-531-09464-2

LC 94-48804

Nine-year-old Booker works with his father and brother at the saltworks, but dreams of the day when he'll be able to read.

"An evocative text combines with well-crafted, dramatic watercolors to provide a stirring, fictionalized account of the early life of Booker T. Washington." Horn Book

Bradford, Wade

Why do I have to make my bed? or, a history of messy rooms. illustrations by Johanna Van der Sterre. Tricycle Press 2011 un il $16.99

Grades: K 1 2   **E**

1. Home economics -- Fiction 2. Mother-son relationship -- Fiction
ISBN 978-1-58246-327-8; 1-58246-327-1

When a boy asks his mother why he must make his bed, she tells him a story about his ancestors who posed the same question through the centuries, going all the way back to a caveboy and his mother.

"While playing up the timelessness and universality of the human condition (at least as far as chores are concerned), the text and pictures underscore the evolving demands and trappings of domestic life. With its clever premise, keenly observed visual comedy, and easygoing pedagogy . . . this book deserves a place next to the Magic School Bus series." Publ Wkly

Bradley, Kimberly Brubaker

Ballerino Nate; illustrated by R.W. Alley. Dial Books for Young Readers 2006 un il $16.99

Grades: PreK K 1 2   **E**

1. Ballet -- Fiction 2. Sex role -- Fiction
ISBN 0-8037-2954-5

LC 2004-17822

After seeing a ballet performance, Nate decides he wants to learn ballet but he has doubts when his brother Ben tells him that only girls can be ballerinas.

"Bradley writes smoothly and insightfully about Nate's experiences. . . . Alley's watercolor-and-pencil contributions, portraying an entirely canine universe, capture both the warm family dynamics and Nate's zooming, irrepressible energy." Booklist

The perfect pony; [by] Kimberly Brubaker Bradley; pictures by Shelagh McNicholas. Dial Books for Young Readers/Penguin Group 2007 un il $16.99

Grades: K 1 2   **E**

1. Horses -- Fiction
ISBN 0-8037-2851-4; 978-0-8037-2851-6

LC 2004024071

While searching for a sleek, fast, and spirited pony to own, a young girl comes to realize that the "perfect" pony is actually very different.

"McNicholas' realistic watercolor illustrations are completely in step with the understated text and the experience itself." Booklist

Brallier, Jess M.

Tess's tree; pictures by Peter H. Reynolds. Harper 2009 un il $16.99

Grades: PreK K 1   **E**

1. Trees -- Fiction 2. Bereavement -- Fiction
ISBN 978-0-06-168752-5; 0-06-168752-9

LC 2009014580

When nine-year-old Tess invites her friends, family, and neighbors to celebrate her beloved maple tree's life before it must be cut down, she learns that it has meant a lot to other people, as well.

"Reynolds's soft watercolor vignettes extend the quiet story. Wispy lines portray a subtle vulnerability; washes of muted blue effectively provide emotional depth as Tess survives grief's powerful storm." Kirkus

Brannen, Sarah S.

Uncle Bobby's wedding; [by] Sarah S. Brannen. G. P. Putnam's Sons 2008 32p il $15.99

Grades: PreK K 1 2   **E**

1. Uncles -- Fiction 2. Weddings -- Fiction 3. Guinea pigs -- Fiction 4. Homosexuality -- Fiction
ISBN 978-0-399-24712-5; 0-399-24712-2

LC 2007-16550

Chloë the guinea pig is jealous and sad when her favorite uncle announces that he will be getting married, but as she gets to know Jamie better and becomes involved in planning the wedding, she discovers that she will always be special to Uncle Bobby—and to Uncle Jamie, too.

"Warmly affectionate watercolor and graphite illustrations accompany this genial story of same-sex marriage." Horn Book Guide

Braun, Sebastien

★ **Back** to bed, Ed! Peachtree Publishers 2010 un il $15.95

Grades: PreK K 1   **E**

1. Mice -- Fiction 2. Sleep -- Fiction 3. Bedtime -- Fiction 4. Parent-child relationship -- Fiction
ISBN 978-1-56145-518-8; 1-56145-518-0

First published 2009 in the United Kingdom

Ed the mouse will not sleep in his own bed, until eventually his exasperated and tired parents find a way to keep him from joining them in the middle of the night.

"Braun's clean illustrations in India ink with markers and colored pencils are bright and bold. . . . They show all the emotions of the characters and many interesting details. . . . The simple text works in tandem with the illustrations to produce a great story that's fun to read." SLJ

Meeow and the big box. Boxer Books 2009 un il lib bdg $12.95

Grades: PreK   **E**

1. Cats -- Fiction 2. Play -- Fiction 3. Imagination -- Fiction
ISBN 978-1-906250-86-7 lib bdg; 1-906250-86-3 lib bdg

"Braun shows a wide-eyed black cat in a red scarf playing with a box. The omniscient narrator carries on a one-way dialogue, describing imaginative Meeow's actions and intentions as he transforms the box into a bright red fire engine. . . . The book is simple and direct, and pulls together all the ingredients (box, red paint, green scissors) in the same methodical way that toddlers hard at work would. Uncluttered pages and primary colors make this a highly attractive book, as does the tactile jacket that allows readers to stroke fuzzy Meeow." SLJ

Other titles about Meeow are:

Meeow and the little chairs (2009)

Meeow and the pots and pans (2010)

Meeow and the blue table (2010)

On our way home. Boxer 2009 un il $14.95

Grades: PreK K   E

1. Bears -- Fiction 2. Father-child relationship -- Fiction

ISBN 978-1-906250-59-1; 1-906250-59-6

"With unadorned, heartfelt prose and idyllic images, Braun . . . conveys just how wonderful it feels to spend a day alone with Daddy. . . . Braun's acrylic pictures strike a lovely balance, as he places his genial, naïf-styled characters within majestically scaled landscapes." Publ Wkly

The **ugly** duckling. Boxer Books 2010 il (A Story House book) lib bdg $16.95

Grades: PreK K   E

1. Fairy tales 2. Ducks -- Fiction 3. Swans -- Fiction

ISBN 978-1-907152-04-7; 1-907152-04-0

A retelling of Hans Christian Andersen's tale of the ugly little duckling who grows up to become a beautiful swan.

"This text presents the highlights of the story in a straightforward fashion that perserves the formal feel of the original. . . . The expressive pictures, though rendered with ink and colored pencil, have the careful lines and bold edges that give them the feel of woodcuts. . . . The large format, combined with bright, bold illustrations and simplified language, makes this ideal for storytime sharing." SLJ

Who can swim? Sebastien Braun. Candlewick Press 2014 14 p. $6.99

Grades: PreK   E

1. Swimming 2. Aquatic animals

ISBN 0763667528; 9780763667528

LC 2013943102

In this children's board book, author and illustrator Sebastien Braun asks "who can swim? . . . Dive with a dolphin, wallow with a whale, and paddle with a polar bear. Who else might be in the water?" (Publisher's note)

Other titles in the series include:

Who can Jump?

Who's Hiding?

Breathed, Berke

Pete & Pickles; [by] Berkeley Breathed. Philomel Books 2008 un il $17.99

Grades: 2 3 4   E

1. Pigs -- Fiction 2. Elephants -- Fiction 3. Friendship -- Fiction

ISBN 978-0-399-25082-8; 0-399-25082-4

LC 2007-50044

When Pickles the elephant turns his life upside-down, Pete the pig comes to realize that a perfectly predictable, practical, and uncomplicated life is not always preferable.

"This heartwarming tale is packed with adventure, imagination, and the all-important message of accepting differences. The illustrations alternate from naturalistic renderings of fantastical scenarios to flat compositions reminiscent of traditional comic strips." SLJ

Breen, Steve

Stick; [by] Steve Breen. Dial Books For Young Readers 2007 un il $16.99

Grades: PreK K 1 2 3   E

1. Frogs -- Fiction 2. Dragonflies -- Fiction

ISBN 978-0-8037-3124-0

LC 2006046318

An independent young frog goes on a wild adventure when he accidentally gets carried away by a dragonfly.

"Breen generates plenty of fun and suspense in the skillfully rendered, animated pictures." Booklist

Violet the pilot; [by] Steve Breen. Dial Books for Young Readers 2008 un il $16.99

Grades: K 1 2 3   E

1. Dogs -- Fiction 2. Air pilots -- Fiction

ISBN 978-0-8037-3125-7

LC 2007022367

Young Violet's only friend is her dog, Orville, until one of her homemade flying machines takes her to the rescue of a Boy Scout troop in trouble.

"An engaging story of a spunky girl who follows her dreams. . . . Done in watercolors, acrylics, and Photoshop, the lively cartoon artwork evokes a nostalgic setting. Violet's various inventions are clever and amusing." SLJ

Brendler, Carol

Not very scary; Carol Brendler; pictures by Greg Pizzoli. Farrar, Straus and Giroux 2014 40 p. color illustrations (hardcover) $12.99

Grades: PreK K 1   E

1. Fear -- Fiction 2. Parties -- Fiction 3. Monsters -- Fiction 4. Halloween -- Fiction 5. Surprise -- Fiction

ISBN 0374355479; 9780374355470

LC 2013011139

In this children's book, by Carol Brendler, "Melly is a brave little monster who is not afraid of anything. She loves surprises, and when her fun-loving cousin invites her over for a big surprise, Melly excitedly sets out for a visit. On her way, she notices skittish skeletons, a coal-black cat, and even ghoulish goblins following her. But Melly is not scared, no she's not! Well, maybe just a teensy bit." (Publisher's note)

"In a delightful Halloween romp that's part counting book, part tongue twister, Brendler and Pizzoli introduce a green-skinned monster named Melly who is heading to her cousin Malberta's house for a 'surprise.' Along the way, Melly realizes an entourage is growing behind her, starting with a 'coal-black cat with an itchy-twitchy tail,' which Melly dismisses as 'not the least bit scary.' But then come 'two skittish skeletons,' 'four mournful ghosts,' and 'seven frenzied fruit bats,' and suddenly Melly isn't feeling so brave. Pizzoli crams the pages with comically ghoulish chaos, and his smiley creatures (Melly included) are more cute than bloodcurdling. Amid the mounting tension (which results in an epic party), readers also get a crash course in adverbs: 'Not significantly scary!' says Melly when six mummies show up. 'Not especially scary!' she shouts on the next page." Pub Wkly

Winnie Finn, worm farmer. Farrar Straus Giroux 2009 un il $15.99

Grades: PreK K 1 2   E
1. Worms -- Fiction
ISBN 978-0-374-38440-1; 0-374-38440-1
LC 2008004255
Winnie Finn raises earthworms, which help her neighbors win prizes at the county fair. Includes instructions on making a worm farm.

"Nimble lines and cool colors depict the energy of the active outdoor scenes. Humorous details abound through animated expressions. . . . Winnie's spunky, good-natured heart anchors a gentle and entertaining read." SLJ

Includes bibliographical references

Brennan, Eileen
Dirtball Pete. Random House 2010 un il $15.99; lib bdg $18.99
Grades: K 1 2 3   E
1. School stories 2. Theater -- Fiction 3. Cleanliness -- Fiction
ISBN 978-0-375-83425-7; 0-375-83425-7; 978-0-375-93425-4 lib bdg; 0-375-93425-1 lib bdg
LC 2006022433
"It's tough to make a book sardonic and heartwarming at the same time, but Brennan nails it." Publ Wkly

Brennan, Rosemarie
Willow; written by Denise Brennan Nelson and Rosemarie Brennan; illustrated by Cyd Moore. Sleeping Bear Press 2008 un il $16.95
Grades: K 1 2 3   E
1. Art -- Fiction 2. Painting -- Fiction 3. Imagination -- Fiction
ISBN 978-1-58536-342-1; 1-58536-342-1
LC 2007034588
In art class, neatness, conformity, and imitation are encouraged, but when Willow brings imagination and creativity to her projects, even straight-laced Miss Hawthorn is influenced

"Soft-toned watercolors contrast colorful, autumn trees with all-the-same green ones. . . . Expressive faces show wonderment and joy as teacher and students discover . . . the intese power of imagination." SLJ

"Another title about Willow is:
Willow and the snow day dance (2011)

Brenner, Barbara
Good morning, garden; illustrated by Denise Ortakales. Northword Press 2004 un il $15.95
Grades: K 1 2 3   E
1. Stories in rhyme 2. Gardens -- Fiction
ISBN 1-55971-888-9
Upon entering a garden one morning, a child greets the flowers, plants, insects, and animals there.

"The alliterative tone and subtle rhyme scheme continue throughout this joyful celebration. . . . Ortakales works with sculpted paper to convey the depth and detail of a garden replete with luscious plants and friendly creatures." SLJ

★ **Wagon** wheels; story by Barbara Brenner; pictures by Don Bolognese. newly il ed; HarperCollins Pubs. 1993 64p il (I can read book) hardcover o.p. pa $3.99
Grades: K 1 2   E
1. African Americans -- Fiction 2. Frontier and pioneer

life -- Fiction
ISBN 0-06-444052-4 pa
LC 92-18780
A newly illustrated edition of the title first published 1978
Shortly after the Civil War a black family travels to Kansas to take advantage of the free land offered through the Homestead Act

"The based-on-fact story . . . is as fascinating as ever. Beautifully narrated with sensitivity, compassion, and just the right amount of suspense, and featuring new full-color illustrations." Horn Book Guide

Brenner, Tom
And then comes Christmas; Tom Brenner, illustrated by Jana Christy. Candlewick Press 2014 32 p. color illustrations $15.99
Grades: PreK K 1 2   E
1. Winter -- Fiction 2. Christmas -- Fiction
ISBN 076365342X; 9780763653422
LC 2013953455
This children's book, by Tom Brenner, is a "lyrical invitation to watch for signs of the approaching season--and revel in the homespun rituals that warm a family celebration. From icicles clinging to roofs and houses strung with colorful lights to visiting Santa and hunting for the perfect tree, this classic-in-the-making celebrates all of the holiday's excitement." (Publisher's note)

"In Brenner's inviting story, chilly weather, holiday decorations, delicious baked goods, and all the other trappings of Christmas act as guideposts for a brother and sister as they eagerly await Christmas morning. Soft-focus digital illustrations in vibrant hues reflect the season's coziness and industry. Those looking for an accessible book about secular celebration of Christmas will enjoy this warm-hearted offering." Horn Book

And then comes Halloween; illustrated by Holly Meade. Candlewick Press 2009 un il $16.99
Grades: PreK K 1 2   E
1. Autumn -- Fiction 2. Halloween -- Fiction
ISBN 978-0-7636-3659-3; 0-7636-3659-2
"When autumn arrives, a group of suburban children and their parents rake leaves, carve pumpkins, decorate yards and porches, and make Halloween costumes. The big day comes at last, and the children go trick-or-treating. . . . The descriptions beautifully evoke the feeling of fall. . . . The watercolor and collage art contributes to the autumnal mood, and the varied perspectives and page design make the story more dynamic. The text and illustrations are a perfect complement to one another." SLJ

Brett, Jan
Cinders; a chicken Cinderella. Jan Brett. G.P. Putnam's Sons, an imprint of Penguin Group (USA) Inc. 2013 32 p.
Grades: K 1 2 3   E
1. Folklore 2. Fairy tales
ISBN 9780399257834
LC 2012048973
"Brett adds to the wide variety of interpretations of the beloved fairy tale with this charming retelling featuring a flock of elegantly attired fowl in an 18th-century Russian setting...he visual heart of the story is a double gatefold spread of the ball, which opens to reveal the cast of elegant

chickens, dancing at the Ice Palace in all their finery. A captivating addition to the "Cinderella" canon." Kirkus

The **Easter** egg. G.P. Putnam's Sons 2010 un il $17.99
Grades: PreK K   E
1. Eggs -- Fiction 2. Easter -- Fiction 3. Rabbits -- Fiction 4. Contests -- Fiction
ISBN 978-0-399-25238-9; 0-399-25238-X
LC 2009-08234
Hoppi the bunny wants to win the egg-decorating contest so the Easter Bunny will choose him to help distribute Easter eggs, but instead, while everyone else is working on their decorations, he finds himself guarding an egg that has fallen from a robin's nest.
"Brett's large watercolors include a few visual puns . . . and lots of woodland detail. . . . A satisfying, gentle tale whose text and images can be enjoyed multiple times over." Booklist

Gingerbread friends; [by] Jan Brett. G.P. Putnam's Sons 2008 un il $17.99
Grades: PreK K 1 2   E
1. Cookies -- Fiction 2. Friendship -- Fiction
ISBN 978-0-399-25161-0; 0-399-25161-8
LC 2007042829
Lonely Gingerbread Baby, having set out to find a friend, enters a bakery where he tries to talk to different cookies and other figures, but winds up leading a crowd back to his house on a chase similar to the one in the familiar tale.
"Brett's highly detailed, luscious illustrations do a fine job telling this story for nonreaders, while readers and listeners will enjoy Gingerbread Baby's energy and enthusiasm." SLJ

★ The **hat**. Putnam 1997 un il $16.95
Grades: PreK K 1 2   E
1. Animals -- Fiction 2. Hedgehogs -- Fiction 3. Clothing and dress -- Fiction
ISBN 0-399-23101-3
LC 96-54015
When Lisa hangs her woolen clothes in the sun to air them out for winter, the hedgehog, to the amusement of the other animals, ends up wearing a stocking on his head
This story "has charm and humor. . . . The setting is the Danish countryside (detailed down to the moss on a tree) on a day when the first snow begins to fall, and Brett conveys the season with such loving spirit that children will almost wish for winter." Booklist

★ **Honey** . . . honey . . . lion! a story from Africa. G.P. Putnam's Sons 2005 un il $16.99
Grades: PreK K 1 2   E
1. Africa -- Fiction 2. Badgers -- Fiction 3. Honeyguides (Birds) -- Fiction
ISBN 0-399-24463-8
LC 2005-00449
After working together to obtain honey, the African honey badger always shares it with his partner, the honeyguide bird, until one day when the honey badger becomes greedy and his feathered friend decides to teach him a lesson.

"Brett has created another lush winner with beautifully detailed illustrations of the animals and a clear, fast-paced story." SLJ

On Noah's ark. Putnam 2003 un il $16.99
Grades: K 1 2 3   E
1. Biblical characters 2. Noah's ark -- Fiction
ISBN 0-399-24028-4
LC 2003-1281
Noah's granddaughter helps him bring the animals onto the ark, calm them down, and get them to sleep
"The words are basic and effective; it's the detailed watercolors of the animals that are the real attraction here. In precise brushstrokes and vivid colors, Brett creates incredibly textured feathers and fur." Booklist

Brian, Janeen
I'm a dirty dinosaur; Janeen Brian. Kane Miller, A Division of EDC Pub. 2014 22 p. col. ill. (hardcover) $11.99
Grades: PreK K 1   E
1. Color 2. Dinosaurs -- Fiction
ISBN 1610672968; 9781610672962
LC 2013949620
In this children's book by Janeen Brian and Ann James "the prehistoric protagonist is drawn with magic pencil (which creates a thin rainbow-hued line) and minimal detail. Slowly, through onomatopoetic, brightly colored, rhyming text, he begins to color himself in with mud." (School Library Journal)
"A buoyant dinosaur revels in the mud in this paper-over-board story, first published in Australia. Brian's repeating rhymes take on the cadence of a song—almost like a mud-themed version of the "Hokey Pokey"—as the raptor-like dinosaur becomes increasingly muddy...Brian's narrative lends itself to reading aloud, and it invites both chiming in and imitating the dinosaur's movements (preferably sans mud). Better still, the sturdy pages are sufficiently coated for easy wiping off if muddy fingers do happen to turn them." PW

Briant, Ed
If you lived here you'd be home by now. Roaring Brook Press 2009 un il $17.99
Grades: PreK K 1 2   E
1. Stories without words 2. Leaves -- Fiction 3. Animals -- Fiction
ISBN 978-1-59643-420-2; 1-59643-420-1
"Crisp colors and bold outlines make the illustrations sing, and tell the story without any words. The linear time line is easy to follow." SLJ
In this "wordless tale, a nature-loving boy visits a city park to look for animals. When he jumps into a pile of leaves, he discovers an enormous, friendly creature made entirely of leaves, who takes the wide-eyed child to see a menagerie of woodland animals, as well as a crew felling trees for a new construction project. The story then fast forwards a few decades to a future filled with flying cars. The now adult boy's son finds a leaf that his father had long ago pressed inside a book, inspiring a trip to the same park, which is now a commercial strip. . . . Father and son travel to a patch of forest where they camp out overnight and encounter wildlife—including the elusive leaf creature." Publ Wkly

Bridges, Shirin Yim

★ **Mary** Wrightly, so politely; by Shirin Bridges; illustrated by Maria Monescillo. Houghton Mifflin Harcourt 2013 32 p. (reinforced) $16.99

Grades: PreK K   E
1. Etiquette -- Fiction 2. Assertiveness (Psychology) -- Fiction
ISBN 9780547342481
LC 2012019633

"Every child will enjoy joining in on this book's irresistible refrain... Understated and sunny." Kirkus

"A gentle storybook about the importance of positive assertiveness introduces little Mary, who is so polite that she apologizes for things that are not her fault and who struggles to speak up when a rude shopper hampers Mary's ability to buy a special toy for her baby brother." Publisher's note

★ **Ruby's** wish; illustrated by Sophie Blackall. Chronicle Bks. 2002 un il $15.95

Grades: K 1 2 3   E
1. China -- Fiction 2. Sex role -- Fiction 3. Education -- Fiction
ISBN 0-8118-3490-5
LC 2001-7406

In China, at a time when few girls are taught to read or write, Ruby dreams of going to the university with her brothers and male cousins

"This true story about Bridges' own grandmother has a gentle momentum. . . . Blackall's gouache illustrations have a quietly historical air, their palette subtly shaded with smoky inks and highlighted with touches of brilliant red." Bull Cent Child Books

The **Umbrella** Queen; illustrations by Taeeun Yoo. Greenwillow Books 2008 un il $16.99; lib bdg $17.89

Grades: K 1 2 3   E
1. Painting -- Fiction 2. Thailand -- Fiction 3. Umbrellas and parasols -- Fiction
ISBN 978-0-06-075040-4; 0-06-075040-5; 978-0-06-075041-1 lib bdg; 0-06-075041-3 lib bdg
LC 2005-35730

In a village in Thailand where everyone makes umbrellas, young Noot dreams of painting the most beautiful one and leading the annual parade as Umbrella Queen, but her unconventional designs, depicting elephants instead of flowers and butterflies, displease her parents.

"Yoo's orange, green, and black colored linoleum prints wonderfully establish the tone for the story, which is related through gracefully told text." SLJ

Briggs, Raymond

★ The **snowman**. Random House 1978 un il $17; pa $6.99; bd bk $4.99

Grades: PreK K 1 2   E
1. Stories without words 2. Snow -- Fiction 3. Dreams -- Fiction
ISBN 0-394-83973-0; 0-394-88466-3 pa; 0-375-81067-6 bd bk
LC 78-55904

"The pastel-toned pencil-and-crayon pictures in their neat rectangular frames will hold the attention of primary 'readers.'" SLJ

Bright, Paul

The **not**-so-scary Snorklum; [illustrations by] Jane Chapman. Good Books 2011 un il $16.99

Grades: PreK K 1   E
1. Fear -- Fiction 2. Animals -- Fiction 3. Mythical animals -- Fiction
ISBN 978-1-56148-728-8; 1-56148-728-7
LC 2011007764

First published in the United Kingdom

As the scary Snorklum stomps home to his cave, he encounters a mole, a rabbit, and a badger, who see through his attempts to frighten them.

"Brisk and bright, yet subtle in its message." Kirkus

Brimner, Larry Dane

Trick or treat, Old Armadillo; illustrated by Dominic Catalano. Boyds Mills Press 2010 un il $16.95

Grades: K 1 2 3   E
1. Animals -- Fiction 2. Halloween -- Fiction 3. Armadillos -- Fiction 4. Spanish language -- Vocabulary
ISBN 978-1-59078-758-8; 1-59078-758-7
LC 2010004342

On Halloween, Old Armadillo sits inside his little house waiting for his friends to come trick-or-treating.

"Brimner infuses this tale with humor and Southwestern flavor. Spanish words are sprinkled throughout and defined in a glossary at the beginning of the book. . . . Catalano's dark pastel illustrations work well with the text." SLJ

Another title about Old Armadillo is:
Merry Christmas, Old Armadillo (1995)

Brisson, Pat

I remember Miss Perry; illustrated by Stéphane Jorisch. Dial Books for Young Readers 2006 un il $16.99

Grades: K 1 2 3   E
1. School stories 2. Death -- Fiction 3. Teachers -- Fiction 4. Bereavement -- Fiction
ISBN 0-8037-2981-2
LC 2004-24070

When his teacher, Miss Perry, is killed in a car accident, Stevie and his elementary school classmates take turns sharing memories of her, especially her fondest wish for each day.

"The delicate pen-and-ink, watercolor, and gouache illustrations reflect the varied emotions evoked by this treasured individual." SLJ

Tap-dance fever; illustrated by Nancy Cote. Boyds Mills Press 2004 un il $15.95

Grades: K 1 2 3   E
1. Tap dancing -- Fiction
ISBN 1-59078-290-9
LC 2004-14575

Annabelle Applegate will not stop tap-dancing no matter what the frustrated citizens of Fiddlers Creek do to make her quit

"A deliciously tall tale with an appealing young heroine, the story of Annabelle's troubles and triumph reads aloud well. Just as amusing are Cote's fanciful watercolor-and-gouache paintings of a multicultural, rural community." Booklist

Broach, Elise

Barnyard baby; Elise Broach, illustrated by Cori Doerrfeld. Little Brown & Co 2013 14 p. col. ill. (Baby Seasons) $7.99

Grades: PreK   E
1. Barns -- Fiction 2. Autumn -- Fiction 3. Infants -- Fiction 4. Stories in rhyme 5. Lift-the-flap books 6. Toy and movable books
ISBN 0316212032; 9780316212038

LC 2012947193

In this children's book by Elise Broach and Cori Doerrfeld, readers join "baby during a day full of fall fun, from hayrides to apple picking. This interactive novelty board book features large lift-the-flaps on each spread, hiding . . . surprises underneath." (Publisher's note)

"The endearing rhymes scan well and read quickly, a great combination for keeping little ones interested." Kirkus

Gumption! with pictures by Richard Egielski. Atheneum Books for Young Readers 2010 un il $16.99

Grades: PreK K   E
1. Africa -- Fiction 2. Uncles -- Fiction 3. Animals -- Fiction 4. Jungles -- Fiction
ISBN 978-1-4169-1628-4; 1-4169-1628-8

LC 2008-49048

"Peter is thrilled when his uncle Nigel invites him on an expedition in search of a rare African gorilla, but making it through the jungle involves lots of challenges. Nigel leads the way, surmounting each obstacle . . . but Egielski's ink-and-watercolor illustrations show a parallel story. As Nigel charges ahead, Peter is swept along by a succession of wild animals. . . . Egielski plays up the comedy with clever, small details, and Broach's repetitive text, with its occasionally vocabulary, is well suited for dramatic read-alouds." Booklist

Brooks, Erik

Polar opposites; written and illustrated by Erik Brooks. Marshall Cavendish 2010 un il $16.99

Grades: PreK K 1   E
1. Opposites 2. Penguins -- Fiction 3. Polar bear -- Fiction
ISBN 978-0-7614-5685-8; 0-7614-5685-6

LC 2009005214

Ambrose, a polar bear, and Zina, a penguin, are very different but they can still find ways to meet in the middle

"The cheerful pencil, charcoal, and watercolor illustrations brim with energy and engaging details. . . . A natural for storytimes or as a lapsit." Booklist

Brooks, Susie

Get into Art! Enjoy Great Art--then Create Your Own! by Susie Brooks. Kingfisher 2013 31 p. col. ill. (hardcover) $14.99

Grades: 3 4 5 6 7   E
1. Art -- Guidebooks 2. Picture books for children
ISBN 0753470586; 9780753470589

For this book, Susie Brooks' "goal is to convince her readers that art is not just something one observes, but rather something that one does. Using a topic beloved by many kids—animals—she presents 13 works by famous artists, each of which incorporates animals into its subject and theme. Each reproduced masterpiece occupies its own two-page spread, and Brooks explores one major art technique for each." (Bookstlist)

Brown, Alan

Love-a-duck; by Alan James Brown; illustrated by Francesca Chessa. Holiday House 2010 un il $16.95

Grades: PreK K 1 2   E
1. Toys -- Fiction 2. Baths -- Fiction 3. Ducks -- Fiction
ISBN 978-0-8234-2263-0; 0-8234-2263-1

After falling out of the window and spending an unforgettable day outdoors, a plastic duck is returned home safely, just in time for little Jane's bath.

"Cheerful, bright illustrations help relate this humorous escapade. Call-and-response portions of the book will engage young listeners." SLJ

Brown, Barbara

Hanukkah in Alaska; Barbara Brown; illustrated by Stacey Schuett. Henry Holt and Company 2013 32 p. (hardcover) $16.99

Grades: K 1 2 3   E
1. Picture books for children 2. Hanukkah -- Fiction 3. Moose -- Fiction 4. Alaska -- Fiction 5. Winter -- Fiction 6. Auroras -- Fiction
ISBN 0805097481; 9780805097481

LC 2013003166

In this children's picture book set in Alaska, a girl and her family want to watch the aurora borealis, or northern lights. Things are complicated by the fact that in their backyard, "a moose has taken up residence. . . . While beautiful, the moose can also be dangerous. Luring him away with apples and carrots does not work, but . . . a trail of latkes on the snow tempts the moose away from the swing," and the family can watch the lights on the last night of Hanukkah. (Kirkus Reviews)

Brown, Calef

Boy wonders. Atheneum Books for Young Readers 2011 un il $16.99

Grades: K 1 2   E
1. Stories in rhyme 2. Questions and answers
ISBN 978-1-4169-7877-0; 1-4169-7877-1

LC 2010020976

A young boy's questions lead to more and more questions, but there do not seem to be any answers.

"The connotations of everyday words and sayings are pondered and turned inside out and upside down in this wholly original paeon to intellectual curiosity. . . . The artist's trademark stylized illustrations, flat, hip, and jazzy, are rendered in a palette of predominantly blue/green/yellow acrylics." SLJ

Pirateria; the wonderful plunderful pirate emporium. written and illustrated by Calef Brown. Atheneum Books for Young Readers 2012 304 p. col. ill. (hardcover) $16.99

Grades: PreK K 1 2   E
1. Stories in rhyme 2. Pirates -- Fiction 3. Picture books for children 4. Stores, Retail -- Fiction
ISBN 141697878X; 9781416978787

LC 2011034023

This rhyming children's book "extols the virtues of the Pirateria," a "one-stop shop [that] carries everything from 'solid maple walking planks' to 'fresh lime quinine/to ward off the scurvy' to eye patches in colors such as 'plunder plum' and 'cannonball black.' However, Pirateria is more than just a store: it provides night classes in subjects such as chart reading, smuggling molasses, and spyglass making." (School Library Journal)

Brown, Heather

The **robot** book. Accord Pub. 2010 un il bd bk $16.99

Grades: PreK K   E

1. Board books for children 2. Robots -- Fiction

ISBN 978-0-7407-9725-5 bd bk; 0-7407-9725-5 bd bk

"'A robot is made of so many parts,' begins this modest board book with movable components. Each spread focuses on a specific feature of a humble red robot that looks very DIY. . . . It's an elegantly simple design with care paid to every detail." Publ Wkly

Brown, Jeff

★ **Flat** Stanley; by Jeff Brown; illustrated by Scott Nash. HarperCollins Pubs. 2006 un il $16.99

Grades: K 1 2 3   E

ISBN 978-0-06-112904-9; 0-06-112904-6

LC 2006019547

Based on the original Flat Stanley by Jeff Brown c1964

A bulletin board falls on Stanley while he is sleeping, and he finds that being flat has its advantages

"Full-page, cartoon illustrations in watercolor and crayon enhance the story while remaining true to the original. This version of an old favorite will introduce a beloved character to a new generation of younger children." SLJ

Brown, Lisa

How to be. HarperCollins Pubs. 2006 un il $15.99

Grades: PreK K 1   E

1. Animals -- Fiction 2. Conduct of life -- Fiction

ISBN 0-06-054635-2

LC 2005-15147

"A girl and a younger boy take turns imitating different animals, including a bear, a snake, and a dog. . . . The final chapter, How to be a PERSON, shows both children embodying all the positive characteristics of the critters with the animals shadowing their actions. . . . The spare text matches the black-and-white drawings, supplemented with well-placed smatterings of bright paint." SLJ

Vampire boy's good night. Harper 2010 un il $16.99

Grades: PreK K 1 2   E

1. Witches -- Fiction 2. Vampires -- Fiction 3. Halloween -- Fiction

ISBN 978-0-06-114011-2; 0-06-114011-2

When Morgan, a young vampire, and his witchy friend Bela set out one night to see if human children really exist, they find themselves at a Halloween party.

"The use of speech balloons adds to the intimacy of Brown's detail-rich scenes, and the absence of parental figures contributes to an exultant mood. The lyrical, understated prose and clever outsider's perspective on the holiday might make this a new seasonal favorite." Publ Wkly

Brown, Marc

★ **In** New York; by Marc Brown. First edition Alfred A. Knopf 2014 40 p. (hardcover) $17.99

Grades: PreK K 1 2 3

1. New York (N.Y.)

ISBN 0375864547; 9780375864544; 9780375964541

LC 2013020158

In this book, author Marc Brown "shares his love for all that the city [of New York] has to offer and all that it stands for, including the way it's always changing and evolving. From its earliest days as New Amsterdam to the contemporary wonders of Central Park, the Statue of Liberty, and the Empire State Building, to the kid-appealing subway, High Line, and so much more, Marc's . . . text and . . . illustrations showcase what he's come to adore about New York." (Publisher's note)

"Just about all of Manhattan's child-pleasing sites get a place in Brown's stupendously detailed gouache and watercolor pictures showing a little boy and his father touring NYC. The text is minimal but inviting ("wherever you walk in New York, you'll see a great parade of people passing by"); endpapers offer additional vignettes and facts. Appended information includes phone numbers and websites for the highlights." Horn Book

Brown, Marc Tolon

Arthur's eyes; [by] Marc Brown. Little, Brown 1979 un il hardcover o.p. pa $6.99

Grades: PreK K 1 2   E

1. Aardvark -- Fiction 2. Eyeglasses -- Fiction

ISBN 0-316-11063-9; 0-316-11069-8 pa

LC 79-11734

His friends tease Arthur when he gets glasses, but he soon learns to wear them with pride.

★ **Arthur's** nose; 25th aniversary limited edition. [by] Marc Brown. Little, Brown and Company 2001 un il $15.95

Grades: PreK K 1 2   E

1. Nose -- Fiction 2. Aardvark -- Fiction

ISBN 0-316-11884-2

LC 00-106832

A reissue of the title first published 1976

Unhappy with his nose, Arthur the aardvark visits the rhinologist to get a new one. In this edition "Brown shows the evolution of his drawings of Arthur from 1976 to the present, along with a sidebar of 'Fun Facts,' . . . followed by a photo gallery of Brown's family with some pretty clear correlations between the author's relatives and Arthur's. Aspiring writers and artists also get a peek at the original manuscript and sketches for Arthur's Nose." Publ Wkly

Arthur's nose

★ **D.W.** all wet; [by] Marc Brown. Little, Brown 1988 un il hardcover o.p. pa $5.95

Grades: PreK K 1 2   E

1. Beaches -- Fiction 2. Aardvark -- Fiction 3. Siblings -- Fiction

ISBN 0-316-11268-2; 0-316-11077-9 pa

LC 87-15752

"A simple, even predictable vignette, but entertaining nonetheless because of Brown's warm pictures." Booklist

Other titles about D.W. are:

D.W. flips (1987)

D.W. go to your room! (1999)

D.W. rides again (1993)

D.W. the picky eater (1995)

D.W. thinks big (1993)
D.W.'s guide to perfect manners (2006)
D.W.'s guide to preschool (2003)
D.W.'s library card (2001)
D.W.'s lost blankie (1998)

Brown, Margaret Wise

★ **Another** important book; pictures by Chris Raschka.
HarperCollins Pubs. 1999 un il $15.99; lib bdg $16.89
Grades: PreK K 1   E
1. Counting 2. Stories in rhyme 3. Growth -- Fiction
ISBN 0-06-026282-6; 0-06-026283-4 lib bdg
                                                            LC 98-7212
Illustrations and simple rhyming text describe how a
child grows from ages one through six
"Raschka assigns each age group a geometric shape: a
simple circle represents age one, pairs of stacked squares
indicate two, a five-pointed star signifies five and so on. . . .
It's a pleasure to hear the organic rhythms of Brown's prose
. . . and Raschka paints in boisterous surprises." Publ Wkly

Big red barn; pictures by Felicia Bond. newly il ed;
Harper & Row 1989 un il $16.99; lib bdg $17.89; bd
bk $7.99
Grades: PreK K 1 2   E
1. Stories in rhyme 2. Animals -- Fiction 3. Farm life
-- Fiction
ISBN 0-06-020748-5; 0-06-020749-3 lib bdg; 0-694-
00624-6 bd bk
                                                           LC 85-45814
A newly illustrated edition of the title first published 1956
Rhymed text and illustrations introduce the many different animals that live in the big red barn
"The large illustrations are somewhat stylized, but still
have a strong sense of detail and reality. The bright colors
will attract young readers. The short text on each page is
superimposed on the picture, but always in a way that is easy
to read. Children will enjoy studying each of the pages as the
day progresses from early morning to night." SLJ

A **child's** good morning book; illustrated by Karen
Katz. newly illustrated ed.; HarperCollins 2009 un il
$17.99; lib bdg $18.89
Grades: PreK   E
1. Animals -- Fiction 2. Morning -- Fiction
ISBN 978-0-06-128864-7; 0-06-128864-0; 978-0-06-
128861-6 lib bdg; 0-06-128861-6 lib bdg
                                                         LC 2008000786
A newly illustrated edition of the title first published 1952
As the sun rises, birds, horses, rabbits, flowers, bugs, and
finally children get up to start their day.
"Katz has reinterpreted the text in her warm and rounded
style. . . . Brightly colored patterns and use of collage add
interest to each page. This book has been popular over the
years." SLJ

Doctor Squash, the doll doctor; illustrated by David
Hitch. Golden Books 2010 un il $17.99; lib bdg $20.99
Grades: PreK K 1   E
1. Dolls -- Fiction 2. Physicians -- Fiction
ISBN 978-0-375-84800-1; 0-375-84800-2; 978-0-375-
95623-2 lib bdg; 0-375-95623-9 lib bdg
A revised and newly illustrated edition of the title first
published 1952

"When dolls are sick or in pain, there's really only one
doctor to call: the good Doctor Squash, who attends to their
every need. . . . And when the doc falls ill, the dolls take care
of him in return. . . . Playing doctor with dolls never falls out
of style, and Hitch's retro style and modern toy updates work
overtime to ensure that this book becomes a classic all over
again. Entertaining and charming." Kirkus

★ The **fierce** yellow pumpkin; story by Margaret Wise
Brown; pictures by Richard Egielski. HarperCollins Pubs.
2003 un il $15.99; lib bdg $16.89
Grades: PreK K 1   E
1. Pumpkin -- Fiction
ISBN 0-06-024479-8; 0-06-024481-X lib bdg
                                                          LC 2002-8338
A little pumpkin dreams of the day when he will be a big,
fierce, yellow pumpkin who frightens away the field mice as
the scarecrow does
"Egielski's artwork features subtle shadings and interesting juxtapositions of colors. . . . The story rolls along
smoothly with a clear plot line and some nice phrasing."
Booklist

★ **Goodnight** moon; by Margaret Wise Brown; pic-
tures by Clement Hurd. rev ed; HarperCollins Publishers
2005 un il $17.99
Grades: PreK K   E
1. Stories in rhyme 2. Bedtime -- Fiction 3. Rabbits
-- Fiction
ISBN 978-0-06-077585-8; 0-06-077585-8
                                                        LC 2005281602
A reissue of the title first published 1947
A little bunny bids goodnight to all the objects in his
room before falling asleep
"Rhythmic, gently lulling words combined with warm
and equally lulling pictures make this beloved classic an
ideal bedtime book." Christ Sci Monit

Goodnight moon ABC; an alphabet book. based on the
book by Margaret Wise Brown; pictures by Clement Hurd.
Harper 2010 un il $16.99
Grades: PreK K   E
1. Alphabet 2. Bedtime -- Fiction
ISBN 978-0-06-189484-8; 0-06-189484-2
"Familiar objects in the classic story are arranged in alphabetical order and accompanied by upper and lowercase
letters in the original style and palette. . . . Endpapers show
the entire alphabet being investigated by two mice. The book
conveys the timeless appeal of the original, and the literacy
skill building will appeal to adults." SLJ

The **little** island; with illustrations by Leonard Weisgard. Doubleday Bks. for Young Readers 2003 un il
$14.95
Grades: PreK K 1 2   E
1. Islands -- Fiction
ISBN 0-385-74640-7
A reissue of the title first published 1946 under the
pseudonym Golden MacDonald
Awarded the Caldecott Medal, 1947
There was a little island in the ocean and his book is
about how the seasons and the storm and the day and night
changed it, how the lobsters and seals and gulls and every-

thing else lived on it, and what the kitten who came to visit found out about it

The **little** scarecrow boy; pictures by David Diaz. newly il ed; HarperCollins Pubs. 1998 un il $15.99; lib bdg $16.89; pa $6.99

Grades: PreK K 1 2   E
1. Scarecrows -- Fiction
ISBN 0-06-026284-2; 0-06-026290-7 lib bdg; 0-06-77891-1 pa

LC 97-32558

Early one morning, a little scarecrow whose father warns him that he is not fierce enough to frighten a crow goes out into the cornfield alone

"Diaz provides wonderful illustrations for a story Brown wrote in the 1940s. . . . Brown's masterful use of repetition and rhythm creates a fine read-aloud story. The warm watercolor illustrations incorporate straw and patchwork." SLJ

★ The **runaway** bunny; pictures by Clement Hurd. HarperCollins Publishers 2005 un il $16.99; lib bdg $17.89

Grades: PreK K   E
1. Rabbits -- Fiction
ISBN 0-06-077582-3; 0-06-077583-1 lib bdg

A reissue, with some illustrations redrawn, of the title first published 1942

"The text has the simplicity of a folk tale and the illustrations are black and white or double page drawings in startling colour." Ont Libr Rev

Sleepy ABC; illustrated by Karen Katz. HarperCollinsPublishers 2010 un il $16.99; lib bdg $17.89

Grades: PreK   E
1. Alphabet 2. Stories in rhyme 3. Bedtime -- Fiction
ISBN 978-0-06-128863-0; 0-06-128863-2; 978-0-06-128865-4 lib bdg; 0-06-128865-9 lib bdg

LC 2008051781

Simple rhymes for each letter of the alphabet are illustrated with an array of toddlers and babies saying goodnight.

"Katz's interpretation of Brown's text . . . is joyful and energetic and features her trademark, round-faced, multicultural children, rendered in collage-like art. . . . Likely to be just what little not-yet-sleeping beauties will want." Booklist

★ **Two** little trains; pictures by Leo and Diane Dillon. HarperCollins Pubs. 2001 un il $15.95; lib bdg $15.89; pa $6.99

Grades: PreK K 1 2   E
1. Railroads -- Fiction
ISBN 0-06-028376-9; 0-06-028377-7 lib bdg; 0-06-443568-7 pa

LC 00-40798

A newly illustrated edition of the title first published 1949 by Scott

Two little trains, one streamlined, the other old-fashioned, puff, puff, puff, and chug, chug, chug, on their way West

"The rhythms, the word sounds and the resonant echo of folk song set up a veritable hypnotic chant. . . . [The] soft-grained paintings . . . are beautifully composed in both form and color. A handsome reinterpretation." Booklist

★ **Where** have you been? pictures by Leo and Diane Dillon. HarperCollins 2004 un il $15.99; lib bdg $16.89

Grades: PreK K 1   E
1. Stories in rhyme 2. Animals -- Fiction
ISBN 0-06-028378-5; 0-06-028379-3 lib bdg

LC 2003-49981

A newly illustrated edition of the title first published 1952 by Crowell

In rhyming verse, various animals tell where they have been.

"Children fond of call-and-response will enjoy this humorous nursery rhyme. . . . The illustrations are as lively as they are charming, and have enough detail to keep children interested." SLJ

Brown, Monica
Chavela and the Magic Bubble; illustrated by Magaly Morales. Clarion Books 2010 un il $16

Grades: K 1 2 3   E
1. Magic -- Fiction 2. Chewing gum -- Fiction 3. Grandmothers -- Fiction 4. Mexican Americans -- Fiction
ISBN 978-0-547-24197-5; 0-547-24197-6

LC 2009015819

When Chavela blows a bubble with a strange new gum, she floats away to Mexico, where her great-grandfather once worked harvesting the tree sap that makes gum chewy.

"Kids will want to chew their own bubblegum as they listen to this exciting, magical journey, handsomely illustrated in brilliantly colored double-page spreads." Booklist

Waiting for the BiblioBurro; illustrations by John Parra. Tricycle Press 2011 un il $16.99; lib bdg $19.99

Grades: PreK K 1   E
1. Reading teachers 2. Colombia -- Fiction 3. Libraries -- Fiction 4. Elementary school teachers 5. Books and reading -- Fiction
ISBN 978-1-58246-353-7; 1-58246-353-0; 978-1-58246-398-8 lib bdg; 1-58246-398-0 lib bdg

LC 2010024183

When a man brings to a remote village two burros, Alfa and Beto, loaded with books the children can borrow, Ana's excitement leads her to write a book of her own as she waits for the BiblioBurro to return. Includes glossary of Spanish terms and a note on the true story of Columbia's BiblioBurro and mobile libraries in other countries.

"Parra's naïve-styled acrylics brim with scenes of country life. A palette of salmon pinks and turquoise and sky blues, painted on board, give the book a roughhewn, handmade quality and an innocent, childlike appeal." Publ Wkly

Brown, Peter
★ **Children** make terrible pets. Little, Brown 2010 un il $16.99

Grades: PreK K 1   E
1. Pets -- Fiction 2. Bears -- Fiction
ISBN 978-0-316-01548-6; 0-316-01548-2

LC 2010-04982

When Lucy, a young bear, discovers a boy lost in the woods, she asks her mother if she can have him as a pet, only to find him impossible to train. "Ages three to six." (N Y Times Book Rev)

"Appealing and humorous, with a lesson to boot!" SLJ

Another title about Lucy the bear is:
You will be my friend! (2011)

Chowder; [by] Peter Brown. Little, Brown 2006 un il $15.99
Grades: PreK K 1 2   E
1. Dogs -- Fiction
ISBN 978-0-316-01180-8; 0-316-01180-0
LC 2005035616

Chowder the bulldog has never fit in with the other neighborhood canines, but he sees a chance to make friends with the animals at the local petting zoo

"The tongue-in-cheek humor melds delightfully with Brown's distinctive acrylic-and-pencil artwork." Booklist
Another title about Chowder is:
The fabulous bouncing Chowder (2007)

★ The **curious** garden. Little, Brown 2009 un il
Grades: K 1 2 3   E
1. Gardens -- Fiction 2. City and town life -- Fiction
ISBN 0-316-01547-4; 978-0-316-01547-9
LC 2008029165

Liam discovers a hidden garden and with careful tending spreads color throughout the gray city.

This "is a quiet but stirring fable of urban renewal, sure to capture imaginations. . . . In Brown's utopian vision, the urban and the pastoral mingle to joyfully harmonious effect." Publ Wkly

★ **Mr.** Tiger goes wild; written and illustrated by Peter Brown. Little Brown & Co 2013 48 p. ill. (reinforced) $18
Grades: PreK K 1 2   E
1. Tigers -- Fiction 2. Picture books for children 3. Etiquette -- Fiction 4. CIty and town life -- Fiction
ISBN 0316200638; 9780316200639
LC 2012048429
Boston Globe-Horn Book Award: Picture Book (2014)

"Mr. Tiger walks upright and wears a top hat and a handsome coat with a bow tie, fitting in with the rest of society. But his orange fur provides the only spot of color in the very drab, very proper community, and Mr. Tiger is bored: 'He wanted to loosen up. He wanted to be wild.' And so, Mr. Tiger drops to all fours and for the first time looks happy. As he gets progressively wilder, roaring and shedding his confining clothes, the town animal-folk are appalled and banish him to the wilderness--which, he decides, is 'a magnificent idea.'" (Horn Book)

★ **My** teacher is a monster! (no, I am not) by Peter Brown. Little Brown & Co 2014 40 p. $18
Grades: PreK K 1 2   E
1. Schools -- Fiction 2. Monsters -- Fiction 3. Teachers -- Fiction
ISBN 0316070297; 9780316070294
LC 2013016664

"A young boy named Bobby has the worst teacher. She's loud, she yells, and if you throw paper airplanes, she won't allow you to enjoy recess. She is a monster! Luckily, Bobby can go to his favorite spot in the park on weekends to play. Until one day . . . he finds his teacher there! Over the course of one day, Bobby learns that monsters are not always what they seem." (Publisher's note)

"Bobby's teacher, Ms. Kirby, is a roaring, teeth-gnashing, galumphing giant green monster. Really! (And it has nothing to do with her reaction to that paper airplane Bobby threw.)...This playful, eye-catching story goes a long way to humanize both teachers and students." Booklist

Brown, Ruth
★ A **dark,** dark tale; story and pictures by Ruth Brown. Dial Bks. for Young Readers 1981 un il hardcover o.p. pa $6.99
Grades: PreK K 1 2   E
1. Cats -- Fiction
ISBN 0-14-054621-9 pa

"The book's mysterious power is engendered by the illustrations of weed-choked gardens and abandoned, echoing halls, of mullioned windows and blowing curtains." Time

Gracie the lighthouse cat. Andersen Press USA 2011 un il $16.95
Grades: K 1 2 3   E
1. Cats -- Fiction 2. Storms -- Fiction 3. Shipwrecks -- Fiction 4. Lighthouses -- Fiction
ISBN 978-0-7613-7454-1; 0-7613-7454-X
LC 2010032950

"Gracie, a cat whose home is in a lighthouse, relaxes alongside her little kitten while in the background Grace, the lighthouse keeper's daughter, spots a ship in trouble on the rocks. The two stories about bravery during a raging storm in 1838 unfold simultaneously. Gracie's story is described in the text, while the human drama is portrayed primarily in the artwork. Attractive, painterly renditions of the treacherous sea as well as the emotional features on the faces of the animals will draw children into the suspenseful tale." SLJ

Brown, Stephanie Gwyn
Bang! Boom! Roar! a busy crew of dinosaurs. by Nate Evans and Stephanie Gwyn Brown; illustrated by Christopher Santoro. Harpercollins Childrens Books 2012 40 p. (trade bdg.) $15.99
Grades: PreK K 1   E
1. Alphabet -- Fiction 2. Picture books for children 3. Stories in rhyme 4. Building -- Fiction 5. Dinosaurs -- Fiction 6. Playgrounds -- Fiction 7. Construction workers -- Fiction
ISBN 0060879602; 9780060879600; 9780060879624
LC 2009005244

In this book by Nate Evans, "[a] teeming dino crew in hard hats and safety vests create organized if frenetic chaos on a mucky construction . . . [A] swarm of grimacing, toothy cartoon monsters convert a trash-filled empty lot into an urban playground. . . . Whether peeking out of a port-a-potty . . . [or] racing lumbering earth movers . . . the well-larded laborers are easily identifiable . . . [a]long with the aforementioned hidden alphabet." (Kirkus)

Brown, Tameka Fryer
Around our way on neighbors' day; illustrated by Charlotte Riley-Webb. Abrams 2010 un il $16.95
Grades: PreK K 1 2   E
1. African Americans -- Fiction 2. City and town life -- Fiction
ISBN 978-0-8109-8971-9; 0-8109-8971-9

"As an African American girl bounces around her urban neighborhood celebrating Neighbors' Day, when everyone comes together for celebration and community bonding, she shares her energetic and enthusiastic observations..... The acrylic art is saturated with rich color, energetic movement, and abstract figures and shapes, all reminiscent of Jacob Lawrence's art. Most scenes are double-page spreads that, together with the words, demonstrate the size and diversity of a joyful world." Booklist

My cold plum lemon pie bluesy mood; by Tameka Fryer Brown; illustrated by Shane Evans. Viking 2013 32 p. (hardcover) $16.99

Grades: PreK K   E
   1. Stories in rhyme 2. African Americans -- Fiction 3. Mood (Psychology) -- Fiction
   ISBN 9780670012855

               LC 2012016781

"A boy describes each of the varying emotions he experiences in terms of color. Listening to music puts him in a purple kind of mood, while being evicted from the couch by his two bossy older brothers makes him feel gray. When his little sister asks him to draw a dragon, a gentle green feeling comes over him, which turns black when his siblings snatch the picture and tease: 'Awww-it's cwayon time.'" (School Library Journal)

"In a free-wheeling style and going far beyond the usual pairings of colors with moods, Jamie describes his day's emotional path. . . . This isn't the easiest scansion to read aloud, but it's worth it. Figurative and grounded--a nicely sophisticated exploration." Kirkus

Browne, Anthony

The **little** bear book; Anthony Browne. 1st Candlewick Press ed. Candlewick Press 2014 [22] p. col. ill. $15.99

Grades: PreK K   E
   1. Bears -- Fiction 2. Drawing -- Fiction
   ISBN 0763670073; 9780763670078
   First published 1988

In this book, "[a] little white bear and his magic pencil make wonderful things happen. . . . As a bear strolls through the forest, he meets a lonely gorilla, a noisy crocodile, a lion, and even an elephant. They all look as if they are missing something, so the bear steps in to save the day, using his magic pencil to draw just what they are looking for." (Publisher's note)

"In this simple yet matter-of-factly bizarre picture book first published in the UK in 1988, Browne makes the surreal accessible. The text consists almost entirely of Bear's musings, which are reminiscent of a young child at play." Horn Book

Little Beauty. Candlewick Press 2008 un il $16.99

Grades: PreK K 1 2 3   E
   1. Cats -- Fiction 2. Zoos -- Fiction 3. Gorillas -- Fiction 4. Sign language -- Fiction
   ISBN 978-0-7636-3959-4; 0-7636-3959-1

               LC 2007051887

When a gorilla who knows sign language tells his keepers that he is lonely, they bring him a small kitten and he names her Beauty

Browne "tells a picture-book story with exquisitely detailed art that blends magic and realism." Booklist

★ **Me** and you. Farrar Straus Giroux 2010 un il

Grades: PreK K 1 2 3   E
   1. Fairy tales 2. Bears -- Fiction 3. Social classes -- Fiction
   ISBN 0-374-34908-8; 978-0-374-34908-0
   Original French edition 2009

In this retelling of "The Three Bears, Goldilocks is a modern-day have-not, while the three bears are haves; their stories unfold separately and receive distinct visual treatments. . . . Primary." (Horn Book) Originally published in France in 2009 under the title Une autre histoire.

This "is a work that's both playfully interpretive and interestingly thought-provoking at a youthful level, raising some easily discussable questions." Bull Cent Child Books

★ **My** brother; [by] Anthony Browne. Farrar, Straus & Giroux 2007 un il $16

Grades: PreK K 1   E
   1. Brothers -- Fiction
   ISBN 978-0-374-35120-5; 0-374-35120-1

               LC 2006050262

"To the younger brother, the older one is coolness personified. . . . Browne . . . takes this universal theme of sibling idolatry and interprets it visually with economy and verve." Booklist

★ **My** dad. Farrar, Straus & Giroux 2001 un il $16

Grades: PreK K 1 2   E
   1. Fathers -- Fiction
   ISBN 0-374-35101-5

               LC 00-37951

First published 2000 in the United Kingdom

A child describes the many wonderful things about "my dad," who can jump over the moon, swim like a fish, and be as warm as toast

"The offhand affection is genuinely moving as well as funny." Booklist

★ **My** mom. Farrar, Straus & Giroux 2005 un il $16; pa $6.95

Grades: PreK K 1 2   E
   1. Mothers -- Fiction
   ISBN 0-374-35098-1; 0-374-40026-1 pa

               LC 2004-47173

A child describes the many wonderful things about "my mom," who can make anything grow, roar like a lion, and be as comfy as an armchair

"Browne's paintings hold attention, whether depicting images true to life or flights of fancy, and the honesty of the narrator's emotions and Mom's devotion shine through." Booklist

Piggybook. Knopf 1986 un il hardcover o.p. pa $7.99

Grades: PreK K 1 2   E
   1. Mothers -- Fiction 2. Family life -- Fiction
   ISBN 0-679-80837-X pa

               LC 86-3008

When Mrs. Piggott unexpectedly leaves one day, her demanding family begins to realize just how much she did for them

"As in most of Browne's art, there is more than a touch of irony and visual humor here, bringing off the didactic

with a light touch and turning the lesson into satire." Bull
Cent Child Books

Silly Billy. Candlewick Press 2006 un il $15.99
Grades: PreK K 1 2   E
1. Dolls -- Fiction 2. Worry -- Fiction
ISBN 0-7636-3124-8
                                          LC 2005-55305
To help with his anxiety, Billy uses the worry dolls his
grandmother recommends, but he finds that they do not quite
solve his problem.
   "The pictures are amazing. In counterpoint to the monochromatic worry scenes are pictures so vivid and colorful
they ease concern and spread cheer with each turn of the
page." Booklist

★ **Voices** in the park. DK Ink 1998 un il hardcover
o.p. pa $7.99
Grades: PreK K 1 2   E
1. Gorillas -- Fiction
ISBN 978-0-7894-8191-7 pa; 978-0-7894-2522-5
                                          LC 97-48730
"A simple outing is described by two parents and two
children, each with a different point of view and emotional
outlook. Intriguing illustrations of the gorilla characters and
surreal touches add layers of visual humor." SLJ

★ **What** if...? Anthony Browne. Candlewick Press
2014 32 p. $16.99
Grades: PreK K 1 2 3   E
1. Anxiety -- Fiction 2. Children's parties -- Fiction 3.
Worry -- Fiction 4. Birthday parties -- Fiction
ISBN 0763674192; 9780763674199
                                          LC 2013952843
This illustrated children's story, by Anthony Browne, the
main character struggles with anxiety only to be reassured
at the end. "What if Joe doesn't like the party he's going to?
What if he doesn't like the food or the games or the people?
As Joe and his mom walk down the darkening street, Joe's
imagination starts to run wild." (Publisher's note)
   "Young Joe is apprehensive about attending his friend
Tom's evening birthday party. He lost the invitation, remembers the street name, but forgot the house number. His
mother assures him they'll find Tom's home if they just walk
along the street and look in windows...he common fear of
dealing with a new situation is handled well, and Browne's
treatment of the topic will have readers nodding with understanding." SLJ

Browning, Diane
   ★ **Signed,** Abiah Rose; written & illustrated by Diane
Browning. Tricycle Press 2009 un il $15.99
Grades: 1 2 3   E
1. Artists -- Fiction 2. Sex role -- Fiction 3. Frontier
and pioneer life -- Fiction
ISBN 978-1-58246-311-7; 1-58246-311-5
                                          LC 2009-22172
In pioneer days, a young girl who is a talented artist is
encouraged to paint portraits, Bible scenes, and other pictures, but told never to sign her work, either because it would
be a sign of pride or because artists are expected to be men.
   "In an engaging narrative, Abiah Rose tells of her experiences. . . . In Browning's pleasing colored-pencil-and-
acrylic illustrations, the formal composition and decorative

elements are reminiscent of folk art, while the softer, more
natural depiction of the characters is all her own." Booklist

Broyles, Anne
   Priscilla and the hollyhocks; [by] Anne Broyles; illustrated by Anna Alter. Charlesbridge 2008 un il $15.95
Grades: 2 3 4   E
1. Slavery -- Fiction 2. Native Americans -- Fiction 3.
African Americans -- Fiction
ISBN 978-1-57091-675-5
                                          LC 2007002281
A young African American girl is sold away from her
mother as a slave, and then later is sold to a Cherokee Indian,
but eventually she is bought by a white man who not only
sets her free, but adopts her into his family of fifteen children. Based on a true story; includes instructions for making
a hollyhock doll.
   "Told in descriptive language accompanied by engaging
acrylic paintings, this fictionalized story about a real child . .
. offers a unique perspective on slavery." SLJ

Bruchac, Joseph
   Crazy Horse's vision; illustrated by S.D. Nelson. Lee
& Low Bks. 2000 un il pa $9.95
Grades: K 1 2 3   E
1. Indian chiefs 2. Oglala Indians -- Fiction
ISBN 9781584302827
                                          LC 99-47451
This is "a fictionalized account of the early life of Lakota
leader Crazy Horse. . . . Grades three to six." (Bull Cent
Child Books)
   "Bruchac has created a memorable tale about Crazy
Horse's childhood. . . . In beautiful illustrations inspired
by the ledger book style of the Plains Indians, Sioux artist
Nelson fills the pages with both action and quiet drama."
Booklist

   My father is taller than a tree; illustrated by Wendy Halperin. Dial Books for Young Readers 2010 un il $16.99
Grades: PreK K 1   E
1. Stories in rhyme 2. Father-son relationship -- Fiction
ISBN 978-0-803-73173-8; 0-803-73173-6
                                          LC 2009-3608
Describes, in rhyming text and illustrations, the many
different ways fathers and sons interact with one another.
   "Short, simple rhymes are highlighted by Halperin's
wonderfully expressive, soft yet colorful crayon and pencil
drawings. . . . A charming celebration of fathers, dads, pops,
papas, and pas." SLJ

Bruel, Nick
   A **Bad** Kitty Christmas. Roaring Brook Press 2011
un il $15.99
Grades: 2 3 4   E
1. Stories in rhyme 2. Cats -- Fiction 3. Christmas
stories 4. Christmas -- Fiction
ISBN 978-1-59643-668-8; 1-59643-668-9
                                          LC 2010037814
After destroying all of the gifts and decorations at
home, Bad Kitty escapes from the car on Christmas Eve and
finds a new friend, who helps her learn the true meaning
of Christmas.

"Kitty's zany antics, three romps through the alphabet, and a warm reunion make this a gift indeed for Bad Kitty fans." Publ Wkly

Bad Kitty; Puppy's big day. Nick Bruel. Roaring Brook Press 2015 160 p. illustrations (Bad Kitty) (hardback) $13.99

Grades: 2 3 4 **E**

1. Cats -- Fiction 2. Dogs -- Fiction 3. Animal shelters -- Fiction 4. Humorous stories

ISBN 9781596439764; 1596439769

LC 2014010357

"Bad Kitty's in a bad mood . . . a very bad mood, and Puppy is not helping. Enter Uncle Murray, who's tasked with taking care of Puppy for the day, but that's when the trouble begins. When they go on a walk through the park, Uncle Murray almost gets himself arrested while Puppy ends up in the pound, where he meets some very peculiar new pals." (Publisher's note)

"Scattered throughout the narrative are interjections from Bad Kitty about the yuckier habits of dogs, and the end matter includes information on adopting pets from shelters. As always, Bruel's writing is hilarious, and his excellent illustrations make the story complete." SLJ

Little red bird; by Nick Bruel. Roaring Brook Press 2008 un il $16.95

Grades: PreK K 1 2 **E**

1. Stories in rhyme 2. Birds -- Fiction

ISBN 978-1-59643-339-7; 1-59643-339-6

LC 2007-13198

After escaping from her cage to see the world, a little red bird finds it difficult to decide whether to stay free or to go home and never fly again.

"The rhyming narrative, . . . is appealingly bouncy and will draw children through the small hero's exciting peregrinations until the final page, which hints at a satisfying conclusion while leaving room to wonder." Booklist

A **wonderful** year; Nick Bruel. Roaring Brook Press 2015 40 p. color illustrations (hardback) $17.99

Grades: PreK K 1 **E**

1. Year -- Fiction 2. Humorous fiction 3. Seasons -- Fiction 4. Humorous stories

ISBN 1596436115; 9781596436114

LC 2014009904

This children's book, by Nick Bruel, is a "comics-style look at the seasons. . . . A girl is excited to play in the snow. However, everyone reminds her to bundle up. Key characters seen again in later stories all pop in to suggest what to wear (the most obvious of her advisers being her mother and father, but a large purple hippo, a tree, a refrigerator and a can of beans weigh in as well). Alas, when she has finally put on all of the clothing, the weather has changed to spring." (Kirkus Reviews)

"Bruel takes readers on a walk through the seasons with a girl and her animal friends...The stylized cartoon illustrations are vividly colored and the panels are easy to follow. This clever, engaging introduction to visual storytelling will hold up through multiple readings." SLJ

Bruel, Robert O.

Bob and Otto; pictures by Nick Bruel. Roaring Brook Press 2007 un il $15.95

Grades: PreK K 1 2 **E**

1. Worms -- Fiction 2. Friendship -- Fiction 3. Butterflies -- Fiction 4. Caterpillars -- Fiction

ISBN 978-1-59643-203-1; 1-59643-203-9

LC 2006012008

Otto the worm is shocked to discover that his best friend Bob is actually a caterpillar who emerges one day as a butterfly.

"Along with the engaging story, the science in the illustrations and text is quite accurate; there are rich, not-to-be missed visual details." Horn Book

Bruins, David

The **legend** of Ninja Cowboy Bear; illustrated by Hilary Leuny. Kids Can Press 2009 un il $16.95

Grades: PreK K 1 2 **E**

1. Bears -- Fiction 2. Ninja -- Fiction 3. Cowhands -- Fiction

ISBN 978-1-55453-486-9; 1-55453-486-0

The ninja, the cowboy and the bear do everything together. But when a contest among themselves leads to resentment, they soon learn that the only way to stop disagreeing is to be considerate of their differences and appreciate one another.

"Readers can take the story a step further with the Ninja Cowboy Bear Game, which is strongly reminiscent of Rock Paper Scissors. The digital-cartoon illustrations are set in comic panels; the art and the occasional Japanese word bubble give the story an anime feel. A fun purchase with a solid message." SLJ

Other titles in this series are:

The way of the ninja (2010)

The call of the cowboy (2011)

Brun-Cosme, Nadine

★ **Big** Wolf & Little Wolf; illustrated by Olivier Tallec. Enchanted Lion Books 2009 un il $16.95

Grades: PreK K 1 **E**

1. Wolves -- Fiction 2. Loneliness -- Fiction

ISBN 978-1-5927-0084-4; 1-5927-0084-5

LC 2008054040

ALA ALSC Batchelder Award Honor Book (2010)

Big Wolf has always lived alone at the top of a hill under a tree, so when a little wolf suddenly arrives one day, he does not know what to think.

"Tallec's colorful illustrations play off the quiet dignity of the text, revealing emotion through the characters' stances and expressions, employing a sketchy painting style that brims with light." SLJ

Other titles about Big Wolf & Little Wolf are:

Big Wolf & Little Wolf, the little leaf that wouldn't fall (2009)

Big Wolf & Little Wolf, such a beautiful orange! (2011)

Brunhoff, Jean de

★ The **story** of Babar, the little elephant; translated from the French by Merle S. Haas. Random House 1937 47p il $15.95; lib bdg $17.99

Grades: PreK K 1 2 **E**

1. Elephants -- Fiction

ISBN 0-394-80575-5; 0-394-90575-X lib bdg

Original French edition, 1931; this is a reduced format version of the 1933 United States edition

"Babar runs away from the jungle and goes to live with an old lady in Paris, where he adapts quickly to French amenities. Later he returns to the jungle and becomes king. Much of the charm of the story is contributed by the author's gay pictures." Hodges. Books for Elem Sch Libr

Other titles about Babar are:

Babar and Father Christmas (1940)
Babar and his children (1938)
Babar the king (1935)
Bonjour, Babar (2000)
Travels of Babar (1934)

Bruss, Deborah

Book! book! book! illustrated by Tiphanie Beeke. Levine Bks. 2001 un il $15.95

Grades: PreK K 1   E
1. Libraries -- Fiction 2. Domestic animals -- Fiction 3. Books and reading -- Fiction
ISBN 0-439-13525-7

LC 99-59758

When the children go back to school, the animals on the farm are bored, so they go into the library in town trying to find something to do

"Soft, naive watercolor paintings illustrate the satisfying story, which, with its witty conclusion, will be a sure winner at story time." Horn Book Guide

Bryant, Jennifer

Abe's fish; a boyhood tale of Abraham Lincoln. by Jen Bryant; illustrated by Amy June Bates. Sterling 2009 un il $15.95

Grades: PreK K 1 2   E
1. Lawyers 2. Presidents 3. State legislators 4. Members of Congress 5. Presidents -- United States -- Fiction
ISBN 978-1-4027-6252-9; 1-4027-6252-6

LC 2008028597

Young Abe Lincoln learns the meaning of selflessness and freedom when he encounters a soldier on a country road and gives up his prized possession: a fish he caught for the family's evening meal. Includes author's note on the early life of the sixteenth president.

"Bates's lively watercolors have rich detail, depicting Abe as a boy in a coonskin hat, still too small to lift his father's ax. The full-spread, sepia-toned paintings capture his rustic lifestyle, the Kentucky landscape, and the reactions of Abe's family to his generosity." SLJ

Includes bibliographical references

Buck, Nola

A **Christmas** goodnight; illustrated by Sarah Jane Wright. Katherine Tegen Books 2011 un il $12.99; lib bdg $13.89

Grades: PreK K   E
1. Stories in rhyme 2. Christmas stories 3. Bedtime -- Fiction 4. Christmas -- Fiction
ISBN 978-0-06-166491-5; 0-06-166491-X; 978-0-06-166492-2 lib bdg; 0-06-166492-8 lib bdg

Illustrations and rhyming text portray characters from the Nativity story, from doves in the stable to the wise men, as they go to sleep on Christmas Eve.

"The double-page-spread format makes this a fine read-aloud for a group of little ones, but it's also a cozy choice as a December bedtime story. A terrific introduction for pre-

schoolers who are just learning about the Nativity story." Kirkus

Buckley, Michael

Kel Gilligan's daredevil stunt show; semiprofessional daredevil. pictures by Dan Santat; written by Michael Buckley. Abrams Books for Young Readers 2012 35 p. (alk. paper) $16.95

Grades: PreK K 1   E
1. Vegetables -- Fiction 2. Picture books for children 3. Toilet training -- Fiction 4. Humorous stories 5. Courage -- Fiction
ISBN 141970379X; 9781419703799

LC 2012001285

In his debut children's picture book, Michael Buckley tells the story of "a child who just loves danger. . . . [Protagonist Kel Gilligan] earnestly recollects his past triumphs in pictures designed to look like freeze frames of his life," discussing the times he successfully ate his broccoli and used the toilet. (School Library Journal)

Budnitz, Paul

The **hole** in the middle; illustrated by Aya Kakeda. Disney/Hyperion Books 2011 un il $16.99

Grades: PreK K 1   E
1. Friendship -- Fiction
ISBN 978-1-4231-3761-0; 1-4231-3761-2

LC 2010036236

Morgan was born with a big hole through his middle that gives him a strange, empty feeling all of the time, but when his good friend Yumi becomes ill, he finds that helping her makes him feel whole.

"The colorful, cheerful spreads depict all sorts of amusements and feature whimsical details that add to the brief text. . . . Focusing on the needs of others is a time-honored solution for those dissatisfied with their own lot in life; here is a motivating parable for contemporary kids." Kirkus

Buehner, Caralyn

Fanny's dream; pictures by Mark Buehner. Dial Bks. for Young Readers 1996 un il $16.99; pa $6.99

Grades: K 1 2 3   E
1. Marriage -- Fiction 2. Farm life -- Fiction
ISBN 0-8037-1496-3; 0-14-250060-7 pa

LC 94-31910

Fanny Agnes is a sturdy farm girl who dreams of marrying a prince, but when her fairy godmother doesn't show up, she decides on a local farmer instead

"Fanny Agnes is a delight: a feminist with a wry sense of humor, she balances her dreams with common sense and a loving heart. What's more, there's plenty for youngsters to enjoy in the robust, bucolic pictures, which seem almost to jump off the page." Booklist

★ **Snowmen** at night; pictures by Mark Buehner. Phyllis Fogelman Bks. 2002 un il $15.99

Grades: PreK K 1 2   E
1. Stories in rhyme 2. Snow -- Fiction
ISBN 0-8037-2550-7

LC 2001-33517

Snowmen play games at night when no one is watching

The "text has bouncy rhymes, but it's the artwork that is spectacular. Acrylic-over-oil paintings feature fat, happy

snowpeople who practically jump—or sled—off the pages."
Booklist

Other titles about the snowmen are:
Snowmen at Christmas (2005)
Snowmen all year (2010)

★ **Superdog**; the heart of a hero. illustrated by Mark
Buehner. HarperCollins 2004 un il $15.99; lib bdg $16.89
Grades: PreK K 1 2   E
1. Dogs -- Fiction
ISBN 0-06-623620-7; 0-06-623621-5 lib bdg
LC 2002-3540
Tired of being overlooked because he is so small, a
big-hearted dog named Dexter transforms himself into
a superhero
"Solid shapings, surprising perspectives, and thick
paints in dynamic colors combine for artwork that practical-
ly jumps off the page. There's plenty of wit, too." Booklist

Buhler, Cynthia von
But who will bell the cats? Houghton Mifflin Books for
Children 2009 un il $16
Grades: K 1 2   E
1. Bats -- Fiction 2. Cats -- Fiction 3. Mice -- Fiction
4. Princesses -- Fiction
ISBN 978-0-618-99718-3; 0-618-99718-0
LC 2008050165
While a princess spoils her eight cats, a mouse and his
friend, a brown bat, live on scraps in the castle cellar, but
Mouse decides to place bells on the cats necks so that he
and Brown Bat might live comfortably, as well. Includes the
Aesop fable on which the story is based.
"Dark, complicated mixed-media illustrations bring a
humorously creepy feel to the tale." Horn Book

Buitrago, Jairo
★ **Jimmy** the greatest! Jairo Buitrago; Rafael Yock-
teng, illustrator; Elisa Amado, translator. Groundwood
Books/House of Anansi Press 2012 48 p. ill. $18.95
Grades: K 1 2 3   E
1. Boxing -- Fiction 2. Poverty -- Fiction 3. Picture
books for children
ISBN 1554981786; 9781554981786
In this book, "[w]ide-eyed Jimmy lives in a ramshackle,
tin-roofed village, painted by [illustrator Rafael] Yockteng
. . . . Jimmy finds out about Muhammad Ali from a box-
ful of old newspapers and, galvanized, starts training in the
local gym. 'He wasn't thinking about what he didn't have
anymore. . . . He didn't need much stuff to run.' . . . But it's
Jimmy's trainer, Don Apolinar, who leaves for the big city,
while Jimmy stays behind; he ends up coaching kids at the
gym." (Publishers Weekly)

Bulla, Clyde Robert
★ The **chalk** box kid; illustrated by Thomas B. Allen.
Random House 1987 un il hardcover o.p. pa $3.99
Grades: K 1 2 3   E
ISBN 0-394-99102-8; 0-394-89102-3 pa
LC 87-4683
"Bulla manages a poignant depth within the confines
of simple style and narrative. Understated and easy to read,
this nevertheless tackles problems that are not easy to solve
without exercising the imagination." Bull Cent Child Books

Bunting, Eve
Baby can; [by] Eve Bunting; illustrated by Maxie
Chambliss. Boyds Mills Press 2007 un il $15.95
Grades: PreK   E
1. Growth -- Fiction 2. Infants -- Fiction 3. Brothers
-- Fiction
ISBN 978-1-59078-322-1
LC 2006011485
Every time his family gets excited over something Baby
James can do, big brother Brendan demonstrates that he can
do even better, from burping to rolling over to walking
"The watercolor illustrations match the light touch of the
spare text." Booklist

The **Banshee**; illustrated by Emily Arnold McCully.
Clarion Books 2009 un il $16
Grades: K 1 2 3   E
1. Fear -- Fiction 2. Ireland -- Fiction 3. Family life
-- Fiction 4. Superstition -- Fiction
ISBN 978-0-618-82162-4; 0-618-82162-7
LC 2008-14581
When Terry wakes up in the middle of the night to horrible screeching, he thinks the Banshee has come to pay his
family a visit.
"This picture book creates a convincing story of bravery in the face of vividly imagined danger. Not a word is
wasted in the first-person text, and the ink-and-watercolor
illustrations show Terry's emotions with clarity and sensitivity." Booklist

Big Bear's big boat; by Eve Bunting; illustrated by
Nancy Carpenter. Clarion Books 2013 32 p. (hardcover)
$12.99
Grades: PreK K 1   E
1. Bears -- Fiction 2. Boats and boating -- Fiction
ISBN 0618585370; 9780618585373
LC 2012003974
In this book by Eve Bunting "Big Bear outgrew his little
boat, so he is building himself a big boat and can't wait till
he's rowing, fishing, and relaxing in it. When his friends
start suggesting improvements, Big Bear obligingly follows
their advice. To his dismay, his big boat is turning out all
wrong. It's because he hasn't followed his own dream, and
he knows exactly how to fix it." (Publisher's note)

★ The **bones** of Fred McFee; illustrated by Kurt
Cyrus. Harcourt 2002 un il hardcover o.p. pa $6
Grades: K 1 2 3   E
1. Stories in rhyme 2. Halloween -- Fiction
ISBN 0-15-202004-7; 0-15-205423-5 pa
LC 2001-2414
A toy skeleton at Halloween provides menace
and mystery
"The story, told in rhyme keeps readers on the edge of
their seats. . . . Cyrus's detailed, realistic illustrations, done
in scratchboard and watercolor, are appropriately dark and
are a perfect complement to the subtly scary mood of the
text." SLJ

Butterfly house; illustrated by Greg Shed. Scholastic
Press 1999 un il $17.99
Grades: K 1 2 3   E
1. Stories in rhyme 2. Butterflies -- Fiction 3.

Grandfathers -- Fiction
ISBN 0-590-84884-4

LC 98-16349

With the help of her grandfather, a little girl makes a house for a larva and watches it develop before setting it free, and every summer after that butterflies come to visit her

"Shed's gouache-on-canvas paintings evoke feelings of warmth and nostalgia suited to the quiet story. Earth tones predominate, especially the browns and oranges found in this species. Appended with directions for raising a butterfly." Booklist

Cheyenne again; illustrated by Irving Toddy. Clarion Bks. 1995 un il $16; pa $5.95

Grades: K 1 2 3   E

1. School stories 2. Cheyenne Indians -- Fiction
ISBN 0-395-70364-6; 0-618-19465-7 pa

LC 94-43287

Young Bull, "a young Cheyenne boy tells how he's taken from his parents on the reservation in the late 1880s and sent to a boarding school, where he's forced to learn white ways. . . . This is a picture book for older readers, a grim story of painful separation and forced assimilation. . . . The short, spare lines of free verse are illustrated by double-page-spread oil and acrylic paintings that contrast the open landscape with the stiffness of figures forced into uniform and regimentation." Booklist

Christmas cricket; illustrated by Timothy Bush. Clarion Bks. 2002 32p il $15

Grades: K 1 2 3   E

1. Crickets -- Fiction 2. Christmas -- Fiction
ISBN 0-618-06554-7

LC 2001-55266

On Christmas Eve, a little cricket finds its way into a house where its singing is thought to be the voice of an angel

"Bush's watercolor pictures celebrate the story's cheerful warmth while their varying sizes and shapes create a cinematic effect that cleverly captures both the rhythm of the text and a cricket's kinetic spirit." Booklist

★ **Flower** garden; written by Eve Bunting; illustrated by Kathryn Hewitt. Harcourt Brace & Co. 1994 un il $16; pa $7; bd bk $10.95

Grades: K 1 2 3   E

1. Stories in rhyme 2. Flowers -- Fiction 3. Birthdays -- Fiction
ISBN 0-15-228776-0; 0-15-202372-0 pa; 0-15-206516-4 bd bk

LC 92-25766

"The simple rhymed verse, which skips along in pace with the child's anticipation, is smoothly integrated with the vibrant, lifelike paintings." Booklist

"The young narrator has, with the help of her father, assembled a 'garden in a shopping cart' to take home and plant in a window box high above the city as a birthday gift for her mother." Horn Book Guide

★ **Fly** away home; illustrated by Ronald Himler. Clarion Bks. 1991 32p il $16; pa $6.99

Grades: K 1 2 3   E

1. Airports -- Fiction 2. Homeless persons -- Fiction
ISBN 0-395-55962-6; 0-395-66415-2 pa

LC 90-42353

A homeless boy who lives in an airport with his father, moving from terminal to terminal and trying not to be noticed, is given hope when he sees a trapped bird find its freedom

"Himler's quiet paintings echo the economy and the touching quality of the story, which is all the more effective in depicting the plight of the homeless because it is so low-keyed." Bull Cent Child Books

Frog and friends; written by Eve Bunting; illustrated by Josee Masse. Sleeping Bear Press 2011 37p il (I am a reader!)

Grades: 1 2   E

1. Frogs -- Fiction 2. Ponds -- Fiction 3. Animals -- Fiction 4. Friendship -- Fiction
ISBN 1-58536-548-3; 1-58536-689-7 pa; 978-1-58536-548-7; 978-1-58536-689-7 pa

LC 2010053706

Frog and his friends are alarmed by a strange object that appears on his pond, share a thoughtful—if scratchy—gift, and meet a hippopotamus that has run away from the zoo.

"This clever beginning reader is divided into three chapters. . . . Repetition, white space, and a large font help prepare children for tackling a smattering of more challenging vocabulary. Bright cartoon illustrations provide some picture clues. Readers will enjoy feeling superior to Frog and his friends." SLJ

Girls A to Z; illustrated by Suzanne Bloom. Boyds Mills Press 2002 un il $15.95

Grades: PreK K 1 2   E

1. Alphabet 2. Occupations
ISBN 1-56397-147-X

Girls with names ranging from Aliki to Zoe imagine themselves in various fun and creative professions

"Bunting has created a winning alphabet book that is playful, inventive, and (coincidentally) politically correct. Accompanied by Bloom's exuberant watercolor portraits." SLJ

★ **Have** you seen my new blue socks? by Eve Bunting; illustrated by Sergio Ruzzier. Clarion Books 2013 32 p. (hardcover) $16.99

Grades: PreK K 1   E

1. Stories in rhyme 2. Ducks -- Fiction 3. Socks -- Fiction 4. Animals -- Fiction 5. Lost and found possessions -- Fiction
ISBN 0547752679; 9780547752679

LC 2012012192

This rhyming children's book, by Eve Bunting, illustrated by Sergio Ruzzier, "spin[s] the tale of a small duck who waddles through the countryside, forlornly searching for his blue socks. . . . Finally, a sharp-eyed peacock sees a bit of blue peeking out of duck's lace-up shoes and the mini-mystery is solved!" (Publisher's note)

Hey diddle diddle; illustrated by Mary Ann Fraser. Boyds Mills Press 2011 un il $16.95

Grades: PreK K   E

1. Stories in rhyme 2. Animals -- Fiction 3. Musicians -- Fiction

ISBN 978-1-59078-768-7; 1-59078-768-4

In this variation on the traditional nursery rhyme, the cat plays the fiddle, the cow plays the silver trombone, and other animals play other musical instruments and join in a band, which is revealed in the end to be a music box wound by a small child.

"Pure whimsy . . . is what [Bunting] delivers here. . . . Fraser's accompanying artwork is cheery and saturated, the colors running from cool to hot. . . . The music made here will be in a sing-along read-aloud, with accompanying guffaws to mark the time." Kirkus

★ **How** many days to America? a Thanksgiving story. illustrated by Beth Peck. Clarion Bks. 1988 un il lib bdg $16; pa $5.95

Grades: K 1 2 3   E

1. Refugees -- Fiction 2. Thanksgiving Day -- Fiction

ISBN 0-89919-521-0 lib bdg; 0-395-54777-6 pa

LC 88-2590

Refugees from an unnamed Caribbean island embark on a dangerous boat trip to America where they have a special reason to celebrate Thanksgiving

"Bunting's simple tale focuses on the hardships of the journey and on the American ideals of freedom and safety. She wisely leaves aside the issues of politics in the homeland or in this country. Her prose is poetically spare. . . . Peck's richly colored crayon drawings yield added enjoyment. . . . A poignant story and a thought-provoking discussion starter." SLJ

Jin Woo; illustrated by Chris K. Soentpiet. Clarion Bks. 2001 30p il $16

Grades: K 1 2 3   E

1. Adoption -- Fiction 2. Brothers -- Fiction 3. Korean Americans -- Fiction

ISBN 0-395-93872-4

LC 00-38408

Davey is dubious about having a new adopted brother from Korea, but when he finds out that his parents still love him, he decides that having a baby brother will be fine

"Soentpiet's watercolors are suffused with light and perfectly capture the characters' expressions. . . . The story's emotional veracity will speak to any new sibling." SLJ

Little Bear's little boat; illustrated by Nancy Carpenter. Clarion Bks. 2003 32p il $12

Grades: PreK K 1 2   E

1. Bears -- Fiction 2. Growth -- Fiction

ISBN 0-395-97462-3

LC 2001-37233

When Little Bear can no longer fit into his boat he finds someone else who can use it

"This is a sensitive, affecting story about growing up and leaving favorite things behind, with charming ink-and-paint illustrations that echo the spare clarity of the words." Booklist

The **memory** string; pictures by Ted Rand. Clarion Bks. 2000 32p il $15

Grades: K 1 2 3   E

1. Memory -- Fiction 2. Stepmothers -- Fiction

ISBN 0-395-86146-2

LC 99-42771

While still grieving for her mother and unable to accept her stepmother, Laura clings to the memories represented by forty-three buttons on a string

"Rand's realistic artwork concentrates on the faces of the family and the emotions that cross them. Some children will find this touches them very deeply." Booklist

My dog Jack is fat; illustrated by Michael Rex. Marshall Cavendish Children 2011 un il $16.99

Grades: PreK K 1   E

1. Dogs -- Fiction 2. Weight loss -- Fiction

ISBN 978-0-7614-5809-8; 0-7614-5809-3

LC 2010018271

Carson does his best to help his dog, Jack, lose weight, with unexpected results.

"This appealing take on a common problem has understated, smooth writing and colorful, digitally rendered cartoons enlivened by Rex's characteristic humor." SLJ

My robot; by Eve Bunting; illustrated by Dagmar Fehlau. Harcourt, Inc. 2006 un il (Green Light readers) $12.95; pa $3.95

Grades: K 1 2   E

1. Robots -- Fiction

ISBN 0-15-205593-2; 0-15-205617-3 pa

LC 2005006936

Cecil the robot is good at playing tag, leading the school band, and performing tricks with the dog, but there is one important thing he does best of all.

"Fehlau's bright, stylized illustrations have a festive feel and infuse the fantastical situations with lighthearted fun." Booklist

My special day at Third Street School; illustrated by Suzanne Bloom. Boyds Mills Press 2004 un il $15.95; pa $9.95

Grades: K 1 2 3   E

1. School stories 2. Authors -- Fiction

ISBN 1-59078-745-5; 1-59078-745-5 pa

A school visit from children's book author Amanda Drake brings a day full of fun.

"Just as Bunting's writing captures the action and the children's emotions in a convincing way, Bloom's gouache, colored pencil, and crayon artwork illustrates the contemporary classroom setting and the children's body language to perfection." Booklist

One candle; illustrated by K. Wendy Popp. HarperCollins Pubs. 2002 un il hardcover o.p. pa $6.99

Grades: K 1 2 3   E

1. Jews -- Fiction 2. Hanukkah -- Fiction 3. Holocaust, 1933-1945 -- Fiction

ISBN 0-06-028115-4; 0-06-028116-2 lib bdg; 0-06-008560-6 pa

LC 2001-47205

Every year a family celebrates Hanukkah by retelling the story of how Grandma and her sister managed to mark the day while in a German concentration camp

"Popp invests her art with all the emotion of Bunting's heartfelt text. . . . A gentle but forthright opening for discussion about the Holocaust." Booklist

★ **One** green apple; illustrated by Ted Lewin. Clarion Books 2006 un il $16
Grades: K 1 2 3   E
   1. School stories 2. Apples -- Fiction 3. Muslims -- Fiction 4. Immigrants -- Fiction
   ISBN 0-618-43477-1
LC 2005011378

While on a school field trip to an orchard to make cider, a young immigrant named Farah gains self-confidence when the green apple she picks perfectly complements the other students' red apples

"Young readers will respond as much to Bunting's fine first-person narrative as to Lewin's double-page, photorealistic watercolors." Booklist

Our library; by Eve Bunting; illustrated by Maggie Smith. Clarion Books 2008 32p il $16
Grades: K 1 2   E
   1. Animals -- Fiction 2. Raccoons -- Fiction 3. Libraries -- Fiction 4. Books and reading -- Fiction
   ISBN 978-0-618-49458-3; 0-618-49458-8
LC 2006009519

A raccoon and his friends go to great lengths to make sure they will always have a library from which to borrow books.

"Bunting's style has a graceful simplicity, descriptive enough to be evocative without overwhelming. . . . Smith's watercolor and acrylic illustrations are charming and should have most children longing to enter the buttercup-yellow library with the grass-green door. An excellent vehicle for discussing the importance of libraries, books, reading, and teamwork." SLJ

Pirate boy; illustrated by Julie Fortenberry. Holiday House 2011 un il $16.95
Grades: PreK K   E
   1. Pirates -- Fiction 2. Imagination -- Fiction 3. Mother-son relationship -- Fiction
   ISBN 978-0-8234-2321-7; 0-8234-2321-2
LC 2010029446

As Colin imagines himself in a series of adventures beginning with joining a pirate crew, his mother assures him that she will always be there to help if he needs her.

"Layers of color and heavily worked figures give Fortenberry's . . . digital art a thick, substantial feel. . . . The book reads like a conversation Bunting . . . might once have had with one of her own children; it's a warmhearted portrait of an endlessly patient parent, ready to help her child work through his fears and desires." Publ Wkly

★ **Pop's** bridge; written by Eve Bunting; illustrated by C. F. Payne. Harcourt, Inc. 2006 un il $17
Grades: 1 2 3 4   E
   1. Fathers -- Fiction 2. San Francisco (Calif.) -- Fiction 3. Golden Gate Bridge (San Francisco, Calif.) -- Fiction
   ISBN 0-15-204773-5
LC 2004-23774

Robert and his friend Charlie are proud of their fathers, who are working on the construction of San Francisco's Golden Gate Bridge.

"Distinguished by its lovely, understated text and Payne's lavish and affectionate mixed-media pictures, this picture book does a quietly successful job of humanizing one of the most important feats of civil engineering in American history." Booklist

★ **Smoky** night; written by Eve Bunting; illustrated by David Diaz. Harcourt Brace & Co. 1994 un il $17; pa $7
Grades: K 1 2 3   E
   1. Riots -- Fiction 2. Korean Americans -- Fiction 3. African Americans -- Fiction 4. Los Angeles (Calif.) -- Fiction
   ISBN 0-15-269954-6; 0-15-201884-0 pa
LC 93-14885

Awarded the Caldecott Medal, 1995

When the Los Angeles riots break out in the streets of their neighborhood, Daniel and his mother, African Americans, make friends with Mrs. Kim, a Korean grocer from across the street

"Thick black lines border vibrant acrylic paintings. . . . Diaz places these dynamic paintings on collages of real objects that, for the most part, reinforce the narrative action. . . . Both author and illustrator insist on a headlong confrontation with the issue of rapport between different races, and the result is a memorable, thought-provoking book." Horn Book

So far from the sea; illustrated by Chris K. Soentpiet. Clarion Bks. 1998 30p il $16; pa $7.99
Grades: K 1 2 3   E
   1. Japanese Americans -- Evacuation and relocation, 1942-1945 -- Fiction
   ISBN 0-395-72095-8; 0-547-23752-9 pa
LC 97-28176

When seven-year-old Laura and her family visit Grandfather's grave at the Manzanar War Relocation Center, the Japanese American child leaves behind a special symbol

"Soentpiet's impressionistic watercolors perfectly complement Bunting's evocative text." SLJ

That's what leprechauns do; illustrated by Emily Arnold McCully. Clarion Books 2005 32p il $16
Grades: K 1 2 3   E
   1. Ireland -- Fiction 2. Leprechauns -- Fiction
   ISBN 0-618-35410-7

When leprechauns Ari, Boo, and Col need to place the pot of gold at the end of the rainbow, they cannot help getting into mischief along the way.

"McCully graces this lighthearted story with her characteristically expressive and charming watercolors that eloquently capture the verdant beauty of the Irish countryside and the irrepressible personalities." SLJ

★ **Tweak,** tweak; illustrated by Sergio Ruzzier. Clarion Books 2011 40p il $14.99
Grades: PreK K 1   E
   1. Elephants -- Fiction 2. Mother-child relationship -- Fiction
   ISBN 978-0-618-99851-7; 0-618-99851-9
LC 2010024651

While out for a walk, Mama Elephant answers her child's questions about a monkey, a frog, a songbird, a butterfly, and a crocodile, all the while teaching about Little Elephant too.

"Young children will enjoy following Little Elephant's fantasies, depicted in the uncluttered, double-page spreads, all the way to the story's climax, which celebrates what Little Elephant really is, as well as the big, strong creature she will grow up to be. Along with imaginative silliness, the nurturing parent-child tenderness is the core of the story." Booklist

Walking to school; by Eve Bunting; illustrated by Michael Dooling. Clarion Books 2008 32p il $16

Grades: 2 3 4   E

1. Prejudices -- Fiction 2. Belfast (Northern Ireland) -- Fiction

ISBN 978-0-618-26144-4; 0-618-26144-3

"The book does an excellent job of presenting the situation from a child's perspective without demonizing either side. . . . Dooling's oil-on-canvas illustrations are realistic enough to resemble stills from documentary footage." SLJ

★ The **Wall**; illustrated by Ronald Himler. Clarion Bks. 1990 un il $16; pa $5.95

Grades: K 1 2 3   E

1. Vietnam Veterans Memorial (Washington, D.C.) -- Fiction

ISBN 0-395-51588-2; 0-395-62977-2 pa

LC 89-17429

"A father and his young son come to the Vietnam Veterans Memorial to find the name of the grandfather the boy never knew. This moving account is beautifully told from a young child's point of view; the watercolors capture the impressive mass of the wall of names as well as the poignant reactions of the people who visit there." Horn Book Guide

Washday; by Eve Bunting; illustrated by Brad Sneed. Holiday House 2014 32 p. (hardcover) $16.95

Grades: K 1 2 3   E

1. Laundry -- Fiction 2. Grandmothers -- Fiction 3. Frontier and pioneer life -- Fiction

ISBN 0823428680; 9780823428687

LC 2012040347

"Lizzie helps her grandma on washday and gets rewarded with a tea party in this historical story celebrating family tradition and hard work," written by Eve Bunting and illustrated by Brad Sneed. (Publisher's note)

"The title page of this charming historical picture book features an image of a monthly calendar with a single date circled, April 20, 1889: Washday. '"Are you ready for work, Lizzie girl?' Grandma asks me." Lizzie is, even though she and her doll are disappointed that their plans for a tea party have been canceled. . . . Lizzie's efforts are rewarded when Grandma surprises her with "a real grown-up doll tea party." Youngsters will savor this best with pearl tea and a snickerdoodle." Booklist

The **Wednesday** surprise; illustrated by Donald Carrick. Clarion Bks. 1989 un il lib bdg $16; pa $5.95

Grades: K 1 2 3   E

1. Reading -- Fiction 2. Grandmothers -- Fiction

ISBN 0-89919-721-3 lib bdg; 0-395-54776-8 pa

LC 88-12117

"Bunting's writing is simple and warm and direct. . . . Carrick's pictures echo the warmth, especially in the faces of the family, painted in realistically detailed watercolors

with a careful attention to familial resemblance. A gentle charmer." Bull Cent Child Books

Will it be a baby brother? illustrated by Beth Spiegel. Boyd Mills Press 2010 un il $16.95

Grades: PreK K   E

1. Infants -- Fiction 2. Siblings -- Fiction

ISBN 978-1-59078-439-6; 1-59078-439-1

A little boy is certain that his expectant mother will give birth to a baby brother.

"The large, bright, watercolor-and-ink cartoon-style pictures skillfully convey the boy's feelings. . . . This warm, reassuring story is about a child's fear of displacement as much as his longing for a sibling just like him." Booklist

Yard sale; Eve Bunting, illustrated by Lauren Castillo. Candlewick Press 2015 32 p.

Grades: PreK K 1   E

1. Garage sales -- Fiction 2. Moving -- Juvenile fiction

ISBN 9780763665425

LC 2014939360

In this children's book, by Eve Bunting, "[a]lmost everything Callie's family owns is spread out in their front yard—their furniture, their potted flowers, even Callie's bike. They can't stay in this house, so they're moving to an apartment in the city. The new place is 'small but nice,' Mom says, and most of their things won't fit, so today they are having a yard sale. But it's kind of hard to watch people buy your stuff, even if you understand why it has to happen." (Publisher's note)

You were loved before you were born; [by] Eve Bunting & [illustrated by] Karen Barbour. Blue Sky Press 2008 un il $16.99

Grades: PreK   E

1. Love -- Fiction 2. Family life -- Fiction

ISBN 978-0-439-04061-7; 0-439-04061-2

LC 2007-9703

A mother shares with her child all the ways in which family members and friends were loving and welcoming before the child was even born

"A marvelous integration of color, image and verbal rhythm sure to delight and to become a must-purchase for newborns and their parents." Kirkus

Burell, Sarah

Diamond Jim Dandy and the sheriff; illustrated by Bryan Langdo. Sterling Pub. 2010 un il $14.95

Grades: K 1 2   E

1. Infants -- Fiction 2. West (U.S.) -- Fiction 3. Rattlesnakes -- Fiction

ISBN 978-1-4027-5737-2; 1-4027-5737-9

LC 2008013767

When a friendly and talented rattlesnake slithers into Dustpan, Texas, he must prove his value to the residents of the town before the sheriff will allow him to stay.

"This charming tale has bright, appealing, kid-friendly illustrations. The lively dialogue combined with the satisfying ending will serve as an excellent storytime read-aloud." SLJ

Burgess, Mark

Where teddy bears come from; written by Mark Burgess; illustrated by Russell Ayto. Peachtree 2009 un il $16.95

Grades: PreK K 1 2   E

1. Wolves -- Fiction 2. Teddy bears -- Fiction

ISBN 978-1-56145-487-7; 1-56145-487-7

LC 2008052705

When Little Wolf cannot fall asleep, he decides that he needs a teddy bear and goes into the woods to see if he can find out where to get one.

"This charming story plays with the conventions of familiar nursery tales. . . . With its lively, bold watercolors filled with humorous details, this tale is likely to be a storytime hit." SLJ

Burkert, Rand

★ **Mouse** & Lion; [by] Aesop; retold by Rand Burkert; picutres by Nancy Ekholm Burkert. Michael di Capua Books 2011 un il $17.95

Grades: 2 3 4 5 6   E

1. Fables 2. Mice -- Fiction 3. Lions -- Fiction 4. Africa -- Fiction

ISBN 978-0-545-10147-9; 0-545-10147-6

This is "a book rich with [Nancy Ekholm Burkert's] signature meticulous brush lines, compelling display of color, and carefully delineated detail. Each page offers dramatic delight that extends the story. In an unusual but fascinating variation on the Aesop tale, Rand Burkert places Mouse at center stage. . . . The illustrations for this spirited tale are nothing less than spectacular. . . . Choosing the Aha Hills (between Botswana and Namibia) for her setting, the artist imbues the scenes with the fauna and flora of this region." SLJ

Burleigh, Robert

Clang-clang! Beep-beep! listen to the city. illustrated by Beppe Giacobbe. Simon & Schuster Books for Young Readers 2009 un il $14.99

Grades: PreK K 1   E

1. Stories in rhyme 2. Noise -- Fiction 3. Sound -- Fiction 4. City and town life -- Fiction

ISBN 978-1-4169-4052-4; 1-4169-4052-9

LC 2007-45844

From morning until night, a city is filled with such sounds as the roars and snores of a subway ride, the flutters and coos of pigeons, and the shouts and beeps of drivers in traffic

"The rhymes that accompany the story are short but evocative. . . . The artist uses a vivid mix of primary and secondary colors to set the stage." SLJ

Good-bye, Sheepie; illustrated by Peter Catalanotto. Marshall Cavendish 2010 un il $16.99

Grades: K 1 2   E

1. Dogs -- Fiction 2. Death -- Fiction 3. Father-son relationship -- Fiction

ISBN 978-0-7614-5598-1; 0-7614-5598-1

LC 2009-5955

A father teaches his young son about death and remembrance as he buries their beloved dog.

"Catalanotto's gentle watercolor-and-gouache paintings give off a yellow glow suggestive of warm sunshine on an autumn day, and are well suited to Burleigh's quiet text." Booklist

Zoom, zoom; sounds of things that go in the city. Robert Burleigh; illustrated by Tad Carpenter. Simon & Schuster Books for Young Readers 2014 32 p. color illustrations (hardcover) $16.99

Grades: PreK K 1   E

1. Noise -- Fiction 2. Stories in rhyme 3. City and town life -- Fiction 4. Sound -- Fiction 5. Vehicles -- Fiction

ISBN 1442483156; 9781442483163; 9781442483156

LC 2012041015

In this children's book, by Robert Burleigh, illustrated by Tad Carpenter, "the sounds of the city come to life in this vivid picture book that's ready-made for repetition and perfect for preschool. From . . . an alarm clock in the morning to the . . . subway and . . . streaming traffic, all the way to the . . . hush of evening, the exciting and lively sounds of the city are vibrantly expressed." (Publisher's note)

"Carpenter's . . . carefree scenes, digitally rendered and saturated in primary colors, are the very picture of urban hustle and bustle, with a jaunty look of 1960s animation. Visual sound effect cues abound in dynamic display type." Pub Wkly

Burn, Doris

Andrew Henry's meadow; Doris Burn. Philomel Books 2012 48 p. ill. $14.99

Grades: K 1 2   E

1. Picture books for children 2. Runaway children -- Fiction 3. Building -- Fiction 4. Self-acceptance -- Fiction

ISBN 0399256083; 9780399256080

LC 2011017476

First published by Coward, McCann (1965)

In this chlidren's picture book reissue, "Andrew Henry has two younger brothers, who are always together, and two older sisters, who are always together. But Andrew Henry is in the middle—and he's always with himself. He doesn't mind this very much, because he's an inventor. But when Andrew Henry's family doesn't appreciate him or his inventions, he decides it's time to run away." (Publisher's note)

Burningham, John

Edwardo; the horriblest boy in the whole wide world. Alfred A. Knopf 2006 un il $16.99; lib bdg $19.99

Grades: PreK K 1 2 3   E

ISBN 978-0-375-84053-1; 0-375-84053-2; 978-0-375-94053-8 lib bdg; 0-375-94053-7 lib bdg

LC 2006-03681

Each time he does something a little bit bad, Edwardo is told that he is very bad and soon his behavior is awful, but when he accidentally does good things and is complimented, he becomes much, much nicer.

"Fans of Burningham will delight in his witty, winsome pictures, so full of animation and expression." SLJ

★ **It's** a secret. Candlewick Press 2009 un il $16.99

Grades: PreK K 1   E

1. Cats -- Fiction 2. Night -- Fiction

ISBN 978-0-7636-4275-4; 0-7636-4275-4

Boston Globe-Horn Book Honor: Picture Book (2010)

"Marie Elaine wonders what her cat, Malcolm, does at night that causes him to sleep all day. When she goes down to the kitchen late one night and finds him all dressed up to go out, she asks to come along. . . . He takes her and her neighbor Norman to a secret cat party on the rooftops, where they dance, feast, and meet the queen of the cats. Burningham's signature sketchy mixed-media illustrations are a good fit for the dreamlike story, as is the off-kilter logic of the text." SLJ

John Patrick Norman McHennessy; the boy who was always late. Alfred A. Knopf 2008 un il $16.99

Grades: PreK K 1 2   E

1. School stories 2. Teachers -- Fiction 3. Truthfulness and falsehood -- Fiction

ISBN 978-0-375-85220-6; 0-375-85220-4

First published 1987 by Crown Publishers

A teacher regrets his decison to disbelieve a student's outlandish excuses for being tardy.

"Burningham uses mixed media here to create boldly-colored illustrations which do a marvelous job of reinforcing the text. The storyline is a simple one, but it is filled with irony." SLJ

Mr. Gumpy's motor car. Crowell 1976 un il lib bdg $18.89

Grades: PreK K 1 2   E

1. Animals -- Fiction 2. Automobiles -- Fiction

ISBN 0-690-00799-X

LC 75-4582

First published 1973 in the United Kingdom

"The strength here is in the rural simplicity and in the colorful illustrations of amiable animals, the countryside in sunshine and under lowering clouds. Those things and the bold type which carries words and phrases for the reader to chew on and roll around on the tongue." N Y Times Book Rev

Another available title in the author's series about Mr. Grumpy

★ **Mr.** Gumpy's outing. Holt & Co. 1971 un il $17.95; pa $7.99; bd bk $6.95

Grades: PreK K 1 2   E

1. Animals -- Fiction

ISBN 0-8050-0708-3; 0-8050-1315-6 pa; 0-8050-6629-2 bd bk

First published 1970 in the United Kingdom

"Mr. Gumpy is about to go off for a boat ride and is asked by two children, a rabbit, a cat, a dog, and other animals if they may come. To each Mr. Gumpy says yes, if—if the children don't squabble, if the rabbit won't hop, if the cat won't chase the rabbit or the dog tease the cat, and so on. Of course each does exactly what Mr. Gumpy forbade, the boat tips over, and they all slog home for tea in friendly fashion." Sutherland. The Best in Child Books

Another title about Mr. Gumpy is:

Mr. Gumpy's motor car (1976)

★ **Picnic**; John Burningham. First U.S. Edition Candlewick Press 2014 32 p. color illustrations (reinforced) $16.99

Grades: PreK K   E

1. Animals -- Fiction 2. Picnics -- Fiction 3. Friendship

-- Fiction

ISBN 9780763669454; 0763669458

LC 2013944024

First U.S. edition

"One day, Boy and Girl head down the hill with a picnic basket and meet a fancily dressed Sheep, Pig, and Duck. They all set off to find the perfect place to sit outside--until they see Bull coming! A short-lived chase segues into a gentle interactive text as the friends wend their way from an idyllic outdoor world to a welcoming house on a hill. (Can you find Pig's ball? Shall we find your bed?)" (Publisher's note)

"Picnic has an interactive quality that encourages readers to find objects easily hidden in the pictures. Each painting is done in bold and bright colors that catch viewers' attention. Reminiscent of a simpler day, this book is a breath of fresh air--a time out of a busy schedule to enjoy the beauty of a picture book with a young child." SLJ

★ **There's** going to be a baby; [illustrated by] Helen Oxenbury. Candlewick Press 2010 un il $16.99

Grades: PreK K 1   E

1. Infants -- Fiction 2. Siblings -- Fiction 3. Imagination -- Fiction

ISBN 978-0-7636-4907-4; 0-7636-4907-4

LC 2009-51509

A young boy imagines what life will be like when his new sibling arrives.

"The handsome, clear-lined images may seem retro at first, but the crispness acts as a containing presence for displacement fears and a source of narrative momentum—all the while allowing Oxenbury to exercise the full power of her visual image." Publ Wkly

The **Way** to the zoo; John Burningham. Candlewick Press 2014 40 p. color illustrations $15.99

Grades: PreK K   E

1. Zoos -- Fiction 2. Humorous fiction 3. Animals -- Fiction 4. Imagination -- Fiction

ISBN 076367317X; 9780763673178

LC 2013952847

This children's book, by John Burningham, asks "[w]hat if you noticed a door in your bedroom that wasn't there before? And what if it led to a passage to . . . the zoo? You might want to take just one little bear back to your room with you, or maybe just all the smaller animals. But how could you resist the penguins and the tigers and the birds?" (Publisher's note)

"Sylvie discovers a door to the zoo in her bedroom and begins bringing animals home, but--being an orderly child--just a few at a time. When she forgets to close the door, a crowd of creatures troops in to watch television. Sylvie's arrangements have both the childlike logic and the solid reality of the best fantasy. Masterfully limned drawings feature harmonious hues." Horn Book

Burton, Virginia Lee

Katy and the big snow; story and pictures by Virginia Lee Burton. Houghton Mifflin 1943 32p il $16; pa $6.95

Grades: PreK K 1   E

1. Snow -- Fiction 2. Tractors -- Fiction

ISBN 0-395-18155-0; 0-395-18562-9 pa

"Katy was a beautiful red crawler tractor. In summer she wore a bulldozer to push dirt with. In winter she wore a snowplow. She was big and strong and the harder the job the better she liked it. When the Big Snow covered the city of Geoppolis like a thick blanket, Katy cleared the city from North to South and East to West." Ont Libr Rev

★ The **little** house; story and pictures by Virginia Lee Burton. Houghton Mifflin 1942 40p il $14.95; pa $5.95
Grades: PreK K 1   E
    1. Houses -- Fiction 2. City and town life -- Fiction
    ISBN 0-395-18156-9; 0-395-25938-X pa
    Awarded the Caldecott Medal, 1943
"The little house was very happy as she sat on the quiet hillside watching the changing seasons. As the years passed, however, tall buildings grew up around her, and the noise of city traffic disturbed her. She became sad and lonely until one day someone who understood her need for twinkling stars overhead and dancing apple blossoms moved her back to just the right little hill." Child Books Too Good to Miss

★ **Mike** Mulligan and his steam shovel; story and pictures by Virginia Lee Burton. Houghton Mifflin 1939 un il $16; pa $6.95
Grades: PreK K 1   E
    1. Steam-shovels -- Fiction
    ISBN 0-395-16961-5; 0-395-25939-8 pa
"One of the most convincing personifications of a machine ever written. Lively pictures, dramatic action, and a satisfying conclusion." Adventuring with Books. 2d edition

Butler, Dori Hillestad
    My grandpa had a stroke; written by Dori Hillestad Butler; illustrated by Nicole Wong. Magination Press 2007 31p il $14.95; pa $8.95
Grades: K 1 2   E
    1. Stroke -- Fiction 2. Fishing -- Fiction 3. Grandfathers -- Fiction
    ISBN 978-1-59147-806-5; 1-59147-806-5; 978-1-59147-807-2 pa; 1-59147-807-3 pa
                                                    LC 2006034528
"Ryan loves spending Saturdays fishing with his grandfather. But when Grandpa suffers a stroke, everything changes. . . . The book, illustrated in soft-edged watercolors, ends on a hopeful note. . . . With quiet prose, this covers most of the emotional and practical hurdles faced by both patient and child." Booklist

Butler, John
    Bedtime in the jungle; [written and illustrated by John Butler] Peachtree 2009 un il $16.95
Grades: PreK K   E
    1. Counting 2. Stories in rhyme 3. Animals -- Fiction 4. Bedtime -- Fiction
    ISBN 978-1-56145-486-0; 1-56145-486-9
                                                    LC 2008040592
As dusk falls in the jungle, animal babies and their parents prepare for bedtime
"What distinguishes this title is its stunning illustrations. . . . The animals are depicted in their natural settings in soothing shades that are sure to bring about the calm that encourages sleep. A lovely addition." SLJ

Butler, M. Christina
    The **smiley** snowman; illustrations by Tina Macnaughton. Good Books 2010 un il $16.99

Grades: PreK K   E
    1. Snow -- Fiction 2. Bears -- Fiction 3. Foxes -- Fiction 4. Rabbits -- Fiction
    ISBN 978-1-56148-696-0; 1-56148-696-5
                                                    LC 2010004916
A bear, a fox, and a rabbit build a snowman, but their efforts to keep it happy and warm almost bring about its demise.
"Silvery blue-green glitter makes the snowman appear to twinkle. And as the lovable animal friends play in the snowy woods, they make winter seem cozy and fun. This book would be a pleasant read-aloud for a winter-themed storytime." SLJ

Button, Lana
    Willow's whispers; illustrated by Tania Howells. Kids Can Press 2010 il $16.95
Grades: PreK K 1   E
    1. Voice -- Fiction
    ISBN 978-1-55453-280-3; 1-55453-280-9

Buxton, Jane
    The **littlest** llama; by Jane Buxton; illustrated by Jenny Cooper. Sterling 2008 un il $9.95
Grades: K 1 2   E
    1. Stories in rhyme 2. Play -- Fiction 3. Andes -- Fiction 4. Llamas -- Fiction
    ISBN 978-1-4027-5277-3; 1-4027-5277-6
                                                    LC 2007036396
High in the Andes Mountains, the littlest llama wants to play but his mother, sisters, gran, and aunt are busy, and so he leaves the herd to seek a playmate and finds adventure, instead.
"The descriptive rhyming text will make a lively read-aloud, while the beautiful, intricately detailed color illustrations extend each scenario." Booklist

Buzzeo, Toni
    Adventure Annie goes to work; illustrated by Amy Wummer. Dial 2009 un il lib bdg $16.99
Grades: PreK K 1   E
    1. Superheroes -- Fiction 2. Lost and found possessions -- Fiction
    ISBN 978-0-8037-3233-9; 0-8037-3233-3
When she goes to work with her mother on a Saturday, Adventure Annie uses her own special methods to help find a missing report.
"The bright, full-color pencil and watercolor pictures are set against ample white space and show the warm relationship between mother and daughter. This is an office adventure that children will want to experience and a heroine they'll love meeting." SLJ
    Another title about Adventure Annie is:
    Adventure Annie goes to kindergarten (2010)

    Inside the books; readers and libraries around the world. Toni Buzzeo; illustrations by Jude Daly. Upstart Books 2012 32 p. col. ill. (hardcover) $17.95
Grades: K 1 2   E
    1. Libraries 2. Stories in rhyme 3. Libraries -- Fiction 4. Bookmobiles -- Fiction 5. Books and reading -- Fiction
    ISBN 1602130582; 9781602130586
                                                    LC 2011287827

This children's book by Toni Buzzeo and illustrated by Jude Daly presents a "gentle homage to books and libraries. . . . [Buzzeo] reminds us of the extraordinary possibilities that lie inside every book and introduces us to many unique places these treasures can be found." (Publisher's note)

My Bibi always remembers; by Toni Buzzeo; illustrated by Mike Wohnoutka. Disney-Hyperion 2014 32 p. color illustrations $16.99
Grades: PreK K 1   E
  1. Elephants -- Fiction 2. Animals -- Infancy -- Fiction
ISBN 1423183851; 9781423183853
                    LC 2013007146
"Little Tembo, a baby elephant, is thirsty and her herd cannot find any water. But Bibi, the matriarch, 'remembers the way to wet.' As Bibi leads them across the parched savannah, Tembo happily follows, every now and then getting distracted by her own memories of games she loves to play." (Publisher's note)
"Wohnoutka's lovely illustrations, in tans, purples and grays, convey the vastness of the setting, along with accurate depictions of the elephants and the other watchful animals. A gentle, loving picture of interaction among generations." Kirkus

★ **One** cool friend; pictures by David Small. Dial Books for Young Readers 2012 32 p. (reinforced) $16.99
Grades: K 1 2   E
  1. Penguins -- Fiction 2. Etiquette -- Fiction 3. Father-son relationship -- Fiction
ISBN 0803734131; 9780803734135
                    LC 2011021637
Caldecott Honor Book (2013)
In this book, "[a]fter Elliott convinces his father to allow him to bring home a penguin (Dad thinks he means a toy) from the aquarium, he sets Magellan (named after the explorer who discovered the species) up in style, creating an ice rink in his bedroom using a wading pool, the garden hose, and the lowest air-conditioning setting. Elliott reads up on his new pet, . . . feeds him anchovy pizza, and lets him hang out in the freezer and the bathtub." (Bulletin of the Center for Children's Books)

Penelope Popper, book doctor; illustrations by Jana Christy. Upstart Books 2011 un il $17.95
Grades: 1 2 3   E
  1. Libraries -- Fiction 2. Books -- Conservation and restoration -- Fiction
ISBN 978-1-60213-054-8; 1-60213-054-X
                    LC 2011283516
In all corners of the library, there are books that need care and Penelope immediately dedicates herself to learning how to mend them.
"The upbeat narrative is . . . enlivened by cheerful illustrations depicting Penelope, an earnest girl with red hair and freckles, in her bright and pleasant classroom and school library. With its soft edges and palette of springtime colors, each painting reflects the positive tone of the story." SLJ

Byars, Betsy Cromer
Boo's surprise; [by] Betsy Byars; illustrated by Erik Brooks. Henry Holt and Co. 2009 45p il $15.99
Grades: K 1 2   E
  1. Siblings -- Fiction 2. Dinosaurs -- Fiction 3.

Imagination -- Fiction
ISBN 978-0-8050-8817-5; 0-8050-8817-2
                    LC 2008048849
Sequel to: Boo's dinosaur (2006)
Boo finds an egg that hatches into a new dinosaur.
"Lively black-and-white drawings extend the fun, with a climactic double-page illustration at the end of each chapter." Booklist

★ The **Golly** sisters go West; by Betsy Byars; pictures by Sue Truesdell. Harper & Row 1986 64p il (I can read book) lib bdg $16.89; pa $3.99
Grades: K 1 2   E
  1. West (U.S.) -- Fiction 2. Entertainers -- Fiction 3. Frontier and pioneer life -- Fiction
ISBN 0-06-020884-8 lib bdg; 0-06-444132-6 pa
                    LC 84-48474
May-May and Rose, the singing, dancing Golly sisters, travel west by covered wagon, entertaining people along the way
"The dialogue and antics are convincingly like those of rivalrous young siblings anywhere on the block. The story lines are cleverer than much easy-to-read fare, and the old-West setting adds flair. The accompanying watercolors, too, add a generous dollop of humor." Bull Cent Child Books
Other titles about the Golly sisters are:
The Golly sisters ride again (1994)
Hooray for the Golly sisters! (1990)

Bynum, Eboni
Jamari's drum; [by] Eboni Bynum and Roland Jackson; pictures on glazed tiles by Baba Wagué Diakité. Groundwood Books 2004 un il $16.95
Grades: K 1 2 3   E
  1. Drums -- Fiction 2. Africa -- Fiction 3. Volcanoes -- Fiction
ISBN 0-88899-531-8
When Jamari forgets to heed Baba Mdogo's warning to play the drum in the village every day, he narrowly averts disaster from a volcano.
"The beautifully executed, folk-style artwork swirls with bold lines and bright patterns, incorporating backgrounds that blend earth tones with the blues and purples of the sky. . . . This book makes an excellent read-aloud." SLJ

Bynum, Janie
Kiki's blankie. Sterling Pub. 2009 un il $14.95
Grades: PreK   E
  1. Monkeys -- Fiction 2. Blankets -- Fiction 3. Lost and found possessions -- Fiction
ISBN 978-1-4027-5910-9; 1-4027-5910-X
                    LC 2008-26837
Kiki the monkey has many daring adventures with her polka-dot 'blankie,' but when it sails away without her and lands above a sleeping crocodile, she may not be brave enough to come to the rescue.
"Brightly colored, uncluttered illustrations are set on large areas of white space, making the objects and action easy for young children to find and follow. Preschoolers will relate to Kiki, her blankie attachment, and to her energy and creative play." SLJ

Byrne, John

Donald & Benoit; written and illustrated by John Patrick Byrne. Rizzoli 2011 un il $17.95

Grades: 2 3 4 5　　　　　　　　　　　　　　E

1. Cats -- Fiction 2. Drums -- Fiction

ISBN 978-0-7893-2084-1; 0-7893-2084-3

"Benoît, the son of a sailor, and Donald, his new kitten, live in an idyllic fishing village. . . . When Benoît's father, Jean-Kiki, disappears at sea and they're left to support themselves, Donald's love of drumming and the timely help of a library book . . . wins him resounding professional triumph—which Jean-Kiki reappears in time to enjoy. With a nod to early cubism, Byrne paints bulky, curvy figures whose swoops and angles have the rhythmic energy of Donald's drums; their impact is heightened by the book's large trim size. Dreamy, melancholy hand-lettering and graceful design add even more charm." Publ Wkly

Cabral, Olga

The **seven** sneezes; illustrated by Bruce Ingman. Golden Books 2009 unp il

Grades: PreK K 1 2　　　　　　　　　　　　E

1. Animals -- Fiction 2. Sneezing -- Fiction

ISBN 9780375835940; 9780375935947 lib bdg

A newly illustrated edition of the title first published 1948

What happens when the local rag man sneezes? The kitten's ears end up on the bunny. The bunny's ears end up on the kitten. The dog meows, the cat barks. But with a little concentration—and a lot of pepper—the rag man tries to sneeze everything right

"At the conclusion of this sweet tale, one feels fully satisfied, as a topsy-turvy situation is resolved and order is regained. First published in 1948, this version preserves the original charm of Cabral's text and introduces Ingman's fresh illustrations, which combine splashes of bright color with simple line drawings." SLJ

Cabrera, Jane

Here we go round the mulberry bush. Holiday House 2010 un il $16.95

Grades: PreK　　　　　　　　　　　　　　E

1. Day -- Fiction 2. Dogs -- Fiction

ISBN 978-0-8234-2288-3; 0-8234-2288-7

LC 2009048137

"This old favorite gets a sprightly new workout in Cabrera's adorable offering. The duo going around the mulberry bush 'on a cold and frosty morning' is a small spotted puppy and an even younger sibling. Lots of verses are added to the familiar refrain. . . . A fun read-aloud, or more aptly put, read-along, because children will want to pick up on the chant." Booklist

★ **If** you're happy and you know it. Holiday House 2005 un il hardcover o.p. board book $7.95

Grades: PreK K　　　　　　　　　　　　　E

1. Songs 2. Animals -- Fiction

ISBN 0-8234-1881-2; 978-0-8234-2227-2 board book

LC 2004-47264

An elephant, a monkey, and a giraffe join other animals to sing different verses of this popular song that encourages everyone to express their happiness through voice and movement.

"Cheerful painterly pictures in a kaleidoscope of colors enhance the jovial mood of the song." SLJ

★ **Mommy,** carry me please! Holiday House 2006 un il $16.95

Grades: PreK K　　　　　　　　　　　　　E

1. Animals -- Fiction 2. Mother-child relationship -- Fiction

ISBN 0-8234-1935-5

LC 2004048862

"On each spread of this warm lapsit book, a baby animal asks its mother to carry me please. Each mother accommodates by transporting the youngster in that animals special way: lemur under its belly, kangaroo in a pouch, tiger in its mouth, crocodile in teeth, penguin on its feet, and so on until the cozy ending when a human child is carried in the mothers arms. The art features Cabrera's trademark breezy, blocky, and bold animals in bright and energetic colors that focus childrens eye and attention." SLJ

One, two, buckle my shoe. Holiday House 2009 un il $16.95

Grades: PreK　　　　　　　　　　　　　　E

1. Counting 2. Stories in rhyme 3. Animals -- Fiction 4. Parties -- Fiction 5. Birthdays -- Fiction

ISBN 978-0-8234-2230-2; 0-8234-2230-5

LC 2008055303

Four chicks have fun hiding while Rabbit and Mommy Hen prepare a party for the little pigs' birthday.

Cabrera's "version of this familiar schoolyard song takes readers all the way up through the number 20. . . . The lively images, thick with paint strokes, create a cheerful atmosphere. Additionally, the opening challenge to find four small chicks on each spread will keep readers entertained as they read along." Publ Wkly

Twinkle, twinkle, little star; by Jane Cabrera. 1st American ed. Holiday House 2012 1 v. (unpaged) ill. (hardcover) $16.95

Grades: PreK K 1　　　　　　　　　　　　E

ISBN 9780823425198

LC 2011044969

Cadena, Beth

Supersister; illustrated by Frank W. Dormer. Clarion Books 2009 un il $16

Grades: K 1 2　　　　　　　　　　　　　　E

1. Pregnancy -- Fiction 2. Mother-daughter relationship -- Fiction

ISBN 978-0-547-01006-9; 0-547-01006-0

LC 2008-11618

A young girl does all kinds of things around the house to help her pregnant mother, proud that when the new baby comes she is going to be 'a super sister.'

"Lively yet thoughtful text and bright, funny illustrations combine beautifully to settle into a pleasing conclusion: a supersister dream that features a superbrother. Highly recommended for children with siblings on the way." Kirkus

Cadow, Kenneth M.

Alfie runs away; pictures by Lauren Castillo. Frances Foster Books 2010 un il $16.99

Grades: PreK K　　　　　　　　　　　　　E

1. Runaway children -- Fiction 2. Mother-son

relationship -- Fiction

ISBN 978-0-374-30202-3; 0-374-30202-2

LC 2008024146

Told he must give up his favorite, now too-small, shoes, Alfie leaves home, but not before his mother persuades him to take all of the things he might need while he is gone

"Castillo's . . . spreads, comfortingly rendered in muted colors, are just right for Cadow's even-tempered narration." Publ Wkly

Calhoun, Mary

★ **Cross**-country cat; illustrated by Erick Ingraham. Morrow 1979 un il hardcover o.p. pa $6.99

Grades: K 1 2 3　　　　　　　　　　　　　　E

1. Cats -- Fiction

ISBN 0-688-22186-6; 0-698-06519-8 pa

LC 78-31718

When he becomes lost in the mountains, Henry, a cat with the unusual ability of walking on two legs finds his way home on cross-country skis

"Only the careful blending of skills by a talented author and illustrator could turn such a farfetched plot into a warm, rich, and rewarding story. The realistic illustrations seem to be enveloped in a glowing light and invite the reader to step right into the story." Child Book Rev Serv

Other titles about Henry the cat are:

Blue-ribbon Henry (1999)

Henry the Christmas cat (2004)

Henry the sailor cat (1994)

High-wire Henry (1991)

Hot-air Henry (1981)

Cali, Davide

The **bear** with the sword; illustrated by Gianluca Foli. Wilkins Farago 2010 un il $15.99

Grades: K 1 2 3　　　　　　　　　　　　　　E

1. Bears -- Fiction 2. Animals -- Fiction

ISBN 978-0-9806-0704-8; 0-9806-0704-3

A bear with a powerful sword goes out into the forest to chop down all of the trees and build on his impregnable home fort. After it is washed away by a flood, he sets out on a journey to find and punish the creature responsible. After accusing an array of unusual creatures, he finally arrives at the truth: the flood was caused by someone with a sword who chopped down all the trees.

"This title features inventive, whimsical mixed-media illustrations that combine black-lined and colored figures, as well as spacious, white backgrounds. An intriguing offering that will open up discussion." Booklist

The **enemy**; a book about peace. written by Davide Cali and illustrated by Serge Bloch. Schwartz & Wade Books 2009 un il $15.99; lib bdg $18.99

Grades: 1 2 3 4　　　　　　　　　　　　　　E

1. War stories 2. Soldiers -- Fiction

ISBN 978-0-375-84500-0; 0-375-84500-3; 978-0-375-93752-1 lib bdg; 0-375-93752-8 lib bdg

LC 2007047974

After watching an enemy for a very long time during an endless war, a soldier finally creeps out into the night to the other man's hole and is surprised by what he finds there.

"Bloch pairs pen-and-ink cartoons with collage elements like family photos, and gives readers a bird's-eye view from which to observe the men's similarities. The point will not be lost on readers." Publ Wkly

I love chocolate; illustrated by Evelyn Daviddi. Tundra Books 2009 un il $12.95

Grades: PreK K　　　　　　　　　　　　　E

1. Chocolate -- Fiction

ISBN 0-88776-912-8; 978-0-88776-912-2

Original Italian edition 2001

"'Why do I love chocolate?' a boy asks as he is about to take a colossal bite of a candy bar. He then lists all the reasons: it crunches and melts, and it can make bad times better. . . . The text captures the essence of chocolate—its varying incarnations and textures—and it will leave everyone salivating. In addition to being a great candidate for programs, the book has potential as an easy reader as well. The art has a European flair." SLJ

Calmenson, Stephanie

Jazzmatazz! by Stephanie Calmenson; illustrated by Bruce Degen. HarperCollinsPublishers 2008 un il $16.99; lib bdg $17.89

Grades: PreK K 1　　　　　　　　　　　　E

1. Stories in rhyme 2. Mice -- Fiction 3. Animals -- Fiction 4. Musicians -- Fiction 5. Jazz music -- Fiction

ISBN 978-0-06-077289-5; 0-06-077289-1; 978-0-06-077290-1 lib bdg; 0-06-077290-5 lib bdg

LC 2007009133

When a mouse scurries into a house and starts to play jazz music, other animals join in, one by one, each using his or her own particular talent

"This cheerful book . . . is full of color and sound. . . . Degen fills the white space . . . with colorful zigzags, curlicues, stars, and other patterns to show how the music is connecting and joining all of the characters together." SLJ

Late for school! by Stephanie Calmenson; illustrated by Sachiko Yoshikawa. Carolrhoda Books 2008 un il lib bdg $16.95

Grades: K 1 2　　　　　　　　　　　　　　E

1. School stories 2. Stories in rhyme 3. Teachers -- Fiction 4. Transportation -- Fiction

ISBN 978-1-57505-935-8 lib bdg; 1-57505-935-5 lib bdg

LC 2007034776

When Mr. Bungles the teacher oversleeps, he goes to great lengths, trying every form of transportation he can find to get to school on time.

"Cartoon characters in scenes of collage and mixed media follow Mr. Bungles's efforts to watch the clock and avoid breaking his own rule, 'Never, ever, ever be late for school!' A colorful selection for all libraries." SLJ

Calvert, Pam

Multiplying menace; the revenge of Rumpelstiltskin. illustrated by Wayne Geehan. Charlesbridge Pub. 2006 32p il $16.95; pa $6.95

Grades: 3 4 5 6　　　　　　　　　　　　　E

1. Fairy tales 2. Multiplication -- Fiction

ISBN 1-57091-889-9; 1-57091-890-2 pa

LC 2004-23072

Ten years after being tricked, Rumpelstiltskin returns to the royal family to wreak vengeance using multiplication.

Includes nonfiction math notes about multiplying by whole numbers and by fractions.

"Calvert has created an interesting vehicle for teaching children about the differences between multiplying with whole numbers and multiplying with fractions. . . . Calvert has written an enjoyable teaching tool, and Geehan's luminous and expressive paintings are perfect for this fairy-tale world." SLJ

Princess Peepers; illustrated by Tuesday Mourning. Marshall Cavendish 2008 un il $16.99

Grades: K 1 2 3   E

1. Eyeglasses -- Fiction 2. Princesses -- Fiction
ISBN 978-0-7614-5437-3; 0-7614-5437-3

           LC 2007022134

When the other princesses make fun of her for wearing glasses, Princess Peepers vows to go without, but after several mishaps—one of which is especially coincidental—she admits that she really does need them if she wants to see.

"Mourning's graphite and digital/collage illustrations combine figures in traditional costumes from different eras with lush backgrounds. The palette of pinks keeps the emphasis on sweet, even when some of the characters are not. Princess Peepers will circulate well and bring laughs during storytimes." SLJ

Another title about Princess Peepers is:
Princess Peepers picks a pet (2011)

Campbell, Bebe Moore

Stompin' at the Savoy; [by] Bebe Moore Campbell; illustrated by Richard Yarde. Philomel Books 2006 un il $16.99

Grades: K 1 2 3   E

1. Dance -- Fiction 2. Jazz music -- Fiction 3. African Americans -- Fiction 4. Harlem (New York, N.Y.) -- Fiction
ISBN 0-399-24197-3

           LC 2005025044

On the night of her jazz dance recital Mindy feels too nervous to go, until a magical drum whisks her away to the Savoy Ballroom in Harlem where she finds her "happy feet"

"Rhythmic gouache and pastel paintings depicting swinging dancers and jiving musicians perfectly complement the lyrical energy and magical realism of the cadenced prose." SLJ

Campbell, K. G.

Lester's dreadful sweaters; Keith Campbell. Kids Can Press 2012 32 p. $16.95

Grades: PreK K 1 2   E

1. Cousins -- Fiction 2. Picture books for children 3. Sweaters -- Fiction
ISBN 1554537703; 9781554537709

In this book, "it's Cousin Clara who knits the dramatically awful, humiliating sweaters of the title. Lester's parents compel him to wear them. . . . One is a 'less-than-pleasant yellow' hoodie with a trailing sleeve and purple pom-poms . . . another has knitted feathers and striped feet. . . . When a group of performing clowns fall in love with the sweaters . . . , Lester is able to offload his entire collection--and Cousin Clara." (Publishers Weekly)

The **Mermaid** and the Shoe; by K G Campbell. Kids Can Pr 2014 32 p. $16.95

Grades: PreK K 1 2   E

1. Mermaids and mermen -- Fiction 2. Mermaids -- Fiction 3. Curiosity -- Fiction
ISBN 1554537711; 9781554537716

In this book, by K G Campbell, "each of King Neptune's 50 mermaid daughters boasts a special talent, except for little Minnow, who seems to be good only at asking questions. When she finds a strange object, Minnow follows her questions to a wondrous place and finds answers, including the answer to the most important question of all: Who am I?" (Publisher's note)

"When a shoe drops into the sea, little mermaid Minnow (least exceptional of King Neptune's fifty daughters) investigates. What she discovers is "an odd creature...a landmaid." Minnow tells her family, and the kingdom's newfound storyteller-adventurer is born. Campbell's tale shows that a little imagination and a lot of inquisitiveness go a long way. The watercolor and pencil-crayon illustrations have a sense of motion and playfulness." Horn Book

Campbell, Nicola I.

Shi-shi-etko; pictures by Kim La Fave. Groundwood Books 2005 un il $16.95

Grades: K 1 2 3   E

1. Canada -- Fiction 2. Native Americans -- Fiction
ISBN 0-88899-659-4

"This is a moving story set in Canada about the practice of removing Native children from their villages and sending them to residential schools to learn the English language and culture. . . . Shi-shi-etko counts down her last four days before going away. . . . The vivid, digital illustrations rely on a red palette, evoking not only the land but also the sorrow of the situation and the hope upon which the story ultimately ends." SLJ

Campbell, Rod

Dear zoo; a pop-up book. Little Simon 2005 un il $12.95

Grades: PreK K   E

1. Pop-up books 2. Animals -- Fiction
ISBN 0-689-87751-X

First published as a board book in the United Kingdom 1982; first published as a pop-up book 2004 in the United Kingdom

Each animal arriving from the zoo as a possible pet fails to suit its prospective owner, until just the right one is found.

Campbell, Scott

Hug machine; by Scott Campbell. 1st ed Atheneum Books for Young Readers 2014 40 p. color illustrations (hardcover) $16.99

Grades: PreK K 1   E

1. Machinery 2. Hugging -- Fiction
ISBN 1442459352; 9781442459359

           LC 2013019664

"Much like cats, young children can be quite persnickety about whom they embrace and when. Not so with this story's protagonist, aka the Hug Machine. This boy takes it upon himself to calm and cheer everyone, and everything (rocks, trees), he encounters with a warm hug. He takes his work quite seriously and no challenge is too tough (a porcupine) or large (a whale) for him to wrap his arms around." (School Library Journal)

"A feel-good ride, full of droll artistic asides and an abundance of caring. . . . Unadorned, hand-lettered text and deliberately muted watercolors increase the warmth of this adorable little fellow." Kirkus

Cannon, A. E.

Sophie's fish; by A.E. Cannon; illustrated by Lee White. Viking 2012 32p.

Grades: PreK K 1 2   **E**

1. Pets -- Fiction 2. Fishes -- Fiction 3. Children's stories 4. Picture books for children 5. Humorous stories 6. Worry -- Fiction

ISBN 9780670012916

     LC 2011016227

In this picture book, "[w]hen schoolmate Sophie asks Jake to care for her fish, Yo-Yo, for a weekend, he agrees, because '[h]ow hard can it be to babysit a fish?' But while waiting for Yo-Yo to arrive, Jake begins to worry. 'What kind of snacks do fish like to eat?' he frets. [Illustrator Lee] White presents a massive Strawberry Worm Cake as a possible fish snack; standing atop the highest layer, Jake offers a slice to a laughing blue fish he finds sitting upright on a wire chair. The fish is as big as Jake. Next, Jake wonders, '[w]hat if Yo-Yo wants to play a game?' Here, the portrayed fish is several times Jake's size, dressed as a pirate and riding an enormous rubber ducky." (Kirkus)

Cannon, Janell

★ **Crickwing**; written and illustrated by Janell Cannon. Harcourt 2000 un il $16; pa $7

Grades: K 1 2 3   **E**

1. Ants -- Fiction 2. Cockroaches -- Fiction

ISBN 0-15-201790-9; 9780152050610

     LC 99-50456

A lonely cockroach named Crickwing has a creative idea that saves the day for the leaf-cutter ants when their fierce forest enemies attack them

"An amusing tale lightly rooted in natural history. . . . Cannon's illustrations skillfully blur the line between fact and fancy." Publ Wkly

★ **Stellaluna**. Harcourt Brace Jovanovich 1993 un il $17

Grades: K 1 2 3   **E**

1. Bats -- Fiction

ISBN 0-15-280217-7

     LC 92-16439

After she falls headfirst into a bird's nest, a baby bat is raised like a bird until she is reunited with her mother

"Cannon's delightful story is full of gentle humor. . . . [She] provides good information about bats in the story, amplifying it in two pages of notes at the end of the book. Her full-page colored-pencil-and-acrylic paintings fairly glow." Booklist

Cantrell, Charlie

A **friend** for Einstein; the smallest stallion. by Charlie Cantrell and Rachel Wagner. Disney/Hyperion 2011 un il $16.99

Grades: PreK K 1 2   **E**

1. Dogs -- Fiction 2. Size -- Fiction 3. Horses -- Fiction

ISBN 978-1-4231-4563-9; 1-4231-4563-1

"With hooves the size of quarters, Einstein, a mini miniature horse, is the smallest horse ever born. . . . Einstein is not tall enough to keep up with other equines, even his fellow miniature horses. The fascinating facts lead into a fictional story line as the presumably lonely horse searches for a playmate. . . . Einsten meets a dog named Lilly . . . who is just his size. Although Lilly and Einstein are actual friends, children will care less about the reality of their meeting and more about this unusual horse and the color photographs. . . . No doubt little Einstein will appeal to big hearts everywhere." Booklist

Caple, Kathy

Duck & Company. Holiday House 2007 32p il $14.95; pa $4.95

Grades: K 1 2   **E**

1. Rats -- Fiction 2. Ducks -- Fiction 3. Booksellers and bookselling -- Fiction

ISBN 978-0-8234-1993-7; 0-8234-1993-2; 978-0-8234-2125-1 pa; 0-8234-2125-2 pa

     LC 2006-12118

Rat and Duck run a bookshop and work to find the right book for each of their customers.

"There are tons of visual clues embedded in the ink and goauche illustrations to help burgeoning readers. . . .Young readers will appreciate both the humor and the diversity of the five included tales." Bull Cent Child Books

Another title about Duck and Rat is:

Duck & Company Christmas (2011)

The **friendship** tree. Holiday House 2000 48p il (Holiday House reader) lib bdg $15.95

Grades: K 1 2   **E**

1. Sheep -- Fiction 2. Trees -- Fiction 3. Friendship -- Fiction

ISBN 0-8234-1376-4

     LC 98-39043

This book "includes four little stories about trees. Best friends Blanche and Otis are sheep who live next door to each other and share their sorrows and joys. . . . The line-and-watercolor illustrations reflect the sweet, gentle tone of the text with the soft, pastel shades." Booklist

Capucilli, Alyssa

Biscuit; pictures by Pat Schories. HarperCollins Pubs. 1996 26p il (My first I can read book) $12.95

Grades: PreK K 1 2   **E**

1. Dogs -- Fiction

ISBN 0-06-026197-8; 0-06-026198-6 lib bdg

     LC 95-9716

"Biscuit is a little yellow puppy. And like most puppies, he would rather play than go to bed. Will Biscuit ever go to sleep? It's Biscuit's bedtime, but this lively little puppy doesn't want to go to sleep! Before he gets into bed, Biscuit plays out the familiar bedtime drama of wanting just one more thing. A perfect story for young readers who won't be able to resist reading about this adorable puppy for themselves." (Publisher's note)

★ **Biscuit's** new trick; story by Alyssa Satin Capucilli; pictures by Pat Schories. HarperCollins Pubs. 2000 24p il (My first I can read book) $12.95; lib bdg $15.89; pa $3.99

Grades: PreK K 1 2   E
1. Dogs -- Fiction
ISBN 0-06-028067-0; 0-06-028068-9 lib bdg; 0-06-444308-6 pa

LC 99-23004

"While his owner tries to teach him to fetch a ball, Biscuit the dog chews his bone or chases the cat—that is, until the ball lands in a mud puddle. . . . The simple language . . . and playful watercolor illustrations make this an appealing choice for beginning readers." Horn Book Guide

Other titles about Biscuit are:
Bathtime for Biscuit (1998)
Biscuit (1996)
Biscuit and the baby (2005)
Biscuit and the lost teddy bear (2011)
Biscuit finds a friend (1997)
Biscuit goes to school (2002)
Biscuit visits the big city (2006)
Biscuit wants to play (2001)
Biscuit wins a prize (2004)
Biscuit's big friend (2003)
Biscuit's day at the farm (2007)
Biscuit's picnic (1998)
Happy birthday, Biscuit! (1999)
Hello, Biscuit! (1998)

Pedro's burro; story by Alyssa Satin Capucilli; pictures by Pau Estrada. HarperCollinsPublishers 2007 32p il (I can read!) $15.99; lib bdg $16.89
Grades: PreK K 1   E
1. Mexico -- Fiction 2. Donkeys -- Fiction
ISBN 978-0-06-056031-7; 0-06-056031-2; 978-0-06-056032-4 lib bdg; 0-06-056032-0 lib bdg

LC 2006036323

Pedro and his papa go to the market to look for the perfect burro

"This winning story is enhanced by Estrada's colorful, inviting illustrations. . . . Featuring repetition and humor, the simple story is set in large type with ample white space." SLJ

Capucilli, Alyssa Satin

Katy Duck and the tip-top tap shoes; by Alyssa Satin Capucilli; illustrated by Henry Cole. Simon Spotlight 2013 24 p. (Ready-to-read. Level one) (hardcover) $15.99
Grades: K 1 2   E
1. Sharing -- Fiction 2. Dance -- Fiction 3. Ducks -- Fiction 4. Ballet -- Fiction 5. Tap dancing -- Fiction
ISBN 1442452455; 1442452463; 1442452471; 9781442452459; 9781442452466; 9781442452473

LC 2011052608

In this book by Alyssa Satin Capucilli "There's a new student in Mr. Tutu's dance class! When dancing diva Katy Duck meets Alice, she thinks Alice has forgotten her ballet slippers! Instead, Alice is ready to make some noise in a pair of tip-top tap shoes! Together, Katy and Alice learn that sharing can be fun—and that there is always more to learn!" (Publisher's note)

Carbone, Elisa

★ **Heroes** of the surf; by Elisa Carbone. Viking 2012 40 p.
Grades: 2 3 4   E
1. Shipwrecks -- Fiction 2. Rescue work -- Fiction 3.

Picture books for children 4. New Jersey -- History -- Fiction 5. United States. Life-Saving Service -- Fiction 6. New Jersey -- History -- 19th century -- Fiction
ISBN 0670063126; 9780670063123

LC 2011012218

The book is "based on a true story of shipwreck and rescue . . . with narration by Anthony, a venturesome lad whose penchant for playing pirates helps him through the harrowing event" aboard the steamship Pliny, which was wrecked in a storm near New Jersey in 1882. Elisa Carbone describes Anthony's rescue with his friend Pedro from the sinking ship: "I swing out into open space. Below me, waves crash and twist like angry snakes. Will the ropes hold?" Illustrator Nancy Carpenter depicts the scene with "a seagoing palette of blue, gray, brown and ochre, crosshatched in black." (Kirkus)

Carbone, Elisa Lynn

★ **Night** running; how James escaped with the help of his faithful dog; based on a true story. [by] Elisa Carbone; illustrated by E.B. Lewis. Alfred A. Knopf 2008 un il $16.99; lib bdg $19.99
Grades: 2 3 4   E
1. Dogs -- Fiction 2. Slavery -- Fiction 3. African Americans -- Fiction
ISBN 0-375-82247-X; 978-0-375-82247-6; 0-375-92247-4 lib bdg; 978-0-375-92247-3 lib bdg

LC 2003014502

A runaway slave makes a daring escape to freedom with the help of his faithful hunting dog, Zeus. Based on the true story of James Smith's journey from Virginia to Ohio in the mid-1800s.

"The watercolor paintings beautifully evoke the sun-drenched cotton fields. Deep purples and rich, dark greens capture the moonlit night. . . . A vividly realized narrative, based on a true story." SLJ

Carle, Eric

★ **10** little rubber ducks. HarperCollins 2005 un il $21.99; bd bk $11.99
Grades: PreK K 1 2   E
1. Counting 2. Toys -- Fiction
ISBN 0-06-074075-2; 0-06-074078-7 bd bk

LC 2004-1420

When a storm strikes a cargo ship, ten rubber ducks are tossed overboard and swept off in ten different directions. Based on a factual incident

"Carle's signature cut-paper collages burst with color, texture, light, and motion, delighting the eye and bringing out the text's nuances." SLJ

★ **The artist** who painted a blue horse. Philomel Books 2011 un il $17.99
Grades: PreK K 1   E
1. Artists 2. Painters 3. Color -- Fiction 4. Animals -- Fiction 5. Artists -- Fiction 6. Painting -- Fiction
ISBN 978-0-399-25713-1; 0-399-25713-6

LC 2011000662

Rather than use the same old colors, a child paints animals and objects in a variety of different hues. Includes biographical information about the German painter Franz Marc, who created unconventional animal paintings in the early 1900s.

"While Carle's creatures are constructed from his familiar, brilliantly colored painted-paper shapes, it is the strength and sinew of their forms that impresses. . . . An homage to Marc becomes testimony to Carle's gifts, too. A short afterword about Marc's life is included." Publ Wkly

★ **Do** you want to be my friend? Crowell 1971 un il $17.99; lib bdg $18.89; pa $6.99; bd bk $7.99
Grades: PreK K   E
1. Stories without words 2. Mice -- Fiction
ISBN 0-690-24276-X; 0-690-01137-7 lib bdg; 0-06-443127-4 pa; 0-694-00709-9 bd bk
"Good material for discussion and guessing games. . . . The pictures tell an amusing story and they are good to look at as well." Times Lit Suppl

Friends; written and illustrated by Eric Carle. Philomel Books 2013 32 p. $17.99
Grades: PreK K   E
1. Picture books for children 2. Friendship -- Fiction 3. Voyages and travels -- Fiction
ISBN 0399165339; 9780399165337
LC 2012048850
In this book, a "describes his devoted affection for a friend with whom he plays, dances, and shares secrets. Then she moves away, and he is all alone. He misses her terribly and vows to find her. Readers will cheer his bravery as he crosses a swift river, climbs over a steep mountain, and travels through a dewy meadow and shadowy forest to find her. Ultimately, he stumbles across a flower garden. With a bouquet in hand, he finds his friend, reunites with her and (playfully) marries her." (School Library Journal)

★ The **grouchy** ladybug. HarperCollins Pubs. 1996 un il $17.99; lib bdg $18.89; pa $7.99; bd bk $8.99
Grades: PreK K 1   E
1. Ladybugs -- Fiction
ISBN 0-06-027087-X; 0-06-027088-8 lib bdg; 0-06-443450-8 pa; 0-694-01320-X bd bk
LC 95-26581
A reissue of the title first published 1977 by Crowell
A grouchy ladybug, looking for a fight, challenges everyone she meets regardless of their size or strength
"The finger paint and collage illustrations—as bold as the feisty hero—are satisfyingly placed on pages sized to suit the successive animals that appear. . . . Tiny clocks show the time of each enjoyable encounter, with the sun rising and setting as the action proceeds." SLJ

★ A **house** for Hermit Crab. Picture Bk. Studio 1988 un il $18.99; pa $7.99; bd bk $8.99
Grades: PreK K 1   E
1. Crabs -- Fiction
ISBN 0-88708-056-1; 0-689-84894-3 pa; 0-689-87064-7 bd bk
LC 87-29261
"The bright illustrations in Carle's familiar style, which seems particularly suited to undersea scenes, and the cumulative story are splendid." Horn Book
"Hermit Crab, having outgrown his old shell, sets out to find a new one. He's a bit frightened at first, but over the course of the next year acquires not only a shell, but also an array of sea creatures to decorate, clean, and protect his new

home. The story ends with him once again outgrowing his shell." SLJ

★ **Mister** Seahorse. Philomel Books 2004 un il $17.99; bd bk $8.99
Grades: PreK K 1   E
1. Fishes -- Fiction 2. Fathers -- Fiction 3. Sea horses -- Fiction
ISBN 0-399-24269-4; 978-0-399-25490-1 bd bk
LC 2003-17125
After Mrs. Seahorse lays her eggs on Mr. Seahorse's belly, he drifts through the water, greeting other fish fathers who are taking care of their eggs
"With each encounter comes a delightful surprise: an acetate overlay camouflages the sea creatures as Mister Seahorse passes by. . . . Awash with the wonders of undersea life, this is a stunning, ingeniously conceived lesson in nature as well as a celebration of fatherly affection." Booklist

★ The **mixed**-up chameleon. Crowell 1984 un il $17.99; lib bdg $18.89; pa $6.99; bd bk $8.99
Grades: PreK K 1   E
1. Chameleons -- Fiction
ISBN 0-690-04396-1; 0-690-04397-X lib bdg; 0-06-443162-2 pa; 0-694-01147-9 bd bk
LC 83-45950
A revised and newly illustrated edition of the title first published 1975
The author "has replaced the heavy-lined, childlike, scrawled colors with crisp, appealing collages and has streamlined the text. The cutaway pages have been retained, and none of the humor has been lost. The simpler text results in a smoother flow, and children will enjoy the resulting repetition." Booklist

Papa, please get the moon for me. Simon & Schuster Books for Young Readers 1991 un il $6.99
Grades: PreK K 1   E
1. Moon -- Fiction
ISBN 0-8870-8177-0
LC 91014561
First published 1986 by Picture Book Studio
Monica's father fulfills her request for the moon by taking it down after it is small enough to carry, but it continues to change in size. Some pages fold out to display particularly large pictures.
This is "drawn in thick, brilliant brushstrokes of blues and greens and reds that dazzle the eye. . . . A splendid introduction to the monthly lunar cycle, this is also a wondrous work of art that will stand up to countless readings." Publ Wkly

★ **Slowly,** slowly, slowly, said the sloth. Philomel Bks. 2002 un il $16.99; pa $7.99
Grades: PreK K 1   E
1. Sloths -- Fiction 2. Animals -- Fiction
ISBN 0-399-23954-5; 0-14-240847-6 pa
LC 2002-16057
Challenged by the other jungle animals for its seemingly lazy ways, a sloth living in a tree explains the many advantages of his slow and peaceful existence

"Carle's art is at its best with a brightly colored selection of painted tissue-paper collage that captures 25 rain-forest denizens." SLJ

★ The **very** busy spider. Philomel Bks. 1984 un il $21.99; bd bk $11.99; oversized bd bk $15.99

Grades: PreK K 1 **E**

1. Spiders -- Fiction

ISBN 0-399-21166-7; 0-399-21592-1 pa; 0-399-22919-1 bd bk; 978-0-399-25601-1 oversized bd bk

LC 84-5907

The farm animals try to divert a busy little spider from spinning her web, but she persists and produces a thing of both beauty and usefulness

This book "has a disarming ingenuousness and a repetitive structure that will capture the response of pre-school audiences. Of special note is the book's use of raised lines for the spider, its web, and an unsuspecting fly. Both sighted and blind children will be able to follow the action with ease." Booklist

★ The **very** clumsy click beetle. Philomel Bks. 1999 un il $22.99

Grades: PreK K 1 **E**

1. Animals -- Fiction 2. Beetles -- Fiction

ISBN 0-399-23201-X

LC 97-33417

A clumsy young click beetle learns to land on its feet with encouragement from various animals and a wise old beetle. An electronic chip with a built-in battery creates clicking sounds to accompany the story

"Done in colored tissue-paper collage, the illustrations burst from the pages and are charmingly rendered. . . . A well-crafted story, joyfully illustrated." SLJ

★ The **very** hungry caterpillar. Philomel Bks. 1981 un il $21.99; bd bk $10.99

Grades: PreK K 1 **E**

1. Caterpillars -- Fiction

ISBN 0-399-20853-4; 0-399-22690-7 bd bk

First published 1970 by World Publishing Company

"This caterpillar is so hungry he eats right through the pictures on the pages of the book—and after leaving many holes emerges as a beautiful butterfly on the last page." Best Books for Child, 1972

★ The **very** lonely firefly. Philomel Bks. 1995 un il $22.99; bd bk $11.99

Grades: PreK K 1 **E**

1. Fireflies -- Fiction

ISBN 0-399-22774-1; 0-399-23427-6 bd bk

LC 94-27827

A lonely firefly goes out into the night searching for other fireflies

"The illustrations are painted cut-paper collages, designed to draw the eye to the page. This is a compelling accomplishment." SLJ

★ The **very** quiet cricket. Philomel Bks. 1990 un il $22.99; bd bk $12.99

Grades: PreK K 1 **E**

1. Crickets -- Fiction

ISBN 0-399-21885-8; 0-399-22684-7 bd bk

LC 89-78317

A very quiet cricket who wants to rub his wings together and make a sound as do so many other animals finally achieves his wish

"The text is skillfully shaped; the illustrations convey energy and immediacy; and, in a surprise ending, a microchip inserted in the last page replicates the cricket's chirp." Horn Book Guide

What's your favorite animal? Eric Carle and friends, Nick Bruel, Lucy Cousins, Susan Jeffers, Steven Kellogg, Jon Klassen, Tom Lichtenheld, Peter McCarty, Chris Raschka, Peter Sís, Lane Smith, Erin Stead, Rosemary Wells, Mo Willems. Henry Holt and Company 2014 40 p. (hardback) $17.99

Grades: PreK K 1 2 **E**

1. Animals in art 2. Animals -- Pictorial works

ISBN 0805096418; 9780805096415

LC 2013018841

This book, by Eric Carle, explains that "everybody has a favorite animal. Some like little white dogs or big black cats or hoppy brown bunnies best. Others prefer squishy snails or tall giraffes or sleek black panthers. With . . . illustrations and . . . personal stories, 14 children's book artists share their favorite animals and why they love them." (Publisher's note)

"Eric Carle and his friends bring a consideration of What's Your Favorite Animal? to the pages of this fine-looking book. Each of fourteen illustrators gets a double-page spread to devote to his or her favorite. Grown-up picture book enthusiasts will appreciate this souvenir of the artists in their singular styles; children will enjoy perusing the spaciously designed pages to decide their own favorites." (Horn Book)

What is your favorite animal?

★ **Where** are you going? To see my friend! [by] Eric Carle & Kazuo Iwamura. Orchard Bks. 2003 un il $19.95

Grades: PreK K 1 **E**

1. Animals -- Fiction 2. Friendship -- Fiction 3. Bilingual books -- English-Japanese

ISBN 0-439-41659-0

LC 2002-70396

Original Japanese edition, 2001

This "bilingual picture book is told in dialogue, with rebuslike symbols used to identify speakers. It details an energetic romp with a dog, cat, rooster, goat, rabbit, and a child, all of whom become friends. Carle's familiar collage technique is employed in the book's first half, while Iwamura's gentle watercolor illustrations, combined with the Japanese text, make up the second half. . . . An irresistible, spirited ode to friendship." SLJ

Carling, Amelia Lau

★ **Mama** & Papa have a store; story and pictures by Amelia Lau Carling. Dial Bks. for Young Readers 1998 un il $16.99

Grades: K 1 2 3 **E**

1. Chinese -- Fiction 2. Guatemala -- Fiction 3. Retail trade -- Fiction

ISBN 0-8037-2044-0

LC 97-10217

A little girl describes what a day is like in her parents' Chinese store in Guatemala City

"Carling's lovingly detailed watercolors in candy-box colors illustrate [the author's] memories. . . . A pleasant family story that should enrich library collections, especially those looking for multicultural themes." SLJ

Carlson, Nancy L.

★ **Get** up and go! by Nancy Carlson. Viking 2006 un il $15.99

Grades: PreK K   E
1. Exercise 2. Pigs -- Fiction 3. Rabbits -- Fiction

ISBN 0-670-05981-1

LC 2005003864

Text and illustrations encourage readers, regardless of shape or size, to turn off the television and play games, walk, dance, and engage in sports and other forms of exercise.

"Bright and sassy, the clearly delineated drawings with vivid washes provide a light, sometimes-comical tone that makes the lessons easier to take. With a short, simple text and a cheerful look, this will suit preschool and kindergarten teachers looking for an accessible book on exercise." Booklist

Henry and the Valentine surprise; [by] Nancy Carlson. Viking 2008 un il $15.99

Grades: PreK K 1 2   E
1. School stories 2. Mice -- Fiction 3. Animals -- Fiction 4. Teachers -- Fiction 5. Valentine's Day -- Fiction

ISBN 978-0-670-06267-6; 0-670-06267-7

LC 2008001283

When Henry the mouse and his first-grade classmates notice a heart-shaped box on their teacher's desk the day before Valentine's Day, they try to find out if he has a girlfriend.

"Told with mounting suspense, this mystery has a delightful and satisfying conclusion. Brightly colored comic illustrations portray the excitement at school as the special day approaches." SLJ

Other titles about Henry are:
Henry's show and tell (2004)
Henry's 100 days of kindergarten (2005)
Henry's amazing imagination! (2008)
Start saving, Henry! (2009)
Henry and the bully (2010)

I like me! [by] Nancy Carlson. Viking Kestrel 1988 un il lib bdg $16.99; pa $6.99

Grades: PreK K 1   E
1. Pigs -- Fiction

ISBN 0-670-82062-8 lib bdg; 0-14-050819-8 pa

LC 87-32616

By admiring her finer points and showing that she can take care of herself and have fun even when there's no one else around, a charming pig proves the best friend you can have is yourself

This book is "visually interesting, with sturdy animals drawn in a deliberately artless style. Simple shapes, strong lines, and clear colors, with lots of pattern mixing, show what is not described in the minimal text. The text is hand-lettered." SLJ

Another title about this pig is:
ABC I like me! (1997)

Carlstrom, Nancy White

It's your first day of school, Annie Claire. Abrams Books for Young Readers 2009 un il $15.95

Grades: PreK K   E
1. School stories 2. Stories in rhyme 3. Dogs -- Fiction 4. Mother-daughter relationship -- Fiction

ISBN 978-0-8109-4057-4; 0-8109-4057-4

LC 2009-2124

Annie Claire the puppy, excited but nervous about her first day of school, is reassured by her mother, whose love always goes with her.

"Sweet, gentle illustrations pair with reassuring text." Booklist

★ **Jesse** Bear, what will you wear? illustrations by Bruce Degen. Macmillan 1986 un il $16.95; pa $6.99; bd bk $7.99

Grades: PreK K   E
1. Stories in rhyme 2. Bears -- Fiction

ISBN 0-02-717350-X; 0-689-80623-X pa; 0-689-80930-1 bd bk

LC 85-10610

"The big, cheerful watercolor paintings show the baby bear in loving relation to his family and world. Without crossing the line into sentimentality, this offers a happy, humorous soundfest that will associate reading aloud with a sense of play." Bull Cent Child Books

Other titles about Jesse Bear are:
Better not get wet, Jesse Bear (1988)
Climb the family tree, Jesse Bear (2004)
Guess who's coming, Jesse Bear (1998)
Happy birthday, Jesse Bear (1994)
How do you say it today, Jesse Bear? (1992)
It's about time, Jesse Bear, and other rhymes (1990)
Let's count it out, Jesse Bear (1996)
What a scare, Jesse Bear! (1999)
Where is Christmas, Jesse Bear? (2000)

Carluccio, Maria

I'm 3! look what I can do. Henry Holt 2010 un il $10.99

Grades: PreK   E
1. Growth -- Fiction 2. Siblings -- Fiction

ISBN 978-0-8050-8313-2; 0-8050-8313-8

"The accomplishments of two young siblings are presented, from morning to night. Short, declarative sentences announce, 'I can sleep in my bed,' 'I can eat with my fork and spoon,' 'I can try different foods.' At preschool, the twins 'read,' paint, and demonstrate social skills such as sharing. At the end of the day they put on their pajamas and kiss their family good night. The bright, cheery digital collages have an eye-catching variety of textures and patterns. An exuberant celebration of three-year-old milestones." SLJ

The **sounds** around town; by Maria Carluccio. Barefoot Books 2008 un il $16.99

Grades: PreK   E
1. Stories in rhyme 2. Day -- Fiction 3. Sound -- Fiction 4. City and town life -- Fiction

ISBN 978-1-905236-28-2; 1-905236-28-X

LC 2007025044

Reveals many things a child might hear during the day, from the singing of birds at dawn to the soft sounds of sleep.

"The text is alive with onomatopoeia, and the visually stimulating cut-paper collages provide myriad sources of the sounds to share and enjoy." Horn Book Guide

Carnesi, Mônica

Sleepover with Beatrice and Bear; Mônica Carnesi. Nancy Paulsen Books, an imprint of Penguin Group (USA) 2014 32 p. col. ill. $15.99

Grades: PreK K 1   E

1. Bears -- Fiction 2. Rabbits -- Fiction 3. Friendship -- Fiction 4. Winter -- Fiction 5. Hibernation -- Fiction 6. Best friends -- Fiction

ISBN 0399256679; 9780399256677

LC 2013034624

In this children's picture book, "Beatrice and Bear meet one spring day and become best buddies. They play together through summer and fall. Then winter comes and Beatrice can't find Bear anywhere. She hears he's gone to hibernate- -but where on earth is that? When Beatrice learns that hibernation is not a place and that Bear will be sleeping all winter long, she fears it will be a lonely season . . . unless she comes up with a brilliant plan to share winter with Bear too." (Publisher's note)

"Carnesi's sweet illustrations perfectly capture the joys of friendship, the frustration at being left behind, and the satisfaction in making something for a friend. The spare text is an excellent complement to the lively illustrations, and the addition of speech balloons for Beatrice's big emotions really lets her perky personality shine." SLJ

Carr, Jan

Greedy Apostrophe; a cautionary tale. by Jan Carr; illustrated by Ethan Long. Holiday House 2007 un il $16.95

Grades: K 1 2 3   E

1. Punctuation -- Fiction

ISBN 978-0-8234-2006-3; 0-8234-2006-X

LC 2006012114

"All the punctuation marks stumble into the Hiring Hall one morning, sipping cocoa and discussing their job prospects. Each receives an important assignment, even Greedy Apostrophe, who has a well-deserved reputation for his bad attitude. . . . Students are asked to be vigilant and to take Greedy away from all the places where he inserts himself but doesn't really belong. With jazzy colors and cartoon-style characters, the upbeat artwork gives personality to the inanimate while underscoring the witty, vivacious tone of the text." Booklist

Carrer, Chiara

Otto Carrotto; written and illustrated by Chiara Carrer. Eerdmans Books for Young Readers 2011 un il $15.99

Grades: K 1 2   E

1. Carrots -- Fiction 2. Rabbits -- Fiction

ISBN 978-0-8028-5393-6; 0-8028-5393-5

LC 2010049546

Otto the rabbit decides to eat nothing but carrots, causing unexpected consequences.

"Sophisticated readers will pore over the thumbnail drawings and speech bubbles within the intricate collage illustrations, and the boldface text emphasizing repetitive words adds visual interest." SLJ

Carrick, Carol

★ **Patrick's** dinosaurs; pictures by Donald Carrick. Clarion Bks. 1983 un il lib bdg $16; pa $5.95

Grades: PreK K 1 2   E

1. Brothers -- Fiction 2. Dinosaurs -- Fiction

ISBN 0-89919-189-4 lib bdg; 0-89919-402-8 pa

LC 83-2049

When his older brother talks about dinosaurs during a visit to the zoo, Patrick is afraid, until he discovers they all died millions of years ago.

"The Carricks do a particularly good job of creating an impressive array of creatures both in text and illustrations— realistic pencil drawings washed in muted greens, browns and oranges." SLJ

Other titles about Patrick's dinosaurs are:

Patrick's dinosaurs on the Internet (1999)

What happened to Patrick's dinosaurs? (1986)

Carter, David A.

600 black spots. Little Simon 2007 un il $19.99

Grades: 2 3 4 5 6   E

1. Puzzles 2. Counting 3. Pop-up books

ISBN 1-4169-4092-8; 978-1-4169-4092-0

In this pop-up book, readers are encouraged to search for the black spots throughout the pages

"This is both simple and stunning. . . . It takes a sophisticated artistic taste to appreciate the modern-art-style creations. . . . Older children will have an interesting time interpreting the artwork and marveling at the skill involved in the construction." Booklist

Blue 2; a pop-up book for children of all ages. Little Simon 2006 un il $10.95

Grades: 2 3 4 5 6   E

1. Puzzles 2. Pop-up books

ISBN 1-4169-1781-0

Each page contains an original piece of artwork that challenges the reader to find the a blue 2.

"Mobiles pop from the pages and readers spin pinwheels and pull tabs to find each elusive numeral two. Another enchanting creation from the inventive paper engineer." Publ Wkly

Hide and Seek. Harry N Abrams Inc 2012 20 p. (hardcover) $25

Grades: K 1 2 3 4 5   E

1. Paper crafts 2. Stories in rhyme 3. Picture books for children

ISBN 1849761019; 9781849761017

This pop-up book "offers six . . . new constructs—each hiding a handful of small cutouts or printed shapes to find. . . . Tallies along the margins invite viewers to spot a 'yellow splat, a red vine, a car and a star. / . . . A sleepy head, in bed, with a red thread on his forehead' and like prizes. These are attached to, dangling from or hidden within the bursts of paper swirls, interlocking mazes and geometrical structures that rise up as each spread opens." (Kirkus)

Lots of bots; a counting pop-up book. Random House/ Corey 2011 un il $14.99

Grades: PreK K 1   E

1. Counting 2. Stories in rhyme 3. Pop-up books 4. Robots -- Fiction

ISBN 978-0-375-86509-1; 0-375-86509-8

This is "a counting book that introduces an eclectic cast of specialized robots that sport antennae, springs, wheels, pincers, and other handy apparatuses. Using a question-and-answer format to count up to 10, the book asks energetic, reader-directed questions like 'Who makes you happy when you are sad?' with the answers appearing in verse.... Carter's quirky robots .... should have effortless appeal for the preschool audience." Publ Wkly

★ **One** red dot; a pop-up book for children of all ages. Little Simon 2005 un il $19.95
Grades: 2 3 4 5 6   E
    1. Puzzles 2. Counting 3. Pop-up books
    ISBN 0-689-87769-2
Original Italian edition 2004
"A graphically bold pop-up book that entices readers to find the one red dot that is hidden on each paper sculpture. Going from 1 to 10, Carter creates a visual hide-and-seek game, ranging from flip-flop flaps to fluttering flicker clickers that really click to orbs that tower above the page. Bold primary colors and a silver-black text give the book a very slick, modern feel." SLJ

White noise; a pop-up book for children of all ages. Little Simon 2009 un il $22.99
Grades: 2 3 4 5 6   E
    1. Pop-up books 2. Noise -- Fiction
    ISBN 978-1-4169-4094-4; 1-4169-4094-4
"Each spread, designed to make crackly, crinkly, creaky, tinkling or snapping noises as the pages are turned, evokes children's construction-paper cutouts.... Carter's creations are akin to fireworks displays, each building in pyrotechnical intensity until the most impressive burst at the end." NY Times Book Rev

Yellow square; a pop-up book for children of all ages. Little Simon 2008 un il $19.99
Grades: 2 3 4 5 6   E
    1. Pop-up books
    ISBN 978-1-4169-4093-7; 1-4169-4093-6
"A yellow square hides in plain sight in or within the paper engineering on each spread; sometimes, the creation of the yellow square is entirely up to the reader. On the first spread, for example, that square exists only when the reader peers through a die-cut while holding the book at the correct angle-in other words, perspective is everything. Captions are variously enigmatic ... or childlike.... Carter confines himself to primary colors, black and white; even with this palette, he alludes to a number of artists, among them Agam, ... Christo, ... Miro, and Calder.... Not all the spreads are equally impressive, but the best are dazzlers." Publ Wkly

Casanova, Mary
The **day** Dirk Yeller came to town; illustrated by Ard Hoyt. Farrar, Straus and Giroux 2011 un il $16.99
Grades: PreK K 1 2   E
    1. Tall tales 2. Libraries -- Fiction 3. West (U.S.) -- Fiction 4. Books and reading -- Fiction
    ISBN 978-0-374-31742-3; 0-374-31742-9
"Dangerous outlaw Dirk Yeller looms into town ... terrifying even the tumbleweeds.... Only one small boy, the narrator of the tale, stands up to Dirk and leads him to, of all places, the public library.... The sandy-hued illustrations are packed with details and humor.... Hoyt's marvelous

caricatures are worth thousands of words, making this hilarious tall tale not only a plug for books and reading but an outsized winner." Kirkus

Some dog! pictures by Ard Hoyt. Farrar, Straus & Giroux 2007 un il $16
Grades: PreK K 1 2   E
    1. Dogs -- Fiction
    ISBN 0-374-37133-4; 978-0-374-37133-3
                        LC 2004053262
A stray dog moves into George's formerly peaceful home, dazzling the man and woman of the house with lively tricks and antics that just leave George exhausted
"The watercolor-and-pencil illustrations perfectly capture the exuberance and spirit of this tale." SLJ

Utterly otterly day; by Mary Casanova; illustrated by Ard Hoyt. Simon & Schuster Books for Young Readers 2008 un il $16.99
Grades: PreK K 1   E
    1. Stories in rhyme 2. Otters -- Fiction
    ISBN 978-1-4169-0868-5; 1-4169-0868-4
                        LC 2007041428
After a day out on his own, Little Otter realizes that he still needs his family no matter how big he grows
"The pen-and-ink-and-watercolor illustrations ... emphasize the quick, exciting movement of the forest's animals, while the text hops with made-up rhyming words.... The adventurous otter and his caring family prove fairly irresistible." Booklist
Another title about Little Otter and his family is:
Utterly Otter night (2011)

Casarosa, Enrico
La **Luna**; story and illustrations by Enrico Casarosa, words by Kiki Thorpe. Disney Press 2012 40 p. $14.99
Grades: PreK K 1   E
    1. Moon -- Fiction 2. Picture books for children 3. Intergenerational relations -- Fiction
    ISBN 1423137663; 9781423137665
This children's book is based on a "Pixar film with an Academy Award nomination for Best Animated Short... . [T]hree characters, a boy, his hugely mustachioed father and his hugely bearded grandfather take their little boat, La Luna, out.... This family's job is to clean up the moon.... A huge star crashes into the moon, and while his father and grandfather argue about how to deal with it, the boy taps it. The star breaks into ... tiny stars, and the three sweep them all up." (Kirkus)

Case, Chris
Sophie and the next-door monsters. Walker 2008 un il $15.99; lib bdg $16.89
Grades: PreK K 1 2   E
    1. Monsters -- Fiction
    ISBN 978-0-8027-9756-8; 0-8027-9756-3; 978-0-8027-9757-5 lib bdg; 0-8027-9757-1 lib bdg
                        LC 2007-49133
When new neighbors move in next door to Sophie, she is startled—and afraid—to discover that they are monsters.
"This is an offbeat delight. The humans matter-or-factness about the monsters' monstrousness intensifies the humor, and the lively text begs to be read aloud. Case layers colors and uses lots of scratchy hatchwork lines and brush-

work to accent the figures and objects in his ink, watercolor, and gouache art." Bull Cent Child Books

Caseley, Judith

★ **On** the town; a community adventure. Greenwillow Bks. 2002 un il $15.95; lib bdg $15.89

Grades: PreK K 1 2   E

1. Community life -- Fiction

ISBN 0-06-029584-8; 0-06-029585-6 lib bdg

LC 2001-23896

Charlie and his mother walk around the neighborhood doing errands so that Charlie can write in his notebook about the people and places that make up his community

"Written from a child's perspective, the story has a cheerful tone and enough variety to keep the expedition interesting. The lively ink, watercolor, and colored-pencil illustrations are full of intriguing details." Booklist

Cash, Megan Montague

★ **Bow**-Wow's nightmare neighbors; Mark Newgarden, Megan Montague Cash. Roaring Brook Press 2014 64 p. chiefly color illustrations (hardcover) $17.99 E

1. Dogs -- Fiction 2. Theft -- Fiction 3. Halloween -- Fiction 4. Neighbors -- Fiction 5. Stories without words

ISBN 1596436409; 9781596436404

LC 2013028312

"As Bow-Wow naps, his neighbors creep in and steal his cozy green bed. When the expressive pup tries to get it back, colorful chaos ensues as the house next door might not be exactly what he thought.'" (Publisher's note)

"In this completely wordless picture book, Newgarden and Cash cue readers with various techniques taken from comics. In some scenes, a series of smaller frames builds to a dramatic turn of events, and page turns are never predictable." Kirkus

Castella, Krystina

Discovering nature's alphabet; [by] Krystina Castella and Brian Boyl. Heyday Books 2005 un il $15.95

Grades: 1 2 3 4   E

1. Alphabet 2. Natural history

ISBN 1-59714-021-X

LC 2005017857

"Castella and Boyl have assembled a portfolio of photographs of natural objects that form individual letters of the alphabet. From beaches to deserts, they discovered letters large and small in vines and flowers, tree trunks and seedpods. The minimal text urges readers to undertake such explorations to find their own hidden patterns." SLJ

Includes bibliographical references

Castellucci, Cecil

Grandma's gloves; illustrated by Julia Denos. Candlewick Press 2010 un il $15.99

Grades: PreK K 1 2   E

1. Death -- Fiction 2. Gardening -- Fiction 3. Grandmothers -- Fiction

ISBN 978-0-7636-3168-0; 0-7636-3168-X

LC 2009015139

When her grandmother, a devoted gardener, dies, a little girl inherits her gardening gloves and feels closer to her memory.

"Castellucci's narrative details give voice to the perspicacity of a sensitive child—the smells, gestures, and alterations of experience that are noticed but rarely articulated. Denos's watercolor, pencil, and digital collage illustrations are bright and charming." SLJ

Odd Duck; by Cecil Castellucci, illustrated by Sara Varon. First Second 2013 96 p. (hardcover) $15.99

Grades: 1 2 3 4 5   E

1. Ducks -- Fiction 2. Friendship -- Fiction 3. Eccentrics and eccentricities -- Fiction

ISBN 1596435577; 9781596435575

In this picture book, by Cecil Castellucci, illustrated by Sara Varon, "Theodora is a perfectly normal duck. She may swim with a teacup balanced on her head and stay north when the rest of the ducks fly south for the winter, but there's nothing so odd about that. Chad, on the other hand, is one strange bird. Theodora quite likes him, but she can't overlook his odd habits. It's a good thing Chad has a normal friend like Theodora to set a good example for him." (Publisher's note)

Castillo, Lauren

Melvin and the boy. Henry Holt 2011 un il $16.99

Grades: PreK K 1   E

1. Pets -- Fiction 2. Turtles -- Fiction

ISBN 978-0-8050-8929-5; 0-8050-8929-2

LC 2010038103

When a boy finds a turtle basking in the sun at the park he thinks he has found the perfect pet, but the turtle only seems happy at bath time. Includes facts about turtles.

"Castillo's . . . gently outlined drawings help to soften a potentially disappointing situation. . . . The boy's parents offer surprising support, allowing their son to bring Melvin home from the park, but the decision to return Melvin is the boy's own. . . . It's an honest account of a small, manageable failure, with a lemonade-from-lemons moment at the end." Publ Wkly

★ **Nana** in the city; by Lauren Castillo. Clarion Books, Houghton Mifflin Harcourt 2014 40 p. (hardcover) $16.99

Grades: PreK K 1   E

1. Grandmothers -- Fiction 2. Cities and towns -- Fiction 3. Courage -- Fiction 4. Grandmothers -- Fiction 5. City and town life -- Fiction

ISBN 0544104439; 9780544104433

LC 2013043953

Caldecott Honor Book (2015)

In this children's book by Lauren Castillo, "a young boy spends an overnight visit with his nana and is frightened to find that the city where she lives is filled with noise and crowds and scary things. But then Nana makes him a special cape to help him be brave, and soon the everyday sights, sounds, and smells of the city are not scary--but wonderful."

""I love my nana," a boy explains, "but I don't love the city." She greets him with a hug, but he's still nervous. "The city is busy," he says (crowds press in). "The city is loud" (a whistle shrieks). "The city is filled with scary things" (the boy shrinks from a homeless man holding out a cup). "It is no place for a nana to live," he concludes. While he sleeps, nana knits him a gift—a big red cape. A series of vignettes shows him wearing it the next morning, striking delighted poses. With new courage, the boy discovers a city he hasn't seen before—one full of life, wonder, and pretzels for homeless men..." PW

The **troublemaker**; by Lauren Castillo. Clarion Books, Houghton Mifflin Harcourt 2014 48 p. (hardcover) $16.99
Grades: PreK K 1   E
1. Bad behavior 2. Toys -- Fiction 3. Siblings -- Fiction 4. Lost and found possessions -- Fiction 5. Behavior -- Fiction
ISBN 054772991X; 9780547729916
                                                    LC 2012039686
In this children's book by Lauren Castillo, "bored and restless on a summer day, a little boy steals his sister's bunny and sends it on an adventure. He is well satisfied with the results--until his own stuffed animal disappears. Could it be that he is not the only troublemaker around . . . ? A case of sibling rivalry is neatly resolved with the 'assistance' of a hilarious raccoon." (Publisher's note)

"The narrator kidnaps his sister's stuffed rabbit, lashes it to his toy boat, and sets it sail on the lake. The boat capsizes, and sister and mom are angry; later when the bunny disappears--again!--they understandably suspect the narrator. (Readers will see that a wild raccoon is the real culprit.) With boldly rendered spreads, the book is at once handsome and child friendly." Horn Book

Caswell, Deanna
Train trip; written by Deanna Caswell; illustrated by Dan Andreasen. Disney Hyperion 2011 un il $16.99
Grades: PreK K   E
1. Railroads -- Fiction
ISBN 978-1-4231-1837-4; 1-4231-1837-5
"A young boy sets off on a solo train trip. As he climbs aboard, he takes in the new sights and sounds. . . . The staccato stop and start iambic verse mimics the rhythm of the train. . . . At the final station, he finds his grandmother waiting. Andreasen's cartoon illustrations have a sentimental, homespun appeal. The anthropomorphized train has a wide, smiling face and even the whistle has goggle eyes and gives a friendly toot. . . . The excitement of the journey rings true." SLJ

Catalanotto, Peter
Emily's art. Atheneum Bks. for Young Readers 2001 un il $16
Grades: PreK K 1   E
1. Artists -- Fiction 2. Contests -- Fiction
ISBN 0-689-83831-X
                                                    LC 00-29293
Emily paints four pictures and enters one in the first-grade art contest, but the judge interprets Emily's entry as a rabbit instead of a dog
"Filled with touches of humor and authentically childlike emotions, this book explores the subjectivity of opinion and the importance of personal conviction." Horn Book Guide

Monkey and Robot; Peter Catalanotto. Atheneum Books for Young Readers 2013 64 p. (hardcover) $12.99
Grades: 1 2   E
1. Robots -- Fiction 2. Monkeys -- Fiction 3. Friendship -- Fiction
ISBN 144242978X; 9781442429789; 9781442430600
                                                    LC 2012003044

This children's chapter book, by Peter Catalanotto, presents four stories which follow a monkey and robot who are friends. "They simply belong together, and it never matters that silly Monkey is furry, or that kind Robot can rust. What matters is their sharing: movies and popcorn, games of hide-and-seek, a fish tank for . . . a hippopotamus?" (Publisher's note)

More of Monkey & Robot; Peter Catalanatto. Atheneum Books for Young Readers 2014 64 p. (hardcover) $14.99
Grades: 1 2   E
1. Adventure and adventurers 2. Robots -- Fiction 3. Monkeys -- Fiction 4. Friendship -- Fiction 5. Best friends -- Fiction
ISBN 144245251X; 9781442452510
                                                    LC 2012051501
In this book, by Peter Catalanatto, "Monkey and Robot . . . return. . . . Divided into four stand-alone chapters, the stories provide kids with . . . antics of two unlikely pals as they plan for Halloween, enjoy a day at the beach, make a new friend, and figure out if it's time for breakfast or bedtime." (School Library Journal)

"In four chapters for new independent readers, Monkey (Monkey & Robot) continues to make a mess, and Robot helps him fix things, at the beach, in the front yard, on Halloween, and while telling time. Catalanotto has created two distinct and likable characters--unlikely pals who understand each other. Black-and-white pencil illustrations provide helpful visual cues for the easy-to-decode text." Horn Book
More of Monkey and Robot

Question Boy meets Little Miss Know-It-All. Atheneum Books for Young Readers 2012 il $16.99 E
1. Humorous fiction 2. Curiosity -- Fiction
ISBN 978-1-4424-0670-4; 1-4424-0670-4
                                                    LC 2011000496
A curious boy with non-stop questions meets a girl who seems to know all the answers.
"Catalanotto creates an intrepid caped crusader for whom no question is too daunting or trivial to ask. Question Boy bests one everyday hero after another with question after question. Parents will identify with the plight of Garbage Man, Police Woman, Mechanic Man, etc. The scenarios build to an absurdist height until, finally, QB meets a worthy opponent who has all the answers and then some." Horn Book

Catchpool, Michael
The **cloud** spinner; by Michael Catchpool; illustrations by Alison Jay. Alfred A. Knopf 2012 32 p.
Grades: K 1 2 3   E
1. Fairy tales 2. Clouds -- Fiction 3. Weaving -- Fiction 4. Kings and rulers -- Fiction 5. Conservation of natural resources -- Fiction 6. Kings, queens, rulers, etc. -- Fiction
ISBN 9780375870118; 9780375970115; 9780375987397
                                                    LC 2011000894
In this book, a "young boy spins clouds into thread, . . . then weaves the thread into cloth. . . . [The] king . . . requests a scarf from the boy, then goes on to demand more and more clothing. . . . [The] king's daughter has been paying attention, and when the king's greedy consumption . . . results in

the disappearance of all the clouds and . . . rain, she brings the clothes back to the spinner so that they can be reverted to clouds." (Bulletin of the Center for Children's Books)

Cate, Annette LeBlanc

The **magic** rabbit; [by] Annette LeBlanc Cate. Candlewick Press 2007 un il $15.99

Grades: K 1 2 3   E

1. Rabbits -- Fiction 2. Magicians -- Fiction 3. Lost and found possessions -- Fiction

ISBN 978-0-7636-6685-9; 978-0-7636-2672-3; 0-7636-2672-4

LC 2007022789

When Bunny becomes separated from Ray, a magician who is his business partner and friend, he follows a crowd to a park where he has a lovely afternoon, and after the people leave and darkness falls, the lonely and frightened Bunny finds a glittering trail of hope

"Embellished only with the gold of 'glittering stars,' Cate's black-and-white drawings perfectly evoke an urban setting in this tale of lost and found." SLJ

Cates, Karin

★ The **Secret** Remedy Book; a story of comfort and love. illustrated by Wendy Anderson Halperin. Orchard Bks. 2003 un il $16.95

Grades: K 1 2 3   E

1. Aunts -- Fiction

ISBN 0-439-35226-6

LC 2002-35475

Although Lolly loves to visit her Auntie Zep's house, she feels homesick when she actually gets there, and so Auntie Zep retrieves the Secret Remedy Book from an old trunk

"This wonderfully warm and satisfying story is paired with Halperin's lovely illustrations. Her trademark details and patterns abound, with softened edges, muted colors, and quiet landscapes." SLJ

Catrow, David

Dinosaur hunt. Orchard Books 2009 un il (Max Spaniel) $6.99

Grades: K 1 2   E

1. Dogs -- Fiction 2. Dinosaurs -- Fiction

ISBN 978-0-545-05748-6; 0-545-05748-5

LC 2008-30144

Max Spaniel searches for dinosaurs in his back yard.

"Washed with colors, the exaggerated, cartoonlike drawings create a zany mood that energizes and extends the deadpan text." Booklist

Other titles about Max Spaniel are:

Funny lunch (2010)

Best in show (2011)

Catusanu, Mircea

The **strange** case of the missing sheep. Viking 2009 un il $16.99

Grades: PreK K 1   E

1. Dogs -- Fiction 2. Sheep -- Fiction 3. Wolves -- Fiction 4. Superheroes -- Fiction

ISBN 978-0-670-01131-5; 0-670-01131-2

LC 2009-12358

When ten sheep go missing in the Dark Forest, Super Sheep Dog Doug comes to the rescue.

"Catusanu's cracked sense of humor and accomplished skills as an illustrator make for a strong authorial debut— readers won't be able to stop giggling." Publ Wkly

Cauley, Lorinda Bryan

Clap your hands. Putnam 1992 un il hardcover o.p. pa $6.99; bd bk $7.99

Grades: PreK K   E

1. Stories in rhyme 2. Animals -- Fiction

ISBN 0-399-22118-2; 0-698-11428-0 pa; 0-399-237100 bd bk

LC 91-12863

Rhyming text instructs the listener to find something yellow, roar like a lion, give a kiss, tell a secret, spin in a circle, and perform other playful activities along with the human and animal characters pictured

"The illustrations feature glowing colors and make good use of Cauley's gift for characterization. . . . Some parts of the book would be fun as action rhymes for preschool story time." Booklist

Cave, Kathryn

One child, one seed; a South African counting book. photographs by Gisèle Wulfsohn. Holt & Co. 2003 un il $16.95

Grades: PreK K 1 2   E

1. Pumpkin 2. Counting 3. South Africa -- Social life and customs

ISBN 0-8050-7204-7

LC 2002-24098

"Children count from 1 to 10 with Nothando as she plants a pumpkin seed that grows to bear fruit for a delicious stew. . . . In a harmonious partnership of narrative and crisp, beautifully composed photographs that show the individuality of each person, readers get a glimpse into the life of an extended family living in a rural South African community. . . . The recipe for isijingi, the pumpkin stew, is included as are some basic geographical facts and a simple map. The writing has good rhythm, and reads aloud well." SLJ

Cazet, Denys

Elvis the rooster almost goes to heaven. HarperCollins Pubs. 2003 48p il (I can read book) lib bdg $16.89

Grades: K 1 2   E

1. Roosters -- Fiction

ISBN 978-0-06-000501-6; 0-06-000501-7

LC 2002-14416

Elvis the rooster thinks he has died when he fails to crow at the rising of the sun but the chickens find a way to restore his cluck

"Cazet's writing is filled with quirky characters, simple wordplay, and gentle humor. The cartoon artwork perfectly reflects the tone of the text." SLJ

Another title about Elvis the rooster is:

Elvis the rooster and the magic words (2004)

Minnie and Moo and the haunted sweater; [by] Denys Cazet. HarperCollinsPublishers 2007 45p il (I can read!) $15.99; lib bdg $16.89

Grades: 1 2 3   E

1. Cattle -- Fiction 2. Birthdays -- Fiction

ISBN 978-0-06-073016-1; 0-06-073016-1; 978-0-06-073017-8 lib bdg; 0-06-073017-X lib bdg

LC 2006036246

Minnie and Moo want to give special presents to the Farmer for his birthday, but something goes awry when Moo knits him a sweater.

This is "an outlandishly hilarious romp. . . . Nonstop action and a clever plot place this title at the top of the list for young readers ready for a slightly more complex story." SLJ

★ **Minnie** and Moo, wanted dead or alive. HarperCollinsPublishers 2006 47p il (I can read book) hardcover o.p. lib bdg $16.89; pa $3.99

Grades: 1 2 3   E
1. Cattle -- Fiction 2. Thieves -- Fiction
ISBN 0-06-073010-2; 978-0-06-073010-9; 0-06-073011-0 lib bdg; 978-0-06-073011-6 lib bdg; 978-0-06-073012-3 pa; 0-06-073012-9 pa
LC 2005-14526

Trying to help Mr. Farmer with his finances, Minnie and Moo (dressed in trenchcoats, ties, and gray fedoras) go to the bank to ask for money and are mistaken for the Bazooka sisters, dangerous outlaws. "Preschool, primary." (Horn Book)

"Cazet's watercolor illustrations of cows dressed as gangsters and cows driving a tractor extend the story's absurd humor and will help move emerging readers through eight chapters of text." Booklist

★ The **octopus**; Grandpa Spanielson's Chicken pox stories, story #1. HarperCollins 2005 46p il (I can read!) $15.99; lib bdg $16.89

Grades: PreK K 1 2   E
1. Dogs -- Fiction 2. Octopuses -- Fiction 3. Chickenpox -- Fiction
ISBN 0-06-051088-9; 0-06-051089-7 lib bdg
LC 2003-26557

Grandpa Spanielson helps his favorite grandpup to avoid scratching his chicken pox by telling how he once had to fight off an octopus during a terrible storm.

"Beginning readers will love the humor, action, and compassion in this story, brought to life in the fun-filled text and superb cartoon illustrations." SLJ

Other titles in Grandpa Spanielson's Chicken pox stories series are:

A snout for chocolate (2006)

The shrunken head (2007)

★ **Will** you read to me? story and pictures by Denys Cazet. Atheneum Books for Young Readers 2007 un il $16.99

Grades: PreK K 1 2   E
1. Pigs -- Fiction 2. Books and reading -- Fiction
ISBN 978-1-4169-0935-4; 1-4169-0935-4
LC 2005024144

Hamlet enjoys reading books and writing poetry, not playing in the mud and fighting over supper like the other pigs, but he finally finds someone who appreciates him just as he is

"Kids will enjoy the uproarious pigsty scenes. . . . But Cazet's simple poetry and soft-toned watercolor-and-colored-pencil spreads also show the beauty of the quiet night . . . and the farm community in solitude. This is not only a celebration of reading but also a moving story about not fitting in, even at home." Booklist

Cech, John

The **nutcracker**; based on the story by E.T.A. Hoffmann; retold by John Cech; illustrated by Eric Puybaret. Sterling 2009 un il $17.95

Grades: 2 3 4 5   E
1. Fairy tales 2. Christmas -- Fiction
ISBN 978-1-4027-5562-0; 1-4027-5562-7
LC 2008043084

In this retelling of the original 1816 German story, Godfather Drosselmeier gives young Marie a nutcracker for Christmas, and she finds herself in a magical realm where she saves a boy from an evil curse

"This beautifully illustrated rendition . . . is wordier than some picture-book adaptations. . . . The language is accessible, though, and lustrous, richly colored paintings cover half, sometimes more, of nearly every spread, providing valuable visual breaks." Booklist

The **princess** and the pea; by Hans Christian Andersen; retold by John Cech; illustrated by Bernhard Oberdieck. Sterling Pub. 2007 un il $14.95

Grades: K 1 2 3   E
1. Authors 2. Novelists 3. Dramatists 4. Fairy tales 5. Children's authors 6. Short story writers
ISBN 978-1-4027-3065-8; 1-4027-3065-9
LC 2006007033

A girl proves that she is a real princess by feeling a pea through twenty mattresses and twenty featherbeds. Includes historical notes about Hans Christian Anderson and the original fairy tale.

"Cech's fluid text sparkles in this well-crafted retelling. . . . The illustrations, created with colored pencils, pastels, and acrylics, glow with lustrous yellow-gold, blue, and green tones." SLJ

Cecil, Randy

Duck; [by] Randy Cecil. Candlewick Press 2008 un il $15.99

Grades: PreK K 1   E
1. Ducks -- Fiction
ISBN 978-0-7636-3072-0
LC 2007040407

Companion volume to: Gator (2007)

Duck happily raises a duckling that has wandered into the amusement park where she is a carousel animal, but finds that she cannot teach what she herself has always longed to do—fly—and sets out to find real ducks to instruct him

"Cecil's illustrations . . . are done in oils. Duck, with her bright, striped scarf, stands out against soft green and gold hues. Many of the paintings are in circles of various sizes on a white background with a gold frame. . . . A beautifully realized friendship story with a happy ending." SLJ

Celenza, Anna Harwell

Duke Ellington's Nutcracker suite; illustrated by Don Tate. Charlesbridge 2011 il lib bdg $19.95

Grades: K 1 2 3   E
1. Pianists 2. Composers 3. Jazz musicians 4. Band leaders 5. Music arrangers 6. Jazz music -- Fiction 7. Jazz musicians -- Fiction 8. African Americans -- Fiction
ISBN 978-1-57091-700-4; 1-57091-700-0
LC 2010023060

Tells the story of how jazz composer and musician Duke Ellington, along with Billy Strayhorn, created his jazz composition based on Tchaikovsky's famous Nutcracker Suite ballet.

"This fictionalization of Ellington and Strayhorn's daring collaboration is well told, and the illustrations convey the hip, cool feeling of the time. An author's note provides more information, and a CD of the piece is included." SLJ

Gershwin's Rhapsody in Blue; [by] Anna Harwell Celenza; illustrated by JoAnn E. Kitchel. Charlesbridge 2006 un il $19.95
Grades: 1 2 3 4   E
1. Composers 2. Music -- Fiction 3. Composers -- Fiction
ISBN 978-1-57091-556-7; 1-57091-556-3
LC 2005006009
In January of 1924, a twenty-six-year-old pianist, George Gershwin, finds himself slated to compose, in only five weeks, a concerto that defines "American music," and the result is his masterpiece, Rhapsody in Blue.

"Celenza's tale, complete with invented dialogue, brings the composer to life. . . . An author's note contains Gershwin's words describing the rhythm of the train ride that freed his mental block. . . . Kitchel's sensitivity to this source material is especially evident in her spread of multifaceted patterns and images. . . . An accompanying CD features Gershwin himself (courtesy of a piano roll)." SLJ

Chabon, Michael, 1963-
★ The **astonishing** secret of Awesome Man; illustrated by Jake Parker. Balzer + Bray 2011 un il $17.99
Grades: K 1 2   E
1. Family life -- Fiction 2. Imagination -- Fiction 3. Superheroes -- Fiction
ISBN 978-0-06-191462-1; 0-06-191462-2
LC 2010041192
A young superhero describes his awesome powers, which he then demonstrates as various foes arrive on the scene.

"Chabon's first picture book discharges delectable language. . . . Things are more likely to skloosh and skarunch than not. Verbiage like this nudges the story into read-aloud territory, and children will be swooping around the room as they listen. But if they stop long enough to peek at the pages, they'll enjoy the way Parker kicks it up another notch with hyperkinetic, hypercolored comic-book action scenes." SLJ

Chaconas, Dori
★ **Cork** & Fuzz; illustrated by Lisa McCue. Viking 2005 32p il (Viking easy-to-read) $13.99
Grades: K 1 2   E
1. Muskrats -- Fiction 2. Opossums -- Fiction 3. Friendship -- Fiction
ISBN 0-670-03602-1
LC 2004-13613
A possum and a muskrat become friends despite their many differences.

"The story's repeated words and entire sentences will help beginning readers feel successful. McCue's endearing drawings add personality and humor to the animals' faces. An excellent addition to easy-reader collections." SLJ

Other titles about Cork & Fuzz are:
Cork & Fuzz: short and tall (2006)
Cork & Fuzz: good sports (2007)

Cork & Fuzz: the collectors (2008)
Cork & Fuzz: finder's keepers (2009)
Cork & Fuzz: the babysitters (2010)
Cork & Fuzz: the swimming lesson (2011)

Don't slam the door! illustrated by Will Hillenbrand. Candlewick Press 2010 un il $15.99
Grades: PreK K 1 2   E
1. Stories in rhyme 2. Doors -- Fiction 3. Animals -- Fiction
ISBN 978-0-7636-3709-5; 0-7636-3709-2
LC 2009015254
A cumulative, rhyming tale of a slamming door which wakes a cat, setting into motion an absurd chain of events and resulting in chaos.

"The author's bouncy couplets are rhythmically consistent all the better for reading aloud. Hillenbrand's mixed-media illustrations with characteristic domestic details and expressive faces on both animal and human figures are a spot-on match to the narrative." SLJ

Mousie love; illustrated by Josee Masse. Bloomsbury U.S.A. Children's Books 2009 un il $16.99; lib bdg $17.89
Grades: K 1 2   E
1. Love -- Fiction 2. Mice -- Fiction
ISBN 978-1-59990-111-4; 1-59990-111-0; 978-1-59990-368-2 lib bdg; 1-59990-368-7 lib bdg
LC 2008-39888
After falling in love at first sight, Tully the mouse strives to prove his devotion to Frill every day—while avoiding the cat—but never gives her a chance to respond to his marriage proposal

"Masse's bright, cheerful acrylic-and-gel illustrations complement the text . . . [and] courtship vignettes alternate with humorous, action-packed chase scenes from a mouse-eye perspective. Mousie love triumphs through adversity in this fetching little romance." Kirkus

Chall, Marsha Wilson
Pick a pup; [by] Marsha Chall; illustrated by Jed Henry. Margaret K. McElderry Books 2011 un il $16.99
Grades: PreK K 1   E
1. Stories in rhyme 2. Dogs -- Fiction 3. Pets -- Fiction 4. Grandmothers -- Fiction
ISBN 978-1-4169-7961-6; 1-4169-7961-1
After observing different types of dogs in his neighborhood, Sam and Gram go to the local pet shelter to choose a puppy.

"Terrific for sharing, with bouncing and memorable phrasing and appealing, energetic illustrations, this sweet and satisfying tale showcases the charm and special qualities of dogs as well as the tenderness of a grandparent-grandchild relationship." Kirkus

Chamberlain, Margaret
Please don't tease Tootsie. Dutton 2008 un il $16.99
Grades: PreK K 1 2   E
1. Stories in rhyme 2. Pets -- Fiction
ISBN 978-0-525-47982-6; 0-525-47982-1
"Tootsie, a disgruntled red cat, is arching her back and glowering at the little girl who is cheerfully threatening to spray her with a hose. On succeeding pages, readers meet a number of animals under siege by naughty preschoolers.

The text consists of brief, alliterative entreaties to mend their ways. . . . The illustrations are droll and stylized, featuring expressive cartoon animals on fields of bright color or flamboyant Art Nouveau patterns." SLJ

Chandra, Deborah

★ **George** Washington's teeth; written by Deborah Chandra & Madeleine Comora; pictures by Brock Cole. Farrar, Straus & Giroux 2003 un il $16

Grades: PreK K 1 2   **E**

1. Teeth 2. Generals 3. Presidents

ISBN 0-374-32534-0

LC 2002-25086

A rollicking rhyme portrays George Washington's life-long struggle with bad teeth. A timeline taken from diary entries and other nonfiction sources follows

This is written "with wit, verve, and a generous amount of sympathy for poor Washington and his dental woes. . . . Illustrator Cole is at his absolute best here, totally at ease with human gesture and expression." Booklist

Chapman, Jane

I'm not sleepy! Jane Chapman. Good Books 2012 32 p. col. ill. (hardcover: alk. paper) $16.99

Grades: PreK K 1   **E**

1. Grandmothers -- Fiction 2. Owls -- Fiction 3. Bedtime -- Fiction

ISBN 1561487651; 9781561487653

LC 2012000185

In author Jeffrey Frank's book, "a little owlet employs a big bag of tricks when Grandma tries to get him to settle down to sleep." Grandma comes "up with a plan. She will go to sleep, and Mo, after putting her to bed, can play to his heart's content. Mo is delighted, but he finds that the effort of arranging a nest for Grandma and flying down to get her bedtime snack has made him...sleepy." (Kirkus Reviews)

Charest, Emily MacLachlan

Before you came; by Patricia MacLachlan & Emily MacLachlan Charest; illustrated by David Diaz. Katherine Tegen Books 2011 un il $16.99; lib bdg $17.89

Grades: PreK K 1   **E**

1. Mother-child relationship -- Fiction

ISBN 978-0-06-051234-7; 0-06-051234-2; 978-0-06-051235-4 lib bdg; 0-06-051235-0 lib bdg

A mother relates how she spent time before her child arrived, then passes on a gift of days paddling a red canoe, reading in a pillow-filled hammock until dark, and watching the moon rise at night.

"Iridescent light, tropical colors, and entwined, nature-themed patterns distinguish Caldecott Medalist Diaz's . . . lavish art, which is the bedrock of this resplendent book. . . . Details of their mothers' and fathers' lives before they became parents are a constant source of fascination for children, and this talented team celebrates the 'before', while emphasizing (and reassuring) that the 'now' is even better." Publ Wkly

Charles, Veronika Martenova

The **birdman**; illustrated by Annouchka Gravel Galouchko & Stéphan Daigle. Tundra Books 2006 un il $17.95

Grades: K 1 2 3   **E**

1. Birds -- Fiction 2. India -- Fiction 3. Bereavement

-- Fiction

ISBN 978-0-88776-740-1; 0-88776-740-0

"In the crowded streets of Calcutta, Nobi, a tailor, works hard to support his family. Then his wife and children are killed. . . . After weeks of immobilizing anguish, Nobi buys some caged birds at the market, sets them free, and finds some of his weighty sorrow released. . . . Charles, who based her vivid, poetic text on a true story (explained in a lengthy afterword), is frank about the pain of loss, but focuses on the uplifting message that acts of kindness can ease grief. The illustrators extend the story's spirit-healing themes in vibrant folk-art paintings, gloriously patterned with flowers, Hindu symbols, and soaring birds." Booklist

Charlip, Remy

Fortunately; written and illustrated by Remy Charlip. Aladdin Books 1993 un il pa $6.99

Grades: PreK K 1   **E**

1. Chance -- Fiction 2. Travel -- Fiction

ISBN 0-689-71660-5; 978-0-689-71660-7

LC 92-22794

First published 1964 by Four Winds Press

Good and bad luck accompany Ned from New York to Florida on his way to a surprise party.

★ A **perfect** day; [by] Remy Charlip. Greenwillow Books 2007 un il $16.99; lib bdg $17.89

Grades: PreK K 1 2   **E**

1. Stories in rhyme 2. Father-son relationship -- Fiction

ISBN 0-06-051972-X; 0-06-051973-8 lib bdg

LC 2004-52350

A father and son's "perfect day consists of doing ordinary things—going for a walk, picnicking with friends, watching the clouds, reading books. . . . The simple illustrations resemble something a youngster might draw, and the palette of soft pastel colors supports the story's comforting atmosphere and the love between these two. . . . Charlip has crafted a cozy story that is a perfect example of parent and child bonding." SLJ

Chase, Kit

Oliver's tree; Kit Chase. G. P. Putnam's Sons 2014 32 p. color illustrations $16.99

Grades: PreK K   **E**

1. Elephants -- Fiction 2. Owls -- Fiction 3. Rabbits -- Fiction 4. Friendship -- Fiction 5. Hide-and-seek -- Fiction

ISBN 0399257004; 9780399257001

LC 2013014667

In this children's book, written and illustrated by Kit Chase, "Oliver, Charlie, and Lulu love to play outside together. Their favorite game is hide-and-seek, but it's not fun for Oliver when his friends hide in the trees--he can't reach them! So the friends set off to find a tree that Oliver can play in." (Publisher's note)

"Suffused with warmth and gentle humor, this deceptively simple story demonstrates the power of friendship, the importance of working together and problem-solving, while simultaneously introducing basic concepts (high/low, tall/short) in a pleasing, organic way." Kirkus

Chast, Roz

★ **Too** busy Marco. Atheneum Books for Young Readers 2010 un il $16.99

Grades: PreK K 1 2   E
1. Birds -- Fiction 2. Bedtime -- Fiction
ISBN 978-1-4169-8474-0; 1-4169-8474-7
LC 2009052481
"Cartoonist Chast brings her affectionate, anxious line and fascination with the eccentrically ordinary to an original riff on bedtime avoidance." Horn Book

"Marco the parrot is too busy for bedtime. Cartoon illustrations in watercolor, gouache, and ink show his human mother from the waist down and a talking alarm clock urging him away from his playthings. Thought bubbles depict his dreams of painting, scientific discoveries, skateboarding, and bowling." SLJ

Chatelain, Jeremy
May the stars drip down; by Jeremy Chatelain; illustrated by Nikki McClure. Abrams Books for Young Readers 2014 40 p. $17.95
Grades: PreK K 1   E
1. Lullabies 2. Songs 3. Children's songs, English -- United States -- Texts
ISBN 1419710249; 9781419710247
LC 2013008241
This book, by musician Jeremy Chatelain, is a "lullaby . . . adapted into a . . . bedtime book with illustrations by . . . cut-paper artist Nikki McClure. McClure's . . . intricate images, inspired by nature and the intense bond between parent and child, . . . complement . . . Chatelain's . . . lyrics. An audio download of the song is also included." (Publisher's note)

"In this achingly loving interpretation of the indie band Cub Country's lullaby, a mother cuddles her sleepy son, picturing his dream wanderings in the natural world and wishing him well on his nighttime journeys...A richly imagined dreamscape in a feat of paper artistry." Kirkus

Chaud, Benjamin
The **bear's** sea escape; Benjamin Chaud. Chronicle Books LLC 2014 32 p. color illustrations $17.99
Grades: PreK K 1 2   E
1. Sea stories 2. Bears -- Fiction 3. Hibernation -- Fiction 4. Lost children -- Fiction 5. Father and child -- Fiction
ISBN 1452127433; 9781452127439
LC 2013037654
"When the bears seek warmth from their chilly perch atop the Paris Opera House, Little Bear is mistaken for a toy bear and whisked away . . . to a tropical island! Papa Bear sets out on a frenzied journey to find Little Bear, traveling to a bustling wharf, beneath a sea brimming with coral and mermaids, onto a busy beach, and all the way to a sun-drenched island." (Publisher's note)

"In delightfully crowded, oversize spreads that jostle with activity and eye-catching colors, Chaud offers another absorbing and cheerful visual feast." Booklist

★ The **bear's** song; by Benjamin Chaud. Chronicle Books 2013 32 p. (alk. paper) $17.99
Grades: PreK K 1 2   E
1. Bears -- Fiction 2. Cities and towns -- Fiction 3. Fathers and sons -- Fiction
ISBN 1452114242; 9781452114248
LC 2012046877

Author Benjamin Chaud presents a "immersive picture book about two bears on a big-city adventure. Papa Bear is searching for Little Bear, who has escaped the den. Little Bear is following a bee, because where there are bees, there is honey! When the quest leads both bears into the bustling city and a humming opera house, theatrical hijinks ensue." (Publisher's note)

Chen, Chih-Yuan
★ **Guji** Guji. Kane/Miller 2004 un il $15.95
Grades: PreK K 1 2   E
1. Ducks -- Fiction 2. Crocodiles -- Fiction
ISBN 1-929132-67-0
Crocodile Guji Guji, who was raised by a family of ducks, meets three crocodiles who tell him that he was not a duck. When the crocodiles ask Guji Guji to help them trap the ducks he saves the duck family.

"This beautifully written story has much to say about appreciating families and differences. . . . Chen's unique illustrations are compelling. . . . The rich blues and earth tones and dramatic page layouts create moving scenes, but the quirky details and characters' expressions are hilarious." SLJ

On my way to buy eggs; written and illustrated by Chih-Yuan Chen. Kane/Miller 2003 un il hardcover o.p. pa $7.99
Grades: PreK K 1 2   E
1. Imagination -- Fiction
ISBN 1-929132-49-2; 1-933605-41-3 pa
LC 2002-117381
First published 2001 in Taiwan
"Sent to the local store to buy eggs, Shau-yu takes a circuitous walk through her neighborhood, 'balancing' on the shadow thrown on the sidewalk by a rooftop, scuffing through fallen leaves, looking at the world through a marble so that everything is transformed into 'a blue ocean world.'. . . Preschool. Primary. " (Horn Book)

"A young girl's errand to the store turns into a sensory adventure. . . . After a make-believe game with the shopkeeper and more adventures along the way, Shau-yu returns home to her loving dad. The story is basic, but the simple words and phrases easily show Shau-yu's delight in transforming small things. The earth-tone colors in the crisp paper-and-pencil collages are as quiet as the story." Booklist

Chen, Yong
A **gift**. Boyds Mills Press 2009 un il $16.95
Grades: K 1 2 3   E
1. Aunts -- Fiction 2. China -- Fiction 3. Uncles -- Fiction 4. Chinese New Year -- Fiction 5. Chinese Americans -- Fiction
ISBN 978-1-59078-610-9; 1-59078-610-6
LC 2009012794
Amy receives a gift for the Chinese New Year from her aunt and uncles who live far away in China.

"Chen's text is spare but, combined with her luscious watercolors, evokes a vivid portrait of rural Chinese culture." SLJ

Cherry, Lynne
★ The **great** kapok tree; a tale of the Amazon rainforest. Harcourt Brace Jovanovich 1990 un il $16; pa $7

Grades: K 1 2 3   E
   1. Rain forests -- Fiction
   ISBN 0-15-200520-X; 0-15-202614-2 pa

                            LC 89-2208

The many different animals that live in a great kapok tree in the Brazilian rainforest try to convince a man with an ax of the importance of not cutting down their home

"A carefully researched picture book. . . . Cherry captures the Amazonian proportions of the plants and animals that live there by using vibrant colors, intricate details, and dramatic perspectives. . . . The writing is simple and clear." Booklist

How Groundhog's garden grew. Blue Sky Press (NY) 2003 un il $15.95
Grades: PreK K 1 2   E
   1. Marmots -- Fiction
   ISBN 0-439-32371-1

                            LC 2002-3428

Squirrel teaches Little Groundhog how to plant and tend a vegetable garden

The author "tells a charming and also informative story about plants, gardening, and environmental respect. Her beautiful, full-color illustrations—realistic and wonderfully detailed—often incorporate spot-art borders of labeled seedlings and plants, highlighting a diverse array of wildlife." Booklist

The **sea,** the storm, and the mangrove tangle. Farrar, Straus and Giroux 2004 un il $16
Grades: K 1 2 3   E
   1. Ecology -- Fiction 2. Wetlands -- Fiction 3. Marine animals -- Fiction 4. Caribbean region -- Fiction
   ISBN 0-374-36482-6

                         LC 2002-29705

A seed from a mangrove tree floats on the sea until it comes to rest on the shore of a faraway lagoon where, over time, it becomes a mangrove island that shelters many birds and animals, even during a hurricane

"Cherry paints lustrous, detailed scenes that, together with her accessible narrative, will spark children's interest in a magnificent, endangered ecosystem." Booklist

Chessa, Francesca
   Holly's red boots; [by] Francesca Chessa. Holiday House 2008 un il $16.95
Grades: PreK K 1   E
   1. Snow -- Fiction 2. Color -- Fiction 3. Shoes -- Fiction
   ISBN 978-0-8234-2158-9; 0-8234-2158-9

                         LC 2007-35516

Holly wants to play in the snow and needs her red boots, so she and her cat Jasper search the house for anything red

"The bright, childlike art uses multiple perspectives and bold swatches of color to portray the freckled preschooler, her patient mom, and the chaotic house search." SLJ

Chichester-Clark, Emma
   Little Miss Muffet counts to ten. Andersen Press 2010 un il pa $9.99
Grades: K 1 2   E
   1. Counting 2. Stories in rhyme 3. Animals -- Fiction 4. Nursery rhymes -- Fiction
   ISBN 978-1-84270-955-9; 1-84270-955-0

"The text is spot-on as Clark keeps the rhyming pattern of the original nursery rhyme and makes it her own. . . . The whimsical illustrations show plenty of activity as the number of characters increases, but they never descend into overwhelming busyness and many invite closer inspection. Perfect for storytime or individual sharing." SLJ

Melrose and Croc; an adventure to remember. Walker & Co. 2008 un il $16.95; lib bdg $17.85
Grades: PreK K 1 2   E
   1. Dogs -- Fiction 2. Birthdays -- Fiction 3. Crocodiles -- Fiction
   ISBN 978-0-8027-9774-2; 0-8027-9774-1; 978-0-8027-9775-9 lib bdg; 0-8027-9775-X lib bdg

                         LC 2007-037146

A friendly crocodile receives the best birthday present ever when he rescues his dear companion, Melrose the dog, during a storm at sea

"This simple story, set in a European seaside village, celebrates two caring individuals who think only of one another. Its gentle, affectionate message and expressive illustrations are a wonderful, reassuring way to lull any child into a peaceful sleep in which all is right with the world." SLJ

   Other titles about Melrose and Croc are:
   Melrose and Croc: a Christmas to remember (2006)
   Melrose and Croc beside the sea (2009)
   Melrose and Croc find a smile (2009)
   Melrose and Croc: friends for life (2009)
   Melrose and Croc go to town (2009)

Piper; [written and illustrated by] Emma Chichester Clark. Eerdmans Books for Young Readers 2007 un il $17
Grades: PreK K 1 2   E
   1. Dogs -- Fiction
   ISBN 978-0-8028-5314-1

                         LC 2006008548

A young dog runs away from its cruel master, but finds a new home after saving the life of an old woman

"Both honorable and adorable, Piper will inspire strong reactions from kids, and Clark's always-impressive watercolors effectively capture both the happy and the dark moments of the tale." Booklist

Child, Lauren
   ★ **I** am too absolutely small for school. Candlewick 2004 un il $16.99; pa $6.99
Grades: PreK K 1 2   E
   1. School stories 2. Siblings -- Fiction
   ISBN 0-7636-2403-9; 0-7636-2887-5 pa

                         LC 2003-65576

When Lola is worried about starting school, her older brother Charlie reassures her

"The children's relationship is refreshingly noncombative. . . . Incorporating photos, fabric, and appealingly childlike cartoon renderings of the siblings, the mixed-media illustrations are a visual treat of color and texture." SLJ

   Other titles about Lola and Charlie are:
   But excuse me that is my book (2006)
   I am not sleepy and I will not go to bed (2001)
   I will never not eat a tomato (2000)
   Say cheese (2007)
   Slightly invisible (2011)
   Snow is my favorite and my best (2006)

Maude the not-so-noticeable Shrimpton; Lauren Child, Trisha Krauss. Candlewick Press 2013 32 p. $16.99
Grades: 1 2 3 **E**
1. Picture books for children 2. Dysfunctional families -- Fiction
ISBN 0763665150; 9780763665159
LC 2012947262

This children's picture book focuses on the dramatic and sometimes ostentatious Shrimpton family. "Readers first see them in a framed photograph, as they ensure their best sides are showing while jostling each other for prominence. Mrs. Shrimpton favors extraordinary hats . . . , her husband has a dramatic mustache, and three of their four children are talented and/or beautiful. Middle daughter Maude is the exception—she literally blends in with the scenery." (Publishers Weekly)

The **New** small person; Lauren Child. Candlewick Press 2015 32 p. $17.99
Grades: PreK K 1 2 **E**
1. Family -- Fiction 2. Brothers and sisters -- Fiction
ISBN 0763678104; 9780763678104
LC 2014939346

"Elmore Green starts life as an only child, as many children do. He has a room to himself, where he can line up his precious things and nobody will move them one inch. But one day everything changes. When the new small person comes along, it seems that everybody might like it a bit more than they like Elmore. Then, one night, everything changes." (Publisher's note)

Chinn, Karen

Sam and the lucky money; illustrated by Cornelius Van Wright, and Ying-Hwa Hu. Lee & Low Bks. 1995 un il hardcover o.p. pa $7.95
Grades: PreK K 1 2 **E**
1. Chinese New Year -- Fiction 2. Chinese Americans -- Fiction
ISBN 1-880000-13-X; 1-880000-53-9 pa
LC 94-11766

"The illustrators masterfully combine Chinatown's exotic setting with the universal emotions of childhood through expressive portraits of the characters." SLJ

Chocolate, Debbi

El barrio; illustrated by David Diaz. Henry Holt 2009 un il $16.95
Grades: PreK K 1 2 **E**
1. Community life -- Fiction 2. City and town life -- Fiction 3. Hispanic Americans -- Fiction
ISBN 978-0-8050-7457-4; 0-8050-7457-0
LC 2008013422

A young boy explores his vibrant Latino neighborhood, with its vegetable gardens instead of lawns, Nativity parades, quinceanera parties, and tejana and salsa music.

"Thick lines surround the woodcut-like artwork imbued with a rainbow of glowing colors. Fascinating mixed-media collages (toy skulls, rocks, beads, shells) border each spread. The whole is an exuberant cacophony of colors and sights." Booklist

Chodos-Irvine, Margaret

Best best friends; [by] Margaret Chodos-Irvine. Harcourt 2006 un il $16

Grades: PreK K 1 **E**
1. School stories 2. Birthdays -- Fiction 3. Friendship -- Fiction
ISBN 0-15-205694-7
LC 2005002251

Mary and Clare do everything together at preschool, but Mary's birthday celebration puts a strain on the girls' friendship.

"In spot-on words and crisp, gaily patterned prints, the [author-illustrator] captures the unselfconscious affection and quicksilver shifts in mood that characterize preschool friendships." Booklist

★ **Ella** Sarah gets dressed. Harcourt 2003 un il $16; bd bk $10.95
Grades: PreK K 1 **E**
1. Clothing and dress -- Fiction
ISBN 0-15-216413-8; 0-15-206486-9 bd bk
LC 2002-5097

A Caldecott Medal honor book, 2004

Despite the advice of others in her family, Ella Sarah persists in wearing the striking and unusual outfit of her own choosing

"With minimal words and her signature art marked by bright, bold prints, Chodos-Irvine perfectly captures a universal childhood struggle." Booklist

Choldenko, Gennifer

A giant crush; illustrated by Melissa Sweet. G.P. Putnam's Sons 2011 un il $16.99
Grades: PreK K 1 2 **E**
1. School stories 2. Rabbits -- Fiction 3. Shyness -- Fiction 4. Valentine's Day -- Fiction
ISBN 978-0-399-24352-3; 0-399-24352-6
LC 2009040110

"Jackson, a young rabbit, has a giant crush on Cami, a bunny in his class, but he's too shy to tell her he likes her. Instead, he leaves her a flower, candy, and a giant valentine. . . . Sweet's watercolor, gouache, and mixed-media illustrations are sunny and expressive, and bring the characters and their world to life. The lighthearted pictures are a perfect match for the breezy text." SLJ

Louder, Lili; [by] Gennifer Choldenko; illustrated by S.D. Schindler. G.P. Putnam's Sons 2007 un il $16.99
Grades: PreK K 1 2 **E**
1. School stories 2. Friendship -- Fiction
ISBN 978-0-399-24252-6
LC 2007007511

Lili is so shy that her voice is never heard in class until the day a good friend needs her help

"This engaging story is well written and even poetic. Lili is a well-developed character, and her growth is believable. The warm, energetic illustrations highlight the elements of humor in the story." SLJ

Chorao, Kay

Ed and Kip; Kay Chorao. Holiday House 2014 32 p. color illustrations (I like to read) (hardcover) $14.95
Grades: PreK K 1 **E**
1. Insects -- Fiction 2. Elephants -- Fiction 3. Friendship -- Fiction 4. Play -- Fiction 5. Rocks --

Fiction 6. Jungle animals -- Fiction

ISBN 0823429032; 9780823429035

LC 2012045920

This children's book, written and illustrated by Kay Chorao, focuses on the adventures of two elephants and their insect friend. "When elephants Ed and Kip get into mischief, their friend Bug uses some quick thinking [and] . . . big brains . . . to get them out of Crocodile's pond . . . [and] save the day!" (Publisher's note)

"Elephants, monkeys, bugs, and crocodiles play games, interact, and experience emotions together in the jungle. Though the text is simple, the panel illustrations tell a more complex story, allowing new readers to enjoy the book on multiple levels. The soft, pastel-colored illustrations in watercolor, gouache, and ink imbue the eponymous elephants with personality. This is an easy reader with substance." Horn Book

Choung, Euh-Hee

Minji's salon. Kane Miller 2008 un il $15.95

Grades: PreK   E

1. Dogs -- Fiction 2. Beauty shops -- Fiction

ISBN 978-1-933605-67-8; 1-933605-67-7

"When Minji's mother heads to the beauty salon, Minji pretends to be her dog's hairdresser. . . . The simply charming story of a young girl using her imagination is accompanied by delightful artwork." Booklist

Christelow, Eileen

The **desperate** dog writes again. Clarion Books 2010 32p il $16.99

Grades: PreK K 1 2   E

1. Dogs -- Fiction

ISBN 978-0-547-24205-7; 0-547-24205-0

When a new girlfriend comes between Emma the dog and her owner George, Emma e-mails "Ask Queenie," an advice column for dogs having problems with difficult humans.

"Christelow's bright, cartoon-like illustrations in comic-book panels humorously display the antics while dialogue bubbles abet easy reading. Pitch perfect for those children adjusting to a new person in their lives." Kirkus

★ **Five** little monkeys jumping on the bed; retold and illustrated by Eileen Christelow. Clarion Bks. 1989 un il $15; pa $5.95; bd bk $11.99

Grades: PreK K 1 2   E

1. Counting 2. Monkeys -- Fiction

ISBN 0-89919-769-8; 0-395-55701-1 pa; 0-547-13176-3 bd bk

LC 88-22839

A counting book in which one by one the five little monkeys jump on the bed only to fall off and bump their heads

"Squiggling, swirling lines of color capture the sense of unbridled motion as the monkeys bounce and, one by one, topple from the bed. After all five bandaged youngsters finally fall asleep, a relaxed mama gratefully retires to her room . . . to bounce on 'her' bed. An amusingly presented counting exercise." Booklist

Other titles about the five little monkeys are:

Don't wake up Mama! (1992)

Five little monkeys go shopping (2007)

Five little monkeys play hide and seek (2004)

Five little monkeys reading in bed (2011)

Five little monkeys sitting in a tree (1991)

Five little monkeys wash the car (2000)

Five little monkeys with nothing to do (1996)

Letters from a desperate dog; [by] Eileen Christelow. Clarion Books 2006 32p il $16

Grades: PreK K 1 2   E

1. Dogs -- Fiction

ISBN 978-0-618-51003-0; 0-618-51003-6

LC 2005032744

Feeling misunderstood and unappreciated by her owner, Emma the dog asks for advice from the local canine advice columnist.

"This is a delightful romp, and Christelow shows Emma's story off to great advantage in an oversize format with comic-book-style watercolor art." Booklist

Another title about Emma the dog is:

The desperate dog writes again (2010)

Christensen, Bonnie

★ **Plant** a little seed; Bonnie Christensen. Roaring Brook Press 2012 32 p.

Grades: 2 3 4 5   E

1. Seeds -- Fiction 2. Seasons -- Fiction 3. Gardening -- Fiction 4. Picture books for children 5. Community gardens -- Fiction

ISBN 159643550X; 9781596435506

LC 2011005202

In this picture book, "a girl narrates the cycle of working a community-garden plot over three productive seasons. She and her friend (a boy) plan, plant, tend and harvest fruits, veggies and flowers. . . . [Bonnie] Christensen's pictures . . . convey visual affirmations of friendship, cooperation and patience through changing seasons. Basic biological facts about plants, arranged on seed packets scattered across a final page, are reinforced visually throughout." (Kirkus Reviews)

Christian, Cheryl

Witches; illustrated by Wish Williams. Star Bright Books 2011 24p il pa $5.95

Grades: PreK   E

1. Stories in rhyme 2. Witches -- Fiction 3. Halloween -- Fiction

ISBN 978-1-59572-283-6; 1-59572-283-1

LC 2010050909

"Children dressed as witches are gathered around a kitchen table putting all sorts of food from the cupboards and refrigerator in a giant black cauldron. This image sets the scene for a very simple story of children (or witches) getting ready for their Halloween outing. The whimsical and vibrant colors in Williams's pictures make this story great fun to view and help to move the rhyming text forward." SLJ

Church, Caroline

One more hug for Madison; by Caroline Jayne Church. Orchard Books 2010 un il lib bdg $16.99

Grades: PreK K   E

1. Mice -- Fiction 2. Bedtime -- Fiction 3. Mother-child relationship -- Fiction

ISBN 978-0-545-16179-4 lib bdg; 0-545-16179-7 lib bdg

LC 2008-52691

Madison the mouse keeps asking her patient mother for just one more thing before she goes to sleep.

"Mouse Madison forestalls bedtime by repeatedly asking Mommy for "just one more thing." The story doesn't distinguish itself from the multitude of like-themed picture book offerings, but the art, which places human-child motifs (Madison picks up her toys, brushes her teeth) within the context of an animal habitat (her bed is a hollowed-out log, her wardrobe a tree branch) invites contemplation." Horn Book

One smart goose; [by] Caroline Jayne Church. Orchard Books 2005 un il $16.95
Grades: PreK K 1 2   E
  1. Foxes -- Fiction 2. Geese -- Fiction
  ISBN 0-439-68765-9
First published 2003 in the United Kingdom
A goose who likes to wash in a muddy pond is teased by the other geese, until they realize that he is the only one not chased by the fox
"The clever story will hold the attention of young children, but the illustrations are the book's most striking feature. Bold black lines define the forms of the geese, the fox, and the setting, while textured papers, buts of smudgy print, and collage elements enrich the simple compositions." Booklist

Claflin, Willy
The **uglified** ducky; a Maynard Moose tale. [by] Willy Claflin; illustrated by James Stimson. August House/Little-Folk 2008 un il $18.95
Grades: K 1 2 3   E
  1. Fairy tales
  ISBN 978-0-87483-858-9; 0-87483-858-4
               LC 2008000974
Resets Hans Christian Andersen's tale, The ugly duckling, in the Northern Piney Woods of Alaska, where a baby moose is raised by a family of ducks who try to teach him to waddle, quack, and fly but cannot see his true beauty.
"Stimson's colorful illustrations are a riot, featuring stylized shapes, funny expressions, and animated scenes. A CD of the story performed hilariously by Claflin is delightful. This fresh, lively story is laugh-out-loud funny." SLJ

Clanton, Ben
Mo's mustache; Ben Clanton. Tundra Books of Northern New York 2013 32 p. (hardcover) $17.95
Grades: PreK K 1   E
  1. Picture books for children 2. Monsters -- Fiction 3. Mustaches -- Fiction
  ISBN 177049538X; 9781770495388; 9781770495401
               LC 2012955642
In this children's picture book, Mo the monster gets a mustache. "All the other monsters are impressed" and soon "each of the monsters appears, be-mustached. Each hairy facial adornment is different." Mo is annoyed and decides to trade his mustache for a scarf. "Every monster follows suit. . . . 'WHY IS EVERYBODY COPYING ME?!' And all the monsters confess that they emulate him because they respect his taste and his style." (Kirkus Reviews)

Clarke, J.
Stuck in the mud; [by] Jane Clarke; illustrations by Garry Parsons. Walker Pub. Co. 2008 un il $16.95
Grades: PreK K 1   E
  1. Stories in rhyme 2. Chickens -- Fiction 3. Domestic

animals -- Fiction
  ISBN 978-0-8027-9758-2; 0-8027-9758-X
               LC 2007032179
"One morning, a hen awakens to find a chick missing from her brood. She spots him in the middle of a patch of 'mucky mud,' assumes he is trapped, and clucks hysterically until her friends come to help pull him out. One by one, the rescuers also become mired in the muck. . . . Bright paintings in solid colors and simple, yet expressive cartoon animals are well suited to very young listeners." SLJ

Clayton, Dallas
An **awesome** book! Dallas Clayton. Harper 2012 64 p. (trd. bdg.) $16.99
Grades: PreK K 1 2   E
  1. Stories in rhyme 2. Creative thinking 3. Dreams -- Fiction
  ISBN 0062114689; 9780062114686
               LC 2011935482
Author and illustrator Dallas Clayton presents a children's picture book about imagination and dreams demonstrated through monsters.
"An awesomely idealistic yet visually exhausting book. "There are places in the world / where people do not dream... / of rocket-powered unicorns / and candy cane machines," it begins. This pro-dreaming, anti-bourgeois manifesto is filled with surrealistic art featuring watermelon boats, a train with a giant birthday-cake car, and other motifs reminiscent of the Beatles film Yellow Submarine." Horn Book

Cleary, Beverly
The **hullabaloo** ABC; illustrated by Ted Rand. rev ed; Morrow Junior Bks. 1998 un il $17.99
Grades: PreK K 1 2   E
  1. Alphabet 2. Stories in rhyme 3. Noise -- Fiction 4. Farm life -- Fiction
  ISBN 0-688-15182-5
               LC 97-6457
A revised and newly illustrated edition of the title first published 1960 by Parnassus Press
An alphabet book in which two children demonstrate all the fun that is to be had by making and hearing every kind of noise as they dash about on the farm
"Rand's expert watercolor illustrations on crisp white backgrounds bring the action to life with just the slightest touch of nostalgia." SLJ

Cleland, Jo
Getting your zzzzs; Jo Cleland; [edited by] Precious McKenzie. Rourke Pub. 2012 24 p. $22.79
Grades: K 1 2   E
  1. Sleep 2. Children's songs 3. Picture books for children
  ISBN 1618100858; 9781618100856
               LC 2011944395
This children's book from Jo Cleland is part of the "Sing and Read: Healthy Habits series, which sets healthful reminders to familiar tunes." Here, the tune of "If You're Happy and You Know It" is used to remind children about the immune system-boosting effects of getting enough sleep. (Booklist)

Clement, Nathan

★ Drive; [by] Nathan Clement. Front Street 2008 un il $16.95

Grades: PreK K   E

1. Trucks -- Fiction 2. Fathers -- Fiction
ISBN 978-1-59078-517-1

LC 2007037469

In brief text with illustrations, a boy describes his father's work as a truck driver

"Working in big, streamlined shapes; flat, bright colors; and shiny, airbrushed-like surfaces, [Clement] evokes a deco-esque world. . . . Unusual and often cinematic perspectives . . . plunge readers into the action and give the compositions a red-blooded energy." Publ Wkly

Job site. Boyds Mills Press 2011 un il

Grades: PreK K 1   E

1. Building -- Fiction 2. Vehicles -- Fiction
ISBN 1-59078-769-2; 978-1-59078-769-4

"Over the course of a day on the job, a burly construction foreman, referred to only as 'Boss,' makes good on his name and bosses around a bulldozer, excavator, dump truck, and other vehicles. . . . Featuring . . . bold digital artwork, . . . this book . . . makes excellent use of perspective to play up the machines' immensity and power." Publ Wkly

Clements, Andrew

Circus family dog; illustrated by Sue Truesdell. Clarion Bks. 2000 32p il $16

Grades: PreK K 1 2   E

1. Dogs -- Fiction 2. Circus -- Fiction
ISBN 0-395-78648-7

LC 99-52657

Grumps is content to do his one trick in the center ring at the circus, until a new dog shows up and steals the show—temporarily

"The combination of Clements's impeccable storyteller pacing and Truesdell's creative and whimsical cartoons create a reading and visual experience second only to actually being at the circus. The illustrator uses a mixture of watercolors with pen and ink to bring the action to life in vibrant colors." SLJ

The **handiest** things in the world; photographs by Raquel Jaramillo. Atheneum 2010 un il $16.99

Grades: PreK K 1 2   E

1. Stories in rhyme 2. Hand -- Fiction
ISBN 978-1-416-96166-6; 1-416-96166-6

"This unusual concept book looks at all the things that hands can do and the tools that help do them better. On a typical double-page spread, two short rhyming sentences are paired with photos. The first shows a child's hands performing a job, while the next shows them using a tool. . . . In the first picture, a girl untangles her hair with her fingers; in the next, with a comb. . . . Excellent color photos of different children engaged in everyday activities enhance the book's appeal." Booklist

Cleminson, Katie

Cuddle up, goodnight. Disney Hyperion Books 2011 un il $15.99

Grades: PreK K   E

1. Stories in rhyme 2. Day -- Fiction 3. Toddlers

-- Fiction
ISBN 978-1-4231-3844-0; 1-4231-3844-9

LC 2010004890

First published 2010 in the United Kingdom with title: Wake up!

Follows, in rhymed text and illustrations, a little boy's activities from the time he wakes up in the morning until he goes to bed at night.

"Boldly outlined illustrations effectively employ spare brush strokes and soft-shaded colors to playfully depict characters, objects, and irrepressibly goofy experiences, such as a hippo slurping spaghetti at the table. . . . Children will enjoy the unexpected antics as well as the reassuring sense of a daily routine." Booklist

Clifton-Brown, Holly

Annie Hoot and the knitting extravaganza. Andersen Press USA 2010 un il $16.95

Grades: PreK K 1 2   E

1. Owls -- Fiction 2. Knitting -- Fiction
ISBN 978-0-7613-6444-3; 0-7613-6444-7

Annie Hoot, an owl, loves to knit, but the other owls in the woods will not wear the clothes she makes for them so she goes off in search of other animals that will appreciate her knitwear.

"The exuberant and joyful tale about finding one's bliss is accompanied by watercolor illustrations full of whimsical details." Horn Book Guide

Cline-Ransome, Lesa

Light in the darkness; a story about how slaves learned in secret. by Lesa Cline-Ransome; illustrations by James E. Ransome. Disney/Jump at the Sun Books 2013 40 p. $16.99

Grades: 2 3 4   E

1. Books and reading -- Fiction 2. Slavery -- United States -- Fiction 3. African Americans -- History -- Fiction 4. Reading -- Fiction 5. Slavery -- Fiction 6. Learning -- Fiction 7. African Americans -- Fiction 8. Southern States -- History -- 1775-1865 -- Fiction
ISBN 1423134958; 9781423134954

LC 2012001834

This children's story, by Lesa Cline-Ransome, illustrated by James E. Ransome, is a historical story of 19th century life in slavery. "Rosa and her mama go to school . . . in the dark of night, silently, afraid that any noise they hear is a patroller on the lookout for escaped slaves. . . . If the Master catches them, it'll mean a whipping--one lash for each letter. No matter how slow and dangerous the process might be, Rosa is determined to learn, and pass on her learning to others." (Publisher's note)

Cobb, Jane

What'll I do with the baby-o? Nursery rhymes, songs and stories for babies. Jane Cobb; illustrated by Kathryn Shoemaker. Black Sheep Press 2012 255 p. ill. (paperback) $39.95; (ebook) $29.95

Grades: Adult Professional   E

1. Children's libraries 2. Children's literature 3. Infants -- Development 4. Early childhood education
ISBN 0969866615; 9780969866619; 9780969866640

This book by Jane Cobb presents "rhymes, songs, and stories . . . to engage . . . babies throughout their first two years of development. All of the activities recommended encourage bonding, fun, and brain and emotional development. . . . This resource contains . . . chapters on a baby's brain, early language, and literacy development; program planning and presentation tips; 350 rhymes and songs arranged by type . . . and other resources and bibliographies for further reading." (Publisher's note)

"Extensive preliminary chapters cover such things as identifying the audience, considering the developmental needs of the babies, and selecting and teaching the rhymes and books. The remainder of the book contains thoughtful suggestions of specific rhymes and songs, as well as comments to use with parents. . . . A musical CD provides samples of songs. . . . This book is a must-have for those embarking upon 'Baby and Me' or 'Mother Goose'-type programs." SLJ

Cobb, Rebecca

★ **Missing** mommy; Rebecca Cobb. Henry Holt and Co. 2013 32 p. (hardcover) $16.99

Grades: K 1 2   E
1. Mother-son relationship 2. Bereavement -- Fiction
3. Death -- Fiction 4. Grief -- Fiction 5. Mothers
-- Fiction
ISBN 0805095071; 9780805095074

LC 2011052417

This children's book, by Rebecca Cobb, "explores the many emotions a bereaved child may experience, from anger and guilt to sadness and bewilderment. Ultimately, [the story] focuses on the positive--the recognition that the child is not alone but still part of a family that loves and supports him." (Publisher's note)

"Told from a young child's point of view, Cobb's moving story respectfully explores the complex emotions a little one may experience while grieving the loss of a parent. ... The artwork, done in a primary palette, skillfully emulates the innocence of a child's drawings... Accessible and tender, this story gives young children a voice and shows how to hold the memory of a loved one close." Kirkus

Cocca-Leffler, Maryann

Princess K.I.M. and the lie that grew. Albert Whitman & Co. 2009 32p $16.99

Grades: PreK K 1 2   E
1. Truthfulness and falsehood -- Fiction
ISBN 978-0-8075-4178-4; 0-8075-4178-8

LC 2008-28056

After new girl Kim tells her classmates she is from a royal family, her lie grows and grows.

"The brightly colored artwork brings the story to life. . . . Varying layouts effectively convey the action." SLJ

Another title about Kim is:
Princess Kim and too much truth (2011)

Rain brings frogs; a little book of hope. Harper 2011 un il $9.99

Grades: PreK K 1   E
1. Hope -- Fiction 2. Happiness -- Fiction
ISBN 978-0-06-196106-9; 0-06-196106-X

"Nate sees everything in a positive light. When Charlie says, 'Keep Out!'/Nate says, 'Room for All.' When Mom says, 'I Hate Rain.' Nate says, 'Rain Brings Frogs!' Green frog endpapers enhance the cheerful colors and cartoonlike characters surrounded by plenty of white space. The font is

large, and the narrative waves through the pages showing action and movement." SLJ

A **vacation** for Pooch; Maryann Cocca-Leffler. Christy Ottaviano Books 2013 32 p. (hardcover) $16.99

Grades: K 1 2 3   E
1. Dogs -- Fiction 2. Vacations -- Fiction
ISBN 0805091068; 9780805091069

LC 2012011271

This children's story, by Maryann Cocca-Leffler, follows a girl and her pet dog going on separate vacations. Violet is "going on vacation to sunny Florida. She packed her bag very carefully. . . ." Pooch is "going on vacation to Grandpa's snowy farm. Violet packed his bag very carefully, too. . . . When their bags get mixed up, Violet thinks Pooch's vacation will be miserable. But Pooch is having a grand old time, so all is very well!" (Publisher's note)

Cochran, Bill

My parents are divorced, my elbows have nicknames, and other facts about me; illustrated by Steve Björkman. HarperCollins 2009 un il $17.99; lib bdg $18.89

Grades: K 1 2 3   E
1. Divorce -- Fiction
ISBN 978-0-06-053942-9; 0-06-053942-9; 978-0-06-053943-6 lib bdg; 0-06-053943-7 lib bdg

While describing his not-so-weird life with his divorced parents, a young boy also describes some other things about himself that could be considered weird.

"This story uses humor to help children cope with the issue of divorce. . . . Ted has a believable voice that children will recognize. . . . The colorful cartoons add to the upbeat nature of the story and make a serious subject a little easier to swallow." SLJ

Codell, Esmé Raji, 1968-

Fairly fairy tales; illustrated by Elisa Chavarri. Aladdin 2011 un il

Grades: PreK K 1   E
1. Fairy tales 2. Books and reading -- Fiction
ISBN 1-4169-9086-0; 978-1-4169-9086-4

LC 2009-16475

This book reimagines six familiar fairy tales. "Ages four to seven." (Bull Cent Child Books)

"In this fanciful collection, Codell takes six familiar fairy tales, lists three known attributes for each . . . then throws in a novel element . . . which provides impetus for a fanciful revisioning depicted in the following spread. . . . It's a great gimmick, and the 'what if?' approach to fairy tales offers heaps of potential for classroom projects and discussions. . . . Chavarri's splashy, digitally rendered illustrations are most notable for their attention to detail: the wordless alternative-story spreads are chock full of minutiae that add considerable humor to the simple text." Bull Cent Child Books

Coerr, Eleanor

The **big** balloon race; pictures by Carolyn Croll. Harper & Row 1981 62p il (I can read book) hardcover o.p. pa $3.99

Grades: K 1 2   E
1. Balloons -- Fiction
ISBN 0-06-444053-2 pa

LC 80-8368

The author "recounts the winning of a hydrogen balloon race by Carlotta Myers, a famous aeronaut, and her stowaway daughter Ariel. Balloon facts are slipped naturally and painlessly into the story, which moves cogently along. The novel subject matter, straightforward mother-daughter relationship, and clear composition of the orange, blue and gray illustrations . . . make for a high-flying new look at a piece of the past." SLJ

The **Josefina** story quilt; pictures by Bruce Degen. Harper & Row 1986 64p il (I can read book) hardcover o.p. pa $3.99

Grades: K 1 2 3   E
1. Quilts -- Fiction 2. Overland journeys to the Pacific -- Fiction
ISBN 0-06-021348-5; 0-06-444129-6 pa

LC 85-45260

While traveling west with her family in 1850, a young girl makes a patchwork quilt chronicling the experiences of the journey and reserves a special patch for her pet hen Josefina

"The story makes the history go down easily, and an author's note at the end fills in facts about the western trip and the place of quilts as pioneer diaries. The charcoal and blue/yellow wash illustrations are clear and natural. . . . A good introduction to historical fiction that children can read for themselves." SLJ

Coffelt, Nancy

Catch that baby! illustrated by Scott Nash. Aladdin 2011 un il $16.99

Grades: PreK K   E
1. Baths -- Fiction 2. Infants -- Fiction 3. Family life -- Fiction
ISBN 978-1-4169-9148-9; 1-4169-9148-4

LC 2009-34934

Everyone from Mom to Grandpa joins the chase when baby Rudy decides he does not want to get dressed after his bath.

"Ebullient in tone and sassy in spirit, this is a romp where both family and action seem quite real." Booklist

★ **Fred** stays with me; illustrated by Tricia Tusa. Little, Brown 2007 un il $16.99

Grades: PreK K 1 2   E
1. Dogs -- Fiction 2. Divorce -- Fiction
ISBN 0-316-88269-0

LC 2005-07973

Boston Globe-Horn Book Award honor book: Picture Book (2008)

A child describes how she lives sometimes with his mother and sometimes with his father, but his dog is his constant companion.

"Coffelt and Tusa have teamed up to create a charming book that meshes text and illustrations seamlessly. . . . Tusa uses gold and brown hues with occasional splashes of red to create a warm tone." SLJ

Cohen, Barbara

★ **Molly's** pilgrim; illustrated by Daniel Mark Duffy. Lothrop, Lee & Shepard Bks. 1998 un il $17.99; pa $3.95

Grades: K 1 2 3   E
1. School stories 2. Jews -- Fiction 3. Immigrants --

Fiction 4. Thanksgiving Day -- Fiction
ISBN 0-688-16279-7; 0-688-16280-0 pa

LC 98-9227

A newly illustrated edition of the title first published 1983

Told to make a Pilgrim doll for the Thanksgiving display at school, Molly is embarassed when her mother tries to help her out by creating a doll dressed as she herself was dressed before leaving Russia to seek religious freedom

Cohen, Caron Lee

Broom, zoom! illustrated by Sergio Ruzzier. Simon & Schuster Books for Young Readers 2010 un il $12.99

Grades: PreK K 1   E
1. Brooms -- Fiction 2. Goblins -- Fiction 3. Witches -- Fiction
ISBN 978-1-4169-9113-7; 1-4169-9113-1

LC 2009000581

One beautiful, starry night, a little witch wants to go for a ride on a broom but first she must help a little monster clean up a mess.

"The text is simple enough for beginning readers, as the characters speak in one and two-word sentences. The illustrations were digitally created in flat, singular colors. . . . . Although Witch and Monster give the story a Halloween feel, it is a simple tale of cooperation and friendship, and youngsters will respond to it as such." SLJ

Cohen, Deborah Bodin

Engineer Ari and the sukkah express; illustrated by Shahar Kober. Kar-Ben Pub. 2010 p. cm. il lib bdg $17.95; pa $7.95

Grades: PreK K 1 2   E
1. Jews -- Fiction 2. Israel -- Fiction 3. Sukkot -- Fiction 4. Railroads -- Fiction
ISBN 978-0-7613-5126-9 lib bdg; 0-7613-5126-4 lib bdg; 978-0-7613-5128-3 pa; 0-7613-5128-0 pa

LC 2009001876

Nachshon, who was afraid to swim; a Passover story. by Deborah Bodin Cohen; illustrations by Jago. Kar-Ben Pub. 2009 un il lib bdg $17.95; pa $8.95

Grades: 1 2 3 4   E
1. Fear -- Fiction 2. Jews -- Fiction 3. Courage -- Fiction 4. Slavery -- Fiction 5. Passover -- Fiction
ISBN 978-0-8225-8764-4 lib bdg; 0-8225-8764-5 lib bdg; 978-0-8225-8765-1 pa; 0-8225-8765-3 pa

LC 2007048359

When the Israelites flee Egypt, Nachshon exhibits great courage by being the first to step into the Red Sea, even though he cannot swim.

"The digitally prepared, mixed-media illustrations utilize muted yellow, orange, and brown tones to depict the sweltering heat of the desert and bright blue and green tones to illustrate the celebration of freedom. They complement and enhance the text marvelously. A wonderful, unique addition." SLJ

Cohen, Miriam

★ **First** grade takes a test; by Miriam Cohen; illustrated by Ronald Himler. Star Bright Books 2006 un il $15.95; pa $5.95

Grades: PreK K 1 2   **E**

1. School stories 2. Examinations -- Fiction
ISBN 978-1-59572-054-2; 1-59572-054-5; 978-1-
59572-055-9 pa; 1-59572-055-3 pa

LC 2006020488

A revised and newly illustrated edition of the title first published 1980 by Greenwillow Bks.

"One day the first-graders are given a special multiple-choice test by the principal. Some kids find the questions puzzling. Then, suddenly, time's up. Anna Maria announces, 'That was easy.' But many kids are confused and upset, and 'You're a dummy!' echoes through the class, which only settles down when the kindly teacher reminds the children of all the things they do understand. . . . Cohen's sensitivity to children's feelings and reactions really shows here. . . . Himler's loose-lined, pencil-and-watercolor pictures skillfully use body language and facial expressions to chart the children's emotional highs and lows." Booklist

My big brother; art by Ronald Himler. Star Bright 2005 un il $15.95

Grades: K 1 2 3   **E**

1. Brothers -- Fiction 2. Soldiers -- Fiction 3. Family life -- Fiction
ISBN 1-59572-007-3

LC 2004-16056

When his big brother leaves to become a soldier, a boy does what he can to take his place in the family.

"This quiet picture book packs a strong emotional wallop. Himler's artwork, pencil with watercolor washes, sensitively depicts each character's emotions through body language and facial expressions." Booklist

★ **Will** I have a friend? by Miriam Cohen; illustrated by Ronald Himler. Star Bright Books 2009 un il $15.95

Grades: PreK K 1   **E**

1. School stories 2. Friendship -- Fiction
ISBN 978-1-59572-069-6; 1-59572-069-3

LC 2008036957

A newly illustrated edition of the title first published 1967 by Macmillan

Jim's anxieties on his first day of school are happily forgotten when he makes a new friend.

The art is "fresh and new. . . . Himler's soft watercolors are . . . contemporary in look, with touches like a recycle mark on the trash bin. . . . Great for combating new-kid-in-school blues." Booklist

Cohn, Diana

Namaste! illustrated by Amy Cordova; with an Afterward by Ang Rita Sherpa of the Mountain Institute. SteinerBooks 2009 un il $17.95

Grades: K 1 2   **E**

1. Nepal -- Fiction
ISBN 978-0-88010-625-2; 0-88010-625-5

LC 2009003216

Whenever Nima meets someone on her long walk to the market village in Nepal, she brings her hands together with her fingers almost touching her chin, bows her head slightly, and says "Namaste," which means "the light in me meets the light in you." Includes information on the geography, culture, and people of Nepal

"The vibrant folk-art illustrations showing the details of Nima's life in her village support the simple story perfectly.

This beautiful book will appeal to primary readers and make an ideal addition to multicultural collections." SLJ

Colato Lainez, Rene

My shoes and I; illustrations by Fabricio Vanden Broeck. Boyds Mills Press 2010 un il $16.95

Grades: K 1 2 3   **E**

1. Shoes -- Fiction 2. Travel -- Fiction 3. Immigrants -- Fiction 4. Central America -- Fiction 5. Father-son relationship -- Fiction
ISBN 978-1-59078-385-6; 1-59078-385-9

LC 2008-30003

As Mario and his Papa travel from El Salvador to the United States to be reunited with Mama, Mario's wonderful new shoes help to distract him from the long and difficult journey.

"Vanden Broeck's color-drenched illustrations on weathered backgrounds add immediacy and detail. This moving, heartfelt tale of courage and perseverance will be embraced by a wide audience of readers, young and old." SLJ

Playing loteria; illustrated by Jill Arena. Luna Rising 2005 un il hardcover o.p. pa $6.95

Grades: PreK K 1 2   **E**

1. Games -- Fiction 2. Mexico -- Fiction 3. Grandmothers -- Fiction 4. Mexican Americans -- Fiction 5. Bilingual books -- English-Spanish
ISBN 0-87358-881-9; 978-0-87358-919-2 pa; 0-87358-919-X pa

A boy has a good time attending a fair with his grandmother in San Luis de La Paz, Mexico, as she teaches him Spanish words and phrases and he teaches her English.

"This is a warm and reassuring story of a boy's involvement not only with his family but also his culture. The prose flows easily in both English and Spanish. [This is illustrated with] spirited primitive acrylics." SLJ

Señor Pancho had a rancho; by René Colato Laínez; illustrated by Elwood Smith. Holiday House 2013 (hardcover) $16.95

Grades: PreK K 1   **E**

1. Farms -- Fiction 2. Bilingual books -- English-Spanish 3. Stories in rhyme 4. Bilingualism -- Fiction 5. Animal sounds -- Fiction 6. Domestic animals -- Fiction
ISBN 0823426327; 9780823426324

LC 2012007672

In this book, by René Colato Laínez, "the barnyard animals on Old MacDonald's and Senor Pancho's farms have a hard time communicating. MacDonald's rooster says cock-a-doodle-doo! While Senor Pancho's gallo says quiquirquí. The English-speaking chick says peep, peep, but el pollito says pio, pio. Then the cow says moo and la vaca says mu! Maybe they're not so different after all! So all the animals come together for a barnyard fiesta, because dancing is a universal language." (Publisher's note)

"Old MacDonald has a farm; Seqor Pancho has a rancho. You'll hear "cock-a-doodle-doo" and "peep" on the farm; Pancho's gallo says "quiquiriqum" and his pollito says "pmo." But when the cow and una vaca get together: "Here a moo, there a muu. / Everywhere a moo muu." The energetic illustrations are a good match for the lively reworked lyrics, which include Spanish words and animal sounds." (Horn Book)

The **Tooth** Fairy meets El Raton Perez; illustrations by Tom Lintern. Tricycle Press 2010 un il $15.99; lib bdg $18.99

Grades: PreK K 1   E
    1. Mice -- Fiction 2. Teeth -- Fiction 3. Fairies -- Fiction 4. Mexican Americans -- Fiction
    ISBN 978-1-58246-296-7; 1-58246-296-8; 978-1-58246-342-1 lib bdg; 1-58246-342-5 lib bdg

                    LC 2009-16782

When Miguel loses a tooth, two legendary characters come to claim it—one who is responsible for collecting teeth in the United States and one who has collected the teeth of the boy's parents and grandparents.

"Lainez's creative story approaches the topic of cultural identity with humor and grace, while newcomer Lintern's colored pencil illustrations give it a sense of nocturnal whimsy." Publ Wkly

Cole, Brock

   ★ **Buttons**. Farrar, Straus & Giroux 2000 un il hardcover o.p. $16

Grades: K 1 2 3   E
    1. Father-daughter relationship -- Fiction
    ISBN 0-374-31001-7; 0-374-41013-5 pa

                    LC 99-27162

When their father eats so much that he pops the buttons off his britches, each of his three daughters tries a different plan to find replacements

"A delectable tall tale. . . . Cole's narrative has a humorous lilt that's as much fun as his rollicking illustrations." Horn Book Guide

   ★ **Good** enough to eat. Farrar, Straus & Giroux 2007 un il $16

Grades: K 1 2 3   E
    1. Fairy tales 2. Orphans -- Fiction 3. Homeless persons -- Fiction
    ISBN 978-0-374-32737-8; 0-374-32737-8

                    LC 2006-37368

When an Ogre comes to town demanding a bride, the mayor sacrifices the homeless girl with no name that everyone thinks is a pest and a bother, but she finds a way to outwit them all.

The illustrations offer "lively line and delicate use of color. The cadenced language and blithe illustrations work perfectly together. . . . With the structure of a fairy tale and the freshness of an original story, Good Enough to Eat is satisfying fare indeed." Horn Book

   ★ **Larky** Mavis. Farrar, Straus & Giroux 2001 un il $16

Grades: K 1 2 3   E
    1. Infants -- Fiction
    ISBN 0-374-34365-9

                    LC 00-51419

Having found a tiny baby in a peanut shell, Larky Mavis calls him Heart's Delight and carries him around as he grows bigger, to the confusion and anger of the adults around her

"The prose is lyrical, peppered with quaint speech patterns and lively dialogue that is a delight to read aloud. . . . The rumpled, animated line-and-watercolor illustrations

extend the charming story beyond his tightly constructed prose." SLJ

   ★ The **money** we'll save. Farrar Straus & Giroux 2011 un il $16.99

Grades: K 1 2   E
    1. Christmas stories 2. Turkeys -- Fiction 3. Christmas -- Fiction 4. Apartment houses -- Fiction 5. New York (State) -- Fiction
    ISBN 978-0-374-35011-6; 0-374-35011-6

                    LC 2010037760

In nineteenth-century New York City, when Pa brings home a young turkey in hopes of saving money on their Christmas dinner, his family faces all sorts of trouble—and expense—in their tiny apartment.

"The cleverly constructed text is full of understated humor and witty dialogue, with a satisfying conclusion describing the family's simple but happy Christmas celebration. Cole's loose watercolor-and-ink illustrations skillfully evoke the old-fashioned setting and busy life of a New York tenement community." Kirkus

Cole, Henry

   Big bug; Henry Cole. Little Simon 2014 32 p. color illustrations (hc: alk. paper) $14.99

Grades: PreK K 1 2   E
    1. Size -- Fiction 2. Farm life -- Fiction 3. English language -- Comparison -- Fiction
    ISBN 1442498978; 9781442498976

                    LC 2013020626

"Beginning with a . . . close-up of a 'big' ladybug, this book," by author and illustrator Henry Cole, "depicts the concept of scale. The book zooms out from the bug, to a flower, to a cow, all the way to an expansive spread of sky. Then . . . zooms back in from that sky, to a tree, to a house, to a window, all the way to the end where [a] . . . dog is taking a 'little' nap." (Publisher's note)

"The concept of scale is brilliantly depicted on the title page (where tiny ladybugs crawl over the title of the book in large font) as well as the endpapers. The different font sizes further highlight the use of scale in his breathtaking illustrations. Big Bug is a unique reading experience with broad appeal." SLJ reviews

   Jack's garden; Henry Cole. Greenwillow Bks. 1995 24 p. $17.99

Grades: PreK K 1   E
    1. Gardening -- Fiction 2. Picture books for children
    ISBN 0688135013; 9780688135010

                    LC 94006249

Author and illustrator Henry Cole features a rhyming children's book that focuses on how to create and maintain a garden. The book chronicles a little boy named Jack as he constructs and plants a flower garden, complete with birds and butterflies. Cole also presents additional and more specific gardening suggestions and guidelines at the back of the book.

   The **littlest** evergreen. Katherine Tegen Books 2011 un il $16.99; lib bdg $18.89

Grades: PreK K 1 2   E
    1. Trees -- Fiction 2. Christmas stories 3. Christmas trees -- Fiction 4. Conservation of natural resources --

Fiction
ISBN 978-0-06-114619-0; 0-06-114619-6; 978-0-06-
114620-6 lib bdg; 0-06-114620-X lib bdg

LC 2008022630

"The littlest evergreen, Cole's narrator, is dug out of the
earth . . . by men searching for Christmas trees. They forgo
using their chainsaw on it, believing it 'too small to
make much of a tree,' but a young family purchases it and, after
Christmas, replants the pine, which thrives. . . . Preschool,
primary." (Horn Book)

"Told from the perspective of a small evergreen, this tale
begins with the narrator as a sprout and continues through
the seasons until men come with their chainsaws. Luckily,
the tree's size saves it from being cut down. . . . Taken to
a Christmas tree lot, it is taken home by a family where it
is decorated with ornaments and begins to feel loved. After
a few weeks, the evergreen is replanted in the yard, where
it grows big and strong. Illustrations are of a contemporary
setting with nature's beauty brought forth through the lush
greenery. A fine Christmas choice with an environmental
message." SLJ

★ **On** Meadowview Street; [by] Henry Cole. Greenwillow Books 2007 un il $17.99; lib bdg $18.89
Grades: K 1 2 3   E
  1. Nature -- Fiction 2. Meadows -- Fiction 3. Suburban
life -- Fiction
ISBN 978-0-06-056481-0; 0-06-056481-4; 978-0-06-
056482-7 lib bdg; 0-06-056482-2 lib bdg

LC 2006023761

Upon moving to a new house, young Caroline and her
parents encourage wildflowers to grow and birds and animals to stay in their yard, which soon has the whole suburban street living up to its name

"Cole's understated watercolors match the tale's gentle
tone." Booklist

On the way to the beach. Greenwillow Bks. 2003 un
il $16.99
Grades: PreK K 1 2   E
  1. Nature -- Fiction 2. Ecology -- Fiction 3. Senses and
sensation -- Fiction
ISBN 0-688-17515-5

LC 2002-23537

On a walk through the woods and a marsh to the seashore, the reader is encouraged to notice all sorts of plants,
animals, insects, and shells

"Each locale . . . is gloriously depicted in a three-page
foldout that is entered through a die-cut. . . . The outstanding realistic acrylic illustrations depict the scenes in an
almost three-dimensional perspective. . . . This beautiful,
interactive book encourages discussion, develops observation skills, and provides a learning experience that will bring
children closer to nature." SLJ

Trudy. Greenwillow Books 2009 un il $17.99; lib
bdg $18.89
Grades: PreK K 1 2   E
  1. Snow -- Fiction 2. Goats -- Fiction
ISBN 978-0-06-154267-1; 0-06-154267-9; 978-0-06-
154268-8 lib bdg; 0-06-154268-7 lib bdg

LC 2007-47641

It seems as though Trudy the goat knows when to expect
snow, but it turns out that she is really expecting something
completely different.

"Cole's acrylic paintings are rounded and soft. They juxtapose muted, earth-toned colors of the environment with
the bright, primary colors of manmade objects. . . . The
steady pace of the text combined with its loosely repetitive
structure creates a calm, reassuring mood, making the book
an excellent bedtime read." SLJ

★ **Unspoken**; a story from the Underground Railroad.
by Henry Cole. Scholastic Press 2012 40 p. (hardcover:
alk. paper) $16.99
Grades: 2 3 4 5   E
  1. Fugitive slaves -- Fiction 2. United States -- History
-- 1861-1865, Civil War 4. Fugitive slaves -- Fiction 5.
African Americans -- Fiction 6. Underground Railroad
-- Fiction
ISBN 0545399971; 9780545399975

LC 2011043583

In this wordless picture book about the Underground
Railroad by Henry Cole, "a farm child and a fugitive [slave]
make an unspoken connection" during the American "Civil
War. Going about her chores after watching a detachment
of mounted soldiers beneath a Confederate flag trot by, the
child is startled and fearful to realize that someone is hiding in a pile of cornstalks in the storehouse. . . . She cou-
rageously ventures out by herself, carrying small gifts of
food." (Kirkus Reviews)

Collard, Sneed B.
  Butterfly count; illustrated by Paul Kratter. Holiday
House 2002 un il $16.95
Grades: K 1 2 3   E
  1. Prairies -- Fiction 2. Butterflies -- Fiction 3. Wildlife
conservation -- Fiction
ISBN 0-8234-1607-0

LC 2001-24114

Amy and her mother look for a very special butterfly
while attending the annual Fourth of July Butterfly Count at
a prairie restoration site. Includes factual information about
butterflies and how to attract and watch them

"A gentle family story with an environmental message. .
. . Soft watercolor illustrations of prairie grasses, plants, and
butterflies quietly illuminate this tranquil tale." SLJ

Collier, Bryan
  ★ **Uptown**. Holt & Co. 2000 un il $16.95
Grades: K 1 2 3   E
  1. African Americans -- Fiction 2. Harlem (New York,
N.Y.) -- Fiction
ISBN 0-8050-5721-8

LC 99-31774

Coretta Scott King Award for illustration
A tour of the sights of Harlem, including the Metro-
North Train, brownstones, shopping on 125th Street, a barber shop, summer basketball, the Boy's Choir, and sunset
over the Harlem River as narrated by a young boy. "Ages
six to nine." (Bull Cent Child Books)

"Collier's evocative watercolor-and-collage illustrations
create a unique sense of mood and place. Bold color choices
for text as well as background pages complement engagingly detailed pictures of city life." SLJ

Collins, Pat Lowery

The **Deer** watch; Pat Lowery Collins, illustrated by David Slonim. Candlewick Press 2013 32 p. ill. (reinforced) $15.99

Grades: K 1 2 3   E

1. Deer -- Fiction 2. Father-son relationship

ISBN 0763648906; 9780763648909

LC 2012942667

In this children's story, by Pat Lowery Collins, illustrated by David Slonim, "a father promises his young son that this summer they will see a deer. They set out over the dunes, through the marsh, and into the woods, searching for a white-flag tail or a set of leaping legs. But deer are hard to find, especially if your feet want to dance and your nose tickles until you sneeze." (Publisher's note)

Collins, Ross

Dear Vampa; written and illustrated by Ross Collins. Katherine Tegen Books 2009 un il $16.99

Grades: K 1 2   E

1. Letters -- Fiction 2. Vampires -- Fiction

ISBN 978-0-06-135534-9; 0-06-135534-8

LC 2008-22631

A young vampire writes a letter to his grandfather bemoaning his new neighbors

"Collins's . . . black, angular vampires lace the comedy with a drop of real creepiness. . . . Young vampire fans will enjoy (and perhaps be secretly relieved by) the vampires' beleaguered state." Publ Wkly

Doodleday. Albert Whitman 2011 un il $16.99

Grades: PreK K   E

1. Drawing -- Fiction 2. Mother-son relationship -- Fiction

ISBN 978-0-8075-1683-6; 0-8075-1683-X

LC 2010-31128

First published in the United Kingdom

Despite his mother's warning, young Harvey draws on Doodleday, but when his drawings come to life in frightening ways, only his mother can help.

"Collins brings to life the always intriguing notion of art brought to life, giving it a movie-blockbuster level of entertaining disaster. Spare, exclamatory text keeps the focus squarely on the action. . . . Any kid who's put crayon to paper will relish the notion that there's having waiting to be caused thereby." Bull Cent Child Books

Collins, Suzanne, 1962-

Year of the jungle; memories from the home front. by Suzanne Collins; illustrated by James Proimos. Scholastic Press 2013 40 p. color illustrations (hc) $17.99

Grades: K 1 2 3   E

1. Vietnam War, 1961-1975 2. Picture books for children 3. Fathers and daughters 4. Separation (Psychology)

ISBN 0545425166; 9780545425162

LC 2012015346

This children's picture book "recounts, through the author's eyes as a child, the year of her father's military tour of duty in Viet Nam. The youngest of four kids growing up in a safe, loving family, Suzy is first seen listening to her dad read Ogden Nash's poem about Custard, the dragon who stays brave despite his inner fears. Thus the stage is set for

her father's imminent deployment," a challenge for Suzy and her father alike. (School Library Journal)

Colon, Edie

Good-bye, Havana! Hola, New York! illustrated by Raúl Colón. Simon & Schuster Books for Young Readers 2011 un il $16.99

Grades: PreK K 1   E

1. Cuba -- Fiction 2. Immigrants -- Fiction 3. Cuban Americans -- Fiction 4. Bronx (New York, N.Y.) -- Fiction

ISBN 978-1-4424-0674-2; 1-4424-0674-7; 9781442406742; 1442406747

LC 2010020932

When Fidel Castro's government takes over their restaurant in 1960, six-year-old Gabriella and her parents move from Cuba to New York City.

"In his signature, almost pointillist style, Raúl Colón's earth-toned artwork imbues the story with a comforting texture and warmth, closely depicting the clothing, hair, and décor of the era. The dialogue is smoothly rendered in Spanish and English, and many Spanish words are defined on the final page. This gentle look back at an important time will also speak to contemporary children whose families are starting anew in the United States." Publ Wkly

Colón, Raúl, 1952-

★ **Draw!** Raul Colon; illustrated by Raul Colon. SSB-FYR 2014 40 p. (hardcover) $17.99

Grades: PreK K 1 2 3   E

1. Safaris 2. Animals -- Fiction 3. Drawing -- Fiction 4. Safaris -- Fiction 5. Stories without words 6. Imagination -- Fiction

ISBN 1442494921; 9781442494923

LC 2013043781

In this children's book by Raúl Colón, "A boy named Leonardo begins to imagine and then draw a world afar - first a rhinoceros, and then he meets some monkeys, and he always has a friendly elephant at his side. Soon he finds himself in the jungle and carried away by the sheer power of his imagination, seeing the world through his own eyes and making friends along the way." (Publisher's note)

"A boy in bed, asthma inhaler within reach, sketchbook at his side, looking at a book about Africa, is not confined by the walls of his room. As he begins to draw, he takes a journey. The palette changes from subdued pen-and-ink with wash in the bedroom to vibrant hues textured with scratched-in lines that seem to pulse, capturing the landscape and animals of Africa...Youngsters will pore over each spread in wonder, soaking up the details...A true celebration of where our imaginations can take us." (Booklist)

Comden, Betty

What's new at the zoo? by Betty Comden and Adolph Green; illustrations by Travis Foster; with an introduction by Phyllis Newman. Blue Apple Books 2011 un il $16.99

Grades: K 1 2 3   E

1. Songs 2. Animals -- Songs

ISBN 978-1-60905-088-7; 1-60905-088-6

LC 2011019080

Presents the lyrics to a song from the Broadway musical, 'Do Re Mi,' in which animals in an overcrowded zoo beg to be let out while accidentally stepping on one anothers trunks, quills, and toes.

"With fun lift-the-flap details and tummy-tickling rhymes, this book will appeal to fans of slapstick humor. The cartoon illustrations really bring the silliness to life." SLJ

Compestine, Ying Chang
★ **Boy** dumplings; illustrated by James Yamasaki. Holiday House 2009 un il $16.95
Grades: PreK K 1 2   E
1. Ghost stories 2. China -- Fiction 3. Cooking -- Fiction
ISBN 978-0-8234-1955-5; 0-8234-1955-X
LC 2006050064

When a hungry ghost threatens to gobble up a plump little boy, the boy tricks the ghost by convincing him to prepare an elaborate recipe first.

"In keeping with the tale's brisk pacing and light tone, Yamasaki depicts the beaming, succulent boy and the menacing but increasingly beleaguered ghost with particularly comical faces in his cartoon illustrations. . . . [This is a] crowd-pleaser." Booklist

★ The **runaway** rice cake; pictures by Tungwai Chau. Simon & Schuster Bks. for Young Readers 2001 un il $16.95
Grades: K 1 2 3   E
1. China -- Fiction 2. Chinese New Year -- Fiction
ISBN 0-689-82972-8
LC 99-462168

After chasing the special rice cake, Nian Gao, that their mother has made to celebrate the Chinese New Year, three poor brothers share it with an elderly woman and have their generosity richly rewarded

"Compestine's engaging tale brims with intriguing details of the traditions that surround the holiday. . . . Chau makes a splash with vibrant acrylics whose textured surface and controlled, sophisticated blending of shades mimic the look of pastels." Publ Wkly

★ The **runaway** wok; a Chinese New Year tale. illustrated by Sebastià Serra. Dutton Children's Books 2011 un il $16.99
Grades: K 1 2 3   E
1. China -- Fiction 2. Magic -- Fiction 3. Chinese New Year -- Fiction
ISBN 978-0-525-42068-2; 0-525-42068-1
LC 2010013473

On Chinese New Year's Eve, a poor man who works for the richest businessman in Beijing sends his son to market to trade their last few eggs for a bag of rice, but instead he brings home an empty—but magic—wok that changes their fortunes forever. Includes information about Chinese New Year and a recipe for fried rice.

"Inspired by the Danish folktale, The Talking Pot, Compestine's . . . jaunty story takes place long ago in Beijing, which Serra . . . portrays as a bustling, cheerful village. . . . The sight of the insouciant wok carrying away the miserly family . . . will make kids snicker. They'll also chime in, since the wok's refrain begs for audience participation." Publ Wkly

Conahan, Carolyn
The **big** wish. Chronicle Books 2011 il $16.99

Grades: PreK K 1   E
1. Wishes -- Fiction
ISBN 978-0-8118-7040-5; 0-8118-7040-5
LC 2010027353

When Molly's neighbor, Pie, tries to mow down her dandelions, Molly insists that dandelions aren't weeds they're wishes in the making! Molly is convinced that if she grows enough dandelions she can make the world's biggest wish ever, a world record!

"Conahan's whimsical watercolors, full of swirl and movement, complement her gentle fable of community harmony. Quirky and full of heart." Kirkus

Connor, Leslie
Miss Bridie chose a shovel; illustrated by Mary Azarian. Houghton Mifflin 2004 un il $16
Grades: K 1 2 3   E
1. Immigrants -- Fiction
ISBN 0-618-30564-5
LC 2003-12290

Miss Bridie emigrates to America in 1856 and chooses to bring a shovel, which proves to be a useful tool throughout her life.

"Azarian's sturdy woodcuts are an excellent choice to illustrate daily life in mid-nineteenth-century America, and her pictures catch some of the emotions that the text shies away from. . . . This is a simple pleasure that will be truly appreciated by those old enough to understand the message." Booklist

Conway, David
The **great** nursery rhyme disaster; illustrated by Melanie Williamson. Tiger Tales 2009 un il $15.95
Grades: PreK K 1   E
1. Nursery rhymes -- Fiction
ISBN 978-1-58925-080-2; 1-58925-080-X
First published 2008 in the United Kingdom

Little Miss Muffet is bored. So she goes off to find a new nursery rhyme to be in. No rhyme seems quite right for Little Miss Muffet. Suddenly life with a scary little spider doesn't seem so bad after all.

"Witty prose and updated interpretations are complemented by Williamson's exuberant illustrations. Colorful, comical, and energetic, the characters race through the pages to the story's end." SLJ

Lila and the secret of rain; [by] David Conway; illustrated by Jude Daly. Frances Lincoln Children's 2007 un il $16.95
Grades: PreK K 1 2   E
1. Rain -- Fiction 2. Kenya -- Fiction 3. Droughts -- Fiction
ISBN 978-1-84507-407-4; 1-84507-407-6

Lila's village in Kenya is experiencing a terrible drought. When Lila's grandfather tells her the secret of rain, she sets off on her own to save her village.

"This quiet story offers inspiration and hope. . . . The illustrations are quite lovely. A huge orange sun in a brilliant blue sky dominates most pages. The prominence of the brown baked earth intensifies the unwanted result of the lack of rain. . . . This story will work well both as a read-aloud and for sharing one-on-one." SLJ

The **most** important gift of all; illustrated by Karin Littlewood. Gingham Dog Press 2006 un il $15.95

Grades: K 1 2 3   **E**

1. Love -- Fiction 2. Kenya -- Fiction 3. Infants -- Fiction 4. Siblings -- Fiction

ISBN 0-7696-4618-2

"Ama is excited when her baby brother is born, and like all the people of her Kenyan village, she wants to bring him a gift. Because Grandma tells her that love is the most important gift of all, the small girl goes in search of it. . . . The beautiful blend of the traditional storytelling pattern and contemporary realism is expressed in Littlewood's double-page spreads." Booklist

Cook, Lisa Broadie

Peanut butter and homework sandwiches; illustrated by Jack E. Davis. G.P. Putnam's Sons 2011 un il $16.99

Grades: K 1   **E**

1. School stories 2. Homework -- Fiction 3. Teachers -- Fiction 4. Family life -- Fiction

ISBN 978-0-399-24533-6; 0-399-24533-2

LC 2010026221

When his teacher is out sick for a week, Martin MacGregor has a difficult time with the homework assigned by the substitute teacher.

"Davis' toothy cartoon characters are wonderfully expressive, especially the hapless Martin. The bright color and humorous situations are certain to keep readers' attention as they try to guess what could possibly happen to Martin next." Kirkus

Cooke, Trish

Full, full, full of love; illustrated by Paul Howard. Candlewick Press 2003 un il hardcover o.p. pa $3.99

Grades: PreK K 1   **E**

1. Grandmothers -- Fiction 2. African Americans -- Fiction

ISBN 0-7636-1851-9; 0-7636-3883-8 pa

LC 2001-43761

For young Jay Jay, Sunday dinner at Gran's house is full of hugs and kisses, tasty dishes, all kinds of fishes, happy faces, and love

"Howard's generous, full-bleed illustrations capture the loving, bountiful spirit of a big family meal with a colorful palette and expressive eyes and smiles." Booklist

Coombs, Kate

The **secret**-keeper; story by Kate Coombs; paintings by Heather M. Solomon. Atheneum Books for Young Readers 2006 un il $16.95

Grades: 1 2 3 4   **E**

1. Fairy tales

ISBN 0-689-83963-4

LC 2003-24695

The people of Maldinga and the surrounding area bring their deep, dark secrets to Kalli, who keeps them all safe until they become too much for her to bear.

"This original fairy tale is elegantly and tenderly told. . . . Solomon's watercolor and oil paintings are lushly colored. . . . The intricate details . . . slow and eye and invite repeated viewings." Bull Cent Child Books

Cooney, Barbara

Chanticleer and the fox; adapted and illustrated by Barbara Cooney. Crowell 1958 un il $16.99; lib bdg $17.89; pa $7.99

Grades: K 1 2 3   **E**

1. Poets 2. Fables 3. Authors 4. Foxes -- Fiction

ISBN 0-690-18561-8; 0-690-18562-6 lib bdg; 0-06-443087-1 pa

Adaptation of the "Nun's Priest's Tale" from the Canterbury Tales. Verso of title page

Awarded the Caldecott Medal, 1959

This adaptation "retains the spirit of the original in its telling and in the beautiful, strongly colored illustrations softened by detailed lines. . . . [It] will be excellent for reading aloud to children." Libr J

Cooper, Elisha

★ **Beach**. Orchard Books 2006 un il $16.99

Grades: PreK K 1 2   **E**

1. Beaches -- Fiction 2. Seashore -- Fiction

ISBN 0-439-68785-3

LC 2005-20195

Women, men, boys, and girls spend a day at the beach enjoying a variety of activities on the sand and in the water.

"Cooper opens with a gorgeous stretch of sand in sun-flecked, amber-white watercolors. . . . His fondness for his subject is evident and infectious." SLJ

Bear dreams. Greenwillow Books 2006 un il $16.99; lib bdg $17.89

Grades: PreK K 1 2   **E**

1. Bears -- Fiction 2. Sleep -- Fiction

ISBN 0-06-087428-7; 0-06-087429-5 lib bdg

After a bear cub persuades his friends to play with him instead of hibernating, he gets very tired and falls asleep

"The watercolor-and-pencil illustrations softly portray the transition from fall to winter as well as from wakefulness to slumber. . . . This quiet book with its dreamlike quality is ideal for bedtime sharing." SLJ

Beaver is lost. Schwartz & Wade Books 2010 un il $17.99; lib bdg $20.99

Grades: PreK K 1   **E**

1. Beavers -- Fiction

ISBN 978-0-375-85765-2; 0-375-85765-6; 978-0-375-95765-9 lib bdg; 0-375-95765-0 lib bdg

LC 2009-24915

A lost beaver looks for the way home.

"Beaver's saga unfolds entirely through Cooper's splendid watercolor-and-pencil illustrations. . . . Stunning in their simplicity, these pictures speak a thousand words." Kirkus

★ **Farm**. Orchard Books 2010 un il $17.99

Grades: K 1 2 3   **E**

1. Farm life -- Fiction

ISBN 0-545-07075-9; 978-0-545-07075-1

LC 2009-04342

This book describes the activities on a family farm from the spring when preparations for planting begin to the autumn when the cats grow winter coats and the cold rains begin to fall. "Ages five to nine." (Bull Cent Child Books)

"Working in his signature style of loosely rendered figures and simple compositions in pencil and watercolor, Cooper combines beautiful expansive views of the farm . . . with small, individual images. . . . Filled with sensory details, the brief text has a poetic, stripped-down simplicity that matches the stark images and will read aloud well." Booklist

A **good** night walk. Orchard Books 2005 un il $16.99
Grades: PreK K 1 2   E
1. Bedtime -- Fiction 2. Walking -- Fiction
ISBN 0-439-68783-7

LC 2004-23571

The reader is taken on a journey through a neighborhood and shown the sights, sounds, and smells as evening approaches.

"The clear, unfussy compositions echo the poetic words' soothing, elemental sounds . . . which beautifully capture the soft, slowdown rhythms of dusk. Children will find much that's cozy, reassuring, and familiar in the scenes, . . . depicted in luminous watercolors and firmly penciled shapes" Booklist

★ **Homer**; Elisha Cooper. Greenwillow Books 2012 32 p. col. ill. (trade bdg.) $16.99
Grades: PreK K 1 2   E
1. Dogs -- Fiction 2. Family -- Fiction 3. Picture books for children 4. Contentment -- Fiction 5. Human-animal relationships -- Fiction
ISBN 0062012487; 9780062012487

LC 2011013453

This picture book tells the story of "an aging yellow Lab named Homer . . . [and his] love for his family. . . . At daybreak Homer is already lying on the front porch. . . . As the family members . . . pass by Homer on their way out, they all invite him to come along to play in the water, dig in the sand or bike to the store. Homer replies to each in turn that he is happy to stay right there on the porch. . . . Homer finally curl[s] up in a cozy armchair for the night, content because 'I have everything I want.'" (Kirkus Reviews)

★ **Magic** thinks big. Greenwillow Books 2004 un il $14.99; lib bdg $15.89
Grades: PreK K 1 2   E
1. Cats -- Fiction
ISBN 0-06-058164-6; 0-06-058165-4 lib bdg

LC 2003-12566

A cat sits in the doorway and tries to decide whether to go inside where he might get fed again, go outside where he might have an adventure, or stay where he is.

"The simple text is full of dry humor and whimsy. The dreamy pencil-and-watercolor illustrations are a pleasing mixture of soft colors and thick lines." SLJ

★ **Train**; by Elisha Cooper. Orchard Books 2013 40 p. $17.99
Grades: PreK K 1 2 3   E
1. Travel 2. Railroads 3. Railroad trains -- Fiction 4. Voyages and travels -- Fiction
ISBN 0545384958; 9780545384957

LC 2012049336

In this book, by Elisha Cooper, readers can "experience [the] sights, sounds, smells [of trains]--and the engineers and conductors who make them go--as they roll across the country. Climb aboard a red-striped Commuter Train in the East. Switch to a blue Passenger Train rolling through midwestern farmland. Then hop on a Freight Train, soar over mountains

on an Overnight Train, and finish on a High-Speed Train as it races to the West Coast." (Publisher's note)

"As five trains (commuter, freight, etc.) overtake each other, we travel with them across the country. Cooper varies his composition throughout, showing close-up interiors, long landscapes, or several vignettes on one spread. He makes sure we hear the trains, too (the passenger train leaving: "like the da dum da dum of a beating heart"). Ideal for poring over. Glos." (Horn Book)

Cooper, Floyd
Max and the tag-along moon; Floyd Cooper. Philomel Books 2012 32 p. ill. (reinforced) $16.99
Grades: PreK K 1   E
1. Picture books for children 2. Grandparent-grandchild relationship -- Fiction 3. Moon -- Fiction 4. Grandfathers -- Fiction
ISBN 0399233423; 9780399233425

LC 2011049784

In this children's picture book, "it's hard to leave Granpa's house, but he has a promise for young Max" the 'big fine moon' in the sky 'will always shine for you . . . on and on!' Granpa seems right for most of the 'swervy-curvy' trip home. . . . Then storm clouds turn the sky dark," and Max begins to worry. "When moon reappears, Max has a deeper understanding of what Granpa's promise means: love, like the moon's light, goes 'on and on.'" (Publishers Weekly)

★ **Willie** and the All-Stars; [by] Floyd Cooper. Philomel Books 2008 un il $16.99
Grades: PreK K 1   E
1. Baseball -- Fiction 2. Chicago (Ill.) -- Fiction 3. Race relations -- Fiction 4. African Americans -- Fiction
ISBN 978-0-399-23340-1; 0-399-23340-7

LC 2007042101

In 1934 Chicago, Willie sees a game between the Negro League All-Star team and the Major League All-Stars, and realizes that his dream of becoming a professional baseball player could come true.

"By looking at race relations through the prism of baseball, Cooper will draw readers. . . . The soft-focus sepia-touched artwork, vintage Cooper, is a nice mix of action and nostalgia." Booklist

Cooper, Helen
★ **Dog** biscuit. Farrar Straus Giroux 2009 un il $16
Grades: PreK K 1   E
1. Dogs -- Fiction 2. Imagination -- Fiction
ISBN 978-0-374-31812-3; 0-374-31812-3

LC 2008-24124

"One day, while Bridget is at Mrs. Blair's house being looked after, she eats a biscuit she finds in the shed—a dog biscuit. Mrs. Blair jokes that she will 'go bowwow and turn into a dog,' and Bridget begins to believe it. . . . A handsome and thoughtfully done layout uses different fonts and sizes for the text, and Cooper's illustrations alternate quiet, ordinary scenes with wild scenes of Bridget's imagination. . . . This is a beautiful and imaginative book for anyone who loves a good story." SLJ

★ **Pumpkin** soup. Farrar, Straus & Giroux 1999 un il hardcover o.p. pa $6.95
Grades: PreK K 1 2   E
1. Cats -- Fiction 2. Ducks -- Fiction 3. Cooking --

Fiction 4. Squirrels -- Fiction

ISBN 0-374-36164-9; 0-374-46031-0 pa

LC 98-18677

First published 1998 in the United Kingdom

The Cat and the Squirrel come to blows with the Duck in arguing about who will perform what duty in preparing their pumpkin soup, and they almost lose the Duck's friendship when he decides to leave them

"Cooper serves up a well-rounded tale told with story-teller's cadences. . . . Rich autumn colors and enchanting details on large spreads and spot illustrations embellish characterizations and setting." SLJ

Other titles about Cat, Squirrel and Duck are:

A pipkin of pepper (2005)

Delicious! (2007)

Cooper, Ilene

The **golden** rule; by Ilene Cooper; illustrated by Gabi Swiatowska. Abrams Books for Young Readers 2007 un il $16.95

Grades: K 1 2 3   E

1. Conduct of life -- Fiction

ISBN 978-0-8109-0960-1; 0-8109-0960-X

LC 2006013333

Grandpa explains that the golden rule is a simple statement on how to live that can be practiced by people of all ages and faiths, then helps his grandson figure out how to apply the rule to his own life.

"The rich, golden paintings and large format reinforce the importance of the topic. . . . Swirling patterns of animal shapes and symbols from various traditions are reminders that the topic is as abstract as the art, with much room for interpretation. This is less a story than a discussion starter, and teachers, parents, and religious leaders will welcome it as a clear introduction to an important subject." SLJ

Copeland, Misty

★ **Firebird**; ballerina Misty Copeland shows a young girl how to dance like the firebird. Misty Copeland; illustrated by Christopher Myers. First edition G.P. Putnam's Sons, an imprint of Penguin Group (USA) 2014 40 p. (hardback) $17.99

Grades: 2 3 4 5 6   E

1. Ballerinas -- Fiction 2. Girls -- Fiction 3. Dance -- Fiction 4. Ballet dancing -- Fiction 5. Self-confidence -- Fiction 6. African Americans -- Fiction

ISBN 0399166157; 9780399166150

LC 2014008878

Coretta Scott King (Illustrator) Book Award (2015)

"In her debut picture book, [author] Misty Copeland tells the story of a young girl--an every girl--whose confidence is fragile and who is questioning her own ability to reach the heights that Misty has reached. Misty encourages this young girl's faith in herself and shows her exactly how, through hard work and dedication, she too can become 'Firebird.'" (Publisher's note)

"Think you can simply write off celebrity books? Think again. American Ballet Theatre soloist Copeland is just as graceful with words as she is with her body....Myers's stunning collages layer strips of thickly painted paper to echo the wings of a firebird (Copeland's signature role), whether they are illustrating the stage curtains or a cloudy sky. His deep, rich colors make even the portraits of the dancers at

rest dramatic, and when the dancers are on stage, they seem to fly." Horn Book

Copp, Jim

Jim Copp, will you tell me a story? three uncommonly clever tales, as told by Jim Copp; illustrated by Lindsay duPont. Harcourt 2008 54p il $17.95

Grades: 2 3 4   E

1. Short stories 2. Stories in rhyme

ISBN 978-0-15-206331-3; 0-15-206331-5

LC 2007033969

"This collection contains three short stories that were originally recordings by Copp, who died in 1999. The humorous tales, some rhyming, have definite kid appeal. In the first, feisty Kate Higgins refuses to take her medicine and suffers the consequences in the morning. . . . [In] 'Miss Goggins and the Gorilla,' . . . a fourth-grade class is saved from a cruel teacher by a visitor in a gorilla suit. In the last story, forgetful Martha Matilda O'Toole has to keep returning home to get school supplies she's left behind—until her teacher reminds her that it is Sunday. . . . DuPont's pen-and-ink and watercolor illustrations are a perfect match for the quirky stories. . . . Copp's narration on the accompanying CD are a refreshing contrast to the commercialized sound of much of today's children's music." SLJ

Cora, Cat

A **suitcase** surprise for Mommy; pictures by Joy Allen. Dial Books for Young Readers 2011 un il $16.99

Grades: PreK K   E

1. Mother-son relationship -- Fiction

ISBN 978-0-8037-3332-9; 0-8037-3332-1

Mommy must travel for business, and Zoran is not happy—he will miss her too much! But what if he gives Mommy one of his special things to take with her so that she will have a part of him with her when she goes?

"The story's concepts and emotions ring true and are accessibly related through the descriptive narrative, which is filled with realistic dialogue and interactions. . . . The brightly colored, cartoon-style, gouache-and-pencil illustrations include many playful touches that reinforce the comforting tone." Booklist

Cordell, Matthew

★ **Another** brother; written and illustrated by Matthew Cordell. Feiwel and Friends 2012 un il $16.99

Grades: PreK K 1 2   E

1. Sheep -- Fiction 2. Brothers -- Fiction 3. Family life -- Fiction

ISBN 978-0-312-64324-9; 0-312-64324-1

LC 2011001135

Davy the sheep wishes he had time alone with his parents, as he did before his twelve brothers came along and started imitating his every move, but when his wish comes true Davy misses playing with the youngsters.

"This is not just another new-baby book: Cordell's humorous text and mischievously silly, expressive cartoon art will have readers bleating to read it again and again." Kirkus

Trouble gum. Feiwel & Friends 2009 un il $16.99

Grades: K 1 2 3   E

1. Pigs -- Fiction 2. Brothers -- Fiction 3. Chewing gum -- Fiction

ISBN 978-0-312-38774-7; 0-312-38774-1

Playing indoors with his little brother on a rainy day, a rambunctious young pig causes a ruckus and then breaks his mother's three chewing gum rules.

"The simple story line and liberal use of white space open plenty of opportunities for Cordell's winsome art to generate laughs. Even better are the sound effects bouncing around each page." Booklist

Corderoy, Tracey

The **little** white owl; illustrated by Jane Chapman. Good Books 2010 un il $16.99

Grades: PreK K 1   E

1. Owls -- Fiction 2. Imagination -- Fiction 3. Storytelling -- Fiction

ISBN 978-1-56148-693-9; 1-56148-693-0

"Living all alone in a snowy landscape under a starry sky, a little white owl imagines himself as a knight or as a rocket, blasting off to the moon. Those empowering fantasies inspire him to take off one day . . . until he reaches a group of big beautiful owls in bright-jewel colors. . . . After he tells the snotty birds his magical stories, . . . they are . . . smitten. . . . [The book offers] tropically hued, textured illustrations. . . . Young children will recognize the pain of loneliness, the power of solitude, and the bliss of imaginative play." Booklist

Cordsen, Carol Foskett

★ **Market** day; illustrated by Douglas B. Jones. Dutton Children's Books 2008 un il $16.99

Grades: PreK K 1   E

1. Stories in rhyme 2. Cattle -- Fiction 3. Markets -- Fiction 4. Farm life -- Fiction

ISBN 978-0-525-47883-6; 0-525-47883-3

LC 2007-28489

The Benson family is so busy preparing for their day at a farmers' market that they not only forget to feed the cow, they leave the farmyard gate open and the hungry cow follows them, making a mess of the market.

"It's not often that words and art mesh as well as they do here. . . . The retro-style artwork . . . mixes striking compositions with tints of glowing peach, vegetable green, honey yellow, and other luscious colors. A delightful read-aloud." Booklist

Corey, Shana

Monster parade; a sticker reader. illustrated by Will Terry. Random House 2009 24p il (Step into reading) lib bdg $11.99; pa $3.99

Grades: PreK K 1   E

1. Stories in rhyme 2. Monsters -- Fiction 3. Halloween -- Fiction

ISBN 0-375-85638-2 pa; 978-0-375-95638-6 lib bdg; 0-375-95638-7 lib bdg; 978-0-375-85638-9 pa

LC 2008009718

Children dressed in monster costumes attend a community party, march in a Halloween parade, and go trick-or-treating.

"The bouncy rhymes, featuring kid-pleasing monster noises, encourage participation. With soft, friendly illustrations showing rounded, silly costumes, this is a decidedly non-scary holiday celebration." Horn Book Guide

Players in pigtails; illustrated by Rebecca Gibbon. Scholastic Press 2003 un il $16.95

Grades: K 1 2 3   E

1. Baseball -- Fiction 2. Sex role -- Fiction 3. All-American Girls Professional Baseball League -- Fiction

ISBN 0-439-18305-7

LC 2002-3445

Katie Casey, a fictional character, helps start the All-American Girls Professional Baseball League, which gave women the opportunity to play professional baseball while America was involved in World War II

"Kids, both girls and boys, will revel in the energy and joy Corey packs into her story. Gibbon's pictures look straight out of the 1940s, with vintage details and an evocative color palette. They also possess a winsome charm that plays nicely with the text." Booklist

Cosentino, Ralph

Superman: the story of the man of steel; written and illustrated by Ralph Cosentino; Superman created by Jerry Siegel & Joe Shuster. Viking 2010 33p il $16.99

Grades: 1 2 3   E

1. Superheroes -- Fiction 2. Superman (Fictional character)

ISBN 978-0-670-06285-0; 0-670-06285-5

"Cosentino acquaints the youngest readers with a comic-book legend. . . . Cosentino presents snapshots that provide a groundwork for understanding Supe's endless print, TV, and movie iterations. Thick-lined new-retro cartoon art in startling primary colors sets off the . . . block-jawed hero. . . . A flashback follows his escape from Krypton, and his boyhood with the Kents features many beloved touchstones. . . . The lineup of his Daily Planet cohorts . . . is followed by the evildoers, who get one double-page spread apiece: Luthor, Metallo, Braniac, and Bizarro." Booklist

Wonder Woman; the story of the Amazon princess. written and illustrated by Ralph Cosentino. Viking 2011 un il $16.99

Grades: 1 2 3   E

1. Wonder Woman (Fictitious character) 2. Superheroes -- Fiction

ISBN 978-0-670-06256-0; 0-670-06256-1

LC 2010024540

Wonder Woman tells how she came to be the protector of humankind, who her enemies are, and how she keeps her identity secret.

"The bold retro artwork has vivid colors and thick black outlines. It's a mix that will work well for the intended audience." SLJ

Cossi, Olga

Pemba Sherpa; Olga Cossi; illustrated by Gary Bernard. Odyssey Books 2009 32p il $15.95

Grades: PreK K 1 2   E

1. Siblings -- Fiction 2. Gender role -- Fiction 3. Tibet (China) -- Fiction 4. Himalaya Mountains -- Fiction

ISBN 9780976865582

LC 2009934415

This book take place "[i]n a Himalayan village in Tibet, [where] a young boy rises before dawn to collect firewood. His younger sister, Yang Ki, longs to join him in his task, which is part of the training to be a Sherpa, but the boy scoffs: it isn't girls' work. One morning, . . . Yang Ki disregards her brother's . . . command to stay home, follows him along the steep mountain path, and saves his life when he loses his footing. When Yang Ki carries his heavy load of firewood home, the villagers are astonished, and she . . . grow[s] up to be a famous guide. . . . [T]his . . . story . . . embeds specifics of Tibetan culture as it captures a child's . . . feelings of frustration when she is . . . underestimated, her determination, and her final pleasure when she triumphs." (Booklist)

Costello, David
I can help; [by] David Hyde Costello. Farrar, Straus & Giroux 2010 un il $12.99
Grades: PreK
E
1. Animals -- Fiction 2. Helping behavior -- Fiction
ISBN 978-0-374-33526-7; 0-374-33526-5
LC 2005044321
When a duck gets lost and a monkey helps him find his way, it starts a chain reaction in which all the young animals help each other solve their problems.
"The ink-and-watercolor artwork features simply drawn, brightly colored focal characters set against landscaped backgrounds. . . . Spare, repetitive text and attractive artwork make this an ideal story hour choice for even the squirmiest group." Booklist

Cote, Genevieve
Goodnight, You; Genevieve Cote, illustrated by Genevieve Cote. Kids Can Press 2014 32 p. $16.95
Grades: PreK K
E
1. Bedtime -- Fiction 2. Monsters -- Fiction 3. Fear -- Fiction 4. Swine -- Fiction 5. Rabbits -- Fiction
ISBN 1771380500; 9781771380508
In this children's book, written and illustrated by Genevieve Cote, part of the Piggy and Bunny series, "the two friends explore what scares them as they prepare for their first campout together. When Bunny admits to being frightened of monsters, Piggy responds that 'even if there WAS a monster, I wouldn't scream like you!' . . . Then, one by one, all of Bunny's questions about what to do if a monster came near are countered confidently by Piggy." (Publisher's note)
"Two friends, a rabbit and a pig, appear in their fourth picture book adventure by the Canadian author/illustrator. As in the earlier titles, this one addresses preschool emotions, in this case, fear...The book's square format is appealing, and the multimedia illustrations—in a simple, soft palette—are charming. The art has a childlike quality and should appeal to the target audience." SLJ
Other titles in the series include:
Me and You (2009)
Starring Me and You (2014)
Without You (2011)

Mr. King's castle; Genevieve Cote. Kids Can Press 2013 32 p. $16.95
Grades: PreK K 1 2
E
1. Castles 2. Conservation of natural resources
ISBN 1554539722; 9781554539727
In this children's picture book by author Genevieve Cote, 'a lion-turned' real estate developer recklessly undermines his own foundations. Fixed on expanding his house into a 'BIG castle' . . . Mr. King chips block-shaped pieces from the surrounding BIG hill. . . . Feeling 'very small' at seeing the hill's other animal residents gathered to protest

. . . Mr. King joins in to reassemble the cutout pieces into seamless slopes." (Kirkus Reviews)

Starring Me and You; by Genevieve Cote. Kids Can Press 2014 32 p. $16.95
Grades: PreK K
E
1. Pigs -- Fiction 2. Rabbits -- Fiction 3. Emotions -- Fiction 4. Children's plays -- Fiction 5. Swine -- Fiction 6. Friendship -- Fiction
ISBN 1894786394; 9781894786393
In this children's story, "two animal friends, a bunny and a pig, explore the world of their emotions as they attempt to put on a play together. Along the way, they must face a few challenges, such as when the bunny wants them to 'be sunflowers and sing a duet,' while the pig would rather 'be pirates on a shipwreck.' As they work their way to a successful collaboration, they take turns describing the different ways they act when they are shy, scared, eager, angry and sad." (Publisher's note)
"The duo from Me and You (2009) and Without You (2011) is back and ready to put on a play. That is, once they get all ready and decide if the play is about pirates or flowers...The illustrations are a simple yet charming mix of crayon and watercolors. Fans of other buddy books, such as the Elephant and Piggie series by Mo Willems or Suzanne Bloom's A Splendid Friend, Indeed (2005), will cheer this team of unlikely friends." Booklist
Other titles include:
Goodnight, You (2014)
Without You (2011)
Me and You (2009)

Cotten, Cynthia
Rain play; [by] Cynthia Cotten; illustrated by Javaka Steptoe. Henry Holt & Co. 2008 un il $16.95
Grades: PreK K 1 2
E
1. Stories in rhyme 2. Play -- Fiction 3. Rain -- Fiction 4. African Americans -- Fiction
ISBN 978-0-8050-6795-8; 0-8050-6795-7
LC 2007012734
Most people leave the park when rain begins to fall, while others enjoy the sights, sounds, and feel of the cool water—until thunder and lightening come near
"The text is written in rhythmic two-line rhymes. . . . Steptoe's cut-paper collages are filled with texture and motion. Facial features rendered in paint show the joy that the youngsters feel. . . . These African-American kids exuberantly jump, splash, run, and puddle-stomp all around the playground." SLJ

This is the stable; illustrated by Delana Bettoli. Holt 2006 un il lib bdg $16.95
Grades: PreK K 1 2
E
1. Stories in rhyme
ISBN 0-8050-7556-9
LC 2005-19904
Recalls, in rhyming text and illustrations, the Nativity story, from the brown and dusty stable to the star shining brightly above.
"This lovely picture book combines beautiful artwork and a seamless, thoughtful . . . style. . . . The rhyme is sweet but never forced. Bettoli uses a mixture of pastels, primary colors, and earth tones." SLJ

Cottin, Menena

★ The **black** book of colors; by Menena Cottin and
Rosana Faria; translated by Elisa Amado. Groundwood/Anansi Books 2008 un il $17.95

Grades: 1 2 3 4   **E**

1. Blind -- Fiction 2. Color -- Fiction

ISBN 978-0-88899-873-6; 0-88899-873-2

Original Spanish edition 2006

"With entirely black pages and a bold white text, this is
not your typical color book. Meant to be experienced with
the fingers instead of the eyes, this extraordinary book allows sighted readers to experience colors the way blind
people do: through the other senses. The text, in both print
and Braille, presents colors through touch . . . taste . . . smell
. . . and sound. . . . Faría's distinctive illustrations present
black shapes embossed on a black background for readers
to feel instead of see. . . . Fascinating, beautifully designed,
and possessing broad child appeal, this book belongs on the
shelves of every school or public library committed to promoting disability awareness and accessibility." SLJ

Cottringer, Anne

Eliot Jones, midnight superhero; illustrated by Alex T.
Smith. Tiger Tales 2009 un il $15.95; pa $7.95

Grades: PreK K 1 2   **E**

1. Superheroes -- Fiction

ISBN 978-1-58925-083-3; 1-58925-083-4; 978-1-
58925-416-9 pa; 1-58925-416-3 pa

"By day, Eliot is a quiet boy who likes to read, but
when the clock strikes midnight, he becomes a superhero.
. . . Eliot's adventures are fast-paced and exciting. A variety
of fonts are used, making the text feel integrated into the
action-packed illustrations. Done in vibrant pastel hues, the
collage-style spreads match the tone of each adventure and
include many details that youngsters will enjoy exploring."
SLJ

Cousins, Lucy

★ **Hooray** for fish! Candlewick Press 2005 un il
$14.99; $8.99

Grades: PreK K 1   **E**

1. Fishes -- Fiction

ISBN 0-7636-2741-0; 978-0-7636-3918-1

Little Fish has all sorts of fishy friends in his underwater
home, but loves one of them most of all

"This winning title . . . features . . . bright hues and
cheerful, childlike creatures. The stars here are fish, and
Cousins matches a gloriously decorated assortment of them
with rhyming text that encourages children to look carefully
and think about similarities and differences." Booklist

★ **I'm** the best. Candlewick Press 2010 un il $14.99

Grades: PreK K 1   **E**

1. Dogs -- Fiction 2. Animals -- Fiction 3. Friendship
-- Fiction

ISBN 978-0-7636-4684-4; 0-7636-4684-9

When Dog's constant boasting makes his friends
sad, they find a way to teach him what it means to be a
good friend.

"The book's large format gives plenty of range for Cousins' naive, expressive pencil-and-ink illustrations. From the
exuberant text to the bold, colorful artwork, a joyous spirit

pervades this picture book and its fallible yet lovable protagonist." Booklist

Maisy goes to preschool. Candlewick Press 2009 un
il $12.99

Grades: PreK   **E**

1. School stories 2. Mice -- Fiction

ISBN 978-0-7636-4254-9; 0-7636-4254-1

"Maisy is confident and acquainted with the routines of
preschool. She clearly has no separation issues. She hangs
up her coat, joins in making music, listens to a story, and so
on. Throughout the day, the young mouse and her friends
have a good time. As always, Cousins's bright color illustrations are simple and appealing." SLJ

Other titles about Maisy are:

Doctor Maisy (2001)

Happy birthday Maisy (2008)

Maisy at the beach (2001)

Maisy at the fair (2001)

Maisy at the farm (2008)

Maisy bakes a cake (2009)

Maisy big, Maisy small (2007)

Maisy, Charlie, and the wobbly tooth (2009)

Maisy cleans up (2002)

Maisy dresses up (1999)

Maisy drives the bus (2000)

Maisy goes camping (2005)

Maisy goes on vacation (2010)

Maisy goes shopping (2001)

Maisy goes swimming (1990)

Maisy goes to bed (2006)

Maisy goes to school (2008)

Maisy goes to the city (2011)

Maisy goes to the hospital (2007)

Maisy goes to the library (2005)

Maisy goes to the museum (2009)

Maisy loves you (2000)

Maisy makes lemonade (2002)

Maisy takes a bath (2000)

Maisy's ABC (2008)

Maisy's amazing book of big words (2007)

Maisy's amazing big book of learning (2011)

Maisy's animals (2007)

Maisy's bedtime (1999)

Maisy's big flap book (2007)

Maisy's book of things that go (2010)

Maisy's Christmas day (2008)

Maisy's favorite animals (2001)

Maisy's morning on the farm (2001)

Maisy's nature walk (1999)

Maisy's pool (2008)

Maisy's show (2010)

Sweet dreams, Maisy (2007)

Vroom, vroom Maisy (2008)

What are you doing, Maisy? (2003)

Where are Maisy's friends? (2000)

Where is Maisy? (2007)

Maisy plays soccer; Lucy Cousins. Candlewick Press
2014 32 p. color illustrations (Maisy first experiences)
(hardcover) $12.99; (pbk.) $6.99

Grades: PreK E

1. Soccer -- Fiction 2. Friendship -- Fiction
ISBN 0763672289; 9780763672287; 9780763672386

LC 2013944013

"Maisy and her friends can't wait to play soccer! Maisy puts on her uniform, laces up her sneakers, and heads to the field. Charlie, Tallulah, and Dotty are on the blue team, while Maisy, Cyril, and Eddie are on the red. Let's play! Soon enough the game heats up, with plenty of action, excitement, and suspense." (Publisher's note)

"The best thing about these books is the distinctive, colorful illustrations. Drenched in primary and secondary colors, the animal characters all display personality and humor." SLJ

Coville, Bruce

Hans Brinker; inspired by the novel by Mary Mapes Dodge; retold by Bruce Coville; illustrated by Laurel Long. Dial Books for Young Readers 2007 un il $16.99

Grades: 3 4 5 E

1. Siblings -- Fiction 2. Ice skating -- Fiction 3. Netherlands -- Fiction
ISBN 978-0-8037-2868-4

LC 2006027109

A Dutch brother and sister work toward two goals, finding the doctor who can restore their father's memory and winning the competition for the silver skates.

"The story's climax . . . is unglamorous yet satisfying. . . . The book's highlight is Long's glowing oil paintings, which are equally effective in illustrating Holland's snowy, glittering landscape and the story's warmer, more intimate family moments." Horn Book

Cowell, Cressida

★ That rabbit belongs to Emily Brown; written by Cressida Cowell; illustrated by Neal Layton. Hyperion Books for Children 2006 un il hardcover o.p. $16.99

Grades: PreK K 1 2 E

1. Play -- Fiction 2. Toys -- Fiction 3. Rabbits -- Fiction
ISBN 978-1-4231-0645-6; 1-4231-0645-8

LC 2006-49046

Emily defends her stuffed rabbit from the naughty queen who is determined to acquire it any way she can. "Ages four to seven." (Bull Cent Child Books)

"The wacky illustrations, done in collage, pen and ink, and watercolor, perfectly depict the joy and energy of the companions' playtime activities. The exuberant text makes use of various fonts and cartoon-bubble dialogue." SLJ

Cowen-Fletcher, Jane

Hello puppy! Candlewick Press 2010 un il $12.99

Grades: PreK K 1 E

1. Dogs -- Fiction
ISBN 978-0-7636-4303-4; 0-7636-4303-3

A child spends time with her new puppy, learning what it means when puppy yawns, stretches, and sniffs.

"The simple sentences are paired with cozy pastel illustrations. The youngster explores the puppy's behavior indoors and out with a special emphasis on play and fun. The story gives young readers a good sense of the responsibility of taking care of a pet." SLJ

Cox, Judy

Carmen learns English; illustrated by Angela N. Dominguez. Holiday House 2010 un il $16.95

Grades: PreK K 1 2 E

1. School stories 2. Sisters -- Fiction 3. Immigrants -- Fiction 4. English language -- Fiction 5. Mexican Americans -- Fiction 6. Spanish language -- Vocabulary
ISBN 978-0-8234-2174-9; 0-8234-2174-0

LC 2008048462

"Older sister Carmen tells Lupita, who is about to enter kindergarten, about her first day of school, when she could speak only Spanish. She recalls other children teasing her about saying the wrong words or mocking her accent. Yet with a kind teacher's help, Carmen mastered English well enough to teach her new language to Lupita and then to begin to use it at school, where classmates learn Spanish from her. Dominguez's . . . paintings convey a childlike energy and effectively express Carmen's moods. This charming celebration of bilingualism captures both the fears and delights of learning a new tongue." SLJ

Go to sleep, Groundhog! illustrated by Paul Meisel. Holiday House 2004 un il $16.95

Grades: PreK K 1 2 E

1. Marmots -- Fiction 2. Groundhog Day -- Fiction
ISBN 0-8234-1645-3

LC 2002-24124

When Groundhog is unable to sleep, he experiences autumn and winter holidays he never knew about, and then he finally falls asleep before Groundhog Day

"An endnote discussing the tradition of using critters as meteorologists makes this a useful as well as a charming answer to the scarcity of engaging material on Groundhog Day." Booklist

My family plays music; illustrated by Elbrite Brown. Holiday House 2003 un il $17.95

Grades: PreK K 1 2 3 E

1. Musicians -- Fiction 2. Family life -- Fiction 3. Musical instruments -- Fiction
ISBN 0-8234-1591-0

LC 00-44903

A musical family with talents for playing a variety of instruments enjoys getting together to celebrate

"The paper-cut illustrations vibrate with color and—almost—with sound. The multiracial family with its rainbow of skin tones is not only a lovely multicultural statement but also a vivid reflection of contemporary families and musical tastes." Booklist

One is a feast for Mouse; a Thanksgiving tale. illustrated by Jeffrey Ebbeler. Holiday House 2008 un il $16.95; pa $6.95

Grades: PreK K 1 2 E

1. Cats -- Fiction 2. Mice -- Fiction 3. Thanksgiving Day -- Fiction
ISBN 978-0-8234-1977-7; 0-8234-1977-0; 978-0-8234-2231-9 pa; 0-8234-2231-3 pa

LC 2007-13972

On Thanksgiving Day while everyone naps, Mouse spots one pea, a perfect feast, but he cannot help adding all of the fixings—until Cat spots him

"Whimsical, large-scale illustrations drawn in acrylics, pastels, and colored pencils are a perfect complement to the story. Plenty of action and humor as well as a thoroughly satisfying ending make this a wonderful holiday read-aloud." SLJ

Other titles about Mouse are:
Cinco de Mouse-O! (2010)
Haunted house, haunted Mouse (2011)

Cox, Lynne

Elizabeth, queen of the seas; Lynne Cox; illustrated by Brian Floca. Schwartz & Wade Books 2014 48 p. $17.99
Grades: K 1 2 3   E
1. New Zealand 2. Seals (Animals) 3. Human-animal relationship 4. Elephant seals -- New Zealand 5. Human-animal relationships -- New Zealand 6. Christchurch (N.Z.) -- Social life and customs
ISBN 0375858881; 9780375858888; 9780375958885
LC 2011023586

This book, by Lynne Cox, "is the incredible story of Elizabeth, a real-life elephant seal who made her home in the Avon River in the city of Christchurch, New Zealand. When Elizabeth decides to stretch out across a two-lane road, the citizens worry she might get hurt or cause traffic accidents, so a group of volunteers tows her out to sea. But Elizabeth swims all the way back to Christchurch. The volunteers catch her again and again . . . but, still, Elizabeth finds her way back home." (Publisher's note)

"Cox opens this fact-based story on just the right note: "There was once a lovely elephant seal who lived in the city.""...Especially effective is a page where Michael, who after nearly three months without his friend, wishes on the stars reflected in the river's water; the page turn reveals the seal's head poking through radiating rings of water while the boy shouts, "Welcome home, Elizabeth!" Children are likely to request multiple readings of this compelling told and lovingly illustrated true story." SLJ

Coy, John

Hoop genius; how a desperate teacher and a rowdy gym class invented basketball. by John Coy; illustrated by Joe Morse. Carolrhoda Books 2013 32 p. (reinforced) $16.95
Grades: 2 3 4 5 6   E
1. Basketball 2. Picture books for children 3. Basketball -- United States -- History
ISBN 0761366172; 9780761366171
LC 2011021235

This children's picture book looks at the invention of basketball. "In 1891, a teacher named James Naismith invented a game that was destined to become a national sensation. The boys' gym class at his school was particularly rowdy. He needed to find an indoor activity for the energetic lads that was fun, but not too rough. Inspired by a favorite childhood game, he stayed up late one night typing the rules of his new game." The class was captivated and the game's popularity spread. (School Library Journal)

★ **Strong** to the hoop; illustrations by Leslie Jean-Bart. Lee & Low Bks. 1999 un il hardcover o.p. pa $8.95
Grades: 2 3 4 5   E
1. Basketball -- Fiction
ISBN 1-880000-80-6; 1-58430-178-3 pa
LC 98-33264

Ten-year-old James tries to hold his own and prove himself on the basketball court when the older boys finally ask him to join them in a game

"Coy's text moves with all the free-wheeling speed of playground ball. . . . Best of all, though, are Jean-Bart's collage-style illustrations, produced by combining Polaroid photographs and scratchboard drawings." Booklist

Craig, Lindsey

Dancing feet! illustrations by Marc Brown. Knopf 2010 un il $16.99
Grades: PreK   E
1. Stories in rhyme 2. Dance -- Fiction 3. Animals -- Fiction
ISBN 978-0-375-86181-9; 0-375-86181-5

"Children are asked to guess who's dancing across a spread by looking at clues in the artwork and listening to the rhymes. . . . Brown uses hand-painted paper collage and primary shapes to create all of the happy dancers. A surprise pairing of partners ends this cheerful story and acts as a motivator to get children moving." SLJ

Farmyard beat; illustrations by Marc Brown. Alfred A. Knopf 2011 un il $15.99; lib bdg $18.99
Grades: PreK K   E
1. Stories in rhyme 2. Bedtime -- Fiction 3. Domestic animals -- Fiction
ISBN 978-0-375-86455-1; 0-375-86455-5; 978-0-375-96455-8 lib bdg; 0-375-96455-X lib bdg
LC 2010016123

The sounds of the farm animals create a lively beat that keep Farmer Sue, the chicks, sheep, and other farm animals awake.

"The repetition, rhythm, and sounds of the words are a big part of the fun in this picture book and will have toddlers chanting along." Booklist

Crews, Donald

★ **Harbor.** Greenwillow Bks. 1982 un il hardcover o.p. pa $6.99
Grades: PreK K 1   E
1. Ships 2. Harbors
ISBN 0-688-00862-3 lib bdg; 0-688-07332-8 pa
LC 81-6607

This book "is an exciting, educational and beautiful show-and-tell. . . . The full-page, full-color paintings will delight children." Publ Wkly

★ **Night** at the fair; pictures and words by Donald Crews. Greenwillow Bks. 1998 un il $17.99
Grades: PreK K 1 2   E
1. Fairs -- Fiction
ISBN 0-688-11483-0
LC 96-48780

Nighttime is a wonderful time to enjoy the lights, the games, and the rides at a fair

"Each borderless double-page spread bursts with color and light and action and noise. . . . A minimal text acts for the most part as captioning or clues us in to what's coming next in this truly spectacular visual experience." Horn Book Guide

★ **Parade.** Greenwillow Bks. 1983 un il hardcover o.p. pa $6.99

Grades: PreK K 1　　　　　　　　E
　　1. Parades
　　ISBN 0-688-01996-X lib bdg; 0-688-06520-1 pa
　　　　　　　　　　　　　　　LC 82-20927
Illustrations and brief text present the various elements
of a parade-the spectators, street vendors, marchers, bands,
floats, and the cleanup afterwards.
　　The author/illustrator's "refined poster-art approach to
evoking an event works again here. . . . A polished assembly of crisp shapes, effective compositions, and pure, bright
color." Booklist

　　★ **Sail** away. Greenwillow Bks. 1995 un il $17.99;
pa $6.99
Grades: PreK K 1　　　　　　　　E
　　1. Sailing -- Fiction
　　ISBN 0-688-11053-3; 0-688-17517-1 pa
　　　　　　　　　　　　　　　LC 94-6004
A family takes an enjoyable trip in their sailboat and
watches the weather change throughout the day
　　"To read any Crews book is to be immersed in sights
and sounds vividly rendered and perfectly phrased, and this
book proves no exception. The paintings move and swell;
the words are haiku-like in their efficiency and implication."
Horn Book

　　★ **School** bus. Greenwillow Bks. 1984 un il $16.99;
lib bdg $17.89; pa $6.99; bd bk $7.99
Grades: PreK K 1　　　　　　　　E
　　1. School stories 2. Buses -- Fiction
　　ISBN 0-688-02807-1; 0-688-02808-X lib bdg; 0-688-
　　12267-1 pa; 0-694-01690-X bd bk
　　　　　　　　　　　　　　　LC 83-18681
Follows the progress of school buses as they take children to school and bring them home again
　　"The author-artist cleverly avoids monotony in his subject matter by using different size buses and a pleasing variety of background, perspectives, and the directions in which
they travel. . . . The . . . yellow of the buses provides both
a unifying element and a contrast for the cheerful colors of
the children's clothing and for the bustle of city streets."
Horn Book

　　★ **Shortcut**. Greenwillow Bks. 1992 un il $17.99;
lib bdg $18.89; pa $6.99
Grades: K 1 2　　　　　　　　　E
　　1. Railroads -- Fiction 2. African Americans -- Fiction
　　ISBN 0-688-06436-1; 0-688-06437-X lib bdg; 0-688-
　　813576-5 pa
　　　　　　　　　　　　　　　LC 91-36312
Children taking a shortcut by walking along a railroad
track find excitement and danger when a train approaches
　　"The story . . . is a perfect foil for the artist's masterful
renderings of trains. . . . Scenes portraying the frightened
children are equally effective in this out of the ordinary drama set forth with uncommon artistry." Publ Wkly

　　Ten black dots; rev ed; Greenwillow Bks. 1986 un il
$16.99; lib bdg $17.89; pa $6.99; bd bk $7.99 E
　　1. Counting 2. Stories in rhyme
　　ISBN 0-688-06067-6; 0-688-06068-4 lib bdg; 0-688-
　　13574-9 pa; 978-0-06-185779-9 bed bk
　　　　　　　　　　　　　　　LC 85-14871

A revision of the title first published 1968
　　"In this basic counting book . . . large black dots appear
as an integral part of each illustrated subject. For example,
'Five dots can make buttons on a coat . . . or the port-holes of
a boat.' This simple concept succeeds admirably through the
bold, flat colors and briskly delineated graphics of Crews'
illustrations." Booklist

　　★ **Truck**. Greenwillow Bks. 1980 un il $16.99; lib
bdg $17.89; pa $6.99; bd bk $7.99
Grades: PreK K 1　　　　　　　　E
　　1. Stories without words 2. Trucks -- Fiction
　　ISBN 0-688-80244-3; 0-688-84244-5 lib bdg; 0-688-
　　10481-9 pa; 0-688-15597-9 bd bk
　　　　　　　　　　　　　　　LC 79-19031
A Caldecott Medal honor book, 1981
　　"Although there is no text, the story is far from word-
less; trucks, buses, and vans are emblazoned with letters and
emblems, the streets are lined with familiar traffic signs, and
a truck stop is festooned with advertisements in neon lights.
. . . [This is] an imaginative, almost pop-art view of mobile
America." Horn Book

Crews, Nina
　　Below. Henry Holt 2006 un il $16.95
Grades: PreK K 1 2　　　　　　　E
　　1. Toys -- Fiction 2. Imagination -- Fiction
　　ISBN 0-8050-7728-6; 978-0-8050-7728-5
　　　　　　　　　　　　　　　LC 2005-12128
　　"Crews uses digitally manipulated photos and line drawings along with brief text to relate the adventures of Jack and
his action-figure toy, Guy. . . . One day Guy falls through
a hole in the stairs. . . . The child uses his crane and other
action figures to effect a rescue. . . . This story . . . will
surely inspire young readers to see everyday objects in a new
light." SLJ
　　Another title about Guy is:
　　Sky-high Guy (2010)

Crimi, Carolyn
　　Dear Tabby; illustrated by David Roberts. Harper
2011 un il $16.99
Grades: PreK K 1 2　　　　　　　E
　　1. Cats -- Fiction 2. Animals -- Fiction 3. Journalists
　　-- Fiction
　　ISBN 978-0-06-114245-1; 0-06-114245-X
　　　　　　　　　　　　　　　LC 2007041935
A feline advice columnist assists other animals with their
problems, such as a parrot whose owners complain that he
talks too much, a groundhog who feels the pressure of pre-
dicting the weather, and a cat who objects to being pampered.
　　"Roberts' playful artwork provides many details that extend and enhance Crimi's clever text." Booklist

　　Rock 'n' roll Mole; pictures by Lynn Munsinger. Dial
Books for Young Readers 2011 il $16.99
Grades: PreK K 1　　　　　　　　E
　　1. Musicians -- Fiction 2. Rock music -- Fiction 3.
　　Moles (Animals) -- Fiction
　　ISBN 978-0-8037-3166-0; 0-8037-3166-3
　　　　　　　　　　　　　　　LC 2010028796
Mole has a "rock-and-roll soul" and the groupies to
prove it, but when his friend Pig organizes a talent show,
Mole's stagefright may prevent him from performing.

"Munsinger's charming band of characters includes a break-dancing pig, a skateboarding raccoon, and a trio of swooning chicks. The watercolor illustrations are full of witty details." SLJ

Cronin, Doreen

The **Chicken** Squad; Case #1, Full house Doreen Cronin; illustrated by Kevin Cornell Atheneum Books for Young Readers. Atheneum Books for Young Readers 2014 112 p. illustrations (A Chicken Squad adventure) $12.99

Grades: 1 2 3   E

1. Mystery fiction 2. Chickens -- Fiction 3. Humorous stories 4. Blue jay -- Fiction 5. Lost and found possessions -- Fiction

ISBN 1442496762; 9781442496767; 9781442496798

LC 2013032099

"Meet the Chicken Squad: Dirt, Sugar, Poppy, and Sweetie. These chicks are not your typical barnyard puffs of fluff, and they are not about to spend their days pecking chicken feed and chasing bugs. No sir, they're too busy solving mysteries and fighting crime." (Publisher's note)

"With its shorter text and larger type, the book will suit somewhat younger readers, those just moving up to chapter books. As in the previous series, some chapters are written in third person, while others are narrated by the dog. Cornell's comical gray-wash illustrations magnify the story's mild humor." Booklist

Full house

Click, clack, boo; Doreen Cronin; illlustrated by Betsy Lewin. Atheneum Books for Young Readers 2014 40 p. (hardcover) $16.99

Grades: PreK K 1   E

1. Farm life -- Fiction 2. Animals -- Fiction 3. Halloween -- Fiction 4. Domestic animals -- Fiction

ISBN 1442465530; 9781442465534; 9781442465541

LC 2012014537

In this Halloween-themed children's book, "Farmer Brown leaves a bowl of candy on the porch . . . puts up a "Do Not Disturb" sign, and prepares to sleep through the holiday, but his animals have other plans for the evening. . . . When he spies a dark, lurking figure through the window, he realizes that his animal friends are at it again. His candy has disappeared and a new note appears on his door--'Halloween Party at the Barn!'" (School Library Journal)

★ **Click,** clack, moo; cows that type. pictures by Betsy Lewin. Simon & Schuster Bks. for Young Readers 2000 un il $15

Grades: PreK K 1 2   E

1. Cattle -- Fiction 2. Farm life -- Fiction

ISBN 0-689-83213-3

LC 97-29718

A Caldecott Medal honor book, 2001

When Farmer Brown's cows find a typewriter in the barn they start making demands, and go on strike when the farmer refuses to give them what they want

"A laugh-out-loud look at life on a very funny farm. . . . Lewin's hilarious cartoons deftly capture the farmer's exasperation and the animals' sheer determination." SLJ

Other titles about Farmer Brown's animals are:

Giggle, giggle, quack (2002)

Click, clack, quackity quack (2005)

Click, clack, splish, splash (2006)

Dooby, dooby, moo (2006)

Thump, quack, moo (2008)

★ **Diary** of a fly; pictures by Harry Bliss. Joanna Cotler Books 2007 un il $15.99; lib bdg $16.89

Grades: PreK K 1 2   E

1. Flies -- Fiction

ISBN 978-0-06-000156-8; 0-06-000156-9; 978-0-06-000157-5 lib bdg; 0-06-000157-7 lib bdg

LC 2006-36064

A young fly discovers, day by day, that there is a lot to learn about being an insect, including the dangers of flyswatters and that heroes come in all shapes and sizes.

"The attention to detail . . . and a lively layout that has a comic-book vibe are sure to appeal." SLJ

★ **Diary** of a spider; pictures by Harry Bliss. Joanna Cotler Books 2005 un il $15.99; lib bdg $16.89

Grades: PreK K 1 2   E

1. Spiders -- Fiction

ISBN 0-06-000153-4; 0-06-000154-2 lib bdg

LC 2004-11549

A young spider discovers, day by day, that there is a lot to learn about being a spider, including how to spin webs and avoid vacuum cleaners.

"The amusing pen-and-ink and watercolor cartoons, complete with funny asides in dialogue balloons, expand the sublime silliness of some of the scenarios." SLJ

★ **Diary** of a worm; pictures by Harry Bliss. HarperCollins Pubs. 2003 un il $15.99; lib bdg $16.89

Grades: PreK K 1 2   E

1. Worms -- Fiction

ISBN 0-06-000150-X; 0-06-000151-8 lib bdg

LC 2002-7949

A young worm discovers, day by day, that there are some very good and some not so good things about being a worm in this great big world

"Bliss's droll watercolor illustrations are a marvel. He gives each worm an individual character with a few deft lines. . . . Inventive and laugh-out-loud funny, this worm's-eye view of the world will be a sure-fire hit." Publ Wkly

★ **Duck** for President; illustrated by Betsy Lewin. Simon & Schuster Books for Young Readers 2004 un il $15.95

Grades: PreK K 1 2   E

1. Ducks -- Fiction 2. Elections -- Fiction

ISBN 0-689-86377-2

LC 2003-21923

When Duck gets tired of working for Farmer Brown, his political ambition eventually leads to his being elected President.

"Lewin's characteristic humorous watercolors with bold black outlines fill the pages with color and jokes. Cronin's text is hilarious for kids and adults and includes a little math and quite a bit about the electoral process." SLJ

Smick; by Doreen Cronin; illustrated by Juana Medina. Viking, published by Penguin Group 2015 40 p. color illustrations (hardcover) $16.99

Grades: PreK K 1 2 3   E

1. Dogs -- Fiction 2. Animals -- Fiction 3. Friendship

-- Fiction 4. Stories in rhyme 5. Chickens -- Fiction 6. Animals -- Infancy -- Fiction

ISBN 0670785784; 9780670785780

LC 2014015658

This book by Doreen Cronin follows a dog named Smick. "Ordered to fetch a stick, Smick complies. . . . Then Smick hears Chick clucking. He curiously approaches the little bird to investigate and receives an alarmed 'No, Smick, no!' As Smick and Chick check each other out, Chick perches on Smick's head until Smick resumes chasing the stick. Eventually, the unlikely pair bond and companionably share the stick as well as a friendly lick." (Kirkus Reviews)

"Smick! It's the perfect name for this dog, who kinda resembles your goofy grandpa. On wide expanses of cream-colored spreads sits Smick, and just a few strokes of black ink outline him—a big old dog with floppy ears...The oversize format makes this great for story time, but independent new readers will also enjoy the story, which may provide their only opportunity to read the word Smick. A great example of how to get maximum fun out of the minimum amount of lines." Booklist

★ **Wiggle**; art by Scott Menchin. Atheneum Books for Young Readers 2005 un il $12.95

Grades: PreK K 1   E

1. Stories in rhyme 2. Dogs -- Fiction

ISBN 0-689-86375-6

LC 2004-3326

"A spotted dog on the cover, vigorously working a hula hoop, leads children through a wiggling world. . . . The delightful cartoon-style, ink-and-watercolor artwork is highlighted by tidbits of collage. . . . Every candy-colored page features the funny, frenetic dog involved in some furious activity, and the sense of motion and movement is palpable each time." Booklist

Other titles about this dog are:

Bounce (2007)

Stretch (2009)

Crosby, Jeff

Wiener wolf. Hyperion Books 2011 32p il $15.99

Grades: PreK K 1   E

1. Dogs -- Fiction 2. Pets -- Fiction 3. Wolves -- Fiction

ISBN 978-1-4231-3983-6; 1-4231-3983-6

Weiner Dog's life of leisure has lost its bite. So when he hears the call of the wild one day, he answers! Thus Weiner Dog becomes Weiner Wolf.

"Crosby employs an array of techniques in his visual storytelling, from the way Wiener Dog appears to run right out of spot illustrations to the hilarious contrast between the turtleneck sweater wearing dog and the slavering wolves. This wiener's a winner." Publ Wkly

Crow, Kristyn

Bedtime at the swamp. HarperCollins Children's 2008 un il $16.99

Grades: PreK K 1 2   E

1. Bedtime -- Fiction 2. Mothers -- Fiction 3. Monsters -- Fiction 4. Wetlands -- Fiction

ISBN 978-0-06-083952-9; 0-06-083952-X

It's bedtime at the swamp—except somebody's not ready. Somebody's still splashing in the water and the mud. Is there a monster on the loose?

"Lively, colorful cartoon characters set in inky black or deep blue moonlit scenes and offset by crisp, white pages add energy and suspense to the story. The repetitive chorus, a simple rhyming story line that will draw readers in, and the perennial appeal of books that are just 'scary' enough make this title an appropriate addition." SLJ

★ **Cool** Daddy Rat; [by] Kristyn Crow; illustrated by Mike Lester. Putnam 2008 un il $16.99

Grades: PreK K 1 2   E

1. Stories in rhyme 2. Rats -- Fiction 3. Musicians -- Fiction 4. Jazz music -- Fiction 5. New York (N.Y.) -- Fiction

ISBN 978-0-399-24375-2; 0-399-24375-5

LC 2006020533

A young rat hides in his father's bass case and tags along as he plays and scats around the big city.

This "hip ode to jazz (and scat in particular) will sweep up its audience in its catchy beat as kinetic cartoon art adds verve and wit. . . . Lester's . . . computer-assisted watercolor illustrations in a heady palette show characters seemingly in perpetual motion." Publ Wkly

The **middle**-child blues; illustrated by David Catrow. G.P. Putnam's Sons 2009 un il $16.99

Grades: K 1 2   E

1. Stories in rhyme 2. Siblings -- Fiction 3. Birth order -- Fiction 4. Blues music -- Fiction

ISBN 978-0-399-24735-4; 0-399-24735-1

LC 2008-30591

A boy named Lee sings about all the miserable aspects of being a middle child.

"Catrow's trademark pencil and watercolor illustrations are perfect for this story. Heads are oversized, and facial expressions exaggerated. The colorful illustrations dance all over the pages. This book is a winner." SLJ

Zombelina; by Kristyn Crow and illustrated by Molly Idle. Walker & Company 2013 32 p. (hardback) $16.99

Grades: PreK K 1 2   E

1. Ballet -- Fiction 2. Stories in rhyme 3. Zombies -- Fiction

ISBN 0802728030; 9780802728036; 9780802728043

LC 2012027333

In this book by Kristyn Crow "Zombelina loves to dance. When Zombelina enrolls in a ballet class for real girls, her dancing gives everyone the chills! But when her first recital brings on a case of stage fright, her zombie moans and ghoulish groans scare her audience away. Only her devoted family's cheers, in their special spooky way, help Zombelina dance the ballet." (Publisher's note)

"Rhymed couplets chronicle a young zombie girl's progression from dancing at home to ballet classes (her detachable limbs give her amazing extension) to a recital. Although Zombelina has a moment of stage fright during her performance, her supportive family's shrieking, howling, and cheering see her through. The charming, funny, and technically accurate dance illustrations outshine the somewhat hokey text." (Horn Book)

Crowley, Ned

Nanook & Pryce; gone fishing. pictures by Larry Day. HarperCollinsPublishers 2009 un il $16.99

Grades: PreK K 1 2   E
1. Stories in rhyme 2. Adventure fiction 3. Friendship
-- Fiction 4. Marine animals -- Fiction 5. Voyages and
travels -- Fiction
ISBN 978-0-06-133641-6; 0-06-133641-6; 978-0-06-
133642-3 lib bdg; 0-06-133642-4 lib bdg
LC 2008032095
Parka-clad friends Nanook and Pryce and their dog Yukon encounter many different types of ocean life and adventure on an unexpected voyage.

"Crowley's perfectly rhymed narrative about an accidental adventure is both minimal and evocative, and Day's
watercolor and line illustrations turn some very funny text
into a hilarious book." SLJ

Crowther, Robert
Amazing pop-up trucks. Candlewick Press 2011 il
$17.99
Grades: PreK K   E
1. Trucks 2. Pop-up books
ISBN 978-0-7636-5587-7; 0-7636-5587-2
"Crowther offers formidable pop-ups of a car transporter, a cement mixer, a monster truck, a 'rubbish' truck,
and truck trains. Each spread contains a description of the
featured vehicle and its primary function, while flaps offer photographs along with additional information about
how the trucks operate. . . . The brightly colored vehicles,
which include working door/window flaps, and real-life details should give truck enthusiasts a gratifying peek into the
world of big rigs." Publ Wkly

The **most** amazing hide-and-seek alphabet book. Candlewick Press 2010 un il $12.99
Grades: PreK K 1   E
1. Alphabet 2. Animals -- Fiction
ISBN 978-0-7636-5030-8; 0-7636-5030-7
First published 1999
This "pull-the-tab [book features a] clean, attractive
[cover] and sturdy paper-on-board construction. The solid
black letters . . . on white pages reveal colorful creatures
when tabs are pulled and animals peek out. [The book is]
cleverly designed and visually appealing." Horn Book Guide

The **most** amazing hide-and-seek numbers book. Candlewick Press 2010 un il $12.99
Grades: PreK K 1   E
1. Numbers 2. Animals -- Fiction
ISBN 978-0-7636-5029-2; 0-7636-5029-3
First published 1999
This "pull-the-tab [book features a] clean, attractive
[cover] and sturdy paper-on-board construction. The solid
black . . . numbers on white pages reveal colorful creatures
when tabs are pulled and animals peek out. [The book is]
cleverly designed and visually appealing." Horn Book Guide

★ **Opposites**. Candlewick Press 2005 un il $12.99
Grades: PreK K 1   E
1. Opposites
ISBN 0-7636-2783-6
"Each page features a word and readers must take some
action—pulling a tab or turning a wheel—to discover its opposite. The pictures incorporate easy-to-understand examples in creative ways. . . . Warmly colored backgrounds and
simply rendered images keep kids' attention focused on the

task at hand, and the volume's sturdy pages and reinforced
tabs will survive lots of use." SLJ

Croza, Laurel
From there to here. Pgw 2014 36 p. $18.95
Grades: K 1 2 3   E
1. Moving -- Fiction 2. Friendship -- Fiction 3. Family
life -- Fiction 4. Toronto (Ont.) -- Fiction 5. Country
life -- Fiction 6. Moving, Household -- Fiction
ISBN 1554983657; 9781554983650
Sequel to: I Know Here (2010)
"A little girl and her family have just moved across the
country by train. Their new neighborhood in the city of Toronto is very different from their home in the Saskatchewan
bush, and at first everything about "there" seems better than
"here". The little girl's dad has just finished building a dam
across the Saskatchewan River, and his new project is to
build a highway through Toronto...Then one day there is a
knock on the door. It is Anne, who lives kitty-corner and
is also eight, going on nine, and suddenly living in Toronto
takes on a whole new light. Laurel Croza and Matt James
have beautifully captured the voice and intense feelings of a
young child who, in the midst of upheaval, finds hope in her
new surroundings." (Publisher's Note)

"In a lovely companion story to 2010's I Know Here,
Croza's heroine and her family have settled in Toronto.
While the girl's references to "here" meant their rural Saskatchewan dwelling in the previous book, Toronto is "here"
for her family now, and their former home has become
"there."... Croza doesn't avoid the reality that some things
were perhaps better in the country ("Here. No stars, no
northern lights"), but readers will come to understand that
while "here" and "there" are different, different is OK, especially when you have the support of a new friend." PW

I know here; pictures by Matt James. Groundwood
Books 2010 un il $18.95
Grades: K 1 2 3   E
1. Moving -- Fiction 2. Saskatchewan -- Fiction
ISBN 978-0-88899-923-8; 0-88899-923-2
Boston Globe-Horn Book Award: Picture Book (2010)
A tale about a young girl whose family moves from the
forests of northeastern Saskatchewan to a strange new place
called "Toronto."

"James's vividly colored, naive-style scenes capture the
bright intensity of the child's inner and outer landscapes and
also the unaffected way in which she observes them. Good
for sharing." Kirkus

Cruise, Robin
Bartleby speaks! pictures by Kevin Hawkes. Farrar,
Straus and Giroux 2009 un il $16.99
Grades: PreK K 1   E
1. Growth -- Fiction 2. Family life -- Fiction 3.
Grandfathers -- Fiction
ISBN 978-0-374-30514-7; 0-374-30514-5
LC 2008-17235
As he grows from infancy to three-years of age, Bartleby
Huddle remains quiet, not speaking a word, until the day
Grampy Huddle arrives and discovers the solution

"Hawkes accompanies Cruise's gently pointed text with
characteristically comic line-and-color cartoons, varying vignettes with full and double-page spreads that focus readers'
attention exactly where it needs to be, modulating noise and

silence through artful pacing. A sweetly underscored paean to the beauty of quiet." Kirkus

Little Mama forgets; illustrated by Stacey Dressen-McQueen. Farrar, Straus and Giroux 2006 32p il $16

Grades: PreK K 1 2   **E**

1. Memory -- Fiction 2. Family life -- Fiction 3. Grandmothers -- Fiction 4. Mexican Americans -- Fiction

ISBN 0-374-34613-5

LC 2004-40462

Although her Mexican-American grandmother now forgets many things, Luciana finds that she still remembers the things that are important to the two of them. Includes glossary of Spanish words used

"The story is bittersweet, but Lucy's ability to look on the bright side, and the obvious love that she and Little Mama share, wrap the events in affection and warmth. Dressen-McQueen's artwork is outstanding. . . . The Mexican family . . . comes alive in pictures that show the vibrancy of the happy household." Booklist

Crum, Shutta

Dozens of cousins; by Shutta Crum; illustrated by David Catrow. Clarion Books 2013 32 p. col. ill. (reinforced) $16.99

Grades: PreK K 1 2   **E**

1. Family reunions -- Fiction 2. Cousins -- Fiction 3. Behavior -- Fiction

ISBN 061815874X; 9780618158744

LC 2012005010

This book, written by Shutta Crum and illustrated by David Catrow, focuses on an "annual family reunion, and . . . dozens of cousins are running wild. They hug fluttering aunts and soft-spoken elders, play in the creek, shimmy up trees [and] take 'double-dog dares.' Hilarious side stories unfold in Catrow's . . . colorful, chaotic spreads that gambol and splash with comical caricatures of grinning kinfolk large and small." (Publisher's note)

★ **Mine!** story by Shutta Crum; pictures by Patrice Barton. Knopf 2011 un il $16.99

Grades: PreK   **E**

1. Infants -- Fiction 2. Siblings -- Fiction

ISBN 978-0-375-86711-8; 0-375-86711-2

A preschooler "and an enthralled baby are placed in a room with a collection of toys and a bemused canine observer. . . . The preschooler quickly lays claim to everything in sight. . . . The discovery of the dog's water dish turns the story into a giddy, soppy free-for-all that culminates in the baby taking its (presumed) first steps to tackle the preschooler, while shrieking 'MINE' in utter adoration. Crum . . . uses only the title word . . . but the various inflections speak volumes about the comic dynamics of sharing. . . . [Barton's] dizzyingly expressive digitized pencil sketches seem to be everywhere at once, continually reframing the action to make sure readers savor every gleefully anarchic moment." Publ Wkly

★ **Thunder**-Boomer! illustrated by Carol Thompson. Clarion Books 2009 32p il $16

Grades: PreK K 1 2   **E**

1. Farm life -- Fiction 2. Family life -- Fiction 3.

Thunderstorms -- Fiction

ISBN 978-0-618-61865-1; 0-618-61865-1

LC 2008-10478

A farm family scurries for shelter from a violent thunderstorm that brings welcome relief from the heat and also an unexpected surprise.

"Thompson's illustrations, done in pastels, ink, and watercolor, are full of motion and capture the sensations. . . . The free-verse storytelling is light, airy, and perfectly matched to the drawings." SLJ

Crummel, Susan Stevens

★ The **Little** Red Pen; written by Janet Stevens and Susan Stevens Crummel; illustrated by Janet Stevens. Harcourt Children's Books 2011 un il $16.99

Grades: PreK K 1 2   **E**

1. School stories 2. Office equipment and supplies -- Fiction

ISBN 978-0-15-206432-7; 0-15-206432-X

LC 2010009062

When a little red pen accidentally falls into the waste basket while trying to correct papers all by herself, the other classroom supplies must cooperate to rescue her.

"Steven's humor-filled watercolors are busy and active, especially since each character is a familiar object with its own personality, facial and body expressions, color, and even typeface. . . . A rollicking read-aloud." Horn Book

Ten-Gallon Bart beats the heat; illustrated by Dorothy Donohue. Marshall Cavendish 2010 il $17.99

Grades: K 1 2 3   **E**

1. Dogs -- Fiction 2. Animals -- Fiction 3. Blizzards -- Fiction

ISBN 978-0-7614-5634-6

LC 2009006342

Tired of the blistering heat in Dog City, Ten-Gallon Bart departs for the frozen north, where he gets lost in a blizzard.

"To escape the oppressive Dog City heat, Ten-Gallon Bart sets off for Alaska, where he encroaches on the fishing pond of three bears, experiences sledding from a sled dog's point of view, and is buried by a freak blizzard while digging for gold...Told in a humorous tall-tale style, the longish story is best suited for school-age children who will enjoy the playful language and silly situations. Collage illustrations feature layers of textured paper that effectively replicate the look and shape of animal fur and feathers. The large pictures are well suited for group sharing and group giggles." Booklist

Cummings, Pat

Harvey Moon, museum boy; written and illustrated by Pat Cummings. HarperCollinsPublishers 2008 un il $16.99; lib bdg $17.89

Grades: PreK K 1 2   **E**

1. Stories in rhyme 2. Lizards -- Fiction 3. Museums -- Fiction 4. African Americans -- Fiction

ISBN 978-0-688-17889-5; 0-688-17889-8; 978-0-06-057861-9 lib bdg; 0-06-057861-0 lib bdg

LC 2004030056

When Harvey and his pet lizard Zippy go on a school field trip, Zippy gets loose in the museum and they have a harrowing adventure

"A lively read-aloud." Booklist

Another title about Harvey Moon is:

Clean your room, Harvey Moon (1991)

Cummings, Phil

Boom bah! [text by Phil Cummings; illustrations by Nina Rycroft] Kane Miller 2010 un il $15.99

Grades: PreK K   **E**

1. Music -- Fiction 2. Orchestra -- Fiction 3. Domestic animals -- Fiction

ISBN 1-935279-22-X; 978-1-935279-22-8

First published 2008 in Australia

After a tiny mouse taps a cup with a spoon and creates a noise, everyone wants to join in. Follow the band as it gathers and grows from a solo perfomance to an explosive, full-scale orchestra.

"Cummings's minimal text moves along in clipped phrases, punctuated by onomatopoeic effects, creating a splendid read-aloud chant. Rycroft's buoyant watercolors, arranged gracefully against expansive white space, add zest. Even the youngest readers should be able to handle the simple text and catch the rhythm." Kirkus

Cummings, Troy

The **eensy** weensy spider freaks out (big time!) written and illustrated by Troy Cummings. Random House 2010 un il $16.99; lib bdg $19.99

Grades: 1 2 3   **E**

1. Fear -- Fiction 2. Spiders -- Fiction 3. Ladybugs -- Fiction

ISBN 978-0-375-86582-4; 0-375-86582-9; 978-0-375-96582-1 lib bdg; 0-375-96582-3 lib bdg

Frightened after the scary waterspout incident, the Eensy Weensy Spider needs some encouragement from her friend the ladybug before she will try climbing again.

"The lively text and whimsical, cartoon-style illustrations include periodic word balloons . . . that advance the story line. The vibrant settings and expressive insects have a retro flair, while the varying perspectives add to the fun." Booklist

Giddy-up, daddy! written and illustrated by Troy Cummings. 1st ed. Random House Inc. 2013 40 p. col. ill. (library) $19.99; (hardcover) $16.99

Grades: PreK K 1 2   **E**

1. Picture books for children 2. Father-child relationship -- Fiction 3. Play -- Fiction 4. Humorous stories 5. Imagination -- Fiction 6. Father and child -- Fiction

ISBN 0375971297; 9780375971297; 9780307978561

LC 2012009236

In this children's picture book, the "childhood game of 'horsey' leaps into outlandish territory as a bespectacled, bald, and very accommodating father eagerly bounds about with his daughter and diapered son riding on his back. . . . When two horse rustlers lure Dad away with sugar cubes, it's up to the kids to rescue him from the rodeo, after which their adventures take them to the Kentucky Derby, a polo match, the circus, and exotic—Canada." (Publishers Weekly)

Cumpiano, Ina

Quinito's neighborhood; story Ina Cumpiano; illustrations by José Ramírez. Children's Book Press 2005 22p il $16.95

Grades: PreK K 1 2   **E**

1. Occupations -- Fiction 2. Bilingual books -- English-

Spanish

ISBN 0-89239-209-6

Quinito not only knows everyone in his neighborhood, he also knows that each person in his community has a different, important occupation

"Ramírez's vibrant acrylic-on-canvas paintings bring this community to life, the primitive forms fairly bursting from the book's pages with their deep hues and sense of emotional warmth. The simple text, equally good in both English and Spanish, is in a font that resembles a child's printing." SLJ

Another title about Quinito is:

Quinito, day and night (2008)

Cunnane, Kelly

★ **Chirchir** is singing. Schwartz & Wade Books 2011 un il $17.99

Grades: PreK K 1 2   **E**

1. Kenya -- Fiction 2. Singing -- Fiction 3. Family life -- Fiction

ISBN 978-0-375-86198-7; 0-375-86198-X

This book, set in Kenya, is "given depth by lyrical prose. . . . Chirchir tries but fails to help her elders and is sent away time after time. . . . Not until Chirchir finds her baby brother, Kip-rop, crying untended does she discover a task she can do as well as the grownups. In an afterword, Cunnane explains that Chirchir is a member of the Kalenjin tribe; the story contains a great deal of information about Kalenjin life, language, customs, and Kenyan flora and fauna. . . . Daly's . . . softly shaded acrylics have much to teach, too. . . . Images of security, dependability, and plenty offer a fresh picture of African life." Publ Wkly

★ **Deep** in the Sahara; Kelly Cunnane; illustrated by Hoda Hadadi. Schwartz & Wade Books 2013 40 p. (g.l.b.) $20.99

Grades: K 1 2 3   **E**

1. Picture books for children 2. Veils -- Religious aspects -- Islam 3. Sahara -- Fiction 4. Muslims -- Fiction 5. Africa, West -- Fiction 6. Coming of age -- Fiction 7. Clothing and dress -- Fiction

ISBN 0375970347; 9780375870347; 9780375970344

LC 2011050245

This book shows "a Mauritanian girl who's fascinated with the malafa, the veil the women in her family wear. The second-person narration . . . presents the veil as desirable rather than confining and describes the girl's wish to wear it so she can be beautiful . . . [and] mysterious. . . . Her relatives reject these superficial reasons. It's not until the girl shows she understands the malafa as a sign of Muslim belief . . . that Mama gives the girl one of her own." (Publishers Weekly)

★ **For** you are a Kenyan child; [by] Kelly Cunnane; art by Ana Juan. Atheneum Books for Young Readers 2005 un il $16.95

Grades: PreK K 1 2   **E**

1. Kenya -- Fiction

ISBN 0-689-86194-X

LC 2004-17060

From rooster crow to bedtime, a Kenyan boy plays and visits neighbors all through his village, even though he is supposed to be watching his grandfather's cows.

This story is told "through vivid, descriptive text. . . . The brilliant, colorful, and humorous illustrations stand out against the white backgrounds and are large enough for group viewing. A gentle story about family, responsibility, and a curious little boy." SLJ

Curtis, Gavin

★ The **bat** boy & his violin; illustrated by E.B. Lewis. Simon & Schuster Bks. for Young Readers 1998 un il hardcover o.p. pa $7.99

Grades: K 1 2 3   E

1. Baseball -- Fiction 2. Violinists -- Fiction 3. African Americans -- Fiction 4. Father-son relationship -- Fiction

ISBN 0-689-80099-1; 0-689-84115-9 pa

LC 97-25417

Reginald is more interested in practicing his violin than in his father's job managing the worst team in the Negro Leagues, but when Papa makes him the bat boy and his music begins to lead the team to victory, Papa realizes the value of his son's passion

"Lewis's soft watercolor illustrations portray the characters with depth and beauty, resulting in a very special book." SLJ

Curtis, Jamie Lee

★ **Big** words for little people; illustrated by Laura Cornell. Joanna Cotler Books 2008 un il $16.99; lib bdg $17.89

Grades: PreK K 1   E

1. Stories in rhyme 2. Conduct of life -- Fiction

ISBN 978-0-06-112759-5; 0-06-112759-0; 978-0-06-112760-1 lib bdg; 0-06-112760-4 lib bdg

LC 2008011856

A big sister teaches her younger siblings some important words, like "responsibility," "perseverance," and "respect"

"Curtis once again demonstrates her trademark sensibility for childhood's simultaneously awkward and silly moments while focusing on the positive values learned from these experiences. Cornell keeps the tone ever lighthearted with her charmingly busy illustrations." SLJ

★ **I'm** gonna like me; letting off a little self-esteem. illustrated by Laura Cornell. HarperCollins Pubs. 2002 un il $16.99; lib bdg $17.89

Grades: PreK K 1 2   E

1. Stories in rhyme

ISBN 0-06-028761-6; 0-06-028762-4 lib bdg

LC 2002-1300

"Though the message is both catchy and effective in its delivery, it's Cornell's humorous, detailed, ink-and-watercolor illustrations that give this volume true pizzazz." Publ Wkly

★ **Is** there really a human race? illustrated by Laura Cornell. Joanna Cotler Books 2006 un il $16.99; lib bdg $17.89

Grades: PreK K 1 2   E

1. Stories in rhyme 2. Conduct of life -- Fiction

ISBN 978-0-06-075346-7; 0-06-075346-3; 978-0-06-075348-1 lib bdg; 0-06-075348-X lib bdg

LC 2006-00274

While thinking about life as a race, a child wonders whether it is most important to finish first or to have fun along the way.

"Curtis writes so very well, in infectious toe-tapping poetic form, of the inner thoughts and worries that children struggle with all too frequently. . . . Cornell's ink-and-color wash cartoons are a perfect match to Curtis's lilting text." SLJ

My mommy hung the moon; a love story. [by] Jamie Lee Curtis & Laura Cornell. HarperCollins 2010 un il $16.99

Grades: PreK K 1   E

1. Stories in rhyme 2. Mothers -- Fiction

ISBN 978-0-06-029016-0; 0-06-029016-1

A hardworking mother's extraordinary accomplishments are listed by her devoted child.

"This is a lively homage to mothers that children and parents alike will enjoy." Booklist

★ **Tell** me again about the night I was born; illustrated by Laura Cornell. HarperCollins Pubs. 1996 un il $16.99; pa $5.99; bd bk $7.99

Grades: PreK K 1 2   E

1. Infants -- Fiction 2. Adoption -- Fiction

ISBN 0-06-024528-X; 0-06-443581-4 pa; 0-694-01215-7 bd bk

LC 95-5412

"The young female narrator asks her adoptive parents to 'tell me again' the story of her birth and introduction into the family she is now a part of. . . . The humorous, cartoon-style pictures by Laura Cornell . . . are a perfect visual counterpart to the text." Horn Book

Cushman, Doug

Christmas Eve good night. Henry Holt 2011 un il $12.99

Grades: PreK K 1   E

1. Stories in rhyme 2. Christmas stories 3. Bedtime -- Fiction 4. Christmas -- Fiction 5. Children's literature -- Works -- Grades two through six

ISBN 978-0-8050-6603-6; 0-8050-6603-9

LC 2010038058

On Christmas Eve, animals at the North Pole, gingerbread men, robots, and more say good night to their mommas, papas, and buddies.

"Cushman's watercolor-and-ink illustrations are full of witty details and hints about the conclusion, but it is his dramatic pacing and skilled balance between art and text that makes this Christmas offering sparkle." Kirkus

Dirk Bones and the mystery of the haunted house; story and pictures by Doug Cushman. HarperCollinsPublishers 2006 31p il (I can read book) $15.99; lib bdg $16.89

Grades: K 1 2   E

1. Ghost stories 2. Mystery fiction

ISBN 978-0-06-073764-1; 0-06-073764-6; 978-0-06-073765-8 lib bdg; 0-06-073765-4 lib bdg

LC 2005019484

"Daily Tombs" newspaper reporter Dirk Bones, who also happens to be a skeleton, investigates when a family of ghosts fears that they are being haunted.

"Cushman's illustrations are delightfully silly and spirited; his hilarious plot will please youngsters who often claim that they want horror but are relieved to get humor instead." SLJ

Another title about Dirk Bones is:

Dirk Bones and the mystery of the missing books (2009)

Halloween goodnight. Henry Holt & Co. 2010 un il $12.99

Grades: PreK K 1   E

1. Bedtime -- Fiction 2. Monsters -- Fiction 3. Halloween -- Fiction

ISBN 978-0-8050-8928-8; 0-8050-8928-4

On Halloween night, monsters, from hairy werewolves on the moors to scaly swamp creatures in a black lagoon, say goodnight to their mommies and daddies.

"The watercolor and ink drawings are colorful and clever. . . . The delightful illustrations make these seasonal monsters not-so-scary for very young readers. This book will fly off your holiday shelves." SLJ

★ **Inspector** Hopper; story and pictures by Doug Cushman. HarperCollins Pubs. 2000 64p il (I can read book) hardcover o.p. pa $3.99

Grades: K 1 2   E

1. Mystery fiction 2. Insects -- Fiction

ISBN 0-06-028382-3; 0-06-028383-1 lib bdg; 0-06-444260-8 pa

LC 99-30878

Inspector Hopper and his perpetually hungry assistant McBugg solve three mysteries for their insect friends

"Beginning readers will find a familiar structure, natural language, compelling plot, supporting illustrations, and engaging characters. . . . The light watercolors define the characters as soft-boiled while slyly playing on stereotypes out of film noir." Horn Book Guide

Another title about Inspector Hopper is:

Inspector Hopper's mystery year (2003)

Mystery at the Club Sandwich; written and illustrated by Doug Cushman. Clarion Books 2004 un il $15

Grades: K 1 2 3   E

1. Mystery fiction 2. Animals -- Fiction 3. Elephants -- Fiction

ISBN 0-618-41969-1

LC 2004-537

When Lola, famous singer at the Club Sandwich, loses her lucky marbles, elephant detective Nick Trunk, lover of peanut butter, takes the case

"Readers will guess the villain early on but that won't interfere with their enjoyment of the droll story, which is greatly enhanced by delightful illustrations. Cushman uses black watercolor washes, colored pencil, and pastel against a stark white background, suggesting the silver nitrate photographs and popular black-and-white movies of the gumshoe era." SLJ

Pigmares; porcine poems of the silver screen. Doug Cushman. Charlesbridge 2012 40 p. col. ill.

Grades: 2 3 4   E

1. Pigs -- Poetry 2. Children's poetry 3. Monsters -- Poetry 4. Swine -- Poetry 5. Children's poetry, American

ISBN 1580894011; 9781580894012

LC 2011025703

This book of children's poems by Doug Cushman "versifies classic movie and literary monsters in 18 single-page poems with accompanying movie-poster-inspired watercolor illustrations starring, of course, pigs rather than people. Plants from outer space (Pigweed), the Yeti (Abominable Snow Pig) and Pig Kong all enjoy the spotlight in turn. All entries are rhymed . . . and each has a humorous twist beyond the punny titles." (Kirkus)

Cutbill, Andy

The **cow** that laid an egg; [by] Andy Cutbill; illustrated by Russell Ayto. HarperCollins Publishers 2008 un il $16.99

Grades: PreK K 1 2   E

1. Eggs -- Fiction 2. Cattle -- Fiction 3. Chickens -- Fiction

ISBN 978-0-06-137295-7; 0-06-137295-1

First published 2006 in the United Kingdom

Marjorie the cow "has no special talents like the rest of the herd, so the chickens hatch a plan. One morning, Marjorie shrieks, 'I've laid an egg!' . . . The bovine endures the taunts of the suspicious cows and the support of the ever-present, silent chickens, until the egg finally hatches a chick with an astonishing 'moo' voice. Cutbill's writing is spare and amusing, and Ayto's goofy, mixed-media collages are a perfect match." SLJ

Another title about Marjorie the cow is:

The cow that was the best moo-ther (2009)

Cutler, Jane

Guttersnipe; pictures by Emily Arnold McCully. Farrar Straus Giroux 2009 un il $16.95

Grades: K 1 2 3   E

1. Jews -- Fiction 2. Canada -- Fiction 3. Poverty -- Fiction 4. Immigrants -- Fiction

ISBN 978-0-374-32813-9; 0-374-32813-7

LC 2007034417

In Canada early in the twentieth century, Ben, the youngest in a family of Jewish immigrants struggling to make ends meet, decides to help out but when a hat maker gives him a chance, disaster strikes and Ben nearly loses hope.

"Detailed watercolors reflect Ben's exhilaration and evoke the early-twentieth-century setting of this unusual story based on true events." Horn Book Guide

★ **Rose** and Riley; pictures by Thomas F. Yezerski. Farrar Straus Giroux 2005 48p il $15

Grades: PreK K 1 2   E

1. Friendship -- Fiction

ISBN 0-374-36340-4

LC 2003-54887

Together, Rose, a vole, and Riley, a groundhog, figure out how to prepare for the possibility of rain, how to celebrate un-birthdays, and what to do with worries.

"Soft pastel illustrations add to the warmth of the text while repetition eases the decoding. A sweet, thoughtful offering with two memorable characters." SLJ

Another title about Rose and Riley is:

Rose and Riley come and go (2005)

Cuyler, Margery

100th day worries; illustrated by Arthur Howard. Simon & Schuster Bks. for Young Readers 2000 un il $16

Grades: K 1 2   E
1. Counting 2. School stories 3. Worry -- Fiction
ISBN 0-689-82979-5

LC 98-52887

Jessica worries about collecting 100 objects to take to class for the 100th day of school

"Energetic pen-and-ink squiggles and bright watercolors fill the pages with round-eyed figures and striped, dotted, and floral patterns as the groups of objects are described and counted." Booklist

Other titles about Jessica are:
Stop, drop, and roll (2001)
Hooray for Reading Day! (2008)
Bullies never win (2009)

The **bumpy** little pumpkin; illustrated by Will Hillenbrand. Scholastic Press 2005 un il $15.95
Grades: PreK K 1 2   E
1. Pumpkin -- Fiction
ISBN 0-439-52835-6

LC 2004-12179

Little Nell chooses an unusual pumpkin for her Halloween jacko-lantern, despite her big sisters' criticisms

"Cuyler's infectious, repetitive text, with its recurrent use of BIG, is perfectly paced for participatory read-alouds, and Hillenbrand's cheery, whimsical mixed-media illustrations show Little Nell's perspective." Booklist

Another title about Little Nell is:
The biggest, best snowman (1998)

Guinea pigs add up; illustrated by Tracey Campbell Pearson. Walker Books for Young Readers 2010 un il $16.99
Grades: PreK K 1   E
1. School stories 2. Stories in rhyme 3. Pets -- Fiction 4. Guinea pigs -- Fiction 5. Mathematics -- Fiction
ISBN 978-0-8027-9795-7; 0-8027-9795-4

"After a teacher announces that a new animal is coming, his young students imagine a giraffe, an elephant, and a snake. What they find, though, is a guinea pig, and the students enjoy petting and feeding him. Because he is lonely, they get him a playmate, who gives birth to three babies, and the numbers start growing. . . . The pen-and-ink, watercolor, and acrylic-gouache pictures show the classroom chaos. . . . The arithmetic exercises—addition, subtraction, multiplication—are woven into the story, and there are surprises right up to the end." Booklist

The **little** dump truck; illustrated by Bob Kolar. Henry Holt and Co. 2009 un il $12.99
Grades: PreK K 1   E
1. Stories in rhyme 2. Trucks -- Fiction
ISBN 978-0-8050-8281-4; 0-8050-8281-6

LC 2008036811

A happy little dump truck, driven by Hard Hat Pete, hauls stones, rocks, and debris from a construction site to a landfill.

"The digital artwork will appeal to young children, who will look for the face depicted on each of the various trucks. The endpapers show all of the vehicles that play a part in the illustrations. The heavy-duty pages are perfect for curious youngsters. Preschoolers will love this book." SLJ

Monster mess! [by] Margery Cuyler; illustrated by S.D. Schindler. Margaret K. McElderry Books 2008 40p il $14.99
Grades: PreK K 1   E
1. Stories in rhyme 2. Monsters -- Fiction 3. Cleanliness -- Fiction
ISBN 0-689-86405-1; 978-0-689-86405-6

LC 2005-012762

A monster sneaks into a boy's room and cleans up while the boy is asleep.

"The watercolor illustrations at times show only part of the creature as its head or other body parts extend off the page. . . . Rhyming, repetitive text and whimsical images whirl on the pages, making this a fun read-aloud." SLJ

Princess Bess gets dressed; illustrated by Heather Maione. Simon & Schuster Books for Young Readers 2009 un il $15.99
Grades: PreK K 1   E
1. Stories in rhyme 2. Princesses -- Fiction 3. Clothing and dress -- Fiction
ISBN 978-1-4169-3833-0; 1-4169-3833-8

LC 2007-25915

A fashionably dressed princess reveals her favorite clothes at the end of a busy day.

This "story brims over with little-girl appeal. Princess Bess [is] depicted in debut artist Maione's zesty ink-and-watercolor art. . . . The well-crafted rhymes roll easily off the tongue; Maione's droll pictures, balancing fashion-loving detail with Bess's brio, are a skillful accompaniment." Publ Wkly

Skeleton hiccups; illustrated by S.D. Schindler. Margaret K. McElderry Books 2002 un il $14.95; pa $6.99
Grades: PreK K 1   E
1. Ghost stories 2. Hiccups -- Fiction 3. Skeleton -- Fiction
ISBN 0-689-84770-X; 1-4169-0276-7 pa

LC 2001-44121

Ghost tries to help Skeleton get rid of the hiccups

"This simple story begs to be read aloud. . . . Schindler's gouache, watercolor, and ink pictures make the most out of each situation, instilling humor in every scene." SLJ

Tick tock clock; pictures by Robert Neubecker. HarperCollins Children's Books 2012 il (My first I can read) $16.99; pa $3.99
Grades: PreK K 1   E
1. Stories in rhyme 2. Time -- Fiction 3. Twins -- Fiction 4. Sisters -- Fiction 5. Grandmothers -- Fiction
ISBN 978-0-06-1363092-; 0-06-136309-X; 978-0-06-136311-5 pa; 0-06-136311-1 pa

LC 2008051780

"Grandma spends a busy day with her twin granddaughters in a day filled with action, rhythm and rhyme. . . . Neubecker's sunny illustrations, in rich reds, yellows and greens, perfectly reflect the spare, very easy-to-read text. Each illustration is set on a white, unframed background and is set apart from the text, making it nicely legible. The repetition of words . . . helps beginning readers build confidence." Kirkus

Cyrus, Kurt

★ **Big** rig bugs. Walker 2010 un il $16.99; lib bdg
$17.89

Grades: PreK K 1   E

1. Stories in rhyme 2. Insects -- Fiction 3. Construction
workers -- Fiction

ISBN 978-0-8027-8674-6; 0-8027-8674-X; 978-0-
8027-8688-3 lib bdg; 0-8027-8688-X lib bdg

"Digital illustrations explore perspective as a crew of
insects joins together to clean up a construction worker's lit-
tered tuna-fish sandwich. Rhymed couplets . . . feature creatures such as an ant, a weevil, a pickleworm, an earwig, and
a dragonfly. The oversize views of bugs will delight many
children, as will the construction analogy." SLJ

★ **Tadpole** Rex; by Kurt Cyrus. Harcourt 2008 un
il $16

Grades: K 1 2 3   E

1. Stories in rhyme 2. Frogs -- Fiction 3. Growth --
Fiction 4. Dinosaurs -- Fiction

ISBN 978-0-15-205990-3; 0-15-205990-3

LC 2006033825

A tiny primordial tadpole grows into a frog, feeling just
as strong and powerful as the huge tyrannosaurus rex that
stomps through the mud

"The rhyming text is image-rich, informational, and fun
to read aloud. . . . Cyrus's oversize artwork conveys information spectacularly. . . . Created in scratchboard and then
colored digitally, the illustrations are luminous and striking."
SLJ

★ The **voyage** of Turtle Rex; written and illustrated
by Kurt Cyrus. Harcourt Children's Books 2011 $16.99

Grades: PreK K 1 2   E

1. Stories in rhyme 2. Sea turtles -- Fiction 3. Marine
animals -- Fiction 4. Prehistoric animals -- Fiction

ISBN 978-0-547-42924-3; 0-547-42924-X;
054742924X; 9780547429243

LC 2010019226

"A tiny prehistoric ancestor to modern sea turtles hatches
from a buried egg, scuttles across a beach into the sea, survives multiple hazards to grow into a mighty two-ton Arche-
lon and then in season returns to shore to lay a clutch of
her own. Injecting plenty of drama into his beach and sunlit
undersea scenes with sudden close-ups and changes of scale,
the illustrator vividly captures the hatchling's vulnerability. .
. . Like it's subject, the rhymed text moves with grand delib-
eration, carrying the primeval story line to a clever transition
between that ancient era and ours." Kirkus

Czekaj, Jef

Call for a new alphabet. Charlesbridge 2011 un il lib
bdg $12.95; pa $5.95

Grades: K 1 2 3   E

1. Alphabet -- Fiction 2. English language -- Fiction

ISBN 978-1-58089-228-5 lib bdg; 1-58089-228-0 lib
bdg; 978-1-58089-229-2 pa; 1-58089-229-9 pa

LC 2010007534

Tired of being near the end of the alphabet, starting few
words, and being governed by grammar rules, X calls for a
vote on a new Alphabet Constitution, then dreams of how
life would be if he became a different letter.

"Written with sly wit and wordplay that will appeal to
the target audience, this little book delves into constitutional

government as well as spelling rules. . . . The upbeat text and
brightly colored, cartoon-like illustrations propel the story,
while the personified letters' grievances will draw a sympathetic response from children struggling with the order of
letters as they learn to read." Booklist

Cat secrets. Balzer + Bray 2011 un il $16.99

Grades: PreK K 1   E

1. Cats -- Fiction

ISBN 978-0-06-192088-2; 0-06-192088-6

LC 2009-49424

Important secrets about how best to live a cat's life
will be revealed only to those who can prove that they are
genuine cats.

"Although the appeals for reader interaction may make
for a rowdy read-aloud, Czekaj cleverly slows the book's
pace at the end by demanding that readers take a catnap. It's
easy to see this one being read just before preschool naptime." Publ Wkly

Hip & Hop, don't stop. Disney/Hyperion 2010 un il
$16.99

Grades: K 1 2   E

1. Rabbits -- Fiction 2. Turtles -- Fiction 3. Contests
-- Fiction 4. Rap music -- Fiction

ISBN 978-1-4231-1664-6; 1-4231-1664-X

LC 2009-20022

A fast rabbit named Hip and a slow turtle named Hop
defy convention when they team up to win a rap music contest in spite of their differences.

"Speech balloons and short rhymes are seamlessly incorporated into the story line. Red text means read fast and
green text means read slowly. . . . The bright colors and engaging characters will grab children's attention." SLJ

Oink-a-doodle-moo; written and illustrated by Jef Czekaj. Balzer + Bray 2012 32 p. (tr. bdg.) $16.99

Grades: PreK K 1   E

1. Games -- Fiction 2. Picture books for children 3.
Domestic animals -- Fiction 4. Humorous stories 5.
Animal sounds -- Fiction 6. Domestic animals -- Fiction

ISBN 0062060112; 9780062060112

LC 2011010065

This barnyard story "is propelled by an old-fashioned
game of telephone. 'I have a secret,' a bubble-gum pink pig
whispers, hoof to mouth, to a blank-eyed rooster: 'Oink.
Pass it on.' The rooster, in turn, relays an 'Oink-a-doodle-
doo' to a cow, whose 'Oink-a-doodle-moo' becomes a frog's
'Oink-a-ribbit-moo,' and so on." (Publishers Weekly)

D'Amico, Carmela

Ella the Elegant Elephant; by Carmela & Steven
D'Amico. Arthur A. Levine Books 2004 un il $16.95

Grades: PreK K 1 2   E

1. School stories 2. Hats -- Fiction 3. Elephants --
Fiction

ISBN 0-439-62792-3

LC 2003-28081

Ella is nervous about the first day of school in her new
town, but wearing her grandmother's good luck hat makes
her feel better—until the other students tease her and call
her names.

"Combining a fairy-tale quality with elements in story
and setting that will be familiar to children, this has a charm-

ing protagonist, as well as lovely, whimsical art, in a soft rich palette. . . . The text is simple, descriptive, and often lively, making a good read-aloud." Booklist

Other titles about Ella are:

Ella takes the cake (2005)

Ella sets the stage (2006)

Ella sets sail (2008)

Suki, the very loud bunny; [by] Carmela & Steven D'Amico. Dutton Children's Books 2011 un il $16.99

Grades: PreK K 1   **E**

1. Noise -- Fiction 2. Rabbits -- Fiction

ISBN 978-0-525-42230-3; 0-525-42230-7

                  LC 2010013470

Unlike most bunnies, Suki loves shouting and playing in the mud, but when she disobeys her mother and leaves the burrow one day, her loud voice is what saves her.

"Appealing for reading in a lap but also well suited to storytimes, this tale of a bunny whose most troublesome traits save the day will ring true with children who have ever been scolded for being noisy or curious." SLJ

D'Aulaire, Ingri

Foxie; the singing dog. [by] Ingri and Edgar Parin d'Aulaire. New York Review Books 2007 un il (New York Review Books children's collection) $14.95

Grades: K 1 2   **E**

1. Dogs -- Fiction

ISBN 978-1-59017-264-3; 1-59017-264-7

                  LC 2007-27028

First published 1949

A lost dog's luck makes him fat and famous, but when given a chance he proves he still thinks there is no place like home.

"Foxie's adventures are illustrated in delightful color." Horn Book Guide

The two cars; [by] Ingri & Edgar Parin d'Aulaire. New York Review Books 2007 un il (The New York Review children's collection) $14.95

Grades: PreK K 1   **E**

1. Fables 2. Automobiles -- Fiction

ISBN 978-1-59017-234-6; 1-59017-234-5

                  LC 2007-2636

First published 1955 by Doubleday

On a magic moonlit night, the sleek, shiny automatic new car and the beat-up old car with many miles on its speedometer go for a drive to see which car is the best.

"A modern adaptation of The Tortoise and the Hare, in which safe and courteous driving wins the day. Delicate pencil illustrations and a plot delivered at a pace fit for a turnpike should prove as enchanting to today's automotively inclined children as when the book was first published in 1955." Pub Wkly

Da Costa, Deborah

Hanukkah moon; [illustrated by] Gosia Mosz. Kar-Ben Pub. 2007 un il lib bdg $17.95; pa $7.95

Grades: PreK K 1 2   **E**

1. Jews -- Fiction 2. Moon -- Fiction 3. Aunts -- Fiction 4. Hanukkah -- Fiction 5. Rosh Hodesh --

Fiction 6. Mexican Americans -- Fiction

ISBN 978-1-58013-244-2 lib bdg; 1-58013-244-8 lib bdg; 978-1-58013-245-9 pa; 1-58013-245-6 pa

                  LC 2006-27430

When Isobel visits her Aunt Luisa, who has just arrived from Mexico, she celebrates Hanukkah with a dreidel-shaped piñata and learns how to celebrate Rosh Hodesh, the women's holiday of the new moon

This is "a valuable contribution to the canon of holiday literature. . . . Mosz's mixed-media pictures . . . feature a cast of doe-eyed, stylized characters golden as Hanukkah lights against the deep purple of moonless night." Bull Cent Child Books

DaCosta, Barbara

★ **Nighttime** Ninja; by Barbara DaCosta; illustrated by Ed Young. Little, Brown 2012 32 p. (hardback) $16.99

Grades: PreK K 1   **E**

1. Ninja -- Fiction 2. Suspense fiction 3. Picture books for children 4. Bedtime -- Fiction 5. Imagination -- Fiction

ISBN 031620384X; 9780316203845

                  LC 2012005492

This children's picture book features a "ninja, a black silhouette, [who] breaks into a house and makes his way silently toward some unknown object: 'He crept down the twisting moonlit hallway, and knelt in the dark shadows, listening.' Suddenly, a huge mother-shaped shadow flicks the light on, and the ninja is revealed as a boy sneaking into the kitchen for ice cream." (Publishers Weekly)

Daddo, Andrew

Goodnight, me; [by] Andrew Daddo; illustrations by Emma Quay. Bloomsbury Children's Books 2007 un il $11.95

Grades: PreK   **E**

1. Bedtime -- Fiction 2. Orangutan -- Fiction

ISBN 978-1-59990-153-4; 1-59990-153-6

                  LC 2007002613

A baby orangutan says goodnight to each and every part of himself until sleep finally comes

"This delightful book has a quiet cadence. . . . Using a mix of pencil, acrylic paints, and watercolors, Quay has created uncluttered spreads that focus on the highlighted body parts. The colors are as soothing as the gentle text." SLJ

Dahl, Michael

Nap time for Kitty; illustrated by Oriol Vidal. Picture Window Books 2011 un il (Hello genius) bd bk $7.99

Grades: PreK   **E**

1. Board books for children 2. Cats -- Fiction 3. Sleep -- Fiction

ISBN 978-1-4048-5216-7; 1-4048-5216-6

                  LC 2010032115

"Toddlers will see themselves in this kitten who just doesn't want to take a nap. When Mama calls him in, he has been busy ogling a bird—and leaping into the birdbath. . . . The cute cats have a slightly stylized and digitized look. Minimal text and plenty of action are just right for the intended age group." Booklist

Daly, Cathleen

Emily's blue period; Cathleen Daly; illustrated by Lisa Brown. Roaring Brook Press 2014 56 p. color illustrations $17.99

Grades: PreK K 1 2 3   E

1. Child artists 2. Art -- Fiction 3. Divorce -- Fiction

ISBN 1596434694; 9781596434691

LC 2013016727

"Emily wants to be an artist. She likes painting and loves the way artists like Pablo Picasso mixed things up. Emily's life is a little mixed up right now. Her dad doesn't live at home anymore, and it feels like everything around her is changing. 'When Picasso was sad for a while,' says Emily, 'he only painted in blue. And now I am in my blue period.' It might last quite some time." (Publisher's note)

"This is a heartfelt, relatable, and even sometimes funny picture book. . . . It's also empowering for even readers struggling with similar situations, as Emily figures out a way to redefine her idea of home." Horn Book

★ Prudence wants a pet. Roaring Brook Press 2011 un il $16.99

Grades: PreK K 1   E

1. Pets -- Fiction

ISBN 978-1-59643-468-4; 1-59643-468-6

LC 2010022001

"Small pen-and-ink and watercolor illustrations on a white background reveal a time progression in vignettes that are spread across the pages. The humorous consequences of Prudence's experiments make this a lighthearted read about never giving up on one's dreams." SLJ

Daly, Jude

Sivu's six wishes; a Taoist tale. retold and illustrated by Jude Daly. Eerdmans Books for Young Readers 2010 un il

Grades: K 1 2   E

1. Africa -- Fiction 2. Taoism -- Fiction 3. Wishes -- Fiction 4. Happiness -- Fiction 5. Stonecutting -- Fiction 6. Folklore

ISBN 0-8028-5369-2; 978-0-8028-5369-1

LC 2010001619

Sivu, an African stonecarver, is not paid well for his work, but through his wishes to become more powerful and live as different people, like the mayor, and things, like the wind, he discovers where real power lies.

"Daly's stylized art, in a rich, clear palette, is quietly stunning. . . . Repetition in both text . . . and art . . . helps make the story easy to follow, and the modern embellishments never obscure its meaning." Horn Book

Daly, Niki

★ Pretty Salma; a Red Riding Hood story from Africa. Clarion Books 2007 29p il $16

Grades: K 1 2 3   E

1. Fairy tales 2. Ghana -- Fiction

ISBN 978-0-618-72345-4; 0-618-72345-5

LC 2006-04249

In this version of "Little Red Riding Hood," set in Ghana, a young girl fails to heed Granny's warning about the dangers of talking to strangers.

"The cartoon-style paintings capture the sights and flavor of the setting and add dimension and humorous details to this modern version of a timeless tale." SLJ

A song for Jamela; story and pictures by Niki Daly. Frances Lincoln Children's Books 2010 un il $16.95

Grades: K 1 2   E

1. Singers -- Fiction 2. Celebrities -- Fiction 3. Beauty shops -- Fiction 4. South Africa -- Fiction

ISBN 978-1-84507-871-3; 1-84507-871-3

It is summer vacation and Jamela is bored, until her Aunt Beauty asks her to come and help her get her hair salon ready for a special client, who turns out to be "Afro-Idols" contestant Miss Bambi Chaka Chaka.

"Daly's humorous and colorful illustrations reflect everyday South African scenes from a child's point of view. The illustrations [are made] utilizing digital art." SLJ

Other titles about Jamela are:

Jamela's dress (1999)

What's cooking Jamela? (2001)

Where's Jamela? (2004)

Happy birthday, Jamela! (2006)

★ Welcome to Zanzibar Road; story and pictures by Niki Daly. Clarion Books 2006 31p il $16

Grades: PreK K 1 2   E

1. Africa -- Fiction 2. Chickens -- Fiction 3. Elephants -- Fiction

ISBN 0-618-64926-3

LC 2005021758

After moving into the house on Zanzibar Road that her neighbors helped her build, Mama Jumbo the elephant decides to share it with Little Chico the chicken.

"Through his warm, expressive watercolors, Daly teaches readers about some of the important things in life—friendship, family, and how to make a house into a home. Details abound, and the animals' patterned clothing adds texture and variety to the pages." SLJ

Danneberg, Julie

The big test; illustrated by Judy Love. Charlesbridge 2011 un il $16.95; pa $6.95

Grades: K 1 2   E

1. School stories

ISBN 1580893600; 1580893619 pa; 9781580893602; 9781580893619 pa; 978-1-58089-360-2; 1-58089-360-0; 978-1-58089-361-9 pa; 1-58089-361-9 pa

Mrs. Hartwell is concerned that preparing her students to take the Big Test is only making them nervous, and so she thinks of a way to help them relax.

"Mrs. Hartwell's students . . . are not sure they can deal with the Big Test. . . . The kids worry and get headaches, stomachaches, and other maladies. On Thursday, Mrs. Hartwell lines up her class and marches them down the hall to the library. The sign on the door says, 'Library Closed: Students Testing.' But inside it's a test party. The students get to play and relax and eat. This works so well that no one is sick anymore and they breeze through the actual Big Test on Friday. The illustrations, done in ink and transparent dyes on watercolor paper, are priceless. The children's faces clearly express all the agony that the situation requires." SLJ

Monet paints a day; Julie Danneberg; illustrated by Caitlin Heimerl. Charlesbridge 2012 48 p. col. ill. (reinforced) $15.95

Grades: 2 3 4   E
1. Plein-air painting 2. Impressionism (Art)
ISBN 1442435798; 9781580892407

LC 2011025789

This book by Julie Danneburg is "written in the voice of the artist and drawn from the letters of the noted French Impressionist Claude Monet. . . . One day, so absorbed in painting as much as he could within a seven-to-15-minute window . . . Monet was actually swept away by a high tide, supplies and all. . . . [Danneburg] integrates details from Monet's letters and minifacts about Impressionism and the exciting practice of plein-air painting." (Kirkus)

Danticat, Edwidge
★ **Eight** days; a story of Haiti. pictures by Alix Delinois. Orchard Books 2010 un il
Grades: K 1 2 3   E
1. Play -- Fiction 2. Haiti -- Fiction 3. Earthquakes -- Fiction 4. Imagination -- Fiction
ISBN 0-545-27849-X; 978-0-545-27849-2

LC 2010035981

Junior tells of the games he played in his mind during the eight days he was trapped in his house after the devastating January 12, 2010 earthquake in Haiti. Includes author's note about Haitian children before the earthquake and her own children's reactions to the disaster.

This is illustrated with "beautiful, bright artwork, in acrylics, pastel, and collage. . . . The narrative's powerful rhythm echoes the Genesis Creation story, giving it even more gravity. . . . Never too sentimental, the story works because of the clear presence of great sadness and loss." Booklist

Danziger, Paula
★ **It's** Justin Time, Amber Brown; illustrated by Tony Ross. Putnam 2001 48p il (A is for Amber) $12.99; pa $3.99
Grades: K 1 2 3   E
1. Time -- Fiction 2. Birthdays -- Fiction 3. Clocks and watches -- Fiction
ISBN 0-399-23470-5; 0-698-11907-X pa

LC 99-89396

Unlike her best friend Justin, Amber Brown loves to measure time and hopes to receive a watch on her seventh birthday

"The illustrations capture the mood of the story, which is playful and spirited. Beginning readers will enjoy sharing Amber's pre-birthday anticipation and older readers may want to go back and see the early years of the characters they know and love." SLJ

Other easy-to-read titles about Amber Brown are:
Get ready for second grade, Amber Brown (2002)
It's a fair day, Amber Brown (2002)
Orange you glad it's Halloween, Amber Brown (2005)
Second grade rules, Amber Brown (2004)
What a trip, Amber Brown (2001)

Darbyshire, Kristen
Put it on the list. Dutton Children's Books 2009 un il $16.99
Grades: PreK K 1   E
1. Week -- Fiction 2. Memory -- Fiction 3. Shopping

-- Fiction 4. Family life -- Fiction
ISBN 978-0-525-47906-2; 0-525-47906-6

LC 2007-28490

"A family of anthropomorphized chickens keeps running out of household staples. Mom tells everyone to put the needed items on the shopping list that's posted on the refrigerator, but they ignore the directive and just complain when supplies run out. . . . The chickens are depicted as stick figures with large round heads. The gouache illustrations are spare, with ink outlines and solid-colored backgrounds. An amusing cautionary tale for families everywhere." SLJ

Darrow, Sharon
Yafi's family; an Ethiopian boy's journey of love, loss, and adoption. by Linda Pettitt and Sharon Darrow; illustrated by Jan Spivey Gilchrist. Amharic 2010 un il
Grades: PreK K 1 2   E
1. Adoption -- Fiction 2. Ethiopia -- Fiction 3. Family life -- Fiction
ISBN 0-979748-14-3; 978-0-979748-14-1

"With his new family in America, Yafi, six, remembers when they first came to his orphanage in Ethiopia. . . . Mom remembers too. . . . They talk about his first mother, who died, and his grandma Elsa, who raised him until she could no longer care for him. . . . Gilchrist's beautiful sepia-toned portraits depict the love Yafi feels for his American family and also his warm remembrances of his birth family. Both words and pictures effectively convey the strong familial ties." Booklist

Daugherty, James Henry
★ **Andy** and the lion; by James Daugherty. Viking 1938 un il hardcover o.p. pa $6.99
Grades: PreK K 1 2   E
1. Lions -- Fiction
ISBN 0-14-050277-7 pa

A Caldecott Medal honor book, 1939

A modern picture story of Androcles and the lion in which Andy, who read a book about lions, was almost immediately plunged into action. The next day he met a circus lion with a thorn in his paw. Andy removed the thorn and earned the lion's undying gratitude

"This is a tall tale for little children. It is typically American in its setting and its fun. The large full page illustrations are in yellow, black and white and the brief, hand-lettered text on the opposite page is clear and readable." Libr J

Davies, Jacqueline
The **night** is singing; illustrations by Kyrsten Brooker. Dial Books for Young Readers 2006 un il $16.99
Grades: PreK K 1   E
1. Stories in rhyme 2. Night -- Fiction 3. Sound -- Fiction
ISBN 0-8037-3004-7; 978-0-8037-3004-5

LC 2004-14161

Rhyming text tells of lullabies that can be heard in the sounds of the night, such as a radiator's hiss, a cat's shadowboxing, and a rainstorm's drumming

This is a "perfect bedtime read. . . . Attractive, full-page folk-art illustrations that combine collage and oil paint on gessoed watercolor paper lend an old-fashioned charm." SLJ

★ **Tricking** the Tallyman; illustrated by S. D. Schindler. Alfred A. Knopf 2009 un il $17.99; lib bdg $20.99

Grades: 1 2 3 4   E
1. Census -- Fiction 2. Vermont -- Fiction 3. United States -- History -- 1783-1809 -- Fiction
ISBN 978-0-375-83909-2; 0-375-83909-7; 978-0-375-93909-9 lib bdg; 0-375-93909-1 lib bdg
LC 2007-45488
In 1790, the suspicious residents of a small Vermont town try to trick the man who has been sent to count their population for the first United States Census.

"This lively, engaging picture book is an outstanding introduction to the concept of census taking and its role in the implementation of the new United States Constitution. . . . Schindler's exceptional illustrations, mainly in earth tones, depict indoor and outdoor scenes that are full of activity. . . . Charming and humorous." SLJ

Davies, Matt

Ben rides on; Matt Davies. 1st ed. Roaring Brook Press 2013 32 p. (reinforced) $16.99
Grades: PreK K 1 2 3   E
1. Picture books for children 2. Bullies -- Fiction 3. Stealing -- Fiction
ISBN 1596437944; 9781596437944
LC 2012013101
In this children's picture book, when "Adrian Underbite takes Ben's bicycle for a joyride and hurtles off a cliff, Ben leans over the edge and sees Adrian clinging to a tiny branch. 'How extraordinarily terrible,' Ben thinks, though his toothy grin conveys quite another emotion. But Ben's conscience smites him, and he goes back to rescue Adrian." (Publishers Weekly)

Davies, Nicola

Outside your window; a first book of nature. Nicola Davies; illustrated by Mark Hearld. Candlewick Press 2012 105 p. il
Grades: K 1 2   E
1. Nature poetry 2. Nature -- Fiction
ISBN 076365549X; 9780763655495
LC 2011046637
This book of poetry has as its subject "the seasons. . . . The year starts with spring (featuring aspects such as "Bulbs," "Lambs' Tails," and "Planting Seeds") and goes on through summer (a bird's "Summer Song," a farm's "Making Hay") and on to fall ("Acorn," "Harvest," "Berry Picking") and finally winter ("Winter Trees," "Snow Song"). The verses, in different forms ranging from prose poems (including craft instructions) to tightly metered rhymes, . . . offer . . . observations ("In the morning, you'll find the snow has kept a diary/ of things that happened when you were asleep" "Snow Song") or invit[e] humor (one of the "Five Reasons to Keep Chickens" is "They look very silly when they are taking a dust bath")." (Bulletin of the Center for Children's Books)

★ **Surprising** Sharks; by Nicola Davies and illustrated by James Croft. Candlewick 2005 29 p. il $6.99
Grades: K 1 2 3   E
1. Sharks
ISBN 0763621854; 0763627429; 9780763627423
LC 200340943
This book, by Nicola Davies and illustrated by James Croft, presents "illustrations, and captivating facts [designed to] reveal that sharks come in all shapes and sizes—and

probably should be more afraid of humans than we are of them." (Publisher's note)

What happens next? Nicola Davies, illustrated by Marc Boutavant. Candlewick Press 2012 24 p. $9.99
Grades: PreK K 1   E
1. Picture books for children 2. Animal behavior -- Fiction 3. Animals 4. Toy and movable books
ISBN 076366264X; 9780763662646
LC 2012942306
Author Nicola Davies' "lift-the-flap book reveals surprises in the animal kingdom. A hungry chameleon spies a juicy grasshopper. Turn the half-page. His long tongue shoots out to catch it. Going on, Davies presents other unexpected animal behaviors. . . . The final spread in this sequencing exercise offers a matching game to remind young viewers of the actions described." (Kirkus Reviews)

What will I be? by Nicola Davies and illustrated by Marc Boutavant. Candlewick 2012 32 p. (alk. paper) $9.99
Grades: PreK K   E
1. Life cycles (Biology) 2. Animals 3. Animal life cycles
ISBN 0763658030; 9780763658038
LC 2011047178
In this book, by Nicola Davies and illustrated by Marc Boutavant, readers "Peek under each large flap and look at colorful spreads to find out how each animal develops. A final spread invites readers to match each fullgrown creature with its beginning stage." (Publisher's note)
Includes bibliographical references and index

★ **White** owl, barn owl; illustrated by Michael Foreman. Candlewick Press 2007 29p il $16.99; pa $6.99
Grades: PreK K 1 2 3   E
1. Owls -- Fiction
ISBN 978-0-7636-3364-6; 0-7636-3364-X; 978-0-7636-4143-6 pa; 0-7636-4143-X pa
"Simple facts about the hunting and nesting habits of barn owls intertwine with the story of two humans who put a nesting box for them high in a tree. Narrated by a girl whose grandfather explains owl behavior as the two watch for avian visitors in the evenings, the story also contains insets of information bits. Well-chosen design elements move both fiction and fact along with clarity and ease. . . . Foreman's artwork includes lovely watercolor and pastel paintings of the birds." SLJ

Who lives here? Nicola Davies, illustrated by Marc Boutavant. Candlewick Press 2012 24 p. $9.99
Grades: PreK K 1   E
1. Children's literature 2. Animals -- Habitations 3. Toy and movable books -- Specimens
ISBN 0763662631; 9780763662639
LC 2012942307
In this children's book by Nicola Davies, illustrated by Marc Boutavant, readers can "lift the flaps and learn about animal life. . . . The jungle is warm and steamy. What kind of animal might live there, a snow goose or a sloth? What about a still, cool pond -- could that be home for a howler monkey? Find out why meerkats like dry sunny grasslands (hint: they

like to dig holes to hide in) or why clown fish feel right at home in a coral reef." (Publisher's note)

Davies, Stephen

Don't spill the milk; by Stephen Davies; illustrated by Christopher Corr. Andersen Press 2013 32 p. (trade hard cover: alk. paper) $16.95

Grades: PreK K   E

  1. Love -- Fiction 2. Responsibility -- Fiction 3. Africa -- Fiction

  ISBN 1467720283; 9781467720281

                         LC 2012049659

Author Stephen Davies presents an illustrated children's picture book about the relationship between a girl and her father in the mountains. "Up the downy dunes, across the dark, wide river and up and down the steep, steep mountain, Penda lovingly carries a bowl of milk to her father in the grasslands. But will she manage to get it there without spilling a single drop?" (Publisher's note)

Davis, Anne

  No dogs allowed! words and pictures by Anne Davis. HarperCollins Children's Books 2011 un il $16.99

Grades: PreK K 1 2   E

  1. Cats -- Fiction 2. Dogs -- Fiction 3. Friendship -- Fiction

  ISBN 978-0-06-075353-5; 0-06-075353-6

                         LC 2010007028

Bud the cat is not happy when his feline companion Gabby befriends a dog.

"Charming illustrations add humor, and young readers will note small details. . . . The kindness-wins-out theme is perfect for storytime." Booklist

Davis, Aubrey

  Kishka for Koppel; illustrated by Sheldon Cohen. Orca Book Publishers 2011 il $19.95

Grades: K 1 2 3   E

  1. Jews -- Fiction 2. Wishes -- Fiction

  ISBN 978-1-55469-299-6; 1-55469-299-7

"In this Jewish retelling of the Grimm Brothers' 'Three Wishes,' Koppel finds a wish-granting meat grinder. The junk man and his wife, Yetta, dream of all the riches they'll wish for, but inevitably they end up wishing for kishka (a kind of sausage), and subsequently wishing it onto and off Koppel's nose. All ends well as the meat grinder points out how lucky they are to have each other (plus a delicious kishka). The naive, folksy cartoon illustrations are expressive and lend a lighthearted air with their varying perspectives and bright acrylic colors. The storytelling is lively and humorous." SLJ

Davis, David

  Fandango stew; illustrated by Ben Galbraith. Sterling Pub. 2011 un il

Grades: PreK K 1 2   E

  1. Folklore 2. West (U.S.) -- Fiction

  ISBN 1402765274; 9781402765278

                         LC 2010004775

Penniless Slim and his grandson Luis ride into the unwelcoming western town of Skinflint, and manage to rustle up a delicious meal for all its citizens out of one lone bean.

"Witty illustrations featuring warm tones and amusing details effectively complement the text. Either alone

or paired with a traditional version, this will make for an appealing read and an even better read-aloud, especially when audiences join in on the chorus: 'Chili's good,/ so is barbecue,/ but nothing's finer than/ fandango stew!'" Libr Media Connect

Davis, Jill

  The **first** rule of little brothers; illustrated by Sarah McMenemy. Alfred A. Knopf 2008 un il $16.99; lib bdg $19.99

Grades: PreK K 1   E

  1. Brothers -- Fiction

  ISBN 978-0-375-84046-3; 0-375-84046-X; 978-0-375-94046-0 lib bdg; 0-375-94046-4 lib bdg

                         LC 2007-44314

A young boy learns that, while his little brother's constant mimicking may be annoying, it is also a sign of admiration.

"Davis makes her point—siblings can drive eachother crazy but also have fun together—credibly and sympathetically with plenty of humor as well. . . . McMenemy's mixed-media art (which looks to incorporate watercolor, ink, and torn paper collage) is sunny and vivid, with lots of crisp white space surrounding the brightly colored figures and backgrounds." Bull Cent Child Books

Davis, Katie

  Little Chicken's big day; [by] Katie Davis and Jerry Davis. Margaret K. McElderry Books 2011 un il $14.99

Grades: PreK K   E

  1. Chickens -- Fiction 2. Mother-child relationship -- Fiction

  ISBN 978-1-4424-1401-3; 1-4424-1401-4

                         LC 2010011826

Little Chicken is tired of being told what to do by Big Chicken, but when they become separated he misses all of the clucking.

"Done in bold lines, simple shapes, and bright colors, the chunky poultry are set against unadorned, mainly white backgrounds. . . . This look at a busy mom and preschooler perfectly echoes a child's experience." SLJ

Day, Alexandra

  ★ **Carl's** sleepy afternoon. Farrar, Straus and Giroux 2005 un il $12.95

Grades: PreK K 1   E

  1. Dogs -- Fiction

  ISBN 0-374-31088-2

Carl's owners have many errands to do and expect Carl to sleep the entire afternoon. Instead, Carl the rottweiler roams the town assisting many people in their daily chores

"The entertaining story is told through the gently detailed, warmly realistic paintings." SLJ

Other titles about Carl are:

Carl and the baby duck (2011)

Carl and the puppies (2011)

Carl goes shopping (1990)

Carl goes to daycare (1993)

Carl makes a scrapbook (1994)

Carl's afternoon in the park (1991)

Carl's birthday (1995)

Carl's Christmas (1990)

Carl's masquerade (1992)

Carl's snowy afternoon (2009)

Carl's summer vacation (2008)

Follow Carl (1998)

Good dog, Carl (1985)

Frank and Ernest. Green Tiger Press 2010 un il
$15.95

Grades: PreK K 1 2   E

1. Bears -- Fiction 2. Elephants -- Fiction 3. Restaurants
-- Fiction

ISBN 978-1-59583-424-9; 1-59583-424-9

LC 2010010747

A reissue of the title first published 1988 by Scholastic

An elephant and a bear take over a diner and find out
about responsibility and food language.

"Day's mock-dignified illustrations, lush and attractive,
add dimension to the entertaining story. A diner glossary is
included to aid comprehension." Horn Book Guide

Another title about Frank and Ernest is:

Frank and Ernest play ball (2011)

Frank and Ernest play ball. Green Tiger Press 2011
un il $15.95

Grades: PreK K 1 2   E

1. Bears -- Fiction 2. Baseball -- Fiction 3. Elephants
-- Fiction

ISBN 978-1-59583-438-6; 1-59583-438-9

LC 2010048046

A reissue of the title first published 1990 by Scholastic

With the help of a baseball dictionary so they can learn
the necessary language, an elephant and a bear take over the
management of a baseball team.

"Sports fans will enjoy the text with its in-the-know
lingo. . . . Day's play-it-straight paintings—except for the
elephant and bear in the infield—convey much of the spirit
of baseball." Horn Book Guide

Day, Nancy Raines

On a windy night; illustrated by George Bates. Abrams
Books for Young Readers 2009 un il $16.95

Grades: PreK K 1   E

1. Stories in rhyme 2. Fear -- Fiction 3. Halloween
-- Fiction

ISBN 978-0-8109-3900-4; 0-8109-3900-2

LC 2008-52532

On a windy Halloween night as a boy is returning home
through the woods after trick-or-treating, he hears scary
noises behind him.

Bates's "pen-and-ink drawings push and pull, creating scariness with forceful hatching and eerie lighting. . .
. There's enough Halloween fright to satisfy adventurous
young readers, and a comforting ending for those with jan-
gled nerves." Publ Wkly

Daywalt, Drew

★ **The day** the crayons quit; Drew Daywalt; illustrated
by Oliver Jeffers. Philomel Books 2013 40 p. $17.99

Grades: PreK K   E

1. Crayon drawing -- Fiction 2. Color -- Fiction 3.
Crayons -- Fiction 4. Letters -- Fiction

ISBN 0399255370; 9780399255373

LC 2012030384

In this children's picture book, by Drew Daywalt, illustrated by Oliver Jeffers, "a schoolboy finds a mysterious
parcel of letters addressed to him in what looks just like a
child's handwriting. The letters, it turns out, are from his

crayons, who deeply resent being typecasst according to
color. Red is tired of drawing apples and fire engines, Green
is bored of coloring dinosaurs and frogs, and so on." (New
York Times Book Review)

"Although the crayons in this inventive catalogue stop
short of quitting, most feel disgruntled. The rank and file
express their views in letters written to a boy, Duncan. Red
complains of having to "work harder than any of your other
crayons" on fire trucks and Santas; a beige crayon declares,
"I'm tired of being called 'light brown' or 'dark tan' because
I am neither." White feels "empty" from Duncan's white-on-
white coloring, and a "naked" Peach wails, "Why did you
peel off my paper wrapping?" ...These memorable personalities will leave readers glancing apprehensively at their
own crayon boxes."

De Groat, Diane

★ **Trick** or treat, smell my feet. Morrow Junior Bks.
1998 un il hardcover o.p. pa $4.95

Grades: K 1 2 3   E

1. Siblings -- Fiction 2. Halloween -- Fiction

ISBN 0-688-15766-1; 0-688-15767-X lib bdg; 0-688-
17061-7 pa

LC 97-32916

"De Groat's funny watercolor pictures capture the various animal creatures' very human expressions and body language." Booklist

Other titles about Gilbert are:

Ants in your pants, worms in your plants! (2011)

April fool!, watch out at school! (2009)

Brand-new pencils, brand-new books (2005)

Good night, sleep tight, don't let the bedbugs bite! (2002)

Happy birthday to you, you belong in the zoo (1999)

Jingle, bells, homework smells (2000)

Last one in is a rotten egg! (2007)

Liar, liar, pants on fire (2003)

Mother, you are the best! (2008)

No more pencils, no more books, no more teacher's dirty
looks! (2006)

Roses are pink, your feet really stink (1996)

We gather together now please get lost! (2001)

De Mouy, Iris

Naptime; Iris de Mouy; translated by Shelley Tanaka.
Groundwood Books 2014 28 p. $16.95

Grades: PreK K   E

1. Sleep -- Fiction 2. Jungle animals -- Fiction

ISBN 1554984874; 9781554984879

In this children's book by Iris de Moüy "all of the animals in the jungle are grumpy--no, they will not take a nap!
But one little girl may know just what to do to make sure
these creatures can get some much-needed shut-eye. Fortunately for these sleepy creatures, a little girl appears who
knows the secret to a good snooze: first close one eye, then
close the other one." (Publisher's note)

"It's naptime, but none of the savannah animals is sleepy-
-that is, until a small girl tricks them into simply shutting
their eyes. The book's wide, horizontal orientation suggests
the act of lying down, while bold colors evoke sunset on the
horizon. Spare text emphasizes the animals' stubbornness,
inviting anyone familiar with the trials of naptime to delight
in this short, clever story." Horn Book

De Regniers, Beatrice Schenk

★ **May** I bring a friend? illustrated by Beni Montresor. Atheneum Pubs. 1964 un il hardcover o.p. pa $7.99

Grades: PreK K   E

1. Animals -- Fiction

ISBN 0-689-20615-1; 0-689-71353-3 pa

Awarded the Caldecott Medal, 1965

"Rich color and profuse embellishment adorn an opulent setting. Absurdities and contrasts are so imaginatively combined in a hilarious comedy of manners that the merriment can be enjoyed on several levels." Horn Book

De Roo, Elena

The **rain** train; illustrated by Brian Lovelock. Candlewick Press 2011 un il $15.99

Grades: PreK K   E

1. Rain -- Fiction 2. Night -- Fiction 3. Railroads -- Fiction

ISBN 978-0-7636-5313-2; 0-7636-5313-6

LC 2010039174

A young boy watches and listens as the Rain Train takes him on a ride past city lights, over rivers, and through tunnels one rainy night.

"De Roo's rhyming, lyrical text never derails; the onomatopoeic verse rolls rhythmically along, both lulling listeners and moving the action forward. . . . Lovelock's misty watercolor and ink illustrations, dominated by dusky purples and blues, convey the excitement of a special nighttime journey." Horn Book

De Seve, Randall

The **Duchess** of Whimsy; an absolutely delicious fairy tale. [by] Randall de Seve; [illustrated by] Peter de Seve. Philomel Books 2009 un il $17.99

Grades: PreK K 1   E

1. Fairy tales

ISBN 978-0-399-25095-8; 0-399-25095-6

LC 2009-2637

The Duchess of Whimsy has absolutely no interest in the Earl of Norm until he makes a sandwich that causes her to look at him in an entirely different way

"Pages burst to life with rich colors whenever the duchess appears and then become comically dull whenever the earl shows up. With a romantic story and smooth art, this charming picture book will appeal to sophisticated young readers who will find the happily-ever-after whimsically ordinary." Booklist

Peanut and Fifi have a ball; by Randall de Sève; illustrations by Paul Schmid. Dial Books for Young Readers 2013 40 p. (hardcover) $15.99

Grades: PreK K   E

1. Sharing -- Fiction 2. Sisters -- Fiction 3. Balls (Sporting goods) -- Fiction

ISBN 0803735782; 9780803735781

LC 2012014355

In this book, "Peanut . . . the little girl is delighted with her new toy. . . . Her sister, pigtailed Fifi, yearns for a piece of the action, but grabbing for the ball, begging, and suggesting shared games don't melt Peanut's resolve to hang on to her toy. Finally Fifi gets wise and presents an attraction all her own: a seal named Bob, and a planned trip around the world for Bob, Fifi, Peanut, and the ball." (Bulletin of the Center for Children's Books)

★ The **toy** boat; [by] Randall DeSeve; [illustrated by] Loren Long. Philomel Books 2007 un il $16.99

Grades: PreK K   E

1. Toys -- Fiction 2. Boats and boating -- Fiction

ISBN 978-0-399-24374-5

LC 2006026281

A toy boat gets separated from its owner and has an adventure on the high seas

"The streamlined text is straightforward, letting the amazing art do much of the work. Long's acrylic, hyperrealistic pictures, awash with many shades of blue, are so substantial they seem to be molded from clay." Booklist

De Smet, Marian

I have two homes; Marian De Smet; [illustrated by] Nynke Talsma. Clavis 2011 32 p. col. ill. $15.95

Grades: PreK K 1 2   E

1. Divorce -- Fiction 2. Picture books for children 3. Children of divorced parents -- Fiction

ISBN 1605371025; 9781605371023

In this children's picture book, "Nina's parents have divorced, and she is dealing with the changes in her life . . . . When they decide to have separate homes, Nina notices changes in their behavior toward her. She misbehaves in an attempt to get their attention but they are often preoccupied. She talks about missing each parent while she is in the home of the other. . . . She finally concludes that her parents aren't happy with each other but they are happy with her." (School Library Journal)

Deacon, Alexis

Beegu. Farrar, Straus & Giroux 2003 un il $16

Grades: PreK K 1 2   E

1. Extraterrestrial beings -- Fiction

ISBN 0-374-30667-2

LC 2002-192738

A small creature from space finds no welcome on Earth, until she meets a group of children on a playground

"Beegu's black outline and solid yellow center evoke a celestial simplicity. . . . The accomplished artwork underscores the children's easy acceptance of Beegu and highlights the book's uplifting message that acts of kindness have lasting effects." Publ Wkly

★ A **place** to call home; Alexis Deacon; illustrated by Viviane Schwarz. Candlewick Press 2011 1 v. col. ill. $15.99

Grades: PreK K 1   E

1. Adventure fiction 2. Hamsters -- Fiction 3. Picture books for children 4. Voyages and travels -- Fiction 5. Home -- Fiction 6. Brothers -- Fiction

ISBN 0-7636-5360-8; 9780763653606

LC 2010040125

This book tells the story of "hamsterlike creatures bumbling across a junkyard . . . [as] they embark on a search for a new home. They cross an ocean (readers can see it's a puddle), a 'desert,' and make their way to the edge of the world--the top of an old dryer. In [various] scenes, . . . [illustrator Viviane] Schwarz's . . . furry animals squabble, fret, and cheer each other on; in sequential panels, their running commentary appears in word balloons above their heads.

When the junkyard dog grabs one of them, they balk, . . . but taking courage from all they've done so far, they tackle the dog and rescue their sibling." (Publishers Weekly)

"In scenes bursting with physical comedy, Schwarz's . . . furry animals squabble, fret, and cheer each other on; in sequential panels, their running commentary appears in word balloons above their heads. . . . While the creatures may trip over themselves, blundering through their tiny lives not knowing quite where they are headed, Deacon . . . and Schwarz never put a foot wrong. Children will clamor for repeats." Publ Wkly

DeFelice, Cynthia C.

★ **Old** Granny and the bean thief; pictures by Cat Bowman Smith. Farrar, Straus and Giroux 2003 un il $16
Grades: K 1 2 3   E
1. Thieves -- Fiction 2. Grandmothers -- Fiction
ISBN 0-374-35614-9

             LC 2002-20770

After a thief steals Old Granny's beans while she is asleep at night, she gets some surprising help with catching him.

"The down-home narrative is folksy and fun to read aloud. . . . Smith uses a Southwestern palette in her cartoon-style paintings." SLJ

★ **One** potato, two potato; pictures by Andrea U'Ren. Farrar, Straus and Giroux 2006 un il $16
Grades: K 1 2 3   E
1. Magic -- Fiction 2. Potatoes -- Fiction
ISBN 978-0-374-35640-8; 0-374-35640-8

             LC 2004-47217

A very poor, humble couple live so simple a life they share everything, until the husband discovers a pot with magical powers buried under the very last potato in the garden.

"U'Ren's large pen-and-gouache illustrations infuse the couple's grim situation with humor. . . . An entertaining tale." SLJ

Degen, Bruce

★ **Jamberry**; story and pictures by Bruce Degen. Harper & Row 1983 un il $17.99; pa $7.99; bd bk $7.99
Grades: PreK K 1 2   E
1. Stories in rhyme 2. Berries -- Fiction
ISBN 0-06-021416-3; 0-06-443068-5 pa; 0-694-00651-3 bd bk

             LC 82-47708

"Berries and jam are roundly celebrated in a lilting rhyme that, coupled with the jaunty colored pictures, makes it . . . a good pick for sharing one on one, or fun to read aloud as a poetry introduction." Booklist

"Boy meets bear, and together they go berry-picking by canoe, through fields and by pony and 'Boys-in-Berries' train, all the way to Berryland." Child Book Rev Serv

Degman, Lori

1 zany zoo. Simon & Schuster Books for Young Readers 2010 un il $15.99
Grades: PreK K 1   E
1. Counting 2. Stories in rhyme 3. Zoos -- Fiction 4. Animals -- Fiction
ISBN 978-1-4169-8990-5; 1-4169-8990-0

             LC 2009003776

When one fearless fox grabs the zookeeper's keys and opens all the cages, increasing numbers of animals behave in most unusual ways.

"Kids will enjoy hearing the catchy rhymes read multiple times. Digital cartoon images, made to appear like hand-drawn ink sketches, capture the swift movement and playful mood." SLJ

DeGroat, Diane

Brand-new pencils, brand-new books. HarperCollins Publishers 2005 il lib bdg $16.89
Grades: K 1 2 3   E
1. School stories
ISBN 0-06-072615-6

             LC 200404179

Gilbert's excitement over starting first grade turns to worry that the teacher will be mean, the work too hard, and his classmates too unfriendly, but throughout the day there are pleasant surprises.

"With its charming, detailed watercolor illustrations, this story has significant child appeal." SLJ

Delessert, Etienne

Big and Bad; [by] Etienne Delessert. Houghton Mifflin 2008 32p il $17
Grades: 1 2 3 4   E
1. Cats -- Fiction 2. Pigs -- Fiction 3. Wolves -- Fiction 4. Animals -- Fiction
ISBN 978-0-618-88934-1; 0-618-88934-5

             LC 2007019291

In this variation on the classic tale of the three little pigs, two clever cats decide to rid their locale of a vicious wolf whose hunger threatens the entire planet, and enlist the help of assorted animals to build houses for the bait—three exquisitely pink pigs.

"Surreal watercolor and colored-pencil scenes are rendered in the artist's signature earthy tones against white backgrounds. . . . Delessert's direct, sophisticated language and unnerving closeups of the 'marauding' felines and their predator are not for the faint of heart, but the message—that the powerless can reverse their fortunes if they unite and use their wits—will resonate with many readers." SLJ

Moon theater. Creative Editions 2009 un il $17.95
Grades: K 1 2 3   E
1. Moon -- Fiction 2. Theater -- Fiction
ISBN 978-1-56846-208-0; 1-56846-208-5

             LC 2008-53991

To prepare for the moon's nightly rising, a young stage-hand performs such tasks as dressing the birds in long dark coats, training wild dogs to howl, and watering the stars.

"Delessert's distinctive, sophisticated style and a dark palette evoke a nighttime theme that turns the onset of evening into a theatrical production. . . . Inventive and dramatic, this has more child appeal than usual from Delessert; although other man-in-the-moon tales exist, they wane alongside this numinous performance." Booklist

Demarest, Chris L.

All aboard! a traveling alphabet; concept by Chris L. Demarest; illustrated by Bill Mayer. Simon & Schuster 2008 un il $17.99

Grades: PreK K 1 2   E
1. Alphabet 2. Travel -- Fiction
ISBN 978-0-689-85249-7; 0-689-85249-5
    LC 2006103006
An alphabet book provides a presentation of the common structures one sees and uses while getting from place to place, using such images as an 'O' for a looped overpass and a 'B' to denote the arches of a bridge.

"Mayer is a master of airbrush and bold design, using striking perspectives and dynamic angles, often evoking a strong sense of motion in this homage to travel posters of the 1920s." Horn Book Guide

Demas, Corinne

Always in trouble; written by Corinne Demas & pictures by Noah Z. Jones. Scholastic Press 2009 un il $16.99
Grades: K 1 2 3   E
1. Dogs -- Fiction
ISBN 978-0-545-02453-2; 0-545-02453-6
    LC 2007-36079
Even after attending obedience school, Emma's dog Toby misbehaves until she takes him back to become a "specially trained dog."

"The story is great for reading aloud, but the many humorous details in the cartoon-style illustrations make it fun for individual reading as well. Text, illustration, and design all work together to create a delightful story." SLJ

Pirates go to school; illustrated by John Manders. Orchard Books 2011 un il $16.99
Grades: K 1 2   E
1. School stories 2. Stories in rhyme 3. Pirates -- Fiction
ISBN 978-0-545-20629-7; 0-545-20629-4
    LC 2010031394
A rhyming tale of pirates who go to school accompanied by their parrots, learn arithmetic and letters, and want to hear sea stories at storytime.

"Boldly colored scenes in watercolor, gouache, and colored pencil are paired with a nonthreatening ensemble, introducing imaginative readers to a typical school day. . . . A humorous read and a general purchase for most libraries." SLJ

Saying goodbye to Lulu; illustrated by Ard Hoyt. Little, Brown 2004 un il hardcover o.p. pa $6.99
Grades: PreK K 1 2   E
1. Dogs -- Fiction 2. Death -- Fiction 3. Bereavement -- Fiction
ISBN 0-316-70278-1; 0-316-04749-X pa
    LC 2003-44690
When her dog Lulu dies, a girl grieves but then continues with her life

"Hoyt's expressive illustrations, ink-and-colored-pencil drawings washed with watercolors, reflect the tone of the text and show the child's sadness without sentimentality. . . . A sensitive, hopeful portrayal." Booklist

Valentine surprise; [by] Corinne Demas; illustrations by R. W. Alley. Walker & Co. 2008 un il $12.95
Grades: PreK K 1   E
1. Valentine's Day -- Fiction 2. Mother-daughter

relationship -- Fiction
ISBN 978-0-8027-9664-6; 0-8027-9664-8
    LC 2007020143
A little girl tries to create the perfect heart-shaped valentine for her mother on Valentine's Day.

"The language is simple enough for beginning readers, and the story will also work well for group sharing. The typeface changes to reflect the adjective relating to each valentine. Cartoon illustrations in pencil, watercolor, and gouache show Lily in a frenzy of activity." SLJ

Another title about Lily is:
Halloween surprise (2011)

Demers, Dominique

Today, maybe; illustrated by Gabrielle Grimard; translated by Sheila Fischman. Orca Book Publishers 2011 un il $19.95
Grades: K 1 2 3   E
1. Fairy tales
ISBN 978-1-55469-400-6; 1-55469-400-0
"A little girl lives alone in a small house in a big forest, where she waits for someone. She doesn't know for whom she waits, nor why. . . . Then a parade of strangers arrives. . . . The girl sends them off . . . explaining that she is waiting for someone else. And, at last, that someone comes. . . . [This] is a work of clever, poetic sweetness, with familiar folktale imagery giving way to tender surprise." Booklist

Demi

★ The **boy** who painted dragons; [by] Demi. Margaret K. McElderry Books 2007 un il $21.99
Grades: 1 2 3 4   E
1. Artists -- Fiction 2. Courage -- Fiction 3. Dragons -- Fiction
ISBN 978-1-4169-2469-2; 1-4169-2469-8
    LC 2005033679
Ping, a painter of dragons—of which he is secretly afraid—is challenged to seek the truth, find the truth, and dare to be true

"Each page contains paintings of gilt-colored creatures and swatches of delicate Chinese silk brocade. The colors range from rich purples and vibrant reds to cool blues and muted beiges. . . . An elegantly told tale, enhanced by exquisite illustrations." SLJ

★ The **emperor's** new clothes; a tale set in China. Margaret K. McElderry Bks. 2000 un il $19.95
Grades: K 1 2 3   E
1. Fairy tales 2. China -- Fiction
ISBN 0-689-83068-8
    LC 99-24883
In this retelling of Hans Christian Andersen's tale, two rascals sell a vain Chinese emperor an invisible suit of clothes

"Demi's retelling is lucid, graceful, and true to the original. . . . Figures are delicately outlined; they are painted with flat, jewel-like colors and metallic gold and set against subtly patterned grounds that resemble silk damask. . . . A lovely and meticulously wrought rendition." Horn Book Guide

The **girl** who drew a phoenix; [by] Demi. Margaret K. McElderry Books 2008 un il $21.99
Grades: 1 2 3   E
1. China -- Fiction 2. Drawing -- Fiction 3. Phoenix

(Mythical bird) -- Fiction
ISBN 978-1-4169-5347-0; 1-4169-5347-7

LC 2007015411

A young Chinese girl acquires the qualities of the miraculous phoenix—wisdom, clear sight, generosity, and right judgment—by practicing drawing the mythical bird

"Created in paint, ink, and Chinese silk brocade, swirling images of phoenixes with long, feathery tails fill the pages, including elegant horizontal foldouts." Booklist

The **greatest** power. Margaret K. McElderry Bks. 2004 un il $19.95
Grades: K 1 2 3   E
1. China -- Fiction 2. Power (Social sciences) -- Fiction
ISBN 0-689-84503-0

LC 2002-10869

Companion volume to The empty pot

Long ago, a Chinese emperor challenges the children of his kingdom to show him the greatest power in the world, and all are surprised at what is discovered

"The text and the handsomely designed, richly colored artwork, which is touched with gold leaf, are set within a circular motif that reinforces the idea of eternity. As usual, Demi ably combines striking artwork and a meaningful story, with quiet dignity and wisdom." Booklist

The **magic** pillow; written and illustrated by Demi. Margaret K. McElderry Books 2008 un il $19.99
Grades: K 1 2   E
1. China -- Fiction 2. Magic -- Fiction 3. Dreams -- Fiction
ISBN 978-1-4169-2470-8; 1-4169-2470-1

LC 2006-029213

A poor young boy in China yearns for wealth and power, until a magician gives him a magic pillow that brings dreams of what would happen if his wishes came true.

"Demi's dainty, jewel-like art is the perfect vehicle for this story, adoped from a Shen Jiji story. Rendered in traditional Chinese paints and inks and framed in her characteristic gold borders." Booklist

Dempsey, Kristy

A **dance** like starlight; one ballerina's dream. Kristy Dempsey; illustrated by Floyd Cooper. Philomel Books 2014 32 p. $16.99
Grades: K 1 2   E
1. Ballerinas -- Fiction 2. Harlem (New York, N.Y.) -- Fiction 3. Ballet dancing -- Fiction 4. Discrimination -- Fiction 5. African Americans -- Fiction 6. New York (N.Y.) -- History -- 1951- -- Fiction
ISBN 0399252843; 9780399252846

LC 2013009520

This book, by Kristy Dempsey and illustrated by Floyd Cooper, "tell[s] the story of one little ballerina who was inspired by Janet Collins, [the first African-American prima ballerina] to make her own dreams come true." (Publisher's note) "When the Ballet Master at the ballet school where Mama works cleaning and sewing costumes notices the girl mimicking dancers backstage, he takes notice" and allows her to join lessons, though she is not allowed to perform with the white students. (Booklist)

"An African American girl from Harlem dreams of becoming a prima ballerina in this beautifully written narrative, which is also a tribute to Janet Collins, who, in 1951,

was the "first colored prima ballerina" to perform at the Metropolitan Opera...hough the narrator is imagined, the inspirational message is real. Cooper's art incorporates his signature subtractive process and mixed media in tones of brown and pink to achieve illustrations as beautiful and transporting as the text. Pair this title with Pam Munoz Ryan and Brian Selznick's When Marian Sang (Scholastic, 2002), and use this poetic offering for units on black history or women's history." (SLJ)

Me with you; illustrated by Christopher Denise. Philomel Books 2009 un il $16.99
Grades: PreK K 1   E
1. Stories in rhyme 2. Bears -- Fiction 3. Grandfathers -- Fiction
ISBN 978-0-399-25017-0; 0-399-25017-4

LC 2008-11751

A little girl bear describes her relationship with her beloved grandfather.

"While the rhyming text is delightful, it is the lush, computer-generated illustrations and the two cozy, endearing characters that children will treasure. The enticing, picturesque scenes will make readers want to climb right into the pages to participate in each charming episode." Booklist

Mini racer; illustrated by Bridget Strevens-Marzo. Bloomsbury USA Children's Books 2011 un il $16.99; lib bdg $17.89
Grades: PreK K 1   E
1. Stories in rhyme 2. Racing -- Fiction 3. Animals -- Fiction 4. Vehicles -- Fiction
ISBN 978-1-59990-170-1; 1-59990-170-6; 978-1-59990-591-4 lib bdg; 1-59990-591-4 lib bdg

LC 2010006950

Animals in a variety of fanciful vehicles, including a snail on a skateboard and rabbits in a carrot-car, race over a difficult course with a suspenseful and surprising outcome.

"Dempsey's rapid text helps spur readers to keep the pages turning. . . . Full of zooming action and fender-bender drama, it has definite appeal for youngsters." Kirkus

Surfer Chick; by Kristy Dempsey; illustrated by Henry Cole. Abrams Books for Young Readers 2012 32 p.
Grades: PreK K 1 2 3   E
1. Stories in rhyme 2. Picture books for children 3. Surfing -- Fiction 4. Chickens -- Fiction 5. Roosters -- Fiction 6. Fathers and daughters -- Fiction
ISBN 1419701886; 9781419701887

LC 2011031798

This children's rhyming picture book tells a story with extensive use of surfing slang of a chicken father and his young daughter "who take to the beach so she can finally learn how to surf." The daughter learns perseverance and how to face new discouraging challenges. "At first Chick's mood is foul as she struggles through some [difficult] waters, but soon she is catching waves on her own board and even doing . . . just like her . . . dad!" (Publisher's note)

Dempsey, Sheena

Bye-bye baby brother! Sheena Dempsey. Candlewick Press 2013 32 p. (reinforced) $15.99

Grades: PreK K 1 2   E
  1. Imagination -- Fiction 2. Sibling rivalry -- Fiction
  ISBN 0763662410; 9780763662417
                                LC 2012942659
In this children's story, by Sheena Dempsey, "Ruby loves nothing more than playing, especially with Mom. But Mom is always so busy with Oliver, Ruby's baby brother . . . and Ruby is tired of waiting. . . . Maybe if Ruby puts her imagination to work, she can invent a way to make Oliver disappear to a place far, far away. Or would it be even more fun if she and Mom climbed aboard and went along for the ride?" (Publisher's note)

Denise, Anika
  Bella and Stella come home; [illustrated] by Christopher Denise. Philomel Books 2010 un il $16.99
Grades: PreK K 1 2   E
  1. Moving -- Fiction 2. Imaginary playmates -- Fiction
  ISBN 978-0-399-24243-4; 0-399-24243-0
"Bella, an endearing girl with a big imagination and lots of personality, is nervous about moving to a new home. Fortunately, her trusted stuffed elephant, Stella, who looms large and lifelike in the child's mind, remains at her side through the upcoming uncertainties. . . . The sweet narrative, told from Bella's point of view, perfectly captures the little girl's psyche. The story is enhanced by luminous, almost photographic illustrations drawn in shades of pink, ivory, and gold." SLJ

  Pigs love potatoes; illustrated by Christopher Denise. Philomel Books 2007 un il $15.99
Grades: PreK K   E
  1. Counting 2. Stories in rhyme 3. Pigs -- Fiction 4. Cooking -- Fiction
  ISBN 978-0-399-24036-2; 0-399-24036-5
                                  LC 2006-20975
A counting book in which increasing numbers of pigs arrive and are recruited to help as Mamma cooks potatoes.
"Charming acrylic and charcoal pictures of a cozy household and a happy family will have wide appeal." SLJ

DePalma, Mary Newell
  Bow-wow wiggle waggle; written and illustrated by Mary Newell DePalma. Eerdmans Books for Young Readers 2012 32 p. col. ill. (reinforced: alk. paper) $14.00
Grades: PreK K 1 2   E
  1. Dogs -- Fiction 2. Animals -- Fiction 3. Picture books for children 4. Stories in rhyme
  ISBN 0802854087; 9780802854087
                                  LC 2011035827
This story is "told exclusively with onomatopoetic narrative and watercolor illustrations." In it, "a boy and his dog encounter other animals while playing outdoors," including a cat, a frog, a butterfly, and other animals. "Geese chase them from the pond, a snake and then rabbits appear from under the bushes, and the dog wanders off from the boy to chase a cat." (School Library Journal)

  A **grand** old tree. Arthur A. Levine Books 2005 un il $16.99
Grades: K 1 2 3   E
  1. Trees -- Fiction
  ISBN 0-439-62334-0

"For many years a tree flourishes. . . . After the old tree dies, it still provides a home to animals and insects as it slowly decomposes. . . . Neither sentimental nor unfeeling, this appealing picture book offers an appreciation of the cycle of life through a story that is accessible to young children." Booklist

  The **Nutcracker** doll. Arthur A. Levine Books 2007 un il $16.99
Grades: K 1 2   E
  1. Ballet -- Fiction
  ISBN 0-439-80242-0; 978-0-439-80242-0
                                  LC 2006-16466
Kepley, a young ballerina, gets to play a flower doll in a professional production of "The Nutcracker."
"Airy pen-and-wash illustrations convey moments both large and small. The text thoughtfully keeps the spotlight on the young dancer's feelings." Horn Book Guide

  The **perfect** gift. Arthur A. Levine Books 2010 un il $16.99
Grades: PreK K 1   E
  1. Gifts -- Fiction 2. Animals -- Fiction 3. Parrots -- Fiction 4. Grandmothers -- Fiction 5. Books and reading -- Fiction
  ISBN 978-0-545-15402-4; 0-545-15402-2
                                  LC 2009006769
Lori the lorikeet wants to give her grandmother a present, but after dropping her beautiful red berry into the river, she and her friends must try to retrieve the berry or find another gift.
"While DePalma uses delightfully expressive, rhythmic language to tell her accessible tale, her acrylic illustrations are the standout." SLJ

  Uh-oh! William B. Eerdmans 2011 un il
Grades: PreK K 1   E
  1. Dinosaurs -- Fiction
  ISBN 0-8028-5372-2; 978-0-8028-5372-1
                                  LC 2010048403
"A young dinosaur gets himself into all kinds of trouble in this clever, nearly wordless book. The little terror is jumping on the couch, which leads to knocking over his siblings' blocks and a plant. This begins a chain of events that culminates in an overflowing dishwasher washing the youngster out the window. . . . The plot is humorously appealing, if deceptively sophisticated. Despite the lack of text, it is likely to appeal most to older preschoolers and early elementary children who will understand the humor." SLJ

dePaola, Tomie, 1934-
  The **art** lesson; written and illustrated by Tomie dePaola. Putnam 1989 un il hardcover o.p. pa $5.99
Grades: PreK K 1 2   E
  1. Art -- Fiction
  ISBN 0-399-21688-X; 0-698-11572-4 pa
                                  LC 88-27617
Having learned to be creative in drawing pictures at home, young Tommy is dismayed when he goes to school and finds the art lesson there much more regimented
This is "engrossing reading. DePaola's characteristic bright illustrations complement and enliven his tale of growing up." Horn Book

The **baby** sister; written and illustrated by Tomie de-Paola. Putnam 1996 un il $16.99; pa $5.99
Grades: PreK K 1 2   **E**
1. Infants -- Fiction 2. Siblings -- Fiction 3. Grandmothers -- Fiction
ISBN 0-399-22908-6; 0-698-11773-5 pa
LC 94-37218

"Tommy's mother is expecting a baby. Tommy helps get the baby's room ready and longs for a sister with a red ribbon in her hair. He's thrilled when the baby is a girl, but while his mother is away in the hospital, his Italian grandmother comes to stay, and he finds it hard to get along with her. . . . Simple lines and warm colors convey the affection in the extended family and the special closeness between Tommy and his parents." Booklist

Four friends at Christmas. Aladdin 2009 un il $12.99
Grades: PreK K 1 2   **E**
1. Frogs -- Fiction 2. Animals -- Fiction 3. Christmas -- Fiction 4. Friendship -- Fiction
ISBN 978-1-4169-9175-5; 1-4169-9175-1

A reissue of the edition published 2002; previously published 1977, in different form, as the chapter entitled Winter in Four Stories for Four Seasons

Mister Frog has slept through Christmas every year and is determined to celebrate this one with his three best friends. But when he takes a short nap that turns into a very long sleep, he wakes up late on Christmas Eve, and there's no one to celebrate with!

"The tale of Frog's first Christmas is charming in its simplicity. The four animal friends' unique personalities come through in dePaola's trademark cozy illustrations." Horn Book Guide

★ **Guess** who's coming to Santa's for dinner? written and illustrated by Tomie dePaola. Putnam's 2004 un il $16.99
Grades: PreK K 1 2   **E**
1. Christmas -- Fiction 2. Family life -- Fiction 3. Santa Claus -- Fiction
ISBN 0-399-24271-6
LC 2003-26638

A houseful of relatives turns "Mrs. C." and Santa's Christmas into a string of surprises, from the arrival of a pet polar bear to Cousin James B.'s flaming plum pudding.

"The part comic strip-style format cleverly reflects the busy, everyone-talk-at-once hum of a big family gathering and serves up plenty of funny asides. Warm and wonderful as Christmas cake fresh out of the oven, dePaola's softly hued, rounded illustrations shine with holiday spirit." Booklist

Jack; Tomie dePaola. Nancy Paulsen Books, an imprint of Penguin Group (USA) 2014 40 p. color illustrations (hbk.) $17.99
Grades: PreK K 1   **E**
1. Animals -- Fiction 2. Friendship -- Fiction 3. Dwellings -- Fiction
ISBN 9780399161544; 0399161546
LC 2013036653

"When Jack sets out to see the world and find a place of his own, he's surprised to attract a following of enthusiastic animal friends eager to join him on his quest. Jack and his

entourage all have high hopes that they will find just what they are looking for as they travel on their merry way." (Publisher's note)

"DePaola dresses the journey in his most sumptuous colors, the carrot-topped hero and his ever-growing group of friends traversing a landscape of deep greens and grays and purple farmhouses to their new home, bright pink in the heart of the city. Storytime audiences will enjoy the trip as well as the sly cameo appearances by nursery-rhyme favorites such as Jack and Jill and Miss Muffet's eight-legged friend." Horn Book

★ **Jamie** O'Rourke and the pooka. Putnam 2000 un il $16.99; pa $6.99
Grades: PreK K 1 2 3   **E**
1. Ireland -- Fiction
ISBN 0-399-23467-5; 0-698-11974-X pa
LC 99-22469

While his wife is away, lazy Jamie O'Rourke relies on a pooka to clean up the messes that he and his friends make

"DePaola's cozy, colorful illustrations are a good match for the lighthearted, rhythmic text." Horn Book Guide

Meet the Barkers; Morgan and Moffat go to school. written and illustrated by Tomie dePaola. Putnam 2001 un il $13.99; pa $5.99
Grades: PreK K 1 2   **E**
1. School stories 2. Dogs -- Fiction 3. Twins -- Fiction
ISBN 0-399-23708-9; 0-14-250083-6 pa
LC 00-55355

Bossy Moffie (a dog) and her quiet twin brother Morgie both enjoy starting school, especially getting gold stars and making new friends

"Genuinely expressive, lovable characters, depicted in warm tones on handmade watercolor paper, make this a great read-aloud." SLJ

Other titles about the Barkers are:
Boss for a day (2001)
Hide-and-seek all week (2001)
A new Barker in the house (2002)
Trouble in the Barkers' class (2003)

★ **Nana** Upstairs & Nana Downstairs; written and illustrated by Tomie dePaola. Putnam 1998 un il $16.99; pa $6.99
Grades: PreK K 1 2   **E**
1. Death -- Fiction 2. Grandmothers -- Fiction
ISBN 0-399-23108-0; 0-698-11836-7 pa
LC 96-31908

A newly illustrated edition of the title first published 1973

"The illustrations are vintage dePaola, and the warm palette conveys the boy's love for his elderly relatives." Horn Book Guide

★ The **night** of Las Posadas; written and illustrated by Tomie dePaola. Putnam 1999 un il $15.99; pa $6.99
Grades: K 1 2 3   **E**
1. Saints 2. Christmas -- Fiction 3. Santa Fe (N.M.) -- Fiction
ISBN 0-399-23400-4; 0-698-11901-0 pa
LC 98-36405

At the annual celebration of Las Posadas in old Santa Fe, the husband and wife slated to play Mary and Joseph are delayed by car trouble, but a mysterious couple appear who seem perfect for the part

"DePaola's talent for crafting folktales is honed to near-perfection, and his pages glow with the soft sun-washed hues of the Southwest." Publ Wkly

Now one foot, now the other. G. P. Putnam's Sons 2005 un il $14.99; pa $7.99
Grades: PreK K 1 2   E
1. Stroke -- Fiction 2. Grandfathers -- Fiction
ISBN 0-399-24259-7; 0-14-240104-8 pa
A newly illustrated edition of the title first published 1981
When his grandfather suffers a stroke, Bobby teaches him to walk, just as his grandfather had once taught him.

"The illustrations have been digitally colorized in this welcome new edition." Horn Book Guide

Pascual and the kitchen angels; written and illustrated by Tomie dePaola. G.P. Putnam 2004 un il hardcover o.p. pa $5.99
Grades: PreK K 1 2   E
1. Angels -- Fiction 2. Cooking -- Fiction 3. Christian life -- Fiction
ISBN 0-399-24214-7; 0-14-240536-1 pa
     LC 2003-8521
Pascual, a boy blessed by angels at his birth, receives divine help when the Franciscan monks make him their cook

"Acrylic illustrations with soft pastel backgrounds show Pascual as a little boy. . . . The winsome paintings capture his serene spirituality as he and the creatures lift their voices toward heaven. Simple, well-chosen words reflect the youngster's sincere love for God and all of His creatures." SLJ

★ The **song** of Francis; [by] Tomie dePaola. G.P. Putnam's Sons 2009 un il $16.99
Grades: PreK K 1 2   E
1. Saints 2. Birds -- Fiction 3. Saints -- Fiction 4. Writers on religion
ISBN 978-0-399-25210-5; 0-399-25210-X
     LC 2008018578
Francis, the Little Poor One, is so filled with the love of God that he bursts into song, and he is joined by birds of every color.

"De Paola's tropical-hued collages convey the magic of this religious interpretation in an appealing way." SLJ

★ **Stagestruck**; written and illustrated by Tomie de-Paola. G.P. Putnam's Sons 2005 un il $16.99
Grades: PreK K 1 2   E
1. School stories 2. Theater -- Fiction
ISBN 0-399-24338-0
     LC 2004-9261
Although Tommy fails to get the part of Peter Rabbit in the kindergarten play, he still finds a way to be the center of attention on stage

"The gently delivered lesson at the end does not dampen the fun of watching this aspiring thespian get carried away. . . . With its warm palette, rounded shapes, and clarity of expression, dePaola's signature style makes Tommy's world an inviting place to visit." Booklist

Strega Nona does it again; written and illustrated by Tomie dePaola. Nancy Paulsen Books 2013 40 p. $17.99

Grades: PreK K 1 2 3   E
1. Cousins -- Fiction 2. Courtship -- Fiction 3. Witches -- Fiction
ISBN 0399257810; 9780399257810
     LC 2012048224
In this book by Tomie dePaola "Angelina is so beautiful that all the young men in the village are chasing her, but the one she has eyes for doesn't know she exists. At his wits' end, her father sends her to his dear cousin--Strega Nona. Strega Nona, Big Anthony and Bambolona are excited to have a houseguest, but they're in for a surprise. Angelina is a spoiled young lady used to being boss. It's up to Strega Nona to devise a plan that will make everyone happy." (Publisher's note)

★ **Strega** Nona: an old tale. Simon & Schuster 1988 un il $18.99; pa $7.99
Grades: PreK K 1 2   E
1. Italy -- Fiction 2. Witches -- Fiction
ISBN 0-671-66283-X; 0-671-66606-1 pa
     LC 88-11438
A reissue of the title first published 1975 by Prentice-Hall
A Caldecott Medal honor book, 1976
"Tomie de Paola has used simple colors, simple line, and medieval costume and architecture in his spaciously composed humorous pictures." Bull Cent Child Books
Other titles about Strega Nona are:
Big Anthony and the magic ring (1979)
Big Anthony: his story (1998)
Brava, Strega Nona (2008)
Merry Christmas, Strega Nona (1986)
Strega Nona: her story (1996)
Strega Nona meets her match (1993)
Strega Nona takes a vacation (2000)
Strega Nona's gift (2011)
Strega Nona's harvest (2009)
Strega Nona's magic lessons (1982)

Derby, Sally
No mush today; by Sally Derby; illustrated by Nicole Tadgell. Lee & Low 2008 un il $16.95
Grades: PreK   E
1. Infants -- Fiction 2. Siblings -- Fiction 3. African Americans -- Fiction
ISBN 978-1-60060-238-2; 1-60060-238-X
"Nonie, a young African-American girl, sits at the breakfast table with her parents and a wailing baby, sulking: 'Not gonna eat my mush. Not gonna eat it!' I say. 'Squishy, yucky, yellow stuff-mush is baby food.' She puts on her shiny black shoes, and, with her chin poked out, stomps off to live with Grandma (next door). . . . The spare text deftly conveys Nonie's reactions and emotions, which are clearly reflected in Tadgell's realistic, folksy watercolors sweeping across double pages." SLJ

Derom, Dirk
Pigeon and Pigeonette; [text by] Dirk Derom; [illustrations by] Sarah Verroken. Enchanted Lion Books 2009 un il $16.95
Grades: K 1 2   E
1. Flight -- Fiction 2. Pigeons -- Fiction 3. Friendship

-- Fiction 4. Disabilities -- Fiction

ISBN 978-1-59270-087-5; 1-59270-087-X

LC 2009-20779

An old, blind pigeon and a young, deformed pigeon become friends as they persevere in their quest to fly.

"The bold woodcuts and limited color palette convey the setting of the woods throughout the seasons. The boot-wearing pigeons are stylized and encourage closer examination. This is a story of overcoming odds and obstacles, and, despite an occasional adult tone, it delivers a positive and important message." SLJ

Derrick, David G.

Animals don't, so I won't! by David G. Derrick. Immedium 2012 36 p. (hardcover) $15.95

Grades: PreK K 1   E

1. Conduct of life -- Fiction 2. Animal behavior -- Fiction 3. Mother-child relationship -- Fiction 4. Behavior -- Fiction 5. Imagination -- Fiction 6. Mother and child -- Fiction 7. Animals -- Habits and behavior -- Fiction

ISBN 159702029X; 9781597020299

LC 2011052797

Author David G. Derrick, Jr. presents a "knowledgeable mother turns the tables on her balky son by pointing out what animals DO. . . . Animal-loving Ben likes to pretend he's wild himself. He won't clean his room until his mother reminds him that as a beetle, he'll have to clean up elephant dung. He pretends to be a penguin that won't eat his lasagna until his mother pretends to barf up fish for him. And so forth . . . [When the story is about to end with] baby chimps rocking in their bedtime nests, there's a surprise: Dawn comes early for roosters." (Kirkus)

Desrosiers, Sylvie

Hocus Pocus. Kids Can Press 2011 un il

Grades: PreK K 1   E

1. Stories without words 2. Dogs -- Fiction 3. Rabbits -- Fiction

ISBN 1-55453-577-8; 978-1-55453-577-4

"This wordless book features a Wile E. Coyote vs. Road Runner-like battle between a rabbit, Hocus Pocus, and a hapless canine. Mr. Magic arrives home one day with a bag of peanuts, greens, and carrots. When he and his pooch settle down for a nap, his rabbit decides to bolt from the magic hat he left on the bureau. . . . The digitally rendered illustrations are suggestive of '60s cartoon storyboards. The drawings are colorful, and the amusing facial expressions and antics of Dog and Hocus Pocus will appeal to children." SLJ

Devlin, Jane

Hattie the bad; [pictures by] Joe Berger. Dial Books for Young Readers 2010 un il $16.99

Grades: PreK K 1   E

1. Good and evil -- Fiction

ISBN 978-0-8037-3447-0; 0-8037-3447-6

LC 2009-09281

A little girl tries to be good but soon discovers that being bad is ever so much more fun.

"Berger's zesty, orange-splashed illustrations hum with energy and comic hyperbole, in perfect sync with the text. . . . This is a romp worth reading time and again." Publ Wkly

Dewan, Ted

One true bear. Walker 2009 un il $14.99

Grades: 1 2 3   E

1. Teddy bears -- Fiction

ISBN 978-0-8027-8495-7; 0-8027-8495-X

LC 2009001807

A brave teddy bear puts his fur on the line when he goes to live with a boy who has a long history of destroying his toys.

"Wonderfully rich and detailed illustrations clearly show an active, rambunctious boy who is also capable of some quiet time with his bear. The placement of the text in and around the illustrations reinforces how well they complement one another." SLJ

Dewdney, Anna

Llama, llama red pajama; by Anna Dewdney. Viking 2005 un il $15.99

Grades: PreK K   E

1. Stories in rhyme 2. Llamas -- Fiction 3. Bedtime -- Fiction 4. Mother-child relationship -- Fiction

ISBN 0-670-05983-8

LC 2004-25149

At bedtime, a little llama worries after his mother puts him to bed and goes downstairs.

"Dewdney gives a wonderfully fresh twist to a familiar nighttime ritual with an adorable bugeyed baby llama, staccato four-line rhymes, and page compositions that play up the drama. The simple rhymes call out for repeating." Booklist

Other titles about Llama are:

Llama Llama mad at Mama (2007)

Llama Llama misses Mama (2009)

Llama Llama holiday drama (2010)

Llama Llama home with Mama (2011)

Nobunny's perfect; by Anna Dewdney. Viking Childrens Books 2008 32p il $12.99

Grades: PreK K 1   E

1. Stories in rhyme 2. Rabbits -- Fiction 3. Etiquette -- Fiction

ISBN 978-0-670-06288-1; 0-670-06288-X

LC 2007-24008

Bunnies, who slurp their juice, forget to say "please," and bite their friends, learn about good manners.

"Dewdney's straightforward text, written in short sentences and rhyme, flows well. Full-color artwork effectively captures the facial expressions, conveys the bunnies' changing emotions, and recreates the activity described in the text." SLJ

Roly Poly pangolin. Viking 2010 un il $16.99

Grades: PreK K   E

1. Stories in rhyme 2. Shyness -- Fiction 3. Pangolins -- Fiction

ISBN 978-0-670-01160-5; 0-670-01160-6

"In this short rhyming story, a small pangolin is afraid of new experiences, including meeting other animals. When he hears an unexpected sound, he runs off in a panic, trips, and rolls into a tight ball to keep himself safe. . . . Dewdney has created a lovable childlike character with whom most pre-schoolers can easily identify. Textured full-bleed pages interspersed with some small action drawings on white space convey movement. Expressive closeup illustrations aptly portray Roly Poly's feelings." SLJ

Dewey, Ariane

Splash! [by] Ariane Dewey and Jose Aruego. Harcourt 2001 un il (Green Light readers) $10.95; pa $3.95
Grades: PreK K 1 2   E
1. Bears -- Fiction 2. Fishing -- Fiction
ISBN 0-15-216256-9; 0-15-216262-3 pa
LC 00-9723
Two clumsy bears join in fishing fun at the river
"This combines big, silly ink-and-watercolor pictures with two or three lines of text on each page. New readers will enjoy the slapstick . . . and the sounds of such words as splash and slip add to the fun of the story." Booklist

Dewey, Jennifer

Once I knew a spider; [by] Jennifer Owens Dewey; illustrated by Jean Cassels. Walker & Co. 2002 un il $16.95; lib bdg $17.85
Grades: PreK K 1 2   E
1. Spiders -- Fiction
ISBN 0-8027-8700-2; 0-8027-8701-0 lib bdg
LC 2001-26345
An expectant mother watches as an orb weaver spider spins a web, lays her eggs, and stays with them over the winter
An "eloquent meditation on the cycle of life. The muted tones of Cassels's . . . austere interiors and the detailed paintings of the spider's behavior complement the calm, contemplative tone of the journal-like text." Publ Wkly

Diakite, Penda

★ I lost my tooth in Africa; by Penda Diakité and Baba Wagué Diakité; illustrated by Baba Wagué Diakité. Scholastic Press 2006 un il $16.99
Grades: PreK K 1 2 3   E
1. Mali -- Fiction 2. Teeth -- Fiction 3. Chickens -- Fiction 4. Family life -- Fiction
ISBN 0-439-66226-5
LC 2004-01933
While visiting her father's family in Mali, a young girl loses a tooth, places it under a calabash, and receives a hen and a rooster from the African Tooth Fairy.
"The vivid ceramic-tile illustrations expand the text, revealing a range of animals, houses, and greenery. At the end are the words to Grandma's Good Night Song, the recipe for African Onion Sauce, and a glossary of Bambara words, all of which add to the authentic feel of the story." SLJ

DiCamillo, Kate

★ Great joy; illustrated by Bagram Ibatoulline. Candlewick Press 2007 un il $16.99
Grades: PreK K 1 2   E
1. Christmas -- Fiction 2. Homeless persons -- Fiction
ISBN 978-0-7636-2920-5; 0-7636-2920-0
LC 2007-29934
Just before Christmas, when Frances sees a sad-eyed organ grinder and his monkey performing near her apartment, she cannot stop thinking about them, wondering where they go at night, and wishing she could do something to help.

"The plotline is simplicity itself, and the text lacks any sentimentality or fluff, allowing the acrylic paintings . . . to enrich and expand the story." SLJ

★ Louise; the adventures of a chicken. written by Kate DiCamillo; pictures by Harry Bliss. Joanna Cotler Books 2008 un il $17.99; lib bdg $18.89
Grades: PreK K 1 2   E
1. Adventure fiction 2. Pirates -- Fiction 3. Chickens -- Fiction
ISBN 978-0-06-075554-6; 0-06-075554-7; 978-0-06-075555-3 lib bdg; 0-06-075555-5 lib bdg
LC 2008-20091
Longing for adventure, intrepid Louise the chicken leaves her comfortable nest and goes to sea.
"DiCamillo's brisk, comic narrative crackles with read-aloud savoriness, and her respect for Louise makes the book all the funnier. . . . Bliss creates a thrilling sense of place and puts his wide-eyed heroine front and center. An enlarged format does justice to the details in the art—and to the grand sweep of the storytelling." Publ Wkly

Dickinson, Rebecca

Over in the hollow; illustrated by Stephan Britt. Chronicle Books 2009 un il $15.99
Grades: PreK K 1 2   E
1. Counting 2. Stories in rhyme 3. Monsters -- Fiction 4. Halloween -- Fiction
ISBN 978-0-8118-5035-3; 0-8118-5035-8
LC 2009000955
A counting book that features a variety of spooky Halloween creatures, from one spider to thirteen ghosts.
"The rhyme and rhythm flow well, making this a good choice for reading aloud. The mixed-media illustrations have a retro cartoon feel and are spooky, but not scary—just like the text." SLJ

Diesen, Deborah

The pout-pout fish; illustrated by Dan Hanna. Farrar, Straus & Giroux 2008 un il $16
Grades: PreK K 1   E
1. Stories in rhyme 2. Fishes -- Fiction 3. Marine animals -- Fiction
ISBN 978-0-374-36096-2; 0-374-36096-0
LC 2007-60730
The pout-pout fish believes he only knows how to frown, even though many of his friends suggest ways to change his expression, until one day a fish comes along that shows him otherwise.
"The bouncy rhythm is appealing [and] . . . the cartoon illustrations of undersea life are bright and clean and the protagonist's exaggerated expressions are entertaining. The layout is attractive, and the three-panel sequences showing the fish moping around during the refrain are especially well done." SLJ
Another title about the pout-pout fish is:
The pout-pout fish in the big-big dark (2010)

The pout-pout fish goes to school; a Pout-pout fish adventure. Deborah Diesen; pictures by Dan Hanna. Farrar Straus & Giroux 2014 32 p. (hardcover) $16.99
Grades: PreK K 1   E
1. School stories 2. Fishes -- Fiction 3. Stories in rhyme 4. Schools -- Fiction 5. Self-confidence --

Fiction 6. First day of school -- Fiction
ISBN 0374360952; 9780374360955

LC 2013001317

In this children's book by Deborah Diesen, illustrated by Daniel X. Hanna, "Mr. Fish is nervously awaiting his first day of school, and he frets about not knowing how to write his name, how to draw shapes, and how to do math--until he's reassured that school is the perfect place to learn how to master all of these new skills, in Pout-Pout Fish Goes to School from Deborah Diesen and Dan Hanna." (Publisher's note)

"In Mr. Fish's latest rhymed tale, he reflects on his first experience at school, where he had to try several different classrooms before he found the right one (marked "Brand-new fish"). Hanna comes through with illustrations of the unlikely hero--just look at the pitiful/hilarious one of an upside-down school-age Mr. Fish trying to negotiate a mind-melting math problem." Horn Book

Diggs, Taye, 1971-

Chocolate me! illustrated by Shane W. Evans. Feiwel and Friends 2011 40p il $16.99

Grades: PreK K 1 2   E

1. Race relations -- Fiction 2. African Americans -- Fiction

ISBN 978-0-312-60326-7; 0-312-60326-6

The boy is teased for looking different than the other kids. His skin is darker, his hair curlier. He tells his mother he wishes he could be more like everyone else. And she helps him to see how beautiful he really, truly is.

"The cartoonlike illustrations are done in bold colors. . . . With its universal themes of wanting to fit in, self-acceptance, and self-esteem, this read-aloud offering is sure to strike a chord with many young readers/listeners, and on a variety subjects, not just race." SLJ

Dipucchio, Kelly

Clink; manufactured by Kelly DiPucchio and [illustrated by] Matthew Myers. Balzer & Bray 2011 un il

Grades: PreK K 1   E

1. Robots -- Fiction

ISBN 006192928X; 9780061929281

While newer, fancier robots are quickly purchased, Clink, an old-fashioned robot who can only make toast and music, gathers dust and feels downhearted until a young boy enters the shop looking for something special.

"The witty text, occasionally interspersed with colorful onomatopoeic robot-centric words . . . is ideal for reading aloud. . . . Myer's paintings . . . burst with loud colors and an energy that's perfect for a store—and story—full of bopping robots and smiling clientele." Horn Book

★ **Gaston**; words by Kelly DiPucchio; pictures by Christian Robinson. First edition Atheneum Books for Young Readers 2014 40 p. (hardcover) $16.99

Grades: PreK K 1 2   E

1. Dogs -- Fiction 2. Bulldog -- Fiction 3. Poodles -- Fiction 4. Individuality -- Fiction

ISBN 1442451025; 9781442451025

LC 2012031987

This children's book, written by Kelly DiPucchio and illustrated by Christian Robinson, "is the story of four puppies: Fi-Fi, Foo-Foo, Ooh-La-La, and Gaston. Gaston works the hardest at his lessons on how to be a proper pooch. . . .

But a chance encounter with a bulldog family in the park - Rocky, Ricky, Bruno, and Antoinette - reveals there's been a mix-up, and so Gaston and Antoinette switch places. The new families look right - but they don't feel right." (Publisher's note)

"Bumptious Gaston looms over his elegant poodle sisters. At the park, they meet a family like theirs but in reverse: bulldogs Rocky, Ricky, and Bruno and their petite sister Antoinette. Were Gaston and Antoinette switched at birth? Should they trade families? DiPucchio's lively text was made to be read aloud. Robinson's elegant illustrations feature dogs with minimal yet wonderfully expressive facial details." (Horn Book)

Grace for president; written by Kelly DiPucchio; pictures by LeUyen Pham. Hyperion Books for Children 2008 un il $15.99

Grades: K 1 2 3   E

1. Elections -- Fiction

ISBN 0-7868-3919-8; 978-0-7868-3919-3

When Grace discovers that there has never been a female U.S. president, she decides to run for school president.

"The illustrations are colorful, and depict the various aspects of political campaigns. While the readership of this title is elementary students, Social Studies teachers at upper levels might consider this as a good way to introduce a concept that isn't always easily understood. This is a timely title, with a likeable heroine." Libr Media Connect

DiPucchio, Kelly S.

★ **Crafty** Chloe; illustrated by Heather Ross. Atheneum Books for Young Readers 2012 il $16.99

Grades: PreK K 1 2   E

1. Gifts -- Fiction 2. Birthdays -- Fiction 3. Handicraft -- Fiction

ISBN 978-1-4424-2123-3; 1-4424-2123-1

LC 2010042811

Chloe is very good at sewing and crafts and when her best friend's birthday approaches, she creates a fabulous gift but also saves the day for a classmate who had been unkind to her.

"DiPucchio is to be commended for providing a simple and strong story with a loving solution that will surprise readers. Strong pacing and fanciful illustrations full of happy yellow highlights capture a delightfully determined and winning child." Kikus

Gilbert Goldfish wants a pet; by Kelly DiPucchio; pictures by Bob Shea. Dial Books for Young Readers 2011 un il $16.99

Grades: PreK K 1   E

1. Pets -- Fiction 2. Fishes -- Fiction 3. Animals -- Fiction 4. Goldfish -- Fiction

ISBN 978-0-8037-3394-7; 0-8037-3394-1

LC 2010028806

Gilbert has everything a goldfish could want except a pet of his own, but none of the animals who come near his fishbowl seem quite right until Fluffy, with his long tail and whiskers, appears.

"The clever text stands on its own, but Shea's bold, expressive illustrations elevate this title to a higher plane. Wavy orange endpapers establish the watery setting and bright palette. Gilbert exudes emotion. . . . Gilbert Goldfish is a perfect choice for storytime and bedtime." SLJ

DiSalvo, DyAnne

A **castle** on Viola Street. HarperCollins Pubs. 2001 un il $16.95; lib bdg $16.89

Grades: K 1 2 3   E

    1. Houses -- Fiction

    ISBN 0-688-17690-9; 0-688-17691-7 lib bdg

               LC 00-40889

A hardworking family gets their own house at last by joining a community program that restores old houses

"DiSalvo-Ryan shares an uplifting story of the importance and impact of community pride and support. . . . The colorful gouache, pen, and pencil pictures are folksy and warm." Booklist

A **dog** like Jack. Holiday House 1999 un il hardcover o.p. $17.95

Grades: K 1 2 3   E

    1. Dogs -- Fiction 2. Death -- Fiction

    ISBN 0-8234-1369-1; 0-8234-1680-1 pa

               LC 97-41949

After a long life of chasing squirrels, licking ice cream cones, and loving his adoptive family, an old dog comes to the end of his days

"Thoughtful words and tender pictures beautifully convey the special relationship between a young boy and his dog." Booklist

Uncle Willie and the soup kitchen. Morrow Junior Bks. 1991 un il hardcover o.p. pa $5.99

Grades: K 1 2 3   E

    1. Uncles -- Fiction 2. Poverty -- Fiction

    ISBN 0-688-15285-6 pa

               LC 90-6375

A boy spends the day with Uncle Willie in the soup kitchen where he works preparing and serving food for the hungry

"The color-pencil and wash illustrations observe . . . [a] balance between attracting the viewer with softly blended colors and avoiding the sentimentality of glamorizing an essentially sad situation. Without sacrifice of story, the total effect leaves young listeners with new considerations of society and social service, a theme too often neglected in picture books." Bull Cent Child Books

Disalvo-Ryan, DyAnne

City green; DyAnne DiSalvo-Ryan. Morrow Junior Bks. 1994 32 p. col il $17.99

Grades: K 1 2 3   E

    1. Community gardens -- Fiction 2. City and town life -- Fiction

    ISBN 0688127878; 068812786X; 9780688127862

               LC 93027117

In this book, by DyAnne DiSalvo-Ryan, "when an abandoned house on her street is torn down, Marcy feels saddened by its loss. But then an idea strikes her: She enlists the aid of several grown-up neighbors and rents the vacant lot from the city for the price of $1. Working together with materials like leftover yellow paint and surplus wood, the residents create a community garden and plant it with a variety of flowers, fruits, and vegetables." (Kirkus Reviews)

Ditchfield, Christin

Cowlick! by Christin Ditchfield; illustrated by Rosalind Beardshaw. Random House 2007 un il $14.99; lib bdg $17.99

Grades: PreK K 1   E

    1. Hair -- Fiction 2. Cattle -- Fiction

    ISBN 0-375-83540-7; 0-375-93540-1 lib bdg

This offers "appealingly rich and textured paintings. . . . The short, lively text makes this fun for sharing aloud." SLJ

Shwatsit! illustrated by Rosalind Beardshaw. Golden Books 2009 un il $15.99

Grades: PreK K 1   E

    1. Siblings -- Fiction 2. Toddlers -- Fiction

    ISBN 978-0-375-84181-1; 0-375-84181-4

As Baby points at everything in sight, she has just one thing to say: "Shwatsit!" But what on earth does it mean? Finally, her older brother solves the mystery.

"The well-designed, expressive illustrations expand on the rhyming text by showing the toddler throughout her day." SLJ

DiTerlizzi, Angela

★ **Some** bugs; words by Angela DiTerlizzi; bugs by Brendan Wenzel. First edition Beach Lane Books 2014 32 p. (hardcover) $17.99

Grades: PreK K   E

    1. Stories in rhyme 2. Insects -- Fiction

    ISBN 1442458801; 9781442458802

               LC 2013006303

This picture book, written by Angela DiTerlizzi and illustrated by Brendan Wenzel, focuses on the "buggy natural world. With minimal words cajoled into loose rhyme . . . each page of this . . . book introduces a different bug's proclivity . . . while a small ladybug saunters past, serving as a cohesive visual element." (Kirkus Reviews)

""Stinging, biting, stinking, fighting, hopping, gliding, swimming, hiding...." Jaunty rhymes describe the many activities of a variety of bugs. The scansion is unstrained, begging to be chanted aloud, and Wenzel's spirited mixed-media illustrations match the text's tone, clarify its meaning, and imbue the bugs with personality. Readers won't hesitate to follow the ending injunction to "find some bugs in your backyard!" Horn Book

Divakaruni, Chitra Banerjee, 1956-

Grandma and the great gourd; a Bengali folk tale. retold by Chitra Divakaruni; illustrated by Susy Waters. Roaring Brook Press 2013 32 p. (hardcover) $17.99

Grades: PreK K 1 2   E

    1. Fairy tales 2. Picture books for children 3. Folklore -- India -- Bengal 4. Bengali (South Asian people) -- Folklore

    ISBN 1596433787; 9781596433786

               LC 2012001392

This children's picture book sets a retelling of "Little Red Riding Hood" in India, "where the forest hides a fox, a bear, and a tiger. Grandma talks the three predators out of eating her during her first trip ("I'll be a lot fatter on my way back from my daughter's house because she's such a good cook"), but she has to innovate on her way back. Grandma rolls herself home in a giant gourd, singing cheerfully," and continues to elude the predators. (Publishers Weekly)

Dobbins, Jan

Driving my tractor; [text by] Jan Dobbins; [illustrations by] David Sim. Barefoot Books 2009 un il $16.99

Grades: PreK K   E

1. Counting 2. Stories in rhyme 3. Color -- Fiction 4. Tractors -- Fiction 5. Domestic animals -- Fiction

ISBN 978-1-84686-358-5; 1-84686-358-9

     LC 2008051065

The reader is invited to count the animal passengers riding in a tractor traveling on a bumpy road.

"This tale is ideal for storytime with its rhyming text, fun sounds, and refrain, 'Chug, chug, clank, clank, toot! It's a very busy day.' This is a jolly read-aloud, and the accompanying CD with a jazzy version adds to the charm, with both an instrumental track and SteveSongs (of PBS fame) singing the text." SLJ

Docherty, Helen

The **Snatchabook**; by Helen Docherty; illustrated by Thomas Docherty. Sourcebooks Jabberwocky 2013 32 p. (hc: alk. paper) $16.99

Grades: PreK K 1   E

1. Bedtime 2. Books -- Fiction 3. Thieves -- Fiction 4. Stories in rhyme 5. Bedtime -- Fiction 6. Forest animals -- Fiction 7. Books and reading -- Fiction

ISBN 1402290829; 9781402290824

     LC 2013012468

In this book by Helen Docherty, "it's bedtime in the woods of Burrow Down, and all the animals are ready for their bedtime story. But books are mysteriously disappearing. [Rabbit] Eliza Brown decides to stay awake and catch the book thief. It turns out to be a little creature called the Snatchabook who has no one to read him a bedtime story. All turns out well when the books are returned and the animals take turns reading bedtime stories to the Snatchabook." (Publisher's note)

Docherty, Thomas

Big scary monster. Candlewick Press 2010 un il

Grades: PreK K   E

1. Fear -- Fiction 2. Monsters -- Fiction 3. Self-perception -- Fiction

ISBN 978-0-7636-4787-2; 0-7636-4787-X

     LC 2009047397

Big Scary Monster learns some surprising things about himself when he goes down his mountain to find the creatures he has frightened away.

"The full-spread watercolor illustrations in deep colors add to the 'scary' element of the story.... The style of these pictures will give young readers an early lesson in perspective. Great as a read-aloud, this book will engage young monster lovers." SLJ

Little boat. Templar Books 2009 un il $15.99

Grades: PreK K   E

1. Boats and boating -- Fiction

ISBN 978-0-7636-4428-4; 0-7636-4428-5

Setting off into the big, wide world, Little Boat runs into treacherous waters, turbulent tides, and seafaring friends. After all his nautical adventures, he finds out that he's no longer such a little boat.

"This simple story of friendship and self-esteem is beautifully illustrated in ink-and-watercolor paintings with a wistful, nostalgic flavor." Booklist

To the beach. Templar Books 2009 un il $15.99

Grades: PreK K 1   E

1. Imagination -- Fiction 2. Voyages and travels -- Fiction

ISBN 978-0-7636-4429-1; 0-7636-4429-3

"A boy packs up all of the necessary gear for a day at the beach, like goggles, snorkel, flippers, bathing suit, and, of course, a big yellow inner tube. The only problem is: it's raining. His imagination then takes over as he secures an airplane, a sailboat, a truck, a camel, and some sand, and finally arrives at the sea.... This clever book is complemented by beautiful ink and watercolor drawings of the landscapes that the boy has created. The simple narrative encourages youngsters to think for themselves and never to limit the places their imaginations will take them." SLJ

Dockray, Tracy

The **lost** and found pony; illustrated by Paul Bachem. Feiwel and Friends 2011 85p il $16.99

Grades: PreK K 1 2   E

1. Horses -- Fiction

ISBN 978-0-312-59259-2; 0-312-59259-0

"The little pony at the heart of this surprisingly affecting story is thrilled when he becomes a little girl's perfect birthday present. He loves jumping and running with her on his back—until the day he encounters a jump too high. The little girl falls, and he is declared too small for her. Her parents sell him to the circus, where he brings joy to thousands of children, but he never forgets his first owner. When the circus closes down and he is sold at auction, who should buy him but the little girl, now an adult and running a stable of her own.... The simple, straightforward narrative in the pony's voice, combined with Dockray's soft, expressive watercolor and ink illustrations, makes it truly heartwarming." SLJ

Dodd, Emma

Forever; Emma Dodd. Candlewick Press 2013 24 p. $12.99

Grades: PreK K   E

1. Picture books for children 2. Parent-child relationship -- Fiction

ISBN 0763671320; 9780763671327

     LC 2013943157

Author and illustrator Emma Dodd's picture book for children focuses on the message that "love between parent and child lasts a lifetime." The book features a family of polar bears and explores the relationships between parents and children and the bonds that tie them together. The book's main idea is that a parent's love lasts forever. (Publisher's note)

Foxy; Emma Dodd. Harper 2012 40 p. (trade bdg.) $14.99

Grades: PreK K 1   E

1. Foxes -- Fiction 2. Magic -- Fiction 3. Picture books for children 4. First day of school -- Fiction

ISBN 0062014196; 9780062014191

     LC 2010045555

In this children's picture book, "Emily cannot go to sleep because she is worried that she won't have all the things she needs for . . . school. Her friend, Foxy, is sure that he can help her with his magic tail, and . . . waves it at Emily's every wish--only, the tail doesn't always work as he hopes. Emily needs a pencil and Foxy's . . . tail produces a penguin. . . . However, second tries work better, and so Emily goes to sleep with all her supplies in her book pack." (School Library Journal)

I am small. Cartwheel Books 2011 il $8.99
Grades: PreK K   E
  1. Penguins -- Fiction
ISBN 978-0-545-35370-0; 0-545-35370-X
"A penguin chick ponders the big, fast, long, steep world around him and notes how small he is in comparison. But when he is with his mother, he knows he is safe. . . . The simple text and easy-to-read block printing make this a good choice for beginning readers. Dodd uses a palette of black, white, and slate blue with touches of silver to evoke the freezing Antarctic habitat." SLJ

★ **I** don't want a cool cat! Little, Brown 2010 un il $15.99
Grades: PreK K 1   E
  1. Cats -- Fiction
ISBN 978-0-316-03674-0; 0-316-03674-9
A little girl "knows what she does not want: 'A stuffy cat. A huffy, over-fluffy cat.' . . . The true-to-life hilarity of the text commands attention, especially when mixed with such smart art. With a combination of paint and collage, the images have a three-dimensional feel as they sit on their smooth, candy-colored backgrounds. . . . Combine the art with the pithy text, and you're got a book that's perfect to read aloud to groups." Booklist

I love bugs. Holiday House 2010 un il $16.95
Grades: PreK K 1 2   E
  1. Insects -- Fiction 2. Spiders -- Fiction
ISBN 978-0-8234-2280-7; 0-8234-2280-1
                      LC 2009-32814
"The text juggles sounds and rhymes skillfully. . . . Varied in composition, palette, and scale, the illustrations have great vitality. . . . Easy to see from a distance, this would be an excellent choice for group sharing." Booklist

Meow said the cow. Arthur A. Levine Books 2011 un il $16.99
Grades: PreK K 1   E
  1. Stories in rhyme 2. Magic -- Fiction 3. Domestic animals -- Fiction
ISBN 978-0-545-31861-7; 0-545-31861-0
                      LC 2010034247
A noisy rooster causes a disgruntled cat to cast a magic spell that creates confusion among the other farm animals.
"The rollicking text is paired with large, colorful digitally produced art that has the kinetic animals fairly popping off the spreads." SLJ

No matter what; [by] Emma Dodd. Dutton Children's Books 2008 un il $10.99
Grades: PreK   E
  1. Stories in rhyme 2. Elephants -- Fiction 3. Parent-child relationship -- Fiction
ISBN 978-0-525-47932-1; 0-525-47932-5
                      LC 2007019207
In rhyming text, a baby elephant is assured of being loved unconditionally.
"Each phrase is supported by a stylized African landscape in muted colors, but with bright touches. . . . The young elephant is simply rendered, too, and quite charming. The art, and the padded cover with metallic accents, is appealing, and the comforting text is perfect for toddlers." SLJ

Dodds, Dayle Ann
Minnie's Diner; a multiplying menu. illustrated by John Manders. Candlewick Press 2004 un il hardcover o.p. pa $6.99
Grades: K 1 2 3   E
  1. Stories in rhyme 2. Restaurants -- Fiction 3. Multiplication -- Fiction
ISBN 0-7636-1736-9; 0-7636-3313-5 pa
                      LC 2002-34756
Rhyming tale of five boys and their father who forget about their chores on the farm to enjoy Minnie's good cooking, each requesting double what the previous one ordered
"Told in jaunty rhymes with varied type sizes for emphasis, this funny story is illustrated with colorful cartoons done in gouache. Children will appreciate the humor and groan with delight when they recognize the math pattern." SLJ

The **prince** won't go to bed; pictures by Kyrsten Brooker. Farrar, Straus & Giroux 2007 un il $16
Grades: PreK K 1 2   E
  1. Stories in rhyme 2. Bedtime -- Fiction 3. Princes -- Fiction
ISBN 0-374-36108-8; 978-0-374-36108-2
                      LC 2005051234
When the young prince refuses to go to bed, assorted members of the royal household offer their ideas on exactly what he needs, but it is his sister, Princess Kate, who learns the truth.
Dodd's "rhymed text abounds with the kind of repetitions in structure and language that make children want to join in. . . . The fonts grow larger and Brooker's hilarious, cock-eyed collages ever more frantic with each repetition." Publ Wkly

Teacher's pets; illustrated by Marylin Hafner. Candlewick Press 2006 un il $15.99
Grades: PreK K 1 2   E
  1. School stories 2. Pets -- Fiction
ISBN 0-7636-2252-4
A teacher invites her students to bring their pets in each Monday for sharing day, but by the end of the year, she has a classroom full of "forgotten" animals.
"This gentle and humorous story has charming watercolor illustrations that reinforce the emotions of the children, the animals, and, of course, the warmhearted teacher." SLJ

Where's Pup? pictures by Pierre Pratt. Dial Bks. for Young Readers 2003 un il $12.99
Grades: PreK K 1   E
  1. Stories in rhyme 2. Dogs -- Fiction 3. Circus -- Fiction 4. Clowns -- Fiction
ISBN 0-8037-2744-5
                      LC 2002-588

A circus clown's search for his partner leads him to the top of an acrobatic pyramid, found by unfolding the book's final page

"Relying on a jeweled palette of acrylic reds and oranges, the images are simple yet arresting and show the action from varying perspectives. A visually exciting charmer." SLJ

Doerrfeld, Cori

   Penny loves pink. Little, Brown 2011 un il $15.99
Grades: PreK K 1   E
   1. Color -- Fiction 2. Infants -- Fiction 3. Siblings -- Fiction
   ISBN 978-0-316-05458-4; 0-316-05458-5
                      LC 2010008632
A little girl who loves pink more than anything must learn to accept the color blue when her baby brother arrives.

"The illustrations are bright and lively. . . . A sweet, satisfying story." SLJ

Dokas, Dara

   Muriel's red sweater; illustrations by Bernadette Pons. Dutton Children's Books 2009 un il $16.99
Grades: PreK K 1   E
   1. Gifts -- Fiction 2. Animals -- Fiction 3. Birthdays -- Fiction 4. Clothing and dress -- Fiction
   ISBN 978-0-525-47962-8; 0-525-47962-7
                      LC 2008020605
"Unbeknownst to duck Muriel, her sweater is unraveling as she delivers invitations to her birthday party. Luckily, her friends have already been working on the perfect present: a new sweater. The cheery illustrations do a good deal of storytelling; readers can spot hints about the new sweater and chuckle at the uses Muriel's friends find for yarn from the old one." Horn Book Guide

Dolan, Elys

   Weasels; Elys Dolan. Candlewick Press 2014 32 p. $17.99
Grades: K 1 2 3 4   E
   1. Weasels -- Fiction 2. Machinery -- Fiction 3. Conspiracies -- Fiction 4. Humorous stories
   ISBN 0763671002; 9780763671006
                      LC 2013943084
In this children's picture book, by Elys Dolan, "ultracaffeinated weasels plotting world domination face a setback when their room-sized, Rube Goldberg-ian machine breaks down. They scurry to troubleshoot, many of them inappropriately insistent on deploying tools like a blow torch, saws and a large electric drill. Luckily, the Health and Safety officer prevails, and the gang repairs to the laboratory to tinker." (Kirkus Reviews)

""Weasels. What do you think they do all day?" asks debut author Dolan, and her answer—which has nothing to do with animal behavior and everything to do with world domination—marks her as a talent to watch...Dolan fills her pages with visual and verbal jokes about coffee obsessions, tech geeks, bureaucracy, and unsafe workplace practices ("I'm entirely confident that this huge drill will fix everything," declares one weasel unconvincingly). Will the weaselly weasels make the fix and carry out their dastardly plan? Dolan leaves readers hanging—but they won't mind a bit." PW

Dominguez, Angela

   Let's go, Hugo! story and pictures by Angela Dominguez. Dial Books for Young Readers 2013 40 p. col. ill. (hardcover) $16.99
Grades: PreK K   E
   1. Fear -- Fiction 2. Birds -- Fiction 3. Artists -- Fiction
   ISBN 9780803738645
                      LC 2012003561

   Maria had a little llama/ María tenía una llamita; Angela Dominguez. Henry Holt and Company 2013 28 p. (hardcover) $16.99
Grades: PreK K 1 2   E
   1. Nursery rhymes 2. Stories in rhyme 3. Llamas as pets -- Fiction 4. Spanish language materials -- Bilingual
   ISBN 0805093338; 9780805093339
                      LC 2012013530
Pura Belpre Illustrator Honor Book (2014)
This book, by Angela Dominguez, is a "bilingual presentation of a classic children's rhyme, set in rural Peru. Dominguez presents a straightforward version of the familiar rhyme, adding just enough new elements to transform it into a story. The text flows rhythmically in both the English and the Spanish, which are placed together on the page with the English in bold and positioned above the Spanish." (Kirkus Reviews)

Maria tenía una llama pequeña

   Santiago stays; by Angela Dominguez. Abrams Books 2013 32 p. bcol. ill. $12.95
Grades: PreK K   E
   1. Dogs 2. Siblings 3. Dogs -- Fiction
   ISBN 141970821X; 9781419708213
                      LC 2012041376
In this children's book, written and illustrated by Angela Dominguez, "Santiago [the French bulldog] stays . . . , despite the growing disappointment of the little boy who is trying to engage him. After several futile attempts, the boy's frustration bubbles over into a yell, which wakes the baby, and the reader realizes whom Santiago has been resolutely guarding all along." (Publisher's note)

"The illustrations, in pencil, marker, ink, tissue paper, and digital color, capture the boy's persistence and the bulldog's dug-in resistance; the warm palette is perfect for this affection-filled, simple, and satisfying family story." - Horn book guide

Domney, Alexis

   Splish, splat! written by Alexis Domney; illustrated by Alice Crawford. Second Story Press 2011 un il $15.95
Grades: PreK K 1   E
   1. Deaf -- Fiction 2. Painting -- Fiction 3. Sign language -- Fiction
   ISBN 978-1-897187-88-3; 1-897187-88-2
"Colin is having nightmares in his yolk-colored room. As he sleeps, eggs over easy zoom around like alien spaceships. It is time for a new paint job, and his mother opts for professionals to do the work. She gets the message relay number of Deaf painters and, via an interpreter, makes an appointment. Whereas this could simply be a didactic picture book on Deaf and hearing etiquette, the humor imbued makes it a delightful story about the joy of communication.

The unique collage illustrations add warmth and render the two women painters in realistic signing stances." SLJ

Don, Lari

Little Red Riding Hood; Lari Don; illustrated by Celia Chauffrey. Barefoot Books 2012 32 p. $16.99

Grades: K 1 2 3   E

1. Fairy tales 2. Wolves -- Fiction 3. Children and strangers -- Fiction 4. Folklore

ISBN 1846867665; 9781846867668

LC 2012009603

In this book by Lari Don, "Little Red Riding Hood loves to visit her Granny's cottage in the forest. Her mother warns her to go straight to Granny's, but when she meets a handsome grey wolf, she doesn't see the harm in stopping for a chat." (Publisher's note) "Although the two leading ladies are gobbled up, legs last, the hunter comes to the rescue. He is rewarded with cakes, Granny learns to lock her door, and Red 'never turned round to talk to strangers again.'" (School Library Journal)

Donaldson, Julia

The **fish** who cried wolf; [by] Julia Donaldson & Axel Scheffler. Arthur A. Levine Books 2008 un il $15.99

Grades: PreK K 1 2   E

1. Stories in rhyme 2. Fishes -- Fiction 3. Storytelling -- Fiction

ISBN 978-0-439-92825-0; 0-439-92825-7

LC 2007-12308

Tiddler the fish is always telling tall tales about why he is late for school, but when he is actually caught in a net and taken far from home, it is his stories that help him find his way back.

"Donaldson's rhyming text is crisp and clean, leaving plenty of metaphorical room for Scheffler's expansively imagined art." Publ Wkly

One Ted falls out of bed; illustrated by Anna Currey. Henry Holt 2006 un il $15.95

Grades: PreK K 1 2   E

1. Counting 2. Stories in rhyme 3. Toys -- Fiction 4. Teddy bears -- Fiction

ISBN 978-0-8050-7787-2; 0-8050-7787-1

LC 2005-12173

"In this rhythmic counting book, a sleeping child's teddy bear falls out of bed and can't climb back up. Three mice invite him to play, racing four cars, counting five stars, sipping tea with six dolls, and so on. . . . The toys in the airy illustrations that sweep across the pages are packed with personality. Perfect for storytimes or one-on-one lapsits, this book can be counted on for a gentle, cozy read." SLJ

Stick Man; illustrated by Axel Scheffler. Arthur A. Levine Books 2009 un il $16.99

Grades: PreK K 1   E

1. Stories in rhyme 2. Christmas -- Fiction 3. Santa Claus -- Fiction

ISBN 978-0-545-15761-2; 0-545-15761-7

LC 2008-48323

First published 2008 in the United Kingdom

Stick Man ends up far away from his family tree when he is fetched by a dog, thrown by a child, used as a snowman's arm, and even put on a fire, but finally Santa Claus steps in to make sure that Stick Man and his family have a joyous Christmas.

"Scheffler's engaging illustrations, Donaldson's irresistible rhyming text and repeated refrains make this a winning read-aloud that will stick around long after the holiday season." Kirkus

Tyrannosaurus Drip; [by] Julia Donaldson; [illustrations by] David Roberts. Feiwel and Friends 2008 un il $16.95

Grades: K 1 2   E

1. Stories in rhyme 2. Dinosaurs -- Fiction

ISBN 978-0-312-37747-2; 0-312-37747-9

LC 2007-40511

A duckbilled dinosaur, accidentally raised by fierce tyrannosauruses who would eat duckbills if only they could reach them, tries to be like his "family" but finally gives up, runs away, and finds a real home with others of his kind.

"The dinosaurs are rendered in an Art Deco-influenced style, and the lines roll off the tongue like the rhymes of Dr. Seuss. Children will enjoy the repetitive lilt, and adults will appreciate how naturally it reads. Expressive characters enhance the humor, and the limited palette helps emphasize just how different the creatures' worlds are. An enjoyable group read-aloud." SLJ

What the ladybug heard; illustrated by Lydia Monks. Henry Holt and Company 2010 un il $16.99

Grades: PreK K 1   E

1. Stories in rhyme 2. Sounds -- Fiction 3. Thieves -- Fiction 4. Ladybugs -- Fiction 5. Domestic animals -- Fiction

ISBN 978-0-8050-9028-4; 0-8050-9028-2

LC 2009005266

First published 2009 in the United Kingdom

Although much quieter than the farm animals that moo, cluck, or oink, a gentle ladybug is instrumental in foiling a plan to steal the farm's prize-winning cow.

"Filled with drama, lively action, and a large supporting cast of characters, this is a mini play more than a fully fleshed story. The appealing and brightly colored collage illustrations, rhyming text, and assorted animal sounds make it a natural for individual or group read-alouds." Booklist

Donaldson, Julia, 1948-

★ The **gruffalo**; Julia Donaldson; pictures by Axel Scheffler. Dial Books for Young Readers 1999 32 p. $6.99

Grades: PreK K 1 2 3   E

1. Mice -- Fiction 2. Animals -- Fiction 3. Stories in rhyme

ISBN 0803723865; 9780803723863; 9789992142226; 9992142227

LC 98033893

"A mouse is taking a stroll through the deep, dark wood when along comes a hungry fox, then an owl, and then a snake. The mouse is good enough to eat but smart enough to know this, so he invents . . . the gruffalo! As Mouse explains, the gruffalo is a creature with terrible claws, and terrible tusks in its terrible jaws, and knobbly knees and turned-out toes, and a poisonous wart at the end of its nose. But Mouse has no worry to show. After all, there's no such thing as a gruffalo. . . ." (Publisher's Note)

The **Highway** Rat; a tale of stolen snacks. by Julia Donaldson and illustrated by Axel Scheffler. 1st American ed. Arthur A. Levine Books 2013 32 p. (reinforced) $16.99

Grades: PreK K 1 2   E

1. Theft -- Fiction 2. Picture books for children 3. Rats -- Fiction 4. Stories in rhyme 5. Animals -- Fiction 6. Robbers and outlaws -- Fiction

ISBN 0545477581; 9780545477581

LC 2012009889

This children's picture book is the tale "of a swashbuckling rat with mask and cape who stops hapless travelers and takes their food at sword point. . . . A brave duck in a red kerchief lures the thief to a distant cave, supposedly full of biscuits and buns. While he follows the echoes of his own voice deeper and deeper into the dark, the duck jumps on Rat's horse and takes the stolen food back to her hungry friends." (School Library Journal)

Superworm; by Julia Donaldson; illustrated by Axel Scheffler. First American Edition Arthur A. Levine Books 2014 32 p. (hardcover: alk. paper) $16.99

Grades: K 1 2 3   E

1. Stories in rhyme 2. Superheroes -- Fiction 3. Worms -- Fiction 4. Heroes -- Fiction 5. Insects -- Fiction 6. Lizards -- Fiction 7. Wizards -- Fiction

ISBN 0545591767; 9780545591768

LC 2013001546

This book, by Julia Donaldson, features a worm superhero who "rescues toads and beetles from peril and young bees from boredom. The insects clap and cheer for their very own invertebrate champion, inciting the ire of the Wizard Lizard and his henchman crow, who kidnap Superworm for their own sinister devices. The toads, slugs, earwigs, and other bugs band together to rescue the hero." (School Library Journal)

Donofrio, Beverly

Where's Mommy? Beverly Donofrio; illustrations by Barbara McClintock. Schwartz & Wade Books 2013 32 p. color illustrations (trade) $17.99

Grades: PreK K 1   E

1. Mice -- Fiction 2. Mothers -- Fiction 3. Friendship -- Fiction 4. Human-animal relationship -- Fiction

ISBN 0375844236; 9780375844232; 9780375944567

LC 2011050242

In this companion to the children's book "Mary and the Mouse, the Mouse and Mary," by Beverly Donofrio, "Maria (Mary's daughter) and Mouse Mouse (Mouse's daughter) are looking for their mothers. They're not in their bedrooms, their car and cart are still in the driveway, and they are not in the gazebo or under the mushroom! Where could they be?" (Publisher's note)

"Donofrio and McClintock offer a companion to 2007's Mary and the Mouse, the Mouse and Mary that's every bit as charming as its predecessor. In the human-scale rooms of her midcentury modern home, Maria spends time with her family; in the subfloor, Mouse Mouse lives with her own. Maria and Mouse Mouse keep their friendship hush-hush, for they fear the adults might acquire a cat. . . . McClintock pictures the cozy, twinned environments in low-lit panels, and her eggshell-white backgrounds and uncluttered pages allow a pleasurable comparison of human and nonhuman habitats (whereas Maria stands on a stool at the kitchen counter,

Mouse Mouse's chairs are jam jars and pill bottles around a plastic berry container). Fans of the original book will revel in the resolution (and the abundance of visual hints), yet the story is no less delightful for newcomers." Pub Wkly

Donovan, Jane Monroe

Small, medium & large; [written and illustrated by] Jane Monroe Donovan. Sleeping Bear Press 2010 un il $15.95

Grades: PreK K 1   E

1. Stories without words 2. Gifts -- Fiction 3. Christmas -- Fiction

ISBN 978-1-58536-447-3; 1-58536-447-9

"A girl who has just moved to a new house mails a letter to Santa, and on Christmas Day her wishes appear under the tree in three appropriately sized boxes–a cat, a dog, and a miniature horse. The new friends play in the snow, make Christmas cookies, and finally snuggle in bed together after a long, wonderful day. This wordless story [is] told in full and half-page illustrations. . . . It's a sure bet that this super-sweet yet cozy story will have kids adding 'a cat, a dog, and a horse–REAL ones' to their Christmas lists." SLJ

Doodler, Todd H.

What color is Bear's underwear? Blue Apple Books 2011 il bd bk $9.99

Grades: PreK K   E

1. Color 2. Stories in rhyme 3. Board books for children 4. Bears -- Fiction 5. Underwear -- Fiction

ISBN 978-1-60905-096-2; 1-60905-096-7

LC 2011018924

Bear wears different colored underwear for every day of the week.

"It's about as an irreverently silly guide to colors as one could want." Publ Wkly

Doremus, Gaetan

Bear despair; Gaetan Doremus. Enchanted Lion Books 2012 32 p. (alk. paper) $14.95

Grades: PreK K 1 2   E

1. Bears -- Fiction 2. Theft -- Fiction 3. Teddy bears -- Fiction

ISBN 1592701256; 9781592701254

LC 2012931209

This book by Gaetan Doreumus, part of the Stories Without Words series, was designated a 2012 "New York Times" Best Illustrated Children's Book. "[B]ear is napping when his teddy bear is taken by a fox who leads him on a merry chase. . . . Since neither animal is particularly good at conflict resolution, bear swallows the fox whole. As he searches, bear is taunted by a series of creatures that play keep-away with his toy. Furious, bear swallows each one." (Children's Literature)

Empty Fridge; by Gaetan Doremus. Trafalgar Square Books 2013 40 p. ill. (hardcover) $19.99

Grades: PreK K 1   E

1. Food -- Fiction 2. Sharing -- Fiction 3. Neighbors -- Fiction

ISBN 0987109936; 9780987109934

In this picture book by Gaetan Doremus,"the many and varied occupants of an apartment house in a French city have been . . . so busy . . . that . . . no one has remembered to buy any food! In a . . . chain of visits, each . . . character makes a trip up to the next floor to explore how they can pool the paltry ingredients they have scavenged to make a meal that everyone can share. . . . A cozy quiche-baking party ensues." (Kirkus Reviews)

Dormer, Frank W.

The **obstinate** pen; Frank W. Dormer. Henry Holt 2012 32 p. (hardcover: alk. paper) $16.99

Grades: K 1 2 3   E

1. Writing -- Fiction 2. Picture books for children 3. Bad behavior -- Fiction 4. Pens -- Fiction 5. Obstinacy -- Fiction

ISBN 0805092951; 9780805092950

LC 2010031794

In this children's story, by Frank W. Dormer, a pen writes what it wants instead of what the writer decides. The pen "speaks the truth to a series of self-involved townsfolk" after it is delivered to Uncle Flood and then passes from person to person through the town, correcting and insulting all who try to use it. (Kirkus)

Socksquatch; words and pictures by Frank W. Dormer. Henry Holt 2010 un il $14.99

Grades: PreK K 1   E

1. Monsters -- Fiction

ISBN 978-0-8050-8952-3; 0-8050-8952-7

LC 2009-27413

Socksquatch tries to find a sock to warm his cold foot.

"The palette contrasts warm-toned monsters with soothing backgrounds of aqua or plain white, and Dormer uses scrawled ink motion and texture lines to great effect to add movement and dimension to the artwork. While youngsters will definitely enjoy listening to this one in a crowd, don't be surprised if they borrow it afterwards to reenact with a friend." Bull Cent Child Books

Dorros, Alex

Numero uno; by Alex Dorros and Arthur Dorros; illustrated by Susan Guevara. Abrams Books for Young Readers 2007 un il $16.95

Grades: K 1 2 3   E

1. Mexico -- Fiction 2. Spanish language -- Vocabulary

ISBN 0-8109-5764-7

Tired of listening to strong Hercules and smart Socrates constantly argue over who is more important to their village, the townspeople devise a test to settle the question once and for all.

"The battle between brains and brawn is entertainingly pitched here. . . . The Spanish dialogue is simple . . . and punctuates the story-hour-ready text with verve. Guevara's tropically accented pastoral oil paintings provide contrast to the often slapstick goings-on but also do their share of storytelling." Horn Book

Dorros, Arthur

★ **Abuela**; illustrated by Elisa Kleven. Dutton Children's Bks. 1991 un il $16.99; pa $7.99

Grades: PreK K 1 2   E

1. Flight -- Fiction 2. Imagination -- Fiction 3. Grandmothers -- Fiction 4. New York (N.Y.) -- Fiction 5. Hispanic Americans -- Fiction

ISBN 0-525-44750-4; 0-14-056225-7 pa

LC 90-21459

While riding on a bus with her grandmother, a little girl named Rosalba imagines that they are carried up into the sky and fly over the sights of New York City

"Each illustration is a masterpiece of color, line, and form that will mesmerize youngsters. . . . The smooth text, interspersed with Spanish words and phrases, provides ample context clues, so the glossary, while helpful, is not absolutely necessary." Booklist

Another title about Rosalba and her grandmother is: Isla (1995)

Julio's magic; collages by Ann Grifalconi. HarperCollins 2005 32p il $15.99; lib bdg $16.89

Grades: PreK K 1 2   E

1. Mexico -- Fiction 2. Wood carving -- Fiction

ISBN 0-06-029004-8; 0-06-029005-6 lib bdg

LC 2004-6616

A young artist in a Mexican village discovers the power of friendship when he helps his mentor win a prestigious wood-carving contest

"Grifalconi's photorealistic collages capture the texture, color, and feel of village life. This book will be excellent for art and social studies classrooms. . . . It is also a compassionate intergenerational story." SLJ

Mama and me; pictures by Rudy Gutierrez. Rayo 2011 un il $16.99; lib bdg $17.89

Grades: PreK K 1 2   E

1. Mother's Day -- Fiction 2. Spanish language -- Vocabulary 3. Mother-daughter relationship -- Fiction

ISBN 0-06-058160-3; 0-06-058161-1 lib bdg; 978-0-06-058160-2; 978-0-06-058161-9 lib bdg

A girl and her mother spend a day together gardening, making cookies, and visiting a neighbor. Includes Spanish words interspersed in the text.

"The first person point of view and smooth integration of informal Spanish terms and phrases provide a comfortable intimacy with the characters, and the vibrant magic realism of the full-page spreads includes elements of street art." Booklist

Papa and me; by Arthur Dorros; illustrated by Rudy Gutierrez. HarperCollinsPublishers 2008 un il $16.99; lib bdg $17.89

Grades: PreK K   E

1. Hispanic Americans -- Fiction 2. Spanish language -- Vocabulary 3. Father-son relationship -- Fiction

ISBN 978-0-06-058156-5; 978-0-06-058157-2 lib bdg

LC 2007011868

A Pura Belpre Illustrator Award honor book, 2009

"From the time they wake up in the morning, a Latino boy and his father have fun. . . . The simple words, in both Spanish and English, and the bright, exuberant unframed double-page pictures celebrate the loving connection between parent and child. . . . The big, swirling circles in the artwork embrace the characters within the widening arcs of sky and waves." Booklist

Doughty, Rebecca

Oh no! Time to go! a book of goodbyes. Schwartz & Wade 2009 un il $15.99; lib bdg $18.99

Grades: PreK K 1 2   **E**
1. Stories in rhyme 2. Family life -- Fiction
ISBN 978-0-375-84981-7; 0-375-84981-5; 978-0-375-95696-6 lib bdg; 0-375-95696-4 lib bdg
LC 2008022462

A young boy presents the different ways his family members and others say goodbye, then describes the worst goodbye he ever experienced.

"Opaque, brightly colored illustrations outlined in black ink are rendered in a spare, stylized manner. . . . This satisfying tale conveys an important truth about how life's goodbyes often lead to new hellos." SLJ

Dowdy, Linda Cress
All kinds of kisses; [illustrated] by Priscilla Lamont. Cartwheel Books 2010 un il bd bk $8.99
Grades: PreK   **E**
1. Stories in rhyme 2. Board books for children 3. Kissing -- Fiction
ISBN 978-0-545-14599-2 bd bk; 0-545-14599-6 bd bk
LC 2010010215

Simple, rhyming text explores different kinds of kisses.

"The padded cover, Lamont's dusky palette, and Dowdy's simple rhymes convey a cozy, loving world, making this a ready choice for easing into bedtime." Publ Wkly

Downing, Julie
No hugs till Saturday; [by] Julie Downing. Clarion Books 2008 31p il lib bdg $16
Grades: PreK K 1   **E**
1. Week -- Fiction 2. Dragons -- Fiction 3. Hugging -- Fiction 4. Mother-son relationship -- Fiction
ISBN 978-0-618-91078-6 lib bdg; 0-618-91078-6 lib bdg
LC 2007010030

When Felix the dragon declares that there will be no hugs, snuggles, or super squeezes for a whole week, both he and his mama have a hard time.

"The soft-edged paintings show a lovable green dragon and humorously depict his antics. . . . Featuring a believably childlike protagonist, a cozy parent-child relationship, and a satisfying resolution, it is a delightfully warmhearted choice for most collections." SLJ

Dowson, Nick
Tracks of a panda; illustrated by Yu Rong. Candlewick Press 2007 un il $16.99
Grades: PreK K 1 2   **E**
1. Giant panda -- Fiction
ISBN 978-0-7636-3146-8; 0-7636-3146-9
LC 2006051836

A mother panda teaches her cub how to survive in their mountain habitat but as the sound of villagers clearing the forest approaches, she knows they must look for a new home.

"The mother panda's endearing facial features—beautifully rendered in black and white in contrast to the delicate watercolor backgrounds of green, blue, brown, and gray—may well elicit an adoring squeal or two. . . . Dowson leaves the reader with the uncertainty of this pair's future and, on a larger scale, the survival of the species as a whole." Horn Book

Doyen, Denise
★ Once upon a twice; illustrated by Barry Moser. Random House Children's Books 2009 un il $16.99; lib bdg $19.99
Grades: PreK K 1   **E**
1. Nonsense verses 2. Stories in rhyme 3. Mice -- Fiction 4. Conduct of life -- Fiction
ISBN 978-0-375-85612-9; 0-375-85612-9; 978-0-375-95612-6 lib bdg; 0-375-95612-3 lib bdg
LC 2008011125

"Doyen's utterly sound and alive story is paired with the perfect illustrator, whose deft touch provides all the eeriness that it begs for. . . . With gloriously nonsensical words and phrases . . . the author manages to get the point across that there is much to fear in the night. . . . This wonderful book is a marvelous read-aloud that children will want to hear again and again." SLJ

Doyle, Malachy
Get happy; illustrated by Caroline Uff. Walker & Co. 2011 un il $15.99
Grades: PreK K   **E**
1. Stories in rhyme 2. Happiness -- Fiction
ISBN 978-0-8027-2271-3; 0-8027-2271-7
LC 2010031000

Simple, rhyming text urges the reader to be happy by making such choices as teasing less and tickling more, or groaning less and giggling more.

"With a short, powerful text and endearing, recognizable children, this book is an excellent discussion starter for the youngest children." Booklist

Doyle, Roddy
Her mother's face; by Roddy Doyle; illustrated by Freya Blackwood. Arthur A. Levine Books 2008 un il $16.99
Grades: K 1 2 3   **E**
1. Ireland -- Fiction 2. Mothers -- Fiction 3. Bereavement -- Fiction
ISBN 978-0-439-81501-7; 0-439-81501-0
LC 2007043660

Siobhan and her father continue to feel sad in the years following the death of Siobhan's mother, until Siobhan follows the advice of a mysterious woman

"The storytelling flows gracefully between the naturalistic details . . . and the magical encounter. Blackwood . . . magnifies Doyle's optimism in her limpid watercolor and charcoal art." Publ Wkly

The dragon & the knight; a pop-up misadventure. Robert Sabuda. Simon & Schuster 2014 22 p. $29.99
Grades: K 1 2 3 4   **E**
1. Fairy tales 2. Dragons -- Fiction 3. Knights and knighthood -- Fiction
ISBN 1416960813; 9781416960812

In this children's book by Robert Sabuda "a Dragon and a Knight race through a fairy tale treasury, visiting the worlds of all of your favorite stories--from Rapunzel to Aladdin, to Cinderella, The Three Little Pigs, and more! With characters who literally pop right off the pages, this tour de force will have readers young and old speeding through the book to see just how this chase will end!" (Publisher's note)

Dragonwagon, Crescent

All the awake animals are almost asleep; written by Crescent Dragonwagon; illustrated by David McPhail. Little, Brown 2012 40 p. $16.99

Grades: PreK   E

1. Sleep -- Fiction 2. Animals -- Fiction 3. Picture books for children 4. Alphabet 5. Stories in rhyme 6. Bedtime -- Fiction

ISBN 0316070459; 9780316070454

LC 2011042734

Author Crescent Dragonwagon "introduces a familiar bedtime battle of wills between a child who resists slumber and a mother trying to lull him to sleep. This introductory section adopts a rhythmic, rhyming text . . . [and e]nsuing pages go through the alphabet using alliterative language to describe animals going to sleep, from" antelopes to zebras. (Kirkus)

Drummond, Allan

Liberty! Farrar, Straus & Giroux 2002 un il pa $6.95

Grades: K 1 2 3   E

1. Statue of Liberty (New York, N.Y.) -- Fiction

ISBN 0-374-34385-3; 0-374-44397-1 pa

LC 2001-18777

"Drummond tells the story of October 28, 1886, the day the Statue of Liberty was first unveiled in New York harbor. A boy, whose name is now lost, is on the ground, ready to signal Bartholdi, the statue's sculptor, to release the tricolor veil that covers the Lady of Liberty's face. . . . This is an unusual offering. Drummond takes a kernel of history . . . and turns it into both a thoughtful lesson and a visual pageant. Scenes of the construction of France's gift to the U.S. are shown in finely wrought, energetic, pen-and-wash images that swirl through the text." Booklist

Drummond, Ree

Charlie the ranch dog; illustrations by Diane deGroat. HarperCollins 2011 un il $16.99

Grades: PreK K 1 2   E

1. Dogs -- Fiction 2. Ranch life -- Fiction

ISBN 978-0-06-199655-9; 0-06-199655-6

LC 2010018435

While Charlie, a sleepy basset hound, tells about the busy life of a ranch dog, his best friend Suzie, a Jack Russell terrier, is getting the work done.

"Charlie seems unaware of the impish chipmunk that deGroat, with characteristic humor, sneaks into each spread. Her paintings drolly portray the discrepancy between reality and Charlie's perceptions of his day. . . . Kids should find it irresistible." Publ Wkly

Dubosarsky, Ursula

The **terrible** plop; pictures by Andrew Joyner. Farrar, Straus and Giroux 2009 un il $15.95

Grades: PreK K   E

1. Stories in rhyme 2. Fear -- Fiction 3. Animals -- Fiction 4. Courage -- Fiction 5. Rabbits -- Fiction

ISBN 978-0-374-37428-0; 0-374-37428-7

LC 2008043323

When a mysterious sound sends the whole forest running away in fear, only the littlest rabbit is courageous enough to discover what really happened.

"Basic, fun rhymes and repetitive, excitable text lend themselves to reading aloud, and the recurring appearance of the word PLOP provides an explosive entree for children to chime in while soaking up Joyner's bouyant mixed-media artwork. In addition, kids will appreciate the easy absurdity of the situation, enjoy the role-reversal in the end, and maybe even come away knowing that most things aren't so scary once you look a little closer." Booklist

Dubuc, Marianne

Animal masquerade; Marianne Dubuc. Kids Can Press 2012 120 p.

Grades: PreK K 1   E

1. Animals -- Fiction 2. Costume -- Fiction 3. Picture books for children

ISBN 1554537827; 9781554537822

In this children's picture book, "[i]t's time for the animal masquerade, and lion begins considering his costume. He settles on . . . an elephant. But what will the elephant be? A parrot. And which costume will the parrot choose? A turn of the page reveals all. Simple text, translated from French, accompanies . . . colored-pencil illustrations of an assortment of animals in and out of costume on white backgrounds. . . . For the most part, each spread features an animal in disguise." (Kirkus)

The **bus** ride; Marianne Dubuc. Kids Can Press 2015 40 p. (hardcover) $15.95

Grades: PreK K 1 2 3   E

1. Animals -- Fiction 2. Automobile travel -- Fiction

ISBN 9781771382090; 1771382090

In this children's story, written and illustrated by Marianne Dubuc, translated by Yvonne Ghione, "while the bus is taking her down the streets, through a forest and into a pitch-black tunnel, the little girl encounters an assortment of animal characters who enliven her journey, including a goat who offers her a flower from a bouquet, a wolf child with whom she happily shares her cookies and a fox who attempts to pickpocket a bear." (Publisher's note)

In front of my house; translated from the French by Yvette Ghione. Kids Can Press 2010 un il $18.95

Grades: PreK K 1 2   E

1. Imagination -- Fiction

ISBN 978-1-55453-641-2; 1-55453-641-3

"In an excursion that starts and ends with a little house on a hill, a child's imagination soars, moving from a rosebush and a bird outside to discover things 'behind the window' and 'in my room,' including a book of fairy tales in which a dragon, a frog prince, and the Big Bad Wolf dwell, as well as the Abominable Snowman, a werewolf, a ghost, and a vampire. Finally, the adventure leads into outer space. . . . While this small picture book is thick, the childlike text is brief. . . . Its size is perfect for one-on-one interaction, and youngsters will enjoy the twists and turns of the trip. . . . The illustrations, rendered in pencil crayon, are appropriately simple. . . . This little gem has everything." SLJ

★ The **lion** and the bird; Marianne Dubuc; translated from the French by Claudia Z. Bedrick. First American edition. Enchanted Lion Books 2014 64 p. (hardback) $17.95

Grades: PreK K 1   E

1. Birds 2. Lions 3. Lion -- Fiction 4. Birds -- Fiction 5. Seasons -- Fiction 6. Friendship -- Fiction

ISBN 1592701515; 9781592701513

LC 2014000317

In this children's book by Marianne Dubuc, "One autumn day, a lion finds a wounded bird in his garden. With the departure of the bird's flock, the lion decides that it's up to him to care for the bird. He does and the two become fast friends. Nevertheless, the bird departs with his flock the following autumn. What will become of Lion and what will become of their friendship?"

"The intimacy of friendship, as well as the bittersweet sweep of time, is exquisitely rendered in this spare story of a kindly lion who rescues an injured bird flying south for winter... The charming depiction of Lion's home will delight sharp-eyed children, and the gentle pace of the story, which takes its time as surely as the plants in Lion's garden take their time to grow, is reassuring. A much needed antidote to the speed of the world, this picture book by French Canadian Dubuc is one to savor." Booklist

Duffy, Carol Ann

The **gift**; [text] by Carol Ann Duffy and [illustrations] by Rob Ryan. Barefoot Books 2010 un il $16.99
Grades: 2 3 4   E
   1. Wishes -- Fiction
   ISBN 978-1-84686-355-4; 1-84686-355-4

After meeting a magical old woman in a clearing in the woods and trading her daisy chain for the granting of a wish, a little girl grows into a young woman and the clearing begins to fill with the loveliest flowers, the most fragrant herbs, and the most perfect stones.

"This original tale is told in simple language and has a clarity and beauty all its own. Ryan's silhouette illustrations are created using hand-cut paper that is painted and photographed, a technique that makes effective use of color and shadows." Booklist

Duke, Kate

Ready for pumpkins; Kate Duke. Knopf Books for Young Readers 2012 40 p. col. ill.
Grades: K 1 2   E
   1. Pumpkin -- Fiction 2. Gardening -- Fiction 3. Guinea pigs -- Fiction
   ISBN 0375870687; 9780307974549; 9780375870682; 9780375970689
                    LC 2011044615

In this children's book by Kate Duke "Hercules, a classroom guinea pig, has a revelation when he watches the first graders grow plants from seeds. He wants to grow things, too! And during summer vacation (spent with the teacher's dad), he gets his chance. With the help of a friendly rabbit, Herky prepares the soil, carefully plants pumpkin seeds, and waits. . . . [I]n October, the teacher's dad arrives with a big pumpkin for her class--that just mysteriously grew in his yard!" (Publisher's note)

Dumbleton, Mike

Cat; written by Mike Dumbleton; illustrated by Craig Smith. Kane/Miller 2008 un il $15.95
Grades: PreK K   E
   1. Cats -- Fiction
   ISBN 978-1-933605-73-9; 1-933605-73-1
   First published 2007 in Australia

As a cat navigates the perils of the outside world, it and its prey all find things to be thankful for

"The humor is elucidated in the richly colored green- and brown-tinged gouache and pen-and-ink illustrations that move the action along from one episode to another." Horn Book Guide

Dumon Tak, Bibi

★ **Mikis** and the donkey; by Bibi Dumon Tak; illustrated by Philip Hopman; translated by Laura Watkinson. Eerdmans Books for Young Readers 2014 93 p. illustrations $13
Grades: 2 3 4   E
   1. Greece -- Fiction 2. Donkeys -- Fiction 3. Grandfathers -- Fiction 4. Corfu Island (Greece) -- Fiction 5. Family life -- Greece -- Fiction
   ISBN 9780802854308
                    LC 2013044666
   Mildred L. Batchelder Award (2015)

In this book by Bibi Dumon Tak, "one day, Mikis's grandfather has a surprise for him: a new donkey waiting! Mikis falls in love with the creature, but his grandparents tell him that the donkey is a working animal, not a pet. However, they still let Mikis choose her name--Tsaki--and allow the two of them to spend their Sundays together. Mikis and Tsaki soon become fast friends, and together the two have some grand adventures." (Publisher's note)

A "quiet story filled with endearing characters, believable situations, and a sense of the importance of caring for other creatures. Short chapters and frequent pencil drawings make the story accessible for beginning chapter-book readers." Booklist

Dumont, Jean-François

The **chickens** build a wall; written and illustrated by Jean Francois Dumont. Eerdmans Books for Young Readers 2013 33 p. ill. (reinforced) $16.00
Grades: PreK K 1   E
   1. Walls -- Fiction 2. Chickens -- Fiction 3. Toleration -- Fiction 4. Domestic animals -- Fiction
   ISBN 9780802854223
                    LC 2012038991

Dunbar, Joyce

The **monster** who ate darkness; illustrated by Jimmy Liao. Candlewick Press 2008 un il $16.99
Grades: PreK K 1   E
   1. Fear -- Fiction 2. Night -- Fiction 3. Bedtime -- Fiction 4. Monsters -- Fiction
   ISBN 978-0-7636-3859-7; 0-7636-3859-5
                    LC 2008-928826

"Under Jo-Jo's bed lurks a 'tiny speck of a monster' with a 'big empty feeling.' This endearingly unscary creature discovers a taste for darkness and eats up even the dimmest corners of the room. . . . Jo-Jo, who is normally afraid of the dark, can't fall asleep in the endless daylight. As the compassionate monster cradles the little boy in his arms and soothes him with a lullaby, the evening shades return. Liao's digitally enhanced pen and watercolor illustrations humorously capture the mayhem caused by lack of darkness." SLJ

Dunbar, Polly

Dog Blue. Candlewick Press 2004 un il hardcover o.p. pa $7.99
Grades: PreK K 1 2   E
   1. Dogs -- Fiction
   ISBN 0-7636-2476-4; 0-7636-3881-1 pa
                    LC 2003-65223

Bertie, who loves the color blue and really wants a dog, finally gets his wish even though the dog he meets is white with black spots

"Dunbar makes clever use of page turns, unfolding the story in pithy, alliterative prose. . . . In the end, the wish fulfillment is gratifying, but it's Bertie's ingenious self-sufficiency that truly resonates." Booklist

★ **Penguin**. Candlewick Press 2007 un il $15.99
Grades: PreK K   E
1. Toys -- Fiction 2. Penguins -- Fiction
ISBN 0-7636-3404-2

"A pajama-clad toddler opens his present to find a toy penguin. Much to Ben's chagrin, the bird doesn't say anything, no matter how hard the boy tries to engage it. . . . It isn't until a blue lion chomps on the child that Penguin jumps into action and rescues his new pal. . . . The attractive, spare illustrations in mixed media are focused and centered on a white background." SLJ

Where's Tumpty? Candlewick Press 2009 un il $12.99
Grades: PreK   E
1. Animals -- Fiction 2. Elephants -- Fiction 3. Friendship -- Fiction
ISBN 978-0-7636-4273-0; 0-7636-4273-8

"After several unsuccessful attempts at hiding, Tumpty the elephant is able to trick his friends into thinking he has disappeared. . . . There are many amusing situations involving Tilly, a little girl, and her animal friends. . . . The background consists of a variety of muted tones, which contrast with the brighter mixed-media drawings. The illustrations are whimsical and detailed. . . . Young children and beginning readers are sure to gravitate to this delightful story that celebrates the joy of friendship." SLJ

Other titles about Tilly and her friends are:
Doodle bites (2009)
Good night, Tiptoe (2009)
Happy Hector (2008)
Hello, Tilly (2008)
Pretty Pru (2009)

Dunklee, Annika
★ **My** name is Elizabeth! written by Annika Dunklee; illustrated by Matthew Forsythe. Kids Can Press 2011 un il $14.95
Grades: PreK K 1 2   E
1. Personal names -- Fiction
ISBN 978-1-55453-560-6; 1-55453-560-3

Elizabeth is not not amused when people insist on using nicknames like "Lizzy" and "Beth." She bears her frustration in silence until an otherwise ordinary autumn day, when she discovers her power to change things once and for all.

"Forsythe's restrained color palette and expressive line contribute to his brilliant rendering of Elizabeth's character, and his whimsical inclusion of a pet duck (unmentioned in the text) adds another layer of idiosyncratic delight." Kirkus

Dunn, Todd
We go together! by Todd Dunn; illustrated by Miki Sakamoto. Sterling 2007 un il $12.95

Grades: PreK K   E
1. Stories in rhyme 2. Vocabulary -- Fiction
ISBN 978-1-4027-3260-7; 1-4027-3260-0
LC 2006023425

A rhyming picture book with pairs of things that go together exceptionally well, like horse and wagon and fire and dragon.

"Using very readable pictures and predictable scheme, children will easily finish the lines. . . . The colorful illustrations are uncomplicated, yet interesting enough to encourage conversation." SLJ

Dunrea, Olivier
Bear Noel. Farrar, Straus & Giroux 2000 un il hardcover o.p. pa $5.95
Grades: PreK K 1 2   E
1. Bears -- Fiction 2. Animals -- Fiction 3. Christmas -- Fiction
ISBN 0-374-39990-5; 0-374-40001-6 pa
LC 99-27600

The animals of the North Woods react with excitement as they hear Bear Noel coming to bring them Christmas

"Dunrea beautifully creates the effect of falling snow throughout the pictures and uses a limited palette of browns, grays, and greens with flashes of fox red to lend a celebratory feel." Booklist

★ **It's** snowing! Farrar, Straus & Giroux 2002 un il hardcover o.p. pa $6.99
Grades: PreK K 1   E
1. Snow -- Fiction 2. Infants -- Fiction 3. Mothers -- Fiction
ISBN 0-374-39992-1; 0-312-60216-2 pa
LC 00-42172

A mother shares the magic of a snowy night with her baby

"The gentle, rhythmical rocking of the text conveys a reassuring message that's beautifully supported by Dunrea's spare, snow-dappled gouache illustrations." Horn Book

Merry Christmas, Ollie! [by] Olivier Dunrea. Houghton Mifflin 2008 un il $12.95
Grades: PreK K 1   E
1. Geese -- Fiction 2. Christmas -- Fiction 3. Santa Claus -- Fiction
ISBN 978-0-618-53242-1; 0-618-53242-0
LC 2004025126

On Christmas Eve, Ollie and the other goslings anxiously await the arrival of Father Christmas Goose.

"First-time readers and those already familiar with Dunrea's goslings will be delighted by this simple story. . . . Remaining true to his uncomplicated watercolor style, Dunrea maintains an element of charm to Ollie's waiting, depicting his impatience as sweet and subdued." SLJ

★ **Old** Bear and his cub. Philomel Books 2010 un il $16.99
Grades: PreK K 1 2   E
1. Bears -- Fiction 2. Parent-child relationship -- Fiction
ISBN 978-0-399-24507-7; 0-399-24507-3
LC 2008-00663

Although they love each other, Old Bear and his little Cub have a tug of war over which one knows best in a variety of situations.

"The adult-child give-and-take in this charming bedtime story will be quite familiar and is bound to bring smiles to both ages. Simplicity at its best." Kirkus

Ollie's Halloween. Houghton Mifflin Books for Children 2010 un il $12.99
Grades: PreK K 1   E
  1. Stories in rhyme 2. Geese -- Fiction 3. Halloween -- Fiction
  ISBN 978-0-618-53241-4; 0-618-53241-2
                         LC 2009-49699
Dressed in their costumes, Ollie and his siblings go out on Halloween night and have a scary but fun adventure.
"As with the previous titles starring this gosling crew, Dunrea's ink and watercolor images beget an understandable and cozy world, this time with just a hint of spookiness and autumnal gloom." Publ Wkly

Dunrea, Olivier, 1953-
  A **Christmas** tree for Pyn. Philomel Books 2011 un il $16.99
Grades: PreK K   E
  1. Trees -- Fiction 2. Christmas stories 3. Christmas -- Fiction 4. Father-daughter relationship -- Fiction
  ISBN 978-0-399-24506-0; 0-399-24506-5
                         LC 2010041653
Little Pyn finally persuades her gruff father to find the perfect Christmas tree in the snowy forest and, after bringing it home, decorates it with him.
Dun-rea's "talent for capturing a mood of majestic stillness in snowy landscapes shines yet again, as does his skill at creating cozy, rustic details—bushy fur coats and boots, tree-stump beds, a stone hearth—that suggest a mythical time. Pyn and Papa's warming relationship is one to celebrate any time of year." Publ Wkly

Gideon; Olivier Dunrea. Houghton Mifflin Books for Children 2012 1 v. (unpaged) col. ill.
Grades: K 1 2 3   E
  1. Geese -- Fiction 2. Children's stories 3. Picture books for children 4. Domestic animals -- Fiction 5. Animals -- Fiction
  ISBN 9780618436613
                         LC 2010044359
This children's book tells the story of "Gideon, 'a small, ruddy gosling who likes to play,' [who] joins Gossie and the other goslings on Dunrea's farm. Always on the move, Gideon chases a piglet, plays 'tag-the-mole,' leaps over a frog, and listens to bees buzzing in their hive—always with his octopus toy in tow. No naps for Gideon, no matter what mother goose says, but a day of barnyard shenanigans has a way of tiring out a gosling." (Publishers Weekly)

Gideon and Otto; Olivier Dunrea. Houghton Mifflin Harcourt 2012 1 v. (unpaged) col. ill.
Grades: K 1 2 3   E
  1. Children's stories 2. Friendship -- Fiction 3. Picture books for children 4. Domestic animals -- Fiction 5. Toys -- Fiction 6. Geese -- Fiction 7. Rabbits -- Fiction
  ISBN 9780618436620
                         LC 2010045844
This children's book tells the story of "Gideon [who] is a 'small ruddy gosling who likes to play. All day.' . . . After climbing to the top of a haystack and snuggling down

in the straw, sleepiness wins out. In Gideon and Otto, children meet the gosling's favorite friend. When the toy octopus goes missing, a search of the leaf pile and pond ensues. Otto's triumphant return is on the back of a turtle." (SLJ)

★ **Gossie**. Houghton Mifflin 2002 un il $9.95
Grades: PreK K 1   E
  1. Geese -- Fiction
  ISBN 0-618-17674-8
                         LC 2002-214
Gossie is a gosling who likes to wear bright red boots every day, no matter what she is doing, and so she is heartbroken the day the boots are missing and she can't find them anywhere. "Ages two to four." (Bull Cent Child Books)
The succinct text uses "repetition and predictability with great skill and will therefore work equally well with early independent readers and preschoolers. . . . The illustrations, focused against restful white space, are spare and expressive, models of composition and clarity." Horn Book
  Other titles about Gossie and her friends are:
  BooBoo (2004)
  Gossie & Gertie (2002)
  Merry Christmas, Ollie (2008)
  Ollie (2003)
  Ollie the stomper (2003)
  Ollie's Easter eggs (2010)
  Ollie's Halloween (2010)
  Peedie (2004)

Jasper & Joop; Olivier Dunrea. Houghton Mifflin Books for Children 2013 32 p. col. ill. (reinforced) $9.99
Grades: PreK K 1   E
  1. Geese -- Fiction 2. Friendship -- Fiction
  ISBN 9780547867625
                         LC 2012018964

Little Cub; Olivier Dunrea. Philomel 2012 32 p. (hardback) $16.99
Grades: PreK K 1 2   E
  1. Adoption -- Fiction 2. Picture books for children 3. Bears -- Fiction 4. Loneliness -- Fiction 5. Foster home care -- Fiction
  ISBN 039924235X; 9780399242359
                         LC 2012015126
In this book, "Little Cub is sad and lonely. He has no one to take care of him, teach him how to catch fish, help him get honey, and be with him during the long dark nights. Old Bear is sad and lonely. He has no one to teach, share his food with, and keep him company during the long dark nights. One day he finds Little Cub . . . . Old Bear names him, takes him home, feeds him, puts him to bed, tells him a story, and the rest is history." (School Library Journal)

Dunston, Marc
  The **magic** of giving; illustrated by Katie Cantrell; foreword by Wally Amos. Pelican 2010 32p il $16.99
Grades: K 1 2   E
  1. School stories 2. Contests -- Fiction 3. Magic tricks -- Fiction
  ISBN 978-1-58980-805-8; 1-58980-805-3
                         LC 2010014648
Little Marc is determined to win his school's talent contest and use the prize money to buy Thanksgiving dinner for his neighbors, but first he must pick a talent and master it.

"The positive, uplifting message encourages children to read and develop their talents not to just help themselves, but to help others. Cantrell's illustrations are bright and sunny and feature a multigenerational, multiethnic cast of characters. The foreward is written by literacy advocate Wally Amos. Literacy awareness is stressed below the storyline on each page with the placement of vocabulary development tools." Libr Media Connect

Durand, Hallie

Mitchell goes bowling; Hallie Durand; illustrated by Tony Fucil. Candlewick Press 2013 40 p. col. ill. $15.99
Grades: PreK K 1   E
1. Bowling -- Fiction 2. Father-son relationship -- Fiction 3. Bowling alleys -- Fiction 4. Picture books for children
ISBN 0763660493; 9780763660499
LC 2012947730
"One Saturday, when Mitchell almost knocks down his dad, his dad catches him and puts him in the car. And when they step into the bowling alley, Mitchell feels right at home. Pizza! Giant crashing noises! Special shoes!" (Publisher's note)
"The story is played for laughs, but, in the process, readers will enjoy the father/son relationship and subtly learning about being a sport. Mitchell's frustration and anger issues are addressed and his dad's patience pays off." SLJ

Mitchell's license; illustrated by Tony Fucile. Candlewick Press 2011 un il $15.99
Grades: PreK K 1   E
1. Bedtime -- Fiction 2. Father-son relationship -- Fiction
ISBN 978-0-7636-4496-3; 0-7636-4496-X
LC 2010039181
Mitchell never wants to go to bed until, at the age of three years, nine months, and five days he gets his license so that he can drive there—at least until he and the car have a disagreement about what fuel goes in the tank.
"Durmand's text will appeal to the active and car obsessed, but Fucile's masterful illustrations, full of expressive characters, great physical comedy and wonderful warmth, will engage readers young and old. . . . An incredibly entertaining ride." Kirkus

Durango, Julia

Angels watching over me; adapted by Julia Durango; illustrated by Elisa Kleven. Simon & Schuster Books for Young Readers 2007 un il $16.99
Grades: PreK K 1 2   E
1. Stories in rhyme 2. Day -- Fiction 3. Angels -- Fiction
ISBN 978-0-689-86252-6; 0-689-86252-0
"Rhyming couplets take a child from sunrise to sunset, imagining all the ways . . . that the angels send their vigilant protection. . . . The melody of the language and its reverence for the natural world are sure to spark interest. Kleven's mixed-media compositions—watercolor, ink, collage and colored pencil—convey an appropriately dream-in-flight feeling." Publ Wkly

Cha-cha chimps; illustrated by Eleanor Taylor. Simon & Schuster Books for Young Readers 2006 un il $15.95

Grades: PreK K 1   E
1. Stories in rhyme 2. Dance -- Fiction 3. Chimpanzees -- Fiction
ISBN 0-689-86456-6
In this counting book, "10 little chimps sneak out of their tree house to go dancing at Mambo Jambas, where a pig band plays music all night long. . . . The rhymes roll easily off the tongue, making the text fun to read aloud. . . . Done in watercolor and pencil, the illustrations are bright and lively." SLJ

Durant, Alan

I love you, Little Monkey; by Alan Durant; illustrated by Katharine McEwen. Simon & Schuster Books for Young Readers 2007 un il $15.99
Grades: PreK K   E
1. Love -- Fiction 2. Monkeys -- Fiction
ISBN 978-1-4169-2481-4; 1-4169-2481-7
First published 2006 in the United Kingdom
"Little Monkey gets into mischief when Big Monkey is too busy to play with him. . . . Little Monkey fears that he is no longer loved when he is sent to bed for punishment, but is reassured that Big Monkey loves him always, even when naughty. . . . The familiar message is always on target for small children. . . . Lively cartoon drawings in watercolor and pencil depict the mischievous animals at play in a colorful jungle setting." SLJ

Duval, Kathy

The **Three** Bears' Halloween; by Kathy Duval; illustrated by Paul Meisel. Holiday House 2007 un il $16.95
Grades: PreK K 1   E
1. Bears -- Fiction 2. Halloween -- Fiction
ISBN 978-0-8234-2032-2; 0-8234-2032-9
LC 2006012120
Is it a witch or a blonde little girl hiding in the bushes of the spooky house when the three bears go trick or treating?
This is a "delightfully presented story, rich with folk-art warmth and whimsical humor." SLJ

Duvoisin, Roger

★ **Petunia**; fiftieth anniversary edition; Knopf 2000 un il $15.95; pa $6.99
Grades: PreK K 1   E
1. Geese -- Fiction 2. Books and reading -- Fiction
ISBN 0-394-90865-7; 0-394-90865-1 lib bdg; 0-440-41754-6 pa
A reissue of the title first published 1950
Petunia, the goose, learns that possessing knowledge involves more than just carrying a book around under her wing
"Duvoisin's energetic drawings perfectly capture Petunia's growing arrogance." Horn Book Guide

DwellStudio (Firm)

Good morning, toucan; by DwellStudio. Blue Apple Books 2011 un il bd bk $8.99
Grades: PreK   E
1. Board books for children 2. Morning -- Fiction 3. Rain forest animals -- Fiction
ISBN 978-1-60905-085-6; 1-60905-085-1
LC 2010046649
Simple text invites the reader to look under lift-up flaps to find various creatures as they awaken in the rain forest.

This is "engaging. . . . [This] visually appealing [book features a] very basic [layout] and graphic-style illustrations that resemble Colorforms, which allow youngsters to focus on the guessing game in [the] book." SLJ

Goodnight, owl; by DwellStudio. Blue Apple Books 2011 un il bd bk $8.99
Grades: PreK   E
1. Board books for children 2. Night -- Fiction 3. Bedtime -- Fiction 4. Forest animals -- Fiction
ISBN 978-1-60905-083-2; 1-60905-083-5
LC 2010046819

Simple text invites the reader to look under lift-up flaps to find various creatures as they go to sleep at night in the forest.

This is "engaging. . . . [This] visually appealing [book features a] very basic [layout] and graphic-style illustrations that resemble Colorforms, which allow youngsters to focus on the guessing game in [the] book." SLJ

Dyckman, Ame
Boy and Bot; by Ame Dyckman; illustrated by Dan Yaccarino. Alfred A. Knopf 2012 32 p.
Grades: PreK K   E
1. Boys -- Fiction 2. Robots -- Fiction 3. Friendship -- Fiction 4. Picture books for children
ISBN 9780375867569; 9780375987243
LC 2011016682

This picture book tells the story of a friendship between a boy and a robot "that prevails over confusion." During the course of author Ame Dyckman's plot, Boy mistakes Bot for another child and later Bot thinks that Boy is also a robot, until an inventor steps in and explains the situation. Illustrator Dan Yaccarino's "stylized gouache paintings" include "final, nearly wordless spreads depicting the two wide-awake friends' happy, ongoing companionship." (Kirkus)

★ **Tea** party rules; by Ame Dyckman; illustrated by K.G. Campbell. Viking, published by Penguin Group 2013 40 p. (hardcover) $16.99
Grades: PreK K 1   E
1. Tea -- Fiction 2. Bears -- Fiction 3. Parties -- Fiction 4. Etiquette -- Fiction 5. Animals -- Infancy -- Fiction
ISBN 0670785016; 9780670785018
LC 2012046989
Ezra Jack Keats New Illustrator Honor Award (2014)
Ezra Jack Keats New Writer Award (2014)

In this children's picture book, by Ame Dyckman, illustrated by K. G. Campbell, "Cub discovers a backyard tea party--with cookies! He is just about to dig in when the hostess of the tea party shows up. And she has several strong opinions on how Tea Party must be played. Cub tries to follow her rules . . . but just how much can one bear take, even for cookies?" (Publisher's note)

"Strong storytelling, pacing, emotive illustrations that match the deceptive plot and an exuberant sense of fun make this little gem a winner." Kirkus

Dyer, Sarah
Batty. Frances Lincoln Children's Books 2011 un il $16.95
Grades: PreK K 1 2   E
1. Bats -- Fiction 2. Zoos -- Fiction 3. Animals --

Fiction
ISBN 978-1-84780-084-8; 1-84780-084-X
"Batty is a zoo-dwelling, long-eared bat. . . . Zoo visitors tend to drift past Batty toward the more popular, talented animals; he tries hanging out with the eager-to-groom gorillas and the raucous birds in the aviary . . . but he doesn't fit in. . . . The spreads in which Batty watches the other animals are upside-down, as a hanging bat would see them, with intervening spreads right-side-up—an entertaining way of representing Batty's point of view. . . . Dyer's understated humor, both in her text and artwork, makes for a winning take on the be-true-to-yourself theme." Publ Wkly

Monster day at work. Frances Lincoln 2010 un il
Grades: PreK K 1   E
1. Monsters -- Fiction
ISBN 1-84780-069-6; 978-1-84780-069-5
Little monster spends a day at work with his father.
"Wide-set eyes, squat statures and two horns that look like party hats worn askew make these monsters anything but scary. Detailed spreads filled with other oddball creatures and quirky touches . . . complete this offbeat monster landscape." Kirkus

Eastman, P. D.
★ **Are** you my mother? written and illustrated by P. D. Eastman. Beginner Bks. 1960 63p il $8.99; lib bdg $12.99; bd bk $4.99
Grades: PreK K 1   E
1. Birds -- Fiction 2. Mother-child relationship -- Fiction
ISBN 0-394-80018-4; 0-394-90018-9 lib bdg; 0-679-89047-5 bd bk
"A small bird falls from his nest and searches for his mother. He asks a kitten, a hen, a dog, a cow, a boat, [and] a plane . . . 'Are you my mother?' Repetition of words and phrases and funny pictures are just right for beginning readers." Chicago. Public Libr

Eaton, Jason Carter
★ **How** to train a train; by Jason Carter Eaton and illustrated by John Rocco. Candlewick Press 2013 48 p. $16.99
Grades: PreK K 1 2   E
1. Pets 2. Railroads
ISBN 0763663077; 9780763663070
LC 2012947747

This book on railroad trains, by Jason Carter, "written as a guidebook for new owners, . . . incorporates language usually associated with pet ownership and child rearing. Digitally colored illustrations [by John Rocco] . . . capture the expressiveness and playfulness of the pet trains." (School Library Journal)

"The ultimate dream for railroad fanatics: pet trains! Eaton offers humorously detailed instructions on how to locate and catch a wild train, with tips on naming and helping your locomotive adjust to life among humans. Digitally colored graphite illustrations have energy and excitement in this fantastical picture book that's sure to be on heavy rotation in train-loving households." (Horn Book)

Eaton, Maxwell
★ **Best** buds; [by] Maxwell Eaton III. Alfred A. Knopf 2007 un il (The adventures of Max and Pinky) $12.99; lib bdg $14.99

Grades: PreK K 1   E
1. Pigs -- Fiction 2. Friendship -- Fiction
ISBN 978-0-375-83803-3; 0-375-83803-1; 978-0-375-93803-0 lib bdg; 0-375-93803-6 lib bdg

LC 2006-02037

Best friends Max and Pinky the pig have an adventure together every Saturday, but one week Max looks everywhere and cannot find Pinky.

"The book is offbeat, irreverent, and affectionate, contrasting the pared-down simplicity of the main text with cheerful dialogue in the speech balloons and the sturdy simplicity of of the flat-planed, digitally colored art with the eccentric actions they depict." Horn Book

Other titles about Max and Pinky are:
Superheroes (2007)
The mystery (2008)

Two dumb ducks. Alfred A. Knopf 2010 un il $12.99; lib bdg $15.99
Grades: PreK K 1 2   E
1. Anger -- Fiction 2. Ducks -- Fiction 3. Gulls -- Fiction 4. Bullies -- Fiction
ISBN 978-0-375-84576-5; 0-375-84576-3; 978-0-375-94576-2 lib bdg; 0-375-94576-8 lib bdg

LC 2010-04959

Steve and Carl, two ducks, decide to get even when the seagulls call them "dumb."

This "is utterly genuine in both its humor and pain; Eaton's bold cartooning and dead-pan, economic storytelling make every page a treat." Publ Wkly

Edgemon, Darcie
Seamore, the very forgetful porpoise; by Darcie Edgemon; illustrated by J. Otto Seibold. HarperCollinsPublishers 2008 un il hardcover o.p. lib bdg $17.89
Grades: K 1 2 3   E
1. Memory -- Fiction 2. Whales -- Fiction 3. Porpoises -- Fiction 4. Friendship -- Fiction
ISBN 978-0-06-085075-3; 0-06-085075-2; 978-0-06-085076-0 lib bdg; 0-06-085076-0 lib bdg

LC 2007010906

Seamore is a very forgetful porpoise and when neither notes to himself nor string around his fins help, he decides to search for his missing memory

This is "effervescent. . . . The straightforward story is buoyed by the polychrome exuberance of Seibold's unmistakable computer-generated illustrations." Booklist

Edmundson, Chris
Yeti, turn out the light! by Greg Long and Chris Edmundson and illustrated by Wednesday Kirwan. Chronicle Books 2013 36 p. (alk. paper) $12.99
Grades: PreK K   E
1. Yeti -- Fiction 2. Sleep -- Fiction 3. Monsters -- Fiction 4. Bedtime -- Fiction 5. Shadows -- Fiction
ISBN 1452111588; 9781452111582

LC 2012049298

In this book, by Greg Long and Chris Edmundson and illustrated by Wednesday Kirwan, "all Yeti wants to do after a long day in the woods is to close his eyes and go to sleep. But something is not right! Shadows lurk, sounds creak, and there are monsters...or are there? This . . . bedtime book featuring the fierce and frenetic GAMAGO Yeti [is designed to]

amuse and delight kids, all while encouraging them to turn out the light and go to sleep!" (Publisher's note)

Edwards, David
The **pen** that Pa built; by David Edwards; illustrations by Ashley Wolff. Tricycle Press 2007 un il $14.95
Grades: PreK K 1 2   E
1. Stories in rhyme 2. Wool -- Fiction 3. Sheep -- Fiction 4. Weaving -- Fiction
ISBN 978-1-58246-153-3; 1-58246-153-8

LC 2006101994

A cumulative, illustrated tale describing the process of raising sheep and using their wool to make warm woolen blankets.

"The language is pleasant and the rhymes clever. What really works here are Wolff's highly textured gesso-and-gouache illustrations." Booklist

Edwards, Michelle
★ **Papa's** latkes; illustrated by Stacey Schuett. Candlewick Press 2004 un il $15.99
Grades: PreK K 1 2   E
1. Jews -- Fiction 2. Hanukkah -- Fiction 3. Bereavement -- Fiction
ISBN 0-7636-0779-7

LC 00-69801

On the first Hanukkah after Mama died, Papa and his two daughters try to make latkes and celebrate without her.

"The poignant text with touches of humor is nicely matched with warm and richly colored oil paintings. . . . A touching and uplifting story." SLJ

Edwards, Pamela Duncan
Jack and Jill's treehouse; illustrated by Henry Cole. Katherine Tegen Books 2008 un il $16.99; lib bdg $17.89
Grades: PreK K 1   E
1. Birds -- Fiction 2. Building -- Fiction 3. Tree houses -- Fiction
ISBN 978-0-06-009077-7; 0-06-009077-4; 978-0-06-009078-4 lib bdg; 0-06-009078-2 lib bdg

A cumulative tale about Jack and Jill who build a treehouse, as a pair of robins make their own home in the same tree.

"Color, spirit, and a sense of satisfaction fill the soft illustrations, which depict idyllic days spent in outdoor amusement. . . . The large images lend themselves well to group sharing, and the text includes small rebus pictures of each added item, allowing listeners to chant along." SLJ

The **leprechaun's** gold; illustrated by Henry Cole. Katherine Tegen Books 2004 un il $15.99; lib bdg $16.89; pa $6.99
Grades: K 1 2 3   E
1. Ireland -- Fiction 2. Musicians -- Fiction 3. Leprechauns -- Fiction
ISBN 0-06-623974-5; 0-06-623975-3 lib bdg; 0-06-443878-3 pa

LC 2002-3150

A leprechaun intervenes with gold and magic when a greedy, boastful young harpist gains an unfair advantage for a royal harping contest

"Cole's imaginative illustrations are a good match for the story, displaying both realism and fantasy. . . . An appealing tale that need not be limited to St. Patrick's Day storytime." Booklist

★ The **mixed**-up rooster; written by Pamela Duncan Edwards; illustrated by Megan Lloyd. Katherine Tegen Books 2006 un il lib bdg $16.89
Grades: PreK K 1 2   E
1. Chickens -- Fiction 2. Roosters -- Fiction
ISBN 978-0-06-028999-7; 0-06-028999-6; 978-0-06-029000-9 lib bdg; 0-06-029000-5 lib bdg
LC 2005014401
Ned the rooster is fired from his job because he cannot wake up in the morning, but he restores his reputation after discovering his usefulness as a night bird
"This lighthearted story is written in an uncomplicated, comical style and has vibrant illustrations that are full of personality and charm." SLJ

The **neat** line; scribbling through Mother Goose. illustrated by Diana Cain Bluthenthal. Katherine Tegan Books 2004 un il hardcover o.p. lib bdg $16.89
Grades: PreK K 1 2   E
1. Nursery rhymes -- Fiction
ISBN 0-06-623970-2; 0-06-623971-0 lib bdg
LC 2002-153424
A young scribble matures into a neat line, then wriggles into a book of nursery rhymes where he transforms himself into different objects to assist the characters he meets there
This is a "brilliantly creative romp. . . . The large cartoon paintings . . . are appropriately outlined with thick, bold lines and are framed by book pages on either side." SLJ

The **old** house; [by] Pamela Duncan Edwards; illustrated by Henry Cole. Dutton Children's Books 2007 un il $16.99; pa $6.99
Grades: PreK K 1   E
1. Houses -- Fiction
ISBN 978-0-525-47796-9; 0-14-241480-8 pa
LC 2006102950
An old empty house feels sorry for itself because it has no family living inside, but with the help of some good friends, its dreams come true
"Edwards colloquial text is accessible for young readers to tackle on their own and would make a lively read-aloud. Cole's energetic cartoon-style artwork gives oodles of personality to this house waiting to shine." SLJ

Princess Pigtoria and the pea; illustrated by Henry Cole. Orchard Books 2010 un il $16.99
Grades: PreK K 1   E
1. Fairy tales 2. Pigs -- Fiction 3. Princesses -- Fiction
ISBN 978-0-545-15625-7; 0-545-15625-4
LC 2008-52693
To make her pigsty of a palace picturesque again, penniless Princess Pigtoria tries to get the pompous porker Prince Proudfoot to propose marriage.
"Fun for listeners and readers alike. . . The scale of the artwork make this a good choice for storytime." Booklist

Some smug slug; illustrated by Henry Cole. HarperCollins Pubs. 1996 32p il $17.99; pa $6.99

Grades: PreK K 1 2   E
1. Animals -- Fiction 2. Slugs (Mollusks) -- Fiction
ISBN 0-06-024789-4; 0-06-443502-4 pa
LC 94-18682
"A slug senses a slope and saunters on up, against the advice of a sparrow, a spider, and a skink, among others, and meets with a sudden, spontaneous demise. Such is the life of a slug told with a multitude of common and not so common 'S' words. . . . Realistically detailed, earth-toned illustrations focus attention on each scene. . . . This slug is so appealing and full of personality that it will certainly garner sympathy." SLJ

While the world is sleeping; illustrated by Dan Kirk. Orchard Books 2010 un il lib bdg $16.99
Grades: PreK K 1   E
1. Stories in rhyme 2. Night -- Fiction 3. Animals -- Fiction 4. Bedtime -- Fiction
ISBN 978-0-545-01756-5; 0-545-01756-4
LC 2007040283
A sleepy child is flown through the night sky to see foxes hunting, rabbits playing, raccoons scrounging, and other animals that are active while people sleep.
"Kirk's illustrations are big and bold, featuring the shimmering light of the moon, animals whose every hair seems distinct, and playful faux-Rousseau forests. The book's mix of the realistic and fantastic seems like a perfect prelude to dream time." Booklist

Edwards, Wallace
Uncle Wally's old brown shoe; Wallace Edwards. Orca Book Publishers 2012 32 p. (hardcover) $19.95
Grades: 3 4 5   E
1. Shoes -- Fiction 2. Picture books for children 3. Animals -- Fiction
ISBN 1459801547; 9781459801547; 9781459801554
LC 2012935414
The protagonist of this book by Wallace Edwards "is a tiger, resplendent in red-and-white-striped pyjamas and a solitary brown oxford. His missing shoe has all the fun in this story, as it is driven by a kitten, who is tickled by a pig in a fancy hat, who is chased by a limber frog on stilts, who —well, you get the idea. Eventually, the reader is treated to the revelation of how the shoe has come to pass through the possession of a menagerie of animals." (Quill & Quire)

Eeckhout, Emmanuelle
There's no such thing as ghosts! Kane/Miller 2008 un il $13.95
Grades: PreK K 1   E
1. Ghost stories
ISBN 978-1-933605-91-3; 1-933605-91-X
"Eager to explore a neighborhood haunted house, a diminutive boy grabs his butterfly net and sets out to catch a ghost. . . . The joke is that readers see the adorable, playful spirits that cavort, tease, and go about their ghostly business, invisible to the boy. Through a simple palette of black, white, yellow, and pink, Eeckhout uses plenty of white space, full spreads, silhouettes, and small vignettes to great advantage." SLJ

Egan, Tim
★ **Dodsworth** in New York; written and illustrated by Tim Egan. Houghton Mifflin 2007 un il $15

Grades: K 1 2   **E**
    1. Ducks -- Fiction 2. New York (N.Y.) -- Fiction 3. Voyages and travels -- Fiction
    ISBN 978-0-618-77708-2; 0-618-77708-3
                          LC 2006-34522

When Dodsworth sets out for adventure, including a stop in New York City before going to Paris, London, and beyond, he does not expect a crazy duck to stow away in his suitcase and lead him on a merry chase.

"Egan favors a palette of golds and clay-browns, and draws pillowy shapes in a gentle, never rigid line. . . . Egan keeps the hijinks low-key, preferring long pauses and slow burns to nutty slapstick." Publ Wkly
    Other titles about Dodsworth are:
    Dodsworth in Paris (2008)
    Dodsworth in London (2009)
    Dodsworth in Rome (2011)

The **pink** refrigerator; [by] Tim Egan, Houghton Mifflin 2007 un il $16
Grades: K 1 2   **E**
    1. Mice -- Fiction
    ISBN 978-0-618-63154-4; 0-618-63154-2
                          LC 2006009816

Dodsworth the mouse does as little work as he can, collecting items from a junkyard and placing them in his thrift store for sale, until he happens upon a pink refrigerator that spurs him to do much more with his life.

"The ink-and-watercolor art mirrors the laid-back tone of the narrative. . . . This offbeat tale is perfect for reading aloud, but will also be appreciated as a read-alone and lap-sit." SLJ

Egielski, Richard

   ★ **Captain** Sky Blue. Michael Di Capua Books 2010 un il $17.95
Grades: PreK K 1 2   **E**
    1. Adventure fiction 2. Toys -- Fiction 3. Christmas -- Fiction 4. Air pilots -- Fiction
    ISBN 978-0-545-21342-4; 0-545-21342-8

Jack's best toy pal is Captain Sky Blue, a pilot. After a thunderstorm separates Sky and his buddy, Sky is abducted by a whale, then left alone to wander a frigid ocean floor until he chances upon a very special place, a place where he's been before.

"Egielski "is in top form in this story. . . . From start to finish, it has the feel of an old-fashioned adventure. . . . Egielski's boldly outlined artwork lends the story a cinematic scope. . . . Airplane-obsessed readers will be thrilled with the aeronautical jargon Sky uses." Publ Wkly

The **sleepless** little vampire. Arthur A. Levine Books 2011 un il $16.99
Grades: PreK K 1   **E**
    1. Bedtime -- Fiction 2. Vampires -- Fiction
    ISBN 978-0-545-14597-8; 0-545-14597-X
                          LC 2010032096

A young vampire, unable to sleep, tries to figure out whether it is the howling of a werewolf, the clacking of skeletons, or something else that is keeping him awake.

"The book closes on a satisfying note, with everyone safe and sound. Egielski's watercolor/ink paintings are superbly executed, with strong colors and bold, expressive lines." SLJ

Ehlert, Lois, 1934-

   Boo to you! Beach Lane Books 2009 un il $17.99
Grades: PreK K 1   **E**
    1. Stories in rhyme 2. Cats -- Fiction 3. Mice -- Fiction 4. Parties -- Fiction
    ISBN 978-1-4169-8625-6; 1-4169-8625-1
                          LC 2008-44352

When the neighborhood cat tries to crash the mice's harvest party, the mice have a plan to scare the intruder away

"Ehlert's use of paper, fruit, seeds, and string is labyrinthine enough to have young children tracing their routes, and so vivid they'll want to touch the page to make sure it's not real." Booklist

   ★ **Circus**. HarperCollins Pubs. 1992 un il $17.99
Grades: PreK K 1   **E**
    1. Circus -- Fiction 2. Animals -- Fiction
    ISBN 0-06-020252-1
                          LC 91-12067

Leaping lizards, marching snakes, a bear on the high wire, and others perform in a somewhat unusual circus

"The book approximates a light show in visual intensity, with neon-bright illustrations set against black or bold backgrounds. . . . The sprightly rhythm of Ms. Ehlert's text complements her Day-Glo palette. Echoing a ringmaster's speech, she's afraid of neither alliteration . . . nor hyperbole." N Y Times Book Rev

   ★ **Feathers** for lunch. Harcourt Brace Jovanovich 1990 un il $17; pa $7
Grades: PreK K 1 2   **E**
    1. Stories in rhyme 2. Cats -- Fiction 3. Birds -- Fiction
    ISBN 0-15-230550-5; 0-15-200986-8 pa
                          LC 89-29459

"Ehlert has attempted many things in these pages—for instance, the birds are all drawn life-size—and has succeeded in all of them; her lavish use of bold color against generous amounts of white space is graphically appealing, and the large type, nearly one-half-inch tall, invites attempts by those just beginning to read. An engaging, entertaining, and recognizably realistic story." Horn Book

   ★ **Hands**; growing up to be an artist. Harcourt 2004 un il $14.95
Grades: PreK K 1 2   **E**
    ISBN 0-15-205107-4
                          LC 2004-1237

A reformatted edition of the title first published 1997

When a child works alongside her parents doing carpentry, sewing, and gardening, she thinks of being an artist as well when she grows up

This edition offers "slightly reworked trimmings, but keeps the same die-cut pages—in the shapes of scissors, seed packets and more—as well as a 'paint box' that opens." Publ Wkly

   ★ **Leaf** Man. Harcourt 2005 un il $16
Grades: PreK K 1 2   **E**
    1. Winds -- Fiction 2. Leaves -- Fiction
    ISBN 0-15-205304-2
                          LC 2004-9981

A man made of leaves blows away, traveling wherever the wind may take him.

This is an "eye-popping book. . . . Scalloped edgings on the tops of the pages, cut at varying heights, artfully give the effect of setting the action against a three-dimensional landscape." Booklist

★ **Lots** of spots. Beach Lane Books 2010 un il $17.99
Grades: PreK K 1   E
   1. Animals
   ISBN 978-1-4424-0289-8; 1-4424-0289-X
                                               LC 2009034361
"Each of the 50 featured creatures in Ehlert's . . . offering sports distinctive markings. . . . Each spread freatures a beautiful collage illustration of an animal, accompanied by a poem of four, short, catchy lines. . . . Children will enjoy paging through and identifying the multitude of brilliantly hued animals that make up this visual zoo." Booklist

★ **Market** day; a story told with folk art. written and designed by Lois Ehlert. Harcourt 2000 un il $17; pa $7
Grades: PreK K 1 2   E
   1. Stories in rhyme 2. Markets -- Fiction 3. Farm life
   -- Fiction
   ISBN 0-15-202158-2; 0-15-216820-6 pa
                                                 LC 99-6252
On market day, a farm family experiences all the fun and excitement of going to and from the farmers' market
"The very young will enjoy the spare, simple rhymes. . . . All ages will appreciate the illustrations, comprising images of folk art, primitive art, and textiles from around the world. An annotated inventory of the featured items is included." Horn Book Guide

★ **Nuts** to you! Harcourt Brace Jovanovich 1993 un il $17; pa $7
Grades: PreK K 1 2   E
   1. Stories in rhyme 2. Squirrels -- Fiction
   ISBN 0-15-257647-9; 0-15-205064-7 pa
                                               LC 92-19441
"A frisky squirrel digs up bulbs and steals birdseed from a nearby feeder; in his boldest act, he enters the young narrator's apartment through a tear in the window screen. The quick-thinking child entices the mischievous squirrel back outside with some peanuts. . . . The story, told in brisk rhyme, is a fast-paced romp, and the large, dramatically styled collages will dazzle even the largest audiences. . . . The four concluding pages offer basic information about squirrels." Horn Book

Oodles of animals. Harcourt 2008 un il $17
Grades: PreK K 1 2   E
   1. Stories in rhyme 2. Animals -- Fiction
   ISBN 978-0-15-206274-3; 0-15-206274-2
                                               LC 2007-17018
Short, easy to read rhymes reveal what is unique about various animals, from ape to wolf.
"The artist uses scissors, pinking shears, and a hole punch to transform brightly colored papers into squares, rectangles, triangles, circles, diamonds, half circles, ovals, hearts, and teardrops of different sizes, which she then fashions into a menagerie guaranteed to spark readers' imagina-

tions. Each creature is coupled with a short, humorous poem that is sure to delight." SLJ

★ **Pie** in the sky. Harcourt 2004 un il $16
Grades: PreK K 1 2   E
   1. Pies -- Fiction 2. Cherries -- Fiction
   ISBN 0-15-216584-3
                                               LC 2003-4986
A father and child watch the cherry tree in their back yard, waiting until there are ripe cherries to bake in a pie. Includes a recipe for cherry pie
"The vibrant collage illustrations, made with an eclectic combination of materials—from paint and handmade papers to sheet metal, wires, and tree branches—celebrate the colors and simplified shapes of birds, insects, the cherry tree, and, yes, kitchen implements." Booklist

★ **Planting** a rainbow; written and illustrated by Lois Ehlert. Harcourt Brace Jovanovich 1988 un il $17; pa $7; bd bk $6.95
Grades: PreK K 1   E
   1. Flowers -- Fiction 2. Gardening -- Fiction
   ISBN 0-15-262609-3; 0-15-262610-7 pa; 0-15-204633-X bd bk
                                               LC 87-8528
A mother and daughter plant a rainbow of flowers in the family garden
"The stylized forms of the plants are clearly and beautifully designed, and the primary, blazing colors of the blossoms dazzle in their resplendence. The minimal text, in very large print, is exactly right to set off the glorious illustrations, making a splendid beginning book of colors and flowers cleverly arranged for young readers." Horn Book

★ **Rrralph**. Beach Lane Books 2011 32p il $17.99
Grades: PreK K 1 2 3   E
   1. Dogs -- Fiction
   ISBN 1-4424-1305-0; 978-1-4424-1305-4
                                               LC 2010006866
The narrator describes discovering how Ralph the dog can talk, appropriately saying words such as "roof," "rough," "bark," and "wolf."
"Created with realia as well as painted and textured papers, the three-dimensional collage illustrations feature zippers for Ralph's mouth, a metal pop-top for his nose, buttons for the bird's eyes, and actual bark for the tree's trunk. The pages, colored in hot-pink, grass-green, and pumpkin, magnify the visual energy of the artwork and graphics. . . . With its appealing jacket art, clever text, and vibrant illustrations, this amusing picture book is a pleasure to read aloud." Booklist

★ The **scraps** book; notes from a colorful life. Lois Ehlert. First edition Beach Lane Books 2013 72 p. (hardcover) $17.99
Grades: K 1 2 3 4   E
   1. Autobiographies 2. Illustration of books 3. Picture
   books for children 4. Illustrators -- United States 5.
   Illustrators -- United States -- Biography
   ISBN 1442435712; 9781442435711
                                               LC 2012041869
Author Lois Ehlert "employs her signature collage technique and images from her past work to explore her lifelong

relationship with creating art in this . . . picture book memoir. The journey begins with Ehlert's early creative inklings, . . . accompanied by family photos, images of the tools she uses today, . . . and a glimpse of her vibrant studio space. She shares thoughts on her varied sources of inspiration . . . . and illustrates how those ideas are translated to the page." (Publishers Weekly)

"In a generously illustrated picture book memoir, Ehlert speaks directly to her audience, particularly readers who like collecting objects and making things. The book is jam-packed with her art and photos from her life: her parents, the house she grew up in, and the small table where she was encouraged to pursue her art; along the way, we see how autobiographical her books have been." Horn Book

★ **Top** cat. Harcourt Brace & Co. 1998 un il $17; pa $7

Grades: PreK K 1 2   **E**

1. Stories in rhyme 2. Cats -- Fiction

ISBN 0-15-201739-9; 0-15-202425-5 pa

LC 97-8818

The top cat in a household is reluctant to accept the arrival of a new kitten but decides to share various survival secrets with it

"Ehlert creates a memorable cat duo in her trademark cut-paper collage style. . . . Children and other feline fans will quickly warm to this spunky story of rivalry and acceptance." Publ Wkly

★ **Wag** a tail; [by] Lois Ehlert. Harcourt, Inc. 2007 un il $16

Grades: PreK K 1 2   **E**

1. Stories in rhyme 2. Dogs -- Fiction

ISBN 978-0-15-205843-2

LC 2006013318

Assorted graduates of the Bow Wow School meet at a farmers market and a dog park, where most of them remember their obedience training.

"This simple story has a rhythmic, jazzy quality that begs to be read aloud. . . . Collages composed of brightly colored buttons and scraps of paper stand out on vivid green backgrounds." SLJ

Ehrhardt, Karen

★ **This** Jazz man; pictures by R. G. Roth. Harcourt 2006 un il $16

Grades: K 1 2 3   **E**

1. Counting 2. Stories in rhyme 3. Jazz musicians -- Fiction 4. African Americans -- Fiction

ISBN 0-15-205307-7

LC 2004-21094

This introduction to jazz is set to the rhythm of the traditional song This Old Man. "Ages five to nine." (Bull Cent Child Books)

"The candy-colored collages burst from the pages, making this addition just right as an up-tempo introduction for youngest music lovers." Publ Wkly

Ehrlich, Amy

Baby Dragon; [by] Amy Ehrlich; illustrated by Will Hillenbrand. Candlewick Press 2008 un il $16.99

Grades: PreK K 1 2   **E**

1. Animals -- Fiction 2. Dragons -- Fiction 3. Mother-child relationship -- Fiction

ISBN 978-0-7636-2840-6; 0-7636-2840-9

LC 2007051883

All day, Baby Dragon turns down other animals' offers to go play or find a snack while he waits for his mother to return for him, but at nightfall, he agrees to go with Crocodile to find her

"Hillenbrand's illustrations, done with ink, colored pencil, finger paint, gouache, and collage, and digitally manipulated, bring to life Baby Dragon's misty tropical forest where water buffaloes wander and storks splash in the river." SLJ

★ The **girl** who wanted to dance; by Amy Ehrlich; illustrated by Rebecca Walsh. Candlewick Press 2009 un il $17.99

Grades: 2 3 4   **E**

1. Fairy tales 2. Dance -- Fiction 3. Loss (Psychology) -- Fiction

ISBN 978-0-7636-1345-7; 0-7636-1345-2

"Both a haunting fairy tale and a parable for families separated by divorce or death, this lyrically rendered story also presents art as a vehicle for transcending pain. . . . Working in a representational style, Walsh . . . adds lush paintings of an idealized old world, and her nighttime scenes glow." Publ Wkly

★ **Thumbelina**; by Hans Christian Andersen; retold by Amy Ehrlich; [illustrated by Susan Jeffers] Dutton Children's Books 2005 32p il $16.99

Grades: K 1 2 3   **E**

1. Authors 2. Novelists 3. Dramatists 4. Fairy tales 5. Children's authors 6. Short story writers

ISBN 0-525-47508-7

LC 2004028979

A reissure of the edition published 1979 by Dial Books for Young Readers

A retelling of Hans Christian Andersen's classic fairy tale about a girl who is only one inch tall.

"This sumputious picture book version the classic Andersen story has been an adapted text that shows some softening of the tale's harsher edges. . . . [Readers will] be caught up in the action as depicted in Jeffers' striking, pastel-dominated pictures." Booklist

Ehrlich, Fred

Does an elephant take a bath? pictures by Emily Bolan. Blue Apple Books 2005 un il (Early experiences) lib bdg $13.50; pa $5.95

Grades: PreK K   **E**

1. Baths 2. Animals 3. Cleanliness

ISBN 1-59354-111-2 lib bdg; 1-59354-123-5 pa

"The humor is just right for the audience . . . and, like the text, the uncluttered illustrations . . . are both informative and amusing." Horn Book Guide

Other titles in the Early experiences series are:

Does a baboon sleep in a bed? (2005)

Does a chimp wear clothes? (2005)

Does a hippo say ahh? (2006)

Does a lion brush? (2005)

Does a panda go to school? (2006)

Does a pig flush? (2005)

Does a seal smile? (2006)

Does a tiger open wide? (2006)

Does a yak get a haircut? (2006)

Ehrlich, H. M.

★ Louie's goose; illustrated by Emily Bolam. Houghton Mifflin 2000 un il $15

Grades: PreK K 1   E

1. Toys -- Fiction 2. Beaches -- Fiction

ISBN 0-618-03023-9

LC 99-28566

While spending the summer at the beach with his parents, Louie has a wonderful time playing with his toy goose and even rescues her from a big wave

"This true-to-life look at a preschooler growing more independent is low-key and natural. . . . Bolam's sunny paintings capture the seashore experience of a charming, lovable family." Booklist

Another title about Louie is:

Gotcha, Louie! (2002)

Eichenberg, Fritz

Ape in a cape; an alphabet of odd animals. Harcourt Brace & Co. 1952 un il hardcover o.p. pa $8

Grades: PreK K 1   E

1. Animals 2. Alphabet

ISBN 0-15-607830-9 pa

A Caldecott Medal honor book, 1953

"The skill of a craftsman distinguishes this picture book illustrated with bold and lively drawings printed in three colors." N Y Public Libr

Eitzen, Ruth

Tara's flight; [by] Ruth Eitzen; illustrated by Allan Eitzen. Boyds Mills Press 2008 un il $16.95

Grades: K 1 2 3   E

1. Birds -- Fiction 2. Noah's ark -- Fiction 3. Grandfathers -- Fiction

ISBN 978-1-59078-563-8

LC 2007018815

Aram, a grandson of Noah, is responsible for taking care of the birds on the ark, including his pet dove Tara, who becomes the first creature to leave after the flood

"Decorated with cut-paper pictures of flying white birds, the endpapers celebrate the dove as the elemental peace symbol then and now." Booklist

Elffers, Joost

Do you love me? [by] Joost Elffers + Curious Pictures. Bowen Press 2009 un il $14.99

Grades: PreK K 1   E

1. Stories in rhyme 2. Love -- Fiction

ISBN 978-0-06-166799-2; 0-06-166799-4

LC 2008005939

Playful creatures called Snuzzles explore the idea of unconditional love

"The gentle, rhyming text is the straightforward stuff of bedtime rituals. But while the questions are expected, the answers feel fresh. . . . Set against high-contrast, single-color backgrounds, the action takes place at close range, so that just their heads, or parts of their heads, are visible." Publ Wkly

Elkin, Mark

Samuel's baby; illustrations by Amy Wummer. Tricycle Press 2010 un il $15.99

Grades: PreK K 1   E

1. School stories 2. Infants -- Fiction 3. Siblings --

Fiction

ISBN 978-1-58246-301-8; 1-58246-301-8

LC 2009-7548

Samuel announces during show-and-tell that he is having a baby and soon his kindergarten classmates are expecting everything from twins to puppies, but while Samuel teaches them how to hold and diaper a newborn, he has some qualms about becoming a big brother.

"A standout original title among new-baby picture books. . . . Wummer's pencil and watercolor illustrations effectively utilize facial expressions to communicate voice and personality." SLJ

Ellery, Amanda

If I were a jungle animal; illustrated by Tom Ellery. Simon & Schuster Books for Young Readers 2009 un il $15.99

Grades: PreK K 1   E

1. Animals -- Fiction 2. Baseball -- Fiction 3. Imagination -- Fiction

ISBN 978-1-4169-3778-4; 1-4169-3778-1

While playing baseball, a boy wonders what it would be like to be different jungle animals.

"Amanda Ellery's tale is simple but delicious, and accessible to very young readers. Husband Tom's expressive, Bill Peet-esque illustrations-in colored pencil, pen and ink-are all they should be: funny, original and so lively they virtually jump off the page." Kirkus

Elliot, David

Henry's map; by David Elliot. Philomel Books 2013 40 p. ill. (reinforced) $16.99

Grades: PreK K 1 2   E

1. Farms -- Fiction 2. Picture books for children 3. Maps -- Fiction 4. Pigs -- Fiction 5. Farm life -- Fiction 6. Domestic animals -- Fiction

ISBN 0399160728; 9780399160721

LC 2012035391

This children's picture book stars a very organized pig named Henry, who "decries the messy state of the farm. . . . Henry decides to draw a map to sort things out and, armed with pencil and paper, makes his way across the barnyard. All the animals are excited to be included, falling in line behind the earnest cartographer." His efforts are less than successful, however, and ultimately all the animals stay where they were originally, "to the relief of all concerned." (Publishers Weekly)

Elliott, David

Finn throws a fit; illustrated by Timothy Basil Ering. Candlewick Press 2009 un il $16.99; pa $6.99

Grades: PreK K 1   E

1. Anger -- Fiction

ISBN 978-0-7636-2356-2; 0-7636-2356-3; 978-0-7636-5604-1 pa; 0-7636-5604-6 pa

LC 2008-21174

A cranky toddler has an enormous tantrum.

"Elliott . . . and Ering . . . operate like the left and right hands of a single comic mind; each tongue-in-cheek line of text is deftly countered with raw charcoal scrawls, wild strokes of paint and crazed scribbles. Small readers will giggle at the realization of their angry feelings—complete with rippling lengths of toilet paper, floods of tears and flying crockery—while parents will blanch at the brilliant exposition of the power their children hold over them." Publ Wkly

Knitty Kitty; illustrated by Christopher Denise. Candlewick Press 2008 un il $16.99
Grades: PreK K 1 2   E
    1. Cats -- Fiction 2. Winter -- Fiction
    ISBN 978-0-7636-3169-7; 0-7636-3169-8
                  LC 2007-52160
Knitty Kitty is knitting a scarf, a hat, and some mittens for her kittens, but when night falls and the snow comes down, the kittens request a blanket to keep them warm Knitty Kitty has a better idea.
"The full-bleed illustrations in acrylic and ink portray an idyllic cottage in a snow-covered countryside. Inside the warmth is made evident with soft golds, browns, and touches of soft color here and there." SLJ

★ **On** the farm; [by] David Elliott; illustrated by Holly Meade. Candlewick Press 2008 un il $16.99; pa $6.99
Grades: PreK K 1 2   E
    1. Domestic animals
    ISBN 978-0-7636-3322-6; 0-7636-3322-4; 978-0-7636-5591-4 pa
                  LC 2007060857
"Elliott looks at a rooster, a cow, a pony, a dog, sheep, a barn cat, a goat, a pig, a snake, bees, a bull, a turtle, a duck, a hen, and a rabbit in verses that are rich in vocabulary and, for the most part, written in rhyme. Large, black typeface mirrors the black lines in Meade's beautiful, color woodblock prints that superbly reflect the mood and action in the poetry." SLJ

One little chicken; a counting book. by David Elliott; illustrated by Ethan Long. Holiday House 2007 un il $16.95
Grades: PreK K   E
    1. Counting 2. Dance -- Fiction 3. Chickens -- Fiction
    ISBN 978-0-8234-1983-8
                  LC 2006037046
"For each number up to 10, funny flapping fowls dance up a storm of different steps—from the hula to the cha cha. . . . The computer-generated cartoon art adds shimmy to the text, with egg-eyed pullets wearing silly attire and equally silly expressions." Booklist

What the grizzly knows; [by] David Elliott; illustrated by Max Grafe. Candlewick Press 2008 un il $16.99
Grades: PreK K   E
    1. Stories in rhyme 2. Bears -- Fiction 3. Teddy bears -- Fiction
    ISBN 978-0-7636-2778-2; 0-7636-2778-X
                  LC 2007052158
When night falls magical things begin to happen to Teddy, taking the reader on an adventure around the countryside and seeing the world through the senses of a bear
"The simple, rhyming text is paired with noteworthy, realistically rendered watercolor art that glows with a dreamlike quality. . . . An engaging fantasy." Booklist

Elliott, Laura
    A **string** of hearts; by Laura Malone Elliott; illustrations by Lynn Munsinger. Katherine Tegen Books 2010 un il $16.99; lib bdg $17.89

Grades: PreK K 1   E
    1. Valentine's Day -- Fiction
    ISBN 978-0-06-000085-1; 0-06-000085-6; 978-0-06-000086-8 lib bdg; 0-06-000086-4 lib bdg
Sam's friend Mary Ann helps him make a special valentine for Tiffany, but when Tiffany does not even notice it, Sam realizes who is really special. Includes facts about the history of Valentine's Day.
"The cheery artwork illustrating this heartwarming love triangle shows fluffy, well-dressed animals in bright colors. Their expressive faces mirror the emotions explored in the narrative. A lovely Valentine story about the real meaning of friendship." SLJ

Elliott, Rebecca
    ★ **Just** because. Trafalgar 2011 un il $14.99
Grades: K 1 2 3   E
    1. Love -- Fiction 2. Siblings -- Fiction 3. Physically disabled -- Fiction
    ISBN 978-0-7459-6267-2; 0-7459-6267-X
Toby describes all the fun he has with Clemmie, his beloved big sister who "can't walk, talk, [or] move around much."
"An endearing and enduring picture book about sibling love. . . . Clemmie's wheelchair plays only a minor role in this story. . . . The double-page spreads burst forth in vibrant colors and energetic streaks and swirls. . . . Full of unconditional love, this is a must-have title." Kirkus

    Zoo girl; Rebecca Elliott. Lion Children's 2012 26 p. col. ill $14.99
Grades: PreK K 1   E
    1. Zoos -- Fiction 2. Orphans -- Fiction 3. Picture books for children 4. Adopted children -- Fiction 5. Families -- Fiction 6. Loneliness -- Fiction
    ISBN 0745963234; 9780745963235
                  LC 2012392527
This children's picture book is the story of a "lonely orphan girl [who] finds her true friends within the walls of the zoo. . . . While the other children play on the swing set and slide outside the orphanage, she sits huddled on the grass far away from them. But the mere sight of the animals at the zoo brings a big smile to her face." After a night where she is accidentally left behind at the zoo, she is adopted by "the pair of zoo workers who find her." (Kirkus)

Elliott, Zetta
    Bird; illustrated by Shadra Strickland. Lee & Low Books Inc. 2008 un il $18.95
Grades: 2 3 4 5   E
    1. Novels in verse 2. Death -- Fiction 3. Drawing -- Fiction 4. Drug abuse -- Fiction 5. Family life -- Fiction 6. African Americans -- Fiction
    ISBN 978-1-60060-241-2; 1-60060-241-X
                  LC 2007-49039
Bird, an artistic young African American boy, expresses himself through drawing as he struggles to understand his older brother's drug addiction and death, while a family friend, Uncle Son, provides guidance and understanding
"This picture book tells a poignant story. . . . A complicated weaving of impressive watercolor, gouache, charcoal and ink drawings amplifies the metaphors and action of the poetic text as it combines black-and-white with color." Publ Wkly

Ellis, Sarah

Ben over night; illustrated by Kim LaFave. Fitzhenry & Whiteside 2005 un il $16.95

Grades: PreK K 1   **E**

1. Fear -- Fiction

ISBN 1-55041-807-6

"Little Ben loves to play at his friend Peter's house across the street, but every time he tries to sleep over, he wakens in the night and chickens out. His supportive parents suggest that he take his flashlight and security blanket, but nothing works until his big sister comes up with more imaginative ideas. Ellis tells Ben's story with economy and understanding. . . . With fresh colors and energetic line work, the apparently digital illustrations do a good job of expressing the characters' emotions as well as defining their actions." Booklist

Elvgren, Jennifer Riesmeyer

Josias, hold the book; [by] Jennifer Riesmeyer Elvgren; illustrated by Nicole Tadgell. Boyds Mills Press 2006 un il $15.95

Grades: PreK K 1 2   **E**

1. Haiti -- Fiction 2. Education -- Fiction 3. Gardening -- Fiction

ISBN 1-59078-318-2

LC 2005024989

Each day Chrislove, who lives in Haiti, asks his friend Josias when he will "hold the book," or join them at school, but Josias can only think of tending the bean garden so that his family will have enough food

"Elvgren has crafted a matter-of-fact snapshot of rural Haitian life. Tadgells muted watercolor spreads set the tone and enhance the text. Emotions are clearly depicted, giving the characters added dimension and believability." SLJ

Elwell, Peter

Adios, Oscar! a butterfly fable. The Blue Sky Press 2009 un il $16.99

Grades: K 1 2   **E**

1. Moths -- Fiction 2. Caterpillars -- Fiction 3. Books and reading -- Fiction

ISBN 978-0-545-07159-8; 0-545-07159-3

LC 2007050842

Despite his friends' teasing, Oscar the caterpillar studies to prepare for becoming a butterfly and migrating to Mexico, so when things do not turn out as he expects, he is still able to make his dream come true.

"This charming story about loving oneself and pursuing one's dreams sends an important message to children without being preachy or pedantic. The bright colors and cartoon-style illustrations enhance its ebullient, optimistic tone." SLJ

Elya, Susan Middleton, 1955-

Adios, tricycle; illustrated by Elisabeth Schlossberg. G. P. Putnam's Sons 2009 un il $16.99

Grades: PreK K   **E**

1. Stories in rhyme 2. Growth -- Fiction 3. Cycling -- Fiction 4. Garage sales -- Fiction 5. Hispanic Americans -- Fiction 6. Spanish language -- Vocabulary

ISBN 978-0-399-24522-0; 0-399-24522-7

LC 2008006562

Even though he has outgrown his tricycle, a young pig hides it at his family's yard sale until just the right smaller child comes along.

"Peppy, rhyming text filled with Spanish vocabulary words tells this entertaining, supportive story. . . . Schlossberg's pastel illustrations capture the mixed emotions in scenes of the diverse animal characters." Booklist

★ Bebe goes shopping; illustrated by Steven Salerno. Harcourt 2006 un il $16

Grades: PreK K 1   **E**

1. Stories in rhyme 2. Infants -- Fiction 3. Shopping -- Fiction 4. Spanish language -- Vocabulary

ISBN 0-15-205426-X

Rhyming text describes a trip to the grocery store for a mamá and her baby boy. Includes Spanish words.

"Almost all the words can be understood from the context or from the pictures. . . . Using gouache, watercolors, colored inks, and pencils, Salerno evokes the hip, retro style of 1950s cartoon-style advertisements. . . . Salerno is also a master at getting motion into his pictures, and his spreads rumble and tumble." Booklist

Another title about Bebé is:

Bebé goes to the beach (2008)

Cowboy Jose; illustrated by Tim Raglin. Putnam's 2005 un il $15.99

Grades: PreK K 1 2   **E**

1. Stories in rhyme 2. Mexico -- Fiction 3. Cowhands -- Fiction 4. Spanish language -- Vocabulary

ISBN 0-399-23570-1

LC 2003-26636

A poor cowboy enters a rodeo to win a date from a pretty señorita, but afterwards wonders if he should spend his winnings on the girl, who is only interested in the money, or on his trusty horse, whose encouragement helped him win.

"Elya's engaging text features snappy rhymes and plenty of contextual clues for the Spanish words that appear in bold type. . . . Raglin's watercolor-and-colored-pencil artwork features bright south-of-the-border colors and characters in traditional dress to accentuate the story's Mexican setting." SLJ

★ F is for fiesta; illustrated by G. Brian Karas. G.P. Putnam's Sons 2006 un il $11.99

Grades: PreK K 1 2   **E**

1. Alphabet 2. Birthdays 3. Stories in rhyme 4. Spanish language -- Vocabulary

ISBN 0-399-24225-2

LC 2004-20478

A rhyming book that outlines the preparations for and celebration of a young boy's birthday, with Spanish words for each letter of the alphabet translated in a glossary.

"At their best, Elya's verses bounce as easily between languages as they did in Oh, No, Gotta Go! (2003), which was also buoyantly illustrated by Karas." Booklist

Fairy trails; a story told in English and Spanish. illustrated by Mercedes McDonald. Bloomsbury Children's Books 2005 un il $17.99

Grades: PreK K 1 2   **E**

1. Fairy tales 2. Stories in rhyme 3. Spanish language

-- Vocabulary

ISBN 1-58234-927-4

Miguel and Maria meet various fairy tale characters as they walk to their aunt's house. Includes some Spanish words

"Done in pastels, the warm and colorful illustrations have an appealing folk-art quality. . . . A glossary of the Spanish words is included, but the rhyming text provides ample context clues so that the story is accessible to non-Spanish speakers. Overall, Fairy Trails would be a great storytime choice for both bilingual and English-only audiences." SLJ

Fire! Fuego! Brave bomberos; by Susan Elya; illustrated by Dan Santat. Bloomsbury Children's Books 2012 40 p. (reinforced: alk. paper) $17.89

Grades: PreK K 1 2   E

1. Spanish language 2. Stories in rhyme 3. Fire fighters -- Fiction

ISBN 1599907593; 9781599904610; 9781599907598

LC 2011004934

This picture book depicts the story of a group of firefighters, "four bomberos and el capitán," as they "race to gear up and get to the fire after the alarm sounds." The book describes various firefighting themes such as the fire station Dalmatian, the fire pole, and rescuing a cat. Author Susan Middleton Elya incorporates Spanish vocabulary words into the text, and adds "context clues as well as words that are close to English [to] make most of the Spanish vocabulary easy to decode." (Kirkus Reviews)

"With more than 20 picture books to her name, Elya has built her career on stories that deftly incorporate Spanish vocabulary words into English verse...The meanings of most of the Spanish words can be inferred from context, and a glossary is also included. The firefighters' determination, grit, and camaraderie—all fully evident in Santat's cinematically action-packed scenes—are sure to bolster childhood ambitions of joining their ranks." PW

Little Roja Riding Hood; Susan Middleton Elya; illustrated by Susan Guevara. G.P. Putnam's Sons 2014 32 p. color illustrations (hardcover) $16.99

Grades: PreK K 1 2   E

1. Folklore 2. Fairy tales 3. Stories in rhyme

ISBN 039924767X; 9780399247675

LC 2012022545

Pura Belpré (Illustrator) Honor Book (2015)

In this book, by Susan Middleton Elya, "while Roja picks flowers on the way to her grandma's, a mean wolf sneaks away with her cape to surprise Abuelita. But Grandma's no fool and Roja's no ordinary chica. They send that hungry lobo packing with a caliente surprise! This . . . retelling of Little Red Riding Hood has accessible Spanish rhymes." (Publisher's note)

"Elya remains a master at blending Spanish and English to create clever, lively verse, and she and Guevara give the story of Little Red Riding Hood an entertaining and thoroughly modern spin." Pub Wkly

N is for Navidad; by Susan Middleton Elya and Merry Banks; illustrated by Joe Cepeda. Chronicle Books 2007 un il $14.95

Grades: PreK K 1   E

1. Alphabet 2. Stories in rhyme 3. Christmas -- Fiction

4. Hispanic Americans -- Fiction 5. Spanish language -- Vocabulary

ISBN 978-0-8118-5205-0; 0-8118-5205-9

LC 2006008169

A rhyming book that outlines the preparations for and celebration of the Christmas season, with Spanish words for each letter of the alphabet translated in a glossary.

"Cepeda's lively paintings take a colorful, dynamic look at a warm Latino neighborhood celebration of the holiday season. . . . This book has potential to provide a springboard for discussion of holiday traditions while keeping children entertained visually." SLJ

No more, por favor; pictures by David Walker. G.P. Putnam's Sons 2010 un il $16.99

Grades: PreK K 1 2   E

1. Stories in rhyme 2. Food -- Fiction 3. Rain forest animals -- Fiction 4. Spanish language -- Vocabulary

ISBN 978-0-399-24766-8; 0-399-24766-1

LC 2008048411

Rain forest parents come up with a solution when all their children become picky eaters at the same time. Spanish words interspersed in the rhyming text are defined in a glossary.

"Walker's acrylic paintings in rich, primary rainforest colors add appeal to the bouncy, sometimes uneven rhyme. Kids with picky palates will appreciate the message and discover new tasty options while training their tongues with morsels of Spanish." Kirkus

Oh no, gotta go! illustrated by G. Brian Karas. Putnam 2003 un il $14.99

Grades: PreK K 1 2   E

1. Stories in rhyme 2. Bathrooms -- Fiction 3. Spanish language -- Vocabulary

ISBN 0-399-23493-4

LC 2002-17703

As soon as she goes out for a drive with her parents, a young girl needs to find a bathroom quickly. Text includes some Spanish words and phrases

"The unexpected rhyming of the English and boldface Spanish words give the rhythmic text an ebullient humor enhanced by Karas' understated gouache, acrylic, pencil, and collage illustrations." Bull Cent Child Books

Another title is:

Oh no, gotta go! #2 (2007)

Emberley, Barbara

Night's nice; [by] Barbara and Ed Emberley. Little, Brown Children 2008 un il $12.99

Grades: PreK K   E

1. Night -- Fiction

ISBN 978-0-316-06623-5; 0-316-06623-0

First published 1962 by Doubleday Books

Moonlit treetops, city lamps aglow, bright fireworks bursting in a dark July sky, and other wondrous illuminated evening sights are captured in a colorful picture book with a die-cut moon and silver foil title type on the cover.

"An inviting exploration of the wonders of nighttime. . . . Thin, sketchlike black line drawings, awash in sumptuous jewel-toned colors, work in tandem with this soothing tale sure to diminish night frights for youngsters concerned about the dark." SLJ

Emberley, Ed

Ed Emberley's bye-bye, big bad bullybug! Little, Brown & Co. 2007 un il $10.99

Grades: PreK K 1 2   E

1. Bullies -- Fiction 2. Insects -- Fiction 3. Monsters -- Fiction

ISBN 978-0-316-01762-6; 0-316-01762-0

LC 2006-15423

Die-cut pages reveal "a mean and scary 'Big Bad Bullybug' from outer space who threatens to bite, pinch, and tickle itty-bitty baby bugs. Luckily for the small fliers, a human with a huge sneaker is willing to do away with the pink-polka-dotted meanie. The cobolt blue backgrounds create a grand contrast for the electric greens, oranges, and yellows." SLJ

★ Go away, big green monster! Little, Brown 1992 un il $10.99

Grades: PreK K 1   E

1. Fear -- Fiction 2. Bedtime -- Fiction 3. Monsters -- Fiction

ISBN 0-316-23653-5

LC 9206231

"Using die-cut, black pages, the book begins with the monster's 'two big yellow eyes' glowing through round holes. Each flip of a page displays more features shining in electric colors through new holes—'a long blue nose/ a big red mouth with sharp white teeth/ two little squiggly ears .. .,' and so on—until the narrator announces, 'You don't scare me! So GO AWAY scraggly purple hair . . .,' and dismisses the monster page by page, feature by feature, like the departing Cheshire Cat." (Booklist) "Preschool." (SLJ)

"In the first half of this fear-dispelling book, graphically distinctive die-cut pages reveal, bit by bit, a monster with 'sharp white teeth' and 'scraggly purple hair.' The process is then reversed as the text commands each scary feature to 'go away,' until there is nothing at all left of the monster but a black page instructing 'Don't Come Back! Until I say so.' Entertaining and empowering for young children." Horn Book Guide

Mice on ice; by Rebecca Emberley and Ed Emberley. Holiday House 2012 32 p. (I like to read) (hardcover) $14.95

Grades: K 1 2   E

1. Ice skating -- Fiction 2. Cats -- Fiction 3. Mice -- Fiction 4. Stories in rhyme

ISBN 0823425762; 9780823425761

LC 2011038812

Authors and illustrators Rebecca Emberley and Ed Emberley present a children's rhyming book about a cat and some mice ice-skating. "Mice skate on ice. As they skate, their blades leave lines that depict a cat. Magically, the cat appears, colorful, graphic, and three-dimensional. What happens next? Why, the cat and the mice skate together!" (Publisher's note)

Nighty night, little green monster; Ed Emberley. Little Brown & Co 2013 32 p. $8.99

Grades: PreK K   E

1. Color -- Fiction 2. Bedtime -- Fiction 3. Monsters

-- Fiction 4. Toy and movable books -- Specimens

ISBN 0316210412; 9780316210416

LC 2012947183

In this picture book, by Ed Emberley, "each turn of the page . . . reveal[s] Little Green Monster's little yellow eyes, his little red mouth, and even a . . . tiny white monster tooth. Then, when the stars begin to appear, it's time for bed... so, nighty night, little yellow eyes. Nighty night, little red mouth. Nighty night, . . . little white tooth. Sweet dreams!" (Publisher's note)

Thanks, Mom! Little, Brown 2003 un il $11.95

Grades: PreK K 1   E

1. Mice -- Fiction 2. Animals -- Fiction

ISBN 0-316-24022-2

LC 2001-50715

Kiko the mouse finds some delicious cheese and gets help from his mother when a group of various animals tries to take it

"Using sunny yellow highlights and creatures constructed from bold, geometric shapes, Emberley creates an exciting, chaotic chase with sparse text and an impressive sense of graphic design." SLJ

Where's my sweetie pie? LB Kids 2010 un il $7.99

Grades: PreK   E

1. Stories in rhyme 2. Board books for children

ISBN 978-0-316-01891-3; 0-316-01891-0

"The book's title becomes a refrain for the short, rhyming text, encouraging kids to lift the flap and discover what's hidden. . . . Bold and colorful, the simple forms that make up the digital illustrations show up clearly against the white backgrounds. . . . As rewarding as a good game of peekaboo." Booklist

Emberley, Rebecca

★ The ant and the grasshopper; Rebecca Emberley and Ed Emberley. Roaring Brook Press 2012 32 p. (alk. paper) $16.99

Grades: PreK K 1 2 3   E

1. Fables 2. Grasshoppers -- Fiction 3. Ants -- Fiction 4. Insects -- Fiction 5. Grasshoppers -- Fiction 6. Bands (Music) -- Fiction

ISBN 1596434937; 9781596434936

LC 2011033800

This children's story, by Rebecca Emberley, illustrated by Ed Emberley, retells the fable of the ant and the grasshopper. "While hard at work on her chores, an ant hears the wonderful clickety click chirrup of music coming from the distance. Although she knows she should focus on the task at hand, she can't help but explore the joyful noise!" (Publisher's note)

★ If you're a monster and you know it; by Rebecca Emberley & Ed Emberley. Orchard Books 2010 un il $16.99

Grades: PreK K 1   E

1. Monsters -- Fiction

ISBN 978-0-545-21829-0; 0-545-21829-2

"In this rollicking interpretation of 'If You're Happy and You Know It,' brightly colored, digitally created monsters .. . run amok, wriggling and roaring, stomping and twitching. The never-frightening creatures are rendered in eye-popping psychedelic colors against a flat black background and fea-

ture horns, antennae, claws, teeth and any number of eyes. . .
. This will be a favorite with adults and children alike, allowing for both imaginative play and a raucous but structured
outpouring of energy." Kirkus

The **lion** and the mice; by Rebecca Emberley and Ed
Emberley. Holiday House 2011 un il (I like to read picture
book) $14.95
Grades: PreK K 1 2   E
   1. Mice -- Fiction 2. Size -- Fiction 3. Lions -- Fiction
   ISBN 978-0-8234-2357-6; 0-8234-2357-3
                                         LC 2010044205
"Aesop's lion and mouse (or mice, as this case has it)
have never looked more stylish. . . . A wacky-hued lion
sleeps. But when a tiny mouse, resplendent in olive-green
heels and a tuft of electric-blue fur, finds herself next to the
lion, he wakes up. The wry narrator intones . . . 'Uh-oh.' But
. . . the lion lets the mouse go, with the mouse squeaking in
reply, 'One day I will help you.' . . . The mouse returns, with
the help of many fashion-forward rodent friends, and fits a
key into a never-before-seen padlock. . . . Fantastic visual
fun." Kirkus

   Ten little beasties; [by] Rebecca Emberley and Ed Emberley. Roaring Brook Press 2011 un il $12.99
Grades: PreK K 1   E
   1. Counting 2. Monsters -- Fiction
   ISBN 978-1-59643-627-5; 1-59643-627-1
                                         LC 2010028118
"Begin with one weird and wacky, black-and-white
beastie, then add an additional, but very different-looking
one, to each subsequent page, and you have the Emberleys'
newest offering, done with their inimitable twist and style.
. . . Each creature is fantastical and geometric, but with a
splotch of color to add to the exotic designs each one sports.
Each spread is of a different vibrant color." SLJ

   ★ **There** was an old monster! [by] Rebecca, Adrian, &
Ed Emberley. Orchard Books 2009 un il lib bdg $16.99
Grades: PreK K   E
   1. Songs 2. Monsters -- Fiction
   ISBN 978-0-545-10145-5; 0-545-10145-X
                                         LC 2008007191
In this variation on the traditional cumulative rhyme, a
monster swallows ants, a lizard, a bat, and other creatures to
try to cure a stomach ache than began when he swallowed
a tick.
   "Individual readers will pore over the illustrations and
enjoy the repetition in the text while the large pictures make
this a natural to share with groups. With the song provided
as a free download at the publisher's Web site, this jazzy
crowd-pleaser will have kids begging for repeat reads." SLJ

Emmett, Jonathan
   The **best** gift of all; illustrated by Vanessa Cabban.
Candlewick Press 2008 un il $15.99
Grades: K 1 2   E
   1. Gifts -- Fiction 2. Animals -- Fiction 3. Moles
   (Animals) -- Fiction
   ISBN 978-0-7636-3860-3; 0-7636-3860-9
                                         LC 2007-52214
Mole has not seen his friend Rabbit for days because it
has been raining, and when he decides to tunnel to her home,

he accidentally meets Squirrel and Hedgehog, who would
like to visit her, as well
   "Children will enjoy this simple tale of friendship. Cabban's cuddly animals drawn in a palette of soft, autumn watercolors reinforce the warm and fuzzy feeling of Emmett's
story. A pleasant selection for fall storytimes and a good
choice for beginning readers." SLJ

   Leaf trouble; illustrated by Caroline Jayne Church.
Chicken House 2009 un il $16.99
Grades: PreK K 1 2   E
   1. Autumn -- Fiction 2. Leaves -- Fiction 3. Squirrels
   -- Fiction
   ISBN 978-0-545-16070-4; 0-545-16070-7
                                         LC 2009008268
A young squirrel panics when the leaves on his tree
change color and fall, but he feels better when his mother
tells him about autumn.
   "The colorful and endearing ink illustrations, placed in a
layered collage using a variety of textures and perspectives,
are a delight." SLJ

   The **princess** and the pig; by Jonathan Emmett; illustrated by Poly Bernatene. Bloomsbury Distributed to the
trade by Macmillan 2011 32 p. col. ill. (hardcover) $16.99
Grades: PreK K 1 2 3 4   E
   1. Humorous fiction 2. Pigs -- Fiction 3. Humorous
   stories 4. Princesses -- Fiction
   ISBN 0802723349; 9780802723345
                                         LC 2010049549
In this children's picture book by Jonathan Emmett,
"There's been a terrible mix-up in the royal nursery. Priscilla
the princess has accidentally switched places with Pigmella,
the farmer's new piglet. The kindly farmer and his wife believe it's the work of a good witch, while the ill-tempered
king and queen blame the bad witch. . . . While Priscilla
grows up on the farm, poor yet very happy, things don't turn
out quite so well for Pigmella." (Publisher's note)

Empson, Jo
   Never Ever; by Jo Empson. Childs Play Intl Ltd 2013
32 p. $7.99
Grades: PreK K 1   E
   1. Children's stories 2. Girls -- Fiction 3. Animals
   -- Pictorial works -- Fiction
   ISBN 184643551X; 9781846435515
In this picture book, by Jo Empson, "a little girl clutches
her toy rabbit and goes for a walk. As a pig with wings takes
to the air, she says, 'Nothing exciting ever happens to me!
Never, ever!' Her eyes are downcast, seeing nothing. . . .
Even the youngest readers . . . will see what the child does
not. . . . Humor builds as the simple text is repeated, leading the way to the next encounter." (School Library Journal)

Enderle, Judith Ross
   Smile, Principessa! by Judith Ross Enderle and Stepha-
nie Jacob Gordon; illustrated by Serena Curmi. Margaret K.
McElderry Books 2007 un il $16.99
Grades: PreK K 1   E
   1. Infants -- Fiction 2. Siblings -- Fiction 3.
   Photography -- Fiction
   ISBN 978-1-4169-1004-6; 1-4169-1004-2
                                         LC 2005012761

A sister is jealous when her baby brother starts getting all the attention in the family photographs

"Featuring characters in snazzy attire, the acrylic and pencil illustrations are delightful. . . . An engaging take on a common family situation." SLJ

Endle, Kate

Bunny Rabbit in the sunlight; [by] Kate Endle & Casper Babypants. Sasquatch Books 2011 il bd bk $9.99 Grades: PreK   **E**

1. Board books for children   2. Sun -- Fiction   3. Animals -- Fiction

ISBN 978-1-57061-749-2; 1-57061-749-X

"Eye-catching collages depict gentle animals whose habitats are brightened by different light sources. . . . Endle varies her compositions with warm and cool colors; visual textures suggest smoothness of glass and the roughness of gravel. When it's time to turn off the lights, readers will likely request a rereading. A recording by Babypants (aka Chris Ballew, lead singer for the Presidents of the United States of America) is available for download." Publ Wkly

Endrulat, Harry

A **bear** in war; [by] Stephanie Innes & Harry Endrulat; illustrated by Brian Deines. Key Porter Books 2009 un il $19.95

Grades: 1 2 3   **E**

1. Teddy bears   2. World War, 1914-1918   3. Father-daughter relationship   4. Soldiers -- Canada

ISBN 1-55470-097-3; 978-1-55470-097-4

"In Quebec during World War I, Aileen Rogers sent her cherished teddy bear overseas to protect her father, a medic, on the front lines. The bear . . . is the narrator. With sensitivity, he describes his experiences. . . . When Lawrence Browning Rogers is killed at the battle of Passchendaele, his uniform, his medal of bravery, and Teddy are sent to his family. [This is illustrated with] Deines's evocative, softly focused pastel illustrations. . . . Inspired by true events, the book includes archival photographs of the Rogers family, a newspaper clipping from 1916, and the Canadian government's report of Lieutenant Rogers's death. A moving remembrance." SLJ

Engle, Margarita

The **drum** dream girl; how one girl's courage changed music. by Margarita Engle; illustrated by Rafael López. Houghton Mifflin Harcourt 2015 48 p. color illustrations $16.99

Grades: K 1 2 3   **E**

1. Drums -- Fiction   2. Girls -- Fiction   3. Sex role -- Fiction   4. Dance music -- Fiction   5. Drummers (Musicians) -- Fiction   6. Cuba -- History -- 1909-1933 -- Fiction

ISBN 0544102290; 9780544102293

LC 2014015056

In this book by Margarita Engle, illustrated by Rafael Lopez, "girls cannot be drummers. Long ago on an island filled with music, no one questioned that rule--until the drum dream girl. In her city of drumbeats, she dreamed of pounding tall congas and tapping small bongós. She had to keep quiet. She had to practice in secret. But when at last her dream-bright music was heard, everyone sang and danced and decided that both girls and boys should be free to drum and dream." (Publisher's note)

"A talented young girl with a passion for drumming dreams of playing music in this upbeat story based on the life of Cuban musician Millo Castro Zaldarriaga. . . . Vibrant, warm, and hopeful, this expressive story shows the power of perseverance and importance of following your dreams. Engle's prose flows easily, with clean but evocative language that will be accessible to a range of young readers." Booklist

Includes bibliographical references

Orangutanka; a story in poems. Margarita Engle; illustrated by Renée Kurilla. Henry Holt & Co. 2015 40 p. color illustrations (hardback) $17.99
Grades: PreK K 1 2   **E**

1. Sleep -- Fiction   2. Stories in rhyme   3. Waka   4. Orangutans -- Fiction   5. Naps (Sleep) -- Fiction   6. Familial behavior in animals -- Fiction

ISBN 0805098399; 9780805098396

LC 2014019224

In this children's story, by Margarita Engle, illustrated by Renée Kurilla, "all the orangutans are ready for a nap in the sleepy depths of the afternoon . . . all except one. This little orangutan wants to dance! A hip-hop, cha-cha-cha dance full of somersaults and cartwheels. But who will dance with her?" (Publisher's note)

"A sprightly introduction to orangutans through nimble wordplay and attractive book design. Kurilla's pen-and-ink illustrations frame Engle's tanka verses, which relate a simple story of an orangutan family in an animal sanctuary in Borneo." SLJ

Includes bibliographical references

English, Karen

★ The **baby** on the way; pictures by Sean Qualls. Farrar, Straus and Giroux 2005 un il $16
Grades: PreK K 1 2   **E**

1. Infants -- Fiction   2. Childbirth -- Fiction   3. Grandmothers -- Fiction   4. African Americans -- Fiction

ISBN 0-374-37361-2

LC 2003-49047

Jamal, a young African American boy, asks his grandmother if she was ever a baby, she tells him the story of how she was born.

"The intimate artwork, in earth colors with pencil-thin line details, shows the loving bond between family members stretching back in time and into the future." Booklist

★ **Hot** day on Abbott Avenue; illustrated by Javaka Steptoe. Clarion Books 2004 32p il $15
Grades: PreK K 1 2   **E**

1. Summer -- Fiction   2. Friendship -- Fiction   3. Rope skipping -- Fiction   4. African Americans -- Fiction

ISBN 0-395-98527-7

LC 2002-09043

After having a fight, two friends spend the day ignoring each other, until the lure of a game of jump rope helps them to forget about being mad.

"Steptoe's found-object and cut-paper collages highlight facial features and depict oppressive summertime weather to perfection. . . . English's simple narrative consists mostly of two to three sentences per page and ends on a gratifying note." SLJ

★ **Speak** to me; (and I will listen between the lines) pictures by Amy June Bates. Farrar Straus Giroux 2004 un il $16

Grades: 2 3 4 5 **E**

1. School stories 2. African Americans -- Fiction 3. San Francisco (Calif.) -- Fiction

ISBN 0-374-37156-3

LC 2002-192895

Describes events of one day at a San Francisco Bay Area school as perceived by different second-graders, from the observations of first to arrive on the playground to the walk home.

"English's rich descriptions and insights bring readers into the world of six inner-city . . . students. . . . Bates's watercolor-and-ink illustrations capture the characters' expressions and moods vividly." SLJ

Ericsson, Jennifer A.

A **piece** of chalk; by Jennifer A. Ericsson; illustrated by Michelle Shapiro. Roaring Brook Press 2007 un il $16.95

Grades: PreK K 1 **E**

1. Drawing -- Fiction

ISBN 978-1-59643-057-0; 1-59643-057-5

LC 2006032178

A little girl creates a colored chalk drawing on her driveway

"This simple, sunny offering captures the delight and escape a child finds in art. . . . The words and rhythms read like poetry, but there are no bouncy rhymes to distract from the story's quiet joy. Shapiro effectively mirrors the girl's art with a childlike style and an appealing palette of bright, opaque colors, muted with chalk white." Booklist

★ **Whoo** goes there? illustrated by Bert Kitchen. Roaring Brook Press 2009 un il $17.99

Grades: K 1 2 3 **E**

1. Owls -- Fiction 2. Night -- Fiction 3. Animals -- Fiction

ISBN 978-1-59643-371-7; 1-59643-371-X

"Finding food involves a long night of waiting and listening that's also filled with disappointment for a handsome owl. . . . Ericsson uses a simple repetitive scheme to introduce an array of small animals that travel through the owl's moonlit world. . . . Kitchen's naturalistic paintings are set in attractive alternating sets. . . . The predictive text and handsome pictures are just right for reading with preschoolers." SLJ

Ering, Timothy Basil

The **Almost** fearless Hamilton Squidlegger; Timothy Basil Ering. Candlewick Press 2013 48 p. $16.99

Grades: PreK K 1 2 **E**

1. Fear -- Fiction 2. Frogs -- Fiction 3. Bedtime -- Fiction 4. Father-son relationship -- Fiction 5. Fathers and sons -- Fiction

ISBN 0763623571; 9780763623579

LC 2012947714

This book, by Timothy Basil Ering, is "an endearing tale of a boy overcoming his bedtime fears with a little help from Dad--and the promise of wormcake in the morning. Hamilton Squidlegger is fearless! Well, almost. During the day he can best all the frackensnappers, skelecragons, and bracklesneeds in the swamp, but at night he quakes in terror. Will

his father be able to help Hamilton remain fearless in his own mud all night?" (Publisher's note)

"Hamilton is "the rippingest, roaringest Squidlegger in the scrintalberry swamp," but his kryptonite is bedtime, when he fears the bracklesneed will strike. Hamilton's father's attempt to bribe him with a double-decker grasshopper worm cake succeeds following a nighttime (or dreamtime? It's rather confusing) multivillain romp in which Hamilton, who resembles a Muppet guppy, cavorts in Ering's fantastically fantastical acrylics." Horn Book

Ernst, Lisa Campbell

The **Gingerbread** Girl. Dutton Children's Books 2006 un il $16.99

Grades: PreK K 1 2 **E**

1. Fairy tales

ISBN 0-525-47667-9; 978-0-525-47667-2

LC 2006004193

Like her older brother, the Gingerbread Boy, who was eventually devoured by a fox, the Gingerbread Girl eludes the many people who would like to eat her but also has a plan to escape her sibling's fate.

"Ernst's familiar art . . . utilizes the oversize format to best advantage, with large characters leaping out of their frames." Booklist

Followed by: Gingerbread Girl goes animal crackers (2011)

The **Gingerbread** Girl goes animal crackers. Dutton Childrens Books 2011 un il $16.99

Grades: PreK K 1 2 **E**

1. Foxes -- Fiction 2. Cookies -- Fiction 3. Birthdays -- Fiction

ISBN 978-0-525-42259-4; 0-525-42259-5

LC 2011005244

Sequel to: The Gingerbread Girl (2006)

The Gingerbread Girl, who once escaped the fox that devoured her brother, must now try to save from a similar fate the animal crackers she received as a birthday gift.

"Ernst's pastel palette is well-suited to this lively story of 'Animal Crackers gone wild,' which, with words like 'menagerie' and 'brouhaha,' scattered throughout, offers a bit of a vocabulary lesson, too." Publ Wkly

Round like a ball! by Lisa Campbell Ernst. Blue Apple Books 2008 un il $15.95 **E**

1. Earth -- Fiction

ISBN 978-1-934706-01-5; 1-934706-01-9

Everyone tries to guess what is round and warm and cold and strong and fragile, until they finally realize it is Earth

"The clues are placed in large letters on the left side of a double-page spread, encircling progressively larger cutout circles. The cutout on each successive page offers a glimpse of the next article guessed. When the pages are flipped, a rainbow of cutout circles, large and small, is created on the previous page. . . . The distinctive illustrations, the guessing element, and the showstopping foldout of the Earth will work well for individual or group viewing." Booklist

Sam Johnson and the blue ribbon quilt. Lothrop, Lee & Shepard Bks. 1983 32p il lib bdg $17.89; pa $6.99

Grades: K 1 2 3   **E**
1. Quilts -- Fiction 2. Sex role -- Fiction
ISBN 0-688-01517-4 lib bdg; 0-688-11505-5 pa
LC 82-9980

While mending the awning over the pig pen, Sam discovers that he enjoys sewing the various patches together but meets with scorn and ridicule when he asks his wife if he could join her quilting club

The illustrations "bring an old-timey, bucolic scene to life and show steps in an equal-rights issue." Publ Wkly

Snow surprise; 1st Green Light Readers ed.; Harcourt 2008 un il $12.95; pa $3.95
Grades: 1 2 3   **E**
1. Snow -- Fiction 2. Siblings -- Fiction
ISBN 978-0-15-206553-9; 0-15-206553-9; 978-0-15-206559-1 pa; 0-15-206559-8 pa
LC 2007-42343

Joan makes a surprise for her little brother, Ben, but in the end, she is the one who is surprised.

Sylvia Jean, scout supreme. Dutton Children's Books 2010 un il $16.99
Grades: PreK K 1 2   **E**
1. Pigs -- Fiction 2. Costume -- Fiction 3. Scouts and scouting -- Fiction
ISBN 978-0-525-47873-7; 0-525-47873-6
LC 2009017919

Sylvia Jean disguises herself in order to assist a neighbor who does not want her enthusiastic help, but she still might be the only one in her Pig Scout Troop who will not earn a Good Deed Badge.

"Expressive faces enhance the gentle narrative; thin lines indicate a quiet vulnerability. Ernst's scenes feature her signature pastel palette even as humorous details advance the energetic tale." Kirkus

Another title about Sylvia Jean is:
Sylvia Jean, drama queen (2005)

The **turn**-around upside-down alphabet book. Simon & Schuster Books for Young Readers 2004 un il $15.95
Grades: PreK K 1 2   **E**
1. Alphabet
ISBN 0-689-85685-7
LC 2003-16318

"With touches of humor and a great deal of creativity, Ernst fashioned this book out of cut paper and surrounded each block with a thick black border that sets off white words. Children will enjoy tilting the pages to see the transformations and will be motivated to come up with ideas of their own." SLJ

Zinnia and Dot. Viking 1992 un il $16.99; pa $5.99
Grades: PreK K 1 2   **E**
1. Chickens -- Fiction
ISBN 0-670-83091-7; 0-14-054199-3 pa
LC 91-36178

Zinnia and Dot, self-satisfied hens who bicker constantly about who lays better eggs, put aside their differences to protect a prime specimen from a marauding weasel.

"Ernst has an easy storytelling style and a flair for grouchy dialogue that clucks to be read aloud, and her line-

and-wash paintings, lighted with gentle yellow tones, warm the comedy." Bull Cent Child Books

Esbaum, Jill

I hatched! by Jill Esbaum; pictures by Jen Corace. Dial Books for Young Readers 2014 40 p. (hardcover) $16.99
Grades: PreK   **E**
1. Chickens -- Fiction 2. Animal babies -- Fiction 3. Birds -- Fiction 4. Stories in rhyme 5. Animals -- Infancy -- Fiction
ISBN 0803736886; 9780803736887
LC 2012006100

In this book, by Jill Esbaum, "a baby chick bursts from his egg and into the world with . . . enthusiasm, awe, and I-can't-help-myself energy. . . . Jen Corace's . . . artwork is alive with critters and curiosities and surprises--the biggest of which? The hatching of a new baby sister, to the absolute delight of her now 'expert' big brother!" (Publisher's note)

Stanza; illustrated by Jack E. Davis. Harcourt Children's Books 2009 un il $16
Grades: PreK K 1 2   **E**
1. Stories in rhyme 2. Dogs -- Fiction 3. Poetry -- Fiction 4. Contests -- Fiction
ISBN 978-0-15-205998-9; 0-15-205998-9
LC 2007051078

Stanza the dog and his two rotten brothers terrorize the streets by day, but at night Stanza secretly writes poetry.

"The message, though well seasoned, is refreshed by lively characterizations of Stanza, his brothers, and the people around them. Children will delight in the details that are often hidden on the page. Rhyming verse makes this an especially fine read-aloud, but the real fun is in upclose scrutiny of the illustrations." SLJ

To the big top; [by] Jill Esbaum; pictures by David Gordon. Farrar Straus Giroux 2008 un il $16.95
Grades: PreK K 1 2   **E**
1. Circus -- Fiction 2. Friendship -- Fiction
ISBN 0-374-39934-4; 978-0-374-39934-4
LC 2006053530

When the circus comes to the small town of Willow Grove in the early 1900s, best friends Benny and Sam enjoy an exciting day helping set up the tent, admiring the various animals, and anticipating the big show.

"Gordon's joyful illustrations capture the appeal traveling entertainers had for small-town residents of the early twentieth century. . . . Esbaum . . . provides a nostalgic trip down memory lane that will give children . . . a good idea of what it was like back then." Booklist

Tom's tweet; illustrated by Kyle M. Stone. Alfred A. Knopf 2010 un il $16.99; lib bdg $19.99
Grades: PreK K 1   **E**
1. Cats -- Fiction 2. Birds -- Fiction
ISBN 978-0-375-85171-1; 0-375-85171-2; 978-0-375-95171-8 lib bdg; 0-375-95171-7 lib bdg
LC 2009017262

When a cat finds a bedraggled baby bird that has fallen from its nest, an unlikely friendship develops between the two.

"Esbaum's tweet tale will have listeners in stitches (especially the wormy bits), and Santat's Photoshopped cartoon illustrations of bulky Tom and the goggle-eyed tweets are as expressive as they are goofy. Totally tweet-rific." Kirkus

Escoffier, Michael

Rabbit and the Not-So-Big-Bad Wolf; by Michaël Escoffier; illustrated by Kris Di Giacomo. Holiday House 2013 32 p.

Grades: PreK K   E

1. Wolves -- Fiction 2. Rabbits -- Fiction
ISBN 9780823428137

LC 2012027931

"As Rabbit gradually discovers in this clever, imaginative book, the Not-So-Big-Bad Wolf is quite different from the Big Bad Wolf, with shorter ears, smaller teeth, and longer hair. Simple, humorous illustrations help build suspense, finally revealing that the Not-So-Big-Bad Wolf is a child in a wolf costume, who catches and squashes Rabbit in "a big hug." Horn Book

Eszterhas, Suzi

Brown bear; by Suzi Eszterhas. Frances Lincoln Children's Books 2012 32 p. ill. (hardcover) $15.99

Grades: K 1 2   E

1. Brown bear
ISBN 1847803024; 9781847803023

This book, part of the Eye on the Wild series, "introduces two little brown bears, . . . and follows them for several years as they grow up and become independent. First seen as cubs closely guarded by their mother, the sisters . . . play fight, and nap under her watchful eye. After more than two years of teaching them how to hunt for food and protect themselves, their mother leaves. They hibernate together before going their separate ways to start families of their own." (Booklist)

Ets, Marie Hall

Play with me; story and pictures by Marie Hall Ets. Viking 1955 31p il hardcover o.p. pa $5.99

Grades: PreK K   E

1. Animals -- Fiction
ISBN 0-14-050178-9 pa

A Caldecott Medal honor book, 1956

On a sunny morning in the meadow an excited little girl tries to catch the meadow creatures and play with them. But, one by one, they all run away. Finally, when she learns to sit quietly and wait, there is a happy ending

The "pictures done in muted tones of brown, gray and yellow . . . accurately reflect the little girl's rapidly changing moods of eagerness, bafflement, disappointment and final happiness." N Y Times Book Rev

Evans, Cambria

Bone soup. Houghton Mifflin 2008 un il lib bdg $16

Grades: K 1 2 3   E

1. Monsters -- Fiction 2. Halloween -- Fiction
ISBN 978-0-618-80908-0 lib bdg; 0-618-80908-2 lib bdg

LC 2008001862

The skeletal Finnigin tricks a town's witches, ghouls, and zombies into helping him make soup

"Even the zombies are lovable in Evans's charming Halloween-themed rendition of 'Stone Soup.' . . . Seasoned with sprightly, luminescent watercolors and the perfect dose

of gross-out factor, this tale has all the right ingredients for a hearty storytime." SLJ

Evans, Freddi Williams

★ **Hush** harbor; praying in secret. illustrated by Erin Bennett Banks. Carolrhoda Books 2008 un il lib bdg $16.95

Grades: K 1 2 3   E

1. Slavery -- Fiction 2. Religion -- Fiction 3. Christian life -- Fiction 4. African Americans -- Fiction
ISBN 978-0-8225-7965-6 lib bdg; 0-8225-7965-0 lib bdg

LC 2007-34777

While Simmy watches for danger from high in a tree, other slaves gather in a hidden spot in the woods to sing and pray together in their own way, risking their lives in pursuit of religious freedom. Includes historical facts about hush, or brush, arbors and the churches that grew from them

This is "a moving narrative. . . . Illustrated with extremely stylized pictures that don't prettify their subjects, this captures some of the fear and horror associated with slavery." Booklist

Evans, Kristina

What's special about me, Mama? words by Kristina Evans; pictures by Javaka Steptoe. Hyperion 2011 un il $16.99

Grades: PreK K   E

1. African Americans -- Fiction 2. Mother-child relationship -- Fiction
ISBN 978-0-7868-5274-1; 0-7868-5274-7

A child wonders what exactly makes him unique. Mama lists her son's many good traits, from physical attributes to behavior. He dismisses each quality as just a little thing, until Mama explains that there is nothing little about love.

"Evans's dialogue swings with an easy back-and-forth rhythm between a mother and her son, and Steptoe's collage illustrations, in deep rich colors, effectively position the characters, harmoniously connecting the two. . . . A heartfelt, comforting tale." SLJ

Evans, Lezlie

Who loves the little lamb? illustrated by David McPhail. Disney-Hyperion Books 2010 un il $15.99

Grades: PreK   E

1. Stories in rhyme 2. Animals -- Fiction 3. Mother-child relationship -- Fiction
ISBN 978-1-4231-1659-2; 1-4231-1659-3

LC 2009015896

Rhyming text reveals that, although baby animals are not always perfect, their mothers love them and help them through difficult moments.

"This has two things going for it that set it apart: Evans' uncommonly clever text and artwork by McPhail. . . . What's so terrific about this . . . is the motherly diversity shown in the art." Booklist

Evans, Michael

Poggle and the treasure. Egmont 2011 il $16.99

Grades: PreK K   E

1. Dragons -- Fiction
ISBN 978-1-4052-4811-2; 1-4052-4811-4

"Poggle is a teddy-bearish blue dragon with a best friend named Henry, who's equally cuddly but of a less determinate species. Inhabiting a cheery world that's given depth and texture by crayon-y black shading, Poggle lives at the beach. . . . It's an ideal setting for making important discoveries, like a mysterious pink egg that the duo uncovers while playing pirates. . . . Evans deftly sidesteps treacle and spins out his stories with a light and distinctly British touch; a few novelty elements . . . provide additional interest. Sweet, expressive, and reassuring." Publ Wkly

Evans, Shane W.

We march; Shane W. Evans. Roaring Brook Press 2012 32 p.

Grades: PreK K 1 2 3   E

1. Family -- Fiction 2. Civil rights demonstrations -- Fiction 3. African Americans -- Civil rights -- Fiction 4. African Americans -- Fiction 5. March on Washington for Jobs and Freedom, Washington, D.C., 1963 -- Fiction

ISBN 9781596435391

LC 2010046862

This illustrated children's book tells the story of "[a]n African-American family [which] awakens before dawn to prepare for the historic March on Washington in August, 1963. In this . . . companion to "Underground" (2011), [author and illustrator Shane W.] Evans captures a pivotal event in the struggle for equality and civil rights in America. The family joins neighbors to pray at their church, paint signs and travel by bus to Washington. They walk and sing and grow tired but "are filled with hope" as they stand together at the Washington Monument to listen to Dr. King speak of dreams and freedom. . . . The March has become synonymous with Dr. King's . . . speech, but Evans reminds readers that ordinary folk were his determined and courageous audience." (Kirkus)

Eversole, Robyn Harbert

East Dragon, West Dragon; story by Robyn Eversole; pictures by Scott Campbell. Atheneum Books for Young Readers 2012 un il $16.99

Grades: PreK K 1 2   E

1. Dragons -- Fiction 2. Prejudices -- Fiction

ISBN 978-0-689-85828-4; 0-689-85828-0

LC 2010039609

East Dragon and West Dragon are suspicious of one another although they have never met, but when the western king is captured in the Eastern Kingdom and West Dragon goes to rescue him, they find they have much in common.

"Eversole's spare narrative mixes tongue-in-cheek exaggeration, childhood fears and adventure, inspiring Campbell to contrast the rough and the refined, designing detailed watercolor worlds brimming with humor and beauty. This primer on friendship wrapped in hijinks is paced for maximum pleasure." Kirkus

Evert, Lori

The Christmas wish; by Lori Evert. Random House Inc 2013 48 p. (trade) $17.99

Grades: PreK K 1 2   E

1. Elves -- Fiction 2. Christmas -- Fiction 3. Santa Claus -- Fiction 4. Arctic regions -- Fiction 5. Tundra animals -- Fiction 6. Voyages and travels -- Fiction

ISBN 0449816818; 9780375971730; 9780375981562; 9780449816813; 9780449819425

LC 2012035529

This book, by Lori Evert, presents the story of "a brave little girl named Anja [who] wanted to be one of Santa's elves. So she leaves a note for her family and helps her elderly neighbor prepare for the holiday, then she straps on her skis, and heads out into the snowy landscape. From a red bird to a polar bear to a reindeer, a menagerie of winter animals help Anja make her way to Santa." (Publisher's note)

Ewart, Claire

Fossil; [by] Claire Ewart. Walker 2004 un il $16.89; lib bdg $17.85

Grades: PreK K 1 2   E

1. Stories in rhyme 2. Fossils -- Fiction 3. Pterosaurs -- Fiction

ISBN 0-8027-8890-4; 0-8027-8891-2 lib bdg

LC 2003-53469

Upon finding a special stone, a child imagines the life of a pterosaur, the ancient flying reptile that lived, died, and was fossilized into that stone. Includes facts about fossils and how they are formed.

"Ewart's inviting text and dramatic artwork work nicely together to describe the fossilization process in an engrossing way." SLJ

Includes bibliographical references

Fackelmayer, Regina

The gifts; illustrated by Christa Unzner. North-South Books 2009 un il $16.95

Grades: K 1 2 3   E

1. Gifts -- Fiction 2. Christmas -- Fiction

ISBN 978-0-7358-2265-8; 0-7358-2265-4

"Mia buys a turkey for dinner, gifts for her dog and cat, a hat for herself, and a Christmas tree. Stopping to help an old man who has slipped on the ice, she leaves her tree outdoors. . . . The story is written with clarity and restraint. . . . The sensitive artwork includes a delicately spattered effect that textures all the illustrations and works particularly well in the snowy outdoor scenes." Booklist

Fagan, Cary

Book of big brothers; pictures by Luc Melanson. Groundwood Books 2010 un il $18.95

Grades: PreK K 1 2   E

1. Brothers -- Fiction

ISBN 978-0-88899-977-1; 0-88899-977-1

"In this fictionalized story, the author reminisces about what it was like to live with two older brothers. The trio will make readers giggle with delight as the boys' escapades, teasing, and love capture the warmth and fireworks of sibling dynamics. The 1970s retro-style illustrations reflect the mood and tone, and color choices accent the setting, creating a shared story from the past. . . . This fresh approach to fraternal relationships makes a welcome purchase." SLJ

Ella May and the wishing stone; illustrated by Geneviève Côté. Tundra Books 2011 un il $17.95

Grades: PreK K 1 2   E

1. Wishes -- Fiction 2. Friendship -- Fiction

ISBN 978-1-77049-225-7; 1-77049-225-9

Ella May finds a stone and makes a wish on it, then refuses to share it with friends who then turn against her, but she finds a way to win them back.

"Fagan believably captures the delicate balance of friendship in the very young and lets the story [play] out with welcome complexity. Côté's illustrations are simple without being cartoonish, demonstrating the same warm understanding of childhood." Kirkus

Mr. Zinger's hat; Cary Fagan. Tundra Books of Northern New York 2012 32 p. (hardcover) $17.95

Grades: K 1 2   E

  1. Imagination -- Fiction 2. Storytelling -- Fiction

  ISBN 1770492534; 9781770492530

LC 2011938764

In this children's book, by Cary Fagan and illustrated by Dusan Petricic, "when old Mr. Zinger's windblown hat lands atop young Leo, the elder's suggestion . . . leads the pair to make up a tale about a rich but bored lad who offers half his possessions to anyone who can cheer him up. . . . Zinger then departs, leaving Leo to continue playing alone . . . until a new friend named Sophie shows up to share both the ball and the creation of a brand new story." (Kirkus Reviews)

Falconer, Ian

  ★ **Olivia**; written and illustrated by Ian Falconer. Atheneum Bks. for Young Readers 2000 un il $17.99; bd bk $7.99

Grades: PreK K 1 2   E

  1. Pigs 2. Behavior 3. Pigs -- Fiction

  ISBN 0-689-82953-1; 0-689-87472-3 bd bk

LC 99-24003

A Caldecott Medal honor book, 2001

Whether at home getting ready for the day, enjoying the beach, or at bedtime, Olivia is a young pig who has too much energy for her own good. "Ages three to seven." (Christ Sci Monit)

"The spacious design of the book; the appeal of the strong, clever art; and the humor that permeates every page make this a standout. . . . Falconer . . . renders Olivia's world in charcoal with dollops of red brightening the pages." Booklist

  Other titles about Olivia are:

  Olivia . . . and the missing toy (2003)

  Olivia forms a band (2006)

  Olivia goes to Venice (2010)

  Olivia helps with Christmas (2007)

  Olivia saves the circus (2001)

Olivia and the fairy princesses; Ian Falconer. Atheneum Books for Young Readers 2012 40 p. (hardback) $17.99

Grades: PreK K 1 2   E

  1. Pigs -- Fiction 2. Princesses -- Fiction 3. Professions -- Fiction 4. Individuality -- Fiction

  ISBN 1442450274; 9781442450271; 9781442450288

LC 2011053046

In this book, the piglet Olivia is "suffering from an identity crisis. While all the other girls she knows, and even some of the boys, dress as ruffled pink princesses for parties and desperately want to be fairy princess ballerinas, Olivia's aspirations are more" unique. Dressed like choreographer Martha Graham, "Olivia explains that she is 'trying to develop a more stark, modern style'...Her ultimate choice is quintessentially Olivia." (Kirkus Reviews)

"Fans will be pleased with this addition to the series." (Booklist)

Falkenstern, Lisa

A **dragon** moves in; written and illustrated by Lisa Falkenstern. Marshall Cavendish Children 2011 il $16.99; ebook $16.99

Grades: PreK K   E

  1. Houses -- Fiction 2. Dragons -- Fiction 3. Rabbits -- Fiction 4. Hedgehogs -- Fiction

  ISBN 978-0-7614-5947-7; 0-7614-5947-2; 978-0-7614-5995-8 e-book; 0-7614-5995-2 e-book

LC 2011001122

When Rabbit and Hedgehog bring home a newly-hatched dragon they all have a wonderful time together, but soon the dragon baby grows too big for their house.

"Falkerstern's oils have depth and warmth, and, though her animals are anthropomorphized, they're closer in authenticity to nature photos than cartoons. Gentle country concoction, two parts Beatrix Potter and one part Cressida Cowell." Kirkus

Faller, Regis

  ★ The **adventures** of Polo. Roaring Brook Press 2006 75p il $16.95

Grades: PreK K 1 2 3   E

  1. Stories without words 2. Dogs -- Fiction

  ISBN 978-1-59643-160-7; 1-59643-160-1

LC 2005055261

Polo the dog sets out from his home and enjoys many adventures, including sailing his boat on top of a whale, roasting hot dogs over a volcano, and taking a ride in a spaceship built from a mushroom.

"Young readers will be charmed by this hound, and be awed by his ingenuity. Somewhat similar to a graphic-novel format, this wordless picture book contains bold, colorful, cartoon panels that are sure to captivate even the most finicky youngster." SLJ

  Other titles about Polo are:

  Polo: the runaway book (2006)

  Polo and the magic flute (2009)

  Polo and Lily (2009)

  Polo and the dragon (2009)

  Polo and the magician (2009)

Falwell, Cathryn

David's drawings; story and pictures by Cathryn Falwell. Lee & Low Bks. 2001 un il hardcover o.p. pa $8.95

Grades: PreK K 1 2   E

  1. School stories 2. Drawing -- Fiction 3. Friendship -- Fiction 4. African Americans -- Fiction

  ISBN 1-58430-031-0; 1-58430-261-5 pa

LC 2001-16450

A shy African American boy arriving at a new school makes friends with his classmates by drawing a picture of a tree

"The cut-paper-and-fabric collages are a good choice for the story. . . . Both theme and execution make this a fine choice for classroom read-alouds." Booklist

Gobble, gobble. Dawn Publications 2011 un il

Grades: PreK K 1   E

  1. Stories in rhyme 2. Turkey -- Fiction

  ISBN 1-58469-148-4; 1-58469-149-2 pa; 978-1-58469-148-8; 978-1-58469-149-5 pa

LC 2011011698

"After discovering a flock of turkeys in her yard in the spring, Jenny continues to watch them thoughout the year. With simple text, mostly rhyming couplets, the young nature watcher describes the turkeys' appearance and behavior as they nest and raise their young in the woods nearby. . . . Falwell augments her multimedia (cut and torn paper and found natural materials) images with overlaid block prints. Leaf prints add further texture. These charming illustrations also show other animals. . . . The author includes suggestions for artwork and other activities." Kirkus

Pond babies. Down East 2011 un il $15.95
Grades: PreK K 1   E
1. Ponds -- Fiction 2. Animals -- Fiction
ISBN 978-0-89272-920-3; 0-89272-920-1
LC 2010043117
"This offering focuses on creatures that live in or near ponds, with a human child included at the end. A simple question-and-answer format presents a single physical characteristic of each one and then inquires, 'Whose baby is this?' Children will quickly catch on to the pattern and the idea that a page turn is necessary to learn the answer. Whether it is white spots that indicate a fawn or a wiggly tail to represent a tadpole, Falwell's colorful collages incorporate the given features. . . . The soft hues of the illustrations evoke the wonder of springtime." SLJ

★ **Scoot!** Greenwillow Books 2008 un il $16.99; lib bdg $17.89
Grades: PreK K 1 2   E
1. Stories in rhyme 2. Ponds -- Fiction 3. Turtles -- Fiction
ISBN 978-0-06-128882-1; 0-06-128882-9; 978-0-06-128883-8 lib bdg; 0-06-128883-7 lib bdg
LC 2007-18355
Six silent turtles sit still as stones on a log, as energetic movement by the other animals in the pond happens all around them
"Extraordinary paper collages accompany a high-spirited romp. . . . Strong, predictable rhymes bounce across the pages. . . . Unusual, lively words extend vocabulary." SLJ

Shape capers; [by] Cathryn Falwell. Greenwillow Books 2007 un il $16.99; lib bdg $17.89
Grades: PreK K   E
1. Stories in rhyme 2. Shape -- Fiction 3. Imagination -- Fiction
ISBN 978-0-06-123699-0; 978-0-06-123700-0 lib bdg
LC 2006043061
A group of children shakes shapes out of a box and discovers the fun of using circles, squares, triangles, semicircles, rectangles, and their imaginations
This is a "bright, playful book, illustrated in whimsical cut-paper collage." Booklist

★ **Turtle** splash! countdown at the pond. Greenwillow Bks. 2001 un il $15.95; lib bdg $15.89
Grades: PreK K 1 2   E
1. Counting 2. Stories in rhyme 3. Turtles -- Fiction
ISBN 0-06-029462-0; 0-06-029463-9 lib bdg
LC 00-30918

As they are startled by the activities of other nearby creatures, the number of turtles on a log in a pond decreases from ten to one
"The rhyming, alliterative text is energized with a rolling rhythm, suspense, and vivid, descriptive words. . . . Evocative woodland scenes spring to life with well-defined animals that are described in a final appended section." Booklist

Fancher, Lou
Star climbing; by Lou Fancher; paintings by Steve Johnson and Lou Fancher. Laura Geringer Books 2006 un il hardcover o.p. lib bdg $16.89
Grades: PreK K   E
1. Stars -- Fiction 2. Bedtime -- Fiction 3. Imagination -- Fiction 4. Constellations -- Fiction
ISBN 978-0-06-073901-0; 0-06-073901-0; 978-0-06-073902-7 lib bdg; 0-06-073902-9 lib bdg
LC 2005005048
When he cannot sleep, a little boy imagines himself on a nighttime journey across the sky where he can run and dance with star constellations
"Ethereal, textured paintings accompany Fancher's rhythmic, lyrical poem." Publ Wkly

Farber, Norma
How the hibernators came to Bethlehem; by Norma Farber; illustrated by Barbara Cooney. Walker 2006 un il $9.95
Grades: K 1 2 3   E
1. Animals -- Fiction 2. Christmas -- Fiction 3. Hibernation -- Fiction
ISBN 0-8027-9610-9
A reissue of the title first published 1980
The Star of Bethlehem awakens the winter-sleeping creatures, such as Bear, Badger, and Raccoon, to send them to visit a newborn baby.
"The simple, unabashed realism of Cooney's art . . . along with Farber's respectful text, celebrates the hibernators as part of a divine plan." Horn Book Guide

Farley, Brianne
★ **Ike's** incredible ink; Brianne Farley. Candlewick Press 2013 32 p. $16.99
Grades: 1 2 3   E
1. Ink -- Fiction 2. Writer's block
ISBN 0763662968; 9780763662967
LC 2012947261
In this children's picture book by Brianne Farley, "Ike-an inkblot . . . is also a blocked writer. Like many before him, he procrastinates . . . and then he decides that his story demands ink made from exceptional ingredients: shadows, the feathers of a booga-bird, and the essence of the dark side of the moon. . . . After some chaotic concocting . . . . Ike sits down to write and, sure enough, a story inspired by his ink quest materializes." (Publishers Weekly)

Farley, Robin
Mia and the too big tutu; pictures by Aleksey and Olga Ivanov. HarperCollins 2010 32p il (I can read) $16.99; pa $3.99

Grades: PreK K 1   E
1. Cats -- Fiction 2. Ballet -- Fiction
ISBN 978-0-06-173302-4; 0-06-173302-4; 978-0-06-173301-7 pa; 0-06-173301-6 pa

LC 2010021960

Mia the kitten is so excited about her first day of ballet class that she accidentally brings her big sister's tutu instead of her own.

"Large, colorful illustrations and an easy-to-read typeface make [this book] visually appealing." SLJ

Farmer, Jacqueline

Valentine be mine; Jacqueline Farmer; illustrated by Megan Halsey and Sean Addy. Charlesbridge 2013 32 p. (reinforced) $17.95; (paperback) $7.95
Grades: 1 2 3   E
1. Valentine's Day
ISBN 1580893902; 9781580893893; 9781580893909

LC 2011049504

This children's book, by Jacqueline Farmer, discusses the history of Valentine's Day. "Influenced by kings, poets, and religious customs, Valentine's Day has changed over the centuries from its origins in ancient Rome. Readers of all ages will learn the history of Valentine's Day as well as its past and present traditions in this informative dual-level text." (Publisher's note)

Farooqi, Musharraf

The **cobbler's** holiday, or, why ants don't have shoes; illustrated by Eugene Yelchin. Roaring Brook Press 2008 un il $16.95
Grades: K 1 2 3   E
1. Ants -- Fiction 2. Shoes -- Fiction 3. Fashion -- Fiction
ISBN 978-1-59643-234-5; 1-59643-234-9

LC 2007044046

At a time when every ant has at least fifteen pairs of shoes and disputes over footwear are common, the one and only ant cobbler decides to take some time off, which leads to many tears until the Red Ant provides an elegant solution.

This is "a dainty, droll fable. . . . Farooqi builds scenarios ripe with comedy. . . . Yelchin . . . contributes decorative initial caps and a modish Jazz Age aesthetic; his spiky-looking ant flappers and dandies sport ritzy top hats and beaded caps, tailored and fur-collared coats, monocles and, of course, elaborate footwear." Publ Wkly

Farrell, Darren

Doug-Dennis and the flyaway fib; words and pictures by Darren Farrell. Dial Books for Young Readers 2010 un il $16.95
Grades: K 1 2   E
1. Sheep -- Fiction 2. Circus -- Fiction 3. Honesty -- Fiction 4. Friendship -- Fiction 5. Truthfulness and falsehood -- Fiction
ISBN 978-0-8037-3437-1; 0-8037-3437-9

LC 2009-12141

Having fibbed about stealing his best friend's popcorn at the circus, Doug-Dennis the sheep finds himself carried far away to a place filled with lies and liars of all sorts and must discover a way to return.

"Sharp-edged irony and wacky cartoon visuals provide newcomer Farrell's moral tale with some serious wattage. . . . Despite the antifib message, the fibs are where all the entertainment is ('I invented the inter-web,' declares a spider), and the ethically unsteady Doug-Dennis has plenty of Homer Simpson–like appeal." Publ Wkly

Thank you, Octopus; story and pictures by Darren Farrell. Dial Books for Young Readers 2014 40 p. color illustrations (hardcover) $16.99
Grades: PreK K 1   E
1. Humorous fiction 2. Bedtime -- Fiction 3. Octopuses -- Fiction
ISBN 0803734387; 9780803734388

LC 2013027093

"It's bedtime, and Octopus is here to help his buddy get ready. First up is a bath (Thank you, Octopus)...in egg salad (No, thank you, Octopus)! Then it's time to brush teeth with paint brushes! And don't worry, Octopus made sure there were no monsters under the bed because they're all in the closet! No, thank you, Octopus!" (Publisher's note)

"Prepare for escalating giggles as a well-meaning octopus takes on bedtime routines with hilarious ineptness. . . . Each page-turn extends the jokes, and the simple recurring refrain adds opportunities for kids to join in." Booklist

Faulkner, Matt

A **taste** of colored water. Simon & Schuster 2008 un il $16.99
Grades: K 1 2 3   E
1. Cousins -- Fiction 2. Civil rights demonstrations -- Fiction 3. African Americans -- Segregation -- Fiction
ISBN 978-1-4169-1629-1; 1-4169-1629-6

In the 1960s two cousins hear of a water fountain labelled "Colored" and imagine a multicolored drink, but they discover the true meaning of the sign when they encounter a Civil Rights demonstration.

"Watercolors decorated with ink crosshatching ably contrast the sweet pastoral fun the children experience with their sudden, terrifying wake up. Faulkner's personal note about his growing up in the north, where segregation was not official but prejudice was always there, will spark discussion." Booklist

Fearing, Mark

The **great** Thanksgiving escape; Mark Fearing. First edition Candlewick Press 2014 32 p. color illustrations $15.99
Grades: K 1 2 3   E
1. Cousins -- Fiction 2. Thanksgiving Day -- Fiction
ISBN 0763663069; 9780763663063

LC 2013955664

"It's another Thanksgiving at Grandma's. Gavin expects a long day of boredom and being pestered by distantly related toddlers, but his cousin Rhonda has a different idea: make a break for it--out of the kids' room to the swing set in the backyard! Gavin isn't so sure, especially when they encounter vicious guard dogs (in homemade sweaters)." (Publisher's note)

"Playing with perspective, Fearing's digitally created cartoons show long lines of pantyhosed legs and an aerial shot of outstretched manicured hands reaching for a hug. Funny play-by-play running commentary describes the action as it unfolds." SLJ

Fearnley, Jan

Martha in the middle; [by] Jan Fearnley. Candlewick Press 2008 40p il $16.99

Grades: PreK K 1   E

1. Mice -- Fiction 2. Frogs -- Fiction 3. Siblings -- Fiction 4. Family life -- Fiction

ISBN 978-0-7636-3800-9; 0-7636-3800-5

Martha, a young mouse with a sensible big sister and a cute little brother, begins to feel invisible and decides to run away, but at the end of the garden she meets a wise frog who points out just how special the middle can be.

"Fearnley's nimble use of line and uncluttered watercolors focus on character and plenty of action. . . . Witty details . . . ramp up the fun." Publ Wkly

Milo Armadillo. Candlewick Press 2009 un il $15.99

Grades: PreK K 1 2   E

1. Toys -- Fiction 2. Armadillos -- Fiction

ISBN 978-0-7636-4575-5; 0-7636-4575-3

               LC 2009004231

When no one can find a pink, fluffy rabbit to give to Tallulah for her birthday, her grandmother knits her a pink, fluffy 'thing' that they name Milo Armadillo, which proves to be a great present.

"Mixed-media collages pay homage to all things handmade by incorporating worked yarn and fabric into the illustrations. This candy-colored picture book tells a simple, sweet story about learning to love what you have." SLJ

Mr. Wolf's pancakes; [by] Jan Fearnley. Tiger Tales 2001 un il $15.95; pa $6.95

Grades: PreK K 1 2 3   E

1. Fairy tales 2. Wolves -- Fiction

ISBN 1-58925-004-4; 1-58925-354-X pa

               LC 2001-834

First published 1999 in the United Kingdom

"Mr. Wolf seeks assistance from his neighbors, but Chicken Little, Wee Willy Winkle, the Gingerbread Man, Little Red Riding Hood and the Three Little Pigs all nastily refuse. Of course, when Mr. Wolf eventually whips up the pancakes all by himself, they demand a share of his culinary creation. Mr. Wolf . . . lets the marauders into the kitchen—and then gobbles them all up. . . . Chipper watercolors depict a sunny storybook town. . . . A gleeful twist on a nursery staple." Publ Wkly

Another title about Mr. Wolf is:

Mr. Wolf and the three bears (2002)

Feder, Jane

Spooky friends; starring Scarlet and Igor. by Jane Feder and illustrated by Julie Downing. Scholastic Press 2013 40 p. (Spooky friends) (hardcover: alk. paper) $16.99

Grades: K 1 2   E

1. Mummies -- Fiction 2. Vampires -- Fiction 3. Friendship -- Fiction 4. Best friends -- Fiction

ISBN 0545478154; 9780545478151; 9780545478168

               LC 2012014786

In this book by Jane Feder and illustrated by Julie Downing "Scarlet is a feisty little Vampire, and her best friend, Igor, is a roly-poly little Mummy. Together, they star in three humorous, heartwarming stories about two friends who never agree on anything. That is--until they discover different ideas can become even better ideas when they cooperate." (Publisher's note)

Feelings, Muriel

★ **Jambo** means hello; Swahili alphabet book. pictures by Tom Feelings. Dial Bks. for Young Readers 1981 un il hardcover o.p. pa $6.99

Grades: PreK K 1 2   E

1. Alphabet 2. Swahili language 3. East Africa

ISBN 0-14-054652-1 pa

A Caldecott Medal honor book, 1975

"Integrated totally in feeling and mood, the book has been engendered by an intense personal vision of Africa—one that is warm, all-enveloping, quietly strong and filled with love." Horn Book

★ **Moja** means one; Swahili counting book. pictures by Tom Feelings. Dial Bks. for Young Readers 1971 un il hardcover o.p. pa $6.99

Grades: PreK K 1 2   E

1. Counting 2. Swahili language 3. East Africa

ISBN 0-14-054662-6 pa

A Caldecott Medal honor book, 1972

"A short introduction explaining the importance of Swahili and providing a map of the areas in which it is spoken expands the book's use beyond the preschool level of the text into the first three school grades." SLJ

Feiffer, Jules

★ **Bark,** George; Jules Feiffer. HarperCollins Publishers 1999 30 p. il $17.99

Grades: PreK K 1 2   E

1. Animal sounds 2. Dogs -- Fiction 3. Humorous stories

ISBN 0062051857; 9780062051851

               LC 98074468

This children's book, by Jules Feiffer, "is a story about a pup whose mother is trying to teach him to bark, but George will only meow, quack, oink and moo. Preschool to grade two." (School Library Journal)

"Feiffer's characters are unforgettable, the text is brief and easy to follow, and the pictures burst with the sort of broad physical comedy that a lot of children just love." Booklist

Rupert Can Dance; Jules Feiffer. Farrar Straus & Giroux 2014 32 p. color illustrations $17.95

Grades: PreK K 1 2   E

1. Cats -- Fiction 2. Dance -- Fiction

ISBN 0374363633; 9780374363635

               LC 2013908976

In this children's book by Jules Feiffer, "Rupert has a big secret. When his owner, Mandy, is fast asleep, he likes to slip on her dancing shoes and dance the night away. Then one night Mandy catches Rupert in the act. She's not upset; she's thrilled! And she's determined to give Rupert dancing lessons so he can hone his talent. Rupert is horrified. Lessons are for dogs. Cats like to do things their own way." (Publisher's note)

"This warmly humorous book may resonate most with those familiar with the love of dance or the delicate dignity of cats, but the story of friendship and shared passion at its heart will appeal to any reader." Horn Book

Feiffer, Kate

But I wanted a baby brother! illustrated by Diane Goode. Simon & Schuster Books for Young Readers 2010 un il $16.99

Grades: PreK K 1   **E**

1. Infants -- Fiction 2. Siblings -- Fiction 3. Family life -- Fiction

ISBN 978-1-4169-3941-2; 1-4169-3941-5

Oliver Keaton wants a baby brother more than anything but when he gets a baby sister instead, he sets out with his dog Chaplin to trade his sister for the perfect baby brother.

"Both text and breezy cartoon illustrations are laced with humor, making this an excellent choice for reading aloud. . . . Feiffer's book is a cut above many of its kind." Booklist

Double pink; illustrated by Bruce Ingman. Simon & Schuster Books for Young Readers 2005 un il $15.95

Grades: PreK K 1   **E**

1. Color -- Fiction

ISBN 0-689-87190-0

LC 2004--06582

Madison covers and surrounds herself with her favorite color, pink, until the day her mother has trouble finding her.

"Feiffer's simple text reads easily, and Ingman's playful acrylic-and-ink paintings take a light approach to this look at childhood obsession." SLJ

Henry, the dog with no tail; illustrated by Jules Feiffer. Simon & Schuster Books for Young Readers 2007 un il $16.99

Grades: PreK K 1 2   **E**

1. Dogs -- Fiction

ISBN 978-1-4169-1614-7; 1-4169-1614-8

LC 2006-13418

Envious of the other dogs that have tails, Henry goes in search of a tail of his own, but in the end he decides he is happy the way he is.

"Feiffer's story features droll humor, wonderfully outlandish plot twists, and a satisfying journey of self-discovery. . . . The charcoal and watercolor illustrations use loose lines and color splashes to convey the action and capture the characters' personalities." SLJ

★ **My** mom is trying to ruin my life; [by] Kate Feiffer; illustrated by Diane Goode. Simon & Schuster Books for Young Readers 2009 un il $16.99

Grades: PreK K 1 2   **E**

1. Father-daughter relationship -- Fiction 2. Mother-daughter relationship -- Fiction

ISBN 978-1-4169-4100-2; 1-4169-4100-2

LC 2007045351

A young girl describes all the ways in which her mother and father conspire to ruin her life

"Feiffer and Goode . . . give the old chestnut of a story line an urbane sheen. . . . [Goode's] watercolor vignettes are gems of wry intelligence and comic understatement." Publ Wkly

★ **My** side of the car; illustrated by Jules Feiffer. Candlewick Press 2011 un il $16.99

Grades: PreK K 1 2   **E**

1. Rain -- Fiction 2. Automobile travel -- Fiction 3.

Father-daughter relationship -- Fiction

ISBN 978-0-7636-4405-5; 0-7636-4405-6

LC 2010039184

Sadie and her father have been planning a trip to the zoo for a long time but something always gets in the way, so when they finally start out and her father sees some raindrops, Sadie insists there is no rain on her side of the car.

"Feiffer's sweet and loopy watercolor-and-pencil drawings follow Sadie's imaginings and explanations for wet car windows. . . . Sadie's cheerful sass and her father's obvious respect for and indulgence of the force of her imagination make this a keeper." Publ Wkly

President Pennybaker; [by] Kate Feiffer; illustrated by Diane Goode. Simon & Schuster Books for Young Readers 2008 un il $16.99

Grades: PreK K 1 2   **E**

1. Politics -- Fiction

ISBN 978-1-4169-1354-2; 1-4169-1354-8

LC 2007004815

Tired of the unfairness of life, young Luke Pennybaker decides to run for president, with his dog Lily as his running mate

"Deadpan narration allows the absurdity of the premise to carry the day, with plenty of help from the illustrations. Goode's breezy watercolors set just the right tone. . . . The humor is deftly understated, both visually and verbally, making this an amusing and appealing send-up of politics and children's chores." SLJ

Feldman, Eve

★ **Billy** and Milly, short and silly! written by Eve Feldman; pictures by Tuesday Mourning. G.P. Putnam's Sons 2009 un il $16.99

Grades: PreK K 1 2   **E**

1. Stories in rhyme

ISBN 978-0-399-24651-7; 0-399-24651-7

LC 2008-26143

"This picture book presents 13 short rhyming stories about Billy and Milly. Most of them are four words long; some, only three. Every word in each selection rhymes. . . . The bright cartoon illustrations done in mixed-media collage are the keys to understanding the stories and the humor. . . . Both clever and slapstick, this book can be read for pleasure or used as a jumping-off point for thinking about rhyme, language, and story." SLJ

Feldman, Thea

Harry Cat and Tucker Mouse: Harry to the rescue! Square Fish 2011 47p (My readers) $15.99; pa $3.99

Grades: 1 2 3   **E**

1. Cats -- Fiction 2. Mice -- Fiction 3. New York (N.Y.) -- Fiction

ISBN 978-0-312-62507-8; 0-312-62507-3; 978-0-312-62509-2 pa; 0-312-62509-X pa

Tucker Mouse spotted a lost penny in the shoeshine store, so he ran in to get it for his collection. Now the store is closed up tight, and Tucker is trapped. Can Harry Cat find a way to get him out?

Harry Cat and Tucker Mouse: starring Harry. Square Fish 2011 32p (My readers) $15.99; pa $3.99

Grades: K 1 2   **E**

1. Cats -- Fiction 2. Mice -- Fiction 3. Theater --

Fiction 4. Friendship -- Fiction 5. New York (N.Y.) -- Fiction

ISBN 978-0-312-68168-5; 978-0-312-68169-2 pa

LC 2010048674

Harry Cat loves the theater, but when he becomes the star of a Broadway play he and his best friend Tucker Mouse miss one another terribly.

Harry Cat and Tucker Mouse: Tucker's beetle band. Square Fish 2011 47p il (My readers) $15.99; pa $3.99
Grades: 1 2 3   E

1. Cats -- Fiction 2. Mice -- Fiction 3. Beetles -- Fiction 4. Crickets -- Fiction 5. Bands (Music) -- Fiction 6. New York (N.Y.) -- Fiction

ISBN 978-0-312-62575-7; 0-312-62575-8; 978-0-312-62576-4 pa; 0-312-62576-6 pa

"Tucker Mouse, Harry Cat, and Chester Cricket contend with a beetle rock band disturbing their sleep under Times Square. The band is practicing to win the Battle of the Bug Bands competition and travel the country. . . . The Ivanovs' intricate ink and watercolor illustrations reflect the charm of Garth Williams's characters and original setting but add many details including varied visual perspectives and characters that exude facial and kinesthetic expression. . . . This well-told tale will appeal to the many young readers and their friends whose family members are in bands, and it serves as a wonderful introduction to the beloved characters in George Selden's The Cricket in Times Square." SLJ

Other titles in this series are:

Harry Cat and Tucker Mouse: Harry to the rescue! (2011)
Harry Cat and Tucker Mouse: Starring Harry! (2011)

Fenton, Joe

What's under the bed? written and illustrated by Joe Fenton. Simon & Schuster for Young Readers un il $15.99
Grades: PreK K 1 2   E

1. Stories in rhyme 2. Fear -- Fiction 3. Bedtime -- Fiction

ISBN 978-1-4169-4943-5; 1-4169-4943-7

When Fred lays down his head, he imagines there is something monstrous under his bed.

"The narrative is accessible, using uncomplicated rhymes. . . . The brooding illustrations would be more unnerving if Fred, diminutive in outsize glasses, weren't so adorably disarming." Horn Book Guide

Ferber, Brenda A.

The **yuckiest,** stinkiest, best Valentine ever; by Brenda A. Ferber; pictures by Tedd Arnold. Dial Books for Young Readers 2012 32 p. col. ill. (hardcover) $16.99
Grades: PreK K 1 2   E

1. Love -- Fiction 2. Valentine's Day 3. Valentine's Day -- Fiction

ISBN 0803735057; 9780803735057

LC 2011047668

In this children's picture book, "Leon makes a very special valentine for his crush, Zoey Maloney, but the valentine has a mind and life of its own. The valentine tells Leon not to tell Zoey that he loves her. In a gingerbread man-like fashion, the valentine dashes out of the house with Leon running after it. During the chase, Leon and the valentine come across different groups of kids who share their opinions about Leon's declaration of love." (Children's Literature)

Fern, Tracey E.

★ **Buffalo** music; illustrated by Lauren Castillo. Clarion Books 2008 31p il $16
Grades: 1 2 3 4   E

1. Teachers 2. Conservationists 3. Ranchers 4. Bison -- Fiction 5. Texas -- Fiction 6. Frontier and pioneer life -- Fiction

ISBN 978-0-618-72341-6; 0-618-72341-2

LC 2007-18435

After hunters kill off the buffalo around her Texas ranch, a woman begins raising orphan buffalo calves and eventually ships four members of her small herd to Yellowstone National Park, where they form the beginnings of newly thriving buffalo herds. Based on the true story of Mary Ann Goodnight and her husband Charles; includes author's note about her work, with websites and a bibliography.

"Fern's lyrical text and Castillo's folk-style artwork beautifully capture the era and events. Done in warm, earthy hues, the mixed-media illustrations depict a rugged landscape of grays and browns speckled with touches of color-wildflowers or bright blooms on a tree." SLJ

★ **Pippo** the Fool; [by] Tracey E. Fern; illustrated by Pau Estrada. Charlesbridge 2009 un il $15.95
Grades: 1 2 3   E

1. Artists 2. Sculptors 3. Architects 4. Florence (Italy) -- Fiction 5. Italy -- History -- 0-1559 -- Fiction 6. Santa Maria del Fiore (Cathedral: Florence, Italy) -- Fiction

ISBN 978-1-57091-655-7; 1-57091-655-1

LC 2007002283

In fifteenth-century Florence, Italy, a contest is held to design a magnificent dome for the town's cathedral, but when Pippo the Fool claims he will win the contest, everyone laughs at him. Based on the true story of Filippo Brunelleschi.

This is "told with a great deal of charm and buttressed by understated humor. . . . Estrada's timeless art highlights Florence's orange-roofed architecture and colorfully attired citizens." Booklist

Fernandes, Eugenie

Kitten's summer; [by] Eugenie Fernandes. Kids Can Press 2011 un il $14.95
Grades: PreK   E

1. Stories in rhyme 2. Cats -- Fiction 3. Summer -- Fiction

ISBN 978-1-55453-342-8; 1-55453-342-2

"As rain begins to fall, Kitten dashes home. . . . Using rhyming couplets, the text tracks her progress and the critters she passes by. . . . Fernandes's clay, acrylic paint, and mixed-media collage artwork creates a unique look for the forest and its denizens. There is a tremendous amount of detail and charm in these realistic vignettes." SLJ

Other titles about Kitten are:

Kitten's autumn (2010)
Kitten's spring (2010)
Kitten's winter (2011)

Kitten's winter; written and illustrated by Eugenie Fernandes. Kids Can Press 2011 un il $14.95
Grades: PreK K 1   E

1. Stories in rhyme 2. Cats -- Fiction 3. Winter --

Fiction

ISBN 978-1-55453-343-5; 1-55453-343-0

Winter comes to Kitten's world, and the little calico leaves her cozy home for an afternoon of exploration and discovery.

"In Kitten's fourth seasonal adventure, the inquisitive feline explores a snowy woodland landscape. Ten simple couplets--"Snow blows, / Kitten hurries. / Pond freezes / Fox scurries"--are accompanied by mixed-media collage illustrations with alluring wood and clay textures. The cross-section visual perspective offers above-and-below-ground vantage points, adding a glimpse at some animals' dens, nests, and hibernation practices." Horn Book

Ferry, Beth

Stick and Stone; by Beth Ferry; illustrated by Tom Lichtenheld. Houghton Mifflin Harcourt 2015 48 p. $16.99

Grades: PreK K 1 2   E

1. Stories in rhyme 2. Stones -- Fiction 3. Friendship -- Fiction 4. Best friends -- Fiction 5. Staffs (Sticks, canes, etc.) -- Fiction

ISBN 054403256X; 9780544032569

LC 2014012651

In this story by Beth Ferry, illustrated by Tom Lichtenheld, "when Stick rescues Stone from a prickly situation with a Pinecone, the pair becomes fast friends. But when Stick gets stuck, can Stone return the favor? . . . [This] warm, rhyming text . . . includes a subtle anti-bullying message even the youngest reader will understand." (Publisher's note)

Finchler, Judy

★ **Miss** Malarkey leaves no reader behind. Walker & Company 2006 un il $16.95; lib bdg $17.85

Grades: K 1 2 3   E

1. School stories 2. Teachers -- Fiction 3. Books and reading -- Fiction

ISBN 978-0-8027-8084-3; 0-8027-8084-9; 978-0-8027-8085-0 lib bdg; 0-8027-8085-7 lib bdg

LC 2005037182

Miss Malarkey vows to find each of her students a book to love by the end of the school year, but one video-game loving boy proves to be a challenge.

"O'Malley's illustrations, done in markers and colored pencils, enhance the text with expressive pictures. . . . A must-have for all libraries." SLJ

Other titles about Miss Malarkey are:

Congratulations, Miss Malarkey! (2009)

Miss Malarkey doesn't live in Room 10 (1995)

Miss Malarkey won't be in today (1998)

Miss Malarkey's field trip (2004)

Testing Miss Malarkey (2000)

You're a good sport, Miss Malarkey (2002)

Fine, Edith Hope

Armando and the blue tarp school; [by] Edith Hope Fine & Judith Pinkerton Josephson; illustrated by Hernan Sosa. Lee & Low 2007 un il lib bdg $16.95

Grades: K 1 2 3   E

1. School stories 2. Mexico -- Fiction 3. Poverty -- Fiction

ISBN 978-1-58430-278-0

"This poignant picture book . . . is based on a true story. . . . [It is illustrated with] clear, unframed, double-page pictures in watercolor and ink with thick white outlines. . . .

Without melodrama, Armando's story shows what poverty means and the hope that things can change." Booklist

Fischer, Scott M.

Jump! [by] Scott Fischer. Simon & Schuster Books for Young Readers 2010 un il $14.99

Grades: PreK K   E

1. Stories in rhyme 2. Fear -- Fiction 3. Animals -- Fiction

ISBN 978-1-4169-7884-8; 1-4169-7884-4

LC 2008025861

From bugs and frogs to alligators and whales, frightened animals always move out of the way of a larger opponent.

"With simple, rhyming text and action-packed artwork, this picture book will appeal to young preschoolers. . . . Even after kids have figured out what is coming, they will enjoy the animals' shifts in power roles, all depicted in lively drawings, rendered in thick black lines and strong, bright colors against blank white space." Booklist

Fisher, Aileen Lucia

The **story** goes on; illustrated by Mique Moriuchi. Roaring Brook Press 2004 un il $16.95

Grades: PreK K 1 2   E

1. Stories in rhyme 2. Food chains (Ecology)

ISBN 1-59643-037-0

LC 2003-18143

An illustrated poem about the cycle of life—bug eats plant, frog eats bug, snake eats frog, hawk eats snake, and so on

"With bright colors, rhyming text, and collage illustrations, this circular tale points out the interdependence of life. . . . This offering is a visual treat and an engaging opportunity to introduce the cycle of life to young readers." SLJ

Fisher, Carolyn

The **Snow** Show; with Chef Kelvin. producer, Carolyn Fisher. Harcourt 2008 un il $17

Grades: K 1 2 3   E

1. Snow -- Fiction 2. Cooking -- Fiction 3. Television programs -- Fiction

ISBN 978-0-15-206019-0; 0-15-206019-7

LC 2007031724

A cooking show goes on location to the North Pole to demonstrate the recipe for making snow.

"The visually dynamic, digitally created art features lettering that helps tell the story. . . . Fisher includes collage, dialogue asides, arrows, onomatopoeic descriptors, and fact boxes, yet maintains clarity, cohesion, and purpose." SLJ

Fisher, Valorie

Everything I need to know before I'm five. Schwartz & Wade 2011 un il $17.99; lib bdg $20.99

Grades: PreK K 1   E

1. Color 2. Numbers 3. Seasons 4. Alphabet 5. Concepts 6. Geometry 7. Opposites

ISBN 978-0-375-86865-8; 0-375-86865-8; 978-0-375-96865-5 lib bdg; 0-375-96865-2 lib bdg

LC 2010031265

Fisher "gives preschoolers a leg up on need-to-know information in this energetic collection. In candy-colored multimedia collages, . . . she presents such topics as weather, seasons, and numbers up to 20. . . . Considering all the titles on just one of these topics, these vintage/tacky photo-spreads are worth several books in one, even as they display the vast potential in rummage sales and vending machines." Publ Wkly

My big brother. Atheneum Bks. for Young Readers 2002 un il $15.95

Grades: PreK K 1   E

1. Brothers -- Fiction

ISBN 0-689-84327-5

LC 2001-22947

Photographs and simple text depict a big brother from the point of view of his baby sibling

"The design is clean and strong, and the colors, textures, and lines all lead the eye to the important parts of the story. Together the text and the pictures tell a funny, very tender story of sibling relationships." Booklist

Fitzpatrick, Marie-Louise

There. Roaring Brook Press 2009 un il $17.95

Grades: K 1 2   E

1. Questions and answers 2. Growth -- Fiction

ISBN 978-1-59643-087-7; 1-59643-087-7

LC 2008-54266

A young girl asks questions about growing up as she walks over rolling hills, climbs a ladder up to the stars, and meets a dragon.

This "is a book for rumination, a rare permission to ask the unanswerable questions. The thoughts that propel it and the images that illuminate it make this volume a small wonder for children." SLJ

Flack, Marjorie

Ask Mr. Bear. Macmillan 1958 un il $15.95; pa $6.99

Grades: PreK K 1   E

1. Animals -- Fiction 2. Birthdays -- Fiction

ISBN 0-02-735390-7; 0-02-043090-6 pa

First published 1932

Danny did not know what to give his mother for a birthday present, so he set out to ask various animals—the hen, the duck, the goose, the lamb, the cow and others, but he met with very little success until he met Mr. Bear

This "will have a strong appeal to very young children because of its repetition, its use of the most familiar animals, its gay pictures and the cumulative effect of the story." N Y Times Book Rev

Flaherty, Alice

The **luck** of the Loch Ness monster; a tale of picky eating. [by] A. W. Flaherty; illustrated by Scott Magoon. Houghton Mifflin 2007 un il $16

Grades: K 1 2 3   E

1. Scotland -- Fiction 2. Ocean travel -- Fiction 3. Loch Ness monster -- Fiction

ISBN 978-0-618-55644-1; 0-618-55644-3

LC 2006026083

"A girl is traveling alone to visit her grandmother in Scotland. . . . She tosses her dreaded morning oatmeal overboard, only to attract the attention of a tiny sea worm that gobbles it up and immediately quadruples in size. . . . This pourquoi tale about how the Loch Ness Monster came to be has a lot of imagination and wonderful storytelling techniques. Dark, cartoonlike watercolors exhibit an excellent use of perspective." SLJ

Fleischman, Paul

The **animal** hedge; illustrated by Bagram Ibatoulline. Candlewick Press 2003 un il $16.99

Grades: K 1 2 3   E

1. Animals -- Fiction 2. Farmers -- Fiction

ISBN 0-7636-1606-0

LC 2002-23751

A newly illustrated edition of the title first published 1983 by Dutton

After being forced to sell the animals he loves, a farmer cuts his hedge to look like them and teaches his sons about following their hearts

"Ibatoulline's watercolor-and-gouache illustrations, inspired by 19th-century American folk-art paintings, are the perfect complement to this simple allegory." SLJ

The **birthday** tree; illustrated by Barry Root. Candlewick Press 2008 un il $16.99

Grades: K 1 2 3   E

1. Trees -- Fiction

ISBN 978-0-7636-2604-4

LC 2007-32344

A newly illustrated edition of the title first published 1979 by Harper & Row

When Jack goes to sea, his parents watch as the tree planted at his birth reflects his fortunes and misfortunes

"Precisely worded and fluid in the telling, the story has a timeless quality that is echoed in the expressive watercolor artwork." Booklist

★ The **Matchbox** diary; Paul Fleischman, illustrated by Bagram Ibatoulline. Candlewick Press 2013 40 p. $16.99

Grades: 1 2 3 4 5   E

1. Memory -- Fiction 2. Diaries -- Fiction 3. Immigrants -- United States -- Fiction

ISBN 0763646016; 9780763646011

LC 2012942613

In this children's story, by Newbery Medalist Paul Fleischman and illustrated by Bagram Ibatoulline, "when a little girl visits her great-grandfather at his curio-filled home, she chooses an unusual object to learn about: an old cigar box. What she finds inside surprises her: a collection of matchboxes making up her great-grandfather's diary. . . . Together they tell of his journey from Italy to a new country, before he could read and write." (Publisher's note)

Sidewalk circus; presented by Paul Fleischman and Kevin Hawkes. Candlewick Press 2004 un il $15.99

Grades: PreK K 1 2 3   E

1. Stories without words 2. Circus -- Fiction 3. City and town life -- Fiction

ISBN 0-7636-1107-7

LC 2002-74168

"As posters advertising the world-renowned Garibaldi circus are put up along a busy city block, a girl waiting for a bus watches the circus of everyday life unfold. There is no actual text to the book, just the words of store signs, a scrolling theater marquee, and the show bills. What the girl imagines is revealed through the playful shadows of the people on the street and the corresponding circus flyers. . . . Hawkes's richly colored acrylic paintings sustain interest and pacing throughout the book. . . . This delightful book will fascinate children and help them to see their world with new eyes." SLJ

★ **Weslandia**; illustrated by Kevin Hawkes. Candlewick Press 1999 un il $15.99; pa $5.99

Grades: K 1 2 3   E

1. Plants -- Fiction 2. Gardening -- Fiction

ISBN 0-7636-0006-7; 0-7636-1052-6 pa

LC 98-30240

Wesley's garden produces a crop of huge, strange plants which provide him with clothing, shelter, food, and drink, thus helping him create his own civilization and changing his life

"This story about a nonconformist creating his own reality resonates with imagination and humor. . . . His natural creativity is reflected in Hawkes' vivid recreations of Wesley's altered environment, lush illustrations that have a realistic whimsy." Bull Cent Child Books

Fleming, Candace

★ **Boxes** for Katje; pictures by Stacey Dressen-McQueen. Farrar, Straus & Giroux 2003 un il $16

Grades: K 1 2 3   E

1. Netherlands -- Fiction 2. World War, 1939-1945 -- Fiction

ISBN 0-374-30922-1

LC 2002-20027

After a young Dutch girl writes to her new American friend in thanks for the care package sent after World War II, she begins to receive increasingly larger boxes

The story is "moving, and Dressen-McQueen's lively illustrations, in colored pencil, oil pastel, and acrylic, pack lots of color, pattern, and historical details onto every expansive page." Booklist

★ **Clever** Jack takes the cake; written by Candace Fleming; illustrated by G. Brian Karas. Schwartz & Wade Books 2010 un il

Grades: K 1 2 3   E

1. Fairy tales 2. Cake -- Fiction 3. Birthdays -- Fiction 4. Princesses -- Fiction 5. Storytelling -- Fiction

ISBN 0375849793; 0375956972 lib bdg; 9780375849794; 9780375956973 lib bdg

LC 2009030030

A poor boy named Jack struggles to deliver a birthday present worthy of the princess. "Ages five to eight." (Bull Cent Child Books)

"Jack accidentally receives an invitation to the princess's birthday party. He . . . bakes a wonderful cake. On his way to the castle, the cake is slowly demolished by crows, a troll, a spooky forest, a dancing bear, and even a palace guard, until the only present Jack has to offer . . . is the story of the cake's demise. . . . This entertaining adventure is packed with action. Karas's scratchy gouache and pencil cartoon illustrations are as detail-rich as the text itself." SLJ

The **hatmaker's** sign; a story. by Benjamin Franklin; retold by Candace Fleming; illustrated by Robert Andrew Parker. Orchard Bks. 1998 un il $16.95; lib bdg $17.99

Grades: K 1 2 3   E

1. Authors 2. Diplomats 3. Inventors 4. Statesmen 5. Architects 6. Presidents 7. Scientists 8. Vice-presidents 9. Essayists 10. Writers on science 11.

Members of Congress

ISBN 0-531-30075-7; 0-531-33075-3 lib bdg

LC 97-27596

To heal the hurt pride of Thomas Jefferson as Congress makes changes to his Declaration of Independence, Benjamin Franklin tells his friend the story of a hatmaker and his sign

"Based on an anecdote in The Papers of ThomasJefferson, the story has a folktale-like quality that lends itself to being read aloud. The illustrations give dimension to the characters and a sense of times past." Horn Book Guide

★ **Imogene's** last stand; written by Candice Fleming; illustrated by Nancy Carpenter. Schwartz & Wade Books 2009 un il $16.99; lib bdg $19.99

Grades: K 1 2   E

1. United States -- History -- Fiction

ISBN 978-0-375-83607-7; 0-375-83607-1; 978-0-375-93607-4 lib bdg; 0-375-93607-6 lib bdg

LC 2008-22458

Enamored of history, young Imogene Tripp tries to save her town's historical society from being demolished in order to build a shoelace factory.

"Fleming's sense of small-town space is impeccable; Carpenter's pen-and-ink art enjoyably scribbly; and the historical facts and quotes that bookend the story are just the thing to get new Imogenes fired up." Booklist

★ **Muncha!** Muncha! Muncha! illustrated by G. Brian Karas. Atheneum Bks. for Young Readers 2002 un il $16; lib bdg $18.63

Grades: PreK K 1 2   E

1. Rabbits -- Fiction 2. Gardening -- Fiction

ISBN 0-689-83152-8; 0-689-93652-X lib bdg

LC 99-24882

After planting the garden he has dreamed of for years, Mr. McGreely tries to find a way to keep some persistent bunnies from eating all his vegetables

"Fleming's text is lilting and deftly paced, with sound effects . . . strategically and enjoyably employed. . . . Karas' mixed-media (gouache, acrylic, and pencil) illustrations offer a cornucopia of plot-enriching details." Bull Cent Child Books

Another title about Mr. Greely and the bunnies is:

Tippy-tippy-tippy-hide! (2007)

★ **Oh,** no! Candace Fleming; [illustrations by Eric Rohmann] Schwartz & Wade Books 2012 40 p. $17.99

Grades: PreK K 1 2   E

1. Rescue work -- Fiction 2. Jungle animals -- Fiction 3. Picture books for children 4. Stories in rhyme 5. Animals -- Fiction

ISBN 0375842713; 9780375842719; 9780375945571

LC 2009045564

In this book, when a "frog falls into a deep hole . . , a . . mouse, . . . loris, . . . sun bear, and . . . monkey all tumble down after him during unsuccessful rescue attempts. . . . The animals face a lurking tiger eager to snack on the helpless group," who, in the end, is himself caught in the hole, seeking help. (School Library Journal)

Papa's mechanical fish; by Candace Fleming; pictures by Boris Kulikov. 1st ed. Margaret Ferguson Books 2013 40 p. ill. (chiefly col.) (reinforced) $16.99

Grades: 2 3 4   E

1. Picture books for children 2. Submarines -- Fiction 3. Inventors -- Fiction 4. Family life -- Fiction 5. Submarines (Ships) -- Fiction

ISBN 0374399085; 9780374399085

LC 2012029659

This children's picture book "profiles a would-be inventor and his indulgent family. Out fishing one day, daughter and narrator Virena happens to ask, "Papa . . . have you ever wondered what it's like to be a fish?"' At this, her "inspired father races for his workshop. To a refrain of 'Clink! Clankety-bang! Thump-whirrrr!' Papa sets to building a series of submarines, which he tests in Lake Michigan." (Publishers Weekly)

Seven hungry babies; illustrated by Eugene Yelchin. Atheneum Books for Young Readers 2010 un il $16.99

Grades: PreK K 1   E

1. Stories in rhyme 2. Birds -- Fiction

ISBN 978-1-4169-5402-6; 1-4169-5402-3

LC 2008-53481

A mother bird frantically tries to keep her seven baby birds fed.

"Fleming's playful text features endearments that will tickle listeners . . . and a rhythm that sweeps the story along. The fresh gouache illustrations are awash in blues and white with fire-bright red and yellow birds and feature expressive faces on the avian stars." SLJ

Sunny Boy! the life and times of a tortoise. pictures by Anne Wilsdorf. Farrar, Straus and Giroux 2005 un il $16

Grades: PreK K 1 2   E

1. Turtles -- Fiction

ISBN 0-374-37297-7

LC 2004-40451

In this fictionalized account, Sunny Boy, a 100-year-old tortoise, describes various events in his long life including the dangerous barrel ride over Niagara Falls that he takes with his daredevil owner on July 5, 1930

"This saga makes for wildly entertaining reading. . . . The comical cartoon narrative . . . enhances the textual flow of the story. Not to be missed is the author's fascinating historical note." SLJ

★ **This** is the baby; pictures by Maggie Smith. Farrar, Straus and Giroux 2004 un il $16.50

Grades: PreK K 1   E

1. Stories in rhyme 2. Infants -- Fiction 3. Clothing and dress -- Fiction

ISBN 0-374-37486-4

LC 2002-70941

A cumulative rhyme enumerating all the items of clothing that go on the baby who hates to be dressed, from the diaper often a mess to the jacket woolen and plaid.

"Smith's naive and rosy-cheeked characters, cozy textures, and crayon-box colors are a perfect accompaniment to Fleming's well-constructed, cumulative, 'House That Jack-Built' patterned story that positively insists on reader interaction." SLJ

Fleming, Denise

★ **Barnyard** banter. Holt & Co. 1994 un il $17.95; pa $7.95; bd bk $7.95

Grades: PreK K 1 2   E

1. Stories in rhyme 2. Animals -- Fiction

ISBN 0-8050-1957-X; 0-8050-5581-9 pa; 0-8050-6594-6 bd bk

LC 93-11032

All the farm animals are where they should be, clucking and mucking, mewing and cooing, except for the missing goose

"Strong rhythm and rhyme, plus fun onomatopoetic animal sounds, demand reading aloud. But even more delightful than the engaging text are Fleming's spectacular illustrations. . . . They create realistically textured, bold, bright settings for the whimsical critters to romp through." SLJ

★ **Beetle** bop. Harcourt 2007 un il $16

Grades: PreK K   E

1. Stories in rhyme 2. Beetles -- Fiction

ISBN 978-0-15-205936-1

LC 2006-09756

Illustrations and rhyming text reveal the great variety of beetles and their swirling, humming, crashing activities.

"Fleming creates a vibrant exciting portrait of often-overlooked creatures. Here she uses expertly crafted fiber collage to celebrate beetles, and both words and pictures vibrate with the relentless energy of the subject." Booklist

Buster. Holt & Co. 2003 un il $16.95; pa $6.95

Grades: PreK K 1 2   E

1. Cats -- Fiction 2. Dogs -- Fiction

ISBN 0-8050-6279-3; 0-8050-8757-5 pa

LC 2002-10857

Buster the dog thinks his perfect life is spoiled when Betty the cat comes to live with him, until he learns not to be afraid of cats

"Fleming's trademark handmade-paper artwork is awash with vibrant colors and dazzling details." SLJ

Another title about Buster is:

Buster goes to Cowboy Camp (2008)

Buster goes to Cowboy Camp. Henry Holt 2008 un il $16.95

Grades: PreK K 1 2   E

1. Dogs -- Fiction 2. Camps -- Fiction 3. West (U.S.) -- Fiction

ISBN 978-0-8050-7892-3; 0-8050-7892-4

LC 2007-12368

When Buster the dog's owner goes away for a few days, he sends Buster to Sagebrush Kennels for Cowboy Camp, where Buster is homesick at first, but then has fun herding balls into the corral, gathering sticks for a campfire, and making wanted posters with his pawprints.

"This sweet, simple story is steeped in the stuff of the Wild West. . . . Fleming extracts remarkable expression from her signature paper-pulp illustrations." Booklist

★ The **cow** who clucked. Henry Holt 2006 un il $16.95

Grades: PreK K 1 2   **E**
  1. Cattle -- Fiction 2. Animals -- Fiction
  ISBN 978-0-8050-7265-5; 0-8050-7265-9

                            LC 2005-22676

When a cow loses her moo, she searches to see if another animal in the barn has it

"The gentle inside jokes, the animal sounds, and the repetitive phrase constitute only a fraction of this book's appeal. Fleming is, after all, a thrilling illustrator whose pulp-painting technique brings subtlety and texture to densely colored art. . . . The layers of subtle humor and visual splendor are truly impressive." SLJ

★ The **everything** book. Holt & Co. 2000 64p il $18.95
Grades: PreK K   **E**
  ISBN 0-8050-6292-0

                            LC 99-53626

Fleming offers an illustrated introduction to such concepts as colors, shapes, numbers, animals, food, and seasons. "Ages two to five." (N Y Times Book Rev)

"The book includes everything needed to make it an anthology of preschool interests and concerns. . . . The very attractive illustrations, done in Fleming's characteristic bold and energetic style, were produced by pouring cotton pulp through hand-cut stencils, the result being simple forms that are attractively textured, with edges that are just fuzzy enough to look soft and friendly." SLJ

★ The **first** day of winter. Henry Holt and Co. 2005 un il $16.95
Grades: PreK K 1   **E**
  1. Snow -- Fiction 2. Winter -- Fiction
  ISBN 0-8050-7384-1

                            LC 2004-22181

A snowman is built and is given special gifts to put on by his best friend each day for ten days with cumulative items of gifts

"Fleming captures the tranquility and light of snowy days with her unique artistic style. Her paper-pulp and stencil illustrations depict a winter wonderland in which vibrant striped scarves, blue mittens, and red hats provide the color in a white, uncluttered landscape. . . . Quietly told and thoughtfully illustrated." SLJ

Go, shapes, go! Denise Fleming. Beach Lane Books 2013 40 p. color illustrations (hardcover) $17.99
Grades: PreK K 1   **E**
  1. Adventure fiction 2. Mice -- Fiction 3. Shape -- Fiction 4. Locomotion -- Fiction
  ISBN 9781442482401; 1442482400

                            LC 2013004899

In this children's book by Denise Fleming, readers join a "creative adventure with a gang of saucy shapes--and a mischievous mouse who wants to play too. Meet circles, rectangles, ovals, arcs, and a triangle and a square as well. Wait till you see what this crowd can make when they're all working together!" (Publisher's note)

"Tiny paper-collage Mouse gives various cut-paper shapes their marching—and rolling, bouncing, and slithering—orders in Fleming's (Underground) celebration of concepts and perception...The shapes themselves, snipped

from decorative handmade paper, are labeled, helping to introduce or reinforce readers' familiarity with them." PW

★ **In** the small, small pond. Holt & Co. 1993 un il $17.95; pa $7.95
Grades: PreK K 1   **E**
  1. Stories in rhyme 2. Pond ecology -- Fiction
  ISBN 0-8050-2264-3; 0-8050-5983-0 pa

                            LC 92-25770

A Caldecott Medal honor book, 1994

Illustrations and rhyming text describe the activities of animals living in and near a small pond as spring progresses to autumn

"The brilliant, primitive illustrations were made by pouring colored cotton pulp through hand-cut stencils. Against the eye-catching colors, the four-word rhymes in bold black print dance, each double-page spread picturing and describing a different creature. Text, pictures, layout, and design are all beautifully done." SLJ

★ **In** the tall, tall grass. Holt & Co. 1991 un il $17.95; pa $7.99
Grades: PreK K 1   **E**
  1. Stories in rhyme 2. Animals -- Fiction
  ISBN 0-8050-1635-X; 0-8050-3941-4 pa

                            LC 90-26444

Rhymed text (crunch, munch, caterpillars lunch) presents a toddler's view of creatures found in the grass from lunchtime till nightfall, such as bees, ants, and moles

"Boldly colored in grassy greens, sunny yellows, and evening blues, the impressionistic illustrations make this a real treat for eyes as well as ears." Booklist

★ **Lunch**. Holt & Co. 1993 un il $17.99; pa $7.99; bd bk $7.95
Grades: PreK K 1   **E**
  1. Color 2. Mice -- Fiction
  ISBN 0-8050-1636-8; 0-8050-4646-1 pa; 0-8050-5696-3 bd bk

                            LC 92-178

"Fleming continues to work in the medium of handmade paper built from layers of colored pulp that has been forced through a stencil. A huge typeface and the judicious use of large blocks of bold, solid color give this book a fresh look. Delectable fun, and, with its simple yet engaging plot, sure to be requested over and over by the youngest readers." Horn Book

★ **Mama** cat has three kittens. Holt & Co. 1998 un il $17.95; pa $7.95
Grades: PreK K 1   **E**
  1. Cats -- Fiction
  ISBN 0-8050-5745-5; 0-8050-7162-8 pa

                            LC 98-12249

While two kittens copy everything their mother does, their brother naps

"Fleming's kittens, created by pouring colored cotton pulp through hand-cut stencils, are large and bold and set against colorful backdrops. An excellent choice for reading aloud to groups." SLJ

★ **Pumpkin** eye. Holt & Co. 2001 un il $16.99; pa $7.95

Grades: PreK K 1   E
1. Stories in rhyme 2. Halloween -- Fiction
ISBN 0-8050-6681-0; 0-8050-7635-2 pa
LC 00-44850

Simple rhymes describe the sights, sounds, and smells of Halloween

"Fleming's homemade paper landscapes set off their midnight-blue—well, probably eight-o'clock blue—backdrops with glowing orange and white accents as well as with the rainbow of colors represented in the trick-or-treaters' costumes. . . . This will be just the shivery ticket for kids looking to move from Halloween giggles to genuine spookiness." Bull Cent Child Books

Shout! Shout it out! Henry Holt 2011 40p il $16.99
Grades: PreK K   E
1. Alphabet 2. Counting 3. Mice -- Fiction 4. Vocabulary -- Fiction
ISBN 978-0-8050-9237-0; 0-8050-9237-4
LC 2010011691

Mouse invites the reader to shout out what he or she knows as they review numbers, letters, and easy words.

"Fleming brings new dimension to her signature pulp-painting technique, using swatches of patterned paper collage and marker accents on her figures. . . . Children just learning their colors, animals, and ABCs will be invigorated, and those who have already mastered these basics will still enjoy the top-of-their lungs review." Publ Wkly

★ **Sleepy,** oh so sleepy. Henry Holt and Company 2010 un il $16.99
Grades: PreK   E
1. Animals -- Fiction 2. Bedtime -- Fiction 3. Mother-child relationship -- Fiction
ISBN 978-0-8050-8126-8; 0-8050-8126-7
LC 2009006151

Depicts a number of animal babies sleeping as a mother puts her own baby to bed.

"Formed using Fleming's signature medium of 'pulp painting,' which simultaneously creates the image and the paper that bears it, and accented with pastel pencil, the large-scale illustrations are bold in form and rich in color. With mesmerizing words rolling along, this large-format book does its job so well that it's hard to repress a contented yawn when the story winds down to its quiet ending." Booklist

★ **Time** to sleep. Holt & Co. 1997 un il $17.95; pa $7.95
Grades: PreK K 1   E
1. Winter -- Fiction 2. Animals -- Fiction 3. Hibernation -- Fiction
ISBN 0-8050-3762-4; 0-8050-6767-1 pa
LC 96-37553

When Bear notices that winter is nearly here he hurries to tell Snail, after which each animal tells another until finally the already sleeping Bear is awakened in his den with the news

"Fleming's simple text is ripe with astute observations of the natural world and animal behavior. . . . Fleming's 'pulp painting' style results in lushly textured handmade paper compositions saturated with earthy browns, reds and golds." Publ Wkly

Underground; Denise Fleming. Beach Lane Books 2012 40 p. (hardcover) $17.99
Grades: PreK K   E
1. Stories in rhyme 2. Animals -- Fiction 3. Burrowing animals -- Fiction 4. Underground areas -- Fiction
ISBN 1442458828; 9781442458826; 9781442458833
LC 2012007083

Fletcher, Ashlee
My dog, my cat. Tanglewood Press 2011 un il $13.95
Grades: PreK K 1   E
1. Cats -- Fiction 2. Dogs -- Fiction
ISBN 978-1-933718-22-4; 1-933718-22-6; 1933718226; 9781933718224
LC 2010032919

A child points out the differences between a dog and a cat, but finds something they have in common, as well.

"Fletcher outlines the friendly blue dog and orange cat in thick, dark lines and surrounds each picture with a wide squiggly frame. The trim size, simple text, predictable story pattern, and obvious picture clues make this book a fine choice for beginning readers." SLJ

Fletcher, Ralph
The **Sandman**; [by] Ralph Fletcher; illustrated by Richard Cowdrey. Henry Holt and Company 2008 un il $16.95
Grades: PreK K 1 2   E
1. Sleep -- Fiction 2. Bedtime -- Fiction 3. Dragons -- Fiction
ISBN 978-0-8050-7726-1; 0-8050-7726-X
LC 2007002831

A tiny little man discovers that sand made from a dragon's scale will send him to dreamland, and begins carrying this magical sand to children each night to give them the gift of sleep

"Fletcher's smoothly written story flows in a thoroughly plausible way and is beautifully served by Cowdrey's vibrant acrylic paintings." SLJ

Fletcher, Susan
Dadblamed Union Army cow; [by] Susan Fletcher; illustrated by Kimberly Bulcken Root. Candlewick Press 2007 un il $16.99
Grades: 2 3 4 5   E
1. Cattle -- Fiction 2. United States -- History -- 1861-1865, Civil War -- Fiction
ISBN 978-0-7636-2263-3; 0-7636-2263-X
LC 2006051833

During the Civil War, a devoted cow follows her owner when he joins the Union Army and, despite all his efforts to send her home, stays with him and his regiment until the end of the war. Based on a true story

"Root's pencil and watercolor drawings vividly render the Civil War landscape. . . . A terrific read-aloud, and a marvelous approach to history." Publ Wkly

Flett, Julie
Wild berries; by Julie Flett; translated by Earl N. Cook. Simply Read Books 2013 32 p. $16.95
Grades: PreK K 1 2 3   E
1. Berries -- Fiction 2. Bilingual books -- English-Cree 3. Grandmothers -- Fiction
ISBN 1897476892; 9781897476895

In this picture book, by Julie Flett, "spend the day picking wild blueberries with Clarence and his grandmother. Meet ant, spider, and fox in a . . . woodland landscape. . . . This book is written in both Enlglish and Cree, in particular the n-dialect, also known as Swampy Cree from the Cumberland House area." (Publisher's note)

"Clarence and his grandma pick "wild berries / pikaciminisa." Each double-page spread describes the sights and sounds and also uses one word in a dialect of Cree (the "n" dialect, known as Swampy Cree), highlighted in red font. The muted earth tones of the watercolor and collage illustrations perfectly complement the quiet story. A pronunciation guide and glossary are appended." (Horn Book)

Floca, Brian

Five trucks; Brian Floca. Simon & Schuster 2014 32 p. il $17.99

Grades: PreK K 1 2   E

1. Counting 2. Trucks -- Fiction 3. Airports -- Fiction
ISBN 1481405934; 9781481405935

LC 9819834

This book, by Brian Floca, "features airport vehicles rarely seen in preschool books as well as the trucks' diverse drivers (men and women of various ethnicities). Unlike most counting books, the story introduces ordinal numbers (first, second, etc.) rather than cardinals (one, two, three). On the second appearance of each truck, the text counts back from the fifth to the first truck, adding another concept covered in the book." (School Library Journal)

"Five drivers for five trucks" begins this concept book, as five workers head out across a tarmac to prepare an airplane for take-off. At close inspection, there's more to see--a boy, his dad, and an overstuffed, rainbow-colored plaid suitcase pop up in various illustrations. The book's simplicity is engaging and age appropriate--even those who are vague about airport operations will catch on quickly." Horn Book

Flood, Nancy Bo

Cowboy up! ride the navajo rodeo. Nancy Bo Flood. WordSong 2013 48 p. (hardcover) $17.95

Grades: 1 2 3 4 5   E

1. Rodeos 2. Navajo Indians
ISBN 1590788931; 9781590788936

LC 2012949009

This book looks at the "history and tradition of the Navajo rodeo" through a day-in-the-life account. "Short narrative poems accompany each spread, recounting the anticipation, determination, danger, and excitement of the day. . . . An announcer guides readers through the book (and each individual event) page by page." (School Library Journal)

Flora, James

The **day** the cow sneezed; story and pictures by James Flora. Enchanted Lion Books 2010 un il $16.95

Grades: K 1 2 3   E

1. Tall tales 2. Cattle -- Fiction 3. Animals -- Fiction 4. Sneezing -- Fiction
ISBN 978-1-59270-097-4; 1-59270-097-7

LC 2010025866

First published 1957 by Harcourt, Brace & World, Inc
A cow sneezes and sets off a series of ridiculous events.
"Flora's illustrations are rich and varied. It doesn't take long to read the text, but children will spend hours with the pictures." Horn Book Guide

Florian, Douglas

★ **Shiver** me timbers; Douglas Florian; illustrated by Robert Neubecker. Beach Lane Books 2012 32 p.

Grades: 2 3 4   E

1. Pirates -- Poetry
ISBN 1442413212; 9781442413214

LC 2010048963

In this collection of "pirate poems and paintings" for children by Douglas Florian, illustrated by Robert Neubecker, "readers will meet scoundrels, scalawags, and scurvy dogs (human and canine). They'll partake in battles, treasure hunts, and some pirate-style grub (flounder, anyone?)" (Publisher's note)

Flournoy, Valerie

The **patchwork** quilt; pictures by Jerry Pinkney. Dial Bks. for Young Readers 1985 un il $16.99

Grades: K 1 2 3   E

1. Quilts -- Fiction 2. Family life -- Fiction 3. African Americans -- Fiction
ISBN 0-8037-0097-0

LC 84-1711

Coretta Scott King Award for illustration

Using scraps cut from the family's old clothing, Tanya helps her grandmother and mother make a beautiful quilt that tells the story of her Afro-American family's life

"Plentiful full-page and double-page paintings in pencil, graphite and watercolor are vivid yet delicately detailed. . . . Giving a sense of dramatization to the text, . . . the illustrations provide just the right style and mood for the story." SLJ

Foggo, Cheryl

Dear baobab; written by Cheryl Foggo; illustrated by Qin Leng. Second Story 2011 il $15.95

Grades: K 1 2 3   E

1. Trees -- Fiction 2. Orphans -- Fiction 3. Immigrants -- Fiction 4. Africans -- United States -- Fiction
ISBN 978-1-8971-8791-3; 1-8971-8791-2

"Maiko used to live in a village in Africa. He misses his home and the 2000-year-old baobab tree beneath which he and other village children sat. . . . Now, since the death of his parents, the lonely child lives in what appears to be a North American city. . . . He likes to sit on the stone steps outside his red brick house where a little spruce tree has sprung up. . . . When its roots begin to threaten the foundation of the house, something needs to be done. . . . The tree is moved and replanted elsewhere, just as Maiko has been. Leng's colorful, cartoonlike watercolor illustrations impart a sense of warmth and emotion to this story of a child's bewildering sense of loss and loneliness, as well as new beginnings." SLJ

Fogliano, Julie

★ **And** then it's spring; Julie Fogliano; illustrated by Erin E. Stead. Roaring Brook Press 2012 32 p.

Grades: PreK K 1   E

1. Seeds -- Fiction 2. Spring -- Fiction 3. Gardening -- Fiction 4. Picture books for children 5. Gardens -- Fiction
ISBN 9781596436244

LC 2010049379

This picture book is about a boy who gardens and explores the seasonal changes of "spring. . . . Amid the brown "all around," he plants seeds, and he waits hopefully for the miracle of their growth; he trudges through in the rain and squelches out in the post-rain puddles to check, but there's no sign of progress. As the weeks of waiting go by and the earth remains stubbornly brown, the boy fears that disaster ("maybe it was the birds . . . or maybe it was the bears and all that stomping") has befallen his would-be crop. Eventually, though, spring, real spring, comes, greening up the earth and sprouting the young gardener's young seedlings." (Bulletin of the Center for Children's Books)

★ **If** you want to see a whale; Julie Fogliano; Erin E. Stead. 1st ed. Roaring Brook Press 2013 32 p. ill. (hardcover) $16.99

Grades: PreK K 1   **E**

1. Patience -- Fiction 2. Whale-watching -- Fiction
ISBN 1596437316; 9781596437319

LC 2012012988

This children's book by Julie Fogliano presents a "story about a boy, his animal friends (a basset hound and a bird) and practicing patience. Whale watching requires lots of resolve to avoid distractions like birds, roses, pirate ships, clouds, pelicans and so on. . . . The poem's unresolved ellipses at the conclusion suggest an unending whale hunt, but [illustrator Erin] Stead's final two images silently deliver what we've been waiting for." (Kirkus Reviews)

Foley, Greg

Purple Little Bird. Balzer + Bray 2011 un il $14.99

Grades: PreK K 1 2   **E**

1. Birds -- Fiction 2. Color -- Fiction 3. Houses -- Fiction 4. Animals -- Fiction 5. Happiness -- Fiction
ISBN 978-0-06-200828-2; 0-06-200828-5

LC 2010030617

Purple Little Bird leaves his almost-perfect purple home in search of a better place, but although Brown Bear, Yellow Camel, and others live in very nice places, none is quite right for him.

"The economical text packs in a surprising amount. . . . Foley uses a crayon palette to good effect, with warm hues and quick strokes that color outside the friendly cartoon lines and fill the page. . . . Satisfying for the very youngest." Kirkus

Thank you Bear; by Greg Foley. Viking 2007 un il $15.99

Grades: PreK K   **E**

1. Mice -- Fiction 2. Bears -- Fiction 3. Boxes -- Fiction 4. Gifts -- Fiction
ISBN 978-0-670-06165-5

LC 2006016881

Despite the criticism of others, a bear finds the perfect gift for his mouse friend

"Bear's journey from euphoria to doubt to euphoria again is gently rendered. . . . Pastels provide the backdrop for the text, while Bear and his detractors stand in contrast on a white page, carrying the story with their expressions and body language." SLJ

Other titles about Bear are:
Don't worry Bear (2008)
Good luck Bear (2009)
I miss you Mouse (2010)

★ **Willoughby** & the lion. Bowen Press 2009 un il $17.99; lib bdg $18.89

Grades: PreK K 1 2   **E**

1. Lions -- Fiction 2. Magic -- Fiction 3. Wishes -- Fiction 4. Friendship -- Fiction
ISBN 978-0-06-154750-8; 0-06-154750-6; 978-0-06-154751-5 lib bdg; 0-06-154751-4 lib bdg

LC 2008000430

When Willoughby moves to a new house far away from his friends, he meets an enchanted lion who shows him what is truly important in life

Foley "scores points for unique visual presentation in this sumptuously produced, two-color book, instantly distinguished by its heavily embossed jacket. . . . With every wish, the ratio of gold to gray increases and Foley's compositions, mingling line drawings with digitally manipulated b&w photos, become more complex. . . . The elegant combination of the two basic colors boosts the visual impact exponentially." Publ Wkly

Another title about Willoughby is:
Willoughby & the moon (2010)

Folgueira, Rodrigo

Ribbit! written by Rodrigo Folguiera; illustrated by Poly Bernatene. Alfred A. Knopf 2013 32 p. (library) $18.99

Grades: PreK K 1   **E**

1. Pigs -- Fiction 2. Animals -- Fiction 3. Friendship -- Fiction
ISBN 9780307981462; 9780307981479; 9780307981509

LC 2012012718

"In a warm, funny and beautifully illustrated story of friendship that is perfect for reading aloud, a group of frogs are living happily in a peaceful pond, until they discover a surprise visitor, a little pink pig, whose behavior causes some misunderstanding." Publisher's note

"When pond frogs discover a croaking piglet in their midst, they assume he is teasing them by using their[cf] sound. Other animals offer opinions but it isn't until they all consult with the wise old beetle that they realize the pig just wants a friend. Bernatene's playful, saturated watercolors bring life and humor to the slightly strained text." Horn Book

Ford, Bernette

★ **First** snow; illustrated by Sebastien Braun. Holiday House 2005 un il $16.95

Grades: PreK K 1 2   **E**

1. Snow -- Fiction 2. Night -- Fiction 3. Rabbits -- Fiction
ISBN 0-8234-1937-1

LC 2004-55257

A family of young rabbits goes into a meadow at night to explore and play in winter's first snow.

"Ford's text has a poetic rhythm that emphasizes the senses as the rabbits explore their wintry world. . . . Braun's illustrations . . . are particularly engaging and complement the story wonderfully." SLJ

No more blanket for Lambkin. Boxer Books 2009 un il $12.95

Grades: PreK   **E**

1. Ducks -- Fiction 2. Sheep -- Fiction 3. Blankets -- Fiction 4. Friendship -- Fiction
ISBN 978-1-906250-28-7; 1-906250-28-6

"One day Lambkin's friend Ducky comes to visit and decides that they should play laundry day, immediately zeroing in on her friend's much-loved and rather-soiled blanket. Lambkin is none too happy, but she decides it is worth it to play with Ducky. Once the blanket is washed, it's cleaner, but it's also smaller and has some holes. Lambkin is upset, but Ducky surprises her by turning the blanket into a little toy lamb. This is a good story to read to young children when it is nearing the time to give up their blankets. . . . The overall feel is one of gentleness, from the soft style of illustrations to the tone of the dialogue between the two friends." SLJ

No more bottles for Bunny! [by] Bernette Ford and [illustrations by] Sam Williams. Sterling Pub. 2007 un il $12.95
Grades: PreK   E
1. Pigs -- Fiction 2. Ducks -- Fiction 3. Growth -- Fiction 4. Rabbits -- Fiction 5. Bottle feeding -- Fiction
ISBN 978-1-905417-34-6; 1-905417-34-9
LC 2007006856
Bunny gives up his bottle so he can have tea and cookies just like the big kids
"This tough topic is handled subtly but the point is made. Complementing this endearing tale are expressive, bright watercolor illustrations with black outlines that make them jump out from the page." SLJ

No more diapers for Ducky! [by] Bernette Ford and [illustrations by] Sam Williams. Sterling Pub. 2006 un il $12.95
Grades: PreK   E
1. Ducks -- Fiction 2. Toilet training -- Fiction
ISBN 1-905417-08-X
When Piggy can't come out to play because he is using the potty, Ducky decides it's time for him to learn to use the potty too.
"The interaction between these toddlers and their implicit support of one another is charming. The dynamic characters, done in thick charcoal outlines and watercolor, are set against a white background." SLJ

Ford, Christine
   Ocean's child; by Chistine Ford and Trish Holland; illustrated by David Diaz. Golden Books 2009 un il $15.99; lib bdg $18.99
Grades: PreK K 1 2   E
1. Inuit -- Fiction 2. Bedtime -- Fiction 3. Marine animals -- Fiction
ISBN 978-0-375-84752-3; 0-375-84752-9; 978-0-375-95752-9 lib bdg; 0-375-95752-9 lib bdg
"As an Inuit mother paddles her baby home at dusk, she identifies baby ocean animals as they prepare for night. . . . The language is warm and assuring bedtime fare with two free-verse lines introducing each animal, followed by a refrain. . . . Close inspection of mother and child's parkas reveal delicate indigenous designs. . . . The soothing flow of rhythmic language and elegant images creates a serenity just right for bedtimes." Booklist

Fore, S. J.
   Read to Tiger; illustrated by R.W. Alley. Viking 2010 un il $15.99

Grades: PreK K 1   E
1. Noise -- Fiction 2. Tigers -- Fiction 3. Books and reading -- Fiction
ISBN 978-0-670-01140-7; 0-670-01140-1
LC 2009-35147
A little boy who wants to read his book keeps being distracted by a tiger who is busy chomping on gum, growling, and practicing karate kicks.
"Fore and Alley play with sound effects and comic expressions, which will please a read-aloud audience. The spare ink drawings expand on Tiger's amusing antics." SLJ
Another title about Tiger is:
Tiger can't sleep (2006)

Foreman, Jack
   Say hello; [by] Jack & Michael Foreman. Candlewick Press 2008 un il $15.99
Grades: PreK K 1 2   E
1. Stories in rhyme 2. Dogs -- Fiction 3. Friendship -- Fiction
ISBN 978-0-7636-3657-9; 0-7636-3657-6
"A simple story about loneliness and the power of friendliness. Spare charcoal, pastel, and colored pencil drawings illustrate [this book]." SLJ

Foreman, Mark
   Grandpa Jack's tattoo tales; [by] Mark Foreman. Farrar, Straus & Giroux 2007 un il $16
Grades: PreK K 1 2   E
1. Sea stories 2. Tattooing -- Fiction 3. Grandfathers -- Fiction 4. Storytelling -- Fiction
ISBN 978-0-374-32768-2; 0-374-32768-8
LC 2006040853
Chloe loves to spend time at her grandparents' restaurant, where she gets to hear Grandpa Jack's stories about the many tattoos that commemorate events in his life at sea
The illustrations are "done in bright crisp watercolors . . . and the pictures are filled with minute details. . . . Children will relish this amusing tall tale and delight in its visual elements." SLJ

Foreman, Michael
   Fortunately, unfortunately. Andersen Press 2011 un il $16.95
Grades: PreK K 1 2   E
1. Adventure fiction
ISBN 0-7613-7460-4; 978-0-7613-7460-2
LC 2010032952
On his way to return his grandmother's umbrella, Milo has a series of unlikely adventures, some more fortunate than others.
"Brightly colored, cartoon-style characters (some large but not too ominous) cavorting across the oversize pages convey the lively action. These eye-catching illustrations and the briskly paced text make this a natural for group sharing." Booklist

   Friends; Michael Foreman. Lerner Pub. Group 2012 32 p. (trade hard cover: alk. paper) $16.95
Grades: PreK K 1   E
1. Picture books for children 2. Animal behavior -- Fiction 3. Conduct of life -- Fiction 4. Cats -- Fiction

5. Fishes -- Fiction 6. Friendship -- Fiction
ISBN 1467703176; 9781467703178

LC 2011051456

Author Michael Foreman presents a picture book on the relationship between a goldfish and a cat. "Bubble is a goldfish who swims around and around unhappily in his tank. Cat is his friend and wishes he could show him the world. One day, Cat has an idea to set Bubble free. But is Bubble ready to swim off into the world and leave his friend behind?" (Publisher's note)

The **littlest** dinosaur's big adventure; written and illustrated by Michael Foreman. Walker & Co. 2009 un il $16.99
Grades: PreK K 1 2   **E**
1. Size -- Fiction 2. Dinosaurs -- Fiction
ISBN 978-0-8027-9545-8; 0-8027-9545-5

LC 2008-40297

The littlest dinosaur discovers the advantages of being small as he frolics among the lily pads with his new frog friends, and then bravely finds his way home after getting lost in the woods

"Foreman's soft and gentle cartoon-style illustrations are tailored for young eyes and hearts. Sharing the book aloud will invite discussion as Foreman leaves readers a well-marked trail for inference and reflection, while the twists and turns of the plot will keep even the youngest audiences riveted." SLJ

Another title about the littlest dinosaur is:
The littlest dinosaur (2008)

Mia's story; a sketchbook of hopes and dreams. Candlewick Press 2006 un il $15.99
Grades: 1 2 3   **E**
1. Dogs -- Fiction 2. Chile -- Fiction 3. Flowers -- Fiction
ISBN 0-7636-3063-2

LC 2005-53183

"Mia's father harvests scrap metal from the nearby dump and sells it in the city. When Mia's dog Poco disappears one winter day, she rides a horse into the mountains to look for him, gathers some flowering plants she has never seen before, and brings them back to her village, where they change the landscape and her fortunes for the better. . . . This unusual book offers an engaging story, graceful illustrations, and a rare glimpse of a child's life in contemporary Chile." Booklist

Forler, Nan
Bird child. Tundra Books 2009 un il $19.95
Grades: K 1 2 3   **E**
1. Bullies -- Fiction 2. Friendship -- Fiction
ISBN 0-88776-894-6; 978-0-88776-894-1

"Silently, Eliza observes new girl Lainey's ostracism due to her unusual appearance, watching as the bullying increases, refraining from intervention when Lainey is brutally pushed in the snow. The authentic voice portrays bullying's devastating impact. . . . Eliza's mother gently guides her daughter to a moral decision. The symbolism of flight is woven through the narrative. Thisdale's vibrant mixed-media art plays with dominance and size in its compositions; drawings, paintings and digital images add layers of context. . . . This is a sensitive account through an empowered youngster's eyes." Kirkus

Formento, Alison
These bees count! Alison Formento; illustrated by Sarah Snow. Albert Whitman & Co. 2012 32 p.
Grades: PreK K 1 2   **E**
1. Counting 2. Bees -- Fiction 3. Honeybee -- Fiction 4. Beekeepers -- Fiction 5. School field trips -- Fiction 6. Human-animal communication -- Fiction
ISBN 0807578681; 9780807578681

LC 2011008567

This children's story by Alison Formento, illustrated by Sarah Snow, provides a lesson both in basic counting and in the ecological importance of bees. "How do bees count? The bees at the Busy Bee Farm buzz through the sky as one big swarm, fly over two waving dandelions, find three wild strawberries dripping tasty nectar." As the children in Mr. Tate's class listen, they learn how bees work to produce honey and make food and flowers grow. Bees count--they're important to us all." (Publisher's note)

This tree counts! illustrated by Sarah Snow. Albert Whitman 2010 un il $16.99
Grades: PreK K 1 2   **E**
1. Counting 2. Trees -- Fiction 3. Ecology -- Fiction
ISBN 0-8075-7890-8; 978-0-8075-7890-2

As Mr. Tate's class prepares to plant saplings, they hear the giant oak tree in their schoolyard tell about all the animal life it supports.

"Snow's collage illustrations add texture and natural beauty to the story. . . . The picture of the industrious kids working together in the grassy field under a bright blue sky epitomizes the story's theme of cooperation and friendship." SLJ

Forward, Toby
What did you do today? the first day of school. illustrated by Carol Thompson. Clarion Books 2004 29p il $15
Grades: PreK K 1   **E**
1. School stories 2. Mother-child relationship -- Fiction
ISBN 0-618-49586-X

LC 2004-2467

A child describes the events of the first day of school, from making sandwiches for lunch to holding a parent's hand on the walk home

"The parallels between a child's day at school and his mother's day at work are shown with insight and love in this cleverly designed book. . . . Thompson varies her pen-and-watercolor illustrations in surprising and eye-catching ways." Booklist

Fox, F. G.
Jean Laffite and the big ol' whale; pictures by Scott Cook. Farrar, Straus & Giroux 2003 un il $16
Grades: K 1 2 3   **E**
1. Tall tales 2. Whales -- Fiction 3. Mississippi River -- Fiction
ISBN 0-374-33669-5

LC 99-43733

When a huge white whale gets stuck between the banks of the Mississippi River causing the water to stop flowing, Jean Laffite finds a way to get the river moving again

"This rollicking good yarn is brought to life with Cook's warm, glowing oil paintings full of action and humor." SLJ

Fox, Lee

Ella Kazoo will not brush her hair; illustrated by Jennifer Plecas. Walker & Co. 2010 un il $15.99; lib bdg $16.89

Grades: PreK K 1   E

1. Stories in rhyme 2. Hair -- Fiction

ISBN 978-0-8027-8836-8; 0-8027-8836-X; 978-0-8027-8755-2 lib bdg; 0-8027-8755-X lib bdg

LC 2009-13329

First published 2007 in Australia

A little girl refuses to brush her hair until it becomes so unruly that it takes over everything.

"Plecas's creative illustrations bring out quirky Ella and her story of stubbornness. The use of rhyme and its overall energy make this book a terrific read-aloud. . . . This book will definitely find fans in libraries serving the young and the young at heart." Libr Media Connect

Fox, Mem

The **goblin** and the empty chair; [illustrated by] Leo & Diane Dillon. Beach Lane Books 2009 un il $17.99

Grades: K 1 2 3   E

1. Monsters -- Fiction

ISBN 978-1-4169-8585-3; 1-4169-8585-9

LC 2008041862

A goblin who for many years has been hiding himself so that he does not frighten anyone finally finds a family

"The all-star team of Fox and the Dillons brings poise and sensitivity to this folksy tale of the pitfalls of self-perception. . . . The ink-and-watercolors are rigidly confined to uniform frames, but even these frames are ornately festooned with not-so-monstrous faces, further developing the story's theme." Booklist

Good night, sleep tight; written by Mem Fox; illustrated by Judy Horacek. Orchard Books 2013 32 p. ill. (reinforced) $16.99

Grades: PreK   E

1. Nursery rhymes -- Fiction 2. Storytelling -- Fiction 3. Nursery rhymes 4. Stories in rhyme 5. Bedtime -- Fiction 6. Babysitters -- Fiction

ISBN 0545533708; 9780545533706

LC 2012032174

In this book, written by Mem Fox and illustrated by Judy Horacek, Bonnie and Ben's favorite babysitter tells them nursery rhymes at bedtime--including "It's raining! It's pouring! The old man is snoring"; "This little piggy went to market"; and more. Bonnie and Ben enjoy the stories so much that they don't want to go to sleep; they want to hear each one again! Instead the babysitter tells them new nursery rhymes until, finally, all three of them fall fast sleep." (Publisher's note)

★ **Hattie** and the fox; illustrated by Patricia Mullins. Bradbury Press 1987 un il $16.95; pa $6.99

Grades: PreK K 1 2   E

1. Foxes -- Fiction 2. Chickens -- Fiction

ISBN 0-02-735470-9; 0-689-71611-7 pa

LC 86-18849

First published 1986 in Australia

"Bright, whimsical tissue collage and crayon illustrations add zest to this simple cumulative tale, and reveal more action than is expressed by the text alone." SLJ

★ **Hello** baby! illustrated by Steve Jenkins. Beach Lane Books 2009 un il $15.99

Grades: PreK K 1   E

1. Stories in rhyme 2. Animals -- Fiction 3. Infants -- Fiction 4. Animals -- Infancy

ISBN 978-1-4169-8513-6; 1-4169-8513-1

LC 2008-34421

A baby encounters a variety of young animals, including a clever monkey, a hairy warthog, and a dusty lion cub, before discovering the most precious creature of all.

This "has all the marks of a lap-sit classic. . . . While Fox is cooing as only she can, Jenkins . . . works his usual magic with cut paper. In many of his large-scale closeups . . . his subjects' big, expressive eyes seem locked in a gaze with the reader." Publ Wkly

Hunwick's egg; illustrated by Pamela Lofts. Harcourt 2005 un il $16

Grades: PreK K 1 2   E

1. Australia -- Fiction 2. Bandicoots -- Fiction

ISBN 0-15-216318-2

LC 2003-16385

When a wild storm sends a beautiful egg to Hunwick the bandicoot's burrow, he decides to give it a home and become its friend.

"This slightly offbeat story . . . is accompanied by glowing watercolor pencil illustrations in orange, pink, and violet tones that showcase the flora and fauna of the Australian landscape, adding an interesting element to this charming title." SLJ

★ **Koala** Lou; illustrated by Pamela Lofts. Harcourt Brace Jovanovich 1989 un il $16.95; pa $6.99

Grades: PreK K 1 2   E

1. Koalas -- Fiction

ISBN 0-15-200502-1; 0-15-200076-3 pa

LC 88-26810

First published 1988 in Australia

"A reassuring story for the child who feels neglected when siblings arrive." Child Book Rev Serv

Let's count goats! illustrated by Jan Thomas. Beach Lane Books 2010 un il $16.99

Grades: PreK K   E

1. Counting 2. Stories in rhyme 3. Goats -- Fiction

ISBN 978-1-4424-0598-1; 1-4424-0598-8

LC 2009-41627

The reader is invited to count goats of many shapes, sizes, hobbies, and professions.

"The traditional counting format receives a charming update as playfully expressive goats mimic human behavior. . . . Fox, an early-literacy specialist to the core, gets each rhyme just right. . . . Thomas's trademark digital spreads provide punch through chunky, dark outlines and zany off-kilter expressions. . . . These wacky goats guarantee a goofy good time." Kirkus

Night noises; written by Mem Fox; illustrated by Terry Denton. Harcourt Brace Jovanovich 1989 un il $16; pa $6

Grades: PreK K 1 2   E
1. Night -- Fiction 2. Sleep -- Fiction
ISBN 0-15-200543-9; 0-15-257421-2 pa

LC 89-2162

Old Lily Laceby dozes by the fire with her faithful dog Butch Aggie at her feet as strange night noises herald a surprising awakening

"With an almost joltingly bright palette . . . Denton has divided up many of the double-page spreads into three scenes: the main one depicting Lily Laceby and Butch Aggie in various stages of alertness, another showing the chronology of Lily's life, and the third cleverly revealing clues to the mysterious activity outdoors. The text, in Mem Fox's Houdini-like hands, reads beautifully—the language, pacing, tension, and sparks of excitement absolutely at one with the artwork." Horn Book

A **particular** cow; [by] Mem Fox; illustrated by Terry Denton. Harcourt 2006 un il $16
Grades: PreK K 1 2   E
1. Cattle -- Fiction
ISBN 0-15-200250-2

LC 2004030060

"When a cow decides to take her usual Saturday constitutional, she accidentally steps through a clothesline and ends up with a pair of bloomers covering her head. Unable to see and running off in a panic, the poor bovine wreaks havoc. . . . The story is told with a dry wit and an economy of words, and the illustrations interpret the action with panache." SLJ

★ **Sleepy** bears; illustrated by Kerry Argent. Harcourt Brace & Co. 1999 un il $16; pa $6
Grades: PreK K 1 2   E
1. Stories in rhyme 2. Bears -- Fiction 3. Bedtime -- Fiction
ISBN 0-15-202016-0; 0-15-216542-8 pa

LC 98-42640

"Mother Bear tucks in her six cubs, sending them off on dreamy adventures. Baxter dreams of pirates, Bella of the circus, Winifred of the jungle, Tosca of kingdoms, Ali of divine foods, and Baby Bear of moonbeams. . . . The rhymes are well written, and the charming pictures, done in gouache, watercolor, and colored pencil, are full of funny details." SLJ

Sophie; illustrated by Aminah Brenda Lynn Robinson. Harcourt Brace & Co. 1994 un il hardcover o.p. pa $7
Grades: PreK K 1 2   E
1. Grandfathers -- Fiction 2. African Americans -- Fiction
ISBN 0-15-277160-3; 0-15-201598-1 pa

LC 94-1976

First published 1989 in Australia

"The artwork is rich, expressionist, heavily lined oil. . . . The oversized hands depicted in many drawings exemplify the handholding theme, and the sunny hues of earth and garden convey with warmth a loving and extended African-American family." Bull Cent Child Books

★ **Ten** little fingers and ten little toes; [illustrations by] Helen Oxenbury. Harcourt 2008 un il $16

Grades: PreK K   E
1. Stories in rhyme 2. Infants -- Fiction
ISBN 978-0-15-206057-2; 0-15-206057-X

LC 2007-10692

Rhyming text compares babies born in different places and in different circumstances, but they all share the commonality of ten little fingers and ten little toes.

"Given their perfect cadences, the rhymes feel as if they always existed in our collective consciousness and were simply waiting to be written down. . . . Oxenbury . . . once again makes multiculturalism feel utterly natural and chummy. As her global brood of toddlers grows . . . readers can savor each addition both as beguiling individualist and giggly, bouncy co-conspirator." Publ Wkly

Tough Boris; illustrated by Kathryn Brown. Harcourt Brace & Co. 1994 un il $16; pa $6
Grades: PreK K 1 2   E
1. Parrots -- Fiction 2. Pirates -- Fiction
ISBN 0-15-289612-0; 0-15-201891-3 pa

LC 92-8015

Boris von der Borch is a tough pirate but he weeps when his parrot dies

"The text is deceptively simple, but the observant child will quickly fill in the details, aptly provided in the illustrations. The reassuring message, although understated, is clear and effective." Horn Book Guide

Two little monkeys; Mem Fox; illustrated by Jill Barton. Beach Lane Books 2010 32 p.
Grades: PreK K 1   E
1. Stories in rhyme 2. Picture books for children 3. Leopard -- Fiction 4. Monkeys -- Fiction
ISBN 1416986871; 9781416986874

LC 2009021995

This preschool children's rhyming picture book by Mem Fox, illustrated by Jill Barton, follows two monkeys hiding from a predator "[w]ith the . . . rhythm of a nursery-school finger game. . . .[T]he text . . . [tells] this story of two little monkeys and their escapades on the plains. Playing among the high grasses and dirt, Cheeky and Chee are frightened by something prowling and take refuge in a nearby tree. . . . Hidden in the landscape are hints of the action to come: a tail in the grass or leopard spots in the brush." (Kirkus)

Where is the green sheep? [by] Mem Fox and [illustrated by] Judy Horacek. Harcourt 2004 un il $15
Grades: PreK K 1 2   E
1. Stories in rhyme 2. Sheep -- Fiction
ISBN 0-15-204907-X

LC 2003-4990

A story about many different sheep, and one that seems to be missing.

"Until the lost sheep turns up, children will have fun with the other sheep that make an appearance and perhaps, unbeknownst to them, also get lessons in colors and comparisons. . . . In this neat and satisfying wedding of text and art, the squat, square format uses wool-white backgrounds to display much of the amusing pen-and-watercolor pictures." Booklist

Where the giant sleeps; [by] Mem Fox; pictures by Vladimir Radunsky. Harcourt 2007 un il $16

Grades: PreK K 1 2   **E**
  1. Stories in rhyme   2. Sleep -- Fiction   3. Bedtime
-- Fiction
ISBN 978-0-15-205785-5
                                   LC 2006020539
Illustrations and rhyming text portray the different residents of fairyland and where each one goes to sleep.
  "The paintings and multifaceted structure of the book inventively translate the puckish text, conjuring misty visions of magical realms." Publ Wkly

Fox, Paula
  Traces. Front Street 2008 un il $16.95
Grades: K 1 2 3   **E**
  1. Nature -- Fiction
ISBN 978-1-932425-43-7; 1-932425-43-8
                              LC 2006-11739
Looks at the traces left behind by a turtle on the sand, a jet in the sky, and even a long-gone dinosaur in loose soil.
  Fox "gives the book an energetic and distilled poetry. . . . The charming medallion sun, torn-paper clouds and watercolor ribbon of the horizon found on these spreads all feel like the naive and studious work of a dedicated seven-year-old. . . . The pictures are much fun and fit the story perfectly." Publ Wkly

Fox, Tamar
  No baths at camp; by Tamar Fox; illustrated by Natalia Vasquez. Kar-Ben Pub. 2013 32 p. col. ill. (reinforced) $17.95
Grades: PreK K 1 2   **E**
  1. Baths -- Fiction 2. Camps -- Fiction 3. Sabbath -- Fiction 4. Jews -- United States -- Fiction
ISBN 9780761381204
                              LC 2012009498

Frame, Jeron Ashford
  ★ **Yesterday** I had the blues; illustrations by R. Gregory Christie. Tricycle Press 2003 un il $14.95
Grades: K 1 2 3   **E**
  1. Emotions -- Fiction 2. Family life -- Fiction 3. African Americans -- Fiction
ISBN 1-58246-084-1
                              LC 2002-155295
A young African American boy ponders a variety of emotions and how different members of his family experience them, from his own blues to his father's grays and his grandmother's yellows
  "Vibrant acrylic-and-gouache spreads give rhythm and meaning to this child's interpretation of everyday life, his neighborhood, and his family. The illustrations effectively express each individual's mood and beautifully capture the cultural and artistic aspects of the family's life, while the expressive text is engaging." SLJ

Franceschelli, Christopher
  (oliver) Lemniscaat 2011 un il bd bk $12.95
Grades: PreK K   **E**
  1. Board books for children 2. Eggs -- Fiction 3. Chickens -- Fiction
ISBN 978-1-9359-5401-9; 1-9359-5401-6
First published in Holland

In this board book, Oliver the egg can't do much but roll from one side to the other, until a miracle happens and he becomes a chick.
  This book "contains crisp, attractive text and drawings, using space, light, and dark elegantly. Small children will delight in pulling open the sturdy pages and experiencing Oliver's transformation over and over." SLJ

  Alphablock; by Christopher Franceschelli. Appleseed 2013 104 p. $16.95
Grades: K 1 2   **E**
  1. Alphabet 2. Toy and movable books 3. Toy and movable books -- Specimens
ISBN 1419709364; 9781419709364
                              LC 2012047783
In this ABC board book, by Christopher Franceschelli, "thick pages [are] cut into the shape of each letter. Sprinkles, hot fudge, and cherries hint at I's ice cream sundae, while aquarium accessories hint at F's fish. As readers interact with the pages, they will familiarize themselves not only with the 26 letters and associated words, but also with each letter's physicality angles, holes, and curves, both front and back." (Publisher's note)

Franco, Betsy
  Bird songs; a backwards counting book. [by] Betsy Franco; [illustrated by] Steve Jenkins. Margaret K. McElderry Books 2006 un il $16.99
Grades: PreK K 1 2   **E**
  1. Counting 2. Day -- Fiction 3. Birds -- Fiction 4. Birdsongs -- Fiction
ISBN 0-689-87777-3; 978-0-689-87777-3
                              LC 2004-25056
Throughout the day and into the night various birds sing their songs, beginning with the woodpecker who taps a pole ten times and counting down to the hummingbird who calls once.
  "In his vivid, realistic-looking collages, Jenkins uses accurate textures and colors for each species, and creates the appearance of depth, light, and warmth. . . . The writing is lyrical and engaging, and quick 'feathery facts' about the creatures are appended." SLJ

  Double play! monkeying around with addition. illustrations by Doug Cushman. Tricycle Press 2011 un il $15.99; lib bdg $18.99
Grades: PreK K 1   **E**
  1. Addition 2. School stories 3. Stories in rhyme 4. Play -- Fiction 5. Monkeys -- Fiction
ISBN 978-1-58246-384-1; 1-58246-384-0; 978-1-58246-396-4 lib bdg; 1-58246-396-4 lib bdg
                              LC 2010024347
Monkey friends Jill and Jake play together at recess, and each game they play provides practice in doubling. Each page displays the matching addition problem.
  "The large watercolor illustrations show a joyous romp. . . . Young students will enjoy the book for its play aspect, not realizing that the math lesson is built into it." SLJ

  Pond circle; illustrated by Stefano Vitale. Margaret K. McElderry Books 2009 un il $16.99
Grades: PreK K 1 2 3   **E**
  1. Animals -- Fiction 2. Ecology -- Fiction 3. Pond

ecology -- Fiction 4. Food chains (Ecology) -- Fiction
ISBN 978-1-4169-4021-0; 1-4169-4021-9
LC 2008016268

In the pond by Anna's house, a food chain begins with algae which is eaten by a mayfly nymph which is eaten by a beetle which is eaten by a bullfrog.

"Vitale's rich, colorful oil-on-wood illustrations are as poetic as the text in their depiction of the natural world. . . . A clear, child-friendly look at ecology." SLJ

Frank, John

How to catch a fish; by John Frank; illustrated by Peter Sylvada. Roaring Brook Press 2007 un il $17.95
Grades: K 1 2   E
1. Stories in rhyme 2. Fishing -- Fiction
ISBN 978-1-59643-163-8; 1-59643-163-6
LC 2006032184

Rhyming text and illustrations describe the ways fish are caught in various locations around the world

"The handsome, full-page oil paintings are rendered in an impressionistic style that evokes the atmospheres of watery, misty, aquatic environments. . . . Resonating poetic vignettes spawn a glinting, striking catch." Booklist

Franson, Scott E.

Un-brella. Roaring Brook Press 2007 un il $15.95
Grades: PreK K   E
1. Stories without words 2. Magic -- Fiction 3. Weather -- Fiction 4. Umbrellas and parasols -- Fiction
ISBN 978-1-59643-179-9; 1-59643-179-2
LC 2006047658

In this wordless book, a little girl uses her magic umbrella to give her the weather she wants, regardless of what the conditions really are outside.

"The crisp, clean pictures have bright colors, exceptional detail, fun patterns, sly repetition, and heaps of whimsy." SLJ

Fraser, Mary Ann

Heebie-Jeebie Jamboree. Boyds Mills Press 2011 un il
Grades: PreK K 1   E
1. Siblings -- Fiction 2. Festivals -- Fiction 3. Halloween -- Fiction
ISBN 1-59078-857-5; 978-1-59078-857-8

"Dressed as a witch and a ghost, Sam and Daphne pull tickets out of thin air to the Heebie-Jeebie Jamboree on Halloween night. They are treated to a magical, good time. . . . Then, in the midst of the festivities, Sam goes missing. . . . The full-bleed illustrations in vibrant colors feature Halloween creatures of all sorts (but none frightening), and the pages are packed with action and energy. Children will love poring over the many details." SLJ

Pet shop follies. Boyd Mills Press 2010 un il $16.95
Grades: PreK K   E
1. Pets -- Fiction 2. Theater -- Fiction
ISBN 978-1-59078-619-2; 1-59078-619-X

"All the pet-shop animals mix and mingle in the front window anxiously awaiting customers, yet no one comes in. The clever hamster takes matters in hand and devises a brilliant plan to get visitors: 'Let's put on a show!' he squeaks. . . . The creamy, rich gouache double-page spreads are uncluttered, allowing each amazing feat its moment in the

spotlight while remaining developmentally appropriate for young readers." Kirkus

Pet shop lullaby. Boyds Mills Press 2009 un il $16.95
Grades: PreK K   E
1. Pets -- Fiction 2. Animals -- Fiction 3. Bedtime -- Fiction
ISBN 978-1-59078-618-5; 1-59078-618-1
LC 2009019661

When the pet store closes for the night, a hamster's activities keep the other animals awake as they try to think of some way to put him to sleep.

"Fraser's tale is brief and to the point, and the comical gouache illustrations infuse energy into the telling. Fun touches abound." SLJ

Another title about the pet shop is:
Pet shop follies (2010)

Frasier, Debra

★ A birthday cake is no ordinary cake; written and illustrated by Debra Frasier. Harcourt 2006 un il $16
Grades: PreK K 1 2   E
1. Cake -- Fiction 2. Year -- Fiction 3. Birthdays -- Fiction
ISBN 978-0-15-205742-8; 0-15-205742-0

A lyrical recipe using the changes in the natural world to explain to a child the time that passes between one birthday and the next. Includes recipe for more traditional birthday cake.

"Pop-off-the-page, vibrant-colored cut-paper collage illustrations capture the fanciful and factual concepts." SLJ

A fabulous fair alphabet. Beach Lane Books 2010 un il $16.99
Grades: PreK K 1   E
1. Alphabet 2. Fairs -- Fiction
ISBN 978-1-4169-9817-4; 1-4169-9817-9
LC 2009038329

Letters of the alphabet in various graphic styles accompany words associated with fairs.

"Despite the flat graphic style, the pages seem to sparkle and blink with the bright lights of a midway. The endpapers are bold collages of photos of signs at fairs. As alphabet books go, this one is delightful. As graphic art goes, it's alive with evocative, almost magical examples." SLJ

★ On the day you were born. Harcourt Brace Jovanovich 1991 un il $16
Grades: K 1 2 3 4   E
1. Childbirth 2. Earth
ISBN 0-15-302160-8
LC 90-36816

This combination of text and paper-collage graphics depicts the earth's preparation for, and celebration of, the birth of a newborn baby

"The text reads like unrhymed poetry, and both parents and educators will find themselves wanting to share this book over and over with individuals and with groups. A three-page appendix that includes miniature versions of each spread elaborates on natural phenomena for older readers—migrating animals, spinning Earth, rising tide, falling rain, growing trees, and more." SLJ

Frazee, Marla

★ **Boot** & Shoe; Marla Frazee. Beach Lane Books 2012 40 p. (hardcover) $16.99
Grades: PreK K 1 2   E
  1. Dogs -- Fiction 2. Solitude -- Fiction
  ISBN 1442422475; 9781442422476
                   LC 2011035990
In this children's picture book by Marla Frazee "Two adorably floppy dogs confront unexpected change. . . . Boot and Shoe were born into the same litter, and now they live in the same house. . . . But they spend their days apart--Boot on the back porch because he's a back porch kind of dog, and Shoe on the front porch because he's a front porch kind of dog. . . . Then a crazy neighborhood squirrel arrives . . . and everything goes topsy-turvy!" (Publisher's note)

★ The **boss** baby. Beach Lane Books 2010 un il $16.99
Grades: PreK K 1   E
  1. Infants -- Fiction
  ISBN 978-1-4424-0167-9; 1-4424-0167-2
From the moment he arrives, it is obvious that the new baby is boss and he gets whatever he wants, from drinks made-to-order around the clock to his executive gym.
"Cartoon vignettes in pencil-streaked gouache hum with a funky, retro style seen in sleek furnishings and the '50s fashions of the accommodating but increasingly exhausted parents. . . . Clever and empathetic." Publ Wkly

★ A **couple** of boys have the best week ever; [by] Marla Frazee. Harcourt 2008 32p il $16
Grades: K 1 2 3   E
  1. Beaches -- Fiction 2. Vacations -- Fiction 3. Friendship -- Fiction 4. Grandparents -- Fiction
  ISBN 978-0-15-206020-6
                   LC 2006-25781
A Caldecott Medal honor book, 2009
Friends James and Eamon enjoy a wonderful week at the home of Eamon's grandparents during summer vacation. "Ages six to nine." (Bull Cent Child Books)
"After Eamon enrolls in nature camp, he spends nights with his grandparents, Bill and Pam, at their beach cottage. Eamon's friend James joins the sleepover. . . . Humorous contradictions arise between the hand-lettered account . . . and voice-bubble exchanges between the boys. . . . Frazee's narrative resembles a tongue-in-cheek travel journal, with plenty of enticing pencil and gouache illustrations of the characters knocking about the shoreline." Publ Wkly

★ The **farmer** and the clown; Marla Frazee. Beach Lane Books 2014 32 p. (hardcover) $17.99
Grades: PreK K 1 2   E
  1. Farmers -- Fiction 2. Stories without words 3. Circus -- Fiction 4. Clowns -- Fiction
  ISBN 1442497440; 9781442497443
                   LC 2013019361
In this picture book, by Marla Frazee, "a baby clown is separated from his family when he accidentally bounces off their circus train and lands in a lonely farmer's vast, empty field. The farmer reluctantly rescues the little clown, and over the course of one day together, the two of them make some surprising discoveries about themselves—and about life!" (Publisher's note)

"Frazee's controlled palette of subdued golds, browns, and grays offers a fitting backdrop for the hard-working farmer foregrounded in this wordless tale. Bent over his wheat, he misses the drama above as sweeping cloud formations bleed off the page. A swiftly moving circus train on the horizon introduces color and an unexpected visitor, when a bump on the tracks ejects a young clown. This is a tender look at light and shadow, the joy and comfort in companionship, the lift that laughter provides, and the friendship possible among generations (and species)." (SLJ)

★ **Roller** coaster. Harcourt 2003 un il
Grades: PreK K 1 2   E
  1. Roller coasters
  ISBN 0-15-204554-6
                   LC 2002-7805
Twelve people set aside their fears and ride a roller coaster, including one who has never done so before. "Ages three to seven." (Christ Sci Monit)
"Frazee does an extraordinary job of conveying motion by the placement of her images, her use of white space, bright colors, and swooshing speed lines. . . . What will keep children coming back for extra looks, however, is Frazee's clever, dramatic depiction of the 12 riders and their wildly and amusingly different reactions to the stomach-churning experience." Booklist

★ **Santa** Claus, the world's number one toy expert. Harcourt 2005 $16
Grades: PreK K 1 2   E
  1. Christmas -- Fiction 2. Santa Claus -- Fiction
  ISBN 0-15-204970-3; 0152049703
                   LC 2004005228
Santa Claus has his own ways of knowing more about children and toys than anyone else in the world. "Ages four to eight." (Bull Cent Child Books)
"Frazee, a master at creating scenes and moods in her energetic drawings and spare text, fills these pages with details and vignettes that readers will want to explore repeatedly." SLJ

★ **Walk** on! a guide for babies of all ages. Harcourt, Inc. 2006 un il $16
Grades: PreK K 1 2   E
  1. Infants -- Fiction 2. Walking -- Fiction
  ISBN 0-15-205573-8
                   LC 2004-29895
"In this how-to for little ones, a baby learns to walk for the first time. . . . The pencil-and-gouache art has the delightful feel of self-help pamphlets from an earlier era. . . . This is one of those rare books that speaks to crawling and walking babies who like to look at pictures of creatures like themselves, preschoolers who enjoy stories about what they were like when they were little, and older children and adults who will appreciate the wry humor." SLJ

Frazier, Craig

Bee & Bird. Roaring Brook Press 2011 un il $16.99
Grades: PreK K 1   E
  1. Adventure fiction 2. Stories without words 3. Bees -- Fiction 4. Birds -- Fiction 5. Travel -- Fiction
  ISBN 978-1-59643-660-2; 1-59643-660-3
                   LC 2010013012

In this wordless picture book, a bumblebee and a bird embark on a travel adventure.

Frazier "uses perspective to great advantage in creating mystery and drawing readers into the story. . . . The vividly colored artwork will immediately snag young readers' attention; the perplexing views will entice them into the plot; and subtle clues . . . will help them make sense of the details in subsequent viewings." Booklist

★ **Hank** finds inspiration; [by] Craig Frazier. Roaring Brook Press 2008 un il $16.95
Grades: K 1 2   E
1. Snakes -- Fiction
ISBN 978-1-59643-358-8; 1-59643-358-2
                              LC 2007047919
Hank the snake and his human friend, Stanley, each go to the city in search of inspiration, but Hank's journey is a failure until he returns home

"Frazier's crisp graphics draw the eye to varied perspectives with bold splashes of color and sharply defined silhouettes and shadings. An 'inspired' addition for all libraries." SLJ

Lots of dots. Chronicle Books 2010 un il
Grades: PreK K 1   E
1. Stories in rhyme 2. Shape -- Fiction
ISBN 0811877159; 9780811877152
Circular shapes are spotted in familiar objects and everyday situations. Buttons are dots. Wheels are dots. Stars are dots. Ladybugs have dots and so do the fried eggs on your plate. Lots of dots!

"Frazier maintains an upbeat tone with tight rhyme and meter throughout; with the exception of one night scene, with dots for stars, the backgrounds are plain white, giving the pages a freshly washed, contemporary feel." Publ Wkly

Frederick, Heather Vogel
Babyberry pie; [illustrations by] Amy Schwartz. Harcourt Children's Books 2010 un il $16.99
Grades: PreK K 1   E
1. Stories in rhyme 2. Bedtime -- Fiction 3. Infants -- Fiction
ISBN 978-0-15-205927-9; 0-15-205927-X
In illustrations and rhyming text, gives the recipe for making "babyberry pie," from picking a baby from the babyberry tree and popping him in the tub to putting powdered sugar on his nose and toes and tucking him into pie crust covers.

"Schwartz brings out her best with these vivid gouache and pen-and-ink illustrations of a family getting a toddler ready for bed. . . . Frederick's rhyming text, repetition, and wordplay amplify the fun in this yummy mix of old-fashioned cozy and modern setting." SLJ

Hide-and-squeak; illustrated by C.F. Payne. Simon & Schuster Books for Young Readers 2011 un il $16.99
Grades: PreK K 1   E
1. Stories in rhyme 2. Mice -- Fiction 3. Bedtime -- Fiction 4. Father-child relationship -- Fiction
ISBN 978-0-689-85570-2; 0-689-85570-2
                              LC 2008039648
A mouse baby leads his father on a merry game of hide-and-squeak at bedtime.

"Payne's settings, amplifying the baby mouse's inexhaustible energy and giddy transgressiveness, while buoying Frederick's . . . rock solid, somewhat quaint rhymes. . . . The spreads are small masterpieces of composition, yet they never feel static; rather, it's as if someone has hit the pause button to briefly allow readers to savor the image's beauty before the story continues on its rollicking way to the bedtime wrap-up." Publ Wkly

Freedman, Claire
Gooseberry Goose; illustrated by Vanessa Cabban. Tiger Tales 2003 un il $15.95
Grades: PreK K 1 2   E
1. Geese -- Fiction 2. Winter -- Fiction 3. Animals -- Fiction
ISBN 1-58925-030-3
                              LC 2003-12960
As Gooseberry Goose practices flying on a beautiful fall morning, his friends are preparing for winter, causing Gooseberry to wonder if there is something else he should be doing

"The text is brought to life through the illustrations, which are loose and lovely. Vibrant red and gold leaves enliven the pages. Gooseberry is a bundle of expression. . . . Readers will be captivated by this irrepressible gosling's infectious charm." SLJ

Freedman, Deborah
★ **Blue** chicken. Viking 2011 un il $15.99
Grades: PreK K 1   E
1. Chickens -- Fiction 2. Farm life -- Fiction 3. Domestic animals -- Fiction
ISBN 978-0-670-01293-0; 0-670-01293-9
                              LC 2011001502
An enterprising chicken attempts to help an artist paint the barnyard and accidentally turns the whole picture blue.

"Watercolor washes and splashes, from pale blue to dark, create wonderful, wet patterns; their liquid edges contrast alluringly with fine pencil lines and shadings. . . . Delicate and durable, visually sophisticated yet friendly: simply exquisite." Kirkus

Freeman, Don
★ **Corduroy**; 40th anniversary edition; Viking Press 2008 32p il $19.99
Grades: PreK K 1   E
1. Teddy bears -- Fiction
ISBN 978-0-670-06336-9; 0-670-06336-3
A reissue of the title first published 1968
A toy bear in a department store wants a number of things, but when a little girl finally buys him he finds what he has always wanted most of all. This edition includes copies of letters and the original manuscript.

"The art and story are direct and just right for the very young who like bears and escalators." Book World
Another title about Corduroy is:
A pocket for Corduroy (1978)

Earl the squirrel. Viking 2005 un il $15.99
Grades: PreK K 1   E
1. Squirrels -- Fiction
ISBN 0-670-06019-4
                              LC 2005-03929
Earl the squirrel learns to gather acorns on his own.

"The pictures are full of energy and detail, and Earl is both cheeky and endearing. . . . The story is gentle, innocent, and funny." SLJ

Quiet! there's a canary in the library; by Don Freeman. Viking Children's Books 2007 un il $15.99
Grades: PreK K 1   E
  1. Animals -- Fiction 2. Libraries -- Fiction
  ISBN 978-0-670-06230-0; 0-670-06230-8
                LC 2006-37904
A reissue of the title first published 1969 by Golden Gate
Cary imagines a special day at the library when she invites only animals and birds to browse.
"Freeman contrasts more detailed drawings of the actual library with childlike crayoned depictions of Cary's day-dreamed adventures." Horn Book Guide

Freeman, Martha
  Mrs. Wow never wanted a cow; by Martha Freeman; illustrated by Steven Salerno. Random House 2006 un il (Beginner books) $8.99; lib bdg $11.99
Grades: K 1 2   E
  1. Cats -- Fiction 2. Dogs -- Fiction 3. Cattle -- Fiction
  ISBN 0-375-83418-4; 0-375-93418-9 lib bdg
                LC 2005006000
When Mrs. Wow takes in a stray cow, her lazy dog and cat hope to train the new household member to catch mice and intimidate the mailman
"The mostly one-syllable words with regular phonetic patterns are spare and natural, and Salerno's brightly colored cartoon illustrations amplify the text's humor." SLJ

Freeman, Tor
  Olive and the big secret; Tor Freeman. Candlewick Press 2012 32 p. $15.99
Grades: PreK K 1 2   E
  ISBN 076366149X; 9780763661496
                LC 2012938740

French, Jackie
  Christmas wombat; by Jackie French; illustrated by Bruce Whatley. Clarion Books 2012 32 p. (hardback) $16.99
Grades: PreK K 1 2   E
  1. Holidays -- Fiction 2. Animals 3. Human-animal relationship -- Fiction 4. Diaries -- Fiction 5. Wombats -- Fiction 6. Christmas -- Fiction
  ISBN 0547868723; 9780547868721
                LC 2011052112
Author Jackie French's story centers on a wombat. "A bearlike Australian animal, the wombat likes to sleep, hide in holes and eat. This wombat especially likes to eat carrots, and the . . . plot focuses on the wombat's intensive search for more and more carrots." The book "describes the wombat's activities and its discovery of carrots set out for some 'strange creatures' (Santa's reindeer). The wombat chomps every carrot in sight, stows away in Santa's sleigh and beats the reindeer to their carrot treats at stops around the world." (Kirkus Reviews)

  Diary of a baby wombat; written by Jackie French; illustrated by Bruce Whatley. Clarion Books 2010 un il $16.99

Grades: PreK K 1 2   E
  1. Wombats -- Fiction
  ISBN 978-0-547-43005-8; 0-547-43005-1
                LC 2009050452
Through a week of diary entries, a wombat describes his life of sleeping, playing, and helping his mother look for a bigger hole in which to make their home.
"Economy of voice is reflected in the understated illustrations. . . . This will be read over and over, providing new laughs each time." Horn Book

  ★ **Diary** of a wombat; illustrated by Bruce Whatley. Clarion Bks. 2003 un il $14
Grades: PreK K 1 2   E
  1. Wombats -- Fiction
  ISBN 0-618-38136-8
                LC 2003-829
First published 2002 in Australia
In his diary, a wombat describes his life of eating, sleeping, and getting to know some new human neighbors
The story is presented in "simple sentences and hilarious yet realistic acrylic illustrations. . . . Whatley gives a sublime balance of the adorable charm of the creature, along with its drawbacks as an acquaintance." SLJ
Another title about the wombat is:
  Diary of a baby wombat (2010)

  Pete the sheep-sheep; illustrated by Bruce Whatley. Clarion Books 2005 32p il $14
Grades: PreK K 1 2   E
  1. Dogs -- Fiction 2. Sheep -- Fiction
  ISBN 0-618-56862-X
                LC 2004-30935
First published 2004 in Australia with title: Pete the sheep
The sheep-shearers in Shaggy Gully all have a sheep dog, but the new guy Shaun uses an extremely polite sheep named Pete.
"Cleanly designed illustrations work well with French's understated text. Strong lines focus attention on the expressive characters." Horn Book Guide

French, Vivian
  The **Daddy** Goose treasury; as told to Vivian French; illustrated by AnnaLaura Cantone . . . [et al.] Scholastic 2006 93p il $18.99
Grades: K 1 2 3   E
  1. Nursery rhymes -- Fiction
  ISBN 0-439-79608-3
"French includes 12 untold stories that give background and context for such familiar rhymes as Little Miss Muffet, Georgie Porgie, Old King Cole, and Hickory, Dickory, Dock. . . . Four European illustrators contribute lively, colorful, and witty illustrations that adeptly articulate the cozy narratives." SLJ

  ★ **Yucky** worms; illustrated by Jessica Ahlberg. Candlewick Press 2010 28p il $16.99; pa $6.99
Grades: PreK K 1 2   E
  1. Worms -- Fiction 2. Gardening -- Fiction 3. Grandmothers -- Fiction 4. Earthworms
  ISBN 978-0-7636-4446-8; 0-7636-4446-3; 978-0-7636-5817-5 pa
                LC 2009-17307

While helping Grandma in the garden, a child learns about the important role of the earthworm in helping plants grow.

"The cheerful pencil-and-gouache artwork shows scenes both above and below the ground and weaves facts into each image, as well as humorous cartoon speech bubbles. . . . Friendly and interactive, this is a great choice for sharing at home and in the classroom." Booklist

Freymann, Saxton

★ **Fast** food; written and illustrated by Saxton Freymann. Arthur A. Levine Books 2006 32p il $12.99

Grades: PreK K 1 2 3   E

1. Transportation

ISBN 0-439-11019-X

"This picture book takes a theme (here, transportation) and illustrates it with exceptionally clear color photos of ephemeral, sometimes whimsical sculptures created from fruits and vegetables. As quietly witty as its title, the book is narrated by a little mushroom man who suggests different ways of getting about. . . . The playful text gallops along smoothly in rhymed couplets, while the illustrations work their inimitable charm." Booklist

★ **Food** for thought; the complete book of concepts for growing minds. written and illustrated by Saxton Freymann. Arthur A. Levine Books 2005 61p il $14.95

Grades: PreK K 1 2 3   E

1. Alphabet 2. Concepts 3. Counting

ISBN 0-439-11018-1

This "covers basic shapes, colors, numbers, letters, and opposites—all introduced through images of artfully manipulated fruits and vegetables. . . . The simple, clean design is ideal for demonstrating the concepts. . . . But it's the playful, wonderfully clever transformation of familiar foods that will win an audience." Booklist

Friedlaender, Linda K.

Look! look! look! by Nancy Elizabeth Wallace with Linda K. Friedlaender; illustrated by Nancy Elizabeth Wallace. Marshall Cavendish 2006 un il $16.95

Grades: K 1 2 3   E

1. Art -- Fiction 2. Mice -- Fiction

ISBN 978-0-7614-5282-9; 0-7614-5282-6

LC 2005016934

Three mice "borrow" a postcard which is a reproduction of a painting, and from it they learn about color, pattern, line, and shape. Includes instructions for making and sending a postcard.

This picture book tells the story of three mice exploring a sculpture exhibit in a museum. "Three frisky mice, sensibilities honed by an exposure to painting in [Linda K. Friedlaender's] 'Look! Look! Look!' (2006), give 3-D art a similarly close once over. The story is centered on an abstract work in slate by Barbara Hepworth in the Yale Center for British Art (where Friedlaender is a curator), but it features sharp color photos of 20 other sculptures from as many eras and cultures." (Kirkus)

"This is not only an amusing, creative story, but also an adventure into art that encourages originality while inspiring creativity." SLJ

Friedman, Caitlin

How do you feed a hungry giant? a munch-and-sip pop-up book. illustrated by Shaw Nielsen. Workman 2011 un il $18.95

Grades: PreK K 1 2   E

1. Pop-up books 2. Giants -- Fiction

ISBN 978-0-7611-5752-6; 0-7611-5752-2

"A gentle giant clothed in patchwork clothing appears in a boy's front yard carrying a sign that says, 'Food Please.' The giant gobbles an entire pizza, slurps up 15 bottles of chocolate milk from a kiddie pool, and consumes 197 cookies, but remains hungry. Luckily, the boy's mother is willing to help. The well-integrated interactive elements—popups, tabs, and flaps—add an extra touch of fun to this lighthearted story." Publ Wkly

Friedman, Darlene

Star of the Week; a story of love, adoption, and brownies with sprinkles. story by Darlene Friedman; illustrations by Roger Roth. HarperCollins 2009 un il $17.99; lib bdg $18.89

Grades: PreK K 1 2 3   E

1. School stories 2. Adoption -- Fiction 3. Chinese Americans -- Fiction

ISBN 978-0-06-114136-2; 0-06-114136-4; 978-0-06-114137-9 lib bdg; 0-06-114137-2 lib bdg

LC 2008-22581

As her turn to be "Star of the Week" in her kindergarten class approaches, Cassidy-Li puts together a poster with pictures of her family, friends, and pets, and wonders about her birthparents in China.

"Roth's vibrant illustrations capture the personality of Cassidy-Li, the six-year-old narrator who tells her story in unaffected language that will appeal to children." SLJ

Friedman, Ina R.

How my parents learned to eat; illustrated by Allen Say. Houghton Mifflin 1984 30p il hardcover o.p. pa $6.99

Grades: K 1 2 3   E

1. Japan -- Fiction 2. Dining -- Fiction

ISBN 0-395-35379-3; 0-395-44235-4 pa

LC 83-18553

An American sailor courts a Japanese girl and each tries, in secret, to learn the other's way of eating

"The illustrations have precise use of line and soft colors, and the composition is economical. A warm and gentle story of an interracial family." Bull Cent Child Books

Friend, Catherine

Eddie the raccoon; illustrated by Wong Herbert Yee. Candlewick Press 2004 40p il (Brand new readers) hardcover o.p. pa $5.99

Grades: K 1 2   E

1. Raccoons -- Fiction

ISBN 0-7636-2331-8; 0-7636-2334-2 pa

LC 2003-69717

"Pleasant watercolors . . . provide ample visual clues to the accompanying sentence—usually comprising four or five basic vocabulary words. . . . Each setup packs a gently humorous punch that's easy enough for children to grasp and sweet enough to make their adult helpers chuckle." Booklist

The **perfect** nest; illustrated by John Manders. Candlewick Press 2007 un il $16.99

Grades: K 1 2   **E**

  1. Cats -- Fiction 2. Chickens -- Fiction
  ISBN 978-0-7636-2430-9; 0-7636-2430-6

               LC 2006047518

Jack the cat gets much more than he bargained for when he decides to build the perfect nest to attract the perfect chicken

This is "highly comical yet heartwarming tale. . . . Manders's gouache illustrations are a perfect complement to the text." SLJ

Friester, Paul

  Owl howl; [illustrated by] Philippe Goossens; [English translation by Erica Stenfalt] NorthSouth Books 2011 un il (Tuff books) pa $6.95

Grades: PreK K   **E**

  1. Owls -- Fiction 2. Forest animals -- Fiction
  ISBN 978-0-7358-4017-1; 0-7358-4017-2

"In response to a little owl's howling, various forest animals take turns trying to determine the problem and stop her tears. The bulbous-eyed owl is uncommonly sympathetic thanks to Goossens's illustrations on sturdy, glossy pages. When the owl is back under her mom's wings, readers will exhale with relief—before they grin at the punch line." Horn Book Guide

Frisch, Aaron

  A **night** on the range; written by Aaron Frisch; illustrated by Chris Sheban. Creative Editions 2010 un il $25.65

Grades: K 1 2 3   **E**

  1. Fear -- Fiction 2. Camping -- Fiction 3. Cowhands -- Fiction 4. Imagination -- Fiction
  ISBN 978-1-56846-205-9; 1-56846-205-0

               LC 2008016595

"Young cowboy-wannabe Cole daydreams about roping strays and hunting down rustlers. He's beyond excited for his first camping experience—that is, until it gets dark. . . . Dreamy, expansive illustrations distinguish between Cole's wild imagination and his reality—a suburban backyard—in this well-done ode to self-fulfillment." Horn Book Guide

"In this story of Western dreaming, a boy and his faithful dog leave indoor comforts behind for their first sleep-out under the stars." Publisher's note

Frost, Helen

  Sweep up the sun; Helen Frost, illustrated by Rick Leider. Candlewick Press 2015 32 p. $15.99

Grades: PreK K 1 2 3   **E**

  1. Birds 2. Nature photography
  ISBN 0763669040; 9780763669041

               LC 2013957345

In this book by Helen Frost, here "commonly seen birds in their natural settings, captured in photographs of rare beauty and grace. In perfect synchrony, a lyrical narrative evokes images of play and flight, perseverance and trust. At the end, readers will find profiles of the featured species. This stunning book is an ideal gift for bird lovers of all ages, graduates, or anyone embarking on an adventure." (Publisher's note)

Fucile, Tony

  ★ **Let's** do nothing! Candlewick Press 2009 un il $16.99; pa $6.99

Grades: PreK K 1 2   **E**

  1. Imagination -- Fiction
  ISBN 978-0-7636-3440-7; 0-7636-3440-9; 978-0-7636-5269-2 pa

               LC 2008-935654

"Frankie and Sal are bored . . . and now there is nothing—which is exactly what they will attempt to do for ten whole seconds. In a series of increasingly hilarious spreads, the two boys . . . are deterred everytime by Frankie's overactive imagination. . . . The imagined scenes employ vibrant color, in effective contrast with the reality sequences. . . . Fucile's figures, ink line with acrylic paints, . . . have a retro touch in their period hues and springy drafting." Bull Cent Child Books

Fuge, Charles

  Astonishing animal ABC. Sterling 2011 un il $14.95

Grades: PreK K 1   **E**

  1. Alphabet 2. Stories in rhyme
  ISBN 978-1-4027-8645-7; 1-4027-8645-X

An alphabet book featuring rhyming text and all sorts of animals.

"The rhyming text is abundant with adjectives and alliteration. Fuge's animals communicate a variety of emotions (fear, happiness and worry), but when they gather together to see the animal that starts with the letter Z zoom past them, they all look surprised. Readers will likely express a similar sentiment." SLJ

Fuller, Sandy Ferguson

  My cat, coon cat; illustrated by Jeannie Brett. Islandport 2011 il $17.95

Grades: PreK K 1 2   **E**

  1. Stories in rhyme 2. Cats -- Fiction
  ISBN 978-1-934031-32-2; 1-934031-32-1

When a young girl moves into a new home, she slowly wins the affection of a shy Maine coon cat, as he meets the girl's kitten, chases dragonflies, and explores the neighborhood.

"The illustrations are full of color and character, capturing with equal charm the bucolic background and the winsome feline. . . . Any reader who has ever known the love of a cat will find much to relate to in this cozy book." SLJ

Funke, Cornelia Caroline

  ★ The **princess** knight; by Cornelia Funke; illustrations by Kerstin Meyer; translated by Anthea Bell. Chicken House/Scholastic 2004 un il $15.95

Grades: PreK K 1 2   **E**

  1. Princesses -- Fiction 2. Knights and knighthood -- Fiction
  ISBN 0-439-53630-8

  Original German edition 2001

"Raised by a widowed king, Princess Violetta is put through the same paces (swordplay, riding, jousting) as her older, brawnier brothers. Her practice pays off when her father holds a tournament—with Violetta as the grand prize—and she handily scuttles his plans. Bell translates Funke's story from the German with aplomb . . . and Meyer's effervescent line-and-watercolor artwork, as funny as it is lovely, stretches across each spread in horizontal strips." Booklist

Princess Pigsty; by Cornelia Funke; illustrated by Kerstin Meyer; translated by Chantal Wright. Chicken House/Scholastic 2007 un il $16.99
Grades: K 1 2   E
1. Fairy tales 2. Princesses -- Fiction
ISBN 0-439-88554-X
LC 2006006294
"Sick of her pampered existence, Princess Isabella tosses aside her tiara, declaring, 'I want to get dirty!' The outraged king prescribes tours of duty in the kitchens and pigsty, but Isabella merely revels in the good, honest work and good, honest mess. . . . Most kids will relate to her spirit of rebellion, especially as embodied in Meyer's ebullient watercolors of the beaming, disheveled girl." Booklist

The **wildest** brother; [by] Cornelia Funke; illustrated by Kerstin Meyer; translated by Oliver Latsch. The Chicken House/Scholastic 2006 un il $16.99
Grades: PreK K 1 2   E
1. Siblings -- Fiction
ISBN 0-439-82862-7
When it comes to protecting his big sister, Anna, young Ben is as brave as a lion. But when the day is over and darkness falls, Ben suddenly doesn't feel quite so brave. Sometimes, he realizes, it's Anna who does the protecting
"Wright's wonderfully expressive acrylic paintings elevate this simple glimpse of sibling play into something special. The animated scenes, filled with Ben's imagined foes, perfectly capture the wild-eyed, physical fun." Booklist

Fusco Castaldo, Nancy
★ **Pizza** for the queen; by Nancy Castaldo; illustrated by Mélisande Potter. Holiday House 2005 un il $16.95
Grades: PreK K 1 2 3   E
1. Italy -- Fiction 2. Pizza -- Fiction 3. Cooking -- Fiction
ISBN 0-8234-1865-0
LC 2004-58134
In 1889 Napoli, Italy, Raffaele Esposito prepares a special pizza for Queen Margherita. Based on a true story. Includes a recipe.
"The richly toned, detailed illustrations . . . extend the action and the sense of history in busy scenes in the kitchen and on the picturesque streets." Booklist

Fyleman, Rose, 1877-1957
Mice; Rose Fyleman; illustrated by Lois Ehlert. Beach Lane Books 2012 p. cm.
Grades: PreK K 1   E
1. Stories in rhyme 2. Picture books for children 3. Mice -- Fiction
ISBN 9781442456846; 9781442456860
LC 2011020555
In this book, "a 1932 poem from [Rose] Fyleman (1877–1957) serves as a springboard for [Lois] Ehlert's" artwork. As "the mice scamper across the pages ('They nibble things they shouldn't touch') Ehlert labels the items they find, turning the story into an introduction to art supplies, household items, and food items that range from mangos and avocadoes to cereal and desserts." (Publishers Weekly)

Gag, Wanda
★ **Millions** of cats. Putnam 2004 un il $13.99

Grades: PreK K 1   E
1. Cats -- Fiction
ISBN 0-399-23315-6
A reissue of the title first published 1928 by Coward-McCann
A Newbery Medal honor book, 1929
It is "a perennial favorite among children and takes a place of its own, both for the originality and strength of its pictures and the living folktale quality of its text." NY Her Trib Books

Gaiman, Neil
Chu's day; Neil Gaiman, Adam Rex; [edited by] Rosemary Brosnan. HarperCollins 2013 32 p. (hardcover bdg.) $17.99
Grades: PreK K 1   E
1. Mystery fiction 2. Sneezing -- Fiction 3. Picture books for children
ISBN 0062017810; 9780062017819
LC 2012942557
In this children's picture book, "[Neil] Gaiman builds suspense from the . . . opening sentence ('When Chu sneezed, bad things happened')." Trips to a dusty library and a diner with peppery air make "Chu's anxious parents ask, 'Are you going to sneeze?' . . . That evening, under a big top . . . , Chu cannot resist, and his true power is revealed." (Publishers Weekly)

Chu's day at the beach; written by Neil Gaiman; illustrated by Adam Rex. Harper, an imprint of HarperCollins Publishers 2015 32 p. color illustrations (hardback) $17.99
Grades: PreK K 1   E
1. Beaches -- Fiction 2. Sneezing -- Fiction 3. Pandas -- Fiction
ISBN 0062223992; 9780062223999
LC 2014034091
"Chu and his family are going to the beach! Chu is excited. He will get to play in the sand and wade in the water. But what will happen if Chu sneezes at the beach? And what will happen if he doesn't?" (Publisher's note)
"In the third tale about Chu, the little panda and his parents visit the beach. . . . Bright colors and the assortment of creatures will enchant children who enjoy poring over pictures, while the type size and short sentences make this a good fit for early readers." Booklist

Crazy hair; illustrated by Dave McKean. HarperCollins Publishers 2009 un il $18.99; lib bdg $19.89
Grades: PreK K 1 2 3   E
1. Stories in rhyme 2. Hair -- Fiction
ISBN 978-0-06-057908-1; 0-06-057908-0; 978-0-06-057909-8 lib bdg; 0-06-057909-9 lib bdg
LC 2008012791
Bonnie encounters all sorts of exotic animals and marvelous things inside a man's crazy hair.
This is a "chaotic picture book popping with bright collage and multimedia imagery. . . . Each page is a veritable feast for the eyes, with frazzled clumps of hair competing for attention with outlandish elements. . . . There's something a little unsettling and unhinged about the imagery, just on the safe side of nightmarish; but the text, for the most part, is delightful and glib." Booklist

The **dangerous** alphabet; by Neil Gaiman; illustrated by Gris Grimly. HarperCollinsPublishers 2008 un il $17.99; lib bdg $18.89

Grades: 2 3 4 5   E

1. Stories in rhyme 2. Pirates -- Fiction 3. Alphabet -- Fiction 4. Monsters -- Fiction
ISBN 978-0-06-078333-4; 0-06-078333-8; 978-0-06-078334-1 lib bdg; 0-06-078334-6 lib bdg

LC 2007-10893

As two children and their pet gazelle sneak out of the house in search of treasure, they come across a world beneath the city that is inhabited with monsters and pirates.

"A sophisticated, interactive alphabet tale in which even the letters break the expected pattern. . . . Skillful narrative and visual storytelling combine to present a complex adventure that unravels through multilayered text and illustrations, challenging readers to ponder the numerous levels of plot. . . . The gothic illustrations, done in sepia tones and faded color washes, ensure that readers remain riveted throughout the story." SLJ

Instructions; written by Neil Gaiman; illustrated by Charles Vess. Harper 2010 un il $14.99; lib bdg $15.89

Grades: 1 2 3 4   E

1. Poetry 2. Voyages and travels -- Poetry
ISBN 978-0-06-196030-7; 0-06-196030-6; 978-0-06-196031-4 lib bdg; 0-06-196031-4 lib bdg

The poem first published 2000 in A Wolf at the Door published by Simon & Schuster

Go on a journey to unknown, but strangely familiar, lands and then travel home again.

"Vess's compositions are distinguished by elegant, winding lines-gnarled vines, plumes of smoke, dragon tails-and intimate frames that evoke moments of gentle wisdom. Young readers should relish the chimerical vision while older Gaiman fans should grasp the underlying suggestion that the compass used to navigate fairy tales can also guide us in the real world." Publ Wkly

The **wolves** in the walls; written by Neil Gaiman; illustrated by Dave McKean. HarperCollins Pubs. 2003 un il $16.99

Grades: 2 3 4   E

1. Wolves -- Fiction
ISBN 0-380-97827-X

LC 2002-192194

Lucy is sure there are wolves living in the walls of her house, although others in her family disagree, and when the wolves come out, the adventure begins

"Gaiman's text rings with energetic confidence and an inviting tone. . . . McKean . . . expertly matches the tale's funny-scary mood . . . against shadow-filled backdrops that blend paint, digital manipulation and photography, his stylized human figures look right at home. His pen-and-inks of the wolves . . . suggest that they inhabit a world apart—or perhaps unreal?" Publ Wkly

Gal, Susan

Day by day; Susan Gal. Alfred A. Knopf 2012 40 p. col. ill. (hardback) $16.99

Grades: PreK K 1 2   E

1. Pigs -- Fiction 2. Family -- Fiction 3. Picture books for children 4. Family life -- Fiction 5. Neighborhoods

-- Fiction
ISBN 037586959X; 9780375869594; 9780375969591; 9780375984334

LC 2011042371

In this children's picture book, "[a]cross a golden prairie, a family of pigs heads west. Their small actions grow in significance as bricks become a house, beloved paraphernalia create a home, neighbors are welcomed and friendships begin." Through daily hard work, "a community is built" and at the end of the book, the pigs gather "under a festive tree at twilight to enjoy the bounty they have grown." (Kirkus)

★ **Night** lights. Alfred A. Knopf 2009 un il $14.99; lib bdg $17.99

Grades: PreK K 1   E

1. Light -- Fiction 2. Night -- Fiction
ISBN 978-0-375-85862-8; 0-375-85862-8; 978-0-375-95862-5 lib bdg; 0-375-95862-2 lib bdg

LC 2008-50909

While preparing for bedtime, a little girl and her dog note all the different kinds of lights that brighten up the night, from headlights to moonlight.

"An appropriately dark palette complements the 15 types of illumination named in this nearly wordless story. Young children will enjoy poring over the rich details in the cozy charcoal and digital collage spreads as they learn to read the simple text." SLJ

Please take me for a walk. Alfred A. Knopf 2010 un il $15.99; lib bdg $18.99

Grades: PreK K 1   E

1. Dogs -- Fiction
ISBN 0375858636; 0375958630 lib bdg; 9780375858635; 9780375958632; 978-0-375-85863-5; 0-375-85863-6; 978-0-375-95863-2 lib bdg; 0-375-95863-0 lib bdg

A dog gives many good reasons it likes to go for a walk—to chase away the neighbor's cat, to greet people on the street, to watch guys shooting hoops, and to feel the wind lifting its ears.

"Gal celebrates the joys of perambulating the neighborhood in simple sentences and mixed-media collage illustrations featuring expressive canines and humans, as well as inventive details." Booklist

Galbraith, Kathryn Osebold

Arbor Day square; written by Kathryn Galbraith; illustrated by Cyd Moore. Peachtree Publishers 2010 un $16.95

Grades: K 1 2 3   E

1. Trees -- Fiction 2. Arbor Day -- Fiction 3. Frontier and pioneer life -- Fiction 4. Father-daughter relationship -- Fiction
ISBN 978-1-56145-517-1; 1-56145-517-2

LC 2009017017

In the mid-nineteenth century, as young Katie and her father help plant and tend trees in their booming frontier town, she doubts that the spindly saplings will ever grow big. Includes facts about Arbor Day.

"Galbraith's poetic text and Moore's soft watercolor and colored-pencil illustrations recreate those spring days on the prairie when planting trees was cause for celebration." SLJ

Boo, bunny! [by] Kathryn O. Galbraith; illustrated by Jeff Mack. Harcourt 2008 un il $16

Grades: PreK K   E

1. Stories in rhyme 2. Fear -- Fiction 3. Rabbits -- Fiction 4. Halloween -- Fiction

ISBN 978-0-15-216246-7; 0-15-216246-1

        LC 2007021426

Two small bunnies face their fears while trick-or-treating on Halloween night

"With very simple, shivery rhyme and bright shapes on black double-page spreads, this picture book brings toddlers the creepy fun of Halloween." Booklist

Gall, Chris

Dear fish; written and illustrated by Chris Gall. Little, Brown 2006 un il $16.99

Grades: 1 2 3 4   E

1. Fishes -- Fiction 2. Beaches -- Fiction

ISBN 0-316-05847-5; 978-0-316-05847-6

        LC 2005-03828

One afternoon at the beach, a small boy puts an invitation to the fish to come for a visit in a bottle and throws it into the ocean, and the results are unprecedented.

"The text has a rich vocabulary. . . . Boldly colored illustrations combine clay-engraved art with digital effects to give the pages a three-dimensional look. Readers who enjoy poring over pictures that are layered with meaning on both the literal and figurative levels will find much to explore here." SLJ

★ **Dinotrux**. Little, Brown 2009 un il $16.99

Grades: PreK K 1 2   E

1. Trucks -- Fiction 2. Dinosaurs -- Fiction

ISBN 978-0-316-02777-9; 0-316-02777-4

        LC 2008-27531

Millions of years ago, the prehistoric ancestors of today's trucks, such as garbageadon, dozeratops, and craneosaurus, roamed the Earth until they rusted out and became extinct.

"Blending the endless appeal of dinosaurs and trucks in one hilarious volume, this title will be hard to keep on the shelves." SLJ

★ **Dog** vs. Cat; Chris Gall. Little Brown & Co 2014 32 p. (hardcover) $17

Grades: PreK K 1 2   E

1. Cats -- Fiction 2. Dogs -- Fiction 3. Friendship -- Fiction 4. Individuality -- Fiction

ISBN 0316238015; 9780316238014

        LC 2013015639

In this children's book, by Chris Gall, "Dog and Cat do not get along. But when they're forced to share a room, they agree to be on their best behavior...until Dog won't stop sniffing. Cat won't stop scratching. And when it comes to the litterbox...sharing is not an option! What will it take to bring Dog and Cat together?" (Publisher's note)

"Starting with illustrations on the endpapers, readers know immediately that they are in for a treat with this picture book...The colored-pencil illustrations are remarkable, and the animals' dialogue, expressions, and body language are priceless, as is the funny conclusion. A terrific addition to any friendship or pet storytime." SLJ

Dog versus Cat

Revenge of the Dinotrux; Chris Gall. Little, Brown & Co 2012 32 p.

Grades: PreK K 1 2   E

1. Picture books for children 2. Dinosaurs -- Fiction 3. Mythical animals -- Fiction 4. Trucks -- Fiction 5. Behavior -- Fiction 6. Imaginary creatures -- Fiction

ISBN 0316132888; 9780316132886

        LC 2011025118

This picture book by Chris Gall is a sequel to his earlier children's book "Dinotrux!" in which the metal dinosaurs escape from their museum. "Exploding through the dino-museum's wall in the wake of a particularly stressful Kindergarten Day, enraged Tyrannosaurus Trux rolls off to climb a skyscraper. . . . Further chaos threatens when they burst out again, though, taking along the children who have introduced them to the wonders of (truck) books and other reading." Gall illustrates the dinotrux as "towering massively atop heavy-duty tires, with wide, headlight eyes and toothy maws agape." (Kirkus)

★ **Substitute** Creacher. Little, Brown 2011 un il $16.99

Grades: K 1 2   E

1. School stories 2. Stories in rhyme 3. Monsters -- Fiction 4. Teachers -- Fiction

ISBN 978-0-316-08915-9; 0-316-08915-X

        LC 2010019758

Mr. Creacher, a multi-tentacled substitute teacher, warns his prankish students not to misbehave, recounting rhyming cautionary tales of the weird, spooky, and unexpected.

Gall "illustrates in explosive, cinematic panels; retro Ben-Day dot patterns allude to classic funnies. If the dire warnings fail to inspire repentance, Mr. Creacher's dilemma—and a conclusion that breaks the spell—may warm the cold hearts of defiant substitute baiters." Publ Wkly

There's nothing to do on Mars; written and illustrated by Chris Gall. Little, Brown 2008 un il $16.99

Grades: PreK K 1 2   E

1. Science fiction 2. Mars (Planet) -- Fiction

ISBN 978-0-316-16684-3; 0-316-16684-7

        LC 2006025290

After moving to Mars with his family, Davey complains of being bored until he begins exploring the planet with his dog Polaris and uncovers a most unusual "treasure"

"The illustrations, created with an engraving technique, are precisely drawn and appropriately painted in scorching reds and oranges. . . . Amusing details . . . extend the text and play off the deadpan humor." SLJ

Gammell, Stephen

★ **Mudkin**. Carolrhoda Books 2011 un il

Grades: PreK K 1   E

1. Play -- Fiction 2. Rain -- Fiction 3. Imagination -- Fiction

ISBN 0-7613-5790-4 lib bdg; 978-0-7613-5790-2 lib bdg

        LC 2010026373

While playing outside on a rainy day, a little girl peers into a puddle and sees Mudkin, who invites her to become his queen.

"Kids love mud, and here's a picture book that positively revels in all its gleefully gloppy glory. . . . The girl has a few lines of dialogue, but Mudkin's responses are all a scrawl of indecipherable brown smears, offering a neat chance for kids to engage and fill in their own ideas for what he's saying. But what will really bring on the squeals is the joyfully messy watercolors that look composed of thick, overhand tosses of mud splatters and heartily ground-in grass stains." Booklist

Once upon MacDonald's farm; rev format ed; Simon & Schuster Bks. for Young Readers 2000 un il $15
Grades: PreK K 1 2   E
1. Animals -- Fiction 2. Farm life -- Fiction
ISBN 0-689-82885-3

LC 99-30691

First published 1981 by Four Winds Press
MacDonald tries farming with exotic circus animals, but has better luck with his neighbor's cow, horse, and chicken—or does he?

"The accomplished, shaded pencil drawings are well suited to this slyly humorous tale with an unexpected twist." Horn Book Guide

Gannij, Joan
Topsy-turvy bedtime; by Joan Levine; illustrated by Tony Auth. Candlewick 2008 un il $14.99
Grades: PreK K 1   E
1. Bedtime -- Fiction 2. Parent-child relationship -- Fiction
ISBN 978-0-7636-3008-9; 0-7636-3008-X

"Arathusela hates going to bed. Her parents are exhausted by day's end, so they reverse roles with her. . . . Kids will appreciate the tables-turned humor ('You forgot to sing us a song') and the reasuring resolution. Auth has a light touch; his watercolors display the particular coziness of domestic life at night." Horn Book Guide

Gantos, Jack
★ **Rotten** Ralph; written by Jack B. Gantos; illustrated by Nicole Rubel. Houghton Mifflin 1976 un il lib bdg $16; pa $7.95
Grades: PreK K 1 2   E
1. Cats -- Fiction
ISBN 0-395-24276-2 lib bdg; 0-395-29202-6 pa
The "bright watercolor scenes . . . capturing Ralph's demonic meanness and his family's chagrin are a perfect complement to the text." SLJ

Other titles about Rotten Ralph are:
Back to school for Rotten Ralph (1998)
Best in show for Rotten Ralph (2005)
Happy birthday Rotten Ralph (1990)
The nine lives of Rotten Ralph (2009)
Not so Rotten Ralph (1994)
Practice makes perfect for Rotten Ralph (2002)
Rotten Ralph helps out (2001)
Rotten Ralph's rotten Christmas (1984)
Rotten Ralph's rotten romance (1997)
Rotten Ralph's show and tell (1989)
Rotten Ralph's trick or treat! (1986)
Three strikes for Rotten Ralph (2011)
Wedding bells for Rotten Ralph (1999)
Worse than rotten, Ralph (1978)

Rotten Ralph feels rotten; written by Jack Gantos; illustrated by Nicole Rubel. Farrar Straus Giroux 2004 47p il $15.99

Grades: PreK K 1 2   E
1. Cats -- Fiction 2. Sick -- Fiction
ISBN 0-374-36357-9

LC 2003-49252

Rotten Ralph comes to appreciate Sarah's healthy cat food after he gets sick from eating out of trash cans.

"The Magic-Marker intensity of Rubel's palette and the undulating quality of her lines are ideal for showing the quavery misery of nausea. . . . Beginning readers will gobble up this third installment of the Rotten Ralph Rotten Reader series." Booklist

Rotten Ralph's rotten family; written by Jack Gantos; illustrated by Nicole Rubel. Farrar Straus & Giroux 2014 48 p. color illustrations (hardback) $16.99
Grades: 1 2 3   E
1. Bad behavior 2. Cats -- Fiction 3. Family -- Fiction 4. Behavior -- Fiction 5. Families -- Fiction
ISBN 0374363536; 9780374363536

LC 2013022076

In this children's book, by Jack Gantos, "Rotten Ralph's owner, Sarah, is fed up with her red rascal's behavior. Ralph is tired of Sarah trying to change him. He misses his cat family, which never made him alter a thing about himself. But in this . . . adventure for newly independent readers, the world's favorite rotten red cat gets tripped up when he runs away for a journey down memory lane." (Publisher's note)

"After finding an old photo album, Ralph visits his family. His mother treats him well, but the other relatives heap humiliation on him. Ralph realizes the reason he is so rotten is that his own family was rotten to him. The longer early-chapter-book format serves Ralph well, allowing a more sophisticated story line to emerge. Lively tongue-in-cheek illustrations extend the action." Horn Book

Three strikes for Rotten Ralph; written by Jack Gantos; illustrated by Nicole Rubel. Farrar Straus Giroux 2011 47p il $16.99
Grades: 1 2 3   E
1. Baseball -- Fiction 2. Squirrels -- Fiction
ISBN 978-0-374-36354-3; 0-374-36354-4
Before he tries out for the new Fighting Squirrels baseball team, Rotten Ralph is sure he is going to be a superstar. Never mind that he doesn't have any skills and doesn't want to practice.

"There is never a dull moment in this colorful and appealing early reader." SLJ

Ganz-Schmitt, Sue
Planet Kindergarten; by Sue Ganz-Schmitt; illustrated by Shane Prigmore. Chronicle Books 2014 40 p. (alk. paper) $16.99
Grades: PreK K 1   E
1. School stories 2. Outer space -- Fiction 3. Kindergarten -- Fiction 4. Imagination -- Fiction 5. First day of school -- Fiction
ISBN 1452118930; 9781452118932

LC 2013011773

This children's book by Sue Ganz-Schmitt, illustrated by Shane Prigmore, encourages "young explorers to boldly go where they have never gone before: Planet Kindergarten. Suit up for a daring adventure as our hero navigates the unknown reaches and alien inhabitants of this strange new world. Hilarious and confidence-boosting, this exciting story will have new kindergarteners ready for liftoff!" (Publisher's note)

"A child bids farewell to his parents (who are sent back to their own planets) and begins his first mission on Planet Kindergarten... With the help of Prigmore's superpowered animation-style illustrations, she offers a story that will help readers understand that kindergarten really is out of this world." SLJ

Garcia, Emma

Tap tap bang bang. Boxer Books 2010 un il $16.95
Grades: PreK K   E
1. Tools -- Fiction 2. Sounds -- Fiction 3. Building -- Fiction
ISBN 978-1-907152-00-9; 1-907152-00-8

"A lively introduction to tools and the sounds that they make. . . . They all work together to make a bright, cherry-red go-kart. . . . Garcia's artwork is clear and colorful, and all of the tools stand out against the stark white backgrounds. . . . There are plenty of opportunities to stretch vocabulary with these building-tool words." SLJ

Garden, Nancy

Molly's family; pictures by Sharon Wooding. Farrar Straus Giroux 2004 un il $16
Grades: PreK K 1 2   E
1. School stories 2. Lesbians -- Fiction 3. Family life -- Fiction
ISBN 0-374-35002-7
LC 2002-29784

When Molly draws a picture of her family for Open School Night, one of her classmates makes her feel bad because he says she cannot have a mommy and a momma

"By tying this specific household to the general diversity within all families, Garden manages to celebrate them all. The soft colored-pencil drawings with their many realistic details depict a room full of active kindergartners." SLJ

Garland, Michael, 1952-

Fish had a wish; by Michael Garland. Holiday House 2012 24p
Grades: PreK K 1 2   E
1. Fishes -- Fiction 2. Wishes -- Fiction 3. Children's stories 4. Picture books for children 5. Animals -- Fiction 6. Contentment -- Fiction 7. Self-acceptance -- Fiction
ISBN 9780823423941
LC 2010050124

In this children's picture book, "Fish has a wish to be some creature other than what he is: a bird, so he can fly high in the sky; a turtle, so he can nap on a sunny rock; a skunk, so he can make a big stink; or a bobcat, a bee, a beaver, a butterfly or a snake. But when a mayfly lands on the water, Fish eats it in one bite and declares: 'That was so good! . . . I wish to stay a fish.' . . . The double-page spreads have wood-grain backgrounds . . . evok[ing] Fish's woodland pond environment." (Kirkus)

Grandpa's tractor. Boyds Mills Press 2011 un il $16.95
Grades: PreK K 1   E
1. Farm life -- Fiction 2. Grandfathers -- Fiction
ISBN 978-1-59078-762-5; 1-59078-762-5

Grandpa Joe brings his grandson Timmy back to the site of the family farm, where the old house and a ramshackle barn still stand. The visit evokes many memories for Grandpa Joe, which he shares with Timmy.

"Garland's artistic genius has never been shown to such advantage as in this book. . . . The text . . . complements the vivid and folksy digitally enhanced artwork. . . . The pictures and text together compose a loving tribute to the heyday of small farms in America." SLJ

Super snow day: seek and find. Dutton Children's Books 2010 un il $16.99
Grades: PreK K 1 2 3   E
1. Picture puzzles 2. Literary recreations 3. Snow -- Fiction 4. Aunts -- Fiction
ISBN 978-0-525-42245-7; 0-525-42245-5
LC 2009-53245

When a heavy snowfall causes schools and businesses to close, Tommy follows a series of notes from his Aunt Jeanne as he explores the frozen landscape, makes new friends, and participates in winter sports. Artwork includes over 200 objects for the reader to find and count.

"Garland's computer-generated illustrations are eye-catching and surreal. . . . They're characterized by bright colors, Claymation-style figures, and an admirable restraint when it comes to clutter." SLJ

Garland, Sarah

Eddie's toolbox; and how to make and mend things. Frances Lincoln 2011 un il $17.95
Grades: K 1 2   E
1. Tools -- Fiction 2. Friendship -- Fiction
ISBN 978-1-84780-053-4; 1-84780-053-X

"Eddie is hoping a boy his age will move in next door, but when he sees the new family unpack, he notices that the only child is a girl his younger sister's age. When the two families meet . . . the two girls form an instant bond. . . . Tilly's dad asks him if he'd like to help him with chores that need to be done. . . . Tom teaches him how to use a saw, a hammer, and a screwdriver. . . . Soon, the two families are completing projects together. . . . This is a lovely story about friendship between neighbors. Garland's watercolor illustrations show scenes in which everyone is helping one another. These two families make lending a hand look fun and rewarding." SLJ

Other titles about Eddie are:
Eddie's kitchen (2004)
Eddie's garden (2008)

Garland, Sherry

The **buffalo** soldier; by Sherry Garland; illustrated by Ronald Himler. Pelican Pub. Co. 2006 un il $15.95
Grades: 2 3 4   E
1. West (U.S.) -- Fiction 2. African American soldiers -- Fiction
ISBN 978-1-58980-391-6
LC 2006012484

Realizing that his future lies in owning land, not just being free, a young man raised as a slave becomes a buffalo soldier—a member of an all-black cavalry regiment formed to protect white settlers from Indians, bandits, and outlaws, and that later fought in the Spanish American War. Includes historical note

"Himler's vibrant illustrations capture the broad vistas of western landscape, the excitement of horseback pursuit, and the hardships of the work, at the same time conveying respect for the loyal soldiers who endured it all." Booklist

Includes bibliographical references

Gary, Meredith

Sometimes you get what you want; art by Lisa Brown; words by Meredith Gary. HarperCollinsPublishers 2008 un il $16.99; lib bdg $17.89

Grades: PreK K   E

1. School stories 2. Siblings -- Fiction 3. Conduct of life -- Fiction

ISBN 978-0-06-114015-0; 978-0-06-114016-7 lib bdg

LC 2007041933

A brother and sister spend a day in preschool learning lessons about boundaries, such as that it is sometimes okay to make a lot of noise, but at other times one must be quiet.

"Gary's concise text conveys an important life lesson about the need to balance fun, responsibility, and respect for others. . . . Appealing illustrations depict each scenario and keep the tone light. Background scenery, props, and adult characters are portrayed in black lines and white and gray shades, while the children are fully fleshed out with a variety of skin tones and bright-hued clothing." SLJ

Garza, Xavier

Juan and the Chupacabras; by Xavier Garza; illustrations by April Ward; Spanish translation by Carolina Villarroel. Pinata Books 2006 un il $15.95

Grades: K 1 2 3   E

1. Monsters -- Fiction 2. Grandfathers -- Fiction 3. Bilingual books -- English-Spanish

ISBN 978-1-55885-454-3; 1-55885-454-1

After hearing about their grandfather's boyhood encounter with the Chupacabras, a green, winged creature with glowing eyes, Juan and his cousin Luz decide to find out if the story could be true.

"The English and Spanish texts appear on the same page, separated by a narrow illustration. The full-page illustration moves the action along nicely. An excellent choice for storytime and classroom sharing." SLJ

Gauch, Patricia Lee

Aaron and the Green Mountain Boys; pictures by Margot Tomes. Boyds Mills Press 2005 64p il $16.95; pa $9.95

Grades: K 1 2   E

1. United States -- History -- 1775-1783, Revolution -- Fiction

ISBN 1-59078-335-2; 1-59078-354-9 pa

A reissue of the title first published 1972 by Coward, McCann & Geohegan

In 1777 nine-year-old Aaron would rather help the Green Mountain Boys fight the British than stay home and bake bread for them.

★ **Tanya** and the red shoes; illustrated by Satomi Ichikawa. Philomel Bks. 2002 un il $16.99

Grades: PreK K 1 2   E

1. Ballet -- Fiction

ISBN 0-399-23314-8

LC 2001-33916

"Tanya confides her dreams of dancing en pointe like the dancer in the movie The Red Shoes. She finally gets her wish but discovers that the seemingly effortless beauty of the dance requires much work (and produces many blisters). The use of the present tense underscores the conversational tone, adding verisimilitude matched by Ichikawa's marvelously agile, expressive illustrations." Horn Book

Other titles about Tanya are:

Bravo Tanya (1992)

Dance Tanya (1989)

Presenting Tanya the Ugly Duckling (1999)

Tanya and the magic wardrobe (1997)

Gauch, Sarah

Voyage to the Pharos; illustrated by Roger Roth. Viking 2009 un il $16.99

Grades: 1 2 3   E

1. Sea stories 2. Egypt -- Fiction 3. Lighthouses -- Fiction

ISBN 978-0-670-06254-6; 0-670-06254-5

LC 2009012345

A young boy in ancient times embarks on an adventurous sea voyage to Alexandria, Egypt, home of the famous Pharos Lighthouse.

"Large-scale illustrations capture the drama of the events to full effect. . . . Roth varies his palette to increase the intensity of the perilous scenes and to highlight the joy of surviving unharmed." SLJ

Gay, Marie-Louise

Caramba and Henry. Groundwood Books 2011 $17.95

Grades: PreK K 1   E

1. Cats -- Fiction 2. Flight -- Fiction 3. Siblings -- Fiction

ISBN 978-1-55498-097-0; 1-55498-097-6; 9781554980970; 1554980976

"Caramba, a zebra-striped cat who lives in a world where cats can fly, has always wanted a brother—but not the one he gets. Henry screams and cries all of the time and, unlike Caramba, Henry isn't having any trouble flying. To Caramba's chagrin, his mother puts him in charge of making sure Henry's fledgling flights don't end in disaster. . . . Gay's watercolors, laced with feathery pencil lines, bring warmth to this fresh spin on a story about learning how to be an older sibling." Publ Wkly

Another title about Caramba is:

Caramba (2005)

★ **Roslyn** Rutabaga and the biggest hole on earth; by Marie-Lou Gay. Groundwood Books/House of Anansi Press 2010 un il $18.95

Grades: PreK K   E

1. Rabbits -- Fiction 2. Father-daughter relationship -- Fiction

ISBN 978-0-88899-994-8; 0-88899-994-1

"The whimsical illustrations, created on Kraft paper and handmade Japanese paper with watercolor, acrylic, pastels, aquarelle crayons, pencil, and collage, are busy without being overdone. Imaginative and adventurous children will identify with Roslyn in this simple, fun story." SLJ

★ **When** Stella was very very small. Groundwood Books 2009 un il $16.95

Grades: PreK K 1 2   E
1. Size -- Fiction 2. Growth -- Fiction
ISBN 978-0-88899-906-1; 0-88899-906-2

"Stella explores her vantage points from each developmental stage to date. As a crawler, she's eye to eye with a
turtle. . . . A goldfish and dog phase follow. Gay's sensitivity
to the rich inner life of childhood flows into her art and language. . . . Gay's mixed-media scenes dance with the energy
of scribbled butterflies on the walls, teetering objects, and a
blanket-turned-turban. . . . Subtle and sweet, yet full of life
and humor, the child's world is a place kids will want to visit
again and again." SLJ

Other titles about Stella are:
Stella, star of the sea (1999)
Stella, queen of the snow (2000)
Stella, fairy of the forest (2002)
Stella, princess of the sky (2004)

Geeslin, Campbell
★ **Elena's** serenade; written by Campbell Geeslin; il-
lustrated by Ana Juan. Atheneum Books for Young Readers
2004 un il $16.95
Grades: K 1 2 3   E
1. Mexico -- Fiction 2. Sex role -- Fiction 3.
Glassblowing -- Fiction
ISBN 0-689-84908-7
                                            LC 2002-3233

In Mexico a little girl disguised as a boy sets out for
Monterrey determined to master the art of glassblowing, and
in the process, experiences self-discovery along the way

"The story flows well and Spanish words are smoothly
incorporated into the text. The alluring acrylic-and-crayon
illustrations have a stylized folk-art quality that helps to set
the stage for the tale." SLJ

Geisert, Arthur
Country road ABC; an illustrated journey through
America's farmland. Houghton Mifflin Harcourt 2010 un
il $17
Grades: K 1 2 3   E
1. Alphabet 2. Farm life -- Fiction
ISBN 978-0-547-19469-1; 0-547-19469-2
                                         LC 2009045450

Arthur Geisert takes readers on a literal journey following a real road in Iowa through the ins and outs of America's farmland.

"Pastoral charm is not Geisert's aim: . . . he begins with
'A is for ammonia fertilizer.' His finely worked etchings,
colored in muted shades, sweep across a sprawl of fields
and roads. . . . Much visual information about farming is provided for lovers of tractors and farm animals, but it's more
than a simple picture book; it's a deeply personal account."
Publ Wkly

Hogwash. Houghton Mifflin 2008 32p il $16
Grades: K 1 2 3   E
1. Stories without words 2. Pigs -- Fiction 3. Machinery
-- Fiction 4. Cleanliness -- Fiction
ISBN 978-0-618-77332-9; 0-618-77332-0
                                           LC 2007-21731

Illustrations without words depict the enormous and
complicated contraption that Mama Pig uses to get her little
piglets clean.

This is illustrated with "intricately detailed colored etchings. . . . A master of the 'page turn,' only Geisert could
take a one-word title and create such an engaging scenario."
Booklist

★ **Ice.** Enchanted Lion Books 2011 un il $14.95
Grades: K 1 2   E
1. Stories without words 2. Ice -- Fiction 3. Pigs
-- Fiction
ISBN 978-1-59270-098-1; 1-59270-098-5
                                          LC 2010-942321

This wordless tale depicts a community of pigs that suffer from the heat and go in search of ice despite the odds
against them.

"This is an especially satisfying Geisert title, because
the task is essential for the pigs' survival and they carry it
off with such élan. And the air-schooner, a charming marriage of sailing and balloon technology, is a standout among
Geisert's many contraptions." Publ Wkly

★ **Lights** out. Houghton Mifflin Co. 2005 32p il $16
Grades: 1 2 3 4   E
1. Pigs -- Fiction 2. Bedtime -- Fiction 3. Inventions
-- Fiction
ISBN 0-618-47892-2
                                           LC 2005-00555

Told by his parents that his light must be out at eight
o'clock, a young piglet who is afraid of the dark devises an
ingenious solution to the problem.

"Fans of roller-coaster construction, marble runs, and
contraption-like machines will be immediately engaged, and
the problem-solving humor is for everyone. The fine lines
and small scale of Geisert's color art work perfectly to give
an effect that is intimate, energetic, and delightful." SLJ

Thunderstorm; Arthur Geisert. 1st ed. Enchanted
Lion Books 2013 32 p. (hardcover) $17.95
Grades: PreK K 1 2   E
1. Farm life 2. Thunderstorms
ISBN 1592701337; 9781592701339
                                          LC 2012952191

This picture book by Arthur Geisert "follows the course
of a storm through midwestern farm country minute-by-
minute, hour-by-hour, from late morning into late afternoon." (Publisher's note) "Cutaway views show the interiors
of buildings and, in the ground below, the burrows of rabbits
and foxes. The story follows a single farming family driving
a red pickup truck hauling a trailer-load of hay; timestamps
('3:00 pm') are the only text." (Publishers Weekly)

Gellman, Ellie B.
Netta and her plant; by Ellie Gellman; illustrated by
Natascia Ugliano. Kar-Ben Publishing 2014 32 p. color
illustrations (lib. bdg) $17.95
Grades: PreK K   E
1. Jews -- Fiction 2. Growth -- Fiction 3. Plants --
Fiction 4. Tu bi-Shevat -- Fiction
ISBN 9781467704229; 1467704229
                                          LC 2013002192

"One Tu B'Shevat day in Israel, little Netta brings a
plant home from preschool. Over time, Netta grows, and the
plant grows too. Soon it is time for both of them to find new
homes and new friends." (Publisher's note)

"A pale springlike palette of greens, yellows and blues in the soft-edged drawings reinforces the symbolism of new growth. A welcome addition to the Judaica and ecology shelves." Kirkus

Genechten, Guido van

  Kai-Mook. Clavis Pub. 2011 il $16.95

Grades: PreK K   E

  1. Zoos -- Fiction 2. Animals -- Fiction 3. Elephants -- Fiction

  ISBN 978-1-60537-096-5; 1-60537-096-7

"When a baby elephant is born, all the animals are smitten. . . . Each creature takes a turn to point out similarities with the new baby and all declare her 'cute.' At last the new baby says, 'I AM NOT CUTE,'. . .'I AM KAI-MOOK!' The friendly collage and pastel cartoon-style animals are just right for toddlers and preschoolers. . . . Bright-eyed, smiling faces and interesting texturing provide visual appeal that earns this book a spot among the pack of baby-in-the-jungle tales." SLJ

  No ghost under my bed. Clavis Pub. 2010 un il $17.95

Grades: PreK K 1 2   E

  1. Fear -- Fiction 2. Bedtime -- Fiction 3. Penguins -- Fiction 4. Father-child relationship -- Fiction

  ISBN 978-1-60537-069-9; 1-60537-069-X

When a little penguin named Jake becomes afraid of strange noises in his room at night, he calls his father to check out the situation, and when everything from the curtain to the wardrobe and toy box has been checked, Jake feels comforted that all of the ghosts are gone and prepares to sleep.

"This story is kept lighthearted with the addition of animated stuffed animals and humorous illustrations of Jake's father looking for ghosts. . . . Told mostly through dialogue between parent and child, this picture book starring two charming penguins dispels bedtime fears by replacing them with belief in a father's love." SLJ

George, Jean Craighead

  ★ **Goose** and Duck; illustrated by Priscilla Lamont. Laura Geringer Books 2008 48p il (I can read!) $16.99; lib bdg $17.89

Grades: PreK K 1 2   E

  1. Ducks -- Fiction 2. Geese -- Fiction

  ISBN 978-0-06-117076-8; 0-06-117076-3; 978-0-06-117077-5 lib bdg; 0-06-117077-1 lib bdg

                  LC 2006-21715

A young boy becomes the "mother" to a goose, who becomes "mother" to a duck, as they learn about the rhythms of nature together.

"Lamont's colorful illustrations combine sensitive line work with appealing color washes. . . . The clearly written story is well suited to beginning readers and, as a read-aloud." Booklist

  Luck; the story of a sandhill crane. by Jean Craighead George; paintings by Wendell Minor. Laura Geringer Books 2006 un il $16.99; lib bdg $17.89

Grades: 1 2 3   E

  1. Cranes (Birds) -- Fiction

  ISBN 0-06-008201-1; 0-06-008202-X lib bdg

                  LC 2004-15628

A young sandhill crane, Luck, finds his place in the ancient crane migration from northern Canada to the Platte River

"Minor's beautifully painted spreads of Luck, including many pictures of the birds in flight, increase the sense of awe that the birds' miraculous journey inspires. A fine title to prompt discussion about local wildlife." Booklist

  Morning, noon, and night; paintings by Wendell Minor. HarperCollins Pubs. 1999 un il $16.99; lib bdg $17.89

Grades: K 1 2 3   E

  1. Day -- Fiction 2. Animals -- Fiction

  ISBN 0-06-023628-0; 0-06-023629-9 lib bdg

                  LC 97-28796

Each day as the sun makes its dawn-to-dusk journey from the Eastern seaboard to the Pacific coast, the animals perform their daily activities

This offers "rhythmic, lyrical text. . . . Minor's lushly detailed paintings capture the beauty of both animals and landscape, elucidating the subtle journey the book makes from east coast to west." Horn Book Guide

  Nutik, the wolf pup; illustrated by Ted Rand. Harper-Collins Pubs. 2001 un il hardcover o.p. lib bdg $18.89

Grades: K 1 2 3   E

  1. Inuit -- Fiction 2. Wolves -- Fiction 3. Arctic regions -- Fiction

  ISBN 0-06-028164-2; 0-06-028165-0 lib bdg

                  LC 99-10501

When his older sister Julie brings home two small wolf pups, Amaroq takes care of the one called Nutik and grows to love it, even though Julie tells him it cannot stay

"Rand's realistic paintings establish the Alaska setting and capture the affection between boy and pup. . . . First told in Julie's Wolf Pack (1997), the story is skillfully telescoped into a picture book with heart-tugging appeal." Booklist

  Another title about Nutik and Amaroq is:

  Nutik & Amaroq play ball (2001)

George, Kristine O'Connell

  Hummingbird nest; a journal of poems. illustrated by Barry Moser. Harcourt 2004 un il $16

Grades: 2 3 4   E

  1. Stories in rhyme 2. Hummingbirds -- Fiction

  ISBN 0-15-202325-9

                  LC 99-50909

When a mother hummingbird builds a nest on a family's porch, they watch and record her actions and the birth and development of her fledglings.

"Moser's quiet, exquisitely detailed pictures show the people watching and the small, delicate creatures. . . . The long, beautifully written notes with astonishing facts about hummingbirds make this a fine choice for both language arts and science classes." Booklist

  Up! illustrated by Hiroe Nakata. Clarion Books 2005 32p il $15

Grades: PreK K   E

  1. Stories in rhyme 2. Father-daughter relationship -- Fiction

  ISBN 0-618-06489-3

                  LC 2004-10729

Rhyming text and illustrations animate the feeling of "up" as experienced by a little girl with her father.

"Nakata's airy, spirited watercolors beautifully expand on the words' carefree, physical elation with skewed angles, glorious fruit-juice colors, and leaping, tumbling toys and figures." Booklist

George, Lindsay Barrett

★ **Inside** mouse, outside mouse. Greenwillow Books 2004 un il $15.99; lib bdg $16.89

Grades: PreK K 1 2   E

1. Mice -- Fiction

ISBN 0-06-000466-5; 0-06-000467-3 lib bdg

LC 2003-48497

Two mice, one who sleeps inside the house in a clock and one who sleeps outside the house in a stump, follow complicated but strangely parallel paths and meet each other at a window.

"The pictures are packed with interesting details just waiting to be explored. The simple text . . . compares and contrasts the animals' environments and lifestyles. The overall effect is mesmerizing" SLJ

Maggie's ball. Greenwillow Books 2010 un il $16.99

Grades: PreK K   E

1. Dogs -- Fiction

ISBN 978-0-06-172166-3; 0-06-172166-2

LC 2008052482

When Maggie the dog goes searching for her missing ball, she finds a lot of different things—including a new friend.

"The illustrations are bright and big, as is the minimal text, making the oversize book a winner for preschool storytimes as well as for individual perusings where the ample small details will fascinate children." SLJ

That pup! Greenwillow Books 2011 un il $16.99

Grades: PreK   E

1. Dogs -- Fiction 2. Squirrels -- Fiction

ISBN 978-0-06-200413-0; 0-06-200413-1

LC 2010012641

After having fun digging up acorns, a little dog decides to bury them all again.

"There is a real story here about taking things that don't belong to you and putting things right after a misunderstanding, right on target for younger preschoolers. Gouache illustrations of the appealing puppy and concerned squirrel use simple layouts and lots of white space." Kirkus

George, Lucy M.

Back to school Tortoise; written by Lucy M. George; illustrated by Merel Eyckerman. Albert Whitman 2011 un il $15.99

Grades: PreK K 1   E

1. School stories 2. Turtles -- Fiction 3. Teachers -- Fiction

ISBN 978-0-8075-0510-6; 0-8075-0510-2

LC 2010046344

Summer is over and Tortoise must summon the courage to go back to school.

"The precisely worded text and amiable mixed-media illustrations work well together. An empathetic read-aloud choice, this book offers a welcome antidote for first-day-of-school jitters." Booklist

George, William T.

Box Turtle at Long Pond; pictures by Lindsay Barrett George. Greenwillow Bks. 1989 un il $17.99

Grades: PreK K 1 2   E

1. Turtles -- Fiction

ISBN 0-688-08184-3

LC 88-18787

On a busy day at Long Pond, Box Turtle searches for food, basks in the sun, and escapes a raccoon

"A beautifully illustrated book that introduces a pond environment. . . . The reader learns of other plants, animals, and insects that inhabit the pond." Sci Child

Other titles about Long Pond are:

Beaver at Long Pond (1988)

Christmas at Long Pond (1992)

Fishing at Long Pond (1991)

Geras, Adele

★ **Little** ballet star; by Adèle Geras; pictures by Shelagh McNicholas. Dial Books for Young Readers 2008 un il $16.99

Grades: PreK K 1 2   E

1. Aunts -- Fiction 2. Ballet -- Fiction

ISBN 978-0-8037-3237-7; 0-8037-3237-6

Tilly is thrilled when she gets to see her aunt perform in the ballet, "The Sleeping Beauty," especially because she gets to go backstage and even on the stage itself.

"This picture book will charm aspiring young dancers. The large format allows plenty of space for the expressive pencil illustrations, tinted with washes in pastel shades." Booklist

Another book about about Tilly is:

Time for ballet (2004)

Gerber, Carole

Leaf jumpers; by Carole Gerber; [illustrated by] Leslie Evans. Charlesbridge 2004 32 p. col ill. $7.95

Grades: PreK K 1 2   E

1. Autumn 2. Leaves

ISBN 1570914974; 1570914982; 9781570914980

LC 200315846

This book, by Carole Gerber, illustrated by Leslie Evans, "celebrates the beauty of autumn leaves, while the . . . text at the end explains why leaves change color. Readers learn how to identify all sorts of leaves from red maple to sycamore by their color, shape, and other characteristics. A great choice for science units and autumn displays." (Publisher's note)

"Gerber's poetic text describes colors, shapes, and characteristics with an abundance of similes and metaphors. . . . Evans' vibrant hand-colored linoleum prints feature scenes of a brother and sister with the family dog enjoying traditional fall activities." Booklist

Seeds, bees, butterflies, and more! poems for two voices. poems by Carole Gerber; illustrated by Eugene Yelchin. 1st ed. Henry Holt and Co. 2013 32 p. col. ill. (reinforced) $17.99

Grades: 2 3 4   E

1. Nature poetry 2. Children's poetry

ISBN 0805092110; 9780805092110

LC 2012011490

This book by Carole Gerber presents a "collection of nature- and spring-themed poems designed to be recited by two readers. The poems' alternating parts are differentiated by color, with multicolored phrases intended to be read in unison." They contain "information about flowers, berries, bugs, and more, as well as topics including germination and pollination." (Publishers Weekly)

Gerdner, Linda

Grandfather's story cloth; written by Linda Gerdner and Sarah Langford; illustrated by Stuart Loughridge. Shen's Books 2008 29p il $16.95

Grades: 2 3 4   E

1. Quilts -- Fiction 2. Grandfathers -- Fiction 3. Laotian Americans -- Fiction 4. Alzheimer's disease -- Fiction 5. Hmong (Asian people) -- Fiction 6. Bilingual books -- English-Hmong

ISBN 978-1-885008-34-3; 1-885008-34-1

Ten-year-old Chersheng helps his beloved grandfather cope with his failing memory, brought on by Alzheimer's disease, by showing him the story quilt Grandfather made after fleeing his homeland, Laos, during wartime.

"The English and Hmong texts face paintings that express the many moods of the characters. Endpapers and the back cover feature numerous geometric patterns that are common in Hmong handicrafts. . . . [The book includes] background information on Alzheimer's disease and the Hmong refugees and their story cloths. . . . A strong family story about difficult social issues relevant to today's society." SLJ

Gerritsen, Paula

Nuts; [by] Paula Gerritsen. Front Street 2006 un il $15.95

Grades: PreK K 1 2   E

1. Mice -- Fiction 2. Nuts -- Fiction 3. Storms -- Fiction

ISBN 1-932425-66-7

LC 2005021491

Original Dutch edition 2005

Mouse braves many dangers while trying to collect nuts before winter sets in, including a sudden storm that first brings her disappointment, then a delightful surprise

"The words are well chosen and the repeated refrain will delight readers. The pencil-and-pastel illustrations are charming, displaying the textures and colors of fall and the foreboding energy of the storm." SLJ

Gershator, Phillis

★ **Listen,** listen; [by] Phillis Gershator; [illustrated by] Alison Jay. Barefoot Books 2007 un il $16.95

Grades: K 1 2 3   E

1. Stories in rhyme 2. Sound -- Fiction 3. Nature -- Fiction 4. Seasons -- Fiction

ISBN 978-1-84686-084-3

LC 2006100351

Illustrations and rhyming text explore the sights and sounds of nature in each season of the year.

"Jay's magical and occasionally eerie crackle-glaze oil paintings furnish a visual feast. The text is built around a series of rhyming, gentile directives to attune one's ears." Publ Wkly

Moo, moo, brown cow, have you any milk? illustrated by Giselle Potter. Random House Children's Books 2011 32p il $16.99; lib bdg $19.99

Grades: PreK K 1   E

1. Stories in rhyme 2. Bedtime -- Fiction 3. Domestic animals -- Fiction

ISBN 978-0-375-86744-6; 0-375-86744-9; 978-0-375-96744-3 lib bdg; 0-375-96744-3 lib bdg

LC 2010018767

Through rhyming text, farm animals are asked if they have items needed to prepare for a snack and bedtime, such as wool for a blanket, down for a pillow, and milk to drink.

"Gershator uses rhyme and the melodic rhythm of 'Baa, Baa, Black Sheep' in her dialogue, making the tale fit for either singing or speaking. Potter uses soft colors for day and rich cobalt and chocolate for night in her folksy paintings." SLJ

Sky sweeper; pictures by Holly Meade. Farrar, Straus & Giroux 2007 un il $16

Grades: 1 2 3 4   E

1. Work -- Fiction 2. Japan -- Fiction 3. Gardens -- Fiction 4. Buddhism -- Fiction

ISBN 978-0-374-37007-7; 0-374-37007-9

LC 2005-49762

Despite criticism for his lack of "accomplishments," Takiboki finds contentment sweeping flower blossoms and raking the sand and gravel in the monks' temple garden. Includes a note on the art and beauty of Japanese gardens

"This is a complex, challenging story. . . . But Meade's beautiful collage illustrations of the earthly garden and glorious afterlife greatly enhance the story's accessibility and will help kids get closer to the text's religious and philosophical themes." Booklist

Time for a hug; by Phillis Gershator & Mim Green; illustrated by David Walker. Sterling Pub. Co. 2012 24 p. $9.95

Grades: PreK K   E

1. Stories in rhyme 2. Hugging -- Fiction 3. Rabbits -- Fiction

ISBN 1402778627; 9781402778629

LC 2011021209

In this children's book, by Phillis Gershator & Mim Green, "two bunnies, one small and orange and the other bigger and gray, wake up at 8:00 to begin a day chock-full of activities that preschoolers will recognize. Washing faces, getting dressed, baking a pie, playing with puppets, reading a book, bathing, brushing teeth and hopping off to bed are all portrayed in [David] Walker's softly colored full-page and double-page spreads or vignettes." (Kirkus Reviews)

"Hour by hour, this bouncy rhyme follows a rabbit parent and child through their day. Every so often, they pause in their many activities--indoors and out--to share a hug. "A hug feels good. / Let's hug again. / We'll hug at nine. / We'll hug at ten." The energetic illustrations, rendered in delicate pastel colors, often include a clock to show the time." Horn Book

Who's awake in springtime? [by] Phillis Gershator and Mim Green; illustrated by Emilie Chollat. Henry Holt & Co. 2010 un il $16.99

Grades: PreK K 1 2   E

1. Stories in rhyme 2. Spring -- Fiction 3. Animals

-- Fiction 4. Bedtime -- Fiction
ISBN 978-0-8050-6390-5; 0-8050-6390-0

LC 2009009224

Describes, in rhymed cumulative text and illustrations, how various young animals and one small human prepare for sleep at the end of a spring day.

"This cumulative tale is simple and accessible by young readers. . . . Adults who share this book with children can engage the students with the rhythmic text, and repetition throughout the book begs for call-backs and other participation activities. . . . Chollat's illustrations offer bold colors and clear lines and strongly support the story." Libr Media Connect

Who's in the forest? [illustrations by] Jill McDonald. Barefoot Books 2010 un il bd bk $14.99

Grades: PreK K   E
1. Stories in rhyme 2. Board books for children 3. Forest animals -- Fiction
ISBN 978-1-84686-476-6; 1-84686-476-3

LC 2010009438

"Simple rhymes tell listeners that the deep and dark forest is home to bears, foxes, squirrels, and all types of birds. The collage illustrations are colorful and childlike, and every other page has a cutout circle that highlights a particular animal. . . . Toddlers, especially, will love the rhyming couplets and enjoy finding the creatures revealed with each page turn of this large-format board book." SLJ

Gerstein, Mordicai

★ **A book**. Roaring Brook 2009 un il

Grades: PreK K 1 2   E
1. Authorship -- Fiction 2. Books and reading -- Fiction
ISBN 1-59643-251-9; 978-1-59643-251-2

"Among a family who lives in a book, the youngest daughter is the only one who doesn't have a story to belong to, so she sets out among fairy tales, adventures, mysteries, histories, science fiction, and others to track down her story." (Publisher's note) "Grades two to four." (Bull Cent Child Books)

"This charming story follows a young girl and her family who live in a book, . . . though she doesn't know what kind of story her book is. . . . She dashes though spreads that take her into nursery rhymes, on the trail of a mystery, across pirate waters, and even into outer space before she ultimately decides to write her own story, which is, of course, this story. . . . The concept is executed with . . . cleverness and gentleness." Booklist

★ **Carolinda** clatter! Roaring Brook Press 2005 un il $16.95

Grades: PreK K 1 2 3   E
1. Fairy tales 2. Giants -- Fiction
ISBN 1-59643-063-X

LC 2004-24258

The excessively quiet town of Pupickton and the sleeping lovesick giant upon which it was built, are both awakened by the joyful noise of a little girl's songs.

"Gerstein tells his whimsical tale with direct humor, and his lovely paint-and-ink illustrations extend the comedy." Booklist

The **first** drawing; by Caldecott Medalist Mordicai Gerstein. Little Brown & Co 2013 40 p. $17

Grades: PreK K 1   E
1. Picture books for children 2. Cave drawings and paintings -- Fiction 3. Drawing -- Fiction 4. Imagination -- Fiction 5. Cave dwellers -- Fiction 6. Cave paintings -- Fiction 7. Prehistoric peoples -- Fiction
ISBN 0316204781; 9780316204781

LC 2013001269

In this picture book, Caldecott Medalist Mordicai Gerstein tells the tale "of a boy living 30,000 years ago with his pet wolf and his very extended family. Using narrative direct address . . . to effectively bridge the gap between prehistoric times and the present, the story follows the boy on his fanciful discoveries of wooly mammoths in clouds, bears in stones and horses galloping on cave walls." (Kirkus Reviews)

How to bicycle to the moon to plant sunflowers; a simple but brilliant plan in twenty-four easy steps. Mordicai Gerstein. Roaring Brook Press 2013 40 p. (hardcover) $16.99

Grades: K 1 2 3   E
1. Moon -- Fiction 2. Picture books for children 3. Voyages and travels -- Fiction
ISBN 1596435127; 9781596435124

LC 2012013787

In this book from Caldecott Medalist Mordicai Gerstein, a "boy with spiky red hair and glasses shares his 24-step plan for planting sunflowers on the moon to cheer it up." The expedition "involves creating a giant sling-shot to launch a flag pole/anchor harpoon into the moon . . . then, wearing a spacesuit kindly donated by NASA, one can simply bicycle up to the moon on the 238,900 miles of garden hose attached to the harpoon." (Publishers Weekly)

Leaving the nest. Farrar, Straus and Giroux 2007 un il $16

Grades: K 1 2 3   E
1. Cats -- Fiction 2. Birds -- Fiction 3. Growth -- Fiction 4. Squirrels -- Fiction
ISBN 978-0-374-34369-9; 0-374-34369-1

LC 2005-51228

The lives of a baby jaybird, a young girl, a kitten, and a small squirrel intersect as they venture out into the world.

"Using dialogue bubbles to reveal conversations and thoughts, Gerstein's realistic illustrations set the backyard stage and choreograph the frenzied acts of the drama, adding touches of humor without diminishing the tension." Booklist

Minifred goes to school. HarperCollins 2009 un il $17.99

Grades: PreK K 1 2   E
1. School stories 2. Cats -- Fiction 3. Animals -- Fiction
ISBN 978-0-06-075889-9; 0-06-075889-9; 978-0-06-075890-5 lib bdg; 0-06-075890-2 lib bdg

LC 2008-13861

When Mr. Portly finds a kitten, he and his wife raise her like a child, but unlike a typical child, Minifred the kitten does not like to follow rules at home or at school.

"Gerstein matches the story's lighthearted mood with action-packed scenes, using playful colors, caricatured figures, and sometimes multiple scenes per page, increasing the sense of action." SLJ

★ The **night** world; by Mordicai Gerstein. Little, Brown & Co. 2015 40 p. (hc) $18

Grades: PreK K 1   E

1. Color -- Fiction 2. Night -- Fiction 3. Cats -- Fiction 4. Colors -- Fiction 5. Animals -- Fiction 6. Sun -- Rising and setting -- Fiction

ISBN 0316188220; 9780316188227

LC 2014006903

In this juvenile story, by Mordicai Gerstein, "the shadows of a summer night sing the promise of morning to a boy and his cat as they venture out into the dark yard surrounding their house. . . . [His cat,] Sylvie, it soon appears, is not ready for sleep and meows insistently until the two tiptoe through the sleeping house and out into the nighttime shadows." (School Library Journal)

"Caldecott Medalist Gerstein delights and inspires readers in this meditation on the night. . . . Glorious sunlit spreads capture not just the look of a breaking dawn but the haunting feel of watching night turn to day. Gerstein is at the top of his game here, capturing a nearly inexpressible mood. Beginning with the very darkest shades while the boy is in the house . . . makes readers look and look again, and once they are outside, the animals' stirrings will have children pointing at the darkened pages with delight. The strong yet simple message impresses: look around; there are so many wonderful things to see." Booklist

Sparrow Jack. Frances Foster Bks. 2003 un il $16

Grades: PreK K 1 2 3   E

1. Photographers 2. Sparrows -- Fiction 3. Immigrants -- Fiction

ISBN 0-374-37139-3

LC 2001-23829

In 1868, John Bardsley, an immigrant from England, brought one thousand sparrows from his home country back to Philadelphia, where he hoped they would help save the trees from the inch-worms that were destroying them

"Though a few imaginative liberties are taken with the facts, Gerstein's cheerful tale is based on a true story. The humor of his whimsically witty text is beautifully captured and expanded by drawings that are filled with comic action and droll details." Booklist

★ The **white** ram; a story of Abraham and Isaac. Holiday House 2006 un il $16.95

Grades: 1 2 3 4   E

1. Prophets 2. Sheep -- Fiction 3. Biblical characters 4. Rosh ha-Shanah -- Fiction

ISBN 0-8234-1897-9; 978-0-8234-1897-8

LC 2005-46001

A white ram, made on the sixth day of creation, waits patiently in the garden of Eden until the time is right, then runs to save a certain child in fulfillment of God's plan.

"This stunningly illustrated picture book is based on a Midrash. . . . The art, done in pen and ink, oils, and colored pencil, is mesmerizing. [This is told] with a captivating use of language along with true drama." SLJ

Ghigna, Charles

Barn storm; by Charles Ghigna and Debra Ghigna; illustrated by Diane Greenseid. Random House 2010 32p il (Step into reading) lib bdg $12.99; pa $3.99

Grades: 1 2 3   E

1. Stories in rhyme 2. Farm life -- Fiction 3. Tornadoes -- Fiction

ISBN 978-0-375-96114-4 lib bdg; 0-375-96114-3 lib bdg; 978-0-375-86114-7 pa; 0-375-86114-9 pa

LC 2009033321

When a tornado touches down in a pond on Farmer Brown's property, it sets off a chain of events among the barnyard animals that soon has every creature displaced, but not unhappy

"The Ghignas' silly rhymes bounce along; Greenseid's textured illustrations will elicit giggles." Horn Book Guide

Gibfried, Diane

Brother Juniper; illustrated by Meilo So. Clarion Books 2006 un il $16

Grades: K 1 2 3   E

1. Saints 2. Clergy -- Fiction 3. Writers on religion

ISBN 0-618-54361-9; 978-0-618-54361-8

LC 2005-10038

Worried about having left the overly-generous Brother Juniper in charge of their chapel when they went out to preach, Father Francis of Assisi and the other friars are not prepared for what they find upon their return.

"Filled with delicate details and gentle humor, the accomplished watercolor paintings add greatly to the book's appeal. . . . This is an excellent choice to open discussion about generosity." SLJ

Giff, Patricia Reilly

Watch out, Ronald Morgan! illustrated by Susanna Natti. Viking Kestrel 1985 24p il hardcover o.p. pa $5.99

Grades: PreK K 1 2   E

1. School stories 2. Eyeglasses -- Fiction

ISBN 0-14-050638-1 pa

LC 84-19623

Ronald has many humorous mishaps until he gets a pair of eyeglasses. Includes a note for adults about children's eye problems

"Told in a forthright manner but with appreciation for children's candor, the book's dialogue rings true with catchy humor. . . . Natti's illustrations show the characters to be bright, colorful informal figures who move with the text." SLJ

Other titles about Ronald Morgan are:

Good luck, Ronald Morgan (1996)

Happy birthday, Ronald Morgan! (1986)

Ronald Morgan goes to bat (1988)

Ronald Morgan goes to camp (1995)

Today was a terrible day (1980)

Gilani-Williams, Fawzia

★ **Nabeel's** new pants; an Eid tale. retold by Fawzia Gilani-Williams; illustrations by Proiti Roy. Marshall Cavendish Children 2010 un il $15.99

Grades: K 1 2 3   E

1. Turkey -- Fiction 2. Muslims -- Fiction 3. Id al-Adha -- Fiction 4. Family life -- Fiction

ISBN 978-0-7614-5629-2; 0-7614-5629-5

First published 2007 in India

"Turkish shoemaker Nabeel buys Eid gifts for his family. . . . The shopkeeper also persuades Nabeel to buy himself new pants, but the pants are too long. His wife, mother, and daughter are all too busy cooking for Eid to shorten his pants, so he cuts a few inches off himself. Later, the women in the house feel guilty and each secretly trims the pants more. . . . Roy's cheerful gouache, watercolor, and ink illustrations show the bonds among family members as they follow their traditions together. Kids will laugh right along with the loving characters." Booklist

Includes glossary

Gilchrist, Jan Spivey

My America; illustrations by Ashley Bryan and Jan Spivey Gilchrist; poem by Jan Spivey Gilchrist. HarperCollins Pubs. 2007 un il $16.99; lib bdg $17.89
Grades: PreK K 1 2　　　　　　　　　　　　　　　E
　1. United States -- Poetry
　ISBN 978-0-06-079104-9; 0-06-079104-7; 978-0-06-079105-6 lib bdg; 0-06-079105-5 lib bdg
　　　　　　　　　　　　　　　　　LC 2006029867
"This unusual tribute celebrates America's diversity in its landscapes, both urban and rural, its wildlife, but most of all its people. . . . Both Bryan and Gilchrist illustrate the poem in alternating spreads: his signature color swirls work in tandem with her muted, blue-toned tableaux and faces. . . . The words have the potential for choral reading or dramatization." Booklist

Gilman, Grace

Dixie; pictures by Sarah McConnell. HarperCollins 2011 30p il (I can read!) $16.99; pa $3.99
Grades: PreK K 1　　　　　　　　　　　　　　　E
　1. School stories 2. Dogs -- Fiction 3. Theater -- Fiction
　ISBN 978-0-06-171914-1; 0-06-171914-5; 978-0-06-171913-4 pa; 0-06-171913-7 pa
　　　　　　　　　　　　　　　　　LC 2010015979
Dixie the puppy plays with Emma every day after school until Emma starts memorizing her lines for the school play. This "should make for a successful experience for the brand-new reader. The simple sentences are accompanied by uncluttered, realistic, brightly colored paintings that complement the story and provide clues to help the reader decipher the text." Booklist

Ginsburg, Mirra

★ The chick and the duckling; translated [and adapted] from the Russian of V. Suteyev; pictures by Jose & Ariane Aruego. Macmillan 1972 un il hardcover o.p. pa $6.99
Grades: PreK K　　　　　　　　　　　　　　　E
　1. Ducks -- Fiction 2. Chickens -- Fiction
　ISBN 0-689-71226-X pa
"The sunny simplicity of the illustrations is just right for a slight but engaging text, and they add a note of humor that is a nice foil for the bland directness of the story." Bull Cent Child Books

Good morning, chick; by Mirra Ginsburg, adapted from a story by Korney Chukovsky; pictures by Byron Barton. Greenwillow Bks. 1980 un il hardcover o.p. pa $6.99
Grades: PreK K　　　　　　　　　　　　　　　E
　1. Chickens -- Fiction
　ISBN 0-688-84284-4 lib bdg; 0-688-08741-8 pa
　　　　　　　　　　　　　　　　　LC 80-11352
"Based upon a tale by the great Russian poet and storyteller, the totally childlike picture book for the very young employs an engaging device: The text, illustrated with

a bright vignette, appears on each of the left-hand pages; then, after pausing briefly and leading the eye to the right, a sentence runs to completion on the opposite page with two words contained in a large storytelling picture done in bold, brilliant color." Horn Book

Giovanni, Nikki

★ The grasshopper's song; an Aesop's fable revisited. by Nikki Giovanni; illustrated by Chris Raschka. Candlewick Press 2008 44p il $16.99
Grades: K 1 2 3　　　　　　　　　　　　　　　E
　1. Ants -- Fiction 2. Trials -- Fiction 3. Grasshoppers -- Fiction
　ISBN 978-0-7636-3021-8; 0-7636-3021-7
Every year the Grasshoppers sing and play their instruments and the Ants work in rhythm to the music. But when winter comes, the Ants turn their backs on the Grasshoppers, and Jimmy Grasshopper finds this unfair. He's hired Robin, Robin, Robin, and Wren to sue Abigail and Nestor Ant for what he deserves—R-E-S-P-E-C-T—and a one-half share of the harvest. But will a jury of his peers agree about the worth of art?

"To illustrate Giovanni's detailed and insightful prose, Raschka . . . creates evocative, earth-tone watercolors that suggest camouflage." Publ Wkly

★ Giving thanks; poems, prayers, and praise songs of thanksgiving. edited and with reflections by Katherine Paterson; illustrated by Pamela Dalton. Chronicle Books LLC 2013 56 p. (alk. paper) $18.99
Grades: 3 4 5 6 7 8 9 10 11 12　　　　　　　　E
　1. Thanksgiving Day 2. Picture books for children 3. Gratitude 4. Children's poetry 5. Children -- Prayers and devotions
　ISBN 1452113394; 9781452113395
　　　　　　　　　　　　　　　　　LC 2013009517
In this illustrated children's book, Wilder Award winner Katherine Paterson presents a collection of speeches, songs, and prayers related to giving thanks. She "offers an essay before each section: 'Gather Around the Table,' 'A Celebration of Life,' 'The Spirit Within' and 'Circle of Community.'" (Kirkus Reviews)

Glaser, Linda

Hoppy Hanukkah! illustrated by Daniel Howarth. Albert Whitman 2009 un il $15.99
Grades: PreK K　　　　　　　　　　　　　　　E
　1. Rabbits -- Fiction 2. Hanukkah -- Fiction 3. Family life -- Fiction
　ISBN 978-0-8075-3378-9; 0-8075-3378-5
　　　　　　　　　　　　　　　　　LC 2008-55696
Two young bunnies learn about the customs of Hanukkah from their parents and grandparents before they light the menorahs, eat potato latkes, and play dreidel.

"Howarth's soft, bright illustrations of an extended floppy-eared family offer details of a Judaic home in this gentle introduction to the rituals of a traditional celebration that young families can follow as they create a Hanukkah atmosphere in their own homes." Kirkus

Hoppy Passover! illustrated by Daniel Howarth. Albert Whitman 2011 un il $15.99
Grades: PreK K　　　　　　　　　　　　　　　E
　1. Jews -- Fiction 2. Rabbits -- Fiction 3. Passover

-- Fiction

ISBN 978-0-8075-3380-2; 0-8075-3380-7

LC 2010024111

Two young bunnies learn about the customs of the Passover seder from their parents and grandparents as they all celebrate the holiday meal.

"Howarth's cozy and colorful illustrations portray a warm and loving family enjoying this holiday and passing their traditions along to a new generation." Booklist

Another title about this rabbit family is:
Hoppy Hanukkah! (2009)

Glass, Beth Raisner

Blue-ribbon dad; illustrated Margie Moore. Harry N Abrams Inc. 2011 un il $14.95

Grades: PreK K 1 E

1. Fathers -- Fiction 2. Squirrels -- Fiction

ISBN 978-0-8109-9727-1; 0-8109-9727-4

"A young squirrel hustles to get a surprise ready before his father comes home. While working on an arts-and-crafts project that necessitates glue, glitter, sequins, stickers, and more, the squirrel reflects on everything his father does for him. . . . Moore's delicately outlined watercolors mirror the coziness of the text." Publ Wkly

Glass, Eleri

The **red** shoes; by Eleri Glass; illustrated by Ashley Spires. Simply Read 2008 un il $16.95

Grades: PreK K 1 2 E

1. Shoes -- Fiction 2. Shopping -- Fiction

ISBN 978-1-894965-78-1; 1-894965-78-7

"Shopping for shoes, a little girl knows that her mother will pick the practical, very dull, lace-ups. Even the palette that Spires uses is dark and drab, and the child's body language screams disappointment. But when she gets to the store, she sees the most wonderful pair of red shoes and wants them more than anything. . . . This sweet story will appeal to little girls who count shoes as something very important indeed." SLJ

Gleeson, Libby

★ **Clancy** & Millie, and the very fine house; [illustrated by] Freya Blackwood. Little Hare Books 2009 un il $16.99

Grades: 1 2 E

1. Moving -- Fiction

ISBN 978-1-921541-19-3; 1-921541-19-9

LC 2010399372

"Australians Gleeson and Blackwood . . . portray with sensitivity a small boy's ambivalence about moving to a new house. . . . Blackwood exaggerates the building's imposing exterior and its rooms, with towering walls, windows that seem miles away, and chilly gray expanses of floor, emphasizing the enormity of the move for Clancy. . . . Though the story deals with a particular childhood dilemma, Clancy's feelings are conveyed with a dignity that should appeal to a wide audience." Publ Wkly

The **great** bear; [illustrations by Armin Greder] Candlewick Press 2011 il $16.99

Grades: PreK K 1 E

1. Bears -- Fiction 2. Freedom -- Fiction

ISBN 978-0-7636-5136-7; 0-7636-5136-2

LC 2010040288

A bear imprisoned in a medieval circus is forced to perform night after night before a mocking crowd, but she finally can no longer stand the torment and determines to set herself free.

"Greder's darkly beautiful charcoal-and-pastel illustrations carry the weight of the storytelling . . . and are abetted by a unique design. . . . Subtle—yet spectacular and deeply moving" Kirkus

★ **Half** a world away; by Libby Gleeson; illustrated by Freya Blackwood. Arthur A. Levine Books 2007 un il hardcover o.p. $15.99

Grades: PreK K 1 2 E

1. Moving -- Fiction 2. Friendship -- Fiction

ISBN 0-439-88977-4; 0-439-88978-2 pa

LC 2006007712

When Louie's best friend Amy moves to the other side of the world, Louie must find a way to reconnect with her

"Blackwood's tender, realistic watercolors reinforce the friends' sweet closeness and magic. . . . Subtle, direct, and profound." Booklist

Glenn, Sharlee Mullins

Just what Mama needs; [by] Sharlee Glenn; illustrated by Amiko Hirao. Harcourt 2008 un il lib bdg $16

Grades: PreK K 1 2 E

1. Dogs -- Fiction 2. Week -- Fiction 3. Imagination -- Fiction

ISBN 978-0-15-205759-6; 0-15-205759-5

LC 2005-25440

Abby the dog assumes a different identity for each day of the week until Sunday, when she is just herself.

"Glenn's descriptive text and use of onomatopoeia provide an ideal read-aloud [and] . . . Hirao's collage and colored-pencil art, expressed on a variety of paper surfaces, alternates stark views as Abby introduces a costume, followed by busy scenes of her imagination and the real-life labors. . . . There's something to please nearly everyone in this tale." SLJ

Gliori, Debi

No matter what. Harcourt Brace & Co. 1999 un il $16; bd bk $6.95

Grades: PreK K 1 E

1. Stories in rhyme 2. Foxes -- Fiction 3. Parent-child relationship -- Fiction

ISBN 0-15-202061-6; 0-15-206343-9 bd bk

LC 98-47277

Small, a little fox, seeks reassurance that Large will always provide love, no matter what

"Gliori's whimsical illustrations use warm, inviting color to invoke the same sense of emotional security as the rhyming text." Booklist

Stormy weather; written and illustrated by Debi Gliori. Walker & Co. 2009 un il $15.99; lib bdg $16.89

Grades: PreK K E

1. Stories in rhyme 2. Foxes -- Fiction 3. Animals -- Fiction 4. Bedtime -- Fiction 5. Mother-child relationship -- Fiction

ISBN 978-0-8027-9419-2; 0-8027-9419-X; 978-0-8027-9422-2 lib bdg; 0-8027-9422-X lib bdg

LC 2008043523

As nighttime approaches, a baby fox and his mother imagine all the different animals around the world preparing for bed and falling asleep.

"The story's lulling pace enhances the quiet bedtime read-aloud. . . . Watercolor-and-ink spreads utilize warm earth tones within the family homes to contrast the sometimes threatening outside elements or cool night backdrops. Nimble lines support the comforting images, and swirling designs and twinkling stars add unique details." SLJ

The **trouble** with dragons; [by] Debi Gliori. Walker & Co. 2008 un il $16.99; lib bdg $17.89

Grades: PreK K 1   E
1. Stories in rhyme 2. Dragons -- Fiction 3. Environmental protection -- Fiction 4. Conservation of natural resources -- Fiction

ISBN 978-0-8027-9789-6; 0-8027-9789-X; 978-0-8027-9790-2 lib bdg; 0-8027-9790-3 lib bdg

LC 2008005389

When dragons cut down too many trees, blow out too much hot air, and do other environmental damage, the future looks grim, but other animals advise them on how to mend their ways and save the planet

This "is magical, thanks to the playful artwork and bouncy rhymes. Though the text sticks to the basics of taking care of the Earth, the illustrations offer fodder for discussion." SLJ

What's the time, Mr. Wolf? by Deb Gliori. Walker 2012 32 p.

Grades: PreK K 1   E
1. Time -- Fiction 2. Wolves -- Fiction 3. Characters and characteristics in literature 4. Characters in literature -- Fiction

ISBN 0802734324; 9780802734327

LC 2012014710

This book by Debi Gliori is "told from the point of view of Mr. Wolf on his birthday. Four and twenty black birds wake him up at seven o'clock, tweeting, 'What's the time, Mr. Wolf?' . . . Little Red Riding Hood, Hickory Dickory Dock . . . Humpty Dumpty, and other favorite nursery rhyme characters make an appearance in the text and/or pictures. Mr. Wolf's day is not going well until six o'clock when his friends surprise him with a birthday party." (School Library Journal)

Global Fund for Children (Organization)

American babies; developed by the Global Fund for Children. Charlesbridge 2010 un il $6.95

Grades: PreK   E
1. Infants 2. Board books for children
ISBN 978-1-58089-280-3; 1-58089-280-9

"This appealing board book offers 17 closeup photos of babies. . . . [It] has a brief text, really a single sentence divided into phrases. . . . From the Hawaiian child on the cover to the African-American girl on the last page, all the babies pictured are beyond early infancy. Their expressive faces and emotions are as varied as their family backgrounds, surroundings, and activities. . . . The pleasing layout places each colorful, full-page photo opposite a page with a slightly smaller photo and large-type text on its bright, solid-color border." Booklist

Global babies; developed by the Global Fund for Children. Charlesbridge 2007 un il $6.95

Grades: PreK   E
1. Infants 2. Board books for children
ISBN 978-1-58089-174-5

This board book offers color photographs of babies from 17 cultures around the world.

★ **Global** baby girls; a Global Fund for Children Book. Global Fund for Children. Charlesbridge 2013 16 p. (board book) $6.95

Grades: PreK   E
1. Girls 2. Board books for children 3. Picture books for children 4. Board books 5. Girls -- Fiction

ISBN 1580894399; 9781580894395

LC 2012007368

Amelia Bloomer List (2014)

This is a children's board book from the nonprofit Global Fund for Children. The "babies' smiling faces and bright-colored clothing (which ranges from everyday jumpers to, in the case of one Russian child, a fur suit) are attention-grabbing, and the overall message ('Baby girls can grow up to change the world') is empowering." (Publishers Weekly)

Goble, Paul

Beyond the ridge; story and illustrations by Paul Goble. Bradbury Press 1989 un il hardcover o.p. pa $6.99

Grades: 2 3 4   E
1. Native Americans -- Fiction
ISBN 0-689-71731-8 pa

LC 87-33113

At her death an elderly Plains Indian woman experiences the afterlife believed in by her people, while the surviving family members prepare her body according to their custom

"Goble's illustrations—in a double spread of gray rocks, smoothly surfaced in a skyscape of flying vultures—make a dignified context for a moving, direct discussion of death." Bull Cent Child Books

Death of the iron horse; story and illustrations by Paul Goble. Bradbury Press 1987 un il hardcover o.p. pa $7.99

Grades: K 1 2 3   E
1. Railroads -- Fiction 2. Cheyenne Indians -- Fiction
ISBN 0-689-71686-9 pa

LC 85-28011

The author "has taken several accounts of the 1867 Cheyenne attack of a Union Pacific freight train . . . and combined them into a story from the Indians' viewpoint. As the Cheyenne Prophet Sweet Medicine had foretold, strange hairy people were invading the land, killing women and children and driving off the horses. Descriptions of the iron horse inspired curiosity and fear in the young braves who decided to go out and protect their village from this new menace. Keeping fairly close to actual Indian accounts, Goble presents the braves' bold attack on the train, glossing over the deaths of the train crew." SLJ

Godden, Rumer

The **story** of Holly & Ivy; [by] Rumer Godden; [pictures by] Barbara Cooney. Viking 2006 31p il $17.99

Grades: K 1 2 3   E
1. Dolls -- Fiction 2. Orphans -- Fiction 3. Christmas

-- Fiction

ISBN 0-670-06219-7; 978-0-670-06219-5

First published 1957; a reissue of the newly illustrated edition published 1985

Orphaned Ivy finds her Christmas wish fulfilled with the help of a lonely couple and a doll named Holly.

"Texturally rich and evocatively wintry, this reissue is timeless." Horn Book Guide

Godin, Thelma Lynne

The **hula** hoopin' queen; by Thelma Lynne Godin; illustrated by Vanessa Brantley-Newton. Lee & Low Books Inc. 2014 40 p. color illustrations (hardcover) $18.95

Grades: K 1 2 3 4   E

1. City and town life -- Fiction 2. Intergenerational relations -- Fiction 3. Parties -- Fiction 4. Birthdays -- Fiction 5. Responsibility -- Fiction 6. African Americans -- Fiction 7. Harlem (New York, N.Y.) -- Fiction 8. Competition (Psychology) -- Fiction

ISBN 1600608469; 9781600608469

LC 2013015548

"A spunky girl has a hula-hooping competition with her friends in Harlem, and soon everyone in the neighborhood--young and old alike--joins in on the fun. . . . Kameeka's disappointed to be stuck at home and can only think about the hoopin' competition. Distracted, Kameeka accidentally ruins Miz Adeline's birthday cake, and has to confess to her that there won't be a cake for her special day." (Publisher's note)

"First-time picture book author Godin's empathic prose and Brantley-Newton's emotionally telegraphic art capture the lively and nurturing Harlem neighborhood and the thrill of competition, whether age nine or 90." Pub Wkly

Godwin, Laura

★ **Happy** and Honey; written by Laura Godwin; pictures by Jane Chapman. Margaret K. McElderry Bks. 2000 un il (Happy Honey) $12.95

Grades: PreK K 1   E

1. Cats -- Fiction 2. Dogs -- Fiction

ISBN 0-689-83406-3

LC 99-46923

Honey the cat is determined to play with Happy the dog, even though he is trying to sleep

"The text is short and effective, and the delightful acrylic paintings, which are set against an expanse of white space, center on Happy and Honey, keeping children as focused on the goings-on as does the just-right text." Booklist

Other titles about Happy and Honey are:

The best fall of all (2002)

Happy Christmas, Honey (2002)

Honey helps (2000)

One moon, two cats; illustrated by Yoko Tanaka. Atheneum Books for Young Readers 2011 un il $16.99

Grades: PreK K 1   E

1. Stories in rhyme 2. Cats -- Fiction 3. Country life -- Fiction 4. City and town life -- Fiction

ISBN 978-1-4424-1202-6; 1-4424-1202-X

LC 2009053697

Two cats, one in the city and one in the country, chase mice before going to sleep.

"The brief, rhymed text changes size to match the rhythms of the cats' adventures, and the rich acrylic paint-

ings create an air of nighttime mystery. An ably told and atmospheric romp." SLJ

Goembel, Ponder

Animal fair; adapted and illustrated by Ponder Goembel. Marshall Cavendish Children 2010 un il $12.99

Grades: PreK K 1   E

1. Stories in rhyme 2. Animals -- Fiction

ISBN 978-0-7614-5642-1; 0-7614-5642-2

LC 2009005937

"Based on the children's song Animal Fair, Goembel's adaptation adroitly posits the wild imaginings of a child: what might go on at a fair apparently run by animals? The answer is nonsense, as virtually nothing the animals do makes a whit of sense. That, of course, is what will make young listeners squeal with glee. The text is wonderfully wordy and tied to an irresistible rhythm. . . . Goembel's ink and acrylic-wash artwork has an appealing orderliness to it." Booklist

Going, K. L.

Dog in charge; by K.L. Going; illustrated by Dan Santat. Dial Books for Young Readers 2012 40 p. col. ill. (hardcover) $16.99

Grades: PreK K 1 2   E

1. Cats -- Fiction 2. Dogs -- Fiction 3. Picture books for children

ISBN 0803734794; 9780803734791

LC 2011035211

This is "Printz-winner [K.L.] Going['s] . . . picture-book debut." It's a "saga of a tutu-wearing bulldog who is the designated cat-sitter while the humans are at the store. Once the car leaves the driveway, five cats of varying breeds skedaddle from the sofa to spill milk, stir up fireplace ash, empty the hamper, disrupt a vanity, and more. Dog worries that their raucous acting out will reflect badly on him: 'Would he still be a good Dog, a smart Dog, the very best Dog?' His idea to entice good behavior with kibbles disappears with his own hunger. As he naps, the cats remember that they love Dog and bring the house back to perfect order as the family arrives." (School Library Journal)

Golan, Avirama

Little Naomi, Little Chick; by Avirama Golan; illustrated by Raaya Karas. Eerdmans Books for Young Readers 2013 34 p. (hbk.) $17

Grades: PreK K   E

1. Schools -- Fiction 2. Chickens -- Fiction 3. Farm life -- Fiction 4. Nursery schools -- Fiction 5. Animals -- Infancy -- Fiction

ISBN 0802854273; 9780802854278

LC 2013000492

In this book, by Avirama Golan, "Little Naomi has a busy day! She gets ready for school, plays with all her friends, builds with blocks, bakes mud pies, colors pictures, eats lunch, and helps mom with the shopping. Little Chick has to stay at home with the other barnyard animals, but that doesn't stop him from having adventures of his own." (Publisher's note)

Gold, August

★ **Thank** you, God, for everything; by August Gold; illustrated by Wendy Anderson Halperin. G.P. Putnam's Sons 2009 un il $16.99

Grades: PreK K 1 2   E
1. God -- Fiction 2. Religious life -- Fiction
ISBN 978-0-399-24049-2; 0-399-24049-7

LC 2008016801

As Daisy watches her parents thanking God everyday, she begins to look at everything around her and realizes she is also thankful for many things.

Gold's "goal here is to 'show young readers how to develop their own thankful eyes.' Both she and artist Halperin do that beautifully in this story. . . . In her signature softly colored style . . . Halperin takes everyday doings and elevates them." Booklist

Goldfinger, Jennifer P.
My dog Lyle. Clarion Books 2007 un il $16
Grades: PreK K 1 2   E
1. Dogs -- Fiction
ISBN 978-0-618-63983-0; 0-618-63983-7

LC 2006-07146

A child provides an ever-increasing list of characteristics that make Lyle a very special dog, despite appearances.

"The lively text matches perfectly with the vibrant, playful illustrations, done in bold, richly hued acrylics and oils." SLJ

Goldin, Barbara Diamond
Cakes and miracles; a Purim tale. [illustrated by] Jaime Zollars. Marshall Cavendish 2010 un il $17.99
Grades: PreK K 1   E
1. Jews -- Fiction 2. Blind -- Fiction 3. Purim -- Fiction
ISBN 978-0-7614-5701-5; 0-7614-5701-1

A revised and newly illustrated edition of the title first published 1991

Young, blind Hershel finds that he has special gifts he can use to help his mother during the Jewish holiday of Purim. Includes author's notes about the holiday and its origins

"Edited significantly from the 1991 edition, the new text is more accessible to a younger audience and works better as a read-aloud. Rich, full-spread illustrations in collage and acrylic paint warmly depict the Eastern European shtetl setting with expression and dimension." SLJ

Goldin, David
Meet me at the art museum; a whimsical look behind the scenes. by David Goldin. Abrams Books for Young Readers 2012 33 p. (hardback) $18.95
Grades: K 1 2 3   E
1. Museums 2. Picture books for children
ISBN 1419701878; 9781419701870

LC 2012019355

In this book, an "anthropomorphized name tag named Daisy gives a discarded 'Admit One' ticket stub (named Stub) a tour of an art museum—doing the same for readers in the process. . . . As Daisy guides Stub through the galleries, she discusses the museum's layout, operations (including security systems and temperature controls), and various staff responsibilities, from conservators to archivists." (Publishers Weekly)

Includes bibliographical references and index

Goldman, Judy
Uncle monarch and the Day of the Dead; [by] Judy Goldman; illustrated by Rene King Moreno. Boyds Mills Press 2008 un il $16.95
Grades: K 1 2 3   E
1. Death -- Fiction 2. Mexico -- Fiction 3. Uncles -- Fiction 4. Butterflies -- Fiction 5. All Souls' Day -- Fiction 6. Spanish language -- Vocabulary
ISBN 978-1-59078-425-9; 1-59078-425-1

LC 2007049322

Upon the death of her beloved Tio Urbano, who has taught her that monarch butterflies are the souls of the dead, young Lupita gains a deeper understanding of Dia de los Muertos, the Day of the Dead, as it is observed in rural Mexico. Includes glossary of Spanish terms and facts about the Day of the Dead

"This lovely picture book effectively blends a poignant story about losing a beloved relative with a lucid description of Día de Muertos. . . . [This features] lovely, bright-hued colored-pencil illustrations. . . . Spanish words are integrated into the text." SLJ

Goldstone, Bruce
Awesome autumn; Bruce Goldstone. 1st ed. Henry Holt and Co. 2012 48 p. ill. (hardcover) $16.99
Grades: K 1 2   E
1. Climate 2. Seasons -- Encyclopedias 3. Autumn
ISBN 0805092102; 9780805092103

LC 2011029043

This book is an educational resource for learning about the Autumn season. "Leaves change color. Animals fly south or get ready to hibernate. People harvest crops and dress up as scary creatures for Halloween. . . . With . . . photographs, . . . explanations, and . . . craft ideas, Bruce Goldstone has created a[n] . . . exploration of autumn." (Publisher's note)

Golenbock, Peter
ABC's of baseball; by Peter Golenbock; illustrated by Dan Andreasen. Dial Books for Young Readers 2012 48 p. col. ill. (reinforced) $16.99
Grades: 3 4 5   E
1. Alphabet 2. Baseball
ISBN 0803737114; 9780803737112

LC 2011021928

In this book, "[Peter] Golenbock defines several baseball terms and phrases for each letter of the alphabet, the entries and their definitions appearing in . . . sidebars that let [illustrator Dan] Andreasen's artwork take center stage. Figures like Babe Ruth and Alexander Cartwright . . . are mentioned alongside terms like 'bases loaded,' 'fielder's choice,' 'line drive' and 'southpaw,' which all receive brief definitions." (Publishers Weekly)

Golson, Terry
Tillie lays an egg; [by] Terry Golson; with photographs by Ben Fink. Scholastic Press 2009 un il $16.99
Grades: PreK K 1 2   E
1. Chickens -- Fiction
ISBN 978-0-545-00537-1; 0-545-00537-X

LC 2008011737

In search of the perfect place to lay her egg, Tillie the chicken leaves the barnyard and explores the farmhouse

"The photographed scenes are packed with Golson's own chicken-motif treasures—glassware, tins, vintage board games—and invite close exploration. Text and photos appear in bordered boxes; these are set against pastel wallpapers with country patterns—a pleasant contrast to Fink's crisp photography. . . . Full of charm." Publ Wkly

Gomi, Taro, 1945-

The **great** day; by Taro Gomi. Chronicle Books LLC. 2014 40 p. color illustrations $16.99

Grades: PreK   E

1. Boys -- Fiction 2. Play -- Fiction 3. Picture books for children 4. Day -- Fiction

ISBN 9781452111254; 1452111251

LC 2013011767

Previously published under the title: First comes Harry

This children's picture book, written and illustrated by Tarō Gomi, depicts "a boy, . . . the first to wake up, get dressed, brush his teeth, eat breakfast, leap out the door, jump over a trash can and run up a slide. . . . He is the first to argue, the first to make up, and the first to march and do a handstand. His frantically busy day tires him out, so naturally, he is the first to finish dinner and the first to fall asleep." (Kirkus Reviews)

"Simple sentences invite readers into the child's daily routine. Gomi's bold, clean design features warm colors and appealing, round-headed characters. A charming celebration of the pleasures of an ordinary day." SLJ

Peekaboo! by Taro Gomi. Chronicle Books 2013 16 p. (alk. paper) $6.99

Grades: PreK K   E

1. Children's costumes 2. Children's literature 3. Board books 4. Toy and movable books 5. Animals

ISBN 1452108358; 9781452108353

LC 2012011703

In this book by Taro Gomi "every spread includes a funny fact about featured creatures, from bears to robots. And young readers will squeal in surprise to find that when this board book is opened, the eye-sized die-cuts allow each spread to become a mask! Kids will have a blast posing as a fly-eating frog or a mouse-chasing cat." (Publisher's note)

Gonzalez, Maya Christina

Call me tree; Maya Christina Gonzalez; translation/traducción, Dana Goldberg. Children's Book Press, an imprint of Lee & Low Books Inc. 2014 24 p. color illustrations (hardcover: alk. paper) $17.95

Grades: PreK K 1 2 3   E

1. Stories in rhyme 2. Trees -- Fiction 3. Bilingual books -- English-Spanish 4. Spanish language materials -- Bilingual

ISBN 0892392940; 9780892392940

LC 2014008759

In this bilingual book, by Maya Christina Gonzalez, "we join a child on a journey of self-discovery. Finding a way to grow from the inside out, just like a tree, the child develops as an individual comfortable in the natural world and in relationships with others. . . . Young readers will be inspired to dream and reach, reach and dream . . . and to be as free and unique as trees." (Publisher's note)

"This bilingual story is an anthem to the innate strength and individuality of children and trees...Many of the children are portrayed in variations of the yoga tree pose—providing an opportunity for inquisitive readers to ask questions in regards to yoga and its practice. Gonzalez's art and text invite

reader participation on multiple levels, thereby appealing to a wider audience." SLJ

Llámame árbol

★ **My** colors, my world. Children's Book Press 2007 23p il $16.95

Grades: PreK K 1 2   E

1. Color -- Fiction 2. Deserts -- Fiction 3. Hispanic Americans -- Fiction 4. Bilingual books -- English-Spanish

ISBN 978-0-89239-221-6; 0-89239-221-5

LC 2007005297

A Pura Belpré Award honor book, 2008

Maya, who lives in the dusty desert, opens her eyes wide to find the colors in her world, from Papi's black hair and Mami's orange and purple flowers to Maya's red swing set and the fiery pink sunset.

"Youngsters will meet curious and playful Maya and, through her vivacious dark eyes, will discover the colors in her world. Sentences are short and simple, yet poetic, placed at the bottom of each page, on a contrasting bold banner... A beautiful and much-needed edition, in a format that youngest patrons will enjoy." SLJ

Goode, Diane

The **most** perfect spot; by Diane Goode. HarperCollins 2006 un il $16.99; lib bdg $17.89

Grades: PreK K 1 2   E

1. Parks -- Fiction 2. Mother-son relationship -- Fiction 3. Brooklyn (New York, N.Y.) -- Fiction

ISBN 0-06-072697-0; 0-06-072698-9 lib bdg

LC 2004030058

"Young Jack wants to go on a picnic with his mother and thinks that he knows the perfect spot in Prospect Park. Maybe it is, but getting there is fraught with problems. . . . When the rain begins to pour down, Mama and Jack decide there's only one perfect spot for a picnic—back home. . . . Goode's art was inspired by the early years of the last century. . . . Full of amusing details and nice touches . . . this book will sustain more readings than one might expect." Booklist

★ **Thanksgiving** is here! HarperCollins Pubs. 2003 un il $15.99; lib bdg $16.89

Grades: PreK K 1 2   E

1. Family life -- Fiction 2. Thanksgiving Day -- Fiction

ISBN 0-06-051588-0; 0-06-051589-9 lib bdg

LC f002-151781

A family gathers to celebrate Thanksgiving at Grandma's house

"The humorously detailed, pen-and-ink and watercolor, cartoon artwork is exuberant, mischievous, and full of surprises. This Thanksgiving book has something for everyone." SLJ

Goodhart, Pippa

Three little ghosties; illustrated by AnnaLaura Cantone. Bloomsbury Children's Books 2007 un il $16.95

Grades: PreK K 1 2   E

1. Ghost stories 2. Stories in rhyme

ISBN 978-1-58234-711-0; 1-58234-711-5

LC 2007-02610

Three mischievous ghosts love scaring little children, until the children decide to take matters into their own hands.

"Goodhart's engagingly silly rhymes are paired with mixed-media illustrations that use dark and spooky colors but feature goofy-looking ghosts." Horn Book

Goodrich, Carter

The **hermit** crab. Simon & Schuster Books for Young Readers 2009 un il $16.99
Grades: K 1 2 3   E
  1. Crabs -- Fiction 2. Marine animals -- Fiction
ISBN 978-1-4169-3892-7; 1-4169-3892-3
                    LC 2007045240

Absorbed in his search for food, a shy hermit crab, disguised in a fancy new shell, inadvertently rescues a flounder caught beneath a trap and wins the admiration of the other marine animals.

"The personal tone engages the audience, bringing immediacy to the plot, and serves as a warm contrast to the cool illustrations. Goodrich's colored pencil and watercolor spreads predominately feature greens and blues to convey the watery depth of the sea." SLJ

Mister Bud wears the cone; Carter Goodrich. Simon & Schuster Books for Young Readers 2014 48 p. color illustrations (hardcover) $16.99
Grades: PreK K 1 2   E
  1. Dogs -- Fiction
ISBN 1442480882; 9781442480889
                    LC 2012040030

"Mister Bud has to wear a dreaded cone to keep him from scratching an itch on his back. It blocks his view and makes it difficult for him to eat, drink, and play with Zorro, the precocious pug with whom he shares a household. Zorro teases and taunts Mister Bud and delights in getting into all kinds of doggie mischief." (School Library Journal)

"Goodrich's watercolors excel at squat doggie bodies, especially the abstract shape of Bud's faceless conehead. This third book featuring the duo is delightfully light on morals and anthropomorphizing. Just weirdo dogs being weird. And therein lies the joy." Booklist

★ **Say** hello to Zorro! Simon & Schuster Books for Young Readers 2010 un il $15.99
Grades: PreK K 1 2   E
  1. Dogs -- Fiction
ISBN 978-1-4169-3893-4; 1-4169-3893-1
                    LC 2009-11484

Mister Bud, the family dog, has a satisfying routine to his life, but when another dog joins the family and disrupts his schedule, Mister Bud must learn to adapt.

"Goodrich has a delightfully economical and humorous voice: trim yet filled with barely contained emotion—kind of like a dog. . . . And the artwork is arresting, done in watercolors of enormous personality and quality." Kirkus

Zorro gets an outfit; Carter Goodrich. Schuster Books for Young Readers 2012 48 p. col. ill. (hardcover) $15.99
Grades: PreK K 1 2   E
  1. Dogs -- Fiction 2. Clothing and dress -- Fiction
ISBN 1442435356; 9781442435360; 9781442435353
                    LC 2011029153

"Zorro and an unwanted gift of a hooded cape similar to that worn by the masked outlaw. When Zorro's owner puts the cape on her dog, the precocious pug hangs his head in embarrassment. . . . The situation improves dramatical-

ly with the arrival of Dart, a dashing dog in a striped coat and bandanna, who makes wearing an outfit seem cool." (Kirkus Reviews)

"With his enormous nose, easygoing mutt Mister Bud supplies the perfect comedic counterpoint to Napoleonic dynamo Zorro in this tale of self-perception and acceptance." Booklist

Gorbachev, Valeri

★ **Christopher** counting; [by] Valeri Gorbachev. Philomel Books 2008 un il $15.99
Grades: PreK K 1   E
  1. Animals -- Fiction 2. Rabbits -- Fiction 3. Counting -- Fiction
ISBN 978-0-399-24629-6
                    LC 2007023642

When Christopher Rabbit learns to count in school, he enjoys it so much that he counts everything in sight, including how many baskets his friends make when they play basketball and how many peas and carrots are on his plate.

"The simplicity of this charming story is what sets it apart from others that aim to introduce this concept. The text's deliberate pace is a perfect match for the pen, ink, and watercolor illustrations." SLJ

Dragon is coming! Harcourt Children's Books 2009 un il $16
Grades: PreK K 1 2   E
  1. Fear -- Fiction 2. Mice -- Fiction 3. Clouds -- Fiction 4. Animals -- Fiction 5. Thunderstorms -- Fiction
ISBN 978-0-15-205196-9; 0-15-205196-1
                    LC 2006101580

Mouse frightens all of the animals she sees by shouting that a dragon is going to eat the sun, and then come after them.

"While the story is familiar, Gorbachev's illustrations revive it with delightful details and humorous poses." SLJ

Me too! by Valeri Gorbachev. Holiday House 2013 32 p. (I like to read) (hardcover) $14.95
Grades: PreK K 1   E
  1. Friendship -- Fiction 2. Snow -- Fiction 3. Bears -- Fiction 4. Chipmunks -- Fiction
ISBN 0823427447; 9780823427444
                    LC 2012039294

In this book, by Valeri Gorbachev, "Chipmunk and Bear have a lot in common, despite their difference in size. And Chipmunk is determined to emulate his big friend. The two dig a path through the snow, build a jolly snowman, have fun skating and skiing—although Chipmunk does need a bit of help from time to time. Warmth and humor fill the snowy-day adventures of two friends who, despite their physical differences, share work and play and true companionship." (Publisher's note)

The **missing** chick. Candlewick Press 2009 un il $15.99
Grades: PreK K 1   E
  1. Ducks -- Fiction 2. Chickens -- Fiction
ISBN 978-0-7636-3676-0; 0-7636-3676-2

"Mother Hen and her seven chicks are hanging the laundry one sunny morning when neighborly Mrs. Duck observes that one chick is missing. Goat, Sheep, and Dog help to search the premises before being joined by the firefighters and the police on the ground and in helicopters. Amid all this noisy commotion, the missing chick wakes up from its napping spot in the laundry basket. . . . The story's simple premise, just-enough page-turning tension, and comical watercolor and ink illustrations add up to a gentle and satisfying tale that will hold up to repeated readings." SLJ

Molly who flew away. Philomel Books 2009 un il $16.99
Grades: PreK K 1 2 E
1. Mice -- Fiction 2. Fairs -- Fiction 3. Animals -- Fiction 4. Balloons -- Fiction
ISBN 978-0-399-25211-2; 0-399-25211-8
     LC 2008-32607
Molly the mouse buys so many balloons for all her animal friends at the fair, she gets carried away into the air.
"Pen-and-ink and watercolor illustrations carry this simple friendship story along to the climactic end. Molly's flight is especially well shown, with a double-page spread with three ascending panels followed by a bird's eye view of the frightened mouse high over the scenery and her friends running to the rescue down below." Booklist
Another title about Molly is:
What's the big idea, Molly? (2010)

★ **Ms.** Turtle the babysitter. HarperCollins Pubs. 2005 64p il (I can read book) hardcover o.p. pa $3.99
Grades: PreK K 1 2 E
1. Frogs -- Fiction 2. Turtles -- Fiction 3. Babysitters -- Fiction
ISBN 0-06-058073-9; 0-06-058074-7 lib bdg; 0-06-058075-5 pa
     LC 2004-6234
Ms. Turtle babysits for three little frogs when their parents go out for the evening
"Beginning readers will enjoy this chapter-style book. . . . The pen-and-ink and watercolor cartoons seamlessly complement the text. The expressions on the faces of these endearing frogs are priceless." SLJ

Shhh! Philomel Books 2011 un il $16.99
Grades: PreK K 1 E
1. Play -- Fiction 2. Noise -- Fiction 3. Sleep -- Fiction 4. Brothers -- Fiction
ISBN 978-0-399-25429-1; 0-399-25429-3
     LC 2010041652
A little boy tries hard to be quiet while his little brother takes a nap.
"The illustrations, done in watercolors, gouache, and ink, are cheerfully rendered in soft tones that capture the calm, then playful, actions in the story. This is a fine book about how a child should behave while a younger sibling is asleep." SLJ

★ **That's** what friends are for. Philomel Books 2005 un il $15.99
Grades: PreK K 1 2 E
1. Pigs -- Fiction 2. Goats -- Fiction 3. Friendship -- Fiction
ISBN 0-399-23966-9
     LC 2004-18118

When Goat finds his friend Pig crying, he imagines all the terrible things that might have happened to cause his distress
"The book is a warm display of friendship and a caution against unnecessary worry. Soft-colored drawings supply details for the simple text." Horn Book Guide

★ **Turtle's** penguin day; [by] Valeri Gorbachev. Alfred A. Knopf 2008 un il $16.99; lib bdg $19.99
Grades: PreK K 1 E
1. School stories 2. Animals -- Fiction 3. Turtles -- Fiction 4. Penguins -- Fiction
ISBN 978-0-375-84374-7; 0-375-84374-4; 978-0-375-94564-9 lib bdg; 0-375-94564-4 lib bdg
     LC 2007037078
After hearing a bedtime story about penguins, Turtle dresses as a penguin for school and soon the entire class is having a penguin day.
"Cheerful watercolors and expressive line art imbue the matter-of-fact narrative with personality. . . . This nurturing tale celebrates the inspiration and information found in books, the invention bubbling up from a child who is read to, and the quality of learning that is possible when a teacher seizes the moment." SLJ

Two little chicks. NorthSouth Books 2011 un il (Tuff books) $6.95
Grades: PreK E
1. Fear -- Fiction 2. Chickens -- Fiction 3. Playgrounds -- Fiction
ISBN 978-0-7358-4018-8; 0-7358-4018-0
First published 2001 with title: Chicken chickens
When two little chicks go to the playground for the very first time, everything looks scary—the seesaw, the merry-go-round, the swings, even the slide. But it takes just one slide down to turn two frightened little chicks into two brave little chicks.
"The new 'Tuff Books' edition of the story . . . sports a smaller trim size and glossy, heavy paper suitable for young hands." Horn Book Guide

What's the big idea, Molly? Philomel Books 2010 un il $16.99
Grades: PreK K 1 2 E
1. Mice -- Fiction 2. Gifts -- Fiction 3. Animals -- Fiction 4. Seasons -- Fiction 5. Turtles -- Fiction 6. Birthdays -- Fiction 7. Books and reading -- Fiction
ISBN 978-0-399-25428-4; 0-399-25428-5
Molly Mouse and her friends struggle to come up with ideas for birthday gifts for their friend Turtle and decide to make a book about the four seasons.
"Written and illustrated with verve and affection, this . . . features a sympathetic protagonist. . . . A fitting tribute to the art of storytelling." Booklist

Gordon, Domenica More
Archie; by Domenica More Gordon. Bloomsbury Childrens Books 2012 48 p. (hardcover) $17.99
Grades: PreK K 1 E
1. Sewing -- Fiction 2. Success -- Fiction 3. Clothing and dress 4. Dogs -- Fiction 5. Humorous stories 6. Stories without words 7. Fashion design -- Fiction
ISBN 1599909367; 9781599909363
     LC 2012009329

Author Domenica More Gordon's character "Archie, a well-dressed dog, receives a sewing machine as a gift. He takes to it immediately, creating smart outfits for his own pet dog, his friends' dogs, and his friends. His phone is ringing off the hook by book's end--the final call comes from a canine monarch with a crown, handbag, and pet corgi . . . Even without the success Archie finds, his life as a clothing designer living alone with his dog is a winning premise." (Publishers Weekly)

Archie's vacation; by Domenica More Gordon; illustrated by Domenica More Gordon. Bloomsbury USA Childrens 2014 32 p. color illustrations (hardback) $17.99
Grades: PreK K 1   E
1. Wit and humor 2. Dogs -- Fiction 3. Vacations -- Fiction 4. Humorous stories 5. Stories without words 6. Luggage -- Packing -- Fiction
ISBN 1619631903; 9781619631908; 9781619631915
LC 2013036177

In this children's book, by Domenica More Gordon, "Archie is taking some much needed some time off. As he prepares for his vacation at the beach, he packs the usual things. But at night he dreams of rain, of snorkeling, and of other fun adventures, convincing him that he'll need to pack everything–just in case! But will his suitcase fit it all?" (Publisher's note)

"In this follow-up to Archie, the dashing canine fashionisto prepares for his coming vacation. But travel anxiety plagues him, causing him to pack for best- and worst-case scenarios until his overflowing suitcase bursts open in a four-page foldout spread. Gordon's loose watercolor illustrations and hand-lettered text capture the excitement and apprehension one often feels before a big trip." Horn Book

Gordon, Gus
★ **Herman** and Rosie; by Gus Gordon. Roaring Brook Press 2013 32 p. (hardcover: alk. paper) $17.99
Grades: K 1 2 3   E
1. Friendship -- Fiction 2. Jazz music -- Fiction 3. Animals -- Fiction 4. Deer -- Fiction 5. Jazz -- Fiction 6. Crocodiles -- Fiction 7. Loneliness -- Fiction 8. New York (N.Y.) -- Fiction
ISBN 1596438568; 9781596438569
LC 2012037557

In author Gus Gordon's book, "once upon a time in a very busy city, on a very busy street, in two very small apartments, lived...Herman and Rosie. Herman liked playing the oboe, the smell of hot dogs in the winter, and watching films about the ocean. Rosie liked pancakes, listening to old jazz records, and watching films about the ocean. They both loved the groovy rhythm of the city, but sometimes the bustling crowds and constant motion left them lonely, until one night" something happens. (Publisher's note)

"In New York City, neighbors Herman (a crocodile) and Rosie (a deer) work boring day jobs but express their true talents at night as a musician and singer. Their disenchantment and the series of romantic comedy style near-misses that stall their meeting will charm adults more than kids. Mixed-media illustrations combine city maps and postcards with quirky drawings of the menagerie of city dwellers." (Horn Book)

Gore, Leonid
Danny's first snow; by Leonid Gore. Atheneum 2007 un il $16.99
Grades: PreK K   E
1. Snow -- Fiction 2. Rabbits -- Fiction 3. Imagination -- Fiction
ISBN 1-4169-1330-0

When he ventures outside to experience his first snowfall, a young rabbit discovers that his world has greatly changed.

"The exquisite illustrations in this story . . . will delight young readers. . . . Gore achieves remarkable shapes and surfaces, with green pines transformed into bears that gradually melt away as the day advances." Publ Wkly

Mommy, where are you? [by] Leonid Gore. Atheneum Books for Young Readers 2009 un il $16.99
Grades: PreK K 1   E
1. Mice -- Fiction 2. Mother-child relationship -- Fiction
ISBN 978-1-4169-5505-4; 1-4169-5505-4
LC 2008-25994

A little mouse wakes up one day and, when he cannot find his mother, goes in search of her.

"Gore skillfully provides both repetition and variety for his audience, so both young listeners and their adults will find the story engaging as well as easy to follow. . . . Acrylic illustrations are simply composed, and the layered colors . . . and textured application of the paint . . . add pleasing depth and sophistication to the images." Bull Cent Child Books

When I grow up. Scholastic Press 2009 un il $16.99
Grades: PreK   E
1. Growth -- Fiction 2. Father-son relationship -- Fiction
ISBN 978-0-545-08597-7; 0-545-08597-7
LC 2008014313

At his drawing table on a rainy day, a boy imagines all the ways in which different things might grow up, and comes to the conclusion that he will grow up to be just like his dad.

"The simple and poetic artwork was done in acrylic and mixed media on die-cut pages. . . . The exploration of his world gives this father-and-son selection a refreshing take on a familiar theme." SLJ

The **wonderful** book. Scholastic Press 2010 un il
Grades: PreK K 1   E
1. Forest animals -- Fiction 2. Books and reading -- Fiction
ISBN 0-545-08598-5; 978-0-545-08598-4
LC 2009026348

When various forest animals discover a mysterious object in the woods, they each use it for a different purpose, until a boy reads stories from it, much to the animals' delight. "Ages three to five." (Bull Cent Child Books)

"Unpretentious watercolor-and-ink illustrations on textured paper suit well, because both text and pictures have a light, unfussy vibe—even while puns lurk unstated, such as the fox treating sheets of paper as bedsheets. Children just beginning to recognize books as objects will appreciate the animals' confusion and their own advanced understanding." Kirkus

Worms for lunch? Scholastic Press 2011 un il $16.99

Grades: PreK K   E
    1. Food -- Fiction 2. Animals -- Fiction 3. Animals -- Food
    ISBN 0-545-24338-6; 978-0-545-24338-4
                       LC 2010004023

In this picture book, readers "follow a curious worm through die-cut pages to discover what different animals like to eat for lunch. 'Who on earth would eat worms for lunch?' the curious little leaf-loving worm wants to know... Not the mouse who likes cheese. Not the little girl, who loves spaghetti and ice cream! Not the cow, nor the bee, nor the monkey... But when a fish reveals what he most desires for lunch, ... our little worm goes quickly on his way." (Publisher's note) "Preschool." (Horn Book)

"In this entertaining primer about what animals like to eat, Gore's bright acrylic paintings are reminiscent of the artwork of Carle and Lionni in their simplicity, textures, and whimsical humor. . . . The clever and effective die-cuts will easily keep readers' interest." Publ Wkly

Gormley, Greg
   ★ **Dog** in boots; illustrated by Roberta Angaramo. Holiday House 2011 un il $17.95
Grades: PreK K 1   E
    1. Dogs -- Fiction 2. Shoes -- Fiction
    ISBN 978-0-8234-2347-7; 0-8234-2347-6
                       LC 2010029889

After reading "Puss in Boots," an adventurous dog sets out to find the perfect pair of shoes to suit his every need.

"Children will identify with Dog's good-natured struggle through trial and error, fall in love with the evocative and funny illustrations and laugh out loud at the satisfying ending. A truly enjoyable selection and a nice follow-up to a favorite fairy tale, just right for reading aloud." Kirkus

Gourley, Robbin
   ★ **Bring** me some apples and I'll make you a pie; a story about Edna Lewis. Clarion Books 2009 45p il $16
Grades: PreK K 1 2   E
    1. Cooks 2. Food -- Fiction 3. Cookbook writers 4. Cooking -- Fiction 5. Virginia -- Fiction 6. Farm life -- Fiction 7. Family life -- Fiction 8. African Americans -- Fiction
    ISBN 978-0-618-15836-2; 0-618-15836-7
                       LC 2007-46978

Edna and members of her family gather fruits, berries, and vegetables from the fields, garden, and orchard on their Virginia farm and turn them into wonderful meals. Includes facts about the life of Edna Lewis, a descendant of slaves who grew up to be a famous chef, and five recipes.

"The cheery watercolor spreads follow Edna and various relatives . . . from spring to first snow. . . . Folk sayings or songs accompany mention of each new food. . . . Dynamic paintings, increasingly lush as summer intensifies, add vigor." Publ Wkly

Gow, Nancy
   Ten big toes and a prince's nose; illustrated by Stephen Costanza. Sterling Pub. 2010 un il $14.95
Grades: PreK K 1 2   E
    1. Stories in rhyme 2. Princes -- Fiction 3. Princesses -- Fiction
    ISBN 978-1-4027-6396-0; 1-4027-6396-4
                       LC 2008031835

A lovely princess with enormous feet and a charming prince with a huge nose meet on a ski lift and, while their flaws are hidden, fall in love.

"Told in chatty rhyme, . . . this cleverly plotted tale conveys its message . . . with aplomb. The saturated colors and folk-like feel of the artwork are just right for this jaunty tale." Kirkus

Gower, Catherine
   Long-Long's New Year; a story about the Chinese spring festival. illustrated by He Zhihong. Tuttle 2005 un il $16.95
Grades: K 1 2 3   E
    1. China -- Fiction 2. Grandfathers -- Fiction 3. Chinese New Year -- Fiction
    ISBN 0-8048-3666-3
                       LC 2004-111580

"Gower's simple, appealing story aptly captures the details of the festival as well as specifics of Chinese life. Zhihong's softly colored, detailed drawings on tan rice paper evoke both the bustle of a preholiday marketplace as well as the gentle warmth shared by grandfather and grandchild." SLJ

Graber, Janet
   Muktar and the camels. Henry Holt and Co. 2009 un il $16.99
Grades: K 1 2 3   E
    1. School stories 2. Kenya -- Fiction 3. Camels -- Fiction 4. Orphans -- Fiction 5. Refugees -- Fiction
    ISBN 978-0-8050-7834-3; 0-8050-7834-7
                       LC 2008038217

Muktar, an eleven-year-old refugee living in a Kenyan orphanage, dreams of tending camels again, as he did with his nomadic family in Somalia, and has a chance to prove himself when a traveling librarian with an injured camel arrives at his school.

"Muktar longs to live the life that is in his blood, and Graber tells his story well. . . . Mack's oil-on-canvas paintings evoke the sun and dust of Kenya, giving readers an impression of the landscape." SLJ

Graham, Bob
   ★ **April** and Esme, tooth fairies. Candlewick Press 2010 un il $16.99
Grades: PreK K 1 2   E
    1. Teeth -- Fiction 2. Fairies -- Fiction 3. Sisters -- Fiction
    ISBN 978-0-7636-4683-7; 0-7636-4683-0

On their first assignment, two young tooth fairy sisters journey by night into the huge world of humans to collect Daniel Dangerfield's tooth and fly it safely home.

"Young audiences will linger over the detailed illustrations that bring to life Graham's gentle tale." Horn Book

A **bus** called Heaven; written and illustrated by Bob Graham. Candlewick Press 2012 40p. ill. $16.99
Grades: PreK K 1   E
    1. Friendship 2. Neighborhood 3. Buses -- Fiction
    ISBN 978-0-7636-5893-9
                       LC 2011278839

This book tells the story of "[a] city neighborhood" which "takes shape around an abandoned school bus." (Kirkus) The bus "becomes a hub of activity. People come together to hold meetings, play games and share stories. . . . But one day a tow truck arrives and threatens to take away not just the bus, but everything everyone has worked so hard to create. . . . This is . . . [a] story about friendship, the strength of a community and a little girl who . . . comes into her own." (Publisher's note)

Dimity Dumpty; the story of Humpty's little sister. Candlewick Press 2006 un il $15.99

Grades: PreK K 1 2   E

1. Eggs -- Fiction 2. Circus -- Fiction 3. Siblings -- Fiction 4. Nursery rhymes -- Fiction

ISBN 0-7636-3078-0

LC 2005-55306

Humpty Dumpty's little sister is too shy to be part of her family's circus act, but she finds courage when her brother needs her help.

"The full-color watercolor illustrations are a delight. . . . The language is lyrical . . . and makes a perfect read-aloud." SLJ

★ **How** to heal a broken wing. Candlewick Press 2008 un il $16.99

Grades: PreK K 1 2   E

1. Birds -- Fiction 2. Rescue work -- Fiction

ISBN 978-0-7636-3903-7; 0-7636-3903-6

LC 2007-40622

When Will finds a bird with a broken wing, he takes it home and cares for it, hoping in time it will be able to return to the sky.

This is a "sparsely worded story. . . . Graham breaks his watercolor-and-ink cartoons into full-bleed spreads and large and small comics-like panels, enabling him to dwell on each moment of tender loving care and to preach patience." Publ Wkly

Let's get a pup, said Kate. Candlewick Press 2001 un il hardcover o.p. pa $6.99

Grades: PreK K 1 2   E

1. Dogs -- Fiction 2. Animal shelters -- Fiction

ISBN 0-7636-1452-1; 0-7636-2193-5 pa

LC 00-57208

When Kate and her parents visit the animal shelter, an adorable puppy charms them, but it is very hard to leave an older dog behind

"Bob Graham's cozy watercolors, lightly held in place by loose, sketchy outlines, contribute to this story's feelings of warmth, family, and belonging." Horn Book

Another title about Kate and her dog is:

"The trouble with dogs," said Dad (2007)

★ **Oscar's** half birthday. Candlewick Press 2005 un il $16.99

Grades: PreK K 1 2   E

1. Birthdays -- Fiction 2. Family life -- Fiction 3. Racially mixed people -- Fiction

ISBN 0-7636-2699-6

LC 2004-57041

"A mixed-race family sets out for a picnic in the park to celebrate baby Oscar's half birthday. . . . The warm, expressive illustrations show a family apartment in which a mop, shoes, and toys all share floor space. . . . This is an effort-

lessly multicultural story, full of the joy of childhood, family, and community." SLJ

★ The **silver** button; written and illustrated by Bob Graham. Candlewick Press 2013 32 p. $16.99

Grades: PreK K 1   E

1. Drawing -- Fiction 2. Walking -- Fiction 3. Everyday life

ISBN 0763664375; 9780763664374

LC 2012947825

In this book, by Bob Graham, "at the same moment that Jodie's baby brother takes his first step, a city's worth of moments unfold. From an ordinary scene of an apartment strewn with child's artwork and toys to a bird's-eye view of a city morning pulsing with life, Bob Graham celebrates a whole world-vision in a single moment, encouraging readers to stop, observe, and savor the world around them." (Publisher's note)

Vanilla ice cream; Bob Graham. Candlewick Press 2014 40 p. color illustrations (reinforced) $16.99

Grades: PreK K 1 2   E

1. Birds -- Fiction 2. Sparrows -- Fiction

ISBN 9780763673772; 0763673773

LC 2013952841

In this book, written and illustrated by Bob Graham, "following some food, a curious young sparrow stows away in the back of a truck and takes an unusual voyage south-- through the lush rice paddies of India, across the rough sea, and all the way into a bright new day. As the sun rises high over the city, he finds little Edie at a café with her grandma and granddad, and for a fleeting instant, his world meets up with hers and changes her life in the most delightful way." (Publisher's note)

Graham's "signature theme, that of connection, remains vibrant and joyous, and we are treated again to his particular loving portraits of people of all shapes, sorts, and conditions." Horn Book

Gralley, Jean

The **moon** came down on Milk Street; written and illustrated by Jean Gralley. Holt 2004 un il $16.95

Grades: PreK K 1 2   E

1. Stories in rhyme 2. Moon -- Fiction 3. Rescue work -- Fiction

ISBN 0-8050-7266-7

When the moon comes down in pieces, different helpers work to set things right again, including the Fire Chief, rescue workers, and helper dogs.

"Gralley presents a perceptive look at how individuals react to an unexpected crisis. . . . Done in gouache and mixed media, the large, uncluttered illustrations on white backgrounds contribute to the gentle nature of the story." SLJ

Gramatky, Hardie

Little Toot; pictures and story by Hardie Gramatky. G.P. Putnam's Sons 2007 86p il $17.99

Grades: PreK K   E

1. Tugboats -- Fiction

ISBN 978-0-399-24713-2; 0-399-24713-0

First published 1939

Little Toot the tugboat conquers his fear of rough seas when he singlehandedly rescues an ocean liner during a storm

"Mr. Gramatky tells his story with humor and enjoyment, giving, too, a genuine sense of the water front in both pictures and story." Horn Book

Grambling, Lois G.

T. Rex and the Mother's Day hug; by Lois G. Grambling; illustrated by Jack E. Davis. HarperCollins 2008 un il $16.99; lib bdg $17.89

Grades: K 1 2   E

1. Dinosaurs -- Fiction 2. Mother's Day -- Fiction

ISBN 978-0-06-053126-3; 0-06-053126-6; 978-0-06-053127-0 lib bdg; 0-06-053127-4 lib bdg

LC 2007-6882

Eager to do something special for Mother's Day, T. Rex decides to surprise his mother by decorating her car.

"Davis's jaunty cartoon illustrations bring these less-than-extinct dinosaurs alive. This fun read-aloud will tickle young children as they prepare for Mother's Day themselves." SLJ

Other titles in this series are:

Here comes T. Rex Cottontail (2007)

T. Rex trick-or-treats (2005)

Grandits, John

★ Ten rules you absolutely must not break if you want to survive the school bus; illustrated by Michael Allen Austin. Clarion Books 2011 32p il $16.99

Grades: K 1 2   E

1. School stories 2. Buses -- Fiction 3. Brothers -- Fiction

ISBN 978-0-618-78822-4; 0-618-78822-0

Before Kyle rides a school bus for the first time, his older brother gives him a list of rules he must follow but after breaking every single one the first day, Kyle discovers the rule his brother left out.

"Austin's acrylic artwork is amazingly lifelike. He is at his best when he illustrates scenes from Kyle's vivid imagination, which has a tendency toward the metaphor. Kyle's every thought and feeling are manifest on the page. . . . Worthy of being shelved next to Jon Scieszka's funniest." Kirkus

The **travel** game; illustrated by R. W. Alley. Clarion Books 2009 32p il $16

Grades: K 1 2 3   E

1. Aunts -- Fiction 2. Games -- Fiction 3. Tailoring -- Fiction 4. Imagination -- Fiction 5. Buffalo (N.Y.) -- Fiction 6. Polish Americans -- Fiction 7. Hong Kong (China) -- Fiction

ISBN 978-0-618-56420-0; 0-618-56420-9

LC 2005017646

To avoid a nap, Tad plays his favorite quiet game with his aunt and together their imaginations take them from their home in Buffalo, New York, to Hong Kong.

"Alley's cheery and busy street, home, and shop scenes in ink, watercolor, and acrylic are filled with the sorts of details that are fully appreciated over multiple readings. Children will be charmed by the warmth and humor of Grandits's wonderful tribute to family memories and the power of imagination." SLJ

Grandpre, Mary

The **sea** chest; illustrated by Mary GrandPré. Dial Bks. for Young Readers 2002 un il $16.99

Grades: K 1 2 3   E

1. Maine -- Fiction 2. Islands -- Fiction 3. Sisters -- Fiction 4. Lighthouses -- Fiction

ISBN 0-8037-2703-8

LC 2001-28255

A young girl listens as her great-aunt, a lighthouse keeper's daughter, tells of her childhood living on a Maine island, and of the infant that washed ashore after a storm

"GrandPré's oil paintings create the dramatic effects of the story. . . . This lovely book has an intimacy that is enhanced by reading it aloud." SLJ

Granstrom, Brita

Baby knows best; illustrated by Brita Granström. Little, Brown 2002 un il $15.95

Grades: PreK K 1 2   E

1. Stories in rhyme 2. Infants -- Fiction

ISBN 0-316-60580-8

LC 00-107325

First published 2001 in the United Kingdom

"The rhyming text is short and fun, and Granström's colorful watercolor illustrations get the point across." Booklist

Grant, Judyann

★ **Chicken** said, Cluck! by Judyann Ackerman Grant; pictures by Sue Truesdell. HarperCollins 2008 32p il (My first I can read book) $16.99; lib bdg $17.89

Grades: K 1 2   E

1. Chickens -- Fiction 2. Gardening -- Fiction 3. Grasshoppers -- Fiction

ISBN 978-0-06-028723-8; 0-06-028723-3; 978-0-06-028724-5 lib bdg; 0-06-028724-1 lib bdg

LC 2001-24016

A Geisel Award honor book, 2009

Earl and Pearl do not want Chicken's help in the garden, until a swarm of grasshoppers arrives and her true talent shines

"This easy reader has short sentences, a variety of verb tenses, and vowel and consonant blends and digraphs. . . . Emergent readers may chime in with their own 'Shoo, Shoos' and 'Cluck, Cluck.' The funny, expressive pen-and-ink drawings support the reading with simple clarity." SLJ

Grant, Karima

Sofie and the city; [by] Karima Grant; illustrated by Janet Montecalvo. Boyds Mills Press 2006 un il $15.95

Grades: PreK K 1 2   E

1. Friendship -- Fiction 2. Immigrants -- Fiction 3. African Americans -- Fiction 4. City and town life -- Fiction

ISBN 1-59078-273-9

LC 2005020116

When Sofie calls her grandmother in Senegal on Sundays, she complains about the ugliness of the city she now lives in, but her life changes when she makes a new friend

"Told in simple language, with dialogue matching that of a child learning English, the text and art show how upsetting any move can be and how it feels to be small in a large and unfamiliar place." SLJ

Graves, Keith

Chicken Big. Chronicle Books 2010 un il $16.99

Grades: PreK K 1 2   E
1. Size -- Fiction 2. Chickens -- Fiction
ISBN 978-0-8118-7237-9; 0-8118-7237-8
"Compared to panicky Chicken Little, Chicken Big is unflappable. . . . This newborn towers over four fellow chickens, who decide he must be an elephant. . . . When something drops on the smallest hen, she yelps 'The sky is falling!' Chicken Big calmly says, 'It's only an acorn. They're actually quite tasty.' He is equally placid and helpful when the ditsy chickens freak out over the rain and wind. . . . Graves . . . renders his fowl in a palette of gray-blue, taupe, and wheat yellow, with exuberant voice bubbles that highlight the ridiculousness of the smaller chickens' assertions." Publ Wkly

The **monsterator**; Keith Graves. Roaring Brook Press 2014 40 p. color illustrations (hardcover) $17.99
Grades: K 1 2 3 4   E
1. Stories in rhyme 2. Monsters -- Fiction 3. Halloween -- Fiction 4. Toy and movable books 5. Toy and movable books -- Specimens
ISBN 159643855X; 9781596438552
LC 2013016728
In this Halloween-themed children's book, written by Keith Graves, "join Master Edgar Dreadbury as he discovers the Monsterator, a machine that changes people into monsters." (Publisher's note)
"Underwhelmed by Halloween costume choices, Master Edgar Dreadbury wants to be "something screamingly scary." The "monsterator" machine fulfills his wish, transforming him into a multicolored creature with fur, horns, fangs, claws, and a tail. Graves's acrylics accentuate the contrast between Edgar's vibrant appearance and his dull surroundings. A five-creature partitioned flipbook creatively extends the humorous rhyming tale so readers can "monsterate" Edgar themselves." Horn Book

Second banana; Keith Graves. Henry Holt & Co 2015 32 p. color illustrations (hardback) $17.99
Grades: K 1 2 3   E
1. Humorous fiction 2. Circus -- Fiction 3. Monkeys -- Fiction 4. Gorillas -- Fiction 5. Humorous stories 6. Gorilla -- Fiction
ISBN 1596438835; 9781596438835
LC 2014009899
This children's book, written and illustrated by Keith Graves, is "about Oop, a gorilla, who is second banana to The Amazing Mr. Bubbles, a monkey, until one day, Mr. Bubbles finds himself in trouble and Oop has to save the day." (Publisher's note)
"Amazing Bubbles is the star of the circus. This monkey is dramatic. He's stylish—he's Top Banana! His sidekick, a gorilla named Oop, is Second Banana...This goofy story about the friendship between a monkey and a gorilla (and a mouse) is a delight." SLJ

Gravett, Emily
Again! Emily Gravett. Simon & Schuster Books for Young Readers 2013 32 p. (hardcover: alk. paper) $17.99
Grades: PreK K 1   E
1. Dragons -- Fiction 2. Storytelling -- Fiction 3. Bedtime -- Fiction 4. Books and reading -- Fiction
ISBN 1442452315; 9781442452312
LC 2012003322

In this book, by Emily Gravett, "it's nearly Cedric the dragon's bedtime, and for Cedric, bedtime means storytime! When his mother reads him his favorite book, he likes the story so much that he wants to hear it again. Cedric's mom understands that the best stories are ripe for repetition, and she tries very hard to be patient. But sometimes dragons will be dragons." (Publisher's note)
"Readers get the feeling that things are not what they appear when a dragon, clutching a book, winks at them. The creature snuggles in to hear its bedtime story--a tale of a dragon who has "never, / His whole life, / (Not once) been to bed." With surprising die-cuts and satisfying metafictive elements, Gravett takes that I-don't-want-to-go-to-sleep trope to a new level." (Horn Book)

Blue chameleon. Simon & Schuster Books for Young Readers 2011 un il $16.99
Grades: PreK K 1   E
1. Chameleons -- Fiction 2. Friendship -- Fiction
ISBN 1-4424-1958-X; 978-1-4424-1958-2
Chameleon can turn himself into anything and appear to fit in anywhere, but it seems that neither the swirly snail, the green grasshopper nor the striped sock want to be friends. Will he ever find someone to talk to? Someone just like him?
"Gravett's art charms; colored pencil lines on rough paper give the pages warmth, and the chameleon's 'disguises' repay attention as readers spot similarities to and differences from the things the chameleon mimics." Publ Wkly

★ **Dogs**. Simon & Schuster 2010 un il $15.99
Grades: PreK K 1   E
1. Opposites 2. Stories in rhyme 3. Dogs -- Fiction
ISBN 978-1-4169-8703-1; 1-4169-8703-7
"In minimal, rhyming text, an unidentified narrator describes its favorite kinds of dogs . . . and, along the way, offers a subtle lesson in the meaning of opposites. Expressive pencil drawings, overlaid with soft washes of watercolor on creamy stock, waggishly animate more than a dozen varieties of dogs. . . . The pacing of the simple text and scale of the drawings lend this title equally well to preschool storytimes, lap-sharing, and emergent-reader[s]." SLJ

★ **Little** Mouse's big book of fears. Simon & Schuster Books for Young Readers 2008 un il $17.99
Grades: K 1 2 3   E
1. Fear -- Fiction 2. Mice -- Fiction
ISBN 978-1-4169-5930-4; 1-4169-5930-0
LC 2008-61104
First published 2007 in the United Kingdom with title: Emily Gravett's big book of fears
Little Mouse draws pictures of some of the many things he is afraid of, including creepy crawlies, sharp knives, and having accidents, and provides the correct scientific name for each of his fears
"Spare text and delightful illustrations chronicle this nervous rodent's journey. . . . The striking mixed-media art captures the humorous adventures of the white mouse and his red pencil." SLJ

Matilda's cat; Emily Gravett. Simon & Schuster Books for Young Readers 2013 32 p. ill. (hardcover) $16.99

Grades: PreK K 1   E
  1. Cats -- Fiction 2. Pets -- Fiction
  ISBN 1442475277; 9781442475274

LC 2012049731

In this book, by Emily Gravett, "Matilda is desperate to figure out what her cat will enjoy. She tries everything she can think of: climbing trees, playing with wool, even tea parties and dress-up games, but as Matilda gets more and more creative in her entertainment attempts, her cat moves from unimpressed to terrified. Will Matilda ever figure out what her cat likes?" (Publisher's note)

"A master of animal countenance, Gravett pairs an expressive cat with a busy kid and winks at the difference between textual and visual message. Matilda likes many things, including riding bikes, climbing trees, funky hats and fighting foes. Each spread shows Matilda playing at one thing while the text claims that her orange tabby enjoys it. "Matilda's cat likes playing with wool," it begins, as rosy-cheeked Matilda romps inside a huge, multicolored wool tangle and launches a ball of yarn toward the cat. . . . On the next page, the words "playing with wool" are neatly crossed out and replaced by the word "boxes." . . . Matilda sports a head-to-toe tabby suit, linking cat and girl all along; the shrewd and skillful art implies sly underlying affection even when the cat's nonplussed, worried or asleep." Kirkus.

Meerkat mail. Simon & Schuster Books for Young Readers 2007 un il $17.99
Grades: PreK K 1   E
  1. Africa -- Fiction 2. Meerkats -- Fiction
  ISBN 978-1-4169-3473-8; 1-4169-3473-1

LC 2007001569

Through a series of flip-up postcards addressed to his family, Sunny Meerkat documents his travels as he searches for the perfect place for him to live.

"Gravett neatly incorporates facts about meerkats, mongooses, and their habitats. She employs a spare narrative, allowing Sunny's postcards to tell most of the story through both the character's distinctive voice and each post card's illustrations." Horn Book

★ **Monkey** and me. Simon & Schuster 2008 un il $15.99
Grades: PreK K   E
  1. Toys -- Fiction 2. Animals -- Fiction 3. Imagination -- Fiction
  ISBN 978-1-4169-5457-6; 1-4169-5457-0

"A little girl pretends that she and her adored stuffed monkey fit right in with tribes of penguins, kangaroos, bats, elephants and . . . monkeys. A catchy refrain sets up each scenario. . . . Working in pencil and watercolor, with a palette limited to red, black and brown, Gravett . . . portrays the action in a series of exuberant spot sketches set against a white sweep." Publ Wkly

★ The **odd** egg. Simon & Schuster Books for Young Readers 2009 un il $15.99
Grades: PreK K 1   E
  1. Eggs -- Fiction 2. Birds -- Fiction 3. Ducks -- Fiction 4. Alligators -- Fiction
  ISBN 978-1-4169-6872-6; 1-4169-6872-5

LC 2008-61108

Duck is trying to hatch the oddest egg of all.

"Using visual suspense and few words, Gravett depicts an alligator bursting from the shell, snapping its jaws and scattering the naysayers. . . . A witty salute to both nature and nurture." Publ Wkly

★ **Orange** pear apple bear. Simon & Schuster Books for Young Readers 2007 un il $12.99
Grades: PreK K   E
  1. Bears -- Fiction 2. Color -- Fiction 3. Shape -- Fiction
  ISBN 978-1-4169-3999-3; 1-4169-3999-7

LC 2006-17964

A "bear changes color and shape as he balances, juggles, and eventually eats the three pieces of fruit before loping off. The front endpapers show oranges, green pears, and green apples with rosy tinges in a line leading readers into the simple and appealing story. . . . Beautiful, softly hued watercolor illustrations loosely outlined in black pen and ink are delightful." SLJ

★ The **rabbit** problem. Simon & Schuster Books for Young Readers 2010 un il $17.99
Grades: K 1 2   E
  1. Counting 2. Months -- Fiction 3. Rabbits -- Fiction 4. Seasons -- Fiction 5. Family life -- Fiction
  ISBN 978-1-4424-1255-2; 1-4424-1255-0

LC 2010009751

In Fibonacci's Field, Lonely and Chalk Rabbit meet, snuggle together, and then spend a year trying to cope with their ever-increasing brood and the seasonal changes that bring a new challenge each month. Presented in calendar format with one pop-up illustration and other special features.

"Whimsical ideas proliferate as fast as rabbits in Gravett's splendid sendup of Fibonacci's query. . . . The only drawback to Gravett's delicious creation is that the moving parts and magnificent final pop-ups are likely to fall prey to small hands. Solution: purchase a duplicate." Publ Wkly

★ **Spells**. Simon & Schuster Books for Young Readers 2009 un il $16.99
Grades: K 1 2 3 4   E
  1. Frogs -- Fiction 2. Magic -- Fiction
  ISBN 978-1-4169-8270-8; 1-4169-8270-1

LC 2008-941243

"A small green frog stumbles on a book of spells, . . . tries to turn himself into a handsome prince, but suffers a series of glitches. Frog transforms himself into a snake, bird, rabbit and other creatures before getting it right. . . . The five pages that show Frog's new forms are cut in half horizontally, and children will delight in turning the half-pages, reading the new spells that appear on the left side of each spread and seeing the combined creatures that emerge (a half-prince, half-newt "prewt," for instance)." Publ Wkly

Wolf won't bite! Emily Gravett. Simon & Schuster Books for Young Readers 2012 32 p.
Grades: PreK K   E
  1. Picture books for children 2. Pigs -- Fiction 3. Circus -- Fiction 4. Wolves -- Fiction
  ISBN 1442427639; 9781442427631

LC 2011000773

In this illustrated children's book by Emily Gravett, "three pigs have captured a wild wolf, and now he's the star of their little circus production as the ringmaster gloatingly presents his patient submission: "I can stand him on a stool! I can dress him in a bow. . . . I can ride him like a horse but WOLF WON'T BITE!" When the trio attempts to place their heads "between his mighty jaws," however, they have tried the wolf's patience too far (. . . not to a fatal degree, as the endpapers show the wolf pursuing the three with a bit of the ringmaster pig's jacket in his mouth)." (Bulletin of the Center for Children's Books)

Wolves; [by] Emily Grrrabbett [i.e. Gravett] Simon & Schuster Books for Young Readers 2006 un il $15.95

Grades: 1 2 3   E
1. Wolves -- Fiction 2. Rabbits -- Fiction 3. Books and reading -- Fiction
ISBN 978-1-4169-1491-4; 1-4169-1491-9
LC 2005027540

When a young rabbit checks out a library book about wolves, he learns much more about their behavior than he wanted to know

"This imaginative, cleverly designed story unfolds in a delectable blend of spare text and eloquent multimedia illustrations." SLJ

Gray, Libba Moore

★ **My** mama had a dancing heart; illustrated by Raúl Colón. Orchard Bks. 1995 un il hardcover o.p. pa $6.99

Grades: K 1 2 3   E
1. Dance -- Fiction 2. Seasons -- Fiction 3. Mother-daughter relationship -- Fiction
ISBN 0-531-09470-7; 0-531-08770-0 lib bdg; 0-531-07142-1 pa
LC 94-48802

"In spring, summer, fall and winter, a mother leads her young daughter in dancing a celebratory ballet, a hymn to the season. When the girl is older, she is a ballerina and remembers that her mother gave her a dancing heart. . . . Colón's etched watercolors in earth and muted jewel tones give the book an old-fashioned ambiance. . . . Gray's writing lends itself to reading aloud, but independent readers will also enjoy it." SLJ

Gray, Luli

★ **Ant** and Grasshopper; written by Luli Gray; illustrated by Giuliano Ferri. Margaret K. McElderry Books 2011 un il $16.99

Grades: K 1 2   E
1. Ants -- Fiction 2. Grasshoppers -- Fiction
ISBN 1-4169-5140-7; 978-1-4169-5140-7

"Industrious Ant and pesty, music-loving Grasshopper move beyond Aesop's pointed lesson on negligence to a quite different moral as Gray further develops their relationship in this engaging, extended story. . . . Ferri expands the funin fulsome watercolor scenes of Ant's glowing home and the changing seasons beyond his door and windows. The sturdy comic insects . . . have expressive eyes and body language. . . . The old tale has a new implied moral about empathy and friendship as the two unlikely fellows learn to care for each other. . . . The humorous, fluent telling and pictures would pair well with terse Aesop versions and stand on their own, offering especially nice read-aloud fare." SLJ

Gray, Rita

Have you heard the nesting bird? by Rita Gray; illustrated by Kenard Pak. Houghton Mifflin Books for Children 2014 32 p. color illustrations $16.99

Grades: PreK K 1 2   E
1. Birds -- Behavior 2. Birdsongs 3. Birds -- Nests
ISBN 054410580X; 9780544105805
LC 2013017621

This children's book, written by poet Rita Dove and illustrated by Kenard Pak, features "all the different bird calls in counterpoint to the pervasive quiet of a mama bird waiting for her eggs to hatch. Fun and informative back matter takes the shape of an interview so that readers learn more right from the bird's bill." (Publisher's note)

"It's a fine first book about watching living beings in the wild, and it also serves as a beginning birders' guide, identifying the features and cries of common backyard birds." Pub Wkly

Green, Alison

The **fox** in the dark; illustrated by Deborah Allwright. Tiger Tales 2010 un il $15.95

Grades: PreK K 1   E
1. Fear -- Fiction 2. Foxes -- Fiction 3. Animals -- Fiction
ISBN 978-1-58925-091-8; 1-58925-091-5

Rabbit, Duck, Mouse and Lamb squish into Rabbit's house to hide from Fox.

"Allwright's warm and comforting mixed-media illustrations are full of soft lines and earth tones, which balance the threat felt by the animals and make Rabbit's home a safe haven. Young children will squeal every time they hear the knock at the door, but will be relieved by the gentle ending." SLJ

Green, Dan

Wild alphabet; an A to zoo pop-up book. [by] Dan Green, [illustrated by] Mike Haines and Julia Frohlich. Kingfisher 2010 un il $19.99

Grades: PreK K 1 2   E
1. Animals 2. Alphabet 3. Pop-up books
ISBN 978-0-7534-6472-4; 0-7534-6472-1

"On each spare, uncluttered spread, a short poem, a small color photo, and a creative paper construction introduce a different animal for each letter of the alphabet. . . . The letters are clearly presented, opening this to a broad audience of both new ABC learners and elementary students, who will appreciate the whimsical, action-filled verse and artistry in the images." Booklist

Greenberg, David

Crocs! by David T. Greenberg; illustrated by Lynn Munsinger. Little, Brown 2008 un il $16.99

Grades: K 1 2 3   E
1. Stories in rhyme 2. Crocodiles -- Fiction
ISBN 978-0-316-07306-6; 0-316-07306-7
LC 2006020571

Having moved from the city to a tropical island to escape such horrifying creatures as bugs and cats, a boy encounters a horde of friendly crocodiles, who drink Tabasco sauce, get tangled in dental floss, and turn the house into a swamp

"The zany illustrations—done in mixed-media, soft-palette watercolors with pen and ink—use plenty of white space and add humor and charm to the perfect-pitch verses." SLJ

Enchanted lions; by David T. Greenberg; illustrated by Kristina Swarner. Dutton Children's Books 2009 un il $16.99
Grades: PreK K 1 2   E
1. Stories in rhyme 2. Constellations -- Fiction 3. Outer space -- Exploration -- Fiction
ISBN 978-0-525-47938-3; 0-525-47938-4
LC 2008-34215

One evening, Rose climbs on the back of an enchanted lion who takes her on a tour of outer space, where they race with Monoceros the unicorn, pass by Pegasus and Pisces, and are rescued from a black hole by Cetus the whale.

"The gentle, rhyming text and the mottled, softly colored scratchboardlike illustrations work together to convey a quiet, calm tone for this heavenly romp." Booklist

Greene, Stephanie
Princess Posey and the first grade boys; Stephanie Greene; illustrated by Stephanie Roth Sisson. G.P. Putnam's Sons, an imprint of Penguin Group (USA) 2014 84 p. illustrations (Princess Posey) (hardcover) $13.99
Grades: K 1 2   E
1. Bad behavior 2. School stories 3. Bullies -- Fiction 4. Schools -- Fiction 5. Teasing -- Fiction 6. Behavior -- Fiction
ISBN 0399163646; 9780399163647
LC 2013020941

In this book, by Stephanie Greene, "will Posey ever be able to get along with boys? Probably not. They barely ever sit still, they make lots of rude noises, and they are just plain annoying. But when Posey teases Henry for being a 'weirdo,' Miss Lee tells her that she's being a (gasp!) bully. Only by calling on the help of the Pink Princess can Posey step back and see that boys have feelings as well. And maybe, in the end, she can be friends with the boys too." (Publisher's note)

Part of the "Princess Posey" series.

Greenfield, Eloise
Africa dream; illustrated by Carole Byard. Crowell 1977 un il hardcover o.p. pa $6.99
Grades: PreK K 1 2   E
1. Africa -- Fiction
ISBN 0-690-04776-2 lib bdg; 0-06-443277-7 pa
LC 77-5080

Coretta Scott King Award for text

"As ethereal as the title implies, this sparsely worded prose-poem relates the benign dream experience of a young child who transports her mind to 'Long-ago Africa.'" Booklist

Grandpa's face; illustrated by Floyd Cooper. Philomel Bks. 1988 un il lib bdg $16.99; pa $6.99
Grades: PreK K 1 2   E
1. Actors -- Fiction 2. Grandfathers -- Fiction
ISBN 0-399-21525-5 lib bdg; 0-399-22106-9 pa
LC 87-16729

"Tamika fears that her grandfather, an actor, is incapable of loving her when she sees him practicing a cruel expression. The young girl's turmoil and its resolution are keenly felt through evocative text and striking pictures." SLJ

Gregorich, Barbara
Waltur paints himself into a corner and other stories; by Barbara Gregorich; illustrated by Kristin Sorra. Houghton Mifflin 2007 un il $15
Grades: K 1 2 3   E
1. Bears -- Fiction 2. Animals -- Fiction 3. Proverbs -- Fiction
ISBN 978-0-618-74796-2; 0-618-74796-6
LC 2006102370

Walter the bear learns more lessons from his friend Matilda, such as "do not put the cart before the horse" and "let sleeping dogs lie."

"Gregorich creates some deliciously sticky, comical situations. . . . Sorra's pen-and-ink and watercolor artwork is a lively mix of spread and panels." Booklist

Another title about Walter is:
Walter buys a pig in a poke and other stories (2006)

Gregory, Nan
Pink; [illustrated by] Luc Melanson. Groundwood 2007 32p il $17.95
Grades: PreK K 1 2   E
1. Dolls -- Fiction
ISBN 978-0-88899-781-4

Vivi loves the color pink. She is working and saving her money in order to buy a pink doll from the store. How does she feel when the doll is sold to someone else?

"Gregory writes with precision and creates apt, sometimes surprising phrases that capture the characters' feelings. Melanson's painterly, digitally assisted pictures create a distinctive look though the elongated forms and faces of the characters." Booklist

Gretz, Susanna
★ **Riley** and Rose in the picture. Candlewick Press 2005 un il $16.99
Grades: PreK K 1 2   E
1. Cats -- Fiction 2. Dogs -- Fiction 3. Friendship -- Fiction
ISBN 0-7636-2681-3
LC 2004-54569

On a rainy day Reilly the dog and Rosa the cat decide to stay indoors and draw a picture together but have trouble agreeing on how to do it

"The lively text is read-aloud friendly, incorporating child-familiar dialogue, interactions, and humor. The colorful gouache art is charming, too, filling the pages with expressive characters and distinctive childlike artwork that perfectly matches the story." Booklist

Grey, Mini
★ The **adventures** of the dish and the spoon. Knopf 2006 un il $16.95; lib bdg $18.99
Grades: PreK K 1 2   E
1. Tableware -- Fiction 2. Nursery rhymes -- Fiction
ISBN 0-375-83691-8; 0-375-93691-2 lib bdg
LC 2005017548

Having run away together, the Dish and the Spoon from the nursery rhyme "The Cat and the Fiddle" become vaudeville stars before turning to a life of crime

"The narrative is packed with tongue-in-cheek humor. The rich art mingles paint with collage, featuring framed scenes and a palette of lush browns dotted with primary reds and blues." Bull Cent Child Books

Egg drop. Alfred A. Knopf 2009 un il $16.99; lib bdg $19.99
Grades: 1 2 3   E
    1. Eggs -- Fiction 2. Flight -- Fiction
    ISBN 978-0-375-84260-3; 0-375-84260-8; 978-0-375-94260-0 lib bdg; 0-375-94260-2 lib bdg
                 LC 2008-24534
Tragedy strikes when an egg, eager to fly like birds, airplanes, and insects, steps off of a tall tower.

"The mixed-media and collage full-color art is quirky and inventive with multiple perspectives, and imbues the Egg with personality." SLJ

★ **Hermelin** the detective mouse; by Mini Grey. Alfred A. Knopf 2014 32 p. (hardcover) $17.99
Grades: PreK K 1 2 3   E
    1. Detectives -- Fiction 2. Mice -- Fiction 3. Neighborhoods -- Fiction 4. Lost and found possessions -- Fiction
    ISBN 0385754337; 9780385754330; 9780385754347
                 LC 2013019508
In this children's book by Mini Grey, "Hermelin is a special little mouse. He was born in a box of cheese and lives in an attic at 33 Offley Street. He can read books and type notes on his typewriter. Most importantly, Hermelin can solve mysteries. And the people of Offley Street are in need of a detective!" (Publisher's note)

"This winning picture book opens with a scene of a tiny community of attached houses on Offley Street, where the residents and their pets are engaged in all sorts of activities simultaneously... Some children will enjoy the challenge of solving the mini-mysteries using clues found in the illustrations, while others will be content to follow the adventures of the amiable mouse as his tale unfolds. An absorbing picture book with a small but worthy hero." SLJ

★ **Three** by the sea. Alfred A. Knopf 2011 un il $17.99; lib bdg $20.99
Grades: K 1 2   E
    1. Cats -- Fiction 2. Dogs -- Fiction 3. Mice -- Fiction 4. Foxes -- Fiction 5. Happiness -- Fiction 6. Friendship -- Fiction 7. Cooperation -- Fiction
    ISBN 978-0-375-86784-2; 0-375-86784-8; 978-0-375-96784-9 lib bdg; 0-375-96784-2 lib bdg
                 LC 2010004084
First published 2010 in the United Kingdom
Cat, Dog, and Mouse live together contentedly in a cottage by the sea, dividing the work between them, until A. Stranger, Esq., a fox from the Winds of Change company, arrives and stirs up trouble.

This is "a beguiling little parable. . . . The artwork is standard-issue outstanding for Grey, with creative dollops of collage, endearing animal characters, and detail-strewn settings. . . . [The] complex resolution . . . refreshingly eschews any simple message." Booklist

Traction Man and the beach odyssey; Mini Grey. Alfred A. Knopf 2012 32 p.
Grades: PreK K 1 2   E
    1. Dolls -- Fiction 2. Toys -- Fiction 3. Beaches --

Fiction 4. Brooms and brushes -- Fiction 5. Action figures (Toys) -- Fiction
    ISBN 0375969527; 9780375869525; 9780375969522; 9780375983641
                 LC 2011020102
In this children's book by Mini Grey, "the action-figure star . . .Traction Man and his trusty sidekick, Scrubbing Brush, are brought to the beach by their boy owner. They explore an underwater world of crabs and cockles, defend their picnic lunch from a hungry dog, and get swept out to sea by a vigorous wave. They're rescued by a girl and squirreled away in a sand castle, where they meet two towering sirens called the Dollies." (Booklist)

★ **Traction** Man is here! Knopf 2005 un il $15.95; lib bdg $17.99
Grades: PreK K 1 2   E
    1. Toys -- Fiction 2. Imagination -- Fiction 3. Superheroes -- Fiction
    ISBN 0-375-83191-6; 0-375-93191-0 lib bdg
                 LC 2004-4452
Traction Man, a boy's courageous action figure, has a variety of adventures with Scrubbing Brush and other objects in the house
And "imaginative and very funny romp. . . . The angular, full-color art sweeps across the pages and perfectly animates the antics of Traction Man and his enemies." SLJ
Followed by: Traction Man meets Turbodog (2008)

Gribnau, Joe
    Kick the cowboy; illustrated by Adrian Tans. Pelican Pub. Co. 2009 un il $15.95
Grades: PreK K 1 2   E
    1. Tall tales 2. Texas -- Fiction 3. Cowhands -- Fiction
    ISBN 978-1-58980-605-4; 1-58980-605-0
                 LC 2009-3950
A cowboy named Kick becomes a mean braggart, driving away all of his friends and terrorizing the people of his Texas town, until a no-nonsense little girl named Belle helps him to mend his ways.

"Gribnau has a real winner here. . . . This above average story will be a real hit with both kids and storytellers. . . . Tans' illustrations are terrific, making the reader really want to see what happens next. This is a fantastic children's story. . . . Highly Recommended." Libr Media Connect

Grifalconi, Ann
    ★ **Ain't** nobody a stranger to me; illustrated by Jerry Pinkney. Hyperion/Jump at the Sun 2007 un il $16.99
Grades: K 1 2 3   E
    1. Slavery -- Fiction 2. Grandfathers -- Fiction 3. African Americans -- Fiction 4. Underground railroad -- Fiction
    ISBN 978-0-7868-1857-0
This story spotlights both the loving rapport between a girl and her grandfather, and the story of his family's escape to freedom.

"Pinkney's watercolor double-paged spreads contrast the sepia-toned gloom of slavery and hiding with the abundant light-filled apple orchard today. . . . Caught by the action, children will hear Finger's shining words across time, race, and generations." Booklist

★ The **village** that vanished; illustrated by Kadir Nelson. Dial Bks. for Young Readers 2002 un il $16.99

Grades: 1 2 3 4   E

  1. Escapes -- Fiction 2. Slave trade -- Fiction 3. Southern Africa -- Fiction 4. Yao (African people) -- Fiction

ISBN 0-8037-2623-6

LC 00-38416

In southeastern Africa, a young Yao girl and her mother find a way for their fellow villagers to escape approaching slave traders

"This story celebrating resourcefulness, quick thinking, and community solidarity may inspire and empower readers. Nelson's pencil drawings enhanced with oil paints are wonderfully evocative of place, mood, posture, and expression." SLJ

Griffin, Kitty

The **ride**; the legend of Betsy Dowdy. illustrated by Marjorie Priceman. Atheneum Books for Young Readers 2010 un il $16.99

Grades: 1 2 3   E

  1. United States -- History -- 1775-1783, Revolution -- Fiction

ISBN 978-1-4169-2816-4; 1-4169-2816-2

"The year is 1775, and teenage Betsy Dowdy secretly sets off on an all-night horseback journey to alert colonial militia to the British advance upon her North Carolina island home. . . . Swirls of deep royal and swaths of magenta evoke the eerie nighttime setting. . . . Griffin's . . . direct yet descriptive narrative recounts the calamities that befall Betsy, while the characters' cartoon styling lessens the tension. Priceman's . . . trademark freeflowing lines speed the story's momentum." Publ Wkly

Griffin, Molly Beth

Loon baby; illustrated by Anne Hunter. Houghton Mifflin Harcourt 2011 un il $16.99

Grades: PreK K 1 2   E

  1. Loons -- Fiction 2. Animals -- Fiction

ISBN 978-0-547-25487-6; 0-547-25487-3

LC 2010006770

A baby loon, afraid that his mother will not return, sets out on his own to find his way across a stormy lake to their home in the great north woods.

This offers "simple text . . . [and] loosely rendered watercolors in blues, greens and grays textured with pen-and-ink cross hatch. . . . Guaranteed to hit the mark with anyone who's ever felt lost and alone." Kirkus

Griffith, Gretchen

When Christmas feels like home; Gretchen Griffith; illustrated by Carolina Farias. Albert Whitman & Company 2013 32 p. $16.99

Grades: PreK K 1 2 3   E

  1. Christmas -- Fiction 2. Immigrants -- United States -- Fiction 3. Immigrants -- Fiction 4. North Carolina -- Fiction 5. Mexican Americans -- Fiction 6. Moving, Household -- Fiction 7. Expectation (Psychology) -- Fiction

ISBN 0807588725; 9780807588727

LC 2013010899

In this book, by Gretchen Griffith, "a little boy named Eduardo moves from a village in an unnamed Latin American country to a town in the United States. . . . Eduardo moves to the U.S. in the fall, bringing along his fútbol (soccer ball) and his family's box of Christmas decorations. . . . He makes friends and participates in family celebrations at Halloween and Thanksgiving. On Christmas, Eduardo sets out the family's Nativity set and announces, 'This is home.'" (Kirkus Reviews)

"Eduardo moves from a village where the kids play futbol to Sleepy Tree Lane, where the kids play football, ride school buses, eat Thanksgiving turkey, and put up Christmas trees. Homesickness aside, Eduardo's immigration experience is conflict-free; but warmly colored, comfortably rounded illustrations ably capture the change of the seasons and the happy anticipation that the wait for Christmas can provide."

Griffith, Helen V.

Moonlight; by Helen V. Griffith; illustrations by Laura Dronzek. Greenwillow Books 2012 1 v. (unpaged) col. ill.

Grades: PreK K   E

  1. Stories in rhyme 2. Dreams -- Fiction 3. Rabbits -- Fiction 4. Picture books for children 5. Moon -- Fiction

ISBN 9780062032850; 9780062032867

LC 2011002149

This children's picture book "tell[s] the . . . story of a rabbit who--too sleepy to wait for the moon to appear-hops into his safe, grass-lined burrow. He dreams of a sky full of veggies, strawberries, and tender flowers, until the moon's buttery light seeps into his burrow, 'spatters him with moondrops/shakes him out of bed--' and draws him out into the bright, flowery field to dance. What Rabbit does not see is the small gray mouse outside his burrow, a raccoon family watching from their hollow tree, and a deer and fawn asleep in the moonlit grass." (School Libr J)

Griffiths, Andy

★ The **big** fat cow that goes kapow; illustrated by Terry Denton. Feiwel & Friends 2009 123p $14.99

Grades: 2 3 4   E

  1. Animals -- Fiction

ISBN 978-0-312-36788-6; 0-312-36788-0

First published 2008 in Australia

In these ten easy-to-read stories there is a mixed-up cow that says "miaow," a mole called Noel who plays rock 'n' roll in a hole, and a boy named Mike who rides a bike with a very big spike

"Broad slapstick humor and galloping, Seuss-like rhymes are just part of the reason this . . . has strong child appeal. Denton's funny illustrations are full of action, and his use of stick figures and stink lines makes the book look as though it had been illustrated by a cheeky but talented kid." SLJ

The **cat** on the mat is flat; [by] Andy Griffiths; illustrated by Terry Denton. Feiwel & Friends 2007 166p il pa $9.95

Grades: 2 3 4   E

  1. Stories in rhyme 2. Animals -- Fiction

ISBN 978-0-312-36787-9

This "innovative book for beginning readers collects nine short, intentionally silly snippets propelled by kid-pleasing, tongue-tripping verse. In the title tale, a cat sitting on a mat decides to chase a rat, who grabs a baseball bat. . . . Other protagonists also encounter tongue-in-cheek adversity. . . .

Denton's edgy, stick-figure-filled sketches enhance the zaniness factor and the offbeat, ironic humor." Publ Wkly

Grigsby, Susan

In the garden with Dr. Carver; illustrated by Nicole Tadgell. Albert Whitman 2010 un il $16.99
Grades: 2 3 4 **E**
1. Botanists 2. Alabama -- Fiction 3. Gardening --
Fiction 4. African Americans -- Fiction
ISBN 978-0-8075-3630-8; 0-8075-3630-X

Sally is a young girl living in rural Alabama in the early 1900s, a time when people were struggling to grow food in soil that had been depleted by years of cotton production. One day, Dr. George Washington Carver shows up to help the grownups with their farms and the children with their school garden.

"Concepts like composting and planting are well conveyed through Sally's descriptive, sometimes lyrical narrative. . . . The colorful watercolor illustrations, featuring soft touches and historical details, depict the rural setting and expressive characters." Booklist

Grimes, Nikki

Oh, brother! [by] Nikki Grimes; illustrations by Mike Benny. 1st ed.; Greenwillow Books 2008 un il $16.99; lib bdg $17.89
Grades: 2 3 4 **E**
1. Brothers -- Fiction 2. Remarriage -- Fiction 3. Stepfamilies -- Fiction 4. Hispanic Americans -- Fiction
ISBN 978-0-688-17294-7; 0-688-17294-6; 978-0-688-17295-4 lib bdg; 0-688-17295-4 lib bdg
LC 2005035645

Xavier is unhappy when his mother remarries and he suddenly has a new stepbrother, as well as a stepfather, in his home.

"Snappy language and varied rhyme schemes energize Grimes's . . . verses. . . . Benny . . . intersperses surreal illustrations with more realistic scenes. . . . The art and poems capture and memorably convey a range of emotions." Publ Wkly

Grindley, Sally

It's my school; [by] Sally Grindley; illustrations by Margaret Chamberlain. Walker & Company 2006 un il $15.95; lib bdg $16.85
Grades: PreK K 1 2 **E**
1. School stories 2. Siblings -- Fiction
ISBN 978-0-8027-8086-7; 0-8027-8086-5; 978-0-8027-8087-4 lib bdg; 0-8027-8087-3 lib bdg
LC 2005037181

Tom is not happy that his younger sister, Alice, is starting kindergarten at his school

"The large illustrations . . . are depicted in soft pastel hues, capturing the siblings' facial expressions and the varying degress of emotion. . . . This is a new take on first-day-of-school stories, and a realistic choice to help children share their lives with a younger sibling." SLJ

Groom, Juliet

Silent night; [illustrated by] Tim Warnes. Good Books 2010 un il $16.99

Grades: PreK K 1 2 **E**
1. Songs 2. Carols 3. Bears -- Fiction
ISBN 978-1-56148-697-7; 1-56148-697-3
LC 2010004919

"This new interpretation of the beloved Christmas carol focuses on an enchanting pair of bears, a parent and cub. The text retains the familiar beginning and then moves on to new words celebrating the beauty of the mountain setting at night under a full moon, as well as peace among the animals and love between parent and child. . . . Warnes masterfully illustrates the charismatic bears, with intimate views of parent and child in close harmony with nature." Kirkus

Guarino, Deborah

Is your mama a llama? illustrated by Steven Kellogg. Scholastic 1989 un il hardcover o.p. pa $6.99; bd bk $6.99
Grades: PreK K **E**
1. Stories in rhyme 2. Llamas -- Fiction 3. Animals -- Fiction
ISBN 0-590-41387-2 lib bdg; 0-439-59842-7 pa; 0-590-25938-5 bd bk
LC 87-32315

A young llama asks his friends if their mamas are llamas and finds out, in rhyme, that their mothers are other types of animals

"The lines are clean as well as exuberant, the colors well-blended as well as bright, and the compositions uncluttered as well as appealing. An ingenious page design invites choral participation, and the ending will encourage a cozy hiatus for bed/nap time." Bull Cent Child Books

Guback, Georgia

Luka's quilt. Greenwillow Bks. 1994 un il $16.99; lib bdg $13.93
Grades: K 1 2 3 **E**
1. Hawaii -- Fiction 2. Quilts -- Fiction 3. Grandmothers -- Fiction
ISBN 0-688-12154-3; 0-688-12155-1 lib bdg
LC 93-12241

When Luka's grandmother makes a traditional Hawaiian quilt for her, she and Luka disagree over the colors it should include

"Eye-catching collages of brightly painted papers, the illustrations express the characters' emotions and show a delight in the Hawaiian landscape and traditions. . . . An involving story that's all the more satisfying because the ending offers no mere emotional patch up but a real solution." Booklist

Gudeon, Adam

Me and Meow. Harper 2011 il
Grades: PreK K **E**
1. Cats -- Fiction 2. Play -- Fiction
ISBN 0061998214; 9780061998218
LC 2010003095

A little girl and her cat enjoy a full day of playing together.

"The primitive figures are expertly posed and arranged with simple props on color-saturated spreads to reflect the joy and devotion the companions share. Children as young as two years will appreciate the brevity, rhythm, onomatopoeia, and repetition in the text. . . . Me and Meow may inspire children to talk about a special friend and events in their day." SLJ

Guest, Elissa Haden

Harriet's had enough; illustrated by Paul Meisel. Candlewick Press 2009 un il $15.99
Grades: PreK K 1 2   **E**
1. Raccoons -- Fiction 2. Family life -- Fiction
ISBN 978-0-7636-3454-4; 0-7636-3454-9

"Harriet refuses to pick up her toys, and her mother is angry. When she tells her grandmother and father that she will run away because 'Mama's mean', they explain that everyone has chores to complete. Grandma succinctly explains, 'That's life, honey-bun.' . . . Harriet's shifting emotions are conveyed through her varied expressions. Intricate strokes add depth and texture to this raccoon family. Soft watercolor, acrylic, and gouache illustrations suit the subject." SLJ

★ **Iris** and Walter; written by Elissa Haden Guest; illustrated by Christine Davenier. Harcourt 2000 43p il $15; pa $5.95
Grades: K 1 2   **E**
1. Friendship -- Fiction 2. Country life -- Fiction 3. City and town life -- Fiction
ISBN 0-15-202122-1; 0-15-216442-1 pa

LC 99-6242

When Iris moves to the country, she misses the city where she formerly lived; but with the help of a new friend named Walter, she learns to adjust to her new home

"Christine Davenier's exuberant pen-and-ink drawings reveal all the delightful things Iris discovers with Walter. . . . An easy-to-read chapter book . . . just right for children ready to step up their skills." Booklist

Other titles about Iris and Walter are:
Iris and Walter and Baby Rose (2002)
Iris and Walter and Cousin Howie (2003)
Iris and Walter and the birthday party (2006)
Iris and Walter and the field trip (2005)
Iris and Walter and the substitute teacher (2004)
Iris and Walter, lost and found (2004)
Iris and Walter, the school play (2003)
Iris and Walter, the sleepover (2002)
Iris and Walter, true friends (2001)

Guidone, Thea

Drum city; illustrations by Vanessa Newton. Tricycle Press 2010 un il $15.99
Grades: PreK K 1 2   **E**
1. Stories in rhyme 2. Drums -- Fiction
ISBN 978-1-58246-308-7; 1-58246-308-5

"Leaning against a tree and beating a kettle with a spoon and whisk, a smiling young drummer seems to be in the zone, mesmerized by his own beats. An exuberant, multicultural crowd quickly gathers, and as hundreds and hundreds of kid drummers march down the streets, they turn the heads of the ho-hum passersby. . . . Guidone's steadily rhythmic, rhyming text captures the allure of a beating drum, and Newton's catchy illustrations echo the cadences of people at work." Booklist

Guthrie, James

★ **Last** song; a poem. illustrated by Eric Rohmann. Roaring Brook Press 2010 un il $10.99
Grades: PreK K   **E**
1. Stories in rhyme 2. Squirrels -- Fiction 3. Family life -- Fiction
ISBN 978-1-59643-508-7; 1-59643-508-9

"Rohmann tenderly interprets a 30-word poem by Scotsman James Guthrie in this attractive offering with a small, easily held trim size and a die-cut cover. One bright day, two squirrels bounce out of their tree to frolic in the meadow, but after the sky darkens, they return home again, where another, parental squirrel awaits them. The watercolor artwork is warm and sweet but never cloying, and it pairs well with the rhythm of the poem. . . . The brevity and calmness of the words make this a good just-one-more book at bedtime, and the depictions of the circle of family love and the cycle of the day will inspire many just-one-more kisses before the lights go out." Booklist

Guy, Ginger Foglesong

★ **Fiesta!** pictures by Rene King Moreno. Greenwillow Bks. 1996 un il $15.99
Grades: PreK K 1 2   **E**
1. Counting 2. Parties -- Fiction 3. Bilingual books -- English-Spanish
ISBN 0-688-14331-8

LC 95-35848

"Three children begin with una canasta (one basket) and proceed to fill it with scrumptious candies, trinkets, and toys in preparation for a Mexican fiesta. . . . A simple bilingual text provides numbers in English and Spanish. The soft-edged full-color illustrations done in pencils, pastels, and watercolors have a subtle folkloric quality." SLJ

★ **Perros!** Perros! Dogs! Dogs! a story in English and Spanish. by Ginger Foglesong Guy; pictures by Sharon Glick. Greenwillow Books 2006 un il $15.99; lib bdg $16.89
Grades: PreK K 1 2   **E**
1. Opposites 2. Dogs -- Fiction 3. Bilingual books -- English-Spanish
ISBN 978-0-06-083574-3; 0-06-083574-5; 978-0-06-083575-0 lib bdg; 0-06-083575-3 lib bdg

This "title makes use of a wide array of breeds to demonstrate the concept of opposites. The story begins with a girl waking up in her bedroom. . . . As she looks out her window, an excited pack of dogs runs by. Big dog. Little dog. . . .Where are they going? . . . What the book lacks in plot development it makes up for in the sheer exuberance of the watercolor cartoons. A must for dog lovers and a good choice for beginning readers in either language." SLJ

Haas, Jessie

Sugaring; pictures by Jos. A. Smith. Greenwillow Bks. 1996 un il $17.99
Grades: PreK K 1 2   **E**
1. Horses -- Fiction 2. Maple sugar -- Fiction 3. Grandfathers -- Fiction
ISBN 0-688-14200-1

LC 95-38139

Nora wants to find a way to give the horses a special treat for helping her grandfather and her gather sap to make maple syrup

"The realistic watercolor illustrations effectively capture the scenes; color and texture are skillfully used to depict the cold, hard job of gathering the sap and the hot steamy atmosphere of the sugar house." SLJ

Haas, Rick de

Peter and the winter sleepers. NorthSouth Books 2011
un il $16.95
Grades: PreK K 1 2   E

1. Snow -- Fiction 2. Animals -- Fiction 3. Lighthouses
-- Fiction

ISBN 978-0-7358-4033-1; 0-7358-4033-4

"When a huge snowstorm hits, sounds of scratching bring
Peter to the door of the lighthouse where he and his grandmother live. First one animal and then another is trapped in
the deep snow and seeking shelter. Peter and Grandma invite
them in, letting them sleep (except the nocturnal ones) in
boxes set up along the stairs. . . . The story is simply told, yet
charming. The illustrations are also inviting, and characters
have expressive faces and animated movements." SLJ

Haber, Tiffany Strelitz

The monster who lost his mean; Tiffany Strelitz
Haber; illustrated by Kirstie Edmunds. Henry Holt 2012
36 p. (hc) $16.99
Grades: PreK K 1 2   E

1. Picture books for children 2. Stories in rhyme 3.
Monsters -- Fiction 4. Conduct of life -- Fiction 5.
Self-acceptance -- Fiction

ISBN 0805093753; 9780805093759

LC 2011029046

In this children's picture book, "monsters are characterized . . . as Mean, Observant, Noisy, Super Strong, Tough-
to-please, Envious, and Remarkable, but what happens if
the letter M for Mean is missing? The multicolored monster
crew of Monsterwood won't tolerate the chartreuse mutant,
not even while eating eyeball soup. Try as he might to find
the M and be mean . . . , Onster's behavior is altered. A new
identity brings an array of friends that leave footprints on his
heart." (Children's Literature)

Hacohen, Dean

★ Tuck me in! [by] Dean Hacohen & Sherry
Scharschmidt. Candlewick Press 2010 un $9.99
Grades: PreK   E

1. Animals -- Fiction 2. Bedtime -- Fiction

ISBN 0-7636-4728-4; 978-0-7636-4728-5

"In a gentle, rhythmic nighttime chant, an unseen narrator asks, 'Who needs to be tucked in?' The next page reveals
a pop-eyed cartoon baby animal, head on a pillow against a
field of white. Readers turn a half-page which is revealed as
a blanket and the baby is tucked in. The opposite page, night
blue with yellow stars, displays the text 'Good night, baby'
and the next request for who needs tucking. . . . The animals
are rendered digitally in a sketchy, jazzy style with swaths of
bright color. Youngsters will delight in covering the babies
and chanting the text in this book that will be re-read endlessly as a comfy prelude to bedtime." SLJ

Haddon, Mark

★ Footprints on the Moon; illustrated by Christian
Birmingham. Candlewick Press 2009 un il $16.99
Grades: K 1 2 3   E

1. Space flight to the moon -- Fiction

ISBN 978-0-7636-4440-6; 0-7636-4440-4

First published 1996 in the United Kingdom with title:
The sea of tranquillity

A man remembers his boyhood fascination with the
Moon and the night mankind first bounced through the dust
in the Sea of Tranquillity.

"Birmingham's nostalgia-tinged illustrations have a
dreamlike quality and provide readers a glimpse into both
the boy's and astronauts' separate worlds until, in a wonderful spread, both worlds join as a third tiny astronaut is
seen bouncing on the Moon with Armstrong and Aldrin. The
pairing of text and art creates a wonderful read-aloud." SLJ

Hader, Berta

The big snow; by Berta and Elmer Hader. Macmillan
1948 un il $18.99; pa $7.99
Grades: PreK K 1   E

1. Winter -- Fiction 2. Animals -- Fiction

ISBN 0-02-737910-8; 0-689-71757-1 pa

Awarded the Caldecott Medal, 1949

This book shows "the birds and animals which come for
the food put out by an old couple after a big snow." Hodges.
Books for Elem Sch Libr

Hafner, Marylin

M & M and the bad news babies; pictures by Marylin
Hafner. Puffin Books 1985 46p il pa $4.99
Grades: K 1 2   E

1. Twins -- Fiction 2. Babysitters -- Fiction

ISBN 0-14-031851-8

LC 84-16557

Mandy and Mimi discover a way to make the unruly
twins for whom they babysit into perfect angels.

Hajdusiewicz, Babs Bell

Sputter, sputter, sput! by Babs Bell; illustrated by Bob
Staake. HarperCollins 2008 un il $16.99; lib bdg $17.89
Grades: PreK K   E

1. Stories in rhyme 2. Automobiles -- Fiction

ISBN 978-0-06-056222-9; 0-06-056222-6; 978-0-06-
056223-6 lib bdg; 0-06-056223-4 lib bdg

A driver happily cruising in his car sputters out of gas,
refills his tank, and zooms right out of town.

"Staake's vibrant, computer-generated geometric art perfectly complements the playfulness of the simple, rhyming
text. Certain to be a favorite among toddler vehicle enthusiasts." SLJ

Hakala, Marjorie

Mermaid dance; by Marjorie Rose Hakala; illustrated
by Mark Jones. Blue Apple 2009 un il $16.99
Grades: PreK K 1 2   E

1. Summer solstice -- Fiction 2. Mermaids and mermen
-- Fiction

ISBN 978-1-934706-47-3; 1-934706-47-7

LC 2008042595

On the first night of summer when high tide brings the
ocean to the edge of the forest, woodland animals watch
mermaids frolicking under a full moon.

"Jones's pastel illustrations show the dreamlike festivities both above and below water. A magical fantasy to celebrate the summer solstice." SLJ

Hale, Dean

The Princess in black; Shannon Hale, Dean Hale, illustrated by LeUyen Pham. Candlewick Press 2014 96 p.
col. ill. $14.99

Grades: K 1 2 3   E

1. Monsters -- Fiction 2. Princesses -- Fiction 3. Superheroes -- Fiction

ISBN 076366510X; 9780763665104

LC 2013955700

In this book, by Shannon Hale and Dean Hale, "Princess Magnolia is having hot chocolate and scones with Duchess Wigtower when . . . . Brring! Brring! The monster alarm! A big blue monster is threatening the goats! Stopping monsters is no job for dainty Princess Magnolia. But luckily Princess Magnolia has a secret—"he's also the Princess in Black, and stopping monsters is the perfect job for her!" (Publisher's note)

"With her cherubic face, gold curls, sparkly tiara, glass slippers, and meringuelike pink-on-pink ensemble, Princess Magnolia seems the epitome of a 'prim and perfect' princess. But she has a secret life, one that involves donning a stylish black costume and defeating monsters (who are more goofy than scary, truth be told) that threaten her kingdom. . . . Pham (A Piece of Cake) offers little jolts of energy and wit on every page, with full-page and spot illustrations that have the vivaciousness and irreverence of contemporary animation." Pub Wkly

Hale, Nathan

The **twelve** bots of Christmas. Walker & Company 2010 un il $14.99; lib bdg $15.89

Grades: PreK K 1 2   E

1. Robots -- Songs 2. Christmas -- Songs

ISBN 978-0-8027-2237-9; 0-8027-2237-7; 978-0-8027-2238-6 lib bdg; 0-8027-2238-5 lib bdg

LC 2010009541

In this variation on the folk song "The Twelve Days of Christmas," Robo-Santa gives gifts that consist of electronic gear, including a cartridge in a gear tree, three wrench hens, and nine droids a-dancing.

"The brightly colored digital artwork pays subtle homage to everything from Star Wars to Dr. Who and rewards careful study with fun details." SLJ

Hall, Bruce Edward

Henry and the kite dragon; illustrated by William Low. Philomel Books 2004 un il $15.99

Grades: K 1 2 3 4   E

1. Kites -- Fiction 2. New York (N.Y.) -- Fiction 3. Chinese Americans -- Fiction 4. Italian Americans -- Fiction

ISBN 0-399-23727-5

LC 2003-16381

In New York City in the 1920s, the children from Chinatown go after the children from Little Italy for throwing rocks at the beautiful kites Grandfather Chin makes, not realizing that they have a reason for doing so.

The author "tells an engaging story about a vibrant community, which is beautifully captured in Low's detailed, dramatic paintings." Booklist

Hall, Donald

Ox-cart man; pictures by Barbara Cooney. Viking 1979 un il $16.99; pa $6.99

Grades: K 1 2 3   E

1. New England -- Fiction

ISBN 0-670-53328-9; 0-14-050441-9 pa

LC 79-14466

Awarded the Caldecott Medal, 1980

"The stunning combination of text and illustrations, suggesting early American paintings on wood, depict the countryside through which [the farmer] travels, the jostle of the marketplace, and the homely warmth of family life." Horn Book

Hall, Michael, 1954-

★ **Cat** tale; Michael Hall. Greenwillow Books 2012 40 p. col. ill. (trade ed.) $16.99

Grades: PreK K 1   E

1. Picture books for children 2. Puns 3. Cats -- Fiction 4. Stories in rhyme 5. Imagination -- Fiction

ISBN 0061915165; 9780061915161

LC 2011033654

In this story, three cats "try to keep up with . . . wordplay as [Michael] Hall . . . explores verbal puns. The . . . text is reinforced by . . . illustrations . . . . Each line ends with a . . . thump: 'They flee a steer. / They steer a plane. / They plane a board. / They board a train.' A huge, blue steer sends the cats dashing into a blobby purple plane. 'They plane a board' explains the verb 'to plane' with vivid red curls of wood; two cats do carpentry" while the third talks to the train driver. (Publishers Weekly)

It's an orange aardvark! Michael Hall. Greenwillow Books, an imprint of HarperCollinsPublishers 2014 40 p. (trade bdg.) $17.99

Grades: PreK K 1 2   E

1. Ants -- Fiction 2. Color -- Fiction 3. Toy and movable books 4. Imagination -- Fiction

ISBN 0062252062; 9780062252067; 9780062252081

LC 2013017265

In this children's book, author Michael Hall "delivers a . . . story about colors, ants, aardvarks, and rainbows. . . . Five carpenter ants at home in their tree stump hear a noise. What is it? One ant thinks it is a hungry aardvark lurking outside the stump, just waiting to eat them. One ant makes a hole in the stump to see. Orange light floods the stump—it's not an aardvark, proclaims the ant chorus. It's orange!" (Publisher's note)

"With an illustration style reminiscent of Lois Ehlert's and storytelling style similar to Eric Carle's, this tale of imagination succeeds in its bold simplicity...The use of color has application to early learning curricular needs, while the pace and flow of the text works well for read-aloud and storytime settings. Get ready to have another go-to favorite to pair with cherished titles like Carle's The Very Hungry Caterpillar (Penguin, 1969) and Ehlert's Color Zoo (HarperCollins, 1989)." SLJ

It is an orange aardvark!

My heart is like a zoo. Greenwillow Books 2010 un il

Grades: PreK K 1   E

1. Stories in rhyme 2. Love -- Fiction 3. Animals -- Fiction

ISBN 0-06-191510-6; 0-06-191511-4 lib bdg; 978-0-06-191510-9; 978-0-06-191511-6 lib bdg

LC 2009017818

Depicts in rhyming text how love can be many different things, such as eager as a beaver, steady as a yak, or silly as a seal.

"The bold digital collages of zoo animals in this debut picture book are clear and bright, and the simple rhymes about feelings will have preschoolers savoring the words, joining in, and pointing at every playful zoo scene, each featuring one animal per page." Booklist

★ **Perfect** square. Greenwillow Books 2011 un il $16.99
Grades: PreK K 1 2   E
1. Shape -- Fiction 2. Square -- Fiction 3. Happiness -- Fiction 4. Color 5. Geometry
ISBN 978-0-06-191513-0; 0-06-191513-0
LC 2010004104
A perfect square that is perfectly happy is torn into pieces, punched with holes, crumpled, and otherwise changed but finds in each transformation that it can be something new, and just as happy.

"This near-perfect concept book incorporates an imaginative exploration of colors, a nice assortment of vivid words, and the tranformational possibilities of a simple-seeming square. . . . Just right for toddlers, but also for those ready for the abstract theme of inventive self-empowerment: a book to revisit often, and with delight." Horn Book

Red; a crayon's story. Michael Hall. Greenwillow Books, an imprint of HarperCollinsPublishers 2015 40 p. color illustrations (trade bdg.) $17.99; (lib. bdg.) $18.89
Grades: PreK K 1 2 3   E
1. Color -- Fiction 2. Crayons -- Fiction 3. Identity -- Fiction
ISBN 0062252097; 9780062252074; 9780062252098
LC 2014010834
In this children's book by Michael Hall, "when a red-labeled crayon discovers he's actually blue, he finds joy, ebullience and acceptance.Red tries to be a quintessential red crayon, coloring fire trucks, strawberries, hearts and cherries, but no matter the object, they all turn blue. . . . Some say he needs to press harder or grow out of it; others say he's lazy or unintelligent. . . . Until Berry asks him to draw something blue. When Red succeeds, he feels free!" (Kirkus Reviews)

"The solid text is matched by the eye-catching artwork. Often placed against pages of shiny white or black, the crayons and their scribblings will charm children (who will also get the message that when it comes to creativity, strawberries and hearts can also be colored blue)." Booklist

Hallowell, George
Wagons ho! by George Hallowell and Joan Holub; illustrated by Lynne Avril. Albert Whitman 2011 il $16.99
Grades: K 1 2   E
1. Moving -- Fiction 2. Automobile travel -- Fiction 3. Overland journeys to the Pacific -- Fiction
ISBN 978-0-8075-8612-9; 0-8075-8612-9
LC 2010050422
Compares the experiences of Jenny Johnson and Katie Miller as their families move from Missouri to Oregon, one in 1846 and one in 2011.

"Carefully chosen facts make contrasts and similarities easy to comprehend. . . . Readers will relate to the travel activities and smile at the humor in the pen-and-ink and watercolor drawings. Together, the art and text make a good introduction to the Westward Movement." SLJ

Hamanaka, Sheila
All the colors of the earth. Morrow Junior Bks. 1994 un il $17.99; pa $6.99
Grades: 1 2 3 4   E
1. Stories in rhyme
ISBN 0-688-11131-9; 0-688-17062-5 pa
LC 93-27118
Reveals in verse that despite outward differences children everywhere are essentially the same and all are lovable

"A poetic picture book and an exemplary work of art. . . . Hamanaka's oil paintings are all double-page spreads filled with the colors of earth, sky, and water, and the texture of the artist's canvas shines through. The text is arranged in undulant waves across each painting." SLJ

Grandparents song. HarperCollins Pubs. 2003 un il $15.99; lib bdg $16.89
Grades: 1 2 3 4   E
1. Stories in rhyme 2. Grandparents -- Fiction 3. Racially mixed people -- Fiction
ISBN 0-688-17852-9; 0-688-17853-7 lib bdg
LC 00-47952
In verse "a young girl recounts the roots of her family tree. Fondly and respectfully, she describes her grandparents—one American Indian, one Irish, one Mexican, and one a descendent of African slaves. Beautifully rendered in calligraphy, the text is clean, simple, and lilting. . . . Filled with magnificent texture, Hamanaka's oil paintings are substantial and striking." SLJ

Hamburg, Jennifer
A **moose** that says moo; Jennifer Hamburg; pictures by Sue Truesdell. Farrar, Straus and Giroux 2013 32 p. (hardcover) $16.99
Grades: PreK K 1   E
1. Animals -- Fiction 2. Zoos -- Fiction 3. Humorous stories 4. Stories in rhyme 5. Zoo animals -- Fiction
ISBN 0374350582; 9780374350581
LC 2013000498
Author Jennifer Hamburg's book focuses on a pretend zoo. "From jump-roping skunks to book-reading sharks, the animals in this girl's make-believe zoo will do whatever she wants. Messing with nature is fun at first, until we see how hilariously wrong things go. Oinking otters! Picketing ground hogs! Stage-crashing pigs! What could be next?" (Publisher's note)

Hamilton, K. R.
★ **Police** officers on patrol; by Kersten Hamilton; pictures by R. W. Alley. Viking 2009 un il $15.99
Grades: PreK   E
1. Stories in rhyme 2. Police -- Fiction
ISBN 978-0-670-06315-4; 0-670-06315-0
LC 2008023240
"Sergeant Santole dispatches Officers Mike, Jan, and Carl to spots around town that require their expertise. Mike in his police car attends to a broken traffic light, Jan on horseback reconnects a small child with his mom, and Carl runs to a crime scene. . . . The hilarious cartoon illustrations effectively convey excitement and brisk movement. . . . Preschoolers will be reassured that special people are there to assist in a variety of circumstances and see that their jobs require all kinds of cool tools." SLJ

★ **Red** Truck; by Kersten Hamilton; illustrated by Valeria Petrone. Viking Childrens Books 2008 un il $15.99
Grades: PreK K   E
  1. Stories in rhyme 2. Buses -- Fiction 3. Trucks -- Fiction
ISBN 978-0-670-06275-1
               LC 2007-22902
When a school bus gets stuck in the mud, Red Truck the tow truck saves the day by pulling it out.

"Strong, flowing lines and highly simplified forms create a certain retro look in the digital artwork. . . . With a well-crafted text spiced with sound effects, this appealing picture book is highly recommended for reading aloud to the truck-loving crowd." Booklist

Hamilton, Virginia
Wee Winnie Witch's Skinny; an original African American scare tale. engravings by Barry Moser. Blue Sky Press 2004 un il $16.95
Grades: 2 3 4 5   E
  1. Witches -- Fiction 2. African Americans -- Fiction
ISBN 0-590-28880-6
               LC 00-67999
James Lee and Uncle Big Anthony become victims of Wee Winnie Witch, who takes them on a ride up into the sky, but Mama Granny saves them.

This "is a wonderful horror story that draws on traditional beliefs about witches. . . . Moser's framed, colored wood engravings do a great job of bringing the wild, shivery adventure close to home, their black backgrounds and strong lines lit with garish Halloween images in green and red." Booklist

Hamlisch, Marvin, 1944-2012
Marvin makes music; Marvin Hamlisch; illustrated by Jim Madsen. Dial Books for Young Readers 2012 32 p. (hardcover) $17.99
Grades: 2 3 4   E
  1. Anxiety 2. Picture books for children 3. Pianists -- Fiction 4. Composers -- Fiction
ISBN 0803737300; 9780803737303
               LC 2011052317
This book, by Marvin Hamlisch, illustrated by Jim Madsen, is the "story of [the author,] . . . who, at the age of six, was . . . accepted into the Juilliard School. . . . Marvin loves to play the piano and compose his own songs. But performing music over and over that's composed by some old guys . . . just gives him knots in his stomach. When . . . he has an audition with the most prestigious music school, how can Marvin overcome his nerves and get swept away by the music?" (Publisher's note)

Hamm, Mia
Winners never quit! illustrated by Carol Thompson. HarperCollins 2004 un il $15.99; lib bdg $16.89
Grades: PreK K 1 2   E
  1. Soccer -- Fiction
ISBN 0-06-074050-7; 0-06-074051-5 lib bdg
"Mia's favorite sport is soccer but she hates losing. In fact, she dislikes it so much that she quits in the middle of a game. . . . Mia learns quickly that there will be times when she will score a goal and those when she will not, but playing the game is the most fun of all. Bright, energetic cartoons depict the child's ups and downs." SLJ

Hammill, Matt
Sir Reginald's logbook. Kids Can Press 2008 un il $17.95
Grades: K 1 2 3   E
  1. Adventure fiction 2. Imagination -- Fiction
ISBN 978-1-55453-202-5; 1-55453-202-7
"Sir Reginald is on a mission to find the Lost Tablet of Illusion. Readers will quickly realize, with the help of Hammill's illustrations, that his dangerous and mysterious quest into the deepest jungle is happening in his imagination. In actuality, he is only searching his home and yard for a missing TV remote control. . . . Hammill's keen sense of humor abounds in both the text and art." SLJ

Hanson, Warren
Bugtown Boogie; illustrated by Steve Johnson and Lou Fancher. Laura Geringer Books 2008 un il $16.99; lib bdg $17.89
Grades: PreK K 1 2   E
  1. Stories in rhyme 2. Dance -- Fiction 3. Insects -- Fiction 4. Parties -- Fiction
ISBN 978-0-06-059937-9; 0-06-059937-5; 978-0-06-059938-6 lib bdg; 0-06-059938-3 lib bdg
               LC 2006029207
While strolling home through the woods one evening, a young boy happens upon a rollicking dancing party in Bugtown

This is written "in jazzy rhyming couplets. . . . Vibrant hues and frenetic energy suffuse the artwork." SLJ

It's Monday, Mrs. Jolly Bones; Warren Hanson; illustrated by Tricia Tusa. Beach Lane Books 2013 32 p. col. ill. (hardcover) $16.99
Grades: PreK K 1 2   E
  1. Ballads 2. Week -- Fiction 3. Humorous stories 4. Stories in rhyme 5. Housekeeping -- Fiction
ISBN 1442412291; 9781442412293
               LC 2010004309
This book-length ballad focuses on "Mrs. Jolly Bones [who] is a woman who keeps a serious housekeeping schedule--in her own peculiar way. Monday is for doing laundry, which concludes with throwing all the clothes out the window; Tuesday's gardening ends with a garden-wrecking dance . . . Wednesday's housecleaning culminates in a toilet-bowl bath, etc. Finally Sunday comes, and a blissful day of rest comes to a celebratory finale." (Bulletin of the Center for Children's Books)

"Mrs. Jolly Bones's life is one of cheerful but determined rule breaking, and readers are guaranteed to laugh out loud at each gag." Pub Wkly

The **Sea** of Sleep; illustrations by Jim LaMarche. Scholastic Press 2010 un il $16.99
Grades: PreK K 1   E
  1. Ocean -- Fiction 2. Sleep -- Fiction 3. Otters -- Fiction 4. Bedtime -- Fiction
ISBN 978-0-439-69735-4; 0-439-69735-2
               LC 2009032602
This "bedtime story follows an otter and its mother on a journey in the Sea of Sleep. They see the moon, myriad examples of marine life, and the personified sea herself. . . . Hanson's musician roots show in the text, which reads very much like lyrics, including a repeating chorus. . . . Young audiences . . . will appreciate the lilting, poetic language. The

Hardin, Melinda

Hero dad; [illustrations by] Bryan Langdo. Marshall
Cavendish 2010 un il $12.99

Grades: PreK K 1 2   E

1. Soldiers -- Fiction 2. Heroes and heroines -- Fiction
3. Father-child relationship -- Fiction

ISBN 978-0-7614-5713-8; 0-7614-5713-5

A child demonstrates that while Dad differs from a traditional superhero, as an American soldier he is a superhero
of a different kind.

"Langdo's watercolor-and-pencil illustrations have an
appealing simplicity and texture, almost as if made by the
boy narrator himself. . . . An important message, delivered
with effective straightforwardness and an abundance of
heart." Kirkus

Hardy, Aurelia

Dancers of the World; by Aurelia Hardy; illustrated by
Sybile; edited by Rebecca Frazer; translated by Susan Allen
Maurin. Innovative Logistics Llc 2013 32 p. ill. (hard-
cover) $19.95

Grades: 3 4 5   E

1. Dogs 2. Dance

ISBN 2733812335; 9782733812334

In this book by Aurelia Hardy, "fifteen young women
worldwide enthusiastically describe the dance form they
love and practice. Each one talks about the music, the steps,
and the dance's history, and imagines herself in a particular
role. In some cases, she describes a real performance. The
styles vary greatly--ballet, ballroom, folk, Kabuki, Senega-
lese, Flamenco, Tahitian, etc." (School Library Journal)

Harley, Bill

Dirty Joe, the pirate; a true story. words by Bill Harley;
pictures by Jack E. Davis. HarperCollinsPublishers 2008
un il $16.99; lib bdg $17.89

Grades: PreK K 1 2   E

1. Stories in rhyme 2. Pirates -- Fiction 3. Clothing
and dress -- Fiction

ISBN 978-0-06-623780-0; 0-06-623780-7; 978-0-06-
623781-7 lib bdg; 0-06-623781-5 lib bdg

LC 2007018377

Dirty Joe and his pirate crew terrorize the seven seas
in their quest for dirty socks, but they meet their match in
Stinky Annie, whose favorite loot is pilfered underwear

"Davis's balloon-headed, goofy characters are just right
for the tale. The chaotic full-color pictures are jam-packed
with pirates and dirty laundry. The crews, dressed in a hilarious mishmash of styles, will have readers poring over the
pages to spot amusing details." SLJ

Harper, Charise Mericle

Gigi in the big city. Random House 2010 un il $12.99

Grades: K 1 2   E

1. City and town life -- Fiction

ISBN 978-0-375-84235-1; 0-375-84235-7

"With an arsenal of flaps, mini-booklets, and wheels,
Harper demonstrates the possibilities cities have to offer, as
readers follow Gigi on a solo journey through a lively metropolis. Harper balances traditionally girly activities (shoe
shopping! makeovers!) with basic information about art,

literature, and more (one wheel rotates through birthstones,
art movements, and mythical creatures; another simply lets
Gigi try different hairstyles). Cheerful cartoons, surprises
aplenty, and a smart design will keep young urbanites occupied." Publ Wkly

Henry's heart. Henry Holt 2011 un il $16.99 E

1. Dogs -- Fiction 2. Heart -- Fiction 3. Family life
-- Fiction

ISBN 978-0-8050-8989-9; 0-8050-8989-6

LC 2010040321

When Henry falls in love with a puppy but his father will
not buy it for him, his heart reacts strangely. Includes facts
about the heart's role within the body.

"Harper's acrylic-and-collage artwork with its filled-in
stick figures is a perfect match for the irreverent humor of
the text." Kirkus

Includes bibliographical references

Mimi and Lulu; three sweet stories: one forever friendship. Balzer & Bray 2009 un il $16.99

Grades: PreK K 1   E

1. Friendship -- Fiction

ISBN 978-0-06-175583-5; 0-06-175583-4

Mimi and Lulu are best friends despite liking different
colors and they love playing together, whether it's pretending to be on a phone or being princesses.

"The dramatic, fuming stand-offs and the fun when
things turn around are playfully illustrated in the bright
scenes of the cartoonish, animal-like figures, set against spacious white pages. A solid offering to add to the picture-book
friendship canon." Booklist

Pink me up. Alfred A. Knopf 2010 un il $16.99; lib
bdg $19.99

Grades: PreK K 1   E

1. Color -- Fiction 2. Father-daughter relationship --
Fiction

ISBN 978-0-375-85607-5; 0-375-85607-2; 978-0-375-
95607-2 lib bdg; 0-375-95607-7 lib bdg

LC 2009-23168

When Mama is too sick to go to the Pink Girls Pink-
nic with Violet, Daddy offers to take her place but, first, he
needs to "pink-up" his clothes.

"Rendered in acrylics, the illustrations are humorous and
lively." SLJ

The power of cute. Robin Corey Books 2011 un il
$10.99

Grades: PreK K   E

1. Size -- Fiction 2. Courage -- Fiction 3. Monsters
-- Fiction

ISBN 978-0-375-85965-6; 0-375-85965-9

In this picture book with lift-the-flaps, pull-tabs, and
simple pop-ups, a small teddy bear-like superhero claims he
is unafraid of a monster because of his "power of cute."

Harper "knows a thing or two about cute; now she shows
it's about being more than a pretty face." Publ Wkly

★ When Randolph turned rotten. Alfred A. Knopf
2007 un il $16.99; lib bdg $19.99

Grades: K 1 2 3   E

1. Geese -- Fiction 2. Beavers -- Fiction 3. Friendship

-- Fiction

ISBN 978-0-375-84071-5; 978-0-375-94071-2 lib bdg

LC 2006-30572

Best friends Randolph, a beaver, and Ivy, a goose, do everything together until Ivy is invited to a girls-only birthday sleepover party and Randolph, full of bad feelings, tries to spoil her fun

This is "irreverent and fun thanks to Harper's exaggerated situations and signature art, with its brightly colored backgrounds and charmingly simple figures." Booklist

Harper, Dan

★ **Sit,** Truman! illustrated by Cara Moser & Barry Moser. Harcourt 2001 un il hardcover o.p. pa $6.99

Grades: PreK K 1 2   E

1. Dogs -- Fiction

ISBN 0-15-202616-9; 0-15-205068-X pa

LC 00-9298

A busy day in the life of Truman the big dog includes walks, play time, and a little dog named Oscar

"Harper's minimal text and the Mosers' watercolor paintings are perfectly paired. Slobbery canine Truman is both exasperating and lovable." SLJ

Harper, Jamie

Miles to go. Candlewick Press 2010 un il $12.99

Grades: PreK   E

1. Automobiles -- Fiction

ISBN 978-0-7636-3598-5; 0-7636-3598-7

Although concerned about a broken horn, young Miles makes his way to preschool in his very own car, with Mom close at hand.

"The rosy-cheeked Miles marvelously embodies the exuberance, imagination and passions of a preschool boy. The block-print, watercolor, ink and cut-paper illustrations create a feast of colors and textures without being overbusy." Kirkus

Miles to the finish; Jamie Harper. Candlewick Press 2013 32 p. $12.99

Grades: PreK K 1   E

1. School stories 2. Racing -- Fiction 3. Conduct of life -- Fiction 4. Play -- Fiction 5. Automobile racing -- Fiction

ISBN 0763655627; 9780763655624

LC 2012950558

In this children's book, by Jamie Harper, "it's race day at the Red Apple School, and Miles and Otto can't wait. But what's that fancy Speedster doing here? It belongs to a girl named Indie, and the boys had better get in shape if they want to win the trophy! Soon everyone is off . . . and Miles takes an early lead. But then Indie is at his side, only to go off the track. Will Miles take his chance for an easy win?" (Publisher's note)

"It's race day, and Miles is pretty pumped, until he sees a new driver with an electric car in the lineup: Indie and her Speedster 660... The book is easy enough for beginning readers, has pictures large and clear enough for a small read-aloud session, and could be a good discussion starter." SLJ

Harper, Lee

The **Emperor's** cool clothes; written and illustrated by Lee Harper. Marshall Cavendish Children's 2011 il $16.99

Grades: PreK K 1 2   E

1. Fairy tales

ISBN 978-0-7614-5948-4; 0-7614-5948-0

LC 2010024234

Two rascally weavers convince the emperor they are making clothing that will make him look "cool" and will let him know who else is "cool," as well, but when he wears them during the Royal Parade, a child cries out that the emperor has nothing on. Includes author's note about the story's origins.

"Humorous details are scattered throughout, some seemingly for the benefit of adult audiences. He uses bright colors in his watercolor-and-pencil artwork and ably conveys the sad fact that the emperor's clothes, no matter how nice, cannot mask his lack of cool. The visual humor makes this a winner, and adults will appreciate the easy segue into conversations about honesty and what defines 'cool' that are sure to follow." Kirkus

Snow! Snow! Snow! Simon & Schuster Books for Young Readers 2009 un il $14.99

Grades: K 1 2 3 4   E

1. Dogs -- Fiction 2. Snow -- Fiction 3. Sledding -- Fiction 4. Father-son relationship -- Fiction

ISBN 978-1-4169-8454-2; 1-4169-8454-2

LC 2008051985

A dog father and his two sons spend a perfect day sledding together.

"Harper's watercolor illustrations are simple, yet effective. Readers get a good sense of the cold, crisp snow and billowing clouds, and the characters' faces are expressive." SLJ

Harrington, Janice N.

Busy-busy Little Chick; Janice Harrington; pictures by Brian Pinkney. Farrar Straus Giroux 2013 32 p. (hardcover) $15.99

Grades: PreK K 1   E

1. Picture books for children 2. Chickens -- Fiction 3. Perseverance (Ethics) -- Fiction

ISBN 0374347468; 9780374347468

LC 2012004871

This children's picture book is "based on a fable of the Nkundo people of Central Africa" about being self-reliant. Mama Nsoso's chicks need a new, warmer nest, but Mama keeps getting distracted by food and doesn't build one. It's up to "persistent, industrious Little Chick" to help. He works "alone and in secret on a new nest for the family. . . . When the nest is ready, Little Chick invites his brothers and sisters in for a good night's rest." (Kirkus Reviews)

★ The **chicken**-chasing queen of Lamar County; pictures by Shelley Jackson. Farrar, Straus and Giroux 2007 un il $16

Grades: K 1 2 3   E

1. Chickens -- Fiction 2. Farm life -- Fiction 3. African Americans -- Fiction

ISBN 0-374-31251-6; 978-0-374-31251-0

LC 2005-52768

A young farm girl tries to catch her favorite chicken, until she learns something about the hen that makes her change her ways.

"Both words and pictures elevate a simple story about a girl's sly barnyard game into a rollicking, well-told delight." Booklist

Going north; pictures by Jerome Lagarrigue. Farrar, Straus and Giroux 2004 un il $16
Grades: 2 3 4 5   **E**
1. Moving -- Fiction 2. African Americans -- Fiction
ISBN 0-374-32681-9

A young African American girl and her family leave their home in Alabama and head for Lincoln, Nebraska, where they hope to escape segregation and find a better life.

"Lagarrigue's paintings are subdued but powerful and well-suited to Harrington's somber, poetic narrative voice." SLJ

Harris, Joe

The **belly** book; [written and illustrated] by Joe Harris. Random House Children's Books 2008 un il (Beginner books) $8.99; lib bdg $12.99
Grades: PreK K 1   **E**
1. Stories in rhyme 2. Stomach -- Fiction
ISBN 978-0-375-84340-2; 0-375-84340-X; 978-0-375-94340-9 lib bdg; 0-375-94340-4 lib bdg
LC 2006016630

Bellies can be used for many things, such as dancing the hula and resting your cup, but it is important to feed them healthy foods, too

"This beginning reader has vibrant illustrations, ample white space, and just two to four lines of simple text per page. . . . [This is a] funny, fast-moving, and original romp." SLJ

Harris, John

Jingle bells; how the holiday classic came to be. written by John Harris; illustrated by Adam Gustavson. Peachtree 2011 un il $16.95
Grades: K 1 2   **E**
1. Clergy 2. Songs 3. Christmas 4. Christmas stories 5. College administrators 6. Jingle bells
ISBN 978-1-56145-590-4; 1-56145-590-3
LC 2010052274

"In 1857, John Lord Pierpont sat down to write a song for his congregation's Thanksgiving program, despite the fact that he was in Savannah, Georgia, struggling with a miserable heat wave and a population that was troubled by his Unitarian church's position on slavery. Homesick for New England (and cool weather), Pierpont ended up writing an enduringly popular holiday song. This is a fictional retelling of the story behind the song's creation." (Publisher's note) "Primary." (Horn Book)

"The oil painting illustrations do right by the story . . . capturing the atmosphere of a community willing to stick together as they journey against the grain, whether that means bringing snow somehow to the South or standing by an unpopular belief." SLJ

Harris, Robie H.

★ The **day** Leo said I hate you; illustrated by Molly Bang. Little, Brown and Co. 2008 un il $16.99
Grades: PreK K 1 2   **E**
1. Love -- Fiction 2. Anger -- Fiction 3. Mother-son

relationship -- Fiction
ISBN 978-0-316-06580-1; 0-316-06580-3
LC 2007-48371

Leo, upset he has been hearing the word "no" all day, lets three words slip out that he wishes he could take back.

The hero is "evoked via vibrant collages of photos and cut paper." Publ Wkly

★ **Goodbye,** Mousie; illustrated by Jan Ormerod. Margaret K. McElderry Bks. 2001 un il hardcover o.p. pa $6.99
Grades: PreK K   **E**
1. Mice -- Fiction 2. Death -- Fiction
ISBN 0-689-83217-6; 0-689-87134-1 pa
LC 99-89167

A boy grieves for his dead pet Mousie, helps to bury him, and begins to come to terms with his loss

"Ormerod's honest pictures, black-pencil line drawings with watercolor washes on buff-colored paper, capture the emotions of the situation and chronicle the boy's move from disbelief to acceptance. . . . This covers all the bases of a frequently asked-for subject." Booklist

I am not going to school today; illustrated by Jan Ormerod. Margaret K. McElderry Bks. 2003 un il $16.95
Grades: PreK K 1 2   **E**
1. School stories
ISBN 0-689-83913-8
LC 00-48053

A little boy decides to skip his very first day of school, because on the first day one doesn't know anything, but on the second, one knows everything

"Children with first-day jitters will take comfort in this story. . . . Ormerod's colorful, expressive illustrations capture a child's anxiety and the warmth of family with equal success." Booklist

★ **Mail** Harry to the moon! [illustrated by] Michael Emberley. Little, Brown and Co. 2008 un il $16.99
Grades: PreK K 1 2   **E**
1. Infants -- Fiction 2. Siblings -- Fiction
ISBN 978-0-316-15376-8; 0-316-15376-1
LC 2007-48369

Harry's older brother, unhappy that the new baby seems to have taken over, dreams up imaginative ways to get rid of him.

"Harris and Emberley . . . are old hands at striking the right balance between comic Sturm and Drang and genuine poignancy, and their considerable talents make this otherwise familiar tale feel fresh and funny—and psychologically true." Publ Wkly

Maybe a bear ate it! by Robie Harris; illustrated by Michael Emberley. Orchard Books 2007 un il lib bdg $15.99
Grades: PreK K 1 2   **E**
1. Animals -- Fiction 2. Bedtime -- Fiction 3. Books and reading -- Fiction
ISBN 978-0-439-92961-5
LC 2006102373

At bedtime, a young boy who cannot find his favorite book imagines the various creatures that might have taken it from him

"Plain white backgrounds allow Emberley, who obviously knows how toddlers move and react, to concentrate closely on his character, whose every beautifully calibrated movement and feeling blasts out across the page." Booklist

Harris, Teresa E.

Summer Jackson: grown up; illustrated by AG Ford. Katherine Tegen Books 2011 un il $16.99
Grades: PreK K 1 2   E
1. Parent-child relationship -- Fiction
ISBN 978-0-06-185757-7; 0-06-185757-2
LC 2010-15962

Seven-year-old Summer Jackson wants to be a grown-up, starting right now.

"Ford's charming and humorous cartoon illustrations are liberally sprinkled throughout the book, ranging from three pictures on a page to full-page images. Although predictable, this story should have wide appeal." SLJ

Harris, Trudy

The **clock** struck one; a time-telling tale. written by Trudy Harris; illustrations by Carrie Hartman. Millbrook Press 2009 31p il (Math is fun) lib bdg $16.95
Grades: K 1 2   E
1. Stories in rhyme 2. Time -- Fiction 3. Animals -- Fiction 4. Clocks and watches -- Fiction
ISBN 978-0-8225-9067-5 lib bdg; 0-8225-9067-0 lib bdg
LC 2008041583

Rhyming text expands on the nursery rhyme, "Hickory Dickory Dock," as a cat chases the mouse up the clock, followed by other animals, until midnight arrives and the tired creatures fall asleep. Includes facts about clocks and basic information about telling time

"The animated romp's peppy verse and colorful art capture the comical bedlam with flair. . . . An entertaining addition to beginning time-telling lessons." Booklist

Say something, Perico; illustrated by Cecilia Rebora. Millbrook Press 2011 un il lib bdg $21.27
Grades: PreK K   E
1. Parrots -- Fiction 2. Bilingualism -- Fiction 3. Spanish language -- Fiction
ISBN 978-0-7613-5231-0; 0-7613-5231-7
LC 2011001114

Perico is a Spanish-speaking parrot who lives in a pet store, and although he works very hard to earn a new home, buyers keep returning him until the bird, now bilingual, finds the perfect owner. Includes Spanish glossary and pronunciation guide.

"The text is well assisted by Rebora's bright, wide-eyed illustrations, which bring out the humor and frustration of Perico's search for a home." Booklist

Tally cat keeps track; illustrated by Andrew N. Harris. Millbrook Press 2011 31p il lib bdg $22.60
Grades: K 1 2 3   E
1. Counting 2. Stories in rhyme 3. Cats -- Fiction 4. Friendship -- Fiction 5. Mathematics -- Fiction
ISBN 978-0-7613-4451-3; 0-7613-4451-9
LC 2009049586

Alley cat Tally McNally loves to tally and loves to win, but when his competitive streak gets him into trouble, he has to rely on his friends for help.

"The illustrations depict a bunch of street savvy, hip cats with great facial expressions. . . . This concept book would work equally well in the classroom or at storytime." SLJ

Harrison, David L.

A **monster** is coming! illustrated by Hans Wilhelm. Random House 2011 32p il (Step into reading) lib bdg $12.99; pa $3.99
Grades: PreK K 1   E
1. Fear -- Fiction 2. Food -- Fiction 3. Animals -- Fiction
ISBN 978-0-375-96677-4 lib bdg; 0-375-96677-3; 978-0-375-86677-7 pa; 0-375-86677-9 pa
LC 2010014513

When Inchworm overhears Mama Bug tell Baby Bug that she eats like a monster, he cries out in fear and sets off a chain reaction of animals trying to hide from the horrible beast they believe is coming.

"Beginning readers who crave suspense will be drawn to this gentle spin on the 'Chicken Little' motif. . . . Wilhelm's expressive, cheerfully colored cartoon illustrations reflect the fact that there is nothing to fear and provide a lot of picture clues to help decode the clever, descriptive text." SLJ

Harrison, Hannah E.

★ **Extraordinary** Jane; by Hannah E. Harrison. Dial Books for Young Readers 2014 40 p. (hardcover: alk. paper) $16.99
Grades: PreK K   E
1. Dogs -- Fiction 2. Circus -- Fiction 3. Self-acceptance -- Fiction
ISBN 0803739141; 9780803739147
LC 2012009713

This book, by Hannah E. Harrison, is a "story set at the circus shows that quiet qualities like friendship, kindness, and loyalty are important and worthy.Jane is an ordinary dog in an extraordinary circus. She isn't strong, graceful, or brave like her family. When she tries to be those things, Jane just doesn't feel like herself, but she also doesn't feel special. Is she really meant for this kind of life? Her Ringmaster thinks so, but not for the reasons Jane believes." (Publisher's note)

"Jane, a small circus dog, doesn't measure up to her talented doggy parents and siblings who can get shot from a cannon, lift an elephant, tightrope walk, etc. The detailed acrylic illustrations set against white backgrounds distinguish the slight story; the colorful circus milieu and aerial perspectives convey Jane's ordinariness, which turns out to be enough for her ringmaster owner." Horn Book

Harrison, Joanna

Grizzly dad. David Fickling Books 2009 un il $16.99; lib bdg $19.99
Grades: PreK K 1   E
1. Bears -- Fiction 2. Father-son relationship -- Fiction
ISBN 978-0-385-75173-5; 0-385-75173-7; 978-0-385-75174-2 lib bdg; 0-385-75174-5 lib bdg
LC 2007049461

First published 2008 in the United Kingdom

One morning Dad wakes up in such a bad mood that he turns into a bear

This "combines appealing text told from the children's point of view with hilarious illustrations that will ring true to parents and caregivers." Booklist

Harshman, Marc

Only one neighborhood; by Marc Harshman & Barbara Garrison; illustrated by Barbara Garrison. Dutton Children's Books 2007 un il $15.99

Grades: PreK K 1 2   E

  1. City and town life -- Fiction

  ISBN 978-0-525-47468-5

                   LC 2006035908

Explores a neighborhood that has only one of several kinds of buildings, but within each there are many things, such as different kinds of breads in the bakery, then shows that the neighborhood itself is just one of many in a world united by a single wish

"Like the best celebrations of unity, this picture book is about the exciting diversity that enriches everyone, and the collagraph illustrations, in warm colors, establish the details and the connections." Booklist

Hartfield, Claire

Me and Uncle Romie; a story inspired by the life and art of Romare Bearden. paintings by Jerome Lagarrigue. Dial Bks. for Young Readers 2002 un il $16.99

Grades: 2 3 4   E

  1. Artists 2. Uncles -- Fiction 3. Artists -- Fiction 4. African Americans -- Fiction

  ISBN 0-8037-2520-5

                   LC 99-41390

A boy from North Carolina spends the summer in New York City visiting the neighborhood of Harlem, where his uncle, collage artist Romare Bearden, grew up. Includes a biographical sketch of Bearden and instructions on making a story collage

This is a "vibrant, evocative picture book. . . . Lagarrigue's lush, acrylic illustrations with collage elements recall the tones, brush strokes, and mixture of media that saturate Bearden's groundbreaking work." SLJ

Hartland, Jessie

Night shift. Bloomsbury Children's Books 2007 un il $16.95; lib bdg $17.85

Grades: PreK K 1 2   E

  1. Night -- Fiction 2. Occupations -- Fiction

  ISBN 978-1-59990-025-4; 1-59990-025-4; 978-1-59990-138-1 lib bdg; 1-59990-138-2 lib bdg

                   LC 2006-102092

Late at night after children have gone to bed, people who work the night shift, like street sweepers, window dressers, newspaper printers, road workers, and donut bakers, are doing their jobs.

"Quirky gouache paintings capture the mood of this alternative world with its vibrant life. . . . Text and illustrations are equally unique." SLJ

Harvey, Jeanne

My hands sing the blues; Romare Bearden's childhood journey. illustrated by Elizabeth Zunon. Marshall Cavendish 2011 40p il

Grades: K 1 2 3   E

  1. Artists 2. Stories in rhyme 3. Artists -- Fiction 4. Blues music -- Fiction 5. North Carolina -- Fiction 6. Harlem (New York, N.Y.) -- Fiction

  ISBN 0-7614-5810-7; 978-0-7614-5810-4

In Harlem, New York City, artist Romare Bearden follows the rhythms of blues music as he recalls his North

Carolina childhood while painting, cutting, and pasting to make art.

"The talented Zunon's pictures intriguingly combine realistic faces, stylized landscapes and photo-collage that pays homage to Bearden's art. . . . The interplay of poetic and visual metaphor makes for a striking presentation; adults who can appreciate and chant the bluesy poem as well as sensitively interpret the pictures together with children are the ideal collaborators in savoring this intriguing work." Kirkus

Harvey, Matt

Shopping with Dad; [by] Matt Harvey and [illustrated by] Miriam Latimer. Barefoot Books 2008 un il $16.99

Grades: PreK K 1 2   E

  1. Stories in rhyme 2. Shopping -- Fiction 3. Father-daughter relationship -- Fiction

  ISBN 978-1-84686-172-7; 1-84686-172-1

                   LC 2007042763

A little girl and her father have a wonderful time in the grocery store until she nearly knocks over a display, then while trying her best to be good she lets out a big sneeze that results in chaos.

"The cartoon mixed-media illustrations depict a lively hubbub amid plenty of color. . . . Funny and warmhearted, this story will be enjoyed one-on-one and handy in classrooms." SLJ

Haseley, Dennis

Twenty heartbeats; [illustrated by] Ed Young. Roaring Brook Press 2008 un il $16.95

Grades: 2 3 4 5   E

  1. Horses -- Fiction 2. Artists -- Fiction

  ISBN 978-1-59643-238-3; 1-59643-238-1

                   LC 2007-13202

After waiting for decades for the portrait of his prize horse to be finished, an angry rich man decides to confront the artist.

"Based on a literary anecdote, the story, like its subject, contains only what is essential. Haseley's minimalist text leaves plenty of room for Young's marvelous collages to set the scene and develop the characters." SLJ

Hassett, Ann

★ Come back, Ben; by Ann & John Hassett. Holiday House 2013 32 p. (I like to read) (hardcover) $14.95

Grades: PreK K   E

  1. Balloons -- Fiction

  ISBN 0823425991; 9780823425990

                   LC 2011049310

In this children's picture book, "happy-go-lucky Ben has a balloon that lifts him up and off the page. With a smile on her face, Ben's sister says, 'Bye, Ben'. . . . As Ben begins his ascent, the window bids him "Come back, Ben," as do the bees, the trees . . . and many more 'friends.' . . . When the child reaches the Moon, he cleverly arranges his descent and down he comes, past all of the friends who await his return." (School Library Journal)

Too many frogs; by Ann and John Hassett. Houghton Mifflin Harcourt 2011 un il $16.99

Grades: PreK K 1   E

  1. Frogs -- Fiction

  ISBN 978-0-547-36299-1; 0-547-36299-4

                   LC 2010006783

With rapidly increasing numbers of frogs coming out of her basement, Nana Quimby asks assorted neighborhood children for help, but finally it is up to her to come up with a solution.

"Delicious to look at—with its explosion of acrobatic frogs, its primitivist-detail décor, its confectionery colors—and a treat to listen to." Horn Book

Hatsue Nakawaki

★ **Wait!** wait! by Hatsue Nakawaki; illustrated by Komako Sakai; translated from the Japanese by Yuki Kaneko. 1st American ed. Enchanted Lion Books 2013 24 p. ill. (hardcover) $14.95

Grades: PreK   E

1. Animals -- Fiction 2. Parent and child -- Fiction

ISBN 1592701388; 9781592701384

LC 2013011003

This book by Hatsue Nawaki "follows a young child's discovery of other creatures. This discovery comes with the recognition that while other creatures can suddenly appear they can also go away and disappear just as quickly. But the delightful appearance of a dad and his playful swoop of his toddler up onto his shoulders will remind little ones that the people who love them will always be there and will never, ever not come back." (Publisher's note)

Haughton, Chris

Little owl lost. Candlewick Press 2010 un il $14.99

Grades: PreK K   E

1. Owls -- Fiction 2. Mothers -- Fiction 3. Forest animals -- Fiction

ISBN 978-0-7636-5022-3; 0-7636-5022-6

While his mother is away finding food, a newborn owl falls out of his nest and anxiously tries to find her, receiving help from various forest animals.

"Haughton's pitch-perfect use of language flows smoothly to the satisfying end. The pencil and digitally rendered illustrations, which have the feel of a mix of woodblock and cut-paper collage, are done in intense, saturated colors of olive, red, orange, fuchsia, blue, and yellow." SLJ

Shh! we have a plan; Chris Haughton. Candlewick Press 2014 40 p. color illustrations $15.99

Grades: PreK K 1 2   E

1. Bird watching 2. Hunting -- Fiction 3. Bird trapping -- Fiction

ISBN 0763672939; 9780763672935

LC 2013955701

In this book by Christ Haughton, "four friends creep through the woods, and what do they spot? An exquisite bird high in a tree! 'Hello birdie,' waves one. 'Shh! We have a plan,' hush the others. They stealthily make their advance, nets in the air. Ready one, ready two, ready three, and go! But as one comically foiled plan follows another, it soon becomes clear that their quiet, observant companion, hand outstretched, has a far better idea." (Publisher's note)

"In spare, humorous text and blocky digital illustrations, four hunters (three of them outfitted with nets) pursue a vibrantly red bird through blue-hued woods. The three larger hunters shush their smallest, netless cohort when he calls to the bird. Subsequent bird-catching attempts result in slapstick pratfalls, but the littlest hunter's methods prevail, charming not only that first red bird, but an entire multicolored flock." Horn Book

Havill, Juanita

Call the horse Lucky; illustrated by Nancy Lane. Gryphon Press 2010 un il $15.95

Grades: K 1 2 3   E

1. Horses -- Fiction

ISBN 978-0-940719-10-1; 0-940719-10-X

"A girl helps a neglected horse in this heartfelt picture book about animal rescue. Bike riding in the country with her grandmother, Mel sees a despondent pinto alone in a corral. When she realizes that the horse is too skinny and moves painfully, her grandmother calls the Humane Society. Lucky, as Mel names him, is taken to a veterinarian and ultimately to a horse therapy ranch where he will live and work. Havill's conversational text keeps the story moving along swiftly without being hindered by a lot of detail, thus keeping the didacticism at a minimum. Lane's watercolor paintings deftly convey the emotions of both the horse and Mel." SLJ

★ **Jamaica's** find; illustrations by Anne Sibley O'Brien. Houghton Mifflin 1986 32p il $16; pa $6.95

Grades: PreK K 1 2   E

1. Toys -- Fiction 2. African Americans -- Fiction

ISBN 0-395-39376-0; 0-395-45357-7 pa

LC 85-14542

"This is a pleasant picture book with warm, expressive pictures and an appealing story line that encourages values clarification." Interracial Books Child Bull

Other titles about Jamaica are:

Brianna, Jamaica, and the Dance of Spring (2002)
Jamaica and Brianna (1993)
Jamaica and the substitute teacher (1999)
Jamaica is thankful (2009)
Jamaica tag-along (1989)
Jamaica's blue marker (1995)

Just like a baby; [by] Juanita Havill; [illustrated by] Christine Davenier. Chronicle Books 2009 un il $15.99

Grades: PreK 1   E

1. Infants -- Fiction 2. Family life -- Fiction

ISBN 978-0-8118-5026-1; 0-8118-5026-9

LC 2008021971

Delighted by the arrival of baby Ellen, extended family members describe their plans for the young one, from becoming a fisherman to playing the saxophone, but baby Ellen prefers other activities.

"Lively dialogue and an upbeat refrain enhance the spare text. Davenier's watercolor-and-ink illustrations seamlessly blend colors; bursts of rosy reds lead to an arresting presentation." Kirkus

Hawkes, Kevin

Remy and Lulu; written and illustrated by Kevin Hawkes; with miniatures by Hannah Harrison. Alfred A. Knopf 2014 40 p. $17.99

Grades: K 1 2 3   E

1. Art -- Fiction 2. Dogs -- Fiction 3. Vision -- Fiction 4. Artists -- Fiction 5. Portraits -- Fiction

ISBN 0449810852; 9780449810859; 9780449810873; 9780449810897

LC 2012021740

In this children's book by Kevin Hawkes, illustrated by Hannah Harrison, "Lulu and her master, Remy, a passionate but struggling portrait painter, wander the French countryside looking for customers. They don't need much business--just enough for some figs and cheese to keep their bellies full--but not many people seem to appreciate Remy's abstract style. Before long, Lulu secretly lends a paw to Remy's work and . . . the pair are the most celebrated artists on the salon circuit." (Publisher's note)

"This is a delightful story that must be viewed and read several times to capture all of its wonderful details, humor, and charm. Remy is an artist who paints "the essence of a person, not their likeness," no doubt because of his very poor eyesight...Children and adults will enjoy giving the two types of paintings a close look and picking up the subtle humor in each. Hawkes has done the illustrations for the story, but Harrison is credited for creating Lulu's miniatures. The contrast of the two types of illustration is what make this book so clever." SLJ

The **wicked** big toddlah. Alfred A. Knopf 2007 un il $16.99; lib bdg $19.99
Grades: PreK K 1 2   E
1. Size -- Fiction 2. Maine -- Fiction 3. Infants -- Fiction
ISBN 978-0-375-82427-2; 0-375-82427-8; 978-0-375-92427-9 lib bdg; 0-375-92427-2 lib bdg
LC 2006-32209
A year in the life of a baby in Maine who is just like any other baby except that he is gigantic.
"Each lush spread . . . uses space and perspective to particular advantage. . . . The many bits of visual humor will keep youngsters poring back and forth over the pages." SLJ
Another title about the wicked big toddlah is:
The wicked big toddlah goes to New York (2011)

The **wicked** big toddlah goes to New York. Alfred A. Knopf 2011 un il $16.99; lib bdg $19.99
Grades: PreK K 1 2   E
1. Size -- Fiction 2. New York (N.Y.) -- Fiction 3. Missing children -- Fiction
ISBN 978-0-375-86188-8; 0-375-86188-2; 978-0-375-96189-2 lib bdg; 0-375-96189-5 lib bdg
LC 2009-48258
A Maine couple and their gigantic toddler take a trip to New York City, where despite his size, the 'wicked big toddlah' becomes lost.
"Hawkes pairs caricaturish sketches of Toddie with gorgeous blue summer skies and skillful renderings of iconic landmarks." Publ Wkly

Hayes, Geoffrey
A **poor** excuse for a dragon. Random House Children's Books 2011 47p il (Step into reading) $12.99; lib bdg $14.99; pa $3.99
Grades: K 1 2   E
1. Dragons -- Fiction
ISBN 978-0-375-87180-1; 0-375-87180-2; 978-0-375-96867-9 lib bdg; 0-375-96867-9 lib bdg; 978-0-375-86867-2 pa; 0-375-86867-4 pa; 978-0-375-89938-6 e-book
LC 2010025000
When Fred the dragon leaves home he learns that he is not very good at roaring or breathing fire and swallowing people only makes him ill, but with help from a witch, a giant, and a wise boy he finds his true calling.

"Entertaining black-line and colored pencil cartoon drawings enliven this Kuklapolitan-esque cast. Part-slapstick, part-fairy tale, the gently humorous plot has enough twists and turns to keep newly independent readers engaged." SLJ

Hayes, Joe
Don't say a word, mamá No digas nada, mamá; No digas nada, mamá. by Joe Hayes; illustrations by Esau Andrade Valencia. Cinco Puntos Press 2013 32 p. (hardcover: alk. paper) $17.95
Grades: K 1 2 3   E
1. Sisters -- Fiction 2. Generosity -- Fiction 3. Farm produce -- Fiction 4. Spanish language materials -- Bilingual
ISBN 1935955292; 9781935955290; 9781935955450
LC 2012004536
In this book, "Rosa and Blanca are loving sisters who grow up and live separately, one by herself and the other with a family, in close proximity to their mother's home. Both have bountiful gardens and decide to share their harvests, in secret, with one another. . . . Only Mamá knows of her daughters' generosity, and she is the recipient of the extra tomatoes and corn. The chile peppers are the last straw, and, finally, Mamá spills the beans about what has been going on." (School Library Journal)

Hayes, Karel
The **summer** visitors. Down East 2011 un il $16.95
Grades: K 1 2 3   E
1. Bears -- Fiction 2. Summer -- Fiction
ISBN 978-0-89272-918-0; 0-89272-918-X
LC 2011014445
During the summer a family of bears enjoys the comforts of life at a cottage by a lake, alongside the human visitors.
"The book is almost wordless. The humorous illustrations, done in pen and ink, cleverly highlight the puzzled family's expressions. Children will enjoy being in on the joke as they watch the bears' antics. A fine vacation choice, especially for one-on-one sharing." SLJ

The **winter** visitors; by Karel Hayes. Down East Books 2007 un il $15.95
Grades: K 1 2 3   E
1. Bears -- Fiction 2. Houses -- Fiction 3. Winter -- Fiction
ISBN 978-0-89272-750-6
LC 2007014051
When the summer visitors leave in the fall, a family of bears moves into the vacation cottage to spend the winter.
"Just five sentences of simple text, spread throughout the book, are a perfect accompaniment to the delightful pen-and-ink and watercolor artwork." SLJ

Hayes, Sarah
Dog day; by Sarah Hayes; illustrated by Hannah Broadway. Farrar Straus and Giroux 2008 un il $16.95
Grades: PreK K 1 2   E
1. School stories 2. Dogs -- Fiction 3. Teachers -- Fiction
ISBN 978-0-374-31810-9; 0-374-31810-7
Ben and Ellie's class has a new teacher, and it's a dog named Riff!

"Colorful full-page illustrations add to the doggone good fun. The placement of the illustrations and text lets readers' eyes scamper across the page." SLJ

Hays, Anna Jane

Kindergarten countdown; written by Anna Jane Hays; illustrated by Linda Davick. Alfred A. Knopf 2007 un il $8.99; lib bdg $11.99

Grades: PreK K   E

1. Counting 2. School stories 3. Stories in rhyme
ISBN 978-0-375-84252-8; 978-0-375-94252-5 lib bdg
     LC 2006024249

Rhyming text follows an excited little girl as she counts down the days before the start of kindergarten

"Both the rhyming verse and the pictures are filled with humor and energy. . . . The computer-generated illustrations are detailed and vibrant." SLJ

★ **Ready,** set, preschool! illustrated by True Kelley. Knopf 2005 30p il $16.95; lib bdg $18.99

Grades: PreK   E

1. School stories
ISBN 0-375-82519-3; 0-375-92519-8 lib bdg

A collection of simple stories, poems, and picture games designed to prepare children for preschool

"With lots of cheerfully illustrated rhymes, stories, and interactive games, this big picture book is an excellent title to prepare kids for preschool." Booklist

Smarty Sara; by Anna Jane Hays; illustrated by Sylvie Wickstrom. Random House 2008 32p il (Step into reading) lib bdg $11.99; pa $3.99

Grades: K 1 2   E

1. Stories in rhyme 2. Diaries -- Fiction
ISBN 978-0-375-95054-4 lib bdg; 0-375-95054-0 lib bdg; 978-0-375-83512-4 pa; 0-375-83512-1 pa
     LC 2007-11068

Everywhere Sara goes she brings along her journal where she jots notes, makes lists, draws pictures and maps, writes poems, and plans a big surprise for her friends.

"The casual, rhyming text has fun with the sound of words as well as their meaning, and the colorful, relaxed pictures, in thick line and watercolor, add to the celebration of reading and writing—not as a duty, but as play." Booklist

Hazen, Barbara Shook

★ **Digby**; story by Barbara Shook Hazen; pictures by Barbara J. Phillips-Duke. HarperCollins Pubs. 1996 32p il (I can read book) hardcover o.p. lib bdg $15.89; pa $4.99

Grades: K 1 2   E

1. Dogs -- Fiction 2. Old age -- Fiction
ISBN 0-06-026253-2; 0-06-026254-0 lib bdg; 0-06-444239-X pa
     LC 95-1689

"A boy wants the family dog to play ball, but his big sister explains that Digby is too old now to run and catch. . . . The story of aging and of time passing is told in very simple conversation . . . and the bright contemporary pictures show the bond between the African American brother and sister and their beloved pet." Booklist

Heap, Sue

Danny's drawing book; by Sue Heap. Candlewick Press 2008 un il $9.99

Grades: PreK K 1   E

1. Zoos -- Fiction 2. Africa -- Fiction 3. Animals -- Fiction 4. Drawing -- Fiction 5. Imagination -- Fiction
ISBN 978-0-7636-3654-8; 0-7636-3654-1
     LC 2007040402

On a trip to the zoo with his friend Ettie, Danny draws pictures of some animals, who then lead the two on an imaginary adventure to Africa and back

This is a "charming picture book, illustrated in a childlike style. . . . Heap's colorful acrylic paintings and pencil sketches differentiate between reality and fantasy, but young children will easily recognize that . . . there's plenty of overlap between the worlds." Booklist

Hector, Julian

The **Gentleman** Bug. Atheneum Books for Young Readers 2010 un il $16.99

Grades: PreK K 1   E

1. Insects -- Fiction 2. Books and reading -- Fiction
ISBN 978-1-4169-9467-1; 1-4169-9467-X
     LC 2009-13177

Teased because he likes to spend all of his time reading, the Gentleman Bug decides to change in order to catch the eye of the new Lady Bug in the garden, but she is not impressed until he goes back to being himself.

"Hector's crisp, utterly charming watercolor-and-colored pencil illustrations have a classic, timeless feel, and the spectacularly detailed scenes, which demand close-up viewing, do the bulk of the storytelling." Booklist

The **Little** Matador; words and pictures by Julian Hector. Hyperion Books for Children 2008 un il $15.99

Grades: PreK K 1 2   E

1. Spain -- Fiction 2. Artists -- Fiction 3. Bullfights -- Fiction
ISBN 978-1-4231-0779-8; 1-4231-0779-9
     LC 2007042072

A young matador who would rather draw pictures than fight bulls finds a new way to entertain the townsfolk

"The old-time setting is well conveyed through illustrations using muted colors for the most part, with the hero in a bright red matador's outfit. The succinct text is enriched by numerous visual touches that help tell the story." SLJ

Hegamin, Tonya

★ **Most** loved in all the world; illustrated by Cozbi Cabrera. Houghton Mifflin 2009 un il $17

Grades: PreK K 1 2   E

1. Slavery -- Fiction 2. African Americans -- Fiction 3. Mother-daughter relationship -- Fiction
ISBN 0-618-41903-9; 978-0-618-41903-6
     LC 2004-13189

Even though Mama is an agent on the Underground Railroad, in order to help others she must remain a slave, but she teaches her daughter the value of freedom through a gift of love and sacrifice.

Cabrera's "broad sweeping paintings—filled with shadowy images, occasionally bordering on the abstract, with some pages merely washes of color—add a deeper note of somberness to the spare text, told in a child's voice." Publ Wkly

Heide, Florence Parry

Always listen to your mother; [by] Florence Parry Heide & Roxanne Heide; pictures by Kyle M. Stone. Disney/Hyperion Books 2010 un il $15.99

Grades: K 1 2	E

1. Monsters -- Fiction

ISBN 978-1-4231-1395-9; 1-4231-1395-0

LC 2010004519

When a new neighbor moves in next door, Ernest's mother, who always insists that he obey all the rules, encourages them to play together every day.

"Young readers will love the contrast in colors from Vlapid's bright and cheery home and the neighbors' dark gray home. This book creates a great opportunity to talk about following directions and how to make chores fun." Libr Media Connect

★ The **day** of Ahmed's secret; [by] Florence Parry Heide & Judith Heide Gilliland; illustrated by Ted Lewin. Lothrop, Lee & Shepard Bks. 1990 un il $16; pa $6.99

Grades: 1 2 3 4	E

1. Cairo (Egypt) -- Fiction

ISBN 0-688-08894-5; 0-688-14023-8 pa

LC 90-52694

"Ahmed has monumental news to share with his family, but first he must complete the age-old duties of a butagaz boy, delivering cooking gas to customers all over Cairo. . . . Enhanced by Lewin's distinguished photorealistic watercolors, the sights, sounds, and smells of the exotic setting come to life. . . . At home at last, surrounded by his loving family, Ahmed demostrates his newly acquired facility, proudly writing his name in Arabic." SLJ

The **one** and only Marigold; written by Florence Parry Heide; illustrated by Jill McElmurry. Schwartz & Wade Books 2009 un il $16.99; lib bdg $19.99

Grades: PreK K 1 2	E

1. Monkeys -- Fiction 2. Friendship -- Fiction 3. Family life -- Fiction 4. Hippopotamus -- Fiction

ISBN 978-0-375-84031-9; 0-375-84031-1; 978-0-375-94051-4 lib bdg; 0-375-94051-0 lib bdg

LC 2007-37840

Relates the misadventures of Marigold the monkey, who does not agree with anyone, as she shops with her mother for a coat, becomes interested in a new hobby, finds a way to "bug" her best friend, Maxine (a hippo), and imaginatively copes with finding the right outfit for the first day of school

"As depicted in McElmurry's . . . stylish spreads, a blend of up-to-the-minute humor and nostalgic, folklike patterning, Marigold has a long prehensile tail and spiky rust-colored hair that she sometimes wears in topknots. Heide . . . introduces a stubborn, potentially maddening character, but Marigold's sunny disposition and creativity make up for her mischief." Publ Wkly

★ **Princess** Hyacinth; (the surprising tale of a girl who floated) illustrated by Lane Smith. Schwartz & Wade Books 2009 un il $17.99; lib bdg $20.99

Grades: PreK K 1 2	E

1. Princesses -- Fiction

ISBN 978-0-375-84501-7; 0-375-84501-1; 978-0-375-93753-8 lib bdg; 0-375-93753-6 lib bdg

LC 2008-39923

Princess Hyacinth is bored and unhappy sitting in her palace every day because, unless she is weighed down by specially-made clothes, she will float away, but her days are made brighter when kite-flying Boy stops to say hello.

"The quirky oil and watercolor illustrations seamlessly match Heide's wry, understated text." Publ Wkly

★ **Sami** and the time of the troubles; [by] Florence Parry Heide & Judith Heide Gilliland; illustrated by Ted Lewin. Clarion Bks. 1992 un il $16; pa $6.95

Grades: 1 2 3 4	E

1. Lebanon -- Fiction 2. Family life -- Fiction

ISBN 0-395-55964-2; 0-395-72085-0 pa

LC 91-14343

A ten-year-old Lebanese boy in Beirut goes to school, helps his mother with chores, plays with his friends, and lives with his family in a basement shelter when bombings occur and fighting begins on his street

This is "a powerful, poignant book. Heide and Gilliland's lyrically written, haunting story makes clear that war threatens not only physical existence but affects the human spirit as well. Lewin's watercolor illustrations capture contemporary Beirut with stunning clarity and drama." SLJ

Heide, Iris van der

A **strange** day; [by] Iris van der Heide; illustrations by Marijke ten Cate. Lemniscaat 2007 un il $15.95

Grades: K 1 2	E

1. Letters -- Fiction

ISBN 978-1-932425-94-9; 1-932425-94-2

LC 2006029265

Original Dutch edition 2006

Upset when an important letter does not arrive in the mail as expected, Jack wanders through the park not even noticing what he is doing and becomes an unwitting hero

"Dutch artist ten Cate's landscapes may be delicate and winsome, but they also brim with scenes of farce and slapstick. . . . It all adds up to a clever comedy of coincidences and misadventures, with ample rewards for attentive youngsters." Publ Wkly

Heilbroner, Joan, 1929-

A **pet** named Sneaker; by Joan Heilbroner; illustrated by Pascal Lemaitre. Random House Children's Books 2013 48 p. (Beginner books) (library binding) $12.99

Grades: K 1 2	E

1. Snakes as pets -- Fiction

ISBN 0375971165; 9780307975805; 9780375971167; 9780375981128

LC 2011047340

This children's book by Joan Heilbroner presents "the story of a pet-store snake who longs for a real home. When he is finally adopted by Pete . . . Sneaker not only proves himself a good pet, but proves to be a good student (sneaking into school with Pete and learning to read and write); a good citizen (saving a drowning toddler at a community pool); and a goodwill ambassador for the entire animal kingdom (inspiring the community to open the pool to all animals)!" (Publisher's note)

Heiligman, Deborah

Cool dog, school dog; illustrated by Tim Bowers. Marshall Cavendish Children 2009 un il $15.99

Grades: PreK K 1   **E**

1. School stories 2. Stories in rhyme 3. Dogs -- Fiction
ISBN 978-0-7614-5561-5; 0-7614-5561-2

LC 2008029398

When Tinka the dog follows her owner to school and creates havoc, the children discover a way to let her stay in the classroom and help.

"Bowers's vivid acrylic illustrations are full of expression. . . . Youngsters will like learning with each turn of the page just what makes this dog so special." SLJ

Helakoski, Leslie Hebert

Big chickens; [by] Leslie Helakoski; illustrated by Henry Cole. Dutton Children's Books 2006 un il $15.99
Grades: PreK K 1 2   **E**

1. Fear -- Fiction 2. Chickens -- Fiction
ISBN 0-525-47575-3

LC 2005003282

While trying to escape from a wolf, four frightened chickens keep getting themselves into the very predicaments they are trying to avoid

"Bright pictures convey the comic events with an exaggerated style just right for the story line. There's a satisfying amount of silliness that will leave children giggling." SLJ

Other titles about the big chickens are:

Big chickens fly the coop (2008)
Big chickens go to town (2009)

Fair cow; written and illustrated by Leslie Helakoski. Marshall Cavendish 2010 un il $16.99
Grades: PreK K 1 2   **E**

1. Pigs -- Fiction 2. Cattle -- Fiction
ISBN 978-0-7614-5684-1; 0-7614-5684-8

LC 2009004789

Effie the cow dreams of winning a blue ribbon at the state fair, while her best friend Petunia the pig advises her to give up all that she truly enjoys in order to prepare for the big day.

"The acrylic on paper illustrations are large, bright, and humorous. The animals' faces are quite expressive. . . . This book will work well for storytimes about barnyard antics and for those always-be-yourself lessons. Besides that, it's just plain fun." SLJ

Helfer, Ralph

World's greatest lion; Ralph Helfer; illustrated by Ted Lewin. Philomel Books 2012 40 p.
Grades: 2 3 4   **E**

1. Lions 2. Mascots 3. Animals in motion pictures 4. Zamba (Lion) 5. Lion -- California -- Los Angeles -- Biography 6. Animal trainers -- California -- Los Angeles -- Biography 7. Animals in motion pictures -- California -- Los Angeles -- Biography
ISBN 039925417X; 9780399254178

LC 2011020681

This children's picture book, by Ralph Helfer, "opens in Zambia, where a woman in a safari camp rescues an orphaned lion cub and names him Zamba. . . . Animal behaviorist [Ralph] Helfer . . . brings the lion to his animal sanctuary in California. . . . He eventually becomes sufficiently gentle to star in Hollywood films. Zamba's heroism emerges in the book's final episode, in which he saves Helfer and the sanctuary animals during a flash flood." (Publishers Weekly)

Heller, Linda

How Dalia put a big yellow comforter inside a tiny blue box; and other wonders of tzedakah. illustrations by Stacey Dressen McQueen. Tricycle Press 2011 un il $16.99; lib bdg $19.99
Grades: K 1 2   **E**

1. Jews -- Fiction 2. Charity -- Fiction 3. Judaism -- Fiction 4. Siblings -- Fiction
ISBN 978-1-58246-378-0; 1-58246-378-6; 978-1-58246-402-2 lib bdg; 1-58246-402-2 lib bdg; 978-1-58246-382-7 e-book; 1-58246-382-4 e-book

LC 2010024325

After learning about the Jewish tradition of tzedakah boxes, Dalia shares her knowledge with her younger brother, Yossi, by telling him what her savings can help to provide for someone in need. Includes a note about the history and customs of tzedakah boxes.

"Dressen-McQueen's fully developed summer scenes in acrylic and oil pastel provide a vivid complement to the often-page-filling text, their naive, folk quality bringing great quantities of love and warmth to the tale." Kirkus

Today is the birthday of the world; by Linda Heller; illustrated by Allison Jay. Dutton Children's Books 2009 un il $16.99
Grades: PreK K 1   **E**

1. God -- Fiction 2. Animals -- Fiction 3. Birthdays -- Fiction
ISBN 978-0-525-47905-5; 0-525-47905-8

LC 2008-34216

On the birthday of the world, all of God's creatures pass before Him as He asks whether each has been the best giraffe, or bee, or child they could be, helping to make the world a better place.

Heller's "repeating form lends the soothing tone of a lullaby, well-matched by Jay's . . . bucolic scenes. . . . Readers will be left feeling connected to the larger world, as one of the 'dear little helpers' God praises." Publ Wkly

Helmore, Jim

Oh no, monster tomato! illustrated by Karen Wall. Egmont 2011 un il pa $8.99
Grades: K 1 2   **E**

1. Plants -- Fiction 2. Siblings -- Fiction 3. Tomatoes -- Fiction
ISBN 978-1-4052-4741-2; 1-4052-4741-X

"Marvin is the smallest child in his family, but when the Great Grislygust Grow-off comes around, he is determined to produce the tastiest tomatoes and win. His brother and sister bait and tease him . . . but he has a potion and a few songs up his sleeve. He grows a plant so large that it shoots its tomatoes—they are the size of beach balls—at his mean siblings. . . . Helmore uses alliteration to make the story sing . . . and the rollicking words dance across the pages. Wall's vibrant, cartoon-style, collage illustrations can seem as fast-growing as Marvin's plant." SLJ

Helquist, Brett

★ **Bedtime** for bear. Harper 2010 un il $16.99
Grades: PreK K 1   **E**

1. Bears -- Fiction 2. Winter -- Fiction 3. Bedtime -- Fiction 4. Hibernation -- Fiction
ISBN 978-0-06-050205-8; 0-06-050205-3

Just after the first snowfall, Bear is ready to go to sleep until spring but his friends encourage him to spend one last day playing with them.

"Helquist's sumptuous paintings and expansive sense of visual comedy make this otherwise familiar hibernation tale a keeper. . . . Reader's will want to jump right into these pages and join in the fun—and they'll close the book agreeing that Bear has truly earned his zzzzs." Publ Wkly

Hemingway, Edward

Bump in the night; [by] Edward Hemingway. G.P. Putnam's Sons 2008 un il $15.99

Grades: PreK K 1 2   E

1. Bedtime -- Fiction 2. Monsters -- Fiction

ISBN 978-0-399-24761-3; 0-399-24761-0

LC 2007013812

After Billy goes to bed one night he hears a scary noise, which, upon investigation turns out to be nothing but a sweet little monster named Bump.

"This lively story meets nighttime fears head-on with the right mix of silliness and reassurance. . . . The acrylic-on-wood illustrations create the perfect mood for this appealing bedtime story." SLJ

Henderson, Kathy

★ **Look** at you! a baby body book. illustrated by Paul Howard. Candlewick Press 2006 un il $15.99

Grades: PreK   E

1. Infants -- Fiction 2. Human body -- Fiction

ISBN 0-7636-2745-3

LC 2005-50792

This "commemorates a small child's amazing feats, from crawling to clapping to exploring food with their entire bodies. . . . The oversize pencil-and-watercolor illustrations are warm and soft, with perfectly captured body movements and facial expressions." SLJ

Hendrix, John

★ **Shooting** at the stars; the Christmas truce of 1914. John Hendrix. Abrams Books for Young Readers 2014 40 p. color illustrations (reinforced) $18.95

Grades: 3 4 5 6   E

1. Christmas -- Fiction 2. World War, 1914-1918 -- Fiction 3. Soldiers -- Fiction 4. Christmas Truce, 1914 -- Fiction

ISBN 9781419711756; 141971175X

LC 2013029535

Written by John Hendrix, "'Shooting at the Stars' is the moving story of a young British soldier on the front lines during World War I who experiences an unforgettable Christmas Eve. In a letter home to his mother, he describes how, despite fierce fighting earlier from both sides, Allied and German soldiers ceased firing and came together on the battlefield to celebrate the holiday. They sang carols, exchanged gifts, and even lit Christmas trees." (Publisher's note)

"A scene of miniature candlelit Christmas trees aglow above the German trench, as the lyrics to 'Silent Night' float across the page, is just one of several powerful images. An author's note, glossary, and bibliography may serve as jumping off points for budding history buffs." Pub Wkly

Includes bibliographical references

Henkes, Kevin

★ **Birds**; illustrated by Laura Dronzek. Greenwillow Books 2009 un il $17.99; lib bdg $18.89

Grades: PreK K 1 2   E

1. Birds -- Fiction

ISBN 978-0-06-136304-7; 0-06-136304-9; 978-0-06-136305-4 lib bdg; 0-06-136305-7 lib bdg

LC 2007-45084

Fascinated by the colors, shapes, sounds, and movements of the many different birds she sees through her window, a little girl is happy to discover that she and they have something in common.

"Henkes' spare, direct words have a lyrical magic, while Dronzek's bright acrylic paintings, in saturated primary color and heavy black outlines, reflect the text's plain elegance while carrying an exuberant energy all their own." Booklist

★ **Chester's** way. Greenwillow Bks. 1988 un il $16.99; lib bdg $17.89; pa $6.99

Grades: PreK K 1 2   E

1. Mice -- Fiction

ISBN 0-688-07607-6; 0-688-07608-4 lib bdg; 0-688-15472-7 pa

LC 87-14882

The mice Chester and Wilson share the same exact way of doing things, until Lilly moves into the neighborhood and shows them that new ways can be just as good

"Henkes' charming cartoons are drawn with pen-and-ink, washed over with cheerful watercolors. They give witty expressions to his characters." SLJ

★ **Chrysanthemum**. Greenwillow Bks. 1991 un il $16.99; lib bdg $17.89; pa $6.99

Grades: PreK K 1 2   E

1. School stories 2. Mice -- Fiction 3. Personal names -- Fiction

ISBN 0-688-09699-9; 0-688-09700-6 lib bdg; 0-688-814732-1 pa

LC 90-39803

Chrysanthemum, a mouse, loves her name, until she starts going to school and the other children make fun of it

"The text, precise and evocative, uses contrast and repetition to achieve rhythm and balance; the illustrations are forthright yet delicately colored, remarkable for the agility of the fine line which creates setting and characters." Horn Book

★ **A good** day. Greenwillow Books 2007 un il $16.99; lib bdg $17.89; bd bk $7.99

Grades: PreK K 1   E

1. Board books for children 2. Animals -- Fiction

ISBN 978-0-06-114018-1; 0-06-114018-X; 978-0-06-114019-8 lib bdg; 0-06-114019-8 lib bdg; 978-0-06-185778-2 bd bk; 0-06-185778-5 bd bk

LC 2005-35923

A bird, a fox, a dog, and a squirrel overcome minor setbacks to have a very good day

"This story works well in every way. As precise, unaffected, and easy for a young child to understand as the text, the illustrations feature forms cleanly defined with thick black lines and brightened with watercolors." Booklist

★ **Jessica**. Greenwillow Bks. 1989 un il $16.99; lib bdg $17.89; pa $6.99

Grades: PreK K 1 2   E

1. Imaginary playmates -- Fiction

ISBN 0-688-07829-X; 0-688-07830-3 lib bdg; 0-688-15847-1 pa

LC 87-38087

"A shy preschooler insists that her friend Jessica is not imaginary—and, in the end, she's absolutely correct. Henkes' depiction of play-alone and play-together time brims with buoyant camaraderie in this upbeat story of friendship fulfilled." SLJ

★ **Julius,** the baby of the world. Greenwillow Bks. 1990 un il $16.99; lib bdg $16.89; pa $5.99

Grades: PreK K 1 2   E

1. Mice -- Fiction

ISBN 0-688-08943-7; 0-688-08944-5 lib bdg; 0-688-14388-1 pa

LC 88-34904

"Magically, Henkes conveys a world of expressions and a wide range of complex emotions with a mere line or two upon the engaging mousey faces of Lilly and her family. A reassuring, funny book for all young children who suffer from new-sibling syndrome." SLJ

★ **Kitten's** first full moon. Greenwillow Books 2004 un il $17.99; lib bdg $16.89

Grades: PreK K 1   E

1. Cats -- Fiction 2. Moon -- Fiction

ISBN 0-06-058828-4; 0-06-058829-2 lib bdg

LC 2003-12564

Awarded the Caldecott Medal, 2005

When Kitten mistakes the full moon for a bowl of milk, she ends up tired, wet, and hungry trying to reach it

"Done in a charcoal and cream-colored palette, the understated illustrations feature thick black outlines, pleasing curves, and swiftly changing expressions that are full of nuance. The rhythmic text and delightful artwork ensure storytime success." SLJ

★ **Lilly's** purple plastic purse. Greenwillow Bks. 1996 un il $17.99; lib bdg $18.89

Grades: PreK K 1 2   E

1. School stories 2. Mice -- Fiction

ISBN 0-688-12897-1; 0-688-12898-X lib bdg

LC 95-25085

"Lilly loves everything about school. . . . But most of all, she loves her teacher, Mr. Slinger. . . . The little mouse will do anything for him—until he refuses to allow her to interrupt lessons to show the class her new movie-star sunglasses, three shiny quarters, and purple plastic purse. Seething with anger, she writes a mean story about him and places it in his book bag at the end of the day. . . . Rich vocabulary and just the right amount of repetition fuse perfectly with the watercolor and black-pen illustrations. . . . Clever dialogue and other funny details will keep readers looking and laughing." SLJ

Another title about Lilly is:

Lilly's big day (2006)

★ **Little** white rabbit. Greenwillow Books 2011 un il $16.99; lib bdg $17.89

Grades: PreK K   E

1. Rabbits -- Fiction 2. Imagination -- Fiction

ISBN 978-0-06-200642-4; 0-06-200642-8; 978-0-06-200643-1 lib bdg; 0-06-200643-6 lib bdg

LC 2010011602

"The colored-pencil-and-acrylic art combines thick outlines with vibrant hues, here mostly in a soothing palette of green that fits the nature setting and the comforting tone." Booklist

★ **My** garden. Greenwillow Books 2010 un il $17.99; lib bdg $18.89

Grades: PreK K 1   E

1. Gardens -- Fiction 2. Imagination -- Fiction

ISBN 978-0-06-171517-4; 0-06-171517-4; 978-0-06-171518-1 lib bdg; 0-06-171518-2 lib bdg

LC 2008-42364

After helping her mother weed, water, and chase the rabbits from their garden, a young girl imagines her dream garden complete with jellybean bushes, chocolate rabbits, and tomatoes the size of beach balls

This is rendered with "thick outlines; boldly applied, ice-cream parlor colors; and simple declarative sentences. . . . [This book is] an enjoyable tour of an imaginary place and will plant creativity in young minds." Booklist

★ **Old** Bear. Greenwillow Books 2008 un il $17.99; lib bdg $18.89

Grades: PreK   E

1. Bears -- Fiction 2. Dreams -- Fiction 3. Seasons -- Fiction 4. Hibernation -- Fiction

ISBN 978-0-06-155205-2; 0-06-155205-4; 978-0-06-155206-9 lib bdg; 0-06-155206-2 lib bdg

LC 2007-35965

Boston Globe-Horn Book Award honor book: Picture Book (2009)

When Old Bear falls asleep for the winter, he has a dream that he is a cub again, enjoying each of the four seasons.

"Every word, line, color choice, and composition element feels essential and fits beautifully into a common theme. . . . The elemental words and graceful pacing make this a perfect read-aloud. . . . [The illustrations are] rendered in bold outlines and color washes." Booklist

★ **Owen**. Greenwillow Bks. 1993 un il $17.99; lib bdg $16.89

Grades: PreK K 1 2   E

1. Blankets -- Fiction

ISBN 0-688-11449-0; 0-688-11450-4 lib bdg

LC 92-30084

A Caldecott Medal honor book, 1994

Owen's parents try to get him to give up his favorite blanket before he starts school, but when their efforts fail, they come up with a solution that makes everyone happy

This is "imbued with Henkes's characteristically understated humor, spry text and brightly hued watercolor-and-ink pictures." Publ Wkly

★ **Penny** and her doll; by Kevin Henkes. Greenwillow Books 2012 32 p. $12.99

Grades: K 1 2   E

1. Mice -- Fiction 2. Dolls -- Fiction 3. Personal names -- Fiction 4. Picture books for children 5. Family life

-- Fiction

ISBN 0062081993; 9780062081995 (trade bdg.))

LC 2011030043

In this children's picture book, Penny the mouse "is delighted to receive a doll from her grandmother ('I love her already,' Penny tells her mother and father separately). But Penny faces a quandary when it comes to naming her doll. As her mother and father attend to 'the babies,' they offer suggestions, but nothing feels right until Penny stops thinking so hard and lets the name come to her." (Publishers Weekly)

★ **Penny** and her marble; by Kevin Henkes. Greenwillow Books 2012 48 p. $12.99

Grades: PreK K 1 2   **E**

1. Mice -- Fiction 2. Marbles -- Fiction 3. Lost and found possessions -- Fiction

ISBN 0062082035; 9780062082039; 9780062082046

LC 2012000708

Theodor Seuss Geisel Honor Book (2014)

In this children's book, written and illustrated by Kevin Henkes, the question of ownership is explored when a mouse finds a marble and discovers the lesson of finding objects which aren't yours. "When Penny spots a marble in Mrs. Goodwin's front yard, she picks it up, puts it in her pocket, and takes it home. . . . but does the marble really belong to Penny?" (Publisher's note)

"Henkes continues to plumb the emotional world of childhood as few author/illustrators can... Another gem." Kirkus

Penny and her song; by Kevin Henkes. Greenwillow Books 2012 32 p.

Grades: PreK K 1 2   **E**

1. Mice -- Fiction 2. Songs -- Fiction 3. Children's stories 4. Singing -- Fiction 5. Family life -- Fiction

ISBN 9780062081957; 9780062081964

LC 2011002154

In this book, "after dinner is done, Penny[, a mouse,] sings her song for her family. They like it so much that they ask her to sing it again, then join her in singing and, on a fourth round, put on silly costumes while belting the tune. In the end, it turns out that Penny's song helped the babies to fall asleep, as they have both dozed off in their basket." (Bulletin of the Center for Children's Books)

★ **Sheila** Rae, the brave. Greenwillow Bks. 1987 un il $16.99; lib bdg $17.89; pa $6.99

Grades: PreK K 1 2   **E**

1. Mice -- Fiction

ISBN 0-688-07155-4; 0-688-07156-2 lib bdg; 0-688-14738-0 pa

LC 86-25761

"Bouncy watercolors in spring-like colors with some pen-and-ink detailing highlight Sheila Rae's bravado in an engaging and amusing way, and Henkes provides Sheila Rae, Louise, and their school friends with highly expressive faces." SLJ

★ **So** happy! pictures by Anita Lobel. Greenwillow Books 2005 un il $15.99; lib bdg $16.89

Grades: PreK K 1 2   **E**

1. Seeds -- Fiction 2. Flowers -- Fiction 3. Rabbits

-- Fiction

ISBN 0-06-056483-0; 0-06-056484-9 lib bdg

"Lobel's vigorous artwork, a riot of color that pays homage to Van Gogh, locates events in a sun-toasted, south-of-the-border landscape, and captures the rhythm of Henkes' splitting, braided narratives in triptychs alternating with cohesive scenes." Booklist

★ **Wemberly** worried. Greenwillow Bks. 2000 un il lib bdg $16.89

Grades: PreK K 1 2   **E**

1. School stories 2. Mice -- Fiction 3. Worry -- Fiction

ISBN 0-688-17028-5

LC 99-34341

A mouse named Wemberly, who worries about everything, finds that she has a whole list of things to worry about when she faces the first day of nursery school.

The author combines "good storytelling, careful characterization, and wonderfully expressive artwork to create an entertaining and reassuring picture book that addresses a common concern." SLJ

Hennessy, B. G.

★ **Because** of you; [by] B.G. Hennessy; illustrated by Hiroe Nakata. Candlewick Press 2005 un il $15.99

Grades: PreK K 1   **E**

1. Kindness -- Fiction 2. Conduct of life -- Fiction

ISBN 0-7636-1926-4

LC 2004-45168

"'Because of you,' Hennessy writes, 'there is one more person who will grow and learn,' but also 'one more person who can teach others.' . . . In an empowering conclusion, Hennessy widens the child's sphere of influence, seeing the 'small and precious' acts at home as the first step toward world peace—an ambitious goal made less daunting by Nakata's billowy, cotton candy-hued watercolors of smiling characters exchanging gestures of help and affection." Booklist

Henrichs, Wendy

When Anju loved being an elephant; written by Wendy Henrichs; illustrated by John Butler. Sleeping Bear Press 2011 il

Grades: K 1 2 3   **E**

1. Elephants -- Fiction

ISBN 1-58536-533-5; 978-1-58536-533-3

LC 2010053708

Anju the Asian elephant recalls her childhood in Sumatra, and the American circuses and zoos in which she toiled for fifty years, when she is loaded into a trailer truck and taken to a sanctuary. Includes advice on helping elephants and 'Elephant Q&A'.

"Butler's realistic paintings in acrylic and colored pencil deliver a soft, hazy muted quality that provides balance to the gentle and often lyrical narration, which highlights Anju's flashback memories of her childhood life with fellow young elephant Lali. . . . This heartfelt, humane vignette provides just the right details to appeal to animal-loving children." Kirkus

Henry, Steve

Happy Cat; Steve Henry. Holiday House 2013 32 p. (I like to read) (hardcover) $14.95

Grades: PreK K   **E**
  1. Cats -- Fiction 2. Animals -- Fiction 3. Apartment houses -- Fiction
  ISBN 0823426599; 9780823426591
                  LC 2012006579

In this children's picture book by Steve Henry, "on a cold night, a chilly kitty slides through the basement window of a house and encounters a rat. As he makes his way up the stairs, he comes upon the other animal residents: a dog, a rabbit, a bird, and an elephant. Each occupant is busy reading, painting, or playing music and presents the feline with a gift. When Cat reaches the top, he settles into his new home and is warm and happy." (School Library Journal)

Henson, Heather
  Grumpy Grandpa; written by Heather Henson; illustrated by Ross MacDonald. Atheneum Books for Young Readers 2009 un il $16.99
Grades: K 1 2   **E**
  1. Fishing -- Fiction 2. Old age -- Fiction 3. Country life -- Fiction 4. Grandfathers -- Fiction
  ISBN 978-1-4169-0811-1; 1-4169-0811-0
                  LC 2008-21543

Jack's grandfather is always grumpy, and a bit scary, too, but during a visit to the country house where "Grumpy Grandpa" lives with the brave Aunt Ellie and Uncle Wilbur, Jack learns that his grandfather was once very different.

"MacDonald's wonderful watercolors have his typical '50s look, and include comic scenes. . . . The pictures are a great match for the text, where the modern elements sit comfortably alongside the old-fashioned ones." SLJ

  ★ **That** Book Woman; pictures by David Small. Atheneum Books for Young Readers 2008 un il $16.99
Grades: K 1 2 3   **E**
  1. Librarians -- Fiction 2. Appalachian region -- Fiction
  ISBN 978-1-4169-0812-8; 1-4169-0812-9
                  LC 2007-18156

A family living in the Appalachian Mountains in the 1930s gets books to read during the regular visits of the "Book Woman"—a librarian who rides a pack horse through the mountains, lending books to the isolated residents.

"Complementing Cal's authentically childlike thoughts, Small's deft, rough-edged lines and masterful watercolors convey even more than Henson's carefully honed text." Horn Book

Heo, Yumi
  Ten days and nine nights; an adoption story. Schwartz & Wade Books 2009 un il $16.99; lib bdg $19.99
Grades: PreK K 1 2   **E**
  1. Sisters -- Fiction 2. Adoption -- Fiction 3. Family life -- Fiction 4. Korean Americans -- Fiction
  ISBN 978-0-375-84718-9; 0-375-84718-9; 978-0-375-94715-5 lib bdg; 0-375-94715-9 lib bdg
                  LC 2007044073

A young girl eagerly awaits the arrival of her newly-adopted sister from Korea, while her whole family prepares.

"The exquisite oil, pencil, and collage illustrations dovetail with the quiet, simple tone of the text." SLJ

Heos, Bridget
  Mustache baby; Bridget Heos; [illustrations by] Joy Ang. Clarion Books 2013 40 p. col. ill. (hardcover) $16.99
Grades: PreK K 1 2   **E**
  1. Mustaches 2. Humorous stories 3. Babies -- Fiction 4. Behavior -- Fiction 5. Mustaches -- Fiction
  ISBN 0547773579; 9780547773575
                  LC 2012008155

In this children's picture book by Bridget Heos, "[w]hen Baby Billy is born with a mustache, his family takes it in stride. They are reassured when he nobly saves the day in imaginary-play sessions as a cowboy or cop. . . . But as time passes, their worst fears are confirmed when little Billy's mustache starts to curl up at the ends in a suspiciously villainous fashion. Sure enough, 'Billy's disreputable mustache led him into a life of dreadful crime.'" (Publisher's note)

Herman, Charlotte
  First rain; illustrated by Kathryn Mitter. Albert Whitman 2010 un il $16.99
Grades: 1 2 3   **E**
  1. Rain -- Fiction 2. Israel -- Fiction 3. Grandmothers -- Fiction
  ISBN 978-0-8075-2453-4; 0-8075-2453-0

When Abby moves with her family to Israel, she misses her grandmother and during the dry Israeli summer, she remembers the fun they used to have splashing in puddles together

"Besides being a realistic look at another culture, this well-written book is heartwarming and reassuring." SLJ

Herman, Emily
  ★ **Hubknuckles**; illustrated by Deborah Kogan Ray. Crown Pubs. 2010 un il $14.99; lib bdg $17.99
Grades: PreK K 1 2   **E**
  1. Ghost stories 2. Halloween -- Fiction
  ISBN 978-0-517-55646-7; 0-517-55646-4; 978-0-375-96687-3 lib bdg; 0-375-96687-0 lib bdg
  A reissue of the title first published 1985

Lee, certain that the Halloween ghost that visits her family is just a trick played by her mother or father, decides one year to go outside and dance with Hubknuckles the ghost.

"Ray's black-and-white drawings of family scenes and costumed children playing Halloween games are warm and friendly, while her pictures o the spectral dance add just the right touch of mystery to the story." Horn Book Guide

Hernandez, Leeza
  Dog gone! Leeza Hernandez. G.P. Putnam's Sons 2012 40 p. (hardcover) $15.99
Grades: PreK K 1 2   **E**
  1. Dogs -- Fiction 2. Pets 3. Picture books for children 4. Lost and found possessions -- Fiction
  ISBN 0399254471; 9780399254475
                  LC 2011013408

In this picture book, a "dog acts up at home and is reprimanded by his human. He runs away, gets lost wandering the streets, and meets a rough crowd of street cats and dogs. They are friendly to him and become envious when the boy comes to find him, using a big flashlight in the pouring rain. As the boy and dog reunite, there are lots of big hugs and sloppy kissing. The two fall asleep together in the boy's bed that night." (School Library Journal)

Herold, Maggie Rugg

★ A **very** important day; illustrated by Catherine
Stock. Morrow Junior Bks. 1995 un il $17.99
Grades: K 1 2 3   E
1. Immigrants -- Fiction 2. Naturalization -- Fiction 3.
New York (N.Y.) -- Fiction
ISBN 0-688-13065-8
LC 94-16647

Two-hundred nineteen people from thirty-two different
countries make their way to downtown New York in a snowstorm to be sworn in as citizens of the United States

"After the first quiet, gray-tone painting . . . this book
bursts forth in a riot of color and activity. . . . A glossary supplies guidance for pronouncing names, and a clear, nicely
detailed overview of the process of naturalization rounds
things out. Pictures and story combine to make the joy of the
day contagious." Booklist

Herthel, Jessica

I am Jazz! by Jessica Herthel and Jazz Jennings; pic-
tures by Shelagh McNicholas. Dial Books for Young Read-
ers 2014 32 p. color illustrations (hardcover) $17.99
Grades: PreK K 1 2   E
1. Autobiographies 2. Transgender people 3.
Transgenderism
ISBN 0803741073; 9780803741072
LC 2013031939

This children's book by Jessica Herthel and Jazz Jennings, illustrated by Shelagh McNicholas, describes how
"from the time she was two years old, Jazz knew that she had
a girl's brain in a boy's body. She loved pink and dressing up
as a mermaid and didn't feel like herself in boys' clothing.
This confused her family, until they took her to a doctor who
said that Jazz was transgender and that she was born that
way." (Publisher's note)

"An autobiographical picture book describes trans-youth
activist Jazz Jennings' story of embracing and asserting her
transgender identity. . . . The story balances . . . acceptance
with honest acknowledgement of others' ongoing confusion
and intermittent cruelty, and it briefly addresses Jazz's exclu-
sion from girls' soccer in her state." Kirkus

Includes bibliographical references and index

Hesse, Karen

★ The **cats** in Krasinski Square; illustrated by Wendy
Watson. Scholastic Press 2004 un il $16.95
Grades: 2 3 4 5   E
1. Cats -- Fiction 2. Jews -- Fiction 3. Poland -- Fiction
4. Holocaust, 1933-1945 -- Fiction
ISBN 0-439-43540-4
LC 2003-27775

Two Jewish sisters, escapees of the infamous Warsaw
ghetto, devise a plan to thwart an attempt by the Gestapo
to intercept food bound for starving people behind the
dark Wall.

"In luminous free verse [this] book tells a powerful story.
. . . In bold black lines and washes of smoky gray and ochre,
Watson's arresting images echo the pared-down language
as well as the hope that shines like glints of sunlight on
Kraskinski Square." Booklist

★ **Come** on, rain! pictures by Jon J. Muth. Scholastic
Press 1999 un il $15.95

Grades: PreK K 1 2   E
1. Rain -- Fiction 2. Summer -- Fiction
ISBN 0-590-33125-6
LC 98-11575

A young girl eagerly awaits a coming rainstorm to bring
relief from the oppressive summer heat

"Beautifully drafted watercolor paintings illustrate the
lyrical text, creating a wonderful sense of atmosphere."
Horn Book Guide

★ **Spuds**; by Karen Hesse; illustrated by Wendy Watson. Scholastic Press 2008 un il $16.99
Grades: PreK K 1 2   E
1. Potatoes -- Fiction 2. Siblings -- Fiction 3. Country
life -- Fiction 4. Great Depression, 1929-1939 -- Fiction
ISBN 978-0-439-87993-4; 0-439-87993-0
LC 2007-24046

Maybelle, Jack, and Eddie want to help Ma by putting
something extra on the table, so they set out in the dark to
take potatoes from a nearby field, but when they arrive home
and empty their potato sacks, they are surprised by what
they see.

"This beautifully crafted picture book features panoramic landscapes and intimate pictures. Watson's pencil, ink,
watercolor, and gouache illustrations, warmly rendered in
earth tones, capture the small figures trudging along under a
huge full moon. . . . This sweetly understated affirmation of
hard work and honesty, neighborliness and family love, will
resonate with a wide audience." SLJ

Hest, Amy

★ **Charley's** first night; Amy Hest, Helen Oxenbury.
Candlewick Press 2012 32 p. $15.99
Grades: PreK K 1   E
1. Dogs -- Fiction 2. Pets -- Fiction 3. Human-animal
relationship -- Fiction
ISBN 0763640557; 9780763640552
LC 2012942295

In this children's picture book by Amy Hest, "on Charley's first night, Henry carries his new puppy . . . all the way
to his house. . . . Henry's parents are very clear about who
will be walking and feeding Charley. . . . They are also very
clear about where Charley will be sleeping . . . the kitchen.
But when the crying starts in the middle of the night, Henry
knows right away that it's Charley! And it looks like his parents' idea . . . may have to change." (Publisher's note)

★ The **dog** who belonged to no one; by Amy Hest;
illustrated by Amy Bates. Abrams Books for Young Readers
2008 un il $15.95
Grades: PreK K 1   E
1. Dogs -- Fiction
ISBN 978-0-8109-9483-6; 0-8109-9483-6
LC 2007012763

The hard-working daughter of two bakers and a perfectly
nice stray dog live lonely lives in the same town, until they
meet one very stormy day.

"The pencil and watercolor illustrations, featuring a palette of golden earth tones, echo the gentle sentiment of the
narrative. Lia in her blue dress, pinafore, and jaunty cap and
the bright-eyed little dog evoke tender sympathy." SLJ

★ **Guess** who, Baby Duck! illustrated by Jill Barton.
Candlewick 2004 un il $15.99

Grades: PreK K   **E**
   1. Ducks -- Fiction 2. Grandfathers -- Fiction
   ISBN 0-7636-1981-7

"Baby Duck has a cold and Grampa comes to visit, bringing a 'cheering-up present,' an album of her baby photos. Together they look at pictures of her on the day she was born, after her first bath, taking her first steps, and on her first birthday. She feels better and draws a picture of Grampa kissing her cheek, which is just what he does. . . . Barton's watercolor-and-pencil art is as warm and playful as Baby Duck herself." SLJ

   Other titles about Baby Duck are:
   Baby Duck and the bad eyeglasses (1996)
   In the rain with Baby Duck (1995)
   Make the team, Baby Duck (2003)
   Off to school, Baby Duck (1999)
   You're the boss, Baby Duck (1997)

Kiss good night; illustrated by Anita Jeram. Candlewick Press 2001 un il $15.99
Grades: PreK K   **E**
   1. Bears -- Fiction 2. Bedtime -- Fiction
   ISBN 0-7636-0780-0

     LC 00-41372
Even after a story, being tucked in, and warm milk, Sam the bear is not ready to go to sleep until his mother kisses him good-night

   "This is an enchanting little story, with homey illustrations that add to its appeal." SLJ

   Other titles about Sam the bear are:
   Don't you feel well, Sam? (2002)
   You can do it, Sam (2003)

★ **Little** Chick; illustrated by Anita Jeram. Candlewick Press 2009 un il $17.99
Grades: PreK K   **E**
   1. Aunts -- Fiction 2. Chickens -- Fiction
   ISBN 978-0-7636-2890-1; 0-7636-2890-5

     LC 2008-935296
"Old-Auntie the hen, endlessly patient, marvelously kind, helps Little Chick deal with frustration in three stories. As depicted in Jeram's . . . watercolor washes, Old-Auntie's feathered bulk dwarfs Little Chick, and her gestures . . . are infused with tenderness. Old-Auntie helps Little Chick deal with her eagerness to harvest the carrot she planted; helps Little Chick endure the long wait until her kite finally flies; and assures Little Chick that the star in the night sky that she wants is better off staying just where it is. . . . Hest's . . . light humor and Jeram's visual charm work . . . harmoniously together." Publ Wkly

★ **Mr.** George Baker; illustrated by Jon J. Muth. Candlewick Press 2004 un il hardcover o.p. pa $6.99
Grades: K 1 2 3   **E**
   1. Old age -- Fiction 2. Reading -- Fiction 3. Friendship -- Fiction 4. African Americans -- Fiction
   ISBN 0-7636-1233-2; 0-7636-3308-9 pa

   Harry sits on the porch with Mr. George Baker, an African American who is one hundred years old but can still dance and play the drums, waiting for the school bus that will take them both to the class where they are learning to read.

This is "beautifully illustrated in subtle watercolors. Hest's understated, unhurried poetry echoes the syncopated rhythms of music. . . . Her book is a simple, sweet, moving portrait of a natural friendship between seniors and children." Booklist

The **purple** coat; pictures by Amy Schwartz. Four Winds Press 1986 un il hardcover o.p. pa $6.99
Grades: PreK K 1 2   **E**
   1. Coats -- Fiction 2. Grandfathers -- Fiction
   ISBN 0-02-743640-3; 0-689-71634-6 pa

     LC 85-29186
"The artwork is full color, and the deep shades and vibrant colors (especially that purple) are arresting. The numerous details and patternings catch the eye and make for pictures that can be looked at over and over; each time the story's satisfying conclusion rings sweetly true." Booklist

When Charley Met Grampa; Amy Hest, illustrated by Helen Oxenbury. Candlewick Press 2013 40 p. $15.99
Grades: PreK K 1   **E**
   1. Dogs -- Fiction 2. Picture books for children
   ISBN 0763653144; 9780763653149

     LC 2012954329
This book is a follow-up to Amy Hest's "Charley's First Night." Here, "Grampa, who admits that he is uncertain about getting to know Henry's puppy, is coming to visit and to meet Charley. The boy and puppy wait for him at the train station while snow gently covers the tracks and the town." When the wind blows Grampa's cap away, "Charley takes off into the white world and it's feared that he's lost in the snow. But the diminutive dog saves the day by bringing the cap back." (School Library Journal)

★ **When** you meet a bear on Broadway; pictures by Elivia Savadier. Farrar, Straus and Giroux 2009 un il $16.99
Grades: PreK K 1   **E**
   1. Bears -- Fiction 2. New York (N.Y.) -- Fiction 3. Mother-child relationship -- Fiction
   ISBN 978-0-374-40015-6; 0-374-40015-6

     LC 2008026053
When a little bear becomes separated from its mother in New York, a sympathetic child explains the proper steps that must be taken to reunite them.

   "The repetitive beat in the sly, humorous words make this a perfect read-aloud, although the irresistible nuances in Savadier's artwork . . . are best viewed at close range." Booklist

Heyward, DuBose
The **country** bunny and the little gold shoes; as told to Jenifer; pictures by Marjorie Flack. Houghton Mifflin 1939 un il lib bdg $15; pa $5.95
Grades: PreK K   **E**
   1. Easter -- Fiction 2. Rabbits -- Fiction
   ISBN 0-395-15990-3 lib bdg; 0-395-18557-2 pa

This is an Easter story for young readers which grew out of a story the author has told and retold to his young daughter. It is of the little country rabbit who wanted to become one of the five Easter bunnies, and how she managed to realize her ambition

   "It is really imaginative and well written. . . . The colored pictures are just right too." New Yorker

Hibbert, Clare

If you were a dog; Jamie Swenson; pictures by Chris Raschka. Farrar, Straus & Giroux 2014 40 p. col. ill. (reinforced) $17.99

Grades: PreK K 1 2 3   E

1. Animals -- Fiction 2. Imagination -- Fiction

ISBN 9780374335304; 0374335303

LC 2011034922

This book by Jamie Swenson and illustrated by Chris Raschka explores the question, "if you could be any kind of animal, what would you be? Would you be a dog . . . ? Or maybe you would be a sharp-toothed dinosaur . . . ! Perhaps you might want to be a hopping frog . . . ? But maybe you would want to be the best kind of animal of all: a child!" (Publisher's note)

"Swenson's rhythmic cadences coupled with Raschka's wry, upbeat illustrations yield a title that's a cheery picker-upper." Kirkus

Hicks, Barbara Jean

Jitterbug jam; pictures by Alexis Deacon. Farrar, Straus and Giroux 2005 un il $16

Grades: K 1 2 3   E

1. Monsters -- Fiction

ISBN 0-374-33685-7

LC 2004-46981

First published 2004 in the United Kingdom

Grandpa Boo-Dad not only believes that Bobo has seen a pink-skinned boy with orange fur on his head hiding under the bed, he knows exactly how a little monster can scare off such a horrible creature

"Printed on luxurious, buff-colored paper, Deacon's line-and-watercolor artwork unites cleverly altered Victorian decorative elements . . . with the striking, varied design of contemporary graphic novels. . . . Hicks' folksy, slightly off-kilter language . . . keeps the sense of an exotic, alternate reality watertight." Booklist

Monsters don't eat broccoli; illustrated by Sue Hendra. Alfred A. Knopf 2009 un il $16.99; lib bdg $19.99

Grades: K 1 2   E

1. Stories in rhyme 2. Food -- Fiction 3. Monsters -- Fiction

ISBN 978-0-375-85686-0; 0-375-85686-2; 978-0-375-95686-7 lib bdg; 0-375-95686-7 lib bdg

LC 2008-24536

Illustrations and rhyming text reveal how imagination can spice up even the healthiest meal

"With a toe-tapping beat and loud, splashy spreads, this paean to mealtime chaos will charm small monsters everywhere. . . . Too much fun to limit to kids who don't like broccoli." Publ Wkly

Highway, Tomson

Caribou Song; Tomson Highway, illustrated by John Rombough. Fifth House 2013 32 p. color illustrations $19.95

Grades: 1 2 3   E

1. Spiritualism 2. Caribou -- Fiction 3. Cree Indians -- Fiction

ISBN 1897252617; 9781897252611

American Indian Youth Literature Award: Picture Book (2014)

In this book by Tomson Highway, "Joe and Cody are young Cree brothers who follow the caribou all year long, tucked into their dog sled with Mama and Papa. To entice the wandering caribou, Joe plays his accordion and Cody dances. Bursting upon the boys, ten thousand animals fill the meadow. And yet what should be a moment of terror turns into something mystical and magical, as the boys open their arms and their hearts to embrace the caribou spirit." (Publisher's note)

"Bilingual in English and Cree, this story of the far north follows a family of four that has a spiritual connection to the caribou of the land. . . . [T]he illustrations forgo snowy whites for deep shades of purple, blue, and orange with shapes delineated by thick black lines; the effect is not unlike a stained-glass window." SLJ

Hill, Isabel

Building stories; Isabel Hill. Star Bright Books 2012 40p. ill. (some col.) $17.95

Grades: 2 3 4   E

1. Buildings 2. City and town life 3. Stories in rhyme

ISBN 9781595722805; 9781595722799

LC 2010050860

"Rhyming text and photographs of icons on buildings invite the reader to guess what was done or made in each building originally. Includes "stories characters and plots" of the buildings, as well as their settings." (Publisher's note)

"The sharp, clear pictures of the ornaments appear opposite those of the exterior and interior of the buildings on which they are found. . . . [This is a] good resource." SLJ

Hill, Susan

Ruby's perfect day; pictures by Margie Moore. HarperCollins 2006 32p il (I can read!) $15.99; lib bdg $16.89

Grades: PreK K 1 2   E

1. Raccoons -- Fiction

ISBN 978-0-06-008982-5; 0-06-008982-2; 978-0-06-008983-2 lib bdg; 0-06-008983-0 lib bdg

LC 2005-14516

When Ruby Raccoon wants to share a perfectly sunny day with her busy woodland friends, she discovers that perfect days can be spent all by yourself.

This "book is perfect for beginning readers. A simple plot and good sentence structure provide repetition without being simplistic, and Ruby is indeed appealing." SLJ

Hill, Susanna Leonard

April Fool, Phyllis! illustrated by Jeffrey Ebbeler. Holiday House 2011 un il

Grades: K 1 2 3   E

1. Snow -- Fiction 2. Marmots -- Fiction 3. Riddles -- Fiction 4. Maple sugar -- Fiction 5. April Fools' Day -- Fiction 6. Weather forecasting -- Fiction

ISBN 0-8234-2270-4; 978-0-8234-2270-8

LC 2010019878

When Punxsutawney Phyllis forecasts a blizzard on April Fools' Day—the same day as the Spring Treasure Hunt—the other groundhogs are convinced that Phyllis is pulling a prank. Includes information of the origins of April Fools' Day and how it is celebrated around the world.

"Warm acrylics, saturated in rich golden tones and creamy tans, offer a cozy look into this furry family's den. .

. . Funny details abound. . . . Here's a lighthearted romp that highlights an often overlooked holiday." Kirkus

Can't sleep without sheep; illustrated by Mike Wohnoutka. Walker & Co. 2010 un il $16.99; lib bdg $17.89
Grades: PreK K 1 2   E
  1. Sheep -- Fiction 2. Sleep -- Fiction 3. Animals -- Fiction 4. Bedtime -- Fiction
  ISBN 978-0-8027-2066-5; 0-8027-2066-8; 978-0-8027-2067-2 lib bdg; 0-8027-2067-6 lib bdg
                                                    LC 2009054215
When counting sheep does not help Ava fall asleep and the sheep complain that they are exhausted, they send in replacements, including cows, horses, penguins, and pigs, but none prove satisfactory.
"Hill's words are simple and effective, and leave room for the art to tell the story. . . . A book that is delightful for the eyes and soothing to the ears, Can't Sleep Without Sheep will quickly become a bedtime favorite." SLJ

Not yet, Rose; written by Susanna Leonard Hill; illustrated by Nicole Rutten. Eerdmans Books for Young Readers 2009 un il $16.50
Grades: PreK K   E
  1. Infants -- Fiction 2. Hamsters -- Fiction 3. Siblings -- Fiction 4. Imagination -- Fiction
  ISBN 978-0-8028-5326-4; 0-8028-5326-9
                                                    LC 2008031736
While impatiently waiting for the birth of a new baby brother or sister, Rose the hamster imagines the things they will do together and how her life will change.
"Rutten's cheery watercolor illustrations, depicting the hamsters' life in their cozy country cottage and later in the hospital, are infused with subtle, appropriate humor. With its thoughtful text and playful art, this book gently helps older siblings confidently adjust to their new roles." SLJ

Punxsutawney Phyllis; illustrated by Jeffrey Ebbeler. Holiday House 2005 un il $16.95
Grades: K 1 2 3   E
  1. Marmots -- Fiction 2. Sex role -- Fiction 3. Groundhog Day -- Fiction
  ISBN 0-8234-1872-3
                                                    LC 2003-67641
Although she can predict the weather much better than the boys in her family, no one thinks that Phyllis the groundhog has a chance of replacing the aging Punxsutawney Phil when Groundhog Day's official groundhog retires
"Details about the origins of Groundhog Day and Punxsutawney Phil are appended. Ebbeler's full-bleed acrylic illustrations show an exuberant Phyllis skipping through a brook, sunbathing, and munching on berries." SLJ
Another title about Punxsutawney Phyllis is:
April fool, Phyllis! (2011)

Hillenbrand, Will
  Cock-a-doodle Christmas! by Will Hillenbrand. Marshall Cavendish 2007 un il $16.99
Grades: PreK K 1   E
  1. Roosters -- Fiction 2. Christmas -- Fiction 3. Farm life -- Fiction
  ISBN 978-0-7614-5354-3
                                                    LC 2006030236

Long ago in the town of Bethlehem, young Harold the rooster keeps failing to wake the other farm animals in the morning, but when a young woman gives birth to a very special baby in the stable, Harold is finally able to crow loudly and help spread the good news
"The text, matter-of-fact and unsentimental, reads like a folktale, making this an excellent story to read aloud, and the gouache, ink, and collage illustrations depict a humble but colorful farm." SLJ

Kite day; a Bear and Mole book. Will Hillenbrand. Holiday House 2012 32 p.
Grades: PreK K 1   E
  1. Bears -- Fiction 2. Kites -- Fiction 3. Storms -- Fiction 4. Moles (Animals) -- Fiction 5. Picture books for children 6. Birds -- Fiction
  ISBN 9780823416035
                                                    LC 2011007269
In this children's picture book, "Bear . . . and his friend Mole work together to construct a lovely yellow [kite] which soars . . . until a storm hits and snaps the kite's string. The two friends rush to extricate their storm-battered creation from a tree but change their minds when they see where it has landed: right above a nest of baby birds, who are now sheltered by its cover." (Bulletin of the Center for Children's Books)

★ **Louie!** Philomel Books 2009 un il $16.99
Grades: PreK K 1 2   E
  1. Pigs -- Fiction 2. Artists -- Fiction 3. Drawing -- Fiction
  ISBN 978-0-399-24707-1; 0-399-24707-6
                                                    LC 2008-19453
Louie the pig loves to draw but it gets him thrown out of every school he attends, so he goes to live with his aunt and uncle who help him realize he has a wonderful talent.
"Using the bare-bones outline of Ludwig Bemelmans's childhood, Hillenbrand brings to life the experience of countless children whose creativity sets them apart in structured environments, especially school. . . . Hillenbrand's gloriously colored, superbly executed illustrations—collages, fingerpaintings, gouache, inks, pencils—magnetically draw readers from page to page." SLJ

Off we go! a Bear and Mole story. Will Hillenbrand. Holiday House 2013 32 p. (hardcover) $16.95
Grades: PreK K   E
  1. Friendship -- Fiction 2. Bears -- Fiction 3. Moles (Animals) -- Fiction 4. Bicycles and bicycling -- Fiction
  ISBN 0823425207; 9780823425204
                                                    LC 2012045823
In this children's picture book by Will Hillenbrand, "Mole is ready to lose the training wheels on his bicycle. . . . After a shaky start, he's on his way. . . . 'Bump. Bump. Bump,' writes Hillenbrand as Mole careens through a field of cattle. 'Scramble. Scramble. Scramble,' he continues as Mole narrowly misses a turtle. . . . All ends well, and Bear remains a supportive, concerned friend through the chaos." (Publishers Weekly)

Spring is here! Holiday House 2011 un il $16.95
Grades: PreK K 1   E
  1. Bears -- Fiction 2. Spring -- Fiction 3. Moles

(Animals) -- Fiction
ISBN 978-0-8234-1602-8; 0-8234-1602-X
                                        LC 2010018883
Excited that spring has finally arrived, Mole tries—unsuccessfully—to wake up Bear, but then he comes up with the perfect plan.

"The repetition, ample onomatopoeia, and tender tone of the spare text, combined with heavily textured mixed-media renderings of this gentle pair of pals, create a sunny welcome to the season." Publ Wkly

Hills, Tad

Drop it, Rocket; Tad Hills. Schwartz & Wade Books 2014 32 p. color illustrations (hardback) $12.99; $3.99
Grades: PreK K 1   E
1. Dogs -- Fiction 2. Birds -- Fiction 3. Vocabulary -- Fiction 4. Books and reading -- Fiction
ISBN 0385372477; 038537254X; 9780385372473; 9780385372480; 9780385372541
                                        LC 2013041866
In this children's book, by Tad Hills, "Rocket [the dog] and the little yellow bird love to collect words for their word tree. Rocket is good at collecting (and dropping) things to add to their tree, until he meets a boot he doesn't want to let go of. He is offered a stick, a ball, and a sock until Bird discovers what he'd like more than a boot - a book! After Rocket lets go of the boot, everyone settles down to enjoy the new book." (School Library Journal)

★ **Duck** & Goose; written and illustrated by Tad Hills. Schwartz & Wade Books 2006 un il $14.95; lib bdg $17.99
Grades: PreK K   E
1. Ducks -- Fiction 2. Geese -- Fiction
ISBN 0-375-83611-X; 0-375-93611-4 lib bdg
                                        LC 2005010849
Duck and Goose learn to work together to take care of a ball, which they think is an egg

"While the narrative is fairly straightforward and has touches of childlike humor throughout, it's the bright and colorful artwork that will attract youngsters' attention. The cartoon-style oil paintings set against soft-focus, almost impressionistic backgrounds keep Duck and Goose center stage, and their expressions are priceless." SLJ

Other titles about Duck and Goose are:
Duck, duck, goose (2007)
Duck & Goose, 1, 2, 3 (2008)
What's up, Duck?: a book of opposites (2008)
Duck & Goose, how are you feeling? (2009)
Duck & Goose find a pumpkin (2009)
Duck & Goose: it's time for Christmas (2010)

How Rocket learned to read. Schwartz & Wade Books 2010 un il
Grades: PreK K 1   E
1. Dogs -- Fiction 2. Birds -- Fiction 3. Reading -- Fiction
ISBN 0-375-85899-7; 0-375-95899-1 lib bdg; 978-0-375-85899-4; 978-0-375-95899-1 lib bdg
                                        LC 2008051015
A little yellow bird teaches Rocket the dog how to read by first introducing him to the "wondrous, mighty, gorgeous alphabet."

The author "offers up an appealing picture of the learning-to-read process. . . . Hills' oil-paint and colored-pencil illustrations nicely capture both the sweetness of pupil and tutor and the prettiness of the changing seasons." Booklist

★ **Rocket** writes a story; Tad Hills. Schwartz & Wade 2012 40 p. col. ill. (hardback) $17.99
Grades: PreK K 1 2   E
1. Dogs -- Fiction 2. Authorship -- Fiction 3. Picture books for children 4. Owls -- Fiction 5. Birds -- Fiction 6. Books and reading -- Fiction
ISBN 0375870865; 9780307974914; 9780375870866; 9780375970863
                                        LC 2011041233
Sequel to: How Rocket learned to read
In this book, "Rocket sniffs out . . . new words in his environment," and his bird friend "helps him create a . . . word tree. Now Rocket searches for ideas for his own story in which he can use his word collection. . . . It's not all smooth sailing; he writes, crosses out, and draws pictures, alternately wagging his tail and growling" but his "finished story wins rave reviews." (Kirkus Reviews)

Rocket's 100th day of school; Tad Hills. Schwartz & Wade Books 2014 32 p. color illustrations $12.99
Grades: K 1 2   E
1. School stories 2. Dogs -- Fiction 3. Squirrels -- Fiction 4. Schools -- Fiction 5. Friendship -- Fiction 6. Collectors and collecting -- Fiction
ISBN 0385390955; 9780385390958; 9780385390965; 9780385390972
                                        LC 2014010940
In this children's book by Tad Hills "Rocket, the beloved dog from the . . . picture books 'How Rocket Learned to Read' and 'Rocket Writes a Story,' is busy collecting 100 things to take to school on his 100th day, and he has the perfect place to keep them safe. That is, until Bella, a squirrel who loves acorns, gets involved." (Publisher's note)

"In the fifth book about Rocket, we discover him searching for 100 things for the one hundredth day of school. He gets help from five friends, including Bella the squirrel, who allows him to store his treasures in her nest...The simple text uses short sentences, repetition, and illustrations that support the emerging reader when more difficult words are introduced. Pair this with 100th Day Worries, by Margery Cuyler, and Emily's First 100 Days of School, by Rosemary Wells (both 2000)." Booklist

Rocket's one hundredth day of school
Other titles in the series include:
How Rocket Learned to Read (2010)
Rocket Writes a Story (2012)
Rocket's Mighty Words (2013)
Drop it, Rocket! (2014)

Himmelman, John

10 little hot dogs. Marshall Cavendish 2010 un $12.99
Grades: PreK K 1   E
1. Counting 2. Dogs -- Fiction
ISBN 978-0-7614-5797-8; 0-7614-5797-6
                                        LC 2009042307
One by one, ten excitable dachshunds pile onto a chair.
"Every page has a watercolor scene of the same chair and the changing number of lively dogs. This book will

work well as a read-aloud with small groups, though the engaging puppies will encourage closer examination." SLJ

★ **Chickens** to the rescue. H. Holt 2006 un il $16.95
Grades: PreK K 1 2   E
    1. Days -- Fiction 2. Chickens -- Fiction 3. Farm life -- Fiction
ISBN 978-0-8050-7951-7; 0-8050-7951-3
                              LC 2005-20044
Six days a week the chickens help the Greenstalk family and their animals recover from mishaps that occur on the farm, but they need one day to rest
"The simplicity of the text allows the sheer brilliance of the colored-pencil and watercolor illustrations to shine through. The details in each rescue scene will have everyone laughing." SLJ
    Other titles in this series are:
Pigs to the rescue (2010)
Cows to the rescue (2011)

Frog in a bog. Charlesbridge 2004 un il $15.95; pa $6.95
Grades: K 1 2 3   E
    1. Marshes -- Fiction
ISBN 1-57091-517-2; 1-57091-518-0 pa
                              LC 2003-3737
"Himmelman leads children through natural events that occur on a typical day in a bog, beginning with a frog hopping into some moss. . . . Throughout, readers are introduced to plant, insect, and animal names that may not be commonly known and the idea that some events trigger others. Some classification lessons are included at the end of the book. The watercolor illustrations are definitely a draw: the effect is soft and delicate. Detail is beautifully rendered. . . . This book will have broad appeal." SLJ
    Includes bibliographical references

Katie loves the kittens. Henry Holt & Co. 2008 un il $16.95
Grades: PreK K 1 2 3   E
    1. Cats -- Fiction 2. Dogs -- Fiction 3. Friendship -- Fiction
ISBN 978-0-8050-8682-9; 0-8050-8682-X
When Sara Ann brings home three little kittens, Katie the dog's enthusiasm frightens the kittens away, until she learns that quiet patience is sometimes needed to begin a friendship.
"Himmelman's charming watercolor-and-ink illustrations depict a character sure to earn the affection of young readers. Katie's expressive movements make both her excitement and her dismay palpable and adorable." SLJ

Himmelman, John, 1959-
    Duck to the rescue; John Himmelman. Henry Holt and Co 2014 32 p. color illustrations (Barnyard Rescue) (hardcover) $16.99
Grades: PreK K 1 2   E
    1. Ducks -- Fiction 2. Farms -- Fiction 3. Humorous stories
ISBN 0805094857; 9780805094855
                              LC 2012027681
    In this children's book, written and illustrated by John Himmelman, "when something goes wrong on the farm, someone is always ready to jump in, and this time Ernie the

duck is determined to help out. But no matter how hard he tries, nothing goes quite right. It takes the clever trick of a kind little lamb for Ernie to finally get his chance to come to the rescue!" (Publishers' note)
"Himmelman's watercolors are sure, whether depicting the brewing crisis or Ernie's inevitable mortification. The artwork also has a comedic clarity that lifts the simple text, enlivening its deadpan humor." Kirkus

Hindley, Judy
    ★ **Baby** talk; a book of first words and phrases. illustrated by Brita Granström. Candlewick Press 2006 un il $15.99
Grades: PreK   E
    1. Stories in rhyme 2. Infants -- Fiction
ISBN 0-7636-2971-5
Rhyming text describes the the activities in a baby's day and the words he says while going to the playground, eating dinner, and taking a bath.
"Hindley's unfussy rhyme offers on-target opportunities for concept development: low, high, bye, out. Granström's festive gouache-and-pencil cartoons shine." SLJ

Hines, Anna Grossnickle
    ★ **1, 2, buckle my shoe.** Harcourt 2008 un il $16
Grades: PreK   E
    1. Counting 2. Nursery rhymes
ISBN 978-0-15-206305-4; 0-15-206305-6
                              LC 2007007022
A child learns to count with the help of a classic nursery rhyme
"The popular verse, included in numerous collections of nursery rhymes, gets the star treatment in this delightful picture book. Illustrated entirely with quilt patches festooned with buttons, the ditty bounces along in bursts of color." SLJ

Daddy makes the best spaghetti. Clarion Bks. 1986 un il hardcover o.p. pa $5.95; bd bk $5.95
Grades: PreK K 1 2   E
    1. Father-son relationship -- Fiction
ISBN 0-89919-794-9 pa; 0-395-98036-4 bd bk
                              LC 85-13993
"Corey and his father enjoy a close relationship that is aptly demonstrated in picture and story. He teases Corey and they spend time together doing things such as shopping for groceries and making a pot of spaghetti or being silly at bath time and getting ready for bed. Hines' simple but warm pencil drawings play out the scenes by capitalizing on the incidents described in the text; the strong sense of family (Mother is here too) is evident." Booklist

I am a backhoe. Tricycle Press 2010 un il $12.99
Grades: PreK K   E
    1. Play -- Fiction 2. Trucks -- Fiction
ISBN 978-1-58246306-3; 1-58246306-9
                              LC 2009007534
A young boy imagines himself to be different types of trucks as he plays in the sand.
"Richly colored, digitally enhanced spreads depict the boy at play, intermingled with illustrations of the actual vehicles. The text is set in white and includes plenty of action words. This is a worthy choice for preschoolers and kindergarteners with a big appetite for truck books." SLJ

I am a Tyrannosaurus. Tricycle Press 2011 un il
$12.99; lib bdg $15.99
Grades: PreK K   E
1. Dinosaurs -- Fiction 2. Imagination -- Fiction
ISBN 978-1-58246-413-8; 1-58246-413-8; 978-1-
58246-414-5 lib bdg; 1-58246-414-6 lib bdg
LC 2010024181

A boy mimics the actions of several different dinosaurs
as he imagines he is one of them.

"Set against bright backdrops, Hines's digital illustrations focus on the boy, and in scenes where he appears with
the various dinos, his poses mimic theirs. Kids are sure to
follow suit." Publ Wkly

Hissey, Jane

Old Bear; Jane Hissey. McClelland & Stewart Ltd
2013 36 p. color illustrations (hardcover) $17.95
Grades: PreK K   E
1. Rescue work -- Fiction 2. Teddy bears -- Fiction 3.
Toys -- Fiction 4. Children's stories
ISBN 9781770494817; 1770494812
LC 2012939438

In this children's story, written and illustrated by Jane
Hissey, "Old Bear has been up in the attic for a very long
time, but he hasn't been forgotten. Bramwell Brown and his
friends Little Bear, Duck, and Rabbit attempt to rescue Old
Bear from the attic and bring him safely back home." (Publisher's note)

"A cast of well-worn stuffed animals populate this story
about rescuing Old Bear from the attic. Though the plot
lacks conflict, the animals' thwarted efforts and eventual victory are fun to follow, and Hissey's detailed pencil drawings
will appeal to fans of old-fashioned toys. This new edition
includes a scrapbook with more information about Hissey
and the real Old Bear's history." Horn Book

Hoban, Lillian

★ **Arthur's** Christmas cookies; words and pictures
by Lillian Hoban. Harper & Row 1972 63p il (I can read
book) hardcover o.p. pa $3.99
Grades: PreK K 1 2   E
1. Christmas -- Fiction 2. Chimpanzees -- Fiction
ISBN 0-06-022368-5 lib bdg; 0-06-444055-9 pa

The characters are chimpanzees but "are endearingly like
human children. . . . The Christmas setting is appealing, the
plot has problem, conflict, and solution yet is not too complex for the beginning independent reader, and the simplicity
and humor make the book an appropriate one for reading
aloud to preschool children also." Bull Cent Child Books

Other titles about Arthur are:
Arthur's back to school day (1996)
Arthur's birthday party (1999)
Arthur's camp-out (1993)
Arthur's funny money (1981)
Arthur's great big valentine (1989)
Arthur's Halloween costume (1984)
Arthur's Honey Bear (1974)
Arthur's loose tooth (1985)
Arthur's pen pal (1976)
Arthur's prize reader (1978)

Silly Tilly's Thanksgiving dinner; story and pictures
by Lillian Hoban. Harper & Row 1990 63p il (I can read
book) hardcover o.p. pa $3.99

Grades: PreK K 1 2   E
1. Animals -- Fiction 2. Moles (Animals) -- Fiction 3.
Thanksgiving Day -- Fiction
ISBN 0-06-022423-1 lib bdg; 0-06-444154-7 pa
LC 89-29287

Forgetful Silly Tilly Mole nearly succeeds in ruining her
Thanksgiving dinner, but her animal friends come to the rescue with tasty treats

"Watercolors in vibrant autumn hues accentuate this
comedy of errors with quirky characterizations and fine
brushwork." Booklist

Other titles about Silly Tilly are:
Silly Tilly and the Easter Bunny (1987)
Silly Tilly's valentine (1998)

Hoban, Russell

★ **Bedtime** for Frances; pictures by Garth Williams.
HarperCollins Pubs. 1995 31p il $16.99; lib bdg $17.89;
pa $6.99
Grades: PreK K 1   E
1. Badgers -- Fiction 2. Bedtime -- Fiction
ISBN 0-06-027106-X; 0-06-027107-8 lib bdg; 0-06-
443451-6 pa
LC 94-43809

A reissue of the title first published 1960

"The soft humorous pictures of these lovable animals in
human predicaments are delightful." Horn Book

Other titles about Frances are:
A baby sister for Frances (1964)
A bargain for Frances (1970)
Best friends for Frances (1969)
A birthday for Frances (1968)
Bread and jam for Frances (1964)

Rosie's magic horse; Russell Hoban, illustrated by
Quentin Blake. Candlewick Press 2013 40 p. $15.99
Grades: PreK K 1 2   E
1. Dreams -- Fiction 2. Picture books for children
ISBN 0763664006; 9780763664008
LC 2012942392

In this children's picture book, "Rosie finds a discarded
ice-pop stick and adds it to the others collected in her cigar
box. . . . The sticks discuss what they can be without their
ice pops. 'Maybe a horse,' muses" one. "Meanwhile, Rosie
overhears her parents say that they can't pay their bills.
Longing to help, she falls asleep and dreams of Stickerino,
a flying, talking horse that gallops out of the cigar box and
takes her on a treasure hunt. The next morning, Rosie surprises her dad with . . . gold." (Booklist)

Hoban, Tana

★ **Black** on white. Greenwillow Bks. 1993 un il bd
bk $5.99
Grades: PreK   E
1. Board books for children
ISBN 0-688-11918-2
LC 92-18897

Black illustrations against a white background depict
such objects as an elephant, butterfly, and leaf

This board book features "the stunning, sophisticated
photography of Tana Hoban. . . . Simply the best for babies."
Horn Book Guide

★ **Is** it red? Is it yellow? Is it blue? an adventure in color. Greenwillow Bks. 1978 un il lib bdg $17.99; pa $6.99
Grades: PreK K   **E**
1. Size 2. Color 3. Shape
ISBN 0-688-84171-6 lib bdg; 0-688-07034-5 pa
                                        LC 78-2549
Illustrations and brief text introduce colors and the concepts of shape and size
"The wordless book is simply designed and opens the eye to the marvelous world of color; each stark-white page contains one photograph which nearly fills it. In the bottom margin the predominant colors in the photograph are indicated by a row of corresponding circles." Horn Book

Over, under & through, and other spatial concepts. Macmillan 1973 un il hardcover o.p. pa $8.99
Grades: PreK K   **E**
1. Vocabulary
ISBN 0-02-744820-7; 1-4169-7541-1 pa
In brief text and photographs, the author depicts several spatial concepts—over, under, through, on, in, around, across, between, beside, below, against, and behind
"Children who are confused by these concepts may need help understanding that many of the pictures illustrate more than one concept. However, both the photographs and the format, with the words printed large on broad yellow bands at the beginning of each section, are uncluttered and appealing." Booklist

★ **White** on black. Greenwillow Bks. 1993 un il bd bk $6.99 **E**
1. Board books for children
ISBN 0-688-11919-0
                                        LC 92-20092
In this board book, white illustrations against a black background depict such objects as a horse, baby bottle, and sailboat
"Hoban's compositions are so supple and her layouts so well balanced that she casts a kind of spell." Publ Wkly

Hobbie, Holly
★ **Everything** but the horse; a childhood memory. Little, Brown 2010 un il $16.99
Grades: PreK K 1 2   **E**
1. Horses -- Fiction 2. Farm life -- Fiction 3. Country life -- Fiction
ISBN 978-0-316-07019-5; 0-316-07019-X
                                        LC 2010006907
When Holly's family moves from the city to a farm, she longs to get a horse for her birthday. Based on events in the author's childhood.
"The simple artwork, done in pen-and-ink and watercolor, beautifully depicts a time when life for a young farm girl was filled with rustic barns, fields, and delightful animals, while her heartwarming text conveys a sense of innocence and dreams." SLJ

Gem; Holly Hobbie. Little, Brown & Co. 2012 32 p.
Grades: PreK   **E**
1. Girls -- Fiction 2. Toads -- Fiction 3. Spring -- Fiction 4. Gardens -- Fiction 5. Picture books for children
ISBN 0316203343; 9780316203340

This picture book "explores the wonders of spring through the eyes of a toad that survives the perils and pleasures of its trek to a country garden, where he encounters the author's granddaughter, Hope. Opening with a letter explaining how Hope's discovery of a toad named Gem inspired her to 'tell the story of Gem's spring journey,' [Holly] Hobbie wordlessly chronicles this odyssey in . . . watercolor, pen and ink illustrations. A palette of fresh greens and yellows heralds springtime, while varying frame sizes and perspectives allow readers to view the . . . toad's cross-country ramble from multiple angles." (Kirkus)

Toot & Puddle; 10th anniversary ed.; Little, Brown Books for Young Readers 2007 un il $16.99; pa $6.99
Grades: PreK K 1 2   **E**
1. Pigs -- Fiction 2. Voyages and travels -- Fiction
ISBN 978-0-316-16702-4; 0-316-16702-9; 978-0-316-08080-4 pa; 0-316-08080-2 pa
A reissue of the title first published 1997
Toot and Puddle pigs are best friends with very different interests, so when Toot spends the year travelling around the world, Puddle enjoys receiving his postcards.
"In Hobbie's expert watercolors are dozens of inventive touches. . . . The book and its heroes are endearing." Kirkus

Toot & Puddle: let it snow. Little, Brown & Co. 2007 un il $16.99
Grades: PreK K 1 2   **E**
1. Pigs -- Fiction 2. Snow -- Fiction 3. Gifts -- Fiction 4. Christmas -- Fiction 5. Friendship -- Fiction
ISBN 978-0-316-16686-7; 0-316-16686-3
Toot and Puddle celebrate Christmas and learn that the best kind of present for the best kind of friend is one that shows just how much you care.
"Hobbie infuses her holiday story of devoted friendship with cozy language . . . all evoked in Hobbie's signature watercolor illustrations." Horn Book
Other titles about Toot & Puddle are:
Toot & Puddle (1997)
Toot & Puddle: a present for Toot (1998)
Toot & Puddle: you are my sunshine (1999)
Toot & Puddle: Puddle's ABC (2000)
Toot & Puddle: I'll be home for Christmas (2001)
Toot & Puddle: top of the world (2002)
Toot & Puddle: charming Opal (2003)
Toot & Puddle: the new friend (2004)
Toot & Puddle: the one and only (2006)

Hoberman, Mary Ann
I like old clothes; by Mary Ann Hoberman; illustrations by Patrice Barton. Alfred A. Knopf 2012 32 p. (hard cover) $16.99
Grades: PreK K 1   **E**
1. Play -- Fiction 2. Picture books for children 3. Clothing and dress -- Fiction 4. Stories in rhyme
ISBN 0375869514; 9780375869518; 9780375969515
                                        LC 2010038292
This children's picture book was "[o]riginally published by Knopf in 1976 (with illustrations by Jacqueline Chwast)," using a poem from "Children's Poet Laureate Mary Ann Hoberman" as its text. The story features a "protagonist who likes old clothes for their 'history' and 'mystery.'" In the update, "[i]llustrator Patrice Barton" offers illustrations of a "little girl and her younger brother playing dress-up, mak-

ing crafts, and happily treasuring their hand-me-downs."
(Barnes and Noble)

The **seven** silly eaters; written by Mary Ann Hoberman; illustrated by Marla Frazee. Browndeer Press 1997 40 p. col. ill. $17
Grades: PreK K 1 2 3   E
1. Food -- Fiction 2. Stories in rhyme 3. Mothers -- Fiction 4. Birthdays -- Fiction 5. Food habits -- Fiction
ISBN 0152000968; 9780152000967
LC 95018186
In this book, by Mary Ann Hoberman, "Peter wants only milk, Lucy won't settle for anything but homemade lemonade, and Jack is stuck on applesauce. . . . What's a mother to do? Even though Mrs. Peters picks, peels, strains, scrapes, poaches, fries, and kneads, the requests for special foods keep coming. It isn't until her birthday arrives that a present from her children solves the problem with a hilarious surprise that pleases everyone." (Publisher's note)

The **two** sillies; illustrated by Lynne Cravath. Harcourt 2000 un il $16
Grades: PreK K 1 2   E
1. Stories in rhyme 2. Cats -- Fiction 3. Mice -- Fiction
ISBN 0-15-202221-X
LC 98-51844
"When Silly Lilly admires Sammy's cat and asks how to get one, he gives her step-by-step instructions that seem to make no sense at all. . . . Short sentences use mono-syllabic words and rhyme to great effect. The brightly colored cartoon-style art adds just the right touch of exaggerated humor." Horn Book Guide

★ **You** read to me, I'll read to you; very short fairy tales to read together (in which wolves are tamed, trolls are transformed, and peas are triumphant) illustrated by Michael Emberley. Little, Brown 2004 32p il $16.95
Grades: K 1 2 3   E
1. Fairy tales
ISBN 0-316-14611-0
LC 2003-47445
"The two voices join seamlessly together to create a truly delightful reading ensemble. Emberley's humorous illustrations feature expressive characters drawn in pen, watercolor, and pastel." SLJ

Hodges, Margaret
The **wee** Christmas cabin; retold by Margaret Hodges; illustrated by Kimberly Bulcken Root. Holiday House 2009 un il $16.95
Grades: K 1 2 3   E
1. Fairies -- Fiction 2. Ireland -- Fiction 3. Christmas -- Fiction
ISBN 978-0-8234-1528-1; 0-8234-1528-7
LC 00044877
A tinker's child who grows up helping everyone in her Irish village is rewarded in her old age with a cabin built by fairies on Christmas Eve.
"Hodges' elegant prose doesn't spell out exactly what happens to Oona, allowing children's imaginations to fill in the rest, and preserving the wonder of the story. Delicate watercolor paintings emphasize the cool dark blues and greens of wintry Ireland against the warm golds and reds of the cheery cabin's hearth." Booklist

Hodgkins, Fran
Who's been here? a tale in tracks. illustrated by Karel Hayes. Down East 2008 un il $15.95
Grades: PreK K 1 2   E
1. Dogs -- Fiction 2. Animal tracks -- Fiction
ISBN 978-0-89272-714-8; 0-89272-714-4
LC 2008015756
"Three children follow golden retriever Willy into the snowy outdoors, seeing not only his paw prints but also those animals he's tracked. Delicate illustrations of snow-covered forest include accurate animal tracks and woodsy borders. The spare text uses repetition effectively in this book for nature lovers." Horn Book Guide

Hodgkinson, Jo
The **talent** show. Andersen 2011 un il $16.95
Grades: PreK K 1   E
1. Stories in rhyme 2. Size -- Fiction 3. Birds -- Fiction 4. Animals -- Fiction
ISBN 0761374876; 9780761374879; 978-0-7613-7487-9; 0-7613-7487-6
LC 2010032965
A tiny red bird wants very much to win the upcoming talent show, but first he must prove that being small does not mean having little talent.
"The rhyming text and dynamic scenes in vivid colors keep the tale rocking. Panels in various sizes are simple compositions that encourage focus on the personalities depicted. From the crooning moose to the singing hippo in a boa, the illustrations don't miss a beat of humor." SLJ

Hodgkinson, Leigh
Limelight Larry. Tiger Tales 2011 un il $15.95
Grades: PreK K 1   E
1. Peacocks -- Fiction 2. Books and reading -- Fiction
ISBN 978-1-58925-102-1; 1-58925-102-4
Limelight Larry the peacock is delighted when he finds an empty book— he can be the star of the story! Then a whole host of storybook characters arrive and Larry, much to his outrage, is pushed out of the limelight.
"Prereaders should be captivated by this cacophony of type and images, and they will certainly identify with the willful peacock." Kirkus

Smile! Balzer & Bray 2010 un il $16.99
Grades: PreK K 1   E
1. Family life -- Fiction
ISBN 978-0-06-185269-5; 0-06-185269-4
LC 2009-14277
A little girl searches all over the house for the smile that seems to have deserted her.
"The childlike illustrations are done in bright colors with collage elements, occasional labels, and sometimes with sound effects. . . . Sunny's imagination enriches her search." SLJ

Hodson, Sally
Granny's clan; a tale of wild orcas. by Sally Hodson; illustrated by Ann Jones. Dawn Publications 2012 32 p. (hardback) $16.95
Grades: 2 3 4   E
1. Killer whales -- Fiction
ISBN 1584691719; 9781584691716; 9781584691723
LC 2011049431

In this book, Sally Hodson offers a "glimpse into the real world of a Pacific Northwest killer whale family or pod. Also known as an orca, 100-year-old granny and her family (the J-pod) interact with one another, just as humans do. Granny teaches her children, grandchildren and great-grandchildren, how and where to locate food, play nicely, avoid danger, sing orca songs, and coexist with people." (Children's Literature)

Hoff, Syd
Danny and the dinosaur; story and pictures by Syd Hoff. Harper & Row 1958 64p il (I can read book) $16.99; pa $3.99
Grades: PreK K 1 2   E
1. Dinosaurs -- Fiction
ISBN 0-06-022465-7; 0-06-444002-8 pa
"The bold, humorous, colored pictures convey the imaginative story.... Because of the simple vocabulary and sentence structure, first-graders can actually read this story." Libr J
Another title about Danny and the dinosaur is:
Happy birthday, Danny and the dinosaur! (1995)

The **littlest** leaguer; story and pictures by Syd Hoff. HarperCollins Childrens Books 2008 48p il (I can read!) $16.99; pa $3.99
Grades: PreK K 1 2   E
1. Baseball -- Fiction
ISBN 978-0-06-053772-2; 0-06-053772-8; 978-0-06-053774-6 pa; 0-06-053774-4 pa
A reissue of the title first published 1976
Littlest of all the little leaguers, Harold has a hard time finding some way to really help his team.
"Hoff's ability to tell an interesting story with a minimum of words is unsurpassed." Horn Book Guide

Oliver; story and pictures by Syd Hoff. HarperCollins Pubs. 2000 64p il (I can read book) lib bdg $17.89; pa $3.99
Grades: PreK K 1 2   E
1. Circus -- Fiction 2. Elephants -- Fiction
ISBN 0-06-028709-8 lib bdg; 0-06-444272-1 pa
LC 99-25591
A newly illustrated edition of the title first published 1960
Oliver the elephant looks elsewhere for employment after learning that the circus already has enough elephants
"One of the most warm-hearted and appealing easy-to-read books available." SLJ

Sammy the seal; story and pictures by Syd Hoff. newly il ed; HarperCollins Pubs. 2000 64p il (I can read book) $16.99; lib bdg $16.89; pa $3.99
Grades: PreK K 1 2   E
1. Zoos -- Fiction 2. Seals (Animals) -- Fiction
ISBN 0-06-028545-1; 0-06-028546-X lib bdg; 0-06-444270-5 pa
LC 99-13805
A newly illustrated edition of the title first published 1959
Anxious to see what life is like outside the zoo, Sammy the seal explores the city, goes to school, and plays with the children but decides that there really is no place like home
"Happy adventures told in entertaining colored cartoon-like drawings and in simple vocabulary and short sentences

which first graders can read with a minimum of help." Booklist

Hoffman, Mary
★ **Amazing** Grace; pictures by Caroline Binch. Dial Bks. for Young Readers 1991 un il $16.99
Grades: K 1 2 3   E
1. Theater -- Fiction 2. African Americans -- Fiction
ISBN 0-8037-1040-2
LC 90-25108
Although her classmates say that she cannot play Peter Pan in the school play because she is black and a girl, Grace discovers that she can do anything she sets her mind to do
"Gorgeous watercolor illustrations portraying a determined, talented child and her warm family enhance an excellent text and positive message of self-affirmation. Grace is an amazing girl and this is an amazing book." SLJ
Other picture book titles about Grace are:
Boundless Grace (1995)
Grace at Christmas (2011)
Princess Grace (2008)

The **color** of home; pictures by Karin Littlewood. Phyllis Fogelman Bks. 2002 un il $15.99
Grades: K 1 2 3   E
1. Somalia -- Fiction 2. Refugees -- Fiction 3. Immigrants -- Fiction
ISBN 0-8037-2841-7
LC 2001-7393
Hassan, newly-arrived in the United States and feeling homesick, paints a picture at school that shows his old home in Somalia as well as the reason his family had to leave
"Readers gain a realistic child's perspective on what it is like to be forced to emigrate from a war-torn country. . . . Littlewood's impressionistic watercolor illustrations . . . beautifully convey Hassan's sadness, fear, and ultimate happiness." SLJ

Grace at Christmas; illustrated by Cornelius Van Wright and Ying-Hwa Hu. Dial Books for Young Readers 2011 il $17.99
Grades: K 1 2 3   E
1. Christmas -- Fiction 2. Family life -- Fiction 3. African Americans -- Fiction
ISBN 978-0-8037-3577-4; 0-8037-3577-4
LC 2011004571
When her grandmother takes in a stranded family at Christmas, Grace is reluctant to share her favorite holiday with strangers, even though the visiting family includes a "real live ballerina."
"Hoffman's empathetic storytelling and Van Wright and Hu's naturalistic illustrations make the most of Grace's abundant humor and personality." Publ Wkly

Hogan, Jamie
Seven days of Daisy. Down East 2012 un il $14.95
Grades: PreK K   E
1. Islands -- Fiction 2. Grandmothers -- Fiction
ISBN 978-0-89272-919-7; 0-89272-919-8
"Counting down the days before Nana comes to visit her island home, young Daisy describes how she fills her time. Sailing, tea parties at the shore, rocking in the hammock, and playing tag all make the wait a bit less tedious. When Nana arrives, Daisy is ready to tell her about her various activities.

. . . The simple sentences and childlike focus stay true to the narrator. . . . The realistic charcoals and pastels offer texture, and colors vary to reflect moods and times of day." SLJ

Hogrogian, Nonny

Cool cat. Roaring Brook Press 2009 un il $17.99
Grades: PreK K 1 2   E
1. Stories without words 2. Cats -- Fiction 3. Animals -- Fiction 4. Painting -- Fiction
ISBN 978-1-59643-429-5; 1-59643-429-5

"A vacant lot strewn with garbage is transformed by an artistic and imaginative black cat in this wordless picture book. Using paints and brushes from his wooden art box, the feline covers his drab surroundings with leaves and sky, enlisting the help of some birds and woodland creatures that take up brushes to add flowers, trees, and a pond. . . . Simple, almost childlike art in the lush colors of summer combines with brilliant composition to tell the story. . . . Both visually and conceptually, this is a gem." SLJ

Holabird, Katharine

★ Angelina Ballerina; story by Katharine Holabird; illustrations by Helen Craig. Viking 2006 un il $12.99
Grades: PreK K 1 2   E
1. Mice -- Fiction 2. Ballet -- Fiction
ISBN 0-670-06026-7

A reissue of the title first published 1983 by Potter
Angelina the mouse loves to dance and wants to become a ballerina more than anything else in the world.

"Touches of humor, attention to detail, a feel for dance and truly anthropomorphic mice make the illustrations a major part of the book." Child Book Rev Serv

Other titles about Angelina are:
Angelina and Alice (1987)
Angelina and Henry (2002)
Angelina and the princess (1984)
Angelina and the royal wedding (2010)
Angelina at the fair (1985)
Angelina on stage (1986)
Angelina, star of the show (2008)
Angelina's baby sister (1991)
Angelina's Christmas (1985)
Angelina's Halloween (2000)

Hole, Stian

★ Garmann's summer. Eerdmans Books for Young Readers 2008 un il $17.50
Grades: 1 2 3   E
1. Fear -- Fiction 2. Aunts -- Fiction 3. Summer -- Fiction 4. Old age -- Fiction 5. Family life -- Fiction
ISBN 978-0-8028-5339-4; 0-8028-5339-0
Original Norwegian edition, 2006

Now that summer is nearly over, Garmann is afraid of starting school. He asks his elderly aunts, and his father, and his mother what they are afraid of.

"The illustrations, spacious, quirky mosaic collages comprising photos, old-fashioned etchings, and wallpaper samples are utterly without a trace of sentimentality. In a feat of deceptive simplicity, Hole has crafted an elegant, fanciful, wholly poetic exploration of the nature of fear and the strength and hope required to conquer it." Booklist

Another title about Garmann is:
Garmann's street (2010)

Holmberg, Bo R.

A day with Dad; illustrations by Eva Eriksson. Candlewick Press 2008 un il $15.99
Grades: K 1 2 3   E
1. Divorce -- Fiction 2. Father-son relationship -- Fiction
ISBN 978-0-7636-3221-2; 0-7636-3221-X
LC 2007034228

Tim waits with excitement for a train to bring his father, who lives in another town, then spends an entire day with him, doing all of their favorite things, until it is time for Dad to catch the train home.

"Eriksson's unfussy colored-pencil illustrations are a good match for Holmberg's straightforward text. . . . This gentle, poignant story offers comfort to readers in similar circumstances and leaves them with a hopeful message." Horn Book

Holmes, Janet A.

Have you seen Duck? [by] Janet A. Holmes and [illustrated by] Jonathan Bentley. Scholastic 2011 un il $8.99
Grades: PreK K   E
1. Toys -- Fiction 2. Lost and found possessions -- Fiction
ISBN 978-0-545-22488-8; 0-545-22488-8
LC 2010-20587

"Holmes offers a fresh spin on an old favorite—the child who can't be away from his stuffed animal. Here that child is the towheaded narrator, and the stuffie, a small yellow duck. But in the boy's mind, it's Duck who needs him. . . . The light, airy ink-and-watercolor artwork, brightened by yellows, keeps its focus on the boy and his duck. Perhaps not as dramatic as Knuffle Bunny (2004) but every bit as moving." Booklist

Holmes, Mary Tavener

A giraffe goes to Paris; by Mary Tavener Holmes and John Harris; illustrated by Jon Cannell. Marshall Cavendish 2010 31p il $16.95
Grades: K 1 2 3   E
1. France -- Fiction 2. Giraffes -- Fiction 3. Voyages and travels -- Fiction
ISBN 978-0-7614-5595-0; 0-7614-5595-7
LC 2009-19047

Recounts the 1827 journey of a young giraffe named Belle, a gift from the Pasha of Egypt to King Charles X of France, as she makes her way by boat and land to Paris, accompanied by her devoted caretaker, Atir.

"Loopy handwritten script is used for emphasis . . . while old maps, photographs, and potraits supplement Cannell's watercolor-and-ink drawings. . . . This is history for children as it ought to be written." Publ Wkly

Holt, Kimberly Willis

The adventures of Granny Clearwater & Little Critter; illustrated by Laura Huliska-Beith. Henry Holt and Company 2010 un il $16.99
Grades: K 1 2 3   E
1. Tall tales 2. West (U.S.) -- Fiction 3. Grandmothers -- Fiction 4. Frontier and pioneer life -- Fiction
ISBN 978-0-8050-7899-2; 0-8050-7899-1
LC 2009-27418

"When the Clearwaters start their journey west in a covered wagon, a mishap separates Granny and her grandson

Little Critter from the others. They travel across the scorching-hot prairie in an effort to find their missing family members. . . . This is a wonderful tall tale, told with plenty of humor and enhanced by colorful collage illustrations. . . . A rip-roaring yarn." SLJ

Holub, Joan

Apple countdown; by Joan Holub; illustrated by Jan Smith. Albert Whitman & Co. 2009 un il $16.99
Grades: PreK K 1 2   E
   1. Counting 2. School stories 3. Stories in rhyme 4. Apples -- Fiction
   ISBN 978-0-8075-0398-0; 0-8075-0398-3
                  LC 2008031705

Rhyming text describes a school field trip to an apple orchard, where the students count down all the things they see, from twenty nametags to one apple pie.

"The vibrant watercolor illustrations are dominated by primary colors, and the excitement shows on the smiling faces of the students." SLJ

The **garden** that we grew; pictures by Hiroe Nakata. Viking 2001 un il (Viking easy-to-read) $13.99
Grades: K 1 2   E
   1. Stories in rhyme 2. Pumpkin -- Fiction 3. Gardening -- Fiction
   ISBN 0-670-89799-X
                  LC 00-10966

Children plant pumpkin seeds, water and weed the garden patch, watch the pumpkins grow, pick them, and enjoy them in various ways

"The text blossoms with the ample warmth, light, and gentle sense of humor in the pictures." Horn Book

★ **Little** Red Writing; by Joan Holub and illustrated by Melissa Sweet. Chronicle Books 2013 36 p. (alk. paper) $16.99
Grades: 1 2 3   E
   1. Humorous stories 2. Pencils -- Fiction 3. Authorship -- Fiction 4. Creative writing -- Fiction
   ISBN 0811878694; 9780811878692
                  LC 2012027737

In this book author Joan Holub and illustrator Melissa Sweet present a "retelling of 'Little Red Riding Hood,' in which a brave, little red pencil finds her way through the many perils of writing a story, faces a ravenous pencil sharpener (the Wolf 3000) . . . and saves the day." (Publisher's note) "Little Red is eager to begin, and knowing that a good story often involves a journey, she sets off, armed with a basket of words for help along the way." (Booklist)

Spring is here! a story about seeds. by Joan Holub; illustrated by Will Terry. Aladdin 2008 un il (Ready-to-read: Ant hill) hardcover o.p. pa $3.99
Grades: PreK K 1   E
   1. Stories in rhyme 2. Ants -- Fiction 3. Seeds -- Fiction 4. Gardening -- Fiction
   ISBN 978-1-4169-5132-2; 1-4169-5132-6 lib bdg; 978-1-4169-5131-5 pa; 1-4169-5131-8 pa
                  LC 2007-17677

In autumn, the little friends from Ant Hill find and plant some seeds, then patiently wait until spring to enjoy the plants that appear.

"The very few words of rhyming text on each spread are supplemented by the book's funny illustrations, which fill the pages and are integral to helping tell the stories. The rhymes and picture clues will help even the newest readers decipher these simplest of tales." Horn Book Guide

Zeus and the thunderbolt of doom; Joan Holub, Suzanne Williams. Aladdin, Simon and Schuster 2012 100 p. (paperback) $5.99; (hardcover) $15.99
Grades: 3 4 5   E
   1. Greek mythology -- Graphic novels 2. Gods and goddesses -- Graphic novels
   ISBN 1442457872; 9781442452633; 9781442457874
                  LC 2012939508

Authors Joan Hollub and Suzanne Williams present a children's story. "After 10-year-old Zeus is plucked from his childhood cave in Crete by armed 'Cronies' of the Titan king, Cronus, he is rescued by harpies. He then finds himself in a Grecian temple where he acquires a lightning bolt with the general personality of a puppy and receives hints of his destiny from an Oracle with fogged eyeglasses. Recaptured and about to be eaten by Cronus, Zeus hurls the bolt down the Titan's throat--causing the king to choke and . . . barf up several previously eaten Olympians." (Kirkus)

Hood, Susan

Pup and Hound hatch an egg; written by Susan Hood; illustrated by Linda Hendry. Kids Can Press 2007 32p il (Kids can read) $14.95; pa $3.95
Grades: PreK K 1   E
   1. Stories in rhyme 2. Dogs -- Fiction 3. Turtles -- Fiction
   ISBN 978-1-55337-974-4; 1-55337-974-8; 978-1-55337-975-1 pa; 1-55337-975-6 pa

"Pup finds an egg in the grass and tries to return it to Duck and then Mother Hen. Both mothers deny ownership, and when the egg eventually hatches, it turns out to be a baby turtle—a new friend for Pup and Hound. [The book has] appealing characters and all of the requisites for a successful beginning reader. . . . Bouncy rhymes add to the fun." SLJ

Other titles about Pup and Hound are:
Pup and Hound (2004)
Pup and Hound at sea (2006)
Pup and Hound catch a thief (2007)
Pup and Hound in trouble (2005)
Pup and Hound lost and found (2006)
Pup and Hound move in (2004)
Pup and Hound play copycats (2007)
Pup and Hound scare a ghost (2007)
Pup and Hound stay up late (2005)

Hooks, Bell

Grump groan growl; illustrated by Chris Raschka. Hyperion Books for Children 2008 un il $16.99
Grades: PreK K 1   E
   1. Emotions -- Fiction
   ISBN 978-0-7868-0816-8; 0-7868-0816-0
                  LC 2007022312

Rhythmic text exposes a bad mood on the prowl, and advises the reader not to hide, but to let those feelings be

"Expressionistic art and economical poetry combine smoothly to create an inspiring model of self-control. . . . Thick, almost tactile lines of paint are slathered onto the

pages with gusto, capturing a feeling of movement and
strong emotion." SLJ

Hooks, Gwendolyn

Pet costume party; a Pet Club story. illustrated by Mike
Byrne. Stone Arch Books 2011 31p il (Stone Arch readers) lib bdg $21.32; pa $3.95

Grades: K 1 2   E

1. Pets -- Fiction 2. Fishes -- Fiction 3. Parties --
Fiction 4. Halloween -- Fiction

ISBN 978-1-4342-2513-9 lib bdg; 1-4342-2513-5 lib
bdg; 978-1-4342-3053-9 pa; 1-4342-3053-8 pa

LC 2010036339

"Andy and his pet goldfish are having a Halloween party
and need costumes. They move through various choices
but the fact that Nibbles can't talk complicates matters. . .
. Byrne's vibrant cartoon drawings offer gentle humor to
Hooks's giggle-worthy story. Basic vocabulary combined
with dialogue and slightly more complex sentence structures
will help stretch beginning readers while keeping them engaged with the familiar. An excellent addition to most collections." SLJ

Hopgood, Tim

Wow! said the owl. Farrar, Straus and Giroux 2009
un il $14.95

Grades: PreK K 1   E

1. Day -- Fiction 2. Owls -- Fiction 3. Color -- Fiction
4. Night -- Fiction

ISBN 978-0-374-38518-7; 0-374-38518-1

LC 2008044038

A curious little owl decides to stay awake to find out how
the things he sees at night look during the daytime.

"Collage-style illustrations done in simple, bright shapes
show little owl in her tree while the changing colors and perspectives keep each page turn 'WOW!'-worthy. . . . Straightforward and flowing, this title makes a satisfying introduction to the colors of the day." SLJ

Hopkins, Lee Bennett, 1938-

Full moon and star; illustrated by Marcellus Hall.
Abrams Books for Young Readers 2011 un il $16.95

Grades: PreK K 1 2   E

1. Moon -- Fiction 2. Stars -- Fiction 3. Theater --
Fiction 4. Authorship -- Fiction 5. Friendship -- Fiction

ISBN 978-1-4197-0013-2; 1-4197-0013-8

"This winsome tale is just another preschool story of
cooperation. Yet the focus on playwriting and performance,
complete with script formatting and special punctuation,
sets a new stage for this common tale. Perfect for budding
thespians, this book in three acts would make an excellent
springboard for classroom explorations of drama." Kirkus

Hopkinson, Deborah

★ **Abe** Lincoln crosses a creek; a tall, thin tale (introducing his forgotten frontier friend) pictures by John Hendrix. Schwartz & Wade Books 2008 un il $16.99; lib
bdg $19.99

Grades: K 1 2 3   E

1. Lawyers 2. Presidents 3. State legislators 4.
Members of Congress 5. Friendship -- Fiction

ISBN 978-0-375-83768-5; 0-375-83768-X; 978-0-
375-93768-2 lib bdg; 0-375-93768-4 lib bdg

LC 2007-35149

In Knob Creek, Kentucky, in 1816, seven-year-old Abe
Lincoln falls into a creek and is rescued by his best friend,
Austin Gollaher.

"Hopkinson has created a lively, participatory tale that
will surely stand out. . . . Hendrix's illustrations have a naive
and rustic flavor that's in perfect harmony with the gravelly,
homespun narrator's voice." SLJ

★ **Apples** to Oregon; being the (slightly) true narrative of how a brave pioneer father brought apples, peaches,
pears, plums, grapes, and cherries (and children) across the
plains. illustrated by Nancy Carpenter. Atheneum Books
for Young Readers 2004 un il map $15.95

Grades: 1 2 3 4   E

1. Tall tales 2. Fruit culture -- Fiction 3. Frontier
and pioneer life -- Fiction 4. Overland journeys to the
Pacific -- Fiction

ISBN 0-689-84769-6

LC 2001-22949

A pioneer father transports his beloved fruit trees and
his family to Oregon in the mid-nineteenth century. Based
loosely on the life of Henderson Luelling

"Carpenter's oil paintings are filled with vivid shades
that reflect the changing scenery. Amusing details abound,
and the slightly exaggerated humor of the pictures is in perfect balance with the tone of the text." SLJ

★ A **band** of angels; a story inspired by the Jubilee Singers. illustrated by Raúl Colón. Atheneum Bks. for
Young Readers 1999 un il hardcover o.p. pa $7.99

Grades: 1 2 3 4   E

1. Pianists 2. Choral conductors 3. Gospel music
-- Fiction 4. African Americans -- Fiction 5. Jubilee
Singers (Musical group) -- Fiction

ISBN 0-689-81062-8; 0-689-84887-0 pa

LC 96-20011

Based on the life of Ella Sheppard Moore. The daughter
of a slave forms a gospel singing group and goes on tour to
raise money to save Fisk University

"Lilting prose, poignant historical details and arresting
portraits of trailblazing singers lost in song contribute to this
triumphant tale." Publ Wkly

★ **Billy** and the rebel; based on a true Civil War story. illustrated by Brian Floca. Atheneum Books for Young
Readers 2002 44p il map (Ready-to-read) $14.95

Grades: 1 2 3 4   E

1. Gettysburg (Pa.), Battle of, 1863 -- Fiction 2. United
States -- History -- 1861-1865, Civil War -- Fiction

ISBN 0-689-83964-2

LC 2001-22982

During the Battle of Gettysburg in 1863, a mother and
son shelter a young Confederate deserter. Includes a historical note on the incident.

"Based on the real William Bayly and his mother, Harriet Hamilton Bayly, [this book] . . . allows beginning readers and researchers some insight into life during the Civil
War. Full-page, full-spread, and spot art, executed mainly in
shades of yellow and tan, add detail and expression to this
story of courage and an unlikely friendship." SLJ

★ **From** slave to soldier; based on a true Civil War story. illustrated by Brian Floca. Atheneum Books for Young Readers 2005 44p il $14.95
Grades: 1 2 3   E
1. Slavery -- Fiction 2. African American soldiers -- Fiction 3. United States -- History -- 1861-1865, Civil War -- Fiction
ISBN 0-689-83965-8

A boy who hates being a slave joins the Union Army to fight for freedom, and proves himself brave and capable of handling a mule team when the need arises

This is written "in simple sentences for those who have just begun to read proficiently. . . . Short chapters and detailed watercolors aid the transition to more difficult text, while an exciting plot . . . keeps readers interested." SLJ

Girl wonder; a baseball story in nine innings. with pictures by Terry Widener. Atheneum Bks. for Young Readers 2003 un il $16.95
Grades: 1 2 3 4   E
1. Baseball -- Fiction
ISBN 0-689-83300-8

LC 99-47052
In the early 1900s, Alta Weiss, a young woman who knows from an early age that she loves baseball, finds a way to show that she can play, even though she is a girl

"Hopkinson tells her story with practiced skill—vivid details, lively language, varied pacing. . . . The illustrations are . . . broad, somewhat exaggerated, but conveying much emotion and narrative content." Horn Book

The **humblebee** hunter; pictures by Jen Corace. Disney Hyperion Books 2010 un il $16.99
Grades: K 1 2   E
1. Naturalists 2. Travel writers 3. Bees -- Fiction 4. Writers on science 5. Great Britain -- History -- 19th century -- Fiction
ISBN 978-1-4231-1356-0; 1-4231-1356-X

LC 2009-33987
On a beautiful day, some of Charles Darwin's many children help him study humblebees (bumblebees) in the garden at their home in the English countryside.

"The delicate, stylized illustrations, outlined in black and washed in natural shades of green and brown with spots of color, depict an amiable country Victorian household. . . . [This is an] inspiring read-aloud." SLJ

Knit your bit; a World War One story. by Deborah Hopkinson; illustrated by Steven Guarnaccia. G.P. Putnam's Sons 2013 32 p. $16.99
Grades: 1 2 3 4   E
1. Historical fiction 2. Knitting -- Fiction 3. Picture books for children 4. Sex role -- Fiction 5. World War, 1914-1918 -- United States -- Fiction 6. New York (N.Y.) -- History -- 1898-1951 -- Fiction 7. World War, 1914-1918 -- New York (State) -- New York -- Fiction
ISBN 039925241X; 9780399252419

LC 2012009635
This children's picture book offers a "story highlighting a patriotic civilian initiative during WWI. After Pop goes overseas, Mikey scoffs at helping Mama and his sister knit clothing for soldiers . . . . But after his teacher announces a knitting competition to benefit soldiers (based on an actual

'Knit-In' held in New York City's Central Park in 1918), Mikey and two friends accept a boys vs. girls challenge to win the knitting bee." (Publishers Weekly)

★ **Sky** boys; how they built the Empire State Building. [by] Deborah Hopkinson & James E. Ransome. Schwartz & Wade Books 2006 un il $16.95
Grades: K 1 2 3 4   E
1. Building -- Fiction 2. New York (N.Y.) -- Fiction 3. Empire State Building (New York, N.Y.) -- Fiction
ISBN 0-375-83610-1

LC 2005010852
In 1931, a boy and his father watch as the world's tallest building, the Empire State Building, is constructed, step-by-step, near their Manhattan home.

"Crisp, lyrical free verse and bold paintings celebrate the skill and daring of those who constructed the Empire State Building. . . . Ransome's powerful acrylic paintings show the building in all stages of construction, and includes the workers' perilous views. A unique, memorable title." Booklist

★ **Sweet** Clara and the freedom quilt; paintings by James Ransome. Knopf 1993 un il hardcover o.p. pa $6.99
Grades: K 1 2 3 4   E
1. Quilts -- Fiction 2. Slavery -- Fiction
ISBN 0-679-82311-5; 0-679-92311-X lib bdg; 0-679-87472-0 pa

LC 91-11601
Clara, a young slave, stitches a quilt with a map pattern which guides her to freedom in the North

"The smooth, optimistic, first-person vernacular of the story is ably accompanied by Ransome's brightly colored, full-page paintings." Horn Book Guide
Another title about Clara is:
Under the quilt of night (2001)

Hoppe, Paul
Hat. Bloomsbury U.S.A Children's Books 2009 un il $14.99
Grades: PreK K 1   E
1. Hats -- Fiction 2. Imagination -- Fiction 3. Lost and found possessions -- Fiction
ISBN 978-1-59990-247-0; 1-59990-247-8; 978-1-59990-248-7 lib bdg; 1-59990-248-6 lib bdg

LC 2008-22357
When Henry finds a hat he is very excited by its possibilities, but becomes worried when he thinks that the hat might belong to someone else

"The text is simple but imaginative. The illustrations bring each imagined scenario to life, and the ink drawings have a slightly retro feel with their subdued colors. The story lends itself to being read aloud, and the red hat pops off the pages." SLJ

The **woods**. Chronicle Books 2011 un il $16.99
Grades: PreK K 1   E
1. Boys -- Fiction 2. Fear -- Fiction 3. Toys -- Fiction 4. Animals -- Fiction 5. Bedtime -- Fiction
ISBN 978-0-8118-7547-9; 0-8118-7547-4

LC 2010039393
"The refrain—'we weren't scared at all. Until...'—sets a comfortable pattern, and the fuzzy watercolors on thick

creamy stock enhance the coziness of the tale. . . . Hoppe's delightfully quirky monsters enhance this pleasant tonic for bedtime fears." Kirkus

Horacek, Petr

★ **Choo** choo. Candlewick Press 2008 un il $5.99
Grades: PreK   E
1. Board books for children 2. Railroads -- Fiction
ISBN 978-0-7636-3477-3; 0-7636-3477-8

"Horácek's cheerful acrylic collage artwork shines in this small, beautifully designed board book about a train that carries cars full of smiling children to the beach. From the sound effects that begin the single line on each spread . . . to the shaped pages that emphasize the curve of mountains or the spikes of treetops, this book begs for interaction." Booklist

★ **Silly** Suzy Goose. Candlewick Press 2006 un il $14.99
Grades: PreK K 1 2   E
1. Geese -- Fiction 2. Lions -- Fiction
ISBN 0-7636-3040-3

Suzy longs to be different from all the other geese, but learns that imitating a lion may not be the best way to express her individuality.

"Created in mixed media, the art jumps off the pages, a fitting verb for a clever, clever book, alive in every way." Booklist

Other titles about Suzy Goose are:
Look out, Suzy Goose (2008)
Suzy Goose and the Christmas star (2009)

Horning, Sandra

Chicks! by Sandra Horning; illustrated by Jon Goodell. Random House 2013 32 p. (Step into Reading. Step 1) (trade pbk.) $3.99
Grades: PreK K 1   E
1. Animal babies 2. Chickens -- Fiction 3. Animals -- Infancy -- Fiction
ISBN 0307932214; 9780307932211; 9780375971174; 9780375981142

LC 2011050438

In this children's book by Sandra Horning, "when a family brings home chicks from a local farm, they must do everything they can to make sure their feathered friends thrive in their new environment. With the help of their knowledgeable parents, the children provide the baby chicks with food, water, warmth, and proper shelter." (Publisher's note)

The **giant** hug; illustrated by Valeri Gorbachev. Knopf 2005 un il $15.95; lib bdg $17.99
Grades: PreK K 1 2   E
1. Pigs -- Fiction 2. Grandmothers -- Fiction 3. Postal service -- Fiction
ISBN 0-375-82477-4; 0-375-92477-9 lib bdg

LC 2003-25883

When Owen the pig sends a real hug to his grandmother for her birthday he inadvertently brings cheer to the postal workers as they pass the hug along

"Gorbachev's cast of animal characters, drawn with a . . . sense of whimsy, are well chosen to emphasize the relevant personality traits." Booklist

Horowitz, Dave

Twenty-six pirates; by Dave Horowitz. Nancy Paulsen Books 2013 32 p. col. ill. (reinforced) $16.99
Grades: PreK K 1   E
1. Alphabet 2. Humorous stories 3. Stories in rhyme 4. Pirates -- Fiction
ISBN 9780399257773

LC 2012023866

This children's book by Dave Horowitz presents "an alphabetical parade of pirates -- by name! . . . Each pirate receives a full-page portrait that depicts him (they are all boys) engaged in the behavior described. Pirate Lee, who needs to pee, quivers outside the head, hands over his crotch. Pirate Quaid, who is not afraid, nevertheless looks a little dubious as giant octopus tentacles loom. Pirate Tony, who is fall of baloney, happily munches a sandwich." (Kirkus Reviews)

Twenty-six princesses. Putnam 2008 un il $15.99
Grades: PreK K 1 2   E
1. Alphabet 2. Fairy tales 3. Princesses -- Fiction
ISBN 978-0-399-24607-4; 0-399-24607-X

LC 2007-13233

Twenty-six princesses, one for each letter of the alphabet, go to a party at the prince's castle.

"Horowitz has a light, witty touch, and the text is rich with puns. The words and the pictures play off one another perfectly, encouraging children to pore over each humorously detailed portrait." SLJ

Includes bibliographical references

Horrocks, Anita

Silas' seven grandparents; story by Anita Horrocks; illustrations by Helen Flook. Orca Book Publishers 2010 un il $19.95
Grades: PreK K   E
1. Family life -- Fiction 2. Grandparents -- Fiction
ISBN 978-1-55143-561-9; 1-55143-561-9

Silas' Seven Grandparents is a fun and loving story about having multiple sets of grandparents and stepgrandparents. When Silas' parents go away on a business trip, all seven grandparents invite Silas to stay with them. How can he choose one without hurting the others' feelings?

"The deftly drawn water-based ink illustrations reflect the story's upbeat tone and portray the widely diverse grandparents in ways that make them distinctive." Booklist

Horse, Harry

Little Rabbit lost. Peachtree Pubs. 2002 un il $15.95; bd bk $9.95
Grades: PreK K 1   E
1. Rabbits -- Fiction 2. Birthdays -- Fiction
ISBN 1-56145-273-4; 1-56145-345-5 bd bk

LC 2002-2697

On his birthday Little Rabbit thinks that he is now a big rabbit, until he gets lost at the Rabbit World amusement park

"The lovely ink-and-watercolor illustrations are filled with clever details kids will enjoy—carrot-shaped paddleboats and bunny roller-coaster cars. Children will welcome this charming story." Booklist

Other titles about Little Rabbit are:
Little Rabbit goes to school (2004)
Little Rabbit runaway (2005)
Little Rabbit's Christmas (2007)
Little Rabbit's new baby (2008)

Horstman, Lisa

Squawking Matilda. Marshall Cavendish Children 2009 un il $17.99

Grades: PreK K 1 2   E

1. Aunts -- Fiction 2. Chickens -- Fiction 3. Farm life -- Fiction

ISBN 978-0-7614-5463-2; 0-7614-5463-2

LC 2008003657

Mae likes starting projects but never seems to finish them, and so when Aunt Susan asks her to take care of a feisty chicken Mae is soon distracted, then must find a way to make up for her neglect before Aunt Susan's visit.

"Handcrafted puppets wearing cheery clothing are posed, photographed, and digitally colored to give this charming selection a down-to-earth quality that matches the story perfectly." SLJ

Horvath, David

What dat? the great big Uglydoll book of things to look at, search for, point to, and wonder about. Random House 2011 il $14.99

Grades: PreK K 1 2 3   E

1. Puzzles 2. Vocabulary

ISBN 978-0-375-86434-6; 0-375-86434-2

"Horvath and Kim have created a word book featuring the Uglyverse. Each spread has bright, labeled cartoon illustrations, and brief paragraphs ask readers to find different things on each page. The scenarios, while full, are not too busy, so the items are easy to find and the labels are easy to read. The scenes are funny, and some jokes are obviously intended for an older audience.... These jokes will be easily passed over by younger children as they are buried within the scenes. The popularity of the toys combined with the fun of a look-and-find word book should make this a popular choice." SLJ

Horáček, Petr

Animal opposites; Petr Horacek. Candlewick Press 2013 20 p. $15.99

Grades: PreK K 1   E

1. Picture books for children 2. Animals 3. Opposites

ISBN 0763667765; 9780763667764

LC 2012950554

In this book from illustrator Petr Horacek, readers can "turn the pages, lift the flaps, and see animals of all shapes and sizes bring the world of opposites to life." Animals "from slow snail to fast cheetah, heavy hippo to light butterfly, smooth frog to prickly porcupine" are covered. (Publisher's note) "Horacek contrasts 20 animals, using flaps, pop-ups, and ... mixed-media paintings to highlight the differences between them." (Publishers Weekly)

One spotted giraffe; a counting pop-up book. Petr Horáček. Candlewick 2012 20 p. (hardback) $18.95

Grades: PreK   E

1. Counting 2. Toy and movable books 3. Pop-up books 4. Animals -- Fiction 5. Numerals -- Fiction

ISBN 0062234897; 9780763661571

LC 2011048376

This pop-up book by Petr Horacek is aimed at helping children "identify animals, count them, and discover numerals.... Spreads filled with realistic depictions of colorful creatures -- everything from pandas to lemurs -- entice readers to count the animals, then flip the flap to reveal a corresponding pop-up numeral. And then the surprise: the numeral looks just like the animal -- fur, spots, stripes, and all!" (Publisher's note)

Hosford, Kate

Infinity and me; written by Kate Hosford; illustrations by Gabi Swiatkowska. Carolrhoda Books 2012 32 p. (lib. bdg.: alk. paper) $16.95

Grades: K 1 2 3 4 5   E

1. Infinite 2. Mathematics 3. Picture books for children 4. Schools -- Fiction 5. Infinity -- Fiction 6. Grandmothers -- Fiction

ISBN 0761367268; 9780761367260

LC 2011044746

In this book, protagonist "Uma's struggle with the meaning of infinity offers readers a[n] ... introduction to the mathematical concept. When little Uma gazes at the vast night sky and wonders how many stars are there, she asks, 'How could I even think about something as big as infinity?' When friends, her grandmother, the school cook and the music teacher offer creative ways of describing infinity, Uma ends up feeling rather overwhelmed." (Kirkus Reviews)

Houston, Gloria

Miss Dorothy and her bookmobile; illustrated by Susan Condie Lamb. Harper 2010 un il $16.99

Grades: K 1 2   E

1. Librarians -- Fiction 2. Bookmobiles -- Fiction 3. Country life -- Fiction 4. Books and reading -- Fiction

ISBN 978-0-06-029155-6; 0-06-029155-9

LC 2005-18630

Dorothy has always wanted to work in a library like the red brick one of her girlhood, but after moving to rural North Carolina she discovers that the type of library is less important than the books and the people who read them.

"Beautiful, soft landscapes of the rugged terrain throughout the seasons serve as a backdrop for this charming story of a librarian on the go." SLJ

The year of the perfect Christmas tree; an Appalachian story. pictures by Barbara Cooney. Dial Bks. for Young Readers 1988 un il $15.99; pa $6.99

Grades: K 1 2 3   E

1. Christmas -- Fiction 2. Appalachian region -- Fiction

ISBN 0-8037-0299-X; 0-14-055827-2 pa

LC 87-24551

"It's 1918 in the mountains of North Carolina, and the custom in the village is for one family to select and donate the Christmas tree each year. In the spring Ruthie and her father select a perfect balsam high on a rocky crag. Then Father goes to war. Still, on Christmas Eve the tree is in the church and Ruthie plays the angel. The winning illustrations perfectly match the tone of this affecting story, which comes from the author's family." NY Times Book Rev

Hovland, Henrik

★ John Jensen feels different; by Henrik Hovland; illustrated by Torill Kove; translated by Don Bartlett. Eerdmans Books for Young Readers 2012 33 p. col. ill. (alk. paper) $16

Grades: PreK K 1 2   E

1. Picture books for children 2. Crocodiles -- Fiction 3.

Individuality -- Fiction
ISBN 0802853994; 9780802853998

LC 2011022446

This children's picture book follows John Jensen, "a well-dressed, well-mannered crocodile living a civilized life in the human world" who worries constantly about being different. "When John Jensen trips and falls after binding up his bulky tail in a futile attempt to conceal it, he meets Dr. Field, whose huge ears and long trunk mean he knows a thing or two about being different. . . . . John Jensen realizes that his tail—and his differentness in general—are all a question of attitude." (Publishers Weekly)

Howard, Arthur

Hoodwinked. Harcourt 2001 un il $16
Grades: PreK K 1   E
1. Pets -- Fiction 2. Witches -- Fiction
ISBN 0-15-202656-8

LC 00-8318

Mitzi, a young witch, searches for a creepy pet, but finds that a cute kitten is perfect for her
"The pictures are perfect for this lively story—lots of fangs and slimy, scaly, weird, and wiggly outlines fill the pages." SLJ

Howard, Elizabeth Fitzgerald

★ **Aunt** Flossie's hats (and crab cakes later) paintings by James Ransome. 10th anniversary ed; Clarion Books 2001 31p il $16; pa $6.95
Grades: K 1 2 3   E
1. Hats -- Fiction 2. Aunts -- Fiction 3. African Americans -- Fiction
ISBN 0-618-12038-6; 0-395-72077-X pa

LC 00-65757

A reissue of the title first published 1991
Sara and Susan share tea, cookies, crab cakes, and stories about hats when they visit their favorite relative, Aunt Flossie.
"This is an affecting portrait of a black American family. . . . Howard's quiet, sure telling is well matched by Ransome's art-elegant, expressive oil paintings that convey warmth, joy, tenderness and love." Publ Wkly

★ **Virgie** goes to school with us boys; illustrated by E.B. Lewis. Simon & Schuster Bks. for Young Readers 1999 un il $17.99; pa $7.99
Grades: K 1 2 3   E
1. African Americans -- Fiction
ISBN 0-689-80076-2; 0-689-87793-5 pa

LC 97-49406

In the post-Civil War South, a young African American girl is determined to prove that she can go to school just like her older brothers
"The story is a superb tribute to the author's great aunt, the inspiration for this book. . . . Lewis's watercolor illustrations capture the characters with warmth and dignity." SLJ

Howatt, Sandra J.

Sleepyheads; by Sandra J. Howatt; illustrated by Joyce Wan. Beach Lane Books 2014 32 p. col. ill. (hardcover) $16.99
Grades: PreK K 1   E
1. Animals -- Fiction 2. Bedtime -- Fiction 3. Sleep -- Fiction 4. Stories in rhyme 5. Babies -- Fiction 6.

Animals -- Sleep behavior -- Fiction
ISBN 1442422661; 9781442422667

LC 2013013607

"The sun has set, and sleepyheads all across the land are tucked into their cozy beds. Rabbit is snoozing in the weeds, and Duck is snuggled in the reeds. Bear is nestled in his cave, and Otter is rocking on a wave. But there's one little sleepyhead who's not in his bed. Where, oh where, could he be?" (Publisher's note)

Gentle narration, soft exclamations and soothing "s" sounds surface again and again, streaming together sweetly. The earthy, mellow artwork, with its dusky greens and browns and thick linework, comforts too. Wan's many circular shapes (all those radiant stars, the creatures' rounded heads, ears, coiled bodies and tails—even dandelion seed-puffs and a lightning bug's glow) recall the warm curve of a caregiver's chest." - Kirkus

Howe, James

★ **Brontorina**; illustrated by Randy Cecil. Candlewick Press 2010 un il $15.99
Grades: PreK K 1 2   E
1. Ballet -- Fiction 2. Dinosaurs -- Fiction
ISBN 978-0-7636-4437-6; 0-7636-4437-4

"Initially turned away from Madame Lucille's Dance Academy for Boys and Girls because she is an enormous dinosaur, Brontorina counters, 'But in my heart I am a ballerina.' . . . Text and illustrations work beautifully together in this witty fantasy. . . . In Cecil's arresting oil paintings, the tawny orange dinosaur stands out boldly against slate blue or white backgrounds, and the unusual texture of the paint creates a distinctive effect." Booklist

★ **Horace** and Morris but mostly Dolores; written by James Howe; illustrated by Amy Walrod. Atheneum Bks. for Young Readers 1999 un il $16; pa $6.99
Grades: PreK K 1 2   E
1. Mice -- Fiction 2. Sex role -- Fiction 3. Friendship -- Fiction
ISBN 0-689-31874-X; 0-689-85675-X pa

LC 96-17645

"Three adventure-loving mice are best friends until gender stereotypes separate them, driving Horace and Morris into a rowdy boys-only clubhouse while Dolores reluctantly goes off to join the ultra-ladylike Cheese Puffs. The bold artwork suits the book's lively protest against conformity." Horn Book Guide

Other titles about Horace, Morris, and Dolores are:
Horace and Morris join the chorus (but what about Dolores?) (2002)
Horace and Morris say cheese (which makes Dolores sneeze!) (2009)

★ **Houndsley** and Catina; illustrated by Marie-Louise Gay. Candlewick Press 2006 36p il $14.99
Grades: PreK K 1 2   E
1. Cats -- Fiction 2. Dogs -- Fiction 3. Friendship -- Fiction
ISBN 0-7636-2404-7

LC 2005-50187

Houndsley, a dog, and Catina, a cat, run into trouble when they decide to prove that they are the best at cooking and writing, respectively.

"The lively, brisk writing is wonderfully extended in Gay's airy watercolor-and-pencil illustrations." Booklist

Other titles about Houndsley and Catina are:
Houndsley and Catina and the birthday surprise (2006)
Houndsley and Catina and the quiet time (2008)
Houndsley and Catina plink and plunk (2009)

Kaddish for Grandpa in Jesus' name, amen; [Illustrated by] Catherine Stock. Atheneum Books for Young Readers 2004 un il $16.95
Grades: K 1 2 3   E
1. Death -- Fiction 2. Judaism -- Fiction 3. Christianity -- Fiction 4. Grandfathers -- Fiction 5. Funeral rites and ceremonies -- Fiction
ISBN 0-689-80185-8
                                                     LC 2002-11569
Five-year-old Emily tries to understand her grandfather's death by exploring the Christian and Jewish rituals that her family practices during and after his funeral

"The soft watercolor illustrations, done in pastel colors, are a perfect accompaniment to the story. This book is a good vehicle to explain the rituals of death to children." SLJ

Otter and odder; James Howe; illustrated by Chris Raschka. 1st ed. Candlewick Press 2012 40 p. ill. (reinforced) $14
Grades: 2 3 4   E
1. Picture books for children 2. Love -- Fiction 3. Fishes -- Fiction 4. Otters -- Fiction
ISBN 076364174X; 9780763641740
                                                     LC 2010048213
In this story, while Otter is hunting for food, "he realizes something unlikely has happened: 'I am in love with my food source.' Myrtle (as Otter hears the fish's name of Gurgle) has fallen for Otter as well, but despite their love the two can't make it work: 'I am no longer sure a fish can love an otter . . . when the way of the otter is to eat fish.' Fortunately, a wise beaver introduces Otter to vegetarianism, and the two 'lived happily ever after.'" (Bulletin of the Center for Children's Books)

★ **Pinky** and Rex; illustrated by Melissa Sweet. Atheneum Pubs. 1990 38p il $15; pa $3.99
Grades: K 1 2   E
1. Toys -- Fiction 2. Museums -- Fiction 3. Friendship -- Fiction
ISBN 0-689-31454-X; 0-689-82348-7 pa
                                                      LC 89-30786
"Sweet's gently washed, jovial illustrations reflect the unpretentious sincerity of Rex and Pinky's relationship, while Howe's readable text blending natural dialogue with narrative, is divided into individual chapters." Booklist

Other titles about Pinky and Rex are:
Pinky and Rex and the bully (1996)
Pinky and Rex and the double-dad weekend (1995)
Pinky and Rex and the just-right pet (2001)
Pinky and Rex and the mean old witch (1991)
Pinky and Rex and the new baby (1993)
Pinky and Rex and the new neighbors (1997)
Pinky and Rex and the perfect pumpkin (1998)
Pinky and Rex and the school play (1998)
Pinky and Rex and the spelling bee (1991)
Pinky and Rex get married (1990)

Pinky and Rex go to camp (1992)

Howland, Naomi
★ **Latkes,** latkes, good to eat; a Chanukah story. Clarion Bks. 1999 31p il $16; pa $5.95
Grades: PreK K 1 2   E
1. Jews -- Fiction 2. Magic -- Fiction 3. Hanukkah -- Fiction
ISBN 0-395-89903-6; 0-618-49295-X pa
                                                      LC 97-50616
In an old Russian village, Sadie and her brothers are poor and hungry until an old woman gives Sadie a frying pan that will make potato pancakes until it hears the magic words that make it stop

"Howland effectively sets her story in a Russian shtetl, using words, intonation, and especially pictures. Working in gouache and colored pencil, she offers a snowy landscape peopled with Jewish villagers who work hard and celebrate harder." Booklist

Princess says goodnight; illustrated by David Small. HarperCollins 2010 un il $16.99; lib bdg $17.89
Grades: PreK K 1 2   E
1. Stories in rhyme 2. Bedtime -- Fiction 3. Princesses -- Fiction
ISBN 978-0-06-145525-4; 0-06-145525-3; 978-0-06-145526-1 lib bdg; 0-06-145526-1 lib bdg
Rhyming text presents what a princess might do between leaving the ball and saying goodnight.

"Sweet and disarmingly infectious without being cloying, this is a bedtime story full of joy and imagination." Publ Wkly

Hubbell, Patricia
Airplanes; soaring! diving! turning! by Patricia Hubbell; illustrated by Megan Halsey and Sean Addy. Marshall Cavendish Children 2008 un il $16.99
Grades: PreK K 1 2   E
1. Stories in rhyme 2. Airplanes -- Fiction
ISBN 978-0-7614-5388-8; 0-7614-5388-1
                                                     LC 2007011721
Illustrations and rhyming text celebrate different kinds of airplanes and what they can do

"This picture book features . . . animated, whimsical art that will delight young would-be jet-setters. . . . The lively, descriptive prose . . . incorporates peppy sounds that amp up the energy that's echoed in the vibrant illustrations." Booklist

★ **Boats;** speeding! sailing! cruising! illustrated by Megan Halsey and Sean Addy. Marshall Cavendish 2009 un il $17.99
Grades: PreK K 1 2   E
1. Stories in rhyme 2. Boats and boating -- Fiction
ISBN 978-0-7614-5524-0; 0-7614-5524-8
                                                      LC 2007-49522
Illustrations and rhyming text celebrate different kinds of boats and what they can do.

"The tight, surprisingly informative rhyming text works so well because it pairs with art that shows off each of these boats to best advantage. The fun part comes in the way the design and the mixed-media art . . . come together." Booklist

Cars; rushing! honking! zooming! illustrated by Megan Halsey and Sean Addy. Marshall Cavendish Children 2006 un il $14.99
Grades: PreK K 1   E
1. Stories in rhyme 2. Automobiles -- Fiction
ISBN 978-0-7614-5296-6; 0-7614-5296-6
Illustrations and rhyming text celebrate different kinds of cars and what they can do
"The rhyming text rolls smoothly along. . . . Color heightens the appeal of the clip art, stamps, etchings, maps, and original drawings, which come together in the paper-collage illustrations." Booklist

Firefighters! speeding! spraying! saving! illustrated by Viviana Garofoli. Marshall Cavendish 2007 un il $14.99; bd bk $7.99
Grades: PreK K 1   E
1. Stories in rhyme 2. Board books for children 3. Fire fighters -- Fiction
ISBN 978-0-7614-5337-6; 0-7614-5337-7; 978-0-7614-5615-5 bd bk; 0-7614-5615-5 bd bk
"The tale begins with the 'Clang! Clang! Clang!' of the alarm. The firefighters rush to get dressed and board their truck, along with Spot, the firehouse Dalmatian. Brief, pulsating, rhythmic text follows across the pages. . . . The digital, cartoon-style artwork is simple. Done in vibrant hues of predominately primary colors." SLJ

Horses; Trotting! Prancing! Racing! illustrated by Joe Mathieu. Marshall Cavendish Children 2011 il $17.99
Grades: PreK K 1   E
1. Stories in rhyme 2. Horses -- Fiction
ISBN 978-0-7614-5949-1; 0-7614-5949-9; 978-0-7614-5997-2 e-book
LC 2010044929
"A simple, rhyming text introduces readers to horses—the different breeds, their abilities in providing transportation, and all else they do. . . . Lovely, action-packed illustrations done in watercolors and colored pencils highlight the different hues and patterns found on the horses' coats. . . . This is an excellent addition for any collection, and it will extend knowledge about transportation that isn't manmade." SLJ

My first airplane ride; by Patricia Hubbell; illustrated by Nancy Speir. Marshall Cavendish 2008 un il $16.99
Grades: PreK K 1   E
1. Stories in rhyme 2. Airplanes -- Fiction
ISBN 978-0-7614-5436-6; 0-7614-5436-5
"Short, rhyming phrases record the events as a boy takes his first plane ride. Every incident along the way is chronicled here: packing, driving to the airport, getting boarding passes, going through security in stocking feet, waiting at the gate, etc. . . . The level of detail is well calibrated to the target audience. . . . Colorful and reassuring." Booklist

Police: hurrying! helping! saving! Marshall Cavendish Children 2008 un il $14.99
Grades: PreK K 1   E
1. Stories in rhyme 2. Police -- Fiction
ISBN 978-0-7614-5421-2; 0-7614-5421-7
Illustrations and rhyming text celebrate police officers and what they do.

"A picture book with a rhyming text, bright colors, and plenty of action." SLJ

Shaggy dogs, waggy dogs; illustrated by Donald Wu. Marshall Cavendish 2011 un il $17.99
Grades: PreK K 1 2   E
1. Dogs -- Fiction
ISBN 978-0-7614-5957-6; 0-7614-5957-X
"An assortment of lovable-looking pooches is pictured in this charming ode to man's best friend. In perfect rhyme, Hubbell describes the canines by their characteristics rather than breeds: shaggy, waggy, thin, saggy, shy, bold, pretty, puppies, full-grown, and more. Next she offers a litany of the things dogs are good at doing. . . . Wu's detailed illustrations drawn with colored pencil over acrylic vividly depict the different textures of each animal's fur as it engages in typical doggie pastimes. Children who love animals will adore this fetching book." SLJ

Snow happy! Tricycle Press 2010 un il $15.99
Grades: PreK K 1   E
1. Stories in rhyme 2. Snow -- Fiction
ISBN 978-1-58246-329-2; 1-58246-329-8
"A rollicking verse about the joys of playing in the snow. Lively children and their parents and grandparents enjoy a day of sledding, making snow angels, building igloos, even shoveling. Hubbell's meter is bouncy. . . . The artwork matches the upbeat mood of the text. . . . The simple watercolor characters are full of activity." SLJ

Hubbell, Will

Pumpkin Jack; written and illustrated by Will Hubbell. Whitman, A. 2000 un il $15.95
Grades: PreK K 1 2 3   E
1. Pumpkin -- Fiction 2. Halloween -- Fiction
ISBN 0-8075-6665-9
LC 00-8282
After Halloween, Tim discards Jack, his jack-o'lantern, in the garden and during the following year it sprouts, blooms, and grows new pumpkins
"Satisfying and surprisingly varied in approach and perspective, Hubbell's colored pencil drawings illustrate the simple story in a series of well-imagined scenes." Booklist

Huckabee, Mike

Can't wait till Christmas; [illustrated by Jed Henry] G. P. Putnam's Sons 2010 un il $17.99
Grades: PreK K 1   E
1. Gifts -- Fiction 2. Siblings -- Fiction 3. Christmas -- Fiction
ISBN 978-0-399-25539-7; 0-399-25539-7
Mike is so eager to open his Christmas gifts that he convinces his older sister, Pam, to unwrap and play with them in advance, but when Christmas morning arrives they are unhappy about what they have done.
"Huckabee's lighthearted cautionary tale is buoyed by zippy digital illustrations that convey both its humor and warmth." Publ Wkly

Hucke, Johannes

Pip in the Grand Hotel; illustrated by Daniel Müller. North-South 2009 un il $16.95

Grades: PreK K 1 2   E
   1. Mice -- Fiction 2. Hotels and motels -- Fiction
   ISBN 978-0-7358-2225-2; 0-7358-2225-5
   Originally published in Sweden
   Mary has a new pet, a mouse named Pip. When she
opens the lid to his box, Pip is off straight into the Grand
Hotel. The reader can search for Pip in the pictures.
   "This lively escapade is heightened by ellipses at the
end of each spread, which create dramatic page turns. As the
children race through this bustling high-end hotel, Müller's
detail-filled watercolor illustrations truly bring the caper to
life." SLJ

Hudes, Quiara Alegria
   Welcome to my neighborhood! a barrio ABC. illus-
trated by Shino Arihara. Arthur A. Levine Books 2010 un
il $16.99
Grades: PreK K   E
   1. Alphabet 2. Stories in rhyme 3. City and town life
-- Fiction 4. Hispanic Americans -- Fiction
   ISBN 978-0-545-09424-5; 0-545-09424-0
   "An expressive girl takes a friend on a poetic tour of
her inner-city neighborhood. 'E is for the echo of the elevated train./ F is for the fire hydrant spraying summer rain.'
Chalky, gouache washes capture both the vital and gently
dilapidated elements of city life. . . . The subtle presence of
the girl's personal narrative and her nuanced understanding
of what makes her neighborhood home set this ABC book
apart." Publ Wkly

Hudson, Katy
   Bear and duck; written and illustrated by Katy Hudson.
Harper, an imprint of HarperCollinsPublishers 2015 32 p.
(hardcover) $17.99
Grades: PreK K 1   E
   1. Bears -- Fiction 2. Ducks -- Fiction 3. Self-
acceptance -- Fiction
   ISBN 0062320513; 9780062320513
                                           LC 2013043137
   In this children's story, written and illustrated by Katy
Hudson, "Bear is sick and tired of being a bear. . . . But when
he sees a line of happy yellow ducklings, he has a thought.
What if he could be a duck? With a few duck lessons from
Duck, Bear learns that being a duck is fun; but as it turns
out, Bear realizes he makes a really good bear." (Publish-
er's note)

Huget, Jennifer LaRue
   The **best** birthday party ever; illustrated by LeUyen
Pham. Schwartz & Wade Books 2011 un il $16.99; lib
bdg $19.99
Grades: PreK K 1 2   E
   1. Parties -- Fiction 2. Birthdays -- Fiction
   ISBN 978-0-375-84763-9; 0-375-84763-4; 978-0-375-
95763-5 lib bdg; 0-375-95763-4 lib bdg
                                           LC 2009-28010
   A child plans an elaborate birthday party and eagerly counts the months, days, hours, and minutes before
the celebration.
   "Pham's watercolor illustrations perfectly capture the
frivolity of the little girl's imagination. . . . . Young birthday enthusiasts will readily identify with the considerable

thought and energy involved in getting ready for the big
day." Bull Cent Child Books

   How to clean your room in 10 easy steps; illustrated
by Edward Koren. Schwartz & Wade Books 2009 un il
$16.99; lib bdg $19.99
Grades: K 1 2   E
   1. Home economics -- Fiction
   ISBN 978-0-375-84410-2; 0-375-84410-4; 978-0-375-
96410-7 lib bdg; 0-375-96410-X lib bdg
                                           LC 2008-48824
   A young girl provides unique advice on how to tidy
a bedroom.
   "Children and their adults are in for a treat with this new
showcase for Koren's illustrations. His wry, bushy, squiggly
style is well-matched by Huget's puckish and not entirely
serious advice. . . . Good for great giggles-and at the end, she
promises even more awesome advice on fixing your hair."
Kirkus

   Thanks a LOT, Emily Post! written by Jennifer LaRue
Huget; illustrated by Alexandra Boiger. Schwartz & Wade
Books 2009 un il $16.99; lib bdg $19.99
Grades: K 1 2 3   E
   1. Novelists 2. Advice columnists 3. Mothers -- Fiction
   4. Etiquette -- Fiction 5. Conduct of life -- Fiction
   ISBN 978-0-375-83853-8; 0-375-83853-8; 978-0-375-
93853-5 lib bdg; 0-375-93853-2 lib bdg
                                          LC 2008004994
   When a mother instructs her children to behave according to Emily Post's rules of etiquette, they respond by insist-
ing that Mother follow the rules, as well. Includes information about Post and selected items from her 1922 book.
   "Written with clarity and wit. . . . The fresh, expressive
watercolors dramatize events through distinctive characters
playing out sometimes-chaotic scenes full of energy, elegance, and entertaining details." Booklist

Hughes, Shirley
   Alfie and the big boys. Bodley Head 2007 un il $17.95
Grades: PreK K 1   E
   1. School stories 2. Friendship -- Fiction
   ISBN 978-0-370-32884-3; 0-370-32884-1
   Alfie and his friends wish they could play with the bigger
boys and one day they get a chance
   This "sensitively portrays children's emotional lives
through everyday events in familiar settings. Ink drawings,
brightened with washes and strokes of color, have the narrative power to tell the basic story on their own. But the book
is richer for the inclusion of a straightforward text." Booklist

   ★ **Annie** Rose is my little sister. Candlewick Press
2003 un il $15.99
Grades: PreK K 1 2   E
   1. Siblings -- Fiction
   ISBN 0-7636-1959-0
                                           LC 2002-67695
   Alfie describes all the things that he and his younger sister Annie Rose do together
   "Few artists have recreated the young child's body
language and surroundings as faithfully as Hughes. The
gouache-and-oil pastel illustrations teem with well-observed
details." Booklist

★ The **Christmas** Eve ghost. Candlewick Press 2010 un il $15.99

Grades: K 1 2 3   E
1. Laundry -- Fiction 2. Christmas -- Fiction 3. Prejudices -- Fiction 4. Great Britain -- Fiction 5. Single parent family -- Fiction
ISBN 978-0-7636-4472-7; 0-7636-4472-2

LC 2009051506

In 1930s Liverpool, England, Bronwen and Dylan live with their widowed mother, who works long hours doing other people's washing, and even though she sometimes must leave the children alone in the house, she cautions them not to speak to the O'Rileys next door, who go to a different church.

"A mixture of full-page and spot illustrations in water-color and ink creates a nostalgic atmosphere. . . . The overall theme of the budding friendship between families of different faiths is subtly and effectively presented." Kirkus

★ **Don't** want to go! Candlewick Press 2010 un il $16.99

Grades: PreK K   E
1. Babysitters -- Fiction
ISBN 978-0-7636-5091-9; 0-7636-5091-9

LC 2010011454

Lily's mother is sick and her father must go to work, but she does not want to stay with a babysitter, even if it means playing with cute baby Sam, sweet little dog Ringo, and fun big brother Jack.

Hughes's "unadorned narration exudes empathy for the dislocated Lily. . . . And her densely textured, saturated gouache images . . . make a strong case that the right people can make any situation feel homey. . . . Lily's gradual acceptance of the situation unfolds naturally and believably." Publ Wkly

Ella's big chance; a Jazz-Age Cinderella. [by] Shirley Hughes. Simon & Schuster Books for Young Readers 2004 un il $16.95

Grades: K 1 2 3   E
1. Fairy tales
ISBN 0-689-87399-9

LC 2003-27274

In this version of the Cinderella tale set in the 1920s, Ella has two men courting her—the handsome Duke of Arc and Buttons the delivery boy

"Hughes's gouache-and-pen-line illustrations exhibit her usual meticulous attention to detail. . . . This insightful re-telling also offers a fascinating visual peek at a glamorous time." SLJ

Jonadab and Rita. Red Fox 2011 il pa $11.99

Grades: PreK K 1   E
1. Toys -- Fiction 2. Magic -- Fiction 3. Fairies -- Fiction
ISBN 978-1-86-230313-3; 1-86-230313-4

Jonadab is a very special toy donkey who can fly. But Minnie has so many other toys that often Jonadab and his friend Rita the mouse find themselves sad and lonely and left behind in the toy box. One moonlit night, tired of being ignored, Jonadab flies away and joins a magical fairy feast. But then he can't get back in to Minnie's room.

"Colorful illustrations cover half of each page while the text is set off in rectangular boxes highlighted with small black pen-and-ink sketches featuring characters from the tale. . . . This quiet fantasy will be welcomed by [Hughes'] many fans." SLJ

Olly and me 1 2 3. Candlewick Press 2009 un il $16.99

Grades: PreK K 1 2   E
1. Counting 2. Siblings -- Fiction
ISBN 978-0-7636-4016-3; 0-7636-4016-6

LC 2008-934556

"Hughes warms up this counting book with appealing characters and colorful action scenes. On the first page, which begins with a big numeral 1 and one large dot, a little girl named Katie introduces herself. On the next, with the numeral 2 and and two large dots, she is joined by her baby brother, Olly. . . . On the pages that follow, more family members, friends, neighbors, and pets join the siblings. . . . The line drawings depict characters with a certain air of rumpled reality that makes Hughes' artwork so endearing and enduring." Booklist

Hughes, Ted, 1930-1998
My brother Bert; pictures by Tracey Campbell Pearson. Farrar, Straus & Giroux 2009 un il $16.95

Grades: PreK K 1   E
1. Stories in rhyme 2. Pets -- Fiction 3. Animals -- Fiction 4. Siblings -- Fiction
ISBN 978-0-374-39982-5; 0-374-39982-4

LC 2007034415

Illustrations and rhyming text portray a hobby gone awry, as Bert's collection of exotic pets seems on the verge of breaking into a quarrel, and perhaps a rumpus, as well.

"Full of action, merriment, and wit, the pictures will occupy children with always one more thing to see. . . . Dizzying and delightful." Booklist

Hughes, Vi
Once upon a bathtime. Tradewind Books 2010 un il $17.95

Grades: PreK K 1   E
1. Baths -- Fiction
ISBN 978-1-896580-5-48; 1-896580-5-48

As a child takes a bath and gets ready for bed, characters from fairy tales accompany the child.

"This picture book is told in simple, elegant verse and illustrated with paper-cut collage artwork." SLJ

Huneck, Stephen
Sally goes to Heaven; Stephen Huneck. Abrams Books for Young Readers 2014 48 p. (Sally the dog) $18.95

Grades: PreK K 1 2 3   E
1. Pets -- Fiction 2. Death -- Fiction 3. Dogs -- Fiction 4. Heaven -- Fiction
ISBN 1419709690; 9781419709692

LC 2013010063

Written by Stephen Huneck, "'Sally Goes to Heaven' is a wonderful, joyous book to help provide gentle insight into the natural cycle of life of a pet, or to share with young children who have recently experienced the loss of a beloved animal. In this book, Sally passes away and goes to heaven, where she lives happily and helps her family on Earth find a new pet." (Publisher's note)

"Huneck, who died in 2010, takes Sally on one last adventure, a trip to heaven. There she finds her aches are gone, there are piles of dirty socks, and there are no fences or animal shelters...Young readers will be reassured that Sally expects to meet her human family in heaven someday, but in the meantime, she hopes they will find a dog to adopt who will look after them." Booklist

Other titles include:
Sally Gets a Job (2008)
Sally Goes to the Beach (2000)
Sally Goes to the Farm (2002)
Sally Goes to the Mountains (2001)
Sally Goes to the Vet (2004)
Sally's Great Balloon Adventure (2009)
Sally's Snow Adventure (2006)

Hunt, Julie

Precious Little; [by] Julie Hunt & Sue Moss; pictures by Gaye Chapman. Allen & Unwin 2011 un il $16.99
Grades: K 1 2 3   E
1. Circus -- Fiction 2. Acrobats and acrobatics -- Fiction
ISBN 978-1-74175-147-5; 1-74175-147-0
LC 2011290332
"A tatterdemalion heroine wearing rags and stars falls into a dream hole and flies through the heavens. Precious Little works for the Light Fantastics, watching the contortionists, Knots-RUs, and the fire-eaters, Flambé and the Infernos, but longing to fly. Her friends Fat Chance and Tough Luck draw a wire across the 'lucky dip,' and she begins to cross it. . . . The text swirls and makes loop-the-loops all over the pages, necessitating constant turning, all the better to pore over the spectacular art. . . . Children (and adults) can be lost for a long and pleasurable time amid the sparkles." Kirkus

Hurd, Edith Thacher

★ **Johnny** Lion's book; pictures by Clement Hurd. new ed.; HarperCollins Pubs. 2001 63p il (I can read book) hardcover o.p. pa $3.99
Grades: PreK K 1   E
1. Lions -- Fiction
ISBN 0-06-029334-9 lib bdg; 0-06-444297-7 pa
A reissue of the title first published 1965
When his parents go out hunting, Johnny Lion stays home and experiences exciting adventures reading a book about a baby lion who goes out into the world and gets lost
"A subtle boost for the joys of reading in a story with engaging illustrations." Booklist
Other titles about Johnny Lion are:
Johnny Lion's bad day (1970)
Johnny Lion's rubber boots (1972)

Hurd, Thacher

★ **Art** dog. HarperCollins Pubs. 1996 un il $15.99; pa $6.99
Grades: PreK K 1 2   E
1. Dogs -- Fiction 2. Artists -- Fiction
ISBN 0-06-024424-0; 0-06-443489-3 pa
LC 95-31092
When the Mona Woofa is stolen from the Dogopolis Museum of Art, a mysterious character who calls himself Art Dog tracks down and captures the thieves
"This is exuberantly drawn by Hurd, who has imbued Art Dog with the flash and dash every artist feels at times;

but Hurd also captures the shyness that comes with displaying your art. Kids will respond not just to the pictures but also to a story that does as well with characters as with plot." Booklist

Bad frogs. Candlewick Press 2009 un il $15.99
Grades: PreK K 1 2   E
1. Frogs -- Fiction
ISBN 978-0-7636-3253-3; 0-7636-3253-8
"Hurd's bad frogs—170 of them—revel in mischievous conduct and generate chaos wherever they go. Whether jumping in muck, slurping ice cream, burping at the dinner table, fighting with toothbrushes, or skateboarding down stair railings, the delightfully green, yellow-tinged characters prance across the pages in an array of costumes, entertaining viewers with their antics. The artwork gleams with Hurd's shiny bright colors, and his swinging text, presented in bold purple, trumpets the frogs' badness as they romp through the action-packed illustrations." SLJ

Mama don't allow; starring Miles and the Swamp Band. Harper & Row 1984 un il hardcover o.p. pa $5.99
Grades: PreK K 1 2   E
1. Alligators -- Fiction 2. Bands (Music) -- Fiction
ISBN 0-06-022690-0 lib bdg; 0-06-443078-2 pa
LC 83-47703
Miles and the Swamp Band have the time of their lives playing at the Alligator Ball, until they discover the menu includes Swamp Band soup
"The multi-colored full-spread watercolor illustrations are stunningly bright and full of movement, far outpacing the story line in energy and imagination." SLJ

The **weaver**; pictures by Elisa Kleven. Farrar Straus Giroux 2010 un il $16.99
Grades: PreK K 1 2   E
1. Dreams -- Fiction 2. Weaving -- Fiction
ISBN 978-0-374-38254-4; 0-374-38254-9
LC 2008028533
High above the world, a weaver spins thread from such things as clouds, dyes it with colors from the sky and grass, and weaves a cloth filled with the emotions she sees throughout the day to make a blanket of dreams.
"The fanciful illustrations reflect the story's sense of celebration, portraying children, their families, and friends sharing small but significant moments in a kaleidoscope of springtime colors. Tiny characters of all nationalities enjoy life in a sun-drenched landscape while the gentle weaver and her adorable gray kitten watch from above. This dreamy story offers a reassuring message of love and security." SLJ

Hurst, Carol Otis

Rocks in his head; pictures by James Stevenson. Greenwillow Bks. 2001 un il $15.99; lib bdg $15.89
Grades: PreK K 1 2   E
1. Rocks -- Collectors and collecting
ISBN 0-06-029403-5; 0-06-029404-3 lib bdg
LC 00-56197
Hurst "recounts the story of her father, an avid rock collector from the time he was a boy. . . . Dominated by earth tones, Stevenson's artwork convincingly evokes both the personality of this endearing protagonist and the period in which he lived." Publ Wkly

★ **Terrible** storm; [illustrated by] S. D. Schindler. Greenwillow Books 2007 un il $16.99; lib bdg $17.89
Grades: K 1 2 3   **E**
  1. Blizzards -- Fiction 2. Grandfathers -- Fiction 3. Massachusetts -- Fiction
  ISBN 978-0-06-009001-2; 0-06-009001-4; 978-0-06-009002-9 lib bdg; 0-06-009002-2 lib bdg
                                              LC 2005-35731
"Humor is everywhere, but the funniest pictures show the men shoveling out of the snow, passing one another through the drifts. This lively, clever story, based on a real storm, neatly captures both the oddities of nature and how differing natures view the same event." Booklist

Hurwitz, Johanna
  New shoes for Silvia; illustrated by Jerry Pinkney. Morrow Junior Bks. 1993 un il $17.99; lib bdg $16.89
Grades: PreK K 1 2   **E**
  1. Shoes -- Fiction 2. Latin America -- Fiction
  ISBN 0-688-05286-X; 0-688-05287-8 lib bdg
                                              LC 92-40868
Silvia receives a pair of beautiful red shoes from her Tia Rosita and finds different uses for them until she grows enough for them to fit
"This simple story, told in spare prose, speaks universally to the imagination and emotions. Pinkney's spirited watercolors animate the narrative and are large enough for group sharing." SLJ

Husband, Amy
  Dear teacher. Sourcebooks Jabberwocky 2010 un il pa $8.99
Grades: K 1 2   **E**
  1. School stories 2. Letters -- Fiction
  ISBN 978-1-4022-4268-7 pa; 1-4022-4268-9 pa
"Each vertical, double-page spread in this inventive title is a letter from young Michael to his new teacher explaining why he may be late for the first day of school. . . . The wild, colorful illustrations show the imaginative play, and kids with back-to-school panic will find comic relief in these over-the-top scenes." Booklist

Hutchins, H. J.
  Mattland; story by Hazel Hutchins and Gail Herbert; art by Dušan Petričić. Annick Press 2008 un il $19.95; pa $8.95
Grades: K 1 2   **E**
  1. Moving -- Fiction 2. Friendship -- Fiction 3. Imagination -- Fiction
  ISBN 978-1-55451-121-1; 1-55451-121-6; 978-1-55451-120-4 pa; 1-55451-120-8 pa
"Matt finds himself in yet another new home. Surrounded by an uninspiring landscape and lacking friends, he begins to poke at the mud outside his house. He quickly notices in his marks the beginning of a landscape. Bit by bit, a miniature world unfolds before Matt. . . . When a rainstorm threatens to flood the newly created 'Mattland,' helping hands appear to route the current safely away. Petričic's understated watercolors are an essential counterpart to Hutchins and Herbert's mature narrative. . . . The illustrator skillfully leads readers from gray, nondescript images to a detailed world brimming with color." SLJ

Hutchins, Pat
  1 hunter. Greenwillow Bks. 1982 un il hardcover o.p. pa $6.99
Grades: PreK K 1 2   **E**
  1. Counting 2. Animals -- Fiction
  ISBN 0-688-00614-0; 0-688-06522-8 pa
                                              LC 81-6352
"Humorous illustrations done in a flat, clear style make an outstanding counting book." Horn Book
This is "a 1 to 10 and back again counting book. . . . Here, a Mr. Magoo-type hunter blunders through the jungle entirely missing the camouflaged elephants (2), giraffes (3), ostriches (4), etc." SLJ

★ The **doorbell** rang. Greenwillow Bks. 1986 un il $15.99; lib bdg $16.89; pa $5.99
Grades: PreK K 1 2   **E**
  1. Cookies -- Fiction 2. Division -- Fiction
  ISBN 0-688-05251-7; 0-688-05252-5 lib bdg; 0-688-09234-9 pa
                                              LC 85-12615
"Bright, joyous, dynamic, this wonderfully humorous piece of realism for the young is presented simply but with style and imagination." Horn Book

★ **Rosie's** walk. Macmillan 1968 un il $16.95; pa $6.99
Grades: PreK K 1   **E**
  1. Foxes -- Fiction 2. Chickens -- Fiction
  ISBN 0-02-745850-4; 0-02-043750-1 pa
"Rosie the hen goes for a walk around the farm and gets home in time for dinner, completely unaware that a fox has been hot on her heels every step of the way. The viewer knows, however, and is not only held in suspense but tickled by the ways in which the fox is foiled at every turn by the unwitting hen. A perfect choice for the youngest." Booklist

Ten red apples. Greenwillow Bks. 2000 un il $17.99; lib bdg $18.89
Grades: PreK K 1   **E**
  1. Counting 2. Stories in rhyme 3. Apples -- Fiction 4. Domestic animals -- Fiction
  ISBN 0-688-16797-7; 0-688-16798-5 lib bdg
                                              LC 99-25065
In rhyming verses, one animal after another neighs, moos, oinks, quacks and makes other appropriate sounds as each eats an apple from the farmer's tree
"A concept book that blends rhyming, counting, repetition, and animal sounds into a charming, folksy story. . . . The gouache paintings are bright and clear." SLJ

★ **We're** going on a picnic! Greenwillow Bks. 2002 un il $15.95; lib bdg $15.89
Grades: PreK K 1 2   **E**
  1. Ducks -- Fiction 2. Chickens -- Fiction
  ISBN 0-688-16799-3; 0-688-16800-0 lib bdg
                                              LC 00-62225
"With an understated humor infusing both narrative and pictures, Hutchins successfully pulls off the child-pleasing contrivance of letting readers in on the secret." Publ Wkly

Hyde, Heidi Smith
  Feivel's flying horses; illustrated by Johanna van der Sterre. Kar-Ben Pub. 2010 un il lib bdg $17.95; pa $7.95

Grades: PreK K 1 2   E
  1. Jews -- Fiction 2. Carousels -- Fiction 3. Immigrants
  -- Fiction 4. Wood carving -- Fiction 5. Coney Island
  (New York, N.Y.) -- Fiction
  ISBN 978-0-7613-3957-1; 0-7613-3957-4; 978-0-
  7613-3959-5 pa; 0-7613-3959-0 pa
                                            LC 2008033480
A Jewish immigrant who is saving money to bring his
wife and children to join him in America creates ornate
horses for a carousel on Coney Island, one for each member
of his family.
  "Watercolor illustrations with ink lines illustrate the immigrant experience on New York's Lower East Side in the
late 1800s and help bring to life the magic of Coney Island."
SLJ

Ian, Janis
  Tiny Mouse; by Janis Ian, illustrated by Ingrid Schubert
and Dieter Schubert. Lemniscaat USA 2013 32 p. $19.95
Grades: PreK K 1 2   E
  1. Ocean travel -- Fiction 2. Mice -- Fiction
  ISBN 193595430X; 9781935954309
This children's book, by Janis Ian and illustrated by Ingrid and Dieter Schubert, "follows the adventures of a bored
mouse who decides to go to sea and narrowly escapes a
grisly death. In his moment of truth, he understands that it's
better to be a whole mouse at home than someone's dinner at
sea." (Publisher's note)
  "In the singer-songwriter's first picture book, a mouse,
bored with his life, stows away on a ship and has an encounter that makes him appreciate what he had. The lyrics
don't quite work without the accompanying CD--the rhyming text's rhythms can be elusive, and some lines pointlessly
repeat--but there's pleasure in Ian's punchy language and
the verging-on-surreal illustrations. Sheet music included."
(Horn Book)

Ichikawa, Satomi
  ★ **Come** fly with me; [by] Satomi Ichikawa. Philomel
Books 2008 un il $15.99
Grades: PreK K 1   E
  1. Dogs -- Fiction 2. Toys -- Fiction 3. France -- Fiction
  4. Airplanes -- Fiction 5. Paris (France) -- Fiction
  ISBN 978-0-399-24679-1
                                            LC 2007023643
Woggy and Cosmos, a toy dog and a toy airplane, go on
an adventure in Paris.
  "The adventure element is perfectly keyed to the age
group. . . . The charming watercolors with their everchang-
ing scenes and skies will pull [children] in." Booklist

  La La Rose. Philomel Books 2004 un il $15.99
Grades: PreK K 1 2   E
  1. Gardens -- Fiction 2. Paris (France) -- Fiction 3.
  Lost and found possessions -- Fiction
  ISBN 0-399-24029-2
                                            LC 2002-15366
  La La Rose, a young girl's stuffed rabbit, gets lost in
Luxembourg Gardens in Paris.
  "Ichikawa's ink-and-watercolor paintings are a wonder-
ful mix of action and thoughtfulness, sweetness and subtlety
that extend the story and give it life past a first reading. . . . A

very satisfying story that also captures the magic and excitement of a special place." Booklist

  My father's shop. Kane/Miller 2006 un il $15.95
Grades: K 1 2 3   E
  1. Morocco -- Fiction 2. Roosters -- Fiction 3. Rugs
  and carpets -- Fiction 4. Father-son relationship --
  Fiction
  ISBN 1-929132-99-9
  "When given a flawed carpet, Mustafa . . . drums up
business for his merchant father by attracting first a similarly colored rooster, then numerous trourists who crow in
their own languages: 'Co-co-ri-co!' 'Qui-qui-ri-qui!' and
'Cock-a-doodle-do!' The multicultural message is light and
the humor contagious. Bright scenes of the crowded Moroc-
can marketplace amplify the story." Horn Book Guide

  My little train. Philomel Books 2010 un il $15.99
Grades: PreK K 1   E
  1. Toys -- Fiction 2. Animals -- Fiction 3. Railroads
  -- Fiction
  ISBN 978-0-399-25453-6; 0-399-25453-6
A little train goes for a ride, taking all the stuffed animals
where they want to go.
  "Ichikawa's soft watercolors reveal destinations that are
ripped from kids' playtime imaginations. . . . Repeated animal noises and train sounds encourage readers to lend their
voices to this whimsical read-aloud." Publ Wkly

  My pig Amarillo. Philomel Bks. 2003 un il $15.99
Grades: PreK K 1 2   E
  1. Pigs -- Fiction 2. Guatemala -- Fiction
  ISBN 0-399-23768-2
                                            LC 2002-7318
Original French edition, 2002
Pablito, a Guatemalan boy whose pet pig Amarillo has
disappeared, uses a kite to send him a message that he still
loves him
  "Ichikawa uses her Guatemalan setting very effectively,
but she also wraps the story in universal emotions: love,
longing, grief, hope. The pen-and-watercolor artwork brings
children close to all facets of Pablito's story." Booklist

Idle, Molly
  ★ **Flora** and the flamingo; by Molly Idle. Chronicle
Books 2013 44 p. col. ill. (reinforced) $16.99
Grades: PreK K 1   E
  1. Stories without words 2. Picture books for children
  3. Dance -- Fiction 4. Flamingos -- Fiction 5. Human-
  animal relationships -- Fiction
  ISBN 1452110069; 9781452110066
                                            LC 2012014608
Caldecott Honor Book (2014)
  "In this . . . wordless picture book with interactive flaps,
[by Molly Idle,] Flora and her graceful flamingo friend explore the trials and joys of friendship through an elaborate
synchronized dance. With a twist, a turn, and even a flop,
these unlikely friends learn at last how to dance together in
perfect harmony." (Publisher's note)

  Flora and the penguin; Molly Idle. Chronicle Books
LLC 2014 40 p. color illustrations (alk. paper) $16.99
Grades: PreK K 1   E
  1. Penguins -- Fiction 2. Stories without words 3. Ice

skating -- Fiction 4. Dance -- fiction 5. Lift-the-flap books 6. Friendship -- Fiction 7. Toy and movable books 8. Conduct of life -- fiction
ISBN 145212891X; 9781452128917

LC 2013042455

In this children's story without words, written and illustrated by Molly Idle, "Flora takes to the ice and forms an unexpected friendship with a penguin. Twirling, leaping, spinning, and gliding, on skates and flippers, the duo mirror each other's graceful dance above and below the ice. But when Flora gives the penguin the cold shoulder, the pair must figure out a way to work together for uplifting results." (Publisher's note)

"Idle reprises the structure and format of her Caldecott Honor–winning Flora and the Flamingo in this wordless wintry companion, which is every bit as graceful a performance for both Flora and her creator. A thick sheet of ice serves as the canvas for Flora's skating performance with a penguin that has climbed up onto the ice; a cutaway view of the pale blue-violet water below shows a school of fish doing a dance of their own. Small glued-in flaps help create a sense of movement, and also explore the brief rift that forms between Flora and the penguin after the bird dives back below the ice in pursuit of a fish. Once again, Idle's elegantly drafted scenes couldn't be more polished, and the foldout sequence that brings this dance to a close feels like a real triumph." Pub Wkly

Tea Rex; by Molly Idle. Viking 2013 40 p. ill. (hardcover) $16.99
Grades: PreK K 1   E
1. Afternoon teas -- Fiction 2. Humorous fiction 3. Humorous stories 4. Parties -- Fiction 5. Dinosaurs -- Fiction 6. Etiquette -- Fiction 7. Tyrannosaurus rex -- Fiction
ISBN 0670014303; 9780670014309

LC 2012016443

This children's story, by Molly Idle, describes a tea party between children and a Tyrannosaurus rex. "Some tea parties are for grown-ups. Some are for girls. But this tea party is for a very special guest. And it is important to follow some rules . . . like providing comfortable chairs, and good conversation, and yummy food. But sometimes that is not enough for special guests, especially when their manners are more Cretaceous than gracious." (Publisher's note)

Il Sung Na

A **book** of babies; by Il Sung Na. Alfred A. Knopf 2014 24 p. (hard cover) $15.99
Grades: PreK   E
1. Animal babies 2. Birth -- Fiction 3. Ducks -- Fiction 4. Animals -- Infancy -- Fiction
ISBN 0385752903; 9780385752909; 9780385752916

LC 2012050490

This picture book, by Il Sung Na, focuses on a "duck [who] leaves his own nest of ducklings to greet new animal babies far and wide. He pops up in . . . locales, observing infant fish, monkeys, zebras, lions, kangaroos, sea horses, polar bears and lizards—all snuggling with mommies and daddies in their habitats." (Kirkus Reviews)

★ **Snow** rabbit, spring rabbit; a book of changing seasons. Alfred A. Knopf 2011 un il $15.99; lib bdg $18.99

Grades: PreK K 1   E
1. Winter -- Fiction 2. Animals -- Fiction 3. Rabbits -- Fiction 4. Seasons 5. Animal behavior
ISBN 0-375-86786-4; 0-375-96786-9 lib bdg; 978-0-375-86786-6; 978-0-375-96786-3 lib bdg

LC 2010-09361

First published 2010 in the United Kingdom with title: A book of winter

While other animals migrate, hibernate, or stay busy all winter, a little white rabbit watches.

"Complex and ethereal at the same time, Na's digitally manipulated spreads feature collage, stenciling, and finger painting over thickly daubed backgrounds; the pages teem with interest and texture." Publ Wkly

Imai, Ayano

Chester. Minedition 2007 un il $16.99
Grades: PreK K   E
1. Dogs -- Fiction
ISBN 978-0-698-40062-7

"Chester, a black-and-white dog with a serious mein, loves his family, but they seem to have forgotten about him. Unhappy, he puts his doghouse on his head and leaves. . . . Imai . . . has produced a small gem. The story . . . is illustrated in delicate watercolors that nonetheless project force both in action and emotion." Booklist

Ingalls, Ann

The **little** piano girl; by Ann Ingalls & Maryann Macdonald; illustrated by Giselle Potter. Houghton Mifflin Books for Children 2010 un il
Grades: K 1 2 3   E
1. Pianists 2. Composers 3. Jazz musicians 4. Pianists -- Fiction 5. Jazz musicians -- Fiction 6. Jazz 7. African American musicians -- Fiction 8. Biography, Individual
ISBN 0-618-95974-2; 978-0-618-95974-7

LC 2008040457

This story depicts the life of the American pianist and composer. "Grades one to five." (SLJ)

Potter's "gouache paintings provide a vivid portrait of industrial Pittsburgh at the beginning of the 20th century, yet have an iconic quality too. Ingalls and MacDonald provide a touching memorial to a jazz great who is not a household name—a valuable contribution." Publ Wkly

Ingman, Bruce

When Martha's away. Candlewick Press 2010 un il $16.99
Grades: PreK K 1 2   E
1. Cats -- Fiction
ISBN 978-0-7636-5135-0; 0-7636-5135-4

A reissue of the title first published 1995 by Houghton Mifflin

Martha's cat reveals that he does not sleep all day, as she believes, but rather has a very busy schedule of activities.

"With humor and sponaneity, the large, spacious illustrations combine line drawings, simple shapes, and bright textured colors." Horn Book Guide

Intriago, Patricia

★ **Dot.** Farrar Straus Giroux 2011 un il $14.99

Grades: PreK K 1   **E**
  1. Opposites
  ISBN 978-0-374-31835-2; 0-374-31835-2
                LC 2010019816

"Even two and three-year-olds will make astute observations. . . . Children will encounter ample ways to interact with this incredibly elegant, clever, and delightful concept book." SLJ

Isaacs, Anne
  ★ **Dust** Devil; illustrated by Paul O. Zelinsky. Schwartz & Wade 2010 un il $17.99
Grades: K 1 2 3   **E**
  1. Tall tales 2. Montana -- Fiction 3. Frontier and pioneer life -- Fiction
  ISBN 0-375-86722-8; 978-0-375-86722-4

Having moved to Montana from Tennessee in the 1830s, fearless Angelica Longrider—also known as Swamp Angel—changes the state's landscape, tames a wild horse, and captures some desperadoes.

"Isaac's far-fetched tall tale is again paired with Zelinsky's stunning American-primitive paintings, framed by the wood upon which they are painted. . . . Zelinsky's action-packed panoramas capture Angel's Paul Bunyanlike strength. . . . Isaacs wraps her narrative in exaggeration that will have kids howling." Publ Wkly

  ★ **Meanwhile,** back at the ranch; by Anne Isaacs and illustrated by Kevin Hawkes. First edition Schwartz & Wade 2014 56 p. color illustrations hardcover $17.99
Grades: K 1 2 3 4   **E**
  1. Texas -- Fiction 2. Widows -- Fiction 3. Ranch life -- Fiction 4. Tall tales 5. Humorous stories 6. Courtship -- Fiction
  ISBN 0375867457; 9780375867453
                LC 2011046490

In this book, by Anne Issacs, "widow Tulip Jones of Bore, England, inherits a ranch in By-Golly Gully, Texas, and moves in with two trunks of tea, twelve pet tortoises, and three servants. The peaceful life suits the wealthy widow fine until word gets out and every unmarried man in Texas lines up to marry her. Widow Tulip and her small staff of three can't possibly run the farm and manage all the suitors, so she devises a plan." (Publisher's note)

"Lively storytelling in colorful, drawn-out sentences, Texas-style, makes for a splendid--albeit lengthy--readaloud. Hawkes' extra-charming soft-focus acrylic-and--colored-pencil artwork on textured paper suits the cactus-filled desert landscape to a T-for-Texas." Kirkus

  Pancakes for supper! illustrated by Mark Teague. Scholastic Press 2006 un il $15.99
Grades: PreK K 1   **E**
  1. Animals -- Fiction 2. New England -- Fiction
  ISBN 0-439-64483-6
                LC 2005-14532

In the backwoods of New England, a young girl cleverly fends off the threats of wild animals by trading her clothes for her safety.

"Isaacs's clever, respectful take on an iconic tale is testament to its appeal. Teague's pictures are brilliant, cinematic full-bleed oil-paint dramas that capture the essence of a nascent New England spring." SLJ

  ★ **Swamp** Angel; illustrated by Paul O. Zelinsky. Dutton Children's Bks. 1994 un il $16.99; pa $6.99
Grades: K 1 2 3   **E**
  1. Tall tales 2. Tennessee -- Fiction 3. Frontier and pioneer life -- Fiction
  ISBN 0-525-45271-0; 0-14-055908-6 pa
                LC 93-43956

A Caldecott Medal honor book, 1995

Along with other amazing feats, Angelica Longrider, also known as Swamp Angel, wrestles a huge bear, known as Thundering Tarnation, to save the winter supplies of the settlers in Tennessee

"Isaacs tells her original story with the glorious exaggeration and uproarious farce of the traditional tall tale and with its typical laconic idiom—you just can't help reading it aloud. . . . Zelinsky's detailed oil paintings in folk-art style are exquisite, framed in cherry, maple, and birch wood grains." Booklist

Another title about Swamp Angel is:
  Dust Devil (2010)

Isadora, Rachel
  Bea at ballet; Rachel Isadora. Nancy Paulsen Books 2012 32 p. col. ill. (hardcover) $12.99
Grades: PreK K 1   **E**
  1. Ballet -- Fiction 2. Picture books for children 3. Dance -- Study and teaching -- Fiction
  ISBN 0399254099; 9780399254093
                LC 2011046803

This children's picture book offers a "primer" about ballet for preschool children. The illustrations "present the preschoolers in black, white, and gray line with bursts of color in wardrobe and accessories, which [author Rachel Isadora] explains piece by piece, for each gender. The class instruction includes labels for the barre, mirror, piano, the five classic positions, and four foot movements (point, flex, flat, relevé)." (School Library Journal)

  ★ **Ben's** trumpet. Greenwillow Bks. 1979 un il $17.99; pa $6.99
Grades: PreK K 1 2   **E**
  1. Musicians -- Fiction 2. African Americans -- Fiction
  ISBN 0-688-80194-3; 0-688-10988-8 pa
                LC 78-12885

A Caldecott Medal honor book, 1980

This is the story of Ben, a boy whose dream is to be a jazz trumpeter but who is too poor to own an instrument until a real musician, remembering his own dreams, puts one into the boy's hands

"The art is astonishingly varied in its brilliant recreation—in the margins, in the urban backgrounds—of the commercial art of the 20's and 30's." N Y Times Book Rev

  Happy belly, happy smile. Harcourt Children's Books 2009 un il $16
Grades: PreK K 1   **E**
  1. Restaurants -- Fiction 2. Grandfathers -- Fiction 3. Chinese Americans -- Fiction
  ISBN 978-0-15-206546-1; 0-15-206546-6
                LC 2008046221

Sitting in the kitchen of his grandfather's Chinese restaurant, a young boy enjoys watching the chefs and waiters prepare and serve mouth-watering dishes

"Isadora's characteristic collage-and-oil illustrations [are] attractive as always. . . . This brief bite of Chinese cuisine will add flavor to cuisine-themed story hours." Booklist

Jake at gymnastics; Rachel Isadora. Nancy Paulsen Books, an imprint of Penguin Group (USA) Inc. 2014 32 p. $14.99

Grades: PreK K 1   E

1. Toddlers -- Fiction 2. Gymnastics -- Fiction

ISBN 0399160485; 9780399160486

LC 2013024243

In this children's book, by Rachel Isadora, "Jake and his diverse group of friend[s] love their action-packed gymnastics class, where they stretch, tumble, balance, turn somersaults and so much more. This is the perfect book to introduce toddlers to the joy of movement and the fun of gymnastics." (Publisher's note)

"Isadora shows a group of roly-poly toddlers enjoying a beginning gymnastics class. Teachers lead five girls and four boys through activities such as stretching, tumbling, walking on a low balance beam, and hanging on a parallel bar. The text is minimal, but the real joy comes through Isadora's sprightly illustrations that combine pencil and ink line drawings with swathes of oil paint." Horn Book

★ **Max**; story & pictures by Rachel Isadora. Macmillan 1976 un il hardcover o.p. pa $5.99

Grades: PreK K 1 2   E

1. Ballet -- Fiction 2. Baseball -- Fiction

ISBN 0-02-043800-1 pa

LC 76-9088

Max "is the star of his baseball team. On a Saturday morning, he has time to spare before his game and accepts (with some hidden disdain) the invitation of his sister, Lisa, to watch her ballet class in action. Max is surprised to find himself interested and happy to join the students at their teacher's suggestion. . . . The experience pays off at the ball park where Max hits a home run. Now he warms up for the game each week at Lisa's dancing class. The pictures are an ebullient combination of grace and comedy, with the leggy students dipping and soaring, in contrast to Max in his uniform." Publ Wkly

Old Mikamba had a farm; Rachel Isadora. Nancy Paulsen Books, An Imprint of Penguin Group (USA) Inc. 2013 40 p. $17.99

Grades: PreK K 1   E

1. Farmers 2. Animals -- Africa 3. Songs 4. Folk songs -- United States 5. Folk songs, English -- United States -- Texts

ISBN 0399257403; 9780399257407

LC 2012049555

"A familiar childhood song gets an African twist in [adaptor and illustrator Rachel] Isadora's latest picture book. She takes readers on safari to the plains of Africa to meet elephants, cheetahs, and dassies. . . . Old Mikamba's farm is a game park, so while there is some interaction between the two small children in the book and the animals, most of them are presented against a backdrop wilder and freer than any space Old MacDonald could offer his domestic stock." (Booklist)

Peekaboo bedtime. G.P. Putnam's Sons 2008 un il $16.99

Grades: PreK   E

1. Bedtime -- Fiction 2. Toddlers -- Fiction

ISBN 978-0-399-24384-4; 0-399-24384-4

LC 2007-34814

A toddler plays peekaboo with parents, grandparents, toys, and the moon while getting ready for bed.

"The pastel illustrations are a delight, a visual celebration of family. . . . Perfect for laptime sharing or calm story hours." Kirkus

Say hello! G.P. Putnam's Sons 2010 un il $16.99

Grades: PreK K 1   E

1. City and town life -- Fiction 2. Language and languages -- Fiction

ISBN 978-0-399-25230-3; 0-399-25230-4

LC 2009011318

A little girl greets people in her neighborhood in many different languages.

"The text is paired down to essentials and the striking collage-style illustrations are colorful and dynamic. Richly patterned with oil paints as well as printed patterns, the cut-paper shapes show up vividly against the white backgrounds." Booklist

The **ugly** duckling; written by Hans Christian Andersen; retold and illustrated by Rachel Isadora. G.P. Putnam's Sons 2009 un il $16.99

Grades: 1 2 3 4   E

1. Fairy tales

ISBN 978-0-399-25029-3; 0-399-25029-8

LC 2008036514

In this retelling of the Ugly Duckling, set on the African continent, the duckling spends an unhappy year ostracized by the other animals before he grows into a beautiful swan.

"What shines in this telling are the illustrations, all collage spreads executed in oil on palette paper and printed paper. . . . Isadora's brilliant colors and broad brushstrokes beautifully capture the unnamed African setting." SLJ

Uh-oh! Harcourt 2008 un il $16

Grades: PreK   E

1. Toddlers -- Fiction 2. African Americans -- Fiction

ISBN 978-0-15-205765-7; 0-15-205765-X

LC 2006039652

As an African American toddler keeps getting into mischief throughout the day, the reader is invited to discover what the trouble is with each page-turn and to say "uh-oh."

This offers "homey, vibrantly colored pastel illustrations. . . . Young listeners . . . [will] get a charge from each thrilling descent into disarray." Horn Book

Ismail, Yasmeen

Time for bed, Fred! Yasmeen Ismail. Bloomsbury/Walker 2014 32 p. color illustrations (hardcover) $14.99; (library reinforced) $15.89

Grades: PreK K 1   E

1. Dogs -- Fiction 2. Bedtime -- Fiction

ISBN 0802735983; 9780802735973; 9780802735980

LC 2013010711

In this children's story, written and illustrated by Yasmeen Ismail, "it's time for [the dog] Fred to go to bed . . . but Fred really, really doesn't want to! From hiding up in trees, to splashing in muddy puddles, to hiding behind bookshelves, Fred will do anything to avoid bedtime. He would even rather have a bath than go to bed . . . but all of this running couldn't possibly have possibly made Fred sleepy-- could it?" (Publisher's note)

"The sophisticated and loose artwork is the ideal match for the simple, emotive text. A perfectly designed read-aloud for the bedtime staller." Kirkus

Isol

It's useful to have a duck; It's useful to have a boy. Groundwood Books 2009 un il $10
Grades: PreK K 1 2 3 **E**
   1. Board books for children 2. Ducks -- Fiction
   ISBN 978-0-88899-927-6; 0-88899-927-5

"Why on earth is it useful to have a duck? In a series of accordioned spreads on yellow board, a little boy reveals the answers, accompanied by swift line sketches that illustrate them. . . . The verso, on blue board, . . . is titled It's Useful to Have a Boy, [and] the identical images receive a very different gloss in the duck's voice. . . . Do not be deceived by the simple-looking board format: This is not for babies. Rather, it challenges children who have accepted the initial premise with developmentally appropriate narcissism to regard the world from the opposite perspective. Gently mind-bending, this playful Mexican import, packaged in a slipcase, will get readers thinking." Kirkus

Petit, the monster; words and pictures by Isol; translated by Elisa Amado. Groundwood Books 2010 un il $16.95
Grades: PreK K **E**
   1. Good and evil -- Fiction
   ISBN 978-0-88899-947-4; 0-88899-947-X

"Poor Petit is a little confused: sometimes he's a good boy and sometimes he's a bad boy, and that's a hard contradiction to work out. . . . Argentinian author-illustrator Isol touches imaginatively on the challenging complexities of behavioral morality, and the book gains special traction from going into failed intentions and contrary correlations . . . while keeping the concept easily kid-accessible. Isol's quirky illustrations feature pencil and oil pastels . . . while computer planes of color fill in figures and backgrounds. . . . Kids will appreciate this playful approach to one of their biggest moral conundrums." Bull Cent Child Books

Isop, Laurie

How do you hug a porcupine? illustrated by Gwen Millward. Simon & Schuster Books for Young Readers 2011 il $15.99
Grades: PreK K 1 **E**
   1. Stories in rhyme 2. Animals -- Fiction 3. Hugging -- Fiction 4. Porcupines -- Fiction
   ISBN 978-1-4424-1291-0; 1-4424-1291-7
                                            LC 2010006941
A child figures out the best way to hug a porcupine as he watches his friends hug other animals.

"The spare, interactive text and clear, uncluttered illustrations . . . make this a natural for group sharing." Booklist

Ives, Penny

★ **Celestine,** drama queen. Arthur A. Levine Books 2009 un il $16.99

Grades: PreK K **E**
   1. Ducks -- Fiction 2. Theater -- Fiction
   ISBN 978-0-545-08149-8; 0-545-08149-1

Celestine the duck is sure that she is destined for stardom, but when her big break comes, she is temporarily stricken with stage fright.

Celestine "captures the essence of children, their emotions, and how they cope. Adorable, annoying, and utterly childlike, Celestine is appealingly portrayed in Ives' funny, sunny watercolors." Booklist

Iwai, Melissa

★ **Soup** day. Henry Holt 2010 un il $12.99
Grades: PreK K 1 2 **E**
   1. Soups -- Fiction 2. Cooking -- Fiction 3. Vegetables -- Fiction 4. Mother-daughter relationship -- Fiction
   ISBN 978-0-8050-9004-8; 0-8050-9004-5
                                            LC 2009029314
A mother and daughter spend a snowy day together buying and preparing vegetables, assembling ingredients, and playing while their big pot of soup bubbles on the stove. Includes a recipe for "Snowy Day Vegetable Soup."

"With economical text and vivid, multitextured collages whose upbeat charm belies their sophistication, the process of preparing the dish unfolds. In one spread, Iwai cleverly offers lessons about numbers, colors, sizes, textures, and what various vegetables look like. . . . A perfect meal and a perfect book." SLJ

Iwamatsu, Atushi Jun

Crow Boy; [by] Taro Yashima. Viking 1955 37p il lib bdg $17.99; pa $5.99
Grades: PreK K 1 2 **E**
   1. School stories 2. Japan -- Fiction
   ISBN 0-670-24931-9 lib bdg; 0-14-050172-X pa
   A Caldecott Medal honor book, 1956

"A moving story interpreted by the author's distinctive illustrations, valuable for human relations and for its picture of Japanese school life." Hodges. Books for Elem Sch Libr

Umbrella; [by] Taro Yashima. Viking 1958 30p il $16.99; pa $6.99
Grades: PreK K 1 **E**
   1. Umbrellas and parasols -- Fiction
   ISBN 0-670-73858-1; 0-14-050240-8 pa
   A Caldecott Medal honor book, 1959

In this simple tale, young children "will be carried along by their identification with the actions of this very real little girl. . . . The beauty of the book makes this worthwhile." Horn Book

Iwamura, Kazuo

Bedtime in the forest. North-South Books 2010 un il $16.95
Grades: PreK K **E**
   1. Owls -- Fiction 2. Bedtime -- Fiction 3. Squirrels -- Fiction
   ISBN 978-0-7358-2310-5; 0-7358-2310-3
   Original Japanese edition 1982

Mick, Mack, and Molly, three young squirrels, find themselves awake and wanting to play all night like the owl children and learn that they should be going to bed instead.

"This unpretentious story with lovely art and endearing animals will be enjoyed by young children." SLJ

Jackson, Alison

The **ballad** of Valentine; illustrated by Tricia Tusa. Dutton Children's Bks. 2001 un il $16.99; pa $6.99

Grades: K 1 2 3   **E**

1. Stories in rhyme 2. Valentines -- Fiction

ISBN 0-525-46720-3; 0-14-240400-4 pa

LC 2001-42737

An ardent suitor tries various means of communication, from smoke signals to Morse code to skywriting, in order to get his message to his Valentine

"Tusa uses sketchy, wispy lines to create loads of droll details that are both funny and subtle. . . . Jackson and Tusa make perfect harmony here—the cadence and rhythm of text and the watercolor artwork are right on pitch." Booklist

Desert Rose and her highfalutin hog; illustrated by Keith Graves. Walker & Co. 2009 un il $16.99; lib bdg $17.89

Grades: K 1 2 3   **E**

1. Tall tales 2. Texas -- Fiction 3. Animals -- Fiction

ISBN 978-0-8027-9833-6; 0-8027-9833-0; 978-0-8027-9834-3 lib bdg; 0-8027-9834-9 lib bdg

LC 2009000206

Upon finding a large gold nugget on her pig farm, Desert Rose sets out to buy the biggest, fattest hog in Texas to enter in the state fair, but first she must get the hog to Laredo and every animal she asks for help is just as "ornery" as the hog

"The cartoon style of the acrylic illustrations accentuates the alliterative text. Youngsters will laugh out loud." SLJ

Thea's tree; [by] Alison Jackson; illustrated by Janet Pedersen. Dutton Children's Books 2008 un il $15.99

Grades: K 1 2 3   **E**

1. Plants -- Fiction 2. Science projects -- Fiction

ISBN 978-0-525-47443-2; 0-525-47443-9

LC 2007-5220

Thea Teawinkle plants an odd, purple, bean-shaped seed in her backyard for her class science project, with astonishing results that even the experts she writes to—including a botanist, an arborist, a museum curator, and a symphony director—cannot offer any explanations for.

"Pedersen's energetic, full-page watercolor illustrations capture the hilarious consequences of Thea's growing crisis." SLJ

Jackson, Shelley

★ **Mimi's** Dada Catifesto. Clarion Books 2009 41p il $17

Grades: 1 2 3 4   **E**

1. Cats -- Fiction 2. Dadaism -- Fiction

ISBN 978-0-547-12681-4; 0-547-12681-6

LC 2008-39486

In Zurich, Switzerland, an artistic cat finds the perfect owner in fellow Dadaist, Mr. Dada. Author's note provides background on the Dadaist art movement.

"Children . . . may not know much about the artistic movement Dada but . . . all (well perhaps not all) becomes clear through Jackson's zingy text and wildly inventive art. . . . With pictures inspired by many artists, including Marcel Duchamp, it's the art that will get kids to sit up and take notice. A mix of collage, fantastical and realistic drawings, and offbeat design work, the illustrations are played against a variety of fonts and typefaces, designed to keep the reader off balance." Booklist

Jacobs, Paul DuBois

The **deaf** musicians; by Pete Seeger and Paul DuBois Jacobs; illustrations by R. Gregory Christie. Putnam 2006 un il $16.99

Grades: K 1 2 3   **E**

1. Deaf -- Fiction 2. Musicians -- Fiction 3. Jazz music -- Fiction

ISBN 0-399-24316-X

LC 2005026901

Lee, a jazz pianist, has to leave his band when he begins losing his hearing, but he meets a deaf saxophone player in a sign language class and together they form a snazzy new band.

"Christie's snazzy style matches perfectly with the book's vivacity. The expressive faces and bold use of color make the story sing. . . . Both uplifting and inclusive, it is a celebration of music and resilience." SLJ

Fire drill; [by] Paul DuBois Jacobs and Jennifer Swender; illustrated by Huy Voun Lee. Henry Holt and Company 2010 un il $15.99

Grades: PreK K 1   **E**

1. School stories 2. Stories in rhyme 3. Fire drills -- Fiction 4. Safety education -- Fiction

ISBN 978-0-8050-8953-0; 0-8050-8953-5

LC 2009005268

In this story told in brief rhyming text, students in a class follow the proper procedures during a fire drill.

"Simple rhyming text paired with colorful, upbeat art offer children an accessible overview of fire-drill rules. . . . Appealing, cheerful illustrations in elemental shapes and colors and vibrant patterns portray the multicultural group and familiar school settings." Booklist

Jadoul, Emile

Good night, Chickie. Eerdmans Books for Young Readers 2011 un il $13.99

Grades: PreK K   **E**

1. Bedtime -- Fiction 2. Chickens -- Fiction 3. Parent-child relationship -- Fiction

ISBN 978-0-8028-5378-3; 0-8028-5378-1

LC 2010024985

Mother Hen reassures Chickie, and Chickie's bunny, that she is nearby and keeping watch over them at bedtime.

"Jadoul is a minimalist, but his big, rounded shapes, thick ink outlines, forceful brushstrokes, and expanses of bright colors do more visual and emotional work than a truckload of detail. . . . Jadoul strikes the right balance between flattering kids' independence and acknowledging their uncertainties." Publ Wkly

Jahn-Clough, Lisa

Felicity & Cordelia; a tale of two bunnies. Farrar Straus and Giroux 2010 un il $16.99

Grades: PreK K 1   **E**

1. Rabbits -- Fiction 2. Balloons -- Fiction 3. Friendship -- Fiction 4. Voyages and travels -- Fiction

ISBN 978-0-374-32300-4; 0-374-32300-3

LC 2009016143

Felicity Rose and Cordelia Bean are best friends, but they are separated when Felicity wants to go on a hot air balloon trip and Cordelia does not want to accompany her.

"Jahn-Clough's illustrations are, as ever, childlike, winsome, and boldly colored. Her story . . . reinforces the importance and interdependence of distinct personalities as well as the beauty of real friendship." SLJ

Little Dog; by Lisa Jahn-Clough. Houghton Mifflin 2006 un il $16
Grades: PreK K   E
1. Dogs -- Fiction 2. Artists -- Fiction
ISBN 978-0-618-57405-6; 0-618-57405-0
LC 2005020455
A lonely stray dog befriends a struggling artist, transforming her art and both their lives.
"The minimal text is accompanied by simple, childlike artwork, framed in and accented by heavy, black brush strokes." SLJ

Jalali, Reza
Moon watchers; Shirin's Ramadan miracle. illustrated by Anne Sibley O'Brien. Tilbury 2010 un il
Grades: 2 3 4   E
1. Maine -- Fiction 2. Muslims -- Fiction 3. Ramadan -- Fiction 4. Siblings -- Fiction 5. Family life -- Fiction
ISBN 0884483215; 9780884483212
Nine-year-old Shirin wants to join her family and other Muslims in fasting for Ramadan but is told she is too young, and so she seeks other ways to participate including, perhaps, getting along better with her older brother, Ali.
"O'Brien's watercolor illustrations evoke a culturally authentic Persian-American aesthetic, depicting warm characters in a family setting. An explanation of Ramadan and Eid is given in the back matter. This is another wonderful contribution to the slowly increasing collection of fictional books on the observance of Ramadan and a great resource for librarians and teachers." SLJ

James, Simon
★ **Baby** Brains. Candlewick Press 2004 un il $15.99; pa $6.99
Grades: PreK K 1 2   E
1. Infants -- Fiction
ISBN 0-7636-2507-8; 0-7636-3682-7 pa
LC 2003-65528
Even though the new baby of Mr. and Mrs. Brains is very intelligent, they realize that he is still just a baby
"This tongue-in-cheek tale will tickle the funny bones of young listeners. The loose and playful lines of the watercolor-and-ink illustrations are used judiciously and to great effect." SLJ
Other titles about Baby Brains are:
Baby Brains superstar (2005)
Baby Brains and RoboMom (2008)

George flies south. Candlewick Press 2011 un il $16.99
Grades: PreK K   E
1. Birds -- Fiction 2. Flight -- Fiction
ISBN 978-0-7636-5724-6; 0-7636-5724-7
LC 2010049468
George does not feel ready to learn to fly, leave his nest, and go south with the other birds, despite his mother's encouragement, but when a strong autumn wind gets hold of the nest, he may have no choice.
This is an "understated yet action-packed story. . . . Beige and pale blue dominate the subtle palette of James's . . . minimalist ink and watercolor pictures, arranged in square

and rectangular panels, full-page scenarios, and—when George at last takes flight—a sprawling double-page vista." Publ Wkly

Little One Step. Candlewick Press 2003 un il $15.99; bd bk $6.99
Grades: PreK K 1   E
1. Ducks -- Fiction 2. Brothers -- Fiction
ISBN 0-7636-2070-X; 0-7636-3520-0 bd bk
LC 2002-71407
As three duckling brothers cross forest and field to return to their mother, the older ones encourage the youngest by teaching him a game that earns him the name of Little One Step
"Abundant white space surrounds the line drawings suffused with buttery yellow and peach watercolor tones. . . . This satisfying tale about perseverance will find an eager audience at storytimes, on a parent's lap, and with independent readers." SLJ

Nurse Clementine; Simon James. Candlewick Press 2013 40 p. (reinforced) $15.99
Grades: PreK K   E
ISBN 9780763663827
LC 2012942668
In this picture book, "young Clementine is thrilled with the nurse's kit she receives for her birthday, so pleased that she starts work immediately when her father bangs his toe on a door, bandaging his leg from toe to knee and admonishing him to keep the bandage on for a week. Her mom gets similar treatment for a headache, and Clementine eagerly waits for her risk-taking little brother, Tommy, to require her medical skills." (Bulletin of the Center for Children's Books)

Jane, Pamela
Little goblins ten; written by Pamela Jane; illustrated by Jane Manning. Harper 2011 un il $16.99; lib bdg $17.89
Grades: K 1 2   E
1. Counting 2. Stories in rhyme 3. Monsters -- Fiction 4. Halloween -- Fiction
ISBN 978-0-06-176798-2; 0-06-176798-0; 978-0-06-176800-2 lib bdg; 0-06-176800-6 lib bdg
LC 2010010169
Ghouls, goblins, ghosts, witches, and other scary creatures cavort in the forest on Halloween, introducing the numbers one through ten.
"Numerous titles interpreting 'Over in the Meadow' have been published, but trust the team of Jane and Manning to conjure up an impressive new vision in time for Halloween. Set in a fantastical land dominated by watery blues, greens and grays and punctuated by warm reds and yellows, Manning's tale presents ethereal ghosts, country-bumpkin werewolves, parading mummies, screeching witches, happy bats and boogieing skeletons that readers will instantly want to have as friends. . . . Truly satisfying." Kirkus

Janni, Rebecca
Every cowgirl needs a horse; illustrations by Lynne Avril. Dutton Children's Books 2010 un il $16.99
Grades: PreK K 1   E
1. Cycling -- Fiction 2. Cowhands -- Fiction 3.

Birthdays -- Fiction 4. Imagination -- Fiction
ISBN 978-0-525-42164-1; 0-525-42164-5
　　　　　　　　　　　LC 2009-12278

Nellie Sue, who fancies herself a real cowgirl, wants a horse for her birthday, but she discovers that a brand new bicycle—her first—takes almost as much taming as a filly.

"The bright, sketchy, watercolor and ink illustrations are suffused with pinks and purples and capture a child who tries to live up to cowgirl ideals of helping others, looking on the bright side, and being strong. The lesson on dealing positively with disappointment is gently delivered." SLJ

Another title about Nellie Sue is:
Every cowgirl needs dancing boots (2011)

Every cowgirl needs dancing boots; illustrated by Lynne Avril. Dutton Children's Books 2011 un il $16.99
Grades: PreK K 1　　　　　　　　　　　　E
1. Dance -- Fiction 2. Cowhands -- Fiction 3. Imagination -- Fiction
ISBN 978-0-525-42341-6; 0-525-42341-9
　　　　　　　　　　　LC 2010037712
Sequel to: Every cowgirl needs a horse (2010)

Nellie Sue hopes to make friends with her new neighbors by hosting a hoedown in her barn, but wonders if the 'glitter girls' will be able to dance in their ballet slippers, rather than in dancing boots like hers.

"Avril's line-and-watercolor cartoons keep the visual tone light. . . . A passel of fun activities—dancing, crafting, biking and dress up—are tucked into Janni's tonic tale of imagination and optimism." Kirkus

Janovitz, Marilyn

Baby baby baby! Sourcebooks 2010 un il bd bk $7.99
Grades: PreK　　　　　　　　　　　　　　E
1. Stories in rhyme 2. Board books for children 3. Infants -- Fiction
ISBN 978-1-4022-4414-8 bd bk; 1-4022-4414-2 bd bk

"Nine stanzas of appealing verse show a baby playing with family members and pets, taking a bath, and going to bed. . . . [This board book's] bouncy verses will hold young children's attention with rhythm, rhyme, repeated phrases, and references to familiar things. . . . The digital artwork illustrates the cheerful characters in squiggly, black line drawings brightened with bold patterns and colors." Booklist

Jarka, Jeff

Love that kitty; the story of a boy who wanted to be a cat. Henry Holt 2010 un il $12.99
Grades: PreK K 1　　　　　　　　　　　　E
1. Cats -- Fiction 2. Imagination -- Fiction
ISBN 978-0-8050-9053-6; 0-8050-9053-3

Tired of being an ordinary boy, Peter decides to become a cat.

"Jarka draws each character and setting with only a few well-placed lines filled in with bright solid colors. Peter's quirky confidence contrasts hilariously with his parents' bewilderment." SLJ

Love that puppy! the story of a boy who wanted to be a dog. Henry Holt 2009 un il $12.95

Grades: PreK K 1
1. Dogs -- Fiction 2. Imagination -- Fiction
ISBN 978-0-8050-8741-3; 0-8050-8741-9
　　　　　　　　　　　LC 2008018333

When his parents want him to change back into a human boy, Peter the dog comes up with a novel solution.

"Jarka's colorful comic-strip-style illustrations drive the humor with one visual joke after another. . . . Children will appreciate both the absurdity of Peter's behavior and Jarka's delivery." SLJ

Another title about Peter is:
Love that kitty (2010)

Jarrett, Clare

★ **Arabella** Miller's tiny caterpillar; [by] Clare Jarrett. Candlewick Press 2008 un il $16.99
Grades: PreK K 1 2　　　　　　　　　　　E
1. Butterflies -- Fiction 2. Caterpillars -- Fiction
ISBN 978-0-7636-3660-9; 0-7636-3660-6

Arabella Miller finds a tiny caterpillar and watches and cares for it until it becomes a butterfly

This is "an engaging, exceptional picture book. . . . Based on the verse about Little Arabella Miller, the story arc is simple but the charm lies in the sketchy, pencil-and-paper collage illustrations." Booklist

Javaherbin, Mina

★ **Goal!** illustrated by A.G. Ford. Candlewick Press 2010 un il $16.99; pa $6.99
Grades: 2 3 4　　　　　　　　　　　　　E
1. Soccer -- Fiction 2. Bullies -- Fiction 3. Friendship -- Fiction 4. South Africa -- Fiction
ISBN 0763645710; 9780763645717; 9780763658229
　　　　　　　　　　　LC 2008047266

In a dangerous alley in a township in South Africa, the strength and unity which a group of young friends feel while playing soccer keep them safe when a gang of bullies arrives to cause trouble.

"Illustrations rendered in oil are impressive. Large and colorful action shots, many full spread, keep the story moving at a quick pace." SLJ

Soccer star; Mina Javaherbin, illustrated by Renato Alarcao. Candlewick Press 2014 40 p. color illustrations (reinforced) $16.99
Grades: K 1 2 3　　　　　　　　　　　　E
1. Brazil -- Fiction 2. Soccer -- Fiction 3. Brothers and sisters -- Fiction 4. Picture books for children
ISBN 9780763660567; 0763660566
　　　　　　　　　　　LC 2013944008

This children's book, by Mina Javaherbin, tells the "story of a Brazilian boy who dreams of being a soccer star--and the sister who steps in to help his team win a game. When Paulo Marcelo Feliciano becomes a soccer star, crowds will cheer his famous name! Then his mother won't have to work long hours, and he won't have to work all day on a fishing boat. . . . But when Jose falls on his wrist, will the team finally break the rules and let a girl show her stuff?" (Publisher's note)

"[I]t's downright refreshing to see illustrations that realistically relay the diversity of shades found among Brazilians. Javaherbin deftly handles Paulo and Maria's poverty with honesty while simultaneously refraining from sugarcoating, overemphasizing or romanticizing it." Kirkus

Javernick, Ellen

The **birthday** pet; illustrated by Kevin O'Malley. Marshall Cavendish 2009 un il $16.99

Grades: PreK K 1 2   **E**
1. Stories in rhyme 2. Pets -- Fiction 3. Turtles -- Fiction 4. Birthdays -- Fiction
ISBN 978-0-7614-5522-6; 0-7614-5522-1

LC 2008010740

Danny can have a pet for his birthday and he knows exactly what he wants, but the other members of his family think differently.

"The colorful, animated illustrations incorporate exaggerated close-ups, unusual perspectives, and witty details that extend the humor in the words. Young readers and listeners will enjoy the simple, well-paced, rhyming text." Booklist

Jay, Alison

★ **1** 2 3; a child's first counting book. Dutton Children's Books 2007 un il $15.99; bd bk $9.99

Grades: PreK K 1 2   **E**
1. Counting
ISBN 978-0-525-47836-2; 978-0-525-42165-8 bd bk

LC 2006035905

"Jay takes readers on an enchanted journey from 1 to 10 and back again, with help from fairy tale figures. A quartet of self-satisfied frog princes impressively embody the number 4, while a plate of gingerbread men . . . represent the number 6. . . . The pictures are a wonder to behold: Jay's flattened perspectives, gently faded colors, crackle-glaze finishes and lean, angular characterizations vaguely evoke the dreamy, ambiguous narrative qualities of medieval art." Publ Wkly

★ **ABC**: a child's first alphabet book. Dutton Children's Bks. 2003 un il hardcover o.p. bd bk $9.99

Grades: PreK K 1 2   **E**
1. Alphabet
ISBN 0-525-46951-6; 0-525-47524-9 bd bk

LC 2003-45218

In this alphabet book, a is for apple and z is for zoo

"This imaginative alphabet book offers visual clues to track and a story to tease out in its beautiful paintings. . . . Older children will flip from page to page, finding the simple story, drawing connections, and naming the letter-related objects. Younger ones can simply enjoy the delightful paintings with their crackle-glazed folk art look and touches of humor." Booklist

Red green blue; a first book of colors. Dutton Children's Books 2010 un il $16.99

Grades: PreK K 1   **E**
1. Stories in rhyme 2. Color -- Fiction 3. Nursery rhymes -- Fiction
ISBN 978-0-525-42303-4; 0-525-42303-6

LC 2009-25098

Characters from nursery rhymes populate this tale, which highlights the colorful aspects of the familiar poems. Includes a key to the nursery rhymes referenced in the story.

"There are numerous opportunities for discussing colors, but as ever, it's Jay's luminous images that steal the show." Publ Wkly

Welcome to the zoo. Dial 2008 un il $16.99

Grades: PreK K 1 2   **E**
1. Stories without words 2. Zoos -- Fiction 3. Animals -- Fiction
ISBN 978-0-8037-3177-6; 0-8037-3177-9

"Jay creates a zoo without the usual barriers between the animals and their visitors. . . . The oil paintings reward close attention with amusing visual details and small wordless dramas that carry through from page to page. . . . Polished yet playful, this nearly wordless picture book is a engaging choice." Booklist

Jeffers, Oliver

The **great** paper caper; [by] Oliver Jeffers. Philomel Books 2009 un il $17.99

Grades: PreK K   **E**
1. Trees -- Fiction 2. Animals -- Fiction
ISBN 978-0-399-25097-2; 0-399-25097-2

LC 2008026192

When tree branches begin disappearing and paper airplanes are left in their place, the forest creatures carry out an investigation to find the culprit who has been stealing their homes.

"Managed forestry is the theme of this book that features folk-art-style animals with funny little stick legs. The mixed-media illustrations nicely complement the spare yet eloquent text." SLJ

The **heart** and the bottle. Philomel Books 2010 un il $17.99

Grades: PreK K 1   **E**
1. Death -- Fiction 2. Emotions -- Fiction 3. Bereavement -- Fiction
ISBN 978-0-399-25452-9; 0-399-25452-8

After safeguarding her heart in a bottle hung around her neck, a girl finds the bottle growing heavier and her interest in things around her becoming smaller.

The "artwork is the sweetness in this bittersweet story. . . . While the subject of loss always has the potential to unsettle young readers, most should find this quietly powerful treatment of grief moving." Publ Wkly

The **Hueys** in The new sweater; Oliver Jeffers. Philomel Books 2012 32 p.

Grades: PreK K 1 2   **E**
1. Children's stories 2. Sweaters -- Fiction 3. Individuality -- Fiction
ISBN 0399257675; 9780399257674

LC 2011048399

In this children's story by Oliver Jeffers ,"each Huey looks the same, thinks the same, and does the same exact things. So you can imagine the chaos when one of them has the idea of knitting a sweater! It seems like a good idea at the time--he is quite proud of it, in fact--but it does make him different from the others. So the rest of the Hueys, in turn, decide that they want to be different too! How? By knitting the exact same sweater, of course!" (Publisher's note)

The **incredible** book eating boy; by Oliver Jeffers. Philomel Books 2007 un il $16.99

Grades: PreK K 1 2 3   **E**
1. Food -- Fiction 2. Books and reading -- Fiction
ISBN 978-0-399-24749-1

LC 2006026279

Henry loves to eat books, until he begins to feel quite ill and decides that maybe he could do something else with the books he has been devouring

"The simple cartoon illustrations twinkle with humor and feeling. Done in paint and pencil on smart backdrops— pages from old books—the pictures set the stage for the quirky story." SLJ

It wasn't me; written and illustrated by Oliver Jeffers. Philomel Books 2014 32 p. (The Hueys) (hardback) $17.99

Grades: PreK K 1 2   E

1. Debates and debating 2. Individuality -- Fiction 3. Brothers and sisters -- Fiction 4. Interpersonal relations -- Fiction

ISBN 0399257683; 9780399257681

LC 2013019164

Author Oliver Jeffers presents another book in his Hueys series. The "egg-shaped creatures may look the same, think the same, and even do the same things, but that doesn't mean they always agree. The only problem is, they can't seem to agree on what they disagreed on in the first place! Which ultimately leads to an even bigger disagreement!" (Publisher's note)

It was not me

★ Once upon an alphabet; Short Stories for All the Letters. Oliver Jeffers. First American edition. Philomel Books, an imprint of Penguin Group (USA) 2014 112 p. $26.99

Grades: PreK K 1 2 3 4   E

1. Alphabet -- Fiction 2. Short stories -- Collections 3. Alphabet

ISBN 9780399167911; 0399167919

LC 2014021089

This children's book, written and illustrated by Oliver Jeffers, presents a collection of short stories from A to Z. "From an Astronaut who's afraid of heights, to a Bridge that ends up burned between friends, to a Cup stuck in a cupboard and longing for freedom, . . . this series of interconnected stories and characters explores the alphabet." (Publisher's note)

"With wry humor, equally droll ink illustrations, and a solid dose of alliteration, Jeffers (the Hueys series) creates delightful mini-narratives for each letter of the alphabet." (Publishers Weekly)

★ Stuck. Philomel Books 2011 un il $16.99

Grades: PreK K   E

1. Kites -- Fiction

ISBN 978-0-399-25737-7; 0-399-25737-3

LC 2011016349

When Floyd's kite gets stuck in a tree, he tries to knock it down with increasingly larger and more outrageous things.

This is "an exuberantly absurd tale. . . . Jeffers . . . pictures the extravagant accumulation in abstract pencil-and-gouache doodles, with hand-lettered text to set a conversational tone." Publ Wkly

This moose belongs to me; Oliver Jeffers. Philomel Books 2012 32 p.

Grades: PreK K 1 2   E

1. Human-animal relationship -- Fiction 2. Pets --

Fiction 3. Moose as pets -- Fiction

ISBN 9780399161032

LC 2012020373

This children's picture book by Oliver Jeffers tells the "tale of a boy and his moose. Wilfred is a boy with rules. He lives a very orderly life. . . . There is, however, one rule that Wilfred's pet has difficulty following: Going whichever way Wilfred wants to go. Perhaps this is because Wilfred's pet doesn't quite realize that he belongs to anyone. . . . Fortunately, the two manage to work out a compromise." (Publisher's note)

★ Up and down. Philomel Books 2010 un il $16.99

Grades: PreK K 1   E

1. Flight -- Fiction 2. Penguins -- Fiction 3. Friendship -- Fiction

ISBN 978-0-399-25545-8; 0-399-25545-1

LC 2010011358

Even though the penguin and the boy are close friends and do many things together, the penguin decides that he wants to fly and he wants to do it on his own.

"Serene white backdrops highlight brilliant compositional choices, while full-page spreads of unconfined color depict dramatic moments with subtle force. Children will intuit, absorb and appreciate this soothing book's heart—the fast, offbeat friendship that makes it so singular and appealing." Kirkus

Another title about Penguin and the boy is:

Lost and found (2006)

The way back home; [by] Oliver Jeffers. Philomel Books 2008 un il $16.99

Grades: PreK K 1 2   E

1. Moon -- Fiction 2. Space flight -- Fiction 3. Extraterrestrial beings -- Fiction

ISBN 978-0-399-25074-3; 0-399-25074-3

LC 2007029570

Stranded on the moon after his extraordinary airplane takes him into outer space, a boy meets a marooned young Martian with a broken spacecraft, and the two new friends work together to return to their respective homes

"The charm of this story is how completely it maintains a childlike perspective. . . . This approach continues in the watercolor, graphite, and collage artwork. Figures consist of circle heads, box bodies, and stick legs; the backgrounds are flat colors with a few scribbled-in clouds or puffs of exhaust. Humorous details abound." SLJ

Jeffers, Susan

My Chincoteague pony. Hyperion Books for Children 2008 un il $16.99

Grades: PreK K 1 2 3   E

1. Horses -- Fiction 2. Chincoteague Island (Va.) -- Fiction

ISBN 1-4231-0023-9; 978-1-4231-0023-2

Julie's "fondest wish is to have a pony of her own. The child convinces her farm-dwelling parents to take her to Chincoteague Island for Pony Penning Day so that she can bid in the auction. Unfortunately, she is continually outbid and realizes that the money she's earned won't be enough. Then one pony is returned and several people in the crowd pitch in to make her dream come true. . . . The lovely illustrations capture Julie's love of horses, the beauty of the ponies, and the excitement of the roundup." SLJ

The **Nutcracker**; [retold and illustrated by] Susan Jeffers. HarperCollinsPublishers 2007 un il $16.99; lib bdg $17.89

Grades: K 1 2   **E**

1. Fairy tales 2. Toys -- Fiction 3. Magic -- Fiction 4. Christmas -- Fiction

ISBN 978-0-06-074386-4; 0-06-074386-7; 978-0-06-074387-1 lib bdg; 0-06-074387-5 lib bdg

LC 2007012489

An abridged version of the story of Marie Stahlbaum, who helps break the spell on her toy nutcracker and watches him change into a handsome prince

"Children who love the traditional Christmas ballet will enjoy this romantic illustrated edition. . . . The illustrations communicate the beauty and the emotional quality of the ballet." SLJ

The **twelve** days of Christmas; written and illustrated by Susan Jeffers. HarperCollins 2013 40 p. (hardcover bdgs) $17.99

Grades: PreK K 1 2   **E**

1. Gifts -- Fiction 2. Magic -- Fiction 3. Christmas -- Fiction 4. Santa Claus -- Fiction

ISBN 0062066153; 9780062066152; 9780062066169

LC 2012050675

In this book, by Susan Jeffers, "a little girl sneaks a look at a wrapped present on the night before Christmas-a snow globe of a partridge in a pear tree-and accidentally breaks it. Falling asleep, she dreams of Santa giving her a ride on his sled, during which he gives her two turtledoves and all the rest of the traditional gifts in the song. Arriving back at his workshop, he repairs the broken gift, and the girl wakes up to Christmas morning to a wrapped-up, unbroken snow globe." (School Library Journal)

Jenkins, Emily

Daffodil, crocodile; pictures by Tomek Bogacki. Farrar, Straus & Giroux 2007 un il $16

Grades: PreK K 1 2   **E**

1. Sisters -- Fiction 2. Triplets -- Fiction 3. Imagination -- Fiction

ISBN 978-0-374-39944-3; 0-374-39944-1

LC 2005-40163

Tired of being one of three look-alike sisters that no one can tell apart, Daffodil puts on a papier mâché crocodile head and has her own individual adventures

"Daffodil's words and actions ring kidlike and true. . . . Colorful art, whimsical and expressive, fills the pages with fanciful patterns, perspectives, and details." Booklist

Five creatures; pictures by Tomek Bogacki. Foster Bks. 2001 un il $16; pa $5.95

Grades: K 1 2 3   **E**

1. Cats 2. Family life 3. Cats -- Fiction 4. Family life -- Fiction

ISBN 0-374-32341-0; 0-374-42328-8 pa

LC 00-28771

In words and pictures, a girl describes the three humans and two cats that live in her house, and details some of the traits that they share

"This clever, multilayered book is as much for sharing and getting little ones on the path to deductive reasoning as it is for reading. . . . The text encourages readers to be observant. . . . Bogacki's colored chalk art . . . is childlike in the best possible way—immediate, identifiable, and executed with soft colors and simple shapes." Booklist

Lemonade in winter; a book about two kids counting money. Emily Jenkins; illustrated by G. Brian Karas. Schwartz & Wade Books 2012 40 p. $16.99

Grades: PreK K 1 2   **E**

1. Siblings -- Fiction 2. Picture books for children 3. Entrepreneurship 4. Winter -- Fiction 5. Addition -- Fiction 6. Lemonade -- Fiction 7. Brothers and sisters -- Fiction 8. Moneymaking projects -- Fiction

ISBN 0375858830; 9780375858833; 9780375958830

LC 2010024135

In this children's picture book, "two young entrepreneurs, Pauline and John-John, ignore the naysayers (their parents) and set up a lemonade stand smack dab on the snowy sidewalk. The lemonade, limeade--and lemon-limeade--are ready. But there are no customers to be seen. Pauline and John-John aren't discouraged. Instead, they improvise by singing a catchy jingle, turning cartwheels to attract attention, decorating their stand and, finally, having a half-price sale." (Kirkus Reviews)

"This quirky tale is a boon for young entrepreneurs, who will enjoy looking at the humorous details in the pictures as much as working out the math after each sale. Abounding with teaching possibilities

Skunkdog; pictures by Pierre Pratt. Farrar, Straus and Giroux 2008 un il $16.95

Grades: K 1 2 3   **E**

1. Dogs -- Fiction 2. Skunks -- Fiction

ISBN 0-374-37009-5; 978-0-374-37009-1

LC 2005-54701

Dumpling, a lonely dog with no sense of smell, moves with his family to the country and makes a new friend who takes some getting used to.

"Jenkins uses a lot of detail and repetition. Pratt's sunlit illustrations are done in oils and portray a white dog with an elongated nose and a furiously wagging black tail who complements the black-and-white skunk. Children will instantly relate to the pup's skunk encounters. . . . Important themes of loneliness, tolerance, friendship, and family emerge from this funny story." SLJ

★ **That** new animal; pictures by Pierre Pratt. Farrar, Straus and Giroux 2005 un il $16

Grades: PreK K 1 2   **E**

1. Dogs -- Fiction 2. Infants -- Fiction

ISBN 0-374-37443-0

LC 2003-44058

The lives of two dogs change after a new animal, a baby, comes to their house.

"Both the author and illustrator demonstrate wonderful insight into pet psychology and family dynamics, and the elongated style of the vibrantly colored artwork strikes just the right note of humor and whimsy." SLJ

Water in the park; a book about water and the times of the day. Emily Jenkins. 1st ed. Schwartz & Wade Books 2013 40 p. ill. (hardcover) $16.99; (library) $19.99
Grades: PreK K 1   E
1. Parks -- Fiction 2. Water -- Fiction
ISBN 0375870024; 9780375870026 trade; 9780375970023
LC 2011050243
This children's picture book, by Emily Jenkins, illustrated by Stephanie Graegin, shows the readers "from the first orange glow on the water in the pond, to the last humans and animals running home from an evening rain shower, . . . a day-in-the-life of a city park, and the playground within it." (Publisher's note)

Jenkins, Steve
★ **Move!** [written by Steve Jenkins and Robin Page; illustrated by Steve Jenkins] Houghton Mifflin 2006 un il $16; bd bk $7.99
Grades: PreK K   E
1. Animal locomotion
ISBN 0-618-64637-X; 0-547-24000-7 bd bk
LC 2005-19082
In this "book illustrated with cut and torn-paper collages, animals leap, swim, slide, swing, and waddle. Each spread contains one action word and two animals for whom that behavior is typical. . . . Jenkins uses brief phrases as captions and provides a well-written, concise appendix. . . . This book is gorgeous and educational." SLJ

Jennings, Sharon
A **Chanukah** Noel; a true story. written by Sharon Jennings; illustrated by Gillian Newland. Second Story Press 2010 un il $15.95
Grades: K 1 2   E
1. Jews -- Fiction 2. France -- Fiction 3. Christmas -- Fiction
ISBN 978-1-897187-74-6; 1-897187-74-2
A young Jewish girl is fascinated by the traditions of Christmas when her family moves to a small town in France.

Jenson-Elliott, Cindy
Weeds find a way; Cynthia Jenson-Elliott; illustrated by Carolyn Fisher. 1st ed. Beach Lane Books 2013 40 p. (hardcover) $16.99
Grades: PreK K 1 2   E
1. Weeds 2. Plants 3. Weeds -- Fiction
ISBN 1442412607; 9781442412606
LC 2011018524
In this book, author Cindy Jenson-Elliott "celebrates weeds for their heartiness and ability to disseminate and adapt. More detailed information about how weeds can actually be useful despite their reputation can be found in the back matter, along with a list both identifying and offering further facts about the plants pictured in the book." (School Library Journal)

Jessell, Tim
Falcon; by Tim Jessell. Random House Inc 2012 40 p. (trade: alk. paper) $17.99; (library) $20.99
Grades: 1 2 3   E
1. Falcons 2. Flight -- Fiction 3. Falcons -- Fiction 4.

Imagination -- Fiction
ISBN 0375868666; 9780375868665; 9780375968662
LC 2011012758
This book looks at falcons, inviting "readers to imagine taking wing. In a series of . . . paintings, [Tim] Jessell provides a bird's-eye view of the raptor in flight, as well as sweeping panoramas that show how it interacts with landscapes as diverse as mountains, sea cliffs, and skyscrapers." (School Library Journal)

Jesset, Aurore
Loopy; by Aurore Jesset; illustrated by Barbara Korthues. North-South 2008 un il $16.95; pa $7.95
Grades: PreK K 1   E
1. Toys -- Fiction 2. Lost and found possessions -- Fiction
ISBN 978-0-7358-2175-0; 0-7358-2175-5; 978-0-7358-2261-0 pa; 0-7358-2261-1 pa
"A child leaves her favorite toy at the doctor's office and ponders its fate should they fail to be reunited 'RIGHT NOW!' On each spread, Jesset's speculation about the beloved stuffed animal's current state is matched with Korthues's Tim Burton-esque illustrations rendered in vibrant colors, often muted to depict the nighttime setting. The simple, rhythmic prose recalls a small child's inner dialogue or storytelling voice." SLJ

Ji Zhaohua
No! that's wrong! [by] Zhaohua Ji and Cui Xu. Kane Miller Book Pub. 2008 un il $15.95
Grades: PreK K 1 2   E
1. Animals -- Fiction 2. Rabbits -- Fiction 3. Clothing and dress -- Fiction
ISBN 978-1-933605-66-1; 1-933605-66-9
"A rabbit has a humorous encounter with a pair of red underpants. Rabbit's not sure how to wear the mysterious garment and tries it on as a hat. He offers the hat in turn to eight different animals until a donkey straightforwardly inquires why the rabbit is wearing underpants on his head. . . . The cartoon-style artwork and the text, consisting primarily of dialogue, work well together. . . . This entertaining picture book stimulates a bit of creative thinking and problem solving." SLJ

Jimenez, Francisco
The **Christmas** gift; El regalo de Navidad; illustrated by Claire B. Cotts. Houghton Mifflin 2000 un il $15; pa $6.99
Grades: K 1 2 3   E
1. Christmas -- Fiction 2. Migrant labor -- Fiction 3. Mexican Americans -- Fiction 4. Bilingual books -- English-Spanish
ISBN 0-395-92869-9; 0-547-13364-2 pa
LC 99-26224
When his family has to move again a few days before Christmas in order to find work, Panchito worries that he will not get the ball he has been wanting
"This story, a version of which appeared in Jiménez's . . . TheCircuit, is presented here in a bilingual picture book format with an excellent Spanish text. . . . Mural-like illustrations soulfully depict the hard life and strong people of the migrant labor camps." Horn Book Guide

Jocelyn, Marthe

Eats; [by] Marthe Jocelyn; [illustrations by] Tom Slaughter. Tundra Books 2007 un il $15.95; bd bk $7.95
Grades: PreK K 1 2   E
    1. Animals -- Food
    ISBN 978-0-88776-820-0; 978-0-88776-988-7 bd bk
"Painted paper cuts in jewel colors graphically portray the principal foods eaten by 14 different animals. . . . Using bold, simple, brightly colored shapes . . . [and] placing them on backgrounds of equally bold contrasting colors, the animals and their dinners are easily identified and, thus, will have instant kid appeal." SLJ

    ★ Ones and twos; by Marthe Jocelyn and Nell Jocelyn. Tundra Books 2011 un il $15.95
Grades: PreK K 1   E
    1. Numbers 2. Stories in rhyme 3. Birds -- Fiction 4. Friendship -- Fiction
    ISBN 978-1-77049-220-2; 1-77049-220-8
"Deceptively simple text accompanied by highly textured, patterned, and colorful collages invite children to consider number relationships, opening with the spread 'One birds, two eggs. One girl, two legs.' The rhyming couplets, akin to terse verse, trace both bird and girl throughout the day. . . . Operating on two levels as a concept book that also tells a story, this delightful picture book will draw readers for many repeat visits." Booklists

    Over under; [illustrated by] Tom Slaughter. Tundra Books 2005 un il $15.95; bd bk $7.95
Grades: PreK   E
    1. Opposites
    ISBN 0-88776-708-7; 0-88776-790-7 bd bk
"Minimal rhyming text and cut-paper illustrations of animals in six basic colors introduce opposites: e.g. 'big' and 'small' are represented by a black elephant and mouse on a vibrant red background." Horn Book Guide

    ★ Same same; Tom Slaughter, illustrator. Tundra Books 2009 un il $15.95; bd bk $7.95
Grades: PreK K 1   E
    1. Concepts 2. Classification
    ISBN 978-0-88776-885-9; 0-88776-885-7; 978-0-88776-987-0 bd bk; 0-88776-987-X bd bk
"Jocelyn and Slaughter . . . strikingly introduce the concept of classification. Slaughter's graphic cut-paper compositions command attention with their paintbox-bright colors. The first spread, for example, shows an apple, a blue-and-green planet Earth and a tambourine. . . 'Round things,' reads the caption. The next pages show the tambourine again, now with a guitar and a bird. This spread is captioned 'things that make music.' Always carrying forward one of the three objects from the previous spread, Jocelyn delivers the vital lesson that everyday objects fall into many categories. The concept is clear and the delivery attractive." Publ Wkly

Johnson, Angela

The day Ray got away; illustated by Luke LaMarca. Simon & Schuster 2010 un il $16.99
Grades: PreK K 1 2   E
    1. Parades -- Fiction 2. Balloons -- Fiction
    ISBN 978-0-689-87375-1; 0-689-87375-1
"In this lighthearted story, the fateful morning begins when Ray wakes up with a smile (he always does) and an-
nounces to his fellow balloons, 'Today is the day.' The parade begins the same as usual, until Ray makes his break and havoc ensues. Cheerful acrylic cartoon illustrations elevate the understated story, adding foreshadowing, drama, and much humor." SLJ

    ★ I dream of trains; illustrated by Loren Long. Simon & Schuster Bks. for Young Readers 2003 un il $16.95
Grades: K 1 2 3   E
    1. Locomotive engineers 2. Railroads -- Fiction 3. African Americans -- Fiction
    ISBN 0-689-82609-5
                 LC 98-52886
The son of a sharecropper dreams of leaving Mississippi on a train with the legendary engineer Casey Jones
"Long's moody acrylic paintings, mainly in subdued tones, are a sterling accompaniment to the book's provocative prose." SLJ

Just like Josh Gibson; written by Angela Johnson; illustrated by Beth Peck. Simon & Schuster Books for Young Readers 2004 un il $15.95; pa $6.99
Grades: K 1 2 3   E
    1. Baseball -- Fiction 2. Grandmothers -- Fiction 3. African Americans -- Fiction
    ISBN 0-689-82628-1; 1-4169-2728-X pa
                 LC 2001-49531
A young girl's grandmother tells her of her love for baseball and the day they let her play in the game even though she was a girl.
"Johnson tempers what could have been a sentimental tale with Grandmama's contagious enthusiasm and sense of empowerment, and her text has a baseball announcer's suspenseful rhythm. . . . Peck's angular pastels . . . skillfully capture the nostalgic sports action and celebration." Booklist

Lottie Paris lives here; illustrated by Scott Fischer. Simon & Schuster Books for Young Readers 2011 un il $16.99
Grades: PreK K 1 2   E
    1. Parks -- Fiction 2. Houses -- Fiction
    ISBN 978-0-689-87377-5; 0-689-87377-8
"Award-winning author Angela Johnson and illustrator Scott Fischer take you inside the mind of a spunky girl and the imaginative world she lives in with this . . . story now available as a Classic Board Book. Lottie Paris may be precocious, but she still knows how to act like a kid. She dresses up, plays on the slide, and prefers to eat cookies instead of vegetables." (Publisher's note)
"Lottie Paris is an exuberant, imaginative, and mischievous girl. . . . Fischer's large gouache images created with brayer, linocut, stamping, airbrush, sandpaper and brush line are endearing. . . . A universal story told through the eyes of a vivacious youngster." SLJ

Wind flyers; illustrated by Loren Long. Simon & Schuster 2006 un il $16.99
Grades: K 1 2 3   E
    1. Air pilots -- Fiction 2. African Americans -- Fiction 3. World War, 1939-1945 -- Fiction
    ISBN 0-689-84879-X
"In spare, poetic lines, a young African American boy introduces his great-great-uncle, who was a Tuskegee airman.

... Johnson introduces the history in oblique, pared-down words. . . . Long's acrylics beautifully extend the evocative words." Booklist

Johnson, Angela, 1961-

★ **All** different now; Juneteenth, the first day of freedom. Angela Johnson; illustrated by E.B. Lewis. Simon & Schuster Books for Young Readers 2014 40 p. (hardcover) $17.99

Grades: K 1 2 3 4   E

1. Juneteenth 2. Slaves -- Emancipation 3. African Americans -- History 4. Slavery -- Fiction 5. Juneteenth -- Fiction 6. African Americans -- Fiction 7. Family life -- Texas -- Fiction 8. Texas -- History -- 1865-1950 -- Fiction

ISBN 068987376X; 9780689873768

LC 2011038273

Written by Angela Johnson and illustrated by E. B. Lewis, "'All Different Now' tells the story of the first Juneteenth, the day freedom finally came to the last of the slaves in the South. Since then, the observance of June 19 as African American Emancipation Day has spread across the United States and beyond." (Publisher's note)

"In exquisite, lyrical text, Johnson reimagines Juneteenth--the date slaves in Texas finally learned of their emancipation--from the perspective of one fictional family. The words build to a crescendo of emotions as these now-free people prepare for a new life. Lewis's soft watercolors mirror the emotion of the text--the sun reflects off the grateful faces, eyes face the future with clarity." Horn Book

Johnson, Crockett

★ **Harold** and the purple crayon. Harper & Row 1955 un il $15.99; lib bdg $15.89; pa $6.99

Grades: PreK K   E

1. Drawing -- Fiction

ISBN 0-06-022935-7; 0-06-022936-5 lib bdg; 0-06-443022-7 pa

"As Harold goes for a moonlight walk, he uses his purple crayon to draw a path and the things he sees along the way, then draws himself back home." Hodges. Books for Elem Sch Libr

Other titles about Harold are:
Harold's ABC (1963)
Harold's circus (1959)
Harold's fairy tale (1986)
Harold's trip to the sky (1957)
A picture for Harold's room (1960)

Johnson, D. B., 1944-

Magritte's marvelous hat; a picture book. by D.B. Johnson. Houghton Mifflin Harcourt 2012 32 p.

Grades: K 1 2 3 4   E

1. Hats -- Fiction 2. Dogs -- Fiction 3. Picture books for children 4. Magic -- Fiction 5. Painting, French -- Fiction

ISBN 9780547558646

LC 2011012242

This picture book "recasts René Magritte as a dapper, blue-eyed hound and incorporates the painter's surreal iconography. . . . The black bowler hat (a familiar, recurrent image in Magritte's paintings) is characterized as a playful muse, engaging the artist in frisky games on walks." Author/illustrator D.B. Johnson depicts the story with "surreal elements," including "four see-through acetate pages . . . [that] transform adjacent spreads," and images inspired by famous Magritte paintings. (Kirkus

Johnson, David

Snow sounds; an onomatopoeic story. [by] David A. Johnson. Houghton Mifflin Company 2006 un il $16

Grades: PreK K 1   E

1. Snow 2. Sound

ISBN 978-0-618-47310-6; 0-618-47310-6

LC 2006-00333

A nearly-wordless book in which a young boy, eager to reach a much-anticipated holiday party on time, listens to the sounds of the shovels, snow plow, and other equipment used to clear his way.

"Full-bleed watercolor spreads capture the light of a wintry morning perfectly. . . . This accomplished offering has a variety of uses and will appeal to a wide age range." SLJ

Johnson, Dinah

★ **Black** magic; illustrated by R. Gregory Christie. Henry Holt and Co. 2010 un il $15.99

Grades: PreK K 1 2   E

1. Black 2. African Americans -- Fiction

ISBN 978-0-8050-7833-6; 0-8050-7833-9

LC 2009-9219

"This expressive book combines well-matched text and pictures to pay tribute to the myriad qualities of blackness. Buoyant yet reflective, Johnson's . . . free-flowing verse presents an imaginative girl's musings on the essence of black, which she sees as containing multitudinous, even oppositional, dimensions. . . . With vibrant colors offsetting velvety black images, Christie's . . . acrylic gouache illustrations playfully tweak perspective and scale, echoing the verse's energy and fluidity." Publ Wkly

Johnson, Donald B.

★ **Henry** hikes to Fitchburg; [by] D. B. Johnson. Houghton Mifflin 2000 un il $16; pa $6.95

Grades: PreK K 1 2   E

1. Authors 2. Naturalists 3. Essayists 4. Pacifists 5. Bears -- Fiction 6. Nature -- Fiction 7. Writers on nature 8. Nonfiction writers 9. Walking -- Fiction

ISBN 0-395-96867-4; 0-618-73749-9 pa

LC 99-35302

While his friend works hard to earn the train fare to Fitchburg, Henry the bear walks the thirty miles through woods and fields, enjoying nature and the time to think great thoughts. Includes biographical information about Henry David Thoreau

"This splendid book works on several levels. Johnson's adaption of a paragraph taken from Thoreau's Walden (set down in an author's note) illuminates the contrast between materialistic and naturalistic views of life without ranting or preaching. His illustrations are breathtakingly rich and filled with lovingly rendered details." Booklist

Other titles about Henry the bear are:
Henry builds a cabin (2002)
Henry climbs a mountain (2003)
Henry works (2004)
Henry's night (2009)

Johnson, Lindsay Lee

Ten moonstruck piglets; illustrated by Carll Cneut. Clarion Books 2011 un il $16.99

Grades: PreK K 1 2   **E**

1. Counting 2. Stories in rhyme 3. Moon -- Fiction 4. Pigs -- Fiction

ISBN 0-618-86866-6; 978-0-618-86866-7

LC 2010-05443

On the night of the full moon, ten piglets go out adventuring while their mother is fast asleep. "Ages four to seven." (Bull Cent Child Books)

"The precise yet playful verse sets the tone and creates the story's structure. Cneut's acrylic paintings give individual traits to the piglets, create a magical moonlit setting, and brilliantly transform it when the moon disappears. . . . An amusing romp and a great opportunity to practice counting from 1 to 10." Booklist

Johnson, Paul Brett

★ **On** top of spaghetti; written and illustrated by Paul Brett Johnson; with lyrics by Tom Glazer. Scholastic Press 2006 un il $15.99

Grades: PreK K 1 2   **E**

1. Songs 2. Dogs -- Fiction 3. Animals -- Fiction 4. Meatballs -- Fiction

ISBN 0-439-74944-1

LC 2005-14311

"Expanding on the popular song, Johnson spins the tale of Yodeler Jones, a hound dog who serves nothing but meatballs and spaghetti at his dining establishment. When business begins to slow, Yodeler concocts a brand-new meatball, but before he can taste it, someone sneezes. . . . With original text printed in black and the lyrics sprinkled throughout in color, this story successfully marries the two. The loony illustrations, full of color and movement, effectively capture the zaniness." SLJ

Johnston, Lynn

Farley follows his nose; story by Lynn Johnston & Beth Cruikshank; illustrations by Lynn Johnston. Bowen Press 2009 un il $17.99

Grades: PreK K 1   **E**

1. Dogs -- Fiction 2. Smell -- Fiction

ISBN 978-0-06-170234-1; 0-06-170234-X

LC 2008-24713

Farley the dog follows his nose from one good smell to another all over town.

"Big-eyed, energetic Farley and his 'sniff snorfle SNUFF' nose will be a big hit with storytimers, and it won't matter a bit that they're too young to recognize the characters. A great addition to storytimes on baths, senses and dogs." Kirkus

Johnston, Tony

The **cat** with seven names; Tony Johnston; illustrated by Christine Davenier. Charlesbridge 2013 36 p. (reinforced for library use) $16.95

Grades: K 1 2 3   **E**

1. Picture books for children 2. Cats -- Fiction 3. Loneliness -- Fiction

ISBN 1580893813; 9781580893817; 9781607346029

LC 2012024434

This picture book shows "six lonely people [who] welcome a large, fat cat into their lives, each giving the feline a

different name and enjoying his company for a while. There is a librarian who loves to read . . . , an old man with a walker, a Latino man and his dog, a policewoman, a homeless ex-soldier, and a mother and her daughter who are new to the area." Ultimately, the cat is found by his owner, but not before all the lonely people have met and begun friendships. (School Library Journal)

★ **Levi** Strauss gets a bright idea or; the positively true and unfabricated story of a pair of pants. written by Tony Johnston; illustrated by Stacy Innerst. Houghton Mifflin Harcourt 2011 il $16.99

Grades: PreK K 1 2   **E**

1. Tall tales 2. California -- Fiction 3. Jeans (Clothing) -- Fiction 4. Clothing industry executives 5. Clothing and dress -- Fiction 6. Gold mines and mining -- Fiction

ISBN 978-0-15-206145-6; 0-15-206145-2

LC 2010043402

Retells, in tall-tale fashion, how Levi Strauss went to California during the Gold Rush, saw the need for a sturdier kind of trouser, and invented jeans.

"Johnston creates an unrepentantly exaggerated version of events that is sure to entertain, offering more factual information about Strauss in an author's note. Using a bright idea of his own, Innerst . . . chronicles the raucous action in acrylic paintings on a canvas of, yes, old Levi's jeans. The denim's texture provides an appropriately rugged tone to the colorful proceedings." Kirkus

★ **My** abuelita; written by Tony Johnston; illustrated by Yuyi Morales; photographed by Tim O'Meara. Harcourt Children's Books 2009 un il $16

Grades: 1 2 3   **E**

1. Grandmothers -- Fiction 2. Storytelling -- Fiction 3. Spanish language -- Vocabulary

ISBN 978-0-15-216330-3; 0-15-216330-1

ALA ALSC Belpre Illustrator Medal Honor Book (2010)

"A boy describes the morning routine he shares with his grandmother as she prepares for work. Flights of fancy enliven the tasks of bathing, eating breakfast, and dressing. When the pair arrive at her workplace, readers discover that Abuelita is a storyteller—a calling that her grandson shares. Spanish words are sprinkled throughout, often followed by brief definitions. . . . Johnston effectively engages young readers' interest. . . . Morales's bold, innovative illustrations brilliantly reinforce the text. . . . Characters molded from polymer clay are dressed in brightly patterned fabrics and placed among images that evoke Mexican art." SLJ

Uncle Rain Cloud; illustrated by Fabricio Vanden Broeck. Charlesbridge Pub. 2001 un il $15.95; pa $7.95

Grades: PreK K 1 2   **E**

1. Uncles 2. English language 3. Mexican Americans 4. Uncles -- Fiction 5. English language -- Fiction 6. Mexican Americans -- Fiction

ISBN 0-88106-371-1; 0-88106-372-X pa

LC 99-54195

Carlos tries to help his uncle, who is frustrated and angry at his inability to speak English, adjust to their new home in Los Angeles

"Brisk pacing, sympathetic characters, and clear prose that uses embedded Spanish words effectively make a winner. VandenBroeck's acrylic and colored-pencil illustrations flesh out the narrative in soft, bright colors enhanced by dramatic shading." SLJ

Winter is coming; Tony Johnston; illustrated by Jim LaMarche. Simon & Schuster Books for Young Readers 2014 40 p. col. ill. (hard cover: alk. paper) $17.99
Grades: PreK K 1 2 3   E
    1. Winter -- Fiction 2. Seasons -- Fiction 3. Autumn -- Fiction 4. Forest animals -- Fiction
    ISBN 1442472510; 9781442472518
                         LC 2012040457
In this children's book by Tony Johnston, illustrated by Jim LaMarche, "Day after day, a girl goes to her favorite place in the woods and quietly watches from her tree house as the chipmunks, the doe, the rabbits prepare for the winter. As the temperature drops, sunset comes earlier and a new season begins. Silently she observes the world around her as it reveals its secrets. It takes time and patience to see the changes as, slowly but surely, winter comes." (Publisher's note)
"On a cold September day, a girl takes her binoculars, sketch pad, and pencils outdoors to draw the wildlife around her family's farm. She returns several times before late November, when the first snowflakes fall...Winter may be in the title, but this evocative picture book is best for reading aloud in the fall, when children can notice the subtle changes happening in their own outdoor spaces. A quiet, beautiful picture book to share." Booklist

Jonas, Ann
    The **quilt**. Greenwillow Bks. 1984 un il $16.99
Grades: PreK K 1 2   E
    1. Quilts -- Fiction
    ISBN 0-688-03825-5
                         LC 83-25385
"The intricate illustrations in Jonas's book can be described only in superlatives. Backed by a length of golden-yellow calico imprinted with small red flowers, a quilt fashioned from squares in a variety of colors is the prize shown to readers by a dear little girl." Publ Wkly

    Round trip. Greenwillow Bks. 1983 un il $15.99; pa $5.99
Grades: PreK K 1 2   E
    1. City and town life -- Fiction
    ISBN 0-688-01772-X; 0-688-09986-6 pa
                         LC 82-12026
Black and white illustrations and text record the sights on a day trip to the city and back home again to the country. The trip to the city is read from front to back and the return trip, from back to front, upside down
"Although one or two pictures too easily suggest their upside-down images and the device is occasionally strained, the author-artist displays a fine sense of graphic design and balance, and pictorial beauty is never sacrificed for mere cleverness." Horn Book

    ★ **Splash!** Greenwillow Bks. 1995 un il $16.99; pa $6.99
Grades: PreK K 1 2   E
    1. Counting 2. Animals -- Fiction
    ISBN 0-688-11051-7; 0-688-15284-8 pa
                         LC 94-4110

A little girl's turtle, fish, frogs, dog, and cat jump in and out of a backyard pond, constantly changing the answer to the question "How many are in my pond?"
"A clever concept book with physical humor and exciting acrylic paintings that capture the heat and drama of a sunny summer day." Booklist

Joosse, Barbara M.
    Friends (mostly) by Barbara Joosse; illustrated by Tomaso Milian. Greenwillow Books 2010 un il $16.99
Grades: K 1 2 3   E
    1. Friendship -- Fiction
    ISBN 978-0-06-088222-8; 0-06-088222-0
                         LC 2009-34951
Henry and Ruby are best friends forever, even though they do not always get along.
"This title provides an excellent springboard for conversations about friendship. . . . Joosse uses some of the text in a dialogue format, the characters responding as if they were being interviewed, providing this picture book with a pre-chapter-book feel. Sections are loosely separated by a rhyme. Lively watercolor illustrations express the children's moods and provide vibrancy to the theme." SLJ

    Higgledy-piggledy chicks; by Barbara Joosse; pictures by Rick Chrustowski. Greenwillow Books 2010 un il $16.99; lib bdg $17.89
Grades: PreK K 1 2   E
    1. Chickens -- Fiction
    ISBN 978-0-06-075042-8; 0-06-075042-1; 978-0-06-075043-5 lib bdg; 0-06-075043-X lib bdg
                         LC 2007047594
Banty Hen keeps her seven new baby chicks safe, even though they like to go exploring.
"Chrustowski's illustrations—done in colorful torn-paper collages—effectively capture the energy of the roaming and curious chicks. Readers will delight in counting the seven chicks on each spread and in predicting what danger might be hiding on the following page." Booklist

    ★ **Hot** city; by Barbara Joosse; illustrated by R. Gregory Christie. Philomel Books 2004 un il $16.99
Grades: PreK K 1 2   E
    1. Summer -- Fiction 2. Libraries -- Fiction 3. African Americans -- Fiction 4. City and town life -- Fiction
    ISBN 0-399-23640-6
                         LC 2002-1254
Mimi and her little brother Joe escape from home and the city's summer heat to read and dream about princesses and dinosaurs in the cool, quiet library.
"This eloquently told story is boldly illustrated with evocative acrylic paintings in shades of orange, red, and yellow." SLJ

    Lovabye dragon; text by Barbara Joosse; illustrations by Randy Cecil. Candlewick 2012 32 p. (hardback) $15.99
Grades: PreK K 1 2   E
    1. Dragons -- Fiction 2. Picture books for children 3. Friendship 4. Friendship -- Fiction 5. Princesses -- Fiction
    ISBN 0763654086; 9780763654085
                         LC 2011046647
In this children's picture book, "[w]hen the tears of a young princess trickle onto a dragon, a sweet friendship is

born. . . . [Barbara] Joosse creates a friendship born out of loneliness and tears between a young princess who longs for a dragon and a friendly dragon who dreams of a girl for a friend." (Kirkus)

★ **Papa,** do you love me? illustrated by Barbara Laval-lee. Chronicle Books 2005 un il $15.95
Grades: PreK K   E
   1. Africa -- Fiction 2. Masai (African people) -- Fiction
   3. Father-son relationship -- Fiction
   ISBN 0-8118-4265-7
                   LC 2003-17344
When a Masai father in Africa answers his son's questions, the boy learns that his father's love for him is unconditional.

"Echoing the soothing rhythm of the poetic narrative, Lavallee's graceful watercolors feature a harmoniously balanced palette." Publ Wkly

Please is a good word to say; by Barbara Joosse; pictures by Jennifer Plecas. Philomel Books 2007 un il $12.99
Grades: PreK K 1 2   E
   1. Etiquette -- Fiction
   ISBN 978-0-399-24217-5
                   LC 2006034508
Harriet gives examples of polite words and expressions to use in various social situations to make them more pleasant.

"Joosse's effective use of speech bubbles in various fonts, in addition to the main text, makes for especially interesting and amusing reading. Plecas's ink-and-watercolor cartoons imbue the already spirited commentary with personality, dimension, and even more energy." SLJ

Roawr! illustrated by Jan Jutte. Philomel Books 2009 un il $16.99
Grades: PreK K   E
   1. Bears -- Fiction
   ISBN 978-0-399-24777-4; 0-399-24777-7
                   LC 2008-16907
When Liam hears a load roar in the middle of the night, he must use all his ingenuity to protect his sleeping mother from a hungry bear.

"This adrenaline-charged romp is, first and foremost, exciting. Jutte's lively cartoon artwork contrasts muted night colors to form powerful images." SLJ

Sleepover at gramma's house; illustrated by Jan Jutte. Philomel Books 2010 un il $17.99
Grades: PreK K 1   E
   1. Elephants -- Fiction 2. Grandmothers -- Fiction
   ISBN 978-0-399-25261-7; 0-399-25261-4
                   LC 2009-31549
A little girl and her grandmother have a rollicking good time during a sleepover.

"Jutte's illustrations are jam-packed full of details. Readers get a clear sense of the child's excitement and activity level, but they will never lose sight of the relationship being celebrated. The colors in the ink, watercolor and acrylic illustrations lend the artwork a retro feel, and the elephants may remind many readers of Babar." Kirkus

Wind-wild dog; written by Barbara Joosse; illustrated by Kate Kiesler. Henry Holt and Company 2006 un il $16.95
Grades: K 1 2 3   E
   1. Dogs -- Fiction 2. Alaska -- Fiction
   ISBN 978-0-8050-7053-8; 0-8050-7053-2
                   LC 2005020055
Ziva, a "wind-wild" young sled dog, decides whether to stay with the man who has trained her or to run free with the wolves and wind

"In spare, precise prose, Ziva's story drives with understated dramatic tension toward a satisfying conclusion. Kiesler's oil paintings capture the clean beauty of the rural Alaska setting as well as the unique qualities of Ziva and the man." Booklist

Jordan, Deloris
★ **Salt** in his shoes; Michael Jordan in pursuit of a dream. by Deloris Jordan with Roslyn M. Jordan; illustrated by Kadir Nelson. Simon & Schuster Bks. for Young Readers 2000 un il $16.95; pa $7.99
Grades: 2 3 4   E
   1. Basketball 2. Baseball players 3. Olympic athletes
   4. Basketball players
   ISBN 0-689-83371-7; 0-689-83419-5 pa
                   LC 00-20539
"This readable and entertaining story will delight the superstar's fans. Nelson's illustrations bring the right blend of vivid color, realism, and personality." SLJ

Jordan, Sandra
★ **Mr.** and Mrs. Portly and their little dog Snack; pictures by Christine Davenier. Farrar Straus Giroux 2009 un il $16.99
Grades: PreK K 1 2   E
   1. Art -- Fiction 2. Dogs -- Fiction
   ISBN 978-0-374-35089-5; 0-374-35089-2
                   LC 2007046663
Snack is a very happy puppy when Mrs. Portly adopts him but when persnickety Mr. Portly returns from a fishing trip, he banishes Snack to a doghouse until their mutual love of art, and a thief, bring them together.

"Davenport's ink-and-watercolor drawings are a delightful mix of sizes and shapes. . . . Exuding warmth, both narrative and pictures transcend the basic plotline, turning this into an irresistible offering." Booklist

Jordan-Fenton, Christy
Not my girl. Firefly Books Ltd 2014 36 p. $21.95
Grades: 1 2 3 4   E
   1. Native American children 2. Mother-daughter relationship -- Fiction 3. Inuit women -- Biography 4. Inuit -- Cultural assimilation -- Canada
   ISBN 1554516250; 9781554516254
   Sequel to: When I was eight
In this children's book by Christy Jordan-Fenton and Margaret Pokiak-Fenton, illustrated by Gabrielle Grimard, "Two years ago, Margaret left her Arctic home for the outsiders' school. Now she has returned and can barely contain her excitement as she rushes towards her waiting family--but her mother stands still as a stone. This strange, skinny child, with her hair cropped short, can't be her daughter. 'Not my girl!' she says angrily." (Publisher's note)

"A poignant picture book memoir about an Inuit girl reconnecting with her culture...Culturally relevant, accurate, and soft, painterly illustrations depict the sequence of events and reinforce the bittersweet and tender reunion of Olemaun with her family...this is an excellent illustrated biography, overall." SLJ

Joubert, Beverly

African animal alphabet; by Beverly and Dereck Joubert. National Geographic 2011 48p il (National Geographic little kids) $16.95

Grades: PreK K 1 2   E

1. Alphabet 2. Animals -- Africa

ISBN 978-1-4263-0781-2; 1-4263-0781-0

"This alphabet book features vivid photographs of African animals. Readers will recognize a cheetah, elephant, and lion, but this husband-and-wife naturalist team also highlights unsung species like the tsessebe, the umbrette, and the dung beetle. . . . Appended animal facts and a glossary for words like 'vociferous' underscore the book's dual focus on diverse animal characteristics and language development." Publ Wkly

Joyce, William

A **day** with Wilbur Robinson; by William Joyce. Laura Geringer Books 2006 un il $16.99

Grades: PreK K 1 2   E

1. Family life -- Fiction 2. Eccentrics and eccentricities -- Fiction

ISBN 978-0-06-089098-8; 0-06-089098-3

LC 2005037287

An expanded version of the title published 1990

While spending the day in the Robinson household, Wilbur's best friend joins in the search for Grandfather Robinson's missing false teeth and meets one wacky relative after another

"The real fun is in the tension between the deadpan words and the fantastical pictures. . . . Save this for small groups, which will most appreciate the wondrous visual details." Booklist

★ **Dinosaur** Bob and his adventures with the family Lazardo; new ed; HarperCollins Pubs. 1995 un il $16.99

Grades: K 1 2 3   E

1. Dinosaurs -- Fiction

ISBN 0-06-021074-5

LC 94-19100

A revised and enlarged edition of the title first published 1988

"The Lazardo family goes on safari to Africa where they find a dinosaur. They name him Bob and take him back to Pimlico Hills. . . . Bob soon becomes famous because he can play the trumpet, dance, and most importantly play baseball." Child Book Rev Serv [review of 1988 edition]

The **fantastic** flying books of Mr. Morris Lessmore; William Joyce. Atheneum Books for Young Readers 2012 56 p. (hardback) $17.99

Grades: PreK K 1 2 3   E

1. Fantasy 2. Libraries -- Fiction 3. Books and reading -- Fiction

ISBN 1442457023; 9781442457027; 9781442464896

LC 2012004465

This children's picture book "follows a dreamy bibliophile named Morris Lessmore, who loses his cherished book collection to a cataclysmic storm. . . . After meeting a 'lovely lady . . . being pulled along by a festive squadron of flying books,' Morris finds an abandoned library whose books are alive and whose covers beat like the wings of birds. They flutter around him protectively, watch as he starts writing again, and care for him as he ages." (Publishers Weekly)

"The message-heavy narrative is lifted by Joyce's superb artwork, presenting nostalgic, picket-fence scenes with a modeled, dimensional feel built on the animation but given a lustrous polish for the printed page." Booklist

★ **George** shrinks; story and pictures by William Joyce. Harper & Row 1985 un il $16.99; pa $6.99

Grades: K 1 2 3   E

1. Fantasy fiction 2. Size -- Fiction

ISBN 0-06-023070-3; 0-06-443129-0 pa

LC 83-47697

"The colorful illustrations, executed with painstaking attention to detail, create a surreal landscape from an ordinary breakfast-cereal world, as familiar objects become monumental structures through which the diminutive George moves with panache." Horn Book

★ The **Man** in the Moon; edited by Laura Geringer Books. Atheneum Books for Young Readers 2011 un il (Guardians of childhood) $17.99

Grades: K 1 2 3   E

1. Fantasy fiction 2. Moon -- Fiction

ISBN 978-1-4424-3041-9; 1-4424-3041-9

LC 2010053985

When a newly orphaned baby in the moon makes friends with the children of Earth, he begins to shine as brightly as possible to ward off their fears.

This "is a rich, cinematic brew of steampunk fancies. [Joyce's] sumptuous spreads are crowded with rotund telescopes, Jules Verne rocket ships, and sherbet-bearing robots, all painted in a superb palette of indigo and gold. . . . Joyce combines elemental fairyland themes . . . into a tale that's warm and fuzzy, swashbuckling, and dazzling inventive all at the same time." Publ Wkly

Joyner, Andrew

Boris for the win; Andrew Joyner. Branches 2013 73 p. (Boris) $15.99

Grades: PreK K 1 2   E

1. Racing -- Fiction 2. Schools -- Fiction 3. Warthogs -- Fiction 4. Friendship -- Fiction 5. Schools -- fiction 6. Running races -- fiction 7. Competition (Psychology) -- Fiction

ISBN 0545484480; 9780545484480; 9780545484497

LC 2012046575

In this book, by Andrew Joyner, "it's Field Day, and Boris is ready to run like he's never run before. All he wants is to beat Eddie, who always wins everything. And all his friend Frederick wants is not to come in last...again. Who will make it across the finish line first? And when Boris is faced with a big decision, will he go for the gold or help a friend in need?" (Publisher's note)

Boris on the move; Andrew Joyner. Branches 2013 80 p. ill. (Boris) (library) $15.99

Grades: PreK K 1 2   E

1. Picture books for children 2. Voyages and travels
Fiction 3. Parks -- Fiction 4. Warthog -- Fiction 5.
Natural areas -- Fiction 6. Parks -- Fiction
ISBN 0545484421; 9780545484428

LC 2012034254

In this book, "Boris, a not-particularly-attractive hog,
is frustrated. Although he and his parents live in a bus that
once took them on fabulous vacations, now the old vehicle
is permanently parked, and he longs for adventure. Finally,
his empathetic parents fire up the engine to bring him on
a journey that, it disappointingly turns out, is only across
town to a nature preserve." Boris still manages to get lost.
(Kirkus Reviews)

Juan, Ana

The **Night** Eater; by Ana Juan. Arthur A. Levine
Books 2004 un il $16.95
Grades: K 1 2 3   E

1. Night -- Fiction
ISBN 0-439-48891-5

LC 2003-20197

The Night Eater, who brings each new day by gobbling
up the darkness, decides he is too fat and stops eating, with
dire consequences

"The sense of magic realism in this story is matched by
in Juan's richly colored acrylic-and-wax paintings. . . . This
delightful tale will definitely appeal to children's imaginations." SLJ

The **pet** shop revolution. Arthur A. Levine 2011
un il
Grades: 1 2 3   E

1. Pets -- Fiction 2. Animals -- Fiction 3. Animal
rescue -- Fiction
ISBN 0-545-12810-2; 978-0-545-12810-0

LC 2010051325

Everyone is afraid of Mr. Walnut, the scowling owner of
the biggest pet store in the city, who sells all kinds of animals
to rich customers from out of town, but when Mina's pet rabbit goes missing she vows to do something about it.

"This intriguing and thought-provoking tale skillfully illustrates the benevolence that is born when one walks in the
shoes of another. It may also generate some activist thinking
among young readers. . . . Juan's beautifully stylized and
deeply expressive acrylic and colored pencil drawings perfectly capture the somber tone that prevails throughout most
of the book." SLJ

Judge, Lita

Flight school; by Lita Judge. Atheneum Books for
Young Readers 2014 40 p. (hardcover) $16.99
Grades: PreK K 1 2   E

1. Animal flight 2. Flight -- Fiction 3. Penguins --
Fiction
ISBN 1442481773; 9781442481770

LC 2012046161

In this book, by Lita Judge, "a persevering penguin is
determined to fly. . . . Although little Penguin has the soul of
an eagle, his body wasn't built to soar. But Penguin has an
irrepressible spirit, and he adamantly follows his dreams to
flip, flap, fly! Even if he needs a little help with the technical parts, this penguin is ready to live on the wind." (Publisher's note)

"Penguin leaves the South Pole for flight school. Though
the other birds are skeptical, Penguin is determined. When
instead of soaring he plunges into the ocean, Penguin sadly
admits defeat and gets ready to head home. Then Flamingo
has an idea. Variations in perspective throughout Judge's
soft watercolor and pencil illustrations add visual interest
to the book, as do parts told entirely through the pictures."
Horn Book

Pennies for elephants. Hyperion Books for Children
2009 un il $16.99
Grades: PreK K 1 2   E

1. Zoos -- Fiction 2. Elephants -- Fiction 3. Boston
(Mass.) -- Fiction
ISBN 978-1-4231-1390-4; 1-4231-1390-X

"In 1914, the children of Boston raised $6,000 to buy
three trained elephants for the Franklin Park Zoo. But told
through the eyes of siblings (and fund-raisers) Dorothy and
Henry, the story expands into an inspired celebration of kid
power. . . . Dollops of historical flavor abound, with watercolors of knickers-clad boys and streets bustling with people, horses and horseless carriages. Warm sepia tones lend
atmosphere." Publ Wkly

Red hat; Lita Judge. Atheneum Books for Young Readers 2013 40 p. (hardcover) $16.99
Grades: PreK K 1 2   E

1. Picture books for children 2. Hats -- Fiction 3. Forest
animals -- Fiction 4. Animals -- Infancy -- Fiction
ISBN 1442442328; 9781442442320; 9781442442337

LC 2012002600

In this children's picture book story, by Lita Judge, "it's
spring-cleaning time now, so the child washes the red hat and
hangs it out to dry. . . . When the critters spy the hat pinned
to the line, . . . an energetic game of keep-away breaks out,
with the accompanying sounds and exclamations of pursuit
and merriment. . . . [Until] the animals' realiz[e] that the hat
is now just one long red strand of yarn with a white pompom
on the end." (Kirkus)

★ **Red** sled. Atheneum Books for Young Readers 2011
un il $16.99
Grades: PreK K 1 2   E

1. Sounds -- Fiction 2. Sledding -- Fiction 3. Forest
animals -- Fiction
ISBN 978-1-4424-2007-6; 1-4424-2007-3

LC 2010033264

At night, a host of woodland creatures plays with a
child's red sled.

"The premise of this book is simple; the execution is
anything but. . . . Pencil and watercolor spreads create a basic wintry mountain environment, but the stars of the show
are the expressive animals. Their childlike delight in each
dynamic scene brings a sense of excitement to the story. The
text consists entirely of sound effects, laid out on the page
in varying font sizes to evoke a sense of movement." SLJ

Jules, Jacqueline

Duck for Turkey Day; illustrated by Kathryn Mitter.
Albert Whitman 2009 un il $16.99
Grades: K 1 2 3   E

1. School stories 2. Thanksgiving Day -- Fiction 3.

Vietnamese Americans -- Fiction
ISBN 978-0-8075-1734-5; 0-8075-1734-8
LC 2008055537

When Tuyet finds out that her Vietnamese family is having duck rather than turkey for Thanksgiving dinner, she is upset until she finds out that other children in her class did not eat turkey either.

"Mitter's acrylic illustrations, in clear bright colors and simple shapes, capture the warmth of the holiday bustle and the affection among family members." Booklist

Juster, Norton

★ The **hello,** goodbye window; story by Norton Juster; pictures by Chris Raschka. Hyperion Books for Children 2005 un il $15.95
Grades: PreK K 1 2   **E**
1. Grandparents -- Fiction
ISBN 0-7868-0914-0
Awarded the Caldecott Medal, 2006

"The window in Nanna and Poppy's kitchen is no ordinary window—it is the place where love and magic happens. . . . The first-person text is both simple and sophisticated, conjuring a perfectly child-centered world. . . . Using a bright rainbow palette of saturated color, Raschka's impressionistic, mixed-media illustrations portray a loving, mixed-race family." SLJ

Another title about Nanna and Poppy and their granddaughter is:
Sourpuss and Sweetie Pie (2008)

★ **Neville**; [illustrations by G. Brian Karas] Schwartz & Wade Books 2011 un il $17.99; lib bdg $20.99
Grades: PreK K 1 2   **E**
1. Moving -- Fiction
ISBN 978-0-375-86765-1; 0-375-86765-1; 978-0-375-96765-8 lib bdg; 0-375-96765-6 lib bdg
LC 2010024119

When a boy and his family move to a new house, he devises an ingenious way to meet people in the neighborhood.

This is an "emotionally authentic tale. . . . Karas's melancholy illustrations brighten and expand as the mood improves; small, quiet type sets the sullen tone, until colorful hand-lettered display type implies the children's collective chatter. . . . Juster . . . identifies a common, stressful situation, and Karas handles the drama with compassion." Publ Wkly

★ The **odious** Ogre; story by Norton Juster; pictures by Jules Feiffer. Michael Di Capua Books 2010 un il $17.95
Grades: K 1 2 3   **E**
1. Fairy tales 2. Monsters -- Fiction
ISBN 978-0-545-16202-9; 0-545-16202-5

An ogre "rampages through the countryside, terrorizing (and eating) the residents with impunity. Until, that is, he is utterly 'confounded, overcome, and undone' by the unexpected kindness and friendly advice of a young woman. . . . Kids might not pick up on all of the philosophical overtones, but they're sure to enjoy Juster's rich wordplay and happily ridiculous story and Feiffer's wonderfully scratchy and energetic watercolors." Kirkus

Kain, Karen

The **Nutcracker**; paintings by Rajka Kupesic. Tundra Books 2005 un il $18.95

Grades: K 1 2 3   **E**
1. Fairy tales 2. Christmas -- Fiction
ISBN 0-88776-696-X

This is a "striking staging of the classic ballet. . . . The narrative reads smoothly, but it's the art that steals the show. Peopled with doll-like folk-art figures, Kupesic's full-page illustrations . . . are intense with luminous colors." Booklist

Kalan, Robert

★ **Jump,** frog, jump! pictures by Byron Baron. Greenwillow Books 1995 un il $16.99; pa $6.99
Grades: PreK K 1   **E**
1. Stories in rhyme 2. Frogs -- Fiction
ISBN 0-688-13954-X; 0-688-09241-1 pa
A reissue of the title first published 1981

"When a frog catches a fly, he sets off a chain of predators. . . . The title answers the repeated refrain 'How did the frog get away?' and children will soon be chanting along with this cumulative tale enhanced by Barton's folk-art-style illustrations." Publ Wkly

Kanevsky, Polly

Sleepy boy; illustrated by Stephanie Anderson. Atheneum Books for Young Readers 2006 un il $15.95
Grades: PreK K   **E**
1. Bedtime -- Fiction 2. Father-son relationship -- Fiction
ISBN 0-689-86735-2

Unable to fall asleep, a little boy lying next to his father experiences the various sensations of his body and remembers a lion cub he saw that day at the zoo

"Simple, physical words and full-page, unframed, sepia-toned watercolor-and-charcoal images combine to create a portrait of blissful intimacy between a toddler and his father." Booklist

Kang, Anna

You are (not) small; by Anna Kang; illustrated by Christopher Weyant. Two Lions 2014 32 p. color illustrations (trade pbk) $16.99
Grades: PreK K 1 2   **E**
1. Size 2. Animals -- Fiction
ISBN 9781477847725; 1477847723
LC 2013958332
Theodor Seuss Geisel Award (2015)

In this children's book by Anna Kang, "two bears argue about perspective. Each is convinced that the other is big or small in comparison to him and his friends ('I am not small. You are big.'; 'I am not big. See?'). Each group argues, until two other creatures (one even bigger and one even smaller) come along and shows them that they can be both big and small at the same time." (School Library Journal)

"While the story itself seems simple, the concepts are pertinent to several important social issues such as bullying and racism, as well as understanding point of view. Charming characters, a clever plot and a quiet message tucked inside a humorous tale." Kirkus

Kanninen, Barbara J.

A **story** with pictures; story by Barbara Kanninen; pictures by Lynn Rowe Reed. Holiday House 2007 un il $16.95
Grades: PreK K 1 2   **E**
1. Authorship -- Fiction 2. Illustration of books --

Fiction

ISBN 978-0-8234-2049-0; 0-8234-2049-3

LC 2006019535

An author forgets to give her manuscript to an illustrator who begins to paint whatever she herself wants, making the author a character in the book, along with a meddlesome duck and other creatures

Reed's "mixed-media compositions expertly contain the antic action. . . . The artist renders the characters in a childlike style, painting them with skewered proportions and in gumdrop-colored clothes, and enhances her spreads with collage elements. . . . Readers will enjoy the wild ride." Publ Wkly

Kantorovitz, Sylvie

★ The **very** tiny baby; Sylvie Kantorovitz. Charlesbridge 2014 32 p. (reinforced for library use) $14.95

Grades: PreK K 1 2   E

1. Infants -- Fiction 2. Jealousy -- Fiction 3. Teddy bears -- Fiction 4. Sibling rivalry -- Fiction 5. Premature babies -- Fiction 6. Jealousy in children -- Fiction

ISBN 1580894453; 9781580894456; 9781607346357

LC 2012038697

In this book, by Sylvie Kantorovitz, "Jacob learns that adults can be scared, too, when his new sibling is born prematurely. While Jacob has his grandma and his faithful teddy bear, Bob, with him at home while his parents are at the hospital, he still feels alone. The Book portrays the range of emotions older siblings often have about a new baby, including fear, anger, and resentment, along with the added challenges of the preemie's health concerns and parents' frequent absences." (Publisher's note)

"Jacob's parents are excited about their expected baby, but the child isn't so sure he wants to share the limelight. Then when the infant arrives too early and everyone-even grandma-is so preoccupied with its survival that they don't pay much attention to him, he's certain that the new baby is a bad idea... Pumping of breast milk, hospital visit precautions, and care of preemies are all depicted. This story can provide information and comfort to youngsters experiencing worry about a sibling born prematurely or even for those who are preparing to share parents with a new brother or sister." SLJ

Kaplan, Bruce Eric

★ **Monsters** eat whiny children. Simon & Schuster Books for Young Readers 2010 un il $15.99

Grades: PreK K 1   E

1. Cooking -- Fiction 2. Monsters -- Fiction 3. Siblings -- Fiction

ISBN 1-4169-8689-8; 978-1-4169-8689-8

LC 2008-50434

Henry and Eve, having ignored their father's warning, are kidnapped by monsters who eat whiny children, but while increasing numbers of monsters argue over how to prepare them, the siblings begin to play nicely. Includes a recipe for cucumber sandwiches.

"For those who like their picture books with a little edge and offbeat humor, this is a surefire hit. . . . Kaplan's minimalist cartoon illustrations bring to mind Quentin Blake's work and complement the humorous, quirky text with its askew frames, thick black lines, and color accents." SLJ

Kaplan, Michael B.

Betty Bunny didn't do it; written by Michael B. Kaplan; illustrated by Stéphane Jorisch. Dial Books for Young Readers 2013 32 p. (hardcover) $16.99

Grades: PreK K 1   E

1. Honesty 2. Rabbits -- Fiction 3. Conduct of life -- Fiction 4. Blame -- Fiction 5. Honesty -- Fiction 6. Behavior -- Fiction 7. Family life -- Fiction

ISBN 0803738587; 9780803738584

LC 2012014367

In this children's book, by Michael Kaplan, illustrated by Stephanie Jorisch, "the value of honesty as seen through the eyes of a . . . precocious preschooler. When Betty Bunny breaks a lamp, she blames it on the Tooth Fairy. Blaming someone else for something she had done seems like such a good idea to Betty Bunny. . . . But when a vase gets broken, everyone blames Betty Bunny, and no one believes her when she says that she really didn't do it." (Publisher's note)

"With humor and some delightful twists, Betty Bunny learns the importance of telling the truth. The peppy ink and watercolor illustrations give Betty and her siblings lots of personality." Horn Book

Betty Bunny did not do it

★ **Betty** Bunny loves chocolate cake; pictures by Stephane Jorisch. Dial Books for Young Readers 2011 un il $16.99

Grades: PreK K 1   E

1. Cake -- Fiction 2. Food -- Fiction 3. Rabbits -- Fiction 4. Family life -- Fiction

ISBN 978-0-8037-3407-4; 0-8037-3407-7

LC 2010-28799

From her first bite, young Betty Bunny likes chocolate cake so much that she claims she will marry it one day, and she has trouble learning to wait patiently until she can have her next taste.

"Readers will delight in feeling older and wiser than Betty, and both Jorisch . . . and debut talent Kaplan demonstrate a sure handle on feisty modern family dynamics." Publ Wkly

Karas, G. Brian

The **Village** Garage. Henry Holt and Company 2010 un il $16.99

Grades: PreK K 1 2 3   E

1. Garages -- Fiction 2. Seasons -- Fiction 3. City and town life -- Fiction

ISBN 0-8050-8716-8; 978-0-8050-8716-1

LC 2009009223

Throughout the seasons the workers at the Village Garage are busy taking care of the town and its residents.

"Adding bits of fun along the way, the simple text explains [the workers'] tasks without too much detail. Nicely varied in composition, the appealing pencil, gouache, and acrylic illustrations offer wonderfully childlike depictions of the workers and their machines." Booklist

Kargman, Jill

Pirates & Princesses; by Jill Kargman & Sadie Kargman; illustrated by Christine Davenier. Dutton Childrens Books 2011 il $16.99

Grades: PreK K 1 2   E

1. School stories 2. Play -- Fiction 3. Sex role -- Fiction

4. Friendship -- Fiction 5. Kindergarten -- Fiction
ISBN 978-0-525-42229-7; 0-525-42229-3

LC 2011005191

Ivy and Fletch have been best friends since they were born but now, at age five, the boys in their kindergarten play Pirates at recess while the girls play Princesses, and the duo is split apart.

"The mother-and-daughter team tells the story, but it's Davenier's energetic pencil-and-watercolor illustrations that give the story its heart. . . . Though the story ends as expected, it's nice to see that they figure out things for themselves, with no adult intervention, giving young readers some good ideas for when gender roles exert themselves in school. Teachers especially will turn to this good-natured story; it will help open up a discussion about friendship that many children will profit from." Kirkus

Kasbarian, Lucine

The **greedy** sparrow; an Armenian tale. illustrated by Maria Zaikina. Marshall Cavendish 2011 un il $17.99
Grades: PreK K 1 2   E
1. Birds -- Fiction 2. Folklore -- Armenia
ISBN 978-0-7614-5821-0; 0-7614-5821-2

LC 2010-18172

A sparrow who is treated kindly by strangers repays each act of kindness with a trick to get more. Will the sparrow's greed get the best of him?

"Zaikina's expressive portrayals of both animal and human characters, rendered in bold outline and rich color, beautifully convey the tale's goofy fun. Her use of wax and oil paint in a kind of scratchboard technique smartly blends folk and cartoon styles." SLJ

Kasza, Keiko

★ The **dog** who cried wolf; [by] Keiko Kasza. G.P. Putnam's Sons 2005 un il $15.99; pa $6.99
Grades: K 1 2 3   E
1. Dogs -- Fiction 2. Wolves -- Fiction
ISBN 0-399-24247-3; 0-14-241305-4 pa

LC 2004-24737

Tired of being a house pet, Moka the dog moves to the mountains to become a wolf but soon misses the comforts of home.

"With an effective variety of page layouts, the expressive pen-and-watercolor pictures show [Moka] dashing off on his adventures. . . . Thanks to excellent pacing, children will get caught up in the childlike Moka's emotions." SLJ

★ **My** lucky day. Putnam 2003 un il $15.99; pa $5.99
Grades: PreK K 1 2   E
1. Pigs -- Fiction 2. Foxes -- Fiction
ISBN 0-399-23874-3; 0-14-240456-X pa

LC 2001-57874

When a young pig knocks on a fox's door, the fox thinks dinner has arrived, but the pig has other plans

"Kasza's gouache art is as buoyant and comical as her narrative." Publ Wkly

Ready for anything. G.P. Putnam's Sons 2009 un il $16.99
Grades: PreK K 1 2   E
1. Ducks -- Fiction 2. Worry -- Fiction 3. Raccoons

-- Fiction
ISBN 978-0-399-25235-8; 0-399-25235-5

LC 2008033615

Raccoon is nervous about all of the things that could spoil a picnic, from bees to dragons, until Duck convinces him that surprises can be fun.

"The characters' dialogue is lively and fun to read aloud; Kasza's affable gouache illustrations spotlight action and emotions." Horn Book

★ The **wolf's** chicken stew. Putnam 1987 un il $16.99; pa $6.99
Grades: K 1 2 3   E
1. Wolves -- Fiction 2. Chickens -- Fiction
ISBN 0-399-21400-3; 0-399-22000-9 pa

LC 86-12303

"Kasza combines quivery line and shaded color to turn Wolf and Chicken into scuptural forms. Landscape images are treated similarly. . . . Wolf is comically and suspensefully visualized, making the flimflamming refrains sound just right." Wilson Libr Bull

Katz, Alan

Stalling; illustrated by Elwood H. Smith. Margaret K. McElderry Books 2010 un il $16.99
Grades: PreK K 1 2   E
1. Stories in rhyme 2. Bedtime -- Fiction
ISBN 978-1-4169-5567-2; 1-4169-5567-4

"Katz's exuberent, ebulliently punctuated tale is enhanced by Smith's humorous art. Cartoon drawings intermixed with digitally collaged items create a visual rhythm for the catchy rhyme." Kirkus

Katz, Bobbi

Nothing but a dog; illustrated by Jane Manning. Dutton Children's Books 2010 un il $16.99
Grades: PreK K 1 2   E
1. Dogs -- Fiction
ISBN 978-0-525-47858-4; 0-525-47858-2

LC 2009017918

"A young girl wishes for a dog while she engages in everyday activities, exclaiming that once the longing for a pup sets in, nothing stops it. Each page gives examples of other kinds of fun . . . but 'a dog is something else.' Subtle images of canines appear in the delightful watercolor illustrations. . . . This is a sweet addition to the child/pet genre." SLJ

Katz, Karen

How Does Baby Feel? A Karen Katz Lift-the-Flap Book. [Karen Katz] Simon & Schuster Merchandise 2013 14 p. $6.99
Grades: PreK K   E
1. Infants -- Fiction 2. Emotions in children 3. Picture books for children 4. Board books 5. Lift-the-flap books -- Specimens 6. Toy and movable books -- Specimens
ISBN 1442452048; 9781442452046

LC 2012277019

In this book, "'Baby wants milk and crackers. How does baby feel?' Lift the picture of a toddler stretching for the goodies on the counter top of the facing page. Now she's in her high chair enjoying her repast under the word 'Hungry.' 'Baby is yawning. How does baby feel?' The little boy in the stroller is clearly 'Sleepy,' as evidenced by his contented snore as he snoozes beneath the picture flap." (Bulletin of the Center for Children's Literature)

My first Chinese New Year; [by] Karen Katz. H. Holt 2004 un il $14.95
Grades: PreK K   E
   1. Chinese New Year -- Fiction 2. Chinese Americans -- Fiction
ISBN 0-8050-7076-1
                      LC 2003-23488
In this "picture book, a young girl prepares for and celebrates the Chinese New Year with her extended family. . . . The tale radiates warmth. . . . The collage illustrations, cut from paper with colorful Asian designs, also include paint and other media to capture the joyful celebrants." SLJ

My first Ramadan; [by] Karen Katz. Henry Holt & Co. 2007 un il $14.95
Grades: PreK K   E
   1. Muslims -- Fiction 2. Ramadan -- Fiction
ISBN 978-0-8050-7894-7; 0-8050-7894-0
                      LC 2006030768
"A young Muslim boy describes the ways his family celebrates the holy month of Ramadan, explaining some of the rituals and symbols of the holiday. Straightforward, easy-to-read text and bright, friendly collage and mixed-media illustrations make this a solid, approachable resource." Horn Book Guide

Now I'm big; Karen Katz. Margaret K. McElderry Books 2013 32 p. (hardcover) $15.99
Grades: PreK   E
   1. Babies -- Fiction 2. Growth -- Fiction
ISBN 9781416935476
                      LC 2011047256
In this picture book, "a multiracial cast of children who note ways they've grown up from babyhood to toddlers/preschoolers. 'I used to be a baby,' the first speaker begins, setting up a pattern: on each spread, the verso lists something the child did as a baby ('When I was a baby, I had to wear diapers') while the recto offers a contrasting ability of the older child ('NOW I'M BIG! I can wear real underpants and poo in the toilet')." (Bulletin of the Center for Children's Books)

Princess Baby; [by] Karen Katz. Schwartz & Wade Books 2008 un il $14.99; lib bdg $17.99
Grades: PreK   E
   1. Nicknames -- Fiction 2. Princesses -- Fiction
ISBN 978-0-375-84119-4; 0-375-84119-9; 978-0-375-94119-1 lib bdg; 0-375-94119-3 lib bdg
                      LC 2007001913
A little girl does not like any of the nicknames her parents have for her she wants to be called by her "real" name, Princess Baby
"Katz has drawn the human and stuffed-animal characters with perfectly rounded heads, and she uses other softly curving lines in rendering motions. . . . The [predominant] color is fuchsia, while other bright hues complement the rosy tones. . . . Toddlers will ask for repeated readings of this cheerful view of a youngster's world." SLJ
   Other titles about Princess Baby are:
   Princess Baby, night-night (2009)

Princess Baby on the go! (2010)

Ten tiny babies; [by] Karen Katz. Margaret K. McElderry Books 2008 un il $14.99
Grades: PreK K 1   E
   1. Counting 2. Stories in rhyme 3. Infants -- Fiction
ISBN 978-1-4169-3546-9; 1-4169-3546-0
                      LC 2007-36061
Babies from one to ten enjoy a bouncy, noisy, jiggly day until they are finally fast asleep at night
"The second half of every couplet is split by a page turn, providing a gentle tease that encourages readers to flip the page and complete the rhyme. Ideally suited for read-aloud in both cadence and content." Publ Wkly

Katz, Susan
   ABC, baby me! by Susan B. Katz; illustrated by Alicia Padrón. Robin Corey Books 2010 un il bd bk $7.99
Grades: PreK   E
   1. Alphabet 2. Board books for children 3. Infants -- Fiction
ISBN 978-0-375-86679-1 bd bk; 0-375-86679-5 bd bk
"This alphabet book is comprised of activities and actions that are presented from the perspective of several babies. For each letter, a simple scene features a child and caregiver from 'Adore me' to 'Zzzz, I'm fast asleep.' The soft-focus watercolor and pencil artwork is done in a predominately pastel palette. The text is simple with a lilting rhyme scheme that will encourge reading aloud." SLJ

Katō, Yukiko, 1936-
   In the meadow; illustrated by Komako Sakai. Enchanted Lion Books 2011 un il $16.99
Grades: PreK   E
   1. Sound -- Fiction 2. Nature -- Fiction 3. Meadows -- Fiction
ISBN 978-1-59270-108-7; 1-59270-108-6
                      LC 2010051988
A little girl named Yu hears the sounds of nature all around her when she follows a butterfly into a meadow.
This is illustrated with "expressionistic acrylic and oil-pencil illustrations in a palette of soft greens, browns, and blues. . . . With her fascination with nature and her first steps into independence and back again, Yu is a relatable, believable preschooler; and illustrator Sakai . . . eloquently captures the facial expressions and postures of the very young." Horn Book

Kaufman, Elliott, 1946-
   Numbers everywhere; by Elliott Kaufman. 1st ed. Abbeville Kids 2013 32 p. (hardback) $12.95
Grades: PreK K 1   E
   1. Numbers 2. Photography 3. Shape 4. Numbers in art 5. Mathematical notation 6. Photography of mathematical notation
ISBN 0789211572; 9780789211576
                      LC 2013027822
This book, by Elliott Kaufman, "reveals how digits and mathematical symbols can be found in the world around us--if we know how to look for them. Kaufman reveals the 'secret' life of numbers through his photographs, showing how they can be found in things we encounter everyday. Each number is represented by multiple images, unintentionally

created by the intersection of architectural details, shadows, light, or natural elements." (Publisher's note)

Kay, Verla

Covered wagons, bumpy trails; illustrated by S.D. Schindler. Putnam 2000 un il $15.99
Grades: K 1 2 3   E
  1. Stories in rhyme 2. Frontier and pioneer life -- Fiction 3. Overland journeys to the Pacific -- Fiction
  ISBN 0-399-22928-0
                                  LC 96-37478
Illustrations and simple rhyming text follow a family as they make the difficult journey by wagon to a new home across the Rocky Mountains

"Schindler handsomely augments the clip-clop rhyme with sweeping vistas and close-up views of the wagons, animals, and people through various stages of the journey." Horn Book Guide

Hornbooks and inkwells; illustrated by S.D. Schindler. G.P. Putnam's Sons 2011 32p il $16.99
Grades: PreK K   E
  1. School stories 2. Stories in rhyme 3. Frontier and pioneer life -- Fiction
  ISBN 978-0-399-23870-3; 0-399-23870-0
                                  LC 2010-13070
John Paul and his older brother Peter spend a year attending a one-room schoolhouse on the frontier.

"In both text and illustrations, the light narrative element is engaging. . . . Schindler's well-composed watercolor-and-gouache paintings offer appealing glimpses of a period that seems distant while portraying the characters as individuals behaving in ways that are wholly recognizable." Booklist

Keane, Dave

Daddy Adventure Day; illustrated by Sue Ramá. Philomel Books 2011 un il $15.99
Grades: PreK K   E
  1. Baseball -- Fiction 2. Father-son relationship -- Fiction
  ISBN 978-0-399-24627-2; 0-399-24627-4
                                  LC 2010024077
Daddy Adventure Days are always special, and this one, featuring a boy's first visit to a baseball stadium, is no exception.

"Ramá's watercolor and digital collage illustrations capture the warm relationship between the wide-eyed boy and his ever-patient dad. . . . A satisfying story about spending time with loved ones." SLJ

Sloppy Joe; illustrated by Denise Brunkus. Harper 2009 un il $16.99; lib bdg $17.89
Grades: PreK K 1 2   E
  1. Cleanliness -- Fiction
  ISBN 978-0-06-171020-9; 0-06-171020-2; 978-0-06-171021-6 lib bdg; 0-06-171021-0 lib bdg
                                  LC 2008020212
Sloppy Joe determines to do everything he can to surprise his family by becoming Neat Joe.

"The illustrations are hilarious. This charming picture book is a wonderful choice for most libraries." SLJ

Kearney, Meg

Trouper; by Meg Kearney; illustrated by E. B. Lewis. Scholastic Press 2013 32 p. (hardcover: alk. paper) $16.99
Grades: K 1 2 3   E
  1. Animal shelters -- Fiction 2. Dogs -- Fiction 3. Novels in verse 4. Feral dogs -- Fiction 5. Pet adoption -- Fiction
  ISBN 0545100410; 9780545100410
                                  LC 2012015730
This book, by Meg Kearney and illustrated by E. B. Lewis, is the "story of a three-legged stray dog who finds a loving boy to call his own. . . . Trouper ran with a mob of mutts. . . . One day, the dogs are captured from off the streets and put in cages in a shelter as they wait to be adopted. Trouper watches . . . as . . . each of his dog friends are chosen. He's the only one left until finally, one lucky day, just the right boy comes around." (Publisher's note)

"This tender story, sensitively illustrated by Lewis's luminous watercolors, is based on the true story of a rescued dog. Trouper himself narrates in free verse, telling of his life on the street and his desolate days and nights in the pound until he's adopted by a gentle boy who is as "skinny as a string bean." It's all quite heartwarming." (Horn Book)

Keats, Ezra Jack

Apt. 3. Viking 1999 un il hardcover o.p. pa $6.99
Grades: PreK K 1 2   E
  1. Blind -- Fiction 2. Brothers -- Fiction 3. City and town life -- Fiction
  ISBN 0-670-88342-5; 0-14-056507-8 pa
                                  LC 98-41043
A reissue of the title first published 1971 by Macmillan
On a rainy day two brothers try to discover who is playing the harmonica they hear in their apartment building

"The well-paced text is illustrated with shadowy paintings that capably convey both the dingy surroundings and the brothers' affection." Horn Book Guide

Hi, cat! Viking 1999 un il $15.99
Grades: PreK K 1 2   E
  1. Cats -- Fiction 2. African Americans -- Fiction
  ISBN 0-670-88546-0
                                  LC 98-37764
A reissue of the title first published 1970 by Macmillan
This book "tells the story of Peter's friend Archie and the inquisitive, nondescript, half-grown alley cat that tags after him and manages to make a shambles out of the boys' street carnival. The text provides an adequate framework for Keats's bold bright paintings of a lively city neighborhood." Horn Book Guide

Another title about Archie is:
Pet show! (1972)

Louie. Viking 2004 un il pa $6.99
Grades: PreK K 1 2   E
  1. Puppets and puppet plays -- Fiction
  ISBN 978-0-14-240080-7 pa; 0-14-240080-7 pa
                                  LC 2003-11378
First published 1975 by Greenwillow Books
Susie and Roberto's puppet show is temporarily interrupted when Louis becomes fascinated by one of the puppets

"This story is illustrated with the same glowing colors . . . and with some of the postercollage that is the artist's trademark. The aura is touching without being maudlin, the writing simple and informal." Sutherland. The Best in Child Books

Other titles about Louie are:
Louie's search (1980)
Regards to the man in the moon (1981)
The trip (1978)

★ **Over** in the meadow; [written and] illustrated by Ezra Jack Keats. Viking 1999 un il $16.99; pa $6.99
Grades: PreK K 1 2   E
1. Counting 2. Nursery rhymes 3. Animals -- Poetry
ISBN 0-670-88344-1; 0-14-056508-6 pa

LC 98-47037
A reissue of the title first published 1971 by Four Winds Press

An old nursery poem introduces animals and their young and the numbers one through ten

"The book features Keats's illustrations that show animals in lively characteristic activity." Horn Book Guide

★ The **snowy** day. Viking 1962 31p il lib bdg $16.99; pa $5.99; bd bk $6.99
Grades: PreK K 1 2   E
1. Snow -- Fiction
ISBN 0-670-65400-0 lib bdg; 0-14-050182-7 pa; 0-670-86733-0 bd bk
Awarded the Caldecott Medal, 1963

A small "boy's ecstatic enjoyment of snow in the city is shown in vibrant pictures. Peter listens to the snow crunch under his feet, makes the first tracks in a clean patch of snow, makes angels and a snowman. At night in his warm bed he thinks over his adventures, and in the morning wakens to the promise of another lovely snowy day." Moorachian. What is a City?

Other titles about Peter are:
Goggles (1969)
A letter to Amy (1968)
Peter's chair (1967)
Whistle for Willie (1964)

Keller, Holly
★ **Geraldine's** blanket. Greenwillow Bks. 1984 un il hardcover o.p. pa $5.99
Grades: PreK K 1 2   E
1. Blankets -- Fiction
ISBN 0-688-07810-9 pa

LC 83-14062
"Simply but wonderfully expressive line drawings washed with pastel colors capture the gentleness and humor of the story." SLJ

Other titles about Geraldine are:
Geraldine and Mrs. Duffy (2000)
Geraldine first (1996)
Geraldine's baby brother (1994)
Geraldine's big snow (1988)
Merry Christmas, Geraldine (1997)

Grandfather's dream. Greenwillow Bks. 1994 un il $16.99
Grades: PreK K 1 2   E
1. Vietnam -- Fiction 2. Grandfathers -- Fiction 3. Cranes (Birds) -- Fiction
ISBN 0-688-12339-2

LC 93-18186

After the end of the war in Vietnam, a young boy's grandfather dreams of restoring the wetlands of the Mekong delta, hoping that the large cranes that once lived there will return

"Keller uses simple, direct storytelling and vivid watercolor and ink illustrations to present a complex theme in a story of hope and rebirth." Horn Book Guide

★ **Help!** a story of friendship. Greenwillow Books 2007 un il $16.99; lib bdg $17.89
Grades: PreK K 1 2   E
1. Fear -- Fiction 2. Animals -- Fiction 3. Friendship -- Fiction
ISBN 978-0-06-123913-7; 0-06-123913-5; 978-0-06-123914-4 lib bdg; 0-06-123914-3 lib bdg

LC 2006-32116
Mouse hears a rumor that snakes do not like mice and while trying to avoid his former friend, Snake, he falls into a hole from which neither Hedgehog, Squirrel, nor Rabbit can help him out

"This story has the simplicity of a fable. The appealing art is done in collographs, which are printed collages, and watercolors." SLJ

Miranda's beach day. Greenwillow Books 2009 un il $17.99; lib bdg $18.89
Grades: PreK K   E
1. Beaches -- Fiction 2. Mother-daughter relationship -- Fiction
ISBN 978-0-06-158298-1; 0-06-158298-0; 978-0-06-158300-1 lib bdg; 0-06-158300-6 lib bdg

LC 2008012645
Miranda and Mama spend a fun day at the beach building castles and catching sand crabs, and Miranda learns that just like the sand and the sea, she and her mother will always be together

"Attractive illustrations in watercolors and printed collages on well-designed spreads capture the children's activities and the vastness of the sand and sea. This is a disarmingly simple and reassuring selection." SLJ

Nosy Rosie; [by] Holly Keller. Greenwillow Books 2006 un il $16.99; lib bdg $17.89
Grades: PreK K 1 2   E
1. Foxes -- Fiction 2. Smell -- Fiction 3. Personal names -- Fiction
ISBN 978-0-06-078758-5; 0-06-078758-9; 978-0-06-078759-2 lib bdg; 0-06-078759-7 lib bdg

LC 2005022183
Rosie the fox's excellent sense of smell is good for finding things, but she stops using it after everyone begins to call her "Nosy Rosie"

"Keller takes on the subject of name calling in a gentle, simple, and compassionate manner. . . . The heartfelt dialogue poignantly conveys the little fox's hurt feelings and reads aloud perfectly. The colorful mixture of robust watercolors and simple black lines touchingly reveals each character's attitude through expressive body movement." SLJ

Pearl's new skates. Greenwillow Books 2005 24p il $15.99

Grades: PreK K 1 2   E
    1. Ice skating -- Fiction
    ISBN 0-06-056280-3
                                        LC 2004-576
Pearl's birthday skates have a single blade and learning
to use them is harder than she expects
    "With her pitch-perfect text and uncluttered watercolor-
and-ink pictures . . . Keller tells a tender story about accepting the failures and frustrations that come with learning
something new." Booklist

Keller, Laurie
    Arnie the doughnut; cooked up by Laurie Keller. 1st
ed; Henry Holt 2003 1 v (unpaged) col il E
    1. Doughnuts
    ISBN 0-8050-6283-1 (alk. paper)
                                        LC 2002-4357
Arnie the talking doughnut convinces Mr. Bing that not
all doughnuts are meant to be eaten.
    "Narrowly escaping the jaws of habitual doughnut eater
Mr. Bing, Arnie is shocked to learn that a doughnut's fate
in life is to be eaten. After sparing him, Mr. Bing realizes
that Arnie could fill a void in his life, and Arnie becomes a
sticky but obedient ""doughnut-dog."" Happily busy acrylic
and collage art sprinkled with humorous, punning asides
complements this silly, satisfying story." Horn Book

    ★ Do unto otters; (a book about manners) by Laurie
Keller. Henry Holt 2007 un il $16.95
Grades: PreK K 1 2   E
    1. Otters -- Fiction 2. Rabbits -- Fiction 3. Etiquette
    -- Fiction
    ISBN 978-0-8050-7996-8; 0-8050-7996-3
                                        LC 2006030505
    Mr. Rabbit wonders if he will be able to get along with
his new neighbors, who are otters, until he is reminded of
the golden rule
    "From the gleeful title pun to the kenetic illustrations,
this clever book . . . introduces the golden rule with irresistible humor." Booklist

    The **scrambled** states of America talent show. Henry
Holt 2008 un il $16.95
Grades: PreK K 1 2   E
    1. United States -- Fiction
    ISBN 978-0-8050-7997-5; 0-8050-7997-1
                                        LC 2007-40907
    The states decide to get together and put on a show fea-
turing their particular talents. Also includes facts about the
history and geography of the states.
    "The snappy dialogue flows effortlessly, the personali-
ties are as winning as ever, and the pictures' energy never
flags. It's e pluribus boffo." Publ Wkly

Kelley, Ellen A.
    My life as a chicken; as told to Ellen A. Kelley; pictures
by Michael Slack. Harcourt, Inc. 2007 un il $16
Grades: PreK K 1 2   E
    1. Stories in rhyme 2. Chickens -- Fiction
    ISBN 0-15-205306-2; 978-0-15-205306-2
                                        LC 2005020051
    After escaping the frying pan, Pauline the chicken has an
adventure that includes pirates, a typhoon, and a balloon ride
before landing happily in a petting zoo.

    "Slack's digital mixed-media illustrations are wacky and
cartoonish, and the text ripples with big, impressive words
befitting the exaggerated nature of Pauline's adventures."
SLJ

Kelley, Marty
    ★ Twelve terrible things. Tricycle Press 2008 un il
$15.99
Grades: 1 2 3 4   E
    1. Courage -- Fiction 2. Monsters -- Fiction
    ISBN 978-1-58246-229-5; 1-58246-229-1
                                        LC 2007-46795
    Grownups who wax nostalgic about their youth are giv-
en a visual tour through twelve terrible experiences of childhood, including bedtime monsters and "atomic wedgies."
    "Realistic, double-page watercolor illustrations use a
clever first-person perspective to render readers the victims
of horrors such as a cheek-pinching lady, an over-the-top
birthday clown, and a hairy-moled lunch lady. . . . Minimal
text and detailed artwork combine to convey a macabre humor that is bound to ensnare even the most hesitant of readers." SLJ

Kelley, True
    Dog who saved Santa. Holiday House 2008 un il
$16.95
Grades: PreK K 1 2   E
    1. Dogs -- Fiction 2. Christmas -- Fiction 3. Santa
    Claus -- Fiction
    ISBN 978-0-8234-2120-6; 0-8234-2120-1
                                        LC 2007-041180
    With the help of his take-charge dog Rodney and a
self-help video, young Santa Claus mends his lazy and
irresponsible ways.
    "The cartoon artwork, done in acrylic, watercolors, and
colored pencils, captures the endearing pup's antics and will
give readers the giggles." SLJ

Kellogg, Steven
    ★ Best friends; story and pictures by Steven Kellogg.
Dial Bks. for Young Readers 1986 un il $16.99; pa $6.99
Grades: PreK K 1 2   E
    1. Friendship -- Fiction
    ISBN 0-8037-0099-7; 0-14-054607-3 pa
                                        LC 85-15971
    Kathy feels lonely and betrayed when her best friend
Louise goes away for the summer and has a wonderful time
    "The watercolor and ink illustrations are appealingly
bright and magical. Kathy and Louise's daydreams are vividly and flamboyantly portrayed, with 'reality' just as attractively pictured." SLJ

    ★ The **missing** mitten mystery; story and pictures by
Steven Kellogg. Dial Bks. for Young Readers 2000 un il
$15.99; pa $6.99
Grades: PreK K 1 2   E
    1. Lost and found possessions -- Fiction
    ISBN 0-8037-2566-3; 0-14-230192-2 pa
                                        LC 99-54777
    First published 1974 with title: The mystery of the miss-
ing red mitten
    Annie searches the neighborhood for her red mitten, the
fifth she's lost this winter

"Kellogg really outdoes himself with pictures that are filled with good cheer, warm spirits, and happy daydreams. . . . A book that's upbeat and touching by turns." Booklist

★ The **mysterious** tadpole; new illustrations and text by Steven Kellogg. 25th anniversary ed; Dial Bks. for Young Readers 2002 un il $16.99; pa $6.99
Grades: PreK K 1 2   E
   1. Pets -- Fiction
   ISBN 0-8037-2788-7; 0-14-240140-4 pa
                LC 2001-53776
   First published 1977
"Louis receives a birthday present from his uncle in Scotland: Alphonse, an amiable tadpole that outgrows his bowl, the bathtub, and even the apartment. . . . The new illustrations are bigger, bolder, brighter, and brimming with lively details." Booklist

The **Pied** Piper's magic. Dial Books for Young Readers 2009 un il $16.99
Grades: PreK K 1   E
   1. Fairy tales 2. Rats -- Fiction 3. Magic -- Fiction
   ISBN 978-0-8037-2818-9; 0-8037-2818-2
                LC 2008-12267
In a story loosely based on The Pied Piper of Hamelin, an elf acquires from a miserable witch a magic pipe that allows him to transform things, including the mean-spirited Grand Duke who rules over a rat-infested town.
"Kellogg depicts the magic-making in bright, buoyant mixed media spreads that show streams of colorful text and corresponding animals pouring from the mouth of the pipe. . . . Far sunnier than the original, this slightly educational adaptation (thanks to the built-in spelling lessons within) should please parents and kids alike." Publ Wkly

★ **Pinkerton**, behave! story and pictures by Steven Kellogg. Dial Books for Young Readers 2002 un il $17.99; pa $6.99
Grades: PreK K 1 2   E
   1. Dogs -- Fiction
   ISBN 0-8037-2722-4; 0-14-230007-1 pa
A reissue of the title first published 1979
"Kellogg wittily captures expressions and movements of animal and human, wisely allowing the focal humor to emanate through the faces and action." Booklist
   Other titles about Pinkerton are:
   A penguin pup for Pinkerton (2001)
   Prehistoric Pinkerton (1987)
   A Rose for Pinkerton (1981)
   Tallyho, Pinkerton (1982)

Kelly, Mij
Where giants hide; illustrated by Ross Collins. Sourcebooks/Jabberwocky 2010 un il
Grades: PreK K 1 2   E
   1. Imagination -- Fiction 2. Voyages and travels -- Fiction
   ISBN 1-4022-4270-0; 978-1-4022-4270-0
"A girl, convinced that all the world's magic has leaked away, is sad because she can't find any giants, fairies, goblins, unicorns, dragons, or genies. . . . By reading the pictures, young children will enjoy the visual joke and find satisfaction in figuring out the mismatch between the girl's narration and what is actually happening. The whimsical,

detailed illustrations, dominated by bright red, yellow, and turquoise, add humor and capture the subtle message of the story" SLJ

Kelly, Sheila M.
Yummy! good food makes me strong. by Shelley Rotner and Sheila M. Kelly; photographs by Shelley Rotner. Holiday House 2013 32 p. col. ill. (reinforced) $16.95
Grades: 1 2 3   E
   1. Food 2. Children -- Nutrition 3. Nutrition
   ISBN 082342426X; 9780823424269
                LC 2012016564
This book by Shelley Rotner presents "color photos of children eating nourishing foods with enjoyment and helping to prepare them. The youngsters are shown in various indoor and outdoor settings, sometimes displaying brightly colored fruits and vegetables. Throughout, text boxes with nutrition tips are clearly meant for adults. The end page includes a handful of additional recommendations . . . and a ChooseMyPlate.gov diagram." (School Library Journal)

Kelsey, Elin
You are stardust; Elin Kelsey, Soyeon Kim. Owlkids Books 2012 32 p. $18.95
Grades: K 1 2 3 4 5   E
   1. Nature 2. Human beings
   ISBN 1926973356; 9781926973357
                LC 2011943505
This book by Elin Kelsey, illustrated by Soyeon Kim, "begins by introducing the idea that every tiny atom in our bodies came from a star that exploded long before we were born. From its opening pages, the book suggests that we are intimately connected to the natural world; it compares the way we learn to speak to the way baby birds learn to sing, and the growth of human bodies to the growth of forests." (Publisher's note)

Kempter, Christa
Wally and Mae; by Christa Kempter; illustrated by Frauke Weldin. North-South 2008 un il $16.95
Grades: PreK K 1 2   E
   1. Bears -- Fiction 2. Rabbits -- Fiction 3. Friendship -- Fiction
   ISBN 978-0-7358-2208-5; 0-7358-2208-5
"A capricious bear named Mae befriends a sensible rabbit named Wally, and this unlikely pair shares an idyllic cottage in the woods. . . . Both of the animals are depicted with tenderness. The colors are bright and many of the scenes show one or both of the characters in full action." SLJ

When Mama can't sleep; illustrated by Natascha Rosenberg. NorthSouth Books 2011 un il (Tuff books) $6.95
Grades: PreK   E
   1. Bedtime -- Fiction 2. Family life -- Fiction
   ISBN 978-0-7358-4015-7; 0-7358-4015-6
When worries keep Mama, Papa, and Max awake, they crawl into bed together with Max's teddy bear for comfort.
"The vibrant speads are filled with color, and the heavy, glossy paper will withstand toddler destruction. Comforting, soothing, and sure to be a hit." SLJ

Kenah, Katharine

The **best** seat in second grade; story by Katharine Kenah; pictures by Abby Carter. HarperCollins Pubs. 2005 48p il (I can read book) $15.99; lib bdg $16.89; pa $3.99
Grades: K 1 2   E
    1. School stories 2. Hamsters -- Fiction
    ISBN 0-06-000734-6; 0-06-000735-4 lib bdg; 0-06-000736-2 pa
                      LC 2004-178

Sam's favorite thing about second grade is the class pet, a hamster named George Washington, so when the class goes on a field trip to a science museum, Sam cannot resist bringing George along

"Kenah has created an appealing cast of characters whose actions ring true. . . . Carter's watercolor illustrations add to the story's appeal." Booklist

Other titles about this second grade are:
The best teacher in second grade (2006)
The best chef in second grade (2007)

Kennedy, Anne Vittur

The **Farmer's** away! baa! neigh! Anne Vittur Kennedy. Candlewick Press 2014 32 p. color illustrations $15.99
Grades: PreK K 1   E
    1. Farms -- Fiction 2. Farm life -- Fiction 3. Domestic animals -- Fiction
    ISBN 0763666793; 9780763666798
                    LC 2013946622

This book, by Anne Vittur Kennedy, explores "what mischief . . . the animals get up to when the farmer's back is turned. . . . Kennedy lets us know in the animals' own words! There will be boating, of course, and a picnic, a rollercoaster ride, Jet Skiing, a hot-air balloon, ballroom dancing." (Publisher's note)

"Babies, toddlers and very young emergent readers will delight in the strong, playful rhythm and energetic and detailed illustrations in this introduction to the noisy world of animal sounds." Kirkus

Kent, Jack

There's no such thing as a dragon. Golden Book 2005 un il hardcover o.p. pa $6.99
Grades: PreK K 1 2   E
    1. Dragons -- Fiction
    ISBN 0-375-83208-4; 0-375-85137-2 pa
                    LC 2004-6123

First published 1975 by Western Pub.

"When Billy Bixbee wakes up and finds a dragon in his room, his mother tells him there is no such thing. The neglected dragon grows larger and larger, eventually walking off with the house, and the Bixbee family is forced to admit his existence. Practically a classic. . . for its neat story line and humorous cartoons of expressively surprised characters." Horn Book Guide

Kerby, Mona

★ **Owney,** the mail-pouch pooch; pictures by Lynne Barasch. Farrar, Straus and Giroux 2008 un il $16.95
Grades: K 1 2 3   E
    1. Dogs -- Fiction 2. Postal service -- Fiction 3. Voyages and travels -- Fiction
    ISBN 0-374-35685-8; 978-0-374-35685-9
                    LC 2006-47605

In 1888, Owney, a stray terrier puppy, finds a home in the Albany, New York, post office and becomes its official mascot as he rides the mail train through the Adirondacks and beyond, criss-crossing the United States, into Canada and Mexico, and eventually traveling around the world by mail boat in 132 days.

"The author does an excellent job of introducing readers to the late-19th century and the system used by the postal service to send mail both nationally and internationally via horse-pulled wagons, trains, and steamships. . . . Barasch's ink and watercolor illustrations complement the narrative with period details. A pair of sepia-toned photographs at the end of the book adds to the authenticity of the tale." SLJ

Another title about Owney is:
The further adventures of a lucky dog: Owney, U.S. rail mail mascot (2009)

Kerley, Barbara

You and me together; moms, dads, and kids around the world. with a note by Marian Wright Edelman. National Geographic 2005 32p il $16.95; lib bdg $25.90
Grades: PreK K 1 2   E
    1. Parent-child relationship
    ISBN 0-7922-8297-3; 0-7922-8298-1 lib bdg

"Using a simple rhyming text, Kerley captures the essence of childhood's special moments, accompanied by superb full-color photos. . . . Diverse cultures in various locations around the world are represented. . . . Children and parents engage in activities such as playing an instrument, taking a walk, making a meal, fishing, and dancing. . . . This book is an excellent tool for raising awareness of cultural differences and similarities." SLJ

Kerr, Judith

One night in the zoo. Kane Miller 2010 un il $15.99
Grades: PreK K   E
    1. Counting 2. Stories in rhyme 3. Children's poetry 4. Zoos -- Fiction 5. Magic -- Fiction 6. Animals -- Fiction
    ISBN 978-1-935279-37-2; 1-935279-37-8

One magical night an elephant jumped in the air and flew. Wild antics, high spirits and silly games of the other zoo animals also occur. Will anyone find out?

"Kerr's softly shaded pencil drawings depict the beasts and birds with all the charm of friendly animal characters come to life. Fresh and simple." Booklist

Kessler, Cristina

The **best** beekeeper of Lalibela; a tale from Africa. by Cristina Kessler; illustrated by Leonard Jenkins. Holiday House 2006 un il $16.95
Grades: K 1 2 3   E
    1. Ethiopia -- Fiction 2. Sex role -- Fiction 3. Beekeeping -- Fiction
    ISBN 978-0-8234-1858-9; 0-8234-1858-8
                    LC 2005046217

In the Ethiopian mountain village of Lalibela a young girl named Almaz determines to find a way to be a beekeeper despite being told that is something only men can do

"Jenkins follows the ups and downs of Almaz's labor in deep-hued, mixed-media scenes spread richly across double pages. . . . Kessler includes well-chosen details about the beekeeping project and a few words from the local Amharic and Tigringna languages." SLJ

Kessler, Leonard P.

★ **Here** comes the strikeout; newly il ed.; HarperCollins Pubs. 1992 64p il (I can read book) hardcover o.p. pa $3.99

Grades: K 1 2   E

1. Baseball -- Fiction

ISBN 0-06-023156-4; 0-06-444011-7 pa

LC 91-14717

A revised and newly illustrated edition of the title first published 1965

This "concerns a boy who can't hit a baseball until he follows the advice of a friend. 'Lucky helmets won't do it. Lucky bats won't do it. Only hard work will do it.' . . . A winner." Booklist

★ **Kick,** pass, and run; story and pictures by Leonard Kessler. newly il ed; HarperCollins Pubs. 1996 64p il (I can read book) hardcover o.p. pa $3.99

Grades: K 1 2   E

1. Football -- Fiction

ISBN 0-06-027105-1; 0-06-444210-1 pa

LC 95-6185

A newly illustrated edition of the title first published 1966

"After a group of animal friends watches a boys' football team play, they are eager to have their own game. An apple serves as a ball until Frog eats it; a paper-bag football works until Duck kicks and pops it. The game is kept alive when a real football from the boys' game sails into the animals' midst. [A] simply told story with plenty of sports action." Horn Book Guide

★ **Last** one in is a rotten egg; newly il ed; HarperCollins Pubs. 1999 64p il (I can read book) hardcover o.p. pa $3.99

Grades: K 1 2   E

1. Swimming -- Fiction

ISBN 0-06-028485-4; 0-06-444262-4 pa

LC 98-50882

A newly illustrated edition of the title first published 1969

After Freddy is pushed into deep water by a couple of toughs, he decides to learn to swim

"This lively . . . . sports story has been newly illustrated with a multicultural cast in a New York City neighborhood." Booklist

Ketteman, Helen

Goodnight, Little Monster; illustrated by Bonnie Leick. Marshall Cavendish 2010 un il $16.99

Grades: PreK K   E

1. Stories in rhyme 2. Bedtime -- Fiction 3. Monsters -- Fiction 4. Mother-child relationship -- Fiction

ISBN 978-0-7614-5683-4; 0-7614-5683-X

LC 2009002185

Rhyming text describes a mother guiding her young monster through bedtime preparations, such as howling at the moon, snacking on worm juice and beetle bread, and choosing a bedtime story.

"While the text is quite fun to read, it is the watercolor illustrations that steal the show. Each page is filled with kid-friendly monster details." SLJ

Swamp song; illustrated by Ponder Goembel. Marshall Cavendish Children 2009 un il $17.99

Grades: PreK K 1 2   E

1. Stories in rhyme 2. Animals -- Fiction 3. Marshes -- Fiction

ISBN 978-0-7614-5563-9; 0-7614-5563-9

LC 2008013810

Down in the swamp where the cypress grows, the animals all come out to enjoy the day.

"The sunny illustrations are done with colored ink lines and acrylic wash paint against mostly white backgrounds. . . . Children will be tapping their toes with Old Man Gator and creating their own cacophony of swamp sounds as they learn about the inhabitants of this habitat." SLJ

The **three** little gators; illustrated by Will Terry. Albert Whitman 2009 un il $16.99

Grades: K 1 2 3   E

1. Folklore 2. Alligators -- Folklore

ISBN 978-0-8075-7824-7; 0-8075-7824-X

LC 2008028085

In this adaptation of the traditional folktale, three little gators each build their house in an east Texas swamp, hoping for protection from the Big-bottomed Boar.

"Ketteman's retelling, including a sassy Texas twang, makes the story hilarious and bright. . . . Terry's illustrations work well with the story. The colors are vibrant yet ominous and swampy." SLJ

Khan, Hena

★ **Night** of the Moon; a Muslim holiday story. illustrated by Julie Paschkis. Chronicle Books 2008 un il $16.99

Grades: PreK K 1 2   E

1. Islam -- Fiction 2. Muslims -- Fiction 3. Ramadan -- Fiction 4. Id al-Adha -- Fiction 5. Pakistani Americans -- Fiction

ISBN 978-0-8118-6062-8; 0-8118-6062-0

LC 2007024962

"A new moon is in the sky, and Yasmeen, identified on the jacket as a seven-year-old Pakistani-American, knows that it is time for the holidays of Ramadan and Eid. . . . Paschkis, borrowing from the arabesque motifs and jeweled colors of Islamic art, portrays the Muslim community as warm, welcoming and multiethnic. . . . Sweet and visually striking, this is a good choice both for children who celebrate these holidays and for others seeking a bridge to their culture." Publ Wkly

Khan, Rukhsana

★ **Big** red lollipop; illustrated by Sophie Blackall. Viking 2010 un il lib bdg $16.99

Grades: PreK K 1 2   E

1. Parties -- Fiction 2. Sisters -- Fiction 3. Birthdays -- Fiction 4. Pakistani Americans -- Fiction

ISBN 978-0-670-06287-4 lib bdg; 0-670-06287-1 lib bdg

LC 2009-22676

"Khan is of Pakistani descent, and this tale of clashing cultural customs is based on an incident from her childhood. The story (and its lesson) comes to like in Blackall's spot-on illustrations. . . . This is an honest, even moving, commentary on sisterly relationships." Booklist

★ **King** for a day; by Rukhsana Khan; illustrations by Christiane Krömer. Lee & Low Books, Inc. 2013 32 p. (hardcover: alk. paper) $17.95

Grades: PreK K 1 2   **E**

1. Picture books for children 2. Kites -- Fiction 3. Pakistan -- Fiction 4. Wheelchairs -- Fiction 5. Basant Festival -- Fiction 6. People with disabilities -- Fiction

ISBN 1600606598; 9781600606595

LC 2013007506

This children's picture book, set in Pakistan during Basant, "focuses on the strength and resourcefulness of a child in a wheelchair as he navigates the skies at the spring kite festival. Perched on the rooftop and assisted by his brother and sister, Malik launches his small but swift creation, named Falcon, into the stratosphere, where it defeats both of the kites that belong to the bully next door." (Kirkus Reviews)

★ **Silly** chicken; illustrated by Yunmee Kyong. Viking 2005 un il $15.99

Grades: K 1 2 3   **E**

1. Chickens -- Fiction 2. Pakistan -- Fiction

ISBN 0-670-05912-9

LC 2004-15830

In Pakistan, Rani believes that her mother loves their pet chicken Bibi more than she cares for her, until the day that a fluffy chick appears and steals Rani's own affections.

"This picture book clearly depicts a child's jealousy. . . . Kyong . . . paints in a naive style, using fresh, warm colors. A pleasing book with an unusual setting." Booklist

Kherdian, David

Come back, Moon; by David Kherdian; illustrated by Nonny Hogrogian. Beach Lane Books 2013 32 p. (hardcover) $16.99

Grades: PreK K 1 2   **E**

1. Picture books for children 2. Moon -- Fiction 3. Bears -- Fiction 4. Forest animals -- Fiction

ISBN 1442458879; 9781442458871

LC 2012037038

In this children's picture book, Bear can't sleep and blames the moon. "He steals it and stuffs it into his pillowcase. Other animals Fox, Skunk, Opossum and Raccoon miss the moon and speculate as to its whereabouts." When they realize Bear has it. "Crow tells Bear a slumber-inducing story, then he and Fox snatch the pillowcase and release the moon." (Kirkus Reviews)

Killen, Nicola

Not me! Egmont USA 2010 un il $13.99

Grades: PreK K 1   **E**

1. Cleanliness -- Fiction

ISBN 978-1-4052-4829-7; 1-4052-4829-7

Not one member of a group of friends admits to having made a big mess, or offers to pitch in to clean it up.

"The illustrations and typeface will melt hearts and delight and inspire potato-printing young readers. The simple, expressive shapes, mostly in muted tones with dapples of red to keep things cheery, are utterly fresh and warm, and the textures feel organic. Children will delight in this sweet-natured picture book." SLJ

Kim, Patti

Here I am; by Patti Kim and illustrated by Sonia Sanchez. Capstone 2013 40 p. $14.95

Grades: 1 2 3   **E**

1. Picture books for children 2. Immigrants -- United States -- Fiction

ISBN 1623700361; 9781404882997; 9781479519316; 9781479519323; 9781623700362

LC 2012051009

In this book by Patti Kim and illustrated by Sonia Sanchez, "newly arrived from their faraway homeland, a boy and his family enter into the lights, noise, and traffic of a busy American city. The language is unfamiliar. Food, habits, games, and gestures are puzzling. They boy clings tightly to his special keepsake from home and wonders how he will find his way. How will he once again become the happy, confident kid he used to be?" (Publisher's note)

Kimmel, Elizabeth Cody

Glamsters; written by Elizabeth Cody Kimmel; illustrated by Jackie Urbanovic. Hyperion Books for Children 2008 un il $16.99

Grades: K 1 2   **E**

1. Hamsters -- Fiction

ISBN 978-1-4231-1148-1; 1-4231-1148-6

LC 2008029692

Harriet the hamster is desperate to be adopted, so she gives her sister Patricia and herself glamorous makeovers in hopes they will get more attention when Hamster World has its huge annual sale.

"The story is filled with clever details and laugh-out-loud humor, but the underlying message of self-acceptance is an important one for children to hear." SLJ

My penguin Osbert; illustrated by H. B. Lewis. Candlewick Press 2004 un il $16.99; pa $6.99

Grades: PreK K 1 2   **E**

1. Penguins -- Fiction 2. Christmas -- Fiction

ISBN 0-7636-1699-0; 0-7636-5730-1 pa

LC 2003-40981

When a boy finally gets exactly what he wants from Santa, he learns that owning a real penguin may not have been a good idea after all

"Kimmel sneaks some sly humor into the well-told, nicely paced story, and Lewis' artwork, executed in watercolor and pastels and enhanced with digital renderings, has a soft look, colored in marshmallow tints." Booklist

Another title about Osbert the penguin is:

My penguin Osbert in love (2009)

The top job; by Elizabeth Cody Kimmel; illustrated by Robert Neubecker. Dutton Children's Books 2007 un il $16.99; pa $6.99

Grades: K 1 2 3   **E**

1. Occupations -- Fiction 2. New York (N.Y.) -- Fiction 3. Father-daughter relationship -- Fiction 4. Empire State Building (New York, N.Y.) -- Fiction

ISBN 978-0-525-47789-1; 0-525-47789-6; 978-0-14-241424-8 pa; 0-14-241424-7 pa

LC 2006039770

On Career Day, a young girl entertains the class with a description of her father's exciting job as light bulb changer at the top of the Empire State Building.

"The pacing and rhythm of the text is impeccable. . . . The stylized, cartoon-style illustrations, rendered in clear colors and bold black outlines, nicely extend the plot." Booklist

Kimmel, Eric A.

★ The **Golem's** latkes; adapted by Eric A. Kimmel; illustrated by Aaron Jasinski. Marshall Cavendish Children 2011 un il $17.99

Grades: K 1 2   E

1. Rabbis 2. Jews -- Fiction 3. Hanukkah -- Fiction 4. Czech Republic -- Fiction 5. Household employees -- Fiction 6. Prague (Czech Republic) -- Fiction

ISBN 978-0-7614-5904-0; 0-7614-5904-9

LC 2010020008

Rabbi Judah Loew ben Bezalel visits the Emperor, leaving a new housemaid to prepare for his Hanukkah party, but returns to find that she has misused the clay man he created. Includes historical and cultural notes.

"Kimmel's storytelling is effective in its use of suspense, humor, trope and repetition, making a fine read-aloud holiday treat." Kirkus

★ **Hershel** and the Hanukkah Goblins; written by Eric A. Kimmel; illustrated by Trina Schart Hyman. 25th anniversary edition Holiday House 2014 32 p. color illustrations (hardcover) $17.95

Grades: K 1 2 3   E

1. Goblins -- Fiction 2. Hanukkah -- Fiction 3. Jews -- Fiction 4. Jews -- Folklore 5. Fairies -- Fiction

ISBN 0823431649; 9780823431649

LC 2013048854

Originally published 1985

This book, by Eric A. Kimmel and illustrated by Trina Schart Hyman, is "the 25th anniversary edition of . . . [a] Caldecott Honor-winning classic. . . . On the first night of Hanukkah, a weary traveler named Hershel of Ostropol eagerly approaches the next village, where . . . the villagers are being tormented by a band of goblins who hate Hanukkah. Brave Hershel leaps to the villagers' rescue." (Publisher's note)

★ **Joha** makes a wish; a Middle Eastern tale. adapted by Eric A. Kimmel; illustrated by Omar Rayyan. Marshall Cavendish Children 2010 un il $17.99

Grades: 1 2 3   E

1. Wishes -- Fiction 2. Middle East -- Fiction

ISBN 978-0-7614-5599-8; 0-7614-5599-X

LC 2009006334

An original story, based on the Joha tales of the Arabic-speaking world, in which a hapless man finds a wishing stick that brings him nothing but bad luck. Includes an author's note about the history of Joha tales.

"Kimmel's well-paced text smoothly builds events and dialogue, leaving the character interpretation to the comic portrayals in Rayyan's energetic watercolors." SLJ

Little Britches and the rattlers; by Eric A. Kimmel; illustrated by Vincent Nguyen. Marshall Cavendish Children 2008 un il $16.99

Grades: PreK K 1 2   E

1. Texas -- Fiction 2. Cowhands -- Fiction 3. Rattlesnakes -- Fiction

ISBN 978-0-7614-5432-8; 0-7614-5432-2

LC 2007030155

As Little Britches, in her best attire, starts for the rodeo in town, she is waylaid by several rattlesnakes wanting to do her harm, but with some quick thinking she finds a way to outsmart them all

"Kimmel's little yarn makes good use of early counting concepts and introduces some western lingo in a leisurely repetitive structure. . . . Nguyen's artwork complements the glib silliness." Booklist

The **mysterious** guests; a Sukkot story. by Eric A. Kimmel; illustrated by Katya Krenina. Holiday House 2008 un il $16.95

Grades: K 1 2 3   E

1. Jews -- Fiction 2. Sukkot -- Fiction 3. Brothers -- Fiction

ISBN 978-0-8234-1893-0; 0-8234-1893-6

LC 2007-43208

Three mysterious guests appear at generous but impoverished Ezra's table on Sukkot and bless him, while they bring curses upon his rich but selfish brother Eben.

This is "a lyrically rendered tale. . . . Krenina's stylized, harvest-toned acrylics and thoughtful, dark-eyed characters evoke a world where the everyday and mystical are intertwined, and righteousness is clear-cut." Publ Wkly

Rip Van Winkle's return; adapted and retold by Eric A. Kimmel from Rip Van Winkle by Washington Irving; pictures by Leonard Everett Fisher. Farrar, Straus and Giroux 2007 un il $17

Grades: 1 2 3 4   E

1. New York (State) -- Fiction 2. Catskill Mountains (N.Y.) -- Fiction

ISBN 978-0-374-36308-6; 0-374-36308-0

LC 2005042922

A man who sleeps for twenty years in the Catskill Mountains wakes to a much-changed world

"Kimmel and Fisher take on an American literary treasure and make it accessible to young children. . . . The drama is nicely played out with Fisher's solid, strategically placed figures." Booklist

Simon and the bear; a Hanukkah tale. by Eric A. Kimmel; illustrated by Matthew Trueman. Disney-Hyperion Books 2014 40 p. $16.99

Grades: PreK K 1 2   E

1. Survival after airplane accidents, shipwrecks, etc. -- Fiction 2. Jews -- Fiction 3. Bears -- Fiction 4. Hanukkah -- Fiction 5. Miracles -- Fiction 6. Survival -- Fiction 7. Polar bear -- Fiction 8. Shipwrecks -- Fiction

ISBN 1423143558; 9781423143550

LC 2013046370

In this children's story, by Eric A. Kimmel, illustrated by Matthew Trueman, "Simon's mother knows he will need a miracle, so she reminds him to celebrate Hanukkah wherever he may be. Little does either of them know that Simon will spend the first night of Hanukkah on an ice floe after his ship sinks. . . . This fanciful Hanukkah tale . . . celebrates eight miracles: family, friendship, hope, selflessness, sharing, faith, courage, and love." (Publisher's note)

Stormy's hat; just right for a railroad man. pictures by Andrea U'Ren. Farrar, Straus and Giroux 2008 un il $16.95

Grades: PreK K 1 2   E

1. Hats -- Fiction 2. Sewing -- Fiction 3. Railroads -- Fiction

ISBN 0-374-37262-4; 978-0-374-37262-0

LC 2005-51233

As Stormy, a railroad engineer, searches for the perfect hat—one that will not blow off, get too hot, or shade his eyes too much—his wife, Ida, becomes increasingly annoyed that he will not let her help. Includes a historical note about the real Stormy and Ida Kromer.

"U'Ren's vibrant paintings capture the palette and motion of Midwestern landscapes and city scenes. . . . With a snappy, high-interest story and connections to hats, history, trains, gender equality, and industrialism, this book is a gem for libraries and classrooms." SLJ

The **three** little tamales; by Eric A. Kimmel; illustrated by Valeria Docampo. Marshall Cavendish 2009 un il $17.99

Grades: K 1 2 3   E

1. Fairy tales 2. Wolves -- Fiction 3. Hispanic Americans -- Fiction

ISBN 978-0-7614-5519-6; 0-7614-5519-1

LC 2008010738

In this variation of 'The Three Little Pigs' set in the Southwest, three little tamales escape from a restaurant before they can be eaten, and set up homes in the prairie, cornfield, and desert.

"Docampo's oil-on-paper illustrations add dimension to the story and bring the three little tamales to life. An excellent addition to collections of fairy-tale retellings." Booklist

★ **Zigazak!** a magical Hanukkah night. illustrated by Jon Goodell. Doubleday Bks. for Young Readers 2001 un il $15.95; lib bdg $19.99

Grades: K 1 2 3   E

1. Jews -- Fiction 2. Magic -- Fiction 3. Hanukkah -- Fiction

ISBN 0-385-32652-1; 0-385-90004-X lib bdg

LC 98-46269

Two evil spirits wreak havoc on the town of Brisk's Hanukkah celebration, until the town's wise rabbi puts a stop to their mischief

"The text is safely boxed away from the devilry in double-page spreads in which intricately detailed art realistically depicts the furnishings, clothing, facial features, and even the townspeople's pets. Storytellers will have fun with the surprise ending." Booklist

Kimmelman, Leslie

★ **Everybody** bonjours! by Leslie Kimmelman; illustrated by Sarah McMenemy. Alfred A. Knopf 2008 un il $16.99; lib bdg $19.99

Grades: PreK K   E

1. Stories in rhyme 2. Paris (France) -- Fiction

ISBN 978-0-375-84443-0; 978-0-375-94443-7 lib bdg

LC 2007006899

"On vacation with her parents . . . and little brother, a girl embraces her role as tourist, savoring all the places where one can say 'Bonjour': On a barge trip down the Seine, at the top of the Tour Eiffel and Notre Dame, in a chic boutique. . . . McMenemy's . . . mixed-media images, mostly full-page

scenes of classic locations, are a stylish yet timeless mélange of fauvist whimsy and affectionate reportage." Publ Wkly

In the doghouse; an Emma and Bo story. by Leslie Kimmelman; illustrated by True Kelley. Holiday House 2006 30p il (Holiday House reader) $14.95

Grades: K 1 2   E

1. Dogs -- Fiction 2. Vacations -- Fiction

ISBN 0-8234-1882-0

LC 2004047466

When the Lewis family goes on vacation to the lake, Emily gets mad at her best friend Bo, the family dog, so he runs away to look for a new best friend

"Kimmelman writes with simplicity and wit, affectionately portraying the main characters' flaws, feelings, and pride. Kelley's cartoonlike ink drawings, brightened with colorful washes, have a carefree air that suits the vacation setting and the tone of the story." Booklist

Mind your manners, Alice Roosevelt! written by Leslie Kimmelman and illustrated by Adam Gustavson. Peachtree Publishers 2009 un il $16.95

Grades: K 1 2 3   E

1. Governors 2. Presidents 3. Vice-presidents 4. Socialites 5. Children of presidents 6. Nobel laureates for peace 7. Presidents -- United States -- Fiction

ISBN 978-1-5614-5492-1; 1-5614-5492-3

LC 2008052837

A brief, fictionalized account of what life was like for Theodore Roosevelt during his political career, with his oldest daughter, Alice, a strong-willed and somewhat wild young woman, who loved to do things that shocked the public, even when she lived in the White House

"Gustavson's energetic oil paintings do justice to Alice's shocking escapades, and parts of the text . . . are cleverly incorporated into the art." Booklist

The **three** bully goats; illustrated by Will Terry. Albert Whitman 2011 un il $16.99

Grades: PreK K 1   E

1. Goats -- Fiction 2. Bullies -- Fiction

ISBN 0-8075-7900-9; 978-0-8075-7900-8

LC 2010024274

Billy goat brothers Gruff, Ruff, and Tuff are bullies who rule their meadow, but when they cross Little Ogre's bridge and are mean to the baby animals on the other side, they are in for a surprise.

"Terry's brilliantly colored acrylics have a soft, out-of-focus look to them, but there is no mistaking the grouchy looks and mean personalities of his Bully Goats. . . . Kimmelman's version stands out even from other nontraditional versions, since the ogre/troll is the good guy and the goats are the villains. A good springboard for both bullying conversations and problem-solving sessions." Kirkus

Kimura, Ken

999 Frogs Wake Up; by Ken Kimura; illustrated by Yasunari Murakami. NorthSouth 2013 48 p. $17.95

Grades: PreK K 1   E

1. Sleep -- Fiction 2. Frogs

ISBN 073584108X; 9780735841086

In this children's book, by Ken Kimura, illustrated by Yasunari Murakami, "it's springtime in the swamp! As 999 young frogs awaken, they panic to find that all of the other animals are still asleep. First they wake the biggest frog . . . then the tortoise, the lizard, and the ladybugs. But when they hop down a hole and all pull together, they find someone they don't want to wake--a big, long snake." (Publisher's note)

★ **999 tadpoles.** NorthSouth Books 2011 un il $16.95
Grades: PreK K 1   E
   1. Frogs -- Fiction 2. Hawks -- Fiction
   ISBN 978-0-7358-4013-3; 0-7358-4013-X
   Original Japanese edition, 2003
"This well-paced journey, with just enough tension to keep young listeners engaged, will be a solid storytime choice." Kirkus

Kinerk, Robert
   Clorinda; illustrated by Steven Kellogg. Simon & Schuster Bks. for Young Readers 2003 un il $15.95; pa $6.99
Grades: PreK K 1 2   E
   1. Stories in rhyme 2. Ballet -- Fiction 3. Cattle -- Fiction
   ISBN 0-689-86449-3; 1-4169-3964-4 pa
               LC 2003-4559
Defying the odds, Clorinda the cow follows her dream of becoming a ballet dancer
"As fine a mix of story and message as this is, it's the irrepressible art that makes this book shine. Kellogg is at the top of his game, finding the humor in every line." Booklist
   Another title about Clorinda is:
   Clorinda takes flight (2007)

King, Dedie
   I see the sun in Afghanistan; illustration by Judith Inglese. Satya House Pub. 2011 40p il $12.95
Grades: PreK K 1   E
   1. Afghanistan -- Fiction 2. Family life -- Fiction 3. Bilingual books -- English-Dari
   ISBN 978-0-9818720-8-7; 0-9818720-8-5
"This simple story follows a young Afghani girl from sunrise to sunset. Living in Bamiyan, a relatively safe city, Habiba fetches water, attends school, and anticipates the arrival of her cousins, who have lost their home because of the war. The story captures the flavor of the culture, and the love and support of this close family is evident. The story is written in both English and Dari (Afghan Farsi), and an author's note provides supplemental information. Inglese's watercolor and collage illustrations are well composed, and color and pattern add richness and texture." SLJ

King, Stephen Michael
   Leaf; ideas, sound effects, and pictures. Roaring Brook 2009 un il $14.95
Grades: K 1 2   E
   1. Dogs -- Fiction 2. Hair -- Fiction 3. Dreams -- Fiction
   ISBN 978-1-59643-503-2; 1-59643-503-8
"A mopheaded child faces a momlike figure with scissors in her hands—definitely time for a haircut. The child, however, has other ideas and runs out to frolic in the grass. . . . Wonderful squiggly line, patches of green and brown, gold and blue and fabulous use of negative white space make this a joy to reread." Kirkus

   Mutt dog! words and pictures by Stephen Michael King. Harcourt 2005 un il $16
Grades: PreK K 1 2   E
   1. Dogs -- Fiction 2. Homelessness -- Fiction
   ISBN 0-15-205561-4
   First published 2004 in Australia
A lonely dog finally finds a home after he makes friends with a woman who works at a homeless shelter.
"The presentation is well done, and the gentle pen-and-ink and watercolor cartoons tell the story beautifully. . . . The book's oversize format and clear wash illustrations on white backgrounds make this a good choice for storytimes." SLJ

   You. Greenwillow Books 2011 un il $14.99
Grades: PreK K 1 2   E
   1. Birds -- Fiction 2. Rabbits -- Fiction 3. Friendship -- Fiction
   ISBN 978-0-06-206014-3
               LC 2010032237
Reveals the world as a colorful, musical, and exciting place where the most special thing of all is a best friend.
King "draws a pup with gravity-defying ears whose best chum is a tiny orange bird; together, they cavort through this free-verse paean to friendship. With curlicue lines and gentle watercolor tints, King creates a winning series of scenarios to accompany his text. . . . The text is good-tempered and reassuring, but it's King's pocket-size, whimsical characters that will endear his creation to readers." Publ Wkly

King-Smith, Dick
   The **twin** giants; [by] Dick King-Smith; illustrated by Mini Grey. Candlewick Press 2008 67p il $16.99
Grades: K 1 2 3   E
   1. Twins -- Fiction 2. Giants -- Fiction
   ISBN 978-0-7636-3529-9; 0-7636-3529-4
Two twin giants do everything together, including looking for the perfect wives.
"This handsomely designed volume offers an original story accompanied by droll illustrations." Booklist

Kinney, Jessica
   The **pig** scramble; written by Jessica Kinney; illustrated by Sarah S. Brannen. Islandport Press 2011 un il $17.95
Grades: PreK K 1   E
   1. Pigs -- Fiction 2. Fairs -- Fiction 3. Brothers -- Fiction 4. Contests -- Fiction
   ISBN 978-1-934031-61-2; 1-934031-61-5
"August is County Fair time in New England, and Clarence, the youngest of three brothers, is looking forward to the Pig Scramble, which involves 10 children and one wily piglet. . . . Clarence thinks that he can be the best, winning the contest and the pig. The story and illustrations match perfectly—they are both timeless and evocative of yesteryear. Brannen's watercolors are detailed. . . . The illustrations are many sizes, keeping the story flowing, and Brannen's pigs are bristly, adorable, and full of life." SLJ

Kinsey-Warnock, Natalie
   ★ **Nora's** ark; illustrated by Emily Arnold McCully. HarperCollins 2005 un il $15.99; lib bdg $16.89
Grades: K 1 2 3   E
   1. Floods -- Fiction 2. Vermont -- Fiction 3. Farm life

-- Fiction 4. Grandparents -- Fiction
ISBN 0-688-17244-X; 0-06-029517-1 lib bdg
LC 2004-3444

During the Vermont flood of 1927, a girl and her grandparents share their new hilltop house with neighbors and animals.

This is a "well-told tale, based on an incident from the author's life. . . . [A] stunning picture is the wild, rainy scene showing houses bobbing along as the water pours down." Booklist

Kipling, Rudyard, 1865-1936

Just So Stories; Volume 2. Rudyard Kipling; illustrated by Ian Wallace. Groundwood Books 2014 88 p. color illustrations (hbk.) $19.95

Grades: K 1 2 3 4 5   E
1. Animals -- Fiction
ISBN 1554982138; 9781554982134

"Six of Kipling's stories, including 'The Beginning of the Armadillos' and 'The Butterfly That Stamped' are featured in this work. Over the years, these tales have delighted young readers with their imaginative pourquoi style, beautiful language, and clever wordplay. Wallace uses mixed media (watercolor, pencil crayon, pastel pencil and chalk) to create glowing, softly colored paintings that successfully capture the essence of the tales." SLJ

Kirk, Connie Ann

Sky dancers; illustrations by Christy Hale. Lee & Low Books 2004 un il $16.95

Grades: 1 2 3 4   E
1. Mohawk Indians -- Fiction 2. Steel construction -- Fiction 3. Father-son relationship -- Fiction 4. Empire State Building (New York, N.Y.) -- Fiction
ISBN 1-58430-162-7
LC 2004-1885

John Cloud, a Mohawk boy, lives in upstate New York, but he goes to visit his father who is working on the Empire State Building

"Rich, sunlit gouache illustrations establish the 1930s setting for this well-told story." Horn Book Guide

Kirk, Daniel

A friend's tale; Daniel Kirk. Abrams Books for Young Readers 2009 32 p. col. ill.

Grades: K 1 2 3   E
1. Mice -- Fiction 2. Authorship -- Fiction 3. Friendship -- Fiction 4. Libraries -- Fiction 5. Bashfulness -- Fiction
ISBN 0810989271; 9780810989276
LC 2008024686

In this book, "Sam, the perky creative mouse hero of 'Library Mouse,' returns. The Writers and Illustrators Club's next project at the library is to be a joint one. Each author is to collaborate with an illustrator. . . . One night, busy researching his next story, Sam falls asleep. He must hide when the children start arriving, and he leaves his notebook behind. Tom finds it. Suspicious, the boy follows inky footprints to Sam's mouse hole and realizes that the mysterious author must be a mouse. When Tom leaves cheese and a cracker for him, Sam hopes that the boy will forget about him. Instead, Tom is inspired to write a story about shy Sam. He leaves the story by the mouse hole, and Sam surprises Tom by illus-

trating it. Together, they keep the secret of Sam's identity." (Children's Literature)

Honk honk! Beep beep! words and pictures by Daniel Kirk. Disney/Hyperion Books 2010 un il $15.99

Grades: PreK K   E
1. Stories in rhyme 2. Toys -- Fiction 3. Vehicles -- Fiction
ISBN 978-1-4231-2486-3; 1-4231-2486-3
LC 2010010275

When a toy father and son set out early one morning for a cross-country drive in their jeep, they see all sorts of vehicles and pick up diverse passengers along the way.

"Bright colors, a rhythmic text, and an imaginative premise make this a winner for kids just starting to find fun in books. . . . The spacious layout and oversize typeface make the story accessible to the youngest readers and listeners, who will want to call out the noisy refrain." Booklist

Keisha Ann can! [by] Daniel Kirk. G.P. Putnam's Sons 2008 un il $15.99

Grades: PreK K 1 2   E
1. School stories 2. Stories in rhyme
ISBN 978-0-399-24179-6; 0-399-24179-5
LC 2007-034815

Keisha Ann is proud of all the things she can do during her day at school.

The "rhyming text . . . is catchy and upbeat. . . . Gouache paintings done in a striking, childlike style are filled with motion and color. . . . The images are clear and crisp, making the book ideal for sharing aloud. The story ends on a positive, all-inclusive note." SLJ

Library mouse; home sweet home. Daniel Kirk. Abrams Books for Young Readers 2013 40 p. (alk. paper) $16.95

Grades: K 1 2 3   E
1. Picture books for children 2. Mice -- Fiction 3. Dwellings -- Fiction 4. Libraries -- Fiction
ISBN 141970544X; 9781419705441
LC 2012039261

This book is part of Daniel Kirk's Library Mouse series. Here, while "Sam the mouse's library is undergoing renovation, he and [his] best friend Sarah . . . want to build the perfect temporary house for themselves, but are having trouble finding it. Sam tries his hand at creating a classical Roman structure, a 'Tudor-style house,' and a bungalow; Sarah . . . gravitates toward a Mongolian yurt, a 'Vietnamese stilt house,' and a geodesic dome worthy of Buckminster Fuller." (Publishers Weekly)

Ten thank-yous; Daniel Kirk. Nancy Paulsen Books, An Imprint of Penguin Group (USA) 2014 32 p. color illustrations $16.99

Grades: PreK K 1 2   E
1. Pigs -- Fiction 2. Rabbits -- Fiction 3. Friendship -- Fiction 4. Gratitude -- Fiction 5. Best friends -- Fiction 6. Thank-you notes -- Fiction
ISBN 0399169377; 9780399169373
LC 2013046403

In this children's book, by Daniel Kirk, "Pig is writing a thank-you note to his grandma when his friend Rabbit comes over to play. Eager to get in on the action, Rabbit writes one of his own . . . and another . . . and another . . . until his flurry of thank-you notes has Pig in a tizzy. Pig just wants to finish writing his note in peace! Fortunately, Rabbit's last thank-you note reminds Pig how lucky he is to have Rabbit as a friend." (Publisher's note)

"This pleasant follow-up to Ten Things I Love about You (2012) again features Pig and Rabbit learning another sweet lesson in thoughtfulness... Kirk's upbeat story is told through dialogue and letters, and his expert combination of old techniques (drawing with ink, painting plywood panels) with new ones (adding colors and textures with Photoshop) nicely highlights the perpetual value of appreciation." Booklist

Kirk, David, 1955-

Oh So Tiny Bunny; David Kirk. Feiwel & Friends 2013 40 p. $16.99

Grades: PreK K   E

1. Size -- Fiction 2. Dreams -- Fiction 3. Rabbits -- Fiction

ISBN 1250016886; 9781250016881

This children's book, by David Kirk, follows a small rabbit who dreams of being larger. "During the day, Oh So Tiny Bunny is very, very small. But at night, he dreams of being . . . as big as a dragon, or even a mountain! At first, that's fine, but then he feels lonely. There's no one to share it with. Are there no other bunnies so big as him? . . . In this book David Kirk reminds us that sometimes . . . it's not so bad being small." (Publisher's note)

Kirk, Katie

Eli, no! Abrams Books for Young Readers 2011 un il $14.95

Grades: PreK K 1   E

1. Dogs -- Fiction

ISBN 978-0-8109-8964-1; 0-8109-8964-6

Eli is a sweet black dog with a knack for getting into huge messes. He makes his disastrous way through the house and the yard, at every turn disobeying his owners.

"There is a retro feel to the minimalist, bold illustrations that match the simple rhyming story. . . . Amusing details . . . make this a fun read-aloud for small groups and lapsits." SLJ

Kirsch, Vincent X.

Forsythia & me. Farrar Straus Giroux 2011 un il $16.99

Grades: PreK K 1   E

1. Friendship -- Fiction

ISBN 978-0-374-32438-4; 0-374-32438-7

LC 2009-53233

Chester has always been in awe of his best friend's accomplishments, but when she becomes ill, he discovers that he is capable of doing amazing things to entertain her while she is bed-ridden.

"The young audience will welcome the wild, imaginative play and the story of loyal friendship, all captured in the winsome ink, watercolor, and pencil illustrations." Booklist

Natalie & Naughtily. Bloomsbury Children's Books 2008 un il $16.99; lib bdg $17.89

Grades: K 1 2 3   E

1. Twins -- Fiction 2. Sisters -- Fiction 3. Department

stores -- Fiction

ISBN 978-1-59990-269-2; 1-59990-269-9; 978-1-59990-320-0 lib bdg; 1-59990-320-2 lib bdg

LC 2007-51098

Natalie and Naughtily Nopps live above their family's department store and love to play there, but one particularly busy day they discover that 'helping' is even better than playing.

"Readers will pore over the intricately detailed watercolor and pencil illustrations of each floor of the department store while chuckling over the girls' ideas of helpfulness." Horn Book Guide

Two little boys from Toolittle Toys. Bloomsbury 2010 un $16.99; lib bdg $17.89

Grades: PreK K 1 2 3   E

1. Play -- Fiction 2. Toys -- Fiction 3. Brothers -- Fiction

ISBN 978-1-59990-428-3; 1-59990-428-4; 978-1-59990-429-0 lib bdg; 1-59990-429-2 lib bdg

LC 2009034583

The Toolittle Toy Company makes toys that children like to play with by making toys that like to play with children.

"Kirsch offers a clever story about the nature and rewards of play, and children will enjoy poring over the wild details of fanciful toys in the watercolor-and-pencil scenes, which culminate in a Toolittle Toy Company catalog at the back of the book." Booklist

Kirwan, Wednesday

Minerva the monster. Sterling 2008 un il $14.95

Grades: PreK K 1 2   E

1. Monsters -- Fiction 2. Family life -- Fiction

ISBN 978-1-4027-5718-1; 1-4027-5718-2

LC 2007043376

Feeling out of sorts, Minerva pretends to be a monster, but after realizing that monsters do not eat cookies, read stories, or sleep in nice warm beds, she decides to rejoin her family.

"The gouache and colored-pencil illustrations are crisp, bright, and full of mischief, much like Minerva herself. This book will be a hit with readers." SLJ

Another title about Minerva is:
Nobody notices Minerva (2007)

Kitamura, Satoshi

Stone Age boy. Candlewick Press 2007 32p il $15.99

Grades: K 1 2 3   E

1. Stone Age -- Fiction 2. Prehistoric peoples -- Fiction

ISBN 978-0-7636-3474-2; 0-7636-3474-3

LC 2007025614

"A boy walking in the woods finds himself falling . . . through time and space, landing in the Stone Age. He befriends a girl named Om and learns about prehistoric society by watching her people make fire, prepare food, use tools, and celebrate a successful hunt. . . . Kitmaura makes Om's society come alive. . . . Sentences are concise and easy to read. . . . The well-designed pages make effective use of white space." Horn Book

Kladstrup, Kristin

★ The **gingerbread** pirates; illustrated by Matt Tavares. Candlewick Press 2009 un il $16.99

Grades: K 1 2 3   E

1. Cookies -- Fiction 2. Pirates -- Fiction 3. Christmas -- Fiction

ISBN 978-0-7636-3223-6; 0-7636-3223-6

LC 2007-23171

When Jim's gingerbread pirate, Captain Cookie, comes alive, the tasty treat prepares to battle Santa Claus, who likes to eat cookies on Christmas Eve.

"An exciting story and full-page, dramatically composed paintings depicting harrowing adventures with a mouse, a cat, and the crew imprisoned in a cookie jar make this a good holiday read-aloud." SLJ

Klassen, Jon

★ **I** want my hat back. Candlewick Press 2011 un il $15.99

Grades: PreK K 1 2   E

1. Hats -- Fiction 2. Bears -- Fiction 3. Animals -- Fiction 4. Lost and found possessions -- Fiction

ISBN 978-0-7636-5598-3; 0-7636-5598-8

LC 2010042793

"Digitally manipulated ink paintings show a slow-witted bear. . . . Unadorned lines of type, printed without quotation marks of attributions, parallel the sparse lines Klassen uses for the forest's greenery. . . . [Klassen creates] skillful characterizations. . . . Each animal emerges fully realized." Publ Wkly

★ **This** is not my hat; Jon Klassen. Candlewick Press 2012 40 p. col. ill. $15.99

Grades: K 1 2 3   E

1. Hats -- Fiction 2. Theft -- Fiction 3. Fishes -- Fiction

ISBN 0763655996; 9780763655990

LC 2012942300

Randolph Caldecott Medal (2013)

In this children's story, written and illustrated by Jon Klassen, a fish steals a hat from a larger fish. "When a tiny fish shoots into view wearing a round blue topper (which happens to fit him perfectly), trouble could be following close behind. So it's a good thing that enormous fish won't wake up. And even if he does, it's not like he'll ever know what happened." (Publisher's note)

Klausmeier, Jesse

★ **Open** this little book; by Jesse Klausmeier; illustrated by Suzy Lee. Chronicle Books 2013 40 p. (alk. paper) $16.99

Grades: PreK K 1 2   E

1. Toy and movable books 2. Board books 3. Color -- Fiction 4. Animals -- Fiction 5. Books and reading -- Fiction

ISBN 0811867838; 9780811867832

LC 2012002129

Boston Globe-Horn Book Honor: Picture Book (2013).

This children's book, by Jesse Klausmeier, illustrated by Suzy Lee, features a series of nested smaller books within itself. The story revolves around a group of animals which each individually read about other animals reading more books until the end where they close their books and find another. The book gives tribute and attention to the joys of reading, colors, and friendship.

Kleven, Elisa

★ The **apple** doll; [by] Elisa Kleven. Farrar, Straus & Giroux 2007 un il $16

Grades: PreK K 1 2   E

1. School stories 2. Dolls -- Fiction 3. Apples -- Fiction

ISBN 978-0-374-30380-8; 0-374-30380-0

LC 2006040981

Lizzy is scared to start school, so she makes a doll out of an apple from her favorite tree to take with her on the first day and keep her company. Includes instructions for making an apple doll

"Kleven's lovely mixed-media collage illustrations . . . are filled with eye-catching detail and activity. A sweet story about accepting change, working together, and forming new friendships." SLJ

The **friendship** wish. Dutton Childrens Books 2011 un il $17.99

Grades: PreK K 1 2   E

1. Dogs -- Fiction 2. Angels -- Fiction 3. Moving -- Fiction 4. Animals -- Fiction 5. Friendship -- Fiction

ISBN 978-0-525-42374-4; 0-525-42374-5

LC 2011005248

Foley the dog has trouble making friends when he moves to a new home, but after an angel visits him in a dream, Foley's neighbors come to hear about the experience and they all begin to share their talents in hopes the angel will return.

Kleven "deftly interweaves fantastic and familiar elements, and kids will recognize how imagination, support, and shared activities can inspire fun and connection. The lively, lyrical prose is illustrated with colorful, intricate mixed-media artwork that includes droll details that invited close viewing." Booklist

Welcome home, Mouse. Tricycle Books 2010 un il $15.99; lib bdg $18.99

Grades: PreK K 1   E

1. Mice -- Fiction 2. Houses -- Fiction 3. Elephants -- Fiction

ISBN 978-1-58246-277-6; 1-58246-277-1; 978-1-58246-364-3 lib bdg; 1-58246-364-6 lib bdg

Stanley the elephant, who is very clumsy, accidentally smashes Mouse's house, then promises to try to make a new one.

"The fascinating illustrations made from watercolors, ink, pastels, and colored pencils feature two simply drawn plump gray elephants and a small tan mouse placed on intricately assembled collage backgrounds. . . . Using one's imagination, repairing a mistake, and making a new friend are some of the themes contained in this charming story." SLJ

Kling, Kevin

Big little brother; illustrations by Chris Monroe. Borealis Books 2011 il $17.95

Grades: PreK K 1 2   E

1. Size -- Fiction 2. Brothers -- Fiction

ISBN 978-0-87351-844-4; 0-87351-844-6

LC 2011018586

A four-year-old boy explains that his little brother is bigger than he is, follows him everywhere, and is annoying, but his presence becomes indispensible when bullies are around.

"Monroe's minimalist, boldly hued cartoons carefully and humorously depict the action. Big Brother's emotional ups and downs are subtly expressed, while Little Brother mostly maintains an even-tempered smile. A sweet-natured tale about negotiating sibling dynamics that is as comforting as a hug." Kirkus

Big little mother; Kevin Kling; illustrated by Chris Monroe. Borealis Books 2013 32 p. (cloth: alk. paper) $17.95
Grades: PreK K 1 2   E
1. Cats -- Fiction 2. Brothers and sisters -- Fiction
ISBN 0873519116; 9780873519113
                                        LC 2013015999
In this book, by Kevin Kling and illustrated by Chris Monroe, "a younger brother has little choice but to look up to his older sister. . . . Big Sister . . . loves to share her knowledge, particularly with her best friend, Kittywumpus, the family cat. However . . . Kittywumpus runs away for a much-needed break, leaving Little Brother as the new target for Big Sister's ministrations. And while it's fun at first, . . . Little Brother think[s] that the cat might have had the right idea." (Publisher's note)

Klinting, Lars

What do you want? [translated from the Swedish by Maria Lundin] Groundwood Books/House of Anansi Press 2006 un il $15.95; board book $7.95
Grades: PreK   E
1. Board books for children 2. Wishes -- Fiction
ISBN 0-88899-636-5; 978-0-88899-988-7 board book
Original Swedish edition 2003
"This diminutive book is mesmerizing in its calm simplicity. Cream-colored pages provide the backdrop to clear, precise color illustrations that are executed with artistic aplomb." SLJ

Klise, Kate

Grammy Lamby and the secret handshake; Kate Klise; illustrated by M. Sarah Klise. Henry Holt 2012 32 p. (hc) $16.99
Grades: K 1 2   E
1. Storms -- Fiction 2. Grandmothers -- Fiction 3. Picture books for children 4. Sheep -- Fiction 5. Repairing -- Fiction 6. Neighborliness -- Fiction
ISBN 0805093133; 9780805093131
                                        LC 2011028532
This is the tale of "Grammy Lamby who arrives for a visit and swoops down on her little grandson Larry. Larry learns her secret handshake is meant to let him know Grammy loves him but he is more than a little intimidated by her. She's very energetic and a trifle overbearing," which "leaves Larry waiting for her visits to end. However, when a terrible storm descends and leaves the house in shambles, Grammy Lamby stays for a month, energetically fixing things." (Children's Literature)

★ **Shall** I knit you a hat? a Christmas yarn. illustrated by M. Sarah Klise. H. Holt 2004 un il $16.95; pa $6.99
Grades: PreK K 1 2   E
1. Hats -- Fiction 2. Animals -- Fiction 3. Rabbits -- Fiction 4. Christmas -- Fiction
ISBN 0-8050-7318-3; 0-312-37139-X pa
                                        LC 2003-22497

When Mother Rabbit knits a warm winter hat for Little Rabbit, he likes it so much that he suggests they make hats for all of their friends as Christmas gifts
"The acrylic artwork glows with humor and radiates warmth." Booklist
Other titles about Little Rabbit are:
Why do you cry?: not a sob story (2006)
Imagine Harry (2007)
Little Rabbit and the night mare (2008)
Little Rabbit and the Meanest Mother on Earth (2010)

★ **Stand** straight, Ella Kate; the true story of a real giant. pictures by M. Sarah Klise. Dial Books for Young Readers 2010 un il $16.99
Grades: K 1 2 3   E
1. Giants 2. Giants -- Fiction
ISBN 978-0-8037-3404-3; 0-8037-3404-2
A fictionalized biography of Ella Kate Ewing, born in 1872, who was eight feet tall by the age of seventeen and who became financially independent by traveling the country for nearly twenty years appearing at museums, exhibitions, and in circus shows.
"The story is well told in straightforward prose with lots of dialogue, and Ella's strength of character shines through. The stylized acrylic illustrations add much to the text, using bright colors and emphasizing Ella's height from various perspectives." SLJ

Kloske, Geoffrey

Once upon a time, the end; (asleep in 60 seconds) by Geoffrey Kloske and Barry Blitt. Atheneum Books for Young Readers 2005 25p il $15.95
Grades: PreK K 1 2   E
1. Fairy tales 2. Bedtime -- Fiction
ISBN 0-689-86619-4
A tired father takes only a few sentences to tell a number of classic tales in order to get the persistent listener to fall asleep.
"Blitt's ink-and-watercolor illustrations are amusing, with fine lines and soothing colors underscoring the comedy in the characters and situations." SLJ

Knapman, Timothy

Guess what I found in Dragon Wood? by Timothy Knapman; illustrated by Gwen Millward. Bloomsbury Children's Books 2008 un il $16.95
Grades: PreK K 1 2   E
1. Dragons -- Fiction
ISBN 978-1-59990-190-9; 1-59990-190-0
                                        LC 2007018847
A young dragon finds a boy and introduces him to his family, friends, and teacher, but it is clear that the boy would like to return to his faraway home
"Executed with humor and cozy, scaly charm. . . . The tidy linework in the line-and-watercolor art adds a certain comic formality to the dragonworld." Bull Cent Child Books

Mungo and the spiders from space; illustrated by Adam Stower. Dial Books for Young Readers 2008 un il $16.99
Grades: PreK K 1 2   E
1. Science fiction 2. Comic books, strips, etc. -- Fiction
ISBN 978-0-8037-3277-3; 0-8037-3277-5
First published 2007 in the United Kingdom

"Mungo discovers the last page is missing from his second-hand picture book; how will he learn what happens to Captain Galacticus and Gizmo? Mungo himself provides the ending when, suddenly, he is pulled into the book and saves the universe. The brightly colored comic-book format, busy with rocket ships, space creatures, and humorous details, weaves Mungo's story into this metafictional adventure." Horn Book Guide

Knapp, Ruthie
★ **Who** stole Mona Lisa? illustrations by Jill McElmurry. Bloomsbury Children's Books 2010 un il $17.99; lib bdg $18.89
Grades: K 1 2 3   **E**
1. Artists 2. Painters 3. Scientists 4. Writers on science 5. Art thefts -- Fiction
ISBN 978-1-59990-058-2; 1-59990-058-0; 978-1-59990-549-5 lib bdg; 1-59990-549-3 lib bdg
LC 2010005512
Tells the story of the famous Leonardo Da Vinci portrait known as the Mona Lisa, including its 1911 theft from the Louvre in Paris, from the point of view of the subject of the painting. Includes an author's note with facts about the painting.
"The engaging, rhythmic-but-not-rhyming text fuses deliciously with McElmurry's marvelous artwork—its flat, decorative style, skewed head angles, strong lines and rich gouache colors echo both illuminated manuscripts and the Sienese school of painting. . . . A gem." Kirkus

Kneen, Maggie
Chocolate moose. Dutton Children's Books 2011 un il $16.99
Grades: PreK K 1   **E**
1. Mice -- Fiction 2. Moose -- Fiction 3. Baking -- Fiction
ISBN 978-0-525-42202-0; 0-525-42202-1
LC 2010013464
When a chocolate-loving moose goes to work in Mrs. Mouse's bakery he does not fit in very well, but Mrs. Mouse discovers that he has other useful talents.
"This is a winsome offering, illustrated in soft-edged shapes and pastel colors. . . . The baby mice are delighted with Moose, and children will be too." Booklist

Knowlton, Laurie Lazzaro
A **young** man's dance; [by] Laurie Knowlton; paintings by Layne Johnson. Boyds Mills Press 2006 un il $15.95
Grades: K 1 2 3   **E**
1. Old age -- Fiction 2. Grandmothers -- Fiction 3. Alzheimer's disease -- Fiction
ISBN 1-59078-259-3
LC 2005021138
Grandma Ronnie's grandson has a hard time adjusting to her needing a wheelchair, living in a nursing home, and not recognizing him when he comes to visit her
"Swirling, dancing colors, both muted and sunny, accompany this lyrical story. . . . Oil paintings reveal clear, expressive faces on soft, fluid backgrounds that breathe action." SLJ

Knudsen, Michelle
Argus; illustrated by Andrea Wesson. Candlewick Press 2011 un il $15.99

Grades: PreK K 1 2   **E**
1. School stories 2. Dragons -- Fiction 3. Chickens -- Fiction 4. Science -- Experiments -- Fiction
ISBN 978-0-7636-3790-3; 0-7636-3790-4
LC 2010-38721
Sallie's class is supposed to be raising chicks as a science project, but although Argus, the large, green, scaly creature that hatches from her egg, causes all sorts of trouble she worries about him when he disappears.
Wesson's "watercolors of the tubby Argus are wonderfully goofy. . . . Knudsen . . . never overplays her hand, but lets the story's laughs unfold naturally from the characters and circumstances. Her grasp of the life of the elementary school classroom is spot-on." Publ Wkly

Bugged! illustrated by Blanche Sims. Kane Press 2008 32p il (Science solves it!) pa $5.95
Grades: 1 2 3   **E**
1. Mosquitoes -- Fiction
ISBN 978-1-57565-259-7 pa; 1-57565-259-5 pa
LC 2007026567
Tired of being covered in itchy mosquito bites, Riley uses science to investigate why mosquitoes are more attracted to him than to his friends.
"Clear and simple sentences, colorful realistic illustrations, and diverse characters all contribute to this appealing easy reader. . . . Riley's activities serve as a great model of the research process as well as the scientific method." SLJ

★ **Library** lion; [by] Michelle Knudsen; illustrated by Kevin Hawkes. Candlewick Press 2006 un il $15.99; pa $6.99
Grades: PreK K 1 2   **E**
1. Lions -- Fiction 2. Libraries -- Fiction
ISBN 978-0-7636-2262-6; 0-7636-2262-1; 978-0-7636-3784-2 pa; 0-7636-3784-X pa
LC 2006042578
A lion starts visiting the local library but runs into trouble as he tries to both obey the rules and help his librarian friend
"Hawkes's deft acrylic-and-pencil pictures have appeal for generations of library lovers. They are rich with expression, movement, and detail. . . . This winsome pairing of text and illustration is a natural for storytime and a first purchase for every collection." SLJ

Marilyn's monster; Michelle Knudsen; illustrated by Matt Phelan. Candlewick Press 2015 40 p. $15.99
Grades: PreK K 1 2 3   **E**
1. School stories 2. Monsters -- Fiction 3. Patience -- Fiction
ISBN 0763660116; 9780763660116
LC 2014944904
In this children's book by Michelle Knudsen, illustrated by Matt Phelan, "some of the kids in Marilyn's class have monsters. Marilyn doesn't have hers yet, but she can't just go out and look for one. Your monster has to find you. That's just the way it works. Marilyn tries to be patient and the kind of girl no monster can resist, but her monster doesn't come. Could she go out and search for him herself? Even if that's not the way it works?" (Publisher's note)

Kockere, Geert De
★ **Willy**; illustrated by Carll Cneut. Eerdmans Books for Young Readers 2011 un il $14

Grades: K 1 2   **E**
1. Elephants -- Fiction
ISBN 978-0-8028-5395-0; 0-8028-5395-1
LC 2010049545

Willy the elephant has everything an elephant should have, from four sturdy legs to a tail with a little brush on the end.

"It is the unexpected turn that De Kockere takes at the story's end that is the showstopper. Suddenly we are all Willy, in one great inclusive hug." Kirkus

Koehler, Fred

How to cheer up dad; story and pictures by Fred Koehler. Dial Books for Young Readers, an imprint of Penguin Group (USA) Inc. 2014 32 p. (hardcover: alk. paper) $16.99

Grades: PreK K 1   **E**
1. Elephants -- Fiction 2. Helping behavior -- Fiction 3. Father-child relationship -- Fiction 4. Behavior -- Fiction 5. Father and child -- Fiction 6. Mood (Psychology) -- Fiction
ISBN 0803739222; 9780803739222
LC 2013008514

In this children's book, by Fred Koehler, "Little Jumbo's Dad is having a bad day. The cereal on the floor, the raisins stuck to the ceiling, and the game of hide-and-seek at bath time are not helping. Little Jumbo spends his timeout thinking of a way to cheer him up. A hug, a game of catch, and some ice cream start to do the trick." (School Library Journal)

"'Little Jumbo's dad was having a bad day.' The joke is that the little elephant is cluelessly responsible for his dad's frustrations--e.g., Jumbo shoots the raisins intended for his oatmeal at the ceiling with his trunk (Dad "should have known what a mess that would make"). Plenty of white space and a modest palette foreground an entertaining father-child dynamic." Horn Book

Kohara, Kazuno

★ **Ghosts** in the house! [by] Kazuno Kohara. Roaring Brook Press 2008 un il $12.95

Grades: PreK K 1   **E**
1. Ghost stories 2. Witches -- Fiction
ISBN 978-1-59643-427-1; 1-59643-427-9
LC 2008018204

Tired of living in a haunted house, a young witch captures, washes, and turns her pesky ghosts into curtains and a tablecloth

"Kohara's wonderfully distinctive art, all orange and black, has the look of woodcuts. . . . A must-have for Halloween." Booklist

Here comes Jack Frost. Roaring Brook Press 2009 un il $12.99

Grades: PreK K 1   **E**
1. Winter -- Fiction
ISBN 978-1-59643-442-4; 1-59643-442-2

"A young boy has nobody to play with until a frosty figure named Jack appears. . . . All the boy has to do to ensure more fun is never mention anything warm. . . . The artwork is divine, beginning with the glittered jacket cover. . . . The simple yet creatively rendered shapes are all icy blues and snowy whites. . . . The artful design . . . is what will draw repeat viewers, young and old." Booklist

The **Midnight** Library; Kazuno Kohara. Roaring Brook Press 2014 32 p. color illustrations (hardcover) $16.99

Grades: PreK K 1   **E**
1. Owls -- Fiction 2. Libraries -- Fiction 3. Animals -- Fiction 4. Books and reading -- Fiction 5. Nocturnal animals -- Fiction
ISBN 1596439858; 9781596439856
LC 2013023154

"There is a little library that only opens at night. In the library there is a little librarian--and her three assistant owls--who helps everyone find the perfect book. The library is always peaceful and quiet . . . until one night when some of the animals stir up a little trouble (and a little fun!) in the Midnight Library." (Publisher's note)

"The jaunty, cartoonish illustrations depict happy animals enjoying the library for more than just reading, and cooperatively respecting everyone's space (is there a more important library lesson?). It goes without saying that this is perfect for storytime." Booklist

Kohuth, Jane

Anne Frank's chestnut tree; by Jane Kohuth; illustrated by Elizabeth Sayles. Random House 2013 48 p. (hardcover: alk. paper) $12.99

Grades: 1 2 3   **E**
1. Nature 2. Amsterdam (Netherlands) -- Biography 3. Jews -- Netherlands -- Amsterdam -- Biography 4. Jewish children in the Holocaust -- Netherlands -- Amsterdam
ISBN 0449812553; 9780307975799; 9780375971150; 9780375981135; 9780449812556
LC 2012034585

Author "Jane Kohuth explores Anne Frank's strong belief in the healing power of nature in this Step 3 leveled reader biography for newly independent readers ages 5-8," which is illustrated by Elizabeth Sayles. It describes how "hidden away in their Secret Annex in Amsterdam during World War II, Anne Frank and her family could not breathe fresh air or see the blue sky for years. . . . This small glimpse of nature gave Anne hope and courage." (Publisher's note)

"Nature, as represented by a chestnut tree outside the Secret Annex, serves as a continuing image for this easy reader. The tree's presence throughout Anne's life in hiding not only gives her a sense of peace but also provides readers a respite from her ordeal. Illustrations are somber except those depicting Anne's pre-war life or Annex visits from helpers bringing food and books." (Horn Book)

Includes bibliographical references and index

Duck sock hop; by Jane Kohuth; illustrated by Jane Porter. Dial Books for Young Readers 2012 32 p. col. ill. (hardcover) $16.99

Grades: PreK K 1   **E**
1. Ducks -- Fiction 2. Stories in rhyme 3. Picture books for children 4. Dance -- Fiction 5. Socks -- Fiction
ISBN 0803737122; 9780803737129
LC 2011029969

This children's picture book "stars a crew of dancing ducks whose webby feet are made even happier by donning all kinds of sprightly socks . . . . No matter that socks prove more of a hindrance than a help when it comes to dancing (the sock hop results in 'big duck flops!' and trips to the first-aid station); at book's end, the dancers are back at the Duck Sock Shop to pick up new pairs for the next soiree." (Publishers Weekly)

Ducks go vroom; illustrated by Viviana Garofoli. Random House 2011 31p il (Step into reading) lib bdg $12.99; pa $3.99

Grades: PreK K 1   E

1. Stories in rhyme 2. Ducks -- Fiction 3. Noise -- Fiction

ISBN 978-0-375-96567-8 lib bdg; 0-375-96567-X lib bdg; 978-0-375-86560-2 pa; 0-375-86560-8 pa

LC 2010002695

Relates three silly ducks' rather impolite visit to their Auntie Goose's house, introducing simple action and noise words.

"Concentrated colored backgrounds add to the visual appeal of the pages, which have either black or white text and bright cartoon illustrations. . . . A solid choice for libraries needing entry-level readers." SLJ

Kolanovic, Dubravka

Everyone needs a friend. Price Stern Sloan 2010 il $9.99

Grades: PreK K 1   E

1. Mice -- Fiction 2. Wolves -- Fiction 3. Friendship -- Fiction

ISBN 978-0-8431-9918-5; 0-8431-9918-0

Jack the wolf has been wishing for a friend, but Walter the dormouse may not be the right choice.

"This simple story is rendered in bright oil pastels, with thoughtful background details that give the illustrations a cozy feel. A tale of friendship that will fit nicely into most collections." SLJ

Kolar, Bob

Big kicks. Candlewick Press 2008 un il $16.99

Grades: PreK K 1 2   E

1. Bears -- Fiction 2. Soccer -- Fiction 3. Animals -- Fiction

ISBN 978-0-7636-3390-5; 0-7636-3390-9

"Biggie Bear's soccer-playing friends appear at his doorstep . . . begging him to join them. . . . Biggie is a jazz fan who collects stamps. . . . Despite his athletic shortcomings, the score is tied until the bear bends over to grasp a rare stamp on the ground and heads the ball into the net for the winning goal. . . . Kolar's soccer story is just rollicking enough for listeners. . . . Digital cartoons of rounded figures with exaggerated features are brightly hued and presented in detailed scenes that are balanced with less complex spreads." SLJ

Komako Sakai

Hannah's Night; Komako Sakai. Lerner Pub Group 2014 32 p. chiefly color illustrations $17.95

Grades: PreK K 1   E

1. Night -- Fiction 2. Bedtime -- Fiction

ISBN 1877579548; 9781877579547

In this book, written and illustrated by Komako Sakai, "when Hannah wakes up and discovers the quiet, exciting night-time world. When Hannah wakes suddenly in the night, she discovers a whole new world of adventure. With nobody awake to tell her off, she can do just as she pleases." (Publisher's note)

"The artist's smoothly drafted drawings capture with aching sweetness all the movements of a very young child the way Hannah's trip down the stairs is an expedition carried out step by step; the way she sits thoughtfully on her haunches to eat the cherries stolen from the refrigerator as Shiro laps milk; the way she reaches stealthily over her sleeping sister to take the older girl's doll. By keeping her focus tight and observing Hannah closely, Sakai's characterization feels natural, light, and true to life." Pub Wkly

Konagaya, Kiyomi

Beach feet; by Kiyomi Konagaya; illustrated by Masamitsu Saito. Enchanted Lion Books 2012 32 p. (hardback) $14.95

Grades: PreK K 1   E

1. Beaches -- Fiction 2. Picture books for children 3. Foot -- Fiction

ISBN 9781592701216

LC 2011052465

In this "installment in the 'Being in the World' series, Japanese collaborators [Kiyomi] Konagaya and [Masamitsu] Saito offer a[n] . . . account of a day in the life of a child at the beach. Cover art depicts . . . toes scrunching down into the sand, and the book opens to a first-person, stream-of-consciousness text detailing the child's seaside experience. It's never clear whether this child is a boy or a girl, but this doesn't matter, as from page to page those feet from the cover art feel the heat of sun-baked sand, the coolness of the ocean waters, and the hard pressure of a seashell underfoot. . . . [N]arration delivers the child's experiences in brief snippets of text that" describe the child's "experiences of the surroundings." (Kirkus)

Konnecke, Ole

Anton can do magic. Gecko Press 2011 il $17.95

Grades: PreK K 1 2   E

1. Magicians -- Fiction

ISBN 978-1-8774-6737-0; 1-8774-6737-5

"Young Anton dons a magician's turban and sets off to prove that he can make things disappear. Because his too-large turban keeps slipping down over his eyes, a few things do indeed go missing. . . . This story is told with a spare, easy-to-read text; it's the illustrations that tell the true story and add much humor." SLJ

Kono, Erin Eitter

Hula lullaby; [by] Erin Eitter Kono. Little, Brown 2005 un il $15.99

Grades: PreK K 1 2   E

1. Hawaii -- Fiction 2. Bedtime -- Fiction 3. Mother-child relationship -- Fiction

ISBN 0-316-73591-4

LC 2004-10270

Against the backdrop of a beautiful Hawaiian landscape, a young girl cuddles and sleeps in her mother's lap

"The rhyming text becomes almost hypnotic as night deepens around the two and, finally, the girl falls asleep. Glowing with warm colors, which seem all the more brilliant in the night scenes, the gouache-and-pencil illustrations create an idyllic vision of Hawaiian culture." Booklist

Kontis, Alethea

Alpha oops! the day Z went first. [by] Alethea Kontis; illustrated by Bob Kolar. Candlewick Press 2006 un il $15.99

Grades: K 1 2   E

1. Alphabet -- Fiction

ISBN 978-0-7636-2728-7; 0-7636-2728-3

LC 2006042310

Chaos ensues when Z thinks that its time for him to go first in the alphabet for a change

"Reflecting the letters' saucy ways, the colorful, stylized artwork dramatizes the action and offers bits of comic byplay for the observant. An alphabet book with attitude." Booklist

★ **AlphaOops!**: H is for Halloween; illustrated by Bob Kolar. Candlewick Press 2010 un il $15.99

Grades: K 1 2 3   E

1. Alphabet 2. Halloween -- Fiction

ISBN 978-0-7636-3966-2; 0-7636-3966-4

LC 2009-14827

While putting on a Halloween pageant, the alphabet mixes things up with some spooky, and funny, results.

"Kontis's text is rhythmic and comical, and readers who are comfortable with the alphabet will delight in the silliness of this story. Kolar's illustrations are imbued with a sense of nighttime theater magic, and the slightly muted jewel-tone hues set the scene perfectly. A winsome union of humorous text and art." SLJ

Kooser, Ted, 1939-

Bag in the wind; illustrated by Barry Root. Candlewick 2010 un il

Grades: 1 2 3   E

1. Bags -- Fiction 2. Landfills -- Fiction 3. Recycling -- Fiction

ISBN 0-7636-3001-2; 978-0-7636-3001-0

One cold, spring morning, an ordinary grocery bag begins blowing around a landfill, then as it travels down a road, through a stream, and into a town, it is used in various ways by different people, many of whom do not even notice it.

"The muted, dappled colors of Root's gouache and watercolor illustrations are a perfect complement to Kooser's lengthy, meditative passages. . . . An excellent opener for discussions about creative reuse and recycling." Booklist

Kornell, Max

Bear with me. Putnam 2011 un il $15.99

Grades: PreK K 1   E

1. Bears -- Fiction 2. Family life -- Fiction

ISBN 978-0-399-25257-0; 0-399-25257-6

LC 2010-23202

A boy at first is angry when his parents suddenly welcome a giant bear named Gary into their family, but eventually he and Gary learn to get along.

"The pleasant watercolor, ink, and acrylic illustrations are expertly drawn, with an interesting use of outlining, perspectives, and layout. . . . This charming offering can be enjoyed even by those whose families are staying just the way they are." SLJ

Korngold, Jamie, 1965-

Sadie and the big mountain; by Jamie Korngold; illustrated by Julie Fortenberry. Kar-Ben Pub. 2012 32 p. (lib. bdg.: alk. paper) $17.95 E

1. Jewish holidays -- Fiction 2. Jewish children -- Fiction 3. Schools -- Fiction 4. Shavuot -- Fiction 5. Nursery schools -- Fiction 6. Ten commandments -- Fiction 7. Jews -- United States -- Fiction

ISBN 0761364927; 9780761364924

LC 2011018797

In this children's book by Jamie Korngold, illustrated by Julie Fortenberry, "When her preschool plans a Shavuot hike just like Moses took up Mt. Sinai, Sadie is afraid she is too little to make it to the top, and tries to think of ways to be absent. But when the day comes, she learns that anyone can climb high enough to reach God." (Publisher's note)

"To celebrate Shavuot, Sadie's class will go on a hike. But Sadie worries that she won't be able to "climb a mountain as big as the one Moses climbed." Unsurprisingly, the rabbi allays Sadie's fears, and she enjoys the day. The formulaic story lacks substance, though the pleasant illustrations suitably convey Sadie's anxiety. A brief explanation of the holiday is included." (Horn Book)

Sadie's almost marvelous menorah; by Jamie Korngold; illustrated by Julie Fortenberry. Kar-Ben Pub. 2013 24 p. $7.95

Grades: PreK K 1   E

1. Menorah -- Fiction 2. Hanukkah -- Fiction

ISBN 0761364935; 0761364951; 9780761364931; 9780761364955

LC 2011029042

In this book, "Sadie works hard to carefully sculpt and paint her clay menorah." She "is eager to show it to her mother on the last day of the week. In her rush, she trips and drops the menorah, which breaks into 'a million, zillion pieces.' Through tears and disappointment, Sadie and her mom realize that while the shattered menorah is not repairable, the shamas remains perfectly intact and becomes 'Sadie's Super Shammash' to light all the menorahs in the home each year." (Kirkus Reviews)

"Sadie has made her own menorah at school. She's thrilled to take home her pink and blue creation, but she trips, shattering the menorah into "a million, zillion pieces." Luckily the shammash remains intact--a Hanukkah miracle!--and a new tradition begins. Illustrations capture both the bustling and the quiet times of Sadie's classroom; light-infused pictures of the family at home radiate warmth." (Horn Book)

Kostecki-Shaw, Jenny Sue

My travelin' eye; [by] Jenny Sue Kostecki-Shaw. Henry Holt 2008 un il $16.95

Grades: K 1 2   E

1. Eye -- Fiction 2. Vision -- Fiction

ISBN 978-0-8050-8169-5; 0-8050-8169-0

LC 2007007224

Jenny Sue loves that her "travelin' eye" lets her see the world in a special way, and so she is not happy when her teacher suggests that her parents take her to an opthamologist to fix the lazy eye

"Bright colors and patterns warm the realistic story, while graphics-style artwork gives a since of [Jenny] Sue's vision." Booklist

Same, same, but different. Henry Holt 2011 un il $16.99

Grades: PreK K 1 2   **E**

1. Friendship -- Fiction

ISBN 978-0-8050-8946-2; 0-8050-8946-2

LC 2010030121

Pen pals Elliott and Kailash discover that even though they live in different countries—America and India—they both love to climb trees, own pets, and ride school buses.

"The imaginative multimedia illustrations, drawn in an animated, childlike style, add vibrant color and rich details to the story. Kostecki-Shaw presents a meaningful message of inclusivity in this engaging title." SLJ

Koster, Gloria

The **Peanut**-Free Cafe; illustrated by Maryann Cocca-Leffler. Whitman, A. 2006 un il $16.95

Grades: K 1 2 3   **E**

1. School stories 2. Allergy -- Fiction 3. Peanuts -- Fiction

ISBN 0-8075-6386-2

When a new classmate has a peanut allergy and has to sit in a special area of the lunchroom, Simon reconsiders his love for peanut butter.

"The cartoon-style art is fun, with some moments of exaggerated drama, as when Grant demonstrates what would happen to him if he ate just one peanut." Booklist

Kraegel, Kenneth

King Arthur's very great grandson; by Kenneth Kraegel. Candlewick 2012 40 p. (hardback) $15.99

Grades: PreK K 1 2   **E**

1. Dragons -- Fiction 2. Picture books for children 3. Knights and knighthood -- Fiction 4. Animals, Mythical -- Fiction 5. Adventure and adventurers -- Fiction

ISBN 076365311X; 9780763653118

LC 2011046646

In this book, "Henry Alfred Grummorson, the great-great-great-great-great-great-great grandson of Arthur, King of Britain, goes in search of adventure. First, he challenges a fire-breathing Dragon that simply blows smoke rings. He announces his presence to the giant Cyclops who, instead of fighting, engages him in a staring contest. . . . Travelling far in search of a worthy adversary, his search leads him past the winged Griffin (who offers a game of chess) to the sea monster Leviathan. Has he finally found something worthy of a fight? . . . Despite the determined lack of conflict, Henry still manages to find a treasure he didn't know he was seeking." (Kirkus)

Krall, Dan

The **great** lollipop caper; Dan Krall. 1st ed. Simon & Schuster Books for Young Readers 2013 48 p. col. ill. (hardcover) $16.99

Grades: PreK K 1 2   **E**

1. Humorous fiction 2. Humorous stories 3. Pickles -- Fiction 4. Lollipops -- Fiction 5. Contentment -- Fiction

ISBN 1442444606; 9781442444607; 9781442444614

LC 2012004041

In this children's story, by Dan Krall, "Mr. Caper . . . wants the children of the world to love him--just as much as they love the sweet, saccharine Lollipop. And thus a plot is hatched: Caper-flavored lollipops are dispatched through-

out the world . . . and everything goes horribly wrong. Will Mr. Caper find a way to repair the havoc he's wreaked by over-reaching? Maybe, if Lollipop helps save the day!" (Publisher's note)

Includes bibliographical references and index

Krasnesky, Thad

I always, always get my way; illustrated by David Parkins. Flashlight 2009 un il $16.95

Grades: PreK K 1 2   **E**

1. Family life -- Fiction

ISBN 978-0-9799746-4-9; 0-9799746-4-X

"Three-year-old Emmy wreaks havoc on her entire household. . . . Krasnesky tells the story with flowing rhyme that accommodates the humor of the plot and heightens Parkins's comical cartoon illustrations." SLJ

That cat can't stay! illustrated by David Parkins. Flashlight 2010 il $16.95

Grades: K 1 2   **E**

1. Cats -- Fiction

ISBN 978-0-9799746-5-6; 0-9799746-5-8

Kraus, Robert

★ **Whose** mouse are you? pictures by José Aruego. 30th anniversary ed.; Simon & Schuster Books for Young Readers 2000 un il $17.95

Grades: PreK K   **E**

1. Stories in rhyme 2. Mice -- Fiction

ISBN 0-689-84052-7

A reissue of the title first published 1970 by Macmillan

A lonely little mouse has to be resourceful in order to bring his family back together

"This is an absolute charmer of a picture book, original, tender, and childlike. The rhyming text is so brief, so catchy, and so right that a child will remember the words after one or two readings, and the large, uncluttered illustrations are gay and appealing." Booklist

Other titles about the mouse and his family are:

Come out and play, little mouse (1987)

Mouse in love (2000)

Where are you going, little mouse? (1986)

Krause, Ute

Oscar and the very hungry dragon. NorthSouth Books 2010 un il $16.95

Grades: PreK K 1 2   **E**

1. Cooking -- Fiction 2. Dragons -- Fiction

ISBN 978-0-7358-2306-8; 0-7358-2306-5

Original German edition, 2007

"When the earth trembles, the villagers at the bottom of the hill know it's time to send the dragon a princess to eat. One day, unfortunately, no princess is available; a child is the next best thing. Village elder Mr. Ballymore holds a lottery and young Oscar . . . is selected. . . . Packed with wit that never descends into camp and illustrated with verve and style in ink-and-watercolor cartoons, Krause's substantial, self-translated fractured fairy tale delights on every level." Kirkus

Krauss, Ruth

And I love you; illustrated by Steven Kellogg. Scholastic Press 2010 un il $16.99

Grades: PreK K 1   E
1. Cats -- Fiction 2. Love -- Fiction 3. Parent-child relationship -- Fiction
ISBN 978-0-439-02459-4; 0-439-02459-5

LC 2010009003

A newly illustrated edition of Big and Little, published 1987

Simple, rhythmic text follows a mother cat and her kitten as they discover the love of big forests for little trees, big skies for little skyscrapers, and parents for their children.

"With lots to look at, talk about and wonder over, this imaginative flight of fancy might also find a place in elementary art or creative-writing classes. Surprisingly and pleasantly offbeat." Kirkus

The **backward** day; story by Ruth Krauss; pictures by Marc Simont. New York Review Children's Collection 2007 un il (New York Review Children's Collection) $14.95
Grades: PreK K 1   E
1. Family -- Fiction 2. Morning -- Fiction
ISBN 978-1-59017-237-7; 1-59017-237-X

LC 2007-6747

A reissue of the title first published 1950 by Harper

Having decided that it is backward day, a boy dresses himself first in his coat, last in his socks, and continues in that way with the cooperation of his family.

"The silliness is enhanced by Simont's bold three-color illustrations showing everyone playing along. The universality of Krauss's work assures that a new generation will want to celebrate backward day." Horn Book Guide

★ **Bears**; story by Ruth Krauss; pictures by Maurice Sendak. HarperCollins Pubs. 2005 un il $14.95
Grades: PreK   E
1. Bears -- Fiction
ISBN 0-06-027994-X

A newly illustrated edition of the title first published 1948

"The 27-word text is full of possibility: 'Bears—Under chairs—Washing hairs—Giving stares—Collecting fares—.' . . . Sendak sets a full-color story in motion on the cover. In a scene both familiar and fresh, a boy in a wolf suit snuggles his stuffed bear in a themed room where the object of his affection is replicated on every conceivable surface. . . . Sure to spark laughter and original wordplay, this is the marriage of two masters." SLJ

★ The **carrot** seed; pictures by Crockett Johnson. Harper & Row 1945 un il $14.99; pa $5.99; bd bk $6.99
Grades: PreK K   E
1. Gardening -- Fiction
ISBN 0-06-023350-8; 0-06-443210-6 pa; 0-06-443210-6 bd bk
Simple text and picture show how the faith of a small boy, who planted a carrot seed, was rewarded

"Crockett Johnson's pictures are perfect and the brief text is just right." Book Week

★ The **growing** story; by Ruth Krauss; illustrated by Helen Oxenbury. HarperCollins 2000 un il $16.99; lib bdg $17.89

Grades: PreK K   E
1. Growth -- Fiction
ISBN 0-06-024716-9; 0-06-024717-7 lib bdg

LC 97-42822

A newly illustrated edition of the title first published 1947

A little boy worries throughout the summer that he's not getting bigger, but at the end of the season he tries on his winter clothes and realizes that he has grown.

"The story gets right to a child's experiences as it expresses both wondering and wonderment. This comes out beautifully in art that captures the affection between a boy and his hardworking mother who makes a bountiful place of the land they farm." Booklist

A **very** special house; by Ruth Krauss; pictures by Maurice Sendak. HarperCollins 1981 un il $16.95
Grades: PreK K   E
1. Imagination -- Fiction
ISBN 0-06-028638-5

LC 2002511422

A reissue of the title first published 1953

A Caldecott Medal honor book, 1954

"The very special house is a house which exists in the imagination of a small boy—a house where the chairs are for climbing, the walls for writing on, and the beds for jumping on; a house where a lion, a giant, or a dead mouse is welcome, and where nobody ever says stop. Told in a chanting rhythm that demands participation by the reader; the imaginary characters, objects, and doings are pictured in line drawings almost as a child would scribble them while the real little boy stands out boldly in bright blue overalls." Booklist

Krebs, Laurie
The **Beeman**; [text by] Laurie Krebs; [illustrations by] Valeria Cis. Barefoot Books 2008 un il $16.99
Grades: PreK K 1 2   E
1. Stories in rhyme 2. Bees -- Fiction 3. Grandfathers -- Fiction
ISBN 978-1-84686-146-8; 1-84686-146-2

A newly illustrated edition of the title first published 2002 by National Geographic

In rhyming text, a child describes the work Grandpa does to take care of honeybees and harvest the honey they make.

"This charming book is visually enticing and just plain fun to read. . . . The acrylic illustrations are done in predominantly muted, pastel shades with occasional touches of bright colors." SLJ

Krensky, Stephen
Hanukkah at Valley Forge; illustrated by Greg Harlin. Dutton Children's Books 2006 un il $17.99
Grades: 1 2 3 4   E
1. Generals 2. Presidents 3. Jews -- Fiction 4. Hanukkah -- Fiction 5. United States -- History -- 1775-1783, Revolution -- Fiction
ISBN 0-525-47738-1
During the Revolutionary War, a Jewish soldier from Poland lights the menorah on the first night of Hanukkah and tells General George Washington the story of the Maccabees and the miracle that Hanukkah celebrates. Based on factual events.

"Harlin's evocative paintings are rich with period details that successfully bring the settings to life. A well-told story." Booklist

★ **How** Santa got his job; illustrated by S.D. Schindler. Simon & Schuster Bks. for Young Readers 1998 un il hardcover o.p. pa $6.99

Grades: PreK K 1 2   E

1. Santa Claus -- Fiction

ISBN 0-689-80697-3; 0-689-84668-1 pa

LC 97-23474

This "peek at Santa's resumé reveals how various odd jobs, like chimney sweep and mail carrier, helped prepare him for his world-famous career. . . . [Schindler's] intricate pen-and-watercolor illustrations make Santa's evolution from boyish redhead to the familiar heavy-set, snowy-bearded character a joy to watch." Publ Wkly

Another title about Santa by this author and illustrator is: How Santa lost his job (2001)

Noah's bark; illustrated by Roge. Carolrhoda Books 2010 un il lib bdg $16.95

Grades: K 1 2   E

1. Sounds -- Fiction 2. Animals -- Fiction 3. Biblical characters 4. Noah's ark -- Fiction

ISBN 978-0-8225-7645-7; 0-8225-7645-7

LC 2007010022

Noah is distracted by animals making whatever sound comes into their heads while he is trying to build, then pilot, the ark, and so he devises a way for each animal to choose only one sound.

"The stylized, brushstroked paintings are embellished with highlighted sound effects and subtle comic expressions. Inventive and sure to elicit a boatload of giggles." Booklist

★ **Play** ball, Jackie! illustrated by Joe Morse. Millbrook Press 2011 un il lib bdg $16.95

Grades: 2 3 4 5   E

1. Baseball players 2. Army officers 3. Baseball -- Fiction 4. Race relations -- Fiction 5. African Americans -- Fiction 6. Brooklyn Dodgers (Baseball team) -- Fiction

ISBN 978-0-8225-9030-9; 0-8225-9030-1

LC 2010027270

On April 15, 1947, Matt Romano and his father watch the Brooklyn Dodgers season-opener, during which Jackie Robinson, a twenty-eight-year-old rookie, breaks the "color line" that had kept black men out of Major League baseball. Includes facts about Jackie Robinson's life and career.

"Morse's dramatically grained, exaggerated artwork plays up the intensity of the era's racial tensions and the dynamism of the game, while Krensky adeptly moves between the action on Ebbets Field and Matty's conversations with his father. An intimate and powerful account of a historic day," Publ Wkly

Sisters of Scituate Light; by Stephen Krensky; illustrated by Stacey Schuett. Dutton Children's Books 2008 un il $16.99

Grades: 1 2 3   E

1. Sisters -- Fiction 2. Lighthouses -- Fiction 3. War of

1812 -- Fiction 4. Massachusetts -- Fiction

ISBN 978-0-525-47792-1; 0-525-47792-6

LC 2007028297

In 1814, when their father leaves them in charge of the Scituate lighthouse outside of Boston, two teenaged sisters devise a clever way to avert an attack by a British warship patrolling the Massachusetts coast

"Krensky's fine telling is well matched by Schuett's illustrations, which are especially effective in capturing the colors of the sea and sky." Booklist

Spark the firefighter; by Stephen Krensky; illustrated by Amanda Haley. Dutton Childrens Books 2008 un il $16.99

Grades: PreK K 1   E

1. Fear -- Fiction 2. Dragons -- Fiction 3. Fire fighters -- Fiction

ISBN 978-0-525-47887-4; 0-525-47887-6

LC 2007050565

Spark's fear of fire has kept him from being a proper dragon, so he takes a job with the Hardscrabble volunteer fire department in hopes of conquering his fear

"Simply told with bright cartoon pictures and a dragon to hold interest, the . . . story teaches fire safety in an appealing way." SLJ

★ **Too** many leprechauns; (or how that pot o' gold got to the end of the rainbow) illustrated by Dan Andreasen. Simon & Schuster Books for Young Readers 2007 un il $12.99

Grades: K 1 2 3   E

1. Ireland -- Fiction 2. Leprechauns -- Fiction

ISBN 0-689-85112-X

LC 2005-20659

Finn O'Finnegan returns home after a year in Dublin and when he finds his village taken over by leprechauns, he must devise a way to get them to leave without making them angry.

"The well-paced story moves along smoothly, enhanced by Andreasen's handsome oil paintings, which picture the setting and characters with equal verve and charm." Booklist

Krilanovich, Nadia

Chicken, chicken, duck! Tricycle Press 2011 un il $16.99

Grades: PreK K   E

1. Ducks -- Fiction 2. Games -- Fiction 3. Sounds -- Fiction 4. Domestic animals -- Fiction

ISBN 978-1-58246-385-8; 1-58246-385-9

LC 2010010773

"A feisty white duck coordinates an impressive stunt amid lots of barnyard noise in Krilanovich's rhythmic book for very young readers. Paintings of the duck with outstretched wings suggest her cheerleader role directing a flock of chickens, a cat, a dog, and assorted other barnyard animals as they prepare to form a Flying Wallendas-style pyramid. The animals appear in tight close-up against clean white pages; they'd look clinical if not for their obvious excitement, the intensity of their interactions, and the painterly attention Krilanovich . . . devotes to their feathers, whiskers, black noses, and furry tails." Publ Wkly

Moon child; illustrations by Elizabeth Sayles. Tricycle Press 2010 un il $15.99; lib bdg $18.99

Grades: PreK K 1   **E**
1. Moon -- Fiction 2. Animals -- Fiction 3. Bedtime -- Fiction
ISBN 978-1-58246-325-4; 1-58246-325-5; 978-1-58246-366-7 lib bdg; 1-58246-366-2 lib bdg
LC 2009032304

"Various animal babies interact with the full moon in this quiet charmer. Otter playfully 'catches' it in order to give the orb a big hug, a raccoon plays with the reflection of its light, and an owl smiles at the stars and pretends she can balance the moon on the tip of her nose. There is very little text—only one sentence per spread—but it works well for this subject matter and mood. Sayles has primarily used dark blue and brown pastels with acrylic ink to set the tone for this peaceful night where all is well. Sweet dreams are sure to follow. Perfect for bedtime or evening storytimes." SLJ

Krishnaswami, Uma
Monsoon; pictures by Jamel Akib. Farrar, Straus & Giroux 2003 un il $16
Grades: K 1 2 3   **E**
1. India -- Fiction 2. Monsoons -- Fiction
ISBN 0-374-35015-9
LC 2001-54753

A child in India describes waiting for the monsoon rains to arrive and the worry that they will not come

"Krishnaswami's poetic text rides faithfully on the child's sensibilities. . . . Akib's impressionistic, pastel illustrations make stunning use of extreme perspectives." SLJ

★ **Out** of the way! Out of the way! story, Uma Krishnaswami; pictures, Uma Krishnaswamy. Groundwood Books/House of Anansi Press 2012 28 p. col. ill. $17.95
Grades: K 1 2 3   **E**
1. India -- Fiction 2. Picture books for children 3. Rural development -- Fiction
ISBN 1554981301 Groundwood Books;
9781554981304 Groundwood Books

In this picture book, "[a] boy in India sees a baby tree growing by the side of a dusty path, and, because he protects it, it flourishes throughout his lifetime despite the changes to the landscape around him." The illustrations "depict the path [by the tree] turning into a lane, then a street, then a road, signaling the rapid development that transforms the landscape from a quiet, sleepy village into a busy town. Meanwhile, the boy grows into a man, and the tree becomes a meeting place for local people." (Kirkus)

Kroll, Steven
The **Hanukkah** mice; by Steven Kroll; illustrated by Michelle Shapiro. Marshall Cavendish Children 2008 un il $14.99
Grades: PreK K 1 2   **E**
1. Mice -- Fiction 2. Hanukkah -- Fiction
ISBN 978-0-7614-5428-1; 0-7614-5428-4
LC 2007035003

A family of mice enjoys the doll house and furnishings that Rachel receives as gifts on the eight nights of Hanukkah

"This book would make a wonderful addition to any holiday collection, and will most likely become a new holiday classic that will be cherished by students for years to come." Libr Media Connect

Stuff! reduce, reuse, recycle. illustrated by Steve Cox. Marshall Cavendish 2009 un il $16.99
Grades: PreK K 1 2   **E**
1. Rats -- Fiction 2. Recycling -- Fiction
ISBN 978-0-7614-5570-7; 0-7614-5570-1
LC 2008-12915

Pinch is a pack rat who does not want to give up the possessions that are cluttering his house, but when he finally is persuaded to sell them at a neighborhood tag sale, he discovers the beauty of recycling. Includes tips on "reducing, reusing, and recycling."

"The bright, bold colors convey the friendly tone of the story and ably show the movement from cluttered to clean as Pinch relinquishes his possessions. An admirable introduction to beginning environmentalism for a young audience." Kirkus

Kroll, Virginia L.
Everybody has a teddy; [by] Virginia Kroll; illustrated by Sophie Allsopp. Sterling Pub. 2007 un il $12.95
Grades: PreK K   **E**
1. Stories in rhyme 2. Teddy bears -- Fiction
ISBN 978-1-4027-3580-6; 1-4027-3580-4
LC 2006005154

A child describes teddy bears owned by other children, from Joshy's giant grizzly to the floppy bear Poppy's grandmother made from socks.

"This light, gentle offering celebrates individuality. . . . The text rolls along with the infectious, easy rhyme and rhythm of a children's song. . . . Cheerful illustrations capture the happy hum of a multicultural classroom filled with kids who paint, play, and look at books." Booklist

Krosoczka, Jarrett J.
Ollie the purple elephant. Knopf 2011 un il $16.99
Grades: PreK K   **E**
1. Elephants -- Fiction
ISBN 978-0-375-86654-8; 0-375-86654-X

"With bright, friendly acrylic art . . . . the author offers a fast-paced and surreal tale with twists aplenty. After Mr. McLaughlin makes good on a silly promise that comes back to bite him ('that should they ever come across a purple elephant, they could keep him'), the McLaughlin family makes room for Ollie. . . . Good times and floor-shaking dance parties follow, upsetting the family cat and the downstairs neighbor, who collude to remove the unwanted pachyderm. . . . Krosoczka's story feels tailor-made for story time, thanks to kid-pleasing plot elements, . . . emphatic prose, . . . and emotive art." Publ Wkly

Krupinski, Loretta
Snow dog's journey. Dutton Children's Books 2010 un il $16.99
Grades: PreK K 1 2   **E**
1. Dogs -- Fiction 2. Love -- Fiction 3. Snow -- Fiction
ISBN 978-0-525-42246-4; 0-525-42246-3
LC 2009-53237

Anna builds a dog of snow, which the Frost King admires and takes away with him, but when Anna's love and faith eventually reunite her with Snow Dog, they each get their fondest wish.

"Krupinski's delightful tale blends fantasy and reality in a familiar, shape-shifting animal story. . . . The softly textured illustrations smoothly convey the characters' individual perspectives and emotions." Booklist

Kruusval, Catarina

Franny's friends. R & S Books 2008 un il $16
Grades: PreK   E
  1. Play -- Fiction 2. Toys -- Fiction 3. Imagination -- Fiction
  ISBN 978-91-29-66836-0; 91-29-66836-0

"Franny is a sweet little girl who plans a picnic for her seven stuffed animals. The simple outing runs into trouble when the two smallest guests, Itty Bitty Kitty and Little Heddy, fall into a hole and can't get out. . . . Kruusval's pastel-shaded illustrations capture the story's charm. . . . Each animal is drawn with a liveliness that will seem wholly believable to a young child engaged in imaginative play." SLJ

Kubler, Annie

Humpty Dumpty; illustrated by Annie Kubler. Child's Play 2010 un il (Baby board books) bd bk $4.99
Grades: PreK   E
  1. Nursery rhymes 2. Board books for children
  ISBN 978-1-84643-339-9 bd bk; 1-84643-339-8 bd bk

"Kubler sets the familiar nursery rhyme in a jolly daycare setting peopled with a multiethnic cast of toddlers. . . . This is a splendid, slightly larger-than-usual contribution that is sure to see many repeated readings." Kirkus

Kulka, Joe

★ Wolf's coming! [by] Joe Kulka. Carolrhoda Books 2007 un il lib bdg $15.95
Grades: PreK K 1   E
  1. Wolves -- Fiction 2. Animals -- Fiction
  ISBN 978-1-57505-930-3 lib. bdg; 1-57505-930-4 lib bdg

                         LC 2006013865

"The simple rhyming text describes the various ways in which the denizens of the forest prepare for Wolf's imminent arrival. . . . Saturated with color, the cartoonlike illustrations depict characters that are more human than animal, but will likely appeal to young children." SLJ

Kulling, Monica

In the bag! Margaret Knight wraps it up. Monica Kulling. Tundra Books of Northern New York 2011 32 p. ill. (Great idea) (hardcover) $17.95
Grades: K 1 2 3 4   E
  1. Women inventors 2. Picture books for children 3. Inventors
  ISBN 1770492399; 9781770492394

                         LC 2010938592

This children's picture book is a "portrait of [Margaret] Knight [that] chronicles her process in inventing the machine that made the flat-bottomed paper bag and, at the age of 12, the shuttle cover for cotton-mill machinery." It points out "the trouble facing female inventors in the 1800s." (School Library Journal)

This is written "in clean, straightforward prose. . . . [The text is] paired with Parkin's detailed and handsome pen-and-ink illustrations." Publ Wkly

The Tweedles Go Electric! by Monica Kulling and Marie Lafrance. Pgw 2014 32 p. $16.95

Grades: 1 2 3   E
  1. Automobiles -- Fiction 2. Family life -- Fiction 3. Electric automobiles -- Fiction
  ISBN 1554981670; 9781554981670

In this book, by Monica Kulling and Marie Lafrance, readers "meet the Tweedles: Papa, Mama, daughter Frances and her brother, Francis. It's the dawn of a new century--the twentieth century!--and the Tweedles have decided to buy a car. . . . Frances is the only member of her eccentric family who is not delighted when Papa decides they need an electric car. . . . But when Mr. Hamm is unable to get to the hospital because his car has run out of gas, Frances saves the day." (Publisher's note)

"In 1903, the Tweedle family eschews the new noisy, dirty, unreliable gas- and steam-powered automobiles, so Papa buys a quiet electric car. Mr. Hamm the butcher tells them to "get a real car," but when his car is out of gas during an emergency, a Tweedle helps out with their trusty electric. Energetic art accompanies the lighthearted story with contemporary relevance." Horn Book

Kumin, Maxine, 1925-2014

Oh, Harry! illustrated by Barry Moser. Roaring Brook Press 2011 un il $16.99
Grades: PreK K   E
  1. Stories in rhyme 2. Horses -- Fiction
  ISBN 978-1-59643-439-4; 1-59643-439-2

                         LC 2010024837

Harry the Horse excels at calming skittish equines in Adams & Son's show-horse barn, but he faces a different challenge when mischievous six-year-old Algernon Adams the Third arrives.

"Moser uses vibrant watercolors from multiple perspectives against dramatic white backgrounds to convey animal personality and movement in an uncluttered way. His Harry grins and rolls his eyes in ways that, like the text, are fanciful but grounded in reality. . . . Good fun for the preschool set and slightly beyond." Kirkus

Kupfer, Wendy

Let's hear it for Almigal. Handfinger Press 2012 32 p. $16.99
Grades: PreK K 1   E
  1. Cochlear implants 2. Picture books for children
  ISBN 0983829403; 9780983829409

This children's picture book follows deaf Almigal, who wants "to hear every single sound in the whole entire universe," so her "doctor suggests cochlear implants. . . . The book gently covers Almigal's trip to the hospital for the operation and the importance of handling the implants carefully. . . . The implants successfully help Almigal hear all the things she'd been missing." (Kirkus)

Kurtz, Jane

Faraway home; illustrated by E.B. Lewis. Harcourt Brace & Co. 2000 un il $16
Grades: PreK K 1 2   E
  1. Ethiopia -- Fiction 2. African Americans -- Fiction 3. Father-daughter relationship -- Fiction
  ISBN 0-15-200036-4

                         LC 96-47664

Desta's father, who needs to return briefly to his Ethiopian homeland, describes what it was like for him to grow up there

"Lewis captures the lyricism and rich imagery of the text with his evocative, realistic watercolors." SLJ

Water hole waiting; by Jane and Christopher Kurtz; illustrated by Lee Christiansen. Greenwillow Bks. 2002 un il $15.95; lib bdg $15.89
Grades: PreK K 1 2   E
1. Animals -- Fiction 2. Monkeys -- Fiction
ISBN 0-06-029850-2; 0-06-029851-0 lib bdg
LC 2001-23040
A thirsty monkey waits as the larger animals drink from the water hole on the African savanna
"Richly colored pastel drawings and precise, surprising word choices make this story a natural for sharing with a group." SLJ

Kushner, Lawrence
In God's hands; [by] Lawrence Kushner and Gary Schmidt; illustrated by Matthew J. Baek. Jewish Lights Pub. 2005 un il $16.99
Grades: K 1 2 3   E
1. Jews -- Fiction 2. Prayer -- Fiction 3. Miracles -- Fiction
ISBN 1-58023-224-8
LC 2005001669
While contemplating their problems in a synagogue, Jacob and David, one man rich, the other poor, come to realize their role in making miracles happen. Inspired by an ancient legend.
"This lovely piece of bookmaking combines a good tale with a strong, easily understood message. Baek's artwork, set against buff-colored pages and highlighted in shades of blue, uses a variety of angles, placements, and design elements to invite interest." Booklist

Kuskin, Karla
A **boy** had a mother who bought him a hat. Harper 2010 un il $16.99
Grades: PreK K 1   E
1. Stories in rhyme 2. Mother-son relationship -- Fiction
ISBN 978-0-06-075330-6; 0-06-075330-7
A newly illustrated edition of the title first published 1976
After a boy's mother buys him a hat, she buys him a mouse, shoes, boots, skis, mask, cello, and an elephant-none of which he is ever without.
This "showcases the late poet's mastery of verse and her acute awareness of both children's sense of humore and the value they place on special belongings. . . . Hawkes' pictures . . . are skillfully executed and include some hidden surprises." Booklist

Green as a bean. Laura Geringer Books 2007 un il $16.99; lib bdg $17.89
Grades: PreK K 1 2   E
1. Stories in rhyme
ISBN 978-0-06-075332-0; 0-06-075332-3; 978-0-06-075334-4 lib bdg; 0-06-075334-X lib bdg
LC 2005017881
First published 1960 with title: Square as a house
Questions in verse about the many things you could be if you were square or soft or loud or red or small or fat or fierce or dark
This "is sure to inspire loud crowd participation. . . . Lines in expertly modulated rhyme and meter . . . are nicely

extended in Iwai's bright, fanciful acrylic paintings." Booklist

I am me. Simon & Schuster Bks. for Young Readers 2000 un il $14.95
Grades: PreK K   E
1. Family life -- Fiction
ISBN 0-689-81473-9
LC 98-7911
After being told how she resembles other members of her family, a young girl states positively and absolutely that she is "NO ONE ELSE BUT ME"
"The illustrations set the story during a family trip to the beach, and in Wolcott's brightly colored double-page spreads, all the rhythmic curves . . . show the natural connections around us, the loving family embrace across generations, and the child's exuberant energy as her own individual self." Booklist

★ **So** what's it like to be a cat? Atheneum Books for Young Readers 2005 un il $15.95; pa $6.99
Grades: PreK K 1 2   E
1. Cats -- Fiction
ISBN 0-689-84733-5; 0-689-85930-9 pa
LC 2003-27338
A cat answers a young child's questions about such things as how much and where it sleeps, and whether or not it likes living with people.
"Lewin's charming, uncluttered watercolors extend the spare poetry's precise wit with swooping bold lines that beautifully capture both characters' movements and moods." Booklist

Kvasnosky, Laura McGee
Really truly Bingo; [by] Laura McGee Kvasnosky. Candlewick Press 2008 un il $15.99
Grades: PreK K 1   E
1. Dogs -- Fiction 2. Imaginary playmates -- Fiction
ISBN 978-0-7636-3210-6; 0-7636-3210-4
LC 2007-40103
When Bea wants to play, her busy mother tells her to use her imagination—outside—and soon Bea and a talking dog, Bingo, are getting into all kinds of mischief.
"This book, with its child-sized problem and child-sized solution, is a fresh take on imaginary friends." Horn Book Guide

★ **Zelda** and Ivy, the runaways. Candlewick Press 2006 42p il $14.99; pa $4.99
Grades: PreK K 1 2   E
1. Foxes -- Fiction 2. Sisters -- Fiction
ISBN 0-7636-2689-9; 978-0-7636-2689-1; 0-7636-3061-6 pa; 978-0-7636-3061-4 pa
LC 2005-54282
In three short stories, fox sisters Zelda and Ivy run away from home, bury a time capsule, and take advantage of some creative juice.
"Bright, expressive cartoon illustrations complement the fine writing in this beginning reader." SLJ
Other titles about Zelda and Ivy are:
Zelda and Ivy (1998)
Zelda and Ivy and the boy next door (1999)
Zelda and Ivy one Christmas (2000)
Zelda and Ivy: keeping secrets (2009)

Zelda and Ivy: the big picture (2010)

Kwon, Yoon-Duck

My cat copies me. Kane/Miller 2007 un il $15.95
Grades: PreK K 1 2   E
1. Cats -- Fiction
ISBN 978-1-933605-26-5
Original Korean edition, 2005

"Kwon tells the story of a little girl and her cat. The pet may act coy and shy when the child seeks its affection, but when she turns away, the feline begins to follow her and mimics her actions. . . . The bright, colorful illustrations feature light gray outlining and accents that add a luminous quality and increase the imaginative nature of the drawings." SLJ

La Chanze

Little diva; illustrated by Brian Pinkney. Feiwel and Friends 2010 un il $16.99
Grades: PreK K   E
1. Theater -- Fiction 2. Mother-daughter relationship -- Fiction
ISBN 978-0-312-37010-7; 0-312-37010-5

"LaChanze, a star of stage and screen herself, supplies a peek at the life of a Broadway performer in this enticing story about a girl's dream of one day conquering the Great White Way. Nena relates her activities from morning to night as she works as a 'D.I.T.—Diva inTraining.' After trying on her mother's clothes, dancing and singing about the house, and watching her mother practice her yoga, the two spend the afternoon at the theater, where the woman is the star. . . . Pinkney catches the mood with sprawling thick black lines and swirling soft hues of pink, lavender, blue, and tawny, bringing a breezy lightness that fits this upbeat tale." SLJ

Labatt, Mary

Pizza for Sam; written by Mary Labatt; illustrated by Marisol Sarrazin. Kids Can Press 2003 32p il (Kids can read) $14.95; pa $3.95
Grades: PreK K 1 2   E
1. Dogs -- Fiction 2. Food -- Fiction
ISBN 1-55337-329-4; 1-55337-331-6 pa

"Sam the dog watches eagerly as [her] owners set out cakes, cookies, and pies for a party. . . . Sam's presented with traditional dog food, but [she] turns up [her] snout, preferring to go hungry . . . until a pizza arrives and he finds [her] perfect puppy chow. Winsome pastel illustrations combine with a few large-type sentences per page in an attractive, uncluttered layout. The basic, repetitive text is filled with action, noise, and enough suspense and silliness to engage new readers." Booklist

Other titles about Sam are:
A friend for Sam (2003)
A parade for Sam (2005)
Sam at the seaside (2006)
Sam finds a monster (2004)
Sam gets lost (2004)
Sam goes next door (2006)
Sam goes to school (2004)
Sam's first Halloween (2003)
Sam's snowy day (2005)

Lacamara, Laura

★ Floating on Mama's song; illustrated by Yuyi Morales. Katherine Tegen Books 2010 un il $16.99
Grades: K 1 2 3   E
1. Mothers -- Fiction 2. Singing -- Fiction 3. Bilingual books -- English-Spanish
ISBN 978-0-06-084368-7; 0-06-084368-3

Anita, a seven-year-old girl, is amazed when her mother's singing suddenly begins to make her listeners float, but Grandma says she must stop, making Mama terribly sad until her daughter makes her smile again.

"Lacámara's debut weaves together a stirring Caribbean tale inspired by her Cuban roots and her mother's opera singing. Both the English and Spanish versions of the story are fun and easy to read, and also well translated. The fusion of Morales's collage illustrations, with bright energetic colors, large warm brown characters, and real photographs interspersed with digitally enhanced foliage, will help children's imaginations take flight." SLJ

Laden, Nina

Peek-a zoo! by Nina Laden. Chronicle Books 2014 22 p. color illustrations (alk. paper) $6.99
Grades: PreK   E
1. Board books 2. Stories in rhyme 3. Animals -- Fiction 4. Toy and movable books
ISBN 1452111758; 9781452111759
                                              LC 2013027686

In this book author Nina Laden presents "a companion to her . . . classic 'Peek-a Who?' Colorful pictures and a . . .rhyming text help children predict what animal is peeking through die-cut windows. The anticipation of what's hiding on the next page and the bright, engaging illustrations [are designed to] keep youngsters laughing and learning." (Publisher's note)

"he follow-up to the long-lived and much-loved Peek-a-Who? (2000) is finally here.As with the first book, a game of peekaboo plays out through die-cut holes that allow readers a glimpse through one right-hand page to the next...Laden's boldly colored gouache art, which has the look of prints, uses the signature style found in the original.While the first book executed this gimmick more successfully (there are only so many words that rhyme with "Boo"), this companion title is a welcome pairing." Kirkus

Follow up to: Peek a Who? (2000)

★ Peek-a-who? by Nina Laden. Chronicle Books 2000 10 p. col. ill. $6.95
Grades: PreK   E
1. Stories in rhyme 2. Board books for children 3. Toy and movable books
ISBN 0811826023; 9780811826020
                                              LC 99044248

The reader can look through die-cut pages for a visual clue to complete a game of peek-a-boo.

"The exuberant illustrations in this guessing-game board book will enchant infants and toddlers. A bright left-hand page with the words "Peek a" faces a right-hand page with die-cut windows through which a visual clue can be seen... Vibrant colors with plenty of black outlines make this a charming visual treat for the youngest patrons." SLJ

LaFaye, A.

Walking home to Rosie Lee; illustrated by Keith D. Shepherd. Cinco Puntos Press 2011 il $16.95

Grades: 2 3 4   **E**

1. Slavery -- Fiction 2. African Americans -- Fiction 3. Voyages and travels -- Fiction 4. Mother-son relationship -- Fiction 5. United States -- History -- 1865-1898 -- Fiction

ISBN 978-1-933693-97-2; 1-933693-97-5

LC 2010037397

At the end of the Civil War, young Gabe meets many other former slaves getting a feel for freedom whose kindness helps him in his quest to find his mother, who was sold away.

This "is distinguished by a vivid narrative voice and page-turning suspense. . . . Shepherd contributes big, dramatic spreads, thickly painted and filled with the blues of night and the yellow light of fires and lanterns." Publ Wkly

Lagercrantz, Rose

My Happy Life. Lerner Pub Group 2013 136 p. (hardcover) $16.95

Grades: 1 2 3   **E**

1. Picture books for children 2. Friendship

ISBN 1877579351; 9781877579356

In this book, "even at a young age, Dani has seen more than her share of heartache: the best friend she meets in chapter four moves away by chapter eight . . . , a departure that prompts the sad revelation that Dani's mother died sometime earlier." But "Dani does indeed have much to be happy about. She has a loving father and extended family, an unflappable teacher . . . , and--above all--an openness to reflection and new possibilities, big and small." (Publishers Weekly)

Lakritz, Deborah

Say hello, Lily; illustrated by Martha Aviles. Kar-Ben Pub. 2010 un il lib bdg $17.95; pa $7.95

Grades: PreK K 1 2   **E**

1. Old age -- Fiction 2. Shyness -- Fiction

ISBN 978-0-7613-4511-4 lib bdg; 0-7613-4511-6 lib bdg; 978-0-7613-4512-1 pa; 0-7613-4512-4 pa

LC 2009001873

Lily wants to go with her mother to visit the people who live at Shalom Home, an assisted living facility, but when they arrive she suddenly feels very shy.

"Pencil-and-gouache illustrations brightly delineate an elder community of kind, thoughtful faces. . . . A gentle and satisfying introduction to a senior residential situation." Kirkus

LaMarche, Jim

Lost and found. Chronicle Books 2009 un il $17.99

Grades: PreK K 1   **E**

1. Short stories 2. Dogs -- Fiction 3. Lost and found possessions -- Fiction

ISBN 978-0-8118-6401-5; 0-8118-6401-4

LC 2008-23009

"In the first story, Anna's retriever Molly leads the way home after the girl runs off in anger and gets lost; in the second, Jules enjoys a happy reunion with his pet Ginger after the scruffy dog disappears in the woods. Jack finds a husky named Yuki, whose owner gives Jack's single mother a fresh start in the final tale. . . . LaMarche's gentle artwork

distinguishes this collection, gracefully rendering the special bond between dogs and children. . . . The soft colors of autumn unite the stories visually, and the pages are full of activity." Publ Wkly

★ The **raft**. Lothrop, Lee & Shepard Bks. 2000 un il $15.99; pa $6.99

Grades: 2 3 4 5   **E**

1. Animals -- Fiction 2. Grandmothers -- Fiction 3. Rafting (Sports) -- Fiction

ISBN 0-688-13977-9; 0-06-443856-2 pa

LC 99-35546

Reluctuant Nicky spends a wonderful summer with Grandma who introduces him to the joy of rafting down the river near her home and watching the animals along the banks

"LaMarche introduces young readers to a visually resplendent, magical world. . . . Nicky's descriptive first-person narration supports the radiant, expressive illustrations." SLJ

Up; by Jim LaMarche. Chronicle Books 2006 un il $16.95

Grades: PreK K 1 2   **E**

1. Whales -- Fiction 2. Fishing -- Fiction 3. Psychokinesis -- Fiction

ISBN 978-0-8118-4445-1; 0-8118-4445-5

LC 2005029793

Tired of being called Mouse and staying home while his brother helps on their father's fishing boat, Daniel proves himself when a problem arises that he can solve using his newly-developed, extraordinary talent.

"The soft acrylics capture the low light, palpable chill, and blue-gray color scheme of Daniel's fishing village. This is an inspiring and (yes) uplifting title about pursuing one's own talents and possibilities." SLJ

Lamb, Albert

The **abandoned** lighthouse; [illustrated by David McPhail] Roaring Brook Press 2011 un il $15.99

Grades: PreK K 1   **E**

1. Dogs -- Fiction 2. Bears -- Fiction 3. Friendship -- Fiction 4. Lighthouses -- Fiction 5. Boats and boating -- Fiction

ISBN 978-1-59643-525-4; 1-59643-525-9

LC un

A bear, followed by a boy and his dog, use a rowboat to float to an abandoned lighthouse where they all spend the day fishing, cooking their catch, and then joining together to make the lighthouse work again.

"Strikingly evocative of the craggy New England coastline and infused with light—from the sun, moon, and lighthouse—McPhail's quaint, jewel-toned paintings anchor the story. The accessible sentences, early-reader trim size, and slightly mysterious setting and adventure are just right for newly independent readers." Publ Wkly

Tell me the day backwards. Candlewick Press 2011 un il $15.99

Grades: PreK K   **E**

1. Day -- Fiction 2. Bears -- Fiction 3. Bedtime -- Fiction 4. Mother-son relationship -- Fiction

ISBN 978-0-7636-5055-1; 0-7636-5055-2

LC 2010039177

"Gentle storytelling and a clever concept set this bedtime book apart from the pack. . . . McPhail's always playful and evocative illustrations set against a beautiful countryside perfectly capture this original way of remembering a day's events. An exceptional idea and a truly fine follow through." Kirkus

Laminack, Lester L.

Three hens and a peacock; written by Lester L. Laminack; illustrated by Henry Cole. Peachtree 2011 un il $15.95

Grades: PreK K 1 2   E

1. Dogs -- Fiction 2. Chickens -- Fiction 3. Peacocks -- Fiction 4. Farm life -- Fiction 5. Happiness -- Fiction

ISBN 978-1-56145-564-5; 1-56145-564-4

LC 2010031989

When life on the Tucker farm is disrupted by the arrival of a peacock, whose shrieking and strutting bring many welcome visitors, the hens complain that they are doing all of the work until the hound suggests a trade.

"Laminack's tale of barnyard envy is a fine addition to farm fables, but it's Cole's signature watercolor, ink, and pencil cartoon illustrations that charm here." Kirkus

Lamorisse, Albert

The red balloon. Doubleday 1957 un il $16.95; pa $12.95

Grades: PreK K 1 2   E

1. Balloons -- Fiction 2. Paris (France) -- Fiction

ISBN 0-385-00343-9; 0-385-14297-8 pa

Original French edition, 1956

"The chief feature of this book is the stunning photographs, many in color, which were taken during the filming of the French movie of the same name. A little French schoolboy Pascal catches a red balloon which turns out to be magic. The streets of Paris form a backdrop for a charming story and superb photographs." Libr J

Lamstein, Sarah Marwil

A big night for salamanders; [by] Sarah Marwil Lamstein; art by Carol Benioff. Boyds Mills Press 2010 un il $17.95

Grades: K 1 2 3   E

1. Salamanders -- Fiction

ISBN 978-1-9324-2598-7; 1-9324-2598-5

"One spring evening . . . spotted salamanders emerge from their winter burrows and make their way to a vernal pool. . . . Young Evan and his parents . . . carry salamanders across the road and even stop cars to ask drivers to slow down and watch out for their amphibian neighbors. . . . The dual text offers Evan's story in plain type and information about salamanders in italics. Readers intrigued by salamanders will learn plenty here and more in the back matter. . . . The gouache paintings add color and drama to this informative picture book." Booklist

Includes glossary and bibliographical references

Landman, Tanya

Mary's penny; written by Tanya Landman; illustrated by Richard Holland. Candlewick Press 2010 un il $15.99

Grades: K 1 2   E

1. Farms -- Fiction 2. Sex role -- Fiction

ISBN 978-0-7636-4768-1; 0-7636-4768-3

A farmer learns that the best man for the job of farm manager is a girl, as his clever daughter bests his brawny sons in a competition.

"The illustrations make this humorous read-aloud even more enjoyable." Libr Media Connect

Landolf, Diane Wright

★ What a good big brother! by Diane Wright Landolf; paintings by Steve Johnson & Lou Fancher. Random House 2009 un il $16.99; lib bdg $19.99

Grades: PreK K 1 2   E

1. Infants -- Fiction 2. Siblings -- Fiction 3. Family life -- Fiction

ISBN 978-0-375-84258-0; 0-375-84258-6; 978-0-375-94258-7 lib bdg; 0-375-94258-0 lib bdg

LC 2006015181

Cameron is always ready to help when his baby sister cries, whether by handing wipes to his father during a diaper change or finding the nursing pillow for his mother, until one day, when no one else can stop Sadie's tears, her big brother succeeds and gets a wonderful reward

Landolf's "simple, descriptive writing should go a long way in alleviating . . . the anxieties of newly minted sibling rivalry. Johnson and Fancher . . . offer a stunning visual counterpoint with their most luxuriant work to date." Publ Wkly

Landry, Leo

Grin and bear it. Charlesbridge 2011 48p il lib bdg $12.95

Grades: K 1 2 3   E

1. Bears -- Fiction 2. Comedians -- Fiction 3. Forest animals -- Fiction

ISBN 978-1-57091-745-5; 1-57091-745-0

LC 2010033633

Will stage fright prevent a very funny bear from becoming a stand-up comedian?

"A deft balance of punchy, dialogue-driven text and expressive, appealingly naïf pencil-and-watercolor pictures make this well suited to newly independent readers. With humor and subtlety, Landry's words and art impart a smart message about partnership, ingenuity, and pursuing one's goals." Publ Wkly

Space boy; written and illustrated by Leo Landry. Houghton Mifflin Company 2007 un il $16

Grades: PreK K 1   E

1. Bedtime -- Fiction 2. Family life -- Fiction 3. Space flight to the moon -- Fiction

ISBN 978-0-618-60568-2; 0-618-60568-1

LC 2006-26081

Having decided not to go to bed because his home is too noisy, Nicholas flies his spaceship to the Moon, where he enjoys a snack, takes a moonwalk, and enjoys the quiet—until he realizes what he is missing at home.

"Simple lines and shapes become much more in the bright watercolor-and-pen paintings. . . . Kids who love outer space and rockets will adore this quiet, imaginative adventure." SLJ

Landström, Lena

A hippo's tale; [by] Lena Landström; translated by Joan Sandin. R&S Books 2007 un il $15

Grades: PreK K 1 2   **E**

1. Africa -- Fiction 2. Hippopotamus -- Fiction
ISBN 978-91-29-66603-8; 91-29-66603-1
Original Swedish edition 1993

Deep in the middle of Africa, Mrs. Hippopotamus enjoys having quiet time all to herself, especially when bathing. But then a monkey shows up and disturbs her solitude.

"This quiet picture book manages to convey a wide range of human emotions through its hippo heroine. . . . The text is simple, and Landstrom's paintings create a pleasing setting and expressive characters with a minimum of fuss." Booklist

Other titles in this series are:
The little hippo's adventure (2002)
The new hippos (2003)

Pom and Pim; by Lena Landstrom; illustrated by Olof Landstrom. Lerner Pub Group 2014 32 p. $16.95
Grades: PreK K   **E**

1. Luck -- Fiction 2. Adventure fiction 3. Friendship -- Fiction 4. Play -- Fiction 5. Fortune -- Fiction 6. Imagination -- Fiction
ISBN 1877579661; 9781877579660

In this children's book, by Lena Landstrom, "Pom and Pim go outside. It's hot. The sun is shining. What luck! Pom and Pim's day full of ups and downs, and luck both good and bad. Is eating a huge ice-cream truly a good idea? Is it really bad luck that it's raining? Or is it good luck...?" (Publisher's note)

"In this simply written picture book, Pom and Pim enjoy the ups and downs of a day together. Pom, a young child, is inseparable from Pim, an unidentifiable stuffed animal with an egg-shaped body, two eyes, and four legs...The Landströms are a Swedish author-illustrator couple, best known in North America for their amusing picture books in the Will series and the Boo and Baa series. Their latest book will engage younger children with its simple, playful story." Booklist

Where is Pim? by Lean Landström; illustrated by Olof Landström. Lerner Pub Group 2015 32 p. (hardcover) $16.99
Grades: PreK K   **E**

1. Pets -- Fiction 2. Hide-and-seek -- Fiction
ISBN 1927271738; 9781927271735

In this children's story, by Lean Landström and illustrated by Olof Landström, "Pom is playing with Pim, until suddenly Pim disappears! Pom and the dog look everywhere. Where is Pim? A wonderfully simple story for toddlers told with few words, humor, unique illustrations, and heart." (Publisher's note)

Lane, Adam J. B.

Stop thief! Adam J.B. Lane. Roaring Brook Press 2012 32 p.
Grades: PreK K 1 2 3 4   **E**

1. Toys -- Fiction 2. Thieves -- Fiction 3. Adventure fiction 4. Growth -- Fiction 5. Robbers and outlaws -- Fiction 6. Adventure and adventurers -- Fiction
ISBN 159643693X; 9781596436930

LC 2011013505

In this children's book, by Adam J. B. Lane, "[o]n the first night that Randall tries to sleep like a big boy, without dear, stuffed Mr. Pigglesworth, he becomes restless. Climb-

ing out of bed, . . . he encounters a thick-necked stranger with the pig in hand. . . . He reels through a zoo, chocolate factory, natural-history museum, and carnival. The . . . chase . . . is traceable with a finger due to the trail of arrow and dash marks on a series of maplike spreads." (School Library Journal)

Langdo, Bryan

Tornado Slim and the magic cowboy hat. Marshall Cavendish un il
Grades: K 1 2   **E**

1. Tall tales 2. Cowhands -- Fiction 3. West (U.S.) -- Fiction
ISBN 0-7614-5962-6; 978-0-7614-5962-0

A coyote gives Tornado Slim at magic hat that stops tornadoes, floods, and fires.

"Colloquially told, with an epistolary twist, this Western tall tale of guileless cowboy Slim, who finds himself thrust into the role of a hero, packs a lot of charm. . . . Langdo's jaunty, energetic pictures employ highlighted circles to zoom in for the occasional telling closeup." Kirkus

LaReau, Kara

Rabbit & Squirrel; a tale of war & peas. [by] Kara LaReau; Scott Magoon. Harcourt 2008 un il $16
Grades: K 1 2 3   **E**

1. Rabbits -- Fiction 2. Gardening -- Fiction 3. Squirrels -- Fiction
ISBN 978-0-15-206307-8; 0-15-206307-2

LC 2006-101618

Rabbit and Squirrel are neighbors who never even say hello until someone starts damaging their gardens, and then they blame one another and start a fight that continues even after they meet the real culprit.

"The textured, earth-tone illustrations assist in identifying the real garden grabber [and] . . . both text and illustration suggest the bickering may become wearisome and the two may actually become friends." Libr Media Connect

LaRochelle, David

1 +1; illustrated by Brenda Sexton. Sterling Pub. Co. 2010 un il
Grades: K 1 2   **E**

1. Mathematics -- Fiction
ISBN 1-4027-5995-9; 978-1-4027-5995-6

"This clever concept book asks children to take a fresh look at simple addition. Are there times when one plus one can equal three and not two? Yes—if you add one unicorn and one goat, you get three horns. Can one plus one ever equal five? Yes, because when you add one set of triplets and one set of twins, you get five babies. After sharing the numerous examples provided, children can be asked to stretch their imaginations and come up with their own quirky equations. Sexton's brightly colored digitally rendered cartoon-like illustrations are not only cheerful and attractive, but they also provide subtle clues." SLJ

★ The **end**; story by David LaRochelle; illustrations by Richard Egielski. Arthur A. Levine Books 2007 un il hardcover o.p. $16.99

Grades: PreK K 1 2 3   **E**
1. Fairy tales
ISBN 978-0-439-64011-4; 0-439-64011-3; 978-0-439-64012-1 pa; 0-439-64012-1 pa

LC 2005-24044

When a princess makes some lemonade, she starts a chain of events involving a fire-breathing dragon, one hundred rabbits, a hungry giant, and a handsome knight

"Turning the standard fairy-tale formula on its head, LaRochelle begins his story at the end. . . . The hand-lettered text, enclosed in streaming banners, consists of terse, declarative statements that are lavishly expounded upon by the illustrations." SLJ

★ The **haunted** hamburger and other ghostly stories; illustrated by Paul Meisel. Dutton Children's Books 2011 un il $16.99
Grades: K 1 2 3   **E**
1. Ghost stories 2. Bedtime -- Fiction 3. Siblings -- Fiction 4. Storytelling -- Fiction
ISBN 978-0-525-42272-3; 0-525-42272-2

LC 2010038179

Father Ghost tells Franny and Frankie Ghost three scary bedtime stories: The Scary Baby, The Haunted Hamburger, and The Big Bad Granny

"Meisel's charming watercolor and ink cartoon illustrations keep the tone light and augment the tongue-in-cheek humor. Smartly written with plenty of unexpected twists, this book is sure to become a year-round bedtime favorite." SLJ

How Martha saved her parents from green beans; by David LaRochelle; illustrated by Mark Fearing. Dial Books for Young Readers 2013 32 p. (hardcover) $16.99
Grades: K 1 2 3   **E**
1. Food -- Fiction 2. Beans -- Fiction 3. Humorous fiction 4. Food habits -- Fiction 5. Parent and child -- Fiction
ISBN 0803737661; 9780803737662

LC 2012014361

In this juvenile story, by David LaRochelle, illustrated by Mark Fearing, "Martha hates green beans. When some mean, green bandits stroll into town, anyone who ever said 'Eat your green beans' is in big trouble. But when the beans kidnap Martha's parents, Martha is forced to take action. She can think of only one way to stop the villainous veggies from taking over her town, and it's not pretty . . . or tasty." (Publisher's note)

Moo! by David LaRochelle; illustrated by Mike Wohnoutka. Walker 2013 40 p. (hardcover) $16.99
Grades: PreK K 1   **E**
1. Cattle 2. Automobile travel -- Fiction 3. Cows -- Fiction 4. Humorous stories 5. Behavior -- Fiction 6. Automobile driving -- Fiction
ISBN 080273409X; 9780802734099; 9780802734105

LC 2013007463

Written by David LaRochelle and illustrated by Mike Wohnoutka, this book features "a complete story with just one word--MOO . . ." as an "imaginative picture book" that "will have readers laughing one moment and on the edge of their seats the next, as it captures the highs and lows of a mischievous cow's very exciting day." (Publisher's note)

Larsen, Andrew
The **imaginary** garden; [by] Andrew Larsen; [illustrated] by Irene Luxbacher. Kids Can Press 2009 un il $16.95
Grades: PreK K 1 2   **E**
1. Gardens -- Fiction 2. Imagination -- Fiction 3. Grandfathers -- Fiction
ISBN 978-1-55453-279-7; 1-55453-279-5

"Theo's Poppa's new apartment has no garden, and the windy balcony does not promise to be a good growing spot. But Theo proposes an imaginary garden, and she and her grandfather begin to fill a large blank canvas with a stone wall for the vines to climb on, early springtime flowers, and a visiting robin. . . . The lively artwork is rendered in pen and ink and multimedia collage. The warmth of the grandparent/grandchild relationship is evident." SLJ

Lasky, Kathryn
Marven of the Great North Woods; written by Kathryn Lasky; illustrated by Kevin Hawkes. Harcourt Brace & Co. 1997 un il hardcover o.p. pa $7
Grades: K 1 2 3   **E**
1. Jews -- Fiction 2. Minnesota -- Fiction 3. Lumber and lumbering -- Fiction
ISBN 0-15-200104-2; 0-15-216826-5 pa

LC 96-2334

When his Jewish parents send him to a Minnesota logging camp to escape the influenza epidemic of 1918, ten-year-old Marven finds a special friend

"Inspired by her father's childhood, Lasky's handsomely crafted picture book is also a captivating survival story. . . . Contributing to the book's vivid sense of time and place are Hawkes' graphically accomplished paintings." Booklist

Last stop on Market Street; by Matt de la Pena; illustrated by Christian Robinson. G.P. Putnam's Sons, an imprint of Penguin Group (USA) 2015 32 p. color illustrations (hardback) $16.99
Grades: PreK K 1 2   **E**
1. City and town life 2. Grandparent-grandchild relationship -- Fiction 3. Buses -- Fiction 4. Grandmothers -- Fiction 5. African Americans -- Fiction 6. City and town life -- Fiction
ISBN 0399257748; 9780399257742

LC 2014019913

In this children's book by Matt De La Peña and illustrated by Christian Robinson "every Sunday after church, CJ and his grandma ride the bus across town. CJ wonders why they don't own a car like his friend Colby. Why doesn't he have an iPod like the boys on the bus? How come they always have to get off in the dirty part of town? Each question is met with an encouraging answer from grandma, who helps him see the beauty--and fun--in their routine and the world around them." (Publisher's note)

"After church on Sundays, CJ and his nana wait for the bus. It's a familiar routine, but this week CJ is feeling dissatisfied...This is an excellent book that highlights less popular topics such as urban life, volunteerism, and thankfulness, with people of color as the main characters. A lovely title." SLJ

Latimer, Alex
The **boy** who cried ninja; written and illustrated by Alex Latimer. Peachtree 2011 un il $15.95

Grades: PreK K 1 2   E
  1. Honesty -- Fiction
  ISBN 978-1-56145-579-9; 1-56145-579-2

                      LC 2010034688

A young boy named Tim is accused of lying when he tells his parents that a ninja ate the last piece of cake and a sunburned crocodile landed on the roof, so he figures out a way to prove that he is telling the truth.

"Latimer has created offbeat digitally colored drawings brimming with quirky, diverse perspectives and hilarious details." SLJ

Laval, Thierry
  ★ **Colors**. Chronicle Books 2011 un il bd bk $6.99
Grades: PreK   E
  1. Color 2. Board books for children
  ISBN 978-0-8118-7952-1; 0-8118-7952-6

                      LC 2010035582

Original French edition 2009

"This zesty book about colors offers genuine surprises. Each page features a flap with a die-cut shape that lets readers view the color and texture beneath. . . . Many of the revealed objects are thematically linked to the main scene. . . . Laval delivers the thrills that a peek-a-boo book should with his charmingly eccentric compositions." Publ Wkly

Lawson, Dorie McCullough
  Tex; a book for little dreamers. Trafalgar Square Books 2011 un il $15.95
Grades: PreK K   E
  1. Cowhands -- Fiction 2. Ranch life -- Fiction
  ISBN 978-1-57076-501-8; 1-57076-501-4

                      LC 2011014775

"Through full-color photographs, each one accompanied by a short sentence or phrase, Lawson tells the story of Luke, a boy who becomes 'Tex' in his dreams each night. He has all sorts of ranch duties like riding horses, digging irrigation trenches, checking the fence, and riding the tractor, and he relaxes for a bit in the pasture. The full-page photos will delight all cowhand enthusiasts." SLJ

Lawson, JonArno
  Sidewalk flowers; by JonArno Lawson, illustrated by Sydney Smith. Groundwood Books 2015 32 p. illustrations $16.95
Grades: PreK K 1 2 3   E
  1. Stories without words 2. Girls -- Fiction 3. Generosity -- Fiction
  ISBN 1554984319; 9781554984312

In this book, by JonArno Lawson, illustrated by Sydney Smith, "a little girl collects wildflowers while her distracted father pays her little attention. Each flower becomes a gift, and whether the gift is noticed or ignored, both giver and recipient are transformed by their encounter." (Publisher's note)

Lazo Gilmore, Dorina K.
  ★ **Cora** cooks pancit; written by Dorina Lazo Gilmore; illustrated by Kristi Valiant. Shen's Books 2009 un il $17.95
Grades: PreK K 1 2 3   E
  1. Cooking -- Fiction 2. Filipino Americans -- Fiction
  ISBN 978-1-885008-35-0; 1-885008-35-X

                      LC 2008045836

When all her older siblings are away, Cora's mother finally lets her help make pancit, a Filipino noodle dish. Includes recipe for pancit.

"Clear expository prose explains how to perform kitchen tasks. . . . These scenes effectively model how adults can introduce children to cooking. The simple, direct style also makes the book equally well suited as a read-aloud and for newly independent readers. The artwork nicely complements the text, as Valiant's warm hues of gold, red, and orange highlight the family's loving relationship." SLJ

Le Guin, Ursula K.
  ★ **Cat** dreams; illustrations by S.D. Schindler. Orchard Books 2009 un il lib bdg $16.99
Grades: PreK K 1   E
  1. Stories in rhyme 2. Cats -- Fiction 3. Dreams -- Fiction
  ISBN 978-0-545-04216-1 lib bdg; 0-545-04216-X lib bdg

                      LC 2008-46299

Presents a feline dreamland where it rains mice, all the dogs have run away, and a big bowl of kibbles and cream is waiting

"Easy rhyming text will be quickly memorized, but the realistic, full-bleed watercolor illustrations will keep youngsters turning the pages. A perfect fit for storytimes on cats, naps and dreams." Kirkus

Leaf, Munro
  ★ **The story** of Ferdinand; illustrated by Robert Lawson. Viking 1936 un il $17.99; pa $6.99
Grades: PreK K 1 2   E
  1. Bulls -- Fiction 2. Spain -- Fiction 3. Bullfights -- Fiction
  ISBN 0-670-67424-9; 0-14-050234-3 pa

"The drawings picture not only Ferdinand but Spanish scenes and characters as well." N Y Public Libr

Leathers, Philippa
  The **Black** rabbit; Philippa Leathers. Candlewick Press 2013 40 p. (reinforced) $14
Grades: PreK K 1 2   E
  1. Children's stories 2. Picture books for children 3. Rabbits -- Fiction 4. Shades and shadows -- Fiction
  ISBN 076365714X; 9780763657147

                      LC 2012942317

In this children's book by Philippa Leathers, part of the Junior Library Guild Selection series, "rabbit has a problem. There's a large black rabbit chasing him. No matter where he runs--behind a tree, over the river--the shadowy rabbit follows. Finally in the deep, dark wood, Rabbit loses his nemesis--only to encounter a real foe!" (Publisher's note)

Lechner, John
  The **clever** stick. Candlewick Press 2009 un il $14.99
Grades: K 1 2 3   E
  1. Drawing -- Fiction 2. Communication -- Fiction
  ISBN 978-0-7636-3950-1; 0-7636-3950-8

                      LC 2008024230

"A clever stick longs to express himself but can't find a way to make his thoughts understood. Discouraged, he drags himself home and discovers that the lines he creates in the sand make shapes and even pictures. . . . Lechner's gently funny ink and watercolor pictures convey the story's meaning." Horn Book Guide

Lee, Ho Baek

While we were out. Kane/Miller 2003 un il $15.95
Grades: PreK K 1 2   E
1. Rabbits -- Fiction
ISBN 1-929132-44-1
LC 2002-112325

"A white rabbit who lives on the patio notices that his family has gone to Grandma's, leaving the house empty. Now the house is hers. Simple line-and-wash pictures alternating with radiant full-page paintings follow the rabbit as she indulges in a multitude of obviously long-held wishes. . . . This Korean import is amusing, yes, but there is also a delicacy and intelligence that pervades the tale. A definite cut above." Booklist

Lee, Mark

★ **Twenty** big trucks in the middle of the street; by Mark Lee; illustrated by Kurt Cyrus. Candlewick Press 2013 32 p. col. ill. (reinforced) $15.99
Grades: PreK K   E
1. Trucks -- Fiction 2. City traffic -- Fiction
ISBN 076365809X; 9780763658090
LC 2012943654

In this children's picture book by Mark Lee, "an ice cream truck breaking down in 'the middle of our street' is a dream come true for many a kid--not to mention the ensuing traffic jam that strands 20 trucks of every shape and purpose. But one boy has something bigger in mind than licking a cone or being a spectator: he wants to solve the problem. That takes some persistence, but he eventually wins over the crowd with a solution that's literally right in front of them." (Publishers Weekly)

Lee, Spike

Giant steps to change the world; [by] Spike and Tonya Lewis Lee; illustrated by Sean Qualls. Simon & Schuster Books for Young Readers 2011 un il $16.99
Grades: PreK K 1 2 3   E
1. Conduct of life -- Fiction
ISBN 978-0-689-86815-3; 0-689-86815-4
LC 2009-27622

"In plainspoken free verse directed right to kids, this title introduces individuals who took 'giant steps to make the world a better place.' . . . Rendered in paint, pencil, and collage, the artwork, featuring often-faceless figures, leaves space for young people to imagine their own stories and, like the poems, will inspire many children to match the pictures with the famous names and find out more." Booklist

Lee, YJ

The **little** moon princess; written and illustrated by YJ Lee. HarperCollins 2010 un il $16.99
Grades: K 1 2   E
1. Stars -- Fiction 2. Sparrows -- Fiction 3. Princesses -- Fiction
ISBN 978-0-06-154736-2; 0-06-154736-0
LC 2009-9294

With the help of a friendly sparrow, the Little Moon Princess, who is afraid of the dark, uses the jewels on the surface of her moon to light up the sky.

"Lee's stunning use of watercolor and ink creates the illusion of light, and her art offers readers a breathtaking view of the night sky. A lovely read-aloud." SLJ

Leedy, Loreen

Crazy like a fox; a simile story. written and illustrated by Loreen Leedy. Holiday House 2008 un il lib bdg $16.95; pa $6.95
Grades: K 1 2   E
1. Foxes -- Fiction 2. Parties -- Fiction 3. Birthdays -- Fiction 4. English language -- Idioms
ISBN 978-0-8234-1719-3 lib bdg; 0-8234-1719-0 lib bdg; 978-0-8234-2248-7 pa; 0-8234-2248-7 pa
LC 2007-051016

"Rufus, a spunky fox in suspenders, rudely startles his friend Babette, a lamb, by roaring 'like...a lion.' She gets 'mad...as a hornet' and chases him, and he eventually leads her to her surprise birthday party. Leedy relates this narrative entirely through similes. Her illustrations emphasize the comparisons as each protagonist is amusingly transformed from one object into another. . . . [Leedy's] vivid illustrations, filled with movement and wide-eyed creatures, will entertain readers." SLJ

The **great** graph contest; written and illustrated by Loreen Leedy. Holiday House 2005 32p il $16.95; pa $6.95
Grades: 1 2 3   E
1. Graphic methods 2. Frogs -- Fiction 3. Snails -- Fiction 4. Lizards -- Fiction
ISBN 0-8234-1710-7; 0-8234-2029-9 pa
LC 2003-62549

Gonk the toad, Chester the snail, and Beezy the lizard hold a contest to see who can make better graphs

"A splashy and colorful offering designed to inform and entertain. . . . The lively text, delivered in large type and contained in dialogue and thought balloons, is engaging and well supported by the vivid, cartoon illustrations." SLJ

Lehman, Barbara

Museum trip. Houghton Mifflin 2006 un il $15
Grades: K 1 2 3   E
1. School stories 2. Stories without words 3. Art museums -- Fiction
ISBN 0-618-58125-1
LC 2005052840

In this wordless picture book, a boy imagines himself inside some of the exhibits when he goes on a field trip to an art museum.

"The sturdiness and clarity of the ink-lined, watercolor-and-gouache art juxtaposes wonderfully with the story's airy world of imagination." Booklist

Rainstorm. Houghton Mifflin 2007 un il $16
Grades: PreK K 1 2   E
1. Stories without words 2. Play -- Fiction
ISBN 978-0-618-75639-1; 0-618-75639-6
LC 2006-49318

In this wordless picture book, a boy finds a mysterious key which leads him on an adventure one rainy day.

"Lehman provides purely colored, precisely rendered artwork that capably captures both adventures and emotions." Booklist

★ The **red** book. Houghton Mifflin 2004 un il $12.95

Grades: K 1 2 3 **E**
1. Stories without words 2. Books and reading -- Fiction
ISBN 0-618-42858-5
A Caldecott Medal honor book, 2005
This "wordless book tells the complex story of a reader who gets lost, literally, in a little book that has the magic to move her to another place. . . . Done in watercolor, gouache, and ink, the simple, streamlined pictures are rife with invitations to peek inside, to investigate further, and—like a hall of mirrors—reflect, refract, repeat, and reveal. Lehman's story captures the magical possibility that exists every time readers open a book." SLJ

★ The **secret** box. Scholastic Press 2011 un il $15.99
Grades: PreK K 1 **E**
1. Stories without words 2. Boys -- Fiction 3. Photography -- Fiction
ISBN 978-0-547-23868-5; 0-547-23868-1
"Here, three boys discover a box in the top floor of their urban boarding school that holds decades-old sepia photographs of a schoolboy, a postcard, and a map leading to a location on the coast. Picking out features of the old landscape amid the built-up, modern city around them, the boys make their way to a boardwalk amusement park, where they find the schoolboy of the photograph with a crowd of children who presumably have made the same trip. . . . A provocative example of the complexity that can be conveyed using only pictures." Publ Wkly

Trainstop. Houghton 2008 un il $16
Grades: PreK K 1 2 **E**
1. Stories without words 2. Railroads -- Fiction 3. Imagination -- Fiction
ISBN 0-618-75640-X
In this wordless picture book, a young girl takes a train and makes a stop at a most unusual place where she has an important task to perform.
Lehman "demonstrates her extraordinary knack for storytelling sans words. . . . Gouache, watercolor, and ink illustrations reveal a bleak cityscape and adults dressed in muted tones—all in pointed contrast to the girl's head-to-toe multicolored outfit. . . . Lehman's true talent is her spot-on depiction of a young child's capacity for criss-crossing the real with the imaginary." Horn Book

Lehrhaupt, Adam
Warning: do not open this book! Adam Lehrhaupt; illustrated by Matthew Forsythe. Simon & Schuster Books for Young Readers 2013 40 p. color illustrations (hardcover) $16.99
Grades: PreK K 1 **E**
1. Monkeys -- Fiction 2. Picture books for children 3. Humorous stories 4. Toucans -- Fiction 5. Alligators -- Fiction
ISBN 9781442435827; 1442435828; 9781442435834
LC 2012014432
In this children's picture book, by Adam Lehrhaput, illustrated by Matthew Forsythe, "the narrator repeatedly warns readers not to open this book. Those who do not heed these pleas release a troop of artistic monkeys that wreak havoc on the book itself. Nothing is safe from these wild invaders--not the art and not the text. When the narrator again urges readers to turn back, toucans join the fracas." (Kirkus Reviews)

"The earth-tone digital illustrations well replicate the messy monkey business of painting all over the trees and pages, and the playful arrangement of text adds greatly to the book's mayhem. Wonderful chaos." Booklist

Lepp, Bil
The **King** of Little Things; by Bil Lepp and illustrated by Daniel T. Wenzel. Peachtree Publishers 2013 32 p. $16.95
Grades: PreK K 1 2 **E**
1. Size -- Fiction 2. Kings, queens, rulers, etc. -- Fiction
ISBN 1561457086; 9781561457083
LC 2012032584
In this book, by Bil Lepp, "when King Normous thinks he has finally become the ruler of all the world, he is enraged to learn that the King of Little Things still reigns happily in his tiny kingdom. Normous sends his army to defeat this upstart, but he finds he cannot outfight or outwit a king who holds sway over the little things of the world." (Publisher's note)

Lerman, Josh
How to raise Mom and Dad; instructions from someone who figured it out. illustrated by Greg Clarke. Dutton Children's Books 2009 un il $16.99
Grades: K 1 2 **E**
1. Parents -- Fiction
ISBN 978-0-525-47870-6; 0-525-47870-1
LC 2008-13886
Advice on how to manipulate your parents in order to avoid eating vegetables, extend your bedtime, or get a puppy.
"The gouache illustrations are as joyful as the text. . . . This is a manual every child will want to read." SLJ

Lester, Alison, 1952-
Noni the pony; Alison Lester. Beach Lane Books 2013 32 p. (hardback) $15.99
Grades: PreK K 1 **E**
1. Stories in rhyme 2. Horses -- Fiction 3. Friendship -- Fiction 4. Ponies -- Fiction
ISBN 144245959X; 9781442459595; 9781442459601
LC 2012004907
This rhyming children's book, by Alison Lester, introduces readers to "Noni, the friendliest, funniest, and friskiest pony you'll ever meet! When she's not racing and chasing with her best pals Dave Dog and Coco the Cat, she's busy making sure they feel cozy and loved. Because Noni isn't just heaps of fun--she's a great friend, too." (Publisher's note)

★ **Running** with the horses. North South Books 2011 un il $16.95
Grades: 2 3 4 **E**
1. Horses -- Fiction 2. Austria -- Fiction 3. World War, 1939-1945 -- Fiction 4. Father-daughter relationship -- Fiction
ISBN 0-7358-4002-4; 978-0-7358-4002-7
First published 2009 in Australia
"Lester crafts a believable wartime adventure. . . . The illustrations, predominately black-and-white drawings layered between photographic and colored-pencil back- and foregrounds, make the historical contemporary." Kirkus

Sophie Scott goes south; Alison Lester. Penguin 2012 [32] p. $17.99
Grades: 1 2 3 4   E
   1. Antarctica -- Fiction 2. Exploration -- Fiction 3. Arctic regions -- Fiction 4. Antarctica
ISBN 0544088956; 9780544088955; 9780670880683
                                              LC 2013433269
In this picture book, by Alison Lester, "nine-year-old Sophie is going on a month-long voyage to Antarctica, with her dad, the captain of an icebreaker. Sailing the frozen seas round-trip from Australia to Mawson Station in the South Pole, Sophie recounts the adventure of a lifetime in her own words, illustrations, and color photographs. She'll show us icebergs, penguins, seals, and whales!" (Publisher's note)

Lester, Helen
   Happy birdday, Tacky! written by Helen Lester; illustrated by Lynn Munsinger. Houghton Mifflin Books for Children 2013 32 p. col. ill. (reinforced) $16.99
Grades: PreK K 1 2   E
   1. Dance -- Fiction 2. Parties -- Fiction 3. Penguins -- Fiction 4. Birthdays -- Fiction
ISBN 0547912285; 9780547912288
                                              LC 2012014847
This children's picture book is part of the Tacky the Penguin series. Here, "everyone is deep into preparations for Tacky's Birdday Party. This includes baking, practicing the special song and making a whole slew of cards for their decidedly odd friend." However, the party goes awry due to Tacky's strange habits and another penguin's injury. Can the party be saved? (Kirkus)

   ★ **Hooway** for Wodney Wat; illustrated by Lynn Munsinger. Houghton Mifflin 1999 32p il $16; pa $5.95
Grades: PreK K 1 2   E
   1. School stories 2. Speech disorders -- Fiction
ISBN 0-395-92392-1; 0-618-21612-X pa
                                              LC 98-46149
All his classmates make fun of Rodney because he can't pronounce his name, but it is Rodney's speech impediment that drives away the class bully.
   "Munsinger's watercolor with pen-and-ink illustrations positively bristle with humor and each rat, mouse, hamster, and capybara is fully realized as both rodent and child." SLJ
   Another title about Rodney is:
   Wodney Wat's wobot (2011)

The **Loch** Mess monster; written by Helen Lester and illustrated by Lynn Munsinger. Houghton Mifflin Books for Children, Houghton Mifflin Harcourt 2014 32 p. color illustrations $16.99
Grades: PreK K 1   E
   1. Orderliness 2. Monsters -- Fiction 3. Scotland -- Fiction 4. Loch Ness monster -- Fiction 5. Humorous stories 6. Orderliness -- Fiction
ISBN 0544099907; 9780544099906
                                              LC 2013017881
In this book, by Helen Lester and illustrated by Lynn Munsinger, "beware the Loch Mess monster! The legend of the Loch Ness monster is not exactly true. There is no single monster; there are three! Nessie, Fergus, and their wee laddie, Angus, live peacefully together beneath the surface of the lake, obeying proper monster etiquette by following five basic monster rules. All is well until Angus'

untidy ways result in a grottie mess and break rule No. 2." (Kirkus Reviews)
   "Legendary monster Nessie's son Angus is banished to his room for being messy. When his personal junk pile bursts through the surface of the loch, one look at 'land-monsters'- -a goat, duck, and cow--scares Angus into cleaning up and remaining in the lake's depths where he belongs. Munsinger's watercolors further the silly humor. A Scottish glossary is included." Horn Book

The **sheep** in wolf's clothing; illustrated by Lynn Munsinger. Houghton Mifflin 2007 32p il $16
Grades: PreK K 1 2   E
   1. Sheep -- Fiction 2. Wolves -- Fiction 3. Clothing and dress -- Fiction
ISBN 978-0-618-86844-5; 0-618-86844-5
                                              LC 2007-00644
Clothing is important to Ewetopia, but her carefully-chosen wolf outfit fails to impress the other sheep at the Woolyones' costume ball until a real wolf appears dressed as a sheep, mistakes her for his mother, and throws a tantrum when she outsmarts him.
   "The playful illustrations, suffused with expression and shades of pink, show sheep outfitted in tutus and an Elvis costume, and the wolf having a tantrum. Lester follows a familiar format in this clever tale." SLJ

Three cheers for Tacky; illustrated by Lynn Munsinger. Houghton Mifflin 1994 32p il $16; pa $5.95
Grades: PreK K 1 2   E
   1. Contests -- Fiction 2. Penguins -- Fiction 3. Cheerleading -- Fiction
ISBN 0-395-66841-7; 0-395-82-740-X pa
                                              LC 93-14342
This "is a smooth, fun read. Munsinger's full-color illustrations are charming and subtle." SLJ
   Other titles about Tacky are:
   Tacky the penguin (1988)
   Tacky in trouble (1998)
   Tacky and the emperor (2000)
   Tackylocks and the three bears (2002)
   Tacky and the winter games (2005)
   Tacky goes to camp (2009)
   Tacky's Christmas (2010)

Wodney Wat's wobot; written by Helen Lester; illustrated by Lynn Munsinger. Houghton Mifflin Books for Children 2011 un il $16.99
Grades: PreK K 1 2   E
   1. School stories 2. Robots -- Fiction 3. Speech disorders -- Fiction
ISBN 978-0-547-36756-9; 0-547-36756-2
                                              LC 2010044363
When Wodney Wat, who cannot pronounce the letter R, gets a talking robot for his birthday, it turns out to be more than just a fun gift.
   "Wodney is a wonderfully quirky character with whom many children will connect. Munsinger's illustrations are joyful and humorous." SLJ

Lester, J. D.
   Daddy calls me doodlebug; illustrations by Hiroe Nakata. Robin Corey Books 2010 un il $7.99

Grades: PreK   **E**
1. Board books for children 2. Animals -- Fiction 3. Father-child relationship -- Fiction
ISBN 978-0-375-85830-7; 0-375-85830-X

Describes the reasons why animal fathers give nick-names to their children based on their characteristics and love for the child.

Grandma calls me gigglepie; illustrations by Hiroe Nakata. Robin Corey Books 2011 un il bd bk $7.99
Grades: PreK   **E**
1. Board books for children 2. Animals -- Fiction 3. Grandmothers -- Fiction
ISBN 978-0-375-85904-5; 0-375-85904-7

"Sprightly watercolors explore the special relationship between grandmothers and their grandchildren. . . . In rhyming couplets, animals share the terms of endearment given to them by their grandmas. . . . Readers for whom a grandparent is a primary caregiver should especially value this buoyant affirmation of affection." Publ Wkly

Mommy calls me monkeypants; illustrations by Hiroe Nakata. Robin Corey Books 2009 un il $7.99
Grades: PreK   **E**
1. Board books for children 2. Animals -- Fiction 3. Mother-child relationship -- Fiction
ISBN 978-0-375-84502-4; 0-375-84502-X

"Through several spreads, each with a different bright background color, animals and insects say their nicknames as they swing, play, chirp, and bounce with their mothers, ending with the girl in bed saying 'Mommy calls me Monkeypants . . . because she loves me so.' The pictures capture the lighthearted mood of the couplets exactly and together they create a perfect foray into toddler territory." SLJ

Lester, Julius
★ **Black** cowboy, wild horses; a true story. [by] Julius Lester, Jerry Pinkney. Dial Bks. 1998 un il $18.99
Grades: 2 3 4   **E**
1. Horses -- Fiction 2. Cowhands -- Fiction 3. African Americans -- Fiction
ISBN 0-8037-1787-3
LC 97-25210

A black cowboy is so in tune with wild mustangs that they accept him into the herd, thus enabling him singlehandedly to take them to the corral

This story is told in "vivid, poetic prose. . . . Pinkney's magnificent earth-toned paintings bring to life the wild beauty of the horses and the western plains." Horn Book Guide

Sam and the tigers; a new telling of Little Black Sambo. pictures by Jerry Pinkney. Dial Bks. for Young Readers 1996 un il $16.99; pa $6.99
Grades: K 1 2 3   **E**
1. Tigers -- Fiction
ISBN 0-8037-2028-9; 0-14-056288-5 pa
LC 95-43080

A boy named Sam, who lives in the land of Sam-sam-sa-mara, gives his new school clothes to tigers who threaten to eat him, but he re-claims them when the tigers chase one another until they turn into butter

"The rolling, lilting narrative is a model of harmony, clarity, and meticulously chosen detail. . . . Pinkney's lively pencil-and-watercolor illustrations sprawl extravagantly

across double spreads and are smoothly integrated with the narrative." SLJ

Leuck, Laura
I love my pirate papa; [by] Laura Leuck; illustrated by Kyle M. Stone. Harcourt 2007 un il $16
Grades: PreK K 1 2   **E**
1. Pirates -- Fiction 2. Father-son relationship -- Fiction
ISBN 978-0-15-205664-3
LC 2006009240

A pirate's son shares the things he loves about his father, including climbing the mast together to yell "Land ho" and sharing the booty when they find buried treasure.

This is written "in well cadenced, rhyming verses. . . . The stylized acrylic paintings, using exaggeration and comical details effectively, create one dramatic double-page scene after another." Booklist

★ **One** witch; illustrations by S.D. Schindler. Walker & Co. 2003 un il hardcover o.p. pa $6.95
Grades: K 1 2   **E**
1. Counting 2. Stories in rhyme 3. Witches -- Fiction 4. Halloween -- Fiction
ISBN 0-8027-8860-2; 0-8027-7729-5 pa
LC 2002-191049

A witch goes around to her fiendish friends—from two cats to ten werewolves—to gather the ingredients to make gruesome stew for her party

"Eerie yet amusing illustrations and a romping, rhyming text add up to fun in this Halloween counting book. Schindler's ink-and-watercolor artwork is a fine fit for Leuck's action-packed, easy-to-read text." SLJ

Levert, Mireille
The **princess** who had almost everything; [text by] Mireille Levert; [illustrations by] Josée Masse. Tundra Books 2008 un il $19.95
Grades: K 1 2 3   **E**
1. Fairy tales 2. Princesses -- Fiction
ISBN 978-0-88776-887-3; 0-88776-887-3

"A princess' parents do everything to make their daughter happy. But Alicia keeps yelling, 'I'M BORED!' . . . When she decides she wants a prince, her parents promise her hand in marriage to anyone who can keep their daughter from tedium. . . . Dramatic angular illustrations in an earth-tone palette let the viewer see the world from contrasting perspectives. . . . The message of the importance of creativity come through loud and clear." Booklist

A **wizard** in love; [written by] Mireille Levert; [illustrated by] Marie Lafrance. Tundra Books 2009 un il $17.95
Grades: PreK K 1 2   **E**
1. Magic -- Fiction 2. Noise -- Fiction 3. Witches -- Fiction
ISBN 978-0-88776-901-6; 0-88776-901-2
Original French edition published 2007 in Canada

Hector, a retired wizard, lives happily and quietly with his cat, Poison, in a dilapidated house at the edge of the forest, until a noisy new neighbor moves into the abandoned house across the road, and things are never the same again.

"Both verbally and visually entirely funny . . . this off-beat import is a sophisticated treat.." Kirkus

Levine, Arthur A.

★ **Monday** is one day; illustrated by Julian Hector. Scholastic Press 2011 un il $16.99

Grades: PreK K 1   E

1. Counting 2. Stories in rhyme 3. Day -- Fiction 4. Week -- Fiction 5. Family life -- Fiction

ISBN 978-0-439-78924-0; 0-439-78924-9

LC 2009011575

A rhyming countdown of the days of the week as families find ways to spend time together while waiting for the weekend.

"Hector's grinning cartoon-style illustrations are delightful, based in reality but accented with unexpected color. . . . But the book's greatest accomplishment might be its cross section of middle America: white, black, old, young, white-collar, blue-collar, straight, and gay. . . . It's that rare book perceptive enough to recognize that the random moments are those we treasure most." Booklist

Levine, Ellen

★ **Henry's** freedom box; illustrated by Kadir Nelson. Scholastic Press 2007 un il $16.99

Grades: 1 2 3   E

1. Slaves 2. Magicians 3. Abolitionists 4. Slavery -- Fiction 5. African Americans -- Fiction 6. Underground railroad -- Fiction

ISBN 0-439-77733-X

LC 2006-09487

A Caldecott Medal honor book, 2008

A fictionalized account of how in 1849 a Virginia slave, Henry "Box" Brown, escapes to freedom by shipping himself in a wooden crate from Richmond to Philadelphia.

"According to the flap copy, an antique lithograph of Brown inspired Nelson's paintings, which use crosshatched pencil lines layered with watercolors and oil paints. . . . Transcending technique is the humanity Nelson imbues in his characters." Booklist

Levine, Gail Carson

Betsy Red Hoodie; illustrated by Scott Nash. HarperCollins Publishers 2010 un il $16.99; lib bdg $17.89

Grades: K 1 2   E

1. Sheep -- Fiction 2. Wolves -- Fiction 3. Grandmothers -- Fiction

ISBN 978-0-06-146870-4; 0-06-146870-3; 978-0-06-146871-1 lib bdg; 0-06-146871-1 lib bdg

LC 2008-27456

In this variation of "Little Red Riding Hood," Betsy Red Hoodie goes to visit her grandma with her friend Zimmo the wolf and her flock of sheep, but Zimmo, her mother, and her grandma have a surprise planned.

"Nash stages the shenanigans in an attractive country landscape, supporting Levine's light tone with comical pen drawings. . . . Good read-aloud fun." Horn Book

Betsy who cried wolf; illustrated by Scott Nash. HarperCollins Pubs. 2002 un lib bdg $16.89

Grades: PreK K 1 2   E

1. Sheep -- Fiction 2. Wolves -- Fiction 3. Shepherds -- Fiction

ISBN 0-06-028763-2; 0-06-028764-0 lib bdg

LC 00-54032

Betsy, a serious young shepherd, finds that there is more than one way to keep a wolf from eating her sheep

"Nash's cartoonlike illustrations, with their clean lines, crisp colors, and folk-art touches, add considerably to the story." SLJ

Levis, Caron

Stuck with the Blooz; Caron Levis; illustrated by Jon Davis. Harcourt Children's Books 2012 40 p. $16.99

Grades: K 1 2 3   E

1. Melancholy 2. Emotions -- Fiction 3. Sadness -- Fiction 5. Monsters -- Fiction

ISBN 0547745605; 9780547745602

LC 2011041938

This children's book, by Caron Lewis, illustrated by Jon Davis, asks "What do you do when you're feeling blue--especially when your mood takes the form of a drippy, oozy monster called the Blooz? Do you ignore it? Do you ask it lots of questions? Do you give it an ice-pop and hope it goes away? Through trial and error, the child in this story discovers that while it may not be easy, it's not impossible to shake the Blooz." (Publisher's note)

Leviton, Michael

My first ghost; illustrated by Stephanie Buscema; text by Margaret Miller & Michael Leviton. 1st ed. Disney/Hyperion Books 2012 40 p.

Grades: PreK K 1 2   E

1. Wit and humor 2. Picture books for children 3. Ghosts -- Fiction

ISBN 1423119495; 9781423119494

LC 2011017596

This children's picture book, by Maggie Miller and Michael Leviton, illustrated by Stephanie Buscema, "comes with a free ghost! But, like any pet, ghosts need special care and attention. . . . [The book] teaches kids everything they need to know about taking care of their very own ghost. . . . [A]uthors Miller and Leviton offer humorous tips on feeding, grooming, and ghostly games which are complemented by . . . illustrations." (Publisher's note)

Levy, Debbie

We Shall Overcome; The Story of a Song. by Debbie Levy; illustrated by Vanessa Brantley-Newton. Disney Press 2013 32 p. $16.99

Grades: 1 2 3 4   E

1. Slavery -- United States -- Songs 2. African Americans -- Civil rights -- Songs 3. African American music

ISBN 1423119541; 9781423119548

This book, written by Debbie Levy and illustrated by Vanessa Brantley-Newton, focuses on the song "We Shall Overcome." "From the song's roots in America's era of slavery through to the civil rights movement of the 1960s and today, 'We Shall Overcome' has come to represent the fight for equality and freedom around the world." (Publisher's note)

"A simple story explains how this rallying song for freedom became the watchword for the civil rights movement in the United States, and from there to countries around the world struggling with human rights issues. Lively digital and mixed-media illustrations convey a joyous mood. Although "No single day marks the birth of the song...", a timeline of highlights is included. Reading list, websites." (Horn Book)

Levy, Janice

Gonzalo grabs the good life; written by Janice Levy; illustrated by Bill Slavin. Eerdmans Books for Young Readers 2009 un il $17.50

Grades: K 1 2 3   E

1. Wealth -- Fiction 2. Roosters -- Fiction
ISBN 978-0-8028-5328-8; 0-8028-5328-5

LC 2008009998

When Gonzalo the rooster wins the lottery, he leaves his job at the farm in search of the good life.

"Acrylic illustrations on gessoed paper animate the humor with fine-feathered cleverness, adding wry details. . . . A vocabulary list defines the six Spanish words sprinkled throughout. This is beak-in-cheek fun with an underlying message." Booklist

Lewin, Betsy, 1937-

★ **Puffling** patrol; Ted and Betsy Lewin. Lee & Low Books 2012 56 p. (hardcover: alk. paper) $19.95

Grades: 2 3 4   E

1. Puffins 2. Heimaey (Iceland) 3. Birds -- Protection 4. Children and animals 5. Wildlife rescue -- Iceland -- Heimaey (Westman Islands) 6. Atlantic puffin -- Infancy -- Iceland -- Heimaey (Westman Islands)
ISBN 1600604242; 9781600604249

LC 2011032248

In this book, "husband and wife team Ted and Betsy Lewin detail their visit to the island of Heimaey (off the coast of Iceland). They accompany two child members of the 'Puffling Patrol' (who rescue newly hatched puffins that become disoriented and lost on their way to the sea) and observe as the children find, care for, and release the baby pufflings." (Bulletin of the Center for Children's Books)

Where is Tippy Toes? [written and] illustrated by Betsy Lewin. Atheneum Books for Young Readers 2010 un il $16.99

Grades: PreK K   E

1. Stories in rhyme 2. Cats -- Fiction
ISBN 978-1-4169-3808-8; 1-4169-3808-7

LC 2009-24455

Although everyone can see how Tippy Toes, a mischievous cat, spends his days, only one knows where he goes after dark.

"Oversize watercolors outlined in a thick black line add humor to the text . . . and the bright hues seen in the flowers, sun, and cat's fur enhance the changing backgrounds. Rhyming sentences come together with the turn of a page and continue to the satisfying page turn at the end. This cat's sun up to sun down routine makes an excellent choice for those looking for a new bedtime story." SLJ

★ **You** can do it! by Betsy Lewin. 1st ed. Holiday House 2013 32 p. (I like to read) (reinforced) $14.95

Grades: K 1 2   E

1. Racing -- Fiction 2. Alligators -- Fiction 3. Self-confidence -- Fiction
ISBN 0823425223; 9780823425228

LC 2011051992

This children's book, by Caldecott Honor-winning illustrator Betsy Lewin, is part of the "I Like to Read" series. "'Can I do it?' wonders the little crocodile when he sees a sign for Sunday's big swimming race. A mean, bigger crocodile tells him he cannot win, but the little crocodile's friend

helps him train and tells him more than once that he can indeed succeed. On the day of the big race, the little crocodile is ready to prove himself." (Publisher's note)

"Limited, repetitive text invites new readers to adopt the same spirit of determination about reading that the protagonist alligator does about swimming... Lewin's restrained watercolor-and-ink artwork matches the control of the text... while delivering engaging and expressive characters. Subtle shifts in the placement of speech balloons provide humor while helping children decode. A winner of an early reader." Kirkus

Lewin, Ted

Animals work; by Ted Lewin. Holiday House 2014 28 p. col. ill., col. map (hardcover) $14.95

Grades: PreK K 1   E

1. Animals 2. Working animals
ISBN 0823430405; 9780823430406

LC 2013014333

"Bursting with detailed illustrations, this picture book not only teaches readers about the variety of work animals perform, but depicts the give-and-take dynamic of human/animal relationships." It "transports readers from an open field to a desert to a snowy tundra as animals of all kinds, from a shaggy pup to a group of camels, perform some very important tasks." (Publisher's note)

"The watercolor illustrations of the various locations and the people that inhabit them are stunningly lifelike, and a world map on the final spread shows where Lewin saw the animals. Easy enough for the very earliest readers." SLJ

Can you see me? by Ted Lewin. Holiday House 2014 32 p. (I like to read) (hardcover) $14.95

Grades: PreK K 1   E

1. Costa Rica 2. Rain forest animals 3. Animals -- Habitations 4. Rain forest animals
ISBN 0823429407; 9780823429400

LC 2013009555

In this children's book, by Ted Lewin, "readers are invited to spot various animals in the Costa Rican rain forest. Lewin . . . . displays . . . mammals, birds and reptiles in their natural habitats. Camouflage is the unspoken theme. . . . . A pictorial guide identifies each of the animals by name." (Kirkus Reviews)

"Lewin camouflages an animal for youngsters to find in each of eleven rainforest scenes. The language ("I am a reptile. Can you see me?") is largely, and appropriately, repetitive, but the challenge of decoding the key word before finding the animal in the illustration adds an extra burden to the target audience of beginning readers. A picture guide with species names is appended." Horn Book

Lewis, J. Patrick

Big is big (and little, little) a book of contrasts. by J. Patrick Lewis; illustrated by Bob Barner. Holiday House 2007 un il $16.95

Grades: PreK K 1   E

1. Opposites 2. Animals -- Poetry
ISBN 978-0-8234-1909-8; 0-8234-1909-6

LC 2005050341

"Wordplay meets playful art in this clever look at opposites. Lewis's bouncy verse and Barner's rollicking illustrations show the contrasts between various animals. . . . Done in a combination of cut-paper collage, bright pastels, and bold black line, Barner's animals cavort against vivid backgrounds." SLJ

Face bug; by J. Patrick Lewis; illustrated by Kelly Murphy; photographs by Frederic B. Siskind. WordSong 2013 36 p. ill. (reinforced) $16.95
Grades: 3 4 5   E
1. Insects -- Poetry
ISBN 1590789253; 9781590789254
LC 2012943510
This book by J. Patrick Lewis "combines poetry, line drawings and scientific facts. . . . A collection of small bugs . . . visits the Face Bug Museum, where they learn to drill like a carpenter bee, experience the stinkbug's stench, sip on nectar at the snack bar and measure the speed of the green darner dragonfly. The insects on display at the 'museum' . . . are portrayed in . . . full-color micrographs by renowned nature photographer [Frederic B.] Siskind." (Kirkus Reviews)

The **Fantastic** 5 & 10[cents] store; a rebus adventure. words by J. Patrick Lewis; pictures by Valorie Fisher. Schwartz & Wade Books 2010 un il $17.99; lib bdg $20.99
Grades: PreK K 1 2   E
1. Riddles 2. Stories in rhyme 3. Department stores -- Fiction
ISBN 978-0-375-85878-9; 0-375-85878-4; 978-0-375-95878-6 lib bdg; 0-375-95878-9 lib bdg
LC 2008048827
Rhymed text, featuring rebuses, describes the wonders of the store run by Mr. Nickel and Mrs. Dime.
"The rebuses appear opposite each image on yellowing lined paper, straight from a vintage school notebook, and for those having trouble guessing, the full text of the rhymes appears at the end of the book. Good, old-fashioned fun, with a surprise ending that reveals Benny's talent for public relations." Publ Wkly

The **kindergarten** cat; illustrated by Ailie Busby. Schwartz & Wade Books 2009 un il $16.99; lib bdg $19.99
Grades: PreK K   E
1. School stories 2. Stories in rhyme 3. Cats -- Fiction
ISBN 978-0-375-84475-1; 0-375-84475-9; 978-0-375-98807-3 lib bdg; 0-375-98807-6 lib bdg
LC 2008006691
A stray cat finds a happy home in a kindergarten classroom.
"Lewis's verse is sweetly complemented by Busby's mixed-media illustrations. Her fat, scruffy orange tiger cat brims with personality, her cartoony roundness matching that of the children neatly. Broad paint strokes accented with swift pencil scribbles lend energy throughout." Kirkus

The **snowflake** sisters; illustrated by Lisa Desimini. Atheneum Bks. for Young Readers 2003 un il $16.95
Grades: K 1 2 3   E
1. Snow -- Fiction 2. New York (N.Y.) -- Fiction
ISBN 0-689-85029-8
LC 2002-6138
Two snowflakes named Crystal and Ivory travel on Santa's sleigh and make their way through the wintry sky until they become part of a snowboy in Central Park

"The setting is New York City, captured through witty collage illustrations that make use of such materials as rice paper, maps, newsprint, and Scrabble letters. Lewis's elegant and fluid rhymed text offers surprises on every page." SLJ

World Rat day; J. Patrick Lewis, illustrated by Anna Raff. Candlewick Press 2013 40 p. (reinforced) $15.99
Grades: K 1 2 3   E
ISBN 9780763654023
LC 2012942612

Lewis, Jill
Don't read this book! illustrated by Deborah Allwright. Tiger Tales 2010 un il $15.95
Grades: 2 3 4   E
1. Fairy tales
ISBN 978-1-58925-094-9; 1-58925-094-X
The king frantically rides throughout his kingdom trying to piece together fragments of his story.
"The collage pictures in blazing colors are just right for scenes of the king threatening to put the reader in the dungeon if he does not go away. . . . Not for the usual picture-book fairy-tale crowd, this is for readers who already know the classic stories and will enjoy the parodies and rebellious chaos, especially their own defiance just by turning the pages." Booklist

Lewis, Kevin
Not inside this house! illustrated by David Ercolini. Orchard Books 2011 un il $16.99
Grades: PreK K   E
1. Stories in rhyme 2. Animals -- Fiction 3. Explorers -- Fiction 4. Mother-son relationship -- Fiction
ISBN 978-0-439-43981-7; 0-439-43981-7
LC 2010033233
Rhyming text follows a young explorer as he discovers bugs and then increasingly larger creatures, brings them home to learn about them, and is warned by his mother that each is unwelcome.
"The precisely composed ink drawing, painting, and Photoshop illustrations, which set the tale in the halcyon age when men wore hats and women donned aprons, add an old-fashioned charm and much humor to the story." SLJ

Lewis, Paeony
No more yawning! by Paeony Lewis; illustrated by Brita Granström. Chicken House/Scholastic 2008 un il $16.99
Grades: PreK K   E
1. Toys -- Fiction 2. Sleep -- Fiction 3. Bedtime -- Fiction
ISBN 0-545-02957; 978-0-545-02957-5
Companion volume to: No more cookies (2005)
Florence and her toy monkey Arnold try to fall asleep but Florence's big yawns keep them awake. Includes tips for falling asleep.
"Florence's childlike voice carries this charming story, and the repetition of her excuses . . . adds humor, as do her crayon drawings, which frequently appear superimposed on the watercolor-and-pencil scenes." Booklist

Lewis, Rose A.
Every year on your birthday; written by Rose Lewis; illustrated by Jane Dyer. Little, Brown 2007 un il $16.99

Grades: PreK K 1 2   E
   1. Adoption -- Fiction 2. Birthdays -- Fiction 3. Mother-daughter relationship -- Fiction
   ISBN 978-0-316-52552-7; 0-316-52552-9
                  LC 2006026467
Each year on the birthday of her adopted Chinese daughter, a mother recalls the moments they have shared, from the first toy to the friends left behind in China

"Expressive watercolors evoke vivid memories. . . . By story's end, readers see a matured parent, secure in her love for her child." Publ Wkly

  I love you like crazy cakes; written by Rose Lewis; illustrated by Jane Dyer. Little, Brown 2000 un il $14.95; bd bk $6.99
Grades: PreK K 1 2   E
   1. Infants -- Fiction 2. Adoption -- Fiction
   ISBN 0-316-52538-3; 0-316-52576-6 bd bk
                  LC 99-34175
A woman describes how she went to China to adopt a special baby girl. Based on the author's own experiences

"Dyer's simple watercolor layouts with expressive characters make this a calming read, befitting the gentle affection in the text." SLJ

Lexau, Joan M.
  Come back, cat; by Joan L. Nodset; pictures by Steven Kellogg. Harper Collins Childrens Books 2008 un il $16.99; lib bdg $17.89
Grades: PreK K 1 2   E
   1. Cats -- Fiction
   ISBN 978-0-06-028081-9; 0-06-028081-6; 978-0-06-028082-6 lib bdg; 0-06-028082-4 lib bdg
                  LC 2007041937
A newly illustrated edition of Come here cat, published 1973
A stray cat and a little girl have their problems getting acquainted.

"This picture book, originally published in two colors and out of print for many years, has been reissued with Kellogg's full-color, mixed-media illustrations. Color is used quite effectively. . . . The text, which consists exclusively of the child's dialogue, is both fresh and timeless." SLJ

  Who took the farmer's [hat]? [by] Joan L. Nodset; pictures by Fritz Siebel. Harper & Row 1963 un il lib bdg $17.89; pa $6.99
Grades: PreK K   E
   1. Animals -- Fiction
   ISBN 0-06-024566-2 lib bdg; 0-06-443174-6 pa
"Away flew the farmer's hat. In his search for it he found that his hat could be many things to many animals including, most permanently, a bird's nest." Publ Wkly

Liao, Jimmy
  The sound of colors; a journey of imagination. [by] Jimmy Liao; English text adapted by Sarah L. Thomson. Little, Brown 2006 un il $16.99
Grades: K 1 2 3 4   E
   1. Blind -- Fiction
   ISBN 0-316-93992-7
                 LC 2004-025100
"A young girl's eyesight began slipping away a year ago. With her white cane in hand, she ventures on a subway trip using her imagination to take herself and readers on a journey. . . . Poetic, lyrical language is used in this translation from Chinese. The girl is strong and admirable. . . . Liao's watercolor illustrations invite readers to take time, slow down, and pore over the details." SLJ

Lichtenheld, Tom
  ★ Bridget's beret. Henry Holt and Company 2010 un il $16.99
Grades: K 1 2   E
   1. Hats -- Fiction 2. Artists -- Fiction 3. Drawing -- Fiction
   ISBN 978-0-8050-8775-8; 0-8050-8775-3
                 LC 2009-12220
When Bridget loses the beret that provides her with artistic inspiration like other great artists, she thinks she will never be able to draw again.

"This smart, saucy book, with its spacious cartoon-style art, is both a spur to artistic endeavor and a message about inspiration and hard work. Yet the motivations are cocooned by a crackin' good tale and tempered by a full-faceted heroine." Booklist

  Cloudette. Henry Holt 2011 un il $16.99
Grades: PreK K 1   E
   1. Rain -- Fiction 2. Size -- Fiction 3. Clouds -- Fiction
   ISBN 978-0-8050-8776-5; 0-8050-8776-1
                 LC 2010011688
Cloudette, the littlest cloud, finds a way to do something big and important as the other clouds do.

"Sprinkled with punny jokes, Lichtenheld's polished spreads show Cloudette as a simple, scalloped-edged puff who looks mighty dejected as she tries to be useful. . . . Neatly constructed and nicely pitched, the message of self-reliance comes through as clear as a cloudless day." Publ Wkly

  ★ E-mergency. Chronicle Books 2011 il $16.99
Grades: 1 2 3   E
   1. Alphabet -- Fiction 2. English language -- Spelling -- Fiction
   ISBN 978-0-8118-7898-2; 0-8118-7898-8
                 LC 2010053591
"Though some of the jokes will be clear only to older brothers and sisters, readers who are in the thick of learning spelling rules will pore over the pages. Comprehensive, witty entertainment from A to Z." Publ Wkly

  ★ Exclamation mark; Amy Krouse Rosenthal, Tom Lichtenheld. Scholastic Press 2013 56 p. (reinforced) $17.99
Grades: PreK K 1 2   E
   1. Self-acceptance -- Fiction 2. Identity (Psychology) -- Fiction
   ISBN 0545436796; 9780545436793
                 LC 2012936803
This children's book, by Amy Krouse Rosenthal, illustrated by Tom Lichtenheld, is a story about an exclamation point that learns to be comfortable with its own identity, different from all the other periods around it. "It's not easy being seen. Especially when you're NOT like everyone else. Especially when what sets you apart is YOU. Sometimes we squish ourselves to fit in. We shrink. Twist. Bend. Until--!--a friend shows the way to endless possibilities." (Publisher's note)

Lies, Brian

Bats at the beach; written and illustrated by Brian Lies. Houghton Mifflin Harcourt 2006 32 p. il $16.99

Grades: PreK K 1 2   **E**

1. Bats -- Fiction 2. Beaches -- Fiction

ISBN 061855744X; 9780618557448

LC 2005010757

This children's book, written and illustrated by Brian Lies, "is the quintessential book about going to the beach complete with overflowing picnic baskets, kite flying, singing around the campfire, and scratchy sand in places where no sand should be.... The rhyming text is grounded in reality with many inventive twists to keep the imagination rolling." (School Library Journal)

"The acrylic paintings capture a moonlit night's deep shadows and reinforce the exuberant rhyming text." Horn Book Guide

Other titles about the bats are:

Bats at the library (2008)

Bats at the ballgame (2010)

Light, Kelly

Louise loves art; Kelly Light. Balzer + Bray, an imprint of HarperCollinsPublishers 2014 40 p. color illustrations (hardcover) $17.99

Grades: K 1 2 3   **E**

1. Imagination -- Fiction 2. Brothers and sisters -- Fiction 3. Art -- Fiction 4. Drawing -- Fiction

ISBN 0062248170; 9780062248176

LC 2013043069

In this children's book by Kelly Light, readers "meet Louise. Louise loves art more than anything. It's her imagination on the outside. She is determined to create a masterpiece. Louise also loves Art, her little brother. This is their story." (Publisher's note)

"Passion is contagious. Fun, focused, and full of flair, Louise anxiously works toward creating her masterpiece. Meanwhile her little brother, tagging along, wants her attention...Younger siblings will appreciate Louise's generosity that transcends the typical dominant older sibling dynamic. Most importantly, budding artists, those not only crazy for art but who have their eyes and heart open, will find a muse and a collaborator." SLJ

Light, Steve

★ The **Christmas** giant. Candlewick Press 2010 un il $15.99

Grades: PreK K 1   **E**

1. Giants -- Fiction 2. Christmas -- Fiction

ISBN 978-0-7636-4692-9; 0-7636-4692-X

When two best friends, a giant and an elf, grow Christmastown's holiday tree, disaster strikes.

"The pen, ink, and pastel artwork is truly lovely. Muted colors and swirly lines evoke old-fashioned folk art while retaining a fresh cartoon whimsy.... The story itself is sweet and economically told, capturing not only the spirit of Christmas, but also of friendship, persistence, and resourcefulness." SLJ

Have you seen my dragon? Steve Light. Candlewick Press 2014 48 p. $16.99

Grades: PreK K 1 2   **E**

1. Dragons -- Fiction 2. Cities and towns -- Fiction 3.

Counting

ISBN 0763666483; 9780763666484

LC 2013943993

In this children's book, by Steve Light, readers "help a boy find his dragon while counting objects from hot dogs to traffic lights. In the heart of the city, among the taxis and towers, a small boy travels uptown and down, searching for his friend. . . . Is the dragon taking the crosstown bus, or breathing his fiery breath below a busy street? Maybe he took a taxi to the zoo or is playing with the dogs in the park." (Publisher's note)

"A dragon is on the loose in New York City, but rather than inciting terror, he provides an opportunity for a gentle quest and counting game. Light (Zephyr Takes Flight, 2012) takes readers on a tour of lower Manhattan with a little boy as he travels from spot to spot looking for his escaped pet... His cityscapes capture the bustle of New York City, and children will have as much fun exploring the city as they do trying to spot the sneaky dragon hidden within. A rough map of the city serves as the book's endpapers, so little eyes can follow along." Booklist

Have you seen my monster? Steve Light. Candlewick Press 2015 48 p. ill (some col) reinforced $16.99

Grades: PreK K 1 2   **E**

1. Pets -- Fiction 2. Monsters -- Fiction 3. Lost and found possessions -- Fiction

ISBN 076367513X; 9780763675134

LC 2013957389

In this story by Steve Light, "a little girl gallivants through a county fair, searching for her furry friend. Readers will surely spot the friendly monster as well as twenty shapes, identified here by their proper names--trapezoids, ellipses, kites, and more--hidden among iconic fair attractions from the fun house to the Ferris wheel." (Publisher's note)

"Simple sentences in large print are prominently placed within the illustrations, and a black banner with white lettering announces the names of brightly colored shapes. A square, rectangle, triangle and circle each make an appearance, along with other familiar shapes. But watch for a quatrefoil, trapezium, nonagon and curvilinear triangle as well." Kirkus

★ **Planes** go; by Steve Light. Chronicle Books LLC 2014 16 p. color illustrations (board bk) $9.99

Grades: PreK   **E**

1. Airplanes 2. Airplanes -- Fiction

ISBN 1452128995; 9781452128993

LC 2013025008

In this children's book, by Steve Light, "the helicopter goes, 'PITTATATATA.' . . . The jumbo jet goes, 'Wheeeeeeeee VRRRRRRRRRRUUUHHHHHHH-HHMMM.' The propeller plane goes, 'HUK HUK HUK WHIRRRRRRR.' . . . Prepare for liftoff with 8 exciting aircraft and the noises they make in this . . . board book!" (Publisher's note)

"The bright and colorful watercolor illustrations zoom across the blue-and-white cloudy backgrounds on wide-trim pages. Buzzy, onomatopoeic sounds in splashy, expressive fonts make this one easily enjoyable with or without a grown-up." Booklist

Trains go; Steve Light. Chronicle Books 2012 16 p. (board) $8.99

Grades: 1 2 3   **E**

    1. Board books for children 2. Sounds 3. Locomotives 4. Railroad trains -- Fiction

ISBN 0811879429; 9780811879422

                            LC 2011008004

This children's story, by Steve Light, describes different types of trains and their sounds. "All aboard! Take a trip on eight noisy trains as they huff, puff, and toot-toot their way through this . . . board book!" Trains described include steam engines, diesel trains, and magnetic high-speed commuter rails. (Publisher's note)

Zephyr takes flight; Steve Light. Candlewick 2012 40 p. (hardcover) $16.99

Grades: PreK K 1   **E**

    1. Flight -- Fiction 2. Imagination -- Fiction 3. Adventure fiction

ISBN 076365695X; 9780763656959

                            LC 2011046669

This children's story, by Steve Light, follows "a clever girl's flight of fancy in a whimsical ode to free spirits, inventiveness, and flying pigs. Zephyr is a girl who loves airplanes . . . and hopes one day to fly one of her own. But when Gramma, Daddy, and Mom are too busy to play airplane with her, Zephyr's excess enthusiasm gets her sent to her room--where she discovers a secret door that leads to the most wondrous place she's ever seen!" (Publisher's note)

Lillegard, Dee

    Tiger, tiger; illustrated by Susan Guevara. Putnam 2002 un il $16.99

Grades: PreK K 1   **E**

    1. Magic -- Fiction 2. Tigers -- Fiction

ISBN 0-399-22633-8

                            LC 2002-272

A bored young boy uses a magic feather to form a tiger, and then must use the feather to save his village when the tiger gets hungry

"The suspenseful story reaches a dramatic climax, made all the more vivid by Guevara's highly charged artwork." Booklist

Lin, Grace

    Bringing in the New Year; [by] Grace Lin. Alfred A. Knopf 2008 un il $15.99; lib bdg $18.99

Grades: PreK K 1 2   **E**

    1. Chinese New Year -- Fiction 2. Chinese Americans -- Fiction

ISBN 978-0-375-83745-6; 0-375-83745-0; 978-0-375-93745-3 lib bdg; 0-375-93745-5

                            LC 2007011687

A Chinese American family prepares for and celebrates the Lunar New Year. End notes discuss the customs and traditions of Chinese New Year.

"The lustrous gouache illustrations are saturated with bold primary colors and deftly convey the joyousness of the festivities. . . . A wonderful and much-needed addition to Chinese New Year literature." SLJ

    ★ **Dim** sum for everyone! written and illustrated by Grace Lin. Knopf 2001 un il $14.95; pa $6.99

Grades: K 1 2 3   **E**

    1. Restaurants -- Fiction 2. Chinese Americans -- Fiction

ISBN 0-375-81082-X; 0-440-41770-8 pa

                            LC 00-34813

A child describes the various little dishes of dim sum that she and her family enjoy on a visit to a restaurant in Chinatown

"Lin's paintings are graphically striking. They combine a simplicity of form and design with a delight of patterning that appears in clothing and in backgrounds. . . . Like the pleasures of dim sum, this is a compact treat." Booklist

    Kite flying. Knopf 2002 un il hardcover o.p. pa $6.99

Grades: K 1 2 3   **E**

    1. Kites -- Fiction

ISBN 0-375-81520-1; 0-553-11254-6 pa

                            LC 2001-33456

"A Chinese girl describes how the members of her family come together to make and fly a dragon kite. . . . The overall simplicity is effective and appealing, and the spare text is accentuated by bright gouache illustrations, in colorful shapes and painted fabric patterns." Booklist

    ★ **Ling** & Ting; not exactly the same! Little, Brown 2010 43p il

Grades: K 1 2   **E**

    1. Twins -- Fiction 2. Sisters -- Fiction

ISBN 031602452X; 9780316024525

"Sticking together through everything from getting haircuts and preparing dumplings to practicing magic tricks and using chopsticks, identical twin sisters Ling and Ting display distinctive differences in personality and preference despite their similar looks." (Publisher's note) "Primary." (Horn Book)

"Sisters Ling and Ting may be twins, but that doesn't mean they're 'exactly the same,' no matter what everyone says upon first meeting them. Children will come to their own conclusions after reading the six short, interconnected stories that make up this pleasing book for beginning readers. . . . Framed with narrow borders, the paintings illustrate the stories with restrained lines, vivid colors, and clarity." Booklist

    Ling & Ting; twice as silly. by Grace Lin. Little, Brown & Co. 2014 48 p. color illustrations

Grades: K 1 2   **E**

    1. Wit and humor 2. Twins -- Fiction 3. Play -- Fiction 4. Humorous stories 5. Sisters -- Fiction 6. Chinese Americans -- Fiction

ISBN 9780316184021; 0316184020

                            LC 2013041479

In this children's book by Grace Lin "Ling & Ting are twins. They like to be silly. They like to tell jokes. Most of all, they like to laugh together. The beloved twins . . . are back to share their favorite funny stories with beginning readers. This collection of six laugh-out-loud stories is [designed] to tickle the funny bone of fans and new readers alike." (Publisher's note)

"Twins Ling and Ting star in six very short stories for beginning readers, who will be charmed by the girls' talent for silliness and by the enjoyable, episodic chapters. The first shows Ting planting a cupcake in the garden, watering it, and waiting in vain for more to grow. In another, Ling fools Ting with a wordplay joke. In the last, titled "Not a Silly Story," the girls pull from their recent experiences to write and illustrate the silliest tale of all. Clean lines, bold accent colors, and beautifully drawn characters make this a handsome addition to the well-crafted Ling & Ting series." Booklist

Ling and Ting, twice as silly
Twice as silly

Thanking the moon; celebrating the Mid-Autumn Moon Festival. Alfred A. Knopf 2010 un il $16.99; lib bdg $19.99

Grades: PreK K 1 2   E
1. Food -- Fiction 2. Moon -- Fiction 3. China -- Fiction 4. Mid-autumn Day -- Fiction
ISBN 978-0-375-86101-7; 0-375-86101-7; 978-0-375-96101-4 lib bdg; 0-375-96101-1 lib bdg
LC 2009052349
Each member of a Chinese family contributes to the celebration of the Mid-Autumn Moon Festival.

"Lin fashions a child-friendly introduction to the mid-autumn harvest moon festival with engagingly simple text and colorful, oversize gouache illustrations. . . . The writing is concise and accessible, and an author's note adds further information on the holiday and its significance. The inviting nocturnal landscapes are vivid with interesting details" SLJ

Lindbergh, Reeve
Homer, the library cat; illustrated by Anne Wilsdorf. Candlewick Press 2011 un il

Grades: PreK K 1   E
1. Stories in rhyme 2. Cats -- Fiction 3. Libraries -- Fiction
ISBN 0-7636-3448-4; 978-0-7636-3448-3
LC 2010048130
A cat's quiet life is disrupted one day when a window is broken, and after several frustrating attempts to find a suitable place, he winds up in the perfect spot.

"Lindbergh's simple rhyming text makes a good match with Wilsdorf's exuberant ink-and-watercolor artwork, which captures all the fun of a cat on the loose." Booklist

My hippie grandmother; illustrated by Abby Carter. Candlewick Press 2003 un il $15.99

Grades: K 1 2 3   E
1. Stories in rhyme 2. Hippies -- Fiction 3. Grandmothers -- Fiction
ISBN 0-7636-0671-5
LC 00-37964
A young girl describes all the things she likes about her grandmother, including the purple bus she drives, growing vegetables, picketing City Hall, and playing the banjo

"A wonderful, poetic portrait. . . . Carter's colorful watercolor-and-gouache illustrations capture the happy mood of the verse." SLJ

Lindenbaum, Pija
Mini Mia and her darling uncle; translated by Elizabeth Kallick Dyssegaard. Farrar, Straus & Giroux 2007 un il $16

Grades: PreK K 1 2   E
1. Uncles -- Fiction 2. Homosexuality -- Fiction
ISBN 978-91-29-66734-9; 91-29-66734-8
LC 2006-93704
"The 'darling uncle' of this . . . title is a gay man, but Lindenbaum . . . focuses not on his identity but on his niece Ella's resentment of his new partner. . . . Lindenbaum paints Uncle Tommy's fabulous shirts and retro furniture with verve, and her pacing is sure. . . . The emotions stay true." Publ Wkly

Lindgren, Astrid
Goran's great escape; translated by Polly Lawson; illustrated by Marit Törnqvist. Floris 2011 il $17.95

Grades: PreK K 1 2   E
1. Bulls -- Fiction 2. Easter -- Fiction 3. Sweden -- Fiction 4. Farm life -- Fiction
ISBN 978-0-86315-793-6; 0-86315-793-9
Original Swedish edition published 1950 as part of a story collection; first English language edition published 1991 with title: The day Adam got mad

"Years ago in Sweden, on an Easter morning, Goran the bull escaped from his barn and might still be at large if 7-year-old Karl hadn't come by and offered to scratch his head. This charming story . . . gets new life with Lawson's translation, which smoothes and slightly modernizes the English. . . . Törnqvist's meticulous watercolor illustrations again complement the story. . . . There are lovely touches of humor. . . . From a beloved author, a tiny gem for reading aloud or reading alone." Kirkus

Lindsey, Kat
Sweet potato pie; by Kathleen D. Lindsey; illustrated by Charlotte Riley-Webb. Lee & Low Books 2003 un il $16.95; pa $7.95

Grades: K 1 2 3   E
1. Pies -- Fiction 2. Farm life -- Fiction 3. Family life -- Fiction 4. African Americans -- Fiction
ISBN 1-58430-061-2; 1-60060-277-0 pa
LC 2002-30164
During a drought in the early 1900s, a large loving African American family finds a delicious way to earn the money they need to save their family farm

"Lindsey's down-home storytelling quality is charming. . . . The artwork's broad, energetic strokes and strong color palette sweep children into this tasty tale, and the included pie recipe makes the experience complete." Booklist

Lionni, Leo
Alexander and the wind-up mouse; by Leo Lionni. Alfred A. Knopf 2006 un il $16.99; lib bdg $18.99; pa $6.99

Grades: PreK K 1 2   E
1. Mice -- Fiction
ISBN 0-394-80914-9; 0-394-90914-3 lib bdg; 0-394-82911-5 pa
A reissue of the title first published 1969 by Pantheon Books
A Caldecott Medal honor book, 1970
The author's "collage illustrations are dazzling in their color and bold design and contribute to a beautiful and appealing picture book." Booklist

★ **Fish** is fish. Alfred A. Knopf 2005 un il $15.95

Grades: PreK K 1 2   E
1. Frogs -- Fiction 2. Fishes -- Fiction
ISBN 0-394-80440-6

A reissue of the title first published 1970 by Pantheon Bks.

The frog tells the fish all about the world above the sea. The fish, however, can only visualize it in terms of fish-people, fish-birds and fish-cows.

"The story is slight but pleasantly and simply told, the illustrations are page-filling, deft, colorful, and amusing." Bull Cent Child Books

★ **Frederick**. Pantheon Bks. 1967 un il $16.95; lib bdg $18.99; pa $5.99
Grades: PreK K 1 2   E
1. Mice -- Fiction
ISBN 0-394-81040-6; 0-394-91040-0 lib bdg; 0-394-82614-0 pa

"This captivating book . . . sings a hymn of praise to poets in a gentle story that is illustrated with gaiety and charm." Saturday Rev

"While other mice are gathering food for the winter, Frederick seems to daydream the summer away. When dreary winter comes, it is Frederick the poet-mouse who warms his friends and cheers them with his words." Wis Libr Bull

★ **Inch** by inch. Alfred A. Knopf 2010 un il $16.99; lib bdg $19.99
Grades: PreK K 1 2   E
1. Birds -- Fiction 2. Measurement -- Fiction 3. Caterpillars -- Fiction
ISBN 978-0-375-85764-5; 0-375-85764-8; 978-0-375-95764-2 lib bdg; 0-375-95764-2 lib bdg
LC 2009-1767

A reissue of the title first published 1960 by Astor-Honor

A Caldecott Medal honor book, 1961

To keep from being eaten, an inchworm measures a robin's tail, a flamingo's neck, a toucan's beak, a heron's legs, and a nightingale's song.

"This is a book to look at again and again. The semi-abstract forms are sharply defined, clean and strong, the colors subtle and glowing, and the grassy world of the inchworm is a special place of enchantment." N Y Times Book Rev

★ **Little** blue and little yellow; a story for Pippo and Ann and other children. 50th anniversary ed.; Alfred A. Knopf 2009 un il $15.99; lib bdg $18.99
Grades: PreK K 1 2   E
1. Color -- Fiction 2. Friendship -- Fiction
ISBN 978-0-375-86013-3; 0-375-86013-4; 978-0-375-96013-0 lib bdg; 0-375-96013-9 lib bdg
LC 2008035932

A reissue of the title first published 1959 by Astor-Honor

A little blue spot and a little yellow spot are best friends, and when they hug each other they become green.

"So well are the dots handled on the pages that little blue and little yellow and their parents seem to have real personalities. It should inspire interesting color play and is a very original picture book by an artist." N Y Her Trib Books

Six crows; a fable. Alfred A. Knopf 2010 un il $16.99; lib bdg $19.99
Grades: PreK K 1 2   E
1. Owls -- Fiction 2. Crows -- Fiction 3. Farm life

-- Fiction
ISBN 978-0-375-84550-5; 0-375-84550-X; 978-0-375-94550-2 lib bdg; 0-375-94550-4 lib bdg

A reissue of the title first published 1988

An owl helps a farmer and some crows reach a compromise over the rights to the wheat crop.

"This brief, simple story works on a literal level as well as on a metaphoric one. It is illustrated with Lionni's usual handsome, colorful collages which project well for reading aloud to groups." SLJ

★ **Swimmy**. Pantheon Bks. 1973 un il $16; pa $5.99
Grades: PreK K 1 2   E
1. Fishes -- Fiction
ISBN 0-394-81713-3; 0-394-82620-5 pa

"To illustrate his clever, but very brief story, Leo Lionni has made a book of astonishingly beautiful pictures, full of undulating, watery nuances of shape, pattern, and color." Horn Book

Lipson, Eden Ross

Applesauce season; illustrated by Mordicai Gerstein. Roaring Brook Press 2009 un il $17.99
Grades: PreK K 1 2   E
1. Apples -- Fiction 2. Family life -- Fiction
ISBN 978-1-59643-216-1; 1-59643-216-0

"Flavored with family tradition and spiced with Gerstein's cheerful illustrations, this account of one family's love of applesauce hits the spot. . . . In a crowded orchard of apple books, this one stands out for home or school apple and/or family-tradition projects. Applesauce recipe appended." Kirkus

Lithgow, John

★ **Micawber**; illustrated by C.F. Payne. Simon & Schuster Bks. for Young Readers 2002 un il $17.95; pa $6.99
Grades: PreK K 1 2   E
1. Stories in rhyme 2. Artists -- Fiction 3. Squirrels -- Fiction 4. New York (N.Y.) -- Fiction
ISBN 0-689-83341-5; 0-689-83542-6 pa
LC 2001-20919

Micawber, a squirrel fascinated by art, leaves the Metropolitan Museum of Art with an art student, secretly uses her supplies to make his own paintings, and starts his own art museum atop Central Park's carousel

"The rhymed text sparkles with pleasing sounds. . . . Lithgow's reading on the CD is brimming with texture and playful pomposity. The mixed-media illustrations depict an utterly fetching protagonist displaying a range of moods and poses." SLJ

Little, Jean

★ **Emma's** yucky brother; story by Jean Little; pictures by Jennifer Plecas. HarperCollins Pubs. 2001 63p il (I can read book) hardcover o.p. pa $3.99
Grades: PreK K 1 2   E
1. Adoption -- Fiction 2. Siblings -- Fiction
ISBN 0-06-028348-3; 0-06-444258-6 pa
LC 99-34515

Emma finds out how hard it is to be a big sister when her family adopts a four-year-old boy named Max

"Heartfelt and honest. . . . Little's simple words and Plecas' clear, expressive line-and-watercolor illustrations tell an intense story." Booklist

Other titles about Emma are:

Emma's magic winter (1998)

Emma's strange pet (2003)

Littlewood, Karin

Immi's gift; written and illustrated by Karin Littlewood. Peachtree 2010 un il $15.95

Grades: K 1 2   E

1. Inuit -- Fiction 2. Fishing -- Fiction

ISBN 978-1-56145-545-4; 1-56145-545-8

Day after day in the frozen north, a young Inuit girl catches brightly-colored objects while ice fishing and uses them to decorate her igloo, until the ice begins to melt and she drops in a gift of her own before leaving for the season.

"A fur-clad Inuit girl searches for the brightest objects she can find in a 'frozen white world,' rendered in smudgy watercolor and gouache with colored pencil detailing. Ice fishing, she finds a painted wooden bird, followed by an orange starfish, a green leaf, and a purple feather, which she uses to adorn her igloo. . . . It's a story with a quiet magic and beauty." Publ Wkly

Litwin, Eric

Pete the cat: I love my white shoes. Harper 2010 un il $16.99

Grades: PreK K 1 2   E

1. Cats -- Fiction 2. Color -- Fiction 3. Shoes -- Fiction

ISBN 978-0-06-190622-0; 0-06-190622-0

First published 2008 by Blue Whiskey Press

Pete the Cat goes walking down the street wearing his brand-new white shoes. Along the way, his shoes change from white to red to blue to brown to WET as he steps in piles of strawberries, blueberries, and other big messes! But no matter what color his shoes are, Pete keeps movin' and groovin' and singing his song . . . because it's all good.

Liu, Jae Soo

Yellow umbrella; written and illustrated by Jae Soo Liu. Kane/Miller 2002 un il $19.95

Grades: PreK K 1   E

1. Stories without words 2. Umbrellas and parasols -- Fiction

ISBN 1-929132-36-0

A story, in pictures and music, of children on their way to school on a rainy day

"Originally published in South Korea, the volume is both delicate and handsome. . . . The joyful hues multiply with each successive spread. Composer Dong Il Sheen gracefully glides between rhythms throughout the 15 tracks here [on the CD] . . . maintaining an overall happy tone." Publ Wkly

Livingston, Myra Cohn

Calendar; by Myra Cohn Livingston; illustrated by Will Hillenbrand. Holiday House 2007 un il $16.95

Grades: PreK K 1 2   E

1. Months -- Poetry

ISBN 978-0-8234-1725-4; 0-8234-1725-5

LC 2006012145

"'January shivers / February shines / March blows off the winter ice / April makes / the mornings nice . . .' First published in 1959 in the collection Wide Awake and Other

Poems, this simple poem by the late Livingston gets its own picture book here with a lively double-page spread for each month of the year. The bright, clear, mixed-media artwork—ink, acrylic, gouache, and collage—extends the words." Booklist

Liwska, Renata

★ **Red** wagon. Philomel Books 2011 un il $16.99

Grades: PreK K   E

1. Play -- Fiction 2. Work -- Fiction

ISBN 978-0-399-25237-2; 0-399-25237-1

LC 2010005393

When Lucy gets a new red wagon she wants to play with it immediately, but first she must use it to bring vegetables home from the market for her mother.

"Liwska's story stays true to the way children see the world, gives the gentlest of pushes toward cooperation, and offers respite from suburban anxiety and busyness." Publ Wkly

Ljungkvist, Laura

★ **Follow** the line; words and art by Laura Ljungkvist. Viking 2006 un il $16.99

Grades: PreK K 1 2   E

1. Counting

ISBN 0-670-06049-6

LC 2005-22701

Invites the reader to visit a wide variety of places and count different objects found in each, from fire hydrants in a big city in the morning, through starfish in the ocean during the day, to babies sleeping in a country village at night.

"An entrancing counting game with a search through detailed art, this title doubles as a vocabulary builder for the youngest readers and includes shapes, colors, and patterns in the search." SLJ

Other titles in this series are:

Follow the line through the house (2007)

Follow the line around the world (2008)

Follow the line to school (2011)

Lloyd, Jennifer

★ The **Best** Thing About Kindergarten. Simply Read Books 2013 36 p. $16.95

Grades: PreK K   E

1. Picture books for children 2. Kindergarten -- Fiction

ISBN 1897476825; 9781897476826

In this children's picture book, the "kids in Mrs. Appleby's kindergarten class are getting ready to graduate, but there's time for one last activity: 'Who can guess what is the best thing about kindergarten?' she asks. Guesses include the playhouse, the writing center, and recess, and Mrs. Appleby affirms each suggestion: 'You are a monkey bar superstar,' she tells a boy named Will, adding, 'We still haven't found the answer' (it turns out to be the children themselves)." (Publishers Weekly)

Lloyd, Sam

Doctor Meow's big emergency. Henry Holt & Co. 2008 un il (Whoops-a-daisy world) $14.95

Grades: PreK K 1 2   E

1. Cats -- Fiction 2. Hospitals -- Fiction 3. Physicians -- Fiction

ISBN 978-0-8050-8819-9; 0-8050-8819-9

First published 2007 in the United Kingdom

"At Kiss-It-Better Hospital, busy Dr. Meow, a cat wearing a pink coat and stethoscope, receives an emergency call from Tom Cat, who has fallen from a tree after a leap toward Mr. Bird. . . . The cartoon-style animal characters and the spare, animated text, filled with sound effects, make for a light and lively read that doesn't downplay the discomfort of being injured and scared. Vibrant, page-spanning illustrations . . . incorporate playful details." Booklist

Followed by: Chief Rhino to the rescue (2009)

Mr. Pusskins and Little Whiskers; another love story. 1st U.S. ed.; Atheneum Books for Young Readers 2008 un il $15.99

Grades: PreK K 1 2   **E**
1. Cats -- Fiction
ISBN 978-1-4169-5796-6; 1-4169-5796-0
LC 2007031911

When Emily brings home a little kitten to be best friends with Mr. Pusskins, the older cat does not appreciate the gesture.

"The combination of bold colors, highly expressive characters, and slightly off-kilter illustrations will pull children in and keep them wanting more." SLJ

Another title about Mr. Pusskins is:
Mr. Pusskins: a love story (2007)

Lloyd-Jones, Sally
★ **How** to be a baby--by me, the big sister; [by] Sally Lloyd-Jones and [illustrated by] Sue Heap. Schwartz & Wade Books 2007 un il $15.99; lib bdg $18.99

Grades: PreK K 1 2   **E**
1. Infants -- Fiction 2. Siblings -- Fiction
ISBN 0-375-83843-0; 978-0-375-83843-9; 0-375-93843-5 lib bdg; 978-0-375-93843-6 lib bdg
LC 2006-02469

"A worldly wise big sister . . . reads from a book she has written for her new sibling. She itemizes a long list of things that babies cannot do. . . . Although she tends to focus on the negatives, in the end the unnamed protagonist admits that babies have some uses. . . . Heap uses acrylic paint, crayon, and felt-tip pen in a pleasing palette of pinks, blues, and yellows to enhance the story with childlike charm." SLJ

Other titles about this character are:
How to get married by me, the bride (2009)
How to get a job by me, the boss (2011)

How to get a job by me, the boss; [written by] Sally Lloyd-Jones and [illustrated by] Sue Heap. Schwartz & Wade Books 2011 un il $17.99; lib bdg $20.99

Grades: PreK K 1 2   **E**
1. Occupations -- Fiction
ISBN 978-0-375-86664-7; 0-375-86664-7; 978-0-375-96664-4 lib bdg; 0-375-96664-1 lib bdg
LC 2009050696

The narrator knows all about how to get a job, and she walks readers through the whole process: from deciding what you want to be all the way to acing the interview.

"The illustrations are perfectly rendered in childlike acrylic paint and crayons and show the fun details of imaginative play on a rainy day." SLJ

Poor Doreen; a fishy tale. by Sally Lloyd-Jones; illustrated by Alexandra Boiger. Schwartz & Wade 2013 40 p. color illustrations $17.99

Grades: PreK K 1 2   **E**
1. Fishes -- Fiction 2. Cousins -- Fiction 3. Fishing -- Fiction
ISBN 0375869182; 9780375869181; 9780375969188
LC 2012047195

In this children's book, written by Sally Lloyd-Jones and illustrated by Alexandra Boiger, "an Ample Roundy Fish called Mrs. Doreen Randolph-Potts is on a mission: to visit her second cousin twice removed who's just welcomed 157 babies. But when she spies what she thinks is a yummy dragonfly--and is actually bait--poor Doreen is lifted out of the water on a fishing pole. Luckily, Doreen is, shall we say, a wee bit clueless about the dire situation." (Publisher's note)

"Delightful illustrations in watercolor, gouache, and colored pencil show a smiling small blue and pink polka-dotted fish wearing a red babushka and sporting a red umbrella. A charming tale with an endearing—and enduring—heroine." -SLJ Reviews

Song of the stars; a Christmas story. illustrated by Alison Jay. Zonderkidz 2011 il $15.99

Grades: PreK K 1   **E**
1. Nature -- Fiction 2. Animals -- Fiction
ISBN 978-0-310-72291-5; 0-310-72291-8
LC 2011006762

Nature and the animal kingdom celebrate the birth of Jesus, while most people do not even notice that a miracle has occurred.

"A subtle, yet satisfying story. . . . Lloyd-Jones's lyrical language . . . and repetitive refrains make the text suitable for reading aloud. Jay's signature-style, crackle-varnish paintings are bright and effective in conveying a sense of eager anticipation and movement among the animals." SLJ

The **ultimate** guide to grandmas and grandpas; by Sally Lloyd-Jones; illustrated by Michael Emberley. HarperCollinsPublishers 2008 un il $14.99; lib bdg $15.89

Grades: PreK K 1 2 3   **E**
1. Family life -- Fiction 2. Grandparents -- Fiction
ISBN 978-0-06-075687-1; 0-06-075687-X; 978-0-06-075688-8 lib bdg; 0-06-075688-8 lib bdg
LC 2007020880

"In this story about how children should treat their elders, grandparents and grandchildren representing all kinds of animal species play together, enjoy snacks, take trips, tell stories, snuggle, and share secrets. Lloyd-Jones's text is both charming and tongue-in-cheek. . . . Emberley's enchanting illustrations mirror each character's personality." SLJ

Lobel, Anita
10 hungry rabbits; by Anita Lobel. Alfred A. Knopf 2012 24 p. (trade hardcover: alk. paper) $9.99

Grades: PreK K   **E**
1. Color 2. Counting 3. Rabbits -- Fiction 4. Hunger -- Fiction 5. Gardens -- Fiction
ISBN 037586864X; 9780375868641; 9780375968648; 9780375987564
LC 2011003514

In this book by Anita Lobel, "one by one, 10 very hungry rabbits find 10 very yummy vegetables for Mama Rabbit's soup pot. Lobel combines learning to count with color concepts in this . . . celebration of good things to eat. Lobel makes a delightful story for preschoolers with the two most basic early learning concepts, counting and color." (Publisher's note)

"In this introduction to numbers and colors which also champions healthful eating poor Mama Rabbit doesn't have anything to feed her hungry brood, so Papa Rabbit sends the little ones out to find the makings for a delicious soup... However, it's the educational components that are rightly front and center here, with both numbers and colors prominently highlighted, close-ups of grouped items for counting, and simple lines of descriptive text (The seventh rabbit spotted SEVEN BROWN mushrooms). An early learning concept book is an obvious choice for one-on-one sharing, but the book's appealing scenes and petite size make it a good fit for little browsers, too." (Booklist)

★ **Hello,** day! Greenwillow Books 2008 un il $16.99; lib bdg $17.89
Grades: PreK   E
1. Sun -- Fiction 2. Animals -- Fiction 3. Morning -- Fiction
ISBN 978-0-06-078765-3; 0-06-078765-1; 978-0-06-078766-0 lib bdg; 0-06-078766-X lib bdg
LC 2007-18361
Various animals greet the sunrise in their own unique voices, except for the owl who welcomes the night.

"The luxuriantly hued, playfully textured portraits will rivet preschoolers and invite them to make animal sounds of their own; the minimal text, set in big, friendly type, may also encourage some simple word recognition." Publ Wkly

Lena's sleep sheep; a going-to-bed book. Anita Lobel. Alfred A. Knopf 2013 24 p. $11.99
Grades: PreK K   E
1. Moon -- Fiction 2. Sheep -- Fiction 3. Bedtime -- Fiction
ISBN 0449810259; 9780449810255; 9780449810262; 9780449810279
LC 2012028378
In this children's picture book by Anita Lobel, "every evening Lena counts her sheep to help her fall asleep, but tonight they are afraid of the 'round monster' in the window. Lena tries to explain that it's just the Moon, but those silly creatures won't listen, so she convinces them to dress up in disguises to scare it away. When a bit of cloud covers it, the sheep finally line up so she can count them properly." (School Library Journal)

★ **Nini** here and there. Greenwillow Books 2007 un il lib bdg $17.89
Grades: PreK K 1 2   E
1. Cats -- Fiction 2. Moving -- Fiction
ISBN 0-06-078767-8; 0-06-078768-6 lib bdg
LC 2005-22186
Fearing at first that her family is going on vacation without her, Nini the cat ends up traveling with her owners to their new home.

"The artwork makes this picture book an endearing delight. Irresistible Nini steals the show in full-page portraits painted with Lobel's usual sensitivity in watercolor and gouache." Booklist

Another title about Nini is:
Nini lost and found (2010)

★ **Nini** lost and found. Alfred A. Knopf 2010 un il $15.99; lib bdg $20.99
Grades: PreK K 1   E
1. Cats -- Fiction 2. Lost and found possessions -- Fiction
ISBN 978-0-375-85880-2; 0-375-85880-6; 978-0-375-95880-9 lib bdg; 0-375-95880-0 lib bdg
LC 2008048721
Nini Cat enjoys her outdoor adventure until she ventures too far and cannot find her way home.

"Told with an elegant simplicity that children will appreciate, . . . this is filled with Lobel's endearing watercolor-and-gouache artwork. . . . A wonderful read-aloud." Booklist

★ **One** lighthouse, one moon. Greenwillow Bks. 2000 40p il hardcover o.p. pa $6.99
Grades: PreK K 1 2   E
1. Counting 2. Days -- Fiction 3. Months -- Fiction
ISBN 0-688-15539-1; 0-06-000537-8 pa
LC 98-50790
This is a "three-part introduction to days, seasons, colors, counting, and other basics. The first section pictures a little girl's feet as they journey through a week, with a different colored shoe marking each day's activity. . . . The second section shows Nini the cat in postcard-size images that reflect those from the 12 months of the year. The title section presents the numbers 1 through 10 in serene images of shoreline activity. . . . The simple phrases are lyrical in places, and Lobel's beautiful paintings, with their rich patterns and textures, luxurious detail, and sophisticated palette, will inspire children to linger over the pages and connect new words with images." Booklist

Lobel, Arnold
★ **Frog** and Toad are friends. Harper & Row 1970 64p il (I can read book) $16.99; lib bdg $17.89; pa $3.99
Grades: K 1 2   E
1. Frogs -- Fiction 2. Toads -- Fiction 3. Friendship -- Fiction
ISBN 0-06-023957-3; 0-06-023958-1 lib bdg; 0-06-444020-6 pa
A Caldecott Medal honor book, 1971
Here are five stories . . . which recount the adventures of two best friends—Toad and Frog. The stories are: Spring; The story; A lost button; A swim; The letter

The stories are told "with humor and perception. Illustrations in soft green and brown enhance the smooth flowing and sensitive story." SLJ
Other titles about Frog and Toad are:
Days with Frog and Toad (1979)
Frog and Toad all year (1976)
Frog and Toad together (1972)

★ **Grasshopper** on the road. Harper & Row 1978 62p il (I can read book) lib bdg $17.89; pa $3.99
Grades: K 1 2   E
1. Animals -- Fiction 2. Grasshoppers -- Fiction
ISBN 0-06-023962-X lib bdg; 0-06-444094-X pa
LC 77-25653
"The contemporary version of the fable of the ant and the grasshopper is told in a repetitive I-Can-Read text and

extended in three-color illustrations which delicately capture the grasshopper's microcosmic world view." Horn Book

Ming Lo moves the mountain; written and illustrated by Arnold Lobel. Greenwillow Bks. 1982 un il hardcover o.p. pa $5.99

Grades: K 1 2 3   E

1. Houses -- Fiction 2. Mountains -- Fiction

ISBN 0-688-10995-0 pa

                  LC 81-13327

"An original tale utilizing folkloric motifs, the book is Chinese-like rather than Chinese, for the artist has created an imagined landscape. The setting, shown in flowing lines and tones of delicate watercolors, provides a source of inspiration drawn from an ancient artistic tradition; particularly effective in conveying a sense of distance are the panoramic double-page spreads." Horn Book

★ **Mouse** soup. Harper & Row 1977 63p il (I can read book) $15.99; lib bdg $16.89; pa $3.99

Grades: K 1 2   E

1. Mice -- Fiction

ISBN 0-06-023967-0; 0-06-023968-9 lib bdg; 0-06-444041-9 pa

                  LC 76-41517

"An artistic triumph with enough suspense, humor and wisdom to hold any reader who has a trace of curiosity and compassion. . . . The little one triumphs over the big one, and every child will rejoice. The exquisite wash drawings in mousey shades of grays, blues, greens and golds, have enough humor and pathos to exact repeated scrutiny. Like the stories, they improve with each reading." N Y Times Book Rev

★ **Mouse** tales. Harper & Row 1972 61p il (I can read book) $15.99; lib bdg $16.89; pa $3.99

Grades: K 1 2   E

1. Mice -- Fiction

ISBN 0-06-023941-7; 0-06-023942-5 lib bdg; 0-06-444013-3 pa

Papa Mouse tells seven bedtime stories, one for each of his sons

"The illustrations have soft colors and precise, lively little drawings of the imaginative and humorous events in the stories. The themes are familiar to children: cloud shapes, wishing, a tall and a short friend who observe-and greet-natural phenomena on a walk, taking a bath, et cetera." Bull Cent Child Books

★ **On** Market Street; pictures by Anita Lobel; words by Arnold Lobel. Greenwillow Bks. 1981 un il $16.99; lib bdg $17.89; pa $6.99

Grades: K 1 2 3   E

1. Alphabet 2. Stories in rhyme 3. Shopping -- Fiction

ISBN 0-688-80309-1; 0-688-84309-3 lib bdg; 0-688-08745-0 pa

                  LC 80-21418

A Caldecott Medal honor book, 1982

"The artist has adapted the style of old French trade engravings, infusing it with a wonderful sense of color and detail. . . . Arnold Lobel's words ring of old rhymes, but it is

these intricate, lovely drawings that take the day, and truly make it brighter." N Y Times Book Rev

★ **Owl** at home. Harper & Row 1982 64p il (I can read book) lib bdg $16.89; pa $3.99

Grades: K 1 2   E

1. Owls -- Fiction

ISBN 0-06-023949-2 lib bdg; 0-06-444034-6 pa

Five stories describe the adventures of a lovably foolish owl

"A child reader or listener in a kind of one-upmanship over wide-eyed tufted Owl will bristle with anxiety to have him perceive what causes two bewildering bumps under the blanket at the foot of his bed. The best scope for Lobel's inventiveness in drawing is, however, the opening episode where 'poor old' Winter makes a pushy entry into Owl's home. Muted browns and greys are countered by an animation that fully reveals Owl's distresses and contentments." Wash Post Child Book World

★ **Small** pig; story and pictures by Arnold Lobel. Harper & Row 1969 63p il (I can read book) lib bdg $16.89; pa $3.99

Grades: K 1 2   E

1. Pigs -- Fiction

ISBN 0-06-023932-8 lib bdg; 0-06-444120-2 pa

This "is the story of a pig who, finding the clean farm unbearable, runs away to look for mud—and ends up stuck in cement. His facial expressions alone are worth the price of the book; the illustrations, in blue, green, and gold, are a perfect complement to the story. Humor, adventure, and short, simple sentences provide a real treat for beginning readers." SLJ

A **treeful** of pigs; pictures by Anita Lobel. Greenwillow Bks. 1979 un il lib bdg $17.89

Grades: K 1 2 3   E

1. Pigs -- Fiction 2. Farm life -- Fiction

ISBN 0-688-84177-5

                  LC 78-1810

"The framed, full-color illustrations, characterized by intricately detailed designs in costumes and setting, are as elaborate as the diction is simple. The total effect, however, is one of unity." Horn Book

★ **Uncle** Elephant. Harper & Row 1981 62p il (I can read book) lib bdg $16.89; pa $3.99

Grades: K 1 2   E

1. Uncles -- Fiction 2. Elephants -- Fiction

ISBN 0-06-023980-8 lib bdg; 0-06-444104-0 pa

                  LC 80-8944

Uncle Elephant takes care of his nephew whose parents are lost at sea. This book describes the way they lived together until the parents are rescued and little elephant rejoins them

"Nine gentle stories for the beginning independent reader; the soft grey, peach, and green tones of the deft pictures are an appropriate echo of the mood." Bull Cent Child Books

Lobel, Gillian

Moonshadow's journey; illustrated by Karin Littlewood. Albert Whitman & Co. 2009 un il $16.99

Grades: K 1 2 3 4   E

1. Death -- Fiction 2. Swans -- Fiction 3. Grandfathers

-- Fiction 4. Birds -- Migration -- Fiction
ISBN 978-0-8075-5273-5; 0-8075-5273-9

LC 2009000004

When his beloved grandfather is killed in a storm while leading the swan flock south for the winter, Moonshadow is reassured by his father that the flock will go on with Grandfather always in their hearts

"Lobel skillfully moves the plot forward while creating appropriate character development for Moonshadow. . . . Littlewood's combination of watercolors and gouache on textured paper of light and dark hues adds to the moods and movement of the book. The pictures capture the elements of nature in both harsh and calm circumstances." SLJ

Loewen, Nancy

The **last** day of kindergarten; illustrated by Sachiko Yoshikawa. Marshall Cavendish 2011 un il $16.99

Grades: PreK K   E

1. School stories 2. Kindergarten -- Fiction
ISBN 978-0-7614-5807-4; 0-7614-5807-7

LC 2010001225

As she prepares for her graduation ceremony, a first grader-to-be remembers her enjoyable year in kindergarten.

"Included in the text are excellent discussion questions that focus on summer plans and first-grade privileges. Yoshikawa's irresistibly sweet illustrations are perfect for children ready to emerge from the kindergarten cocoon and rejoice in their achievements." SLJ

Logan, Bob

The **Sea** of Bath. Sourcebooks Jabberwocky 2010 un il $16.99

Grades: PreK K   E

1. Toys -- Fiction 2. Baths -- Fiction 3. Boats and boating -- Fiction
ISBN 978-1-4022-4185-7; 1-4022-4185-2

"A ship captain, commander of the S.S. Rubb A. Dubb, navigates 'a curious sea indeed!' Full of unusual creatures (e.g., rubber duckies) and unpredictable conditions (e.g., bubbles), the setting makes itself known to readers as a bathtub. . . . Logan's eye-pleasing illustrations of animated-looking bath toys support a satisfying preschooler-friendly text." Horn Book Guide

Logue, Mary

★ **Sleep** like a tiger; written by Mary Logue and illustrated by Pamela Zagarenski. Houghton Mifflin Harcourt 2012 40 p. $16.99

Grades: PreK K 1 2   E

1. Sleep -- Fiction 2. Bedtime -- Fiction 3. Animals -- Sleep behavior -- Fiction
ISBN 0547641028; 9780547641027

LC 2011044881

Caldecott Honor Book (2013)

This picture book features a "little girl" whose "wise parents sidestep her protestation of not being sleepy ('They nodded their heads and said she didn't have to go to sleep. But she had to put her pajamas on'), but once she's in bed she starts a new delaying tactic, inquiring about sleeping habits in the animal kingdom. After exploring the sleep habits of bats, whales, and tigers, she's inspired enough by their snoozes to fall asleep herself." (Bulletin of the Center for Children's Books)

London, Jonathan

★ **Baby** whale's journey; illustrated by Jon Van Zyle. Chronicle Bks. 1999 un il $15.95; pa $6.95

Grades: K 1 2 3   E

1. Whales -- Fiction
ISBN 0-8118-2496-9; 0-8118-5761-1 pa

LC 99-13020

Off the Pacific coast of Mexico, a baby sperm whale is born, feeds, speaks to her mother in clicks, and spends her days diving, spy-hopping, lob-tailing, and rolling as she grows and learns the ways of the sea

This book offers "London's lyrical text and Van Zyle's dramatic paintings dominated by blues and purples. . . . An informative afterword supplies additional facts about sperm whales, and a reader's guide offers thoughtful ideas for discussion of both the scientific and poetic aspects of the text." Horn Book Guide

Froggy learns to swim; illustrated by Frank Remkiewicz. Viking 1995 un il $15.99; pa $5.99

Grades: PreK K 1 2   E

1. Frogs -- Fiction 2. Swimming -- Fiction
ISBN 0-670-85551-0; 0-14-055312-6 pa

LC 94-43077

Froggy is afraid of the water until his mother, along with his flippers, snorkle, and mask, help him learn to swim

"Vivid watercolor cartoons add the humor, showing the comical facial expressions and hilarious beachwear. Froggy's childlike dialogue and the sound words—'zook! zik!'; 'flop flop . . . splash!'—make this story a wonderful read-aloud." SLJ

Other titles about Froggy are:
Froggy bakes a cake (2000)
Froggy builds a treehouse (2011)
Froggy eats out (2001)
Froggy gets dressed (1992)
Froggy goes to bed (2000)
Froggy goes to camp (2008)
Froggy goes to Hawaii (2011)
Froggy goes to school (1996)
Froggy goes to the doctor (2002)
Froggy plays in the band (2002)
Froggy plays T-Ball (2007)
Froggy plays soccer (1999)
Froggy's baby sister (2003)
Froggy's best Christmas (2000)
Froggy's day with Dad (2004)
Froggy's first kiss (1998)
Froggy's Halloween (1999)
Froggy's sleepover (2005)
Let's go, Froggy! (1994)

I'm a truck driver; illustrated by David Parkins. Henry Holt 2010 26p il $12.99

Grades: PreK K 1   E

1. Stories in rhyme 2. Trucks -- Fiction
ISBN 978-0-8050-7989-0; 0-8050-7989-0

LC 2009009220

"This is a wonderful picture book about trucks. . . . On every other spread, a girl and a boy take turns driving each of the vehicles. The trucks are described in rhyming couplets. . . . The alternating voices of the children help to enhance the rhythm and rhyme of the story. . . . The acrylic illustrations are vibrant, cartoonlike, and friendly." SLJ

A **plane** goes ka-zoom! illustrated by Denis Roche. Henry Holt & Co. 2010 un il $15.99
Grades: PreK   **E**
1. Airplanes -- Fiction
ISBN 978-0-8050-8970-7; 0-8050-8970-5
"Simple enough for toddlers, the rhythmic, rhyming text comments on what planes do as well as how they look, sound, and move. . . . The naive gouache paintings invite kids to stop along the way and talk about who's doing what in each colorful illustration. A engaging choice." Booklist

A **train** goes clickety-clack; by Jonathan London; illustrated by Denis Roche. Henry Holt 2007 un il $15.95
Grades: PreK K   **E**
1. Stories in rhyme 2. Railroads -- Fiction
ISBN 978-0-8050-7972-2; 0-8050-7972-6
       LC 2006030765
Easy-to-read, rhyming text describes the sounds of, and uses for, different kinds of trains
"Brief sentences and bright gouache artwork in primary hues capture the excitement and attraction of trains. The text is filled with appealing rhythms and rhymes." SLJ

★ A **truck** goes rattley-bumpa; illustrated by Denis Roche. Henry Holt and Co. 2005 un il $14.95
Grades: PreK K   **E**
1. Stories in rhyme 2. Trucks -- Fiction
ISBN 0-8050-7233-0
       LC 2004-22174
"Short, rhyming couplets tell about a variety of trucks: what they look like, what sounds they make, where they go, and what they do. Meanwhile, childlike gouache paintings clearly illustrate the brief sentences or phrases on each page." Booklist

Long, Ethan
Bird & Birdie in a fine day. Ten Speed Press 2010 un il $14.99
Grades: PreK K 1   **E**
1. Birds -- Fiction 2. Friendship -- Fiction
ISBN 978-1-5824-6321-6; 1-5824-6321-2
"Three separate stories introduce two bug-eyed cartoon birds (Bird is blue, while Birdie, who is yellow, sports eyelashes and a pink ribbon) interacting over the course of a day. In 'A Beautiful Morning,' they meet, exchange pleasantries, are briefly separated by a storm, and happily join up again. In 'A Wonderful Afternoon,' Bird tries to concentrate on getting a worm out of the ground but is distracted by Birdie. In 'A Marvelous Night,' Birdie can't get comfortable in her nest until Bird helps out. . . . The fetching Bird and Birdie will hit the right note with many preschoolers and beginning readers." Booklist

The **Croaky** Pokey! Holiday House 2011 un il $14.95
Grades: PreK K 1   **E**
1. Frogs -- Fiction
ISBN 978-0-8234-2291-3; 0-8234-2291-7
"Inspired by a tasty-looking dragonfly, a group of frogs decides to perform their own version of the Hokey Pokey. The first part of the song is familiar ('Put your right hand in...'), but each verse is intended to end with a snack: 'Hop

the Croaky Pokey/ As we chase a fly around,/ Right in the froggy's mouth!/ Whap!') The problem is, not a single member of the froggy chorus can catch the fly. . . . Long . . . has a gift for conveying manic, obsessive personalities . . . and he has found a great match in a song of relentless, rote cheeriness." Publ Wkly

Max & Milo go to sleep! by Heather & Ethan Long. Aladdin 2013 32 p. (hardcover edition) $14.99
Grades: PreK K 1 2   **E**
1. Bedtime 2. Humorous fiction 3. Humorous stories 4. Beavers -- Fiction 5. Bedtime -- Fiction 6. Brothers -- Fiction
ISBN 1442451432; 9781442451438
       LC 2012011458
This children's story, by Heather Long and Ethan Long, follows "Max and Milo, two . . . beaver brothers who make going to sleep an up-all-night adventure. Milo can't get to sleep, . . . but no matter what helpful sleeping tip Max suggests, Milo turns it riotously on its head and is as far from rest as ever. Will Milo finally get to sleep? Will he ever stop driving Max crazy?" (Publisher's note)

My dad, my hero. Sourcebooks Jabberwocky 2011 un il $12.99
Grades: PreK K 1   **E**
1. Father-son relationship -- Fiction
ISBN 978-1-4022-4239-7; 1-4022-4239-5
A child describes his dad, who may not have super powers, but is still wonderful.
"Powered by a Roy Lichtenstein meets Sunday funnies aesthetic and a self-effacing sense of humor, Long's story is sincere without being saccharine—which dads will appreciate." Publ Wkly

One drowsy dragon. Orchard Books 2010 un il $16.99
Grades: PreK K 1 2   **E**
1. Counting 2. Stories in rhyme 3. Noise -- Fiction 4. Sleep -- Fiction 5. Dragons -- Fiction
ISBN 978-0-545-16557-0; 0-545-16557-1
       LC 2009032861
As one dragon tries to take a nap, his ten little dragons, in increasing numbers, disturb his sleep by making milk shakes, screaming at scary movies, and playing loud games.
"The digital art features clean lines and distinct colors. . . . Big round eyes and slightly goofy expressions lend an air of silliness to the cartoon figures. . . . A solid storytime choice that covers several popular picture-book topics, including counting, colors, dragons, and bedtime." SLJ

Up, tall and high; Ethan Long. G.P. Putnam's Sons 2012 p. cm.
Grades: K 1 2 3   **E**
1. Vocabulary 2. Birds -- Fiction 3. Altitudes -- Fiction
ISBN 9780399256110
       LC 2011003291
Theodor Seuss Geisel Award (2013)
This children's picture book presents "three tiny tales of a flock of bird buddies. 'I Am Tall' centers on boasting about stature . . . 'I Can Go High' finds the birds outdoing each other on altitude attempts . . . In 'I Am Up,' two birds 'up' in a nest collapse the branch and are now decidedly 'down,' until their friends arrive to help them 'up' on their feet again

. . . each tale's punchline is delivered with a visual gag revealed with a lifted or pulled flap." (Bulletin of the center for Children's Books)

Long, Loren

★ **Otis**. Philomel Books 2009 un il $17.99; board bk $8.99

Grades: PreK K 1 2   **E**

1. Tractors -- Fiction 2. Farm life -- Fiction

ISBN 978-0-399-25248-8; 0-399-25248-7; 978-0-399-25600-4 board bk; 0-399-25600-8 board bk

LC 2008-50020

When a big new yellow tractor arrives, Otis the friendly little tractor is cast away behind the barn, but when trouble occurs Otis is the only one who can help.

"Long's gouache and pencil artwork is stunning with a red and cream main character against a sepia-toned monochromatic background. The overall effect is nostalgic and comforting." SLJ

Followed by: Otis and the tornado (2011)

Otis and the puppy; Loren Long. Philomel Books 2013 40 p. $17.99

Grades: PreK K 1 2   **E**

1. Fear of the dark 2. Dogs 3. Farms 4. Dogs -- Fiction 5. Tractors -- Fiction 6. Farm life -- Fiction 7. Fear of the dark -- Fiction 8. Animals -- Infancy -- Fiction

ISBN 0399254692; 9780399254697

LC 2012013312

In this book by Loren Long "Otis and his farm friends love to play hide-and-seek. When the newest addition to the farm—a bounding puppy . . . "tries to hide, he finds his attention wandering and is soon lost in the forest. Night falls and Otis, knowing his new friend is afraid of the dark, sets out to find him. Otis is also afraid of the dark. His friend is alone and in need, though, so Otis takes a deep breath, counts to ten, and sets off on a different game of hide-and-seek." (Publisher's note)

Otis and the tornado. Philomel Books 2012 il $17.99

Grades: PreK K 1 2   **E**

1. Tractors -- Fiction 2. Farm life -- Fiction 3. Tornadoes -- Fiction 4. Domestic animals -- Fiction

ISBN 978-0-399-25477-2; 0-399-25469-2

LC 2010036770

Sequel to: Otis (2009)

When a tornado threatens his farm, Otis the tractor must try to save the animals, including an unfriendly bull.

"Long's sepia-tinged, rolling croplands evoke Dust Bowl paintings and photos, and Otis's heroism is steeped in old-fashioned Americana, from 1930s picture books to 1960s TV dramas." Publ Wkly

Long, Melinda

★ **How** I became a pirate; written by Melinda Long; illustrated by David Shannon. Harcourt 2003 un il $16

Grades: K 1 2 3   **E**

1. Pirates -- Fiction

ISBN 0-15-201848-4

LC 2002-6308

Jeremy Jacob joins Braid Beard and his pirate crew and finds out about pirate language, pirate manners, and

other aspects of their life. "Ages four to seven." (Bull Cent Child Books)

"Jeremy spies a pirate ship. When he's asked to join its crew, he can't resist. On board, he does all sorts of fun pirate stuff. . . . But, alas, Jeremy soon discovers, there's no good-night kiss or bedtime story, so there's something to be said for home. . . . The rollicking tale is a charmer, with a lively, witty, first-person narrative, highly expressive characters, and farcical elements. . . . Shannon's acrylic art is marvelously animated, with bright, bold colors and extraordinary details." Booklist

Another title about Jeremy is:
Pirates don't change diapers (2007)

Long, Sylvia

Sylvia Long's Thumbelina. Chronicle Books 2010 un $17.99

Grades: 1 2 3 4   **E**

1. Fairy tales

ISBN 978-0-8118-5522-8; 0-8118-5522-8

LC 2009-04369

A tiny girl no bigger than a thumb is stolen by a great ugly toad and subsequently has many adventures and makes many animal friends, before finding the perfect mate in a warm and beautiful southern land.

"While following the familiar story line of Hans Christian Andersen's original, Long effectively condenses the narrative and gives a contemporary touch to the wording. . . . Thumbelina's adventures with the beautifully drawn toad, beetles, mouse, mole, and swallow unfold in jewel-like colors, defined textures, and well-imagined details to complete the surroundings." SLJ

Longstreth, Galen Goodwin

Yes, let's; by Galen Goodwin Longstreth; illustrated by Maris Wicks. Tanglewood Publishing 2013 32 p. (hardcover) $15.95

Grades: PreK K 1 2   **E**

1. Stories in rhyme 2. Camping -- Fiction 3. Family life -- Fiction 4. Outdoor life -- Fiction

ISBN 1933718870; 9781933718873

LC 2012045312

This children's book, by Galen Goodwin Longstreth, illustrated by Maris Wicks, is "about a family's camping trip." Activities such as driving, singing, taking pictures and hiking are all included. "The . . . rhyming text is enhanced by comical illustrations. . . . This little book serves as a loving tribute to family togetherness." (Publisher's note)

Look, Lenore

★ **Brush** of the gods; by Lenore Look; illustrated by Meilo So Sandford. 1st ed. Schwartz & Wade Books 2013 40 p. ill. (hardcover) $17.99; (library) $20.99

Grades: K 1 2 3   **E**

1. Picture books for children 2. Artists -- Fiction 3. Painting -- Fiction 4. China -- History -- Tang dynasty, 618-907 -- Fiction

ISBN 0375870016; 9780375870019; 9780375970016

LC 2012006442

In this children's picture book, Lenore Look "blends mystical realism and biography to create a magical portrait of one of ancient China's famous artists, Wu Daozi. As a boy during the T'ang Dynasty in the seventh century, Daozi is unable to conform in calligraphy class. . . . Later known for his dynamic murals, Daozi paints subjects so realistically they seem to come alive." (Publishers Weekly)

★ **Henry's** first-moon birthday; illustrated by Yumi Heo. Atheneum Bks. for Young Readers 2001 un il $16
Grades: PreK K 1 2   **E**
  1. Infants -- Fiction 2. Grandmothers -- Fiction 3. Chinese Americans -- Fiction
  ISBN 0-689-82294-4

LC 98-21626

Jen helps her grandmother with preparations for the traditional Chinese celebration to welcome her new baby brother
  "The words are clear and basic as well as creative . . . and Jen's chatty narration infuses the book with the cozy immediacy that's beautifully picked up in Heo's swirling paint-and-paper collages." Booklist

★ **Love** as strong as ginger; illustrated by Stephen T. Johnson. Atheneum Pubs. 1999 un il $15
Grades: PreK K 1 2   **E**
  1. Work -- Fiction 2. Grandmothers -- Fiction 3. Chinese Americans -- Fiction
  ISBN 0-689-81248-5

LC 96-43459

A Chinese American girl comes to realize how hard her grandmother works to fulfill her dreams when they spend a day together at the grandmother's job cracking crabs
  "Inspired by the author's memories of her grandmother, this gentle story is carefully and precisely told. . . . Johnson's expressive pastel-and-watercolor illustrations are rendered in muted colors and set within wide, softly colored margins." SLJ

Polka Dot Penguin Pottery; illustrated by Yumi Heo. Schwartz & Wade Books 2011 un il $16.99
Grades: PreK K 1 2   **E**
  1. Artists -- Fiction 2. Pottery -- Fiction 3. Authorship -- Fiction 4. Chinese Americans -- Fiction
  ISBN 978-0-375-86332-5; 0-375-86332-X

A visit to a pottery shop and the encouragement of family and friends not only provide Aspen the opportunity to paint something beautiful, they also help her get past her writer's block.
  "Naïve-style oil, pencil, and collage illustrations are unpredictably laid out in a top-to-bottom format rather than side-to-side. The girl's frustration and eventual pleasure as she works through her writer's and painter's blocks are revealed in single-page and full-spread pictures. Good motivation for children who need to activate their artistic side." SLJ

★ **Uncle** Peter's amazing Chinese wedding; illustrated by Yumi Heo. Atheneum Books for Young Readers 2006 un il $16.95
Grades: PreK K 1 2   **E**
  1. Uncles -- Fiction 2. Weddings -- Fiction 3. Chinese Americans -- Fiction
  ISBN 0-689-84458-1

LC 2002-10740

Companion volume to Henry's first-moon birthday
  Jenny, a Chinese American girl, describes the festivities of her uncle's Chinese wedding and the customs behind them.

"Heo's child-inspired illustrations contribute to the story's strong appeal with lively colors, perspectives, and details that accentuate both Jenny's feelings and the wedding traditions. A delightful invitation to learn more about Chinese traditions." SLJ

Lopez, Mario
  Mario and baby Gia; [illustrations by Maryn Roos] Celebra Childrens Books 2011 il $17.99
Grades: PreK K   **E**
  1. Cousins -- Fiction 2. Infants -- Fiction 3. Birthdays -- Fiction 4. Babysitters -- Fiction 5. Family life -- Fiction
  ISBN 978-0-451-23417-9; 0-451-23417-0

LC 2011005235

Unable to find anyone to play with, Mario agrees to help his Nana by watching cousin Gia, but caring for the toddler is challenging and Mario is near the end of his rope when he gets a reminder that spending time with family is a gift.
  "Roos continues the commercial-looking cartoon-style illustrations from the earlier Mario book, which work well with the story, particularly during Mario's stories. A good choice for children with younger siblings and cousins, especially Latinos." Kirkus
  Another title about Mario is:
  Mud tacos (2009)

Lopez, Susana
  The **best** family in the world; [illustrated by] Ulises Wensell. Kane Miller un il $15.99
Grades: PreK K 1 2   **E**
  1. Orphans -- Fiction 2. Adoption -- Fiction 3. Family life -- Fiction
  ISBN 978-1-935279-47-1; 1-935279-47-5

Carlota is anxiously awaiting the arrival of the family who is adopting her. She imagines that they might be astronauts, pastry chiefs or even pirates. And then Carlota finds out that the Lopez family is the best family in the world.
  "The telling is clear and lively, while the artwork glows with warmth and light. . . . A lovely, thought-provoking picture book to share and discuss." Booklist

Lorbiecki, Marybeth
  Paul Bunyan's sweetheart; written by Marybeth Lorbiecki; illustrated by Renee Graef. Sleeping Bear Press 2007 un il $16.95
Grades: 1 2 3 4   **E**
  1. Tall tales 2. Bunyan, Paul (Legendary character) 3. Love -- Fiction 4. Nature -- Fiction 5. Minnesota -- Fiction 6. Environmental protection -- Fiction
  ISBN 1-58536-289-1; 978-1-58536-289-9

LC 2006026583

When legendary logger Paul Bunyan falls in love with Lucette Diana Kensack, he will do whatever it takes to win her heart, including trying to restore the Minnesota environment to its previous condition as part of Lucette's "love test."
  "The prose is just right for the genre. . . . The paintings extend the story's humorous images, while firmly placing the action in a mythical time." SLJ

Lord, Cynthia
  Happy birthday, Hamster; pictures by Derek Anderson. Scholastic Press 2011 un il $16.99

Grades: PreK K 1 **E**
1. Dogs -- Fiction 2. Hamsters -- Fiction 3. Birthdays -- Fiction 4. Friendship -- Fiction
ISBN 978-0-545-25522-6; 0-545-25522-8
LC 2010018989
Follows Hamster and his friend Dog as they prepare for a birthday party.
"Those who miss the clues the first time, should enjoy being privy to them upon rereading." Publy Wkly

Hot rod hamster; monster truck mania! by Cynthia Lord; pictures by Derek Anderson. Scholastic Press 2014 40 p. color illustrations (hardcover: alk. paper) $16.99
Grades: PreK K 1 **E**
1. Fairs -- Fiction 2. Hamsters -- Fiction 3. Amusement rides -- Fiction
ISBN 0545462614; 9780545462617
LC 2013008570
In this book, by Cynthia Lord and illustrated by Derek Anderson, "it's Fair Day, and Fearless Franco's famous Monster Truck Mania has come to town. Hot Rod Hamster and his friends are geared up for a roaring, soaring great time, so they set out to find the best ride at the fair. The water boats, spinning teacups, and bumper cars are great, but Hamster can't seem to find the BEST ride. That is, of course, until Fearless Franco needs a last-minute back-up driver for his monster truck." (Publisher's note)
"Hot Rod Hamster and his bulldog buddy (and readers, too) have myriad choices of rides and food at the fair: 'Slurp treats, lick treats, eat it on a stick treats. Which would you choose?' Ultimately, Hot Rod's biggest thrill is filling in for driver Fearless Franco in Monster Truck Mania. Colorful acrylics complement the peppy rhymes and the boisterous good time." Horn Book
Monster truck mania

Lord, Janet
★ **Albert** the Fix-it Man; story by Janet Lord; pictures by Julie Paschkis. Peachtree 2008 un il $15.95
Grades: PreK K 1 2 **E**
1. Repairing -- Fiction 2. Community life -- Fiction
ISBN 978-1-56145-433-4
LC 2007-29465
A cheerful repairman fixes squeaky doors, leaky roofs, and crumbling fences for his neighbors, who return the kindness when he catches a terrible cold
"Lord's rhythmic, simple text is perfectly cadenced for reading aloud, while Paschkis' cheerful illustrations, filled with scrolling designs and smiling friends, reinforce the sense of the close, busy community working together." Booklist

Here comes Grandma! [by] Janet Lord; illustrated by Julie Paschkis. Henry Holt and Co. 2005 un il $12.95
Grades: PreK K 1 **E**
1. Grandmothers -- Fiction 2. Transportation -- Fiction
ISBN 0-8050-7666-2
LC 2004-22179
Grandma is coming to visit and she will use any possible method of transport, including a horse and a hot air balloon, to get there

"The simple, rhythmic text suits the mood of the story, and the vivid gouache illustrations have a warm, folklike quality." SLJ

Where is Catkin? written by Janet Lord; illustrated by Julie Paschkis. Peachtree Publishers 2010 un il $16.95
Grades: PreK K 1 **E**
1. Cats -- Fiction 2. Animals -- Fiction
ISBN 978-1-56145-523-2; 1-56145-523-7
"In this picture-book hide-and-seek game, feline Catkin jumps off young Amy's lap and goes hunting into the grass, by a pond, through rocks, and up a tree, looking for Cricket, then Frog, Mouse, Snake, and Bird. Where are they? Children will enjoy searching through the busy, bright, stylized pictures in ink and gouache and pointing to the creatures hiding where Catkin doesn't see them." Booklist

Lord, John Vernon
The **giant** jam sandwich; story and pictures by John Vernon Lord, with verses by Janet Burroway. Houghton Mifflin 1973 32p il lib bdg $17; pa $6.95; bd bk $6.99
Grades: K 1 2 3 **E**
1. Stories in rhyme 2. Wasps -- Fiction
ISBN 0-395-16033-2 lib bdg; 0-395-44237-0 pa; 0-547-15077-6 bd bk
First published 1972 in the United Kingdom
"Highly amusing in the details of John Vernon Lord's illustrations. . . . The figures are deliciously grotesque, their expressions wickedly accurate and the colours cheerfully vivid." Jr Bookshelf

Lorig, Steffanie
Such a silly baby! by Steffanie and Richard Lorig; illustrated by Amanda Shepherd. Chronicle Books 2008 un il $15.99
Grades: PreK **E**
1. Stories in rhyme 2. Animals -- Fiction 3. Infants -- Fiction
ISBN 978-0-8118-5134-3; 0-8118-5134-6
LC 2007-13135
Rhyming text and illustrations follow the adventures of a baby who on excursions to the zoo, the circus, or the farm manages to get switched with an animal.
"Each time [the baby] greets Mom again, he adds a new phrase learned from his animal friends, for a cumulative festival of animal sounds that storytime listeners will love. Shepherd's bright, wildly cartoonlike oil paintings perfectly reflect the wackiness of the text." SLJ

Loth, Sebastian
Clementine. North-South 2011 un il $14.95
Grades: PreK K 1 2 **E**
1. Shape -- Fiction 2. Worms -- Fiction 3. Snails -- Fiction
ISBN 978-0-7358-4009-6; 0-7358-4009-1
Clementine the snail loves all things round and dreams of flying to the moon. Her earthworm friend Paul helps her fly a rocket in orbit around the Earth, and she discovers that the Earth is round too.
"Loth's illustrations carry the weight of the offbeat story, featuring rich colors, beautiful compositions and a cinematic sense of movement." Kirkus

Remembering Crystal. NorthSouth 2010 un il $14.95

Grades: PreK K 1 2   E
1. Death -- Fiction 2. Ducks -- Fiction 3. Turtles -- Fiction 4. Friendship -- Fiction
ISBN 978-0-7358-2300-6; 0-7358-2300-6

Zelda is a young duck that lives in the garden. Her friend Crystal is a turtle who is growing old. The two do many things together. One day Crystal is not in the garden. But friendship never dies.

"This gets high points for the simplicity of the text . . . and the handsomeness of the design. Buff, mottled pages serve as the background for illustrations that are elegant in their spareness. . . . Despite the somber subject, moments of humor escape into the art. . . . This story of a final friendship touches the heart." Booklist

Zelda the Varigoose; Sebastian Loth. NorthSouth Books 2012 32 p. $15.95
Grades: PreK K   E
1. Geese -- Fiction 2. Imagination -- Fiction 3. Picture books for children
ISBN 0735840768; 9780735840768

This children's picture book is about Zelda the goose who "enjoys changing her persona as she allows her imagination to take flight. The left side of each spread features a digitalized photo of the habitat of a different creature. Opposite, Zelda becomes a different animal through the assistance of an overlay. . . . After the little bird transforms into a "Chamelegoose," a 'Goosquid,' and so on, she is also perfectly content to just be herself." (School Library Journal)

Lottridge, Celia Barker
One watermelon seed. Fitzhenry & Whiteside 2008 un il $17.95
Grades: PreK K 1 2   E
1. Counting 2. Gardening -- Fiction
ISBN 978-1-55455-034-0; 1-55455-034-3
First published 1986 by Oxford University Press

"Numbers, colors, and gardening are combined in this vividly illustrated counting book. The story starts as Max and Josephine plant a garden, first 1 watermelon seed, then 2 pumpkin seeds, and so on all the way to 10. The phrase, 'and they grew' follows mention of each new set of seeds. The graphic-style illustrations depict the seedlings as they grow. . . . The vibrant colors and closeup views of the produce make it look delicious and irresistible." SLJ

Lotu, Denize
★ **Running** the road to ABC; by Denizé Lauture; illustrated by Reynold Ruffins. Simon & Schuster Bks. for Young Readers 1996 un il hardcover o.p. pa $6.99
Grades: PreK K 1 2   E
1. School stories 2. Haiti -- Fiction
ISBN 0-689-80507-1; 0-689-83165-X pa
       LC 95-38290
A Coretta Scott King honor book for illustration, 1997
Long before the sun even thinks of rising the Haitian children run to school where they learn the letters, sounds, and words of their beautiful books

"The rich lyrical language used by the author, a Haitian poet, creates a strong sense of place. . . . The lush, green country and sense of hope are reflected and enhanced by stylized, warmly detailed gouache paintings." Horn Book

Loupy, Christophe
Hugs and kisses; [by] Christophe Loupy, Eve Tharlet; translated by J. Alison James. North-South Bks. 2001 un il $15.95; bd bk $6.95
Grades: PreK   E
1. Dogs -- Fiction 2. Animals -- Fiction
ISBN 0-7358-1484-8; 0-7358-2019-8 bd bk
       LC 2001-42595
Original German edition published 2001 in Switzerland
Hugs the puppy sets out to collect lots of wonderful kisses from his animal friends, but in the end he discovers that the best kiss of all is the one he gets from his loving mother

"With fur that seems real enough to touch, a sunny disposition, and sweet manners, Hugs is a real charmer." Booklist

Low, William
★ **Machines** go to work in the city; William Low. 1st ed. Henry Holt and Company 2012 48 p.
Grades: PreK K   E
1. Lift-the-flap books 2. Machinery 3. Cities and towns
ISBN 0805090509; 9780805090505
       LC 2011029045
This children's book by William Low focuses on "Trains, planes, trucks and cranes and the people who make them work [and] keep the city moving. . . . Low presents each vehicle, with an appropriate onomatopoetic sound, in two double-page spreads wherein a simply stated question is posed with the answer appearing on a gate-fold that enlarges the view even further." (Kirkus)

Lowell, Susan
The **elephant** quilt; stitch by stitch to California! pictures by Stacey Dressen-McQueen. Farrar, Straus and Giroux 2008 un il $16.95
Grades: K 1 2 3   E
1. Quilts -- Fiction 2. Overland journeys to the Pacific -- Fiction
ISBN 0-374-38223-9; 978-0-374-38223-0
       LC 2005-51227
Lily Rose and Grandma stitch a quilt that tells the story of their family's journey from Missouri to California by covered wagon in 1859.

"Dramatic, mixed-media paintings portray majestic landscapes and frontier dangers, as well as moments of family merriment. An earthly color palette and brightly patterned quilt pieces add warmth and vibrancy to the 'bodacious' journey." Booklist

Lowry, Lois
★ **Crow** call; illustrated by Bagram Ibatoulline. Scholastic Press 2009 un il $16.99
Grades: 1 2 3 4   E
1. Crows -- Fiction 2. Hunting -- Fiction 3. Veterans -- Fiction 4. Pennsylvania -- Fiction 5. Father-daughter relationship -- Fiction
ISBN 978-0-545-03035-9; 0-545-03035-8
       LC 2008-30158
Nine-year-old Liz accompanies the stranger who is her father, just returned from the war, when he goes hunting for crows in Pennsylvania farmland.

"Beautifully written. . . . Lowry's narrative, dense with sensory details, is based on her own life's events. Fittingly,

Ibatoulline's muted, earth-toned palette is reminiscent of vintage, faded photographs." Kirkus

Lucas, David

A **Letter** for Bear; David Lucas. Flying Eye Books 2013 32 p. $14.95

Grades: PreK K 1   E

1. Bears -- Fiction 2. Postal service -- Fiction

ISBN 1909263133; 9781909263130

This picture book, written and illustrated by David Lucas, tells the story of Bear. "Come rain or shine, he works so hard delivering the post to all the animals of the wood but he never receives anything himself. Hardly surprising since he's never actually sent a message! One day Bear decides to write some mail of his own, inviting all the forest animals to a party." (Publisher's note)

The **Skeleton** pirate; David Lucas. Candlewick Press 2013 30 p. ill. (reinforced) $15.99

Grades: PreK K 1 2   E

1. Picture books for children 2. Pirates -- Fiction

ISBN 0763661074; 9780763661076

LC 2012942674

This children's picture book, by David Lucas, follows "the Skeleton Pirate . . . , and he'll never be beaten! That is, until he gets beaten by an unruly bunch of pirates and is thrown overboard. Down in the depths of the sea, he is rescued by a beautiful mermaid, only to be swallowed by a whale. But the whale has a tummy ache from all the other things he has swallowed--like a golden ship full of treasure." (Publisher's note)

Something to do. Philomel Books 2009 un il $14.99

Grades: PreK K   E

1. Bears -- Fiction 2. Imagination -- Fiction 3. Parent-child relationship -- Fiction

ISBN 978-0-399-25247-1; 0-399-25247-9

LC 2009-1821

A parent and child bear must use their imaginations to find something to do.

"Young readers will instantly relate to the richly textured crayon drawings, which illustrate the expressiveness of the story and complement its softness with their deceptively simple, fuzzy-edged forms. . . . This stands out as a unique work because of its emotionally simple charm." Kirkus

Lucke, Deb

Sneezenesia. Clarion Books 2010 un il $17

Grades: K 1 2   E

1. Sneezing -- Fiction

ISBN 978-0-547-33006-8; 0-547-33006-5

Young Zack sneezes so hard, over and over, that he sneezes all memories out of his head, leaving everything he once knew standing before him, trying to figure out how to get back inside.

"The artwork, done in paint, collage, and Photoshop, jumps off the page and adds pace and animation to the story. The supermarket mothers are worth a giggle with their retro outfits and accessories. This funny read-aloud could be paired with any version of 'I Know an Old Lady Who Swallowed a Fly' for a rousing storytime." SLJ

Ludwig, Trudy

Better than you; illustrations by Adam Gustavson. Tricycle Press 2011 un il $15.99; lib bdg $18.99

Grades: PreK K 1 2   E

1. Friendship -- Fiction

ISBN 978-1-58246-380-3; 1-58246-380-8; 978-1-58246-407-7 lib bdg; 1-58246-407-3 lib bdg

LC 2010033224

Tyler's friend Jake continually boasts about his abilities, making Tyler feel bad about himself until his Uncle Kevin and new neighbor Niko help him see that Jake is the one with the problem.

"Focusing on a subject not often written about for children, Ludwig's story may be helpful to youngsters dealing with braggarts. . . . Well-executed paintings are appealing and portray the characters' emotions clearly." SLJ

★ The **invisible** boy; by Trudy Ludwig. Alfred A. Knopf Books for Young Readers 2013 40 p. (hardcover) $16.99; (library binding) $19.99

Grades: K 1 2 3   E

1. Picture books for children 2. School stories 3. Schools -- Fiction 4. Friendship -- Fiction 5. Popularity -- Fiction

ISBN 1582464502; 1582464510; 9780449818206; 9781582464503; 9781582464510

LC 2012042631

In this children's picture book, timid schoolchild "Brian wants to join in but is overlooked, even ostracized, by his classmates. . . . High-maintenance children get the teacher's attention; team captains choose kickball players by popularity and athletic ability; chatter about birthday parties indicates they are not inclusive events." Ultimately, Brian's creative drawings help him win his classmates' attention. (Kirkus Reviews)

Lum, Kate

What! cried Granny; an almost bedtime story. pictures by Adrian Johnson. Dial Bks. for Young Readers 1999 un il hardcover o.p. pa $6.99

Grades: K 1 2 3   E

1. Bedtime -- Fiction 2. Grandmothers -- Fiction

ISBN 0-8037-2382-2; 0-14-230092-6 pa

LC 98-19642

First published 1998 in the United Kingdom with title: What!

This "combines the deadpan and the surreal in wild words and neon-colored acrylic illustrations." Booklist

Lumry, Amanda

Safari in South Africa; by Amanda Lumry and Laura Hurwitz; illustrated by Sarah McIntyre. Scholastic 2008 32p il map (Adventures of Riley) $16.99; pa $6.99

Grades: 1 2 3 4   E

1. Game reserves 2. Animals -- Africa 3. South Africa -- Fiction 4. Wildlife conservation -- Fiction

ISBN 978-0-545-06827-7; 0-545-06827-4; 978-0-545-06826-0 pa; 0-545-06826-6 pa

First published 2003 by Eaglemont Press

Riley travels with his Uncle Max to check on the animal population at a South African game reserve.

"Combining whimsical cartoons and striking photographs of animals in the bush, this title is a marvelous intermingling of adventure and science. . . . Boxes presenting significant facts about the animals appear next to their photographs." SLJ

Other titles in this series are:
Amazon River rescue (2004)
Dolphins in danger (2009)
Mission to Madagascar (2005)
Operation Orangutan (2007)
Polar bear puzzle (2008)
Project Panda (2008)
Riddle of the reef (2009)
South Pole penguins (2008)
Tigers in Terai (2009)

Lund, Deb
Monsters on machines; [by] Deb Lund; illustrated by Robert Neubecker. Harcourt 2008 un il $16
Grades: PreK K 1 2   E
1. Stories in rhyme 2. Monsters -- Fiction 3. Construction workers -- Fiction 4. Construction equipment -- Fiction
ISBN 978-0-15-205365-9; 0-15-205365-4
LC 2006037393
Construction crew monsters arrive on the scene with tractors, cranes, and grader machines, and after a gruesome site is created as their routine, they straighten it up and leave everything clean.
"The India-ink drawings colored digitally in neon-bright hues exude a jazzy, busy look that brings to life the chaos that results when monsters and machines meet." SLJ

Lunde, Darrin
Monkey colors; Darrin Lunde; illustrated by Patricia J. Wynne. Charlesbridge 2011 48 p. col. ill.
Grades: PreK K 1 2   E
1. Color 2. Monkeys 3. Picture books for children
ISBN 1570917418; 9781570917417; 9781570917424
LC 2011000669
In this children's picture book, "[Darrin] Lunde and [Patricia] Wynne describe 12 monkey species in simple sentences. The monkeys are grouped into three categories: four whose fur is a single all-over color (yellow, red, brown, orange); four who have colorful features or stripes; and four whose colors vary with sex or age or gender or who are truly multicolored." (Kirkus)

Lunde, Stein Erik
★ **My** father's arms are a boat; Stein Erik Lunde; [illustrated by] Oyvind Torseter; [translated by Kari Dickson] Enchanted Lion Books 2013 40 p. (hardback) $15.95
Grades: K 1 2 3   E
1. Death -- Fiction 2. Emotions -- Fiction 3. Father-son relationship -- Fiction 4. Fathers and sons -- Fiction
ISBN 1592701248; 9781592701247
LC 2012022767
Mildred L. Batchelder Honor Book (2014)
In author Stein Erik Lunde's book, "it's quieter than it's ever been. Unable to sleep, a young boy climbs into his father's arms. Feeling the warmth and closeness of his father, he begins to ask about the birds, the foxes . . . and whether his mother will ever wake up. Even in the face of absence and loss, the cycles of life continue unabated. We know in the end everything will somehow be all right." (Publisher's note)

Lundquist, Mary
Cat & Bunny; by Mary Lundquist. Balzer + Bray, an imprint of HarperCollins Publishers 2014 32 p. color illustrations (hardcover) $17.99
Grades: PreK K 1   E
1. Cats -- Fiction 2. Play -- Fiction 3. Rabbits -- Fiction 4. Friendship -- Fiction 5. Animals -- Fiction 6. Best friends -- Fiction
ISBN 006228780X; 9780062287809
LC 2013051216
This children's book, by Mary Lundquist, is about "Cat and Bunny. . . . It's always been just the two of them - daydreaming, having adventures, playing their special game. Until the day someone else asks, 'Can I play?'" (Publisher's note)
"Lundquist's sympathetic debut introduces inseparable friends, one in a zippered cat costume and the other in a white, long-eared bunny outfit: "Right from the start, they did everything together."... While developing independent identities and adjusting their expectations, Cat and Bunny demonstrate how to admit new friends into a tight circle." PW
Cat and Bunny

Luxbacher, Irene
Mattoo, let's play! written and illustrated by Irene Luxbacher. Kids Can Press 2010 un il $16.95
Grades: PreK K 1   E
1. Cats -- Fiction 2. Play -- Fiction
ISBN 978-1-55453-424-1; 1-55453-424-0
"Highly imaginative Ruby wants to play with Mattoo, her 'shy' cat, who shuns her attempts at entertainment. As the child crashes and clangs pots and pans, or jumps up and down on her bed . . . readers will understand his 'shyness.'. . . This clever, unique tale illustrates how 'play' can be fun for humans but not so great for pets. Ruby is delightful, full of creativity and imagination. The use of acrylic ink and collage makes for stunning illustrations." SLJ

Mr. Frank; by Irene Luxbacher. Pgw 2014 32 p. mostly color illustrations $16.95
Grades: PreK K 1   E
1. Sewing -- Fiction 2. Tailoring -- Fiction 3. Retirement -- Fiction
ISBN 1554984351; 9781554984350
LC bl2014038746
In this children's book, by Irene Luxbacher, "on his last day before retirement, Mr. Frank is sewing the most wonderful outfit of his long career. Who could it be for? In all his years working as a tailor, Mr. Frank has made all kinds of clothes. From the practical uniforms of the 1940s to the wild and weird designs of the 1960s and 1970s, he has seen (and sewn) just about everything. But today's project is especially close to Mr. Frank's heart." (Publisher's note)
"Outstanding mixed-media collages and a thoughtful text create a distinctive book that rises far above most tributes to grandparental love. "Mr. Frank was a tailor," proclaims the first page, in bold, unambiguous lettering. . . . The double-page spreads that follow are perfect examples of artwork extending text, as each decade of Mr. Frank's long career reveals the fashions he helped to create and promulgate. . . The entirely wordless climax hints that the book may be turning maudlin, until the turn of the page reveals a hu-

morous and heartwarming denouement. It's a perfect ending to a perfect book. " Kirkus

Lynn, Sarah

Tip-Tap Pop; illustrated by Valeria Docampo. Marshall Cavendish 2010 un il $17.99

Grades: PreK K 1   E

1. Dance -- Fiction 2. Old age -- Fiction 3. Grandfathers -- Fiction

ISBN 978-0-7614-5712-1; 0-7614-5712-7

Emma and Pop have been tap dancing together since before she could talk, but Pop becomes very forgetful and can no longer dance until one special day when he hears Emma's steps and they find a way for him to join in.

"Short text and attention-grabbing words combine with colorful gouache and pencil illustrations. . . . With Docampo's inclusion of a gramophone, bowties, and suspenders, Tip-Tap Pop has a nostalgic feel and leisurely pace. A first purchase." SLJ

Lyon, George Ella

My friend, the starfinder; by George Ella Lyon; pictures by Stephen Gammell. Atheneum Books for Young Readers 2008 un il $16.99

Grades: PreK K 1 2   E

1. Storytelling -- Fiction

ISBN 978-1-4169-2738-9; 1-4169-2738-7

LC 2006032026

A child relates some of the wondrous tales told by an old man who once found a falling star and stood at the end of a rainbow.

This is a "sumptuously illustrated book. . . . Text and art are sure to evoke wonder in young readers." Publ Wkly

The pirate of kindergarten; illustrated by Lynne Avril. Atheneum Books for Young Readers 2010 un il $16.99

Grades: PreK K 1 2   E

1. School stories 2. Vision disorders -- Fiction

ISBN 978-1-4169-5024-0; 1-4169-5024-9

Ginny's eyes play tricks on her, making her see everything double, but when she goes to vision screening at school and discovers that not everyone sees this way, she learns that her double vision can be cured.

"Lyon's short, descriptive sentences set up the situation deftly, and Avril's astute chalk, pencil, and acrylic drawings of 'two of everything' provide a vivid window into Ginny's pretreatment world." SLJ

Planes fly! George Ella Lyon; illustrated by Mick Wiggins. Atheneum Books for Young Readers 2013 40 p. (hardcover: alk. paper) $17.99

Grades: PreK K   E

1. Picture books for children 2. Airplanes 3. Air travel 4. Stories in rhyme 5. Airplanes -- Fiction

ISBN 1442450258; 9781442450257; 9781442450264

LC 2012030310

This children's picture book by George Ella Lyon looks at planes. Rhyming "text names aircraft parts, lists different kinds of planes, and describes passenger air-travel experiences, repeating the upbeat refrain, 'Planes fly!' throughout." A "reassuring rundown of events that happen between buckling the seatbelt and touching down for landing (includ-

ing a snack and a nap) makes this title helpful to those new to flying." (School Library Journal)

Trucks roll! words by George Ella Lyon; art by Craig Frazier. Atheneum Books for Young Readers 2007 un il $14.99

Grades: PreK   E

1. Stories in rhyme 2. Trucks -- Fiction

ISBN 978-1-4169-2435-7; 1-4169-2435-3

LC 2006-10811

Illustrations and simple, rhyming text reveal many different—and sometimes silly—items that trucks can haul.

"Solid, up-to-date information about a major preschool enthusiasm is leavened with lively verse and touch of whimsey." Horn Book

You and me and home sweet home; illustrated by Stephanie Anderson. Atheneum Books for Young Readers 2009 un il $17.99

Grades: PreK K 1 2 3   E

1. Houses -- Fiction 2. Building -- Fiction 3. Volunteer work -- Fiction 4. African Americans -- Fiction

ISBN 978-0-689-87589-2; 0-689-87589-4

LC 2008010414

Third-grader Sharonda and her mother help volunteers from their church to build the house that will be their very own.

"Sharonda narrates in clean, simple prose. . . . Varied in composition and perspective, the watercolor-and-pastel-pencil illustrations center on the nicely individualized characters . . . and readers will share Sharonda's quiet glow of happiness at the end." Booklist

Lyon, Tammie

Olive and Snowflake; written and illustrated by Tammie Lyon. Marshall Cavendish Children 2011 il

Grades: PreK K 1   E

1. Dogs -- Fiction

ISBN 0761459553; 9780761459552; 9780761460695 e-book

LC 2011001124

When her parents threaten to send away the dog if he cannot learn to behave, Olive is worried they will both be sent to live with a new family.

"Bold text and vibrant cartoon-style illustrations make this a great read-aloud or lap read. Children will delight in the happy ending and will appreciate this simple tale of love, responsibility, and growing up." SLJ

Lyons, Kelly Starling

Ellen's broom; Kelly Starling Lyons; illustrated by Daniel Minter. G. P. Putnam's Sons 2012 32 p.

Grades: K 1 2 3   E

1. Brooms -- Fiction 2. Picture books for children 3. Reconstruction (1865-1876) -- Fiction 4. Slaves -- Emancipation -- Fiction 5. Marriage customs and rites -- Fiction 6. Slavery -- Fiction 7. Marriage -- Fiction 8. African Americans -- Fiction 9. Brooms and brushes -- Fiction

ISBN 9780399250033

LC 2011047101

Coretta Scott King Illustrator Honor Book (2013)

This picture book, "[s]et during Reconstruction, . . . [is] based on a historical event, [and] opens with a preacher's announcement to his black congregation that "all former slaves living as husband and wife shall be registered and seen as married in the eyes of the law." Young Ellen doesn't quite understand what this means until her mother explains to her that during slavery, slave couples like Ellen's mother and father were only allowed "broom weddings," wherein couples would jump over a broom. . . . Ellen grabs the marriage broom, ... decorates it with flowers, and hands it to her parents during the[ir] ceremony. . . . [T]he story touches . . . on how formerly enslaved people . . . found . . . ways to celebrate their freedoms during . . . Reconstruction." (Bulletin of the Center for Children's Books)

Hope's gift; Kelly Starling Lyons; illustrated by Don Tate. G.P. Putnam's Sons 2012 32 p. (hardcover) $16.99
Grades: 1 2 3   E
    1. Slaves -- Emancipation -- Fiction 2. Slavery -- Fiction 3. African Americans -- Fiction 4. Emancipation Proclamation -- Fiction 5. United States -- History -- Civil War, 1861-1865 -- Fiction
    ISBN 0399160019; 9780399160011
                 LC 2012014587
In this children's story, by Kelly Starling Lyons, illustrated by Don Tate, "it's 1862. . . . Hope's father . . . decides to join the Union army to fight for freedom. He slips away one tearful night, leaving Hope, . . . with only a conch shell for comfort. . . . But then Lincoln finally does it: on January 1, 1863, he issues the Emancipation Proclamation, freeing the slaves, and a joyful Hope finally spies the outline of a familiar man standing on the horizon." (Publisher's note)

Maass, Robert
  A is for autumn. Henry Holt 2011 un il $16.99
Grades: PreK K 1 2   E
    1. Alphabet 2. Autumn -- Fiction
    ISBN 978-0-8050-9093-2; 0-8050-9093-2
                 LC 2010040333
Photographs and simple text present a variety of things seen in the fall.
"Vivid photography brings the autumn season to life in an alphabet book with thoughtful descriptions of nature, changing weather, and leisure activities. . . . Maass delivers a vibrant tribute to Autumn." Publ Wkly

Macaulay, David
  Why the chicken crossed the road. Houghton Mifflin 1987 31p il lib bdg $16
Grades: 3 4 5   E
    1. Chickens -- Fiction
    ISBN 0-395-44241-9 lib bdg
                 LC 87-2908
"A ridiculous chicken sets off a circular story involving a herd of cows, a bridge, a train, a robber, the fire department and some hydrangeas. Chaos. The illustrations are suitably wild—painted with brilliant color and almost palpable energy." N Y Times Book Rev

Maccarone, Grace
  ★ **Miss** Lina's ballerinas; illustrated by Christine Davenier. Feiwel and Friends 2010 un il $16.99
Grades: PreK K 1   E
    1. Stories in rhyme 2. Ballet -- Fiction
    ISBN 0-312-38243-X; 978-0-312-38243-8
                 LC 2009-49367

Ballet instructor Miss Lina has a solution when her eight students, who always dance in pairs, are distraught when a ninth girl joins the class.
"The rhymic rhyming text flows beautifully throughout the book. . . . Davenier's free-spirited drawings and color washes add a sense of music as well as movement to the scenes." Booklist
Another title about Miss Lina is:
  Miss Lina's ballerinas and the prince (2011)

  Miss Lina's ballerinas and the prince; illustrated by Christine Davenier. Feiwel & Friends 2011 $16.99
Grades: PreK K 1   E
    ISBN 978-0-312-64963-0; 0-312-64963-0
Miss Lina's ballerinas have all learned how to dance as a group. But now Miss Lina has a new surprise for them—a boy will be joining their class and performing in their end-of-year show.
"Maccarone has fashioned another charming story in rhyme for young readers that integrates ballet terminology into the narrative and provides a very positive reinforcement for boys interested in the arts. The pastel drawings with swirls of crayon lines provide just the right touch of ambiance and energy." Kirkus

MacDonald, Ross
  ★ **Another** perfect day. Millbrook Press 2002 un il hardcover o.p. pa $6.95
Grades: PreK K 1 2   E
    1. Heroes and heroines -- Fiction
    ISBN 0-7613-1595-0; 1-59643-079-6 pa
                 LC 2002-18798
What started out as another perfect day for Jack the superhero performing heroic feats suddenly goes awry
"With a beefy hero and graphics inspired by 1930-40s comic books, this impeccably designed volume features a forthright text that comically counterpoints a livelier tale told through the pictures." Publ Wkly
Another title about Jack is:
  Bad baby (2005)

Macdonald, Suse
  Circus opposites; an interactive extravaganza. Little Simon 2010 un il $11.99
Grades: PreK K 1 2   E
    1. Opposites 2. Circus -- Fiction
    ISBN 978-1-4169-7154-2; 1-4169-7154-8
"Macdonald's crisp trademark paper collages are the main event, as she uses the sights of the circus to explore the concept of opposites. Readers kick things off by pulling a tab to let 11 clowns 'out' of a tiny yellow car. They can also literally turn a clown's frown upside down. . . . The elaborate costumes and variety of interactive elements should prove kid-pleasing." Publ Wkly

Machado, Ana Maria
  What a party! Ana Maria Machado, illustrated by Helene Moreau. Groundwood Books 2013 32 p. ill. (hardcover) $18.95
Grades: PreK K 1 2   E
    1. Cooking 2. Children's parties -- Fiction
    ISBN 1554981689; 9781554981687
This children's book, by Ana Maria Machado, illustrated by Helene Moreau, warns that "if it is just a few days until

your birthday, and your mother says you can invite anyone you like to come over to play, be careful! . . . In a celebration of neighbors and diversity, an open-ended party invitation results in a raucous gathering of children, pets, and parents (plus salsa dancers and a reggae band!), all feasting on food from all over the world." (Publisher's note)

MacHale, D. J.

The **monster** princess; written by D.J. MacHale; illustrated by Alexandra Boiger. Aladdin Paperbacks 2010 un il $17.99

Grades: PreK K   **E**

1. Stories in rhyme 2. Monsters -- Fiction 3. Princesses -- Fiction 4. Self-acceptance -- Fiction

ISBN 978-1-4169-4809-4; 1-4169-4809-0

LC 2008037933

Unhappy with her life in a dark cave, Lala longs to live like the princesses far, far above but after venturing into their world, she finds contentment at home.

"A potentially didactic story . . . is saved by a wry text . . . and endearing illustrations. . . . The resolution satisfies." Booklist

MacIver, Juliette, 1972-

The **Frog** who lost his underpants; Juliette MacIver, illustrated by Cat Chapman. Candlewick Press 2014 32 p. $14.99

Grades: PreK K 1   **E**

1. Frogs -- Fiction 2. Underwear -- Fiction 3. Stories in rhyme 4. Teddy bears -- Fiction 5. Jungle animals -- Fiction

ISBN 076366782X; 9780763667825

LC 2013944130

In this children's book by Juliette MacIver, illustrated by Cat Chapman, "Frog is in a frenzy, scattering the ants. . . . Poor Frog. Someone stole his underpants! Good thing Teddy Bear, Little Chimp, and Big Gray Elephant are there to help--although they may find it hard to hide their smiles. A jungle frog in underpants? Now that is something to see." (Publisher's note)

"The silliness begins with the book's title and cover image, which features a big teddy bear helping a woebegone frog through the jungle...When the elephant, chimpanzee, bear, and a hundred jungle frogs find the pair of red undies, chaos ensues, followed by a suitably silly solution. Frog distinguishes himself from the other jungle frogs not by his taste in skivvies but by the friendships he has made." Booklist

Mack, Jeff

Ah ha! Jeff Mack. Chronicle Books 2013 40 p. (alk. paper) $16.99

Grades: PreK K 1   **E**

1. Frogs -- Fiction 2. Picture books for children

ISBN 1452112657; 9781452112657

LC 2012040903

"This nearly wordless book . . . follows the adventures of a frog who is caught in a jar by a boy and his dog ('AH HA!'). Don't worry, he escapes ('AAHH!') but lands on the back of a hungry turtle ('AH HA!') from whom he leaps away to escape being eaten ('AAHH!'), only to find himself on the back of an even hungrier crocodile ('AH HA!'). And

so it goes from croc to flamingo leg and then back into the jar to the final escape ('AH HA!')." (School Library Journal)

Good news, bad news; Jeff Mack. Chronicle Books 2012 40 p. (alk. paper) $16.99

Grades: PreK K 1   **E**

1. Rain -- Fiction 2. Picnics -- Fiction 3. Picture books for children 4. Mice -- Fiction 5. Rabbits -- Fiction 6. Optimism -- Fiction 7. Pessimism -- Fiction

ISBN 1452101108; 9781452101101

LC 2011016710

In this book, "[w]hen optimistic Rabbit and unlucky Mouse go on a picnic, there is plenty of good news and bad news. Some good news-umbrella, apples, cake, cave. Some bad news-rain, worms, bees, bear. Unfortunately, all the bad seems to happen to Mouse, who eventually has a hissy fit that makes Rabbit cry. But as the sun breaks through the clouds, Mouse makes it all better with a peace offering of the picnic basket and a hug" (School Library Journal)

Hippo and Rabbit in 3 more tales: brave like me. Scholastic Inc. 2011 32p pa $3.99

Grades: K 1 2   **E**

1. Fear -- Fiction 2. Courage -- Fiction 3. Rabbits -- Fiction 4. Hippopotamus -- Fiction

ISBN 978-0-545-28360-1; 0-545-28360-4

Hippo is scared of everything. He worries his balloon will pop and make a big noise. He's nervous about taking a bath. And he is so very afraid of spiders. Rabbit tells him not to worry—to just be brave, like him.

Hippo and Rabbit in three short tales. Scholastic/Cartwheel Books 2011 32p il pa $3.99

Grades: K 1 2   **E**

1. Graphic novels 2. Humorous graphic novels 3. Rabbits -- Fiction 4. Friendship -- Fiction 5. Hippopotamus -- Fiction

ISBN 978-0-545-27445-6; 0-545-27445-1

LC 2010-13567

Friends Hippo and Rabbit are very different in size, but they have fun together as they eat breakfast (Rabbit eats vegetables, Hippo has a cheeseburger), play on the swing (Rabbit has to try very hard to push Hippo), and then comfort each other during a thunderstorm at night.

"With a low word count and simple sentences [this is] suitable for newly independent readers. . . . . The book can be used as a supplemental reader in the classroom, but the stories are fun enough for recreational reading at home. " Booklist

Hush little polar bear; [by] Jeff Mack. Roaring Brook Press 2008 un il $16.95

Grades: PreK K   **E**

1. Stories in rhyme 2. Adventure fiction 3. Dreams -- Fiction 4. Bedtime -- Fiction 5. Polar bear -- Fiction

ISBN 978-1-59643-368-7; 1-59643-368-X

LC 2007044049

A little girl invites her plush polar bear to dream of all of the places where sleeping bears go, from the high seas to a starry desert and back home

"The richly textured spreads are bright and imaginative, perfectly complementing the simple, lyrical text." SLJ

Look! Jeff Mack. Philomel Books, an imprint of Penguin Group (USA) 2015 32 p. color illustrations (hardback) $16.99

Grades: PreK K 1   E

1. Humorous fiction 2. Gorillas -- Fiction 3. Friendship -- Fiction 4. Books and reading -- Fiction 5. Humorous stories

ISBN 0399162054; 9780399162053

LC 2014020636

"Everyone needs a little attention from time to time. Just ask our gorilla who will stop at nothing to be noticed by the boy with his eyes glued to the TV set. . . . Using only two words--LOOK and OUT--[author] Jeff Mack relates an adorably hilarious story about an attention-loving gorilla, a television-loving boy, and a friendship that develops over books." (Publisher's note)

"Bright, mostly monochrome page bac kgrounds evoke clothbound book covers and distressed old pages; minimal set dressing (a door, a stool, the TV) keeps the focus on the zany interaction. The personalities and emotions of the chunky, fluffy ape and the TV-entranced boy nearly vibrate off the page." Kirkus

Mackall, Dandi Daley

First day; illustrated by Tiphanie Beeke. Harcourt 2003 un il $16

Grades: PreK K   E

1. School stories 2. Stories in rhyme

ISBN 0-15-216577-0

LC 2002-933

The first day of school starts out filled with doubt, but after facing fear of the big kids, reciting the alphabet with ease, and learning about recess, a child can't help but look forward to day two.

"The rhyming text gives the story a sweet, singsong quality. . . . The softly colored, reassuring art works well with the simple text that is set on pastel backgrounds." SLJ

Listen to the silent night; illustrated by Steve Johnson and Lou Fancher. Dutton Childrens Books 2011 un il $16.99

Grades: PreK K 1   E

1. Stories in rhyme 2. Noise -- Fiction 3. Sound -- Fiction 4. Christmas stories

ISBN 978-0-525-42276-1; 0-525-42276-5

LC 2011005243

Rhyming text reveals many sounds heard on the night of Jesus' birth, such as the flapping of Joseph's sandals as he walks into Bethlehem, the lowing of a cow in the stable, and the flutter of angels' wings as they proclaim the news.

"Johnson and Fancher's lovely artwork is filled with warm welcoming colors and highly textured details. A noisy account of the miraculous night." SLJ

Macken, JoAnn Early

Baby says moo! written by JoAnn Early Macken; illustrated by David Walker. Disney Hyperion Books 2011 un il lib bdg $15.99

Grades: PreK   E

1. Stories in rhyme 2. Sounds -- Fiction 3. Animals -- Fiction 4. Infants -- Fiction

ISBN 978-1-4231-3400-8 lib bdg; 1-4231-3400-1 lib bdg

LC 2009-52504

A cumulative, rhyming tale of a baby who sees many animals while out with her family, only one of which makes her favorite sound.

"The rhyming text reads smoothly, and the acrylic illustrations are childlike and cheerful, making the book exactly right for toddlers." SLJ

★ **Waiting** out the storm; illustrated by Susan Gaber. Candlewick Press 2010 un il $15.99

Grades: PreK K 1 2   E

1. Stories in rhyme 2. Rain -- Fiction 3. Storms -- Fiction 4. Mother-child relationship -- Fiction

ISBN 978-0-7636-3378-3; 0-7636-3378-X

LC 2008030746

A mother reassures her child about the wind, lightning, and thunder when a storm passes through.

"The text creates a natural-sounding rhythm and flow of dialogue. . . . Gaber's captivating artwork, combining watercolor, pencil, and charcoal with digital renderings, is simultaneously strong and delicate." Booklist

Mackintosh, David

Marshall Armstrong is new to our school. Abrams 2011 il

Grades: PreK K 1 2   E

1. School stories 2. Parties -- Fiction 3. Birthdays -- Fiction 4. Friendship -- Fiction

ISBN 1-4197-0036-7; 978-1-4197-0036-1

Marshall Armstrong is new to school and definitely stands out from the crowd, with his pale skin, perpetual hats, and special "space food" lunches that come in silver wrappers. He doesn't play sports, and he doesn't watch television. So when he invites everyone in class over for his birthday party, it's sure to be a disaster. Or is it?

"Macintosh's beautifully underplayed text and genial drawings manage to be empathic to both the leery narrator and the serenely outré object of his misapprehension." Publ Wkly

MacLachlan, Patricia

Lala salama; a Tanzanian lullaby. illustrated by Elizabeth Zunon. Candlewick Press 2011 il $16.99

Grades: PreK K 1   E

1. Lullabies 2. Tanzania -- Fiction 3. Family life -- Fiction 4. Mother-child relationship -- Fiction

ISBN 978-0-7636-4747-6; 0-7636-4747-0

LC 2010040465

A mother relates the events of a peaceful day along the banks of Lake Tanganyika to her baby, wrapped up and ready for sleep.

"Zunon's lush, softly textured oil paintings on watercolor paper reflect the warmth of the African setting and emotion-imbued prose. . . . Share this with preschoolers who may enjoy a peek into another culture's family life or keep at hand for the tired child, who will most appreciate this quietly sentimental offering." Kirkus

Painting the wind; by Patricia MacLachlan & Emily MacLachlan; illustrated by Katy Schneider. J. Cotler Bks. 2003 un il $15.99; pa $7.99

Grades: K 1 2 3   E

1. Artists -- Fiction 2. Painting -- Fiction

ISBN 0-06-029798-0; 0-06-443825-2 pa

LC 2001-47549

Several artists who paint different things, with different kinds of paint, and at different times of the day, all paint the same island that they visit each summer

"The gentle prose pairs well with handsome artwork that evokes warm, strong sensory impressions through a combination of thick brushwork, texture, and a vibrant color palette." Booklist

Your moon, my moon; a grandmother's words to a faraway child. illustrated by Bryan Collier. Simon & Schuster Books for Young Readers 2011 un il $16.99
Grades: PreK K 1 2   E
  1. Africa -- Fiction 2. New England -- Fiction 3. Grandmothers -- Fiction
  ISBN 978-1-4169-7950-0; 1-4169-7950-6
                   LC 2008050451

Although their homes are different, a grandmother in New England and her loving grandson in Africa share the same moon.

"Collier's vibrant illustrations are a blend of watercolor and his trademark collage. This is a wonderful book to contrast different lifestyles." SLJ

Maclear, Kyo
  Spork; written by Kyo Maclear; illustrated by Isabelle Arsenault. Kids Can Press 2010 un il $16.95
Grades: PreK K 1 2   E
  1. Cutlery -- Fiction 2. Prejudices -- Fiction 3. Identity (Psychology) -- Fiction 4. Racially mixed people -- Fiction
  ISBN 978-1-55337-736-8; 1-55337-736-2

His mum is a spoon. His dad is a fork. And he's a bit of both. He's Spork! The spoons think he's too pointy, while the forks find him too round.

"Maclear's text feels nearly effortless. The inanimate-object identification . . . pairs brilliantly with Arsenault's melding of mixed media and digital art. . . . A sublime little parable." Kirkus

MacLennan, Cathy
  ★ **Chicky** chicky chook chook. Boxer 2007 un il $12.95; bd bk $7.95
Grades: PreK K 1   E
  1. Stories in rhyme 2. Bees -- Fiction 3. Cats -- Fiction 4. Chickens -- Fiction 5. Farm life -- Fiction
  ISBN 978-1-905417-40-3; 1-905417-40-3; 978-1-906250-55-3 bd bk; 1-906250-55-3 bd bk

Chicks, chickens, cats, and bees on a farm enjoy an active, busy day playing, snoozing, and getting drenched in a thunderstorm before finally going to sleep at night

"This rambunctious story has an onomatopoeic rhyming text that children will love to hear again and again. . . . Inspired by the art and culture of her native Zimbabwe, MacLennan dabs, swirls, and sponges bright splashes of paint on brown butcher paper." SLJ

MacLeod, Doug
  Heather Fell in the Water; by Doug MacLeod; illustrated by Craig Smith. Independent Pub Group 2013 32 p. ill. (hardcover) $16.99
Grades: PreK K   E
  1. Picture books for children 2. Swimming -- Fiction
  ISBN 1742376487; 9781742376486

In this children's picture book, "everywhere Heather goes, from farms to art galleries, she falls in the water. As a result, her parents make her wear water wings at all times, even in bed. Then one day they determine that their child needs to learn how to swim. Unsurprisingly, Heather is frightened, convinced that the water dislikes her. But she climbs into the shallow end of a pool with her mother and father," and finds that she loves the water and it loves her. (School Library Journal)

Mader, C. Roger
  ★ **Tiptop** cat; written and illustrated by C. Roger Mader. Houghton Mifflin Books for Children, Houghton Mifflin Harcourt 2014 40 p. color illustrations $17.99
Grades: PreK K 1 2   E
  1. Cats -- Fiction
  ISBN 0544147995; 9780544147997
                   LC 2013038998

In this children's book, by Roger Mader, "a curious cat plus a big fall leads to squashed confidence. How this cat bounces back will encourage readers everywhere to try, try again. Eye-catching art and crisp graphic paneling invite even the youngest of children to get back on their feet to explore the city alongside TipTop Cat." (Publisher's note)

"A Parisian cat that has enjoyed touring rooftops is terrified when he falls from a sixth-floor balcony, only to have his confidence later restored. Arresting, detailed pastels capture feline behavior and also steep heights and angles. The simple narrative's tone is light rather than didactic as we cheer on the unnamed hero's triumphant return to the "top of the world." Horn Book

Madison, Alan
  ★ **Velma** Gratch & the way cool butterfly; written by Alan Madison; illustrated by Kevin Hawkes. Schwartz & Wade Books 2007 un il $16.99; lib bdg $19.99
Grades: PreK K 1 2   E
  1. School stories 2. Sisters -- Fiction 3. Butterflies -- Fiction
  ISBN 978-0-375-83597-1; 978-0-375-93597-8 lib bdg
                   LC 2006030978

Velma starts first grade in the shadow of her memorable older sisters, and while her newfound interest in butterflies helps her to stand out, it also leads to an interesting complication

"With humorous wordplay and electric cartoon art, this is an uplifting and way-cool look at one child's metamorphosis." SLJ

Madrigal, Antonio Hernandez
  Erandi's braids; written by Antonio Hernandez Madrigal; illustrated by Tomie dePaola. Putnam 1999 un il $15.99; pa $6.99
Grades: K 1 2 3   E
  1. Hair -- Fiction 2. Mexico -- Fiction 3. Mother-daughter relationship -- Fiction
  ISBN 0-399-23212-5; 0-698-11885-5 pa
                   LC 97-49631

In a poor Mexican village, Erandi surprises her mother by offering to sell her long, beautiful hair in order to raise enough money to buy a new fishing net

"This tale of love and sacrifice is based on an actual Mexican practice in the 1940s and 50s. The facial expressions in dePaola's warm illustrations add to the poignancy of the story." Horn Book Guide

Magoon, Scott

The **boy** who cried Bigfoot! Scott Magoon. Simon & Schuster Books for Young Readers 2012 48 p. color illustrations $16.99

Grades: PreK K 1   E

1. Yeti -- Fiction 2. Honesty -- Fiction

ISBN 1442412577; 9781442412576

LC 2010031149

In this children's book, written and illustrated by Scott Magoon, "a friendly Sasquatch narrates this twist on 'The Boy Who Cried Wolf,' relating his introduction to young Ben, who has a habit of making up stories about spying Bigfoot near the woods. When no Bigfoot ever actually appears, Ben's believers predictably lose faith. As Ben sits dejectedly near the woods one evening, Bigfoot makes his presence known and borrows Ben's bike for a ride." (Bulletin of the Center for Children's Books)

"Digitally rendered illustrations are done in mostly green hues. Bigfoot is charming and goofy-looking with his smiles and manners, asking if he can 'borrow' Ben's bike, and the child's expressions are priceless." SLJ

Breathe; Scott Magoon. Simon & Schuster Books for Young Readers 2014 40 p. (hardcover) $16.99

Grades: PreK K 1   E

1. Whales -- Fiction 2. Animals -- Infancy -- Fiction

ISBN 1442412585; 9781442412583

LC 2013017696

This children's book, by Scott Magoon, "follows a young whale on a journey of discovery as he experiences his first day at sea on his own! He swims, explores, and makes friends in his marine habitat. After a day of independence, this little whale delights in returning home to his mother." (Publisher's note)

"With the encouragement of its mother, a young whale spends the day exploring, making new friends, finding shipwrecks, and swimming past glaciers, while intermittently pausing to "breathe" during its busy day...The minimal text is laid out in clear, big font, supporting the impressive illustrations without ever overshadowing them. With its succinct text and sprawling pictures, this story is perfectly suitable as a read-aloud." SLJ

Mahy, Margaret, 1936-2012

★ **Bubble** trouble; illustrated by Polly Dunbar. Clarion Books 2009 37p il $16

Grades: PreK K 1   E

1. Stories in rhyme 2. Bubbles -- Fiction

ISBN 978-0-547-07421-4; 0-547-07421-2

LC 2008-07244

Boston Globe-Horn Book Award: Picture Book (2009)

Mabel blows a bubble that captures Baby and wafts him away, resulting in a wild chase that involves the whole neighborhood.

"Mahy is a master at creating verse that is as light and airy as the baby's bubble. Filled with lovely Briticisms, alliterative nonsense words, double, triple and internal rhymes, it's meant to be read aloud. . . . Dunbar's joyous watercolor-and-cut-paper illustrations are wonderfully expressive, a visual treat moving apace with the text." Kirkus

The **green** bath; Margaret Mahy; illustrated by Steven Kellogg. Arthur A. Levine Books 2013 40 p. (hardcover: alk. paper) $16.99

Grades: PreK K 1 2   E

1. Picture books for children 2. Baths -- Fiction 3. Bathtubs -- Fiction 4. Adventure and adventurers -- Fiction

ISBN 0545206677; 9780545206679; 9780545206686

LC 2012013239

In this children's picture book, Sammy's father buys a "clunky, green bathtub" at the flea market. "This is no ordinary tub: for one, it has an expressive, wide-eyed face, and Sammy hears the tub 'give a gurgle as if it were laughing.'" During Sammy's bath, the tub comes to life and "Sammy sails out to sea in the tub and, with the help of a friendly sea serpent, engages in 'a wonderful bath-and-buccaneer battle' with pirates." (Publishers Weekly)

The **man** from the land of Fandango; Margaret Mahy; illustrations by Polly Dunbar. Clarion Books 2012 32 p. (hardback) $16.99

Grades: PreK K 1 2   E

1. Picture books for children 2. Imagination 3. Adventure fiction 4. Stories in rhyme 5. Imagination -- Fiction

ISBN 0547819889; 9780547819884

LC 2011052109

In this children's book by Margaret Mahy, illustrated by Polly Dunbar, "two children paint Mr. Fandango to life, and together the trio has a tremendous adventure with baboons and bisons, dinosaurs and kangaroos . . . [in] a playful imaginary world. . . . Even the lines of type curve and tango." (Publisher's note)

Mair, J. Samia

The **perfect** gift; illustrated by Craigh Howarth. Kube Pub. 2010 29p il $8.95

Grades: 1 2 3 4   E

1. Gifts -- Fiction 2. Muslims -- Fiction 3. Id al-Adha -- Fiction 4. Family life -- Fiction

ISBN 978-0-86037-438-1; 0-86037-438-6

Sarah is sad because she cannot find an Eid gift for her mother, so she takes a walk along the secret path in the woods that always makes her feel better. There she finds the first flower of spring—God's perfect gift to the world. Leaving her gift in its place to share with her entire family, Sarah grows in her understanding and appreciation of nature and what it means to live in submission to God.

"Howarth's watercolor illustrations effectively portray a contemporary Muslim family living in North America or Europe. This realistic picture book, one of the few stories on Eid-ul-Adha, is a solid purchase for many collections." SLJ

Mak, Kam

★ **My** Chinatown; one year in poems. HarperCollins Pubs. 2002 un il $16.95

Grades: 2 3 4   E

1. Immigrants -- Fiction 2. Chinese Americans -- Fiction 3. Chinatown (New York, N.Y.) -- Fiction

ISBN 0-06-029190-7; 0-06-029191-5 lib bdg

LC 2001-16686

A boy adjusts to life away from his home in Hong Kong, in the Chinatown of his new American city

"Extraordinary photo-realistic paintings and spare, free-verse poems bring New York's Chinatown to life in this picture book with appeal to a wide age group." Booklist

Malaspina, Ann

★ **Heart** on fire; Susan B. Anthony votes for president. by Ann Malaspina; illustrated by Steve James. Albert Whitman & Co. 2012 32 p. col. ill. (hardcover) $16.99

Grades: 2 3 4   E

1. Elections 2. Voter registration 3. Women's rights -- History 4. Election law -- New York (State) -- Criminal provisions 5. Trials (Political crimes and offenses) -- New York (State) 6. Women -- Suffrage -- United States -- History -- 19th century

ISBN 080753188X; 9780807531884

LC 2011034179

Author Ann Malaspina tells the story of Susan B. Anthony. "On November 5, 1872, Susan B. Anthony made history--and broke the law--when she voted in the US presidential election, a privilege that had been reserved for men. She was arrested, tried, and found guilty . . . It wasn't until 1920 that women were granted the right to vote, but the civil rights victory would not have been possible without Susan B. Anthony's leadership and passion to stand up for what was right." (Publisher's note)

"Incisive storytelling and luminous oil paintings make for a memorable, important read." SLJ

Includes bibliographical references.

Maloney, Peter

★ **One** foot two feet; an exceptional counting book. [by] Peter Maloney & Felicia Zekauskas. G.P. Putnam's Sons 2011 un il $12.99

Grades: PreK K   E

1. Counting 2. English language -- Grammar

ISBN 978-0-399-25446-8; 0-399-25446-3

LC 2010028172

"Preschoolers will enjoy pointing at the pictures and turning the pages in this simple, interactive counting book that is also a game of wordplay. Along with the numbers, the spreads introduce the vocabulary changes from single to plural nouns. Each brightly colored page has a central cut-out window of a single object, beginning with one foot. Turn the page, and there are two feet. . . . The playful cartoon pictures on thick paper with lots of white space will draw kids with the humorous details." Booklist

Mandel, Peter

Jackhammer Sam; illustrated by David Catrow. Roaring Brook Press 2011 un il $16.99

Grades: PreK K 1 2   E

1. Stories in rhyme 2. Construction workers -- Fiction

ISBN 978-1-59643-034-1; 1-59643-034-6

LC 2010036341

A jackhammer operator boasts about his loud, sidewalk-blasting skills.

"The sing-song text is punctuated by onomatopoeia and nonsense words, and it is as loud and brash as the illustrations or, for that matter, a jackhammer." Horn Book

Manger; edited by Lee Bennett Hopkins; illustrated by Helen Cann. Eerdmans Books for Young Readers 2014 34 p. color illustrations $16

Grades: K 1 2 3   E

1. Children's poetry 2. Christmas -- Poetry 3. Jesus Christ -- Nativity -- Poetry

ISBN 0802854192; 9780802854193

LC 2013044516

This collection of children's poetry, selected by author Lee Bennett Hopkins, focuses on the "legend that describes how, at midnight on Christmas Eve, all creatures are granted the power of speech for one hour. . . . The poems represent a diverse group of animals, but all come together with one singular purpose: celebrating the joy of the miraculous event. This collection of graceful poems provides readers with a Nativity story unlike any other." (Publisher's note)

""What gifts have I / to give / this Child? // No gold, / no frankincense, / no myrrh, / only my quiet / soothing purr." Fourteen poems, each told from the perspective of an animal present at Jesus' birth, are here collected. The poems convey both the majesty and intimacy of that night; decorative mixed-media illustrations highlight each animal on its own double-page spread." Horn Book

Mann, Jennifer K.

Two speckled eggs; Jennifer K. Mann. Candlewick Press 2014 32 p. $14.99

Grades: K 1 2 3   E

1. Birthdays -- Fiction 2. Self-acceptance -- Fiction 3. Eccentrics and eccentricities -- Fiction 4. Birthday parties -- Fiction

ISBN 0763661686; 9780763661687

LC 2013944009

In this book, by Jennifer K. Mann, "it's Ginger's birthday, and she has to invite all the girls in her class to her party, including Lyla Browning. Lyla isn't like the other girls. . . . But . . . Ginger's party doesn't go quite the way she'd hoped. . . . By the time Lyla gives Ginger her present—a tiny homemade nest with two delicious malted-milk eggs—Ginger begins to wonder: is being different really such a bad thing?" (Publisher's note)

"Ginger does not want strange Lyla Browning to come to her birthday party. But when her other friends disrupt Ginger's party plans, she discovers that she and Lyla have some things in common after all. Mann infuses a simple text with humorous details and insights, and her art combines pencil, paint, and digital collage to produce a quietly complex backdrop that echoes the story." Horn Book

Manning, Jane

Millie Fierce Sleeps Out; by Jane Manning. Penguin Group USA 2014 32 p. $16.99

Grades: PreK K 1 2   E

1. Courage -- Fiction 2. Emotions -- Fiction 3. Temper -- Fiction 4. Camping -- Fiction 5. Sleepovers -- Fiction

ISBN 0399160930; 9780399160936

In this children's book, by Jane Manning, "Millie is strong. Millie is fierce. But Millie has learned to keep her fierceness in check. And since she's been sweet all summer long, Millie gets to have a sleepout with her friends. . . . [S]he tries her best to keep her fierceness inside. But when the scary dog from next door howls at the girls' tent, Millie's ferocity saves them all!" (Publisher's note)

"In this follow-up to Millie Fierce, the protagonist hosts a backyard sleepover for her friends. Millie is determined to control her temper and keep herself "fierce-free." She manages to do so until a snarling dog scares her friends (an authorial voice obtrusively ends the narrative with "Sometimes it takes a little ferocity to set things right"). Outdoorsy watercolor illustrations set the scene." Horn Book

Follow up to:

Millie Fierce (2012)

Manning, Maurie

Kitchen dance; by Maurie J. Manning. Clarion Books 2008 un il $16

Grades: PreK K 1   E

1. Dance -- Fiction 2. Bedtime -- Fiction 3. Family life -- Fiction 4. Hispanic Americans -- Fiction

ISBN 978-0-618-99110-5; 0-618-99110-7

LC 2007036838

"Drawn from their beds by noises downstairs, the narrator and her little brother, Tito, peer into the kitchen to find that their parents have turned dinner cleanup into a rambunctious, Latin-flavored song and dance number. . . . As the rounded, sculptural bodies of the couple move about the kitchen with humor and grace, the illustrations take on a cinematic sense of motion and space." Publ Wkly

Manning, Maurie J.

Laundry day; by Maurie J. Manning. Houghton Mifflin Harcourt 2012 40 p.

Grades: K 1 2 3 4   E

1. Scarves 2. Picture books for children 3. City and town life -- Fiction 4. Lost and found possessions -- Fiction 5. New York (N.Y.) -- History -- Fiction 6. Graphic novels 7. Neighborhoods -- Fiction 8. Tenement houses -- Fiction 9. New York (N.Y.) -- History -- 1898-1951 -- Fiction

ISBN 0547241968; 9780547241968

LC 2010043252

This picture book depicts the events of "one windy day [when] a young shoeshine boy makes a world of new friends. Unable to make a sale, he looks up to see a long, bright-red scarf drifting down to him as he sits dejectedly on the curb. The story of his search for the owner is told with dialogue balloons in comic-book style. Text and illustrations are mutually dependent as one panel follows another, moving the story along. . . . [Maurie J.] Manning's . . . detailed digital pencil, watercolor and pastel drawings depict an unnamed but unmistakable turn-of-the-20th-century New York City. Laundry whips in the wind, and busy people on every floor of the buildings are shown from multiple perspectives." (Kirkus)

Mannis, Celeste Davidson

One leaf rides the wind; counting in a Japanese garden. by Celeste Davidson Mannis, pictures by Susan Kathleen Hartung. Viking 2002 un il $15.99; pa $6.99

Grades: PreK K 1 2   E

1. Haiku 2. Counting 3. Gardens -- Poetry

ISBN 0-670-03525-4; 0-14-240195-1 pa

LC 2002-1024

In this collection of haiku poems, a young girl walks through a Japanese garden and discovers many delights, from one leaf to ten stone lanterns. Includes notes about Japanese religion and philosophy

"The book as a whole is elegantly and respectfully presented and the counting aspect is especially well crafted, capturing the meandering focus of a small child. Mannis's simple verses are complemented by Hartung's pleasing and evocative pen-and-ink and watercolor art." SLJ

Manushkin, Fran

The **belly** book; illustrated by Dan Yaccarino. Feiwel and Friends 2011 il $16.99

Grades: PreK K   E

1. Stories in rhyme 2. Abdomen

ISBN 978-0-312-64958-6; 0-312-64958-4

"A meditation on the middle for beginning readers and younger listeners supports some appealingly merry illustrations. Manushkin's rhyming text is an invitation to a general celebration of abdomens—readers' own or other peoples', and occasionally those of beasts and birds. . . . The art. . . is the real treat here, Yaccarino's clever, energetic, lighthearted illustration. . . . His playful full-page gouaches zip nimbly from thought to thought and invest the whole with a generous dollop of whimsy." Kirkus

How Mama brought the spring; [by] Fran Manushkin; illustrated by Holly Berry. Dutton 2008 un il $16.99

Grades: K 1 2 3   E

1. Russia -- Fiction 2. Spring -- Fiction 3. Cooking -- Fiction 4. Family life -- Fiction

ISBN 978-0-525-42027-9; 0-525-42027-4

LC 2007-05217

A mother in Chicago tells her daughter how Grandma used to make a special surprise on the freezing cold winter mornings in Belarus—so special that it seemed to bring spring with it.

"This tale is filled with rich language and imagery. The illustrations fill the page with great detail and show images of the Russian culture. A recipe for cheese blintzes is included. This book would be a great addition." Libr Media Connect

★ The **Shivers** in the fridge; illustrated by Paul O. Zelinsky. Dutton Children's Books 2006 un il $16.99

Grades: PreK K 1 2   E

1. Magnets -- Fiction 2. Refrigeration -- Fiction

ISBN 0-525-46943-5

LC 2006-03867

One-by-one, the members of the Shivers family disappear from the inside of their chilly refrigerator home

"The story's humor is matched by Zelinsky's inventive artwork, which picks up on the wit and slyness of the text." Booklist

Marceau, Fani

★ **Panorama**; a foldout book. [illustrated by] Joëlle Jolivet. Abrams Books for Young Readers 2009 un il $19.95

Grades: 1 2 3   E

1. Travel -- Fiction 2. Voyages around the world -- Fiction

ISBN 978-0-8109-8332-8; 0-8109-8332-X

LC 2008022166

Original French edition 2007

Illustrations and simple text invite the reader to visit different places around the world, then to view the same scenes at night on the reverse of the fanfolded page.

This is a "stunning travelogue. . . . Each oversize page is grounded by a poetic fragment evoking each locale. . . . A faint ecological bent further enriches the descriptions. But the main event is the alternately dizzying and mysterious black-and-white woodcut illustrations. They can be flipped through like an ordinary book, though the full impact is felt only through unfurling all 15 pages so that they lay flat in a seamless panorama." Booklist

Marcellino, Fred

I, crocodile. HarperCollins Pubs. 1999 un il hardcover o.p. pa $6.99

Grades: 1 2 3 4   E

  1. Emperors 2. Crocodiles -- Fiction

  ISBN 0-06-205168-7; 0-06-008859-1 pa

"The text is reportorial in tone, a perfect complement to the extravagant, expressive illustrations. . . . A sophisticated picture book, this is one publication with appeal to many different audiences." Horn Book

Marciano, John Bemelmans

Madeline at the White House; story and pictures by John Bemelmans Marciano. Viking Children's Books 2011 un il $17.99

Grades: PreK K 1   E

  1. Stories in rhyme 2. Easter -- Fiction 3. Orphans -- Fiction 4. Presidents -- Fiction 5. Washington (D.C.) -- Fiction

  ISBN 978-0-670-01228-2; 0-670-01228-9

                        LC 2010025110

Madeline and the other orphans of the vine-covered house in Paris spend Easter at the White House visiting with the President's daughter.

"Based on an idea Bemelmans was working on at the time of his 1962 death, grandson Marciano has done a credible job copying the rhythms and artistic style of the originals." Booklist

Marcus, Kimberly

Scritch-scratch a perfect match; illustrated by Mike Lester. G.P. Putnam's Sons 2011 un il $16.99

Grades: PreK K   E

  1. Stories in rhyme 2. Dogs -- Fiction 3. Fleas -- Fiction

  ISBN 978-0-399-25004-0; 0-399-25004-2

                        LC 2008-30482

When a flea lands on a stray dog, it starts a chain of events that ends with the dog happily adopted by a pet-loving man.

"Abundant motion lines, copious scrawled hatch and crosshatch details, and heaps of sly character humor . . . all work together to support the playful text. Those who like their friendship tales with a touch of chaos will gladly take a bite out of this mischievous offering." Bull Cent Child Books

Mariconda, Barbara

Sort it out! illustrated by Sherry Rogers. Sylvan Dell 2008 un il $16.95; pa $8.95

Grades: PreK K 1 2   E

  1. Rats -- Fiction 2. Collectors and collecting -- Fiction

  ISBN 978-1-934359-11-2; 1-934359-11-4; 978-1-934359-32-7 pa; 1-934359-32-7 pa

"When Pack rat comes home with a cart full of stuff— a locket, a book, an umbrella, a pinecone, and many more

random items—his mother admonishes him to sort it all out and put it away. Packy does just that, cleverly sorting things with like characteristics such as where they're found, their color, shape, etc. . . . The illustrations are brightly colored, large, and very clear. Careful readers will notice a subplot in the pictures and find satisfaction in seeing its resolution on the final page. In addition, the rhyming text prompts them to guess the word that defines each collection. Back matter has activities to extend the experience." SLJ

Ten for me; illustrated by Sherry Rogers. Sylvan Dell 2011 il $16.95; pa $8.95

Grades: 2 3 4   E

  1. Stories in rhyme 2. Butterflies -- Fiction 3. Mathematics -- Fiction

  ISBN 978-1-60718-074-6; 1-60718-074-X; 978-1-60718-085-2 pa; 1-60718-085-5 pa

"Rose and Ed learn much more than expected on their butterfly hunt. . . . Each day is seen as a double-page spread of the duo hunting in field and garden. As Rose's totals grow, Ed's shrink. The totals in the text are mirrored in a tally of 'Butterflies Captured and Released' in the illustrations. . . . An excellent rhyming tale that doubles as math lesson and triples as a butterfly-biology primer." Kirkus

Marino, Gianna

Following Papa's song; by Gianna Marino. Viking, published by Penguin Group 2014 40 p. (hardback) $16.99

Grades: PreK K   E

  1. Whales -- Fiction 2. Humpback whale -- Fiction 3. Father and child -- Fiction 4. Animals -- Migration -- Fiction

  ISBN 0670013153; 9780670013159

                        LC 2013024213

"Two whales swim together through the big ocean," in this children's book by Gianna Marino. "Little Blue has many questions for Papa, especially ones about the long migration. How will they know the way? Will he be able to keep up? What will they see along the way? Papa has answers for all these questions, but Little Blue remains curious as they begin their journey." (Publisher's note)

"Little Blue, a young humpback whale, is worried about his first long migration up the coast, and he is scared he will be separated from Papa in the big ocean. As with human families on adventures, Little Blue has many questions that need to be answered and needs to be reassured that everything will be fine...This is a story for all ages to enjoy. What a wonderful way to use science in the lower grades. A top choice for any library." SLJ

Meet me at the moon; by Gianna Marino. Viking 2012 40p. illustrations (hardcover) $16.99

Grades: PreK K   E

  1. Elephants -- Fiction 2. Picture books for children 3. Mother-child relationship -- Fiction 4. Africa -- Fiction 5. Drought -- Fiction 6. Separation (Psychology) -- Fiction

  ISBN 9780670013135

                        LC 2011013210

A "mother elephant tells her Little One that she must leave and 'climb the highest mountain to ask the skies for rain.' 'What if I can't hear you, Mama?' Little One asks. 'Listen for my sound on the wind,' she answers. . . . When rain finally arrives but Mama doesn't return, Little One is bereft until he remembers to 'sing the calling song' that brings her back." (Publishers Weekly)

"Marino impresses with her lyrical language, conveying it in a perfect tone to allay young readers' feelings of separation anxiety. The textured mixed-media art paired with the flowing text elevates this title above most missing-mama fare." Kirkus

One too many; a seek & find counting book. Chronicle Books 2010 un il
Grades: PreK K 1 2   E
    1. Counting 2. Animals -- Fiction
    ISBN 0-8118-6908-3; 978-0-8118-6908-9

Children count from one jumping flea to twelve frisky animals until, at last, they reach one too many.

"Marino's naturalistic illustrations are done in gouache in this remarkable counting book. . . . Young readers will find much to discover as they revisit the book time after time." SLJ

Markes, Julie
    Good thing you're not an octopus! story by Julie Markes; pictures by Maggie Smith. HarperCollins Pubs. 2001 un il $14.95; pa $6.99
Grades: PreK K   E
    1. Animals -- Fiction
    ISBN 0-06-028465-X; 0-06-443586-5 pa
                                                                          LC 99-37139

"A boy who complains about getting dressed, riding in his car seat, and more is answered with funny worst-case scenarios: 'You don't like to take a nap? It's a good thing you're not a bear. If you were a bear, you would have to nap all winter long!' The tone is silly, and the cheerful illustrations convey the absurdity in the text." Horn Book Guide

    Shhhhh! Everybody's sleeping; illustrated by David Parkins. HarperCollins 2005 un il $14.99; lib bdg $15.89
Grades: PreK K 1   E
    1. Stories in rhyme 2. Sleep -- Fiction 3. Bedtime -- Fiction
    ISBN 0-06-053790-6; 0-06-053791-4 lib bdg
                                                                          LC 2003-27854

A young child is encouraged to go to sleep by the thought of everyone else sleeping, from teacher to baker to postman

"The text satisfyingly moves along while the artwork soars. . . . Glowing with warm colors in subdued hues, the sturdy pictures stretch wide across double-page spreads, offering surprisingly energetic, varied compositions." Booklist

Markle, Sandra, 1946-
    Butterfly tree; written by Sandra Markle; illustrated by Leslie Wu. Peachtree 2010 32 p. ill.
Grades: K 1 2   E
    1. Clouds -- Fiction 2. Monarch butterflies 3. Lake Erie -- Fiction 4. Butterflies -- Fiction 5. Picture books for children
    ISBN 1561455393; 9781561455393
                                                                          LC 2009040526

In this picture book, "[a] black rain that becomes a mysterious orange cloud over Lake Erie is the beginning for of a magical encounter with monarch butterflies for Jilly, her dog, Fudge, and her mother. Veteran nature-writer [Sandra] Markle . . . offers a gentle free-verse narrative based on a never-to-be-forgotten experience from her own Ohio child-

hood. . . . At first, Jilly is worried, hesitant about following the cloud into the woods with her mother, wanting to turn back. [In illustrator Leslie] Wu's hazy pastel paintings . . . the monarchs explode from the tree where they were resting and Jilly realizes what they are. . . . Author's notes, a map showing monarch migration and a list of books and websites for further exploration add . . . information." (Kirkus)

"What looks dark and indistinct closeup shows surprisingly well at a distance; the text reads aloud smoothly, suiting this especially well for use with a group. Author's notes, a map showing monarch migration and a list of books and websites for further exploration add helpful information. Even collections with many monarch titles will want to add this one for its masterful evocation of a child's sense of wonder at the natural world." Kirkus

Includes bibliographical references

★ **Family** pack; illustrated by Alan Marks. Charlesbridge 2011 un il lib bdg $15.95
Grades: K 1 2 3   E
    1. Wolves -- Fiction 2. Yellowstone National Park -- Fiction
    ISBN 978-1-58089-217-9 lib bdg; 1-58089-217-5 lib bdg
                                                                          LC 2010-07548

A young wolf, taken from her pack in Canada to Yellowstone National Park, struggles alone to master the skills of hunting and survival until she finds a lone male and begins a new pack with him.

"Without a hint of anthropomorphism but with vivid, poetic language, [Markle] shows readers the wolves bound only by nature. . . . The illustrator's watercolors add drama and energy. . . . An excellent story for wolf-lovers and a welcome addition to elementary-school science shelves." Kirkus

    Race the wild wind; a story of the Sable Island horses. Sandra Markle; paintings by by Layne Johnson. Walker 2011 1 v. (unpaged) $17.99
Grades: K 1 2 3   E
    1. Horses -- Fiction 2. Nova Scotia -- Fiction 3. Wild horses -- Fiction 4. Sable Island (N.S.) -- fiction
    ISBN 978-0-8027-9766-7; 0-8027-9766-0; 9780802797667; 9780802797674
                                                                          LC 2010036013

"After being lowered into the frigid Atlantic by a schooner, a young stallion and his equine companions swim to Sable Island in this poetic tale that imagines how wild horses first came to live on this isolated island off of Nova Scotia. . . . Dramatic oil spreads depict his survival and transformation from domestic to wild horse amid this beautiful yet harsh environment." Booklist

Includes bibliographical references

    Snow school; Sandra Markle; illustrated by Alan Marks. Charlesbridge 2013 32 p. (reinforced) $16.95
Grades: PreK K 1 2   E
    1. Snow leopard 2. Animal behavior 3. Learning in animals 4. Snow leopard -- Infancy
    ISBN 1580894100; 9781580894104
                                                                          LC 2012000790

In this children's book, by Sandra Markle, illustrated by Alan Marks, "readers are introduced to twin snow leopard cubs and their mother from the Hindu Kush mountains of Pakistan. . . . Text and . . . watercolor illustrations lead readers through the struggles these snow leopards face from finding food to bearing harsh weather conditions and the lessons the young cubs learn as they prepare for a life on their own, out from underneath the watchful, caring eye of their mother." (Publisher's note)

Includes bibliographical references

What If You Had Animal Teeth? by Sandra Markle; illustrated by Howard McWilliam. Scholastic 2013 32 p. ill. (paperback) $3.99

Grades: K 1 2   E
1. Teeth 2. Comparative anatomy
ISBN 0545484383; 9780545484381

In this book by Sandra Markle, readers "explore what it would be like if their own front teeth were replaced by those of a different animal. Featuring a dozen animals (beaver, great white shark, narwhal, elephant, rattlesnake, naked mole rat, hippopotamus, crocodile, and more), this book explores how different teeth are especially adapted for an animal's survival. At the end of the book, children will discover why their own teeth are just right for them." (Publisher's note)

Marko, Cyndi
Let's get cracking! by Cyndi Marko. Branches Scholastic Inc. 2014 80 p. (Kung Pow Chicken) (hardcover) $15.99

Grades: 1 2 3   E
1. Humorous stories 2. Cookies -- Fiction 3. Chickens -- Fiction 4. Superheroes -- Fiction
ISBN 0545610621; 9780545610612; 9780545610629
LC 2013018130

In this book, by Cyndi Marko, "Gordon Blue transforms into Kung Pow Chicken, an avian superhero who fights crime in the city of Fowladelphia. The first book in the series kicks off when Gordon's birdy senses lead him to a festival. Suddenly, POOF! Feathers fill the air and shivering naked chickens are everywhere. Why have all these chickens lost their feathers? Forced to wear wooly sweaters, the city itches for a hero. Kung Pow Chicken hops into his Beakmobile to save the day!" (Publisher's note)

Marlow, Layn
★ **Hurry** up and slow down; [by] Layn Marlow. Holiday House 2009 un il $16.95

Grades: PreK K 1   E
1. Bedtime -- Fiction 2. Rabbits -- Fiction 3. Turtles -- Fiction 4. Books and reading -- Fiction
ISBN 978-0-8234-2178-7; 0-8234-2178-3
LC 2008010796

First published 2008 in the United Kingdom

Hare likes to hurry through the day, unlike Tortoise, but manages to slow down for his favorite bedtime story

"This delightful spinoff of 'The Tortoise and the Hare' follows a typical day in the lives of these two friends. . . . The illustrations of Hare, Tortoise, their animal companions, and their environment are rounded and softly colored, creating a comforting world for young children. An endearing story that will no doubt become a bedtime favorite." SLJ

Marsalis, Wynton, 1961-
Squeak! rumble! whomp! whomp! whomp! a sonic adventure. Wynton Marsalis; illustrated by Paul Rogers. Candlewick 2012 40 p. (hardback) $15.99

Grades: PreK K 1   E
1. Music -- Fiction 2. Sound -- Fiction 3. Neighborhoods -- Fiction
ISBN 9780763639914; 0763639915
LC 2011048367

This children's book, by Wynton Marsalis, illustrated by Paul Rogers, explores various sounds in everyday life in a neighborhood. "What's that sound? The back door squeeeaks open, sounding like a noisy mouse nearby--eeek, eeeek, eeeek! Big trucks on the highway rrrrrrrumble, just as hunger makes a tummy grrrrumble." (Publisher's note)

Marshall, Edward
★ **Fox** and his friends; pictures by James Marshall. Dial Bks. for Young Readers 1982 56p il (Dial easy-to-read) hardcover o.p. pa $3.99

Grades: K 1 2   E
1. Foxes -- Fiction
ISBN 0-14-037007-2 pa
LC 81-68769

"The sibling exchanges and situations are comically true to life. . . . The red, green and black illustrations . . . pick the story up and add character embellishment and humor." SLJ

Other titles about Fox are:
Fox in love (1982)
Fox on wheels (1983)
Fox at school (1983)
Fox all week (1984)
Foc on the job (1988)
Fox be nimble (1990)
Fox outfoxed (1992)
Fox on stage (1993)

★ **Space** case; pictures by James Marshall. Dial Bks. for Young Readers 1980 un il hardcover o.p. pa $6.99

Grades: PreK K 1 2   E
1. Science fiction 2. Halloween -- Fiction
ISBN 0-8037-8005-2; 0-14-054704-5 pa
LC 80-13369

"The open ending of the brief story is as satisfying as it is original, for the small space traveler is thoroughly childlike in its insouciance, curiosity, and concern for self-gratification. The text is an economical, tongue-in-cheek accompaniment to the various levels of humor depicted in the illustrations." Horn Book

Three by the sea; pictures by James Marshall. Dial Bks. for Young Readers 1981 48p il (Dial easy-to-read) hardcover o.p. pa $3.99

Grades: K 1 2   E
1. Storytelling -- Fiction
ISBN 0-14-037004-8 pa

"The mild lunacy of the illustrations (an almost vertical hill, a neatly striped cat) with their ungainly, comical figures is nicely matched with the bland directness of the writing. This is good-humored and amusing." Bull Cent Child Books

Other titles about Spider, Sam, and Lolly are:
Four on the shore (1985)
Three up a tree (1986)

Marshall, James

Fox be nimble; written and illustrated by James Marshall. Dial Books for Young Readers 1990 48p il (Dial easy-to-read) hardcover o.p. pa $3.99

Grades: K 1 2   E

1. Foxes -- Fiction

ISBN 0-8037-0760-6; 0-8037-0761-4 lib bdg; 0-14-036842-6 pa

LC 89-7933

Fox babysits for the miserable Ling children, makes a big scene when he slips on a skate and hurts himself, and gets to lead the band in the big parade

"Marshall's wit is evidenced through the antics of all his zany characters. Without using difficult words, he extends new readers' understanding of the text through his bright, colorful, and very funny watercolors." SLJ

Fox on stage. Dial Books for Young Readers 1993 48p il (Dial easy-to-read) hardcover o.p. pa $3.99

Grades: K 1 2   E

1. Foxes -- Fiction

ISBN 0-8037-1356-8; 0-8037-1357-6 lib bdg; 0-14-038032-9 pa

LC 91-46740

Fox makes a film for Grannie, takes part in a magic show, and puts on a play

"The hilarious volume is all that a beginning reader should be—accessible, enjoyable, and flawlessly written and illustrated." Horn Book

Fox on the job. Dial Books for Young Readers 1988 48p il (Dial easy-to-read) hardcover o.p. pa $3.99

Grades: K 1 2   E

1. Foxes -- Fiction

ISBN 0-8037-0350-3; 0-8037-0351-1 lib bdg; 0-14-037602-X pa

LC 87-15589

Fox tries to earn the money for a new bicycle in several different jobs.

"This book is populated with Marshall's typically amusing animal characters. The watercolor illustrations aid readers in understanding Fox's business attempts." SLJ

Fox outfoxed. Dial Bks. for Young Readers 1992 48p il (Dial easy-to-read) hardcover o.p. pa $3.99

Grades: K 1 2   E

1. Foxes -- Fiction

ISBN 0-8037-1036-4; 0-8037-1037-2 lib bdg; 0-14-038113-9 pa

LC 91-21815

Fox competes in a big race, gives away his comic books, and goes trick-or-treating on Halloween with his friends

"With its straightforward plot and dialogue, Marshall's text is just right for new readers. Most of the humor comes from the delightful pen-and-ink and watercolor illustrations—great facial expressions (appearing so simply created with lines and dots) and often funny poses of characters." SLJ

★ George and Martha; written and illustrated by James Marshall. Houghton Mifflin 1972 46p il lib bdg $16; pa $6.95

Grades: PreK K 1 2   E

1. Friendship -- Fiction 2. Hippopotamus -- Fiction

ISBN 0-395-16619-5 lib bdg; 0-395-19972-7 pa

In these five short episodes which include a misunderstanding about split pea soup, invasion of privacy and a crisis over a missing tooth, two not very delicate hippopotamuses reveal various aspects of friendship

"The pale pictures of these creatures and their adventures—in yellows, pinks, greens, and grays—capture the directness and humor of the stories." Horn Book

Other titles about George and Martha are:

George and Martha back in town (1984)

George and Martha encore (1973)

George and Martha, one fine day (1978)

George and Martha rise and shine (1976)

George and Martha round and round (1988)

George and Martha, tons of fun (1980)

★ Swine Lake; [pictures by] Maurice Sendak. HarperCollins Pubs. 1999 un il $16.95

Grades: PreK K 1 2   E

1. Pigs -- Fiction 2. Ballet -- Fiction 3. Wolves -- Fiction

ISBN 0-06-205171-7

LC 98-73253

A hungry wolf attends a performance of Swine Lake, performed by the Boarshoi Ballet, intending to eat the performers, but he is so entranced by the story unfolding that he forgets about his meal

"Both Marshall and Sendak are cleverly comic here . . . the text shines. Sendak's art captures the nuance as well as all the humor of the story." Booklist

Marshall, Linda Elovitz

Talia and the rude vegetables; illustrated by Francesca Assirelli. Kar-Ben 2011 un il lib bdg $16.95

Grades: PreK K 1 2   E

1. Jews -- Fiction 2. Gardening -- Fiction 3. Vegetables -- Fiction 4. Rosh ha-Shanah -- Fiction

ISBN 978-0-7613-5217-4; 0-7613-5217-1

LC 2010020301

City-girl Talia misunderstands her grandmother's request that she go to the garden for "root vegetables" for a Rosh Hashanah stew but manages to find some she thinks are rude, as well as a good use for the rest she harvests. Includes a recipe for Rude Vegetable Stew.

"This laugh-out-loud title keeps the little jokes coming. . . . Quirky, cool-palette color illustrations by Italian artist Assirelli perfectly convey the whimsical narrative." Publ Wkly

Marshall, Natalie

Colors; Natalie Marshall. Little Brown & Co 2013 12 p. color illustrations (My turn to learn) $6.99

Grades: PreK   E

1. Color 2. Picture books for children

ISBN 0316251631; 9780316251631

LC 2012953594

Written by Natalie Marshall and part of the My Turn to Learn series, in this book "The tabbed edges and thick, strong pages make it easy for young readers to flip through the book by themselves, revealing fun, colorful answers on every spread." It offers "an interactive reading and learning experience that can withstand even the most 'hands-on' readers." (Publisher's note)

"Marshall's illustrations are a friendly jumble of clean lines and mixed textures, and the tabs are tailor-made for little fingers to help turn pages." Pub Wkly

My turn to learn opposites; Natalie Marshall. Little, Brown and Co. 2013 12 p. color illustrations (My turn to learn) $6.99
Grades: PreK   E
1. Opposites 2. Toy and movable books
ISBN 0316251658; 9780316251655
LC 2012953392

In this book, part of the My Turn To Learn series, by Natalie Marshall, children can "explore the exciting world of numbers, brought to life through this . . . tabbed board book." The book aims to "teach early counting concepts." It is an "interactive reading and learning experience." (Publisher's note)

My turn to learn shapes; Natalie Marshall. Little, Brown and Co. 2013 12 p. col. ill. (My turn to learn) $6.99
Grades: PreK   E
1. Shape
ISBN 0316251666; 9780316251662
LC 2012953593

In this book, part of the My Turn To Learn series, by Natalie Marshall, children can "explore the exciting world of numbers, brought to life through this . . . tabbed board book." The book aims to "teach early counting concepts." It is an "interactive reading and learning experience." (Publisher's note)

Numbers; Natalie Marshall. Little Brown & Co 2013 12 p. $6.99
Grades: PreK   E
1. Numbers 2. Counting 3. Children's literature
ISBN 031625164X; 9780316251648
LC 2012953545

Written by Natalie Marshall and part of the My Turn to Learn series, this book "uses simple, colorful images and bold, lively scenes to teach early counting concepts. The tabbed edges and thick, strong pages make it easy for young readers to flip through the book by themselves, revealing fun, colorful answers on every spread." (Publisher's note)

Martin, Amy

Symphony city; written and illustrated by Amy Martin. McSweeney's 2011 un il $17.95
Grades: 2 3 4 5   E
1. Music -- Fiction 2. Sounds -- Fiction 3. City and town life -- Fiction
ISBN 978-1-936365-39-5; 1-936365-39-1

A young girl, lost in a big city, makes her way home by following the rich and vibrant music of the streets.

"The story is told visually through the gradual outpouring of color; the division of space in surprising vertical and horizontal lines, with cityscape backgrounds like blueprints; and colors layered as if silk-screened. . . . The economical text is a paean to music. . . . Craftsmanship reigns in this title. A flock of birds embossed in gold flies from the back to the front of the textured orange binding, and the jacket folds out into a two-sided poster. A perfect book for music lovers and bibliophiles." SLJ

Martin, Bill

Baby Bear, Baby Bear, what do you see? by Bill Martin, Jr.; pictures by Eric Carle. Henry Holt & Co. 2007 un il $16.95; My first reader ed. $8.99
Grades: PreK K   E
1. Stories in rhyme 2. Bears -- Fiction 3. Animals -- Fiction
ISBN 978-0-8050-8336-1; 0-8050-8336-7; 978-0-8050-9291-2 My first reader ed.
LC 2006037769

Written by Bill Martin and illustrated by Eric Carle, part of the Brown Bear and Friends series, "'Baby Bear, Baby Bear, What Do You See?' is the final collaboration from this bestselling author-illustrator team. Young readers will enjoy Baby Bear's quest to find Mama, and they'll revel in identifying each of the native North American animals that appear along the way. The central focus on the special bond between mama and baby makes a fitting finale to a beloved series." (Publisher's note)

"Creative action words and renderings of the various creatures in motion give the book a pleasing energy, while Mama Bear's obvious delight at finding her cub provides an endearing poignancy. [An] elegant balance of art, text, emotion and exposition." Publ Wkly

Barn dance! by Bill Martin, Jr. and John Archambault; illustrated by Ted Rand. Holt & Co. 1986 un il $16.95; pa $6.95
Grades: PreK K 1 2   E
1. Stories in rhyme 2. Dance -- Fiction 3. Country life -- Fiction
ISBN 0-8050-0089-5; 0-8050-0799-7 pa
LC 86-14225

Unable to sleep on the night of a full moon, a young boy follows the sound of music across the fields and finds an unusual barn dance in progress

"The bouncy rhyme will be a pleasure for listeners and tellers as they pick up the twang and the barn-dance beat. Rand's raucous two-page watercolor spreads are as spirited as the story poem." Booklist

★ A **beasty** story; [written by] Bill Martin, Jr. & [illustrated by] Steven Kellogg. Harcourt Brace & Co. 1999 un il $16; pa $7
Grades: PreK K 1 2   E
1. Stories in rhyme 2. Mice -- Fiction 3. Color -- Fiction
ISBN 0-15-201683-X; 0-15-216560-6 pa
LC 97-49519

A group of mice venture into a dark, dark woods where they find a dark brown house with a dark red stair leading past other dark colors to a spooky surprise

"A rhymed narrative tells the story along the top of the pages, with the mice commenting in rhymed conversation as they move through the adventure. The silly resolution will appeal to young children. . . . Kellogg's lively ink-and-watercolor art strikes just the right note for the gently suspenseful story." Booklist

★ **Brown** bear, brown bear what do you see? pictures by Eric Carle. Holt & Co. 1992 un il $16.99; bd bk $7.95; $8.99

Grades: PreK K   E

1. Stories in rhyme 2. Color -- Fiction 3. Animals
-- Fiction

ISBN 0-8050-1744-5; 0-8050-4790-5 bd bk; 978-0-
8050-9244-8 My first reader ed.; 0-8050-9244-7 My
first reader ed.

LC 91-29115

A newly illustrated edition of the title first published
1967 by Holt, Rinehart & Winston

A chant in which a variety of animals, each one a different color, answers the question, "What do you see?"

"Carle's large, brilliantly colored animals set against a
white background make the book perfect for sharing with
a group of preschoolers, while Martin's repetitious text
is eminently chantable—a boon for beginning readers."
Horn Book

★ **Chicka** chicka 1, 2, 3; [by] Bill Martin, Jr. & Michael Sampson; illustrated by Lois Ehlert. Simon & Schuster Books for Young Readers 2004 un il $15.95

Grades: PreK K 1   E

1. Counting 2. Stories in rhyme

ISBN 0-689-85881-7

LC 2003-19106

Numbers from one to one hundred climb to the top of an
apple tree in this rhyming chant.

"The chanting rhyme and eye-popping images have a
contagious energy youngsters will find irresistible." Booklist

★ **Chicka** chicka boom boom; [by] Bill Martin, Jr. and
John Archambault; illustrated by Lois Ehlert. anniversary
edition; Beach Lane Books 2009 un il $17.99 E

1. Alphabet 2. Stories in rhyme

ISBN 978-1-4169-9091-8; 1-4169-9091-7

LC 2009-626

A reissue of the title first published 1989

An alphabet rhyme/chant that relates what happens
when the whole alphabet tries to climb a coconut tree.

"Ehlert's illustrations-bold, colorful shapes-are contained by broad polka-dotted borders, like a proscenium
arch through which the action explodes. Tongue-tingling,
visually stimulating, with an insistent repetitive chorus of
'chicka chicka boom boom,' the book demands to be read
again and again and again." Horn Book

★ The **ghost**-eye tree; by Bill Martin, Jr. and John
Archambault; illustrated by Ted Rand. Holt & Co. 1985 un
il $16.95; pa $6.95

Grades: K 1 2 3   E

1. Ghost stories 2. Fear -- Fiction

ISBN 0-8050-0208-1; 0-8050-0947-7 pa

LC 85-8422

"On a dark and ghostly night a brother and sister are sent
to fetch a pail of milk from the other end of town. They must
pass the fearful ghost-eye tree, old and horribly twisted,
looking like a monster, with a gap in the branches where the
moon shines through like an eye. . . . The story is rhythmically told, sometimes rhyming, always moving ahead, sharp
with the affectionate teasing of the brother and sister. The realistic watercolor illustrations are superb—strong, striking,
very dark, with highlights of moonlight and lantern light that

cast a spooky, scary spell. A splendidly theatrical book for
storytelling and reading aloud." Horn Book

Kitty cat, kitty cat, are you going to sleep? by Bill Martin Jr. and Michael Sampson; illustrated by Laura J. Bryant.
Marshall Cavendish Children's 2011 un il $15.99

Grades: PreK K   E

1. Stories in rhyme 2. Cats -- Fiction 3. Bedtime
-- Fiction

ISBN 978-0-7614-5946-0; 0-7614-5946-4

LC 2010025274

A young cat is distracted by many things while getting
ready for bed at night.

"A simple rhyming exchange alternates between parent
and child as it playfully follows the usual bedtime routine
and stall tactics. . . . Adorable colored pencil and watercolor
illustrations support the conversation and take Kitty from
wide awake to sleeping sooo tight. The soft palette and simple details have the perfect calming effect." SLJ

Kitty Cat, Kitty Cat, are you waking up? by Bill Martin
Jr. & Michael Sampson; illustrated by Laura J. Bryant. Marshall Cavendish 2008 un il $14.99

Grades: PreK K 1   E

1. Stories in rhyme 2. Cats -- Fiction

ISBN 978-0-7614-5438-0; 0-7614-5438-1

LC 2007041987

Kitty Cat is distracted by many things as she gets ready
for school in the morning

This is a "delightfully comic rhyming book.. . . . A tiny
mouse serves as an interested observer in each watercolor,
until he becomes prey, and then a very relieved escapee, as
the kitten is finally swept off to school." Booklist

★ **Knots** on a counting rope; by Bill Martin, Jr. and
John Archambault; illustrated by Ted Rand. Holt & Co.
1987 un il $16.95; pa $6.95

Grades: K 1 2 3   E

1. Blind -- Fiction 2. Grandfathers -- Fiction 3. Native
Americans -- Fiction

ISBN 0-8050-0571-4; 0-8050-5479-0 pa

LC 87-14858

A different version of the title illustrated by Joe Smith
was published in 1966

"The powerful spare poetic text is done full justice by
Rand's fine full-color illustrations, which capture both the
drama and brilliance of vast southwestern space and the intimacy of starlit camp-fire scenes." Booklist

Panda bear, panda bear, what do you see? by Bill Martin Jr.; pictures by Eric Carle. Henry Holt & Co. 2003 un il
$15.95; bd bk $7.95; My first reader ed. $8.99

Grades: PreK K   E

1. Stories in rhyme 2. Animals -- Fiction 3. Endangered
species -- Fiction

ISBN 0-8050-1758-5; 0-8050-8078-3 bd bk; 978-0-
8050-9292-9 My first reader ed.

LC 2002-10855

In this board book in the Bear series, "A Bald Eagle
soars, a Spider Monkey swings, a Macaroni Penguin struts,
and a Red Wolf sneaks through [author] Bill Martin Jr's
rhythmic text and [illustrator] Eric Carle's vibrant images,

and all are watched over by our best hope for the future--a dreaming child." (Publisher's note)

"The pictures, featuring animals strolling, splashing, and soaring, are brilliant lessons in the application of color, shape, form, and texture. . . . A fine read-aloud with a subtle, yet clear, message." Booklist

Polar bear, polar bear, what do you hear? by Bill Martin, Jr.; pictures by Eric Carle. Holt & Co. 1991 un il $16.95; bd bk $7.95
Grades: PreK K E
1. Stories in rhyme 2. Animals -- Fiction
ISBN 0-8050-1759-3; 0-8050-5388-3 bd bk
LC 91-13322

Zoo animals from polar bear to walrus make their distinctive sounds for each other, while children imitate the sounds for the zookeeper

"Carle's characteristically inventive, jewel-toned artwork forms a seamless succession of images that fairly leap off the pages." Publ Wkly

★ **Ten** little caterpillars; [by] Bill Martin Jr.; illustrated by Lois Ehlert. Beach Lane Books 2011 40p il
Grades: PreK K E
1. Stories in rhyme 2. Caterpillars -- Fiction
ISBN 1-4424-3385-X; 978-1-4424-3385-4
LC 2011002156

A newly illustrated edition of the title first published 1967

Illustrations and rhyming text follow ten caterpillars as one wriggles up a flower stem, another sails across a garden pool, and one reaches an apple leaf, where something amazing happens.

"Martin's caterpillar counting rhyme has been given new life with gorgeous and bold watercolor collages from . . . Ehlert. . . . This is a graphically sumptuously book, but the lesson is clear: nature is one tough town." Publ Wkly

★ **Trick** or treat? [by] Bill Martin, Jr. and Michael Sampson; illustrated by Paul Meisel. Simon & Schuster Bks. for Young Readers 2002 un il hardcover o.p. pa $6.99
Grades: PreK K 1 2 E
1. Magic -- Fiction 2. Halloween -- Fiction
ISBN 0-689-84968-0; 1-4169-0262-7 pa
LC 2002-70646

A child has a wonderful time collecting treats from the wacky neighbors until Magic Merlin decides that a trick would be more fun

"Meisel's cartoon illustrations take full advantage of the topsy-turvy story, adding lots of comic holiday detail to keep little ones alert. The fun is in the pictures, and the challenge is in figuring out the visual joke and the backward names." Booklist

Martin, David
Christmas tree; illustrated by Melissa Sweet. Candlewick Press 2009 un il bd bk $5.99
Grades: PreK E
1. Board books for children 2. Trees -- Fiction 3. Christmas -- Fiction
ISBN 978-0-7636-3030-0 bd bk; 0-7636-3030-6 bd bk

At Christmastime, a tree from the outside comes inside, just waiting to be decorated

This "attractive board [book features] simple, [a] clear [concept] and delightful pencil-and-watercolor illustrations enhanced with patterned fabric swatches." SLJ

Hanukkah lights; illustrated by Melissa Sweet. Candlewick Press 2009 un il bd bk $5.99
Grades: PreK E
1. Board books for children 2. Hanukkah -- Fiction
ISBN 978-0-7636-3029-4 bd bk; 0-7636-3029-2 bd bk

Children celebrate Hanukkah by lighting candles, eating latkes, spinning a dreidel, and giving presents

This "attractive board [book features] simple, clear concepts and delightful pencil-and-watercolor illustrations enhanced with patterned fabric swatches." SLJ

Peep and Ducky; David Martin, illustrated by David Walker. Candlewick Press 2013 32 p. (reinforced) $14.99
Grades: PreK K E
1. Stories in rhyme 2. Play -- Fiction 3. Friendship -- Fiction
ISBN 0763650390; 9780763650391
LC 2012942391

In this children's book, by David Martin, illustrated by David Walker, "when Peep goes to the playground with his mommy and runs into Ducky and his daddy, the result is definitely lucky. In . . . rhyming verse, the two encounter the usual highs and lows of playground adventures. . . . After a long bout of play, it's time to go home, but the two don't whine, promising instead to play together another time." (Kirkus)

Piggy and Dad go fishing; illustrated by Frank Remkiewicz. Candlewick Press 2005 un il $14.99
Grades: PreK K 1 2 E
1. Pigs -- Fiction 2. Fishing -- Fiction 3. Father-son relationship -- Fiction
ISBN 0-7636-2506-X
LC 2004-51941

When his dad takes Piggy fishing for the first time and Piggy ends up feeling sorry for the worms and the fish, they decide to make some changes.

"The summery watercolor-and-pencil cartoon illustrations clue listeners into Piggy's emotions and create a bit of tension in the nicely paced story." Horn Book Guide
Other titles about Piggy and Dad are:
Piggy and Dad (2001)
Piggy and Dad play (2002)

Martin, Emily Winfield
Dream animals; by Emily Winfield Martin. Random House Inc 2013 32 p. (hc) $17.99
Grades: PreK E
1. Stories in rhyme 2. Dreams -- Fiction 3. Animals -- Fiction 4. Bedtime -- Fiction
ISBN 0449810801; 9780375971495; 9780375981371; 9780449810804
LC 2012029945

Author and illustrator Emily Winfield Martin "convinces children to close their eyes and discover who their dream animal might be--and what dream it might take them to." This rhyming picture book story for children also includes illustrations of multiple animals and acts as a bedtime story for children, parents, and readers of all ages. (Publisher's note)

Martin, Jacqueline Briggs

Grandmother Bryant's pocket; pictures by Petra Mathers. Houghton Mifflin 1996 48p il hardcover o.p. pa $5.95

Grades: K 1 2 3   E

1. Fear -- Fiction 2. Maine -- Fiction 3. Grandmothers -- Fiction

ISBN 0-395-68984-8; 0-618-03309-2 pa

LC 94-31309

"Appealingly structured in one-and two-page chapters, the book is illustrated with watercolor paintings. Executed in naive style, the artwork has an unassuming sweetness." Booklist

On Sand Island; illustrated by David Johnson. Houghton Mifflin 2003 un il $16

Grades: 1 2 3   E

1. Islands -- Fiction

ISBN 0-618-23151-X

LC 2002-5090

In 1916 on an island in Lake Superior, Carl builds himself a boat by bartering with the other islanders for parts and labor

"Martin's simple, poetic text deftly balances small, revealing details about the island's characters and Carl's life with the particulars of boat building. . . . The illustrations . . . capture the lake's translucent light and the story's nostalgic mood in expert, geometric line drawings washed with watery blue-green and sunset-orange colors." Booklist

Martin, Rafe

Will's mammoth; illustrated by Stephen Gammell. Putnam 1989 un il $16.99

Grades: K 1 2 3   E

1. Mammoths -- Fiction

ISBN 0-399-21627-8

LC 88-11651

"Gammell's depiction of a child's rich imagination is illustrated in vivid colors. The fantasy spreads use winter whites and blues as background for subtly individualized animals who move energetically across the pages." Booklist

Martin, Ruth

Moon dreams; illustrated by Olivier Latyk. Templar Books 2010 un il $15.99

Grades: PreK K 1   E

1. Day -- Fiction 2. Moon -- Fiction 3. Night -- Fiction 4. Dreams -- Fiction

ISBN 978-0-7636-5012-4; 0-7636-5012-9

LC 2010003808

Published in the United Kingdom with title: Where on earth is the moon?

Luna, who loves to look at the moon, wonders where it goes during the day.

"Latyk's lush artwork, well-executed and incredibly tasteful, is a visual treat. Composed of graphic shapes in a retro-cool style, the digital illustrations flow with Martin's words as the story progresses. . . . A lovely, slumberous story." Kirkus

Martin, Steve

The **alphabet** from A to Y with bonus letter, Z! by Steve Martin & [illustrated by] Roz Chast. Doubleday/Flying Dolphin Press 2007 un il $17.95; lib bdg $17.95

Grades: K 1 2 3   E

1. Alphabet 2. Stories in rhyme

ISBN 978-0-385-51662-4; 978-0-385-52377-6 lib bdg

LC 2006102543

Presents a rhyming couplet featuring each letter of the alphabet, with such characters as David the dog-faced boy, who dons a derby despite being dirty, and Victor, whose frequent victories have made him vainglorious

"Martin and Chast show their mettle as each other's wacky sidekicks. . . . [A] peculiar and funny book." Publ Wkly

Martins, Isabel Minhós

My neighbor is a dog; Isabel Minhos Martins. Owlkids Books 2013 32 p. $16.95

Grades: K 1 2   E

1. Dogs -- Fiction 2. Picture books for children

ISBN 1926973682; 9781926973685

LC 2012943001

In this children's picture book, apartment building residents "are shocked when a blue dog moves into a vacant apartment. 'My parents thought it was very strange to have a dog as a neighbor,' says the young narrator. 'They said he would leave his hair all over the place . . . .' (Meanwhile, the dog's habits actually involve reading the newspaper and playing saxophone.) Additional animals move in, but while the girl befriends them, her parents are having none of it." (Publishers Weekly)

"Stylish and understated, this argument for tolerance is a welcome one." Kirkus

★ **Where** do we go when we disappear? Isabel Minhos Martins, Madalena Matoso. Abrams 2013 44 p. $14.95

Grades: K 1 2 3   E

1. Picture books for children 2. Change

ISBN 1849761604; 9781849761604

LC 2013933771

This children's picture book offers a "rumination on the idea that disappearance is really only change. For someone to disappear, [Isabel Minhós] Martins begins, someone else has to be left behind with questions: '"Where has she gone?" "Will we ever see each other again?"' But from leaves and rain puddles to the sand on beaches and the noise of children at play, everything in this world disappears, going somewhere else or taking some new form." (Kirkus Reviews)

Marzollo, Jean

Help me learn numbers 0-20; photographs by Chad Phillips. Holiday House 2011 un il $15.95

Grades: PreK K   E

1. Numbers 2. Counting

ISBN 978-0-8234-2334-7; 0-8234-2334-4

LC 2010029892

"Marzollo and Phillips team up for an idiosyncratic and eye-catching counting book featuring photographic compositions of miscellaneous objects including vintage toy cars, Dalmatian figurines, and rubber finger-puppet monsters. In one spread, 10 glass animals are clustered atop white steps, while the verse hints at the answer. . . . The playful displays suggest that number sense isn't just a classroom tool, but a way in which to explore and engage with one's environment." Publ Wkly

Ten little Christmas presents. Scholastic 2008 un il pa $9.99

Grades: PreK K   E

1. Counting 2. Stories in rhyme 3. Gifts -- Fiction 4. Animals -- Fiction 5. Christmas -- Fiction 6. Santa Claus -- Fiction

ISBN 978-0-545-02791-5 pa; 0-545-02791-8 pa

LC 2007-21572

A counting-down book in which ten forest animals find unexpected Christmas presents, left for them by a Secret Santa

"Toddlers will like the simple, rhyming story and the sketchy, childlike illustrations, and preschoolers will like the reverse counting game. Teachers and librarians will find this a good fit for story hours about counting or Christmas presents." Kirkus

Mason, Margaret H.

These hands. Houghton Mifflin Harcourt 2011 un il $16.99

Grades: PreK K 1 2 3   E

1. Hand -- Fiction 2. Grandfathers -- Fiction 3. African Americans -- Fiction 4. African Americans -- Civil rights -- Fiction

ISBN 978-0-547-21566-2; 0-547-21566-5

LC 2010006782

"Cooper's signature style of softly blurred illustrations in sepia shades shows the bonds in a loving family.... The story's roots in rarely told history will widen the audience of this moving title to older readers, too." Booklist

Mathers, Petra

★ **Lottie's** new beach towel. Atheneum Bks. for Young Readers 1998 un il hardcover o.p. pa $6.99

Grades: PreK K 1 2   E

1. Beaches -- Fiction 2. Chickens -- Fiction

ISBN 0-689-81606-5; 0-689-84441-7 pa

LC 97-6689

Lottie the chicken has a number of adventures at the beach, during which her new towel, a gift from her friend Herbie the duck, comes in handy.

"Pure fun, with a resourceful, big-hearted main character; humor in both text and pictures; and a good story, elegantly shaped." Horn Book

Other titles about Lottie and Herbie are:

A cake for Herbie (2000)

Herbie's secret Santa (2002)

Lottie's new friend (1999)

When Aunt Mattie got her wings; by Petra Mathers. Beach Lane Books 2014 32 p. color illustrations (hardcover) $17.99

Grades: PreK K 1 2   E

1. Grief -- Fiction 2. Chickens -- Fiction 3. Death -- Fiction 4. Ducks -- Fiction 5. Friendship -- Fiction

ISBN 148141044X; 9781481410441

LC 2013037476

In this book, written and illustrated by Petra Mathers, "Aunt Mattie has died. But before she went, she got to say good-bye to Lottie. Then she got to follow a light to a bustling gate. (A gate that sounded a lot like a busy airport!) And there she found a crew of friends who were waiting to take off with her on a new journey. Will Lottie and Herbie be

able to overcome their sadness? They will, with time, and by taking a journey of their own." (Publisher's note)

"Lucid and insightful, Mathers presents death and grief as natural processes with compassion and great care." Kirkus

Matsuoka, Mei

★ **Footprints** in the snow. Henry Holt & Co. 2008 un il $16.95

Grades: PreK K 1 2 3   E

1. Wolves -- Fiction 2. Storytelling -- Fiction

ISBN 978-0-8050-8792-5; 0-8050-8792-3

Wolf is feeling offended and indignant: All the wolves he's ever read about are nasty, scary, and greedy! To set the record straight he decides to write a story about a nice wolf. But will his wolfish instincts get the better of him after all?

"Both plot and pictures . . . take a surprising turn, which will delight young readers. Replete with visual allusions to popular wold stories, the folk-art style illustrations set up the scenario for this story-within-stories." Booklist

Matthews, Tina

Out of the egg. Houghton Mifflin 2007 un il $12.95

Grades: K 1 2 3   E

1. Animals -- Fiction 2. Chickens -- Fiction

ISBN 978-0-618-73741-3; 0-618-73741-3

LC 2006-09812

When the barnyard animals who refused to help her plant and tend a seed ask to play under the "great green whispery tree" that Little Red Hen grew, she says no, but her chick thinks that answer is mean.

"This gritty, sharply graphic woodcut version of the time-honored tale sets our feathered friend and her slothful sidekicks squarely in the present. . . . Matthews's hand-painted Japanese woodblock illustrations, black and white and red all over—with, of course, an important touch of green—are striking editorial panoramas." SLJ

Matthies, Janna

★ The **Goodbye** Cancer garden; illustrated by Kristi Valiant. Albert Whitman 2011 un il $16.99

Grades: K 1 2 3   E

1. Cancer -- Fiction 2. Gardens -- Fiction 3. Gardening -- Fiction 4. Family life -- Fiction

ISBN 978-0-8075-2994-2; 0-8075-2994-X

LC 2010024069

When a mother is diagnosed with breast cancer, she and her family plant a garden and watch it grow through the seasons as she undergoes treatments and gets better.

"Smoothly told in a reassuringly matter-of-fact and understated way. . . . Details about the treatment and the woman's physical reactions to it are worked in unobtrusively. . . . Realistic emotions like her general sadness or Janie's brother's dismay at his mom's baldness are included, but are downplayed. The sketchy illustrations are tender and sweet. . . . An uplifting, hopeful story, well told and beautifully illustrated." SLJ

Mayer, Mercer

★ A **boy,** a dog, and a frog. Dial Bks. for Young Readers 1967 un il hardcover o.p. $6.99

Grades: PreK K 1   E

1. Stories without words 2. Frogs -- Fiction

ISBN 0-8037-2880-8

"Without the need for a single word, humorous, very engaging pictures tell the story of a little boy who sets forth with his dog and a net on a summer day to catch an enterprising and personable frog. Even very young preschoolers will 'read' the tiny book with the greatest satisfaction and pleasure." Horn Book

Other titles in this series are:

A boy, a dog, a frog, and a friend (1971)

Frog goes to dinner (1974)

Frog on his own (1973)

Frog, where are you? (1969)

One frog too many (1975)

The **bravest** knight; story and pictures by Mercer Mayer. Dial Books for Young Readers 2007 un il $16.99

Grades: PreK K 1 2   E

1. Play -- Fiction 2. Knights and knighthood -- Fiction

ISBN 978-0-8037-3206-3

LC 2006021321

First published 1968 by Dial Press with title: Terrible Troll

A little boy imagines the adventures he would have if he lived a thousand years ago and was the squire of a bold knight who fought dragons and trolls.

"Funny details abound in every picture. . . . This fresh version of an old favorite should find a place in all picture-book collections." SLJ

Octopus soup. Marshall Cavendish Children 2011 un il $16.99

Grades: PreK K 1 2   E

1. Stories without words 2. Animals -- Fiction 3. Octopuses -- Fiction

ISBN 978-0-7614-5812-8; 0-7614-5812-3

LC 2010021232

An octopus struggles with misadventure when he leaves home but is relieved to know how and where to find a safe haven.

"The artist's signature cartoons are colorful, whimsical, and entertaining. Mayer continues to enchant." SLJ

★ **There's** a nightmare in my closet. Dial Bks. for Young Readers 1968 un il $16.99; pa $6.99

Grades: PreK K 1   E

1. Fear -- Fiction

ISBN 0-8037-8682-4; 0-14-054712-6 pa

"Childhood fear of the dark and the resulting exercise in imaginative exaggeration are given that special Mercer Mayer treatment in this dryly humorous fantasy. Young children will easily empathize with the boy and can be comforted by his experience." SLJ

Another title about this boy is:

There's an alligator under my bed (1987)

Too many dinosaurs. Holiday House 2011 un il $16.95

Grades: PreK K 1   E

1. Pets -- Fiction 2. Dinosaurs -- Fiction

ISBN 978-0-8234-2316-3; 0-8234-2316-6

LC 2010029442

A little boy really wants a dog, but instead he gets dinosaurs!

"Mayer's colloquial text and unmistakable illustrative style are both present here. The illustrations are full-page or cutouts surrounded by white space and done in rich colors. The text is placed in and around them to good effect. Plenty of background details spice up the very funny scenes for observant readers, and wild action and chases abound." SLJ

Mayo, Margaret

Choo choo clickety-clack! written by Margaret Mayo; illustrated by Alex Ayliffe. Carolrhoda Books 2005 un il lib bdg $14.95

Grades: PreK K   E

1. Noise -- Fiction 2. Transportation -- Fiction

ISBN 1-57505-819-7

LC 2004-11976

First published 2004 in the United Kingdom

Rhythmic sounds imitate trains, planes, and other busy transports that come and go

"Short and snappy, four lines of text encapsulate the excitement that comes with getting in a car, sailing on a lake, or floating in a hot-air balloon. The graphic-style artwork is executed in a melange of pure colors." Booklist

Roar! [by] Margaret Mayo & [illustrated by] Alex Ayliffe. Carolrhoda Books 2007 un il lib bdg $15.95

Grades: PreK K 1   E

1. Animals -- Fiction

ISBN 978-0-7613-9473-0

LC 2006029853

First published 2006 in the United Kingdom

Text and pictures describe the things which different kinds of animals like to do

"The creatures each get a spread with a rhythmic, fun-to-read narrative. . . . The malleable lines of type stretch with the giraffes, wave with the hippos, and jump with the kangaroos. Ayliffe's illustrations have bright, bold colors and simple, but effective depictions of the animals and landscapes that fairly leap off the pages." SLJ

Zoom, rocket, zoom! by Margaret Mayo; illustrated by Alex Ayliffe. Walker Books for Young Readers 2012 32 p. $16.99

Grades: PreK K 1 2   E

1. Stories in rhyme 2. Outer space -- Exploration 3. Astronauts -- Fiction 4. Space vehicles -- Fiction 5. Outer space -- Exploration -- Fiction

ISBN 0802727905; 9780802727909; 9780802727916

LC 2011024959

This children's picture book by Margaret Mayo "introduces youngsters to the jobs various space vehicles do and to the astronauts that explore outer space. . . . Lunar modules and moon buggies allow them to explore the moon. And space stations are a home away from home for astronauts who need to work in space. Mayo also devotes pages to unmanned space vehicles, including satellites, robotic spacecraft and rovers, all the while explaining in simple language what each does." (Kirkus Reviews)

Mayr, Diane

Run, Turkey run; [by] Diane Mayr; illustrated by Laura Rader. Walker Pub. Co. 2007 un il $15.95; lib bdg $16.85

Grades: PreK K 1 2   **E**
1. Turkeys -- Fiction 2. Thanksgiving Day -- Fiction
ISBN 978-0-8027-9630-1; 0-8027-9630-3; 978-0-
8027-9631-8 lib bdg; 0-8027-9631-1 lib bdg
LC 2006036190
The day before Thanksgiving, Turkey tries to disguise
himself as other animals in order to avoid being caught by
the farmer.

"This fast-paced romp is as much fun to read as it is to
listen to. . . . The illustrations are light and humorous." SLJ

Mazer, Norma Fox
Has anyone seen my Emily Greene? [by] Norma Fox
Mazer; illustrated by Christine Davenier. Candlewick Press
2007 un il $15.99
Grades: PreK K 1 2   **E**
1. Stories in rhyme 2. Play -- Fiction 3. Father-
daughter relationship -- Fiction
ISBN 978-0-7636-1384-6; 0-7636-1384-3
LC 2006051828
Emily decides to play hide and seek when her father calls
her for lunch

This is a "picture-book romp that reads with the hand-
clapping, foot-stomping rhythm of a rowdy folk song and
includes lots of sound effects that kids will want to shout out
loud. Davenier's sweeping ink lines, dabbed with watercolors, match the energy in the rhyming words." Booklist

McAlister, Caroline
Brave Donatella and the Jasmine thief; illustrated by
Donald Hendricks. Charlesbridge 2010 un il $16.95
Grades: 1 2 3   **E**
1. Princes 2. Love -- Fiction 3. Italy -- Fiction 4.
Middle Ages -- Fiction
ISBN 978-1-57091-729-5; 1-57091-729-9
In sixteenth-century Florence, in what would become
Italy, Antonio and Donatella flee the wrath of Duke Cosimo
de Medici from whom Antonio has stolen a sprig of jasmine,
and they use that rare plant to make a fresh start. Includes
facts about the duke and Italian history.

"The illustrations have a soft quality to them and fit the
time period perfectly. . . . This story could be used in a world
history class for older students, as well as in a class studying legends around the world. And of course, it can be read
aloud to younger students." Libr Media Connect

McAlister, Angela
Little Mist; illustrated by Sarah Fox-Davies. Alfred A.
Knopf 2011 un il $16.99; lib bdg $19.99
Grades: PreK K 1   **E**
1. Snow leopard -- Fiction
ISBN 978-0-375-86788-0; 0-375-86788-0; 978-0-375-
96788-7 lib bdg; 0-375-96788-5 lib bdg
LC 2010-28822
Little Mist, a young snow leopard, is filled with won-
der when his mother introduces him to the world for the
first time.

"Young readers will be lulled by the incantatory quality of the text and drawn to the snow leopards, who look as
friendly and welcoming as they do dignified." SLJ

My mom has x-ray vision; illustrated by Alex T. Smith.
Tiger Tales 2011 un il $15.95; pa $7.95

Grades: PreK K 1 2   **E**
1. Mothers -- Fiction 2. Superheroes -- Fiction
ISBN 978-1-58925-097-0; 1-58925-097-0; 978-1-
58925-428-2 pa; 1-58925-428-7 pa
"Matthew is certain that his mother has superhuman
abilities. She might have 'ordinary hair, ordinary clothes,
and a nice smile,' but she also seems to have x-ray vision.
So Matthew decides to test his hypothesis. He disobeys her
request to bring in the groceries and hides in a closet, waiting to see if she knows where he is. . . . Matthew's logical
thought processes pull youngsters along through bright full-
page cartoons with visual details like the dragon in his fantasies or a superhero costume hanging on the clothesline while
font changes add emphasis. . . . Young readers will recognize
this puzzled child's analysis of an age-old mystery." SLJ

Yuck! That's not a monster! illustrated by Alison Edgson. Good Books 2010 un il $16.99
Grades: PreK K   **E**
1. Monsters -- Fiction 2. Parent-child relationship --
Fiction
ISBN 978-1-56148-683-0; 1-56148-683-3
LC 2009-33696
As Mr. and Mrs. Monster's three eggs begin to hatch,
they happily welcome the first two ugly little monsters to
come out, but are shocked and disappointed when they see
what pops out of their last egg.

"The large format and brightly colored cartoons lend
themselves well to group sharing. Edgson's monsters are
like plush toys with coy expressions, more funny than fierce.
McAllister offers fresh descriptions touched with humor."
SLJ

McBratney, Sam
★ **Guess** how much I love you; illustrated by Anita
Jeram; paper engineering by Corina Fletcher. pop-up edi-
tion; Candlewick Press 2011 un il $19.99
Grades: PreK K   **E**
1. Pop-up books 2. Love -- Fiction 3. Rabbits --
Fiction 4. Father-son relationship -- Fiction
ISBN 978-0-7636-5378-1; 0-7636-5378-0
First published 1995
During a bedtime game, every time Little Nutbrown Hare
demonstrates how much he loves his father, Big Nutbrown
Hare gently shows him that the love is returned even more

"It's hard to believe that a pop-up wasn't the creators'
original intention, so seamlessly do moveable parts dovetail into this modern classic's storyline. . . . The figures here
move on every page, and with an unusually graceful naturalism to boot. . . . All of Little Nutbrown Hare's hops, stretches
and small gestures serve the poetically spare text. . . . The
book is available in just about every format—but this is the
perfect one." Kirkus

When I'm big; illustrated by Anita Jeram. Candlewick
2007 un il bd bk $7.99
Grades: PreK   **E**
1. Board books for children 2. Growth -- Fiction 3.
Rabbits -- Fiction
ISBN 978-0-7636-3546-6 bd bk
Little Nutbrown Hare loves playing in the spring, when
everything is growing and changing, but what will a little
brown hare grow into?

"Jeram's sunny ink-and-watercolor illustrations—sprightly spot art and spreads—offer subtle yet solid reinforcement of the text." Publ Wkly

McCarthy, Mary
★ A **closer** look. Greenwillow Books 2007 un il $16.99; lib bdg $17.89
Grades: PreK K 1 2   E
1. Nature -- Fiction
ISBN 978-0-06-124073-7; 0-06-124073-7; 978-0-06-124074-4 lib bdg; 0-06-124074-5 lib bdg
LC 2006-29459
Detailed collage illustrations accompanied by simple text present expanding views of familiar objects in nature, such as a bug and a flower.
"Rendered from handmade papers and collage, the bold artwork is elegant and eye-catching. The broad lines, simple graphic images, and textured details suit the magnified perspectives, while the more expansive scenes are beautifully composed." SLJ

McCarthy, Meghan
Daredevil; by Meghan McCarthy. 1st ed. Simon & Schuster Books for Young Readers 2013 48 p. col. ill. (reinforced) $16.99
Grades: K 1 2   E
1. Women air pilots 2. Skelton, Betty, 1926-2011 3. Air pilots -- United States -- Biography 4. Women air pilots -- United States -- Biography 5. Automobile racing drivers -- United States -- Biography 6. Women automobile racing drivers -- United States -- Biography
ISBN 1442422629; 9781442422629
LC 2012023603
This biographical "portrait of Betty June Skelton (1926-2011) reveals a woman who embodies a 'need for speed.' . . . She was obsessed with flying from an early age, and she made the newspapers for a solo flight on her 16th birthday--never mind that her father had already plopped her into a cockpit four years earlier. . . . Skelton went on to break records on land, sea, and air, and she even had a shot at becoming the first woman in space." (Publishers Weekly)

McCarty, Peter
Chloe; Peter McCarty. Balzer + Bray 2012 40 p.
Grades: PreK K 1   E
1. Play -- Fiction 2. Rabbits -- Fiction 3. Siblings -- Fiction 4. Television -- Fiction 5. Family life -- Fiction 6. Brothers and sisters -- Fiction
ISBN 0061142913; 9780061142918; 9780061142925
LC 2011019346
"Chloe is the middle rabbit child, with 10 older brothers and sisters and 10 younger. One of the best things about so many siblings is family fun time. When Dad brings home a television set, all the siblings are delighted except for Chloe and baby Bridget, who are less enthused. Why watch a piece of pound cake attack a city onscreen when you could do something else--like play inside the box the TV came in?" (Booklist)

First snow for Pedro; Peter McCarty. Balzer + Bray, an imprint of HarperCollins Publishers 2015 40 p. color illustrations (hardcover) $16.99

Grades: PreK K 1   E
1. Snow -- Fiction 2. Cousins -- Fiction
ISBN 0062189964; 9780062189967
LC 2013037211
In this children's picture book, written and illustrated by Peter McCarty, "it's a day of firsts for Pedro . . . First snowfall. First snow angel. First taste of a snowflake. First sled run. First snowball fight!" (Publisher's note)
"Pedro, a young anthropomorphic dog, has traveled from far away, and his cousins Sancho, Bella, Lola, Ava, and Maria are eager to introduce him to snow—something he's never before experienced...Through it all, a message emphasizing the importance of trying new things is unobtrusively folded in, but most of all, readers will come away with a genuine sense of fun and the joy of family and friends. A delightful winter excursion." SLJ

★ **Henry** in love. Balzer & Bray 2009 un il $16.99; lib bdg $17.89
Grades: PreK K 1   E
1. School stories 2. Cats -- Fiction 3. Love -- Fiction 4. Rabbits -- Fiction
ISBN 978-0-06-114288-8; 0-06-114288-3; 978-0-06-114289-5 lib bdg; 0-06-114289-1 lib bdg
LC 2009-14412
On the first day of school, Henry the cat vies for the attention of the most amazing girl in class, Chloe Rabbit.
"This gentle, pitch-perfect romance will have readers' hearts thumping with the thrill of first love." Publ Wkly

★ **Hondo** and Fabian. Holt & Co. 2002 un il $16.95; pa $6.95
Grades: PreK K 1 2   E
1. Cats -- Fiction 2. Dogs -- Fiction
ISBN 0-8050-6352-8; 0-312-36747-3 pa
LC 2001-1884
A Caldecott Medal honor book, 2003
Hondo the dog gets to go to the beach and play with his friend Fred, while Fabian the cat spends the day at home
"McCarty's staccato text, one line to a page, captures a lot of action in a few words, but it is the pencil-on-watercolor-paper art that makes this so arresting. Each carefully shaded picture, in muted tones, has a smooth, solid look." Booklist
Another title about Hondo and Fabian is:
Fabian escapes (2007)

Jeremy draws a monster. Henry Holt 2009 un il $16.99 E
1. Drawing -- Fiction 2. Monsters -- Fiction
ISBN 978-0-8050-6934-1; 0-8050-6934-8
LC 2008-36813
A young boy who spends most of his time alone in his bedroom makes new friends after the monster in his drawing becomes a monstrous nuisance.
"The finely rendered pen-and-ink and watercolor illustrations skillfully delineate characters and objects. . . . [This is] top-notch." Booklist

★ **Moon** plane; written and illustrated by Peter McCarty. Henry Holt 2006 un il $16.95
Grades: PreK K   E
1. Moon -- Fiction 2. Flight -- Fiction 3. Airplanes

-- Fiction

ISBN 978-0-8050-7943-2; 0-8050-7943-2

LC 2005016244

A young boy looks at a plane in the sky and imagines flying one all the way to the moon

"Using only pencils, McCarty creates soft-edged, silvertone artwork notable for its elegant simplicity. . . . McCarty catches both the way children's imaginations work and the connections they make." Booklist

T is for terrible; written and illustrated by Peter McCarty. Henry Holt 2004 un il $15.95; pa $6.99

Grades: PreK K 1   E

1. Dinosaurs -- Fiction

ISBN 0-8050-7404-X; 0-312-38423-8 pa

LC 2003-18246

A tyrannosaurus rex explains that he cannot help it that he is enormous and hungry and is not a vegetarian.

"Filled with textured lines and soft shading, the artwork glows with warmth and vitality. This beautifully formatted and well-conceived offering has creamy ivory pages that frame the subtle illustrations and spare text." SLJ

McClatchy, Lisa

Dear Tyrannosaurus Rex; illustrated by John Manders. Random House 2010 un il $16.99; lib bdg $19.99

Grades: PreK K 1 2   E

1. Parties -- Fiction 2. Birthdays -- Fiction 3. Dinosaurs -- Fiction

ISBN 978-0-375-85608-2; 0-375-85608-0; 978-0-375-95608-9 lib bdg; 0-375-95608-5 lib bdg

LC 2009005038

Enamored of dinosaurs, Erin writes a letter inviting a real one to her sixth birthday party.

"Enthusiastic descriptions of games, treats, the cake, party favors, etc., are accompanied by large cartoonlike illustrations featuring the T. rex as if he were in attendance. Each spread is filled with humor. . . . Perfect for reading aloud." SLJ

McClements, George

★ **Dinosaur** Woods; can seven clever critters save their forest home? Beach Lane Books 2009 un il $16.99

Grades: PreK K 1 2   E

1. Animals -- Fiction 2. Dinosaurs -- Fiction 3. Endangered species -- Fiction 4. Environmental protection -- Fiction

ISBN 978-1-4169-8626-3; 1-4169-8626-X

LC 2008-33084

To save their homes from being destroyed by developers, a fanciful group of endangered animals constructs a fearsome dinosaur.

"This title's generous trim size, cleanly rendered illustrations, and fast-paced text are perfect for group read-alouds or one-on-one sharing." SLJ

Night of the Veggie Monster. Bloomsbury Children's Books 2008 un il $14.95; lib bdg $15.85

Grades: K 1 2 3   E

1. Food -- Fiction 2. Family life -- Fiction

ISBN 978-1-59990-061-2; 1-59990-061-0; 978-1-59990-234-0 lib bdg; 1-59990-234-6 lib bdg

LC 2007017850

Every Tuesday night, while his parents try to enjoy their dinner, a boy turns into a monster the moment a pea touches his lips

"Illustrations are a creative medley of photographed realia . . . cut-out brown paper . . . and simple pastel lines and textural elements, . . . resulting in a spare vigor that nicely supports the textual humor." Bull Cent Child Books

McClintock, Barbara

★ **Adele** & Simon. Farrar, Straus & Giroux 2006 un il $16

Grades: PreK K 1 2   E

1. Siblings -- Fiction 2. Paris (France) -- Fiction 3. Lost and found possessions -- Fiction

ISBN 0-374-38044-9

LC 2002-35311

When Adele walks her little brother Simon home from school he loses one more thing at every stop: his drawing of a cat at the grocer's shop, his books at the park, his crayons at the art museum, and more.

"Set in Paris during the early 20th century, this simple story is the basis for some remarkable illustrations. McClintock's pen-and-ink with watercolor technique has the feel of illustrated children's books from that period. . . . A beautiful example of bookmaking, with plenty to charm children, this is a visual delight." SLJ

Another title about Adele and Simon is:

Adele & Simon in America (2008)

★ **Dahlia**. Farrar, Straus & Giroux 2002 un il $16

Grades: PreK K 1   E

1. Dolls -- Fiction

ISBN 0-374-31678-3

LC 2001-18778

"Charlotte doesn't want a doll for a playmate. . . . She prefers to climb trees, make mud pies, and dig in the dirt. When her Aunt Edme sends her a doll that's dressed in lace, ribbons, and gloves, Charlotte wrinkles her nose and informs the doll that there will be no tea parties or riding in 'frilly prams!' . . . McClintock tells an engaging story about an unusual character. . . . In her trademark delicate pen-and-ink outline art—filled with soft watercolors—McClintock delightfully juxtaposes spirited Charlotte within the old-fashioned setting." Booklist

McCloskey, Robert

★ **Blueberries** for Sal. Viking 1948 54p il $16.99; pa $7.99

Grades: PreK K 1 2   E

1. Bears -- Fiction 2. Maine -- Fiction

ISBN 0-670-17591-9; 0-14-050169-X pa

A Caldecott Medal honor book, 1949

"The author-artist tells what happens on a summer day in Maine when a little girl and a bear cub, wandering away from their blueberry-picking mothers, each mistakes the other's mother for its own. The Maine hillside and meadows are real and lovely, the quiet humor is entirely childlike, and there is just exactly the right amount of suspense for small children." Wis Libr Bull

Another title about Sal is:

One morning in Maine (1952)

Lentil. Viking 1940 un il $18.99; pa $5.99

Grades: PreK K 1 2   **E**
   1. Ohio -- Fiction   2. Harmonicas -- Fiction
   ISBN 0-670-42357-2; 0-14-050287-4 pa

Picture-story book about a small boy who could not sing, but who could work wonders on a simple harmonica, especially on the day when the great Colonel Carter returned to his home town

"Big, vigorous, amusing pictures in black-and-white, with an Ohio small-town background." New Yorker

★ **Make** way for ducklings. Viking 1941 un il $17.99; pa $7.99
Grades: PreK K 1 2   **E**
   1. Ducks -- Fiction   2. Boston (Mass.) -- Fiction
   ISBN 0-670-45149-5; 0-14-056434-9 pa
   Awarded the Caldecott Medal, 1942

"There are some very beautiful drawings in this book." Horn Book

★ **Time** of wonder. Viking 1957 63p il $18.99; pa $6.99
Grades: K 1 2 3   **E**
   1. Maine -- Fiction
   ISBN 0-670-71512-3; 0-14-050201-7 pa
   Awarded the Caldecott Medal, 1958

"A summer on an island in Maine is described through the simple everyday experiences of children, but also reveals the author's deep awareness of an attachment to all the shifting moods of season and weather, and the salty, downright character of the New England people." Top News

McClure, Nikki
   Apple; Nikki McClure. Abrams Appleseed 2012 40 p. $12.95
Grades: PreK K 1   **E**
   1. Apples   2. Plants -- Growth   3. Picture books for children   4. Apples -- Fiction
   ISBN 9781419703782
          LC 2011052130

This picture book by cut-paper artist Nikki McClure "follows the life of an apple throughout the year, demonstrating the cyclical patterns in nature. . . . [R]eaders will . . . follow[. . .] the journey of the bright red apple—the only splash of color in the otherwise black-and-white illustrations—as it travels from tree, to harvest, to snack, to compost, and finally to sprout. A single word complements each illustration, urging early readers to reflect on each stage in the apple's life." (Amazon.com)

How to be a cat; Nikki McClure. Abrams Books for Young Readers 2013 40 p. $16.95
Grades: PreK K 1   **E**
   1. Cats   2. Picture books for children   3. Cats -- Fiction   4. Animals -- Infancy -- Fiction
   ISBN 1419705288; 9781419705281
          LC 2012021633

This children's picture book from Nikki McClure includes cut-paper illustrations that "show nothing more than cats being cats, with a single word describing each of their actions." Words illustrated include "stretch," "wait," "find," "feast," and "dream." (Publishers Weekly)

"The expressive, striking cut-paper illustrations are entirely black and white except for well-placed touches of sky blue, which reinforce the natural setting. Very new readers

will enjoy navigating the simple story arc on their own." Horn Book

In; by Nikki McClure. Abrams Appleseed 2015 36 p. illustrations hbk $16.95
Grades: PreK K   **E**
   1. Play -- Fiction   2. Imagination -- Fiction   3. Contentment -- Fiction   4. English language -- Prepositions -- Fiction
   ISBN 1419714864; 9781419714863
          LC 2014027139

In this story by Nikki McClure, "for a boy and his toy giraffe, today is the perfect day to stay in. Snug in his pajamas, he reads books, bakes popovers, and plays with a big wicker basket--that he transforms into a rocket ship to fly in 'innerspace.' But soon, the outdoors is too tempting to resist, and he takes his wild imagination into nature. That is, until it's time to come inside again." (Publisher's note)

"Using only yellow, black, and white, McClure's cut-paper illustrations are filled with amazing detail. Readers will have fun spotting the yellow giraffe in every picture and following the boy from one activity to the next." Booklist

Mama, is it summer yet? Abrams Books for Young Readers 2010 un il $17.95
Grades: PreK K 1   **E**
   1. Summer -- Fiction   2. Mother-son relationship -- Fiction
   ISBN 978-0-8109-8468-4; 0-8109-8468-7

"Repetition of this book's title question ties together responses and scenes of a child and his mother as they wait for warmer weather. . . . The days pass with a graceful swirl as the most delicate of paper-cuts detail budding trees, squirrels nesting, soft earth for seedlings, young ducklings following their mother, swallows circling overhead, and blossoming trees, culminating in the anticipated delight of summer berries. . . . Simple black paper contrasts with a light, neutral background, highlighting spare use of digitally added color accents; solid-color sheets underscore the repeated text. . . . Children will appreciate the simple sentences and lyrical verse that relate the seasonal passing of time." SLJ

McCormack, Caren McNelly
   The **fiesta** dress; a quinceanera tale. illustrated by Martha Aviles. Marshall Cavendish 2009 un il $17.99
Grades: K 1   **E**
   1. Sisters -- Fiction   2. Family life -- Fiction   3. Hispanic Americans -- Fiction   4. Quinceañera (Social custom) -- Fiction
   ISBN 0-7614-5467-5; 978-0-7614-5467-0
          LC 2008-10781

While Eva and her family prepare for her quinceanera, no one is paying attention to her younger sister, but when the dog gets out of the laundry room and steals Eva's sash, her little sister comes to the rescue.

"Aviles incorporates a warm palette of roses, aquas, deep oranges and springy greens to illustrate the story; her acrylic and watercolor compositions have a somewhat old fashioned feel. . . . There is abundant joy in this tale of a big extended family preparing for an exciting event, and audience members will relish being included." Bull Cent Child Books

McCourt, Frank

Angela and the baby Jesus; illustrated by Raúl Colón. Simon & Schuster Books for Young Readers 2007 un il $17.99

Grades: K 1 2 3   E

  1. Ireland -- Fiction 2. Christmas -- Fiction

  ISBN 978-1-4169-3789-0; 1-4169-3789-7

"The six-year-old heroine is McCourt's mother, Angela, who is disturbed that the Baby Jesus must be cold as he lies outside in a Nativity scene. . . . Angela steals the baby so she get hime home and warm him in her bed. . . . McCourt writes with the lilt of the Irish and the ability to get inside a child's mind. . . . Painted with a glow that comes from street lamps or candlelight, Colon's artwork showcases the warmth that a caring family radiates." Booklist

McCue, Lisa

Quiet Bunny. Sterling 2009 un il $14.95

Grades: PreK K   E

  1. Sounds -- Fiction 2. Rabbits -- Fiction

  ISBN 978-1-4027-5719-8; 1-4027-5719-0

                         LC 2008-32903

Quiet Rabbit enjoys listening to the night song of the other animals every evening and wishes he could join them, but no matter how hard he tries he is unable to copy their sounds.

"The text is full of onomatopoeic words, often incorporated into the illustrations, creating a pleasing link between story and picture." SLJ

Other titles about Quiet Bunny are:

Quiet Bunny's many colors (2011)

Quiet Bunny & Noisy Puppy (2011)

McCully, Emily Arnold

★ **Beautiful** warrior; the legend of the nun's kung fu. Levine Bks. 1998 un il $18.95

Grades: 1 2 3 4   E

  1. China -- Fiction 2. Martial arts -- Fiction

  ISBN 0-590-37487-7

                         LC 97-3823

"Born near the end of the Ming Dynasty, a girl grows up to become a fighting nun, renowned for her martial arts. Later, when a timid village girl asks for help in deterring her loutish husband-to-be, the nun teaches her kung fu so she can save herself. The story is intriguing, and the watercolors . . . are filled with dramatic motion." Horn Book Guide

The **bobbin** girl. Dial Bks. for Young Readers 1996 un il $15.99

Grades: 3 4 5   E

  1. Strikes -- Fiction 2. Factories -- Fiction 3. Massachusetts -- Fiction 4. United States -- History -- 1815-1861 -- Fiction

  ISBN 0-8037-1827-6

                         LC 95-6997

Rebecca, a ten-year-old bobbin girl working in a textile mill in Lowell, Massachusetts, in the 1830s, must make a difficult decision—will she participate in the first workers' strike in Lowell?

"McCully weaves historical facts and fictional characters into an intriguing story. The author's note details the background, incidents, and people who inspired the book. Beautifully composed watercolor paintings give a vivid impression of America in the 1830s and bring the period to life." Booklist

★ **First** snow. HarperCollins Publishers 2004 un il $15.99

Grades: PreK K   E

  1. Mice -- Fiction 2. Snow -- Fiction 3. Sledding -- Fiction

  ISBN 0-06-623852-8

                         LC 2003-44971

A timid little mouse discovers the thrill of sledding in the first snow of the winter.

"First published as a wordless picture book in 1985, First Snow is back with a brief text, enhanced illustrations, and a larger trim size. . . . This new edition has brighter, deeper colors. . . . Full of exuberance and excitement." SLJ

Other titles about this young mouse are:

Picnic (2003)

School (2005)

★ The **grandma** mix-up; story and pictures by Emily Arnold McCully. Harper & Row 1988 63p il (I can read book) hardcover o.p. pa $5.99

Grades: PreK K 1 2   E

  1. Grandmothers -- Fiction

  ISBN 0-06-444150-4 pa

                         LC 87-29378

Young Pip doesn't know what to do when two very different grandmothers come to baby sit, each with her own way of doing things

"McCully's two-color, line-and-wash drawings emphasize the personality differences by consciously flouting stereotypes: Pip's laid-back Grandma Sal has white hair and glasses, while his strict Grandma Nan dresses like a teenager. Choice of words and sentence length will make the sly humor easy for beginning readers to grasp." Booklist

Other titles about Pip and his grandmothers are:

Grandmas at bat (1993)

Grandmas at the lake (1990)

★ **Mirette** on the high wire. Putnam 1992 un il hardcover o.p. pa $6.99

Grades: K 1 2 3   E

  1. Paris (France) -- Fiction 2. Tightrope walking -- Fiction

  ISBN 0-399-22130-1; 0-698-11443-4 pa

                         LC 91-36324

Awarded the Caldecott Medal, 1993

Mirette learns tightrope walking from Monsieur Bellini, a guest in her mother's boarding house, not knowing that he is a celebrated tightrope artist who has withdrawn from performing because of fear

"With a rich palette of deep colors, the artist immerses the reader in 19th-century Paris. Colorful theatrical personalities . . . fill the glowing interiors with robust life. And the exterior scenes . . . are filled with the magic of a Paris night when anything can happen. . . . An exuberant and uplifting picture book." N Y Times Book Rev

Other titles about Mirette and Bellini are:

Mirette & Bellini cross Niagra Falls (2000)

Starring Mirette and Bellini (1997)

★ The **secret** cave; discovering Lascaux. Farrar Straus Giroux 2010 un il $16.99
Grades: 1 2 3 4   **E**
   1. France -- Fiction 2. Prehistoric art -- Fiction 3. Cave drawings and paintings -- Fiction
   ISBN 978-0-374-36694-0; 0-374-36694-2
"This mesmerizing look at the discovery of the prehistoric cave paintings of Lascaux invites today's readers to experience the wonder of the event. McCully has written and drawn a stunning fictionalized account based on historical records and interviews. The endpapers entice with the rendering of the maps of the caves, and soft wide watercolor strokes capture the essence of the prehistoric art. . . . The Caldecott winner gets the emotions of the secret decent for buried treasure just right." Kirkus
   Includes bibliographical references

Squirrel and John Muir. Farrar Straus Giroux 2004 un il $16
Grades: K 1 2 3   **E**
   1. Authors 2. Naturalists 3. Writers on nature 4. California -- Fiction
   ISBN 0-374-33697-0
             LC 2003-45511
In the early 1900s, a wild little girl nicknamed Squirrel meets John Muir, later to become a famous naturalist, when he arrives at her parents' hotel in Yosemite Valley seeking work and knowledge about the natural world.
"The afterword explains how this fictionalized retelling of an actual relationship reveals much about the compelling founder of the Sierra Club. . . . McCully's sure watercolors capture the stunning natural beauty of the area and provide a majestic backdrop for the small figure of Squirrel." SLJ
   Includes bibliographical references

★ **Wonder** horse. Henry Holt and Company 2010 un il $16.99
Grades: K 1 2 3   **E**
   1. Slaves 2. Veterinarians 3. Animal trainers 4. Horses -- Fiction 5. African Americans -- Fiction
   ISBN 978-0-8050-8793-2; 0-8050-8793-1
             LC 2009006208
A fictionalized account of Bill "Doc" Key, a former slave who became a veterinarian, trained his horse, Jim Key, to recognize letters and numbers and to perform in skits around the country, and moved the nation toward a belief in treating animals humanely. Includes an author's note.
"McCully's storytelling is as sensitive, engaging, and well paced as her brightly colored, expressive artwork." Booklist
   Includes bibliographical references

McDermott, Gerald
   Creation. Dutton Children's Bks. 2003 un il $16.99
Grades: 2 3 4   **E**
   1. Creation -- Fiction
   ISBN 0-525-46905-2
The author's meditation on the creation story based on Genesis I of Hebrew Bible. In it man and woman are created last to be the keepers of all this beauty

"McDermott casts the story of creation in strong poetic text and sweeping vibrant views. . . . Sumptuous, rhythmic, and mystical, this book is arresting and evocative." SLJ

Papagayo; the mischief maker. written and illustrated by Gerald McDermott. Harcourt Brace Jovanovich 1992 un il hardcover o.p. pa $8
Grades: 2 3 4   **E**
   1. Parrots -- Fiction
   ISBN 0-15-259465-5; 0-15-259464-7 pa
             LC 91-40364
A reissue of the title first published 1980 by Windmill Bks.
Papagayo, the noisy parrot, helps the night animals save the moon from being eaten up by the moon dog
"McDermott's original story assumes folktale proportions. . . . Art for the story is striking; deep tropical colors seem intensified by glossy page surfaces, and they nearly vibrate against the intermittent deep-blue backdrop of a night sky." Booklist

McDonald, Megan
   Ant and Honey Bee; a pair of friends at Halloween. illustrated by G. Brian Karas. new ed.; Candlewick Press 2010 44p il $14.99
Grades: K 1 2   **E**
   1. Ants -- Fiction 2. Bees -- Fiction 3. Costume -- Fiction 4. Halloween -- Fiction 5. Friendship -- Fiction
   ISBN 978-0-7636-4662-2; 0-7636-4662-8
             LC 2009021485
A new edition of Ant and Honey Bee: what a pair! published 2005
Best friends Ant and Honey Bee, who think of themselves as quite a pair, become matching home appliances on Halloween.
"With its open format, large type, judious use of repetition, and plentiful, narrative-laden mixed-media illustrations, this book functions well both as a picture book and an easy reader." Horn Book Guide

Hen hears gossip; illustrated by Joung Un Kim. HarperCollins 2008 un il $17.99; lib bdg $17.89
Grades: PreK K   **E**
   1. Gossip -- Fiction 2. Animals -- Fiction
   ISBN 978-0-06-113876-8; 0-06-113876-2; 978-0-06-113877-5 lib bdg; 0-06-113877-0 lib bdg
             LC 2007027137
When Hen overhears some news on the farm, she runs to tell Duck, who tells another animal, and as the gossip is repeated from one animal to the next, it becomes unrecognizable
"The simple prose incorporates capitals and punctuation that offer guidance for animated read-alouds. The colorful, mixed-media collages . . . blend bold, blocky shapes with vivid, intricate patterns and textures. Children will enjoy the farcical fun." Booklist

It's picture day today! illustrated by Katherine Tillotson. Atheneum Books for Young Readers 2009 un il $16.99
Grades: PreK K   **E**
   1. School stories 2. Artists' materials -- Fiction
   ISBN 978-1-4169-2434-0; 1-4169-2434-5
             LC 2007-46435
A classroom of art supplies gathers for their picture day.

"Tillotson's collage work, both creative and endearingly clunky, will awaken the inner cutter-and-paster in almost any young child. An ideal book to pair with a craft session." Booklist

McDonald, Megan, 1959-

Ant and honey bee; a pair of friends in winter. Megan McDonald, illustrated by G. Brian Karas. Candlewick Press 2013 64 p. $14.99

Grades: K 1 2   E

1. Ants -- Fiction 2. Bees -- Fiction 3. Friendship -- Fiction

ISBN 0763657123; 9780763657123

LC 2012947754

"Can Ant brave the cold for one last surprise visit before the snow flies? And will Honey Bee welcome an interruption of her peace and quiet? The author of the Judy Moody series [Megan McDonald] teams up again with award-winning illustrator G. Brian Karas to show that true friends can weather whatever comes their way--even if one is feeling antsy and the other has . . . hibernation in mind." (Publisher's note)

Jessica Finch in Pig Trouble; by Megan McDonald; illustrated by Erwin Madrid; based on the characters created by Peter H. Reynolds. Candlewick Press 2014 64 p. color illustrations (Judy Moody and Friends) (pbk) $4.99; (reinforced) $12.99

Grades: K 1 2   E

1. Pigs -- Fiction 2. Gifts -- Fiction 3. Birthdays -- Fiction 4. Female friendship -- Fiction

ISBN 9780763670276; 9780763657185; 0763657182; 0763670278

LC 2012947726

In this book, by Megan McDonald, "readers meet Jessica Finch, a friend of Judy Moody who loves pigs and hopes to get one as a pet for her upcoming birthday. Jessica asks Judy to snoop around and find out what her birthday present will be and is upset when she does not help her. When Judy later appears at the birthday party with a baby potbellied pig, Jessica realizes that Judy is her best friend ever." (School Library Journal)

"Full-bleed color illustrations (modeled after Peter H. Reynolds's originals) add to the fun. The easy-to-read books are great for newly independent readers not quite ready for the longer Judy Moody chapter books." Horn Book

Shoe dog; Megan McDonald; illustrated by Katherine Tillotson. Atheneum Books for Young Readers 2014 40 p. color illustrations (hardcover) $17.99

Grades: PreK K 1 2   E

1. Dogs 2. Dog adoption -- Fiction 3. Dogs -- Training -- Fiction

ISBN 1416979328; 9781416979326

LC 2012051499

In this book, by Megan McDonald, illustrated by Katherine Tillotson, "Shoe Dog likes to chew. And chew and chew. But he doesn't chew a boring old bone. Not a squeaky old toy. Not a smelly old sock. Nope. Shoe Dogs chews well, take a guess! Chewing shoes poses a problem, however, and Shoe Dog needs help to solve it. Good thing there's... Shoe Cat!" (Publisher's note)

"McDonald's lively word choices inject plenty of life into the repetitive storyline, and Tillotson's crayon, charcoal, and digital illustrations give it a goofy spark, depicting Shoe Dog as a zig-zag pattern that looks drawn from a single, thick line." Booklist

McDonnell, Christine

Dog wants to play; illustrated by Jeff Mack. Viking Children's Books 2009 un il $15.99

Grades: PreK K   E

1. Dogs -- Fiction 2. Play -- Fiction

ISBN 978-0-670-01126-1; 0-670-01126-6

LC 2009001955

Dog is eager to have fun, but no one in the barnyard will play with him except one special friend.

"Textured, sun-kissed painted images put bounce into the simple story and capture Dog's realistic body poses." Booklist

★ **Goyangi** means cat; Christine McDonnell; pictures Steve Johnson & Lou Fancher. Viking Children's Books 2011 1 v. (unpaged) $16.99

Grades: PreK K 1 2   E

1. Cats -- Fiction 2. Home -- Fiction 3. Adoption -- Fiction 4. Korean Americans -- Fiction 5. Intercountry adoption -- Fiction

ISBN 978-0-670-01179-7; 0-670-01179-7; 9780670011797

LC 2010043325

An understanding cat helps a young Korean girl named Soo Min adjust to her new home and adopted family in America.

"Soft-focus collage-and-paint illustrations show the family members getting to know one another. . . . Korean words in hanja (characters) incorporated into the pictures' backgrounds and the presence of Korean words in the Western alphabet interspersed throughout the text make this an excellent choice to share with children like Soo Min. . . . A sensitive portrayal of international adoption, authentically and realistically done." Kirkus

McDonnell, Patrick

★ The **monsters'** monster; Patrick McDonnell. Little, Brown 2012 40 p. $16.99

Grades: PreK   E

1. Monsters -- Fiction 2. Conduct of life -- Fiction 3. Behavior -- Fiction

ISBN 0316045470; 9780316045476

LC 2011042742

In this children's picture book by Patrick McDonnell, a National Parenting Publications Award Silver Winner, a trio of monsters "bicker about who is the most impressive monster." When they decide to create "'the biggest, baddest monster EVER!'" they discover that "they cannot change their creation's pleasant nature . . . and learn that respectful, mannerly companionship can lead to fulfilling and sunny results." (Kirkus Reviews)

A **perfectly** messed-up story; by Patrick McDonnell. Little, Brown & Co. 2014 40 p. color illustrations (hardcover) $17

Grades: PreK K 1   E

1. Perfection 2. Storytelling -- Fiction 3. Orderliness -- fiction 4. Anger in children -- fiction 5. Books and reading -- Fiction 6. Characters and characteristics in

literature
ISBN 0316222585; 9780316222587

LC 2013041668

In this children's story, written and illustrated by Patrick McDonnell, "little Louie's story keeps getting messed up, and he's not happy about it! What's the point of telling his tale if he can't tell it perfectly? But when he stops and takes a deep breath, he realizes that everything is actually just fine, and his story is a good one--imperfections and all." (Publisher's note)

"Here's an existential dilemma: What if you were a character in a book, and sandwich fillings fell onto your page from above? . . . The ultrarealistic digitally collaged PB&J splotches retain their exact shape from spread to spread; McDonnell also uses pen and ink, brush pen, crayon and watercolor. More messes deface the idyllic countryside—fingerprints, juice, scribbles and, worst of all, a paper towel that smears rather than cleaning—and Louie has a meltdown. The blank backgrounds that throw Louie's freakout in relief, the interplay between narrative text and Louie's frantic speech bubbles, and Louie's prostrate despair are all brilliant. Happily, the backgrounds reappear (clean, but what's that on the endpaper?), and so does Louie's equilibrium. A playful, funny and friendly treatment of anxiety and life's unpredictable messes." Kirkus

★ South; [by] Patrick McDonnell. Little, Brown and Co. 2008 un il $14.99
Grades: PreK K 1 2   E
    1. Stories without words 2. Cats -- Fiction 3. Birds -- Fiction
    ISBN 978-0-316-00509-8; 0-316-00509-6

LC 2007048373

Mooch the cat helps a lonely bird find its flock, which has flown south for the winter

"McDonnell's comfort with unfilled expanses, his beautifully balanced compositions, and the nature of his brushwork evoke the feel of traditional Chinese art. Tan recycled paper provides warmth in keeping with this tender, compact story." SLJ

McElligott, Matthew
    ★ Bean thirteen. G. P. Putnam's Sons 2007 un il lib bdg $15.99
Grades: K 1 2 3   E
    1. Insects -- Fiction 2. Division -- Fiction
    ISBN 978-0-399-24535-0 lib bdg; 0-399-24535-9 lib bdg

LC 2006-26295

Two bugs, Ralph and Flora, try to divide thirteen beans so that the unlucky thirteenth bean disappears, but they soon discover that the math is not so easy.

"Done in pen and ink with digital effects, the cartoon illustrations feature bright hues and slightly off-kilter perspectives that will appeal to children. Youngsters will undoubtedly enjoy this funny tale; teachers will truly appreciate the connections it makes to their curriculum and the use of manipulatives in math." SLJ

Even monsters need haircuts. Walker & Co. 2010 un il $16.99
Grades: PreK K 1   E
    1. Monsters -- Fiction 2. Barbers and barbershops --

Fiction
    ISBN 978-0-8027-8819-1; 0-8027-8819-X

At night under a full moon, a child operates a barber shop with a monstrous clientele.

"With the distinctive combination of the freakish and the humdrum, it's a good candidate for the stack of battered bedtime favorites." Publ Wkly

★ The lion's share; [by] Matt McElligott. Walker & Co. 2009 un il $16.99; lib bdg $17.89
Grades: PreK K 1 2   E
    1. Ants -- Fiction 2. Lions -- Fiction 3. Etiquette -- Fiction 4. Mathematics -- Fiction
    ISBN 978-0-8027-9768-1; 0-8027-9768-7; 978-0-8027-9769-8 lib bdg; 0-8027-9769-5 lib bdg

LC 2008013358

Ant is honored to receive an invitation to lion's annual dinner party, but is shocked when the other guests behave rudely and then accuse her of thinking only of herself.

"McElligott's digitally touched ink-and-watercolor artwork combines expressive animal characters with clear groupings of objects that illustrated the embedded arithmetic exercises. While the story will find an obvious place in early elementary math or character education units, the lively illustrations amplify the story's slapstick humor and will easily entertain story hour crowds." Booklist

McElmurry, Jill
    Mario makes a move; Jill McElmurry. Schwartz & Wade Books 2012 32 p. (glb) $19.99
Grades: K 1   E
    1. Dance -- Fiction 2. Squirrels -- Fiction 3. Picture books for children
    ISBN 0375968547; 9780375868542; 9780375968549

LC 2011011014

In this children's picture book, "Mario is a frenetic squirrel whose 'amazing' acrobatic high jinks impress his family but not his . . . friend Isabelle. Not only does she put down his best trick, but she also comes up with a more impressive one of her own and points out that everyone can have special moves. Crushed, Mario abandons his beloved but no longer unique hobby . . . . Isabelle persuades him to return to his spiffy move-making. Teaming up, they teach each other new stunts." (School Library Journal)

McEvoy, Anne
    Betsy B. Little; by Anne McEvoy; illustrated by Jacqueline Rogers. HarperCollinsPublishers 2009 un il $17.99; lib bdg $18.89
Grades: PreK K 1 2   E
    1. Stories in rhyme 2. Size -- Fiction 3. Ballet -- Fiction 4. Giraffes -- Fiction
    ISBN 978-0-06-059337-7; 0-06-059337-7; 978-0-06-059338-4 lib bdg; 0-06-059338-5 lib bdg

LC 2008010569

Betsy the giraffe longs to be a ballerina, so when her dance class does not work out, she discovers another way to make her dreams come true

"The rhyming text is fairly smooth and has a satisfying ending. . . . Watercolor illustrations show Betsy's uniqueness and awkwardness with sympathy and wit." SLJ

McGhee, Alison

Always; illustrated by Pascal Lemaitre. Simon & Schuster Books for Young Readers 2009 un il $15.99

Grades: PreK K 1   E

1. Dogs -- Fiction

ISBN 978-1-4169-7481-9; 1-4169-7481-4

LC 2008-42624

A loyal dog promises to protect his young mistress and her home from any danger.

"Succinct, funny and, in its way, action-packed, this is written in the universal language of affection—only the stonyhearted could withstand its charms." Publ Wkly

★ **Bye**-bye, crib; illustrated by Ross MacDonald. Simon & Schuster Books for Young Readers 2008 un il $16.99

Grades: PreK   E

1. Beds -- Fiction 2. Growth -- Fiction

ISBN 978-1-4169-1621-5; 1-4169-1621-0

LC 2006-10583

A big boy and his best stuffed friend seek the courage to move to a gigantic new bed.

"MacDonald's evocative art . . . employs the comic-book conventions, visual wit, and pulp-art palette fans know and love, and the animation in both the text and the pictures turns what might have been a ho-hum tale of trepidation into a proactive adventure with a winsome wee hero." SLJ

The **case** of the missing donut; by Alison McGhee; pictures by Isabel Roxas. Dial Books for Young Readers 2013 32 p. (hardcover) $16.99

Grades: PreK K 1   E

1. Food -- Fiction 2. Sheriffs -- Fiction 3. Donuts -- Fiction

ISBN 0803739257; 9780803739253

LC 2012017460

In this book by Alison Mcghee and illustrated by Isabel Roxas "the sheriff and his deputy dog have been charged with a mission: to bring a dozen donuts home safely. The young sheriff peeks inside the box to check on the tasty treats. They're practically calling his name, and in the blink of an eye (and with just a few nibbles), a donut disappears! Wherever could that missing donut be? Luckily, this is one mystery the sheriff and his deputy are sure to bring to a close." (Publisher's note)

Little boy; [by] Alison McGhee and [illustrated by] Peter H. Reynolds. Atheneum Books for Young Readers 2008 un il $15.99

Grades: PreK K 1   E

1. Father-son relationship -- Fiction

ISBN 978-1-4169-5872-7; 1-4169-5872-X

LC 2007029625

A father reflects on how the future depends upon the all of the little things in his son's world, from his yellow drinking cup to a big cardboard box

"There is ample white space around the charming pen, ink, and watercolor illustrations. The artwork bursts with energy. . . . The straightforward text, written from the dad's perspective, recounts the simple things that are important to his child." SLJ

Making a friend; illustrated by Marc Rosenthal. Atheneum Books for Young Readers 2011 40p il $16.99

Grades: K 1 2   E

1. Snow -- Fiction 2. Seasons -- Fiction 3. Friendship -- Fiction

ISBN 978-1-4169-8998-1; 1-4169-8998-6

LC 2010041661

When the snow falls, a young boy makes a snowman that becomes his friend until the seasons change

This is written "in minimal but evocative text. . . . This gentle story offers [an] opportunity to discuss the cycle of love, loss, and emotional renewal. The digitally manipulated pencil illustrations have a retro look. . . . A simple but deeply nuanced story that should resonate with children." SLJ

Mrs. Watson wants your teeth; story by Alison McGhee; pictures by Harry Bliss. Harcourt 2004 un il $16; pa $6

Grades: K 1 2 3   E

1. School stories 2. Teeth -- Fiction 3. Teachers -- Fiction

ISBN 0-15-204931-2; 0-15-206348-X pa

LC 2003-21267

A first grader is frightened on her first day of school after hearing a rumor that her teacher is a 300-year-old alien with a purple tongue who steals baby teeth from her students.

"McGhee has the pulse of this blue-ribbon worrier. . . . Bliss's watercolor and black-ink illustrations feature distinctive, large-eyed classmates and a number of humorous toothy references on the walls in the hall and in the classroom." SLJ

★ **Only** a witch can fly; illustrated by Taeeun Yoo. Feiwel and Friends 2009 un il $16.99

Grades: K 1 2   E

1. Stories in rhyme 2. Flight -- Fiction 3. Witches -- Fiction

ISBN 978-0-312-37503-4; 0-312-37503-4

LC 2008-28542

A young girl wants to fly like a witch on a broom, and one special night, through enormous effort and with the help of her brother, her black cat, and an owl, she fulfills her dream.

"Yoo's illustrations are linoleum block prints done in shades of green and brown with black and white details, adding a wonderful simplicity to this beautiful story." Libr Media Connect

So many days; with illustrations by Taeeun Yoo. Atheneum Books for Young Readers 2010 un il $15.99

Grades: PreK K 1   E

1. Conduct of life -- Fiction 2. Parent-child relationship -- Fiction

ISBN 978-1-4169-5857-4; 1-4169-5857-6

LC 2008038300

Through rhythmic text, a parent reflects on the options and opportunities possible in a beloved child's future.

"This book seamlessly pairs lyrical text and digitally manipulated linocut illustrations in a philosophical offering that encourages youngsters to face life head on." SLJ

Song of middle C; illustrated by Scott Menchin. Candlewick Press 2009 un il $16.99

Grades: K 1 2 3   **E**

   1. Fear -- Fiction 2. Pianists -- Fiction

   ISBN 978-0-7636-3013-3; 0-7636-3013-6

"One little girl uses imagination, bravado and her lucky underwear to overcome a colossal case of stage fright. She has practiced 'Dance of the Wood Elves' diligently [on the piano]. . . . When she steps confidently onto the stage, however, she totally forgets everything she rehearsed. . . . The only note she can manage is Middle C, so she plays it in several different ways with gusto, verve and true artistry, earning great applause. McGhee . . . employs a first-person narration to tell the story in direct, vivid, fast-paced colloquial language. Menchin's digitally colored pen-and-ink cartoons are remarkably detailed while appearing deceptively simple and childlike." Kirkus

A **very** brave witch; [by] Alison McGhee; [illustrated by] Harry Bliss. Simon & Schuster Books for Young Readers 2006 un il lib bdg $12.95

Grades: PreK K 1 2   **E**

   1. Witches -- Fiction 2. Halloween -- Fiction

   ISBN 0-689-86730-1

"A friendly young witch describes what she likes most about Halloween. . . . After boarding her broom, she zooms in a circle, becomes dizzy, and crashes near some trick-or-treaters. She soon discovers that a brave witch and a brave human girl dressed as a witch are not so very different. . . . The chatty text appears in dialogue balloons. Done in black ink and watercolor, the cartoon artwork captures the holiday's spirit with crisp fall colors and amusing details." SLJ

McGinley, Phyllis

A **year** without a Santa Claus; illustrated by John Manders. Marshall Cavendish 2010 un il $16.99

Grades: PreK K 1 2   **E**

   1. Christmas -- Fiction 2. Santa Claus -- Fiction

   ISBN 978-0-7614-5799-2; 0-7614-5799-2

A newly illustrated edition of the title first published 1957 by Lippincott

"This newly illustrated edition maintains all of the original's read-aloud charm while accentuating its playfulness with Mander's vibrant gouache and pencil illustrations." Horn Book Guide

McGinness, Suzanne

My bear Griz. Frances Lincoln Children's Books 2011 un il $17.95

Grades: PreK K   **E**

   1. Bears -- Fiction 2. Teddy bears -- Fiction

   ISBN 978-1-84780-113-5; 1-84780-113-7

Billy has a bear called Griz. A Grizzly Bear. And the two friends have all kinds of wonderful adventures together. Is he a real Grizzly Bear or a teddy bear? Well, that's for every reader to decide.

"A bear of imposing presence provides safety and joy in this visually distinctive debut. . . . Griz is striking, drawn in densely hatched and layered pen lines of browns and blacks, too big to fit on the page yet dominating the space. . . . Backgrounds are abstract, mellow watercolor, balancing the energetic lines of Griz's fur. . . . A winner for read-alouds, whether in groups or one-on-one." Kirkus

McGinty, Alice B.

Eliza's kindergarten pet. Marshall Cavendish 2010 un il $15.99

Grades: K 1 2   **E**

   1. School stories 2. Guinea pigs -- Fiction

   ISBN 978-0-7614-5702-2; 0-7614-5702-X

When the kindergarten classroom gets a pet guinea pig Eliza is afraid, but when the guinea pig gets lost, Eliza helps find her.

"This is a heartwarming story, enhanced by bright illustrations, about facing one's fears." SLJ

Eliza's kindergarten surprise; illustrated by Nancy Speir. Marshall Cavendish 2007 un il $14.99

Grades: PreK K   **E**

   1. School stories 2. Mother-daughter relationship -- Fiction

   ISBN 978-0-7614-5351-2; 0-7614-5351-2

               LC 2006022415

On her first day of school, Eliza fills her pocket with objects—buttons, a pebble, a napkin, and a piece of yarn—that remind her of her mother, whom she misses very much

"McGinty avoids overly sweet clichés with a strong concept and smooth telling, and Speir's cartoonlike illustrations balance scenes showing Eliza's anguish with brightly colored views of a welcoming classroom and pictures of a loving mother and daughter that reinforce the warm, reassuring words." Booklist

   Another title about Eliza is:

   Eliza's kindergarten pet (2010)

McGowan, Michael

Sunday is for God; illustrated by Lou Fancher and Steve Johnson. Schwartz & Wade Books 2010 un il $17.99; lib bdg $20.99

Grades: 1 2 3   **E**

   1. Church -- Fiction 2. Family life -- Fiction 3. African Americans -- Fiction

   ISBN 978-0-375-84188-0; 0-375-84188-1; 978-0-375-94591-5 lib bdg; 0-375-94591-1 lib bdg

               LC 2008-48828

"It's Sunday morning and a young African American boy knows what that means: 'Sunday is for God. That's what Momma says.' . . . McGowan unleashes a wealth of sensory details. . . . Johnson and Facher's artwork . . . gets a lift from its textured mix of acrylic and collage. . . . A tender reflection of many children's Sunday experience." Booklist

McGrath, Barbara Barbieri

The **little** red elf; illustrated by Rosalinde Bonnet. Charlesbridge 2009 un il lib bdg $14.95

Grades: PreK K 1   **E**

   1. Fairies -- Fiction 2. Christmas -- Fiction 3. North Pole -- Fiction

   ISBN 978-1-58089-236-0; 1-58089-236-1

               LC 2008-25340

In this version of "The Little Red Hen," set at the North Pole, a penguin and a hare refuse to help an elf plant, grow, and decorate an evergreen tree but nevertheless expect to open the presents found under its branches on Christmas Day.

"The acrylic and ballpoint-pen illustrations are full of childlike humor, depicting cute North Pole characters who look like toys themselves. This is that rare beast—an endearing holiday book without a hint of treacle." SLJ

Teddy bear counting; illustrated by Tim Nihoff. Charlesbridge 2010 il lib bdg $16.95; pa $7.95 **E**
1. Color 2. Shape 3. Counting 4. Stories in rhyme 5. Teddy bears -- Fiction
ISBN 978-1-58089-215-5 lib bdg; 978-1-58089-216-2 pa
LC 2008025339

Teddy bears introduce numbers from one to twelve, as well as colors and shapes.

McGrory, Anik
Quick, slow, mango! Bloomsbury Books for Young Readers 2011 un il $16.99; lib bdg $17.89
Grades: PreK K 1   **E**
1. Speed -- Fiction 2. Africa -- Fiction 3. Monkeys -- Fiction 4. Elephants -- Fiction
ISBN 978-1-59990-242-5; 1-59990-242-7; 978-1-59990-592-1 lib bdg; 1-59990-592-2 lib bdg
LC 2010025975

"The attractive pencil-and-watercolor artwork features bright, soft colors and rounded, smiling animals, while the variety of sizes and layouts match and enhance the pace of this simple, utterly charming story." Kirkus

McGuirk, Leslie
★ If rocks could sing. Tricycle Press 2011 un il $15.99; lib bdg $18.89
Grades: PreK K 1 2   **E**
1. Alphabet 2. Rocks -- Fiction
ISBN 1-58246-370-0; 1-58246-395-6 lib bdg; 978-1-58246-370-4; 978-1-58246-395-7 lib bdg
LC 2010019206

"This unique alphabet book features photos of ocean-sculpted rocks lovingly collected over the course of a decade by the author. McGuirk amassed a complete alphabet of letter-shaped rocks, which she pairs with other humorously representational geologic findings. She puts the emphasis on the rocks themselves, employing simple text, solid backgrounds, and spare, yet engaging layouts to showcase her finds. . . . Sure to spark imaginative rock-finding hunts and found-object art projects, this quirky title will earn its place in any picture-book collection." SLJ

McKee, David
★ **Elmer**; by David McKee. Lothrop, Lee & Shepard Books 1989 [31] p. $16.99
Grades: PreK K 1   **E**
1. Laughter -- Fiction 2. Individuality -- Fiction 3. Elephants -- Fiction
ISBN 0688091717; 0688091725; 9780688091712
LC 89002285

In this picture book, by David McKee, "Elmer the elephant is bright-colored patchwork all over. No wonder the other elephants laugh at him! If he were ordinary elephant color, the others might stop laughing. That would make Elmer feel better, wouldn't it? The . . . conclusion . . . is a celebration of individuality and the power of laughter." (Publisher's note)

"Elmer the elephant is a colorful character. His heady optimism and unbridled sense of humor keep the entire community in a cheery mood...McKee's gentle humor and love

of irony are in full force in this celebration of individuality and laughter. Well-designed spreads are washed with stunning color and the use of textured, painted and airbrushed surfaces contributes to the powerful visual impression." (Publishers Weekly)

McKissack, Pat, 1944-
The **all-**I'll-ever-want Christmas doll; written by Patricia C. McKissack; illustrated by Jerry Pinkney. Schwartz & Wade Books 2007 1 v. (unpaged) col. ill.
Grades: PreK K 1 2 3 4 5   **E**
1. Dolls -- Fiction 2. Sisters -- Fiction 3. Christmas -- Fiction 4. Sharing -- Fiction 5. African Americans -- Fiction 6. Depressions -- 1929 -- Fiction
ISBN 9780375836152
LC 2006030981

In this children's book, a recipient of a starred review by "Booklist" and "Kirkus Reviews" in 2007, "[i]t's Christmas and Nella is beside herself with excitement! She and her sisters have been given a real gift—a beautiful Baby Betty doll. But it's hard to share something you've waited your whole seven-year-old life for, and Nella grabs the doll for herself. It isn't long before she discovers that a doll can't do the fun things she and her sisters do together. So, as Christmas day fades, Nella shares it with her sisters." (Publisher's note)

★ **Flossie** & the fox; pictures by Rachel Isadora. Dial Bks. for Young Readers 1986 un il $15.99
Grades: K 1 2 3   **E**
1. Foxes -- Fiction 2. African Americans -- Fiction
ISBN 0-8037-0250-7
LC 86-2024

A wily fox notorious for stealing eggs meets his match when he encounters a bold little girl in the woods who insists upon proof that he is a fox before she will be frightened

"The watercolor and ink illustrations, with realistic figures set on impressionistic backgrounds, enliven this humorous and well-structured story which is told in the black language of the rural south." SLJ

★ **Goin'** someplace special; [illustrated by] Jerry Pinkney. Atheneum Bks. for Young Readers 2001 un il $16; pa $6.99
Grades: K 1 2 3   **E**
1. Libraries -- Fiction 2. Tennessee -- Fiction 3. Segregation -- Fiction 4. African Americans -- Fiction
ISBN 0-689-81885-8; 1-4169-2735-2 pa
LC 99-88258

Coretta Scott King Award for illustration
In segregated 1950s Nashville, a young African American girl braves a series of indignities and obstacles to get to one of the few integrated places in town: the public library

"Pinkney's watercolor paintings are lush and sprawling as they evoke southern city streets and sidewalks as well as Tricia Ann's inner glow. . . . This book carries a strong message of pride and self-confidence as well as a pointed history lesson." Booklist

★ **Mirandy** and Brother Wind; illustrated by Jerry Pinkney. Knopf 1988 un il $17; pa $6.99
Grades: K 1 2 3   **E**
1. Dance -- Fiction 2. Winds -- Fiction 3. African

Americans -- Fiction

ISBN 978-0-394-88765-4; 0-394-88765-4; 978-0-679-88333-3 pa; 0-679-88333-9 pa

LC 87-349

A Caldecott Medal honor book, 1989

Coretta Scott King Award for illustration

"Ms. McKissack and Mr. Pinkney's ebullient collaboration captures the texture of rural life and culture 40 years after the end of slavery." N Y Times Book Rev

"Mirandy is sure that she'll win the cake walk if she can catch Brother Wind for her partner, but he eludes all the tricks her friends advise." Bull Cent Child Books

★ **Ol'** Clip-Clop; a ghost story. by Patricia C. McKissack; illustrated by Eric Velasquez. Holiday House 2013 32 p. (hardcover) $16.95

Grades: 1 2 3 4 5   E

1. Ghost stories 2. Historical fiction 3. Ghosts -- Fiction 4. Conduct of life -- Fiction

ISBN 0823422658; 9780823422654

LC 2010029448

In this ghost story, "an 18th-century miser, John Leep, rides on horseback to evict a woman from her residence. But as darkness falls over the forest . . . Leep hears the 'Clip, Clop' of a ghostly rider behind him. After cruelly deceiving his desperate tenant ('You're short. This isn't everything you owe me!'), he journeys home, again pursued by the invisible horseman." (Publishers Weekly)

★ **Precious** and the Boo Hag; [by] Patricia C. McKissack and Onawumi Jean Moss; illustrated by Kyrsten Brooker. Atheneum Books for Young Readers 2004 un il $16.95

Grades: K 1 2 3   E

1. Monsters -- Fiction 2. African Americans -- Fiction

ISBN 0-689-85194-4

LC 2002-1571

Home alone with a stomachache while the family works in the fields, a young girl faces up to the horrifying Boo Hag that her brother warned her about.

"With the grand feel of a folktale, this lively story speaks to choosing right in a world full of temptation and peril. . . . Expressive and fluid, Brooker's mixed-media art, comical yet scary, too, pops from the pages." Booklist

McLeod, Heather

Kiss me! (I'm a prince!) illustrated by Brooke Kerrigan. Fitzhenry & Whiteside 2011 un il $18.95

Grades: K 1 2   E

1. Fairy tales 2. Frogs -- Fiction 3. Princes -- Fiction

ISBN 978-1-55455-161-3; 1-55455-161-7

"This clever variation on the classic 'Frog Prince' features a modern girl wearing a red ball cap, a striped T-shirt, purple pants, and red sneakers. She is carrying a basketball, ready to shoot hoops, when a little green frog with a crown on his head wants a kiss to become a prince. . . . The uncluttered artwork uses a pastel palette and makes good use of white space. Whether read independently or shared at storytime, this breezy tale of a frog who comes to value being a boy as much as being a prince will elicit smiles." SLJ

McLerran, Alice

Roxaboxen; illustrated by Barbara Cooney. Lothrop, Lee & Shepard Bks. 1991 un il $16.99; pa $6.99

Grades: K 1 2 3   E

1. Imagination -- Fiction

ISBN 0-688-07592-4; 0-06-052633-5 pa

LC 89-8057

A hill covered with rocks and wooden boxes in the desert becomes an imaginary town named Roxaboxen for Marian, her sisters, and their friends

"A celebration of the transforming magic of the imagination, the story was inspired by McLerran's mother's reminiscences of her childhood in Yuma, Arizona. . . . The story, told as though from the memory of a Roxaboxenite, brings their play to life through concrete details and a spare, understated style. Equally vivid, Cooney's full-color artwork evokes the striking variety of colors and moods found in the desert landscape." Booklist

McLimans, David

★ **Gone** wild; an endangered animal alphabet. Walker & Company 2006 un il $16.95; lib bdg $17.85

Grades: 1 2 3 4   E

1. Animals 2. Alphabet 3. Endangered species

ISBN 978-0-8027-9563-2; 978-0-8027-9564-9 lib bdg; 0-8027-9563-3; 0-8027-9564-1 lib bdg

LC 2006-44702

A Caldecott Medal honor book, 2007

"Although organized as a conventional alphabet book, the letters here are far from ordinary. McLimans has created a black-and-white iconic representation of 26 endangered animals, and his art is striking. . . . The arresting graphics and clean design will hold viewers' attention and create interest in the topic." SLJ

Includes bibliographical references

McMillan, Bruce

★ **How** the ladies stopped the wind; illustrated with paintings by Gunnella. Houghton Mifflin 2007 32p il $16

Grades: K 1 2 3   E

1. Sheep -- Fiction 2. Trees -- Fiction 3. Winds -- Fiction 4. Iceland -- Fiction 5. Chickens -- Fiction

ISBN 978-0-618-77330-5; 0-618-77330-4

LC 2007-04207

The women of one village in Iceland decide to plant trees to stop the powerful winds that make it difficult even to go for a walk, but first they must find a ways to prevent sheep from eating all of their saplings, while encouraging chickens to fertilize them.

"The team that made stars of a group of Icelandic ladies in The Problem with Chickens returns for another winning round. . . . Gunnella's flat, deadpan oil portraits of the ladies, their polka-dot aprons and their hapless chickens are inherently funny, and every page contains another visual poke in the ribs." Publ Wkly

★ **The problem** with chickens; illustrated with paintings by Gunnella. Houghton Mifflin 2005 32p il $16

Grades: K 1 2 3   E

1. Iceland -- Fiction 2. Chickens -- Fiction

ISBN 0-618-58581-8

LC 2005-01225

When women in an Icelandic village buy chickens to lay eggs for them to use, the chickens follow them, adopting human ways and forgetting their barnyard roots, until the ladies hatch a clever plan.

"The playful text is both silly and joyous, without a wasted word. Gunnella's enchanting oil paintings are full of childlike humor and saturated with appealing primary colors." SLJ

McMullan, Kate

★ **Bulldog's** big day; pictures by Pascal Lemaitre. Orchard Books 2011 un il $16.99
Grades: PreK K   E
1. Dogs -- Fiction 2. Animals -- Fiction 3. Occupations -- Fiction
ISBN 0-545-17155-5; 978-0-545-17155-7
LC 2010-26235

While looking for a job, Bulldog tries being a firefighter, a window washer, a sign painter, and a bookseller before finding just the right job for himself. "Ages four to seven." (Bull Cent Child Books)

"The illustrations were created in pen and ink, colored in Adobe Photoshop. . . . There are five or six scenes per spread. Everything is outlined in a thin black line and colored in flat hues. There's a lot to look at on each page, and children will enjoy poring over all the details." SLJ

★ **I** stink! [by] Kate & Jim McMullan. HarperCollins Pubs. 2002 un il $15.95; lib bdg $15.89; pa $6.99
Grades: PreK K 1 2   E
1. Refuse and refuse disposal -- Fiction
ISBN 0-06-029848-0; 0-06-029849-9 lib bdg; 0-06-443836-8 pa
LC 00-54229

A big city garbage truck makes its rounds, consuming everything from apple cores and banana peels to leftover ziti with zucchini

"Kate McMullan creates an automotive beast whose narrative style reeks of personality, and Jim McMullan's renderings are a perfect match, coaxing steely features into flexible, expressive shapes." Bull Cent Child Books

★ **I'm** bad; [by] Kate & Jim McMullan. Joanna Cotler Books 2008 un il $16.99; lib bdg $17.89
Grades: PreK K 1   E
1. Dinosaurs -- Fiction
ISBN 978-0-06-122971-8; 0-06-122971-7; 978-0-06-122972-5 lib bdg; 0-06-122972-5 lib bdg
LC 2007032020

A hungry Tyrannosaurus rex searches for food in the prehistoric forest but is thwarted in its attempts to find something to eat

"The high-energy illustrations and macho narrator's words create a rowdy, crowd-pleasing whole. Children will delight in the dinosaur's wild expressions and the dynamic text, filled with comic-book sound effects." Booklist

★ **I'm** big! [by] Kate & Jim McMullan. Balzer + Bray 2010 un il $16.99; lib bdg $17.89
Grades: PreK K 1   E
1. Dinosaurs -- Fiction
ISBN 978-0-06-122974-9; 0-06-122974-1; 978-0-06-122975-6 lib bdg; 0-06-122975-X lib bdg

A young Sauropod encounters friends and foes while searching for his pack, who left while he was oversleeping.

"This tale of a young dinosaur finding his inner power is told through childlike vernacular with varying type sizes and colors to emphasize mood. The full-color watercolor illus-

trations feature plenty of action and multiple perspectives. . . . Perfect as a read-aloud or a read-alone." SLJ

★ **I'm** dirty! [by] Kate & Jim McMullan. Joanna Cotler Books 2006 un il $16.99; lib bdg $17.89
Grades: PreK K 1 2   E
1. Cleanliness -- Fiction 2. Construction equipment -- Fiction
ISBN 978-0-06-009293-1; 0-06-009293-9; 978-0-06-009294-8 lib bdg; 0-06-009294-7 lib bdg
LC 2005-17919

A busy backhoe loader describes all the items it hauls off a lot and all the fun it has getting dirty while doing so

"With its saucy tone and dynamic color cartoon illustrations, this picture book exudes energy." SLJ

I'm mighty! [by] Kate & Jim McMullan. Joanna Cotler Bks. 2003 un il $17.99
Grades: PreK K 1 2   E
1. Tugboats -- Fiction
ISBN 0-06-009290-4
LC 2002-7948

A little tugboat shows how he can bring big ships into the harbor even though he is small

"The tugboat that narrates this picture book tells his story with more than a splash of moxie. Strong ink drawings define the harbor setting from a variety of perspectives and show the emotions of the anthropomorphic figures of boats and trucks, while color brightens the scenes and heightens the drama." Booklist

★ **Pearl** and Wagner: one funny day. Dial Books for Young Readers 2009 40p (Dial easy-to-read) $14.99
Grades: K 1 2   E
1. School stories 2. Mice -- Fiction 3. Animals -- Fiction 4. Rabbits -- Fiction 5. April Fools' Day -- Fiction
ISBN 978-0-8037-3085-4; 0-8037-3085-3
LC 2008007699

ALA ALSC Geisel Award Honor Book (2010)

April Fools' Day is not a happy one for Wagner the mouse because his best friend, Pearl the rabbit, and other children and adults at school keep tricking him.

"Alley's expressive ink-and-watercolor illustrations portray Wagner's shifting emotions with clarity and finesse." Booklist

Other titles about Pearl and Wagner are:
Pearl and Wagner: two good friends (2003)
Pearl and Wagner: three secrets (2004)
Pearl and Wagner: four eyes (2010)

McNamara, Margaret
The **apple** orchard riddle; Margaret McNamara; pictures by G. Brian Karas. Schwartz & Wade 2013 40 p. $15.99
Grades: K 1 2   E
1. Apples -- Fiction 2. Field trips 3. Riddles -- Fiction 4. School field trips -- Fiction
ISBN 0375847448; 9780375847448; 9780375957444
LC 2011008742

This book, by Margaret McNamara and illustrated by G. Brian Karas, is "about a school trip to an apple orchard! The students learn a lot about apples and apple orchards--including how apples are harvested, how cider is made, and what the different varieties of apples are--while trying to solve a riddle. The book also celebrates how some children learn differently than others." (Publisher's note)

How many seeds in a pumpkin? illustrated by G. Brian Karas. Schwartz & Wade Books 2007 un il $14.99
Grades: K 1 2   E
1. School stories 2. Size -- Fiction 3. Pumpkin -- Fiction 4. Counting -- Fiction
ISBN 978-0-375-84014-2; 0-375-84014-1; 978-0-375-94014-9 lib bdg; 0-375-94014-6 lib bdg
LC 2006-16866
Charlie, the smallest child in his first grade class, is amazed to discover that of the three pumpkins his teacher brings to school, the tiniest one has the most seeds.
"Karas's characteristic watercolor illustrations done in a fall palette depict a diverse, modern classroom full of warm and humorous details. . . . This enjoyable story, sprinkled with math and science lessons, should be a first-purchase consideration." SLJ

The **three** little aliens and the big bad robot; written by Margaret McNamara; illustrated by Mark Fearing. Schwartz & Wade Books 2011 un il $16.99; lib bdg $19.99
Grades: PreK K 1 2   E
1. Robots -- Fiction 2. Siblings -- Fiction 3. Extraterrestrial beings -- Fiction 4. Outer space -- Exploration -- Fiction
ISBN 978-0-375-86689-0; 0-375-86689-2; 978-0-375-96689-7 lib bdg; 0-375-96689-7 lib bdg
LC 2010050153
Three aliens set off to find a new planet for themselves but soon Bork and Gork have forgotten all of their mother's good advice and only Nklxwcyz builds a home safe enough to withstand the Big Bad Robot.
"With its broad humor and a knowing wink to folktale conventions, this delightful reworking of 'The Three Little Pigs' has potential to become a crowd-pleasing favorite. . . . Fearing's hand-drawn cartoon illustrations rendered digitally with collage techniques offer bugeyed, green aliens and an enjoyable mix of science and playful details." SLJ

The **whistle** on the train; [by] Margaret McNamara; illustrated by Richard Egielski; paper engineering by Gene Vosough. Hyperion 2008 un il $18.99
Grades: PreK   E
1. Songs 2. Pop-up books 3. Railroads -- Fiction
ISBN 978-0-7868-4890-4; 0-7868-4890-1
"Here's a great concept, handsomely executed. Take a song known to virtually every preschooler, 'The Wheels on the Bus,' and update it with a vehicle much more widely adored by this group, a train, then soup it up with lavish but resilient paper engineering. Involving plenty of repetition, McNamara's lyrics are easy to learn. . . . The pop-ups, mostly stationary, are multidimensional renderings of Egielski's cheery cartoons." Publ Wkly

McNaughton, Colin
★ **Not** last night but the night before; illustrated by Emma Chichester Clark. Candlewick Press 2009 un il $16.99
Grades: PreK K 1 2   E
1. Fairy tales 2. Stories in rhyme 3. Parties -- Fiction

4. Birthdays -- Fiction 5. Nursery rhymes -- Fiction
ISBN 978-0-7636-4420-8; 0-7636-4420-X
"Rhyming, repetitive text tells of a boy who reluctantly welcomes a parade of nursery-rhyme characters into his home. Everyone from the man in the moon to Little Miss Muffet bursts through the entryway wearing party clothes and carrying presents. . . . Colorful pencil and acrylic illustrations alternate between scallop-edged vignettes and full-bleed scenes rife with excitement. Preschoolers will enjoy the predictability of this tale." SLJ

Once upon an ordinary school day; story by Colin McNaughton; pictures by Satoshi Kitamura. Farrar, Straus & Giroux 2005 un il $16
Grades: K 1 2   E
1. School stories 2. Teachers -- Fiction 3. Imagination -- Fiction
ISBN 0-374-35634-3
LC 2004-105656
First published 2004 in the United Kingdom
"An ordinary boy awakens to an ordinary school day. The story opens with drab scenes depicted in shades of gray that turn to Technicolor several pages in, with the arrival of a new teacher in a yellow suit. . . . Deftly rendered cartoon drawings convey the expressive gestures and transformation of the characters and scenes. . . . An excellent selection to start the creative juices flowing or to enliven an ordinary day." SLJ

McPhail, David
Baby Pig Pig talks; David McPhail. Charlesbridge 2014 14 p. color illustrations (board book) $6.95
Grades: PreK   E
1. Pigs -- Fiction 2. Animals -- Fiction 3. Board books for children 4. Board books 5. Speech -- Fiction
ISBN 1580895972; 9781580895972; 9781607347033
LC 2013020489
In this children's book, "David McPhail takes readers back in time to when Pig Pig, star of the popular picture-book series, was a baby. Baby Pig Pig tries to copy his mother's speech as she points out the animals and objects around them, but nothing he says seems to come out right. What will Baby Pig Pig's first real word be?" (Publisher's note)
"McPhail's picture book hero Pig Pig is back—as a baby. As his mother pushes him around in his stroller, she introduces words for things they see... McPhail's watercolors exude warmth and quiet humor, and the aural sources for many of Baby Pig Pig's words ("Dinga" for tricycle, "Quacka" for duck) hint at how the gears are turning in his young porcine brain. Simultaneously available: Baby Pig Pig Walks. " PW

Baby Pig Pig walks; David McPhail. Charlesbridge 2014 14 p. color illustrations (board book) $6.95
Grades: PreK   E
1. Pigs -- Fiction 2. Walking -- Fiction 3. Board books for children 4. Board books
ISBN 1580895964; 9781580895965; 9781607347040
LC 2013020490
In this children's story, by David McPhail, "takes readers back in time to when Pig Pig, star of the popular picture-book series, was a baby. Baby Pig Pig is learning to walk. After a few rough starts, he makes his way out of the playpen and into the kitchen, right into his mother's waiting arms." (Publisher's note)

"A piglet toddler learns to walk. After growing bored, Baby Pig Pig learns to pull himself up, climb out of his playpen and walk out of the living room into the kitchen, all in the course of a day...Phail understands the simplicity required for a story for the youngest toddlers. Clarity and humor carry the day." Kirkus

Bad dog; by David McPhail. Holiday House 2014 32 p. (I like to read) (hardcover) $14.95
Grades: PreK K 1 **E**
1. Dogs -- Fiction 2. Bad behavior -- Fiction
ISBN 0823428524; 9780823428526
LC 2012038836

"Forgiveness and love triumph at the end of this . . . easy-to-read story of a family dog who is rarely on his best behavior," written and illustrated by David McPhail, and part of the I Like to Read series. (Publisher's note) The dog "irks the family cat, Kit, who one night escapes. Tom is threatened with eviction from the family but is redeemed when he helps the boy see where Kit is hiding." (Kirkus Reviews)

"Tom is a bad dog; he makes the narrator's mom, dad, and cat Kit mad. Just when "Dad says that Tom must go," Kit goes missing, and it's Tom to the rescue. Simple, repetitive text; mild tension; pen-and-ink and watercolor illustrations with plenty of details for kids to notice; and lots of clean white space make this a good pick for beginning readers." Horn Book

Bella loves Bunny; by David McPhail. Abrams Appleseed 2013 22 p. (alk. paper) $8.95
Grades: PreK **E**
1. Picture books for children 2. Toys -- Fiction 3. Friendship -- Fiction
ISBN 1419705431; 9781419705434
LC 2012035411

This children's picture book is David McPhail's "companion title to 'Ben Loves Bear'" and "follows a similar day-in-the-life format." Here, a "young girl enjoys the company of her stuffed rabbit from sunup to sundown. . . . Bella and Bunny do some gardening, enjoy a picnic and play the piano." (Kirkus Reviews)

★ **Ben** loves Bear; by David McPhail. Abrams Appleseed 2013 22 p. $8.95
Grades: PreK **E**
1. Toys 2. Picture books for children 3. Friendship -- Fiction 4. Teddy bears -- Fiction
ISBN 1419703862; 9781419703867
LC 2012003527

In this children's picture book by David McPhail, "Ben and his favorite stuffed toy are together from morning to night, and they seem to exist contentedly in their own little world. They wake up together and then, 'Ben has cereal. Bear has honey' at the kitchen table. They play hide-and-seek, Ben gets dressed while Bear watches, they play outdoors, Bear waits patiently while Ben bathes, and the day winds down as the two snuggle up for bedtime, complete with a story." (School Library Journal)

"McPhail, in top form here, has created soft watercolors with rounded lines that adroitly capture Ben's toddler movements. The artist's use of full spreads and smaller visual vignettes spotlighted in hazy, round borders gives the simple, easy-reader–like text rhythm and balance. Already a gifted

artist, McPhail proves here that he intrinsically understands what the youngest readers want and need." Kirkus

Big Brown Bear's up and down day; [written and illustrated by] David McPhail. Harcourt 2003 un il $16; pa $6
Grades: PreK K 1 2 **E**
1. Rats -- Fiction 2. Bears -- Fiction
ISBN 0-15-216407-3; 0-15-205684-X pa
LC 2002-15854

Big Brown Bear is visited by a rat who wants to use one of his slippers for a bed

"A warm and gentle story. . . . Beautiful watercolor and pen-and-ink paintings make the most of the size difference between the characters and help to create real personalities by capturing the emotions they experience." SLJ

Other titles about Big Brown Bear are:
Big Brown Bear goes to town (2006)
Big Brown Bear's birthday surprise (2007)

Big Pig and Little Pig; [by] David McPhail. Harcourt 2003 un il (Green light readers) $11.95; pa $3.95
Grades: PreK K 1 **E**
1. Pigs -- Fiction
ISBN 978-0-15-204818-1; 0-15-204818-9; 978-0-15-204857-0 pa; 0-15-204857-X pa
A reissue of the title first published 2001

Big Pig and Little Pig enjoy spending time together, though they take different approaches to the same task

"McPhail's signature illustrations fill each page as he once again successfully manages to transfer human emotions to his lovable cartoon pigs. Well-chosen vocabulary and repetition of words make this story a suitable choice for those just learning to read." SLJ

Boy, Bird, and Dog; by David McPhail. Holiday House 2011 il (I like to read picture book) $14.95
Grades: PreK K 1 2 **E**
1. Dogs -- Fiction 2. Birds -- Fiction 3. Tree houses -- Fiction
ISBN 978-0-8234-2346-0; 0-8234-2346-8
LC 2010029435

In this story for beginning readers, Boy, Bird, and Dog have lots of fun in their tree house.

"The story is told in the sparest of language. . . . It reads smoothly with a clear plot, likable characters and an interesting setting. . . . McPhail's signature watercolor-and-ink illustrations are large scale with soft edges. The action and characters are well defined and appealing." Kirkus

★ **Drawing** lessons from a bear; [by] David McPhail. Little, Brown 2000 un il $14.95
Grades: PreK K 1 **E**
1. Bears -- Fiction 2. Artists -- Fiction
ISBN 0-316-56345-5
LC 98-54966

A bear explains how he became an artist, first experimenting with simple drawings, then continuing to draw both things around him and things in his imagination. Includes tips for drawing

"This gentle story combines a humorous tone with warm, cozy watercolors to create inspiration for budding artists." SLJ

★ **Emma** in charge; by David McPhail. Dutton Children's Books 2005 un il $12.99

Grades: PreK K 1   E

  1. Play -- Fiction 2. Bears -- Fiction

  ISBN 0-525-47411-0

                  LC 2004-21580

Emma the bear pretends that she and her dolls spend a day at school.

"McPhail's watercolors are . . . expressive and winsome . . . and the short sentences, printed in bold type, are just right for read-alouds or for emerging readers to follow along." Booklist

  Other titles about Emma are:

  Emma's pet (1985)

  Emma's vacation (1987)

  Fix-it (1984)

Mole music; written and illustrated by David McPhail. Holt & Co. 1999 un il $15.95; pa $7.99

Grades: PreK K 1 2   E

  1. Music -- Fiction 2. Violins -- Fiction 3. Moles (Animals) -- Fiction

  ISBN 0-8050-2819-6; 0-8050-6766-3 pa

                  LC 98-21318

Feeling that something is missing in his simple life, Mole acquires a violin and learns to make beautiful, joyful music

"McPhail's delicate watercolor-and-ink illustrations work with the simple text to create a lyrical celebration of music and musicians." Booklist

No! Roaring Brook Press 2009 un il $16.95

Grades: K 1 2 3   E

  1. War stories 2. Stories without words 3. Bullies -- Fiction

  ISBN 978-1-59643-288-8; 1-59643-288-8

                  LC 2008054607

"In this dark, nearly wordless allegory, the power of a single word ripples outward, stopping a bully, an army, a war. . . . McPhail's . . . delicately tinted crosshatching gives poignancy to the violence the boy witnesses without minimizing it. The idea of taking effective action without fighting is a powerful one, and children and adults alike will find that McPhail's images linger." Publ Wkly

Pig Pig meets the lion; David McPhail. Charlesbridge 2012 32p.

Grades: PreK K   E

  1. Lions -- Fiction 2. Children's stories 3. Picture books for children 4. Lion -- Fiction 5. Pigs -- Fiction 6. Friendship -- Fiction 7. Friendship -- Fiction 8. English language -- Prepositions -- Fiction 9. English language -- Prepositions

  ISBN 9781580893589

                  LC 2011009031

This book "starring . . . Pig Pig begins wordlessly on the pre-title page and continues onto the opening pages, as a lion escapes from a zoo and climbs up the tree outside Pig Pig's bedroom window. From there, the friendly lion enters Pig Pig's room, much to the delight of Pig Pig, who jumps '"out" of bed' and runs '"down" the stairs,' followed by the lion. Pig Pig and the lion continue their romp through the house, unbeknownst to his ever-distracted mother, and though Pig Pig longs to keep the lion, it must skedaddle

when the zookeepers show up on the doorstep on the book's closing endpapers. There's a manifestly educational bent to this escapade, as prepositions are printed in boldfaced type." (Bulletin of the Center for Children's Books)

Pig Pig returns; [by] David McPhail. Charlesbridge 2011 un il lib bdg $15.95

Grades: PreK K 1   E

  1. Pigs -- Fiction 2. Aunts -- Fiction 3. Uncles -- Fiction 4. Vacations -- Fiction 5. Automobile travel -- Fiction

  ISBN 978-1-58089-356-5; 1-58089-356-2

                  LC 2010023528

Initially reluctant to leave his mother and cat, Pig Pig spends his summer vacation road tripping with his Aunt Wilma and Uncle Fred across the country in their teal-green camper.

"The line-and-watercolor art is drawn with sweetness and humor. Many kids (and adults) will see their mixed feelings about travel here." Booklist

★ **Pigs** aplenty, pigs galore! [by] David McPhail. Dutton Children's Bks. 1993 un il hardcover o.p. pa $6.99

Grades: PreK K 1 2   E

  1. Stories in rhyme 2. Pigs -- Fiction

  ISBN 0-525-45079-3; 0-14-055313-4 pa

                  LC 92-27986

"The rhyme is bouncy enough, but it's the pictures that will have parents and kids howling. Using deep watercolors set against a black background, McPhail presents a magnificent group of porkers, whose capacity for costumes and capers is truly wondrous." Booklist

  Other titles about the pigs are:

  Pigs ahoy! (1995)

  Those can-do pigs (1996)

★ **Sylvie** & True; [by] David McPhail. Farrar, Straus, & Giroux 2007 31p il lib bdg $15

Grades: PreK K 1 2   E

  1. Snakes -- Fiction 2. Rabbits -- Fiction 3. Friendship -- Fiction

  ISBN 978-0-374-37364-1 lib bdg; 0-374-37364-7 lib bdg

                  LC 2006048979

In four vignettes, Sylvie the rabbit and her friend True, a giant water snake, share a small apartment in a big city, cook, go bowling, and have a good time together

The scenarios are "simple . . . occasioning affectionate dialogue and terrific sight gags. . . . [This is a] charmer." Publ Wkly

The **teddy** bear; written and illustrated by David McPhail. Holt & Co. 2002 un il $15.95; pa $7.99

Grades: PreK K 1 2   E

  1. Teddy bears -- Fiction 2. Homeless persons -- Fiction

  ISBN 0-8050-6414-1; 0-8050-7882-7 pa

                  LC 2001-1500

"By accident a boy leaves his beloved bear in a diner. A homeless man finds it in the garbage and loves the bear as much as the boy did. Then one day the boy sees the bear on a park bench and joyfully grabs it. But when he recognizes the lonely man's sorrow at losing his friend, the child returns the toy. . . . It works because McPhail's beautiful soft-toned watercolor pictures with detailed ink cross-hatching tell the elemental story of shelter and love through the child's eyes." Booklist

Waddles; by David McPhail. Abrams Books for Young Readers 2011 un il $15.95
Grades: PreK K 1 2   E
1. Ducks -- Fiction 2. Raccoons -- Fiction 3. Friendship -- Fiction
ISBN 0-8109-8415-6; 978-0-8109-8415-8
LC 2010023699

Waddles, a very plump and furry raccoon, helps his best friend Emily, a duck, hatch and raise her ducklings, and discovers what makes him truly happy.

"McPhail's ink-and-watercolor illustrations elevate the familiar story of mismatched, devoted friends, coaxing expertly drawn emotion from his endearing characters." Booklist

Water boy; [by] David McPhail. Abrams Books for Young Readers 2007 un il $15.95
Grades: PreK K 1 2   E
1. Magic -- Fiction 2. Water -- Fiction
ISBN 978-0-8109-1784-2; 0-8109-1784-X
LC 2006013578

Fascinated by the fact that humans are made mostly of water, a boy develops an unusual relationship with it once he stops being afraid.

"Beautifully written, illustrated, and designed, this small gem of a book calls to be opened, touched, and read from its texturally and visually appealing cover . . . to the rich, color-drenched pictures of the real and the fantastic inside." SLJ

Weezer changes the world; [by] David McPhail. Beach Lane Books 2009 un il $15.99
Grades: PreK K 1   E
1. Dogs -- Fiction
ISBN 978-1-4169-9000-0; 1-4169-9000-3
LC 2009005537

After an ordinary puppyhood, Weezer develops extraordinary skills that make him a major influence in the world.

"McPhail's amusing tale will inspire young children to consider how they can make the world a better place, and his droll ink-and-watercolor illustrations reinforce the book's simple but powerful message." Booklist

McQuinn, Anna
★ **Leo** loves baby time; Anna McQuinn; illustrated by Ruth Hearson. 1st U.S. edition Charlesbridge 2014 24 p. (reinforced for library use) $9.95
     E
1. Play -- Fiction 2. Babies -- Fiction 3. Infants -- Fiction 4. Play groups -- Fiction
ISBN 1580896650; 9781580896658; 9781607346654
LC 2013004292

In this children's picture book, "Leo . . . attends a baby program with his mother. He and his fellow sitting-up babes enjoy singing and playing on their grown-ups' laps, as well as exploring books and toys. The single- and double-page spreads include one or two sentences describing the action written in a bold, black type. . . . The setting of this program is left unclear, but it could easily be a public library

or a community center in a very diverse neighborhood." (Kirkus Reviews)

Lola at the library; [by] Anna McQuinn; illustrated by Rosalind Beardshaw. Charlesbridge 2006 un il lib bdg $15.95; pa $6.95
Grades: PreK K 1 2   E
1. Libraries -- Fiction 2. Books and reading -- Fiction
ISBN 978-1-58089-113-4 lib bdg; 1-58089-113-6 lib bdg; 978-1-58089-142-4 pa; 1-58089-142-X pa
LC 2005019620

Published in the United Kingdom with title: Layla loves the library

Every Tuesday Lola and her mother visit their local library to return and check out books, attend story readings, and share a special treat

"Simple text and large, bright acrylic illustrations of this engaging African-American child make this selection just right for sharing" SLJ

"Another title about Lola is:
Lola loves stories (2010)

My friend Jamal; by Anna McQuinn; illustrated by Ben Frey. Annick 2008 un il (My friend) lib bdg $17.95; pa $8.95
Grades: K 1 2 3   E
1. Friendship -- Fiction 2. Immigrants -- Fiction 3. Africans -- United States -- Fiction
ISBN 978-1-55451-123-5 lib bdg; 1-55451-123-2 lib bdg; 978-1-55451-122-8 pa; 1-55451-122-4 pa

"Joseph describes his friendship with Jamal, a boy whose family immigrated to the United States from Somalia. . . . He discusses their similarities . . . as well as their differences. . . . The lively, brightly colored collages consist of original photographs of the main characters and stock photos of food or objects with thickly painted outlines and accents added. Both text and pictures project an energetic, friendly tone." SLJ

My friend Mei Jing; text by Anna McQuinn; artwork by Ben Frey; photography by Irvin Cheung. Annick Press 2009 un il (My friend) $17.95; pa $8.95
Grades: K 1 2 3   E
1. Friendship -- Fiction 2. African Americans -- Fiction 3. Chinese Americans -- Fiction
ISBN 978-1-55451-153-2; 1-55451-153-4; 978-1-55451-152-5 pa; 1-55451-152-6 pa

"In this large, colorful book, a Nigerian-American second-grader tells the story of her best friend from school, who is Chinese-American. The girls share a love of arts and crafts, dressing up, and a desire to become veterinarians. Monifa describes aspects of Mei Jing's culture. . . . The story's authentic voice comes from simple declarative sentences. . . . The brightly colored collages combine photographs of the girls' heads and hands with their cartoon bodies and depict them as they work with clay in arts and crafts at school or walk through an outdoor market with Mei Jing's grandma." SLJ

The **sleep** sheep; [by] Anna McQuinn and [illustrated by] Hannah Shaw. Chicken House 2010 un il $17.99
Grades: PreK K 1   E
1. Sheep -- Fiction 2. Sleep -- Fiction 3. Bedtime

-- Fiction

ISBN 978-0-545-23145-9; 0-545-23145-0

LC 2009051481

When Sylvie cannot fall asleep and her mother suggests that she try counting sheep, the sheep do not cooperate.

"The cartoon pen-and-ink drawings paint vivid scenes of Sylvie's imagination and are flush with fun details. Readers will linger over each page. . . . The Sleep Sheep moves along at a rapid clip and with enough humor to be successful read-aloud." SLJ

Meade, Holly

★ **If** I never forever endeavor. Candlewick Press 2011 un il $15.99

Grades: PreK K 1 2   E

1. Birds -- Fiction 2. Flight -- Fiction

ISBN 978-0-7636-4071-2; 0-7636-4071-9

LC 2010-39182

"To fly or not to fly is the question for a little bird weighing the pros and cons of launching into the unknown. . . . Meade effectively uses rhyme . . . onomatopoeia . . . and repetition to accentuate the fledgling's inner conflict. . . . Stunning collages of textured linoleum block prints and watercolors span double-page spreads. . . . An irresistible invitation to test those wings and fly." Kirkus

Inside, inside, inside; written and illustrated by Holly Meade. Marshall Cavendish 2005 un il $16.95

Grades: PreK K 1 2   E

1. Games -- Fiction 2. Siblings -- Fiction

ISBN 0-7614-5125-0

LC 2004-19321

Noah and Jenny play a game in which they place one item inside another, over and over, until they place it all in the shower, then imagine and draw the shower inside the house, inside the neighborhood, and all the way to the solar system

"Meade cheerfully mixes cut-paper collage and watercolor, and sprinkles many homey details into the large and small scenes. . . . The messy game is fun, and the concept draws a useful lesson from creative play." SLJ

★ **John** Willy and Freddy McGee. Marshall Cavendish 1998 un il hardcover o.p. pa $5.95

Grades: PreK K 1 2   E

1. Guinea pigs -- Fiction

ISBN 0-7614-5033-5; 0-7614-5143-9 pa

LC 97-50362

Two guinea pigs escape from their safe but boring cage and have an adventure in the tunnels of the family's pool table

"Zesty cut-paper collages track all of the details of this funny outing." SLJ

Meadows, Michelle

Hibernation station; illustrated by Kurt Cyrus. Simon and Schuster Books for Young Readers 2010 un il $16.99

Grades: PreK K 1 2   E

1. Stories in rhyme 2. Sleep -- Fiction 3. Animals -- Fiction

ISBN 978-1-4169-3788-3; 1-4169-3788-9

LC 2008042141

"The hibernation train, fashioned of hollow logs, is filled with all sorts of animals. . . . On its way to the station, it hits

a few snags: crowded conditions, leakage from a stream, and a lack of snacks and pillows. As the snow falls heavier and heavier, the bears in charge manage to get everyone squared away. . . . The enjoyable rhyming text provides the perfect platform for the wonderful illustrations that accompany it. Cyrus blends realistic depictions of the animals with just the right anthropomorphic touches." SLJ

Piggies in pajamas; Michelle Meadows; illustrated by Ard Hoyt. 1st ed. Simon & Schuster Books for Young Readers 2012 32 p. col. ill. (hardcover) $15.99

Grades: PreK K 1   E

1. Stories in rhyme 2. Pigs -- Fiction 3. Bedtime -- Fiction

ISBN 1416949828; 9781416949824

LC 2010024472

In this children's story, by Michelle Meadows, illustrated by Ard Hoyt, "after Mama has put her kids to bed, she settles in to make some phone calls. But she keeps hearing things from upstairs. Could her little piggies be jumping on the bed or playing dress-up instead of sleeping? But every time Mama goes up to check on them, they are all tucked in . . . until the noises begin again!" (Publisher's note)

Piggies in the kitchen; illustrated by Ard Hoyt. Simon & Schuster 2011 un il $14.99

Grades: PreK K 1   E

1. Stories in rhyme 2. Pigs -- Fiction 3. Baking -- Fiction

ISBN 978-1-4169-3787-6; 1-4169-3787-0

"Five little porkers and their father wave Mama off one bright, sunny day as she leaves the house. Daddy goes to cut the grass while his children enthusiastically descend upon the kitchen. Rhyming couplets filled with onomatopoeia tell the tale of the frenetic piglets making a mess plus a pleasant surprise for their mother. Pen-and-ink with watercolor illustrations in pastel hues humorously reveal the raucous goings-on." SLJ

Meddaugh, Susan

The **best** place. Houghton Mifflin 1999 un il $15

Grades: PreK K 1 2   E

1. Wolves -- Fiction 2. Animals -- Fiction

ISBN 0-395-97994-3

LC 98-50184

After traveling around the world to make sure that the view from his screen porch is the best, an old wolf tries drastic measures to get his house back from the rabbit family that had bought it

"Meddaugh combines understated humor with her expressive watercolor illustrations to produce a delightful book." SLJ

★ **Cinderella's** rat. Houghton Mifflin 1997 32p il $15; pa $5.95

Grades: PreK K 1 2   E

1. Fairy tales 2. Rats -- Fiction

ISBN 0-395-86833-5; 0-618-12540-X pa

LC 97-2156

One of the rats that was turned into a coachman by Cinderella's fairy godmother saves his rat sister's life, but an inept magician turns her into a girl who says "woof."

"The telling is a perfect example of a successful fractured fairy tale, with switched point of view. . . . The buoyant line drawings capture the whimsy." SLJ

★ **Harry** on the rocks. Houghton Mifflin 2003 32p il hardcover o.p. pa $6.95
Grades: PreK K 1 2   E
1. Shipwrecks -- Fiction
ISBN 0-618-27603-3; 0-618-84068-0 pa
                                LC 2002-9740
Harry and his boat become stranded on an island, where he discovers an egg which hatches into a strange lizard with wings

This is "a well-paced, cleanly wrought piece of storytelling. The cheerful watercolor and colored-pencil art has a sturdy matter-of-factness that makes the fantasy endearingly domestic." Bull Cent Child Books

★ **Hog**-eye. Houghton Mifflin 1995 32p il hardcover o.p. pa $5.95
Grades: PreK K 1 2   E
1. Pigs -- Fiction 2. Wolves -- Fiction
ISBN 0-395-74276-5; 0-395-93746-9 pa
                                LC 95-3951
Meddaugh presents a "story within a story as a piglet tells her family how she was caught by a wolf and nearly made into soup. Seeing that her captor is illiterate . . . she reads him a recipe that sends him on a wild wolf chase." SLJ

★ **Martha** speaks. Houghton Mifflin 1992 un il hardcover o.p. pa $6.99
Grades: PreK K 1 2   E
1. Dogs -- Fiction
ISBN 0-395-63313-3; 0-395-72952-1 pa
                                LC 91-48455
Problems arise when Martha, the family dog, learns to speak after eating alphabet soup

"Good-natured and amusing, with cheerful illustrations of the delightfully stocky Martha and her amazed family." Horn Book

"Other titles about Martha are:
Martha and Skits (2000)
Martha and Skits out West (2011)
Martha blah blah (1996)
Martha calling (1994)
Martha walks the dog (1998)
Perfectly Martha (2004)

The **witch's** walking stick. Houghton Mifflin 2005 32p il $16
Grades: K 1 2 3   E
1. Magic -- Fiction 2. Witches -- Fiction
ISBN 0-618-52948-9
                             LC 2004-17509
When a witch loses her magic walking stick, which has been used over the years to grant hundreds of miserable wishes, she tricks a young girl into finding and returning it, with unexpected results.

"Illustrated with watercolor and ink in a style that will put readers in mind of William Steig, Meddaugh's dry, quirky tale of the little guy triumphing over adversity will have children smiling and cheering." SLJ

Medearis, Angela Shelf
Seven spools of thread; a Kwanzaa story. illustrated by Daniel Minter. Whitman, A. 2001 un il $15.95; pa $6.95
Grades: K 1 2 3   E
1. Ghana -- Fiction 2. Blacks -- Fiction 3. Kwanzaa -- Fiction 4. Brothers -- Fiction
ISBN 0-8075-7315-9; 0-8075-7316-7 pa
                             LC 00-8101
When they are given the seemingly impossible task of turning thread into gold, the seven Ashanti brothers put aside their differences, learn to get along, and embody the principles of Kwanzaa. Includes information on Kwanzaa, West African cloth weaving, and instructions for making a belt

"Well-paced, the story incorporates the Kwanzaa values without spelling them out too much. Minter's attractively composed, dramatic painted linocuts, with strong community images and lively, silhouetted figures, root the story in a sun-drenched, magical landscape." Booklist

Medina, Meg
Tia Isa wants a car. Candlewick Press 2011 un il $15.99
Grades: K 1 2   E
1. Aunts -- Fiction 2. Money -- Fiction 3. Automobiles -- Fiction 4. Family life -- Fiction 5. Hispanic Americans -- Fiction
ISBN 978-0-7636-4156-6; 0-7636-4156-1
                           LC 2010040128
"Always true to the child's viewpoint, the story shows how hard it is to be separated from loved ones and how long it can take to reunite, and the lively, unframed illustrations in pencil, watercolor, and ink extend the sense of warmth and longing." Booklist

Meinderts, Koos
On My Street; Koos Meinderts, illustrated by Annette Fienieg. Lemniscaat USA 2013 32 p. ill. (hardcover) $12.95
Grades: PreK K   E
1. Neighbors 2. Neighborhood
ISBN 1935954245; 9781935954248
In this children's book, by Koos Meinderts, illustrated by Annette Fienieg, characters created by the illustrator are presented in one story. "For every child born to one of her friends, Annette Fienieg used to make a colorfully decorated teeshirt, with a character you would fall in love with. Now it is time to introduce those creations--Mrs. McQueen Fifi LaPointe, Johnny Deck, Lightfingers Louie and more--to a wider audience." (Publisher's note)

Meisel, Paul
See me dig; by Paul Meisel. Holiday House 2013 32 p. (I like to read) (hardcover) $14.95
Grades: PreK K 1   E
1. Pirates -- Fiction 2. Dogs -- Fiction
ISBN 0823427439; 9780823427437
                           LC 2012016549
This children's story, by Paul Meisel, is part of the "I Like to Read" series. "A crew of happy dogs dig merrily in the dirt. But the groundhogs, mice, and moles don't like it. The animals chase the dogs away to another digging spot. This time the dogs dig up a box--a treasure chest--

from which ghostly pirates emerge. The dogs are on the run again!" (Publisher's note)

See me run. Holiday House 2011 un il $14.95
Grades: PreK K 1   E
1. Dogs -- Fiction 2. Parks -- Fiction
ISBN 978-0-8234-2349-1; 0-8234-2349-2
LC 2010029445

"Cartoon drawings done in acrylic ink, pen and colored pencils offer a variety of dog breeds; eyes are wide and tongues hang out in their expressive faces as they frolic through the pale green, grassy park. Formatted in a larger trim than the usual early reader, this imaginary rumpus is just right for beginners to successfully read and reread." Kirkus

Meister, Cari
My pony Jack; illustrated by Amy Young. Viking 2005 32p il (Viking easy-to-read) $13.99
Grades: PreK K 1 2   E
1. Stories in rhyme 2. Horses -- Fiction
ISBN 0-670-05917-X
LC 2004-21417

Easy-to-read, rhyming text follows Lacy as she spends a day with her pony, giving him exercise, grooming him, and feeding him oats and hay.

"The book has an attractive format, with colorful cartoon artwork and a small amount of text on each page. . . . A solid addition to easy-reader collections." SLJ

Other titles about Jack the pony are:
My pony Jack at riding lessons (2005)
My pony Jack at the horse show (2006)

★ **Tiny's** bath; illustrated by Rich Davis. Viking 1998 un il (Viking easy-to-read) hardcover o.p. pa $3.99
Grades: PreK K 1   E
1. Dogs -- Fiction 2. Baths -- Fiction
ISBN 0-670-87962-2; 0-14-130267-4 pa
LC 98-3844

Tiny is a very big dog who loves to dig, and when it is time for his bath, his owner has trouble finding a place to bathe him

"In this book for the least sophisticated beginning readers, each sentence appears on a single line, and only one sentence appears on a page. Illustrations mirror text, providing clues that support readers as they decipher both words and events. Add Tiny to the roll call of great dogs in children's literature." Horn Book Guide

Other titles about Tiny are:
Tiny goes camping (2006)
Tiny goes to the library (2000)
Tiny on the farm (2008)
Tiny the snow dog (2001)
When Tiny was tiny (1999)

Melanson, Luc
Topsy-Turvy Town. Tundra Books 2010 un il $17.95
Grades: PreK K   E
1. Imagination -- Fiction
ISBN 978-0-88776-920-7; 0-88776-920-9

Original French language edition published 2004 in Canada

A boy lives in a town where it rains broccoli that crunches when it lands on the tops of umbrellas, where police offi-

cers march to a very different beat, where you can go fishing in your living room or even juggle a wildcat before bedtime.

"This highly imaginative tale is told in simple text with outstanding illustrations. Round-headed humans and buildings with harlequin faces abound, as well as a menagerie of animals reminiscent of classic wooden toys." SLJ

Melling, David
Don't worry, Douglas! Tiger Tales 2011 il $12.95
Grades: PreK K 1   E
1. Hats -- Fiction 2. Bears -- Fiction 3. Gifts -- Fiction 4. Animals -- Fiction
ISBN 978-1-58925-106-9; 1-58925-106-7

"Douglas the bear loves the fuzzy orange hat that his father gives him, but when the hat snags on a branch, it turns into a 'long string of spaghetti.' Douglas's friends offer suggestions—the sheep try to wind it into a ball, a cow demonstrates how it can still be worn like a wig—but when it starts to rain, Douglas takes Rabbit's advice to tell his father the truth about what happened. Melling's artwork brims with physical comedy as he delivers his message about coming clean with sensitivity and good humor." Publ Wkly

"Another title about Douglas is:
Hugless Douglas (2010)

Hugless Douglas. Tiger Tales 2010 un il $15.95
Grades: PreK K 1   E
1. Bears -- Fiction 2. Hugging -- Fiction
ISBN 978-1-58925-098-7; 1-58925-098-2

"Melling gives new meaning to the phrase, 'a big bear hug' with this tale of a cub who sets off one morning in search of that special feeling he needs. A gigantic boulder is too heavy to hug and a tree trunk is too splintery. Douglas knows that a hug feels comfy, and he is not having an easy time locating one. Colorful illustrations enhance the humor." SLJ

★ The **Scallywags**. Barron's 2006 un il $14.99
Grades: K 1 2 3   E
1. Wolves -- Fiction 2. Animals -- Fiction 3. Etiquette -- Fiction
ISBN 0-7641-5991-7

"This hilarious story is accompanied by equally lively and humorous pictures that fill the pages with images worthy of close perusal." SLJ

"The animals in the neighborhood are disgusted by the Wolf family, known collectively as the Scallywags. . . . After the wolves are sent packing, they finally . . . improve their manners." Booklist

Melmed, Laura Krauss
Hurry! Hurry! Have you heard? illustrated by Jane Dyer. Chronicle Books 2008 un il $16.99
Grades: PreK K 1 2   E
1. Stories in rhyme 2. Birds -- Fiction 3. Animals -- Fiction
ISBN 978-0-8118-4225-9
LC 2007021062

A small bird, her heart filled with love, hurries from her perch above the manger to spread the news to creatures of the field and forest that a child, to whom all are precious, has been born.

"This contemporary-set Nativity story, featuring seasonally clad but otherwise realistic-looking animals, has energy and movement." Horn Book Guide

Meltzer, Lynn

The **construction** crew; illustrated by Carrie Eko-Burgess. Henry Holt 2011 un il $12.99

Grades: PreK K   E

1. Stories in rhyme 2. Tools -- Fiction 3. Trucks -- Fiction 4. Building -- Fiction 5. Construction equipment -- Fiction

ISBN 978-0-8050-8884-7; 0-8050-8884-9

LC 2010039763

A construction crew tears down an old building and builds a new house in its place.

"Truck and construction fans will find an energetic exploration of both in this square-format volume. . . . Crisp, electric digital illustrations spotlight vehicles, construction equipment, and workers who resemble fleshed-out Lego characters. . . . The rhyming text offers variations on the same question ('Tons of dirt/ And lots of muck/ What do we need?/ DUMP TRUCK!'), . . . a narrative device that will have children shouting out the answers in no time." Publ Wkly

Melvin, Alice

Counting birds; written and illustrated by Alice Melvin. Tate 2010 un il $14.50

Grades: K 1 2   E

1. Counting 2. Day -- Fiction 3. Birds -- Fiction

ISBN 978-1-85437-855-2; 1-85437-855-4

"This is a charming counting book, replete with lilting text and exquisite illustrations. Beginning at dawn with one cockerel, the narration moves through the day and into the evening, counting birds from 1 to 20. . . . The text, which is composed in couplets, counts birds both inside and outside a stately country house. . . . In her bright and cheerful illustrations, Melvin employs geometric designs and patterns that bring to mind the warmth and comfort of a favorite quilt." SLJ

Menchin, Scott

What if everything had legs? Candlewick Press 2010 un il $15.99

Grades: PreK K 1   E

1. Imagination -- Fiction

ISBN 978-0-7636-4220-4; 0-7636-4220-7

LC 2010038719

Feeling too tired to walk the rest of the way home, a little girl wonders why the house cannot have legs to come to her and her mother, then imagines what else would change if everything had legs.

"The simple text and wacky, hybrid illustrations of objects sprouting legs (and arms) combine for an entertaining read-aloud that will engage young children and stir up their own creative juices." SLJ

Meng, Cece

I will not read this book; written by Cece Meng; illustrated by Joy Ang. Clarion Books 2011 32p il $15.99

Grades: K 1 2   E

1. Books and reading -- Fiction

ISBN 978-0-547-04971-7; 0-547-04971-4

LC 2010043175

A child adamantly refuses to read a book, regardless of the increasingly outrageous circumstances that might occur.

"Oh, yes, you will read this book. You'll be reeled in by the feisty, angular, frequently exciting digital illustrations, not to mention that confrontational title." Booklist

Merlin, Christophe

Under the hood; [by] Merlin. Candlewick Press 2011 il $14.99

Grades: PreK   E

1. Animals -- Fiction 2. Automobiles -- Fiction

ISBN 978-0-7636-5535-8; 0-7636-5535-X

LC 2010042743

A mechanic welcomes the reader to his garage where he will try to fix his car, but first needs help in finding his friends, Mouse, Crocodile, and Bird under lift-up flaps and fold-out pages.

"The large, humorous illustrations are done in vivid hues set against cream-colored backgrounds. Children will delight in the mystery of what lies beneath all those flaps." SLJ

Meschenmoser, Sebastian

★ **Waiting** for winter. Kane Miller 2009 un il $15.99

Grades: PreK K 1 2   E

1. Snow -- Fiction 2. Forest animals -- Fiction

ISBN 978-1-935279-04-4; 1-935279-04-1

LC 2009-922111

Deer has told Squirrel how wonderful snow is. But Squirrel gets bored with the wait. With his friend Hedgehog they pass the time by singing and waking Bear. Soon things are falling from the sky, but they aren't snow. But eventually they find what snow is.

"The illustrations are deftly drawn in colored pencils, complete with sketching lines that give the renderings depth and maturity. . . . This is a beautiful title to share with children on a lap or with a small group." SLJ

Meserve, Jessica

Bedtime without Arthur; illustrated by Jessica Meserve. Andersen Press USA 2009 un il $16.95

Grades: K 1 2   E

1. Fear -- Fiction 2. Bedtime -- Fiction 3. Siblings -- Fiction 4. Teddy bears -- Fiction

ISBN 978-0-7613-5497-0; 0-7613-5497-2

Arthur, Bella's very special bear, protects her from monsters while she sleeps, but when Arthur goes missing one night, Bella makes an interesting discovery.

Meshon, Aaron

★ **Take** me out to the Yakyu; Aaron Meshon. Atheneum Books for Young Readers 2013 40 p. (hardcover) $15.99

Grades: PreK K 1   E

1. Picture books for children 2. Japan -- Fiction 3. Baseball -- Fiction 4. Grandfathers -- Fiction 5. Racially mixed people -- Fiction

ISBN 1442441771; 9781442441774; 9781442441781

LC 2011050907

In this children's book by Aaron Meshon readers can "join one little boy and his family for two ballgames--on opposite sides of the world! Come along with one little boy and his grandfathers, one in America and one in Japan, as he learns about baseball and its rich, varying cultural traditions." (Publisher's note)

Tools rule! by Aaron Meshon. Atheneum Books for Young Readers 2014 40 p. (hardcover) $16.99

Grades: PreK K 1 2   E
    1. Tools -- Fiction
    ISBN 1442496010; 9781442496019
                   LC 2013009361

This children's book, by Aaron Meshon, "features animated tool characters, each with its own individual traits. T Square rounds up a crew of tools to clean up a messy yard and build a tool shed. T Square and Pencil draft plans; Wheelbarrow gathers materials; Saw saws Wood; Drill drills Screws; Level inspects; Glue glues on Roof Tiles, etc. Together, they work hard, and when the project is finished, they go to sleep in an organized toolshed feeling satisfied." (Kirkus Reviews)

"A diligent T-square rallies its fellow tools to get to work building a shed. One helpful illustration shows the tools, strewn about the lawn, but with captionlike arrows to identify what's what. Meshon's lively text is full of tool-centric wordplay; a detailed note describes his process for creating the digitally colored mixed-media illustrations of smiley tools with a can-do attitude." Horn Book

Metaxas, Eric
It's time to sleep, my love (a lullabye) illustrated by Nancy Tillman. Feiwel and Friends 2008 un il $16.95; bd bk $7.99

Grades: PreK K   E
    1. Lullabies 2. Stories in rhyme 3. Animals -- Fiction 4. Bedtime -- Fiction
    ISBN 978-0-312-38371-8; 0-312-38371-1; 978-0-312-67336-9 bd bk; 0-312-67336-1 bd bk
                   LC 2008028550

At bedtime, birds, bees, fishes, and other creatures urge their tired children to go to sleep

"Mextaxas' words set the sleepy-time tone with lulling sounds, repetition, and rhythms in short lines that read like poetry. . . . Tillman combines vibrantly colored photos and textured paintings in digital collages of the detailed animals." Booklist

Metropolitan Museum of Art (New York, N.Y.)
★ **Museum** shapes. Little, Brown 2005 un il $16.99

Grades: PreK K 1 2   E
    1. Shape 2. Art appreciation
    ISBN 0-316-05698-7

"The concept is simple; what makes this book so wonderful is the art, which is varied in content, style, medium, culture, and period, and is beautifully reproduced." SLJ

Metzger, Steve, 1949-
★ **Detective** Blue; illustrated by Tedd Arnold. Orchard Books 2011 un il $16.99

Grades: PreK K 1 2   E
    1. Mystery fiction 2. Nursery rhymes -- Fiction
    ISBN 0545172861; 9780545172868

"Metzger and Arnold display a consistent wit on every page, tucking in manifold nursery rhyme references for readers to tease out. Children will enjoy recognizing familiar stories, as well as the satisfying surprise conclusion." Publ Wkly

"The story of Detective Blue (the kid formerly known as Little Boy—'At one time I blew a horn and looked after cows and sheep. That's in the past!')—and his search for a missing person: Miss Muffet." Kirkus

Meyer, Susan Lynn
New shoes; by Susan Lynn Meyer; illustrated by Eric Velasquez. Holiday House 2015 40 p. col. ill. (hardcover) $16.95

Grades: K 1 2 3   E
    1. Shoes -- Fiction 2. Picture books for children 3. African Americans -- Segregation -- Fiction 4. Segregation -- Fiction 5. Discrimination -- Fiction
    ISBN 0823425282; 9780823425280
                   LC 2012019673

This history story, by Susan Lynn Meyer and illustrated by Eric Velasquez, is "set in the [American] South during the time of segregation. This lushly illustrated picture book brings the civil rights era to life for contemporary readers as two young girls find an inventive way to foil Jim Crow laws." (Publisher's note)

"The tale stands out from other stories of children overcoming obstacles, emphasizing how resistance and transformation can be found in the smallest of actions. An author's note gives readers background on Jim Crow and the Civil Rights and Voting Rights acts." Kirkus

Meyers, Susan
Bear in the air; illustrated by Amy Bates. Abrams Books for Young Readers 2010 il $15.95

Grades: PreK K 1   E
    1. Stories in rhyme 2. Adventure fiction 3. Teddy bears -- Fiction 4. Lost and found possessions -- Fiction
    ISBN 978-0-8109-8398-4; 0-8109-8398-2

When a teddy bear is lost by the child who loves him, the bear begins an adventurous journey to get back home again.

"Words are almost unnecessary as the pencil and watercolor illustrations, in appealing beach tones of blue, brown, and tan, tell the story of the lost, bewildered-looking bear and his surprising journey. . . . A sweet story that will capture the imaginations of young children." SLJ

★ **Everywhere** babies; illustrated by Marla Frazee. Harcourt 2001 un il $16; bd bk $6.95

Grades: PreK K 1   E
    1. Infants 2. Stories in rhyme
    ISBN 0-15-202226-0; 0-15-205315-8 bd bk
                   LC 99-6288

Describes babies and the things they do from the time they are born until their first birthday

"The rhythmic rhyming text hums along pleasantly. . . . The many moods, expressions, and body movements of babies are faithfully, gracefully rendered in the pencil drawings, and brightened with watercolors in rather muted hues." Booklist

★ **Kittens!** Kittens! Kittens! by Susan Meyers; illustrated by David Walker. Abrams Books for Young Readers 2007 un il $15.95

Grades: PreK K   E
    1. Cats -- Fiction
    ISBN 978-0-8109-1218-2; 0-8109-1218-X
                   LC 2006013575

Illustrations and rhyming text portray kittens as they go from nestling newborns to proud, independent, and ready to have kittens of their own.

"Cheerful rhymes, with the title used as a satisfying refrain, are expanded on by Walker's acrylic artwork in soft-toned, thickly applied colors that have the look of sunny chalks." Booklist

Michalak, Jamie

Joe and Sparky go to school; Jamie Michalak, illustrated by Frank Remkiewicz. Candlewick Press 2013 48 p. (Joe and Sparky) $15.99

Grades: K 1 2 3   E

    1. School stories 2. Friendship -- Fiction 3. Giraffe -- Fiction 4. Turtles -- Fiction 5. High interest-low vocabulary books

    ISBN 076366278X; 9780763662783

                       LC 2012943657

In this children's book by Jamie Michalak, "Joe Giraffe and Sparky, a turtle, live in Safari Land, 'the famous cageless zoo.' In four chapters they see a school bus and climb on to satisfy their curiosity; end up at school with the 'noisy short people'; try to blend in but the 'magic pond' (the toilet) provides some silliness; and Joe attempts to get a star for good work since Sparky has earned several. The animals experience the ups and downs of friendship." (School Library Journal)

Joe and Sparky, superstars! illustrated by Frank Remkiewicz. Candlewick Press 2011 37p il $15.99

Grades: K 1 2   E

    1. Turtles -- Fiction 2. Giraffes -- Fiction 3. Friendship -- Fiction

    ISBN 978-0-7636-4578-6; 0-7636-4578-8

                       LC 2009006425

When Joe the giraffe and his friend Sparky, a turtle, see a television talent show, Joe tries to find Sparky's talent so that they can compete.

"The font is large and at times changes in appearance to reflect emotion and sound. Michalak and Remkiewicz have written another enjoyable book about two friends who bring out the best in each other." SLJ

Michelson, Richard

Across the alley; [by] Richard Michelson; illustrated by E. B. Lewis. G. P. Putnam's Sons 2006 un il $16.99

Grades: K 1 2 3   E

    1. Jews -- Fiction 2. Baseball -- Fiction 3. Friendship -- Fiction 4. Violinists -- Fiction 5. African Americans -- Fiction

    ISBN 0-399-23970-7

                       LC 2005032656

Jewish Abe's grandfather wants him to be a violinist while African-American Wille's father plans for him to be a great baseball pitcher, but it turns out that the two boys are more talented when they switch hobbies.

"The poignancy of two boys who can be friends only at night is revealed brilliantly in both text and rich watercolor art." SLJ

    ★ Busing Brewster; illustrated by R. G. Roth. Knopf 2010 un il $16.99

Grades: 1 2 3   E

    1. School stories 2. African Americans -- Fiction 3.

School integration -- Fiction

    ISBN 978-0-375-83334-2; 0-375-83334-X; 978-0-375-93334-9 lib bdg; 0-375-93334-4 lib bdg

                       LC 2009-22626

Bused across town to a school in a white neigborhood of Boston in 1974, a young African American boy named Brewster describes his first day in first grade. Includes historical notes on the court-ordered busing.

"This title will make a good addition for libraries that want to strengthen their picture book collection by adding material on this period in the African-American experience. " Libr Media Connect

Miché, Mary

Nature's patchwork quilt; understanding habitats. by Mary Miché; illustrated by Consie Powell. Dawn Publications 2012 32 p.

Grades: 1 2 3   E

    1. Nature 2. Habitat (Ecology) 3. Natural history 4. Nature study -- Activity programs

    ISBN 1584691697; 9781584691693; 9781584691709

                       LC 2011048064

This children's book by Mary Miché "presents [natural] habitats while introducing environmental vocabulary: interdependence, niche, food chain, adaptations, biodiversity, deforestation and domestication, among others. . . . [W]atercolor quilts of different patterns dominate Powell's double-page compositions. A large center scene is surrounded by tiny blocks that each house lifelike depictions of the plants and animals that make up a habitat: forest, desert, ocean, rainforest, etc." (Kirkus)

Includes bibliographical references

Micklethwait, Lucy

    ★ I spy: an alphabet in art; devised & selected by Lucy Micklethwait. Greenwillow Bks. 1992 un il $19.99; pa $10.99

Grades: K 1 2 3   E

    1. Alphabet 2. Art appreciation

    ISBN 0-688-11679-5; 0-688-14730-5 pa

                       LC 91-42212

Presents objects for the letters of the alphabet through paintings by such artists as Magritte, Picasso, Botticelli, and Vermeer

"The author's stated intention of introducing young children to fine art, her choice of paintings, the handsome book design, and the quality of paper and reproduction take this beyond the usual alphabet book." Booklist

Other titles in this series are:

I spy a freight train: transportation in art (1996)

I spy a lion: animals in art (1994)

I spy colors in art (2007)

I spy shapes in art (2004)

I spy two eyes: numbers in art (1993)

Middleton, Charlotte

Nibbles: a green tale. Marshall Cavendish Children 2010 un il $17.99

Grades: PreK K 1 2   E

    1. Dandelions -- Fiction 2. Guinea pigs -- Fiction 3. Plant conservation -- Fiction

    ISBN 978-0-7614-5791-6; 0-7614-5791-7

"A guinea pig loves dandelions, just like everyone else in his town. The plants are eaten for breakfast, lunch, dinner, and all snacks in between until they slowly disappear. . . . Luckily Nibbles discovers a lone dandelion survivor growing under his bedroom window. With great patience and the help of a library book, he cares for his secret treasure until it has a full head of billowy white seeds. Then . . . he blows the precious seeds all over Dandeville. . . . Middleton's tale of overconsuming and scarcity is direct but not preachy. . . . The text is simple and age appropriate, but the mixed-media illustrations steal the show." SLJ

Middleton, Julie

Are the dinosaurs dead, Dad? written by Julie Middleton; illustrated by Russell Ayto. Peachtree Publishers 2013 32 p. ill. (reinforced) $16.95
Grades: K 1 2   E
1. Museums -- Fiction 2. Dinosaurs -- Fiction 3. Father and child -- Fiction
ISBN 156145690X; 9781561456901
LC 2012025716
"This story follows Dave and his dad to a natural history museum, where dinosaurs on exhibit come alive when Dad's back is turned, winking at Dave, tickling him, and attempting to snag a bite of his burger. Dave's dad dismisses questions . . . with the classic parental response, 'It's just your imagination.' But when a Tyrannosaurus rex follows the pair out of the exhibit and lets loose with an ear-splitting roar, Dad changes his mind at a dead run." (School Library Journal)

Miles, Victoria

Old Mother Bear; by Victoria Miles; illustrated by Molly Bang. Chronicle Books 2007 un il $16.95
Grades: 1 2 3 4   E
1. Bears -- Fiction
ISBN 978-0-8118-5033-9; 0-8118-5033-1
LC 2006011651
A twenty-four-year-old grizzly bear gives birth to her last litter of cubs, then spends three years teaching them what they need to know to survive in their southern British Columbia home before they go off on their own. Includes facts about grizzlies and the Khutzeymateen Grizzly Bear Sanctuary.
"The detailed zoology facts are the gripping story in this realistic picture book, which is based on true events and illustrated in beautifully textured, closeup, oil-and-chalk artwork by . . . artist Bang." Booklist

Milgrim, David

Eddie gets ready for school. Cartwheel Books 2011 un il $8.99
Grades: PreK K 1   E
1. School stories 2. Mother-son relationship -- Fiction
ISBN 978-0-545-27329-9; 0-545-27329-3
LC 2010016779
As young Eddie goes through his checklist to get ready for school, his mother does not agree with all of his choices.
"Big, bold cartoons make their lighthearted tug-of-war the center of attention, as grinning Eddie sheepishly responds to the amended checklist. . . . Readers accustomed to chasing the bus with one shoe on will relate." Publ Wkly

My dog, Buddy. Scholastic 2008 un il pa $3.99
Grades: K 1 2   E
1. Dogs -- Fiction 2. Family life -- Fiction
ISBN 978-0-545-03593-4 pa; 0-545-03593-7 pa
LC 2007-22795
Mom, Dad, and brother Pete all try to get Buddy to obey, but only one family member understands how to communicate with the mischievous canine.
"Digitally created art suggests line and watercolor in its smooth planes of color neatly bordered by slightly off-kilter lines. . . . Packed with pithy humor, sly irreverence, and rampant usefulness, this is a beginning reader's best friend." Bull Cent Child Books

★ Santa Duck. G.P. Putnam's Sons 2008 un il lib bdg $16.99
Grades: PreK K 1 2   E
1. Ducks -- Fiction 2. Animals -- Fiction 3. Christmas -- Fiction 4. Santa Claus -- Fiction
ISBN 978-0-399-25018-7; 0-399-25018-2
LC 2007-43162
When Nicholas Duck, wearing a Santa hat and coat he found on his doorstep, goes looking for Santa to tell him what he wants for Christmas, all the other animals mistake him for Mr. Claus.
"Nicholas's silliness and frustration will appeal to youngsters as will the simple message. Milgrim's charming digital ink and oil pastel illustrations use a successful mix of narrative text and cartoon balloons to move the story along at a brisk pace." SLJ
Another title about Santa Duck is:
Santa Duck and his merry helpers (2010)

Santa Duck and his merry helpers. G.P. Putnam's Sons 2010 un il $12.99
Grades: PreK K 1 2   E
1. Ducks -- Fiction 2. Christmas -- Fiction 3. Santa Claus -- Fiction
ISBN 978-0-399-25473-4; 0-399-25473-0
It's Christmastime, so Nicholas Duck puts on his Santa's helper suit and proudly starts gathering wish lists for Santa. But this year, Nicholas's little brothers and sister want to help.
"A multifaceted plot and some succinct lessons are skillfully conveyed in just a few pages, with the funny dialogue contained in speech balloons within the holiday-bright, cartoon-style illustrations." Kirkus

Time to get up, time to go. Clarion Books 2006 32p il $15
Grades: PreK K   E
1. Stories in rhyme 2. Day -- Fiction 3. Dolls -- Fiction
ISBN 0-618-51998-X; 978-0-618-51998-9
LC 2005011359
"From early morning to bedtime, a boy whirls through his day's activities, taking care of his stuffed blue doll. . . . Milgrim's digital oil-paint illustrations have muted, pleasant shades with the figures crisply outlined in black. They work well with the minimal text, in which not a word is wasted." SLJ

Milich, Zoran

City 1 2 3. Kids Can Press 2005 un il $15.95; pa $6.95

Grades: PreK K 1 2   E
  1. Counting
  ISBN 1-55337-540-8; 1-55453-163-2 pa
Photographs of objects such as skyscrapers, bags of leaves, fire trucks, and taxis illustrate numbers from 1 to 10
"An excellent, well-constructed concept book. . . . The superb pictures feature not only the required number of items, but the corresponding numeral as well." SLJ

City colors. Kids Can Press 2004 un il $14.95; pa $5.95
Grades: PreK K 1 2   E
  1. Color
  ISBN 1-55337-542-4; 1-55337-981-0 pa
This is a collection of color photographs of objects found in cities such as a red bus, a blue warehouse wall, and a yellow highway cone, a green swing, an orange cylindrical curb block, and a purple playground stool.
This is "a dazzling . . . concept book. . . . Precise partial photos inspire speculation on each verso with the recto revealing the complete image." SLJ

Millen, C. M.
The **ink** garden of brother Theophane; illustrated by Andrea Wisnewski. Charlesbridge 2010 un il $17.95
Grades: 1 2 3 4   E
  1. Stories in rhyme 2. Monks -- Fiction 3. Middle Ages -- Fiction 4. Illumination of books and manuscripts -- Fiction
  ISBN 978-1-58089-179-0; 1-58089-179-9
In medieval Ireland, Theophane's boredom with his duties as a scribe distracts the other monks, but when he is sent to the kitchens he discovers that he can make inks of many colors from plants, allowing the others to illustrate their work. Includes facts about the history of monasteries, scriptoriums, and illuminated manuscripts.
"Written in rhythmic, rhyming, and rear-rhyming verse, the simple story unfolds in a satisfying way, accompanied by short poems inspired by the writings of Irish monks. The richly detailed illustrations were created by using a papercut design to print bold, black lines and brightening the pictures with watercolors." Booklist

Miller, Pat
Squirrel's New Year's resolution; illustrated by Kathi Ember. Albert Whitman & Co. 2010 un il $16.99
Grades: PreK K 1   E
  1. New Year -- Fiction 2. Squirrels -- Fiction 3. Forest animals -- Fiction
  ISBN 978-0-8075-7591-8; 0-8075-7591-7
                    LC 2009-49305
Squirrel cannot think of a New Year's resolution until she realizes that by helping her friends, she has made one after all.
"The simple dialogue and predictable plot make this a good read-aloud, and the brightly colored, acrylic cartoons are full of fun details and expression, giving the woodland creatures anthropomorphic characteristics." SLJ

Miller, Pat Zietlow
★ **Sophie's** squash; Pat Zietlow Miller; [illustrations by] Anne Wilsdorf. Schwartz & Wade 2013 40 p. $16.99
Grades: PreK K 1 2   E
  1. Picture books for children 2. Squashes -- Fiction 3.

Friendship -- Fiction
  ISBN 0307978966; 9780307978967; 9780307978974
                    LC 2012006438
In this children's picture book, when "Sophie selects a butternut squash at the farmer's market, her parents assume they will be having it for dinner. Sophie, however, quashes that plan by adopting the vegetable as her new best friend and naming her Bernice . . . . Despite gentle prodding to relinquish Bernice before she rots, Sophie brings her deteriorating pal to the library and somersaults with her in the yard." (Publishers Weekly)

Miller, Sara Swan
★ **Three** more stories you can read to your dog; illustrated by True Kelley. Houghton Mifflin 2000 un il $14; pa $5.95
Grades: PreK K 1 2   E
  1. Dogs -- Fiction
  ISBN 0-395-92293-3; 0-618-15244-X pa
                    LC 99-39880
Stories addressed to dogs and written from a dog's point of view, featuring such topics as going to the vet, making friends with a rocklike creature, and getting a bath
"The witty, believable portrayal of canine thoughts and behavior will amuse readers. . . . True Kelley's lively ink-and-watercolor illustrations brighten every page." Booklist
  Other titles in this series are:
  Three more stories you can read to your cat (2002)
  Three stories you can read to your cat (1997)
  Three stories you can read to your dog (1995)
  Three stories you can read to your teddy bear (2004)

Miller, William
★ **Night** golf; illustrated by Cedric Lucas. Lee & Low Bks. 1999 un il hardcover o.p. pa $8.95
Grades: K 1 2 3   E
  1. Golf -- Fiction 2. Prejudices -- Fiction 3. African Americans -- Fiction
  ISBN 1-880000-79-2; 1-58430-056-6 pa
                    LC 98-47168
Despite being told that only whites can play golf, James becomes a caddy and is befriended by an older African American man who teaches him to play on the course at night
"Gentle paste and pencil illustrations support this quietly powerful story." Horn Book Guide

★ **Rent** party jazz; illustrated by Charlotte Riley-Webb. Lee & Low Bks. 2001 un il $16.95; pa $7.95
Grades: K 1 2 3   E
  1. Jazz music -- Fiction 2. New Orleans (La.) -- Fiction
  ISBN 1-58430-025-6; 1-60060-344-0 pa
                    LC 2001-16449
When Sonny's mother loses her job in New Orleans during the Depression, Smilin' Jack, a jazz musician, tells him how to organize a rent party to raise the money they need
"Miller uses folksy dialogue to tell the story that celebrates both community and the uplifting power of music. Evocative artwork, done in broad, swirling strokes, fills pages with color and motion." Booklist

Millman, Isaac
★ **Moses** goes to school. Farrar, Straus & Giroux 2000 un il $16

Grades: PreK K 1 2   E
1. School stories 2. Deaf -- Fiction 3. Sign language
-- Fiction
ISBN 0-374-35069-8

LC 99-40582

Moses and his friends enjoy the first day of school at
their special school for the deaf and hard of hearing, where
they use sign language to talk to each other

"Child-friendly cartoon illustrations do a marvelous job
of emphasizing the normalcy and charm of these youngsters.
. . . The double-page layouts nicely accommodate the primary pictorial action along with written text and ASL inserts. .
. . [This is a] great contribution to children's education about
disabilities that also succeeds as effective storytelling in its
own right." SLJ

Other titles about Moses are:
Moses goes to a concert (1998)
Moses goes to the circus (2003)
Moses sees a play (2004)

Mills, Claudia
★ **Gus** and Grandpa and the two-wheeled bike; pictures by Catherine Stock. Farrar, Straus & Giroux 1999
47p il hardcover o.p. pa $7.99
Grades: K 1 2 3   E
1. Cycling -- Fiction 2. Grandfathers -- Fiction
ISBN 0-374-32821-8; 0-374-42816-6 pa

LC 97-44203

Gus doesn't want to give up the training wheels on his
bike, even for a new five-speed bicycle, until Grandpa helps
him learn how to get along without them

"Mills conveys strong sentiment without a trace of
mawkishness, and Stock's illustrations in loose line and watercolor augment the story of this childhood rite of passage
expressively." Horn Book Guide

Other titles about Gus and Grandpa are:
Gus and Grandpa (1997)
Gus and Grandpa and show-and-tell (2000)
Gus and Grandpa and the Christmas cookies (1997)
Gus and Grandpa and the Halloween costume (2002)
Gus and Grandpa and the piano lesson (2004)
Gus and Grandpa at basketball (2001)
Gus and Grandpa at the hospital (1998)
Gus and Grandpa go fishing (2003)
Gus and Grandpa ride the train (1998)

Milord, Susan
Happy 100th day! illustrated by Mary Newell DePalma. Scholastic Press 2011 37p il $16.99
Grades: PreK K 1 2   E
1. School stories 2. Birthdays -- Fiction 3. Books and
reading -- Fiction
ISBN 978-0-439-88281-1; 0-439-88281-8

LC 2010009848

"Graham is a reluctant student at the start of the new
school year. His irritability is compounded by the fact that
his teacher is gung-ho about the 100th day, an event that
just happens to fall on Graham's birthday, threatening to
overshadow his own celebration. In addition Miss Currier
assigns everyone a 100th day goal; Graham's is to complete
100 books despite the fact that he is a 'lousy' reader. In
timeline fashion, Milord shows his progress. DePalma's delightful cartoon illustrations perfectly capture the boy's frustration and eventual pride, and the pages are chock-full of

graphic elements that mirror the wall art and teaching tools
of a typical first-grade classroom." SLJ

Love that baby! written and illustrated by Susan Milord.
Houghton Mifflin 2005 un il $7.95
Grades: PreK K 1   E
1. Infants -- Fiction
ISBN 0-618-56323-7

LC 2004-25119

"Each folded-over page poses a situation to ponder,
while the unfolded spread beneath it suggests what to do
next. A drawing of a . . . child . . . is accompanied by the
words: 'Baby is hungry,' while the picture of father . . . gives
the advice, 'Feed that baby!' Other pages offer suggested
actions to take if the baby is napping, hiding, scared, sad,
or sleepy. Simple drawings, soft colors in offbeat combinations, and a variety of patterns give this simple picture
book visual appeal, while the lift-the-flap game will make it
enjoyable for toddlers to revisit again and again." Booklist

Milton, Joyce
Dinosaur days; Joyce Milton; illustrated by Franco
Tempesta. Random House Inc 2014 48 p. (Step into read-
ing. Step 3) (pbk.) $3.99
Grades: 1 2 3   E
1. Readers 2. Dinosaurs
ISBN 0385379234; 9780307978707; 9780375973383;
9780385379236

LC 2013044052

This book, written by Joyce Milton and illustrated by
Franco Tempesta, "highlights or at least names over a dozen
dinos, from the diminutive Citipati to the humongous Argentinosaurus. . . . Prehistoric contemporaries that were
not dinosaurs also get nods, as do modern paleontology,
the great extinction and the continued survival of birds."
(Kirkus Reviews)

Milway, Katie Smith
One hen; how one small loan made a big difference.
written by Katie Smith Milway; illustrated by Eugenie Fer-
nandes. Kids Can Press 2008 32p il $18.95
Grades: 2 3 4   E
1. Eggs -- Fiction 2. Ghana -- Fiction 3. Loans --
Fiction 4. Chickens -- Fiction
ISBN 978-1-55453-028-1; 1-55453-028-8

"In Ghana, young Kojo has a business idea, borrowing
a small bit of money from his mother to purchase a hen,
intending to sell her extra eggs at the market. Slowly his
income grows so that he can not only pay his mother back
but he can also buy more hens; eventually, he has enough
money to go back to school. . . . [This gains] power from its
modeling on a real Ghanian entrepeneur, Kwabena Darko. .
. The beneficial effects of small loans and small projects are
thoughtfully and carefully explained in the extensive text.
. . . Acrylic illustrations, vivid and lively with an emphasis
on sunny hues and warm earthtones, balance out the large
blocks of text." Bull Cent Child Books

Includes glossary

Minarik, Else Holmelund
★ **Little** Bear; pictures by Maurice Sendak. Harper
& Row 1957 63p il (I can read book) $16.95; lib bdg
$17.89; pa $3.95

Grades: PreK K 1 2   **E**

1. Bears -- Fiction

ISBN 0-06-024240-X; 0-06-024241-8 lib bdg; 0-06-444004-4 pa

The pictures "depict all the warmth of feeling and the special companionship that exists between a small child and his mother." Publ Wkly

Other titles about Little Bear are:

Father Bear comes home (1959)

A kiss for Little Bear (1968)

Little Bear's friend (1960)

Little Bear's visit (1961)

Little Bear and the Marco Polo (2010)

★ No fighting, no biting! pictures by Maurice Sendak. Harper & Row 1958 62p il (I can read book) lib bdg $17.89; pa $3.95

Grades: PreK K 1 2   **E**

1. Alligators -- Fiction

ISBN 0-06-024291-4 lib bdg; 0-06-444015-X pa

"A young lady who is unable to read in peace because of two children squabbling beside her tells them a story about two little alligators whose fighting and biting almost lead to disastrous consequences with a big hungry alligator. Children are sure to accept and enjoy the lesson in this little adventure tale and be amused by the expressive old-fashioned drawings." Booklist

Mineko Mamada

Which is round? Which is bigger? written and illustrated by Mineko Mamada. Kids Can Press 2013 24 p. $16.95

Grades: PreK K   **E**

1. Concept learning 2. Size

ISBN 1554539730; 9781554539734

This book by Mineko Mamada is a "concept book [that] prompts the reader to compare pairs of objects and then choose which one has a particular attribute. At first the answer seems obvious until the page is turned to reveal a delightful twist!" (Publisher's note) "Other comparisons include longer and faster. The question 'What do you think?' creates opportunity for discussion. Simple text and color cartoon animals on solid backgrounds allow children to focus on the investigations." (School Library Journal)

Minor, Florence

If you were a panda bear; Wendell and Florence Minor. Katherine Tegen Books, an imprint of HarperCollinsPublishers 2013 32 p. (hardcover bdg.) $17.99

Grades: PreK K 1   **E**

1. Stories in rhyme 2. Bears -- Fiction

ISBN 0061950904; 9780061950902

       LC 2012040150

This book, written by Florence Minor and illustrated by Wendell Minor, "introduces different types of bears to young children. Through the poems in this . . . storybook, kids will learn that pandas are shy and eat bamboo, black bears love to climb trees, and grizzly bears can be up to ten feet tall. A section at the back includes even more . . . animal facts." (Publisher's note)

Includes bibliographical references

Minor, Wendell

My farm friends. G.P. Putnam's Sons 2011 un il $16.99

Grades: PreK K   **E**

1. Stories in rhyme 2. Farm life -- Fiction 3. Domestic animals -- Fiction

ISBN 0399244778; 9780399244773

       LC 2010014793

Simple, rhyming text describes the characteristics of different farm animals. Includes 'Farm friends fun facts' and books and websites for further reading.

"Drawing on childhood memories of his family's Illinois farm, Minor celebrates farm animals—furry, feathered, hairy, and woolly—with warm watercolor-and-gouache artwork and cozy, playful rhymes that young children will love to hear many times over." Booklist

Miranda, Anne

★ To market, to market; written by Anne Miranda; illustrated by Janet Stevens. Harcourt Brace & Co. 1997 un il $16; pa $7

Grades: PreK K 1 2   **E**

1. Stories in rhyme 2. Animals -- Fiction

ISBN 0-15-200035-6; 0-15-216398-0 pa

       LC 95-26326

"Patterned, staccato verses tell the zany tale, but it is Stevens's wonderfully wild illustrations that bring it to life." SLJ

In this "riff on the old nursery rhyme, 'To market, to market, to buy a fat pig,' a plump matron makes a series of increasingly calamitous purchases of animals at the supermarket. Hungry and cranky after the raucous menagerie turns her house topsy-turvy, the lady . . . wisely decides to make vegetable soup instead." Publ Wkly

Miron, Marie-Charlotte

My Little Handbook of Experiments; Physics, Water and Light, Ecology. by Marie-Charlotte Miron and Melanie Perez; illustrated by Vincent Hubert and Sandrine Lamour; translated by Susan Allen Maurin. Innovative Logistics Llc 2012 144 p. ill. (hardcover) $12.95

Grades: 2 3 4   **E**

1. Science -- Experiments 2. Science -- Study and teaching

ISBN 2733821474; 9782733821473

This book packs a "collection of science activities into three sections. . . . The unspecified 'Sciences' section is . . . approximately 18 activities including color, electricity and magnets, plus photography, astronomy, meteorology, and more. 'Water and Light' and 'Ecology' are" also included. (School Library Journal)

Mitchell, Margaree King

★ Uncle Jed's barbershop; illustrated by James Ransome. Simon & Schuster Bks. for Young Readers 1993 un il hardcover o.p. pa $6.99

Grades: PreK K 1 2   **E**

1. Uncles -- Fiction 2. African Americans -- Fiction 3. Barbers and barbershops -- Fiction

ISBN 0-671-76969-3; 0-689-81913-7 pa

       LC 91-44148

Despite serious obstacles and setbacks Sarah Jean's Uncle Jed, the only black barber in the county, pursues his dream of saving enough money to open his own barbershop

"The author's convivial depictions of family life are enhanced by Ransome's . . . spirited oil paintings, which set the affectionate intergenerational cast against brightly patterned walls and crisp, leaf-strewn landscapes." Publ Wkly

When grandmama sings; illustrated by James Ransome. HarperCollins/Amistad 2011 un il $16.99
Grades: 2 3 4   **E**
   1. Singers -- Fiction 2. Jazz music -- Fiction 3. Segregation -- Fiction 4. Grandmothers -- Fiction 5. Race relations -- Fiction 6. African Americans -- Fiction
   ISBN 978-0-688-17563-4; 0-688-17563-5
"Set in the segregated South of the 1950s, Mitchell's poignant story features eight-year-old Belle and her loving, stalwart African-American family. When Grandmama, who can't read but whose singing voice captures the hearts of all who hear her, joins a jazz band for a tour of the South, Belle pleads to go along. . . . She experiences firsthand the difficulties her people face: hotels marked 'White Only,' diners that refuse them service, police who search their cars and luggage for no reason. . . . Ransome's full-page images, rich in color and feeling, portray the landscapes of the South and the individual emotions of the characters with equal aplomb." SLJ

Mitchell, Stephen
   The **ugly** duckling; retold by Stephen Mitchell; illustrated by Steve Johnson and Lou Fancher. Candlewick Press 2008 un il $16.99
Grades: K 1 2 3   **E**
   1. Fairy tales 2. Swans -- Fiction
   ISBN 978-0-7636-2159-9
                   LC 2007-34235
An ugly duckling spends an unhappy year ostracized by the other animals before he grows into a beautiful swan.
"Mitchell retells the familiar story, preserving just enough of the character of Andersen's narrative voice to give his adaptation a tart, bracing flavor. . . . Johnson and Fancher's lacy, luminous art, rich with underwaterlike greens, gives [the swan's transformation] all the visual splendor it deserves." Horn Book

Miura, Taro
   ★ **Tools**. Chronicle Books 2006 un il $15.95
Grades: PreK K 1   **E**
   1. Tools
   ISBN 978-0-8118-5519-8; 0-8118-5519-8
                   LC 2005-34057
"Miura shows a distinctive set of tools on a double-page spread, identifying items such as a clamp, a saw, and nails. A turn of the page reveals the worker using them. Prereading children will enjoy identifying the tools, but their biggest challenge will be guessing the occupation represented. . . . The guessing-game aspect adds an element of fun to this beautifully designed and distinctively illustrated book." Booklist

Mobin-Uddin, Asma
   ★ The **best** Eid ever; [by] Asma Mobin-Uddin; illustrated by Laura Jacobsen. Boyds Mills Press 2007 un il $16.95
Grades: K 1 2 3   **E**
   1. Muslims -- Fiction 2. Id al-Adha -- Fiction 3. Grandmothers -- Fiction 4. Pakistani Americans --

Fiction
   ISBN 978-1-59078-431-0; 1-59078-431-6
                   LC 2006037945
Eid is the Islamic holiday that marks the end of Ramadan. In this story, young Aneesa meets two girls at the prayer hall dressed in ill-fitting clothes and discovers they are refugees. Aneesa comes up with a plan to make this the best Eid ever
"This is a heartwarming tale of a child's generosity, and Jacobsen's illustrations flesh out the warmth and tenderness of the characters' interaction." SLJ

   A **party** in Ramadan; illustrated by Laura Jacobsen. Boyds Mills Press 2009 un il $16.95
Grades: K 1 2 3   **E**
   1. Muslims -- Fiction 2. Parties -- Fiction 3. Ramadan -- Fiction
   ISBN 978-1-59078-604-8; 1-59078-604-1
                   LC 2008-43890
"With lively pastel-and-pencil artwork, this warm picture book shows and tells the observance and meaning of Ramadan through the viewpoint of a Muslim child. Leena is happy to be invited to her friend's birthday party, although it turns out that the event is on a day during Ramadan when Leena plans to fast with her family. . . . The blend of the upbeat with challenging moments will spark discussion, and a final note fills in more about the holy month." Booklist

Mochizuki, Ken
   ★ **Baseball** saved us; written by Ken Mochizuki; illustrated by Dom Lee. Lee & Low Bks. 1993 un il $16.95; pa $6.95
Grades: K 1 2 3   **E**
   1. Baseball -- Fiction 2. Prejudices -- Fiction 3. World War, 1939-1945 -- Fiction 4. Japanese Americans -- Evacuation and relocation, 1942-1945 -- Fiction
   ISBN 1-880000-01-6; 1-880000-19-9 pa
                   LC 92-73215
The narrator, Shorty, interned with his family in a camp for Japanese Americans during World War II, "tells how baseball was used as a diversion from the dire situation in which the camp's inhabitants found themselves. . . . {In one game}, the usually weak-hitting Shorty catches a glimpse of one of the ever-present guards and channels his anger toward the man into his swing, resulting in a winning home run. After the war and his return home, he continues to play ball while at the same time being subjected to racial taunts, again refocusing his anger to produce positive results on the diamond. . . . Grades two to four." (SLJ)
"Fences and watchtowers are in the background of many of Lee's moving illustrations, some of which were inspired by Ansel Adams' 1943 photographs of Manzanar. . . . The baseball action will grab kids—and so will the personal experience of bigotry." Booklist

   Heroes; written by Ken Mochizuki; illustrated by Dom Lee. Lee & Low Bks. 1995 un il hardcover o.p. pa $6.95
Grades: K 1 2 3   **E**
   1. Prejudices -- Fiction 2. Japanese Americans -- Fiction
   ISBN 1-880000-16-4; 1-880000-50-4 pa
                   LC 94-26541
"The book is a powerful exploration of the cruelty children can inflict upon one another and of the confusion

and pain borne by the target of such unthinking racism."
Horn Book

Modarressi, Mitra

Taking care of Mama. G.P. Putnam's Sons 2010 un
il $16.99
Grades: PreK K 1 2   E
1. Stories in rhyme 2. Sick -- Fiction 3. Raccoons --
Fiction 4. Family life -- Fiction
ISBN 978-0-399-25216-7; 0-399-25216-9
LC 2009011315

When Mama raccoon gets sick, Papa and the kids wear
themselves out doing the cooking and cleaning for the day.

"The watercolor scenes . . . capture cozy family chaos,
while the smooth text make this a good read-aloud choice."
Booklist

Moerbeek, Kees

★ **Count** 1 to 10. Abrams 2011 un il
Grades: K 1 2 3 4   E
1. Counting 2. Pop-up books
ISBN 0-8109-9644-8; 978-0-8109-9644-1
LC 2010928779

"A showpiece of popup design features the numbers one
through 10 worked into multileveled constructs of dazzling
virtuosity. Made from brightly colored digits floating over
contrasting monochromatic backgrounds . . . the pop-ups
range from a die-cut '1' that rotates into place and a pair of
'2's folding out from behind a screen to phalanxes of '9's
and '10's floating up as thier spreads open. . . . Every opening provides initial surprises, plenty of angles and spaces to
explore and a rich visual experience."

"A showpiece of popup design features the numbers one
through 10 worked into multileveled constructs of dazzling
virtuosity. Made from brightly colored digits floating over
contrasting monochromatic backgrounds . . . the pop-ups
range from a die-cut '1' that rotates into place and a pair of
'2's folding out from behind a screen to phalanxes of '9's
and '10's floating up as thier spreads open. . . . Every opening provides initial surprises, plenty of angles and spaces to
explore and a rich visual experience." Kirkus

Mol, Sine van

Meena; illustrated by Carianne Wijffels. Eerdmans
Books for Young Readers 2011 un il $17
Grades: 1 2 3   E
1. Fear -- Fiction 2. Old age -- Fiction 3. Prejudices
-- Fiction 4. Grandmothers -- Fiction
ISBN 978-0-8028-5394-3; 0-8028-5394-3
LC 2010049547

The children of Fly Street fear and taunt their neighbor Meena, thinking she is a witch, but when they meet
her granddaughter and taste her red currant pie, they learn
the truth.

"Simple sentences and a lot of dialogue will appeal to
emerging readers. Wijffels uses childlike line drawings to
show the youngsters' fevered imaginings. . . . Collage elements, children's art, and blue line drawings on uncluttered
white space give the story unexpected depth." SLJ

Mollel, Tololwa M.

★ **My** rows and piles of coins; illustrated by E. B.
Lewis. Clarion Bks. 1999 32p il $15

Grades: K 1 2 3   E
1. Money -- Fiction 2. Bicycles -- Fiction 3. Tanzania
-- Fiction
ISBN 0-395-75186-1
LC 98-21586

A Coretta Scott King honor book for illustration, 2000

A Tanzanian boy saves his coins to buy a bicycle so that
he can help his parents carry goods to market, but then he
discovers that in spite of all he has saved, he still does not
have enough money

"The story is natural and never excessively moralistic.
The fluid, light-splashed watercolor illustrations lend a sense
of place and authenticity." SLJ

Monari, Manuela

Zero kisses for me! illustrated by Virginie Soumagnac.
Tundra Books 2010 un il $12.95
Grades: PreK K   E
1. Kissing -- Fiction 2. Parent-child relationship --
Fiction
ISBN 978-1-77049-208-0; 1-77049-208-9

"A little one goes on strike against kisses. . . . Told mostly in a loving dialogue between mother and child, the language and syntax are true to life and utterly believable. Soumagnac's cartoon-style illustrations are a perfect match. . . .
This is a sit-on-your-lap, kiss-and-hug read-aloud." Kirkus

Monfreid, Dorothee de

Dark night. Random House Children's Books 2009 un
il $14.99; lib bdg $17.99
Grades: PreK K 1 2   E
1. Fear -- Fiction 2. Night -- Fiction 3. Animals --
Fiction
ISBN 978-0-375-85687-7; 0-375-85687-0; 978-0-375-
95687-4 lib bdg; 0-375-95687-5 lib bdg
LC 2008011257

Original French edition, 2007

When he wanders into the forest at night, Felix, terrified
by the ferocious animals he sees, finds refuge in an unusual
undergound house.

"De Monfreid's watercolor-and-ink illustrations are simple, charming, and extraordinarily expressive, making this a
lovely book to add to any collection." SLJ

Monjo, F. N.

★ The **drinking** gourd; a story of the Underground
Railroad. pictures by Fred Brenner. newly il ed.; Harp-
erCollins Pubs. 1993 62p il (I can read book) pa $3.99
Grades: K 1 2 3   E
1. Underground railroad -- Fiction
ISBN 0-06-444042-7 pa
LC 92-10823

First published 1970

Set in New England in the decade before the Civil War.
For mischievous behavior in church, Tommy is sent home
to his room, but wanders instead into the barn. There he
discovers that his father is helping runaway slaves escape
to Canada

"The simplicity of dialogue and exposition, the level of
concepts, and the length of the story [makes] it most suitable
for the primary grades reader. The illustrations are deftly representational, the whole a fine addition to the needed body of
historical books for the very young." Bull Cent Child Books

Monroe, Chris

Monkey with a tool belt. Carolrhoda 2008 un il lib bdg $16.95

Grades: K 1 2 3   E

1. Tools -- Fiction 2. Monkeys -- Fiction

ISBN 978-0-8225-7631-0; 0-8225-7631-7

LC 2007-10020

Clever monkey Chico Bon Bon builds lots of things with his many tools, and when he is captured by an organ grinder, he uses them to help him escape and get back home.

"Slightly edgy, highly detailed comics-style art will have readers poring over the pages. . . . Not only gadget jockeys will enjoy this visually polished tale." Publ Wkly

Other titles about Chico are:

Monkey with a tool belt and the noisy problem (2009)

Monkey with a tool belt and the seaside shenanigans (2011)

★ Sneaky sheep. Carolrhoda Books 2010 un il lib bdg $16.95

Grades: PreK K 1 2   E

1. Sheep -- Fiction

ISBN 978-0-7613-5615-8 lib bdg; 0-7613-5615-0 lib bdg

LC 2009040852

Blossom and Rocky, two sneaky and not very bright sheep, keep trying to get away from the rest of the flock, in spite of the dangers they encounter.

"Monroe's pen-and-ink and watercolor illustrations are entertaining; kids will enjoy following Rocky and Blossom's antics both in and out of panels." SLJ

Montes, Marisa

★ Los gatos black on Halloween; illustrated by Yuyi Morales. Henry Holt and Company 2006 un il $16.95

Grades: PreK K 1 2   E

1. Stories in rhyme 2. Halloween -- Fiction 3. Spanish language -- Vocabulary

ISBN 978-0-8050-7429-1; 0-8050-7429-5

LC 2005-20049

A Pura Belpré Author Award honor book, 2008

Easy to read, rhyming text about Halloween night incorporates Spanish words, from las brujas riding their broomsticks to los monstruos whose monstrous ball is interrupted by a true horror.

"Montes smoothly incorporates Spanish terms into a rhythmic poem. . . . The full-bleed paintings create a creepy mood with curving lines, fluid textures, and dusky hues. . . . The pictures are eerie enough to tingle spines, but the effect is leavened with bits of humor." SLJ

Montijo, Rhode

The Halloween Kid. Simon & Schuster 2010 un il $12.99

Grades: PreK K 1 2   E

1. Cowhands -- Fiction 2. Halloween -- Fiction

ISBN 978-1-4169-3575-9; 1-4169-3575-4

The brave and trusty Halloween Kid saves trick-or-treaters from a crowd of sweet-stealing Goodie Goblins.

"This rollicking story projects a delightfully retro style and sensibility, aided by black, white, and orange brush-and-ink illustrations. . . . A treat for storytime as well as for independent reading and a must for Halloween picture-book collections." SLJ

Moore, Eva

Lucky Ducklings; by Eva Moore; illustrations by Nancy Carpenter. Orchard Books 2013 32 p. (hardcover: alk. paper) $16.99

Grades: K 1 2 3   E

1. Animal rescue 2. Ducks -- Fiction 3. Animal babies -- Fiction 4. Rescues -- Fiction 5. Animals -- Infancy -- Fiction

ISBN 0439448611; 9780439448611

LC 2012002444

Author Eva Moore presents a children's picture book on ducks. "Early one morning, Mama Duck takes her babies for a walk. They follow safely behind her as they leave their pond, waddle through the park, and stop in the little sunlit town's parking lot for yummy breakfast. But one by one, Mama's little ducklings get separated when they disappear into the slats of the town's storm drain." Moore describes "how three firemen and a pickup truck rush to their rescue." (Publisher's note)

Moore, Genevieve

Catherine's story; illustrated by Karin Littlewood. Frances Lincoln Children's 2010 un il $17.95

Grades: 1 2 3   E

1. People with disabilities -- Fiction

ISBN 978-1-84507-655-9; 1-84507-655-9

"Catherine, who wears leg braces, has a special walk and a special way of clapping her hands (so quietly, no one ever hears them). Her cousin Frances thinks she can walk like Catherine but when she tries, she falls over. When she says that Catherine can't talk, Catherine's dad says, 'lots and lots of people talk . . . too much . . . Catherine listens—really, really hard.' Catherine is loved and valued. . . . The lovely watercolor illustrations capture joy and optimism. With subtlety and grace, they perfectly depict a child with disabilities." SLJ

Moore, Inga

A house in the woods. Candlewick Press 2011 il $16.99

Grades: PreK K 1   E

1. Building -- Fiction 2. Friendship -- Fiction 3. Forest animals -- Fiction 4. House construction -- Fiction

ISBN 978-0-7636-5277-7; 0-7636-5277-6

LC 2010050827

Two Little Pigs whose small homes in the woods have been accidentally destroyed by Bear and Moose decide to build a house they can all share, and with the help of Beaver Builders they soon have a fine new home.

"The gentle arc of the story about a warm friendship is perfectly echoed by the large, detailed illustrations. The pencil, pastel, and wash art is full of autumn colors and delicate touches and details that bring the woods and the animals to life." SLJ

Moore, Jodi

When a dragon moves in; written by Jodi Moore; illustrated by Howard McWilliam. Flashlight Press 2011 un il $16.95

Grades: PreK K 1   E

1. Beaches -- Fiction 2. Dragons -- Fiction 3. Family life -- Fiction 4. Imagination -- Fiction

ISBN 978-0-979974-67-0; 0-979974-67-4

"While enjoying a day at the beach with his family, a boy builds a perfect sand castle and a dragon promptly moves in toting a well-worn suitcase. The youngster can't believe his luck while the rest of the family can't believe him. Mischief blamed on the dragon eventually gets the child in trouble. . . . While the text is fun, the story is truly told through the comical illustrations. The friendly red dragon's expressions are hilarious. . . . This story of a runaway imagination will make for an entertaining storytime as well as an enjoyable one-on-one read." SLJ

Mora, Pat

Abuelos; story by Pat Mora; pictures by Amelia Lau Carling. Groundwood Books 2008 un il $18.95
Grades: PreK K 1 2   E
1. Winter -- Fiction 2. New Mexico -- Fiction 3. Hispanic Americans -- Fiction
ISBN 978-0-88899-716-6; 0-88899-716-7
Mora "introduces the intriguing midwinter New Mexican festival of 'los abuelos' in this playful tale. The narrator, Amelia, is about to experience the spooky-sounding tradition for the first time, and Papá offers reassurances. . . . Played by costumed villagers in scary masks, the abuelos chase the children around bonfires; when one snatches her brother, Amelia grabs the abuelo's mask, only to discover her uncle beneath it. Carling's . . . watercolor and pastel illustrations impart Amelia's apprehension as well as family togetherness." Publ Wkly

★ Book fiesta! celebrate Children's Day/Book Day. illustrated by Rafael Lopez. HarperCollins 2009 un il $17.99
Grades: PreK K 1 2 3   E
1. Books and reading -- Fiction 2. Bilingual books -- English-Spanish
ISBN 978-0-06-128877-7; 0-06-128877-2
ALA ALSC Belpre Illustrator Medal (2010)
"Mora encourages teachers, parents, and librarians to celebrate Children's Day/Book Day and includes ideas for observing the festivities. Written in English and Spanish, the text shows children reading in a variety of places, going to the library, listening to stories, and enjoying books. López's acrylic illustrations fill the pages with color. His upbeat iconic style shows how much fun this celebration can be." SLJ

★ Dona Flor; a tall tale about a giant woman with a great big heart. illustrated by Raul Colón. Knopf 2005 un il $15.99; lib bdg $17.99
Grades: K 1 2 3   E
1. Tall tales 2. Pumas -- Fiction 3. Giants -- Fiction
ISBN 0-375-82337-9; 0-375-92337-3 lib bdg
Doña Flor, a giant woman with a big heart, sets off to protect her neighbors from what they think is a dangerous animal, but soon discovers the tiny secret behind the huge noise.
"A charming tall tale. . . Colón uses his signature mix of watercolor washes, etching, and litho pencils for the art. There is great texture and movement on each page in the sunbaked tones of the landscape." SLJ

★ Gracias; Thanks. ilustraciones por John Parra; traducción por Adriana Domínguez; illustrations by John Parra; translation by Adriana Dominguez. Lee & Low Books 2009 un il

Grades: PreK K 1 2   E
1. Hispanic Americans -- Fiction 2. Racially mixed people -- Fiction 3. Bilingual books -- English-Spanish
ISBN 1600602584; 9781600602580
LC 2009013060
ALA ALSC Belpre Illustrator Medal Honor Book (2010)
In this bilingual picture book, a young boy says thank you for many things in his life. "Primary." (Horn Book)
"From the sun waking him up in the morning to a cricket chirping him to sleep at night, a young boy gives thanks for the many things and people who enrich his life. These blessings are remarkable for their childlike imagination and fresh imagery. . . . The bilingual format features Spanish on the left-hand page and English on the right. . . . Parra's vivid acrylic illustrations have the feel of folk-art woodcuts and whimsically portray the details of the boy's world." Booklist

Here, kitty, kitty; illustrated by Maribel Suarez. Rayo 2008 un il (My family, mi familia) $14.99; lib bdg $15.89
Grades: PreK K   E
1. Cats -- Fiction 2. Bilingual books -- English-Spanish
ISBN 978-0-06-085044-9; 0-06-085044-2; 978-0-06-085045-6 lib bdg; 0-06-085045-0 lib bdg
"This joyful picture book tells a lively story of a young girl who gets a shy new kitten that hides and makes trouble. With English and Spanish text on each double-page spread, the line-and-watercolor pictures show the loving family as the kitten hides under the sofa, under sister's bed, in a flowerpot, until finally the soft friend snuggles up on the girl's lap." Booklist

Tomas and the library lady; illustrated by Raúl Colón. Knopf 1997 un il $17; pa $6.99
Grades: K 1 2 3   E
1. Poets 2. Authors 3. Novelists 4. Essayists 5. College teachers 6. Libraries -- Fiction 7. College administrators 8. Migrant labor -- Fiction 9. Books and reading -- Fiction 10. Mexican Americans -- Fiction
ISBN 0-679-80401-3; 0-375-80349-1 pa
LC 89-37490
While helping his family in their work as migrant laborers far from their home, Tomás finds an entire world to explore in the books at the local public library
"Mora's story is based on a true incident in the life of the famous writer Tomás Rivera, the son of migrant workers who became an education leader and university president. . . . Colón's beautiful scratchboard illustrations, in his textured, glowingly colored, rhythmic style, capture the warmth and the dreams that the boy finds in the world of books." Booklist

Uno, dos, tres: one, two, three; illustrated by Barbara Lavallee. Clarion Bks. 1996 43p il hardcover o.p. pa $6.95
Grades: PreK K 1 2   E
1. Counting 2. Stories in rhyme 3. Mexico -- Fiction 4. Bilingual books -- English-Spanish
ISBN 0-395-67294-5; 0-618-05468-5 pa
LC 94-15337
"Two girls search a Mexican market for gifts for their mother's birthday in this counting book in both English and Spanish. . . . Cheerful stylized paintings in muted reds, blues,

and yellows depict designs from Mexican art and use pattern to highlight the number sequence." Horn Book Guide

Wiggling pockets. Rayo 2009 un il (My family, mi familia) $12.99

Grades: PreK K   E

1. Frogs -- Fiction 2. Family life -- Fiction 3. Bilingual books -- English-Spanish

ISBN 978-0-06-085047-0; 0-06-085047-7

"When Danny comes to the table with wiggling pockets, Mom and Dad ask what he has in them. Four frogs jump out and cause minor chaos. The simple text in both English and Spanish and the warm illustrations portray a loving family." Horn Book Guide

Morales, Melita

Jam & honey; illustrations by Laura J. Bryant. Tricycle Press 2011 un il $15.99

Grades: PreK K 1   E

1. Stories in rhyme 2. Bees -- Fiction

ISBN 978-1-58246-299-8; 1-58246-299-2

Tells the story of a young girl and a honeybee who learn to coexist peacefully in the same garden as they go about their respective tasks.

"Simple, bouncing rhymes switch from the child's viewpoint . . . to the bee's voice. . . . The whimsical, uncluttered watercolor-and-pencil illustrations show each character busy at first, then scared of the other, and finally safe and satisfied on their way home." Booklist

Morales, Yuyi

★ **Just** in case; a trickster tale and Spanish alphabet book. Roaring Brook Press 2008 un il $16.95

Grades: 1 2 3   E

1. Ghost stories 2. Gifts -- Fiction 3. Alphabet -- Fiction 4. Birthdays -- Fiction

ISBN 978-1-59643-329-8; 1-59643-329-9

LC 2007-44061

A Pura Belpre Author Award honor book, 2009

Awarded the Pura Belpre Illustrator Award, 2009

As Senor Calavera prepares for Grandma Beetle's birthday he finds an alphabetical assortment of unusual presents, but with the help of Zelmiro the Ghost, he finds the best gift of all.

"Luminous, jewel-tone spreads chronicle the collection of gifts and pay homage to a rich Mexican culture. . . . Part ghost story and part alphabet book, this trickster tale transcends both. Librarians will want to share it for the beautiful language, the spirited artwork, and the rightness of the ending." SLJ

Little Night. Roaring Brook Press 2006 un il $16.95

Grades: PreK K   E

1. Sky -- Fiction 2. Night -- Fiction 3. Bedtime -- Fiction 4. Mother-daughter relationship -- Fiction

ISBN 978-1-59643-088-4; 1-59643-088-5

LC 2006011571

At the end of a long day, Mother Sky helps her playful daughter, Little Night, to get ready for bed

"Morales has created a sumptuous feast of metaphors in her text: a bathtub filled with falling stars, a dress crocheted from clouds. The equally splendid illustrations effectively

convey each of the images and heighten the comfort and serenity inspired by the text." Booklist

★ **Niño** wrestles the world; Yuyi Morales. 1st ed. Roaring Brook Press 2013 40 p. ill. (hardcover) $16.99

Grades: PreK K 1 2 3   E

1. Picture books for children 2. Monsters -- Fiction 3. Wrestling -- Fiction 4. Imagination -- Fiction 5. Brothers and sisters -- Fiction

ISBN 1596436042; 9781596436046

LC 2012012989

Pura Belpre Illustrator Award (2014)

In this children's picture book, "playing alone in his room, Niño dons his Lucha Libre mask and lets his imagination take flight. (According to an endnote, Lucha Libre is a dramatic form of professional wrestling followed by fans in Mexico.) The young hero is then ready to take on an eclectic cast of monstrous opponents. Spurred on by chanting crowds, the boy handily defeats the Guanajuato Mummy (La Momia de Guanajuato), Olmec Head (Cabeza Olmeca), and the Weeping Woman (La Llorona)." (School Library Journal)

★ **Viva** Frida! Yuyi Morales; photography by Tim O'Meara. Roaring Brook Press 2014 40 p. color illustrations (hardcover) $17.99

Grades: K 1 2 3   E

1. Artists 2. Painters -- Mexico -- Biography

ISBN 1596436034; 9781596436039

LC 2013044236

Pura Belpré (Illustrator) Award (2015)

Caldecott Honor Book (2015)

Written by Yuyi Morales, with photography by Tim O'Meara, this children's book describes how "Frida Kahlo, one of the world's most famous and unusual artists is revered around the world. Her life was filled with laughter, love, and tragedy, all of which influenced what she painted on her canvases." (Publisher's note)

"Morales layers English and Spanish words--never more than four to a page--to depict a Frida who is curious, playful, wise, and inspired. Rather than tell a story, the text captures fragments of Frida's life, like snapshots with bilingual captions." Booklist

Morgan, Sally

Me and my dad; [by] Sally Morgan and Ezekiel Kwaymullina; illustrated by Matt Ottley. Little Hare Books 2011 un il $16.99

Grades: PreK K 1   E

1. Fear -- Fiction 2. Birds -- Fiction 3. Beaches -- Fiction 4. Father-son relationship -- Fiction

ISBN 978-1-921541-81-0; 1-921541-81-4

"During an action-filled day at the beach, a boy recounts everything his father isn't afraid of. . . . Making dynamic use of perspective and scale, Ottley shows the boy's father laughing as a skyscraper-high sandcastle tumbles down on him, flexing his bicep while a surging wave threatens to swallow him up, and confidently swimming amid transparent jellyfish to unhook a fishing line. There's a cartoonish sense of playfulness throughout, right up to the final scene in which the father's sole, improbable fear—seagulls— is revealed, giving the boy a chance to be the brave one." Publ Wkly

Sam's bush journey; [by] Sally Morgan and Ezekiel Kwaymullina; illustrated by Bronwyn Bancroft. Little Hare Books 2010 un il $15.99; pa $8.99

Grades: PreK K 1   E

1. Australia -- Fiction 2. Grandmothers -- Fiction 3. Aboriginal Australians -- Fiction

ISBN 978-1-921541-04-9; 1-921541-04-0; 978-1-921541-72-8 pa; 1-921541-72-8 pa

"Living in Australia, Sam's grandmother loves the bush that surrounds her house. On their long walks into the gum forest to the waterhole, spiky shrubs scratch the boy's legs and mosquitoes bite him. Though Nanna tells him about the many good things there, Sam would be happy if they all disappeared. One night he dreams of wandering in the bush lost and alone. Remembering what Nanna has told him, he finds edible berries when his stomach grumbles and shelter in a hollow gum tree during a storm. . . . Stunning illustrations feature thick black outlines and intricate patterns, evoking the Aboriginal culture of the book's creators. The story can be read independently, and the vivid illustrations will nurture an appreciation of the ecology of the Australian bush." SLJ

Morpurgo, Michael

Mirror. Seven Footer Kids 2010 un il $15.95

Grades: PreK K 1 2   E

1. Mirrors -- Fiction

ISBN 978-1-934734-39-1; 1-934734-39-X

In this wordless book "a small girl sits in the corner of a spread, her isolation and loneliness underscored by her head-down, hunkered-over posture as well as the austere palette . . . and stark white backdrop. Her mood . . . changes to surprise when she catches sight of her likeness in a mirror . . . and eventually transforms into playful exuberance as she makes faces at and dances with her reflected double. . . . A blank spread provides a narrative beat, and when the action resumes, the child's reflection no longer parallels her movements, taking on a life of its own. Enraged, the protagonist seems to push at the mirror, which shatters. . . . Lee's illustrations cut to the core to express deep-seated feelings." SLJ

★ **Wave.** Chronicle Books 2008 un il $15.99

Grades: PreK K   E

1. Stories without words 2. Ocean -- Fiction 3. Beaches -- Fiction

ISBN 978-0-8118-5924-0; 0-8118-5924-X

LC 2007-62026

A wordless picture book that shows a little girl's first experiences at the beach, as she goes from being afraid of the roaring waves to playing on the shore while gulls soar overhead.

"A panoramic trim size beautifully supports the expansiveness of the beach. . . . Loosely rendered charcoal and acrylic images curl and flow like water and reflect playfulness, especially in the facial and bodily expressions of the child and seagulls. . . . A simple, well-crafted story." SLJ

Morris, Jackie

I am cat; by Jackie Morris. Frances Lincoln Children's Books 2013 32 p. ill. (hardcover) $17.99

Grades: 1 2 3 4   E

1. Cats -- Poetry 2. Picture books for children

ISBN 1847801358; 9781847801357

In this children's picture book, "Cat, curled tight on a round tasseled pillow, sleeps and dreams. The tabby's poetic

musings accompany . . . watercolor paintings of 10 great cats." Among the cats included are the Siberian tiger, the cheetah, and the lynx. "Cat also dreams of the Scottish wildcat on the verge of extinction and the regal Amur leopard, its 'thick coat coloured like leaves in autumn,/ almost the last' of its kind." (School Library Journal)

Morris, Richard T.

Bye-bye, baby! by Richard Morris; illustrated by Larry Day. Walker & Co. 2009 un il $16.99; lib bdg $17.89

Grades: PreK   E

1. Infants -- Fiction 2. Siblings -- Fiction

ISBN 978-0-8027-9772-8; 0-8027-9772-5; 978-0-8027-9773-5 lib bdg; 0-8027-9773-3 lib bdg

LC 2008044318

Felix does not like his new baby sister and thinks his parents should take her back, until a trip to the zoo makes him realize that she might not be as bad as he thought.

"Outstanding illustrations are done in pen, ink, watercolor, and gouache. The characters' expressions and body language could tell this story alone, but wonderfully enhance the strong and simple text." SLJ

This is a moose; by Richard Morris; illustrated by Tom Lichtenheld. Little, Brown & Co. 2014 48 p. $18

Grades: PreK K 1   E

1. Documentary films -- Fiction 2. Humorous stories 3. Moose -- Fiction 4. Animals -- Habits and behavior -- Fiction 5. Documentary films -- Production and direction -- Fiction

ISBN 0316213608; 9780316213608

LC 2013015681

In this children's book, by Richard Morris and illustrated by Tom Lichtenheld, "a movie director tries to capture the life of a moose on film. . . . It turns out the moose has a dream bigger then just being a moose–he wants to be an astronaut and go to the moon. His forest friends step in to help him, and action ensues. Lots of action. Like a lacrosse-playing grandma, a gigantic slingshot into space, and a flying, superhero chipmunk." (Publisher's note)

"This romp chronicles the making of a documentary about a moose. The hapless (and visually absent, until book's end) director grows increasingly frustrated as silly situations ("would someone kindly get the moose out of the space suit?") and interjections from offstage interrupt filming. Energy and over-the-top hilarity abound, but there are some befuddling plot details. Ever-changing fonts and text formats hamper readability." Horn Book

Morrow, Barbara Olenyik

A good night for freedom; illustrated by Leonard Jenkins. Holiday House 2004 un il $16.95

Grades: K 1 2 3   E

1. Abolitionists 2. Slavery -- Fiction 3. Underground railroad -- Fiction

ISBN 0-8234-1709-3

LC 2002-192207

Hallie discovers two runaway slaves hiding in Levi Coffin's home and must decide whether to turn them in or help them escape to freedom. Includes historical notes on the Underground Railroad and abolitionists Levi and Catharine Coffin.

"The well-written text smoothly blends fact and fiction. . . . Jenkins's mixed-media illustrations capture the emotions

of the characters as well as the details of pre-Civil War life."
SLJ

Includes bibliographical references

Mr. Mosquito put on his tuxedo; illustrated by Ponder
Goembel. Holiday House 2009 un il $16.95
Grades: K 1 2 3   E
    1. Stories in rhyme 2. Bears -- Fiction 3. Insects --
Fiction 4. Mosquitoes -- Fiction
ISBN 978-0-8234-2072-8; 0-8234-2072-8
                                  LC 2007025486
    Mr. Mosquito saves the insect ball from an intruding bear.
"The abundant and rhyming text is only half of this sto-
ry; the illustrations tell the rest. Using lush colors befitting a
royal ball and excellent attention to detail, Goembel brings
this idiosyncratic tale to life." SLJ

Morstad, Julie
    How to. Simply Read Books 2013 36 p. (hardcover)
$16.95
Grades: PreK K 1   E
    1. Picture books for children
ISBN 1897476574; 9781897476574
    This children's picture book by Julie Morstad "explores
whimsical ways of doing a host of different tasks, including
'how to wonder,' 'how to see the breeze,' and 'how to be
brave.'" (Publisher's note) "Morstad explores topics of interest to children, from 'staying close' (two girls sharing one
braid) to disappearing—a scene in which meaning comes
first from the curtained image; the text is nearly invisible."
(Kirkus)

Mortensen, Denise Dowling
    Bug patrol; by Denise Dowling Mortensen; illustrated
by Cece Bell. Clarion Books 2012 32 p. col. ill. (hardcover) $16.99
Grades: PreK K 1 2   E
    1. Stories in rhyme 2. Police -- Fiction 3. Insects --
Fiction 4. Police -- Fiction 5. Insects -- Fiction
ISBN 0618790241; 9780618790241
                                    LC 2011041586
    In this children's book, by Denise Dowling Mortensen,
illustrated by Cece Bell, "bugs are a misbehaving bunch, so
Captain Bob, insect cop, has a busy beat. The beetles are
using their bug mobiles like bumper cars, the roaches are
protesting for better housing . . . , and the crickets are up late,
partying. Can Captain Bob keep the peace and maintain law
and order?" (Publisher's note)

Mortensen, Lori
    Cowpoke Clyde and Dirty Dawg; by Lori Mortensen;
illustrated by Michael Allen Austin. Clarion Books 2013
32 p. (hardcover) $16.99
Grades: PreK K 1 2   E
    1. Dogs -- Fiction 2. Baths -- Fiction 3. Stories in
rhyme 4. Cowboys -- Fiction
ISBN 0547239939; 9780547239934
                                    LC 2011052429
    This book, by Lori Mortensen, tells "the tale of a cowboy
who likes to keep things clean and tidy. Clyde tries tactic after tactic to catch his dog for a scrub down, each new method
adding another layer of mayhem to the scene . . . . Finally
Clyde takes a bath in the moonlight by himself while singing

. . . and that is the winning lure that gets the dirty Dawg into
the washtub." (Kirkus)

Mortimer, Anne
    Pumpkin cat; written & illustrated by Anne Mortimer.
Katherine Tegen Books 2011 un il $14.99; lib bdg $15.89
Grades: PreK K 1   E
    1. Cats -- Fiction 2. Mice -- Fiction 3. Pumpkin --
Fiction
ISBN 978-0-06-187485-7; 0-06-187485-X; 978-0-06-
187486-4 lib bdg; 0-06-187486-8 lib bdg
    "One morning in May, Cat wondered, 'How do pump-
kins grow?' 'I know,' said Mouse. 'And I will show you
how.' Mouse proceeds to guide Cat through the various steps
and stages, one phase featured on each spread, until October
arrives and they are rewarded with a large orange pumpkin.
. . . Mortimer has masterfully captured the texture of her
subjects—the softness of the animals' fur, the scratchiness
of burlap bags, the silkiness of delicate flower petals, etc. . . .
A lovely addition that should be popular in any season." SLJ

Mortiz, Dianne
    Hush little beachcomber; illustrated by Holly McGee.
Kane Miller 2011 un il $14.99
Grades: PreK K 1   E
    1. Stories in rhyme 2. Seashore -- Fiction
ISBN 978-1-935279-81-5; 1-935279-81-5
    "'Hush, Little Baby' receives a bright makeover, with
seagulls and sand pies replacing mockingbirds and diamond
rings. Repetitive phrases may mirror the soothing lullaby's
format, but this blissful beach day opens with a more enthusiastic call for action. . . . The cheerful voice remains optimistic throughout. . . . . The lilting text naturally progresses through each experience. . . . Pastel spreads flash with
smudges of golden color, with their hazy hues dominating
each page, the brief rhyming text highlighting each featured
activity." Kirkus

Morton, Carlene
    The **library** pages; illustrated by Valeria Docampo.
UpstartBooks 2010 un il $17.95
Grades: K 1 2 3   E
    1. School stories 2. Libraries -- Fiction
ISBN 978-1-60213-045-6; 1-60213-045-0
    While Mrs. Heath, the school librarian, is on maternity
leave, the library pages put all the thin books together, shelve
the books by color, mend them with duct tape, cut pictures
out of encyclopedias, shelve every third book with the pages
pointing out, and borrow books without checking them out.
    "Docampo's colorful combination of manual and digital
illustrations sets a perfectly mood for this story. This is an
entertaining read-aloud, a humorous joke, and an excellent
starter for library orientation." SLJ

Moser, Lisa
    Cowboy Boyd and Mighty Calliope; by Lisa Moser;
illustrated by Sebastiaan Van Doninck. 1st ed. Random
House Inc 2013 40 p. ill. (hardcover) $17.99; (library)
$20.99; (ebook) $53.97
Grades: PreK K 1   E
    1. Picture books for children 2. Cowboys -- Fiction 3.

Ranch life -- Fiction 4. Rhinoceroses -- Fiction
ISBN 0375870563; 0375970568; 9780375870569;
9780375970566; 9780375980794

LC 2012025379

In this picture book, "Rancher Rose and her hired hands are skeptical when Cowboy Boyd and his unusual mount arrive for a job at the Double R Ranch. As it happens, Calliope is a sensitive and affectionate rhinoceros, though she is not a very good ranch horse. Each task that she attempts ends in failure and, unsurprisingly, the very night that Rancher Rose tells Boyd and Calliope to 'roll on,' a situation arises where only her unique talents can provide a happy ending." (School Library Journal)

Kisses on the wind; illustrated by Kathryn Brown. Candlewick Press 2009 un il $15.99
Grades: K 1 2 3   E
1. Moving -- Fiction 2. West (U.S.) -- Fiction 3. Grandmothers -- Fiction 4. Frontier and pioneer life -- Fiction
ISBN 978-0-7636-3110-9; 0-7636-3110-8

LC 2008-53490

Young Lydia struggles to say goodbye to her grandmother as her parents finish packing their wagon for the long journey to Oregon in the nineteenth century.

"Moser and Brown tell a wise, gentle story about goodbyes. . . . The fluid watercolors amplify the story's mood of transition." Booklist

Perfect Soup; illustrated by Ben Mantle. Random House 2010 un il $16.99; lib bdg $19.99
Grades: PreK K 1 2   E
1. Mice -- Fiction 2. Snow -- Fiction 3. Soups -- Fiction
ISBN 978-0-375-86014-0; 0-375-86014-2; 978-0-375-96014-7 lib bdg; 0-375-96014-7 lib bdg

LC 2009052846

Murray the mouse goes into town for the carrot he needs to make Perfect Soup, and soon finds himself with a chain of favors that will work only if a friendly snowman can help him gets things started

"Mantle's illustrations cheer, comedically maximizing Murray's diminutive size and adding gently whimsical touches." Kirkus

Railroad Hank; by Lisa Moser; illustrations by Benji Davies. Random House Children's Books 2012 40 p. col. ill. (trade) $16.99
Grades: PreK K 1 2   E
1. Farm life -- Fiction 2. Railroads -- Fiction 3. Humorous fiction 4. Humorous stories 5. Railroad trains -- Fiction
ISBN 0375868496; 9780375868498; 9780375968495

LC 2011030231

In this children's story, by Lisa Moser, illustrated by Benji Davies, "Railroad Hank is headed up the mountain in his . . . little train to see Granny Bett. . . . Along the way, he stops to talk to Missy May, Country Carl, Cinnamon Cobbler, and Reel-'Em-In Sam. Each friend offers up something to cheer Granny Bett. . . . By the time he reaches the mountaintop, his train is bursting with crazy cargo! And Granny Bett has a great idea for what to do with it all." (Publisher's note)

"Moser's folksy writing style is paired well with Davies's perky acrylic illustrations... This satisfying, good-humored picture book sends a worthy message about looking after other people." SLJ

★ **Squirrel's** world; illustrated by Valeri Gorbachev. Candlewick Press 2007 44p il $14.99; pa $4.99
Grades: 1 2 3   E
1. Animals -- Fiction 2. Squirrels -- Fiction
ISBN 978-0-7636-2929-8; 0-7636-2929-4; 978-0-7636-4088-0 pa; 0-7636-4088-3 pa

LC 2007-60859

Squirrel's well-meaning attempts to help his forest friends do not always turn out as planned.

"Gorbachev's loosely hatched linework provides apealing informal texture to the forest clan, and his illustrations offer plenty of decoding clues for novices. . . . Early independent readers will revel in the abundant repetition." Bull Cent Child Books

Moses, Will
Mary and her little lamb; the true story behind the nursery rhyme. Philomel Books 2011 36p il $17.99
Grades: 1 2 3   E
1. School stories 2. Sheep -- Fiction 3. Farm life -- Fiction 4. Massachusetts -- Fiction
ISBN 978-0-399-25154-2; 0-399-25154-5

LC 2010037445

In 1810s Massachusetts, young Mary Elizabeth Sawyer nurses a sickly lamb back to health and becomes the subject of a famous nursery rhyme. Includes facts about the real Mary, John Roulstone who wrote the rhyme, and Lowell Mason who set it to music.

"Moses's rich oil paintings, rendered in his characteristic folk-art style, beautifully depict rural 19th-century life. They include spreads, framed pictures with images of books and hens in the margins, and vignettes accompanying the lengthy text." SLJ

Moss, Lloyd
★ **Zin!** zin! zin! a violin; illustrated by Marjorie Priceman. Simon & Schuster Bks. for Young Readers 1995 un il $17.95; pa $6.99
Grades: K 1 2 3   E
1. Counting 2. Stories in rhyme 3. Musical instruments
ISBN 0-671-88239-2; 0-689-83524-8 pa

LC 93-37902

A Caldecott Medal honor book, 1996

"Rhyming couplets present 10 instruments and their characteristics. . . . In the process of adding instruments, the book teaches the names of musical groups up to a chamber group of 10 as well as the categories into which the instruments fall: strings, reeds, and brasses. Amazingly, Moss conveys this encyclopedic information while keeping the poem streamlined and peppy. Priceman's sprightly, sunny hued gouache paintings should take a bow, too." Booklist

Moss, Peggy
One of us; illustrated by Penny Weber. Tilbury House 2010 un il $16.95
Grades: 1 2 3   E
1. School stories 2. Moving -- Fiction 3. Friendship -- Fiction 4. Individualism -- Fiction
ISBN 978-0-88448-322-9; 0-88448-322-3

Roberta is welcomed by different groups on her first day at a new school, only to be told she does not fit in with them for some reason, but by the next day, members of each group have begun to see that they do not have to be alike in every way.

"Expressive eyes, happy faces, and rosy cheeks are indicative of the engaging illustrations that complement this winning color picture book. It can be used to supplement guidance lessons, welcome new students, or just as a fun discussion after a read-aloud session." Libr Media Connect

Most, Bernard

ABC T-Rex. Harcourt Brace & Co. 2000 un il $14; pa $6

Grades: PreK K 1   E

1. Alphabet 2. Dinosaurs -- Fiction

ISBN 0-15-202007-1; 0-15-205028-0 pa

LC 98-51128

A young T-Rex loves his ABCs so much that he eats them up, experiencing on each letter a word that begins with that letter

"Heavy black lines define the cartoonlike drawings, brightened with a colorful palette emphasizing shades of green, purple, and orange. Fun for alphabetically inclined preschoolers." Booklist

★ **Whatever** happened to the dinosaurs? written and illustrated by Bernard Most. Harcourt Brace Jovanovich 1984 un il hardcover o.p. pa $4.95

Grades: PreK K 1   E

1. Dinosaurs -- Fiction

ISBN 0-15-295295-0; 0-15-295296-9 pa

LC 84-3779

"A hilarious book, sure to be popular for individual reading or with groups." Child Book Rev Serv

The author "offers various fantastic explanations to answer his title question. 'Did the dinosaurs go to another planet? . . . did a magician make them disappear? . . . Are the dinosaurs in the hospital?'" SLJ

Moulton, Mark Kimball

The **very** best pumpkin; written by Mark Kimball Moulton; illustrated by Karen Hillard Good. Simon & Schuster Books for Young Readers 2010 un il $12.99

Grades: PreK K 1   E

1. Autumn -- Fiction 2. Pumpkin -- Fiction 3. Friendship -- Fiction

ISBN 978-1-4169-8288-3; 1-4169-8288-4

LC 2008046639

While Peter carefully tends a special pumpkin on his grandparents' farm, quiet Meg watches from her new home next door.

"Illustrations, rendered in watercolors mottled by instant coffee and bleach, are full of life and happy moments. The iconic symbols of the season—falling leaves, acorns, ripe apples—help provide an idyllic autumnal setting for the appealing friendship story." Booklist

Moundlic, Charlotte

The **bathing** costume, or, The worst vacation of my life; by Charlotte Moundlic; illustrated by Olivier Tallec; translated by Claudia Zoe Bedrick. Enchanted Lion Books 2013 40 p. ill. (hardcover) $15.95

Grades: K 1 2 3   E

1. Summer -- Fiction 2. Cousins -- Fiction 3. Vacations -- Fiction 4. Grandparents -- Fiction

ISBN 1592701418; 9781592701414

LC 2013011002

Mildred L. Batchelder Honor Book (2014)

In this children's story, by Charlotte Moundlic, illustrated by Olivier Tallec, "this summer, Michel will go away alone . . . to stay with his grandparents while his parents move apartments. To add to the horror, Michel's older boy cousins will be going, too. . . . Between a competition to see who can shower the least, wild bike rides without gear, and a tooth that finally falls out, Michel discovers both independence and real moments of happiness." (Publisher's note)

The **scar**; [illustrations by Olivier Tallec] Candlewick Press 2011 il $14.99

Grades: K 1   E

1. Death -- Fiction 2. Mothers -- Fiction 3. Bereavement -- Fiction

ISBN 978-0-7636-5341-5; 0-7636-5341-1

LC 2010042792

When his mother dies, a little boy is angry at his loss but does everything he can to hold onto the memory of her scent, her voice, and the special things she did for him, even as he tries to help his father and grandmother cope.

"Rendered in pencil and wash in a limited palette of reds and yellows, simple illustrations stress the boy's distress and isolation while powerfully conveying his progression from anger and fear to sadness and acceptance. A sympathetic exploration of the stages of grief through the eyes of one little boy." Kirkus

Mozelle, Shirley

Zack's alligator and the first snow; story by Shirley Mozelle; pictures by James Watts. Harper 2011 32p il (I can read!) $16.99; pa $3.99

Grades: PreK K 1 2   E

1. Snow -- Fiction 2. Alligators -- Fiction

ISBN 978-0-06-147370-8; 0-06-147370-7; 978-0-06-147372-2 pa; 0-06-147372-3 pa

LC 2008034359

Zack and Bridget, his alligator keychain that grows into a fun-loving, full-sized alligator when it gets wet, enjoy the day playing in the snow, ice-fishing, and sledding.

"Watts' softly-colored illustrations reflect the joy and exuberance that snow brings, while Bridget's innocence is charming. . . . Simple sentences and vocabulary and a lively story make this just right for developing readers." Kirkus

Other titles about Zack's alligator are:

Zack's alligator (1989)

Zack's alligator goes to school (1994)

Muir, Leslie

The **little** bitty bakery; illustrations by Betsy Lewin. Disney-Hyperion Books 2011 il $16.99

Grades: PreK K 1   E

1. Stories in rhyme 2. Cake -- Fiction 3. Mice -- Fiction 4. Birthdays -- Fiction 5. Bakers and bakeries -- Fiction

ISBN 978-1-4231-1640-0; 1-4231-1640-2

LC 2011012267

When a pastry chef works straight through her birthday with no time for birthday cake, some industrious mice make good use of her kitchen and bake a delicious surprise.

"This delightful read-aloud, with its enticing cover featuring an array of sparkling baked goods, works well on many levels. Muir's sweet, engaging story is sprinkled with French words throughout, and Lewin's charming cartoon art, in nighttime shades of blue and purple, uses thick and thin brush lines to capture the action." SLJ

Muldrow, Diane

We planted a tree; illustrated by Bob Staake. Golden Books 2010 un il $17.99; lib bdg $20.99

Grades: PreK K 1 2   **E**

1. Trees -- Fiction 2. Growth -- Fiction 3. Ecology -- Fiction

ISBN 978-0-375-86432-2; 0-375-86432-6; 978-0-375-96432-9 lib bdg; 0-375-86432-6 lib bdg

LC 2009000394

"A family in Brooklyn plants a tree in their small backyard; turn the page and a Kenyan family plants a tree on the bare African savanna. Then in Paris, Tokyo, and more places across the globe, each newly planted tree grows up, as the children in the family do. Muldow weaves some science into the lines. . . . Illustrating the simple poetry are clean-lined digital illustrations that show the botany details and celebrate the connections between plants and people, present and long-term, across time and space." Booklist

Munari, Bruno

Bruno Munari's zoo; [by] Bruno Munari. Chronicle Books 2005 un il $17.95

Grades: PreK K   **E**

1. Zoos 2. Animals

ISBN 0-8118-4830-2

LC 2004-21214

A reissue of the title first published 1963 by World Publishing

Illustrations and brief text introduce more than twenty zoo animals, including a rhinoceros that is always ready to fight and a peacock that struts proudly because he is the peacock.

"A stunning picture book of birds and beasts original in design, brilliant with color, and touched with humor." Booklist

Muncaster, Harriet

I am a witch's cat; by Harriet Muncaster. Harper 2014 32 p. col. ill. (hardcover bdg.) $15.99

Grades: PreK K 1 2   **E**

1. Cats -- Fiction 2. Witches -- Fiction

ISBN 0062229141; 9780062229144

LC 2012022152

In this children's book, by Harriet Muncaster, "a little girl believes her mother is a good witch—and she is a special witch's cat! After all, every good witch needs a black cat. Together, this playful girl and her loving mom are a perfect twosome, whether they are mixing potions, growing magical plants, or dreaming of wild broomstick rides under a full moon." (Publisher's note)

"In Muncaster's tongue-in-cheek debut, a girl dressed in a head-to-toe cat costume explains how she knows her mother is actually a witch. For starters, she keeps 'strange potion bottles in the bathroom that I am NOT allowed to touch,'

and 'when her friends come over, they sit in a circle and cackle and swap spell books.' . . . Muncaster's miniatures create an alluring backdrop for this ode to creative, capable mothers and their adoring familiars... er, children. And the story doesn't shut the door to the possibility of real magic, either. " Pub Wkly

Munro, Roxie

Circus. Chronicle Books 2006 un il $15.95

Grades: PreK K 1 2   **E**

1. Puzzles 2. Stories in rhyme 3. Circus -- Fiction

ISBN 0-8118-5209-1

Flaps open to reveal circus acts, from astounding acrobats to elegant elephants, and rhyming text lists objects hidden within each performance

"The detailed ink and watercolor illustrations are bold and lively." Horn Book Guide

★ Go! go! go! with more than 70 flaps to uncover & discover. Sterling 2009 un il $15.95

Grades: PreK K 1 2   **E**

1. Fires -- Fiction

ISBN 978-1-4027-3773-2; 1-4027-3773-4

Gatefolds, layers of lift-the-flaps and complex fold-outs take the reader on a race of a fire truck to battle a blaze, to gallop to the finish line on the favorite horse and riding the race course in a car.

This is a "fascinating picture book. . . . Text is kept to a minimum while full-spread artwork carries the story. . . . The full-color illustrations are loaded with pertinent details." SLJ

Muntean, Michaela

★ Do not open this book! illustrated by Pascal LeMaitre. Scholastic Press 2006 un il $15.99

Grades: PreK K 1 2   **E**

1. Pigs -- Fiction 2. Authorship -- Fiction 3. Books and reading -- Fiction

ISBN 0-439-69839-1

As Pig tries to write a book, he chastises the reader who keeps interrupting him by turning the pages.

"Along with hand lettering Muntean's text, LeMaitre contributes bright, comics-style pictures that clarify the occasionally dizzying concepts. . . . Children will be . . . enraptured by the irreverent, interactive premise and will emerge with a fresh understanding of the powerful qualities of words." Booklist

Muon Van

In a village by the sea; by Muon Van; illustrated by April Chu. Creston Books 2015 32 p. (hardback) $16.95

Grades: PreK K 1 2   **E**

1. Vietnam -- Fiction 2. Homesickness -- Fiction 3. Seafaring life -- Fiction

ISBN 1939547156; 9781939547156

LC 2015006486

This children's story, by Muon Van, illustrated by April Chu, "set[s] human and animal characters into seascapes and interior scenes in an almost timeless Vietnam and extend the story far beyond the words. A wife and a baby are in their traditional kitchen anxiously awaiting the fisherman-husband's return. He is in his boat, fearfully viewing the dark waves and black clouds but also looking at family photos (a hint of modernity)." (Kirkus Reviews)

Murphy, Claire Rudolf

Marching with Aunt Susan; Susan B. Anthony and the fight for women's suffrage. written by Claire Rudolf Murphy; illustrated by Stacey Schuett. Peachtree 2011 un il $16.95

Grades: 1 2 3 4   E

1. Suffragists 2. Abolitionists 3. Sex role -- Fiction 4. Women's rights -- Fiction 5. Women -- Suffrage -- Fiction

ISBN 978-1-56145-593-5; 1-56145-593-8

LC 2011002703

Not allowed to go hiking with her father and brothers because she is a girl, Bessie learns about women's rights when she attends a suffrage rally led by Susan B. Anthony.

"Schuett's somewhat impressionistic gouache paintings effectively capture the time and place and convey the emotionally charged tenor of the campaign. The endnotes, accompanied by photographs, provide factual material about the real Bessie Keith Pond, Anthony, and the suffrage movement, especially in California." SLJ

Murphy, Mary

★ **I** kissed the baby. Candlewick Press 2003 un il hardcover o.p. bd bk $6.99

Grades: PreK K 1   E

1. Ducks -- Fiction 2. Animals -- Fiction

ISBN 0-7636-2122-6; 0-7636-2443-8 bd bk

LC 2002-31419

Various animals tell how they saw, fed, sang to, tickled, and kissed the new duckling

"Murphy makes creative use of color on the edges of the black-and-white pages, until the duckling appears in a splash of vibrant yellow, and the text changes to hot pink. This is an ideal book for little eyes and ears, for text, illustrations, and design meld perfectly." SLJ

A **Kiss** like this; Mary Murphy. Candlewick Press 2012 32 p. $12.99

Grades: PreK K   E

1. Animals -- Fiction 2. Kissing -- Fiction 3. Parent-child relationship -- Fiction

ISBN 0763661821; 9780763661823

LC 2012942308

In this children's picture book by Mary Murphy, "split-page flaps reveal . . . a silly series of animal kisses. . . . Each spread features a vibrantly hued child/parent pair of creatures, including giraffes, mice, fish, bees, elephants, owls and bunnies. The black, smudgy hand-lettered text describes the different kinds of kisses. . . . Each phrase ends with an ellipsis prompting readers to flip the half page to reveal 'like this!' and an eyes-closed buss." (Kirkus Reviews)

Say hello like this; Mary Murphy. Candlewick Press 2014 32 p. color illustrations $12.99

Grades: PreK K   E

1. Animals 2. Etiquette 3. Animal sounds

ISBN 0763669512; 9780763669515

LC 2013943080

In this children's concept book, written and illustrated by Mary Murphy, "different kinds of animals say hello in their own way. . . . Full of funny adjectives and sound words, this . . . companion to Mary Murphy's 'A Kiss Like This' is a . . . read-aloud for the very youngest of listeners." (Publisher's note)

"Each spread offers just enough detail to pique interest due to some clever bookmaking; when youngsters flip a flap, they will observe that the scene has changed considerably. . . . The repetitive phrasing acts as a prompt, encouraging youngsters to chime in." Booklist

Murphy, Stuart J.

Emma's friendwich. Charlesbridge Pub. 2010 un il (I see I learn) $14.95; pa $6.95

Grades: PreK K   E

1. Animals -- Fiction 2. Friendship -- Fiction

ISBN 978-1-58089-450-0; 1-58089-450-X; 978-1-58089-451-7 pa; 1-58089-451-8 pa

LC 2009027784

After moving to a new home, Emma makes friends with the girl next door. Includes questions about the text and notes to parents about visual learning.

"Murphy folds his educational points into a warm stand-alone story, and the cheerful, uncluttered, jellybean-colored spreads clearly illustrate friend-making steps." Booklist

Freda is found. Charlesbridge 2011 un il (I see I learn) $14.95; pa $6.95

Grades: PreK K   E

1. School stories 2. Animals -- Fiction 3. Missing children -- Fiction

ISBN 978-1-58089-462-3; 1-58089-462-3; 978-1-58089-463-0 pa; 1-58089-463-1 pa

On a field trip, Freda is separated from her class, but she remembers just what to do. Includes questions about the text and a note to parents about visual learning.

The book has "vibrant, playful illustrations featuring animated characters that reinforce the story [line]. The highlighted text and expanded captions convey the action." SLJ

★ **Leaping** lizards; illustrated by JoAnn Adinolfi. HarperCollins Pubs. 2005 33p il (MathStart) hardcover o.p. pa $4.99

Grades: 1 2 3   E

1. Addition 2. Counting 3. Stories in rhyme 4. Lizards -- Fiction

ISBN 0-06-000130-5; 0-06-000132-1 pa

LC 2004-22470

"This book introduces the multiples of five, as lizards of different colors travel through the pages on unicycles, a hot-air balloon, an airplane, and other modes of transport, while a green snake looks on. Finally, the number 50 is reached, and lizards explode in all directions. . . . An intelligent blending of white space and colors make each double-page spread visually stand out. A box on one side of each page helps children keep track of the multiplying lizards, and a closing section offers adults a few more ideas for easy math education." Booklist

Same old horse; illustrated by Steve Björkman. HarperCollins Pubs. 2005 31p il (Mathstart) hardcover o.p. pa $4.99

Grades: K 1 2 3   E

1. Horses -- Fiction

ISBN 0-06-055770-2; 0-06-055771-0 pa

Hankie wants to be unpredictable, but the other horses are sure he'll always be the same old Hankie. Someone's in for a surprise in this story about making predictions

This "is a lively story that encourages kids to work with numbers to find out what happens next. Bjorkman's clear, funny ink-and-watercolor pictures show horses in a barnyard acting just like children on a school playground." Booklist

Write on, Carlos! illustrated by Tim Jones. Charlesbridge 2011 un il $14.95; pa $6.95
Grades: PreK K   E
  1. Literacy -- Fiction 2. Personal names -- Fiction
  ISBN 978-1-58089-464-7; 1-58089-464-X; 978-1-58089-465-4 pa; 1-58089-465-8 pa
                 LC 2010023522
With his mother's help, Carlos learns to write his name, as some of his friends can do.
This book has "vibrant, playful illustrations featuring animated characters that reinforce the story [line]. The highlighted text and expanded captions convey the action." SLJ

Murphy, Yannick
  Baby Polar; illustrated by Kristen Balouch. Clarion Books 2009 un il $16 E
  1. Storms -- Fiction 2. Polar bear -- Fiction 3. Arctic regions -- Fiction 4. Mother-child relationship -- Fiction
  ISBN 978-0-618-99850-0; 0-618-99850-0
                 LC 2008011619
Even though his mother warns him of a coming storm, Baby Polar goes outside to play, but when he cannot see his own paw he realizes that he now faces danger.
"The illustrations are digitally produced and beautifully designed. Stylized white snowflakes and polar bear figures set against a blue gray background convey well the icy coldness of the storm. . . . The book's reassuring conclusion offers a satisfying story for that audience, as well as an introduction to polar bears and their Arctic world." SLJ

Murray, Alison
  ★ **Apple** pie ABC. Disney Hyperion 2011 un il $16.99
Grades: PreK K   E
  1. Alphabet 2. Dogs -- Fiction 3. Pies -- Fiction
  ISBN 978-1-4231-3694-1; 1-4231-3694-2
"It all starts with 'A apple pie' in this terse, alphabetically organized story: a towheaded little girl, accompanied by her loyal pooch, bakes that pie, cools it, then dishes out a piece for herself. And that's when her dog develops his obsssesion: he tries to get at the treat. . . . The illustrations, retro-touched digital art with a strong graphic sensibility and a hearkening back to block prints, take this neat concept and joyously gallop with it." Bull Cent Child Books

  Little mouse; Alison Murray. 1st U.S. ed. Disney-Hyperion Books 2013 32 p. ill. (reinforced) $16.99
Grades: PreK   E
  1. Picture books for children 2. Animals -- Fiction 3. Mother-daughter relationship -- Fiction 4. Nicknames -- Fiction 5. Mother and child -- Fiction
  ISBN 1423143302; 9781423143307
                 LC 2012006147
In this book, "Mommy sometimes calls her daughter little mouse, which amuses the spirited child because her self-perception is that she's strong as an ox and brave as a lion and that she can howl like a wolf. But when bedtime nears and the sprightly child gets sleepy, she is more than happy

to curl up in her mother's arms and be that little mouse." (Kirkus)

  One two that's my shoe! Alison Murray. Disney-Hyperion Books 2012 32 p.
Grades: PreK   E
  1. Counting 2. Stories in rhyme 3. Picture books for children 4. Dogs -- Fiction 5. Animals -- Infancy -- Fiction
  ISBN 1423143299; 9781423143291
                 LC 2011013171
This preschool children's story, written and illustrated by Alison Murray, is a rhyming picture book describing a "mischievous puppy [who] runs off with his owner's shoe, it's a race from one to ten to get it back again!" (Publisher's note) Each page illustrates an exercise of counting household objects, animals, or landscape pieces. "The brief, rhymed text is . . . placed to allow viewers time to count the teddy bears, flowers, etc., along the way." (Kirkus Reviews)

Murray, Laura
  The **gingerbread** man loose in the school; illustrated by Mike Lowery. G. P. Putnam's 2011 il $16.99
Grades: PreK K 1   E
  1. School stories 2. Stories in rhyme 3. Cookies -- Fiction
  ISBN 978-0-399-25052-1; 0-399-25052-2
                 LC 2009006642
A gingerbread man searches all over the school for the group of children that made him and then left him behind.
"With a little practice to get the beats just right, the text can be easily read aloud, and youngsters can be invited to chime in on the refrain: 'I'm the Gingerbread Man/and I'm trying to find,/the children who made me,/but left me behind.' A variety of fonts is used to indicate differences between speakers and the narration. The cartoon illustrations are primitive in style, but suit the story to a tee." SLJ

Murray, Marjorie Dennis
  Halloween night; by Marjorie Dennis Murray; illustrations by Brandon Dorman. Greenwillow Books 2008 un il $16.99; lib bdg $17.89
Grades: K 1 2 3   E
  1. Stories in rhyme 2. Parties -- Fiction 3. Monsters -- Fiction 4. Halloween -- Fiction
  ISBN 978-0-06-135186-0; 0-06-135186-5; 978-0-06-135187-7 lib bdg; 0-06-135187-3 lib bdg
                 LC 2007027686
Loosely based on "The Night Before Christmas," this rhyming story tells of a group of animals, monsters, and witches who prepare such a frightening Halloween party that their expected trick-or-treaters all run away.
"Murray's smooth rhyming text combines well with Dorman's vibrant and extraordinarily detailed digital art, with surprises on every page. This is an energetic romp with a satisfying conclusion that will be a fun read-aloud." SLJ

  Mustache! illustrations by Kevin Cornell. Disney/Hyperion Books 2011 un il $16.99
Grades: 1 2 3   E
  1. Kings and rulers -- Fiction 2. Personal appearance -- Fiction
  ISBN 978-1-4231-1671-4; 1-4231-1671-2
                 LC 2011008462

When extremely good-looking King Duncan builds more and more tributes to his handsome face, neglecting kingdom projects and repairs, his loyal subjects find a mustachioed solution.

"The large cartoon illustrations, mostly spreads, are framed in gold with a peacock motif along the bottom. The brief, humorous text appears in scrolls superimposed on the paintings. . . . This royal romp of a story contains some subtle messages behind the hilarity." SLJ

Muth, Jon J.
Zen ghosts. Scholastic Press 2010 un il $17.99
Grades: K 1 2 3   E
1. Siblings -- Fiction 2. Halloween -- Fiction 3. Giant panda -- Fiction 4. Storytelling -- Fiction 5. Zen Buddhism -- Fiction
ISBN 978-0-439-63430-4; 0-439-63430-X
LC 2009-31236
On Halloween night, Stillwater the giant panda tells Karl, Addy, and Michael a spooky and unusual story. Based on a Zen koan.

"Haunting in multiple senses of the word, this tale should captivate thoughtful readers, as Muth's watercolors convey a world of infinite possibility and gentle enchantment." Publ Wkly

★ **Zen** shorts; illustrated by Jon Muth. Scholastic Press 2005 un il $16.95
Grades: K 1 2 3   E
1. Giant panda -- Fiction 2. Storytelling -- Fiction 3. Zen Buddhism -- Fiction
ISBN 0-439-33911-1
LC 2003-20471
A Caldecott Medal honor book, 2006
When Stillwater the panda moves into the neighborhood, the stories he tells to three siblings teach them to look at the world in new ways.

This "is both an accessible, strikingly illustrated story and a thought-provoking mediation." Booklist

Other titles about Stillwater the panda are:
Zen ties (2008)
Zen ghosts (2010)

Myers, Christopher
★ **Black** cat. Scholastic Press 1999 un il $16.95
Grades: PreK K 1 2   E
1. Cats -- Fiction 2. City and town life -- Fiction
ISBN 0-590-03375-1
LC 98-28609
A Coretta Scott King honor book for illustration, 2000
A black cat wanders through the streets of a city
"With striking photo-collages enhanced with gouache and ink, this book captures the gritty beauty of the city." Horn Book Guide

My pen; Christopher Myers. Disney-Hyperion 2015 32 p. illustrations hbk $16.99
Grades: K 1 2 3 4 5   E
1. Drawing -- Fiction 2. Imagination -- Fiction 3. Pens -- Fiction
ISBN 1423103718; 9781423103714
LC 2013047312
"Aurelio is a young artist with big eyes, a fedora, and, most importantly, a vivid imagination. In ink renderings on

pages that maintain interest by alternating between black on white and the perception of the reverse, the boy contrasts the sense of being small--evoked when he sees rich and famous people--with the power he wields with his pen." (School Library Journal)

"Highly sophisticated concepts and art invite the long and close examination of older readers. Poignant, vulnerable, wise." Kirkus

Wings. Scholastic Press 2000 un il $16.95
Grades: K 1 2 3   E
1. Flight -- Fiction 2. Classical mythology -- Fiction
ISBN 0-590-03377-8
LC 99-87389
"Myers retells the myth of Icarus through the story of Ikarus Jackson, the new boy on the block, who can fly above the rooftops and over the crowd. In this contemporary version, the winged kid nearly falls from the sky . . . because jeering kids in the schoolyard and repressive adults don't like his being different and try to break his soaring spirit. . . . Myers' beautiful cut-paper collages are eloquent and open." Booklist

Myers, Tim
Basho and the river stones; illustrations by Oki S. Han. Marshall Cavendish 2004 un il $16.95
Grades: K 1 2 3   E
1. Poets 2. Authors 3. Foxes -- Fiction 4. Japan -- Fiction 5. Poetry -- Fiction
ISBN 0-7614-5165-X
LC 2003-26245
Tricked by a fox into giving up his share of cherries, a famous Japanese poet is inspired to write a haiku and the fox, ashamed of his actions, must devise another trick to set things right

"Han's expressive watercolors, with an unusual variety of perspectives, keep the story lively. A clever original fable." Booklist

Another title about Basho by this author and illustrator is:
Basho and the fox (2000)

Myers, Walter Dean, 1937-2014
★ The **blues** of Flats Brown; illustrated by Nina Laden. Holiday House 2000 un il $16.95; pa $6.95
Grades: 1 2 3 4   E
1. Dogs -- Fiction 2. Blues music -- Fiction
ISBN 0-8234-1480-9; 0-8234-1679-8 pa
LC 99-16695
To escape an abusive master, a junkyard dog named Flats runs away and makes a name for himself from Mississippi to New York City playing blues on his guitar

"The narrator's vernacular, rhythmic and easy-rolling, has the feel of a timeless legend, and the vibrant, jewel-toned illustrations, dominated by moody, bittersweet, tonal variations of blue, are filled with rich detail, expressive characters, and fantastic landscapes." Booklist

Looking for the easy life; illustrated by Lee Harper. Harper 2010 un il $16.99
Grades: K 1 2 3   E
1. Work -- Fiction 2. Animals -- Fiction 3. Monkeys

-- Fiction 4. Conduct of life -- Fiction
ISBN 978-0-06-054375-4; 0-06-054375-2; 978-0-06-065476-1 lib bdg; 0-06-054376-0 lib bdg

LC 2008-34360

Five monkeys go in search of the easy life, but find that "easy ain't always good" and "a little work ain't always bad."

"Myers . . . offers deft characterizations and quick retorts . . . and Harper's . . . animals grin and flirt engagingly. . . . Myers demonstrates a profound talent for kid-pleasing humor—it's a story-time natural." Publ Wkly

★ **Looking** like me; illustrated by Christopher Myers. Egmont USA 2009 un il
Grades: 1 2 3   E
1. Family life -- Fiction 2. African Americans -- Fiction 3. Harlem (New York, N.Y.) -- Fiction
ISBN 1-60684-001-0; 1-60684-041-X lib bdg; 978-1-60684-001-6; 978-1-60684-041-2 lib bdg

LC 2009-14640

Jeremy sets out to discover all of the different people that make him who he is, including brother, son, writer, and runner. "Grades two to four." (Bull Cent Child Books)

"The innovative art and design represent different identities with colorful silhouettes placed against photos of people, places, and icons. . . . This very contemporary work is encouraging, energetic, and inspired." Booklist

★ **Patrol**; an American soldier in Vietnam. collages by Ann Grifalconi. HarperCollins Pubs. 2002 un il hardcover o.p. lib bdg $16.89; pa $6.99
Grades: 3 4 5 6   E
1. Vietnam War, 1961-1975 -- Fiction 2. African American soldiers -- Fiction
ISBN 0-06-028363-7; 0-06-028364-5 lib bdg; 0-06-073159-1 pa

LC 00-35009

A frightened American soldier faces combat in the lush forests of Vietnam and sees a young enemy soldier who is as frightened as he is

The story is told "in free verse that is at once ethereal and white-knuckle tense. . . . Grifalconi's intricate paper and photo collages juxtapose snips of explosion smoke, snapshot images of fleeing villagers, and paper constructions of burning huts against a landscape that approaches fantasy in its lush beauty." Bull Cent Child Books

Na, Il Sung
A **book** of sleep. Alfred A. Knopf 2009 un il $15.99; lib bdg $18.99; bd bk $6.99
Grades: PreK K 1   E
1. Owls -- Fiction 2. Sleep -- Fiction 3. Animals -- Fiction
ISBN 978-0-375-86223-6; 0-375-86223-4; 978-0-375-96223-3 lib bdg; 0-375-96223-9 lib bdg; 978-0-375-86618-0 bd bk; 0-375-86618-3 bhd bk

LC 2008-47865

First published 2007 in the United Kingdom with title: Zzzz: a book of sleep

While other animals sleep at night, some quietly and others noisily, some alone and others huddled together, a wide-eyed owl watches.

"Na's textural images recall the lightheartedness and limpid charm of Paul Klee. . . . It's the rare picture book that,

upon arrival, feels as though it has been around for years already; Na's belongs to this group." Publ Wkly

★ **Hide** & seek; by Il Sung Na. Alfred A. Knopf 2012 32 p.
Grades: PreK K   E
1. Games -- Fiction 2. Rain forests -- Fiction 3. Picture books for children 4. Rain forest animals -- Fiction 5. Animals -- Fiction 6. Elephants -- Fiction 7. Chameleons -- Fiction 8. Hide-and-seek -- Fiction
ISBN 0375870784; 9780307974600; 9780375870781; 9780375970788

LC 2011021740

This picture book describes the action when "a group of animals plays a rainforest game of hide-and-seek," as the elephant counts and the flamingo, giraffe, rhino, and others find hiding places. Il Sung Na's artwork depicts a "tie-dyed rainforest awash in reds, yellows, greens and blues" and uses a "fusion of painterly textures, soft patterns and fine outlines . . . with dappled colors that shine like light through a leaf." (Kirkus)

The **thingamabob**. Alfred A. Knopf 2010 un il $15.99; lib bdg $18.99
Grades: PreK K   E
1. Elephants -- Fiction 2. Umbrellas and parasols -- Fiction
ISBN 978-0-375-86106-2; 0-375-86106-8; 978-0-375-96106-9 lib bdg; 0-375-96106-2 lib bdg

LC 2009003120

First published 2008 in the United Kingdom

An elephant finds a "thingamabob" and experiments until he discovers what to do with it.

"Sumptuous colors and swirling textures turn this slight, silly story into a visual feast, buoyed by a handful of great sight gags and the hands-down adorableness of the animals." Booklist

Nakagawa, Chihiro
★ **Who** made this cake? text and English translation by Chihiro Nakagawa; illustrations by Junji Koyose. Front Street 2008 un il $16.95
Grades: PreK K 1   E
1. Cake -- Fiction 2. Size -- Fiction 3. Baking -- Fiction 4. Construction equipment -- Fiction
ISBN 978-1-59078-595-9; 1-59078-595-9

LC 2008003070

While a boy and his parents go for an outing, little people invade the house and use their big construction equipment to bake a cake.

"The understated text is almost unnecessary, as the pictures easily tell the story and then some. . . . Truck fans will naturally pore over every busy, action-filled scene." Horn Book

Namioka, Lensey
The **hungriest** boy in the world; illustrated by Aki Sogabe. Holiday House 2001 un il $16.95
Grades: K 1 2 3   E
1. Japan -- Fiction 2. Hunger -- Fiction
ISBN 0-8234-1542-2

LC 00-25142

After swallowing the Hunger Monster, Jiro begins eating everything in sight, until his family finds a way to lure the monster out of Jiro's stomach

"The story is told economically but with wit and humor. Sogabe's illustrations, created using cut paper over rice paper that has been colored by airbrush or watercolor, complement the text with their elegant simplicity." SLJ

Napoli, Donna Jo

★ **Albert**; illustrated by Jim LaMarche. Silver Whistle Bks. 2001 un il $16; pa $7

Grades: K 1 2 3   E

1. Birds -- Fiction

ISBN 0-15-201572-8; 0-15-205249-6 pa

LC 97-7089

One day when Albert is at his window, two cardinals come to build a nest in his hand, an event that changes his life

"Napoli has written a pleasing modern fairy tale, transformed into a picture book by LaMarche's appealing, shaded pencil drawings." Booklist

★ The **crossing**; [illustrated by Jim Madsen] Atheneum Books for Young Readers 2011 un il $16.99

Grades: K 1 2   E

1. Trappers 2. Fur traders 3. Interpreters 4. Guides (Persons) 5. Native Americans -- Fiction 6. Shoshoni Indians -- Fiction 7. Overland journeys to the Pacific -- Fiction 8. Lewis and Clark Expedition (1804-1806) -- Fiction

ISBN 978-1-4169-9474-9; 1-4169-9474-2

LC 2010-08368

In 1805, Sacagawea, a woman of the Shoshoni tribe, helps Meriwether Lewis and William Clark find a passage to the West Coast, in this story told through the eyes of the baby boy on Sacagawea's back.

"Short, poetic descriptions of the landscape and journey . . . close with onomatopoetic phrases that refer to the many animals they meet during the journey. . . . Madsen's . . . full-bleed full and half-spread digital artwork is rendered in warm, earthy hues, shot through with tiny, crackling lines that give the images an aura of old oil paintings. . . . A refreshing new angle on a familiar story of American history." Publ Wkly

The **Earth** shook; a Persian tale. illustrations by Gabi Swiatkowska. Hyperion Books for Children 2009 un il $15.99

Grades: K 1 2 3   E

1. Iran -- Fiction 2. Animals -- Fiction 3. Earthquakes -- Fiction

ISBN 978-1-4231-0448-3; 1-4231-0448-X

"In this Persian-inspired tale (based on a 2003 earthquake in Bam, Iran), Parisa desperately seeks the company of another human being when her village is destroyed. She knocks on door after door, but hostile animals now occupy any still-standing homes. . . . Swiatkowska's extraordinary artwork—textured oil paintings, decorative designs, splendid palette and artfully spare compositions—adds power and beauty to the poetic text that echoes Rumi. A gorgeous, discussion-provoking read-aloud." Kirkus

The **Wishing** Club; a story about fractions. Henry Holt 2007 un il $16.95

Grades: 1 2 3   E

1. Wishes -- Fiction 2. Siblings -- Fiction 3. Fractions -- Fiction

ISBN 978-0-8050-7665-3; 0-8050-7665-4

LC 2006030767

When four siblings wish on a star, each gets only a fraction of what he or she wanted, but when they combine their wishes, they just might get a whole new pet.

"Napoli's story moves smoothly between the magic of wishes granted and the reality of working with fractions. . . . Currey's watercolor-and-ink illustrations evoke summer nights when barefoot youngsters lean on porch railings and look at the stars." SLJ

Nargi, Lela

★ The **Honeybee** Man; illustrated by Kyrsten Brooker. Schwartz & Wade Books 2011 un il $17.99; lib bdg $20.99

Grades: PreK K 1 2   E

1. Bees -- Fiction 2. Beekeeping -- Fiction 3. Brooklyn (New York, N.Y.) -- Fiction

ISBN 978-0-375-84980-0; 0-375-84980-7; 978-0-375-95695-9 lib bdg; 0-375-95695-6 lib bdg

LC 2009044216

Fred, a beekeeper whose hives are on the roof of his Brooklyn, New York, apartment building, tends his bees and distributes their honey to his neighbors. Includes facts about bees and beekeepers.

"Copious details are carefully woven into descriptions of Fred's day-today activities. . . . In sunny, oil-and-collage compositions, Brooker . . . captures the bustle of sidewalks and storefronts, as well as the serenity of Fred's rooftop and a green expanse of park. She also does a fine job demonstrating the steps of collecting honey. . . . Kids should find this easygoing blend of fiction and fact fascinating." Publ Wkly

Nascimbeni, Barbara

Animals and their families; Barbara Nascimbeni. Owlkids Books, Inc. 2012 72 p. ill. (hardcover) $17.95

Grades: K 1 2   E

1. Animal behavior 2. Animals 3. Animal babies

ISBN 1926973321; 9781926973326

LC 2011935958

Parents' Choice Awards - Picture Books: 2012

Author Barbara Nascimbeni's book helps children "explore the animal kingdom . . . . A new creature is introduced in silhouette, while the facing page shows that same creature in its natural habitat, playing with, caring for, or teaching its young. All members of the animal family--male and female, adult and baby--are illustrated in warm colors and identified by the proper term. Small bits of text share the sound each animals makes, where it lives, and what it eats with young readers." (Publisher's note)

Nazoa, Aquiles

A **small** Nativity; by Aquiles Nazoa; illustrated by Ana Palmero Cáceres; translated by Hugh Hazelton. Groundwood Books 2007 44p il $9.95

Grades: 1 2 3   E

ISBN 0-88899-839-2

"Venezuelan poet Nazoa's unadorned retelling of the Nativity story offers a homely approach to the familiar tale. . . . Palmero Cáceres illustrates this humble text with devotional pictures inspired by medieval illuminated manuscripts. Her richly colored art successfully combines traditional symbols of Christianity with images of Latin American flora and fauna." Horn Book

Nelson, Kadir

★ **Baby** Bear; words and paintings by Kadir Nelson. Balzer + Bray 2014 40 p. (hardcover bdg.) $17.99
Grades: PreK K 1   E
1. Home -- Fiction 2. Bears -- Fiction 3. Lost children -- Fiction 4. Forest animals -- Fiction
ISBN 0062241729; 9780062241726
LC 2013003083

This children's book, by Kadir Nelson, is "about a lost little bear searching for home." It functions "as the tale of a bear who finds his way home with the help of his animal friends; as a reassuring way to show children how to comfort themselves and find their way in everyday life; . . . as a method of teaching readers that by listening to your heart and trusting yourself, you will always find a true home within yourself." (Publisher's note)

Nelson, Marilyn

★ **Snook** alone; illustrated by Timothy Basil Ering. Candlewick Press 2010 48p il $16.99
Grades: K 1 2 3   E
1. Dogs -- Fiction 2. Monks -- Fiction 3. Islands -- Fiction
ISBN 978-0-7636-2667-9; 0-7636-2667-8
LC 2009-49040

"Snook is a rat terrier who lives with a monk on an island hermitage. . . . He gleefully munches rats while his companion works and prays. This simple, wonderful life is interrupted when a storm strands Snook on a tiny nearby atoll. Nelson writes in delicate stanzas of effortless poetry. . . . Ering's acrylic-and-ink artwork fades from the bright palette of the monk's abode to a nearly two-tone earthiness and creates a style both realistic and emotional. . . . The final reuniting is sudden yet as genuine as everything else about the book." Booklist

Nelson, Vaunda Micheaux

★ **Who** will I be, Lord? illustrated by Sean Qualls. Random House 2009 un il $16.95; lib bdg $19.99
Grades: PreK K 1 2   E
1. Family life -- Fiction 2. Occupations -- Fiction 3. African Americans -- Fiction
ISBN 978-0-375-84342-6; 0-375-84342-6; 978-0-375-94342-3 lib bdg; 0-375-94342-0 lib bdg
LC 2008035186

"An African-American girl looking to the future has a broad range of relatives to emulate—a banjo-playing mailman, a housewife who broke the color barrier, a pool shark, and a burger-flipping aspiring jazzman. Nelson's rhythmic and colloquial first-person narrative introduces the characters not only in terms of the jobs they hold, but also the kind of people they are. . . . Qualls's mixed-media illustrations combine muted and bright elements and feature full-spread renditions of each relative at home or work, followed by a page showing surreal floating heads of the girl and the featured role model as she repeats the title's query. Nelson shows respect for all the ways people live and work." SLJ

Nelson-Schmidt, Michelle

Cats, cats! Kane Miller 2011 un il pa $5.99

Grades: PreK K 1   E
1. Cats -- Fiction
ISBN 978-1-61067-042-5; 1-61067-042-6

"After initially establishing that cats . . . are everywhere, [this] title presents nine different types. . . . Timid, nosy, stubborn, sad-these are animals as defined by a set of descriptors that children might recognize in themselves. . . . Text set against plenty of white space, with a few sophisticated words to challenge youngsters, make [this a] good [choice] for emerging readers. The bright, crisp illustrations are cheerful and attractive. . . . [This book is] also useful as [an introduction] to adjectives." SLJ

Dogs, Dogs! Kane Miller 2011 un il pa $5.99
Grades: PreK K 1   E
1. Dogs -- Fiction
ISBN 978-1-61067-041-8; 1-61067-041-8

"After initially establishing that . . . . dogs are everywhere, [this] title presents nine different types. . . . Timid, nosy, stubborn, sad-these are animals as defined by a set of descriptors that children might recognize in themselves. . . . . Text set against plenty of white space, with a few sophisticated words to challenge youngsters, make [this a] good [choice] for emerging readers. The bright, crisp illustrations are cheerful and attractive. . . . [This book is] also useful as [an introduction] to adjectives." SLJ

Nesbitt, Kenn

More bears! illustrated by Troy Cummings. Sourcebooks/Jabberwocky 2010 un il $12.99
Grades: PreK K 1   E
1. Bears -- Fiction 2. Authors -- Fiction
ISBN 978-1-4022-3835-2; 1-4022-3835-5

When an author starts writing, children yell that they want more bears in the story.

"Cummings's smooth, digitally rendered artwork does the job admirably. There is strong color on every page, and the bears are infused with zaniness and fun. The participatory refrain of 'More Bears' will bring this selection to life at storytimes." SLJ

Nesquens, Daniel

My tattooed dad; [by] Daniel Nesquens; & [illustrated by] Magicomora; translated by Elisa Amado. Groundwood Books 2011 un il $18.95
Grades: 3 4 5   E
1. Fathers -- Fiction 2. Tattooing -- Fiction
ISBN 978-1-55498-109-0; 1-55498-109-3

"Loved without judgment despite his frequent absences, this larger-than-life figure dotes on his family while at home, cooking, gardening, and filling the space with his incredible stories. Like The Illustrated Man, his manifold tattoos provide a springboard for the narrative. . . . Magicomora's cameos and full spreads, a combination of folk art and caricatures, are drawn with pencil and colored digitally on backgrounds simulating antique wood, replete with stains and cracks. Not for the faint of heart, Nesquens's highly original anecdotes, narrated jointly by father and son in an aura of mystery, will be appreciated by fans of magical realism." SLJ

Ness, Evaline

★ **Sam,** Bangs & Moonshine; written and illustrated by Evaline Ness. Holt & Co. 1966 un il $17.95; pa $6.95

Grades: PreK K 1 2   E
  1. Imagination -- Fiction
ISBN 0-8050-0314-2; 0-8050-0315-0 pa
Awarded the Caldecott Medal, 1967
"In this unusually creative story the fantasy in which many, many children indulge is presented in a realistic and sympathetic context. The illustrations in ink and pale color wash (mustard, grayish-aqua) have a touching realism, too. This is an outstanding book." SLJ

Neubecker, Robert
  What little boys are made of; by Robert Neubecker. Balzer + Bray 2012 32 p.
Grades: PreK K 1 2   E
  1. Boys -- Fiction 2. Play -- Fiction 3. Stories in rhyme 4. Imagination -- Fiction 5. Picture books for children
ISBN 9780062023551

LC 2011016612

In this children's picture book, the "half-pint hero imagines his way through most boys' obsessions. Astronaut, sports star, knight, dinosaur-tamer--they're all there, presented in action-packed, energetic illustrations. . . . Each verse begins with the boy and his toys in a plain and simple environment. But in resolving the verse ('That's what little boys are made of') . . . visually complex, full spreads are offered, giving readers insight into the boy's rollicking fantasies. . . . The illustrator also pays homage to a certain visual aesthetic for each of the youth's adventures." (Kirkus) "By the end, the text speculates that a boy's makeup consists of sugar and spice or puppy-dogs' tails but decides ultimately on snuggles and love." (School Libr J)

★ **Wow!** America! Hyperion Books for Children 2006 un il $16.99
Grades: PreK K 1 2   E
  1. United States -- Description and travel
ISBN 0-7868-3816-7

LC 2005-44735

"This companion to Wow! City! follows country girl Izzy on another journey, this time with her little sister and dog. Each spread reveals a location in the U.S. . . . Each spread also contains brief informational text. The drawings are as energetic as the exclamation-enhanced text." Horn Book Guide

★ **Wow!** city! Hyperion 2004 un il $16.99
Grades: PreK K 1 2   E
  1. City and town life -- Fiction
ISBN 0-7868-0951-5

Two-year-old toddler Izzy goes on a trip with her father and experiences in what she sees in the hustling-and-bustling, gigantic, crowded, loud, and colorful city.

"Drawn in India ink and vividly colored on a Macintosh computer using Adobe Photoshop, the illustrations are full of life, action, and detail." SLJ

Wow! Ocean! Disney/Hyperion Books 2011 un il
Grades: PreK K 1 2   E
  1. Ocean -- Fiction 2. Beaches -- Fiction 3. Marine animals
ISBN 1-4231-3113-4; 978-1-4231-3113-7

"When Izzy and her sister Jo travel from the mountains to the ocean they find a wealth of things to be excited about." (Publisher's note) "Preschool." (Horn Book)

"Izzy visits a beach with her family. Izzy's exclamations appear in colorful, chalky font in the borders ('Wow! Beach!'), as she and her sister peer at a treasure trove of shells and tide pool species; plunge underwater to swim and scuba dive among rays, whales, and sharks (all labeled for readers); and have a tea party on the ocean floor next to a sunken pirate ship. Foldout spreads, an abundance of whimsical details, and bold artwork that lives up to Izzy's repeated 'wows' make this a rewarding mix of fact and fancy." Publ Wkly

★ **Wow!** school! Hyperion Books for Children 2007 un il $16.99
Grades: PreK K 1   E
  1. School stories
ISBN 0-7868-3896-5; 978-0-7868-3896-7

LC 2006-49569

Izzy finds many things to be excited about on the first day of school.

"The bold, crayonlike lines of Neubecker's India-ink drawings contrast pleasingly with the computer-generated color. This is a wonderful book for sharing with groups of emergent readers, who will enjoy chiming along, and it is well suited to the attention spans of children just beginning preschool or kindergarten." SLJ

Nevius, Carol
  Building with Dad; by Carol Nevius; illustrated by Bill Thomson. Marshall Cavendish 2006 un il $16.99
Grades: PreK K 1 2   E
  1. Stories in rhyme 2. Building -- Fiction 3. Construction equipment -- Fiction 4. Father-son relationship -- Fiction
ISBN 978-0-7614-5312-3; 0-7614-5312-1

LC 2005027311

A father and his young child watch the construction of the new school, from the bulldozing of earth and mixing of the concrete for the foundation to the hanging of the new sign.

This is an "energetic picture book with visual punch. . . . The spreads spill down the page vertically, rather than horizontally, for maximum impact. . . . Thomson uses full color, and his photo-realistic paintings bring viewers close up to, sometimes even under, giant machines." Booklist

★ **Karate** hour; illustrated by Bill Thomson. Marshall Cavendish 2004 un il $14.95
Grades: PreK K 1 2   E
  1. Stories in rhyme 2. Karate -- Fiction
ISBN 0-7614-5169-2

LC 2003-27122

Rhyming text portrays the exuberance of an hour of karate class. Includes nonfiction information at end

Nevius "deftly captures the excitement and energy of the experience as well as the discipline and commitment required to rise in rank. Thomson's realistic mixed-media artwork is a standout, using light, shadow, and perspective in a variety of interesting ways." SLJ

Soccer hour; illustrated by Bill Thomson. Marshall Cavendish 2010 un il $16.99

Grades: PreK K 1 2   **E**
1. Stories in rhyme 2. Soccer -- Fiction
ISBN 978-0-7614-5689-6; 0-7614-5689-9
LC 2009014112

Pictures and rhyming text describe the drills and scrimmages of a team at soccer practice.

"This book offers a winning combination of rhyming couplets and striking artwork to describe an hour of practice among boys and girls. While the text reads in bursts of active statements . . . the extraordinary illustrations are the essence of the book. Thomson uses acrylics and colored pencils to create realistic paintings that almost resemble sepia photographs." SLJ

Newberry, Clare Turlay
April's kittens. HarperCollins Pubs. 1993 32p il
$16.99
Grades: PreK K 1 2   **E**
1. Cats -- Fiction
ISBN 0-06-024400-3

A reissue of the title first published 1940
A Caldecott Medal honor book, 1941

"Though old-fashioned, the story of a small girl's yearning to keep both a mother cat and one of her kittens still speaks to pet owners young and old. Newberry's simple, charcoal drawings of the felines are as elegant and endearing as ever." Horn Book

Marshmallow; story and pictures by Clare Turlay Newberry. rev ed.; HarperCollinsPublishers 2008 un il $16.99; lib bdg $17.89; pa $6.99
Grades: K 1 2   **E**
1. Cats -- Fiction 2. Rabbits -- Fiction
ISBN 978-0-06-072486-3; 0-06-072486-2; 978-0-06-072487-0 lib bdg; 0-06-072487-0 lib bdg; 978-0-06-072488-7 pa; 0-06-072488-9 pa
LC 2007-30888

First published 1942
A Caldecott Medal honor book, 1943

A cat who is used to being the center of attention learns to share his home with a rabbit

Newbery, Linda
★ Posy! illustrated by Catherine Rayner. Atheneum Books for Young Readers 2009 un il $16.99
Grades: PreK K   **E**
1. Stories in rhyme 2. Cats -- Fiction
ISBN 978-1-4169-7112-2; 1-4169-7112-2
LC 2008-03807

Posy the kitten has lots of adventures catching spiders, swiping crayons, tangling yarn, and cuddling

"Rendered in watercolor pencil crayons, acrylic, and India inks, [Posy] sometimes dominates the broad cream-colored spreads or divides a page into several vignettes with her actions. . . . While grownups, particularly cat lovers, will be charmed by the stylized art, children will notice in the kitten's daily activities much of what interests them." SLJ

Newgarden, Mark
★ Bow-Wow bugs a bug; [by] Mark Newgarden and Megan Montague Cash. Harcourt 2007 un il $12.95
Grades: K 1 2 3   **E**
1. Stories without words 2. Dogs -- Fiction 3. Insects

-- Fiction
ISBN 978-0-15-205813-5
LC 2006-11026

A wordless picture book about a persistent terrier who follows a bug through his neighborhood.

"The clever circular plot is funny, quirky, and even suspenseful. . . . The simple, bold, expressive illustrations, outlined with heavy black line, challenge viewers to follow the visual story line and sequences of events." SLJ

Other titles about Bow-Wow are:
Bow-Wow naps by number (2007)
Bow-Wow orders lunch (2007)
Bow-Wow attracts opposites (2008)
Bow-Wow hears things (2008)
Bow-Wow 12 months running (2009)
Bow-Wow's colorful life (2009)

Newman, Jeff
The boys; written by Jeff Newman; illustrated by Jeff Newman. Simon & Schuster Books for Young Readers 2009 un il $15.99
Grades: 1 2 3   **E**
1. Stories without words 2. Old age -- Fiction 3. Shyness -- Fiction 4. Baseball -- Fiction
ISBN 1-4169-5012-5; 978-1-4169-5012-7
LC 2007-47985

A shy boy, seeking the courage to play baseball with the other children in a park, is coaxed out of his shell by some "old-timers" sitting nearby. "Ages six to nine." (Bull Cent Child Books)

"Employing sly visual humor, Newman . . . presents the narrative in sketchy, retro-flavored gouache brushstrokes on a white background. This is a quirky book, but sensitive readers will appreciate the child's shyness and the men's efforts to help him remember what it means to be a kid." Publ Wkly

★ Hand book. Simon & Schuster Books for Young Readers 2011 il $15.99
Grades: PreK K 1 2   **E**
1. Stories in rhyme 2. Hand -- Fiction 3. Growth -- Fiction
ISBN 978-1-4169-5013-4; 1-4169-5013-3
LC 2010007017

Follows a person's journey through life, focusing on the hands and what they do, from babyhood to adulthood when a new pair of hands comes into existence.

"Telegraphic verse and line drawings celebrate the many things hands can do. . . . Newman challenges readers to consider their hands as intricate and capable tools, instruments of emotion, creation, and tenderness; children will almost certainly see them with new respect." Publ Wkly

Newman, Leslea
The best cat in the world; written by Lesléa Newman; illustrated by Ronald Himler. Eerdmans Books for Young Readers 2004 un il $16; pa $8
Grades: K 1 2 3   **E**
1. Cats -- Fiction 2. Death -- Fiction
ISBN 0-8028-5252-1; 0-8028-5294-7 pa
LC 2003-13028

A young boy deals with the loss of his beloved cat Charlie, eventually accepting the arrival of another, very different cat.

"Himler's warm pencil-and-watercolor illustrations generously fill the pages. They portray the casually clad characters with tenderness and contrast the shape of the old and sick animal with that of the young and playful one. . . . For comfort and catharsis, Newman's fine story is the cat's pajamas." SLJ

Daddy, papa, and me; illustrated by Carol Thompson. Tricycle Press 2009 un il bd bk $7.99

Grades: PreK   E

1. Board books for children 2. Homosexuality -- Fiction 3. Father-child relationship -- Fiction

ISBN 978-1-58246-262-2 bd bk; 1-58246-262-3 bd bk

ALA GLBTRT Stonewall Book Award Honor Book (2010)

"A smiling tot describes his role within a nurturing two-dad family. . . . Thompson provides warm, mixed-media illustrations of the happy trio against clean white backgrounds as they play and keep house together. . . . It gives children with single-sex parents validation of their family structures in a healthy, positive way." Kirkus

Donovan's big day. Tricycle Press 2011 un il $15.99; lib bdg $18.99

Grades: PreK K   E

1. Stories in rhyme 2. Lesbians -- Fiction 3. Weddings -- Fiction 4. Mother-son relationship -- Fiction

ISBN 978-1-58246-332-2; 1-58246-332-8; 978-1-58246-392-6 lib bdg; 1-58246-392-1 lib bdg

LC 2009048488

"Plain and poetic, the swiftly flowing free verse perfectly captures the day's excitement, as does Dutton's digitally touched gouache artwork. . . . A welcome addition to the still short shelf of picture books featuring same-sex parents." Booklist

A **fire** engine for Ruthie; illustrated by Cyd Moore. Clarion Books 2004 32p il $16

Grades: PreK K 1 2   E

1. Play -- Fiction 2. Sex role -- Fiction 3. Grandmothers -- Fiction

ISBN 0-618-15989-4

LC 2003-22791

Ruthie's Nana suggests playing tea party and fashion show during their visit, but Ruthie is much more interested in the vehicles that a neighbor boy is playing with as they pass his house each day.

"This book hits the mark on three solid counts—a real story, good pacing, and deliciously full artwork that has its own momentum." Booklist

Miss Tutu's star; illustrated by Carey Armstrong-Ellis. Abrams 2010 un il $16.95

Grades: PreK K 1 2   E

1. Ballet -- Fiction

ISBN 978-0-8109-8396-0; 0-8109-8396-6

Young Selena, who would rather twirl than walk, begins to study ballet and, after years of practice and a great deal of encouragement from Miss Tutu, finally makes her stage debut.

"Armstrong-Ellis's gouache and colored-pencil illustrations add comic touches. . . . The protagonist is a likable character with lots of heart. Many children will recognize themselves in this agreeable offering." SLJ

★ **Mommy,** mama, and me; illustrated by Carol Thompson. Tricycle Press 2009 un il (My family tree) bd bk $7.99

Grades: PreK   E

1. Board books for children 2. Lesbians -- Fiction 3. Mother-child relationship -- Fiction

ISBN 978-1-58246-263-9 bd bk; 1-58246-263-1 bd bk

ALA GLBTRT Stonewall Book Award Honor Book (2010)

"A curly-haired toddler . . . celebrates 'mommy' and 'mama,' and the activities and tender moments they share. . . . The bright colors . . . and pleasing verse offer a simple lesson about love that same-sex parents should embrace." Publ Wkly

Newman, Patricia

Nugget on the flight deck; illustrated by Aaron Zenz. Walker & Co. 2009 un il $16.99; lib bdg $17.89

Grades: 1 2 3   E

1. Air pilots -- Fiction 2. Aircraft carriers -- Fiction

ISBN 978-0-8027-9735-3; 0-8027-9735-0; 978-0-8027-9736-0 lib bdg; 0-8027-9736-9 lib bdg

LC 2008044673

Aboard an aircraft carrier, a lieutenant introduces a new aviator to the 'lingo' and layout before taking him on a practice dogfight.

"Military jargon appears in boldface in the text and is defined in a separate pictorial area on each spread. Colored-pencil illustrations show many essential components of the carrier and the planes that take off and land on its deck. . . . Anyone interested in planes will appreciate the high level of information provided in an attractive, accessible format." SLJ

Includes bibliographical references

Newman, Robin

The **case** of the missing carrot cake; by Robin Newman; illustrated by Deborah Zemke. Creston Books 2015 40 p. (hardback) $15.95

Grades: K 1 2 3 4   E

1. Farm life -- Fiction 2. Mystery fiction -- Fiction

ISBN 1939547172; 9781939547170

LC 2015006474

In this children's story, by Robin Newman, illustrated by Deborah Zemke, part of the "Wilcox and Griswold mystery" series, "when Miss Rabbit leaves her carrot cake (with cream-cheese icing) out to cool and returns later to find only a mess of crumbs, she calls Detective Wilcox and Capt. Griswold. Over 100 animals on Ed's farm means there's a lot of suspects." (Kirkus Reviews)

Nichols, Lori

Maple; written and illustrated by Lori Nichols. Nancy Paulsen Books 2014 32 p.

Grades: PreK K 1   E

1. Maple -- Fiction 2. Trees -- Fiction 3. Babies -- Fiction 4. Sisters -- Fiction 5. Friendship -- Fiction

ISBN 9780399160851; 039916085X

LC 2013013715

In this book, by Lori Nichols, "when Maple is tiny, her parents plant a maple tree in her honor. She and her tree grow up together, and even though a tree doesn't always make an ideal playmate, it doesn't mind when Maple is in the mood to be loud. Then Maple becomes a big sister, and finds that babies have their loud days, too. Fortunately, Maple and her beloved tree know just what the baby needs." (Publisher's note)

Maple and Willow together; Lori Nichols. Nancy Paulsen Books, an imprint of Penguin Group (USA) 2014 32 p. color illustrations $16.99
Grades: PreK K 1   E
1. Sisters -- Fiction 2. Friendship -- Fiction 3. Nature -- Fiction
ISBN 0399162836; 9780399162831
           LC 2013043045
Sequel to: Maple (2014)
This children's book by Lori Nichols examines "the dynamics of siblings and their ability to figure things out on their own and find a way to meet halfway. Maple and Willow . . . love playing outside. But it's not always sunshine and rainbows, because sometimes big sisters can be bossy--and sometimes little sisters can be frustrating--and even the best of friends need a break from each other . . . at least until they can no longer bear to be apart." (Publisher's note)
"This paean to sisterhood reintroduces the title character in Maple (2014), whose parents planted a maple tree before she was born. They did the same for Willow, who is a most satisfactory younger sister...Nichols is clever enough to build the sisters' subtle differences, so their breakup comes from somewhere. Children will feel all that the girls do: love, anger, and the happiness that comes with making up." Booklist

Niemann, Christoph
     Pet dragon; a story about adventure, friendship, and Chinese characters. by Christoph Niemann. Greenwillow Books 2008 un il $16.99; lib bdg $17.89
Grades: K 1 2 3   E
1. Chinese language 2. China -- Fiction 3. Dragons -- Fiction 4. Witches -- Fiction
ISBN 978-0-06-157776-5; 0-06-157776-6; 978-0-06-157777-2 lib bdg; 0-06-157777-4 lib bdg
When Lin's beloved pet dragon disappears, she searches for him far and wide until a witch helps her to reach the dragon's new home. Introduces a different Chinese character on each step of Lin's adventure.
"The book is clever. Its purpose is to introduce the Chinese language, and it succeeds admirably. Each page contains one or more Chinese characters, which appear not only at the bottom with the English translation, but also superimposed on the drawings. . . . The stylized illustrations are jaunty and appealing, and the use of red, a color representing good fortune in China, visually unifies the tale from beginning to end. Playful and humorous." SLJ

     The **police** cloud. Schwartz & Wade Books 2007 un il $15.99; lib bdg $17.99
Grades: PreK K 1   E
1. Clouds -- Fiction 2. Police -- Fiction
ISBN 0-375-83963-1; 978-0-375-83963-4; 0-375-93963-6 lib bdg; 978-0-375-93963-1 lib bdg
           LC 2006-06415

A small cloud that has always dreamed of becoming a police officer discovers that he might not be suited to the job.
"The computer-enhanced illustrations have a very simple, bold graphic design and feature basic colors. . . . The illustrations do such a good job of telling the story, the concise text is almost unnecessary." Booklist

★ **Subway**. Greenwillow Books 2010 un il $16.99; lib bdg $17.89
Grades: PreK K 1 2   E
1. Stories in rhyme 2. Subways -- Fiction 3. New York (N.Y.) -- Fiction
ISBN 978-0-06-157779-6; 0-06-157779-0; 978-0-06-157780-2 lib bdg; 0-06-157780-4 lib bdg
           LC 2009-18756
"This colorful, vivacious, child-centered title began with a post on Niemann's blog, Abstract City, in which he describes a day of riding the subway with his two sons just for fun. The artist uses thick gouache paint to render his characters as standard pictograms, akin to those on city signs, with curved edges for hands and feet, and the technique creates a chalky texture that looks like correction fluid. . . . A sure hit with most youngsters, especially those who are transfixed by trains." SLJ

That's how! Greenwillow Books 2011 un il $16.99
Grades: PreK K 1   E
1. Vehicles -- Fiction 2. Imagination -- Fiction
ISBN 978-0-06-201963-9; 0-06-201963-5
           LC 2010017216
"A boy entertains his friend with cleverly imagined ideas about how a number of vehicles work. When she asks about a truck, he responds, 'Hmmm. . . let me think.' A flip of the page shows a yellow lion pedaling a bicyclelike chain and gears inside a black truck. . . . The freighter is run by an octopus winding a whale's tale, the steamroller by a bird tickling two bears, and so forth. . . . The mixed-media digital illustrations are saturated full-bleed spreads. . . . Boy, girl, animals, and vehicles are all done in bold colors and have a cartoonish, childlike sensibility. The large trim size, popular topic, and brightly colored artwork will work well in storytimes. . . . A surefire hit." SLJ

Nikola-Lisa, W.
     Magic in the margins; a medieval tale of bookmaking. by W. Nikola-Lisa; illustrated by Bonnie Christensen. Houghton Mifflin 2007 un il $17
Grades: 1 2 3 4   E
1. Artists -- Fiction 2. Orphans -- Fiction 3. Apprentices -- Fiction 4. Middle Ages -- Fiction 5. Illumination of books and manuscripts -- Fiction
ISBN 978-0-618-49642-6; 0-618-49642-4
           LC 2006017060
At a medieval monastery, orphaned Simon, who is apprenticing in illumination, dreams of the day he can create his own pictures, but finds he must first complete a strange and unusual assignment that Father Anselm has given him.
"Many kids . . . will be drawn in by the appealing story of a child's empowerment and the glimpse of the medieval world. Christensen extends the story with strong, clear scenes, bordered by botanical patterns and executed in ink and egg-tempura pigments." Booklist

Setting the turkeys free; written by W. Nikola-Lisa; illustrated by Ken Wilson-Max. Jump at the Sun/Hyperion Books for Children 2004 un il $15.99
Grades: PreK K 1   E
1. Foxes -- Fiction 2. Artists -- Fiction 3. Turkeys -- Fiction
ISBN 0-7868-1952-9
LC 2003-50928
When a sly, hungry fox threatens a flock of turkeys, the young artist who drew the birds must find a way to save them.
"Right at a preschooler's level, the artwork . . . has humor as well as momentum. . . . This clever mixing of art and a spot-on text provides a fun story as well as a surefire craft idea that kids will want to try." Booklist

Nobisso, Josephine
Francis woke up early; illuminations, Maureen Hyde. Gingerbread House 2011 un il $17.95; pa $9.95
Grades: K 1 2 3   E
1. Saints 2. Italy -- Fiction 3. Saints -- Fiction 4. Wolves -- Fiction 5. Writers on religion 6. Farm life -- Fiction
ISBN 978-0-940112-20-9; 0-940112-20-5; 978-0-940112-22-3 pa; 0-940112-20-5 pa
LC 2011015539
Imagines a moment in the boyhood of Saint Francis of Assisi, in which he befriends a wild she-wolf by sharing with her his breakfast, gathered on his family's farm.
"A beautiful marriage of author, illustrator, and subject. . . . Hyde's work . . . perfectly captures early morning light in 13th-century Assisi. The bordered paintings are filled with tender detail. . . . This exquisite book will make peaceful family reading." Publ Wkly

Noble, Trinka Hakes
★ The **day** Jimmy's boa ate the wash; pictures by Steven Kellogg. Dial Bks. for Young Readers 1980 un il $16.99; pa $6.99
Grades: PreK K 1 2   E
1. School stories 2. Snakes -- Fiction 3. Farm life -- Fiction
ISBN 0-8037-1723-7; 0-8037-0094-6 pa
LC 80-15098
"The illustrations, which depict disgruntled chickens, expressive pigs, and smiling cats as well as other individualized animal and human characters, show the artist's flair for humorous detail." Horn Book
Other titles about Jimmy's boa are:
Jimmy's boa and the big splash birthday bash (1989)
Jimmy's boa and the bungee jump slam dunk (2003)
Jimmy's boa bounces back (1984)

The **last** brother; a Civil War tale. illustrated by Robert Papp. Sleeping Bear Press 2006 un il $17.95
Grades: 2 3 4 5   E
1. Brothers -- Fiction 2. Gettysburg (Pa.), Battle of, 1863 -- Fiction 3. United States -- History -- 1861-1865, Civil War -- Fiction
ISBN 1-58536-253-0
Eleven-year-old Gabe enlists in the Union Army in Pennsylvania along with his older brother Davy and, as bugler, does his best to protect Davy during the Battle of Gettysburg.

This "story resonates with courage and fear, love and loyalty. . . . The well-rendered paintings are hauntingly detailed and place readers right in the action." SLJ

Nolan, Dennis
Hunters of the great forest; Dennis Nolan. Roaring Brook Press 2014 40 p. color illustrations (hardcover) $17.99
Grades: PreK K 1 2   E
1. Hunting -- Fiction 2. Stories without words 3. Adventure stories
ISBN 1596438967; 9781596438965
LC 2013044241
In this children's book, by Dennis Nolan, "On a warm night, a band of hunters sets out on a journey. As they travel over hills, through thickets of trees, and around mountains, nothing will keep them from their ultimate goal. What that goal is may surprise you." (Publisher's note)
"In this wordless picture book, insect-sized explorers set off from their village to go on an adventure. Along the way, they must overcome several perils, such as a hungry blue jay and an angry chipmunk. Though teamwork and blind luck, they arrive at their destination, an unguarded bag of marshmallows, and take one back to their village for a feast. Nolan's illustrations are wonderfully detailed and textured, from the jagged roots and tree bark the group climbs to the wings of the dragonfly that soars overhead. His work with shadows is exceptionally impressive; as the characters run for their lives, the hunters' oblong shadows accentuate their various actions. However, very young readers may be frightened by the team's antics, as the backyard animals that chase the travelers come across as monsterlike. Overall, this is a good adventure story that's silly and original. Fans of David Wiesner's imaginative works may want to give it a try." SLJ

★ **Sea** of dreams. Roaring Brook Press 2011 il $16.99
Grades: PreK K 1   E
1. Stories without words 2. Beaches -- Fiction
ISBN 978-1-59643-470-7; 1-59643-470-8
LC 2010037815
A wordless picture book featuring a sandcastle that takes on a life of its own.
"Nolan's enchanting artwork creates a gorgeous, wordless nautical fantasy infused with the thrill of life-or-death adventure. . . . Readers will never look at the beach the same way." Publ Wkly

Nolen, Jerdine
★ **Big** Jabe; illustrations by Kadir Nelson. Lothrop, Lee & Shepard Bks. 2000 un il hardcover o.p. pa $6.99
Grades: K 1 2 3   E
1. Slavery -- Fiction 2. African Americans -- Fiction
ISBN 0-688-13662-1; 0-06-054061-3 pa
LC 99-38001
Momma Mary tells stories about a special young man who does wondrous things, especially for the slaves on the Plenty Plantation
"Nolen recounts her original tale with a light touch and lyrical voices that add depth and resonance to its imagery and serious overtones. The gouache and watercolor illustrations convey both the lush summer and the rigorous life of the slaves. This powerful story will be particularly effective shared aloud." Horn Book Guide

Christmas in the time of Billy Lee; illustrated by Barry Moser. Disney/Jump at the Sun Books 2010 un il $16.99
Grades: PreK K 1   **E**
   1. Wishes -- Fiction 2. Christmas -- Fiction 3. Imaginary playmates -- Fiction
   ISBN 978-0-7868-1871-6; 0-7868-1871-9
                       LC 91-38129

When Ellie makes three wishes and begins to believe in the magic of Christmas, all kinds of miracles occur, from broken tree lights twinkling again, to angel shapes appearing in snow, to the biggest of all: a baby brother arriving soon.

"The acknowledgment of money troubles and other concerns makes the magic feel all the sweeter, as Moser's bucolic winter landscapes and cozy portraits convey a hushed wonderment and warm family bonds." Publ Wkly

Harvey Potter's balloon farm; [illustrated by] Mark Buehner. Lothrop, Lee & Shepard Bks. 1994 un il $16.99; lib bdg $15.93; pa $5.99
Grades: PreK K 1 2   **E**
   1. Tall tales 2. Balloons -- Fiction 3. Farm life -- Fiction
   ISBN 0-688-07887-7; 0-688-07888-5 lib bdg; 0-688-15845-5 pa
                       LC 91-38129

"Harvey Potter's unusual crop is balloons—which grow just like corn on long, sturdy stalks. Harvey Potter himself is not at all unusual, and his friend, a young African-American girl, is determined to uncover the secret of his curious harvest. The story is lively, but of even greater attraction are the vivid, air-brushed illustrations of balloons with expressive faces in every size, color, and shape." Horn Book Guide

★ **Hewitt** Anderson's great big life; illustrated by Kadir Nelson. Simon & Schuster Books for Young Readers 2005 un il $16.95
Grades: PreK K 1 2   **E**
   1. Size -- Fiction 2. Giants -- Fiction
   ISBN 0-689-86866-9
                       LC 98-14039

When tiny Hewitt is born into a family of giants, everyone learns that sometimes small is best of all.

"Nelson's funny, larger-than-life oil paintings warmly depict this African-American family and give readers a real sense of gigantic proportions. . . . Told in colorful language that begs to be read aloud, this humorous, oversize book offers a gentle look at accepting others as they are." SLJ

Pitching in for Eubie; illustrated by E.B. Lewis. Amistad 2007 un il $16.99; lib bdg $17.89
Grades: PreK K 1 2   **E**
   1. Sisters -- Fiction 2. Family life -- Fiction 3. African Americans -- Fiction 4. Money-making projects for children -- Fiction
   ISBN 978-0-688-14917-8; 978-0-06-056960-0 lib bdg
                       LC 2007-06995

Lily tries to find a way to pitch in and help her family make enough money to send her older sister, Eubie, to college

"Imbued with warmth, Nolen's . . . story about a family working together toward a common goal will appeal to many audiences. . . . Each painting helps advance the action and delineate the characters." Publ Wkly

Raising dragons; illustrated by Elise Primavera. Silver Whistle Bks. 1998 un il $16; pa $7
Grades: PreK K 1 2   **E**
   1. Dragons -- Fiction 2. Farm life -- Fiction
   ISBN 0-15-201288-5; 0-15-216536-3 pa
                       LC 95-43307

A farmer's young daughter shares numerous adventures with the dragon that she raises from infancy

"Nolen's chimerical text meets its match in Primavera's imaginative and bold illustrations." Horn Book Guide

★ **Thunder** Rose; illustrated by Kadir Nelson. Harcourt 2003 un il $16; pa $7
Grades: K 1 2 3   **E**
   1. Tall tales 2. West (U.S.) -- Fiction 3. African Americans -- Fiction
   ISBN 0-15-216472-3; 0-15-206006-5 pa
                       LC 2002-12287

Unusual from the day she is born, Thunder Rose performs all sorts of amazing feats, including building fences, taming a stampeding herd of steers, capturing a gang of rustlers, and turning aside a tornado

"Nolen and Nelson offer up a wonderful tale of joy and love, as robust and vivid as the wide West. The oil, watercolor, and pencil artwork is outstanding." SLJ

Norac, Carl

My daddy is a giant; illustrated by Ingrid Godon. Clarion Books 2005 29p il $16
Grades: PreK K 1 2   **E**
   1. Father-son relationship -- Fiction
   ISBN 0-618-44399-1
                       LC 2004-12093

A little boy's father seems so large to him that he needs a ladder to cuddle him and birds nest in his father's hair

"The simple premise captures the little boy's idolization of his dad well. . . . With the man so large that he often has to bend his head or crouch down to fit onto the page, and the full-bleed spreads overflowing the book, these pictures will engage even the children in the last row of storytime." SLJ

My mommy is magic; by Carl Norac; illustrated by Ingrid Godon. Clarion Books 2007 29p il $16
Grades: PreK K   **E**
   1. Mothers -- Fiction
   ISBN 978-0-618-75766-4; 0-618-75766-X
                       LC 2006007149

First published 2006 in the United Kingdom with title: My mummy is magic

A child lists things a mommy does, such as chasing monsters away, that show she is magic, even if she does not have a wand or magic hat

"Godon's pastel-and-paint, full-bleed spreads in gentle hues exude warmth. They complement the text and the resulting mood is sweet without being cloying." SLJ

Swing Cafe; translated from the French by Jacob Homel; illustrated by Rebecca Dautremer. The Sacred Mountain 2010 un il $16.95
Grades: K 1 2 3   **E**
   1. Insects -- Fiction 2. Crickets -- Fiction 3. Jazz music -- Fiction 4. New York (N.Y.) -- Fiction
   ISBN 978-2-923163-62-8; 2-923163-62-1

"Norac's story stars a Brazilian jazz-singing cricket named Zaz who dreams of New York City. The death of her butterfly friend Miro releases her; she hops a ride in a flowered hat, befriends a blue fly, and arrives at last at the Swing Cafe. Zaz and the other characters are portrayed as stylish humans with just a trace of their insect nature. . . . Dautremer's visual imagination taps the subconscious brilliantly. . . . Norac's writing is equally arresting. . . . An enclosed CD supplies cherished jazz gems from Ellington, Calloway, Fitzgerald, and more, which accompany a lovely audio recording of the story. Intelligent, poetic, and provocative entertainment." Publ Wkly

Nordqvist, Sven

Tomtes' Christmas porridge; translated by Polly Lawson. Floris 2011 il $17.95

Grades: PreK K 1 2   E
   1. Sweden -- Fiction 2. Christmas -- Fiction
   ISBN 978-0-86315-824-7; 0-86315-824-2

"Nordqvist's amusing watercolor-and-ink illustrations are full of distinct personalities and tiny details in costumes and settings. . . . A charming and sprightly story with the flavor of a traditional tale." Kirkus

Norman, Kimberly

I know a wee piggy; by Kim Norman; pictures by Henry Cole. Dial Books for Young Readers 2014 32 p. col. ill. (hardcover) $16.99

Grades: PreK K 1   E
   1. Pigs -- Fiction 2. Animals -- Color -- Fiction 3. Color -- Fiction 4. Stories in rhyme 5. Agricultural exhibitions -- Fiction
   ISBN 0803737351; 9780803737358
                     LC 2011029977

This children's book is the story of a "little piggy [who] has escaped from his owner and is running riot through the county fair, getting covered in gunk, globs, and other stuff representing nine colors: brown from the muddy pig pen, red from the tomato canning display, yellow from the broken yolks in the chicken coop . . . and so forth. By the time the wee piggy proudly wins a blue ribbon," he's very dirty indeed. Author Kimberly E. Norman's text riffs on the folk song "I Know an Old Lady." (Publishers Weekly)

"The star's earnestness is irresistible, and both text and pictures are rich and energetic." (Booklist)

Ten on the sled; by Kim Norman; illustrated by Liza Woodruff. Sterling 2010 un il $14.95

Grades: PreK K 1   E
   1. Counting 2. Stories in rhyme 3. Animals -- Fiction 4. Sledding -- Fiction
   ISBN 978-1-4027-7076-0; 1-4027-7076-6
                     LC 2009-11501

Animals fall off a speeding sled one by one until only a lonely caribou is left, chasing a giant snowball that has engulfed the falling animals.

"What with animal identification, counting, vocabulary building and print awareness all scaffolded on a can't-lose rhyme, this one's a keeper." Kirkus

North, Sherry

Champ's story; dogs get cancer too! Sylvan Dell 2010 un il $16.95; pa $8.95

Grades: 1 2 3   E
   1. Dogs -- Fiction 2. Cancer -- Fiction
   ISBN 978-1-60718-077-7; 1-60718-077-4; 978-1-60718-088-3 pa; 1-60718-088-X pa

"While practicing for the upcoming agility show, Cody notices a lump on his dog's belly, which turns out to be cancer. The treatment is similar to what a human endures, and Cody is filled with worry for his pet. Champ is able to participate in the show, but it is Cody who has trouble when he trips and hurts his ankle. Now it's Champ's turn to take care of Cody, and she proves she is a real champion. Children will have empathy for both characters. . . . A sincere, caring story told with a straightforward, honest approach." SLJ

Noullet, Georgette

Bed hog; illustrated by David Slonim. Marshall Cavendish 2011 un il $12.99

Grades: PreK K   E
   1. Dogs -- Fiction 2. Sleep -- Fiction
   ISBN 978-0-7614-5823-4; 0-7614-5823-9
                     LC 2010008089

"Every night, Bailey, the family dog, travels from room to room trying to find a comfortable place to sleep. Although his owners call him a 'bed hog,' readers will see early on that the pup is not the one taking up all the space. . . . Gentle humor and spare wording with repetitive phrasing will allow pre-readers to retell the simple tale after hearing it once. The colorful cartoonlike illustrations in acrylic and charcoal will put a smile on the face of any family member who frequently finds a dog sleeping in the bed." SLJ

Novak, B. J.

The book with no pictures; B.J. Novak. Dial Books for Young Readers, an imprint of Penguin Group (USA) 2014 48 p. (hardcover) $17.99

Grades: PreK K 1 2 3   E
   1. Humorous fiction 2. Books and reading -- Fiction
   ISBN 0803741715; 9780803741713
                     LC 2014000725

This children's book, by B. J. Novak, has no pictures. "You might think a book with no pictures seems boring and serious. Except . . . here's how books work. Everything written on the page has to be said by the person reading it aloud. Even if the words say . . . BLORK. Or BLUURF. Even if the words are a preposterous song about eating ants for breakfast, or just a list of astonishingly goofy sounds like BLAGGITY BLAGGITY and GLIBBITY GLOBBITY." (Publisher's note)

"On crisp white pages, in a large black font, listeners and readers are clued in: 'Here is how books work: Everything the words say, the person reading the book has to say.' Listeners will be tickled when adults say ridiculous things and then whine about it, as the text directs. Comic pacing and theatrics ensure a silly trip; visual cues keep (pictureless) pages lively." Horn Book

Novak, Matt

A wish for you. Greenwillow Books 2010 un il $16.99

Grades: PreK K   E
   1. Stories in rhyme 2. Infants -- Fiction 3. Family life -- Fiction
   ISBN 978-0-06-155202-1; 0-06-155202-X
                     LC 2008052485

"In this bouncy story, a man and woman meet, court, marry, and prepare for their new baby. . . . Half-page pictures zip through scenes of preparation for the infant's arrival. Then, when the baby joins them on their vacation adventures. . . . Novak's soft-edged digitally enhanced artwork perfectly portrays the merry mood of his pudgy characters. This is a great choice for cozy sharing with a beloved child." SLJ

Novesky, Amy

Georgia in Hawaii; when Georgia O'Keeffe painted what she pleased. written by Amy Novesky; illustrated by Yuyi Morales. Houghton Mifflin Harcourt 2012 40 p.
Grades: K 1 2 3 4   E
1. Painting -- Fiction 2. Flowers in art -- Fiction 3. Hawaii -- History -- Fiction 4. Artists -- Fiction 5. Obstinacy -- Fiction 6. Hawaii -- History -- 1900-1959 -- Fiction
ISBN 9780152054205
LC 2010043401
This book tells how in "1939, Georgia O'Keefe was commissioned by the Hawaiian Pineapple Company (later Dole Pineapple) to create two paintings to promote and market pineapple juice. She spent nine weeks traveling around the islands. . . . During that time, she decided she did not want to paint the way the pineapple company wanted her to paint, and they rejected some of the art she created. She discovered and fell in love with the lush greenery and flowers and waterfalls and all the beauty Hawaii had to offer, but she refused to paint a pineapple. . . . After the Hawaiian Pineapple Company airlifted a pineapple plant to her in New York, she agreed to paint what she would call "Pineapple Bud," which became part of their advertising campaign." (International Reading Association)

★ Me, Frida; illustrated by David Diaz. Abrams Books for Young Readers 2010 un il $16.95
Grades: K 1 2 3   E
1. Artists 2. Painters 3. Artists -- Fiction 4. Women artists -- Fiction 5. San Francisco (Calif.) -- Fiction
ISBN 978-0-8109-8969-6; 0-8109-8969-7
Pura Belpré Award honor book (Illustrator), 2011
Artist Frida Kahlo finds her own voice and style when her famous husband, Diego Rivera, is commissioned to paint a mural in San Francisco, California, in the 1930s and she finds herself exploring the city on her own.
"Overflowing with compelling imagery, . . . the story also incorporates the motif of Kahlo as a tiny bird. . . . Vibrant spreads feature backdrops of warm colors dripping into cooler ones (and vice versa). . . . Diaz's . . . overlapping complementary colors add a gorgeous yet slightly unsettling visual element, his intense hues and folk/naive style recalling Kahlo's work." Publ Wkly

Noyes, Deborah

★ Red butterfly; how a princess smuggled the secret of silk out of China. illustrated by Sophie Blackall. Candlewick Press 2007 un il $16.99
Grades: 1 2 3   E
1. China -- Fiction 2. Silkworms -- Fiction 3. Princesses -- Fiction
ISBN 978-0-7636-2400-2; 0-7636-2400-4
LC 2006-52931

In long-ago China, as a young princess prepares to leave her parents' kingdom to travel to far-off Khotan where she is to marry the king, she decides to surreptitiously take with her a precious reminder of home.
"Noyes' graceful text includes allusions to nature and the shifting seasons in a style reminiscent of Chinese poetry. . . . [This is illustrated with] beautiful, ink-and-watercolor illustrations in rich, jewel colors." Booklist

Numberman, Neil

Do not build a Frankenstein! Greenwillow Books 2009 un il $16.99
Grades: K 1   E
1. Moving -- Fiction 2. Monsters -- Fiction
ISBN 978-0-06-156816-9; 0-06-156816-3
LC 2008-20751
A boy warns his new neighbors of the trouble that comes with building a monster, including having to move to a different town in hopes of escaping his creation
"Numberman is a nimble, funny writer, and he opts for showing rather than telling, his naif watercolors scoring a punch line every time." Publ Wkly

Numeroff, Laura Joffe

Beatrice doesn't want to; illustrated by Lynn Munsinger. Candlewick Press 2004 un il $15.99; pa $6.99
Grades: PreK K 1 2   E
1. Libraries -- Fiction 2. Books and reading -- Fiction
ISBN 0-7636-1160-3; 0-7636-3843-9 pa
LC 2002-73908
A newly illustrated edition of the title first published 1981 by Watts
On the third afternoon of going to the library with her brother Henry, Beatrice finally finds something she enjoys doing.
"Done in watercolor, ink, and pencil and featuring floppy-eared canine characters, the expressive illustrations perfectly capture the humor of the text." SLJ

The Chicken sisters; by Laura Numeroff; pictures by Sharleen Collicott. HarperCollins Pubs. 1997 un il $15.99; pa $6.95
Grades: PreK K 1 2   E
1. Wolves -- Fiction 2. Sisters -- Fiction 3. Chickens -- Fiction
ISBN 0-06-026679-1; 0-06-443520-2 pa
LC 96-30297
"Violet, Poppy, and Babs, the chicken sisters, possess talents that annoy the neighbors until a threatening wolf moves into the neighborhood. The illustrations achieve a captivating sense of texture that adds immediacy to the humorous story." Horn Book Guide

★ If you give a mouse a cookie; by Laura Numeroff; illustrated by Felicia Bond. Harper & Row 1985 un il $15.99; lib bdg $16.89
Grades: PreK K 1   E
1. Mice -- Fiction
ISBN 0-06-024586-7; 0-06-024587-5 lib bdg
LC 84-48343
Relating the cycle of requests a mouse is likely to make after you give him a cookie takes the reader through a young child's day

"Children love to indulge in supposition or to ask 'what will happen if . . .?' and here there is a long, satisfying chain of linked and enjoyably nonsensical causes and effects. . . . The illustrations, neatly drawn, spaciously composed, and humorously detailed, extend the story just the way picture book illustrations should." Bull Cent Child Books

Other titles in this series are:

If you give a cat a cupcake (2008)
If you give a dog a donut (2011)
If you give a moose a muffin (1991)
If you give a pig a pancake (1998)
If you give a pig a party (2005)
If you take a mouse to school (2002)
If you take a mouse to the movies (2000)

The **Jellybeans** and the big Book Bonanza. Abrams 2010 il $15.95
Grades: PreK K 1 2   E
1. School stories 2. Animals -- Fiction 3. Friendship -- Fiction 4. Books and reading -- Fiction
ISBN 978-0-8109-8412-7; 0-8109-8412-1
"Anna and her friends Emily, Nicole, and Bitsy remain, like the candies, 'differenct flavors [that] go well together.' When their class has a Book Bonanza, book-loving Anna is excited, but her friends' expressions suggest they would rather be doing other things. Luckily, the librarian helps each Jellybean find the perfect book. . . . The characters sweetly express friendship dynamics in a group setting." Publ Wkly

The **Jellybeans** and the big camp kickoff; [by] Laura Numeroff, Nate Evans; illustrated by Lynn Munsinger. Abrams Books for Young Readers 2011 un il $16.95
Grades: PreK K 1 2   E
1. Camps -- Fiction 2. Animals -- Fiction 3. Friendship -- Fiction
ISBN 978-0-8109-9765-3; 0-8109-9765-7
LC 2010023698
When four friends with different talents and abilities go to summer camp together, they use their strengths to make camp fun for all.
"Though it's a simple story, readers who value their close friendships should appreciate how the girls encourage one another to succeed." Publ Wkly

Otis & Sydney and the best birthday ever; illustrated by Dan Andreasen. Abrams Books for Young Readers 2010 un il $16.95
Grades: PreK K 1 2   E
1. Bears -- Fiction 2. Parties -- Fiction 3. Birthdays -- Fiction 4. Friendship -- Fiction
ISBN 978-0-8109-8959-7; 0-8109-8959-X
LC 2009-47199
Otis plans a surprise party for his best friend, Sydney, and although he has put the wrong date on the invitations and no one else comes, the two still have a wonderful time together.
Andreasen's "digitally colored pen and ink art echoes the old-fashioned tenor of Numeroff's . . . story; strong hatching for shading and texture leads the eye and gives the bears' fur a dapper, well-groomed quality. . . . The honeyed story never strays far from its warm and fuzzy core." Publ Wkly

Ponyella; [by] Laura Numeroff and Nate Evans; pictures by Lynn Munsinger. Disney/Hyperion Books 2011 un il $16.99
Grades: PreK K 1   E
1. Fairy tales 2. Horses -- Fiction
ISBN 978-1-4231-0259-5; 1-4231-0259-2
LC 2010-23406
Ponyella's dream of showing Princess Penelope her tricks at the pony championship comes true with the help of her fairy godmare.
"Cinderella gets a peppy makeover in this pony tale. . . . The frillier moments in Munsinger's pastel-dominated paintings are offset by lightly comedic particulars. . . . A sweet, playful adaptation." Publ Wkly

When sheep sleep; by Laura Numeroff; illustrated by David McPhail. Abrams Books for Young Readers 2006 un il $15.95
Grades: PreK K 1 2   E
1. Counting 2. Stories in rhyme 3. Sleep -- Fiction 4. Animals -- Fiction 5. Bedtime -- Fiction
ISBN 0-8109-5469-9
LC 2005022544
Rhyming text suggests other options when one tries to count sheep but discovers that they are all asleep.
"McPhail's charming watercolor-and-ink illustrations are infused with warmth and are a lovely complement to the gentle, rhyming lullaby." SLJ

Would I trade my parents? by Laura Numeroff; illustrated by James Bernardin. Abrams Books for Young Readers 2009 un il $16.95
Grades: PreK K 1 2   E
1. Parents -- Fiction
ISBN 978-0-8109-0637-2; 0-8109-0637-6
LC 2008030381
A young boy considers what is special about all of his friends' parents, and realizes that his own are the most wonderful of all.
"The illustrations are large and clear, made with acrylics and a digital paint program. They simply illustrate the text. . . . This is a straightforward retelling of a common childhood exercise in wishful thinking." SLJ

Nutt, Robert

Amy's light; written and illustrated by Robert Nutt. Dawn 2010 un il (Sharing nature with children) $16.95; pa $8.95
Grades: K 1 2   E
1. Stories in rhyme 2. Fear -- Fiction 3. Fireflies -- Fiction
ISBN 978-1-58469-128-0; 1-58469-128-X; 978-1-58469-129-7 pa; 1-58469-129-8 pa
A young girl discovers a light in nature that helps her overcome her fear of the dark. Includes an author's note about fireflies.
"Told in lyrical poetry, the author has created the magic of lightning bugs. His photo-illustrations capture Amy's fear, delight and joy." Libr Media Connect

Nyeu, Tao

Bunny days. Dial Books for Young Readers 2010 un il $16.99

Grades: PreK K   E
1. Bears -- Fiction 2. Goats -- Fiction 3. Rabbits -- Fiction
ISBN 978-0-8037-3330-5; 0-8037-3330-5
LC 2009-23060
As a pair of busy goats inadvertently cause trouble for six bunnies, their neighbor Bear comes to the rescue.
"Nyeu's illustrations are silk-screened using water-based ink. . . . The simple language and layout of the book make it suitable for beginning readers." SLJ

Squid and Octopus; friends for always. Tao Nyeu. Dial Books for Young Readers 2012 40 p. col. ill. (hardcover) $16.99
Grades: PreK K 1 2   E
1. Squids -- Fiction 2. Octopuses -- Fiction 3. Friendship -- Fiction 4. Best friends -- Fiction
ISBN 0803735650; 9780803735651
LC 2011033194
This children's picture book presents "four stories about the relationship between two eccentric sea creatures. When Squid knits socks for his multiple limbs and Octopus tells him they wear mittens, not socks, the buddies argue. Next, Squid is sad to have lost the X-ray vision bestowed while dreaming--and his status as 'Super Squid.' . . . Octopus then mistakes a cowboy boot for a hat; finally, the duo reads a fortune about everlasting friendship." (Kirkus Reviews)

O Flatharta, Antoine
★ **Hurry** and the monarch; illustrated by Meilo So. Knopf 2005 un il $14.95; pa $7.99
Grades: K 1 2   E
1. Turtles -- Fiction 2. Butterflies -- Fiction
ISBN 0-375-83003-0; 0-385-73719-X pa
LC 2004-15984
Hurry the tortoise befriends a monarch butterfly when she stops in his garden in Wichita Falls, Texas, during her migration from Canada to Mexico. Includes facts about monarch butterflies
"Veined with a tracery of inked details, So's subtle watercolors reference both Asian nature-painting traditions and the limited palette of artwork in the early days of color printing. Together with its informative afterword, this is a particularly attractive, affecting introduction to the wonder of species diversity and the elegant continuum of life." Booklist

O'Callahan, Jay
★ **Raspberries!** [illustrated by] Will Moses. Philomel Books 2009 un il $17.99
Grades: K 1 2 3   E
1. Baking -- Fiction 2. Raspberries -- Fiction
ISBN 978-0-399-25181-8; 0-399-25181-2
LC 2008048085
Once a famous baker but now down on his luck, Simon makes a living selling eggs until he is given some very special raspberry plants.
"Faithful to narrative details, the energetic folk-art style illustrations capture the personalities, exuberance, and flavor of a story that celebrates a persevering, kindhearted entrepreneur." Booklist

O'Connell, Rebecca
The **baby** goes beep; pictures by Ken Wilson-Max. Albert Whitman 2010 un il bd bk $7.99

Grades: PreK   E
1. Board books for children 2. Sound -- Fiction 3. Infants -- Fiction 4. Parent-child relationship -- Fiction
ISBN 978-0-8075-0508-3 bd bk; 0-8075-0508-0 bd bk
LC 2010002094
First published 2003 by Roaring Book Press
A baby makes various sounds as he explores the world around him.
"Wilson-Max's heavy black outlines and bright, thickly applied colors provide the perfect definition for the images. This pink baby (with a tuft of black hair) is clearly the best thing that ever happened to this set of parents, and this book is one of the best things to happen to those babies lucky enough to encounter it." Kirkus

Danny is done with diapers; a potty ABC. illustrated by Amanda Gulliver. Albert Whitman & Co. 2010 un il $16.99
Grades: PreK   E
1. Alphabet 2. Toilet training -- Fiction
ISBN 978-0-8075-1466-5; 0-8075-1466-7
"This book gently encourages, commends, and celebrates 26 youngsters who are in the process of being toilet trained. It begins 'A is for Accident, Adam had an accident. It's all right Adam.' Sweet, brightly colored acrylic illustrations discreetly show the kids using a potty chair or a toilet, washing hands, and pulling on clothing, with only a few bare bottoms revealed. . . . Written at a young child's level of understanding, this title will be useful in showing toddlers how others have accomplished this feat." SLJ

O'Connor, George
If I had a raptor; George O'Connor. Candlewick Press 2014 32 p. $15.99
Grades: PreK K 1 2   E
1. Pets -- Fiction 2. Dinosaurs -- Fiction 3. Birds of prey -- Fiction
ISBN 0763660124; 9780763660123
LC 2013944012
In this children's picture book, by George O'Connor, an "imaginative little girl dreams of the best pet ever—a fuzzy baby raptor to snuggle. Our heroine can't think of anything better than bringing home a baby raptor. . . . It would cuddle and play, stalk birds and dust bunnies, and curl up on laps. In short, it would be the perfect pet! Readers may notice striking similarities between the raptor's behavior and that of a more common house pet." (Publisher's note)
"This story is a welcome addition to the dinosaur-as-pet genre, in which a girl imagines all of the fun she would have with a dinosaur of her very own...The text is lively and simple enough to make a great read-aloud. O'Connor's charming protagonist is an African American girl, a fact that is not integral to the story but simply wonderful for readers to see. A fun story for any dinosaur fan." SLJ

O'Connor, Jane
Fancy Nancy; pictures by Robin Preiss Glasser. HarperCollins 2006 un il $17.99; lib bdg $17.89
Grades: PreK K   E
1. Family life -- Fiction 2. Clothing and dress -- Fiction
ISBN 0-06-054209-8; 0-06-054210-1 lib bdg
LC 2004-28662

A young girl who loves fancy things helps her family to be fancy for one special night. "Ages four to seven." (N Y Times Book Rev)

"For Nancy, there's no such thing as too, too much; she loves her frilly bedroom, her lace-trimmed socks, and her pen with a plume. Nancy teaches her family how to be fancy, too. . . . Nancy's perky narrative, in short, simple sentences, incorporates some 'fancy' vocabulary for kids to absorb (stupendous, posh), along with a sense of the rewards of a family doing things together. The cheerfully colored art is aptly exuberant, a riotous blending of color and pattern and action." Booklist

Other titles about Fancy Nancy are:
Fancy Nancy and the posh puppy (2007)
Fancy Nancy and the boy from Paris (2008)
Fancy Nancy at the museum (2008)
Fancy Nancy: Bonjour, butterfly (2008)
Fancy Nancy's favorite fancy words (2008)
Fancy Nancy sees stars (2009)
Fancy Nancy: poison ivy expert (2009)
Fancy Nancy: explorer extraordinaire! (2009)
Fancy Nancy tea parties (2009)
Fancy Nancy: the dazzling book report (2009)
Fancy Nancy: splendiferous Christmas (2009)
Fancy Nancy: poet extraordinaire! (2010)
Fancy Nancy: the 100th day of school (2010)
Fancy Nancy: ooh la la! It's beauty day (2010)
Fancy Nancy and the delectable cupcakes (2010)
Fancy Nancy and the fabulous fashion boutique (2010)
Fancy Nancy: aspiring artist (2011)
Fancy Nancy: stellar stargazer (2011)

The **perfect** puppy for me; by Jane O'Connor and Jessie Hartland; illustrated by Jessie Hartland. Viking 2003 un il $15.99
Grades: PreK K 1 2   **E**
1. Dogs -- Fiction
ISBN 0-670-03614-5
LC 2002-15568
While waiting to get his very own puppy, a young boy spends time with various dogs and describes what the different breeds are like

"Each page is jam-packed with good advice, useful information, and bright and cleverly detailed paintings that successfully reflect the pertinent traits of the different canines." SLJ

★ **Ready,** set, skip! illustrated by Ann James. Viking 2007 un il $15.99; pa $6.99
Grades: PreK K   **E**
1. Stories in rhyme 2. Mother-daughter relationship -- Fiction
ISBN 978-0-670-06216-4; 978-0-14-241423-1 pa
LC 2006-08632
A little girl cannot skip until her mother shows her a special trick.

"Exuberant color and black line illustrations on a white background depict the actions with élan and convey the special camaraderie between girl and dog and mother and daughter." SLJ

O'Hair, Margaret
My kitten; illustrated by Tammie Lyon. Marshall Cavendish Childrens 2011 un il $15.99

Grades: PreK   **E**
1. Stories in rhyme 2. Cats -- Fiction
ISBN 978-0-7614-5811-1; 0-7614-5811-5
LC 2009052902
Brief rhyming text and illustrations show a kitten's activities, from dreaming in the sunlight to playing with a ball of yarn.

This is "toe-tapping and easy to read. . . . The watercolor-and-colored-pencil illustrations are both spot and full-bleed, and they match the action of the text wonderfully. . . . Repeated readings will be required." Kirkus

My pup; by Margaret O'Hair; illustrated by Tammie Lyon. Marshall Cavendish 2008 un il $14.99; bd bk $7.99
Grades: PreK   **E**
1. Stories in rhyme 2. Dogs -- Fiction
ISBN 978-0-7614-5389-5; 0-7614-5389-X; 978-0-7614-5644-5 bk bk; 0-7614-5644-9 bd bk
LC 2007011719
"Bouncy text and simple rhyming couplets take readers through a day in the life of a little girl and her pet as they play in the mud, enjoy a car ride, get in the way of the cat, go for a walk, and finally cuddle up together in bed. . . . Children will delight in the expressive, brightly colored gouache and pencil spreads of a smiling, round-faced youngster with large, oval animal-print glasses and her pup." SLJ

O'Hora, Zachariah
No fits, Nilson! by Zachariah OHora. Dial Books for Young Readers 2013 32 p. ill. (reinforced) $16.99
Grades: PreK K 1   **E**
1. Picture books for children 2. Temper tantrums -- Fiction 3. Gorilla -- Fiction 4. Behavior -- Fiction
ISBN 0803738528; 9780803738522
LC 2012021514
In this children's picture book, "Amelia helps a 9-foot blue gorilla named Nilson avoid tantrums by repeatedly reminding him, 'No fits, Nilson!' . . . Illustrations depict age-old meltdown triggers: a toppled block tower, uncooperative sneakers that just (eeergh!) won't get (oof!) on your feet and boring grownup errands." (Kirkus Reviews)

Stop snoring, Bernard. Henry Holt & Co. 2011 un il $16.99
Grades: PreK K 1 2   **E**
1. Zoos -- Fiction 2. Sleep -- Fiction 3. Otters -- Fiction 4. Animals -- Fiction 5. Snoring -- Fiction
ISBN 978-0-8050-9002-4; 0-8050-9002-9
Bernard the otter snores so loudly that he keeps all of the otters at the zoo awake during naptime and Grumpy Giles tells Bernard to move his snoring somewhere else!

Ohora's "bright, flat paintings, saturated in the limited palette of red, teal, gold, gray, and black, convey depths of emotion in simple strokes and heavy outlines. Jaunty compositions, with animal characters busting out of the frames, make for audacious humor, and hand-painted lettering signifying Bernard's snoring and the animals' admonitions adds visual zing." Booklist

O'Malley, Kevin
★ **Animal** crackers fly the coop. Walker & Co. 2010 un il $16.99; lib bdg $17.89

Grades: 2 3 4   E

1. Animals -- Fiction 2. Comedians -- Fiction
ISBN 978-0-8027-9837-4; 0-8027-9837-3; 978-0-8027-9838-1 lib bdg; 0-8027-9838-1 lib bdg
LC 2009018188

In this humorous take-off of 'The Bremen Town Musicians,' four animals that aspire to make it big as comedians leave their owners and seek their fortunes.

"Full of puns, this . . . is clever, well executed, and loaded with laughs. O'Malley's expressive black-line illustrations over deep-hued colors bring the large images of the animals and robbers up-front on the page, increasing the interaction with his audience and enhancing the humor." SLJ

Captain Raptor and the moon mystery; illustrations by Patrick O'Brien. Walker & Co. 2005 un il $16.95; lib bdg $17.85

Grades: PreK K 1 2 3 4   E

1. Graphic novels 2. Science fiction graphic novels 3. Dinosaurs -- Graphic novels
ISBN 0-8027-8935-8; 0-8027-8936-6 lib bdg
LC 2004-53624

When something lands on one of the moons of the planet Jurassica, Captain Raptor and his spaceship crew go to investigate

"An action-packed science-fiction romp starring a cast of dinosaur characters. . . . Presented in comic-book style, this story blends an eye-catching layout with a quick-moving plot, tongue-in-cheek humor, and an imaginative setting." SLJ

Another title about Captain Raptor is:
Captain Raptor and the space pirates (2007)

Captain Raptor and the space pirates; [by] Kevin O'Malley and Patrick O'Brien; illustrations by Patrick O'Brien. Walker & Co. 2007 un il $16.95; lib bdg $17.85

Grades: 1 2 3   E

1. Science fiction 2. Pirates -- Fiction 3. Dinosaurs -- Fiction
ISBN 978-0-8027-9571-7; 0-8027-9571-4; 978-0-8027-9572-4 lib bdg; 0-8027-9572-2 lib bdg
LC 2006101182

Captain Raptor and the crew of the Megatooth are called back into action to save the planet Jurassica from rogue space pirates.

This "comes alive with O'Brien's watercolor and gouache illustrations. The action moves quickly in small frames dense with realistic dinosaurs in armor and the inner workings of spaceships." SLJ

★ **Gimme** cracked corn and I will share. Walker & Co. 2007 un il $16.95; lib bdg $17.85

Grades: 2 3 4   E

1. Chickens -- Fiction
ISBN 978-0-8027-9684-4; 0-8027-9684-2; 978-0-8027-9685-1 lib bdg; 0-8027-9685-0 lib bdg
LC 2007-03706

Chicken dreams about a treasure and sets off on a dangerous journey to find it

"Fans of corny humor and 'punny yolks' will welcome this tale. . . . The unique illustrations are a combination of pen, ink, and Photoshop." SLJ

Lucky leaf. Walker & Co. 2004 un il hardcover o.p. pa $6.95

Grades: PreK K 1 2   E

1. Leaves -- Fiction
ISBN 0-8027-8924-2; 0-8027-8925-0 lib bdg; 0-8027-9647-8 pa
LC 2003-68868

After his mother tells him to stop playing video games and go outside, a young boy tries to catch the last leaf on a tree, thinking it will bring him luck

"Done in pen and ink and colored in PhotoShop, the illustrations feature crisp, vibrant colors that create a vivid setting. . . . The story is told through spare, but effective, dialogue presented in speech bubbles." SLJ

Once upon a royal superbaby; written and illustrated by Kevin O'Malley; illustrated by Carol Heyer & Scott Goto. Walker & Co. 2010 un il lib bdg $17.89; $16.99

Grades: K 1 2 3   E

1. Infants -- Fiction 2. Authorship -- Fiction 3. Imagination -- Fiction 4. Superheroes -- Fiction 5. Kings and rulers -- Fiction
ISBN 978-0-8027-2165-5 lib bdg; 0-8027-2165-6 lib bdg; 978-0-8027-2164-8; 0-8027-2164-8
LC 2009054216

Cooperatively writing a story for school, a girl imagines a king and queen who have a baby named Sweet Piper who can talk to birds, while a boy names the baby Sweet Viper and gives him super-strength, cool wrestling moves, and a motorcycle and sunglasses.

"The boy and the girl are illustrated by O'Malley. Goto and Heyer's hyperrealistic art functions well to depict the imaginations of the narrators; and children of both genders will relate to the ongoing debate between the boy and girl." SLJ

O'Neill, Alexis

★ **Estela's** swap; illustrated by Enrique O. Sanchez. Lee & Low Bks. 2002 un il hardcover o.p. pa $7.95

Grades: K 1 2 3   E

1. Mexican Americans -- Fiction
ISBN 1-58430-044-2; 1-60060-253-3 pa
LC 2001-38785

A young Mexican American girl accompanies her father to a swap meet, where she hopes to sell her music box for money for dancing lessons

"This is a warm, nicely paced story about sharing and bartering that's filled with sensory descriptions of the vibrant open market. The textured acrylics capture the hum and bustle of the stalls." Booklist

O'Neill, Catharine

Annie & Simon; the sneeze and other stories. Catharine O'Neill. 1st ed. Candlewick Press 2013 64 p. col. ill. (reinforced) $15.99

Grades: 1 2   E

1. Pets -- Fiction 2. Siblings -- Fiction 3. Dogs -- Fiction 4. Brothers and sisters -- Fiction
ISBN 076364921X; 9780763649210
LC 2011046618

This story collection is the second in Catharine O'Neill's Annie and Simon series. Here, "Simon's sneeze unleashes a patiently borne flood of little-sister TLC; Annie's efforts to get her dog Hazel to purr end abruptly when she sees the neighbor's cat stroll by with a mouse in his mouth; and the sudden disappearance of a wagonload of horse chestnuts left on the porch sparks a bit of detective work." (Kirkus)

Annie and Simon. Candlewick Press 2008 57p il $15.99
Grades: 1 2   E
   1. Dogs -- Fiction 2. Siblings -- Fiction
   ISBN 978-0-7636-2688-4; 0-7636-2688-0
                    LC 2006-47521
Recounts four adventures of Annie, her big brother, Simon, and their dog, Hazel.
   "Annie and Simon's four stories collected here will ring true for most newly independent readers. The watercolor illustrations of the two and their bark-full dog Hazel are full of humor and detail. . . . O'Neill's first solo effort in some years is well worth adding to the first-chapter-book collection." Kirkus

O'Neill, Gemma
   Monty's magnificent mane; Gemma O'Neill. Templar 2015 40 p. color illustrations $15.99
Grades: PreK K   E
   1. Lions -- Fiction 2. Animals -- Fiction 3. Meerkat -- Fiction 4. Crocodiles -- Fiction 5. Friendship -- Fiction
   ISBN 0763675938; 9780763675936
                  LC 2014939340
   In this children's book by Gemma O'Neill "Monty the lion loves his long, golden mane, so he's not happy when his meerkat friends mess it up. Stomping off to the waterhole, he's cheered up by the flattery of a new friend . . . a green friend . . . a big, green friend. With a SNAP Monty realizes that his flattering pal is actually a giant crocodile looking for dinner." (Publisher's note)
   "A lion named Monty is so proud of his mane that he nearly causes disaster for himself and his little meerkat friends. A charming double-page spread shows Monty relaxing on his back and happily fiddling with a lock of his autumn-hued tresses with one padded paw...The tried-and-true fable about curbing vanity and appreciating friends enjoys a fresh touch with these ebullient African animals." Kirkus

Oakley, Graham
   The **church** mouse. Kane Miller 2010 un il $16.99 E
   1. Cats -- Fiction 2. Mice -- Fiction 3. Church -- Fiction
   ISBN 978-1-935279-69-3; 1-935279-69-6
A reissue of the title first published 1972 by Atheneum
Arthur, a lonely mouse living in a church with only Sampson, a friendly, sleepy cat, for company devises a plan to get all the mice in town to move in with him.
   "The cover of this reissue is different from the 1972 original, but inside can be found the same detailed illustrations and child appealing events (e.g., mid-sermon melees, burglars, acrobatics)." Horn Book Guide

Obed, Ellen Bryan
   ★ **Who** would like a Christmas tree? illustrated by Anne Hunter. Houghton Mifflin Books for Children 2009 un il $16
Grades: 1 2 3   E
   1. Trees -- Fiction 2. Months -- Fiction 3. Nature --

Fiction 4. Animals -- Fiction 5. Christmas -- Fiction
   ISBN 978-0-547-04625-9; 0-547-04625-1
                  LC 2008052302
Describes the flora and fauna that inhabit a Christmas tree farm throughout the year and use the growing trees for a variety of purposes. Includes section on how the farmer takes care of the farm through the year.
   "Though presented as a Christmas book, this informative introduction to the different animals inhabiting a Maine tree plantation can be enjoyed year round. . . . The charming watercolor and ink illustrations are rendered in naturalistic fashion using nature's hues and cross-hatching techniques for shading and depth. . . . An excellent resource for getting youngsters enthused about nature." SLJ

Oberman, Sheldon
   The **always** prayer shawl; illustrated by Ted Lewin. Boyds Mills Press 1994 un il $15.95; pa $10.95
Grades: 1 2 3 4   E
   1. Jews -- Fiction 2. Immigrants -- Fiction
   ISBN 1-878093-22-3; 1-59078-332-8 pa
This story "tells of the Jewish boy Adam, growing up in a shtetl, whose life drastically changes when famine and chaos in old Russia force his parents to immigrate to America. At parting, Adam's beloved grandfather gives the boy a gift, a prayer shawl . . . which was presented to the grandfather by his grandfather. . . . The watercolors are abundantly detailed and wonderfully expressive. . . . The pictures enrich the tranquil telling . . . as it movingly depicts how memory and tradition add texture and richness to our lives." Booklist

Ochiltree, Dianne
   Molly, by golly! the legend of Molly Williams, America's first female firefighter. Dianne Ochiltree; illustrated by Kathleen Kemly. Boyds Mills Press 2012 32 p. ill. (reinforced) $16.95
Grades: 2 3 4   E
   ISBN 1590787218; 9781590787212
                  LC 2012933452
   This children's book by Diane Ochiltree tells the story of Molly Williams, "The first American female firefighter [and] an African-American cook in the first quarter of the 19th century. . . . Molly cooked for Mr. Aymar, who was also a volunteer firefighter for the Oceanus Engine Company No. 11. A heavy snowstorm and a wave of influenza laid many of the volunteers low, so Molly . . . put on a leather helmet and gloves and worked beside the men . . . until finally the blaze was out." (Kirkus Reviews)

Odanaka, Barbara
   Crazy day at the Critter Cafe; illustrated by Lee White. Margaret K. McElderry Books 2009 un il $16.99
Grades: K 1 2   E
   1. Stories in rhyme 2. Animals -- Fiction 3. Restaurants -- Fiction
   ISBN 978-1-4169-3914-6; 1-4169-3914-8
A quiet morning in a roadside cafe turns to chaos when a bus breaks down and a managerie of noisy, rude animals enters, demanding to be fed.
   "The rhymed text emphasizes the zany sound effects as the mixed-media illustrations comically exaggerate the scenes. Kids will giggle over the heightened food mess the animals leave behind." Booklist

Oelschlager, Vanita

A **tale** of two daddies; illustrated by Kristin Blackwood and Mike Blanc. Vanita 2010 il $15.95

Grades: PreK K 1 2   **E**

1. Homosexuality -- Fiction 2. Father-daughter relationship -- Fiction

ISBN 9780981971452; 0981971458

Ofanansky, Allison

Harvest of light; by Allison Ofanansky; photos by Eliyahu Alpern. Kar-Ben Pub. 2008 un il (Nature in Israel) lib bdg $15.95

Grades: 1 2 3   **E**

1. Jews -- Fiction 2. Israel -- Fiction 3. Olives -- Fiction 4. Hanukkah -- Fiction

ISBN 978-0-8225-7389-0 lib bdg; 0-8225-7389-X lib bdg

LC 2007-43133

"In this wonderfully different Hanukkah book, an Israeli family harvests olives to be processed into the oil. The daughter provides a simple narrative, which is clearly written and accompanied by full-color photographs depicting each step in the process from gathering and sorting the olives to pressing them and using the oil to light the menorah. Resonating with familial warmth and a shared purpose, this is a fine offering." SLJ

The **patchwork** Torah; Allison Ofanansky; illustrated by Elsa Oriol. Kar-Ben Publishing 2014 32 p. (lib. bdg.: alk. paper) $17.95

Grades: K 1 2 3 4   **E**

1. Grandfathers -- Fiction 2. Torah scrolls -- Fiction 3. Jews -- United States -- Fiction

ISBN 1467704261; 9781467704267

LC 2013002194

"Fragments of damaged and rescued Torahs from several periods of history are woven together in this . . . tale of four generations of a Torah scribe and his family," written by Allison Ofanansky and illustrated by Elsa Oriol. (Publisher's note)

"Inspired by tradition, deep faith, and an understanding that to "repair and reuse things" makes the world a better place, a sofer (the Hebrew word for a craftsman-scribe who transcribes sacred documents) takes pieces of four damaged Torah scrolls—ravaged by old age, the Holocaust, fire, and Hurricane Katrina—and creates a wonderful new Torah... Surprisingly inventive and genuinely uplifting, this story beautifully and subtly ties together two key Jewish precepts: l'dor v'dor (generation to generation) and tikkum olam (repair the world)." PW

Sukkot treasure hunt; photographs by Eliyahu Alpern. Kar-Ben 2009 un il (Nature in Israel) $15.95

Grades: PreK K 1 2   **E**

1. Jews -- Fiction 2. Israel -- Fiction 3. Sukkot -- Fiction

ISBN 978-0-8225-8763-7; 0-8225-8763-7

LC 2008-31202

In Israel, a young girl and her family go on a scavenger hunt to find the 'four species' they will use in their celebration of the Jewish holiday, Sukkot. Includes facts about plants named in the story.

"Straightforward first-person text and clear photographs encourage readers to join the family on their search for palm, willow, myrtle, and etrog." Horn Book Guide

What's the buzz? honey for a sweet new year. photographed by Eliyahu Alpern. Kar-Ben 2011 il (Nature in Israel) lib bdg $15.95

Grades: K 1 2 3   **E**

1. School stories 2. Bees -- Fiction 3. Honey -- Fiction 4. Israel -- Fiction 5. Rosh ha-Shanah -- Fiction

ISBN 978-0-7613-5640-0; 0-7613-5640-1

LC 2010026181

A class in Israel tours a farm to learn how honey is made and used to celebrate the Jewish New Year, Rosh Hashanah.

"Ofanansky and Alpern offer a fresh take on Rosh Hashanah. . . . Color photographs and a running narrative combine to produce an easy-to-grasp book that is about science but also about culture." Publ Wkly

Offill, Jenny

11 experiments that failed; written by Jenny Offill; pictures by Nancy Carpenter. 2011 un il $16.99

Grades: PreK K 1 2   **E**

1. Science -- Experiments -- Fiction

ISBN 978-0-375-84762-2; 0-375-84762-6

"The curious and mischief-minded heroine from 17 Things I'm Not Allowed to Do Anymore turns her attention to the scientific method. A typical experiment: 'Question: Do dogs like to be covered in glitter? Hypothesis: Dogs like everything.' Offill's matter-of-fact recounting . . . make for very funny reading and allow Carpenter to go all out with her collages, which create especially lively depictions of the protagonist's misadventures." Publ Wkly

★ **17** things I'm not allowed to do anymore. Schwartz & Wade Books 2006 un il $15.99

Grades: PreK K 1 2   **E**

1. Behavior -- Fiction

ISBN 0-375-83596-2

LC 2005-16414

A young girl lists the sixteen things she is not allowed to do anymore, including not being able to make ice after freezing a fly in one of the cubes.

"Ingenious artwork—a flawless marriage of digital imagery and pen-and-ink—is indisputably the focus of this winning title." SLJ

Another title about this girl is:

11 experiments that failed (2011)

Sparky; by Jenny Offill; illustrated by Chris Appelhans. Schwartz & Wade Books 2013 40 p. $16.99

Grades: PreK K 1   **E**

1. Pets -- Fiction 2. Sloths -- Fiction 3. Sloths as pets

ISBN 0375870237; 9780375870231; 9780375970238

LC 2012047196

In this book, by Jenny Offill, "a young girl desperately wants a pet but has to find one that will meet her mother's low-maintenance stipulations, so she's delighted to discover that a sloth would fill the bill nicely. . . . Know-it-all peer Mary Potts is dismissive of Sparky. . . . The girl, however, doesn't let that ruin her outlook and continues to love Sparky just as he is." (Bulletin of the Center for Children's Books)

"A girl tries to teach her new pet sloth, Sparky, to play hide-and-seek, roll over, fetch: nothing. After a misguided pseudo-talent show, the girl accepts that, while Sparky is no whirling dervish, he is an endearing companion. Appelhans's striking watercolor and pencil illustrations, in a muted color palette of pinks, browns, and green-blues, do much of the story's heavy lifting." Horn Book

While you were napping; Jenny Offill. Schwartz & Wade 2014 40 p. color illustrations $16.99

Grades: K 1 2 3   E

    1. Humorous fiction 2. Sleep -- Fiction 3. Brothers and sisters -- Fiction 4. Humorous stories 5. Naps (Sleep) -- Fiction

    ISBN 0375865721; 9780375865725; 9780375965722

LC 2010048532

This children's book, by Jenny Offill, "featur[es] robots, fire trucks, and pirates, meet an older sister who's more than happy to fill her little brother in on all he missed while he was napping. Since none of the other neighborhood kids had to nap, they came over. Then came the robots, and of course the astronauts. It was tons of fun . . . and luckily for the boy (right?!), he slept through it all!" (Publisher's note)

"A big sister tells her brother everything he missed during his nap: bulldozer-driving, dinosaur fossils, pirates, space travel, and more. That her yarn is based on specific items in her brother's room--toy truck, dinosaur model, pirate book--adds insult to injury. The conversational text gets that teasing big-sisterly tone just right. The illustrations combine child-centered nonsense imagery with wicked humor adults will appreciate." Horn Book

Ogburn, Jacqueline K.

    The **bake** shop ghost; illustrated by Marjorie Priceman. Houghton Mifflin 2005 un il $16; pa $6.99

Grades: K 1 2 3   E

    1. Ghost stories 2. Cake -- Fiction 3. Bakers and bakeries -- Fiction

    ISBN 0-618-44557-9; 0-547-07677-0 pa

Miss Cora Lee Meriweather haunts her bake shop after her death, until Annie Washington, the new shop owner, makes a deal with her.

"Priceman's illustrations are charming, with dashes of color and humor and a sense of action in each one. . . . This is a delightful story with a satisfying conclusion." SLJ

    The **magic** nesting doll; illustrated by Laurel Long. Dial Bks. 2000 un il $16.99

Grades: K 1 2 3   E

    1. Fairy tales 2. Russia -- Fiction

    ISBN 0-8037-2414-4

LC 98-34397

After her grandmother dies, Katya finds herself in a kingdom where the Tsarvitch has been turned into living ice and she uses the magic nesting dolls her babushka had given her to try to break the curse

"The writings is filled with description and poetic images. . . . Created using oil paints on paper primed with gesso, the illustrations are alive with detail and reminiscent of the miniaturist style used in Russian decorative items." SLJ

Ohi, Debbie Ridpath

    Where are my books? Debbie Ridpath Ohi. Simon & Schuster Books for Young Readers 2015 40 p. (hardcover: alk. paper) $17.99

Grades: PreK K 1   E

    1. Squirrels -- Fiction 2. Books and reading -- Fiction 63 Lost and found possessions -- Fiction

    ISBN 144246741X; 9781442467415

LC 2014015990

In this children's book, by Debbie Ridpath Ohi, "Spencer loves to read. He reads a book every night. But one morning his favorite book goes missing, and in its place is a tulip. Spencer searches high and low, but he can't find his book. The next morning another book is missing, a nut in its place. And the morning after that, another book is missing. What is happening to Spencer's books?" (Publisher's note)

Ohi, Ruth

    Chicken, pig, cow and the class pet. Annick Press 2011 un il lib bdg $19.95; pa $6.95

Grades: PreK K 1 2   E

    1. School stories 2. Toys -- Fiction 3. Hamsters -- Fiction

    ISBN 1-55451-346-4 pa; 978-1-55451-347-5 lib bdg; 1-55451-347-2 lib bdg; 978-1-55451-346-8 pa

"Three toys take an unexpected field trip. Huddled in close quarters, Cow, Pig and Chicken try to dissect the sounds around them. Readers see that their temporary housing (a makeshift Popsicle-stick barn) confines them to a classroom while their beloved young owner enjoys her day at school. The friends' introduction to the imposing class pet, dubbed Furface by the anxious critters, leads to some wacky interactions. . . . Humorous watercolors splashed against open white backgrounds extend the visual humor, depicting the classroom environment from a toy's-eye point of view." Kirkus

    Kenta and the big wave; by Ruth Ohi. Annick Press 2013 32 p. $9.95

Grades: PreK K 1 2   E

    1. Japan -- Fiction 2. Tsunamis -- Fiction 3. Evacuation of civilians

    ISBN 1554515769; 1554515777; 9781554515769; 9781554515776

In this book by Ruth Ohi, "when tragedy strikes Kenta's small village in Japan, he does all he can to hang on to the things that matter to him most. But amidst the chaos of an emergency evacuation brought on by the tsunami, Kenta and his family must quickly leave their home. Climbing to safer ground, Kenta watches helplessly as his prized soccer ball goes bouncing down a hill and gets swept away by the waves . . . into the hands of a child who takes it upon himself to return the ball to [Kenta]." (Publisher's note)

Oldland, Nicholas

    ★ **Big** bear hug. Kids Can Press 2009 un il $16.95

Grades: PreK K   E

    1. Bears -- Fiction 2. Trees -- Fiction 3. Hugging -- Fiction

    ISBN 978-1-55453-464-7; 1-55453-464-X

A bear who loves to hug everything meets a human who is about to chop down a tree, and the bear must make a decision on how to save his forest.

"Oldland's rustic-styled digital artwork looks like a hip flannel pajama print . . . and his pictures play sly comic foil to the earnest text." Publ Wkly

    The **busy** beaver. Kids Can Press 2011 un il

Grades: PreK K 1   E
  1. Animals -- Fiction 2. Beavers -- Fiction
  ISBN 1554537495; 9781554537495

A "busy but careless beaver spends his days following random impulses, . . . and leaving in his wake a devastated forest filled with stumps, half-nibbled trees and injured, homeless animals. But then one day the beaver finds himself on the wrong side of a falling tree, which as it turns out, is just the thing to knock some sense into him. After reflecting on his behavior, he decides to make some changes. Soon, the now wiser and gentler beaver is getting down to the business of making things right, much to the delighted surprise of his forest friends." (Publisher's note) "Ages three to five." (Quill Quire)

"Beaver's exuberance for his work leads to careless accidents for a bear, moose, and bird's nest, and eventually for himself. . . . Beaver realizes he has a great deal for which to atone. He exercises, reads a how-to book, and practices apologies. His return is greeted by fear until he shows his newfound consideration with gifts and kind deeds. . . . The comic Photoshop illustrations have a stop-action effect and creative attention to detail." SLJ

Making the moose out of life. Kids Can Press 2010 un il $16.95
Grades: PreK K 1 2   E
  1. Moose -- Fiction 2. Friendship -- Fiction
  ISBN 978-1-55453-580-4; 1-55453-580-8

"Mild-mannered Moose never joins his friends when they go puddle jumping, kite flying, or skiing. . . . When he sets out alone in a sailboat, he . . . is washed away to a deserted island. It's here that he learns how to fend for himself and he meets a new friend, a tortoise named Tuesday. . . . When Moose is rescued by a cruise ship, he embraces shipboard life, taking part in all of the activities. Finally, he returns to his former friends and is now ready to join them and have some fun. . . . The illustrations are in muted outdoorsy colors of brown, green, and blue with a contemporary folk-art look. . . . Charming and simply told." SLJ

Oliver, Lin
  ★ **Little** Poems for Tiny Ears; by Lin Oliver; illustrated by Tomie dePaola. Nancy Paulsen Books 2013 32 p. $16.99
Grades: PreK   E
  1. Children's poetry
  ISBN 039916605X; 9780399166051
                   LC 2013014049

In this children's picture book, "twenty-three short poems written in the first-person viewpoints of infants and toddlers muse on the small discoveries and quietly joyful moments that are part of early childhood. Among them: learning to make new sounds; discovering one's toes, bellybutton, mouth, and nose . . . cozying up to a parent; and making messes." (Publishers Weekly)

"Everything about this book is child friendly, beginning with its charming cover. Oliver has written 23 highly readable poems about almost every familiar aspect of a young child's life, from belly buttons and diapers to noises and the kitchen drawer...Each poem and illustration is framed to highlight chubby babies and toddlers of all ethnic backgrounds at the center of their world, being active and being loved. Pair with Mem Fox's Ten Little Fingers and Ten Little

Toes (2008) for another rhyming celebration of babies and their worlds." (Booklist)

Olshan, Matthew
  The **mighty** Lalouche; Matthew Olshan; illustrated by Sophie Blackall. Schwartz & Wade Books 2012 40 p. (hardcover) $17.99; (library) $20.99
Grades: PreK K 1 2   E
  1. Boxing -- Fiction 2. Letter carriers -- Fiction 3. Paris (France) -- History -- 20th century -- Fiction 4. France -- History -- Third Republic, 1870-1940 -- Fiction
  ISBN 0375862250; 9780375862250; 9780375962257
                   LC 2010031825

This children's story, by Matthew Olshan, illustrated by Sophie Blackall, begins "in Paris, France, [where] there lived a humble postman named Lalouche. He was small, but his hands were nimble, his legs were fast, and his arms were strong. When his job was replaced by an electric car, he turned to boxing to support himself and his pet finch, Genevieve." (Publisher's note)

Olson, Julie
  Tickle, tickle! itch, twitch! written and illustrated by Julie Olson. Marshall Cavendish 2010 un il $12.99
Grades: PreK K   E
  1. Mice -- Fiction 2. Marmots -- Fiction
  ISBN 978-0-7614-5714-5; 0-7614-5714-3

Gus the groundhog desperately needs to scratch his back after a mouse tickles him with a feather, but the stick, bush, and log he tries to scratch against are not what they appear to be.

"Olson has created a book that just begs to be read aloud. . . . This story is simple and repetitive, allowing for audience participation and many different storytelling techniques such as reader's theater or flannel-board retelling. Young children will enjoy the simple and silly humor and the bright, colorful illustrations that fill the pages." SLJ

Olson-Brown, Ellen
  Ooh la la polka dot boots; illustrations by Christiane Engel. Tricycle Press 2010 il $14.99
Grades: PreK   E
  1. Stories in rhyme 2. Clothing and dress -- Fiction
  ISBN 9781582462875; 1582462879
                   LC 2009007547

Illustrations and brief rhyming text sing the praises of polka dot boots, which add panache to any outfit.

Omololu, Cynthia Jaynes
  When it's six o'clock in San Francisco; a trip through time zones. illustrated by Randy DuBurke. Clarion Books 2009 31p il map $16
Grades: K 1 2 3   E
  1. Time -- Fiction
  ISBN 978-0-618-76827-1; 0-618-76827-0
                   LC 2007012721

When Jared wakes up in San Francisco at six o'clock in the morning, children in other parts of the world are doing other things, like going to school in Buenos Aires, Argentina, playing soccer in London, England, and eating dinner in Lahore, Pakistan, because of the difference in time zones around the globe. Includes factual material about telling time and time zones.

"The diversity and connections across the globe are the story, with warm, colorful, individual portraits that move beyond cultural stereotypes. . . . This is a great choice for science classes and for today's international families." Booklist

Onishi, Satoru
★ **Who's** hiding? Kane/Miller 2007 31p il $14.95
Grades: PreK K 1 2　　　　　　　　　　　　　E
1. Puzzles 2. Animals -- Fiction
ISBN 978-1-933605-24-1
"Eighteen simply drawn, brightly colored animals are laid out in the same order on each spread. . . . The first spread shows the creatures and their names and asks, Who is hiding? The next spread shows all of them except for the reindeer who is invisible except for his antlers. This question alternates with others. . . . This is a clever puzzle book for caregivers and young children to share and to learn animals, colors, concepts." SLJ

Onyefulu, Ifeoma
Play; Ifeoma Onyefulu. Frances Lincoln Children's Books 2013 32 p. chiefly color illustrations (Look at this) $17.99
Grades: PreK K 1　　　　　　　　　　　　　E
1. Play 2. Games
ISBN 1847802672; 9781847802675
"Hopscotch, cat's cradle, the mud game, football, Way. . . . Many different ways to play, with games that are familiar all over the world as well as some traditional African games. Photographed in Mali by an award-winning photographer, this is a unique and culturally diverse word book, with lots to look at and talk about." (Publisher's note)

Oppel, Kenneth
★ **The king's** taster; paintings by Steve Johnson & Lou Fancher. HarperCollinsPublishers 2008 un il $17.99; lib bdg $18.89
Grades: K 1 2 3　　　　　　　　　　　　　E
1. Diet -- Fiction 2. Dogs -- Fiction 3. Food -- Fiction 4. Kings and rulers -- Fiction
ISBN 978-0-06-075372-6; 0-06-075372-2; 978-0-06-075373-3 lib bdg; 0-06-075373-0 lib bdg
LC 2008000779
The royal chef takes Max the dog, the royal taster, on several international journeys to find a dish for the land's pickiest king.
"The mixed-media illustrations are deliciously capricious with clever collage details. . . . Kids will relish this comic culinary calamity." Booklist

Orloff, Karen Kaufman
I wanna go home; Karen Kaufman Orloff; illustrated by David Catrow. G. P. Putnam's Sons, an imprint of Penguin Group (USA) 2014 32 p. color illustrations (hardcover) $16.99
Grades: PreK K 1 2　　　　　　　　　　　　　E
1. Humorous fiction 2. Letters -- Fiction 3. Family life -- Fiction 4. Grandparents -- Fiction 5. Humorous stories
ISBN 0399254072; 9780399254079
LC 2013039319
In this children's book, by Karen Kaufman Orloff & illustrated by David Catrow, "Alex is not happy about being sent to his grandparents' retirement community while his

parents go on a fabulous vacation. . . . But as the week goes on, Alex's desperate emails to his parents turn into stories about ice cream before dinner and stickball with Grandpa. Before he knows it, Alex has made a surprising discovery: grandparents are way cooler than he thought!" (Publisher's note)
"Previously seen in I Wanna Iguana and I Wanna New Room, Alex is still exchanging plaintive missives with his parents in his third picture book, though he has upgraded to email, out of necessity—Alex and his siblings are staying in Florida with their grandparents while their parents are in Bora Bora. Alex is miserable: it's raining, it's boring, and he's unnerved by seeing Grandpa's false teeth on his bedside table (a scene that Catrow, no surprise, delights in making as icky as possible). But a square dancing class, Grandma and Grandpa's laissez-faire attitude toward mealtime (at a diner, Alex turns nine corn dogs into an impressive statue of a poodle), and a (very) old-fashioned game of stickball soon have the boy singing another tune. Orloff skillfully expresses Alex's gradually shifting attitude, while Catrow's comically exaggerated art provides a hyperbolic sense of fun." Pub Wkly

★ **I** wanna iguana; illustrated by David Catrow. Putnam 2004 un il $15.99
Grades: PreK K 1 2　　　　　　　　　　　　　E
1. Pets -- Fiction 2. Iguanas -- Fiction
ISBN 0-399-23717-8
LC 2002-10895
Alex and his mother write notes back and forth in which Alex tries to persuade her to let him have a baby iguana for a pet.
"This funny story is told through an amusing exchange of notes. . . . Featuring his signature cartoon characters, Catrow's illustrations provide a hilarious extension of the text." SLJ
Another title about Alex is:
I wanna new room (2010)

I wanna new room; illustrated by David Catrow. Putnam 2010 un il $16.99
Grades: PreK K 1 2　　　　　　　　　　　　　E
1. Infants -- Fiction 2. Letters -- Fiction 3. Brothers -- Fiction 4. Family life -- Fiction
ISBN 978-0-399-25405-5; 0-399-25405-6
LC 2009040106
Through a series of brief letters to his parents, Alex presents all the reasons why he should not have to share a room with his younger brother
"The slapstick, sibling anger, and crowding issues are all spot-on." Booklist

Ormerod, Jan
101 things to do with baby; Jan Ormerod. Pgw 2014 32 p. col il $16.95
Grades: PreK　　　　　　　　　　　　　E
1. Picture books for children 2. Siblings -- Graphic novels 3. Infants -- Fiction 4. Play
ISBN 1554983797; 9781554983797
LC 844401
In this picture book, by Jan Ormerod, "a little girl and her family find 101 things to do with their new baby. . . . What do you do with a new baby? An imaginative older sister and her parents explore this question in this sweet and

authentic depiction of a day in the life of a young family." (Publisher's note)

"This charming and innovative sibling story came out in 1984 and is back in hardcover to celebrate its 30th anniversary With homey, pastel-hued illustrations arranged in graphic novel-esque panels, a new big sister demonstrates for readers 101 daily activities that she can do with her baby brother, from sharing her morning egg to helping keep baby entertained while Mom does the wash...The text is minimal; the art tells the deeper story here. One of the very best books for new siblings." SLJ

The **baby** swap; by Jan Ormerod; illustrated by Andrew Joyner. Little Simon 2015 32 p. (hardcover) $16.99
Grades: PreK K 1   E
1. Babies -- Fiction 2. Jealousy -- Fiction 3. Crocodiles -- Fiction 4. Animals -- Infancy -- Fiction 5. Brothers and sisters -- Fiction
ISBN 1481419145; 9781481419147
LC 2013047673
"Caroline Crocodile is not thrilled with her baby brother. He drools. A lot. But all Mama Crocodile ever says is how GORGEOUS he is! And so Caroline ventures into a baby shop to swap out her brother. Unfortunately, the baby panda is a fussy eater, the giraffe is missing scales, and the piglet isn't green. Turns out, the best younger sibling around might just be her own yellow-eyed, sharp-clawed, drooling baby brother." (Publisher's note)

Ballet sisters: the duckling and the swan. Scholastic 2007 32p il $5.99
Grades: PreK K 1 2   E
1. Ballet -- Fiction 2. Sisters -- Fiction 3. Imagination -- Fiction
ISBN 978-0-439-82281-7; 0-439-82281-5
LC 2006-02575
Sylvie and her older sister dance their way through make-believe adventures that include princesses, fairy queens, swans, and ducklings.

"The language . . . is clear, concise, and descriptive— essential qualities for beginning readers. The watercolor illustrations place the girls and their mother on a clean white background, which effectively highlights the expressive detail in their faces and postures." SLJ

Another title about Sylvie and her sister is:
Ballet sisters: the newest dancer (2008)

If you're happy and you know it! [by] Jan Ormerod, Lindsey Gardiner. Star Bright Books 2003 un il $15.95; pa $5.95
Grades: PreK   E
1. Stories in rhyme 2. Animals -- Fiction
ISBN 1-932065-07-5; 1-932065-10-5 pa
LC 2002-13692
A little girl and various animals sing their own versions of this popular rhyme

"Delightful, colorful animal figures cavort through the pages of this book that puts a twist on the familiar song. . . . The action on each spread gives the story a great deal of energy and the backgrounds are washes of color, from dark pink to yellow to blue." SLJ

★ **Lizzie** nonsense; a story of pioneer days. Clarion Books 2005 32p il lib bdg $15
Grades: PreK K 1 2   E
1. Australia -- Fiction 2. Family life -- Fiction 3. Imagination -- Fiction
ISBN 0-618-57493-X lib bdg
LC 2004-26642
First published 2004 in Australia
"Lizzie lives with her mother, father, and baby brother in a small, isolated house in the Australian bush. Her father has taken his sandalwood into town to sell and will be gone for weeks. Lizzie passes the lonely days by indulging in flights of fancy. . . . The text is simple yet evocative . . . while the skillfully rendered watercolors bring the unique setting to life." SLJ

Miss Mouse's day. HarperCollins Pubs. 2001 un il hardcover o.p. lib bdg $14.89
Grades: PreK   E
1. Day -- Fiction 2. Mice -- Fiction
ISBN 0-688-16333-5; 0-688-16334-3 lib bdg
LC 99-27641
"The illustrations, in panels of varying sizes, brim with pattern, detail, and bright splashes of color. . . . Ormerod delightfully and realistically illustrates the challenges of energetic toddlerhood." Booklist

Another title about Miss Mouse is:
Miss Mouse takes off (2001)

Orr, Wendy
The **princess** and her panther; illustrated by Lauren Stringer. Simon & Schuster 2010 un il $16.99
Grades: K 1 2   E
1. Fear -- Fiction 2. Camping -- Fiction 3. Sisters -- Fiction 4. Panthers -- Fiction 5. Princesses -- Fiction
ISBN 978-1-4169-9780-1; 1-4169-9780-6
LC 2009034359
A brave princess and a panther who tries to be brave cross the desert together and settle into a red silk tent, in which they listen to "leaf-snakes," an "owl-witch," and other frightening creatures until the princess frightens them away.

"Deep-hued, textured acrylics ably reflect the imaginative story's drama and its nighttime setting." Horn Book Guide

Osborne, Mary Pope
★ **New** York's bravest; paintings by Steve Johnson & Lou Fancher. Knopf 2002 un il $15.95; pa $6.99
Grades: PreK K 1 2   E
1. Fire fighters -- Fiction 2. New York (N.Y.) -- Fiction
ISBN 0-375-82196-1; 0-375-83841-4 pa
LC 2002-455
Tells of the heroic deeds of the legendary New York firefighter, Mose Humphreys

"Boldly executed art supports the tall-tale flavor of a story that is both powerful and humane." Booklist

Oskarsson, Bardur
The **flat** rabbit; Bardur Oskarsson, translated by Marita Thomsen. Owlkids Books, Inc. 2014 40 p. color illustrations hardcover $16.95
Grades: K 1 2 3   E
1. Dogs -- Fiction 2. Rats -- Fiction 3. Rabbits --

Fiction

ISBN 9781771470599; 1771470593

LC 2014932277

"When a dog and a rat come upon a rabbit flattened on the road in their neighborhood, they contemplate her situation, wondering what they should do to help her. They decide it can't be much fun to lie there; she should be moved. But how? And to where? Finally, the dog comes up with an inspired and unique idea and they work together through the night to make it happen." (Publisher's note)

"Although they depict a gruesome subject (r oadkill), there's nothing grotesque about the images. . . . Oskarsson offers a pleasing vision of the afterlife, as the dog and rat try to give the rabbit a gift--an experience it didn't have during its lifetime." Kirkus

Otoshi, Kathryn

★ **One**. KO Kids Books 2008 un il $16.95

Grades: PreK K 1   E

1. Counting 2. Color -- Fiction 3. Bullies -- Fiction 4. Courage -- Fiction

ISBN 0972394648; 9780972394642

Blue is a quiet color. Red's a hothead who likes to pick on Blue. Yellow, Orange, Green, and Purple don't like what they see, but what can they do? When no one speaks up, things get out of hand—until One comes along and shows all the colors how to stand up, stand together, and count.

"The use of colors and numbers gives the story a much-needed universality. . . . Otoshi cleverly offers a way to talk to very young children about the subject of bullying, even as she helps put their imaginations to work on solutions." Booklist

Two; by Kathryn Otoshi. Pgw 2014 40 p. color illustrations hbk $18.95

Grades: PreK K 1   E

1. Numbers 2. Friendship

ISBN 0972394664; 9780972394666

In this book by Kathryn Otoshi, "two is best friends with One. Whenever they'd get the chance, they'd dance! She'd sing and snap. He'd tappity-tap. What a pair they made! At the end of each day, they'd always say, 'ONE, TWO, I'll count on you, 'til the end, we'll be best friends.' Until Three jumps in between them . . . Suddenly One only wants to play with Three." (Publisher's note)

"Although the main storyline is simple, students will quickly pick up on the more complex mathematical and social relationships that unfold. This is certain to generate some teachable moments." Lib Med Con

★ **Zero**. Ko Kids Books 2010 un il $17.95

Grades: PreK K 1   E

1. Counting 2. Courage -- Fiction

ISBN 978-0-9723946-3-5; 0-9723946-3-X

Zero, dismayed by her big, empty, roundness, tries to force herself into the shape of the much-admired One, but must finally accept that she can only be Zero.

"What could have been a pedestrian just-be-yourself tale is distinguished by Otoshi's simple and lucid text, judicious use of white space, and a voice that stays sincere without becoming overly moralistic." Publ Wkly

Owen, Karen

I could be, you could be; [text by] Karen Owen; [illustrations by] Barroux. Barefoot Books 2009 un il $16.99

Grades: PreK K 1   E

1. Stories in rhyme 2. Imagination -- Fiction

ISBN 978-1-84686-405-6; 1-84686-405-4

LC 2008039825

"A boy and a girl make believe they are everything from astronauts to animals in the jungle. Each spread has a rhyming couplet that begins either with 'I' or 'You.' . . . This simple formula and clear writing make the story accessible for listeners who love to play pretend games as well as for beginning readers. Barroux's eye-catching acrylic and pencil illustrations are filled with vibrant color and evoke a joyful feeling." SLJ

Pace, Anne Marie

Vampirina ballerina; Anne Marie Pace; illustrated by LeUyen Pham. Disney Hyperion Books 2012 40 p. $14.99

Grades: PreK K   E

1. Ballet -- Fiction 2. Vampires -- Fiction 3. Picture books for children 4. Ballet dancing -- Fiction

ISBN 1423157532; 9781423157533

LC 2011026660

In this children's picture book, "a pale little vampire with tiny fangs and a black cape enrolls in an evening class at Madame Sang's Dance Studio. . . . Vampirina does her best to fit in" with the other girls. "The aspiring ballerina practices and practices until she is ready for her debut. On the big night, she dons her costume, overcomes stage fright, and takes a well-earned bow after the performance." (School Library Journal)

Pak, Soyung

Dear Juno; illustrated by Susan Kathleen Hartung. Viking 1999 un il hardcover o.p. pa $5.99

Grades: PreK K 1 2   E

1. Letters -- Fiction 2. Grandmothers -- Fiction 3. Korean Americans -- Fiction

ISBN 0-670-88252-6; 0-14-230017-9 pa

LC 98-43408

Although Juno, a Korean American boy, cannot read the letter he receives from his grandmother in Seoul, he understands what it means from the photograph and dried flower that are enclosed and decides to send a similar letter back to her

"The handsome layout, featuring ample white space and illustrations that cover anywhere from one page to an entire spread, perfectly suit the gentle, understated tone of the text." SLJ

Pal, Erika

Azad's camel. Frances Lincoln Children's Books 2010 un il $17.95

Grades: PreK K 1 2   E

1. Camels -- Fiction 2. Orphans -- Fiction 3. Arabian Peninsula -- Fiction

ISBN 1-84507-982-5; 978-1-84507-982-6

In a big Arabian city, an orphan boy is forced to work as a camel jockey—a dangerous job he doesn't like. But a new friendship and a magical escape into the desert are about to change his life .

"Pal's striking illustrations in watercolor and ink position sharply delineated characters in the foreground against soft, blurry desert backgrounds. Her heart-tugging tale also folds in a succint social-studies lesson, and a brief afterword explains the controversial 'sport' of camel racing." Kirkus

Palatini, Margie

Bad boys get henpecked! illustrated by Henry Cole. Katherine Tegen Books 2009 un il $17.99; lib bdg $18.89
Grades: PreK K 1 2   E
 1. Wolves -- Fiction 2. Chickens -- Fiction
 ISBN 978-0-06-074433-5; 0-06-074433-2; 978-0-06-074434-2 lib bdg; 0-06-074434-0 lib bdg
          LC 2008-11771

Bad boy wolves Willy and Wally try to get a chicken dinner by disguising themselves as the Handy-Dandy Lupino Brothers and going to work for a hen in need of household help.

"With its fast-paced language and witty narrative paired with lively alliteration and puns, the Bad Boys' latest tale will entertain and capture youngsters' imaginations. Cole deftly expresses humor and the power of understatement in his pencil and watercolor illustrations. Expressive facial expressions and body language tell all." SLJ

Boo-hoo moo; illustrated by Keith Graves. Katherine Tegen Books 2009 un il $17.99; lib bdg $18.89
Grades: K 1 2   E
 1. Cattle -- Fiction 2. Farm life -- Fiction
 ISBN 978-0-06-114375-5; 0-06-114375-8; 978-0-06-114376-2 lib bdg; 0-06-114376-6 lib bdg
          LC 2007024417

When Hilda Mae Heifer's trademark 'moo' starts sounding even worse, the other animals decide she is lonely and hold auditions to find her some singing partners.

"Palatini's prose is poetic, quirky, inventive, and just plain fun. . . . Graves escalates the sophisticated silliness with his wacky, superbly crafted, almost 3D illustrations." SLJ

★ The **cheese**; paintings by Steve Johnson and Lou Fancher. Katherine Tegan Books 2007 un il $16.99; lib bdg $17.89
Grades: K 1 2 3   E
 1. Nursery rhymes -- Fiction
 ISBN 978-0-06-052630-6; 0-06-052630-0; 978-0-06-052631-3 lib bdg; 0-06-052631-9 lib bdg
          LC 2006-18163

After they all agree to ignore the story of "The Farmer in the Dell," the rat, cat, dog, child, farmer, and his wife have a party featuring the tempting hunk of cheese.

"The folk-art quality of the illustrations is rich with country colors—barn reds, field greens, and earthy yellows, and the cartoon animals are funny and expressive. A smattering of words and music from the song is worked in effectively on most pages, and the full lyrics are printed on the last page." SLJ

Earthquack! illustrated by Barry Moser. Simon & Schuster Bks. for Young Readers 2002 un il $15.95; pa $6.99
Grades: PreK K 1 2   E
 1. Domestic animals -- Fiction
 ISBN 0-689-84280-5; 1-4169-0260-0 pa
          LC 2001-31302

When Chucky Ducky feels the earth beneath him grumble and rumble, he runs to alert the other barnyard animals to the coming earthquake, but just as a wily weasel is about to take advantage of their fears, the true source of the rumbling is revealed

"Moser captures the essence of Weasel's dark determination as well as the bug-eyed hysteria of the farm animals in his expressive graphite and transparent watercolor illustrations. . . . Palatini's text is funny, with contemporary dialogue, puns, and a fast-paced narrative rich in rhythm and alliteration." SLJ

Goldie and the three hares; illustrated by Jack E. Davis. Katherine Tegen Books 2010 un il $16.99
Grades: K 1 2 3   E
 1. Fairy tales 2. Rabbits -- Fiction
 ISBN 978-0-06-125314-0; 0-06-125314-6
          LC 2008036910

When Goldilocks, running from the three bears, falls down a rabbit hole and hurts her foot, a family of hares tries to help but she proves to be a very loud, demanding, and tenacious guest.

"The zingy prose begs for full-throttled performance . . . and there are plenty of visual laughs in both the Hares' wide-eyed, innocent dismay and Goldilocks' overweening narcissism." Publ Wkly

Gorgonzola; a very stinkysaurus. by Margie Palatini; illustrated by Tim Bowers. Katherine Tegen Books 2008 un il $16.99; lib bdg $17.89
Grades: PreK K 1 2   E
 1. Birds -- Fiction 2. Smell -- Fiction 3. Dinosaurs -- Fiction 4. Cleanliness -- Fiction
 ISBN 978-0-06-073897-6; 0-06-073897-9; 978-0-06-073898-3 lib bdg; 0-06-073898-7 lib bdg
          LC 2006002191

When Gorgonzola the dinosaur learns that everyone runs from him to avoid his smell, rather than out of fear, he is grateful to the little bird who shows him how to brush his teeth and wash

"The over-the-top illustrations of the grossed-out dinosaurs . . . will bring belly laughs to children and inspiration to the grownups who have to wrestle them into the bathtub or dentist's chair. Witty dialogue and an effective layout get the personal hygiene message across without being preachy or didactic." SLJ

Hogg, Hogg & Hog. Simon & Schuster Books for Young Readers 2011 un il $15.99
Grades: PreK K 1 2   E
 1. Pigs -- Fiction 2. Fashion -- Fiction 3. Domestic animals -- Fiction 4. City and town life -- Fiction
 ISBN 1-4424-0322-5; 978-1-4424-0322-2
          LC 2009053646

Three pigs achieve success in the big city by making oinking the ultimate in fashion, but their fresh, new idea captures the attention of some friends from back on the farm.

"Palatini's smart storytelling bustles with all the ringing phones and over-the-top bluster of 'big business' speech. Attentive text design places the emphasis in all the right places, making this a fun read-aloud. . . . Palatini has created a hilariously relatable tale by including all the old barnyard favorites. . . . Quirky illustrations rendered digitally and mainly in pinks, lavenders, and grays suit this unusual story." SLJ

No nap! yes nap! by Margie Palatini; illustrated by Dan Yaccarino. Little, Brown & Co. 2014 32 p. color illustrations (hardcover) $17
Grades: PreK   E
   1. Infants -- Fiction 2. Mother-child relationship -- Fiction 3. Stories in rhyme 4. Babies -- Fiction 5. Naps (Sleep) -- Fiction
ISBN 0316248215; 9780316248211
                             LC 2013024729
In this children's picture book with illustrator Dan Yaccarino, author "Margie Palatini brings her signature humor to this rollicking sing-song read-along, inviting readers on a fast-paced chase through every room in the house as we follow Mommy on her quest to settle Baby down for nap." (Publisher's note)

"Babies and toddlers will enjoy the rhythm and upbeat tempo of the text, and the oversize font and repetitive phrases will encourage emerging readers to participate. Both children and adults will enjoy the humorous touches in the cartoonlike drawings." Booklist

Piggie pie! illustrated by Howard Fine. Clarion Bks. 1995 un il $15; pa $5.95
Grades: PreK K 1 2   E
   1. Pigs -- Fiction 2. Wolves -- Fiction 3. Witches -- Fiction
ISBN 0-395-71691-8; 0-395-86618-9 pa
                             LC 94-19726
"Gritch the Witch sets out for Old MacDonald's Farm to get herself a meal of plump piggies. Alerted, however, . . . the swine hastily don sheep, cow, and other barnyard disguises and fool her. . . . The still-hungry Gritch is persuaded to give up by a Big Bad Wolf . . . and the two go off for lunch, each picturing the other made into a sandwich. . . . The exuberant illustrations are colorful and action-filled. Greedy (but not too bright) witch and wolf both get what they deserve in this thoroughly enjoyable romp." SLJ

★ **Three** French hens; a holiday tale. illustrations by Richard Egielski. Hyperion Books for Children 2005 un il $15.99
Grades: PreK K 1 2   E
   1. Foxes -- Fiction 2. Chickens -- Fiction 3. Christmas -- Fiction 4. New York (N.Y.) -- Fiction
ISBN 0-7868-5167-8
"The three French hens from the familiar Christmas song are sent by a Parisian lady to her boyfriend, Philippe Renard, in New York. Alas, the hens wind up in lost mail, and when they can't find Philippe in the phone book, they think perhaps they should translate his name: Phil Fox. They find Phil Fox, but he's a downtrodden fox living in the Bronx. . . . [This] is so much fun, it's hard to imagine an artist milking more laughs from it than Egielski. . . . Something really fresh for the holiday season." Booklist

The **three** silly billies; illustrated by Barry Moser. Simon & Schuster Books for Young Readers 2005 un il $15.95

Grades: PreK K 1 2   E
   1. Goats -- Fiction
ISBN 0-689-85862-0
                           LC 2002-155835
Three billy goats, unable to cross a bridge because they cannot pay the toll, form a car pool with The Three Bears, Little Red Riding Hood, and Jack of beanstalk fame to get past the rude Troll.

"Painted in cheery watercolors, Moser's figures are in contemporary dress and pop out from the white backgrounds. There is plenty of visual humor. . . . Palatini's hip and punny text is fun to read aloud." SLJ

Pallotta, Jerry
  Ocean counting; odd numbers. illustrated by Shennen Bersani. Charlesbridge 2004 un il $16.95; pa $6.95
Grades: PreK K 1   E
   1. Counting 2. Marine animals
ISBN 0-88106-151-4; 0-88106-150-6 pa
                            LC 98-46035
"Bersani's bright, realistic colored-pencil illustrations will lure readers into perusing the factoid-loaded, simple, conversational text. . . . This book offers a colorful, engaging, and intriguing slant on the technique of counting." SLJ

Pamintuan, Macky
  Twelve haunted rooms of Halloween. Sterling Children's Books 2011 un il $14.95
Grades: PreK K 1   E
   1. Counting 2. Ghost stories 3. Picture puzzles 4. Stories in rhyme 5. Halloween -- Fiction
ISBN 978-1-4027-7935-0; 1-4027-7935-6
A small bear journeys through a haunted house as rhyming text encourages readers to find and count holiday inspired items that have been hidden by the silly monsters.

"What raises this title above other books of this type . . . is the 'I Spy' type format. Each picture includes all of the items mentioned previously along with the new addition, and readers are invited to search each spread to find them. Children will want to pore over the not-too-scary pictures until they find every creature mentioned in the rhyme." SLJ

Panahi, H. L.
  Bebop Express; illustrated by Steve Johnson and Lou Fancher. Laura Geringer Books 2005 un il $15.99
Grades: K 1 2 3   E
   1. Stories in rhyme 2. Railroads -- Fiction 3. Jazz music -- Fiction
ISBN 0-06-057190-X
                           LC 2003-24244
A rollicking rhythmic express train takes passengers on a jazzy journey that celebrates the United States and its unique musical culture.

"The intricate collages use old photographs and vintage fabrics to obtain a unique look. Teeming with life, the art visually complements the noisy text." Booklist

Pancheri, Jan
  Brother William's year; a monk at Westminster Abbey. Frances Lincoln 2010 36p il $17.95
Grades: 2 3 4   E
   1. Year -- Fiction 2. Monks -- Fiction 3. Middle Ages -- Fiction 4. Westminster Abbey -- Fiction
ISBN 978-1-84507-953-6; 1-84507-953-1

"Narrated by a fourteenth-century monk, this lightly informative picture book takes readers through his activities during 12 months at Westminster Abbey. . . . Written and illustrated by the current head gardener at Westminster Abbey, this attractive picture book captures the rhythm of a monastery year." Booklist

Panzieri, Lucia

The **kindhearted** crocodile; by Lucia Panzieri; illustrated by AntonGionata Ferrari. Holiday House 2013 24 p. (hardcover) $16.95

Grades: PreK K 1 2   E

1. Pets -- Fiction 2. Crocodiles -- Fiction 3. Crocodiles as pets -- Fiction

ISBN 0823427676; 9780823427673

LC 2012025486

This children's story, by Lucia Panzieri, illustrated by Anton Gionata Ferrari, follows "a crocodile with the kindest of hearts that was gentle and sensitive, and dreamed of one day being a beloved pet in a happy family. Through the magic of a picture book and with an irrepressible desire to please, this ferocious-looking crocodile that tidies toys, washes dishes, and even fights monsters in bad dreams makes his own dream come true." (Publisher's note)

Parenteau, Shirley

Bears on chairs; illustrated by David Walker. Candlewick Press 2009 un il $15.99

Grades: PreK K   E

1. Stories in rhyme 2. Bears -- Fiction

ISBN 978-0-7636-3588-6; 0-7636-3588-X

LC 2008-937035

Four bears are happily seated on four chairs until Big Brown Bear shows up and demands a seat.

"Between the unerringly positive approach to a common early-childhood dilemma and the can't miss rhyme, this volume will likely find its place on many a daycare shelf." Kirkus

Parish, Herman

Amelia Bedelia bakes off; pictures by Lynn Sweat. Greenwillow Books 2010 64p il (An I can read book) $17.99

Grades: K 1 2   E

1. Cake -- Fiction 2. Baking -- Fiction 3. Contests -- Fiction 4. Household employees -- Fiction

ISBN 978-0-06-084358-8; 0-06-084358-6

Literal-minded housekeeper Amelia Bedelia lends a hand at the bakery and enters a cakemaking contest, with unexpected results.

Amelia Bedelia's first apple pie; pictures by Lynne Avril. Greenwillow Books 2010 un il $16.99; lib bdg $17.89

Grades: PreK K 1   E

1. Pies -- Fiction 2. Apples -- Fiction 3. Baking -- Fiction 4. Grandparents -- Fiction

ISBN 978-0-06-196409-1; 0-06-196409-3; 978-0-06-196410-7 lib bdg; 0-06-196410-7 lib bdg

LC 2010009379

While visiting her grandparents, literal-minded Amelia Bedelia finally learns, despite some mishaps, how to bake an apple pie.

"Children will find the humor relevant and funny. The illustrations flow well with the text." SLJ

Other titles about Amelia Bedelia as a child are:

Amelia Bedelia's first day of school (2009)

Amelia Bedelia's first valentine (2009)

Amelia Bedelia's first field trip (2011)

Go west, Amelia Bedelia! pictures by Lynn Sweat. Greenwillow Books 2011 64p il $17.99; lib bdg $18.89

Grades: K 1 2   E

1. Ranch life -- Fiction 2. West (U.S.) -- Fiction

ISBN 978-0-06-084361-8; 0-06-084361-6; 978-0-06-084362-5 lib bdg; 0-06-084362-4 lib bdg

LC 2010012429

Amelia Bedelia visits her uncle's dude ranch and makes herself at home on the range, getting all tied up (by her own lasso) and stopping a stampede (with only her own two hands)!

Parish, Peggy

★ **Amelia** Bedelia; pictures by Fritz Siebel. Newly illustrated I can read ed.; HarperCollins 1992 63p il (I can read book) $16.99; lib bdg $17.89; pa $3.99

Grades: K 1 2   E

1. Household employees -- Fiction

ISBN 0-06-020186-X; 0-06-020187-8 lib bdg; 0-06-444155-5 pa

LC 91010163

A newly illustrated edition of the title first published 1963

A literal-minded housekeeper causes chaos in the Rogers household when she attempts to make sense of some instructions.

Other titles in this series are:

Thank you, Amelia Bedelia (1993)

Good driving, Amelia Bedelia (1995) by Herman Parish

Come back, Amelia Bedelia (1995)

Amelia Bedelia and the surprise shower (1995)

Play ball, Amelia Bedelia (1996)

Bravo, Amelia Bedelia (1997) by Herman Parish

Amelia Bedelia 4 mayor (1999) by Herman Parish

Calling Doctor Amelia Bedelia (2002) by Herman Parish

Amelia Bedelia, bookworm (2003) by Herman Parish

Amelia Bedelia and the Christmas list (2003) by Herman Parish

Amelia Bedelia goes camping (2003) by Herman Parish

Happy haunting, Amelia Bedelia (2004) by Herman Parish

Amelia Bedelia, rocket scientist (2005) by Herman Parish

Be my valentine, Amelia Bedelia (2005) by Herman Parish

Amelia Bedelia under construction (2006) by Herman Parish

Amelia Bedelia's masterpiece (2007) by Herman Parish

Amelia Bedelia and the cat (2008) by Herman Parish

Amelia Bedelia talks turkey (2008) by Herman Parish

An Amelia Bedelia celebration [Contents: Amelia Bedelia Good work, Amelia Bedelia

Good driving, Amelia Bedelia

Bravo, Amelia Bedelia] (2009)

Amelia Bedelia bakes off (2010) by Herman Parish

Go west, Amelia Bedelia! (2011) by Herman Parish

An **Amelia** Bedelia celebration; four stories tall. [by] Peggy Parish & Herman Parish; [illustrated by] Lynn Sweat & Fritz Siebel. Greenwillow Books 2009 214p il $19.99
Grades: PreK K 1 2   **E**
1. Household employees -- Fiction
ISBN 978-0-06-171030-8; 0-06-171030-X
LC 2008043826
Four previously published stories featuring the extremely literal-minded Amelia Bedelia, with related activities and recipes. Includes CD.

Park, Frances
Good-bye, 382 Shin Dang Dong; [by] Frances and Ginger Park; illustrated by Yangsook Choi. National Geographic Soc. 2002 un il $16.95
Grades: K 1 2 3   **E**
1. Korea -- Fiction 2. Immigrants -- Fiction
ISBN 0-7922-7985-9
LC 2001-2976
Jangmi finds it hard to say goodbye to relatives and friends, plus the food, customs, and beautiful things of her home in Korea, when her family moves to America
"The oil paintings done in a simple, childlike style are formally framed with white space. . . . Children will find the details of cultural differences and the immigrant experience well evoked." SLJ

Park, Linda Sue
★ **Bee**-bim bop! illustrated by Ho Baek Lee. Clarion Books 2005 32p il $15; pa $6.99
Grades: PreK K 1 2   **E**
1. Stories in rhyme 2. Cooking -- Fiction 3. Korean Americans -- Fiction
ISBN 0-618-26511-2; 0-547-07671-1 pa
LC 2003027697
"Playful, cartoonlike drawings portray a round-faced girl helping her mother. . . . The illustrations . . . are very appealing. . . . The rhyme works well. A recipe follows the story." SLJ

★ The **firekeeper's** son; illustrated by Julie Downing. Clarion Books 2004 37p il $16; pa $6.99
Grades: 1 2 3 4   **E**
1. Korea -- Fiction
ISBN 0-618-13337-2; 0-547-23769-3 pa
LC 2002-13917
In eighteenth-century Korea, after Sang-hee's father injures his ankle, Sang-hee attempts to take over the task of lighting the evening fire which signals to the palace that all is well. Includes historical notes.
"Park's command of place, characterization, and language is as capable and compelling in this picture book as it is in her novels. . . . [This offers] lyrical prose and deftly realized watercolors and pastels." SLJ

★ The **third** gift. Clarion Books 2011 il $16.99
Grades: K 1 2   **E**
1. Magi -- Fiction 2. Father-son relationship -- Fiction
ISBN 978-0-547-20195-5; 0-547-20195-8;
9780547201955; 0547201958
LC 2010050819
"The hyperrealistic acryl-gouache illustrations depict the sandy beige hues and nuanced textures of a dry and inhospitable land, contrasting with the smooth skin and rounded cheeks of the young boy and his loving relationship with his father. This gorgeous picture book sheds thoughtful light on a fascinating facet of the Christmas story." SLJ

Xander's panda party; by Linda Sue Park and illustrated by Matt Phelan. Clarion Books 2013 40 p. (hardcover) $16.99
Grades: PreK K 1   **E**
1. Zoos -- Fiction 2. Parties -- Fiction 3. Stories in rhyme 4. Pandas -- Fiction 5. Zoo animals -- Fiction
ISBN 0547558651; 9780547558653
LC 2012039662
In this book by Linda Sue Park "the zoo's paucity of pandas doesn't impede Xander's party planning for long. He decides to invite all the bears. But Koala protests. She's not a bear--she's a marsupial! Does that mean she can't come? Xander rethinks his decision to invite only bears, and 'Calling all bears' evolves into 'Calling all creatures'" (Publisher's note)

Parker, Marjorie Blain
A **paddling** of ducks; animals in groups from A to Z. written by Marjorie Blain Parker; illustrated by Joseph Kelly. Kids Can Press 2010 il $16.95
Grades: PreK K 1   **E**
1. Animals 2. Alphabet
ISBN 978-1-55337-682-8; 1-55337-682-X
"This ABC book provides a delightfully offbeat introduction to collective nouns, featuring groups of animals at a Riviera-like resort locale with palm trees and a seaside Ferris wheel. . . . Even better than learning some of the unusual ways to refer to multiple animals is the way Kelly's soft-focus oil and acrylic paintings riff on the terms themselves. . . . The anthropomorphic animals feel anatomically authentic, but with exaggerated joie de vivre to spare." Publ Wkly

Parker, Michael
You are a star! Michael Parker; illustrations by Judith Rossell. Walker 2012 40 p. (hardback) $16.99
Grades: PreK K 1 2 3   **E**
1. Fear -- Fiction 2. Stars -- Fiction 3. Astronomy -- Fiction 4. Life (Biology) -- Fiction
ISBN 0802728413; 9780802728418; 9780802728425
LC 2011050073
In this children's bedtime story, by Michael Parker, illustrated by Judith Rossell, "readers take a journey through the night sky to the moment a star is born. Starting as a fire in the sky that explodes into millions of pieces, stars eventually become part of Earth with all the living things on it-meaning that everyone has a little bit of stardust inside them." (Publisher's note)

Parkhurst, Carolyn
★ **Cooking** with Henry and Elliebelly; illustrations by Dan Yaccarino. Feiwel and Friends 2010 un il $16.99
Grades: PreK K 1   **E**
1. Cooking -- Fiction 2. Siblings -- Fiction 3. Imagination -- Fiction
ISBN 978-0-312-54848-3; 0-312-54848-6
LC 2009050247
Five-year-old Henry, along with his two-year-old sister, pretend to make waffles on a make-believe television show.
"The entire story is written in dialogue and the sibling relationship is presented with skill. . . . The pure adventure

of creative play and experimentation will be a treat for any reader. . . . Yaccarino has created characters and an environment that grab readers' attention and won't let go." SLJ

Parnell, Peter

★ **And** Tango makes three; by Justin Richardson and Peter Parnell; illustrated by Henry Cole. Simon & Schuster Bks. for Young Readers 2005 un il $14.95
Grades: PreK K 1 2　　　　　　　　　　　　　　E
　1. Penguins -- Fiction 2. Homosexuality -- Fiction
ISBN 0-689-87845-1

At New York City's Central Park Zoo, two male penguins fall in love and start a family by taking turns sitting on an abandoned egg until it hatches

"Done in soft watercolors, the illustrations set the tone for this uplifting story, and readers will find it hard to resist the penguins' comical expressions. . . . This joyful story about the meaning of family is a must for any library." SLJ

Parot, Annelore

Kimonos. Chronicle Books 2011 un il
Grades: PreK K 1　　　　　　　　　　　　　　E
　1. Dolls -- Fiction 2. Japan -- Fiction
ISBN 145210493X; 9781452104935
　　　　　　　　　　　　　　　　LC 2011008003

Original French edition 2009

Inspired by traditional Japanese dolls, this story introduces readers to the Kokeshis' kimonos and hair-dos as well as Japanese culture. Contains die-cut pages, flaps and gatefolds.

"Sharp-eyed children will enjoy poring over the pages again and again. Scenes that evoke everyday life in Japan . . . add delightfully authentic cultural texture, while lift-the-flap and die-cut panels enhance the book's interactivity." SLJ

Partridge, Elizabeth

Oranges on Golden Mountain; illustrated by Aki Sogabe. Dutton Children's Bks. 2001 un il hardcover o.p. pa $6.99
Grades: K 1 2 3　　　　　　　　　　　　　　E
　1. China -- Fiction 2. Immigrants -- Fiction 3. Chinese Americans -- Fiction 4. San Francisco (Calif.) -- Fiction
ISBN 0-525-46453-0; 0-14-250033-X pa
　　　　　　　　　　　　　　　　LC 99-462287

When hard times fall on his family, Jo Lee is sent from China to San Francisco, where he helps his uncle fish and dreams of being reunited with his mother and sister

"The spirited story is beautifully written. . . . The striking, skillful paper-cut illustrations . . . create a vivid sense of place and do much to explain and extend the story's action." Booklist

Paschkis, Julie

Mooshka; written and illustrated by Julie Paschkis. Peachtree Publishers 2012 35 p.
Grades: PreK K 1　　　　　　　　　　　　　　E
　1. Magic -- Fiction 2. Quilts -- Fiction 3. Infants -- Fiction 4. Sisters -- Fiction 5. Picture books for children 6. Babies -- Fiction 7. Sharing -- Fiction
ISBN 9781561456208
　　　　　　　　　　　　　　　　LC 2011020463

In this picture book, "Karla loves her quilt, and Mooshka makes Karla feel safe, brightening dark days. Made by Karla's grandmother from scraps of old fabric, Mooshka is un-

usual because it talks to Karla, telling her the stories behind each piece of the quilt. . . . When Karla's life changes--her mother's bulging belly is a hint of baby Hannah's arrival--Mooshka goes strangely silent. . . . Soon, both children curl up under the quilt with Karla retelling the family stories." (Horn Book Magazine)

★ **P.** Zonka lays an egg; by Julie Paschkis. Peachtree Publishers 2015 32 p. color illustrations $16.95
Grades: PreK K 1 2　　　　　　　　　　　　　　E
　1. Eggs -- Fiction 2. Color -- Fiction 3. Chickens -- Fiction
ISBN 1561458198; 9781561458196
　　　　　　　　　　　　　　　　LC 2014006507

In this children's story, by Julie Paschkis, the "hen [named] P. Zonka spends her time taking in the beauty around her. . . . The other hens can't understand why she never lays eggs like they do. Finally, P. Zonka gives in and lays an egg. To everyone's delight, she produces a wondrous egg that contains all the colors and designs that she has stored in her creative imagination." (Publisher's note)

"Paschkis's watercolors are filled with repeated patterns and a beautiful use of black outlines. Some pages contain brightly colored backgrounds while on others, colors pop off bright white backgrounds. . . . P. Zonka's lesson is gently delivered: take time to produce something you will be proud of." Horn Book

Paterson, Katherine

★ **Brother** Sun, Sister Moon; Saint Francis of Assisi's Canticle of the Creatures. retold by Katherine Paterson; illustrated by Pamela Dalton. Chronicle Books 2011 un il
Grades: PreK K 1　　　　　　　　　　　　　　E
　1. Nature -- Fiction 2. Prayer -- Fiction
ISBN 0-8118-7734-5; 978-0-8118-7734-3
　　　　　　　　　　　　　　　　LC 2010035120

Reimagines Francis of Assisi's 1224 prayer of praise in celebration of God's gifts throughout the universe.

"As Paterson expresses thankfulness to God for various forces of creation . . . debut artist Dalton offers delicately detailed, loosely symmetrical cut-paper tableaus, set against black backdrops and framed by birds' nests, willow trees, vines, and branches." Publ Wkly

Patricelli, Leslie

Be quiet, Mike! Candlewick Press 2011 un il $14.99
Grades: PreK K 1 2　　　　　　　　　　　　　　E
　1. Stories in rhyme 2. Drums -- Fiction 3. Noise -- Fiction 4. Monkeys -- Fiction 5. Musicians -- Fiction
ISBN 978-0-7636-4477-2; 0-7636-4477-3
　　　　　　　　　　　　　　　　LC 2010044814

Monkey Mike is reprimanded for making noise when he taps pencils and clangs trash cans until he sees a drum set in the music store and puts his hands-on talents to work in a most impressive way.

"This rhythmic, rhyming romp about a youngster who must drum is illustrated with bold lines and colors in acrylic that suggest a jazzy ease. The bright, ever-changing background hues keep the focus on Mike and the onomatopoeic words scattered throughout the story." SLJ

The **birthday** box. Candlewick Press 2007 un il $15.99; bd bk $6.99

Grades: PreK   E
1. Boxes -- Fiction 2. Birthdays -- Fiction 3. Imagination -- Fiction
ISBN 978-0-7636-2825-3; 0-7636-2825-5; 978-0-7636-4449-9 bd bk; 0-7636-4449-8 bd bk
LC 2006-49084
"A child wearing only a diaper and a striped party hat gets a present from Grandma. . . . The toddler takes off the wrapping paper . . . and discovers A big brown box! A box is full of possibilities and this child lets imagination reign. . . . Patricelli's simple, first-person narration is refreshing. With bold black outlines, the acrylic paintings are rudimentary but nonetheless expressive and endearing." SLJ

★ **Higher!** higher! Candlewick Press 2009 un il $15.99; bd bk $6.99
Grades: PreK K 1   E
1. Play -- Fiction 2. Imagination -- Fiction
ISBN 978-0-7636-3241-0; 0-7636-3241-4; 978-0-7636-4433-8 bd bk; 0-7636-4433-1 bd bk
Boston Globe-Horn Book Award honor book: Picture Book (2009)
"As an adult pushes a pigtailed girl in a striped sweater and socks on a swing, the child calls out: 'Higher! Higher!' The ride gradually takes her from a giraffe's-eye view, to a mountaintop, to an airplane, and finally high enough to trade high fives with a one-eyed, green alien. . . . The repetitive text is ideal for new readers, and the cartoon paintings, though spare, provide plenty of room for imagination." SLJ

Potty. Candlewick Press 2010 un il $6.99
Grades: PreK   E
1. Board books for children 2. Toilet training -- Fiction
ISBN 978-0-7636-4476-5; 0-7636-4476-5
LC 2009-49045
Baby, a toddler, decides to use the potty for the first time.
This "appealing [book features] simple text, bright acrylic illustrations, and [an] everyday [situation] that [is] certain to engage the very young." SLJ

Tubby. Candlewick Press 2010 un il $6.99
Grades: PreK   E
1. Board books for children 2. Baths -- Fiction 3. Infants -- Fiction
ISBN 978-0-7636-4567-0; 0-7636-4567-2
LC 2009-49046
Baby loves playing during bath time.
This "appealing [book features] simple text, bright acrylic illustrations, and [an] everyday [situations] that [is] certain to engage the very young." SLJ

Patten, Brian
The **big** snuggle-up; [written by] Brian Patten & [illustrated by] Nicola Bayley. Kane Miller 2011 un il
Grades: PreK K 1   E
1. Stories in rhyme 2. Animals -- Fiction 3. Scarecrows -- Fiction
ISBN 1-61067-036-1; 978-1-61067-036-4
It all started with the scarecrow coming into the house out of the snow and bringing with him the mouse that lived up his sleeve. But it wasn't only these two who were looking for a warm place to snuggle up!
"The text is printed in a large, easy-to-read font on a cream-colored background and surrounded by Bayley's col-

ored pencil and crayon illustrations. The art is meticulously crafted, with attention given to every hair and whisker. . . . A lovely book about sharing and compassion." SLJ

Pattison, Darcy S.
19 girls and me; [by] Darcy Pattison; illustrated by Steven Salerno. Philomel Books 2006 un il $16.99
Grades: PreK K 1 2   E
1. School stories 2. Sex role -- Fiction
ISBN 0-399-24336-4
LC 2005020501
John Hercules is worried about being the only boy in his kindergarten class, but after the first week he stops worrying.
"The mixed-media illustrations include wild color combinations and dizzying perspectives that provide the backdrops for the children, drawn in a stylishly simple but endearing cartoon style." SLJ

The **journey** of Oliver K. Woodman; written by Darcy Pattison; illustrated by Joe Cepeda. Harcourt 2003 un il $16; pa $6.99
Grades: K 1 2 3   E
1. Travel -- Fiction
ISBN 0-15-202329-1; 0-15-206118-5 pa
LC 2001-5320
Oliver K. Woodman, a man made of wood, takes a remarkable journey across America, as told through the postcards and letters of those he meets along the way
"The boldly colored, textured illustrations were made with oils over an acrylic under-painting on boards. . . . A fresh, unusual tale." SLJ
Another title about Oliver K. Woodman is:
Searching for Oliver K. Woodman (2005)

Patz, Nancy
Babies can't eat kimchee! by Nancy Patz & [illustrated by] Susan L. Roth. Bloomsbury Children's Books 2007 un il $16.95
Grades: PreK K 1 2   E
1. Infants -- Fiction 2. Sisters -- Fiction 3. Korean Americans -- Fiction
ISBN 1-59990-017-3
A baby sister must wait to grow up before doing big sister things, such as ballet dancing and eating spicy Korean food.
This book's "Korean-American perspective and mixed-media collage illustrations set the title apart. . . . The illustrations use just the right colors and lines to capture the child's changing emotions." SLJ

Paul, Ann Whitford
Count on Culebra; go from 1 to 10 in Spanish. Holiday House 2008 un il $16.95
Grades: PreK K 1   E
1. Counting 2. Iguanas -- Fiction 3. Rattlesnakes -- Fiction 4. Desert animals -- Fiction 5. Spanish language -- Vocabulary
ISBN 978-0-8234-2124-4; 0-8234-2124-4
LC 2007017303
When Iguana stubs her toe and cannot make her popular candies known as cactus butter dulces, Culebra the rattlesnake finds a cure that introduces the Spanish words for the numbers from one to ten.
"The well-paced story exudes a charming silliness and invites participation. Bright cartoon-style illustrations,

rendered in gouache and colored pencil, nicely depict the foolishness and are large enough for group sharing. . . . The introduction of Spanish words and counting concepts along with the appealing art and offbeat story make this a treat." Booklist

Fiesta fiasco; illustrated by Ethan Long. Holiday House 2007 un il $16.95
Grades: PreK K 1 2 3   E
1. Gifts -- Fiction 2. Rabbits -- Fiction 3. Desert animals -- Fiction 4. Spanish language -- Vocabulary
ISBN 0-8234-2037-X; 978-0-8234-2037-7
LC 2006-12112
When shopping for Culebra's birthday, Conejo convinces his friends Iguana and Tortuga to buy all the wrong presents. Includes a glossary of Spanish words used.
"A fiery palette enlivens the simple cartoon artwork set in the desert. The scenes are fun to look at." SLJ
Other titles about these characters are:
Mañana Iguana (2004)
Tortuga in trouble (2009)

If animals kissed good night-- [by] Ann Whitford Paul; pictures by David Walker. Farrar, Straus and Giroux 2008 un il $16.95
Grades: PreK K 1   E
1. Stories in rhyme 2. Animals -- Fiction 3. Kissing -- Fiction 4. Parent-child relationship -- Fiction
ISBN 0-374-38051-1; 978-0-374-38051-9
LC 2006051108
Rhyming text explores what would happen if animals kissed like humans do, from a slow kiss between a sloth and her cub to a mud-happy kiss from a hippo calf to his father
Walker "gets great emotional mileage from his rounded, stuffed toy-like shapes, velvety colors, and tiny dot eyes; the characters radiate unconditional love. There's a lot to go 'Ahhhh' over." Publ Wkly

Snail's good night; by Ann Whitford Paul; illustrated by Rosanne Litzinger. Holiday House 2008 32p il $14.95
Grades: PreK K 1   E
1. Snails -- Fiction 2. Bedtime -- Fiction
ISBN 978-0-8234-1912-8; 0-8234-1912-6
LC 2007-614
When Snail realizes that his friends are going to bed, he begins a very long, very slow slide to wish them all good night.
"Created using watercolor, gouache, and colored pencil, the fanciful artwork features mild-mannered animal characters and a benevolent moon shining down on the world. . . . The large type and short sentences make this gently amusing story just right for beginning readers." Booklist

Word builder; illustrated by Kurt Cyrus. Simon & Schuster Books for Young Readers 2009 un il $16.99
Grades: PreK K 1   E
1. Authorship -- Fiction
ISBN 978-1-4169-3981-8; 1-4169-3981-4
LC 2007045244
Text explains how putting letters into words, words into sentences, sentences into paragraphs, and paragraphs into chapters ends up creating a book

"This oversize book uses direct language and terrific artwork to show children how literal and figurative construction works. . . . The art, rendered in pencil and digital color, seems almost three-dimensional and will fascinate readers." Booklist

Payne, Emmy
Katy No-Pocket; pictures by H. A. Rey. Houghton Mifflin 1944 un il lib bdg $17; pa $5.95
Grades: PreK K 1 2   E
1. Animals -- Fiction 2. Kangaroos -- Fiction
ISBN 0-395-17104-0 lib bdg; 0-395-13717-9 pa
Katy Kangaroo was most unfortunately unprovided with a pocket in which to carry her son Freddy. She asked other animals with no pockets how they carried their children but none of their answers seemed satisfactory. Finally a wise old owl advised her to try to find a pocket in the City, and so off she went and in the City she found just what she and Freddy needed

Peacock, Carol Antoinette
Mommy far, Mommy near; an adoption story. written by Carol Antoinette Peacock; illustrated by Shawn Brownell. Whitman, A. 2000 un il $16.99
Grades: PreK K 1 2   E
1. Adoption -- Fiction 2. Chinese Americans -- Fiction 3. Mother-child relationship -- Fiction
ISBN 0-8075-5234-8
LC 99-36108
Elizabeth, who was born in China, describes the family who has adopted her and tries to sort out her feelings for her mother back in China
"The situation is handled sensitively by the author, who writes from personal experience. . . . The faces deftly show the strong emotional bond between adoptive mother and daughter." Horn Book Guide

Pearce, Emily Smith
Slowpoke; illustrated by Scot Ritchie. Boyds Mills Press 2010 39p il $16.95
Grades: K 1 2 3   E
1. Speed -- Fiction 2. Family life -- Fiction
ISBN 978-1-59078-705-2; 1-59078-705-6
LC 2009033955
After pokey Fiona attends Speed School, where she learns to wash dishes, brush her teeth, and clean her room at the same time, she decides to demonstrate to her family the value of sometimes doing things more slowly.
"The text is interspersed with black-and-white illustrations that do a stellar job of conveying both leisure and frenzy. A clever early reader with challenging vocabulary and some food for thought to boot." Kirkus

Pearce, Philippa
The **squirrel** wife; illustrated by Wayne Anderson. Candlewick Press 2007 un il $16.99
Grades: K 1 2 3   E
1. Fairy tales 2. Fairies -- Fiction 3. Brothers -- Fiction 4. Squirrels -- Fiction 5. Forests and forestry -- Fiction
ISBN 978-0-7636-3551-0; 0-7636-3551-0
LC 2006052454
As a reward for saving the life of one of the feared green people, Jack acquires a beautiful and loving squirrel wife, knowledgeable in the secrets of the forest.

"Anderson's mixed-media illustrations strengthen the story's connections while amplifying the sense of enchantment with images of the elfin, lime-colored folk and the forest scenes, rendered in feathery strokes and an earthy green palette of moss and mushrooms. An intriguing, atmospheric offering." Booklist

Pearle, Ida

A **child's** day; an alphabet of play. Harcourt 2008 un il $12.95

Grades: PreK K
E

1. Alphabet 2. Play -- Fiction

ISBN 978-0-15-206552-2; 0-15-206552-0

LC 2007-33966

"This simple, attractive alphabet of action words and pictures depicts children engaged in play and other activities. . . . The design is particularly effective. Large, colorful cut-paper collages of multiethnic children feature interesting patterns that stand out against solid backgrounds." SLJ

Pearson, Debora

Sophie's wheels; by Debora Pearson; art by Nora Hilb. Annick Press 2006 un il lib bdg $18.95; pa $6.95

Grades: PreK
E

1. Growth -- Fiction 2. Wheels -- Fiction

ISBN 978-1-55451-038-2 lib bdg; 1-55451-038-4 lib bdg; 978-1-55451-037-5 pa; 1-55451-037-6 pa

"The language is descriptive. . . . The text is accompanied by simple, soft-washed watercolor illustrations. . . . This [is a] satisfying, peaceful tale." SLJ

Pearson, Susan

How to teach a slug to read; illustrated by David Slonim. Marshall Cavendish Children's 2011 un il $16.99

Grades: PreK K 1 2
E

1. Reading -- Fiction 2. Slugs (Mollusks) -- Fiction

ISBN 978-0-7614-5805-0; 0-7614-5805-0

LC 2010-24289

Provides simple, step-by-step instructions for teaching a slug how to read, including using Mother Slug rhymes, helping your slug sound out words, and making vocabulary lists.

"The two main slug characters are portrayed both affectionately and creatively. The literary references are fast and furious . . . and, fortunately, very accessible to current listeners. . . . Slonim's acrylic-and-charcoal illustrations have a pleasantly informal silliness, with rough, sketchy charcoal lines partnering with the paint." Bull Cent Child Books

We're going on a ghost hunt; by Susan Pearson; illustrated by S.D. Schindler. Marshall Cavendish 2012 32 p. (hardcover) $16.99

Grades: K 1 2 3
E

1. Children's poetry 2. Picture books for children 3. Ghost stories -- Fiction 4. Ghosts -- Fiction 5. Adventure and adventurers -- Fiction

ISBN 0761463070; 9780761463078; 9780761463085

LC 2011031815

In this children's picture book, the "familiar cadence and words associated with 'We're Going on a Bear Hunt' are giving a seasonal twist by [Susan] Pearson. These kids are heading off on a ghost hunt. . . . But when they reach the graveyard and a ghost appears, their courage wavers and they make a fast trip back home retracting their steps

through the woods, across the stream, cornfield and swamp to race into their beds." (Children's Literature)

Pearson, Tracey Campbell

★ **Bob**. Farrar, Straus & Giroux 2002 un il $16; pa $6.95

Grades: PreK K 1 2
E

1. Animals -- Fiction 2. Roosters -- Fiction

ISBN 0-374-39957-3; 0-374-40871-8 pa

LC 2001-40439

While looking for someone to teach him how to crow, a rooster learns to sound like many different animals and finds that his new skills come in handy

"The droll, repetitious text, perfect for reading aloud, is delightfully complemented by bright, lively watercolor illustrations." SLJ

Myrtle. Farrar, Straus and Giroux 2004 un il $15

Grades: PreK K 1 2
E

1. Mice -- Fiction 2. Aunts -- Fiction

ISBN 0-374-35157-0

LC 2003-44059

With the help of her favorite Aunt Tizzy, Myrtle the mouse learns to overcome her fear of the mean next-door neighbor. "Ages three to six." (Bull Cent Child Books)

"Pearson uses a fruit-colored palette with lots of design work to showcase her delightful mouse characters, brimming with personality." Booklist

Peet, Bill

Big bad Bruce. Houghton Mifflin 1977 38p il $17; pa $8.95

Grades: PreK K 1 2
E

1. Bears -- Fiction 2. Witches -- Fiction

ISBN 0-395-25150-8; 0-395-32922-1 pa

LC 76-62502

Bruce, a bear bully, never picks on anyone his own size until he is diminished in more ways than one by a small but very independent witch

"The language of the text is almost musical, with lots of words used for the sheer pleasure or appropriateness of their sounds. The illustrations are colorful and amusing." Child Book Rev Serv

Huge Harold; written and illustrated by Bill Peet. Houghton Mifflin 1961 un il hardcover o.p. pa $8.95

Grades: PreK K 1 2
E

1. Stories in rhyme 2. Rabbits -- Fiction

ISBN 0-395-18449-5; 0-395-32923-X pa

This story, "told in rhyming couplets and colored drawings, is action filled and laughable." Booklist

The **whingdingdilly**; written and illustrated by Bill Peet. Houghton Mifflin 1970 60p il $17; pa $9.95

Grades: PreK K 1 2
E

1. Dogs -- Fiction 2. Witches -- Fiction

ISBN 0-395-24729-2; 0-395-31381-3 pa

"Scamps, the dog, wants to be a horse, but a well-meaning witch turns him into a Whingdingdilly with the hump of a camel, zebra's tail, giraffe's neck, elephant's front legs and ears, rhinoceros' nose, and reindeer's horns." Adventuring With Books. 2d edition

Peete, Holly Robinson

My brother Charlie; written by Holly Robinson Peete and Ryan Elizabeth Peete with Denene Millner; pictures by Shane W. Evans. Scholastic Press 2010 un il

Grades: 1 2 3 4   E
1. Twins -- Fiction 2. Autism -- Fiction 3. Siblings -- Fiction
ISBN 0-545-09466-6; 978-0-545-09466-5
LC 2009005589

A girl tells what it is like living with her twin brother who has autism and sometimes finds it hard to communicate with words, but who, in most ways, is just like any other boy. Includes authors' note about autism

"The authors, a mother-daughter team, based this story on personal experience. Evans's bright, mixed-media illustrations skillfully depict the family's warmth and concern." SLJ

Pelham, David

★ **Trail**; paper poetry. Little Simon/Simon & Schuster Books for Young Readers 2007 un il $26.99

Grades: 1 2 3 4   E
1. Pop-up books 2. Snails -- Fiction
ISBN 978-1-4169-4894-0

In five pop-up spreads a silver line of poetry on white paper follows a small snail through its day, from roots and leaf on the forest floor to a pond at sunset. Pelham lays the verse out on a paper wheel that must be turned to be read in its entirety.

Pelley, Kathleen T.

Magnus Maximus, a marvelous measurer; [pictures by] S.D. Schindler. Farrar Straus Giroux 2010 un il $16.99

Grades: K 1 2   E
1. Counting -- Fiction 2. Measurement -- Fiction
ISBN 978-0-374-34725-3; 0-374-34725-5
LC 2006-51714

As the town's official measurer, Magnus Maximus is consumed with measuring and counting everything and everyone, missing out on life's simple pleasures, until one day when he breaks his glasses.

"Children will enjoy the humor in this eccentric's ever-increasing obsession. Fine ink lines and muted watercolors fill the illustrations with small details, add humor, and complete the story. The art firmly places it in the Victorian era, a time of scientific exploration. The style perfectly captures the focus of the marvelous measurer and his scientific obsession." SLJ

Raj, the bookstore tiger; illustrated by Paige Keiser. Charlesbridge 2011 un il lib bdg $15.95

Grades: K 1 2 3   E
1. Cats -- Fiction 2. Tigers -- Fiction 3. Books and reading -- Fiction
ISBN 978-1-58089-230-8; 1-58089-230-2
LC 2010007585

When a new manager brings Snowball, a grouchy cat, to the shop where Raj and his owner live and work, Snowball informs Raj that he is not the tiger everyone believes him to be.

"The lively, descriptive narrative will provide an entertaining read-aloud, while the cheery watercolor-and-pencil illustrations feature expressive feline and human characters. . . . A whimsical title with a positive message." Booklist

Pendziwol, Jean

Marja's skis; [by] Jean E. Pendziwol; pictures by Jirina Marton. Groundwood 2007 un il $17.95

Grades: 1 2 3   E
1. Canada -- Fiction 2. Skiing -- Fiction 3. Fathers -- Fiction 4. Immigrants -- Fiction 5. Lumber and lumbering -- Fiction
ISBN 978-0-88899-674-9

"Marja can hardly wait to be big and strong enough to help with Father's horses and attend school. . . . But after her father dies . . . being strong seems too hard. One day . . . Marja sees someone who has fallen through the ice and . . . she finds the courage to help him. . . . Evocative oil-pastels illustrate the text. . . . A simply told, emotionally resonant tale." Booklist

Penn, Audrey

A **bedtime** kiss for Chester Raccoon; illustrated by Barbara Gibson. Tanglewood 2011 il $7.95

Grades: PreK   E
1. Stories in rhyme 2. Board books for children 3. Fear -- Fiction 4. Bedtime -- Fiction 5. Raccoons -- Fiction
ISBN 978-1-933718-52-1; 1-933718-52-8
LC 2010046711

"As Chester Raccoon nestles into his lair, he begins to imagine frightening creatures in the light that streams across his bedroom. . . . The ink and watercolor illustrations are realistic and reassuringly expressive. . . . Designed for younger children, this board book features rounded corners, rhyming couplets, and a simpler text than the earlier books in the series. It should find an audience in most public libraries." SLJ
Other titles about Chester Raccoon are:
Chester Raccoon and the acorn full of memories (2009)
Chester Raccoon and the big bad bully (2008)
The kissing hand (2006)

Pennypacker, Sara

Pierre in love; pictures by Petra Mathers. Orchard Books 2007 un il $16.99

Grades: K 1 2   E
1. Love -- Fiction 2. Mice -- Fiction 3. Rabbits -- Fiction
ISBN 0-439-51740-0

Feeling "bloopy and love-swoggled" in the presence of Catherine, the elegant ballet teacher, a humble fisherman tries to muster the courage to reveal his affection for her.

"Subtleties abound, and the emotions may affect adults more than children. But the purity of the love will touch children, too, and both the words and the art are delightful." Booklist

★ **Sparrow** girl; illustrated by Yoko Tanaka. Hyperion 2009 un il $16.99

Grades: 1 2 3 4   E
1. Birds -- Fiction 2. Sparrows -- Fiction 3. China -- History -- 1949-1976 -- Fiction
ISBN 978-1-4231-1187-0; 1-4231-1187-7
LC 2009-6758

When China's leader declares war on sparrows in 1958, everyone makes loud noise in hopes of chasing the hungry birds from their land except for Ming-Li, a young girl whose compassion and foresight prevent a disaster

"Pennypacker strikes a suitably moralistic tone and tells her story with rich, descriptive detail. Tanaka matches the somber elegance of the text with opaque, folk-inspired paintings in a subdued palette. An author's note explains the difficult facts behind the story." Booklist

Perez, Amada Irma

My diary from here to there; story, Amada Irma Pérez; illustrations, Maya Christina Gonzalez. Children's Bk. Press 2002 un il $16.95

Grades: 2 3 4   E
1. Immigrants -- Fiction 2. Mexican Americans -- Fiction 3. Bilingual books -- English-Spanish
ISBN 0-89239-175-8

LC 2001-58251

A young girl describes her feelings when her father decides to leave their home in Mexico to look for work in the United States

"The diary entries, written in conversational English and Spanish, resonate with the tensions of the experience. . . . The full-page, bright acrylic paintings complement the text, with the blocky primitive forms adding a reassuring note to the whole." SLJ

★ **My** very own room; story by Amada Irma Pérez; illustrations by Maya Christina Gonzalez. Children's Bk. Press 2000 30p il $16.95

Grades: PreK K 1 2   E
1. Family life -- Fiction 2. Mexican Americans -- Fiction 3. Bilingual books -- English-Spanish
ISBN 0-89239-164-2

LC 00-20769

With the help of her family, a resourceful Mexican American girl realizes her dream of having a space of her own to read and to think

"Gonzalez' palette is replete with joyfully exuberant colors; rich magentas, purples, and blues contrast with the warm golds of faces and arms, and the dark eyes and hair offer further contrast with the backgrounds and skin colors. Pérez based this story on her own life . . . and the text . . . exudes a comfortably familiar, accessible voice." Bull Cent Child Books

Perez, L. King

First day in grapes; illustrated by Robert Casilla. Lee & Low Bks. 2002 un il $16.95

Grades: K 1 2 3   E
1. School stories 2. California -- Fiction 3. Migrant labor -- Fiction 4. Mexican Americans -- Fiction
ISBN 1-58430-045-0

LC 2001-38787

When Chico starts the third grade after his migrant worker family moves to begin harvesting California grapes, he finds that self confidence and math skills help him cope with the first day of school

This story "sheds light on the life of migrant children in a poignant, balanced manner. . . . The watercolor, colored-pencil, and pastel illustrations bring warmth and color to this portrait of life in rural California." SLJ

Pericoli, Matteo

Tommaso and the missing line. Alfred A. Knopf 2008 un il $15.99; lib bdg $18.99

Grades: K 1 2 3   E
1. Italy -- Fiction 2. Drawing -- Fiction 3. Lost and found possessions -- Fiction
ISBN 978-0-375-84102-6; 0-375-84102-4; 978-0-375-94102-3 lib bdg; 0-375-94102-9 lib bdg

When Tommaso discovers that a line is missing from his favorite drawing, he goes looking for it all around town and notices many lines he never saw before.

Pericoli "demonstrates remarkable draftsmanship and a vivid eye for detail and perspective; the mostly black-and-white pictures combine the elegant extravagance of architectural engravings with the playfulness and spontaneity of a great doodle. The Italian setting adds to the charm. . . . The design is striking. . . . Facing each illustration, the text drops out from solid orange; the effect is eye-popping." Publ Wkly

The **true** story of Stellina. Knopf 2006 un il $15.95; lib bdg $17.99

Grades: PreK K 1 2   E
1. Finches 2. New York (N.Y.)
ISBN 0-375-83273-4; 0-375-93273-9 lib bdg

The true story of a baby finch rescued and raised by the author and his wife when no zoo would take the abandoned bird fallen from her nest onto a busy street in the middle of New York City.

"A precise linguistic lyricism is at play. . . . The art is sophisticated and spare, but utterly accessible." Booklist

Perkins, Lynne Rae

★ The **cardboard** piano. Greenwillow Books 2008 un il $17.99; lib bdg $18.89

Grades: PreK K 1 2   E
1. Pianos -- Fiction 2. Friendship -- Fiction
ISBN 978-0-06-154265-7; 0-06-154265-2; 978-0-06-154266-4 lib bdg; 0-06-154266-0 lib bdg

LC 2007-39194

When Debbie tries to interest Tina in playing the piano by creating a cardboard keyboard, they find not only does it not have the same appeal but also that they do not need to share everything to be best friends.

"Perkins engages her young audience on three levels: the straightforward yet emotionally complex text; conversational asides in word balloons that develop characterization; and intricate pen-and-ink and watercolor illustrations. . . . Perkins presents the delicate nature of friendship without patronizing." Horn Book

Snow music. Greenwillow Bks. 2003 un il $15.99

Grades: PreK K 1   E
1. Snow -- Fiction 2. Sound -- Fiction
ISBN 0-06-623956-7

LC 2002-192758

When a dog gets loose from the house on a snowy day, his owner searches for him and experiences the sounds of various animals and things in the snow

"With whispery, musical words and detailed, soft-focus images that depict typical winter scenes, this gentle book gives children a sense of what snow is." SLJ

Perl, Erica S.

Dotty; illustrated by Julia Denos. Abrams Books for Young Readers 2010 un il $16.95

Grades: PreK K 1   E
1. School stories 2. Imaginary playmates -- Fiction 3. Teacher-student relationship -- Fiction
ISBN 978-0-8109-8962-7; 0-8109-8962-X

Ida's imaginary friend, Dotty, is tied to her with a blue string and when Ida's classmates tease her about Dotty, Ida is surprised to discover that her teacher carries a red string with her wherever she goes.

"Denos's illustrations subtly show the characters and the seasons changing, and the pressures of growing up. The text is best suited for one-on-one reading as the pictures have hidden nuggets of information for those who look carefully. This enjoyable tale of maturing at one's own pace and on one's own terms will resonate with children and parents alike." SLJ

Perlman, Janet

The **delicious** bug. Kids Can Press 2009 un il $16.95
Grades: PreK K 1 2 3   **E**
1. Insects -- Fiction 2. Chameleons -- Fiction
ISBN 978-1-55337-996-6; 1-55337-996-9

"With a flick of the tongue, two hungry chameleons catch the same bumblebug. Neither is willing to let go, and they have a knockdown-dragout fight to claim the snack. Eventually they realize, thanks to some equally hungry crocodiles, how much they need each other. The snappy story . . . is accompanied by cartoony digital illustrations bordered by panel drawings." Horn Book Guide

Perlman, Willa

Good night, world; illustrated by Carolyn Fisher. Beach Lane Books 2011 il $16.99
Grades: PreK K   **E**
1. Stories in rhyme 2. Bedtime -- Fiction
ISBN 978-1-4424-0197-6; 1-4424-0197-4
LC 2009053078

Rhyming text bids goodnight to the world and everything that is in it, including stars, streams, animals, and roads.

"The evocative rhyme scans perfectly. . . . Each verse is grandly illustrted with a large, double-page painting. Fisher's multicolored, textured paintings match the expansive tone of the book with a wide palette of swirling colors and layed details." SLJ

Perlov, Betty Rosenberg

Rifka takes a bow; by Betty Rosenberg Perlov; illustrated by Cosei Kawa. Kar-Ben Publishing 2013 32 p. $7.95
Grades: K 1 2 3   **E**
1. Picture books for children 2. Historical fiction 3. Theater, Yiddish -- Fiction 4. Jews -- United States -- Fiction
ISBN 0761381287; 9780761381273; 9780761381280
LC 2012028985

In this book, "Rifka lives in early 20th-century New York City with her glamorous, devoted parents, who are stars of the Yiddish theater. She marvels at the transformations that they undergo and revels in backstage life, with its dressing rooms filled with makeup, ribbons, and beads; its clever props . . . and even its rules for how to perform a kiss. . . . When Rifka accidentally ends up on stage during a performance, she blanches only for a minute." (Publishers Weekly)

Perret, Delphine

The **Big** Bad Wolf and me; [by] Delphine Perret. Sterling Pub. 2006 un il $9.95

Grades: K 1 2 3   **E**
1. Wolves -- Fiction
ISBN 978-1-4027-3725-1; 1-4027-3725-4
LC 2005031460

Original French edition 2005

When the Big Bad Wolf is mistaken for a dog, he comes to live in a boy's closet and eat chocolate chip cookies.

"Told in witty, thumbnail-size line drawings accompanied by brief text in very small type. . . . The story's humor, absurdity, and heart will please a wide readership." Booklist

The **Big** Bad Wolf Goes on Vacation; Delphine Perret. Sterling 2013 64 p. (hardcover) $12.95
Grades: K 1 2 3   **E**
1. Picture books for children 2. Summer -- Fiction 3. Voyages and travels 4. Humorous stories 5. Wolves -- Fiction 6. Vacations -- Fiction 7. Grandfathers -- Fiction 8. Characters in literature -- Fiction
ISBN 1402786336; 9781402786334
LC 2012009933

This book is Delphine Perret's sequel to "The Big Bad Wolf and Me" and "again stars Louis and his wolf friend, Bernard." Here, Louis and Bernard go on a summer trip with Louis's Grandpa. "During their travels, the three enjoy lunch in a park when they can't take Bernard into a restaurant, come upon a herd of odiferous cows blocking the roadway, and stop to stretch their legs near woods. Arriving at the seaside, Louis and Bernard partake of plenty of interactive seaside fun." (School Library Journal)

Perrin, Martine

Look who's there! Albert Whitman 2011 un il
Grades: PreK   **E**
1. Stories in rhyme 2. Board books for children 3. Animals -- Fiction
ISBN 080757676X; 9780807576762
LC 2010037841

Original French edition 2005

Text and images on die-cut pages lead the reader to discover the hiding places of a variety of animals in the water and near the shore.

This is a "striking hide-and-seek book. . . . A stylish presentation." Publ Wkly

What do you see? Albert Whitman 2011 un il
Grades: PreK   **E**
1. Board books for children 2. Animals -- Fiction
ISBN 0807567124; 9780807567128
LC 2010037477

Original French editiion 2005

Text and images on die-cut pages lead the reader to discover the hiding places of a variety of small animals.

"Kids will appreciate the objects profiled: boots, buckets, bibs, cribs, and the like." Booklist

Perry, Andrea

The **Bicklebys'** birdbath; illustrated by Roberta Angaramo. Atheneum 2010 un il $16.99
Grades: PreK K 1 2   **E**
1. Stories in rhyme
ISBN 978-1-4169-0624-7; 1-4169-0624-X

A cumulative rhyme in the style of "The House That Jack Built," describing the antics that occur when a mailman lands in a birdbath causing it to break.

"This jaunty cumulative tale has a pleasingly playful complexity, both in the wording and in its sense of time. Perry concocts a rhythmic text with unexpected twists and turns, and rather than moving the story forward, it works backward. . . . Sweetly clever." Kirkus

Peterkin, Allan

The flyaway blanket; illustrated by Emmeline Pidgen. Magination Press 2011 un il $14.95; pa $9.95

Grades: PreK K 1 2   E

1. Blankets -- Fiction 2. Mother-child relationship -- Fiction

ISBN 978-1-4338-1047-3; 1433810476; 978-1-4338-1046-6 pa; 1-4338-1046-8 pa

LC 2011011079

"In a sensitive lullaby, a small boy and his mother hang the laundry to dry on the clothesline, as she sings, 'time to fly, touch the sky, fly up, high up, wave goodbye.' Jake doesn't want to let go of his comforting blue blanket, but his mother assures him that it will soon be dry. As they sit together in the sun, Jake falls asleep, and a gust of wind sends the blanket sailing. . . . Pidgen's cheerful artwork is reassuring, with a bright palette, loose, sweeping lines, and plenty of attention on mother-child tenderness, human and animal alike. The message about attachment, security, and sometimes letting go is conveyed subtly and organically." Publ Wkly

Peters, Lisa Westberg

★ Cold little duck, duck, duck; pictures by Sam Williams. Greenwillow Bks. 2000 un il $15.99

Grades: PreK K 1   E

1. Stories in rhyme 2. Ducks -- Fiction 3. Spring -- Fiction

ISBN 0-688-16178-2

LC 99-29880

Early one spring a little duck arrives at her pond and finds it still frozen, but not for long

"The poetic text, well served by expressive watercolors, is set in a large black typeface (inviting letter and word recognition); colorful and playful typefaces are used for the rhythmic three-word refrains." Horn Book Guide

Frankie works the night shift; illustrated by Jennifer Taylor. Greenwillow Books 2010 un il $16.99

Grades: PreK K   E

1. Counting 2. Cats -- Fiction 3. Night -- Fiction

ISBN 978-0-06-009095-1; 0-06-009095-2

LC 2008012644

In this counting book, Frankie the cat's night prowling causes a ruckus, waking sleeping neighbors who do not share Frankie's love of the "night shift."

"Peters's spare text, full of exclamatory statements in the second half . . . moves the story forward with energy and speed, but Taylor's artwork is the showstopper, creating a surreal environment for Frankie's nocturnal adventures." Publ Wkly

Petersen, David

Snowy Valentine; written and illustrated by David Petersen. Harper 2011 un il $14.99

Grades: PreK K 1   E

1. Love -- Fiction 2. Gifts -- Fiction 3. Rabbits -- Fiction 4. Forest animals -- Fiction 5. Valentine's Day

-- Fiction

ISBN 978-0-06-146378-5; 0-06-146378-7

LC 2009027197

Jasper Bunny spends a snowy Valentine's Day visiting his forest friends in hopes of finding the perfect gift for his beloved Lilly.

"Petersen's whimsical, full-bleed illustrations with Victorian-pattern details add warmth and gentle humor to the story. . . . The timeless quality of the theme and perfect cast of supporting characters make this valentine story a head (or at least two rabbit ears) above the rest." SLJ

Peterson, Brenda

Seal pup rescue; by Brenda Peterson. Square Fish 2013 32 p. $15.99

Grades: K 1 2   E

1. Marine animals 2. Seals (Animals)

ISBN 1250027756; 9781250027757

This book, by Brenda Peterson, presents an "adaptation of the picture book 'Leopard & Silkie' [and is designed] for new readers who love animals. [Noting that] baby seals can swim soon after they are born, but they also need to rest on shore [it asks] how can they stay safe if the beach is full of dogs and people?" (Publisher's note)

Pfeffer, Wendy

★ Light is all around us; by Wendy Pfeffer; illustrated by Paul Meisel. First edition Harper, an imprint of HarperCollinsPublishers 2014 40 p. (hardback) $17.99

Grades: K 1 2 3   E

1. Light

ISBN 0060291214; 9780060291211; 9780064409247

LC 2013021512

This children's book, by Wendy Pfeffer and illustrated by Paul Meisel, shows children that light "comes in many forms: Light from the sun brightens our day, firelight flickers in the night, electric lights fill our homes--and some animals even make the sea glow! . . . This is a Stage 2 Let's-Read-and-Find-Out, which means the book explores more challenging concepts for children in the primary grades and supports the Common Core Learning Standards and Next Generation Science Standards." (Publisher's note)

"This strong series entry introduces youngsters to light: where it comes from, how fast it travels, and how it enables us to see. The prose is generally lively, but Pfeffer is all business when it comes to scientific explanations. Lighthearted paintings, outlined in pen and ink, add humor but never distract from the text. Three simple experiments are appended." Horn Book

Pfister, Marcus

Questions, questions; [translated by NordSüd Verlag; English adaptation by Marcus Pfister and Susan Pearson] NorthSouth 2011 un il $16.95

Grades: PreK K   E

1. Nature 2. Questions and answers

ISBN 978-0-7358-4000-3; 0-7358-4000-8

First published in Switzerland

Questions on nature.

"Pfister has created images as pithy as they are poignant, boldly graphic and dramatically cropped against white backgrounds. A blue-headed songbird is reminiscent of Asian watercolor; a storm cloud looks like it's been fashioned from salt dough; falling leaves seem cut from pieces of thickly tufted carpet. Although each was created using the same painted paper method (explained on the final page), the results are as varied as the questions." Publ Wkly

Snow puppy. North-South 2011 il $16.95
Grades: PreK K 1   E
1. Dogs -- Fiction 2. Snow -- Fiction 3. Christmas -- Fiction
ISBN 978-0-7358-4031-7; 0-7358-4031-8
A puppy is lost in the snowy woods and needs to make his way home.
"Rascal is a big-nosed scamp, full of curiosity and joy. Pfister's scenes are speckled throughout with the falling snow, wintry whites contrasting with the forest browns. This nicely captures a puppy's (or a child's) distractibility." Kirkus

Pham, LeUyen
★ **All** the things I love about you; written and illustrated by LeUyen Pham. Balzer + Bray 2010 un il $16.99
Grades: PreK K 1 2   E
1. Love -- Fiction 2. Mother-son relationship -- Fiction
ISBN 978-0-06-199029-8; 0-06-199029-9
LC 2009054255
A mother relates some of the many things that she loves about her young son.
"In capturing the goofy spontaneity of affection and everyday family life without a whiff of treacle, Pham proves once again that she's among the most natural and gifted illustrators working today." Publ Wkly

Phillipps, Julie C.
★ **Wink**: the ninja who wanted to be noticed. Viking Children's Books 2009 un il $15.99
Grades: K 1 2 3   E
1. School stories 2. Ninja -- Fiction
ISBN 978-0-670-01092-9; 0-670-01092-8
LC 2008-23238
Although ninjas should be silent and use stealth, Wink finds his enthusiasm gets him into trouble with his teacher until he finds the perfect way to express both traits.
"The story's oft-told message of acceptance has been invigorated with originality and humor. The collage-style illustrations often appear to have a three-dimensional effect and Wink practically bounds off the pages with barely contained energy." SLJ
Another title about Wink is:
Wink: the ninja who wanted to nap (2011)

Wink: the ninja who wanted to nap; by J.C. Phillipps. Viking 2011 un il $15.99
Grades: K 1 2 3   E
1. Fame -- Fiction 2. Japan -- Fiction 3. Ninja -- Fiction 4. Sleep -- Fiction
ISBN 978-0-670-01192-6; 0-670-01192-4
LC 2010025107
Wink loves being the most famous ninja in Japan but when he needs a nap his fans will not leave him alone, and so he seeks guidance from his former teacher, Master Zutsu.
"Phillipps offers wit aplenty in cut-paper compositions that match Wink's boundless energy and bravado. Even when sleepy, her hero demands to be noticed." Publ Wkly

Pichon, Liz
Penguins. Orchard Books 2008 un il lib bdg $12.99
Grades: PreK K   E
1. Zoos -- Fiction 2. Cameras -- Fiction 3. Penguins -- Fiction
ISBN 978-0-545-02215-6 lib bdg; 0-545-02215-0 lib bdg
LC 2007-40419
Penguins at the zoo have an exciting afternoon when one finds a camera left behind by a visitor.
"The cartoon style of these pastel illustrations is as light and playful as the text. The sweet faces show a lot of expression, while the aqua and purple backgrounds highlight their antics." SLJ

The **three** horrid little pigs; by Liz Pichon. Tiger Tales 2008 un il $15.95
Grades: PreK K 1 2   E
1. Pigs -- Fiction 2. Wolves -- Fiction
ISBN 978-1-58925-077-2; 1-58925-077-X
When their mother sends them packing, three pigs find despicable ways to find new accommodations, but when the big, friendly wolf tries to show them the error of their ways, the pigs respond by huffing and puffing.
"The lively narrative, printed in playfully arranged text of varying size, is well suited for spirited read-alouds, as are the colorful illustrations that add to the hilarity with expressive characters. Children will enjoy the clever twist on a familiar story." Booklist

Pien, Lark
★ **Mr.** Elephanter. Candlewick Press 2010 un il $14.99
Grades: PreK K   E
1. Nannies -- Fiction 2. Elephants -- Fiction
ISBN 978-0-7636-4409-3; 0-7636-4409-9
LC 2010-07577
From early morning until sunset, beloved Mr. Elephanter takes care of the rambunctious youngsters of the Elephantery, preparing their breakfast, taking them to the park, tucking them in for naps, and joining them at play.
"The simple story will speak to youngsters, and Pien's clever wording captures the humor in daily life. The sketchy watercolor illustrations portray both movement and story well." SLJ

Pilkey, Dav
The **Hallo-wiener**. Blue Sky Press (NY) 1995 un il $16.95; pa $5.99
Grades: PreK K 1 2   E
1. Dogs -- Fiction 2. Halloween -- Fiction
ISBN 0-590-41703-7; 0-439-07946-2 pa
LC 94-40949
All the other dogs make fun of Oscar the dachshund until one Halloween when, dressed as a hot dog, Oscar bravely rescues the others
"Pilkey's bold, colorful illustrations add life to his simple tale of courage and friendship." Horn Book Guide

★ The **paperboy**; story and paintings by Dav Pilkey. Orchard Bks. 1996 un il $16.95; pa $6.99

Grades: PreK K 1 2   E
1. Newspaper carriers -- Fiction
ISBN 0-531-09506-1; 0-531-07139-1 pa
                                                    LC 95-30641
A Caldecott Medal honor book, 1997
"The palette of the artwork is rich and inviting, and an emphasis is put on balance and geometric form, giving solidity to this celebration of routine. A meditative evocation of the extraordinary aspects of ordinary living." Horn Book Guide

Pinder, Eric
If all the animals came inside; by Eric Pinder; illustrated by Marc Brown. Little, Brown and Company 2012 40 p.
Grades: PreK K 1 2   E
1. Home -- Fiction 2. Stories in rhyme 3. Animals -- Fiction 4. Picture books for children
ISBN 0316098833; 9780316098830
                                                   LC 2011020100
In this picture book, a "young boy imagines the riot that would ensue if his house were overrun with wild animals. . . . The hodgepodge of animals ranges from forest chipmunks and savanna giraffes to Australian kangaroos and even an octopus. And they all come with mischief in mind. . . . From ruining the furniture and eating all the food to taking up the comfiest places, they would eventually leave no room for the boy and his family, relegating them to sleeping outside. And in fact, the boy wisely decides in the end that, as much fun as all the animals might be, he will be satisfied with just his cat and dog." (Kirkus)

Pinfold, Levi
Black dog; Levi Pinfold. Candlewick Press 2012 32 p. ill. (hardcover) $15.99
Grades: PreK K 1 2   E
1. Dogs -- Fiction 2. Fear -- Fiction 3. Picture books for children 4. Family life -- Fiction
ISBN 0763660973; 9780763660970
                                                   LC 2011048380
Boston Globe-Horn Book Honor: Picture Book (2013).
This book tells how "when the Hope family wakes up one morning, they're stunned to see 'a black dog the size of an elephant' outside their house. . . . The youngest Hope, known as Small, fearlessly marches out to meet the humongous pooch. Singing a taunting rhyme, she entices him to chase her, darting under the bridge, through the playground slide, and back home through the cat flap in the door. With each obstacle negotiated, the dog shrinks somewhat, until . . . he clearly has become the new house pet." (Bulletin of the Center for Children's Books)

★ The Django. Templar Books 2010 un il $16.99
Grades: K 1 2   E
1. Banjos -- Fiction 2. Gypsies -- Fiction 3. Musicians -- Fiction 4. Imaginary playmates -- Fiction
ISBN 978-0-7636-4788-9; 0-7636-4788-8
A young Gypsy boy named Jean has an imaginary friend, Django, who keeps getting him in trouble and eventually is "sent away," but whenever Jean plays the banjo he continues to feel close to Django. Inspired by the life of jazz musician Django Reinhardt; includes facts about his life.
"Fish-eyed perspectives and generous detailing almost suck readers' gazes into Pinfold's exotic and pastoral artwork. Once in, children will revel in the bouncy rhythms and

nonsense words sprinkled throughout the fun-to-read-and-hear narrative." Booklist

Pinkney, Andrea Davis
★ Boycott blues; how Rosa Parks inspired a nation. illustrations by Brian Pinkney. Greenwillow Books 2008 un il $16.99; lib bdg $17.89
Grades: 1 2 3 4   E
1. Civil rights activists 2. African Americans -- Fiction 3. Montgomery (Ala.) -- Fiction
ISBN 978-0-06-082118-0; 0-06-082118-3; 978-0-06-082119-7 lib bdg; 0-06-082119-1 lib bdg
                                                   LC 2006-38273
Illustrations and rhythmic text recall the December, 1955, bus boycott in Montgomery, Alabama.
"Color and movement are vibrant components in this extraordinary book. . . . Text and illustration work in perfect sync. Andrea Pinkney chose the rhythm of the blues as cadence for the guitar-strumming hound-dog narrator. . . . The evocative text is bolstered by Brian Pinkney's perceptive vision. . . . Against electric blues and greens diffused with streaks of black line, Pinkney's artwork rivets the eye." SLJ
Includes bibliographical references

★ Peggony-Po; a whale of a tale. illustrated by Brian Pinkney. Jump at the Sun/Hyperion Books for Children 2006 un il $16.99
Grades: K 1 2 3   E
1. Tall tales 2. Whales -- Fiction 3. Whaling -- Fiction 4. African Americans -- Fiction
ISBN 0-7868-1958-8
                                                   LC 2005047537
Peggony-Po, carved out of wood by his father, a one-legged whaler, determines to catch the huge whale that ate his father's leg.
"Told with humor and verve, this [is a] rollicking tall tale. . . . The illustrations brim with activity and energy." SLJ

Pinkney, Jerry
The grasshopper & the ants; Jerry Pinkney. Little, Brown & Co. 2015 40 p. (hardcover) $18
Grades: PreK K 1 2   E
1. Ants 2. Fables 3. Winter 4. Grasshoppers 5. Folklore
ISBN 0316400815; 9780316400817
                                                   LC 2013042074
In this fable, by Jerry Pinkney, "a playful grasshopper wonders why the busy ants around him won't join in his merrymaking as the seasons pass by. But when winter arrives, he soon sees the value of his friends' hard work--just as the ants learn the value of sharing what they've worked for." (Publisher's note)
"Moving right up Maslow's hierarchy of needs, Pinkney transforms Aesop's harsh fable about the consequences of improvidence into one celebrating the value of the arts. . . . Pinkney's woodland scenes, in his signature style, teem with recognizable flora, insects, and seasonal activity; once again, there's a wealth of variety in the endpapers plus both jacket and binding art, none of it to be missed. A genial note apologizes for depicting ants and grasshopper in different scale. No need; it's all just right as it is." Horn Book
Grasshopper and the ants

★ The **lion** & the mouse. Little, Brown Books for Young Readers 2009 un il $16.99

Grades: PreK K 1 2   E

1. Fables 2. Authors 3. Folklore 4. Stories without words 5. Storytellers

ISBN 978-0-316-01356-7; 0-316-01356-0

LC 2008-43852

Awarded the Caldecott Medal (2010)

Boston Globe-Horn Book Award honor book: Picture Book (2010)

In this wordless retelling of an Aesop fable, an adventuresome mouse proves that even small creatures are capable of great deeds when he rescues the King of the Jungle.

Young readers will be drawn "into watercolors of . . . detail and splendor. Pinkney's soft, multihued strokes make everything in the jungle seem alive. . . . His luxuriant use of close-ups humanizes his animal characters without idealizing them." Booklist

The **little** match girl; [by] Hans Christian Andersen; adapted and illustrated by Jerry Pinkney. Phyllis Fogelman Books 1999 un il hardcover o.p. pa $6.99

Grades: 1 2 3 4   E

1. Fairy tales

ISBN 0-8037-2314-8; 0-14-230188-4 pa

LC 99-13814

The wares of the poor little match girl illuminate her cold world, bringing some beauty to her brief, tragic life

"A faithful retelling of a classic tale. . . . The story's haunting death imagery . . . may disturb the very young, but ultimately Pinkney's vision proves as transcendent as Andersen's." Publ Wkly

★ The **nightingale**; [by] Hans Christian Andersen; adapted and illustrated by Jerry Pinkney. Phyllis Fogelman Bks. 2002 un il $16.99

Grades: 2 3 4   E

1. Nightingales -- Fiction

ISBN 0-8037-2464-0

LC 2001-47601

Despite being neglected by the emperor for a jewel-studded bird, the little nightingale revives the dying ruler with its beautiful song. A retelling set in Morocco

This "is a pleasing version of the classic, fresh in its interpretation but true to the spirit of the original. . . . Each double-page spread is illuminated by artwork that glows with rich colors and teems with lively details. Done in graphic, gouache, and watercolor, the large, gracefully composed illustrations feature a profusion of patterns." Booklist

★ **Rikki**-tikki-tavi; by Rudyard Kipling; adapted and illustrated by Jerry Pinkney. Morrow Junior Bks. 1997 un il $16.99; pa $6.99

Grades: 1 2 3 4   E

1. Poets 2. Authors 3. Novelists 4. Memoirists 5. India -- Fiction 6. Cobras -- Fiction 7. Children's authors 8. Short story writers 9. Mongooses -- Fiction 10. Nobel laureates for literature

ISBN 0-688-14320-2; 0-06-058785-7 pa

LC 96-51194

This is a retelling of the story from Rudyard Kipling's The jungle book in which a mongoose saves an English boy and his family from cobras in their garden in India

"Dramatic in content, sensitive in line, and rich with color, the illustrations in this picture book make full use of the broad, double-page spreads. Children who are not familiar with the story will be captivated; those who have had the story read to them before will find new things to shiver over." Booklist

★ The **tortoise** & the hare; Jerry Pinkney. Little, Brown and Co. 2013 40 p. $18

Grades: PreK K   E

1. Fables 2. Animals -- Fiction 3. Folklore

ISBN 0316183563; 9780316183567

LC 2012048426

In this book, by Jerry Pinkney, "even the slowest tortoise can defeat the quickest hare, and even the proudest hare can learn a timeless lesson from the most humble tortoise: Slow and steady wins the race! Here is a . . . journey from starting line to finish that embodies the bravery, perseverance, and humility we can all find inside ourselves." (Publisher's note)

"Following up on his superb rendition of The Lion & the Mouse (Little, Brown, 2009), Pinkney has created yet another stunning interpretation of a classic tale in this virtually wordless picture book... Tortoise and Hare, each sporting a bandana, are joined by their animal friends at the starting line for the famous race...Pinkney uses watercolor, colored pencil, and pastel paintings to create vibrant characters that are in colorful contrast to the tans and natural browns of the desert... Pinkney takes care to show Tortoise overcoming challenges and Hare demonstrating good sportsmanship and healthy competition. An artist's note explains the creative process and motivation for retelling the well-known tale. This spectacular success is certain to become a classic in its own right." (School Library Journal)

★ **Twinkle,** twinkle, little star. Little, Brown Books 2011 un il $16.99

Grades: PreK   E

1. Nursery rhymes 2. Stars -- Fiction 3. Chipmunks -- Fiction

ISBN 978-0-316-05696-0; 0-316-05696-0

"The song 'Twinkle, Twinkle, Little Star' proves lines of text for this imaginative picture book, in which a little chipmunk emerges from the safety of its burrow to discover the natural world. . . . This appropriate theme for young children finds expression in a series of vividly imagined, gracefully composed, and beautifully detailed illustrations, created using pencil, watercolors, and colored pencils. . . . This evocative picture book offers a rewarding reading experience at bedtime, or any time." Booklist

★ The **ugly** duckling; [by] Hans Christian Andersen; adapted and illustrated by Jerry Pinkney. Morrow Junior Bks. 1999 un il $16.99; lib bdg $17.89

Grades: 1 2 3 4   E

1. Fairy tales 2. Swans -- Fiction

ISBN 0-688-15932-X; 0-688-15933-8 lib bdg

LC 98-23604

A Caldecott Medal honor book, 2000

An ugly duckling spends an unhappy year ostracized by the other animals before he grows into a beautiful swan

"This is an elegantly accessible retelling, with illustrations full of lively, emotive animals and the kind of vigorous

movement that young children are bound to find appealing."
Bull Cent Child Books

Pinkney, Sandra L.

Read and rise; photographs by Myles C. Pinkney; foreword by Maya Angelou. Scholastic 2006 un il $15.99
Grades: PreK K 1   E
1. Reading 2. African American children
ISBN 0-439-30929-8

Photographs and poetic text celebrate reading as a means of encouraging African American children to pursue their dreams

"Powerful verbs match the vivid portrayal of children succeeding." SLJ

Pinkwater, Daniel Manus

★ **Beautiful** Yetta; the Yiddish chicken. by Daniel Pinkwater; illustrated by Jill Pinkwater. Feiwel and Friends 2010 un il $16.99
Grades: PreK K 1 2   E
1. Parrots -- Fiction 2. Chickens -- Fiction 3. Spanish language -- Vocabulary 4. Yiddish language -- Vocabulary 5. Brooklyn (New York, N.Y.) -- Fiction
ISBN 978-0-312-55824-6; 0-312-55824-4

"With wry humor, this multilingual picture book tells the story of a brave chicken, Yetta. Determined that she will not be soup, she escapes from a delivery crate and runs into the streets of Brooklyn. . . . She saves a little green parrot from a pouncing cat, and the wild parrots who witness the act welcome her and show her how to find food. Yetta speaks Yiddish (gevahlt!), and her speech is printed in both Hebrew and English alphabets with the English translation. The rich language mix does not stop there, though. The parrots speak Spanish, and their dialogue, shown in italics, includes a pronunciation guide. A warm twist on the immigration story that celebrates the richness of urban diversity." Booklist

I am the dog; by Daniel Pinkwater; illustrated by Jack E. Davis. Harper 2010 un il $16.99
Grades: PreK K 1   E
1. Dogs -- Fiction
ISBN 978-0-06-055505-4; 0-06-055505-X

Jacob the boy trades places with Max the dog.

"This amiable and impressive walk for Pinkwater breezily showcases his skill as a comic storyteller. . . . Davis keeps the dry humor right up on the surface, the tone bright . . . but not frantic." Kirkus

Pinkwater, Daniel Manus, 1941-

Bear in love; by Daniel Pinkwater; illustrations by Will Hillenbrand. 1st ed. Candlewick Press 2012 40 p. col. ill. (reinforced) $15.99
Grades: PreK K 1 2   E
1. Bears -- Fiction 2. Friendship -- Fiction 3. Picture books for children 4. Humorous stories 5. Rabbits -- Fiction
ISBN 0763645699; 9780763645694
LC 2011046620

This picture book is the story of an "impulsive, happy-go-lucky bear [who] keeps finding carrots on a flat rock outside his cave, left by some anonymous well-wisher. After days of this, the bear places honeycomb on the rock as a lure

. . . , and pretty soon there's a full-scale war of random acts of kindness going on." (Publishers Weekly)

★ **Bear's** picture; written by Daniel Pinkwater; illustrated by D. B. Johnson. Houghton Mifflin Company 2008 un il $16
Grades: K 1 2 3   E
1. Bears -- Fiction 2. Painting -- Fiction
ISBN 978-0-618-75923-1; 0-618-75923-9
LC 2007-15149

A newly illustrated editition of the title first published 1972 by Holt, Rinehart and Winston

A bear continues to paint what he likes despite criticism from two passing gentlemen.

This is "a quirky, sardonic, and highly entertaining view of what makes art. . . . Johnson . . . provides . . . fabulous mixed-media artwork, including paper sculptures that add both angular dimension and a wry touch to the simple story." Booklist

Beautiful Yetta's Hanukkah Kitten; by Daniel Manus Pinkwater; illustrated by Jill Pinkwater. Feiwel & Friends 2014 32 p. color illustrations $17.99
Grades: PreK K 1 2   E
1. Cats -- Fiction 2. Parrots -- Fiction 3. Hanukkah -- Fiction 4. Chickens -- Fiction 5. City and town life -- Fiction
ISBN 0312621345; 9780312621346

In this children's book, by Daniel Pinkwater, illustrated by Jill Pinkwater, "Yetta, beautiful Yetta, manages to escape from the butcher's shop. But now she is lost in Brooklyn - a strange place filled with rude rats and dangerous buses! . . . But then, brave Yetta saves a small green bird from a sneaky cat, and his friends, the wild parrots of Brooklyn, are very grateful. . . . Has beautiful Yetta found her new home?" (Publisher's note)

"In her second book, the Brooklyn-based Jewish-mama hen and her Spanish-speaking parrot pals find a lost kitten during Hanukkah. Yetta knows what to do: 'take her to the old grandmother!' Kitten and Bubbie find companionship--and the birds benefit from homemade latkes. The speech-bubble text is in English and Spanish or Yiddish (phonetic pronunciation included). Energetic limited-palette illustrations fly off the pages." Horn Book

Piper, Watty

★ The **little** engine that could; retold by Watty Piper; illustrated by George & Doris Hauman. Grosset & Dunlap 2009 un il $17.99
Grades: PreK K 1 2   E
1. Toys -- Fiction 2. Railroads -- Fiction
ISBN 978-0-448-45257-9; 0-448-45257-X
LC 2009-9031

First published 1930

"When a train carrying good things to children breaks down, the little blue engine proves his courage and determination. The rhythmic, repetitive text encourages children to help tell the story." Hodges. Books for Elem Sch Libr

Pitman, Gayle E.

This day in June; by Gayle E. Pitman; illustrated by Kristyna Litten. Magination Press 2014 32 p. color illustrations (hardcover) $14.95

Grades: PreK K 1 2   **E**
1. LGBT people 2. Stories in rhyme 3. Parades -- Fiction 4. Gay pride parades -- Fiction
ISBN 143381658X; 1433816598; 9781433816581; 9781433816598

LC 2013021623

Stonewall Book Award: Children's & Young Adult Literature (2015)

This children's picture book, by Gayle E. Pitman, illustrated by Kristyna Litten, "welcomes readers to experience a pride celebration and share in a day when we are all united. Also included is a Reading Guide chock-full of facts about LGBT history and culture, as well as a Note to Parents and Caregivers with information on how to talk to children about sexual orientation and gender identity in age-appropriate ways." (Publisher's note)

"Filled with saturated colors and vivid illustrations, this picture book uses rhyming couplets to convey the fun and exuberant feelings associated with a pride parade for lesbian, gay, bisexual, and transgender (LGBT) people and families. . . . The diversity shown at the pride parade is realistic; both homosexual and heterosexual people, young and old, are depicted as well as individuals, couples, and families." SLJ

Piven, Hanoch

My best friend is as sharp as a pencil; and other funny classroom portraits. Schwartz & Wade 2010 un il $17.99
Grades: K 1 2 3   **E**
1. Portraits -- Fiction
ISBN 0375853383; 9780375853388; 978-0-375-85338-8; 0-375-85338-3

"Vibrant portraits in words and realia-collage illustrations, purportedly created by the child narrator in anticipation of her grandmother's inevitable questions about school, will delight readers. One double-page spread gives each new character's traits, expressed in several verbal metaphors . . . and in photos of objects. . . . On the next spread, a painting incorporating those objects forms an eye-catching, idiosyncratic portrait."

"Vibrant portraits in words and realia-collage illustrations, purportedly created by the child narrator in anticipation of her grandmother's inevitable questions about school, will delight readers. One double-page spread gives each new character's traits, expressed in several verbal metaphors . . . and in photos of objects. . . . On the next spread, a painting incorporating those objects forms an eye-catching, idiosyncratic portrait." Booklist

My dog is as smelly as dirty socks; and other funny family portraits. Schwartz & Wade 2007 un il $16.99; lib bdg $18.99
Grades: PreK K 1 2   **E**
1. Portraits -- Fiction 2. Family life -- Fiction
ISBN 978-0-375-84052-4; 0-375-84052-4; 978-0-375-94052-1 lib bdg; 0-375-94052-9 lib bdg

LC 2006-21936

A young girl draws a family portrait, then makes it more accurate by adding common objects to show aspects of each member's personality, such as her father's playfulness, her mother's sweetness, and her brother's strength

"Childlike line drawings are paired with the more creative portraits, in which representational objects are glued on gouache-and-watercolor backgrounds to make the figures. Children will get caught up in this playful, fun, cre-

ative, and easy-to-do art concept and will want to follow through with their own creations." Booklist

Pizzoli, Greg

★ **Number** one Sam; Greg Pizzoli. Disney-Hyperion 2014 40 p. $16.99
Grades: PreK K   **E**
1. Dogs -- Fiction 2. Automobile racing -- Fiction 3. Chickens -- Fiction 4. Dogs -- Fiction 5. Competition (Psychology) -- Fiction
ISBN 142317111X; 9781423171119

LC 2013021231

In this children's book, by Greg Pizzoli, "Sam is used to winning everything, including car racing, his sport of choice. His wall of trophies and trinkets show off his talent for success until the day the unthinkable happens: the pup loses the big race because he stops for a group of oblivious chickens in the middle of the track. Then his cheering friends and the chickens let him know that he is still number one with them." (Publisher's note)

"Sam is used to winning everything, including car racing, his sport of choice. His wall of trophies and trinkets show off his talent for success until the day the unthinkable happens: the pup loses the big race because he stops for a group of oblivious chickens in the middle of the track... Pizzoli's use of four-color art provides an airy, uncluttered vision for his story that will definitely attract children. The simple yet exciting text drives the story forward and will make it a popular choice at storytimes." SLJ

The **watermelon** seed; Greg Pizzoli. 1st ed. Disney Hyperion Books 2013 40 p. ill. (reinforced) $16.99
Grades: PreK K   **E**
1. Humorous fiction 2. Humorous stories 3. Seeds -- Fiction 4. Crocodiles -- Fiction 5. Imagination -- Fiction 6. Watermelons -- Fiction
ISBN 1423171012; 9781423171010

LC 2012020297

Theodor Seuss Geisel Award (2014)

This children's story, written and illustrated by Greg Pizzoli, "introduces us to one funny crocodile who has one big fear: swallowing a watermelon seed. What will he do when his greatest fear is realized? Will vines sprout out his ears? Will his skin turn pink? This crocodile has a wild imagination." (Publisher's note)

Platt, Cynthia

A **little** bit of love; illustrated by Hannah Whitty. Tiger Tales 2011 il $15.95
Grades: PreK K   **E**
1. Food -- Fiction 2. Love -- Fiction 3. Mice -- Fiction 4. Baking -- Fiction 5. Mother-child relationship -- Fiction
ISBN 978-1-58925-095-6; 1-58925-095-8

"Small Mouse is tired of plain old cheese and crumbs and wants something new and sweet to eat, so her mother takes her on a journey, gathering ingredients to make something out of love. . . . Together they make a pie, and the youngster understands how good things are made with a mother's love. This is a sweet story that not only teaches a child how a pie is made, but also how each ingredient comes from nature. . . . The colors in the art are soft but sunny, making this a cozy read. The loving facial expressions between the mice are endearing." SLJ

Platt, Mary

The **Scoop** on Poop; Lifting the lid on the science of poo and wee. by Mary & Richard Platt; illustrated by John Kelly. Kingfisher 2012 48 p. ill. (chiefly col.) (hardcover) $15.99; (paperback) $7.99

Grades: 4 5 6   E

1. Feces 2. Urine

ISBN 0753468867; 0753469235; 9780753468869; 9780753469231

This children's picture book by Richard Platt looks at bodily waste. "'Gathering Gold' is about manure as fertilizer," while "'Garden Growers' is a bit about that as well. There are also two-page spreads on 'Pooper Paper,' (making paper from waste), 'Scent or Stink,' 'Dangerous Dung,'" and "'Backside Buffet,' which notes worldwide dishes that include poop and pee." (Booklist)

Player, Micah

Chloe, instead; by Micah Player. Chronicle Books 2012 32 p. (alk. paper) $15.99

Grades: PreK K 1 2   E

1. Picture books for children 2. Family life -- Fiction 3. Sisters -- Fiction 4. Individuality -- Fiction 5. Individuality in children

ISBN 0811878651; 9780811878654

LC 2011012717

This children's book, by Micah Player, follows "Molly[, who] always dreamed of having a sister who is just like her. But she got Chloe, instead. These two sisters are nothing alike: Molly loves to color with crayons. Chloe prefers the taste of wax. . . . Molly is frustrated! But then she realizes that maybe sisters aren't the ones next to you on the piano bench, they're the ones dancing to the music you play!" (Publisher's note)

Plecas, Jennifer

Pretend! Philomel Books 2011 un il $15.99

Grades: PreK K 1   E

1. Imagination -- Fiction 2. Father-son relationship -- Fiction

ISBN 978-0-399-23430-9; 0-399-23430-6

LC 2010-19288

A father and son embark on an imaginary adventure and discover how much they love each other.

"The breezy writing and lighthearted watercolor cartoons make this father-son bonding story fly by; with occasional reminders of where Jimmy and Dad really are, readers gain a full appreciation for the powers of the boy's imagination." Publ Wkly

Plourde, Lynn

Dino pets go to school; illustrated by Gideon Kendall. Dutton Children's Books 2011 il $16.99

Grades: PreK K   E

1. School stories 2. Stories in rhyme 3. Pets -- Fiction 4. Dinosaurs -- Fiction

ISBN 978-0-525-42232-7; 0-525-42232-3

LC 2010038065

A boy brings various dinosaurs to school, but discovers that neither the loudest, nor the tallest, nor the smartest is suited to the classroom. Includes facts about dinosaurs.

"Exuberant illustrations bring a sense of whimsy to the story. The facial expressions are both comical and endear-ing. Children will love the dino baseball game at the conclusion." SLJ

Field trip day; illustrated by Thor Wickstrom. Dutton Children's Books 2010 un il $16.99

Grades: PreK K 1 2   E

1. School stories 2. Farm life -- Fiction

ISBN 978-0-525-47994-9; 0-525-47994-5

Today is Field Trip Day at school, and everyone in Mrs. Shepherd's class is excited to visit Fandangle's Farm, especially Juan, who loves to explore. But Juan just might be too good at exploring, and Mrs. Shepherd and the chaperones have trouble keeping track of him!

"This good-natured story . . . will appeal to children, especially those who adore farm animals. The watercolor-and-ink cartoons are lively and depict a diverse class that lauds thinking and questioning over strict rule-keeping." SLJ

Grandpappy snippy snappies; illustrated by Christopher Santoro. HarperCollinsPublishers 2009 un il $17.99

Grades: PreK K 1 2   E

1. Stories in rhyme 2. Farmers -- Fiction 3. Clothing and dress -- Fiction

ISBN 978-0-06-028050-5; 0-06-028050-6

LC 2001-24328

When things go wrong around his farm Grandpappy sets them right with a snap of his suspenders, but Grandmammy is in trouble and the suspenders are all worn out

"This whimsical tale of an everyday hero has a rhyming text and lively illustrations. . . . Santoro's digital mixed-media illustrations animate the tale in a wonderful way. Together the cartoon and realistic elements add depth, detail, and humor to the tale." SLJ

A **mountain** of mittens; [by] Lynn Plourde; illustrated by Mitch Vane. Charlesbridge 2007 un il $15.95; pa $7.95

Grades: PreK K 1   E

1. Clothing and dress -- Fiction 2. Lost and found possessions -- Fiction

ISBN 978-1-57091-585-7; 978-1-57091-466-9 pa

LC 2006021253

Molly's parents try various methods to help her remember her mittens but nothing seems to work.

"Readers will chuckle as they recognize what a problem mateless mittens can become. Vane's watercolor-and-ink drawings have a jaunty air." Booklist

You're wearing that to school?! by Lynn Plourde; illustrated by Sue Cornelison. Disney-Hyperion Books 2013 32 p. (hardcover) $16.99

Grades: PreK K 1   E

1. Picture books for children 2. School stories 3. Mice -- Fiction 4. Schools -- Fiction 5. Hippopotamus -- Fiction 6. Individuality -- Fiction 7. First day of school -- Fiction

ISBN 1423155106; 9781423155102

LC 2011031614

This children's picture book follows hippo Penelope, who's "excited about starting school. Her retiring friend Tiny, a mouse, is a pessimistic first-grader determined to prevent what he expects would be gaffes on her first day. Penelope plans to wear her favorite outlandish outfit, bring her

well-worn stuffed toy for show-and-tell, and pack a picnic
lunch. Tiny quashes her cheerful plans, dialing her down to
jeans and a T-shirt, a rock, and PB&J. Undeterred, the hippo
ignores Tiny." (School Library Journal)

Pochocki, Ethel

The **blessing** of the beasts; by Ethel Pochocki; illustrated by Barry Moser. Paraclete Press 2007 39p il $18.95
Grades: K 1 2 3   E
    1. Skunks -- Fiction 2. Animals -- Fiction 3. Religion
-- Fiction 4. Cockroaches -- Fiction 5. New York
(N.Y.) -- Fiction
    ISBN 978-1-55725-502-0; 1-55725-502-4
                                        LC 2007002231
    Martin the skunk and Francesca the cockroach wend
their way across the city to attend the blessing of the animals
celebration on the Feast of St. Francis at the Cathedral of St.
John the Divine.
    This is a "a delightful fantasy. . . . Cats and dogs are
the usual celebrants at the real service; here they are joined
by lions, bears, and falcons. . . . Funny, sly, and noble, the
animal pictures range from amusing takeoffs to moving tributes." Booklist

Polacco, Patricia

Babushka's doll. Simon & Schuster Bks. for Young
Readers 1990 un il hardcover o.p. pa $6.95
Grades: K 1 2 3   E
    1. Dolls -- Fiction
    ISBN 0-671-68343-8; 0-689-80255-2 pa
                                          LC 89-6122
    "Polacco's distinctive artwork interprets the story with
style and verve. Using pencil, marker, and paint, she creates
a series of varied compositions, highlighting muted shades
with an occasional flare of bright colors and strong patterns. .
. . A good, original story, illustrated with panache." Booklist

The **blessing** cup; Patricia Polacco. Simon & Schuster
Books for Young Readers 2013 48 p. (hardcover) $17.99
Grades: 1 2 3 4 5   E
    1. Picture books for children 2. Heirlooms 3. Jews
-- Fiction 4. Family life -- Fiction 5. Drinking cups
-- Fiction
    ISBN 1442450479; 9781442450479; 9781442450486
                                        LC 2012023596
    This book is Patricia Polacco's prequel to "The Keep-
ing Quilt." Here, "readers learn how Polacco's great-grandmother Anna and her parents were forced from their shtetl
in Czarist Russia and made their way to America. Among
the few treasures the family took with them was a vibrantly
painted tea set, a kind of familial talisman . . . , which also
served as a reminder that they would always be rich in what
matters: resilience and love." (Publishers Weekly)

Bun Bun Button. G. P. Putnam's Sons 2011 il $17.99
Grades: PreK K 1   E
    1. Toys -- Fiction 2. Grandmothers -- Fiction 3. Lost
and found possessions -- Fiction
    ISBN 978-0-399-25472-7; 0-399-25472-2
                                        LC 2010047740
    Paige Darling loves the stuffed rabbit her grandmother
has made for her, but when she ties a helium-filled balloon
to Bun Bun Button the toy gets loose and goes floating away,
and it may take some Darling luck to bring her home.

"Brimming with nostalgia, heartfelt sentimentality, and
eccentricity, this portrait of a tight-knit intergenerational
bond will charm Polacco enthusiasts with its old-fashioned
tone and bright illustrations. Even when she is illustrating a
picture of a grandmother reading to her granddaughter, Polacco fills the pages with tumbling action, familial warmth,
and love." Publ Wkly

The **butterfly**. Philomel Bks. 2000 un il $16.99; pa
$7.99
Grades: 2 3 4   E
    1. Jews -- Fiction 2. France -- Fiction 3. World War,
1939-1945 -- Fiction
    ISBN 0-399-23170-6; 0-14-241306-2 pa
                                          LC 99-30038
    During the Nazi occupation of France, Monique's moth-
er hides a Jewish family in her basement and tries to help
them escape to freedom
    "Polacco's use of color has never been more effective. .
. . The bold pattern and heightened color of the insect provides a counterpoint to the equally dynamic black-on-red
swastikas. Convincing in its portrayal of both the disturbing
and humanitarian forces of the time." SLJ

★ **Chicken** Sunday. Philomel Bks. 1992 un il
$16.99; pa $6.99
Grades: K 1 2 3   E
    1. Jews -- Fiction 2. Easter -- Fiction 3. Friendship
-- Fiction 4. African Americans -- Fiction
    ISBN 0-399-22133-6; 0-698-11615-1 pa
                                        LC 91-16030
    To thank old Eula for her wonderful Sunday chicken
dinners, her two grandsons and their friend, a girl who has
"adopted" her since her own "babushka" died, sell decorated
eggs and buy her a beautiful Easter hat
    "Without being heavy-handed, Polacco's text conveys a
tremendous pride of heritage as it brims with rich images
from her characters' African American and Russian Jewish
cultures. Her vibrant pencil-and-wash illustrations glow—
actual family photographs have been worked into several
spreads." Publ Wkly

★ **G** is for goat. Philomel Bks. 2003 un il $16.99;
pa $6.99; bd bk $6.99
Grades: PreK K 1 2   E
    1. Goats 2. Alphabet 3. Stories in rhyme
    ISBN 0-399-24018-7; 0-14-240550-7 pa; 0-399-
24530-8 bd bk
                                        LC 2002-11551
    A rhyming celebration of goats and their antics, from A
to Z
    "The charming animals will energize any storytime. . . .
The pencil-and-watercolor illustrations against white backgrounds steal the spotlight, with charming details." SLJ

★ **Ginger** and Petunia; [by] Patricia Polacco. Philomel
Books 2007 un il $16.99
Grades: K 1 2 3   E
    1. Pigs -- Fiction
    ISBN 978-0-399-24539-8
                                        LC 2006024878
    When her beloved Ginger, a piano-playing socialite and
very snappy dresser, makes a last-minute trip to London not

knowing her housesitter has cancelled, Petunia the pig does more than fend for herself, she becomes Ginger.

"Polacco's comic portrayal of pampered pet and attentive owner is spot-on—and her characteristic watercolor illustrations highlight both characters' sense of fashion and joie de vivre. . . . A delight from start to finish." Booklist

In our mothers' house. Philomel Books 2009 un il $17.99
Grades: 1 2 3 4   **E**
  1. Mothers -- Fiction 2. Adoption -- Fiction 3. Lesbians -- Fiction 4. Family life -- Fiction
  ISBN 978-0-399-25076-7; 0-399-25076-X
                                           LC 2008-32615
"The oldest of three adopted children recalls her childhood with mothers Marmee and Meema, as they raised their African American daughter, Asian American son, and Caucasian daughter in a lively, supportive neighborhood. . . . The energetic illustrations in pencil and marker, . . . teem with family activities and neighborhood festivity." Booklist

★ **John** Philip Duck. Philomel Books 2004 un il $16.99
Grades: K 1 2 3   **E**
  1. Ducks -- Fiction 2. Memphis (Tenn.) -- Fiction 3. Hotels and motels -- Fiction
  ISBN 0-399-24262-7
During the Depression, a young Memphis boy trains his pet duck to do tricks in the fountain of a grand hotel and ends up becoming the Duck Master of the Peabody Hotel

"This is Polacco at the height of her form in terms of both text and illustration. The story moves smoothly from start to finish and has a refreshing air of innocence. The artwork is simply beautiful as the artist orchestrates a harmonious symphony of color." SLJ

★ The **keeping** quilt; rev format ed; Simon & Schuster Bks. for Young Readers 1998 un il $17.95; pa $6.99
Grades: K 1 2 3   **E**
  1. Jews -- Fiction 2. Quilts -- Fiction
  ISBN 0-689-82090-9; 0-689-84447-6 pa
                                           LC 97-47690
A reissue of the title first published 1988

A homemade quilt ties together the lives of four generations of an immigrant Jewish family, remaining a symbol of their enduring love and faith

"Jewish customs and the way they've shifted through the years are portrayed unobtrusively in the story, which is illustrated in sepia pencil, except for the quilt, which sparks every page with its strong colors." Booklist

★ The **Lemonade** Club; [by] Patricia Polacco. Philomel Books 2007 un il $16.99
Grades: 2 3 4   **E**
  1. School stories 2. Cancer -- Fiction 3. Teachers -- Fiction 4. Friendship -- Fiction
  ISBN 978-0-399-24540-4
                                           LC 2007011440
When Marilyn and her teacher, Miss Wichelman, both get cancer, they encourage each other and, aided by medical treatments and support from friends, they get better. Based on a true story.

"Polacco continues to draw from rich family experiences to weave satisfying, inspirations stories. . . . Pencil-and-marker illustrations in Polacco's usual free style gently convey the emotions." Booklist

★ **Mr.** Lincoln's way. Philomel Bks. 2001 un il $16.99
Grades: K 1 2 3   **E**
  1. School stories 2. Prejudices -- Fiction
  ISBN 0-399-23754-2
                                           LC 00-66939
When Mr. Lincoln, "the coolest principal in the whole world," discovers that Eugene, the school bully, knows a lot about birds, he uses this interest to help Eugene overcome his intolerance

"The book may be useful to schools in need of a springboard for discussion of the topic and is graced with impressive watercolors." SLJ

Mr. Wayne's masterpiece; Patricia Polacco. G. P. Putnam's Sons 2014 40 p. color illustrations (reinforced) $17.99
Grades: 2 3 4 5   **E**
  1. School stories 2. Theater -- Fiction 3. Schools -- Fiction 4. Teachers -- Fiction 5. Public speaking -- Fiction
  ISBN 0399160957; 9780399160950
                                           LC 2013046428
"Speaking in front of an audience terrifies Trisha. Ending up in Mr. Wayne's drama class is the last thing she wants! But Mr. Wayne gives her a backstage role painting scenery for the winter play. As she paints, she listens to the cast rehearse, memorizing their lines without even realizing it." (Publisher's note)

"Early elementary readers will relate to the self-doubt Polacco expresses, and they will also find vicarious comfort through her supportive relationships with teachers, as well as her ultimate triumph over fear." Booklist

Mrs. Katz and Tush. Doubleday Books for Young Readers 1992 un il $16.99; lib bdg $19.99; pa $6.99
Grades: K 1 2 3   **E**
  1. Jews -- Fiction 2. Friendship -- Fiction 3. African Americans -- Fiction
  ISBN 0-553-08122-5; 0-385-90650-1 lib bdg; 0-440-40936-5 pa
                                           LC 91-18710
A long-lasting friendship develops between Larnel, a young African-American, and Mrs. Katz, a lonely, Jewish widow, when Larnel presents Mrs. Katz with a scrawny kitten without a tail

"Polacco has used loving details in both words and art work to craft a moving and heartfelt story of a friendship that reaches across racial and generational differences." Horn Book

My rotten redheaded older brother. Simon & Schuster Bks. for Young Readers 1994 un il $17.95; pa $6.99
Grades: PreK K 1 2 3   **E**
  1. Siblings -- Fiction
  ISBN 0-671-72751-6; 0-689-82036-4 pa
                                           LC 93-13980

"Featuring an obnoxious, freckle-faced, bespectacled boy and a comforting, tale-telling grandmother, this autobiographical story is as satisfying as a warm slice of apple pie. Patricia can't quite understand how anyone could possibly like her older brother Richard. Whether picking blackberries or eating raw rhubarb, he always manages to outdo her, rubbing it in with one of his 'extra-rotten, weasel-eyed, greeny-toothed grins.' When their Bubbie teaches Patricia to wish on a falling star, she knows just what to ask for." SLJ

★ **Oh,** look! Philomel Books 2004 un il $16.99
Grades: PreK K 1 2   E
1. Goats -- Fiction
ISBN 0-399-24223-6

Three goats visit a fair but run home after they seem to encounter a troll.

"In this colorful picture book, the . . . author transfers the rhythms and movement of the traditional bear-hunt chant to safer ground. . . . Polacco's signature pencil-and-watercolor paintings cascade across the pages, creating festive scenes and bright hues." SLJ

★ **Pink** and Say. Philomel Bks. 1994 un il $16.99
Grades: 2 3 4   E
1. Friendship -- Fiction 2. African American soldiers -- Fiction 3. United States -- History -- 1861-1865, Civil War -- Fiction
ISBN 0-399-22671-0
                                                     LC 93-36340
Say Curtis describes his meeting with Pinkus Aylee, a black soldier, during the Civil War, and their capture by Southern troops

"Polacco pulls out all the stops in this heart-wrenching tale . . . which has been passed through several generations of the author's family. . . . Polacco's signature line-and-watercolor paintings epitomize heroism, tenderness, and terror. . . . Unglamorized details of the conventions and atrocities of the Civil War target readers well beyond customary picture book age." Horn Book

★ **Rechenka's** eggs; written and illustrated by Patricia Polacco. Philomel Bks. 1988 un il lib bdg $16.99; pa $6.99
Grades: K 1 2 3   E
1. Eggs -- Fiction 2. Geese -- Fiction 3. Easter -- Fiction
ISBN 0-399-21501-8 lib bdg; 0-698-11385-3 pa
                                                     LC 87-16588
An injured goose rescued by Babushka, having broken the painted eggs intended for the Easter Festival in Moscva, lays thirteen marvelously colored eggs to replace them, then leaves behind one final miracle in egg form before returning to her own kind

"Polacco achieves optimal dramatic contrast by using bold shapes against uncluttered white space and by contrasting rich colors and design details with faces in black and white." Bull Cent Child Books

Someone for Mr. Sussman; [by] Patricia Polacco. Philomel Books 2008 un il $16.99
Grades: 2 3 4   E
1. Grandmothers -- Fiction 2. Jews -- United States --

Fiction 3. Dating (Social customs) -- Fiction
ISBN 978-0-399-25075-0; 0-399-25075-1
                                                     LC 2008000660
Although she is the best matchmaker in the neighborhood, Jerome's Bubbie has a hard time finding a match for the fussy Mr. Sussman.

"The author brings in homey, Fiddler on the Roof syntax . . . along with words like 'oy' and 'farklempt,' illustrating the story in her signature style of comfortable caricatures and broad strokes. A good-natured spirit percolates throughout." Publ Wkly

★ **Thank** you, Mr. Falker. Philomel Bks. 1998 un il $16.99
Grades: K 1 2 3   E
1. Reading -- Fiction 2. Teachers -- Fiction 3. Learning disabilities -- Fiction
ISBN 0-399-23166-8
                                                     LC 97-18685
At first, Trisha loves school, but her difficulty learning to read makes her feel dumb, until, in the fifth grade, a new teacher helps her understand and overcome her problem

"Young readers struggling with learning difficulties will identify with Trisha's situation and find reassurance in her success. Polacco's gouache-and-pencil compositions deftly capture the emotional stages—frustration, pain, elation—of Trisha's journey." Publ Wkly

★ The **trees** of the dancing goats. Simon & Schuster Bks. for Young Readers 1996 un il hardcover o.p. pa $6.99
Grades: K 1 2 3   E
1. Jews -- Fiction 2. Hanukkah -- Fiction 3. Christmas -- Fiction
ISBN 0-689-80862-3; 0-689-83857-3 pa
                                                     LC 95-26670
"On the family farm in Michigan, Trisha and Richard watch as Babushka and Grampa prepare for Hanukkah in their native Russian way. . . . When scarlet fever debilitates their neighbors, Trisha's whole family pitches in to make and deliver holiday dinners and Christmas trees." Publ Wkly

When lightning comes in a jar. Philomel Bks. 2002 un il $16.99; pa $6.99
Grades: 2 3 4   E
1. Family life -- Fiction 2. Grandmothers -- Fiction 3. Family reunions -- Fiction
ISBN 0-399-23164-1; 0-14-240350-4 pa
                                                     LC 2001-45925
A young girl describes the family reunion at her grandmother's house, from the food and baseball and photos to the flickering fireflies on the lawn

"The watercolor-and-pencil illustrations, skillfully composed on the pages, expressively sketch the characters. . . . This autobiographical story will convey the joys of family." Booklist

Polhemus, Coleman
The **crocodile** blues; [by] Coleman Polhemus. Candlewick Press 2007 un il $16.99
Grades: PreK K   E
1. Stories without words 2. Eggs -- Fiction 3.

Crocodiles -- Fiction
ISBN 978-0-7636-3543-5; 0-7636-3543-X

LC 2006051848

A wordless tale in which a man and his pet cockatoo discover, much to their dismay, the true nature of the egg they bring home from the store

"Youngsters will laugh at both the story line and the characters depicted in this zany book. The simple royal blue and black silhouettes capture the feeling of the dark night, and the bright yellow of the daylight offers a realistic contrast." SLJ

Politi, Leo

Emmet. Getty Publications 2009 un il $16.95
Grades: PreK K 1 2   E
1. Dogs -- Fiction
ISBN 978-0-89236-992-8; 0-89236-992-2
A reissue of the title first published 1971 by Scribner
Emmet, one of the many stray dogs taken in by old Mr. Winkel, was always the troublemaker of the lot. Mr. Winkel's neighbors are ready to call the dogcatcher when the rascally dog saves the grocer's shop from a fire set by a prowler.

Juanita. Getty Publications 2009 un il $16.95
Grades: K 1 2 3   E
1. Easter -- Fiction 2. Birthdays -- Fiction 3. Mexican Americans -- Fiction 4. Los Angeles (Calif.) -- Fiction
ISBN 978-0-89236-991-1; 0-89236-991-4
A reissue of the title first published 1948 by Scribner
A Caldecott honor book, 1949
Juanita, a Mexican girl of Olvera Street in Los Angeles, brings the dove she received for her birthday to the Blessing of the Animals on the day before Easter.
"The pictures in soft colors have a warmth and tenderness." Horn Book

Pedro, the angel of Olvera Street. Getty Publications 2009 un il $14.96
Grades: K 1 2 3   E
1. Christmas -- Fiction 2. Mexican Americans -- Fiction 3. Los Angeles (Calif.) -- Fiction
ISBN 978-0-89236-990-4; 0-89236-990-6
A reissue of the title first published 1946 by Scribner
A Caldecott Medal honor book, 1947
Little Pedro, who sings like an angel, is allowed to lead the Christmas procession, known as La Posada, through the old Mexican section of downtown Los Angeles.
"Beguiling both in text and in the pictures with their soft, rich colors." Bookmark

Song of the swallows. Getty Publications 2009 un il $16.98
Grades: 2 3 4   E
1. Missions -- Fiction 2. Swallows -- Fiction 3. California -- Fiction
ISBN 978-0-89236-989-8; 0-89236-989-2
A reissue of the title first published 1949 by Scribner
Awarded the Caldecott Medal, 1950
Sad when the swallows leave for the winter, young Juan prepares to welcome them back to the old California Mission at Capistrano on St. Joseph's Day the next spring.
This is a "tender poetic story. . . Lovely pictures in soft colors bring out the charm of the southern California land-

scape and the melody of the swallow song adds to the feeling of Spring." Horn Book

Pomerantz, Charlotte

The **chalk** doll; pictures by Frané Lessac. Lippincott 1989 30p il hardcover o.p. pa $6.99
Grades: K 1 2 3   E
1. Dolls -- Fiction 2. Jamaica -- Fiction 3. Mother-daughter relationship -- Fiction
ISBN 0-06-443333-1 pa

LC 88-872

"The stylized illustrations by the West Indian artists Frané Lessac are primitive in bright, oscillating colors, evoking poverty in a tropical paradise as well as mother-daughter affection in a well-appointed home." N Y Times Book Rev

Poole, Amy Lowry

★ The **pea** blossom; retold and illustrated by Amy Poole. Holiday House 2005 un il hardcover o.p. pa $6.95
Grades: K 1 2 3   E
1. Fairy tales 2. China -- Fiction
ISBN 0-8234-1864-2; 0-8234-2018-3 pa

LC 2003-67544

In a garden near Beijing, five peas in a shell grow and wait to discover what fate has in store for them.

"Choosing to set her version in Beijing, China, Poole illustrates her simple, elegant prose with watercolors on rice paper that are clearly reminiscent of Chinese paintings." Booklist

Portis, Antoinette

Froodle; Antoinette Portis. Roaring Brook Press 2014 32 p. (hardback) $16.99
Grades: PreK K 1 2   E
1. Birds -- Fiction 2. Birdsongs -- Fiction 3. Individuality -- Fiction
ISBN 159643922X; 9781596439221

LC 2013032417

In this book, by Antoinette Portis, "a little brown bird is sick of peeping like she's supposed to and lets out an unexpected 'Froodle.' Her other bird friends are shocked, but soon Cardinal is spouting 'Ickle zickle' instead of 'Chirp,' and Dove sings 'Oobly snoobly' instead of 'Coo.' Crow, who is not silly, tries to keep the other birds in line, but they're having too much fun to listen, and Crow flies off... . Silliness is contagious, though, and Crow can't stay away for long." (Booklist)

"All of the birds say, "caw," "coo," "chip," or "peep," except Little Brown Bird, who wants to try something different. She finds it more enjoyable to say things like, "Froodle sproodle" and "Tiffle biffle./just a little/miffle!" Crow is annoyed, especially when the other birds join in, but who could resist participating in fun like this?...The cadence of the birds' dialogue might take a few read-throughs to get used to, but that will only provide more laughs in the meantime. This book will work in many settings and is certain to prompt giggles from young audiences." SLJ

Kindergarten diary; as told to Antoinette Portis by me, Annalina. Harper 2010 un il $12.99; lib bdg $14.89

Grades: PreK K   E

1. School stories

ISBN 978-0-06-145691-6; 0-06-145691-8; 978-0-06-145692-3 lib bdg; 0-06-145692-6 lib bdg

"Imaginative, spirited Annalina narrates a month of days in her life, beginning with the day before she starts kindergarten. . . . Realistic and gorgeously patterned collage items outlined in black are mingled with simple paintings to create an explosion of color, shape, and texture. The narrative and illustrations are gently funny and filled with little details and jokes." SLJ

★ **Not** a box. HarperCollins 2007 un il $12.99; lib bdg $14.89

Grades: PreK K   E

1. Boxes -- Fiction 2. Rabbits -- Fiction 3. Imagination -- Fiction

ISBN 978-0-06-112322-1; 0-06-112322-6; 978-0-06-112323-8 lib bdg; 0-06-112323-4 lib bdg

LC 2006002477

To an imaginative bunny, a box is not always just a box.

"The spare, streamlined design and the visual messages about imagination's power will easily draw young children, who will recognize their own flights of fantasy." Booklist

★ **Not** a stick. HarperCollinsPublishers 2008 un il $12.99; lib bdg $14.89

Grades: PreK K   E

1. Pigs -- Fiction 2. Play -- Fiction 3. Imagination -- Fiction

ISBN 978-0-06-112325-2; 0-06-112325-0; 978-0-06-112326-9 lib bdg; 0-06-112326-9 lib bdg

LC 2007-14475

An imaginative young pig shows some of the many things that a stick can be.

"Portis's simple color palette and playful drawings with never a line out of place represent the best in children's illustration." SLJ

★ A **penguin** story. HarperCollins 2009 un il $17.99; lib bdg $18.89

Grades: PreK K 1 2   E

1. Color -- Fiction 2. Penguins -- Fiction

ISBN 978-0-06-145688-6; 0-06-145688-8; 978-0-06-145689-3 lib bdg; 0-06-145689-6 lib bdg

LC 2008020210

Edna the penguin tries to find something in her surroundings that is not black, white, or blue.

"This gentle tribute to dreamers crackles with quiet humor, and the art's limited palette both parallels the plot and lends the book a classic feel. Portis's ability to convey emotion and character through the slightest change in Edna's beady eyes and flippers is extraordinary, and the interplay of the text and pictures nears perfection. A delightful story, delightfully told." SLJ

Princess Super Kitty. Harper 2011 il $14.99

Grades: K 1 2   E

1. Imagination -- Fiction

ISBN 978-0-06-182725-9; 0-06-182725-8

LC 2010032230

Maggie, a little girl with a huge imagination, becomes a cat, a superhero, a princess, and more in the course of a day.

"This girl is bouncy, delightful and not to be easily typed or contained. Bold lines and solid colors—not overly dominated by pink—surrounded by plenty of empty space keep the focus firmly on the girl and her props. Readers and listeners both bold and retiring will find much to like in this charming depiction of a child with a strong sense of self and confidence in her imaginative makeovers." Kirkus

Portnoy, Mindy Avra

Tale of two Seders; illustrated by Valeria Cis. Kar-Ben Pub. 2010 32p il lib bdg $17.95; pa $7.95

Grades: PreK K 1 2   E

1. Jews -- Fiction 2. Divorce -- Fiction 3. Passover -- Fiction 4. Family life -- Fiction

ISBN 978-0-8225-9907-4; 0-8225-9907-4; 978-0-8225-9931-9 pa; 0-8225-9931-7 pa

LC 2008033570

After her parents' divorce, a young girl experiences a variety of Passover seders. Includes recipes and facts about Passover.

"Cis's delightful acrylic paintings beautifully complement the text. . . . [This is a] realistic, contemporary story." SLJ

The potato king; Christoph Niemann. Owlkids Books, Inc. 2015 32 p. (hardcover) $17.95

Grades: K 1 2 3   E

1. Potatoes 2. Kings and rulers

ISBN 1771471395; 9781771471398

LC 2014950139

This children's book, illustrated by Christoph Niemann, describes how "once upon a time there was a Prussian King, Frederick, . . . who saw potential in the lowly potato. . . . However, it quickly became clear that his subjects didn't like being told what to eat. Determined to see the potato thrive, Fritz cleverly used reverse psychology to pique his people's curiosity and make the crop popular, and the potato has flourished ever since." (Publisher's note)

Potter, Beatrix

The **story** of Miss Moppet. Warne 2002 32p il $6.99

Grades: PreK K 1 2 3   E

1. Cats -- Fiction 2. Mice -- Fiction

ISBN 0-7232-4790-0

First published 1906

Miss Moppet is a kitten who uses her wiles to capture a curious mouse. But her trickery amounts to naught when she herself is outwitted

Other titles about Moppet's brother Tom and sister Mittens are:

The complete adventures of Tom Kitten and his friends (1984)

The roly-poly pudding (1908)

The tale of Tom Kitten (1935)

★ The **tailor** of Gloucester. Warne 2002 56p il $6.99

Grades: PreK K 1 2 3   E

1. Mice -- Fiction 2. Christmas -- Fiction 3. Tailoring -- Fiction

ISBN 0-7232-4772-2

First published in 1903

"A read-aloud classic in polished style, perfectly complemented by the author's exquisite watercolor illustrations." Hodges. Books for Elem Sch Libr

★ The **tale** of Jemima Puddle-duck. Warne 2002 56p il $6.99; bd bk $6.99
Grades: PreK K 1 2 3   E
1. Ducks -- Fiction
ISBN 0-7232-4778-1; 0-7232-6434-1 bd bk
First published 1908
"Jemima Puddle-duck's obstinate determination to hatch her own eggs, makes a story of suspense and sly humor." Toronto Public Libr. Books for Boys & Girls

★ The **tale** of Mr. Jeremy Fisher. Warne 2002 56p il $6.99
Grades: PreK K 1 2 3   E
1. Frogs -- Fiction
ISBN 0-7232-4776-5
First published 1906
A frog fishing from his lilly pad boat doesn't catch any fish, but one catches him

★ The **tale** of Mrs. Tiggy-Winkle. Warne 2002 56p il $6.99
Grades: PreK K 1 2 3   E
1. Hedgehogs -- Fiction
ISBN 0-7232-4775-7
First published 1905
Lucie visits the laundry of Mrs. Tiggy-Winkle, a hedgehog, and finds her lost handerchiefs

The **tale** of Mrs. Tittlemouse. Warne 2002 56p il $6.99
Grades: PreK K 1 2 3   E
1. Mice -- Fiction
ISBN 0-7232-3470-1
First published 1910
The story of a little mouse's funny house, the visitors she has there, and how she finally rids herself of the untidy, messy ones

★ The **tale** of Peter Rabbit. Warne 2002 69p il $6.99
Grades: PreK K 1 2 3   E
1. Rabbits -- Fiction
ISBN 0-7232-4770-6
First published 1903
All about the famous rabbit family consisting of Flopsy, Mopsy, Cotton-tail and especially Peter Rabbit who disobeys Mother Rabbit's admonishment not to go into Mr. McGregor's garden
"Distinctive writing and a strong appeal to a small child's sense of justice and his sympathies make this an outstanding story. The water color illustrations add charm to the narrative by their simplicity of detail and delicacy of color." Child Books Too Good to Miss
Other titles about Peter Rabbit and his family are:
The tale of Benjamin Bunny (1904)
The tale of Mr. Tod (1912)
The tale of the flopsy bunnies (1909)

★ The **tale** of Pigling Bland. Warne 2002 80p il $6.99

Grades: PreK K 1 2 3   E
1. Pigs -- Fiction
ISBN 0-7232-4784-6
First published 1913
"Pigling's story ends happily with a perfectly lovely little black Berkshire pig called Pigwig." Toronto Public Libr. Books for Boys & Girls

★ The **tale** of Squirrel Nutkin. Warne 2002 56p il $6.99
Grades: PreK K 1 2 3   E
1. Squirrels -- Fiction
ISBN 0-7232-4771-4
First published 1903
Each day the squirrels gather nuts, Nutkin propounds a riddle to Mr. Brown, the owl, until impertinent Nutkin, overestimating Mr. Brown's patience, gets his due

★ The **tale** of Timmy Tiptoes. Warne 2002 56p il $6.99
Grades: PreK K 1 2 3   E
1. Squirrels -- Fiction
ISBN 0-7232-4781-1
First published 1911
An innocent squirrel accused of stealing nuts is forced down a hole in a tree, where he meets a friendly chipmunk

★ The **tale** of two bad mice. Warne 2002 56p il $6.99
Grades: PreK K 1 2 3   E
1. Mice -- Fiction
ISBN 0-7232-4774-9
First published 1904
"Two mischievous little mice pilfer a doll's house to equip their own. They are caught and finally make amends for what they have done. Perfectly charming illustrations and a most enticing tale." Adventuring With Books. 2d edition

Pow, Tom
Tell me one thing, Dad; illustrated by Ian Andrew. Candlewick Press 2004 un il $15.99
Grades: PreK K 1 2 3   E
1. Bedtime -- Fiction 2. Father-daughter relationship -- Fiction
ISBN 0-7636-2474-8
LC 2003-65272
Molly and her father play a bedtime game that shows how much they love each other
"The sharp yet simple text avoids the obvious, going for interesting images. . . . The watercolor-and-ink artwork . . . brims with whimsy in both design and execution." Booklist

Poydar, Nancy
★ The **biggest** test in the universe. Holiday House 2005 un il $16.95
Grades: K 1 2 3   E
1. School stories 2. Examinations -- Fiction
ISBN 0-8234-1944-4
Sam and his classmates dread Friday, the day they are to take the infamous Big Test.
"Enlivened by colorful and humorous illustrations depicting the students' worries, this book is fun and cheerful, as well as unique in its subject." SLJ

Fish school. Holiday House 2009 un il $16.95
Grades: PreK K 1 2   **E**
1. School stories 2. Goldfish -- Fiction 3. Marine aquariums -- Fiction
ISBN 978-0-8234-2140-4; 0-8234-2140-6
LC 2008022576
Charlie tries to educate his pet goldfish by taking him to school and to the aquarium on a class trip. Includes tips on the care and feeding of goldfish.

"Filled with lively and amusing details, this is a good choice for one-on-one or independent reading." SLJ

No fair science fair. Holiday House 2011 32p il $14.95
Grades: K 1 2   **E**
1. School stories 2. Birds -- Fiction 3. Science projects -- Fiction
ISBN 978-0-8234-2269-2; 0-8234-2269-0
LC 2010023224
As the judging of his class's science fair approaches, Otis has trouble even thinking of an idea but once he has built a bird feeder he is determined to make some good observations, no matter how long it takes.

"A great book for sharing with classes on many levels, this is both a good primer for science fairs and for skills such as being a good friend, appreciating differences and persistence." Kirkus

Prahin, Andrew
Brimsby's hats; Andrew Prahin. Simon & Schuster Books for Young Readers 2013 40 p. col. ill. (hardcover: alk. paper) $15.99
Grades: K 1 2   **E**
1. Hats -- Fiction 2. Friendship -- Fiction 3. Creative ability -- Fiction
ISBN 1442481471; 9781442481473; 9781442481480
LC 2012024049
In this picture book by Andrew Prahin, "a lonely hat maker uses quirky creativity to make friends. Brimsby is a happy hat maker--until his best friend goes off to find adventure at sea. Now Brimsby is a lonely hat maker, unsure of what to do. But since making hats is what he does best, perhaps his talents can help him find some friends." (Publisher's note)

"There's no dialogue—Prahin narrates the whole story comfortingly in the third person, softening Brimsby's feelings of loss—and much of the humor appears in the stylish spreads. In one, a bison tries on a comically small hat; in another, Brimsby and his friend fantasize in pictorial dialogue balloons about fighting a pirate octopus." Pub Wkly

Preller, James
Home sweet horror; James Preller; illustrated by Iacopo Bruno. Feiwel and Friends 2013 97 p. illustrations (Scary tales) (pbk.) $5.99
Grades: 3 4 5   **E**
1. Ghost stories 2. Horror fiction 3. Haunted houses -- Fiction 4. Horror stories 5. Ghosts -- Fiction 6. Moving, Household -- Fiction 7. Moving, Household -- Fiction
ISBN 1250018862; 1250018870; 9781250018861; 9781250018878
LC 2012286525
Cybil Award: Early Chapter Book (2013)

In this horror story, by James Preller and illustrated by Iacopo Bruno, "Meet Liam Finn, who's just moved into a new home with his father and sister. But this old house that seems empty, isn't . . . Bloody Mary is here. Called back from the dead by a game, she's just dying to talk." (Publisher's note)

"These two horror novels for middle-grade readers cover the legend of Bloody Mary (Home) and a terrifying amusement park ride (Scream). While the writing and plot construction are nicely targeted to a young audience, there are genuinely terrifying elements in both that make these a good match only for readers who are seeking a true scare." Horn Book

Mighty Casey; by James Preller; illustrated by Matthew Cordell. Feiwel and Friends 2008 un il $16.95
Grades: K 1 2 3   **E**
1. Stories in rhyme 2. Baseball -- Fiction
ISBN 978-0-312-36764-0; 0-312-36764-3
LC 2007-47331
The Delmar Dogs baseball team is terrible, especially Casey Jenkins, but with a little bit of faith in themselves, they finally manage to win a game.

"Set against ample white space, Cordell's endearingly geeky kids take center stage. . . . It's hard to envision a reader who won't take to these underdogs." Publ Wkly

★ A **pirate's** guide to first grade; illustrated by Greg Ruth. Feiwel and Friends 2010 un il $16.99
Grades: PreK K 1   **E**
1. School stories 2. Pirates -- Fiction 3. Imagination -- Fiction
ISBN 978-0-312-36928-6; 0-312-36928-X
"Throughout his first day of first grade, a young boy describes his everyday actions in briny pirate terms, from breakfasting on grub in the galley to meeting Cap'n Silver (his new teacher) and walking the plank (seesaw) at recess. Each sharply rendered, full-color scene shows a crew of imagined pirates, differentiated in gray-toned drawings, who follow the boy and provide friendly company throughout the day. Young would-be buccaneers facing their own first-day jitters will enjoy this droll title." Booklist

Prelutsky, Jack
★ The **wizard**; by Jack Prelutsky; illustrations by Brandon Dorman. Greenwillow Books 2007 un il $16.99; lib bdg $17.89
Grades: K 1 2 3   **E**
1. Stories in rhyme 2. Magic -- Fiction
ISBN 978-0-06-124076-8; 978-0-06-124077-5 lib bdg
The verse originally appeared in the 1976 collection Nightmares: Poems to Trouble Your Sleep

An illustrated, rhyming tale of a wicked wizard and his evil deeds, as he uses "elemental sorcery" to change a bullfrog into a series of objects, from a flea to a flame.

"The illustrator's digital artwork has all the burnished lushness and radiance of oil paintings. . . . Dorman proves his mettle as a marvelous visual storyteller." Publ Wkly

Preus, Margi
The **Peace** Bell; illustrated by Hideko Takahashi. Henry Holt and Co. 2008 un il $16.95
Grades: K 1 2 3   **E**
1. Bells -- Fiction 2. Japan -- Fiction 3. Peace --

Fiction 4. New Year -- Fiction 5. Friendship -- Fiction 6. Grandmothers -- Fiction

ISBN 978-0-8050-7800-8; 0-8050-7800-2

LC 2007040897

Yoko's grandmother tells about how the bell in their town that would ring on New Year's Eve is given up during the war for scrap metal, finds its way back to their village, and becomes known as the Peace Bell.

"The simple plot is clearly developed with descriptive language, and an author's note provides more historical details. Done in Japanese acrylic paints, the realistic illustrations accurately portray the setting and capture the characters' various emotions." SLJ

Prevert, Jacques

★ **How** to paint the portrait of a bird; translated and illustrated by Mordicai Gerstein. Roaring Brook 2007 un il $14.95

Grades: K 1 2 3   E

1. Birds -- Fiction

ISBN 1-59643-215-2; 978-1-59643-215-4

LC 2006-32183

"This petite, elegant picture book . . . delivers a mind-stretching allegory of artistic creation. First, a wordless sequence shows a mopheaded boy awakening to a bluebird's trill. Palette in hand, he follows a peculiar series of instructions for capturing its likeness: paint a cage; lure the bird into it; . . . erase the cage, replacing it with a forest; then see if the bird will sing. It's a delight to see how Gerstein's scribbly lines and loose washes cohere into playful, accessible images." Booklist

Priceman, Marjorie

★ **Hot** air; the (mostly) true story of the first hot-air balloon ride. Atheneum Books for Young Readers 2005 un il $16.95

Grades: K 1 2 3   E

1. Balloons

ISBN 0-689-82642-7

LC 2004-14743

A Caldecott Medal honor book, 2006

"With vibrant colors and varied use of panels, full-page illustrations, and spreads, Priceman paces the tale perfectly." SLJ

How to make a cherry pie and see the U.S.A. Alfred A. Knopf 2008 un il $16.99; lib bdg $19.99

Grades: PreK K 1 2   E

1. Baking -- Fiction 2. United States -- Fiction 3. Voyages and travels -- Fiction

ISBN 978-0-375-81255-2; 0-375-81255-5; 978-0-375-91255-9 lib bdg; 0-375-91255-X lib bdg

LC 2007-46064

Since the Cook Shop is closed, the reader is led around the United States to gather coal, cotton, granite, and other natural resources needed to make the utensils for preparing a cherry pie

"The trip is a madcap adventure. . . . The art brims with good cheer and excites with detail." Booklist

★ **How** to make an apple pie and see the world. Knopf 1994 un il $16; pa $6.99

Grades: PreK K 1 2   E

1. Baking -- Fiction 2. Voyages and travels -- Fiction

ISBN 0-679-83705-1; 0-679-88083-6 pa

LC 93-12341

Since the market is closed, the reader is led around the world to gather the ingredients for making an apple pie

"The perfect blend of whimsical illustrations and tongue-in-cheek humor makes this an irresistable offering. The recipe is included." Child Book Rev Serv

Prigger, Mary Skillings

Aunt Minnie McGranahan; illustrated by Betsy Lewin. Clarion Bks. 1999 31p il $15; pa $5.95

Grades: K 1 2 3   E

1. Aunts -- Fiction 2. Orphans -- Fiction

ISBN 0-395-82270-X; 0-618-60488-X pa

LC 98-33501

The townspeople in St. Clere, Kansas, are sure it will never work out when the neat and orderly spinster, Minnie McGranahan, takes her nine orphaned nieces and nephews into her home in 1920

"In a dexterous style, Prigger employs repetitive elements to establish and maintain a spry tempo in clipped, spruce sentences. . . . The black outlines of Lewin's . . . witty, loose watercolors punctuate the pages in a flurry of scribbles, suggesting the kind of bursting-at-the-seams activity." Publ Wkly

Another title about Aunt Minnie is:

Aunt Minnie and the twister (2002)

Primavera, Elise

Louise the big cheese: divine diva; illustrated by Diane Goode. Simon & Schuster Books for Young Readers 2009 un il $16.99

Grades: PreK K 1 2   E

1. Theater -- Fiction 2. Friendship -- Fiction

ISBN 978-1-4169-7180-1; 1-4169-7180-7

LC 2008-23608

When she learns her class will be doing a play, little Louise Cheese has big dreams of being the star, but when her best friend is given the lead she learns that even the small roles count

"Primavera's breezy story . . . and Goode's distinctive artwork intermingle wonderfully. In both story and art, Louise makes a splash. . . . Goode is at her best here." Booklist

Other titles about Louise are:

Louise the big cheese and the la-di-da shoes (2009)

Louise the big cheese and the back-to-school smarty-pants (2011)

Louise the big cheese and the Ooh-la-la Charm School; Elise Primavera; illustrated by Diane Goode. Simon & Schuster Books for Young Readers 2012 40 p.

Grades: PreK K 1 2   E

1. Etiquette -- Fiction 2. Popularity -- Fiction 3. Picture books for children 4. Female friendship -- Fiction 5. Friendship -- Fiction

ISBN 1442405996; 9781442405998

LC 2009047236

This picture book tells the story of "Louise, the little girl with big ideas about getting noticed. . . . A new kid, Claire Eclaire, takes Louise under her wing and shows her how life is lived in Paris. . . . When it becomes clear that Claire is from Paris, Maine, Louise not only knows she's been duped

but regrets her treatment of best-friend Fern." (Booklist) ".
. . Louise has high hopes of improving her status that don't
quite work out as planned. . . . [T]here's also a villain of
sorts who leads her astray: snooty Claire . . . [who] uses the
promise of "charm school" lessons to coerce Louise into doing her chores and letting her win at games. In the process,
Louise . . . embarrasses herself in front of family and friends
as usual." (Kirkus)

Thumb love. Robin Corey Books 2010 un il $16.99;
lib bdg $19.99
Grades: PreK K 1   E
1. Thumb sucking -- fiction
ISBN 978-0-375-84481-2; 0-375-84481-3; 978-0-375-
95182-4 lib bdg; 0-375-95182-2 lib bdg

Prince, April Jones
★ **Twenty**-one elephants and still standing; written by
April Jones Prince; illustrated by Francois Roca. Houghton
Mifflin 2005 un il $16
Grades: K 1 2 3 4   E
1. Circus executives 2. Elephants -- Fiction 3.
Brooklyn Bridge (New York, N.Y.) -- Fiction
ISBN 0-618-44887-X
                                            LC 2004-05229
Upon completion of the Brooklyn Bridge, P.T. Barnum
and his twenty-one elephants parade across to prove to ev-
eryone that the bridge is safe.
A "well-researched, handsomely illustrated picture book.
. . . The sparse, yet powerful text contains both alliteration
and occasional rhyme, making it a pleasure for readers and
listeners alike. Roca's masterful paintings capture both the
spirit of the times and of the expansive bridge." SLJ

Princess pistachio; Marie-Louise Gay; translated from
French by Jacob Homel. Pajama Press 2015 46 p.
color illustrations hardcover $10.95
Grades: K 1 2 3   E
1. Birthdays -- Fiction 2. Princesses -- Fiction
ISBN 192748569X; 9781927485699
"Pistachio has always known she was a princess. When a
mysterious gift turns up on her birthday, she's sure it's only
a matter of time before her real parents, the king and queen
of Papua, arrive to take her away. But in the meantime, she
still has to eat her spinach and get up for school." (Publisher's note)
"The skillful combination of text and illustrations addresses many serious concerns of early childhood--and even
of parenthood--without straying from the book's tone of fun
and frivol ity. (Among the issues so adeptly addressed are
adoption, sibling relationships, classmate rejection and a
missing child.)" Kirkus

Princesse Camcam, 1982-
Fox's garden; Princesse Camcam. Enchanted Lion
Books 2014 32 p. color illustrations (Stories without
words) (alk. paper) $14.95
Grades: K 1 2 3   E
1. Foxes -- Fiction 2. Kindness -- Fiction 3. Stories
without words 4. Boys 5. Animal Welfare
ISBN 1592701671; 9781592701674
                                            LC 2014934817
In this children's book, by Princesse Camcam, "[o]ne
snowy night, a fox loses its way, entering a village. Chased

away by the grown ups, Fox takes shelter in a greenhouse. A
little boy sees this from his window. Without hesitating, he
brings a basket of food to the greenhouse, where he leaves
it for the fox. His gift is noticed and the night becomes a
garden of new life, nourished by compassion and kindness."
(Publisher's note)
"An act of tender compassion is given (and repaid) in
secret during an icy winter night in this memorable addition
to the Stories Without Words series, the U.S. debut for this
French artist, born Camille Garoche. The story concerns a
sleek, rust-colored fox seen darting through a gnarled forest of pale lavender trees beneath swirling snowy skies. .
. . Camcam creates her images by assembling cut-paper
dioramas, which are then lit and photographed. The resulting images possess a subtle dimensionality while the story
exudes a haunting winter magic and a strong sense of the
way a small kindness can make an enormous difference. "
Pub Wkly

Pritchett, Dylan
★ The **first** music; as told by Dylan Pritchett; illustrated by Erin Bennett Banks. August House Little Folk 2006
un il $16.95
Grades: PreK K 1 2   E
1. Music -- Fiction 2. Animals -- Fiction
ISBN 0-87483-776-6
A series of accidents in the jungle proves that everyone
has something special to add when it comes to making music.
"Fresh and intriguing, this African cumulative tale of the
origin of music unfolds in a vibrant storyteller's voice. . . .
The message (everyone has something to add to the mix) is
subtle, but clear enough for children to understand. However, it's the stylized, earth-toned illustrations, resembling
carved wooden figures, that really rock and roll, evoking the
synergy of the forest animals." Booklist

Prochovnic, Dawn Babb
Hip hip hooray! it's Family Day! sign language for
family. by Dawn Babb Prochovnic; illustrated by Stephanie
Bauer. ABDO/Magic Wagon 2012 32 p. col. ill. $28.50
Grades: K 1 2   E
1. Family 2. Counting 3. Sign language 4. Stories in
rhyme 5. Sign Language 6. Families -- Fiction
ISBN 1616418370; 9781616418373
                                            LC 2011027065
Author Dawn Babb Prochovnic "invites readers to
chant along and learn American Sign Language signs for
the members of a family including grandma, grandpa, cousins, siblings, and pets. . . . [The] literacy-based, finger-play
[teaches signing for children]. . . . [Included are] illustrated
handshapes for the alphabet, numbers 1-10, and signs from
the stories." (Publisher's note)
"Despite the somewhat bland text, the childlike, cheerful
art (including a small demo diagram) and familiar themes
(e.g., the alphabet, Halloween, and counting) will make this
series welcome in classrooms looking to explore American
Sign Language." Horn Book
Includes bibliographical references (p. 32).

Proimos, James, 1958-
The **best** bike ride ever; James Proimos; [pictures by]
Johanna Wright. Dial Books for Young Readers 2012 32 p.
col. ill. (hardcover) $16.99

Grades: PreK K 1   **E**
1. Bicycles -- Fiction 2. Imagination -- Fiction 3. Humorous stories 4. Bicycles and bicycling -- Fiction
ISBN 0803738501; 9780803738508

LC 2011035449

In this children's picture book by James Proimos, "Bonnie O'Boy is so excited about her new pink polka-dotted bike that she hops on without asking how to use the brakes. As a result, she goes 'all willy-nilly. In fact, she had willy-nillied herself right down the hill.' From there, it's a long, strange trip, one that includes riding up to the top of the Statue of Liberty, down to the bottom of the Grand Canyon, and through a scene straight out of Jurassic Park." (Publishers Weekly)

Patricia von Pleasantsquirrel. Dial Books for Young Readers 2009 un il $15.99
Grades: K 1 2   **E**
1. Princesses -- Fiction
ISBN 978-0-8037-3066-3; 0-8037-3066-7

LC 2008015776

After failing to convince her parents that she is a princess, Patricia von Pleasantsquirrel leaves her moatless house in search of a "princessdom."

"Proimos's story plays 'cheeky homage' to Sendak and Max, but the bold-lined, cartoon-style illustrations and Patricia's postmodern sassiness also owe a debt to James Marshall, calling to mind his bossy Goldilocks." SLJ

Paulie Pastrami achieves world peace. Little Brown Books for Young Readers 2009 un il $15.99
Grades: K 1 2 3   **E**
1. Peace -- Fiction 2. Kindness -- Fiction 3. Conduct of life -- Fiction
ISBN 978-0-316-03292-6; 0-316-03292-1

LC 2008043800

Seven-year-old Paulie, an ordinary boy, brings peace to his home and school through small acts of kindness, but needs help to achieve his goal of world peace

"The peppy, colorful cartoon art incorporates witty, sometimes hyperbolic details. . . . The positive story conveys how small, individual actions can have a large, ripple effect." Booklist

Swim! swim! [by Lerch; illustrations by James Proimos] Scholastic Inc. 2010 un il $16.99
Grades: PreK   **E**
1. Fishes -- Fiction
ISBN 978-0-545-09419-1; 0-545-09419-4
"Lerch the goldfish wants a friend, which is difficult since he's the only fish in his tank. . . . Just when he thinks he's as lonely as a fish can be . . . a cat arrives outside the tank and talks to Lerch. But, uh-oh, he calls him Lunch. . . . Though Lerch gets the credit for this picture book, James Proimos is responsible for the art and story. He uses the comic-book format, with panels and word balloons, to great effect here. . . . The bright colors and clear art match the simple story." Booklist

Todd's TV. Katherine Tegen Books 2010 un il $15.99

Grades: PreK K 1 2   **E**
1. Parents -- Fiction 2. Television -- Fiction
ISBN 978-0-06-170985-2; 0-06-170985-9

LC 2009-18507

When Todd's parents are too busy to take care of him, his television steps in to handle the parenting.

"With broad strokes and witty slapdashery, Proimos's light cartoon art and plotline carry some weighty themes. . . . Amusing cartoon drawings in shades of gray, black, and persimmony-red against a white background and a satiric twist at the story's end further enhance this funny-scary cautionary tale." SLJ

Prokofiev, Sergey
Peter and the wolf; translated by Maria Carlson; illustrated by Charles Mikolaycak. Viking 1982 un il hardcover o.p. pa $5.99
Grades: K 1 2 3 4   **E**
1. Fairy tales 2. Wolves -- Fiction
ISBN 0-14-050633-0 pa

LC 81-70402

This book retells the orchestral fairy tale of the boy who, ignoring his grandfather's warnings, proceeds to capture a wolf

"Prokofiev's classic, designed to teach children the instruments of an orchestra, has been published in picture book form before, but never better illustrated. The translation is smooth. . . . The paintings are rich in color, dramatic in details of costume or architecture, strong in composition, with distinctive individuality in the faces of people and of the wolf." Bull Cent Child Books

Prosek, James
★ **Bird,** butterfly, eel; story and paintings by James Prosek. Simon & Schuster Books for Young Readers 2009 un il map $16.99
Grades: K 1 2 3   **E**
1. Eels -- Fiction 2. Birds -- Fiction 3. Butterflies -- Fiction
ISBN 978-0-689-86829-0; 0-689-86829-4

LC 2007-15734

Follows a bird, a monarch butterfly, and an eel from summer on a farm until they make their respective fall voyages south, and then later begin to return north again when the weather warms.

"A well-designed and useful resource to pique curiosity about an amazing aspect of the lives of many animals." SLJ

A **good** day's fishing. Simon & Schuster Bks. for Young Readers 2004 un il $15.95
Grades: 1 2 3 4   **E**
1. Fishing -- Fiction
ISBN 0-689-85327-0

LC 2003-7383

A child searches through the hooks, lures, bobbers, and other paraphernalia in his tacklebox for the one thing he needs to ensure a good day's fishing. Includes a detailed glossary

"A beautifully illustrated, simple story. . . . Young fishing enthusiasts will certainly learn more about which tackle works best to catch particular kinds of fish, while the wonderfully detailed, gentle watercolor illustrations of fish and gear offer a lovely introduction." Booklist

Protopopescu, Orel

★ **Thelonious** Mouse; [by] Orel Protopopescu; pictures by Anne Wilsdorf. Farrar Straus Giroux 2011 un il $16.99

Grades: PreK K 1   E

1. Cats -- Fiction 2. Mice -- Fiction

ISBN 978-0-374-37447-1; 0-374-37447-3

Thelonious is a hipster mouse who cannot keep himself from taunting the cat of the house, but once Thelonious discovers a toy piano, he and the cat make some beautiful music together.

"Plenty of action and droll interior details to spy should capture kids' fancy, while grown-ups trying this as a read-aloud might need to pause to untangle their tongues. . . . Replete with scat-y, cat-and-mouse-y wordplay, this is giggle-worthy fun." Kirkus

Provensen, Alice

★ **A day** in the life of Murphy. Simon & Schuster Bks. for Young Readers 2003 un il $16.95; pa $6.99

Grades: PreK K 1 2 3   E

1. Dogs -- Fiction 2. Farm life -- Fiction

ISBN 0-689-84884-6; 1-4169-1800-0 pa

LC 2002-4309

Murphy, a farm terrier, describes a day in his life as he gets fed in the kitchen, hunts mice, goes to the vet, returns to the house for dinner, investigates a noise outside, and retires to the barn for sleep

"With charming, lively illustrations and peppy, descriptive prose, Provensen portrays the smells, sounds, and activities of a delightful, active pup." Booklist

Pullen, Zachary

★ **Friday** my Radio Flyer flew; [by] Zachary Pullen. Simon & Schuster Books for Young Readers 2008 un il $16.99 E

1. Days -- Fiction 2. Flight -- Fiction 3. Imagination -- Fiction 4. Father-son relationship -- Fiction

ISBN 978-1-4169-3983-2; 1-4169-3983-0

LC 2007041852

A father and son find an old Radio Flyer wagon when cleaning out the attic and, through the course of a week, turn it back into a wonderful toy

"Subtle alliteration moves the story through the week. . . . Full-color spreads are oversize and beautifully done in oil paints. . . . The final spread . . . is take-your-breath-away wonderful. This is a strong first purchase, affirming the bond between boys and their fathers as well as the power of imagination." SLJ

Pulver, Robin

Christmas kitten; home at last. illustrated by Layne Johnson. Albert Whitman 2010 un il $16.99

Grades: PreK K 1 2   E

1. Cats -- Fiction 2. Christmas -- Fiction 3. Santa Claus -- Fiction

ISBN 978-0-8075-1157-2; 0-8075-1157-9

When Santa's allergies prevent him from keeping a homeless kitten, he and Mrs. Claus find it a perfect home.

"Johnson's oil paintings are rich with detail and expression, giving life to Cookie and all the North Pole denizens. The artist's careful attention to light and shadow, along with the use of bold primary colors, gives the book a perfect blend of warmth and exuberance. This is a sweet, fun read-aloud." SLJ

Never say boo! Holiday House 2009 un il $16.95

Grades: PreK K 1 2   E

1. Ghost stories 2. School stories

ISBN 978-0-8234-2110-7; 0-8234-2110-4

LC 2008022609

When Gordon, a ghost, moves to a new school, everyone is afraid of him until they learn that he is not as scary as they thought he was.

"In Lucke's creepy and comical gouache illustrations, Gordon's bulging eyes and pasty white skull stand out on the mostly black background and are in contrast to his orange-yellow striped shirt and human classmates. Add in Pulver's straightforward dialogue and you have an amusing read-aloud." SLJ

Punctuation takes a vacation; illustrated by Lynn Rowe Reed. Holiday House 2003 un il $16.95; pa $6.95

Grades: 2 3 4   E

1. School stories 2. Punctuation -- Fiction

ISBN 0-8234-1687-9; 0-8234-1820-0 pa

LC 2002-68915

When all the punctuation marks in Mr. Wright's class decide to take a vacation, the students discover just how difficult life can be without them

"Pulver's clever story moves along at a nice clip and makes its point without belaboring the matter. Reed's acrylics-on-canvas illustrations are rich in color and texture, and add to the amusement of the story." SLJ

Other titles in the author's series about Mr. Wright's class are:

Nouns and verbs have a field day (2006)

Silent letters loud and clear (2008)

Happy endings (2011)

Saturday is Dadurday; by Robin Pulver; illustrated by R.W. Alley. Walker Books For Young Readers Distrib. to the trade by Macmillan Publishers 2013 32 p. (hardcover) $16.99

Grades: PreK K 1 2   E

1. Father-daughter relationship -- Fiction 2. Fathers -- Fiction

ISBN 080278691X; 9780802786098; 9780802786913

LC 2012032293

In this book, written by Robin Pulver and illustrated by R.W. Alley, "the best day of the week [for Mimi] is always Saturday, because she gets to spend it with just her Dad. Every 'Dadurday' begins the same way--Mimi and Dad make silly-shaped pancakes, read the comics section of the newspaper and make lists of fun things to do together. But when Dad gets a new work schedule, 'Dadurday' is ruined. Can Mimi find a way to still make it a special day for her and dad?" (Publisher's note)

Thank you, Miss Doover; illustrated by Stephanie Roth Sisson. Holiday House 2010 un il $16.95

Grades: K 1 2 3   E

1. School stories 2. Letters -- Fiction 3. Teachers -- Fiction 4. Authorship -- Fiction

ISBN 978-0-8234-2046-9; 0-8234-2046-9

Jack learns the value of revision as he practices Miss Doover's lesson on how to write a proper thank-you note.

"Pulver's characterization of the elementary schoolers' thought processes and lack of tact is spot-on. Sisson's colored pencil-and-acrylic illustrations go hand-in-hand with the funny text." Kirkus

Purmell, Ann

Apple cider making days; illustrated by Joanne Friar. Millbrook Press 2002 un il lib bdg $21.90

Grades: K 1 2 3   E

  1. Apples -- Fiction 2. Farm life -- Fiction

  ISBN 0-7613-2364-3

                  LC 2001-44920

Alex and Abigail join the whole family in processing and selling apples and apple cider at their grandfather's farm

"The comfortable, colorful art brings little ones up close to the process and gives them a good look at the conveyor belts and presses and other machinery involved. . . . A double-page spread, 'Cider Lore,' following the story, provides wonderful tidbits about the cider-making process. An excellent resource for autumn units or to use in preparation for a trip to the orchard." Booklist

Christmas tree farm; by Ann Purmell; illustrated by Jill Weber. Holiday House 2006 un il $16.95

Grades: K 1 2 3   E

  1. Farm life -- Fiction 2. Family life -- Fiction 3. Grandfathers -- Fiction 4. Christmas tree growing -- Fiction

  ISBN 978-0-8234-1886-2; 0-8234-1886-3

                  LC 2004-47502

A boy describes how he, his grandfather, and the rest of his family work on their tree farm throughout the year to prepare Christmas trees

"Purmell packs the friendly story with plenty of information. . . . The text makes the book interesting; the art gives it charm. The simply drawn, sometimes diminutive characters exude warmth and exemplify the work that goes into any kind of farming." Booklist

Maple syrup season; by Ann Purmell; illustrated by Jill Weber. Holiday House 2008 un il $16.95

Grades: K 1 2 3   E

  1. Family life -- Fiction 2. Maple sugar -- Fiction 3. Grandfathers -- Fiction

  ISBN 978-0-8234-1891-6; 0-8234-1891-X

                  LC 2006-03455

Grandpa leads the way as his family works together to tap maple trees, collect sap, and make syrup.

"This gentle story has a straightforward text and folksy, colorful gouache illustrations. . . . A glossary and two pages of maple syrup lore are appended. This book would be a great addition to units on seasons, farms, or plants and trees." SLJ

Puttock, Simon

Little lost cowboy; illustrated by Caroline Jayne Church. Egmont USA 2011 un il $16.99

Grades: PreK K 1 2   E

  1. Coyotes -- Fiction 2. West (U.S.) -- Fiction

  ISBN 978-1-60684-259-1; 1-60684-259-5

                  LC 2010050495

A kindly toad helps a "lonesome and lost" young coyote find his mother.

"The repetitive text is accessible and child-friendly, and the desert setting is skillfully evoked with warm, earth-toned illustrations created from beautifully textured handmade paper, finished with bold black lines." SLJ

Pym, Tasha

★ **Have** you ever seen a sneep? pictures by Joel Stewart. Farrar, Straus and Giroux 2009 un il $16.95

Grades: PreK K 1 2   E

  1. Stories in rhyme 2. Monsters -- Fiction

  ISBN 978-0-374-32868-9; 0-374-32868-4

                  LC 2008042985

"In rhyming text, a boy relates a woeful tale of trying to have fun but being plagued by monsters that ruin his every pleasure. Each encounter begins with the child asking readers if they've experienced a similar situation. . . . The pleasing and unexpected conclusion is sure to be met with a smile. The muted, almost fuzzy-looking illustrations feature the small barefoot and straw-hatted boy. . . . The artwork alternates between full-color washes that cover the pages completely and spreads that isolate the boy against expanses of white space. Perfectly paced and quietly dramatic." SLJ

Qiong, Yu Li

★ **A New** Year's reunion. Candlewick Press 2011 un il $15.99

Grades: PreK K 1 2   E

  1. China -- Fiction 2. Fathers -- Fiction 3. Family life -- Fiction 4. Chinese New Year -- Fiction

  ISBN 978-0-7636-5881-6; 0-7636-5881-2

  First published 2008 in Taipei

"Two things make this Chinese New Year story remarkable—Zhu's meticulously observed gouaches and the family's poignant backstory." Publ Wkly

Quackenbush, Robert M.

First grade jitters; written by Robert Quackenbush; illustrated by Yan Nascimbene. Harper 2010 un il $16.99

Grades: PreK K   E

  1. School stories 2. Worry -- Fiction

  ISBN 978-0-06-077632-9; 0-06-077632-3

                  LC 2009007290

A newly illustrated edition of the title first published 1982

Aidan is about to enter first grade and doesn't know quite what to expect. Will his friends be there? Will he have to know how to read and spell? What if he can't understand anything his teacher says?

"The text and pictures explore this common anxiety effectively and with a touch of humor." SLJ

Quattlebaum, Mary

The **hungry** ghost of Rue Orleans; illustrated by Patricia Castelao. Random House 2011 un il $15.99; lib bdg $18.99

Grades: PreK K 1 2   E

  1. Ghost stories 2. Restaurants -- Fiction 3. New Orleans (La.) -- Fiction

  ISBN 978-0-375-86207-6; 0-375-86207-2; 978-0-375-96207-3 lib bdg; 0-375-96207-7 lib bdg

                  LC 2010037063

Fred the ghost is perfectly happy haunting his ramshackle New Orleans house until Pierre and his daughter Marie move in and turn the house into a restaurant.

"Castelao's illustrations have an ethereal, quirky quality that complements the story, and the details she includes help anchor its New Orleans setting." Kirkus

Jo MacDonald saw a pond; by Mary Quattlebaum; illustrated by Laura J. Bryant. Dawn Publications 2011 il $16.95; pa $8.95

Grades: PreK K 1   E

1. Pond ecology -- Fiction 2. Folk songs -- United States

ISBN 978-1-58469-150-1; 1-58469-150-6; 978-1-58469-151-8 pa; 1-58469-151-4 pa

LC 2011011700

In this version of the classic song 'Old MacDonald Had a Farm,' the farmer's granddaughter discovers the creatures living at a pond. End notes present facts, outdoor activities, and games related to this lively ecosystem.

"The familiar tune starts on page one and never misses a beat, begging kids to participate. . . . Observant readers will notice the clever design of the illustrations that hides the last-mentioned animal and the next one within the spread. Bryant's softly colored watercolor creatures echo Jo's rosy-cheeked childhood innocence and have just a touch of expression in their faces." Kirkus

Includes bibliographical references

Pirate vs. pirate; the terrific tale of a big, blustery maritime match. written by Mary Quattlebaum; illustrated by Alexandra Boiger. Disney Hyperion Books 2011 un il $16.99

Grades: PreK K 1   E

1. Pirates -- Fiction

ISBN 978-1-4231-2201-2; 1-4231-2201-1

"Quattlebaum litters the pages with robust buccaneer lingo. . . . Boiger expertly blends droll humor with dramatic seascapes and detailed ship settings." SLJ

Quay, Emma

Yummy ice cream; a book about sharing. [illustrated by] Anna Walker. Board book ed.; Dial books for Young Readers 2011 un il (Hello friends!) bd bk $5.99

Grades: PreK   E

1. Board books for children 2. Owls -- Fiction 3. Sheep -- Fiction 4. Giant panda -- Fiction 5. Ice cream, ices, etc. -- Fiction

ISBN 978-0-8037-3568-2; 0-8037-3568-5

LC 2010020618

First published 2009 in Australia

Owl wishes he had some ice cream like his friends, and so Panda and Sheep find a way to share.

"Walker incorporates collaged fabric prints into creamy, sage backdrops, . . . providing a gentle contrast with the muted colors of the animals. Quay and Walker nicely convey both Owl's longing and joy when Panda and Sheep finally share. The well-trod message is delivered with panache and abundant sweetness." Publ Wkly

Other titles in this series are:

Let's play house (2011)

Puddle jumping (2011)

Good night, sleep tight (2011)

Rabinowitz, Alan

★ **A boy** and a jaguar; written by Alan Rabinowitz; illustrated by Catia Chien. First edition Houghton Mifflin Books for Children 2013 32 p. color illustrations $16.99

Grades: PreK K 1 2 3   E

1. Human-animal relationship 2. Panthera -- Conservation 3. Wildlife conservationists -- United States

ISBN 054787507X; 9780547875071

LC 2012025531

Schneider Family Book Award (2015)

In this children's book by Alan Rabinowitz, illustrated by Catia Chen, "Alan loves animals, but the great cat house at the Bronx Zoo makes him sad. Why are they all alone in empty cages? Are they being punished? More than anything, he wants to be their champion--their voice--but he stutters uncontrollably. . . . He searches for his voice and fulfills a promise to speak for animals, and people, who cannot speak for themselves." (Publisher's note)

"An unusual picture book autobiography, written by an animal scientist who began his lifelong interest in big cats when he found he could communicate more easily with animals than with people due to his stuttering. Rabinowitz's commitment to petitioning for wildlife conservation has helped him communicate more comfortably. This accessible story, with quietly emotive, impressionistic art, will help children understand both concerns." Horn Book

Raczka, Bob

Fall mixed up; illustrations by Chad Cameron. Carolrhoda Books 2011 un il lib bdg $17.95

Grades: PreK K 1 2   E

1. Stories in rhyme 2. Autumn -- Fiction

ISBN 978-0-7613-4606-7; 0-7613-4606-6

LC 2009038922

The delights of autumn are described in mixed-up verse and illustrations, and the reader is challenged to uncover the errors.

"Silly as the rhyming verses are, they need Cameron's zany illustrations to truly make them come alive. . . . Digital paintings with photo-collage elements draw readers' eye through the scenes. . . . A true celebration of fall certain to be a winner." Kirkus

Snowy, blowy winter; [by] Bob Raczka; illustrated by Judy Stead. Albert Whitman & Co. 2008 un il $16.99

Grades: PreK K 1 2   E

1. Stories in rhyme 2. Snow -- Fiction 3. Winter -- Fiction

ISBN 978-0-8075-7526-0; 0-8075-7526-7

LC 2007052608

Illustrations and simple rhyming text portray winter activities, from snowman-building, sledding, and sitting by a fire to feeding birds

"The text is simple and bouncy, and the cartoon illustrations are bright, clear, and inclusive. The book's quick pace and cheerful pictures make it a perfect choice for seasonal storytimes." SLJ

Spring things; by Bob Raczka; illustrated by Judy Stead. Albert Whitman 2007 un il $16.95

Grades: PreK K 1 2   E
1. Spring -- Fiction
ISBN 978-0-8075-7596-3
LC 2006023403

Winter melts into spring with the sights and sounds of hopping and skipping, sowing and mowing, and blading and lemonading

"Stead's paintings add an entertaining element and useful clarification to the active text." SLJ

Summer wonders; illustrated by Judy Stead. Albert Whitman & Co. 2009 un il $16.99
Grades: PreK K 1 2   E
1. Stories in rhyme 2. Summer -- Fiction
ISBN 0-8075-7653-0; 978-0-8075-7653-3
LC 2008031037

Illustrations and rhyming text celebrate the sights and sounds of summer, from days of diving and swimming to nights of stargazing and fireflies.

"Bright-hued acrylic illustrations bring the expressive verbal images to life. The paintings are festive and entertaining." SLJ

Who loves the fall? by Bob Raczka; illustrated by Judy Stead. Albert Whitman 2007 un il $16.95
Grades: PreK K 1 2   E
1. Stories in rhyme 2. Autumn -- Fiction
ISBN 978-0-8075-9037-9; 0-8075-9037-1
LC 2007001506

Rhyming text and illustrations portray the sights and sounds of autumn, from "rakers, leapers, and corn crop reapers" to "trickers, treaters, and turkey eaters"

"The brightly colored, well-designed illustrations pulsate with energy, movement, and charm." SLJ

Radunsky, Vladimir

The **mighty** asparagus. Silver Whistle/Harcourt 2004 un il $16
Grades: K 1 2 3   E
1. Italy -- Fiction 2. Asparagus -- Fiction
ISBN 0-15-216743-9
LC 2003-12241

In Renaissance Italy, a large asparagus appears suddenly in the king's back yard, and he enlists the help of several people and animals, including a songbird, in order to get rid of it

"The lowbrow humor, the blind silliness, and the quirky exaggerations are childishness itself. For older children there is the appeal of random sarcasm and funky, distorted illustrations." SLJ

What does peace feel like? by V. Radunsky and children just like you from around the world. Atheneum Books for Young Readers 2004 un il $14.95
Grades: K 1 2 3   E
1. Peace
ISBN 0-689-86676-3
LC 2003-11506

Simple text and illustrations portray what peace looks, sounds, tastes, feels, and smells like to children around the world.

"As much a celebration of the five senses as an antiwar message, this bright picture book combines Radunsky's playful gouache double-page scenarios with quotes from grade-schoolers at an international school in Rome." Booklist

You? translated from Dog-ese to English by my learned dog, Tsetsa. Harcourt, Inc. 2009 un il $16
Grades: PreK K 1 2   E
1. Dogs -- Fiction
ISBN 978-0-15-205177-8; 0-15-205177-5
LC 2008-3281

A lonely girl and a stray dog find one another in a park.

"Radunsky makes the most of his canvas. . . . Thin, energetic lines define the forms minimally on gouache blobs of color, all arrayed on a generous expanse of buff-colored handmade paper. . . . The heartfelt, plaintive dialogue will hold readers' interest, and the wait makes the inevitable discovery—'Woof! YOU!'—all the sweeter." Kirkus

Rahaman, Vashanti

Divali rose; [by] Vashanti Rahaman; illustrated by Jamel Akib. Boyds Mills Press 2008 un il $16.95
Grades: 2 3 4   E
1. Divali -- Fiction 2. Trinidad -- Fiction 3. Prejudices -- Fiction 4. East Indians -- Fiction 5. Grandparents -- Fiction
ISBN 978-1-59078-524-9; 1-59078-524-X
LC 2007049686

As the festival of Divali approaches, Ricki wants to confess that he accidentally broke a rosebud off the bush he and his grandfather planted, but grandfather is busy blaming the neighbors who are newly arrived in Trinidad from India. Includes facts about Divali and the people and language of Trinidad

"This appealing, multilayered story will provoke discussion about resentments between different generations of immigrants. . . . Akib's impressionistic pastel paintings portray the tropical setting and Ricki's feelings of guilt." SLJ

Ramirez, Antonio

Napi; story by Antonio Ramirez; pictures by Domi. Groundwood Books 2004 un il $15.95
Grades: K 1 2 3   E
1. Dreams -- Fiction 2. Herons -- Fiction 3. Mexico -- Fiction 4. Mazatec Indians -- Fiction 5. Native Americans -- Mexico -- Fiction
ISBN 0-88899-610-1

Napi is a Mazatec Indian girl who loves to dream. One day, she dreams of becoming a heron and flying over the river.

"The clear, lyrical prose has a childlike charm that brilliantly recreates the joys of this child's experience. . . . Domi's primitive acrylic artwork enhances the sense of the story." SLJ

Other titles about Napi are:
Napi goes to the mountain (2006)
Napi makes a village (2010)

Ramos, Jorge

I'm just like my mom/I'm just like my dad; illustrated by Akemi Gutierrez. Rayo 2008 un il $16.99
Grades: PreK K   E
1. Bilingual books -- English-Spanish 2. Father-son relationship -- Fiction 3. Mother-daughter relationship -- Fiction
ISBN 978-0-06-123968-7; 0-06-123968-2

In two stories in English and Spanish, printed back to back, children reflect on how much they resemble their parents.

"This is a comforting celebration of family. . . . Spare illustrations is subtle colors completely fill each double-page spread and feature pleasant figures with enlarged oval heads, giving a happy, open, comfortable feel to the narratives." Booklist

Ramos, Mario

I am so strong; [translated by Jean Anderson] Gecko Press 2011 il

Grades: PreK K 1   E

1. Wolves -- Fiction

ISBN 0-9582-7877-6; 978-0-9582-7877-5

Original French edition, 2001

"This offering from Belgian author/illustrator Ramos is a single, drawn-out joke, but achieves keeper status with intelligent dialogue and Gallic sophistication. A megalomaniacal wolf strolls through the forest buttonholing fairy tale creatures and asking them to burnish his ego. . . . Ramos's thickly brushed paintings alternate between woodland scenes suggestive of stage scenery and closer shots of the wolf and other creatures against white backdrops, the better to appreciate the comic tension. . . . The wolf's comeuppance is deeply satisfying; the only disappointment is that the book is over so soon. Better read it again." Publ Wkly

Ramsey, Calvin Alexander

Belle, the last mule at Gee's Bend; [by] Calvin Alexander Ramsey and Bettye Stroud; illustrated by John Holyfield. Candlewick Press 2011 un il $15.99

Grades: PreK K 1 2   E

1. Clergy 2. Mules -- Fiction 3. Alabama -- Fiction 4. Nonfiction writers 5. Civil rights activists 6. Nobel laureates for peace 7. African Americans -- Civil rights -- Fiction

ISBN 978-0-7636-4058-3; 0-7636-4058-1

LC 2010048132

In Gee's Bend, Alabama, Miz Pettway tells young Alex about the historic role her mule played in the struggle for civil rights led by Dr. Martin Luther King, Jr. Includes factual information about the community of Gee's Bend and Martin Luther King, Jr.

"Holyfield's intense acrylic paintings, in blues, yellows and browns, evoke the heat and the drama. . . . A solid choice for parents and teachers who are introducing the 1960s to young children. An intergenerational story filled with heart and soul." Kirkus

★ **Ruth** and the Green Book; [by] Calvin Alexander Ramsey, with Gwen Strauss; illustrations by Floyd Cooper. Carolrhoda Books 2010 un il

Grades: K 1 2 3   E

1. Segregation -- Fiction 2. Southern States -- Fiction 3. Automobile travel -- Fiction 4. African Americans -- Segregation -- Fiction

ISBN 0761352554; 9780761352556

LC 2009034284

When Ruth and her parents take a motor trip from Chicago to Alabana to visit her grandmother, they rely on a pamphlet called "The Negro Motorist Green Book" to find places that will serve them. This title concludes with a historical note on the Green Book itself. "Ages five to nine." (Bull Cent Child Books)

This is a "powerful picture book. . . . Cooper's glowing, unframed, sepia-toned artwork delivers a strong sense of the period from a child's viewpoint. . . . This is a compelling addition to U.S. history offerings." Booklist

Rand, Ann

I know a lot of things; by Ann & Paul Rand. Chronicle Books 2009 un il $16.99

Grades: PreK K 1   E

1. Growth -- Fiction

ISBN 978-0-8118-6615-6

LC 2008020680

A reissue of the title first published 1956

Celebrates the many things young children know about their world, while looking forward to a time when they will know more

This is written "in poetic text. . . . Paul Rand's simply composed, ahead-of-their-time illustrations don't look the least bit dated and perfectly reflect the concepts in the text." Horn Book Guide

Sparkle and spin; a book about words. by Ann & Paul Rand. Chronicle Books 2006 un il $15.95

Grades: PreK K 1   E

1. Communication 2. English language

ISBN 978-0-8118-5003-2; 0-8118-5003-X

LC 2004-23260

A reissue of the title first published 1957 by Harcourt, Brace, and World

Lyrical text explores what words are and how they are used, highlighting such characteristics as that some words are spoken softly, some are shouted, some sound like their meaning, and some evoke certain feelings.

This "is a vibrantly eye-catching collection of visual puns and graphic double-entendres." NY Times Book Rev

Rand, Betseygail

Big Bunny; written by Betseygail Rand and Colleen Rand; illustrated by C. S. W. Rand. Tricycle Press 2011 un il $14.99; lib bdg $17.99

Grades: PreK K   E

1. Size -- Fiction 2. Easter -- Fiction 3. Rabbits -- Fiction

ISBN 978-1-58246-376-6; 1-58246-376-X; 978-1-58246-386-5 lib bdg; 1-58246-386-7 lib bdg

LC 2010018017

At first Big Bunny loves being big, taking the other little Easter bunnies for rides on her back throughout the countryside. When she accidentally breaks some of the Easter eggs she is helping decorate, she begins to feel clumsy and frustrated by her tremendous size. Happily, her little bunny friends show her how to help with her Easter tasks in a way only she can.

"This thoughtful, understated book with intriguing minimalist illustrations provides both an interesting Easter Bunny tale and a quiet message about helping someone who is different. . . . The unusual illustrations use simple, stylized shapes against whit backgrounds with bold colors and a minimum of detail." Kirkus

Randall, Alison L.

The **wheat** doll; [by] Alison L. Randall; illustrated by Bill Farnsworth. Peachtree Publishers 2008 30p il $16.95

Grades: K 1 2 3   E

1. Dolls -- Fiction 2. Storms -- Fiction 3. Frontier and pioneer life -- Fiction 4. Lost and found possessions -- Fiction

ISBN 978-1-56145-456-3; 1-56145-456-7

LC 2008-4562

On the nineteenth-century Utah frontier, Mary Ann is heartbroken when her doll Betty is lost during a fierce storm and her sadness lasts all winter long, until spring brings a wonderful surprise.

"This is a sweet story of loss and renewal told with empathy and feeling that is never heavy-handed. . . . Farnsworth's realistic oil paintings have a warm, soft quality that matches the tone of the text. . . . This picture book is a great addition." SLJ

Rania

The **sandwich** swap; by Her Majesty Queen Rania; with Kelly DiPucchio; illustrations by Tricia Tusa. Disney-Hyperion Books 2010 un il $16.99

Grades: PreK K 1 2   E

1. School stories 2. Food -- Fiction 3. Friendship -- Fiction 4. Toleration -- Fiction

ISBN 978-1-4231-2484-9; 1-4231-2484-7

LC 2009018673

"The day Lily stops eating her peanut butter and jelly sandwich to tell Salma her hummus and pita sandwich looks yucky—and vice versa—is the day they stop being friends. . . . When the two girls get caught in the middle of a food fight and called to the principal's office, they decide it's time to make some changes. . . . Soft watercolor cartoon illustrations portray a lively student body and a slightly forbidding principal. This engaging title reminds children that having the courage to try new things can result in positive experiences." SLJ

Rankin, Laura

Ruthie and the (not so) teeny tiny lie; [by] Laura Rankin. Bloomsbury Children's Books 2007 un il $15.95

Grades: PreK K   E

1. School stories 2. Foxes -- Fiction 3. Truthfulness and falsehood -- Fiction

ISBN 978-1-59990-010-0; 1-59990-010-6

LC 2006013192

Ruthie the fox loves tiny things and when she finds a tiny camera on the playground she is very happy, but after she lies and says the camera belongs to her, nothing seems to go right

"Emotionally authentic in text and art, this story gets its message across without preaching." SLJ

Ruthie and the (not so) very busy day; by Laura Rankin; illustrated by Laura Rankin. Bloomsbury 2014 32 p. col. ill. (hardcover) $17.99

Grades: PreK K   E

1. Girls -- Fiction 2. Parent-child relationship -- Fiction 3. Family life -- Fiction 4. Parent and child -- Fiction

ISBN 1599900521; 9781599900520; 9781619631625; 9781619632127

LC 2013034315

"It's Saturday morning--Ruthie's very favorite day. No school. No homework. No practices. Just a day to be with Mom and Dad. And Ruthie has BIG plans with her day off. But they keep getting interrupted. Dad has to go off to help Grandma. Mom has errands to run. Poor Ruthie is suddenly having the worst day ever!" (Publisher's note)

"Endearing illustrations of an anthropomorphized fox family depict both the chaos and pathos that are inevitable with this kind of day. Readers of all ages will easily identify with Ruthie's trying day." -Kirkus

Ransom, Candice F.

The **old** blue pickup truck; written by Candice F. Ransom; illustrated by Jenny Mattheson. Walker & Co. 2009 un il $16.99; lib bdg $17.89

Grades: PreK K 1   E

1. Trucks -- Fiction 2. Father-daughter relationship -- Fiction

ISBN 978-0-8027-9591-5; 0-8027-9591-9; 978-0-8027-9592-2 lib bdg; 0-8027-9592-7 lib bdg

LC 2008-40316

As a girl and her father run errands in their old blue pickup, she discovers how many different ways they can use their truck.

"This enjoyable story is accompanied by oil on primed paper illustrations that have a bright and clean feel." SLJ

Ransome, James

Gunner, football hero; [by] James E. Ransome. Holiday House 2010 un il $16.95

Grades: PreK K 1   E

1. Football -- Fiction

ISBN 978-0-8234-2053-7; 0-8234-2053-1

LC 2008-48487

When short, round Gunner, the third-string quarterback, finally gets to play in a big game, everyone treats him like a hero.

"The simple, economical narrative supposes a fair amount of familiarity with football but certainly conveys the thrill of Gunner's short time on the field. . . . Ransome's watercolor-and-line drawings as well as page layouts are appropriately full of action, and the faces of the players and crowds engagingly expressive and humorous." Kirkus

New red bike! [by] James E. Ransome. Holiday House 2011 un il $16.95

Grades: PreK K 1   E

1. Cycling -- Fiction 2. Bicycles -- Fiction 3. Friendship -- Fiction

ISBN 978-0-8234-2226-5; 0-8234-2226-7

Tom enjoys the thrill of riding his brand new bicycle, and then shares it with a friend.

"Story takes a backseat to a bigger emotional truth: a bike is an awesome thing. Wearing a bright red helmet that matches the bike's frame, Tom is truly at one with his machine, and Ransome . . . provides Zenlike text to match. . . . Each moment of action . . . gets its own watercolor and pencil image and perspective. . . . Newbie bikers should find that this book gives full voice to the joys of having wheels of one's own." Publ Wkly

Rao, Sandhya

My mother's sari; illustrated by Nina Sabnani. North South Books 2006 un il $14.95; pa $6.95

Grades: PreK K 1 2   E
1. India -- Fiction 2. Clothing and dress -- Fiction 3. Mother-daughter relationship -- Fiction
ISBN 0-7358-2101-1; 0-7358-2233-6 pa
First published in India

A little girl is fascinated by her mother's sari and finds many uses for it.

"Subtle backgrounds, lightly decorated with objects from nature, provide a gentle showcase for the children and the saris. Rao [uses] . . . childlike drawings to represent the kids and photographs of the cloths, bringing the fabric designs, colors, and folds up close. A winsome look at a fresh subject." Booklist

Rappaport, Doreen
★ The **secret** seder; illustrated by Emily Arnold McCully. Hyperion Books for Children 2005 un il $16.99
Grades: 2 3 4   E
1. Jews -- Fiction 2. France -- Fiction 3. Passover -- Fiction 4. Holocaust, 1933-1945 -- Fiction
ISBN 0-7868-0777-6
LC 2003-57115

During the Nazi occupation of France, a boy and his father slip out of their village and into the mountains, where they join a group of fellow Jews at a humble seder table

"Rappaport interweaves themes and descriptive text to create a meaningful story in a distinctive setting. An excellent discussion starter." SLJ

Raschka, Chris
★ A **ball** for Daisy; by Chris Raschka. Schwartz & Wade Books 2011 1 v. col. ill. $16.99; lib bdg $19.99
Grades: PreK K 1   E
1. Stories without words 2. Dogs -- Fiction 3. Play -- Fiction
ISBN 978-0-375-85861-1; 0-375-85861-X; 978-0-375-95861-8 lib bdg; 0-375-95861-4 lib bdg
LC 2010024132

Caldecott Medal (2012)

In this wordless picture book, Daisy the dog "loves playing with her ball . . . until the fateful moment that another dog bites too hard on the ball and deflates it. . . . Raschka uses fairly sophisticated comic-book arrangements . . . but masks them with soft watercolor edges instead of sharp corners. The result feels like something made of pure emotion, a pretty close approximation of what it's probably like to be a dog." Booklist

★ **Daisy** gets lost; Chris Raschka. Schwartz & Wade Books 2013 32 p. (glb) $20.99
Grades: PreK K   E
1. Stories without words 2. Dogs -- Fiction 3. Lost and found possessions -- Fiction
ISBN 0449817423; 9780449817414; 9780449817421
LC 2012049221

Author Chris Raschka's book will "follow Daisy the dog on her next adventure. . . . Raschka has created a story that explores fear as only he can. Any child who has ever felt lost will relate to Daisy's despair upon finding herself in an unfamiliar part of the park after chasing a squirrel. In a nearly wordless picture book, Daisy encounters the unease of being lost and the joys of being found." (Publisher's note)

★ **Everyone** can learn to ride a bicycle; Chris Raschka. Schwartz & Wade Books 2013 32 p. (hardcover) $16.99
Grades: PreK K 1 2   E
1. Picture books for children 2. Bicycles -- Fiction 3. Father-daughter relationship -- Fiction 4. Fathers and daughters -- Fiction 5. Bicycles and bicycling -- Fiction
ISBN 0375870075; 9780375870071; 9780375970078
LC 2012009172

In this children's picture book, by Chris Raschka, "a father takes his daughter through all the steps in the process [of riding a bike]--from choosing the perfect bicycle to that triumphant first successful ride. . . . [The] picture book . . . not only shows kids how to learn to ride, but captures what it feels like to fall . . . get up . . . fall again . . . and finally . . . ride a bicycle!" (Publisher's note)

"Rendered in Raschka's signature style of fluid, kinetic brushstrokes, the ink-and-watercolor illustrations beautifully capture the action and emotion in each scene...Deceptively simple and perfectly paced for read-alouds, this latest from the two-time Caldecott medalist captures a child's everyday experience with gentle, joyful sensitivity." Booklist

Farmy farm; by Chris Raschka. Orchard Books 2011 il $8.99
Grades: PreK   E
1. Stories in rhyme 2. Sounds -- Fiction 3. Farm life -- Fiction 4. Domestic animals -- Fiction
ISBN 978-0-545-21981-5
LC 2010039061

Rhyming text and touch-and-feel illustrations introduce a variety of farm animals and the sounds they make.

"The book's repeated verse, buoyant palette, and soft texture should find an enthusiastic toddler-aged audience." Publ Wkly

Five for a little one; [by] Chris Raschka. Atheneum Books for Young Readers 2006 un il $16.95
Grades: PreK K   E
1. Counting 2. Stories in rhyme 3. Rabbits -- Fiction 4. Senses and sensation -- Fiction
ISBN 978-0-689-84599-4; 0-689-84599-5
LC 2005-08963

"A buoyant bunny, drawn in thick ink outline with a fuzzy body and delightfully mismatched ears (one downy and one plain), introduces readers to the senses, numbering them one through five. The rhyming verses and ebullient artwork convey a child's curiosity and enthusiasm for investigating the world in various ways." SLJ

Hip hop dog; words by Chris Raschka; pictures by Vladimir Radunsky. Harper 2010 un il $16.99; lib bdg $17.89
Grades: PreK K 1 2   E
1. Stories in rhyme 2. Dogs -- Fiction 3. Hip-hop -- Fiction 4. Rap music -- Fiction
ISBN 978-0-06-123963-2; 0-06-123963-1; 978-0-06-123964-9 lib bdg; 0-06-123964-X lib bdg
LC 2008031449

A neglected dog finds his purpose through rapping and rhyming.

"This is great for reading aloud. . . . The well-matched mixed-media illustrations show lively urban scenes. . . . Kids will chant along to the text, which slides and whirls across the pages." Booklist

John Coltrane's Giant steps; remixed by Chris Raschka. Atheneum Bks. for Young Readers 2002 33p il $17
Grades: K 1 2 3   E
    1. Jazz music
    ISBN 0-689-84598-7
       LC 2001-33755
John Coltrane's musical composition is performed by a box, a snowflake, some raindrops, and a kitten

"Like Coltrane, Raschka is creating something deeply personal here that we don't need to understand fully to appreciate. Instead, he asks us to trust our own understanding of raindrops, snowflakes, kittens, and music to experience the book. Anyone who's still intimidated by jazz after giving this book a chance is probably just trying too hard." Horn Book

★ **Little** black crow; [by] Chris Raschka. Atheneum Books for Young Readers 2010 un il $16.99
Grades: K 1 2 3   E
    1. Stories in rhyme 2. Crows -- Fiction
    ISBN 978-0-689-84601-4; 0-689-84601-0
       LC 2009032110
A boy thinks about the life of a little black crow that he sees, wondering where it goes in the snow, where it sleeps, and whether or not it worries like he does.

"Impressionistic watercolor landscapes perfectly set the mood and style for these awe-filled inquiries of a curious child." SLJ

New York is English, Chattanooga is Creek; by Chris Raschka. Atheneum Books for Young Readers 2005 un il $16.95
Grades: K 1 2 3   E
    1. Cities and towns -- Fiction 2. Geographic names -- Fiction
    ISBN 0-689-84600-2
       LC 2004-23188
New York City, though a bit boastful, decides to throw a party to make new friends of other unique cities like Chattanooga and Minneapolis

"This is both a fascinating exploration of the etymology and derivation of American city names and a characteristic Raschka farcical flight-of-fancy. . . . Raschka's illustrations rendered in ink and watercolor employ his loose, impressionistic, brushy style to perfect effect, giving the book its humor while artfully delivering his message and entertaining information." SLJ

★ **Peter** and the wolf; retold by Chris Raschka. Atheneum Books for Young Readers 2008 un il $17.99
Grades: PreK K 1 2   E
    1. Fairy tales 2. Wolves -- Fiction
    ISBN 978-0-689-85652-5; 0-689-85652-0
       LC 2008-04472
Retells the orchestral fairy tale in which a boy ignores his grandfather's warnings and captures a wolf with the help of a bird, a duck, and a cat

"Raschka conveys the mounting suspense in lilting words, swerving zigzags and curves. . . . Raschka's pictures—of characters venturing close to the wolf's bear-trap

jaws, of the cat's enormous face looming over a tiny Peter—gain extra energy from geometrically shaped color blocks on the same spreads. . . . One reading will not be enough to appreciate the artist's keen attention to detail." Publ Wkly

★ **Yo!** Yes? by Chris Raschka. Orchard Bks. 1993 un il $15.95
Grades: PreK K 1 2   E
    1. Friendship -- Fiction 2. Race relations -- Fiction 3. African Americans -- Fiction
    ISBN 0-531-05469-1
       LC 92-25644
A Caldecott Medal honor book, 1994
Two lonely characters, one black and one white, meet on the street and become friends

"The design and drawing are bold, spare and expressive; the language has the strength and rhythm of a playground chant." Bull Cent Child Books
Another title about these characters is:
Ring! Yo? (2000)

Rathmann, Peggy
★ **10** minutes till bedtime. Putnam 1998 un il $16.99; pa $6.99; bd bk $7.99
Grades: PreK K 1 2   E
    1. Bedtime -- Fiction 2. Hamsters -- Fiction
    ISBN 0-399-23103-X; 0-14-240024-6 pa; 0-399-23770-4 bd bk
       LC 97-51295
A boy's hamster leads an increasingly large group of hamsters on a tour of the boy's house, while his father counts down the minutes to bedtime

"Children will pore over the comical details and follow closely the antics of the numbered hamsters, each one with a personality of its own." SLJ

★ **The day** the babies crawled away. Putnam 2003 un il $16.99
Grades: PreK K 1 2   E
    1. Stories in rhyme 2. Infants -- Fiction
    ISBN 0-399-23196-X
       LC 2002-152002
A boy follows fives babies who crawl away from a picnic and saves the day by bringing them back

This is a "rollicking rhyming tale, illustrated in needle-sharp, atmospheric silhouettes against twilight skies." Publ Wkly

★ **Good** night, Gorilla. Putnam 1994 un il
Grades: PreK K 1 2   E
    1. Zoos -- Fiction 2. Animals -- Fiction
    ISBN 0-399-22445-9; 0-399-23003-3 bd bk; 0-698-11649-6 pa
       LC 92-29020
In this picture book, "a zookeeper makes his final rounds of the day, bidding his charges good night, while unbeknownst to him the gorilla, who has taken his keys, lets each animal out after the keeper has passed. . . . {They} follow the zookeeper home to his house and curl up for the night in his room, undiscovered until his wife says 'Good night, dear' and gets more responses than she had bargained for. Mrs. Zookeeper then trudges back to the zoo and returns the would-be guests, but the gorilla and his mouse side-

kick sneak back again.... Ages two to five." (Bull Cent Child Books)

"In a book economical in text and simple in illustration, the many amusing, small details, as well as the tranquil tone of the story, make this an outstanding picture book." Horn Book Guide

★ **Officer** Buckle and Gloria. Putnam 1995 un il
Grades: PreK K 1 2   E
   1. School stories 2. Dogs -- Fiction 3. Safety education -- Fiction
   ISBN 0399226168

                                LC 93-43887
Awarded the Caldecott Medal, 1996

"When rotund, good-natured Officer Buckle visits school assemblies to read off his sensible safety tips, the children listen, bored and polite, dozing off one by one. But when the new police dog, Gloria, stands behind him, secretly miming the dire consequences of acting imprudently, the children suddenly become attentive, laughing uproariously and applauding loudly. The good policeman is first gratified with the response, then deflated to learn that Gloria was stealing the show. Finally, he realizes that he and Gloria make a great team, and they take their show on the road again, adding a new message, 'Always Stick With Your Buddy!'" (Booklist) "Kindergarten to grade three." (SLJ)

"When rotund, good-natured officer Buckle visits school assemblies to read off his sensible safety tips, the children listen, bored and polite, dozing off one by one. But when the new police dog, Gloria, stands behind him, secretly miming the dire consequences of acting imprudently, the children suddenly become attentive, laughing uproariously and applauding loudly.... The deadpan humor of the text and slapstick wit of the illustrations make a terrific combination. Large, expressive line drawings illustrate the characters with finesse, and the Kool-Aid-bright washes add energy and pizzazz." Booklist

Rattigan, Jama Kim
   Dumpling soup; illustrated by Lillian Hsu-Flanders. Little, Brown 1993 un il hardcover o.p. pa $6.99
Grades: K 1 2 3   E
   1. Hawaii -- Fiction 2. New Year -- Fiction 3. Family life -- Fiction
   ISBN 0-316-73445-4; 0-316-73047-5 pa
                                LC 91-42949
"Marisa, a seven-year-old Asian-American girl who lives in Hawaii, explains the traditions that exist in her family to celebrate the New Year. Her family ... consists of people who are Japanese, Chinese, Korean, Hawaiian, and haole (Hawaiian for white person).... A glossary of English, Hawaiian, Japanese, and Korean words provides pronunciations and definitions for many of the possibly unfamiliar terms that weave in and out of the text. A thoroughly enjoyable celebration of family warmth and diverse traditions, illustrated with cheery watercolors." Horn Book

Rau, Dana Meachen, 1971-
   Robot, Go Bot! by Dana Meachen Rau; illustrated by Wook Jin Jung. Random House Inc. 2013 32 p. col. ill. (paperback) $3.99; (library) $12.99
Grades: PreK K 1   E
   1. Robots -- Fiction 2. Cartoons and comics 3. Robots

-- Cartoons and comics
   ISBN 0375870830; 9780375870835; 9780375970832
                                LC 2012027691
In this book for beginning readers, "a girl assembles a robot and then treats it like a slave until it goes on strike. Having put the robot together from a jumble of loose parts, the budding engineer issues an increasingly peremptory series of rhymed orders--'Throw, Bot. / Row, Bot'--that turn from playful activities like chasing bubbles in the yard to tasks like hoeing the garden, mowing the lawn and towing her around in a wagon." (Kirkus Reviews)

Rausch, Molly
   My cold went on vacation; [by] Molly Rausch and [illustrated by] Nora Krug. G.P. Putnam's Sons 2011 un il $16.99
Grades: PreK K   E
   1. Sick -- Fiction 2. Cold (Disease) -- Fiction
   ISBN 978-0-399-25474-1; 0-399-25474-9
A little boy is curious about all the places his cold might go after it leaves him.

"Bold, whimsical art neatly complements the text, adding fantastical details and additional humor. ... A perfect choice for readers with the sniffles and those who enjoy their stories with a twist." SLJ

Raven, Margot
   ★ **Circle** unbroken; the story of a basket and its people. [by] Margot Theis Raven; pictures by E. B. Lewis. Farrar, Straus and Giroux 2004 un il $16; pa $7.99
Grades: K 1 2 3   E
   1. Baskets -- Fiction 2. Gullahs -- Fiction 3. African Americans -- Fiction
   ISBN 0-374-31289-3; 0-312-37603-0 pa
                                LC 2002-24009
A grandmother tells the tale of Gullahs and their beautiful sweetgrass baskets that keep their African heritage alive

"Raven's text masterfully frames several hundred years of African-American history within the picture-book format. Lewis's double-page, watercolor images are poignant and perfectly matched to the text and mood." SLJ

   ★ **Night** boat to freedom; [by] Margot Theis Raven; pictures by E. B. Lewis. Farrar, Straus and Giroux 2006 un il $16; pa $6.99
Grades: 1 2 3 4   E
   1. Quilts -- Fiction 2. Slavery -- Fiction 3. African Americans -- Fiction 4. Underground railroad -- Fiction
   ISBN 978-0-374-31266-4; 0-374-31266-4; 978-0-312-55018-9 pa; 0-312-55018-9 pa
At the request of his fellow slave Granny Judith, Christmas John risks his life to take runaways across a river from Kentucky to Ohio.

"The older mentor is as tough as the young boy, and Lewis' beautiful, unframed double-page spreads depict the bond between them. ... Words and pictures work perfectly together." Booklist

Ravishankar, Anushka
   ★ **Elephants** never forget; illustrated by Christiane Pieper. Houghton Mifflin Company 2008 un il $16
Grades: PreK K 1 2   E
   1. Stories in rhyme 2. Elephants -- Fiction 3. Water

buffalo -- Fiction

ISBN 978-0-618-99784-8; 0-618-99784-9

LC 2007-25745

A lonely elephant meets a herd of buffaloes and decides to stay with them, but when they meet up with some elephants, he must make an important decision

The "story is full of good read-aloud noises. . . . Pieper . . . produces digital woodcuts that . . . [eschew] cuteness in favor of strength and clarity. A two-color scheme—black and periwinkle on cream-colored paper—and bold, simple spreads focus attention on the ponderous forms of the elephant and buffalo. Varied compositions as well as printed letters that grow and shrink and dance across the pages match the dexterity of the text with a visual sprightliness." Publ Wkly

★ **Tiger** on a tree; [by] Anushka Ravishankar, Pulak Biswas. Farrar, Straus and Giroux 2004 un il $15

Grades: PreK K 1 2   E

1. Stories in rhyme 2. Tigers -- Fiction

ISBN 0-374-37555-0

LC 2003-49050

First published 1997 in India

After trapping a tiger in a tree, a group of men must decide what to do with it

"This very simple chanting story is perfect for reading aloud with young preschoolers. . . . The thickly stroked illustrations, mostly black and white, have occasional splashes of orange." Booklist

Rawlinson, Julia

★ **Fletcher** and the falling leaves; pictures by Tiphanie Beeke. Greenwillow Books 2006 un il $16.99; pa $6.99

Grades: PreK K 1 2   E

1. Foxes -- Fiction 2. Trees -- Fiction 3. Autumn -- Fiction 4. Leaves -- Fiction

ISBN 978-0-06-113401-2; 0-06-113401-5; 978-0-06-157397-2 pa; 0-06-157397-3 pa

LC 2005-34348

When his favorite tree begins to lose its leaves, Fletcher the fox worries that it is sick, but instead a magical sight is in store for him.

"This potent synthesis of art and prose conveys a child's first awareness of the changing seasons with reverence and wonder. . . . Beeke's resplendent watercolors work beautifully with the book's tone, content, layout, and design." SLJ

Other titles about Fletcher the fox are:

Fletcher and the springtime blossoms (2009)

Fletcher and the snowflake Christmas (2010)

Ray, Jane

Ahmed and the feather girl. Frances Lincoln Children's 2010 un il $17.95

Grades: K 1 2 3   E

1. Magic -- Fiction 2. Circus -- Fiction 3. Orphans -- Fiction

ISBN 978-1-84507-988-8; 1-84507-988-4

Ahmed is a poor orphan who lives with a travelling circus and works for cruel Madame Saleem. His life is changed forever when he finds a beautiful egg in the forest and brings it back to the circus. From the egg hatches a little girl called Aurelia, and as she grows she sprouts soft feathers that turn into wings.

"The moving story, layered with magical moments, is truly expressed in Ray's triumphant art. With her signature mix of patterning, collage, and golden flourishes, the spreads have much to look at." Booklist

★ The **apple**-pip princess. Candlewick Press 2008 un il $16.99

Grades: PreK K 1 2   E

1. Fairy tales 2. Seeds -- Fiction 3. Apples -- Fiction 4. Princesses -- Fiction

ISBN 978-0-7636-3747-7; 0-7636-3747-5

LC 2007-34239

In a land that has stood barren, parched by drought and ravaged by frosts since the Queen's death, the King sets his three daughters the task of making the kingdom bloom again, and discovers that sometimes the smallest things can make the biggest difference.

"Ray's rich language and sure pacing create a winning read-aloud, but it's the shining collage artwork that really stands out. Mixing color photos into her typically fine, elaborately decorated illustrations, Ray creates dramatic scenes." Booklist

The **dollhouse** fairy. Candlewick Press 2009 un il $16.99

Grades: PreK K 1 2   E

1. Sick -- Fiction 2. Fairies -- Fiction 3. Dollhouses -- Fiction 4. Father-daughter relationship -- Fiction

ISBN 978-0-7636-4411-6; 0-7636-4411-0

LC 2009-18405

Worried about her father's trip to the hospital, Rosy goes to play with the special dollhouse he built for her and finds Thistle, a very messy and mischievous fairy who needs a place to stay while her injured wing mends.

"The story unfolds with subtlety and sensitivity to the emotional issues at its heart. The book's large format gives plenty of space for the vibrant mixed-media artwork." Booklist

Ray, Mary Lyn

★ **Christmas** farm; illustrated by Barry Root. Harcourt 2008 un il $17

Grades: K 1 2   E

1. Trees -- Fiction 2. Gardening -- Fiction

ISBN 978-0-15-216290-0; 0-15-216290-9

LC 2007-15216

Wilma decides to plant Christmas trees with the help of her young neighbor, Parker.

"Root's appealing watercolor-and-gouache illustrations invite inspection. . . . [This is] a story that lovingly depicts the hard work, cooperation, and patience necessary to grow crops." Booklist

Deer dancer; Mary Lyn Ray; illustrated by Lauren Stringer. Beach Lane Books 2014 40 p. col. ill. (hardcover) $17.99

Grades: PreK K 1 2   E

1. Deer -- Fiction 2. Dance -- Fiction

ISBN 144243421X; 9781442434219; 9781442434226

LC 2012042214

In this picture book, by Mary Lyn Ray and illustrated by Lauren Stringer, "a young ballerina finds dancing inspiration in the natural world. 'There's a place I go that's green and grass, a place I thought that no one knew—until the deer came.'" (Publisher's note)

"Poetic text and soft, sun-dappled acrylic illustrations capture the enchantment of their duet, the hidden clearing, and the girl's love of movement." Horn Book

★ **Stars**. Beach Lane Books 2011 un il $16.99
Grades: PreK K 1　　　　　　　　　　　　　E
　1. Stars -- Fiction
　ISBN 978-1-4424-2249-0; 1-4424-2249-1
　　　　　　　　　　　　　　LC 2010033253
"A poetic paean to stars both real and metaphorical brings the heavenly down to readers without robbing it of mystery. . . . Frazee excels at illustrating textual details in fresh ways, keeping young children engaged and curious. . . . Her pictures ebb and flow with the text, alternating charming spots of self-possessed, spirited youngsters with ink-black or gloriously blue, starry heavens inviting dreamy meditation." Kirkus

Rayner, Catherine
　★ The **bear** who shared. Dial Books for Young Readers 2011 un il $16.99
Grades: PreK K 1　　　　　　　　　　　　　E
　1. Mice -- Fiction 2. Bears -- Fiction 3. Raccoons -- Fiction 4. Friendship -- Fiction
　ISBN 978-0-8037-3576-7; 0-8037-3576-6
　　　　　　　　　　　　　　LC 2010012142
First published 2010 in the United Kingdom with title: Norris, the bear who shared

Norris the bear has been waiting patiently for the last ripe fruit to fall from the tree, and when it does he decides to share it with his two new friends, Tulip the raccoon and Violet the mouse.

"Rayner's quirky illustrations are the real star of the book; deceptively basic compositions with barely-there watercolor strokes that manage to look simultaneously haphazard and carefully applied. . . . The minimal text is accessible to the very youngest readers." Kirkus

　★ **Ernest,** the moose who doesn't fit. Farrar, Straus and Giroux 2010 un il $16.99
Grades: PreK K 1　　　　　　　　　　　　　E
　1. Size -- Fiction 2. Moose -- Fiction 3. Chipmunks -- Fiction
　ISBN 978-0-374-32217-5; 0-374-32217-1
A rather large moose who cannot fit on the page teams up with his little chipmunk friend to find a solution. Final pages form a gatefold.

"The collage illustrations on a background of a softly hued green grid contrast the moose's grand dimensions with that of the tiny chipmunk in a gently humorous fashion. . . . The language is engaging and inventive." Kirkus

　Solomon Crocodile. Farrar Straus & Giroux 2011 un il $15.99
Grades: PreK K 1　　　　　　　　　　　　　E
　1. Play -- Fiction 2. Crocodiles -- Fiction 3. Friendship -- Fiction
　ISBN 978-0-374-38064-9; 0-374-38064-3
　　　　　　　　　　　　　　LC 2010045855
Solomon Crocodile's rough play prevents him from making friends down by the river until a stranger comes stomping through the reeds!

"Rayner's lush illustrations reflect the tension between the puppyish croc and his staider neighbors. . . . Solomon practically vibrates energy. . . . The well-paced story has just enough tension to draw in little troublemakers who will cheer for Solomon's eventual triumph." Horn Book

Reagan, Jean
　How to babysit a grandma; by Jean Reagan; illustrated by Lee Wildish. Alfred A. Knopf 2014 32 p. (hardcover library binding) $19.99
Grades: PreK K 1 2　　　　　　　　　　　　E
　1. Humorous fiction 2. Babysitters -- Fiction 3. Grandmothers -- Fiction
　ISBN 0385753853; 9780385753845; 9780385753852
　　　　　　　　　　　　　　LC 2013019509
In this children's book, written by Jean Reagan and illustrated by Lee Wildish, "a young girl heads over to her grandma's house for a sleepover babysitting session-with the child providing clear and humorous instructions to readers on how to care for a grandma. The to-do list contains many choices for Grandma to select from, including a walk to the park, reading, taking photos, playing dress-up, and adding sugary sprinkles to her meal items." (School Library Journal)

"In this companion to How to Babysit a Grandpa (2012), Reagan offers a fun, relatable story about the qualities of being a good babysitter, told from the perspective of a little girl who is spending quality time with her grandmother...Particularly clear in an evening scene as the girl and her grandma observe the stars in the purplish night sky, the mood of kindness, love, and togetherness comes through on every page." Booklist

　How to babysit a grandpa; by Jean Reagan; illustrated by Lee Wildish. Alfred A. Knopf 2012 32 p. (hard cover) $16.99
Grades: PreK K 1 2　　　　　　　　　　　　E
　1. Humorous fiction 2. Babysitters -- Fiction 3. Grandfathers -- Fiction 4. Humorous stories
　ISBN 0375867139; 9780375867132; 9780375967139
　　　　　　　　　　　　　　LC 2010052507
This children's book, written by Jean Reagan and illustrated by Lee Wildish, is "about a child spending time with his grandpa. Written in a how-to style, the narrator gives important tips for 'babysitting' a grandpa, including what to eat for snack, . . . what to do on a walk, . . . and how to play with a grandpa." (Publisher's note)

"A boy's tips for babysitting a grandpa include hiding when he arrives; fixing snacks such as "anything dipped in ketchup"; looking for "lizards, cool rocks, and dandelion puffs" on walks; and so on...The humorous illustrations include a snoozing grandpa with a meowing cat atop his head to wake him up. Youngsters will recognize some of the sayings they've heard from their own grandparents and will thoroughly enjoy the tongue-in-cheek role reversal." SLJ

Reasoner, Charles
　One blue fish; a colorful counting book. Little Simon 2010 un il $9.99
Grades: PreK　　　　　　　　　　　　　　E
　1. Color 2. Counting
　ISBN 978-1-4169-9672-9; 1-4169-9672-9
"Combining counting and color identification, this book introduces various pond-dwelling creatures. On the left side of the spread, a number from 1 to 10 is spelled out. On the

right, the die-cut numeral is on a foldout flap. When the page is opened, a creature in the corresponding color and quantity is depicted with identifying text, such as '10 yellow ducks.' The layout successfully reinforces the simple concepts, and the bold digital illustrations are set against a solid background." SLJ

Recorvits, Helen

★ **My** name is Yoon; pictures by Gabi Swiatkowska. Frances Foster Bks. 2002 un il $16

Grades: PreK K 1 2   **E**

1. Immigrants -- Fiction 2. Korean Americans -- Fiction
ISBN 0-374-35114-7

LC 00-51395

Disliking her name as written in English, Korean-born Yoon, or "shining wisdom," refers to herself as "cat," "bird," and "cupcake," as a way to feel more comfortable in her new school and new country

"Swiatkowska's stunningly spare, almost surrealistic paintings enhance the story's message. . . . A powerful and inspiring picture book." SLJ

Other titles about Yoon are:
Yoon and the Christmas mitten (2006)
Yoon and the jade bracelet (2008)

Reed, Lynn Rowe

Basil's birds. Marshall Cavendish Children 2010 un il $17.99

Grades: K 1 2   **E**

1. Birds -- Fiction 2. Janitors -- Fiction
ISBN 978-0-7614-5627-8; 0-7614-5627-9

LC 2009007071

While Basil the school janitor is napping, birds build a nest atop his head and when the eggs hatch, he becomes a proud 'dad' to the chicks.

"Brightly painted clay birds and photographs of the nest and worms are scanned into Reed's gouache illustrations. Her childlike paintings are done in flat spring colors, often showing faces in profile and bodies so loose jointed that they hardly seem earthbound." SLJ

Color chaos! Holiday House 2010 un il $16.95

Grades: PreK K 1 2   **E**

1. School stories 2. Color -- Fiction 3. Illustrators -- Fiction
ISBN 978-0-8234-2257-9; 0-8234-2257-7

LC 2009029053

"The narrator, an aspiring illustrator who is itching to use his new box of 64 crayons, runs afoul of 'substitute principal' Mr. Greystone . . . who furiously confiscates all coloring tools and bans 'color of any kind.' With the school suddenly a sea of gray—not an ideal turn of events given that the day's guest is a famous illustrator, Maurice Coleur—can the discarded crayons, markers, and paints overcome their bickering . . . and stage a comeback? Reed's . . . terse, reportorial prose is the perfect counterfoil to the subtly controlled chaos of her collage and acrylic illustrations." Publ Wkly

Roscoe and the pelican rescue. Holiday House 2011 un il $14.95

Grades: PreK K 1   **E**

1. Pelicans -- Fiction 2. Vacations -- Fiction 3. Oil spills -- Fiction 4. Wildlife conservation -- Fiction 5.

Gulf of Mexico oil spill, 2010 -- Fiction
ISBN 978-0-8234-2352-1; 0-8234-2352-2

LC 2010045005

The Gulf Coast oil spill turns Tony's summer vacation into an animal rescue mission.

"Reed's narrative is straightforward, ending happily. . . . Reed's illustrations are deliberately child-like. . . . This . . . should appeal to many young nature lovers." Booklist

Rees, Douglas

Jeannette Claus saves Christmas; illustrated by Olivier Latyk. Margaret K. McElderry Books 2010 un il $16.99

Grades: PreK K 1 2   **E**

1. Reindeer -- Fiction 2. Christmas -- Fiction 3. Santa Claus -- Fiction
ISBN 978-1-4169-2686-3; 1-4169-2686-0

LC 2008023021

When Santa falls sick on Christmas Eve, his feisty daughter Jeannette takes his place in the sleigh and saves the day, despite rebellious reindeer.

"The Photoshop-rendered artwork has a retro cut-paper feel and is filled with implausibly pastel animals and romantic big-city backdrops. With its unlikely antagonists and plucky heroine, this has the potential to be a fan favorite." Booklist

Regan, Dian Curtis

The **Snow** Blew Inn; illustrated by Doug Cushman. Holiday House 2011 un il $16.95

Grades: PreK K 1   **E**

1. Snow -- Fiction 2. Animals -- Fiction 3. Cousins -- Fiction 4. Hotels and motels -- Fiction
ISBN 0-8234-2351-4; 978-0-8234-2351-4

Emma can't wait to have a sleepover with her cousin Abby! But snow is falling outside the Snow Blew Inn where Emma is waiting. Stranded travelers arrive seeking shelter, and soon the inn is packed. Emma even gives up her own room for the Fox family. When Abby finally arrives, she and Emma camp out on the parlor floor and have their sleepover at last!

"Regan and Cushman . . . pull readers into the story with strong atmospherics. With simple prose and crisp but warm watercolors, they conjure up the ever accumulating snow and guests—an array of anthropomorphized animals, dressed in vivid Victorian garb—and a palpable spirit of hospitality that turns a shelter into an arklike community brimming with Dickensian bonhomie and gratitude." Publ Wkly

Reibstein, Mark

★ **Wabi** Sabi; art by Ed Young. Little, Brown 2008 un il $16.99

Grades: 2 3 4   **E**

1. Cats -- Fiction 2. Japan -- Fiction 3. Animals -- Fiction 4. Aesthetics -- Fiction
ISBN 978-0-316-11825-5; 0-316-11825-7

LC 2007-50895

Wabi Sabi, a cat living in the city of Kyoto, learns about the Japanese concept of beauty through simplicity as she asks various animals she meets about the meaning of her name.

"Young's beautiful collages have an almost 3D effect and perfectly complement the spiritual, lyrical text." SLJ

Reich, Susanna

★ **Minette's** feast; the delicious story of Julia Child and her cat. by Susanna Reich; illustrated by Amy Bates. Abrams Books for Young Readers 2012 40 p.

Grades: K 1 2 3   E

1. Cats -- Fiction 2. French cooking -- Fiction 3. Paris (France) -- Fiction 4. Picture books for children 5. France -- Fiction 6. Food habits -- Fiction

ISBN 1419701770; 9781419701771

LC 2011034275

This biographical picture book "introduces the iconic American chef Julia Child to a new audience of young readers through the story of her spirited cat, Minette, whom Julia adopted when living in Paris. While Julia is in the kitchen learning to master delicious French dishes, the only feast Minette is truly interested in is that of fresh mouse!" (Publisher's note)

Includes bibliographical references.

Reid, Alastair

Supposing; illustrated by Bob Gill. New York Review Books 2010 il (New York Review Children's Collection) $15.95

Grades: PreK K 1   E

1. Imagination -- Fiction

ISBN 978-1-59017-369-5; 1-59017-369-4

LC 2010016522

First published 1960 by Little, Brown

A child imagines many silly, impossible, and even naughty things and their possible consequences, from learning unusual languages to building a tiny boat and sailing around the world.

"The scenarios are (often surreal) springboards for readers' imaginations. . . . There's an understated but fitting whimsy in Gill's artwork." Publ Wkly

Reid, Barbara

★ **Perfect** snow. Albert Whitman & Company 2011 un il

Grades: K 1 2   E

1. School stories 2. Snow -- Fiction 3. Friendship -- Fiction

ISBN 0-8075-6492-3; 978-0-8075-6492-9

LC 2010045643

On the first snow of the season, Jim and Scott and their classmates build an enormous snowman fort.

"The boys' personality differences are marked throughout the book, but their rock-solid friendship is at the heart of the understated, but satisfying story. Reid's artwork takes two forms; large, colorful plasticine illustrations, and small ink drawings with sepia-toned, watercolor washes. In either medium, the figures of children are expressive and pleasing." Booklist

★ **Picture** a tree; Barbara Reid. Albert Whitman 2013 32 p. (hardcover) $16.99

Grades: PreK K 1   E

1. Picture books for children 2. Trees -- Fiction

ISBN 0807565261; 9780807565261

LC 2012019530

In this children's picture book, "viewers are invited to think about how trees can be pictured: as a drawing on the sky, a skeleton, a tunnel, an ocean, a pirate ship, and more. . . . The book is not a guide to learning about trees but rather

a lyrical request to explore them in our personal worlds." (School Library Journal)

"The book is not a guide to learning about trees but rather a lyrical request to explore them in our personal worlds... The vibrant pictures will draw in readers, while the text will encourage them to view the world in a different way." SLJ

The **Subway** mouse. Scholastic Press 2005 un il $15.95

Grades: PreK K 1 2   E

1. Mice -- Fiction 2. Subways -- Fiction

ISBN 0-439-72827-4

First published 2003 in Canada

Remembering childhood stories of a beautiful but dangerous place called Tunnel's End, a mouse named Nib leaves his dirty, crowded home under a busy subway station and sets out on a long journey, joined by Lola, a mouse he meets along the way.

"Reid creates a charming, lively adventure in short, smoothly paced sentences, but it's her marvelous collage illustrations that really bring the characters and richly imagined world to life. Working in found materials and expertly molded, brightly colored plasticine, she sculpts remarkably expressive characters and a vivid, subterranean world." Booklist

Reid, Rob

Comin' down to storytime; pictures by Nadine Bernard Westcott. Upstart Books 2009 32p il $17.95

Grades: PreK K 1   E

1. Songs 2. Farm life -- Fiction 3. Libraries -- Fiction 4. Storytelling -- Fiction

ISBN 978-1-60213-039-5; 1-60213-039-6

"Building on the familiar song 'She'll Be Coming 'Round the Mountain,' Reid's animal version begins, 'We'll be comin' down to storytime when we come. Yee ha!' as all the farm animals run excitedly to the barn. It ends with 'We will check out lots of books when we leave. Bye now!' . . . Illustrations fit the rollicking mood perfectly. Westcott imbues each scene with plenty of color and lively action." SLJ

Reidy, Jean

All through my town; by Jean Reidy; illustrated by Leo Timmers. Bloomsbury Childrens 2013 32 p. col. ill. (hardcover) $14.99; (library) $15.89

Grades: PreK   E

1. Stories in rhyme 2. Neighborhoods -- Fiction 3. City and town life -- Fiction

ISBN 9781599907857; 9781619630291

LC 2012023304

Light up the night; illustrations by Margaret Chodos-Irvine. Disney/Hyperion Books 2011 un il $16.99

Grades: PreK K 1 2   E

1. Stories in rhyme 2. Bedtime -- Fiction 3. Universe -- Fiction

ISBN 978-1-4231-2024-7; 1-4231-2024-8

LC 2011008523

In this cumulative, rhyming story, a young boy takes a nighttime ride from the distant stars in the Milky Way galaxy to his cozy bed, as his blanket becomes a rocket, a plane, and a skateboard.

"Soft assonant sounds soothe the cumulative rhyme that parallels nighttime routines through its repetition and structure. . . . Double-page spreads of bright but not overpowering collages depict [the boy's] journey, while the opening and closing actions (of going to bed and going to sleep) are shown in wordless panels, bringing the story full circle." Horn Book

Time (out) for monsters! by Jean Reidy; pictures by Robert Neubecker. Disney-Hyperion Books 2012 32 p.
Grades: K 1 2   **E**
   1. Picture books for children 2. Monsters -- Fiction 3. Behavior -- Fiction 4. Imagination -- Fiction
ISBN 1423131274; 9781423131274
                LC 2011013049
In this children's book, by Jean Reidy, illustrated by Robert Neubecker, a young boy is dissatisfied with the decor of his "time-out corner. 'Mom says it's fine, but I know better. I spend a LOT of time there.' . . . So he conjures up a world of excitement that includes a killer view, a fire brigade, a dump truck full of ice cream, and some kingly accoutrements." (Publishers Weekly)

Too purpley! illustrated by Genevieve Leloup. Bloomsbury Children's Books 2010 un il $11.99; lib bdg $12.89
Grades: PreK K 1 2   **E**
   1. Stories in rhyme 2. Clothing and dress -- Fiction
ISBN 978-1-59990-307-1; 1-59990-307-5; 978-1-59990-437-5 lib bdg; 1-59990-437-3 lib bdg
                LC 2009004741
A young girl rejects many outfits before finding the perfect clothes to wear
"This fun book has lots of descriptive words that tickle the ear, great colors and patterns, and a charming protagonist." SLJ

Reiser, Lynn
   My baby and me; concept and words by Lynn Reiser; photographs by Penny Gentieu. Alfred A. Knopf 2008 un il $16.99
Grades: PreK   **E**
   1. Stories in rhyme 2. Infants -- Fiction 3. Siblings -- Fiction
ISBN 978-0-375-85205-3; 0-375-85205-0
                LC 2007031949
Photographs and simple text portray interactions between babies and their toddler siblings.
"The photographs are just right for the very youngest, with each double-page spread foregrounding a pair of siblings and a few baby-friendly objects." Horn Book

★ **Tortillas** and lullabies. Tortillas y cancioncitas; pictures by Corazones Valientes; coordinated and translated by Rebecca Hart. Greenwillow Bks. 1998 40p il $16.99; pa $6.99
Grades: PreK K 1 2   **E**
   1. Grandmothers -- Fiction 2. Bilingual books -- English-Spanish 3. Mother-daughter relationship -- Fiction
ISBN 0-688-14628-7; 0-06-089185-8 pa
                LC 97-7096
Companion volume to Cherry pies and lullabies
In this "picture book, four everyday activities are depicted—making tortillas, gathering flowers, washing clothes, and singing a lullaby—as they are repeated by the women of a family over the last four generations. . . . Six Costa Rican

women worked together to produce the striking acrylic folk-art paintings. With deeply saturated, glowing tones and a decidedly Central American style, the pictures enhance and extend the lyrical narrative, which is printed in English and in Spanish." SLJ

Rennert, Laura Joy
   Buying, training & caring for your dinosaur; written by Laura Joy Rennert; pictures by Marc Brown. Alfred A. Knopf 2009 un il $16.99; lib bdg $19.99
Grades: PreK K 1 2   **E**
   1. Pets -- Fiction 2. Dinosaurs -- Fiction
ISBN 978-0-375-83679-4; 0-375-83679-9; 978-0-375-93679-1 lib bdg; 0-375-93679-3 lib bdg
                LC 2008-50680
Includes instructions for choosing and caring for a pet dinosaur
"This features funny, colorful illustrations. . . . Youngsters will quickly become absorbed in this enjoyable mix of facts, fantasy, and fossils." Booklist

Rex, Adam
   Pssst! Harcourt 2007 un il $16
Grades: PreK K 1 2   **E**
   1. Zoos -- Fiction 2. Animals -- Fiction
ISBN 978-0-15-205817-3; 0-15-205817-6
                LC 2006-24551
"A zoo-going girl talks to the animals, but the novelty wears off when the pushy beasts send her on errands. . . . Rex packs increasingly crisp conversations into tight six-panel comics, relaxing into airy spreads as the girl meanders along zoo paths. . . . A very funny excursion." Publ Wkly

Rex, Michael
   Goodnight goon; a petrifying parody. [by] Michael Rex. G.P. Putnam's Sons 2008 un il $14.99
Grades: K 1 2 3   **E**
   1. Stories in rhyme 2. Bedtime -- Fiction 3. Monsters -- Fiction
ISBN 978-0-399-24534-3; 0-399-24534-0
                LC 2007-16585
A young monster says goodnight to all of the other monsters in his bedroom.
"This book is a hilarious adaptation of the classic bedtime story, Goodnight Moon. . . . This is a delightfully funny and witty story containing adorable illustrations with tons of details. . . . Author and illustrator Michael Rex has created a wonderful page-by-page companion to the original." Libr Media Connect

   Truck Duck; [by] Michael Rex. G.P. Putnam's Sons 2004 un il hardcover o.p. bd bk $7.99
Grades: PreK K 1 2   **E**
   1. Stories in rhyme 2. Animals -- Fiction 3. Vehicles -- Fiction
ISBN 0-399-24009-8; 0-399-25092-1 bd bk
                LC 2003-707
A variety of animals drive vehicles whose names rhyme with their own
"This is the stuff of toddlers' play, with vrooming action and small characters in charge. The sounds of the words add to the fun, and to little ones' vocabularies. The vehicles are big, bright, and clear." Booklist
A companion to this title is:

Dunk skunk (2005)

Rey, H. A.

★ **Curious** George. Houghton Mifflin 1941 un il $16; pa $6.95

Grades: PreK K 1   E

1. Monkeys -- Fiction

ISBN 0-395-15993-8; 0-395-15023-X pa

Colored picture book, with simple text, describing the adventures of a curious small monkey, and the difficulties he had in getting used to city life, before he went to live in the zoo

"The bright lithographs in red, yellow, and blue, are gay and lighthearted, following the story closely with the same speed and animated humour." Ont Libr Rev

Other titles about Curious George are:

Curious George flies a kite (1958)

Curious George gets a medal (1957)

Curious George goes to the hospital (1966)

Curious George learns the alphabet (1963)

Curious George rides a bike (1952)

Curious George takes a job (1947)

Curious George: Cecily G. and the 9 monkeys; written and illustrated by H. A. Rey; afterword by Louise Borden. Houghton Mifflin Company 2007 un il $16; pa $6.99

Grades: PreK K 1   E

1. Monkeys -- Fiction 2. Giraffes -- Fiction

ISBN 978-0-618-80066-7; 0-618-80066-2; 978-0-618-99794-7 pa; 0-618-99794-6 pa

LC 2006-38698

First published 1942

A lonely giraffe teams up with the nine playful monkeys. "This edition of the first story to feature Curious George includes a new afterword." Horn Book Guide

Rey, Margret

Whiteblack the penguin sees the world; [by] Margret & H. A. Rey. Houghton Mifflin 2000 un il $15; pa $5.95

Grades: PreK K 1   E

1. Penguins -- Fiction

ISBN 0-618-07389-2; 0-618-07390-6 pa

LC 00-23196

In search of new stories for his radio program, Whiteblack the penguin sets out on a journey and has some interesting adventures

"The plot is very well crafted, and Whiteblack's adventures are appealingly silly, almost slapstick. H. A. Rey's watercolors make great use of the white paper, contrasting it with deep hues of yellow, red, and ultramarine blue and thick black outlines." Booklist

Reynolds, Aaron

★ **Back** of the bus; illustrated by Floyd Cooper. Philomel Books 2010 un il $16.99

Grades: K 1 2 3   E

1. Civil rights activists 2. Race relations -- Fiction 3. African Americans -- Fiction 4. African Americans -- Civil rights -- Fiction

ISBN 978-0-399-25091-0; 0-399-25091-3

LC 2008018109

From the back of the bus, an African American child watches the arrest of Rosa Parks.

Reynolds's "lyrical yet forceful text conveys the narrator's apprehension and Park's calm resolve. . . . Cooper's . . . filmy oil paintings are characterized by a fine mistlike texture, which results in warm, lifelike portraits that convincingly evoke the era, the intense emotional pitch of this incident, and the everyday heroism it embodied." Publ Wkly

Carnivores; by Aaron Reynolds; illustrated by Dan Santat. Chronicle Books 2012 40 p. $16.99

Grades: 1 2 3   E

1. Picture books for children 2. Carnivorous animals -- Fiction 3. Clubs -- Fiction 4. Animals -- Fiction 5. Food chains (Ecology) -- Fiction

ISBN 0811866904; 9780811866903

LC 2008035029

In this children's book, three carnivores including "a lion . . . , great white shark . . . and timber wolf . . . take up vegetarianism in an effort to fit in and then try donning disguises. When neither strategy butters the biscuit, they turn to a great horned owl as a carnivore consultant," who tells them to own their carnivore status. (Kirkus Reviews)

★ **Creepy** carrots! words Aaron Reynolds; pictures Peter Brown. Simon & Schuster Books for Young Readers 2012 40 p. (hardcover: alk. paper) $16.99

Grades: PreK K 1 2   E

1. Carrots -- Fiction 2. Rabbits -- Fiction 3. Picture books for children 4. Humorous stories

ISBN 1442402970; 9781442402973

LC 2010035099

Odyssey Honor Recording (2014)

Caldecott Honor Book (2013)

In this book, "Jasper Rabbit [didn't] think twice about plundering the carrots of Crackenhopper Field 'until they started following him.' Jasper glimpses three jack-o-lantern-jawed carrots behind him in the bathroom mirror (when he turns around it's just a washcloth, shampoo bottle, and rubber duck--or is it?), and he yells for his parents when a carrot shadow looms on his bedroom wall." (Publishers Weekly)

Here comes Destructosaurus! by Aaron Reynolds; illustrated by Jeremy Tankard. Chronicle Books 2014 32 p. (alk. paper) $16.99

Grades: PreK K   E

1. Orderliness 2. Monsters -- Fiction 3. Dinosaurs -- Fiction 4. Children -- Conduct of life -- Fiction 5. Conduct of life -- Fiction

ISBN 145212454X; 9781452124544

LC 2013015843

In this children's book, written by Aaron Reynolds and illustrated by Jeremy Tankard, "a baby dinosaur emerges from the sea and goes on a rampage across New York City, tracking seaweed and dead fish all over the tourists and setting fire to every ship in the harbor. His tail the size of a small planet, Destructosaurus is chastised by the narrator for his lack of self-control and for his sassy attitude, much like a mother would speak to a wild child." (School Library Journal)

"Tankard's cartoon-style art is the perfect foil for Reynolds' seemingly rational text. His humorous illustrations feature boldly outlined characters, vivid colors, and rich backgrounds. The compositions are often cluttered (apropos to the mayhem depicted) but Destructosaurus (and the child's perspective) remain clear focal points." Booklist

Metal man; illustrated by Paul Hoppe. Charlesbridge 2008 un il lib bdg $15.95; pa $7.95
Grades: PreK K 1 2   E
  1. Metalwork -- Fiction 2. Sculpture -- Fiction 3. African Americans -- Fiction
  ISBN 978-1-58089-150-9 lib bdg; 1-58089-150-0 lib bdg; 978-1-58089-151-6 pa; 1-58089-151-9 pa
                                LC 2007-17187
One hot summer day, a man who makes sculpture out of junk helps a boy create what he sees in his mind's eye.
"Beautifully understated, the story is about the capacity of art to empower the artist and to affect how others see the world. The poetic text is visceral. . . . The cartoon illustrations, in rusty browns and shiny blues, depict the metal man as tall, strong, gentle, and wise, a larger-than-life hero. . . . A wonderful example of sensory writing and colloquial storytelling." SLJ

Snowbots; illustrated by David Barneda. Alfred A. Knopf 2010 un il $16.99; lib bdg $19.99
Grades: PreK K 1 2   E
  1. Stories in rhyme 2. Snow -- Fiction 3. Robots -- Fiction
  ISBN 978-0-375-85873-4; 0-375-85873-3; 978-0-375-95873-1 lib bdg; 0-375-95873-8 lib bdg
Rhyming tale of a fun day young robots spend playing in new-fallen snow.
"The acrylic and colored pencil artwork features an array of mechanical kids and household props and plug-ins. The cool, blue-tinged snow scenes contrast with the warm yellows and browns of the house interiors. Libraries with robot fans won't want to pass on this snowy fun." SLJ

Superhero School; illustrated by Andy Rash. Bloomsbury Children's Books 2009 un il $16.99; lib bdg $17.89
Grades: K 1 2 3 4   E
  1. School stories 2. Mathematics -- Fiction 3. Superheroes -- Fiction
  ISBN 978-1-59990-166-4; 1-59990-166-8; 978-1-59990-346-0 lib bdg; 1-59990-346-6 lib bdg
                                  LC 2008031374
When Leonard starts attending Superhero School he is disappointed to find that all they learn is math, but when the ice zombies strike, Leonard and his classmates put their newly-acquired knowledge to good use
"Rash's illustrations in digital collage of gouache and Sharpies create his trademark cartoons that pulsate with energy and engage readers. Reynolds creatively blends the use of math skills in word-problem superhero settings that are playful, smart, and positive." SLJ

Reynolds, Peter
  The dot; [by] Peter H. Reynolds. Candlewick Press 2003 un il $14
Grades: PreK K 1 2   E
  1. School stories 2. Drawing -- Fiction
  ISBN 0-7636-1961-2
                                LC 2002-041113
Vashti believes that she cannot draw, but her art teacher's encouragement leads her to change her mind

"In this engaging, inspiring tale, Reynolds . . . demonstrates the power of a little encouragement. . . . Rendered in watercolor, ink and tea, Reynolds's spare, wispy illustrations exude a fresh, childlike quality pleasingly in sync with his hand-lettered text." Publ Wkly

★ **I'm** here; [by] Peter H. Reynolds. Atheneum Books for Young Readers 2011 il $15.99
Grades: PreK K 1 2   E
  1. Parks -- Fiction 2. Friendship -- Fiction
  ISBN 978-1-4169-9649-1; 1-4169-9649-4
                                LC 2010038962
In a crowded park, a boy makes an airplane out of a piece of paper carried to him by a gentle breeze, sends it on its way, and watches a new friend bring it back to him.
"Though back matter explains that the book was written 'to help us all reach out, embrace, and appreciate children in the autism spectrum,' the pared-down prose and artwork, painted in Reynolds's typical loose style, are open to multiple interpretations and may facilitate conversations about reaching out to others who are different—and alone—for many reasons." Publ Wkly

Ish; [by] Peter H. Reynolds. Candlewick Press 2004 un il $14
Grades: PreK K 1 2 3   E
  1. Drawing -- Fiction 2. Siblings -- Fiction
  ISBN 0-7636-2344-X
                                LC 2003-66196
Ramon loses confidence in his ability to draw, but his sister gives him a new perspective on things
"The overriding theme about creativity versus exactitude will resonate with many. The line-and-color artwork is simple, but it has great emotion and warmth." Booklist

Rose's garden; [by] Peter H. Reynolds. Candlewick Press 2009 un il $15.99
Grades: K 1 2 3   E
  1. Flowers -- Fiction 2. Gardens -- Fiction
  ISBN 978-0-7636-4641-7; 0-7636-4641-5
                                LC 2009-24175
Rose finds a neglected patch of earth in the middle of a bustling city where she can plant the flower seeds collected from her travels in her magical teapot
"This inspiring fable will capture the hearts and imaginations of readers and show them that anything is possible. . . . Reynolds's outstanding illustrations done in watercolor and ink begin in shades of gray and then explode with color and joy as the garden evolves and people come to enjoy it." SLJ

Rice, Eve
  Sam who never forgets. Greenwillow Bks. 1977 un il hardcover o.p. pa $5.99
Grades: PreK K   E
  1. Zoos -- Fiction 2. Animals -- Fiction
  ISBN 0-688-07335-2 pa
                                LC 76-30370
"A simple, unpretentious story with child appeal that lies in the naive, straightforward telling and elemental emotional interactions of the characters. . . . Rice has forsaken her pen drawings for bright, unlined colored shapes. The figures are pleasantly stylized, the scenes evenly composed." Booklist

Richards, Beah

★ **Keep** climbing, girls; by Beah E. Richards; illustrated by R. Gregory Christie; introduction by LisaGay Hamilton. Simon & Schuster Books for Young Readers 2006 un il $15.95
Grades: PreK K 1 2   E
1. Girls -- Poetry
ISBN 1-4169-0264-3
LC 2004-29153
"In this picture-book rendition of Richards's 1951 poem of the same name, girls are urged to 'keep climbing' no matter what obstacles get in the way. Bold gouache illustrations create a beguiling green-and-gold landscape with an irresistible tree and a determined little girl who climbs it higher and higher with every page turn." SLJ

Richards, Chuck

Critter sitter; [by] Chuck Richards. Walker & Company 2008 un il $16.99; lib bdg $17.89
Grades: 1 2 3 4   E
1. Pets -- Fiction
ISBN 978-0-8027-9595-3; 0-8027-9595-1; 978-0-8027-9596-0 lib bdg; 0-8027-9596-X lib bdg
LC 2008004314
When the Mahoney family hires Henry the Critter Sitter to watch their dog, cat, bird, fish, frog, and snake, he thinks he is up for the challenge since creature control is his game, but the pets have a different idea.
"The storytelling is well paced and amusing, but the artwork is the real grabber here. Created with colored-pencil and watercolor, the illustrations cleverly mix realism with humorous exaggeration." SLJ

Richards, Keith, 1943-

Gus & me; the story of my granddad and my first guitar. Keith Richards, Theodora Richards. Little, Brown & Co. 2014 32 p. color illustrations (hardcover) $18
Grades: PreK K 1 2 3 4   E
1. Musicians 2. Grandfathers 3. Musical instruments 4. Grandparent and child
ISBN 031632065X; 9780316281911; 9780316320634; 9780316320658
LC 2014936772
This children's book is a "look into the childhood of the legendary Keith Richards through this poignant and inspiring story that is lovingly illustrated with Theodora Richards's exquisite pen-and-ink collages. This unique autobiographical picture book honors the special bond between a grandfather and grandson and celebrates the artistic talents of the Richards family." (Publisher's note)
"Rolling Stones guitarist Keith Richards has penned a poignant picture book depicting his close relationship with his grandfather Gus...Loose black-and-white pen-and-ink illustrations, done by Keith's daughter, affectionately depict the title characters, as well as the various objects in their orbit (musical instruments, Big Ben, tea kettles, a double-decker bus), while backgrounds provide rich washes of purples, blues, yellows, and green, emphasizing the beauty and the sense of magic of the music. A gentle story celebrating the importance of family." SLJ

Richards, Lucy

Ollie and the lost toy; a lift-the-flap story. Sterling Pub. 2011 un il $9.95

Grades: PreK K   E
1. Fear -- Fiction 2. Toys -- Fiction 3. Lost and found possessions -- Fiction
ISBN 978-1-4027-7754-7; 1-4027-7754-X
LC 2010037979
First published 2006 in the United Kingdom
Ollie must face his fear of the dark to find Snaily, his favorite toy that has been missing all day.
"The soft, colorful illustrations will elicit an emotional response from children. . . . The book has many lift-the-flap elements." SLJ

Richardson, Justin

Christian, the hugging lion; [by] Justin Richardson and Peter Parnell; illustrated by Amy Bates. Simon & Schuster Books for Young Readers 2010 un il $16.99
Grades: PreK K 1 2   E
1. Kenya -- Fiction 2. Lions -- Fiction 3. London (England) -- Fiction
ISBN 978-1-4169-8662-1; 1-4169-8662-6
LC 2009002297
When Ace and John find a lion cub for sale at Harrods department store, they buy him, name him Christian, and the three live happily for a year in a London apartment, but eventually Christian grows too big and they must let him go to live the life of a wild cat. Based on a true story; includes an author's note.
"Bates captures the friendship and love between Christian, Ace and John when they go visit him years later. Justin Richardson and Peter Parnell write this story like a fairy tale—whimisical and entertaining." Libr Media Connect

Richardson, Nan

The **pearl**; written by Nan Richardson; illustrations by Alexandra Young. Umbrage Editions, Inc. 2011 il $17
Grades: K 1 2   E
1. Actors 2. Opera -- Fiction 3. Russia -- Fiction 4. Singers -- Fiction
ISBN 978-1-884167-24-9; 1-884167-24-1
Tells the love story of Nicolas Cheremeteff, a wealthy courtier and Praskovia, a serf girl in eighteenth-century Russia.
"Richly illustrated in bold pen-and-ink and watercolor, the story is brought to life in sumptuous detail and precisely placed splashes of color. Readers will relish this unique, Russian Cinderella tale." SLJ

Ries, Lori

★ **Aggie** and Ben; three stories. illustrated by Frank W. Dormer. Charlesbridge 2006 48p il lib bdg $12.95; pa $5.95
Grades: K 1 2   E
1. Dogs -- Fiction
ISBN 978-1-57091-549-9 lib bdg; 1-57091-594-6 lib bdg; 978-1-57091-649-6 pa; 1-57091-649-7 pa
LC 2005-28702
After choosing a new dog, Ben describes what the pet Aggie can do and should not do around the house
"Funky but tender, Dormer's pen-and-ink cartoons with watercolor washes add depth to the simple story and provide that perfect illustration-to-text match that one seeks in successful easy readers." SLJ
Other titles about Aggie and Ben are:
Good dog, Aggie (2009)

Aggie the brave (2010)
Aggie gets lost (2011)

Punk wig; illustrated by Erin Eitter-Kono. Boyds Mills Press 2008 un il $16.95
Grades: PreK K 1 2   E
  1. Wigs -- Fiction 2. Cancer -- Fiction 3. Mother-son relationship -- Fiction
ISBN 978-1-59078-486-0; 1-59078-486-3
              LC 2007-17688
A little boy does helpful things for his mother as she undergoes chemotherapy, and goes with her as she picks out a wig, which together they call her "punk wig."
"The story handles a tough subject with sensitivity, grace, and a sense of fun. It covers some of the issues facing families without giving too much information that might overwhelm a young child, and provides a good introduction to a hard subject. The watercolor pictures fit well with the text, portraying both the mother's treatment and her fun with the family." Libr Media Connect

Riggs, Shannon
  ★ **Not** in Room 204; illustrated by Jaime Zollars. Albert Whitman 2007 un il $15.95
Grades: K 1 2 3   E
  1. School stories 2. Child sexual abuse -- Fiction
ISBN 978-0-8075-5764-8
              LC 2006023402
"Quiet Regina feels comfortable in her classroom, where Mrs. Salvador runs a tight ship and insists on hard work and fair play. When the teacher starts the annual Stranger Danger unit, she departs from the usual script by saying that most often an adult who touches a child inappropriately is not a stranger but someone known to the child. . . . The next morning, Regina arrives early at Room 204 to confide her secret, which involves her father. . . . This picture book's strength is in the forthrightness of its message and the sensitivity of its presentation. . . . The text and digitally enhanced artwork work together well to express the book's message smoothly. . . . This helpful picture book will raise children's awareness of sexual abuse without raising anxiety." Booklist

Riley, Linnea Asplind
  Mouse mess; [by] Linnea Riley. Blue Sky Press (NY) 1997 un il $16.95
Grades: PreK K 1   E
  1. Stories in rhyme 2. Food -- Fiction 3. Mice -- Fiction
ISBN 0-590-10048-3
              LC 96-49499
A hungry mouse leaves a huge mess when it goes in search of a snack
"Cut-paper collages, set against black backgrounds, depict a chubby-cheeked mouse spilling, cutting, and eating a variety of colorful foods. . . . The rhyming text, filled with crunching and munching sounds, is rhythmic and fun to read aloud." SLJ

Rim, Sujean
  Birdie's big-girl dress. Little, Brown 2011 il $16.99
Grades: PreK K   E
  1. Parties -- Fiction 2. Birthdays -- Fiction 3. Clothing

and dress -- Fiction
ISBN 978-0-316-13287-9; 0-316-13287-X
              LC 2010049435
Birdie's excitement over her approaching birthday party fades when she finds that her favorite party dress is too small, and nothing at her mother's favorite boutique is quite right.
"As Birdie shimmies into each potentially restrictive outfit, Rim's illustrations capture each halfhearted shrug and sucked-in breath. Collage and watercolor accents lend a sensory feel to chromatic, textured design . . . [and] canine companion Monster remains a supportive secondary choice, dressed to the nines in his top hat to rave reviews." Kirkus

  Birdie's big-girl hair; Sujean Rim. Little, Brown and Co. 2013 40 p. color illustrations $17
Grades: PreK K   E
  1. Hair -- Fiction 2. Fashion -- Fiction 3. Identity -- Fiction 4. Hairstyles -- Fiction 5. Individuality -- Fiction 6. Mothers and daughters -- Fiction
ISBN 0316227919; 9780316227919
              LC 2012039921
In this book, by Sujean Rim, "It's time for Birdie's very first haircut, and the miniature fashionista yearns for more than just a simple trim. . . . She looks through pictures . . . to find the best new look, and she and Mommy head to the salon. Her haircut looks fantastic, but begins to sag later on at the playground... because Birdie doesn't just love fashion - she likes to run and jump and play! . . . Mommy reminds her that the most perfect Birdie look is the one that lets her be herself." (Publisher's note)
"Birdie needs a haircut and wants a new look. She spends most of the book agonizing about what look to try; the adorable mixed-media art has Birdie with Betty Draper, Holly Golightly, Princess Leia, and Farrah Fawcett dos. Though this third Birdie vehicle will be relatable and appealing to a fashionista readership, the "be yourself" message feels rather obligatory." Horn Book

  Birdie's big-girl shoes. Little, Brown Books for Young Readers 2009 un il $15.99
Grades: PreK K   E
  1. Play -- Fiction 2. Shoes -- Fiction 3. Mother-daughter relationship -- Fiction
ISBN 978-0-316-04470-7; 0-316-04470-9
              LC 2008-43799
Five-year-old Birdie loves her mother's shoes, but when she is finally granted permission to wear some for a little while, she discovers that her 'barefoot shoes' are best of all
"The bold, stylized watercolor and collage illustrations, paired with spare, simple text, are set against ample white space and burst with bright, attractive textile patterns. A light confection for the preschool dress-up set." SLJ
  Another title about Birdie is:
  Birdie's big-girl dress (2011)

Rinck, Maranke
  I feel a foot! [by] Maranke Rinck & Martijn van der Linden. Lemniscaat 2008 un il $16.95
Grades: PreK K 1   E
  1. Animals -- Fiction 2. Imagination -- Fiction
ISBN 978-1-59078-638-3; 1-59078-638-6
              LC 2008000917

Five animal friends, awakened by a strange noise, discover a creature in the dark that seems to be a giant-sized version of each of them.

"With simple wording, Rinck injects personality into each animal and van der Linden's images interact well with the text. His stark black backgrounds spotlight expressively imagined animals that appear in psychedelic colors and patterns reminiscent of a kaleidoscope." SLJ

Ringgold, Faith

★ **Tar** Beach. Crown 1991 un il $18; lib bdg $18.99; pa $6.99
Grades: PreK K 1 2   **E**
1. Dreams -- Fiction 2. African Americans -- Fiction 3. Harlem (New York, N.Y.) -- Fiction
ISBN 0-517-58030-6; 0-517-58031-4 lib bdg; 0-517-88544-1 pa
LC 90-40410
A Caldecott Medal honor book, 1992
Eight-year-old Cassie dreams of flying above her Harlem home, claiming all she sees for herself and her family. Based on the author's quilt painting of the same name
"Part autobiographical, part fictional, this allegorical tale sparkles with symbolic and historical references central to African-American culture. The spectacular artwork, a combination of primitive naive figures in a flattened perspective against a boldly patterned cityscape, resonates with color and texture." Horn Book
Another title about Cassie is:
Cassie's word quilt (2002)

Rinker, Sherri Duskey

★ **Goodnight,** goodnight, construction site; illustrated by Tom Lichtenheld. Chronicle Books 2011 un il $16.99
Grades: PreK K 1   **E**
1. Stories in rhyme 2. Trucks -- Fiction 3. Bedtime -- Fiction 4. Construction equipment -- Fiction
ISBN 0-8118-7782-5; 978-0-8118-7782-4
LC 2010025008
At sunset, when their work is done for the day, a crane truck, a cement mixer, and other pieces of construction equipment make their way to their resting places and go to sleep.
"Lichtenheld's detailed and textured illustrations, rendered in wax oil pastels on vellum paper, perfectly complement the fun, rhyming text, cleverly personifying each truck with expressive eyes and amusing details." SLJ

★ **Steam** train, dream train; by Sherri Duskey Rinker; illustrated by Tom Lichtenheld. Chronicle Books 2013 40 p. ill. (hardcover) $16.99
Grades: PreK K 1   **E**
1. Bedtime -- Fiction 2. Railroads -- Fiction 3. Stories in rhyme 4. Animals -- Fiction 5. Railroad trains -- Fiction
ISBN 1452109206; 9781452109206
LC 2012030942
In this children's story, by Sherri Duskey Rinker, illustrated by Tom Lichtenheld, "the dream train pulls into the station, and one by one the train cars are loaded: polar bears pack the reefer car with ice cream, elephants fill the tanker cars with paints, tortoises stock the auto rack with race cars, bouncy kangaroos stuff the hopper car with balls." (Publisher's note)

"The strength of this book is in the striking spreads in wax oil pastel. ... The beginning and end of the book are filled with expressive and enjoyable railroad sounds, yet the rhyming text loses a bit of steam in the middle, describing but not always enhancing the activity depicted in the illustrations. Still, this is a book that will...be embraced as a nighttime standard, particularly among train lovers everywhere." SLJ

Riphagen, Loes

Animals home alone. Seven Footer Press 2011 il $15.95
Grades: PreK K 1   **E**
1. Stories without words 2. Animals -- Fiction
ISBN 1-93473455-1; 978-193473455-1
This picture book introduces readers to fifteen animals who begin to act in unusual ways when the humans are away,. In wordless pages, each animal finds a unique activity or bit of mischief to get into. At the book's conclusion, readers are asked questions about what the animals have done.
"This wordless picture book is a playful romp. . . . The little dramas will have children (and adults) flipping back and forth for more whimsical and hilarious details." SLJ

Ritchie, Alison

Duck says don't! Alison Ritchie; [illustrated by] Hannah George. Good Books 2012 26 p. col. ill. (hardcover: alk. paper) $16.99
Grades: K 1 2   **E**
1. Picture books for children 2. Animals 3. Friendship -- Fiction 4. Ducks -- Fiction 5. Geese -- Fiction 6. Ponds -- Fiction 7. Bossiness -- Fiction 8. Pond animals -- Fiction
ISBN 9781561487455; 1561487457
LC 2011031770
Author Alison Ritchie presents a children's picture book. "Goose leaves Duck in charge when she leaves her pond, with unhappy results. Power goes immediately to Duck's head. First, he stops the dragonflies from racing, although they point out that flying is what they do . . . Soon he forbids the kingfishers from fishing and the frogs from diving, and . . . signs appear forbidding, well, everything. Then Duck realizes all his friends have gone . . . and [he] welcomes everyone back to do what they do." (Kirkus)

Ritz, Karen

Windows with birds; written and illustrated by Karen Ritz. Boyds Mills Press 2010 un il $16.95
Grades: PreK K 1 2   **E**
1. Cats -- Fiction 2. Moving -- Fiction
ISBN 978-1-59078-656-7; 1-59078-656-4
LC 2009-19504
"This delicate and understated book tells a simple story about a striped cat with green eyes that loves a boy and a house. All of the feline's comforts are in that house, but one day the boy takes it to live in an apartment. The cat sulks and hides, while the boy tries to coax it out. . . . By morning, the cat realizes that the things it loves best—hiding places, windows with birds, and the boy—are in the new environment as well. . . . The realistic, closeup watercolors convey many emotions. . . . This is a beautiful book for cat lovers and for those who are uncomfortable with change." SLJ

Robbins, Jacqui

The **new** girl . . . and me; story by Jacqui Robbins; with art by Matt Phelan. Atheneum 2006 un il $16.95

Grades: K 1 2   E

  1. School stories 2. Iguanas -- Fiction 3. Friendship -- Fiction

ISBN 0-689-86468-X

                   LC 2004-09931

Two girls named Shakeeta and Mia become friends when Shakeeta boasts that she has a pet iguana and Mia learns how to help Shakeeta "feel at home" even when she is in school.

"The characters are realistically and sympathetically portrayed, and the conversations and actions of the children are natural. Phelan's cartoon-style watercolors depict a realistic-looking classroom with a mix of children from a variety of backgrounds." SLJ

  Two of a kind; [by] Jacqui Robbins and Matt Phelan. Atheneum Books for Young Readers 2008 un il $16.99

Grades: K 1 2   E

  1. School stories 2. Friendship -- Fiction

ISBN 978-1-4169-2437-1; 1-4169-2437-X

                   LC 2006033210

When Anna abandons her best friend, Julisa, to spend time with Kayla and Melanie, whose friendship is considered very special, she soon learns that she has little in common with her new friends.

"Phelan's restrained watercolor-and-pencil illustrations are particularly apt at capturing the emotions at play in the story, while Kayla and Melanie's devilish expressions provide a gentle comic lift. A great introduction to early converations are character, bullying, and peer pressure." Booklist

Robert, Francois

  ★ **Find** a face; by François and Jean Robert, with Jane Gittings. Chronicle Books 2004 un il $15.95

Grades: PreK K 1 2   E

  1. Face in art

ISBN 0-8118-4338-6

                   LC 2003-17593

Presents, with accompanying rhyming text, photographs of everyday objects depicting faces

This is "a fun book that demonstrates that faces can be found anywhere if you look hard enough. . . . The photographs are clear and bright, and set against boldly colored backgrounds. Youngsters will never again look at a light switch in the same way." SLJ

Robert, Na'ima bint

  Ramadan moon; by Na'íma B. Robert; illustrated by Shirin Adl. Frances Lincoln Children's Books 2009 un il $17.99

Grades: K 1 2 3   E

  1. Muslims -- Fiction 2. Ramadan -- Fiction

ISBN 978-1-84507-922-2; 1-84507-922-1

This "follows a Muslim family through its observance of the 'Month of Mercy.' . . . This book's poetic words and playful, patterned collage artwork capture both the solemnity and joy of religious practice and, in a series of scenes of worshippers of every type and hue, show the diversity of the Muslim community around the world." Booklist

Roberton, Fiona

  Wanted: the perfect pet. G.P. Putnam's Sons 2010 un il $16.99

Grades: K 1 2   E

  1. Dogs -- Fiction 2. Pets -- Fiction 3. Ducks -- Fiction

ISBN 978-0-399-25461-1; 0-399-25461-7

A boy who desperately wants a pet dog ends up with a duck instead.

"Roberton's line drawings have a palette of mostly of black and white, gray, and touches of green and yellow. They are very effective in conveying mood, action, and humor. The amusing text is placed in and among the illustrations for a seamless partnership between the two. An excellent tale about not getting what you thought you wanted but loving it anyway." SLJ

Roberts, Lynn

  Little Red; a fizzingly good yarn. retold by Lynn Roberts; illustrated by David Roberts. Harry N. Abrams 2005 32p il $16.95

Grades: PreK K 1 2   E

  1. Fairy tales 2. Wolves -- Fiction 3. Grandmothers -- Fiction

ISBN 0-8109-5783-3

                   LC 2004-29534

This adaptation of Little Red Riding Hood is set in "late eighteenth-century America. In this version Little Red is a young boy named Thomas, who sets out to visit Grandma with delicious treats and a keg of his innkeeper parents' famous ginger ale. . . . Ages six to nine." (Bull Cent Child Books)

"The real strength of the book is David Roberts' stylish pen-and-ink and watercolor art, which creates a shadowy, detailed work that is deliciously creepy yet packed with humor." Bull Cent Child Books

Robinson, Fiona

  What animals really like; a new song composed & conducted by Mr. Herbert Timterteeth. Abrams 2011 un il

Grades: 1 2   E

  1. Animals -- Fiction

ISBN 0-8109-8976-X; 978-0-8109-8976-4

"This amusing story begins when readers open two foldouts to part a pair of red curtains. On stage is a large group of animals ready to give voice to the composer/conductor's new song. Unfortunately, his preconceived notions about the creatures are evident. . . . The pen, ink and marker-pens illustrations show a number of animals dressed in their finest. They become livelier and bolder as their performance goes on. Although Robinson keeps the focus and humor on the well-lit stage, she occasionally pans over to the audience where all readers see are the many colorful eyeballs peering out of the darkness. Sublime silliness." SLJ

Robinson, Michelle

  What to do if an elephant stands on your foot; by Michelle Robinson; pictures by Peter H. Reynolds. Dial 2012 32 p. (hardback) $16.99

Grades: PreK K   E

  1. Elephants -- Fiction 2. Jungle animals -- Fiction 3. Picture books for children 4. Humorous stories

ISBN 9780803733985

                   LC 2011035450

This children's picture book offers tongue-in-cheek information about "[s]afari etiquette . . . . From what to do if an elephant stands on your foot . . . to how to escape the attentions of a crocodile . . . , our . . . guide leads our unlucky hero on a jungle adventure, barely avoiding tigers, a rhino," and "snakes." (Amazon.com

Robinson, Sharon

Jackie's gift; a true story of Christmas, Hanukkah, and Jackie Robinson. illustrated by E. B. Lewis. Viking 2010 un il $16.99
Grades: K 1 2 3   E
1. Baseball players 2. Army officers 3. Jews -- Fiction 4. Hanukkah -- Fiction 5. Christmas -- Fiction 6. Race relations -- Fiction
ISBN 978-0-670-01162-9; 0-670-01162-2
When young Steve, who is Jewish, tells his new neighbor, Jackie Robinson, that his family does not have a Christmas tree, Jackie brings one to his neighbors, not knowing that they celebrate Hanukkah instead of Christmas. Based on a true story.
"What could have been an awkward moment becomes a lesson in tolerance and friendship. Lewis's lovely paintings do a fine job of conveying the time and place in this heartwarming story." SLJ

Rocco, John

★ **Blackout**. Disney/Hyperion Books 2011 un il lib bdg $16.99
Grades: K 1 2 3   E
1. Night -- Fiction 2. Summer -- Fiction 3. Family life -- Fiction 4. City and town life -- Fiction 5. Electric power failures -- Fiction
ISBN 978-1-4231-2190-9 lib bdg; 1-4231-2190-2 lib bdg
"The plot line, conveyed with just a few sentences, is simple enough, but the dramatic illustrations illuminate the story. . . . Page composition effectively intermingles boxed pages and panels with double-page spreads, generating action. Brilliant designed, with comic bits." Kirkus

Blizzard; by John Rocco. Disney-Hyperion Books 2014 40 p. color illustrations (hardback) $17.99
Grades: PreK K 1 2 3   E
1. Blizzards -- Fiction 2. Heroes and heroines -- Fiction 3. Snow -- Fiction 4. Heroes -- Fiction
ISBN 1423178653; 9781423178651
     LC 2014003220
This children's book "is based on John Rocco's childhood experience during the now infamous Blizzard of 1978, which brought fifty-three inches of snow to his town in Rhode Island. . . . The book opens with a boy's excitement upon seeing the first snowflake fall outside his classroom window. It ends with the neighborhood's immense relief upon seeing the first snowplow break through on their street." (Publisher's note)
"Young readers will be tickled by a young boy's resourcefulness in this story of how he and his family survive a monumental blizzard. The first flake falls on Monday while the young narrator is at school, and by the time he and his sister make it home after being dismissed early, the snow is over their boots. On Tuesday, the family's door won't open, and the kids climb out the window to play outside (though it's too deep for sledding and even walking). Wednesday,

Dad shovels, but the snowplows don't come (though the kids can now build snow tunnels and forts). . . . The Caldecott honoree's pencil, watercolor and digital paint illustrations are reminiscent of Steven Kellogg in their light and line and detail, and readers will pore over the pages as they vicariously live through a blizzard. An author's note explains that the story is based on his own experience in the New England blizzard of 1978. A kid is the hero in this tale of ingenuity and bravery." Kirkus

Moonpowder; story and pictures by John Rocco. Hyperion Books for Children 2008 un il $15.99
Grades: K 1 2   E
1. Dreams -- Fiction 2. Bedtime -- Fiction
ISBN 978-1-4231-0011-9; 1-4231-0011-5
     LC 2007-042236
Even though Eli is the "Fixer of all things fixable," one thing he cannot fix is his bad dreams, until one night when Mr. Moon appears and asks him to come fix the Moonpowder factory, where sweet dreams are created.
"Steeped in dreamy sepia tones suffused with golden light and brightened by unexpected patches of electric blue, the illustrations are lush and painterly. Using spreads combined with comic-style panels, Rocco creates a hint of a graphic novel for the youngest readers." SLJ

Wolf! wolf! Hyperion Books for Children 2007 un il $15.99
Grades: K 1 2 3   E
1. China -- Fiction 2. Goats -- Fiction 3. Wolves -- Fiction
ISBN 1-4231-0012-3
     LC 2007-04636
"This twisted treatment of Aesop's fable flips everything readers know about the boy who cried wolf on its head. . . . Ancient China unfolds as the stage and setting for this story. In this variant, children get a little insight into the wolf's point of view. . . . The purposeful use of frames, unusual setting, and visual humor makes this an excellent addition to any collection." SLJ

Rockliff, Mara

The **case** of the July 4th jinx; by Lewis B. Montgomery; illustrated by Amy Wummer. Kane Press 2010 96p il (The Milo & Jazz mysteries) lib bdg $22.60; pa $6.95
Grades: 1 2 3   E
1. Mystery fiction
ISBN 978-1-57565-315-0 lib bdg; 1-57565-315-X lib bdg; 978-1-57565-308-2 pa; 1-57565-308-7 pa
     LC 2009049886
With the help of ace detective Dash Marlowe, sleuths-in-training Mio and Jazz investigate a so-called jinx at the local Fourth of July fair
"The story is simple, and children will enjoy solving the mystery. Black-and-white spot art appears frequently throughout, creating a text that will not intimidate children just starting to read chapter books." SLJ

Chik Chak Shabbat; by Mara Rockliff; illustrated by Kyrsten Brooker. First edition. Candlewick Press 2014 32 p. color illustrations $15.99
Grades: PreK K 1 2   E
1. Jewish cooking 2. Cooking -- Fiction 3. Neighbors -- Fiction 4. Jewish holidays -- Fiction 5. Dinners and

dining 6. children's stories
ISBN 0763655287; 9780763655280

LC 2013953462

In this children's book, by Mara Rockliff and illustrated by Kyrsten Brooker, "Goldie Simcha doesn't joyfully throw open her door to welcome everyone in to her apartment for a meal of her famous cholent. . . . Little Lali Omar knocks on the door to 5-A, only to learn that Goldie was feeling too sick on Friday to cook, and everyone knows you can't make cholent in a hurry. . . . But it just isn't Shabbat without cholent. What can her neighbors do to save the day?" (Publisher's note)

"Designed to cook unattended for 12 hours over the Sabbath, when observant Jews cannot perform work, cholent is a fragrant stew. Goldie Simcha, a youngish woman living in a big-city apartment building, 'doesn't celebrate Shabbat exactly as my grandma did,' but she honors her memory (the book's title is a colloquialism for 'hurry up') by inviting her neighbors to feast on cholent every Saturday. The dish (a recipe concludes the book) is such a mainstay of building life that when Goldie gets sick and can't fix cholent, her neighbors bring dishes from their own homelands . . . lovely, unassuming story of tradition and multicultural community is smartly paired with Brooker's (The Honeybee Man) oil and collages. At once homespun and stylish, the pictures speak to the possibilities for human connection in a modern, urban setting." Pub Wkly

The **Grudge** Keeper; written by Mara Rockliff; illustrated by Eliza Wheeler. Peachtree Publishers 2014 32 p. $16.95

Grades: K 1 2 3 4   E
1. Children's stories 2. City and town life -- Fiction 3. Forgiveness -- Fiction
ISBN 1561457299; 9781561457298

LC 2012048880

"No one in the town of Bonnyripple ever kept a grudge. No one, that is, except old Cornelius, the Grudge Keeper. Ruffled feathers, petty snits, minor tiffs and major huffs, insults, umbrage, squabbles, dust-ups, and imbroglios-the Grudge Keeper received them all, large and small, tucking each one carefully away in his ramshackle cottage." (Publisher's note)

"Wheeler's strong, witty ink-and-watercolor illustrations combine with the text to humorously demonstrate that "holding a grudge" is a bad thing. Wordplay and humor provide an effective vehicle for a valuable moral." Kirkus

Me and Momma and Big John; text by Mara Rockliff; illustrations by William Low. Candlewick 2012 32 p. (hardback) $16.99

Grades: PreK K 1 2   E
1. Mothers -- Fiction 2. Cathedrals -- Fiction 3. Picture books for children 4. Building -- Fiction 5. Stonecutters -- Fiction 6. New York (N.Y.) -- Fiction 7. Mothers and sons -- Fiction 8. African Americans -- Fiction
ISBN 0763643599; 9780763643591

LC 2011046649

In this story, "our narrator . . . greets his mother . . . when she returns from work, tired and covered with gray dust. She has been hired to cut stone for the cathedral in the city called Big John." She spends many days on just one stone. "John expects to see his mother's name on the stone . . . . When the stone is finished, the whole" family goes to see it, and though "her name is not on it, Momma knows that many people will come and see it, high atop the cathedral." (Children's Literature)

My heart will not sit down; illustrations by Ann Tanksley. Alfred A. Knopf 2012 un il $17.99; lib bdg $20.99

Grades: K 1 2 3   E
1. School stories 2. Charity -- Fiction 3. Cameroon -- Fiction 4. New York (N.Y.) -- Fiction 5. Great Depression, 1929-1939 -- Fiction
ISBN 978-0-375-84569-7; 0-375-84569-0; 978-0-375-94569-4 lib bdg; 0-375-94569-5 lib bdg; 978-0-375-98728-1 ebook

LC 2011001117

In 1931 Cameroon, young Kedi is upset to learn that children in her American teacher's village of New York are going hungry because of the Great Depression, and she asks her mother, neighbors, and even the headman for money to help. Includes historical notes.

"Inspired by a true incident, [this] story demonstrates what real generosity looks like. . . . Rendered in watercolor, pen-and-ink, and oils, Tanksley's . . . pared-down, childlike pictures provide a sketch of Cameroon village life, their electric hues of orange, magenta, and scarlet jumping from the pages." Publ Wkly

Rockwell, Anne F.

Apples and pumpkins; illustrated by Lizzy Rockwell. Simon & Schuster 2011 il $14.99

Grades: PreK   E
1. Apples -- Fiction 2. Autumn -- Fiction 3. Pumpkin -- Fiction
ISBN 978-1-4424-0350-5; 1-4424-0350-0

A reissue of the title first published 1989

A little girl spends a glorious Fall day picking apples and searching for the perfect pumpkin.

This edition "has new cover art that punches up the fall colors, adds a chicken, and features apples and pumpkins in the foreground. The text's typeface has changed, but everything else is kept in its original perfection so that yet another generation of youngsters will celebrate autumn, from orchard visits to trick-or-treating." SLJ

At the supermarket. Henry Holt 2010 un il $16.99

Grades: PreK   E
1. Shopping -- Fiction 2. Birthdays -- Fiction 3. Supermarkets -- Fiction
ISBN 0-8050-7662-X; 978-0-8050-7662-2

LC 2009009221

A revised and newly illustrated edition of The Supermarket, published 1979 by MacMillan

A boy and his mother fill a cart at the supermarket with everything from grapes to paper towels, finishing off with ingredients for a birthday cake.

"The well-written narration explains their trip from start to finish, including how the checkout line works. The brightly colored gouache illustrations on white backgrounds show the child helping to fill the cart and feature such items as produce and a container of ice cream alone on the page, making identification easy. This is a fun, educational read-aloud." SLJ

Big wheels; by Anne Rockwell. Walker & Co. 2003 un il $14.95; bd bk $6.95

Grades: PreK K 1   E

1. Vehicles 2. Machinery

ISBN 0-8027-8882-3; 0-8027-8903-X bd bk

LC 2002-34348

A reissue of the title first published 1986 by Dutton Children's Bks.

Introduces a number of big-wheeled trucks, such as bulldozers, power shovels, and dump trucks, and explains what they do

"Although the author-artist has supplied a very brief text, she uses active, vivid verbs, such as dig, dump, and chop up, effectively conveying a sense of the machinery in the fewest words necessary. Likewise, her illustrations contain exactly the right amount of detail to satisfy but not confuse." Horn Book

★ **Father's** Day; by Anne Rockwell; pictures by Lizzy Rockwell. HarperCollins 2005 un il $14.99

Grades: PreK K 1   E

1. Fathers -- Fiction 2. Father's Day -- Fiction

ISBN 0-06-051377-2

LC 2004-6243

For Fathers' Day, the students in Mrs. Madoff's class write and illustrate books about their dads.

"The best part of the book is the way it reflects the differences in dads. . . . The artwork, with rounded shapes and smooth colors, has a simple, friendly look that puts the focus on the characters." Booklist

Other titles about Mrs. Madoff's class are:

100 school days (2002)

Career day (2000)

First day of school (2011)

Halloween day (1997)

Mother's Day (2004)

Presidents' Day (2007)

St. Patrick's Day (2010)

Thanksgiving Day (1999)

Valentine's Day (2001)

★ **Four** seasons make a year; pictures by Megan Halsey. Walker & Co. 2004 un il $15.95; lib bdg $16.85

Grades: PreK K 1   E

1. Seasons

ISBN 0-8027-8883-1; 0-8027-8885-8 lib bdg

LC 2003-57171

Describes the passing of the seasons through the changes in plants and animals that occur on a farm

"The first-person text is simple and childlike, a tone reflected in the clearly delineated collages. Combining ink drawings with acrylic paintings on torn paper, these illustrations create eye-catching compositions." Booklist

My preschool; [by] Anne Rockwell. Holt 2008 un il $16.95

Grades: PreK   E

1. School stories

ISBN 978-0-8050-7955-5; 0-8050-7955-6

LC 2007002834

Follows a little boy during his day at preschool, from cheerful hellos in circle time, to painting colorful pictures and playing at the water table, to passing out paper cups for snack

In the illustrations Rockwell uses "colorful inks and traditional Japanese woodblock printing. . . . The detail and realistic depiction of the preschool experience will help to calm some newcomers' trepidations about attending school for the first time." SLJ

★ The **toolbox**; by Anne & Harlow Rockwell. Walker & Company 2004 un il hardcover o.p. bd bk $6.95

Grades: PreK K 1   E

1. Tools

ISBN 0-8027-8930-7; 0-8027-9609-5 bd bk

LC 2003-66562

A reissue of the title first published 1971 by Macmillan

An easy-to-read description of the basic tools found in a toolbox

"The brief text is printed in clear, handsome type. . . . [The illustrations] make ingenious use of watercolor to show textures and surfaces of wood and metal." Horn Book

Rodman, Mary Ann

First grade stinks; written by Mary Ann Rodman; illustrated by Beth Spiegel. Peachtree 2006 un il $15.95; pa $8.95

Grades: K 1 2   E

1. School stories

ISBN 1-56145-377-3; 1-56145-462-1 pa

LC 2006-02711

First-grader Haley wishes she were back having fun in kindergarten with her old teacher, until she finds out that first-grade is special, too

"The scratchy, fluid, full-color watercolor-and-ink illustrations feature plenty of white space. Perfect as a read-aloud." SLJ

★ **My** best friend; illustrated by E.B. Lewis. Viking 2005 un il $14.99; pa $5.99

Grades: PreK K 1   E

1. Friendship -- Fiction

ISBN 0-670-05989-7; 0-14-240806-9 pa

LC 2004-22778

Six-year-old Lily has a best friend all picked out for play group day, but unfortunately the differences between first-graders and second-graders are sometimes very large

"Rodman's honest text captures the girl's heartbroken disappointment and makes it real for young readers, and Lewis's shining, sun-drenched illustrations convey both the harshness and warmth of the bright days at the pool." SLJ

★ **Surprise** soup; illustrated by G. Brian Karas. Viking 2009 un il $15.99

Grades: PreK K 1   E

1. Bears -- Fiction 2. Soups -- Fiction 3. Cooking -- Fiction 4. Brothers -- Fiction 5. Family life -- Fiction

ISBN 978-0-670-06274-4; 0-670-06274-X

LC 2008-22548

"Frequent, playful sound effects . . . will make read-alouds fun, and Rodman perfectly captures the rhythm and words of family dialogue. . . . Kara's collage artwork combines thickly lined, expressive figures with patterned details." Booklist

A **tree** for Emmy; written by Mary Ann Rodman; illustrated by Tatjana Mai-Wyss. Peachtree 2009 un il $15.95
Grades: K 1 2   E
1. Trees -- Fiction 2. Birthdays -- Fiction
ISBN 978-1-56145-475-4; 1-56145-475-3
LC 2008036745
Emmy loves the mimosa tree in her grandmother's yard and asks for one for her birthday, only to find that stores do not sell wild trees.

"The repetition of phrases, the cadence of the text, and the understanding of a child's emotions make this picture book a fine choice for reading aloud." Booklist

Rodriguez, Beatrice
★ The **chicken** thief. Enchanted Lion Books 2010 un il $14.95
Grades: PreK K 1   E
1. Stories without words 2. Foxes -- Fiction 3. Chickens -- Fiction
ISBN 978-1-59270-092-9; 1-59270-092-6
"In Rodriguez's wordless debut, a bear and rabbit are enjoying a peaceful lunch in the garden outside their cottage when a fox makes off with one of their hens. The rooster wrings his wings melodramatically, and all three give chase. . . . Rodriguez succeeds in creating a distinctive personality for each of the characters, and her ability to capture the players' emotions via body language is masterful. . . . For readers who love a good chase—and who doesn't?—this one is a delight from beginning to end." Publ Wkly
Other titles in this series are:
Fox and Hen together (2011)
Rooster's revenge (2011)

Rogers, Gregory
The **boy,** the bear, the baron, the bard. Roaring Brook 2004 un il $15.95; pa $7.95
Grades: K 1 2 3   E
1. Poets 2. Authors 3. Dramatists 4. Stories without words
ISBN 1-59643-009-5; 1-59643-267-5 pa
A boy playing among the warehouses of London kicks a soccer ball into an abandoned theater. There he finds an enchanted cape that transports him back in time right onto the stage of one of William Shakespeare's plays
"The plot in this wordless picture book unfolds straightforwardly. . . . The full watercolor-and-ink panels give kids . . . the chance to peek into another era while sympathizing with a contemporary young protagonist." Booklist
Another title about these characters is:
Midsummer knight (2007)

The **hero** of Little Street; Gregory Rogers. Roaring Brook Press 2012 32 p.
Grades: PreK K 1 2 3   E
1. Stories without words 2. Picture books for children 3. Art museums -- Fiction 4. Dogs -- Fiction 5. England -- Fiction 6. Painting -- Fiction 7. Time travel -- Fiction 8. London (England) -- Fiction 9. Netherlands -- History -- 17th century -- Fiction 10. Delft (Netherlands) -- History -- 17th century -- Fiction
ISBN 1596437294; 9781596437296
LC 2010042371
This children's book by Gregory Rogers is the final entry in the "Boy, Bear" trilogy. "Narrowly escaping from a gang of bullies, a boy slips into a grand old gallery--the perfect hiding place, full of mystery and treasures. Suddenly, a painting comes to life and the boy finds himself on an adventure led by a mischievous dog that has leapt from the canvas. The two slip into a Vermeer painting and are transported to Little Street, Delft in seventeenth-century Holland, where the boy has to use every ounce of his ingenuity to rescue his new friend from an untimely fate." (Publisher's note)

★ **Midsummer** knight. Roaring Brook Press 2007 un il $16.95
Grades: K 1 2 3 4 5   E
1. Stories without words 2. Bears -- Fiction 3. Fairies -- Fiction 4. Heroes and heroines -- Fiction
ISBN 978-1-59643-183-6; 1-59643-183-0
LC 2006-51013
First published in Australia 2006
A bear is rescued by a fairy in an enchanted wood and agrees to return the favor by leading the battle against a usurper who has imprisoned the king and queen, along with their loyal subjects, in the dungeon of their castle
"This is another wordless adventure, depicted in colorful, comics-style panels that will delight young readers." Booklist

Rogerson, Gillian
You can't eat a Princess! written by Gillian Rogerson; illustrated by Sarah McIntyre. Price Stern Sloan 2011 un il $9.99
Grades: PreK K 1 2   E
1. Chocolate -- Fiction 2. Princesses -- Fiction 3. Extraterrestrial beings -- Fiction
ISBN 978-0-8431-9881-2; 0-8431-9881-8
LC 2010008352
Princess Spaghetti blasts off into space to save her kidnapped father, King Cupcake, from hungry aliens, who are introduced to a wonderful new food: chocolate.
"Pastel hues, comical cartoon creatures, and zippy dialogue make this, on one level, a lighthearted story. But when young children beg to hear it again and again, it will undoubtedly be for the power conveyed by a shrewd little princess who can tame aliens and get them to eat chocolates out of her hand." SLJ

Rohmann, Eric
★ **Bone** dog. Roaring Brook Press 2011 un il $16.99
Grades: K 1 2   E
1. Dogs -- Fiction 2. Death -- Fiction 3. Skeleton -- Fiction 4. Halloween -- Fiction
ISBN 978-1-59643-150-8; 1-59643-150-4
LC 2010045142
Although devastated when his pet dog dies, a young boy goes trick-or-treating and receives a timely visit from an old friend during a scary encounter with graveyard skeletons.
"Rohmann's . . . friendly figures and soft, autumnal colors give this spooky story an overlay of tranquility. . . . It's an offbeat mixture of humor and sadness." Publ Wkly

★ **Clara** and Asha. Roaring Brook 2005 un il $16.95
Grades: PreK K 1 2   E
1. Fishes -- Fiction 2. Bedtime -- Fiction 3. Imaginary playmates -- Fiction
ISBN 1-59643-031-1
LC 2005-04677

Young Clara would rather play with her imaginary giant fish, Asha, than settle down to sleep.

"The oil paintings portray a natural world in all its glorious seasons, brimming with mystery and delight. . . . Children will revel in the opportunity to see their dreams and longings realized so enchantingly." SLJ

★ A **kitten** tale. Alfred A. Knopf 2008 un il $15.99; lib bdg $18.99
Grades: PreK   E
1. Cats -- Fiction 2. Snow -- Fiction 3. Seasons -- Fiction
ISBN 978-0-517-70915-3; 978-0-517-70916-0 lib bdg
LC 2007-11093

As four kittens who have never seen winter watch the seasons pass, three of them declare the reasons they will dislike snow when it arrives, while the fourth cannot wait to experience it for himself

This is a "marvel of sly simplicity for the very young. . . . [Rohmann's] uncluttered, inventive scenes masterfully echo the repetitive rhythm in the words." Booklist

★ **My** friend Rabbit. Roaring Brook Press 2002 un il $15; pa $6.99
Grades: PreK K 1 2   E
1. Mice -- Fiction 2. Rabbits -- Fiction 3. Friendship -- Fiction
ISBN 0-7613-1535-7; 0-312-36752-X pa
LC 2002-17764

Awarded the Caldecott Medal, 2003
Something always seems to go wrong when Rabbit is around, but Mouse lets him play with his toy plane anyway because he is his good friend

"The double-page, hand-colored relief prints with heavy black outlines are magnificent, and children will enjoy the comically expressive pictures of the animals." SLJ

Time flies. Crown 1994 un il $17; lib bdg $17.99; pa $6.99
Grades: PreK K 1 2   E
1. Stories without words 2. Birds -- Fiction 3. Dinosaurs -- Fiction
ISBN 0-517-59598-2; 0-517-59599-0 lib bdg; 0-517-88555-7 pa
LC 93-28200

A Caldecott Medal honor book, 1995
A wordless tale in which a bird flying around the dinosaur exhibit in a natural history museum has an unsettling experience when the dinosaur seems to come alive and view the bird as a potential meal

"The handsome, atmospheric paintings heighten the drama as they tell their simple, somewhat mysterious, and quite short story." Booklist

Roode, Daniel
Little Bea. Greenwillow Books 2011 un il $12.99
Grades: PreK   E
1. Day -- Fiction 2. Bees -- Fiction 3. Animals -- Fiction 4. Friendship -- Fiction
ISBN 978-0-06-199392-3; 0-06-199392-1
LC 2009053681

From morning to night, Little Bea buzzes through her neighborhood helping friends and having fun.

"Roode's computer-generated images are highly stylized. . . . The text is full of sounds . . . internal rhymes, . . . and the simple pleasures of knock-knock jokes and games of 'duck, duck, goose' and 'peekaboo' . . . There's reassurance and contentment throughout. Friendly, fuzzy creatures abound; the lives of characters who live in a tightly knit community of friends they see and enjoy every day is a satisfying theme." Publ Wkly

Another title about Little Bea is:
Little Bea and the snowy day (2011)

Little Bea and the snowy day. Greenwillow Books 2011 32p il $12.99
Grades: PreK   E
1. Bees -- Fiction 2. Snow -- Fiction 3. Animals -- Fiction
ISBN 978-0-06-199395-4; 0-06-199395-6
LC 2010032236

Little Bea and her friends enjoy a day of snow angels, skating, and even making a new snow friend.

"The simplistic text and singsong rhyme are best suited for two-year-olds. . . . Children will delight in the bright, animated digital art and large, two-dimensional perspective." SLJ

Roop, Peter
Down East in the ocean; a Maine counting book. written by Peter and Connie Roop; illustrated by Nicole Fazio. Down East 2011 il $16.95
Grades: PreK K 1   E
1. Counting 2. Stories in rhyme 3. Maine -- Fiction 4. Seashore -- Fiction 5. Marine animals -- Fiction
ISBN 978-0-89272-709-4; 0-89272-709-8

"This rhyming counting book features animals associated with the Maine seashore, but that can also be found on many other beaches. Each spread tells a mini story of parent and offspring while introducing the concept of counting. . . . This is an engaging way to learn numbers and a great beach book. Music notations are included at the end to put the verses to song." SLJ

Roosa, Karen
Pippa at the parade; illustrated by Julie Fortenberry. Boyds Mills Press 2009 un il $16.95
Grades: PreK K   E
1. Stories in rhyme 2. Parades -- Fiction
ISBN 978-1-59078-567-6; 1-59078-567-3
LC 2008028127

A young child has a fun-filled day with her parents at the big parade

"Bursting with movement, the spirited and free-flowing watercolors capture cartwheeling gymnasts and marching scout troops. . . . The brief rhyming verses . . . include a few onomatopoeic phrases that invite young listeners to join in." Booklist

Root, Phyllis
Big Momma makes the world; written by Phyllis Root; illustrated by Helen Oxenbury. Candlewick Press 2003 un il $16.99; pa $6.99
Grades: PreK K 1 2   E
1. Creation -- Fiction
ISBN 0-7636-1132-8; 0-7636-2600-7 pa
LC 2002-17498

Big Momma, with a baby on her hip and laundry piling up, makes the world and everything in it and, at the end of the sixth day, tells the people she has made that they must take care of her creation

"Root's text is strong and sassy, with a down-home cadence that has immediate appeal, and Oxenbury's Big Momma is the perfect embodiment of the story's earth mother." Booklist

Creak! said the bed; illustrated by Regan Dunnick. Candlewick Press 2010 un il $15.99
Grades: PreK K E
1. Beds -- Fiction 2. Noise -- Fiction
ISBN 978-0-7636-2004-2; 0-7636-2004-1

"The increasingly crowded bed . . . is by now a standard picture-book plotline. Fresh takes on the subject are hard to come by, but Root manages to make it feel new by punctuating the story with the sounds of impending disaster. . . . The economy of the story line is paralleled by gouache illustrations . . . that reinforce the bed-centered tale but also pull in and zoom out on its inhabitants for different perspectives. The lantern-jawed, snub-nosed family is cartoon cute, making for a perfect storytime read." Booklist

Flip, flap, fly! illustrated by David Walker. Candlewick 2009 un il $14.99
Grades: PreK E
1. Stories in rhyme 2. Animals -- Fiction
ISBN 978-0-7636-3109-3; 0-7636-3109-4

An "assortment of baby animals flap, wiggle and splash their way through the forest, spotting each other in turn as they play with their mamas. Human babies and toddlers will love guessing which animal comes next as they follow clues from Root's contagious, rhyming text and Walker's bright and warm acrylic illustrations." Kirkus

Kiss the cow; illustrated by Will Hillenbrand. Candlewick Press 2000 un il hardcover o.p. pa $6.99
Grades: K 1 2 3 E
1. Cattle -- Fiction
ISBN 0-7636-0298-1; 0-7636-2003-3 pa
LC 00-20926

Annalisa, the most curious and stubborn of Mama May's children, disobeys her mother and upsets the family's magic cow by refusing to kiss her in return for the milk she gives

"Elements of folklore echo through the story that reads aloud rhythmically with a satisfying, folksy sound. . . . The well-conceived illustrations, warm in color and graceful in line, depict a variety of scenes with style and panache." Booklist

★ **Lucia** and the light; illustrated by Mary Grandpré. Candlewick Press 2006 un il $16.99
Grades: PreK K 1 2 E
1. Sun -- Fiction 2. Cats -- Fiction 3. Trolls -- Fiction 4. Winter -- Fiction
ISBN 978-0-7636-2296-1; 0-7636-2296-6

One winter in the Far North the sun disappears and Lucia, accompanied by her milk-white cat, braves the freezing cold and trolls who want to eat her, trying to find the sun and bring it back.

"Grandpré's evocative, dimly lit acrylics capture the eerie mystery and shivery suspense of the adventure. . . .

Root's rich language and well-paced story are sure to capture a young crowd of eager listeners." Booklist

The **name** quilt; pictures by Margot Apple. Farrar, Straus & Giroux 2003 un il $16
Grades: K 1 2 3 E
1. Quilts -- Fiction 2. Grandmothers -- Fiction
ISBN 0-374-35484-7
LC 2002-69328

One of Sadie's favorite things to do when she visits her grandmother is to hear stories about the family members whose names are on a special quilt that Grandma had made, so Sadie is very sad when the quilt is blown away in a storm

"Root makes the most of the simple, intimate anecdotes that flow between generations, and the crayon-looking drawings bespeak a rustic informality." Publ Wkly

Paula Bunyan; illustrated by Kevin O'Malley. Farrar, Straus and Giroux 2009 un il $16.95
Grades: K 1 2 3 E
1. Tall tales 2. Size -- Fiction
ISBN 978-0-374-35759-7; 0-374-35759-5
LC 2007-43728

Recounts the exploits of Paul Bunyan's "little" sister, Paula, who lived in the North Woods, sang three-part harmony with the wolves, and used an angry bear for a foot warmer.

"O'Malley's white-framed, woodcutlike pictures, heavily outlined with intricate line shading, appear throughout this appropriately tall book. Sweeping panoramic views, Paula's thunderous voice depicted in large speech bubbles, bear-carrying mosquitoes, comical animal expressions, and energetic black-and-white drawings add to the fun. The timely environmental message is an added plus." SLJ

Scrawny cat; illustrated by Alison Friend. Candlewick Press 2011 un il $16.99
Grades: PreK K 1 2 E
1. Cats -- Fiction
ISBN 978-0-7636-4164-1; 0-7636-4164-2
LC 2010047671

A lost, lonely, and scrawny cat, hungry and afraid, unexpectedly meets someone who takes him in and loves him.

"Delicious language and a winsome feline ensure that this new iteration of an oft-told plot will find an appreciative audience. . . . Friend's gouache paintings, including vignettes, single pages and double page spreads, illuminate the straightforward action. . . . She captures the fluctuating reactions of the cat perfectly." Kirkus

Thirsty Thursday; illustrated by Helen Craig. Candlewick Press 2009 un il $9.99
Grades: PreK K E
1. Rain -- Fiction 2. Flowers -- Fiction 3. Farm life -- Fiction
ISBN 978-0-7636-3628-9; 0-7636-3628-2

"It's Thursday on Bonnie Bumble's farm, and everyone is thirsty—especially the flowers. . . . Not a drop of rain is in sight, but luckily Bonnie has an idea. She puts the sheep on top of the cow and the pig on top of the sheep, and she climbs on top of the pig . . . and tickles the cloud with a feather. . . . Short, sweet and unabashedly darling, Root's text employs just the right amount of repetition to get toddlers chiming in by the second reading. Craig's ink, watercolor and pencil illustrations lend Bonnie, animals and flowers expressive personalities." Kirkus

Toot toot zoom! illustrated by Matthew Cordell. Candlewick Press 2009 un il $15.99

Grades: PreK K   **E**

1. Animals -- Fiction 2. Friendship -- Fiction 3. Automobiles -- Fiction

ISBN 978-0-7636-3452-0; 0-7636-3452-2

LC 2008-934781

"A simple storyline, great sound effects, a touch of humor, and big, bold illustrations make this a lively choice for storytime." Bull Cent Child Books

Rose, Deborah Lee

All the seasons of the year; illustrated by Kay Choaro. Abrams Books for Young Readers 2010 un il $16.95

Grades: PreK K 1   **E**

1. Stories in rhyme 2. Cats -- Fiction 3. Seasons -- Fiction 4. Mother-child relationship -- Fiction

ISBN 978-0-8109-8395-3; 0-8109-8395-8

"This rhyming story portrays a mother cat's love for her child. . . . With two spreads devoted to each season, the first-person narrative describes some of their favorite activities. Chorao's lush illustrations in gouache, colored pencils, and ink fill the pages with colorful pastel depictions of the momma and her kitten diving into a pile of autumn leaves, sledding down a winter slope, flying kites in the spring, watering summer blossoms, and celebrating the youngster's birthday in the fall." SLJ

Birthday zoo; written by Lee Rose; illustrated by Lynn Munsinger. Whitman, A. 2002 un il $15.95; pa $6.95

Grades: PreK K 1 2   **E**

1. Stories in rhyme 2. Zoos -- Fiction 3. Animals -- Fiction 4. Birthdays -- Fiction

ISBN 0-8075-0776-8; 0-8075-0777-6 pa

LC 2002-1726

Rhyming text describes the preparations made for a boy's birthday party by his hosts, the animals at the zoo

"While Rose's strong rhythm and rhymes will charm youngsters in a storytime, Munsinger's lively pen-and-ink and watercolor illustrations beg for closer inspection." SLJ

The **twelve** days of winter; a school counting book. illustrated by Carey Armstrong-Ellis. Abrams 2006 un il lib bdg $14.95

Grades: PreK K 1 2   **E**

1. Counting 2. Winter -- Fiction

ISBN 0-8109-5472-9

A cumulative counting verse in which a child lists items pertaining to winter given to him by his teacher, from twelve treats for tasting to one bird feeder in a snowy tree.

"While the book would work well as a read or sing-aloud, with so much to pore over and absorb in the art, it is best used for one-on-one sharing. A surefire choice to spice up the dreariest winter day." SLJ

Rose, Naomi C.

Tashi and the Tibetan flower cure. Lee & Low Books 2011 il $18.95

Grades: 1 2 3   **E**

1. Sick -- Fiction 2. Flowers -- Fiction 3. Grandfathers

-- Fiction 4. Community life -- Fiction

ISBN 978-1-60060-425-6; 1-60060-425-0

LC 2011010556

"The softly brushed paintings have a naive, self-tutored look, but suit the text's homespun tone. The story, outwardly realistic, turns on two charming ideas: that of a child using ancient wisdom to restore the health of a relative, and that of a sterile American suburb becoming as close-knit as a Tibetan village." Publ Wkly

Rosen, Michael

Bear flies high; [illustrated by Adrian Reynolds] Bloomsbury 2009 un il $16.99; lib bdg $17.89

Grades: PreK K 1 2   **E**

1. Bears -- Fiction 2. Flight -- Fiction

ISBN 978-1-59990-386-6; 1-59990-386-5; 978-1-59990-387-3 lib bdg; 1-59990-387-3 lib bdg

LC 2008-55015

Bear usually spends his days on the beach, singing and watching birds, but when he leaves to visit a carnival, his dream of flying may just come true.

"The lyrical call-and-response and glowing illustrations give the book a cadence that's perfect for afternoon naps or lazy days." Publ Wkly

I'm number one; illustrated by Bob Graham. Candlewick Press 2009 un il $16.99

Grades: PreK K 1 2   **E**

1. Toys -- Fiction

ISBN 978-0-7636-4535-9; 0-7636-4535-4

LC 2009004246

A wind-up soldier bosses and berates the other toys, making them feel terrible, until they suddenly start to rebel.

"The pen-and-watercolor illustrations are filled with expressive characters and Graham's signature, whimsical details, such as the stuffed pig's snout ring. This simple, affecting story will be welcome anywhere that more than two young kids are gathered together and where laughter, not mean words, is the lingua franca." Booklist

★ **Michael** Rosen's sad book; words by Michael Rosen; pictures by Quentin Blake. Candlewick Press 2005 un il $16.99; pa $6.99

Grades: K 1 2 3   **E**

1. Bereavement -- Fiction

ISBN 0-7636-2597-3; 0-7636-4104-9 pa

LC 2004-45787

A man tells about all the emotions that accompany his sadness over the death of his son, and how he tries to cope

"Blake's evocative watercolor-and-ink illustrations use shades of gray for the pictures where sadness has taken hold but brighten with color at the memory of happy times. This story is practical and universal and will be of comfort to those who are working through their bereavement. A brilliant and distinguished collaboration." SLJ

Red Ted and the lost things; illustrated by Joel Stewart. Candlewick Press 2009 40p il

Grades: PreK K 1 2   **E**

1. Toys -- Fiction 2. Teddy bears -- Fiction 3. Lost and found possessions -- Fiction

ISBN 0-7636-4537-0; 0-7636-4624-5 pa; 978-0-7636-4537-3; 978-0-7636-4624-0 pa

LC 2009-02992

When a teddy bear is accidentally left on the seat of a train, he uses his ingenuity—and some new friends—to search for the little girl who lost him. "Grades two to three." (Bull Cent Child Books)

"Rosen's quirky combination of characters is matched by Stewart's muted colors and deliberately hazy backgrounds, which nicely spotlight the stuffed animals. . . . The plucky and determined Red Ted deserves a place among the many lost-toys books on library shelves." SLJ

Send for a superhero! Michael Rosen, illustrated by Katharine McEwen. Candlewick Press 2014 40 p. color illustrations $16.99
Grades: PreK K 1 2 3   E
    1. Bedtime -- Fiction 2. Superheroes -- Fiction 3. Comic books, strips, etc.
    ISBN 0763664383; 9780763664381
                   LC 2013944084

"Comic-book action meets picture-book adventure in this . . . new outing from beloved author Michael Rosen and illustrator Katharine McEwen. Tune in as a father reads his children a bedtime story about the exploits of two villains, Filth and Vacuum, and their wicked plan to suck all the money out of the banks and cover everything with muck and slime." (Publisher's note)

" The comic adventure is laid out in frames with urgent declarations and sound effects, with a printed-on-newsprint effect, whereas the scenes with Elmer and Emily are often on full-bleed pages and pulse with saturated colors. Although this approach has been used before, rarely has it been executed with such hilarious results." - Kirkus

★ **Tiny** Little Fly; words by Michael Rosen; pictures by Kevin Waldron. Candlewick Press 2010 un il $15.99
Grades: PreK K   E
    1. Stories in rhyme 2. Flies -- Fiction 3. Tigers -- Fiction 4. Elephants -- Fiction 5. Hippopotamus -- Fiction
    ISBN 978-0-7636-4681-3; 0-7636-4681-4
                   LC 2010-07549

With a tramp and a roll and a swat, Great Big Elephant, Great Big Hippo, and Great Big Tiger try to capture Tiny Little Fly as he teases each one in turn.

"The consistently patterned, simple rhyming text is accompanied by rustic, large-scale, digitally enhanced pencil-and-gouache art. . . . The words and images create an easily absorbed, enjoyable adventure." Booklist

★ **Totally** wonderful Miss Plumberry; [by] Michael Rosen; illustrated by Chinlun Lee. Candlewick Press 2006 un il $15.99
Grades: PreK K 1 2   E
    1. School stories 2. Teachers -- Fiction
    ISBN 0-7636-2744-5
                   LC 2005045392

Molly's day turns from totally wonderful to totally horrible when her classmates are not interested in the special crystal she has brought to school, until Miss Plumberry steps in to help

"This gentle picture book captures the impact a sensitive teacher has on the lives of her students. . . . The soft watercolor-and-pencil illustrations reveal [Molly's] emo-

tions and expose the fickle attention of children in engaging . . . spreads." SLJ

★ **We're** going on a bear hunt; anniversary edition of a modern classic. retold by Michael Rosen; illustrated by Helen Oxenbury. Margaret K. McElderry Books 2009 un il $18.99
Grades: PreK K 1 2   E
    1. Bears -- Fiction 2. Hunting -- Fiction
    ISBN 978-1-4169-8711-6; 1-4169-8711-8
                   LC 2008-53214

First published 1989

Brave bear hunters go through grass, a river, mud, and other obstacles before the inevitable encounter with the bear forces a headlong retreat

"Glorious puddles of watercolor alternate with impish charcoal sketches in this refreshing interpretation of an old hand rhyme in which a man, four children, and a dog stalk the furry beast through mud and muck, high and low. A book with a genuine atmosphere of togetherness and boundless enthusiasm for the hunt." SLJ

Rosen, Michael J.
★ **Chanukah** lights; illustrations by Robert Sabuda. Candlewick Press 2011 un il $34.99
Grades: K 1 2   E
    1. Counting 2. Pop-up books 3. Jews -- Fiction 4. Hanukkah stories 5. Hanukkah -- Fiction
    ISBN 978-0-7636-5533-4; 0-7636-5533-3
                   LC 2011013664

Counts the candles of a menorah on each night of Hanukkah while recalling images of Jewish life in different places and times, such Herod's temple in Jerusalem, a shtetl in Russia, and a refugee ship bound for the New World.

"This is a gorgeous and fragile holiday book for adults and children to enjoy together." SLJ

Night of the pumpkinheads; illustrations by Hugh McMahon. Dial Books for Young Readers 2011 il $16.99
Grades: K 1 2   E
    1. Pumpkin -- Fiction 2. Halloween -- Fiction 3. Vegetables -- Fiction
    ISBN 978-0-8037-3452-4; 0-8037-3452-2
                   LC 2010039314

Determined to make Halloween a frightening night of the pumpkinheads, the pumpkins transform themselves into a variety of scary monsters and then head for town hoping to terrify everyone they meet.

"Digitally assembled with photographs of McMahon's work and pencil drawings, the illustrations treat readers to spirited images of spunky pumpkins rising up to take an active part in trick-or-treating instead of remaining parked on porches. . . . A solid addition to the Halloween shelf, especially for those who have graduated from safer, sweeter stories." Kirkus

Rosenberg, Liz
Nobody; illustrated by Julie Downing. Roaring Brook Press 2010 un il $16.99
Grades: PreK K   E
    1. Morning -- Fiction 2. Imaginary playmates -- Fiction 3. Parent-child relationship -- Fiction
    ISBN 978-1-59643-120-1; 1-59643-120-2

"Young George wakes up early one morning while his parents are asleep. His imaginary companion, Nobody, is there to keep him company and inspires plenty of mischief. . . . Color pops off the page with playful illustrations done in watercolor, colored pencil, pastels, and china marker. Downing cleverly contrasts Nobody in black and white. The visual impact is strong but simple and underscores the tightly written text, and the facial expressions are priceless. Perspective is creatively used, particularly in a spread where George and Nobody are exploring the contents of the refrigerator. Kids and their parents will love this one." SLJ

Tyrannosuarus dad. Roaring Brook Press 2011 il $16.99
Grades: PreK K 1 2   E
1. Fathers -- Fiction 2. Dinosaurs -- Fiction
ISBN 9781596435315; 1596435313
Tobias's father is a lot like other fathers—he likes corny jokes, and doing magic tricks, and works really hard at the office. But there the resemblance ends. He has teeth as sharp as steak knives, is forty feet high, and weighs as much as a locomotive. He is, in fact, a tyrannosaurus.
"Rosenberg's well-paced dialogue and succinct descriptions result in a most engaging read. Myers' oil paintings truly amaze." Kirkus

Rosenberg, Madelyn
Happy birthday, Tree; a Tu B'Shevat story. by Madelyn Rosenberg; illustrated by Jana Christy. Albert Whitman & Co. 2012 24 p. (hardcover) $15.99
Grades: PreK K 1 2   E
1. Jews -- Fiction 2. Trees -- Fiction 3. Tu bi-Shevat -- Fiction
ISBN 0807531510; 9780807531518
LC 2011034187
In this children's picture book by Madelyn Rosenberg, illustrated by Jana Christy, "Joni strives to create a celebration befitting her old majestic tree . . . on the Jewish holiday of Tu B'Shevat, the birthday of the trees. . . . Determined to find the right gift for her leafy friend, Joni concludes that a new tree planted close by and a promise to continue to nurture her arboreal companions is the best way to observe the holiday." (Kirkus)

The **Schmutzy** Family; by Madelyn Rosenberg; illustrated by Paul Meisel. Holiday House 2012 32 p. (hardcover) $16.95
Grades: PreK K 1   E
1. Jews -- Fiction 2. Picture books for children 3. Sabbath -- Fiction 4. Cleanliness -- Fiction 5. Family life -- Fiction
ISBN 0823423719; 9780823423712
LC 2011040341
In this children's picture book, "wading in Feldman Swamp, making mud pies, painting with tomato sauce, and other messy activities are a part of the Schmutzy family activities. Despite how grimy the playing gets, Mama Schmutzy does not mind one bit except on Friday when" they must prepare for the Sabbath. (Children's Literature)

Rosenberry, Vera
★ **Vera's** first day of school. Holt & Co. 1999 un il hardcover o.p. pa $6.95

Grades: PreK K 1 2   E
1. School stories
ISBN 0-8050-5936-9; 0-8050-7269-1 pa
LC 98-43347
Vera cannot wait for the day when she starts school, but the first day does not go exactly as she has anticipated
"Rosenberry's playful, brightly colored gouache illustrations capture Vera's jubilation-turned-dismay." Horn Book Guide
Other titles about Vera are:
Vera goes to the dentist (2002)
Vera rides a bike (2004)
Vera runs away (2000)
Vera's baby sister (2005)
Vera's Halloween (2008)
Vera's new school (2006)
When Vera was sick (1998)

Rosenstock, Barbara
The **littlest** mountain; illustrated by Melanie Hall. Kar-Ben Pub. 2011 un il $17.95; pa $7.95
Grades: PreK K 1 2 3   E
1. Jewish legends 2. God -- Fiction 3. Mountains -- Fiction
ISBN 978-0-7613-4495-7; 0-7613-4495-0; 978-0-7613-4497-1 pa; 0-7613-4497-7 pa
LC 2010021249
"This pourquoi story about why God chose Mount Sinai as the location for giving the Ten Commandments has its roots in Jewish legend. Various mountains in the land of Israel list their best qualities and argue over which should be chosen. In the end, God picks humble, faithful Mount Sinai. . . . This is a lovely tale. . . . Kids will get a kick out of the folktale feeling and the talking mountains, caregivers will like the lesson on the value of being humble and faithful, and Jewish educators will be thrilled to have a great read-aloud for the holiday of Shavuot, which commemorates the receiving of the Ten Commandments." SLJ

Rosenthal, Amy Krouse
Al Pha's bet; illustrated by Delphine Durand. G. P. Putnam's Sons 2011 un il $16.99
Grades: PreK K   E
1. Alphabet -- Fiction
ISBN 978-0-399-24601-2; 0-399-24601-0
LC 2010028171
Al Pha makes a bet with himself that he can invent the perfect order for the twenty-six letters.
Durand's "loopy acrylic paintings carry the story through a long, long middle section about how Al comes to arrange each of the letters as he does . . . populating Al's world with a wacky assortment of proto-trees and flowers, as well as a cast of equally goofy-looking villagers and animals. Pages are well designed and visually lively throughout, the text peppered with spot illustrations. . . . Fans of dopey puns everywhere, rejoice!" Publ Wkly

Bedtime for Mommy; illustrated by LeUyen Pham. Bloomsbury 2010 un il $16.99; lib bdg $17.89
Grades: PreK K 1 2   E
1. Bedtime -- Fiction 2. Mother-daughter relationship

-- Fiction

ISBN 978-1-59990-341-5; 1-59990-341-5; 978-1-59990-465-8 lib bdg; 1-59990-465-9 lib bdg

LC 2009-18205

In a reversal of the classic bedtime story, a child helps her mommy get ready for bed, enduring pleas for one more book, five more minutes of play time, and a glass of water before the lights go out.

"The facial expressions throughout are priceless, and the final illustration showing the parents peeking in at a sleeping daughter round out this tale. This very visual story will appeal to beginning readers as well as parents and librarians looking for a fun bedtime read-aloud." Libr Media Connect

Chopsticks; illustrated by Scott Magoon. Disney/Hyperion 2012 un il $16.99

Grades: PreK K 1 2   E

1. Chopsticks -- Fiction 2. Friendship -- Fiction

ISBN 978-1-4231-0796-5; 1-4231-0796-9

LC 2011010269

This book "outlines the . . . activities of a pair of chopsticks who are not only working partners but also BFFs. Then the tip of one chopstick is broken in an unfortunate encounter with an asparagus spear, and after getting medical attention (the glue bottle mends him and wraps the 'wound' with a bandage) the injured chopstick must 'stay off it until it sets.' At first, the non-injured chopstick stays close by his friend's side, but the injured one finally tells him, 'You need to get out . . . venture off on your own a bit.' The chopsticks discover that time away from each other can also be a good thing." (Bulletin of the Center for Children's Books)

"The marriage of text, digital art, and design provide plentiful puns and laugh-out-laud humor." Publ Wkly

★ **Cookies**; bite-size life lessons. written by Amy Krouse Rosenthal; illustrated by Jane Dyer. HarperCollins Publishers 2006 un il $12.99; lib bdg $13.89

Grades: PreK K 1 2   E

1. Cookies 2. Conduct of life

ISBN 978-0-06-058081-0; 0-06-058081-X; 978-0-06-058082-7 lib bdg; 0-06-058082-8 lib bdg

LC 2005-15134

"Using the activity of making and eating cookies, the author defines some important concepts for young children, such as respect, trustworthiness, patience, politeness, loyalty, etc. . . . Lovely pastel watercolor illustrations show appealing children and anthropomorphic animals interacting with one another and the treats. . . . The utilization of the cookies to explain the concepts is a brilliant idea and works well on a child's level. The text is short and clear, and the book is delightful to look at and browse through." SLJ

Other titles in this series are:

Christmas cookies (2008)

Sugar cookies (2009)

One smart cookie (2010)

★ **Duck!** Rabbit! [illustrated by] Tom Lichtenheld. Chronicle Books 2009 un il $16.99

Grades: PreK K 1 2   E

1. Ducks -- Fiction 2. Rabbits -- Fiction

ISBN 978-0-8118-6865-5; 0-8118-6865-6

LC 2008-28102

This children's book by Amy Krouse Rosenthal, illustrated by Tom Lichtenheld, asks "Is it a duck or a rabbit? Depends on how you look at it . With more than 100,000 copies sold, this classic picture book is now available in a sturdy board book that little ones will love holding in their own two hands." (Publisher's note)

Rosenthal and Lichtenheld play "with perspective and visual trickery, . . . using a classic image that looks like either a rabbit (with long ears) or a duck (with a long bill). . . . Two off-stage speakers, their words appearing on either side of the animal's head, argue their points of view. The snappy dialogue makes for [a] fine read-aloud." Publ Wkly

I scream ice cream! a book of wordles. by Amy Krouse Rosenthal and illustrated by Serge Bloch. Chronicle Books 2013 40 p. (alk. paper) $16.99

Grades: K 1 2   E

1. English language -- Terms and phrases 2. Word games -- Fiction 3. Plays on words -- Fiction

ISBN 1452100047; 9781452100043

LC 2013011487

This book, by Amy Krouse Rosenthal and illustrator Serge Bloch, examines English language words that sound the same. "Amy Krouse Rosenthal unleashes her . . . wit in this . . . book of wordplay. Complemented by . . . illustrations from Serge Bloch, this . . . book will have young readers thinking about words in an entirely new way! (Publisher's note)

★ **Little** Hoot; illustrated by Jen Corace. Chronicle Books 2008 un il $12.99

Grades: PreK K   E

1. Owls -- Fiction 2. Bedtime -- Fiction

ISBN 978-0-8118-6023-9; 0-8118-6023-X

LC 2007-24960

Little Hoot wants to go to bed early, like all of his friends do, and he is hopping mad when Mama and Papa Owl insist that he stay up late and play.

The "owl family . . . feels recognizable. . . . This outing is not to be missed." Publ Wkly

Other titles in the series are:

Little oink (2009)

Little pea (2005)

The **OK** book; [by] Amy Krouse Rosenthal & Tom Lichtenheld. HarperCollins 2007 un il $12.99

Grades: PreK K 1 2   E

1. Ability -- Fiction 2. Self-acceptance -- Fiction

ISBN 978-0-06-115255-9; 0-06-115255-2

LC 2006030432

"The book's hero is a little stick figure whose head is the O of OK, and whose arms and legs are the K. . . . I like to try a lot of different things, the OK figure says. I'm not great at all of them, but I enjoy them all the same. . . . One day, I'll grow up to be really excellent at something, OK says, while lying in bed. . . . It can't hurt to remind kids that the pleasure we take in simple activities is what makes life worthwhile." Publ Wkly

★ **This** plus that; life's little equations. Amy + Krouse + Rosenthal = writer; Jen + Corace = artist. Harper 2011 un il $14.99

Grades: PreK K 1 2   **E**
1. Mathematics -- Fiction 2. Conduct of life -- Fiction
3. Addition
ISBN 978-0-06-172655-2; 0-06-172655-9
                        LC 2008-34357

"Two pigtailed girls squabble, then reason with each other. The outcome is a simple sum: 'yes + no = maybe.' The same two girls gossip through a tin-can telephone: 'laughter + keeping secrets + sharing = best friend.' Witty observations—'anything + sprinkles = better'—alternate with improving messages as well as nods to the seasons, arts, and kid-friendly activities. . . . Corace's stylized pen and ink vignettes show a world that's safe and secure; the same family members appear throughout. . . . It's the kind of math that children won't have any trouble comprehending." Publ Wkly

Uni the unicorn; by Amy Krouse Rosenthal; illustrated by Brigette Barrager. Random House Inc. 2014 48 p. col. ill. (hardcover) $17.99; (library) $20.99
Grades: PreK K 1   **E**
1. Girls -- Fiction 2. Unicorns -- Fiction 3. Picture books for children
ISBN 0385375557; 9780385375559; 9780375972065
                        LC 2013009884

In this story by Amy Krouse Rosenthal, illustrated by Brigette Barrager, "Uni the unicorn is told there's no such thing as little girls! No matter what the grown-up unicorns say, Uni believes that little girls are real. Somewhere there must be a smart, strong, wonderful, magical little girl waiting to be best friends." (Publisher's note)

"The book features Rosenthal's familiar mix of humor and wit, making this book ideal for reading out loud or independently. Barrager's illustrations offer full page spreads of whimsical, dreamlike images that will make every reader want to believe in unicorns (or little girls)." SLJ

Yes Day! [by] Amy Krouse Rosenthal & [illustrated by] Tom Lichtenheld. HarperCollins 2009 un il $14.99; lib bdg $15.89
Grades: PreK K 1   **E**
1. Day -- Fiction 2. Wishes -- Fiction
ISBN 978-0-06-115259-7; 0-06-115259-5; 978-0-06-115260-3 lib bdg; 0-06-115260-9 lib bdg
                        LC 2008-20219

A little boy gets everything he asks for on Yes Day, a special day that only comes once a year.

"Lichtenheld's bright and funny cartoons bring the story to life, with character expressions that are right on the mark." SLJ

Rosenthal, Betsy R.
Which shoes would you choose? illustrated by Nancy Cote. G. P. Putnam's Sons 2010 un il $15.99
Grades: PreK   **E**
1. Shoes -- Fiction
ISBN 978-0-399-25013-2; 0-399-25013-1

"This picture book invites children to enjoy a shoe-themed guessing game as they follow a boy named Sherman through his day. The question-and-answer text alternates between two types of queries. The first asks Which shoes does he choose? A situation is described, followed by an answer and a reason for the choice. The second sort of question begins with the last shoes chosen and asks if they are worn in

an amusingly inappropriate situation. . . . The questions are sure to garner responses from individual children or story hour crowds. . . . Almost cartoonlike in their simplicity, the pleasant gouache and watercolor-pencil drawings feature tousle-haired Sherman sporting an extraordinarily large wardrobe of footwear." Booklist

Rosenthal, Eileen
I must have Bobo! illustrated by Marc Rosenthal. Atheneum Books for Young Readers 2010 un il $14.99
Grades: PreK K 1   **E**
1. Cats -- Fiction 2. Toys -- Fiction 3. Lost and found possessions -- Fiction
ISBN 978-1-4424-0377-2; 1-4424-0377-2
                        LC 2010-04963

When Willy wakes up without his favorite toy, he looks everywhere until he finds it.

"Illustrator Marc Rosenthal's . . . ability to capture Earl's feline deviousness—the way Earl cranes his neck to see if Willy is coming, or hides under the covers with Bobo—is one of the book's chief charms. . . . Soft pencil drawings on cream-colored pages add to the generally calm, bedtime atmosphere." Publ Wkly

I'll save you Bobo! Eileen Rosenthal; illustrated by Marc Rosenthal. Atheneum Books for Young Readers 2012 40 p.
Grades: PreK K 1 2 3   **E**
1. Cats -- Fiction 2. Toys -- Fiction 3. Drawing -- Fiction 4. Picture books for children 5. Adventure fiction -- Fiction 6. Fear -- Fiction 7. Storytelling -- Fiction
ISBN 1442403780; 9781442403789
                        LC 2011278288

This picture book tells the story of Willy, the young boy introduced in Eileen Rosenthal's previous book "'I Must Have Bobo!" and his companions, his favorite toy Bobo and Earl the cat. "Willy . . . here puts down the book he's reading in order to create a more exciting story himself, while his sock monkey Bobo serves as audience for his crayon drawings and narrative about a jungle adventure. . . . The cartoon illustrations create a kind of spotlight for the story: boy, drawing table and crayons, armchair, Bobo and cat." (Kirkus)

I will save you Bobo!

Rosenthal, Marc
Archie and the pirates. Joanna Cotler Books 2009 un il $16.99
Grades: K 1 2 3   **E**
1. Islands -- Fiction 2. Monkeys -- Fiction 3. Pirates -- Fiction 4. Friendship -- Fiction
ISBN 978-0-06-144164-6; 0-06-144164-3
                        LC 2008-35251

When Archie the monkey finds himself on a strange island, he makes a multitude of new friends who help him defend their home from intruding pirates.

"Rosenthal relates the adventure in a simple, matter-of-fact way and pairs the narrative to neatly drawn . . . cartoons. . . . Loaded with child appeal." Booklist

Rosner, Jennifer
The **mitten** string; repairing the world, a stitch at a time. by Jennifer Rosner; illustrated by Kristina Swarner.

Random House Inc 2014 32 p. color illustrations (jacketed hardcover: alk. paper) $17.99
Grades: 1 2 3   E
  1. Jewish legends 2. Deaf -- Fiction 3. Jews -- Fiction 4. People with disabilities -- Fiction 5. Mittens -- Fiction
ISBN 0385371187; 9780375971860; 9780385371186
                                                      LC 2013018685

This children's book, by Jennifer Rosner and illustrated by Kristina Swarner, is a "Jewish folktale about a girl who knits, a deaf woman, and a piece of blue yarn. When her family invites a deaf woman and her baby to stay, Ruthie, a talented knitter of mittens, wonders how the mother will know if her child wakes in the night. The surprising answer inspires Ruthie to knit a special gift that offers great comfort to mother and baby--and to Ruthie herself." (Publisher's note)

"The Tobers raise sheep, and young Ruthie loves to knit mittens from their wool for the villagers. When her family befriends a deaf woman whose wagon has broken down and her baby, the child observes how the mother, Bayla, sleeps with a string tied between her own wrist and Aaron's, to alert her if her son wakes up in the night...The "old country" Jewish setting is subtle, giving the story flavor without dominating it. Knitting and sign-language glossaries round out this attractive title. This beautiful story of kindness, acceptance, and resourcefulness will have wide appeal." SLJ

Rosoff, Meg
  ★ **Jumpy** Jack and Googily; [by] Meg Rosoff; illustrated by Sophie Blackall. Henry Holt 2008 un il $16.95
Grades: PreK K 1   E
  1. Fear -- Fiction 2. Snails -- Fiction 3. Monsters -- Fiction 4. Friendship -- Fiction
ISBN 978-0-8050-8066-7; 0-8050-8066-X
                                                      LC 2007-07227

Jumpy Jack the snail is terrified that there are monsters around every corner despite the reassurances of his best friend, Googily.

"The interplay between the two creates a wonderfully safe space for children to explore their fears. . . . The text . . . employs a formal elevated tone that gently chides Jumpy Jack's childish fears, adding an element of dry humor. The illustrations are filled with whimsical details." SLJ

  ★ **Meet** wild boars; [written by] Meg Rosoff and [illustrated by] Sophie Blackall. Henry Holt & Co. 2005 un il $15.95; pa $6.99
Grades: PreK K 1 2   E
  1. Boars -- Fiction
ISBN 0-8050-7488-0; 0-312-37963-3 pa
                                                      LC 2004-8985

It is very hard to be friends with wild boars because they are dirty and smelly, bad-tempered, and rude

This is "bitingly funny and deeply satisfying. . . . Blackall's roll-on-the-ground-in-laughter illustrations are incisively rendered in ink and gouache." Booklist

Another title about the wild boars is:
Wild boars cook (2008)

Ross, Fiona
  Chilly Milly Moo. Candlewick Press 2011 il $15.99
Grades: PreK K   E
  1. Milk -- Fiction 2. Cattle -- Fiction 3. Weather --

Fiction
ISBN 978-0-7636-5693-5; 0-7636-5693-3
                                                      LC 2010051446

While the other cows are enjoying the sun and making plenty of milk, Milly Moo is too hot to make a drop but when the temperature falls, Milly Moo shows the farmer and the rest of the herd what she can do.

"This is a great addition to read-alouds centered on the theme of individuality (with a snack tie-in built right in). Delightfully different, just like Milly Moo." Kirkus

Ross, Michael Elsohn
  Mama's milk; by Michael Elsohn Ross; illustrated by Ashley Wolff. Tricycle Press 2007 un il $12.95
Grades: PreK K   E
  1. Stories in rhyme 2. Animals -- Fiction 3. Mammals -- Fiction 4. Breast feeding -- Fiction
ISBN 978-1-58246-181-6; 1-58246-181-3
                                                      LC 2006020873

"From humans to a variety of aquatic and land animals, Ross's rhyming text describes the different ways that mothers nurse their babies. . . . The pastel-infused watercolor illustrations tastefully depict the nursing pairs." SLJ

Ross, Pat
  Meet M & M; pictures by Marylin Hafner. Pantheon Bks. 1980 41p il hardcover o.p. pa $4.99
Grades: K 1 2   E
  1. Friendship -- Fiction
ISBN 0-14-038731-5
                                                      LC 79-190

"Beginning readers will have no difficulty with the humorously told, very real incidents. . . . The many black-and-white pencil drawings capture the girls' facial expressions especially well." Horn Book

Other titles about M and M (Mandy and Mimi) are:
M and M and the bad news babies (1983)
M and M and the Halloween monster (1991)
M and M and the haunted house game (1980)
M and M and the mummy mess (1986)

Ross, Tony
  I want a party! written and illustrated by Tony Ross. Andersen Press 2011 un il $16.95
Grades: PreK K 1 2   E
  1. Parties -- Fiction 2. Princesses -- Fiction
ISBN 978-0-7613-8089-4; 0-7613-8089-2
                                                      LC 2011001597

Little Princess discovers that she can have a lovely party with just one guest.

"Ross's illustrations are produced in colorful ink and watercolors. The whimsy and simple story line will appeal to young children." SLJ

  I want two birthdays! Andersen Press 2010 un il $16.95
Grades: PreK K 1 2   E
  1. Birthdays -- Fiction 2. Princesses -- Fiction
ISBN 978-0-76135-495-6; 0-76135-495-6
First published 2008 in the United Kingdom
A little princess decides that two birthdays would be better than one, and three better than two, until every day becomes her birthday, but she soon realizes that the more birthdays she has, the less special they are.

"Ross's bright, cheerful trademark watercolor illustrations add much humor to this already funny tale about having too much of a good thing." SLJ

Other titles about the little princess are:

I want my light on! (2010)

I want to do it myself! (2011)

Rossell, Judith

Oliver; written and illustrated by Judith Rossell. Harper 2012 32 p.

Grades: PreK K 1 2   E

1. Boys -- Fiction 2. Imagination -- Fiction 3. Picture books for children 4. Penguins -- Fiction 5. Mothers and sons -- Fiction

ISBN 0062022105; 9780062022103

LC 2011019368

This picture book tells the story of a curious young boy named Oliver, who wonders about where penguins go on vacation and especially about what lives in the drain. His mother won't let him feed a banana to whatever is down there making gurgling noises, "so Oliver builds a submarine and takes it for a ride to see just what the drain is harboring. Here Oliver turns into a kid's drawing . . . in watercolor and pencil, with a touch of collage elsewhere; maybe this is all in his head? And what's down the drain? Penguins, of course." (Kirkus)

Rostoker-Gruber, Karen

★ Bandit; illustrated by Vincent Nguyen. Marshall Cavendish Children's Books 2008 un il $15.99

Grades: PreK K 1 2   E

1. Cats -- Fiction 2. Moving -- Fiction

ISBN 978-0-7614-5382-6; 0-7614-5382-2

LC 2007011720

When Bandit's family moves to a new house, the cat runs away and returns to the only home he knows, but after he is brought back, he understands that the new house is now home

"By telling the story from the point of view of an extremely territorial pet, Rostoker-Gruber approaches the issue of moving in a fresh way. . . . Nguyen's mixed-media illustrations have an attractive Pop Art style. . . . A funny, stylish book." SLJ

Another title about Bandit is:

Bandit's surprise (2010)

★ Ferret fun; illustrated by Paul Ratz de Tagyos. Marshall Cavendish Children's 2011 un il

Grades: PreK K 1 2   E

1. Cats -- Fiction 2. Ferrets -- Fiction

ISBN 0-7614-5817-4; 978-0-7614-5817-3

LC 2010-21301

Two nervous pet ferrets named Fudge and Einstein try to convince a visiting cat that they are not rats. "Grades two to four." (Bull Cent Child Books)

"Rátz de Tagyos's magic-marker-and-ink graphic-novel-style illustrations are the real draw; the bouncy, fanged trio are a terrific balance between Saturday morning cartoon and real animals. Just enough lesson hidden in the fun." Kirkus

Tea time; [illustrated by] Viviana Garofoli. Marshall Cavendish 2010 un il (Board buddies) bd bk $7.99

Grades: PreK   E

1. Stories in rhyme 2. Board books for children 3. Tea

-- Fiction 4. Parties -- Fiction

ISBN 978-0-7614-5638-4 bd bk; 0-7614-5638-4 bd bk

A young girl dresses up and prepares tea and cookies for her teddy bear and her mother.

"It's a just-right mix of text and illustration to coax the youngest readers into following a narrative; the familiarity of the activity serves to reinforce this. A sweet little beginning story." Kirkus

Roth, Carol

The little school bus; illustrated by Pamela Paparone. North-South Bks. 2002 un il hardcover o.p. pa $6.95

Grades: PreK K   E

1. Stories in rhyme 2. Buses -- Fiction 3. Animals -- Fiction

ISBN 0-7358-1646-8; 0-7358-1905-X pa

LC 2002-71417

An assortment of animals, including a goat in a coat, a quick chick, and a hairy bear, ride the bus to and from school

"Paparone's bright, sprightly illustrations feature plenty of cheery mugging out the windows and other amusing side business. . . . This will take children on a verbal and visual ride that they'll want to repeat as often as possible." Booklist

Will you still love me? illustrated by Daniel Howarth. Albert Whitman 2010 un il $15.99

Grades: PreK K   E

1. Love -- Fiction 2. Animals -- Fiction 3. Siblings -- Fiction 4. Parent-child relationship -- Fiction

ISBN 978-0-8075-9114-7; 0-8075-9114-9

Young animals and a little boy are reassured that their mothers will still love them after a new baby arrives.

"Howarth's sunny watercolor and ink illustrations match the upbeat tone of the bouncy, rhyming text." SLJ

Roth, Susan L.

Hard hat area; [by] Susan Roth. Bloomsbury Children's Books 2004 un il $17.95

Grades: PreK K 1 2   E

1. Building -- Fiction 2. Construction workers -- Fiction

ISBN 1-58234-946-0

LC 2003-65343

Construction workers ask Kristen, a young apprentice, to bring them snacks and supplies

"Stunning collages showcase the workers, their jobs, and their equipment in situ; clear explanatory notes describe the work and responsibilities for each person involved in the construction." Horn Book Guide

Rotner, Shelley

Senses at the seashore. Millbrook Press 2006 un il lib bdg $22.60

Grades: PreK K 1 2   E

1. Seashore 2. Senses and sensation

ISBN 978-0-7613-2897-1 lib bdg; 0-7613-2897-1 lib bdg

LC 2005-06151

"This picture book tells what children see, hear, smell, touch, and taste at the beach. . . . A few of the clear, colorful photos show adults (fishermen, a lifeguard) at work, but most of the illustrations are closeups of children at play. An inviting, kid-friendly introduction to the senses and the seashore." Booklist

Senses in the city; by Shelley Rotner. Millbrook Press 2008 un il (Shelley Rotner's early childhood library) lib bdg $23.93

Grades: PreK K 1   **E**

1. City and town life 2. Senses and sensation

ISBN 978-0-8225-7502-3 lib bdg; 0-8225-7502-7 lib bdg

"Both an exciting celebration of city life and a show-and-tell about the five senses, this photo-essay will draw even very young children. Clear, direct words and unframed pictures show children in the packed streets of an unnamed city, where they see the skyline and hear trains passing by, go inside tall buildings, and travel in a subway car." Booklist

Shades of people; by Shelley Rotner and Sheila M. Kelly; photographs by Shelley Rotner. Holiday House 2009 un il $16.95

Grades: PreK K 1   **E**

1. Race 2. Skin 3. Color

ISBN 978-0-8234-2191-6; 0-8234-2191-0

LC 2008022574

Explores the many different shades of human skin, and points out that skin is just a covering that does not reveal what someone is like inside.

"Filled with smiles and hugs, the pictures prove an upbeat confirmation of the book's central idea. . . . This will enrich and spark discussions of diversity." Booklist

Rowand, Phyllis

It is night; by Phyllis Rowand; illustrated by Laura Dronzek. Greenwillow Books, an imprint of HarperCollinsPublishers 2014 32 p. (trade ed.) $16.99

Grades: PreK K   **E**

1. Toys -- Fiction 2. Animals -- Fiction 3. Bedtime -- Fiction

ISBN 0062250248; 9780062250247

LC 2013028060

In this children's book, written by Phyllis Rowand and illustrated by Laura Dronzek, "A little girl says good-night and finds the perfect beds for each and every animal, for dolls big and small, and even for a railroad train. . . . In a gentle surprise ending, no matter where their beds should be, each animal or object is a toy. And so they all belong tucked into bed with the little girl because she loves them all." (Publisher's note)

"A series of bedtime questions ("Where does a railroad train go at night?") receive answers in this book first published in 1953 with illustrations by Rowand. The lulling litany is sweetly updated in Dronzek's blanket-soft, moon-drenched art. Some unlikely groupings (tiger and giraffe) presage the satisfying conclusion in which it is shown that the creatures are dolls, toys, and pets." Horn Book

Rubel, David

The carpenter's gift; a Christmas tale about the Rockefeller Center tree. illustrated by Jim LaMarche. Random House 2011 un il $17.99; lib bdg $20.99

Grades: K 1 2 3   **E**

1. Trees -- Fiction 2. Christmas stories 3. Kindness -- Fiction 4. Christmas -- Fiction 5. Rockefeller Center

-- Fiction.

ISBN 978-0-375-86922-8; 0-375-86922-0; 978-0-375-96922-5 lib bdg; 0-375-96922-5 lib bdg; 978-0-375-98933-9 e-book

LC 2010033203

In Depression-era New York City, construction workers at the Rockefeller Center site help a family in need—a gift that is repaid years later in the donation of an enormous Christmas tree.

"Rubel's story . . . puts the now magnificent symbol in perspective. LaMarche conveys emotional resonance with gauzy, soft-hued paintings of the inspirational proceedings." Publ Wkly

Rubin, Adam

Those darn squirrels and the cat next door; illustrated by Daniel Salmieri. Clarion Books 2011 32p il $16.99

Grades: K 1 2 3   **E**

1. Cats -- Fiction 2. Birds -- Fiction 3. Squirrels -- Fiction

ISBN 0-547-42922-3; 978-0-547-42922-9

"Mr. Fookwire, his beloved backyard birds, and his relentlessly clever squirrel frenemies are united against a new neighbor and common enemy: a corpulent, take-no-prisoners cat named Muffins, whose idea of fun is giving the squirrels noogies, wet willies, and wedgies. . . . Rubin's sly ironies and Salmieri's spare but deeply goofy aesthetic is child-friendly urbanity at its best." Publ Wkly

Those darn squirrels! by Adam Rubin; illustrated by Daniel Salmieri. Clarion Books 2008 32p il $16

Grades: K 1 2 3   **E**

1. Birds -- Fiction 2. Old age -- Fiction 3. Squirrels -- Fiction

ISBN 978-0-547-00703-8; 0-547-00703-5

LC 2007040110

When grumpy Old Man Fookwire builds feeders to try to keep birds—the only creatures he likes—from leaving for the winter, he finds himself in a battle with clever, crafty squirrels who want a share of the abundant food

"This simple tale has a sneaky, edgy humor that erupts into hilarity. . . . [The] paintings [are] reminiscent of some of the best European children's book illustrations." SLJ

Another title about these characters is:

Those darn squirrels and the cat next door (2011)

Ruddell, Deborah

Who said coo? illustrated by Robin Luebs. Beach Lane Books 2010 un il $16.99

Grades: PreK K 1   **E**

1. Stories in rhyme 2. Pigs -- Fiction 3. Sounds -- Fiction 4. Animals -- Fiction 5. Bedtime -- Fiction

ISBN 978-1-4169-8510-5; 1-4169-8510-7

LC 2009000929

"Unbeknownst to Lulu the pig, Pigeon and Owl have shown up on her doorstep at bedtime. . . . Lulu's slumber is interrupted by a loud 'Cooooo' and then a 'Whooooo.' Lulu confronts the likely culprits, but Pigeon and Owl refuse to fess up. . . . Luebs's acrylic paintings feature a luminescent pastel palette, which makes the story's nighttime scenes glow. A few deft strokes convey Lulu's contentedness, exasperation, and anger." Publ Wkly

Ruddra, Anshumani

Dorje's stripes; illustrated by Gwangjo and Jung-a-Park. Kane Miller 2010 un il $15.99

Grades: 1 2 3 4   E

1. Monks -- Fiction 2. Tigers -- Fiction 3. Monasteries -- Fiction 4. Tibet (China) -- Fiction

ISBN 978-1-935279-98-3; 1-935279-98-X

Dorje is a beautiful Royal Bengal tiger but he has no stripes. In a small Buddhist monastery in Tibet, Master Wu explains the reasons behind Dorje's missing stripes, and offers hope for the future.

"This heartwarming story is enhanced by stunning watercolors that add to its peaceful tone and suggest a quiet beauty as well as depict the action and emotions of each character." SLJ

Rueda, Claudia

My little polar bear. Scholastic Press 2009 un il $16.99

Grades: PreK K 1 2   E

1. Polar bear -- Fiction 2. Mother-child relationship -- Fiction

ISBN 978-0-545-14600-5; 0-545-14600-3

LC 2008043079

When a cub asks if he is a polar bear, his mother describes what a polar bear is and does, reassuring him that she will teach him to hunt, walk securely on ice, and otherwise be true to his breed, and that she will always love him.

"The striking, minimalist style of illustration seem well suited to the Arctic scenes. Despite the cold setting, the story generates its own warmth." Booklist

★ **No**; translated by Elisa Amado. Groundwood Books/House of Anansi Press 2010 un il $18.95

Grades: PreK K   E

1. Snow -- Fiction 2. Bears -- Fiction 3. Winter -- Fiction 4. Hibernation -- Fiction 5. Mother-child relationship -- Fiction

ISBN 978-0-88899-991-7; 0-88899-991-7

Original Spanish edition 2009

"Mother suggests that it is time to hibernate for the winter, but little bear has other ideas. . . . But when a blinding snowstorm practically buries little bear, he realizes mother might have known best. . . . Flat figures in a minimal wintry palette nevertheless burst with personality, abetted by clever compositions." Kirkus

Ruelle, Karen Gray

★ The **Thanksgiving** beast feast. Holiday House 1999 32p il (Holiday House reader) $15.95

Grades: PreK K 1 2   E

1. Cats -- Fiction 2. Animals -- Fiction 3. Thanksgiving Day -- Fiction

ISBN 0-8234-1511-2

LC 98-51339

Harry the cat and his sister Emily celebrate Thanksgiving by making a holiday feast for the animals in their yard

"Simple and child-centered, the story reads well and uses repetition in ways that sound natural, while reinforcing word recognition. Pleasantly childlike, the naive ink drawings are tinted with gentle washes." Booklist

Other titles about Harry and Emily are:

April fool (2002)

The crunchy, munchy Christmas tree (2003)

Dear Tooth Fairy (2006)

Easter egg disaster (2004)

Easy as apple pie (2002)

Great groundhogs! (2005)

Just in time for New Year's (2004)

The monster in Harry's backyard (1999)

Mother's Day mess (2003)

Snow valentines (2000)

Spookier than a ghost (2001)

Rumford, James

From the good mountain; how Gutenberg changed the world. James Rumford. 1st ed. Roaring Brook Press 2012 40 p. (reinforced: alk. paper) $17.99

Grades: 3 4 5   E

1. Riddles 2. Book industry 3. Printing -- History 4. Books -- History 5. Printers -- Germany -- Biography 6. Printing -- History -- Origin and antecedents

ISBN 1596435429; 9781596435421

LC 2011033796

Author James Rumford presents a history on printmaking. "What was made of rags and bones, soot and seeds? What took a mountain to make? For the answer, travel back to the fifteenth century—to a time when books were made by hand and a man named Johannes Gutenberg invented a way to print books with movable type . . . [The book is w]ritten as a series of riddles . . . [with things] to learn about how the very thing you are holding in your hands came to be." (Publisher's note)

Includes bibliographical references and index.

★ **Rain** school; written and illustrated by James Rumford. Houghton Mifflin Books for Children 2010 un il $16.99

Grades: PreK K 1 2   E

1. School stories 2. Chad -- Fiction 3. Rain -- Fiction

ISBN 0-547-24307-3; 978-0-547-24307-8

LC 2009-49701

Thomas, who lives in Chad in Africa is ready for his first day of school, but "when he arrives at the schoolyard he finds that there is no school. . . . After Thomas and his schoolmates build the school from mud and grass, they're ready for their nine-month school year. . . . Ages five to eight." (Bull Cent Child Books)

"While serving as a Peace Corps volunteer, Rumford was a teacher in Chad, and the authentic details illuminate the spare text and beautiful artwork. . . . The colored-pencil, ink, and pastel images echo the words' elemental rhythms. . . . This moving offering will leave kids thinking about the daily lives of other young people around the world." Booklist

★ **Silent** music; a story of Baghdad. Roaring Brook Press 2008 un il $17.95

Grades: K 1 2 3   E

1. Iraq -- Fiction 2. Calligraphy -- Fiction 3. Baghdad (Iraq) -- Fiction 4. Iraq War, 2003- -- Fiction

ISBN 978-1-59643-276-5; 1-59643-276-4

LC 2007-23600

As bombs and missiles fall on Baghdad in 2003, a young boy named Ali uses the art of calligraphy to distance himself from the horror of war.

"Art sings on the pages of this visual celebration of Arabic calligraphy as Rumford's . . . collages of floral and geometric designs and flowing lines deftly echo Arabic language and patterns. . . . Spreads incorporating stamps, money and postcards reinforce the Baghdad setting and complement representational scenes." Publ Wkly

Tiger and turtle. Roaring Brook 2010 un il $17.99
Grades: 1 2 3   E
   1. Tigers -- Fiction 2. Turtles -- Fiction 3. Friendship -- Fiction
   ISBN 978-1-59643-416-5; 1-59643-416-3

When a tiger and a turtle both want a flower that has fallen to the ground, they argue over it until a fight breaks out between them.

"The brief text is well paced, with repeated rising and falling action, and the resolution of the most suspenseful moments requires a page turn. Read this tale aloud . . . for a lively storyhour." SLJ

Runton, Andy
   Owly and Wormy, friends all aflutter! Atheneum Books for Young Readers 2011 un il $15.99
Grades: PreK K 1 2   E
   1. Stories without words 2. Owls -- Fiction 3. Worms -- Fiction 4. Butterflies -- Fiction
   ISBN 978-1-4169-5774-4; 1-4169-5774-X
                       LC 2010-06123

Good friends Owly and Wormy are disappointed when their new plant attracts fat, green, bug-like things, instead of butterflies, until a metamorphosis occurs.

"Even very young children will be able to puzzle out the story's details from the expressions on the characters' faces, and Runton's unvarnished sentimentality creates an atmosphere of absolute security." Publ Wkly

Russell, Natalie
   Moon rabbit. Viking Children's Books 2009 un il $16.99
Grades: PreK K 1   E
   1. Rabbits -- Fiction 2. Friendship -- Fiction 3. City and town life -- Fiction
   ISBN 978-0-670-01170-4; 0-670-01170-3
                       LC 2008022799

A city rabbit befriends a country rabbit, but soon she misses her home with its cafes and bright lights

"The story's considerable appeal is amplified by Russell's exceptional artwork. Using her skills as a printmaker, she places her endearing characters on beautifully colored backgrounds so smooth they resemble suede." Booklist

Another title about these rabbits is:
Brown Rabbit in the city (2010)

Russo, Marisabina
   ★ The **big** brown box. Greenwillow Bks. 2000 un il $16.99
Grades: PreK K 1 2   E
   1. Boxes -- Fiction 2. Brothers -- Fiction
   ISBN 0-688-17096-X
                       LC 99-14871

As he plays in a very large box in his room and turns it into a house, then a cave, then a boat, Sam is reluctant to let his little brother Ben join him, but then he finds the perfect way for them to share.

"The well-paced, child-centered text is complemented by Russo's trademark two-dimensional gouache illustrations that realistically capture the creative play of children." SLJ

   ★ **I** will come back for you; a family in hiding during World War II. Schwartz & Wade 2011 un il $17.99; lib bdg $20.99
Grades: K 1 2 3   E
   1. Italy -- Fiction 2. Bracelets -- Fiction 3. Grandmothers -- Fiction 4. Jews -- Italy -- Fiction 5. World War, 1939-1945 -- Italy -- Fiction
   ISBN 978-0-375-86695-1; 0-375-86695-7; 978-0-375-96695-8 lib bdg; 0-375-96695-1 lib bdg
                       LC 2010044523

A grandmother tells her granddaughter the story of the charm bracelet that represent her own childhood experiences while she and her family tried to evade the Nazis in Italy during World War II.

"Russo bases this book on her own family history. Her writing is direct but always reassuring, and her naif [gouache] illustrations, rendered in saturated autumnal tones, feel very close to the actual family photographs that serve as the book's endpapers. Ingenuity and compassion are recurring themes in this eloquent portrayal of a family's struggle for freedom." Publ Wkly

   Little Bird takes a bath; Marisabina Russo. Schwartz & Wade Books 2015 40 p. color illustrations (hc) $16.99; (glb) $19.99
Grades: PreK K 1   E
   1. Rain -- Fiction 2. Baths -- Fiction 3. Birds -- Fiction 4. New York (N.Y.) -- Fiction 5. Rain and rainfall -- Fiction 6. City and town life -- New York (State) -- New York -- Fiction
   ISBN 0385370156; 9780385370141; 9780385370158
                       LC 2013018300

In this book by Marisabina Russo, "a little bird in the big city searches for the perfect puddle. . . . He searches far and wide, but some puddles are too big, some are too small, and some are already crowded with bathers. . . . When Little Bird finds a good-looking puddle in a city park, one surprise after another spoils his bath. . . . But soon, Little Bird finds the perfect puddle to call his own." (Publisher's note)

"Without stretching a point too far, the interconnectedness of nature and city, the consequences of action and play, the sounds and sense of an urban environment make for a really nice story whose words and images repay repeated readings." Kirkus

   Peter is just a baby; written and illustrated by Marisabina Russo. Eerdmans Books for Young Readers 2011 un il $16
Grades: PreK K 1   E
   1. Infants -- Fiction 2. Siblings -- Fiction 3. French language -- Vocabulary
   ISBN 978-0-8028-5384-4; 0-8028-5384-6
                       LC 2011022480

"The title is the favorite refrain of the narrator, an anthropomorphized six-year-old bear and Peter's big sister. . . . Delineating Peter's babyish ways . . . lets her cite all the ways she is more mature and sophisticated. . . . With help from her tutor, the narrator learns to say 'Bon appetit!' before eating and 'Quel dommage!' when disappointed. . . .

This worldly-wise and ultimately accepting attitude, combined with the parallel story of learning French . . . gives an otherwise typical tale of sibling rivalry a stylish, refreshing twist. . . . [The book is illustrated with] cheery, naif gouache pictures." Publ Wkly

A **very** big bunny. Schwartz & Wade Books 2010 un il $17.99; lib bdg $20.99

Grades: PreK K 1 2   E
1. School stories 2. Size -- Fiction 3. Rabbits -- Fiction 4. Friendship -- Fiction
ISBN 978-0-375-84463-8; 0-375-84463-5; 978-0-375-94463-5 lib bdg; 0-375-94463-X lib bdg
LC 2008-39924

Amelia is so big that she is always last in line at school and none of the other students will play with her, but a special new classmate teaches her that size is not always the most important thing.

"Russo's tale about unlikely friends executes a familiar theme with abundant charm and humor. . . . Featuring a saturated palate, Russo's matte gouache illustrations amplify the snappy storytelling." Publ Wkly

Ruth, Greg

★ **Coming** Home; by Greg Ruth. Feiwel & Friends 2014 32 p. color illustrations $16.99

Grades: PreK K 1 2 3   E
1. Veterans 2. Soldiers -- Fiction 3. Mothers and Sons -- Fiction 4. Children of military personnel -- Fiction 5. Families of military personnel -- Fiction
ISBN 1250055474; 9781250055477

In this picture book, by Greg Ruth, "readers follow the anxious progress of a young boy in a red T-shirt as he looks through the crowds of returning veterans and their loved ones. Along with him, there's a border collie dashing into its owner's arms, a man tenderly touching the belly of a pregnant woman, tight embraces, and comradely photo shoots." (School Library Journal)

"This affecting picture book is simplicity itself. Nuanced drawings drive the action, with only occasional words appearing every other page or so...This gently reassuring selection will resonate with children who have parents in the military or with anyone who is separated from a family member for any reason..." Booklist

Ruzzier, Sergio

Amandina. Roaring Brook Press 2008 un il $16.95

Grades: K 1 2 3   E
1. Dogs -- Fiction 2. Theater -- Fiction
ISBN 978-1-59643-236-9; 1-59643-236-5
LC 2007047914

Amandina decides to overcome her shyness and show the town what a talented little dog she is, but when no one shows up for her performance, she finds that she also has a lot of perseverance.

"The artwork combines delicate lines and faded colors to create a fanciful stage for this likable character." SLJ

Hey rabbit! Roaring Brook Press 2010 un il $16.99

Grades: K 1 2   E
1. Gifts -- Fiction 2. Magic -- Fiction 3. Animals -- Fiction 4. Rabbits -- Fiction
ISBN 978-1-59643-502-5; 1-59643-502-X

"Instead of a magician pulling a rabbit out of a hat, here we have a rabbit magically producing all sorts of things from a suitcase. An ode to gift giving, Ruzzier's latest picture book showcases his charming illustrations without letting a complicated plot get in the way. . . . Ruzzier's animals are a very appealing group . . . and each wish leads to a colorful and lively scene." Booklist

Ryan, Candace

Ribbit rabbit; illustrated by Mike Lowery. Walker Books for Young Readers 2011 un il

Grades: PreK K 1   E
1. Frogs -- Fiction 2. Rabbits -- Fiction 3. Friendship -- Fiction
ISBN 0-8027-2180-X; 0-8027-2181-8 lib bdg; 978-0-8027-2180-8; 978-0-8027-2181-5 lib bdg
LC 2010-08418

Frog and Bunny are the best of friends, even though they sometimes get into fights. "Ages three to five." (Bull Cent Child Books)

"The rhythmic, onomatopoetic text is a pretty music, the kind of song you'd sing in the dark to lift your spirits. Equally joyful and engaging—and that's a tall order—is Lowery's artwork. It has a childlike, elemental tone, with neat planes of color, but it is wonderfully, touchingly emotive." Kirkus

Ryan, Pam Muñoz

★ **Tony** Baloney; illustrated by Edwin Fotheringham. Scholastic Press 2011 un il $16.99

Grades: PreK K 1   E
1. Penguins -- Fiction 2. Siblings -- Fiction
ISBN 0-545-23135-3; 978-0-545-23135-0
LC 2009-51693

Tony, a macaroni penguin, is a middle child with very exasperating siblings, and although he never looks for trouble, it often finds him.

"Dominated by bold primary colors, Fotheringham's . . . hyperbolic digital illustrations counterbalance the slyly understated narrative, portraying Tony's (and Dandelion's) antics with humor." Publ Wkly

Tony Baloney; buddy trouble. by Pam Muñoz Ryan; illustrated by Edwin Fotheringham. Scholastic Press 2014 40 p. color illustrations (alk. paper) $6.99

Grades: K 1 2 3   E
1. Penguins -- Fiction 2. Brothers and sisters -- Fiction 3. Behavior -- Fiction 4. Helpfulness -- Fiction
ISBN 0545481694; 9780545481694
LC 2012026700

This book, written by Pam Munoz Ryan and illustrated by Edwin Fotheringham, is the author's second early reader featuring the penguin Tony. "Tony Baloney and his best friend, Bob, can't wait for tonight. It's Books and Buddies, the best school event ever! But will a fight with Big Sister ruin everything?" (Publisher's note)

"Fotheringham's macaroni penguins are as delightful as ever, their every facial expression and gesture broadcasting their feelings and personalities." Kirkus

Ryder, Joanne

Dance by the light of the moon; written by Joanne Ryder; illustrated by Guy Francis. Hyperion Books for Children 2007 un il $15.99

Grades: PreK K 1 2   **E**
1. Dance -- Fiction 2. Animals -- Fiction
ISBN 0-7868-1820-4

"Buffalo Flo gets an invitation to 'come out tonight and dance by the light of the moon' and proceeds to collect her friends Goose, Cat, and Pig for the occasion. . . . The rhymes dance, and so do Francis's paintings. Detailed moonlit landscapes are filled with animal characters that seem to leap from the pages." SLJ

Each living thing; illustrations by Ashley Wolff. Harcourt 2000 un il $16
Grades: K 1 2 3   **E**
1. Stories in rhyme 2. Animals -- Fiction
ISBN 0-15-201898-0

LC 98-51832

Celebrates the creatures of the earth, from spiders dangling in their webs to owls hooting and hunting out of sight, and asks that we respect and care for them

"Wolff's intense gouache paintings, outlined in black, are as lyrical as the text, with just the right balance of simplicity and subtle detail." Booklist

My father's hands; illustrated by Mark Graham. Morrow Junior Bks. 1994 un il $16.99
Grades: PreK K 1 2   **E**
1. Gardening -- Fiction 2. Father-daughter relationship -- Fiction
ISBN 0-688-09189-X

LC 93-27116

"A little girl and her father share the wonders of nature as they examine several small creatures in the garden—a pink worm, a golden beetle, a sliding snail, and a praying mantis. Graham's lovely double-page, impressionistic oil paintings clearly focus on the man and his daughter, with closeups of faces and hands in nearly every illustration. The garden in the background, lush with flowers and vegetable plants, provides a picturesque setting for this simple, straightforward description of a special parent/child outing." SLJ

Rylant, Cynthia
★ **All** in a day; illustrated by Nikki McClure. Abrams Books for Young Readers 2009 un il $17.95
Grades: PreK K 1 2   **E**
1. Stories in rhyme 2. Day -- Fiction
ISBN 978-0-8109-8321-2; 0-8109-8321-4

LC 2008030527

Illustrations and rhyming text pay homage to a new day, with promises for the future in its "perfect piece of time."

"Alternating backdrops of color, finch-yellow and a soft, muted blue, allow for a whole new outlook with every page turn. This uplifting picture book succeeds in introducing children to the perennial promise of tomorrow through lithe language and honed imagery." Kirkus

Alligator boy; [by] Cynthia Rylant & [illustrated by] Diane Goode. Harcourt 2007 un il $16
Grades: PreK K   **E**
1. Stories in rhyme 2. Alligators -- Fiction
ISBN 978-0-15-206092-3

LC 2006006049

A boy puts on an alligator head and tail and is transformed into an alligator boy.

"Goode's watercolor and gouache cartoon vignettes on white ground are reminiscent of the artist's other work in which she evokes a former time. . . . . [A] charming story." SLJ

★ **Annie** and Snowball and the dress-up birthday; the first book of their adventures. illustrated by Suçie Stevenson. Simon & Schuster Books for Young Readers 2007 40p il (Ready-to-read) $15.95; pa $3.99
Grades: K 1 2   **E**
1. Parties -- Fiction 2. Rabbits -- Fiction 3. Birthdays -- Fiction
ISBN 978-1-4169-0938-5; 1-4169-0938-9; 978-1-4169-1459-4 pa; 1-4169-1459-5 pa

LC 2006-02516

Annie and her pet bunny, Snowball, love living next door to Annie's favorite cousin, Henry and his dog, Mudge. Whether it's playing Frisbee or watching old movies, there's no shortage of fun to be had when these four are together.

"Stevenson's lively pen-and-ink and watercolor illustrations depict lots of action in the story's four short chapters, and amplify the characters' warmth, affection, and laughter." SLJ

Other titles about Annie and Snowball are:
Annie and Snowball and the prettiest house (2007)
Annie and Snowball and the pink surprise (2008)
Annie and Snowball and the teacup club (2008)
Annie and Snowball and the cozy nest (2009)
Annie and Snowball and the shining star (2009)
Annie and Snowball and the magical house (2010)
Annie and Snowball and the wintry freeze (2010)
Annie and Snowball and the Book Bugs Club (2011)

Brownie & Pearl go for a spin; by Cynthia Rylant; pictures by Brian Biggs. Beach Lane Books 2012 24 p.
Grades: PreK K   **E**
1. Cats -- Fiction 2. Automobiles -- Fiction 3. Picture books for children 4. Automobile travel -- Fiction
ISBN 1416986332; 9781416986331

LC 2010018320

This children's book is part of Cynthia Rylant's "Brownie and Pearl" series in which, "Brownie and her cat are taking a spin in the girl's pink convertible. Pearl loves riding in the car and retrieving and delivering mail so much that she doesn't want to get out when they return home. Brownie finds a solution through a delicious "takeout" meal that they can enjoy together on the grass. With its simple story line, ample white space, and vivid digitally rendered illustrations, this is a welcome addition to a popular series." (School Libr J)

Brownie and Pearl go for a spin

Brownie & Pearl step out; pictures by Brian Biggs. Beach Lane Books 2010 un il $12.99
Grades: PreK K   **E**
1. Cats -- Fiction 2. Parties -- Fiction 3. Birthdays -- Fiction
ISBN 978-1-4169-8632-4; 1-4169-8632-4

LC 2008032804

A little girl named Brownie arrives at a birthday party feeling shy while her cat Pearl confidently enters through the "kitty door."

"Rylant addresses the challenges and rewards of facing new social situations in short, conversational text perfectly suited to its young audience. Biggs' digitally rendered, cartoonlike illustrations . . . make this first title in the Brownie and Pearl series as delicious and appealing as a triple-layered birthday cake." Booklist

Other titles about Brownie & Pearl are:
Brownie & Pearl get dolled up (2010)
Brownie & Pearl see the sights (2010)
Brownie & Pearl take a dip (2011)
Brownie & Pearl grab a bite (2011)
Brownie & Pearl hit the hay (2011)

★ The **case** of the missing monkey; story by Cynthia Rylant; pictures by G. Brian Karas. Greenwillow Bks. 2000 48p il (High-rise private eyes) pa $3.99
Grades: K 1 2   E
1. Mystery fiction
ISBN 0-06-444306-X
    LC 99-16878
While having breakfast at their favorite diner, two detectives, Bunny and Jack, find a missing glass monkey

"The full-color illustrations, rendered in acrylic gouache, and pencil, capture the cartoonlike animals' animated expressions and poses. . . . Children will enjoy searching the pages for the reported clues." SLJ

Other titles in the High-rise private eyes series are:
The case of the baffled bear (2004)
The case of the climbing cate (2000)
The case of the desperate duck (2005)
The case of the fidgety fox (2003)
The case of the puzzling possum (2001)
The case of the sleepy sloth (2002)
The case of the troublesome turtle (2001)

Cat Heaven; written and illustrated by Cynthia Rylant. Blue Sky Press (NY) 1997 40 p. col il $17.99
Grades: PreK K 1 2   E
1. Cats -- Fiction 2. Heaven -- Fiction 3. Stories in rhyme
ISBN 0590100548; 9780590100540
    LC 96049501
In this book, "Writing in rhyme, [author and illustrator Cynthia] Rylant assures readers that all cats already know the way to heaven's yellow door, and once past it will never want for laps, toys, or full kitty dishes. Rylant paints in the same extremely naive style of the first book, with large brushes and bright, opaque colors; heaven is a place with trees and clouds to perch on, fields to leap through--and a garden full of tall flowers, where God walks." (Kirkus)

★ **Dog** Heaven; written and illustrated by Cynthia Rylant. Blue Sky Press (NY) 1995 40 p. col il $17.99
Grades: PreK K 1 2   E
1. Heaven -- Fiction 2. Dogs -- Fiction
ISBN 0590417010; 9780590417013
    LC 94040950
This picture book by Cynthia Rylant tells of a place called "Dog Heaven, where there are endless fields for running; clear lakes filled with teasing, honking geese; and loving angel children playing everywhere. There are tasty biscuits shaped like cats and fluffy cloud beds for sleeping, memory trips back to favorite spots and people, and cozy

homes with petting hands. . . . Preschool to grade two." (SLJ)

★ **Henry** and Mudge; the first book of their adventures. story by Cynthia Rylant; pictures by Suçie Stevenson. Simon & Schuster Books for Young Readers 1996 39p il (Ready-to-read) $15.99; pa $3.99
Grades: K 1 2   E
1. Dogs -- Fiction
ISBN 0-689-81004-0; 0-689-81005-9 pa
First published 1987 by Bradbury Press
Henry, feeling lonely on a street without any other children, finds companionship and love in a big dog named Mudge.

"The stories are lighthearted and affectionate. Backed by line-and-wash cartoon drawings, they celebrate the familiar in a down-to-earth way that will please young readers." Booklist

Other titles about Henry and Mudge are:
Henry and Mudge and a very Merry Christmas (2004)
Henry and Mudge and Annie's good move (1998)
Henry and Mudge and Annie's perfect pet (2000)
Henry and Mudge and Mrs. Hopper's house (2003)
Henry and Mudge and the bedtime thumps (1991)
Henry and Mudge and the best day of all (1995)
Henry and Mudge and the big sleepover (2006)
Henry and Mudge and the careful cousin (1994)
Henry and Mudge and the forever sea (1989)
Henry and Mudge and the funny lunch (2004)
Henry and Mudge and the great grandpas (2005)
Henry and Mudge and the happy cat (1990)
Henry and Mudge and the long weekend (1992)
Henry and Mudge and the sneaky crackers (1998)
Henry and Mudge and the Snowman plan (1999)
Henry and Mudge and the starry night (1998)
Henry and Mudge and the tall tree house (1999)
Henry and Mudge and the tumbling trip (2005)
Henry and Mudge and the wild goose chase (2003)
Henry and Mudge and the wild wind (1993)
Henry and Mudge get the cold shivers (1989)
Henry and Mudge in puddle trouble (1987)
Henry and Mudge in the family trees (1997)
Henry and Mudge in the green time (1987)
Henry and Mudge in the sparkle days (1988)
Henry and Mudge take the big test (1991)
Henry and Mudge under the yellow moon (1987)

Moonlight: the Halloween cat; illustrated by Melissa Sweet. HarperCollins Pubs. 2003 un il $14.99; lib bdg $15.89; pa $6.99
Grades: PreK K 1 2   E
1. Cats -- Fiction 2. Halloween -- Fiction
ISBN 0-06-029711-5; 0-06-029712-3 lib bdg; 0-06-443814-7 pa
    LC 2001-39511
Moonlight the cat loves everything about Halloween, from pumpkins to children to candy

"In simple, poetic prose, Rylant tracks the meandering cat's night journey. . . . Sweet's endearingly childlike, color-rich paintings convey an appreciation for the ever-deepening night. . . . A soothing, ghoul-free, utterly noncreepy Halloween picture book for the preschool set." Booklist

★ **Mr.** Putter & Tabby pour the tea; illustrated by Arthur Howard. Harcourt Brace & Co. 1994 un il $14; pa $5.95

Grades: K 1 2   E

1. Cats -- Fiction 2. Old age -- Fiction
ISBN 0-15-256255-9; 0-15-200901-9 pa

LC 93-21470

"Rylant's charming story of two elderly characters is complemented and enhanced by Howard's delightful illustrations, done in pencil, watercolor, and gouache." SLJ

Other titles about Mr. Putter and Tabby are:

Mr. Putter & Tabby bake the cake (1994)
Mr. Putter & Tabby walk the dog (1994)
Mr. Putter & Tabby pick the pears (1995)
Mr. Putter & Tabby row the boat (1997)
Mr. Putter & Tabby fly the plane (1997)
Mr. Putter & Tabby take the train (1998)
Mr. Putter & Tabby toot the horn (1998)
Mr. Putter & Tabby paint the porch (2000)
Mr. Putter & Tabby feed the fish (2001)
Mr. Putter & Tabby catch the cold (2002)
Mr. Putter & Tabby stir the soup (2003)
Mr. Putter & Tabby write the book (2004)
Mr. Putter & Tabby make a wish (2005)
Mr. Putter & Tabby spin the yarn (2006)
Mr. Putter & Tabby see the stars (2007)
Mr. Putter & Tabby run the race (2008)
Mr. Putter & Tabby spill the beans (2009)
Mr. Putter & Tabby clear the decks (2010)
Mr. Putter & Tabby ring the bell (2011)

★ **Poppleton**; book one. illustrated by Mark Teague. Blue Sky Press (NY) 1997 48p il hardcover o.p. pa $3.99

Grades: K 1 2   E

1. Pigs -- Fiction 2. Friendship -- Fiction
ISBN 0-590-84783-X; 0-590-84782-1 pa

LC 96-3365

"City pig Poppleton adjusts to small-town life in this . . . chapter book. In 'Neighbors,' the polite Poppleton tries to think up a polite way to say 'no thanks' to Cherry Sue, a friendly llama who invites him to breakfast, lunch and dinner every single day. . . . The second vignette, 'The Library,' details Poppleton's reading ritual, which demands solitude. Finally, 'The Pill' introduces Fillmore, a sick goat who refuses to take his pill unless Poppleton hides it in a cake. . . . [Rylant's] concise sentences mimic the characters' good manners and wryly point up the failures of etiquette. Teague contributes fetching watercolor-and-pencil images of the pudgy pig, slender llama and dignified goat." Publ Wkly

Other titles about Poppleton are:

Poppleton and friends (1997)
Poppleton everyday (1998)
Poppleton forever (1998)
Poppleton has fun (2000)
Poppleton in Fall (1999)
Poppleton in Spring (1999)
Poppleton in Winter (2001)
Poppleton through and through (2000)

Puppies and piggies; illustrated by Ivan Bates. Harcourt 2008 32p il $16

Grades: PreK   E

1. Stories in rhyme 2. Animals -- Fiction
ISBN 978-0-15-202321-8; 0-15-202321-6

LC 2004-3136

Rhyming text describes what various animals do and what they love, as well as a baby who loves his bed and his mother.

"Told in reassuring rhyme, the simple upbeat text showcases happy animals doing what comes naturally while Bates's idyllic watercolor and crayon illustrations present a bucolic barnyard teeming with contented critters. . . . Comforting and carefree fare for tiny tots." Kirkus

★ The **relatives** came; story by Cynthia Rylant; illustrated by Stephen Gammell. rev format ed.; Atheneum Books for Young Readers 2001 un il $16.95; pa $6.99

Grades: PreK K 1 2   E

1. Family life -- Fiction
ISBN 0-689-84508-1; 0-689-71738-5 pa

A reformatted edition of the title first published 1985 by Bradbury Press

A Caldecott Medal honor book, 1986

"If there's anything more charming than the tone of voice in this story, it's the drawings that go with it. Stephen Gammell . . . fills the pages with bright, crayony pictures teeming with details that children should enjoy poring over for hours." NY Times Book Rev

★ **Snow**; illustrated by Lauren Stringer. Harcourt 2008 un il $17

Grades: PreK K 1 2   E

1. Snow -- Fiction
ISBN 978-0-15-205303-1; 0-15-205303-4

LC 2006-06171

Celebrates the beauty of a snowfall and its happy effects on children.

"Snow is not an uncommon subject in picture books, but few have both the grace and exuberance of this lovely collaboration featuring Rylant's evocative words and Stringer's entrancing paintings." Booklist

When I was young in the mountains; illustrated by Diane Goode. Dutton 1982 un il $15.99; pa $6.99

Grades: K 1 2 3   E

1. Appalachian region -- Fiction
ISBN 0-525-42525-X; 0-525-44198-0 pa

LC 81-5359

A Caldecott Medal honor book, 1983

"The people in the story are poor in material things, but rich in family pleasures. The title becomes a pleasing refrain. . . . Illustrations and text are placed on a bed of white space, without borders, which makes them look uncrowded and imparts a great feeling of freedom." SLJ

Saab, Julie

Little Lola; by Julie Saab; pictures by David Gothard. Greenwillow Books, an imprint of HarperCollinsPublishers 2014 32 p. (trade ed.) $16.99

Grades: PreK K 1 2   E

1. School stories 2. Cats -- Fiction 3. Schools -- Fiction
ISBN 0062274570; 9780062274571

LC 2013030016

In this children's book, by Julie Saab, "Lola is curious about everything . . . especially school. What is school like?

Find out when Lola the cat heads to school herself and gets a paw (or two) into just about everything." (Publisher's note)

"Little Lola, a cat, "has big plans." She dresses herself as a kid, hops on the bus, and goes to school. Lola manages to fit right in...until her show-and-tell mouse gives her away and disrupts everything. Gothard's watercolor art combines a retro look with comic action and brings Lola vividly to life, though her human counterparts appear stiff in comparison." Horn Book

Sabuda, Robert

Alice's adventures in Wonderland; a pop-up adaptation of Lewis Carroll's original tale. illustrated by Robert Sabuda. Little Simon 2003 un il $25.95

Grades: 1 2 3 4   E
   1. Fantasy fiction 2. Pop-up books
   ISBN 0-689-84743-2

A pop-up version of Lewis Carroll's classic tale of Alice who falls down the rabbit hole to find a new world.

"Sabuda brings Alice's world to life with breathtaking, three-dimensional images that are incredibly imaginative, intricately detailed, and perfectly executed. Carroll's text has been significantly abridged, and . . . the quickly paced narrative retains the flavor of the original." SLJ

The **Christmas** alphabet; deluxe anniversary edition; Orchard Books 2004 un il $22.95

Grades: K 1 2 3 4   E
   1. Alphabet 2. Christmas 3. Pop-up books
   ISBN 0-439-67256-2
   First published 1994

"Four large flaps per spread—each representing a letter of the alphabet—open to reveal sophisticated 3D images, some with parts that move in uncommonly inventive ways. Many of the pop-ups are obvious Christmas symbols. . . . Others have ambiguous—but resourceful—ties to the holiday. . . . A yuletide gem." Publ Wkly

The **Little** Mermaid; a pop-up adaptation of the classic fairytale. by Robert Sabuda. 1st ed. Simon & Schuster 2013 12 p. $29.99

Grades: 2 3 4 5   E
   1. Toy and movable books 2. Fairy tales 3. Princes -- Fiction 4. Mermaids -- Fiction
   ISBN 1416960805; 144245086X; 9781416960805; 9781442450868

This pop-up book, by Robert Sabuda, is an "adaptation of the beloved fairy tale 'The Little Mermaid.' . . . Amazing three-dimensional paper structures pop off each page, bringing this classic underwater adventure to life. This [is a] visually stunning tale of adventure, true love, and sacrifice." (Publisher's note)

"Sabuda graces Andersen's dark tale with enormous, elaborate pop-up illustrations. Each of five double-page spreads contains one large construction; sidebars open to additional pop-ups. The paper engineering is more remarkable for its intricacy and atmosphere-building than its role in the storytelling. Children familiar with Disney's version may be surprised at the tragedy in this adaptation, which stays close to Andersen's original." (Horn Books)

★ **Peter** Pan: a classic collectible pop-up. Simon & Schuster Children's Pub. 2008 un il $29.99

Grades: 2 3 4 5 6   E
   1. Fairy tales 2. Pop-up books
   ISBN 978-0-689-85364-7; 0-689-85364-5

"Sabuda enhances the already powerful enchantments of J. M. Barrie's classic 1902 tale with astonishing paper engineering. Illustrations suggest a hybrid of period styles, somewhere between arts and crafts, with their rich patterning, and art nouveau, with their Tiffany glass-like outlines and colorations. . . . Not to be missed." Publ Wkly

Sacre, Antonio

La Noche Buena; a Christmas story. illustrated by Angela Dominguez. Abrams Books for Young Readers 2010 un il $16.95

Grades: K 1 2 3   E
   1. Florida -- Fiction 2. Christmas -- Fiction 3. Family life -- Fiction 4. Grandmothers -- Fiction 5. Cuban Americans -- Fiction
   ISBN 978-0-8109-8967-2; 0-8109-8967-0
                      LC 2009052204

While spending Christmas with her Cuban American grandmother in Miami, Florida, young Nina misses her usual New England holiday but enjoys learning about the foods and other traditions her father knew as a child.

"Attractive paintings with simple lines and bright, solid colors help tell this warm, loving story in an understated way." Kirkus

A **mango** in the hand; a story told through proverbs. illustrated by Sebastia Serra. Abrams Books for Young Readers 2011 un il $16.95

Grades: K 1 2 3   E
   1. Cuba -- Fiction 2. Mangoes -- Fiction 3. Proverbs -- Fiction 4. Family life -- Fiction 5. Spanish language -- Vocabulary
   ISBN 978-0-8109-9734-9; 0-8109-9734-7
                      LC 2010024423

Guided by proverbs from his father and other relatives, Francisco makes several attempts to bring ripe mangoes home for dessert on his saint day, and in the process learns lessons in love and generosity. Includes glossary of Spanish terms.

"Sacre's snappy storytelling avoids being overly moralistic, and Serra's digitally colored pencil-and-ink artwork creates a friendly, close-knit neighborhood for Francisco, the kind in which food, conversation—and proverbs—can be found in abundance." Publ Wkly

Saint-Lot, Katia Novet

Amadi's snowman; illustrated by Dimitrea Tokunbo. Tilbury House 2008 un il $16.95

Grades: PreK K 1 2   E
   1. Nigeria -- Fiction 2. Books and reading -- Fiction 3. Igbo (African people) -- Fiction
   ISBN 978-0-88448-298-7; 0-88448-298-7
                      LC 2007043343

As a young Igbo man, Amadi does not understand why his mother insists he learn to read, since he already knows his numbers and will be a businessman one day, but an older boy teaches him the value of learning about the world through books

"Children will enjoy reading about Amadi's life in the village, depicted in the earth-toned, intimate scenes." Booklist

Sakai, Komako

Emily's balloon. Chronicle Books 2006 un il $14.95
Grades: PreK K 1   E
  1. Balloons -- Fiction
ISBN 0-8118-5219-9
                                          LC 2005-11283
A little girl's new friend is round, lighter than air, and
looks like the moon at night.

"The yellow balloon and its blue string stand out in a
simple color palette of white, gray, and tan with a few accents of red. The illustrations, rendered in watercolor and
charcoal, are placed on tan pages and surrounded by unadorned thin, round-edged black frames. A tale of a common
childhood experience, tenderly and sweetly told." SLJ

★ **Mad** at Mommy. Arthur A. Levine Books 2010
un il $16.99
Grades: PreK K 1   E
  1. Anger -- Fiction 2. Rabbits -- Fiction 3. Mother-
child relationship -- Fiction
ISBN 978-0-545-21209-0; 0-545-21209-X
Original Japanese edition, 2000
A little rabbit is very angry at his mother, and he tells her
the reasons why.

"Sakai's paintings are simply composed and staged, allowing rabbit's expressive poses to shine. . . . A playful story
that offers young readers—and their big feelings—a serious
voice. Charming, classy and current." Kirkus

★ The **snow** day. Arthur A. Levine Books 2009 un
il $16.99
Grades: PreK K   E
  1. Snow -- Fiction 2. Rabbits -- Fiction
ISBN 978-0-545-01321-5; 0-545-01321-6
                                          LC 2007-49949
Original Japanese edition 2005
A little rabbit enjoys having a day off from kindergarten and spending time with his mother during a snowstorm,
but his father's flight home is cancelled until the snow
stops falling.

Sakai's "subdued palette and minimalist text suggest the
blanketed sound produced by a heavy snowfall. . . . The layers of paint are applied to a black ground with a combination
of wet and dry brushes, producing a convincing depth and
texture. . . . The sentences are appropriately concise, yet with
lovely rhythms and interesting details." SLJ

Salas, Laura Purdie

A **leaf** can be; by Laura Purdie Salas; illustrations by
Violeta Dabija. Millbrook Press 2012 32 p. (lib. bdg.: alk.
paper) $17.95
Grades: K 1 2 3   E
  1. Stories in rhyme 2. Leaves -- Fiction
ISBN 0761362037; 9780761362036
                                          LC 2011022227
In this book of poetry, by Laura Purdie Salas, rhyming
text explores the many roles a leaf can play, from providing
shelter for animals in the rain . . . to housing cocoons, . . . to
purifying the air, . . . to providing autumnal entertainment
for children. . . . [The] book offers abundant opportunity
for discussion of scientific concepts from photosynthesis
("Sun taker/ Food maker") to camouflage ("Moth matcher"
and "Snake concealer"). (Bulletin of the Center for Children's Books)

"In a simple rhyming text, Salas examines the ways that
leaves play a part in our world's ecosystem... A lovely observation about nature, suitable for a variety of science units or
individual sharing." SLJ
  Includes bibliographical references [p. 31]

★ **Water** can be; by Laura Purdie Salas; illustrations
by Violeta Dabija. Millbrook Press 2014 32 p. (lib. bdg.:
alk. paper) $17.95
Grades: PreK K 1 2 3 4   E
  1. Water
ISBN 1467705918; 9781467705912
                                          LC 2013017772
"Water can be a thirst quencher, kid drencher, cloud fluffer, fire snuffer. Find out about the many roles water plays in
this poetic exploration of water throughout the year," written by Laura Purdie Salas and illustrated by Violeta Dabija.
(Publisher's note)

"Calling attention to water helps children appreciate
this necessary and ubiquitous resource. In lilting rhymed
text, Salas shows readers that water can be "many things":
a "thirst quencher" and "kid drencher"; a "cloud fluffer"
and "fire snuffer." Each couplet is attractively illustrated,
predominantly in various shades of blues and greens. Appended "More About Water" explanations help extend the
text." Honor Book

Salerno, Steven

Harry hungry! written and illustrated by Steven Salerno. Harcourt 2009 un il $16
Grades: PreK K   E
  1. Hunger -- Fiction 2. Infants -- Fiction
ISBN 978-0-15-206257-6; 0-15-206257-2
                                          LC 2007-04375
Harry is a baby so hungry that he eats all the food in his
house, then goes outside to find more.

"Done in his trademark retro style, Salerno's bright,
sweeping illustrations and offbeat perspectives instantly
capture this tiny tot's insatiable energy. . . . Children will delight in growling loudly along with Harry's tummy." Kirkus

Salley, Coleen

Epossumondas plays possum; written by Coleen Salley; illustrated by Janet Stevens. Harcourt Children's Books
2009 un il $16
Grades: K 1 2 3   E
  1. Fear -- Fiction 2. Marshes -- Fiction 3. Opossums
-- Fiction 4. Louisiana -- Fiction
ISBN 978-0-15-206420-4; 0-15-206420-6
                                          LC 2009-7976
Forgetting his mother's warnings, Epossumondas goes
into the swamp alone then must pretend to be dead time and
again as he hears frightening sounds and fears they are being
made by the dreaded loup garou.

"Rich with Southern flavor . . . it's an immersive piece of
storytelling." Pub Wkly

Epossumondas saves the day; written by Coleen Sal-
ley; illustrated by Janet Stevens. Harcourt 2006 un il $16
Grades: K 1 2 3   E
  1. Turtles -- Fiction 2. Opossums -- Fiction 3.
Birthdays -- Fiction
ISBN 0-15-205701-3
                                          LC 2005-27538

In this variation on the folktale, Sody Salyraytus, each of Epossumondas's birthday guests disappears until it is finally up to him to rescue them all and bring home the "sody" for his birthday biscuits.

"Salley's text is alive with the colorful expressions of the South . . . which make the story a delight to read aloud. Stevens's hilarious mixed-media illustrations are a perfect match for the narrative." SLJ

Saltzberg, Barney

Beautiful oops! Workman 2010 un il $11.95
Grades: PreK K 1 2   E
 1. Errors -- Fiction 2. Creative ability -- Fiction
 ISBN 978-0-7611-5728-1; 0-7611-5728-X

"A celebration of creative thinking, Saltzberg's small-format book encourages readers to view mistakes not as failures but opportunities. . . . Various spills and blobs are transformed into animals, a crumpled piece of paper becomes wool for a sheep, and . . . a panel with a hole in the center telescopes outward, accordian-style, to reveal a tiny creature way at the bottom. Inspirational without being saccharine." Publ Wkly

Chengdu could not, would not, fall asleep; written and illustrated by Barney Saltzberg. Disney-Hyperion Books 2014 48 p. (hardback) $16.99
Grades: PreK K   E
 1. Sleep -- Fiction 2. Bedtime -- Fiction 3. Pandas -- Fiction
 ISBN 142316721X; 9781423167211
                                            LC 2013029121

In this children's book, written and illustrated by Barney Saltzberg, "a young panda named Chengdu lies awake, even though everyone around him is quietly sleeping. He tosses and he turns. He scrunches and he squirms, until he finally finds the perfect spot." (Publisher's note)

"All the pandas are sleeping peacefully except for little Chengdu. Saltzberg gives the book an old-fashioned look by limiting the colors to black, white, gray, and the green of the bamboo trees, catching the soft textures of a dark forest at night. Gentle sight gags add humor without breaking the calming mood, making this an ideal nighttime book for the very young." Horn Book

I want a dog! Random House Children's Books 2009 un il $11.99
Grades: PreK K   E
 1. Pop-up books 2. Dogs -- Fiction
 ISBN 978-0-375-85783-6; 0-375-85783-4

"The earnest speaker in this fun story, based on the author's song of the same title, pleads for a dog, promising that it 'will never, ever make a mess' (via a pull tab, she sweeps his 'mess' into a dustpan as she holds her nose). Other animals—a hippo, a pig—won't do (turning a wheel helps the girl feed an endless bucket of slop to a tubby swine). On a final pop-up spread, she embraces a dog, surrounded by blooming, red hearts. Effective interactive elements and simple humor will charm." Publ Wkly

Stanley and the class pet; [by] Barney Saltzberg. Candlewick Press 2008 un il $16.99
Grades: PreK K 1 2   E
 1. School stories 2. Birds -- Fiction 3. Hamsters --

Fiction
 ISBN 978-0-7636-3595-4; 0-7636-3595-2
                                            LC 2007-40541

Stanley is excited about bringing the class pet, a bird, home for the weekend, but when his friend Larry urges him to open the cage and let Figgy out to fly, it is hard to know who is to blame for the ensuing disaster.

"With clearly lined acrylic paintings and a smoothly paced text that avoids a too-heavy message, Saltzberg deftly turns a common classroom scenario into a gentle story about peer pressure and responsibility." Booklist

Other titles about Stanley are:
 Crazy hair day (2003)
 Star of the week (2006)

Salzano, Tammi

One rainy day; illustrated by Hannah Wood. Tiger Tales 2011 un bd bk $8.95
Grades: PreK   E
 1. Board books for children 2. Rain -- Fiction 3. Color -- Fiction 4. Ducks -- Fiction
 ISBN 978-1-58925-860-0; 1-58925-860-6

"Beneath light showers of foil raindrops, a duckling sporting red boots and an orange umbrella happily encounters a green frog, pink worms, yellow flowers, and other color-linked items. The text in this padded-cover board book runs to just a short phrase per spread, and the fuzzy yellow duck's joie de vivre glows in each simply composed scene." Booklist

Samuels, Barbara

 ★ The **trucker**. Farrar, Straus and Giroux 2010 un il $16.99
Grades: PreK K 1   E
 1. Cats -- Fiction 2. Toys -- Fiction 3. Trucks -- Fiction
 ISBN 978-0-374-37804-2; 0-374-37804-5
                                            LC 2007029266

A boy who loves trucks is disappointed when he receives a cat named Lola instead of a toy fire truck, but Lola proves to be a "trucker" after all.

"A winner for young children, this offers a real story along with all of the vehicle action. Kids will enjoy the combination of active play and cozy snuggling." Booklist

Sandall, Ellie

Birdsong. Egmont USA 2011 un il $16.99
Grades: PreK   E
 1. Birds -- Fiction 2. Birdsongs -- Fiction
 ISBN 978-1-60684-193-8; 1-60684-193-9
                                            LC 2010017006

A crowd of birds lands in a tree, sharing their different songs, until one last winged creature proves to be too much.

"The book has rhythm, bird sounds that are great fun to hear and say, and illustrations that depict each cast member as a winged creature of distinction." Horn Book Guide

Sandemose, Iben

Gracie & Grandma & the itsy, bitsy seed; translated from Norwegian by Tonje Vetleseter. MacKenzie Smiles 2009 un il $14.95
Grades: PreK K 1 2   E
 1. Growth -- Fiction 2. Plants -- Fiction 3. Grandmothers -- Fiction
 ISBN 978-0-9790347-5-6; 0-9790347-5-2

"Spunky and imaginative Gracie presents her equally exuberant grandmother with a surprise–an itsy, bitsy seed. But what will it grow into? As the plant gets larger and larger, Grandma incorrectly guesses that it is a banana, lemon, fried mackerel, balloon, jungle, cow, or ghost tree until she spots a large red dot growing at the top and shouts: 'A big tomato!' . . . The simple yet expressive text, in a large, bold typeface, perfectly complements the wacky, exaggerated, dazzlingly bright colored ink and marker cartoon illustrations." SLJ

Other titles in this series are:
Gracie & Grandma (2008)
Gracie & Grandma under water (2008)

Sanders-Wells, Linda

Maggie's monkeys; illustrated by Abby Carter. Candlewick Press 2009 un il $16.99
Grades: K 1 2   E
1. Siblings -- Fiction 2. Family life -- Fiction 3. Imagination -- Fiction
ISBN 978-0-7636-3326-4; 0-7636-3326-7
LC 2008-28711

When Maggie reports that pink monkeys have moved into the refrigerator, her mother and father play along and accomodate the invisible visitors, much to the frustration of Maggie's older, reality-obsessed brother.

"Sanders-Wells wonderfully encapsulates the difficulties of being a middle child—simultaneously too old and too young. Carter's masterful facial expressions reflects this inner battle. Her gouache artwork is done in a bright, tropical palette that emphasizes the imaginative theme. . . . A humorous tale sure to make siblings smile, even as they inwardly groan." Kirkus

Santat, Dan

★ The **adventures** of Beekle; the unimaginary friend. Dan Santat. First edition Little, Brown and Co. 2014 40 p. $17
Grades: PreK K 1 2   E
1. Friendship -- Fiction 2. Imaginary playmates -- Fiction
ISBN 0316199982; 9780316199988
LC 2013017700
Caldecott Medal (2015)

In this book by Dan Santat, "an imaginary friend . . . longs for the day when a child will 'imagine' him, and thus choose and name him. As the days pass and he remains unchosen, the intrepid fellow goes in search of his intended child, leaving his imaginary home for the real world. . . . Finally a girl named Alice chooses him; once she dubs him 'Beekle' a bond is formed, and the two go on to have adventures, both real and imaginary, together." (Bulletin of the Center for Children's Books)

"Imaginary friend Beekle waits and waits for a child to think him into existence. When it doesn't happen, Beekle sails off to the real world--a city full of boring adults--to find her. Santat's bright digital illustrations capture the vivid land of imagination, the drab adult world, and the giggle-inducing expressions on marshmallow-like Beekle's pudgy white face." Horn Book

Sarcone-Roach, Julia

The **bear** ate your sandwich; by Julia Sarcone-Roach. Alfred A. Knopf 2015 40 p. color illustrations (lib. bdg.) $19.99
Grades: PreK K 1 2   E
1. Bears -- Fiction 2. City and town life 3. Dogs -- Fiction 4. Humorous stories 5. Sandwiches -- Fiction 6. City and town life -- Fiction
ISBN 0375958606; 9780375858604; 9780375958601
LC 2014013199

Written by Julia Sarcone-Roach, this children's book tells the "tale of a bear, lost in the city, who happens upon an unattended sandwich in the park. The bear's journey from forest to city and back home again is full of happy accidents, funny encounters, and sensory delights. The story is so engrossing, it's not until the very end that we begin to suspect this is a TALL tale." (Publisher's note)

"By now I think you know what happened to your sandwich," begins the very unreliable narrator in this amusing picture book. His story? A woodland bear fell asleep in the back of a truck and awoke to find himself in the city... The city scenes reward attention with intriguing, sometimes comical details. This is a picture book that kids will want to hear again immediately, once they know who is telling the story." Booklist

The **secret** plan. Alfred A. Knopf 2009 un il $16.99; lib bdg $19.99
Grades: PreK K 1 2   E
1. Cats -- Fiction 2. Play -- Fiction 3. Bedtime -- Fiction 4. Elephants -- Fiction
ISBN 978-0-375-85858-1; 0-375-85858-X; 978-0-375-95858-8 lib bdg; 0-375-95858-4 lib bdg
LC 2008-39291

Continually thwarted in their efforts to escape bedtime and continue playing, Milo the elephant and three kittens named Henry, Hildy, and Harriet finally find a "perfect late night bedtime-free hideout."

"The age-old dilemma of wanting to stay up and play just a bit longer finds a gently humorous treatment in this tale, accompanied by swirly acrylic paintings that evoke dreamy nighttime fantasy." SLJ

Subway story. Alfred A. Knopf 2011 un il $16.99; lib bdg $19.99
Grades: PreK K   E
1. Subways -- Fiction 2. New York (N.Y.) -- Fiction
ISBN 978-0-375-85859-8; 0-375-85859-8; 978-0-375-95859-5 lib bdg; 0-375-95859-2 lib bdg
LC 2010045487

Jessie, a subway car 'born' in St. Louis, Missouri, enjoys many years as an important part of the New York City subway system, and after she is replaced by more modern cars she begins another important job.

"The author's acrylics gently anthropomorphize Jessie, giving her headlight-eyes and a winsome smile. Immensely readable and surprisingly touching, this large heft of metal totes a lot of charm." Kirkus

Includes bibliographical references

Sartell, Debra

Time for bed, baby Ted; illustrations by Kay Chorao. Holiday House 2010 un il $16.95

Grades: PreK   E
1. Stories in rhyme 2. Bedtime -- Fiction
ISBN 978-0-8234-1968-5; 0-8234-1968-1
LC 2008-48652

At bedtime, Baby Ted finds many ways to avoid going to bed.

"The various animal sounds and action words in the short text, coupled with Chorao's pleasing illustrations, featuring a mop-topped Ted and his pretend menagerie, make this a fun read-aloud for parent and child and a natural for sharing with a young group of children." Booklist

Sasso, Sandy Eisenberg

The **Shema** in the mezuzah; listening to each other. Sandy Eisenberg Sasso; Illustrations by Joani Keller Rothenberg. Jewish Lights Pub. 2012 30 p. col. ill. $18.99
Grades: K 1 2 3   E
1. Mezuzah -- Fiction 2. Listening -- Fiction 3. Jews -- Fiction 4. Judaism -- Customs and practices -- Fiction
ISBN 1580235069; 9781580235068
LC 2012007709

National Jewish Book Awards: Illustrated Children's Book (2012)

This Jewish children's story, by Rabbi Sandy Eisenberg Sasso, is about "compromise and listening. The townspeople have mezuzahs but cannot agree on how to put them up on their doorways. . . . To end their arguing, they consult the wise rabbi of the town, who advises them to carefully read the Shema in the mezuzah to find the answer. This . . . tale [is] based on a twelfth-century rabbinic debate." (Publisher's note)

Sattler, Jennifer

★ **Pig** kahuna. Bloomsbury Children's Books 2011 un il $14.99; lib bdg $15.89
Grades: PreK K 1 2   E
1. Pigs -- Fiction 2. Surfing -- Fiction
ISBN 978-1-59990-635-5; 1-59990-635-X; 978-1-59990-636-2 lib bdg; 1-59990-636-8 lib bdg
LC 2010035629

Fergus is afraid to go in the water, but he and his baby brother Dink find a surfboard while collecting treasures along the seashore.

"The briskly paced text . . . offers alliteration and deadpan humor. Together words and pictures create an utterly engaging picture-book experience—eye-catching, thought-provoking and just plain fun." Kirkus

Pig kahuna pirates! Jennifer Sattler. Bloomsbury 2014 32 p. (hardback) $16.99
Grades: PreK K 1 2   E
1. Pigs -- Fiction 2. Play -- Fiction 3. Beaches -- Fiction 4. Brothers -- Fiction
ISBN 1619632004; 9781619632004; 9781619632011; 9781619632035
LC 2013028954

In this children's book, by Jennifer Sattler, "Fergus and Dink love playing at the beach. But when Dink wakes up from his nap in a crabby mood, it's up to big brother Fergus to pull him out of it. Does the little fella want to take a swim? Build a sand castle? Have a juice box? Aaargh! Only one thing will tame the tantrum: When Fergus invites Dink to play with his new pirate ship of sand, and gives him the starring role as pirate captain." (Publisher's note)

"Fergus likes swimming in the ocean, but his young brother, Dink, who wakes up from his nap out of sorts, finds it too cold. He's in a horrible mood, and Fergus can't seem to cheer him up...The detail and line of the pigs make them pop to the forefront of the summery seaside scene. The large font and short sentences make this book easy to share with a group, and the subject matter and the single plotline are a great match for a preschool audience." SLJ

Sylvie. Random House 2009 un il $15.99; lib bdg $18.99
Grades: PreK K 1   E
1. Food -- Fiction 2. Color -- Fiction 3. Flamingos -- Fiction
ISBN 978-0-375-85708-9; 0-375-85708-7; 978-0-375-95708-6 lib bdg; 0-375-95708-1 lib bdg
LC 2008-11259

When Sylvie the pink flamingo learns her color comes from the little pink shrimp she eats, she decides to expand her choices, trying everything under the sun and, unfortunately, overdoing it.

"Sattler's art steals the show; the colors are eye-popping and vibrant, right to the swirling bright endpapers. . . . This title is sure to create storytime magic." SLJ

Uh-oh, dodo! Jennifer Sattler. Boyds Mills Press 2013 32 p. (reinforced) $15.95
Grades: PreK K   E
1. Dodo -- Fiction 2. Picture books for children
ISBN 9781590789292; 1590789296
LC 2012947460

In this children's story, written and illustrated by Jennifer Sattler, Dodo "loves an adventure. He is always willing to try new things. He enjoys making new friends. But not everything turns out the way Dodo expects. Even a walk with his Mama turns into a topsy-turvy day of discoveries, challenges, and surprises. Good thing Dodo has a sense of humor!" (Publisher's note)

Sauer, Tammi

Chicken dance; illustrated by Dan Santat. Sterling 2009 un il $14.95
Grades: PreK K 1   E
1. Chickens -- Fiction 2. Contests -- Fiction 3. Domestic animals -- Fiction
ISBN 978-1-4027-5366-4; 1-4027-5366-7
LC 2008-50578

Determined to win tickets to an Elvis Poultry concert, hens Marge and Lola enter the Barnyard Talent Show, then, while the ducks who usually win the contest jeer, they test out their abilities.

"The zippy narrative features punchy dialogue and witty interactions. . . . Santat's rich ink-and-acrylic designs provide a humorous context through animated expressions. . . . Fly the coop to enjoy this hilarious adventure." Kirkus

Mostly monsterly; illustrated by Scott Magoon. Simon & Schuster Books for Young Readers 2010 un il $14.99
Grades: PreK K 1   E
1. School stories 2. Monsters -- Fiction
ISBN 978-1-4169-6110-9; 1-4169-6110-0
LC 2008-48676

On the outside, Bernadette is a lot like the other monsters in her class but when she shows that she can be sweet, her classmates reject her until she finds a way to fit in again.

"Sauer tells a well-paced story in simple, repetitive phrases. The writing reveals just enough, allowing the artwork to fill in the rest of the story. . . . This artistic style proves effective in conveying the look of monsters without the frightening attributes. In fact, the art complements the humorous tone of the story." SLJ

Nugget and Fang; friends forever--or snack time? Tammi Sauer; illustrated by Michael Slack. Harcourt Children's Books 2013 40 p. (reinforced) $16.99

Grades: PreK K 1 2   E

    1. Humorous stories 2. Fishes -- Fiction 3. Sharks -- Fiction 4. Minnows -- Fiction 5. Friendship -- Fiction 6. Peer pressure -- Fiction

ISBN 0547852851; 9780547852850

LC 2012025329

Savage, Stephen

    ★ **Little** Tug; Stephen Savage. Roaring Book Press 2012 32 p. (alk. paper) $12.99

Grades: PreK K 1   E

    1. Picture books for children 2. Boats and boating -- Fiction 3. Tugboats -- Fiction

ISBN 1596436484; 9781596436480

LC 2011033799

This children's picture book "depicts Little Tug as beloved and helpful from the start. The story has the tempo of a waltz, as readers meet three other ships (a sailboat, a speedboat, and an ocean liner), each of which get into trouble of a sort, and are rescued in turn by Little Tug." (Publishers Weekly)

"Little Tug isn't the tallest, fastest, or biggest boat in the harbor, but he's very helpful when the other boats need a push, a pull, or a guide. Savage's illustrations give the boats distinct personalities and provide punch for the story. Tug's busy day will resonate with children, especially toddlers who also spend their days measuring up, helping out, and thoroughly exhausting themselves." Horn Book

Supertruck; Stephen Savage. Roaring Brook Press 2015 32 p. color illustrations (hardback) $12.99

Grades: PreK K 1   E

    1. Snow -- Fiction 2. Trucks -- Fiction 3. Heroes and heroines -- Fiction 4. Heroes -- Fiction 5. Snow removal -- Fiction 6. Refuse collection vehicles -- Fiction

ISBN 1596438215; 9781596438217

LC 2014009901

In this children's book, by Stephen Savage, "the city is hit by a colossal snowstorm [and] only one superhero can save the day. But who is this mysterious hero, and why does he disappear once his job is done? Find out in this snowy tale about a little truck with a very big job." (Publisher's note)

"When a blizzard stops the mighty trucks of the city from working, it's Supertruck to the rescue! In this metropolis, a cadre of brave trucks fixes electrical lines, extinguishes fires, and tows buses in need...sing a cool palette, Savage exploits shapes and colors to create interesting imagery and atmospheric environme nts for the truck that show that col-

lecting trash is just as heroic as powerfully plowing through snow. A serious treat for truck lovers." Kirkus

Ten orange pumpkins; by Stephen Savage. Dial Books for Young Readers 2013 48 p. (hardcover) $16.99

Grades: PreK K 1 2   E

    1. Counting 2. Stories in rhyme 3. Pumpkin -- Fiction 4. Halloween -- Fiction

ISBN 0803739389; 9780803739383

LC 2012042091

Author Stephen Savage presents a "counting book [that] opens with 10 orange pumpkins on a farm. As the rhyming, rhythmic verses roll along, one pumpkin after another disappears, but observant children will be able to figure out what happens to each." (Publisher's note)

★ **Where's** Walrus? Scholastic Press 2011 un il

Grades: PreK K 1   E

    1. Stories without words 2. Zoos -- Fiction 3. Walruses -- Fiction 4. Children's literature -- Works -- Preschool through grade two

ISBN 0-439-70049-3; 978-0-439-70049-8

LC 2010-922375

"With the zookeeper on his trail, an escaped walrus hides out in the city. . . . His trick is to blend in to each particular scene. However, he can't help but stand out in a diving competition where he wins a gold medal. . . . The collagelike illustrations in this wordless book were created in Adobe Illustrator. They are large, clear, and simple; the colors are bright, although flat. Young children will take delight in their ability to spot the wandering walrus." SLJ

Say, Allen

    ★ **Allison**. Houghton Mifflin 1997 32p il $17; pa $6.95

Grades: PreK K 1 2   E

    1. Adoption -- Fiction 2. Japanese Americans -- Fiction

ISBN 0-395-85895-X; 0-618-49537-1 pa

LC 97-7528

When Allison realizes that she looks more like her Japanese doll than like her parents, she comes to terms with this unwelcomed discovery through the help of a stray cat

"A subtle, sensitive probing of interracial adoption, this exquisitely illustrated story will encourage thoughtful adult-child dialogue on a potentially difficult issue." Publ Wkly

The **bicycle** man. Parnassus Press 1982 un il lib bdg $16; pa $5.95

Grades: K 1 2 3   E

    1. Japan -- Fiction 2. Cycling -- Fiction

ISBN 0-395-32254-5 lib bdg; 0-395-50652-2 pa

LC 82-2980

The amazing tricks two American soldiers do on a borrowed bicycle are a fitting finale for the school sports day festivities in a small village in occupied Japan

"The kindly, openhearted story is beautifully pictured in a profusion of delicate pen-and-ink drawings washed in gentle colors." Horn Book

★ **Boy** in the garden; written and illustrated by Allen Say. Houghton Mifflin Harcourt 2010 un il $17.99

Grades: PreK K 1 2   E

    1. Japan -- Fiction 2. Dreams -- Fiction 3. Cranes

(Birds) -- Fiction
ISBN 978-0-547-21410-8; 0-547-21410-3

After Jiro encounters a life-like garden statue of a tall bird, he falls asleep and dreams of the story his mother once told him about a grateful crane.

"Say is a master of composition. . . . Positions and postures are eloquent. . . . A gently unsettling tale of the power of the imagination." Horn Book

★ **Erika**-san. Houghton Mifflin Books for Children 2009 un il $17
Grades: 2 3 4   E
1. Japan -- Fiction 2. Teachers -- Fiction
ISBN 978-0-618-88933-4; 0-618-88933-7
LC 2008-00601

After falling in love with Japan as a little girl, Erika becomes a teacher and fulfills her childhood dream by moving to a remote Japanese island.

"With luminous watercolors and economical text . . . Say . . . tells of an American girl whose ingenuous hopes of reaching 'old Japan' are finally realized." Publ Wkly

The **favorite** daughter; Allen Say. Arthur A. Levine Books 2013 32 p. (hardcover) $17.99
Grades: K 1 2 3   E
1. Picture books for children 2. Artists -- Fiction 3. Schools -- Fiction 4. Teasing -- Fiction 5. Japanese Americans -- Fiction 6. Fathers and daughters -- Fiction 7. San Francisco (Calif.) -- Fiction
ISBN 054517662X; 9780545176620
LC 2012026830

In this children's picture book, by Allen Say, "Yuriko hates her name when the children make fun of it. . . . The teasing makes her want to hide, to retreat even from the art projects she used to love. Fortunately she has a patient, kind father who finds gentle ways of drawing her out and reminding Yuriko of the traditions they share that have always brought her joy." (Publisher's note)

★ **Grandfather's** journey; written and illustrated by Allen Say. Houghton Mifflin 1993 32p il $16.95; pa $7.99
Grades: 1 2 3 4   E
1. Japan -- Fiction 2. Grandfathers -- Fiction 3. Japanese Americans -- Fiction 4. Voyages and travels -- Fiction
ISBN 0-395-57035-2; 0-547-07680-0 pa
LC 93-18836

Awarded the Caldecott Medal, 1994

A Japanese American man recounts his grandfather's journey to America which he later also undertakes, and the feelings of being torn by a love for two different countries

"The brief text is simple and unaffected, but the emotions expressed are deeply complex. The paintings are astonishingly still, like the captured moments found in a family photo album. Each translucent watercolor is suffused with light." SLJ

★ **Kamishibai** man; written and illustrated by Allen Say. Houghton Mifflin Co. 2005 32p il $17
Grades: PreK K 1 2 3   E
1. Japan -- Fiction 2. Entertainers -- Fiction
ISBN 0-618-47954-6

After many years of retirement, an old Kamishibai man—a Japanese street performer who tells stories and sells candies—decides to make his rounds once more even though such entertainment declined after the advent of television.

"The quietly dramatic, beautifully evocative tale contains a cliffhanger of its own, and its exquisite art, in the style of Kamishibai picture cards, will attract even the most jaded kid away from the TV to enjoy a good, good book." Booklist

The **lost** lake. Houghton Mifflin 1989 32p il $16; pa $6.95
Grades: K 1 2 3   E
1. Camping -- Fiction 2. Father-son relationship -- Fiction
ISBN 0-395-50933-5; 0-395-63036-3 pa
LC 89-11026

"Using colors as crisp and clean as the outdoors, Say effectively alternates between scenes where father and son are the focus and those where the landscape predominates. Both in story and art, a substantial piece." Booklist

★ **Tea** with milk. Houghton Mifflin 1999 32p il $17; pa $6.99
Grades: K 1 2 3 4   E
1. Japan -- Fiction 2. Japanese Americans -- Fiction
ISBN 0-395-90495-1; 0-547-23747-2 pa
LC 98-11667

After growing up near San Francisco, Masako (or May) returns with her parents to their native Japan, but she feels foreign and out of place until she finds a job in Osaka and marries a man with a similarly mixed background

"Say's masterfully executed watercolors tell as much of this story . . . as his eloquent prose." Publ Wkly

Tree of cranes; written and illustrated by Allen Say. Houghton Mifflin 1991 32p il $17.95; pa $7.99
Grades: K 1 2 3   E
1. Japan -- Fiction 2. Christmas -- Fiction 3. Mother-son relationship -- Fiction
ISBN 0-395-52024-X; 0-547-24830-X pa
LC 91-14107

A Japanese boy learns of Christmas when his mother decorates a pine tree with paper cranes

"The quiet, graciously told picture book is a perfect blend of text and art. Fine-lined and handsome, Say's watercolors not only capture fascinating details of the boy's far away home . . . but also depict, with simple grace, the rich and complex bond between mother and child that underlies the story." Booklist

Sayre, April Pulley
Dig, wait, listen; a desert toad's tale. pictures by Barbara Bash. Greenwillow Bks. 2001 un il $15.95
Grades: PreK K 1 2   E
1. Toads -- Fiction 2. Desert animals -- Fiction
ISBN 0-688-16614-8
LC 00-32111

A spadefoot toad waits under the sand for the rain, hears the sounds of other desert animals, and eventually mates and spawns other toads

"Created with pencil, pen and ink, and watercolor, Bash's pictures illustrate the desert scenes with pleasingly varied colors, perspectives, and layouts. Preschool and primary-grade children will find this well-crafted book a wholly satisfying introduction to the spadefoot toad in particular and desert animals and the idea of life cycles in general." Booklist

★ **Eat** like a bear; by April Pulley Sayre; illustrated by Steve Jenkins. Henry Holt and Company 2013 32 p. (hardback) $16.99
Grades: PreK K 1 2 3   E
    1. Picture books for children 2. Bears -- Fiction 3. Grizzly bear -- Fiction
    ISBN 0805090398; 9780805090390
                                LC 2013015686
This children's picture book by April Pulley, a "grizzled, lumbering bear wakes up in the springtime. What is there to eat? . . . 'With long, strong claws, / dig in. Dig down. / Paw and claw and pull. / Find . . . // . . . ants! / Chew them, / sour and squirming. / Lick your lips.' As the months go by, bears eat many different types of food." (Kirkus Reviews)

If you're hoppy; pictures by Jackie Urbanovic. Greenwillow Books 2011 un il $16.99
Grades: PreK K 1   E
    1. Stories in rhyme 2. Animals -- Fiction
    ISBN 978-0-06-156634-9; 0-06-156634-9
                                LC 2010-04103
In rhyming text reminiscent of the traditional song, "If you're happy and you know it," presents various animals that are hoppy, sloppy, growly, flappy, or slimy, scaly and mean.
    "Urbanovic's sprightly watercolor-and-ink cartoons add humor and vivacious energy. . . . Sure to be a storytime staple, with many requests for repeat performances." SLJ

One is a snail, ten is a crab; a counting by feet book. [by] April Pulley Sayre and Jeff Sayre; illustrated by Randy Cecil. Candlewick Press 2003 un il hardcover o.p. pa $6.99
Grades: PreK K 1 2   E
    1. Foot 2. Animals 3. Counting
    ISBN 0-7636-1406-8; 0-7636-2631-7 pa
                                LC 2001-52494
A counting book featuring animals with different numbers of feet
    "Very simple text in large type is appropriate for group use as well as beginning readers. Uncluttered, black-outlined, oil-on-paper pictures clearly illustrate the concepts, and Cecil's googly-eyed snails, sports-minded crabs, and other animals add a touch of humor." SLJ

Turtle, turtle, watch out! illustrated by Annie Patterson. Charlesbridge 2010 un il lib bdg $17.95; pa $7.95
Grades: K 1 2   E
    1. Sea turtles -- Fiction
    ISBN 978-1-58089-148-6 lib bdg; 1-58089-148-9 lib bdg; 978-1-58089-149-3 pa; 1-58089-149-7 pa
                                LC 2008025338
A newly illustrated edition of the title first published 2000 by Orchard Books
    From before the time she hatches until she returns to the same beach to lay eggs of her own, a sea turtle is helped to escape from danger many times by different human hands.
    "The simple, direct text reads aloud well, drawing readers into the turtles' story without anthropomorphism. Im-

pressive pastel illustrations, including many dramatic double-page spreads, depict with power and beauty the turtles' world of sand and shore." Booklist

Scanlon, Liz Garton
The **Good**-Pie Party; by Liz Garton Scanlon; illustrated by Kady Macdonald Denton. Arthur A. Levine Books, An Imprint of Scholastic Inc. 2014 32 p. color illustrations (hardcover: alk. paper) $17.99
Grades: PreK K 1 2 3   E
    1. Baking -- Fiction 2. Moving -- Fiction 3. Female friendship -- Fiction 4. Pies -- Fiction 5. Parties -- Fiction 6. Friendship -- Fiction 7. Moving, Household -- Fiction
    ISBN 0545448700; 9780545448703
                                LC 2013006975
In this children's book, by Liz Garton Scanlon, "Posy, Megan, and Mae have always been the best of friends--but now Posy has to move away. Only their favorite activity can comfort the girls: baking pie! And when they realize they can host a good-pie party instead of a good-bye party, the sad situation becomes a sweet gathering for their entire community." (Publisher's note)
    "Posy is feeling the moving blues. Lamenting her near departure, Posy and her two best friends decide to make a pie amidst the packed boxes. Inspired by their 'hot, sweet, good pie' they elect to throw a 'good-pie party' rather than a 'good-bye' one. Soft, emotionally detailed ink and watercolor illustrations lighten up the stressful subject and capture the warmth of childhood friendship." Horn Book

Noodle & Lou. Beach Lane Books 2011 un il $15.99
Grades: PreK K 1   E
    1. Birds -- Fiction 2. Worms -- Fiction 3. Friendship -- Fiction
    ISBN 978-1-4424-0288-1; 1-4424-0288-1
                                LC 2009-42950
Noodle and Lou are unlikely friends. One is a worm and one is a bird. When Noodle is having a bad day, Lou knows just what to say to cheer up his wormy friend and help him see what it means to be liked just the way you are.
    "Howard's cartoon-style illustrations match the bouncy rhythm of Scanlon's couplets perfectly and keep the tone light. . . . Chirpy, instructive and fun." Kirkus

Schachner, Judith Byron
The **Grannyman**. Dutton Children's Bks. 1999 un il $15.99; pa $6.99
Grades: PreK K 1 2   E
    1. Cats -- Fiction 2. Old age -- Fiction
    ISBN 0-525-46122-1; 0-14-250062-3 pa
                                LC 98-52964
Simon the cat is so old that most of his parts have stopped working, but just when he is ready to breathe his last breath, his family brings home a new kitten for him to raise
    "Schachner's expressive watercolor-and-mixed-media artwork mirrors the affection, humor, and warmth of her finely crafted text." Booklist

Schachner, Judy
Skippyjon Jones class action; by Judy Schachner. Dutton Children's Books 2011 un il $16.99

Grades: PreK K 1   E
1. School stories 2. Cats -- Fiction 3. Dogs -- Fiction
ISBN 0-525-42228-5; 978-0-525-42228-0
LC 2009053293

Skippyjon Jones, a Siamese cat who would rather be his Chihuahua alter ego, is determined to attend dog obedience school.

"Schachner's style, the book has hilarious songs, wild antics, a smattering of Spanish words, and humor that everyone can appreciate. The zany illustrations add to its exuberant nature. Children will enjoy the amusing details on each page. As with the earlier books, this one makes for a wonderful read-aloud that will have young audiences laughing out loud." SLJ

Schaefer, Carole Lexa

Big Little Monkey; illustrated by Pierre Pratt. Candlewick Press 2008 un il $16.99
Grades: PreK K 1 2   E
1. Monkeys -- Fiction
ISBN 978-0-7636-2006-6; 0-7636-2006-8
LC 2007052024

When Little Monkey decides to venture out into the jungle alone, beyond the gaze of his watchful Mama, he discovers that other animals are not as friendly and warm as his own family and that independence is not altogether a good thing

"Schaefer's text has the style and cadences of a folktale with the effective refrain 'bim-ba-lah, bim-ba-lah' appearing as the protagonist swings through the trees. . . . Pratt's stylized animals, done in sweeping, brightly colored acrylics . . . and the mostly full-bleed illustrations with their color-saturated backgrounds are eye-catching and will carry well in storytimes." SLJ

Dragon dancing; illustrated by Pierr Morgan. Viking 2007 un il $16.99
Grades: PreK K 1   E
1. School stories 2. Dragons -- Fiction 3. Birthdays -- Fiction 4. Imagination -- Fiction
ISBN 0-670-06084-9

A group of children pretend that they are a dragon to celebrate their classmate's birthday.

"An excellent choice for storytime, the text features . . . many fun sounds. . . . The color of the gouache-and-marker illustrations increases in brightness as the students transition gradually from the classroom into their imaginative fantasy. . . . Pleasing to the eye and the ear." SLJ

Schaefer, Lola M.

Frankie Stein; illustrated by Kevan J. Atteberry. Marshall Cavendish 2007 un il $14.99; pa $6.99
Grades: PreK K 1   E
1. Monsters -- Fiction 2. Family life -- Fiction
ISBN 978-0-7614-5358-1; 978-0-7614-5608-7 pa
LC 2007000256

"Frankie Stein is nothing like his monstrous, green-skinned parents. Instead, he is cute, with a pink face and golden hair. . . . In the end, little Frankie discovers his own way of being scary, which frightens even his parents. Purples and greens dominate the illustrations, emphasizing the cartoony creepiness of the Stein house." SLJ

Another title about Frankie Stein is:

Frankie Stein starts school (2010)

★ **Loose** tooth; story by Lola M. Schaefer; pictures by Sylvie Wickstrom. HarperCollinsPublishers 2004 31p il (My first I can read book) hardcover o.p. pa $3.99
Grades: PreK K 1 2   E
1. Stories in rhyme 2. Teeth -- Fiction
ISBN 0-06-052776-5; 0-06-052778-1 pa
LC 2003-6322

A young child experiences a loose tooth for the first time and eagerly waits for it to come out

"With a few words, lots of repetition, some rhyme, and good rhythm, this story is perfect for beginning readers. The cartoon illustrations add details to the plot and create interest." SLJ

Mittens; story by Lola M. Schaefer; pictures by Susan Kathleen Hartung. HarperCollinsPublishers 2006 25p il (I can read!) $16.99; lib bdg $15.89; pa $3.99
Grades: PreK K 1 2   E
1. Cats -- Fiction
ISBN 0-06-054659-X; 0-06-054660-3 lib bdg; 0-06-054661-1 pa

Nick helps Mittens the kitten adjust to life in a new home

"The controlled vocabulary in this gentle, unassuming story is made up primarily of one-syllable words, and the sentence structure is very basic. The soft pastel illustrations are simple and uncluttered and enhance the quiet tone of the text." SLJ

Other titles about Mittens are:
Follow me, Mittens (2007)
What's that, Mittens (2008)
Happy Halloween, Mittens (2010)
Mittens, where is Max? (2011)

One busy day; A Story for Big Brothers and Sisters. written by Lola Schaefer; illustrated by Jessica Meserve. First edition Disney-Hyperion Books 2014 40 p. color illustrations $16.99
Grades: PreK K 1   E
1. Play -- Fiction 2. Imagination -- Fiction 3. Brothers and sisters -- Fiction
ISBN 1423171128; 9781423171126
LC 2013000494

In this children's book, written by Lola Schaefer and illustrated by Jessica Meserve, "all Mia wants is for her big brother, Spencer, to play with her. But he's always too busy! So Mia paints, and dances, and explores, and keep busy all by herself. But with a little imagination and a lot of love, Mia might just be able to show Spencer that it's a lot more fun to be busy together." (Publisher's note)

"Schaefer and Meserve depict a growing sibling bond between big brother Spencer and little sister Mia. No longer a baby, Mia longs to play with Spencer. . . . Meserve's art cleverly extends the text to expound upon plucky Mia's imaginative flights of fancy. . . . The pleasing text culminates in a circular ending that showcases the pair as 'busy. Very, very busy—together.' Throughout, Meserve's digitally rendered illustrations employ soft visual texture and bold colors to create a cheery, charming world for the two children to enjoy. Hooray for sibling revelry!" Kirkus

One special day; by Lola Schaefer; illustrated by Jessica Meserve. Disney/Hyperion Books 2012 40p. col. ill. Grades: PreK K 1 **E**

1. Siblings -- Fiction 2. Picture books for children 3. Babies -- Fiction 4. Behavior -- Fiction 5. Brothers -- Fiction

ISBN 1423137604; 9781423137603

LC 2011015977

In this book, "Spencer . . . [is] fast as a horse, tall as a giraffe, funny as a monkey and more. Yet when his parents come home with a new arrival, Spencer finds a new way to describe himself. He may be like animals in many respects, but now he"s gentle, just as a big brother should be. . . .The text allows readers to guess what animal Spencer will come to resemble next, until finally there is only one thing left to be." (Kirkus Reviews)

"With a simple interactive text and thoroughly engaging illustrations, this book is a perfect blending of words and pictures." SLJ

This is the sunflower; pictures by Donald Crews. Greenwillow Bks. 2000 un il $15.99 Grades: PreK K 1 2 **E**

1. Stories in rhyme 2. Sunflowers -- Fiction

ISBN 0-688-16413-7

LC 98-46682

A cumulative verse describing how a sunflower in a garden blossoms and, with the help of the birds, spreads its seeds to create an entire patch of sunflowers

"A beautiful, noteworthy title. The velvety watercolors are clearly defined and saturated with color. . . . This is perfect for story hours; also recommend it to budding ornithologists, who will appreciate the illustrated key identifying the birds pictured in the text." Booklist

What's up, what's down? pictures by Barbara Bash. Greenwillow Bks. 2002 un il $15.99; lib bdg $17.89 Grades: PreK K 1 2 **E**

1. Nature

ISBN 0-06-029757-3; 0-06-029758-1 lib bdg

"On each page is the question 'What's up if you're ...?' from the viewpoint of various flora and fauna: a mole, a root, grass, a toad. . . . The highest thing 'up' is the moon, and then it's time to turn the book upside down and move down through sky and water to see 'what's down.' Children will have a chance to stretch their imaginations as they get a rudimentary idea of how the natural world works. The artwork, executed in chalks, has a muscular look that brings nature home." Booklist

Scheer, Julian

Rain makes applesauce; by Julian Scheer & Marvin Bileck. Holiday House 1964 un il $16.95 Grades: PreK K 1 2 **E**

ISBN 0-8234-0091-3

A Caldecott Medal honor book, 1965

"A book of original nonsense, illustrated with intricate drawings. Small children live the refrains, 'Rain makes applesauce' and 'You're just talking silly talk,' and enjoy the fantastic details in the pictures." Hodges. Books for Elem Sch Libr

Schertle, Alice

1, 2, I love you; illustrated by Emily Arnold McCully. Chronicle Books 2004 un il $16.95 Grades: PreK K **E**

1. Counting 2. Stories in rhyme 3. Elephants -- Fiction

ISBN 0-8118-3518-9

LC 2003-21245

"A mother elephant addresses her little one as they engage in a variety of child-centered activities. . . . The numbers climb from 1 to 10 in the first half of the book, then descend until the end, when the little elephant goes to bed and to sleep. The rhythmic, rhyming verses are . . . engaging. . . . The colorful artwork features playful, large-scale paintings." Booklist

★ **Little** Blue Truck; illustrated by Jill McElmurry. Harcourt Children's Books 2008 un il $16 Grades: PreK K 1 2 **E**

1. Trucks -- Fiction 2. Animals -- Fiction 3. Friendship -- Fiction

ISBN 0-15-205661-0; 978-0-15-205661-2

LC 2006-29445

A small blue truck finds his way out of a jam, with a little help from his friends. "Ages three to six." (Bull Cent Child Books)

"Schertle contrasts a huge dump truck, hurtling self-importantly down a country road, with a small pickup that greets each farm animal. . . . When the dump truck bogs down in a deep slough, its cries of distress go unanswered. When the pickup gets stuck while trying to help, the animals rush in to lend a hearty push. . . . McElmurry creates crisply drawn rural scenes. . . . Along with being a natural for storytime, this upbeat tale may spark a discussion about friendships and helping one another." Booklist

Another title about Little Blue Truck is:

Little Blue Truck leads the way (2009)

Such a little mouse; [text] Alice Schertle; [illustrations] Stephanie Yue. Orchard Books 2015 32 p. $16.99 Grades: PreK K **E**

1. Mice -- Fiction 2. Seasons -- Fiction

ISBN 0545649293; 9780545649292

LC 2014022920

"With Alice Schertle's sweet descriptive language and touching illustrations from Stephanie Yue, a little mouse interacts with the world around him. Every season of the year, 'such a little mouse' pops out of his hole and goes out to explore the wider world." (Publisher's note)

Schimel, Lawrence

Let's go see Papa! translated from Spanish by Elisa Amado; illustrated by Alba Marina Rivera. Groundwood Books 2011 un il $18.95 Grades: 1 2 3 **E**

1. Spain -- Fiction 2. Immigrants -- Fiction 3. Father-daughter relationship -- Fiction

ISBN 978-1-55498-106-9; 1-55498-106-9

"A young girl waits by the telephone every Sunday for a call from Papá. He left 'one year, eight months and twenty two days' ago to find work in the United States. . . . When Papá asks her and Mamá to join him, she is thrilled to be reunited, but also sad to leave her abuela and friends. Rivera's pencil, crayon, and watercolor illustrations capture the daily details of a loving extended family. . . . . The feelings of missing a loved one are realistically conveyed and will resonate with children." SLJ

Schmid, Paul

Hugs from Pearl; story and pictures by Paul Schmid. Harper 2011 un il $14.99

Grades: PreK K   E

1. School stories 2. Hugging -- Fiction 3. Porcupines -- Fiction

ISBN 978-0-06-180434-2; 0-06-180434-7

LC 2010015906

A friendly porcupine figures out how to give hugs without hurting others with her sharp quills.

"With his simple pastel and charcoal illustrations set against pale green and blue pages, Schmid brings just the right touch of sweetness to this charming tale." SLJ

★ **Oliver** and his alligator; Paul Schmid. Disney-Hyperion Books 2013 40 p. $15.99

Grades: PreK K 1   E

1. School children -- Fiction 2. Fear -- Fiction 3. Schools -- Fiction 4. Alligators -- Fiction 5. First day of school -- Fiction

ISBN 1423174372; 9781423174370

LC 2012020298

This book by Paul Schmid is a "tale about overcoming first day of school jitters. Oliver is nervous about the first day of school, so he picks up an alligator at the swamp, just in case. Whenever anything scares Oliver-be it a teacher, a classmate, or the prospect of learning everything-the alligator makes the problem go away. Quickly, school becomes much simpler . . . and a little lonely. But Oliver knows just what to do!" (Publisher's note)

★ A **pet** for Petunia. Harper 2011 un il $12.99

Grades: PreK K 1   E

1. Pets -- Fiction 2. Skunks -- Fiction 3. Parent-child relationship -- Fiction

ISBN 978-0-06-196331-5; 0-06-196331-3

Petunia so desperately wants a pet skunk that she refuses to believe her parents when they say skunks stink.

Schmid's "line drawings are simple, fluid, and convey lots of valuable information. . . . Enthusiastic and single-minded, Petunia makes delightful company; kids will recognize themselves and clamor for rereads." Publ Wkly

Petunia goes wild; by Paul Schmid. HarperCollins 2012 40 p.

Grades: PreK K 1 2   E

1. Temper tantrums 2. Tigers -- Fiction 3. Temper tantrums -- Fiction 4. Children's costumes -- Fiction 5. Parent-child relationship -- Fiction 6. Humorous stories 7. Behavior -- Fiction 8. Parent and child -- Fiction

ISBN 9780061963346; 9780061963353

LC 2011001888

In this children's book, "Petunia . . . would much rather be an animal than a human girl, a preference that she expresses by wearing a tiger tail, roaring at passersby, and pleading with her parents for a cave in which to live. As a compromise, she offers to be their pet, an offer that provokes a page-long parental lecture: "No, you may NOT! Where did you get such an idea? Of all the crazy things! That is NOT how nice little girls behave." Feeling completely misunderstood, Petunia addresses a packing box to Africa and climbs

in, only to have second thoughts when she overhears her mother singing in the kitchen ("Tigers did not sing, thought Petunia. Or tickle at bedtime, neither"), and she decides to stay." (Bulletin of the Center for Children's Books)

Schneider, Josh

Bedtime monsters; Josh Schneider. Clarion Books, Houghton Mifflin Harcourt 2013 32 p. (hardcover) $16.99

Grades: PreK K 1   E

1. Picture books for children 2. Bedtime -- Fiction 3. Monsters -- Fiction 4. Fear of the dark -- Fiction

ISBN 0544002709; 9780544002708

LC 2012036483

In this book, "Arnold knows he has nothing more to be afraid of at bedtime after the winged fargle, the horrible tooth gnasher, the grozny buzzler, and other monsters with their own fears crawl into his bed. These colorful figures lurk in the darkest corners of bedrooms, but, as Arnold discovers, the scary creatures have more in common with him than he could have imagined." (School Library Journal)

The **meanest** birthday girl; by Josh Schneider. Clarion Books 2013 48 p. col. ill. (hardcover) $14.99

Grades: 1 2 3   E

1. Conduct of life -- Fiction 2. Gifts -- Fiction 3. Birthdays -- Fiction 4. Elephants -- Fiction

ISBN 054783814X; 9780547838144

LC 2011041587

In this children's story, by Josh Schneider, "it's Dana's birthday, so she can do what she likes. And what Dana likes to do is pinch. And call people names. And steal her classmates' desserts. You probably know a kid like Dana. What can stop her from being so mean? . . . Sometimes, it takes a little creativity (and possibly a very large pet) to change a mean kid's ways." (Publisher's note)

★ **Princess** Sparkle-Heart gets a makeover; Josh Schneider. Clarion Books, Houghton Mifflin Harcourt 2014 32 p. (hardcover) $16.99

Grades: PreK K 1 2   E

1. Dogs -- Fiction 2. Jealousy -- Fiction 3. Dolls -- Repairing -- Fiction

ISBN 0544142284; 9780544142282

LC 2013004355

In this book, by Josh Schneider, "Amelia and her dog are best friends . . . until Princess Sparkle-Heart comes along. Soon, Amelia and Princess Sparkle-Heart are doing everything together: having tea parties, attending royal weddings, keeping each other's secrets. Princess Sparkle-Heart may be an awesome princess doll - but is she any match for a jealous canine?" (Publisher's note)

"Amelia's jealous dog hates Amelia's beloved princess doll. Following "an accident" (read: the dog destroys the doll), Amelia rebuilds Princess Sparkle-Heart, but readers don't see until book's end that it now resembles a dog-repelling Raggedy Ann like horror-movie creation. Schneider plays it perfectly: Amelia is mellow throughout, and he never tips his hand regarding her sinister side. The droll art is pleasantly sparkle-light." Horn Book

Schnur, Steven

Winter; an alphabet acrostic. illustrated by Leslie Evans. Clarion Bks. 2002 un il $15

Grades: K 1 2 3 **E**
1. Winter 2. Alphabet 3. Acrostics
ISBN 0-618-02374-7

LC 2001-17358

"On each page, a winter-related word provides the basis for an acrostic that reads like a short poem. . . . A striking, hand-colored linoleum print illustrates each small, boxed acrostic." Booklist

Schnur, Susan
Tashlich at Turtle Rock; by Susan Schnur and Anna Schnur-Fishman; illustrated by Alex Steele-Morgan. Kar-Ben Pub. 2010 un il lib bdg $17.95; pa $7.95
Grades: K 1 2 3 **E**
1. Jews -- Fiction 2. Rosh ha-Shanah -- Fiction
ISBN 978-0-7613-4509-1 lib bdg; 0-7613-4509-4 lib bdg; 978-0-7613-4510-7 pa; 0-7613-4510-8 pa

LC 2009001871

Annie leads her family on a Rosh Hashanah hike to observe tashlich, where each person will ask God's forgiveness for the things they regret doing the previous year. Includes facts about this Jewish custom.

"Throughout, the authors empahsize environmental awareness . . . and Steele-Morgan's boldly colored heavily textured illustrations highlight the rich colors of autumn. . . . Handled with a light touch, this is secular enough to make it useful for general as well as religious collections." Booklist

Schoenherr, Ian
★ Don't spill the beans! Greenwillow Books 2010 un il $16.99; lib bdg $17.89
Grades: PreK **E**
1. Stories in rhyme 2. Bears -- Fiction 3. Animals -- Fiction 4. Birthdays -- Fiction
ISBN 978-0-06-172457-2; 0-06-172457-2; 978-0-06-172458-9 lib bdg; 0-06-172458-0 lib bdg

LC 2008042363

A bear tries hard to keep a birthday surprise a secret.

"The story is told in short rhyming sentences of large, colorful, hand-lettered text. The ink and acrylic paint illustrations depict cheerfully clothed animals with expressive faces." SLJ

★ Read it, don't eat it! Greenwillow Books 2009 un il $17.99; lib bdg $18.89
Grades: PreK K **E**
1. Stories in rhyme 2. Books and reading -- Fiction
ISBN 978-0-06-172455-8; 0-06-172455-6; 978-0-06-178034-9 lib bdg; 0-06-178034-0 lib bdg

LC 2008027716

Rhyming advice on how to take care of a library book
"One white, hand-lettered sentence per page is set against a bold color, and the ink and acrylic art features endearing animal library users on an expansive white space. The book is simple enough to use with preschool children and funny enough to be appreciated by early readers." SLJ

Schoettler, Joan
Good fortune in a wrapping cloth; illustrated by Jessica Lanan. Shen's Books 2011 il $17.95
Grades: 2 3 4 **E**
1. Korea -- Fiction 2. Sewing -- Fiction 3. Clothing and dress -- Fiction 4. Mother-daughter relationship --

Fiction
ISBN 978-1-885008-40-4; 1-885008-40-6

LC 2011001702

When Ji-su's mother is chosen by the emperor to be a seamstress in his court, Ji-su vows to learn to sew the beautiful Korean bojagi, or wrapping cloths, just as well so that she will also be summoned to the palace and be reunited with her mother.

"Descriptive language and stunning watercolor paintings show the seasons passing as Ji-su works toward her goal. With a masterful eye for color and skillful use of perspective, Lanan brings the text to life and adds depth to Ji-su's emotions." SLJ

Schofield-Morrison, Connie
I got the rhythm; by Connie Schofield-Morrison; illustrated by Frank Morrison. Bloomsbury 2014 32 p. (hardback) $16.99
Grades: PreK K 1 **E**
1. Dance -- Fiction 2. Musical meter and rhythm 3. Parks -- Fiction 4. Rhythm -- Fiction
ISBN 1619631784; 9781619631786; 9781619631793; 9781619632103

LC 2013038025

In this children's book, written by Connie Schofield-Morrison and illustrated by Frank Morrison, "the joy of music overtakes a mother and daughter. The little girl hears a rhythm coming from the world around her - from butterflies, to street performers, to ice cream sellers everything is musical! She sniffs, snaps, and shakes her way into the heart of the beat, finally busting out in an impromptu dance, which all the kids join in on!" (Publisher's note)

"Music is everywhere in the city, but a warm summer day in the park makes it downright infectious. A young African American girl leaves the house with her mother, using all her senses to find rhythm everywhere as they walk... With text like "STOMP STOMP" and "BEAT BOP" strewn across the pages, the book begs readers to sing and move along with this little dancer as she "pops and locks, hips and hops" her way through the sunny afternoon." Booklist

Schoonmaker, Elizabeth
Square cat; written and illustrated by Elizabeth Schoonmaker. Aladdin 2011 un il $14.99
Grades: PreK K 1 **E**
1. Cats -- Fiction 2. Shape -- Fiction 3. Individualism -- Fiction
ISBN 978-1-4424-0619-3; 1-4424-0619-4

Eula the cat is square, and while she longs to be round like other cats, her friends show her the benefits of the shape she has. "Ages four to seven." (Bull Cent Child Books)

"This title gently packs a powerful message about self-acceptance and friendship. . . . Ink and bright watercolor illustrations using basic shapes with simple and engaging facial expressions steal the show." SLJ

Schories, Pat
Jack wants a snack. Front Street 2008 un il $13.95
Grades: PreK K 1 **E**
1. Stories without words 2. Dogs -- Fiction 3. Chipmunks -- Fiction
ISBN 978-1-59078-546-1; 1-59078-546-0

LC 2007-52154

Jack the dog discovers that he is not the only uninvited guest at a tea party

"Schories does a masterful job of creating a clear plot that children will be able to follow despite the absence of text clues. The illustrations are warm, friendly, and full of movement." SLJ

Schotter, Roni

★ The **boy** who loved words; pictures by Giselle Potter. Schwartz & Wade Books 2006 un il $16.95; lib bdg $18.99

Grades: K 1 2 3   E

1. English language -- Fiction

ISBN 0-375-83601-2; 0-375-93601-7 lib bdg

LC 2005-10850

Selig, who loves words and copies them on pieces of paper that he carries with him, goes on a trip to discover his purpose.

"Potter's signature naive-style art is light and comical, while Schotter's words are a lovely celebration of the power and the music of language." Booklist

★ **Doo-**Wop Pop; by Roni Schotter; illustrated by Bryan Collier. Amistad/HarperCollins 2008 un il $16.99; lib bdg $17.89

Grades: K 1 2 3   E

1. School stories 2. Stories in rhyme 3. Singing -- Fiction 4. Janitors -- Fiction

ISBN 978-0-06-057968-5; 0-06-057968-4; 978-0-06-057974-6 lib bdg; 0-06-057974-9 lib bdg

LC 2008015212

A school janitor teaches children to sing and have confidence in themselves

"Schotter stacks the prose with rhymes, giving the first-person narrative an authentic, contemporary freestyle flow that begs to be read aloud. Collier's trademark collage paintings, shaded with bursts of yellow and green, hum with the students' energy and pride." Booklist

★ **Mama,** I'll give you the world; by Roni Schotter; illustrated by S. Saelig Gallagher. Schwartz & Wade Books 2006 un il $16.95

Grades: K 1 2 3   E

1. Birthdays -- Fiction 2. Beauty shops -- Fiction 3. Mother-daughter relationship -- Fiction

ISBN 978-0-375-83612-1; 0-375-83612-8

At Walter's World of Beauty, Luisa's secret plans are underway to create a very special birthday celebration for her hardworking, single mother who is employed there as a stylist.

"Gallagher's bright-eyed, smiling, subtly modeled faces light up this loving mother-daughter tale." Booklist

Schroeder, Alan

★ **Satchmo's** blues; illustrated by Floyd Cooper. Doubleday Bks. for Young Readers 1996 un il hardcover o.p. pa $6.99

Grades: 1 2 3 4   E

1. Singers 2. Jazz musicians 3. Band leaders 4. Trumpet players 5. New Orleans (La.) -- Fiction 6. African American musicians -- Fiction

ISBN 0-385-32046-9; 0-440-41472-5 pa

LC 93-41082

A fictional recreation of the youth of trumpeter Louis Armstrong in New Orleans

"This book is full of gorgeous writing, accompanied by Cooper's atmospheric paintings." SLJ

Schubert, Ingrid

The **umbrella**; [by] Ingrid & Dieter Schubert. Lemniscaat 2011 il $16.95

Grades: PreK K 1 2   E

1. Stories without words 2. Dogs -- Fiction 3. Voyages and travels -- Fiction 4. Umbrellas and parasols -- Fiction

ISBN 978-1-9359-5400-2; 1-9359-5400-8

A little dog finds an umbrella in the garden on a windy day. The moment the dog picks up the umbrella, it catches the wind and pulls the dog skywards. The wind carries the umbrella and the dog all over the world, from the desert to the sea, from the jungle to the north pole.

"The illustrations easily tell the story; there's no need for words. The paintings excel at showing the different landscapes and depicting movement. What a great journey!" SLJ

Schubert, Leda

Feeding the sheep; pictures by Andrea U'Ren. Farrar Straus Giroux 2010 un il $16.99

Grades: PreK K 1 2   E

1. Stories in rhyme 2. Wool -- Fiction 3. Sheep -- Fiction 4. Weaving -- Fiction 5. Mother-daughter relationship -- Fiction

ISBN 978-0-374-32296-0; 0-374-32296-1

LC 2007-48843

In pictures and rhythmic text, a mother relates to her daughter all the steps involved in making her a snug, wooly sweater, starting at the very beginning with feeding the sheep

"The physicality of the words, . . . the fascinating facts, and the action-filled, brightly colored illustrations will capture kids' attention, as will the cozy family bond between parent and child." Booklist

★ The **Princess** of Borscht; illustrated by Bonnie Christensen. Roaring Brook Press 2011 un il $17.99

Grades: PreK K 1 2   E

1. Sick -- Fiction 2. Soups -- Fiction 3. Cooking -- Fiction 4. Grandmothers -- Fiction

ISBN 978-1-59643-515-5; 1-59643-515-1

LC 2010014520

Ruthie's grandmother, who is in the hospital with pneumonia, says she needs homemade borscht by five o'clock and young Ruthie, with the help of her neighbors, tries to make some even without the secret recipe.

"Of course, it's not just about borscht or even about cooking, though there's a great recipe included. Schubert has concocted a sweet mixture of traditions that bind and give comfort, along with love in many forms. . . . Christensen's heavily outlined, strongly colored illustrations emphasize equally strong personalities. The paintings are filled with details that add interest to the proceedings." Kirkus

Reading to Peanut; illustrated by Amanda Haley. Holiday House 2011 un il $16.95

Grades: PreK K 1 2   E

1. Dogs -- Fiction 2. Reading -- Fiction 3. Birthdays

-- Fiction 4. Family life -- Fiction
ISBN 978-0-8234-2339-2; 0-8234-2339-5

LC 2010031412

Lucy works hard to learn to read and write before her dog's birthday.

"Colorful, energetic acrylics show Lucy and her ever-present pup Peanut in motion. . . . The appealing character, lively pictures and mild suspense make for a warm family story that shows the fun of having a pet and provides a strategy for learning to read that youngsters will eagerly embrace." Kirkus

Schuch, Steve

★ A **symphony** of whales; illustrated by Peter Sylvada. Harcourt Brace & Co. 1999 un il hardcover o.p. pa $7
Grades: 1 2 3 4.   E
1. Music -- Fiction 2. Whales -- Fiction
ISBN 0-15-201670-8; 0-15-216548-7 pa

LC 98-17248

Young Glashka's dream of the singing of whales, accompanied by a special kind of music, leads to the rescue of thousands of whales stranded in a freezing Siberian bay

"This is a quiet, powerful story, beautifully extended by Sylvada's paintings of ghostly whale shapes and glowing, fin-shaped skies." Booklist

Schwartz, Amy, 1954-

100 things that make me happy; by Amy Schwartz. Abrams Appleseed 2014 40 p. color illustrations $16.95
Grades: PreK K 1   E
1. Stories in rhyme 2. Happiness -- Fiction
ISBN 1419705180; 9781419705182

LC 2013042633

This children's book, by Amy Schwartz, is "tribute to 100 everyday things worth celebrating. The list, in rhyming couplets, draws directly from a preschooler's world--from slippery floors to dinosaurs, from goldfish to a birthday wish." (Publisher's note) "Each vignette is illustrated with pictures of smiley kids of different ethnicities following their bliss." (Horn Book Magazine)

"Lollipop colors and utterly cheery simplicity make for a rousing read-aloud chant. A multiethnic cast of small children and adults lists happy-making small joys in rhyme. . . . The pictures range from multiple small vignettes on a spread to full-page illustrations. . . . Fine line and strong color make each image a joy: There's lots of pattern and movement to every figure, therefore muc h to revel in visually. All 100 things are numbered and reproduced as a poster on the inside of the dust jacket, and the endpapers are striped in every color used. It is a book chock-full of fun—what more could one want?" Kirkus

One hundred things that make me happy

Dee Dee and me; written and illustrated by Amy Schwartz. 1st ed. Holiday House 2013 32 p. ill. (reinforced) $16.95
Grades: PreK K 1 2   E
1. Picture books for children 2. Sisters -- Fiction
ISBN 082342524X; 9780823425242

LC 2012016565

In this children's picture book, "Hannah is an easy target for Dee Dee. She's younger and shorter (Dee Dee says the brains are in the 5 1/2 inches of height Hannah's missing),

and she longs for her sister's acceptance. But after one too many manipulations, Hannah learns to assert herself--and now she's sure her brains are growing!" (Kirkus Reviews)

Tiny and Hercules. Roaring Brook Press 2009 un il $16.95
Grades: K 1 2 3   E
1. Mice -- Fiction 2. Elephants -- Fiction 3. Friendship -- Fiction
ISBN 978-1-59643-253-6; 1-59643-253-5

LC 2008-54268

Five short stories about the lives of two unusual friends: Tiny, an elephant with a fear of ice skating and a newfound love of knitting, and Hercules, a mouse with a heart of gold and a desire to learn to paint.

"Even the most sidesplitting moments in these stories . . . are secondary to the touching portrait of a devoted friendship." SLJ

★ **What** James likes best. Atheneum Bks. for Young Readers 2003 un il $16.95
Grades: PreK K 1 2   E
1. Transportation -- Fiction
ISBN 0-689-84059-4

LC 2001-22988

James goes with his parents on an express bus to visit twins, in a taxi to visit Grandma, and in a car to see the county fair, then walks next door with his mother for a play date

"Schwartz's pristine illustrations are streamlined and clean; the lucid, transparent colors make her gouache and pen-and-ink illustrations . . . seem almost weightless. This is a terrifically simple, successful way to get readers and listeners to interact with printed text." Bull Cent Child Books

Willie and Uncle Bill; Amy Schwartz. 1st ed. Holiday House 2012 40 p. col. ill. (hardcover) $16.95
Grades: K 1 2   E
1. Picture books for children 2. Uncles -- Fiction 3. Babysitters -- Fiction
ISBN 0823422038; 9780823422036

LC 2011007274

In this picture book, "[e]ach of the three stories . . . begins 'The doorbell rang three times,' and in comes Uncle Bill to babysit. In the first story, as Uncle Bill . . . makes tacos and chocolate pudding for lunch. . . . The second story features a concoction they call 'Icky Stew.' . . . In the third story, the two of them go out at night and ride the subway to go listen to--and play along with--a garage band." (Horn Book Magazine)

Schwartz, Betty Ann

The **splendid** spotted snake. Workman 2011 un il $13.95
Grades: PreK K   E
1. Snakes -- Fiction
ISBN 978-0-7611-6360-2; 0-7611-6360-3

"A yellow snake, made from a ribbon that is woven through slots in the pages, is born with red spots, but as he gets longer, he gains additional spots of different colors. . . . Turning the pages pulls a new section of ribbon through, making the winding snake grow. Schwartz and Wilensky combine a satisfying tactile experience with a lighthearted lesson on size and color recognition, well-suited for preschoolers." Publ Wkly

Schwartz, Corey Rosen

The **three** ninja pigs; Corey Rosen Schwartz; illustrated by Dan Santat. G.P. Putnam's Sons 2012 40 p. (hardcover) $16.99

Grades: PreK K 1 2 3   E

1. Pigs -- Fiction 2. Fractured fairy tales 3. Martial arts -- Fiction 4. Ninja -- Fiction 5. Stories in rhyme

ISBN 0399255141; 9780399255144

LC 2011037111

In this fractured fairy tale for children by Corey Rosen Schwartz, illustrated by Dan Santat, "These three little pigs just aren't going to take it from that bully anymore! The first starts aikido lessons--he'll make mincemeat out of that wolf! His brother learns a little jujitsu--he'll chop that guy to pieces! But when the wolf actually appears, it turns out these two pigs aren't quite ready after all. Good thing their sister has been training every day." (Publisher's note)

"In this fractured fairy tale, three little pigs are portrayed as frustrated siblings fed up with a wolf that loves to huff and puff and blow houses down. In an attempt to protect their homes in their Japanese village, they train at a Ninja school...Youngsters with an interest in martial arts and those seeking strong female characters will relish this picture book." SLJ

Schwartz, Howard

Gathering sparks; illustrated by Kristina Swarner. Roaring Brook Press 2010 un il $16.99

Grades: K 1 2 3   E

1. Jews -- Fiction 2. Love -- Fiction 3. Stars -- Fiction 4. Kindness -- Fiction 5. Grandfathers -- Fiction 6. Conduct of life -- Fiction

ISBN 978-1-59643-280-2; 1-59643-280-2

Based on the Jewish concept of Tikkun olam, "the narration begins when 'you' ask 'your grandfather' about the origin of the stars. He responds that before people were created, God sent ships carrying light sailing across the sky. These fragile vessels broke apart, scattering their precious cargo across the Earth and sky. It is the job of the human race to gather the 'sparks of light' and restore them to their proper place by doing acts of kindness and love. . . . Schwartz's language is simple, personal, and poetic, and his use of the second person adds a sense of intimacy. . . . Swarner's stylized, painterly artwork is soft and gentle and complements the peaceful mood of the text. . . . This is a handsome book with a timeless message." SLJ

Schwartz, Joanne

★ **City** alphabet; words by Joanne Schwartz; photos by Matt Beam. Groundwood Books 2009 un il $18.95; pa $12.95

Grades: K 1 2 3 4   E

1. Alphabet 2. City and town life

ISBN 978-0-88899-928-3; 0-88899-928-3; 978-0-88899-962-7 pa; 0-88899-962-3 pa

"Stark, metallic and urban, these images may encourage children to think about alternate ways of seeing their surroundings." Publ Wkly

★ **Our** corner grocery store; illustrated by Laura Beingessner. Tundra Books 2009 un il $19.95

Grades: K 1 2 3   E

1. Family life -- Fiction 2. Grandparents -- Fiction 3.

Retail trade -- Fiction 4. Italian Americans -- Fiction

ISBN 978-0-88776-868-2; 0-88776-868-7

"This sweet story takes readers through young Anna Maria's Saturday as she helps her grandparents in their neighborhood store. The day is special for its simplicity; the book is special for its rich evocation of the delights of a little Italian market and the loving relationships between a girl and her grandparents. Beingessner's folksy illustrations and Schwartz's easy text fit well together and are filled with details." SLJ

Schwartz, Roslyn

Splat! starring the vole brothers. by Roslyn Schwartz. Pgw 2014 32 p. $16.95

Grades: PreK K   E

1. Humorous fiction 2. Pigeons -- Fiction 3. Brothers -- Fiction 4. Adventure and adventurers 5. Humorous stories 6. Voles -- Fiction

ISBN 1771470097; 9781771470094

In this book, by Roslyn Schwartz, "the Vole Brothers, are on their next adventure. . . . In signature cinematic style, one half of the loveable bickering duo finds himself at the mercy of a flying pigeon as it flap, flap, flaps by and then drops in, literally with a splat! . . . Nearly wordless and told entirely through sight-gags and sound effects, this easy-to-read adventure." (Publisher's note)

"This slapstick comedy plays out primarily in spare ink and pencil-crayon illustrations, especially in Schwartz's expressive characters. Two vole brothers look up to see a pigeon flying overhead: "Ooooooo..." But then--"SPLAT!" The clueless pigeon drops a bird-poo bomb on one brother's head. The silliness continues with a banana-peel pratfall and more bird poo--it's a recipe for a rollicking if low-brow storytime." Horn Book

Schwarz, Viviane

Is there a dog in this book? Viviane Schwarz. Candlewick Press 2014 32 p. color illustrations $16.99

Grades: PreK   E

1. Cats -- Fiction 2. Dogs -- Fiction 3. Toys and moveable

ISBN 0763669911; 9780763669911

LC 2013955681

This children's story, written and illustrated by Viviane Schwarz, asks "can cats and dogs share the same turf? Revisit the age-old dilemma with a hide-and-seek romp among furry friends. Brimming with humor . . . , here is a lively interactive exploration of the surprising joys of unlikely friendships." (Publisher's note)

"With the uncertainty of There Are Cats in This Book (2008) and There Are No Cats in This Book (2010) behind us, our trio of flighty felines have a new problem: someone drank their milk, chewed their toy, and left behind a peculiar odor. Horrors! It must be a 'snappy and yappy, smelly and noisy, hair and scary' dog. By directly asking the reader for help lifting flaps, the cats go into hiding, first behind a sofa, then a piano, in a closet. . . . With sturdy construction nearly worthy of a board book, this ought to withstand plenty of repeat abuse, which it will get, thanks to Schwarz's gregarious dialogue-only text and her adorably simple pen-and-inks. Let the fur fly." Booklist

There are no cats in this book! Candlewick Press 2010 un il $16.99

Grades: PreK   E
1. Pop-up books 2. Cats -- Fiction 3. Books and reading -- Fiction
ISBN 978-0-7636-4954-8; 0-7636-4954-6
LC 2009-51510
Companion volume to: There are cats in this book (2008)
Filled with the spirit of adventure, three cats pack their suitcases and try to escape from their book.

"This explores on the notion that the book—or at least the cats in it—are looking back at the viewers and interacting with them, and the paper-engineering elements such as foldouts and popups add playful entertainment. . . . The illustrations are uncomplicated yet fluid, with saturated watercolor pigments . . . against warm-toned pages, and elements of layered-paper collage adding dimension." Bull Cent Child Books

Scieszka, Jon
★ **Baloney** (Henry P.) received and decoded by Jon Scieszka; visual recreation by Lane Smith. Viking 2001 un il $15.99
Grades: K 1 2 3   E
1. Life on other planets -- Fiction
ISBN 0-670-89248-3
LC 00-12041
A transmission received from outer space in a combination of different Earth languages tells of an alien schoolboy's fantastic excuse for being late to school again

"Every Earth kid will immediately recognize a soul mate in this extraterrestrial truth-stretcher and tall-tale teller. . . . Illustrator Smith has been having equal fun stretching the visual truth to create a vision of space that is not only artfully outer but also utterly outre. The result is wacky fun for everyone." Booklist

Battle Bunny; by Jon Scieszka and Mac Barnett and Alex; pictures by Matthew Myers but mostly Alex. Simon & Schuster Books for Young Readers 2013 32 p. (hardcover) $14.99
Grades: K 1 2   E
1. Drawing 2. Humorous stories 3. Parties -- Fiction 4. Rabbits -- Fiction 5. Birthdays -- Fiction 6. Supervillains -- Fiction 7. Forest animals -- Fiction
ISBN 1442446730; 9781442446731; 9781442446748
LC 2012025515
In this book, by Jon Scieszka, "Alex has been given a saccharine, sappy, silly-sweet picture book about Birthday Bunny that his grandma found at a garage sale. Alex isn't interested--until he decides to make the book something he'd actually like to read. So he takes out his pencil, sharpens his creativity, and totally transforms the story!" (Publisher's note)

★ The **Frog** Prince continued; story by Jon Scieszka; paintings by Steve Johnson. Viking 1991 un il $15.99; pa $6.99
Grades: 2 3 4 5   E
1. Fairy tales 2. Frogs -- Fiction
ISBN 0-670-83421-1; 0-14-054285-X pa
LC 90-26537
After the frog turns into a prince, he and the Princess do not live happily ever after and the Prince decides to look for a witch to help him turn back into a frog

"The dialogue is witty; the plot, as logical as it is offbeat. Steve Johnson's paintings, executed in a rich and somber palette, are like stage settings; his depiction of the various characters is inspired." Horn Book

Pete's party; written by Jon Scieszka; characters and environments developed by the Design Garage: David Gordon, Loren Long, David Shannon. Aladdin 2008 un il (Jon Scieszka's Trucktown: Ready-to-roll) lib bdg $13.89; pa $3.99
Grades: PreK K 1   E
1. Trucks -- Fiction 2. Signs and signboards -- Fiction
ISBN 978-1-4169-4149-1 lib bdg; 1-4169-4149-5 lib bdg; 978-1-4169-4138-5 pa; 1-4169-4138-X pa
LC 2007027154
The Trucktown trucks follow the road signs directing them to Pete's party

This title "will draw beginning readers into the zany world of anthropomorphic trucks, whose distinct personalities and endearing facial expressions roll across the colorful pages." SLJ
Other titles in this series are:
Dizzy Izzy (2010)
Kat's mystery (2009)
Melvin's valentine (2009)
Snow trucking! (2008)
Zoom! boom? bully (2008)
The spooky tire (2009)
Uh-oh Max (2009)

★ **Robot** Zot! illustrated by David Shannon. Simon & Schuster Books for Young Readers 2009 un il $17.99
Grades: K 1 2   E
1. Robots -- Fiction
ISBN 978-1-4169-6394-3; 1-4169-6394-4
LC 2008-20031
On a mission to conquer planet Earth, tiny but fearless Robot Zot and his mechanical sidekick leave a path of destruction as they battle kitchen appliances.

"Scieszka laces his action-filled narrative with rhymes and repetitive robot phrases. . . . Shannon's acrylic artwork offers bright colors and plenty of humor." Publ Wkly

★ **Science** verse; illustrated by Lane Smith. Viking 2004 un il $16.99
Grades: 2 3 4 5   E
1. Poetry -- Fiction 2. Science -- Fiction
ISBN 0-670-91057-0
LC 2004-1641
Companion volume to Math curse
When the teacher tells his class that they can hear the poetry of science in everything, a student is struck with a curse and begins hearing nothing but science verses that sound very much like some well known poems.

"Children need not be familiar with the works upon which the spoofs are based to enjoy the humor, but this is a perfect opportunity to introduce the originals and to discuss parody as a poetic form. The dynamic cartoons are an absolute delight." SLJ

Smash! crash! illustrated by David Shannon, Loren Long, and David Gordon. Simon & Schuster 2008 un il (Jon Scieszka's Trucktown) $16.99

Grades: PreK K   **E**
1. Trucks -- Fiction
ISBN 1-4169-4133-9

"Jack Truck, a red flatbed with chrome exhaust stacks, and best friend Dump Truck Dan, a blue guy with a yellow cab and mud flaps, adore the smash and crash of work in progress. . . . Scieszka . . . revs readers up with gear-grinding noise and rowdy antics. . . . Illustrators Shannon, Long and Gordon embed mechanical shapes in their punchy display type, and they contribute panoramic vistas." Publ Wkly

Other titles in this series are:
Melvin might? (2008)
Truckery rhymes (2009)

Uh-oh Max; written by Jon Scieszka; characters and environments developed by the Design Garage: David Shannon, Loren Long, David Gordon. Aladdin Paperbacks 2009 un il (Jon Scieszka's Trucktown: Ready-to-roll) $13.25; pa $3.99
Grades: PreK K 1   **E**
1. Trucks -- Fiction 2. Traffic accidents -- Fiction
ISBN 978-1-4169-4152-1; 1-4169-4152-5; 978-1-4169-4141-5 pa; 1-4169-4141-X pa
     LC 2007027809
When Max gets in trouble after speeding up a ramp, all of his Trucktown friends try to help out.

Scillian, Devin
Pappy's handkerchief; by Devin Scillian; illustrated by Chris Ellison. Sleeping Bear Press 2007 un il (Tales of young Americans) $17.95
Grades: 2 3 4   **E**
1. Oklahoma -- Fiction 2. Family life -- Fiction 3. African Americans -- Fiction 4. Frontier and pioneer life -- Fiction
ISBN 978-1-58536-316-2
     LC 2007006394
In 1889, young Moses and his family sell everything they own and leave their Baltimore, Maryland, home to join many other settlers—black and white—in a race to claim land in the newly-opened territory of Oklahoma.

"This history of a unique and interesting part of the settling of the West is illustrated in beautiful paintings of warm, soft browns, yellows, and blues that complement the narrative, together creating a fascinating look at the past." SLJ

Scott, Ann Herbert
On Mother's lap; illustrated by Glo Coalson. Clarion Bks. 1992 32p il $16; pa $6.95; bd bk $5.95
Grades: PreK K   **E**
1. Inuit -- Fiction 2. Mother-child relationship -- Fiction
ISBN 0-395-58920-7; 0-395-62976-4 pa; 0-618-05159-7 bd bk
     LC 91-17765
A newly illustrated edition of the title first published 1972 by McGraw-Hill

"Sitting on his mother's lap, a young Eskimo boy gathers his belongings until he, some toys, his puppy, and a blanket are all crowded together in the rocking chair. When his baby sister cries, the boy claims there is no room for her, but Mother proves him wrong, and the threesome settle comfortably in the chair. Soft illustrations depict a cozy scene and a loving family." Horn Book

Scotton, Rob
Russell the sheep; by Rob Scotton. HarperCollins 2005 un il $17.99; lib bdg $18.89
Grades: PreK K 1 2   **E**
1. Sheep -- Fiction 2. Bedtime -- Fiction
ISBN 0-06-059848-4; 0-06-059849-2 lib bdg
     LC 2003-24274
Russell the sheep tries all different ways to get to sleep

"Scotton makes a captivating debut with this comical tale. He illustrates it with a witty, engaging, and fluffy character bathed in calming blue hues." SLJ

Other titles about Russell are:
Russell and the lost treasure (2006)
Russell's Christmas magic (2007)

Splat the cat. HarperCollins 2008 un il $16.99; lib bdg $17.89
Grades: K 1 2   **E**
1. School stories 2. Cats -- Fiction 3. Friendship -- Fiction
ISBN 978-0-06-083154-7; 0-06-083154-5; 978-0-06-083155-4 lib bdg; 0-06-083155-3 lib bdg
     LC 2008-20218
"The fuzzy black feline is worried about his first day of school, and despite determined attempts to avoid the inevitable, he ends up there. . . . This lighthearted story, told with a generous helping of humor and goofy characterizations, will have broad appeal." SLJ

Other titles about Splat are:
Love, Splat (2008)
Merry Christmas, Splat (2009)
Scaredy-cat, Splat! (2010)
Splat the cat sings flat (2011)
Splish, splash, Splat! (2011)

Sebe, Masayuki
Let's count to 100! Kids Can Press 2011 il $16.95
Grades: PreK K 1 2   **E**
1. Counting
ISBN 978-1-55453-661-0; 1-55453-661-8
"Every spread in this high-energy counting book contains 100 cartoon people, objects, or animals, as Sebe provides enthusiastic prompts. . . . Conversations and interactions between the creatures add to the fun. . . . With much to discover, a wry sense of humor, and a clean aesthetic, it's a lively pick for readers ready for more adventurous counting challenges." Publ Wkly

Seder, Rufus Butler
Gallop! [by] Rufus Butler Seder. Workman Pub. 2007 un il $12.95
Grades: PreK K 1 2   **E**
1. Stories in rhyme 2. Animals -- Fiction 3. Animal locomotion -- Fiction
ISBN 978-0-7611-4763-3
     LC 2007024247
"Readers will gasp with delight when they open this book." Publ Wkly

"A first book of motion for kids, [this book] shows a horse in full gallop and a turtle swimming up the page. A dog runs, a cat springs, an eagle soars, and a butterfly flutters. Created by Rufus Butler Seder . . . Scanimation is a state-of-the-art six-phase animation process that combines the 'persistence of vision' principle with a striped acetate overlay to give the illusion of movement." Publisher's note

Swing! Workman Pub. 2008 un il $12.95
Grades: PreK K 1 2   E
  1. Sports -- Fiction
  ISBN 978-0-7611-5127-2; 0-7611-5127-3

"Open the die-cut cover and see a baseball player swing his bat at a ball, then watch as the ball zooms ever-larger to fit the acetate window showcasing all this action. . . . Colored fonts and multicolored borders offset the severity of the b&w pictures and generate reader participation. . . . On other spreads, child athletes perform soccer drills, run, cartwheel, twirl on ice skates, shoot hoops, swim and lead cheers—it's all jaw-dropping, even if the novelty technology has yet to find its most imaginative application." Publ Wkly

Waddle! Workman Pub. 2009 un il $12.95
Grades: PreK K 1 2   E
  1. Animals -- Fiction 2. Animal locomotion -- Fiction
  ISBN 978-0-7611-5112-8; 0-7611-5112-5

Text asks if the reader can move like a variety of animals. Striped acetate overlays on board pages give illustrations the illusion of movement.

"The level of detail . . . is striking . . . [and the] readers should find the animations mesmerizing." Publ Wkly

Seeger, Laura Vaccaro
  ★ **Black?** white! day? night! a book of opposites.
Roaring Brook Press 2006 20p il $16.95
Grades: PreK K 1 2   E
  1. Opposites
  ISBN 978-1-59643-185-0; 1-59643-185-7

LC 2005-32378

On the first page of this picture book "a large black flap with a cutout [reveals] a black bat set against a pure white background. The single word black? printed in white, stands out clearly on the page. When kids lift the flap, they'll see the word white! (in white type) and discover that what appeared to be a bat is really the mouth of a ghost. Each of 18 opposites is similarly conveyed using only one word and the lift of a flap. . . . Each flap is a different bold color . . . and the scenes under the flaps are in keeping with the simple yet sophisticated graphic design of the book. Thick, shiny pages add to the sense of richness." Booklist

Bully; by Laura Vaccaro Seeger. 1st ed. Roaring Brook Press 2013 40 p. ill. (reinforced) $16.99
Grades: PreK K 1 2   E
  1. Invective -- Fiction 2. Bulls -- Fiction 3. Bullies -- Fiction 4. Domestic animals -- Fiction
  ISBN 1596436301; 9781596436305

LC 2012012991

In this book, author Laura Vaccaro Seeger "uses . . . barnyard animals to tell her story about bullying, casting a bull in the title role. The trouble starts when the young bull is rejected by an older one: 'Go away!' it shouts. The young bull is shaken, but he's learned something--how to hurt others. . . . The more he abuses the others, the larger he grows, his angry bluster feeding his self-importance. At last a goat speaks truth to power: 'Bully!'" (Publishers Weekly)

Dog and Bear; tricks and treats. Laura Vaccaro Seeger. Roaring Brook Press 2014 32 p. color illustrations (hardcover) $14.99
Grades: PreK K 1   E
  1. Dogs -- Fiction 2. Bears -- Fiction 3. Halloween -- Fiction 4. Friendship -- Fiction 5. Teddy bears -- Fiction
  ISBN 1596436328; 9781596436329

LC 2013016658

In this book, written and illustrated by Laura Vaccaro Seeger, part of the Dog and Bear Series, "Dog and Bear are back in three new Halloween stories that are sure to delight their many fans and win them new ones. Join them as they search for the perfect costume, hand out candy to trick-or-treaters (or not!), and then go trick-or-treating themselves." (Publisher's note)

"The humor strengthens the friendship of the eager and fun-loving characters in an amusing and inclusive way. The acrylic paint and India ink illustrations are painterly with broad brushstrokes and thick black outlines, while the simple white background keeps the spotlight on the action." SLJ

  ★ **Dog** and Bear: two friends, three stories. Roaring Brook Press 2007 un il $12.95
Grades: PreK K 1   E
  1. Dogs -- Fiction 2. Bears -- Fiction 3. Friendship -- Fiction
  ISBN 978-1-59643-053-2; 1-59643-053-2

LC 2006-11687

"Bear is a multicolored stuffed toy; Dog is a playful, rowdy dachshund. . . . In the first episode, Dog helps timid Bear down from a high stool. In the second, Dog wants to play, but Bear needs some quiet time alone. And in the final story, Dog suffers a small identity crisis, but Bear helps him recognize that he is just fine as he is. . . . Seeger's minimal text is perfectly paced for new readers, who will love the dose of humor at each story's close. In pictures as spare and charming as the text, Seeger captures preschoolers' expressions and body language." Booklist

Other titles about Dog and Bear are:
Dog and Bear: two's company (2008)
Dog and Bear: three to get ready (2009)

  ★ **Dog** and Bear: two's company. Roaring Brook Press 2008 un il $12.95
Grades: PreK K 1   E
  1. Dogs -- Fiction 2. Bears -- Fiction 3. Friendship -- Fiction
  ISBN 978-1-59643-273-4; 1-59643-273-X

LC 2007-10038

Companion volume to: Dog and Bear: two friends, three stories (2007)

Dog and Bear celebrate Bear's birthday, have their first falling out, and take care of each other when Dog is under the weather.

"Seeger employs casual gouaches in terracotta, ochre and olive green on a white background. . . . Her rough-hewn ink outlines and unpolished brushwork have homespun warmth." Publ Wkly

  ★ **First** the egg. Roaring Brook Press 2007 un il $14.95

Grades: PreK K   **E**
1. Growth
ISBN 978-1-59643-272-7; 1-59643-272-1

LC 2006-32924

A Caldecott Medal honor book, 2008

"Pages are color-saturated and as minimalist as the text.
. . . Cleverly conceived and executed cutouts reinforce the
book's tactile appeal. . . . The best picture books creat a
world in themselves, and this tour de force is one of them."
Horn Book

★ **Green**; Laura Vaccaro Seeger. Roaring Brook Press
2012 40 p.
Grades: PreK K 1 2   **E**
1. Plants -- Color 2. Animals -- Color 3. Stories in
rhyme 4. Picture books for children 5. Green -- Fiction
ISBN 9781596433977

LC 2011013495

Caldecott Honor Book (2013)

This picture book is an exploration of the color green.
"In four simple quatrains, two-word lines each suggest a
kind of green, introducing a scene that might show natural,
domestic or built elements. . . . [Laura Vaccaro] Seeger's
paintings vary in perspective; in their portrayal of animals
such as fish, a tiger, and a lizard, trees and flowers, and children. The die-cuts reveal green-related words demonstrated
by the vignettes within the paintings." (Kirkus Reviews)

★ **Lemons** are not red. Roaring Brook Press 2004
un il $14.95
Grades: PreK K 1 2   **E**
1. Color
ISBN 1-59643-008-7

"The first spread reads, 'Lemons are not/ RED.' The
word 'RED' appears on a bright yellow page beneath the
die-cut shape of a lemon with a red background showing
through. When the page is turned, the die-cut shape falls
on the correct yellow background, with the words 'Lemons
are YELLOW' underneath. . . . This framework continues
throughout the book. . . . Illustrated with richly colored yet
simple oil paintings, this offering will delight preschoolers."
SLJ

★ **One** boy. Roaring Brook Press 2008 un il $14.95
Grades: PreK K 1 2   **E**
1. Counting 2. Painting -- Fiction 3. Vocabulary --
Fiction
ISBN 978-1-59643-274-1; 1-59643-274-8

LC 2007-45941

A Geisel Award honor book, 2009

A boy creates ten paintings in this counting book that
also explores the relationship of words within words.

Seeger "crafts another nifty peek-a-boo book, counting
to 10 and identifying new words by exposing or covering
letters with die-cuts. . . . Seeger uses pared-down digital art
and flat saturated colors." Publ Wkly

★ **Walter** was worried. Roaring Book Press 2005 un
il $15.95
Grades: PreK K 1 2   **E**
1. Storms -- Fiction 2. Emotions -- Fiction
ISBN 1-59643-066-8

LC 2004-024558

Children's faces, depicted with letters of the alphabet,
react to the onset of a storm and its aftermath in this picture
book, accompanied by simple alliterative text.

"The artwork uses bold colors with wide brush marks as
backdrops and primary colors with almost graphic shapes
to represent rain, snow flakes, leaves, and branches. With
only one sentence per page, there is surprising depth in this
wonderful collaboration of art and story." SLJ

★ **What** if? Roaring Brook Press 2010 un il $15.99
Grades: PreK K   **E**
1. Beaches -- Fiction 2. Seals (Animals) -- Fiction 3.
Choice (Psychology)
ISBN 978-1-59643-398-4; 1-59643-398-1

This book presents three different scenarios which show
what happens when different choices are made. "Ages three
to six." (Bull Cent Child Books)

"What if a boy found a beach ball and kicked it into the
ocean? What if two seals found it and began to play? What
if a third seal appeared on the beach looking for a friend?
In this . . . book, Laura Vaccaro Seeger shows us the same
story with three different outcomes, each highlighting the
possibility in possibilities." Publisher's note

Segal, John
Alistair and Kip's great adventure; written and illus-
trated by John Segal. Margaret K. McElderry Books 2008
un il $15.99
Grades: PreK K 1 2   **E**
1. Cats -- Fiction 2. Dogs -- Fiction 3. Whales --
Fiction 4. Boats and boating -- Fiction
ISBN 978-1-4169-0280-5; 1-4169-0280-5

LC 2006019870

Alistair the cat and Kip the dog build a boat and soon find
themselves sailing down the creek to the river to the bay and
out to sea where a violent storm threatens to capsize them

"The quick-paced story is told through both dialogue and
simple narrative. Beautifully rendered watercolors in bright
hues comically depict the self-confident cat and his smaller
canine pal." SLJ

Carrot soup; written and illustrated by John Segal.
Margaret K. McElderry Books 2006 un il $12.95
Grades: PreK K 1 2   **E**
1. Carrots -- Fiction 2. Rabbits -- Fiction 3. Gardening
-- Fiction
ISBN 0-689-87702-1

LC 2004-16963

After working hard on his garden all spring and summer, Rabbit looks forward to harvest time when he can make
soup, but every carrot disappears and Rabbit must find out
who has taken them. Includes a recipe for carrot soup

"The clues are in Segal's stylized pencil and watercolor
pictures, and observant children won't have any trouble determining where the carrots went. The delicate springtime
greens and browns used in the background contrast nicely
with Rabbit's comically expressive face." Booklist

Far far away. Philomel Books 2009 un il $16.99
Grades: PreK K 1   **E**
1. Pigs -- Fiction 2. Runaway children -- Fiction 3.
Mother-child relationship -- Fiction
ISBN 978-0-399-25007-1; 0-399-25007-7

LC 2008035855

When an unhappy young pig decides to run away, his mother helps him to see that everything he needs and wants is right there at home.

"Segal's art, executed in pencil and watercolors, features stylized pigs set against backgrounds that alternate between mottled colors and pure white. The pictures make good use of space and squeeze every bit of humor out of a familiar situation." Booklist

Seibold, J. Otto

★ **Olive** the other reindeer; by J. Otto Seibold and Vivian Walsh. Chronicle Bks. 1997 un il $15.99

Grades: PreK K 1 2   E

    1. Dogs -- Fiction 2. Reindeer -- Fiction 3. Christmas -- Fiction 4. Santa Claus -- Fiction

    ISBN 0-8118-1807-1

                    LC 97-9876

Thinking that "all of the other reindeer" she hears people singing about include her, Olive the dog reports to the North Pole to help Santa Claus on Christmas Eve

"Seibold has developed a signature style with computer digitized art, and his playful skewed lines and warm shades of ochre, pimento and olive green are user-friendly." Publ Wkly

Seki, Sunny

Yuko-chan and the Daruma doll; the adventures of a blind Japanese girl who saves her village. story and illustrations by Sunny Seki. Tuttle Pub. 2012 32 p.

Grades: 1 2 3   E

    1. Fables 2. Blind -- Fiction 3. Dolls -- Fiction 4. Japan -- Fiction

    ISBN 4805311878; 9784805311875

                    LC 2011031332

In this children's story, by Sunny Seki, "Yuko-chan, an adventurous blind orphan, . . . trips and tumbles down a snowy cliff. She discovers . . . her tea gourd, regardless of how she drops it, always lands right-side-up. . . . Inspired by this, she creates the famous Daruma doll toy, which rights itself when tipped--a true symbol of resilience. Thanks to Yuko-chan's invention, the villagers are able to earn a living and feed themselves by selling the dolls." (Publisher's note)

Selbert, Kathryn

War dogs; Churchill and Rufus. Kathryn Selbert. Charlesbridge 2013 48 p. ill. (reinforced) $17.95

Grades: 2 3 4   E

    1. World War, 1939-1945 -- Great Britain 2. Dogs -- Great Britain 3. Great Britain -- History -- George VI, 1936-1952

    ISBN 1580894143; 9781580894142

                    LC 2012000794

This children's book, by Kathryn Selbert, profiles Winston Churchill and his dog. "Churchill, often noted for his tenacious, bulldog-like personality, was one of the greatest wartime leaders of the modern era. But few people know that he was also a devoted poodle owner. The friendship between the British Bulldog and his faithful miniature poodle, Rufus, spans World War II and takes readers through the bombings of London, the invasion of Normandy, and postwar reconstruction." (Publisher's note)

Includes bibliographical references

Sendak, Maurice

★ **Alligators** all around; an alphabet. Harper & Row 1962 un il lib bdg $16.89; pa $5.95

Grades: PreK K 1 2   E

    1. Alphabet

    ISBN 0-06-025530-7 lib bdg; 0-06-443254-8 pa

Originally published in smaller format as volume one of the Nutshell library

An alphabet book of alligators doing dishes, juggling jelly beans, throwing tantrums and wearing wigs, all from A to Z

★ **Bumble**-Ardy. HarperCollins 2011 un il $17.95

Grades: PreK K 1 2   E

    1. Counting 2. Stories in rhyme 3. Pigs -- Fiction 4. Parties -- Fiction 5. Birthdays -- Fiction

    ISBN 978-0-06-205198-1; 0-06-205198-9

Bumble-Ardy is a mischievous pig who has reached the age of nine without ever having had a birthday party. But all that changes when Bumble throws a party for himself and invites all his friends, leading to a wild masquerade that quickly gets out of hand.

"Savvy readers will notice references to Sendak's previous books and an ebullient cameo; scholars will undoubtedly discover personal iconography in the densely populated watercolors. Familiar themes abound: the quest for home, the capacity children have for navigating their circumstances, the pleasure of cake, the presence of death. . . . Nobody does naughty quite like [Sendak] does." SLJ

★ **Chicken** soup with rice; a book of months. Harper & Row 1962 30p il lib bdg $16.89; pa $5.95

Grades: PreK K 1 2   E

    1. Stories in rhyme 2. Seasons -- Fiction

    ISBN 0-06-025535-8 lib bdg; 0-06-443253-X pa

Originally published in smaller format as volume two of the Nutshell library

Pictures and verse illustrate the delight of eating chicken soup with rice in every season of the year

★ **In** the night kitchen; 25th anniversary ed; HarperCollins Pubs. 1996 un il $17.95; lib bdg $18.89; pa $6.95

Grades: PreK K 1 2 3   E

    1. Fantasy fiction

    ISBN 0-06-026668-6; 0-06-026669-4 lib bdg; 0-06-443436-2 pa

First published 1970

A Caldecott Medal honor book, 1971

"A perfect midnight fantasy. The feelings, smells, sights, and comforting emotions which young children experience are here in lovely dream colors." Brooklyn. Art Books for Child

★ **Mommy?** [art by Maurice Sendak; scenario by Arthur Yorinks; paper engineering by Matthew Reinhart] Scholastic 2006 un il $24.95

Grades: PreK K 1 2   E

    1. Pop-up books 2. Monsters -- Fiction

    ISBN 0-439-88050-5

"This pop-up tour de force abounds with humor, vibrant artwork, and visual fireworks." SLJ

★ **One** was Johnny; a counting book. Harper & Row 1962 un il lib bdg $16.89; pa $5.95

Grades: PreK K 1 2   E

   1. Counting

   ISBN 0-06-025540-4 lib bdg; 0-06-443251-3 pa

Originally published in smaller format as volume three of the Nutshell library

Counting from one to ten and back again to one, Johnny, who starts off alone, acquires too many numbered visitors for his own comfort, until they disappear one by one

★ **Outside** over there. Harper & Row 1981 un il $22.95; pa $9.95

Grades: K 1 2 3   E

   1. Fairy tales 2. Sisters -- Fiction

   ISBN 0-06-025523-4; 0-06-443185-1 pa

                            LC 79-2682

A Caldecott Medal honor book, 1982

With Papa off to sea and Mama despondent, Ida must go outside over there to rescue her baby sister from goblins who steal her to be a goblin's bride

"A gentle yet powerful story in the romantic tradition. . . . Soft in tones, rich in the use of light and color . . . the pictures are particularly distinctive for the tenderness with which the children's faces are drawn; the classic handling of texture, the imaginative juxtaposition of infant faces and the baroque landscape details that might have come from Renaissance paintings." Bull Cent Child Books

★ **Pierre**; a cautionary tale in five chapters and a prologue. Harper & Row 1962 48p il lib bdg $16.89; pa $5.95

Grades: PreK K 1 2   E

   1. Stories in rhyme

   ISBN 0-06-025965-5 lib bdg; 0-06-443252-1 pa

Originally published in smaller format as volume four of the Nutshell library

A story in verse about a little boy called Pierre who insisted upon saying 'I don't care' until he said it once too often and learned a well needed lesson

★ **Where** the wild things are; story and pictures by Maurice Sendak. Harper & Row 1963 un il $17.95; lib bdg $18.89; pa $8.95

Grades: PreK K 1 2   E

   1. Fantasy fiction

   ISBN 0-06-025492-0; 0-06-025493-9 lib bdg; 0-06-443178-9 pa

Awarded the Caldecott Medal, 1964

"This vibrant picture book in luminous, understated full color has proved utterly engrossing to children with whom it has been shared. . . . A sincere, preceptive contribution which bears repeated examination." Horn Book

Senior, Olive

Anna Carries Water; by Olive Senior; illustrated by Laura James. Tradewind Books 2014 40 p. $18.95

Grades: PreK K 1 2   E

   1. Water -- Fiction 2. Jamaica -- Fiction 3. Family life -- Fiction 4. Brothers and sisters -- Fiction

   ISBN 1896580602; 9781896580609

In this book, by Olive Senior and illustrated by Laura James, "Anna fetches water from the spring every day, but she can't carry it on her head like her older brothers and sisters can. In this charming and poetic family story set in Jamaica, . . . Senior shows young readers the power of determination, as Anna achieves her goal and overcomes her fear." (Publisher's note)

"Anna, the youngest in a large family, desperately wants to carry her coffee can of water on her head. She doesn't yet have this skill that all her siblings have mastered. Why, Karen can even read while she carries a water container on her head, a detail noted in the exuberant paintings accompanying the simple text, ideal for reading aloud...When water easily comes out of a faucet, young readers rarely think about the difficult chore of carrying water, but they will empathize with Anna's desire to reach an important milestone." (Kirkus)

Birthday suit; by Olive Senior; paintings by Eugenie Fernandes. Annick Press 2012 32 p.

Grades: PreK K   E

   1. Nudity 2. Picture books for children 3. Children's clothing -- Fiction

   ISBN 1554513685; 9781554513680

This book tells the story of "Johnny, [who] likes to run around naked . . . . But now that he's 4, mom insists on clothes at all times. She buys him red trunks for playing in the water. As soon as her back is turned, however, he's out of them and back to the titular birthday suit. . . . It takes a man-to-man talk with dad for Johnny to realize that he really does want to be a big boy. He puts on his overalls and everybody claps. Now he has fun with clothes, zipping and tying and snapping." (Kirkus Reviews)

Senir, Mirik

When I first held you; a lullaby from Israel. [by] Mirik Snir; [illustrated by] Eleyor Snir; translated from the Hebrew by Mary Jane Shubow. Kar-Ben 2009 un il $9.95

Grades: PreK K 1   E

   1. Lullabies 2. Stories in rhyme 3. Nature -- Fiction 4. Parent-child relationship -- Fiction

   ISBN 978-0-7613-5098-9; 0-7613-5098-5

                            LC 2008-53741

A parent describes, in rhyming text, the beauty of the world on the day a young child is born

"The unassuming and calming melodious text, fluidly translated by Shubow, will certainly encourage serenity and comfort at the end of each day." Kirkus

Serfozo, Mary

Plumply, dumply pumpkin; written by Mary Serfozo; illustrated by Valeria Petrone. Margaret K. McElderry Bks. 2001 un il hardcover o.p. pa $6.99; bd bk $6.99

Grades: PreK K 1 2   E

   1. Stories in rhyme 2. Pumpkin -- Fiction 3. Halloween -- Fiction

   ISBN 0-689-83834-4; 0-689-87135-X pa; 0-689-86277-6 bd bk

                            LC 00-32421

Peter finds the perfect pumpkin so that he and his Dad can make a jack-o-lantern

"Toddlers will relish the bouncy, rhyming stanzas and silly wordplay, which help make this a great, nonspooky Halloween storytime choice. The subtly textured computer-generated art has solid child appeal." Booklist

Serrano, Francisco

La Malinche; the princess who helped Cortés conquer the Aztec Empire. Francisco Serrano. Groundwood Books/House of Anansi Press 2012 37 p. $18.95

Grades: 4 5 6   **E**

1. Picture books for children

ISBN 1554981115; 9781554981113

This is a "picture-book biography about the controversial Mexican figure 'La Malinche.' Malinali, a Nahuatl princess, was sold into slavery and eventually traded to Spanish explorer Hernán Cortés." (School Library Journal) "Presented here as an enigma La Malinche is viewed by some as the mother of a new culture and by others as a traitor who helped Cortes defeat an indigenous people of which she was a part. What is agreed upon is that Cortes . . . may not have had success without her." (Children's Literature)

Seto, Loretta

Mooncakes; Loretta Seto, Renne Benoit. Orca Book Publishers 2013 32 p. (hardcover) $19.95

Grades: PreK K 1 2   **E**

1. Moon -- Folklore 2. Festivals -- Fiction

ISBN 1459801075; 9781459801073

LC 2012952944

This children's story, by Loretta Seto, illustrated by Renné Benoit, follows "a young girl who shares the special celebration of the Chinese Moon Festival with her parents. As they eat mooncakes, drink tea and watch the night sky together, Mama and Baba tell ancient tales of a magical tree that can never be cut down, the Jade Rabbit who came to live on the moon and one brave woman's journey to eternal life." (Publisher's note)

Seuss, Dr., 1904-1991

The **500** hats of Bartholomew Cubbins. Random House 1990 un il $14.95

Grades: PreK K 1 2 3   **E**

1. Hats -- Fiction

ISBN 0-394-84484-X

LC 88-38412

A reissue of the title first published 1938 by Vanguard Press

"It is a lovely bit of tomfoolery which keeps up the suspense and surprise until the last page, and of the same ingenious and humorous imagination are the author's black and white illustrations in which a red cap and then an infinite number of red caps titillate the eye." N Y Times Book Rev

★ **And** to think that I saw it on Mulberry Street. Random House 1989 un il $14.95; lib bdg $15.99

Grades: PreK K 1 2   **E**

1. Stories in rhyme

ISBN 0-394-84494-7; 0-394-94494-1 lib bdg

LC 88-38411

A reissue of the title first published 1937 by Vanguard Press

"A fresh, inspiring picture-story book in bright colors. . . . As convincing to a child as to the psychologist in quest of a book with an appeal to the child's imaginations." Horn Book

Bartholomew and the oobleck; written and illustrated by Dr. Seuss. Random House 1949 un il $14.95; lib bdg $15.99

Grades: PreK K 1 2   **E**

ISBN 0-394-80075-3; 0-394-90075-8 lib bdg

A Caldecott Medal honor book, 1950

"Bored with the same old kinds of weather, the King of Didd commanded his magicians to stir up something new and different. What they produced was a gooey, gummy green stuff which might have wrecked the kingdom had it not been for Bartholomew Cubbins, the page boy." Booklist

The **Bippolo** Seed and other lost stories; by Dr. Seuss; introduction by Charles D. Cohen. Random House 2011 69p il $15

Grades: K 1 2 3 4   **E**

1. Short stories 2. Stories in rhyme

ISBN 978-0-375-86435-3; 0-375-86435-0

LC 2009052588

Presents seven Dr. Seuss stories first published in magazines between 1948 and 1959, with an introduction and commentary on each.

"The stories' rhymed couplets are pitch-perfect, the verse's rhythm as snappy as in any of Seuss's better-known works. . . . Fans old and young will deem these 'lost' stories a tremendous find." Publ Wkly

★ The **cat** in the hat; by Dr. Seuss. 50th anniversary ed.; Random House 2007 61p il $8.99 **E**

1. Stories in rhyme 2. Cats -- Fiction

ISBN 978-0-394-80001-1

A reissue of the title first published 1957

A nonsense story in verse illustrated by the author about an unusual cat and his tricks which he displayed for the children one rainy day

Another title about The cat in the hat is:

The cat in the hat comes back (1958)

★ **Green** eggs and ham. Beginner Bks. 1960 62p il $8.99; lib bdg $11.99; pa $9.95

Grades: PreK K 1 2   **E**

1. Stories in rhyme 2. Food -- Fiction

ISBN 0-394-80016-8; 0-394-90016-2 lib bdg; 0-394-89220-8 pa

"The happy theme of refusal-to-eat changing to relish will be doubly enjoyable to the child who finds many common edibles as nauseating as the title repast. The pacing throughout is magnificent, and the opening five pages, on which the focal character introduces himself with a placard: 'I am Sam,' are unsurpassed in the controlled-vocabulary literature." Saturday Rev

Hooray for Diffendoofer Day! [by] Dr. Seuss with some help from Jack Prelutsky & Lane Smith. Knopf 1998 un il $17; lib bdg $18.99

Grades: PreK K 1 2   **E**

1. School stories 2. Stories in rhyme

ISBN 0-679-89008-4; 0-679-99008-9 lib bdg

LC 97-39725

The students of Diffendoofer School celebrate their unusual teachers and curriculum, including Miss Fribble who teaches laughing, Miss Bonkers who teaches frogs to dance, and Mr. Katz who builds robotic rats

"Given an unfinished manuscript (some sketches, snippets of verse, and jottings of names—but no plot) retrieved after Seuss's death, Prelutsky and Smith have brought this fragment to fruition in a style that does credit to all three artists." Horn Book Guide

Horton and the Kwuggerbug and more lost stories; by Dr. Seuss; introduction by Charles D. Cohen. Random House Inc 2014 56 p. (trade) $15

Grades: K 1 2 3 4   E
   1. Stories in rhyme 2. Children's stories 3. Short stories 4. Children's stories, American
   ISBN 0385382987; 9780375973420; 9780385382984
            LC 2014003038

In this children's book by Dr. Seuss, "Seuss fans will learn more about Horton's integrity, Marco's amazing imagination, a narrowly avoided disaster on Mullbery Street, and a devious Grinch." The book features "a color palette enhanced beyond that of the magazines in which the stories originally appeared." (Publisher's note)

"Readers will delight in this book of "lost" stories, told in Seuss's signature inventive rhyme...The introduction, by scholar Charles D. Cohen, is chock-full of background and offers the provenance of these stories collected from a variety of magazines. Dr. Seuss stories are irresistible, and this collection is no exception." SLJ

★ **Horton** hatches the egg. Random House 1940 un il $14.95; lib bdg $15.99

Grades: PreK K 1 2   E
   1. Stories in rhyme 2. Elephants -- Fiction
   ISBN 0-394-80077-X; 0-394-90077-4 lib bdg

"Horton, the elephant, is faithful one hundred percent as he carries out his promise to watch a bird's egg while she takes a rest. Hilarious illustrations and a surprise ending." Adventuring with Books. 2d edition

★ **Horton** hears a Who! Random House 1954 un il $14.95; lib bdg $16.99

Grades: PreK K 1 2   E
   1. Stories in rhyme 2. Elephants -- Fiction
   ISBN 0-394-80078-8; 0-394-90078-2 lib bdg

"The verses are full of the usual lively, informal language and amazing rhymes that have delighted such a world-wide audience in the good 'doctor's' other books." N Y Her Trib Books

"Although considered the biggest blame fool in the Jungle of Nool, the faithful and kindhearted elephant of 'Horton hatches the egg' believing that a person's a person no matter how small, stanchly defends the Whos, too-small-to-be-seen inhabitants of Whoville, a town which exists on a dust speck." Booklist

★ **How** the Grinch stole Christmas. Random House 1957 un il $15; lib bdg $18

Grades: PreK K 1 2   E
   1. Stories in rhyme 2. Christmas -- Fiction
   ISBN 0-394-80079-6; 0-394-90079-0 lib bdg

"The verse is as lively and the pages are as bright and colorful as anyone could wish." Saturday Rev

★ **If** I ran the circus. Random House 1956 un il $14.95; lib bdg $15.99

Grades: PreK K 1 2   E
   1. Stories in rhyme 2. Circus -- Fiction
   ISBN 0-394-80080-X; 0-394-90080-4 lib bdg

The author-illustrator "presents the fabulous Circus Mc-Gurkus with its highly imaginative young owner, Morris McGurk and its intrepid performer, Sneelock, behind whose store the circus is to be housed. There are the expected number of strange creatures with nonsensical names, but the real humor lies in the situations, and especially those involving Mr. Sneelock. There is fun for the entire family here." Bull Cent Child Books

★ **If** I ran the zoo. Random House 1950 un il $14.95; lib bdg $16.99

Grades: PreK K 1 2   E
   1. Stories in rhyme 2. Zoos -- Fiction
   ISBN 0-394-80081-8; 0-394-90081-2 lib bdg
   A Caldecott Medal honor book, 1951

"As you turn the pages, the imaginings get wilder and funnier, the rhymes more hilarious. There will be no age limits for this book, because families will be forced to share rereading and quotation, for a long long time." NY Her Trib Books

McElligot's pool; written and illustrated by Dr. Seuss. Random House 1947 un il $14.95; lib bdg $16.99

Grades: PreK K 1 2   E
   1. Stories in rhyme 2. Fishing -- Fiction
   ISBN 0-394-80083-4; 0-394-90083-9 lib bdg
   A Caldecott Medal honor book, 1948

"Fine color surrounding a host of strange creatures enlivens this amazing fish story for all ages." Horn Book

Yertle the turtle and other stories; A 50th anniversary retrospective. with 32 pages of rarely seen Seuss images and commentary by Charles D. Cohen. 50th anniversary ed.; Random House 2008 114p il $24.99; lib bdg $27.99

Grades: PreK K 1 2   E
   1. Stories in rhyme 2. Turtles -- Fiction
   ISBN 978-0-375-83850-7; 0-375-83850-3; 978-0-375-93850-4 lib bdg; 0-375-93850-8 lib bdg
            LC 2007033486

A reissue of the title first published 1958

Includes three humorous stories in verse, Yertle the Turtle, Gertrude McFuzz, and The Big Brag, followed by commentary and end notes, reproductions of illustrations from other Dr. Seuss books, and two poems, 'The Ruckus' and 'The Kindly Snather'

Includes bibliographical references

Seven, John

Happy punks 1 2 3; A Counting Story. Manic D Press 2013 32 p. $15.95

Grades: PreK K   E
   1. Counting -- Fiction 2. Punk culture -- Fiction
   ISBN 1933149671; 9781933149677

This "counting book . . . takes readers up to 12 as musicians prepare to give a free concert. . . . 'Six happy punks go to the thrift store. . . . Perry buys a funny jacket. Siobhan loves that strange gizmo.' The book doesn't get specific about what punk means, but the diversity of characters (including a second-wave ska fan, anthropomorphic animals and robots, and a jetpack-wearing punk of the steam variety) hint at a be-yourself, anything-goes mentality." (Publishers Weekly)

The **ocean** story; written by John Seven; illustrated by Jana Christy. Picture Window Books 2011 un il

Grades: PreK K 1 2   **E**

1. Ocean -- Fiction 2. Water -- Fiction 3. Oil spills -- Fiction 4. Marine animals -- Fiction 5. Water pollution -- Fiction

ISBN 1-4048-6785-6; 978-1-4048-6785-7

LC 2011006480

Relates the story of the oceans that are home to so many creatures, that are part of the water cycle which produces rain, and that can become very messy if we do not take care of them.

"Endpapers filled with images of ocean life are the auspicious beginning of this beautiful eco-tale. . . . This splendid call to stewardship is gloriously illustrated with paintings, each a gift of color and texture that encourages lingering. . . . This book is a perfect blend of poetry, visual art, and science." SLJ

Shahan, Sherry

Spicy hot colors: colores picantes; illustrated by Paula Barragan. August House 2004 un il $16.95

Grades: PreK K 1 2   **E**

1. Color 2. Bilingual books -- English-Spanish

ISBN 0-87483-741-3

This is an "introduction to the names of nine colors in Spanish. Snappy, image-filled verses bring to life some of the hues and traditions of Latino culture. . . . Vibrant paintings that have both ethnic and fine-art references are appealing and attention grabbing." SLJ

Shange, Ntozake, 1948-

★ **Ellington** was not a street; written by Ntozake Shange; illustrations by Kadir Nelson. Simon & Schuster Bks. for Young Readers 2004 un il $15.95

Grades: K 1 2 3 4   **E**

1. Children's poetry 2. African Americans -- Poetry 3. Children's literature -- Works -- Grades two through six

ISBN 0-689-82884-5

LC 00-45060

"Shange's poem 'Mood Indigo,' an adult recollection of a childhood spent 'in the company of men/ who changed the world,' receives a . . . treatment through illustrations that follow a demure little girl who nonchalantly interacts with the mid-twentieth-century African-American luminaries who visit her father. . . . Grades three to six." (Bull Cent Child Books)

"Nelson illustrates the noted poet's 'Mood Indigo,' from her collection entitled A Daughter's Geography. . . . In the poem, Shange recalls her childhood when her family entertained many of the . . . 'men/who changed the world,' including Paul Robeson, W.E.B. DuBois, Ray Barretto, Dizzy Gillespie, 'Sonny Til' Tilghman, Kwame Nkrumah, and Duke Ellington. Both the words and the rich, nostalgic illustrations are a tribute to these visionaries. . . . A biographical sketch of each man appears at the end, along with the poem reprinted on a single page." SLJ

Shannon, David

★ **Alice** the fairy. Blue Sky Press 2004 un il $15.95

Grades: PreK K 1 2   **E**

1. Fairies -- Fiction 2. Imagination -- Fiction

ISBN 0-439-49025-1

LC 2003-23478

Alice, who claims to be a Temporary Fairy, still has a lot to learn, such as how to make her clothes put themselves away in the closet.

"Kids will find most of the humor right at their level, in terms of both wit and imagination. The pictures are richly colored, some almost effervescent in their playfulness." Booklist

★ **Bugs** in My Hair! David Shannon. Blue Sky Press 2013 32 p. (hardcover: alk. paper) $17.99

Grades: K 1 2 3   **E**

1. Hair -- Fiction 2. Lice -- Fiction 3. Humorous stories

ISBN 0545143136; 9780545143134

LC 2012042220

In this children's picture book by David Shannon, "there's a Lice-a-Palooza going on-right on top of the narrator's head. Our hero . . . has head lice. His ever-attentive mother is on the attack, with stinky stuff and a nit comb. Head lice may have taken over the boy's life, but his mom can conquer just about anything. . . . The book imparts . . . information while revealing the humiliation, embarrassment, frustration, and downright itchiness of these little nasties." (School Library Journal)

★ **Duck** on a bike. Blue Sky Press (NY) 2002 un il $15.95

Grades: PreK K 1 2   **E**

1. Ducks -- Fiction 2. Cycling -- Fiction 3. Domestic animals -- Fiction

ISBN 0-439-05023-5

LC 2001-35992

A duck decides to ride a bike and soon influences all the other animals on the farm to ride bikes too

"This delightful story will have youngsters chiming in on the repeated phrases and predicting, in no time, what will happen next, and the many animal sounds provide ample opportunities for role-playing. Shannon's brightly colored spreads are filled with humor." SLJ

★ **Good** boy, Fergus! Blue Sky Press 2006 un il $15.99

Grades: PreK K 1 2   **E**

1. Dogs -- Fiction

ISBN 0-439-49027-8

LC 2005-08541

Except for his bath, Fergus experiences the perfect doggy day, from chasing cats and motorcycles to being scratched on his favorite tickle spot.

"This book is all about the impressive, oversize visuals—pictures that show the adorable doggie in full canine-caper mode." Booklist

★ **No,** David! Blue Sky Press (NY) 1998 un il $16.99

Grades: PreK K 1 2   **E**

1. Behavior -- Fiction 2. Mother-son relationship -- Fiction

ISBN 0-590-93002-8

LC 97-35125

A Caldecott Medal honor book, 1999

A young boy is depicted doing a variety of naughty things for which he is repeatedly admonished, but finally he gets a hug. "Preschool to grade two." (SLJ)

"The vigorous and wacky full-color acrylic paintings portray a lively and imaginative boy whose stick-figure body conveys every nuance of anger, exuberance, defiance, and best of all, the reassurance of his mother's love." SLJ

Other titles about David are:
David goes to school (1999)
David gets in trouble (2002)
It's Christmas, David! (2010)

★ The **rain** came down. Blue Sky Press (NY) 2000 un il lib bdg $15.95
Grades: PreK K 1 2   E
1. Quarreling 2. Rain -- Fiction 3. Rain and rainfall
ISBN 0-439-05021-9
                                              LC 99-86363
An unexpected rain shower causes quarreling and confusion among the members of a small community. However, when the sun comes out, everyone feels better. "Ages five to eight." (Bull Cent Child Books)

"This deceptively simple story showcases Shannon's quirky humor and offbeat illustrations." SLJ

★ **Too** many toys. Blue Sky Press 2008 un il $16.99
Grades: PreK K 1 2   E
1. Toys -- Fiction
ISBN 0-439-49029-4; 978-0-439-49029-0
                                           LC 2007-44753
Although he finally agrees that he has too many toys and needs to give them away, there is one toy that Spencer absolutely cannot part with. "Ages six to nine." (Bull Cent Child Books)

"A master at capturing the workings of a young mind, Shannon combines realistic dialogue with his boisterous illustrations to create another surefire hit." SLJ

Shannon, George
★ **One** family; George Shannon; pictures by Blanca Gomez. Farrar, Straus & Giroux 2015 32 p. color illustrations (hardcover) $17.99
Grades: PreK K 1   E
1. Counting 2. Family -- Fiction 3. Families -- Fiction
ISBN 0374300038; 9780374300036
                                           LC 2014040391
This children's book, by George Shannon, "celebrates family and community, while also offering young readers a chance to practice counting. Each spread features an increasing number of people who form a family. From babies in buggies to white-haired elders holding hands, families stretch across generations and races.." (School Library Journal)

"A playful counting book also acts as a celebration of family and human diversity. Shannon's text is delivered in spare, rhythmic, lilting verse that begins with one and counts up to 10 as it presents different groupings of things and people in individual families, always emphasizing the unitary nature of each combination. . . . Interracial families are included, as are depictions of men with their arms around each other, and a Sikh man wearing a turban. This inclusive spirit supports the text's culminating assertion that "One is one and everyone. One earth. One world. One family." A visually striking, engaging picture book that sends the message that everyone counts." Kirkus

Tippy-toe chick, go! pictures by Laura Dronzek. Greenwillow Bks. 2003 un il $15.99; lib bdg $16.89

Grades: PreK K 1 2   E
1. Dogs -- Fiction 2. Chickens -- Fiction
ISBN 0-06-029823-5; 0-06-029824-3 lib bdg
                                           LC 2002-17509
When a mean dog blocks the path to the garden where a delicious breakfast awaits, Little Chick shows her family how brave and clever she is

"The narrative has a fresh, buoyant vitality that begs to be read aloud. . . . The bright, uncluttered acrylic illustrations neatly match the spare text." Booklist

★ **Tomorrow's** alphabet; pictures by Donald Crews. Greenwillow Bks. 1996 un il $17; pa $6.99
Grades: PreK K 1 2 3   E
1. Alphabet
ISBN 0-688-13504-8; 0-688-16424-2 pa
                                           LC 94-19484
"In 26 double-page spreads, the letters of the alphabet are used to demonstrate where things come from. 'A is for seed' is followed on the next page with 'tomorrow's APPLE.' 'D is for puppy—tomorrow's DOG.'. . . All of the combinations are clever, well chosen, and well within youngsters' experience. . . . Each two-page spread offers brightly colored, large and realistic depictions of the objects named." SLJ

Turkey Tot; by George Shannon; illustrated by Jennifer K. Mann. Holiday House 2013 32 p. color illustrations (hardcover) $16.95
Grades: PreK K 1   E
1. Turkeys -- Fiction 2. Inventions -- Fiction 3. Picture books for children 4. Animals -- Fiction 5. Determination (Personality trait) -- Fiction
ISBN 0823423794; 9780823423798
                                           LC 2011022103
In this picture book, written by George Shannon and illustrated by Jennifer K. Mann, "Turkey Tot thinks outside the box. He's hopeful, imaginative, and persistent, refusing to let his Debbie Downer friends in the farmyard discourage him. He's determined to retrieve juicy blackberries that hang just out of reach, but he needs a little help to implement the plans he makes to get within range." (School Library Journal)

"Big, comic-style thought balloons show the friends imagining each of the turkey's schemes failing, their round eyes with black dots somehow giving away their thoughts. With its short words and sentences and humorous repetition, this makes a good early reader as well as an entertaining storytime book." Horn Book

A **very** witchy spelling bee; George Shannon; illustrated by Mark Fearing. HMH Books for Young Readers 2013 32 p. $16.99
Grades: 1 2 3 4   E
1. Picture books for children 2. Witches -- Fiction 3. Spelling bees -- Fiction 4. English language -- Spelling -- Fiction
ISBN 0152066969; 9780152066963
                                           LC 2012045935
This children's picture book is a "story about a purple-haired witch named Cordelia who loves spelling words and casting spells . . . . After Cordelia enters a spelling bee, the mean-spirited 203-year-old reigning champ, Beulah Divine, vows to defeat the young witch; Cordelia wins by adding the

letter R to the word 'F-I-E-N-D,' turning her rival into an ally." (Publishers Weekly)

★ **White** is for blueberry; pictures by Laura Dronzek. Greenwillow Books 2005 un il $17.99; lib bdg $17.89 Grades: PreK K 1 2 3   E
   1. Color
   ISBN 0-06-029275-X; 0-06-029276-8 lib bdg
                         LC 2004-10147
"The bold, uncluttered scenes, rendered in acrylics, have a sweetness and strength that is quite pleasing to the eye. Easy to read and fun to share, this paean to the wonder of cycles and the rewards of close observation is the perfect prelude to a thoughtful excursion." SLJ

Sharmat, Marjorie Weinman
Gila monsters meet you at the airport; pictures by Byron Barton. Macmillan 1980 un il hardcover o.p. pa $5.99
Grades: PreK K 1 2   E
   1. Moving -- Fiction 2. West (U.S.) -- Fiction
   ISBN 0-02-782450-0; 0-689-71383-5 pa
                          LC 80-12264
A New York City boy's preconceived ideas of life in the West make him very apprehensive about the family's move there
"The exaggeration is amusing, the style yeasty, with a nice final touch; the illustrations are comic and awkward, but add little that's not inherent in the story." Bull Cent Child Books

★ **Nate** the Great; illustrated by Marc Simont. Delacorte Press 2002 60p il $13.95; pa $4.50
Grades: K 1 2   E
   1. Mystery fiction
   ISBN 978-0-385-73017-4; 0-385-73017-9; 978-0-440-46126-5 pa; 0-440-46126-X pa
A reissue of the title first published 1972 by McCann & Geoghegan
Nate the Great, a junior detective who has found missing balloons, books, slippers, chickens and even a goldfish, is now in search of a painting of a dog by Annie, the girl down the street.
"The illustrations capture the exaggerated, tongue-in-cheek humor of the story." Booklist
Other titles about Nate the Great are:
Nate the Great and me: the case of the fleeing fang (1998)
Nate the Great and the big sniff (2001)
Nate the Great and the boring beach bag (1987)
Nate the Great and the crunchy Christmas (1996)
Nate the Great and the fishy prize (1985)
Nate the Great and the Halloween hunt (1989)
Nate the Great and the hungry book club (2009)
Nate the Great and the lost list (1975)
Nate the Great and the missing key (1981)
Nate the Great and the monster mess (1999)
Nate the Great and the mushy valentine (1994)
Nate the Great and the musical note (1990)
Nate the Great and the phony clue (1977)
Nate the Great and the pillowcase (1993)
Nate the Great and the snowy trail (1982)
Nate the Great and the sticky case (1978)
Nate the Great and the stolen base (1992)
Nate the Great and the tardy tortoise (1995)

Nate the Great goes down in the dumps (1989)
Nate the Great goes undercover (1974)
Nate the Great on the Owl Express (2003)
Nate the Great, San Francisco detective (2000)
Nate the Great saves the King of Sweden (1997)
Nate the Great stalks stupidweed (1986)
Nate the Great talks turkey (2006)

Sharmat, Mitchell
Gregory, the terrible eater; illustrated by Jose Aruego and Ariane Dewey. Four Winds Press 1985 un il $16.95
Grades: PreK K 1 2   E
   1. Diet -- Fiction 2. Goats -- Fiction
   ISBN 0-02-782250-8
                         LC 85-29290
A reissue of the title first published 1980
"Aruego and Dewey's illustrations are highly amusing, thanks to their goats' dot-eyed facial expressions. . . . There is energy in the pictures; they are beguiling and help to carry the humor." Booklist

Sharratt, Nick
What's in the witch's kitchen? Candlewick Press 2011 un il $12.99
Grades: PreK K   E
   1. Stories in rhyme 2. Pop-up books 3. Witches -- Fiction 4. Halloween -- Fiction
   ISBN 978-0-7636-5224-1; 0-7636-5224-5
                       LC 2010042323
The contents of the witch's kitchen are hidden by flaps that can be opened either to the left or right to reveal pop-up illustrations of either a delight or a nasty fright.
"Sharratt's digital illustrations are colorful and large. . . . Humorous contrasts, cheery colors, and smiling bats and ghosts make this book a perfect fit for storytimes about homes, rhymes, or surprises." SLJ

Shaskan, Stephen
A **dog** is a dog. Chronicle Books 2011 un il $14.99
Grades: PreK K 1   E
   1. Stories in rhyme 2. Animals -- Fiction
   ISBN 978-0-8118-7896-8; 0-8118-7896-1
                       LC 2010041949
Using various animals as examples, this rhyming picture book explores what makes them the same and what makes them different.
This "looks simple, but it's in fact a polished and controlled piece of work. . . . There's a chunky, woodcut feel to Shaskan's hip and cheery art, and he gives each of the animals abundant personality. Children attracted to Escher-like paradoxes will appreciate the endless loop of animal costumes and low-key surprises." Publ Wkly

Shaw, Charles
★ **It** looked like spilt milk. Harper & Row 1947 un il $16.99; lib bdg $18.89; pa $6.99; bd bk $6.99
Grades: PreK K 1   E
   ISBN 0-06-025566-8; 0-06-025565-X lib bdg; 0-06-443159-2 pa; 0-694-00491-X bd bk
White silhouettes on a blue background with simple captions: "sometimes it looked like a tree," "Sometimes it looked like a bird," etc. lead to a surprise ending "sometimes it looked like split milk, but what it was was—"

"What one thing could look like all of these? On the last page you are told, and I could no more tell you now than I could spoil an adult mystery by a review that gives away its solution." N Y Her Trib Books

Shaw, Hannah

★ **School** for bandits. Alfred A. Knopf 2011 un il $16.99

Grades: K 1 2   E

1. Raccoons -- Fiction 2. Etiquette -- Fiction
ISBN 978-0-375-86768-2; 0-375-86768-6
LC 2010039516

Ralph Raccoon is too polite so his parents send him to Bandit School to learn to behave like a properly bad raccoon.

"This clever story is packed with childlike humor. The pen-and-ink drawings are in bold colors and are full of action and creative details." SLJ

Shaw, Nancy

★ **Sheep** in a jeep; illustrated by Margot Apple. Houghton Mifflin 1986 32p il lib bdg $15; pa $5.95; bd bk $5.95

Grades: PreK K 1 2   E

1. Stories in rhyme 2. Sheep -- Fiction
ISBN 0-395-41105-X lib bdg; 0-395-47030-7 pa; 0-395-86786-X bd bk
LC 86-3101

"Shaw demonstrates a promising capacity for creating nonsense rhymes. . . . Veteran illustrator Apple's whimsical portraits of the sheep bring the story to life. Pleasing and lighthearted, this has much appeal for young readers." Publ Wkly

Other titles about the sheep are:
Sheep blast off! (2008)
Sheep in a shop (1991)
Sheep on a ship (1989)
Sheep out to eat (1992)
Sheep take a hike (1994)
Sheep trick or treat (1997)

Shea, Bob

★ **Big** plans; [illustrated by] Lane Smith. Hyperion 2008 42p il $17.99

Grades: 1 2 3 4   E

1. School stories 2. Imagination -- Fiction
ISBN 1-4231-1100-1; 978-1-4231-1100-9
LC 2008-00707

A little boy sits in the corner of his classroom dreaming about his big plans for his future.

"Smith is the perfect artist for this illogically logical scenario, with retro tones of gold and avocado predominating in his carefully disorganized oversized compositions. . . . An escapist adventure, a victory over important adults, and a new catch-phrase to triumphantly wield." Bull Cent Child Books

Cheetah can't lose; Bob Shea. Balzer + Bray 2013 40 p. (trade bdg.) $17.99

Grades: K 1 2   E

1. Racing -- Fiction 2. Animal babies -- Fiction 3. Humorous fiction 4. Cats -- Fiction 5. Humorous stories 6. Cheetah -- Fiction 7. Animals -- Infancy

-- Fiction 8. Winning and losing -- Fiction
ISBN 0061730831; 9780061730832
LC 2012008407

Author Bob Shea presents a children's story about a cheetah. "It's race day, and once and for all, it's time to determine the better feline: little cats or big cheetah. Cheetah might be bigger, taller, stronger, faster . . . but the little cats have some tricks up their sleeves, so don't count them out!" Shea presents a "story about the difference between brains and brawn." (Publisher's note)

★ **Dinosaur** vs. bedtime. Hyperion Books for Children 2008 un il $15.99

Grades: PreK K   E

1. Bedtime -- Fiction 2. Dinosaurs -- Fiction
ISBN 978-1-4231-1335-5; 1-4231-1335-7

"Incorporating paper, paint, photo collage and quick strokes of crayon, Shea's freewheeling compositions convey both a beguiling spontaneity and a preschooler's sense of invincibility." Publ Wkly

Other titles about Dinosaur are:
Dinosaur vs. the potty (2010)
Dinosaur vs. the library (2011)

Dinosaur vs. Santa; Bob Shea. Disney-Hyperion 2012 40 p. (hardback) $15.99

Grades: PreK K   E

1. Humorous fiction 2. Christmas -- Fiction 3. Dinosaurs -- Fiction 4. Santa Claus -- Fiction 5. Humorous stories
ISBN 1423168062; 9781423168065
LC 2011051350

In this book, by Bob Shea, "Dinosaur is getting ready for Santa! He tackles many challenges - decorating, making presents for Mom and Dad, trying not to be naughty - and defeats each one with his trademark ROAR! But on Christmas Eve, when he hears some rustling downstairs, he can't resist a peek. Will our feisty red friend meet his match in the man in the red suit?" (Publisher's note)

"In this follow-up to Dinosaur vs. the Potty (2010), the rebellious little monster creature gets ready for Christmas... The red and green colors make this a fun Christmas read-aloud for toddlers who will recognize how hard it is not to get things wrong as tension rises during holiday preparations. The climax is when the choo-choo that Dinosaur asked for in his letter appears." Booklist

Companion to:
Dinosaur vs. the Potty (2010)

Dinosaur vs. school; Bob Shea. Disney-Hyperion 2014 40 p. $16.99

Grades: PreK K   E

1. School stories 2. Dinosaurs -- Fiction 3. Humorous stories 4. Schools -- Fiction 5. Nursery schools -- Fiction
ISBN 1423160878; 9781423160878
LC 2013025784

In this children's book written and illustrated by Bob Shea, "Dinosaur is starting preschool today. ROAR! There are new friends to meet, dress-up outfits to wear, glitter and googly eyes to paste, musical instruments to play, and snacks to eat. What's not to like? But then, oh, no! It's Dinosaur vs. Clean-up Time! Fortunately, when friends work together, EVERYONE WINS!" (Publisher's note)

""Roar! Roar! Roar!" The diminutive red dinosaur (Dinosaur vs. Bedtime) romps and stomps its way through the school day, making friends, playing dress-up, etc. The fun comes to a halt at clean-up time: "OH, NO! It's too much for one dinosaur!" But there's a lesson to be learned: "When everyone helps...EVERYONE WINS!" The mixed-media illustrations contain lots of color and motion." Horn Book

Dinosaur versus school

I'm a shark! Balzer + Bray 2011 un il $16.99

Grades: PreK K 1   E

1. Fear -- Fiction 2. Sharks -- Fiction 3. Courage -- Fiction

ISBN 978-0-06-199846-1; 0-06-199846-X

LC 2010-21850

A boastful shark is not afraid of anything, which impresses his underwater friends until they ask about spiders.

"Witty banter begs for audience participation. . . . Thick, dark crayon strokes convey both Shark's powerful physique and his endearing vulnerability. . . . Bold, uncluttered mixed-media spreads emphasize this predator's sharp-toothed, goofy grin." Kirkus

Kid sheriff and the terrible Toads; written by Bob Shea; illustrated by Lane Smith. Roaring Brook Press 2014 32 p. color illustrations (hardback) $17.99

Grades: K 1 2 3   E

1. Toads -- Fiction 2. Sheriffs -- Fiction 3. Humorous stories 4. Dinosaurs -- Fiction 5. West (U.S.) -- Fiction 6. Robbers and outlaws -- Fiction

ISBN 1596439750; 9781596439757

LC 2014001767

In this book by Bob Shea, illustrated by Lane Smith, "Sheriff Ryan might only be seven years old, and he might not know much about shooting and roping. But he knows a lot about dinosaurs. Yes, dinosaurs. And it turns out that knowing a thing or two about paleontology can come in handy when it comes to hoodwinking and rounding up a few no-good bandits." (Publisher's note)

"Shea's enjoyably bizarre take on a good old fashioned hoodwinkin' finds a perfect executor in Smith, whose desert-hued illustrations have all the hard corners and sneering lines of a wanted poster." Booklist

★ **Oh,** Daddy! Balzer + Bray 2010 un il $16.99

Grades: PreK K   E

1. Hippopotamus -- Fiction 2. Father-child relationship -- Fiction

ISBN 978-0-06-173080-1; 0-06-173080-7

A young hippopotamus shows his father the right way to do things, such as getting dressed, watering the flowers, and especially giving big hugs.

"The concise text captures the child's voice perfectly. . . . The mixed-media illustrations incorporate collage elements into a spare, cartoonlike world. . . . The gentle humor . . . will keep kids entertained." SLJ

Race you to bed. Katherine Tegen Books 2010 un il $16.99

Grades: PreK K 1   E

1. Stories in rhyme 2. Bedtime -- Fiction 3. Rabbits

-- Fiction

ISBN 978-0-06-170417-8; 0-06-170417-2

LC 2008044525

"A fuzzy white rabbit with an oversize head races readers to bed, but he finds many reasons to delay bedtime. Animals, toys, and other objects divert his attention. . . . The singsong rhyme flows as the rabbit cavorts through the flat colored pages. The backgrounds are all done in soothing pastel colors, with the exuberant youngster cavorting across the pages. Clever details in the art enhance the telling." SLJ

★ **Unicorn** thinks he's pretty great; by Bob Shea. Disney-Hyperion 2013 40 p. $15.99

Grades: PreK K 1 2   E

1. Picture books for children 2. Jealousy -- Fiction 3. Envy -- Fiction 4. Goats -- Fiction 5. Unicorns -- Fiction 6. Friendship -- Fiction

ISBN 1423159527; 9781423159520

LC 2012047987

In this children's book, a goat is jealous of a unicorn. "The goat bakes marsh-mallow squares. The unicorn can make it rain cupcakes! The goat tries a magic trick. The unicorn can turn things into gold! . . . It turns out that the unicorn actually has some goat envy," himself, and the two become friends. (Publishers Weekly)

"Rainbows, smiling cupcakes, and flying unicorns in one picture book can be a recipe for a cutesy-wootsy disaster, but not so in this hilarious friendship story... An ideal choice for fans of silliness." SLJ

Shea, Susan A.

★ **Do** you know which ones will grow? Blue Apple Books 2011 un il $16.99

Grades: PreK K 1   E

1. Life (Biology) 2. Stories in rhyme 3. Growth -- Fiction

ISBN 978-1-60905-062-7; 1-60905-062-2

"Shea's book debut is a clever, rhymed test of kids' notions of living and nonliving things that's great for both lap and group sharing. . . . [The book offers] a terrific interplay of rhyming questions and cunningly designed gatefold illustrations: 'If a calf grows and becomes a cow, / can a shovel grow and become . . . a plow?', . . . Other rhymes include duck and truck, bear and chair, cat and hat . . . and kangaroo and you. . . . Slaughter's illustrations bring pop art to mind: vivid reds, blues, yellows and greens, few details, simple backgrounds and blocks of color." Kirkus

Shelby, Anne

★ **The man** who lived in a hollow tree; by Anne Shelby and Cor Hazelaar. Atheneum Books for Young Readers 2009 un il $17.99

Grades: K 1 2 3   E

1. Tall tales 2. Trees -- Fiction 3. Ecology -- Fiction 4. Carpentry -- Fiction

ISBN 978-0-689-86169-7; 0-689-86169-9

LC 2008-10369

Carpenter Harlan Burch, who builds everything from cradle to casket, plants two trees for every one he cuts down, and when he is very old his sap begins to rise, he grows young again, and starts a family that still lives all over the mountains.

"The storyteller's voice is vibrant, and the earth-toned acrylics on textured backgrounds of cardboard and linen have a quaint, collage-like feel." Booklist

Sheridan, Sara

I'm me! illustrated by Margaret Chamberlain. Chicken House 2011 un il $15.99

Grades: PreK K 1   E

1. Play -- Fiction 2. Aunts -- Fiction 3. Imagination -- Fiction

ISBN 978-0-545-28222-2; 0-545-28222-5

"Imogen's visits to her aunt's house are always an adventure. As the child rushes in, Auntie Sara asks her what she wants to play. 'Can we play pretend?' And the woman replies 'Yes, yes, yes, we can!' A turn of each page reveals a suggestion. . . . But to each inquiry, Imogen smilingly replies 'No! Today I want to be....' and she reveals she just wants to be herself. . . . The exuberant, candy-colored illustrations show the pair delighting in each other as they cavort across the spreads. There are few books starring an aunt and her niece, and this playful gem that explores pretending and being oneself will find a welcome place in libraries." SLJ

Sherman, Pat

Ben and the Emancipation Proclamation; written by Pat Sherman; illustrated by Floyd Cooper. Eerdmans Books for Young Readers 2010 un il $16.99

Grades: 3 4 5   E

1. Slaves 2. Teachers 3. Slavery -- Fiction 4. African Americans -- Fiction 5. Books and reading -- Fiction 6. Emancipation Proclamation (1863) -- Fiction

ISBN 978-0-8028-5319-6; 0-8028-5319-6

"Based on the life of Benjamin Holmes, a slave who taught himself to read at a young age, this picture book is an inspiring account of overcoming oppression. Sherman's fictionalized telling is stirring, especially when Holmes revels in the discovery of new words. . . . Sherman's text has a stately simplicity. Cooper's paintings glow with a hopeful, golden warmth. . . . This is a powerful tale of a bright ray of light in a very dark period in America." SLJ

Includes bibliographical references

Sherry, Kevin

I'm the biggest thing in the ocean. Dial Books for Young Readers 2007 un il $16.99

Grades: PreK   E

1. Size -- Fiction 2. Squids -- Fiction 3. Marine animals -- Fiction

ISBN 978-0-8037-3192-9; 0-8037-3192-2

LC 2006-27815

A giant squid brags about being bigger than everything else in the ocean—almost.

"A lighthearted, clever story presented in an oversize, colorful package." SLJ

Another title about the giant squid is:

I'm the best artist in the ocean (2008)

Turtle Island; story and pictures by Kevin Sherry. Dial Books for Young Readers, an imprint of Penguin Group (USA) Inc. 2014 32 p. color illustrations (hardcover) $16.99

Grades: PreK K 1   E

1. Family -- Fiction 2. Animals -- Fiction 3. Turtles -- Fiction 4. Islands -- Fiction 5. Friendship -- Fiction

6. Loneliness -- Fiction

ISBN 0803733917; 9780803733916

LC 2013027091

Publishers Weekly (March 10, 2014)

"Turtle is big. But the ocean is bigger. And Turtle is all alone. Until four shipwrecked folks--a bear, an owl, a frog, and a cat--climb to safety on his shell. Before long, they're fast friends, and the sea doesn't seem so vast anymore. But when Frog confides that he misses his family, Turtle doesn't understand. Isn't he their family?" (Publisher's note)

"Sherry uses brilliant, speckled watercolor washes for the ocean and sky, while the creatures are rendered in simple, colorful shapes with thick outlines and cartoonishly big eyes. Lovable Turtle and his happy, friend-filled future will likely strike a chord with little ones feeling lonely." - Booklist

Sheth, Kashmira

Monsoon afternoon; written by Kashmira Sheth; illustrated by Yoshiko Jaeggi. Peachtree 2008 un il $16.95

Grades: PreK K 1 2   E

1. Rain -- Fiction 2. India -- Fiction 3. Monsoons -- Fiction 4. Grandfathers -- Fiction

ISBN 978-1-56145-455-6; 1-56145-455-9

LC 2008004565

A young boy and his grandfather find much they can do together on a rainy day during monsoon season in India

"Jaeggi's atmospheric watercolors nicely translate the sensory details in the words. . . . The scenes give a strong sense of everyday life in the boy's Indian community, as well as the sweet bond between grandfather and grandson." Booklist

My Dadima wears a sari; written by Kashmira Sheth; illustrated by Yoshiko Jaeggi. Peachtree 2007 un il $16.95

Grades: K 1 2 3   E

1. Grandmothers -- Fiction 2. Clothing and dress -- Fiction 3. East Indians -- United States -- Fiction

ISBN 1-56145-392-7

LC 2006024334

Two young sisters raised in America learn about the beauty and art of wearing a sari from their wise Indian grandmother.

"Soft watercolor paintings capture the magnificent fabrics of Dadima's saris and accentuate the loving story." SLJ

★ Tiger in my soup; written by Kashmira Sheth; illustrated by Jeffrey Ebbeler. Peachtree Publishers 2013 32 p. (reinforced) $15.95

Grades: PreK K 1   E

1. Siblings 2. Imagination -- Fiction 3. Babysitters -- Fiction 4. Books and reading -- Fiction 5. Brothers and sisters -- Fiction

ISBN 1561456969; 9781561456963

LC 2012025539

In this book by Kashmira Sheth, "[a]n unnamed narrator is left in the care of his older sister. . . . Although he asks her to read him a book about a tiger, she would rather read her own book. He captures her attention long enough to get her to heat up some alphabet soup, but she . . . doesn't even notice when a tiger rises up out of the steaming bowl. The boy uses . . . handy utensils to fend off the raging beast until his sister finally . . . agrees to read to him." (School Library Journal)

"Ebbeler truly knocks it out of the park, gleefully building on Sheth's prose with dynamic perspectives, a realistically detailed (and menacing) tiger, abundant visual hyperbole, and unexpected delights on nearly every page." Pub Wkly

Shields, Carol Diggory

★ **Baby's** got the blues; Carol Diggory Shields, illustrated by Lauren Tobia. Candlewick Press 2014 32 p. $16.99

Grades: PreK K 1　　　　　　　　　　　　　　E

1. Infants -- Fiction

ISBN 0763632600; 9780763632601

LC 2013943085

This book, by Carol Diggory Shields, illustrated by Lauren Tobia, is a "tale of soggy diapers, mushy meals, and sleepin' behind bars. . . . Babies can't talk, can't walk, can't even really chew. It's enough to make the baby in this story blue, blue, blue." The book "gives a tip of the fedora to B.B. King in an ode to babyhood." (Publisher's note)

"Who can blame a baby for singing the blues? Representative lyrics from this soulfully silly book (with more parent- than kid appeal): "I'd like to eat some pizza, / Macaroni, or beef stew, / But I haven't got a single tooth, / So I can't even chew." Happily, the conclusion is pop-song upbeat. Tobia uses spare lines to capture the baby's emotions." (Horn Book)

Wombat walkabout; illustrated by Sophie Blackall. Dutton Children's Books 2009 un il $16.99

Grades: PreK K　　　　　　　　　　　　　　E

1. Counting 2. Stories in rhyme 3. Animals -- Fiction 4. Wombats -- Fiction 5. Australia -- Fiction

ISBN 978-0-525-47865-2; 0-525-47865-5

LC 2008013885

Rhyming text follows six little wombats on walkabout and a hungry dingo following, envisioning them as his lunch until the wombats turn the tables on him.

"This picture book offers a nicely cadenced, rhyming story with a solid base in folklore and a distinctive locale. . . . The pleasing double-page paintings . . . use color sparingly but well." Booklist

Shields, Gillian

Library Lily; illustrated by Francesca Chessa. William B. Eerdmans 2011 un il $16

Grades: PreK K 1 2　　　　　　　　　　　　E

1. Play -- Fiction 2. Libraries -- Fiction 3. Friendship -- Fiction 4. Books and reading -- Fiction

ISBN 978-0-8028-5401-8; 0-8028-5401-X

LC 2010053737

From the day her mother introduces her to the library, Lily wants to spend all of her time reading until she meets Milly, who hates reading but loves adventure.

"The simple text includes some dialogue and quotes from the books that Lily is reading and is placed attractively around the illustrations. Bright, vibrant, cartoon artwork enhances the text and evokes a cheerful feeling." SLJ

When the world is ready for bed. Bloomsbury 2009 un il $14.99; lib bdg $15.89

Grades: PreK K　　　　　　　　　　　　　　E

1. Stories in rhyme 2. Bedtime -- Fiction 3. Rabbits

-- Fiction

ISBN 978-1-59990-339-2; 1-59990-339-3; 978-1-59990-385-9 lib bdg; 1-59990-385-7 lib bdg

LC 2009002858

"This calming tale follows three brown bunnies as their day draws to a close. They have dinner, tidy up, tell dad about the fun they've had, brush their teeth, and listen to one last story. . . . The gentle singsong text makes for excellent bedtime reading, and the homey watercolors are equally pleasant. The bunnies wear distinctive outfits and have a variety of expressions." SLJ

Another title about this rabbit family is:

When the world was waiting for you (2011)

When the world was waiting for you; illustrated by Anna Currey. Bloomsbury Childrens Books 2011 un il $14.99; lib bdg $15.89

Grades: PreK K　　　　　　　　　　　　　　E

1. Stories in rhyme 2. Infants -- Fiction 3. Rabbits -- Fiction

ISBN 978-1-59990-531-0; 1-59990-531-0; 978-1-59990-532-7 lib bdg; 1-59990-532-9 lib bdg

LC 2010029861

Illustrations and simple rhyming text tell the story of a rabbit family anticipating the birth of a baby.

"With just a few rhyming lines of text, this story . . . makes a memorable addition to the welcoming-the-new-baby subgenre. . . . The large-format watercolor illustrations of the rabbits are done in a loose style with delightful details." Kirkus

Shireen, Nadia

Good little wolf. Alfred A. Knopf 2011 il

Grades: K 1 2　　　　　　　　　　　　　　E

1. Wolves -- Fiction

ISBN 0-375-86904-2; 0-375-96904-7 lib bdg; 978-0-375-86904-4; 978-0-375-96904-1 lib bdg

LC 2011003517

Rolf is proud when his friend, Mrs. Boggins, calls him a good little wolf, but when the Big Bad Wolf teases him Rolf tries to prove himself by howling at the moon and blowing down Little Pig's house.

"Simple, strikingly colored illustrations, rendered in pencil, ink, and collage with digital enhancements, feature the characters against bare backgrounds, allowing them to pop off the pages. . . . These bold illustrations, as well as the short text, make this a good read-aloud for audiences old enough to understand the tongue-in-cheek humor." Booklist

Shirley, Debra

Best friend on wheels; by Debra Shirley; illustrated by Judy Stead. Albert Whitman & Co. 2008 un il $15.95

Grades: K 1 2 3　　　　　　　　　　　　　　E

1. Stories in rhyme 2. Friendship -- Fiction 3. Physically disabled children -- Fiction

ISBN 978-0-8075-8868-0; 0-8075-8868-7

LC 2007024252

A young girl relates all the ways she and her best friend, Sarah, are alike, in spite of the fact that Sarah uses a wheelchair.

"The colorful cartoon illustrations delightfully capture [the friends] in their favorite activities. . . . The rhyme moves quickly yet touches on many aspects of life for people in wheelchairs. . . . The artwork conveys the same positive fun as the text. The book's lesson is evident without being didactic." SLJ

Shulevitz, Uri

Dusk; Uri Shulevitz. Farrar, Straus & Giroux (BYR) 2013 32 p. (hardcover) $17.99

Grades: PreK K 1   E

1. Picture books for children 2. Cities and towns -- Fiction 3. Night -- Fiction 4. City and town life -- Fiction

ISBN 0374319030; 9780374319038

LC 2012045967

In this companion to Uri Shulevitz's Caldecott Honor-winning book "Snow," a boy and his dog who are "out for a walk with his 'grandfather with beard,' comes to realize that a city (especially if it's New York City) can come alive in magical ways at dusk. The sidewalks and streets fill with people (and one extraterrestrial) headed home or out for a night's adventure." (Publishers Weekly)

★ **How** I learned geography. Farrar, Straus & Giroux 2008 un il $16.95

Grades: PreK K 1 2   E

1. Maps -- Fiction 2. Refugees -- Fiction 3. Geography -- Fiction 4. Kazakhstan -- Fiction 5. Imagination -- Fiction

ISBN 978-0-374-33499-4; 0-374-33499-4

LC 2007-11889

A Caldecott Medal honor book, 2009

As he spends hours studying his father's world map, a young boy escapes the hunger and misery of refugee life. Based on the author's childhood in Kazakhstan, where he lived as a Polish refugee during World War II.

The "text is clear and straightforward but vivid, and small memorable touches . . . add dimensionality. Watercolor illustrations avoid demonizing the boy's real-life: the town (Turkestan, according to Shulevitz' note) looks like an interesting place. . . . Chunky lines and sweeps of washy watercolor gain additional textures in the map worlds." Bull Cent Child Books

★ **Snow**. Farrar, Straus & Giroux 1998 un il $16; pa $6.99

Grades: PreK K 1 2   E

1. Snow -- Fiction

ISBN 0-374-37092-3; 0-374-46862-1 pa

LC 97-37257

A Caldecott Medal honor book, 1999

As snowflakes slowly come down, one by one, people in the city ignore them, and only a boy and his dog think that the snowfall will amount to anything

"Passersby are caricatured into humorous figures bent into impossible postures, their tall hats, parasols, and funny shoes giving them an almost circus-clown appearance. . . . The elegantly stark text suits the elegant architectural lines of the cityscape." Bull Cent Child Books

★ **So** sleepy story. Farrar Straus Giroux 2006 un il $16

Grades: PreK K 1 2   E

1. Night -- Fiction 2. Sleep -- Fiction

ISBN 0-374-37031-1

LC 2005-51146

"A sleepy sleepy boy is fast asleep in his sleepy sleepy bed along with everything else in his sleepy sleepy house until music comes drifting in, in ever louder tones. Then the child and his surroundings gradually come alive, dance, and shake to the beat, and drift back to sleep as the notes and instruments depart. The brief repetitive text takes a backseat to the whimsical watercolor-and-ink cartoon illustrations." SLJ

Troto and the trucks; Uri Shulevitz. Margaret Ferguson Books, Farrar, Straus & Giroux 2015 32 p. (hardback) $17.99

Grades: PreK K 1   E

1. Size -- Fiction 2. Trucks -- Fiction 3. Teasing -- Fiction 4. Automobiles -- Fiction 5. Automobile racing -- Fiction

ISBN 0374300801; 9780374300807

LC 2014040549

In this children's story, by Uri Shulevitz, "Troto is a happy little car who likes to go places. One day after a long drive, he arrives in Cactusville, where he meets some big trucks. But when those big trucks laugh at how small Troto is, Troto doesn't feel very happy anymore, so he challenges them to a race to show them just what a little car can do." (Publisher's note)

When I wore my sailor suit. Farrar, Straus & Giroux 2009 un il $16.95

Grades: K 1 2 3   E

1. Adventure fiction 2. Sailors -- Fiction 3. Imagination -- Fiction

ISBN 978-0-374-34749-9; 0-374-34749-2

LC 2008016187

A young child spends the day imagining himself to be a sailor on a grand adventure.

"Shulevitz combines child-size sentences with words that stretch and please. . . . The artist's mastery of the medium produces both warm, dappled interiors and Old Master severity, with convincing fades into the fantastic. . . . This is the work of a wise and wonderful storyteller." SLJ

Shulman, Mark

★ **Mom** and Dad are palindromes; a dilemma for words . . . and backwards. by Mark Shulman; illustrated by Adam McCauley. Chronicle Books 2006 un il $15.95

Grades: 1 2 3 4   E

1. Palindromes -- Fiction

ISBN 978-0-8118-4328-7; 0-8118-4328-9

LC 2005023614

When Bob realizes that he is surrounded by palindromes, from his mom, dad, and sis Anna to his dog Otto, he discovers a way to deal with the palindrome puzzle

"In all, Shulman cleverly weaves over 101 palindromes into the text. . . . The mixed-media cartoon art amplifies the zany situation." SLJ

Siddals, Mary McKenna

Compost stew; an A to Z recipe for the earth. illustrated by Ashley Wolff. Tricycle Press 2010 un il $15.99; lib bdg $18.99

Grades: PreK K 1 2   E

1. Alphabet 2. Stories in rhyme 3. Compost -- Fiction

ISBN 978-1-58246-316-2; 1-58246-316-6; 978-1-58246-341-4 lib bdg; 1-58246-341-7 lib bdg

LC 2009016300

"With bouncing, rhyming lines, this cheerful title uses the alphabet to introduce children to ingredients that make great compost, from apple cores to zinnias. . . . A short supplementary note about what compost is and why it is beneficial is included. . . . This title . . . provides a light-hearted introduction to an earth- and kid-friendly activity. The brightly patterned collage artwork featuring a cast of multicultural kids working together will easily draw a young audience." Booklist

Shivery Shades of Halloween; by Mary McKenna Siddals; illustrated by Jimmy Pickering. Random House Childrens Books 2014 32 p. color illustrations $12.99
Grades: PreK K 1 2   E
1. Color -- Fiction 2. Halloween -- Fiction
ISBN 0385369999; 9780385369992
This book, by Mary McKenna Siddals, illustrated by Jimmy Pickering, asks "[w]hat color is Halloween? Why, it's as green as an 'eerie glow, evil grin, vile brew, clammy skin,' as white as 'cobwebs clinging, a misty trail, a skull, a spook, a face gone pale . . .' Children will learn their colors as they follow a cute little creature on his adventure through haunted halls, moonlit forests . . . perhaps even a Halloween party!" (Publisher's note)
"Can colors other than orange and black be associated with Halloween? Upbeat rhymes make the case for a multihued holiday...A nice summary of all the colors appears at the end, as if the aforementioned wizard conjured up a spell to make a perfect Halloween. A solid and fun read-aloud." SLJ

Sidman, Joyce
★ **Red** sings from treetops; a year in colors. illustrated by Pamela Zagarenski. Houghton Mifflin Harcourt 2009 un il $16
Grades: PreK K 1   E
1. Color -- Fiction 2. Nature -- Fiction 3. Seasons -- Fiction
ISBN 978-0-547-01494-4; 0-547-01494-5
LC 2008-35947
ALA ALSC Caldecott Medal Honor Book (2010)
Nature displays different colors to announce the seasons of the year.
"Fresh descriptions and inventive artistry are a charming inspiration to notice colors and correlate emotions. Details in the artwork will invite repeated readings and challenge kids to muse about other color icons." Kirkus

Siegel, Mark
★ **Moving** house. Roaring Brook Press 2011 il $16.99
Grades: PreK K 1   E
1. Home -- Fiction 2. Moving -- Fiction
ISBN 978-1-59643-635-0; 1-59643-635-2
LC 2010036602
When Joey and Chloe and their family are getting ready to move, their house decides it wants to go too.
"Siegel's . . . background as an illustrator (and an editor) serve him well; his vignettes and spreads are drafted in clean ink lines, with watercolor washes of blue and red signaling the clean skies above Foggytown. He's crafted a strong story, too." Publ Wkly

Siegel, Randy
Grandma's smile; illustrated by Dyanne DiSalvo. Roaring Brook Press 2010 32p il $15.99
Grades: PreK K 1 2   E
1. Airports -- Fiction 2. Grandmothers -- Fiction
ISBN 978-1-59643-438-7; 1-59643-438-4
DiSalvo's "sketch-style watercolors achieve an authenticity and immediacy that should give even infrequent fliers a shudder of recognition. . . . This is a wry and contemporary reality check on the going-to-Grandma's genre." Publ Wkly

My snake Blake; Randy Siegel; illustrations by Serge Bloch. Roaring Brook Press 2012 32 p. $16.99
Grades: PreK K   E
1. Pets -- Fiction 2. Snakes -- Fiction 3. Picture books for children 4. Snakes as pets -- Fiction 5. Human-animal relationships -- Fiction
ISBN 1596435844; 9781596435841
LC 2011018402
This book "tell[s] the story of a 'super-long, bright green snake' who wows the young narrator by helping him with his homework, eating rejected Brussels sprouts, and fighting bullies. 'He's a perfectly polite, delightful snake,' the boy says." The illustrations show "Blake engaged in a series of charmingly unsnakelike activities: he cooks, finds lost keys, and enjoys cuddling on park benches." (Publishers Weekly)

Sierra, Judy
Ballyhoo Bay; illustrated by Derek Anderson. Simon & Schuster Books for Young Readers 2009 un il $16.99
Grades: K 1 2   E
1. Stories in rhyme 2. Artists -- Fiction 3. Beaches -- Fiction 4. Social action -- Fiction 5. Environmental protection -- Fiction
ISBN 978-1-4169-5888-8; 1-4169-5888-6
LC 2007-49720
Mira Bella mobilizes her art students, from grandmothers to children, crabs to seagulls, to stop a dastardly plan for turning the beach at Ballyhoo Bay into an exclusive resort, and offers an alternative—leave the beach as it is
"Lively, humorous acrylic cartoons have a buoyancy that captures the sparkle of the seaside setting and the exaggerated antics of the characters. This upbeat ecological message is delivered with plenty of panache. Told in rhyming couplets, the story reads aloud well." SLJ

Born to read; story by Judy Sierra; pictures by Marc Brown. Alfred A. Knopf 2008 un il $16.99; lib bdg $19.99
Grades: PreK K 1 2   E
1. Stories in rhyme 2. Reading -- Fiction
ISBN 978-0-375-84687-8; 0-375-84687-5; 978-0-375-94687-5 lib bdg; 0-375-94687-X lib bdg
LC 2007-2306
A little boy named Sam discovers the many unexpected ways in which a love of reading can come in handy, and sometimes even save the day
This is written "in quick, quirky rhymed couplets. . . . Brown's gouache illustrations are cheery, and each page pours into the next through the use of subtly repeated background motifs. . . . This is an easy, obvious choice for events with literacy and early learning as their themes." SLJ

E-I-E-I-O! how Old MacDonald got his farm with a little help from a hen. Judy Sierra, illustrated by Matthew Myers. Candlewick Press 2014 32 p. (hbk.) $16.99
Grades: PreK K 1 2 3   E
1. Farms -- Fiction 2. Gardening -- Fiction 3. Stories in rhyme 4. Domestic animals -- Fiction
ISBN 0763660434; 9780763660437
LC 2013934306
In this book, by Judy Sierra, "Little Red Hen gives old MacDonald some pointers on composting—and a legendary farm is born. . . . Once upon a time, Old MacDonald didn't have a farm. He just had a yard—a yard he didn't want to mow. But under the direction of . . . Little Red Hen, Mac learns to look at the environment in a very different way, and whole new worlds start to bloom with the help of some mud, garbage, horse poop, and worms!" (Publisher's note)
"Most children know about Old MacDonald and his animals, but did they ever wonder how he got that farm? Sierra imagines a rollicking suburban scenario that starts when MacDonald gets tired of mowing the lawn and begins to seek out creative alternatives...This title offers a great way to extend the song into a lesson about the plant cycle and suburban farming. An excellent purchase for general collections as well as curriculum support." (SLJ)

Preschool to the rescue; illustrated by Will Hillenbrand. Harcourt 2001 un il $15
Grades: PreK   E
1. Stories in rhyme 2. Vehicles -- Fiction
ISBN 0-15-202035-7
LC 99-6475
When a mud puddle traps a pizza van, police car, tow truck, and other vehicles, a group of preschoolers comes along and saves the day
"The repetition and rhyme carry the story along and the fun doesn't stop until the book is closed. The artwork is perfect." SLJ

Sleepy little alphabet; a bedtime story from Alphabet Town. written by Judy Sierra; illustrated by Melissa Sweet. Alfred A. Knopf 2009 un il $16.99; lib bdg $19.99
Grades: PreK K 1   E
1. Alphabet 2. Stories in rhyme 3. Bedtime -- Fiction
ISBN 978-0-375-84002-9; 0-375-84002-8; 978-0-375-94002-6 lib bdg; 0-375-94002-2 lib bdg
LC 2008-24526
Sleepy letters of the alphabet get ready for bed
"The bounce of Sierra's meter, the time-for-bed theme and Sweet's offhand pencil and watercolor drawings make the story feel fresh. Throughout, Sierra inserts vocabulary items that incorporate the letters . . . while Sweet provides the laughs." Pub Wkly

Tell the truth, B.B. Wolf; written by Judy Sierra; illustrated by J. Otto Seibold. Alfred A. Knopf 2010 un il $16.99; lib bdg $19.99
Grades: PreK K 1 2 3   E
1. Wolves -- Fiction 2. Honesty -- Fiction
ISBN 978-0-375-85620-4; 0-375-85620-X; 978-0-375-95620-1 lib bdg; 0-375-95620-4 lib bdg
LC 2009030778
When Big Bad Wolf, who now lives at the Villain Villa Retirement Residence, is invited to tell his story at the li-

brary, he faces the truth about what he did to the three little pigs and decides to make amends.
"This brilliant retelling deserves a place at the head of the fractured-fairy-tale pack. . . . Seibold's vivid computer illustrations, replete with comic touches, are a perfect match for Sierra's zany tale." SLJ
Another title about B. B. Wolf is:
Mind your manners, B. B. Wolf (2007)

★ **Thelonius** Monster's sky-high fly pie; illustrations by Edward Koren. Knopf 2006 un il $16.95; lib bdg $18.99
Grades: K 1 2 3   E
1. Stories in rhyme 2. Pies -- Fiction 3. Flies -- Fiction 4. Monsters -- Fiction
ISBN 0-375-83218-1; 0-375-93218-6 lib bdg
LC 2005-16773
A good-natured monster thinks a pie made out of flies would be a good dessert, and invites all his friends and relatives over to try it.
"An incomparable rhymester has teamed up with a master cartoonist to conjure up some haute cuisine on the fly. . . . The words are carefully chosen. . . . A lovable and entertaining work of art." SLJ

We love our school! illustrated by Linda Davick. Alfred A. Knopf 2011 il $7.99; lib bdg $10.99
Grades: PreK K   E
1. Riddles 2. School stories 3. Stories in rhyme 4. Animals -- Fiction
ISBN 978-0-375-86728-6; 0-375-86728-7; 978-0-375-96728-3 lib bdg; 0-375-96728-1 lib bdg
Rhyming text with rebuses follows a group of animals through their first day of school.
"This is a simple but thoroughly charming little gem of a book. . . . For one thing, Sierra has told the tale in effortless rhyme. For another, the rebus format makes it a perfect lapsit choice with a parent or caregiver reading the words and a child 'reading' the easily decipherable pictures. The illustrations have a flat quality and appear to be digitally done, but they are bright and cheerful and should have considerable appeal for the new-to-school set." SLJ

★ **Wild** about books; by Judy Sierra; pictures by Marc Brown. Knopf 2004 un il $16.95
Grades: PreK K 1 2   E
1. Stories in rhyme 2. Animals -- Fiction 3. Libraries -- Fiction 4. Books and reading -- Fiction
ISBN 0-375-82538-X
A librarian named Mavis McGrew introduces the animals in the zoo to the joy of reading when she drives her bookmobile to the zoo by mistake.
"Sierra's text has a wacky verve and enough clever asides and allusions to familiar characters to satisfy bibliophiles of all ages. . . . Brown's cheerful, full-color illustrations stretch his trademark art with ever-so-slightly stylized spreads that are rich in pattern, texture, and nuance." SLJ

Wild about you! Judy Sierra; pictures by Marc Brown. Alfred A. Knopf 2012 40 p. (library binding) $20.99
Grades: PreK K 1   E
1. Zoos -- Fiction 2. Picture books for children 3. Animal babies -- Fiction 4. Stories in rhyme 5. Zoo

animals -- Fiction 6. Animals -- Infancy -- Fiction
ISBN 0375971076; 9780307931788; 9780375971075
LC 2011029010

This children's picture book looks at zoo animals. All the animals are "having babies, all except the tree kangaroo and the pandas. Even though some parents say that the babies are bothersome, none of them will give theirs up to the childless ones. When a van from Animal Rescue delivers an endangered egg, all of the birds refuse it, but the tree kangaroo offers her pouch." A baby penguin hatches, and all the animals pitch in to help the kangaroo feed it. (School Library Journal)

★ **ZooZical**; pictures by Marc Brown. Alfred A. Knopf 2011 un il $17.99; lib bdg $20.99
Grades: PreK K 1   E
1. Stories in rhyme 2. Zoos -- Fiction 3. Animals -- Fiction 4. Theater -- Fiction
ISBN 978-0-375-86847-4; 0-375-86847-X; 978-0-375-96847-1 lib bdg; 0-375-96847-4 lib bdg
LC 2010038565

When the winter doldrums arrive at the zoo, a very small hippo and a young kangaroo decide to stage a "ZooZical," a show to display their singing, dancing, acrobatic, and other talents to the people of Springfield.

"With humor and gusto, Brown's richly textured folk art-inspired pictures convey the characters' dramatic shift in moods and imbue them with abundant personality. Meanwhile, Sierra's riffs on familiar tunes guarantee that readings will be very musical affairs, with children enthusiastic participants." Publ Wkly

Silsbe, Brenda
The **bears** we know; [text by] Brenda Silsbe; [art by] Vlasta van Kampen. Annick Press 2009 un il $19.95; pa $7.95
Grades: PreK K 1 2   E
1. Bears -- Fiction
ISBN 978-1-55451-167-9; 1-55451-167-4; 978-1-55451-166-2 pa; 1-55451-166-6 pa

Nobody has seen the bears, but everybody knows where they live that their house is a mess, they eat bagfuls of chips, jump on the furniture, decorate with sawdust, and sing songs that make them cry.

"The warm, funny watercolors are a great match for the goofy creatures and their various antics. Their great brown bodies sprawl across the page (and the couches), and the simple text is clearly printed on a field of white." SLJ

Silverman, Erica
★ **Cowgirl** Kate and Cocoa; written by Erica Silverman; painted by Betsy Lewin. Harcourt 2005 un il $15
Grades: K 1 2   E
1. Horses -- Fiction 2. Cowhands -- Fiction
ISBN 0-15-202124-8
LC 2004-5739

Cowgirl Kate and her cowhorse Cocoa, who is always hungry, count cows, share a story, and help each other fall asleep.

"Children will . . . recognize the friends' good-natured banter and lively dialogue. . . . Lewin's bold-lined illustrations extend the comedy and the affectionate friendship." Booklist

Other titles about Kate and Cocoa are:

Cowgirl Kate and Cocoa: partners (2006)
Cowgirl Kate and Cocoa: school days (2007)
Cowgirl Kate and Cocoa: rain or shine (2008)
Cowgirl Kate and Cocoa: horse in the house (2009)
Cowgirl Kate and Cocoa: spring babies (2010)

The **Hanukkah** hop; written by Erica Silverman; illustrated by Steven D'Amico. Simon & Schuster 2011 un il $12.99
Grades: PreK K 1   E
1. Hanukkah stories 2. Parties -- Fiction 3. Hanukkah -- Fiction 4. Jews -- United States -- Fiction
ISBN 978-1-4424-0604-9

Rhymed text and illustrations follow a family's activities as they prepare to celebrate Hanukkah.

"Like the enthusiastic revelers, Silverman's gleeful text has rhythm. D'Amico's angular illustrations, with their circa-1950s flair, keep up the pace. . . . Readers' toes are sure to be tapping throughout this unabashedly joyful Hanukkah romp." Horn Book

Silverstein, Shel
Who wants a cheap rhinoceros? by Shel Silverstein. 50th anniversary edition Simon & Schuster Books for Young Readers 2014 un illustrations hbk $17.99
Grades: K 1 2 3   E
1. Pets -- Fiction 2. Rhinoceros -- Fiction
ISBN 9781481415934; 148141593X
First published 1964

"Silverstein's economical black-line drawings illustrate the joys of owning a rhinoceros. . . . The deadpan text belies the goofiness of the pictures, with the rhinoceros jumping rope, playing pirates, and opening a soda can with his horn." Horn Book Guide

Siminovich, Lorena
★ **Alex** and Lulu: two of a kind. Templar Books 2009 un il $14.99
Grades: PreK K 1   E
1. Cats -- Fiction 2. Dogs -- Fiction 3. Friendship -- Fiction
ISBN 978-0-7636-4423-9; 0-7636-4423-4

"Alex, a white dog with a large black spot over one eye, is best friends with a white cat with black markings. One day, Lulu gets her pal thinking about the ways in which they are different. . . . He worries that their relationship is in jeopardy. To reassure him, Lulu offers several examples of true opposites . . . and reminds Alex that they share many interests in common. . . . Siminovich's spare scenes offer patterned backgrounds and an occasional charming detail. . . . With their retro feel and lack of fuss, the artwork is delectable." SLJ

You are my baby; garden. Lorena Siminovich. Chronicle Books 2014 10 p. color illustrations (alk. paper) $8.99
Grades: PreK   E
1. Animal babies 2. Gardens -- Fiction 3. Board books
ISBN 1452126496; 9781452126494
LC 2013025142

"Two books in one introduce youngsters to garden critters and their babies. An ingenious cutaway design separates the book into two distinct, connected pieces, creating a small book that sits nestled inside a larger one. . . . Each striking double-page spread has a distinct design, making it easy for children to match the baby animals in the smaller book with the adults on the larger pages." Kirkus

You know what I love? by Lorena Siminovich. Dial Books for Young Readers 2013 32 p. (hardcover) $16.99
Grades: PreK K   E
    1. Love -- Fiction 2. Dolls -- Fiction
    ISBN 0803737777; 9780803737778
                     LC 2012035617
This book, by Lorena Siminovich, is "one doll's . . . tribute to her little girl. From playing dress up to finding hidden treasures, these two always have fun because it turns out that what they love most of all is each other." (Publisher's note)
"A doll describes what she loves about her owner. The bland valentine of a narrative hinges on the crisp digital-collage art: "That we always make new friends together" has doll and girl seated before food arranged to look like faces; "Singing songs very loudly while we wait in traffic" spurs a cute image of the doll "riding" in a shoe." (Horn Book)

Simms, Laura
    Rotten teeth; illustrated by David Catrow. Houghton Mifflin 1998 un il $16
Grades: K 1 2 3   E
    1. School stories 2. Teeth -- Fiction
    ISBN 0-395-82850-3
                     LC 97-2528
When Melissa takes a big glass bottle of authentic pulled teeth from her father's dental office for a show-and-tell presentation, she becomes a first-grade celebrity
"Catrow's watercolors are a suitably twisted complement to Simms' somewhat warped sense of humor (actually, it's perfect for this audience)." Bull Cent Child Books

Simon, Norma
    All kinds of friends; by Norma Simon; illustrated by Cherie Zamazing. Albert Whitman 2013 32 p. (hardcover) $16.99
Grades: PreK K 1 2   E
    1. Friendship
    ISBN 9780807502839
                     LC 2012017376
"Simon . . . offers an unassuming exploration of friendship. The text conveys information in a straightforward, simple way. . . . The illustrations also make the point that friendships can thrive across gender, age and ethnic boundaries, and children are sure to recognize themselves and others they know in the diverse array of characters that populate the pages." Kirkus

Simont, Marc
    Nate the Great and the stolen base; illustrations by Marc Simont. Coward-McCann 1992 47p il hardcover o.p. pa $4.50
Grades: K 1 2   E
    1. Mystery fiction
    ISBN 0-698-20708-4; 0-440-40932-2 pa
                     LC 91-26153
Nate the Great investigates the mysterious disappearance of the purple plastic octopus that his baseball team uses for second base
"Sharmat does not condescend to her audience, and readers are provided with enough information to find the an-

swer themselves. Subtle humor sparkles through the young detective's narration." SLJ

    ★ The **stray** dog; retold and illustrated by Marc Simont from a true story by Reiko Sassa. HarperCollins Pubs. 2001 un il $16.99; lib bdg $18.89
Grades: PreK K 1 2   E
    1. Dogs -- Fiction
    ISBN 0-06-028933-3; 0-06-028934-1 lib bdg
A Caldecott Medal honor book, 2002
"Simont's art and narrative play off each other strategically, together imparting the tale's humor and tenderness." Publ Wkly

Simpson, Lesley
    Yuvi's candy tree; illustrated by Janice Lee Porter. KarBen Pub. 2011 un il lib bdg $17.95; pa $7.95
Grades: K 1 2 3   E
    1. Trees -- Fiction 2. Israel -- Fiction 3. Ethiopia -- Fiction 4. Jewish refugees -- Fiction 5. Jews -- Ethiopia -- Fiction
    ISBN 978-0-7613-5651-6; 0-7613-5651-7; 978-0-7613-5652-3 pa; 0-7613-5652-5 pa
                     LC 2010003880
Fleeing famine in her native Ethiopia, five-year-old Yuvi is sure she will have a candy tree when she arrives in Jerusalem.
"Flowing illustrations in browns, blues, and oranges bring this story, based on one woman's experience with Operation Moses, to life." Horn Book Guide

Singer, Marilyn
    I'm your bus; pictures by Evan Polenghi. Scholastic Press 2009 un il $16.99
Grades: PreK   E
    1. Buses -- Fiction
    ISBN 978-0-545-08918-0; 0-545-08918-2
                     LC 2008017870
In rhyming text, a school bus describes its busy day transporting children to and from school.
"The digitally rendered pictures, composed of bold black outlines and bright colors, create a wholly endearing character. . . . Both energetic and reassuring." Booklist

    Tallulah's Nutcracker; by Marilyn Singer; illustrated by Alexandra Boiger. Clarion Books 2013 48 p. (hardcover) $16.99
Grades: PreK K 1 2   E
    1. School stories 2. Ballet -- Fiction 3. Christmas -- Fiction 4. Ballet dancing -- Fiction 5. Nutcracker (Choreographic work) -- Fiction
    ISBN 054784557X; 9780547845579
                     LC 2012034744
In this book by Marilyn Singer, "it's Christmastime, and Tallulah finally gets what she's been wishing for--a part in a real ballet, a professional production of The Nutcracker. She's only a mouse, but she works as hard as if she had been cast as the Sugar Plum Fairy. On the night of the show, everything is perfect. But then disaster strikes! Does Tallulah have what it takes to become a real ballerina?" (Publisher's note)

    Tallulah's solo; written by Marilyn Singer; illustrated by Alexandra Boiger. Clarion Books 2012 40 p. $16.99

Grades: PreK K 1 2   **E**

1. School stories 2. Ballet -- Fiction 3. Ballet dancing -- Fiction 4. Brothers and sisters -- Fiction
ISBN 0547330049; 9780547330044

LC 2011025729

In this book by Marilyn Singer, "Tallulah is certain she will have a solo in her dance school's upcoming performance of The Frog Prince. After all, she is now an excellent ballerina. And she's proud that her little brother, Beckett, has started taking ballet too. But then Tallulah gets an unexpected surprise . . . and not the good kind. What's a ballerina to do when everything does not go as planned?" (Publisher's note)

Tallulah's toe shoes; by Marilyn Singer; illustrated by Alexandra Boiger. Clarion Books 2013 48 p. (hardcover) $16.99

Grades: PreK K 1 2   **E**

1. Shoes -- Fiction 2. Ballet -- Fiction 3. Ballet dancing -- Fiction 4. Ballet slippers -- Fiction
ISBN 054748223X; 9780547482231

LC 2012010869

In this book by Marilyn Singer "Tallulah is back in ballet class and now she wants to go en pointe—to dance up on the tips of her toes in pink satin toe shoes, like a real ballerina. But going en pointe is not good for growing feet, and her ballet teacher says her feet aren't ready yet. Oh, yes, they are, Tallulah thinks. Not only is she ready, she's determined. And nothing stops Tallulah when her mind is made up!" (Publisher's note)

Tallulah's tutu; illustrated by Alexandra Boiger. Clarion Books 2011 un il $16.99

Grades: PreK K 1 2   **E**

1. Ballet -- Fiction
ISBN 978-0-547-17353-5; 0-547-17353-9

LC 2010-05441

Tallulah takes ballet lessons and eagerly awaits her coveted tutu, which, she learns, she must work hard to earn.

"Even children who don't share Tallulah's ballet dreams may long for such an idyllic world. . . . Boiger's expressive paintings emphasize Tallulah's enthusiasm, grace, and large-eyed innocence." Booklist

What is your dog doing? illustrated by Kathleen Habbley. Atheneum Books for Young Readers 2011 il $12.99

Grades: PreK K 1   **E**

1. Stories in rhyme 2. Dogs -- Fiction
ISBN 978-1-4169-7931-9; 1-4169-7931-X

LC 2010016351

Illustrations and simple, rhyming text reveal that dogs do much more than sit, stay, and roll over.

"This fun look at canine activities will be a hit with dog people, cat people, and all people at storytime or anytime." SLJ

Siomades, Lorianne

Katy did it! Boyds Mills Press 2009 un il $16.95

Grades: PreK K 1   **E**

1. Katydids -- Fiction
ISBN 978-1-59078-602-4; 1-59078-602-5

LC 2008028133

A katydid named Katy, who upsets other insects as she bounces through the garden, saves the day for a colony of ants

"Digitally created jewel-tone illustrations are airy and uncluttered against a pure white background. . . . Sound effects . . . mimic Katy's hops, ever advancing the story, and the insect's simplified face with round, googly eyes is especially expressive. This bright, bouncy story will be a favorite with youngsters." SLJ

Sis, Peter

★ **Ballerina!** Greenwillow Bks. 2001 un il $14.95; bd bk $7.99

Grades: PreK K 1   **E**

1. Color 2. Ballet -- Fiction
ISBN 0-688-17944-4; 0-06-075966-6 bd bk

LC 00-35401

A little girl puts on costumes of different colors and imagines herself dancing on stage

Sis "creates a beautifully realized spot-on view of creative kids at play." Booklist

★ **Dinosaur!** Greenwillow Bks. 2000 un il $15.99; bd bk $7.99

Grades: PreK K 1   **E**

1. Dinosaurs 2. Stories without words
ISBN 0-688-17049-8; 0-06-075967-4 bd bk

LC 99-32923

While taking a bath, a young boy is joined by all sorts of dinosaurs

"A wordless picture book that takes readers on a wild adventure of the imagination. . . . This imaginative story with wonderful end-papers naming the creatures should appeal to all young dinosaur lovers. Sis's barely fleshed-out, cookie-cutter cartoons tell the story." SLJ

★ **Fire** truck. Greenwillow Bks. 1998 un il $15.99; bd bk $6.99

Grades: PreK K 1   **E**

1. Fire engines -- Fiction
ISBN 0-688-15878-1; 0-06-056259-5 bd bk

LC 97-29320

Matt, who loves fire trucks, wakes up one morning to find that he has become a fire truck, with one driver, two ladders, three hoses, and ten boots. Features a gate-fold illustration that opens into a three-page spread

"Sis blends simple text with bold pictures to give insight into one boy's vivid imagination." SLJ

Komodo! Greenwillow Bks. 1993 un il $17.99

Grades: K 1 2 3   **E**

1. Indonesia -- Fiction 2. Komodo dragon -- Fiction
ISBN 0-688-11583-7; 0-688-11584-5 lib bdg

LC 92-25811

"Mad about dragons, the boy who narrates this picture book is pleased when his doting parents decide to take him to Indonesia, home of the Komodo dragon (aka monitor lizard). When the family disembarks on the Island of Komodo, the parents join a throng of tourists waiting for the Dragon Show, but the shy lizard never ventures out of its leafy shelter. Their adventuresome son, however, takes the road less traveled through the jungle, where he encounters the dragon of his dreams." (Booklist) "Ages five to eight." (Bull Cent Child Books)

"The story, assisted by the art in its moodily surreal tone, is simply written buy implies worlds." Bull Cent Child Books

Madlenka. Farrar, Straus & Giroux 2000 un il $17
Grades: PreK K 1 2 3   E
  1. Teeth -- Fiction 2. New York (N.Y.) -- Fiction
  ISBN 0-374-39969-7
                      LC 99-57730

Madlenka, whose New York City neighbors include the French baker, the Indian news vendor, the Italian ice-cream man, the South American grocer, and the Chinese shopkeeper, goes around the block to show her friends her loose tooth and finds that it is like taking a trip around the world

"The real magic comes in the cleverly cut-away windows in each storefront through which children glimpse complex, global dreamscapes. Madlenka journeys through these mystical places, too, and it is these surreal, wordless stories-within-the-story that will excite a wide range of children, launching them in their own imagined departures." Booklist

Other titles about Madlenka are:
Madlenka's dog (2002)
Madlenka, soccer star (2010)

★ **Trucks**, trucks, trucks. Greenwillow Bks. 1999 un il $16.99; bd bk $7.99
Grades: PreK K   E
  1. Trucks -- Fiction
  ISBN 0-688-16276-2; 0-06-056258-7 bd bk
                      LC 98-4482

A little boy cleans up his room using a variety of trucks and gives a one word description of their work such as hauling, plowing, and loading. Features a gate-fold illustration that opens into a three-page spread

"Sis creates a simple, bold look. . . . Gouache paints in yellow, black, and gray are set off by plenty of white space. The single verbs on each page are rendered in shades of blue, purple, green, and orange. This cheery romp is perfect for toddlers." SLJ

Sit, Danny
  Tucker; little dog lost and found. Sterling 2011 un il $9.95
Grades: PreK K   E
  1. Dogs -- Fiction 2. Beaches -- Fiction 3. Lost and found possessions -- Fiction
  ISBN 978-1-4027-5999-4; 1-4027-5999-1
                    LC 2010031378

Tucker the Jack Russell terrier packs his bags and takes the train to the beach for an adventure, but after a fun day he discovers that he does not know how to get home.

"A strong narrative voice, charming photographs and an utterly appealing little dog protagonist coalesce to create a winning story about a Jack Russell terrier named Tucker. . . . Each page contains only a few sentences, making this a good choice for younger preschoolers and a possible selection for newly independent readers as well. Tucker's charming personality and the quality of the photographic illustrations help this stand out from the pack." Kirkus

Skofield, James
  Detective Dinosaur; pictures by R.W. Alley. HarperCollins Pubs. 1996 46p il (I can read book) hardcover o.p. pa $3.99
Grades: K 1 2   E
  1. Mystery fiction 2. Dinosaurs -- Fiction
  ISBN 0-06-024907-2; 0-06-024908-0 lib bdg; 978-0-06-444235-0 pa; 0-06-444235-7 pa
                    LC 94-42296

Detective Dinosaur and Officer Pterodactyl are challenged to solve three cases when a hat is missing, a shoe squeaks, and a loud clanging comes from a dark alley at night

"The various plots are pleasantly silly and uncomplicated, and what kids may not grasp from the text . . . can easily be gleaned from the artwork, which is warm, lively, and lots of fun. Enlarged type and extra leading make the reading easier." Booklist

  Detective Dinosaur undercover; illustrated by R. W. Alley. HarperCollins 2010 36p il (I can read) $16.99
Grades: K 1 2   E
  1. Mystery fiction 2. Dinosaurs -- Fiction
  ISBN 978-0-06-623878-4; 0-06-623878-1

In three brief mysteries, Detective Dinosaur learns about doing undercover work, gets chased by strange blobs, and finds rain on a sunny day.

"The dino's genial expressions projected in colorful pen-and-ink and watercolor cartoons follow the action. Conversation and onomatopoeia spice up the text, presented in large font. . . . His innocent confusion creates entertaining problems with simple solutions." SLJ

Other titles in this series are:
Detective Dinosaur (1996)
Detective Dinosaur: lost and found (1998)

  Detective Dinosaur: lost and found; pictures by R.W. Alley. HarperCollins Pubs. 1998 46p il (I can read book) $14.95; pa $3.99
Grades: K 1 2   E
  1. Mystery fiction 2. Dinosaurs -- Fiction
  ISBN 0-06-026784-4; 0-06-026785-2 lib bdg; 978-0-06-444257-2 pa; 0-06-444257-8 pa
                    LC 97-2725

After Detective Dinosaur and Officer Pterodactyl find a missing baby wearing pink diapers and a home for Cadet Kitty, they lose and rediscover each other

"The watercolor-and-ink illustrations add visual interest and, in the case about the lost baby, reveal her location to alert readers. The humor is right on target for beginning readers." SLJ

Slack, Michael
  Elecopter; Michael Slack. Henry Holt and Company 2013 32 p. (hardcover) $15.99
Grades: PreK   E
  1. Heroes and heroines -- Fiction 2. Stories in rhyme 3. Heroes -- Fiction 4. Elephants -- Fiction 5. Helicopters -- Fiction
  ISBN 0805093044; 9780805093049
                    LC 2012046317

This children's picture book by Michael Slack focuses on "a hybrid elephant/helicopter who patrols the savannah. . . . In the story's tensest sequence, Elecopter rescues a group of animals from wildfire: 'Flying into danger, she's first on the scene/ to airlift a rhino from a rocky ravine.' She also escorts to safety a cheetah, a passel of baboons, and a giraffe, and, best of all, she works for peanuts." (Publishers Weekly)

Slack, Michael H.

Monkey Truck; [by] Michael Slack. Henry Holt & Co. 2011 un il $12.99

Grades: PreK K 1   E

1. Stories in rhyme 2. Trucks -- Fiction 3. Jungles -- Fiction 4. Monkeys -- Fiction

ISBN 978-0-8050-8878-6; 0-8050-8878-4

         LC 2010011687

Monkey Truck comes racing to the rescue anytime there is trouble in the jungle.

"Slack produces a zippy jungle jaunt with enough action and rhythm for any preschooler in his first solo effort. The bright, blocky and, above all, goofy digitally painted illustrations will grab attention, and Monkey Truck's hooting mug (and tooting bottom) will keep the giggles flowing." Kirkus

Slate, Jenny

Marcel the Shell with shoes on; things about me. by Jenny Slate & Dean Fleischer-Camp; paintings by Amy Lind. Razorbill 2011 un il $18.99

Grades: K 1 2   E

1. Fantasy fiction 2. Shells -- Fiction

ISBN 978-1-59514-455-3; 1-59514-455-2

"Like the popular Internet video it's based on, this picture book stars a pink-shod, one-eyed snail shell who is happy to discuss his habits, preferences, and inner life, while revealing a life that's both miniature and writ large. . . . The artwork trades the jerky animation of the original for Lind's thick, luminous oil paintings, which provide a fittingly off-kilter realism." Publ Wkly

Slate, Joseph

★ **I** want to be free; illustrated by E. B. Lewis. G.P. Putnam's Sons 2009 un il $16.99

Grades: 2 3 4   E

1. Stories in rhyme 2. Slavery -- Fiction 3. African Americans -- Fiction

ISBN 978-0-399-24342-4; 0-399-24342-9

         LC 2007-38356

Based on a sacred Buddhist tale as related in Rudyard Kipling's novel "Kim," tells of an escaped slave who rescues an abandoned baby from slave hunters

"The spare words and pictures never sensationalize the drama or the universal themes of cruelty, courage, and kindness." Booklist

Miss Bindergarten celebrates the 100th day of kindergarten; illustrated by Ashley Wolff. Dutton Children's Bks. 1998 un il $16.99; pa $6.99

Grades: PreK K 1   E

1. Stories in rhyme 2. Animals -- Fiction 3. Kindergarten -- Fiction

ISBN 0-525-46000-4; 0-14-250005-4 pa

         LC 98-10486

To celebrate one hundred days in Miss Bindergarten's kindergarten class, all her students bring one hundred of something to school, including a one hundred-year-old relative, one hundred candy hearts, and one hundred polka dots

"Wolff's sturdy, genially observed illustrations prove a perfect match for Slate's rhyming text." Publ Wkly

Other titles about Miss Bindergarten are:

Miss Bindergarten celebrates the last day of kindergarten (2006)

Miss Bindergarten gets ready for kindergarten (1996)

Miss Bindergarten has a wild day in kindergarten (2005)

Miss Bindergarten stays home from kindergarten (2000)

Miss Bindergarten takes a field trip with kindergarten (2001)

Miss Bindergarten's craft center (1999)

Slater, Dashka

Baby shoes; by Dashka Slater; pictures by Hiroe Nakata. Bloomsbury Children's Books 2006 un il $15.95

Grades: PreK   E

1. Stories in rhyme 2. Color -- Fiction 3. Shoes -- Fiction

ISBN 978-1-58234-684-7; 1-58234-684-4

         LC 2005053581

After taking a walk with his mother, Baby's new white shoes with the blue stripe are covered with a variety of colors

"In the text, loping lines of rhymed couplets are interspersed with staccato sections, followed by a refrain that reins in the pace. . . . The changing rhythm creates a pleasing pattern and gives listeners places to chime in. Setting a sunny tone for the excursion, Nakata's airy watercolor artwork sympathetically depicts an increasingly scruffy toddler and his tired but resilient mother." Booklist

Slater, David Michael

The **boy** & the book; David Michael Slater; illustrated by Bob Kolar. Charlesbridge 2015 32 p. (reinforced) $16.95

Grades: PreK K   E

1. Stories without words 2. Libraries -- Fiction 3. Books and reading -- Fiction

ISBN 158089562X; 9781580895620

         LC 2013049017

In this story without words, by David Michael Slater, illustrated by Bob Kolar, "a library book tries desperately to evade the destructive clutches of a little boy. What drives the Boy, however, is enthusiasm and love--not malice--and the Book eventually responds in kind, accepting his rough but worthy fate." (Publisher's note)

Boy and the book

Slater, Kate

Magpie's treasure. Andersen 2011 un il $16.99

Grades: PreK K   E

1. Moon -- Fiction 2. Birds -- Fiction 3. Thieves -- Fiction

ISBN 978-1-84939-008-8; 1-84939-008-8

"Magnus Magpie, a bird with an eye for burglary, steals the shiniest, most dazzling things and stashes them secretly. . . . What he wants most of all, though, is the shining moon. . . . With a sweet final twist, he find that home and a family of his own are what he wants most. . . . The energetic text is well paced for read-alouds, and kids will enjoy picking out the objects in Slater's vibrant, mixed-media collage illustrations." Booklist

Slater, Teddy

Smooch your pooch; illustrations by Arthur Howard. Scholastic Inc. 2010 un il $14.99

Grades: PreK K   E

1. Stories in rhyme 2. Dogs -- Fiction

ISBN 978-0-545-16736-9; 0-545-16736-1

"A winning cast of fun-loving children cavorts with an assortment of equally engaging dogs in this rhyming tale. Describing how to show love to a favorite four-legged friend, the short, punchy lines beg to be read aloud, engaging listeners and moving the action right along. . . . The cartoon illustrations, rendered in black line and watercolors, pair perfectly with the text in their movement and energy and are sure to prompt many giggles." SLJ

Slegers, Liesbet

Bathing. Clavis 2011 un il bd bk $5.95

Grades: PreK   E

1. Board books for children 2. Baths -- Fiction

ISBN 978-1-60537-092-7; 1-60537-092-4

"A smiling toddler makes bath time seem easy and fun in this warm board book. . . . He uses his orange washcloth, happily lets his mother shampoo his hair, and sails his red boat in the bathwater, finishing up with a cuddly towel. Slegers's characteristically bright, smudgy paintings convey a common experience with a light, appealing touch." Publ Wkly

Katie goes to the doctor. Clavis Pub. 2011 un il $12.95

Grades: PreK   E

1. Sick -- Fiction 2. Physicians -- Fiction

ISBN 978-1-60537-076-7; 1-60537-076-2

Katie doesn't feel well—she has a cough, a runny nose, and she feels dizzy. Her mother explains that she has a fever and takes Katie to see the doctor.

This "presents a common childhood experience through a friendly narrator who explains step-by-step what is happening. [It] will guide parents through a discussion of what to expect as they prepare and reassure their children. Large, colorful illustrations support the [text]." SLJ

Kevin goes to the library. Clavis 2011 un il $12.95

Grades: PreK   E

1. Libraries -- Fiction 2. Books and reading -- Fiction

ISBN 978-1-60537-075-0; 1-60537-075-4

Explores the cyclical nature of borrowing library books and emphasizes the many joys of reading as Kevin, a young boy, describes his experiences at the library

"Toddlers should be drawn to this straightforward depiction of a common experience." Publ Wkly

Sloat, Teri

Berry magic; written by Teri Sloat and Betty Huffmon; illustrated by Teri Sloat. Alaska Northwest Books 2004 un il hardcover o.p. $15.95

Grades: K 1 2 3   E

1. Inuit -- Fiction 2. Alaska -- Fiction 3. Berries -- Fiction

ISBN 0-88240-575-6; 0-88240-576-4 pa

LC 2003-70851

Long ago, the only berries on the tundra were hard, tasteless, little crowberries. When Anana sings, she turns four dolls into little girls who run and tumble over the tundra cre-

ating patches of fat, juicy berries: blueberries, cranberries, salmonberries, and raspberries

"Done in a palette of deep, earthy hues, ethereal blues, and bright highlights, Sloat's pictures are vibrant and engaging. . . . The rich language enlightens readers to different elements of the Eskimo culture." SLJ

I'm a duck! story and pictures by Teri Sloat. G.P. Putnam's Sons 2006 un il hardcover o.p. pa $6.99

Grades: PreK K 1 2   E

1. Stories in rhyme 2. Ducks -- Fiction

ISBN 0-399-24274-0; 0-14-241062-4 pa

LC 2004-20479

"From the moment he hatches, a duckling celebrates his duck-ness–his webbed feet, his perfect waddle, his strong quack, and his flapping wings. As he grows, he meets a mate, becomes a father, and continues his zestful take on life. Sloat's rhymed text captures the exuberance of this eternal optimist and gives a glimpse into the life cycle of a mallard. The full-color art is rendered in pastels and has bold lines and a variety of perspectives and page layouts." SLJ

There was an old man who painted the sky; illustrated by Stefano Vitale. Henry Holt 2009 32p il $16.95

Grades: PreK K 1 2   E

1. Songs 2. Prehistoric art -- Fiction 3. Cave drawings and paintings -- Fiction

ISBN 978-0-8050-6751-4; 0-8050-6751-5

LC 2008-18340

In this song based on 'The Old Woman Who Swallowed a Fly,' a prehistoric man, contemplating the creation of the world, paints images on the ceiling of a cave, that are later discovered by a young Spanish girl in 1879

"Vitale's vibrant illustrations, in mixed media on board, reference both cave drawings and folk art. Appropriate for a wide audience, this will find its ideal fit with families wishing to impart diverse beliefs about the Earth's beginnings to their children." Booklist

Slobodkina, Esphyr

★ **Caps** for sale; a tale of a peddler, some monkeys & their monkey business. told and illustrated by Esphyr Slobodkina. Addison Wesley Longman 1947 un il $17.99; pa $6.99

Grades: PreK K   E

1. Monkeys -- Fiction 2. Peddlers and peddling -- Fiction

ISBN 0-201-09147-X; 0-06-443143-6 pa

A picture book story which "provides hilarious confusion. A cap peddler takes a nap under a tree. When he wakes up, his caps have disappeared. He looks up in the tree and sees countless monkeys, each wearing a cap and grinning." Parent's Guide To Child Read

Small, David

George Washington's cows. Farrar, Straus and Giroux 1994 un il hardcover o.p. pa $6.95

Grades: PreK K 1 2   E

1. Generals 2. Presidents 3. Stories in rhyme 4. Animals -- Fiction

ISBN 0-374-32535-9; 0-374-42534-5 pa

LC 93-39989

Humorous rhymes about George Washington's farm where the cows wear dresses, the pigs wear wigs, and the sheep are scholars

"Small's watercolors immeasurably extend his zany poem and make maximum use of the double-page spreads. Cleverly designed and well-executed scenes are filled with silly details that children will love." Booklist

Imogene's antlers; written and illustrated by David Small. Crown 2000 un il $16.99; pa $6.99
Grades: PreK K 1 2   E
1. Humorous fiction 2. Metamorphosis -- Fiction
ISBN 978-0-375-81048-0; 0-375-81048-X; 978-0-517-56242-0 pa; 0-517-56242-1 pa
First published 1985

One Thursday Imogene wakes up with a pair of antlers growing out of her head and causes a sensation wherever she goes

The author "maximizes the inherent humor of the absurd situation by allowing the imaginative possibilities of Imogene's predicament to run rampant. The brief text is supported by Small's expansive watercolors. They brim with humorous details." SLJ

Smallcomb, Pam
Earth to Clunk; pictures by Joe Berger. Dial Books for Young Readers 2011 un il $16.99
Grades: PreK K 1   E
1. Siblings -- Fiction 2. Extraterrestrial beings -- Fiction
ISBN 978-0-8037-3439-5; 0-8037-3439-5
LC 2010-20621

For a school assignment, a boy reluctantly writes a letter to Clunk of the planet Quazar, sending his older sister with it, but as more letters and packages are exchanged, he realizes that having an alien pen pal can be fun.

"The boy narrates in pitch-perfect deadpan style; the comedy lurks just below the surface, and the spare details leave boundless room for listeners' imaginations. . . . Berger's illustrations, composed in pencil, pen, and ink and colored digitally, are candy toned, with copious use of yellow, chartreuse, aqua, and bright orange." Bull Cent Child Books

★ **I'm** not; not drawn by Pam Smallcomb; not written by Robert Weinstock. Schwartz & Wade Books 2010 un il $15.99; lib bdg $18.99
Grades: PreK K 1   E
1. Friendship -- Fiction
ISBN 0-375-86115-7; 0-375-96115-1 lib bdg; 978-0-375-86115-4; 978-0-375-96115-1 lib bdg
LC 2009-46742

Our shy narrator lists all the things that her best friend, Evelyn, is good at—from jumping on the bed to roller skating really fast. Luckily, Evelyn points out what makes her so special: she's a one-of-a-kind true blue best friend.

"Weinstock captures the friends as rotund, squat reptiles who suggest trash-compacted dragons, and the scenes are confidently laced with absurdity. . . . This offers a nice reminder that good friendships always offer mutual benefits." Bull Cent Child Books

Smee, Nicola
What's the matter, Bunny Blue? Boxer Books 2010 un il $14.95

Grades: PreK   E
1. Animals -- Fiction 2. Rabbits -- Fiction 3. Grandmothers -- Fiction
ISBN 978-1-906250-91-1; 1-906250-91-X

"A wide-eyed little blue bunny . . . calls, 'Granny! Granny! Where are you?' No sooner does he explain his dilemma to Duck and Bee than the tears begin. A series of animals—a tiger, alligator, bear, and fox—ask the despondent bunny what Granny looks like. . . . All the animals join the ultimately successful search for Granny. The very real, small details of twinkly eyes, a big smile, and soft furry arms are just what matter to children when they experience separation anxiety. The uncluttered pages with lots of white space and sympathetic, childlike animals are perfect for the toddler set." Booklist

Smith, Alex T.
Foxy and Egg; a book by Alex T. Smith. Holiday House 2011 un il $17.95
Grades: K 1 2   E
1. Eggs -- Fiction 2. Foxes -- Fiction 3. Alligators -- Fiction
ISBN 978-0-8234-2330-9; 0-8234-2330-1
LC 2010026416
First published 2010 in the United Kingdom

"Foxy DuBois gives Egg shelter for the evening, but as a chicken connoisseur, she plots to fatten up her guest and make a tasty meal out of him. Her plans run afowl—sorry, afoul—when Egg cracks open and reveals a sizable, mustachioed alligator named Alphonso hankering for a taste of fox. Children will have fun poring over the spreads to find silly touches like chicken wallpaper, fork and spoon finials on the guest bed, and, in a neat little turn, the silhouettes of a fox on Alphonso's teacup. Smith's art . . . [mixes] cartoon-like sketches with photographs of patterns and objects." SLJ

Smith, Cynthia Leitich
Jingle dancer; illustrated by Cornelius Van Wright and Ying-Hwa Hu. Morrow Junior Bks. 2000 un il $17.99; lib bdg $18.89
Grades: K 1 2 3   E
1. Creek Indians -- Fiction 2. Native American dance -- Fiction
ISBN 0-688-16241-X; 0-688-16242-8 lib bdg
LC 99-15503

Jenna, a member of the Muscogee, or Creek, Nation, borrows jingles from the dresses of several friends and relatives so that she can perform the jingle dance at the powwow. Includes a note about the jingle dance tradition and its regalia

"The colorful, well-executed watercolor illustrations lend warmth to the story." Booklist

Smith, Danna
Pirate nap; a book of colors. illustrated by Valeria Petrone. Clarion Books 2011 il $14.99
Grades: PreK K 1   E
1. Color 2. Stories in rhyme 3. Play -- Fiction 4. Pirates -- Fiction 5. Brothers -- Fiction 6. Imagination -- Fiction
ISBN 978-0-547-57531-5; 0-547-57531-9
LC 2010043253

Two brothers use their imaginations to turn their surroundings--from a white bandana and yellow coins to a red blanket and even their baby sister-- into a colorful pirate adventure before naptime.

"Clever rhyming text in 'pirate speak' and colorful, digital gouache illustrations in muted tones create a standout concept book. . . . The eight basic colors are introduced in the humorous text and in the imaginative pictures. . . . Children will pore over the small and large details in the artwork. This title inspires creative play, and is likely to be a treasure for years to come." SLJ

Two at the zoo; illustrated by Valeria Petrone. Clarion 2009 32p il $16
Grades: PreK K   E
1. Stories in rhyme 2. Zoos -- Fiction 3. Animals -- Fiction 4. Grandfathers -- Fiction
ISBN 978-0-547-04982-3; 0-547-04982-X
A grandfather and grandchild go to the zoo, where they count animals from one to ten.

"The digital gouache illustrations have vibrant colors, clean lines, and palpable texture. . . . An engaging read-aloud for storytime and one-on-one sharing." SLJ

Smith, Lane
★ **Abe** Lincoln's dream; written and illustrated by Lane Smith. 1st ed. Roaring Brook Press 2012 32 p. col. ill. (hardcover) $16.99
Grades: 1 2 3   E
1. Ghost stories 2. United States -- Fiction 3. Ghosts -- Fiction 4. White House (Washington, D.C.) -- Fiction
ISBN 1596436085; 9781596436084
LC 2012020110
In this children's picture book by Lane Smith, "when a schoolgirl gets separated from her tour of the White House and finds herself in the Lincoln bedroom, she also discovers the ghost of the great man himself. Together they embark on a journey across the country to answer [Abraham] Lincoln's questions and quiet his concerns about the nation for which he gave his life." (Publisher's note)

★ **Grandpa** Green. Roaring Brook Press 2011 un il $16.99
Grades: K 1 2   E
1. Gardens -- Fiction 2. Old age -- Fiction 3. Grandfathers -- Fiction
ISBN 978-1-59643-607-7; 1-59643-607-7
LC 2010038729
"The idea of a garden as a lockbox of memories is not a new one, but rarely is it pulled off with this kind of panache. . . . Sketched with a finely lined fairy-tale wispiness and dominated by verdant green, the illustrations are not just creative but poignant. . . . The perfect book to help kids understand old age." Booklist

★ **It's** a book. Roaring Book Press 2010 un il $12.99
Grades: PreK K 1 2   E
1. Animals -- Fiction 2. Electronic books -- Fiction 3. Books and reading -- Fiction
ISBN 978-1-59643-606-0; 1-59643-606-9
"Smith jump-starts the action on the title page where readers meet the characters—a mouse, a jackass, and a monkey. . . . Slapstick humor ensues in an armchair face-off when one character, reared on a diet of Web 2.0 and gaming, cannot fathom what to do with a book and slings a barrage of annoying questions, 'Can you blog with it? How do you

scroll down? Can you make the characters fight?' Readers know who is speaking by each animal's unique font type and color, achieving economy and elegance on each page. . . . A clever choice for readers, young and old, who love a good joke and admire the picture book's ability to embody in 32 stills the action of the cinema." SLJ

★ **John,** Paul, George & Ben. Hyperion Books for Children 2006 un il $16.99
Grades: 2 3 4   E
1. Authors 2. Generals 3. Diplomats 4. Governors 5. Inventors 6. Statesmen 7. Presidents 8. Scientists 9. Vice-presidents 10. Artisans 11. Essayists 12. Metalworkers 13. Revolutionaries 14. Colonial leaders 15. Members of Congress 16. United States -- History -- 1775-1783, Revolution -- Fiction
ISBN 0-7868-4893-6
LC 2005-52735
This is a humorous look at George Washington, John Hancock, Paul Revere, Benjamin Franklin, and Thomas Jefferson. "Grades three to five." (Bull Cent Child Books)

"Describing each man in turn as either bold, noisy, honest, clever, or independent, and taking many liberties with the truth, Smith relates how the Founding Fathers of the title [John Hancock, Paul Revere, George Washington, Benjamin Franklin]—and [Thomas] Jefferson, too—played a part in securing America's freedom. . . . The pen-and-ink cartoon illustrations, richly textured with various techniques, add to the fun. . . . A true-and-false section in the back separates fact from fiction." SLJ

★ **Madam** President. Hyperion Books for Children 2008 un il lib bdg $16.99
Grades: K 1 2   E
1. Sex role -- Fiction 2. Presidents -- Fiction 3. Children's literature -- Works -- Grades two through six
ISBN 1-4231-0846-9 lib bdg; 978-1-4231-0846-7 lib bdg
LC 2008-04509
Katy imagines what her day would be like if she were President of the United States. "Ages six to ten." (Bull Cent Child Books)

This is a "sly, witty recitation of a president's responsibilities. . . . The list . . . does grow rather long. But the stretch can be forgiven because it provides more opportunity to enjoy Smith's amazing artwork. Madam President, with her boxy head and triangular body appears against a variety of backgrounds . . . with disparate uses of materials and images that often give the look of collage." Booklist

Smith, Maggie
Christmas with the Mousekins. Alfred A. Knopf 2010 un il $15.99; lib bdg $18.99
Grades: PreK K 1   E
1. Mice -- Fiction 2. Christmas -- Fiction 3. Family life -- Fiction
ISBN 978-0-375-83330-4; 0-375-83330-7; 978-0-375-93330-1 lib bdg; 0-375-93330-1 lib bdg
LC 2010003878
A mouse family tells stories, bakes cookies, makes crafts, and more as they prepare for Christmas. Includes directions for each of the crafts and recipes for cookies.

"The cheerful text and busy, colorful illustrations combine for a charmingly old-fashioned overall tone." Booklist

Snell, Gordon

The **King** of Quizzical Island; illustrated by David McKee. Candlewick Press 2009 un il

Grades: K 1 2 3   E

1. Stories in rhyme 2. Earth -- Fiction 3. Explorers -- Fiction 4. Kings and rulers -- Fiction 5. Voyages and travels -- Fiction

ISBN 0-7636-3857-9; 978-0-7636-3857-3

LC 2008-26510

When no one can answer his question about what is at the edge of the world, the King of Quizzical Island builds a boat and sets sail to find out for himself, despite the objections of his fearful people. "Ages six to nine." (Bull Cent Child Books)

"The text is a case study in clever rhyme, and the pen-and-ink and watercolor illustrations—in black-and-white except for the king—show readers that curiosity is like a light in the darkness." Horn Book Guide

Snicket, Lemony, 1970-

13 words; [illustrated by] Maira Kalman. HarperCollins 2010 un il

Grades: K 1 2   E

1. Vocabulary -- Fiction

ISBN 0061664650; 0061664669 lib bdg; 9780061664656; 9780061664663 lib bdg

LC 2009039671

A dog attempts to cheer up his friend, a despondent bird, in a tale that introduces a series of words from "baby" to "haberdashery."

"Snicket and Kalman are perfectly matched here, both revelers in life's delicious . . . details and things best left unexplained. . . . This charming chef-d'oeuvre sings like a mezzo-soprano." Kirkus

★ The **composer** is dead; written by Lemony Snicket; with music composed by Nathaniel Stookey and illustrations by Carson Ellis. HarperCollinsPublishers 2008 un il $17.99; lib bdg $18.89

Grades: K 1 2 3   E

1. Mystery fiction 2. Orchestra -- Fiction 3. Musical instruments -- Fiction

ISBN 978-0-06-123627-3; 0-06-123627-6; 978-0-06-123628-0 lib bdg; 0-06-123628-4 lib bdg

LC 2007-20834

An inspector seeks to solve a murder mystery at the symphony by questioning each of the musical instruments.

This offers "witty wordplay. . . . Ellis . . . brightens the heavily black stage scenes with coral, gold and sepia accents against expansive white backgrounds. . . . The accompanying CD features Snicket narrating and the San Francisco Symphony Orchestra performing Stookey's original score." Publ Wkly

★ The **dark**; by Lemony Snicket; illustrated by Jon Klassen. Little, Brown and Co. 2013 40 p. (reinforced) $16.99

Grades: K 1 2   E

1. Picture books for children 2. Fear of the dark -- Fiction

ISBN 0316187488; 9780316187480

LC 2012026498

This children's picture book by Lemony Snicket offers a "suspenseful take on childhood fear. Laszlo, a solemn boy in blue pajamas, is scared of the dark, and it's easy to see why. He lives in a house with 'a creaky roof, smooth, cold windows, and several sets of stairs.' The floors are bare, the halls are empty, and the windows are uncurtained. And the dark in his house is not just any dark--it has a will of its own." (Publishers Weekly)

★ The **latke** who couldn't stop screaming; a Christmas story. by Lemony Snicket; illustrations by Lisa Brown. McSweeney's Books 2007 43p il $9.95

Grades: K 1 2 3 4   E

1. Hanukkah -- Fiction 2. Christmas -- Fiction

ISBN 978-1-932416-87-9

"The miraculous birth here is of a potato pancake, which . . . begins screaming the moment it gets cooked. Leaping out of the frying pan and into the great white spaces of Brown's retro-cool graphics, the latke screams even louder as it tries in vain to explain itself and its role at Hanukkah to flashing colored lights . . . and an equally Christmas-centric candy cane and tree. Embedding the satirical sting in his elegantly cadenced prose, the author . . . up-ends any number of conventions in what may be his funniest book yet." Publ Wkly

Snyder, Betsy E.

Sweet dreams lullaby. Random House Children's Books 2010 un il $15.99

Grades: PreK K   E

1. Lullabies 2. Stories in rhyme 3. Dreams -- Fiction 4. Nature -- Fiction 5. Bedtime -- Fiction 6. Rabbits -- Fiction

ISBN 978-0-375-85852-9; 0-375-85852-0

LC 2008-52265

A young bunny goes to sleep and dreams of the soothing colors, shapes, sights, and sounds of nature.

Snyder, Laurel

Baxter, the pig who wanted to be kosher; illustrated by David Goldin. Tricycle Press 2010 un il $15.99; lib bdg $18.99

Grades: PreK K 1   E

1. Pigs -- Fiction 2. Sabbath -- Fiction 3. Jews -- United States -- Fiction

ISBN 978-1-58246-315-5; 1-58246-315-8; 978-1-58246-360-5 lib bdg; 1-58246-360-3 lib bdg

When Baxter the pig hears about the joys of Shabbat dinner he tries to become kosher so that he can participate.

"The delightfully expressive and comical pen-and-ink illustrations are digitally enhanced with photographs of storefronts, deli counters, pickle jars, and traditional Jewish foods. . . . The idea of a pig wanting to become kosher will entertain children and the adults reading to them, especially those familiar with Jewish traditions." SLJ

The **longest** night; a Passover story. Laurel Snyder; [illustrations by] Catia Chien. Schwartz & Wade Books 2013 40 p. col. ill. (hardcover) $17.99; (library) $20.99

Grades: K 1 2 3 4   E

1. Stories in rhyme 2. Picture books for children 3. Passover -- Fiction 4. Slavery -- Fiction 5. Jews -- History -- To 1200 B.C. -- Fiction 6. Bible O.T. -- History of Biblical events -- Fiction 7. Egypt -- History

-- Eighteenth dynasty, ca. 1570-1320 B.C. -- Fiction
ISBN 0375869425; 037596942X; 9780375869426; 9780375969423

LC 2011011009

This children's picture book, by Laurel Snyder, illustrated by Catia Chien, offers a Passover story. "This . . . book in verse follows the actual story of the Exodus. Told through the eyes of a young slave girl, [the] author . . . and illustrator . . . skillfully and gently depict the story of Pharoah, Moses, the 10 plagues, and the parting of the Red Sea." (Publisher's note)

Soetoro-NG, Maya

★ **Ladder** to the moon; illustrated by Yuyi Morales. Candlewick Press 2011 un il $16.99
Grades: K 1 2 3   E
1. Moon -- Fiction 2. Compassion -- Fiction 3. Grandmothers -- Fiction
ISBN 0-7636-4570-2; 978-0-7636-4570-0

LC 2010039183

Suhaila's wish to know her deceased grandmother is granted when a golden ladder appears at her window and Grandma Annie invites her on a journey to the moon, where they welcome people who are facing tragedy. Includes facts about the painting and woman who inspired the story.

This is "a lush, haunting story. . . . It's hard to imagine a more perfect illustrator for this text than Morales, whose rounded shapes, sunset colors, and softness and strength mirror the words." Booklist

Solheim, James

Born yesterday; the diary of a young journalist. illustrated by Simon James. Philomel Books 2010 un il lib bdg $15.99
Grades: PreK K   E
1. Diaries -- Fiction 2. Infants -- Fiction 3. Siblings -- Fiction
ISBN 978-0-399-25155-9 lib bdg; 0-399-25155-3 lib bdg

LC 2009006251

A baby who plans to grow up to be a writer records thoughts and events in a private journal.

"The watercolor and ink illustrations . . . faithfully follow the humorous text. . . . The book is a fresh and amusing slant on sibling adjustment." SLJ

Soltis, Sue

Nothing like a puffin; illustrated by Bob Kolar. Candlewick Press 2011 un il $15.99
Grades: PreK K 1 2   E
1. Puffins -- Fiction
ISBN 978-0-7636-3617-3; 0-7636-3617-7

LC 2010040796

A narrator sets out to prove that there is nothing like a puffin but discovers that many things, including a newspaper and a helicopter, are a little bit like one and that a penguin is very much like a puffin.

"Kolar's . . . bold, cheerful cartoons show the bird causing lighthearted havoc. . . . What's more, his restrained palette reinforces the similarities Soltis so effectively uncovers. . . . Delightful, thought-provoking fun." Publ Wkly

Soman, David

The **amazing** adventures of Bumblebee Boy; by David Soman & Jacky Davis. Dial Books for Young Readers 2011 il $16.99
Grades: PreK K 1   E
1. Play -- Fiction 2. Brothers -- Fiction 3. Imagination -- Fiction 4. Superheroes -- Fiction
ISBN 978-0-8037-3418-0; 0-8037-3418-2

LC 2011004567

As imaginary superhero Bumblebee Boy, Sam rejects his pesky little brother's help in defeating pirates, dragons, and saber-toothed lions, but when Sam comes up against some scary aliens, he discovers the advantage of having a sidekick.

"The contrast between Sam's brawny superhero exploits and the humble domestic scenes from which they derive . . . will charm readers, and so will the cute-as-a-button Owen in his blankie cape and aviator's hat with flaps." Publ Wkly

Ladybug Girl; [by] David Soman and Jacky Davis. Dial Books for Young Readers 2008 un il $16.99
Grades: PreK K   E
1. Play -- Fiction 2. Siblings -- Fiction 3. Imagination -- Fiction 4. Superheroes -- Fiction
ISBN 978-0-8037-3195-0

LC 2007008619

After her brother tells her she is too little to play with him, Lulu, dressed as Ladybug Girl, makes her own fun.

"Readers' eyes are inexorably drawn to Lulu's red ladybug costume, which sets off the subdues earth tones. . . . Simple sentences throughout the story usually express just one thought or directive at a time, usually in just one sentence per page. A super book for lapsits and storyhours." SLJ

Other titles about Ladybug Girl are:
Ladybug Girl and Bumblebee Boy (2009)
Ladybug Girl at the beach (2010)
Ladybug Girl and the bug squad (2011)

★ **Three** bears in a boat; by David Soman. Dial Books for Young Readers, an imprint of Penguin Group (USA) Inc. 2014 40 p. (hardcover) $17.99
Grades: PreK K 1   E
1. Bears -- Fiction 2. Boats and boating -- Fiction 3. Brothers and sisters -- Fiction 4. Adventure and adventurers -- Fiction
ISBN 0803739931; 9780803739932

LC 2013017796

In this book, by David Soman, "three bear siblings break their mother's favorite blue seashell, and rather than tell her, they decide to set out in their sailboat to find her a new one. On their quest they encounter salty sailors, strange new islands, huge whales, and vast seas but no blue seashells. When a treacherous storm suddenly blows in, the three bears find themselves tossed about in their little boat, far from Mama." (Publisher's note)

"Breaking a prized blue seashell while their mother is away and knowing they'll be in big trouble, three mischievous bears set out to sea to find a replacement. The plot is simple, yet the bears don't find what they're looking for immediately...The gorgeous, bright and detailed illustrations are a perfect fit for the text. A first purchase for all." SLJ

Soto, Gary

Too many tamales; illustrated by Ed Martinez. Putnam 1992 un il $16.99; pa $7.99

Grades: PreK K 1 2　　　　　　　　E
1. Christmas -- Fiction 2. Mexican Americans -- Fiction
ISBN 0-399-22146-8; 0-698-11412-4 pa
LC 91-19229
Maria tries on her mother's wedding ring while helping make tamales for a Christmas family get together, but panic ensues when hours later, she realizes the ring is missing

This is "a very funny story, full of delicious surprise. The handsome, realistic oil paintings, in rich shades of brown, red, and purple, are filled with light, evoking the togetherness of an extended family." Booklist

Souhami, Jessica
Foxy! written and illustrated by Jessica Souhami. Frances Lincoln Children's Books 2013 32 p. ill. (hardcover) $17.99
Grades: PreK K 1 2　　　　　　　　E
1. Tricksters -- Folklore 2. Foxes -- Fiction 3. Picture books for children
ISBN 1847802184; 9781847802187
In this children's picture book, a trickster fox "catches a bee in the opening scene and places it in a sack." When he meets a woman with a fine rooster, he "asks the woman to watch after his sack, cautioning her not to look inside. Of course, the woman does just that, and after the rooster chases away the bee, Foxy claims the rooster as recompense. The pattern repeats, with Foxy trading up to gain a pig and then a small boy before he meets his match in a woman who turns the tables on him." (Publishers Weekly)

Spanyol, Jessica
★ **Little** neighbors on Sunnyside Street; [by] Jessica Spanyol. Candlewick Press 2007 un il $16.99
Grades: PreK K　　　　　　　　E
1. Day -- Fiction 2. Animals -- Fiction
ISBN 978-0-7636-2986-1; 0-7636-2986-3
LC 2005053641
On Sunnyside Street "the animal and insect residents enjoy doing their own things. . . . [The] peek into their everyday activities is accompanied with boisterous word sounds [and] playful typefaces. . . . Pen-and-gouache illustrations are a melding of . . . simple shapes, flat dimension, and busy pages with plenty of preschool child appeal." SLJ

Sperring, Mark
The **sunflower** sword; illustrated by Miriam Latimer. Andersen 2011 un il $16.95
Grades: PreK K 1 2　　　　　　　　E
1. Fairy tales 2. Dragons -- Fiction 3. Knights and knighthood -- Fiction
ISBN 0-7613-7486-8; 978-0-7613-7486-2
LC 2010032954
In a land marked by endless fighting between knights and dragons, a mother gives her eager little boy a sunflower rather than the sword he requests, and when he wields it against a real dragon, new understanding begins.

This is a "charming tale. . . . The cheerful patchwork illustrations painted in bright, springtime colors add touches of humor to the story." SLJ

Spiegelman, Art
Jack and the box; a toon book. Raw Junior 2008 32p il (Toon books) $12.95

Grades: K 1　　　　　　　　E
1. Toys -- Fiction 2. Rabbits -- Fiction
ISBN 978-0-9799238-3-8; 0-9799238-3-2
"Spiegelman has produced a polished and fun story following a young bunny's struggle with his new jack-in-the-box, which proves to be hyperactive and rather argumentative. [This is filled] with plenty of word repetition and age-appropriate humor to keep pre- and early readers engaged and curious." Booklist

Spinelli, Eileen
The **best** story; [by] Eileen Spinelli; illustrations by Anne Wilsdorf. Dial Books for Young Readers 2008 un il $16.99
Grades: 1 2 3　　　　　　　　E
1. Authorship -- Fiction
ISBN 978-0-8037-3055-7; 0-8037-3055-1
LC 2007028478
When a contest at the local library offers a prize for the best story, a girl tries to write one using her family's suggestions, but her story does not seem right until she listens to her heart.

"Lively energy and imagination permeate both the watercolor and ink illustrations and the warm text." Horn Book Guide

Buzz; illustrated by Vincent Nguyen. Simon & Schuster Books for Young Readers 2010 un il $15.99
Grades: PreK K 1　　　　　　　　E
1. Bees -- Fiction 2. Flight -- Fiction 3. Animals -- Fiction
ISBN 978-1-4169-4925-1; 1-4169-4925-9
LC 2008042191
After learning that a bee's body is too chunky for flight, Buzz the bumblebee defies the laws of aerodynamics to save a friend in need.

"Delightful mixed-media illustrations incorporate painted oils and Photoshop to show the pixie-faced Buzz and stage the uncluttered story line with gentle and luminous images." Booklist

Cold snap; by Eileen Spinelli; illustrated by Marjorie Priceman. Alfred A. Knopf 2012 40 p. $17.99
Grades: PreK K 1　　　　　　　　E
1. Picture books for children 2. Winter -- Fiction 3. City and town life -- Fiction 4. Cold -- Fiction 5. Community life -- Fiction
ISBN 0375857001; 9780375857003; 9780375957000
LC 2011013290
In author Eileen Spinelli's book, "[t]he Toby Mills cold snap begins innocently enough on a Friday, with snow angels, sledding and an icicle on the nose of the statue of the town founder . . . By [next] Friday, the statue's icicle reaches the ground, along with everyone's patience. But the mayor's wife has just the solution—a warm winter surprise that brings out the best in everyone and makes them forget the cold." (Kirkus)

Do you have a cat? illustrated by Geraldo Valerio. Eerdmans Books for Young Readers 2010 un il $15.99
Grades: PreK K 1 2　　　　　　　　E
1. Stories in rhyme 2. Cats -- Fiction 3. History --

Fiction 4. Biography -- Fiction
ISBN 978-0-8028-5351-6; 0-8028-5351-X

LC 2010001642

Simple, rhyming text introduces historical figures through the cats each owned. Includes facts about each person.

"Delightful, whimsical paintings contribute to this joyous portrait of pet ownership. The historical figures are as diverse as their feline companions. . . . Animal lovers are sure to enjoy this charming story." SLJ

Do you have a dog? illustrated by Geraldo Valerio. Eerdmans Books for Young Readers 2011 un il $16
Grades: PreK K 1 2   E
1. Stories in rhyme 2. Dogs -- Fiction
ISBN 978-0-8028-5387-5; 0-8028-5387-0

LC 2011005650

Rhyming text describes some famous historical figures, from Annie Oakley and Merriwether Lewis to Sigmund Freud and Billie Holiday, and their beloved dogs. Includes facts about the people cited in the book.

"Young readers itching for a furry friend will find only the benefits of dog ownership in Spinelli's buoyant verse and Valério's cheerful acrylics. Endpapers provide further details about the historical figures mentioned within." Publ Wkly

I know it's autumn; illustrated by Nancy Hayashi. HarperCollinsPublishers 2004 un il $15.99; lib bdg $16.89
Grades: PreK K 1 2   E
1. Stories in rhyme 2. Autumn -- Fiction
ISBN 0-06-029422-1; 0-06-029423-X lib bdg

LC 2003-4099

A rhyming celebration of the sights, smells, and sounds of autumn, such as pumpkin muffins, turkey stickers on spelling papers, and piles of raked leaves

"Large enough for group sharing and as quiet and comfortable as the text, Hayashi's illustrations feature rounded lines, soft shading, and gentle colors." Booklist

Miss Fox's class goes green; illustrated by Anne Kennedy. Albert Whitman 2009 un il $16.99
Grades: K 1 2   E
1. School stories 2. Animals -- Fiction 3. Environmental protection -- Fiction
ISBN 978-0-8075-5166-0; 0-8075-5166-X

LC 2008055693

The students in Miss Fox's class lead their school in making choices to help keep the planet healthy, such as turning off lights when leaving a room, taking shorter showers, and using cloth bags instead of plastic ones

"The best part of this, besides Kennedy's exuberant watercolor pictures, is the way the kids consider their actions." Booklist

Other titles about Miss Fox's class are:
Peace Week in Miss Fox's class (2009)
Miss Fox's class earns a field trip (2010)
Miss Fox's class shapes up (2011)

Night shift daddy; illustrated by Melissa Iwai. Hyperion Bks. for Children 2000 un il $14.99
Grades: PreK K 1 2   E
1. Stories in rhyme 2. Bedtime -- Fiction 3. Father-daughter relationship -- Fiction
ISBN 0-7868-0495-5

LC 98-52499

A father shares dinner and bedtime rituals with his daughter before going out to work the night shift

"The rhyming text manages to convey many feelings—love, loneliness, anticipation—in few words; the mood is reinforced beautifully by the rich, detailed illustrations, especially those depicting a child's room at night." Horn Book Guide

Nora's ark; written by Eileen Spinelli; illustrated by Nora Hilb. Zonderkidz 2013 32 p. (hardcover) $14.99
Grades: PreK K 1   E
1. Play -- Fiction 2. Noah's ark -- Fiction 3. Imagination -- Fiction
ISBN 0310720060; 9780310720065

LC 2011023551

In this children's book, by Eileen Spinelli, illustrated by Nora Hilb, "the weatherman predicted rain. So Nora built an ark. . . . Nora's passenger list includes two backyard spiders, a pair of battery-operated monkeys, and a couple of unimpressed cats. Nora also employs her little brother, some dusty wooden boxes, and a sizeable dose of contagious imagination in her distinctive re-creation of the timeless story." (Publisher's note)

Silly Tilly; by Eileen Spinelli; illustrated by David Slonim. Marshall Cavendish Children 2009 un il $16.99
Grades: PreK K 1 2   E
1. Stories in rhyme 2. Geese -- Fiction 3. Animals -- Fiction
ISBN 978-0-7614-5525-7; 0-7614-5525-6

LC 2008022880

"Tilly, a goose, bathes in apple juice, wears a pancake as a hat, and likes to tickle frogs. But her ways raise the ire of the other farm animals, who demand that she cease all silliness. . . . The acrylic, pencil, and ballpoint pen illustrations complement the rhyming text and do a nice job of conveying the animals' varying levels of frustration. Some pictures are laugh-out-loud funny." SLJ

★ **Sophie's** masterpiece; a spider's tale. illustrations by Jane Dyer. Simon & Schuster Bks. for Young Readers 2001 un il $16
Grades: PreK K 1 2   E
1. Spiders -- Fiction
ISBN 0-689-80112-2

LC 95-44063

Sophie the spider makes wondrous webs, but the residents of Beekman's Boarding House do not appreciate her until at last, old and tired, she weaves her final masterpiece

"The graceful telling glimmers with feeling and occasional humor, while the full-page watercolors and lacy spot art capture the delicate magic of Sophie's webs and enhance the tale's quiet mood." Horn Book Guide

Wanda's monster; written by Eileen Spinelli; illustrated by Nancy Hayashi. Whitman, A. 2002 un il $15.95; pa $6.95

Grades: PreK K 1 2 E
1. Monsters -- Fiction 2. Grandmothers -- Fiction
ISBN 0-8075-8656-0; 0-8075-8657-9 pa
LC 2002-1955
When Wanda fears that she has a monster in her closet, she takes her grandmother's advice and begins to look at things from the monster's point of view
"Hayashi's watercolor and colored-pencil illustrations do a great job of melding the real and the imaginary in Spinelli's story, staying true to the child's fearful fantasies and transforming them with warmth and affection." Booklist

When Papa comes home tonight; illustrated by David McPhail. Simon & Schuster Books for Young Readers 2009 un il $16.99
Grades: PreK E
1. Stories in rhyme 2. Bedtime -- Fiction 3. Father-child relationship -- Fiction
ISBN 978-1-4169-1028-2; 1-4169-1028-X
LC 2008008860
A father and child enjoy a range of activities together before bedtime.
"A sweet ode to family life, beautifully illustrated in pencil, pen-and-ink, and watercolor. . . . The rhyming phrases are gentle but not cloying." SLJ

When you are happy; illustrated by Geraldo Valério. Simon & Schuster Books for Young Readers 2006 un il $16.95
Grades: PreK K 1 E
1. Emotions -- Fiction 2. Family life -- Fiction
ISBN 0-689-86251-2
"Using a comforting refrain (When you are . . .) , each member of the young girl's family reassures her when she is cold, sick, lonely, tired, grumpy, lost, and happy. . . . Appealingly offbeat, whimsical illustrations characterize the girl's emotions." Booklist

Spinelli, Jerry
I can be anything; illustrated by Jimmy Liao. Little, Brown 2010 un il $16.99
Grades: PreK K E
1. Stories in rhyme 2. Occupations -- Fiction
ISBN 0-316-16226-4; 978-0-316-16226-5
A little boy ponders the many possible jobs in his future, from paper-plane folder and puppy-dog holder to mixing-bowl licker and tin-can kicker.
"Aided by Liao's cleverly integrated full-bleed mixed-media illustrations, which radiate every hue of the rainbow, and dynamic typesetting with words that swoop and dive, the author's perspective on this adult-inspired question yields some refreshingly child-oriented answers. . . . An inspired take on a timeless question." Kirkus

Spinner, Stephanie
It's a miracle! a Hanukkah storybook. written by Stephanie Spinner; illustrated by Jill McElmurry. Atheneum Bks. for Young Readers 2003 un il $16.95
Grades: K 1 2 3 E
1. Hanukkah -- Fiction 2. Grandmothers -- Fiction
ISBN 0-689-84493-X
LC 2002-6137
"Owen Block, aged six and a half, has just been named O.C.L.-Official Candle Lighter. Each night, as he performs

his duty, he listens to Grandma Karen's cozy stories of family life. . . . A brief retelling of the Hanukkah legend and blessings in Hebrew, English, and transliteration appear at the end of the book. McElmurry's gouache illustrations add a light, humorous touch. Adults will appreciate the lessons gracefully imparted, and children will enjoy the silliness of Grandma's fanciful, zany family stories." SLJ

The **Nutcracker**; retold by Stephanie Spinner; illustrated by Peter Malone; with a fully orchestrated CD of Peter Ilyich Tchaikovsky music. Alfred A. Knopf 2008 un il $16.99; lib bdg $19.99
Grades: K 1 2 3 4 E
1. Fairy tales 2. Christmas -- Fiction
ISBN 978-0-375-84464-5; 0-375-84464-3; 978-0-375-94464-2 lib bdg; 0-375-94464-8 lib bdg
LC 2007041524
In this retelling of the original 1816 German story, Godfather Drosselmeier gives young Marie a nutcracker for Christmas, and she finds herself in a magical realm where she saves the nutcracker and sees him change into a handsome prince
"Malone's richly colored, opaque watercolors embellish the dancers' magic. . . . This book, which comes with a CD, provides a good entry-point before attending a performance as well as a chance to relive the experience afterward." Horn Book

Spires, Ashley
The **Most** Magnificent Thing; Ashley Spires. Kids Can Press 2014 32 p. color illustrations $16.95
Grades: PreK K 1 2 E
ISBN 1554537045; 9781554537044
2015 ALA Notable Children's Book
"Award-winning author and illustrator Ashley Spires has created a charming picture book about an unnamed girl and her very best friend, who happens to be a dog. The girl has a wonderful idea. . . . But making her magnificent thing is anything but easy, and the girl tries and fails, repeatedly. Eventually, the girl gets really, really mad." (Publisher's note)
"he colorful caricatures and creations contrast with the digital black outlines on a white background that depict an urban neighborhood. Intermittent blue-gray panels break up the white expanses on selected pages showing sequential actions. When the first piece doesn't turn out as desired, the protagonist tries again, hoping to achieve magnificence." Kirkus

Spirin, Gennady
Martha. Philomel Books 2005 un il $14.99
Grades: K 1 2 3 E
1. Crows 2. Russia
ISBN 0-399-23980-4
LC 2004-6735
The author relates how he and his Moscow family rescued Martha, a crow with a broken wing, and how she joined their household.
"The story will appeal to the picture book audience. . . . The lush art set in plentiful white space beautifully portrays a Moscow of a few decades ago." Horn Book Guide

Spohn, Kate
★ **Turtle** and Snake's day at the beach. Viking 2003 32p il (Viking easy-to-read) hardcover o.p. pa $3.99

Grades: K 1 2   E

1. Snakes -- Fiction 2. Beaches -- Fiction 3. Turtles -- Fiction

ISBN 0-670-03628-5; 0-14-240157-9 pa

LC 2002-153376

Turtle and Snake go to the beach, where they and some other animals participate in a sandcastle-making contest

"Brightly colored, simple drawings capture the pleasure of this fun-in-the-sun day at the beach. . . . It's difficult to find easy-to-read books that have charm and a real story, and this one does." SLJ

Other titles about Turtle and Snake are:

Turtle and Snake and the Christmas tree (2000)

Turtle and Snake at work (1999)

Turtle and Snake fix it (2002)

Turtle and Snake go camping (2000)

Turtle and Snake's spooky Halloween (2002)

Turtle and Snake's Valentine's Day (2003)

Springett, Martin

Kate and Pippin; Martin Springett; photos by Isobel Springett. Henry Holt 2012 32 p.

Grades: K 1 2 3   E

1. Deer 2. Dogs 3. Friendship 4. Animal babies 5. Picture books for children 6. Deer -- Fiction 7. Dogs -- Fiction 8. Great Dane -- Fiction 9. Fawns -- Fiction 10. Animals -- Infancy -- Fiction 11. Parental behavior in animals -- Fiction

ISBN 0805094873; 9780805094879

LC 2011033499

In this picture book, "[w]hen Pippin, a fawn abandoned by her mother, cries out for help, she is found by author Isobel Springett. After carrying the tiny fawn back to her home, Isobel places Pippin next to Kate, a Great Dane who has never had puppies of her own. What follows is a remarkable and unlikely friendship. Kate successfully raises Pippin to be an independent deer, and Pippin always returns from the forest to visit her best friend." (Publisher's note) "Pippin learns to negotiate a milk-bottle nipple and later a set of porch steps. . . . [T]he two plainly enjoy each other's company, and the pictures underscore their closeness at rest or play. . . . [T]he narrative . . . notes that Pippin is a wild animal 'but she and Kate remain the best of friends.'" (Kirkus)

Srinivasan, Divya

Little Owl's day; by Divya Srinivasan. Viking 2014 32 p. chiefly color illustrations (hardcover) $16.99

Grades: PreK K 1   E

1. Owls -- Fiction 2. Bedtime -- Fiction 3. Forest animals -- Fiction 4. Forests and forestry -- Fiction

ISBN 0670016500; 9780670016501

LC 2013047053

"A squirrel is chittering. Bees are buzzing. The sun is high in the sky. And Little Owl is supposed to be asleep, but when he wakes up early, he's just too curious to close his eyes again. The forest he knows so well at nighttime is completely different--and exciting--in the day!" (Publisher's note)

"Through carefully controlled application of color washes and linear patterns, Srinivasan conveys the magic of a fantasy world that will delight very young children and their caregivers." Kirkus

★ **Little** Owl's night. Viking Childrens Books 2011 un il $16.99

Grades: PreK K 1   E

1. Owls -- Fiction 2. Night -- Fiction 3. Forest animals -- Fiction 4. Forests and forestry -- Fiction

ISBN 978-0-670-01295-4; 0-670-01295-5

LC 2010049513

Little Owl enjoys a lovely night in the forest visiting his friend the raccoon, listening to the frogs croak and the crickets chirp, and watching the fog that hovers overhead.

"The story's chief virtue is its graceful, balletic prose; the [artwork has] crisp edges and cold greens and blacks. . . . It's a provocative inversion of the classic bedtime story, and a solid first outing. Srinavasan's message is that night is a delightful place, and that's useful knowledge for small children." Publ Wkly

Octopus alone; by Divya Srinivasan. Viking 2013 40 p. (hardcover) $16.99

Grades: PreK K   E

1. Shyness -- Fiction 2. Octopuses -- Fiction 3. Bashfulness -- Fiction 4. Marine animals -- Fiction

ISBN 0670785156; 9780670785155

LC 2012029678

This children's picture book, by Divya Srinivasan, is "about shy Octopus who lives on a lively reef, and what happens when she finds herself in a new place far from home, wonderfully, peacefully alone." In it the octopus is constantly interrupted by other sea creatures who live in the reef and she learns to appreciate her neighbors. (Publisher's note)

Staake, Bob

★ **Bluebird**; Bob Staake. 1st ed. Schwartz & Wade Books 2013 40 p. col. ill. (hardcover) $17.99; (library) $20.99

Grades: PreK K 1 2 3   E

1. Stories without words 2. Human-animal relationship -- Fiction 4. Bluebirds -- Fiction 5. Friendship -- Fiction

ISBN 0375870377; 9780375870378; 9780375970382

LC 2012007043

This children's picture book, by Bob Staake, "explores . . . loneliness, bullying, and the importance of friendship. In this emotional picture book, readers will . . . follow the journey of a bluebird as he develops a friendship with a young boy and ultimately risks his life to save the boy from harm." (Publisher's note)

"Color changes, from blue to near black to white to blue again, allow readers to feel every emotion, including the devastating climax and the begs-to-be-discussed ending." Kirkus

The **donut** chef. Random House 2008 un il $14.99; lib bdg $17.99

Grades: PreK K 1 2   E

1. Stories in rhyme 2. Baking -- Fiction

ISBN 978-0-375-84403-4; 0-375-84403-1; 978-0-375-94716-2 lib bdg; 0-375-94716-7 lib bdg

A baker hangs out his shingle on a small street and soon the line for his donuts stretches down the block. But it's not long before the competition arrives and a battle of the bakers ensues.

"The entire book has a retro tone, from its lengthy rhyming text to its Art Deco-style illustrations, which are updated with more modern-looking graphic shapes and a multicolored palette. . . . The story's lively rhythmic text and colorful artwork should make it a good pick for storytime." SLJ

★ **Look!** A book! a zany seek-and-find adventure. Little, Brown 2011 un il $16.99
Grades: K 1 2   E
1. Picture puzzles 2. Stories in rhyme 3. Books and reading -- Fiction
ISBN 0-316-11862-1; 978-0-316-11862-0
LC 2010001540
Easy-to-read, rhyming text invites the reader to search for items on a different theme on each page, while celebrating the wonder of a picture book.
"With polished typography, minty-fresh layout, and crisp-edged figures, the book stays tidy despite the frenetic action, and the rhymed and metered text is carefully wrought." Publ Wkly

★ **Look!** Another book! Bob Staake. Little, Brown 2012 48 p. $16.99
Grades: PreK   E
1. Paper crafts 2. Picture books for children 3. Picture puzzles 4. Stories in rhyme 5. Books and reading -- Fiction
ISBN 0316204595; 9780316204590
LC 2011053200
This book is the sequel to Bob Staake's "Look! A Book!" The "solid-colored pages are graced with small die cuts that reveal little tidbits of the busy scenes hiding on the following spreads. Sometimes the page turns make the images blend seamlessly into the busy new scene . . . . The die cuts themselves also seem to disappear with the page turn, leading readers to touch the pages to find the circles and to prove that they are still there." (Kirkus)

The **red** lemon. Golden Books 2006 un il $14.95; lib bdg $16.99
Grades: PreK K 1   E
1. Stories in rhyme 2. Lemons -- Fiction
ISBN 0-375-83593-8; 0-375-93593-2 lib bdg
LC 2005-09854
Farmer McPhee's yellow lemons are ready to be picked and made into lemonade, pies, and muffins, but when a red lemon is found in the crop and discarded, it eventually yields some surprises.
"Bold, enticing illustrations dominate the pages. Staake creates a fun, dynamic world . . . in its sweeping arcs, bright colors, multicolored cartoon people, and effortlessly rhyming text." SLJ

Stamp, Jorgen
Flying high. Enchanted Lion 2009 un il $16.95
Grades: K 1 2   E
1. Turtles -- Fiction 2. Giraffes -- Fiction 3. Air pilots -- Fiction
ISBN 978-1-59270-089-9; 1-59270-089-6
"Walter is a giraffe who wishes he could fly. He finds himself a book, and begins to build an airplane for himself. When Sonny the turtle meanders over and asks if he, too, can go flying, Walter tells his friend he's too slow and cowardly and hurts his feelings. . . . When his plane is hit by lightning

and crashes into the lake, it is Sonny who swims out and saves him. . . . The colorful cartoon illustrations convey the fast pace of the tale and do a suitable job of moving things along to a satisfying conclusion." SLJ

Stanley, Diane
The **Giant** and the beanstalk; written and illustrated by Diane Stanley. HarperCollinsPublishers 2004 un il $17.99; lib bdg $17.89
Grades: K 1 2 3   E
1. Fairy tales
ISBN 0-06-000010-4; 0-06-000011-2 lib bdg
LC 2003-1818
In this version of the traditional tale, a young giant chases Jack down the beanstalk to rescue his beloved hen and meets other Jacks from various nursery rhymes along the way
"Stanley injects her characteristic, understated humor into both text and art, and young ones will take pleasure in identifying the individual elements of the thoroughly mixed-up story." Booklist

Goldie and the three bears. HarperCollins Pubs. 2003 un il $15.99; lib bdg $17.89; pa $6.99
Grades: K 1 2 3   E
1. Bears -- Fiction 2. Friendship -- Fiction
ISBN 0-06-000008-2; 0-06-000009-0 lib bdg; 0-06-113611-5 pa
LC 2002-23843
In this story, loosely based on that of Goldilocks, Goldie, who has yet to find a friend to "love with all her heart," makes an unplanned visit to the house of some bears
"The writing is smooth, concise, and rhythmic. . . . The pictures are marvelous, with fine lines; soft, glowing colors; and winsome, telling details." SLJ

★ **Rumpelstiltskin's** daughter. Morrow Junior Bks. 1997 un il $17.99; lib bdg $16.89; pa $7.99
Grades: K 1 2 3   E
1. Fairy tales
ISBN 0-688-14327-X; 0-688-14328-8 lib bdg; 0-06-441095-1 pa
LC 96-14834
"Rumpelstiltskin's daughter relies on her cleverness instead of magic. When the king orders her to spin straw into gold, she tricks him out of his greedy ways and becomes prime minister of his kingdom. The illustrations provide splendid, detailed palace interiors and endow the characters, especially the king and his minions, with comically exaggerated features." Horn Book Guide

Saving Sweetness; illustrated by G. Brian Karas. Putnam 1996 un il $16.99; pa $5.99
Grades: K 1 2 3   E
1. Orphans -- Fiction 2. West (U.S.) -- Fiction
ISBN 0-399-22645-1; 0-698-11767-0 pa
LC 95-10621
The sheriff of a dusty western town rescues Sweetness, an unusually resourceful orphan, from nasty old Mrs. Sump and her terrible orphanage
"Telling the tale from the sheriff's point of view, Stanley packs this fast-paced adventure full of language that begs to be read aloud. . . . Combining gouache, acrylic, and pencil drawings with cyanotype photographs, Karas's illustrations

evoke the arid landscape of the West yet remain wonderfully original." SLJ

Another title about Sweetness is:

Raising Sweetness (1999)

★ The **trouble** with wishes. HarperCollins Pubs. 2007 un il $16.99; lib bdg $17.89
Grades: 1 2 3 4   **E**
1. Wishes -- Fiction 2. Sculpture -- Fiction 3. Classical mythology -- Fiction
ISBN 0-06-055451-7; 0-06-055452-5 lib bdg

Jane wishes she were more like her friend Pyg the sculptor until Pyg's statue of a beautiful goddess comes to life and teaches them both to be careful what they wish for. Based on the Greek myth of Pygmalion

"Stanley's fresh artwork, which mixes the grandeur of old classical forms and the absurdity of the new, is in perfect balance with the parody." Booklist

Stanley, Malaika Rose

Baby Ruby bawled; with illustrations by Ken Wilson-Max. Transworld Publishers 2011 32p il pa $9.99
Grades: PreK   **E**
1. Infants -- Fiction 2. Siblings -- Fiction 3. Family life -- Fiction 4. Racially mixed people -- Fiction
ISBN 978-1-84-853017-1; 1-84-853017-X

"Theo's baby sister cries and cries whenever it is time to go to sleep. Dad tries soothing Ruby with a bath, Mum feeds her, Nana takes her for a ride in the car, Grandad carries her around in the baby backpack, and Uncle Clyde pushes her in the buggy. Nothing works until Theo sings her a lullaby. . . . Bright, bold painterly illustrations, sharply outlined in black, beautifully depict the love, and frustration, of this mixed-race family. Anyone who has ever struggled to get a fussy baby to sleep will relate to this British import, and the ending will give older siblings a sense of pride and empowerment." SLJ

Stanton, Karen

Monday, Wednesday, and Every Other Weekend; by Karen Stanton. 1st ed. Feiwel & Friends 2014 40 p. $16.99
Grades: PreK K 1   **E**
1. Dogs -- Fiction 2. Parent-child relationship -- Fiction 3. Children of divorced parents -- Fiction 4. Divorce -- Fiction
ISBN 1250034892; 9781250034892

In this book, by Karen Stanton, "Henry Cooper and his dog Pomegranate have two houses. On Mondays, Wednesdays, and every other weekend, they live with Mama in her new apartment, but on Tuesdays, Thursdays, and every other weekend, they live with Papa in his new house. Henry knows that sometimes Pomegranate gets confused and just wants to go . . . home. [Stanton presents a] story about dealing with the many changes that come with divorce." (Publisher's note)

Papi's gift; by Karen Stanton; illustrated by Rene King Moreno. Boyds Mills Press 2007 un il $16.95
Grades: K 1 2 3   **E**
1. Droughts -- Fiction 2. Birthdays -- Fiction 3. Latin America -- Fiction 4. Father-daughter relationship -- Fiction
ISBN 978-1-59078-422-8; 1-59078-422-7
LC 2006011569

Graciela's Papi has been working in the United States for so long that she has almost forgotten his face, so when the box he promised for her seventh birthday does not arrive, she is very upset and nearly loses hope that he— and the rain—will someday return

"A few Spanish words and phrases add authenticity to the engaging text. Moreno uses pastels to render soothing, warm illustrations that have a Latin American flavor and elements of folk art." SLJ

Staub, Leslie

Everybody gets the blues; written by Leslie Staub; pictures by R.G. Roth. Houghton Mifflin Harcourt 2012 un il $16.99 **E**
1. Stories in rhyme 2. Emotions -- Fiction 3. Blues music -- Fiction
ISBN 978-0-15-206300-9; 0-15-206300-5
LC 2010043400

"Writing cheerfully about sadness sounds like an oxymoron, but Staub . . . performs this balancing act with casual grace. . . . Blues Guy, a sweet-faced, bulky gentleman dressed in tweed, sits with the boy, radiating sympathy and asking nothing. They sing together ('I've got the blues so bad,/ I want to cry, cry, cry'), and the strength of their song lifts them into the sky to bring comfort to 'everyone who's feeling low.' . . . Roth's . . . flat, cutout figures have a retro feel, but reflect the present-day world with figures of many ages, colors, and sizes. Staub's verses scan as neatly as an old radio hit." Publ Wkly

Stead, Philip C.

Bear has a story to tell; Philip C. Stead; illustrated by Erin E. Stead. 1st ed. Roaring Brook Press 2012 32 p. ill. (reinforced: alk. paper) $16.99
Grades: PreK K 1   **E**
1. Bears -- Fiction 2. Hibernation -- Fiction 3. Storytelling -- Fiction 4. Picture books for children 5. Animals -- Fiction
ISBN 1596437456; 9781596437456
LC 2011033795

In this children's picture book, "Bear wants to tell a story, but his friends Mouse, Duck, Frog, and Mole are busy preparing for winter. . . . Instead, Bear offers help to his friends." He "raises a great paw to check the wind for Duck and tucks Frog tenderly into his hole. When winter passes, the animals are reunited, but Bear has forgotten his story; now it's his friends' turn to help him." (Publishers Weekly)

Hello, my name is Ruby; Philip C. Stead. 1st ed. Henry Holt & Co 2013 40 p. (hardcover) $16.99
Grades: PreK K 1   **E**
1. Picture books for children 2. Birds -- Fiction 3. Friendship -- Fiction
ISBN 1596438096; 9781596438095
LC 2012046929

In this children's picture book, "Ruby is a diminutive, yellow bird whose frequent introductions are a touch formal: 'I am glad to meet you.' She fearlessly initiates conversation with much bigger birds and is the kind of friend who offers ideas and is willing to try the suggestions of others. In the process, much is gleaned about avian (and human) behavior." (Kirkus Reviews)

A **home** for Bird; Philip C. Stead. Roaring Brook Press 2012 32 p.

Grades: PreK K   E

1. Home -- Fiction 2. Birds -- Fiction 3. Toads -- Fiction 4. Picture books for children 5. Clocks and watches -- Fiction 6. Cuckoos -- Fiction

ISBN 1596437111; 9781596437111

LC 2011012742

In this picture book for children, "Vernon is both a toad and a forager for found objects. Ambling along with his latest haul, he chances upon a creature he seeks to know and then to help. . . . Vernon observes that 'Bird is shy . . , but also a very good listener,' when he introduces Bird to his friends. He and his pals conclude that Bird is lost and unhappy, so the thoughtful, resourceful amphibian readies a teacup boat for the journey to help this quiet stranger return home." (Kirkus Reviews)

Jonathan and the big blue boat; [by] Philip Christian Stead. Roaring Brook Press 2011 un il $16.99

Grades: K 1 2   E

1. Teddy bears -- Fiction 2. Boats and boating -- Fiction 3. Voyages and travels -- Fiction

ISBN 978-1-59643-562-9; 1-59643-562-3

LC 2010012952

When Jonathan's parents decide that he has gotten too old to have a stuffed animal, they trade his favorite bear, Frederick, for a toaster, so he sets off aboard a boat, looking for Frederick.

"Stead . . . uses squiggly ink lines and washes of warm color against a background of collaged newsprint, charts, and stamps that underscore the nautical theme and distance traveled. Frederick shows up at the end in the nicest possible way, and Jonathan's slow, reflective journey-filled with pitch-perfect details, sound effects, and vocabulary . . . offers a lovely, gentle adventure for younger readers." Publ Wkly

Sebastian and the balloon; Philip C. Stead. Roaring Brook Press 2014 40 p. color illustrations (hardcover) $17.99

Grades: PreK K 1 2   E

1. Balloons -- Fiction 2. Voyages and travels -- Fiction 3. Hot air balloons -- Fiction

ISBN 1596439300; 9781596439306

LC 2013044240

"On a boring day, on a dull street, Sebastian sat high atop his roof--something he was never supposed to do. When he launched himself into the air in his balloon made of Grandma's afghans and patchwork quilts, his journey took on a life of its own and his boring day turned into the adventure of a lifetime." (Publisher's note)

"The sophisticated nature of the book requires readers to slow down and read the pictures as carefully as the text--and both carry equal, impressive weight." Kirkus

★ A **sick** day for Amos McGee; written by Philip C. Stead; illustrated by Erin E. Stead. Roaring Brook Press 2010 un il $16.99

Grades: PreK K 1 2   E

1. Sick -- Fiction 2. Zoos -- Fiction 3. Animals -- Fiction

ISBN 978-1-59643-402-8; 1-59643-402-3

Awarded the Caldecott Medal, 2011

Amos McGee he spends a little bit of time each day with each of his friends at the zoo, running races with the tortoise, keeping the shy penguin company, and even reading bedtime stories to the owl. But when Amos is too sick to make it to the zoo, his animal friends decide it's time they returned the favor.

"The artwork in this quiet tale of good deeds rewarded uses woodblock-printing techniques, soft flat colors, and occasional bits of red. Illustrations are positioned on the white space to move the tale along and underscore the bonds of friendship and loyalty. Whether read individually or shared, this gentle story will resonate with youngsters." SLJ

Special delivery; Philip C. Stead; illustrated by Matthew Cordell. Roaring Brook Press 2015 40 p. (hardback) $17.99

Grades: PreK K 1 2   E

1. Elephants -- Fiction 2. Transportation -- Fiction 3. Voyages and travels -- Fiction

ISBN 1596439319; 9781596439313

LC 2014009900

In this children's book by Philip C. Stead, illustrated by Matthew Cordell, "Sadie is on her way to deliver an elephant to her Great-Aunt Josephine, who lives completely alone and can really use the company. She tries everything from mailing the elephant to boarding a plane, a train, and an alligator to get to her aunt's home. Along the way she meets an array of interesting characters, including an odd postal worker and a gang of bandit monkeys." (Publisher's note)

Steggall, Susan

Following the tractor; by Susan Steggall. Frances Lincoln Children's Books 2014 32 p. color illustrations $17.99

Grades: PreK K 1   E

1. Farms -- Fiction 2. Tractors -- Fiction 3. Seasons -- Fiction

ISBN 1847804896; 9781847804891

In this children's book, by Susan Steggall, "follow the hard-working tractor on its journey as it plows, sows, and harvests the fields throughout the course of a year. With a whole host of farm machinery to pore over . . . this richly illustrated book will be read time and time again." (Publisher's note)

"Steggall follows a bright red tractor throughout the seasons, introducing children to a variety of farm equipment... The book's large size and vivid spreads make it an excellent choice for storytimes, and its clear font and simple rhyming text make it a good early-reader choice. Recommended for all kids who love farms and big vehicles." SLJ

Steig, William

★ The **amazing** bone. Farrar, Straus & Giroux 1976 un il $17.99; pa $7.99

Grades: PreK K 1 2 3   E

1. Pigs -- Fiction 2. Bones -- Fiction

ISBN 0-374-30248-0; 0-374-40358-9 pa

A Caldecott Medal honor book, 1977

On her way home from school, Pearl finds an unusual bone that has unexpected powers

"Steig's marvelously straightfaced telling comes with a panoply of ultra-spring landscapes for pink-dressed Pearl to tiptoe through. And there's no holding back the chortles at the wonderfully expressive faces the artist delights in. This is a tight mesh of witty storytelling and art bound to please any audience." Booklist

★ **Brave** Irene. Farrar, Straus & Giroux 1986 un il
Grades: PreK K 1 2 3   **E**
1. Courage -- Fiction 2. Blizzards -- Fiction
ISBN 0-374-30947-7; 0-374-40927-7 pa
LC 86-80957
Plucky Irene, a dressmaker's daughter, braves a fierce snowstorm to deliver a new gown to the duchess in time for the ball. "Ages five to nine." (N Y Times Book Rev)
"With sure writing and well-composed, riveting art, Steig keeps readers with Irene every step of the long way. The pictures . . . are done in winter blues, purples, and grays that gradually get darker as Irene trudges on." Booklist

Caleb & Kate. Farrar, Straus & Giroux 1977 un il
hardcover o.p. pa $6.95
Grades: PreK K 1 2 3   **E**
1. Dogs -- Fiction 2. Witches -- Fiction
ISBN 0-374-41038-0 pa
LC 77-4947
"The well-cadenced storytelling has a certain old-fashioned elegance of language, and the humor is emphasized by an atmosphere of mock-pathos." Horn Book
"Though Caleb the carpenter loves Kate the weaver very much, he leaves her one day because of a quarrel. In the deep woods where he is resting Yedida the witch turns him into a dog. The tale of his faithfulness and love for his wife, even though he is a dog, is . . . told. Their love is shared to the end, when a remarkable turn of events enables him to return to his former self." Child Book Rev Serv

★ **Doctor** De Soto. Farrar, Straus & Giroux 1982 un il $17; pa $7.99
Grades: PreK K 1 2   **E**
1. Mice -- Fiction 2. Animals -- Fiction 3. Dentists -- Fiction
ISBN 0-374-31803-4; 0-374-41810-1 pa
LC 82-15701
A Newbery Medal honor book, 1983
"The story achieves comic heights partly through the delightful irony of the situation. . . . Watercolor paintings, with the artist's firm line and luscious color, depict with aplomb the eminently dentistlike mouse as he goes about his business." Horn Book
Another title about Doctor De Soto is:
Doctor De Soto goes to Africa (1992)

★ **Pete's** a pizza. HarperCollins Pubs. 1998 un il $16.99; lib bdg $17.89
Grades: PreK K 1 2   **E**
1. Father-son relationship -- Fiction
ISBN 0-06-205157-1; 0-06-205158-X lib bdg
LC 97-78384
"The watercolor illustrations are executed in a clean palette with precise lines in tightly controlled compositions, the semi-formality of which only add to the hilarity. . . . This is a jolly, affectionate story." Bull Cent Child Books

Shrek! twentieth anniversary edition; Farrar Straus Giroux 2010 un il $16.99

Grades: K 1 2 3 4   **E**
1. Monsters -- Fiction
ISBN 978-0-374-36879-1; 0-374-36879-1
A reissue of the title first published 1990
"The pictures are just as nutty as the story, blending with the text so thoroughly, sometimes echoing, sometimes expanding it, that it's hard to imagine one without the other. . . . The fast-forward movement of the story and the inventive challenging language, full of surprises, make this especially fun to read aloud." SLJ

★ **Sylvester** and the magic pebble. Simon & Schuster Books for Young Readers 2005 un il $16.95
Grades: PreK K 1 2 3   **E**
1. Donkeys -- Fiction
ISBN 1-4169-0206-6
LC 2004-15445
A reissue of the title first published 1969
Awarded the Caldecott Medal, 1970
In a moment of fright, Sylvester the donkey asks his magic pebble to turn him into a rock but then can not hold the pebble to wish himself back to normal again
"A remarkable atmosphere of childlike innocence pervades the book; beautiful pictures in full, natural color show daily and seasonal changes in the lush countryside and greatly extend the kindly humor and the warm, unselfconscious tenderness." Horn Book

When everybody wore a hat. Joanna Cotler Bks. 2003 un il $17.99; pa $8.99
Grades: PreK K 1 2 3   **E**
ISBN 0-06-009700-0; 0-06-009702-7 pa
LC 2002-6512
"In 1916, Steig was eight years old. This autobiography describes that year of his life. . . . The childlike, watercolor artwork that accompanies the memories features flattened tables, nostrils on the sides of noses, and a sidewalk extending up into the air. Yet the illustrations' naiveté belies their underlying sophistication. With a few spare lines, the artist manages to convey body language, facial expression, and gesture." SLJ

Stein, David Ezra
Cowboy Ned and Andy; [by] David Ezra Stein. Simon & Schuster Books for Young Readers 2006 un il $14.95
Grades: PreK K 1 2   **E**
1. Horses -- Fiction 2. Cowhands -- Fiction 3. Birthdays -- Fiction 4. West (U.S.) -- Fiction
ISBN 978-1-4169-0041-2; 1-4169-0041-1
LC 2005006969
On a cattle drive in the desert on the night before Cowboy Ned's birthday, his horse Andy goes in search of a birthday cake, which he thinks will make Ned's birthday complete
"Stein's language is simple yet expressive. . . . Done in ink and watercolor, the cartoon illustrations make the most of the Western landscape." SLJ
Another title about Cowboy Ned and Andy is:
Ned's new friend (2007)

Dinosaur kisses; by David Ezra Stein. Candlewick Press 2013 32 p. ill. (reinforced) $15.99

Grades: PreK   E
1. Kissing 2. Dinosaurs
ISBN 076366104X; 9780763661045

LC 2012954335

In this book, written and illustrated by David Ezra Stein, "an energetic young dinosaur figures out her own way to give a kiss. For newly hatched dinosaur Dinah, the world is an exciting place. After a few disastrous attempts, can she figure out how to give someone a kiss without whomping, chomping, or stomping them first?" (Publisher's note)

I'm my own dog; David Ezra Stein. Candlewick Press 2014 32 p. color illustrations $15.99
Grades: PreK K 1   E
1. Dogs -- Fiction 2. Pets -- Fiction
ISBN 0763661392; 9780763661397

LC 2013952833

"Many dogs have human owners. Not this dog. He fetches his own slippers, curls up at his own feet, and gives himself a good scratch. But there is one spot, in the middle of his back, that he just can't reach. So one day, he lets a human scratch it. And the poor little fella follows him home. What can the dog do but get a leash to lead the guy around with?" (Publisher's note)

"The cartoonlike drawings perfectly illuminate the life and attitudes of this canine character, from his contented chewing on a slipper to his joyful, bowlegged run during a game of fetch. Minimal text makes this a great read-aloud for listeners with short attention spans, while the humor will tickle older kids and grown-ups." SLJ

★ **Interrupting** chicken. Candlewick Press 2010 un il $16.99
Grades: PreK K 1 2   E
1. Bedtime -- Fiction 2. Chickens -- Fiction 3. Storytelling -- Fiction 4. Father-daughter relationship -- Fiction
ISBN 978-0-7636-4168-9; 0-7636-4168-5

LC 2009017523

A Caldecott Medal honor book, 2011
Little Red Chicken wants Papa to read her a bedtime story, but interrupts him almost as soon as he begins each tale.
"Stein's droll cartoons use watercolor, crayon, china marker, pen, and tea. The rich colors of the characters perfectly contrast with the sepia pages of the storybooks." SLJ

★ **Leaves**. Putnam 2007 un il $15.99
Grades: PreK K 1 2   E
1. Bears -- Fiction 2. Leaves -- Fiction 3. Seasons -- Fiction
ISBN 978-0-399-24636-4; 0-399-24636-3

LC 2006-24753

A curious bear observes how leaves change throughout the seasons.
"Bamboo pen and earth-toned watercolors are used to great effect. . . . The serene scenes and streamlined story line reflect perfectly the gentle passage of time." SLJ

★ **Love,** Mouserella. Nancy Paulsen Books un il $15.99
Grades: PreK K   E
1. Mice -- Fiction 2. Letters -- Fiction 3. Grandmothers

-- Fiction
ISBN 978-0-399-25410-9; 0-399-25410-2

Mouserella misses her grandmouse, so she writes her a letter. At first she can't think of anything to say, but once she starts, the news begins to flow.

"Showing his customary gift for spot-on evocations of childlike voice and sensibility, . . . Stein . . . interweaves Mouserella's loosely connected comments with decorative crayon sketches, relatively more finished vignettes representing pictures in her imagination or scenes she is describing and painted 'photos' of a pet chrysalis, Dadmouse and other subjects. . . . Sometimes snail mail is just better. Here's proof." Kirkus

★ **Pouch!** G.P. Putnam's Sons 2009 un il $15.99
Grades: PreK K 1   E
1. Growth -- Fiction 2. Kangaroos -- Fiction 3. Mother-child relationship -- Fiction
ISBN 978-0-399-25051-4; 0-399-25051-4

LC 2008-53558

A baby kangaroo takes his first tentative hops outside of his mama's pouch, meeting other creatures and growing bolder each time.

"The short, pithy text tells a story young listeners will immediately understand. . . . Done in marker, watercolor, and crayon, the artwork has a fresh energetic quality that suits the story well." Booklist

Stein, Peter
Cars galore; illustrated by Bob Staake. Candlewick Press 2011 un il $15.99
Grades: PreK K 1 2   E
1. Stories in rhyme 2. Vehicles -- Fiction 3. Automobiles -- Fiction
ISBN 978-0-7636-4743-8; 0-7636-4743-8

LC 2010038923

"Rhythmic verse and lively illustrations showcase autos of every color, size, style, and speed. . . . The illustrator's familiar cartoon style easily matches the text. Crisp, clean lines and bright colors pop against the white background, while black traffic-filled roads crisscross and loop around the pages. Readers will eagerly search for and find every vehicle mentioned." SLJ

Stephens, Helen
The **big** adventure of the Smalls; Helen Stephens. Aladdin 2012 32 p. col. ill. $15.99
Grades: K 1 2   E
1. Adventure fiction 2. Adventure stories 3. Children's stories
ISBN 1442450584; 9781442450585

LC 2011277645

In this children's book by Helen Stephens "it's the night of the Small Hall Ball, and everyone in the Small family is getting ready for one of the BIGGEST parties of the year. Everyone, that is, except for Paul and Sally Small, who are too young to join in the fun. But when Paul's tiny teddy bear goes missing, he and Sally have no choice but to sneak into the festivities, and nothing . . . will stop the smallest of the Smalls from finding Paul's furry little friend." (Publisher's note)

How to hide a lion; Helen Stephens. Henry Holt and Company 2013 32 p. (hardcover) $16.99

Grades: PreK K 1 2   E
1. Picture books for children 2. Lion -- Fiction
ISBN 0805098348; 9780805098341
LC 2013001930

"In this children's picture book, a girl named Iris secretly cares for a lion she knows to be kind--a lion who eventually saves the town from burglary. All the lion wants as he strolls into town is to purchase a hat, but he soon finds himself fleeing from terrified, broom-and-rolling-pin-armed townspeople. . . . Iris recognizes his gentleness, but it isn't easy to hide him." (Kirkus Reviews)

Stevens, April
★ **Edwin** speaks up; written by April Stevens; illustrated by Sophie Blackall. Schwartz & Wade Books 2011 un il $16.99; lib bdg $19.99
Grades: PreK K 1   E
1. Ferrets -- Fiction 2. Infants -- Fiction 3. Shopping -- Fiction 4. Birthdays -- Fiction 5. Family life -- Fiction
ISBN 978-0-375-85337-1; 0-375-85337-5; 978-0-375-95633-1 lib bdg; 0-375-95633-6 lib bdg
LC 2009-28009

Before his family leaves the grocery store, Baby Edwin (a ferret) makes sure their grocery cart contains the last ingredient needed to make his birthday celebration complete.

"Stevens' spot-on story about every mother's nightmare, the group grocery-store shop, is matched by Blackall's delicious art. . . . This is a book that's clever in every sense of the word: skillful, original, and witty." Booklist

Stevens, Janet
★ **Cook-a-doodle-doo!** [by] Janet Stevens and Susan Stevens Crummel; illustrated by Janet Stevens. Harcourt Brace & Co. 1999 un il $17; pa $7
Grades: PreK K 1 2   E
1. Animals -- Fiction 2. Cooking -- Fiction
ISBN 0-15-201924-3; 0-15-205658-0 pa
LC 98-8853

With the questionable help of his friends, Big Brown Rooster manages to bake a strawberry shortcake which would have pleased his great-grandmother, Little Red Hen.

"With the main story and each hilarious, mouthwatering double-page picture of pandemonium, there is a quiet sidebar in small type that explains what recipes are, what ingredients are, what measuring and baking means, and how to make a strawberry shortcake, step by step. The luscious illustrations on hand-made paper are beautifully drawn and deliciously textured. . . . The full recipe is printed on the last page." Booklist

★ **The great** fuzz frenzy; written by Janet Stevens and Susan Stevens Crummel; illustrated by Janet Stevens. Harcourt 2005 un il $17
Grades: PreK K 1 2 3   E
1. Prairie dogs -- Fiction
ISBN 0-15-204626-7

When a fuzzy tennis ball lands in a prairie-dog town, the prairie dogs discover that their newfound frenzy for fuzz creates no end of trouble.

"The marvelously rendered mixed-media illustrations, with vivid blues, earthy browns, and that luminescent green, capture the true fuzzy nature and greenish glow of the ball." SLJ

Help me, Mr. Mutt! expert answers for dogs with people problems. written by Janet Stevens and Susan Stevens Crummel; illustrated by Janet Stevens. Harcourt 2008 un il $17
Grades: 1 2 3   E
1. Dogs -- Fiction
ISBN 978-0-15-204628-6; 0-15-204628-3
LC 2007020549

Dogs across the United States write to Mr. Mutt, a people expert, for help with their humans.

"Art and text work seemlessly, with plenty of visual and verbal jokes . . . to entice repeated readings." Booklist

Stevenson, James
No laughing, no smiling, no giggling. Farrar, Straus and Giroux 2004 un il $16
Grades: PreK K 1 2   E
1. Animals -- Fiction
ISBN 0-374-31829-8
LC 2003-45508

Companion volume to Don't make me laugh (1999)

The reader joins Freddy Fafnaffer the pig as he deals with Mr. Frimdimpny, a crocodile who never laughs and who decides on the rules for reading this book.

"Children will enjoy the humorous cartoons and delight in helping Freddy out of his predicament. The act of inviting readers to actively participate in the plot has great appeal." SLJ

Stevenson, Robert Louis
Block city; illustrated by Daniel Kirk. Simon & Schuster Books for Young Readers 2005 un il $14.95
Grades: PreK K 1   E
1. Play -- Fiction
ISBN 0-689-86964-9

A child creates a world of his own which has mountains and sea, a city and ships, all from toy blocks.

"This colorfully illustrated version of Stevenson's poem is as relevant today as when it was written for A Child's Garden of Verses in 1883. . . . Done in colored pencils and gouache in rich, deep colors, the large, clear pictures have a retro feel." SLJ

★ **The moon**; [by] Robert Louis Stevenson; pictures by Tracey Campbell Pearson. Farrar, Straus and Giroux 2006 un il $16
Grades: PreK K 1 2   E
1. Moon -- Poetry
ISBN 0-374-35046-9
LC 2005040067

"Stevenson's famous 12-line poem, which begins 'The moon has a face / like the clock in the hall,' becomes the text of a picture-book depiction of the nighttime outing of a contemporary father and his child. Leaving Mother and Baby behind, they climb into a truck with the dog, the cat, and some provisions; travel to the dock; and take their boat across a cove and back again while they watch the places and creatures illuminated by the moon. The pictured journey creates a vivid, visual counterpoint to the poetry, which flows as magically as an incantation. . . . The luminous ink-and-watercolor illustrations reflect Pearson's creative imagination and her sure sense of what is visually interesting to young children." Booklist

Stewart, Joel

Addis Berner Bear forgets; [by] Joel Stewart. Farrar, Straus and Giroux 2008 un il $16.95

Grades: K 1 2 3   E

1. Bears -- Fiction 2. Memory -- Fiction 3. Musicians -- Fiction 4. City and town life -- Fiction

ISBN 978-0-374-30036-4; 0-374-30036-4

     LC 2007044778

A musical bear visits the city and finds the experience a bit overwhelming until he remembers the reason for his trip

"The delicate artwork fascinates, sometimes exacerbating, sometimes ameliorating the bleakest parts of the story. But there's happiness here as well in the vignettes and full-page art." Booklist

Stewart, Sarah

The **library**; pictures by David Small. Farrar, Straus & Giroux 1995 un il $16.50; pa $6.95

Grades: K 1 2 3   E

1. Stories in rhyme 2. Books and reading -- Fiction

ISBN 0-374-34388-8; 0-374-44394-7 pa

     LC 94-30320

Elizabeth Brown loves to read more than anything else, but when her collection of books grows and grows, she must make a change in her life

"Framed watercolors give the book an old-fashioned, scrapbooklike appearance.... Small black-ink line drawings decorate the verses below and often add an additional touch of humor. This is a funny, heartwarming story about a quirky woman with a not-so-peculiar obsession." SLJ

★ The **friend**; pictures by David Small. Farrar, Straus and Giroux 2004 un il $16

Grades: K 1 2 3   E

1. Household employees -- Fiction

ISBN 0-374-32463-8

     LC 2003-64352

With Mom too busy and Dad away much of the time, Belle finds companionship with a household employee who after each day's work takes Belle "hand in hand" to the beach

"David Small's elegant, moving illustrations . . . show the twosome touchingly small on the vast beach. . . . In both illustrations and text, Bea is not merely a playmate but her own person." NY Times Book Rev

★ The **gardener**; pictures by David Small. Farrar, Straus & Giroux 1997 un il $16; pa $6.95

Grades: K 1 2 3   E

1. Letters -- Fiction 2. Gardening -- Fiction 3. Great Depression, 1929-1939 -- Fiction

ISBN 0-374-32517-0; 0-374-42518-3 pa

     LC 96-30894

A Caldecott Medal honor book, 1998

"Stewart's quiet story, relayed in the form of letters written by a little girl, focuses on a child who literally makes joy blossom. Small's illustrations . . . [offer] wonderfully expressive characters, ink-line details, and patches of pastel." Booklist

★ The **journey**; pictures by David Small. Farrar, Straus & Giroux 2001 un il $16; pa $6.95

Grades: K 1 2 3   E

1. Amish -- Fiction 2. City and town life -- Fiction

ISBN 0-374-33905-8; 0-374-40010-5 pa

     LC 99-31001

A young Amish girl tells her "silent friend," her diary, about all the wonderous experiences she has on her first trip to the city

"This title offers so much: a glimpse into Amish culture and Chicago treasures; a winsome main character and many sensitively depicted supporting personalities; a fresh, authentic voice; and a design perfectly melded to its subtle message." SLJ

The **quiet** place; Sarah Stewart; pictures by David Small. Margaret Ferguson Books 2012 44 p. $16.99

Grades: K 1 2 3   E

1. Aunts -- Fiction 2. Letters -- Fiction 3. Immigrants -- Fiction 4. Homesickness -- Fiction 5. Mexican Americans -- Fiction

ISBN 0374325650; 9780374325657

     LC 2011031768

This children's story, by Sarah Stewart, illustrated by David Small, is the winner of the "Kirkus Reviews" Best Children's Book award of 2012. "When Isabel and her family move to the United States, Isabel misses all the things she left behind in Mexico. . . . But she also experiences some wonderful new things. . . . Even better, Papa and her brother Chavo help her turn a big box into her own quiet place, where she keeps her books and toys and writes letters to Aunt Lupita." (Publisher's note)

Stiegemeyer, Julie

Gobble-gobble crash! by Julie Stiegemeyer; illustrated by Valeri Gorbachev. Dutton Childrens Books 2008 un il $16.99

Grades: PreK K 1   E

1. Counting 2. Stories in rhyme 3. Turkeys -- Fiction 4. Domestic animals -- Fiction

ISBN 978-0-525-47959-8; 0-525-47959-7

     LC 2008003012

A flock of clumsy turkeys disrupts a quiet night on the farm, but when the farmer threatens them, all the barnyard animals help the noisy birds hide

"In rhythmic couplets, a numbers game unfolds..... Gorbachev's action-filled illustrations add to the fun. His animals cavort against moonlit teal backgrounds, with the text printed in white." SLJ

Seven little bunnies; pictures by Laura J. Bryant. Marshall Cavendish Children 2010 un il $15.99

Grades: PreK K   E

1. Counting 2. Stories in rhyme 3. Bedtime -- Fiction 4. Rabbits -- Fiction

ISBN 978-0-7614-5600-1; 0-7614-5600-7

     LC 2009006337

Seven bunnies find many other things to do when it is time for them to go to bed.

"The sounds and action will appeal to young preschoolers in this lively bedtime rhyme that includes a counting exercise. . . . The words are lively . . . and as kids chant along, they'll also follow the subtraction and addition as seamless parts of the story." Booklist

Stier, Catherine

Bugs in my hair?! written by Catherine Stier; illustrated by Tammie Lyon. Albert Whitman & Co. 2008 un il $15.95
Grades: K 1 2 3   E
1. School stories 2. Lice -- Fiction
ISBN 0807509086; 9780807509081

LC 2007024250

When immaculately groomed Ellie gets head lice she is terribly upset, but once she learns some facts about the creatures, she calms down and figures out a way to help her classmates.

"Stier has taken a difficult topic and turned it into a charming story that demystifies the fears and false information surrounding lice infestation. The writing . . . comes across simply without sounding didactic. Cartoon illustrations capture Ellie's emotions." SLJ

Today on election day; Catherine Stier; illustrated by David Leonard. A. Whitman & Co. 2012 32 p. (hardcover) $16.99
Grades: 2 3 4   E
1. Picture books for children 2. Elections -- United States 3. Election Day -- History 4. Elections -- United States -- History
ISBN 0807580082; 9780807580080

LC 2011035248

This informational picture book about U.S. election day offers children a "salute to the first Tuesday after the first Monday in November." It presents "information . . . [on] political parties, campaigns, Congress, the history of the vote, Constitutional amendments, debates and voting." Author Catherine Stier "situates the activity around the children's school." (Kirkus Reviews)

Stileman, Kali

Roly-poly egg. Tiger Tales 2011 un il $12.95
Grades: PreK K 1   E
1. Eggs -- Fiction 2. Birds -- Fiction 3. Mother-child relationship -- Fiction
ISBN 978-1-58925-852-5; 1-58925-852-5

"Mother love leads to near tragedy in this tale of an egg. Rendered in smears of fiery red paint, Splotch the bird personifies her name. She learns the true testament of a mother's love after she lays a magnificent polka-dotted egg. . . . In her utter joy, she bounces her branch—and the egg falls off into the lush jungle habitat. Met with ambivalence by some and threat from others, the little one is tossed until it's gently returned to her grateful mom. . . . Paint streaks collide with textured papers, creating a bright array of rainbow hues. Spare, crisp sentences describe each action, leaving lots of room for expansion in the bold mixed-media spreads. Vibrant designs breathe life into this mama." Kirkus

Stimpson, Colin

Jack and the baked beanstalk; Colin Stimpson. Candlewick Press 2012 40 p. col. ill. (hardback) $15.99
Grades: K 1 2 3 4   E
1. Fairy tales 2. Restaurants -- Fiction 3. Picture books for children 4. Magic -- Fiction 5. Giants -- Fiction 6. Cooking -- Fiction 7. Characters in literature -- Fiction
ISBN 0763655635; 9780763655631

LC 2011047003

In this children's picture book, "Jack and his mother live and work in a broken-down burger truck parked at the edge of town. When a new overpass diverts traffic away from their location, business dries up. Jack is sent to the store with their last pennies for milk and coffee beans, but instead buys a can of magic baked beans from a mysterious stranger and is tossed out by his angry mother. After the purchase grows into a vine sprouting shiny cans of this delicious staple, the boy climbs up and meets a fearsome-looking giant, but soon discovers that this lonely individual would rather cook for him than eat him." (School Library Journal)

Stinson, Kathy

Big or little? Kathy Stinson [text]; Toni Goffe [illustrations] Annick Press 2009 un il $19.95; pa $6.95
Grades: PreK   E
1. Size -- Fiction 2. Growth -- Fiction
ISBN 978-1-55451-169-3; 1-55451-169-0; 978-1-55451-168-6 pa; 1-55451-168-2 pa

"Toby, a preschooler with flyaway hair, considers the benefits and responsibilities of being big, as well as the frustrations of being small. The mishaps of spilled milk or a wet bed, for instance, are balanced by the joys of helping to wash the car and remembering to return library books. Goffe's line drawings in a pastel palette depict a traditional family of five in a messy home. . . . Plenty of children will relate to [Toby]." SLJ

Stock, Catherine

A **porc** in New York; [by] Catherine Stock. Holiday House 2007 un il $16.95
Grades: PreK K 1 2   E
1. Animals -- Fiction 2. Vacations -- Fiction 3. New York (N.Y.) -- Fiction
ISBN 978-0-8234-1994-4; 0-8234-1994-0

LC 2006002015

Monsieur Monmouton and his dog Cabot fly from France to New York City in pursuit of his farm animals, who are taking a vacation to see such sights as Blooming Dells and MOOMA

"The story is fun, and the expansive, exuberant artwork shows Stock at the top of her game." Booklist

Stoeke, Janet Morgan

★ A **hat** for Minerva Louise. Dutton Children's Bks. 1994 un il hardcover o.p. pa $5.99
Grades: PreK K 1 2   E
1. Hats -- Fiction 2. Chickens -- Fiction
ISBN 0-525-45328-8; 0-14-055666-4 pa

LC 94-2139

Minerva Louise, a snow-loving chicken, mistakes a pair of mittens for two hats to keep both ends warm

This "is a rare find: a picture book exactly on target for preschoolers that sacrifices none of the essential elements of plot, character, and humor. . . . The pictures, in large rectangles of bright primary colors, are easy for preschoolers to 'read' and contain most of the book's considerable humor." Horn Book

Other titles about Minerva Louise are:
A friend for Minerva Louise (1997)
Minerva Louise (1988)
Minerva Louise and the colorful eggs (2006)
Minerva Louise at school (1996)
Minerva Louise at the fair (2000)

Minerva Louise on Christmas Eve (2007)
Minerva Louise on Halloween (2009)

★ The **Loopy** Coop hens. Dutton Children's Books 2011 un il $16.99
Grades: PreK K   E
  1. Chickens -- Fiction 2. Roosters -- Fiction
  ISBN 0-525-42190-4; 978-0-525-42190-0
                LC 2010-13354
Chickens Pip, Midge, and Dot admire Rooster Sam and his ability to fly up to the barn roof, but when they spy on him to see how he does it, they get a big surprise. "Grades one to two." (Bull Cent Child Books)
"The simple text and sentences are ideal for new readers, but it is Stoeke's loose, unfussy artwork that emphasizes the slapstick humor and carries much of the character development. The fowls' body language is especially hilarious in scenes where they attempt to fly and find themselves flat on the ground, or when overconfident Rooster Sam strolls by." Publ Wkly

Minerva Louise and the red truck. Dutton Children's Bks. 2002 un il $14.99
Grades: PreK K 1 2   E
  1. Trucks -- Fiction 2. Chickens -- Fiction
  ISBN 0-525-46909-5
Minerva Louise the chicken "goes for a ride in the farmer's red truck. . . . She fits everything she sees into her own limited experience, so a backyard swimming pool becomes a beautiful lake, a church with a steeple is a 'silly barn wearing a hat,' and a construction site is a truck farm/playground. Kids who know just a little bit more about the world than Minerva Louise will delight in their superior knowledge. . . . The brief text and vibrant, well-composed illustrations are once again ideal for the intended audience." Horn Book

Stohner, Anu
  Brave Charlotte; [illustrated by Henrike Wilson; translated from the German by Alyson Cole] Bloomsbury Children's Bks. 2005 un il $16.95
Grades: PreK K 1 2   E
  1. Sheep -- Fiction
  ISBN 1-58234-690-9
Charlotte, a headstrong sheep, rescues the flock when their shepherd is injured.
"There is a lot to like in 'Brave Charlotte': the gentle way the story unfolds, and the lovely way the illustrator . . . expresses an inviting, dingy fluffiness. . . . Each dreamlike image is suffused with colors that are rich yet subdued." NY Times Book Rev
  Another title about Charlotte is:
  Brave Charlotte and the wolves (2009)

Stojic, Manya
  ★ **Rain**; written and illustrated by Manya Stojic. Crown 2000 un il $15.95
Grades: PreK K 1 2   E
  1. Rain -- Fiction 2. Africa -- Fiction 3. Animals -- Fiction
  ISBN 0-517-80085-3; 0-517-80086-1 lib bdg
                LC 99-35298
The animals of the African savanna use their senses to predict and then enjoy the rain

"The brilliant double-page spreads, the play on the five senses, and a text that invites participation make this one trip to Africa you can't afford to miss!" SLJ

Stone, Kate
  One spooky night; a Halloween adventure. Accord Publishing 2011 36p il pa $11.99
Grades: PreK K 1   E
  1. Fear -- Fiction 2. Monsters -- Fiction 3. Halloween -- Fiction
  ISBN 978-1-4494-0330-0; 1-4494-0330-1
"Cut pages and vellum layers combine to striking effect in this story about a little monster's nocturnal journey. The monster isn't afraid when an owl hoots, and he doesn't cower at grinning jacko'lanterns or ghosts. The transparent layers and stained glass-style cutouts with black, yellow, and purple accents create dramatic dimension. When the monster finally arrives at a haunted house, a bright foldout reveals that he is really a boy in costume." Publ Wkly

Stone, Tanya Lee
  Who says women can't be doctors? the story of Elizabeth Blackwell. Tanya Lee Stone; illustrated by Marjorie Priceman. 1st ed. Christy Ottaviano Books/Henry Holt and Co. 2013 40 p. (reinforced) $16.99
Grades: K 1 2 3   E
  1. Women -- History 2. Women physicians -- United States -- Biography
  ISBN 0805090487; 9780805090482
                LC 2011043528
This children's book, by Tanya Lee Stone, illustrated by Marjorie Priceman, is a biographical story of Elizabeth Blackwell. "In the 1830s, . . . women were supposed to be wives and mothers. . . . Certainly no women were doctors. But Elizabeth refused to accept the common beliefs that women weren't smart enough to be doctors, or that they were too weak for such hard work. . . . Although she faced much opposition, she worked hard and finally . . . proved her detractors wrong." (Publisher's note)
  Includes bibliographical references.

Stoop, Naoko
  Red Knit Cap Girl; by Naoko Stoop. Little, Brown & Co. 2012 40 p. (Red Knit Cap Girl) $15.99
Grades: PreK K 1   E
  1. Picture books for children 2. Moon -- Fiction 3. Forest animals -- Fiction 4. Forests and forestry -- Fiction
  ISBN 0316129461; 9780316129466
                LC 2011025121
This children's picture book by Naoko Stoop, illustrated on wood grain, follows the character of "Red Knit Cap Girl [who] lives with her animal friends in an enchanted forest. There is so much to see and do, but more than anything Red Knit Cap Girl wishes she could talk to the Moon. . . . Red Knit Cap Girl's curiosity, imagination, and joy" are the focus of the tale, "offer[ing] a . . . reminder to appreciate the beauty of the natural world around us." (Publisher's note)

Storad, Conrad J.
  Rattlesnake rules; illustrated by Nathaniel P. Jensen. Five Star Publications 2009 40p il $16.95
Grades: PreK K 1   E
  1. Stories in rhyme 2. Snakes -- Fiction 3. Rattlesnakes

-- Fiction
ISBN 978-1-58985-161-0; 1-58985-161-7

LC 2009-27518

A mother rattlesnake who can locate food with her tongue and swallow prey in one gulp shares survival tips with her babies—and with humans.

"Nathaniel Jensen's illustrations are playfully rendered showcasing the love a mother rattlesnake has for her babies. The skillful combination of fiction and fact in this cleverly conceived story is sure to engage children and teachers alike." Libr Media Connect

Stott, Ann

Always; illustrated by Matt Phelan. Candlewick Press 2008 un il $15.99
Grades: PreK   E
1. Love -- Fiction 2. Mother-son relationship -- Fiction
ISBN 978-0-7636-3232-8; 0-7636-3232-5

LC 2007052020

A child is reassured by his mother that she will love him even when he misbehaves.

"A sweet, understated story. . . . Phelan's illustrations bring this quiet text to exuberant life with pastel watercolors." SLJ

I'll be there; [illustration by Matt Phelan] Candlewick Press 2011 un il $14.99
Grades: PreK K 1 2   E
1. Growth -- Fiction 2. Mother-son relationship -- Fiction
ISBN 978-0-7636-4711-7; 0-7636-4711-X

LC 2010039180

A young boy and his mother talk about what she did for him as a baby, what he can do for himself now, and that she will always be there when he needs her.

"Phelan's warm, sketchy watercolors in a restrained palette of blues, greens, and grays with orange accents reinforce the sweet sentiment. While the touching story, with its simple text and accessible images, is easily suitable for story hour, this will doubtless be a favorite for sharing at home, as well." Booklist

Stringer, Lauren

★ **Winter** is the warmest season; by Lauren Stringer. Harcourt 2006 un il $16
Grades: PreK K 1 2   E
1. Winter -- Fiction
ISBN 0-15-204967-3

LC 2005005723

A child describes pleasant ways to stay warm during the winter, from sipping hot chocolate and eating grilled cheese sandwiches to wearing wooly sweaters and sitting near a glowing fireplace.

"It takes special art to accentuate the evocative words, and Stringer . . . provides distinctive pictures for herself. . . . The deeply hued acrylic artwork ranges from friendly to joyous. . . . A special book worthy of many readings, this radiates warmth." Booklist

Strom, Kellie

Sadie the air mail pilot. David Fickling Books 2007 un il $17.78

Grades: K 1 2 3   E
1. Cats -- Fiction 2. Air pilots -- Fiction
ISBN 978-0-385-60506-9; 0-385-60506-4

Although her day got off to a bad start, Sadie, a highflying cat, is confident that she can make the air mail run to Knuckle Peak Weather Station, even after the station reports that a storm is headed their way.

"Strom peppers the narrative with memorable rhymes. . . . Children will be fascinated by the courage of this determined pilot. They will pore over the antique-appearing illustrations that glow in an orangish-red palette with rusty browns and golden yellows." SLJ

Stroud, Bettye

The **patchwork** path; a quilt map to freedom. illustrated by Erin Susanne Bennett. Candlewick Press 2005 32p il $15.99
Grades: K 1 2 3   E
1. Quilts -- Fiction 2. Slavery -- Fiction 3. African Americans -- Fiction 4. Underground railroad -- Fiction
ISBN 0-7636-2423-3

LC 2004-45786

While her father leads her toward Canada and away from the plantation where they have been slaves, a young girl thinks of the quilt her mother used to teach her a code that will help guide them to freedom.

"The exciting escape story makes the history immediate, and the fascinating quilt-code messages will have children revisiting the page that shows each symbol and its secret directions. Bennett's bright oil paintings make dramatic use of collage." Booklist

Stuchner, Joan Betty

Can hens give milk? illustrated by Joe Weissmann. Orca Book Publishers 2011 un il $19.95
Grades: PreK K 1   E
1. Jews -- Folklore 2. Chickens -- Fiction
ISBN 978-1-55469-319-1; 1-55469-319-5

"On this visit to Chelm, which in Jewish folklore is the hotbed for all things silly, readers meet Shlomo and Rivka, a kindly couple who have 'five children, twelve scrawny hens, one rooster and not much money.' Yearning for a little milk and cheese and unable to afford a cow, Shlomo engages in some magical thinking of the animal husbandry kind. Since cows eat grass, he reasons, '...if we feed grass to our hens, they will still lay eggs, but they will also give us milk.'" Publ Wkly

Sturges, Philemon

I love planes! illustrated by Shari Halpern. HarperCollins Pubs. 2003 un il $12.99; lib bdg $14.89
Grades: PreK K   E
1. Airplanes -- Fiction
ISBN 0-06-028898-1; 0-06-028899-X lib bdg

LC 2001-26483

A child celebrates his love of planes by naming his favorite kinds and their notable characteristics

"The simplicity of the child's words is well matched by the colorful, uncluttered images, outlined in black." Booklist

I love school! illustrated by Shari Halpern. HarperCollins Pubs. 2004 un il $12.99; lib bdg $14.89

Grades: PreK K   E
1. School stories 2. Stories in rhyme
ISBN 0-06-009284-X; 0-06-009285-8 lib bdg
LC 2002-68554
A brother and sister describe the things they love to do during their day at kindergarten

This book "is a good way to prepare nervous new preschoolers and kindergartners. . . . [It features] simple, rhymed text and big, clear color pictures outlined in thick black line." Booklist

I love trains! illustrated by Shari Halpern. HarperCollins Pubs. 2001 un il $12.95; lib bdg $13.89
Grades: PreK K   E
1. Stories in rhyme 2. Railroads -- Fiction
ISBN 0-06-028900-7; 0-06-028901-5 lib bdg
LC 99-86367
A boy expresses his love of trains, describing many kinds of train cars and their special jobs

This offers "clear, bright, double-page pictures with thick black lines and neon colors. . . . Toddlers will enjoy making the hoot, roar, and rumble sounds and identifying the various cars." Booklist

Stutson, Caroline
  ★ **By** the light of the Halloween moon; illustrated by Kevin Hawkes. Marshall Cavendish 2009 un il $16.99
Grades: PreK K 1 2   E
1. Stories in rhyme 2. Halloween -- Fiction
ISBN 978-0-7614-5553-0; 0-7614-5553-1
LC 2008022965
A reissue of the title first published 1993 by Lothrop, Lee, & Shepherd Books

In this cumulative tale, a host of Halloween spooks, including a cat, a witch, and a ghoul, are drawn to the tapping of a little girl's toe.

"Not only is the text rhythmically bouncy and appealing, but the illustrations are of the least fearful and most amusing of ghastly creatures, very effectively set against a black and gloomy background. A sure Halloween hit." Horn Book

Cats' night out; illustrated by J. Klassen. Simon & Schuster Books for Young Readers 2010 un il $15.99
Grades: K 1 2 3   E
1. Stories in rhyme 2. Cats -- Fiction 3. Dance -- Fiction 4. City and town life -- Fiction
ISBN 978-1-4169-4005-0; 1-4169-4005-7
LC 2008-52268
Cats dance the night away out on the town, doing the tango, rumba, twist, fox trot, and more

"Klassen's eye-catching digitally rendered urban streetscapes resemble the sets of classic musical theater. . . . The finely detailed illustrations feature a subdued palette of brown, gray, and charcoal enlivened by splashes of color. The subtle charms of this lighter-than-air confection should delight young connoisseurs of dance and style." SLJ

Suen, Anastasia
  ★ **Subway**; written by Anastasia Suen; illustrated by Karen Katz. Viking 2004 un il $15.99
Grades: PreK K 1 2   E
1. Stories in rhyme 2. Subways -- Fiction
ISBN 0-670-03622-6
LC 2003-14020

"In brief, rhyming verses, an African-American child describes her ride on the subway. . . . The rhythmic language captures the feel of her journey and a repeated refrain invites readers to participate in the telling of the story. The bright, bold artwork depicts each scene in a realistic manner from the child's point of view." SLJ

Sullivan, Mary
  Ball; word and pictures by Mary Sullivan. Houghton Mifflin Harcourt 2013 40 p. $12.99
Grades: PreK K 1   E
1. Dogs -- Fiction 2. Picture books for children
ISBN 0547759363; 9780547759364
Theodor Seuss Geisel Honor Book (2014)
This children's picture book is about a ball-obsessed dog. "The dog's curly headed owner is delighted to play with him, but after she leaves for school he's stuck with her meditating mother and a squalling baby. He tries listlessly to amuse himself, then dozes off. His dreams are a parade of mad, creative whimsy. A tiered cake dotted with balls, a monstrous baby, and an interstellar game of chase climax with a journey down the toilet and through a maze of pipes." (Publishers Weekly)

Sullivan, Sarah
  Once upon a baby brother; pictures by Tricia Tusa. Farrar Straus Giroux 2010 un il $16.99
Grades: PreK K 1 2   E
1. Infants -- Fiction 2. Siblings -- Fiction 3. Authorship -- Fiction 4. Storytelling -- Fiction
ISBN 978-0-374-34635-5; 0-374-34635-6
LC 2008016791
Lizzie, who loves to tell and write stories, is surprised to discover that much of her storytelling inspiration comes from her messy baby brother.

"Sullivan has found an oblique way to write about the ups and downs of a school-age child adjusting to a much younger sibling, and she carries it out with skill. Bringing the story to life, Tusa's strong, quirky line-and-wash drawings define characters and settings, add bits of visual humor, amplify the book's emotional content, and give the jacket its winsome appeal." Booklist

  Passing the music down; illustrated by Barry Root. Candlewick Press 2010 un il $16.99
Grades: K 1 2 3   E
1. Folk music -- Fiction 2. Violinists -- Fiction 3. Country life -- Fiction
ISBN 978-0-7636-3753-8; 0-7636-3753-X
LC 2008037104
A boy and his family befriend a country fiddler, who teaches the boy all about playing the old tunes, which the boy promises to help keep alive. Inspired by Melvin Wine and Jake Krack.

"Root's sweet illustrations in watercolor and gouache show the man and boy in an almost grandfather-grandson setting, making pancakes, hunting ginseng, and picking beans, and at the end of their hard day's work, they make music together. . . . Told in free verse, this picture book would be a good accompaniment to music-appreciation lessons focused on American roots music." SLJ

Surgal, Jon

Have you seen my dinosaur? illustrated by Joe Mathieu. Random House Children's Books 2010 un il $8.99

Grades: PreK K 1 2   E

1. Stories in rhyme 2. Dinosaurs -- Fiction 3. Lost and found possessions -- Fiction

ISBN 978-0-375-85639-6; 978-0-375-95639-3 lib bdg
LC 2007043166

A five-year-old boy searches high and low for his missing dinosaur, and the people he asks for help do not believe such a creature actually exists.

"A boy looks for his dinosaur at the zoo, the museum, and other places. No one can help him, but readers will easily see the large green reptile in the illustrations. While the rhyming text strains to tell the story, the generic-looking cartoony illustrations are mildly diverting." Horn Book

Surovec, Yasmine

I see Kitty; Yasmine Surovec. Roaring Brook Press 2013 40 p. (hardcover) $15.99

Grades: PreK K 1   E

1. Imagination -- Fiction 2. Cats -- Fiction 3. Animals -- Infancy -- Fiction

ISBN 1596438622; 9781596438620
LC 2012050306

In this children's picture book, " Chloe, a petite preschooler in a polka-dot dress, eyes a 'Pet Adoptions' sign and beams with joy at the sight of an orange-and-white kitten. Her mother says, 'Not today,' but her coy smile does not rule out the possibility of a future pet. 'Now Chloe sees Kitty everywhere she goes,' writes Surovec as Chloe points out cat shapes in a cloud, the auburn bouffant of a woman waiting for the bus, a tower of pink cotton candy, and her bubble bath." (Publishers Weekly)

Sussman, Michael B.

Otto grows down; illustrated by Scott Magoon. Sterling Pub. Co. 2009 un il $14.95

Grades: PreK K 1   E

1. Growth -- Fiction 2. Wishes -- Fiction 3. Infants -- Fiction 4. Siblings -- Fiction

ISBN 978-1-4027-4703-8; 1-4027-4703-9
LC 2008028229

When time goes backwards, granting six-year-old Otto his wish that his attention-stealing baby sister was never born, it keeps going backwards, and Otto finds himself getting younger and younger.

"A refreshing take on the arrival of a new sibling and the rivalry that frequently follows. . . . Exaggerated cartoon art captures his predicament. With humor and poignancy, author and illustrator portray an age-old rite of passage." SLJ

Sutton, Sally

Construction; Sally Sutton, illustrated by Brian Lovelock. Candlewick Press 2014 34 p. color illustrations $15.99

Grades: PreK K 1   E

1. Construction workers -- Fiction 2. Construction equipment -- Fiction 3. Building -- fiction 4. Building sites -- fiction

ISBN 0763673250; 9780763673253
LC 2013953459

This children's book, by Sally Sutton, illustrated by Brian Lovelock, describes the construction of a library build-

ing. "Thonk! Clonk! Clap! The team behind 'Roadwork' and 'Demolition' returns to the construction site, where big machines and busy workers dig, hoist, and hammer away." (Publisher's note)

"The New Zealand duo who created Roadwork (2008) and Demolition (2012, both Candlewick) turn their considerable talents to the building of a library. The foundation is prepared, the holes are filled with concrete, and the building rises. Clad in safety gear, men and women of different ethnic backgrounds cut the planks, raise the roof, fit the doors and windows, lay the pipes, and run the wires. . . . Printed in large, clear letters, the rhythmic text uses basic vocabulary, strong verbs, and onomatopoeia, making it wonderful to read aloud. Artwork is done in ink, acrylic, and colored pencil on full-bleed spreads where pigmented inks and a variety of perspectives are used to great effect. A picture vocabulary at the end identifies excavators, cranes, and trucks on site as well as the safety equipment worn by workers. The simplicity of the telling and the rich details in the spreads make this a must-have for all libraries serving young children." SLJ

Roadwork! [by] Sally Sutton; illustrated by Brian Lovelock. Candlewick Press 2008 32p il $15.99

Grades: PreK   E

1. Stories in rhyme 2. Trucks -- Fiction 3. Construction equipment -- Fiction

ISBN 978-0-7636-3912-9; 0-7636-3912-5

"Kids who love trucks and construction will find an ideal vehicle for their passions in this exuberant book from New Zealand, which uses full-bleed art and rhyming text to show how each of seven machines functions in the building of a road. Sutton's rhythms invite audience participation, as do the sound effects that end each verse . . . Using ink, acrylics and colored pencils, Lovelock conjures artful landscapes with visible brushwork, reserving a speckling effect not unlike concrete for the road." Publ Wkly

"No construction detail is ignored in this rhythmic readaloud. . . . Extensive use of action verbs and onomatopoeic exclamations guide youngsters through packing the ground, rolling the tar, raising the signs, and even planting trees along the side on the route. Angular road lines . . . traverse each spread, often guiding viewers eyes in the direction of the next page." SLJ

Suzuki, David T.

There's a barnyard in my bedroom; [by] David Suzuki; Eugenie Fernandes, illustrator. Greystone Books 2010 un il $12.95

Grades: K 1 2   E

1. Imagination -- Fiction 2. Natural history -- Fiction

ISBN 978-1-55365-532-9; 1-55365-532-X

With the help of their parents and their own imaginations, Jamie and Megan discover that natural magic is all around them, even in their own home. Sheets and pillows, fruits and furniture—they all come from nature. What's more, the air isn't just empty space—it's full of smells, sounds, water, and life-giving gases.

Suzuki "presents a whimsical and beautifully illustrated children's book that speaks to a child's imagination and creativity. . . . The illustrations are lively and boldly colored." Sci Books Films

Swain, Gwenyth

Riding to Washington; written by Gwenyth Swain; illustrated by David Geister. Sleeping Bear Press 2008 un il (Tales of young Americans) $17.95

Grades: 1 2 3 4   E

1. Clergy 2. Nonfiction writers 3. Civil rights activists 4. Nobel laureates for peace 5. Race relations -- Fiction 6. African Americans -- Fiction

ISBN 978-1-58536-324-7; 1-58536-324-3

"The illustrations provide a strong sense of the period. The soft earth tones and rounded forms create a mood of safety and stability. This heartfelt tale provides an unusual and compelling perspective on a historical event." SLJ

"A young white girl rides the bus with her father to the March on Washington in 1963—at which Dr. Martin Luther King, Jr., would give his 'I Have a Dream' speech. She comes to see that Dr. King's dream belongs not just to Blacks but to all Americans." Publisher's note

Swallow, Pamela Curtis

Groundhog gets a say; as told to Pamela Curtis Swallow; illustrated by Denise Brunkus. G.P. Putnam's Sons 2005 un il $15.99

Grades: PreK K 1 2   E

1. Crows -- Fiction 2. Marmots -- Fiction 3. Squirrels -- Fiction

ISBN 0-399-23876-X

A groundhog describes his various characteristics to a skeptical squirrel and crow. Text includes various facts about groundhogs

"The humorous text is completed by Brunkus's finely executed, animated, watercolor-and-colored-pencil drawings." SLJ

Swanson, Susan Marie

★ The house in the night; written by Susan Marie Swanson and illustrated by Beth Krommes. Houghton Mifflin Company 2008 un il $16

Grades: PreK K 1   E

1. Light -- Fiction 2. Night -- Fiction 3. Houses -- Fiction

ISBN 978-0-618-86244-3; 0-618-86244-7

LC 2007012921

Awarded the Caldecott Medal, 2009

Illustrations and easy-to-read text explore the light that makes a house in the night a home filled with light.

"Inspired by traditional cumulative poetry, Swanson weaves a soothing song that is as luminescent and soulful as the gorgeous illustrations that accompany her words. . . . Krommes's folk-style black-and-white etchings with touches of yellow-orange make the world of the poem an enchanted place." SLJ

Sweeney, Linda Booth

When the wind blows; Linda Booth Sweeney; illustrated by Jana Christy. G. P. Putnam's Sons 2014 32 p. (hardcover) $16.99

Grades: PreK K 1   E

1. Spring -- Fiction 2. Kites -- Juvenile fiction 3. Winds -- Juvenile fiction 4. Stories in rhyme 5. Storms -- Fiction 6. Family life -- Fiction

ISBN 0399160159; 9780399160158

LC 2013040049

In this children's book by Linda Booth Sweeney, illustrated by Jana Christy, "when wind chimes start singing and clouds race across the sky, one little guy knows just what to do--grab his kite! But as the kite soars, the wind picks up even more, and soon he and his grandma are chasing the runaway kite into town. As they pass swirling leaves, bobbing boats, and flapping scarves, . . . the sky darkens. Can they squeeze in one more adventure before the downpour?" (Publisher's note)

Sweet, Melissa

Carmine; a little more red. by Melissa Sweet. Houghton Mifflin 2005 un il $16

Grades: PreK K 1 2   E

1. Alphabet 2. Fairy tales 3. Dogs -- Fiction 4. Wolves -- Fiction

ISBN 0-618-38794-3

LC 2004-9212

While a little girl who loves red—and loves to dillydally—stops to paint a picture on the way to visit her grandmother, her dog Rufus meets a wolf and leads him directly to Granny's house.

"A fetching retelling of 'Little Red Riding Hood' that also works as an effective alphabet book. . . . The fresh and imaginative mixed-media art imitates the sketchbook of a child artist." SLJ

★ Tupelo rides the rails; written and illustrated by Melissa Sweet. Houghton Mifflin Company 2008 un il $17

Grades: K 1 2 3   E

1. Dogs -- Fiction 2. Stars -- Fiction 3. Tramps -- Fiction 4. Wishes -- Fiction 5. Railroads -- Fiction

ISBN 978-0-618-71714-9; 0-618-71714-5

LC 2007012924

After being left by the side of a road with nothing but her favorite sock toy, Tupelo meets a pack of dogs named the BONEHEADS (The Benevolent Order of Nature's Exalted Hounds Earnest And Doggedly Sublime), led by a hobo named Garbage Pail Tex. Tupelo joins them as they are wishing on Sirius, the Dog Star, for new homes, and as they catch a passing train.

"Sweet's beautifully detailed artwork, in watercolor and mixed-media, is packed with feeling and story." Booklist

Swenson, Jamie A.

Big rig; by Jamie Swenson; illustrated by Ned Young. Disney-Hyperion Books 2014 32 p. $16.99

Grades: PreK K   E

1. Traffic accidents 2. Trucks -- Fiction 3. Tractor trailers -- Fiction

ISBN 1423163303; 9781423163305

LC 2013012223

In this book, by Jamie A. Swenson, readers "come along for the ride as Frankie the big rig truck takes us on the job, driving past kiddie cars (school buses) and land yachts (RVs). [After] a blow-out . . . a service truck saves the day so we can get the job done and make a very special delivery." (Publisher's note)

"This bright, colorful look at an eighteen-wheeler surely will be a hit with young audiences...The big and bold cartoon illustrations and the text's use of sound effects and a few unusual phrases should make this a fun read-aloud for toddlers and a good storytime participation book as well. Given the number of books on cars and trucks available, this might not be a necessary purchase, but it will be a popular one." (School Library Journal)

Swiatkowska, Gabi

Queen on Wednesday; Gabi Swiatkowska. Frances Foster Books, Farrar Straus Giroux 2014 40 p. color illustrations (hardcover) $17.99

Grades: K 1 2 3   **E**

1. Pets -- Fiction 2. Queens -- Fiction 3. Kings, queens, rulers, etc. -- Fiction

ISBN 0374374465; 9780374374464

LC 2013019719

"On Wednesday, Thelma is bored--so she decides to become a queen. She makes the royal announcement on Thursday and chooses the royal pets on Friday. But she needs a castle to keep the pets, and royally qualified trainers to tame them, and of course someone to clean up after the messes. . . . Filled with playful humor and stunning artwork, 'Queen on Wednesday' marks renowned illustrator Gabi Swiatkowska's debut as a picture book author." (Publisher's note)

" The children in her delightfully weird paintings look like they have stepped out of a nineteenth-century painting and into an absurd wonderland full of odd animals and objects that juxtapose amusingly. It's a familiar story of imaginative play, but Swiatkowska's whimsical pictures set it apart." Booklist

Swift, Hildegarde Hoyt

★ The **little** red lighthouse and the great gray bridge; by Hildegarde H. Swift and [illustrated by] Lynd Ward. Harcourt 2002 un il $16

Grades: PreK K 1 2   **E**

1. Lighthouses -- Fiction 2. George Washington Bridge (N.Y. and N.J.) -- Fiction

ISBN 0-15-204571-6

LC 2001-7106

A reissue of the title first published 1942

"The story is written with imagination and a gift for bringing alive this little lighthouse and its troubles. . . . [Lynd Ward's] illustrations have some distinction and one in particular, the fog creeping over the river clutching at the river boats, has atmosphere, rhythm and good colour." Ont Libr Rev

Swinburne, Stephen R.

Whose shoes? a shoe for every job. Boyds Mills Press 2010 un il $16.95

Grades: PreK   **E**

1. Shoes

ISBN 978-1-59078-569-0; 1-59078-569-X

Swinburne "offers a guessing game in which a photo on the right-hand page shows a person below the knees and asks, Whose shoes? A turn of the page gives the answer and a full-length photo of a ballerina (or farmer, Army National Guard soldier, post office worker, clown . . .) on the left. The facing page repeats the question Whose Shoes? with a new photo. . . . The clear, colorful photos provide plenty of talking points, while the short text flows in a conversational way." Booklist

Swope, Sam

Gotta go! Gotta go! pictures by Sue Riddle. Farrar, Straus & Giroux 2000 un il hardcover o.p. pa $5.95

Grades: PreK K 1 2   **E**

1. Butterflies -- Fiction 2. Caterpillars -- Fiction

ISBN 0-374-32757-2; 0-374-427867-0 pa

LC 99-28503

Although she does not know why or how, a caterpillar who becomes a monarch butterfly is certain that she must make her way to Mexico

"The rhythm and repetition are infectious; and the pen-and-ink and watercolor illustrations, set against expanses of white space, enlarge the book remarkably." Horn Book Guide

Sydor, Colleen

Timmerman was here; illustrated by Nicolas Debon. Tundra Books 2009 un il $19.95

Grades: K 1 2 3   **E**

1. Friendship -- Fiction

ISBN 978-0-88776-890-3; 0-88776-890-3

"A little girl is forced to contend with a boarder, Timmerman, when she temporarily occupies the bedroom of her Granddad, who has moved to a senior citizens' home. Despite her resentment, the little girl begins to appreciate the boarder's kindness, diligence, helpfulness and soft-spoken demeanor. But Timmerman's mysterious late-night walks, carrying a spade and burlap sack, raise everyone's suspicions. . . . Debon's deep, dark, Depression-era-style paintings rendered in gouache and colored and wax pencils show one man's work ethic opposite a child's intuitive yet waning confidence in a story filled with mystery, misperceptions, doubt and friendship. . . . Readers' and listeners' predictions will abound as will discussion of how one's actions should be interpreted and noted. Provocative." Kirkus

Sylvester, Kevin

Splinters; (this girl needs a miracle. . . .) Tundra Books 2010 un il $17.95

Grades: K 1 2 3   **E**

1. Fairy tales 2. Hockey -- Fiction

ISBN 978-0-88776-944-3; 0-88776-944-6

"Cindy is a destitute but excellent hockey player who can't catch a break. When she finally saves enough money to join a league, it's dominated by two evil sisters and their mother, the coach. They keep Cindy on the bench and nickname her 'Splinters.' When the acclaimed coach Charmaine Prince holds tryouts for the All-Star team, Cindy needs the help of her Fairy Goaltender to get to the rink on time on a new Zamboni. . . . The watercolor and pencil illustrations depict the actions and emotions of the characters perfectly. The facial expressions are spot-on." SLJ

Symes, Ruth

Harriet dancing; by Ruth Symes; illustrated by Caroline Jayne Church. Chicken House 2008 un il $16.99

Grades: PreK K 1   **E**

1. Dance -- Fiction 2. Hedgehogs -- Fiction 3. Butterflies -- Fiction

ISBN 978-0-545-03204-9; 0-545-03204-0

LC 2007015258

Harriet the hedgehog learns that dancing is for everyone, big and small

"Church's collage illustrations are charming and vibrant, and children will love the depictions of the protagonist as she progresses through the story." SLJ

Taback, Simms

★ **I** miss you every day; by Simms Taback. Viking Children's Books 2007 un il $16.99

Grades: PreK K 1 2   E
  1. Stories in rhyme 2. Postal service -- Fiction
  ISBN 978-0-670-06192-1

LC 2007008046

A little girl misses someone so much that she wraps herself up like a package and sends herself through the mail.

"Anyone who has ever yearned for an absent loved one will treasure this beautifully simple picture book. . . . Taback's trademark wavy outlines and simple shapes . . . add both whimsy and wide appeal." SLJ

Simms Taback's farm animals. Blue Apple Books 2011 un bd bk $12.99

Grades: PreK   E
  1. Board books for children 2. Farm life -- Fiction 3. Domestic animals -- Fiction
  ISBN 978-1-60905-078-8; 1-60905-078-9

LC 2011019081

The reader is invited to guess which farm animal is hiding beneath fold-outs that reveal a succession of clues.

"The simple, boldly outlined and brightly colored illustrations portray each animal standing against a monochromatic sky ranging in color from yellow to blue to purple. The pages are constructed of sturdy card stock, allowing small fingers to practice unfolding and re-folding the flaps. An amusing and instructive story." SLJ

Tafolla, Carmen

★ **Fiesta** babies; illustrated by Amy Cordova. Tricycle Press 2010 un il $12.99

Grades: PreK K   E
  1. Stories in rhyme 2. Infants -- Fiction 3. Mexican Americans -- Fiction
  ISBN 978-1-5824-6319-3; 1-5824-6319-0

LC 2009016301

Pura Belpré Award honor book (Illustrator), 2011

"Short lines of bouncy, rhyming text describe how several adorable, chubby babies and toddlers participate in their local Hispanic celebration. . . . The length and rhythm of the text make this book an excellent choice for toddler and preschool storytimes. Córdova once again demonstrates how her award-winning style brilliantly brings an author's words to life. Her bold acrylic colors and brisk brushstrokes capture the fiesta's energy and good cheer." SLJ

What can you do with a rebozo? by Carmen Tafolla; illustrations by Amy Cordova. Tricycle Press 2007 un il $14.95

Grades: PreK K 1   E
  1. Stories in rhyme 2. Mexican Americans -- Fiction 3. Clothing and dress -- Fiction
  ISBN 978-1-58246-220-2; 1-58246-220-8

LC 2006-39624

A Pura Belpre Illustrator Award honor book, 2009

A spunky, young Mexican American girl explains the many uses of her mother's red rebozo, or long scarf.

"Bright, textured acrylic illustrations with a strong sense of line decorate this celebration of cultural heritage. An author's note gives more information about the rebozo as well as asking readers what they might do with one." Horn Book Guide

Tafuri, Nancy

All kinds of kisses. Little, Brown 2012 un il $16.99

Grades: PreK   E
  1. Bedtime -- Fiction 2. Kissing -- Fiction 3. Domestic animals -- Fiction
  ISBN 978-0-316-12235-1; 0-316-12235-1

LC 2010049433

Each barnyard animal has its favorite kind of kiss, but the best of all is a mother's goodnight kiss.

"Using her distinctively recognizable artwork rendered in watercolor and colored pencil, Tafuri has created another loving book for toddlers." SLJ

The **big** storm; a very soggy counting book. Simon & Schuster Books for Young Readers 2009 un il $15.99

Grades: PreK K   E
  1. Counting 2. Storms -- Fiction 3. Animals -- Fiction
  ISBN 978-1-4169-6795-8; 1-4169-6795-8

LC 2007047989

Ten animals find shelter in a hill hollow one by one, but when the storm is over, a rumbling tells them there is still danger afoot.

"This title accomplishes much with simplicity. Repetitive words . . . add tension to the plot. Dramatic poses picture the animals' wariness of the storm ahead. . . . An autumn-colored palette with orange-and-yellow leaves swirling across a spread is rendered in watercolor and watercolor pencils." SLJ

★ **Blue** Goose. Simon & Schuster Books for Young Readers 2008 un il $15.99

Grades: PreK K   E
  1. Color -- Fiction 2. Animals -- Fiction 3. Farm life -- Fiction
  ISBN 978-1-4169-2834-8; 1-4169-2834-0

LC 2006-38368

When Farmer Gray goes away for the day, Blue Goose, Red Hen, Yellow Chick, and White Duck get together and paint their black and white farm.

"The scenes have the bold, graphic punch of murals. . . . [The] generously sized animals and pithy text extend a warm welcome to readers." Publ Wkly

The **busy** little squirrel; [by] Nancy Tafuri. Simon & Schuster Books for Young Readers 2007 un il $15.99

Grades: PreK K   E
  1. Autumn -- Fiction 2. Animals -- Fiction 3. Squirrels -- Fiction
  ISBN 978-0-689-87341-6; 0-689-87341-7

LC 2005015520

Squirrel is too busy getting ready for winter to nibble a pumpkin with Mouse, run in the field with Dog, or otherwise play with any of the other animals

"The ink-and-watercolor pictures show squirrel's flurry of activity. . . . The basic words and large, clearly defined pictures of familiar animals are perfectly suited for pre-school read-alouds." Booklist

★ **Five** little chicks. Simon & Schuster Books for Young Readers 2006 un il $14.95

Grades: PreK K   E
  1. Chickens -- Fiction
  ISBN 0-689-87342-5

Five chicks and their mother peck in the corn patch in search of breakfast.

"Created with brush pen, watercolor pencils, and ink, the gorgeous double-page spreads, in warm shades of red, yellow, and brown, manage to be both clear and fuzzy, simple and rich." Booklist

★ **Have** you seen my duckling? Greenwillow Bks. 1984 un il $16.99; lib bdg $17.89; pa $6.99; bd bk $6.99
Grades: PreK K   E
    1. Ducks -- Fiction
    ISBN 0-688-02797-0; 0-688-02798-9 lib bdg; 0-688-10994-2 pa; 0-688-14899-9 bd bk
                                             LC 83-17196
A Caldecott Medal honor book, 1985
"Tafuri's artwork . . . features clean lines, generous figures, and clear, cool colors. She also adds nice detail—feathers, for instance, that you can almost feel under your hands." Booklist

★ **This** is the farmer. Greenwillow Bks. 1994 un il $16.99
Grades: PreK K 1 2   E
    1. Farm life -- Fiction
    ISBN 0-688-09468-6
                                             LC 92-30082
A farmer's kiss causes an amusing chain of events on the farm
"The well-defined, watercolor-and-ink double-spread illustrations are . . . of the highest quality. The brief story is rhythmic, predictable, and printed in extra-large type." SLJ

Whose chick are you? Greenwillow Books 2007 un il $16.99; lib bdg $17.89
Grades: PreK K   E
    1. Birds -- Fiction 2. Swans -- Fiction
    ISBN 0-06-082514-6; 0-06-082515-4 lib bdg
Goose, Duck, Hen, Bird and the little chick, itself, cannot tell to whom a new hatchling belongs, but its mother knows.
"The artwork's close-up perspective and the combination of large type, onomatopoeia, and the clues to Little Chick's parents scattered through the pictures will draw children into the scenes." Booklist

Tallec, Olivier
    Waterloo & Trafalgar; Olivier Tallec. Enchanted Lion Books 2012 64 p. (alk. paper) $17.95
Grades: 1 2 3 4 5   E
    1. War stories 2. Soldiers
    ISBN 1592701272; 9781592701278
                                             LC 2012937561
This children's picture book by Olivier Tallec "portrays two characters, separated only by narrow walls, who watch each other ceaselessly through the seasons. Moving between day and night . . . they fight their cold war, full of suspicion, never daring to bridge the gap between them. As time passes, a snail shows up, and then a bird, and one day, to their utter surprise, they come face-to-face in a different way, and they discover that their differences don't make them enemies."(Publisher's note)

Tan, Shaun
    ★ **Rules** of summer; Shaun Tan. Arthur A. Levine Books 2014 48 p. (hardcover: alk. paper) $18.99

Grades: 3 4 5 6 7 8 9   E
    1. Summer -- Fiction 2. Conduct of life -- Fiction 3. Picture books for children 4. Friendship -- Fiction
    ISBN 0545639123; 9780545639125
                                             LC 2013040915
Boston Globe-Horn Book Honor: Picture Book (2014)
In this picture book, written and illustrated by Shaun Tan, "one summer, two brothers live by mysteriously dire rules laid down by the older of the pair. The little one lists what he learned. . . . What if you break a rule? You risk facing monstrous red rabbits, crow armies, teetering robots, lumbering metal dinosaurs, large lizards, overgrown fungus and more." (Publisher's note)
"On left-hand pages the narrator enumerates a series of 'rules' ('Never eat the last olive at a party'). The right-hand pages depict, in thickly textured paintings, a young boy (presumably the narrator) and an older boy (perhaps his brother) in a variety of enigmatically surreal situations. The book delivers superb artwork that elicits both a cerebral and emotional response." Horn Book

Tankard, Jeremy
    Grumpy Bird. Scholastic Press 2007 un il $12.99
Grades: K 1 2 3   E
    1. Birds -- Fiction 2. Emotions -- Fiction
    ISBN 0-439-85147-5; 978-0-439-85147-3
                                             LC 2006-03770
Feeling too grumpy to fly, Bird begins to walk and finds that his mood changes as other animals join him.
"This straightforward story is enlivened by unusual mixed-media illustrations. Each scene consists of sketches of farmland or trees, layered over photographs of real farms and trees. Cheerful flowers and stars are scribbled throughout. The animal characters are simplistic cartoons with thick black outlines and comical facial expressions." SLJ
Another title about Bird is:
Boo hoo Bird (2009)

    Me hungry! Candlewick Press 2008 un il $15.99
Grades: PreK K   E
    1. Animals -- Fiction 2. Prehistoric peoples -- Fiction
    ISBN 978-0-7636-3360-8; 0-7636-3360-7
                                             LC 2007-35735
A little prehistoric boy decides to hunt for his own food, and makes a new friend in the process.
"Tankard's bold, thick black lines, done in ink and digital media, outline the youngster and his many choices for a snack, allowing the characters to jump off the monochromatic pages. Minimal but effective text perfectly complements the expressive prehistoric family. This energetic story comes full circle with a humorous punch line that will make all children with busy parents laugh out loud." SLJ

Tarlow, Ellen
    Pinwheel days; by Ellen Tarlow; art by Gretel Parker. Star Bright Books 2007 56p il pa $6.95
Grades: K 1 2   E
    1. Animals -- Fiction 2. Donkeys -- Fiction 3. Squirrels -- Fiction 4. Friendship -- Fiction
    ISBN 978-1-59572-059-7 pa; 1-59572-059-6 pa
In four separate stories, Pinwheel the donkey learns about friendship when his loneliness ends after meeting his "echo," a lovely picnic stems from a mistake, his rubbing on a tree seems to break it, and his best dream ever comes true

"The four easy-to-read chapters feature abundant dialogue and humorous plots. Complementing the text, the watercolor illustrations are characterized by round figures, warm earth tones, and decorative elements such as multiple patterns." SLJ

Taro Miura

The tiny king; Taro Miura. Candlewick Press 2013 32 p. $14.99

Grades: PreK K 1 2   E

1. Happiness -- Fiction 2. Family life 3. Kings and rulers -- Fiction

ISBN 0763666874; 9780763666873

LC 2012955151

In this children's picture book by Taro Miura "the Tiny King lives all alone in his big castle with too much space, accompanied only by an army. When he falls in love with a big princess, they soon have 10 children who share his massive table, ride in a carriage pulled by his giant white horse, splash in the gigantic bathtub, and fill up the once-empty bed. The king is so happy that he sends his army marching home for a holiday." (School Library Journal)

Tarpley, Natasha

Bippity Bop barbershop; by Natasha Anastasia Tarpley; illustrated by E.B. Lewis. Little, Brown 2002 un il $15.95

Grades: PreK K 1 2   E

1. African Americans -- Fiction 2. Barbers and barbershops -- Fiction

ISBN 0-316-52284-8

LC 00-30188

A story celebrating a young African-American boy's first trip to the barbershop

"Expressive watercolors showcase [the child's] curiosity, fear, and satisfaction, as well as a close father-son relationship." Horn Book Guide

Tarshis, Lauren

I survived the Battle of Gettysburg, 1863; Lauren Tarshis. Scholastic 2013 89 p. (paperback) $4.99

Grades: 3 4 5 6   E

1. Fugitive slaves -- Fiction 2. Gettysburg (Pa.), Battle of, 1863 -- Fiction

ISBN 0545459362; 9780545459365

This children's book, by Lauren Tarshis, is book 7 in the "I Survived" series. "It's 1863, and Thomas and his little sister, Birdie, have fled the farm where they were born and raised as slaves. . . . They soon cross paths with a Union soldier . . . , marching with the army. But then orders come through: The men are called to battle in Pennsylvania. Thomas has made it so far . . . but does he have what it takes to survive Gettysburg?" (Publisher's note)

Tavares, Matt

Mudball; [by] Matt Tavares. Candlewick Press 2005 un il $15.99

Grades: K 1 2 3   E

1. Baseball -- Fiction

ISBN 0-7636-2387-3

LC 2004-40671

During a rainy Minneapolis Millers baseball game in 1903, Little Andy Oyler has the chance to become a hero by hitting the shortest and muddiest home run in history

"The large-scale, softly shaded pencil drawings have plenty of motion, just right for a sports story. . . . An attractive book for baseball fans who enjoy watching small heroes triumph and don't mind a bit of nostalgia." Booklist

Taxali, Gary

This is silly! Scholastic Press 2010 un il $17.99

Grades: PreK K   E

1. Stories in rhyme

ISBN 978-0-439-71836-3; 0-439-71836-8

Billy, Willy, Dilly, and Lilly take turns being silly.

"The rhyming text is not plot-driven but revels in phonemic silliness, with lots of action and playful turns of phrase. . . . The combination of vibrant illustrations with rollicking rhymes will engage young readers and art buffs alike." SLJ

Taylor, Debbie A.

Sweet music in Harlem; illustrated by Frank Morrison. Lee & Low Books 2004 un il $16.95

Grades: K 1 2 3   E

1. Jazz musicians -- Fiction 2. African Americans -- Fiction 3. Harlem (New York, N.Y.) -- Fiction

ISBN 1-58430-165-1

LC 2003-8994

C.J., who aspires to be as great a jazz musician as his uncle, searches for Uncle Click's hat in preparation for an important photograph and inadvertently gathers some of the greatest musicians of 1950s Harlem to join in on the picture

"This dazzling tale is filled with energy, rhythm, and style from its attention-grabbing cover to its satisfying ending. . . . The acrylic illustrations make the text come alive." SLJ

Taylor, Sean

Hoot owl, master of disguise; Sean Taylor, illustrated by Jean Jullien. Candlewick Press 2015 48 p. color illustrations reinforced $15.99

Grades: PreK K 1 2   E

1. Owls -- Fiction 2. Humorous fiction 3. Disguise -- Fiction

ISBN 0763675784; 9780763675783

LC 2013957281

In this story by Sean Taylor, illustrated by Jean Jullien, "Hoot Owl is no ordinary owl. He is a master of disguise! In the blackness of night, he's preparing to swoop on his prey before it can realize his dastardly tricks. Look there--a tasty rabbit for him to eat! Hoot Owl readies his costume, disguising himself as . . . a carrot!" (Publisher's note)

"Smart pacing, easy-to-read spreads, and complete confidence that no animals will be hurt in the reading of this book make it a winner." Pub Wkly

Huck runs amuck! story by Sean Taylor; art by Peter H. Reynolds. Dial Books for Young Readers 2011 un il $16.99

Grades: PreK K 1 2   E

1. Goats -- Fiction

ISBN 0-8037-3261-9; 978-0-8037-3261-2

"Huck is a goat with an eclectic appetite. . . . His all-time favorite tasty treats are flowers. . . . Even flower patterns on clothing or table linens call to him. Huck tries, but each attempt to reach those elusive flowers leads to disaster. . . . Taylor employs simple, conversational language in a fast-paced, almost breathless, easy-breezy cadence that draws readers right into Huck's adventures. Double-page spreads of Reynolds' detailed, cartoon-like, watercolor, ink and tea illustrations on a bright, white background surround the large-print text. . . . [Huck's] expressions are wildly enthusiastic, goofy and totally demented. Hilarious, laugh-out-loud fun." Kirkus

When a monster is born; [illustrated by] Nick Sharratt. Roaring Brook Press 2007 un il $16.95
Grades: PreK K 1   **E**
   1. Monsters -- Fiction
   ISBN 978-1-59643-254-3; 1-59643-254-3
               LC 2006-20890
Explores the options available to a monster from the time it is born, such as becoming the scary monster under someone's bed or playing on the school basketball team.
   "The words have the rhythm of a chant. . . . Sharratt's neon-toned artwork, which has the look of computer-generated collage, features a furry, round, lime-green monster, whose pink horns and buck teeth make an endearingly goofy star. Bright, funny, and interactive." Booklist

The **world** champion of staying awake; [illustrations by] Jimmy Liao. Candlewick Press 2011 il $15.99
Grades: PreK K 1   **E**
   1. Toys -- Fiction 2. Bedtime -- Fiction
   ISBN 978-0-7636-4957-9; 0-7636-4957-0
               LC 2009051511
At bedtime, Stella must find a way to make her toys fall asleep before she can go to sleep.
   "In contrast to the spot illustrations of the main story, which are set against white backgrounds, the characters' imagined expeditions are rich, full-bleed watercolor scenes, accompanied by rhymed couplets that balance the rowdiness of the bedtime preparations with cozy imagery and soothing rhythms. It's just the thing for testing the mettle of those who would lay claim to the titular honorific." Publ Wkly

Teague, Mark
   Dear Mrs. LaRue; letters from obedience school, written and illustrated by Mark Teague. Scholastic Press 2002 un il $15.95
Grades: PreK K 1 2 3   **E**
   1. Dogs -- Fiction
   ISBN 0-439-20663-4
               LC 2001-43479
Gertrude LaRue receives typewritten and paw-written letters from her dog Ike, entreating her to let him leave the Igor Brotweiler Canine Academy and come back home
   "The humorous acrylic illustrations are, at times, a howl and the over-sized format is well-suited to storytelling." SLJ
   Other titles about Mrs. LaRue and her dog Ike are:
   Detective LaRue (2004)
   LaRue for mayor (2008)
   LaRue across America: postcards from the vacation (2011)

   Funny Farm. Orchard Books 2009 un il $16.99
Grades: PreK K   **E**
   1. Dogs -- Fiction 2. Animals -- Fiction 3. Farm life -- Fiction
   ISBN 978-0-439-91499-4; 0-439-91499-X
               LC 2008-02477

"When Edward, a city-slicker dog, arrives at his canine relatives' farm for a visit, Teague provides the perfect setup for this goofily sweet fish-out-of-water tale. . . . The narrative nature of the crisp oil illustrations reveals a much more entertaining version of the story than does the straightforward text. . . . Young readers will find plenty to revisit in the humorous bucolic scenes of barnyard creatures at work and play." Publ Wkly
   Another title about Edward is:
   Firehouse! (2010)

   Pigsty. Scholastic 1994 un il hardcover o.p. pa $6.99
Grades: PreK K 1 2 3   **E**
   1. Pigs -- Fiction 2. Cleanliness -- Fiction
   ISBN 0-590-45915-5; 0-439-59843-5 pa
               LC 93-21179
When Wendell doesn't clean up his room, a whole herd of pigs comes to live with him
   "Much of the tale's fun resides in Teague's quirky acrylic art. . . . Whether Wendell and his friends are jumping on the bed or playing Monopoly on the rug, their antics are rendered in the bold palette of a gleefully inventive imagination. Highly recommended for neat-freaks and mess-makers alike." Publ Wkly

Teckentrup, Britta
   Big Smelly Bear; [by] Britta Teckentrup. Sterling Pub. 2007 un il $12.95
Grades: PreK K   **E**
   1. Bears -- Fiction 2. Cleanliness -- Fiction
   ISBN 978-1-905417-37-7
               LC 2006101350
Big Fluffy Bear insists that Big Smelly Bear visit the pond for a bath before she will scratch the itch he cannot reach
   "This charming oversize book is accompanied by watercolor illustrations." SLJ

   Little wolf's song. Boxer Books 2010 un il $16.95
Grades: PreK K 1   **E**
   1. Wolves -- Fiction
   ISBN 978-1-907152-33-7; 1-907152-33-4
Even though Little Wolf's mom, dad, sister, and brothers all have their own special song, he can only manage a poor, pitiful squeak. But one snowy day, Little Wolf finds himself lost and alone in the woods and he discovers his own special, beautiful voice.
   "This effective picture book touches on many issues that children experience. . . . Created using digital collage of hand-printed paper, the large-scale illustrations feature clean lines, simple forms, and restrained use of color." Booklist

Tegen, Katherine
   The **story** of the Jack O'Lantern; illustrated by Brandon Dorman. Harper 2010 un il $12.99; lib bdg $14.89
Grades: K 1 2 3   **E**
   1. Devil -- Fiction 2. Pumpkin -- Fiction 3. Halloween -- Fiction
   ISBN 978-0-06-143088-6; 0-06-143088-9; 978-0-06-143090-9 lib bdg; 0-06-143090-0 lib bdg
               LC 2008046150
On Halloween night, Jack—a stingy and mean man—makes a deal with the devil for a free dinner, only to regret his choice many years later when the devil comes to collect.

"Lavish, carefully composed, full-page illustrations with the look of oil paintings clearly depict the actions of the despicable characters against pleasingly detailed backgrounds. . . . Well suited for use in a pumpkin-decorating program— or any Halloween program." Booklist

The **story** of the leprechaun; illustrated by Sally Anne Lambert. Harper 2011 un il $12.99; lib bdg $14.89
Grades: PreK K 1 2   E
  1. Magic -- Fiction 2. Wishes -- Fiction 3. Fairies -- Fiction 4. Leprechauns -- Fiction
  ISBN 978-0-06-143086-2; 0-06-143086-2; 978-0-06-143085-5 lib bdg; 0-06-143085-4 lib bdg
                         LC 2008034358
A clever leprechaun who has amassed a pot of gold by making beautiful shoes for people decides to hide his money at the end of a rainbow, knowing that no one will find it there.

"The descriptive, entertaining narrative is well paced and read-aloud-friendly, and enchanting color illustrations, with soft textures and patterns, portray characters, settings, and events in both small vignettes and page-filling spreads." Booklist

Tekavec, Heather
  Storm is coming! pictures by Margaret Spengler. Dial Bks. for Young Readers 2002 un il $14.99
Grades: PreK K 1 2   E
  1. Storms -- Fiction 2. Domestic animals -- Fiction
  ISBN 0-8037-2626-0
                         LC 00-34622
The animals misunderstand the farmer's "Storm" warning and expect someone scary and mean

"Children will giggle over the animals' confusion and enjoy the well-paced buildup of suspense. Inviting pastel illustrations feature round, cartoonlike animals and dramatic use of perspective." Horn Book Guide

Tenzing Norbu
  Secret of the snow leopard; [by] Tenzing Norbu, Lama with Stéphane Frattini. Douglas & McIntyre 2004 un il $16.95
Grades: 1 2 3 4   E
  1. Nepal -- Fiction 2. Himalaya Mountains -- Fiction
  ISBN 0-88899-544-X
Tsering, a boy from a small Nepali village, and "his stepfather accompany the village healer, who is gravely ill, on a journey to the monastery where he will seek a cure. . . . On the way home, Tsering . . . asserts his independence by climbing the dangerous pass where his father . . . lost his life. . . . Handsome earth-tone paintings, stylized and carefully composed, portray the people and animals that belong to this stark landscape. . . . The quiet authority of the artwork and the drama of the story will engage children emotionally." SLJ
  Another title about Tsering is:
  Himalaya (2002)

Thayer, Jane
  The **popcorn** dragon; written by Jane Thayer; illustrated by Lisa McCue. Morrow Junior Bks. 1989 un il $17.99
Grades: PreK K 1 2   E
  1. Dragons -- Fiction
  ISBN 0-688-08340-4
                       LC 88-39855

A newly illustrated edition of the title first published 1953
Though his hot breath is the envy of all the other animals, a young dragon learns that showing off does not make friends

"McCue's new full-color illustrations capture the whimsical mood of the fable. The animals, although too coy, have appealing humanlike expressions which convey their envy and contempt." SLJ

The **puppy** who wanted a boy; illustrated by Lisa McCue. HarperCollins Pubs. 2003 un il $14.99; lib bdg $15.89
Grades: PreK K 1 2   E
  1. Dogs -- Fiction 2. Christmas -- Fiction
  ISBN 0-06-052696-3; 0-06-052697-1 lib bdg
A reissue of the edition published 1986 by Morrow; story first published 1958 with different illustrations

When Petey the puppy decides that he wants a boy for Christmas, he discovers that he must go out and find one on his own

"It is the same, somewhat sentimental but certainly appealing tale that Thayer fashioned in 1958, when this was originally published; however, McCue's affectionately drawn, warmly colored illustrations go a long way toward perking up the story." Booklist

Thisdale, François, 1964-
  Nini. Tundra Books 2011 un il $15.95
Grades: PreK K 1   E
  1. Adoption -- Fiction
  ISBN 978-1-77049-270-7; 1-77049-270-4
  Original French edition published 2009 in Canada
Long before Nini was born, she was in a safe place where a familiar voice promised her a loving home. But once she was born, that soft voice was replaced by the words of care givers in an orphanage. Then, one day, a man and a woman on the other side of the world learned that their dreams were about to come true. They would finally have a baby to love.

This is a "heart-warming poetic story of adoption. . . . Thisdale's imaginative use of traditional drawing and painting, digitally manipulated, produces double pages that suggest rather than stipulate the images." SLJ

Thomas, Jan
  Can you make a scary face? Beach Lane Books 2009 un il $12.99
Grades: PreK K 1   E
  1. Frogs -- Fiction 2. Ladybugs -- Fiction 3. Imagination -- Fiction
  ISBN 978-1-4169-8581-5; 1-4169-8581-6
                       LC 2008-38288
A ladybug invites the reader to play a game of "let's pretend."

"This book will have youngsters jumping, wiggling, dancing, pretending, and laughing. . . . The expressive ladybug is outlined in broad black lines and seems only inches away from readers. Adults will enjoy using this title to encourage lively activity and imaginative games. Children will love everything about it—especially the surprise ending." SLJ

The **doghouse**. Harcourt 2008 un il $12.95
Grades: PreK K   E
  1. Dogs -- Fiction 2. Fear -- Fiction 3. Animals --

Fiction
ISBN 978-0-15-206533-1; 0-15-206533-4
LC 2007038355

Cow, Pig, Duck, and Mouse are afraid to retrieve their ball when it goes into the dog's house, but when they do go in they are pleasantly surprised.

"The simple cartoon characters, scenery, and dialogue balloons are outlined in thick, bold lines. Colors are smooth and flat, with backgrounds done in bright blues, purple, and lime green. The pictures are large and distinct, and will work well with a group." SLJ

Another title about Cow, Pig, Duck, and Mouse is:
A birthday for Cow! (2008)
Pumpkin trouble (2011)

Is everyone ready for fun? Beach Lane Books 2011 un il $12.99
Grades: PreK K 1   E
1. Cattle -- Fiction 2. Chickens -- Fiction
ISBN 978-1-4424-2364-0; 1-4424-2364-1
LC 2011005212

Chicken's cow visitors try to jump, dance, and wiggle on his couch, which is much too tiny for such exuberant activities.

"Thomas's illustrations energetically emphasize the cows' frenetic energy and the chicken's frustration, which are sure to draw giggles." Publ Wkly

Pumpkin trouble. Harper 2011 un il $9.99; lib bdg $12.99
Grades: PreK K   E
1. Mice -- Fiction 2. Pigs -- Fiction 3. Ducks -- Fiction 4. Pumpkin -- Fiction
ISBN 978-0-06-169284-0; 0-06-169284-0; 978-0-06-169285-7 lib bdg; 0-06-169285-9 lib bdg
LC 2010007029

When Duck decides to make a jack-o-lantern, he and his friends Pig and Mouse are in for a scary adventure.

"With well-paced, slapstick action and opportunities for children to practice making predictions, this story features characters who can hold their own. . . . A terrific Halloween read-aloud." Booklist

★ **Rhyming** dust bunnies. Atheneum Books for Young Readers 2009 un il $12.99
Grades: K 1 2   E
1. Dust -- Fiction 2. Rhyme -- Fiction
ISBN 978-1-4169-7976-0; 1-4169-7976-X
LC 2008-28779

As three dust bunnies, Ed, Ned, and Ted, are demonstrating how much they love to rhyme, a fourth, Bob, is trying to warn them of approaching danger.

"The simple text and rhyming game-playing make this a natural as an early reader while also offering entertaining opportunities for readers-aloud. Digitally rendered art offers coloring-book strength and simplicity." Bull Cent Child Books

Another title about the dust bunnies is:
Here comes the big, mean dust bunny! (2009)

What will Fat Cat sit on? Harcourt 2007 un il $12.95

Grades: PreK K   E
1. Cats -- Fiction 2. Animals -- Fiction
ISBN 978-0-15-206051-0; 0-15-206051-0
LC 2006-24558

A group of animals is terrified at the prospect of being sat upon by the imposing Fat Cat, until the mouse comes up with a solution that satisfies everyone.

"Thomas . . . makes this book a laugh-out-loud pas de deux between Dick-and-Jane-get-stylish typography . . . and the supremely silly visual evocation of high anxiety. . . . She renders her barnyard characters in super-saturated colors and thick, bold outlines." Publ Wkly

Thomas, Patricia
Red sled; [by] Patricia Thomas; illustrated by Chris L. Demarest. Boyds Mills Press 2008 un il $16.95
Grades: PreK K 1   E
1. Stories in rhyme 2. Sledding -- Fiction 3. Father-son relationship -- Fiction
ISBN 978-1-59078-559-1; 1-59078-559-2
LC 2007-50838

A boy and his father lift one another's spirits by going sledding on a winter's night.

"The brief text consists of easy-to-read words in rhyming pairs. . . . Bright watercolor pictures capture perfectly the downcast faces of the characters when they are stuck inside during a snowstorm, . . . their expressions of happiness and excitement during their nocturnal adventure on the red sled." SLJ

Thomas, Shelley Moore
★ **Good** night, Good Knight; pictures by Jennifer Plecas. Dutton Children's Bks. 2000 47p il (Dutton easy reader) $13.99
Grades: PreK K 1 2   E
1. Bedtime -- Fiction 2. Dragons -- Fiction 3. Knights and knighthood -- Fiction
ISBN 0-525-46326-7
LC 99-28415

A Good Knight helps three little dragons who are having trouble getting to sleep.

"The short, simple, repetitive phrases are sure to capture the imaginations of young children. . . . With a palette dominated by the blues, grays, and purples of the nightime setting, Plecas's illustrations are a wonderful complement to this endearing tale." SLJ

Other titles about the Good Knight are:
A cold winter's Good Knight (2008)
Get well, Good Knight (2002)
Happy birthday, Good Knight (2006)
Take care Good Knight (2006)
A Good Knight's rest (2011)

Thomassie, Tynia
Feliciana Feyra LeRoux; a Cajun tall tale. illustrated by Cat Bowman Smith. Pelican 2005 un il $15.95
Grades: K 1 2 3   E
1. Cajuns -- Fiction 2. Louisiana -- Fiction 3. Alligators -- Fiction
ISBN 1-58980-286-1

A reissue of the title first published 1995 by Little, Brown

This "combines breezy watercolors and a swinging text that's perfect for reading aloud. A note on Cajun culture, a glossary, and a pronunciation guide are included." Booklist

Another title about Feliciana is:

Feliciana meets d'Loup Garou (1998)

Thompson, Carol

I like you the best. Holiday House 2011 un il

Grades: PreK K 1   **E**

1. Pigs -- Fiction 2. Rabbits -- Fiction 3. Friendship -- Fiction 4. Meditation -- Fiction

ISBN 0823423417; 9780823423415

LC 2010030747

Dolly the pig and Jack Rabbit are best friends, even after they have a fight. "Ages five to seven." (Bull Cent Child Books)

"Dolly and Jack overcome their feelings, thanks to some basic meditative skills. . . . Thompson's drawings, mostly spot images, are gems. Smudgy and rough-edged, they have a sketchbooklike immediacy and eloquently articulate two personalities who like to turn the emotional dial up to 11." Publ Wkly

Thompson, Emma, 1959-

The **Further** Tale of Peter Rabbit. Penguin Group USA 2012 72 p. $20.00

Grades: PreK K   **E**

1. Rabbits -- Fiction 2. Scotland -- Fiction 3. Voyages and travels -- Fiction

ISBN 0723269106; 9780723269106

This book is a "new adventure of the mischievous bunny who first appeared 110 years ago in Beatrix Potter's original tale. . . . Peter (again) wriggles under Mr. McGregor's gate, this time into an 'interesting basket smelling of onions.' After eating the picnic lunch within, he nods off, awakened later by the jostling of a horse-drawn cart he's been loaded onto, which is en route to, of all places, Scotland," where he meets his cousin and has an adventure in the Highland Games. (Publishers Weekly)

Thompson, Kay

Kay Thompson's Eloise; a book for precocious grown ups. drawings by Hilary Knight. Simon & Schuster 1995 65p il $17 **E**

1. New York (N.Y.) -- Fiction 2. Hotels and motels -- Fiction

ISBN 0-671-22350-X

LC 96-103190

A reissue of the title first published 1955

This is the "tale of the little girl who makes merry mayhem from her digs on the top floor of New York's Plaza Hotel." Horn Book

Other titles about Eloise are:

Eloise at Christmastime (1958)

Eloise in Paris (1957)

Eloise in Moscow (1959)

Eloise's guide to life (2000)

Eloise takes a bawth (2002)

Thompson, Lauren

★ The **apple** pie that Papa baked; illustrated by Jonathan Bean. Simon & Schuster Books for Young Readers 2007 un il $15.99

Grades: PreK K 1   **E**

1. Pies -- Fiction 2. Trees -- Fiction 3. Apples -- Fiction

ISBN 1-4169-1240-1; 978-1-4169-1240-8

"A pigtailed girl introduces the apple pie 'warm and sweet that Papa baked.' Then moving backward, the girl runs . . . out to the tree 'crooked and strong,' where shiny red apples are waiting to be picked. The roots 'deep and fine,' feed the tree. . . . Rain waters the roots, clouds drop the rain, the sky carries the clouds, the sun lights the sky. . . . The text is clear, and it's well matched by delightful illustrations . . . The intricately detailed art is reminiscent of the time when picture books were rarely full color." Booklist

The **Christmas** magic; illustrated by Jon J. Muth. Scholastic Press 2009 un il $16.99

Grades: K 1 2 3   **E**

1. Magic -- Fiction 2. Christmas -- Fiction 3. Santa Claus -- Fiction

ISBN 978-0-439-77497-0; 0-439-77497-7

LC 2008-43308

As Santa prepares for the upcoming holiday season, it is the Christmas magic that truly makes everything happen.

"Muth's haunting watercolor and pastel illustrations bring the simple story to magical life. . . . This gentle and lovely book is sheer enchantment." SLJ

How many cats? pictures by Robin Eley. Disney Hyperion Books 2009 un il $15.99

Grades: K 1 2   **E**

1. Counting 2. Stories in rhyme 3. Cats -- Fiction

ISBN 978-1-4231-0801-6; 1-4231-0801-9

LC 2008-46540

From zero to twenty, a house becomes filled with frolicking cats, who then leave alone or in groups

"Eley paints exuberant bundles of fun that dance and leap across the pages of Thompson's joyous and slyly math-infused counting tale. . . . Sure to be a call-and-response crowd-pleaser at any kitty-cat storytime." Kirkus

★ **Leap** back home to me; illustrated by Matthew Cordell. Margaret K. McElderry Books 2011 un il $15.99

Grades: PreK K   **E**

1. Stories in rhyme 2. Frogs -- Fiction 3. Mother-child relationship -- Fiction

ISBN 978-1-4169-0664-3; 1-4169-0664-9

LC 2009-53708

A little frog makes increasingly bold leaps out into the world, and then comes back to his mother after each excursion.

"Sweet and simple, lively and expressive, this picture book provides a loving template for parents who want to encourage their children to explore an ever-widening world without losing their connection to home and family." Publ Wkly

Little Quack; pictures by Derek Anderson. Simon & Schuster Bks. for Young Readers 2003 un il $14.95

Grades: PreK K   **E**

1. Counting 2. Ducks -- Fiction

ISBN 0-689-84723-8

LC 2002-5567

One by one, four ducklings find the courage to jump into the pond and paddle with Mama Duck, until only Little Quack is left in the nest, trying to be brave

"Here's a familiar story kicked up a notch by a counting element and irresistible art. The story is reassuring and utterly straightforward. . . . The charm is in Anderson's comical, eye-commanding acrylics." Booklist

Other titles about Little Quack are:
Little Quack's bedtime (2005)
Little Quack's hide and seek (2004)
Little Quack's new friend (2006)

★ **One** starry night; illustrated by Jonathan Bean. Margaret K. McElderry Books 2011 un il $16.99
Grades: PreK K 1   E
1. Stories in rhyme 2. Christmas stories 3. Animals -- Fiction 4. Christmas -- Fiction
ISBN 978-0-689-82851-5; 0-689-82851-9
LC 2011008776

One starry night, as all sorts of animals watch over their young, Mary and Joseph watch over their baby boy, Jesus, in Bethlehem.

"This tender, poetic retelling of the age-old story takes the form of a whispered prayer as it highlights the nurturing given to babies of many species. The art and the words strike just the right tone of reverence and delight. A lovely offering." SLJ

Polar bear morning; by Lauren Thompson; pictures by Stephen Savage. Orchard Books 2013 32 p. (alk. paper) $16.99
Grades: PreK K 1 2   E
1. Bears -- Fiction 2. Friendship -- Fiction 3. Polar bear -- Fiction
ISBN 0439698855; 9780439698856
LC 2012024848

Polar bear night; illustrated by Stephen Savage. Scholastic Press 2004 un il $15.95
Grades: PreK K 1 2   E
1. Night -- Fiction 2. Polar bear -- Fiction
ISBN 0-439-49524-5
LC 2003-27538

After wandering out at night to watch a magical star shower, a polar bear cub returns home to snuggle with her mother in their warm den.

"With comforting, carefully chosen words and soft pastels shading linocut prints, this book has all the elements to make it a bedtime favorite." SLJ

Wee little bunny; illustrated by John Butler. Simon & Schuster Books for Young Readers 2010 un il $14.99
Grades: PreK   E
1. Animals -- Fiction 2. Rabbits -- Fiction
ISBN 978-1-4169-7937-1; 1-4169-7937-9
LC 2008044911

A young rabbit enjoys a 'busy, dizzy' day of playing in the meadow near his home

"This sweet follow-up to Little Chick and Little Lamb is ideal for kids who like adventures, but like coming home even more." Publ Wkly

Wee little chick; by Lauren Thompson; illustrated by John Butler. Simon & Schuster Books for Young Readers 2008 un il $14.99
Grades: PreK   E
1. Size -- Fiction 2. Animals -- Fiction 3. Chickens

-- Fiction
ISBN 978-1-4169-3468-4; 1-4169-3468-5
LC 2007016411

When the other barnyard animals comment on how tiny the littlest chick is, the proud little one peeps louder, stands taller, and runs faster than any of them

"Thompson's simple, rhythmic text moves the action along at a brisk, even pace. Butler's bright acrylic and pencil illustrations artistically portray the story's springtime mood and warmhearted tone." SLJ

Wee little lamb; by Lauren Thompson; illustrated by John Butler. Simon & Schuster Books for Young Readers 2009 un il $14.99
Grades: PreK   E
1. Sheep -- Fiction 2. Animals -- Fiction
ISBN 978-1-4169-3469-1; 1-4169-3469-3
LC 2008004428

A little, newborn lamb, too shy to say hello to the rabbit or sing with the robin, is finally drawn out by a tiny fieldmouse

"This gentle, reassuring tale tells youngsters that they can explore their world at their own speed. The eye-catching spreads and simple language make this book a natural for toddler storytime." SLJ

Thomson, Bill
★ **Chalk**. Marshall Cavendish Children 2010 un il $15.99
Grades: PreK K 1 2   E
1. Stories without words 2. Drawing -- Fiction
ISBN 978-0-7614-5526-4; 0-7614-5526-4
LC 2009014141

A wordless picture book about three children who go to a park on a rainy day, find some chalk, and draw pictures that come to life.

"With eye-catching, realistic illustrations, clever details, and some dramatic suspense, this wordless picture book offers a fresh take on the drawings-come-to-life theme. . . . Vibrant acrylic and colored-pencil illustrations, rendered with intricate precision, nearly leap off the page." Booklist

Thomson, Sarah L.
Cub's big world; Sarah L. Thomson; illustrated by Joe Cepeda. Harcourt Children's Books, Houghton Mifflin Harcourt 2013 32 p. $16.99
Grades: PreK K   E
1. Arctic regions -- Fiction 2. Polar bear -- Fiction 3. Mother and child -- Fiction 4. Animals -- Infancy -- Fiction
ISBN 0544057392; 9780544057395
LC 2012045056

In this picture book, by Sarah L. Thomson, "Cub knows all about the familiar world in the snow den where she was born. When she follows Mom out of their den, tumbling into the Arctic wilderness, she finds that the world under the wide blue sky is big, big, BIG! It's easy to be curious when there's so much to explore—and when Mom is nearby. But when she thinks she's all alone, can Cub be brave?" (Publisher's note)

Imagine a night; paintings by Rob Gonsalves; text by Sarah L. Thomson. Atheneum Books for Young Readers 2003 un il $16.95

Grades: 2 3 4 5 6   E
    1. Night -- Fiction 2. Imagination -- Fiction
    ISBN 0-689-85218-5
                   LC 2002-10718

Presents a night when imagination takes over and gravity does not work quite as expected.

"Magical realism permeates Gonsalves's large acrylic paintings, and they are essential to the lyrical text. . . . This is a fascinating foray into the imagination and a fine discussion starter for older children." SLJ

Other titles in this series are:

Imagine a day (2005)

Imagine a place (2008)

Pirates, ho! by Sarah L. Thomson; illustrated by Stephen Gilpin. Marshall Cavendish 2008 un il $14.99
Grades: K 1 2   E
    1. Stories in rhyme 2. Pirates -- Fiction
    ISBN 978-0-7614-5435-9; 0-7614-5435-7
                   LC 2007-29792

Pirates Peg-Leg Tom, Angus Black, Dreadful Nell, and One-Eyed Jack chase ships on the high seas, tell ghost stories, and fall asleep counting gold instead of sheep.

"Gilpin's wacky cartoons have a retro, take-no-prisoners abandon. . . . This funny, fabulously illustrated rhyme is certainly worth adding." SLJ

Thong, Roseanne

Fly free! illustrated by Eujin Kim Neilan. Boyds Mills Press 2010 un il $17.95
Grades: 3 4 5   E
    1. Vietnam -- Fiction 2. Buddhism -- Fiction 3. Kindness -- Fiction 4. Conduct of life -- Fiction
    ISBN 978-1-59078-550-8; 1-59078-550-9
                   LC 2009020248

When Mai feeds the caged birds at a Buddhist temple in Vietnam, her simple act of kindness starts a chain of thoughtful acts that ultimately comes back to her. Includes author's note explaining the Buddhist concepts of karma and samsara, or the wheel of life.

"The lesson of this simple story, that helping others is helpful to you, is universal. The muted and warm watercolor-on-board illustrations glow with gold, orange, red, and brown tones." SLJ

★ **Green** is a chile pepper; a book of colors. by Roseanne Greenfield Thong; illustrated by John Parra. Chronicle Books 2014 40 p. color illustrations (alk. paper) $16.99
Grades: PreK K 1 2   E
    1. Color -- Fiction 2. Latin America -- Civilization 3. Stories in rhyme 4. Hispanic American children 5. Hispanic Americans -- Fiction
    ISBN 1452102031; 9781452102030
                   LC 2013021561

Pura Belpré (Illustrator) Honor Book (2015)

In this children's book by Roseanne Greenfield Thong, illustrated by John Parra, "children discover a world of colors all around them: red is spices and swirling skirts, yellow is masa, tortillas, and sweet corn cake. Many of the featured objects are Latino in origin, and all are universal in appeal." (Publisher's note)

"Each double-page spread introduces a color in rhyming, explanatory verse; attractive art; and a colored bubble with the word in English and Spanish." Booklist

One is a drummer; written by Roseanne Thong; illustrated by Grace Lin. Chronicle Books 2004 un il $14.95; pa $6.99
Grades: PreK K 1 2   E
    1. Counting 2. Stories in rhyme 3. Chinese Americans -- Fiction
    ISBN 0-8118-3772-6; 0-8118-6482-4 pa
                   LC 2003-10810

A young girl numbers her discoveries in the world around her, from one dragon boat to four mahjong players to ten bamboo stalks

"The rhymes provide a pleasing framework for the book, and Lin's striking artwork gives it great visual appeal. . . . An appealing counting book, particularly for Chinese American children who want to learn a little about their heritage." Booklist

Red is a dragon; a book of colors. written by Roseanne Thong; illustrated by Grace Lin. Chronicle Bks. 2001 un il hardcover o.p. pa $6.99
Grades: PreK K 1 2   E
    1. Color 2. Stories in rhyme 3. Asian Americans 4. Chinese Americans -- Fiction
    ISBN 0-8118-3177-9; 0-8118-6481-2 pa
                   LC 2001-93

A Chinese American girl provides rhyming descriptions of the great variety of colors she sees around her, from the red of a dragon, firecrackers, and lychees to the brown of her teddy bear

"Lin's simply drawn gouache illustrations, outlined in black, fairly explode with color. . . . This is a must-have for libraries serving Chinese American populations, and it will be a welcome addition to preschool story hours for children of all backgrounds." Booklist

Round is a mooncake; a book of shapes. written by Roseanne Thong; illustrated by Grace Lin. Chronicle Books 2000 un il $15.99
Grades: PreK K 1 2   E
    1. Shape 2. Stories in rhyme 3. Chinese Americans -- Fiction
    ISBN 0-8118-2676-7
                   LC 99-50852

As a little girl discovers things round, square, and rectangular in her urban neighborhood, she is reminded of her Chinese American culture

"Lin's gouache paintings are bright and arresting, presenting scenes that have an interest beyond shape identification." Booklist

★ **Round** is a tortilla; by Roseanne Greenfield Thong; illustrated by John Parra. Chronicle Books 2013 40 p. col. ill. (reinforced) $16.99
Grades: PreK K 1 2   E
    1. Stories in rhyme 2. Hispanic Americans -- Fiction 4. Shape -- Fiction
    ISBN 9781452106168 (alk. paper); 1452106169
                   LC 2012013341

In this children's picture book, by Roseanne Greenfield Thong, illustrated by John Parra, "children discover a world of shapes all around them: rectangles are ice-cream carts and stone metates, triangles are slices of watermelon and quesadillas. Many of the featured objects are Latino in origin, and all are universal in appeal." (Publisher's note)

Thornhill, Jan

The **wildlife** 1 2 3; a nature counting book. by Jan Thornhill. Owlkids Books 2012 32 p. $14.95; $7.95

Grades: PreK K   E

1. Counting 2. Animals

ISBN 0671679260; 1926973461; 9781926973463

LC 89005970

This book, by Jan Thornhill, "communicates simple information through colorful illustrations and classic design; every page [is designed to engage] young readers' interest and imagination. At the end of the book, 'Nature Notes' provide additional information on each of the featured animals and their habitats." (Publisher's note)

Thurber, James

★ **Many** moons; illustrated by Louis Slobodkin. Harcourt Brace Jovanovich 1943 un il $17; pa $7

Grades: 1 2 3 4   E

1. Fairy tales 2. Moon -- Fiction 3. Princesses -- Fiction

ISBN 0-15-251873-8; 0-15-656980-9 pa

Awarded the Caldecott Medal, 1944

"Louis Slobodkin's pictures float on the pages in four colors: black and white cannot represent them. They are the substance of dreams . . . the long thoughts little children, and some adults wise as they, have about life." N Y Her Trib Books

Thurlby, Paul

★ **Paul** Thurlby's alphabet. Candlewick Press 2011 un il $16.99

Grades: PreK K   E

1. Alphabet

ISBN 978-0-7636-5565-5; 0-7636-5565-1

LC 2010045400

"From a cover that features a boy's head and arms on a body shaped like the letter A to Z for zipper, the illustrator explains that he 'pursues the challenge of fusing the object of the word with the shape of the letter.' His approach succeeds in a fascinating way. The lower and uppercase letter is centered on the verso pages against textured, vividly colored papers, while the letter designs appear on the recto and have a posterlike quality. . . . The digital-media artwork has a distinctive look that will be best appreciated by young ones who already know the ABCs. Skillfully constructed and cleverly composed, it's an awesome alphabet book." Kirkus

Tibo, Gilles

My diary; the totally true story of me! illustrations by Josee Bisaillon. Magination Press 2011 un il pa $12.95

Grades: K 1 2   E

1. Diaries -- Fiction

ISBN 978-1-4338-095-83; 1-4338-0958-3

LC 2011007778

A young girl shares many things, including thoughts on becoming a big sister, freedom, joy, death, peace, and

hope, through secrets, lists, poems, and inventions recorded in her diary.

"This well-crafted book would be useful as an example for a writing workshop. Others may find it equally as helpful as a means to begin discussions about emotions." SLJ

Tierney, Fiona

Lion's lunch? illustrated by Margaret Chamberlain. Chicken House 2010 un il $17.99

Grades: K 1 2 3   E

1. Lions -- Fiction 2. Animals -- Fiction 3. Drawing -- Fiction

ISBN 978-0-545-17691-0; 0-545-17691-3

LC 2009-08267

When Lion comes upon Sarah walking in the jungle, he threatens to eat her unless she shows that she can do something none of the other animals can do.

"Vibrant, brightly colored illustrations of the lively animals and cheerful child fill every bit of space on the spreads and are sure to engage readers. This clever tale of courage and confidence teaches an important life lesson in a fun way." SLJ

Tillman, Nancy

On the night you were born. Feiwel & Friends 2006 un il $16.95

Grades: K 1 2   E

1. Stories in rhyme 2. Nature -- Fiction 3. Childbirth -- Fiction

ISBN 0-312-34606-9

First published 2005 by Darling Press

The moon, wind, rain, and a variety of animals celebrate the special occasion that is the birth of a child.

Tillman's "writing has the authenticity of whispered conversation. . . . The pictures subtly radiate golden glints of moonlight, and her almost sculptural rendering style gives her characters a hefty physicality that counterbalances the ethereal sentiments being expressed." Publ Wkly

The **spirit** of Christmas. Feiwel and Friends 2009 un il $16.99

Grades: PreK K 1 2   E

1. Stories in rhyme 2. Christmas -- Fiction

ISBN 978-0-312-54965-7; 0-312-54965-2

LC 2008-48139

Despite the arrival of the Spirit of Christmas, who brings all sorts of trimmings and reminders of seasonal joys, something is still lacking.

"Realism and fantasy are satisfyingly paired to bring the mixed-media illustrations of treasured holiday scenes to life. . . . A beautiful and timeless book." SLJ

Timberlake, Amy

The **dirty** cowboy; pictures by Adam Rex. Farrar, Straus & Giroux 2003 un il $16

Grades: K 1 2 3   E

1. Dogs -- Fiction 2. Cowhands -- Fiction

ISBN 0-374-31791-7

LC 2001-53224

Telling his faithful dog to make sure nobody touches his clothes but him, a cowboy jumps into a New Mexico river for a bath, not realizing just how much the scrubbing will change his scent

"Told in descriptive language that rolls off the tongue, this story makes the most of a humorous situation. . . . The paintings have a gritty, sinewy look that matches the earthy tone of the tale." SLJ

Tinkham, Kelly

Hair for Mama; [by] Kelly A. Tinkham; illustrated by Amy June Bates. Dial Books for Young Readers 2007 un il $16.99

Grades: K 1 2 3   E

1. Hair -- Fiction 2. Cancer -- Fiction 3. African Americans -- Fiction 4. Mother-son relationship -- Fiction

ISBN 0-8037-2955-3; 978-0-8037-2955-1

LC 2005-10621

When Marcus's mother has chemotherapy for her cancer and loses her hair, he tries to find new hair for her to make her well again.

"This is a beautifully written story about an African-American family dealing with cancer. . . . The lovely watercolor illustrations fit the text well, using gold, brown, orange, and green tones to show a family going through tough times together." SLJ

Titcomb, Gordon

The **last** train; paintings by Wendall Minor. Roaring Brook Press 2010 un il $16.99

Grades: PreK K 1 2   E

1. Railroads -- Fiction

ISBN 978-1-59643-164-5; 1-59643-164-4

"Based on musician Titcomb's 2005 song, this stunning book both celebrates and eulogizes the golden era of railway travel. Minor's luminous, occasionally almost photographic, paintings portray the adult narrator as a boy, surrounded by a ghostly haze as he walks along the tracks." Publ Wkly

Titherington, Jeanne

Pumpkin, pumpkin. Greenwillow Bks. 1986 23p il $16.99; pa $6.99

Grades: PreK K 1 2   E

1. Pumpkin -- Fiction 2. Gardening -- Fiction

ISBN 0-688-05695-4; 0-688-09930-0 pa

LC 84-25334

Jamie "plants a seed, then grows and harvests a pumpkin from which he saves seeds for next year. The large, detailed drawings capture Jamie's anticipation and pleasure just right. . . . Nonreaders can easily follow the story in pictures alone. Very large, clear print on facing pages makes the simple narrative inviting for beginning readers, too." SLJ

Tobin, Jim

The **very** inappropriate word; Jim Tobin; illustrated by Dave Coverly. Christy Ottaviano Books 2013 40 p. (hardcover) $16.99

Grades: K 1 2 3 4   E

1. Picture books for children 2. Schools -- Fiction 3. Swearing -- Fiction 4. Vocabulary -- Fiction

ISBN 0805094741; 9780805094749

LC 2012021084

In this children's picture book, "Michael is a budding logophile: 'He picked up new words at practice and downtown and even in school, where Mrs. Dixon gave the kids one new spelling word every day.' But when Michael picks up an 'inappropriate' word (albeit one that grownups use with impunity) on the school bus, he can't resist helping it go viral ('Michael could see there was some thing kind of bad about it. But there was also something about it that he kind of liked')." (Publishers Weekly)

Tolman, Marije

The **tree** house; [by] Marije Tolman & Ronald Tolman. Lemniscaat un il $17.95

Grades: PreK K 1   E

1. Stories without words 2. Animals -- Fiction

ISBN 978-1-59078-806-6; 1-59078-806-0

Original Dutch edition 2009

"A wordless picture book about an elaborate wooden structure in the tree. Three stories tall, it soaks up the water surrounding its base as animals inhabit its various nooks and crannies. Bears, peacocks, and owls, and a hippo all find different ways to amuse themselves while up so high. . . . Soft pastel spreads allow readers to see all the activity in and around the tree. . . . Children will gaze in wonder at this tree house. . . . This oversize picture book celebrates acceptance of others and the splendor of nature." SLJ

Tomoko Ohmura

The **long,** long line; Tomoko Ohmura. Owlkids Books 2013 40 p. $16.95

Grades: PreK K 1 2   E

1. Picture books for children 2. Amusement parks -- Fiction 3. Animals -- Fiction

ISBN 1926973925; 9781926973920

LC 2013930499

The story of this children's picture book "starts opposite the title page with a small frog looking up at a sign that requests 'Please line up in single file.' Turn the page, and animals stand politely, clearly wondering what's at the front of the line. As the numbers decrease, the size of the animals increases: #4 is hippo. Turn the page after #1, elephant, to a gatefold sign: JUMBO COASTER," which turns out to be a whale giving rides. (Kirkus Reviews)

"In this Japanese import, fifty animals stand in a line, roughly in size order, waiting for...what? Readers wait alongside and guess at what lies ahead as small dramas unfold. The illustrations are simple and bright, rendered in saturated colors and outlined with thick black brushstrokes against ample white space. The wealth of storytelling detail on each double-page spread rewards repeat viewing." (Horn Book)

Tompert, Ann

Little Fox goes to the end of the world; illustrated by Laura J. Bryant. Marshall Cavendish 2010 un il $16.99

Grades: PreK K 1 2   E

1. Foxes -- Fiction 2. Mother-child relationship -- Fiction

ISBN 978-0-7614-5703-9; 0-7614-5703-8

A newly illustrated edition of the title first published 1976 by Crown

"Capturing a young child's yearning for independence, Tompert describes the story of Little Fox, who tells her mother, 'Some day . . . I'm going to travel to the end of the world.' Her mother's wise reply encourages Little Fox's imagination and conversation by asking appropriate questions such as, 'What will you see?' 'Won't you be scared?' Bryant's dramatic watercolor artwork frequently fills the spreads." SLJ

Tonatiuh, Duncan

★ **Dear** Primo; a letter to my cousin. Abrams 2010
un il $15.95
Grades: 1 2 3   E
    1. Mexico -- Fiction 2. Cousins -- Fiction 3. Country
life -- Fiction 4. Mexican Americans -- Fiction 5. City
and town life -- Fiction
ISBN 978-0-81093-872-4; 0-81093-872-3
Pura Belpré Award honor book (Illustrator), 2011

Two cousins, one in Mexico and one in New York City,
write to each other and learn that even though their daily
lives differ, at heart the boys are very similar.

"The digitally enhanced collage illustrations are based
on traditional Mixtec art, and show the characters posed in
profile in simply composed scenes. This useful method of
comparing and contrasting can serve as a fine general introduction to contemporary rural life in Mexico, while it also
demonstrates the fun of having a pen pal and reinforces the
sense that kids around the world are more alike than different." Booklist

★ **Pancho** Rabbit and the coyote; a migrant's tale. by
Duncan Tonatiuh. Abrams Books for Young Readers 2013
32 p. ill. (reinforced) $16.95
Grades: K 1 2   E
    1. Allegories 2. Coyote -- Fiction 3. Rabbits -- Fiction
4. Migrant labor -- Fiction 5. Voyages and travels --
Fiction
ISBN 1419705830; 9781419705830
                 LC 2012022573
Pura Belpre Author Honor Book (2014)
Pura Belpre Illustrator Honor Book (2014)

"In this allegorical picture book, [by Duncan Tonatiuh,] a
young rabbit named Pancho eagerly awaits his papa's return.
Papa Rabbit traveled north two years ago to find work in the
great carrot and lettuce fields. . . . When Papa does not return, Pancho sets out to find him. . . . He meets a coyote, who
offers to help Pancho in exchange for some of Papa's food.
They travel together until the food is gone and the coyote
decides he is still hungry . . . for Pancho!" (Publisher's note)

Torrey, Rich

Almost. HarperCollinsPublishers 2009 un il $17.99;
lib bdg $18.89
Grades: PreK K   E
    1. Growth -- Fiction
ISBN 978-0-06-156166-5; 0-06-156166-5; 978-0-06-
156167-2 lib bdg; 0-06-156167-3 lib bdg
                 LC 2008011724
Almost six-year-old Jack lists all the ways in which he is
almost a grown-up.

"The large, cartoonlike spreads have plenty of pleasing
color and detail, and expand on the simple text. . . . This
simple story addresses both the desire of children to be older
and sibling rivalry. It's sure to be a hit at storytime." SLJ
    Other titles about Jack are:
    Why? (2010)
    Because (2011)

Toscano, Charles

Papa's pastries; illustrated by Sonja Lamut. Zonderkidz
2010 un il $15.99
Grades: PreK K 1 2   E
    1. Baking -- Fiction 2. Poverty -- Fiction 3. Kindness

-- Fiction
ISBN 978-0-310-71602-0; 0-310-71602-0
Miguel sees the results of his father's faith and generosity when, although his own family is facing the oncoming
winter with threadbare clothing, a leaky roof, and no firewood, Papa gives away the pastries he has baked.

"Effective use of repetition and a pleasing rhythm in-
vigorate . . . Toscano's predictable but touching tale. . . . The
illustrations . . . effectively convey communal warmth and
industry against a backdrop of poverty and looming fear."
Publ Wkly

Tougas, Chris

Art's supplies; by Chris Tougas. Orca Book Publishers
2008 un il $19.95
Grades: 1 2 3   E
    1. Art -- Fiction
ISBN 978-1-55143-920-4; 1-55143-920-4
"Bright colors, heavy doses of humor, and puns to make
readers groan fill the pages as a boy's art supplies prepare
for a personality-plus party. . . . Art's endearing, off-centered
features combine with google-eyed markers, crayons, boxes,
brushes, tapes, scissors, and glue. . . . This lively title is sure
to be a favorite of youngsters learning to appreciate both
subtle humor and engaging cartoon art." SLJ

Tourville, Jacqueline

Albie's first word; a tale inspired by Albert Einstein's
childhood. Jacqueline Tourville; illustrated by Wynne Evans. Schwartz & Wade books 2014 40 p. color illustrations
(glb) $20.99
Grades: PreK K 1 2   E
    1. Speech 2. Children 3. Speech -- Fiction
ISBN 030797894X; 9780307978936; 9780307978943
                 LC 2013007891

This book, by Jacqueline Tourville, is a "historical fiction picture book that provides a rare glimpse into the early
childhood of Albert Einstein. . . . Three-year-old Albie has
never said a single word. When his worried mother and father consult a doctor, he advises them to expose little Albie
to new things: a trip to the orchestra, an astronomy lecture,
a toy boat race in the park. But though Albie dances with
excitement at each new experience, he remains silent." (Publisher's note)

"Spun from a remark of Albert Einstein's that he took
several years to begin talking, this mostly extrapolated tale
takes a silent yet expressive lad through a series of experiences: family outings, concerts, a science lecture, and a
model boat race... An extended note introduces Einstein in
greater detail and explains that while many of the story's
specifics are invented, its core, his parents' fear he might
never learn, is true. A reassuring episode for late bloomers,
and their parents, too." Booklist

Townsend, Michael

Billy Tartle in Say Cheese! Alfred A. Knopf 2007 un
il $15.99; lib bdg $18.99
Grades: K 1 2 3   E
    1. School stories 2. Photography -- Fiction
ISBN 978-0-375-83932-0; 0-375-83932-1; 978-0-375-
93932-7 lib bdg; 0-375-93932-6 lib bdg
                 LC 2006-24354
Billy is determined to find a way to make his school picture day less boring than usual.

The story "unfolds in comic-strip panels that effectively juggle their multitude of elements and palette of high-voltage colors with strategic design. Billy's . . . adventurous take on reality fits the comic-strip medium perfectly." Bull Cent Child Books

Trapani, Iza

Haunted party. Charlesbridge 2009 un il lib bdg $15.95; pa $7.95

Grades: PreK K 1 2   E

1. Counting 2. Ghost stories 3. Stories in rhyme 4. Parties -- Fiction 5. Halloween -- Fiction 6. Supernatural -- Fiction

ISBN 978-1-58089-246-9 lib bdg; 1-58089-246-9 lib bdg; 978-1-58089-247-6 pa; 1-58089-247-7 pa

LC 2008025330

In this counting book that introduces the numbers from one to ten, a ghost and his supernatural friends have a party on Halloween night.

This is a "rollicking Halloween tale. . . . Rhyming stanzas build steadily then shrink to single lines, adding to the guests' speedy departure. Humor abounds . . . in the watercolor, colored-pencil, and ink illustrations." Horn Book Guide

Tresselt, Alvin R.

Hide and seek fog; by Alvin Tresselt; illustrated by Roger Duvoisin. Lothrop, Lee & Shepard Bks. 1965 un il lib bdg $18.89; pa $6.99

Grades: PreK K 1   E

1. Fog

ISBN 0-688-51169-4 lib bdg; 0-688-07813-3 pa

A Caldecott Medal honor book, 1966

"This is . . . a mood picture book . . . describing a fog which rolls in from the sea to veil an Atlantic seacoast village for three days. The beautiful paintings . . . and the brief, poetic text sensitively and effectively evoke the atmosphere of the 'worst fog in twenty years' and depict the reactions of children and grown-ups to it." Booklist

★ **White** snow, bright snow; by Alvin Tresselt; illustrated by Roger Duvoisin. Lothrop, Lee & Shepard Bks. 1988 un il $17.99; lib bdg $18.89; pa $6.99

Grades: PreK K 1   E

1. Snow -- Fiction

ISBN 0-688-41161-4; 0-688-51161-9 lib bdg; 0-688-08294-7 pa

LC 88-10018

A reissue of the title first published 1947

Awarded the Caldecott Medal, 1948

When it begins to look, feel, and smell like snow, everyone prepares for a winter blizzard

Trewin, Trudie

I lost my kisses; [by] Trudie Trewin; illustrations by Nick Bland. Scholastic 2008 32p il $14.99

Grades: PreK K   E

1. Kissing -- Fiction 2. Lost and found possessions -- Fiction

ISBN 0-545-05557-1; 978-0-545-05557-4

Matilda Rose loves to kiss hello, goodbye, good morning, and goodnight, but on the day her father is to return from a trip, she cannot find her kisses anywhere, despite knowing how they feel, taste, and sound.

"Bland's striking black-and-white pencil illustrations have splashes of watercolor highlighting the wide-eyed cow's polka-dotted tights as she searches high and low. . . . Matilda Rose has a whimsical charm." SLJ

Trottier, Maxine

★ **Migrant**; pictures by Isabelle Arsenault. Groundwood Books/House of Anansi Press 2011 un il $18.95

Grades: K 1 2 3   E

1. Mennonites -- Fiction 2. Migrant agricultural laborers -- Fiction

ISBN 978-0-88899-975-7; 0-88899-975-5

"Each spring Anna leaves her home in Mexico and travels north with her family where they will work on farms harvesting fruits and vegetables. Sometimes she feels like a bird, flying north in the spring and south in the fall. Sometimes she feels like a jack rabbit living in an abandoned burrow, as her family moves into an empty house near the fields. But most of all she wonders what it would be like to stay in one place. The Low German-speaking Mennonites from Mexico are a unique group of migrants who moved from Canada to Mexico in the 1920s and became an important part of the farming community there. But it has become increasingly difficult for them to earn a livelihood, and so they come back to Canada each year as migrant workers in order to survive." (Publisher's note) "Ages four to seven." (Quill Quire)

"Trottier frames the outlook of a child in a family of migrant workers within a series of metaphors and similes. Anna sees herself as part of a flock that travels its seasonal round from Mexico to Canada like migratory geese. . . . Arsenault's mixed-media images of doll-like figures in overalls and long print dresses, hats and headscarves effectively capture both Anna's sense of isolation and the close family ties that keep her immediate family and larger community together. [Anna] . . . belongs to a group of Low German-speaking Mennonite farmers who emigrated to Mexico in the early 20th century but kept their Canadian citizenship and still travel northward each summer. . . . [This] is a moving, inventive and thoughtful look at a way of life many people share" Kirkus

The **paint** box; [illustrations by] Stella East. Fitzhenry & Whiteside 2003 32p il $16.95; pa $8.95

Grades: 2 3 4   E

1. Painters 2. Artists -- Fiction 3. Venice (Italy) -- Fiction

ISBN 1-55041-801-7; 1-55041-808-4 pa

LC 2003-464840

"'Long ago in Venice there was a girl named Marietta who loved to paint. She was the daughter of the great artist Tintoretto,' With her father's help, she disguises herself as a boy in order to explore the art world of Venice. . . . Marietta befriends an enslaved cabin boy and they spend their days sketching and exploring the city, and telling one another about their lives. When it is time for Piero's owner to leave the city, Marietta helps him escape and return to his family. This poignant tale has its roots in historical fact. . . . Trottier's fictional story about Marietta and her friend seems plausible, due in part to her descriptive and expressive writing style. East's painterly illustrations are magnificent. Each spread captures the feeling of Renaissance Venice and supports the accompanying text." SLJ

Tryon, Leslie

Albert's birthday; written and illustrated by Leslie Tryon. Atheneum Bks. for Young Readers 1999 un il $16; pa $6.99

Grades: PreK K 1 2   E

1. Animals -- Fiction 2. Birthdays -- Fiction

ISBN 0-689-82296-0; 0-689-85251-7 pa

LC 98-36621

Patsy Pig plans a surprise birthday party for her friend Albert, giving careful instructions to all their friends, but she forgets to invite the guest of honor

"The prose is personable and engaging, and colorful, exquisitely detailed illustrations portray the animal cast in such familiar human settings as a classroom and a town." Booklist

Other titles about Albert are:

Albert's alphabet (1991)

Albert's ballgame (1996)

Albert's Christmas (1997)

Albert's field trip (1993)

Albert's Halloween (1998)

Albert's play (1992)

Albert's Thanksgiving (1994)

Tseng, Kevin

Ned's new home. Tricycle Press 2009 un il $14.99

Grades: PreK K 1   E

1. Home -- Fiction 2. Fruit -- Fiction 3. Worms -- Fiction

ISBN 978-1-58246-297-4; 1-58246-297-6

LC 2008-42385

A worm tries out a variety of new homes when the apple he has been living in starts to rot, but none—from a lemon to a watermelon—is satisfactory.

"The cartoon illustrations are filled with warm colors and comic touches. Endpapers depict the life cycle of the apple from seed to fruit and back to seed. This reassuring tale will be appreciated by the read-aloud crowd while also supplying a subtle lesson in ecology." SLJ

Tsiang, Sarah

A flock of shoes; story by Sarah Tsiang; art by Qin Leng. Annick Press 2010 un il lib bdg $19.95; pa $8.95

Grades: PreK K 1 2   E

1. Shoes -- Fiction 2. Seasons -- Fiction

ISBN 978-1-55451-249-2 lib bdg; 1-55451-249-2 lib bdg; 978-1-55451-248-5 pa; 1-55451-248-4 pa

"At the end of summer, Abby refuses to give up her sandals despite all her mother's reasons for letting them go. But while Abby's playing at the park . . . her flip-flops slip off her feet and fly away, joining other sandals headed southward in a V formation. At first, she grudgingly puts on boots and wears them all winter, though she imagines her sandals vacationing at the beach and sending her fond postcards. . . . Tsiang expresses childlike emotions and thoughts in a simple text that reads aloud well. Washed with cheerful colors, Leng's cartoon-style drawings interpret the story with originality and wit." Booklist

Tuck, Justin

Home-field advantage; illustrated by Leonardo Rodriguez. Simon & Schuster 2011 il $16.99

Grades: PreK K 1   E

1. Football players 2. Hair -- Fiction 3. Twins --

Fiction 4. Football -- Fiction 5. Siblings -- Fiction 6. Family life -- Fiction

ISBN 978-1-4424-0369-7; 1-4424-0369-1

LC 2010043733

New York Giants defensive end Justin Tuck observes that growing up with five sisters helped make him tough, and tells of when twins Christale and Tiffany gave him an unforgettable haircut.

"The plot is realistic and believable. Rodríguez's comical watercolor illustrations match well with the text." SLJ

Tucker, Kathy

The seven Chinese sisters; written by Kathy Tucker; illustrated by Grace Lin. Whitman, A. 2003 un il $15.95; pa $6.99

Grades: K 1 2 3   E

1. China -- Fiction 2. Dragons -- Fiction 3. Sisters -- Fiction

ISBN 0-8075-7309-4; 0-8075-7310-5 pa

LC 2002-11330

When a dragon snatches the youngest of seven talented Chinese sisters, the other six come to her rescue

Lin "expertly captures the drama and humor of the story with delightful paintings that reveal lovely Chinese landscapes and a quirky, not-too-scary dragon. A wonderful read-aloud." Booklist

Tucker, Lindy

Porkelia; a pig's tale. written and illustrated by Lindy Tucker. Mackinac Island Press, Inc. 2011 il $9.95

Grades: PreK K 1 2   E

1. Stories in rhyme 2. Pigs -- Fiction 3. Dancers -- Fiction

ISBN 978-1-934133-28-6; 1-934133-28-0

Porkelia has always wanted to be a dancer, but not just any dancer—a Rockette! But Porkelia is a pig. Everyone laughs and makes fun of her, but she sets out on her own to be discovered and become famous.

"Tucker tells this appealing sty-to-Broadway fame story with an appealingly silly, rhyming text. . . . The spare pictures, rendered in clean black lines and pink accents, extend the fun." Booklist

Tudor, Tasha

1 is one. Simon & Schuster Bks. for Young Readers 2000 un il $16

Grades: PreK K 1 2   E

1. Counting

ISBN 0-689-82843-8

LC 99-31290

A reissue of the title first published 1956 by Oxford University Press

A Caldecott Medal honor book, 1957

"The author-artist has with characteristic charming quaintness written and illustrated a counting book. Delicately tinted, decoratively bordered pictures and rhyming lines of text count from one to twenty." Booklist

Corgiville fair; by Tasha Tudor. Little, Brown & Company 1998 1v. (unpg) col. ill. $12.23; pa $6.95

Grades: PreK K 1 2   E

1. Fairs -- Fiction 2. Animals -- Fiction 3. Picture

books for children 4. Cats -- Fiction 5. Dogs -- Fiction
ISBN 0-316-85312-7; 0-316-85329-1 pa;
9780316853125

LC 97029665

This picture book takes place in the "village of Corgiville, 'west of New Hampshire and east of Vermont,' the population of cats, rabbits, corgis ('enchanted' small dogs the color of foxes), and boggarts (toy-like 'trolls') turn out for the annual country fair. The plan of young Caleb Brown, a corgi, to ride his goat Josephine in the Grand Race, is almost foiled by rival Edgar Tomcat who feeds Caleb a soporific hot dog and stuffs Josephine with mince pies and cigars. But Caleb's resourceful buddy Merton Boggart gets the groaning Josephine going by feeding her the rockets for his fireworks display. . . . Caleb wins the race, leads the grand parade, starts off the Virginia Reel with Miss Corgiville, . . . and applauds Merton's closing fireworks display." (Kirkus)

Tullet, Herve
The **book** with a hole. Abrams 2011 un il pa $14.50
Grades: PreK K 1 2   E
1. Imagination -- Fiction
ISBN 978-1-85437-946-7; 1-85437-946-1
"As the title suggests, this oversize book has a die-cut hole—a large semicircle is cut out of the book's spine, which becomes a full circle in the center of the book when opened, serving different interactive functions in a series of spare b&w scenes. . . . Tullet's simple innovation allows readers to become active participants in the experience of reading." Publ Wkly

The **game** of finger worms. Phaedon Press 2011 un il bd bk $8.95
Grades: PreK K   E
1. Games 2. Board books for children
ISBN 978-0-7148-6071-8; 0-7148-6071-9

LC 2011289051

Invites the reader to complete the illustrations by drawing eyes and a mouth on one's finger and inserting it through the die-cut hole in each page as a "finger worm."
The book has "whimsical art done in bold watercolors. The [book is] appropriate for hands-on learning in early education settings or one-on-one with an adult to help youngsters develop finger dexterity and fine motor skills." SLJ

The **game** of let's go! Phaedon Press 2011 un il bd bk $8.95
Grades: PreK K   E
1. Games 2. Board books for children
ISBN 978-0-7148-6075-6; 0-7148-6075-1

LC 2011289050

Invites the reader to close one's eyes and follow a felt line through the book with one's finger, around and through various die-cut holes, imagining where the journey leads.
The book has "whimsical art done in bold watercolors. The [book is] appropriate for hands-on learning in early education settings or one-on-one with an adult to help youngsters develop finger dexterity and fine motor skills." SLJ

The **game** of light. Phaidon 2011 un il bd bk $8.95
Grades: PreK K   E
1. Games 2. Board books for children
ISBN 978-0-7148-6189-0; 0-7148-6189-8

This board book "makes for a fun nighttime activity as simple cutout shapes on each page can be illuminated with a flashlight. . . .The [book has] whimsical art done in bold watercolors. The [book is] appropriate for hands-on learning in early education settings or one-on-one with an adult to help youngsters develop finger dexterity and fine motor skills." SLJ

The **game** of mix and match. Phaidon 2011 un il bd bk $8.95
Grades: PreK K   E
1. Games 2. Board books for children
ISBN 978-0-7148-6073-2; 0-7148-6073-5
In this board book, "each page contains four flaps that children can mix and match to create more than 50 pictures among familiar objects such as hearts, stars, and the sun. . . .The [book has] whimsical art done in bold watercolors. The [book is] appropriate for hands-on learning in early education settings or one-on-one with an adult to help youngsters develop finger dexterity and fine motor skills." SLJ

The **game** of mix-up art. Phaidon 2011 un il bd bk $8.95
Grades: PreK K   E
1. Games 2. Board books for children
ISBN 978-0-7148-6188-3; 0-7148-6188-X
This board book "contains colorful shapes and obscure patterns among zigzagged cut-page flaps that create new artwork and designs as different flaps are turned. . . . The [book has] whimsical art done in bold watercolors. The [book is] appropriate for hands-on learning in early education settings or one-on-one with an adult to help youngsters develop finger dexterity and fine motor skills." SLJ

The **game** of patterns. Phaidon 2011 un il bd bk $8.95
Grades: PreK K   E
1. Games 2. Board books for children
ISBN 978-0-7148-6187-6; 0-7148-6187-1
This board book "provides the opportunity to point out as many patterns and similarities children can find on each spread. They increase in difficulty as the book progresses. The [book has] whimsical art done in bold watercolors. The [book is] appropriate for hands-on learning in early education settings or one-on-one with an adult to help youngsters develop finger dexterity and fine motor skills." SLJ

Tullet, Hervé
10 times 10; Herve Tullet. Abrams 2014 128 p. illustrations $15.95
Grades: 1 2   E
1. Counting -- Fiction
ISBN 1849762473; 9781849762472

LC 2013949412

In this children's book, author Herve Tullet asks "[h]ow many ways can you count to 10? With numbers, fingers, paints? How about with racing cars or with a fairy tale? In fact, you can do it almost any way you like!" (Publisher's note) "A wordless retelling of the Genesis creation story adds elements of nature through to Adam, Eve, and the serpent. Cubist-inspired art is achieved by adding multiple body parts to a giant pink head." (Bulletin of the Center for Children's Books)

"Tullet counts to 10 in 10 wildly eccentric ways, channeling the energy of a messy preschool art room... A riff on the Biblical story of creation and a fairy tale about two princes, three princesses, four witches, and so on are just a couple of the ways Tullet takes something as simple as counting to 10 and uses it as a springboard for loopy, creative experimentation." PW

★ **I** Am Blop! Hervé Tullet. Phaidon Inc Ltd 2013 110 p. col. ill. (hardcover) $19.95
Grades: PreK K   E
1. Color 2. Shape
ISBN 0714865338; 9780714865331
LC 2012285660

This children's story, by Hervé Tullet, explores "the world of Blop! A Blop is a simple shape, somewhere between a flower and a butterfly, a sponge and a drawing of a little man -- above all Blop is whatever you want it to be . . . explor[ing] many concepts encountered for the first time by young children, including up and down, single and plural, individual and family, city and countryside etc." (Publisher's note)

"The latest in a series of offbeat, imaginative creations by renowned French artist Tullet will intrigue children and encourage them to think outside the blop... Any child bored with standard activity-book fare will love using this open-ended, imaginative tool for creating their own universe...[T]aps directly into the heart of a child's natural creativity by avoiding the didactic explanatory tone of similar books." Kirkus

Mix it up! Hervé Tullet; translated by Christopher Franceschelli. Chronicle Books 2014 56 p. color illustrations (reinforced) $15.99
Grades: PreK K 1   E
1. Art 2. Color 3. Color -- Fiction 4. Imagination -- Fiction
ISBN 9781452137353; 1452137358
LC 2014006665

In this book by Hervé Tullet, readers will "follow the artist's simple instructions, and suddenly colors appear, mix, splatter, and vanish in a world powered only by the reader's imagination." It "sets readers on an extraordinary interactive journey all within the printed page." (Publisher's note)

"Franceschelli is a talented translator, and the book's conversational tone is an important part of its charm. It's an effective presentation of basic color mixing, and great fun for paint lovers in places where paints can't be used." Pub Wkly

★ **Press** here; [translated by Christopher Franceschelli] Chronicle Books 2011 un il
Grades: PreK K 1 2   E
1. Toy and movable books 2. Imagination -- Fiction
ISBN 0-8118-7954-2; 978-0-8118-7954-5
LC 2010035579

Original French edition 2010

Instructs the reader on how to interact with the illustrations to create imaginative images.

"Tullet's brilliant creation proves that books need not lose out to electronic wizardry. . . . The fun continues as the dots proliferate, travel around the page, grow and shrink in

response to commands to clap, shake, and tilt the book, etc." Publ Wkly

Turner, Ann Warren
★ **Dust** for dinner; story by Ann Turner; pictures by Robert Barrett. HarperCollins Pubs. 1995 64p il (I can read book) hardcover o.p. pa $3.99
Grades: K 1 2 3   E
1. Farm life -- Fiction 2. Family life -- Fiction 3. Great Depression, 1929-1939 -- Fiction
ISBN 0-06-023377-X lib bdg; 0-06-444225-X pa
LC 93-34634

Jake narrates the story of his family's life in the Oklahoma dust bowl and the journey from their ravaged farm to California during the Great Depression

"Turner takes a sad episode in history and fashions it into a story that has some depth as well as some drama. . . . Realistic, nicely executed illustrations decorate every page." Booklist

Tusa, Tricia
★ **Follow** me; written and illustrated by Tricia Tusa. Harcourt Children's Books 2011 un il $16.99
Grades: PreK K 1 2   E
1. Color -- Fiction 2. Imagination -- Fiction
ISBN 978-0-547-27201-6; 0-547-27201-4
LC 2010009061

A girl travels through an imaginative world of colors by way of a swing.

"The beautiful etchings are rich in color and alive with vibrant line. . . . A glorious visual meditation on light, color and home for even the smallest child and artist." Kirkus

Twohy, Mike
★ **Poindexter** makes a friend. Simon & Schuster Books for Young Readers 2011 un il $15.99
Grades: K 1 2   E
1. Pigs -- Fiction 2. Shyness -- Fiction 3. Turtles -- Fiction 4. Libraries -- Fiction 5. Friendship -- Fiction 6. Books and reading -- Fiction
ISBN 978-1-4424-0965-1; 1-4424-0965-7
LC 2010018489

Poindexter is a very shy pig who, while helping out at the library, meets a turtle who is also shy, and together they read a book about making a friend in four easy steps.

"The watercolor illustrations in this gentle story are done in a cartoon style. Humorous details . . . will bring smiles. The pals' pleasure in sharing books with a dim-eyed mole and each other is palpable. . . . This reassuring story will envelop youngsters like a warm, cozy blanket." SLJ

Uchida, Yoshiko
The **bracelet**; story by Yoshiko Uchida; illustrated by Joanna Yardley. Philomel Bks. 1993 un il $17.99; pa $6.99
Grades: K 1 2 3   E
1. Friendship -- Fiction 2. World War, 1939-1945 -- Fiction 3. Japanese Americans -- Evacuation and relocation, 1942-1945 -- Fiction
ISBN 0-399-22503-X; 0-698-11390-X pa
LC 92-26196

Emi, a Japanese American in the second grade, is sent with her family to an internment camp during World War II, but the loss of the bracelet her best friend has given her proves that she does not need a physical reminder of that friendship

This "is a gentle, honest introduction to the treatment of the Japanese-Americans during the war, and Yardley's delicate pencil-and-watercolor paintings are cleanly drawn and richly colored." Bull Cent Child Books

Udry, Janice May

The **moon** jumpers; Pictures by Maurice Sendak. Harper 1959 31 p. ill. (hardcover) $17.95

Grades: PreK K 1 2   E

1. Night -- Fiction

ISBN 0060284609; 9780060284602

LC 58007757

"A full moon on a summer night turns an ordinary landscape into a world of mystery and the uninhibited caperings of children into a joyous dance. There are black-and-white drawings and brief text in between double-page spreads in full ... color." (Horn Bk)

★ A **tree** is nice; pictures by Marc Simont. Harper & Row 1956 un il $17.99; lib bdg $18.89; pa $6.99

Grades: PreK K 1 2   E

1. Trees -- Fiction

ISBN 0-06-026155-2; 0-06-026156-0 lib bdg; 0-06-443147-9 pa

Awarded the Caldecott Medal, 1957

"In childlike terms and in enticing pictures, colored and black and white, author and artist set forth reasons why trees are nice to have around—trees fill up the sky, they make everything beautiful, cats get away from dogs in them, leaves come down and can be played in, and trees are nice to climb in, to hang a swing in, or to plant. A picture book sure to please young children." Booklist

Uegaki, Chieri

Rosie and Buttercup; written by Chieri Uegaki; illustrated by Stéphane Jorisch. Kids Can Press 2008 un il $17.95

Grades: PreK K 1 2   E

1. Sisters -- Fiction

ISBN 978-1-55337-997-3

"At first Rosie's perfect life seems even more perfect when little sister Buttercup arrives. . . . In time, Rosie becomes disenchanted and gives Buttercup away—to her sitter, Oxford. . . . Predictably, she is soon sorry. . . . Uegaki's assured text assumes an intelligent reader. . . . Jorisch's watercolor illustrations, uncluttered but dense with patterns, are crisp against generous fields of white space." Publ Wkly

Suki's kimono; written by Chieri Uegaki; illustrated by Stephane Jorisch. Kids Can Press 2003 un il hardcover o.p. pa $7.95

Grades: PreK K 1 2   E

1. Japanese -- Fiction

ISBN 1-55337-752-4 pa; 1-55337-084-8

LC 2003-495264

"On her first day of first grade [Suki] chooses to wear her beloved Japanese kimono to school, despite the objections of her older sisters and the initial laughter of other children on the playground. . . . Her day ends in triumph, with her teacher and classmates won over by her impromptu dance performance. . . . This is an appealing story of courage and independence. Delicate, playful watercolor-and-ink illus-

trations perfectly capture the child's neighborhood and the characters' facial expressions." SLJ

Uhlberg, Myron

Dad, Jackie, and me; illustrated by Colin Bootman. Peachtree Publishers 2005 un il $16.95

Grades: K 1 2 3   E

1. Baseball players 2. Army officers 3. Deaf -- Fiction 4. Baseball -- Fiction 5. Father-son relationship -- Fiction 6. Brooklyn (New York, N.Y.) -- Fiction

ISBN 1-56145-329-3

LC 2004-16711

In Brooklyn, New York, in 1947, a boy learns about discrimination and tolerance as he and his deaf father share their enthusiasm over baseball and the Dodgers' first baseman, Jackie Robinson.

"Bootman's lovely watercolor paintings add detail and wistful nostalgia. . . . [Readers] will appreciate the story's insightful treatment of deafness as viewed through the eyes of a child." SLJ

★ A **storm** called Katrina; written by Myron Uhlberg; illustrated by Colin Bootman. Peachtree 2010 un il $17.95

Grades: 1 2 3 4   E

1. Floods -- Fiction 2. African Americans -- Fiction 3. New Orleans (La.) -- Fiction 4. Hurricane Katrina, 2005 -- Fiction

ISBN 978-1-56145-591-1; 1-56145-591-1

LC 2009024518

When flood waters submerge their New Orleans neighborhood in the aftermath of Hurricane Katrina, a young cornet player and his parents evacuate their home and struggle to survive and stay together.

"Bootman's dramatic oil paintings and the boy's first-person narration provide realistic immediacy. . . . Readers are in for a deeply personal and sometimes uncomfortable look at a disaster whose ramifications are still being felt." Publ Wkly

Ulmer, Wendy K.

A **isn't** for fox; an isn't alphabet. written by Wendy K. Ulmer; illustrated by Laura Knorr. Sleeping Bear Press 2008 un il $16.95

Grades: PreK K   E

1. Alphabet

ISBN 978-1-58536-319-3; 1-58536-319-7

LC 2007006436

"Though the entertaining non-examples show an appreciation for the audience's sense of the silly, Knorr's charming paintings of winking cats, smiling jellyfish, trumpeting lions, and pillow-fighting llamas are worth the purchase price alone." SLJ

"This book points out first what each letter of the alphabet is not for and then gives an example of a word that does begin with the letter." Publisher's note

Uman, Jennifer

Jemmy button; Jennifer Uman, Valerio Vidali. Candlewick Press 2013 48 p. (reinforced) $16.99

Grades: K 1 2 3   E

ISBN 9780763664879

LC 2012942662

"Exchanged for the single mother-of-pearl button that gave him his nickname, an indigenous Tierra del Fuegan boy named Orundellico spent many years in England in the early 1800s as part of a failed experiment in forced civilization. Less a biography than an attempt to represent this alienating experience from Jemmy's point of view, it is distinguished by lyrical prose-poetry...and intensely creative and beautifully conceived paintings." Publ Wkly

Underwood, Deborah

★ **Bad** bye, good bye; written by Deborah Underwood; illustrated by Jonathan Bean. Houghton Mifflin Books for Children, Houghton Mifflin Harcourt 2014 32 p. $16.99
Grades: PreK K 1 2   E
1. Stories in rhyme 2. Moving, Household -- Fiction
ISBN 0547928521; 9780547928524
LC 2013017616

In this children's book, written by Deborah Underwood and illustrated by Jonathan Bean, "a boy and his family are packing up their old home, and the morning feels scary and sad. But when he arrives at his new home, an evening of good byes awaits: bye to new friends, bye to glowing fireflies, bye to climbing trees." (Publisher's note)

"An upset little boy sees nothing good about his family's move: "Bad truck / Bad guy / Bad wave / Bad bye." But the journey to and exploration of his new house are full of good experiences, including making a friend. Bean's dynamic ink and Prismacolor-tone illustrations creatively highlight the passage of time, and Underwood's simple rhymes skillfully address common emotions about moving." Horn Book

A **balloon** for Isabel; illustrations by Laura Rankin. Greenwillow Books 2010 un il $16.99
Grades: K 1 2   E
1. School stories 2. Candy -- Fiction 3. Balloons -- Fiction 4. Porcupines -- Fiction
ISBN 978-0-06-177987-9; 0-06-177987-3
LC 2009018759

As graduation day approaches, Isabel tries to convince her teacher that she and Walter, both porcupines, should receive balloons on the big day just like the other children.

"Illustrations full of color and personality add to the story's depth and appeal. Authentic dialogue, a touch of humor, and Isabel's ingenious invention make this title of desire and determination a keeper." SLJ

The **Christmas** quiet book; by Deborah Underwood; illustrated by Renata Liwska. Houghton Mifflin Books for Children 2012 32 p. $12.99
Grades: PreK K 1   E
1. Christmas 2. Quietude -- Fiction 3. Sound -- Fiction 4. Animals -- Fiction
ISBN 0547558635; 9780547558639
LC 2011040920

In this children's book by Deborah Underwood, illustrated by Renata Liwska, "the holidays are filled with joyful noise. But Christmas is sometimes wrapped in quiet: 'Searching for presents quiet,' 'Getting caught quiet,' and 'Hoping for a snow day quiet.' . . . The book features "soft colored pencil illustrations of bunnies, bears, and more." (Publisher's note)

Here comes Santa Cat; by Deborah Underwood; pictures by Claudia Rueda. Dial Books for Young Readers, an imprint of Penguin Group (USA) Inc. 2014 88 p. color illustrations (hardcover) $16.99

Grades: PreK K 1 2   E
1. Cats -- Fiction 2. Gifts -- Fiction 3. Humorous fiction 4. Santa Claus -- Fiction 5. Conduct of life -- Fiction 6. Humorous stories
ISBN 0803741006; 9780803741003
LC 2013035538

In this children's book, by Deborah Underwood, "Cat has a hunch he's not on Santa's 'nice' list. Which means? No presents for Cat. So he tries to be good, but children, it seems, aren't wild for his brand of gift-giving. Still, Cat might surprise himself, and best of all, he may just get to meet the man in the red suit himself - and receive a holiday surprise of his own." (Publisher's note)

"Naughty Cat (Here Comes the Easter Cat) figures that if he dresses up as Santa Claus, he can give himself a present. But he quickly abandons the idea when he realizes Santa's job entails not only getting sooty but also delivering gifts to others. Underwood and Rueda's spot-on use of comedic timing, page turns, and layout creates another holiday winner." Horn Book

★ **Here** comes the Easter Cat! by Deborah Underwood; pictures by Claudia Rueda. Dial Books for Young Readers 2014 80 p. (hardcover) $16.99
Grades: PreK K 1 2   E
1. Humorous fiction 2. Cats -- Fiction 3. Humorous stories 4. Easter Bunny -- Fiction
ISBN 0803739397; 9780803739390
LC 2012038134

This book, by Deborah Underwood and illustrated by Claudia Rueda, tells the story of a cat that attempts to deliver eggs on Easter. "He dons his sparkly suit, jumps on his Harley, and roars off into the night. But it turns out delivering Easter eggs is hard work. And it doesn't leave much time for naps (of which Cat has taken five--no, seven). So when a pooped-out Easter Bunny shows up, and with a treat for Cat, what will Cat do?" (Publisher's note)

"In this witty offering, Cat is unhappy about the Easter Bunny's arrival. The text addresses jealous Cat directly, and he responds using placards, humorous expressions, and body language. Rueda expertly uses white space and page turns to focus attention on Cat and the repartee. Underwood's knowledgeable authorial voice and Rueda's loosely sketched, textured ink and colored-pencil illustrations make this an entertaining tale." Horn Book

★ The **loud** book! illustrated by Renata Liwska. Houghton Mifflin Harcourt 2011 un il $12.99
Grades: PreK K   E
1. Day -- Fiction 2. Noise -- Fiction
ISBN 978-0-547-39008-6; 0-547-39008-4
LC 2010006784

From the blare of an alarm clock in the morning to snores and crickets in the evening, simple text explores the many loud noises one might hear during the course of a day.

"Fortified with the same charm and humor as the first book, this has enough activity and drama to elicit interesting observations and reactions from young audiences." Booklist

★ The **quiet** book; illustrated by Renata Liwska. Houghton Mifflin Books for Children 2010 un il $12.95

Grades: PreK K   E

1. Noise -- Fiction 2. Animals -- Fiction

ISBN 978-0-547-21567-9; 0-547-21567-3

From the quiet of being the first one awake in the morning to "sweet dreams quiet" when the last light is turned off, simple text explores the many kinds of quiet that can exist during the day.

"The soft, matte feel of the illustrations, created with pencil, are digitally enhanced, and are priceless. The animals' facial expressions and body language are endearing. . . . All of the scenarios are child-centric and realistic." SLJ

Ungerer, Tomi

Adelaide; the flying kangaroo. Phaidon Press 2011 un il $14.95

Grades: K 1 2   E

1. Flight -- Fiction 2. Kangaroos -- Fiction 3. Paris (France) -- Fiction

ISBN 978-0-7148-6083-1; 0-7148-6083-2

First published 1959 by Harper

Adelaide is a little bit different to most kangaroos because most kangaroos don't have wings.

"Ungerer remains a master of suggestion: with marvelous skill, his agile pen embellishes the straightforward visual narrative, arrayed on spacious white, with a wealth of comical details of posture and countenance." Horn Book

★ **Crictor**. Harper & Row 1958 32p il $17.99; pa $6.99

Grades: PreK K 1 2   E

1. Snakes -- Fiction

ISBN 0-06-026180-3; 0-06-443044-8 pa

A story "about the boa constrictor that was sent to Madame Bodot, who lived and taught school in a little French town. . . . The boys used him for a slide and the girls for a jump-rope. When Crictor captured a burglar by coiling around him until the police came, he was awarded impressive tokens of esteem and affection of the townspeople. Engaging line drawings echo the restrained and elegant absurdities of the text." Bull Cent Child Books

★ **Otto**; the autobiography of a teddy bear. Phaidon Press 2010 un il $16.95

Grades: 1 2 3   E

1. Jews -- Fiction 2. Soldiers -- Fiction 3. Friendship -- Fiction 4. Teddy bears -- Fiction 5. Holocaust, 1933-1945 -- Fiction 6. World War, 1939-1945 -- Fiction

ISBN 978-0-7148-5766-4; 0-7148-5766-1

First published 1999 by Robert Rinehard

Otto the teddy bear belongs to David, a Jewish boy in Germany. When David and his parents are taken away by the Nazis, David gives Otto to his friend Oskar, whose father goes to war. After a bombing raid, Otto is found by an American soldier. Years later Oskar rediscovers Otto in antique store in the U.S. and David finds them too.

"Ungerer's illustrations—expressive, carefully worked paintings . . . —present some potentially scary images; parents and teachers should prepare for questions. But Otto's tranquil voice allows Ungerer to tell his story at a safe remove, and his unvarnished honesty makes this a vital account." Publ Wkly

Urban, Linda

Little Red Henry; Linda Urban, illustrated by Madeline Valentine. Candlewick Press 2015 40 p. $16.99

Grades: PreK K 1 2 3   E

1. Growth 2. Family life -- Fiction 3. Brothers and sisters -- Fiction

ISBN 0763661767; 9780763661762

LC 2014939355

In this children's book, written by Linda Urban and illustrated by Madeline Valentine, "Little redheaded Henry's family treats him like a baby. They dress him. They feed him. They brush his 'widdle toofers.' But he's not a baby anymore. He's a little boy who wants to do things for himself. So with his family watching anxiously from the wings, Henry sets out on a glorious day of independence." (Publisher's note)

Mouse was mad; illustrated by Henry Cole. Harcourt Children's Books 2009 un il $16

Grades: PreK K 1 2   E

1. Mice -- Fiction 2. Anger -- Fiction 3. Animals -- Fiction

ISBN 978-0-15-205337-6; 0-15-205337-9

LC 2007045081

Mouse struggles to find the right way to express his anger, modeling the behavior of Hare, Bear, Hedgehog, and Bobcat, only to discover that his own way may be the best way of all.

"Through playful language and expressive watercolors with colored pencil and ink, this story about anger management proves to be both entertaining and therapeutic." SLJ

Urbanovic, Jackie

Duck at the door. HarperCollins 2007 un il $16.99; lib bdg $17.89

Grades: PreK K 1 2   E

1. Ducks -- Fiction 2. Winter -- Fiction 3. Animals -- Fiction

ISBN 0-06-121438-8; 0-06-121439-6 lib bdg

When Max the duck decides to stay behind when his flock flies south, Irene invites him to stay with her for the winter.

"Urbanovic's animals, with their expressive, engaging facial features, take center stage in the open, cheery illustrations. . . . Great fun for storyhours." SLJ

Other titles about Max the duck are:

Duck soup (2008)

Duck and cover (2009)

Sitting duck. Harper 2010 un il $17.99; lib bdg $18.89

Grades: PreK K 1 2   E

1. Dogs -- Fiction 2. Ducks -- Fiction 3. Animals -- Fiction 4. Babysitters -- Fiction

ISBN 978-0-06-176583-4; 0-06-176583-X; 978-0-06-176584-1 lib bdg; 0-06-176584-8 lib bdg

LC 2009014565

Max the duck volunteers to babysit for puppy Anabel, unaware of all the mischief a puppy can get into.

"Young Max fans will enjoy the cartoon-style visual humor, which ramps up the energy was well as the chaos as the story unfolds." Booklist

Urdahl, Catherine

Polka-dot fixes kindergarten; illustrated by Mai S. Kemble. Charlesbridge 2011 un il $16.95; pa $7.95; e-book $6.99

Grades: PreK K   E

1. School stories 2. Kindergarten -- Fiction

ISBN 978-1-57091-737-0; 1-57091-737-X; 978-1-57091-738-7 pa; 1-57091-738-8 pa; 978-1-60734-312-7 e-book

On the first day of kindergarten, Polka-dot uses the fix-it kit her grandpa has prepared for her to help her make a friend.

"The colorful watercolor illustrations support the text well. Kemble does a particularly good job of rendering facial expressions to mirror the children's emotions: worry, anger, hopefulness, shame, discomfort, and ultimately, kindness. Character education is becoming increasingly important in schools, and this book will make a solid addition to the resource shelf." SLJ

Vail, Rachel

Sometimes I'm Bombaloo; illustrated by Yumi Heo. Scholastic Press 2001 un il $15.95

Grades: PreK K 1 2   E

1. Anger -- Fiction

ISBN 0-439-08755-4

LC 99-58709

When Katie Honors feels angry and out of control, her mother helps her to be herself again

"Vail captures the intensity of emotion that children (and many adults) feel when they are angry, and then distills it with laughter. Heo uses lots of stripes and splotches of color to match Katie's emotions. . . . Kudos to Vail and Heo for making a scary subject manageable." Booklist

Vainio, Pirkko

Who hid the Easter eggs? NorthSouth Books 2011 un il $16.95

Grades: PreK K   E

1. Eggs -- Fiction 2. Birds -- Fiction 3. Easter -- Fiction 4. Squirrels -- Fiction 5. Grandmothers -- Fiction

ISBN 978-0-7358-2304-4; 0-7358-2304-9

"A loving grandmother . . . hides her beautiful, hand-painted Easter eggs for her five grandchildren to find. The story focuses on a charming squirrel named Harry who lives in the grandmother's backyard. He is horrified to discover that a jackdaw (a European bird like a crow) has stolen all the eggs and hidden them in his nest. . . . The simple story is predictable and sweet, but the large-format watercolor illustrations . . . elevate this effort beyond the usual Easter Bunny adventure. . . . The Easter eggs are painted in traditional Ukrainian style, with tiny geometric prints and patterns that add a special touch to this story." Kirkus

Valdivia, Paloma

Up above and down below; Paloma Valdivia. Owlkids Books, Inc. 2012 32 p. col. ill., maps $15.95

Grades: PreK K   E

1. Earth 2. Geography 3. Picture books for children

ISBN 1926973399; 9781926973395

LC 2011943194

This children's picture book "highlights the notion that although different kinds of people live in different places around the world, we share many things in common. The ti-

tle subtly references the Earth's northern and southern hemispheres, launching readers into a picture book with spreads characterized by a line bisecting each page into upper and lower halves." (Kirkus)

Vamos, Samantha R.

★ The cazuela that the farm maiden stirred. Charlesbridge 2011 un il lib bdg $17.95

Grades: PreK K 1 2   E

1. Cooking -- Fiction 2. Domestic animals -- Fiction 3. Spanish language -- Vocabulary

ISBN 978-1-58089-242-1; 1-58089-242-6

LC 2010007547

"Inspired by 'The House that Jack Built,' Vamos offers a fresh, new twist, playfully introducing Spanish into this cumulative tale. . . . Lopez's artwork, with its desert palette punctuated by brilliant primary colors and its graphic, hard edges, suggestive of folk art, is a perfect match. . . . A wonderful read-aloud, filled with merriment and conviviality." Kirkus

Van Allsburg, Chris

★ Ben's dream; story and pictures by Chris Van Allsburg. Houghton Mifflin 1982 31p il lib bdg $16.95

Grades: K 1 2 3 4   E

1. Dreams -- Fiction

ISBN 0-395-32084-4

LC 81-20029

"When rain spoils Ben's ball game with Margaret, he returns to an empty house, falls asleep in his father's chair, and embarks on a dream. In a marvelous series of double-page black-and-white pictures meticulously textured with hatching, one shares Ben's voyage past such sights as the Statue of Liberty, the Sphinx, and the Mount Rushmore presidents, all with flood waters lapping about their respective chins and waists. . . . A visual tour de force." Horn Book

The garden of Abdul Gasazi; written and illustrated by Chris Van Allsburg. Houghton Mifflin 1979 un il lib bdg $18.95

Grades: 1 2 3 4   E

1. Dogs -- Fiction 2. Magic -- Fiction

ISBN 0-395-27804-X

A Caldecott Medal honor book, 1980

When the dog he is caring for runs away from Alan into the forbidden garden of a retired dog-hating magician, a spell seems to be cast over the contrary dog

The full page "lithographlike drawings are astonishing—eerie, monumental, surreal and witty all at once—and the effect of the whole is original and unforgettable." Books of the Times

★ Jumanji; written and illustrated by Chris Van Allsburg. 30th anniversary edition Houghton Mifflin Books for Children 2011 1 v. (unpaged) ill. (book and CD) $18.99

Grades: K 1 2 3 4   E

1. Play -- Fiction 2. Games -- Fiction

ISBN 9780547608389

LC 2011456885

Originally published 1981

Caldecott Medal (1982)

Left on their own for an afternoon, two bored and restless children find more excitement than they bargained for in a mysterious and mystical jungle adventure board game.

"Through the masterly use of light and shadow, the interplay of design elements, and audacious changes in perspective and composition, the artist conveys an impression of color without losing the dramatic contrast of black and white." Horn Book

Just a dream. Houghton Mifflin 1990 un il $18.95
Grades: K 1 2 3 4 E
1. Dreams -- Fiction 2. Pollution -- Fiction 3. Environmental protection -- Fiction
ISBN 0-395-53308-2
LC 90-41343

When he has a dream about a future Earth devastated by pollution, Walter begins to understand the importance of taking care of the environment.

"Van Allsburg demonstrates his unique artistic magic in combining foresight, wisdom and striking artwork to deliver an ecological message concerning conservation and renewal." Child Book Rev Serv

The **mysteries** of Harris Burdick. Houghton Mifflin 1984 un il lib bdg $18.95
Grades: 1 2 3 4 E
1. Imagination -- Fiction 2. Storytelling -- Fiction
ISBN 0-395-35393-9
LC 84-9006

Presents a series of loosely related drawings each accompanied by a title and a caption which the reader may use to make up his or her own story

Rendered in the author's "signature velvet black and white . . . the pictures are nothing short of spectacular. . . . While some may find this just an excuse for handsome artwork, others will see its great potential for stretching a child's imagination. Although the book could be used in countless ways, primarily it will make storytellers of children." Booklist

★ The **Polar** Express; written and illustrated by Chris Van Allsburg. Twentieth anniversary ed.; Houghton Mifflin 2005 un il $35
Grades: PreK K 1 2 3 E
1. Christmas -- Fiction 2. North Pole -- Fiction 3. Santa Claus -- Fiction
ISBN 978-0-618-61169-0; 0-618-61169-X
LC 2005281613

A reissue of the title first published 1985
Awarded the Caldecott Medal, 1986

A magical train ride on Christmas Eve takes a boy to the North Pole to receive a special gift from Santa Claus.

This offers "stunning paintings in which Van Allsburg uses dark, rich colors and misty shapes in contrast with touches of bright white-gold light to create scenes, interior and exterior, that have a quality of mystery that imbues the strong composition to achieve a soft, evocative mood." Bull Cent Child Books

The **stranger**. Houghton Mifflin 1986 un il lib bdg $18.95
Grades: 1 2 3 4 E
1. Seasons -- Fiction
ISBN 0-395-42331-7
LC 86-15235

The enigmatic origins of the stranger Farmer Bailey hits with his truck and brings home to recuperate seem to have a mysterious relation to the weather.

"The full-color illustrations, framed in white, evoke an old-fashioned New England landscape at the end of summer; some are remarkably peaceful in tone, others slightly spooky by virtue of brooding colors, unexpected perspectives, or the stranger's peculiar expressions." Bull Cent Child Books

The **sweetest** fig. Houghton Mifflin 1993 un il $18.95
Grades: 1 2 3 4 E
1. Dogs -- Fiction 2. Magic -- Fiction 3. Dreams -- Fiction
ISBN 0-395-67346-1
LC 93-12692

After being given two magical figs that make his dreams come true, Monsieur Bibot sees his plans for future wealth upset by his long-suffering dog

"The full-color, expressive illustrations are filled with nuance, detail and mystery. Once again, Van Allsburg weaves a spell with ultimate skill and creativity." Child Book Rev Serv

The **widow's** broom. Houghton Mifflin 1992 un il $18.95
Grades: 1 2 3 4 E
1. Magic -- Fiction 2. Witchcraft -- Fiction
ISBN 0-395-64051-2
LC 92-7110

A witch's worn-out broom serves a widow well, until her neighbors decide the thing is wicked and dangerous

"In addition to being a neatly understated piece of storytelling, this fuels Van Allsburg's best kind of illustration—darkly rounded, speckle-textured art with eerie effects." Bull Cent Child Books

The **wretched** stone. Houghton Mifflin 1991 un il $18.95
Grades: 1 2 3 4 E
1. Sea stories
ISBN 0-395-53307-4
LC 91-11525

This book chronicles the "events that occur during the last voyage of the Rita Anne. . . . One month into the journey, an uncharted island is explored . . . {and} the captain brings aboard a strange, heavy object; one surface of the rock is flat and glassy and emits a 'glowing light that is quite beautiful and pleasing to look at.' . . . A trip into the hold, where the sailors have barricaded themselves with the stone, reveals . . . {that} the men have turned into grinning monkeys, and they are unable to understand their captain's words. After a lightning storm disables the stone, the captain discovers that when he reads to the sailors, they recover some of their alertness." (Horn Book) "Grades two to four." (SLJ)

"Although Van Allsburg clearly has a message to convey, he has added to the book an enjoyable and necessary dollop of humor. The story has a quiet, understated, yet suspenseful tone; most of the plot's considerable drama is conveyed in the impressive illustrations." Horn Book

Zathura; a space adventure. written and illustrated by Chris Van Allsburg. Houghton Mifflin 2002 un il $18

Grades: 1 2 3 4   **E**
1. Games -- Fiction
ISBN 0-618-25396-3

LC 2002-1751

"Van Allsburg illustrates the surreal events in a grainy charcoal-black that seems to shimmer on a rough, cream-colored ground. His deathly quiet images . . . have a frozen stillness that leaves all color and activity to the imagination; with each new threat, the book seems to hold its breath. . . . Zathura, like Jumanji, is a satisfying enigma." Publ Wkly

Van Camp, Katie

Cookiebot! a Harry and Horsie adventure. [by] Katie Van Camp and [illustrated by] Lincoln Agnew. Balzer + Bray 2011 un il $16.99
Grades: PreK K 1 2   **E**
1. Robots -- Fiction 2. Cookies -- Fiction 3. Imagination -- Fiction
ISBN 978-0-06-197445-8; 0-06-197445-5

LC 2010017684

When Harry and his best friend Horsie build a robot that can reach the cookie jar for them, it goes out of control and wreaks havoc around the city.

"Iconic splash pages capture the scope of Harry's spirited imagination, while detailed illustrations offer clever, hidden humor. Once again, friendship rules for Harry and Horsie; and for Van Camp and Agnew, their seemingly seamless collaboration perfectly tells the story." Kirkus

Harry and Horsie; illustrated by Lincoln Agnew. Balzer & Bray 2009 un il $16.99
Grades: PreK K 1 2   **E**
1. Imagination -- Fiction
ISBN 978-0-06-175598-9; 0-06-175598-2

When a boy named Harry sneaks out of bed one night with his best friend, Horsie, to play with his Super Duper Bubble Blooper—an out-of-this-world adventure begins!

"Agnew's art uses an effectively limited color palette, faded dot patterns, and crisp lines to create a retro-cartoon feel. . . . With dashing visuals that capture Harry's deep-space adventure with verve to spare, and a comforting resolution, this has potential to be a bedtime favorite." Booklist

Another title about Harry and Horsie is:
Cookiebot! A Harry and Horsie adventure (2011)

Van Camp, Richard

★ **Little** you; Richard Van Camp, Julie Flett. Orca Book Publishers 2013 24 p. (hardcover) $9.95
Grades: PreK   **E**
1. Infants -- Fiction 2. Parent-child relationship -- Fiction
ISBN 1459802489; 9781459802483; 9781459802490

LC 2012952954

In this book, by Richard Van Camp and illustrated by Julie Flett, "a mother and father profess their love for their little one. With Van Camp's spare second-person verse on the left-hand page and Flett's graphic art in various shades of red, orange, tan, gray, black and orange against a white background on the facing page, the spreads . . . depict a young child growing from infancy to toddlerhood." (Kirkus Reviews)

Van Dusen, Chris

The **circus** ship. Candlewick Press 2009 un il $16.99

Grades: PreK K 1 2 3   **E**
1. Stories in rhyme 2. Circus -- Fiction 3. Animals -- Fiction 4. Shipwrecks -- Fiction
ISBN 978-0-7636-3090-4; 0-7636-3090-X

LC 2008938402

Van Dusen "uses an actual 1836 shipwreck as the seed for this charming and humorous picture book. . . . The rhyming text provides the structure for the story; however, the vividly colored, meticulously drawn illustrations articulate the story so well that they could practically stand on their own." Booklist

King Hugo's huge ego. Candlewick Press 2011 il
Grades: PreK K 1   **E**
1. Stories in rhyme 2. Kings and rulers -- Fiction
ISBN 0-7636-5004-8; 978-0-7636-5004-9

LC 2010040458

When haughty King Hugo tangles with a sorceress, she causes him to see himself in a more realistic light.

"A life lesson and true love tie up the loose ends, but not before readers are treated to a terrific mélange of satire, slapstick, and caricature, all served up with expert comic timing." Publ Wkly

Learning to ski with Mr. Magee. Chronicle Books 2010 un il $15.99
Grades: PreK K 1   **E**
1. Stories in rhyme 2. Dogs -- Fiction 3. Skiing -- Fiction
ISBN 978-0-8118-7495-3; 0-8118-7495-8

An encounter with a moose while they are learning to ski provides Mr. Magee and his dog with some unexpected excitement.

"The gouache illustrations are clean, crisp, and colorful. Various shades of blue, green, and purple nicely show the chill of the winter day. The rhyming text, with occasional bolded words, scans easily. Fans of Mr. Magee will feel at home with this one." SLJ

Other titles about Mr. Magee are:
A camping spree with Mr. Magee (2003)
Down to the sea with Mr. Magee (2000)

Van Fleet, Matthew

Heads. Simon & Schuster 2010 un il $17.99
Grades: PreK K   **E**
1. Pop-up books 2. Animals -- Fiction
ISBN 978-1-4424-0379-6; 1-4424-0379-9

"Children begin the safari that celebrates the traits of diverse animals by pulling a tab that allows a giraffe, elephant, rhino, tiger, and alligator to assemble jumbled letters to create the title. On each busy page, more tabs open a platypus egg, enlarge a frog's throat, and wiggle an elephant's ears. Watercolor cartoon critters rock the pages with greedy grins, loving licks, and astonished yelps. . . . This fun board book is designed to entertain toddlers time and again." SLJ

Moo; photos by Brian Stanton. Simon & Schuster 2011 il $16.99
Grades: PreK   **E**
1. Board books for children 2. Domestic animals -- Fiction
ISBN 978-1-4424-3503-2; 1-4424-3503-8

"Van Fleet's interactive board book identifies farm animals using simple, playful rhymes. . . . Textures—a woolly sheep, a duck's downy chest feathers—provide a touch-and-feel aspect, while flaps and pop-ups make this a playful excursion." Publ Wkly

Van Hout, Mies

Happy; Mies van Hout. Lemniscaat 2012 52 p.
Grades: PreK K 1 2 3   E
   1. Fishes -- Fiction 2. Emotions -- Fiction 3. Vocabulary -- Fiction 4. Animals -- Pictorial works 5. Picture books for children
   ISBN 1935954148; 9781935954149

In this picture book, "vibrant fish--although not ones found in nature--illustrate emotions in this art piece for children and for adults translated from the Dutch. Each double-page spread is constructed with an image of a fish on one side, in what looks like a chalk drawing on a blackboard. Opposite is a single hand-lettered word, also drawn in chalk or crown, on a jewel-toned, textured sheet. "Brave" is a very small pale fish with a tentative smile, isolated in the lower corner of the black page. . . . The "content" green fish aligns itself in the precise middle of the page; one can almost see it wriggling in its satisfaction. The "shocked" square-ish fish is shocking pink and purple and prickly, with open mouth and round eyes." (Kirkus)

Van Laan, Nancy

Nit-pickin' [by] Nancy Van Laan and [illustrated by] George Booth. Atheneum Books for Young Readers 2008 un il $15.99
Grades: PreK K 1   E
   1. Stories in rhyme 2. Lice -- Fiction
   ISBN 0-689-83898-0; 978-0-689-83898-9
                              LC 00-062077
Family members go to great lengths to rid their child of head lice.

"The lively text is complemented by the over-the-top antics observed in Booth's cartoon illustrations." SLJ

When winter comes; illustrated by Susan Gaber. Atheneum Bks. for Young Readers 2000 un il $16
Grades: PreK K 1 2   E
   1. Stories in rhyme 2. Winter -- Fiction 3. Animals -- Fiction
   ISBN 0-689-81778-9
                              LC 97-32914
Rhyming text asks what happens to different animals and plants "when winter comes and the cold wind blows"

"The rhyming answers use simple and accessible language. Gaber's exuberant acrylic paintings show a child, mother, father, and dog taking a walk through the woods during a snowfall." SLJ

Van Leeuwen, Jean

★ **Amanda** Pig and the awful, scary monster; pictures by Ann Schweninger. Phyllis Fogelman Bks. 2003 48p il (PJF easy-to-read) hardcover o.p. pa $3.99
Grades: K 1 2   E
   1. Pigs -- Fiction 2. Bedtime -- Fiction 3. Monsters -- Fiction
   ISBN 0-8037-2766-6; 0-14-240203-6 pa
                              LC 2001-33519
Amanda pig sees monsters at night, but her parents and her brother find different ways to convince her that there are no monsters

"Van Leeuwen captures childhood emotions perfectly and includes just the right amount of humor. With bright illustrations done in carbon pencil, colored pencils, and watercolor washes on every page, this book will delight the piglet's many fans." SLJ

Other titles about Amanda Pig are:
Amanda Pig and her big brother Oliver (1982)
Tales of Amanda Pig (1983)
More tales of Amanda Pig (1985)
Oliver, Amanda, and Grandmother Pig (1987)
Oliver and Amanda's Christmas (1989)
Amanda Pig on her own (1991)
Oliver and Amanda's Halloween (1992)
Oliver and Amanda and the big snow (1995)
Amanda Pig, school girl (1997)
Amanda Pig and her best friend Lollipop (1998)
Amanda Pig and the really hot day (2005)
Amanda Pig, first grader (2007)
Amanda Pig and the wiggly tooth (2008)

Chicken soup; by Jean Van Leeuwen; illustrated by David Gavril. Abrams Books for Young Readers 2009 un il $16.95
Grades: PreK K 1   E
   1. Chickens -- Fiction 2. Farm life -- Fiction
   ISBN 978-0-8109-8326-7; 0-8109-8326-5
                              LC 2008030824
When they hear that Mrs. Farmer is making soup, all the frightenened chickens run for their lives, but Mr. Farmer finds Little Chickie, who has a bad cold, and he takes her to the kitchen for some nice hot vegetable soup.

"This simple, just-scary-enough story will appeal to preschoolers with its repetition and bright, childlike pen and watercolor illustrations." SLJ

Van Lieshout, Maria

Bloom! a little book about finding love. written and illustrated by Maria van Lieshout. Feiwel and Friends 2008 un il $12.95
Grades: PreK K 1   E
   1. Love -- Fiction 2. Pigs -- Fiction 3. Friendship -- Fiction 4. Butterflies -- Fiction
   ISBN 978-0-312-36913-2; 0-312-36913-1
                              LC 2007-33411
Bloom, a pig who prefers flowers to mud puddles, falls in love with a flying flower," but when the butterfly leaves she is brokenhearted until a friend gives her a reason to smile again.

"Van Lieshout's loosely drawn pen and ink illustrations, mostly on stark white pages, wring Oscar-winning expressions from the slenderest curves and squiggles. The minimalist text begins before the title page, when Bloom's faithful friend urges her to join him playing in a puddle. . . . This paper-overboard book's stylish design and small square format designate it as a natural for Valentine's Day." Publ Wkly

Flight 1-2-3; by Maria van Lieshout. Chronicle Books 2013 40 p. (hardcover) $14.99
Grades: PreK K 1   E
   1. Picture books for children 2. Air travel -- Fiction 4. Airports -- Fiction 5. Counting -- Fiction 6. Airplanes -- Fiction
   ISBN 1452116628; 9781452116624
                              LC 2012033606

This children's counting story, by Maria van Lieshout, follows a boy on a airplane. "What can you see when you go on an airplane journey? 1 airplane, 2 luggage carts, 3 check-in counters, and so much more! Using familiar airport signs, this . . . book introduces little ones not only to numbers, but to the world around them." (Publisher's note)

Hopper and Wilson. Philomel Books 2011 un il $16.99

Grades: PreK K 1   E

1. Mice -- Fiction 2. Sailing -- Fiction 3. Elephants -- Fiction

ISBN 978-0-399-25184-9; 0-399-25184-7

LC 2010-19396

An elephant and a mouse embark on a journey to discover what it looks like at the end of the world.

Van Lieshout "plays up the suspense of the separation with lots of space in the spreads and long waits. . . . [The] story is filled with adventure, emotion, and imagery that supplies lots of effervescent warmth." Publ Wkly

Tumble; a little book about having it all. written and illustrated by Maria van Lieshout; designed by Molly Leach. Feiwel & Friends 2010 un il $12.99

Grades: PreK K 1   E

1. Polar bear -- Fiction

ISBN 978-0-312-54859-9; 0-312-54859-1

When three little bears find a red toy to play with and Tumble claims it for his own, this proves to be not such a good idea.

"This title gently reminds youngsters about the rewards of sharing. . . . The pencil, ink, and watercolor artwork is digitally enhanced and done in van Lieshout's expressive trademark style. . . . A perfect choice for a wintertime story-hour or one-on-one sharing." SLJ

Van Steenwyk, Elizabeth

Prairie Christmas; written by Elizabeth Van Steenwyk; illustrated by Ronald Himler. Eerdmans 2006 un il $17

Grades: 1 2 3 4   E

1. Midwives -- Fiction 2. Nebraska -- Fiction 3. Christmas -- Fiction 4. Mother-daughter relationship -- Fiction

ISBN 0-8028-5280-7

On the Nebraska prairie in 1880, eleven-year-old Emma finds a way to celebrate the spirit of Christmas while her mother, a midwife, delivers a baby on Christmas Eve.

"This memorable tale is beautifully told in clear and simple prose, which is complemented perfectly by the uncluttered, colored-pencil and watercolor drawings." SLJ

Vander Zee, Ruth

Always with you; written by Ruth Vander Zee; illustrated by Ronald Himler. Eerdmans Books for Young Readers 2008 un il $17

Grades: 2 3 4   E

1. Orphans -- Fiction 2. Vietnam -- Fiction 3. Mother-daughter relationship -- Fiction

ISBN 978-0-8028-5295-3

LC 2007009354

Orphaned at the age of four when her village in Vietnam is bombed, Kim is rescued by soldiers and raised in an or-phanage, always finding comfort in her mother's last words "Don't be afraid. I will always be with you."

Mississippi morning; written by Ruth Vander Zee; illustrated by Floyd Cooper. Eerdmans Books for Young Readers 2004 un il $16

Grades: 1 2 3 4   E

1. Mississippi -- Fiction 2. Ku Klux Klan -- Fiction 3. Race relations -- Fiction 4. Father-son relationship -- Fiction

ISBN 0-8028-5211-4

LC 2002-151212

Amidst the economic depression and the racial tension of the 1930s, a boy discovers a horrible secret of his father's involvement in the Ku Klux Klan.

"Cooper's large, warm oil paintings create the perfect sense of time, place, and atmosphere. . . . A sad and poignant story." SLJ

Vanderwater, Amy Ludwig

Forest has a song; poems. by Amy Ludwig VanDerwater; illustrations by Robbin Gourley. Clarion Books 2013 40 p. col. ill. (reinforced) $16.99

Grades: 2 3 4   E

1. Seasons -- Poetry 2. Picture books for children

ISBN 0618843493; 9780618843497

LC 2011052433

In this children's picture book, moving "through the seasons. newcomer [Amy Ludwig] VanDerwater shares a girl's experience of what the forest has to offer. On a chilly spring day, she 'stop[s] to read/ the Forest News! in mud or fallen snow./ Articles are printed/ by critters on the go.'" She encounters the forest in summer, autumn, and winter as well. (Publishers Weekly)

VanHecke, Susan

An **apple** pie for dinner; retold by Susan VanHecke; illustrated by Carol Baicker-McKee. Marshall Cavendish Children 2009 un il $17.99

Grades: K 1 2 3   E

1. Apples -- Fiction 2. Baking -- Fiction 3. Barter -- Fiction

ISBN 978-0-7614-5452-6; 0-7614-5452-7

LC 2008003664

Wishing to bake an apple pie, Old Granny Smith sets out with a full basket, trading its contents for a series of objects until she gets the apples she needs.

"The bas-relief illustrations, made from baked clay and mixed-media of found objects, create a 3-D, Claymation effect. . . . The fascinating tactile details will have young and old poring over the pages. . . . Complete with a pie recipe and notes from both the author and illustrator that cite the origin of the tale (the English folktale 'An Apple Dumpling') and directions on how to make bas-reliefs, the book is a delicious treat to be shared anytime. " Booklist

Varela, Barry

Gizmo; [by] Barry Varela; illustrations by Ed Briant. Roaring Brook Press 2007 un il $16.95

Grades: K 1 2 3   E

1. Stories in rhyme 2. Machinery -- Fiction

ISBN 978-1-59643-115-7; 1-59643-115-6

LC 2006012007

When Professor Ludwig von Glink's contraption gets so out of hand that the City Buildings and Permits Inspector condemns his home, the City Contemporary Art Museum comes to the rescue

"The animation inherent in Briant's colorful line-and-wash artwork bolsters the humor, while Varela's playful sense of language leads to some inspired wordplay." Booklist

Velasquez, Eric

★ **Grandma's** gift. Walker 2010 un il $16.99; lib bdg $17.89

Grades: K 1 2 3   E

1. Gifts -- Fiction 2. Artists -- Fiction 3. Christmas -- Fiction 4. Grandmothers -- Fiction 5. Puerto Ricans -- Fiction 6. New York (N.Y.) -- Fiction 7. African Americans -- Fiction 8. Metropolitan Museum of Art (New York, N.Y.) -- Fiction

ISBN 978-0-8027-2082-5; 0-8027-2082-X; 978-0-8027-2083-2 lib bdg; 0-8027-2083-8 lib bdg

LC 2010005326

Prequel to: Grandma's records (2004)

Pura Belpré Award for illustration, 2011

The author describes Christmas at his grandmother's apartment in Spanish Harlem the year she introduced him to the Metropolitan Museum of Art and Diego Velazquez's portrait of Juan de Pareja, which has had a profound and lasting effect on him.

"The realistic oil paintings reveal a strong and stylish grandmother of great character and a polite child. . . . The sweetly understated story has Spanish words and sentences skillfully woven into the text throughout with translations provided in parenthesis." Kirkus

Veldkamp, Tjibbe

Tom the tamer; illustrated by Philip Hopman. Lemniscaat USA 2011 32p il

Grades: PreK K   E

1. Fear -- Fiction 2. Animals -- Fiction 3. Father-son relationship -- Fiction

ISBN 1-9359-5405-9; 978-1-9359-5405-7

"This tender, loopy, and unconventional work . . . stars a boy who wants to lure his phobic father away from his model railway and into the backyard so that the father can meet the animals he's frightened of face-to-face. . . . Tom purchases a polar bear from the local pet store and discovers that the bear can do an uncanny imitation of an armchair. . . . This success sets the stage for a full-scale animal-furniture renovation. . . . The episodes recall gentler moments from Roald Dahl or Russell Hoban. Similarly, Hopman's illustrations are first cousin to Quentin Blake's, full of fanciful color and a jumble of imagined detail."

"This tender, loopy, and unconventional work . . . stars a boy who wants to lure his phobic father away from his model railway and into the backyard so that the father can meet the animals he's frightened of face-to-face. . . . Tom purchases a polar bear from the local pet store and discovers that the bear can do an uncanny imitation of an armchair. . . . This success sets the stage for a full-scale animal-furniture renovation. . . . The episodes recall gentler moments from Roald Dahl or Russell Hoban. Similarly, Hopman's illustrations are first cousin to Quentin Blake's, full of fanciful color and a jumble of imagined detail." Publ Wkly

Verburg, Bonnie

The **kiss** box; illustrated by Henry Cole. Orchard Books 2011 un il lib bdg $16.99

Grades: PreK   E

1. Love -- Fiction 2. Bears -- Fiction 3. Kissing -- Fiction 4. Mother-child relationship -- Fiction

ISBN 978-0-545-11284-0; 0-545-11284-2

LC 2009012102

As they prepare for a short separation, Mama Bear and Little Bear find a way to reassure each other while they are apart.

"Cole's charming and cheery watercolor and colored-pencil illustrations of Mama Bear and Little Bear enjoying the day before she leaves do much to make this title appealing." SLJ

Verde, Susan

The **museum**; written by Susan Verde; art by Peter H. Reynolds. Abrams Books for Young Readers 2013 32 p. (reinforced) $16.95

Grades: PreK K 1 2   E

1. Picture books for children 2. Stories in rhyme 3. Museums -- Fiction 4. Art museums -- Fiction 5. Art appreciation -- Fiction

ISBN 1419705946; 9781419705946

LC 2012022518

This children's picture book focuses on a girl's experience at an art museum. "A girl in pigtails embodies the emotions elicited by the paintings she sees, leaping, twirling, giggling, and—inspired by the famous Munch work—even shrieking, as she tours a museum gallery filled with European and American masterpieces." (Publishers Weekly)

Verdick, Elizabeth

Mealtime; illustrated by Marieka Heinlen. Free Spirit Pub. 2011 un il bd bk $7.95

Grades: PreK   E

1. Food 2. Etiquette 3. Nutrition 4. Board books for children

ISBN 978-1-57542-366-1; 1-57542-366-9

LC 2010045051

"Pretty much every main lesson adults try to impart about mealtime is covered here: washing hands, using utensils, displaying manners, trying new food, sitting still, and cleaning up. This . . . list of demands is relayed via a group of four beaming multicultural children wearing wild color and set before even more wildly colored backdrops." Booklist

Vere, Ed

Banana! Henry Holt & Co. 2010 un il $12.99

Grades: PreK K 1   E

1. Banana -- Fiction 2. Monkeys -- Fiction

ISBN 978-0-8050-9214-1; 0-8050-9214-5

LC 2009-936514

"Especially noteworthy are the bold graphic illustrations: the digitally scrawled figures are oversized, and in each spread they're set against a different field of solid color. . . . [The monkeys'] faces are remarkably expressive, showing a range of emotions from frustration to desperation to fury. . . . This would be a lively title to share in a toddler storytime, but its simplicity and illustratively conveyed plot make it an enjoyable work for youngsters to pore over solo." Bull Cent Child Books

Vernick, Audrey

Is your buffalo ready for kindergarten? illustrated by Daniel Jennewein. Balzer + Bray 2010 un il $16.99

Grades: PreK K   E

1. School stories 2. Bison -- Fiction

ISBN 978-0-06-176275-8; 0-06-176275-X

LC 2009-11841

"This is a silly book about the first day of kindergarten with one's own buffalo. . . . The story prompts readers to remind the buffalo that finger painting is fun and it's okay to get messy; those hooves could create a masterpiece. Buffaloes (and children) learn how to get along without using their horns. . . . This wacky picture book, with its bold cartoon-like illustrations of a buffalo that snorts, dances, and makes faces, may help apprehensive youngsters to be more at ease about going to school." SLJ

Another title about the buffalo is:

Teach you buffalo to play drums (2011)

Teach your buffalo to play drums; written by Audrey Vernick; illustrated by Daniel Jennewein. Balzer + Bray 2011 un il $16.99

Grades: PreK K 1 2   E

1. Bison -- Fiction 2. Drums -- Fiction 3. Musicians -- Fiction

ISBN 978-0-06-176253-6; 0-06-176253-9

LC 2010007478

Encourages the reader, through practical advice, to support his or her buffalo's desire to play the drums, even if he has quickly lost interest in other activities in the past.

"Several small pictures appear on most pages . . . showing the huge animal trying to engage in human activities like skateboarding and showering, resulting in some very funny scenarios. His expressions are priceless." SLJ

Verplancke, Klaas

Applesauce; Klaas Verplancke, Helen Mixter. Groundwood Books/House of Anansi Press 2012 40 p. $18.95

Grades: PreK K 1   E

1. Anger -- Fiction 2. Picture books for children 3. Fathers -- Fiction 4. Father-son relationship -- Fiction

ISBN 1554981867; 9781554981861

This children's book by Klaas Verplancke is about a father-son relationship. "Johnny's daddy has smooth cheeks, an apple in his throat and sounds like a mom when he sings in the bath. . . . Other times his hands are cold and flash like lightning, and he becomes a thunder-daddy. When this happens Johnny wants to find a new daddy, but he eventually realizes that thunder-daddies don't last forever. And that there's nothing like the comfort that comes from those we love." (Publisher's note)

Vestergaard, Hope

Potty animals; what to know when you've gotta go! illustrated by Valeria Petrone. Sterling Pub. 2010 un il $14.95

Grades: PreK   E

1. Stories in rhyme 2. Animals -- Fiction 3. Toilet training -- Fiction

ISBN 978-1-4027-5996-3; 1-4027-5996-7

"Petrone's cheery digital characters and Vestergaard's decorous yet humorous rhymes invite readers to help civilize the bathroom habits of some uncouth preschool-age animals.

. . . Petrone's wide-eyed cartoon animals capture a broad spectrum of toddler emotions." Publ Wkly

Villeneuve, Anne

Loula is leaving for Africa; by Anne Villeneuve. Kids Can Press 2013 32 p. $16.95

Grades: PreK K 1 2   E

1. Africa -- Fiction 2. Brothers and sisters -- Fiction 3. Adventure and adventurers -- Fiction

ISBN 1554539412; 9781554539413

In this book, by Anne Villeneuve, "Loula has had enough of her terrible triplet brothers and decides to run away to Africa. Luckily, her mother's chauffeur, Gilbert, knows just how to get there. Together, Loula and Gilbert ride camels, cross a desert and, most important, use heaps of imagination in this . . . adventure." (Publisher's note)

"Villeneuve has created a sensitive tale about running away from home. Feeling neglected and ignored, Loula is sitting in a tree with her three favorite possessions and is happy to be away from her "mean, horrible, stinky" brothers. When Gilbert, the family's chauffeur, sees her, he looks up and asks, "What are you doing up in a tree?" She replies, "This is not a tree. This is AFRICA!" What follows is an afternoon of imaginary travel across oceans, jungles, deserts, and restaurants that serve grasshopper sandwiches and ostrich egg soufflé...The ink and watercolor illustrations have the classic look of Ludwig Bemelmans's "Madeline" series (Viking)..." (Library Journal)

Villnave, Erica Pelton

Sophie's lovely locks. Marshall Cavendish 2011 un il $16.99

Grades: PreK K 1 2   E

1. Hair -- Fiction

ISBN 978-0-7614-5820-3; 0-7614-5820-4

LC 2010010055

Sophie loves her long hair, but when it becomes too hard to manage and she decides to get it cut, she finds something generous to do with it. Includes list of organizations that make wigs from donated hair.

"Soft lines in the watercolor illustrations show [the hair's] movement and [Sophie's] delight in it as she twirls and swirls. . . . The playful main character presents the obvious message in a joyous, engaging way." SLJ

Viorst, Judith

★ **Alexander** and the terrible, horrible, no good, very bad day; illustrated by Ray Cruz; with a new preface by Judith Viorst and Ray Cruz. Special limited ed.; Atheneum Books for Young Readers 2009 un il $17.99

Grades: PreK K 1 2   E

1. Day -- Fiction

ISBN 978-1-4169-8595-2; 1-4169-8595-6

LC 2008049478

A reissue of the title first published 1972

On a day when everything goes wrong for him, Alexander is consoled by the thought that other people have bad days too.

"Small listeners can enjoy the litany of disaster, and perhaps be stimulated to discuss the possibility that one contributes by expectation. The illustrations capture the grumpy dolor of the story, ruefully funny." Sutherland. The Best In Child Books

Other titles about Alexander are:

Alexander, who is not (do you hear me?) going (I mean it) to move (1995)

Alexander, who used to be rich last Sunday (1978)

And two boys booed; Judith Viorst; pictures by Sophie Blackall. Margaret Ferguson Books, Farrar Straus Giroux 2014 32 p. (hardcover) $16.99

Grades: PreK K 1 2   **E**

1. Anxiety -- Fiction 2. Talent shows -- Fiction 3. Fear -- Fiction 4. Stage fright -- Fiction

ISBN 0374303029; 9780374303020

LC 2013007871

In this children's book by Judith Viorst, illustrated by Sophie Blackall, "on the day of the talent show, a boy is ready to sing his song, and he isn't one bit scared because he has practiced a billion times, plus he's wearing his lucky blue boots and his pants with all ten pockets. But as all of the other kids perform before him, he gets more and more nervous." (Publisher's note)

"It's the day of the class talent show, and our little-boy protagonist is ready. He's last to go, though, and the nerves sneak up. He freezes, "...and two boys booed." Viorst uses repetition to create a cumulative pattern that she then breaks as the protagonist's confidence falters. Blackall's art masterfully captures the boy's ambivalence. Occasional lift-the-flaps pace the story and offer unexpected visual treats." Horn Book

Earrings! illustrated by Nola Langner Malone. Atheneum Books for Young Readers 2010 un il $16.99

Grades: 1 2 3   **E**

1. Earrings -- Fiction

ISBN 978-1-4424-1281-1; 1-4424-1281-X

LC 2010502964

A reissue of the title first published 1990

A young girl uses various arguments to convince her parents to let her have her ears pierced.

"Viorst homes in on minor childhood crises with the perfect blend of humor and insight, and Malone's expressive and comic figures are miniature character studies in themselves." Horn Book

Just in case; written by Judith Viorst; illustrated by Diana Cain Bluthenthal. Atheneum Books for Young Readers 2006 un il $15.95

Grades: PreK K 1 2   **E**

1. Worry -- Fiction

ISBN 0-689-87164-3

LC 2003-26068

Charlie likes to be ready for anything, imagining that his house could be flooded or a mermaid might kidnap him, but he learns that it is sometimes good to be unprepared

"Blumenthal's colorful, mixed-media illustrations add some good cheer, sly wit, . . . and a companionable canine to the catalog of Charlie's hypothetical 'just in case' concerns." Booklist

The **tenth** good thing about Barney; illustrated by Erik Blegvad. Atheneum Pubs. 1971 25p il $15.95; pa $5.99

Grades: PreK K 1 2   **E**

1. Cats -- Fiction 2. Death -- Fiction

ISBN 0-689-20688-7; 0-689-71203-0 pa

"The author succinctly and honestly handles both the emotions stemming from the loss of a beloved pet and the questions about the finality of death . . . An unusually good book that handles a difficult subject straightforwardly." Horn Book

Viva, Frank

★ **Along** a long road. Little, Brown 2011 un il $16.99

Grades: PreK K 1 2   **E**

1. Cycling -- Fiction

ISBN 978-0-316-12925-1; 0-316-12925-9

LC 2010019751

Illustrations and brief text evoke a bicycle ride, with its ups and downs, sweeping turns, and vivid views.

"Viva's artwork combines supple curves, big areas of soft black background, light blue for water and shading, and the occasional brick-red accent; it's simultaneously stylish and restrained. Simple, lilting text reproduces the smooth, rhythmic pace of cycling and the meditative state of mind it induces. . . . It's the kind of book that creates a mood rather than telling a story, evoking the freedom of traveling, the joy of movement, and the exhilaration of being outside." Publ Wkly

★ A **long** way away; Frank Viva. Little, Brown Books for Young Readers 2013 40 p. (hardback) $16.99

Grades: PreK K 1   **E**

1. Outer space -- Fiction 2. Voyages and travels -- Fiction 3. Ocean -- Fiction 4. Upside-down books 5. Upside-down books -- Specimens 6. Interplanetary voyages -- Fiction

ISBN 0316221961; 9780316221962

LC 2012028757

This children's picture book follows an alien family's journey. "Their alien child starts a downward slide along a yellow path past celestial bodies (and a shoe), through the Earth's atmosphere, past a whale and school of dapper fish, and into the blackest ocean depths. 'Deep asleep,' the final page reads, as the alien lodges on an underwater cliff. The return trip shows the creature rising up through the ocean and back through deep space . . . before being reunited with his family." (Publishers Weekly)

Vogel, Amos

★ **How** little Lori visited Times Square; pictures by Maurice Sendak. HarperCollins Pubs. 2001 un il $14.95

Grades: PreK K 1 2   **E**

1. New York (N.Y.) -- Fiction

ISBN 0-06-028462-5

A reissue of the title first published 1963

This "tells the story of Lori's many misadventures trying to get to Times Square on various modes of transportation, with a slow-moving turtle finally bearing him off." Horn Book Guide

Vries, Anke de

Raf; [illustrated by] Charlotte Dematons. Lemniscaat 2009 un il $16.95

Grades: PreK K   **E**

1. Toys -- Fiction 2. Africa -- Fiction 3. Voyages and travels -- Fiction

ISBN 978-1-59078-749-6

Original Dutch edition, 2008

This "follows a toy giraffe that spontaneously disappears from his child's room to travel through Africa. . . . In postcards sent to his owner/pal, Ben . . . Raf tells of encounters with camels, flamingos, elephants, monkeys, and giraffes. . . . Just in time for Ben's birthday, the toy arrives in the mail, dressed in kente cloth and colored beads. . . . In addition to being a great success with preschool fans of toy tales, this story could also be shared with primary-grade children in conjunction with units on biome study or continents." SLJ

Waber, Bernard

Ask me; by Bernard Waber; illustrated by Suzy Lee. Houghton Mifflin Harcourt 2015 40 p. $16.99

Grades: PreK K 1 2   E

1. Questions and answers 2. Parent-child relationship 3. Parent and child -- Fiction 4. Questions and answers -- Fiction

ISBN 0547733941; 9780547733944

LC 2014009668

In this children's story, by Bernard Waber and illustrated by Suzy Lee, "a father and daughter walk through their neighborhood, brimming with questions as they explore their world. With so many things to enjoy, and so many ways to ask--and talk--about them, it's a snapshot of an ordinary day in a world that's anything but." (Publisher's note)

The **house** on East 88th Street. Houghton Mifflin 1962 48p il lib bdg $16.95; pa $6.95

Grades: PreK K 1 2   E

1. Crocodiles -- Fiction 2. New York (N.Y.) -- Fiction

ISBN 0-395-18157-7; 0-395-19970-0 pa

LC 62-8144

"In an amusing fantasy, Mr. and Mrs. Joseph F. Primm and their young son Joshua move into a new home in New York City and discover a crocodile [named Lyle] in the bathtub. The illustrations detail the wrought iron railings, the graceful doorway with its fanlight, the sweeping staircase, elaborate fireplaces, and ornate chandeliers, characteristic of a comfortable old brownstone dwelling."

"Illustrations have verve and are a perfect complement to the story. Highly recommended." SLJ

★ **Ira** sleeps over. Houghton Mifflin 1972 48p il lib bdg $16; pa $6.95

Grades: PreK K 1 2   E

1. Friendship -- Fiction 2. Teddy bears -- Fiction

ISBN 0-395-13893-0 lib bdg; 0-395-20503-4 pa

Ira is excited at the prospect of spending the night at his friend's house but worries how he'll get along without his teddy bear

"An appealing picture book which depicts common childhood qualms with empathy and humor in brief text and colorful illustrations." Booklist

Another title about Ira is:

Ira says goodbye (1988)

★ **Lyle,** Lyle, crocodile. Houghton Mifflin 1965 48p il $16; pa $6.95

Grades: PreK K 1 2   E

1. Crocodiles -- Fiction 2. New York (N.Y.) -- Fiction

ISBN 0-395-16995-X; 0-395-13720-9 pa

"The illustrations are cartoon-like, lively, and colorful. . . . The situation is nicely exploited with a bland daffiness." Bull Cent Child Books

Other titles about Lyle are:

Funny, funny Lyle (1987)

The house on East 88th Street (1962)

Lovable Lyle (1969)

Lyle and the birthday party (1966)

Lyle at Christmas (1998)

Lyle at the office (1994)

Lyle finds his mother (1974)

Lyle walks the dogs (2010)

Waddell, Martin

Can't you sleep, Little Bear? illustrated by Barbara Firth. special anniversary edition; Candlewick Press 2002 un il $15.99

Grades: PreK   E

1. Bears -- Fiction 2. Bedtime -- Fiction

ISBN 978-0-76361-929-9; 0-76361-929-9

First published 1988 in the United Kingdom

When bedtime comes Little Bear is afraid of the dark, until Big Bear brings him lights and love.

"Firth's brightly lit watercolor and soft pencil illustrations, framed in the dark blue of the night, capture the cozy, physical affection of the story, the playfulness of Little Bear, . . . the shadowy mystery of the moonlit landscape, and the huge comforting presence of a parent who is always there when you call." Booklist

Other titles about Little Bear are:

Good job, Little Bear! (1999)

Let's go home, Little Bear (1993)

Little Bear's baby book (2000)

Sleep tight Little Bear (2005)

Well done, Little Bear (1999)

You and me, Little Bear (1996)

★ **Captain** Small Pig; illustrated by Susan Varley. Peachtree Pubs. 2009 un il $15.95

Grades: PreK K   E

1. Pigs -- Fiction 2. Goats -- Fiction 3. Turkeys -- Fiction 4. Boats and boating -- Fiction

ISBN 978-1-56145-519-5; 1-56145-519-9

Small Pig persuades Old Goat and Turkey to go out on Blue Lake in a row boat with him and fish for whales

"This book pleases at every level. The simplicity of its concept, the ease of its words, and the ink-and-watercolor art's subtle mix of wit and whimsy combine in a comfortable way." Booklist

★ **Farmer** duck; illustrated by Helen Oxenbury. Candlewick Press 1992 un il hardcover o.p. pa $5.99; bd bk $6.99

Grades: PreK K 1 2   E

1. Ducks -- Fiction 2. Farm life -- Fiction

ISBN 1-56402-009-6; 1-56402-596-9 pa; 0-7636-2167-6 bd bk

LC 91-71855

First published 1991 in the United Kingdom

When a kind and hardworking duck nearly collapses from overwork, while taking care of a farm because the owner is too lazy to do so, the rest of the animals get together and chase the farmer out of town

"Hilarious art masterfully captures the expressions of the put-upon duck, the supportive cast, and the slovenly ergophobic who reads the newspaper and chomps on bonbons in bed. . . . With its lilting, large-print text and satisfying resolution, it's as perfect for beginning readers as it is for story hours." SLJ

It's quacking time! illustrated by Jill Barton. Candlewick Press 2005 un il $15.99
Grades: PreK K 1   E
  1. Eggs -- Fiction 2. Ducks -- Fiction
  ISBN 0-7636-2738-0
                                              LC 2004-57039
A duckling and all his family happily await the hatching of his parents' new egg
  "A warm tale. . . . Barton's expressive watercolor and pencil illustrations are appropriately full of life." Horn Book Guide

★ **Owl** babies; illustrated by Patrick Benson. Candlewick Press 1992 un il hardcover o.p. pa $6.99; bd bk $6.99
Grades: PreK K 1 2   E
  1. Owls -- Fiction
  ISBN 1-56402-101-7; 0-7636-1710-5 pa; 1-56402-965-4 bd bk
                                              LC 91-58750
Three owl babies whose mother has gone out in the night try to stay calm while she is gone
  "The illustrations, executed in black ink and watercolor, capture in every feather and expression the little owls' worry and watchfulness as well as their complete joy when Owl Mother returns." Horn Book

The **super** hungry dinosaur; pictures by Leonie Lord. Dial Books for Young Readers 2009 un il $16.99
Grades: PreK K 1   E
  1. Dinosaurs -- Fiction
  ISBN 978-0-8037-3446-3; 0-8037-3446-8
                                              LC 2008-51099
  "When a Super Hungry Dinosaur charges into Hal's backyard, it's up to Hal to teach it some manners and keep himself, his parents, and even his dog from becoming lunch. The charming, naive illustrations look as though they are done in pencil and crayon. . . . Great fun." Booklist

★ **Tiny's** big adventure; illustrated by John Lawrence. Candlewick Press 2004 un il $15.99; pa $6.99
Grades: PreK K   E
  1. Mice -- Fiction 2. Siblings -- Fiction 3. Country life -- Fiction
  ISBN 0-7636-2170-6; 0-7636-3819-6 pa
                                              LC 2002-35004
Katy Mouse teaches her younger brother, Tiny, the names of some of the things they see, including a boot, a snail, and a pheasant, when they go to the cornfield to play games
  "The rich mixture of vinyl engravings, watercolor washes, and printed wood textures gives a timeless flavor to the adventure, as do Waddell's sweet story line and clear sentences." Booklist

Wadham, Tim
★ The **Queen** of France; illustrated by Kady MacDonald Denton. Candlewick Press 2011 un il $16.99
Grades: PreK K 1   E
  1. Imagination -- Fiction 2. Kings and rulers -- Fiction

  3. Parent-child relationship -- Fiction
  ISBN 978-0-7636-4102-3; 0-7636-4102-2
                                              LC 2010039185
Rose wakes up one morning feeling royal and, donning jewels and a crown, she seeks her parents who behave as her royal subjects, causing Rose to wonder what they would think if the queen traded places with their daughter.
  Wadham's "rhythmic prose and comic pacing feel elegant and effortless. . . . Denton . . . wonderfully conveys the story's impishness, emotional subtleties, and familial affections." Publ Wkly

Wadsworth, Ginger
Yosemite's songster; one coyote's story. Ginger Wadsworth, Daniel San Souci. Yosemite Conservancy 2013 32 p. $15.95
Grades: PreK K 1 2   E
  1. Picture books for children 2. Yosemite National Park (Calif.)
  ISBN 1930238347; 9781930238343
                                              LC 2012952115
In this children's picture book, Ginger Wadsworth follows "a coyote that has been separated from her mate. A rock slide divides the pair, and Coyote dashes away, first taking refuge underneath a canvas cabin in Curry Village, and then exploring further. Coyote's travels give Wadsworth many opportunities to point out the park's highlights and show how visitors are enjoying it." (Publishers Weekly)

Wadsworth, Olive A.
★ **Over** in the meadow; a counting rhyme. illustrated by Anna Vojtech. North-South Bks. 2002 un il $15.95
Grades: PreK K 1 2   E
  1. Counting 2. Nursery rhymes
  ISBN 0-7358-1596-8; 0-7358-1597-6 lib bdg
                                              LC 2001-51434
An old nursery poem introduces animals and their young and the number one through ten
  "Although many versions of the verse, both traditional and nontraditional, are available, this is an accessible rendition that children will enjoy in storytime and on their own." SLJ

Waechter, Philip
Bravo! illustrated by Moni Port; [translated from German by Sally-Ann Spencer] Gecko Press 2011 un il $17.95
Grades: PreK K 1   E
  1. Cats -- Fiction 2. Noise -- Fiction 3. Trumpet -- Fiction 4. Listening -- Fiction 5. Family life -- Fiction 6. Father-daughter relationship -- Fiction
  ISBN 978-1-8774-6771-4; 1-8774-6771-5
  "Helena, a trumpet-playing kitten who lives with her mother, father, and little brother, has almost a perfect life, except for one thing. Her father is a shouter who comes from a long line of shouters. She dislikes his yelling so much that she leaves home to find another person with whom to live. . . . The muted, full-color art is delicate and sketchy. The illustrations feature plenty of white space and large vistas that focus the action on the family. Children will respond to Helena." SLJ

Wahl, Jan
The **art** collector; illustrated by Rosalinde Bonnet. Charlesbridge 2011 un il $15.95

Grades: K 1 2 3   E
1. Art appreciation -- Fiction 2. Collectors and collecting -- Fiction
ISBN 978-1-58089-270-4; 1-58089-270-1
LC 2010022760
Oscar is not pleased with his own artistic efforts but treasures his great-grandmother's drawing goes on to collect art throughout his life.

"Created with acrylic paint, pencil, and collage, the precisely drawn illustrations offer pleasing views of Oscar's world. An unusual, potentially eye-opening picture book." Booklist

★ Candy shop; illustrated by Nicole Wong. Charlesbridge 2004 un il lib bdg $15.95
Grades: K 1 2 3   E
1. Toleration -- Fiction 2. African Americans -- Fiction 3. Taiwanese Americans -- Fiction
ISBN 1-57091-508-3
LC 2003-3695
When a boy and his aunt find that a bigot has written hurtful words on the sidewalk just outside the candy shop owned by "Miz Chu," a new immigrant from Taiwan, they set out to comfort her

"The clean hues and supple lines of the pictures support Wahl's gentle message of comfort and tolerance." Booklist

The golden Christmas tree; illustrated by Leonard Weisgard. Golden Book 2010 un il $8.99; lib bdg $11.99
Grades: PreK K 1   E
1. Trees -- Fiction 2. Animals -- Fiction 3. Christmas -- Fiction
ISBN 978-0-375-82747-1; 0-375-82747-1; 978-0-375-92747-8 lib bdg; 0-375-92747-6 lib bdg
A reissue of the title first published 1988 by Western Pub.
"Animals gather to decorate a fir tree and celebrate Christmas together. Wahl's quiet, reverent text is extended by Weisgard's art in which the lines of the animals' fur connect them visually with the fir tree's needles, unifying the pages." Horn Book Guide

Wahman, Wendy
A cat like that. Henry Holt 2011 il
Grades: PreK K 1   E
1. Cats -- Fiction 2. Friendship -- Fiction
ISBN 0-8050-8942-X; 978-0-8050-8942-4
LC 2010026952
A cat presents the characteristics of a perfect human friend.

"Executed with the Photoshop lasso tool, the graphic elements here are standouts. . . . An attractive primer for kids who love cats—or may some day." Booklist

Waldron, Kevin
Mr. Peek and the misunderstanding at the zoo. Candlewick Press 2010 il $15.99
Grades: PreK K 1 2   E
1. Zoos -- Fiction 2. Worry -- Fiction 3. Animals -- Fiction
ISBN 978-0-7636-4549-6; 0-7636-4549-4
LC 2009015137
First published 2008 in the United Kingdom
"Poor Mr. Peek thinks he has suddenly gained a tremendous amount of weight when he puts on his zookeeper jacket

and a button pops off. As he makes his morning rounds, he complains to himself about how fat and wrinkled he is. . . . He does not notice that the zoo animals are worried because they think he is talking to them. Luckily, he returns home to discover that he had inadvertently switched jackets with his son. . . . Waldron's digital-media illustrations humorously convey the alarmed expressions of the animals while the quirky font and creative text placement reinforce Mr. Peek's stream-of-consciousness muttering." SLJ

Walker, Anna
I love Christmas. Simon & Schuster Books for Young Readers 2009 un il $9.99
Grades: PreK K 1   E
1. Stories in rhyme 2. Dogs -- Fiction 3. Zebras -- Fiction 4. Christmas -- Fiction
ISBN 978-1-4169-8317-0; 1-4169-8317-1
"A zebra named Ollie runs down some of his favorite holiday activities. Sweet, soft watercolors show Ollie and his dog decorating the Christmas tree, baking holiday treats with Nanna, and waiting for Santa, creating a cozy, merry accompaniment to the simple rhyming text. This is a great choice for a lap-sit and also as a read-alone for beginning readers." SLJ
Other titles about Ollie are:
I love to dance (2009)
I love to sing (2009)
I love my dad (2010)
I love my mom (2010)
I love birthdays (2010)
I love vacations (2011)

Peggy; a brave chicken on a big adventure. by Anna Walker. Clarion Books, Houghton Mifflin Harcourt 2014 32 p. (hardback) $16.99
Grades: PreK K 1 2   E
1. Chickens -- Fiction 2. City and town life -- Fiction 3. Adventure and adventurers -- Fiction
ISBN 0544259009; 9780544259003
LC 2013034562
In this book, by Anna Walker, "Peggy the hen is contented with her quiet existence and daily routine. When a powerful gust of wind sweeps her up and deposits her in the midst of a busy city, she explores her new surroundings, makes new friends, and cleverly figures out how to get home—with a newly kindled appetite for adventure." (Publisher's note)

"After a gust of wind transports her to the big city, suburban chicken Peggy explores her new surroundings. Walker's ink and photo-collage art is full of clever details that add levity to the story. The subtle color palette remains constant, regardless of Peggy's surroundings, exuding a calm throughout that is emulated by the varied illustration formats, the text, and Peggy herself." Horn Book

Walker, Rob D.
★ Mama says; a book of love for mothers and sons. by Rob D. Walker; illustrations by Leo & Diane Dillon. The Blue Sky Press 2008 un il $16.99
Grades: K 1 2 3   E
1. Faith 2. Stories in rhyme 3. Conduct of life -- Fiction 4. Mother-son relationship -- Fiction
ISBN 978-0-439-93208-0; 0-439-93208-4
LC 2007029827

"This elegantly designed book pairs a series of poems with stunning illustrations to celebrate the bond between mothers and sons. . . . The poems appear in English as well as another language (among them Cherokee, Danish, Hebrew, and Inuktitut). . . . The illustrations . . . are well-researched and lavish, showing mothers in traditional dress lovingly engaged with their sons. . . . The Dillons' breathtaking paintings and the quiet dignity of the poems merit a wide audience." Publ Wkly

Walker, Sally M.

Druscilla's Halloween; illustrations by Lee White. Carolrhoda Books 2009 un il lib bdg $16.95

Grades: PreK K   E
1. Old age -- Fiction 2. Witches -- Fiction 3. Halloween -- Fiction
ISBN 978-0-8225-8941-9 lib bdg; 0-8225-8941-9 lib bdg
      LC 2008-41163

In the time when witches tiptoe about to have their Halloween fun, ancient Druscilla knows her creaking knees will prevent her from being sneaky and sets out to find a silent conveyance for herself, her cat, and her jack-o-lantern

"Walker shows her lighter side in this witty picture book. White's expressive paintings, wonderfully varied in size and approach but unified by style, capture both the comedy and the pathos of Druscillas's predicament." Booklist

★ **Freedom** song; the story of Henry 'Box' Brown. by Sally M. Walker; illlustrated by Sean Qualls. 1st ed. Harper 2012 40 p. col. ill. (hardcover) $17.99

Grades: 2 3 4   E
1. Slaves -- Fiction 2. Gospel music -- Fiction 3. Historical fiction 4. Slaves 5. Magicians 6. Abolitionists 7. Singing -- Fiction 8. Slavery -- Fiction 9. Virginia -- Fiction 10. African Americans -- Fiction 11. Underground railroad -- Fiction
ISBN 006058310X; 9780060583101
      LC 2010024448

In this book, author Sally M. Walker discusses the "rhythm and song sustained [Henry] Brown throughout his years of enslaved labor and inspired him to seek his freedom when his wife and children were sold away from Virginia. [She looks at Brown, a slave who shipped himself to New York, and how he] sang for many years in a church choir." (Bulletin of the Center for Children's Books)

The **Vowel** family; a tale of lost letters. by Sally M. Walker; illustrated by Kevin Luthardt. Carolrhoda Books 2008 un il lib bdg $16.95

Grades: 1 2 3   E
1. English language -- Fiction
ISBN 978-0-8225-7982-3 lib bdg; 0-8225-7982-0 lib bdg
      LC 2007-9952

The members of the Vowel family have a hard time talking until their children, Alan, Ellen, Iris, Otto, and Ursula, are born, and when one of them gets lost one day, it takes their Aunt Cyndy to fix the problem

"Luthardt's bright illustrations, featuring people with cartoonish balloon heads, ably echo the story's silliness. This clever approach to learning vowels will prove far more fun than just the basic recitation that's commonly taught." Booklist

Wallace, Carol

The **pumpkin** mystery. Holiday House 2010 37p il (Holiday House reader) $15.95

Grades: 1 2 3 4   E
1. Mystery fiction 2. Cats -- Fiction 3. Dogs -- Fiction 4. Pumpkin -- Fiction 5. Rabbits -- Fiction 6. Halloween -- Fiction
ISBN 978-0-8234-2219-7; 0-8234-2219-4

Louie Rabbit helps Mocha the dog and Scruffy the cat solve the mystery of why the pumpkins don't grow in the human family's plot in time for Halloween.

★ **Turkeys** together; illustrated by Jacqueline Rogers. Holiday House 2005 38p il (Holiday house reader) $15.95

Grades: K 1 2   E
1. Dogs -- Fiction 2. Eggs -- Fiction 3. Turkeys -- Fiction
ISBN 0-8234-1895-2
      LC 2004-52392

A pointer dog puppy helps a mother turkey figure out how to protect her eggs from being stolen.

"A sweet tale about cooperation and friendship, with a satisfying conclusion. . . . Soft watercolor illustrations add meaning to the text and provide clues for some of the more difficult words. . . . The expressive animal faces are charming and realistic." SLJ

Wallace, Nancy Elizabeth

Pond walk; written and illustrated by Nancy Elizabeth Wallace. Marshall Cavendish Children's 2011 un il $17.99

Grades: PreK K 1 2   E
1. Ponds -- Fiction 2. Animals -- Fiction 3. Pond ecology -- Fiction
ISBN 978-0-7614-5816-6; 0-7614-5816-6
      LC 2010025281

One summer day, Buddy Bear and his mother take a walk around a pond and observe the animals and insects that live there.

"Interspersed in the sequential text are Buddy's love of food and his sense of humor in the form of some nature jokes and puns. Wallace's familiar mixed-media collage illustrations (cut paper, photographs, and colored pencil) make this a visually appealing and informative look at limnology." SLJ

Pumpkin day! written and illustrated by Nancy Elizabeth Wallace. Marshall Cavendish 2002 un il $16.95

Grades: PreK K 1 2   E
1. Pumpkin -- Fiction 2. Rabbits -- Fiction
ISBN 0-7614-5128-5
      LC 2002-834

Companion volume to Apples, apples, apples (2000)

A bunny family picks pumpkins at a local farm and learns pumpkin facts in the process

"Although there are many other books on the topic, this one stands apart because of its simple, yet dynamic collage artwork and the quality and quantity of information that is tucked into the text in all sorts of interesting ways." Booklist

Ready! Set! 100th day! written and illustrated by Nancy Elizabeth Wallace. Marshall Cavendish Children 2011 il $17.99

Grades: K 1   E
1. School stories 2. Rabbits -- Fiction 3. Set theory

-- Fiction 4. Family life -- Fiction

ISBN 978-0-7614-5956-9; 0-7614-5956-1; 978-0-7614-6070-1 e-book

LC 2011001128

Minna's family pitches in to help her come up with the perfect project for the hundredth day of school, from twenty sets of five sticks to two sets of fifty pieces of pasta.

"This is definitely a book that will appeal to children. All of the characters are anthropomorphic brown rabbits done in large, colorful collages. The concepts are shown in a straightforward way that will be useful for introducing and reinforcing the number sets." SLJ

Recycle every day! written and illustrated by Nancy Elizabeth Wallace. Marshall Cavendish 2003 un il $16.95

Grades: PreK K 1 2   E

1. Rabbits -- Fiction 2. Recycling -- Fiction

ISBN 0-7614-5149-8

LC 2001-26050

When Minna has a school assignment to make a poster about recycling, her entire rabbit family spends the week practicing various kinds of recycling and suggesting ideas for her poster

"Using found materials to create the lovely art, the author/illustrator practices what she preaches and invites readers to search for the recycled materials. An activity and a game are appended. While the book's message is obvious, there is enough of a story to keep youngsters interested." SLJ

Other titles about Minna are:

The kindness quilt (2006)

Stars! Stars! Stars! (2009)

Seeds! Seeds! Seeds! written and illustrated by Nancy Elizabeth Wallace. Marshall Cavendish 2004 un il hardcover o.p. pa $5.99

Grades: PreK K 1 2   E

1. Bears -- Fiction 2. Seeds -- Fiction

ISBN 0-7614-5159-5; 0-7614-5366-0 pa

LC 2003-9318

Buddy Bear learns about different kinds of seeds and their uses when he opens a package sent by his grandfather

"The artwork consists of cut-paper collages with shadowing and life-sized photos of real seeds that look as though they can be picked right off the pages. The story is entertaining and educational." SLJ

Walsh, Barbara

★ **Sammy** in the sky; paintings by Jamie Wyeth. Candlewick Press 2011 un il $16.99

Grades: PreK K 1 2   E

1. Dogs -- Fiction 2. Death -- Fiction

ISBN 978-0-7636-4927-2; 0-7636-4927-9

LC 2010040744

A little girl tells about her special pet, Sammy, "the best hound dog in the whole world," and how, after he becomes sick and dies, she comes to know the truth of her mother's words, that Sammy's spirit is everywhere.

"This timeless story, told in straightforward prose, is brought to life in textured, soft-edged watercolor paintings in a predominant palette of blue, green, and gold. The feelings of the protagonist and the playful personality of the dog are palpably rendered in their facial expressions and body language." SLJ

Walsh, Ellen Stoll

Balancing act. Beach Lane 2010 un $16.99

Grades: PreK K   E

1. Mice -- Fiction 2. Animals -- Fiction 3. Balance -- Fiction

ISBN 978-1-4424-0757-2; 1-4424-0757-3

"This deceptively simple and creative book is loaded with fun. Two adorable mice create a teeter-totter using a stick balanced on a rock. A salamander joins one side, creating an imbalance, but then another one of equal weight joins the other mouse, and all is in order—until it happens again with a frog and a bird. . . . Observant children will want to converse about animal and color identification, as well as why the actions and reactions of the animals are creating balances/imbalances on the teeter-totter. The delightful illustrations were done using cut-paper collage and then splattered with acrylic paints. . . . This book is full of wonder and can be used at storytime or one-on-one." SLJ

Hop Jump. HMH Books for Young Readers 1996 32 p. $6.99 E

1. Dance -- Fiction 2. Frogs -- Fiction

ISBN 015201375X; 9780152013752

LC 9221037

Author Ellen Stoll Walsh's book focuses on a frog named Betsy. "Tired of hopping and jumping, Betsy the frog sees the leaves float down from the trees and is inspired to leap and twirl--she calls it dancing. At first the other frogs tell her there is no room for dancing. But she eventually teaches everyone that there is room for hopping, jumping, and dancing." (Publisher's note)

★ **Mouse** shapes. Harcourt 2007 un il $16

Grades: PreK K   E

1. Mice -- Fiction 2. Shape -- Fiction

ISBN 978-0-15-206091-6

LC 2006-13695

Three mice make a variety of things out of different shapes as they hide from a scary cat

"The collage technique works well for distinguishing the brightly colored shapes, and the simple story is pitched perfectly for sharing with the youngest of listeners." SLJ

Other titles about the mice are:

Mouse paint (1989)

Mouse count (1991)

Walsh, Joanna

The **biggest** kiss; illustrated by Judi Abbot. Simon & Schuster Books for Young Readers 2011 il $12.99 E

1. Stories in rhyme 2. Kissing -- Fiction

ISBN 978-1-4424-2769-3; 1-4424-2769-8

LC 2011019442

A celebratioin of kisses from the sleepy goodnight kiss and the splishy splashy fish kiss to the sticky lipstick kiss and finally the best kiss of all.

"The engaging rhymes are perfectly complemented by the colorful, whimsical illustrations. A wonderful cuddle-up-and-read choice." SLJ

Walsh, Melanie

Living with mom and living with dad; Melanie Walsh. Candlewick Press 2012 40 p.

Grades: PreK K   E

1. Toy and movable books 2. Parent-child relationship

3. Children of divorced parents 4. Divorce -- Fiction
ISBN 0763658693; 9780763658694

LC 2011047029

This children's picture book follows a little girl whose parents are divorced. "Sometimes she lives with her mom, and sometimes with her dad. . . . [A] lift-the-flap design juxtaposes how things are in one home versus the other. On her birthday, the girl's mother makes a cake, and the flap lifts to show her dad taking her bowling. . . . Other pages show joint activities--both parents attend a school play, and both are included in a photo album that the girl can look at if she misses one of them." (Kirkus Reviews)

Walter, Mildred Pitts

Alec's primer; illustrated by Larry Johnson. Vermont Folklife Center 2004 un il (Vermont Folklife Center children's book series) $15.95

Grades: K 1 2 3   **E**

1. Reading -- Fiction 2. Slavery -- Fiction 3. African Americans -- Fiction
ISBN 0-916718-20-4

LC 2003-27716

A young slave's journey to freedom begins when a plantation owner's granddaughter teaches him how to read. Based on the childhood of Alec Turner (1845-1923) who escaped from slavery by joining the Union Army during the Civil War and later became a landowner in Vermont

"Walter's spare, dramatic words and Johnson's stirring double-page paintings present a glimpse of the history in a brutal world." Booklist

Walters, Eric

My name is Blessing; Eric Walters. Tundra Books of Northern New York 2013 32 p. (hardcover) $17.95

Grades: PreK K 1 2   **E**

1. Picture books for children 2. People with disabilities -- Fiction
ISBN 1770493018; 9781770493018; 9781770493971

LC 2012955581

In this book, "physically disabled child Baraka and eight cousins live with their grandmother. She gives them boundless love, but there is never enough money or food, and life is hard-love doesn't feed hungry stomachs or clothe growing bodies, or school keen minds. Baraka is too young, and, with his disability, needs too much, and she is too old. A difficult choice must be made, and grandmother and grandchild set off on a journey to see if there is a place at the orphanage for Baraka." (Publisher's note)

Walters, Virginia

Are we there yet, Daddy? illustrated by S.D. Schindler. Viking 1999 un il hardcover o.p. pa $6.99

Grades: PreK K 1 2   **E**

1. Stories in rhyme 2. Maps -- Fiction 3. Automobile travel -- Fiction
ISBN 0-670-87402-7; 0-14-230013-6 pa

LC 97-18220

A young boy describes the trip he and his father make to Grandma's house, measuring how many miles are left at various points on the trip

"This unique picture book combines maps and counting skills with a bouncy refrain that invites kids to join in. . . . The flat, pastel pictures add enlivening details to the repetitive text." SLJ

Wang Xiaohong

One year in Beijing; written by Xiaohong Wang; illustrated by Grace Lin. ChinaSprout 2006 un il map $16.95

Grades: PreK K 1 2   **E**

1. China -- Fiction
ISBN 0-97473-025-4; 978-0-97473-025-7

In this introduction to China and Chinese culture, an eight-year-old girl named "Ling Ling points out famous places as well as some of her favorite spots, describes foods eaten during special occasions, and explains traditions associated with particular celebrations throughout the year. . . . Grace Lin's bright, colorful illustrations and accompanying cartoonlike ink sketches accentuate the narrative's informality and make this engaging personal tour an excellent supplement to classroom textbooks." Booklist

Warburton, Tom

1000 times no; as told by Mr. Warburton. Laura Geringer Books 2009 un il $17.99

Grades: PreK K 1   **E**

1. Polyglot materials
ISBN 978-0-06-154263-3; 0-06-154263-6

LC 2007044270

When Noah's mother tells him that it is time to go, he finds more than a few ways to refuse.

"Gouache cartoon scenes visually reinforce Noah's multilingual vetoes, from a full-page sphinx and hieroglyphics to a small square panel with a text message. Endpapers provide identification of the languages, pronunciations, and cultures that the precocious youngster employs. Delightful fun in its theme and delivery, this story will be asked for again and again." SLJ

Ward, Helen, 1962-

★ The **town** mouse and the country mouse; an Aesop fable. Helen Ward. Candlewick Press 2012 48 p. $16.99

Grades: PreK K 1 2   **E**

1. Fables 2. Mice -- Fiction 3. City and town life -- Fiction
ISBN 0763660981; 9780763660987

LC 2012942271

This children's fable, retold by Helen Ward, is "set in a 1930s-era city at Christmastime. . . . Beguiled by his cousin's amazing tales, the country mouse visits the electric city. Unfortunately the town mouse forgot to mention that the city has a lot of noise, tall buildings . . . and dangerous dogs! . . . In the end the reader understands both why the town mouse loves his exciting life and why the country mouse is content with his peaceful home." (Publisher's note)

Ward, Jennifer

The **busy** tree; illustrated by Lisa Falkenstern. Marshall Cavendish Children 2009 un il $17.99

Grades: PreK K 1 2   **E**

1. Stories in rhyme 2. Trees -- Fiction 3. Forest animals -- Fiction
ISBN 978-0-7614-5550-9; 0-7614-5550-7

LC 2008006005

"In rhyming couplets, an old oak introduces children to the wildlife that lives and feeds in and around it. . . . Handsome realistic oil paintings set on white pages show details of the tree and its denizens in daytime, at sunset, and at night, in fall and in summer. . . . Children will enjoy this brief glimpse at a familiar species that reinforces much that they have already observed." SLJ

What will hatch? by Jennifer ward; illustrated by Susie Ghahremani. 1st ed. Walker & Company 2013 40 p. col. ill. (hardcover) $12.99; (library) $13.89

Grades: 1 2 3   E

1. Animal reproduction 3. Eggs -- Incubation
ISBN 080272311X; 9780802723116; 9780802723123
LC 2011046330

In this children's picture book, "[Jennifer] Ward introduces seven animals that hatch from eggs-sea turtle, penguin, tadpole, crocodile, robin, caterpillar, and platypus. The first spread includes a two to three word 'clue,' and the question, 'What Will Hatch?' On the second spread, the clue's rhyme is completed and the answer is provided in words and illustration (e.g., 'SANDY ball./WHAT will HATCH?/PADDLE and CRAWL-/SEA TURTLE.')." (School Library Journal)

Ward, Lynd Kendall

The **biggest** bear; by Lynd Ward. Houghton Mifflin 1988 84p il lib bdg $16; pa $6.95

Grades: PreK K 1 2   E

1. Bears -- Fiction
ISBN 0-395-14806-5 lib bdg; 0-395-15024-8 pa
LC 88-176366

A reissue of the title first published 1952

Awarded the Caldecott Medal, 1953

"Johnny Orchard never did acquire the bearskin for which he boldly went hunting. Instead, he brought home a cuddly bear cub, which grew in size and appetite to mammoth proportions and worried his family and neighbors half to death." Child Books Too Good to Miss

Wardlaw, Lee

Red, white, and boom! Lee Wardlaw; illustrated by Huy Voun Lee. Henry Holt 2012 32 p. col. ill. (hc: reinforced binding) $16.99

Grades: PreK K 1   E

1. Fourth of July -- Fiction 2. Holidays -- United States 3. Picture books for children 4. Stories in rhyme
ISBN 0805090657; 9780805090659
LC 2011018541

In this children's picture book from author Lee Wardlaw, "[i]t's the Fourth of July! [Readers can] [t]ravel across the country for a city parade, a beach picnic, and fireworks in the park in this . . . celebration of the many cultures and traditions that make America's birthday BOOM!" (Amazon. com)

★ **Won** Ton; a cat tale told in haiku. illustrated by Eugene Yelchin. Henry Holt & Co. 2011 40 p. il $16.99

Grades: PreK K 1   E

1. Haiku -- Fiction 2. Children's poetry 3. Haiku 4. Cats -- Fiction 5. Animal shelters -- Fiction
ISBN 0805089950; 9780805089950
LC 2009029414

A cat arrives at a shelter, arranges to go home with a good family, and settles in with them, all the while letting them know who is boss and, finally, sharing his real name.

"Wardlaw . . . has a fine understanding of the feline mind, and each 17-syllable poem packs a big impact—especially in the first section, which imagines the emotional life of a cat in a shelter. . . . The Japanese haiku theme . . . is

carried through with elements and backgrounds lifted from old woodblock prints. The final page, a delicate painting of the boy nuzzling the cat, is a fitting reward for the boy's patience and Won Ton's resilience. A surprisingly powerful story in verse." Publ Wkly

Wargin, Kathy-Jo

Moose on the loose; written by Kathy-jo Wargin; illustrated by John Bendall-Brunello. Sleeping Bear Press 2009 un il $15.95

Grades: PreK K 1   E

1. Stories in rhyme 2. Moose -- Fiction
ISBN 978-1-58536-427-5; 1-58536-427-4
LC 2009004803

Rhyming text poses a series of questions about how the reader would deal with a moose that is on the loose, in the yard, in the house, or taking a bath

"Children will delight in the antics of both the moose and its young human companion. Bold, bright, cartoonlike illustrations capture the action in a humorous style." SLJ

Warhola, James

Uncle Andy's. Putnam 2003 un il $16.99

Grades: K 1 2 3   E

1. Artists 2. Artists -- United States 3. Motion picture directors
ISBN 0-399-23869-7
LC 2002-7766

The author describes a trip to see his uncle, the soon-to-be-famous artist Andy Warhol, and the fun that he and his family had on the visit

"This catches the excitement that the creative process can engender, both for the established artist and for the dreamer." Booklist

Another title about Uncle Andy is:
Uncle Andy's cats (2009)

Waring, Geoffrey

Oscar and the bat; a book about sound. [by] Geoff Waring. Candlewick Press 2008 27p il (Start with science) $14.99

Grades: PreK K 1 2   E

1. Bats -- Fiction 2. Cats -- Fiction 3. Sound -- Fiction
ISBN 978-0-7636-4025-5; 0-7636-4025-5
LC 2007052195

First published 2006 in the United Kingdom

Bat teaches Oscar the kitten to hear and identify the sounds around him, whether they are made by animals and birds or by a passing thunderstorm

This is "clear and immediate. . . . Spacious digital color illustrations show Oscar the Cat in a meadow with his friend, Bat, who answers Oscar's questions with fascinating scientific detail." Booklist

Other titles about Oscar are:
Oscar and the bird (2009)
Oscar and the cricket (2008)
Oscar and the frog (2007)
Oscar and the moth (2007)
Oscar and the snail (2009)

Warnes, Tim

Chalk and Cheese. Simon & Schuster Books for Young Readers 2008 un il $16.99

Grades: K 1 2   **E**

1. Dogs -- Fiction 2. Mice -- Fiction 3. Friendship -- Fiction 4. New York (N.Y.) -- Fiction

ISBN 978-1-4169-1378-8; 1-4169-1378-5

LC 2007-18332

Cheese, an English country mouse, goes to visit his best friend, Chalk, a dog who lives in New York City, and even though the two of them are very different, they have a great time.

This is illustrated with "expansive, humor-laden art, some drawn in cartoon-strip style. . . . What's best is the sheer exuberance both feel about New York. . . . Kids . . . will enjoy both the travelogue and the unlikely friendship." Booklist

Daddy hug; by Tim Warnes; illustrated by Jane Chapman. HarperCollins 2008 un il $16.99; lib bdg $17.89

Grades: PreK K   **E**

1. Stories in rhyme 2. Animals -- Fiction 3. Fathers -- Fiction

ISBN 978-0-06-058950-9; 0-06-058950-7; 978-0-06-058951-6 lib bdg; 0-06-058951-5 lib bdg

LC 2005017867

"In a jolly, rhyming text, this book describes various animal fathers. . . . The vibrant, painterly illustrations, featuring fathers interacting with their offspring, are filled with action and color. . . . The simple text and warm-hued artwork create a feeling of security that will appeal to children." SLJ

Washington, Donna L.

★ **Li'l** Rabbit's Kwanzaa; illustrated by Shane W. Evans. Katherine Tegen Books 2010 un il $12.99

Grades: PreK K 1   **E**

1. Gifts -- Fiction 2. Kwanzaa -- Fiction 3. Rabbits -- Fiction 4. Grandmothers -- Fiction

ISBN 978-0-06-072816-8; 0-06-072816-7

L'il Rabbit searches for a gift for his grandmother when she is sick during Kwanzaa, and surprises her with the best gift of all. Includes 'The Nguzo Saba' The Seven Principles of Kwanzaa.

"The yellow undertones . . . add warmth to the cartoon artwork. Sweetly capturing the spirit of the season, the story comes in handy as a lovely supplement to resources that provide straightforward facts about Kwanzaa." SLJ

Watson, Renee

A **place** where hurricanes happen; illustrated by Shadra Strickland. Random House 2010 un il lib bdg $20.99

Grades: 1 2 3 4   **E**

1. New Orleans (La.) -- Fiction 2. Hurricane Katrina, 2005 -- Fiction

ISBN 978-0-375-85609-9; 0-375-85609-9; 978-0-375-95609-6 lib bdg; 0-375-95609-3 lib bdg

LC 2009017826

Told in alternating voices, four friends from the same New Orleans neighborhood describe what happens to them and their community when they are separated, then reunited, as a result of Hurricane Katrina.

"The text is lyrical and realistically portrays a child's point of view, deftly describing in a few words how the children are affected. . . . The evocative watercolor-and-ink illustrations in soft pastels and grays limn the devastation but also the good times of the neighborhood to great effect." SLJ

Watson, Wendy

★ **Bedtime** bunnies; story and pictures by Wendy Watson. Clarion Books 2010 un il $16

Grades: PreK K   **E**

1. Bedtime -- Fiction 2. Rabbits -- Fiction

ISBN 978-0-547-22312-4; 0-547-22312-9

Bunnies scamper, scurry, splash, zip, and snuggle as they get ready for bed.

"Rendered in pencil, watercolor, and acrylic paint, Watson's buoyant, gauzy pictures reveal several 'oops' moments: one bunny spills juice down the front of his overalls, and another drops a bar of soap while taking a bath. . . . At once soothing and spirited, this is a charmingly crafted bedtime tale for cold winter nights." Publ Wkly

Watt, Melanie

Have I got a book for you! Kids Can Press 2009 un il $16.95

Grades: PreK K 1 2   **E**

1. Selling -- Fiction 2. Books and reading -- Fiction

ISBN 978-1-55453-289-6; 1-55453-289-2

Mr. Al Foxword is one persistent salesman! He will do just about anything to sell you this book. Al tries every trick of the trade. But just when you're ready to close the book on him, he comes up with a clever tactic you simply can't refuse!

"Charcoal pencil illustrations are digitally assembled and feature bright orange, yellow, and green. Foxword's clever sales techniques make this book funny to the hilt." SLJ

Scaredy Squirrel has a birthday party. Kids Can Press 2011 un il $16.95

Grades: PreK K 1 2   **E**

1. Animals -- Fiction 2. Parties -- Fiction 3. Birthdays -- Fiction 4. Squirrels -- Fiction

ISBN 978-1-55453-468-5; 1-55453-468-2

Scaredy Squirrel would rather celebrate his birthday alone quietly in the safety of his nut tree and avoid any pesky party animals. When all his excessive plans are thrown up in the air like confetti, will Scaredy play dead and cancel, or will he face the music?

"The story unfolds with both humor and some useful etiquette tips. . . . Kids will find much to laugh at and think about. . . . Watt's wry digital illustrations make the most of the perceived mayhem, using a host of graphic conventions to tell her story." Kirkus

Watt, Mélanie, 1975-

Chester; written and illustrated by Melanie Watt. Kids Can Press 2007 un il $16.95

Grades: PreK K 1 2   **E**

1. Cats -- Fiction 2. Authorship -- Fiction

ISBN 1-55453-140-3; 978-1-55453-140-0

"Watt presents audiences with the story of a mouse—or she tries to, but her cat Chester has a red marker and his own idea about the subject of the story: himself. . . . Grades two to four." (Bull Cent Child Books)

"Watt presents audiences with the story of a mouse—or she tries to, but her cat Chester has a red marker and his own idea about the subject of the story: himself. . . . The notion is entertaining and its execution . . . is frequently hilarious. . . . This entertains both as a cat story and as an entry-level metatextual narrative." Bull Cent Child Books

Other titles about Chester are:
Chester's back! (2008)
Chester's masterpiece (2010)

Scaredy Squirrel. Kids Can Press 2006 un il $14.95
Grades: PreK K 1 2   E
1. Fear -- Fiction 2. Squirrels -- Fiction
ISBN 1-55337-959-4
Scaredy Squirrel never leaves his nut tree because he's
afraid of the unknown "out there." But then, something unexpected happens that may just change his outlook.

"With his iconic nervous grin and over-the-top punctili-
ousness, Scaredy Squirrel is an endearing character. Thick-
lined cartoons with bold patches of color, quirky charts and
graphs, and clever asides provide humor that will appeal to
children." SLJ

"Other titles about Scaredy Squirrel are:
Scaredy Squirrel makes a friend (2007)
Scaredy Squirrel at the beach (2008)
Scaredy Squirrel at night (2009)
Scaredy Squirrel has a birthday party (2011)

Scaredy Squirrel Goes Camping; Melanie Watt. Kids
Can Press 2013 32 p. (hardcover) $16.95
Grades: PreK K 1 2   E
1. Fear -- Fiction 2. Camping -- Fiction 3. Squirrels
-- Fiction
ISBN 1894786866; 9781894786867
In this children's story, by Melanie Watt, "Scaredy
Squirrel is not too comfortable with the idea of camping .
. . unless it's on his couch! There will be no mosquitoes,
skunks or zippers to worry about when he watches a show
about the joys of camping on his brand-new TV. But first
Scaredy must find an electrical outlet, and that means going
into the woods!" (Publisher's note)

Scaredy Squirrel Prepares for Halloween; A Safety
Guide for Scaredies. Mélanie Watt. Kids Can Press 2013
64 p. $17.95
Grades: PreK K 1 2   E
1. Picture books for children 2. Halloween -- Fiction
ISBN 1894786874; 9781894786874
This book looks at celebrating Halloween. In eight chapters, Scaredy Squirrel "explains how best to carve pumpkins
(don't use an ax or chainsaw, and 'always go with a friendly
look'), decorate one's home (stick to 'unscary' black and orange items like top hats and popsicles), pick a costume, and
host a party ('Pipe organ music makes a great soundtrack
for dancing. The very gloomy tempo will slow festivities
down.')." (Publishers Weekly)

Watts, Bernadette
The **Smallest** Snowflake. North-South 2009 un il
$16.95
Grades: PreK K 1 2   E
1. Snow -- Fiction 2. Spring -- Fiction 3. Winter
-- Fiction
ISBN 978-0-7358-2258-0; 0-7358-2258-1
"Smallest Snowflake, longing for 'someplace special,'
drifts along through the air until she lands in the window box
of a little cottage. . . . Finally, green shoots push up through
the dirt and snowdrop flowers open on the stalks. . . . Watts
writes a tale as sturdy yet delicate as her artwork. . . . This

quiet yet involving picture book is highly recommended for
reading aloud as winter turns to spring." Booklist

The **ugly** duckling; by Hans Christian Andersen; adapted and illustrated by Bernadette Watts. North-South Bks.
2000 un il $15.95; lib bdg $16.95
Grades: K 1 2 3 4   E
1. Fairy tales 2. Swans -- Fiction
ISBN 0-7358-1388-4; 0-7358-1389-2 lib bdg
LC 00-35125
An ugly duckling spends an unhappy year ostracized by
the other animals before he grows into a beautiful swan
The "detailed double-paged spreads are beautiful. . . .
Watts' active pastoral landscapes, filled with light and movement, capture the changing seasons and the sturdy, unwanted
outsider's search for home." Booklist

Wax, Wendy
City witch, country switch; illustrated by Scott Gibala-
Broxholm. Marshall Cavendish 2008 un il $16.99
Grades: K 1 2 3   E
1. Stories in rhyme 2. Cousins -- Fiction 3. Witches
-- Fiction 4. Country life -- Fiction 5. City and town
life -- Fiction
ISBN 978-0-7614-5429-8; 0-7614-5429-2
LC 2007-28355
While paying a surprise visit to her city-dwelling cousin,
Muffletump misses her home in the country but when Mitzi
leaves the city to see where Muffletump lives, she is just
as uncomfortable until the two, together, conjure a solution.
"Told in rollicking, lyrical text accompanied by bright,
colorful illustrations. . . . Children will want to check this
book out again and again." Libr Media Connect

Wayland, April Halprin
New Year at the pier; a Rosh Hashanah story. illustrated by Stephane Jorisch. Dial Books for Young Readers
2009 un il $16.99
Grades: K 1 2 3   E
1. Jews -- Fiction 2. Rosh ha-Shanah -- Fiction
ISBN 978-0-8037-3279-7; 0-8037-3279-1
LC 2007039812
On Rosh Hashanah, Izzy and his family make lists of the
wrongs they have committed over the past year, and after
they have apologized, they throw pieces of bread into the
water to 'clean their hearts' in a ceremony called tashlich.
"The empathetic, low-key prose makes important points
about personal responsibility without pummeling readers,
while the stylish, keenly observed watercolors convey both
Izzy's sheepish chagrin and the joys of communal tradition."
Publ Wkly

Weatherford, Carole Boston
★ **Freedom** on the menu; the Greensboro sit-ins.
paintings by Jerome Lagarrigue. Dial Books for Young
Readers 2005 un il $16.99
Grades: K 1 2 3   E
1. North Carolina -- Fiction 2. Race relations --
Fiction 3. African Americans -- Fiction 4. Civil rights
demonstrations -- Fiction
ISBN 0-8037-2860-3
LC 2002-13226

The 1960 civil rights sit-ins at the Woolworth's lunch counter in Greensboro, North Carolina, are seen through the eyes of a young Southern black girl.

"Simple and straightforward, the first-person narrative relates events within the context of one close-knit family. . . . The well-composed, painterly illustrations show up well from a distance. A handsome book." Booklist

Sugar Hill; Harlem's historic neighborhood. Carole Boston Weatherford; illustrated by R. Gregory Christie. Albert Whitman & Company 2014 32 p. color illustrations (hardback) $16.99

Grades: 2 3 4   E

1. Harlem (New York, N.Y.) -- Fiction 2. African Americans -- Harlem (New York, N.Y.) 3. Stories in rhyme 4. African Americans -- Fiction 5. New York (N.Y.) -- History -- 1898-1951 -- Fiction 6. African Americans -- New York (State) -- New York -- Fiction 7. Harlem (New York, N.Y.) -- History -- 20th century -- Fiction

ISBN 0807576506; 9780807576502

LC 2013030748

In this book, by Carole Boston Weatherford, "take a walk through Harlem's Sugar Hill and meet all the . . . people who made this neighborhood legendary. . . . Includes brief biographies of jazz [musicians] Duke Ellington, Count Basie, Sonny Rollins, and Miles Davis; artists Aaron Douglas and Faith Ringgold; entertainers Lena Horne and the Nicholas Brothers; writer Zora Neale Hurston; civil rights leader W. E. B. DuBois and lawyer Thurgood Marshall." (Publisher's note)

"Weatherford's poetic, swinging textual rhythms meet Christie's artistic razzmatazz to create one hot picture book. A historic and cultural tour of Harlem's famous neighborhood, the book drops names aplenty. Miles Davis, Lena Horne, Zora Neale Hurston, Thurgood Marshall and W.E.B. Du Bois, among others . . . Sparsely detailed but action-packed, Christie's illustrations echo the lives of the star-studded cast of characters. . . . The backmatter offers biographical blurbs that emphasize the longitudinal impact this neighborhood has had on Harlem and on the nation; birthdates begin in 1868 (Du Bois) and end in the present . . . A fine tribute to the local color of Sugar Hill, who have made America a better and more interesting country for almost a century." Kirkus

Weatherly, Lee

The **scariest** monster in the world; [by] Lee Weatherly & [illustrated by] Algy Craig Hall. Boxer Books 2009 un il $14.95

Grades: K 1 2   E

1. Monsters -- Fiction

ISBN 978-1-906250-40-9; 1-906250-40-5

"A scary, hairy monster with green teeth chases and frightens all of the woodland creatures. One day, he comes down with the hiccups. . . . When the other animals see him sitting on a rock and crying, they develop a novel idea for curing the problem. . . . The large illustrations, done in graphite stick and watercolor paints, are lively, fresh, and expressive, giving personality to the story." SLJ

Weaver, Tess

Cat jumped in! by Tess Weaver; illustrated by Emily Arnold McCully. Clarion Books 2007 32p il $16

Grades: PreK K 1 2   E

1. Cats -- Fiction

ISBN 978-0-618-61488-2

LC 2006039217

An inquisitive feline walks through the rooms of a house, jumping into one mess after another, before landing in the loving arms of its owner.

"Some 26 different verbs describe the cat's movements, infusing the story with plenty of action, and the bright watercolors seem quickly carefully rendered." Booklist

Frederick Finch, loudmouth; by Tess Weaver; illustrated by Debbie Tilley. Clarion Books 2008 un il $16

Grades: K 1 2   E

1. Fairs -- Fiction 2. Contests -- Fiction

ISBN 0-618-45239-7; 978-0-618-45239-2

LC 2007019114

After trying and trying to win a ribbon at the state fair, Frederick finally is rewarded for his true talent.

"This title uses humor to illustrate how even an unusual and often-considered-negative talent can be useful. . . . The watercolor-and-ink illustrations humorously depict the boy's trials without giving away the surprise ending." SLJ

Weber, Elka

One little chicken; illustrations by Elisa Kleven. Tricycle Press 2011 un il $16.99

Grades: K 1 2 3   E

1. Jews -- Fiction 2. Goats -- Fiction 3. Chickens -- Fiction 4. Conduct of life -- Fiction 5. Lost and found possessions -- Fiction

ISBN 1-58246-374-3; 978-1-58246-374-2

LC 2010008918

Retells a story in the Talmud about a family that cares for a lost chicken, turning its eggs into a profit which they later give to its owner.

"Kleven's engaging mixed-media folk-art collages brim with details like a border of cakes and pies, or a coy goat offering a bouquet to Leora. The colors are rich; the textures and patterns beg to be touched, and the ending is likely to leave readers pondering this story." SLJ

Webster, Sheryl

Noodle's knitting; [illustrated by] Caroline Pedler. Good Books 2010 un il $16.99

Grades: PreK K 1   E

1. Mice -- Fiction 2. Animals -- Fiction 3. Knitting -- Fiction

ISBN 978-1-56148-694-6; 1-56148-694-9

LC 2010004920

A mouse named Noodle finds a ball of wool and decides to knit a scarf, which grows so big that she is trapped inside her house.

"Webster's prose makes for a fluid read-aloud, and Pedler's full and double-page paintings are playful, warm, and cozy." SLJ

Weeks, Sarah

Drip, drop; story by Sarah Weeks; pictures by Jane Manning. HarperCollins Pubs. 2000 32p il (I can read book) hardcover o.p. pa $3.99

Grades: PreK K 1 2   E
    1. Stories in rhyme 2. Mice -- Fiction 3. Rain -- Fiction
    ISBN 0-06-028523-0; 0-06-028524-9 lib bdg; 0-06-
    443597-0 pa

                        LC 00-21652

Pip Squeak the mouse is kept awake all night by the drips from his leaky roof

"Short, simple sentences keep the action moving along while a single problem focuses readers' attention. The snappy narrative is coupled with expressive, silly illustrations." SLJ

    Another title about Pip Squeak is:
    Pip Squeak (2007)

    Ella, of course! written by Sarah Weeks; illustrated by Doug Cushman. Harcourt 2007 un il $16
Grades: PreK K   E
    1. Pigs -- Fiction 2. Dance -- Fiction
    ISBN 978-0-15-204943-0; 0-15-204943-6

                    LC 2005-25910

When Ella the pig is banned from bringing her umbrella to the dance recital, she comes up with an ingenious solution to the problem

"Weeks' short text includes lots of repetitive phrases and sound effects that will easily encourage participation. Cushman adds slapstick humor with double-page scenes." Booklist

    Mac and Cheese; illustrated by Jane Manning. Laura Geringer Books 2010 32p il $16.99; pa $3.99
Grades: K 1 2   E
    1. Stories in rhyme 2. Cats -- Fiction 3. Friendship -- Fiction
    ISBN 978-0-06-117079-9; 0-06-117079-8; 978-0-06-
    117081-2 pa; 0-06-117081-X pa

                    LC 2008014199

Two cats that are as different as night and day are nevertheless best friends.

"The simple sentences with ample white space suit the brief snippets of rhyming dialogue between the two characters, and brightly colored watercolor illustrations of the feline alley friends reveal expressions ranging from Mac's sheer glee to Cheese's exasperated disgust. Simplicity of text, action illustrated to lead readers in turning the page, and a satisfying conclusion makes this easy reader a solid selection for all libraries." SLJ

    ★ **Sophie** Peterman tells the truth! illustrated by Robert Neubecker. Beach Lane Books 2009 un il $16.99
Grades: PreK K 1 2   E
    1. Infants -- Fiction 2. Siblings -- Fiction
    ISBN 978-1-4169-8686-7; 1-4169-8686-3

                    LC 2008-51058

A disgruntled big sister reveals unpleasant facts about babies.

This offers "thick-lined cartoon illustrations in bright colors and clear bold type that gets bigger and bigger. . . . The details of messy daily life and the honest, unsentimental expressions of rage and bonding are just right for young children to recognize and laugh about together." Booklist

Two eggs, please; written by Sarah Weeks; illustrated by Betsy Lewin. Atheneum Bks. for Young Readers 2003 un il $15.95
Grades: PreK K 1 2   E
    1. Eggs -- Fiction 2. Animals -- Fiction 3. Restaurants -- Fiction
    ISBN 0-689-83196-X

                    LC 2002-5291

"An all-night diner attracts a wide variety of customers in the middle of the night, including a rhino cab driver, two wolf police officers, and a crocodile street performer and his snake. One by one, they take stools at the counter and order the same thing, 'Two eggs, please,' but each order is different: soft-boiled, hard-boiled, poached, raw (for the snake). The premise is as basic as fried eggs, and handled with a light touch, but Lewin's inviting watercolor and ink illustrations add flavor and expand the story to involve young listeners and readers." Horn Book

    ★ **Woof;** a love story. illustrated by Holly Berry. Laura Geringer Books 2009 un il $16.99
Grades: PreK K 1 2   E
    1. Stories in rhyme 2. Cats -- Fiction 3. Dogs -- Fiction
    4. Love -- Fiction 5. Communication -- Fiction
    ISBN 978-0-06-025007-2; 0-06-025007-0

                    LC 2006022295

Despite a language barrier, a dog and cat fall in love with the help of a buried trombone.

"This affectionate and funny story is told almost musically, in rhythmic . . . verse by expert storyteller Weeks. Berry's exuberant collage illustrations spill over the pages, gorgeously chaotic and filled with heart." SLJ

Weis, Carol
    When the cows got loose; [by] Carol Weis; [illustrated by] Ard Hoyt. Simon & Schuster Books for Young Readers 2006 un il $16.95
Grades: K 1 2 3   E
    1. Cattle -- Fiction 2. Circus -- Fiction
    ISBN 0-689-85166-9

"When a family of big-top performers' eccentric cow herd is on the loose, it's young Ida Mae's job to perform the roundup. . . . Ida Mae narrates in a droll, colloquial voice . . . . and the tension between what her words leave out and what the pictures show makes most of the fun. . . . The expressive mixed-media images . . . will easily draw interest, giggles, and requests for repeated viewings." Booklist

Weiss, Ellen
    Porky and Bess; by Ellen Weiss and Mel Friedman; illustrated by Marsha Winborn. Random House 2010 il $12.99
Grades: K 1 2 3   E
    1. Cats -- Fiction 2. Pigs -- Fiction 3. Poetry -- Fiction
    4. Friendship -- Fiction
    ISBN 9780375854583; 9780375961137 lib bdg;
    9780375861130 pa

                    LC 2009013384

Despite their differences, Porky the messy pig and Bess the fussy cat are best friends and support each other in all their endeavors, from poetry writing to cake baking.

"In between outings with his best friend Bess (a meticulous cat, mother of three kittens), Porky (a messy, disorganized, bachelor pig) is trying to write a special poem for Poem-Reading Day. By book s end, Porky has found the perfect words to celebrate their friendship. Gently humorous and expressive pictures illustrate this odd-couple pair." Horn Book

The **taming** of Lola; a shrew story; a picture book in five acts. illustrated by Jerry Smath. Abrams Books for Young Readers 2010 un il $15.95
Grades: PreK K 1 2   E
1. Shrews -- Fiction 2. Cousins -- Fiction 3. Grandmothers -- Fiction
ISBN 978-0-8109-4066-6; 0-8109-4066-3
LC 2009-00617
Lola, a shrew, is famous all over West Meadow for her temper tantrums, but when her cousin Lester comes for a visit and gets special treatment just because he demands it, Lola begins to rethink her behavior.
"Screwball dialogue and banter, . . . asides from the narrator, and details about the shrew diet . . . combine to keep action and laughs coming. The pacing is even, the goody-goody peacemaking is leavened by the wisecracks, and there's even a surprise ending." Publ Wkly

Weitzman, Jacqueline Preiss
Superhero Joe; written by Jacqueline Preiss; drawn by Ron Barrett. Simon & Schuster Books for Young Readers 2011 un il $16.99
Grades: K 1 2   E
1. Fear -- Fiction 2. Imagination -- Fiction 3. Superheroes -- Fiction
ISBN 978-1-4169-9157-1; 1-4169-9157-3
LC 2009034390
Five-year-old Joey uses his super powers to help his parents out of a sticky situation.
"Barrett's line drawings are rendered in ink and colored digitally. The crisp text is hand lettered. The graphic-novel format and retro atmosphere mimic the comic books whose heroes Joe emulates. Weitzman acknowledges the boy's feelings and provides imaginative solutions followed by more practical ones. An upbeat, humorous selection." SLJ

Superhero Joe and the creature next door; by Jacqueline Preiss Weitzman and illustrated by Ron Barrett. Simon & Schuster Books for Young Readers 2013 32 p. (hardcover) $16.99
Grades: 1 2 3   E
1. Fear -- Fiction 2. Neighbors -- Fiction 3. Imagination -- Fiction 4. Superheroes -- Fiction 5. Tree houses -- Fiction 6. Moving, Household -- Fiction
ISBN 1442412682; 9781442412682; 9781442450752
LC 2012023608
In this book, by Jaqueline Preiss Weitzman, "a moving van arrives and brings the creature next door! Where did it come from? Why is it here? From his window Joe can't see the creature's face, but he can imagine the neighborhood will never be the same. Who can help? It's Superhero Joe to the rescue! But could it be that Joe's fears are much wilder than his new neighbor?" (Publisher's note)

★ **You** can't take a balloon into the Metropolitan Museum; story by Jacqueline Preiss Weitzman; pictures by Robin Preiss Glasser. Dial Bks. for Young Readers 1998 37p il hardcover o.p. pa $7.99

Grades: K 1 2 3   E
1. Stories without words 2. New York (N.Y.) -- Fiction 3. Metropolitan Museum of Art (New York, N.Y.) -- Fiction
ISBN 0-8037-2301-6; 0-14-056816-6 pa
LC 97-31629
In this wordless story, a young girl and her grandmother view works inside the Metropolitan Museum of Art, while the balloon she has been forced to leave outside floats around New York City causing a series of mishaps that mirror scenes in the museum's artworks
"Lively, squiggly ink sketches with characters picked out in watercolor and gouache for accent, along with reproductions of art from the Met . . ., tell a vivid, happy tale." Booklist
Other titles in this series are:
You can't take a balloon into the Museum of Fine Arts (2002)
You can't take a balloon into the National Gallery (2000)

Weller, Frances Ward
The **day** the animals came; a story of Saint Francis Day. illustrated by Loren Long. Philomel Bks. 2003 un il $16.99
Grades: K 1 2 3   E
1. Animals -- Fiction 2. New York (N.Y.) -- Fiction 3. Hispanic Americans -- Fiction
ISBN 0-399-23630-9
LC 2002-6297
A young girl who misses her former home and her animal friends left behind in the West Indies makes new friends at the blessing of the animals at a cathedral in New York City on the Feast of St. Francis
"The acrylic paintings soar as Long looks at goings-on from many different perspectives. . . . Children will like seeing so many animals in such an unexpected place, and Ria's feeling of acceptance makes for a satisfying conclusion." Booklist

Wellington, Monica
Apple farmer Annie. Dutton Children's Bks. 2001 un il $14.99
Grades: PreK K 1 2   E
1. Apples -- Fiction
ISBN 0-525-46727-0
LC 00-46203
Annie the apple farmer saves her most beautiful apples to sell fresh at the farmers' market
"Charming and cheery, [this] story makes a great read-aloud. The illustrations seem to step right out of a coloring book with simple shapes, objects, and bright, crayon-box colors." SLJ

★ **Mr.** Cookie Baker; [by] Monica Wellington. rev ed.; Dutton Children's Books 2006 un il $15.99
Grades: PreK   E
1. Baking -- Fiction 2. Cookies -- Fiction
ISBN 0-525-47763-2
First published 1992
After a day of making and selling cookies, Mr. Baker gets to enjoy one himself. Includes cookie recipes.

"Done in gouache and colored pencil, the artwork features clean lines and flat colors that are as cheery as the cookies' sugar sprinkles." Booklist

Pizza at Sally's; [by] Monica Wellington. Dutton Children's Books 2006 un il $14.99
Grades: PreK K 1 2   E
   1. Pizza -- Fiction 2. Cooking -- Fiction 3. Restaurants -- Fiction
   ISBN 978-0-525-47715-0; 0-525-47715-2
                                        LC 2005026498
With vegetables from her own garden and other fresh ingredients, Sally mixes and bakes hot and bubbly pizzas for her customers to take home or eat in her pizzeria
   "Cheerful, precisely composed gouache paintings accented with photo collages of fresh ingredients add warmth and humor to the story." SLJ

Riki's birdhouse. Dutton Children's Books 2009 un il $15.99
Grades: PreK K 1 2   E
   1. Birds -- Fiction 2. Birdhouses -- Fiction
   ISBN 978-0-525-42079-8; 0-525-42079-7
                                        LC 2008013890
Riki, who loves to watch, feed, and listen to the birds that come to his garden, decides to build a birdhouse
   "Riki's passion for birds is evident, and likely to be contagious. . . . The bold colors, simple shapes and clean lines of the gouache illustrations are in sharp contrast to the details found in the photographic elements cut out and glued onto the artwork. . . . Backmatter includes instructions for building and installing a birdhouse, a recipe for bird-food cupcakes and information about birdbaths, feeders and bluebirds." Kirkus

Truck driver Tom; [by] Monica Wellington. Dutton Children's Books 2007 un il $15.99
Grades: PreK K   E
   1. Trucks -- Fiction
   ISBN 978-0-525-47831-7
                                        LC 2006035911
The driver of a tractor-trailer picks up a load of fresh fruits and vegetables, then drives through the countryside, past small towns, and into the big city, passing farms, construction sites, and many other vehicles, then delivers the produce and relaxes with other drivers
   "The simple text is printed in a large block font that is just right for beginning readers. . . . Clearly drawn gouache paintings are enhanced with meticulously cut photos to add texture and character to the scene." SLJ

Wells, Rosemary
   ★ **Emily's** first 100 days of school. Hyperion Bks. for Children 2000 un il hardcover o.p. pa $7.99
Grades: PreK K   E
   1. Counting 2. School stories 3. Rabbits -- Fiction
   ISBN 0-7868-0507-2; 0-7868-1354-7 pa
                                        LC 99-27021
Starting with number one for the first day of school, Emily the rabbit learns the numbers to one hundred in many different ways
   "Wells manages to find fresh, engaging presentations for that many numbers. Alive with color and thematically relevant decoration, the oversized pages are sometimes di-

vided into several panels, but never feel too busy." Horn Book Guide
   Another title about Emily and her school is:
   My kindergarten (2004)

Hands off, Harry! Katherine Tegen Books 2011 un il (Kindergators) $14.99
Grades: K 1 2   E
   1. School stories 2. Alligators -- Fiction 3. Kindergarten -- Fiction
   ISBN 978-0-06-192112-4; 0-06-192112-2
                                        LC 2010016046
Harry has trouble keeping his hands off his classmates until Tina thinks of the perfect piece of gym equipment to teach him about personal space.
   Wells "builds a sense of drama while showing that she knows kindergarten inside and out. Kids will appreciate her faith in their inventiveness and sense of community—and they'll also enjoy the genial, neatly framed collaged images, which use textured materials to convey the alligators' bumpy skin and vibrant wardrobe." Publ Wkly

   ★ **Love** waves. Candlewick Press 2011 un il $15.99
Grades: PreK K   E
   1. Stories in rhyme 2. Love -- Fiction 3. Parent-child relationship -- Fiction
   ISBN 978-0-7636-4989-0; 0-7636-4989-9
                                        LC 2010040460
While they are at work a mother and father send powerful "love waves" to their child at home, offering reassurance and comfort in their absence.
   "With cozy pastel scenes and gentle verse, Wells makes tangible the powerful emotional connection between parent and child, reminding children that longing and, more importantly, love are both two-way streets." Publ Wkly

Max & Ruby's bedtime book. Viking Children's Books 2010 un il $17.99
Grades: PreK K 1 2   E
   1. Bedtime -- Fiction 2. Rabbits -- Fiction 3. Siblings -- Fiction 4. Grandmothers -- Fiction
   ISBN 978-0-670-01141-4; 0-670-01141-X
                                        LC 2009-49441
At bedtime, Grandma tells Max and Ruby three favorite stories about themselves
   "Brightly illustrated and filled with her customary cheer, Wells's latest Max and Ruby book should entertain both old and new fans of these lively siblings." Publ Wkly

Max & Ruby's treasure hunt; by Rosemary Wells. Viking 2012 32 p. (hardcover) $17.99
Grades: PreK K   E
   1. Rabbits -- Fiction 2. Grandmothers -- Fiction 3. Brothers and sisters -- Fiction 4. Treasure hunt (Game) -- Fiction
   ISBN 0670063177; 9780670063178
                                        LC 2011048535
This children's book by Rosemary Wells presents a "return adventure for Max and Ruby. . . . When a thunderstorm ruins Ruby's tea party, Grandma suggests the four bunnies have a treasure hunt. . . . The final treasure box has five gold coins filled with chocolate -- but wait, there are only four bunnies! They decide to give the fifth to Lily's doll, Dagmar,

but where is she? . . . [T]he bunnies retrace their steps and clues to find the doll." (Kirkus)

Max and Ruby at the Warthogs' wedding; by Rosemary Wells. Viking 2014 40 p. color illustrations (hardcover) $17.99
Grades: PreK K 1   E
    1. Rabbits -- Fiction 2. Warthogs -- Fiction 3. Weddings -- Fiction 4. Lost and found possessions -- Fiction
    ISBN 0670784613; 9780670784615
             LC 2014001450
    In this children's book, by Rosemary Wells, "Max has lost the wedding ring! How can the Warthogs wedding go on without the ring? Max and Ruby lead the search through the grand hotel. Down to the laundry, up to the towers, back to the conservatory they run, following the map in Grandmother's Bunnyphone." (Publisher's note)
    "Max isn't excited to be a ring bearer, so he stashes his Gob Smacker in his pocket to play with. When the toy ejects the wedding ring, Max, Ruby, and Louise consult Grandma's cellphone map to track it down. Wells's beloved characters are their usual entertaining selves, and readers will enjoy navigating through the timely adventure via maps under 'iBunny' lift-the-flaps." Horn Book

★ **Morris's** disappearing bag. Viking 1999 un il hardcover o.p. pa $6.99
Grades: PreK K 1 2   E
    1. Rabbits -- Fiction 2. Christmas -- Fiction
    ISBN 0-670-88721-8; 0-14-230004-7 pa
             LC 00-267633
    First published 1975 by Dial Bks. for Young Readers
    Morris is so disappointed with his Christmas present that he invents a disappearing bag, which gives him a chance to share his brother's and sister's gifts
    In this version "Morris re-appears in a full-color, full-size edition of the Christmas day story." Horn Book Guide

★ **Noisy** Nora; with all new illustrations [by] Rosemary Wells. Dial Bks. for Young Readers 1997 un il $15.99; pa $6.99
Grades: PreK K 1 2   E
    1. Stories in rhyme 2. Mice -- Fiction
    ISBN 0-670-88722-6; 0-14-056728-3 pa
    A newly illustrated edition of the title first published 1973
    Little Nora, tired of being ignored, tries to gain her family's attention by being noisy. When this doesn't work Nora disappears but returns when she is sure she has been missed
    "All new illustrations infuse this much-loved picture book . . . . with energy. Vibrant colors and a larger format make the characters seem to jump out at readers." SLJ

Otto runs for President. Scholastic Press 2008 un il $15.99
Grades: K 1 2   E
    1. School stories 2. Dogs -- Fiction 3. Politics -- Fiction
    ISBN 978-0-545-03722-8; 0-545-03722-0
             LC 2007024816
    While the popular Tiffany and athletic Charles make increasingly outrageous promises in their campaigns for President of Canine Country Day School, Otto quietly enters the race, vowing only to try to do what students really want.

"Wells' canine coterie . . . is satisfyingly personable and appealing, and kids will find the knowledge they accrue from the book very useful." Booklist

Read to your bunny. Scholastic 1998 un il $7.95; pa $3.99
Grades: PreK K   E
    1. Stories in rhyme 2. Rabbits -- Fiction 3. Books and reading -- Fiction
    ISBN 0-590-30284-1; 0-439-08717-1 pa
             LC 97-17704
    Brief rhyming text and colorful illustrations tell what happens when parents and children share twenty minutes a day reading
    "Each line of text gets one of Wells' delightful bordered pictures of parents and children at all sorts of activities, from bathing to skating, but always with a book in hand." Booklist

★ **Ruby's** beauty shop. Viking 2002 un il $16.99; pa $6.99
Grades: PreK K 1 2   E
    1. Rabbits -- Fiction 2. Siblings -- Fiction 3. Beauty shops -- Fiction
    ISBN 0-670-03553-X; 0-14-240194-3 pa
             LC 2001-7730
    Louise and Ruby use Louise's "Deluxe Beauty Kit" to give Max a make-over, but when Grandma calls to schedule her own make-over, she makes an appointment with Max
    "Wells is in top form. . . . The author's affinity for kid-based glee is playfully evident." Bull Cent Child Books
    Other titles about Max and Ruby are:
Bunny cakes (1997)
Bunny mail (2004)
Bunny money (1997)
Bunny party (2001)
Max and Ruby's bedtime book (2010)
Max and Ruby's first Greek myth: Pandora's box (1993)
Max and Ruby's Midas: another Greek myth (1995)
Max cleans up (2000)
Max counts his chickens (2007)
Max's ABC (2006)
Max's bath (1985)
Max's bedtime (1985)
Max's birthday (1985)
Max's breakfast (1985)
Max's bunny business (2008)
Max's chocolate chicken (1989)
Max's Christmas (1986)
Max's dragon shirt (1991)
Max's first word (1979)
Max's new suit (1979)
Max's ride (1979)
Max's toys (1979)

Shy Charles; [by] Rosemary Wells. Viking 2001 un il hardcover o.p. pa $5.99
Grades: PreK K 1 2   E
    1. Stories in rhyme 2. Mice -- Fiction
    ISBN 0-670-88729-3; 0-14-056843-3 pa
             LC 2001-271649
    A reissue of the title first published 1988 by Dial Books for Young Readers

Stella's starliner; Rosemary Wells. Candlewick Press 2014 32 p. color illustrations $15.99

Grades: PreK K 1 2 3   E

1. Mobile homes 2. Bullies -- Fiction 3. Family life -- Fiction

ISBN 0763614955; 9780763614959

LC 2013943104

In this children's book, by Rosemary Wells, "Stella lives in a sparkling home on wheels. . . . Her home is called the Starliner, and it has everything Stella and her mama and daddy need to be happy. Until, that is, some big weasels pop up along the road, saying mean things about the Starliner. Mama comes to soothe away the hurt, and Daddy hitches their home to a truck and drives it away to a brand-new place, where Stella meets friends who are as enchanted as she is with her shiny home." (Publisher's note)

"A little fox lives contentedly with her family in Airstream-style trailer, a small but ingenious living space . . . Stella's sense of security evaporates when a gang of weasels mocks the Starliner . . . but when Stella's Daddy hitches the trailer to his pickup truck and moves the family to a place where there are palm trees and shimmering water, Stella makes new friends who think her life in the Starliner is worthy of 'A squillionaire!' Curiously, Wells never clarifies the reason behind the relocation, and so a story that draws so much power from its sense of emotional truth concludes with an ending that seems almost too magical. . . . as income inequality takes it toll on more and more children, this story and its heroine are an important reminder of just how resilient families can and must be." Pub Wkly

★ **Time**-out for Sophie; by Rosemary Wells. Viking Childrens books 2013 32 p. (hardcover) $15.99

Grades: PreK K 1   E

1. Mice -- Fiction 2. Picture books for children 3. Bad behavior -- Fiction 4. Behavior -- Fiction 5. Family life -- Fiction

ISBN 0670785113; 9780670785117

LC 2012015263

In this children's book, "after getting sent to time-out for unnecessary roughness during dinner with Mama . . . and upsetting the laundry Daddy has folded . . . , Sophie comes up against a master: Granny. Instead of giving Sophie a time-out for repeated eyeglasses-snatching, Granny gives herself one, moving from the sofa to the rocking chair, where she sits implacably, arms folded." (Publishers Weekly)

Use your words, Sophie; Rosemary Wells. Viking, published by Penguin Group 2015 32 p. (hardcover) $16.99

Grades: PreK K   E

1. Language and languages 2. Speech -- Fiction 3. Babies -- Fiction 4. Sisters -- Fiction 5. Communication -- Fiction 6. Names, Personal -- Fiction

ISBN 0670016632; 9780670016631

LC 2014011450

In this children's book by Rosemary Wells "Sophie knows lots of words, but she doesn't always use them. It's more fun to speak in hyena talk or space language. But when her new baby sister arrives, Sophie is the only one who can find out what she really wants." (Publisher's note)

A **Visit** to Dr. Duck; Rosemary Wells. 1st board book edition Candlewick Press 2014 30 p. color illustrations (board book) $7.99

Grades: PreK   E

1. Ducks -- Fiction 2. Physician-patient relationship -- Fiction

ISBN 9780763672294; 0763672297

LC 2013948640

"Little guinea pig Felix eats too many "chocolate blimpies" and doesn't feel well the next day. His mama tries chamomile tea and fresh air; finally, she takes him to see Dr. Duck." (Horn Book)

"The lovely illustrations are rendered in watercolor, ink, and other media. This soothing book will resonate with its young audience who will inevitably be in Felix's position one day." SLJ

★ **Yoko**. Hyperion Bks. for Children 1998 un il $14.95; pa $6.99

Grades: PreK K 1 2   E

1. School stories 2. Cats -- Fiction 3. Food -- Fiction 4. Japanese Americans -- Fiction

ISBN 0-7868-0395-9; 1-4231-1983-5 pa

LC 98-12342

When Yoko the cat brings sushi to school for lunch, her classmates make fun of what she eats—until one of them tries it for himself

"Wells sets the story in an active preschool classroom, and her clear ink-and-watercolor pictures have never been more expressive and tender, with a range of animal characters that are endearingly human in body language and expression." Booklist

Other titles about Yoko are:

Yoko writes her name (2008)

Yoko's paper cranes (2001)

Yoko's world of kindness (2005)

Yoko's show and tell (2010)

Yoko learns to read; Rosemary Wells. Disney-Hyperion Books 2012 32 p.

Grades: PreK K 1   E

1. Cats -- Fiction 2. Schools -- Fiction 3. Books and reading -- Fiction 4. Japanese Americans -- Fiction 5. Mothers and daughters -- Fiction

ISBN 1423138236; 9781423138235

LC 2011010868

This children's story by Rosemary Wells tells of a cat learning how to read. "Like her classmates, Yoko yearns to see her name on the "book tree" at school. . . . Her mother only reads Japanese, and, oddly, they own just the three books. A trip to the library solves at least one of these problems, and Yoko's determination carries her along as she sounds out words and uses pictures to predict plot. . . . The final picture shows Yoko beginning to teach her mother the English alphabet." (Kirkus)

Wentworth, Marjory

Shackles; by Marjory Heath Wentworth; illustration by Leslie Darwin Pratt-Thomas. Legacy 2009 un il $16.99

Grades: 2 3 4 5   E

1. Slavery -- Fiction 2. South Carolina -- Fiction 3. African Americans -- Fiction

ISBN 978-0-93310-106-7; 0-93310-106-6

"Hunter, 11, watches his pesky little brothers dig for buried treasure in their backyard on Sullivan's Island, South Carolina. When they dig up 'an armful of mud and metal,' their neighbor . . . explains to them that what they have found are shackles used on slaves to prevent their escape. . . . Based on a true story, this compelling picture book speaks in clear, lyrical prose, true to Hunter's perspective, with beautiful oil paintings." Booklist

Wewer, Iris

My wild sister and me. North-South 2011 un il $16.95

Grades: PreK K 1 2   E

1. Siblings -- Fiction

ISBN 978-0-7358-4003-4; 0-7358-4003-2

Having a wild big sister—who can be a giraffe one day, a giant bear the next, and a racing rabbit the day after that—is just about the very best thing that can happen to little brother.

"With great sensitivity and sweetness, German writer Wewer probes the never-quite-settled nature of sibling relationships. . . . Wewer doesn't promise an end to the hostilities, but her honesty will touch siblings on both sides of the age divide." Publ Wkly

Whatley, Bruce

Clinton Gregory's secret; [by] Bruce Whatley. Abrams Books for Young Readers 2008 un il $15.95

Grades: K 1 2   E

1. Dreams -- Fiction

ISBN 978-0-8109-9364-8; 0-8109-9364-3

LC 2007012760

Clinton Gregory has fantastic adventures every night, from fighting dragons to flying around the world with his friends, and he keeps each one a secret.

"Everything is big in Whatley's colorful and fantastical spreads, which include details sure to appeal to children. . . . An entertaining addition to help wind down the day." SLJ

Wait! No paint! written and illustrated by Bruce Whatley. HarperCollins Pubs. 2001 31p il hardcover o.p. pa $6.99

Grades: PreK K 1 2   E

1. Pigs -- Fiction 2. Wolves -- Fiction 3. Illustrators -- Fiction

ISBN 0-06-028270-3; 0-06-028271-1 lib bdg; 0-06-443546-6 pa

LC 00-61351

The three little pigs are in their usual trouble with the big bad wolf, until a mysterious Voice gets involved and mixes things up

"The 'Voice' is the careless illustrator of the story, and . . . he's run out of red paint! . . . A quirky retelling of a perennial favorite, this may appeal most to early-elementary-age children, who will delight in the picture's conceptual surprises." Booklist

Wheeler, Lisa

★ **Boogie** knights; words by Lisa Wheeler; pictures by Mark Siegel. Atheneum Books for Young Readers 2008 un il $16.99

Grades: PreK K 1   E

1. Stories in rhyme 2. Parties -- Fiction 3. Monsters -- Fiction 4. Knights and knighthood -- Fiction

ISBN 978-0-689-87639-4; 0-689-87639-4

LC 2007-24158

When the knights of the castle are awakened by the noise from the Madcap Monster Ball, they decide to join the party.

"Wheeler's rhythmic text is filled with taut rhymes, alliteration, and vivid images. . . . Done in charcoal, pencil, and Photoshop, Siegel's sophisticated, graphic-novel-style artwork . . . demands a second look. . . . Sepia tones, splashes of color, silhouettes, and outline sketches cleverly underscore the plot elements and keep the pages interesting." SLJ

Bubble gum, bubble gum; illustrated by Laura Huliska-Beith. Little, Brown and Co. 2004 un il $15.99

Grades: PreK K 1 2   E

1. Stories in rhyme 2. Animals -- Fiction

ISBN 0-316-98894-4

LC 2002-16268

After a variety of animals get stuck one by one in bubble gum melting in the road, they must survive encounters with a big blue truck and a burly black bear.

"A fast-paced, rhyming story with vibrant, bouncing illustrations." SLJ

Castaway cats; story by Lisa Wheeler; art by Ponder Goembel. Atheneum Books for Young Readers 2006 un il $16.95

Grades: PreK K 1 2   E

1. Stories in rhyme 2. Cats -- Fiction 3. Survival after airplane accidents, shipwrecks, etc. -- Fiction

ISBN 0-689-86232-6

LC 2004-541

Fifteen felines find themselves marooned on an island and are not sure what to do.

"This delightful book is told in verses that become smoother as the cats cooperate and find their groove. . . . Goembel's illustrations, done in acrylic and ink, are fantastic and provide wonderful insight into the side stories developing as the book progresses." SLJ

★ **Jazz** baby; illustrations by R. Gregory Christie. Harcourt 2007 un il $16

Grades: PreK K 1   E

1. Stories in rhyme 2. Infants -- Fiction 3. Jazz music -- Fiction 4. Family life -- Fiction

ISBN 0-15-202522-7; 978-0-15-202522-9

LC 2006-09236

Baby and the family make music. "Ages one to three." (Bull Cent Child Books)

"The percussive text scans like a musical dream, a nearly flawless scat on music, dance, and the contagious joy of jazz. Christie's gouache illustrations—in a sixties palette of olive, gold, and brick—feature characters with fluid bodies and mobile faces that fill the images with movement and energy." Booklist

★ **Old** Cricket; illustrations by Ponder Goembel. Atheneum Bks. for Young Readers 2003 un il $16.95

Grades: PreK K 1 2   **E**
    1. Crickets -- Fiction
    ISBN 0-689-84510-3
                     LC 2002-2199
Old Cricket doesn't feel like helping his wife and neighbors to prepare for winter and so he pretends to have all sorts of ailments that require the doctor's care, but hungry Old Crow has other ideas
    "Wheeler invests her delightful tale with all the characteristics of a good fable, and Goembel's sharp, highly detailed acrylic artwork gives a clever, humorous bug's-eye view of the world." Booklist

The **pet** project; cute and cuddly vicious verses. by Lisa Wheeler; illustrated by Zachariah OHora. Atheneum Books for Young Readers 2013 40 p. col. ill. (hardcover) $16.99
Grades: K 1 2 3 4 5   **E**
    1. Stories in rhyme 2. Pets -- Fiction 3. Animals -- Fiction
    ISBN 1416975950; 9781416975953
                     LC 2011029647
This children's book, by Lisa Wheeler, illustrated by Zachariah O'Hora, presents a series of poems focused on animals and pets. "If you think you'd like a cute and cuddly pet, you may need to do some research. . . . Join one budding young scientist as she catalogs the pros and pitfalls of potential pet ownership in this assortment of zany . . . poems that will change the way you look at cuddly animals--and give you the giggles." (Publisher's note)

Ugly Pie; illustrated by Heather Solomon. Harcourt 2010 un il $16
Grades: PreK K 1   **E**
    1. Pies -- Fiction 2. Bears -- Fiction
    ISBN 978-0-15-216754-7; 0-15-216754-4
                     LC 2008-4535
After baking a scrumptious Ugly Pie, made from ingredients donated by his neighbors, Ol' Bear invites everyone over for a slice. Includes pie recipe.
    "Large, bright watercolors, acrylics, and collage trace the bear's search as he goes from house to house. . . . This humorous tale should appeal greatly to little cubs everywhere." SLJ

Whelan, Gloria
The **listeners**; written by Gloria Whelan; illustrated by Mike Benny. Sleeping Bear Press 2009 un il $17.95
Grades: 1 2 3   **E**
    1. Slavery -- Fiction 2. African Americans -- Fiction
    ISBN 978-1-58536-419-0; 1-58536-419-3
                     LC 2009005436
After a day of picking cotton in late 1860, Ella May, a young slave, joins her friends Bobby and Sue at their second job of listening outside the windows of their master's house for useful information
    This is "a spare, lyrical narrative. . . . Benny's unframed, dusk-toned, double-page paintings emphasize the stark contrast between slave shacks and plantation mansion." Booklist

★ **Queen** Victoria's Bathing Machine; by Gloria Whelan; illustrated by Nancy Carpenter. Simon & Schuster 2014 40 p. $17.99

Grades: K 1 2 3   **E**
    1. Swimming 2. .Swimming
    ISBN 1416927530; 9781416927532
In this picture book, by Gloria Whelan, "Prince Albert comes up with a royally creative solution to Queen Victoria's modesty. . . . She loves to swim, but can't quite figure out how to get to the water without her devoted subjects glimpsing her swimming suit. (Because, of course, such a sight would compromise her regal dignity.) Fortunately for the water-loving monarch, it's Prince Albert to the rescue with an invention fit for a queen!" (Publisher's note)
    "Modesty decreed that Queen Victoria mustn't be seen in her bathing costume. It's Prince Albert to the rescue with a queen-sized bathing machine. This entertaining story nicely encapsulates a curious bit of social history, with a jaunty tall-tale tone governing a rhymed text. The stifling frills of Victorian dress; the loving couple's delight in each other--Carpenter renders each in comical detail." Horn Book

Waiting for the owl's call; [illustrated by] Pascal Milelli. Sleeping Bear Press 2009 un il (Tales of the world) $17.95
Grades: 2 3 4 5   **E**
    1. Weaving -- Fiction 2. Afghanistan -- Fiction 3. Child labor -- Fiction 4. Rugs and carpets -- Fiction
    ISBN 978-1-58536-418-3; 1-58536-418-5
                     LC 2009005437
For generations the women of Zulviya's family have earned their living by weaving rugs by hand. During one work day, Zulviya will tie thousands of knots. As she sits at her work, Zulviya weaves not one but two patterns. The pattern on the loom will become a fine rug. She weaves a second pattern in her mind.
    "Impressionistic paintings in muted colors accompany Zulviya's lyrical description of her Afghan homeland and her yearning to escape 'the shadow of the loom.' An author's note provides details about illegal child labor in the Afghani rug-making industry." Horn Book Guide

Yuki and the one thousand carriers; written by Gloria Whelan; illustrated by Yan Nascimbene. Sleeping Bear Press 2008 un il (Tales of the world) $17.95
Grades: 1 2 3   **E**
    1. Haiku -- Fiction 2. Japan -- Fiction 3. Voyages and travels -- Fiction
    ISBN 978-1-58536-352-0; 1-58536-352-9
                     LC 2007046318
In Japan, as a provincial governor, his wife, and daughter Yuki, followed by 1,000 attendants, travel the historic Tokaido Road to the Shogun's palace in Edo, Yuki keeps up with her lessons by writing poems describing the journey
    "Nascimbene stays true to Yuki's childish perspective. . . . Accompanying the simple prose narrative, are haiku . . . that express intense feelings in clear, casual words." Booklist

Whitaker, Zai
Kali and the rat snake; story by Zai Whitaker; illustrations by Srividya Natarajan. Kane/Miller 2006 un il $15.95
Grades: 1 2 3   **E**
    1. School stories 2. India -- Fiction 3. Snakes -- Fiction 4. Prejudices -- Fiction
    ISBN 1-933605-10-3

First published 2000 in India

"Kali has always been proud of his father, who is the best snake catcher in their Indian village. But when he attends school, the children make fun of his Irula ways. . . . But one day the classroom is visited by a six-foot-long rat snake. . . . Kali grabs it and becomes the class hero. The text is smoothly written, with lots of cultural details. . . . Natarajan's stylized illustrations are a mixture of smaller pencil drawings and luscious larger paintings that seem to be done on silk." SLJ

White, Dianne

★ **Blue** on blue; Dianne White; illustrated by Beth Krommes. Beach Lane Books 2014 48 p. (hardcover) $17.99

Grades: PreK K 1 2   E

1. Stories in rhyme 2. Rain -- Fiction 3. Storms -- Fiction 4. Rain and rainfall -- Fiction

ISBN 1442412674; 9781442412675; 9781442456877

LC 2012014239

In this children's book by Dianne White, illustrating by Beth Krommes, readers will "Join a farming family as they experience the full range of a thrilling seaside thunderstorm--from the wild wind and the very first drops; to the pouring, pouring rain; to the wonderful messy mud after the sun returns!" (Publisher's note)

"A beautiful sunny day darkens as clouds gather and rain arrives. From morning till bedtime, the story follows a young family on their farm. Rhyming, spare text augments the striking scratchboard and watercolor illustrations...The combination of limited, strong text; rich illustrations; and child-centric perspective make this a strong choice for storytimes and one-on-one sharing." SLJ

White, Linda

Too many turkeys; illustrated by Megan Lloyd. Holiday House 2010 un il $16.95

Grades: K 1 2 3   E

1. Turkeys -- Fiction 2. Farm life -- Fiction

ISBN 978-0-8234-2084-1; 0-8234-2084-1

LC 2008049210

Chaos ensues when Farmer Fred's wife fertilizes her beautiful garden with an secret ingredient that attracts turkeys from miles around.

"Bright watercolors wash over detailed illustrations. . . . Text moves readers forward with italicized first-person ruminations and the occasional 'but then . . .' encouragement to turn the page. An engaging story, . . . this book is a welcome addition for all libraries." SLJ

Whiting, Sue

The **firefighters**; [by] Sue Whiting; illustrated by Donna Rawlins. Candlewick Press 2008 un il $15.99

Grades: PreK K 1 2   E

1. School stories 2. Imagination -- Fiction 3. Fire fighters -- Fiction

ISBN 978-0-7636-4019-4; 0-7636-4019-0

LC 2007051895

After dressing up as fire fighters, building a fire truck out of a cardboard box, and extinguishing imaginary fires on the playground, Mrs. Iverson's students are surprised by the arrival of a real fire engine with real fire fighters on board

"Rawlins's acrylic illustrations feature bright, primary colors that stand out against the clean, white backgrounds. . .

. A great choice for introducing not only fire safety, but also creative play." SLJ

Whitman, Candace

Lines that wiggle; illustrations by Steve Wilson. Blue Apple Books 2009 un il $14.99

Grades: K 1 2 3   E

1. Stories in rhyme 2. Monsters -- Fiction

ISBN 978-1-934706-54-1; 1-934706-54-X

LC 2008042383

A variety of monsters and other creatures demonstrate some of the different things that lines can do, from curve and curl to zig-zag

"Through bouncy verse and lively artwork, this creative collaboration explores the many different ways that lines are used. . . . Children will enjoy this book on many levels." SLJ

Whitman, Walt

When I heard the learn'd astronomer; words by Walt Whitman; pictures by Loren Long. Simon & Schuster Books for Young Readers 2004 un il $16.95

Grades: 1 2 3 4   E

1. Astronomy -- Poetry

ISBN 0-689-86397-7

LC 2004-7538

"A little boy obsessed with outer space has been dragged to an astronomy lecture. . . . The fidgety youngster takes his toy rocket ship outside, where he marvels at the 'perfect silence of the stars, casting a decisive vote for creative speculation over chilly analysis.' The painterly artwork . . . gets its own injection of childlike wonder through playful doodles contributed by Long's two children." Booklist

Whybrow, Ian

The **noisy** way to bed; illustrated by Tiphanie Beeke. Arthur A. Levine Books 2004 un il $15.95

Grades: PreK K 1 2   E

1. Stories in rhyme 2. Animals -- Fiction 3. Bedtime -- Fiction

ISBN 0-439-55689-9

LC 2003-2785

As a sleepy boy decides it is bedtime and sets out across the farm toward home, he meets several animals who, in their noisy way, express the same idea

"This engaging bedtime story begs for participation from children. . . . [Beeke's] full-page, mixed-media pictures are captivating, providing an eye-pleasing blend of colors, textures, and facial expressions." SLJ

Wiesner, David

★ **Art** & Max. Clarion Books 2010 un il $17.99

Grades: K 1 2 3   E

1. Artists -- Fiction 2. Lizards -- Fiction 3. Painting -- Fiction 4. Artists' materials -- Fiction

ISBN 978-0-618-75663-6; 0-618-75663-9

LC 2010005205

Max the lizard wants to be an artist like Arthur, but his first attempt at using a paintbrush sends the two friends on a whirlwind trip through various media, with unexpected consequences.

"This small-scale and surprisingly comedic story takes place against a placid backdrop of pale desert colors, which recedes to keep the focus squarely on the dynamic between the two lizards and the wide range of emotions that Wiesner masterfully evokes." Publ Wkly

★ **Flotsam**. Clarion Books 2006 un il $17
Grades: K 1 2 3 4   E
   1. Stories without words 2. Beaches -- Fiction 3. Cameras -- Fiction 4. Children's literature -- Works -- Grades two through six
   ISBN 0-618-19457-6
   Awarded the Caldecott Medal, 2007
"A wave deposits an old-fashioned contraption at the feet of an inquisitive young beachcomber. It's a Melville underwater camera, and the excited boy quickly develops the film he finds inside. The photos are amazing. . . . This wordless books vivid watercolor paintings have a crisp realism that anchors the elements of fantasy. . . . Filled with inventive details and delightful twists, each snapshot is a tale waiting to be told." SLJ

   Free fall. Lothrop, Lee & Shepard Bks. 1988 un il lib bdg $18.89; pa $6.99
Grades: K 1 2 3 4   E
   1. Stories without words 2. Dreams -- Fiction
   ISBN 0-688-05584-2 lib bdg; 0-688-10990-X pa
                LC 87-22834
   A Caldecott Medal honor book, 1989
A young boy dreams of daring adventures in the company of imaginary creatures inspired by the things surrounding his bed
"Technical virtuosity is the trademark of the double-page watercolor spreads. Especially notable is the solidity of forms and architectural details." SLJ

   Hurricane. Clarion Bks. 1990 un il $16; pa $6.95
Grades: K 1 2 3   E
   1. Brothers -- Fiction 2. Hurricanes -- Fiction
   ISBN 0-395-54382-7; 0-395-62974-8 pa
                LC 90-30070
"A family weathers a hurricane; the next day, in the post-hurricane yard, the two boys in the family play on a great fallen elm, imagining it to be a jungle, a pirate ship, and a space ship. A handsome book, affording opportunities for sharing fears and dreams of adventure." Horn Book Guide

   June 29, 1999. Clarion Bks. 1992 un il $16; pa $5.95
Grades: K 1 2 3 4   E
   1. Vegetables -- Fiction
   ISBN 0-395-59762-5; 0-395-72767-7 pa
                LC 91-34854
"Here an understated, fairly straightforward text is a perfect foil for the outrageous scenes of vegetables run amok. Realistic watercolors reveal red peppers that need to be roped down, beans with bemused Arizona sheep clambering over them, and gargantuan peas floating down the Mississippi like logs to the sawmill. Fans of Wiesner's offbeat sense of humor will be delighted." Horn Book

   ★ **Mr.** Wuffles! by David Wiesner. Clarion Books, Houghton Mifflin Harcourt 2013 32 p ill. (hardcover) $17.99
Grades: PreK K 1 2 3   E
   1. Cats 2. Picture books for children 3. Cats -- Fiction

   4. Toys -- Fiction 5. Extraterrestrial beings -- Fiction
   ISBN 0618756612; 9780618756612
                LC 2012046025
   Caldecott Honor Book (2014)
In this children's picture book, a housecat is battling some tiny aliens. The aliens' "initial celebration at landing turns to mayhem as their craft is buffeted by Mr. Wuffles. The aliens assess a smoldering engine part and disembark for help. . . . A ladybug and several ants assist them, and the repair's successfully made by harvesting cross sections of detritus: pencil eraser, M&M, marble and metal screw." (Kirkus Reviews)

   ★ **Sector** 7. Clarion Bks. 1999 un il $16
Grades: K 1 2 3 4   E
   1. Stories without words 2. Clouds -- Fiction 3. Empire State Building (New York, N.Y.) -- Fiction
   ISBN 0-395-74656-6
                LC 96-40343
   A Caldecott Medal honor book, 2000
While on a school trip to the Empire State Building, a boy is taken by a friendly cloud to visit Sector 7, where he discovers how clouds are shaped and channeled throughout the country
"Wiesner's lofty watercolors render words superfluous as he transforms the sky into magical scenes of marine life, reminding children of the innate power of their own imagination." Publ Wkly

   ★ **The three** pigs. Clarion Bks. 2001 un il $16
Grades: K 1 2 3 4   E
   1. Pigs 2. Pigs -- Fiction 3. Characters in literature
   ISBN 0618007016
                LC 00-57016
   Awarded the Caldecott Medal, 2002
The three pigs escape the wolf by going into another world where they meet the cat and the fiddle, the cow that jumped over the moon, and a dragon. "Ages four to eight." (NY Times Book Rev)
"Wiesner's brilliant use of white space and perspective evokes a feeling that the characters can navigate endless possibilities—and that the range of story itself is limitless." Publ Wkly

   ★ **Tuesday**. Clarion Bks. 1991 un il $17; pa $6.95
Grades: K 1 2 3 4   E
   1. Frogs -- Fiction
   ISBN 0-395-55113-7; 0-395-87082-8 pa
                LC 90-39358
   Awarded the Caldecott Medal, 1992
Frogs rise on their lily pads, float through the air, and explore the nearby houses while their inhabitants sleep
"Wiesner offers a fantasy watercolor journey accomplished with soft-edged realism. Studded with bits of humor, the narrative artwork tells a simple, pleasant story with a consistency and authenticity that makes the fantasy convincing." Booklist

Wigger, J. Bradley, 1958-
   Thank you, God; by J. Bradley Wigger; illustrated by Jago. Eerdmans Books for Young Readers 2014 26 p. $16
Grades: PreK K 1 2   E
   1. Gratitude 2. Children -- Religious life 3. Gratitude -- Prayers and devotions 4. Christian children -- Prayers

and devotions
ISBN 0802854249; 9780802854247

LC 2013044346

A children's book written by J. Bradley Wigger and illustrated by Jago "'Thank You, God' is a celebration of family and friends, of homes and food to share, and of the wonder of creation from the first light of day to the calm, peaceful night." It "offers readers of all ages and backgrounds the perfect chance to reflect on all the things that they have to be grateful for." (Publisher's note)

"Created with digital paints and photographic textures, this religious picture book is elegant and enjoyable... The diversity is refreshing and reflective of many families, a pleasure to see in children's books. This book would be a great tool for devotions in the home, classroom, or church." SLJ

Wild, Margaret

★ **Harry** & Hopper. Feiwel & Friends 2011 un il $16.99

Grades: PreK K   E

1. Dogs -- Fiction 2. Pets -- Fiction 3. Bereavement -- Fiction

ISBN 978-0-312-64261-7; 0-312-64261-X

"Redheaded Harry and his spotted dog, Hopper, are constant companions, accomplices . . . and bedmates. The dog's sudden death (an accident that happens while Harry is at school), leaves the boy devastated. . . . Wild's . . . understated, empathic prose offers both a voice for a child unable to articulate his grief and the reassurance that those we love never really disappear. Blackwood's . . . predominantly charcoal drawings are equally eloquent, particularly in her use of texture to capture the emotional essence of good and sad times." Publ Wkly

Itsy-bitsy babies; illustrated by Jan Ormerod. Little Hare Books 2010 un il $15.99

Grades: PreK   E

1. Stories in rhyme 2. Infants -- Fiction

ISBN 978-1-9215413-6-0; 1-9215413-9-X

"This picture book introduces a multicultural cast of babies and toddlers engaged in everyday activities. . . . Short and precise, Wild's rhyming couplets offer plenty of chances for children to chime in with the end words. . . . Ormerod's clean, crayonlike drawings illustrate one or more babies with a few props . . . and create a sense of changing settings with flat, toned color above and below the horizon line in each picture." Booklist

Kiss kiss! [by] Margaret Wild & Bridget Strevens-Marzo. Simon & Schuster Books for Young Readers 2004 un il $12.95

Grades: PreK K   E

1. Hippopotamus -- Fiction 2. Mother-child relationship -- Fiction

ISBN 0-689-86279-2

LC 2002-154516

First published 2003 in Australia

Baby Hippo is in such a rush to play one morning he forgets to kiss his mama, but strangely all the jungle noises seem to remind him

"This is a story filled with movement and physical affection. The lap-sit audience will love the squishy, lumpy

sounds and the repetition of the text as they point to the animals in the clear, bright pictures." Booklist

★ **Our** granny; story by Margaret Wild; pictures by Julie Vivas. Ticknor & Fields 1994 un il $17; pa $6.95

Grades: PreK K 1 2   E

1. Grandmothers -- Fiction

ISBN 0-395-67023-3; 0-395-88395-4 pa

LC 93-11950

First published 1993 in Australia

"Two young children present a catalog of all the varying sizes, shapes, and types of grandmothers, interspersed with loving comments about their own granny, who has 'a wobbly bottom' and wears a funny bathing suit. . . . Vivas's lively illustrations capture the grandmothers in their most comic moments." Horn Book Guide

★ **Piglet** and Mama; illustrated by Stephen Michael King. Harry N. Abrams 2005 un il $14.95

Grades: PreK K   E

1. Pigs -- Fiction 2. Mothers -- Fiction 3. Farm life -- Fiction

ISBN 0-8109-5869-4

LC 2004-19497

When Piglet cannot find her mother, all of the barnyard animals try to make her feel better, but Piglet wants nothing but Mama.

"The text is reassuring and rhythmic. . . . The cheery watercolor cartoons depict farm life on a bright, sunny day, and the gentle pastel color scheme matches the tender tone of the text." SLJ

Other titles about Piglet are:
Piglet and Papa (2007)
Piglet and Granny (2009)

Wildsmith, Brian

Brian Wildsmith's ABC. Star Bright Bks. 1995 un bd bk $6.95

Grades: PreK K   E

1. Alphabet 2. Board books for children

ISBN 978-1-88773-402-8 bd bk; 1-88773-402-3 bd bk

LC 95-31730

First published 1962 in the United Kingdom; first U.S. edition 1963 by Watts

"From A/apple to Z/zebra, Wildsmith's 26 playful renderings of objects and animals are highlighted with an eye-catching, colorful design; kaleidoscopic animals constructed from bold circles, triangles and squares add an unexpected geometric element to the counting book." Publ Wkly

Brian Wildsmith's Amazing animal alphabet. Star Bright Books 2009 un $17.95; pa $7.95

Grades: PreK K   E

1. Animals 2. Alphabet

ISBN 978-1-59572-104-4; 1-59572-104-5; 978-1-59572-185-3 pa; 1-59572-185-1 pa

LC 2007033811

"Wildsmith's distinctive, detailed animals pop against brightly colored backgrounds as they illustrate each letter of the alphabet. Preschoolers will easily recognize most of the creatures, with a few refreshingly unusual exceptions (quetzel for Q, vole for V, xenops for X). Four pages of

'Amazing Animal Facts' conclude the animal parade." Horn Book Guide

Jungle party. Star Bright Books 2006 un il $16.95; pa $6.95

Grades: PreK K 1 2   **E**

1. Animals -- Fiction 2. Parties -- Fiction 3. Pythons -- Fiction

ISBN 978-1-59572-052-8; 1-59572-052-9; 978-1-59572-053-5 pa; 1-59572-053-7 pa

First published 1974 by Oxford University Press with title: Python's party

Although he is hungry, Python tries to prove his goodwill by throwing a party for all the jungle animals

"Wildsmith excels at bold, brightly colored illustrations of animals, and this cautionary tale is a visual delight." Horn Book Guide

Wiles, Deborah

Freedom Summer; illustrated by Jerome Lagarrigue. Atheneum Bks. for Young Readers 2001 un il $16

Grades: K 1 2 3   **E**

1. Friendship -- Fiction 2. Race relations -- Fiction 3. African Americans -- Fiction

ISBN 0-689-87829-X

LC 98-52805

In 1964, Joe is pleased that a new law will allow his best friend John Henry, who is colored, to share the town pool and other public places with him, but he is dismayed to find that prejudice still exists

"The text, though concise, is full of nuance, and the oil paintings shimmer with the heat of the South in summer." Horn Book Guide

Willems, Mo

★ A **big** guy took my ball! text and illustrations by Mo Willems. Hyperion Books for Children 2013 64 p. ill. (reinforced) $8.99

Grades: K 1 2 3   **E**

1. Picture books for children 2. Bullies -- Fiction 3. Pigs -- Fiction 4. Play -- Fiction 5. Whales -- Fiction 6. Animals -- Fiction 7. Elephants -- Fiction 8. Friendship -- Fiction

ISBN 1423174917; 9781423174912

LC 2012010899

Theodor Seuss Geisel Honor Book (2014)

In this book, author and illustrator Mo "Willems observes truths about human behavior through the eyes of Gerald, an elephant, and Piggie. The premise this time is that Piggie's recently acquired ball has been snatched by some unknown creature, one so big that Piggie begs Gerald to intervene. But Gerald's perceived power and genuine desire to help his smaller friend cannot provide him with sufficient courage once he sees that he'll have to confront an enormous whale." (School Library Journal)

"This morality play in false assumptions and relativity unfurls with Willems' customary command of visual pacing; gags are spaced just right to keep the pages turning and readers giggling." Kirkus

Can I play too? Hyperion Books for Children 2010 57p il (Elephant & Piggie book) $8.99

Grades: PreK K 1 2   **E**

1. Pigs -- Fiction 2. Play -- Fiction 3. Snakes -- Fiction

4. Elephants -- Fiction 5. Friendship -- Fiction

ISBN 978-1-4231-1991-3; 1-4231-1991-6

Elephant and Piggie learn to play catch with their new friend Snake, in spite of the fact that Snake has no hands.

"Page turns and placement of speech bubbles are customarily flawless, yielding multiple guffaws, but this story also provides much-needed guidance to kids who are navigating the etiquette minefield of friendship among peers of differing abilities. Brilliantly subtle and spot-on." Kirkus

★ **Cat** the Cat, who is that? Balzer & Bray 2010 un il $12.99; lib bdg $14.89

Grades: PreK K 1   **E**

1. Cats -- Fiction 2. Animals -- Fiction 3. Friendship -- Fiction

ISBN 978-0-06-172840-2; 0-06-172840-3; 978-0-06-172841-9 lib bdg; 0-06-172841-1 lib bdg

LC 2008-46187

An exuberant cat introduces readers to her friends.

"Willems provides just enough humor and surprise to entertain youngest audiences and . . . Cat could become another favorite; her personality sparkles in expansive gestures and gleeful interactions." Publ Wkly

Other titles about Cat the Cat and her friends are:

Let's say hi to friends who fly! (2010)

What's your sound, Hound the Hound ?(2010)

Time to sleep, Sheep the Sheep! (2010)

★ **City** Dog, Country Frog; words, Mo Willems; pictures, Jon J. Muth. Hyperion Books for Children 2010 un il

Grades: PreK K 1 2   **E**

1. Dogs -- Fiction 2. Frogs -- Fiction 3. Seasons -- Fiction 4. Friendship -- Fiction

ISBN 1423103009; 9781423103004

City Dog and Country Frog play together in the spring and summer and fall, but in winter Country Frog is gone. Then when spring comes again City Dog makes a new friend.

Willems "is gracefully spare here, making every word count. That leaves room for Muth's watercolors, richly seasonal, which fill every page. The pictures are imbued with hope and happiness, leaving and longing. This wonderful collaboration makes a significant impact with subtlety and wit." Booklist

★ **Don't** let the pigeon drive the bus! words and pictures by Mo Willems. Hyperion Bks. for Children 2003 un il $12.99

Grades: PreK K 1 2   **E**

1. Buses -- Fiction 2. Pigeons -- Fiction

ISBN 0-7868-1988-X

A Caldecott Medal honor book, 2004

"An unflinching and hilarious look at a child's potential for mischief. In a plain palette, with childishly elemental line drawings, Willems has captured the essence of unreasonableness in the very young." SLJ

"When a bus driver goes on break, he asks the audience to keep an eye on his vehicle and the daft, bug-eyed pigeon who desperately wants to drive it. The pigeon then relentlessly begs readers for some time behind the wheel." Publ Wkly

Other titles about the pigeon are:

The pigeon finds a hot dog! (2004)

Don't let the pigeon stay up late (2006)

The pigeon wants a puppy (2008)

The **duckling** gets a cookie!? words and picture by Mo Willems. Hyperion Books for Children 2012 40 p.
Grades: PreK K 1 2   **E**
  1. Ducks -- Fiction 2. Cookies -- Fiction 3. Pigeons -- Fiction 4. Etiquette -- Fiction 5. Temper tantrums -- Fiction 6. Humorous stories
ISBN 9781423151289
               LC 2011012304
As this book "opens, the yellow Duckling requests a cookie, receives one immediately, and graciously thanks the unseen provider with a "flappy flip flap!" The Pigeon, whom the Duckling cajoled into sharing a hot dog in the earlier book, soon arrives to express astonishment. Multipanel spreads and emphatic voice balloons reveal his outrage as The Pigeon throws a colossal tantrum ("I ask for things all the time!/ I ask to drive the bus! . . . I've asked for a walrus! . . . But do I get what I ask for? Noooooo!"). In an unexpected turn, the Duckling gives the Pigeon the entire cookie, shocking the bird." (Publishers Weekly)

Edwina, the dinosaur who didn't know she was extinct; words and pictures by Mo Willems. Hyperion 2006 un il $16.99
Grades: PreK K 1   **E**
  1. Dinosaurs -- Fiction
ISBN 0-7868-3748-9
Everyone in town loves Edwina the dinosaur except Reginald, who is determined to prove to everyone, including Edwina, that dinosaurs are extinct.
"Set against plain, light-blue backdrops, the pictures, in Willem's familiar cartoon style, show Reginald up to his dastardly deeds. . . . Consider this an enjoyable visit to a happy community that has no room for curmudgeons." Booklist

★ **Goldilocks** and the three dinosaurs; as retold by Mo Willems. Balzer + Bray 2012 40 p. $17.99
Grades: PreK K 1 2 3   **E**
  1. Dinosaurs -- Fiction 2. Fairy tales -- Fiction 3. Picture books for children
ISBN 0062104187; 9780062104182
In this book, Goldilocks "ventures into the home of three diabolical dinosaurs. Having cooked up three bowls of chocolate pudding and arranged their house 'just so,' the two olive-green T. rexes and smaller brown dino lick their lips. . . . Goldilocks doesn't hesitate to enter the dinos' house or stick her whole head in their food . . . and she wises up just in time to give herself, if not the dinosaurs, a happy ending." (Publishers Weekly)

Happy Pig Day! Hyperion Books for Children 2011 57p il $8.99
Grades: PreK K   **E**
  1. Pigs -- Fiction 2. Parties -- Fiction 3. Elephants -- Fiction 4. Friendship -- Fiction
ISBN 978-1-4231-4342-0; 1-4231-4342-6
               LC 2010034326
Piggie celebrates her favorite day of the year, but Gerald the elephant is sad, thinking that he cannot join the fun.
"The elements that have made this series so successful and enduring are all present once again: a clean design (white background, lack of extraneous details, large type in

word bubbles, etc.), a friendship theme and a satisfying resolution." Kirkus

★ **Hooray** for Amanda & her alligator! words and pictures by Mo Willems. Balzer + Bray 2011 68p $17.99
Grades: PreK K 1 2   **E**
  1. Toys -- Fiction 2. Alligators -- Fiction 3. Friendship -- Fiction
ISBN 978-0-06-200400-0; 0-06-200400-X; 006200400X; 9780062004000
               LC 2010009633
Amanda and her alligator have lots of fun together, but when Amanda's grandfather buys her a panda, Alligator must learn to make new friends.
"With the book's minimal backgrounds and roomy page design, the focus falls squarely on Willems' cleanly styled characters, whose facial expressions are carried in the simplest of just-so lines. Willems may not have the market cornered on best friends, but few do them better." Booklist

I broke my trunk! Hyperion Books for Children 2011 57p il $8.99
Grades: PreK K 1 2   **E**
  1. Pigs -- Fiction 2. Elephants -- Fiction 3. Storytelling -- Fiction
ISBN 978-1-4231-3309-4; 1-4231-3309-9
               LC 2010035528
"Willems' use of pastel colors and vast white backdrops work minimalist wonders." Booklist

★ **Knuffle** Bunny; a cautionary tale. Hyperion Books for Children 2004 un il $15.99
Grades: PreK K 1 2   **E**
  1. Lost and found possessions -- Fiction
ISBN 0-7868-1870-0
A Caldecott Medal honor book, 2005
After Trixie and daddy leave the laundromat, something very important turns up missing.
A "concise, deftly told narrative. . . . Printed on olive-green backdrops, the illustrations are a combination of muted, sepia-toned photographs upon which bright cartoon drawings of people have been superimposed. . . . A seamless and supremely satisfying presentation of art and text." SLJ
Other titles about Knuffle Bunny are:
Knuffle Bunny too (2007)
Knuffle Bunny free (2010)

★ **Leonardo,** the terrible monster. Hyperion 2005 un il $16.99
Grades: PreK K 1 2   **E**
  1. Monsters -- Fiction
ISBN 0-7868-5294-1
Leonardo is a terrible monster he can't seem to frighten anyone. When he discovers the perfect nervous little boy, will he scare the lunch out of him? Or will he think of something better?
"Willems's familiar cartoon drawings work hand in glove with the brief text to tell this perfectly paced story." SLJ

Let's go for a drive! by Mo Willems. Hyperion Books for Children 2012 57 p. (hardback) $8.99

Grades: PreK K 1 2   **E**
1. Picture books for children 2. Pigs -- Fiction 3.
Humorous stories 4. Elephants -- Fiction 5. Automobile
travel -- Fiction
ISBN 1423164822; 9781423164821

LC 2011053285

Theodor Seuss Geisel Honor Book (2013)

In this children's picture book, "Gerald the elephant
and Piggie decide to go for a drive, [but] they find that all
the planning in the world can't replace one crucial ingredient. . . . Gerald, a touch on the OCD side, insists on a plan
that includes a number of items: map, sunglasses, umbrellas, bags and, as there will be 'a lot of driving on [their]
drive,' a car. Oops. Piggie doesn't have one; '[a] pig with a
car would be silly." Neither does Gerald. Whatever will they
do?" (Kirkus)

★ **Naked** Mole Rat gets dressed; words and pictures
by Mo Willems. Hyperion Books for Children 2009 un
il $16.99
Grades: PreK K 1 2   **E**
1. Naked mole rat -- Fiction
ISBN 978-1-4231-1437-6; 1-4231-1437-X

LC 2008-48251

Willems "informs readers that 'for this story' they need
only know three things about naked mole rats: '1. They are
a little bit rat. 2. They are a little bit mole. 3. They are all naked.' The exception to point number three, however, is Wilbur, who revels in a wardrobe that ranges from a turtleneck
and beret to an astronaut suit—infuriating his brethren. . . .
[Willems'] legion of emotive, square-headed rodents . . . are
paired successfully with droll prose." Publ Wkly

The **pigeon** needs a bath! words and pictures by Mo
Willems. Hyperion Books for Children, an imprint of Dis-
ney Book Group 2014 40 p. color illustrations $16.99
Grades: PreK K 1 2   **E**
1. Baths -- Fiction 2. Pigeons -- Fiction
ISBN 1423190874; 9781423190875

LC 2013003178

"The Pigeon really needs a bath! Except, the Pigeon's
not so sure about that. Besides, he took a bath last month!
Maybe. It's going to take some serious convincing to try and
get the Pigeon to take the plunge." (Publisher's note)

"The details fans have come to expect are all present,
from the simple, expressive drawings on blank grounds
(though the customary pastel backdrops have been replaced
by a variety of muddy browns and greys) to the before-and-
after endpapers, complete with a rubber-ducky Easter egg."
- Booklist

Should I share my ice cream? Hyperion Books for
Children 2011 57p il $8.99
Grades: PreK K 1 2   **E**
1. Pigs -- Fiction 2. Elephants -- Fiction 3. Friendship
-- Fiction 4. Ice cream, ices, etc. -- Fiction
ISBN 978-1-4231-4343-7; 1-4231-4343-4

LC 2011014860

"Children will delight in this perfect drama for hot
weather. . . . Willems's simple text allows beginning readers
independent success, although the text and illustrations also

work well as a read-aloud. Fans of the series will not want to
miss this offering." SLJ

★ **That** is not a good idea! Mo Willems. Balzer + Bray
2013 48 p. ill. $17.99
Grades: PreK K 1 2   **E**
1. Motion pictures -- Fiction 2. Humorous fiction 3.
Foxes -- Fiction 4. Geese -- Fiction 5. Humorous
stories 6. Dinners and dining -- Fiction
ISBN 0062203096; 9780062203090

LC 2012277475

This children's story, by Mo Willems, "presents itself
as a movie in book form, observed not only by readers, but
by a gaggle of excitable goslings. The action begins when
a dapper fox and a plump goose meet . . . as the wide-eyed
goose follows the fox from the city to his home in the woods.
The goslings' antics grow progressively frantic . . . as their
warnings increase in intensity. The climax proves that appearances can be deceiving." (Kirkus Reviews)

"This charmer is lovingly composed as an homage to silent movies and the concept of picture books as the "theater
of the lap." Readers will become totally involved as they
watch, along with several chicks, a drama unfolding, certain
to end in tragedy... Children and adults will relish being
taken for such a thrilling, suspenseful ride again and again."
SLJ

There is a bird on your head! Hyperion Books for Chil-
dren 2007 57p il $8.99
Grades: PreK K 1 2   **E**
1. Pigs -- Fiction 2. Birds -- Fiction 3. Elephants --
Fiction 4. Friendship -- Fiction
ISBN 978-1-4231-0686-9; 1-4231-0686-5

Gerald the elephant discovers that there is something
worse than a bird on your head two birds on your head! Piggie will try to help her best friend.

"The conversation between the friends flows smoothly
and allows beginning readers to practice expression as they
read. [This] appealing [title] will tickle the funny bones of
children." SLJ

★ **Today** I will fly! Hyperion Books for Children 2007
57p il $8.99
Grades: PreK K 1 2   **E**
1. Pigs -- Fiction 2. Elephants -- Fiction 3. Friendship
-- Fiction
ISBN 978-14231-0295-3; 1-4231-0295-9

LC 2006-49621

While Piggie is determined to fly, Elephant is skeptical, but when Piggie gets a little help from others, amazing
things happen.

"Characters zip in and out of white space, proffer speech-
bubble remarks, and express emotion through spot-on body
language. . . . Accessible, appealing, and full of authentic
emotions." Booklist

Other titles in this series are:
My friend is sad (2007)
I am invited to a party! (2007)
There is a bird on your head (2007)
I love my new toy! (2008)
I will surprise my friend! (2008)
Are you ready to play outside? (2008)
Elephants cannot dance! (2009)

Pigs make me sneeze! (2009)

Watch me throw the ball! (2009)

I am going! (2010)

Can I play too? (2010)

We are in a book! (2010)

I broke my trunk! (2011)

Should I share my ice cream? (2011)

Happy Pig Day! (2011)

Waiting is not easy! by Mo Willems. First edition Hyperion Books for Children 2014 57 p. color illustrations (Elephant and Piggie) hc $8.99

Grades: PreK K 1 2   E

1. Pigs -- Fiction 2. Elephants -- Fiction 3. Humorous stories 4. Patience -- Fiction

ISBN 142319957X; 9781423199571

LC 2014007802

Theodor Seuss Geisel Honor Book (2015)

In this book, part of Mo Willems' "Elephant and Piggie" series, "Gerald loses patience with Piggie when he is told that a surprise is in store but that he must wait for it. His reactions include producing several loud GROANS and reminding Piggie repeatedly that waiting is NOT easy. Piggie knows that the surprise is worth the wait, but she has to keep Gerald there to see it." (School Library Journal)

"A lesson that never grows old, enacted with verve by two favorite friends." Kirkus

We are in a book! Hyperion Books for Children 2010 57p il (Elephant & Piggie book) $8.99

Grades: PreK K 1 2   E

1. Pigs -- Fiction 2. Elephants -- Fiction 3. Friendship -- Fiction 4. Books and reading -- Fiction

ISBN 978-1-4231-3308-7; 1-4231-3308-0

"Stalwart friends Piggie and Gerald the elephant push the metafictive envelope in a big way when they realize that 'someone is looking at us.' . . . Emergent readers just beginning to grapple one-on-one with the rules of the printed codex will find the friends' antics both funny and provocative. . . . Willems displays his customary control of both body language and pacing even as he challenges his readers to engage with his characters and the physicality of their book." Kirkus

Willey, Margaret

A **Clever** Beatrice Christmas; illustrated by Heather M. Solomon. Atheneum Books for Young Readers 2006 un il $16.95

Grades: K 1 2 3   E

1. Christmas -- Fiction 2. Santa Claus -- Fiction

ISBN 0-689-87017-5

LC 2005-10281

As Christmas approaches, Clever Beatrice sets out to prove the existence of Père Noël to three questioning children

This is "a pleasing, seasonal picture book. Solomon's appealing artwork combines elements of acrylic and oil painting with fluid watercolors and collage elements that add unexpected textures to the illustrations." Booklist

Williams, Barbara

Albert's impossible toothache; illustrated by Doug Cushman. Candlewick Press 2003 un il $15.99

Grades: PreK K 1 2   E

1. Turtles -- Fiction

ISBN 0-7636-1723-7

LC 2002-67059

A newly illustrated edition of Albert's toothache, published 1974 by Dutton

When Albert the turtle complains of a toothache, no one in his family believes him, until his grandmother takes the time to really listen to him

"This title is a worthwhile addition to any picture-book collection." SLJ

Another title about Albert is:

Albert's gift for grandmother (2006)

Williams, Brenda

Lin Yi's lantern; a Moon Festival tale. [text by] Brenda Williams; [illustrations by] Benjamin Lacombe. Barefoot Books 2009 un il $16.99

Grades: K 1 2 3   E

1. China -- Fiction 2. Shopping -- Fiction 3. Festivals -- Fiction

ISBN 978-1-84686-147-5; 1-84686-147-0

LC 2008043900

When his mother sends him to the market to buy necessities for the upcoming festival, Lin Yi is certain his bargaining skills will get him the best prices and he will have money left over for his coveted red rabbit lantern

"Handsome, stylized gouache illustrations portray the Chinese characters and scenes from a variety of perspectives. . . . The length of the narrative and accompanying cultural information make this an excellent supplement for primary multicultural units." Booklist

Williams, C. K.

A **not** scary story about big scary things; illustrated by Gabi Swiatkowska. Harcourt Children's Books 2010 un il $16.99

Grades: PreK K 1 2   E

1. Fear -- Fiction 2. Monsters -- Fiction

ISBN 978-0-15-205466-3; 0-15-205466-9

A little boy walking through an ordinary forest encounters an extraordinary monster.

"Sharing a surreal sense of logic and elegance, Williams and Swiatkowska convey a mood that's both dreamy and reassuringly matter-of-fact. Swiatkowska . . . is in particularly fine form, with wry drawings that range from florid to schematic, and clever collages that underscore the silliness of conventional wisdom." Publ Wkly

Williams, Emma

The **story** of Hurry; Emma Williams, Ibrahim Quraishi. Seven Stories Press 2014 36 p. illustrations $16.95

Grades: K 1 2 3 4   E

1. Zoos 2. Israel-Arab conflicts 3. Zoos -- Fiction 4. Donkeys -- Fiction 5. Poverty -- Fiction 6. Gaza Strip -- Fiction 7. Arab-Israeli conflict -- Fiction

ISBN 1609805895; 9781609805890

LC 2014005764

This children's story, by Emma Williams, illustrated by Ibrahim Quraishi, recounts how "after a major invasion of the Gaza Strip in late 2008, twenty-year-old Mahmoud Barghout decided to become a zookeeper. . . . But the war made feeding and caring for the animals impossible. . . . So Mr. Barghout came up with a solution for at least one animal: he dyed two local white donkeys with dark stripes, to create zebras, which visiting children could touch and even ride." (Publisher's note)

"Williams, a physician and journalist who witnessed the second Palestinian intifada while living in Jerusalem, bases this haunting, hopeful, and relevant story on an incident that took place in the Gaza Strip in 2008...An assemblage of photos, stark silhouettes, and abstract flourishes, the pictures mesh comforting and disturbing images—Hurry himself appears as a wooden toy, a striking symbol of innocence in a story built around children forced to grow up quickly." PW

Williams, Karen Lynn
★ A **beach** tail; illustrated by Floyd Cooper. Boyds Mills Press 2010 un il $17.95
Grades: PreK K 1 2   E
1. Beaches -- Fiction 2. African Americans -- Fiction 3. Father-son relationship -- Fiction
ISBN 978-1-59078-712-0; 1-59078-712-9

"At the beach with his father, Greg strays from his beach umbrella, but stays calm and remembers the two things Dad told him: 'Don't go in the water, and don't leave Sandy.' Sandy is a lion Greg has drawn in the sand, and because Greg hasn't lifted the stick with which he has drawn Sandy's long, long tail . . . he's able to retrace his steps to find his father. . . . Cooper . . . draws a startlingly real Greg in a series of tight closeups, . . . Grainy pastel and washed-out color evoke the seashore's bleached palette. . . . Williams's . . . even pacing and soothing text reassure children without losing momentum." Publ Wkly

Four feet, two sandals; written by Karen Lynn Williams and Khadra Mohammed; illustrated by Doug Chayka. Eerdmans Books for Young Readers 2007 un il $17
Grades: 2 3 4   E
1. Shoes -- Fiction 2. Pakistan -- Fiction 3. Refugees -- Fiction 4. Friendship -- Fiction 5. Afghanistan -- Fiction
ISBN 978-0-8028-5296-0
                                        LC 2006002635

Two young Afghani girls living in a refugee camp in Pakistan share a precious pair of sandals brought by relief workers

"The thickly brushed, double-page paintings show the long lines of desperate refugees and then close-ups of the two Muslim girls. . . . This is a personal drama behind the daily news." Booklist

Galimoto; illustrated by Catherine Stock. Lothrop, Lee & Shepard Bks. 1990 un il $16.95; pa $6.99
Grades: PreK K 1 2   E
1. Toys -- Fiction 2. Malawi -- Fiction
ISBN 0-688-08789-2; 0-688-10991-8 pa
                                            LC 89-2258

"In Malawi, Africa, according to the author's note, galimoto are intricate and popular push toys crafted by children. Williams tells the story of seven-year-old Kondi's quest to find ample scrap material to fashion his own toy pickup truck. . . . Kondi's perseverance and the pleasure he takes in his accomplishment are just two of the delights of this appealing story. Stock's graceful watercolors portray life in a bustling village and include enough detail . . . to give

readers the flavor of a day in this southern African nation." Horn Book

My name is Sangoel; written by Karen Lynn Williams and Khadra Mohammed; illustrated by Catherine Stock. Eerdmans Books for Young Readers 2009 un il $17
Grades: 1 2 3   E
1. Refugees -- Fiction 2. Immigrants -- Fiction 3. Personal names -- Fiction 4. Sudanese Americans -- Fiction
ISBN 978-0-8028-5307-3; 0-8028-5307-2
                                        LC 2008-31735

As a refugee from Sudan to the United States, Sangoel is frustrated that no one can pronounce his name correctly until he finds a clever way to solve the problem.

"Stock's bright watercolor scenarios, accentuated with thick black lines, express the wrenching leave-taking and then the combination of exciting new things, . . . as well as disorienting ones. . . . [This is a] moving story." Booklist

Painted dreams; pictures by Catherine Stock. Lothrop, Lee & Shepard Bks. 1998 un il hardcover o.p. lib bdg $15.93
Grades: PreK K 1 2   E
1. Haiti -- Fiction 2. Artists -- Fiction
ISBN 0-688-13901-9; 0-688-13902-7 lib bdg
                                            LC 97-32920

Because her Haitian family is too poor to be able to buy paints for her, eight-year-old Ti Marie finds her own way to create pictures that make the heart sing

"Beautifully composed and full of life, Stock's watercolors suggest the personalities of the characters through their expressions and gestures." Booklist

Williams, Laura E.
The **Can** Man; illustrated by Craig Orback. Lee & Low 2010 un il $18.95
Grades: K 1 2 3   E
1. Homeless persons -- Fiction
ISBN 1-60060-266-5; 978-1-60060-266-5

"Tim wants a skateboard badly, but money is tight. Watching a homeless man every calls the Can Man . . . collect cans to redeem for cash, Tim decides to do the same to bankroll his skateboard. . . . Orback's . . . realistic oil paintings on canvas bring the tale's urban setting into clear focus in warmly lit scenes that illuminate the characters' feelings." Publ Wkly

Williams, Linda
★ The **little** old lady who was not afraid of anything; illustrated by Megan Lloyd. Crowell 1986 un il
Grades: PreK K 1 2   E
1. Fear -- Fiction
ISBN 0-06-443183-5 pa; 0-690-04584-0; 0-690-04586-7 lib bdg
                                            LC 85-48250

Coming home late to her cabin by the woods, a fearless little old lady "sees two big shoes in her path. . . . She tells them to get out of the way, but they follow her, going 'CLOMP, CLOMP.' Shoes are followed by pants, 'WIGGLE, WIGGLE'; shirt, 'SHAKE, SHAKE'; gloves, 'CLAP, CLAP'; hat, 'NOD, NOD'; and, finally, a scary pumpkin, 'BOO, BOO.' Even the intrepid little old lady is a little shaken by this, and she runs home. She finally helps them all . . . by suggesting they become a scarecrow." (Horn Book) "Preschool to grade two." (SLJ)

"A delightful picture book, perfect for both independent reading pleasure and for telling aloud." SLJ

Williams, Sherley Anne

Working cotton; written by Sherley Anne Williams; illustrated by Carole Byard. Harcourt Brace Jovanovich 1992 un il hardcover o.p. pa $7

Grades: PreK K 1 2   E
   1. Cotton -- Fiction 2. Migrant labor -- Fiction 3. African Americans -- Fiction
   ISBN 0-15-299624-9; 0-15-201482-9 pa

                     LC 91-21586

A Caldecott Medal honor book, 1993

A young black girl relates the daily events of her family's migrant life in the cotton fields of central California

"Byard's acrylic paintings contribute weight and emotion to Williams's spare text. The fields and family members fill each full-page spread, drawing the reader very close to the action of the story. The mural-like paintings glow with blue and brown tones, recreating the textures and hues of the cotton fields. Williams's text, based on her poems, has a lyrical, rhythmic quality." Horn Book

Williams, Sue

Let's go visiting; written by Sue Williams; illustrated by Julie Vivas. Harcourt Brace & Co. 1998 un il hardcover o.p. pa $7; bd bk $6.95

Grades: PreK K   E
   1. Counting 2. Stories in rhyme 3. Domestic animals -- Fiction
   ISBN 0-15-201823-9; 0-15-202410-7 pa; 0-15-204638-0 bd bk

                     LC 97-34398

A counting story in which a boy visits his farmyard friends, from one brown foal to six yellow puppies

"The bold illustrations, simple yet full of motion, combine with a lively text to make this perfect for toddler story hours." Booklist

Williams, Suzanne

Library Lil; illustrated by Steven Kellogg. Dial Bks. for Young Readers 1997 un il $16.99; pa $6.99

Grades: PreK K 1 2 3   E
   1. Tall tales 2. Librarians -- Fiction 3. Books and reading -- Fiction
   ISBN 0-8037-1698-2; 0-14-056837-9 pa

                     LC 95-23490

A formidable librarian makes readers not only out of the once resistant residents of her small town, but out of a tough-talking, television-watching motorcycle gang as well

"The silliness of both story and pictures are perfectly matched. Kellogg's distinctive toothy kids and laughing cats crowd the pages, fitting right in with the baby-faced biker banditos." SLJ

Williams, Vera B.

★ **Cherries** and cherry pits. Greenwillow Bks. 1986 un il hardcover o.p. $17.99; pa $6.99

Grades: PreK K 1 2 3   E
   1. Drawing -- Fiction 2. African Americans -- Fiction
   ISBN 0-688-05145-6; 0-688-05146-4 lib bdg; 0-688-10478-9 pa

                     LC 85-17156

"Williams' portraits of Bidemmi drawing are done in watercolor; the drawings Bidemmi makes are done with bright markers, some being simple sketches, others filling the page with color, looking like naive, but glorious icons. The interior stories are well integrated with each other, and the whole adds up to a study of child as artist that is fresh, vibrant, and exciting." Bull Cent Child Books

Lucky song. Greenwillow Bks. 1997 un il $16.99

Grades: PreK K 1   E
   1. Day -- Fiction 2. Kites -- Fiction 3. Songs -- Fiction
   ISBN 0-688-14459-4

                     LC 96-7151

"Evie flies the kite made by her grandfather until it's time to go home for supper all tired and ready for bed. This patterned story, showing a little girl surrounded by a loving family, ends by circling back to the beginning. It is illustrated using brilliantly colored watercolors." Child Book Rev Serv

★ **More** more more said the baby; 3 love stories. Greenwillow Bks. 1990 un il $17.99; lib bdg $18.89; pa $6.99; bd bk $7.99

Grades: PreK K 1   E
   1. Infants -- Fiction 2. Family life -- Fiction
   ISBN 0-688-09173-3; 0-688-09174-1 lib bdg; 0-688-814736-4 pa; 0-688-15634-7 bd bk

                     LC 89-2023

A Caldecott Medal honor book, 1991

Three babies are caught up in the air and given loving attention by a father, grandmother, and mother

"The pages reverberate with bright colors and vigorous forms, and the rhythmic language begs to be read aloud." Horn Book Guide

★ **Stringbean's** trip to the shining sea; greetings from Vera B. Williams, story and pictures; and Jennifer Williams, more pictures. Greenwillow Bks. 1987 un il hardcover o.p. $18.99; pa $7.99

Grades: K 1 2 3   E
   1. West (U.S.) -- Fiction 2. Automobile travel -- Fiction
   ISBN 0-688-07161-9; 0-688-07162-7 lib bdg; 0-688-16701-2 pa

                     LC 86-29502

"The use of mixed media—watercolors, Magic Markers, and colored pencils—is as aesthetically pleasing as it is skillful. Nothing has been forgotten; nothing more needs to be added. Not for the usual picture-book set, this travelogue storybook will appeal to slightly older audiences." Horn Book

Three days on a river in a red canoe. Greenwillow Bks. 1984 un il hardcover o.p. pa $6.99

Grades: K 1 2 3   E
   1. Camping -- Fiction 2. Canoes and canoeing -- Fiction
   ISBN 0-688-84307-7 lib bdg; 0-688-04072-1 pa

                     LC 80-23893

In this book, a "canoe trip for two children and two adults is recorded with all its interesting detail in a spontaneous first-person account and engaging full-color drawings on carefully designed pages. Driving to a river site, making camp, paddling the craft, negotiating a waterfall, swimming, fishing, dealing with a sudden storm, and even rescuing one overboard child are all described as important incidents in a summertime adventure." Horn Book

Willis, Jeanne

★ The **bog** baby; written by Jeanne Willis; illustrated by Gwen Millward. Schwartz & Wade Books 2009 un il $16.99; lib bdg $19.99
Grades: K 1 2   E
  1. Magic -- Fiction 2. Sisters -- Fiction
  ISBN 978-0-375-86176-5; 0-375-86176-9; 978-0-375-96176-2 lib bdg; 0-375-96176-3 lib bdg
                                        LC 2008-47635
First published 2008 in the United Kingdom
When two sisters go fishing in a magic pond, they find a winged blue bog baby and take it home with them.
  "The glorious illustrations reveal a lush dreamscape of a backyard flush with tendrils, bluebells, Queen Anne's lace, birch trees, cherry trees, dragonflies, ladybugs, and more, all delicately and minutely drawn, and painted in watercolors. The child-voiced, economical narrative transports readers into the squelches and squeaks of tromping through the mud and spring plants." SLJ

  Gorilla! Gorilla! [by] Jeanne Willis and [illustrated by] Tony Ross. Simon & Schuster 2006 un il $15.95
Grades: PreK K 1 2   E
  1. Mice -- Fiction 2. Gorillas -- Fiction
  ISBN 978-1-4169-1490-7; 1-4169-1490-0
  "While searching for her lost baby, a mouse is chased by a great, big, hairy, scary ape! . . . Young readers will guess what the mother mouse, in her terror, can't see—that the seemingly fierce gorilla is simply trying to return her baby to her. The brief, lively text and the melodramatic refrain make for a humorous and boisterous read-aloud. Ross's bright pastel illustrations capture the mouse's fear and the gorilla's determination with verve." SLJ

  ★ **Susan** laughs; illustrated by Tony Ross. Holt & Co. 2000 un il $15
Grades: PreK K 1   E
  1. Stories in rhyme 2. Play -- Fiction 3. Physically disabled -- Fiction
  ISBN 0-8050-6501-6
                                        LC 99-59560
Rhyming couplets describe a wide range of common emotions and activities experienced by a little girl who uses a wheelchair
  "Without being condescending or preachy, the words, pictures, and design of this very simple picture book show that a physically disabled child is 'just like me, just like you.' Only on the very last page do we discover that Susan uses a wheelchair." Booklist

Wilson, Karma
  ★ **Bear** snores on; illustrations by Jane Chapman. Margaret K. McElderry Bks. 2002 un il $16; bd bk $7.99
Grades: PreK K 1   E
  1. Stories in rhyme 2. Bears -- Fiction 3. Animals --

Fiction 4. Parties -- Fiction
  ISBN 0-689-83187-0; 1-4169-0272-4 bd bk
                                        LC 00-28371
On a cold winter night many animals gather to party in the cave of a sleeping bear, who then awakes and protests that he has missed the food and the fun
  "The characters are infused with warmth and humor. . . . The warm, soft tones of these acrylic illustrations perfectly capture the coziness of Bear's lair and capture the action." SLJ

Other titles in this series are:
Bear feels scared (2008)
Bear feels sick (2007)
Bear stays up for Christmas (2004)
Bear wants more (2003)
Bear's new friend (2006)

  Bear's loose tooth; [illustrated by] Jane Chapman. Margaret K. McElderry Books 2011 il $16.99
Grades: K 1 2   E
  1. Stories in rhyme 2. Bears -- Fiction 3. Teeth -- Fiction 4. Animals -- Fiction
  ISBN 978-1-4169-5855-0; 1-4169-5855-X
                                        LC 2009045690
When Bear discovers he has a loose tooth, his friends try to help make it fall out.
  "With warm prose, comforting acrylics, and a healthy dose of physical comedy, the tale should amuse young readers." Publ Wkly

  The **cow** loves cookies; illustrated by Marcellus Hall. Margaret K. McElderry Books 2010 un il $16.99
Grades: PreK K 1 2   E
  1. Stories in rhyme 2. Cattle -- Fiction 3. Cookies -- Fiction 4. Farmers -- Fiction 5. Domestic animals -- Fiction
  ISBN 978-1-4169-4206-1; 1-4169-4206-8
                                        LC 2009-00742
While all the other animals on the farm enjoy eating their regular food, the cow chooses to eat the one thing that she loves best.
  "The big, clear watercolor pictures with thick ink lines leave lots of white space, and the simple rhyming lines, with descriptive words and messy action, will encourage preschoolers to join in." Booklist

  A **frog** in the bog; [illustrated by] Joan Rankin. Margaret K. McElderry Bks. 2003 un il $16.95
Grades: PreK K 1   E
  1. Counting 2. Stories in rhyme 3. Frogs -- Fiction 4. Insects -- Fiction
  ISBN 0-689-84081-0
                                        LC 2002-5903
A frog in the bog grows larger and larger as he eats more and more bugs, until he attracts the attention of an alligator who puts an end to his eating
  "This gastronomic adventure is told in catchy rhyming verse, complemented by soft, dreamy watercolors that perfectly recreate the bog. The illustrations are enhanced by humorous details." SLJ

  Hogwash; illustrated by Jim McMullan. Little, Brown 2011 un il $16.99

Grades: PreK, K   E

1. Stories in rhyme 2. Pigs -- Fiction 3. Baths -- Fiction 4. Farmers -- Fiction 5. Cleanliness -- Fiction

ISBN 978-0-316-98840-7; 0-316-98840-5

LC 2010019754

When his stubborn pigs refuse a sudsy cleaning, a determined farmer learns that mud baths can be just as fun.

"Kids will be plenty entertained by the lanky, bespectacled Farmer's many disguises (and escalating frustration), but the crafty, confident, and expressive pigs hog the spotlight in every scene. It's a highly satisfying story." Publ Wkly

How to bake an American pie; illustrated by Raul Colón. Simon & Schuster 2007 un il $16.99

Grades: K 1 2 3   E

1. Stories in rhyme 2. Patriotism -- Fiction

ISBN 0-689-86506-6; 978-0-689-86506-0

Rhyming text and illustrations present a recipe for how to bake a pie from all the things that make America great.

"In these watercolor-and-ink paintings, the action rolls across the spreads in all sorts of fantastical ways. Purple mountain majesties grow out of teacups, and the cooks pull rainbows out of a sky studded with stars and stripes. . . . [This is a] wild, wonderful celebration." Booklist

Mama, why? illustrations by Simon Mendez. Margaret K. McElderry Books 2011 un il $16.99

Grades: PreK, K 1   E

1. Stories in rhyme 2. Sky -- Fiction 3. Night -- Fiction 4. Bedtime -- Fiction 5. Polar bear -- Fiction 6. Mother-child relationship -- Fiction

ISBN 978-1-4169-4205-4; 1-4169-4205-X

A sleepy polar bear cub asks his mother questions about the night sky as he gets ready to go to sleep.

"Wilson's conversational style beautifully captures a homespun imagination and the feel of a mother's end-of-day murmurs to her 'dearest one.' There's genuine magic in Mendez's soft-focus arctic scenes, particularly the way his lighting conveys the warm glow of the moon, the glittering night, and the glacial air." Publ Wkly

Where is home, Little Pip? [by] Karma Wilson; illustrated by Jane Chapman. Margaret K. McElderry Books 2008 un il $16.99

Grades: PreK, K 1   E

1. Animals -- Fiction 2. Penguins -- Fiction 3. Antarctica -- Fiction

ISBN 978-0-689-85983-0; 0-689-85983-X

LC 2006019094

After Little Pip the penguin gets lost she meets a whale, a kelp gull, and sled dogs who cannot help her, but with the aid of her family's song, home finds her.

"Well-structured text, genuine emotions, and beautiful full-bleed illustrations in a palette that ranges from cool whites and blues to warm pinks, corals, and tans combine to produce a wonderful story of a loving family separated and then reunited." SLJ

Other titles about Little Pip are:

Don't be afraid, Little Pip (2009)

What's in the egg, Little Pip? (2010)

Whopper cake; [by] Karma Wilson; [illustrated by] Will Hillenbrand. Margaret K. McElderry Books 2007 un il $16.99

Grades: PreK, K 1 2   E

1. Tall tales 2. Stories in rhyme 3. Cake -- Fiction 4. Birthdays -- Fiction

ISBN 0-689-83844-1

LC 00058742

Grandad bakes Grandma a whopper of a birthday cake. Includes recipe and directions for chocolate cake.

"Rendered in ink and egg tempera, Hillenbrand's illustrations spill off the spreads." SLJ

Wimmer, Sonja

The **word** collector. Cuento de Luz 36 p. $15.95

Grades: 1 2 3   E

1. New words 2. Picture books for children

ISBN 8415241348; 9788415241348

This children's picture book tells of Luna, who lives in the sky and collects words. "But one day the words stop coming. Luna learns that the people have become too busy to remember the importance of words. With her collection, she travels across the land. Where Luna finds darkness and despair she plants words of compassion and love. When her words run out, people begin to create—and generously share—new words." (Kirkus)

Wing, Natasha

Go to bed, monster! written by Natasha Wing; illustrated by Sylvie Kantorovitz. Harcourt 2007 un il $16

Grades: PreK, K 1   E

1. Bedtime -- Fiction 2. Monsters -- Fiction

ISBN 978-0-15-205775-6

LC 2006010849

Trying to avoid bedtime, Lucy uses her imagination and some crayons to draw a monster to play with.

"Kantorovitz's whimsical ink-and-watercolor pictures on open white backgrounds . . . are perfectly paired to Wing's engaging and breezy text and characters." SLJ

Winstanley, Nicola

Cinnamon baby; [text by] Nicola Winstanley; [illustrations by] Janice Nadeau. Kids Can Press 2011 un il $16.95

Grades: PreK, K 1 2   E

1. Baking -- Fiction 2. Infants -- Fiction 3. Racially mixed people -- Fiction

ISBN 1-55337-821-0; 978-1-55337-821-1

Miriam the baker marries Sebastian and they have a baby who won't stop crying, until the smell of Miriam's cinnamon bread calms it.

"Both the words and pictures engage the senses in a heady, tangled mix. . . . Miriam is paper white, Sebastian is cocoa brown, and their cinammon-colored child gives the title a sly double meaning. A charming offering infused with warmth, romantic whimsy, and love." Booklist

Winstead, Rosie

Sprout helps out; Rosie Winstead. Dial Books for Young Readers, an imprint of Penguin Group (USA) Inc. 2013 32 p. color illustrations (hardcover) $16.99

Grades: PreK, K   E

1. Helping behavior -- Fiction 2. Mother-daughter

relationship -- Fiction 3. Helpfulness -- Fiction
ISBN 0803730721; 9780803730724

LC 2013008765

This children's book, by Rosie Winstead, is "about helping Mom and making a sweet, sweet mess of it. . . . Sprout's small, but she's good at helping. She makes the bed (with Mom still in it), cooks (if cooking is overflowing the cereal bowl), vacuums (up the cat--almost), and looks after her baby sister Bea (like a champ). Sure, sometimes Sprout's plans backfire, but good intentions go a long way--and make life interesting." (Publisher's note)

"Ironic narration, primly positive and perky, allows playful pictures to reveal how much (or little) Sprout really helps around her house. She brushes her teeth without being reminded and then takes care of the forgetful dog's teeth, for instance—with her mother's toothbrush. She conscientiously does the laundry after getting dirty—but her baby sister needs to rescue the cat from the washing machine! Simple sentences imbued with wide-eyed innocence work alongside illustrations showing Sprout's misguided household management to winning comedic effect. Winstead's breezy pencil, gouache and watercolor illustrations suit Sprout's comfortable household, with its charming wallpapers, art supplies and scattered toys. . . . High, sly entertainment for troublemakers and helpers alike." Kirkus

Winter, Jeanette

★ **Biblioburro**; a true story from Colombia. Beach Lane Books 2010 un il
Grades: PreK K 1 2   E
1. Libraries 2. Books and reading 3. Colombia 4. Reading teachers 5. Elementary school teachers
ISBN 1416997784; 9781416997788

"After amassing piles of books, Luis, a voracious reader, dreams up a way to share his collection with 'faraway villages.' He starts with two burros—one for himself, one for books—and heads off. Tough terrain and menacing bandits challenge him along the way, but at last he reaches a remote town, where he holds a story hour and loans titles to eager kids before returning home to his wife and reading late into the night. Winter's captivating paintings evoke a South American feel in their brilliant palette and dense, green tropical scenes teeming with creatures, including large, orange-winged butterflies on every page. . . . Winter's text is spare and streamlined, as usual, and here it has a particularly engaging, repetitive rhythm that builds into a lulling bedtime beat." Booklist

★ **Calavera** abecedario; a Day of the Dead alphabet. Harcourt 2004 un il $16
Grades: PreK K 1 2   E
1. Alphabet 2. All Souls' Day -- Fiction 3. Spanish language -- Vocabulary 4. Mexico -- Social life and customs
ISBN 0-15-205110-4

LC 2004-1554

Every year Don Pedro makes papier-mache skeletons, or calaveras, for Mexico's Day of the Dead fiesta. From Angel to Unicornio, each letter of the alphabet has its own special calavera. Spanish words illustrate each letter of the alphabet.

This "features jaunty illustrations inspired by Mexican folk art. . . . This is a lovely book that approaches the Day of the Dead from an unusual angle." SLJ

★ **Follow** the drinking gourd; story and pictures by Jeanette Winter. Alfred A. Knopf 2008 un il hardcover o.p. pa $7.99
Grades: K 1 2 3   E
1. Slavery -- Fiction 2. African Americans -- Fiction 3. Underground railroad -- Fiction
ISBN 978-0-394-89694-6; 978-0-679-81997-4 pa
A reissue of the title first published 1988

By following directions in a song, taught them by an old sailor, runaway slaves journey north along the Underground Railroad to freedom in Canada.

"Complementing the few lines of text per page are dark-hued illustrations horizontally framed with a fine black line and plenty of white space. . . . The art carries the weight of introducing children to a riveting piece of U.S. history, and the music included at the end of the book will fix it in their minds." Bull Cent Child Books

Kali's song; Jeanette Winter. Schwartz & Wade Books 2012 40 p.
Grades: PreK K 1 2   E
1. Music -- Fiction 2. Mammoths -- Fiction 3. Bow and arrow -- Fiction 4. Picture books for children 5. Prehistoric peoples -- Fiction 6. Hunting -- Fiction 7. Cave dwellers -- Fiction
ISBN 9780375870224; 9780375970221

LC 2011009357

In this illustrated children's book, "[w]hen young Kali . . . is given a bow to practice hunting, he discovers that if he puts it to his mouth and plucks the string he can make music. . . . [W]hen the big hunt occurs, Kali stuns everyone by playing his bow so musically that even the herd of mammoths is entranced. The people decide that Kali is a shaman . . . and he lives out his days healing and guiding his community." (Bulletin of the Center for Children's Books)

Winter, Jonah

★ **The fabulous** feud of Gilbert & Sullivan; illustrated by Richard Egielski. Arthur A. Levine Books 2009 un il hardcover o.p. $16.99
Grades: K 1 2 3   E
1. Authors 2. Composers 3. Dramatists 4. Librettists 5. Authors -- Fiction 6. Operetta -- Fiction 7. Composers -- Fiction 8. Theatrical directors 9. Great Britain -- History -- 19th century -- Fiction
ISBN 978-0-439-93050-5; 0-439-93050-2; 978-0-439-93051-2 pa; 0-439-93051-0 pa

LC 2008-27027

In the late nineteenth century, Mr. Gilbert and Mr. Sullivan, who write operas together for a theater called Topsy-Turvydom, have a falling-out when Mr. Sullivan refuses to write music for another ridiculous story that is like all the others.

"The clearly written story comes alive in a series of distinctive ink-and-watercolor illustrations that are full of intriguing details and show great skill in the use of color, shading, and composition." Booklist

★ **Here** comes the garbage barge! written by Jonah Winter; illustrated by Red Nose Studio. Schwartz & Wade Books 2010 un il $17.99; lib bdg $20.99
Grades: K 1 2   E
1. Long Island (N.Y.) -- Fiction 2. Voyages and travels

-- Fiction 3. Refuse and refuse disposal -- Fiction
ISBN 978-0-375-85218-3; 0-375-85218-2; 978-0-375-95218-0 lib bdg; 0-375-95218-7 lib bdg
LC 2008-40709

In the spring of 1987, the town of Islip, New York, with no place for its 3,168 tons of garbage, loads it on a barge that sets out on a 162-day journey along the east coast, around the Gulf of Mexico, down to Belize, and back again, in search of a place willing to accept and dispose of its very smelly cargo

"A fictionalized account of real events. . . . The illustrations are photographs of objects made from garbage. The people, full of personality and expression, were made from polymer clay, and wire, wood scraps, and leftover materials of all kinds were used for the tugboat and barge. The inside of the paper jacket explains how the art was done. This title should be a part of every elementary school ecology unit." SLJ

★ **Steel** Town; illustrated by Terry Widener. Atheneum Books for Young Readers 2008 un il $16.99
Grades: 2 3 4 E
1. Factories -- Fiction 2. Steel industry -- Fiction 3. Cities and towns -- Fiction
ISBN 978-1-4169-4081-4; 1-4169-4081-2
LC 2006-29284

In Steel Town, it's always raining, freight trains come and go, the big furnace roars, and the steel mill never sleeps.

"The acrylic artwork creates an atmosphere of gloom with fiery furnaces and gray skies. Against this backdrop is the rhythmic, repetitious language detailing a day in the life of Steel Town. . . . Both informative and visually stunning, . . . beautifully written and powerfully illustrated." SLJ

Winters, Kay
My teacher for President; illustrated by Denise Brunkus. Dutton Children's Books 2004 un il $14.99
Grades: PreK K 1 2 E
1. Teachers -- Fiction 2. Presidents -- Fiction
ISBN 0-525-47186-3
LC 2003-19222

A second-grader writes a television station with reasons why his teacher would make a good president, but only if she can continue teaching till the end of the year

"Brunkus' cheerful illustrations show a gray-haired woman in large, round glasses. . . . The humorous tone brings lofty ideals about desirable presidential qualities down to an everyday, accessible level." Booklist

This school year will be the best! illustrated by Renée Andriani. Dutton Children's Books 2010 un il $16.99
Grades: K 1 2 E
1. School stories
ISBN 978-0-525-42275-4; 0-525-42275-7

When a teacher asks her students on the first day of school what they wish for in the coming year, the answers range from having a good school picture to receiving a perfect report card.

"The short text leaves plenty of space for Andriani to work in, and she uses it imaginatively, creating upbeat and sometimes comical ink-and-wash illustrations. A good discussion starter for the beginning of the school year." Booklist

Whooo's that? Harcourt Children's Book 2009 un il $9.99
Grades: PreK E
1. Halloween -- Fiction
ISBN 978-0-15-206480-8; 0-15-206480-X
LC 2007039823

"'Whooo's that prancing . . . in the park?/Whooo's that . . . prowling in the dark?' Why, it's trick-or-treaters, of course, as revealed on the book's final page. The volume is enhanced by its appealing trim size, the many engaging lift-the-flaps, and the softly spooky and expressive characters waiting to be uncovered from behind toothy jack-o-lanterns." Horn Book Guide

Winthrop, Elizabeth
Shoes; illustrated by William Joyce. Harper & Row 1986 19p il lib bdg $16.89; pa $6.99
Grades: PreK K E
1. Stories in rhyme 2. Shoes -- Fiction
ISBN 0-06-026592-2 lib bdg; 0-06-443171-1 pa
LC 85-45841

"This lilting rhyme about shoes and feet easily pleases. . . . Backing the verses are full-color drawings of children busily involved with one kind of shoe or another. Joyce's pictures are animated, energetic, and warmly colored." Booklist

Wiseman, Bernard
Morris and Boris at the circus; by B. Wiseman. Harper & Row 1988 64p il (I can read book) hardcover o.p. pa $3.99
Grades: PreK K 1 2 E
1. Bears -- Fiction 2. Moose -- Fiction 3. Circus -- Fiction
ISBN 0-06-026478-0 lib bdg; 0-06-444143-1 pa
LC 87-45682

"The cartoon illustrations with bold colors provide ample context clues for beginning readers. This delightful combination of text and illustrations will entice children to read and re-read this book." SLJ

Wishinsky, Frieda
Maggie can't wait; illustrated by Dean Griffiths. Fitzhenry & Whiteside 2009 un il $17.95
Grades: PreK K 1 E
1. Cats -- Fiction 2. Infants -- Fiction 3. Sisters -- Fiction 4. Adoption -- Fiction
ISBN 978-1-55455-103-3; 1-55455-103-X

Maggie the cat "is excited about the arrival of her newly adopted baby sister. But when she takes a picture of Rose to school, a mean-spirited nemesis dubs the baby ugly. . . . The drama of a cruel comment is fully realized in a manner and tone that children will identify with; Maggie's mortification is as believable as her triumph." SLJ

Another title about Maggie is:
Give Maggie a chance (2002)

Please, Louise! [by] Frieda Wishinsky; illustrated by Marie-Louise Gay. Groundwood Books 2007 un il $17.95
Grades: PreK K 1 2 E
1. Dogs -- Fiction 2. Siblings -- Fiction
ISBN 0-88899-796-5; 978-0-88899-796-8

Jake is annoyed that his little sister Louise won't leave him alone. He wishes Louise were a dog. Suddenly Louise is gone and a little dog appears to be in her place. Jake is worried that his wish may have come true.

"Deft pencil drawings, brightened with watercolor washes and collage elements, capture every nuance of the characters' emotions. . . . [The] story . . . unfolds with surprise and wit." Booklist

You're mean, Lily Jean! illustrated by Kady MacDonald Denton. Albert Whitman 2011 un il $16.99
Grades: PreK K 1 2   E
1. Play -- Fiction 2. Sisters -- Fiction 3. Friendship -- Fiction
ISBN 0-8075-9476-8; 978-0-8075-9476-6
LC 2010027028

Sisters Carly and Sandy have always played together, but when Lily moves in next door she only wants to play with Sandy, and insists that if Carly joins them she must be a baby, or a cow, or a dog.

"Wishinsky re-creates a common childhood experience through realistic dialogue and actions that convery every emotional shift. Just as engaging, Denton's watercolor illustrations capture the girls' attitudes with gestures and facial expressions that speak volumes. Well paced and fine for reading aloud." Booklist

Witte, Anna
★ **Lola's** fandango; written by Anna Witte; illustrated by Micha Archer. Barefoot Books 2010 un il $16.99
Grades: K 1 2 3   E
1. Dance -- Fiction 2. Flamenco -- Fiction 3. Hispanic Americans -- Fiction
ISBN 978-1-84686-174-1; 1-84686-174-8
LC 2008028143

After learning how to dance a style of flamenco known as the fandango, Lola plans a surprise for her mother's birthday.

"Witte and Archer hit all the right notes here. The text dances across the pages, with 'tacs' and 'tocs' and 'ticas' beating out the rhythm. The action, both external and internal, is visualized in the charming collage-style artwork. . . . A CD is included, and a Spanish-language version is also available." Booklist

The **parrot** Tico Tango; written and illustrated by Anna Witte. Barefoot Books 2004 un il $15.99; pa $6.99
Grades: PreK K 1 2   E
1. Stories in rhyme 2. Parrots -- Fiction 3. Rain forest animals -- Fiction
ISBN 1-84148-243-9; 1-84148-890-9 pa
LC 2004-17922

A cumulative rhyme in which a greedy parrot keeps taking fruit from the other creatures of the rainforest until he can hold no more.

"The rhymes are unusually taut and rhythmic, and the mixed-media art, which features fabric swatches, amounts to a feast of tropical colors." Horn Book Guide

Wiviott, Meg
★ **Benno** and the Night of Broken Glass; illustrated by Josee Bisallion. Kar-Ben Pub. 2010 un il lib bdg $17.95; pa $7.95
Grades: 2 3 4 5   E
1. Cats -- Fiction 2. Jews -- Germany -- Fiction 3. Kristallnacht, 1938 -- Fiction 4. Holocaust, 1933-1945

-- Fiction 5. Germany -- History -- 1933-1945 -- Fiction
ISBN 978-0-8225-9929-6 lib bdg; 0-8225-9929-5 lib bdg; 978-0-8225-9975-3 pa; 0-8225-9975-9 pa
LC 2008033482

In 1938 Berlin, Germany, a cat sees Rosenstrasse change from a peaceful neighborhood of Jews and Gentiles to an unfriendly place where, one November night, men in brown shirts destroy Jewish-owned businesses and arrest or kill Jewish people. Includes facts about Kristallnacht and a list of related books and web resources.

"The straightforward text describes events without sentimentality. . . . But what truly distinguishes this book is the striking multimedia artwork composed of paper, fabric, and drawn images in hues of olive, brown, and red. Interesting angles, textures, and patterns add to the visual effect throughout. . . . The message of terror and sadness that marks the beginning of the Holocaust is transmitted in a way that is both meaningful and comprehensible." SLJ

Includes bibliographical references

Wohl, Lauren L.
The **eighth** menorah; by Lauren L. Wohl and illustrated by Laura Hughes. Albert Whitman & Company 2013 32 p.
Grades: PreK K 1   E
1. Jews -- Fiction 2. Hanukkah -- Fiction 3. Jewish holidays -- Fiction 4. Menorah -- Fiction 5. Jews -- United States -- Fiction
ISBN 9780807518922
LC 2013005188

In this book, by Lauren L. Wohl, "Hanukkah is a few weeks away, and Sam can't wait to celebrate with his family, especially his grandma. At Sunday school, everyone in his class is busy making clay menorahs to give as Hanukkah gifts! Sam likes how his menorah is turning out, but he's worried--his family already has seven menorahs! His teacher reassures him that his parents will love it, but Sam is determined to solve this problem on his own and find the perfect home for his menorah." (Publisher's note)

Wojciechowski, Susan
The **Christmas** miracle of Jonathan Toomey; illustrated by P. J. Lynch. Candlewick Press 2004 un il $12.99
Grades: 1 2 3 4   E
1. Christmas -- Fiction 2. Friendship -- Fiction 3. Wood carving -- Fiction
ISBN 0-7636-2621-X
A reissue of the title first published 1995

The widow McDowell and her seven-year-old son Thomas ask the gruff Jonathan Toomey, the best woodcarver in the valley, to carve the figures for a Christmas creche

"The story verges on the sentimental, but it's told with feeling and lyricism. . . . Lynch's sweeping illustrations, in shades of wood grain, are both realistic and gloriously romantic, focusing on faces and hands at work before the fire and in the lamplight." Booklist

A **fine** St. Patrick's day; illustrated by Tom Curry. Random House 2004 un il hardcover o.p. pa $6.99
Grades: K 1 2 3   E
1. Ireland -- Fiction 2. Saint Patrick's Day -- Fiction
ISBN 0-375-82386-7; 978-0-385-73640-4 pa; 0-385-73640-1 pa
LC 2002-11684

Two towns, Tralee and Tralah, compete in an annual St. Patrick's Day decorating contest which Tralah boastfully always wins, but when their hearts are put to the test by a little man with pointed ears, Tralee wins with no effort at all

"Wojciechowski's charming tale is beautifully complemented by Curry's stylized depictions of green rolling hills and thatched-roof houses. Both text and art convey a sturdy feeling about community and charity, brushed with touch of whimsy." Booklist

Wolf, Sallie

Truck stuck; illustrated by Andy Robert Davies. Charlesbridge 2008 un il $14.95

Grades: PreK K 1   E

1. Stories in rhyme 2. Trucks -- Fiction 3. Vehicles -- Fiction

ISBN 978-1-58089-119-6; 1-58089-119-5

"A red 18-wheeler gets stuck under a viaduct and causes a huge traffic jam. Nearby, two children who have a lemonade stand observe the incident and try to keep everyone cool by selling their wares. . . . Eventually, a huge tow truck arrives and, after the air has been let out of the semi's tires, the road is cleared for traffic to resume just in time, because the children are out of lemonade. The bright, flat, cartoon art brings the minimal rhyming text to life and really tells the story." SLJ

Wolff, Ashley, 1956-

Baby Bear sees blue; Ashley Wolff. Beach Lane Books 2012 40 p.

Grades: PreK K 1   E

1. Bears -- Fiction 2. Color -- Fiction 3. Nature -- Fiction 4. Picture books for children 5. Mother-child relationship -- Fiction

ISBN 1442413069; 9781442413061

LC 2010005992

This picture book about a "mother bear and cub . . . introduces colors and images from the natural world. Between awakening in the den and cuddling down for the night, Baby Bear's day is full of new experiences and prescient questions. "A glow creeps in. / 'Who is warming me, Mama?'/ asks Baby Bear. / 'That is the sun,' Mama says." Page turns . . . deliver the color lessons: Silhouetted against the golden light of dawn, "Baby Bear sees yellow." The cub sees green oak leaves waving, smells fragrant red strawberries, and hears the growl of thunder against a stormy gray sky. [Ashley] Wolff's . . . compositions feature inked linoleum block prints that render those bears a strikingly deep, matte black. . . . [W]atercolors illuminate the scenes--colors in the downpour's puddles reflect a rainbow." (Kirkus)

Wolff, Ferida

It is the wind; illustrated by James Ransome. HarperCollins 2005 un il $14.99; lib bdg $15.89

Grades: PreK K 1 2   E

1. Sound -- Fiction 2. Bedtime -- Fiction

ISBN 0-06-028191-X; 0-06-028192-8 lib bdg

LC 00-63197

"In his room at night, a boy looks outside and tries to imagine what is making the noise he hears. . . . The mesmerizing effect of the verse makes this a good bedtime story. . . . Ransome makes the most of the simple story with grace-

ful scenes of the African American boy and the rural night scenes he sees and imagines." Booklist

The **story** blanket; [written by Ferida Wolff and Harriet May Savitz; illustrated by Elena Odriozola] Peachtree 2008 un il $16.95

Grades: K 1 2 3   E

1. Gifts -- Fiction 2. Blankets -- Fiction 3. Storytelling -- Fiction

ISBN 978-1-56145-466-2; 1-56145-466-4

LC 2008-08627

With no wool to be found in the village, Babba Zarrah, the storyteller, starts unraveling her story blanket bit by bit, to secretly supply the needs of the community, and when the villagers realize what is happening they return the favor.

"Colorful illustrations accompany this story of generosity and ingenuity. Rosy-cheeked children and the bright folk art quilt suggest a timelessness to the story as well as the underlying message." Libr Media Connect

Wolfie the bunny; Ame Dyckman; illustrated by Zachariah OHora. Little Brown & Co 2015 40 p. (hardcover) $17

Grades: PreK K 1 2   E

1. Adoption -- Fiction 2. Animal babies -- Fiction 3. Wolves -- Fiction 4. Rabbits -- Fiction 5. Animals, Infancy -- Fiction

ISBN 0316226149; 9780316226141

LC 2013034213

In this children's book by Ame Dyckman, illustrated by Zachariah OHora, "The Bunny family has adopted a wolf son, and daughter Dot is the only one who realizes Wolfie can--and might--eat them all up! Dot tries to get through to her parents, but they are too smitten to listen. A new brother takes getting used to, and when (in a twist of fate) it's Wolfie who's threatened, can Dot save the day?" (Publisher's note)

Won, Brian

Hooray for hat! Brian Won. Harcourt Children's Books, Houghton Mifflin Harcourt 2014 40 p. $16.99

Grades: PreK K 1 2   E

1. Hats -- Fiction 2. Animals -- Fiction 3. Elephants -- Fiction 4. Mood (Psychology) -- Fiction

ISBN 0544159039; 9780544159037

LC 2013020189

In this children's book, by Brian Won, "Elephant wakes up grumpy - until ding, dong! What's in the surprise box at the front door? A hat! HOORAY FOR HAT! Elephant marches off to show Zebra, but Zebra is having a grumpy day, too -until Elephant shares his new hat and cheers up his friend. Off they march to show Turtle! The parade continues as every animal brightens the day of a grumpy friend. An irresistible celebration of friendship, sharing, and fabulous hats." (Publisher's note)

"As everyone well knows, there's nothing so cheering as a good fashion accessory...HOORAY FOR FRIENDS! Won's expressively posed animal figures and the spare narrative are placed on white backgrounds that both brighten the colors and give each scene a clean, spacious look. Moreover, the repeated chorus endows the episode with storytime-friendly rhythm and predictability. A tip of the hat to this buoyant debut." Booklist

Wondriska, William

A **long** piece of string. Chronicle Books 2010 un il $15.99

Grades: PreK K 1   **E**

1. Alphabet 2. String figures -- Fiction

ISBN 978-0-8118-7493-9; 0-8118-7493-1

First published 1963 by Holt

Follows a piece of string through images that correspond to the letters of the alphabet.

"The string's journey is a page-turning visual narrative that subtly reveals the connections among the various objects throughout the book." Horn Book Guide

Wong, Janet S.

Apple pie 4th of July; pictures by Margaret Chodos-Irvine. Harcourt 2002 un il $16

Grades: PreK K 1 2   **E**

1. Fourth of July -- Fiction 2. Chinese Americans -- Fiction

ISBN 0-15-202543-X

LC 2001-1313

A Chinese American girl fears that the food her parents are preparing to sell on the Fourth of July will not be eaten

"An appealing story with believable characters and emotions, written in the girl's spare, lyrical voice. Chodos-Irvine . . . captures the story's uncluttered, elemental qualities in opaque prints that resemble paper cutouts." Booklist

Homegrown house; illustrated by E.B. Lewis. Margaret K. McElderry Books 2009 un il $16.99

Grades: K 1 2 3   **E**

1. Home -- Fiction 2. Moving -- Fiction 3. Grandmothers -- Fiction

ISBN 978-0-689-84718-9; 0-689-84718-1

LC 2006038599

A young girl describes her grandmother's comfortable, long-time home, and wishes that she and her parents could stay in the same house instead of moving so often.

"Wong's poignant poem nicely captures a child's sense of powerlessness and disorientation. With his usual mastery and sensitivity, Lewis creates a true story from the words in sensitive scenes." Booklist

This next New Year; pictures by Yangsook Choi. Foster Bks. 2000 un il $16

Grades: PreK K 1 2   **E**

1. Chinese New Year -- Fiction

ISBN 0-374-35503-7

LC 99-22377

"Choi's smooth, brightly colored paintings . . . ably illustrate the optimistic activity and the yearning in the accessible, rhythmic text." Booklist

"A Chinese-Korean boy reflects on what Chinese New Year means to him. By sweeping last year's mistakes and bad luck out of the house, he hopes to make room for 'a fresh start, my second chance.'" Horn Book Guide

Wood, Audrey

Blue sky; Audrey Wood. The Blue Sky Press 2012 32p

Grades: PreK K 1 2 3   **E**

1. Children's stories 2. Picture books for children 3.

Sky -- Fiction 4. Nature -- Fiction

ISBN 9780545316101

LC 2011010374

In this children's picture book, "a child and his family experience the fun of a sunny-sky day at the beach, then the electricity of a thunder-storm sky, and finally the magical delight of a rainbow sky. . . . Using only two words per page -- 'Blue Sky,' 'Cloud Sky,' 'Storm Sky' . . . [the book] will encourage young readers to make up their own simple descriptions of the sky above." (Publisher's note) Other illustrations depict "Wish Sky/ Sleep Sky/ Dream Sky." The illustrations were created with "pastel paper in deep colors for the backgrounds . . . [and] gouache highlights and colored pencils." (Kirkus)

The **deep** blue sea; a book of colors. story by Audrey Wood; pictures of Bruce Wood. Blue Sky Press 2005 un il $15.99

Grades: PreK K   **E**

1. Color

ISBN 0-439-75382-1

Introduces various colors by presenting a colorful scene on a rock in the deep blue sea.

"Sharply focused, vividly hued artwork makes this concept book a standout. . . . The rhythmic text is enticing and reads aloud smoothly." SLJ

Elbert's bad word; illustrated by Audrey and Don Wood. Harcourt Brace Jovanovich 1988 un il hardcover o.p. pa $7

Grades: K 1 2 3 4   **E**

1. Parties -- Fiction

ISBN 0-15-225320-3; 0-15-201367-9 pa

LC 86-7557

"A bad word, spoken by a small boy at a fashionable garden party, creates havoc, and the child, Elbert, gets his mouth scrubbed out with soap. The bad word, in the shape of a long-tailed furry monster, will not go away until a wizard-gardener cooks up some really delicious, super-long words that everyone at the party applauds. This single-idea cautionary tale has lively, absurdist pictures of tiara-crowned, formally dressed adults recoiling in horror or cavorting with glee when Elbert, the only child at the party, speaks a word." SLJ

★ **Heckedy** Peg; illustrated by Don Wood. Harcourt Brace Jovanovich 1987 un il lib bdg $17; pa $7

Grades: K 1 2 3 4   **E**

1. Fairy tales 2. Witches -- Fiction

ISBN 0-15-233678-8 lib bdg; 0-15-233679-6 pa

LC 86-33639

"The poor mother of seven children, each named for a day of the week, goes off to market promising to return with individual gifts that each child has requested and admonishing them to lock the door to strangers and not to touch the fire. The gullible children are tricked into disobeying their mother by the witch, Heckedy Peg, who turns them all into various kinds of food. The mother can rescue her children only by guessing which child is the fish, the roast rib, the bread. . . . This story, deep and rich with folk wisdom, is stunningly illustrated with Don Wood's luminous paintings.

. . . With variety of color and line he enhances every nuance of the text." SLJ

★ **King** Bidgood's in the bathtub; written by Audrey Wood; illustrated by Don Wood. Harcourt Brace Jovanovich 1985 un il lib bdg $17

Grades: K 1 2 3 4   E

1. Baths -- Fiction 2. Kings and rulers -- Fiction
ISBN 0-15-242730-9

LC 85-5472

A Caldecott Medal honor book, 1986

Despite pleas from his court, a fun-loving king refuses to get out of his bathtub to rule his kingdom

"The few simple words of text per large, well-designed page invite story-telling—but keep the group very small, so the children can be close enough to pore over the brilliant, robust illustrations." SLJ

Piggy Pie Po; 3 little stories. written by Audrey Wood; pictures drawn by Audrey Wood and painted by Don Wood. Harcourt Children's Books 2010 un il $16.99

Grades: PreK K   E

1. Stories in rhyme 2. Pigs -- Fiction
ISBN 978-0-15-202494-9; 0-15-202494-8

LC 2001-01312

"Three vignettes follow the antics of an active and curious piglet. In the first narrative, the lovable character displays some of his special clothes and what he likes to do while wearing them. . . . In the next, children hear about all the things the little piggy is good at. . . . In the last tale, Piggy Pie Po arrives at dinner before the other guests and helps himself to the delicious feast but regrets his final, unfortunate sampling of a red hot pepper. The jolly, alliterative rhyme dances merrily on the tongue, and the paintings of the endearing pig's adventures are surrounded by generous white space." SLJ

Wood, Don

★ The **napping** house. Harcourt Children's Books 2009 un il $17.99

Grades: K 1 2 3   E

1. Sleep -- Fiction
ISBN 978-0-15-256708-8; 0-15-256708-9

A reissue, with new audio CD, of the title first published 1984

"The cool blues and greens are superseded by warm colors and bursts of action as each sleeper wakes, ending in an eruption of color and energy as naptime ends. A deft matching of text and pictures adds to the appeal of cumulation, and to the silliness of the mound of sleepers—just the right kind of humor for the lap audience." Bull Cent Child Books

★ **Piggies**; written by Don and Audrey Wood; illustrated by Don Wood. Harcourt Brace Jovanovich 1991 un il $17; pa $8; bd bk $5.95

Grades: PreK K 1 2   E

1. Pigs -- Fiction 2. Bedtime -- Fiction
ISBN 0-15-256341-5; 0-15-200217-0 pa; 0-15-202638-X bd bk

LC 89-24598

Ten little piggies dance on a young child's fingers and toes before finally going to sleep

"A happy text and luxuriant, witty pictures make this a book to pore over again and again." Booklist

Wood, Douglas

Miss Little's gift; illustrated by Jim Burke. Candlewick Press 2009 un il $16.99

Grades: 1 2 3   E

1. Reading 2. Teachers 3. Hyperactive children 4. Attention deficit disorder
ISBN 978-0-7636-1686-1; 0-7636-1686-9

LC 2008-17915

"This autobiographical picture book chronicles the author's struggles in second grade. Smaller than everyone else, new in town, and speaking with an unfamiliar Southern accent, Wood also found reading to be a chore. . . . . The story works as a tribute to those unsung teacher heroes whose dedication to their craft and native intuition about children have changed lives. . . . Burke's large, realistic oils, with their rich greens and blues, complement the story nicely." SLJ

What dads can't do; pictures by Doug Cushman. Simon & Schuster Bks. for Young Readers 2000 un il $14

Grades: PreK K   E

1. Fathers -- Fiction
ISBN 0-689-82620-6

LC 98-41773

"This amusing picture book will tickle youngsters' funny bones and make every parent and child smile with recognition. . . . Cushman's large, delightful, pen-and-ink and watercolor cartoons . . . capture perfectly the father-and-son interactions." SLJ

Other titles in this series are:
What grandmas can't do (2005)
What moms can't do (2000)
What Santa can't do (2003)
What teachers can't do (2000)

When a dad says "I love you" Douglas Wood; illustrated by Jennifer A. Bell. 1st ed. Simon & Schuster Books for Young Readers 2013 32 p. col. ill. (hardcover) $16.99

Grades: PreK K   E

1. Father-child relationship 2. Love -- Fiction 3. Fathers -- Fiction 4. Father and child -- Fiction
ISBN 0689875320; 9780689875328

LC 2012013268

This children's picture book, by Douglas Wood, illustrated by Jennifer A. Bell, shows how "dads know how to do everything. They can help with homework and carry you on their shoulders. They can make pancakes and teach you how to sing songs. These loving actions are just some of the ways dads show how much they care." (Publisher's note)

When a grandpa says "I love you" Douglas Wood; illustrated by Jennifer A. Bell. Simon & Schuster Books for Young Readers 2014 32 p. color illustrations (hardcover) $16.99

Grades: PreK K 1 2   E

1. Love -- Fiction 2. Grandparent-grandchild relationship -- Fiction 3. Grandfathers -- Fiction
ISBN 0689815123; 9780689815126

LC 2012047773

In this book by Douglas Wood, illustrated by Jennifer A. Bell, "discover all the wonderful ways grandfathers show grandchildren their love. . . . Everyone knows grandpas are best at spoiling their grandkids, but it's just because they love them so much! Whether by attending a tea party or getting an extra scoop of ice cream, there is nothing grandpas won't do to say 'I love you!'" (Publisher's note)

"With an 'actions speak louder than words' theme, the grandfathers depicted here speak volumes and confirm the importance of spending quality time with their grandchildren." SLJ

Where the sunrise begins; words by Douglas Wood; art by Wendy Popp. Simon & Schuster Books for Young Readers 2010 un il $16.99
Grades: PreK K 1   E
1. Sun -- Fiction 2. Nature -- Fiction
ISBN 978-0-689-86172-7; 0-689-86172-9

Reveals the part that each of us plays in the beginning of every day.

"Science is in full view as the author searches for the place where the sunrise begins. The beautiful watercolor drawings complement the simple but rich text. Not only are different cultures revealed, but geography is also put on display as the author, a naturalist, explores the world trying to find exactly where the sunrise begins. What the book unveils will amaze and delight the reader." Libr Media Connect

Wood, Nancy C.
Mr. and Mrs. God in the Creation Kitchen; illustrated by Timothy Basil Ering. Candlewick Press 2006 un il $16.99
Grades: K 1 2   E
1. Creation -- Fiction
ISBN 0-7636-1258-8
                                          LC 2005-53187
"Mr. and Mrs. God putter in the Creation Kitchen, first roasting Sun and Earth in their enormous oven, then whipping up Earth's creatures in between marital tiffs, finishing off with two jut-jawed humans and speculations about 'how they'll turn out.' . . . Ering's artwork captures the puckish spirit of Wood's telling. Spattered with dribbles and cluttered with gadgets, this chaotic kitchen reinforces the creators' portrayal as anything but perfect." Booklist

Woodruff, Elvira
The **memory** coat; story by Elvira Woodruff; illustrations by Michael Dooling. Scholastic Press 1999 un il $17.99
Grades: K 1 2 3   E
1. Jews -- Fiction 2. Immigrants -- Fiction 3. Ellis Island Immigration Station -- Fiction
ISBN 0-590-67717-9
                                          LC 95-30048
In the early 1900s, cousins Rachel and Grisha leave their Russian shtetl with the rest of their family to come to America, hopeful that they will all pass the dreaded inspection at Ellis Island

This offers "warm, realistic period paintings, some in color, some in sepia shades. . . . In a long, interesting author's note, Woodruff discusses the shtetl and immigrant history." Booklist

Woodson, Jacqueline
★ **Coming** on home soon; illustrated by E.B. Lewis. Putnam's 2004 un il $16.99
Grades: K 1 2 3   E
1. Grandmothers -- Fiction 2. African Americans -- Fiction 3. World War, 1939-1945 -- Fiction 4. Mother-

child relationship -- Fiction
ISBN 0-399-23748-8
                                          LC 2003-21949
A Caldecott Medal honor book, 2005
After Mama takes a job in Chicago during World War II, Ada Ruth stays with Grandma but misses her mother who loves her more than rain and snow.

"Woodson and Lewis tell a moving historical story of longing and separation. . . . Lewis' beautiful watercolors establish the setting. . . . Period and place are wonderfully specific." Booklist

★ **Each** kindness; Jacqueline Woodson; illustrated by E.B. Lewis. Nancy Paulsen Books 2012 32 p. $16.99
Grades: 1 2 3 4   E
1. Bullies 2. Schools -- Fiction 3. Kindness -- Fiction 4. Friendship -- Fiction
ISBN 0399246525; 9780399246524
                                          LC 2011046800
Coretta Scott King Author Honor Book (2013)
Charlotte Zolotow Award (2012)
In this book, "Chloe, Kendra, and Sophie are a tight trio, and when new girl Maya arrives, with her shabby clothes and obvious desperation, they resist her overtures of friendship. . . . When their teacher leads an exercise about kindness and its effects, Chloe realizes she can't think of any kind act she's ever done, and when Maya leaves her classroom never to return, Chloe realizes that she'll never be able to rectify her rejection." (Bulletin of the Center for Children's Books)

★ The **other** side; illustrations by E. B. Lewis. Putnam 2001 un il $16.99
Grades: K 1 2 3   E
1. Summer 2. Friendship 3. Race relations 4. Friendship -- Fiction 5. Race relations -- Fiction 6. African Americans -- Fiction
ISBN 0-399-23116-1; 978-0-399-23116-2
                                          LC 99-42055
Two girls, one white and one black, gradually get to know each other as they sit on the fence that divides their town. "Ages six to nine." (Bull Cent Child Books)

"Lewis' watercolors provide a telling backdrop to the action. . . . This is an emotionally intricate tale presented simply and intimately." Bull Cent Child Books

★ **Pecan** pie baby; illustrated by Sophie Blackall. G.P. Putnam's Sons 2010 un il
Grades: PreK K 1   E
1. Infants -- Fiction 2. Siblings -- Fiction 3. Pregnancy -- Fiction 4. African Americans -- Fiction 5. Mother-daughter relationship -- Fiction
ISBN 0-399-23987-1; 978-0-399-23987-8
When Mama's pregnancy draws attention away from Gia, she worries that the special bond they share will disappear forever once the baby is born. "Preschool, primary." (Horn Book)

"Blackall's apt watercolor-and-ink pictures capture the grounded serenity of a multiracial family (and community) with its priorities on straight. . . . Fresh and wise." Kirkus

★ **Show** way; illustrated by Hudson Talbott. G. P. Putnam's Sons 2005 un il $16.99

Grades: K 1 2 3   E
1. Quilts -- Fiction 2. Slavery -- Fiction 3. African
Americans -- Fiction
ISBN 0-399-23749-6

LC 2004-28093

A Newbery Medal honor book, 2006

The making of "Show ways," or quilts which once
served as secret maps for freedom-seeking slaves, is a tradition passed from mother to daughter in the author's family.

"The gorgeous, multimedia art includes chalk, watercolors, and muslin. An outstanding tribute, perfectly executed
in terms of text, design, and illustration." SLJ

Visiting day; illustrated by James E. Ransome. Scho-
lastic Press 2002 un il $15.95
Grades: K 1 2 3   E
1. Fathers -- Fiction 2. Prisoners -- Fiction 3. African
Americans -- Fiction
ISBN 0-590-40005-3

LC 00-35772

A young girl and her grandmother visit the girl's father
in prison

"The text is spare, gentle, and reassuring. . . . Ransome's
vibrant acrylic paintings fill each page at home with intense
pinks, yellows, greens, and blues in contrast to the monotone
hue of the prison walls. Both author and illustrator provide
notes that relate this story to their own personal experiences." SLJ

Wormell, Christopher

George and the dragon; [by] Chris Wormell. Knopf
2006 un il $16.95
Grades: PreK K 1 2   E
1. Mice -- Fiction 2. Dragons -- Fiction
ISBN 0-375-83315-3

First published in 2002 in the United Kingdom

A dragon terrorizes the kingdom until he is frightened by
George the mouse.

Wortche, Allison

Rosie Sprout's time to shine; story by Allison Wortche; pictures by Patrice Barton. Alfred A. Knopf 2011 il
$17.99; lib bdg $20.99
Grades: K 1 2 3   E
1. School stories 2. Plants -- Fiction
ISBN 978-0-375-86721-7; 978-0-375-96721-4 lib
bdg; 978-0-375-98459-4 e-book

LC 2011004092

Rosie's rival, Violet, outdoes her in everything until the
class plants seeds for a unit on gardening.

"Wortche possesses both a refreshing directness and a
willingness to trust her readers. She also has the courage to
conclude not with reconciliation, but with a bittersweet and
profoundly wise acknowledgment that it takes all kinds. This
impressive new author is well served by Barton . . . whose
digital classroom sketches convey a tumult of emotion and
have just the right amounts of energy and vulnerability."
Publ Wkly

The wreck of the Zephyr; Chris Van Allsburg. 30th anniversary edition Houghton Mifflin Harcourt 2013 un
color illustrations hbk $18.99
Grades: 1 2 3 4   E
1. Fantasy fiction 2. Imagination -- Fiction 3. Boats
and boating -- Fiction
ISBN 9780544050051; 0544050053

First published 1983

A boy's ambition to be the greatest sailor in the world
brings him to ruin when he misuses his new ability to sail
his boat in the air.

This "displays recognizable hallmarks of the artist's
work: beauty of composition, striking contrasts of light and
shadow, and especially the fascinating ambiguity of illusion
and reality." Horn Book

Wright, Johanna

The **secret** circus. Roaring Brook Press 2009 un il
$16.95
Grades: PreK K 1   E
1. Mice -- Fiction 2. Circus -- Fiction 3. France --
Fiction 4. Paris (France) -- Fiction
ISBN 978-1-59643-403-5; 1-59643-403-1

LC 2008-54261

Mice carefully dress for an evening out, journey across
Paris in a hot air balloon, and finally arrive at a secret place
to see the circus.

This is written in "simple, rhythmic prose. . . . Rustic
canvas paintings done in a subdued palette cast a mood of
quiet mystery over the nocturnal activities of the mice. The
artwork provides the clever details that the text never reveals." SLJ

Wright, Maureen

★ **Sleep,** Big Bear, sleep! illustrated by Will Hillen-
brand. Marshall Cavendish Children 2009 un il $16.99
Grades: PreK K 1   E
1. Stories in rhyme 2. Bears -- Fiction 3. Winter --
Fiction 4. Hibernation -- Fiction
ISBN 978-0-7614-5560-8; 0-7614-5560-4

LC 2008029402

As winter comes and Big Bear prepares to hibernate,
he keeps thinking he hears Old Man Winter giving him exhausting orders that prevent him from sleeping.

"The text moves at a steady clip, and the refrain will encourage child participation. . . . The story reads aloud well,
and the limited text and oversize illustrations will be effective in storytime. The artwork is the real star here, though.
Hillenbrand imbues his characters with motion and personality." SLJ

Another title about Big Bear is:
Sneeze, Big Bear, Sneeze (2011)

Sneeze, Big Bear, sneeze! illustrated by Will Hillenbrand. Marshall Cavendish Children 2011 un il $16.99
Grades: PreK K 1   E
1. Stories in rhyme 2. Bears -- Fiction 3. Winds --
Fiction 4. Autumn -- Fiction 5. Sneezing -- Fiction
ISBN 978-0-7614-59590; 0-7614-5959-6; 978-0-
7614-6074-9 e-book

LC 2011001125

Big Bear thinks that his tremendous sneezes are causing
the leaves and apples to fall off the trees and the geese to fly
away, but when the wind finally convinces him otherwise,
he knows what to do.

"Hillenbrand's sweeping mixed-media spreads should
stir up anticipation for apple-picking season." Publ Wkly

Wright, Michael

Jake goes peanuts. Feiwel and Friends 2010 un il $16.99

Grades: PreK K   **E**
1. Stories in rhyme 2. Peanuts -- Fiction
ISBN 978-0-312-54967-1; 0-312-54967-9

In an effort to get Jake to eat something other than peanut butter, his parents declare it "Peanut Butter Week" and create such dishes as peanut butter soup, peanut butter pot roast, and even peanut butter dog food for their pet.

"Wright's crisp rhymes and droll cartoons should make picky eaters smile, and perhaps consider a little diversity in their own diets." Publ Wkly

Another title about Jake is:
Jake starts school (2008)

Wright, Randall

The geezer in the freezer; illustrated by Thor Wickstrom. Bloomsbury USA Children's Books 2009 un il $16.99; lib bdg $17.89

Grades: PreK K 1 2   **E**
1. Stories in rhyme
ISBN 978-1-59990-135-0; 1-59990-135-8; 978-1-59990-390-3 lib bdg; 1-59990-390-3 lib bdg
LC 2009004631

Stuck between a rump roast and a pie, the old man living in the freezer finally gets to tell his tale of woe.

"The horror-story premise is played beautifully for laughs, thanks to the expertly sustained country-flavored rhymes. Wickstrom's slathered-on oils capture the situation's absurdity—and tenderness, when the geezer is telling his tale of star-crossed love." Horn Book Guide

Wyatt, Valerie

Boy meets dog; a word-game adventure. Kids Can Press 2013 32 p. $16.95

Grades: K 1 2   **E**
1. Word games
ISBN 1554538246; 9781554538249

In this children's picture book, author "[Valerie] Wyatt introduces kids to word ladders, in which a starting word leads step by step, by the substitution of one letter at a time, to a final word. . . . The artwork . . . borrows from conventions of animation to provide two-page scenes that carry readers on each word journey, and there is a little narrative twist at the end, about whether or not a character is real or just a toy (boy into toy)." (Kirkus Reviews)

Wynne Pechter, Lesley

Alligator, bear, crab; a baby's ABC. Orca Book Publishers 2011 un il bd bk $9.95

Grades: PreK   **E**
1. Alphabet 2. Board books for children 3. Animals -- Fiction
ISBN 978-1-55469-360-3; 1-55469-360-8
LC 2010-941967

"Endearing animals introduce the ABCs in an inviting board book. Pechter's organic paintings feature soft lines, kindly faces, and a soothing palette of creamy sunset colors and sky blues. . . . Uncommon additions like an urchin and a vole broaden the menagerie. . . . With care paid to each image, this is a charming, distinctive primer." Publ Wkly

Xinran

★ **Motherbridge** of love; text provided by Mother Bridge of Love; illustrated by Josee Masse. Barefoot 2007 un il $16.99

Grades: PreK K 1 2   **E**
1. Mothers -- Fiction 2. Adoption -- Fiction
ISBN 978-1-84686-047-8

Celebrates the bond between parent and child as the adoptive parent of a little Chinese girl speaks about her love for her adopted daughter.

"Simple, lyrical language and gorgeous art make this more than just another adoption story. . . . The sentiment is exactly right—loving, caring, and thoughtful—and the stylized acrylic illustrations, in thick brush strokes and swirling shapes, evoke the lyrical tone with grace and elegance." Booklist

Yaccarino, Dan

★ **Doug** unplugged! Dan Yaccarino. Alfred A. Knopf 2013 40 p. (trade) $16.99

Grades: K 1 2 3 4   **E**
1. Robots -- Fiction 2. City and town life -- Fiction
ISBN 0375866434; 9780375866432; 9780375966439
LC 2011047496

This children's book, by Dan Yaccarino, follows a robot named Doug. "His parents want him to be smart, so each morning they plug him in and start the information download. After a morning spent learning facts about the city, Doug suspects he could learn even more about the city by going outside and exploring it. And so Doug . . . unplugs. What follows is an exciting day of adventure and discovery." (Publisher's note)

Every Friday. Henry Holt and Company 2007 32p il $16.95

Grades: PreK K 1 2   **E**
1. Father-son relationship -- Fiction
ISBN 978-0-8050-7724-7; 0-8050-7724-3
LC 2005020253

A "boy describes the route that he and his dad walk on their way to their weekly Friday breakfast at the corner diner. . . . Yaccarino's clean lines, saturated colors, and very simple words distill the story's emotions into clear, understated sweetness that's not too sugary." Booklist

Lawn to lawn. Alfred A. Knopf 2010 un il $17.99; lib bdg $20.99

Grades: K 1 2 3   **E**
1. Adventure fiction 2. Gardens -- Fiction 3. Voyages and travels -- Fiction
ISBN 0-375-85574-2; 0-375-95574-7 lib bdg; 978-0-375-85574-0; 978-0-375-95574-7 lib bdg
LC 2009002303

When their family moves away and leaves them behind, a group of lawn ornaments sets out on a dangerous trek across the country to try to find them.

"Yaccarino's clean, bright illustrations have an appealing retro look, and the trek through suburbs, swamps, fields, and city is a visual treat." Booklist

Yamasaki, Katie

Fish for Jimmy; based on one family's experience in a Japanese American internment camp. Katie Yamasaki. Holiday House 2013 40 p. (reinforced) $16.95

Grades: 1 2 3 4 5   E
1. Historical fiction 2. Picture books for children 3. Brothers -- Fiction 4. Japanese Americans -- Evacuation and relocation, 1942-1945 -- Fiction
ISBN 0823423751; 9780823423750
LC 2012006584

In this children's picture book, "following the bombing of Pearl Harbor, Taro's father is taken away for questioning by the FBI, and Taro, his younger brother, and their mother are transported to an internment camp. Jimmy refuses to eat and becomes withdrawn and listless. Taro finds a way to slip outside the camp fences to obtain fresh fish to entice his brother to eat." (School Library Journal)

Yamashita, Haruo
Seven little mice go to school; illustrated by Kazuo Iwamura. NorthSouth 2011 un il $16.95
Grades: PreK K 1 2   E
1. School stories 2. Mice -- Fiction
ISBN 978-0-7358-4012-6; 0-7358-4012-1
Original Japanese edition 1981

"Mama Mouse has seven little mice who are about to start school. . . . The septuplets are reluctant to go. Clever Mama gets an idea. . . . She takes two blue balls of yarn and makes a path through the forest all the way to school. The next morning she announces, 'All aboard! The train for school is leaving now!.' . . . The children eagerly pick up on the game and follow along. . . . The pen-and-ink and watercolor illustrations perfectly complement the story. The mice are individualized with gently humorous details. . . . This clever take on the afraid-to-go-to-school theme should have broad appeal." SLJ

Another title about the seven little mice is:
Seven little mice have fun on the ice (2011)

Seven little mice have fun on the ice; illustrated by Kazuo Iwamura. NorthSouth 2011 un il $16.95
Grades: PreK K 1 2   E
1. Mice -- Fiction 2. Ice fishing -- Fiction
ISBN 978-0-7358-4048-5; 0-7358-4048-2

"Following an afterschool ice-skating excursion, the [seven little mice] are anxious to go ice fishing, just like Little Weasel and his father. However, Father has to work, and Mother is too afraid of slipping on the ice. . . . The softly colored illustrations are extremely detailed, giving readers much to peruse. . . . The mice are adorable and expressive." Kirkus

Yang, Belle
Foo, the flying frog of Washtub Pond. Candlewick 2009 un il $16.99
Grades: PreK K 1 2   E
1. Size -- Fiction 2. Frogs -- Fiction 3. Ponds -- Fiction 4. Animals -- Fiction 5. Friendship -- Fiction
ISBN 978-0-7636-3615-9; 0-7636-3615-0

"Gouache illustrations made up of buoyant, spontaneous, and comedic strokes match the exaggeration of this foolish frog." Booklist

Hannah is my name. Candlewick Press 2004 un il $16.99
Grades: K 1 2 3   E
1. Immigrants -- Fiction 2. Chinese Americans --

Fiction 3. San Francisco (Calif.) -- Fiction
ISBN 0-7636-2223-0
LC 2003-69675

A young Chinese girl and her parents emigrate to the United States and try their best to assimilate into their San Francisco neighborhood while anxiously awaiting the arrival of their green cards.

"The bright gouache pictures of San Francisco draw strongly on Chinese and American traditions. . . . The struggle with documentation and the celebration when the green cards finally arrive in the mail is a drama many immigrant families will recognize." Booklist

Yankovic, Al
When I grow up; illustrations by Wes Hargis. Harper 2011 un il $17.99
Grades: PreK K 1 2   E
1. School stories 2. Stories in rhyme 3. Occupations -- Fiction
ISBN 978-0-06-192691-4; 0-06-192691-4
LC 2010021966

An exuberant eight-year-old details for his teacher and classmates the astonishing variety of inventive careers he is thinking of pursuing when he grows up.

"As the boy's fantasies about his future get wilder and wilder, Hargis' hilarious, detailed illustrations in clear line and watercolor extend the uproarious nonsense. . . . Along with the imaginative play, the farce and parody make this a rare book with appeal to both kids and adults." Booklist

Yarrow, Peter
Puff the magic dragon pop-up book; [by] Peter Yarrow, Lenny Lipton; with paintings by Eric Puybaret and paper engineering by Bruce Foster. Sterling 2011 un il $26.95
Grades: PreK K 1 2   E
1. Pop-up books 2. Dragons -- Fiction
ISBN 978-1-4027-8711-9; 1-4027-8711-1

"Puybaret's capricious paintings combine elegantly with pop-up engineering by Bruce Foster in a condensed, interactive version of this bestselling 2007 picture book. The story unfolds in six graceful pop-up scenes, some of which have side panels that conceal additional pop-up effects. . . . Includes a four-song CD recording." Publ Wkly

Yates, Louise
★ **Dog** loves books. Alfred A. Knopf 2010 un il $16.99; lib bdg $19.99
Grades: PreK K 1 2   E
1. Dogs -- Fiction 2. Books and reading -- Fiction
ISBN 978-0-375-86449-0; 0-375-86449-0; 978-0-375-96449-7 lib bdg; 0-375-96449-5 lib bdg
LC 2009-11097

Dog loves books so much that he decides to open a book store.

"The simple story is accompanied by soft pastel pencil and watercolor drawings that give the book a whimsical, dreamy quality. Dog is surrounded by nonthreatening dinosaurs, space aliens, and other creatures when he is reading about them. Young children can enjoy the book by themselves by following the charming illustrations." SLJ

Dog loves drawing; Louise Yates. Alfred A. Knopf 2012 32 p. (trade) $16.99; $16.99

Grades: PreK K 1 2   E
1. Dogs -- Fiction 2. Drawing -- Fiction 3. Picture books for children 4. Animals -- Fiction
ISBN 9780307974495; 9780375870675; 9780375970672; 0375870679
LC 2011032353
In "this follow-up to the . . . 'Dog Loves Books' . . . the pup receives a blank book as a gift. He quickly realizes that it's a sketchbook, and though initially struck by artist's block, he soon uses his pencils and pens to draw himself some friends, a boat and a train to ride, and food for them to feast on, all of which magically come to life on the page. When one of Dog's new friends draws a monster, though, Dog must quickly use his skills to contain it and create an escape route." (School Library Journal)

A **small** surprise. Alfred A. Knopf 2009 un il $16.99; lib bdg $19.99
Grades: PreK K 1   E
1. Size -- Fiction 2. Circus -- Fiction 3. Rabbits -- Fiction
ISBN 978-0-375-85698-3; 0-375-85698-6; 978-0-375-95698-0 lib bdg; 0-375-95698-0 lib bdg
LC 2008024535
A little rabbit, too small even to wipe his own nose, is just the right size to do one very special thing
"The illustrations are rendered in soft hues that are soothing yet colorful. The animals . . . have wonderfully expressive eyes and gestures. There are a few words in a large font on each page, making it easy for young children to follow along." SLJ

Yee, Wong Herbert
Tracks in the snow. H. Holt 2003 un il $15.95
Grades: PreK K 1 2   E
1. Stories in rhyme 2. Snow -- Fiction 3. Animal tracks -- Fiction
ISBN 0-8050-6771-X
LC 2002-10854
A little girl investigates tracks in the snow, trying to determine what could have made them.
"The gentle, rhyming text makes an ideal read-aloud, and young listeners will chime in on the repeated phrases. The soft-focus, colored-pencil illustrations portray a small Asian girl exploring her safe world, but a world transformed by the fresh snowfall." SLJ

Upstairs Mouse, downstairs Mole. Houghton Mifflin Co. 2005 un il $15
Grades: K 1 2 3   E
1. Mice -- Fiction 2. Friendship -- Fiction 3. Moles (Animals) -- Fiction
ISBN 0-618-47313-0
LC 2004-5238
Mouse and her downstairs neighbor, Mole, discover that when they help each other, housecleaning and other daily tasks are much easier
"The expressive bamboo-pen and watercolor with colored-pencil illustrations capture the humor of the situations as well as the emotions of the characters. . . . A real winner." SLJ
Other titles about Mouse and Mole are:
Abracadabra! Magic with Mouse and Mole (2007)
A brand-new day with Mouse and Mole (2008)

Mouse and Mole: fine feathered friends (2009)
Mouse and Mole: a winter wonderland (2010)
Mouse and Mole: a perfect Halloween (2011)

Who likes rain? Holt & Co. 2007 un il $14.95
Grades: PreK K 1   E
1. Rain -- Fiction
ISBN 978-0-8050-7734-6; 0-8050-7734-0
LC 2006-03429
As a young girl splashes in the rain, she plays a guessing game with the reader about other living things that enjoy a cloudburst.
"The rhyming text tells the story as naturally as if the rhythm and rhyme just fell into place. . . . Fine strokes of color softly define the shapes of characters and settings." Booklist

Yee, Wong Herbert, 1953-
Mouse and Mole, secret valentine; Wong Herbert Yee. Houghton Mifflin Books for Children 2014 48 p. $15.99
Grades: K 1 2 3   E
1. Moles (Animals) -- Fiction 2. Mice -- Fiction 3. Friendship -- Fiction 4. Best friends -- Fiction 5. Valentine's Day -- Fiction
ISBN 0547887191; 9780547887197
LC 2012041660
In this picture book, by Wong Herbert Yee, "Mouse and Mole are best friends, but with Valentine's Day coming soon, each has a peculiar feeling of butterflies in the stomach when thinking of the other. . . . As Valentine's Day nears, Mouse and Mole get together to decorate cards. Mouse is good at making a list of friends and writing the words, while Mole's specialty is cutting out paper hearts and sprinkling glitter over glue to create a sparkly message." (Kirkus Review)
Secret valentine

Summer days and nights; Wong Herbert Yee. Henry Holt 2012 32 p. (hc) $14.99
Grades: PreK K 1   E
1. Stories in rhyme 2. Day -- Fiction 3. Night -- Fiction 4. Summer -- Fiction
ISBN 0805090789; 9780805090789
LC 2011028598
In this children's picture book by Wong Herbert Lee, "a little girl finds ways to entertain herself and stay cool. She catches a butterfly, sips lemonade, jumps in a pool, and goes on a picnic. At night, she sees an owl in a tree and a frog in a pond, and hears leaves rustling. Before long, she's fast asleep, dreaming about more summer days and summer nights." (Publisher's note)

Yeoman, John
The **wild** washerwomen; illustrated by Quentin Blake. Andersen 2009 un il lib bdg $16.95
Grades: K 1 2 3   E
1. Laundresses -- Fiction
ISBN 978-0-7613-5152-8; 0-7613-5152-3
LC 2008055432
A reissue of the title first published 1979 by Greenwillow Books
Seven washerwomen, sick of their work, go on an uncontrollable rampage, only to meet their match in seven very dirty woodcutters.

"The expressive illustrations—caricature line drawings washed with color—continuously echo and expand the preposterous, joyful text's often understated humor." Horn Book Guide

Yep, Laurence, 1948-
Auntie Tiger; pictures by Insu Lee. HarperCollinsPublishers 2009 un il $17.99; lib bdg $18.89
Grades: K 1 2 3   E
   1. Fairy tales 2. China -- Fiction 3. Tigers -- Fiction 4. Sisters -- Fiction
   ISBN 978-0-06-029551-6; 0-06-029551-1; 978-0-06-029552-3 lib bdg; 0-06-029552-X lib bdg
                        LC 2006-28649
In this version of Red Riding Hood set in China, Big Sister sets aside her differences with Little Sister to rescue her from a tiger in disguise.

"Bright, energetic illustrations done in jewel tones bring this story to life. The cunning tiger with his large head, bulging eyes, and small pointy teeth is scarcely contained in three of the spreads." SLJ

Yin
Coolies; illustrated by Chris K. Soentpiet. Philomel Bks. 2001 un il $16.99
Grades: 2 3 4   E
   1. Brothers -- Fiction 2. Chinese Americans -- Fiction 3. Central Pacific Railroad -- Fiction
   ISBN 0-399-23227-3
                        LC 98-40403
A young boy hears the story of his great-great-great-grandfather and his brother who came to the United States to make a better life for themselves helping to build the transcontinental railroad

"Soentpiet's strong, realistic watercolor paintings, in shades of blue and gold, show the bond between the brothers. . . . The American history is powerful. Yin provides notes and a bibliography for readers who want to know more." Booklist

Yolen, Jane
   ★ **Baby** Bear's books; written by Jane Yolen; illustrated by Melissa Sweet. Harcourt 2006 un il $16
Grades: PreK K   E
   1. Stories in rhyme 2. Bears -- Fiction 3. Books and reading -- Fiction
   ISBN 0-15-205290-9
                     LC 2005019203
Throughout the day, Baby Bear finds a book to fit every special moment.

"Mixed-media and collage illustrations create a warm and comfortable world. . . . The charming double-page pictures are large enough to share with groups, and the rhymes will engage listeners." SLJ
Other titles about Baby Bear are:
Baby Bear's chairs (2005)
Baby Bear's big dreams (2007)

Come to the fairies' ball; illustrated by Gary Lippincott. Wordsong 2009 un il $17.95
Grades: 1 2 3 4   E
   1. Stories in rhyme 2. Fairies -- Fiction
   ISBN 978-1-59078-464-8; 1-59078-464-2
                    LC 2009018247

All the fairies are excited to be invited to the King's ball, except for one young fairy whose only party dress is in tatters.

"An enchanting picture book full of whimsy and magic. . . . Lippincott's paintings take the forefront in this book, while Yolen's clever verse adds to the unfolding pictorial drama." SLJ

Commander Toad and the voyage home; pictures by Bruce Degen. Putnam 1998 64p il hardcover o.p. pa $5.99
Grades: 1 2 3 4   E
   1. Science fiction 2. Toads -- Fiction
   ISBN 0-399-23122-6; 0-698-11602-X pa
                    LC 96-21739
Commander Toad leads the lean green space machine "Star Warts" to find new worlds but runs into trouble when he sets course for home

"Yolen captures the high drama of space fiction in a delightful story that never loses sight of developing readers, who will be old enough to get the jokes but still young enough to relish the goofiness." Booklist
Other titles about Commander Toad are:
Commander Toad and the big black hole (1996)
Commander Toad and the dis-asteroid (1996)
Commander Toad and the intergalactic spy (1997)
Commander Toad and the Planet of the Grapes (1996)
Commander Toad and the space pirates (1997)
Commander Toad in space (1996)

Creepy monsters, sleepy monsters; a lullaby. illustrated by Kelly Murphy. Candlewick Press 2011 32p il $14.99
Grades: PreK K 1   E
   1. Stories in rhyme 2. Bedtime -- Fiction 3. Monsters -- Fiction
   ISBN 978-0-7636-4201-3; 0-7636-4201-0
                    LC 2010040342
Two rambunctious monsters creep, gurgle, crawl, and tumble before falling asleep.

This is a "whimsical, warmhearted rhyme, which turns bumps in the night into the sweetest sounds of all. . . . Murphy's oil, acrylic, and gel illustrations instantly grab attention with their unusual points of view. . . . Bedtime fare you can count on." Booklist

★ The **day** Tiger Rose said goodbye; illustrations by Jim LaMarche. Random House 2011 un il
Grades: PreK K 1 2   E
   1. Cats -- Fiction 2. Death -- Fiction 3. Country life -- Fiction
   ISBN 0-375-86663-9; 0-375-96663-3 lib bdg; 978-0-375-86663-0; 978-0-375-96663-7 lib bdg
                    LC 2010013548
A cat whose kitten days are far behind her says goodbye to her human family, and the animals and places that have made her life special, before leaving this life behind.

"The calm tone of the text is just right: matter-of-fact but compassionate. Reflecting the delicate beauty of the writing, LaMarche's mixed-media illustrations show equal finesse in line, color, texture, and composition." Booklist

★ **Elsie's** bird; illustrated by David Small. Philomel Books 2010 un il $17.99
Grades: K 1 2 3   E
1. Canaries -- Fiction 2. Nebraska -- Fiction 3. Frontier and pioneer life -- Fiction
ISBN 978-0-399-25292-1; 0-399-25292-4

Young Elsie must find a way to adapt to her new home on the Nebraska prairie after she and her father leave their comfortable city life in Boston.

"Yolen's evocative story, full of wonder and warmth, rolls smoothly along on carefully worded phrases, capturing the child's emotions as well as the flavor of the time and setting in a simple yet heartfelt way. Small's delivery, completely in sync with the author's, brings Elsie deftly to life. The illustrations, rendered in brush and ink with watercolor and pastel, realize both the streets of Boston and the grasslands of Nebraska with equal ease and aplomb." SLJ

How do dinosaurs act when they're mad? Jane Yolen; illustrated by Mark Teague. The Blue Sky Press 2013 40 p. (hardcover: alk. paper) $16.99
Grades: PreK K   E
1. Picture books for children 2. Anger -- Fiction 3. Stories in rhyme 4. Behavior -- Fiction 5. Emotions -- Fiction 6. Dinosaurs -- Fiction 7. Temper tantrums -- Fiction
ISBN 0545143152; 9780545143158

LC 2012040941

This children's picture book "features angry dinosaurs acting out and, with the help of human parents, learning how to cope with this powerful emotion. A different dino is featured in each rhyming scenario. . . . After he is told to take a time-out, the Afrovenator counts to 10 and breathes calmly. The Sauropelta proceeds to clean up the mess he made; Beipiaosaurus apologizes to his mom and gives her a hug." (School Library Journal)

★ **How** do dinosaurs say goodnight? illustrated by Mark Teague. Blue Sky Press (NY) 2000 un il $15.95
Grades: PreK K 1 2 3   E
1. Stories in rhyme 2. Bedtime -- Fiction 3. Dinosaurs -- Fiction
ISBN 0-590-31681-8

LC 98-56134

Mother and child ponder the different ways a dinosaur can say goodnight, from slamming his tail and pouting to giving a big hug and kiss

"The text is sweet and simple—just right for the wonderful pictures that really make this picture book special. . . . Endpapers introduce the critter cast in all their gorgeous glory: tyrannosaurus rex, dimetrodon, and more, in vivid, yet still earthbound colors." Booklist

Other titles in this series are:
How do dinosaurs eat their food? (2005)
How do dinosaurs get well soon? (2003)
How do dinosaurs go to school? (2007)
How do dinosaurs say happy birthday? (2011)
How do dinosaurs say I love you? (2009)

How do dinosaurs stay safe? Jane Yolen; illustrated by Mark Teague. Blue Sky Press, an imprint of Scholastic Inc. 2015 40 p. color illustrations (hardcover) $16.99

Grades: PreK K   E
1. Stories in rhyme 2. Dinosaurs -- Fiction 3. Safety education -- Fiction 4. Safety -- Fiction
ISBN 0439241049; 9780439241045

LC 2014012577

In this book, written by Jane Yolen and illustrated by Mark Teague, "a young dinosaur takes precautions in order to stay safe throughout the day, both at home and at play." (Publisher's note)

"Yolen's rhyming text tackles recreational safety ('He wears/a good helmet/when riding his bike/takes bottles of water/when on a long hike.'), safety at home ('Is he rough with the cat?/Does he stand up/on chairs?/When Mama says 'No!'/does he run down the stairs?'), and a reminder that every 'dinosaur' should know when and how to dial 911. Teague's bright illustrations are wonderfully whimsical, with colorful dinosaurs taking up the bulk of the spreads." SLJ

Hush, little horsie; written by Jane Yolen; illustrated by Ruth Sanderson. Random House 2010 un il $16.99; lib bdg $19.99
Grades: PreK K   E
1. Stories in rhyme 2. Horses -- Fiction 3. Bedtime -- Fiction
ISBN 978-0-375-85853-6; 0-375-85853-9; 978-0-375-95853-3 lib bdg; 0-375-95853-3 lib bdg

LC 2008030184

"In this gentle picture book, a variety of mares stand guard as their foals and fillies play, run, leap, and finally sleep. . . . The horses are introduced in simple rhyme. In each case, readers are reassured that the mothers will always take care of their babies. . . . The book ends with a human mother and her daughter nestled beneath blankets at bedtime, reading stories and preparing for sleep. . . . Sanderson's lush and lovely paintings are an ideal match for the reflective text. With text and illustrations as tender as a lullaby, this picture book is ideal for bedtime sharing." SLJ

My father knows the names of things; illustrated by Stephane Jorisch. Simon & Schuster Books for Young Readers 2010 un il $15.99
Grades: PreK K 1   E
1. Stories in rhyme 2. Father-child relationship -- Fiction
ISBN 978-1-4169-4895-7; 1-4169-4895-3

LC 2007-41840

Rhyming text depicts a father sharing with his child such things as seven words that all mean blue and the name of every kind of cloud.

"Yolen's easeful rhymes and Jorisch's warm illustrations craft a bighearted tribute to fathers' seemingly infinite capacities for information—and their willingness to share it." Publ Wkly

Naming Liberty; by Jane Yolen; illustrated by Jim Burke. Philomel Books 2008 un il $16.99
Grades: 1 2 3   E
1. Artists 2. Sculptors 3. Jews -- Fiction 4. Immigrants -- Fiction 5. Statue of Liberty (New York, N.Y.) -- Fiction 6. United States -- History -- 1865-1898 -- Fiction
ISBN 978-0-399-24250-2; 0-399-24250-3

In parallel stories, a Ukrainian Jewish family prepares to emigrate to the United States in the late 1800s, and Frederic Auguste Bartholdi designs, raises funds for, and builds the Statue of Liberty in honor of the United States' centennial.

"Burke's luminous paintings, designed on burnt sienna oil-washed boards, convey the landscapes and details of nineteenth-century Europe and New York. . . . An ideal choice for introducing the concepts of immigration and liberty to young listeners." Booklist

Not all princesses dress in pink; [by] Jane Yolen and Heidi Stemple Yolen; illustrated by Anne-Sophie Lanquetin. Simon & Schuster Books for Young Readers 2010 un il $15.99
Grades: PreK K 1 E
1. Stories in rhyme 2. Girls -- Fiction 3. Sex role -- Fiction 4. Princesses -- Fiction
ISBN 978-1-4169-8018-6; 1-4169-8018-0
LC 2008-38122
Rhyming text affirms that girls can pursue their many interests, from playing sports to planting flowers in the dirt, without giving up their tiaras.

"The snappy, upbeat illustrations and blithely confident characters are plenty of fun." Publ Wkly

Off we go! illustrated by Laurel Molk. Little, Brown 2000 un il lib bdg $12.95
Grades: PreK K E
1. Stories in rhyme 2. Animals -- Fiction 3. Grandmothers -- Fiction
ISBN 0-316-90228-4
LC 98-6893
One by one, baby woodland creatures leave home and sing their way to visit grandma

"Rhyme, repetition, and the playful, onomatopoeic language make this especially appealing for read-alouds. Large watercolors in earthy tones of gray, green, and brown are soft and fluid." Horn Book Guide

★ **Owl** moon; illustrated by John Schoenherr. 20th anniversary edition; Philomel 2007 un il $16.99
Grades: PreK K 1 2 E
1. Owls -- Fiction 2. Father-daughter relationship -- Fiction
ISBN 978-0-399-24799-6; 0-399-24799-8
A reissue of the title first published 1987
Awarded the Caldecott Medal, 1988
On a winter's night under a full moon, a father and daughter trek into the woods to see the great horned owl

This book "conveys the scary majesty of winter woods at night in language that seldom overreaches either character or subject. . . . This book has a magic that is extremely rare in books for any age." NY Times Book Rev

Pretty princess pig; by Jane Yolen and Heidi E. Y. Stemple; illustrated by Sam Williams. Little Simon 2011 un il $9.99
Grades: PreK K 1 E
1. Stories in rhyme 2. Pigs -- Fiction 3. Parties -- Fiction
ISBN 978-1-4424-0833-3; 1-4424-0833-2

Follows Pretty Princess Pig as she gets ready to throw a party by painting the dining room, baking, and digging up flowers.

"With their pastel palette and nimble linework, Williams's watercolors match this princess's verve." Publ Wkly

Sleep, black bear, sleep; by Jane Yolen and Heidi E. Y. Stemple; illustrated by Brooke Dyer. HarperCollins 2007 un il $15.99; lib bdg $16.89
Grades: PreK K 1 E
1. Stories in rhyme 2. Winter -- Fiction 3. Animals -- Fiction 4. Bedtime -- Fiction 5. Hibernation -- Fiction
ISBN 978-0-06-081560-8; 0-06-081560-4; 978-0-06-081561-5 lib bdg; 0-06-081561-2 lib bdg
LC 2006000344
As winter's chill spreads, different animals settle into their cozy homes for a long sleep

"The rhyme scheme is as lilting as a lullaby, and Dyer's ineffably sweet watercolor illustrations enrich this bedtime story." Booklist

Yolleck, Joan
★ **Paris** in the spring with Picasso; illustrated by Marjorie Priceman. Schwartz & Wade Books 2010 un il $17.99; lib bdg $20.99
Grades: K 1 2 3 E
1. Poets 2. Artists 3. Authors 4. Painters 5. Novelists 6. Dramatists 7. Essayists 8. Memoirists 9. Art critics 10. Literary critics 11. Private secretaries 12. Paris (France) -- Fiction
ISBN 978-0-375-83756-2; 0-375-83756-6; 978-0-375-93756-9 lib bdg; 0-375-93756-0 lib bdg
LC 2008-05867
Describes how some of Paris's famous artists and writers, such as Pablo Picasso, Max Jacob, and Guillaume Apollinaire, spend their day before preparing to attend a party at Gertrude Stein's apartment.

"Priceman's brightly colored illustrations exhibit energy, creativity, and general joie de vivre. . . . This whirlwind tour flows easily thanks to clear writing and carefully chosen details." SLJ

Yoon, Salina
Found; by Salina Yoon; illustrated by Salina Yoon. Walker & Co 2014 40 p. (hardback) $14.99
Grades: PreK K 1 E
1. Toys -- Fiction 2. Bears -- Fiction 3. Moose -- Fiction 4. Lost and found possessions -- Fiction
ISBN 0802735592; 9780802735591; 9780802735607
LC 2013029206
In this children's story, written and illustrated by Salina Yoon, "when Bear finds a lost stuffed toy bunny in the forest, he begins to worry. After all, the stuffed bunny must feel lonely and want to return safely to its owner and home! But as Bear diligently searches for the bunny's owner, posting notices high and low, he begins to grow attached to his newfound friend. What will happen when the bunny's owner finally comes forward?" (Publisher's note)

"Wishing he could keep the found bunny for himself, Bear searches high and low for the stuffed animal's original owner. When grown-up Moose recognizes his old toy, he also recognizes the opportunity to pass it on to someone younger who will love it like he did. Simple, colorful, bold-lined digital illustrations evoke the complex and conflicting feelings about letting something go." Horn Book

One, two, buckle my shoe; a counting nursery rhyme. Robin Corey Books 2011 un il bd bk $6.99
Grades: PreK   E
1. Counting 2. Board books for children 3. Circus -- Fiction
ISBN 978-0-375-86479-7; 0-375-86479-2

"Square die-cut windows offer clues about what comes next in this Big Top twist on the classic nursery rhyme. The opening spread places one purple square opposite a die-cut that frames two yellow circles. Turning the page reveals a polka-dotted clown's shoe, with the purple square becoming the buckle.... Watching abstract images turn into concrete shapes should please toddlers, and the inclusion of the words and numerals for each number cements the concept." Publ Wkly

Opposnakes; a lift-the-flap book about opposites. Little Simon 2009 un il $9.99
Grades: PreK K   E
1. Opposites 2. Snakes -- Fiction
ISBN 978-1-4169-7875-6; 1-4169-7875-5

"Yoon introduces opposites via friendly snakes. The spare text focuses on simple concepts: 'Cold snake/Hot snake,' 'Skinny snake/Plump snake,' 'One snake/Many snakes!' Brightly colored, cartoonlike reptiles stretch across the double-foldout spreads and are set against a white background. They are full of amusing details.... A book that entertains as it informs." SLJ

Penguin and Pinecone; a friendship story. Salina Yoon. Walker & Co. 2012 40 p. $12.99
Grades: PreK K 1 2   E
1. Trees -- Fiction 2. Penguins -- Fiction 3. Friendship -- Fiction 4. Pine cones -- Fiction
ISBN 080272843X; 9780802728432; 9780802728449
LC 2011037221

In this children's book, by Salina Yoon, "when Penguin finds a lost pinecone one day, an unlikely friendship blooms. But Grandpa reminds Penguin that pinecones can't live in the snow--they belong in the warm forest far away. Though he will miss his friend, Penguin returns Pinecone to his home, dreaming of the day they can reunite. And when he finally returns to the forest to check on his friend, Penguin discovers that love only grows over time-and so do little pinecones!" (Publisher's note)

Penguin on vacation; by Salina Yoon. "Walker Books For Young Readers Distributed to the trade by Macmillan Publishers" 2013 40 p. (hardcover) $14.99
Grades: PreK K 1 2   E
1. Penguins -- Fiction 2. Beaches -- Fiction 3. Vacations -- Fiction 4. Friendship -- Fiction
ISBN 0802733972; 9780802733962; 9780802733979
LC 2012032284

In this book written and illustrated by Salina Yoon, "Penguin is tired of the snow and cold—so he decides to visit the beach! But when his favorite activities like skiing and skating don't work so well on sand, can a new friend help

Penguin learn how to have fun in the sun?" Ultimately, Penguin befriends a Crab. (Publisher's note)

Super babies on the move; Mia on the move. G.P. Putnam's Sons 2009 un il $14.99
Grades: PreK   E
1. Infants -- Fiction
ISBN 978-0-399-24755-2; 0-399-24755-6
LC 2008000706

After following Baby Mia as she sneaks out during naptime to go to the playground, the reader may turn the book upside down to watch Baby Max skip bathtime to join in a backyard animal chase.

"Toddlers will like these stories, both for the bright but simply styled visuals and the text." SLJ

Who do I see? Robin Corey Books 2011 un il bd bk $6.99
Grades: PreK   E
1. Color 2. Animals 3. Board books for children
ISBN 978-0-375-87309-6; 0-375-87309-0

"This guess-the-animal book contains circular die-cut windows that offer a peek at bright animal prints adorned with shimmery holographic foil. Prompts encourage readers to guess what animal appears on the next page.... Friendly-looking naïf animals and an eye-catching design make this a gentle introduction to colors and patterns." Publ Wkly

Yorinks, Arthur

Flappy and Scrappy; story by Arthur Yorinks; pictures by Aleksey and Olga Ivanov. HarperCollinsPublishers 2011 42p il (I can read!) $16.99
Grades: K 1 2   E
1. Dogs -- Fiction 2. Play -- Fiction 3. Parties -- Fiction 4. Birthdays -- Fiction
ISBN 978-0-06-205117-2; 0-06-205117-2
LC 2008027467

After canine friends Scrappy and Flappy play an unusual game of catch, Scrappy complains that everyone has forgotten his birthday, but Flappy surprises him.

"Emerging readers will enjoy the Ivanovs' cheerful, expressive illustrations, which are thoughtfully placed with the text in spot or full-spread layouts. Beginning readers in the city, suburbs, or country will enjoy these engaging animals and the very simple text." SLJ

★ **Happy** bees; by Arthur Yorinks; illustrated by Carey Armstrong-Ellis. Harry N. Abrams 2005 un il $15.95
Grades: PreK K 1 2   E
1. Bees -- Fiction
ISBN 0-8109-5866-X
LC 2004-15454

Rhythmic text describes the carefree life of bees as they sting knees, munch on Swiss cheese, and laugh in the breeze.

"The nonsensical text doubles as the lyrics of the first tune on the accompanying CD.... The happy-go-lucky insects have loads of personality.... Listeners will enjoy the romp, whether spoken or sung, and can discover more beeguiling silliness in the other selections on the CD." SLJ

★ **Hey,** Al; story by Arthur Yorinks; pictures by Richard Egielski. Farrar, Straus & Giroux 1986 un il $17; pa $7.99

Grades: PreK K 1 2 3   **E**
1. Fantasy fiction 2. Birds -- Fiction
ISBN 0-374-33060-3; 0-374-42985-5 pa
LC 86-80955

Awarded the Caldecott Medal, 1987
"Egielski's solid naturalism provides just the visual foil needed to establish the surreal character of this fantasy. . . . Text and pictures work together to challenge readers' concept of reality." SLJ

Homework; illustrations by Richard Egielski. Walker & Co. 2009 un il $16.99; lib bdg $17.89
Grades: K 1 2   **E**
1. Homework -- Fiction 2. Writing -- Materials and instruments -- Fiction
ISBN 978-0-8027-9585-4; 0-8027-9585-4; 978-0-8027-9586-1 lib bdg; 0-8027-9586-2 lib bdg
LC 2008-28011

When Tony's pens, along with his pencil and eraser, come to life, the squabbling set of writing tools tries to complete Tony's neglected homework
"Yorinks has devised a pleasing homage to the creative process and uses a light touch to show how inspiration can derive from the unlikeliest of places. . . . A simple but amusing winner." Booklist

★ The **invisible** man; illustrated by Doug Cushman. Harper 2011 un il $16.99
Grades: PreK K 1 2   **E**
1. Fruit -- Fiction 2. Supernatural -- Fiction
ISBN 978-0-06-156148-1; 0-06-156148-7
LC 2009-1404

Sy Kravitz, a Brooklyn fruit seller, explains why becoming invisible should never happen to you.
"Yorinks employs a narrative tone that's a cross between an old Jewish comedian and The Twilight Zone's Rod Serling, which adds to the deadpan humor, while Cushman's splendid watercolor art becomes ever more clever the closer you look. A fine bit of funnery." Booklist

The **witch's** child; by Arthur Yorinks; illustrated by Jos. A. Smith. Abrams Books for Young Readers 2007 un il $16.95
Grades: K 1 2 3   **E**
1. Fairy tales 2. Witches -- Fiction
ISBN 978-0-8109-9349-5
LC 2006031980

Desiring a child of her own, Rosina the witch fashions one out of straw and scraps, but when she cannot bring the rag child to life she becomes enraged and turns the village children into shrubs, where they stay until a kind girl discovers the discarded doll and saves her.
"Yorinks's flowing language is evocative, and the plot builds steadily to an exciting climax. Smith's detailed paintings depict Rosina with jet-black standing-on-end hair and exaggerated facial features that vividly—and frighteningly—express her emotions." SLJ

★ **You** read to me & I'll read to you; 20th-century stories to share. selected by Janet Schulman. Knopf 2001 250p il $34.95
Grades: PreK K 1 2   **E**
1. Short stories
ISBN 0-375-81083-8
LC 2001-29211

Companion volume to The 20th century children's book treasury (1998)
This is a collection of 26 picture books and selections from early chapter books by such authors as Maurice Sendak, William Steig, Dr. Seuss, and Florence Parry Heide
"A great choice for family or classroom sharing." SLJ

Young, Amy
Belinda, the ballerina. Viking 2002 un il $15.99
Grades: PreK K 1 2   **E**
1. Ballet -- Fiction
ISBN 0-670-03549-1
LC 2001-8395

When Belinda auditions for the Spring Ballet Recital and the judges tell her she can not be a ballerina because her feet are too big, she tries to forget about dancing
This offers "spirited gouache paintings that capture the sadness, the humor and the triumph of Belinda's story. . . . The story puts physical defects into perspective and offers something to laugh about at the same time." Booklist
Other titles about Belinda are:
Belinda and the glass slipper (2006)
Belinda begins ballet (2008)
Belinda in Paris (2005)

Young, Cybèle
A **few** bites; by Cybele Young. Groundwood Books/House of Anansi Press 2012 48 p. col. ill. (hardcover) $18.95
Grades: K 1 2   **E**
1. Siblings -- Fiction 2. Vegetables -- Fiction 3. Imagination -- Fiction
ISBN 1554982952; 9781554982950
Author Cybele Young tells a story of a sister who tries to entice her brother to eat his lunch by making up stories about the food. "Viola has made lunch for her little brother Ferdie: broccoli, carrot sticks, ravioli . . . . Ferdie does not want this lunch . . . [so] Viola launches into a brilliant saga of dinosaurs [and] . . . aliens and their Orange Power Sticks." (Kirkus)

★ A **few** blocks. Groundwood Books 2011 un il $18.95
Grades: K 1 2   **E**
1. Siblings -- Fiction 2. Imagination -- Fiction
ISBN 978-0-88899-995-5; 0-88899-995-X

"It's time for school, but Viola's younger brother, Ferdie, isn't interested. . . . Resourceful and creative, Viola uses Ferdie's jacket, a leaf, and a piece of cardboard to turn their short walk into three heroic adventures, as they become superheroes, seek buried treasure, and prepare to battle a dragon. . . . Young's collages cast shadows on the white background below, with silhouettes of curling waves, sea creatures, and blobby monsters painted in pale blues, greens, and reds and filled in with crisp imagery of the duo's urban neighborhood. With empathy and respect for both charac-

ters' emotions, Young presents a loving story of sibling camaraderie." Publ Wkly

★ **Nancy** knows; Cybele Young. Tundra Books of
Northern New York 2014 40 p. (hardcover) $17.99
Grades: PreK K 1 2 3 4   **E**
     1. Memory -- Fiction 2. Elephants -- Fiction
     ISBN 1770494820; 9781770494824; 9781770494831
                      LC 2013943888
     In this children's book by Cybele Young, "Nancy knows
she's forgotten something. Something important. When she
tries to remember, she thinks of all kinds of other things
instead. She remembers things she knows and things she
doesn't quite know. She remembers things one way, then another. . . . Nancy Knows is the . . . story of an elephant who
remember lots of things, except the very thing she is trying
to remember." (Publisher's note)
     "Nancy, an elephant, knows that she has forgotten some-
thing important, but she can't for the life of her think what it
is...Her elephantine shape is filled with colorful Japanese paper sculptures that reflect what's on her mind. For example,
when she thinks of things with wheels, her shape is filled
with a paper bicycles, a scooter, a wheelbarrow, a unicycle,
and a shopping cart. Nancy is a charming protagonist with a
memory like an elephant. She won't be soon forgotten." SLJ

★ **Ten** birds. Kids Can Press 2011 un il $18.95
Grades: 1 2 3 4   **E**
     1. Counting 2. Birds -- Fiction 3. Problem solving
     -- Fiction
     ISBN 978-1-55453-568-2; 1-55453-568-9
     "Ten birds are trying to figure out how to get to the other
side of the river. The bird they call 'Brilliant' devises a pair
of stilts. The bird they call 'Highly Satisfactory' engineers a
raft. One by one, nine resourceful birds make the crossing
until a single bird is left behind—the one they call 'Needs
Improvement.' This bird's solution proves surprising—and
absurdly simple." (Publisher's note) "Primary." (Horn Book)
     "Ten small birds . . . need to get across a river and have
only a deserted lot full of discarded odds and ends—and their
own ingenuity—to help them. . . . The straightforward text
provides structure and clarity, while the striking and intricate
pen-and-ink illustrations perfectly capture the stillness of a
night full of wintry snow, show the birds' innovative and
slightly mystical solutions to the problem at hand and seamlessly depict the decreasing numbers that represent the birds
who have yet to cross. . . . This quietly dazzling selection is
a subtle celebration of individuality and creativity." Kirkus

Young, Jessica
     My blue is happy; Jessica Young, illustrated by Catia
Chien. Candlewick Press 2013 32 p. $15.99
Grades: PreK K 1   **E**
     1. Color -- Fiction 2. Emotions -- Fiction
     ISBN 0763651257; 9780763651251
                      LC 2012950616
     In this children's picture book by Jessica Young, "a little
girl realizes that not everyone feels the same about colors.
Her sister sees blue as sad and associates it with lonely songs.
But the protagonist sees it as happy because it reminds her
of her favorite jeans and the pool on a hot day. Dad says
brown is ordinary like a paper bag but chocolate syrup is the
association that the child makes." (School Library Journal)

Young, Judy Dockrey
     A **pet** for Miss Wright; written by Judy Young; illus-
trated by Andrea Wesson. Sleeping Bear Press 2011 un il
$15.95
Grades: PreK K 1   **E**
     1. Pets -- Fiction 2. Authorship -- Fiction
     ISBN 978-1-58536-509-8; 1-58536-509-2
                      LC 2010034399
     A lonely writer searches for the perfect pet to keep her
company in her solitary work.
     "Both the story and the illustrations have a light, charm-
ing flavor, with understated humor and a sophisticated air
that assumes that intelligent children will enjoy this story."
Kirkus

Yuly, Toni
     ★ **Early** Bird; by Toni Yuly. First edition Feiwel &
Friends 2014 40 p. $15.99
Grades: PreK   **E**
     1. Birds
     ISBN 1250043271; 9781250043276
     This children's book, by Toni Yuly, tells the "story of
an early-rising red bird, which also introduces a handful of
directional prepositions. . . .After awakening, she stretches,
'takes a deep breath of fresh morning air and then Early Bird
gets going!' The bird's rambles take her 'across the grass/
through the flowerbed/ under the spiderweb/up the path' and
beyond." (Publishers Weekly)
     "A little red bird wakes early and goes on a preposition-
laden journey: "Across...through...under...up...and over"
until she finds the Early Worm. Readers may think they
know the little worm's fate, but Early Bird gets the worm--
and shares a strawberry breakfast. The large-size type plays
around, under, and over the bold shapes and colors in this
simple, pleasing story." Horn Book

     Night owl; Toni Yuly. Feiwel & Friends 2015 40 p.
color illustrations (hardback) $15.99; (board book) $7.99
Grades: PreK   **E**
     1. Owls -- Fiction 2. Sound -- Fiction 3. Board books
     for children 4. Animals -- Infancy -- Fiction
     ISBN 1250054575; 9781250054579; 9781250072917
                      LC 2014045970
     In this children's book by Toni Yuly, "little Night Owl
happily greets the night. But where is his mother? In a series
of onomatopoeic moments, the owlet hears different sounds
and wonders if it's his mother's. Alas, each one reveals a
cricket, a train, a toad or other source of the sound--but no
mother. When a storm crashes in, the owlet wings bravely
home to his tree where his mother soon joins him." (School
Library Journal)
     "Although Night Owl is portrayed as independent, curi-
ous, and brave, toddlers and preschoolers will understand
that he really wants his mother during the storm. . . . With
its question-and-response text, this is a satisfying choice for
reading aloud." Booklist

Yum, Hyewon
     ★ **Mom,** it's my first day of kindergarten! Hyewon
Yum. Frances Foster Books 2012 40 p. col. ill. $16.99
Grades: PreK K   **E**
     1. School stories 2. Picture books for children 3.
     Mother-son relationship -- Fiction 4. Worry -- Fiction
     5. Schools -- Fiction 6. Kindergarten -- Fiction 7.

Mothers and sons -- Fiction 8. First day of school -- Fiction

ISBN 0374350043; 9780374350048

LC 2011018294

This book "looks at the first day of school from two points of view—that of a little boy who is more than ready and a nervous mother not quite prepared to let him go. . . . [T]he 5-year-old shakes his mother awake on the first day of school." The text "enumerates her worries (that he won't have time to eat, she forgot some vital supply, he'll be late, he'll get lost, he won't have any friends)" but when "they reach his classroom door . . . [h]e quickly gets over it and has a great day at school." (Kirkus)

This is our house; Hyewon Yum. Frances Foster Books 2013 40 p. (hardcover) $16.99

Grades: PreK K 1 2   E

1. Picture books for children 2. Home -- Fiction 3. Dwellings -- Fiction 4. Family life -- Fiction

ISBN 0374374872; 9780374374877

LC 2012029684

In this children's picture book, a "small girl with twin braids narrates her family's history with pride, starting with when her grandparents arrived at a brick rowhouse on a leafy street, coming from 'far away with just two suitcases in hand.' Since then, three generations have marked the seasons and personal milestones outside the house's front door . . ., found snug shelter within its walls . . ., and consumed homemade soup in its kitchen." (Publishers Weekly)

★ The **twins'** blanket. Farrar Straus Giroux 2011 un il $16.99

Grades: PreK K   E

1. Twins -- Fiction 2. Sisters -- Fiction 3. Blankets -- Fiction

ISBN 978-0-374-37972-8; 0-374-37972-6

Two twin girls, who have always shared everything, sleep in separate beds with their own blankets for the first time.

"It's an exquisitely designed book: lots of white space focuses attention on unexpected pleasures, like the feet of the twins as they stomp on the fabric in a wash basin. The book's inherent symmetry, with the twins mirroring each other on the left and right sides of the spreads, is a treat as well." Publ Wkly

The **twins'** little sister; Hyewon Yum. Frances Foster Books, Farrar Straus Giroux 2014 40 p. color illustrations (hardcover) $17.99

Grades: PreK K   E

1. Twins -- Fiction 2. Sisters -- Fiction 3. Babies -- Fiction 4. Mother and child -- Fiction

ISBN 0374379734; 9780374379735

LC 2013013078

Sequel to: The Twins' Blanket

"In 'The Twins' Little Sister' by . . . picture book author Hyewon Yum, being twins means having two of almost everything: two twin beds, two polka-dot dresses, two dolls. But these two little girls have only one mom. This is a big problem. Soon there will be an even bigger problem: Mom is having a baby, and the twins will have a little sister." (Publisher's note)

"Those strong-willed sisters from The Twins' Blanket are fighting over Mom's attention. The situation worsens when Mom brings home a new baby sister. Yum's twins are believably childlike in their directness and their unshakable belief that the world revolves around them. Collage elements add texture and interest to the gouache illustrations. This is a fresh take on both the sibling-rivalry and new-baby themes." Horn Book

Zalben, Jane Breskin

★ **Baby** shower. Roaring Brook Press 2010 un il $16.99

Grades: PreK K 1 2   E

1. Dogs -- Fiction 2. Pets -- Fiction 3. Aunts -- Fiction 4. Animals -- Fiction

ISBN 978-1-5964-3465-3; 1-5964-3465-1

"Zoe wants a pet. . . . To get her mind off dogs . . . and cats . . . Mama suggests that Zoe help with her aunt's baby shower. That night in bed Zoe . . . [dreams] about a baby shower—of puppies, kittens, and even piglets and ducklings. . . . Much of the charm comes from Zalben's sweet and funny ink-and-watercolor pictures, filled with delicious detail in both the homey scenes and windswept expanses of tumbling babies." Booklist

Mousterpiece; Jane Breskin Zalben. Roaring Brook Press 2012 30 p. $16.99

Grades: PreK K 1 2   E

1. Mice -- Fiction 2. Painting -- Fiction 3. Picture books for children 4. Artists -- Fiction 5. Museums -- Fiction 6. Art museums -- Fiction

ISBN 1596435496; 9781596435490

LC 2011021755

In this book, "Janson the mouse lives in an art museum . . . . When she happens upon the modern wing, she is mesmerized. Paintings by Picasso and Matisse, Munch and Pollack, Van Gogh and Warhol spark her creative talents and she emulates them all. When the wing is closed for renovation, Janson is bereft. . . . Rather than leave the space empty, she paints . . . until the room is once again filled with art. The museum director happens upon her work and mounts a show for her." (School Library Journal)

Zemach, Kaethe

Ms. McCaw learns to draw; by Kaethe Zemach. Arthur A. Levine Books 2008 un il $16.99

Grades: 1 2 3   E

1. School stories 2. Drawing -- Fiction 3. Teachers -- Fiction 4. Learning disabilities -- Fiction

ISBN 978-0-439-82914-4; 0-439-82914-3

LC 2006016465

Dudley Ellington struggles to learn anything at school, but when his very patient teacher, Mrs. McGraw, is unable to draw a face on the board, he helps her figure out how to do it

"Because the text is simple and straightforward, the book is a good choice to read aloud. . . . The pen and watercolor illustrations are expressive and full of energy." SLJ

Zia, F.

Hot, hot roti for Dada-ji; art by Ken Min. Lee & Low Books 2011 il $17.95

Grades: K 1 2   E

1. Grandfathers -- Fiction 2. East Indian Americans

-- Fiction
ISBN 978-1-60060-443-0; 1-60060-443-9
LC 2010034694

Aneel and his grandfather, Dada-ji, tell stories, use their imaginations, and make delicious roti, a traditional Indian flatbread.

"Min echoes the narrative's exuberance with bright, blocky acrylic scenes of an Indian family in Western surroundings, dressed in a mix of contemporary and traditional styles and headlined by the lad and his elder. . . . A natural for reading aloud, laced with great tastes, infectious sound effects and happy feelings." Kirkus

Includes glossary

Ziefert, Harriet

Bunny's lessons; paintings by Barroux. Blue Apple 2011 un il $16.99
Grades: PreK K 1 2   E
1. Toys -- Fiction 2. Rabbits -- Fiction
ISBN 978-1-60905-028-3; 1-60905-028-2
LC 2010046645

A stuffed rabbit learns much from Charlie, his constant companion, including the meaning of the words "loud," "ouch," and "messy," but also about saying you are sorry and knowing you are loved.

"With simple lines, Barroux creates emotions of surprise, anger, joy, and sadness in his childlike paintings. Thick paper and a matte finish give the book a sturdy, solid feel that complements the sturdy, solid message of friendship." Booklist

Lucy rescued; Harriet Ziefert; paintings by Barroux. Blue Apple Books 2012 40 p. (hardback) $16.99
Grades: PreK K 1 2   E
1. Dogs -- Fiction 2. Toys -- Fiction 3. Picture books for children 4. Animals -- Infancy -- Fiction
ISBN 1609051874; 9781609051877
LC 2011039015

In this children's picture book, a family adopts a puppy named Lucy from the pound. "Out of nowhere that evening Lucy begins to howl a horrific howl. Morning, noon and night the howling went on and on. The little girl and her parents tried everything to stop it. . . . One night the little girl presented Lucy with a simple toy for her to snuggle with and the howling stopped. . . . But when one of Lucy's favorite toys comes up missing, the howling begins again." (Children's Literature)

My dog thinks I'm a genius; illustrated by Barroux. Blue Apple Books 2011 il $16.99
Grades: PreK K   E
1. Dogs -- Fiction 2. Painting -- Fiction
ISBN 978-1-60905-059-7; 1-60905-059-2
LC 2011018936

A budding artist goes to school after painting a picture with input from his dog Louie, and returns home to find that the dog has some talent, as well.

"Both the text and illustrations are true to the voice of an eight-year-old boy. . . . The colors in the illustrations are perfectly suited to the story. . . . Share this book as an introduction to art, or simply as a sweet dog story." SLJ

Zimmerman, Andrea Griffing

★ **Dig!** [by] Andrea Zimmerman and David Clemesha; illustrated by Marc Rosenthal. Harcourt 2004 un il $16
Grades: PreK K   E
1. Dogs -- Fiction 2. Construction workers -- Fiction 3. Excavating machinery -- Fiction
ISBN 0-15-216785-4
LC 2003-4373

Follows Mr. Rally and his dog, Lightning, as they travel the town on a big yellow digging machine, taking care of five important jobs

"Earth-tone illustrations are created with watercolor and Prismacolor pencil. . . . The pace, repetition, and word choices make the book appropriate for beginning readers. The uncluttered art, catchy refrain, and focus on heavy machinery make it a natural for storytimes." SLJ

★ **Digger** man; [by] Andrea Zimmerman & David Clemesha. Holt & Co. 2003 un il $15.95
Grades: PreK K   E
1. Brothers -- Fiction 2. Steam-shovels -- Fiction
ISBN 0-8050-6628-4
LC 2002-10856

A young boy imagines how he will use his digger to make a park where he and his little brother can play

"The joyful acrylic illustrations and the sparse, confident text will delight other digger-wannabes." Booklist

Fire engine man; [by] Andrea Zimmerman & [illustrated by] David Clemesha. Henry Holt 2007 un il $15.95
Grades: PreK K   E
1. Brothers -- Fiction 2. Imagination -- Fiction 3. Fire fighters -- Fiction
ISBN 978-0-8050-7905-0
LC 2006007909

A young boy imagines the work he will do and the safety gear he will wear when he becomes a fireman some day, as his younger brother first watches then joins him on the job

"The brothers from Digger Man (Holt, 2003) are back. . . . The same colorful acrylic illustrations greet readers, and have enough detail to interest yet not overwhelm them. The text moves at a brisk pace." SLJ

★ **Trashy** town; [by] Andrea Zimmerman and David Clemesha; illustrated by Dan Yaccarino. HarperCollins Pubs. 1999 un il $17.99
Grades: PreK K   E
1. Refuse and refuse disposal -- Fiction
ISBN 0-06-027139-6
LC 98-27495

Little by little, can by can, Mr. Gillie, the trash man, cleans up his town

"Short energetic sentences propel the tale. . . . Employing primary colors dominated by bold blues, Yaccarino's vibrant art has a retro look." Booklist

Zion, Gene

★ **Harry** the dirty dog; pictures by Margaret Bloy Graham. Harper & Row 1956 un il $17.99; lib bdg $17.89; pa $6.99; bd bk $7.99
Grades: PreK K   E
1. Dogs -- Fiction
ISBN 0-06-026865-4; 0-06-026866-2 lib bdg; 0-06-443009-X pa; 0-06-084244-X bd bk

"A runaway dog becomes so dirty his family almost doesn't recognize him. Harry's flight from scrubbing brush and bath water takes him on a tour of the city." Moorachian. What is a City?

Other titles about Harry are:

Harry and the lady next door (1960)

Harry by the sea (1965)

No roses for Harry! (1958)

Zoehfeld, Kathleen Weidner

★ **Secrets** of the seasons; orbiting the sun in our backyard. Kathleen Weidner Zoehfeld; illustrated by Priscilla Lamont. First edition Alfred A. Knopf 2014 40 p. (trade) $16.99

Grades: K 1 2 3　　　　　　　　　　　　　　　　E

1. Sun -- Fiction 2. Earth -- Fiction 3. Seasons -- Fiction

ISBN 0517709945; 9780517709948; 9780517709955

LC 2013021351

This book, written by Kathleen Weidner Zoehfeld and illustrated by Priscilla Lamont, is "about backyard science that explains why the seasons change. Alice and her friend Zack explore the reasons for the seasons. Alice's narrative is all about noticing the changes as fall turns into winter, spring, and then summer. She explains how the earth's year-long journey around the sun, combined with the tilt in the earth's axis, makes the seasons happen." (Publisher's note)

"Alice and friends from Secrets of the Garden return to enjoy her nature-filled backyard. This time, she learns to notice and welcome differences in weather, plants, and animal life in each of the four seasons of the temperate northern hemisphere. Throughout, airy pen and watercolor illustrations make the appeal of nature accessible to even the youngest readers." Horn Book

Zolotow, Charlotte

Mr. Rabbit and the lovely present; pictures by Maurice Sendak. Harper & Row 1962 un il $16.99; pa $5.99

Grades: PreK K 1 2　　　　　　　　　　　　　　　E

1. Color -- Fiction 2. Rabbits -- Fiction 3. Birthdays -- Fiction

ISBN 0-06-026945-6; 0-06-443020-0 pa

A Caldecott Medal honor book, 1963

"The quiet story, told in dialogue, is illustrated in richly colored pictures which exactly fit the fanciful mood." Hodges. Books for Elem Sch Libr

"A serious little girl and a tall, other-worldly white rabbit converse about a present for her mother. 'But what?' said the little girl. 'Yes, what?' said Mr. Rabbit. It requires a day of searching—for red, yellow, green, and blue, all things the mother likes, to make a basket of fruit for the present." Horn Book

When the wind stops; illustrated by Stefano Vitale. rev and newly illustrated ed; HarperCollins Pubs. 1995 un il hardcover o.p. pa $6.99

Grades: PreK K　　　　　　　　　　　　　　　　E

1. Nature -- Fiction

ISBN 0-06-025425-4; 0-06-443472-9 pa

LC 94-14477

A revised and newly illustrated edition of the title first published 1962 by Abelard-Schuman

This is a revised edition of Zolotow's 1962 title, with a new illustrator. "A little boy feels sorry when the day is over, but his mother explains that day is beginning somewhere else, and that 'Nothing ends . . . It begins in another place or in a different way.'" (Bull Cent Child Books) "Ages four to eight." (Booklist)

"The full-color scenes, painted on wood, gloriously depict heaven and earth and give concrete meaning to abstract concepts. Not only wonderful for lap sharing, this beautiful book will also be a rich supplement for a science unit on the elements or the seasons." Booklist

★ **William's** doll; pictures by William Pène Du Bois. Harper & Row 1972 30p il $16.99; pa $6.99

Grades: PreK K 1 2　　　　　　　　　　　　　　　E

1. Dolls -- Fiction 2. Sex role -- Fiction

ISBN 0-06-027047-0; 0-06-027048-9 lib bdg; 0-06-443067-7 pa

When little William asks for a doll, the other boys scorn him and his father tries to interest him in conventional boys' playthings such as a basketball and a train. His sympathetic grandmother buys him the doll, explaining his need to have it to love and care for so that he can practice being a father

"Very, very special. The strong, yet delicate pictures . . . convey a gentleness of spirit and longing most effectively, as William pantomimes his craving." N Y Times Book Rev

Zuckerman, Andrew

★ **Creature** ABC. Chronicle Books 2009 un il $19.99

Grades: PreK K 1 2　　　　　　　　　　　　　　　E

1. Animals 2. Alphabet

ISBN 978-0-8118-6978-2; 0-8118-6978-4

LC 2009-04365

"This is a first choice for libraries." Bull Cent Child Books

Includes glossary

Zuffi, Stefano

Art 123; count from 1 to 12 with great works of art. Abrams Books for Young Readers 2011 32p $12.95

Grades: K 1 2　　　　　　　　　　　　　　　　　E

1. Counting 2. Art appreciation

ISBN 978-1-4197-0100-9; 1-4197-0100-2

LC 2011009728

"From Caravaggio to Lichtenstein, this enriching counting book features a different work of Western art for numbers one through 12, accompanied by a brief, descriptive rhyme. . . . In addition to introducing numbers and counting, the book works well as a basic primer on viewing (and thinking about) art." SLJ

Zullo, Germano

Little bird; Germano Zullo; illustrated by Albertine. Enchanted Lion Books 2012 72 p.

Grades: PreK K 1 2　　　　　　　　　　　　　　　E

1. Birds -- Fiction 2. Flight -- Fiction 3. Friendship -- Fiction 4. Picture books for children

ISBN 1592701183; 9781592701186

LC 2011052462

This picture book, a French Caldecott Medal winner, tells the story of a man who frees a group of birds from his truck so that they can fly away. When one small bird remains, he keeps it company and tries to show it how to fly. The little bird returns later with the entire flock, lifting up the man and flying with him. The story "suggests that little things can change lives--and perhaps even the world. Placing small, uncomplicated shapes against large fields of uniform color . . . [illustrator] Albertine provides a visual plot for [Germano] Zullo's meditative abstractions . . . the characters express fear, friendship, yearning and delight through glances, posture and other cues." (Kirkus)

Zuravicky, Oril

★ C is for city; an alphabet book. illustrated by Giuseppe Castellano. Little Simon 2011 il $7.99

Grades: PreK K   **E**

1. Alphabet 2. Stories in rhyme 3. Board books for children

ISBN 978-1-4424-2049-6; 1-4424-2049-9

"Mister Doodle may be a simple stick figure, but he lives in a vibrant photo-collage world. In this alphabet book, he and his dog, Sketch, share a new noun for every letter of the alphabet. . . . Mister Doodle's adventures unfold in bouncy, playful rhymes. . . . A great little introduction to the alphabet, this lively outing . . . should inspire kids to notice details." Publ Wkly